THE ZONDERVAN

Greek AND English Interlinear New Testament (NASB/NIV)

THE ZONDERVAN

Greek AND English Interlinear New Testament (NASB/NIV)

GENERAL EDITORS

William D. Mounce AND Robert H. Mounce

ZONDERVAN EDITOR

Verlyn D. Verbrugge

ASSISTANT EDITOR

D. Matthew Smith

ZONDERVAN

The Zondervan Greek and English Interlinear New Testament (NASB/NIV)

This edition replaces ISBN 978-0-310-24139-3.

Requests for information should be addressed to:
Zondervan, *Grand Rapids, Michigan 49530*

ISBN 978-0-310-49296-2

Typeset: Teknia Software

Printed in the United States of America

---

14 15 /DCI/ 27 26 25 24 23 22 21 20 19 18 17 16 15 14 13 12 11 10 9 8 7 6 5 4

Table of Contents

Abbreviations

a. Most parsing codes first list the type of word following by a period.

n.	Noun	r.	Pronoun	v.	Verb	f.	Infinitive
a.	Adjective	d.	Definite article	pt.	Participle		

b. Substantives are parsed as case–number–gender. "n.asm" means "noun . accusative singular masculine"

n	Nominative	s	Singular	m	Masculine
g	Genitive	p	Plural	f	Feminine
d	Dative			n	Neuter
a	Accusative				
v	Vocative				

Adjectives can be followed by ".c" ("Comparative") or ".s" ("superlative"). "a.gpn.c" means "adjective . genitive plural neuter . comparative."

Personal pronouns are parsed "case–number–gender . person–number." "r.apf.3p" means "pronoun . accusative plural feminine . third person plural."

c. Verbs are parsed "tense–voice–mood . person–number." "v.pai.1s" means "verb . present active indicative . first person singular."

p	Present	a	Active	i	Indicative	1	First
i	Imperfect	m	Middle	s	Subjunctive	2	Second
f	Future	p	Passive	o	Optative	3	Third
a	Aorist			m	Imperative		
r	Perfect					s	Singular
l	Pluperfect					p	Plural

Participles are parsed "tense–voice . case–number–gender." "pt.pa.nsm" means "participle . present active . nominative singular masculine."

Infinitives are parsed "tense–voice." "f.ra" means "infinitive . perfect active."

d. The following codes are used by themselves for other parsing tags.

adv	Adverb	cj	Conjunction
adv.c	Comparative adverb	j	Interjection
adv.s	Superlative adverb	pl	Particle
p.g	Preposition with the genitive		
p.d	Preposition with the dative		
p.a	Preposition with the accusative		

Preface

Greek tools are like some medicines: you wish you didn't have to use them, but you're glad they're there when you need them. In a perfect world we would all know biblical Greek and not need any help reading the New Testament as it was originally written. But it is not a perfect world, and many people do need help.

I have long considered interlinears to be a questionable form of help because they engender so many false notions about language. They make it appear that one word in Greek corresponds to one and only one English word. It appears, because of the nature of most interlinears, that one Greek word always has the same meaning in English. Not only are these assumptions false, but they are misleading and, to anyone conversant with a foreign language, foolish. And because most interlinears follow the Greek word order, their English translations are almost worthless.

John 3:16 in a traditional interlinear: "For thus loved God the world, so as the Son the only begotten he gave, that everyone believing in him may not perish but may have life eternal."

John 3:16 in our interlinear: "For this is how God loved the world: he gave his one and only Son that everyone who believes in him should not perish but have eternal life."

I have already addressed most of these issues when I created my "reverse interlinear," an interlinear that follows the English word order and alters the order of the Greek words (*Interlinear for the Rest of Us* [Grand Rapids: Zondervan, 2006]). For someone who has never learned Greek, this is the better volume to purchase, especially if you study from the NIV translation.

So when Zondervan asked me to write some new interlinears that were still traditional in their approach, at first I hesitated. Why reinvent my own wheel, so to speak? Then I realized that with a special typesetting format and just the right translation, I could write an interlinear that would not perpetrate the myths created by traditional interlinears and instead produce a work that would make it easy to see both the Greek and the English in their respective word order. I also wanted to work on a project with my father, and as a result of his many years of translation expertise, this seemed to be the right thing to do.

What is distinctive about this interlinear?

1. As with traditional interlinears, it follows the word order of the Greek text. You can scan along the Greek line, and at any point drop down and see how that word is translated. κόσμος means "world." Nothing new here.

ὁ	κόσμος			δι᾽	αὐτοῦ	ἐγένετο,	καὶ	ὁ	κόσμος				αὐτὸν	οὐκ	ἔγνω.	11		εἰς	τὰ	
the	world	was	created	by	him,	*was created*	but	the	world	did	not	know	him.	*not*	*did know*	He	came	to	⸤that which⸥	was
3836	3180	1181	1181	1328	899	1181	2779	3836	3180	1182	4024	1182	899	4024	1182	2262	2262	1650	3836	
d.nsm	n.nsm			p.g	r.gsm.3	v.ami.3s	cj	d.nsm	n.nsm				r.asm.3	pl	v.aai.3s			p.a	d.apn	

2. The second line of each staff is a brand new translation done by my father, Robert Mounce. My goal was to have a translation that would make good sense while at the same time illustrate how translation work should be done. This is unique in the history of traditional interlinears.

In the example above, a traditional interlinear following Greek word order would translate, "the world by him was created but the world him not did know." As I will discuss below, if you want to read the English, just ignore any word that is in superscript italics: "the world was created by him, but the world did not know him." (I boxed in the text to read just for this example.)

ὁ	κόσμος			δι᾽	αὐτοῦ	ἐγένετο,	καὶ	ὁ	κόσμος				αὐτὸν	οὐκ	ἔγνω.	11		εἰς	τὰ	
the	world	was	created	by	him,	*was created*	but	the	world	did	not	know	him.	*not*	*did know*	He	came	to	⸤that which⸥	was
3836	3180	1181	1181	1328	899	1181	2779	3836	3180	1182	4024	1182	899	4024	1182	2262	2262	1650	3836	
d.nsm	n.nsm			p.g	r.gsm.3	v.ami.3s	cj	d.nsm	n.nsm				r.asm.3	pl	v.aai.3s			p.a	d.apn	

But there is more that is new in this translation besides word order. Contrary to normal practice, the same Greek word is not always translated with the same English word. That simply is not the way language functions. ὁ does not always mean "the"; sometimes, in context, it means "you" or "my" or some other word. Often, it has no translation equivalent because it is performing a grammatical function. For example, a common Greek construction is "article ('the') — noun — article — adjective"; for example, "the person the good." It is simply wrong to translate the second article as "the." Its function is to tell the reader that the following adjective modifies the preceding noun. Nothing more.

There are words like δέ, which may be translated by a punctuation mark, ὅτι, which may be translated with quotation marks, or καί, which may be translated as a new paragraph.

And then there are idioms. εἰς ("into") τῶν ("the") αἰῶνα ("age") does not mean "into the age." It means "forever," just as the German "Ich ('I') habe ('have') Hunger ('hunger')" does not mean "I have hunger"; rather, it means, "I am hungry."

3. The third line contains the GK number for the word. Ed Goodrick and John Kohlenberger developed this numbering system as an improvement over the more familiar Strong's numbering system. This means that without any knowledge of Greek you can find the English word you want to study, drop down and get its number, and then use that number to look up the meaning of the Greek word (not the English word) in a reference book such as my *Mounce's Complete Expository Dictionary of Old and New Testament Words*, or the fuller *New International Dictionary of New Testament Theology; Abridged Edition* by my good friend Verlyn Verbrugge (who is also my Zondervan editor). In the example below, "grace" is from the Greek word #5921.

ἐδόθη,	ἡ	χάρις	καὶ	ἡ	ἀλήθεια		διὰ	Ἰησοῦ	Χριστοῦ	ἐγένετο.	18						θεὸν	οὐδεὶς	ἑώρακεν	πώποτε·
was given	*{the}*	grace	and	*{the}*	truth	came	through	Jesus	Christ.	*came*		No	one	has	ever	seen	God.	*No one*	*has seen*	*ever*
1443	3836	5921	2779	3836	237	1181	1328	2652	5986	1181		4029	4029	3972	4799	3972	2536	4029	3972	4799
v.api.3s	d.nsf	n.nsf	cj	d.nsf	n.nsf		p.g	n.gsm	n.gsm	v.ami.3s							n.asm	a.nsm	v.rai.3s	adv

4. The fourth line of each staff "parses" each word. In other words, it tells you the case, number, and gender of the noun, or the person, number, tense, voice, mood of the verb. For someone who has had a little Greek, this line may be your favorite. In the example above, the Greek word translated "has seen" is a verb, perfect active indicative, 3rd person singular ("v.rai.3s").

5. At the end of the book is an updated Greek dictionary for quick reference. This is the same dictionary that is included in my *Mounce's Complete Expository Dictionary of Old and New Testament Words*. In the Greek dictionary, references such as "See *king; leader*" refer to the main entries in the *Expository Dictionary*.

These interlinears are truly a group project. Stan Gundry (Senior Vice President and Editor in Chief at Zondervan) approached me with the idea. I (Bill) designed the basic approach with much help from my editor (Verlyn Verbrugge). Dad (Robert) did the translation. I wrote the software that enabled Matt Smith (a former student and now good friend and colaborer with me at BiblicalTraining.org) to connect each Greek word to its English counterpart. I made the software to typeset the book.

I hope to create a short class on how to use this tool and the others I have written, to be published at www.BiblicalTraining.org. I would encourage you to go there often, not only for this class but for all the other classes the website has to offer.

My thanks to all involved. Without each of you, the interlinears would not exist. May our work help all of you who are using this new interlinear to understand the wonderful truths of God's Word, every word proceeding from God's very mouth, and may you by God's enabling grace be transformed as you grow in your knowledge of him.

Bill Mounce
Spokane, 2007

Technical Comments

This section will be of interest primary to those who have learned Greek.

Greek text

This is a unique Greek text and one that I trust will prove helpful. It is a compilation of four Greek texts.

1. The UBS (United Bible Society), which is the same as NA[27], is the standard Greek text used today. This is the text followed by most modern translations such as the RSV, NRSV, ESV, and the NASB. Prof. Bruce Metzger played a significant role in the UBS, RSV, and NRSV, and so it should be of no surprise to see the latter's use of the UBS text. The ESV differs from the UBS text at only one place (Jude 1:5).

2. The TNIV Greek text is not publicly available, but Gordon Fee (one of the NIV and TNIV translators and one of today's top textual critics) gave Zondervan a marked-up Greek text so we could see the textual basis for the TNIV, which is relatively close to that of the Greek text behind the NIV.

3. The NET Bible (available at www.NETBible.org) has a wealth of discussion of the New Testament Greek text. Behind much of the notes lies the work of Daniel B. Wallace, another top textual critic today. In the Preface we read that the NET "agrees for the most part with NA[27]" and the differences "are due to a slightly different emphasis on the role of internal evidence (such as scribal tendencies, author's style, and context). The NET New Testament puts more emphasis on internal evidence than does the NA[27], so that both external and internal evidence are generally given equal weight." Their work therefore makes for a helpful comparison with the more externally-based text-critical work of the UBS. Every place the NET differs from the UBS is marked in the NET with a double dagger ("‡") in a bolded footnote "**tc**." There are approximately 119 places where this occurs.

4. The TR is the Textus Receptus, the Greek textual tradition behind the King James version. I used the version of the TR included with the software program Accordance, which was "based upon the text compiled by Dr. Maurice A. Robinson" (version 3.2).

Please note that I am not a textual critic. It is beyond my expertise to evaluate the manuscript tradition and make a choice. Rather, the text I have included here is simply a compilation of the first three with notes from the TR. Differences among these four sources are listed in the footnotes. My original goal had been to produce a Greek text that would show the Greek variations that would explain some the differences among the major English translations; however, most translations follow the UBS so closely that my work would simply have produced the UBS. Please attach no text-critical significance to my choice of English words in the footnotes such as "omitted" and "inserted." I am not passing text-critical judgment.

The TR is different from the first three Greek texts in so many places that I could not include every variation. However, I focused on those verses that are significantly different in the TR and would most likely affect someone preaching from the KJV. As a preacher, you would not want to spend a significant amount of your sermon time talking about the angel that descended into the Pool of Bethesda (John 5:4) only to find out that anyone using a modern translation doesn't have that verse.

For the UBS I assumed the full reading of any form they include. The UBS brackets certain words to show that there is some uncertainty about whether they were part of the original text or not. Unfortunately, sometimes these words range from "most likely not original" to "very certain they are original" (my appraisal). I have removed all brackets from the text and listed the word with brackets in the footnotes. The UBS also uses brackets within a word to indicate uncertainty. These are especially confusing words and again I assumed the fuller form of the word. For example, in the UBS we see "αὐτό[ν]" in Matthew 14:12. We list the UBS reading as αὐτόν and then footnote the bracketed form as "αὐτό[ν]."

As far as the NET is concerned, unless a footnote indicates differently we list the NET as in agreement with the UBS. At times this feels a little uncertain, especially when the UBS has a bracketed form. For example, at times the article with a proper name is bracketed ([ὁ] Ἰησοῦς), and there often is no reference to this in the NET's footnotes, and yet this is relatively unimportant and does not affect the translation. In other words, there are situations in which the NET may simply have decided not to comment on a word. In these cases, I assume the NET agrees with the UBS. (What brought this situation to my attention was when Fee would cross out the article, indicating that he felt it was not original. I could not tell whether the NET agreed with his assessment or not.) Upon correspondence with Dan Wallace, I learned that the formal Greek text behind the NET is different from the UBS in about 400 places, but many of these readings have no noticeable impact on the translation.

I decided to keep capitalization to a minimum. Unlike the UBS, which capitalizes the first letter of the first word in a paragraph, and often the first word after a semicolon when they felt the following text was a direct citation, I simply kept everything lowercase except for proper names and place names.

A "crasis" is a Greek word in which two words are written as one. There are several in the New Testament and I simply parsed them as "crasis." Here is a list of all crasis forms. The first word is usually the conjunction καί; the second word is listed below.

Crasis	*Two parts*	
κἀγώ	καὶ ἐγώ	ἐγώ is a first person singular nominative personal pronoun
κἀμοί	καὶ ἐμοί	ἐμοί is a first person singular dative personal pronoun
κἀμέ	καὶ ἐμέ	ἐμοί is a first person singular accusative personal pronoun
κἀκεῖ	καὶ ἐκεῖ	ἐκεῖ is an adverb
κἀκεῖνος	καὶ ἐκεῖνος	ἐκεῖνος is a demonstrative adjective/pronoun
κἀκεῖνον		Nominative or accusative singular masculine
κἀκεῖνα		Nominative or accusative plural neuter
κἀκεῖνοι		Nominative plural masculine
κἀκείνους		Accusative plural masculine
κἀκεῖθεν	καὶ ἐκεῖθεν	ἐκεῖθεν is an adverb
κἄν	καὶ ἐάν or ἄν	ἐάν and ἄν are a conjunction and particle (respectively)
τοὐναντίον	τό and ἐαντίον	Nominative or accusative singular neuter
τοὔνομα	τό and ὄνομα	Nominative or accusative singular neuter

The Special Formatting

As mentioned above, the interlinear translation is a special translation specifically developed for these interlinears. I asked Dad to use his years of experience to produce a somewhat dynamic translation that could still function within the context of an interlinear. As you watch Dad work with the different Greek constructions in their different contexts, you not only can see what each word means but can also receive an excellent lesson in how translation should be done (within, of course, the limitations of the interlinear).

But notice that *the translation actually makes sense*. The meaning of the special formatting may not be obvious at first, but within a few minutes it should be clear. *And so, if you want to just read through the English, the key is to ignore any word that is superscript.* Here is a short passage from John 3.

ζωὴν	αἰώνιον.	16	οὕτως	γὰρ		ἠγάπησεν	ὁ	θεὸς	τὸν	κόσμον,	ὥστε			τὸν				υἱὸν	τὸν	μονογενῆ
life."	*eternal*	For	this is how	*For*	God	loved	*{the}*	*God*	the	world:	*{that}*	he	gave	his	one	and	only	Son	*{the}*	*one and only*
2437	173	1142	4048	1142	2536	26	3836	2536	3836	3180	6063	1443	1443	3836	3666	3666	3666	5626	3836	3666
n.asf	a.asf		adv	cj		v.aai.3s	d.nsm	n.nsm	d.asm	n.asm	cj			d.asm				n.asm	d.asm	a.asm

ἔδωκεν,	ἵνα	πᾶς	ὁ	πιστεύων	εἰς	αὐτὸν	↱	μὴ	ἀπόληται	ἀλλ᾽	ἔχῃ		ζωὴν	αἰώνιον.	17		↱	οὐ	γὰρ
he gave	that	everyone	who	believes	in	him	should	not	perish	but	have	eternal	life.	*eternal*	For	God	did	not	*For*
1443	2671	4246	3836	4409	1650	899	660	3590	660	247	2400	173	2437	173	1142	2536	690	4024	1142
v.aai.3s	cj	a.nsm	d.nsm	pt.pa.nsm	p.a	r.asm.3		pl	v.ams.3s	cj	v.pas.3s		n.asf	a.asf				pl	cj

ἀπέστειλεν	ὁ	θεὸς	τὸν	υἱὸν	εἰς	τὸν	κόσμον	ἵνα	κρίνῃ	τὸν	κόσμον,	ἀλλ᾽	ἵνα			σωθῇ	ὁ	κόσμος	δι᾽
send	*{the}*	*God*	his	Son	into	the	world	to	condemn	the	world,	but	so that	the	world	⌞might be saved⌟	*the*	*world*	through
690	3836	2536	3836	5626	1650	3836	3180	2671	3212	3836	3180	247	2671	3836	3180	5392	3836	3180	1328
v.aai.3s	d.nsm	n.nsm	d.asm	n.asm	p.a	d.asm	n.asm	cj	v.aas.3s	d.asm	n.asm	cj	cj			v.aps.3s	d.nsm	n.nsm	p.g

αὐτοῦ.	18 ὁ	πιστεύων	εἰς	αὐτὸν ↱		οὐ	κρίνεται·		ὁ	δὲ	↱	↱	↱	μὴ	πιστεύων			ἤδη
him.	The	one who believes	in	him	is	not	condemned,	but	the	*but*	one	who	does	not	believe	is	condemned	already,
899	3836	4409	1650	899	3212	4024	3212	1254	3836	1254	4409	4409	4409	3590	4409	3212	3212	2453
r.gsm.3	d.nsm	pt.pa.nsm	p.a	r.asm.3		pl	v.ppi.3s		d.nsm	cj				pl	pt.pa.nsm			adv

1. A normal situation. Below every Greek word is an English word. It may be in regular Roman type or perhaps superscript in italics, sometimes with curly brackets around the word. In any case, that word is what that Greek means in that context.

In John 3:16, οὕτως means "this is how," γάρ means "for," and ὁ means "the."

2. The straight arrow in the Greek line. The arrow tells you that the English word under it comes from the next Greek word toward which the arrow is pointing. In Mark 1:3, "of" (in the phrase "of the Lord") is derived from κυρίου.

ἐρήμῳ·	ἑτοιμάσατε	τὴν	ὁδὸν	→	κυρίου,	εὐθείας	ποιεῖτε	τὰς		τρίβους	αὐτοῦ,		4 ἐγένετο	Ἰωάννης	ὁ	βαπτίζων
wilderness:	'Prepare	the	way	of the	Lord,	*straight*	make	*{the}*	his	paths	*his*	straight.'"	*appeared*	John	the	baptizer
2245	2286	3836	3847		3261	2318	4472	3836	899	5561	899	2318	1181	2722	3836	966
n.dsf	v.aam.2p	d.asf	n.asf		n.gsm	a.apf	v.pam.2p	d.apf		n.apf	r.gsm.3		v.ami.3s	n.nsm	d.nsm	pt.pa.nsm

3. The bent arrow in the Greek line. If an English word is derived from a Greek word, but if there is an intervening Greek word between the English and its Greek counterpart such that a straight arrow would point to the wrong word, the bent arrow points in the correct direction and the GK numbers will help you connect the correct English and Greek words together.

In John 3:18 above, the first "is" (#3212) is derived from κρίνεται. In other words, κρίνεται means "is condemned."

4. Corner brackets in the Greek line. When the Greek phrase was too idiomatic to translate word for word, we bracketed the phrase and defined it as a unit. If you still want to know what each word means, then use the GK numbers and look the word up in the Greek dictionary in the back of the book. αὐλὴν τῶν προβάτων means "courtyard of the sheep," hence, "sheepfold."

⌞αὐλὴν	τῶν	προβάτων⌟	ἀλλὰ	ἀναβαίνων	ἀλλαχόθεν	ἐκεῖνος			κλέπτης	ἐστὶν	καὶ		λῃστής·	2	ὁ	δὲ
sheepfold			but	climbs in	⌞by some other way,⌟	*{that one}*	is	a	thief	*is*	and	a	robber.	But	the	*But*
885	3836	4585	247	326	249	1697	1639		3095	1639	2779		3334	1254	3836	1254
n.asf	d.gpn	n.gpn	cj	pt.pa.nsm	adv	r.nsm			n.nsm	v.pai.3s	cj		n.nsm		d.nsm	cj

5. Italicized superscripted words with curly brackets in the English line. When a Greek word cannot be translated, such as when it has no true English equivalent or it is performing a grammatical function, Dad left it out of the translation and you should skip it when reading the English. However, if you are looking at the Greek and want to know what each word basically means, we included its meaning this way.

In John 3:16. ὁ means "the" but is not translated because we do not say, "The God so loved the world."

6. Italicized superscripted words in the English line. Greek word order is often different from English. So if we were to produce an interlinear that actually made sense when reading the English, we had to find some method to indicate English word order but still connect the English to the Greek word. Here's what we did. Where the English word needs to appear, we include the English word and the GK number for its corresponding Greek form. This enables you to find the Greek word without any difficulty. When you get to the Greek word, the English word is under it but is in superscripted italics; so if you are just reading the English, you can skip the word. This may seem complicated at first, but you will adjust to it quickly.

John 3:16 reads, "For this is how God loved the world: he gave his one and only Son that everyone who believes in him should not perish but have eternal life."

7. Corner brackets in the English line. When an English phrase is needed to translate a single Greek word, we often put the English phrase in corner brackets so it would be clear which words come from the Greek. Without the corner brackets, the English words farthest to the right might appear to be disconnected to any Greek word. In John 3:17, σωθῇ means "might be saved"; "saved" comes from σωθῇ.

8. If there is an English word with nothing over it in the Greek line, that means the word was added to make sense of the Greek sentence although it is not connected to any one Greek word. This is a common and necessary practice, and all translations do it. The KJV and NASB put this type of word in italics.

In John 3:16, this rule does not apply to "For." The GK number under it tells you it has been separated from the Greek word it translates. However, in Mark 1:3 below, "a" in the phrase "a voice" is added, because that is how we speak in English.

ἀποστέλλω τὸν ἄγγελόν μου πρὸ προσώπου σου, ὃς κατασκευάσει τὴν ὁδόν σου· 3 φωνὴ βοῶντος ἐν τῇ
I am sending *{the}* my messenger *my* before your face, *your* who will prepare *{the}* your way, *your* a voice calling out in the
690 3836 1609 34 1609 4574 5148 4725 5148 4005 2941 3836 5148 3847 5148 5889 1066 1877 3836
v.pai.1s d.asm n.asm r.gs.1 p.g n.gsn r.gs.2 r.nsm v.fai.3s d.asf n.asf r.gs.2 n.nsf pt.pa.gsm p.d d.dsf

9. Tilde. When a Greek cannot be translated without using tortorous English, and when it is performing a grammatical function, we often put a tilde (~) under the Greek word. We used the tilde mostly in the folowing situations.

When ὅτι is translated with quotation marks.

Γαλιλαίαν κηρύσσων τὸ εὐαγγέλιον τοῦ θεοῦ 15 καὶ λέγων ὅτι πεπλήρωται ὁ καιρὸς καὶ ἤγγικεν ἡ βασιλεία
Galilee, proclaiming the gospel of God, and saying, ~ "The time is fulfilled *The time* and *is at hand* the kingdom
1133 3062 3836 2295 3836 2536 2779 3306 4022 3836 2789 4444 3836 2789 2779 1581 3836 993
n.asf pt.pa.nsm d.asn n.asn d.gsm n.gsm cj pt.pa.nsm cj v.rpi.3s d.nsm n.nsm cj v.rai.3s d.nsf n.nsf

When the article is part of an "articular infinitive."

ἐν τῇ διδαχῇ αὐτοῦ· 3 ἀκούετε. ἰδοὺ ἐξῆλθεν ὁ σπείρων σπεῖραι. 4 καὶ ἐγένετο ἐν τῷ σπείρειν ὃ
in {the} teaching his "Listen! *{behold}* A sower went out *{the} sower* to sow. And *{it happened that}* as ~ he was sowing, some
1877 3836 1439 899 201 2627 5062 2002 3836 5062 5062 2779 1181 1877 3836 5062 4005
p.d d.dsf n.dsf r.gsm.3 v.pam.2p j v.aai.3s d.nsm pt.pa.nsm f.aa cj v.ami.3s p.d d.dsn f.pa r.nsn

ἄν introduces an element of contingency, often with the subjunctive. It can sometimes be translated with "would," or with the relative pronoun ὅς ("who") becomes "whoever," but other times it is omitted.

βλασφημίαι ⌞ὅσα ἐὰν⌟ βλασφημήσωσιν· 29 ὃς δ' ἂν βλασφημήσῃ εἰς τὸ πνεῦμα τὸ ἅγιον, ↱ οὐκ ἔχει
blasphemies *whatever* they may utter; but whoever *but* ~ blasphemes against the Holy Spirit *{the} Holy* will not have
1060 4012 1569 1059 1254 4005 1254 323 1059 1650 3836 41 4460 3836 41 2400 4024 2400
n.npf r.apn pl v.aas.3p r.nsm cj pl v.aas.3s p.a d.asn n.asn d.asn a.asn pl v.pai.3s

We had to use the tilde in various other situations as well. For example, δυναται οὐδείς means "no one is able" and the preceding οὐ ("not") strengthens the negation. It is a nuance difficult to bring into English.

ἔχει. 27 ἀλλ' οὐ δύναται οὐδεὶς εἰς τὴν οἰκίαν τοῦ ἰσχυροῦ εἰσελθὼν τὰ σκεύη
is coming to But ~ no one can *no one {into}* enter the house of the strong man *enter* and carry off *{the}* his possessions
2400 247 4024 4029 4029 1538 4029 1650 1656 3836 3864 3836 2708 1656 1395 1395 3836 899 5007
v.pai.3s cj pl v.ppi.3s a.nsm p.a d.asf n.asf d.gsm a.gsm pt.aa.nsm d.apn n.apn

μέν can indicate the first in a series and is often untranslated.

μὲν ἔπεσεν παρὰ τὴν ὁδόν, καὶ ἦλθεν τὰ πετεινὰ καὶ κατέφαγεν αὐτό. ↰ 5 καὶ ἄλλο ἔπεσεν ἐπὶ τὸ πετρῶδες
~ seed fell along the path, and birds came *{the} birds* and ate it up. *{and}* Other seed fell on *{the}* rocky
3525 4406 4123 3836 3847 2779 4374 2262 3836 4374 2779 2983 899 2983 2779 257 4406 2093 3836 4378
pl v.aai.3s p.a d.asf n.asf cj v.aai.3s d.npn n.npn cj v.aai.3s r.asn.3 cj r.nsn v.aai.3s p.a d.asn n.asn

10. Quotation marks in the English line. We decided not to paragraph the interlinear text in order to save space. However, we followed the standard procedure of using quotation marks in English as if the interlinear English translation were divided into paragraphs. If there is a series of paragraphs, all of which is a single citation, we start each paragraph with a double quotation mark and include the closing quotation mark only with the final paragraph.

11. Idioms. Idioms are collections of words that together mean something different than what the individuals words mean. εἰς ("into") τῶν ("the") αἰῶνα ("age") does not mean "into the age." It means "forever." The interlinear format simply fails at this point. If you know a little Greek, you should be able to see what we are doing; but if you don't know Greek, it will make little sense. Such is the limitation of an interlinear.

Matthew

NIV

Matthew

The Genealogy of Jesus the Messiah

1 This is the
genealogy[a] of
Jesus the Messiah[b]
the son of David,
the son of Abra-
ham:

[2]Abraham was
the father of Isaac,
Isaac the father of
Jacob, Jacob the
father of Judah and
his brothers, [3]Ju-
dah the father of
Perez and Zerah,
whose mother was
Tamar,Perez the
father of Hezron,
Hezron the father
of Ram, [4]Ram the
father of Ammin-
adab, Amminadab
the father of Nah-
shon, Nahshon the
father of Salmon,
[5]Salmon the father
of Boaz, whose
mother was Rahab,
Boaz the father
of Obed, whose
mother was Ruth,
Obed the father of
Jesse, [6]and Jesse
the father of King
David.

David was the
father of Solomon,
whose mother had
been Uriah's wife,
[7]Solomon the fa-
ther of Rehoboam,
Rehoboam the
father of Abijah,
Abijah the father
of Asa, [8]Asa the
father of Jehosha-
phat, Jehoshaphat
the father of Je-
horam, Jehoram
the father of Uz-

[a] 1 Or *is an account of the origin*
[b] 1 Or *Jesus Christ. Messiah* (Hebrew) and *Christ* (Greek) both mean *Anointed One*; also in verse 18.

1:1 βίβλος → γενέσεως Ἰησοῦ Χριστοῦ υἱοῦ Δαυὶδ υἱοῦ Ἀβραάμ.
The record of the origin of Jesus Christ, the son of David, the son of Abraham.
1047 1161 2652 5986 5626 1253 5626 11
n.nsf n.gsf n.gsm n.gsm n.gsm n.gsm n.gsm n.gsm

2 Ἀβραὰμ ἐγέννησεν τὸν Ἰσαάκ, Ἰσαὰκ δὲ ἐγέννησεν τὸν Ἰακώβ,
Abraham ⌊was the father of⌋ *{the}* Isaac, Isaac *{and}* ⌊was the father of⌋ *{the}* Jacob, and
11 1164 3836 2693 2693 1254 1164 3836 2609 1254
n.nsm v.aai.3s d.asm n.asm n.nsm cj v.aai.3s d.asm n.asm

Ἰακὼβ δὲ ἐγέννησεν τὸν Ἰούδαν καὶ τοὺς ἀδελφοὺς αὐτοῦ, 3 Ἰούδας δὲ
Jacob *and* ⌊was the father of⌋ *{the}* Judah and *{the}* his brothers, *his* Judah *{and}*
2609 1254 1164 3836 2683 2779 3836 899 81 899 2683 1254
n.nsm cj v.aai.3s d.asm n.asm cj d.apm n.apm r.gsm n.nsm cj

ἐγέννησεν τὸν Φάρες καὶ τὸν Ζάρα ἐκ τῆς Θαμάρ, Φάρες δὲ
⌊was the father of⌋ *{the}* Perez and *{the}* Zerah by *{the}* Tamar, Perez *{and}*
1164 3836 5756 2779 3836 2406 1666 3836 2500 5756 1254
v.aai.3s d.asm n.asm cj d.asm n.asm p.g d.gsf n.gsf n.nsm cj

ἐγέννησεν τὸν Ἑσρώμ, Ἑσρὼμ δὲ ἐγέννησεν τὸν Ἀράμ, 4 Ἀρὰμ δὲ
⌊was the father of⌋ *{the}* Hezron, and Hezron *and* ⌊was the father of⌋ *{the}* Ram, Ram *{and}*
1164 3836 2272 1254 2272 1254 1164 3836 730 730 1254
v.aai.3s d.asm n.asm n.nsm cj v.aai.3s d.asm n.asm n.nsm cj

ἐγέννησεν τὸν Ἀμιναδάβ, Ἀμιναδὰβ δὲ ἐγέννησεν τὸν Ναασσών,
⌊was the father of⌋ *{the}* Amminadab, Amminadab *{and}* ⌊was the father of⌋ *{the}* Nahshon, and
1164 3836 300 300 1254 1164 3836 3709 1254
v.aai.3s d.asm n.asm n.nsm cj v.aai.3s d.asm n.asm

Ναασσὼν δὲ ἐγέννησεν τὸν Σαλμών, 5 Σαλμὼν δὲ ἐγέννησεν τὸν Βόες
Nahshon *and* ⌊was the father of⌋ *{the}* Salmon, Salmon *{and}* ⌊was the father of⌋ *{the}* Boaz
3709 1254 1164 3836 4891 4891 1254 1164 3836 1067
n.nsm cj v.aai.3s d.asm n.asm n.nsm cj v.aai.3s d.asm n.asm

ἐκ τῆς Ῥαχάβ, Βόες δὲ ἐγέννησεν τὸν Ἰωβὴδ ἐκ τῆς Ῥούθ, Ἰωβὴδ δὲ
by *{the}* Rahab, Boaz *{and}* ⌊was the father of⌋ *{the}* Obed by *{the}* Ruth, and Obed *and*
1666 3836 4829 1067 1254 1164 3836 2725 1666 3836 4858 1254 2725 1254
p.g d.gsf n.gsf n.nsm cj v.aai.3s d.asm n.asm p.g d.gsf n.gsf n.nsm cj

ἐγέννησεν τὸν Ἰεσσαί, 6 Ἰεσσαὶ δὲ ἐγέννησεν τὸν Δαυὶδ τὸν
⌊was the father of⌋ *{the}* Jesse, and Jesse *and* ⌊was the father of⌋ *{the}* David the
1164 3836 2649 1254 2649 1254 1164 3836 1253 3836
v.aai.3s d.asm n.asm n.nsm cj v.aai.3s d.asm n.asm d.asm

βασιλέα. Δαυὶδ δὲ ἐγέννησεν τὸν Σολομῶνα ἐκ τῆς τοῦ Οὐρίου,
king. David *{and}* ⌊was the father of⌋ *{the}* Solomon by the wife of Uriah.
995 1253 1254 1164 3836 5048 1666 3836 3836 4043
n.asm n.nsm cj v.aai.3s d.asm n.asm p.g d.gsf d.gsm n.gsm

7 Σολομὼν δὲ ἐγέννησεν τὸν Ῥοβοάμ, Ῥοβοὰμ δὲ ἐγέννησεν τὸν
Solomon *{and}* ⌊was the father of⌋ *{the}* Rehoboam, Rehoboam *{and}* ⌊was the father of⌋ *{the}*
5048 1254 1164 3836 4850 4850 1254 1164 3836
n.nsm cj v.aai.3s d.asm n.asm n.nsm cj v.aai.3s d.asm

Ἀβιά, Ἀβιὰ δὲ ἐγέννησεν τὸν Ἀσάφ, 8 Ἀσὰφ δὲ ἐγέννησεν τὸν
Abijah, and Abijah *and* ⌊was the father of⌋ *{the}* Asaph, Asaph *{and}* ⌊was the father of⌋ *{the}*
7 1254 7 1254 1164 3836 811 811 1254 1164 3836
n.asm n.nsm cj v.aai.3s d.asm n.asm n.nsm cj v.aai.3s d.asm

NASB

The Genealogy of Jesus the Messiah

1:1 The record of
the genealogy of
Jesus the Messiah,
the son of David,
the son of Abra-
ham:
[2]Abraham was the
father of Isaac,
Isaac the father of
Jacob, and Jacob
the father of [a]Judah
and his brothers.
[3]Judah was the
father of Perez and
Zerah by Tamar,
Perez was the fa-
ther of Hezron, and
Hezron the father
of Ram. [4]Ram
was the father
of Amminadab,
Amminadab the
father of Nahshon,
and Nahshon the
father of Salmon.
[5]Salmon was the
father of Boaz by
Rahab, Boaz was
the father of Obed
by Ruth, and Obed
the father of Jesse.
[6]Jesse was the
father of David the
king.

David was the
father of Solomon
by [b]Bathsheba who
had been the wife
of Uriah. [7]Solomon
was the father of
Rehoboam, Reho-
boam the father of
Abijah, and Abijah
the father of Asa.
[8]Asa was the father
of Jehoshaphat,

[a] Gr *Judas;* names of people in the Old Testament are given in their Old Testament form
[b] Lit *her of Uriah*

NIV

ziah, 9 Uzziah the
father of Jotham,
Jotham the fa-
ther of Ahaz,
Ahaz the father of
Hezekiah, 10 Hez-
ekiah the father of
Manasseh, Manas-
seh the father of
Amon, Amon the
father of Josiah, 11
and Josiah the fa-
ther of Jeconiah[a]
and his brothers at
the time of the ex-
ile to Babylon.
12 After the ex-
ile to Babylon:
Jeconiah was the
father of Shealtiel,
Shealtiel the father
of Zerubbabel, 13
Zerubbabel the
father of Abihud,
Abihud the father
of Eliakim, Elia-
kim the father of
Azor, 14 Azor the
father of Zadok,
Zadok the father of
Akim, Akim the
father of Elihud, 15
Elihud the father
of Eleazar, Eleazar
the father of Mat-
than, Matthan the
father of Jacob, 16
and Jacob the fa-
ther of Joseph, the
husband of Mary,
and Mary was the
mother of Jesus
who is called the
Messiah.

[a] *11* That is, Jehoiachin; also in verse 12

Ἰωσαφάτ,	Ἰωσαφὰτ	δὲ	ἐγέννησεν	τὸν	Ἰωράμ,		Ἰωρὰμ	δὲ
Jehoshaphat,	Jehoshaphat	*{and}*	⌞was the father of⌟	*{the}*	Joram,	and	Joram	*and*
2734	2734	1254	1164	3836	2732	1254	2732	1254
n.asm	n.nsm	cj	v.aai.3s	d.asm	n.asm		n.nsm	cj

ἐγέννησεν	τὸν	Ὀζίαν,	9 Ὀζίας	δὲ	ἐγέννησεν	τὸν	Ἰωαθάμ,	Ἰωαθὰμ	δὲ
⌞was the father of⌟	*{the}*	Uzziah,	Uzziah	*{and}*	⌞was the father of⌟	*{the}*	Jotham,	Jotham	*{and}*
1164	3836	3852	3852	1254	1164	3836	2718	2718	1254
v.aai.3s	d.asm	n.asm	n.nsm	cj	v.aai.3s	d.asm	n.asm	n.nsm	cj

ἐγέννησεν	τὸν	Ἀχάζ,		Ἀχὰζ	δὲ	ἐγέννησεν	τὸν	Ἐζεκίαν,	10 Ἐζεκίας
⌞was the father of⌟	*{the}*	Ahaz,	and	Ahaz	*and*	⌞was the father of⌟	*{the}*	Hezekiah,	Hezekiah
1164	3836	937	1254	937	1254	1164	3836	1614	1614
v.aai.3s	d.asm	n.asm		n.nsm	cj	v.aai.3s	d.asm	n.asm	n.nsm

δὲ	ἐγέννησεν	τὸν	Μανασσῆ,	Μανασσῆς	δὲ	ἐγέννησεν	τὸν	Ἀμώς,	
{and}	⌞was the father of⌟	*{the}*	Manasseh,	Manasseh	*{and}*	⌞was the father of⌟	*{the}*	Amos,	and
1254	1164	3836	3442	3442	1254	1164	3836	322	1254
cj	v.aai.3s	d.asm	n.asm	n.nsm	cj	v.aai.3s	d.asm	n.asm	

Ἀμὼς	δὲ	ἐγέννησεν	τὸν	Ἰωσίαν,	11 Ἰωσίας	δὲ	ἐγέννησεν	τὸν	Ἰεχονίαν
Amos	*and*	⌞was the father of⌟	*{the}*	Josiah,	Josiah	*{and}*	⌞was the father of⌟	*{the}*	Jechoniah
322	1254	1164	3836	2739	2739	1254	1164	3836	2651
n.nsm	cj	v.aai.3s	d.asm	n.asm	n.nsm	cj	v.aai.3s	d.asm	n.asm

καὶ	τοὺς		ἀδελφοὺς	αὐτοῦ	ἐπὶ	τῆς	μετοικεσίας	Βαβυλῶνος.	12 μετὰ	δὲ
and	*{the}*	his	brothers	*his*	⌞at the time⌟	of the	deportation	to Babylon.	After	*{and}*
2779	3836	899	81	899	2093	3836	3578	956	3552	1254
cj	d.apm		n.apm	r.gsm	p.g	d.gsf	n.gsf	n.gsf	p.a	cj

τὴν	μετοικεσίαν	Βαβυλῶνος	Ἰεχονίας	ἐγέννησεν	τὸν	Σαλαθιήλ,		Σαλαθιὴλ
the	deportation	to Babylon,	Jechoniah	⌞was the father of⌟	*{the}*	Shealtiel,	and	Shealtiel
3836	3578	956	2651	1164	3836	4886	1254	4886
d.asf	n.asf	n.gsf	n.nsm	v.aai.3s	d.asm	n.asm		n.nsm

δὲ	ἐγέννησεν	τὸν	Ζοροβαβέλ,	13 Ζοροβαβὲλ	δὲ	ἐγέννησεν	τὸν	Ἀβιούδ,
and	⌞was the father of⌟	*{the}*	Zerubbabel,	Zerubbabel	*{and}*	⌞was the father of⌟	*{the}*	Abiud,
1254	1164	3836	2431	2431	1254	1164	3836	10
cj	v.aai.3s	d.asm	n.asm	n.nsm	cj	v.aai.3s	d.asm	n.asm

Ἀβιοὺδ	δὲ	ἐγέννησεν	τὸν	Ἐλιακίμ,		Ἐλιακὶμ	δὲ	ἐγέννησεν	τὸν
Abiud	*{and}*	⌞was the father of⌟	*{the}*	Eliakim,	and	Eliakim	*and*	⌞was the father of⌟	*{the}*
10	1254	1164	3836	1806	1254	1806	1254	1164	3836
n.nsm	cj	v.aai.3s	d.asm	n.asm		n.nsm	cj	v.aai.3s	d.asm

Ἀζώρ,	14 Ἀζὼρ	δὲ	ἐγέννησεν	τὸν	Σαδώκ,	Σαδὼκ	δὲ	ἐγέννησεν	τὸν
Azor,	Azor	*{and}*	⌞was the father of⌟	*{the}*	Zadok,	Zadok	*{and}*	⌞was the father of⌟	*{the}*
110	110	1254	1164	3836	4882	4882	1254	1164	3836
n.asm	n.nsm	cj	v.aai.3s	d.asm	n.asm	n.nsm	cj	v.aai.3s	d.asm

Ἀχίμ,		Ἀχὶμ	δὲ	ἐγέννησεν	τὸν	Ἐλιούδ,	15 Ἐλιοὺδ	δὲ	ἐγέννησεν
Achim,	and	Achim	*and*	⌞was the father of⌟	*{the}*	Eliud,	Eliud	*{and}*	⌞was the father of⌟
943	1254	943	1254	1164	3836	1809	1809	1254	1164
n.asm		n.nsm	cj	v.aai.3s	d.asm	n.asm	n.nsm	cj	v.aai.3s

τὸν	Ἐλεάζαρ,	Ἐλεάζαρ	δὲ	ἐγέννησεν	τὸν	Ματθάν,		Ματθὰν	δὲ
{the}	Eleazar,	Eleazar	*{and}*	⌞was the father of⌟	*{the}*	Matthan,	and	Matthan	*and*
3836	1789	1789	1254	1164	3836	3474	1254	3474	1254
d.asm	n.asm	n.nsm	cj	v.aai.3s	d.asm	n.asm		n.nsm	cj

ἐγέννησεν	τὸν	Ἰακώβ,	16 Ἰακὼβ	δὲ	ἐγέννησεν	τὸν	Ἰωσὴφ	τὸν	ἄνδρα
⌞was the father of⌟	*{the}*	Jacob,	Jacob	*{and}*	⌞was the father of⌟	*{the}*	Joseph	the	husband
1164	3836	2609	2609	1254	1164	3836	2737	3836	467
v.aai.3s	d.asm	n.asm	n.nsm	cj	v.aai.3s	d.asm	n.asm	d.asm	n.asm

Μαρίας,	ἐξ	ἧς		ἐγεννήθη	Ἰησοῦς	ὁ	λεγόμενος	χριστός.	17	πᾶσαι	οὖν
of Mary,	from	whom	Jesus	was born,	*Jesus*	who	is called	Christ.	So	all	*So*
3451	1666	4005	2652	1164	2652	3836	3306	5986	4036	4246	4036
n.gsf	p.g	r.gsf		v.api.3s	n.nsm	d.nsm	pt.pp.nsm	n.nsm		a.npf	cj

NASB

Jehoshaphat the fa-
ther of Joram, and
Joram the father
of Uzziah. 9Uzziah
was the father of
Jotham, Jotham the
father of Ahaz, and
Ahaz the father of
Hezekiah. 10Heze-
kiah was the father
of Manasseh, Ma-
nasseh the father of
Amon, and Amon
the father of Josiah.
11Josiah became the
father of Jeconiah
and his brothers,
at the time of the
deportation to
Babylon.
12After the
deportation to
Babylon: Jeconiah
became the father
of Shealtiel, and
Shealtiel the father
of Zerubbabel.
13Zerubbabel was
the father of Abi-
hud, Abihud the
father of Eliakim,
and Eliakim the
father of Azor.
14Azor was the
father of Zadok,
Zadok the father of
Achim, and Achim
the father of Eliud.
15Eliud was the
father of Eleazar,
Eleazar the father
of Matthan, and
Matthan the father
of Jacob. 16Jacob
was the father of
Joseph the husband
of Mary, by whom
Jesus was born,
who is called the
Messiah.

NIV

[17]Thus there were
fourteen genera-
tions in all from
Abraham to David,
fourteen from Da-
vid to the exile to
Babylon, and four-
teen from the exile
to the Messiah.

Joseph Accepts Jesus as His Son

[18]This is how
the birth of Jesus
the Messiah came
about[a]: His mother
Mary was pledged
to be married to
Joseph, but before
they came togeth-
er, she was found
to be pregnant
through the Holy
Spirit. [19]Because
Joseph her hus-
band was faithful
to the law, and
yet[b]did not want
to expose her to
public disgrace, he
had in mind to di-
vorce her quietly.
[20]But after he
had considered
this, an angel of
the Lord appeared
to him in a dream
and said, "Joseph
son of David, do
not be afraid to
take Mary home as
your wife, because
what is conceived
in her is from the
Holy Spirit. [21]She
will give birth to a
son, and you are to
give him the name
Jesus,[c] because
he will save his
people from their
sins."
[22]All this took
place to fulfill
what the Lord had
said through the
prophet: [23]"The

[a] 18 Or *The origin of Jesus the Messiah was like this*
[b] 19 Or *was a righteous man and*
[c] 21 *Jesus* is the Greek form of *Joshua,* which means *the* LORD *saves.*

αἱ γενεαὶ ἀπὸ Ἀβραὰμ ἕως Δαυὶδ γενεαὶ δεκατέσσαρες, καὶ ἀπὸ
the generations from Abraham to David were fourteen generations, *fourteen* and from
3836 1155 608 11 2401 1253 1280 1155 1280 2779 608
d.npf n.npf p.g n.gsm p.g n.gsm n.npf a.npf cj p.g

Δαυὶδ ἕως τῆς μετοικεσίας Βαβυλῶνος γενεαὶ δεκατέσσαρες, καὶ ἀπὸ τῆς
David to the deportation to Babylon fourteen generations, *fourteen* and from the
1253 2401 3836 3578 956 1280 1155 1280 2779 608 3836
n.gsm p.g d.gsf n.gsf n.gsf n.npf a.npf cj p.g d.gsf

μετοικεσίας Βαβυλῶνος ἕως τοῦ Χριστοῦ γενεαὶ δεκατέσσαρες. [18]
deportation to Babylon to the Christ fourteen generations. *fourteen* Now
3578 956 2401 3836 5986 1280 1155 1280 1254
n.gsf n.gsf p.g d.gsm n.gsm n.npf a.npf

τοῦ δὲ Ἰησοῦ Χριστοῦ ἡ γένεσις οὕτως ἦν. →
the birth of *Now* Jesus Christ *the birth* took place ⌊in this way:⌋ *took place* When his
3836 1161 3836 1254 2652 5986 3836 1161 1639 1639 4048 1639 899
d.gsm cj n.gsm n.gsm d.nsf n.nsf adv v.iai.3s

μνηστευθείσης τῆς μητρὸς αὐτοῦ Μαρίας τῷ Ἰωσήφ, ⌊πρὶν ἢ⌋
mother Mary was pledged in marriage *{the} mother his Mary* to Joseph, before
3613 3451 3650 3836 3613 899 3451 3836 2737 4570 2445
pt.ap.gsf d.gsf n.gsf r.gsm n.gsf d.dsm n.dsm cj pl

συνελθεῖν αὐτοὺς εὑρέθη ἐν γαστρὶ ἔχουσα ἐκ
they had come together, *they* ⌊she was found⌋ to be with child *to be* by the Holy
899 5302 899 2351 2400 2400 1877 1143 2400 1666 41
f.aa r.apm v.api.3s p.d n.dsf pt.pa.nsf p.g

πνεύματος ἁγίου. [19] Ἰωσὴφ δὲ ὁ ἀνὴρ αὐτῆς, δίκαιος
Spirit. *Holy* Because her husband Joseph *{and} {the} husband her* was a just man
4460 41 899 467 2737 1254 3836 467 899 1639 1465
n.gsn a.gsn n.nsm cj d.nsm n.nsm r.gsf a.nsm

ὢν καὶ ⌊μὴ θέλων⌋ αὐτὴν δειγματίσαι, ἐβουλήθη
was and unwilling to disgrace her *to disgrace in public* in public, he planned
1639 2779 3590 2527 1258 1258 899 1258 1258 1258 1089
pt.pa.nsm cj pl pt.pa.nsm r.asf f.aa v.api.3s

λάθρα ἀπολῦσαι αὐτήν. [20] ↱ ταῦτα δὲ αὐτοῦ
quietly to release her quietly. But as he pondered this, *But he*
3277 668 899 3277 1254 1926 899 1926 4047 1254 899
adv f.aa r.asf r.apn cj r.gsm

ἐνθυμηθέντος ἰδοὺ ἄγγελος → κυρίου κατ' ὄναρ ἐφάνη αὐτῷ
pondered behold, an angel of the Lord appeared to him in a dream, *appeared to him*
1926 2627 34 3261 5743 899 899 2848 3941 5743 899
pt.ap.gsm j n.nsm n.gsm p.a n.asn v.api.3s r.dsm

λέγων, Ἰωσὴφ υἱὸς Δαυίδ, ↱ μὴ φοβηθῇς παραλαβεῖν Μαρίαν τὴν ↱
saying, "Joseph, son of David, do not be afraid to take Mary *{the}* as your
3306 2737 5626 1253 5828 3590 5828 4161 3451 3836 1222 5148
pt.pa.nsm n.vsm n.nsm n.gsm pl v.aps.2s f.aa n.asf d.asf

γυναῖκά σου· τὸ γὰρ ↰ ἐν αὐτῇ γεννηθὲν ἐκ
wife; *your* for that *for* which has been conceived in her *has been conceived* is by
1222 5148 1142 3836 1142 3836 1164 1164 1164 1877 899 1164 1639 1666
n.asf r.gs.2 d.nsn cj p.d r.dsf pt.ap.nsn p.g

πνεύματός ἐστιν ἁγίου. [21] τέξεται δὲ υἱόν, καὶ καλέσεις τὸ
the Holy Spirit. *is Holy* And ⌊she will bear⌋ *And* a son, and ⌊you are to call⌋ *{the}*
41 4460 1639 41 1254 5503 1254 5626 2779 2813 3836
n.gsn v.pai.3s a.gsn v.fmi.3s cj n.asm cj v.fai.2s d.asn

ὄνομα αὐτοῦ Ἰησοῦν· αὐτὸς γὰρ σώσει τὸν λαὸν αὐτοῦ ἀπὸ τῶν
{name} him Jesus, for he *for* will save *{the}* his people *his* from *{the}* their
3950 899 2652 1142 899 1142 5392 3836 899 3295 899 608 3836 899
n.asn r.gsm n.asm r.nsm cj v.fai.3s d.asm n.asm r.gsm.3 p.g d.gpf

ἁμαρτιῶν αὐτῶν. [22] τοῦτο δὲ ὅλον γέγονεν ἵνα πληρωθῇ τὸ ῥηθὲν
sins." *their* All this *{and} All* took place so that *might be fulfilled* what was spoken
281 899 3910 4047 1254 3910 1181 2671 4444 3836 3306
n.gpf r.gpm.3 r.nsn cj a.nsn v.rai.3s cj v.aps.3s d.nsn pt.ap.nsn

ὑπὸ κυρίου διὰ τοῦ προφήτου λέγοντος, [23] ἰδοὺ ἡ
by the Lord through the prophet might be fulfilled: *{saying}* "Behold, the
5679 3261 1328 3836 4737 4444 4444 4444 3306 2627 3836
p.g n.gsm p.g d.gsm n.gsm pt.pa.gsm j d.nsf

NASB

[17]So all the
generations from
Abraham to Da-
vid are fourteen
generations; from
David to the depor-
tation to Babylon,
fourteen genera-
tions; and from the
deportation to
Babylon to the
Messiah, fourteen
generations.

Conception and Birth of Jesus

[18]Now the birth of
Jesus Christ was
as follows: when
His mother Mary
had been betrothed
to Joseph, before
they came together
she was found to
be with child by
the Holy Spirit.
[19]And Joseph her
husband, being
a righteous man
and not wanting
to disgrace her,
planned [a]to send
her away secretly.
[20]But when he had
considered this,
behold, an angel of
the Lord appeared
to him in a dream,
saying, "Joseph,
son of David, do
not be afraid to
take Mary as your
wife; for the Child
who has been
[b]conceived in her is
of the Holy Spirit.
[21]She will bear a
Son; and you shall
call His name
Jesus, for He will
save His people
from their sins."
[22]Now all this took
place to fulfill what
was spoken by the
Lord through the
prophet: [23]"BEHOLD,

[a] Or *to divorce her*
[b] Lit *begotten*

NIV

virgin will con-
ceive and give
birth to a son,
and they will call
him Immanuel"[a]
(which means
"God with us").
24 When Joseph
woke up, he did
what the angel
of the Lord had
commanded him
and took Mary
home as his wife.
25 But he did not
consummate their
marriage until she
gave birth to a son.
And he gave him
the name Jesus.

The Magi Visit the Messiah

2 After Jesus
was born in
Bethlehem in Ju-
dea, during the
time of King Her-
od, Magi[b] from the
east came to Jeru-
salem 2 and asked,
"Where is the one
who has been born
king of the Jews?
We saw his star
when it rose and
have come to wor-
ship him."
3 When King Her-
od heard this he
was disturbed, and
all Jerusalem with
him. 4 When he had
called together all
the people's chief
priests and teach-
ers of the law, he
asked them where
the Messiah was
to be born. 5 "In
Bethlehem in Ju-
dea," they replied,
"for this is what
the prophet has
written:

6 " 'But you,
Bethlehem,
in the land
of Judah,
are by no
means least
among the
rulers of
Judah;
for out of you
will come a

[a] 23 Isaiah 7:14
[b] 1 Traditionally *wise men*

παρθένος ⌞ἐν γαστρὶ ἕξει⌟ καὶ τέξεται υἱόν, καὶ καλέσουσιν τὸ
virgin shall conceive and ⌞give birth to⌟ a son, and they shall call *{the}*
4221 1877 1143 2400 2779 5503 5626 2779 2813 3836
n.nsf p.d n.dsf v.fai.3s cj v.fmi.3s n.asm cj v.fai.3p d.asn

ὄνομα αὐτοῦ Ἐμμανουήλ, ὅ ἐστιν μεθερμηνευόμενον μεθ' ἡμῶν ὁ θεός.
{name} him Emmanuel," which is translated "God is with us." *{the}* *God*
3950 899 1842 4005 1639 3493 2536 3552 7005 3836 2536
n.asn r.gsm.3 n.asm r.nsn v.pai.3s pt.pp.nsn p.g r.gp.1 d.nsm n.nsm

24 → ἐγερθεὶς δὲ ὁ Ἰωσὴφ ἀπὸ τοῦ ὕπνου ἐποίησεν ὡς
When Joseph arose *{and}* *{the}* *Joseph* from *{the}* sleep, he did what the angel of
2737 1586 1254 3836 2737 608 3836 5678 4472 6055 34 3261
pt.ap.nsm cj d.nsm n.nsm p.g d.gsm n.gsm v.aai.3s cj

προσέταξεν αὐτῷ ὁ ἄγγελος κυρίου καὶ παρέλαβεν τὴν γυναῖκα
the Lord had told him, *{the}* *angel* *of Lord* and he took her as *{the}* his wife,
3261 4705 899 3836 34 3261 2779 4161 3836 899 1222
v.aai.3s r.dsm.3 d.nsm n.nsm n.gsm cj v.aai.3s d.asf n.asf

αὐτοῦ, 25 καὶ ↱ ↱ οὐκ ἐγίνωσκεν αὐτὴν ⌞ἕως οὗ⌟ ἔτεκεν
his but he had no ⌞marital relations with⌟ her until ⌞she had given birth to⌟ a
899 2779 1182 1182 4024 1182 899 2401 4005 5503
r.gsm.3 cj adv v.iai.3s r.asf.3 p.g r.gsm v.aai.3s

υἱόν·[a] καὶ ἐκάλεσεν τὸ ὄνομα αὐτοῦ Ἰησοῦν.
son; and he called *{the}* *{name}* him Jesus.
5626 2779 2813 3836 3950 899 2652
n.asm cj v.aai.3s d.asn n.asn r.gsm.3 n.asm

2:1 τοῦ δὲ ↱ Ἰησοῦ γεννηθέντος ἐν Βηθλέεμ τῆς Ἰουδαίας ἐν ἡμέραις
{the} *{and}* After Jesus was born in Bethlehem of Judea in the days
3836 1254 1164 2652 1164 1877 1033 3836 2677 1877 2465
d.gsm cj n.gsm pt.ap.gsm p.d n.dsf d.gsf n.gsf p.d n.dpf

Ἡρῴδου τοῦ βασιλέως, ἰδοὺ μάγοι ἀπὸ ἀνατολῶν παρεγένοντο εἰς
of Herod the king, behold, wise men from the East came to
2476 3836 995 2627 3407 608 424 4134 1650
n.gsm d.gsm n.gsm j n.npm p.g n.gpf v.ami.3p p.a

Ἱεροσόλυμα 2 λέγοντες, ποῦ ἐστιν ὁ τεχθεὶς βασιλεὺς τῶν
Jerusalem, saying, "Where is the ⌞one who has been born⌟ king of the
2642 3306 4544 1639 3836 5503 995 3836
n.apn pt.pa.npm adv v.pai.3s d.nsm pt.ap.nsm n.nsm d.gpm

Ἰουδαίων; εἴδομεν γὰρ αὐτοῦ τὸν ἀστέρα ἐν τῇ ἀνατολῇ καὶ ἤλθομεν
Jews? For we saw *For* his *{the}* star at its rising and have come
2681 1142 1625 1142 899 3836 843 1877 3836 424 2779 2262
a.gpm v.aai.1p cj r.gsm.3 d.asm n.asm p.d d.dsf n.dsf cj v.aai.1p

προσκυνῆσαι αὐτῷ. 3 → ἀκούσας δὲ ὁ βασιλεὺς Ἡρῴδης
to worship him." Now when king Herod heard this, *Now* *{the}* *king* *Herod*
4686 899 1254 995 2476 201 1254 3836 995 2476
f.aa r.dsm.3 pt.aa.nsm cj d.nsm n.nsm n.nsm

ἐταράχθη καὶ πᾶσα Ἱεροσόλυμα μετ' αὐτοῦ, 4 καὶ συναγαγὼν πάντας τοὺς
he was troubled, and all Jerusalem with him; and gathering all the
5429 2779 4246 2642 3552 899 2779 5251 4246 3836
v.api.3s cj a.nsf n.nsf p.g r.gsm.3 cj pt.aa.nsm a.apm d.apm

ἀρχιερεῖς καὶ γραμματεῖς τοῦ λαοῦ ἐπυνθάνετο παρ' αὐτῶν ποῦ ὁ χριστὸς
ruling priests and scribes of the people, he inquired of them where the Messiah
797 2779 1208 3836 3295 4785 4123 899 4544 3836 5986
n.apm cj n.apm d.gsm n.gsm v.imi.3s p.g r.gpm.3 adv d.nsm n.nsm

γεννᾶται. 5 οἱ δὲ εἶπαν αὐτῷ, ἐν Βηθλέεμ τῆς Ἰουδαίας· οὕτως γὰρ
was to be born. They *{and}* told him, "In Bethlehem of Judea, for thus *for*
1164 3836 1254 3306 899 1877 1033 3836 2677 1142 4048 1142
v.ppi.3s d.npm cj v.aai.3p r.dsm.3 p.d n.dsf d.gsf n.gsf adv cj

γέγραπται διὰ τοῦ προφήτου, 6 καὶ σὺ Βηθλέεμ, γῆ Ἰούδα,
it is written by the prophet: 'And you, Bethlehem, in the land of Judah, are by
1211 1328 3836 4737 2779 5148 1033 1178 2683 1639
v.rpi.3s p.g d.gsm n.gsm cj r.ns.2 n.vsf n.vsf n.gsm

οὐδαμῶς ἐλαχίστη εἶ ἐν τοῖς ἡγεμόσιν Ἰούδα· ἐκ σοῦ γὰρ ἐξελεύσεται
no means least *are* among the rulers of Judah; for from you *for* will come a
4027 1788 1639 1877 3836 2450 2683 1142 1666 5148 1142 2002
adv a.nsf.s v.pai.2s p.d d.dpm n.dpm n.gsm p.g r.gs.2 cj v.fmi.3s

[a] αὐτῆς τὸν πρωτότοκον included by TR after υἱόν.

NASB

THE VIRGIN SHALL
BE WITH CHILD
AND SHALL BEAR
A SON, AND THEY
SHALL CALL HIS
NAME IMMANUEL,"
which translated
means, "GOD WITH
US." 24 And Joseph
awoke from his
sleep and did as the
angel of the Lord
commanded him,
and took *Mary* as
his wife, 25 [a]but kept
her a virgin until
she gave birth to a
Son; and he called
His name Jesus.

The Visit of the Magi

2:1 Now after Jesus
was born in Beth-
lehem of Judea in
the days of Herod
the king, [b]magi
from the east ar-
rived in Jerusalem,
saying, 2 "Where is
He who has been
born King of the
Jews? For we saw
His star in the east
and have come
to worship Him."
3 When Herod the
king heard *this,* he
was troubled, and
all Jerusalem with
him. 4 Gathering to-
gether all the chief
priests and scribes
of the people, he
inquired of them
where the Messiah
was to be born.
5 They said to him,
"In Bethlehem of
Judea; for this is
what has been writ-
ten by the prophet:
6 ' AND YOU,
BETHLEHEM,
LAND OF JU-
DAH,
ARE BY NO
MEANS LEAST
AMONG THE
LEADERS OF
JUDAH;
FOR OUT OF
YOU SHALL
COME FORTH A
RULER

[a] Lit *and was not knowing her*
[b] A caste of wise men specializing in astronomy, astrology, and natural science

NIV

ruler
who will
shepherd
my people
Israel.'[a] "

[7]Then Herod
called the Magi
secretly and found
out from them the
exact time the star
had appeared. [8]He
sent them to Beth-
lehem and said,
"Go and search
carefully for the
child. As soon as
you find him, re-
port to me, so that
I too may go and
worship him."
[9]After they had
heard the king,
they went on their
way, and the star
they had seen
when it rose went
ahead of them un-
til it stopped over
the place where the
child was. [10]When
they saw the star,
they were over-
joyed. [11]On com-
ing to the house,
they saw the child
with his mother
Mary, and they
bowed down and
worshiped him.
Then they opened
their treasures
and presented him
with gifts of gold,
frankincense and
myrrh. [12]And hav-
ing been warned
in a dream not to
go back to Herod,
they returned to
their country by
another route.

The Escape to Egypt

[13]When they had
gone, an angel
of the Lord ap-
peared to Joseph
in a dream. "Get
up," he said, "take
the child and his
mother and escape
to Egypt. Stay
there

ἡγούμενος, ὅστις ποιμανεῖ τὸν λαόν μου τὸν Ἰσραήλ. [7]τότε Ἡρῴδης λάθρᾳ
ruler who will shepherd {the} my people my {the} Israel.'" Then Herod secretly
2451 4015 4477 3836 1609 3295 1609 3836 2702 5538 2476 3277
pt.pm.nsm r.nsm v.fai.3s d.asm n.asm r.gs.1 d.asm n.asm adv n.nsm adv

καλέσας τοὺς μάγους ἠκρίβωσεν παρ' αὐτῶν ↰ τὸν χρόνον τοῦ
called for the magi and found out from them exactly what {the} time the star {the}
2813 3836 3407 208 4123 899 208 3836 5989 843 3836
pt.aa.nsm d.apm n.apm v.aai.3s p.g r.gpm.3 d.asm n.asm d.gsm

φαινομένου ἀστέρος, [8]καὶ πέμψας αὐτοὺς εἰς Βηθλέεμ εἶπεν, πορευθέντες
had appeared. star Then he sent them to Bethlehem, saying, "Go and
5743 843 2779 4287 899 1650 1033 3306 4513
pt.pm.gsm n.gsm cj pt.aa.nsm r.apm.3 p.a n.asf v.aai.3s pt.ap.npm

ἐξετάσατε ἀκριβῶς περὶ τοῦ παιδίου· ἐπὰν δὲ εὕρητε, ἀπαγγείλατέ
search diligently for the child; and when and ⌞you have found⌟ him, report back
2004 209 4309 3836 4086 1254 2054 1254 2351 550
v.aam.2p adv p.g d.gsn n.gsn cj cj v.aas.2p v.aam.2p

μοι, ὅπως κἀγὼ ἐλθὼν προσκυνήσω αὐτῷ. [9]οἱ δὲ ἀκούσαντες τοῦ
to me, so that I also may go and worship him." they And ⌞having listened to⌟ the
1609 3968 2743 2262 4686 899 3836 1254 201 3836
r.ds.1 cj crasis pt.aa.nsm v.aas.1s r.dsm.3 d.npm cj pt.aa.npm d.gsm

βασιλέως ἐπορεύθησαν καὶ ἰδοὺ ὁ ἀστήρ, ὃν εἶδον ἐν τῇ
king, they ⌞continued their journey,⌟ and {behold} the star that ⌞they had seen⌟ in its
995 3836 4513 2779 2627 3836 843 4005 1625 1877 3836
n.gsm v.api.3p cj j d.nsm n.nsm r.asm v.aai.3p p.d d.dsf

ἀνατολῇ, προῆγεν αὐτούς, ἕως ἐλθὼν ἐστάθη ἐπάνω οὗ
rising went before them until {having arrived} it stopped over the place where the child
424 4575 899 2401 2262 2705 2062 4023 3836 4086
n.dsf v.iai.3s r.apm.3 cj pt.aa.nsm v.api.3s p.g adv

ἦν τὸ παιδίον. [10]ἰδόντες δὲ τὸν ἀστέρα ἐχάρησαν
was. the child And ⌞when they caught sight of⌟ And the star, they rejoiced
1639 3836 4086 1254 1625 1254 3836 843 5897
v.iai.3s d.nsn n.nsn pt.aa.npm cj d.asm n.asm v.api.3p

χαρὰν μεγάλην σφόδρα. [11]καὶ ⌞ἐλθόντες εἰς⌟ τὴν οἰκίαν
exceedingly with great joy. great exceedingly {and} Upon entering the house
5379 3489 5915 3489 5379 2779 2262 1650 3836 3864
n.asf a.asf adv cj pt.aa.npm p.a d.asf n.asf

εἶδον τὸ παιδίον μετὰ Μαρίας τῆς μητρὸς αὐτοῦ, καὶ πεσόντες
they saw the child with Mary {the} his mother, his and falling to their knees
1625 3836 4086 3552 3451 3836 899 3613 899 2779 4406
v.aai.3p d.asn n.asn p.g n.gsf d.gsf n.gsf r.gsm.3 cj pt.aa.npm

προσεκύνησαν αὐτῷ καὶ ἀνοίξαντες τοὺς θησαυροὺς αὐτῶν προσήνεγκαν αὐτῷ
they worshiped him. Then opening {the} their treasure chests, their they presented him
4686 899 2779 487 3836 899 2565 899 4712 899
v.aai.3p r.dsm.3 cj pt.aa.npm d.apm n.apm r.gpm.3 v.aai.3p r.dsm.3

↰ δῶρα, χρυσὸν καὶ λίβανον καὶ σμύρναν. [12]καὶ χρηματισθέντες κατ' ὄναρ
with gifts, gold and frankincense and myrrh. And being warned in a dream
4712 1565 5996 2779 3337 2779 5043 2779 5976 2848 3941
n.apn n.asm cj n.asm cj n.asf cj pt.ap.npm p.a n.asn

μὴ ἀνακάμψαι πρὸς Ἡρῴδην, δι' ἄλλης ὁδοῦ
not to return to Herod, they left for their own country by another way.
3590 366 4639 2476 432 432 1650 899 899 6001 1328 257 3847
pl f.aa p.a n.asm p.g r.gsf n.gsf

ἀνεχώρησαν εἰς τὴν χώραν αὐτῶν. [13]→ ἀναχωρησάντων δὲ αὐτῶν ἰδοὺ
they left for {the} country their own After they had gone, {and} they {behold}
432 1650 3836 6001 899 899 432 1254 899 2627
v.aai.3p p.a d.asf n.asf r.gpm.3 pt.aa.gpm cj r.gpm.3 j

ἄγγελος → κυρίου φαίνεται κατ' ὄναρ τῷ Ἰωσὴφ λέγων, ἐγερθεὶς παράλαβε
an angel of the Lord appeared in a dream to Joseph, saying, "Rise, take
34 3261 5743 2848 3941 3836 2737 3306 1586 4161
n.nsm n.gsm v.pmi.3s p.a n.asn d.dsm n.dsm pt.pa.nsm pt.ap.nsm v.aam.2s

τὸ παιδίον καὶ τὴν μητέρα αὐτοῦ καὶ φεῦγε εἰς Αἴγυπτον καὶ ἴσθι ἐκεῖ
the child and {the} his mother, his {and} flee to Egypt, and stay there
3836 4086 2779 3836 899 3613 899 2779 5771 1650 131 2779 1639 1695
d.asn n.asn cj d.asf n.asf r.gsm.3 cj v.pam.2s p.a n.asf cj v.pam.2s adv

NASB

WHO WILL
SHEPHERD
MY PEOPLE
ISRAEL.'"
[7]Then Herod
secretly called the
magi and deter-
mined from them
the exact time
the star appeared.
[8]And he sent them
to Bethlehem and
said, "Go and
search carefully
for the Child; and
when you have
found *Him,* report
to me, so that I
too may come and
worship Him."
[9]After hearing the
king, they went
their way; and
the star, which
they had seen in
the east, went on
before them until
it came and stood
over *the place*
where the Child
was. [10]When they
saw the star, they
rejoiced exceed-
ingly with great
joy. [11]After coming
into the house they
saw the Child with
Mary His mother;
and they fell to
the ground and
worshiped Him.
Then, opening
their treasures, they
presented to Him
gifts of gold, frank-
incense, and myrrh.
[12]And having been
warned *by God* in a
dream not to return
to Herod, the magi
left for their own
country by another
way.

The Flight to Egypt

[13]Now when they
had gone, behold,
an angel of the
Lord *appeared to
Joseph in a dream
and said, "Get up!
Take the Child and
His mother and
flee to Egypt, and
remain there until I
tell you; for Herod

[a] 6 Micah 5:2,4

NIV

until I tell you, for
Herod is going to
search for the child
to kill him."
14 So he got up,
took the child and
his mother dur-
ing the night and
left for Egypt,
15 where he stayed
until the death of
Herod. And so
was fulfilled what
the Lord had said
through the proph-
et: "Out of Egypt I
called my son."[a]
16 When Herod
realized that he
had been outwitted
by the Magi, he
was furious, and
he gave orders to
kill all the boys
in Bethlehem and
its vicinity who
were two years
old and under, in
accordance with
the time he had
learned from the
Magi. 17 Then what
was said through
the prophet Jere-
miah was fulfilled:

18 "A voice is
heard in
Ramah,
weeping
and great
mourning,
Rachel weeping
for her
children
and refusing
to be
comforted,
because they
are no
more."[b]

The Return to Nazareth

19 After Herod
died, an angel of
the Lord appeared
in a dream to Jo-
seph in Egypt
20 and said, "Get
up, take the child
and his mother
and go to the land
of Israel, for those
who were trying to
take the child's life
are dead."
21 So he got up,

⌊ἕως ἂν⌋ εἴπω σοι, μέλλει γὰρ Ἡρῴδης ζητεῖν τὸ παιδίον τοῦ
until I tell you; for Herod is going {for} {Herod} ⌊to search for⌋ the child {the}
2401 323 3306 5148 1142 2476 3516 1142 2476 2426 3836 4086 3836
cj pl v.aas.1s r.ds.2 v.pai.3s cj n.nsm f.pa d.asn n.asn d.gsn

ἀπολέσαι αὐτό. 14 ὁ δὲ ἐγερθεὶς παρέλαβεν τὸ παιδίον καὶ τὴν μητέρα
to destroy him." So he {So} got up, took the child and {the} his mother
660 899 1254 3836 1254 1586 4161 3836 4086 2779 3836 899 3613
f.aa r.asn.3 d.nsm cj pt.ap.nsm v.aai.3s d.asn n.asn cj d.asf n.asf

αὐτοῦ νυκτὸς καὶ ἀνεχώρησεν εἰς Αἴγυπτον, 15 καὶ ἦν ἐκεῖ ἕως τῆς τελευτῆς
{his} by night, and left for Egypt, and was there until the death
899 3816 2779 432 1650 131 2779 1639 1695 2401 3836 5463
r.gsm.3 n.gsf cj v.aai.3s p.a n.asf cj v.iai.3s adv p.g d.gsf n.gsf

Ἡρῴδου· ἵνα πληρωθῇ τὸ ῥηθὲν ὑπὸ κυρίου διὰ τοῦ προφήτου
of Herod. This was to fulfill what was spoken by the Lord through the prophet:
2476 2671 4444 3836 3306 5679 3261 1328 3836 4737
n.gsm cj v.aps.3s d.nsn pt.ap.nsn p.g n.gsm p.g d.gsm n.gsm

λέγοντος, ἐξ Αἰγύπτου ἐκάλεσα τὸν υἱόν μου. 16 τότε Ἡρῴδης ἰδὼν
{saying} "Out of Egypt I have called {the} my son." {my} Then Herod, ⌊when he saw⌋
3306 1666 131 2813 3836 1609 5626 1609 5538 2476 1625
pt.pa.gsm p.g n.gsf v.aai.1s d.asm n.asm r.gs.1 adv n.nsm pt.aa.nsm

ὅτι ἐνεπαίχθη ὑπὸ τῶν μάγων ⌊ἐθυμώθη λίαν,⌋ καὶ ↱ ἀποστείλας
that ⌊he had been tricked⌋ by the wise men, became furious; and he sent and
4022 1850 5679 3836 3407 2597 3336 2779 359 690
cj v.api.3s p.g d.gpm n.gpm v.api.3s adv cj pt.aa.nsm

ἀνεῖλεν πάντας τοὺς παῖδας τοὺς ἐν Βηθλέεμ καὶ ἐν πᾶσι τοῖς ὁρίοις
killed all the male children {the} in Bethlehem and in all {the} her regions
359 4246 3836 4090 3836 1877 1033 2779 1877 4246 3836 899 3990
v.aai.3s a.apm d.apm n.apm d.apm p.d n.dsf cj p.d a.dpn d.dpn n.dpn

αὐτῆς ἀπὸ διετοῦς καὶ κατωτέρω, κατὰ τὸν χρόνον ὃν
{her} who were {from} ⌊two years old⌋ or under, ⌊according to⌋ the time that
899 608 1453 2779 3006 2848 3836 5989 4005
r.gsf.3 p.g a.gsm cj adv.c p.a d.asm n.asm r.asm

ἠκρίβωσεν παρὰ τῶν μάγων. 17 τότε ἐπληρώθη τὸ ῥηθὲν διὰ
he had determined from the wise men. Then was fulfilled what was spoken by the prophet
208 4123 3836 3407 5538 4444 3836 3306 1328 3836 4737
v.aai.3s p.g d.gpm n.gpm adv v.api.3s d.nsn pt.ap.nsn p.g

Ἰερεμίου τοῦ προφήτου λέγοντος, 18 φωνὴ ἐν Ῥαμὰ ἠκούσθη,
Jeremiah: {the} {prophet} {saying} "A voice was heard in Ramah, {was heard}
2635 3836 4737 3306 5889 201 201 1877 4821 201
n.gsm d.gsm n.gsm pt.pa.gsm n.nsf p.d n.dsf v.api.3s

κλαυθμὸς καὶ ὀδυρμὸς πολύς· Ῥαχὴλ κλαίουσα τὰ τέκνα αὐτῆς, καὶ
weeping and loud lamentation, {loud} Rachel weeping for {the} her children; {her} {and}
3088 2779 4498 3851 4498 4830 3081 3836 899 5451 899 2779
n.nsm cj n.nsm a.nsm n.nsf pt.pa.nsf d.apn n.apn r.gsf.3 cj

⌊οὐκ ἤθελεν⌋ παρακληθῆναι, ὅτι οὐκ εἰσίν. 19 →
she refused to be comforted, because they were no more." {they were} But when Herod
4024 2527 4151 4022 1639 1639 4024 1639 1254 2476
adv v.iai.3s f.ap cj adv v.pai.3p

τελευτήσαντος δὲ τοῦ Ἡρῴδου ἰδοὺ ἄγγελος → κυρίου φαίνεται κατ᾽
died, {But} {the} {Herod} {behold} an angel of the Lord appeared in a
5462 1254 3836 2476 2627 34 3261 5743 2848
pt.aa.gsm cj d.gsm n.gsm j n.nsm n.gsm v.pmi.3s p.a

ὄναρ τῷ Ἰωσὴφ ἐν Αἰγύπτῳ 20 λέγων, ἐγερθεὶς παράλαβε τὸ παιδίον καὶ τὴν
dream to Joseph in Egypt, saying, "Rise, take the child and {the}
3941 3836 2737 1877 131 3306 1586 4161 3836 4086 2779 3836
n.asn d.dsm n.dsm p.d n.dsf pt.pa.nsm pt.ap.nsm v.aam.2s d.asn n.asn cj d.asf

μητέρα αὐτοῦ καὶ πορεύου εἰς γῆν Ἰσραήλ· τεθνήκασιν γὰρ οἱ
his mother, {his} and go to the land of Israel, {are dead} for those
899 3613 899 2779 4513 1650 1178 2702 2569 1142 3836
n.asf r.gsm.3 cj v.pmm.2s p.a n.asf n.gsm v.rai.3p cj d.npm

ζητοῦντες τὴν ψυχὴν τοῦ παιδίου. 21 ὁ δὲ ἐγερθεὶς
who were seeking the child's life {the} {child's} are dead." {the} So Joseph got up,
2426 3836 4086 6034 3836 4086 2569 2569 3836 1254 1586
pt.pa.npm d.asf n.asf d.gsn n.gsn d.nsm cj pt.ap.nsm

NASB

is going to search
for the Child to
destroy Him."
14 So Joseph got
up and took the
Child and His
mother while it
was still night, and
left for Egypt. 15 He
remained there
until the death of
Herod. *This was*
to fulfill what had
been spoken by the
Lord through the
prophet: "OUT OF
EGYPT I CALLED MY
SON."

Herod Slaughters Babies

16 Then when
Herod saw that he
had been tricked
by the magi, he
became very en-
raged, and sent and
slew all the male
children who were
in Bethlehem and
all its vicinity, from
two years old and
under, according
to the time which
he had determined
from the magi.
17 Then what had
been spoken
through Jeremiah
the prophet was
fulfilled:

18 "A VOICE WAS
HEARD IN RA-
MAH,
WEEPING AND
GREAT MOURN-
ING,
RACHEL WEEP-
ING FOR HER
CHILDREN;
AND SHE RE-
FUSED TO BE
COMFORTED,
BECAUSE THEY
WERE NO
MORE."

19 But when Herod
died, behold, an
angel of the Lord
*appeared in a
dream to Joseph
in Egypt, and said,
20 "Get up, take
the Child and His
mother, and go
into the land of Is-
rael; for those who
sought the Child's
life are dead." 21 So

---

[a] 15 Hosea 11:1
[b] 18 Jer. 31:15

NIV

took the child and
his mother and
went to the land
of Israel. 22 But
when he heard
that Archelaus
was reigning in
Judea in place of
his father Herod,
he was afraid to
go there. Having
been warned in a
dream, he with-
drew to the district
of Galilee, 23 and
he went and lived
in a town called
Nazareth. So was
fulfilled what was
said through the
prophets, that he
would be called a
Nazarene.

John the Baptist Prepares the Way

3 In those days
John the Bap-
tist came, preach-
ing in the wilder-
ness of Judea 2 and
saying, "Repent,
for the kingdom of
heaven has come
near." 3 This is he
who was spoken of
through the proph-
et Isaiah:

"A voice of one
calling
in the
wilderness,
'Prepare the
way for the
Lord,
make straight
paths for
him.'"[a]

4 John's clothes
were made of cam-
el's hair, and he
had a leather belt
around his waist.
His food was lo-
custs and wild
honey. 5 People
went out to him
from Jerusalem
and all Judea and
the whole region of
the Jordan.

[a] 3 Isaiah 40:3

παρέλαβεν τὸ παιδίον καὶ τὴν μητέρα αὐτοῦ καὶ εἰσῆλθεν εἰς γῆν Ἰσραήλ.
took the child and {the} his mother, his and went into the land of Israel.
4161 3836 4086 2779 3836 899 3613 899 2779 1656 1650 1178 2702
v.aai.3s d.asn n.asn cj d.asf n.asf r.gsm.3 cj v.aai.3s p.a n.asf n.gsm

22 ἀκούσας δὲ ὅτι Ἀρχέλαος βασιλεύει τῆς Ἰουδαίας ἀντὶ τοῦ
But when he heard But that Archelaus ⌞was reigning over⌟ {the} Judea ⌞in place of⌟ {the}
1254 201 1254 4022 793 996 3836 2677 505 3836
pt.aa.nsm cj cj n.nsm v.pai.3s d.gsf n.gsf p.g d.gsm

πατρὸς αὐτοῦ Ἡρῴδου ἐφοβήθη ἐκεῖ ἀπελθεῖν· χρηματισθεὶς δὲ
his father his Herod, he was afraid to go there, to go and being warned and
899 4252 899 2476 5828 599 599 1695 599 1254 5976 1254
n.gsm r.gsm.3 n.gsm v.api.3s adv f.aa pt.ap.nsm cj

κατ᾽ ὄναρ ἀνεχώρησεν εἰς τὰ μέρη τῆς Γαλιλαίας, 23 καὶ ➝ ἐλθὼν
in a dream he went into the region of Galilee. And he went and
2848 3941 432 1650 3836 3538 3836 1133 2779 2997 2262
p.a n.asn v.aai.3s p.a d.apn n.apn d.gsf n.gsf cj pt.aa.nsm

κατῴκησεν εἰς πόλιν λεγομένην Ναζαρέτ, ὅπως πληρωθῇ τὸ ῥηθὲν διὰ
settled in a town called Nazareth, that might be fulfilled what was spoken by
2997 1650 4484 3306 3715 3968 4444 3836 3306 1328
v.aai.3s p.a n.asf pt.pp.asf n.asf cj v.aps.3s d.nsn pt.ap.nsn p.g

τῶν προφητῶν ὅτι Ναζωραῖος κληθήσεται.
the prophets might be fulfilled: ~ "He will be called a Nazarene." He will be called
3836 4737 4444 4444 4444 4022 2813 2813 2813 2813 3717 2813
d.gpm n.gpm cj n.nsm v.fpi.3s

3:1 ἐν δὲ ταῖς ἡμέραις ἐκείναις παραγίνεται Ἰωάννης ὁ
In {and} {the} those days those John the Baptist began John the
1877 1254 3836 1697 2465 1697 2722 3836 969 4134 2722 3836
p.d cj d.dpf n.dpf r.dpf v.pmi.3s n.nsm d.nsm

βαπτιστὴς κηρύσσων ἐν τῇ ἐρήμῳ τῆς Ἰουδαίας 2 καὶ [a]
Baptist proclaiming his mission in the wilderness of Judea, proclaiming, {and}
969 3062 1877 3836 2245 3836 2677 3062 2779
n.nsm pt.pa.nsm p.d d.dsf a.dsf d.gsf n.gsf cj

λέγων, μετανοεῖτε· ἤγγικεν γὰρ ἡ βασιλεία τῶν
{saying} "Repent, for the kingdom of heaven is at hand. for the kingdom of
3306 3566 1142 3836 993 3836 4041 1581 1142 3836 993 3836
pt.pa.nsm v.pam.2p v.rai.3s cj d.nsf n.nsf d.gpm

οὐρανῶν. 3 οὗτος γάρ ἐστιν ὁ ῥηθεὶς διὰ Ἠσαΐου τοῦ προφήτου
heaven For this For is he ⌞who was spoken of⌟ by Isaiah the prophet
4041 1142 4047 1142 1639 3836 3306 1328 2480 3836 4737
n.gpm r.nsm cj v.pai.3s d.nsm pt.ap.nsm p.g n.gsm d.gsm n.gsm

λέγοντος, φωνὴ βοῶντος ἐν τῇ ἐρήμῳ, ἑτοιμάσατε τὴν ὁδὸν ➝
when he said, 'The voice ⌞of one crying out⌟ in the wilderness: Prepare the way of the
3306 5889 1066 1877 3836 2245 2286 3836 3847
pt.pa.gsm n.nsf pt.pa.gsm p.d d.dsf a.dsf v.aam.2p d.asf n.asf

κυρίου, εὐθείας ποιεῖτε τὰς τρίβους αὐτοῦ. 4 αὐτὸς δὲ ὁ
Lord; make his paths straight.'" make {the} paths his {himself} Now {the}
3261 4472 899 5561 2318 4472 3836 5561 899 899 1254 3836
n.gsm a.apf v.pam.2p d.apf n.apf r.gsm.3 r.nsm cj d.nsm

Ἰωάννης εἶχεν τὸ ἔνδυμα αὐτοῦ ἀπὸ τριχῶν καμήλου καὶ ζώνην
John wore {the} clothing {his} made of camel's hair, camel's with a leather belt
2722 2400 3836 1903 899 608 2823 2582 2823 2779 1294 2438
n.nsm v.iai.3s d.asn n.asn r.gsm.3 p.g n.gpf n.gsf cj n.asf

δερματίνην περὶ τὴν ὀσφὺν αὐτοῦ, ἡ δὲ τροφὴ ἦν αὐτοῦ ἀκρίδες καὶ
leather about {the} his waist; his {the} and his food was his locusts and
1294 4309 3836 899 4019 899 3836 1254 899 5575 1639 899 210 2779
a.asf p.a d.asf n.asf r.gsm.3 d.nsf cj n.nsf v.iai.3s r.gsm.3 n.npf cj

μέλι ἄγριον. 5 τότε ἐξεπορεύετο πρὸς αὐτὸν ↞ Ἱεροσόλυμα καὶ
wild honey. wild ⌞At that time⌟ people were going out to him from Jerusalem and
67 3510 67 5538 1744 4639 899 1744 2642 2779
n.nsn a.nsn adv v.imi.3s p.a r.asm.3 n.npn cj

πᾶσα ἡ Ἰουδαία καὶ πᾶσα ἡ περίχωρος τοῦ Ἰορδάνου, 6 καὶ
all {the} Judea and all the region along the Jordan, and
4246 3836 2677 2779 4246 3836 4369 3836 2674 2779
a.nsf d.nsf n.nsf cj a.nsf d.nsf a.nsf d.gsm n.gsm cj

[a] [καὶ] UBS.

NASB

Joseph got up, took
the Child and His
mother, and came
into the land of Is-
rael. 22 But when he
heard that Arche-
laus was reigning
over Judea in place
of his father Herod,
he was afraid to go
there. Then after
being warned *by
God* in a dream, he
left for the regions
of Galilee, 23 and
came and lived
in a city called
Nazareth. *This was*
to fulfill what was
spoken through the
prophets: "He shall
be called a Naza-
rene."

The Preaching of John the Baptist

3:1 Now in those
days John the Bap-
tist *came, preach-
ing in the wilder-
ness of Judea,
saying, 2 "Repent,
for the kingdom of
heaven is at hand."
3 For this is the
one referred to by
Isaiah the prophet
when he said,

"THE VOICE OF
ONE CRYING IN
THE WILDER-
NESS,
'MAKE READY
THE WAY OF
THE LORD,
MAKE HIS
PATHS
STRAIGHT!'"

4 Now John himself
had a garment of
camel's hair and a
leather belt around
his waist; and his
food was locusts
and wild honey.
5 Then Jerusalem
was going out to
him, and all Judea
and all the district
around the Jordan;
6 and they were
being baptized by
him in the Jordan
River, as they con-
fessed their sins.

NIV

6 Confessing their
sins, they were
baptized by him in
the Jordan River.
7 But when he
saw many of the
Pharisees and Sad-
ducees coming to
where he was bap-
tizing, he said to
them: "You brood
of vipers! Who
warned you to flee
from the coming
wrath? 8 Produce
fruit in keeping
with repentance.
9 And do not think
you can say to
yourselves, 'We
have Abraham as
our father.' I tell
you that out of
these stones God
can raise up chil-
dren for Abraham.
10 The ax is already
at the root of the
trees, and every
tree that does not
produce good fruit
will be cut down
and thrown into
the fire.
11 "I baptize you
with[a] water for re-
pentance. But after
me comes one who
is more power-
ful than I, whose
sandals I am not
worthy to carry.
He will baptize
you with[b] the Holy
Spirit and fire.
12 His winnow-
ing fork is in his
hand, and he will
clear his threshing
floor, gathering
his wheat into the
barn and burning
up the chaff with
unquenchable
fire."

The Baptism of Jesus

13 Then Jesus
came from Galilee
to the Jordan to be
baptized by John.

[a] 11 Or *in*
[b] 11 Or *in*

ἐβαπτίζοντο ἐν τῷ Ἰορδάνῃ ποταμῷ ὑπʼ αὐτοῦ ἐξομολογούμενοι
⌊they were being baptized⌋ by him in the Jordan River, *by* *him* confessing
966 5679 899 1877 3836 2674 4532 5679 899 2018
v.ipi.3p p.d d.dsm n.dsm n.dsm p.g r.gsm.3 pt.pm.npm

τὰς ἁμαρτίας αὐτῶν. 7 ἰδὼν δὲ πολλοὺς τῶν Φαρισαίων καὶ
{the} their sins. *their* But ⌊when he saw⌋ *But* many of the Pharisees and
3836 899 281 899 1254 1625 1254 4498 3836 5757 2779
d.apf n.apf r.gpm.3 pt.aa.nsm cj a.apm d.gpm n.gpm cj

Σαδδουκαίων ἐρχομένους ἐπὶ τὸ βάπτισμα αὐτοῦ εἶπεν αὐτοῖς, γεννήματα ἐχιδνῶν,
Sadducees coming for *{the}* baptism, *{his}* he said to them, "You brood of vipers!
4881 2262 2093 3836 967 899 3306 899 1165 2399
n.gpm pt.pm.apm p.a d.asn n.asn r.gsm.3 v.aai.3s r.dpm.3 n.vpn n.gpf

τίς ὑπέδειξεν ὑμῖν φυγεῖν ἀπὸ τῆς μελλούσης ὀργῆς; 8 ποιήσατε οὖν
Who warned you to flee from the coming wrath? Therefore bear *Therefore*
5515 5683 7007 5771 608 3836 3516 3973 4036 4472 4036
r.nsm v.aai.3s r.dp.2 f.aa p.g d.gsf pt.pa.gsf n.gsf v.aam.2p cj

καρπὸν ἄξιον τῆς μετανοίας 9 καὶ ↱ μὴ δόξητε λέγειν ἐν ἑαυτοῖς, πατέρα
fruit worthy of repentance, and do not presume ⌊you can say⌋ to yourselves, *father*
2843 545 3836 3567 2779 1506 3590 1506 3306 1877 1571 4252
n.asm a.asm d.gsf n.gsf cj pl v.aas.2p f.pa p.d r.dpm.2 n.asm

ἔχομεν τὸν Ἀβραάμ. λέγω γὰρ ὑμῖν ὅτι δύναται ὁ θεὸς
'We have *{the}* Abraham as our father'; for I say *for* to you that God is able *{the}* *God*
2400 3836 11 4252 1142 3306 1142 7007 4022 2536 1538 3836 2536
v.pai.1p d.asm n.asm v.pai.1s cj r.dp.2 cj v.ppi.3s d.nsm n.nsm

ἐκ τῶν λίθων τούτων ἐγεῖραι τέκνα τῷ Ἀβραάμ. 10 ἤδη δὲ ἡ
from *{the}* these stones *these* to raise up children to Abraham. Even now *Even* the
1666 3836 4047 3345 4047 1586 5451 3836 11 1254 2453 1254 3836
p.g d.gpm n.gpm r.gpm f.aa n.apn d.dsm n.dsm adv cj d.nsf

ἀξίνη πρὸς τὴν ῥίζαν τῶν δένδρων κεῖται· πᾶν οὖν δένδρον ↱ μὴ
axe is lying at the root of the trees; *is lying* so any *so* tree that does not
544 3023 3023 4639 3836 4844 3836 1285 3023 4036 4246 4036 1285 4472 3590
n.nsf p.a d.asf n.asf d.gpn n.gpn v.pmi.3s a.nsn cj n.nsn pl

ποιοῦν καρπὸν καλὸν ἐκκόπτεται καὶ εἰς πῦρ βάλλεται. 11 ἐγὼ μὲν
bear good fruit *good* will be cut down and thrown into the fire. *thrown* "I ~
4472 2819 2843 2819 1716 2779 965 1650 4786 965 1609 3525
pt.pa.nsn n.asm a.asm v.ppi.3s cj p.a n.asn v.ppi.3s r.ns.1 pl

ὑμᾶς βαπτίζω ἐν ὕδατι εἰς μετάνοιαν, ὁ δὲ ὀπίσω
baptize you *baptize* with water for repentance, but the *but* one who comes after
966 7007 966 1877 5623 1650 3567 1254 3836 1254 2262 2262 2262 3958
r.ap.2 v.pai.1s p.d n.dsn p.a n.asf d.nsm cj p.g

μου ἐρχόμενος ἰσχυρότερός μού ἐστιν, οὗ οὐκ εἰμὶ ἱκανὸς
me *one who comes* is greater than I *is* — *his* I am not *I am* worthy even
1609 2262 1639 2708 1609 1639 4005 1639 1639 4024 1639 2653
r.gs.1 pt.pm.nsm a.nsm.c r.gs.1 v.pai.3s r.gsm adv v.pai.1s a.nsm

τὰ ὑποδήματα βαστάσαι· αὐτὸς ὑμᾶς βαπτίσει ἐν
to remove his *{the}* sandals. *to remove* He will baptize you *will baptize* with the
1002 1002 4005 3836 5687 1002 899 966 966 7007 966 1877
d.apn n.apn f.aa r.nsm r.ap.2 v.fai.3s p.d

πνεύματι ἁγίῳ καὶ ↰ πυρί· 12 οὗ τὸ πτύον ἐν τῇ χειρὶ
Holy Spirit *Holy* and with fire. His *{the}* ⌊winnowing fork⌋ is in *{the}* his hand,
41 4460 41 2779 1877 4786 4005 3836 4768 1877 3836 899 5931
n.dsn a.dsn cj n.dsn r.gsm d.nsn n.nsn p.d d.dsf n.dsf

αὐτοῦ καὶ διακαθαριεῖ τὴν ἅλωνα αὐτοῦ καὶ συνάξει τὸν σῖτον
his and he will clean out *{the}* his ⌊threshing floor⌋ *his* and gather *{the}* his wheat
899 2779 1351 3836 899 272 899 2779 5251 3836 899 4992
r.gsm.3 cj v.fai.3s d.asf n.asf r.gsm.3 cj v.fai.3s d.asm n.asm

αὐτοῦ εἰς τὴν ἀποθήκην, τὸ δὲ ἄχυρον κατακαύσει → πυρὶ
his into the barn; but the *but* chaff he will burn up with unquenchable fire."
899 1650 3836 630 1254 3836 1254 949 2876 812 4786
r.gsm.3 p.a d.asf n.asf d.asn cj n.asn v.fai.3s n.dsn

ἀσβέστῳ. 13 τότε παραγίνεται ὁ Ἰησοῦς ἀπὸ τῆς Γαλιλαίας ἐπὶ
unquenchable Then Jesus came *{the}* *Jesus* from *{the}* Galilee to John at
812 5538 2652 4134 3836 2652 608 3836 1133 4639 2722 2093
a.dsn adv v.pmi.3s d.nsm n.nsm p.g d.gsf n.gsf p.a

NASB

7 But when he
saw many of the
Pharisees and Sad-
ducees coming for
baptism, he said to
them, "You brood
of vipers, who
warned you to flee
from the wrath to
come? 8 Therefore
bear fruit in keep-
ing with repen-
tance; 9 and do not
suppose that you
can say to your-
selves, 'We have
Abraham for our
father'; for I say to
you that from these
stones God is able
to raise up children
to Abraham. 10 The
axe is already laid
at the root of the
trees; therefore
every tree that
does not bear good
fruit is cut down
and thrown into
the fire.
11 "As for me, I
baptize you [a]with
water for repen-
tance, but He who
is coming after me
is mightier than
I, and I am not
fit to remove His
sandals; He will
baptize you with
the Holy Spirit and
fire. 12 His winnow-
ing fork is in His
hand, and He will
thoroughly clear
His threshing floor;
and He will gather
His wheat into the
barn, but He will
burn up the chaff
with unquenchable
fire."

The Baptism of Jesus

13 Then Jesus *ar-
rived from Galilee

[a] The Gr here can be translated *in*, *with* or *by*

NIV

14But John tried
to deter him, say-
ing, "I need to be
baptized by you,
and do you come
to me?"
15Jesus replied,
"Let it be so now;
it is proper for us
to do this to fulfill
all righteousness."
Then John con-
sented.
16As soon as
Jesus was bap-
tized, he went up
out of the water. At
that moment heav-
en was opened,
and he saw the
Spirit of God de-
scending like a
dove and alighting
on him. 17And a
voice from heaven
said, "This is my
Son, whom I love;
with him I am well
pleased."

Jesus Is Tested in the Wilderness

4 Then Jesus
was led by
the Spirit into the
wilderness to be
tempted[a] by the
devil. 2After fast-
ing forty days and
forty nights, he
was hungry. 3The
tempter came to
him and said, "If
you are the Son
of God, tell these
stones to become
bread."
4Jesus answered,

[a] 1 The Greek for *tempted* can also mean *tested.*

τὸν Ἰορδάνην πρὸς τὸν Ἰωάννην τοῦ βαπτισθῆναι ὑπ᾽ αὐτοῦ. 14 ὁ δὲ
the Jordan river *to* *{the}* *John* *{the}* to be baptized by him. *{the}* But
3836 2674 4639 3836 2722 3836 966 5679 899 3836 1254
d.asm n.asm p.a d.asm n.asm d.gsn f.ap p.g r.gsm.3 d.nsm cj

Ἰωάννης[a] διεκώλυεν αὐτὸν λέγων, ἐγὼ ⌊χρείαν ἔχω⌋ ὑπὸ σοῦ
John tried to prevent him, saying, "I need to be baptized by you,
2722 1361 899 3306 1609 5970 2400 966 966 966 5679 5148
n.nsm v.iai.3s r.asm.3 pt.pa.nsm r.ns.1 n.asf v.pai.1s p.g r.gs.2

βαπτισθῆναι, καὶ ↱ σὺ ἔρχῃ πρός με; 15 ἀποκριθεὶς δὲ ὁ
to be baptized and yet do you come to me?" But Jesus answered *But* *{the}*
966 2779 2262 5148 2262 4639 1609 1254 2652 646 1254 3836
f.ap cj r.ns.2 v.pmi.2s p.a r.as.1 pt.ap.nsm cj d.nsm

Ἰησοῦς εἶπεν πρὸς αὐτόν, ἄφες ἄρτι, οὕτως γὰρ πρέπον
Jesus *{said}* *{to}* him, ⌊"Let it be so⌋ now; *in this way* for in this way it is fitting
2652 3306 4639 899 918 785 4048 1142 4048 4048 4048 1639 1639 4560
n.nsm v.aai.3s p.a r.asm.3 v.aam.2s adv adv cj pt.pa.nsn

ἐστὶν ἡμῖν πληρῶσαι πᾶσαν δικαιοσύνην. τότε ἀφίησιν αὐτόν. 16 →
it is for us to fulfill all righteousness." Then he allowed him. And when Jesus
1639 7005 4444 4246 1466 5538 918 899 1254 2652
v.pai.3s r.dp.1 f.aa a.asf n.asf adv v.pai.3s r.asm.3

βαπτισθεὶς δὲ ὁ Ἰησοῦς εὐθὺς ἀνέβη ἀπὸ τοῦ ὕδατος· καὶ ἰδοὺ
was baptized, *And* *{the}* *Jesus* just as ⌊he was coming up⌋ from the water, *{and}* *{behold}*
966 1254 3836 2652 2318 326 608 3836 5623 2779 2627
pt.ap.nsm cj d.nsm n.nsm adv v.aai.3s p.g d.gsn n.gsn cj j

ἠνεῴχθησαν[b] οἱ οὐρανοί, καὶ εἶδεν τὸ[c] πνεῦμα τοῦ[d] θεοῦ καταβαῖνον
the heavens were opened, *the* *heavens* and he saw the Spirit of God descending
3836 4041 487 3836 4041 2779 1625 3836 4460 3836 2536 2849
v.api.3p d.npm n.npm cj v.aai.3s d.asn n.asn d.gsm n.gsm pt.pa.asn

ὡσεὶ περιστερὰν καὶ[e] ἐρχόμενον ἐπ᾽ αὐτόν· 17 καὶ ἰδοὺ φωνὴ ἐκ τῶν
like a dove and lighting on him. And *{behold}* a voice from *{the}*
6059 4361 2779 2262 2093 899 2779 2627 5889 1666 3836
pl n.asf cj pt.pm.asn p.a r.asm.3 cj j n.nsf p.g d.gpm

οὐρανῶν λέγουσα, οὗτός ἐστιν ὁ υἱός μου ὁ ἀγαπητός, ἐν ᾧ
heaven said, "This is *{the}* my Son, *my* the Beloved, in whom
4041 3306 4047 1639 3836 1609 5626 1609 3836 28 1877 4005
n.gpm pt.pa.nsf r.nsm v.pai.3s d.nsm n.nsm r.gs.1 d.nsm a.nsm p.d r.dsm

εὐδόκησα.
I delight."
2305
v.aai.1s

4:1 τότε ὁ Ἰησοῦς ἀνήχθη εἰς τὴν ἔρημον ὑπὸ τοῦ πνεύματος
Then *{the}* Jesus was led by the Spirit into the wilderness *by* *the* *Spirit*
5538 3836 2652 343 5679 3836 4460 1650 3836 2245 5679 3836 4460
adv d.nsm n.nsm v.api.3s p.a d.asf n.asf p.g d.gsn n.gsn

πειρασθῆναι ὑπὸ τοῦ διαβόλου. 2 καὶ νηστεύσας ἡμέρας τεσσεράκοντα καὶ
to be tempted by the devil. And after fasting forty days *forty* and forty
4279 5679 3836 1333 2779 3764 5477 2465 5477 2779 5477
f.ap p.g d.gsm n.gsm cj pt.aa.nsm n.apf a.apf cj

νύκτας τεσσεράκοντα, ὕστερον ἐπείνασεν. 3 καὶ προσελθὼν ὁ
nights, *forty* *{afterwards}* he was hungry. And the tempter came *the*
3816 5477 5731 4277 2779 3836 4279 4665 3836
n.apf a.apf adv.c v.aai.3s cj pt.aa.nsm d.nsm

πειράζων ↰ εἶπεν αὐτῷ, εἰ υἱὸς εἶ τοῦ θεοῦ, εἰπὲ ἵνα
tempter to him and said, *him* "If you are the Son *you are* of God, command *{that}*
4279 4665 899 3306 899 1623 1639 1639 5626 1639 3836 2536 3306 2671
pt.pa.nsm v.aai.3s r.dsm.3 cj n.nsm v.pai.2s d.gsm n.gsm v.aam.2s cj

οἱ λίθοι οὗτοι ἄρτοι γένωνται. 4 ὁ δὲ ἀποκριθεὶς εἶπεν,
{the} these stones *these* to become bread." *to become* But he *But* replied, *{saying}*
3836 4047 3345 4047 1181 1181 788 1181 1254 3836 1254 646 3306
d.npm n.npm r.npm n.npm v.ams.3p d.nsm cj pt.ap.nsm v.aai.3s

[a] Ἰωάννης omitted by NET.
[b] αὐτῷ included by UBS after ἠνεῴχθησαν.
[c] [τὸ] UBS, omitted by TNIV.
[d] [τοῦ] UBS, omitted by TNIV.
[e] [καὶ] UBS.

NASB

at the Jordan *com-
ing* to John, to be
baptized by him.
14But John tried to
prevent Him, say-
ing, "I have need
to be baptized by
You, and do You
come to me?" 15But
Jesus answering
said to him, "Per-
mit *it* at this time;
for in this way it
is fitting for us to
fulfill all righteous-
ness." Then he
*permitted Him.
16After being bap-
tized, Jesus came
up immediately
from the water; and
behold, the heav-
ens were opened,
and he saw the
Spirit of God de-
scending as a dove
and lighting on
Him, 17and behold,
a voice out of the
heavens said, "This
is [a]My beloved
Son, in whom I am
well-pleased."

The Temptation of Jesus

4:1Then Jesus was
led up by the Spirit
into the wilderness
to be tempted by
the devil. 2And
after He had
fasted forty days
and forty nights,
He [b]then became
hungry. 3And the
tempter came and
said to Him, "If
You are the Son
of God, command
that these stones
become bread."
4But He answered
and said, "It is

[a] Or *My Son, the Beloved*
[b] Lit *later became;* or *afterward became*

NIV

"It is written:
'Man shall not live
on bread alone, but
on every word that
comes from the
mouth of God.'[a] "
5Then the devil
took him to the
holy city and had
him stand on the
highest point of
the temple. 6"If
you are the Son
of God," he said,
"throw yourself
down. For it is
written:
" 'He will
command
his angels
concerning
you,
and they will
lift you
up in their
hands,
so that you
will not
strike your
foot against
a stone.'[b]"
7Jesus answered
him, "It is also
written: 'Do not
put the Lord your
God to the test.'[c]"
8Again, the devil
took him to a very
high mountain and
showed him all
the kingdoms of
the world and their
splendor. 9"All this
I will give you,"
he said, "if you
will bow down and
worship me."
10Jesus said to
him, "Away from
me, Satan! For it is
written: 'Worship
the Lord your God,
and serve him
only.'[d]"
11Then the devil
left him, and an-
gels came and at-
tended him.

Jesus Begins to Preach

12When Jesus
heard that John
had been put in
prison, he with-
drew to

a 4 Deut. 8:3
b 6 Psalm 91:11,12
c 7 Deut. 6:16
d 10 Deut. 6:13

γέγραπται, ↱ οὐκ ἐπ᾿ ἄρτῳ μόνῳ ζήσεται ὁ ἄνθρωπος, ἀλλ᾿ ἐπὶ
"It stands written, "Man does not live on bread alone, *live* *{the}* *Man* but on
1211 476 2409 4024 2409 2093 788 3668 2409 3836 476 247 2093
v.rpi.3s adv p.d n.dsm a.dsm v.fmi.3s d.nsm n.nsm cj p.d

παντὶ ῥήματι ἐκπορευομένῳ διὰ στόματος θεοῦ. 5 τότε παραλαμβάνει
every word that comes from the mouth of God." Then the devil took
4246 4839 1744 1328 5125 2536 5538 3836 1333 4161
a.dsn n.dsn pt.pm.dsn p.g n.gsn n.gsm adv v.pai.3s

αὐτὸν ὁ διάβολος εἰς τὴν ἁγίαν πόλιν καὶ ἔστησεν αὐτὸν ἐπὶ τὸ πτερύγιον
him *the* *devil* into the holy city, *{and}* placed him on the pinnacle
899 3836 1333 1650 3836 41 4484 2779 2705 899 2093 3836 4762
r.asm.3 d.nsm n.nsm p.a d.asf a.asf n.asf cj v.aai.3s r.asm.3 p.a d.asn n.asn

τοῦ ἱεροῦ 6 καὶ λέγει αὐτῷ, εἰ υἱὸς εἶ τοῦ θεοῦ, βάλε σεαυτὸν
of the temple, and said to him, "If you are the Son *you are* of God, throw yourself
3836 2639 2779 3306 899 1623 1639 1639 5626 1639 3836 2536 965 4932
d.gsn n.gsn cj v.pai.3s r.dsm.3 cj n.nsm v.pai.2s d.gsm n.gsm v.aam.2s r.asm.2

κάτω· γέγραπται γὰρ ὅτι τοῖς ἀγγέλοις αὐτοῦ
down, for it stands written: *for* ~ 'He will command *{the}* his angels *his*
3004 1142 1211 1142 4022 1948 1948 1948 3836 899 34 899
adv v.rpi.3s cj cj d.dpm n.dpm r.gsm.3

ἐντελεῖται περὶ σοῦ καὶ ἐπὶ χειρῶν ἀροῦσίν σε, ↰ μήποτε
He will command concerning you,' and, 'on their hands ⌊they will hold⌋ you up, lest
1948 4309 5148 2779 2093 5931 149 5148 149 3607
v.fmi.3s p.g r.gs.2 cj p.g n.gpf v.fai.3p r.as.2 cj

προσκόψῃς πρὸς λίθον τὸν πόδα σου. 7 ἔφη αὐτῷ ὁ Ἰησοῦς,
you strike your foot against a stone.'" *{the}* *foot* *your* Jesus said to him, *{the}* *Jesus*
4684 5148 4546 4639 3345 3836 4546 5148 2652 5774 899 3836 2652
v.aas.2s p.a n.asm d.asm n.asm r.gs.2 v.iai.3s r.dsm.3 d.nsm n.nsm

↱ πάλιν γέγραπται, ↱ ↱ οὐκ ἐκπειράσεις κύριον τὸν θεόν σου. ↰
"It also stands written: 'You shall not put the Lord *{the}* your God *your* to
1211 4099 1211 1733 1733 4024 1733 3261 3836 5148 2536 5148 1733
adv v.rpi.3s adv v.fai.2s n.asm d.asm n.asm r.gs.2

↰ ↰ 8 πάλιν παραλαμβάνει αὐτὸν ὁ διάβολος εἰς
the test.'" Again, the devil took him *the* *devil* to a very high
1733 1733 4099 3836 1333 4161 899 3836 1333 1650 3336 5734
adv v.pai.3s r.asm.3 d.nsm n.nsm p.a

ὄρος ὑψηλὸν λίαν καὶ δείκνυσιν αὐτῷ πάσας τὰς βασιλείας τοῦ κόσμου καὶ
mountain, *high* *very* and showed him all the kingdoms of the world and
4001 5734 3336 2779 1259 899 4246 3836 993 3836 3180 2779
n.asn a.asn adv cj v.pai.3s r.dsm.3 a.apf d.apf n.apf d.gsm n.gsm cj

τὴν δόξαν αὐτῶν 9 καὶ εἶπεν αὐτῷ, ταῦτά σοι πάντα
{the} their splendor; *their* and he said to him, "All these I will give you, *All*
3836 899 1518 899 2779 3306 899 4246 4047 1443 1443 1443 5148 4246
d.asf n.asf r.gpf.3 cj v.aai.3s r.dsm.3 r.apn r.ds.2 a.apn

δώσω, ἐὰν ↱ ↱ πεσὼν προσκυνήσῃς μοι. 10 τότε λέγει αὐτῷ ὁ
I will give if you will fall down and worship me." Then Jesus said to him, *{the}*
1443 1569 4686 4686 4406 4686 1609 5538 2652 3306 899 3836
v.fai.1s cj pt.aa.nsm v.aas.2s r.ds.1 adv v.pai.3s r.dsm.3 d.nsm

Ἰησοῦς, ὕπαγε, σατανᾶ· γέγραπται γάρ, κύριον
Jesus "Away with you, Satan! For it stands written, *for* 'You shall worship the Lord
2652 5632 4928 1142 1211 1142 4686 4686 4686 3261
n.nsm v.pam.2s n.vsm v.rpi.3s cj n.asm

τὸν θεόν σου προσκυνήσεις καὶ αὐτῷ μόνῳ λατρεύσεις. 11 τότε
{the} your God *your* *You shall worship* and serve him alone.'" *serve* Then the devil
3836 5148 2536 5148 4686 2779 3302 899 3668 3302 5538 3836 1333
d.asm n.asm r.gs.2 v.fai.2s cj r.dsm.3 a.dsm v.fai.2s adv

ἀφίησιν αὐτὸν ὁ διάβολος, καὶ ἰδοὺ ἄγγελοι προσῆλθον καὶ διηκόνουν
left him, *the* *devil* and behold, angels came and ⌊began to take care of⌋
918 899 3836 1333 2779 2627 34 4665 2779 1354
v.pai.3s r.asm.3 d.nsm n.nsm cj j n.npm v.aai.3p cj v.iai.3p

αὐτῷ. 12 → ἀκούσας δὲ ὅτι Ἰωάννης παρεδόθη ἀνεχώρησεν εἰς
him. Now when Jesus heard *Now* that John had been arrested, he withdrew into
899 1254 201 1254 4022 2722 4140 432 1650
r.dsm.3 pt.aa.nsm cj cj n.nsm v.api.3s v.aai.3s p.a

NASB

written, 'MAN
SHALL NOT LIVE ON
BREAD ALONE, BUT
ON EVERY WORD
THAT PROCEEDS OUT
OF THE MOUTH OF
GOD.'"
5Then the devil
*took Him into the
holy city and had
Him stand on the
pinnacle of the
temple, 6and *said
to Him, "If You are
the Son of God,
throw Yourself
down; for it is
written,
'HE WILL COM-
MAND HIS
ANGELS CON-
CERNING YOU';
and
'ON *their* HANDS
THEY WILL
BEAR YOU UP,
SO THAT YOU
WILL NOT
STRIKE YOUR
FOOT AGAINST
A STONE.'"
7Jesus said to him,
"On the other hand,
it is written, 'YOU
SHALL NOT PUT THE
LORD YOUR GOD TO
THE TEST.'"
8Again, the devil
*took Him to a
very high mountain
and *showed Him
all the kingdoms
of the world and
their glory; 9and he
said to Him, "All
these things I will
give You, if You
fall down and wor-
ship me." 10Then
Jesus *said to him,
"Go, Satan! For
it is written, 'YOU
SHALL WORSHIP THE
LORD YOUR GOD,
AND SERVE HIM
ONLY.'" 11Then the
devil *left Him;
and behold, angels
came and *began* to
minister to Him.

Jesus Begins His Ministry

12Now when Jesus
heard that John
had been taken into
custody, He

NIV

Galilee. 13 Leaving
Nazareth, he went
and lived in Caper-
naum, which was
by the lake in the
area of Zebulun
and Naphtali—
14 to fulfill what
was said through
the prophet Isaiah:

15 "Land of Zebulun
and land of
Naphtali,
the Way of the
Sea, beyond
the Jordan,
Galilee of the
Gentiles—
16 the people living
in darkness
have seen a
great light;
on those living in
the land of
the shadow
of death
a light has
dawned."[a]

17 From that time
on Jesus began to
preach, "Repent,
for the kingdom of
heaven has come
near."

Jesus Calls His First Disciples

18 As Jesus was
walking beside the
Sea of Galilee, he
saw two brothers,
Simon called Pe-
ter and his brother
Andrew. They
were casting a net
into the lake, for
they were fish-
ermen. 19 "Come,
follow me," Jesus
said, "and I will
send you out to
fish for people."
20 At once they left
their nets and fol-
lowed him.
21 Going on from
there, he saw two
other brothers,
James son of Zebe-
dee and his brother
John. They were
in a boat with their
father Zebedee,
preparing their
nets. Jesus called
them, 22 and imme-
diately they

[a] 16 Isaiah 9:1,2

τὴν Γαλιλαίαν. 13 καὶ καταλιπὼν τὴν Ναζαρὰ ↱ ἐλθὼν κατῴκησεν εἰς
{the} Galilee. And leaving {the} Nazareth he went and lived in
3836 1133 2779 2901 3836 3711 2997 2262 2997 1650
d.asf n.asf cj pt.aa.nsm d.asf n.asf pt.aa.nsm v.aai.3s p.a

Καφαρναοὺμ τὴν παραθαλασσίαν ἐν ὁρίοις Ζαβουλὼν καὶ Νεφθαλίμ· 14 ἵνα
Capernaum {the} by the sea, in the region of Zebulun and Naphtali, so that
3019 3836 4144 1877 3990 2404 2779 3750 2671
n.asf d.asf a.asf p.d n.dpn n.gsm cj n.gsm cj

πληρωθῇ τὸ ῥηθὲν διὰ Ἠσαΐου τοῦ προφήτου λέγοντος,
might be fulfilled what was spoken by Isaiah the prophet might be fulfilled: {saying}
4444 3836 3306 1328 2480 3836 4737 4444 4444 4444 3306
v.aps.3s d.nsn pt.ap.nsn p.g n.gsm d.gsm n.gsm pt.pa.gsm

15 γῆ Ζαβουλὼν καὶ γῆ Νεφθαλίμ, ὁδὸν θαλάσσης, πέραν τοῦ Ἰορδάνου,
"Land of Zebulun and land of Naphtali, toward the sea, beyond the Jordan,
1178 2404 2779 1178 3750 3847 2498 4305 3836 2674
n.nsf n.gsm cj n.nsf n.gsm n.asf n.gsf p.g d.gsm n.gsm

Γαλιλαία τῶν ἐθνῶν, 16 ὁ λαὸς ὁ καθήμενος ἐν σκότει
Galilee of the Gentiles — the people {the} living in darkness have seen a great
1133 3836 1620 3836 3295 3836 2764 1877 5030 1625 1625 3489
n.nsf d.gpn n.gpn d.nsm n.nsm d.nsm pt.pm.nsm p.d n.dsn

φῶς εἶδεν μέγα, καὶ τοῖς καθημένοις ἐν χώρᾳ καὶ σκιᾷ θανάτου φῶς
light, *have seen* *great* and on those living in the region and shadow of death, a light
5890 1625 3489 2779 3836 2764 1877 6001 2779 5014 2505 5890
n.asn v.aai.3s a.asn cj d.dpm pt.pm.dpm p.d n.dsf cj n.dsf n.gsm n.nsn

ἀνέτειλεν αὐτοῖς. 17 ἀπὸ τότε ἤρξατο ὁ Ἰησοῦς κηρύσσειν καὶ λέγειν,
has dawned." {on them} From ⌞then on⌟ Jesus began {the} *Jesus* to proclaim, {and} {saying}
422 899 608 5538 2652 806 3836 2652 3062 2779 3306
v.aai.3s r.dpm.3 p.g adv v.ami.3s d.nsm n.nsm f.pa cj f.pa

μετανοεῖτε· ἤγγικεν γὰρ ἡ βασιλεία τῶν οὐρανῶν.
"Repent, *is at hand* for the kingdom of heaven is at hand."
3566 1581 1142 3836 993 3836 4041 1581 1581 1581
v.pam.2p v.rai.3s cj d.nsf n.nsf d.gpm n.gpm

18 περιπατῶν δὲ παρὰ τὴν θάλασσαν τῆς Γαλιλαίας εἶδεν δύο ἀδελφούς,
As he was walking {and} by the Sea of Galilee, he saw two brothers,
4344 1254 4123 3836 2498 3836 1133 1625 1545 81
pt.pa.nsm cj p.a d.asf n.asf d.gsf n.gsf v.aai.3s a.apm n.apm

Σίμωνα τὸν λεγόμενον Πέτρον καὶ Ἀνδρέαν τὸν ἀδελφὸν αὐτοῦ, βάλλοντας
Simon who was called Peter and Andrew {the} his brother, *his* casting a
4981 3836 3306 4377 2779 436 3836 899 81 899 965
n.asm d.asm pt.pp.asm n.asm cj n.asm d.asm n.asm r.gsm.3 pt.pa.apm

ἀμφίβληστρον εἰς τὴν θάλασσαν· ἦσαν γὰρ ἁλιεῖς. 19 καὶ λέγει αὐτοῖς,
net into the sea, for they were *for* fishermen. And he said to them,
312 1650 3836 2498 1142 1639 1142 243 2779 3306 899
n.asn p.a d.asf n.asf v.iai.3p cj n.npm cj v.pai.3s r.dpm.3

δεῦτε ὀπίσω μου, καὶ ποιήσω ὑμᾶς ἁλιεῖς ἀνθρώπων. 20 οἱ δὲ
"Come, follow me, and I will make you fishers of men." Immediately they {and}
1307 3958 1609 2779 4472 7007 243 476 2311 3836 1254
adv p.g r.gs.1 cj v.fai.1s r.ap.2 n.apm n.gpm d.npm cj

εὐθέως ἀφέντες τὰ δίκτυα ἠκολούθησαν αὐτῷ. 21 καὶ προβὰς ἐκεῖθεν
Immediately left their nets and followed him. And going on from there,
2311 918 3836 1473 199 899 2779 4581 1696
adv pt.aa.npm d.apn n.apn v.aai.3p r.dsm.3 cj pt.aa.nsm adv

εἶδεν ἄλλους δύο ἀδελφούς, Ἰάκωβον τὸν τοῦ Ζεβεδαίου καὶ Ἰωάννην
he saw two other *two* brothers, James the son of Zebedee and John
1625 1545 257 1545 81 2610 3836 3836 2411 2779 2722
v.aai.3s r.apm a.apm n.apm n.asm d.asm d.gsm n.gsm cj n.asm

τὸν ἀδελφὸν αὐτοῦ, ἐν τῷ πλοίῳ μετὰ Ζεβεδαίου τοῦ πατρὸς αὐτῶν
{the} his brother, *his* in a boat with Zebedee {the} their father, *their*
3836 899 81 899 1877 3836 4450 3552 2411 3836 899 4252 899
d.asm n.asm r.gsm.3 p.d d.dsn n.dsn p.g n.gsm d.gsm n.gsm r.gpm.3

καταρτίζοντας τὰ δίκτυα αὐτῶν, καὶ ἐκάλεσεν αὐτούς. 22 οἱ δὲ
preparing {the} their nets. *their* And he called to them. Immediately they {and}
2936 3836 899 1473 899 2779 2813 899 2311 3836 1254
pt.pa.apm d.apn n.apn r.gpm.3 cj v.aai.3s r.apm.3 d.npm cj

NASB

withdrew into
Galilee; 13 and leav-
ing Nazareth, He
came and settled in
Capernaum, which
is by the sea, in the
region of Zebulun
and Naphtali.
14 *This was* to fulfill
what was spoken
through Isaiah the
prophet:
15 "THE LAND OF
ZEBULUN AND
THE LAND OF
NAPHTALI,
BY THE WAY
OF THE SEA,
BEYOND THE
JORDAN, GALI-
LEE OF THE
[a]GENTILES—
16 "THE PEOPLE
WHO WERE SIT-
TING IN DARK-
NESS SAW A
GREAT LIGHT,
AND THOSE
WHO WERE
SITTING IN THE
LAND AND
SHADOW OF
DEATH,
UPON THEM
A LIGHT
DAWNED."
17 From that time
Jesus began to
preach and say,
"Repent, for the
kingdom of heaven
is at hand."

The First Disciples

18 Now as Jesus
was walking by
the Sea of Galilee,
He saw two broth-
ers, Simon who
was called Peter,
and Andrew his
brother, casting a
net into the sea; for
they were fisher-
men. 19 And He
*said to them, "Fol-
low Me, and I will
make you fishers
of men." 20 Immedi-
ately they left their
nets and followed
Him. 21 Going on
from there He saw
two other brothers,
James the *son* of
Zebedee, and John
his brother, in the
boat with Zebedee

[a] Lit *nations*, usually non-Jewish

NIV

left the boat and their
father and followed
him.

Jesus Heals the Sick

23 Jesus went
throughout Galilee,
teaching in their syn-
agogues, proclaim-
ing the good news
of the kingdom, and
healing every disease
and sickness among
the people. 24 News
about him spread all
over Syria, and peo-
ple brought to him
all who were ill with
various diseases,
those suffering se-
vere pain, the demon-
possessed, those
having seizures, and
the paralyzed; and he
healed them. 25 Large
crowds from Galilee,
the Decapolis,[a] Jeru-
salem, Judea and the
region across the Jor-
dan followed him.

Introduction to the Sermon on the Mount

5 Now when Jesus
saw the crowds,
he went up on a
mountainside and sat
down. His disciples
came to him, 2 and he
began to teach them.

The Beatitudes

He said:

3 "Blessed are the poor in spirit,
for theirs is the kingdom of heaven.
4 Blessed are those who mourn,
for they will be comforted.
5 Blessed are the meek,
for they will inherit the earth.
6 Blessed are those who hunger and thirst for righteous–ness,
for they will be filled.
7 Blessed are the merciful,
for they will

[a] 25 That is, the Ten Cities

εὐθέως ἀφέντες τὸ πλοῖον καὶ τὸν πατέρα αὐτῶν ἠκολούθησαν αὐτῷ.
Immediately left the boat and *{the}* their father *their* and followed him.
2311 918 3836 4450 2779 3836 899 4252 899 199 899
adv pt.aa.npm d.asn n.asn cj d.asm n.asm r.gpm.3 v.aai.3p r.dsm.3

23 καὶ περιῆγεν ἐν ὅλῃ τῇ Γαλιλαίᾳ διδάσκων ἐν ταῖς συναγωγαῖς
And Jesus went throughout all *{the}* Galilee, teaching in *{the}* their synagogues
2779 4310 1877 3910 3836 1133 1438 1877 3836 899 5252
cj v.iai.3s p.d a.dsf d.dsf n.dsf pt.pa.nsm p.d d.dpf n.dpf

αὐτῶν καὶ κηρύσσων τὸ εὐαγγέλιον τῆς βασιλείας καὶ θεραπεύων πᾶσαν νόσον
their and proclaiming the gospel of the kingdom and healing every disease
899 2779 3062 3836 2295 3836 993 2779 2543 4246 3798
r.gpm.3 cj pt.pa.nsm d.asn n.asn d.gsf n.gsf cj pt.pa.nsm a.asf n.asf

καὶ πᾶσαν μαλακίαν ἐν τῷ λαῷ. 24 καὶ ἀπῆλθεν ἡ ἀκοὴ αὐτοῦ
and every sickness among the people. And *spread* the report about him spread
2779 4246 3433 1877 3836 3295 2779 599 3836 198 899 599
cj a.asf n.asf p.d d.dsm n.dsm cj v.aai.3s d.nsf n.nsf r.gsm.3

⸤εἰς ὅλην⸥ τὴν Συρίαν· καὶ προσήνεγκαν αὐτῷ πάντας τοὺς κακῶς
throughout *{the}* Syria, and they brought to him all who were suffering
1650 3910 3836 5353 2779 4712 899 4246 3836 2400 2809
p.a a.asf d.asf n.asf cj v.aai.3p r.dsm.3 a.apm d.apm adv

ἔχοντας ποικίλαις νόσοις καὶ βασάνοις συνεχομένους καὶ [a] δαιμονιζομένους καὶ
were with various diseases and pains, *with* *{and}* demoniacs, *{and}*
2400 5309 4476 3798 2779 992 5309 2779 1227 2779
pt.pa.apm a.dpf n.dpf cj n.dpf pt.pp.apm cj pt.pp.apm cj

σεληνιαζομένους καὶ παραλυτικούς, καὶ ἐθεράπευσεν αὐτούς. 25 καὶ
epileptics, and paralytics, and he healed them. And great crowds
4944 2779 4166 2779 2543 899 2779 4498 4063
pt.pp.apm cj a.apm cj v.aai.3s r.apm.3 cj

ἠκολούθησαν αὐτῷ ὄχλοι πολλοὶ ἀπὸ τῆς Γαλιλαίας καὶ Δεκαπόλεως καὶ ↰
followed him *crowds great* from *{the}* Galilee and the Decapolis, *{and}* from
199 899 4063 4498 608 3836 1133 2779 1279 2779 608
v.aai.3p r.dsm.3 n.npm a.npm p.g d.gsf n.gsf cj n.gsf cj

Ἱεροσολύμων καὶ Ἰουδαίας καὶ ↰ πέραν τοῦ Ἰορδάνου.
Jerusalem and Judea, and from beyond the Jordan.
2642 2779 2677 2779 608 4305 3836 2674
n.gpn cj n.gsf cj p.g d.gsm n.gsm

5:1 ἰδὼν δὲ τοὺς ὄχλους ἀνέβη εἰς τὸ ὄρος, καὶ →
And seeing *And* the crowds, Jesus went up on the mountainside; and when he
1254 1625 1254 3836 4063 326 1650 3836 4001 2779 899
pt.aa.nsm cj d.apm n.apm v.aai.3s p.a d.asn n.asn cj

καθίσαντος αὐτοῦ προσῆλθαν αὐτῷ οἱ μαθηταὶ⸥ αὐτοῦ· 2 καὶ ↱
had sat down, *he* his disciples came to him. *{the}* *disciples* *his* And he
2767 899 899 3412 4665 899 3836 3412 899 2779 1438
pt.aa.gsm r.gsm.3 v.aai.3p r.dsm.3 d.npm n.npm r.gsm.3 cj

ἀνοίξας τὸ στόμα αὐτοῦ ἐδίδασκεν αὐτοὺς λέγων, 3 μακάριοι οἱ
opened *{the}* his mouth *his* and began to teach them, saying: "Blessed are the
487 3836 899 5125 899 1438 899 3306 3421 3836
pt.aa.nsm d.asn n.asn r.gsm.3 v.iai.3s r.apm.3 pt.pa.nsm a.npm d.npm

πτωχοὶ τῷ πνεύματι, ὅτι αὐτῶν ἐστιν ἡ βασιλεία τῶν οὐρανῶν. 4 μακάριοι
poor in spirit, for theirs is the kingdom of heaven. Blessed are
4777 3836 4460 4022 899 1639 3836 993 3836 4041 3421
a.npm d.dsn n.dsn cj r.gpm.3 v.pai.3s d.nsf n.nsf d.gpm n.gpm a.npm

οἱ πενθοῦντες, ὅτι αὐτοὶ παρακληθήσονται. 5 μακάριοι οἱ πραεῖς, ὅτι αὐτοὶ
those who mourn, for they will be comforted. Blessed are the meek, for they
3836 4291 4022 899 4151 3421 3836 4558 4022 899
d.npm pt.pa.npm cj r.npm v.fpi.3p a.npm d.npm a.npm cj r.npm

κληρονομήσουσιν τὴν γῆν. 6 μακάριοι οἱ πεινῶντες καὶ διψῶντες τὴν
will inherit the earth. Blessed are those who hunger and thirst for *{the}*
3099 3836 1178 3421 3836 4277 2779 1498 3836
v.fai.3p d.asf n.asf a.npm d.npm pt.pa.npm cj pt.pa.npm d.asf

δικαιοσύνην, ὅτι αὐτοὶ χορτασθήσονται. 7 μακάριοι οἱ ἐλεήμονες, ὅτι αὐτοὶ
righteousness, for they will be fully satisfied. Blessed are the merciful, for they
1466 4022 899 5963 3421 3836 1798 4022 899
n.asf cj r.npm v.fpi.3p a.npm d.npm a.npm cj r.npm

[a] [καὶ] UBS.

NASB

their father, mend-
ing their nets; and
He called them.
22 Immediately they
left the boat and
their father, and
followed Him.

Ministry in Galilee

23 Jesus was go-
ing throughout all
Galilee, teaching
in their synagogues
and proclaiming
the gospel of the
kingdom, and heal-
ing every kind of
disease and every
kind of sickness
among the people.
24 The news
about Him spread
throughout all
Syria; and they
brought to Him all
who were ill, those
suffering with vari-
ous diseases and
pains, demoniacs,
epileptics, paralyt-
ics; and He healed
them. 25 Large
crowds followed
Him from Galilee
and *the* Decapolis
and Jerusalem and
Judea and *from* be-
yond the Jordan.

The Sermon on the Mount; The Beatitudes

5:1 When Jesus
saw the crowds,
He went up on the
mountain; and after
He sat down, His
disciples came to
Him. 2 He opened
His mouth and *be-
gan* to teach them,
saying,
3 "Blessed are the
poor in spirit, for
theirs is the king-
dom of heaven.
4 "Blessed are
those who mourn,
for they shall be
comforted.
5 "Blessed are the
[a] gentle, for they
shall inherit the
earth.
6 "Blessed are
those who hunger
and thirst for righ-
teousness, for they
shall be satisfied.
7 "Blessed are

[a] Or *humble, meek*

NIV

be shown
mercy.
8 Blessed are the
pure in heart,
for they will see
God.
9 Blessed are the
peace–
makers,
for they will
be called
children of
God.
10 Blessed are those
who are
persecuted
because of
righteous–
ness,
for theirs is the
kingdom of
heaven.

11 “Blessed are
you when people
insult you, perse-
cute you and false-
ly say all kinds of
evil against you
because of me.
12 Rejoice and be
glad, because great
is your reward in
heaven, for in the
same way they
persecuted the
prophets who were
before you.

Salt and Light

13 “You are the
salt of the earth.
But if the salt loses
its saltiness, how
can it be made
salty again? It is
no longer good for
anything, except
to be thrown out
and trampled un-
derfoot.
14 “You are the
light of the world.
A town built on a
hill cannot be hid-
den. 15 Neither do
people light a lamp
and put it under a
bowl. Instead they
put it on its stand,
and it gives light
to everyone in the
house. 16 In the
same way, let your
light shine before
others, that they
may see your good
deeds and glori-
fy your Father in
heaven.

ἐλεηθήσονται. 8 μακάριοι οἱ καθαροὶ τῇ καρδίᾳ, ὅτι αὐτοὶ τὸν
will be shown mercy. Blessed are the pure in heart, for they will see {the}
1796 3421 3836 2754 3836 2840 4022 899 3972 3972 3836
v.fpi.3p a.npm d.npm a.npm d.dsf n.dsf cj r.npm d.asm

θεὸν ὄψονται. 9 μακάριοι οἱ εἰρηνοποιοί, ὅτι αὐτοὶ υἱοὶ θεοῦ
God. will see Blessed are the peacemakers, for they will be called sons of God.
2536 3972 3421 3836 1648 4022 899 2813 2813 2813 5626 2536
n.asm v.fmi.3p a.npm d.npm n.npm cj r.npm n.npm n.gsm

κληθήσονται. 10 μακάριοι οἱ δεδιωγμένοι ἕνεκεν δικαιοσύνης, ὅτι
will be called Blessed are those who are persecuted ⌊for the sake of⌋ righteousness, for
2813 3421 3836 1503 1914 1466 4022
v.fpi.3p a.npm d.npm pt.rp.npm p.g n.gsf cj

αὐτῶν ἐστιν ἡ βασιλεία τῶν οὐρανῶν. 11 μακάριοί ἐστε ὅταν ὀνειδίσωσιν
theirs is the kingdom of heaven. Blessed are you when others revile
899 1639 3836 993 3836 4041 3421 1639 4020 3943
r.gpm.3 v.pai.3s d.nsf n.nsf d.gpm n.gpm a.npm v.pai.2p cj v.aas.3p

ὑμᾶς καὶ διώξωσιν καὶ εἴπωσιν πᾶν πονηρὸν καθ᾽ ὑμῶν ψευδόμενοι[a]
you and persecute you and say ⌊all kinds of⌋ evil against you falsely
7007 2779 1503 2779 3306 4246 4505 2848 7007 6017
r.ap.2 cj v.aas.3p cj v.aas.3p a.asn a.asn p.g r.gp.2 pt.pm.npm

ἕνεκεν ἐμοῦ. 12 χαίρετε καὶ ἀγαλλιᾶσθε, ὅτι ὁ μισθὸς ὑμῶν πολὺς
⌊on account of⌋ me. Rejoice and be very glad because {the} your reward your is great
1914 1609 5897 2779 22 4022 3836 7007 3635 7007 4498
p.g r.gs.1 v.pam.2p cj v.pmm.2p cj d.nsm n.nsm r.gp.2 a.nsm

ἐν τοῖς οὐρανοῖς· οὕτως γὰρ ἐδίωξαν τοὺς προφήτας τοὺς πρὸ
in {the} heaven; for that is how for they persecuted the prophets who were before
1877 3836 4041 1142 4048 1142 1503 3836 4737 3836 4574
p.d d.dpm n.dpm adv cj v.aai.3p d.apm n.apm d.apm p.g

ὑμῶν. 13 ὑμεῖς ἐστε τὸ ἅλας τῆς γῆς· ἐὰν δὲ τὸ ἅλας μωρανθῇ, ⌊ἐν
you. “You are the salt of the earth, but if but {the} salt ⌊has lost its taste,⌋ how
7007 7007 1639 3836 229 3836 1178 1254 1569 1254 3836 229 3701 1877
r.gp.2 r.np.2 v.pai.2p d.nsn n.nsn d.gsf n.gsf cj cj d.nsn n.nsn v.aps.3s p.d

τίνι⌋ ἁλισθήσεται; εἰς οὐδὲν ἰσχύει ἔτι ⌊εἰ
⌊will it be made salty⌋ again? It is no longer good for anything It is good no longer but
5515 245 2710 2710 2285 2285 2710 1650 4029 2710 2285 1623
r.dsn v.fpi.3s p.a a.asn v.pai.3s adv cj

μὴ⌋ βληθὲν ἔξω καταπατεῖσθαι ὑπὸ τῶν ἀνθρώπων. 14 ὑμεῖς ἐστε τὸ φῶς
to be thrown out and trampled under foot by {the} people. You are the light
3590 965 2032 2922 5679 3836 476 7007 1639 3836 5890
pl pt.ap.asn adv f.pp p.g d.gpm n.gpm r.np.2 v.pai.2p d.nsn n.nsn

τοῦ κόσμου. ⌊οὐ δύναται⌋ πόλις κρυβῆναι ἐπάνω ὄρους
of the world. A city built on a hill cannot city be hidden on hill
3836 3180 4484 3023 2062 4001 4024 1538 4484 3221 2062 4001
d.gsm n.gsm adv v.ppi.3s n.nsf f.ap p.g n.gsn

κειμένη· 15 οὐδὲ → καίουσιν λύχνον καὶ τιθέασιν αὐτὸν ὑπὸ τὸν
built be hidden. Nor do people light a lamp and put it under the
3023 3221 3221 4028 2794 3394 2779 5502 899 5679 3836
pt.pm.nsf cj v.pai.3p n.asm cj v.pai.3p r.asm.3 p.a d.asm

μόδιον ἀλλ᾽ ἐπὶ τὴν λυχνίαν, καὶ λάμπει πᾶσιν τοῖς ἐν τῇ οἰκίᾳ. 16 οὕτως
meal-tub, but on a stand, and ⌊it gives light⌋ to all {the} in the house. like that
3654 247 2093 3836 3393 2779 3290 4246 3836 1877 3836 3864 4048
n.asm cj p.a d.asf n.asf cj v.pai.3s a.dpm d.dpm p.d d.dsf n.dsf adv

→ λαμψάτω τὸ φῶς ὑμῶν ἔμπροσθεν τῶν ἀνθρώπων, ὅπως
Let your light shine {the} light your like that before {the} others, so that
7007 5890 3290 3836 5890 7007 4048 4048 1869 3836 476 3968
v.aam.3s d.nsn n.nsn r.gp.2 p.g d.gpm n.gpm cj

ἴδωσιν ὑμῶν τὰ καλὰ ἔργα καὶ δοξάσωσιν τὸν πατέρα ὑμῶν τὸν ἐν
⌊they may see⌋ your {the} good works and glorify {the} your Father your who is in
1625 7007 3836 2819 2240 2779 1519 3836 7007 4252 7007 3836 1877
v.aas.3p r.gp.2 d.apn a.apn n.apn cj v.aas.3p d.asm n.asm r.gp.2 d.asm p.d

τοῖς οὐρανοῖς. 17 ↱ μὴ νομίσητε ὅτι ἦλθον καταλῦσαι τὸν νόμον ἢ τοὺς
{the} heaven.” “Do not think that I came to abolish the law or the
3836 4041 3787 3590 3787 4022 2262 2907 3836 3795 2445 3836
d.dpm n.dpm pl v.aas.2p cj v.aai.1s f.aa d.asm n.asm cj d.apm

[a] [ψευδόμενοι] UBS, omitted by TNIV.

NASB

the merciful, for
they shall receive
mercy.
8 “Blessed are the
pure in heart, for
they shall see God.
9 “Blessed are the
peacemakers, for
they shall be called
sons of God.
10 “Blessed are
those who have
been persecuted
for the sake of
righteousness, for
theirs is the king-
dom of heaven.
11 “Blessed are you
when *people* insult
you and persecute
you, and falsely
say all kinds of evil
against you be-
cause of Me. 12 Re-
joice and be glad,
for your reward in
heaven is great; for
in the same way
they persecuted the
prophets who were
before you.

Disciples and the World

13 “You are the
salt of the earth;
but if the salt has
become tasteless,
how can it be made
salty *again?* It is
no longer good for
anything, except
to be thrown out
and trampled under
foot by men.
14 “You are the
light of the world.
A city set on a hill
cannot be hidden;
15 nor does *anyone*
light a lamp and
put it under a
basket, but on the
lampstand, and
it gives light to
all who are in the
house. 16 Let your
light shine before
men in such a way
that they may see
your good works,
and glorify your
Father who is in
heaven.
17 “Do not think
that I came to abol-
ish the Law or the

NIV

The Fulfillment of the Law

[17]"Do not think
that I have come
to abolish the Law
or the Prophets; I
have not come to
abolish them but to
fulfill them. [18]For
truly I tell you,
until heaven and
earth disappear,
not the small-
est letter, not the
least stroke of a
pen, will by any
means disappear
from the Law un-
til everything is
accomplished.
[19]Therefore any-
one who sets aside
one of the least of
these commands
and teaches others
accordingly will
be called least in
the kingdom of
heaven, but who-
ever practices
and teaches these
commands will be
called great in the
kingdom of heav-
en. [20]For I tell you
that unless your
righteousness sur-
passes that of the
Pharisees and the
teachers of the law,
you will certainly
not enter the king-
dom of heaven.

Murder

[21]"You have
heard that it was
said to the people
long ago, 'You
shall not murder,[a]
and anyone who
murders will be
subject to judg-
ment.' [22]But I tell
you that anyone
who is angry with
a brother or sis-
ter[b,c] will be sub-
ject to judgment.
Again, anyone

[a] *21* Exodus 20:13
[b] *22* The Greek word for *brother or sister* (*adelphos*) refers here to a fellow disciple, whether man or woman; also in verse 23.
[c] *22* Some manuscripts *brother or sister without cause*

προφήτας· ↱ ↱ οὐκ ἦλθον καταλῦσαι ἀλλὰ πληρῶσαι. 18 ἀμὴν
prophets. I did not come to abolish, but to fulfill. I tell you the truth,
4737 2262 2262 4024 2262 2907 247 4444 3306 3306 7007 297
n.apm adv v.aai.1s f.aa cj f.aa pl

γὰρ λέγω ὑμῖν, ⸤ἕως ἂν⸥ παρέλθῃ ὁ οὐρανὸς καὶ ἡ γῆ,
{for} *I tell* *you* until *pass away* *{the}* heaven and *{the}* earth pass away, not a single
1142 3306 7007 2401 323 4216 3836 4041 2779 3836 1178 4216 4216 4024 1651
cj v.pai.1s r.dp.2 cj pl v.aas.3s d.nsm n.nsm cj d.nsf n.nsf

ἰῶτα ἓν ἢ μία κεραία ⸤οὐ μὴ⸥ παρέλθῃ ἀπὸ τοῦ νόμου, ⸤ἕως ἂν⸥ πάντα
iota *single* or one little stroke *not* will pass from the law until everything
2740 1651 2445 1651 3037 4024 3590 4216 608 3836 3795 2401 323 4246
n.nsn a.nsn cj a.nsf n.nsf adv pl v.aas.3s p.g d.gsm n.gsm cj pl a.npn

γένηται. 19 ⸤ὃς ἐὰν⸥ οὖν λύσῃ μίαν τῶν → ἐντολῶν
takes place. Therefore whoever *Therefore* relaxes one of the least of these commandments
1181 4036 4005 1569 4036 3395 1651 3836 1788 4047 1953
v.ams.3s r.nsm pl cj v.aas.3s a.asf d.gpf n.gpf

τούτων τῶν ἐλαχίστων καὶ διδάξῃ οὕτως τοὺς ἀνθρώπους,
these *{the}* *least* and teaches others to do the same *{the}* *others* will be called
4047 3836 1788 2779 1438 476 4048 3836 476 2813 2813 2813
r.gpf d.gpf a.gpf.s cj v.aas.3s adv d.apm n.apm

ἐλάχιστος κληθήσεται ἐν τῇ βασιλείᾳ τῶν οὐρανῶν· ὃς δ' ἂν ποιήσῃ
least *will be called* in the kingdom of heaven; but whoever *but* ~ does
1788 2813 1877 3836 993 3836 4041 1254 4005 1254 323 4472
a.nsm.s v.fpi.3s p.d d.dsf n.dsf d.gpm n.gpm r.nsm cj pl v.aas.3s

καὶ διδάξῃ, οὗτος μέγας κληθήσεται ἐν τῇ βασιλείᾳ
them and teaches others, this person will be called great *will be called* in the kingdom
2779 1438 4047 2813 2813 2813 3489 2813 1877 3836 993
cj v.aas.3s r.nsm a.nsm v.fpi.3s p.d d.dsf n.dsf

τῶν οὐρανῶν. 20 λέγω γὰρ ὑμῖν ὅτι ⸤ἐὰν μὴ⸥ περισσεύσῃ
of heaven. For I tell *For* you that unless your righteousness exceeds
3836 4041 1142 3306 1142 7007 4022 1569 3590 7007 1466 4355
d.gpm n.gpm v.pai.1s cj r.dp.2 cj cj pl v.aas.3s

ὑμῶν ἡ δικαιοσύνη πλεῖον τῶν γραμματέων καὶ Φαρισαίων, ↱ ↱ ⸤οὐ
your *{the}* *righteousness* beyond that of the scribes and Pharisees, you will never
7007 3836 1466 4498 3836 1208 2779 5757 1656 1656 4024
r.gp.2 d.nsf n.nsf adv.c d.gpm n.gpm cj n.gpm adv

μὴ⸥ εἰσέλθητε εἰς τὴν βασιλείαν τῶν οὐρανῶν. 21 ἠκούσατε ὅτι ἐρρέθη
enter *{into}* the kingdom of heaven. ⸤"You have heard⸥ that it was said
3590 1656 1650 3836 993 3836 4041 201 4022 3306
pl v.aas.2p p.a d.asf n.asf d.gpm n.gpm v.aai.2p cj v.api.3s

τοῖς ἀρχαίοις, ↱ ↱ οὐ φονεύσεις· ὃς δ' ἂν φονεύσῃ, ἔνοχος ἔσται
to those of old, 'You shall not murder,' and, 'whoever *and* ~ murders *liable* will be
3836 792 5839 5839 4024 5839 1254 4005 1254 323 5839 1944 1639
d.dpm a.dpm adv v.fai.2s r.nsm cj pl v.aas.3s a.nsm v.fmi.3s

τῇ κρίσει. 22 ἐγὼ δὲ λέγω ὑμῖν ὅτι πᾶς ὁ ὀργιζόμενος τῷ
liable to judgment.' But I *But* say to you that anyone who is angry with his
1944 3836 3213 1254 1609 1254 3306 7007 4022 4246 3836 3974 3836 899
d.dsf n.dsf r.ns.1 cj v.pai.1s r.dp.2 cj a.nsm d.nsm pt.pp.nsm d.dsm

ἀδελφῷ αὐτοῦ ἔνοχος ἔσται τῇ κρίσει· ὃς δ' ἂν εἴπῃ τῷ
brother *his* will be liable *will be* to judgment; and whoever *and* ~ says to his
81 899 1639 1639 1944 1639 3836 3213 1254 4005 1254 323 3306 3836 899
n.dsm r.gsm.3 a.nsm v.fmi.3s d.dsf n.dsf r.nsm cj pl v.aas.3s d.dsm

ἀδελφῷ αὐτοῦ, ῥακά, ἔνοχος ἔσται τῷ συνεδρίῳ· ὃς δ' ἂν
brother, *his* 'Raka,' will be liable *will be* ⸤to the⸥ council; and whoever *and* ~
81 899 4819 1639 1639 1944 1639 3836 5284 1254 4005 1254 323
n.dsm r.gsm.3 n.vsm a.nsm v.fmi.3s d.dsn n.dsn r.nsm cj pl

εἴπῃ, μωρέ, ἔνοχος ἔσται εἰς τὴν γέενναν τοῦ πυρός. 23 ἐὰν
says, 'You fool!' will be liable *will be* to the hell of fire. Therefore if
3306 3704 1639 1639 1944 1639 1650 3836 1147 3836 4786 4036 1569
v.aas.3s a.vsm a.nsm v.fmi.3s p.a d.asf n.asf d.gsn n.gsn cj

οὖν προσφέρῃς τὸ δῶρόν σου ἐπὶ τὸ θυσιαστήριον κἀκεῖ μνησθῇς
Therefore you are bringing *{the}* your gift *your* to the altar and there remember
4036 4712 3836 5148 1565 5148 2093 3836 2603 2795 3630
cj v.pas.2s d.asn n.asn r.gs.2 p.a d.asn n.asn crasis v.aps.2s

---

NASB

Prophets; I did not
come to abolish
but to fulfill. [18]For
truly I say to you,
until heaven and
earth pass away,
not the smallest let-
ter or stroke shall
pass from the Law
until all is accom-
plished. [19]Whoever
then annuls one of
the least of these
commandments,
and teaches others
to do the same,
shall be called least
in the kingdom
of heaven; but
whoever keeps
and teaches *them,*
he shall be called
great in the king-
dom of heaven.
[20]"For I say to you
that unless your
righteousness sur-
passes *that* of the
scribes and Phari-
sees, you will not
enter the kingdom
of heaven.

Personal Relationships

[21]"You have heard
that the ancients
were told, 'YOU
SHALL NOT COM-
MIT MURDER' and
'Whoever commits
murder shall be [a]li-
able to the court.'
[22]But I say to you
that everyone who
is angry with his
brother shall be
guilty before the
court; and whoever
says to his brother,
'[b]You good-for-
nothing,' shall be
guilty before [c]the
supreme court;
and whoever says,
'You fool,' shall be
guilty *enough to go*
into the [d]fiery hell.
[23]Therefore if you
are presenting your
offering at the altar,
and there remem-
ber that your

[a] Or *guilty before*
[b] Or *empty-head;* Gr *Raka (Raca)* fr Aram *reqa*
[c] Lit *the Sanhedrin*
[d] Lit *Gehenna of fire*

NIV

your gift at the
altar and there
remember that
your brother or
sister has some-
thing against you,
24 leave your gift
there in front of
the altar. First go
and be reconciled
to them; then come
and offer your gift.
25 "Settle matters
quickly with your
adversary who
is taking you to
court. Do it while
you are still to-
gether on the way,
or your adversary
may hand you
over to the judge,
and the judge may
hand you over to
the officer, and
you may be thrown
into prison. 26 Truly
I tell you, you will
not get out until
you have paid the
last penny.

Adultery

27 "You have
heard that it was
said, 'You shall not
commit adultery.'[a]
28 But I tell you that
anyone who looks
at a woman lust-
fully has already
committed adul-
tery with her in
his heart. 29 If your
right eye causes
you to stumble,
gouge it out and
throw it away. It
is better for you
to lose one part of
your body than for
your whole body
to be thrown into
hell. 30 And if your
right hand causes
you to stumble, cut
it off and throw
it away. It is bet-
ter for you to lose
one part of your
body than for your
whole body to go
into hell.

[a] 27 Exodus 20:14

ὅτι ὁ ἀδελφός σου ἔχει τι κατὰ σοῦ, 24 ἄφες ἐκεῖ τὸ
that {the} your brother your has something against you, leave your gift there {the}
4022 3836 5148 81 5148 2400 5516 2848 5148 918 5148 1565 1695 3836
cj d.nsm n.nsm r.gs.2 v.pai.3s r.asn p.g r.gs.2 v.aam.2s adv d.asn

δῶρόν σου ἔμπροσθεν τοῦ θυσιαστηρίου καὶ ὕπαγε πρῶτον διαλλάγηθι τῷ
gift your before the altar and first go first and be reconciled to
1565 5148 1869 3836 2603 2779 4754 5632 4754 1367 3836
n.asn r.gs.2 p.g d.gsn n.gsn cj v.pam.2s adv v.apm.2s d.dsm

ἀδελφῷ σου, καὶ τότε ἐλθὼν πρόσφερε τὸ δῶρόν σου. 25 ἴσθι εὐνοῶν
your brother, your and then come and offer {the} your gift. your Come to terms
5148 81 5148 2779 5538 2262 4712 3836 5148 1565 5148 1639 2333
n.dsm r.gs.2 cj adv pt.aa.nsm v.pam.2s d.asn n.asn r.gs.2 v.pam.2s pt.pa.nsm

τῷ ἀντιδίκῳ σου ταχύ, ⌞ἕως ὅτου⌟ εἶ ↰ μετ' αὐτοῦ ἐν τῇ ὁδῷ,
quickly with your accuser your quickly while ⌞you are⌟ still with him on the way,
5444 3836 5148 508 5148 5444 2401 4015 1639 2401 3552 899 1877 3836 3847
d.dsm n.dsm r.gs.2 adv p.g r.gsn v.pai.2s p.g r.gsm.3 p.d d.dsf n.dsf

μήποτέ σε παραδῷ ← ὁ ἀντίδικος τῷ κριτῇ καὶ ὁ
to court, or you your accuser may hand you over {the} accuser ⌞to the⌟ judge, and the
3607 5148 508 4140 5148 3836 508 3836 3216 2779 3836
cj r.as.2 v.aas.3s d.nsm n.nsm d.dsm n.dsm cj d.nsm

κριτὴς τῷ ὑπηρέτῃ καὶ εἰς φυλακὴν βληθήσῃ· 26
judge ⌞to the⌟ guard, and you be thrown into prison. you be thrown I tell you
3216 3836 5677 2779 965 965 965 1650 5871 965 3306 3306 5148
n.nsm d.dsm n.dsm cj p.a n.asf v.fpi.2s

ἀμὴν λέγω σοι, ↱ ↱ ⌞οὐ μὴ⌟ ἐξέλθῃς ἐκεῖθεν, ⌞ἕως ἂν⌟ ἀποδῷς
the truth, I tell you you will certainly not get out of there until ⌞you have paid⌟
297 3306 5148 3119 2002 4024 3590 2002 1696 2401 323 625
pl v.pai.1s r.ds.2 adv pl v.aas.2s adv cj pl v.aas.2s

τὸν ἔσχατον κοδράντην. 27 ἠκούσατε ὅτι ἐρρέθη, ↱ ↱ οὐ
the last penny. ⌞"You have heard⌟ that it was said, 'You shall not
3836 2274 3119 201 4022 3306 3658 3658 4024
d.asm a.asm n.asm v.aai.2p cj v.api.3s adv

μοιχεύσεις. 28 ἐγὼ δὲ λέγω ὑμῖν ὅτι πᾶς ὁ βλέπων γυναῖκα πρὸς
commit adultery.' But I But say to you that whoever {the} looks at a woman to
3658 1254 1609 1254 3306 7007 4022 4246 3836 1063 1222 4639
v.fai.2s r.ns.1 cj v.pai.1s r.dp.2 cj a.nsm d.nsm pt.pa.nsm n.asf p.a

τὸ ἐπιθυμῆσαι αὐτὴν ↱ ἤδη ἐμοίχευσεν αὐτὴν ἐν τῇ καρδίᾳ
{the} lust after her has already ⌞committed adultery with⌟ her in {the} his heart.
3836 2121 899 3658 2453 3658 899 1877 3836 899 2840
d.asn f.aa r.asf.3 adv v.aai.3s r.asf.3 p.d d.dsf n.dsf

αὐτοῦ. 29 εἰ δὲ ὁ ὀφθαλμός σου ὁ δεξιὸς σκανδαλίζει σε, ↰ ↰
his If {and} {the} your right eye your {the} right causes you to sin,
899 1623 1254 3836 5148 1288 4057 5148 3836 1288 4997 5148 4997 4997
r.gsm.3 cj cj d.nsm n.nsm r.gs.2 d.nsm a.nsm v.pai.3s r.as.2

ἔξελε αὐτὸν ↰ καὶ βάλε ἀπὸ σοῦ· συμφέρει γάρ σοι ἵνα ἀπόληται
gouge it out and throw it ⌞away from⌟ you, for it is better for ⌞for you⌟ to lose
1975 899 1975 2779 965 608 5148 1142 5237 1142 5148 2671 660
v.aam.2s r.asm.3 cj v.aam.2s p.g r.gs.2 v.pai.3s cj r.ds.2 cj v.ams.3s

ἓν τῶν μελῶν σου ↰ ⌞καὶ μὴ⌟ ὅλον τὸ σῶμά σου βληθῇ εἰς
a {the} part of your body than to have your whole {the} body your thrown into
1651 3836 3517 5148 3517 2779 3590 5148 3910 3836 5393 5148 965 1650
a.nsn d.gpn n.gpn r.gs.2 cj pl a.nsn d.nsn n.nsn r.gs.2 v.aps.3s p.a

γέενναν. 30 καὶ εἰ ἡ δεξιά σου χεὶρ σκανδαλίζει σε, ↰ ↰ ἔκκοψον αὐτὴν
hell. And if {the} your right your hand causes you to sin, cut it
1147 2779 1623 3836 5148 1288 5148 5931 4997 5148 4997 4997 1716 899
n.asf cj cj d.nsf a.nsf r.gs.2 n.nsf v.pai.3s r.as.2 v.aam.2s r.asf.3

↰ καὶ βάλε ἀπὸ σοῦ· συμφέρει γάρ σοι ἵνα ἀπόληται ἓν τῶν
off and throw it ⌞away from⌟ you; for it is better for ⌞for you⌟ to lose a {the}
1716 2779 965 608 5148 1142 5237 1142 5148 2671 660 1651 3836
cj v.aam.2s p.g r.gs.2 v.pai.3s cj r.ds.2 cj v.ams.3s a.nsn d.gpn

μελῶν σου ↰ ⌞καὶ μὴ⌟ ὅλον τὸ σῶμά σου εἰς γέενναν
part of your body than to have your whole {the} body your thrown into hell.
3517 5148 3517 2779 3590 5148 3910 3836 5393 5148 599 1650 1147
n.gpn r.gs.2 cj pl a.nsn d.nsn n.nsn r.gs.2 p.a n.asf

NASB

brother has some-
thing against you,
24 leave your offer-
ing there before
the altar and go;
first be reconciled
to your brother,
and then come and
present your offer-
ing. 25 Make friends
quickly with your
opponent at law
while you are with
him on the way, so
that your opponent
may not hand you
over to the judge,
and the judge to the
officer, and you be
thrown into prison.
26 Truly I say to you,
you will not come
out of there until
you have paid up
the last [a]cent.
27 "You have heard
that it was said,
'YOU SHALL NOT
COMMIT ADULTERY';
28 but I say to you
that everyone who
looks at a woman
with lust for her
has already com-
mitted adultery
with her in his
heart. 29 If your right
eye makes you
stumble, tear it out
and throw it from
you; for it is bet-
ter for you to lose
one of the parts of
your body, than for
your whole body
to be thrown into
hell. 30 If your right
hand makes you
stumble, cut it off
and throw it from
you; for it is better
for you to lose one
of the parts of your
body, than for your
whole body to go
into hell.

[a] Lit *quadrans* (equaling two mites); i.e. 1/64 of a daily wage

NIV

Divorce
31 "It has been
said, 'Anyone who
divorces his wife
must give her a
certificate of di-
vorce.'[a] 32 But I tell
you that anyone
who divorces his
wife, except for
sexual immorali-
ty, makes her the
victim of adultery,
and anyone who
marries a divorced
woman commits
adultery.

Oaths
33 "Again, you
have heard that
it was said to the
people long ago,
'Do not break your
oath, but fulfill to
the Lord the vows
you have made.'
34 But I tell you,
do not swear an
oath at all: either
by heaven, for it is
God's throne; 35 or
by the earth, for it
is his footstool; or
by Jerusalem, for
it is the city of the
Great King. 36 And
do not swear by
your head, for you
cannot make even
one hair white or
black. 37 All you
need to say is sim-
ply 'Yes' or 'No';
anything beyond
this comes from
the evil one.[b]

Eye for Eye
38 "You have
heard that it was
said, 'Eye for
eye, and tooth for
tooth.'[c] 39 But I tell
you, do not resist
an evil person. If
anyone slaps you
on the right cheek,
turn to them the
other cheek also.

[a] 31 Deut. 24:1
[b] 37 Or *from evil*
[c] 38 Exodus 21:24; Lev. 24:20; Deut. 19:21

ἀπέλθῃ. 31 ἐρρέθη δέ, ⌞ὃς ἂν⌟ ἀπολύσῃ τὴν γυναῖκα αὐτοῦ,
thrown "And it was said, *And* 'Whoever divorces *{the}* his wife, *his*
599 1254 3306 1254 4005 323 668 3836 899 1222 899
v.aas.3s v.api.3s cj r.nsm pl v.aas.3s d.asf n.asf r.gsm.3

δότω αὐτῇ ἀποστάσιον. 32 ἐγὼ δὲ λέγω ὑμῖν ὅτι πᾶς ὁ
⌞let him give⌟ her a ⌞written notice of divorce.'⌟ But I *But* say to you that anyone who
1443 899 687 1254 1609 1254 3306 7007 4022 4246 3836
v.aam.3s r.dsf.3 n.asn r.ns.1 cj v.pai.1s r.dp.2 cj a.nsm d.nsm

ἀπολύων τὴν γυναῖκα αὐτοῦ παρεκτὸς λόγου πορνείας ποιεῖ
divorces *{the}* his wife, *his* except ⌞on the ground of⌟ sexual immorality, makes
668 3836 899 1222 899 4211 3364 4518 4472
pt.pa.nsm d.asf n.asf r.gsm.3 p.g n.gsm n.gsf v.pai.3s

αὐτὴν μοιχευθῆναι, καὶ ⌞ὃς ἐὰν⌟ ἀπολελυμένην γαμήσῃ,
her commit adultery, and whoever marries a divorced woman *marries*
899 3658 2779 4005 1569 1138 668 1138
r.asf.3 f.ap cj r.nsm pl pt.rp.asf v.aas.3s

μοιχᾶται. 33 πάλιν ἠκούσατε ὅτι ἐρρέθη τοῖς ἀρχαίοις, ↱
⌞is made to commit adultery.⌟ "Again, you have heard that it was said to those of old, 'You
3656 4099 201 4022 3306 3836 792 2155
v.ppi.3s adv v.aai.2p cj v.api.3s d.dpm a.dpm

↱ οὐκ ἐπιορκήσεις, ἀποδώσεις δὲ τῷ κυρίῳ τοὺς
shall not break an oath, but carry out *but* the vows you made ⌞to the⌟ Lord.' *the*
2155 4024 2155 1254 625 1254 3836 3992 5148 3836 3261 3836
adv v.fai.2s v.fai.2s cj d.dsm n.dsm d.apm

ὅρκους σου. 34 ἐγὼ δὲ λέγω ὑμῖν ↱ μὴ ὀμόσαι ὅλως· μήτε ἐν τῷ
vows *you* But I *But* say to you, do not ⌞take an oath⌟ at all; neither by *{the}*
3992 5148 1254 1609 1254 3306 7007 3923 3590 3923 3914 3612 1877 3836
n.apm r.gs.2 r.ns.1 cj v.pai.1s r.dp.2 pl f.aa adv cj p.d d.dsm

οὐρανῷ, ὅτι θρόνος ἐστὶν τοῦ θεοῦ, 35 μήτε ἐν τῇ γῇ, ὅτι
heaven, for it is the throne *it is* of God, nor by the earth, for it is a
4041 4022 1639 1639 2585 1639 3836 2536 3612 1877 3836 1178 4022 1639 1639
n.dsm cj n.nsm v.pai.3s d.gsm n.gsm cj p.d d.dsf n.dsf cj

ὑποπόδιόν ἐστιν τῶν ποδῶν αὐτοῦ, μήτε εἰς Ἱεροσόλυμα, ὅτι πόλις
footstool *it is* for his feet, *his* nor by Jerusalem, for it is the city
5711 1639 3836 899 4546 899 3612 1650 2642 4022 1639 1639 4484
n.nsn v.pai.3s d.gpm n.gpm r.gsm.3 cj p.a n.apn cj n.nsf

ἐστὶν τοῦ μεγάλου βασιλέως, 36 μήτε ἐν τῇ κεφαλῇ
it is of the great King. Nor shall you take an oath by *{the}* your head,
1639 3836 3489 995 3612 3923 3923 3923 3923 3923 1877 3836 5148 3051
v.pai.3s d.gsm a.gsm n.gsm cj p.d d.dsf n.dsf

σου ὀμόσῃς, ὅτι ⌞οὐ δύνασαι⌟ μίαν τρίχα λευκὴν ποιῆσαι
your *shall you take an oath* because you cannot make a single hair white *make*
5148 3923 4022 4024 1538 4472 1651 2582 3328 4472
r.gs.2 v.aas.2s cj adv v.ppi.2s a.asf n.asf a.asf f.aa

ἢ μέλαιναν. 37 → ἔστω δὲ ὁ λόγος ὑμῶν ναὶ ναί,
or black. But let what you say be *But* *what* *say* *you* a simple 'Yes, Yes,'
2445 3506 1254 3836 7007 3364 1639 1254 3836 3364 7007 3721 3721
cj a.asf v.pam.3s cj d.nsm n.nsm r.gp.2 pl pl

οὒ οὔ· τὸ δὲ περισσὸν τούτων ἐκ τοῦ πονηροῦ ἐστιν.
or 'No, No;' *{the}* *{and}* anything more than this comes from the evil one. *comes*
4024 4024 3836 1254 4356 4047 1639 1666 3836 4505 1639
pl pl d.nsn cj a.nsn r.gpn p.g d.gsm a.gsm v.pai.3s

38 ἠκούσατε ὅτι ἐρρέθη, ὀφθαλμὸν ἀντὶ ὀφθαλμοῦ καὶ ὀδόντα ἀντὶ
⌞"You have heard⌟ that it was said, 'An eye for an eye and a tooth for a
201 4022 3306 4057 505 4057 2779 3848 505
v.aai.2p cj v.api.3s n.asm p.g n.gsm cj n.asm p.g

ὀδόντος. 39 ἐγὼ δὲ λέγω ὑμῖν ↱ μὴ ἀντιστῆναι τῷ πονηρῷ· ἀλλ᾽ ὅστις
tooth.' But I *But* say to you, do not resist the evildoer; but whoever
3848 1254 1609 1254 3306 7007 468 3590 468 3836 4505 247 4015
n.gsm r.ns.1 cj v.pai.1s r.dp.2 pl f.aa d.dsn a.dsn cj r.nsm

σε ῥαπίζει εἰς τὴν δεξιὰν σιαγόνα σου,[a] στρέψον αὐτῷ καὶ
slaps you *slaps* on *{the}* your right cheek, *your* turn to him the other as well.
4824 5148 4824 1650 3836 5148 1288 4965 5148 5138 899 3836 257 2779
r.as.2 v.pai.3s p.a d.asf a.asf n.asf r.gs.2 v.aam.2s r.dsm.3 adv

[a] [σου] UBS, omitted by TNIV, NET.

NASB

31 "It was said,
'WHOEVER SENDS
HIS WIFE AWAY, LET
HIM GIVE HER A
CERTIFICATE OF DI-
VORCE'; 32 but I say
to you that every-
one who divorces
his wife, except
for *the* reason of
unchastity, makes
her commit adul-
tery; and whoever
marries a divorced
woman commits
adultery.
33 "Again, you
have heard that the
ancients were told,
'YOU SHALL NOT
MAKE FALSE VOWS,
BUT SHALL FULFILL
YOUR VOWS TO THE
LORD.' 34 But I say
to you, make no
oath at all, either
by heaven, for it is
the throne of God,
35 or by the earth,
for it is the foot-
stool of His feet,
or by Jerusalem,
for it is THE CITY
OF THE GREAT KING.
36 Nor shall you
make an oath by
your head, for you
cannot make one
hair white or black.
37 But let your state-
ment be, 'Yes, yes'
or 'No, no'; any-
thing beyond these
is of evil.
38 "You have heard
that it was said,
'AN EYE FOR AN
EYE, AND A TOOTH
FOR A TOOTH.' 39 But
I say to you, do
not resist an evil
person; but who-
ever slaps you on
your right cheek,
turn the other to
him also. 40 If any-
one wants to sue
you and take your
[a]shirt, let him have
your [b]coat also.
41 Whoever forces
you to go one mile,
go with him two.
42 Give to him who
asks of you, and do

[a] Lit *tunic;* i.e. a garment worn next to the body
[b] Lit *cloak;* i.e. an outer garment

NIV

[40]And if any-
one wants to sue
you and take your
shirt, hand over
your coat as well.
[41]If anyone forces
you to go one mile,
go with them two
miles. [42]Give to
the one who asks
you, and do not
turn away from the
one who wants to
borrow from you.

Love for Enemies

[43]"You have
heard that it was
said, 'Love your
neighbor[a] and hate
your enemy.' [44]But
I tell you, love
your enemies and
pray for those who
persecute you,
[45]that you may be
children of your
Father in heaven.
He causes his sun
to rise on the evil
and the good, and
sends rain on the
righteous and the
unrighteous. [46]If
you love those who
love you, what
reward will you
get? Are not even
the tax collectors
doing that? [47]And
if you greet only
your own people,
what are you doing
more than others?
Do not even pa-
gans do that? [48]Be
perfect, therefore,
as your heavenly
Father is perfect.

τὴν ἄλλην· 40 καὶ ↱ τῷ θέλοντί σοι κριθῆναι καὶ τὸν
the *other* And let the ⌞one who wants⌟ to sue you *to sue* and take *{the}* your
3836 257 2779 918 3836 2527 3212 3212 5148 3212 2779 3284 3836 5148
d.asf r.asf cj d.dsm pt.pa.dsm r.ds.2 f.ap cj d.asm

χιτῶνά σου λαβεῖν, ἄφες αὐτῷ καὶ τὸ ἱμάτιον· 41 καὶ ὅστις σε
shirt *your* *take* have your coat as well. *{the}* *coat* And whoever compels you
5945 5148 3284 918 899 2668 2779 3836 2668 2779 4015 30 5148
n.asm r.gs.2 f.aa v.aam.2s r.dsm.3 adv d.asn n.asn cj r.nsm r.as.2

ἀγγαρεύσει μίλιον ἕν, ὕπαγε μετ' αὐτοῦ δύο. 42 τῷ αἰτοῦντί
compels to go one mile, *one* go with him two. Give ⌞to the⌟ ⌞one who asks of⌟
30 1651 3627 1651 5632 3552 899 1545 1443 3836 160
v.fai.3s n.asn a.asn v.pam.2s p.g r.gsm.3 a.apn d.dsm pt.pa.dsm

σε δός, καὶ τὸν θέλοντα ἀπὸ σοῦ δανίσασθαι
you, *Give* and do not turn down the one who wants to borrow from you. *to borrow*
5148 1443 2779 695 3590 695 695 3836 2527 1244 1244 608 5148 1244
r.as.2 v.aam.2s cj d.asm pt.pa.asm p.g r.gs.2 f.am

μὴ ἀποστραφῇς. 43 ἠκούσατε ὅτι ἐρρέθη, ἀγαπήσεις τὸν πλησίον σου
not *do turn down* ⌞"You have heard⌟ that it was said, 'You shall love *{the}* your neighbor *your*
3590 695 201 4022 3306 26 3836 5148 4446 5148
pl v.aps.2s v.aai.2p cj v.api.3s v.fai.2s d.asm adv r.gs.2

καὶ μισήσεις τὸν ἐχθρόν σου. 44 ἐγὼ δὲ λέγω ὑμῖν, ἀγαπᾶτε τοὺς
and hate *{the}* your enemy.' *your* But I *But* say to you, love *{the}* your
2779 3631 3836 5148 2398 5148 1254 1609 1254 3306 7007 26 3836 7007
cj v.fai.2s d.asm a.asm r.gs.2 r.ns.1 cj v.pai.1s r.dp.2 v.pam.2p d.apm

ἐχθροὺς ὑμῶν[a] καὶ προσεύχεσθε ὑπὲρ τῶν διωκόντων ὑμᾶς, 45 ὅπως γένησθε
enemies *your* and pray for those who persecute you, so that ⌞you may be⌟
2398 7007 2779 4667 5642 3836 1503 7007 3968 1181
a.apm r.gp.2 cj v.pmm.2p p.g d.gpm pt.pa.gpm r.ap.2 cj v.ams.2p

υἱοὶ τοῦ πατρὸς ὑμῶν τοῦ ἐν οὐρανοῖς, ὅτι ↱ ↱ τὸν ἥλιον αὐτοῦ
sons of your Father *your* who is in heaven, for he makes *{the}* his sun *his*
5626 3836 7007 4252 7007 3836 1877 4041 4022 422 422 3836 899 2463 899
n.npm d.gsm n.gsm r.gp.2 d.gsm p.d n.dpm cj d.asm n.asm r.gsm.3

ἀνατέλλει ἐπὶ πονηροὺς καὶ ↰ ἀγαθοὺς καὶ βρέχει ἐπὶ δικαίους καὶ
rise on the evil and on the good, and sends rain on the just and
422 2093 4505 2779 2093 19 2779 1101 2093 1465 2779
v.pai.3s p.a a.apm cj a.apm cj v.pai.3s p.a a.apm cj

↰ ἀδίκους. 46 ἐὰν γὰρ ἀγαπήσητε τοὺς ἀγαπῶντας ὑμᾶς, τίνα μισθὸν
on the unjust. For if *For* you love those who love you, what reward
2093 96 1142 1569 1142 26 3836 26 7007 5515 3635
a.apm cj cj v.aas.2p d.apm pt.pa.apm r.ap.2 r.asm n.asm

ἔχετε; ↱ οὐχὶ καὶ οἱ τελῶναι τὸ αὐτὸ ποιοῦσιν; 47 καὶ ἐὰν
⌞do you have?⌟ Do not even the tax collectors do the same? *do* And if
2400 4472 4049 2779 3836 5467 4472 3836 899 4472 2779 1569
v.pai.2p pl adv d.npm n.npm d.asn r.asn v.pai.3p cj cj

ἀσπάσησθε τοὺς ἀδελφοὺς ὑμῶν μόνον, τί περισσὸν
you greet only *{the}* your brothers, *your* *only* what are you doing more than others?
832 3667 3836 7007 81 7007 3667 5515 4472 4472 4472 4356
v.ams.2p d.apm n.apm r.gp.2 adv r.asn a.asn

ποιεῖτε; ↱ οὐχὶ καὶ οἱ ἐθνικοὶ τὸ αὐτὸ ποιοῦσιν; 48 ἔσεσθε
are you doing Do not even the Gentiles do the same? *do* You, however, are
4472 4472 4049 2779 3836 1618 4472 3836 899 4472 7007 4036 1639
v.pai.2p pl cj d.npm a.npm d.asn r.asn v.pai.3p v.fmi.2p

οὖν ὑμεῖς ↰ ↰ τέλειοι ὡς ὁ πατὴρ ὑμῶν ὁ οὐράνιος
however *You* to be perfect, as *{the}* your heavenly Father *your* *{the}* *heavenly* is
4036 7007 1639 1639 5455 6055 3836 7007 4039 4252 7007 3836 4039 1639
cj r.np.2 a.npm cj d.nsm n.nsm r.gp.2 d.nsm a.nsm

τέλειός ἐστιν.
perfect. *is*
5455 1639
a.nsm v.pai.3s

NASB

not turn away from
him who wants to
borrow from you.
[43]"You have heard
that it was said,
'YOU SHALL LOVE
YOUR NEIGHBOR and
hate your enemy.'
[44]But I say to you,
love your enemies
and pray for those
who persecute
you, [45]so that you
may be sons of
your Father who
is in heaven; for
He causes His sun
to rise on *the* evil
and *the* good, and
sends rain on *the*
righteous and *the*
unrighteous. [46]For
if you love those
who love you,
what reward do
you have? Do not
even the tax collec-
tors do the same?
[47]If you greet only
your brothers, what
more are you doing
than others? Do
not even the Gen-
tiles do the same?
[48]Therefore you are
to be perfect, as
your heavenly Fa-
ther is perfect.

[a] 43 Lev. 19:18

[a] εὐλογεῖτε τοὺς καταρωμένους included by TR after ὑμῶν.

NIV

Giving to the Needy

6 "Be careful
not to practice
your righteousness
in front of others
to be seen by them.
If you do, you will
have no reward
from your Father
in heaven.
2"So when you
give to the needy,
do not announce it
with trumpets, as
the hypocrites do
in the synagogues
and on the streets,
to be honored by
others. Truly I tell
you, they have
received their re-
ward in full. 3But
when you give to
the needy, do not
let your left hand
know what your
right hand is do-
ing, 4so that your
giving may be in
secret. Then your
Father, who sees
what is done in
secret, will reward
you.

Prayer

5"And when you
pray, do not be like
the hypocrites, for
they love to pray
standing in the
synagogues and
on the street cor-
ners to be seen by
others. Truly I tell
you, they have re-
ceived their reward
in full. 6But when
you pray, go into
your room, close
the door and pray
to your Father,
who is unseen.

6:1 προσέχετε[a] τὴν δικαιοσύνην[b] ὑμῶν μὴ ποιεῖν
"Take care not to perform *{the}* your good deeds *your not to perform*
4668 3590 4472 4472 3836 7007 1466 7007 3590 4472
v.pam.2p d.asf n.asf r.gp.2 pl f.pa

ἔμπροσθεν τῶν ἀνθρώπων πρὸς τὸ θεαθῆναι αὐτοῖς· ⸤εἰ δὲ μή γε,⸥
before *{the}* others so as *{the}* to be seen by them; otherwise you have
1869 3836 476 4639 3836 2517 899 1623 1254 3590 1145 2400 2400
p.g d.gpm n.gpm p.a d.asn f.ap r.dpm.3 cj cj pl pl

μισθὸν οὐκ ἔχετε παρὰ τῷ πατρὶ ὑμῶν τῷ ἐν τοῖς οὐρανοῖς. 2
no reward *no you have* from *{the}* your Father *your* who is in *{the}* heaven. So
4024 3635 4024 2400 4123 3836 7007 4252 7007 3836 1877 3836 4041 4036
n.asm adv v.pai.2p p.d d.dsm n.dsm r.gp.2 d.dsm p.d d.dpm n.dpm

ὅταν οὖν ποιῇς ἐλεημοσύνην, ↱ μὴ σαλπίσῃς ἔμπροσθέν σου, ὥσπερ οἱ
whenever *So* you give alms do not sound a trumpet before you, as the
4020 4036 4472 1797 4895 3590 4895 1869 5148 6061 3836
cj cj v.pas.2s n.asf pl v.aas.2s p.g r.gs.2 cj d.npm

ὑποκριταὶ ποιοῦσιν ἐν ταῖς συναγωγαῖς καὶ ἐν ταῖς ῥύμαις, ὅπως δοξασθῶσιν
hypocrites do in the synagogues and in the streets, so that they may be praised
5695 4472 1877 3836 5252 2779 1877 3836 4860 3968 1519
n.npm v.pai.3p p.d d.dpf n.dpf cj p.d d.dpf n.dpf cj v.aps.3p

ὑπὸ τῶν ἀνθρώπων· ἀμὴν λέγω ὑμῖν, ἀπέχουσιν τὸν
by *{the}* others. I tell you the truth, *I tell you* they have received *{the}* their
5679 3836 476 3306 3306 7007 297 3306 7007 600 3836 899
p.g d.gpm n.gpm pl v.pai.1s r.dp.2 v.pai.3p d.asm

μισθὸν αὐτῶν. 3 ↱ σοῦ δὲ ποιοῦντος ἐλεημοσύνην ↱ μὴ ↱
reward. *their* But when you *But* are giving alms, do not let your left hand
3635 899 1254 4472 5148 1254 4472 1797 1182 3590 1182 5148 754 754
n.asm r.gpm.3 r.gs.2 cj pt.pa.gsm n.asf pl

γνώτω ἡ ἀριστερά σου τί ποιεῖ ἡ δεξιά σου, 4ὅπως
know *{the} left hand your* what your right hand is doing, *{the} right hand your* so that your
1182 3836 754 5148 5515 5148 1288 1288 4472 3836 1288 5148 3968 5148
v.aam.3s d.nsf a.nsf r.gs.2 r.asn v.pai.3s d.nsf a.nsf r.gs.2 cj

ᾖ σου ἡ ἐλεημοσύνη ἐν τῷ κρυπτῷ· καὶ ὁ πατήρ σου
almsgiving ⸤may be⸥ *your {the} almsgiving* in *{the}* secret; and *{the}* your Father *your*
1797 1639 5148 3836 1797 1877 3836 3220 2779 3836 5148 4252 5148
v.pas.3s r.gs.2 d.nsf n.nsf p.d d.dsn a.dsn cj d.nsm n.nsm r.gs.2

ὁ βλέπων ἐν τῷ κρυπτῷ ἀποδώσει σοι. 5καὶ ὅταν προσεύχησθε, ↱ οὐκ
who sees in *{the}* secret will reward you. "And when you pray, do not
3836 1063 1877 3836 3220 625 5148 2779 4020 4667 1639 4024
d.nsm pt.pa.nsm p.d d.dsn a.dsn v.fai.3s r.ds.2 cj cj v.pms.2p adv

ἔσεσθε ὡς οἱ ὑποκριταί, ὅτι φιλοῦσιν ἐν ταῖς συναγωγαῖς καὶ
be like the hypocrites, for they love to pray standing in *{the}* synagogues and
1639 6055 3836 5695 4022 5797 4667 4667 2705 1877 3836 5252 2779
v.fmi.2p cj d.npm n.npm cj v.pai.3p p.d d.dpf n.dpf cj

ἐν ταῖς γωνίαις τῶν πλατειῶν ἑστῶτες προσεύχεσθαι, ὅπως φανῶσιν
on *{the}* street corners *{the} street standing to pray* that ⸤they may be seen⸥
1877 3836 4426 1224 3836 4426 2705 4667 3968 5743
p.d d.dpf n.dpf d.gpf n.gpf pt.ra.npm f.pm cj v.aps.3p

τοῖς ἀνθρώποις· ἀμὴν λέγω ὑμῖν, ἀπέχουσιν τὸν μισθὸν
by others. I tell you the truth, *I tell you* they have received *{the}* their reward.
3836 476 3306 3306 7007 297 3306 7007 600 3836 899 3635
d.dpm n.dpm pl v.pai.1s r.dp.2 v.pai.3p d.asm n.asm

αὐτῶν. 6 σὺ δὲ ὅταν προσεύχῃ, εἴσελθε εἰς τὸ ταμεῖόν σου καὶ
their But when you *But when* pray, go into *{the}* your room, *your* and
899 1254 4020 5148 1254 4020 4667 1656 1650 3836 5148 5421 5148 2779
r.gpm.3 r.ns.2 cj cj v.pms.2s v.aam.2s p.a d.asn n.asn r.gs.2 cj

κλείσας τὴν θύραν σου πρόσευξαι τῷ πατρί σου τῷ ἐν τῷ κρυπτῷ·
shuting *{the}* your door, *your* pray to your Father *your* who is in *{the}* secret;
3091 3836 5148 2598 5148 4667 3836 5148 4252 5148 3836 1877 3836 3220
pt.aa.nsm d.asf n.asf r.gs.2 v.amm.2s d.dsm n.dsm r.gs.2 d.dsm p.d d.dsn a.dsn

NASB

Giving to the Poor and Prayer

6:1"Beware of
practicing your
righteousness
before men to be
noticed by them;
otherwise you have
no reward with
your Father who is
in heaven.
2"So when you
give to the poor, do
not sound a trum-
pet before you, as
the hypocrites do
in the synagogues
and in the streets,
so that they may be
honored by men.
Truly I say to you,
they have their
reward in full. 3But
when you give to
the poor, do not
let your left hand
know what your
right hand is doing,
4so that your giving
will be in secret;
and your Father
who sees *what is
done* in secret will
reward you.
5"When you pray,
you are not to be
like the hypocrites;
for they love to
stand and pray in
the synagogues
and on the street
corners so that they
may be seen by
men. Truly I say
to you, they have
their reward in full.
6But you, when you
pray, go into your
inner room, close
your door and pray
to your Father who
is in secret, and

[a] δὲ included by UBS after προσέχετε.
[b] δικαιοσύνην UBS, TNIV, NET. ἐλεημοσύνην TR.

NIV

Then your Father,
who sees what is
done in secret, will
reward you. 7And
when you pray, do
not keep on bab-
bling like pagans,
for they think
they will be heard
because of their
many words. 8Do
not be like them,
for your Father
knows what you
need before you
ask him.
9"This, then, is
how you should
pray:

"'Our Father in
heaven,
hallowed be your
name,
10your kingdom
come,
your will be done,
on earth as it is
in heaven.
11Give us today our
daily bread.
12And forgive us our
debts,
as we also have
forgiven our
debtors.
13And lead us
not into
temptation,[a]
but deliver us
from the evil
one.[b]'

14For if you forgive
other people when
they sin against
you, your heaven-
ly Father will also
forgive you. 15But
if you do not for-
give others their
sins, your Father
will not forgive
your sins.

Fasting

16"When you fast,
do not

[a] 13 The Greek for *temptation* can also mean *testing.*
[b] 13 Or *from evil*; some late manuscripts *one, / for yours is the kingdom and the power and the glory forever. Amen.*

καὶ ὁ πατήρ σου ὁ βλέπων ἐν τῷ κρυπτῷ ἀποδώσει σοι.[a] 7
and {the} your Father your who sees in {the} secret will reward you. "And
2779 3836 5148 4252 5148 3836 1063 1877 3836 3220 625 5148 1254
cj d.nsm n.nsm r.gs.2 d.nsm pt.pa.nsm p.d d.dsn a.dsn v.fai.3s r.ds.2

προσευχόμενοι δὲ ↱ μὴ βατταλογήσητε ὥσπερ οἱ ἐθνικοί, δοκοῦσιν
when you are praying, And do not babble on, as the Gentiles do, for they think
4667 1254 1006 3590 1006 6061 3836 1618 1142 1506
pt.pm.npm cj pl v.aas.2p cj d.npm a.npm v.pai.3p

γὰρ ὅτι ἐν τῇ πολυλογίᾳ αὐτῶν εἰσακουσθήσονται. 8 ↱
for that they will be heard for {the} their many words. their they will be heard Do
1142 4022 1653 1653 1653 1653 1877 3836 899 4494 899 1653 3929
cj cj p.d d.dsf n.dsf r.gpm.3 v.fpi.3p

μὴ οὖν ὁμοιωθῆτε αὐτοῖς· οἶδεν γὰρ ὁ πατὴρ ὑμῶν ὧν ⌞χρείαν
not {thus} be like them, for your Father knows for {the} Father your what you need
3590 4036 3929 899 1142 7007 4252 3857 1142 3836 4252 7007 4005 5970
pl cj v.aps.2p r.dpm.3 v.rai.3s cj d.nsm n.nsm r.gp.2 r.gpn n.asf

ἔχετε⌟ πρὸ τοῦ ὑμᾶς αἰτῆσαι αὐτόν. 9 οὕτως οὖν προσεύχεσθε ὑμεῖς·
before {the} you ask him. Pray then like this: then Pray {you} 'Our
2400 4574 3836 7007 160 899 4667 4036 4048 4036 4667 7007 7005
v.pai.2p p.g d.gsn r.ap.2 f.aa r.asm.3 adv cj v.pmm.2p r.np.2

Πάτερ ἡμῶν ὁ ἐν τοῖς οὐρανοῖς· → ἁγιασθήτω τὸ ὄνομά σου·
Father Our {the} in {the} heaven, may your name be revered, {the} name your
4252 7005 3836 1877 3836 4041 5148 3950 39 3836 3950 5148
n.vsm r.gp.1 d.vsm p.d d.dpm n.dpm v.apm.3s d.nsn n.nsn r.gs.2

10 → ἐλθέτω ἡ βασιλεία σου· → γενηθήτω τὸ θέλημά σου,
may your kingdom come, {the} kingdom your may your will be done, {the} will your
5148 993 2262 3836 993 5148 5148 2525 1181 3836 2525 5148
v.aam.3s d.nsf n.nsf r.gs.2 v.apm.3s d.nsn n.nsn r.gs.2

ὡς ἐν οὐρανῷ καὶ ἐπὶ γῆς· 11 τὸν ἄρτον
on earth as it is in heaven. {also} on earth Give us today {the} our daily bread,
2093 1178 6055 1877 4041 2779 2093 1178 1443 7005 4958 3836 7005 2157 788
cj p.d n.dsm adv p.g n.gsf d.asm n.asm

ἡμῶν τὸν ἐπιούσιον δὸς ἡμῖν σήμερον· 12 καὶ ἄφες ἡμῖν τὰ ὀφειλήματα
our {the} daily Give us today and forgive us {the} our sins,
7005 3836 2157 1443 7005 4958 2779 918 7005 3836 7005 4052
r.gp.1 d.asm a.asm v.aam.2s r.dp.1 adv cj v.aam.2s r.dp.1 d.apn n.apn

ἡμῶν, ὡς καὶ ἡμεῖς ἀφήκαμεν τοῖς ὀφειλέταις ἡμῶν· 13 καὶ ↱ μὴ
our as we also we forgive those who sin against us. And do not
7005 6055 7005 2779 7005 918 3836 4050 7005 2779 1662 3590
r.gp.1 cj adv r.np.1 v.aai.1p d.dpm n.dpm r.gp.1 cj pl

εἰσενέγκῃς ἡμᾶς εἰς πειρασμόν, ἀλλὰ ῥῦσαι ἡμᾶς ἀπὸ τοῦ πονηροῦ.[b] 14 ἐὰν
bring us into temptation, but deliver us from the evil one.' "For if
1662 7005 1650 4280 247 4861 7005 608 3836 4505 1142 1569
v.aas.2s r.ap.1 p.a n.asm cj v.amm.2s r.ap.1 p.g d.gsn a.gsn cj

γὰρ ἀφῆτε τοῖς ἀνθρώποις τὰ παραπτώματα αὐτῶν, →
For you forgive {the} others {the} their offenses, their your heavenly Father will
1142 918 3836 476 3836 899 4183 899 7007 4039 4252
cj v.aas.2p d.dpm n.dpm d.apn n.apn r.gpm.3

ἀφήσει καὶ ὑμῖν ὁ πατὴρ ὑμῶν ὁ οὐράνιος· 15 ἐὰν δὲ ↱ ↱ μὴ
also forgive also you; {the} Father your {the} heavenly but if But you do not
2779 918 2779 7007 3836 4252 7007 3836 4039 1254 1569 1254 918 918 3590
v.fai.3s adv r.dp.2 d.nsm n.nsm r.gp.2 d.nsm a.nsm cj cj pl

ἀφῆτε τοῖς ἀνθρώποις,[c] οὐδὲ ↱ ὁ πατὴρ ὑμῶν ἀφήσει τὰ
forgive {the} others their offenses, neither will {the} your Father your forgive {the} your
918 3836 476 4028 918 3836 7007 4252 7007 918 3836 7007
v.aas.2p d.dpm n.dpm cj d.nsm n.nsm r.gp.2 v.fai.3s d.apn

παραπτώματα ὑμῶν. 16 ὅταν δὲ νηστεύητε, ↱ μὴ γίνεσθε ὡς οἱ
offenses. your "And when And you fast, do not put on as the
4183 7007 1254 4020 1254 3764 1181 3590 1181 6055 3836
n.apn r.gp.2 cj cj v.pas.2p pl v.pmm.2p conj d.npm

[a] ἐν τῷ φανερῷ included by TR after σοι.
[b] ὅτι σοῦ ἐστιν ἡ βασιλεία καὶ ἡ δύναμις καὶ ἡ δόξα εἰς τοὺς αἰῶνας. ἀμήν. included by TR after πονηροῦ.
[c] τὰ παραπτώματα αὐτῶν included by TNIV after ἀνθρώποις.

NASB

your Father who
sees *what is done*
in secret will re-
ward you.
7"And when you
are praying, do not
use meaningless
repetition as the
Gentiles do, for
they suppose that
they will be heard
for their many
words. 8So do not
be like them; for
your Father knows
what you need be-
fore you ask Him.
9"Pray, then, in
this way:
'Our Father
who is in
heaven,
Hallowed be
Your name.
10'Your kingdom
come.
Your will be
done,
On earth as it
is in heaven.
11'Give us this
day our daily
bread.
12'And forgive us
our debts, as
we also have
forgiven our
debtors.
13'And do not
lead us into
temptation,
but deliver
us from evil.
[For Yours is
the kingdom
and the pow-
er and the
glory forever.
Amen.']
14For if you forgive
others for their
transgressions,
your heavenly
Father will also
forgive you. 15But
if you do not for-
give others, then
your Father will
not forgive your
transgressions.

Fasting; The True Treasure; Wealth (Mammon)

16"Whenever you
fast, do not put on
a gloomy face as

NIV

look somber as
the hypocrites do,
for they disfigure
their faces to show
others they are
fasting. Truly I tell
you, they have re-
ceived their reward
in full. 17 But when
you fast, put oil
on your head and
wash your face,
18 so that it will
not be obvious to
others that you are
fasting, but only to
your Father, who is
unseen; and your
Father, who sees
what is done in
secret, will reward
you.

Treasures in Heaven

19 "Do not store
up for yourselves
treasures on earth,
where moths and
vermin destroy,
and where thieves
break in and steal.
20 But store up for
yourselves trea-
sures in heaven,
where moths and
vermin do not de-
stroy, and where
thieves do not
break in and steal.
21 For where your
treasure is, there
your heart will be
also.
22 "The eye is the
lamp of the body.
If your eyes are
healthy,[a] your
whole body will be
full of light. 23 But
if your eyes are
unhealthy,[b] your
whole body will be
full of darkness. If
then the light with-
in you is darkness,
how great is that
darkness!
24 "No one can
serve two masters.
Either you will
hate

[a] 22 The Greek for *healthy* here implies *generous*.
[b] 23 The Greek for *unhealthy* here implies *stingy*.

ὑποκριταὶ σκυθρωποί, ἀφανίζουσιν γὰρ τὰ πρόσωπα
hypocrites a gloomy face as the hypocrites do, for they disfigure *for* *{the}* their faces
5695 5034 6055 3836 5695 1142 906 1142 3836 899 4725
n.npm a.npm v.pai.3p cj d.apn n.apn

αὐτῶν ὅπως φανῶσιν τοῖς ἀνθρώποις νηστεύοντες· ἀμὴν λέγω
their so that they will appear to others as fasting; I tell you the truth, *I tell*
899 3968 5743 3836 476 3764 3306 3306 7007 297 3306
r.gpm.3 cj v.aps.3p d.dpm n.dpm pt.pa.npm pl v.pai.1s

ὑμῖν, ἀπέχουσιν τὸν μισθὸν αὐτῶν. 17 ↱ σὺ δὲ νηστεύων ἄλειψαί σου
you they have *{the}* their reward. *their* But when you *But* fast, anoint your
7007 600 3836 899 3635 899 1254 3764 5148 1254 3764 230 5148
r.dp.2 v.pai.3p d.asm n.asm r.gpm.3 r.ns.2 cj pt.pa.nsm v.amm.2s r.gs.2

τὴν κεφαλὴν ↰ ↰ καὶ τὸ πρόσωπόν σου νίψαι, 18 ὅπως ↱ ↱ μὴ
{the} head with oil and wash *{the}* your face, *your* *wash* so that you will not
3836 3051 230 230 2779 3782 3836 5148 4725 5148 3782 3968 5743 5743 3590
d.asf n.asf cj d.asn n.asn r.gs.2 v.amm.2s cj pl

φανῇς τοῖς ἀνθρώποις νηστεύων ἀλλὰ τῷ πατρί σου τῷ ἐν τῷ κρυφαίῳ·
appear to others as fasting, but by your Father *your* who is in *{the}* secret;
5743 3836 476 3764 247 3836 5148 4252 5148 3836 1877 3836 3224
v.aps.2s d.dpm n.dpm pt.pa.nsm cj d.dsm n.dsm r.gs.2 d.dsm p.d d.dsn a.dsn

καὶ ὁ πατήρ σου ὁ βλέπων ἐν τῷ κρυφαίῳ ἀποδώσει σοι.[a] 19 ↱ μὴ
and *{the}* your Father *your* who sees in *{the}* secret will reward you. "Do not
2779 3836 5148 4252 5148 3836 1063 1877 3836 3224 625 5148 2564 3590
cj d.nsm n.nsm r.gs.2 d.nsm pt.pa.nsm p.d d.dsn a.dsn v.fai.3s r.ds.2 pl

θησαυρίζετε ὑμῖν θησαυροὺς ἐπὶ τῆς γῆς, ὅπου σὴς καὶ βρῶσις ἀφανίζει
lay up for yourselves treasures on *{the}* earth, where moth and rust destroy,
2564 7007 2565 2093 3836 1178 3963 4962 2779 1111 906
v.pam.2p r.dp.2 n.apm p.g d.gsf n.gsf pl n.nsm cj n.nsf v.pai.3s

καὶ ὅπου κλέπται διορύσσουσιν καὶ κλέπτουσιν· 20 θησαυρίζετε δὲ ὑμῖν
and where thieves break in and steal; but lay up *but* for yourselves
2779 3963 3095 1482 2779 3096 1254 2564 1254 7007
cj pl n.npm v.pai.3p cj v.pai.3p v.pam.2p cj r.dp.2

θησαυροὺς ἐν οὐρανῷ, ὅπου οὔτε σὴς οὔτε βρῶσις ἀφανίζει καὶ ὅπου κλέπται
treasures in heaven, where neither moth nor rust destroys, and where thieves
2565 1877 4041 3963 4046 4962 4046 1111 906 2779 3963 3095
n.apm p.d n.dsm pl cj n.nsm cj n.nsf v.pai.3s cj pl n.npm

↱ οὐ διορύσσουσιν οὐδὲ κλέπτουσιν· 21 ὅπου γάρ ἐστιν ὁ
do not break in and steal. For where *For* your treasure is, *{the}*
1482 4024 1482 4028 3096 1142 3963 1142 5148 2565 1639 3836
adv v.pai.3p cj v.pai.3p cj cj v.pai.3s d.nsm

θησαυρός σου, ἐκεῖ ἔσται καὶ ἡ καρδία σου. 22 ὁ λύχνος τοῦ
treasure *your* there your heart will be also. *{the}* *heart* *your* "The lamp of the
2565 5148 1695 5148 2840 1639 2779 3836 2840 5148 3836 3394 3836
n.nsm r.gs.2 adv v.fmi.3s adv d.nsf n.nsf r.gs.2 d.nsm n.nsm d.gsn

σώματός ἐστιν ὁ ὀφθαλμός. ἐὰν οὖν ᾖ ὁ ὀφθαλμός σου ἁπλοῦς,
body is the eye. If then your eye is *{the}* *eye* *your* healthy,
5393 1639 3836 4057 1569 4036 5148 4057 1639 3836 4057 5148 606
n.gsn v.pai.3s d.nsm n.nsm cj cj v.pas.3s d.nsm n.nsm r.gs.2 a.nsm

ὅλον τὸ σῶμά σου φωτεινὸν ἔσται· 23 ἐὰν δὲ ὁ
your whole *{the}* body *your* will be ⌊filled with light;⌋ *will be* but if *but* *{the}* your
5148 3910 3836 5393 5148 1639 1639 5893 1639 1254 1569 1254 3836 5148
a.nsn d.nsn n.nsn r.gs.2 a.nsn v.fmi.3s cj cj d.nsm

ὀφθαλμός σου πονηρὸς ᾖ, ὅλον τὸ σῶμά σου σκοτεινὸν
eye *your* is evil, *is* your whole *{the}* body *your* will be filled with darkness.
4057 5148 1639 4505 1639 5148 3910 3836 5393 5148 1639 1639 5027
n.nsm r.gs.2 a.nsm v.pas.3s a.nsn d.nsn n.nsn r.gs.2 a.nsn

ἔσται. εἰ οὖν τὸ φῶς τὸ ἐν σοὶ σκότος ἐστίν, τὸ σκότος
will be If then the light that is in you is darkness, *is* how great is that darkness!
1639 1623 4036 3836 5890 3836 1877 5148 1639 5030 1639 4531 4531 3836 5030
v.fmi.3s cj cj d.nsn n.nsn d.nsn p.d r.ds.2 n.nsn v.pai.3s d.nsn n.nsn

πόσον. 24 οὐδεὶς δύναται δυσὶ κυρίοις δουλεύειν· ἢ γὰρ
how great "No one can serve two masters, *serve* for either *for* he will hate
4531 4029 1538 1526 1545 3261 1526 1142 2445 1142 3631 3631 3631
r.nsn a.nsm v.ppi.3s a.dpm n.dpm f.pa cj cj

[a] ἐν τῷ φανερῷ included by TR after σοι.

NASB

the hypocrites *do,*
for they neglect
their appearance
so that they will
be noticed by men
when they are fast-
ing. Truly I say
to you, they have
their reward in full.
17 But you, when
you fast, anoint
your head and
wash your face 18 so
that your fasting
will not be noticed
by men, but by
your Father who is
in secret; and your
Father who sees
what is done in
secret will reward
you.
19 "Do not store
up for yourselves
treasures on earth,
where moth and
rust destroy, and
where thieves
break in and steal.
20 But store up for
yourselves trea-
sures in heaven,
where neither moth
nor rust destroys,
and where thieves
do not break in or
steal; 21 for where
your treasure is,
there your heart
will be also.
22 "The eye is the
lamp of the body;
so then if your eye
is clear, your whole
body will be full of
light. 23 But if your
eye is bad, your
whole body will be
full of darkness. If
then the light that
is in you is dark-
ness, how great is
the darkness!
24 "No one can
serve two masters;
for either he will

NIV

the one and love
the other, or you
will be devoted
to the one and de-
spise the other.
You cannot serve
both God and
money.

Do Not Worry

25 "Therefore I tell
you, do not worry
about your life,
what you will eat
or drink; or about
your body, what
you will wear.
Is not life more
than food, and the
body more than
clothes? 26 Look at
the birds of the air;
they do not sow or
reap or store away
in barns, and yet
your heavenly Fa-
ther feeds them.
Are you not much
more valuable than
they? 27 Can any
one of you by wor-
rying add a single
hour to your life[a]?
28 "And why do
you worry about
clothes? See how
the flowers of the
field grow. They
do not labor or
spin. 29 Yet I tell
you that not even
Solomon in all
his splendor was
dressed like one of
these. 30 If that is
how God clothes
the grass of the
field, which is here
today and tomor-
row is thrown into
the fire, will he not
much more clothe
you—you of lit-
tle faith? 31 So do
not worry, saying,
'What

[a] 27 Or *single cubit to your height*

τὸν ἕνα μισήσει καὶ τὸν ἕτερον ἀγαπήσει, ἢ ἑνὸς ἀνθέξεται
the one *he will hate* and love the other, *love* or *one* ⌊he will be devoted to⌋ the one
3836 1651 3631 2779 26 3836 2283 26 2445 1651 504 1651
d.asm a.asm v.fai.3s cj d.asm r.asm v.fai.3s cj a.gsm v.fmi.3s

καὶ τοῦ ἑτέρου καταφρονήσει. ⌊οὐ δύνασθε⌋ θεῷ δουλεύειν καὶ
and despise the other. *despise* You cannot serve God *serve* and
2779 2969 3836 2283 2969 4024 1538 1526 2536 1526 2779
cj d.gsm r.gsm v.fai.3s adv v.ppi.2p n.dsm f.pa cj

μαμωνᾷ. 25 ⌊διὰ τοῦτο⌋ λέγω ὑμῖν, ↱ μὴ μεριμνᾶτε τῇ ψυχῇ
possessions. "Therefore I say to you, 'Do not ⌊be anxious about⌋ *{the}* your life,
3440 1328 4047 3306 7007 3534 3590 3534 3836 7007 6034
n.dsm p.a r.asn v.pai.1s r.dp.2 pl v.pam.2p d.dsf n.dsf

ὑμῶν τί φάγητε [a]ἢ τί πίητε, μηδὲ τῷ σώματι ὑμῶν τί
your what ⌊you will eat⌋ or what ⌊you will drink,⌋ or about your body, *your* what
7007 5515 2266 2445 5515 4403 3593 3836 7007 5393 7007 5515
r.gp.2 r.asn v.aas.2p cj r.asn v.aas.2p cj d.dsn n.dsn r.gp.2 r.asn

ἐνδύσησθε. οὐχὶ ἡ ψυχὴ πλεῖόν ἐστιν τῆς τροφῆς καὶ τὸ σῶμα ↰ ↰
you will put on. Is not *{the}* life more than *Is* *{the}* food and the body more than
1907 1639 4049 3836 6034 4498 1639 3836 5575 2779 3836 5393 4498 4498
v.ams.2p pl d.nsf n.nsf a.nsn.c v.pai.3s d.gsf n.gsf cj d.nsn n.nsn

τοῦ ἐνδύματος; 26 ἐμβλέψατε εἰς τὰ πετεινὰ τοῦ οὐρανοῦ ὅτι ↱ οὐ
{the} clothing? Look at the birds of the air, *{that}* they neither
3836 1903 1838 1650 3836 4374 3836 4041 4022 5062 4024
d.gsn n.gsn v.aam.2p p.a d.apn n.apn d.gsm n.gsm cj adv

σπείρουσιν οὐδὲ θερίζουσιν οὐδὲ συνάγουσιν εἰς ἀποθήκας, καὶ ὁ
sow nor reap nor gather into barns, and yet *{the}* your heavenly
5062 4028 2545 4028 5251 1650 630 2779 3836 7007 4039
v.pai.3p cj v.pai.3p cj v.pai.3p p.a n.apf cj d.nsm

πατὴρ ὑμῶν ὁ οὐράνιος τρέφει αὐτά· ↱ οὐχ ὑμεῖς μᾶλλον διαφέρετε αὐτῶν;
Father *your* *{the}* *heavenly* feeds them. Are you not *you* more valuable than they?
4252 7007 3836 4039 5555 899 1422 7007 4024 7007 3437 1422 899
n.nsm r.gp.2 d.nsm a.nsm v.pai.3s r.apn.3 pl r.np.2 adv.c v.pai.2p r.gpn.3

27 τίς δὲ ἐξ ὑμῶν μεριμνῶν δύναται προσθεῖναι ἐπὶ τὴν
And which *And* of you by being anxious can add a single cubit to *{the}* his
1254 5515 1254 1666 7007 3534 1538 4707 1651 4388 2093 3836 899
r.nsm cj p.g r.gp.2 pt.pa.nsm v.ppi.3s f.aa p.a d.asf

ἡλικίαν αὐτοῦ πῆχυν ἕνα; 28 καὶ περὶ ἐνδύματος τί
height? *his* *cubit* *single* And why are you anxious about clothing? *why*
2461 899 4388 1651 2779 5515 3534 3534 3534 4309 1903 5515
n.asf r.gsm.3 n.asm a.asm cj p.g n.gsn r.asn

μεριμνᾶτε; καταμάθετε τὰ κρίνα τοῦ ἀγροῦ πῶς αὐξάνουσιν· ↱ ↱ οὐ
are you anxious Consider the lilies of the field, how they grow; they do not
3534 2908 3836 3211 3836 69 4802 889 3159 3159 4024
v.pai.2p v.aam.2p d.apn n.apn d.gsm n.gsm pl v.pai.3p adv

κοπιῶσιν οὐδὲ νήθουσιν· 29 λέγω δὲ ὑμῖν ὅτι οὐδὲ Σολομὼν ἐν πάσῃ τῇ
toil nor do they spin; but I say *but* to you that not even Solomon in all *{the}*
3159 4028 3756 1254 3306 1254 7007 4022 4028 5048 1877 4246 3836
v.pai.3p cj v.pai.3p v.pai.1s cj r.dp.2 cj adv n.nsm p.d a.dsf d.dsf

δόξῃ αὐτοῦ περιεβάλετο ὡς ἓν τούτων. 30 εἰ δὲ
his ⌊royal splendor⌋ *his* was clothed like one of these. Now if *Now* God so clothes
899 1518 899 4314 6055 1651 4047 1254 1623 1254 2536 4048 314
n.dsf r.gsm.3 v.ami.3s conj a.nsn r.gpn cj cj

τὸν χόρτον τοῦ ἀγροῦ σήμερον ὄντα καὶ αὔριον εἰς
the grass of the field, which is here today *which is here* but tomorrow is thrown into
3836 5965 3836 69 1639 1639 1639 4958 1639 2779 892 965 965 1650
d.asm n.asm d.gsm n.gsm adv pt.pa.asm cj adv p.a

κλίβανον βαλλόμενον ὁ θεὸς οὕτως ἀμφιέννυσιν, οὐ πολλῷ μᾶλλον
the oven, *is thrown* *{the}* *God* *so* *clothes* will he not much more
3106 965 3836 2536 4048 314 4024 4498 3437
n.asm pt.pp.asm d.nsm n.nsm adv v.pai.3s pl a.dsn adv.c

ὑμᾶς, ὀλιγόπιστοι; 31 ↱ μὴ οὖν μεριμνήσητε λέγοντες, τί
clothe you, ⌊O you of little faith?⌋ So then, do not *So then* be anxious, saying, 'What
7007 3899 4036 4036 3534 3590 4036 3534 3306 5515
r.ap.2 a.vpm pl cj v.aas.2p pt.pa.npm r.asn

[a] [ἢ τί πίητε] UBS.

NASB

hate the one and
love the other, or
he will be devoted
to one and despise
the other. You can-
not serve God and
[a]wealth.

The Cure for Anxiety

25 "For this reason
I say to you, do not
be worried about
your life, *as to*
what you will eat
or what you will
drink; nor for your
body, *as to* what
you will put on. Is
not life more than
food, and the body
more than cloth-
ing? 26 Look at the
birds of the air, that
they do not sow,
nor reap nor gather
into barns, and
yet your heavenly
Father feeds them.
Are you not worth
much more than
they? 27 And who
of you by being
worried can add a
single hour to his
life? 28 And why are
you worried about
clothing? Observe
how the lilies of
the field grow;
they do not toil nor
do they spin, 29 yet
I say to you that
not even Solomon
in all his glory
clothed himself
like one of these.
30 But if God so
clothes the grass of
the field, which is
alive today and to-
morrow is thrown
into the furnace,
will He not much
more *clothe* you?
You of little faith!
31 Do not worry
then,

[a] Gr *mamonas,* for Aram *mamon* (mammon); i.e. wealth, etc., personified as an object of worship

NIV

shall we eat?' or
'What shall we
drink?' or 'What
shall we wear?'
32For the pagans
run after all these
things, and your
heavenly Father
knows that you
need them. 33But
seek first his king-
dom and his righ-
teousness, and all
these things will
be given to you as
well. 34Therefore
do not worry about
tomorrow, for to-
morrow will worry
about itself. Each
day has enough
trouble of its own.

Judging Others

7 "Do not judge,
or you too will
be judged. 2For in
the same way you
judge others, you
will be judged, and
with the measure
you use, it will be
measured to you.
3"Why do you
look at the speck
of sawdust in your
brother's eye and
pay no attention to
the plank in your
own eye? 4How
can you say to
your brother, 'Let
me take the speck
out of your eye,'
when all the time
there is a plank
in your own eye?
5You hypocrite,
first take the plank
out of your own
eye, and then you
will see clearly to
remove the speck
from your broth-
er's eye.
6"Do not give
dogs what is sa-
cred;

φάγωμεν; ἤ, τί πίωμεν; ἤ, ↱ τί περιβαλώμεθα; 32
shall we eat?' or, 'What ⌞shall we drink?'⌟ or, 'With what shall we clothe ourselves?' — for
2266 2445 5515 4403 2445 4314 5515 4314 1142
v.aas.1p cj r.asn v.aas.1p cj r.asn v.ams.1p

πάντα γὰρ ταῦτα τὰ ἔθνη ἐπιζητοῦσιν·
the Gentiles pursue all *for* these things *the* *Gentiles* *pursue* — for your heavenly
3836 1620 2118 4246 1142 4047 3836 1620 2118 1142 7007 4039
a.apn cj r.apn d.npn n.npn v.pai.3p

οἶδεν γὰρ ὁ πατὴρ ὑμῶν ὁ οὐράνιος ὅτι χρῄζετε τούτων ἁπάντων.
Father knows *for* *{the}* *Father* *your* *{the}* *heavenly* that you need them all.
4252 3857 1142 3836 4252 7007 3836 4039 4022 5974 4047 570
v.rai.3s cj d.nsm n.nsm r.gp.2 d.nsm a.nsm cj v.pai.2p r.gpn a.gpn

33 ζητεῖτε δὲ πρῶτον τὴν βασιλείαν [a]τοῦ θεοῦ καὶ τὴν δικαιοσύνην αὐτοῦ,
But seek *But* first the kingdom of God and *{the}* his righteousness, *his*
1254 2426 1254 4754 3836 993 3836 2536 2779 3836 899 1466 899
v.pam.2p cj adv d.asf n.asf d.gsm n.gsm cj d.asf n.asf r.gsm.3

καὶ ταῦτα πάντα προστεθήσεται ὑμῖν. ↰ ↰ 34 ↱ μὴ οὖν
and all these things *all* will be given to you as well. Therefore do not *Therefore*
2779 4246 4047 4246 4707 7007 4707 4707 4036 3534 3590 4036
cj r.npn a.npn v.fpi.3s r.dp.2 pl cj

μεριμνήσητε εἰς τὴν αὔριον, ἡ γὰρ αὔριον μεριμνήσει ἑαυτῆς· ἀρκετὸν
be anxious about *{the}* tomorrow, *{the}* for tomorrow ⌞will be anxious about⌟ itself. Sufficient
3534 1650 3836 892 3836 1142 892 3534 1571 757
v.aas.2p p.a d.asf adv d.nsf cj adv v.fai.3s r.gsf.3 a.nsn

τῇ ἡμέρᾳ ἡ κακία αὐτῆς.
⌞for the⌟ day is *{the}* its own trouble. *its own*
3836 2465 3836 899 899 2798 899
d.dsf n.dsf d.nsf n.nsf r.gsf.3

7:1 ↱ μὴ κρίνετε, ἵνα ↱ ↱ μὴ κριθῆτε· 2 ⌞ἐν ᾧ⌟
"Do not judge others, so that you will not be judged. For by the standard
3212 3590 3212 2671 3212 3212 3590 3212 1142 1877 4005 3210
pl v.pam.2p cj pl v.aps.2p p.d r.dsn

γὰρ κρίματι κρίνετε κριθήσεσθε, καὶ ⌞ἐν ᾧ⌟ μέτρῳ μετρεῖτε μετρηθήσεται
For *standard* you judge you will be judged, and with the measure you use it will be measured
1142 3210 3212 3212 2779 1877 4005 3586 3582 3582
cj n.dsn v.pai.2p v.fpi.2p cj p.d r.dsn n.dsn v.pai.2p v.fpi.3s

ὑμῖν. 3 τί δὲ βλέπεις τὸ κάρφος τὸ ἐν τῷ ὀφθαλμῷ
to you. And why *And* ⌞do you look at⌟ the speck *{the}* in your brother's *{the}* eye
7007 1254 5515 1254 1063 3836 2847 3836 1877 5148 81 3836 4057
r.dp.2 r.asn cj v.pai.2s d.asn n.asn d.asn p.d d.dsm n.dsm

τοῦ ἀδελφοῦ σου, τὴν δὲ ἐν τῷ σῷ ὀφθαλμῷ
{the} *brother's* *your* *{the}* but pay no attention to the log in *{the}* ⌞your own⌟ eye?
3836 81 5148 3836 1254 2917 4024 2917 2917 1512 1877 3836 5050 4057
d.gsm n.gsm r.gs.2 d.asf cj p.d d.dsm r.dsm.2 n.dsm

δοκὸν οὐ κατανοεῖς; 4ἢ πῶς ἐρεῖς τῷ ἀδελφῷ σου, ἄφες ἐκβάλω
log *no* *pay attention to* Or how dare you say to your brother, *your* 'Let me remove
1512 4024 2917 2445 4802 3306 3836 5148 81 5148 918 1675
n.asf adv v.pai.2s cj pl v.fai.2s d.dsm n.dsm r.gs.2 v.aam.2s v.aas.1s

τὸ κάρφος ἐκ τοῦ ὀφθαλμοῦ σου, καὶ ἰδοὺ ἡ δοκὸς ἐν τῷ
the speck from *{the}* your eye,' *your* and look, there is a log in *{the}* your
3836 2847 1666 3836 5148 4057 5148 2779 2627 3836 1512 1877 3836 5148
d.asn n.asn p.g d.gsm n.gsm r.gs.2 cj j d.nsf n.nsf p.d d.dsm

ὀφθαλμῷ σοῦ; 5ὑποκριτά, ἔκβαλε πρῶτον ἐκ τοῦ
own eye? *your own* You hypocrite! First take *First* the log out of your own
5148 4057 5148 5695 4754 1675 4754 3836 1512 1666 3836 5148 5148
n.dsm r.gs.2 n.vsm v.aam.2s adv p.g d.gsm

ὀφθαλμοῦ σοῦ τὴν δοκόν, καὶ τότε διαβλέψεις ἐκβαλεῖν τὸ κάρφος
eye, *your own* *the* *log* and then ⌞you will be able to see clearly⌟ to remove the speck
4057 5148 3836 1512 2779 5538 1332 1675 3836 2847
n.gsm r.gs.2 d.asf n.asf cj adv v.fai.2s f.aa d.asn n.asn

ἐκ τοῦ ὀφθαλμοῦ τοῦ ἀδελφοῦ σου. 6↱ μὴ δῶτε τὸ ἅγιον τοῖς
out of your brother's eye. *{the}* *brother's* *your* "Do not give what is holy to
1666 3836 5148 81 4057 3836 81 5148 1443 3590 1443 3836 41 3836
p.g d.gsm n.gsm d.gsm n.gsm r.gs.2 pl v.aas.2p d.asn a.asn d.dpm

[a] [τοῦ θεοῦ] UBS, omitted by NET.

NASB

saying, 'What will
we eat?' or 'What
will we drink?'
or 'What will we
wear for clothing?'
32For the Gentiles
eagerly seek all
these things; for
your heavenly
Father knows that
you need all these
things. 33But seek
first His kingdom
and His righteous-
ness, and all these
things will be
added to you.
34"So do not wor-
ry about tomorrow;
for tomorrow will
care for itself. Each
day has enough
trouble of its own.

Judging Others

7:1"Do not judge
so that you will not
be judged. 2For in
the way you judge,
you will be judged;
and by your stan-
dard of measure, it
will be measured to
you. 3Why do you
look at the speck
that is in your
brother's eye, but
do not notice the
log that is in your
own eye? 4Or how
can you say to your
brother, 'Let me
take the speck out
of your eye,' and
behold, the log is
in your own eye?
5You hypocrite,
first take the log
out of your own
eye, and then you
will see clearly to
take the speck out
of your brother's
eye.
6"Do not give
what is holy to

NIV

do not throw your
pearls to pigs. If
you do, they may
trample them un-
der their feet, and
turn and tear you
to pieces.

Ask, Seek, Knock

7“Ask and it will
be given to you;
seek and you will
find; knock and
the door will be
opened to you.
8For everyone who
asks receives; the
one who seeks
finds; and to the
one who knocks,
the door will be
opened.
9“Which of you,
if your son asks
for bread, will give
him a stone? 10Or
if he asks for a
fish, will give him
a snake? 11If you,
then, though you
are evil, know how
to give good gifts
to your children,
how much more
will your Father in
heaven give good
gifts to those who
ask him! 12So in
everything, do to
others what you
would have them
do to you, for this
sums up the Law
and the Prophets.

The Narrow and Wide Gates

13“Enter through
the narrow gate.
For wide is the
gate and broad is
the road that leads
to destruction,
and many enter
through it. 14But
small is the gate
and narrow the
road that leads to
life, and only a few
find it.

κυσὶν μηδὲ ↱ ↰ βάλητε τοὺς μαργαρίτας ὑμῶν ἔμπροσθεν τῶν χοίρων, μήποτε
dogs, and do not throw *{the}* your pearls *your* in front of pigs, lest
3264 3593 965 3593 965 3836 7007 3449 7007 1869 3836 5956 3607
n.dpm cj v.aas.2p d.apm n.apm r.gp.2 p.g d.gpm n.gpm cj

καταπατήσουσιν αὐτοὺς ἐν τοῖς ποσὶν αὐτῶν καὶ στραφέντες
the pigs trample them under *{the}* their feet, *their* and the dogs turn
2922 899 1877 3836 899 4546 899 2779 5138
v.fai.3p r.apm.3 p.d d.dpm n.dpm r.gpm.3 cj pt.ap.npm

ῥήξωσιν ὑμᾶς. ↰ ↰ 7αἰτεῖτε καὶ δοθήσεται ὑμῖν, ζητεῖτε καὶ εὑρήσετε,
and tear you to pieces. “Ask and it will be given to you, seek and you will find,
4838 7007 4838 4838 160 2779 1443 7007 2426 2779 2351
v.aas.3p r.ap.2 v.pam.2p cj v.fpi.3s r.dp.2 v.pam.2p cj v.fai.2p

κρούετε καὶ ἀνοιγήσεται ὑμῖν· 8 πᾶς γὰρ ὁ αἰτῶν λαμβάνει καὶ
knock and it will be opened for you. For everyone *For* who asks receives, and
3218 2779 487 7007 1142 4246 1142 3836 160 3284 2779
v.pam.2p cj v.fpi.3s r.dp.2 a.nsm cj d.nsm pt.pa.nsm v.pai.3s cj

↰ ὁ ζητῶν εὑρίσκει καὶ ↱ ↰ τῷ κρούοντι ἀνοιγήσεται. 9ἢ
everyone who seeks finds, and for everyone who knocks it will be opened. Or is
4246 3836 2426 2351 2779 3836 4246 3836 3218 487 2445 1639
d.nsm pt.pa.nsm v.pai.3s cj d.dsm pt.pa.dsm v.fpi.3s cj

τίς ἐστιν ἐξ ὑμῶν ἄνθρωπος, ὃν αἰτήσει ὁ υἱὸς αὐτοῦ
there any man *is there* among you *man* who, if his son should ask *{the}* *son* *his*
1639 5515 476 1639 1666 7007 476 4005 899 5626 160 3836 5626 899
r.nsm v.pai.3s p.g r.gp.2 n.nsm r.asm v.fai.3s d.nsm n.nsm r.gsm.3

↰ ἄρτον, μὴ λίθον ἐπιδώσει αὐτῷ; 10ἢ καὶ
for bread, ~ would give him a stone? *would give* *him* Or *{also}* if he should ask for a
160 788 3590 2113 2113 899 3345 2113 899 2445 2779 160 160 160 160
n.asm pl n.asm v.fai.3s r.dsm.3 cj adv

ἰχθὺν αἰτήσει, μὴ ὄφιν ἐπιδώσει αὐτῷ; 11εἰ οὖν ὑμεῖς
fish, *he should ask for* ~ would give him a snake? *would give* *him* If then you, who
2716 160 3590 2113 2113 899 4058 2113 899 1623 4036 7007 1639
n.asm v.fai.3s pl n.asm v.fai.3s r.dsm.3 cj cj r.np.2

πονηροὶ ὄντες οἴδατε δόματα ἀγαθὰ διδόναι τοῖς τέκνοις
are evil, *who are* know how to give good gifts *good* *to give* to your children,
1639 4505 1639 3857 1443 1443 19 1517 19 1443 3836 7007 5451
a.npm pt.pa.npm v.rai.2p n.apn a.apn f.pa d.dpn n.dpn

ὑμῶν, πόσῳ μᾶλλον ↱ ὁ πατὴρ ὑμῶν ὁ ἐν τοῖς οὐρανοῖς δώσει
your how much more will *{the}* your Father *your* *{the}* in *{the}* heaven give
7007 4531 3437 1443 3836 7007 4252 7007 3836 1877 3836 4041 1443
r.gp.2 r.dsn adv.c d.nsm n.nsm r.gp.2 d.nsm p.d d.dpm n.dpm v.fai.3s

ἀγαθὰ τοῖς αἰτοῦσιν αὐτόν. 12πάντα οὖν ⌞ὅσα ἐὰν⌟ θέλητε
good things to those who ask him! *{all things}* “So whatever ⌞you would like⌟ others
19 3836 160 899 4246 4036 4012 1569 2527 476
a.apn d.dpm pt.pa.dpm r.asm.3 a.apn cj r.apn pl v.pas.2p

ἵνα ποιῶσιν ὑμῖν οἱ ἄνθρωποι, οὕτως καὶ ὑμεῖς ποιεῖτε αὐτοῖς· οὗτος
to do to you, *{the}* *others* *{likewise}* do also *{you}* *do* to them, for this
2671 4472 7007 3836 476 4048 4472 2779 7007 4472 899 1142 4047
cj v.pas.3p r.dp.2 d.npm n.npm adv adv r.np.2 v.pam.2p r.dpm.3 r.nsm

γάρ ἐστιν ὁ νόμος καὶ οἱ προφῆται. 13εἰσέλθατε διὰ τῆς στενῆς πύλης· ὅτι
for is the law and the prophets. “Enter through the narrow gate. For
1142 1639 3836 3795 2779 3836 4737 1656 1328 3836 5101 4783 4022
cj v.pai.3s d.nsm n.nsm cj d.npm n.npm v.aam.2p p.g d.gsf a.gsf n.gsf cj

πλατεῖα ἡ πύλη καὶ εὐρύχωρος ἡ ὁδὸς ἡ ἀπάγουσα εἰς τὴν ἀπώλειαν καὶ
wide is the gate and easy the way that leads to *{the}* destruction, and
4426 3836 4783 2779 2353 3836 3847 3836 552 1650 3836 724 2779
a.nsf d.nsf n.nsf cj a.nsf d.nsf n.nsf d.nsf pt.pa.nsf p.a d.asf n.asf cj

πολλοί εἰσιν οἱ εἰσερχόμενοι δι᾽ αὐτῆς· 14τί στενὴ ἡ πύλη καὶ
many are those who enter through it. How narrow is the gate and
4498 1639 3836 1656 1328 899 5515 5101 3836 4783 2779
a.npm v.pai.3p d.npm pt.pm.npm p.g r.gsf.3 r.asn a.nsf d.nsf n.nsf cj

τεθλιμμένη ἡ ὁδὸς ἡ ἀπάγουσα εἰς τὴν ζωὴν καὶ ὀλίγοι εἰσὶν οἱ εὑρίσκοντες
difficult the way that leads to *{the}* life, and few are those who find
2567 3836 3847 3836 552 1650 3836 2437 2779 3900 1639 3836 2351
pt.rp.nsf d.nsf n.nsf d.nsf pt.pa.nsf p.a d.asf n.asf cj a.npm v.pai.3p d.npm pt.pa.npm

NASB

dogs, and do not
throw your pearls
before swine, or
they will trample
them under their
feet, and turn and
tear you to pieces.

Prayer and the Golden Rule

7“Ask, and it will
be given to you;
seek, and you will
find; knock, and it
will be opened to
you. 8For everyone
who asks receives,
and he who seeks
finds, and to him
who knocks it will
be opened. 9Or
what man is there
among you who,
when his son asks
for a loaf, will give
him a stone? 10Or if
he asks for a fish,
he will not give
him a snake, will
he? 11If you then,
being evil, know
how to give good
gifts to your chil-
dren, how much
more will your
Father who is in
heaven give what
is good to those
who ask Him!
12“In everything,
therefore, treat
people the same
way you want them
to treat you, for
this is the Law and
the Prophets.

The Narrow and Wide Gates

13“Enter through
the narrow gate;
for the gate is wide
and the way is
broad that leads to
destruction, and
there are many
who enter through
it. 14For the gate is
small and the way
is narrow that leads
to life, and there
are few who find it.

NIV

True and False Prophets

15 “Watch out for
false prophets.
They come to you
in sheep’s cloth-
ing, but inwardly
they are ferocious
wolves. 16 By their
fruit you will rec-
ognize them. Do
people pick grapes
from thornbushes,
or figs from this-
tles? 17 Likewise,
every good tree
bears good fruit,
but a bad tree
bears bad fruit. 18 A
good tree cannot
bear bad fruit, and
a bad tree cannot
bear good fruit.
19 Every tree that
does not bear good
fruit is cut down
and thrown into
the fire. 20 Thus, by
their fruit you will
recognize them.

True and False Disciples

21 “Not everyone
who says to me,
‘Lord, Lord,’ will
enter the kingdom
of heaven, but
only the one who
does the will of
my Father who is
in heaven. 22 Many
will say to me on
that day, ‘Lord,
Lord, did we not
prophesy in your
name and in your
name drive out de-
mons and in your
name perform
many miracles?’
23 Then I will tell
them plainly, ‘I
never knew you.
Away from me,
you evildoers!’

αὐτήν. 15 προσέχετε ἀπὸ τῶν ψευδοπροφητῶν, οἵτινες ἔρχονται πρὸς ὑμᾶς ἐν
it! “Beware of {the} false prophets; they come to you in sheep’s
899 4668 608 3836 6021 4015 2262 4639 7007 1877 4585
r.asf.3 v.pam.2p p.g d.gpm n.gpm r.npm v.pmi.3p p.a r.ap.2 p.d

ἐνδύμασιν προβάτων, ἔσωθεν δέ εἰσιν λύκοι ἅρπαγες. 16 ἀπὸ τῶν
clothing, sheep’s but inwardly but are ravenous wolves. ravenous By {the} their
1903 4585 1254 2277 1254 1639 774 3380 774 608 3836 899
n.dpn n.gpn adv cj v.pai.3p n.npm a.npm p.g d.gpm

καρπῶν αὐτῶν ἐπιγνώσεσθε αὐτούς. μήτι → συλλέγουσιν ἀπὸ ἀκανθῶν
fruits their you will know them. ~ Do people gather grapes from thornbushes,
2843 899 2105 899 3614 5198 5091 608 180
n.gpm r.gpm.3 v.fmi.2p r.apm.3 pl v.pai.3p p.g n.gpf

σταφυλὰς ἢ ἀπὸ τριβόλων σῦκα; 17 οὕτως πᾶν δένδρον ἀγαθὸν
grapes or figs from thistles? figs So, every healthy tree healthy bears
5091 2445 5192 608 5560 5192 4048 4246 19 1285 19 4472
n.apf cj p.g n.gpm n.apn adv a.nsn n.nsn a.nsn

καρποὺς καλοὺς ποιεῖ, τὸ δὲ σαπρὸν δένδρον καρποὺς πονηροὺς
good fruit, good bears but the but unhealthy tree bears bad fruit. tree
2819 2843 2819 4472 1254 3836 1254 4911 1285 4472 4505 2843 4505
n.apm a.apm v.pai.3s d.nsn cj a.nsn n.nsn n.apm a.apm

ποιεῖ. 18 ⌊οὐ δύναται⌋ δένδρον ἀγαθὸν καρποὺς πονηροὺς
fruit A healthy tree cannot tree healthy bear bad fruit, bad
4472 19 1285 4024 1538 1285 19 4472 4505 2843 4505
v.pai.3s adv v.ppi.3s n.nsn a.nsn n.apm a.apm

ποιεῖν οὐδὲ ↰ δένδρον σαπρὸν καρποὺς καλοὺς ποιεῖν.
bear nor can an unhealthy tree unhealthy bear good fruit. good bear
4472 4028 1538 4911 1285 4911 4472 2819 2843 2819 4472
f.pa cj n.nsn a.nsn n.apm a.apm f.pa

19 πᾶν δένδρον ↱ μὴ ποιοῦν καρπὸν καλὸν ἐκκόπτεται καὶ εἰς
Every tree that does not bear good fruit good is cut down and thrown into the
4246 1285 4472 3590 4472 2819 2843 2819 1716 2779 965 1650
a.nsn n.nsn pl pt.pa.nsn n.asm a.asm v.ppi.3s cj p.a

πῦρ βάλλεται. 20 ἄρα γε ἀπὸ τῶν καρπῶν αὐτῶν ἐπιγνώσεσθε αὐτούς.
fire. thrown So then, So by {the} their fruits their you will know them.
4786 965 1145 726 1145 608 3836 899 2843 899 2105 899
n.asn v.ppi.3s cj pl p.g d.gpm n.gpm r.gpm.3 v.fmi.2p r.apm.3

21 οὐ πᾶς ὁ λέγων μοι, κύριε κύριε, ⌊εἰσελεύσεται εἰς⌋ τὴν βασιλείαν τῶν
“Not everyone who says to me, ‘Lord, Lord,’ will enter the kingdom of
4024 4246 3836 3306 1609 3261 3261 1656 1650 3836 993 3836
adv a.nsm d.nsm pt.pa.nsm r.ds.1 n.vsm n.vsm v.fmi.3s p.a d.asf n.asf d.gpm

οὐρανῶν, ἀλλ᾽ ὁ ποιῶν τὸ θέλημα τοῦ πατρός μου τοῦ ἐν τοῖς
heaven, but the ⌊one who does⌋ the will of my Father my {the} in {the}
4041 247 3836 4472 3836 2525 3836 1609 4252 1609 3836 1877 3836
n.gpm cj d.nsm pt.pa.nsm d.asn n.asn d.gsm n.gsm r.gs.1 d.gsm p.d d.dpm

οὐρανοῖς. 22 πολλοὶ ἐροῦσίν μοι ἐν ἐκείνῃ τῇ ἡμέρᾳ, κύριε κύριε,
heaven. On that day many will say to me, On that {the} day ‘Lord, Lord,
4041 1877 1697 2465 4498 3306 1609 1877 1697 3836 2465 3261 3261
n.dpm a.npm v.fai.3p r.ds.1 p.d r.dsf d.dsf n.dsf n.vsm n.vsm

οὐ τῷ σῷ ὀνόματι ἐπροφητεύσαμεν, καὶ τῷ σῷ ὀνόματι
did we not prophesy in your name, did we prophesy and in your name cast
4736 4736 4024 4736 3836 5050 3950 4736 2779 3836 5050 3950 1675
pl d.dsn r.dsn.2 n.dsn v.aai.1p cj d.dsn r.dsn.2 n.dsn

δαιμόνια ἐξεβάλομεν, καὶ τῷ σῷ ὀνόματι δυνάμεις πολλὰς
out demons, cast out and in your name do many mighty works?’ many
1675 1228 1675 2779 3836 5050 3950 4472 4498 1539 4498
n.apn v.aai.1p cj d.dsn r.dsn.2 n.dsn n.apf a.apf

ἐποιήσαμεν; 23 καὶ τότε ὁμολογήσω αὐτοῖς ὅτι ↱ οὐδέποτε ἔγνων ὑμᾶς· ἀποχωρεῖτε
do And then will I declare to them, ~ ‘I never knew you; go away
4472 2779 5538 3933 899 4022 1182 4030 1182 7007 713
v.aai.1p cj adv v.fai.1s r.dpm.3 cj adv v.aai.1s r.ap.2 v.pam.2p

ἀπ᾽ ἐμοῦ οἱ ἐργαζόμενοι τὴν ἀνομίαν. 24 πᾶς οὖν ὅστις
from me, you who practice {the} lawlessness.’ “Therefore everyone Therefore who
608 1609 3836 2237 3836 490 4036 4246 4036 4015
p.g r.gs.1 d.vpm pt.pm.vpm d.asf n.asf a.nsm cj r.nsm

NASB

A Tree and Its Fruit

15 “Beware of the
false prophets, who
come to you in
sheep’s clothing,
but inwardly are
ravenous wolves.
16 You will know
them by their
fruits. Grapes are
not gathered from
thorn *bushes* nor
figs from thistles,
are they? 17 So ev-
ery good tree bears
good fruit, but the
bad tree bears bad
fruit. 18 A good tree
cannot produce bad
fruit, nor can a bad
tree produce good
fruit. 19 Every tree
that does not bear
good fruit is cut
down and thrown
into the fire. 20 So
then, you will
know them by their
fruits.

21 “Not everyone
who says to Me,
‘Lord, Lord,’ will
enter the kingdom
of heaven, but he
who does the will
of My Father who
is in heaven *will
enter.* 22 Many will
say to Me on that
day, ‘Lord, Lord,
did we not proph-
esy in Your name,
and in Your name
cast out demons,
and in Your name
perform many
miracles?’ 23 And
then I will declare
to them, ‘I never
knew you; DEPART
FROM ME, YOU WHO
PRACTICE LAWLESS-
NESS.’

NIV

The Wise and Foolish Builders

[24]"Therefore
everyone who
hears these words
of mine and puts
them into prac-
tice is like a wise
man who built his
house on the rock.
[25]The rain came
down, the streams
rose, and the
winds blew and
beat against that
house; yet it did
not fall, because it
had its foundation
on the rock. [26]But
everyone who
hears these words
of mine and does
not put them into
practice is like a
foolish man who
built his house on
sand. [27]The rain
came down, the
streams rose, and
the winds blew
and beat against
that house, and it
fell with a great
crash."

[28]When Jesus
had finished say-
ing these things,
the crowds were
amazed at his
teaching, [29]be-
cause he taught
as one who had
authority, and not
as their teachers of
the law.

Jesus Heals a Man With Leprosy

8 When Jesus
came down
from the moun-
tainside, large
crowds followed
him. [2]A man with
leprosy[a] came and
knelt before him
and said, "Lord,
if you are willing,
you can make me
clean."

ἀκούει μου τοὺς λόγους τούτους καὶ ποιεῖ αὐτούς, ὁμοιωθήσεται
hears these words of mine, {the} words these and does them, is like the
201 4047 3364 1609 3836 3364 4047 2779 4472 899 3929
v.pai.3s r.gs.1 d.apm n.apm r.apm cj v.pai.3s r.apm.3 v.fpi.3s

ἀνδρὶ φρονίμῳ, ὅστις ᾠκοδόμησεν αὐτοῦ τὴν οἰκίαν ἐπὶ τὴν πέτραν· [25] καὶ
wise man, wise who built his {the} house upon {the} rock. When
5861 467 5861 4015 3868 899 3836 3864 2093 3836 4376 2779
n.dsm a.dsm r.nsm v.aai.3s r.gsm.3 d.asf n.asf p.a d.asf n.asf cj

κατέβη ἡ βροχὴ καὶ ἦλθον οἱ ποταμοὶ καὶ
the rain came down, the rain and the waters rose, the waters and the winds
3836 1104 2849 3836 1104 2779 3836 4532 2262 3836 4532 2779 3836 449
v.aai.3s d.nsf n.nsf cj v.aai.3p d.npm n.npm cj

ἔπνευσαν οἱ ἄνεμοι καὶ προσέπεσαν τῇ οἰκίᾳ ἐκείνῃ, καὶ ↱ ↱ οὐκ
blew the winds and beat against {the} that house, that {and} it did not
4463 3836 449 2779 4700 3836 1697 3864 1697 2779 4406 4406 4024
v.aai.3p d.npm n.npm cj v.aai.3p d.dsf n.dsf r.dsf cj adv

ἔπεσεν, τεθεμελίωτο γὰρ ἐπὶ τὴν πέτραν. [26] καὶ πᾶς ὁ ἀκούων
collapse because it had been founded because on {the} rock. But everyone who hears
4406 1142 2530 1142 2093 3836 4376 2779 4246 3836 201
v.aai.3s v.lpi.3s cj p.a d.asf n.asf cj a.nsm d.nsm pt.pa.nsm

μου τοὺς λόγους τούτους καὶ ↱ μὴ ποιῶν αὐτοὺς ὁμοιωθήσεται
these words of mine, {the} words these and does not do them, will be like the
4047 3364 1609 3836 3364 4047 2779 4472 3590 4472 899 3929
r.gs.1 d.apm n.apm r.apm cj pl pt.pa.nsm r.apm.3 v.fpi.3s

ἀνδρὶ μωρῷ, ὅστις ᾠκοδόμησεν αὐτοῦ τὴν οἰκίαν ἐπὶ τὴν ἄμμον· [27] καὶ
foolish man foolish who built his {the} house on {the} sand. When the
3704 467 3704 4015 3868 899 3836 3864 2093 3836 302 2779 3836
n.dsm a.dsm r.nsm v.aai.3s r.gsm.3 d.asf n.asf p.a d.asf n.asf cj

κατέβη ἡ βροχὴ καὶ ἦλθον οἱ ποταμοὶ καὶ ἔπνευσαν
rain came down, the rain and the waters rose, the waters and the winds blew
1104 2849 3836 1104 2779 3836 4532 2262 3836 4532 2779 3836 449 4463
v.aai.3s d.nsf n.nsf cj v.aai.3p d.npm n.npm cj v.aai.3p

οἱ ἄνεμοι καὶ προσέκοψαν τῇ οἰκίᾳ ἐκείνῃ, καὶ ἔπεσεν καὶ ἦν
the winds and beat against {the} that house, that {and} it collapsed — and great was
3836 449 2779 4684 3836 1697 3864 1697 2779 4406 2779 3489 1639
d.npm n.npm cj v.aai.3p d.dsf n.dsf r.dsf cj v.aai.3s cj v.iai.3s

ἡ πτῶσις αὐτῆς μεγάλη. [28] ⌊καὶ ἐγένετο⌋ ὅτε ἐτέλεσεν ὁ Ἰησοῦς
its {the} fall!" its great Now when Jesus had finished {the} Jesus
899 3836 4774 899 3489 2779 1181 4021 2652 5464 3836 2652
d.nsf n.nsf r.gsf.3 a.nsf cj v.ami.3s cj v.aai.3s d.nsm n.nsm

τοὺς λόγους τούτους, ἐξεπλήσσοντο οἱ ὄχλοι ἐπὶ τῇ διδαχῇ
{the} these words, these the crowds were amazed the crowds at {the} his teaching,
3836 4047 3364 4047 3836 4063 1742 3836 4063 2093 3836 899 1439
d.apm n.apm r.apm v.ipi.3p d.npm n.npm p.d d.dsf n.dsf

αὐτοῦ· [29] ἦν γὰρ διδάσκων αὐτοὺς ὡς ἐξουσίαν ἔχων καὶ
his for ⌊he was⌋ for teaching them as one who had authority, one who had and
899 1142 1639 1142 1438 899 6055 2400 2400 2400 2026 2400 2779
r.gsm.3 v.iai.3s cj pt.pa.nsm r.apm.3 conj n.asf pt.pa.nsm cj

οὐχ ὡς οἱ γραμματεῖς αὐτῶν.
not as {the} their scribes. their
4024 6055 3836 899 1208 899
adv conj d.npm n.npm r.gpm.3

8:1 → καταβάντος δὲ αὐτοῦ ἀπὸ τοῦ ὄρους ἠκολούθησαν
When he came down {and} he from the mountain, large crowds were following
899 2849 1254 899 608 3836 4001 4498 4063 199
pt.aa.gsm cj r.gsm.3 p.g d.gsn n.gsn v.aai.3p

αὐτῷ ὄχλοι πολλοί. [2] καὶ ἰδοὺ λεπρὸς προσελθὼν προσεκύνει αὐτῷ
him. crowds large {and} {behold} A leper came up to him, knelt down, him and
899 4063 4498 2779 2627 3320 4665 899 4686 899
r.dsm.3 n.npm a.npm cj j a.nsm pt.aa.nsm v.iai.3s r.dsm.3

λέγων, κύριε, ἐὰν θέλῃς δύνασαί ↱ με καθαρίσαι. [3] καὶ
said, "Lord, if ⌊you are willing,⌋ you can make me clean." {and} Jesus
3306 3261 1569 2527 1538 2751 1609 2751 2779
pt.pa.nsm n.vsm cj v.pas.2s v.ppi.2s r.as.1 f.aa cj

NASB

The Two Foundations

[24]"Therefore
everyone who
hears these words
of Mine and acts
on them, may be
compared to a wise
man who built
his house on the
rock. [25]And the
rain fell, and the
floods came, and
the winds blew and
slammed against
that house; and *yet*
it did not fall, for it
had been founded
on the rock. [26]Ev-
eryone who hears
these words of
Mine and does not
act on them, will
be like a foolish
man who built his
house on the sand.
[27]The rain fell, and
the floods came,
and the winds
blew and slammed
against that house;
and it fell—and
great was its fall."
[28]When Jesus
had finished these
words, the crowds
were amazed at His
teaching; [29]for He
was teaching them
as *one* having au-
thority, and not as
their scribes.

Jesus Cleanses a Leper; The Centurion's Faith

[8:1]When Jesus
came down from
the mountain, large
crowds followed
Him. [2]And a leper
came to Him and
bowed down be-
fore Him, and said,
"Lord, if You are
willing, You can
make me clean."

[a] 2 The Greek word traditionally translated *leprosy* was used for various diseases affecting the skin.

NIV

[3]Jesus reached
out his hand and
touched the man.
"I am willing," he
said. "Be clean!"
Immediately he
was cleansed of
his leprosy. [4]Then
Jesus said to him,
"See that you don't
tell anyone. But
go, show yourself
to the priest and
offer the gift Mo-
ses commanded,
as a testimony to
them."

The Faith of the Centurion

[5]When Jesus had
entered Caperna-
um, a centurion
came to him,
asking for help.
[6]"Lord," he said,
"my servant lies at
home paralyzed,
suffering terribly."
[7]Jesus said to
him, "Shall I come
and heal him?"
[8]The centurion
replied, "Lord, I
do not deserve to
have you come un-
der my roof. But
just say the word,
and my servant
will be healed.
[9]For I myself am
a man under au-
thority, with sol-
diers under me. I
tell this one, 'Go,'
and he goes; and
that one, 'Come,'
and he comes. I
say to my servant,
'Do this,' and he
does it."
[10]When Jesus
heard this, he was
amazed and said
to those following
him, "Truly I tell
you, I have not
found anyone in
Israel with such
great faith. [11]I say
to you

ἐκτείνας τὴν χεῖρα ἥψατο αὐτοῦ λέγων, θέλω, καθαρίσθητι· καὶ
⌞stretched out⌟ his hand and touched him, saying, ⌞"I am willing;⌟ be made clean." And
1753 3836 5931 721 899 3306 2527 2751 2779
pt.aa.nsm d.asf n.asf v.ami.3s r.gsm.3 pt.pa.nsm v.pai.1s v.apm.2s cj

εὐθέως ἐκαθαρίσθη αὐτοῦ ἡ λέπρα. [4]καὶ λέγει αὐτῷ ὁ
immediately his leprosy was cleansed. *his* *{the}* *leprosy* Then Jesus said to him, *{the}*
2311 899 3319 2751 899 3836 3319 2779 2652 3306 899 3836
adv v.api.3s r.gsm.3 d.nsf n.nsf cj v.pai.3s r.dsm.3 d.nsm

Ἰησοῦς, ὅρα μηδενὶ εἴπῃς, ἀλλὰ ὕπαγε σεαυτὸν δεῖξον τῷ
Jesus "See that you tell no one; *you tell* but go, show yourself *show* ⌞to the⌟
2652 3972 3306 3306 3594 3306 247 5632 1259 4932 1259 3836
n.nsm v.pam.2s a.dsm v.aas.2s cj v.pam.2s r.asm.2 v.aam.2s d.dsm

ἱερεῖ καὶ προσένεγκον τὸ δῶρον ὃ προσέταξεν Μωϋσῆς, εἰς μαρτύριον
priest, and offer the gift that Moses commanded, *Moses* as a testimony
2636 2779 4712 3836 1565 4005 3707 4705 3707 1650 3457
n.dsm cj v.aam.2s d.asn n.asn r.asn v.aai.3s n.nsm p.a n.asn

αὐτοῖς. [5]→ εἰσελθόντος δὲ αὐτοῦ εἰς Καφαρναοὺμ προσῆλθεν
to them." When Jesus entered *{and}* *Jesus* *{into}* Capernaum, a centurion came
899 899 1656 1254 899 1650 3019 1672 4665
r.dpm.3 pt.aa.gsm cj r.gsm.3 p.a n.asf v.aai.3s

αὐτῷ ἑκατόνταρχος παρακαλῶν αὐτὸν [6]καὶ λέγων, κύριε, ὁ παῖς μου
to him *centurion* and pleaded with him, *{and}* saying, "Lord, *{the}* my servant *my*
899 1672 4151 899 2779 3306 3261 3836 1609 4090 1609
r.dsm.3 n.nsm pt.pa.nsm r.asm.3 cj pt.pa.nsm n.vsm d.nsm n.nsm r.gs.1

βέβληται ἐν τῇ οἰκίᾳ παραλυτικός, δεινῶς βασανιζόμενος. [7]καὶ
is lying at *{the}* home paralyzed, suffering terribly." *suffering* And Jesus
965 1877 3836 3864 4166 989 1267 989 2779
v.rpi.3s p.d d.dsf n.dsf a.nsm adv pt.pp.nsm cj

λέγει αὐτῷ, ἐγὼ ↱ ἐλθὼν θεραπεύσω αὐτόν. [8]καὶ ἀποκριθεὶς
said to him, "I will come and heal him." But the centurion replied,
3306 899 1609 2543 2262 2543 899 2779 3836 1672 646
v.pai.3s r.dsm.3 r.ns.1 pt.aa.nsm v.fai.1s r.asm.3 cj pt.ap.nsm

ὁ ἑκατόνταρχος ἔφη, κύριε, οὐκ εἰμὶ ἱκανὸς ἵνα μου
the *centurion* *{said}* "Lord, I am not *I am* worthy for you to come under my
3836 1672 5774 3261 1639 1639 4024 1639 2653 2671 1656 1656 1656 5679 1609
d.nsm n.nsm v.iai.3s n.vsm adv v.pai.1s a.nsm cj r.gs.1

ὑπὸ τὴν στέγην εἰσέλθῃς, ἀλλὰ μόνον εἰπὲ λόγῳ, καὶ ἰαθήσεται
under *{the}* roof, *you to come* but just say the word, and my servant will be healed.
5679 3836 5094 1656 247 3667 3306 3364 2779 1609 4090 2615
p.a d.asf n.asf v.aas.2s cj adv v.aam.2s n.dsm cj v.fpi.3s

ὁ παῖς μου. [9] καὶ γὰρ ἐγὼ ἄνθρωπός εἰμι ὑπὸ ἐξουσίαν, ἔχων
{the} *servant* *my* For I too *For* *I* am a man *am* under authority, with
3836 4090 1609 1142 1609 2779 1142 1609 1639 476 1639 5679 2026 2400
d.nsm n.nsm r.gs.1 adv cj r.ns.1 n.nsm v.pai.1s p.a n.asf pt.pa.nsm

ὑπ' ἐμαυτὸν στρατιώτας, καὶ λέγω τούτῳ, πορεύθητι, καὶ πορεύεται, καὶ
soldiers under me. *soldiers* *{and}* I say to this one, 'Go!' and he goes, and
5132 5679 1831 5132 2779 3306 4047 4513 2779 4513 2779
p.a r.asm.1 n.apm cj v.pai.1s r.dsm v.apm.2s cj v.pmi.3s cj

ἄλλῳ, ἔρχου, καὶ ἔρχεται, καὶ τῷ δούλῳ μου· ποίησον τοῦτο, καὶ ποιεῖ.
to another, 'Come!' and he comes, and to my servant, *my* 'Do this!' and he does it."
257 2262 2779 2262 2779 3836 1609 1529 1609 4472 4047 2779 4472
r.dsm v.pmm.2s cj v.pmi.3s cj d.dsm n.dsm r.gs.1 v.aam.2s r.asn cj v.pai.3s

[10]→ ἀκούσας δὲ ὁ Ἰησοῦς ἐθαύμασεν καὶ εἶπεν τοῖς
When Jesus heard *{and}* *{the}* *Jesus* this, he was amazed and said to those
2652 201 1254 3836 2652 2513 2779 3306 3836
pt.aa.nsm cj d.nsm n.nsm v.aai.3s cj v.aai.3s d.dpm

ἀκολουθοῦσιν, ἀμὴν λέγω ὑμῖν, ↱
who were following, "I tell you the truth, *I tell* *you* I have not found faith like this
199 3306 3306 7007 297 3306 7007 2351 2351 4029 2351 4411 5537 5537
pt.pa.dpm pl v.pai.1s r.dp.2

παρ' οὐδενὶ τοσαύτην πίστιν ἐν τῷ Ἰσραὴλ εὗρον. [11]λέγω δὲ ὑμῖν ὅτι
in anyone *like this* *faith* in *{the}* Israel. *I have found* I tell *{and}* you, ~
4123 4029 5537 4411 1877 3836 2702 2351 3306 1254 7007 4022
p.d a.dsm r.asf n.asf p.d d.dsm n.dsm v.aai.1s v.pai.1s cj r.dp.2 cj

NASB

[3]Jesus stretched
out His hand and
touched him, say-
ing, "I am willing;
be cleansed."
And immediately
his leprosy was
cleansed. [4]And
Jesus *said to him,
"See that you tell
no one; but go,
show yourself to
the priest and pres-
ent the offering
that Moses com-
manded, as a testi-
mony to them."
[5]And when
Jesus entered
Capernaum, a
centurion came to
Him, imploring
Him, [6]and saying,
"Lord, my servant
is lying paralyzed
at home, fearfully
tormented." [7]Jesus
*said to him, "I
will come and heal
him." [8]But the cen-
turion said, "Lord,
I am not worthy
for You to come
under my roof, but
just say the word,
and my servant
will be healed. [9]For
I also am a man
under authority,
with soldiers under
me; and I say to
this one, 'Go!' and
he goes, and to
another, 'Come!'
and he comes, and
to my slave, 'Do
this!' and he does
it." [10]Now when Je-
sus heard *this,* He
marveled and said
to those who were
following, "Truly I
say to you, I have
not found such
great faith with
anyone in Israel. [11]I
say to you that

NIV

that many will
come from the
east and the west,
and will take their
places at the feast
with Abraham,
Isaac and Jacob
in the kingdom
of heaven. 12 But
the subjects of the
kingdom will be
thrown outside,
into the darkness,
where there will
be weeping and
gnashing of teeth."
13 Then Jesus said
to the centurion,
"Go! Let it be
done just as you
believed it would."
And his servant
was healed at that
moment.

Jesus Heals Many

14 When Jesus
came into Peter's
house, he saw
Peter's mother-in-
law lying in bed
with a fever. 15 He
touched her hand
and the fever left
her, and she got up
and began to wait
on him.
16 When evening
came, many who
were demon-
possessed were
brought to him,
and he drove out
the spirits with a
word and healed
all the sick. 17 This
was to fulfill
what was spoken
through the proph-
et Isaiah:

> "He took up our
> infirmities
> and bore our
> diseases."[a]

The Cost of Following Jesus

18 When Jesus saw
the crowd around
him, he gave or-
ders to cross to
the other side of
the lake. 19 Then a
teacher of the law
came to him and
said, "Teacher,

[a] 17 Isaiah 53:4 (see Septuagint)

πολλοὶ ἀπὸ ἀνατολῶν καὶ δυσμῶν ἥξουσιν καὶ ἀνακλιθήσονται μετὰ
many will come from the east and west *will come* *{and}* to recline at table with
4498 2457 2457 608 424 2779 1553 2457 2779 369 3552
a.npm p.g n.gpf cj n.gpf v.fai.3p cj v.fpi.3p p.g

Ἀβραὰμ καὶ Ἰσαὰκ καὶ Ἰακὼβ ἐν τῇ βασιλείᾳ τῶν οὐρανῶν, 12 οἱ δὲ
Abraham and Isaac and Jacob in the kingdom of heaven, but the *but*
11 2779 2693 2779 2609 1877 3836 993 3836 4041 1254 3836 1254
n.gsm cj n.gsm cj n.gsm p.d d.dsf n.dsf d.gpm n.gpm d.npm cj

υἱοὶ τῆς βασιλείας ἐκβληθήσονται εἰς τὸ σκότος τὸ ἐξώτερον· ἐκεῖ
sons of the kingdom will be cast out into *{the}* outer darkness, *{the}* *outer* where
5626 3836 993 1675 1650 3836 2035 5030 3836 2035 1695
n.npm d.gsf n.gsf v.fpi.3p p.a d.asn n.asn d.asn a.asn.c adv

ἔσται ὁ κλαυθμὸς καὶ ὁ βρυγμὸς τῶν ὀδόντων. 13 καὶ εἶπεν ὁ
⌊there will be⌋ *{the}* weeping and *{the}* gnashing of teeth." And Jesus said *{the}*
1639 3836 3088 2779 3836 1106 3836 3848 2779 2652 3306 3836
v.fmi.3s d.nsm n.nsm cj d.nsm n.nsm d.gpm n.gpm cj v.aai.3s d.nsm

Ἰησοῦς τῷ ἑκατοντάρχῃ, ὕπαγε, ὡς ἐπίστευσας
Jesus ⌊to the⌋ centurion, "Go; it will be done for you ⌊just as⌋ you believed."
2652 3836 1672 5632 1181 1181 1181 1181 5148 5148 6055 4409
n.nsm d.dsm n.dsm v.pam.2s cj v.aai.2s

γενηθήτω σοι. καὶ ἰάθη ὁ παῖς αὐτοῦ[a] ἐν τῇ ὥρᾳ
it will be done *for you* And his servant was healed *{the}* *servant* *his* at that very hour.
1181 5148 2779 899 4090 2615 3836 4090 899 1877 1697 3836 6052
v.apm.3s r.ds.2 cj v.api.3s d.nsm n.nsm r.gsm.3 p.d d.dsf n.dsf

ἐκείνῃ. 14 καὶ → ἐλθὼν ὁ Ἰησοῦς εἰς τὴν οἰκίαν Πέτρου εἶδεν
that And when Jesus entered *{the}* *Jesus* *{into}* *{the}* Peter's house, *Peter's* he saw
1697 2779 2652 2262 3836 2652 1650 3836 4377 3864 4377 1625
r.dsf cj pt.aa.nsm d.nsm n.nsm p.a d.asf n.asf n.gsm v.aai.3s

τὴν πενθερὰν αὐτοῦ βεβλημένην καὶ πυρέσσουσαν· 15 καὶ ἥψατο τῆς
{the} his mother-in-law *his* lying *{and}* sick with a fever. *{and}* He touched *{the}* her
3836 899 4289 899 965 2779 4789 2779 721 3836 899
d.asf n.asf r.gsm.3 pt.rp.asf cj pt.pa.asf cj v.ami.3s d.gsf

χειρὸς αὐτῆς, καὶ ἀφῆκεν αὐτὴν ὁ πυρετός, καὶ ἠγέρθη καὶ
hand, *her* and her fever left her. *her* *fever* Then ⌊she got up⌋ and
5931 899 2779 3836 4790 918 899 3836 4790 2779 1586 2779
n.gsf r.gsf.3 cj v.aai.3s r.asf.3 d.nsm n.nsm cj v.api.3s cj

διηκόνει αὐτῷ. 16 ↱ ὀψίας δὲ γενομένης προσήνεγκαν αὐτῷ
began to serve him. Now when evening *Now* came, they brought to him many
1354 899 1254 1181 4068 1254 1181 4712 899 4498
v.iai.3s r.dsm.3 n.gsf cj pt.am.gsf v.aai.3p r.dsm.3

δαιμονιζομένους πολλούς· καὶ ἐξέβαλεν τὰ πνεύματα → λόγῳ καὶ
⌊who were possessed by demons,⌋ *many* and he drove out the spirits with a word and
1227 4498 2779 1675 3836 4460 3364 2779
pt.pp.apm a.apm cj v.aai.3s d.apn n.apn n.dsm cj

πάντας τοὺς κακῶς ἔχοντας ἐθεράπευσεν, 17 ὅπως πληρωθῇ τὸ
healed all who were ill. *were* *healed* ⌊In this way⌋ *was fulfilled* what
2543 4246 3836 2400 2809 2400 2543 3968 4444 3836
a.apm d.apm adv pt.pa.apm v.aai.3s cj v.aps.3s d.nsn

ῥηθὲν διὰ Ἠσαΐου τοῦ προφήτου λέγοντος, αὐτὸς τὰς
was spoken by Isaiah the prophet was fulfilled: *{saying}* "He took *{the}* our
3306 1328 2480 3836 4737 4444 4444 3306 899 3284 3836 7005
pt.ap.nsn p.g n.gsm d.gsm n.gsm pt.pa.gsm r.nsm d.apf

ἀσθενείας ἡμῶν ἔλαβεν καὶ τὰς νόσους ἐβάστασεν. 18 → ἰδὼν
illnesses *our* *took* and carried our diseases." *carried* Now when Jesus saw
819 7005 3284 2779 1002 3836 3798 1002 1254 2652 1625
n.apf r.gp.1 v.aai.3s cj d.apf n.apf v.aai.3s pt.aa.nsm

δὲ ὁ Ἰησοῦς ὄχλον[b] περὶ αὐτὸν ἐκέλευσεν ἀπελθεῖν εἰς τὸ πέραν.
Now *{the}* *Jesus* a crowd around him, he gave orders to go to the other side of the
1254 3836 2652 4063 4309 899 3027 599 1650 3836 4305
cj d.nsm n.nsm n.asm p.a r.asm.3 v.aai.3s f.aa p.a d.asn adv

19 καὶ προσελθὼν εἷς γραμματεὺς εἶπεν αὐτῷ, διδάσκαλε,
lake. *{and}* A scribe came to him *A* *scribe* and said, *to him* "Teacher,
2779 1651 1208 4665 899 899 1651 1208 3306 899 1437
cj pt.aa.nsm a.nsm n.nsm v.aai.3s r.dsm.3 n.vsm

[a] [αὐτοῦ] UBS, omitted by NET.
[b] ὄχλον UBS, TNIV. πολλοὺς ὄχλους NET.

NASB

many will come
from east and west,
and [a]recline *at the*
table with Abra-
ham, Isaac and Ja-
cob in the kingdom
of heaven; 12 but the
sons of the king-
dom will be cast
out into the outer
darkness; in that
place there will
be weeping and
gnashing of teeth."
13 And Jesus said to
the centurion, "Go;
it shall be done for
you as you have
believed." And the
servant was healed
that *very* moment.

Peter's Mother-in-law and Many Others Healed

14 When Jesus
came into Peter's
home, He saw his
mother-in-law
lying sick in bed
with a fever. 15 He
touched her hand,
and the fever left
her; and she got
up and waited on
Him. 16 When eve-
ning came, they
brought to Him
many who were
demon-possessed;
and He cast out the
spirits with a word,
and healed all who
were ill. 17 *This was*
to fulfill what was
spoken through
Isaiah the prophet:
"HE HIMSELF TOOK
OUR INFIRMITIES AND
CARRIED AWAY OUR
DISEASES."

Discipleship Tested

18 Now when Je-
sus saw a crowd
around Him, He
gave orders to
depart to the other
side *of the sea.*
19 Then a scribe
came and said to
Him, "Teacher,

[a] Or *dine*

NIV

I will follow you
wherever you go."
[20] Jesus replied,
"Foxes have dens
and birds have
nests, but the Son
of Man has no
place to lay his
head."
[21] Another dis-
ciple said to him,
"Lord, first let me
go and bury my
father."
[22] But Jesus told
him, "Follow me,
and let the dead
bury their own
dead."

Jesus Calms the Storm

[23] Then he got
into the boat and
his disciples fol-
lowed him. [24] Sud-
denly a furious
storm came up on
the lake, so that
the waves swept
over the boat.
But Jesus was
sleeping. [25] The
disciples went and
woke him, say-
ing, "Lord, save
us! We're going to
drown!"
[26] He replied,
"You of little faith,
why are you so
afraid?" Then he
got up and rebuked
the winds and the
waves, and it was
completely calm.
[27] The men were
amazed and asked,
"What kind of
man is this? Even
the winds and the
waves obey him!"

Jesus Restores Two Demon-Possessed Men

[28] When he ar-
rived at the other
side in the region
of the Gadarenes,[a]
two demon-pos-
sessed men com-
ing from the tombs
met him. They
were so violent

[a] 28 Some manuscripts *Gergesenes*; other manuscripts *Gerasenes*

ἀκολουθήσω σοι ⌞ὅπου ἐὰν⌟ ἀπέρχῃ. [20] καὶ λέγει αὐτῷ ὁ Ἰησοῦς, αἱ
I will follow you wherever you go." And Jesus said to him, *{the}* *Jesus* *{the}*
199 5148 3963 1569 599 2779 2652 3306 899 3836 2652 3836
v.fai.1s r.ds.2 cj pl v.pms.2s cj v.pai.3s r.dsm.3 d.nsm n.nsm d.npf

ἀλώπεκες φωλεοὺς ἔχουσιν καὶ τὰ πετεινὰ τοῦ οὐρανοῦ ↰ κατασκηνώσεις,
"Foxes have lairs *have* and *{the}* birds of the air have nests,
273 2400 5887 2400 2779 3836 4374 3836 4041 2400 2943
n.npf n.apm v.pai.3p cj d.npn n.npn d.gsm n.gsm n.apf

ὁ δὲ υἱὸς τοῦ ἀνθρώπου οὐκ ἔχει ποῦ τὴν κεφαλὴν κλίνῃ.
but the *but* Son of Man has no *has* place to lay his head." *to lay*
1254 3836 1254 5626 3836 476 2400 4024 2400 4543 3111 3111 3836 3051 3111
d.nsm cj n.nsm d.gsm n.gsm adv v.pai.3s adv d.asf n.asf v.pas.3s

[21] ἕτερος δὲ τῶν μαθητῶν[a] εἶπεν αὐτῷ, κύριε, ἐπίτρεψόν μοι πρῶτον ἀπελθεῖν καὶ
Another *{and}* of his disciples said to him, "Lord, permit me first to go and
2283 1254 3836 3412 3306 899 3261 2205 1609 4754 599 2779
r.nsm cj d.gpm n.gpm v.aai.3s r.dsm.3 n.vsm v.aam.2s r.ds.1 adv f.aa cj

θάψαι τὸν πατέρα μου. [22] ὁ δὲ Ἰησοῦς λέγει αὐτῷ, ἀκολούθει μοι καὶ
bury *{the}* my father." *my* *{the}* And Jesus said to him, "Follow me, and
2507 3836 1609 4252 1609 3836 1254 2652 3306 899 199 1609 2779
f.aa d.asm n.asm r.gs.1 d.nsm cj n.nsm v.pai.3s r.dsm.3 v.pam.2s r.ds.1 cj

ἄφες τοὺς νεκροὺς θάψαι τοὺς ἑαυτῶν νεκρούς. [23] καὶ ἐμβάντι αὐτῷ εἰς τὸ
let the dead bury *{the}* their own dead." Then he got *he* into the
918 3836 3738 2507 3836 1571 3738 2779 899 1832 899 1650 3836
v.aam.2s d.apm a.apm f.aa d.apm r.gpm.3 a.apm cj pt.aa.dsm r.dsm.3 p.a d.asn

πλοῖον ἠκολούθησαν αὐτῷ οἱ μαθηταὶ αὐτοῦ. [24] ⌞καὶ ἰδοὺ⌟
boat and his disciples followed him. *{the}* *disciples* *his* Suddenly a
4450 899 3412 199 899 3836 3412 899 2779 2627
n.asn v.aai.3p r.dsm.3 d.npm n.npm r.gsm.3 cj j

σεισμὸς μέγας ἐγένετο ἐν τῇ θαλάσσῃ, ὥστε τὸ πλοῖον καλύπτεσθαι
violent storm *violent* arose on the sea, so that the boat was being swamped
3489 4939 3489 1181 1877 3836 2498 6063 3836 4450 2821
n.nsm a.nsm v.ami.3s p.d d.dsf n.dsf cj d.asn n.asn f.pp

ὑπὸ τῶν κυμάτων, αὐτὸς δὲ ἐκάθευδεν. [25] καὶ προσελθόντες
by the waves; but he *but* was asleep. *{and}* The disciples went to him
5679 3836 3246 1254 899 1254 2761 2779 4665
p.g d.gpn n.gpn r.nsm cj v.iai.3s cj pt.aa.npm

ἤγειραν αὐτὸν λέγοντες, κύριε, σῶσον, ἀπολλύμεθα. [26] καὶ λέγει αὐτοῖς,
and woke him, crying out, "Lord, save us! We are perishing!" And he said to them,
1586 899 3306 3261 5392 660 2779 3306 899
v.aai.3p r.asm.3 pt.pa.npm n.vsm v.aam.2s v.pmi.1p cj v.pai.3s r.dpm.3

τί δειλοί ἐστε, ὀλιγόπιστοι; τότε ↱ ἐγερθεὶς ἐπετίμησεν τοῖς
"Why are you so afraid, *are you* you of little faith?" Then he rose and rebuked the
5515 1639 1639 1264 1639 3899 5538 2203 1586 2203 3836
r.asn a.npm v.pai.2p a.vpm adv pt.ap.nsm v.aai.3s d.dpm

ἀνέμοις καὶ τῇ θαλάσσῃ, καὶ ἐγένετο γαλήνη μεγάλη. [27] οἱ δὲ
winds and the sea, and there was a great calm. *great* And the *And*
449 2779 3836 2498 2779 1181 3489 1132 3489 1254 3836 1254
n.dpm cj d.dsf n.dsf cj v.ami.3s n.nsf a.nsf d.npm cj

ἄνθρωποι ἐθαύμασαν λέγοντες, ποταπός ἐστιν οὗτος ὅτι καὶ οἱ
men were amazed and said, ⌞"What sort of⌟ man is this that even the
476 2513 3306 4534 1639 4047 4022 2779 3836
n.npm v.aai.3p pt.pa.npm r.nsm v.pai.3s r.nsm cj adv d.npm

ἄνεμοι καὶ ἡ θάλασσα αὐτῷ ὑπακούουσιν; [28] Καὶ → ἐλθόντος αὐτοῦ
winds and the sea obey him?" *obey* And when he came *he*
449 2779 3836 2498 5634 899 5634 2779 899 2262 899
n.npm cj d.nsf n.nsf r.dsm.3 v.pai.3p cj pt.aa.gsm r.gsm.3

εἰς τὸ πέραν εἰς τὴν χώραν τῶν Γαδαρηνῶν ὑπήντησαν αὐτῷ δύο
to the other side, to the region of the Gadarenes, there met him two
1650 3836 4305 1650 3836 6001 3836 1123 5636 899 1545
p.a d.asn adv p.a d.asf n.asf d.gpm a.gpm v.aai.3p r.dsm.3 a.npm

δαιμονιζόμενοι ἐκ τῶν μνημείων ἐξερχόμενοι, χαλεποὶ λίαν,
demoniacs coming out from the tombs. *coming out* They were so violent *so*
1227 2002 2002 1666 3836 3646 2002 3336 5901 3336
pt.pp.npm p.g d.gpn n.gpn pt.pm.npm a.npm adv

[a] αὐτοῦ included by UBS after μαθητῶν.

NASB

I will follow You
wherever You go."
[20] Jesus *said to
him, "The foxes
have holes and
the birds of the air
have nests, but the
Son of Man has
nowhere to lay His
head." [21] Another of
the disciples said to
Him, "Lord, permit
me first to go and
bury my father."
[22] But Jesus *said to
him, "Follow Me,
and allow the dead
to bury their own
dead."
[23] When He got
into the boat, His
disciples followed
Him. [24] And behold,
there arose a great
storm on the sea,
so that the boat
was being covered
with the waves; but
Jesus Himself was
asleep. [25] And they
came to *Him* and
woke Him, saying,
"Save *us,* Lord;
we are perishing!"
[26] He *said to them,
"Why are you
afraid, you men of
little faith?" Then
He got up and
rebuked the winds
and the sea, and it
became perfectly
calm. [27] The men
were amazed, and
said, "What kind of
a man is this, that
even the winds and
the sea obey Him?"

Jesus Casts Out Demons

[28] When He came
to the other side
into the country
of the Gadarenes,
two men who were
demon-possessed
met Him as they
were coming out
of the tombs. *They
were* so extremely
violent that no one

NIV

that no one could
pass that way.
29"What do you
want with us, Son
of God?" they
shouted. "Have
you come here to
torture us before
the appointed
time?"
30Some distance
from them a large
herd of pigs was
feeding. 31The
demons begged
Jesus, "If you
drive us out, send
us into the herd of
pigs."
32He said to them,
"Go!" So they
came out and went
into the pigs, and
the whole herd
rushed down the
steep bank into the
lake and died in
the water. 33Those
tending the pigs
ran off, went into
the town and re-
ported all this,
including what had
happened to the
demon-possessed
men. 34Then the
whole town went
out to meet Jesus.
And when they
saw him, they
pleaded with him
to leave their re-
gion.

Jesus Forgives and Heals a Paralyzed Man

9 Jesus stepped
into a boat,
crossed over and
came to his own
town. 2Some men
brought to him a
paralyzed man,
lying on a mat.
When Jesus saw
their faith, he said
to the man, "Take
heart, son; your
sins are forgiven."

ὥστε μὴ ἰσχύειν τινὰ παρελθεῖν διὰ τῆς ὁδοῦ ἐκείνης. 29 καὶ ἰδοὺ
that no one could *one* pass by *{the}* that way. *that* *{and}* *{behold}*
6063 3590 5516 2710 5516 4216 1328 3836 1697 3847 1697 2779 2627
cj pl f.pa r.asm f.aa p.g d.gsf n.gsf r.gsf cj j

ἔκραξαν λέγοντες, τί ἡμῖν καὶ σοί, υἱὲ τοῦ θεοῦ;
⌊They cried out,⌋ *{saying}* "What do you have to do ⌊with us,⌋ *{and}* *you* Son of God?
3189 3306 5515 5148 7005 2779 5148 5626 3836 2536
v.aai.3p pt.pa.npm r.nsn r.dp.1 cj r.ds.2 n.vsm d.gsm n.gsm

ἦλθες ὧδε πρὸ καιροῦ βασανίσαι ἡμᾶς; 30 ἦν δὲ
⌊Have you come⌋ here before the ⌊appointed time⌋ to torment us?" *there was* *{and}*
2262 6045 4574 2789 989 7005 1639 1254
v.aai.2s adv p.g n.gsm f.aa r.ap.1 v.iai.3s cj

μακρὰν ἀπ' αὐτῶν ἀγέλη χοίρων πολλῶν βοσκομένη. 31 οἱ
Some distance from them there was a large herd of pigs *large* feeding. And the
3426 608 899 1639 1639 4498 36 5956 4498 1081 1254 3836
adv p.g r.gpm.3 n.nsf n.gpm a.gpm pt.pp.nsf d.npm

δὲ δαίμονες παρεκάλουν αὐτὸν λέγοντες, εἰ ἐκβάλλεις ἡμᾶς, ↰ ἀπόστειλον ἡμᾶς
And demons begged him, saying, "If you drive us out, send us
1254 1230 4151 899 3306 1623 1675 7005 1675 690 7005
cj n.npm v.iai.3p r.asm.3 pt.pa.npm cj v.pai.2s r.ap.1 v.aam.2s r.ap.1

εἰς τὴν ἀγέλην τῶν χοίρων. 32 καὶ εἶπεν αὐτοῖς, ὑπάγετε. οἱ δὲ ἐξελθόντες
into the herd of pigs." And he said to them, "Be gone." So they *So* came out
1650 3836 36 3836 5956 2779 3306 899 5632 1254 3836 1254 2002
p.a d.asf n.asf d.gpm n.gpm cj v.aai.3s r.dpm.3 v.pam.2p d.npm cj pt.aa.npm

ἀπῆλθον εἰς τοὺς χοίρους· καὶ ἰδοὺ ὥρμησεν πᾶσα ἡ ἀγέλη
and went into the pigs. Then *{behold}* the entire herd rushed *entire* *the* *herd*
599 1650 3836 5956 2779 2627 3836 4246 36 3994 4246 3836 36
v.aai.3p p.a d.apm n.apm cj j v.aai.3s a.nsf d.nsf n.nsf

κατὰ τοῦ κρημνοῦ εἰς τὴν θάλασσαν καὶ ἀπέθανον ἐν τοῖς ὕδασιν. 33 οἱ δὲ
down the steep bank into the sea and drowned in the waters. The *{and}*
2848 3836 3204 1650 3836 2498 2779 633 1877 3836 5623 3836 1254
p.g d.gsm n.gsm p.a d.asf n.asf cj v.aai.3p p.d d.dpn n.dpn d.npm cj

βόσκοντες ἔφυγον, καὶ ἀπελθόντες εἰς τὴν πόλιν ἀπήγγειλαν πάντα καὶ
herdsmen fled, *{and}* went into the town, and told everything *{even}*
1081 5771 2779 599 1650 3836 4484 550 4246 2779
pt.pa.npm v.aai.3p cj pt.aa.npm p.a d.asf n.asf v.aai.3p a.apn cj

τὰ τῶν δαιμονιζομένων. 34 καὶ ἰδοὺ πᾶσα ἡ πόλις ἐξῆλθεν
that had happened to the demoniacs. Then *{behold}* the entire *the* town went out
3836 3836 1227 2779 2627 3836 4246 3836 4484 2002
d.apn d.gpm pt.pp.gpm cj j a.nsf d.nsf n.nsf v.aai.3s

εἰς ὑπάντησιν τῷ Ἰησοῦ καὶ ἰδόντες αὐτὸν παρεκάλεσαν ὅπως μεταβῇ
to meet *{the}* Jesus; and ⌊when they saw⌋ him, they begged him to leave
1650 5637 3836 2652 2779 1625 899 4151 3968 3553
p.a n.asf d.dsm n.dsm cj pt.aa.npm r.asm.3 v.aai.3p cj v.aas.3s

ἀπὸ τῶν ὁρίων αὐτῶν.
{from} *{the}* their region. *their*
608 3836 899 3990 899
p.g d.gpn n.gpn r.gpm.3

9:1 καὶ ἐμβὰς εἰς πλοῖον διεπέρασεν καὶ ἦλθεν εἰς τὴν ἰδίαν
So Jesus got into a boat, ⌊crossed to the other side,⌋ and went to *{the}* his own
2779 1832 1650 4450 1385 2779 2262 1650 3836 2625
cj pt.aa.nsm p.a n.asn v.aai.3s cj v.aai.3s p.a d.asf a.asf

πόλιν. 2 καὶ ἰδοὺ προσέφερον αὐτῷ παραλυτικὸν ἐπὶ κλίνης
town. And *{behold}* some people brought to him a paralyzed man lying on a stretcher.
4484 2779 2627 4712 899 4166 965 2093 3109
n.asf cj j v.iai.3p r.dsm.3 a.asm p.g n.gsf

βεβλημένον. καὶ → ἰδὼν ὁ Ἰησοῦς τὴν πίστιν αὐτῶν εἶπεν τῷ
lying *{and}* When Jesus saw *{the}* *Jesus* *{the}* their faith, *their* he said ⌊to the⌋
965 2779 2652 1625 3836 2652 3836 899 4411 899 3306 3836
pt.rp.asm cj pt.aa.nsm d.nsm n.nsm d.asf n.asf r.gpm.3 v.aai.3s d.dsm

παραλυτικῷ, θάρσει, τέκνον, ἀφίενταί σου αἱ ἁμαρτίαι. 3 ⌊καὶ
paralytic, "Take courage, my son; your sins are forgiven." *your* *{the}* *sins* At this,
4166 2510 5451 5148 281 918 5148 3836 281 2779
a.dsm v.pam.2s n.vsn v.ppi.3p r.gs.2 d.npf n.npf cj

NASB

could pass by that
way. 29And they
cried out, saying,
"What business do
we have with each
other, Son of God?
Have You come
here to torment us
before the time?"
30Now there was
a herd of many
swine feeding at
a distance from
them. 31The de-
mons *began* to en-
treat Him, saying,
"If You *are going*
to cast us out, send
us into the herd of
swine." 32And He
said to them, "Go!"
And they came
out and went into
the swine, and the
whole herd rushed
down the steep
bank into the sea
and perished in
the waters. 33The
herdsmen ran
away, and went
to the city and re-
ported everything,
including what had
happened to the
demoniacs. 34And
behold, the whole
city came out to
meet Jesus; and
when they saw
Him, they implored
Him to leave their
region.

A Paralytic Healed

9:1Getting into a
boat, Jesus crossed
over *the sea* and
came to His own
city.
2And they brought
to Him a paralytic
lying on a bed.
Seeing their faith,
Jesus said to the
paralytic, "Take
courage, son; your
sins are forgiven."

NIV

[3]At this, some
of the teachers
of the law said to
themselves, "This
fellow is blas-
pheming!"
[4]Knowing their
thoughts, Jesus
said, "Why do
you entertain evil
thoughts in your
hearts? [5]Which
is easier: to say,
'Your sins are for-
given,' or to say,
'Get up and walk'?
[6]But I want you
to know that the
Son of Man has
authority on earth
to forgive sins."
So he said to the
paralyzed man,
"Get up, take your
mat and go home."
[7]Then the man got
up and went home.
[8]When the crowd
saw this, they were
filled with awe;
and they praised
God, who had giv-
en such authority
to man.

The Calling of Matthew

[9]As Jesus went
on from there, he
saw a man named
Matthew sitting at
the tax collector's
booth. "Follow
me," he told him,
and Matthew got
up and followed
him.
[10]While Jesus
was having din-
ner at Matthew's
house, many tax
collectors and sin-
ners came and ate
with him and his
disciples. [11]When
the Pharisees saw
this, they asked his
disciples, "Why
does your teacher
eat with tax collec-
tors and sinners?"

ἰδού⌋ τινες τῶν γραμματέων εἶπαν ἐν ἑαυτοῖς, οὗτος βλασφημεῖ. 4 καὶ
some of the scribes said to themselves, "This man is blaspheming." And Jesus,
2627 5516 3836 1208 3306 1877 1571 4047 1059 2779 2652
j r.npm d.gpm n.gpm v.aai.3p p.d r.dpm.3 r.nsm v.pai.3s cj

ἰδὼν[a] ὁ Ἰησοῦς τὰς ἐνθυμήσεις αὐτῶν εἶπεν, ἱνατί ἐνθυμεῖσθε πονηρὰ
knowing {the} Jesus {the} their thoughts, *their* said, "Why are you harboring evil
1625 3836 2652 3836 899 1927 899 3306 2672 1926 4505
pt.aa.nsm d.nsm n.nsm d.apf n.apf r.gpm.3 v.aai.3s cj v.pmi.2p a.apn

↰ ἐν ταῖς καρδίαις ὑμῶν; 5 τί γάρ ἐστιν εὐκοπώτερον, εἰπεῖν,
thoughts in {the} your hearts? *your* For which *For* is easier; to say, 'Your
1926 1877 3836 7007 2840 7007 1142 5515 1142 1639 2324 3306 5148
p.d d.dpf n.dpf r.gp.2 r.nsn cj v.pai.3s a.nsn.c f.aa

ἀφίενταί σου αἱ ἁμαρτίαι, ἢ εἰπεῖν, ἔγειρε καὶ περιπάτει; 6 ἵνα δὲ
sins are forgiven,' *Your* {the} *sins* or to say, ⌊'Stand up⌋ and walk'? But so *But*
281 918 5148 3836 281 2445 3306 1586 2779 4344 1254 2671 1254
v.ppi.3p r.gs.2 d.npf n.npf cj f.aa v.pam.2s cj v.pam.2s cj cj

εἰδῆτε ὅτι ἐξουσίαν ἔχει ὁ υἱὸς τοῦ ἀνθρώπου ἐπὶ
⌊you may know⌋ that the Son of Man has authority *has* *the* *Son* *of* *Man* on
3857 4022 3836 5626 3836 476 2400 2026 2400 3836 5626 3836 476 2093
v.ras.2p cj n.asf v.pai.3s d.nsm n.nsm d.gsm n.gsm p.g

τῆς γῆς ἀφιέναι ἁμαρτίας ↱ τότε λέγει τῷ παραλυτικῷ, ἐγερθεὶς ἆρόν σου
the earth to forgive sins" — he then said ⌊to the⌋ paralytic, "Get up, pick up your
3836 1178 918 281 3306 5538 3306 3836 4166 1586 149 5148
d.gsf n.gsf f.pa n.apf adv v.pai.3s d.dsm a.dsm pt.ap.nsm v.aam.2s r.gs.2

τὴν κλίνην καὶ ὕπαγε εἰς τὸν οἶκόν σου. 7 καὶ ↱ ἐγερθεὶς ἀπῆλθεν εἰς
{the} stretcher, and go to {the} your home." *your* So he got up and went to
3836 3109 2779 5632 1650 3836 5148 3875 5148 2779 599 1586 599 1650
d.asf n.asf cj v.pam.2s p.a d.asm n.asm r.gs.2 cj pt.ap.nsm v.aai.3s p.a

τὸν οἶκον αὐτοῦ. 8 → ἰδόντες δὲ οἱ ὄχλοι
{the} his home. *his* When the crowds saw {and} *the* *crowds* it,
3836 899 3875 899 3836 4063 1625 1254 3836 4063
d.asm n.asm r.gsm.3 pt.aa.npm cj d.npm n.npm

ἐφοβήθησαν καὶ ἐδόξασαν τὸν θεὸν τὸν δόντα ἐξουσίαν τοιαύτην
⌊they were struck with awe⌋ and glorified {the} God who had given such authority *such*
5828 2779 1519 3836 2536 3836 1443 5525 2026 5525
v.api.3p cj v.aai.3p d.asm n.asm d.asm pt.aa.asm n.asf r.asf

τοῖς ἀνθρώποις. 9 καὶ → παράγων ὁ Ἰησοῦς ἐκεῖθεν εἶδεν ἄνθρωπον
to men. {and} As Jesus went on {the} *Jesus* from there, he saw a man
3836 476 2779 2652 4135 3836 2652 1696 1625 476
d.dpm n.dpm cj pt.pa.nsm d.nsm n.nsm adv v.aai.3s n.asm

καθήμενον ἐπὶ τὸ τελώνιον, Μαθθαῖον λεγόμενον, καὶ λέγει αὐτῷ,
named Matthew sitting at the tax booth, *Matthew* *named* and he said to him,
3306 3414 2764 2093 3836 5468 3414 3306 2779 3306 899
pt.pm.asm p.a d.asn n.asn n.asm pt.pp.asm cj v.pai.3s r.dsm.3

ἀκολούθει μοι. καὶ ἀναστὰς ἠκολούθησεν αὐτῷ. 10 καὶ ἐγένετο
"Follow me." So Matthew got up and followed him. And {it happened that}
199 1609 2779 482 199 899 2779 1181
v.pam.2s r.ds.1 cj pt.aa.nsm v.aai.3s r.dsm.3 cj v.ami.3s

↱ αὐτοῦ ἀνακειμένου ἐν τῇ οἰκίᾳ, καὶ ἰδοὺ πολλοὶ τελῶναι καὶ
as Jesus sat at table in the house, {and} {behold} many tax collectors and
367 899 367 1877 3836 3864 2779 2627 4498 5467 2779
r.gsm.3 pt.pm.gsm p.d d.dsf n.dsf cj j a.npm n.npm cj

ἁμαρτωλοὶ ἐλθόντες συνανέκειντο τῷ Ἰησοῦ καὶ τοῖς μαθηταῖς αὐτοῦ.
sinners came and were eating with Jesus and {the} his disciples. *his*
283 2262 5263 3836 2652 2779 3836 899 3412 899
a.npm pt.aa.npm v.imi.3p d.dsm n.dsm cj d.dpm n.dpm r.gsm.3

11 καὶ → ἰδόντες οἱ Φαρισαῖοι ἔλεγον τοῖς μαθηταῖς
{and} When the Pharisees saw *the* *Pharisees* this, they said to his disciples,
2779 3836 5757 1625 3836 5757 3306 3836 899 3412
cj pt.aa.npm d.npm n.npm v.iai.3p d.dpm n.dpm

αὐτοῦ, ⌊διὰ τί⌋ μετὰ τῶν τελωνῶν καὶ ἁμαρτωλῶν ἐσθίει
his "Why does your teacher eat with {the} tax collectors and sinners?" *does eat*
899 1328 5515 2266 7007 1437 2266 3552 3836 5467 2779 283 2266
r.gsm.3 p.a r.asn p.g d.gpm n.gpm cj a.gpm v.pai.3s

NASB

[3]And some of
the scribes said
to themselves,
"This *fellow* blas-
phemes." [4]And
Jesus knowing
their thoughts
said, "Why are
you thinking evil
in your hearts?
[5]Which is easier,
to say, 'Your sins
are forgiven,' or to
say, 'Get up, and
walk'? [6]But so that
you may know that
the Son of Man has
authority on earth
to forgive sins"—
then He *said to
the paralytic, "Get
up, pick up your
bed and go home."
[7]And he got up and
went home. [8]But
when the crowds
saw *this,* they were
awestruck, and
glorified God, who
had given such au-
thority to men.

Matthew Called

[9]As Jesus went
on from there, He
saw a man called
Matthew, sitting in
the tax collector's
booth; and He *said
to him, "Follow
Me!" And he got
up and followed
Him.
[10]Then it hap-
pened that as Jesus
was reclining *at the
table* in the house,
behold, many tax
collectors and
sinners came and
were dining with
Jesus and His dis-
ciples. [11]When the
Pharisees saw *this,*
they said to His
disciples, "Why
is your Teacher
eating with the tax
collectors and sin-
ners?"

[a] ἰδὼν UBS, NET. εἰδὼς TNIV.

NIV

[12]On hearing this,
Jesus said, "It is
not the healthy
who need a doc-
tor, but the sick.
[13]But go and learn
what this means: 'I
desire mercy, not
sacrifice.'[a] For I
have not come to
call the righteous,
but sinners."

Jesus Questioned About Fasting

[14]Then John's
disciples came and
asked him, "How
is it that we and
the Pharisees fast
often, but your dis-
ciples do not fast?"
[15]Jesus an-
swered, "How can
the guests of the
bridegroom mourn
while he is with
them? The time
will come when
the bridegroom
will be taken from
them; then they
will fast.
[16]"No one sews
a patch of un-
shrunk cloth on
an old garment,
for the patch will
pull away from the
garment, making
the tear worse.
[17]Neither do peo-
ple pour new wine
into old wineskins.
If they do, the
skins will burst;
the wine will
run out and the
wineskins will be
ruined. No, they
pour new wine
into new wine-
skins, and both are
preserved."

ὁ διδάσκαλος ὑμῶν; 12 ↱ ὁ δὲ ἀκούσας εἶπεν,
{the} teacher your But when Jesus But heard it, he said, "Those who are well
3836 1437 7007 1254 201 3836 1254 201 3306 3836 2710 2710 2710
d.nsm n.nsm r.gp.2 d.nsm cj pt.aa.nsm v.aai.3s

οὐ χρείαν ἔχουσιν οἱ ἰσχύοντες → ἰατροῦ ἀλλ᾽ οἱ κακῶς ἔχοντες.
have no need have Those who are well of a doctor, but those who are sick. who are
2400 4024 5970 2400 3836 2710 2620 247 3836 2400 2400 2809 2400
adv n.asf v.pai.3p d.npm pt.pa.npm n.gsm cj d.npm adv pt.pa.npm

13 πορευθέντες δὲ μάθετε τί ἐστιν· ἔλεος θέλω καὶ οὐ θυσίαν·
Go {and} and learn what this means, 'I desire mercy, I desire {and} not sacrifice.'
4513 1254 3443 5515 1639 2527 2527 1799 2527 2779 4024 2602
pt.ap.npm cj v.aam.2p r.nsn v.pai.3s n.asn v.pai.1s cj adv n.asf

↱ ↱ οὐ γὰρ ἦλθον καλέσαι δικαίους ἀλλὰ ἁμαρτωλούς.
For I did not For come to call the pious, but sinners, to repentance."
1142 2262 2262 4024 1142 2262 2813 1465 247 283
adv cj v.aai.1s f.aa a.apm cj a.apm

14 τότε προσέρχονται αὐτῷ οἱ μαθηταὶ Ἰωάννου λέγοντες,
Then the disciples of John came to him the disciples of John and asked,
5538 3836 3412 2722 2722 4665 899 3836 3412 2722 3306
adv v.pmi.3p r.dsm.3 d.npm n.npm n.gsm pt.pa.npm

⌞διὰ τί⌟ ↱ ἡμεῖς καὶ οἱ Φαρισαῖοι νηστεύομεν πολλά,[a] οἱ δὲ μαθηταί
"Why do we and the Pharisees fast regularly, {the} but your disciples
1328 5515 3764 7005 2779 3836 5757 3764 4498 3836 1254 5148 3412
p.a r.asn r.np.1 cj d.npm n.npm v.pai.1p a.apn d.npm cj n.npm

σου ↱ οὐ νηστεύουσιν; 15 καὶ εἶπεν αὐτοῖς ὁ Ἰησοῦς, ⌞μὴ δύνανται⌟
your do not fast?" And Jesus said to them, {the} Jesus can't
5148 3764 4024 3764 2779 2652 3306 899 3836 2652 3590 1538
r.gs.2 adv v.pai.3p cj v.aai.3s r.dpm.3 d.nsm n.nsm pl v.ppi.3p

οἱ υἱοὶ τοῦ νυμφῶνος πενθεῖν ⌞ἐφ᾽ ὅσον⌟
"Certainly the wedding guests {the} wedding can't mourn as long as the bridegroom
3836 3813 5626 3836 3813 3590 4291 2093 4012 3836 3812
d.npm n.npm d.gsm n.gsm f.pa p.a r.asm

μετ᾽ αὐτῶν ἐστιν ὁ νυμφίος; ἐλεύσονται δὲ ἡμέραι ὅταν
is still with them? is the bridegroom The days will come {and} days when the
1639 3552 899 1639 3836 3812 2465 2262 1254 2465 4020 3836
p.g r.gpm.3 v.pai.3s d.nsm n.nsm v.fmi.3p cj n.npf pl

ἀπαρθῇ ἀπ᾽ αὐτῶν ὁ νυμφίος, καὶ τότε νηστεύσουσιν. 16 οὐδεὶς
bridegroom is taken away from them, the bridegroom and then they will fast! No one
3812 554 608 899 3836 3812 2779 5538 3764 4029
v.aps.3s p.g r.gpm.3 d.nsm n.nsm cj adv v.fai.3p a.nsm

δὲ ἐπιβάλλει ἐπίβλημα → ῥάκους ἀγνάφου ἐπὶ ἱματίῳ παλαιῷ·
{and} sews a piece of unshrunk cloth unshrunk on an old garment, old
1254 2095 2099 47 4820 47 2093 4094 2668 4094
cj v.pai.3s n.asn n.gsn a.gsn p.d n.dsn a.dsn

αἴρει γὰρ τὸ πλήρωμα αὐτοῦ ἀπὸ τοῦ ἱματίου καὶ
because the patch ⌞will pull away⌟ because the patch {it's} from the garment, and the
1142 3836 4445 149 1142 3836 4445 899 608 3836 2668 2779
v.pai.3s cj d.asn n.asn r.gsn.3 p.g d.gsn n.gsn cj

χεῖρον σχίσμα γίνεται. 17 οὐδὲ → βάλλουσιν οἶνον νέον εἰς
tear will be worse. tear will be Neither is new wine poured wine new into
5388 1181 1181 5937 5388 1181 4028 3742 3885 965 3885 3742 1650
a.nsn.c n.nsn v.pmi.3s cj v.pai.3p n.asm a.asm p.a

ἀσκοὺς παλαιούς· ⌞εἰ δὲ μή γε,⌟ ῥήγνυνται οἱ
old wineskins. old If that happens, the wineskins split, the
4094 829 4094 1623 1254 3590 1145 3836 829 4838 3836
n.apm a.apm cj cj pl pl v.ppi.3p d.npm

ἀσκοὶ καὶ ὁ οἶνος ἐκχεῖται καὶ οἱ ἀσκοὶ ἀπόλλυνται· ἀλλὰ
wineskins {and} the wine pours out, and the wineskins are ruined. Instead, new wine
829 2779 3836 3885 1772 2779 3836 829 660 247 3742 3885
n.npm cj d.nsm n.nsm v.ppi.3s cj d.npm n.npm v.ppi.3p cj

βάλλουσιν οἶνον νέον εἰς ἀσκοὺς καινούς, καὶ ἀμφότεροι συντηροῦνται.
is put wine new into fresh wineskins, fresh ⌞and so⌟ both are preserved."
965 3885 3742 1650 2785 829 2785 2779 317 5337
v.pai.3p n.asm a.asm p.a n.apm a.apm cj a.npm v.ppi.3p

NASB

[12]But when Jesus
heard *this,* He said,
"*It is* not those who
are healthy who
need a physician,
but those who are
sick. [13]But go and
learn what this
means: 'I DESIRE
COMPASSION, [a]AND
NOT SACRIFICE,' for
I did not come to
call the righteous,
but sinners."

The Question about Fasting

[14]Then the dis-
ciples of John
*came to Him,
asking, "Why do
we and the Phari-
sees fast, but Your
disciples do not
fast?" [15]And Jesus
said to them, "The
attendants of the
bridegroom can-
not mourn as long
as the bridegroom
is with them, can
they? But the days
will come when
the bridegroom is
taken away from
them, and then
they will fast. [16]But
no one puts a patch
of unshrunk cloth
on an old garment;
for the patch pulls
away from the
garment, and a
worse tear results.
[17]Nor do *people* put
new wine into old
wineskins; other-
wise the wineskins
burst, and the wine
pours out and the
wineskins are
ruined; but they
put new wine into
fresh wineskins,
and both are pre-
served."

[a] 13 Hosea 6:6

[a] [πολλά] UBS.

[a] I.e. more than

NIV

Jesus Raises a Dead Girl and Heals a Sick Woman

18While he was
saying this, a syn-
agogue leader
came and knelt
before him and
said, "My daugh-
ter has just died.
But come and put
your hand on her,
and she will live."
19Jesus got up and
went with him,
and so did his dis-
ciples.
20Just then a
woman who had
been subject
to bleeding for
twelve years came
up behind him and
touched the edge
of his cloak. 21She
said to herself, "If
I only touch his
cloak, I will be
healed."
22Jesus turned
and saw her. "Take
heart, daughter,"
he said, "your faith
has healed you."
And the woman
was healed at that
moment.
23When Jesus
entered the syn-
agogue leader's
house and saw the
noisy crowd and
people playing
pipes, 24he said,
"Go away. The
girl is not dead but
asleep." But they
laughed at him.
25After the crowd
had been put out-
side, he went in
and took the girl
by the hand, and
she got up. 26News
of this spread
through all that
region.

Jesus Heals the Blind and the Mute

27As Jesus went
on from there,

18 ταῦτα αὐτοῦ λαλοῦντος αὐτοῖς, ἰδοὺ ἄρχων εἷς
As he was saying these things *he* *As was saying* to them, *{behold}* a ruler *a*
3281 899 3281 3281 4047 899 3281 899 2627 1651 807 1651
r.apn r.gsm.3 pt.pa.gsm r.dpm.3 j n.nsm a.nsm

ἐλθὼν προσεκύνει αὐτῷ λέγων ὅτι ἡ θυγάτηρ μου ↱ ἄρτι
came and ⌊bowed down before⌋ him, saying, ~ *{the}* "My daughter *My* has just
2262 4686 899 3306 4022 3836 1609 2588 1609 5462 785
pt.aa.nsm v.iai.3s r.dsm.3 pt.pa.nsm cj d.nsf n.nsf r.gs.1 adv

ἐτελεύτησεν· ἀλλὰ ἐλθὼν ἐπίθες τὴν χεῖρά σου ἐπ' αὐτήν, καὶ ζήσεται.
died; but come, lay *{the}* your hand *your* on her and she will live again."
5462 247 2262 2202 3836 5148 5931 5148 2093 899 2779 2409
v.aai.3s cj pt.aa.nsm v.aam.2s d.asf n.asf r.gs.2 p.a r.asf.3 cj v.fmi.3s

19 καὶ ἐγερθεὶς ὁ Ἰησοῦς ἠκολούθησεν αὐτῷ καὶ οἱ μαθηταὶ
So Jesus got up *{the}* *Jesus* and followed him, and so did *{the}* his disciples.
2779 2652 1586 3836 2652 199 899 2779 3836 899 3412
cj pt.ap.nsm d.nsm n.nsm v.aai.3s r.dsm.3 cj d.npm n.npm

αὐτοῦ. 20 ⌊καὶ ἰδοὺ⌋ γυνὴ αἱμορροοῦσα δώδεκα ἔτη
his Just then a woman ⌊who had suffered from severe bleeding⌋ for twelve years
899 2779 2627 1222 137 1557 2291
r.gsm.3 cj j n.nsf pt.pa.nsf a.apn n.apn

προσελθοῦσα ὄπισθεν ἥψατο τοῦ κρασπέδου τοῦ ἱματίου αὐτοῦ· 21
came up behind him and touched the fringe of his cloak, *his* for
4665 3957 721 3836 3192 3836 899 2668 899 1142
pt.aa.nsf adv v.ami.3s d.gsn n.gsn d.gsn n.gsn r.gsm.3

ἔλεγεν γὰρ ἐν ἑαυτῇ, ἐὰν ↱ ↱ μόνον ἅψωμαι τοῦ ἱματίου αὐτοῦ
⌊she was saying⌋ *for* to herself, "If I can only touch *{the}* his garment, *his*
3306 1142 1877 1571 1569 721 721 3667 721 3836 899 2668 899
v.iai.3s cj p.d r.dsf.3 cj adv v.ams.1s d.gsn n.gsn r.gsm.3

σωθήσομαι. 22 ὁ δὲ ↱ Ἰησοῦς στραφεὶς καὶ ἰδὼν αὐτὴν εἶπεν,
I will be healed." *{the}* And when Jesus turned and saw her, he said,
5392 3836 1254 5138 2652 5138 2779 1625 899 3306
v.fpi.1s d.nsm cj n.nsm pt.ap.nsm cj pt.aa.nsm r.asf.3 v.aai.3s

θάρσει, θύγατερ· ἡ πίστις σου σέσωκέν σε. ↰ καὶ
"Take courage, my daughter; *{the}* your faith *your* has made you well." And the woman
2510 2588 3836 5148 4411 5148 5392 5148 5392 2779 3836 1222
v.pam.2s n.vsf d.nsf n.nsf r.gs.2 v.rai.3s r.as.2 cj

ἐσώθη ἡ γυνὴ ἀπὸ τῆς ὥρας ἐκείνης. 23 καὶ → ἐλθὼν ὁ
was healed *the* *woman* from *{the}* that hour. *that* *{and}* When Jesus arrived *{the}*
5392 3836 1222 608 3836 1697 6052 1697 2779 2652 2262 3836
v.api.3s d.nsf n.nsf p.g d.gsf n.gsf r.gsf cj pt.aa.nsm d.nsm

Ἰησοῦς εἰς τὴν οἰκίαν τοῦ ἄρχοντος καὶ ἰδὼν τοὺς αὐλητὰς καὶ τὸν
Jesus at the ruler's house *{the}* *ruler's* and saw the flute players and the
2652 1650 3836 807 3864 3836 807 2779 1625 3836 886 2779 3836
n.nsm p.a d.asf n.asf d.gsm n.gsm cj pt.aa.nsm d.apm n.apm cj d.asm

ὄχλον θορυβούμενον 24 ἔλεγεν, ἀναχωρεῖτε, οὐ γὰρ → ἀπέθανεν
noisy crowd, *noisy* he said, "Leave now, *not* for the girl is not dead
2572 4063 2572 3306 432 4024 1142 3836 3166 4024 633
n.asm pt.pp.asm v.iai.3s v.pam.2p adv cj v.aai.3s

τὸ κοράσιον ἀλλὰ καθεύδει. καὶ κατεγέλων αὐτοῦ. 25 ὅτε δὲ
the *girl* but only sleeping." And ⌊they began to ridicule⌋ him. But when *But*
3836 3166 247 2761 2779 2860 899 1254 4021 1254
d.nsn n.nsn cj v.pai.3s cj v.iai.3p r.gsm.3 cj cj

ἐξεβλήθη ὁ ὄχλος εἰσελθὼν ἐκράτησεν τῆς χειρὸς
the crowd had been removed, *the* *crowd* Jesus went in and took her by the hand,
3836 4063 1675 3836 4063 1656 3195 899 3836 5931
v.api.3s d.nsm n.nsm pt.aa.nsm v.aai.3s d.gsf n.gsf

αὐτῆς, καὶ ἠγέρθη τὸ κοράσιον. 26 καὶ ἐξῆλθεν ἡ φήμη αὕτη
her and the girl arose. *the* *girl* And *spread* the report of this spread
899 2779 3836 3166 1586 3836 3166 2779 2002 3836 5773 4047 2002
r.gsf.3 cj v.api.3s d.nsn n.nsn cj v.aai.3s d.nsf n.nsf r.nsf

εἰς ὅλην τὴν γῆν ἐκείνην. 27 καὶ → παράγοντι ἐκεῖθεν τῷ Ἰησοῦ
through all *{the}* that region. *that* And as Jesus went on from there, *{the}* *Jesus*
1650 3910 3836 1697 1178 1697 2779 2652 4135 1696 3836 2652
p.a a.asf d.asf n.asf r.asf cj pt.pa.dsm adv d.dsm n.dsm

NASB

Miracles of Healing

18While He was
saying these things
to them, a *syna-
gogue* official came
and bowed down
before Him, and
said, "My daugh-
ter has just died;
but come and lay
Your hand on her,
and she will live."
19Jesus got up and
began to follow
him, and *so did* His
disciples.
20And a woman
who had been
suffering from a
hemorrhage for
twelve years, came
up behind Him and
touched the fringe
of His cloak; 21for
she was saying to
herself, "If I only
touch His garment,
I will get well."
22But Jesus turn-
ing and seeing her
said, "Daughter,
take courage; your
faith has made you
well." At once the
woman was made
well.
23When Jesus
came into the
official's house,
and saw the flute-
players and the
crowd in noisy
disorder, 24He said,
"Leave; for the girl
has not died, but is
asleep." And they
began laughing at
Him. 25But when
the crowd had
been sent out, He
entered and took
her by the hand,
and the girl got up.
26This news spread
throughout all that
land.
27As Jesus went
on from there, two
blind men followed
Him, crying out,
"Have mercy on
us, Son of David!"
28When He entered
the house,

NIV

two blind men fol-
lowed him, calling
out, "Have mercy
on us, Son of Da-
vid!"
28 When he had
gone indoors, the
blind men came to
him, and he asked
them, "Do you be-
lieve that I am able
to do this?"
"Yes, Lord," they
replied.
29 Then he
touched their eyes
and said, "Accord-
ing to your faith
let it be done to
you"; 30 and their
sight was restored.
Jesus warned them
sternly, "See that
no one knows
about this." 31 But
they went out and
spread the news
about him all over
that region.
32 While they
were going out,
a man who was
demon-possessed
and could not talk
was brought to
Jesus. 33 And when
the demon was
driven out, the
man who had been
mute spoke. The
crowd was amazed
and said, "Noth-
ing like this has
ever been seen in
Israel."
34 But the Phar-
isees said, "It is
by the prince of
demons that he
drives out de-
mons."

ἠκολούθησαν αὐτῷ[a] δύο τυφλοὶ κράζοντες καὶ λέγοντες,
two blind men followed him, *two* *blind men* calling out, *{and}* *{saying}*
1545 5603 5603 199 899 1545 5603 3189 2779 3306
v.aai.3p r.dsm.3 a.npm a.npm pt.pa.npm cj pt.pa.npm

ἐλέησον ἡμᾶς, υἱὸς Δαυίδ. 28 ἐλθόντι δὲ εἰς τὴν οἰκίαν
⌞"Have mercy on⌟ us, Son of David!" ⌞When he had gone⌟ *{and}* into the house, the blind
1796 7005 5626 1253 2262 1254 1650 3836 3864 3836 5603
v.aam.2s r.ap.1 n.nsm n.gsm pt.aa.dsm cj p.a d.asf n.asf

προσῆλθον αὐτῷ οἱ τυφλοί, καὶ λέγει αὐτοῖς ὁ Ἰησοῦς, πιστεύετε
men came to him; *the* *blind men* and Jesus said to them, *{the}* *Jesus* "Do you believe
5603 4665 899 3836 5603 2779 2652 3306 899 3836 2652 4409
v.aai.3p r.dsm.3 d.npm a.npm cj v.pai.3s r.dpm.3 d.nsm n.nsm v.pai.2p

ὅτι δύναμαι τοῦτο ποιῆσαι; λέγουσιν αὐτῷ, ναὶ κύριε. 29 τότε ἥψατο
that I am able to do this?" *to do* They said to him, "Yes, Lord." Then he touched
4022 1538 4472 4472 4047 4472 3306 899 3721 3261 5538 721
cj v.ppi.1s r.asn f.aa v.pai.3p r.dsm.3 pl n.vsm adv v.ami.3s

τῶν ὀφθαλμῶν αὐτῶν λέγων, κατὰ τὴν πίστιν ὑμῶν γενηθήτω
{the} their eyes *their* and said, ⌞"According to⌟ *{the}* your faith *your* may it be done
3836 899 4057 899 3306 2848 3836 7007 4411 7007 1181
d.gpm n.gpm r.gpm.3 pt.pa.nsm p.a d.asf n.asf r.gp.2 v.apm.3s

ὑμῖν. 30 καὶ ἠνεῴχθησαν αὐτῶν οἱ ὀφθαλμοί. καὶ ἐνεβριμήθη
to you." And their eyes were opened. *their* *{the}* *eyes* Then Jesus sternly charged
7007 2779 899 4057 487 899 3836 4057 2779 2652 1839
r.dp.2 cj v.api.3p r.gpm.3 d.npm n.npm cj v.api.3s

αὐτοῖς ὁ Ἰησοῦς λέγων, ὁρᾶτε μηδεὶς γινωσκέτω. 31 οἱ δὲ
them, *{the}* *Jesus* *{saying}* "See that no one knows about this." But they *But*
899 3836 2652 3306 3972 3594 1182 1254 3836 1254
r.dpm.3 d.nsm n.nsm pt.pa.nsm v.pam.2p a.nsm v.pam.3s d.npm cj

ἐξελθόντες διεφήμισαν αὐτὸν ἐν ὅλῃ τῇ γῇ ἐκείνῃ.
went out and spread the news about him throughout that entire *{the}* region. *that*
2002 1424 899 1877 1697 3910 3836 1178 1697
pt.aa.npm v.aai.3p r.asm.3 p.d a.dsf d.dsf n.dsf r.dsf

32 ↱ αὐτῶν δὲ ἐξερχομένων ἰδοὺ προσήνεγκαν αὐτῷ ἄνθρωπον
As they *{and}* were going away, *{behold}* others brought to him a man
2002 899 1254 2002 2627 4712 899 476
r.gpm.3 cj pt.pm.gpm j v.aai.3p r.dsm.3 n.asm

κωφὸν δαιμονιζόμενον. 33 καὶ → ἐκβληθέντος
⌞who could not speak⌟ and was demon-possessed. And when the demon ⌞had been driven out,⌟
3273 1227 2779 3836 1228 1675
a.asm pt.pp.asm cj pt.ap.gsn

τοῦ δαιμονίου ἐλάλησεν ὁ κωφός. καὶ
the *demon* *began to speak* the ⌞man who had been mute⌟ began to speak. *{and}* The crowds
3836 1228 3281 3836 3273 3281 3281 3281 2779 3836 4063
d.gsn n.gsn v.aai.3s d.nsm a.nsm cj

ἐθαύμασαν οἱ ὄχλοι λέγοντες, οὐδέποτε → ἐφάνη οὕτως ἐν
were amazed *The* *crowds* and said, "Never has anything like this been seen *like this* in
2513 3836 4063 3306 4030 4048 4048 5743 4048 1877
v.aai.3p d.npm n.npm pt.pa.npm adv v.api.3s adv p.d

τῷ Ἰσραήλ. 34 οἱ δὲ Φαρισαῖοι ἔλεγον, ἐν τῷ ἄρχοντι τῶν
{the} Israel." But the *But* Pharisees kept saying, "It is by the ruler of
3836 2702 1254 3836 1254 5757 3306 1877 3836 807 3836
d.dsm n.dsm d.npm cj n.npm v.iai.3p p.d d.dsm n.dsm d.gpn

δαιμονίων ἐκβάλλει τὰ δαιμόνια. 35 καὶ περιῆγεν ὁ Ἰησοῦς
demons that he drives out *{the}* demons." And Jesus went throughout *{the}* *Jesus* all
1228 1675 3836 1228 2779 2652 4310 3836 2652 4246
n.gpn v.pai.3s d.apn n.apn cj v.iai.3s d.nsm n.nsm

τὰς πόλεις πάσας καὶ τὰς κώμας διδάσκων ἐν ταῖς συναγωγαῖς αὐτῶν καὶ
their cities *all* and *{the}* towns, teaching in *{the}* their synagogues, *their* *{and}*
3836 4484 4246 2779 3836 3267 1438 1877 3836 899 5252 899 2779
d.apf n.apf a.apf cj d.apf n.apf pt.pa.nsm p.d d.dpf n.dpf r.gpm.3 cj

κηρύσσων τὸ εὐαγγέλιον τῆς βασιλείας καὶ θεραπεύων πᾶσαν νόσον καὶ πᾶσαν
preaching the gospel of the kingdom, and healing every disease and every
3062 3836 2295 3836 993 2779 2543 4246 3798 2779 4246
pt.pa.nsm d.asn n.asn d.gsf n.gsf cj pt.pa.nsm a.asf n.asf cj a.asf

[a] [αὐτῷ] UBS.

NASB

the blind men came
up to Him, and
Jesus *said to them,
"Do you believe
that I am able to
do this?" They
*said to Him, "Yes,
Lord." 29 Then He
touched their eyes,
saying, "It shall
be done to you
according to your
faith." 30 And their
eyes were opened.
And Jesus sternly
warned them:
"See that no one
knows *about this!*"
31 But they went
out and spread the
news about Him
throughout all that
land.
32 As they were
going out, a mute,
demon-possessed
man was brought
to Him. 33 After
the demon was
cast out, the mute
man spoke; and
the crowds were
amazed, *and were*
saying, "Noth-
ing like this has
ever been seen in
Israel." 34 But the
Pharisees were
saying, "He casts
out the demons
by the ruler of the
demons."
35 Jesus was go-
ing through all the
cities and villages,
teaching in their
synagogues and
proclaiming the
gospel of the king-
dom, and healing
every kind of dis-
ease and every

NIV

The Workers Are Few

35 Jesus went
through all the
towns and villag-
es, teaching in
their synagogues,
proclaiming the
good news of
the kingdom and
healing every dis-
ease and sickness.
36 When he saw
the crowds, he
had compassion
on them, because
they were harassed
and helpless, like
sheep without a
shepherd. 37 Then
he said to his disci-
ples, "The harvest
is plentiful but the
workers are few.
38 Ask the Lord of
the harvest, there-
fore, to send out
workers into his
harvest field."

Jesus Sends Out the Twelve

10 Jesus called
his twelve
disciples to him
and gave them au-
thority to drive out
impure spirits and
to heal every dis-
ease and sickness.
2 These are the
names of the
twelve apostles:
first, Simon (who
is called Peter) and
his brother An-
drew; James son
of Zebedee, and
his brother John;
3 Philip and Bar-
tholomew; Thom-
as and Matthew
the tax collector;
James son of Al-
phaeus, and Thad-
daeus; 4 Simon the
Zealot and Judas
Iscariot, who be-
trayed him.
5 These twelve
Jesus sent out with
the following in-
structions: "Do
not go among the
Gentiles or enter
any town of the
Samaritans. 6 Go
rather to the

μαλακίαν. 36 ἰδὼν δὲ τοὺς ὄχλους ἐσπλαγχνίσθη περὶ αὐτῶν, ὅτι
sickness. And ˻when he saw˼ *And* the crowds, he had compassion on them, because
3433 1254 1625 1254 3836 4063 5072 4309 899 4022
n.asf pt.aa.nsm cj d.apm n.apm v.api.3s p.g r.gpm.3 cj

ἦσαν ἐσκυλμένοι καὶ ἐρριμμένοι ὡσεὶ πρόβατα ˻μὴ ἔχοντα˼ ποιμένα. 37 τότε
they were distressed and dejected, like sheep without a shepherd. Then
1639 5035 2779 4849 6059 4585 3590 2400 4478 5538
v.iai.3p pt.rp.npm cj pt.rp.npm pl n.npn pl pt.pa.npn n.asm adv

λέγει τοῖς μαθηταῖς αὐτοῦ, ὁ μὲν θερισμὸς πολύς, οἱ δὲ ἐργάται
he said to his disciples, *his* "The ~ harvest is great but the *but* workers are
3306 3836 899 3412 899 3836 3525 2546 4498 1254 3836 1254 2239
v.pai.3s d.dpm n.dpm r.gsm.3 d.nsm pl n.nsm a.nsm d.npm cj n.npm

ὀλίγοι· 38 δεήθητε οὖν τοῦ κυρίου τοῦ θερισμοῦ ὅπως ἐκβάλῃ ἐργάτας εἰς τὸν
few; so pray to *so* the Lord of the harvest to send out workers into *{the}*
3900 4036 1289 4036 3836 3261 3836 2546 3968 1675 2239 1650 3836
a.npm v.apm.2p cj d.gsm n.gsm d.gsm n.gsm cj v.aas.3s n.apm p.a d.asm

θερισμὸν αὐτοῦ.
his harvest." *his*
899 2546 899
n.asm r.gsm.3

10:1 καὶ προσκαλεσάμενος τοὺς δώδεκα μαθητὰς αὐτοῦ ἔδωκεν
{and} Jesus gathered *{the}* his twelve disciples *his* and gave
2779 4673 3836 899 1557 3412 899 1443
cj pt.am.nsm d.apm a.apm n.apm r.gsm.3 v.aai.3s

αὐτοῖς ἐξουσίαν → πνευμάτων ἀκαθάρτων ὥστε ἐκβάλλειν αὐτὰ ↰ καὶ
them authority over unclean spirits *unclean* so that they could drive them out and
899 2026 176 4460 176 6063 1675 899 1675 2779
r.dpm.3 n.asf n.gpn a.gpn cj f.pa r.apn.3 cj

θεραπεύειν πᾶσαν νόσον καὶ πᾶσαν μαλακίαν. 2
heal ˻every kind of˼ disease and *{every kind of}* sickness. These are the names
2543 4246 3798 2779 4246 3433 4047 1639 3836 3950
f.pa a.asf n.asf cj a.asf n.asf

τῶν δὲ δώδεκα ἀποστόλων τὰ ὀνόματά ἐστιν ταῦτα· πρῶτος Σίμων ὁ
of the *{and}* twelve apostles: *the names are These* first, Simon, who
3836 1254 1557 693 3836 3950 1639 4047 4755 4981 3836
d.gpm cj a.gpm n.gpm d.npn n.npn v.pai.3s r.npn a.nsm n.nsm d.nsm

λεγόμενος Πέτρος καὶ Ἀνδρέας ὁ ἀδελφὸς αὐτοῦ, καὶ Ἰάκωβος ὁ τοῦ
is called Peter, then Andrew *{the}* his brother; *his* *{and}* James the son of
3306 4377 2779 436 3836 899 81 899 2779 2610 3836 3836
pt.pp.nsm n.nsm cj n.nsm d.nsm n.nsm r.gsm.3 cj n.nsm d.nsm d.gsm

Ζεβεδαίου καὶ Ἰωάννης ὁ ἀδελφὸς αὐτοῦ, 3 Φίλιππος καὶ Βαρθολομαῖος,
Zebedee, and John *{the}* his brother; *his* Philip and Bartholomew;
2411 2779 2722 3836 899 81 899 5805 2779 978
n.gsm cj n.nsm d.nsm n.nsm r.gsm.3 n.nsm cj n.nsm

Θωμᾶς καὶ Μαθθαῖος ὁ τελώνης, Ἰάκωβος ὁ τοῦ Ἀλφαίου καὶ[a]
Thomas and Matthew the tax collector; James the son of Alphaeus, and
2605 2779 3414 3836 5467 2610 3836 3836 271 2779
n.nsm cj n.nsm d.nsm n.nsm n.nsm d.nsm d.gsm n.gsm cj

Θαδδαῖος, 4 Σίμων ὁ Καναναῖος καὶ Ἰούδας ὁ Ἰσκαριώτης ὁ καὶ παραδοὺς
Thaddaeus; Simon the Cananaean, and Judas *{the}* Iscariot, who *{also}* betrayed
2497 4981 3836 2831 2779 2683 3836 2697 3836 2779 4140
n.nsm n.nsm d.nsm n.nsm cj n.nsm d.nsm n.nsm d.nsm adv pt.aa.nsm

αὐτόν. 5 τούτους τοὺς δώδεκα ἀπέστειλεν ὁ Ἰησοῦς παραγγείλας αὐτοῖς
him. These *{the}* twelve Jesus sent out *{the} Jesus* after instructing them
899 4047 3836 1557 2652 690 3836 2652 4133 899
r.asm.3 r.apm d.apm a.apm v.aai.3s d.nsm n.nsm pt.aa.nsm r.dpm.3

λέγων, ˻εἰς ὁδὸν˼ ἐθνῶν μὴ ἀπέλθητε καὶ εἰς
as follows: "Do not go among the Gentiles *not Do go* and do not enter *{into}*
3306 599 3590 599 1650 3847 1620 3590 599 2779 1656 3590 1656 1650
pt.pa.nsm p.a n.asf n.gpn pl v.aas.2p cj p.a

πόλιν Σαμαριτῶν μὴ εἰσέλθητε· 6 πορεύεσθε δὲ μᾶλλον πρὸς τὰ
any Samaritan town; *Samaritan* *not do enter* but go *but* rather to the
4901 4484 4901 3590 1656 1254 4513 1254 3437 4639 3836
n.asf n.gpm pl v.aas.2p v.pmm.2p cj adv.c p.a d.apn

[a] Λεββαῖος ὁ ἐπικληθεὶς included by TR after καὶ.

NASB

kind of sickness.
36 Seeing the
people, He felt
compassion for
them, because they
were distressed
and dispirited like
sheep without a
shepherd. 37 Then
He *said to His
disciples, "The
harvest is plentiful,
but the workers are
few. 38 Therefore
beseech the Lord
of the harvest to
send out workers
into His harvest."

The Twelve Disciples; Instructions for Service

10:1 Jesus sum-
moned His twelve
disciples and gave
them authority over
unclean spirits,
to cast them out,
and to heal every
kind of disease and
every kind of sick-
ness.
2 Now the names
of the twelve
apostles are these:
The first, Simon,
who is called Pe-
ter, and Andrew
his brother; and
James the son of
Zebedee, and John
his brother; 3 Philip
and Bartholomew;
Thomas and Mat-
thew the tax collec-
tor; James the son
of Alphaeus, and
Thaddaeus; 4 Simon
the Zealot, and
Judas Iscariot, the
one who betrayed
Him.
5 These twelve
Jesus sent out
after instructing
them: "Do not go
in *the* way of *the*
Gentiles, and do
not enter *any* city
of the Samaritans;
6 but rather go to the

NIV

lost sheep of Is-
rael. 7 As you go,
proclaim this mes-
sage: 'The king-
dom of heaven has
come near.' 8 Heal
the sick, raise
the dead, cleanse
those who have
leprosy,[a] drive out
demons. Freely
you have received;
freely give.
9 "Do not get any
gold or silver or
copper to take
with you in your
belts— 10 no bag
for the journey
or extra shirt or
sandals or a staff,
for the worker is
worth his keep.
11 Whatever town
or village you en-
ter, search there
for some worthy
person and stay
at their house
until you leave.
12 As you enter the
home, give it your
greeting. 13 If the
home is deserving,
let your peace rest
on it; if it is not, let
your peace return
to you. 14 If anyone
will not welcome
you or listen to
your words, leave
that home or town
and shake the
dust off your feet.
15 Truly I tell you, it
will be more bear-
able for Sodom
and Gomorrah on
the day of judg-
ment than for that
town.

[a] 8 The Greek word traditionally translated *leprosy* was used for various diseases affecting the skin.

πρόβατα τὰ ἀπολωλότα οἴκου Ἰσραήλ. 7 πορευόμενοι δὲ κηρύσσετε
lost sheep *{the}* *lost* ⌞of the house⌟ of Israel. As you go, *{and}* proclaim the
660 4585 3836 660 3875 2702 4513 1254 3062
n.apn d.apn pt.ra.apn n.gsm n.gsm pt.pm.npm cj v.pam.2p

λέγοντες ὅτι ἤγγικεν ἡ βασιλεία τῶν οὐρανῶν.
message, saying, ~ 'The kingdom of heaven is at hand.' *The kingdom of heaven*
3306 4022 3836 993 3836 4041 1581 3836 993 3836 4041
pt.pa.npm cj v.rai.3s d.nsf n.nsf d.gpm n.gpm

8 ἀσθενοῦντας θεραπεύετε, νεκροὺς ἐγείρετε, λεπροὺς
Heal the sick, *Heal* raise the dead, *raise* cleanse the lepers,
2543 820 2543 1586 3738 1586 2751 3320
pt.pa.apm v.pam.2p a.apm v.pam.2p a.apm

καθαρίζετε, δαιμόνια ἐκβάλλετε· δωρεὰν ἐλάβετε, δωρεὰν δότε. 9 ↱
cleanse drive out demons. *drive out* Freely you received, freely give. Do
2751 1675 1675 1228 1675 1562 3284 1562 1443 3227
v.pam.2p n.apn v.pam.2p adv v.aai.2p adv v.aam.2p

μὴ κτήσησθε χρυσὸν μηδὲ ἄργυρον μηδὲ χαλκὸν εἰς τὰς ζώνας ὑμῶν,
not take gold, or silver, or copper in *{the}* your ⌞money belts,⌟ *your*
3590 3227 5996 3593 738 3593 5910 1650 3836 7007 2438 7007
pl v.ams.2p n.asm cj n.asm cj n.asm p.a d.apf n.apf r.gp.2

10 μὴ πήραν εἰς ὁδὸν μηδὲ δύο χιτῶνας μηδὲ ὑποδήματα μηδὲ ῥάβδον·
or a bag for your journey, or two tunics, or sandals, or a staff; for
3590 4385 1650 3847 3593 1545 5945 3593 5687 3593 4811 1142
pl n.asf p.a n.asf cj a.apm n.apm cj n.apn cj n.asf

ἄξιος γὰρ ὁ ἐργάτης τῆς τροφῆς αὐτοῦ. 11 εἰς ⌞ἣν δ'
the worker deserves *for the worker* *{the}* his keep. *his* *{into}* And whatever
3836 2239 545 1142 3836 2239 3836 899 5575 899 1650 4005 1254
a.nsm cj d.nsm n.nsm d.gsf n.gsf r.gsm.3 p.a r.asf cj

ἂν⌟ πόλιν ἢ κώμην εἰσέλθητε, ἐξετάσατε τίς ἐν αὐτῇ ἄξιός ἐστιν· κἀκεῖ
town or village you enter, find out who in it is worthy *is* and
323 4484 2445 3267 1656 2004 5515 1877 899 1639 545 1639 2795
pl n.asf cj n.asf v.aas.2p v.aam.2p r.nsm p.d r.dsf.3 a.nsm v.pai.3s crasis

μείνατε ↰ ⌞ἕως ἂν⌟ ἐξέλθητε. 12 → ↱ εἰσερχόμενοι δὲ εἰς τὴν οἰκίαν
stay there until you leave. And when you enter *And* *{into}* a house,
3531 2795 2401 323 2002 1254 832 1656 1254 1650 3836 3864
v.aam.2p cj pl v.aas.2p pt.pm.npm cj p.a d.asf n.asf

ἀσπάσασθε αὐτήν· ↰ ↰ 13 καὶ ἐὰν μὲν ᾖ ἡ οἰκία
give it your greeting. *{and}* If ~ the household is *the household*
832 899 832 832 2779 1569 3525 3836 3864 1639 3836 3864
v.amm.2p r.asf.3 cj cj pl v.pas.3s d.nsf n.nsf

ἀξία, → ἐλθάτω ἡ εἰρήνη ὑμῶν ἐπ' αὐτήν, ἐὰν δὲ
worthy, let your greeting of peace come *{the}* *peace* *your* upon it; but if *but* it
545 7007 1645 2262 3836 1645 7007 2093 899 1254 1569 1254 1639
a.nsf v.aam.3s d.nsf n.nsf r.gp.2 p.a r.asf.3 cj cj

μὴ ᾖ ἀξία, ἡ εἰρήνη ὑμῶν πρὸς ὑμᾶς ἐπιστραφήτω. 14 καὶ
is not *it is* worthy, let *{the}* your peace *your* return to you. *let return* And
1639 3590 1639 545 2188 3836 7007 1645 7007 2188 4639 7007 2188 2779
pl v.pas.3s a.nsf d.nsf n.nsf r.gp.2 p.a r.ap.2 v.apm.3s cj

⌞ὃς ἂν⌟ ↱ μὴ δέξηται ὑμᾶς μηδὲ ἀκούσῃ τοὺς λόγους ὑμῶν, ἐξερχόμενοι
if anyone will not receive you or listen to *{the}* your message, *your* as you leave
4005 323 1312 3590 1312 7007 3593 201 3836 7007 3364 7007 2002
r.nsm pl pl v.ams.3s r.ap.2 cj v.aas.3s d.apm n.apm r.gp.2 pt.pm.npm

ἔξω τῆς ↱ οἰκίας ἢ τῆς πόλεως ἐκείνης ἐκτινάξατε τὸν κονιορτὸν τῶν
{outside} *{the}* that house or *{the}* that town *that* shake off the dust from
2032 3836 1697 3864 2445 3836 1697 4484 1697 1759 3836 3155 3836
p.g d.gsf n.gsf cj d.gsf n.gsf r.gsf v.aam.2p d.asm n.asm d.gpm

ποδῶν ὑμῶν. 15 ἀμὴν λέγω ὑμῖν, ἀνεκτότερον
your feet. *your* I tell you the truth, *I tell* *you* it will be more bearable
7007 4546 7007 3306 3306 7007 297 3306 7007 1639 1639 1639 445
n.gpm r.gp.2 pl v.pai.1s r.dp.2 a.nsn.c

ἔσται → γῇ Σοδόμων καὶ Γομόρρων ἐν ἡμέρᾳ κρίσεως ἢ ↱ τῇ
it will be for the land of Sodom and Gomorrah in the day of judgment than for *{the}* that
1639 1178 5047 2779 1202 1877 2465 3213 2445 4484 3836 1697
v.fmi.3s n.dsf n.gpn cj n.gpn p.d n.dsf n.gsf pl d.dsf

NASB

lost sheep of the
house of Israel.
7 And as you go,
preach, saying,
'The kingdom of
heaven is at hand.'
8 Heal *the* sick, raise
the dead, cleanse
the lepers, cast out
demons. Freely
you received,
freely give. 9 Do not
acquire gold, or sil-
ver, or copper for
your money belts,
10 or a bag for *your*
journey, or even
two coats, or san-
dals, or a staff; for
the worker is wor-
thy of his support.
11 And whatever
city or village you
enter, inquire who
is worthy in it, and
stay at his house
until you leave *that*
city. 12 As you enter
the house, give it
your greeting. 13 If
the house is wor-
thy, give it your
blessing of peace.
But if it is not
worthy, take back
your *blessing of*
peace. 14 Whoever
does not receive
you, nor heed your
words, as you go
out of that house
or that city, shake
the dust off your
feet. 15 Truly I say to
you, it will be more
tolerable for *the*
land of Sodom and
Gomorrah in the
day of judgment
than for that city.

NIV

16"I am sending
you out like sheep
among wolves.
Therefore be as
shrewd as snakes
and as innocent
as doves. 17Be on
your guard; you
will be handed
over to the local
councils and be
flogged in the syn-
agogues. 18On my
account you will
be brought before
governors and
kings as witness-
es to them and to
the Gentiles. 19But
when they arrest
you, do not worry
about what to say
or how to say it. At
that time you will
be given what to
say, 20for it will not
be you speaking,
but the Spirit of
your Father speak-
ing through you.
21"Brother will
betray brother to
death, and a father
his child; children
will rebel against
their parents and
have them put to
death. 22You will
be hated by ev-
eryone because
of me, but the one
who stands firm
to the end will be
saved. 23When you
are persecuted in
one place, flee to
another. Truly I
tell you, you will
not finish going
through the towns
of Israel before the
Son of Man comes.
24"The student is

πόλει ἐκείνῃ. 16 ἰδοὺ ἐγὼ ἀποστέλλω ὑμᾶς ↰ ὡς πρόβατα ἐν μέσῳ λύκων·
town. *that* "Behold, I am sending you out as sheep in the midst of wolves;
4484 1697 2627 1609 690 7007 690 6055 4585 1877 3545 3380
n.dsf r.dsf j r.ns.1 v.pai.1s r.ap.2 conj n.apn p.d n.dsn n.gpm

γίνεσθε οὖν φρόνιμοι ὡς οἱ ὄφεις καὶ ἀκέραιοι ὡς αἱ περιστεραί. 17
so be *so* shrewd as *{the}* serpents and innocent as *{the}* doves. And
4036 1181 4036 5861 6055 3836 4058 2779 193 6055 3836 4361 1254
v.pmm.2p cj a.npm conj d.npm n.npm cj a.npm conj d.npf n.npf

προσέχετε δὲ ἀπὸ τῶν ἀνθρώπων· παραδώσουσιν γὰρ ὑμᾶς ↰ εἰς
beware *And* of *{the}* men, for they will hand *for* you over to the
4668 1254 608 3836 476 1142 4140 1142 7007 4140 1650
v.pam.2p cj p.g d.gpm n.gpm v.fai.3p cj r.ap.2 p.a

συνέδρια καὶ ἐν ταῖς συναγωγαῖς αὐτῶν μαστιγώσουσιν ὑμᾶς·
courts, and they will flog you in *{the}* their synagogues; *their* *they will flog* *you*
5284 2779 3463 3463 3463 7007 1877 3836 899 5252 899 3463 7007
n.apn cj p.d d.dpf n.dpf r.gpm.3 v.fai.3p r.ap.2

18 καὶ ἐπὶ ἡγεμόνας δὲ καὶ βασιλεῖς ἀχθήσεσθε ἕνεκεν ἐμοῦ
and you will be brought before governors *{and}* and kings *you will be brought* for my
2779 72 72 72 72 2093 2450 1254 2779 995 72 1914 1609
cj p.a n.apm cj adv n.apm v.fpi.2p p.g r.gs.1

↰ εἰς μαρτύριον αὐτοῖς καὶ τοῖς ἔθνεσιν. 19 ὅταν δὲ παραδῶσιν ὑμᾶς,
sake, as a testimony to them and to the Gentiles. But when *But* they hand you
1914 1650 3457 899 2779 3836 1620 1254 4020 1254 4140 7007
p.a n.asn r.dpm.3 cj d.dpn n.dpn cj cj v.aas.3p r.ap.2

↰ ↱ μὴ μεριμνήσητε πῶς ἢ τί λαλήσητε·
over, do not worry about how you are to speak or what you are to say; for what you are
4140 3534 3590 3534 4802 2445 5515 3281 1142 5515 3281 3281
pl v.aas.2p cj cj r.asn v.aas.2p

δοθήσεται γὰρ ὑμῖν ἐν ἐκείνῃ τῇ ὥρᾳ τί λαλήσητε· 20
to say will be given *for* to you at that *{the}* time. *what you are to say* For it will
3281 3281 1443 1142 7007 1877 1697 3836 6052 5515 3281 1142 1639 1639
v.fpi.3s cj r.dp.2 p.d r.dsf d.dsf n.dsf r.asn v.aas.2p

οὐ γὰρ ὑμεῖς ἐστε οἱ λαλοῦντες ἀλλὰ τὸ πνεῦμα τοῦ πατρὸς ὑμῶν
not *For* be you *it will be* *{the}* speaking but the Spirit of your Father *your*
4024 1142 1639 7007 1639 3836 3281 247 3836 4460 3836 7007 4252 7007
adv cj r.np.2 v.pai.2p d.npm pt.pa.npm cj d.nsn n.nsn d.gsm n.gsm r.gp.2

τὸ λαλοῦν ἐν ὑμῖν. 21 παραδώσει δὲ ἀδελφὸς ἀδελφὸν εἰς θάνατον
{the} speaking through you. "Brother will hand over *{and}* *Brother* brother to death,
3836 3281 1877 7007 81 4140 1254 81 81 1650 2505
d.nsn pt.pa.nsn p.d r.dp.2 v.fai.3s cj n.nsm n.asm p.a n.asm

καὶ πατὴρ τέκνον, καὶ ἐπαναστήσονται τέκνα ἐπὶ γονεῖς καὶ ↱
and a father his child, and children will rise up *children* against parents and have them
2779 4252 5451 2779 5451 2060 5451 2093 1204 2779 899
cj n.nsm n.asn cj v.fmi.3p n.npn p.a n.apm cj

θανατώσουσιν αὐτούς. 22 καὶ ἔσεσθε μισούμενοι ὑπὸ πάντων διὰ τὸ
put to death. *them* And ⌞you will be⌟ hated by all ⌞on account of⌟ *{the}*
2506 899 2779 1639 3631 5679 4246 1328 3836
v.fai.3p r.apm.3 cj v.fmi.2p pt.pp.npm p.g a.gpm p.a d.asn

ὄνομά μου· ὁ δὲ ὑπομείνας εἰς τέλος οὗτος σωθήσεται. 23 ὅταν
my name. *my* But the *But* one who endures to the end, this one will be saved. When
1609 3950 1609 1254 3836 1254 5702 1650 5465 4047 5392 4020
n.asn r.gs.1 d.nsm cj pt.aa.nsm p.a n.asn r.nsm v.fpi.3s cj

δὲ διώκωσιν ὑμᾶς ἐν τῇ πόλει ταύτῃ, φεύγετε εἰς τὴν ἑτέραν· ἀμὴν γὰρ
{and} they persecute you in *{the}* one town, *one* flee to *{the}* another; *the truth* for
1254 1503 7007 1877 3836 4047 4484 4047 5771 1650 3836 2283 297 1142
cj v.pas.3p r.ap.2 p.d d.dsf n.dsf r.dsf v.pam.2p p.a d.asf r.asf pl cj

λέγω ὑμῖν, ↱ ↱ ⌞οὐ μὴ⌟ τελέσητε τὰς πόλεις τοῦ
I tell you the truth, you will not finish going through all the towns of
3306 7007 297 297 5464 5464 4024 3590 5464 3836 4484 3836
v.pai.1s r.dp.2 adv pl v.aas.2p d.apf n.apf d.gsm

Ἰσραὴλ ⌞ἕως ἂν⌟ ἔλθῃ ὁ υἱὸς τοῦ ἀνθρώπου. 24
Israel before the Son of Man comes. *the* *Son* *of* *Man* "A disciple is
2702 2401 323 3836 5626 3836 476 2262 3836 5626 3836 476 3412 1639
n.gsm cj pl v.aas.3s d.nsm n.nsm d.gsm n.gsm

NASB

A Hard Road before Them

16"Behold, I send
you out as sheep
in the midst of
wolves; so be
shrewd as serpents
and innocent as
doves. 17But be-
ware of men, for
they will hand you
over to *the* courts
and scourge you in
their synagogues;
18and you will even
be brought before
governors and
kings for My sake,
as a testimony to
them and to the
Gentiles. 19But
when they hand
you over, do not
worry about how
or what you are to
say; for it will be
given you in that
hour what you are
to say. 20For it is
not you who speak,
but *it is* the Spirit
of your Father who
speaks in you.
21"Brother will
betray brother to
death, and a father
his child; and
children will rise
up against parents
and cause them to
be put to death.
22You will be hated
by all because of
My name, but it is
the one who has
endured to the end
who will be saved.
23"But whenever
they persecute you
in one city, flee to
the next; for truly
I say to you, you
will not finish *go-
ing through* the
cities of Israel until
the Son of Man
comes.

The Meaning of Discipleship

24"A disciple

NIV

not above the
teacher, nor a
servant above
his master. 25 It is
enough for stu-
dents to be like
their teachers, and
servants like their
masters. If the
head of the house
has been called
Beelzebul, how
much more the
members of his
household!
26 "So do not be
afraid of them, for
there is nothing
concealed that will
not be disclosed,
or hidden that
will not be made
known. 27 What
I tell you in the
dark, speak in the
daylight; what
is whispered in
your ear, proclaim
from the roofs.
28 Do not be afraid
of those who kill
the body but can-
not kill the soul.
Rather, be afraid
of the One who
can destroy both
soul and body in
hell. 29 Are not two
sparrows sold for
a penny? Yet not
one of them will
fall to the ground
outside your Fa-
ther's care.[a] 30 And
even the very hairs
of your head are
all numbered. 31 So
don't be afraid;
you are worth
more than many
sparrows.
32 "Whoever ac-
knowledges me be-
fore others, I will
also acknowledge
before my Father

οὐκ ἔστιν μαθητὴς ὑπὲρ τὸν διδάσκαλον οὐδὲ δοῦλος ὑπὲρ τὸν κύριον αὐτοῦ.
not *is* *disciple* above his teacher, nor a servant above *{the}* his master. *his*
4024 1639 3412 5642 3836 1437 4028 1529 5642 3836 899 3261 899
adv v.pai.3s n.nsm p.a d.asm n.asm cj n.nsm p.a d.asm n.asm r.gsm.3

25 ἀρκετὸν τῷ μαθητῇ ἵνα γένηται ὡς ὁ διδάσκαλος αὐτοῦ καὶ ὁ
It is enough ⌊for the⌋ disciple that he be as *{the}* his teacher, *his* and the
757 3836 3412 2671 1181 6055 3836 899 1437 899 2779 3836
a.nsn d.dsm n.dsm cj v.ams.3s pl d.nsm n.nsm r.gsm.3 cj d.nsm

δοῦλος ὡς ὁ κύριος αὐτοῦ. εἰ τὸν οἰκοδεσπότην Βεελζεβοὺλ
servant as *{the}* his master. *his* If they have called the head of the house 'Beelzebul,'
1529 6055 3836 899 3261 899 1623 2126 2126 2126 3836 3867 1015
n.nsm pl d.nsm n.nsm r.gsm.3 cj d.asm n.asm n.asm

ἐπεκάλεσαν, πόσῳ μᾶλλον τοὺς οἰκιακοὺς αὐτοῦ. ↰
they have called how much more will they revile the members of his household!
2126 4531 3437 3836 3865 899 3865
v.aai.3p r.dsn adv.c d.apm n.apm r.gsm.3

26 ↱ μὴ οὖν φοβηθῆτε αὐτούς· οὐδὲν γάρ ἐστιν
"Therefore do not *Therefore* be afraid of them; for there is nothing *for* *there is*
4036 5828 3590 4036 5828 899 1142 1639 1639 4029 1142 1639
pl cj v.aps.2p r.apm.3 a.nsn cj v.pai.3s

κεκαλυμμένον ὃ ↱ οὐκ ἀποκαλυφθήσεται καὶ κρυπτὸν ὃ ↱ οὐ γνωσθήσεται.
covered that will not be uncovered, and hidden that will not be made known.
2821 4005 636 4024 636 2779 3220 4005 1182 4024 1182
pt.rp.nsn r.nsn adv v.fpi.3s cj a.nsn r.nsn adv v.fpi.3s

27 ὃ λέγω ὑμῖν ἐν τῇ σκοτίᾳ εἴπατε ἐν τῷ φωτί, καὶ ὃ εἰς τὸ
What I say to you in the darkness, speak in the light; and what you hear in the
4005 3306 7007 1877 3836 5028 3306 1877 3836 5890 2779 4005 201 201 1650 3836
r.asn v.pai.1s r.dp.2 p.d d.dsf n.dsf v.aam.2p p.d d.dsn n.dsn cj r.asn p.a d.asn

οὖς ἀκούετε κηρύξατε ἐπὶ τῶν δωμάτων. 28 καὶ ↱ μὴ φοβεῖσθε ἀπὸ τῶν
ear *you hear* proclaim from the housetops. *{and}* Do not be afraid of ⌊those who⌋
4044 201 3062 2093 3836 1560 2779 5828 3590 5828 608 3836
n.asn v.pai.2p v.aam.2p p.g d.gpn n.gpn cj pl v.ppm.2p p.g d.gpm

ἀποκτεννόντων τὸ σῶμα, τὴν δὲ ψυχὴν μὴ δυναμένων⌋
can kill the body but cannot kill the *but* soul. *cannot*
650 3836 5393 1254 3590 650 3836 1254 6034 3590 1538
pt.pa.gpm d.asn n.asn d.asf cj n.asf pl pt.pp.gpm

ἀποκτεῖναι· φοβεῖσθε ⌊δὲ μᾶλλον⌋ τὸν δυνάμενον καὶ ψυχὴν καὶ σῶμα
kill *fear* Rather, fear the one who can destroy both soul and body
650 5828 1254 3437 5828 3836 1538 660 2779 6034 2779 5393
f.aa v.ppm.2p cj adv.c d.asm pt.pp.asm cj n.asf cj n.asn

ἀπολέσαι ἐν γεέννῃ. 29 οὐχὶ δύο στρουθία ἀσσαρίου πωλεῖται; καὶ
destroy in hell. Are not two sparrows sold for a penny? *Are sold* Yet not
660 1877 1147 4797 4049 1545 5141 4797 837 4797 2779 4024
f.aa p.d n.dsf pl a.npn n.npn n.gsn v.ppi.3s cj

ἓν ἐξ αὐτῶν οὐ πεσεῖται ἐπὶ τὴν γῆν ἄνευ τοῦ πατρὸς ὑμῶν.
one of them *not* will fall to the ground ⌊apart from⌋ *{the}* your Father. *your*
1651 1666 899 4024 4406 2093 3836 1178 459 3836 7007 4252 7007
a.nsn p.g r.gpn.3 adv v.fmi.3s p.a d.asf n.asf p.g d.gsm n.gsm r.gp.2

30 ὑμῶν δὲ καὶ αἱ τρίχες τῆς κεφαλῆς ↱ πᾶσαι ἠριθμημέναι εἰσίν.
your But even the hairs of your head have all been counted. *been*
7007 1254 2779 3836 2582 3836 7007 3051 1639 4246 1639 749 1639
r.gp.2 cj adv d.npf n.npf d.gsf n.gsf a.npf pt.rp.npf v.pai.3p

31 ↱ μὴ οὖν φοβεῖσθε· πολλῶν στρουθίων
So do not *So* be afraid; you are of greater value than many sparrows.
4036 5828 3590 4036 5828 7007 1422 1422 1422 1422 4498 5141
pl cj v.ppm.2p a.gpn n.gpn

διαφέρετε ὑμεῖς. 32 πᾶς οὖν ὅστις ὁμολογήσει ἐν ἐμοὶ ἔμπροσθεν
are of greater value *you* So everyone *So* who will acknowledge *{in}* me before
1422 7007 4036 4246 4036 4015 3933 1877 1609 1869
v.pai.2p r.np.2 a.nsm cj r.nsm v.fai.3s p.d r.ds.1 p.g

τῶν ἀνθρώπων, ὁμολογήσω κἀγὼ ἐν αὐτῷ ἔμπροσθεν τοῦ πατρός μου
{the} others, I will acknowledge *I* *{in}* him before *{the}* my Father *my*
3836 476 2743 3933 2743 1877 899 1869 3836 1609 4252 1609
d.gpm n.gpm v.fai.1s crasis p.d r.dsm.3 p.g d.gsm n.gsm r.gs.1

NASB

is not above his
teacher, nor a slave
above his master.
25 It is enough for
the disciple that
he become like
his teacher, and
the slave like his
master. If they have
called the head of
the house Beel-
zebul, how much
more *will they ma-
lign* the members
of his household!
26 "Therefore do
not fear them, for
there is nothing
concealed that will
not be revealed, or
hidden that will not
be known. 27 What
I tell you in the
darkness, speak in
the light; and what
you hear *whis-
pered* in *your* ear,
proclaim upon the
housetops. 28 Do not
fear those who kill
the body but are
unable to kill the
soul; but rather fear
Him who is able
to destroy both
soul and body in
hell. 29 Are not two
sparrows sold for a
[a]cent? And *yet* not
one of them will
fall to the ground
apart from your
Father. 30 But the
very hairs of your
head are all num-
bered. 31 So do not
fear; you are more
valuable than many
sparrows.
32 "Therefore
everyone who con-
fesses Me before
men, I will also
confess him before

[a] 29 Or *will*; or *knowledge*

[a] Gr *assarion*, the smallest copper coin

NIV

in heaven. 33But
whoever disowns
me before others,
I will disown be-
fore my Father in
heaven.
34"Do not sup-
pose that I have
come to bring
peace to the earth.
I did not come to
bring peace, but a
sword. 35For I have
come to turn

"'a man against
his father,
a daughter
against her
mother,
a daughter-in-law
against her
mother-in-
law—
36 a man's enemies
will be the
members
of his own
household.'[a]

37"Anyone who
loves their father
or mother more
than me is not
worthy of me;
anyone who loves
their son or daugh-
ter more than me is
not worthy of me.
38Whoever does
not take up their
cross and follow
me is not worthy
of me. 39Whoever
finds their life will
lose it, and whoev-
er loses their life
for my sake will
find it.
40"Anyone who
welcomes you
welcomes me,
and anyone who
welcomes me wel-
comes the one who
sent me. 41Who-
ever welcomes a
prophet as a proph-
et will receive a
prophet's reward,
and whoever wel-
comes a righteous
person as a righ-
teous person will
receive a righteous
person's reward.

[a] 36 Micah 7:6

τοῦ ἐν τοῖς[a] οὐρανοῖς· 33 ὅστις δ᾽ ἂν ἀρνήσηταί με ἔμπροσθεν τῶν
who is in *{the}* heaven; but whoever *but* ~ disowns me before *{the}*
3836 1877 3836 4041 1254 4015 1254 323 766 1609 1869 3836
d.gsm p.d d.dpm n.dpm r.nsm cj pl v.ams.3s r.as.1 p.g d.gpm

ἀνθρώπων, ἀρνήσομαι κἀγὼ αὐτὸν ἔμπροσθεν τοῦ πατρός μου τοῦ ἐν
others, I will disown *I* him before *{the}* my Father *my* who is in
476 2743 766 2743 899 1869 3836 1609 4252 1609 3836 1877
n.gpm v.fmi.1s crasis r.asm.3 p.g d.gsm n.gsm r.gs.1 d.gsm p.d

τοῖς[b] οὐρανοῖς. 34 ↱ μὴ νομίσητε ὅτι ἦλθον βαλεῖν εἰρήνην ἐπὶ τὴν γῆν·
{the} heaven. "Do not think that ⌊I have come⌋ to bring peace to the earth.
3836 4041 3787 3590 3787 4022 2262 965 1645 2093 3836 1178
d.dpm n.dpm pl v.aas.2p cj v.aai.1s f.aa n.asf p.a d.asf n.asf

↱ ↱ οὐκ ἦλθον βαλεῖν εἰρήνην ἀλλὰ μάχαιραν. 35 ἦλθον γὰρ διχάσαι
I did not come to bring peace, but a sword. For I came *For* to turn a
2262 2262 4024 2262 965 1645 247 3479 1142 2262 1142 1495
adv v.aai.1s f.aa n.asf cj n.asf v.aai.1s cj f.aa

ἄνθρωπον κατὰ τοῦ πατρὸς αὐτοῦ καὶ θυγατέρα κατὰ τῆς μητρὸς αὐτῆς
man against *{the}* his father, *his* and a daughter against *{the}* her mother, *her*
476 2848 3836 899 4252 899 2779 2588 2848 3836 899 3613 899
n.asm p.g d.gsm n.gsm r.gsm.3 cj n.asf p.g d.gsf n.gsf r.gsf.3

καὶ νύμφην κατὰ τῆς πενθερᾶς αὐτῆς, 36 καὶ ἐχθροὶ τοῦ
and a daughter-in-law against *{the}* her mother-in-law; *her* and a man's enemies *{the}*
2779 3811 2848 3836 899 4289 899 2779 476 2398 3836
cj n.asf p.g d.gsf n.gsf r.gsf.3 cj a.npm d.gsm

ἀνθρώπου οἱ οἰκιακοὶ αὐτοῦ. ↰ 37 ὁ φιλῶν πατέρα ἢ
man's will be *{the}* members of his own household. Whoever loves father or
476 3836 3865 899 3865 3836 5797 4252 2445
n.gsm d.npm n.npm r.gsm.3 d.nsm pt.pa.nsm n.asm cj

μητέρα ὑπὲρ ἐμὲ οὐκ ἔστιν μου ἄξιος, καὶ ὁ φιλῶν υἱὸν ἢ
mother ⌊more than⌋ me is not *is* worthy of me, *worthy* and whoever loves son or
3613 5642 1609 1639 4024 1639 545 1609 545 2779 3836 5797 5626 2445
n.asf p.a r.as.1 adv v.pai.3s r.gs.1 a.nsm cj d.nsm pt.pa.nsm n.asm cj

θυγατέρα ὑπὲρ ἐμὲ οὐκ ἔστιν μου ἄξιος· 38 καὶ ὃς ↱ οὐ
daughter ⌊more than⌋ me is not *is* worthy of me. *worthy* And whoever does not
2588 5642 1609 1639 4024 1639 545 1609 545 2779 4005 3284 4024
n.asf p.a r.as.1 adv v.pai.3s r.gs.1 a.nsm cj r.nsm adv

λαμβάνει τὸν σταυρὸν αὐτοῦ καὶ ἀκολουθεῖ ὀπίσω μου, οὐκ ἔστιν
take up *{the}* his cross *his* and follow *{after}* me is not *is* worthy
3284 3836 899 5089 899 2779 199 3958 1609 1639 4024 1639 545
v.pai.3s d.asm n.asm r.gsm.3 cj v.pai.3s p.g r.gs.1 adv v.pai.3s

μου ἄξιος. 39 ὁ εὑρὼν τὴν ψυχὴν αὐτοῦ ἀπολέσει αὐτήν, καὶ ὁ
of me. *worthy* Whoever finds *{the}* his life *his* will lose it, but whoever
1609 545 3836 2351 3836 899 6034 899 660 899 2779 3836
r.gs.1 a.nsm d.nsm pt.aa.nsm d.asf n.asf r.gsm.3 v.fai.3s r.asf.3 cj d.nsm

ἀπολέσας τὴν ψυχὴν αὐτοῦ ἕνεκεν ἐμοῦ ↰ εὑρήσει αὐτήν. 40 ὁ
loses *{the}* his life *his* for my sake will find it. "Whoever
660 3836 899 6034 899 1914 1609 1914 2351 899 3836
pt.aa.nsm d.asf n.asf r.gsm.3 p.g r.gs.1 v.fai.3s r.asf.3 d.nsm

δεχόμενος ὑμᾶς ἐμὲ δέχεται, καὶ ὁ ἐμὲ δεχόμενος δέχεται τὸν
receives you receives me, *receives* and whoever receives me *receives* receives the
1312 7007 1312 1609 1312 2779 3836 1312 1609 1312 1312 3836
pt.pm.nsm r.ap.2 r.as.1 v.pmi.3s cj d.nsm r.as.1 pt.pm.nsm v.pmi.3s d.asm

ἀποστείλαντά με. 41 ὁ δεχόμενος προφήτην εἰς ὄνομα προφήτου
one who sent me. Whoever welcomes a prophet because he is a prophet will
690 1609 3836 1312 4737 1650 3950 4737 3284
pt.aa.asm r.as.1 d.nsm pt.pm.nsm n.asm p.a n.asn n.gsm

μισθὸν προφήτου λήμψεται, καὶ ὁ δεχόμενος δίκαιον
receive a prophet's reward, *prophet's* *will receive* and whoever welcomes a ⌊righteous person⌋
3284 4737 3635 4737 3284 2779 3836 1312 1465
n.asm n.gsm v.fmi.3s cj d.nsm pt.pm.nsm a.asm

εἰς ὄνομα δικαίου μισθὸν δικαίου
because he is a ⌊righteous person⌋ will receive a righteous person's reward. *righteous person's*
1650 3950 1465 3284 3284 1465 1465 3635 1465
p.a n.asn a.gsm n.asm a.gsm

[a] [τοῖς] UBS.
[b] [τοῖς] UBS.

NASB

My Father who is
in heaven. 33But
whoever denies
Me before men, I
will also deny him
before My Father
who is in heaven.
34"Do not think
that I came to
bring peace on
the earth; I did
not come to bring
peace, but a sword.
35For I came to
SET A MAN AGAINST
HIS FATHER, AND A
DAUGHTER AGAINST
HER MOTHER, AND A
DAUGHTER-IN-LAW
AGAINST HER MOTH-
ER-IN-LAW; 36and A
MAN'S ENEMIES WILL
BE THE MEMBERS OF
HIS HOUSEHOLD.
37"He who loves
father or mother
more than Me is
not worthy of Me;
and he who loves
son or daughter
more than Me is
not worthy of Me.
38And he who does
not take his cross
and follow after
Me is not worthy
of Me. 39He who
has found his life
will lose it, and he
who has lost his
life for My sake
will find it.

The Reward of Service

40"He who re-
ceives you receives
Me, and he who re-
ceives Me receives
Him who sent Me.
41He who receives
a prophet in *the*
name of a prophet
shall receive a
prophet's reward;
and he who re-
ceives a righteous
man in the name
of a righteous man
shall receive a
righteous man's

NIV

[42]And if anyone
gives even a cup of
cold water to one
of these little ones
who is my disciple,
truly I tell you,
that person will
certainly not lose
their reward."

Jesus and John the Baptist

11 After Jesus
had finished
instructing his
twelve disciples,
he went on from
there to teach
and preach in the
towns of Galilee.[a]
[2]When John,
who was in pris-
on, heard about
the deeds of the
Messiah, he sent
his disciples [3]to
ask him, "Are you
the one who is to
come, or should
we expect some-
one else?"
[4]Jesus replied,
"Go back and re-
port to John what
you hear and see:
[5]The blind receive
sight, the lame
walk, those who
have leprosy[b] are
cleansed, the deaf
hear, the dead
are raised, and
the good news is
proclaimed to the
poor. [6]Blessed is
anyone who does
not stumble on ac-
count of me."
[7]As John's dis-
ciples were leav-
ing, Jesus began
to speak to the
crowd about John:
"What did you go
out into the wil-
derness to see? A
reed swayed by the
wind? [8]If not,

λήμψεται. [42] καὶ ⌞ὃς ἂν⌟ ποτίσῃ ἕνα τῶν
will receive And whoever, because he is a disciple, gives one of these
3284 2779 4005 323 1650 3950 3950 3412 4540 1651 3836 4047
v.fmi.3s cj r.nsm pl v.aas.3s a.asm d.gpm

μικρῶν τούτων ποτήριον ψυχροῦ μόνον ↰ ↰ εἰς ὄνομα μαθητοῦ,
little ones *these* even a cup of cold water *even* to drink, *because* *he is* *disciple*
3625 4047 3667 4539 6037 3667 4540 4540 1650 3950 3412
a.gpm r.gpm n.asn n.gsn adv p.a n.asn n.gsm

ἀμὴν λέγω ὑμῖν, ↱ ↱ ⌞οὐ μὴ⌟ ἀπολέσῃ τὸν μισθὸν
I tell you the truth, *I tell* *you* he will by no means lose *{the}* his reward."
3306 3306 7007 297 3306 7007 660 660 4024 3590 660 3836 899 3635
pl v.pai.1s r.dp.2 adv pl v.aas.3s d.asm n.asm

αὐτοῦ.
his
899
r.gsm.3

[11:1] καὶ ἐγένετο ὅτε ἐτέλεσεν ὁ Ἰησοῦς διατάσσων τοῖς
Now *{it happened that}* when Jesus had finished *{the}* *Jesus* giving instructions to his
2779 1181 4021 2652 5464 3836 2652 1411 3836 899
cj v.ami.3s cj v.aai.3s d.nsm n.nsm pt.pa.nsm d.dpm

δώδεκα μαθηταῖς αὐτοῦ, μετέβη ἐκεῖθεν τοῦ διδάσκειν καὶ κηρύσσειν
twelve disciples, *his* ⌞he went on⌟ from there *{the}* to teach and proclaim his message
1557 3412 899 3553 1696 3836 1438 2779 3062
a.dpm n.dpm r.gsm.3 v.aai.3s adv d.gsn f.pa cj f.pa

ἐν ταῖς πόλεσιν αὐτῶν. [2] ὁ δὲ ↱ Ἰωάννης ἀκούσας ἐν τῷ δεσμωτηρίῳ
in *{the}* their towns. *their* *{the}* Now when John heard in *{the}* prison
1877 3836 899 4484 899 3836 1254 201 2722 201 1877 3836 1303
p.d d.dpf n.dpf r.gpm.3 d.nsm cj n.nsm pt.aa.nsm p.d d.dsn n.dsn

↰ τὰ ἔργα τοῦ Χριστοῦ πέμψας διὰ τῶν μαθητῶν αὐτοῦ [3] εἶπεν
about the works of the Messiah, he sent word through *{the}* his disciples, *his* asking
201 3836 2240 3836 5986 4287 1328 3836 899 3412 899 3306
d.apn n.apn d.gsm n.gsm pt.aa.nsm p.g d.gpm n.gpm r.gsm.3 v.aai.3s

αὐτῷ, σὺ εἶ ὁ ἐρχόμενος ἢ ἕτερον
him, "Are you *Are* the ⌞one who is to come,⌟ or should we wait for ⌞someone else?"⌟
899 1639 5148 1639 3836 2262 2445 4659 4659 4659 4659 2283
r.dsm.3 r.ns.2 v.pai.2s d.nsm pt.pm.nsm cj r.asm

προσδοκῶμεν; [4] καὶ ἀποκριθεὶς ὁ Ἰησοῦς εἶπεν αὐτοῖς, πορευθέντες
should we wait for And Jesus answered *{the}* *Jesus* them, saying, *them* "Go
4659 2779 2652 646 3836 2652 899 3306 899 4513
v.pai.1p cj pt.ap.nsm d.nsm n.nsm v.aai.3s r.dpm.3 pt.ap.npm

ἀπαγγείλατε Ἰωάννῃ ἃ ἀκούετε καὶ βλέπετε· [5] τυφλοὶ ἀναβλέπουσιν καὶ
and tell John what you hear and see: the blind receive their sight and
550 2722 4005 201 2779 1063 5603 329 2779
v.aam.2p n.dsm r.apn v.pai.2p cj v.pai.2p a.npm v.pai.3p cj

χωλοὶ περιπατοῦσιν, λεπροὶ καθαρίζονται καὶ κωφοὶ ἀκούουσιν, καὶ
the lame walk, lepers are cleansed and the deaf hear, *{and}* the
6000 4344 3320 2751 2779 3273 201 2779
a.npm v.pai.3p a.npm v.ppi.3p cj a.npm v.pai.3p cj

νεκροὶ ἐγείρονται καὶ πτωχοὶ εὐαγγελίζονται· [6] καὶ μακάριός ἐστιν
dead are raised and the poor ⌞are being told the good news.⌟ And blessed is the
3738 1586 2779 4777 2294 2779 3421 1639
a.npm v.ppi.3p cj a.npm v.ppi.3p cj a.nsm v.pai.3s

⌞ὃς ἐὰν⌟ ↱ μὴ σκανδαλισθῇ ἐν ἐμοί. [7] ↱ τούτων δὲ πορευομένων
one who does not stumble ⌞because of⌟ me." As they *{and}* went away,
4005 1569 4997 3590 4997 1877 1609 4513 4047 1254 4513
r.nsm pl pl v.aps.3s p.d r.ds.1 r.gpm cj pt.pm.gpm

ἤρξατο ὁ Ἰησοῦς λέγειν τοῖς ὄχλοις περὶ Ἰωάννου, τί ἐξήλθατε εἰς
Jesus began *{the}* *Jesus* to speak to the crowds about John: "What ⌞did you go out⌟ into
2652 806 3836 2652 3306 3836 4063 4309 2722 5515 2002 1650
v.ami.3s d.nsm n.nsm f.pa d.dpm n.dpm p.g n.gsm r.asn v.aai.2p p.a

τὴν ἔρημον θεάσασθαι; κάλαμον ὑπὸ ἀνέμου σαλευόμενον; [8] ἀλλὰ
the wilderness to look at? A reed shaken by the wind? *shaken* What then
3836 2245 2517 2812 4888 5679 449 4888 5515 247
d.asf n.asf f.am n.asm p.g n.gsm pt.pp.asm cj

NASB

reward. [42]And who-
ever in the name of
a disciple gives to
one of these little
ones even a cup of
cold water to drink,
truly I say to you,
he shall not lose his
reward."

John's Questions

[11:1]When Jesus
had finished giving
instructions to His
twelve disciples,
He departed from
there to teach and
preach in their
cities.
[2]Now when John,
while imprisoned,
heard of the works
of Christ, he sent
word by his dis-
ciples [3]and said to
Him, "Are You the
Expected One, or
shall we look for
someone else?"
[4]Jesus answered
and said to them,
"Go and report to
John what you hear
and see: [5]*the* BLIND
RECEIVE SIGHT and
the lame walk, *the*
lepers are cleansed
and *the* deaf hear,
the dead are raised
up, and *the* POOR
HAVE THE GOSPEL
PREACHED TO THEM.
[6]And blessed is he
who does not take
offense at Me."

Jesus' Tribute to John

[7]As these men
were going *away,*
Jesus began to
speak to the
crowds about John,
"What did you go
out into the wil-
derness to see? A
reed shaken by the
wind? [8]But what

[a] 1 Greek *in their towns*
[b] 5 The Greek word traditionally translated *leprosy* was used for various diseases affecting the skin.

NIV

what did you go
out to see? A
man dressed in
fine clothes? No,
those who wear
fine clothes are
in kings' palaces.
9Then what did
you go out to see?
A prophet? Yes, I
tell you, and more
than a prophet.
10This is the one
about whom it is
written:

"'I will send my
messenger
ahead of you,
who will
prepare your
way before
you.'[a]

11Truly I tell you,
among those born
of women there
has not risen any-
one greater than
John the Baptist;
yet whoever is
least in the king-
dom of heaven is
greater than he.
12From the days
of John the Bap-
tist until now, the
kingdom of heaven
has been subject-
ed to violence,[b]
and violent people
have been raiding
it. 13For all the
Prophets and the
Law prophesied
until John. 14And if
you are willing to
accept it, he is the
Elijah who was to
come. 15Whoever
has ears, let them
hear.
16"To what can I
compare this gen-
eration? They are
like children sit-
ting in the market-
places and calling
out to others:

17"'We played the
pipe for you,
and you did not
dance;
we sang a dirge,
and you did not
mourn.'

18For John came
neither

[a] 10 Mal. 3:1
[b] 12 Or *been forcefully advancing*

τί ἐξήλθατε ἰδεῖν; ἄνθρωπον ἐν μαλακοῖς ἠμφιεσμένον; ἰδοὺ οἱ
What ⌊did you go out⌋ to see? A man dressed in soft clothing? *dressed* Behold, those
5515 2002 1625 476 314 1877 3434 314 2627 3836
r.asn v.aai.2p f.aa n.asm p.d a.dpn pt.rp.asm j d.npm

τὰ μαλακὰ φοροῦντες ἐν τοῖς οἴκοις τῶν βασιλέων εἰσίν. 9
who wear *{the}* soft clothing *who wear* are in the courts of kings. *are* What
5841 5841 3836 3434 5841 1639 1877 3836 3875 3836 995 1639 5515
d.apn a.apn pt.pa.npm p.d d.dpm n.dpm d.gpm n.gpm v.pai.3p

ἀλλὰ τί ἐξήλθατε ἰδεῖν; προφήτην; ναὶ λέγω ὑμῖν, καὶ περισσότερον →
then *What* ⌊did you go out⌋ to see? A prophet? Yes, I tell you, and more than a
247 5515 2002 1625 4737 3721 3306 7007 2779 4358
cj r.asn v.aai.2p f.aa n.asm pl v.pai.1s r.dp.2 cj adv.c

προφήτου. 10 οὗτός ἐστιν περὶ οὗ γέγραπται, ἰδοὺ ἐγὼ ἀποστέλλω
prophet. This is the one about whom it stands written, 'Behold, I send
4737 4047 1639 4309 4005 1211 2627 1609 690
n.gsm r.nsm v.pai.3s p.g r.gsm v.rpi.3s j r.ns.1 v.pai.1s

τὸν ἄγγελόν μου πρὸ ⌊προσώπου σου,⌋ ὃς κατασκευάσει τὴν ὁδόν σου
{the} my messenger *my* ahead of you, who will prepare *{the}* your way *your*
3836 1609 34 1609 4574 4725 5148 4005 2941 3836 5148 3847 5148
d.asm n.asm r.gs.1 p.g n.gsn r.gs.2 r.nsm v.fai.3s d.asf n.asf r.gs.2

ἔμπροσθέν σου. 11 ἀμὴν λέγω ὑμῖν, ↱ ↱ οὐκ ἐγήγερται ἐν
before you.' "I tell you the truth, *I tell* *you* there has not risen among
1869 5148 3306 3306 7007 297 3306 7007 1586 1586 4024 1586 1877
p.g r.gs.2 pl v.pai.1s r.dp.2 adv v.rpi.3s p.d

γεννητοῖς γυναικῶν μείζων Ἰωάννου τοῦ βαπτιστοῦ· ὁ δὲ
those born of women anyone greater than John the Baptist; yet the *yet*
1168 1222 3489 2722 3836 969 1254 3836 1254
n.dpm n.gpf a.nsm.c n.gsm d.gsm n.gsm d.nsm cj

μικρότερος ἐν τῇ βασιλείᾳ τῶν οὐρανῶν μείζων αὐτοῦ ἐστιν. 12 ἀπὸ δὲ
one who is least in the kingdom of heaven is greater than he. *is* From *{and}*
3625 1877 3836 993 3836 4041 1639 3489 899 1639 608 1254
a.nsm.c p.d d.dsf n.dsf d.gpm n.gpm a.nsm.c r.gsm.3 v.pai.3s p.g cj

τῶν ἡμερῶν Ἰωάννου τοῦ βαπτιστοῦ ἕως ἄρτι ἡ βασιλεία τῶν οὐρανῶν
the days of John the Baptist until now the kingdom of heaven
3836 2465 2722 3836 969 2401 785 3836 993 3836 4041
d.gpf n.gpf n.gsm d.gsm n.gsm p.g adv d.nsf n.nsf d.gpm n.gpm

βιάζεται καὶ βιασταὶ ἁρπάζουσιν αὐτήν. ↰ ↰ 13 πάντες γὰρ
⌊has suffered violence,⌋ and the violent are taking it by force. For all *For*
1041 2779 1043 773 899 773 773 1142 4246 1142
v.ppi.3s cj n.npm v.pai.3p r.asf.3 a.npm cj

οἱ προφῆται καὶ ὁ νόμος ἕως Ἰωάννου ἐπροφήτευσαν· 14 καὶ εἰ
the prophets and the law prophesied until John; *prophesied* and if
3836 4737 2779 3836 3795 4736 2401 2722 4736 2779 1623
d.npm n.npm cj d.nsm n.nsm p.g n.gsm v.aai.3p cj cj

θέλετε δέξασθαι, αὐτός ἐστιν Ἠλίας ὁ μέλλων ἔρχεσθαι. 15 ὁ ἔχων
⌊you are willing⌋ to accept it, he is Elijah who is to come. He ⌊who has⌋
2527 1312 899 1639 2460 3836 3516 2262 3836 2400
v.pai.2p f.am r.nsm v.pai.3s n.nsm d.nsm pt.pa.nsm f.pm d.nsm pt.pa.nsm

ὦτα ἀκουέτω. 16 τίνι δὲ ὁμοιώσω τὴν γενεὰν ταύτην;
ears, let him hear! ⌊"To what⌋ *{and}* shall I compare *{the}* this generation? *this* It is
4044 201 5515 1254 3929 3836 4047 1155 4047 1639 1639
n.apn v.pam.3s r.dsn cj v.fai.1s d.asf n.asf r.asf

ὁμοία ἐστὶν παιδίοις καθημένοις ἐν ταῖς ἀγοραῖς ἃ προσφωνοῦντα τοῖς
like *It is* children sitting in the marketplaces who cry to their
3927 1639 4086 2764 1877 3836 59 4005 4715 3836
a.nsf v.pai.3s n.dpn pt.pm.dpn p.d d.dpf n.dpf r.npn pt.pa.npn d.dpn

ἑτέροις 17 λέγουσιν, ηὐλήσαμεν ὑμῖν καὶ ↱ ↱ οὐκ ὠρχήσασθε,
friends, *{saying}* ⌊'We played the flute⌋ for you, and you did not dance;
2283 3306 884 7007 2779 4004 4004 4024 4004
r.dpn v.pai.3p v.aai.1p r.dp.2 cj adv v.ami.2p

ἐθρηνήσαμεν καὶ ↱ ↱ οὐκ ἐκόψασθε. 18 ἦλθεν γὰρ Ἰωάννης μήτε
we sang a dirge, and you did not mourn.' For John came *For* *John* neither
2577 2779 3164 3164 4024 3164 1142 2722 2262 1142 2722 3612
v.aai.1p cj adv v.ami.2p v.aai.3s cj n.nsm cj

NASB

did you go out to
see? A man dressed
in soft *clothing?*
Those who wear
soft *clothing* are
in kings' palaces!
9But what did you
go out to see? A
prophet? Yes, I
tell you, and one
who is more than
a prophet. 10This
is the one about
whom it is written,

'BEHOLD, I SEND
MY MESSEN-
GER AHEAD OF
YOU,
WHO WILL
PREPARE YOUR
WAY BEFORE
YOU.'

11Truly I say to you,
among those born
of women there has
not arisen *anyone*
greater than John
the Baptist! Yet the
one who is least
in the kingdom of
heaven is greater
than he. 12From
the days of John
the Baptist until
now the kingdom
of heaven suffers
violence, and vio-
lent men take it by
force. 13For all the
prophets and the
Law prophesied
until John. 14And if
you are willing to
accept *it,* John him-
self is Elijah who
was to come. 15He
who has ears to
hear, let him hear.
16"But to what
shall I compare this
generation? It is
like children sitting
in the market plac-
es, who call out to
the other *children,*
17and say, 'We
played the flute for
you, and you did
not dance; we sang
a dirge, and you
did not mourn.'
18For John came
neither eating

NIV

eating nor drink-
ing, and they say,
'He has a demon.'
[19]The Son of Man
came eating and
drinking, and
they say, 'Here
is a glutton and a
drunkard, a friend
of tax collectors
and sinners.' But
wisdom is proved
right by her
deeds."

Woe on Unrepentant Towns

[20]Then Jesus be-
gan to denounce
the towns in
which most of
his miracles had
been performed,
because they did
not repent. [21]"Woe
to you, Chora-
zin! Woe to you,
Bethsaida! For if
the miracles that
were performed in
you had been per-
formed in Tyre and
Sidon, they would
have repented long
ago in sackcloth
and ashes. [22]But
I tell you, it will
be more bearable
for Tyre and Si-
don on the day of
judgment than for
you. [23]And you,
Capernaum, will
you be lifted to
the heavens? No,
you will go down
to Hades.[a] For if
the miracles that
were performed
in you had been
performed in Sod-
om, it would have
remained to this
day. [24]But I tell
you that it will be
more bearable for
Sodom on the day
of judgment than
for you."

The Father Revealed in the Son

[25]At that time
Jesus said, "I
praise you, Father,
Lord of heaven
and earth,

[a] 23 That is, the realm of the dead

ἐσθίων μήτε πίνων, καὶ λέγουσιν, δαιμόνιον ἔχει. 19
eating nor drinking, and they say, 'He has a demon!' *He has* The Son of Man
2266 3612 4403 2779 3306 2400 2400 1228 2400 3836 5626 3836 476
pt.pa.nsm cj pt.pa.nsm cj v.pai.3p n.asn v.pai.3s

ἦλθεν ὁ υἱὸς τοῦ ἀνθρώπου ἐσθίων καὶ πίνων, καὶ λέγουσιν, ἰδοὺ ἄνθρωπος
came *The Son of Man* eating and drinking, and they say, ⌊'Look at⌋ him!
2262 3836 5626 3836 476 2266 2779 4403 2779 3306 2627 476
v.aai.3s d.nsm n.nsm d.gsm n.gsm pt.pa.nsm cj pt.pa.nsm cj v.pai.3p j n.nsm

φάγος καὶ οἰνοπότης, τελωνῶν φίλος καὶ ἁμαρτωλῶν. καὶ
A glutton and a drunkard, a friend of tax collectors *friend* and sinners!' Yet wisdom
5741 2779 3884 5813 5467 5813 2779 283 2779 5053
n.nsm cj n.nsm n.gpm n.nsm cj a.gpm cj

ἐδικαιώθη ἡ σοφία ἀπὸ τῶν ἔργων[a] αὐτῆς. 20 τότε ἤρξατο ὀνειδίζειν
⌊is shown to be right⌋ *{the} wisdom* by what she does." *she* Then he began to reprimand
1467 3836 5053 608 3836 899 2240 899 5538 806 3943
v.api.3s d.nsf n.nsf p.g d.gpn n.gpn r.gsf.3 adv v.ami.3s f.pa

τὰς πόλεις ἐν αἷς ἐγένοντο αἱ πλεῖσται δυνάμεις
the towns in which most of his mighty works had been done, *{the} most mighty works*
3836 4484 1877 4005 4498 899 1539 1539 1181 3836 4498 1539
d.apf n.apf p.d r.dpf v.ami.3p d.npf a.npf.s n.npf

αὐτοῦ, ὅτι ↱ ↱ οὐ μετενόησαν· 21 οὐαί σοι, Χοραζίν, οὐαί σοι,
his because they did not repent: "Woe to you, Chorazin! Woe to you,
899 4022 3566 3566 4024 3566 4026 5148 5960 4026 5148
r.gsm.3 cj adv v.aai.3p j r.ds.2 n.vsf j r.ds.2

Βηθσαϊδά· ὅτι εἰ ἐν Τύρῳ καὶ Σιδῶνι ἐγένοντο αἱ δυνάμεις αἱ γενόμεναι
Bethsaida! For if in Tyre and Sidon had been done the mighty works that were done
1034 4022 1623 1877 5602 2779 4972 1181 3836 1539 3836 1181
n.vsf cj cj p.d n.dsf cj n.dsf v.ami.3p d.npf n.npf d.npf pt.am.npf

ἐν ὑμῖν, πάλαι ἂν ἐν σάκκῳ καὶ σποδῷ μετενόησαν.
in you, they would have repented long ago *would* in sackcloth and ashes. *they have repented*
1877 7007 3566 323 3566 3566 4093 323 1877 4884 2779 5075 3566
p.d r.dp.2 adv pl p.d n.dsm cj n.dsf v.aai.3p

22 πλὴν λέγω ὑμῖν, Τύρῳ καὶ Σιδῶνι ἀνεκτότερον
Nevertheless I tell you, it will be more bearable for Tyre and Sidon *more bearable*
4440 3306 7007 1639 1639 1639 445 445 5602 2779 4972 445
cj v.pai.1s r.dp.2 n.dsf cj n.dsf a.nsn.c

ἔσται ἐν ἡμέρᾳ κρίσεως ἢ ὑμῖν. 23 καὶ σύ, Καφαρναούμ,
it will be on the day of judgment than for you. And as for you, Capernaum, will you
1639 1877 2465 3213 2445 7007 2779 5148 3019 5738 5738
v.fmi.3s p.d n.dsf n.gsf pl r.dp.2 cj r.ns.2 n.vsf

μὴ ἕως οὐρανοῦ ὑψωθήσῃ; ἕως
be exalted to heaven? No, *to heaven will you be exalted* you will be brought down to
5738 5738 2401 4041 3590 2401 4041 5738 2849 2849 2849 2849 2849 2401
pl p.g n.gsm v.fpi.2s p.g

ᾅδου καταβήσῃ· ὅτι εἰ ἐν Σοδόμοις ἐγενήθησαν αἱ δυνάμεις αἱ
Hades! *you will be brought down* For if in Sodom had been done the mighty works that
87 2849 4022 1623 1877 5047 1181 3836 1539 3836
n.gsm v.fmi.2s cj cj p.d n.dpn v.api.3p d.npf n.npf d.npf

γενόμεναι ἐν σοί, → ἔμεινεν ἂν μέχρι τῆς σήμερον. 24 πλὴν λέγω
were done in you, it would have remained *would* to this day. Nevertheless I tell
1181 1877 5148 323 3531 323 3588 3836 4958 4440 3306
pt.am.npf p.d r.ds.2 v.aai.3s pl p.g d.gsf adv cj v.pai.1s

ὑμῖν ὅτι γῆ Σοδόμων ἀνεκτότερον ἔσται ἐν
you that it will be more bearable for the land of Sodom *more bearable it will be* on the
7007 4022 1639 1639 1639 445 445 1178 5047 445 1639 1877
r.dp.2 cj n.dsf n.gpn a.nsn.c v.fmi.3s p.d

ἡμέρᾳ κρίσεως ἢ σοί. 25 ἐν ἐκείνῳ τῷ καιρῷ ἀποκριθεὶς ὁ Ἰησοῦς
day of judgment than for you." At that *{the}* time Jesus declared, *{the} Jesus*
2465 3213 2445 5148 1877 1697 3836 2789 2652 646 3836 2652
n.dsf n.gsf pl r.ds.2 p.d r.dsm d.dsm n.dsm pt.ap.nsm d.nsm n.nsm

εἶπεν, ἐξομολογοῦμαί σοι, πάτερ, κύριε τοῦ οὐρανοῦ καὶ τῆς γῆς, ὅτι
{saying} "I praise you, Father, Lord of heaven and *{the}* earth, because
3306 2018 5148 4252 3261 3836 4041 2779 3836 1178 4022
v.aai.3s v.pmi.1s r.ds.2 n.vsm n.vsm d.gsm n.gsm cj d.gsf n.gsf cj

[a] ἔργων UBS, TNIV. τέκνων NET.

NASB

nor drinking, and
they say, 'He has a
demon!' [19]The Son
of Man came eat-
ing and drinking,
and they say, 'Be-
hold, a gluttonous
man and a drunk-
ard, a friend of tax
collectors and sin-
ners!' Yet wisdom
is vindicated by her
deeds."

The Unrepenting Cities

[20]Then He began
to denounce the cit-
ies in which most
of His miracles
were done, because
they did not repent.
[21]"Woe to you,
Chorazin! Woe to
you, Bethsaida!
For if the miracles
had occurred in
Tyre and Sidon
which occurred in
you, they would
have repented long
ago in sackcloth
and ashes. [22]Nev-
ertheless I say to
you, it will be more
tolerable for Tyre
and Sidon in *the*
day of judgment
than for you. [23]And
you, Capernaum,
will not be exalted
to heaven, will
you? You will de-
scend to Hades; for
if the miracles had
occurred in Sodom
which occurred in
you, it would have
remained to this
day. [24]Nevertheless
I say to you that it
will be more toler-
able for the land of
Sodom in *the* day
of judgment, than
for you."

Come to Me

[25]At that time Je-
sus said, "I praise
You, Father, Lord
of heaven and
earth, that You

NIV

because you have
hidden these
things from the
wise and learned,
and revealed them
to little children.
26Yes, Father, for
this is what you
were pleased to do.
27"All things have
been committed to
me by my Father.
No one knows the
Son except the Fa-
ther, and no one
knows the Father
except the Son and
those to whom the
Son chooses to re-
veal him.
28"Come to me,
all you who are
weary and bur-
dened, and I will
give you rest.
29Take my yoke
upon you and learn
from me, for I am
gentle and humble
in heart, and you
will find rest for
your souls. 30For
my yoke is easy
and my burden is
light."

Jesus Is Lord of the Sabbath

12 At that time
Jesus went
through the grain-
fields on the Sab-
bath. His disciples
were hungry and
began to pick some
heads of grain and
eat them. 2When
the Pharisees saw
this, they said to
him, "Look! Your
disciples are doing
what is unlawful
on the Sabbath."
3He answered,
"Haven't you
read what David
did when he and
his companions
were hungry? 4He
entered the

ἔκρυψας ταῦτα ἀπὸ σοφῶν καὶ συνετῶν καὶ ἀπεκάλυψας αὐτὰ
you have hidden these things from the wise and clever and revealed them
3221 4047 608 5055 2779 5305 2779 636 899
v.aai.2s r.apn p.g a.gpm cj a.gpm cj v.aai.2s r.apn.3

νηπίοις· 26 ναὶ ὁ πατήρ, ὅτι οὕτως εὐδοκία ἐγένετο ἔμπροσθέν
to little children; yes, {the} Father, for such was your gracious will. *was* *{before}*
3758 3721 3836 4252 4022 4048 1181 5148 2306 1181 1869
a.dpm pl d.vsm n.nsm cj adv n.nsf v.ami.3s p.g

σου. 27 πάντα μοι παρεδόθη ὑπὸ τοῦ πατρός μου, καὶ
your All things were handed over to me *were handed over* by *{the}* my Father, *my* and
5148 4246 4140 4140 4140 1609 4140 5679 3836 1609 4252 1609 2779
r.gs.2 a.npn r.ds.1 v.api.3s p.g d.gsm n.gsm r.gs.1 cj

οὐδεὶς ἐπιγινώσκει τὸν υἱὸν ⸤εἰ μὴ⸥ ὁ πατήρ, οὐδὲ τὸν
no one knows the Son except the Father; neither does anyone know the
4029 2105 3836 5626 1623 3590 3836 4252 4028 2105 5516 2105 3836
a.nsm v.pai.3s d.asm n.asm cj pl d.nsm n.nsm cj d.asm

πατέρα τις ἐπιγινώσκει ⸤εἰ μὴ⸥ ὁ υἱὸς καὶ ⸤ᾧ ἐὰν⸥
Father *anyone does know* except the Son and the one to whom the Son
4252 5516 2105 1623 3590 3836 5626 2779 4005 1569 3836 5626
n.asm r.nsm v.pai.3s cj pl d.nsm n.nsm cj r.dsm pl

βούληται ὁ υἱὸς ἀποκαλύψαι. 28 δεῦτε πρός με πάντες οἱ κοπιῶντες καὶ
chooses *the* *Son* to reveal him. Come to me, all you who are weary and
1089 3836 5626 636 1307 4639 1609 4246 3836 3159 2779
v.pms.3s d.nsm n.nsm f.aa adv p.a r.as.1 a.vpm d.vpm pt.pa.vpm cj

πεφορτισμένοι, κἀγὼ ἀναπαύσω ὑμᾶς. 29 ἄρατε τὸν ζυγόν μου ἐφ' ὑμᾶς
carrying heavy burdens, and I will refresh you. Take *{the}* my yoke *my* upon you
5844 2743 399 7007 149 3836 1609 2433 1609 2093 7007
pt.rp.vpm crasis v.fai.1s r.ap.2 v.aam.2p d.asm n.asm r.gs.1 p.a r.ap.2

καὶ μάθετε ἀπ' ἐμοῦ, ὅτι πραΰς εἰμι καὶ ταπεινὸς τῇ καρδίᾳ, καὶ
and learn from me, for I am gentle *I am* and lowly in heart, and
2779 3443 608 1609 4022 1639 1639 4558 1639 2779 5424 3836 2840 2779
cj v.aam.2p p.g r.gs.1 cj a.nsm v.pai.1s cj a.nsm d.dsf n.dsf cj

εὑρήσετε ἀνάπαυσιν ταῖς ψυχαῖς ὑμῶν· 30 ὁ γὰρ ζυγός μου χρηστὸς
you will find rest for your souls. *your* *{the}* For my yoke *my* is easy
2351 398 3836 7007 6034 7007 3836 1142 1609 2433 1609 5982
v.fai.2p n.asf d.dpf n.dpf r.gp.2 d.nsm cj n.nsm r.gs.1 a.nsm

καὶ τὸ φορτίον μου ἐλαφρόν ἐστιν.
and *{the}* my burden *my* is light." *is*
2779 3836 1609 5845 1609 1639 1787 1639
cj d.nsn n.nsn r.gs.1 a.nsn v.pai.3s

12:1 ἐν ἐκείνῳ τῷ καιρῷ ἐπορεύθη ὁ Ἰησοῦς τοῖς
At that *{the}* time Jesus went *{the}* *Jesus* through the grainfields on the
1877 1697 3836 2789 2652 4513 3836 2652 1328 3836 5077 3836
p.d r.dsm d.dsm n.dsm v.api.3s d.nsm n.nsm d.dpn

σάββασιν διὰ τῶν σπορίμων· οἱ δὲ μαθηταὶ αὐτοῦ ἐπείνασαν καὶ ἤρξαντο
Sabbath; *through the grainfields* *{the}* and his disciples *his* were hungry, and they began
4879 1328 3836 5077 3836 1254 899 3412 899 4277 2779 806
n.dpn p.g d.gpn n.gpn d.npm cj n.npm r.gsm.3 v.aai.3p cj v.ami.3p

τίλλειν στάχυας καὶ ἐσθίειν. 2 ↱ οἱ δὲ Φαρισαῖοι ἰδόντες εἶπαν
to pluck heads of grain and eat. But when the *But* Pharisees saw this, they said
5504 5092 2779 2266 1254 1625 3836 1254 5757 1625 3306
f.pa n.apm cj f.pa d.npm cj n.npm pt.aa.npm v.aai.3p

αὐτῷ, ἰδοὺ οἱ μαθηταί σου ποιοῦσιν ὃ ↱ οὐκ ἔξεστιν ποιεῖν ἐν
to him, "Look, *{the}* your disciples *your* are doing what is not lawful to do on a
899 2627 3836 5148 3412 5148 4472 4005 1997 4024 1997 4472 1877
r.dsm.3 j d.npm n.npm r.gs.2 v.pai.3p r.asn adv v.pai.3s f.pa p.d

σαββάτῳ. 3 ὁ δὲ εἶπεν αὐτοῖς, ↱ ↱ οὐκ ἀνέγνωτε τί ἐποίησεν
Sabbath." But he *But* said to them, "Have you not read what David did
4879 1254 3836 1254 3306 899 336 336 4024 336 5515 1253 4472
n.dsn d.nsm cj v.aai.3s r.dpm.3 pl v.aai.2p r.asn v.aai.3s

Δαυὶδ ὅτε ἐπείνασεν ← καὶ οἱ μετ' αὐτοῦ, 4 πῶς ⸤εἰσῆλθεν εἰς⸥
David when *were hungry* he and those with him were hungry, how he entered
1253 4021 4277 2779 3836 3552 899 4277 4277 4802 1656 1650
n.nsm cj v.aai.3s cj d.npm p.g r.gsm.3 cj v.aai.3s p.a

NASB

have hidden these
things from *the*
wise and intelligent
and have revealed
them to infants.
26Yes, Father, for
this way was well-
pleasing in Your
sight. 27All things
have been handed
over to Me by My
Father; and no one
knows the Son ex-
cept the Father; nor
does anyone know
the Father except
the Son, and any-
one to whom the
Son wills to reveal
Him.
28"Come to Me,
all who are weary
and heavy-laden,
and I will give
you rest. 29Take
My yoke upon
you and learn
from Me, for I am
gentle and humble
in heart, and YOU
WILL FIND REST FOR
YOUR SOULS. 30For
My yoke is easy
and My burden is
light."

Sabbath Questions

12:1At that time
Jesus went through
the grainfields
on the Sabbath,
and His disciples
became hungry
and began to pick
the heads *of grain*
and eat. 2But when
the Pharisees saw
this, they said to
Him, "Look, Your
disciples do what
is not lawful to do
on a Sabbath." 3But
He said to them,
"Have you not read
what David did
when he became
hungry, he and his
companions, 4how
he entered the

NIV

house of God,
and he and his
companions ate
the consecrated
bread—which was
not lawful for them
to do, but only for
the priests. 5Or
haven't you read
in the Law that the
priests on Sabbath
duty in the temple
desecrate the Sab-
bath and yet are
innocent? 6I tell
you that something
greater than the
temple is here. 7If
you had known
what these words
mean, 'I desire
mercy, not sacri-
fice,'[a] you would
not have con-
demned the inno-
cent. 8For the Son
of Man is Lord of
the Sabbath."
9Going on from
that place, he went
into their syna-
gogue, 10and a man
with a shriveled
hand was there.
Looking for a
reason to bring
charges against
Jesus, they asked
him, "Is it lawful
to heal on the Sab-
bath?"
11He said to them,
"If any of you has
a sheep and it falls
into a pit on the
Sabbath, will you
not take hold of
it and lift it out?
12How much more
valuable is a per-
son than a sheep!
Therefore it is law-
ful to do good on
the Sabbath."
13Then he said to
the man, "Stretch
out your hand." So
he stretched

τὸν οἶκον τοῦ θεοῦ καὶ τοὺς ἄρτους τῆς προθέσεως ἔφαγον, ὃ
the house of God and they ate the sacred bread, {the} sacred they ate which
3836 3875 3836 2536 2779 2266 2266 3836 4606 788 3836 4606 2266 4005
d.asm n.asm d.gsm n.gsm cj d.apm n.apm d.gsf n.gsf v.aai.3p r.asn

οὐκ ἐξὸν ἦν αὐτῷ φαγεῖν οὐδὲ τοῖς μετ' αὐτοῦ ⌊εἰ μὴ⌋
it was not lawful it was for him to eat nor ⌊for those who⌋ were with him, but
1639 1639 4024 1997 1639 899 2266 4028 3836 3552 899 1623 3590
adv pt.pa.nsn v.iai.3s r.dsm.3 f.aa cj d.dpm p.g r.gsm.3 cj pl

τοῖς ἱερεῦσιν μόνοις; 5 ἢ ↱ ↱ οὐκ ἀνέγνωτε ἐν τῷ νόμῳ ὅτι τοῖς
for the priests alone? Or have you not read in the law that on the
3836 2636 3668 2445 336 336 4024 336 1877 3836 3795 4022 3836
d.dpm n.dpm a.dpm cj pl v.aai.2p p.d d.dsm n.dsm cj d.dpn

σάββασιν οἱ ἱερεῖς ἐν τῷ ἱερῷ τὸ σάββατον βεβηλοῦσιν καὶ
Sabbath the priests in the temple break the Sabbath break and yet are
4879 3836 2636 1877 3836 2639 1014 3836 4879 1014 2779 1639
n.dpn d.npm n.npm p.d d.dsn n.dsn d.asn n.asn v.pai.3p cj

ἀναίτιοί εἰσιν; 6 λέγω δὲ ὑμῖν ὅτι τοῦ ἱεροῦ μεῖζόν ἐστιν
not guilty? are But I say But to you that something greater ⌊than the⌋ temple greater is
360 1639 1254 3306 1254 7007 4022 3489 3836 2639 3489 1639
a.npm v.pai.3p v.pai.1s cj r.dp.2 cj d.gsn n.gsn a.nsn.c v.pai.3s

ὧδε. 7 εἰ δὲ ἐγνώκειτε τί ἐστιν· ἔλεος θέλω καὶ οὐ
here. And if And you had known what this means, 'I desire mercy I desire and not
6045 1254 1623 1254 1182 5515 1639 2527 2527 1799 2527 2779 4024
adv cj cj v.lai.2p r.nsn v.pai.3s n.asn v.pai.1s cj adv

θυσίαν, ↱ οὐκ ἂν κατεδικάσατε τοὺς ἀναιτίους. 8 κύριος γάρ
sacrifice,' you would not would have condemned the guiltless. lord For the Son of
2602 2868 323 4024 323 2868 3836 360 3261 1142 3836 5626 3836
n.asf adv pl v.aai.2p d.apm a.apm n.nsm cj

ἐστιν τοῦ σαββάτου ὁ υἱὸς τοῦ ἀνθρώπου. 9 καὶ ↱ μεταβὰς ἐκεῖθεν
Man is lord of the Sabbath." the Son of Man Then he left that place
476 1639 3261 3836 4879 3836 5626 3836 476 2779 2262 3553 1696
v.pai.3s d.gsn n.gsn d.nsm n.nsm d.gsm n.gsm cj pt.aa.nsm adv

ἦλθεν εἰς τὴν συναγωγὴν αὐτῶν· 10 καὶ ἰδοὺ ἄνθρωπος
and went into {the} their synagogue, their and ⌊there he saw⌋ a man with a
2262 1650 3836 899 5252 899 2779 2627 476 2400
v.aai.3s p.a d.asf n.asf r.gpm.3 cj j n.nsm

χεῖρα ἔχων ξηράν. καὶ ἐπηρώτησαν αὐτὸν λέγοντες, εἰ ἔξεστιν
withered hand. with withered And they asked him, {saying} {if} "Is it lawful to heal
3831 5931 2400 3831 2779 2089 899 3306 1623 1997 2543 2543
n.asf pt.pa.nsm a.asf cj v.aai.3p r.asm.3 pt.pa.npm cj v.pai.3s

τοῖς σάββασιν θεραπεῦσαι; ἵνα κατηγορήσωσιν αὐτοῦ.
on the Sabbath?" to heal — so ⌊they might have a charge to bring against⌋ him.
3836 4879 2543 2671 2989 899
d.dpn n.dpn f.aa cj v.aas.3p r.gsm.3

11 ὁ δὲ εἶπεν αὐτοῖς, τίς ἔσται ἐξ ὑμῶν ἄνθρωπος ὃς ἕξει
But he But said to them, "What man is there among you man who has only
1254 3836 1254 3306 899 5515 476 1639 1666 7007 476 4005 2400
d.nsm cj v.aai.3s r.dpm.3 r.nsm v.fmi.3s p.g r.gp.2 n.nsm r.nsm v.fai.3s

πρόβατον ἓν καὶ ἐὰν ἐμπέσῃ τοῦτο τοῖς σάββασιν εἰς βόθυνον,
one sheep, one and if it falls it into a pit on the Sabbath, into pit
1651 4585 1651 2779 1569 4047 1860 4047 1650 1073 3836 4879 1650 1073
n.asn a.asn cj cj v.aas.3s r.nsn d.dpn n.dpn p.a n.asm

↱ ↱ οὐχὶ κρατήσει αὐτὸ καὶ ἐγερεῖ; ← 12 πόσῳ οὖν διαφέρει ←
will he not take hold of it and lift it out? How much then more valuable then is a
3195 3195 4049 3195 899 2779 1586 4531 4036 1422 4036
pl v.fai.3s r.asn.3 cj v.fai.3s r.dsn cj v.pai.3s

ἄνθρωπος → προβάτου. ὥστε ἔξεστιν τοῖς σάββασιν καλῶς
man than a sheep! So then, it is lawful to do good on the Sabbath." good
476 4585 6063 1997 4472 4472 2822 3836 4879 2822
n.nsm n.gsn cj v.pai.3s d.dpn n.dpn adv

ποιεῖν. 13 τότε λέγει τῷ ἀνθρώπῳ, ἔκτεινόν σου τὴν χεῖρα. καὶ ἐξέτεινεν
to do Then he said ⌊to the⌋ man, "Stretch out your {the} hand." And the man stretched
4472 5538 3306 3836 476 1753 5148 3836 5931 2779 1753
f.pa adv v.pai.3s d.dsm n.dsm v.aam.2s r.gs.2 d.asf n.asf cj v.aai.3s

NASB

house of God, and
they ate the conse-
crated bread, which
was not lawful for
him to eat nor for
those with him,
but for the priests
alone? 5Or have
you not read in the
Law, that on the
Sabbath the priests
in the temple break
the Sabbath and
are innocent? 6But
I say to you that
something greater
than the temple
is here. 7But if
you had known
what this means,
'I DESIRE COMPAS-
SION, AND NOT A
SACRIFICE,' you
would not have
condemned the in-
nocent.

Lord of the Sabbath

8For the Son of
Man is Lord of the
Sabbath."
9Departing from
there, He went into
their synagogue.
10And a man *was
there* whose hand
was withered. And
they questioned
Jesus, asking, "Is
it lawful to heal on
the Sabbath?"—so
that they might
accuse Him. 11And
He said to them,
"What man is there
among you who
has a sheep, and if
it falls into a pit on
the Sabbath, will
he not take hold of
it and lift it out?
12How much more
valuable then is a
man than a sheep!
So then, it is lawful
to do good on the
Sabbath." 13Then
He *said to the
man, "Stretch out
your hand!" He
stretched it out,

[a] 7 Hosea 6:6

NIV

it out and it was
completely re-
stored, just as
sound as the other.
14 But the Pharisees
went out and plot-
ted how they might
kill Jesus.

God's Chosen Servant

15 Aware of this,
Jesus withdrew
from that place.
A large crowd
followed him,
and he healed all
who were ill. 16 He
warned them not
to tell others about
him. 17 This was to
fulfill what was
spoken through the
prophet Isaiah:

18 "Here is my
servant
whom I have
chosen,
the one I love,
in whom I
delight;
I will put my Spirit
on him,
and he will
proclaim
justice to the
nations.
19 He will not quarrel
or cry out;
no one will hear
his voice in
the streets.
20 A bruised reed
he will not
break,
and a
smoldering
wick he will
not snuff out,
till he has brought
justice
through to
victory.
21 In his name
the nations
will put their
hope."[a]

Jesus and Beelzebul

22 Then they
brought him a de-
mon-possessed
man who was
blind and mute,
and Jesus healed
him, so that he
could both talk
and see. 23 All the
people were as-
tonished and said,
"Could this be the
Son of David?"

[a] 21 Isaiah 42:1-4

← καὶ ἀπεκατεστάθη ὑγιὴς ὡς ἡ ἄλλη. 14 ἐξελθόντες δὲ
it out, and it was restored, sound like the other. Then the Pharisees went *Then*
2779 635 5618 6055 3836 257 1254 3836 5757 2002 1254
cj v.api.3s a.nsf pl d.nsf r.nsf pt.aa.npm cj

οἱ Φαρισαῖοι ⌊συμβούλιον ἔλαβον⌋ κατ' αὐτοῦ ὅπως ↱ ↱ ↱
the Pharisees and plotted against him ⌊in order that⌋ they might put
3836 5757 5206 3284 2848 899 3968 660 660 660
d.npm n.npm n.asn v.aai.3p p.g r.gsm.3 cj

αὐτὸν ἀπολέσωσιν. 15 ὁ δὲ Ἰησοῦς γνοὺς ἀνεχώρησεν ἐκεῖθεν. καὶ
him to death. *{the}* But Jesus, ⌊aware of⌋ this, withdrew from there. And large
899 660 3836 1254 2652 1182 432 1696 2779 4498
r.asm.3 v.aas.3p d.nsm cj n.nsm pt.aa.nsm v.aai.3s adv cj

ἠκολούθησαν αὐτῷ ὄχλοι[a] πολλοί, καὶ ἐθεράπευσεν αὐτοὺς πάντας 16 καὶ
crowds followed him, *crowds large* and he healed them all. And
4063 199 899 4063 4498 2779 2543 899 4246 2779
v.aai.3p r.dsm.3 n.npm a.npm cj v.aai.3s r.apm.3 a.apm cj

ἐπετίμησεν αὐτοῖς ἵνα μὴ φανερὸν αὐτὸν ποιήσωσιν,
he sternly warned them that they should not make him known *him they should make*
2203 899 2671 4472 4472 3590 4472 899 5745 899 4472
v.aai.3s r.dpm.3 cj pl a.asm r.asm.3 v.aas.3p

17 ἵνα πληρωθῇ τὸ ῥηθὲν διὰ Ἠσαΐου τοῦ προφήτου
so that *might be fulfilled* what was written by Isaiah the prophet might be fulfilled:
2671 4444 3836 3306 1328 2480 3836 4737 4444 4444 4444
cj v.aps.3s d.nsn pt.ap.nsn p.g n.gsm d.gsm n.gsm

λέγοντος, 18 ἰδοὺ ὁ παῖς μου ὃν ᾑρέτισα, ὁ ἀγαπητός μου
{saying} "Here is *{the}* my servant *my* whom I have chosen, *{the}* my beloved *my*
3306 2627 3836 1609 4090 1609 4005 147 3836 1609 28 1609
pt.pa.gsm j d.nsm n.nsm r.gs.1 r.asm v.aai.1s d.nsm a.nsm r.gs.1

εἰς ὃν εὐδόκησεν ἡ ψυχή μου· θήσω τὸ πνεῦμά μου ἐπ'
with whom my soul is well pleased. *{the} soul my* ⌊I will put⌋ *{the}* my Spirit *my* upon
1650 4005 1609 6034 2305 3836 6034 1609 5502 3836 1609 4460 1609 2093
p.a r.asm v.aai.3s d.nsf n.nsf r.gs.1 v.fai.1s d.asn n.asn r.gs.1 p.a

αὐτόν, καὶ κρίσιν τοῖς ἔθνεσιν ἀπαγγελεῖ. 19 ↱ ↱ οὐκ ἐρίσει
him, and he will proclaim justice to the nations. *he will proclaim* He will not quarrel,
899 2779 550 550 550 3213 3836 1620 550 2248 2248 4024 2248
r.asm.3 cj n.asf d.dpn n.dpn v.fai.3s adv v.fai.3s

οὐδὲ κραυγάσει, οὐδὲ → ἀκούσει τις ἐν ταῖς πλατείαις τὴν
nor will he cry out, nor will anyone hear *anyone* his voice in the streets. *{the}*
4028 3198 4028 5516 201 5516 899 5889 1877 3836 4426 3836
cj v.fai.3s cj v.fai.3s r.nsm p.d d.dpf n.dpf d.asf

φωνὴν αὐτοῦ. 20 κάλαμον συντετριμμένον ↱ ↱ οὐ κατεάξει καὶ
voice his A shattered reed *shattered* he will not break, and a
5889 899 5341 2812 5341 2862 2862 4024 2862 2779
n.asf r.gsm.3 n.asm pt.rp.asm adv v.fai.3s cj

λίνον τυφόμενον ↱ ↱ οὐ σβέσει, ⌊ἕως ἂν⌋ ἐκβάλῃ εἰς νῖκος
smoldering wick *smoldering* he will not snuff out, until he brings justice to victory.
5606 3351 5606 4931 4931 4024 4931 2401 323 1675 3213 1650 3777
n.asn pt.pp.asn adv v.fai.3s cj pl v.aas.3s p.a n.asn

τὴν κρίσιν. 21 καὶ τῷ ὀνόματι αὐτοῦ ἔθνη ἐλπιοῦσιν. 22 τότε
{the} justice And in his name *his* the nations ⌊will put their hope."⌋ Then a blind
3836 3213 2779 3836 899 3950 899 1620 1827 5538 5603
d.asf n.asf cj d.dsn n.dsn r.gsm.3 n.npn v.fai.3p adv

προσηνέχθη αὐτῷ δαιμονιζόμενος τυφλὸς καὶ κωφός, καὶ
and mute demoniac was brought to him, *demoniac blind and mute* and
2779 3273 1227 4712 899 1227 5603 2779 3273 2779
v.api.3s r.dsm.3 pt.pm.nsm a.nsm cj a.nsm cj

ἐθεράπευσεν αὐτόν, ὥστε τὸν κωφὸν → λαλεῖν καὶ[b] βλέπειν. 23 καὶ
he healed him so that the mute could both speak and see. And all the
2543 899 6063 3836 3273 3281 2779 1063 2779 4246 3836
v.aai.3s r.asm.3 cj d.asm a.asm f.pa cj f.pa cj

ἐξίσταντο πάντες οἱ ὄχλοι καὶ ἔλεγον, μήτι οὗτός ἐστιν ὁ υἱὸς
crowds were astonished *all the crowds* and were saying, "Could this be the Son
4063 2014 4246 3836 4063 2779 3306 3614 4047 1639 3836 5626
v.imi.3p a.npm d.npm n.npm cj v.iai.3p pl r.nsm v.pai.3s d.nsm n.nsm

[a] [ὄχλοι] UBS.
[b] κωφὸν καὶ λαλεῖν καὶ included by TR after καί.

NASB

and it was restored
to normal, like the
other. 14 But the
Pharisees went
out and conspired
against Him, *as to*
how they might
destroy Him.
15 But Jesus, aware
of *this,* withdrew
from there. Many
followed Him, and
He healed them all,
16 and warned them
not to tell who He
was. 17 *This was* to
fulfill what was
spoken through
Isaiah the prophet:
18 "BEHOLD, MY
SERVANT
WHOM I HAVE
CHOSEN;
MY BELOVED
IN WHOM MY
SOUL is WELL-
PLEASED;
I WILL PUT MY
SPIRIT UPON
HIM,
AND HE SHALL
PROCLAIM
JUSTICE TO THE
GENTILES.
19 "HE WILL NOT
QUARREL, NOR
CRY OUT;
NOR WILL ANY-
ONE HEAR HIS
VOICE IN THE
STREETS.
20 "A BATTERED
REED HE WILL
NOT BREAK
OFF,
AND A SMOL-
DERING WICK
HE WILL NOT
PUT OUT,
UNTIL HE
LEADS JUSTICE
TO VICTORY.
21 "AND IN HIS
NAME THE
GENTILES WILL
HOPE."

The Pharisees Rebuked

22 Then a demon-
possessed man
who was blind and
mute was brought
to Jesus, and He
healed him, so
that the mute man
spoke and saw.
23 All the crowds
were amazed, and
were saying, "This
man cannot be the
Son of David, can

NIV

24But when the
Pharisees heard
this, they said, "It
is only by Beelze-
bul, the prince of
demons, that this
fellow drives out
demons."
25Jesus knew
their thoughts
and said to them,
"Every kingdom
divided against it-
self will be ruined,
and every city or
household divid-
ed against itself
will not stand. 26If
Satan drives out
Satan, he is divid-
ed against himself.
How then can his
kingdom stand?
27And if I drive out
demons by Beel-
zebul, by whom
do your people
drive them out?
So then, they will
be your judges.
28But if it is by the
Spirit of God that I
drive out demons,
then the kingdom
of God has come
upon you.
29"Or again, how
can anyone enter a
strong man's house
and carry off his
possessions unless
he first ties up the
strong man? Then
he can plunder his
house.
30"Whoever is not
with me is against
me, and whoever
does not gather
with me scatters.
31And so I tell you,
every kind of sin
and slander can be
forgiven,

Δαυίδ; 24 ↱ οἱ δὲ Φαρισαῖοι ἀκούσαντες εἶπον, οὗτος ↱
of David?" But when the *But* Pharisees heard this, they said, "This fellow does
1253 1254 201 3836 1254 5757 201 3306 4047 1675
n.gsm d.npm cj n.npm pt.aa.npm v.aai.3p r.nsm

οὐκ ἐκβάλλει τὰ δαιμόνια ⌊εἰ μὴ⌋ ἐν τῷ Βεελζεβοὺλ ἄρχοντι τῶν
not cast out *{the}* demons except by *{the}* Beelzebul, the ruler of the
4024 1675 3836 1228 1623 3590 1877 3836 1015 807 3836
adv v.pai.3s d.apn n.apn cj pl p.d d.dsm n.dsm n.dsm d.gpn

δαιμονίων. 25 ↱ εἰδὼς δὲ τὰς ἐνθυμήσεις αὐτῶν εἶπεν αὐτοῖς, πᾶσα
demons." But he knew *But* *{the}* their thoughts *their* and said to them, "Every
1228 1254 3306 3857 1254 3836 899 1927 899 3306 899 4246
n.gpn pt.ra.nsm cj d.apf n.apf r.gpm.3 v.aai.3s r.dpm.3 a.nsf

βασιλεία μερισθεῖσα καθ' ἑαυτῆς ἐρημοῦται καὶ πᾶσα πόλις ἢ οἰκία
kingdom divided against itself ⌊is brought to ruin,⌋ and *{each}* no city or house
993 3532 2848 1571 2246 2779 4246 4024 4484 2445 3864
n.nsf pt.ap.nsf p.g r.gsf.3 v.ppi.3s cj a.nsf n.nsf cj n.nsf

μερισθεῖσα καθ' ἑαυτῆς οὐ σταθήσεται. 26 καὶ εἰ ὁ σατανᾶς τὸν
divided against itself *no* will stand. So if *{the}* Satan casts out *{the}*
3532 2848 1571 4024 2705 2779 1623 3836 4928 1675 1675 3836
pt.ap.nsf p.g r.gsf.3 adv v.fpi.3s cj cj d.nsm n.nsm d.asm

σατανᾶν ἐκβάλλει, ἐφ' ἑαυτὸν ἐμερίσθη· πῶς οὖν →
Satan, *casts out* he is divided against himself; *he is divided* how then will his kingdom
4928 1675 3532 3532 3532 2093 1571 3532 4802 4036 899 993
n.asm v.pai.3s p.a r.asm.3 v.api.3s cj cj

σταθήσεται ἡ βασιλεία αὐτοῦ; 27 καὶ εἰ ἐγὼ ἐν Βεελζεβοὺλ
stand? *{the}* *kingdom* *his* And if I cast out demons by Beelzebul,
2705 3836 993 899 2779 1623 1609 1675 1675 1228 1877 1015
v.fpi.3s d.nsf n.nsf r.gsm.3 cj cj r.ns.1 p.d n.dsm

ἐκβάλλω τὰ δαιμόνια, ↱ οἱ υἱοὶ ὑμῶν ἐν τίνι ἐκβάλλουσιν;
cast out *{the}* *demons* by whom do *{the}* your sons *your* *by* *whom* cast
1675 3836 1228 1877 5515 1675 3836 7007 5626 7007 1877 5515 1675
v.pai.1s d.apn n.apn d.npm n.npm r.gp.2 p.d r.dsm v.pai.3p

← διὰ τοῦτο αὐτοὶ κριταὶ ἔσονται ὑμῶν. 28 εἰ δὲ
them out? For this reason they will be your judges. *will be* *your* But if *But* I
1328 4047 899 1639 1639 7007 3216 1639 7007 1254 1623 1254 1609
p.a r.asn r.npm n.npm v.fmi.3p r.gp.2 cj cj

ἐν πνεύματι θεοῦ ἐγὼ ἐκβάλλω τὰ δαιμόνια, ἄρα
cast out demons by the Spirit of God, *I* *cast out* *{the}* *demons* then the kingdom
1675 1675 1228 1877 4460 2536 1609 1675 3836 1228 726 3836 993
p.d n.dsn n.gsm r.ns.1 v.pai.1s d.apn n.apn cj

ἔφθασεν ἐφ' ὑμᾶς ἡ βασιλεία τοῦ θεοῦ. 29 ἢ πῶς δύναταί τις
of God has come upon you. *the* *kingdom* *of* *God* Or how can someone
3836 2536 5777 2093 7007 3836 993 3836 2536 2445 4802 1538 5516
v.aai.3s p.a r.ap.2 d.nsf n.nsf d.gsm n.gsm cj cj v.ppi.3s r.nsm

⌊εἰσελθεῖν εἰς⌋ τὴν οἰκίαν τοῦ ἰσχυροῦ καὶ τὰ σκεύη
enter the strong man's house *{the}* *strong man's* and carry off *{the}* his belongings,
1656 1650 3836 2708 2708 3864 3836 2708 2779 773 773 3836 899 5007
f.aa p.a d.asf n.asf d.gsm a.gsm cj d.apn n.apn

αὐτοῦ ἁρπάσαι, ⌊ἐὰν μὴ⌋ ↱ πρῶτον δήσῃ τὸν ἰσχυρόν; καὶ τότε
his *carry off* unless he first ties up the strong man? And then he will ransack
899 773 1569 3590 1313 4754 1313 3836 2708 2779 5538 1395 1395 1395
r.gsm.3 f.aa cj pl adv v.aas.3s d.asm a.asm cj adv

τὴν οἰκίαν αὐτοῦ διαρπάσει. 30 ὁ μὴ ὢν μετ' ἐμοῦ
his *{the}* house. *his* *he will ransack* The one who is not *one who is* with me is
899 3836 3864 899 1395 3836 1639 1639 1639 3590 1639 3552 1609 1639
d.asf n.asf r.gsm.3 v.fai.3s d.nsm pl pt.pa.nsm p.g r.gs.1

κατ' ἐμοῦ ἐστιν, καὶ ὁ ↱ ↱ ↱ μὴ συνάγων μετ' ἐμοῦ σκορπίζει. 31 διὰ
against me, *is* and the one who does not gather with me scatters. "For
2848 1609 1639 2779 3836 5251 5251 5251 3590 5251 3552 1609 5025 1328
p.g r.gs.1 v.pai.3s cj d.nsm pl pt.pa.nsm p.g r.gs.1 v.pai.3s p.a

τοῦτο λέγω ὑμῖν, πᾶσα ἁμαρτία καὶ βλασφημία ἀφεθήσεται τοῖς ἀνθρώποις,
this reason I say to you, every sin and blasphemy will be forgiven *{the}* people,
4047 3306 7007 4246 281 2779 1060 918 3836 476
r.asn v.pai.1s r.dp.2 a.nsf n.nsf cj n.nsf v.fpi.3s d.dpm n.dpm

NASB

he?" 24But when
the Pharisees heard
this, they said,
"This man casts
out demons only
by Beelzebul the
ruler of the de-
mons."
25And knowing
their thoughts Jesus
said to them, "Any
kingdom divided
against itself is laid
waste; and any city
or house divided
against itself will
not stand. 26If Satan
casts out Satan, he
is divided against
himself; how then
will his kingdom
stand? 27If I by
Beelzebul cast out
demons, by whom
do your sons cast
them out? For this
reason they will be
your judges. 28But
if I cast out de-
mons by the Spirit
of God, then the
kingdom of God
has come upon
you. 29Or how can
anyone enter the
strong man's house
and carry off his
property, unless
he first binds the
strong *man?* And
then he will plun-
der his house.

The Unpardonable Sin

30He who is not
with Me is against
Me; and he who
does not gather
with Me scatters.
31"Therefore I say
to you, any sin and
blasphemy shall be
forgiven people,

NIV

but blasphemy
against the Spirit
will not be for-
given. 32 Anyone
who speaks a word
against the Son
of Man will be
forgiven, but any-
one who speaks
against the Holy
Spirit will not be
forgiven, either in
this age or in the
age to come.
33 "Make a tree
good and its fruit
will be good, or
make a tree bad
and its fruit will
be bad, for a tree is
recognized by its
fruit. 34 You brood
of vipers, how
can you who are
evil say anything
good? For the
mouth speaks what
the heart is full
of. 35 A good man
brings good things
out of the good
stored up in him,
and an evil man
brings evil things
out of the evil
stored up in him.
36 But I tell you that
everyone will have
to give account on
the day of judg-
ment for every
empty word they
have spoken. 37 For
by your words you
will be acquitted,
and by your words
you will be con-
demned."

The Sign of Jonah

38 Then some of
the Pharisees and
teachers of the
law said to him,
"Teacher, we want
to see a sign from
you."

ἡ δὲ τοῦ πνεύματος βλασφημία ↱ οὐκ ἀφεθήσεται. 32 καὶ
but the *but* blasphemy ⌊against the⌋ Spirit *blasphemy* will not be forgiven. And
1254 3836 1254 1060 3836 4460 1060 918 4024 918 2779
d.nsf cj d.gsn n.gsn n.nsf adv v.fpi.3s cj

⌊ὃς ἐὰν⌋ εἴπῃ λόγον κατὰ τοῦ υἱοῦ τοῦ ἀνθρώπου, ἀφεθήσεται αὐτῷ·
whoever speaks a word against the Son of Man will be forgiven; *{to him}* but
4005 1569 3306 3364 2848 3836 5626 3836 476 918 899 1254
r.nsm pl v.aas.3s n.asm p.g d.gsm n.gsm d.gsm n.gsm v.fpi.3s r.dsm.3

ὃς δ᾽ ἂν εἴπῃ κατὰ τοῦ πνεύματος τοῦ ἁγίου, ↱ οὐκ ἀφεθήσεται
whoever *but* ~ speaks against the Holy Spirit *{the} Holy* will not be forgiven,
4005 1254 323 3306 2848 3836 41 4460 3836 41 918 4024 918
r.nsm cj pl v.aas.3s p.g d.gsn n.gsn d.gsn a.gsn adv v.fpi.3s

αὐτῷ οὔτε ἐν τούτῳ τῷ αἰῶνι οὔτε ἐν τῷ ↰ μέλλοντι. 33 ἢ ποιήσατε
{to him} neither in this *{the}* age nor in the age to come. "Either make
899 4046 1877 4047 3836 172 4046 1877 3836 172 3516 2445 4472
r.dsm.3 cj p.d r.dsm d.dsm n.dsm cj p.d d.dsm pt.pa.dsm cj v.aam.2p

τὸ δένδρον καλὸν καὶ τὸν καρπὸν αὐτοῦ καλόν, ἢ ποιήσατε τὸ δένδρον
the tree good and *{the}* its fruit *its* good, or make the tree
3836 1285 2819 2779 3836 899 2843 899 2819 2445 4472 3836 1285
d.asn n.asn a.asn cj d.asm n.asm r.gsn.3 a.asm cj v.aam.2p d.asn n.asn

σαπρὸν καὶ τὸν καρπὸν αὐτοῦ σαπρόν· ἐκ γὰρ τοῦ
rotten and *{the}* its fruit *its* rotten; *by* for the tree is known by its
4911 2779 3836 899 2843 899 4911 1666 1142 3836 1285 1182 1182 1666 3836
a.asn cj d.asm n.asm r.gsn.3 a.asm p.g cj d.gsm

καρποῦ τὸ δένδρον γινώσκεται. 34 γεννήματα ἐχιδνῶν, πῶς δύνασθε
fruit. *the tree is known* You offspring of snakes! How can you, being evil, speak
2843 3836 1285 1182 1165 2399 4802 1538 1639 4505 3281
n.gsm d.nsn n.nsn v.ppi.3s n.vpn n.gpf cj v.ppi.2p

ἀγαθὰ λαλεῖν πονηροὶ ὄντες; ἐκ γὰρ τοῦ περισσεύματος τῆς καρδίας
good things? *speak evil being* For ⌊out of⌋ *For* the abundance of the heart
19 3281 4505 1639 1142 1666 1142 3836 4354 3836 2840
a.apn f.pa a.npm pt.pa.npm p.g cj d.gsn n.gsn d.gsf n.gsf

τὸ στόμα λαλεῖ. 35 ὁ ἀγαθὸς ἄνθρωπος ἐκ τοῦ ἀγαθοῦ
the mouth speaks. The good man brings good things ⌊out of⌋ his good
3836 5125 3281 3836 19 476 1675 19 19 1666 3836 19
d.nsn n.nsn v.pai.3s d.nsm a.nsm n.nsm p.g d.gsm a.gsm

θησαυροῦ ἐκβάλλει ἀγαθά, καὶ ὁ πονηρὸς ἄνθρωπος ἐκ τοῦ
treasure, *brings good things* and the evil man brings evil things ⌊out of⌋ his
2565 1675 19 2779 3836 4505 476 1675 4505 4505 1666 3836
n.gsm v.pai.3s a.apn cj d.nsm a.nsm n.nsm p.g d.gsm

πονηροῦ θησαυροῦ ἐκβάλλει πονηρά. 36 λέγω δὲ ὑμῖν ὅτι
evil treasure. *brings evil things* But I say *But* to you that on the day of
4505 2565 1675 4505 1254 3306 1254 7007 4022 1877 2465 3213
a.gsm n.gsm v.pai.3s a.apn v.pai.1s cj r.dp.2 cj

πᾶν ῥῆμα ἀργὸν ὃ λαλήσουσιν οἱ
judgment, people will give an account for every careless word *careless {that}* they speak. *{the}*
3213 476 625 625 3364 4246 734 4839 734 4005 3281 3836
a.asn n.asn a.asn r.asn v.fai.3p d.npm

ἄνθρωποι ἀποδώσουσιν περὶ αὐτοῦ λόγον ἐν ἡμέρᾳ κρίσεως· 37 ἐκ γὰρ τῶν
people will give {about} {it} account on day of judgment For by *For {the}*
476 625 4309 899 3364 1877 2465 3213 1142 1666 1142 3836
n.npm v.fai.3p p.g r.gsn.3 n.asm p.d n.dsf n.gsf p.g cj d.gpm

λόγων σου δικαιωθήσῃ, καὶ ἐκ τῶν λόγων σου καταδικασθήσῃ.
your words *your* you will be justified, and by *{the}* your words *your* you will be condemned."
5148 3364 5148 1467 2779 1666 3836 5148 3364 5148 2868
n.gpm r.gs.2 v.fpi.2s cj p.g d.gpm n.gpm r.gs.2 v.fpi.2s

38 τότε ἀπεκρίθησαν αὐτῷ τινες τῶν γραμματέων καὶ Φαρισαίων
Then *answered him* some of the scribes and Pharisees answered him,
5538 646 899 5516 3836 1208 2779 5757 646 899
adv v.api.3p r.dsm.3 r.npm d.gpm n.gpm cj n.gpm

λέγοντες, διδάσκαλε, θέλομεν ἀπὸ σοῦ σημεῖον ἰδεῖν. 39 ὁ δὲ
saying, "Teacher, we wish to see a sign from you." *sign to see* But he *But*
3306 1437 2527 1625 1625 4956 608 5148 4956 1625 1254 3836 1254
pt.pa.npm n.vsm v.pai.1p p.g r.gs.2 n.asn f.aa d.nsm cj

NASB

but blasphemy
against the Spirit
shall not be for-
given. 32 Who-
ever speaks a word
against the Son of
Man, it shall be
forgiven him; but
whoever speaks
against the Holy
Spirit, it shall not
be forgiven him,
either in this age or
in the *age* to come.

Words Reveal Character

33 "Either make the
tree good and its
fruit good, or make
the tree bad and
its fruit bad; for
the tree is known
by its fruit. 34 You
brood of vipers,
how can you, being
evil, speak what
is good? For the
mouth speaks out
of that which fills
the heart. 35 The
good man brings
out of *his* good
treasure what is
good; and the evil
man brings out of
his evil treasure
what is evil. 36 But
I tell you that ev-
ery careless word
that people speak,
they shall give
an accounting for
it in the day of
judgment. 37 For by
your words you
will be justified,
and by your words
you will be con-
demned."

The Desire for Signs

38 Then some of
the scribes and
Pharisees said to
Him, "Teacher, we
want to see a sign
from You." 39 But

NIV

[39]He answered,
"A wicked and
adulterous gen-
eration asks for
a sign! But none
will be given it
except the sign of
the prophet Jonah.
[40]For as Jonah was
three days and
three nights in the
belly of a huge
fish, so the Son of
Man will be three
days and three
nights in the heart
of the earth. [41]The
men of Nineveh
will stand up at
the judgment with
this generation
and condemn it;
for they repented
at the preaching
of Jonah, and now
something greater
than Jonah is here.
[42]The Queen of the
South will rise at
the judgment with
this generation and
condemn it; for
she came from the
ends of the earth to
listen to Solomon's
wisdom, and now
something greater
than Solomon is
here.
[43]"When an im-
pure spirit comes
out of a person, it
goes through arid
places seeking rest
and does not find
it. [44]Then it says, 'I
will return to the
house I left.' When
it arrives, it finds
the house unoccu-
pied, swept clean
and put in order.
[45]Then it goes and
takes with it seven
other spirits more
wicked than itself,
and they go in and
live there. And the
final condition of
that person is

ἀποκριθεὶς εἶπεν αὐτοῖς, γενεὰ πονηρὰ καὶ μοιχαλὶς
answered {he said} them, "An evil and adulterous generation *evil* *and* *adulterous* asks
646 3306 899 4505 2779 3655 1155 4505 2779 3655 2118
pt.ap.nsm v.aai.3s r.dpm.3 n.nsf a.nsf cj a.nsf

σημεῖον ἐπιζητεῖ, καὶ σημεῖον οὐ δοθήσεται αὐτῇ ⸤εἰ μὴ⸥ τὸ σημεῖον
for a sign, *asks for* but no sign *no* will be given to it except the sign
2118 4956 2118 2779 4024 4956 4024 1443 899 1623 3590 3836 4956
n.asn v.pai.3s cj n.nsn adv v.fpi.3s r.dsf.3 cj pl d.nsn n.nsn

Ἰωνᾶ τοῦ προφήτου. 40 ὥσπερ γὰρ ἦν Ἰωνᾶς ἐν τῇ κοιλίᾳ τοῦ
of Jonah the prophet. For just as *For* Jonah was *Jonah* in the belly of the
2731 3836 4737 1142 6061 1142 2731 1639 2731 1877 3836 3120 3836
n.gsm d.gsm n.gsm cj cj v.iai.3s n.nsm p.d d.dsf n.dsf d.gsn

κήτους τρεῖς ἡμέρας καὶ τρεῖς νύκτας, οὕτως ἔσται ὁ υἱὸς τοῦ ἀνθρώπου ↰
great fish for three days and three nights, so will the Son of Man be
3063 5552 2465 2779 5552 3816 4048 1639 3836 5626 3836 476 1639
n.gsn a.apf n.apf cj a.apf n.apf adv v.fmi.3s d.nsm n.nsm d.gsm n.gsm

ἐν τῇ καρδίᾳ τῆς γῆς τρεῖς ἡμέρας καὶ τρεῖς νύκτας. 41 ἄνδρες Νινευῖται
in the heart of the earth for three days and three nights. The men of Nineveh
1877 3836 2840 3836 1178 5552 2465 2779 5552 3816 467 3780
p.d d.dsf n.dsf d.gsf n.gsf a.apf n.apf cj a.apf n.apf n.npm n.npm

ἀναστήσονται ἐν τῇ κρίσει μετὰ τῆς γενεᾶς ταύτης καὶ κατακρινοῦσιν
will stand up at the judgment with *{the}* this generation *this* and condemn
482 1877 3836 3213 3552 3836 4047 1155 4047 2779 2891
v.fmi.3p p.d d.dsf n.dsf p.g d.gsf n.gsf r.gsf cj v.fai.3p

αὐτήν, ὅτι μετενόησαν εἰς τὸ κήρυγμα Ἰωνᾶ, καὶ ἰδοὺ πλεῖον Ἰωνᾶ
it, for they repented at the preaching of Jonah; and look, ⸤something greater⸥ than Jonah
899 4022 3566 1650 3836 3060 2731 2779 2627 4498 2731
r.asf.3 cj v.aai.3p p.a d.asn n.asn n.gsm cj j a.nsn.c n.gsm

ὧδε. 42 βασίλισσα → νότου ἐγερθήσεται ἐν τῇ κρίσει μετὰ τῆς
is here! The queen of the South will rise up at the judgment with *{the}* this
6045 999 3803 1586 1877 3836 3213 3552 3836 4047
adv n.nsf n.gsm v.fpi.3s p.d d.dsf n.dsf p.g d.gsf

γενεᾶς ταύτης καὶ κατακρινεῖ αὐτήν, ὅτι ἦλθεν ἐκ τῶν περάτων τῆς γῆς
generation *this* and condemn it, because she came from the ends of the earth
1155 4047 2779 2891 899 4022 2262 1666 3836 4306 3836 1178
n.gsf r.gsf cj v.fai.3s r.asf.3 cj v.aai.3s p.g d.gpn n.gpn d.gsf n.gsf

ἀκοῦσαι τὴν σοφίαν Σολομῶνος, καὶ ἰδοὺ πλεῖον Σολομῶνος ὧδε.
to hear the wisdom of Solomon; and look, ⸤something greater⸥ than Solomon is here!
201 3836 5053 5048 2779 2627 4498 5048 6045
f.aa d.asf n.asf n.gsm cj j a.nsn.c n.gsm adv

43 ὅταν δὲ τὸ ἀκάθαρτον πνεῦμα ἐξέλθῃ ἀπὸ τοῦ ἀνθρώπου, διέρχεται δι'
"When *{and}* an unclean spirit comes out of a person, it wanders through
4020 1254 3836 176 4460 2002 608 3836 476 1451 1328
cj cj d.nsn a.nsn n.nsn v.aas.3s p.g d.gsm n.gsm v.pmi.3s p.g

ἀνύδρων τόπων ζητοῦν ἀνάπαυσιν καὶ οὐχ εὑρίσκει. 44 τότε λέγει,
waterless regions ⸤in search of⸥ a resting place, but finds none. *finds* Then it says, 'I
536 5536 2426 398 2779 2351 4024 2351 5538 3306 2188
a.gpm n.gpm pt.pa.nsn n.asf cj adv v.pai.3s adv v.pai.3s

εἰς τὸν οἶκόν μου ἐπιστρέψω ὅθεν ἐξῆλθον· καὶ ἐλθὸν
will return to *{the}* my house *my* *I will return* ⸤from which⸥ I came.' And ⸤when it arrives,⸥
2188 2188 1650 3836 1609 3875 1609 2188 3854 2002 2779 2262
p.a d.asm n.asm r.gs.1 v.fai.1s cj v.aai.1s cj pt.aa.nsn

εὑρίσκει σχολάζοντα σεσαρωμένον καὶ κεκοσμημένον. 45 τότε πορεύεται καὶ
it finds the house unoccupied, swept, and put in order. Then it goes and
2351 5390 4924 2779 3175 5538 4513 2779
v.pai.3s pt.pa.asm pt.rp.asm cj pt.rp.asm adv v.pmi.3s cj

παραλαμβάνει μεθ' ἑαυτοῦ ἑπτὰ ἕτερα πνεύματα πονηρότερα ἑαυτοῦ καὶ εἰσελθόντα
brings along with it seven other spirits more evil than itself, and they enter
4161 3552 1571 2231 2283 4460 4505 1571 2779 1656
v.pai.3s p.g r.gsn.3 a.apn r.apn n.apn a.apn.c r.gsn.3 cj pt.aa.npn

κατοικεῖ ἐκεῖ· καὶ γίνεται τὰ ἔσχατα τοῦ ἀνθρώπου ἐκείνου
and settle down there; and *turns out to be* the last state of that person *that* turns out
2997 1695 2779 1181 3836 2274 3836 1697 476 1697 1181 1181
v.pai.3s adv cj v.pmi.3s d.npn a.npn d.gsm n.gsm r.gsm

NASB

He answered and
said to them, "An
evil and adulter-
ous generation
craves for a sign;
and *yet* no sign
will be given to
it but the sign of
Jonah the prophet;
[40]for just as JONAH
WAS THREE DAYS
AND THREE NIGHTS
IN THE BELLY OF
THE SEA MONSTER,
so will the Son of
Man be three days
and three nights
in the heart of the
earth. [41]The men
of Nineveh will
stand up with this
generation at the
judgment, and will
condemn it because
they repented at the
preaching of Jonah;
and behold, some-
thing greater than
Jonah is here. [42]*The*
Queen of *the* South
will rise up with
this generation at
the judgment and
will condemn it,
because she came
from the ends of
the earth to hear
the wisdom of Sol-
omon; and behold,
something greater
than Solomon is
here.
[43]"Now when
the unclean spirit
goes out of a man,
it passes through
waterless places
seeking rest, and
does not find *it*.
[44]Then it says, 'I
will return to my
house from which
I came'; and when
it comes, it finds *it*
unoccupied, swept,
and put in order.
[45]Then it goes and
takes along with it
seven other spirits
more wicked than
itself, and they go
in and live there;
and the last state of
that man becomes

NIV

worse than the
first. That is how
it will be with this
wicked genera-
tion."

Jesus' Mother and Brothers

[46]While Jesus
was still talking
to the crowd, his
mother and broth-
ers stood outside,
wanting to speak
to him. [47]Someone
told him, "Your
mother and broth-
ers are standing
outside, wanting to
speak to you."
[48]He replied to
him, "Who is my
mother, and who
are my brothers?"
[49]Pointing to his
disciples, he said,
"Here are my
mother and my
brothers. [50]For
whoever does the
will of my Father
in heaven is my
brother and sister
and mother."

The Parable of the Sower

13 That same
day Jesus
went out of the
house and sat by
the lake. [2]Such
large crowds gath-
ered around him
that he got into a
boat and sat in it,
while all the peo-
ple stood on the
shore. [3]Then he
told them many
things in parables,
saying: "A farmer
went out to sow
his seed. [4]As he
was scattering the
seed, some fell
along the path, and
the birds came and
ate it up. [5]Some
fell on rocky plac-
es, where it

χείρονα τῶν πρώτων. οὕτως ἔσται καὶ τῇ
to be worse ⌊than the⌋ first. So ⌊will it be⌋ for this evil generation as well." *for*
1181 1181 5937 3836 4755 4048 1639 3836 4047 4505 1155 2779 3836
a.npn.c d.gpn a.gpn adv v.fmi.3s cj d.dsf

γενεᾷ ταύτῃ τῇ πονηρᾷ. [46]ἔτι ↱ αὐτοῦ → λαλοῦντος τοῖς ὄχλοις
generation this {the} evil *still* While he was still speaking to the people,
1155 4047 3836 4505 2285 3281 899 2285 3281 3836 4063
n.dsf r.dsf d.dsf a.dsf adv r.gsm.3 pt.pa.gsm d.dpm n.dpm

ἰδοὺ ἡ μήτηρ καὶ οἱ ἀδελφοὶ αὐτοῦ εἱστήκεισαν ἔξω ζητοῦντες
{behold} {the} his mother and *{the}* his brothers *his* stood outside, wanting to
2627 3836 899 3613 2779 3836 899 81 899 2705 2032 2426 3281
j d.nsf n.nsf cj d.npm n.npm r.gsm.3 v.lai.3p adv pt.pa.npm

αὐτῷ λαλῆσαι. [48]ὁ δὲ ἀποκριθεὶς εἶπεν τῷ λέγοντι αὐτῷ,
speak to him. *to speak* But he *But* answered, saying ⌊to the⌋ ⌊one who had told⌋ him,
3281 899 3281 1254 3836 1254 646 3306 3836 3306 899
r.dsm.3 f.aa d.nsm cj pt.ap.nsm v.aai.3s d.dsm pt.pa.dsm r.dsm.3

τίς ἐστιν ἡ μήτηρ μου καὶ τίνες εἰσὶν οἱ ἀδελφοί μου; [49]καὶ
"Who is *{the}* my mother? *my* And who are *{the}* my brothers?" *my* And
5515 1639 3836 1609 3613 1609 2779 5515 1639 3836 1609 81 1609 2779
r.nsf v.pai.3s d.nsf n.nsf r.gs.1 cj r.npm v.pai.3p d.npm n.npm r.gs.1 cj

ἐκτείνας τὴν χεῖρα αὐτοῦ ἐπὶ τοὺς μαθητὰς αὐτοῦ εἶπεν, ἰδοὺ
⌊stretching out⌋ *{the}* his hand *his* toward *{the}* his disciples, *his* he said, "Look, here are
1753 3836 899 5931 899 2093 3836 899 3412 899 3306 2627
pt.aa.nsm d.asf n.asf r.gsm.3 p.a d.apm n.apm r.gsm.3 v.aai.3s j

ἡ μήτηρ μου καὶ οἱ ἀδελφοί μου. [50]ὅστις γὰρ ἂν ποιήσῃ τὸ
{the} my mother *my* and *{the}* my brothers! *my* For whoever *For* ~ does the
3836 1609 3613 1609 2779 3836 1609 81 1609 1142 4015 1142 323 4472 3836
d.nsf n.nsf r.gs.1 cj d.npm n.npm r.gs.1 r.nsm cj pl v.aas.3s d.asn

θέλημα τοῦ πατρός μου τοῦ ἐν οὐρανοῖς αὐτός μου ἀδελφὸς καὶ ἀδελφὴ
will of my Father *my {the}* in heaven, he is my brother and sister
2525 3836 1609 4252 1609 3836 1877 4041 899 1639 1609 81 2779 80
n.asn d.gsm n.gsm r.gs.1 d.gsm p.d n.dpm r.nsm r.gs.1 n.nsm cj n.nsf

καὶ μήτηρ ἐστίν.
and mother." *is*
2779 3613 1639
cj n.nsf v.pai.3s

13:1 ἐν τῇ ἡμέρᾳ ἐκείνῃ ἐξελθὼν ὁ Ἰησοῦς τῆς οἰκίας
That same *{the}* day *That* Jesus went out *{the} Jesus* of the house and
1697 1877 3836 2465 1697 2652 2002 3836 2652 3836 3864
p.d d.dsf n.dsf r.dsf pt.aa.nsm d.nsm n.nsm d.gsf n.gsf

ἐκάθητο παρὰ τὴν θάλασσαν· [2]καὶ συνήχθησαν πρὸς αὐτὸν ὄχλοι
was sitting by the sea. And great crowds gathered around him *crowds*
2764 4123 3836 2498 2779 4498 4063 5251 4639 899 4063
v.imi.3s p.a d.asf n.asf cj v.api.3p p.a r.asm.3 n.npm

πολλοί, ὥστε αὐτὸν εἰς πλοῖον ἐμβάντα καθῆσθαι, καὶ πᾶς ὁ ὄχλος
great so that he got into a boat *got* and sat down, and all the crowd
4498 6063 899 1832 1650 4450 1832 2764 2779 4246 3836 4063
a.npm cj r.asm.3 p.a n.asn pt.aa.asm f.pm cj a.nsm d.nsm n.nsm

ἐπὶ τὸν αἰγιαλὸν εἱστήκει. [3]καὶ ἐλάλησεν αὐτοῖς πολλὰ ἐν παραβολαῖς
stood on the beach. *stood* And he told them many things in parables,
2705 2093 3836 129 2705 2779 3281 899 4498 1877 4130
p.a d.asm n.asm v.lai.3s cj v.aai.3s r.dpm.3 a.apn p.d n.dpf

λέγων, ἰδοὺ ἐξῆλθεν ὁ σπείρων τοῦ σπείρειν. [4]καὶ ἐν τῷ
saying: *{behold}* "A sower went out *{the} sower* to sow. And as *{the}* he
3306 2627 5062 2002 3836 5062 3836 5062 2779 1877 3836 899
pt.pa.nsm j v.aai.3s d.nsm pt.pa.nsm d.gsn f.pa cj p.d d.dsn

σπείρειν αὐτὸν ἃ μὲν ἔπεσεν παρὰ τὴν ὁδόν, καὶ ἐλθόντα τὰ
sowed, *he* some ~ seeds fell along the path, and the birds came *the*
5062 899 4005 3525 4406 4123 3836 3847 2779 3836 4374 2262 3836
f.pa r.asm.3 r.npn pl v.aai.3s p.a d.asf n.asf cj pt.aa.npn d.npn

πετεινὰ κατέφαγεν αὐτά. [5]ἄλλα δὲ ἔπεσεν ἐπὶ τὰ πετρώδη ὅπου ↱
birds and devoured them. Other *{and}* seed fell on *{the}* rocky places, where it
4374 2983 899 257 1254 4406 2093 3836 4378 3963 2400
n.npn v.aai.3s r.apn.3 r.npn pl v.aai.3s p.a d.apn n.apn cj

NASB

worse than the first.
That is the way it
will also be with
this evil genera-
tion."

Changed Relationships

[46]While He was
still speaking to
the crowds, be-
hold, His mother
and brothers
were standing
outside, seeking
to speak to Him.
[47]Someone said
to Him, "Behold,
Your mother and
Your brothers are
standing outside
seeking to speak to
You." [48]But Jesus
answered the one
who was telling
Him and said,
"Who is My moth-
er and who are My
brothers?" [49]And
stretching out His
hand toward His
disciples, He said,
"Behold My moth-
er and My broth-
ers! [50]For whoever
does the will of My
Father who is in
heaven, he is My
brother and sister
and mother."

Jesus Teaches in Parables

[13:1]That day Jesus
went out of the
house and was
sitting by the sea.
[2]And large crowds
gathered to Him, so
He got into a boat
and sat down, and
the whole crowd
was standing on
the beach.
[3]And He spoke
many things to
them in parables,
saying, "Behold,
the sower went out
to sow; [4]and as he
sowed, some *seeds*
fell beside the
road, and the birds
came and ate them
up. [5]Others fell on
the rocky places,
where they

NIV

did not have much
soil. It sprang up
quickly, because
the soil was shal-
low. 6But when
the sun came up,
the plants were
scorched, and they
withered because
they had no root.
7Other seed fell
among thorns,
which grew up and
choked the plants.
8Still other seed
fell on good soil,
where it produced
a crop—a hun-
dred, sixty or thir-
ty times what was
sown. 9Whoever
has ears, let them
hear."
10The disciples
came to him and
asked, "Why do
you speak to the
people in para-
bles?"
11He replied,
"Because the
knowledge of the
secrets of the king-
dom of heaven has
been given to you,
but not to them.
12Whoever has will
be given more, and
they will have an
abundance. Who-
ever does not have,
even what they
have will be taken
from them. 13This
is why I speak to
them in parables:

"Though seeing,
they do not
see;
though hearing,
they do
not hear or
understand.

14In them is ful-
filled the prophecy
of Isaiah:

"'You will be ever
hearing but
never under-
standing;
you will be
ever seeing
but never
perceiving.

↱ οὐκ εἶχεν γῆν πολλήν, καὶ εὐθέως ἐξανέτειλεν διὰ τὸ μὴ
did not have much soil; *much* and immediately it sprouted because *{the}* it had no
2400 4024 2400 4498 1178 4498 2779 2311 1984 1328 3836 2400 3590
adv v.iai.3s n.asf a.asf cj adv v.aai.3s p.a d.asn pl

ἔχειν βάθος γῆς· 6 ↱ ἡλίου δὲ ἀνατείλαντος ἐκαυματίσθη καὶ διὰ
had depth of soil. But when the sun *But* came up it was scorched; and because
2400 958 1178 1254 422 2463 1254 422 3009 2779 1328
f.pa n.asn n.gsf n.gsm cj pt.aa.gsm v.api.3s cj p.a

τὸ μὴ ἔχειν ῥίζαν ἐξηράνθη. 7 ἄλλα δὲ ἔπεσεν ἐπὶ τὰς
{the} it had no *had* root, ⌊it withered away.⌋ Other *{and}* seed fell among *{the}*
3836 2400 3590 2400 4844 3830 257 1254 4406 2093 3836
d.asn pl f.pa n.asf v.api.3s r.npn pl v.aai.3s p.a d.apf

ἀκάνθας, καὶ ἀνέβησαν αἱ ἄκανθαι καὶ ἔπνιξαν αὐτά. 8 ἄλλα δὲ
thorns, and the thorns grew up *the thorns* and choked it. Other *{and}* seed
180 2779 3836 180 326 3836 180 2779 4464 899 257 1254
n.apf cj v.aai.3p d.npf n.npf cj v.aai.3p r.apn.3 r.npn pl

ἔπεσεν ἐπὶ τὴν γῆν τὴν καλὴν καὶ ἐδίδου καρπόν, ὃ μὲν ἑκατόν, ὃ
fell on *{the}* good soil *{the} good* and produced grain, some ~ a hundredfold, some
4406 2093 3836 2819 1178 3836 2819 2779 1443 2843 4005 3525 1669 4005
v.aai.3s p.a d.asf n.asf d.asf a.asf cj v.iai.3s n.asm r.nsn pl a.apm r.nsn

δὲ ἑξήκοντα, ὃ δὲ τριάκοντα. 9 ὁ ἔχων ὦτα ἀκουέτω. 10 καὶ
{and} sixty, and some *and* thirty. He ⌊who has⌋ ears, let him hear!" And the
1254 2008 1254 4005 1254 5558 3836 2400 4044 201 2779 3836
pl a.apm r.nsn pl a.apm d.nsm pt.pa.nsm n.apn v.pam.3s cj

προσελθόντες οἱ μαθηταὶ εἶπαν αὐτῷ, ⌊διὰ τί⌋
disciples came *the disciples* to him and said, *to him* "Why do you speak
3412 4665 3836 3412 899 899 3306 899 1328 5515 3281 3281 3281
pt.aa.npm d.npm n.npm v.aai.3p r.dsm.3 p.a r.asn

ἐν παραβολαῖς λαλεῖς αὐτοῖς; 11 ὁ δὲ ἀποκριθεὶς εἶπεν
to them in parables?" *do you speak to them* He *{and}* answered them, saying,
899 899 1877 4130 3281 899 3836 1254 646 899 3306
p.d n.dpf v.pai.2s r.dpm.3 d.nsm cj pt.ap.nsm v.aai.3s

αὐτοῖς, ὅτι ὑμῖν δέδοται γνῶναι τὰ μυστήρια τῆς βασιλείας τῶν
them "Because to you ⌊it has been given⌋ to know the mysteries of the kingdom of
899 4022 7007 1443 1182 3836 3696 3836 993 3836
r.dpm.3 cj r.dp.2 v.rpi.3s f.aa d.apn n.apn d.gsf n.gsf d.gpm

οὐρανῶν, ἐκείνοις δὲ ↱ ↱ οὐ δέδοται. 12 ὅστις γὰρ ἔχει,
heaven, but to them *but* it has not been given. For to the one who *For* has,
4041 1254 1697 1254 1443 1443 4024 1443 1142 899 899 4015 1142 2400
n.gpm r.dpm cj adv v.rpi.3s r.nsm cj v.pai.3s

δοθήσεται αὐτῷ καὶ περισσευθήσεται· ὅστις δὲ ↱ οὐκ
more will be given, *to one* and he will have an abundance; but from the one who *but* does not
1443 899 2779 4355 1254 608 899 4015 1254 2400 4024
v.fpi.3s r.dsm.3 cj v.fpi.3s r.nsm cj adv

ἔχει, καὶ ὃ ἔχει ἀρθήσεται ἀπ᾽ αὐτοῦ. 13 ⌊διὰ τοῦτο⌋
have, even what he has ⌊will be taken away.⌋ *from one* This is why I speak to
2400 2779 4005 2400 149 608 899 1328 4047 3281 3281 899
v.pai.3s adv r.asn v.pai.3s v.fpi.3s p.g r.gsm.3 p.a r.asn

ἐν παραβολαῖς αὐτοῖς λαλῶ, ὅτι βλέποντες ↱ ↱ οὐ βλέπουσιν καὶ
them in parables, *to them I speak* because seeing they do not see and
899 1877 4130 899 3281 4022 1063 1063 1063 4024 1063 2779
p.d n.dpf r.dpm.3 v.pai.1s cj pt.pa.npm adv v.pai.3p cj

ἀκούοντες ↱ ↱ οὐκ ἀκούουσιν οὐδὲ συνίουσιν, 14 καὶ ἀναπληροῦται αὐτοῖς
hearing they do not hear nor do they understand. And *is being fulfilled* in them
201 201 201 4024 201 4028 5317 2779 405 899
pt.pa.npm adv v.pai.3p cj v.pai.3p cj v.ppi.3s r.dpm.3

ἡ προφητεία Ἠσαΐου ἡ λέγουσα, ↱ ↱ ἀκοῇ ἀκούσετε καὶ
the prophecy of Isaiah is being fulfilled that says: 'You will surely hear but
3836 4735 2480 405 405 405 3836 3306 201 201 198 201 2779
d.nsf n.nsf n.gsm d.nsf pt.pa.nsf n.dsf v.fai.2p cj

⌊οὐ μὴ⌋ συνῆτε, καὶ ↱ ↱ βλέποντες βλέψετε καὶ ⌊οὐ μὴ⌋ ἴδητε.
never understand, and you will surely see but never perceive.
4024 3590 5317 2779 1063 1063 1063 1063 2779 4024 3590 1625
adv pl v.aas.2p cj pt.pa.npm v.fai.2p cj adv pl v.aas.2p

NASB

did not have much
soil; and immedi-
ately they sprang
up, because they
had no depth of
soil. 6But when the
sun had risen, they
were scorched;
and because they
had no root, they
withered away.
7Others fell among
the thorns, and the
thorns came up and
choked them out.
8And others fell on
the good soil and
*yielded a crop,
some a hundred-
fold, some sixty,
and some thirty.
9He who has ears,
let him hear."

An Explanation

10And the dis-
ciples came and
said to Him, "Why
do You speak to
them in parables?"
11Jesus answered
them, "To you it
has been granted to
know the myster-
ies of the kingdom
of heaven, but to
them it has not
been granted. 12For
whoever has, to
him *more* shall be
given, and he will
have an abundance;
but whoever does
not have, even
what he has shall
be taken away from
him. 13Therefore I
speak to them in
parables; because
while seeing they
do not see, and
while hearing they
do not hear, nor do
they understand.
14In their case the
prophecy of Isaiah
is being fulfilled,
which says,

'YOU WILL KEEP
ON HEARING,
BUT WILL NOT
UNDERSTAND;
YOU WILL KEEP
ON SEEING,
BUT WILL NOT
PERCEIVE;

NIV

[15] For this people's
heart has
become
calloused;
they hardly
hear with
their ears,
and they have
closed their
eyes.
Otherwise they
might see
with their
eyes,
hear with their
ears,
understand with
their hearts
and turn, and I
would heal
them.'[a]

[16] But blessed are
your eyes because
they see, and your
ears because they
hear. [17] For truly
I tell you, many
prophets and
righteous people
longed to see what
you see but did not
see it, and to hear
what you hear but
did not hear it.
[18] "Listen then
to what the para-
ble of the sower
means: [19] When
anyone hears the
message about the
kingdom and does
not understand it,
the evil one comes
and snatches away
what was sown in
their heart. This
is the seed sown
along the path.
[20] The seed falling
on rocky ground
refers to some-
one who hears the
word and at once
receives it with
joy. [21] But since
they have no root,
they last only a
short time. When
trouble or perse-
cution comes be-
cause of the word,
they quickly

[a] 15 Isaiah 6:9,10
(see Septuagint)

---

15 ἐπαχύνθη γὰρ ἡ καρδία τοῦ λαοῦ τούτου, καὶ τοῖς
has become dull For the heart of this people *this* has become dull, and ⌊with their⌋
4266 1142 3836 2840 3836 4047 3295 4047 4266 4266 4266 2779 3836
v.api.3s cj d.nsf n.nsf d.gsm n.gsm r.gsm cj d.dpn

ὠσὶν ↱ βαρέως ἤκουσαν καὶ τοὺς ὀφθαλμοὺς αὐτῶν ἐκάμμυσαν, μήποτε
ears they scarcely hear, and *{the}* their eyes *their* they have closed, lest
4044 201 977 201 2779 3836 899 4057 899 2826 3607
n.dpn adv v.aai.3p cj d.apm n.apm r.gpm.3 v.aai.3p cj

ἴδωσιν τοῖς ὀφθαλμοῖς καὶ τοῖς ὠσὶν ἀκούσωσιν καὶ
⌊they should see⌋ ⌊with their⌋ eyes and hear ⌊with their⌋ ears *hear* and understand
1625 3836 4057 2779 201 3836 4044 201 2779 5317
v.aas.3p d.dpm n.dpm cj d.dpn n.dpn v.aas.3p cj

τῇ καρδίᾳ συνῶσιν καὶ ἐπιστρέψωσιν καὶ ἰάσομαι αὐτούς. 16
⌊with their⌋ hearts *understand* and turn, and I would heal them.' But blessed are
3836 2840 5317 2779 2188 2779 2615 899 1254 3421
d.dsf n.dsf v.aas.3p cj v.aas.3p cj v.fmi.1s r.apm.3

ὑμῶν δὲ μακάριοι οἱ ὀφθαλμοὶ ὅτι βλέπουσιν καὶ τὰ ὦτα ὑμῶν ὅτι
your *But* *blessed* *{the}* eyes, because they see, and *{the}* your ears, *your* because
7007 1254 3421 3836 4057 4022 1063 2779 3836 7007 4044 7007 4022
r.gp.2 cj a.npm d.npm n.npm cj v.pai.3p cj d.npn n.npn r.gp.2 cj

ἀκούουσιν. 17 ἀμὴν γὰρ λέγω ὑμῖν ὅτι πολλοὶ προφῆται καὶ
they hear. I tell you the truth, *{for}* *I tell* *you* *{that}* many prophets and
201 3306 3306 7007 297 1142 3306 7007 4022 4498 4737 2779
v.pai.3p pl cj v.pai.1s r.dp.2 cj a.npm n.npm cj

δίκαιοι ἐπεθύμησαν ἰδεῖν ἃ βλέπετε καὶ ↱ οὐκ εἶδαν, καὶ
⌊righteous people⌋ longed to see ⌊the things⌋ you are seeing but did not see them, and
1465 2121 1625 4005 1063 2779 1625 4024 1625 2779
a.npm v.aai.3p f.aa r.apn v.pai.2p cj adv v.aai.3p cj

ἀκοῦσαι ἃ ἀκούετε καὶ ↱ οὐκ ἤκουσαν. 18 ὑμεῖς οὖν
to hear ⌊the things⌋ you are hearing but did not hear them. *{you}* "Hear then
201 4005 201 2779 201 4024 201 7007 201 4036
f.aa r.apn v.pai.2p cj adv v.aai.3p r.np.2 cj

ἀκούσατε τὴν παραβολὴν τοῦ σπείραντος. 19 ↱ παντὸς ἀκούοντος τὸν λόγον
Hear the parable of the sower: When anyone hears the message
201 3836 4130 3836 5062 201 4246 201 3836 3364
v.aam.2p d.asf n.asf d.gsm pt.aa.gsm a.gsm pt.pa.gsm d.asm n.asm

τῆς βασιλείας καὶ ↱ μὴ συνιέντος ἔρχεται ὁ πονηρὸς καὶ
of the kingdom and does not understand it, the evil one comes *the* *evil one* and
3836 993 2779 5317 3590 5317 3836 4505 4505 2262 3836 4505 2779
d.gsf n.gsf cj pl pt.pa.gsm v.pmi.3s d.nsm a.nsm cj

ἁρπάζει τὸ ἐσπαρμένον ἐν τῇ καρδίᾳ αὐτοῦ, οὗτός ἐστιν ὁ
⌊snatches away⌋ that which was sown in *{the}* his heart. *his* This is what was
773 3836 5062 1877 3836 899 2840 899 4047 1639 3836 5062
v.pai.3s d.asn pt.rp.asn p.d d.dsf n.dsf r.gsm.3 r.nsm v.pai.3s d.nsm

παρὰ τὴν ὁδὸν σπαρείς. 20 ὁ δὲ ἐπὶ τὰ
sown along the path. *was sown* As for the *As for* one who was sown on *{the}*
5062 4123 3836 3847 5062 1254 1254 3836 1254 5062 5062 5062 5062 2093 3836
p.a d.asf n.asf pt.ap.nsm d.nsm cj p.a d.apn

πετρώδη σπαρείς, οὗτός ἐστιν ὁ τὸν λόγον ἀκούων καὶ
rocky places, *one who was sown* this is the one who hears the message *one who hears* and
4378 5062 4047 1639 3836 201 201 201 3836 3364 201 2779
n.apn pt.ap.nsm r.nsm v.pai.3s d.nsm d.asm n.asm pt.pa.nsm cj

εὐθὺς μετὰ χαρᾶς λαμβάνων αὐτόν, 21 οὐκ ἔχει δὲ
immediately receives it with joy; *receives* *it* yet he has no *he has* *yet*
2318 3284 899 3552 5915 3284 899 1254 2400 2400 4024 2400 1254
adv p.g n.gsf pt.pa.nsm r.asm.3 adv v.pai.3s cj

ῥίζαν ἐν ἑαυτῷ ἀλλὰ πρόσκαιρός ἐστιν, →
root in himself but lasts only a short time, *lasts* and when suffering or persecution
4844 1877 1571 247 1639 4672 1639 1254 2568 2445 1501
n.asf p.d r.dsm.3 cj a.nsm v.pai.3s

γενομένης δὲ θλίψεως ἢ διωγμοῦ διὰ τὸν λόγον εὐθὺς
arises *and* *suffering* *or* *persecution* ⌊on account of⌋ the message, immediately
1181 1254 2568 2445 1501 1328 3836 3364 2318
pt.am.gsf cj n.gsf cj n.gsm p.a d.asm n.asm adv

NASB

[15] FOR THE HEART
OF THIS PEOPLE
HAS BECOME
DULL,
WITH THEIR
EARS THEY
SCARCELY
HEAR,
AND THEY HAVE
CLOSED THEIR
EYES,
OTHERWISE
THEY WOULD
SEE WITH THEIR
EYES,
HEAR WITH
THEIR EARS,
AND UNDER-
STAND WITH
THEIR HEART
AND RETURN,
AND I WOULD
HEAL THEM.'
[16] But blessed are
your eyes, because
they see; and your
ears, because they
hear. [17] For truly
I say to you that
many prophets
and righteous men
desired to see what
you see, and did
not see *it,* and to
hear what you hear,
and did not hear *it.*

The Sower Explained

[18] "Hear then the
parable of the
sower. [19] When
anyone hears the
word of the king-
dom and does not
understand it, the
evil *one* comes
and snatches away
what has been
sown in his heart.
This is the one on
whom seed was
sown beside the
road. [20] The one on
whom seed was
sown on the rocky
places, this is the
man who hears
the word and im-
mediately receives
it with joy; [21] yet he
has no *firm* root in
himself, but is *only*
temporary, and
when affliction or
persecution arises
because of the
word, immediately
he falls away.

NIV

fall away. 22 The
seed falling among
the thorns refers
to someone who
hears the word,
but the worries of
this life and the
deceitfulness of
wealth choke the
word, making it
unfruitful. 23 But
the seed falling on
good soil refers
to someone who
hears the word
and understands
it. This is the one
who produces a
crop, yielding a
hundred, sixty or
thirty times what
was sown."

The Parable of the Weeds

24 Jesus told them
another parable:
"The kingdom of
heaven is like a
man who sowed
good seed in his
field. 25 But while
everyone was
sleeping, his en-
emy came and
sowed weeds
among the wheat,
and went away.
26 When the wheat
sprouted and
formed heads, then
the weeds also ap-
peared.
27 "The owner's
servants came
to him and said,
'Sir, didn't you
sow good seed in
your field? Where
then did the weeds
come from?'
28 " 'An enemy did
this,' he replied.
"The servants
asked him, 'Do
you want us to go
and pull them up?'

σκανδαλίζεται. 22 ὁ δὲ εἰς τὰς ἀκάνθας
he falls away. As for the *As for* one who was sown among *{the}* thorns,
4997 1254 1254 3836 1254 5062 5062 5062 5062 1650 3836 180
v.ppi.3s d.nsm cj p.a d.apf n.apf

σπαρείς, οὗτός ἐστιν ὁ τὸν λόγον ἀκούων, καὶ ἡ
one who was sown this is the one who hears the message, *one who hears* but *{the}* worldly
5062 4047 1639 3836 201 201 201 3836 3364 201 2779 3836 172
pt.ap.nsm r.nsm v.pai.3s d.nsm d.asm n.asm pt.pa.nsm cj d.nsf

μέριμνα τοῦ αἰῶνος καὶ ἡ ἀπάτη τοῦ πλούτου συμπνίγει τὸν λόγον καὶ
anxiety *{the}* *worldly* and the deception of wealth choke the message and it
3533 3836 172 2779 3836 573 3836 4458 5231 3836 3364 2779 1181
n.nsf d.gsm n.gsm cj d.nsf n.nsf d.gsm n.gsm v.pai.3s d.asm n.asm cj

ἄκαρπος γίνεται. 23 ὁ δὲ ἐπὶ τὴν καλὴν γῆν
becomes unfruitful. *it becomes* As for the *As for* one who was sown on *{the}* good soil,
1181 182 1181 1254 1254 3836 1254 5062 5062 5062 5062 2093 3836 2819 1178
a.nsm v.pmi.3s d.nsm cj p.a d.asf a.asf n.asf

σπαρείς, οὗτός ἐστιν ὁ τὸν λόγον ἀκούων καὶ συνιείς,
one who was sown this is the one who hears the message *one who hears* and understands
5062 4047 1639 3836 201 201 201 3836 3364 201 2779 5317
pt.ap.nsm r.nsm v.pai.3s d.nsm d.asm n.asm pt.pa.nsm cj pt.pa.nsm

ὃς δὴ καρποφορεῖ καὶ ποιεῖ ὃ μὲν ἑκατόν, ὃ δὲ ἑξήκοντα,
it, who indeed bears fruit and produces, some ~ a hundredfold, some *{and}* sixty, and
4005 1314 2844 2779 4472 4005 3525 1669 4005 1254 2008 1254
r.nsm pl v.pai.3s cj v.pai.3s r.nsn pl a.apn r.nsn pl a.apn

ὃ δὲ τριάκοντα. 24 ἄλλην παραβολὴν παρέθηκεν αὐτοῖς λέγων,
some *and* thirty." Jesus put another parable *put before* before them, saying:
4005 1254 5558 4192 257 4130 4192 4192 899 3306
r.nsn pl a.apn r.asf n.asf v.aai.3s r.dpm.3 pt.pa.nsm

ὡμοιώθη ἡ βασιλεία τῶν οὐρανῶν ἀνθρώπῳ σπείραντι καλὸν σπέρμα
is like "The kingdom of heaven is like a man sowing good seed
3929 3836 993 3836 4041 3929 3929 476 5062 2819 5065
v.api.3s d.nsf n.nsf d.gpm n.gpm n.dsm pt.aa.dsm a.asn n.asn

ἐν τῷ ἀγρῷ αὐτοῦ. 25 ἐν δὲ τῷ καθεύδειν τοὺς ἀνθρώπους
in *{the}* his field. *his* But while *But* *{the}* everyone was sleeping, *{the}* *everyone*
1877 3836 899 69 899 1254 1877 1254 3836 476 2761 3836 476
p.d d.dsm n.dsm r.gsm.3 p.d cj d.dsn f.pa d.apm n.apm

ἦλθεν αὐτοῦ ὁ ἐχθρὸς καὶ ἐπέσπειρεν ζιζάνια ⌞ἀνὰ μέσον⌟ τοῦ σίτου
his enemy came *his* *{the}* *enemy* and sowed weeds among the wheat
899 2398 2262 899 3836 2398 2779 2178 2429 324 3545 3836 4992
v.aai.3s r.gsm.3 d.nsm a.nsm cj v.aai.3s n.apn p.a n.asn d.gsm n.gsm

καὶ ἀπῆλθεν. 26 ὅτε δὲ ἐβλάστησεν ὁ χόρτος καὶ καρπὸν
and went away. When *{and}* the plants came up *the* *plants* and bore grain,
2779 599 4021 1254 3836 5965 1056 3836 5965 2779 4472 2843
cj v.aai.3s cj cj v.aai.3s d.nsm n.nsm cj n.asm

ἐποίησεν, τότε ἐφάνη καὶ τὰ ζιζάνια. 27 προσελθόντες δὲ οἱ
bore then the weeds appeared as well. *the* *weeds* *came* And the
4472 5538 3836 2429 5743 2779 3836 2429 4665 1254 3836
v.aai.3s adv v.api.3s adv d.npn n.npn pt.aa.npm cj d.npm

δοῦλοι τοῦ οἰκοδεσπότου εἶπον αὐτῷ, κύριε, οὐχὶ καλὸν
servants of the master of the house came and said to him, 'Sir, did you not sow good
1529 3836 3867 4665 3306 899 3261 5062 5062 4049 5062 2819
n.npm d.gsm n.gsm v.aai.3p r.dsm.3 n.vsm pl a.asn

σπέρμα ἔσπειρας ἐν τῷ σῷ ἀγρῷ; πόθεν οὖν ἔχει ζιζάνια; 28 ὁ
seed *did you sow* in *{the}* your field? Why then ⌞does it have⌟ weeds?' And he
5065 5062 1877 3836 5050 69 4470 4036 2400 2429 1254 3836
n.asn v.aai.2s p.d d.dsm r.dsm.2 n.dsm cj cj v.pai.3s n.apn d.nsm

δὲ ἔφη αὐτοῖς, ἐχθρὸς ἄνθρωπος τοῦτο ἐποίησεν. οἱ δὲ δοῦλοι
And said to them, 'An enemy *{person}* has done this!' *has done* And the *And* servants
1254 5774 899 2398 476 4472 4472 4047 4472 1254 3836 1254 1529
cj v.iai.3s r.dpm.3 a.nsm n.nsm r.asn v.aai.3s d.npm cj n.npm

λέγουσιν αὐτῷ, θέλεις οὖν ἀπελθόντες συλλέξωμεν αὐτά; 29 ὁ
said to him, 'So ⌞do you want⌟ *So* us to go and gather them?' But he
3306 899 4036 2527 4036 599 5198 899 1254 3836
v.pai.3p r.dsm.3 v.pai.2s cj pt.aa.npm v.aas.1p r.apn.3 d.nsm

NASB

22 And the one on
whom seed was
sown among the
thorns, this is the
man who hears the
word, and the wor-
ry of the world and
the deceitfulness
of wealth choke
the word, and it
becomes unfruit-
ful. 23 And the one
on whom seed was
sown on the good
soil, this is the man
who hears the word
and understands it;
who indeed bears
fruit and brings
forth, some a
hundredfold, some
sixty, and some
thirty."

Tares among Wheat

24 Jesus presented
another parable
to them, saying,
"The kingdom of
heaven may be
compared to a man
who sowed good
seed in his field.
25 But while his
men were sleeping,
his enemy came
and sowed [a]tares
among the wheat,
and went away.
26 But when the
wheat sprouted and
bore grain, then
the tares became
evident also. 27 The
slaves of the land-
owner came and
said to him, 'Sir,
did you not sow
good seed in your
field? How then
does it have tares?'
28 And he said to
them, 'An enemy
has done this!' The
slaves *said to him,
'Do you want us,
then, to go and
gather them up?'

[a] Or *darnel*, a weed resembling wheat

NIV

29 "'No,' he an-
swered, 'because
while you are
pulling the weeds,
you may uproot
the wheat with
them. 30 Let both
grow together un-
til the harvest. At
that time I will
tell the harvesters:
First collect the
weeds and tie them
in bundles to be
burned; then gath-
er the wheat and
bring it into my
barn.'"

The Parables of the Mustard Seed and the Yeast

31 He told them
another parable:
"The kingdom
of heaven is like
a mustard seed,
which a man took
and planted in his
field. 32 Though
it is the smallest
of all seeds, yet
when it grows, it
is the largest of
garden plants and
becomes a tree, so
that the birds come
and perch in its
branches."
33 He told them
still another para-
ble: "The kingdom
of heaven is like
yeast that a wom-
an took and mixed
into about sixty
pounds[a] of flour
until it worked
all through the
dough."
34 Jesus spoke all
these things to the
crowd in parables;
he did not say
anything to them
without using a
parable. 35 So was
fulfilled what was
spoken through the
prophet:

δέ φησιν, οὔ, μήποτε συλλέγοντες τὰ ζιζάνια ἐκριζώσητε ἅμα
But replied, 'No, lest in gathering the weeds you uproot the wheat ⌊along with⌋
1254 5774 4024 3607 5198 3836 2429 1748 3836 4992 275
cj v.pai.3s pl cj pt.pa.npm d.apn n.apn v.aas.2p p.d

αὐτοῖς τὸν σῖτον. 30 ἄφετε συναυξάνεσθαι ἀμφότερα ἕως τοῦ θερισμοῦ, καὶ
them. *the* *wheat* Let both grow together *both* until the harvest; and
899 3836 4992 918 317 5277 317 2401 3836 2546 2779
r.dpn.3 d.asm n.asm v.aam.2p f.pp a.apn p.g d.gsm n.gsm cj

ἐν καιρῷ τοῦ θερισμοῦ ἐρῶ τοῖς θερισταῖς, συλλέξατε πρῶτον τὰ
at harvest time *{the}* *harvest* ⌊I will tell⌋ the harvesters, "First gather *First* the
1877 2546 2789 3836 2546 3306 3836 2547 4754 5198 4754 3836
p.d n.dsm d.gsm n.gsm v.fai.1s d.dpm n.dpm v.aam.2p adv d.apn

ζιζάνια καὶ δήσατε αὐτὰ εἰς δέσμας πρὸς τὸ κατακαῦσαι αὐτά, τὸν δὲ
weeds and bind them into bundles to *{the}* be burned, *{them}* then gather the *then*
2429 2779 1313 899 1650 1299 4639 3836 2876 899 1254 5251 3836 1254
n.apn cj v.aam.2p r.apn.3 p.a n.apf p.a d.asn f.aa r.apn.3 d.asm cj

σῖτον συναγάγετε εἰς τὴν ἀποθήκην μου. 31 ἄλλην παραβολὴν
wheat *gather* into *{the}* my barn."'" *my* He gave them another parable,
4992 5251 1650 3836 1609 630 1609 4192 4192 899 257 4130
n.asm v.aam.2p p.a d.asf n.asf r.gs.1 r.asf n.asf

παρέθηκεν αὐτοῖς λέγων, ὁμοία ἐστὶν ἡ βασιλεία τῶν
He gave *them* saying: "The kingdom of heaven is like *is* *The* *kingdom* *of*
4192 899 3306 3836 993 3836 4041 1639 3927 1639 3836 993 3836
v.aai.3s r.dpm.3 pt.pa.nsm a.nsf v.pai.3s d.nsf n.nsf d.gpm

οὐρανῶν κόκκῳ σινάπεως, ὃν λαβὼν ἄνθρωπος ἔσπειρεν ἐν τῷ
heaven a mustard seed *mustard* that a man took *man* and sowed in *{the}*
4041 4983 3133 4983 4005 476 3284 476 5062 1877 3836
n.gpm n.dsm n.gsn r.asm pt.aa.nsm n.nsm v.aai.3s p.d d.dsm

ἀγρῷ αὐτοῦ· 32 ὃ μικρότερον μέν ἐστιν πάντων τῶν σπερμάτων,
his field. *his* It is the smallest ~ *is* of all the seeds; but
899 69 899 4005 1639 3625 3525 1639 4246 3836 5065 1254
n.dsm r.gsm.3 r.nsn a.nsn.c pl v.pai.3s a.gpn d.gpn n.gpn

ὅταν δὲ αὐξηθῇ μεῖζον → τῶν λαχάνων ἐστὶν καὶ γίνεται
when *but* it is grown, it is larger than all the garden plants *it is* and becomes a
4020 1254 889 1639 1639 3489 3836 3303 1639 2779 1181
cj cj v.aps.3s a.nsn.c d.gpn n.gpn v.pai.3s cj v.pmi.3s

δένδρον, ὥστε ἐλθεῖν τὰ πετεινὰ τοῦ οὐρανοῦ καὶ κατασκηνοῦν ἐν τοῖς
tree so that *come* the birds of the air come and nest in *{the}*
1285 6063 2262 3836 4374 3836 4041 2262 2779 2942 1877 3836
n.nsn cj f.aa d.apn n.apn d.gsm n.gsm cj f.pa p.d d.dpm

κλάδοις αὐτοῦ. 33 ἄλλην παραβολὴν ἐλάλησεν αὐτοῖς·
its branches." *its* He spoke another parable *He spoke* to them: "The kingdom of
899 3080 899 3281 3281 257 4130 3281 899 3836 993 3836
n.dpm r.gsn.3 r.asf n.asf v.aai.3s r.dpm.3

ὁμοία ἐστὶν ἡ βασιλεία τῶν οὐρανῶν ζύμῃ, ἣν λαβοῦσα
heaven is like *is* *The* *kingdom* *of* *heaven* leaven, which a woman took
4041 1639 3927 1639 3836 993 3836 4041 2434 4005 1222 3284
a.nsf v.pai.3s d.nsf n.nsf d.gpm n.gpm n.dsf r.asf pt.aa.nsf

γυνὴ ἐνέκρυψεν εἰς ἀλεύρου σάτα τρία ⌊ἕως οὗ⌋ → →
woman and put into three measures of flour, *measures* *three* until it was all
1222 1606 1650 5552 4929 236 4929 5552 2401 4005 3910
n.nsf v.aai.3s p.a n.gsn n.apn a.apn p.g r.gsm

ἐζυμώθη ὅλον. 34 ταῦτα πάντα ἐλάλησεν ὁ Ἰησοῦς
leavened." *all* All these things *All* Jesus spoke *{the}* *Jesus* to the crowds
2435 3910 4246 4047 4246 2652 3281 3836 2652 3836 3836 4063
v.api.3s a.nsn r.apn a.apn v.aai.3s d.nsm n.nsm

ἐν παραβολαῖς τοῖς ὄχλοις καὶ χωρὶς παραβολῆς οὐδὲν ἐλάλει
in parables, *to the* *crowds* and without a parable he told them nothing; *he told*
1877 4130 3836 4063 2779 6006 4130 3281 3281 899 4029 3281
p.d n.dpf d.dpm n.dpm cj p.g n.gsf a.asn v.iai.3s

αὐτοῖς, 35 ὅπως πληρωθῇ τὸ ῥηθὲν διὰ τοῦ προφήτου
them so that *might be fulfilled* what was spoken by the prophet might be fulfilled,
899 3968 4444 3836 3306 1328 3836 4737 4444 4444 4444
r.dpm.3 cj v.aps.3s d.nsn pt.ap.nsn p.g d.gsm n.gsm

NASB

29 But he *said, 'No;
for while you are
gathering up the
tares, you may up-
root the wheat with
them. 30 Allow both
to grow together
until the harvest;
and in the time of
the harvest I will
say to the reapers,
"First gather up the
tares and bind them
in bundles to burn
them up; but gather
the wheat into my
barn."'"

The Mustard Seed

31 He presented
another parable to
them, saying, "The
kingdom of heaven
is like a mustard
seed, which a man
took and sowed
in his field; 32 and
this is smaller than
all *other* seeds,
but when it is full
grown, it is larger
than the garden
plants and becomes
a tree, so that THE
BIRDS OF THE AIR
come and NEST IN
ITS BRANCHES."

The Leaven

33 He spoke an-
other parable to
them, "The king-
dom of heaven is
like leaven, which
a woman took and
hid in three pecks
of flour until it was
all leavened."
34 All these things
Jesus spoke to
the crowds in
parables, and He
did not speak to
them without a
parable. 35 *This was*
to fulfill what was
spoken through the
prophet:

[a] 33 Or about 27 kilograms

NIV

"I will open my
mouth in
parables,
I will utter
things
hidden since
the creation
of the
world."[a]

The Parable of the Weeds Explained

36 Then he left the
crowd and went
into the house. His
disciples came to
him and said, "Ex-
plain to us the par-
able of the weeds
in the field."
37 He answered,
"The one who
sowed the good
seed is the Son of
Man. 38 The field is
the world, and the
good seed stands
for the people of
the kingdom. The
weeds are the peo-
ple of the evil one,
39 and the enemy
who sows them
is the devil. The
harvest is the end
of the age, and
the harvesters are
angels.
40 "As the weeds
are pulled up and
burned in the fire,
so it will be at the
end of the age.
41 The Son of Man
will send out his
angels, and they
will weed out of
his kingdom ev-
erything that caus-
es sin and all who
do evil. 42 They
will throw them
into the blazing
furnace, where
there will be weep-
ing and gnashing
of teeth. 43 Then
the righteous will
shine like the sun
in the kingdom of
their Father.

λέγοντος, ἀνοίξω ἐν παραβολαῖς τὸ στόμα μου, ἐρεύξομαι
saying, "I will open my mouth in parables; {the} mouth my I will utter
3306 487 1609 5125 1877 4130 3836 5125 1609 2243
pt.pa.gsm v.fai.1s p.d n.dpf d.asn n.asn r.gs.1 v.fmi.1s

κεκρυμμένα ἀπὸ καταβολῆς → κόσμου.[a] 36 τότε ↱ ἀφεὶς τοὺς ὄχλους
things kept secret from the foundation of the world." Then he left the crowds and
3221 608 2856 3180 5538 2262 918 3836 4063
pt.rp.apn p.g n.gsf n.gsm adv pt.aa.nsm d.apm n.apm

ἦλθεν εἰς τὴν οἰκίαν. καὶ προσῆλθον αὐτῷ οἱ μαθηταὶ αὐτοῦ
went into the house. And his disciples came to him, {the} disciples his
2262 1650 3836 3864 2779 899 3412 4665 899 3836 3412 899
v.aai.3s p.a d.asf n.asf cj v.aai.3p r.dsm.3 d.npm n.npm r.gsm.3

λέγοντες, διασάφησον ἡμῖν τὴν παραβολὴν τῶν ζιζανίων τοῦ ἀγροῦ. 37 ὁ
saying, "Explain to us the parable of the weeds in the field." And he
3306 1397 7005 3836 4130 3836 2429 3836 69 1254 3836
pt.pa.npm v.aam.2s r.dp.1 d.asf n.asf d.gpn n.gpn d.gsm n.gsm d.nsm

δὲ ἀποκριθεὶς εἶπεν, ὁ σπείρων τὸ καλὸν σπέρμα ἐστὶν ὁ υἱὸς τοῦ
And answered, saying, "The one who sows the good seed is the Son of
1254 646 3306 3836 5062 3836 2819 5065 1639 3836 5626 3836
cj pt.ap.nsm v.aai.3s d.nsm pt.pa.nsm d.asn a.asn n.asn v.pai.3s d.nsm n.nsm d.gsm

ἀνθρώπου, 38 ὁ δὲ ἀγρός ἐστιν ὁ κόσμος, τὸ δὲ καλὸν
Man; and the and field is the world; and as for the and good
476 1254 3836 1254 69 1639 3836 3180 1254 3836 1254 2819
n.gsm d.nsm cj n.nsm v.pai.3s d.nsm n.nsm d.nsn cj a.nsn

σπέρμα οὗτοί εἰσιν οἱ υἱοὶ τῆς βασιλείας· τὰ δὲ ζιζάνιά εἰσιν οἱ υἱοὶ
seed, these are the sons of the kingdom; and the and weeds are the sons
5065 4047 1639 3836 5626 3836 993 1254 3836 1254 2429 1639 3836 5626
n.nsn r.npm v.pai.3p d.npm n.npm d.gsf n.gsf d.npn cj n.npn v.pai.3p d.npm n.npm

τοῦ πονηροῦ, 39 ὁ δὲ ἐχθρὸς ὁ σπείρας αὐτά ἐστιν ὁ διάβολος,
of the evil one; and the and enemy who sowed them is the devil; and
3836 4505 1254 3836 1254 2398 3836 5062 899 1639 3836 1333 1254
d.gsm a.gsm d.nsm cj a.nsm d.nsm pt.aa.nsm r.apn.3 v.pai.3s d.nsm n.nsm

ὁ δὲ θερισμὸς συντέλεια → αἰῶνός ἐστιν, οἱ δὲ θερισταὶ
the and harvest is the end of the age; is and the and harvesters are
3836 1254 2546 1639 5333 172 1639 1254 3836 1254 2547 1639
d.nsm cj n.nsm n.nsf n.gsm v.pai.3s d.npm cj n.npm

ἄγγελοί εἰσιν. 40 ὥσπερ οὖν συλλέγεται τὰ ζιζάνια καὶ
the angels. are Therefore just as Therefore the weeds are gathered the weeds and
34 1639 4036 6061 4036 3836 2429 5198 3836 2429 2779
n.npm v.pai.3p cj cj v.ppi.3s d.npn n.npn cj

→ πυρὶ κατακαίεται, οὕτως ἔσται ἐν τῇ συντελείᾳ τοῦ αἰῶνος·
burned in the fire, burned so ⌊it will be⌋ at the end of the age.
2876 4786 2876 4048 1639 1877 3836 5333 3836 172
n.dsn v.ppi.3s adv v.fmi.3s p.d d.dsf n.dsf d.gsm n.gsm

41 ἀποστελεῖ ὁ υἱὸς τοῦ ἀνθρώπου τοὺς ἀγγέλους αὐτοῦ, καὶ
will send The Son of Man will send {the} his angels, his and
690 3836 5626 3836 476 690 690 3836 899 34 899 2779
v.fai.3s d.nsm n.nsm d.gsm n.gsm d.apm n.apm r.gsm.3 cj

συλλέξουσιν ἐκ τῆς βασιλείας αὐτοῦ πάντα τὰ σκάνδαλα καὶ τοὺς
they will gather out of his kingdom his everything that causes sin and those
5198 1666 3836 899 993 899 4246 3836 4998 2779 3836
v.fai.3p p.g d.gsf n.gsf r.gsm.3 a.apn d.apn n.apn cj d.apm

ποιοῦντας τὴν ἀνομίαν 42 καὶ βαλοῦσιν αὐτοὺς εἰς τὴν κάμινον τοῦ πυρός·
who break his laws. And they will throw them into the fiery furnace, {the} fiery
4472 3836 490 2779 965 899 1650 3836 4786 2825 3836 4786
pt.pa.apm d.asf n.asf cj v.fai.3p r.apm.3 p.a d.asf n.asf d.gsn n.gsn

ἐκεῖ ἔσται ὁ κλαυθμὸς καὶ ὁ βρυγμὸς τῶν ὀδόντων. 43 τότε οἱ
where ⌊there will be⌋ {the} weeping and {the} gnashing of teeth. Then the
1695 1639 3836 3088 2779 3836 1106 3836 3848 5538 3836
adv v.fmi.3s d.nsm n.nsm cj d.nsm n.nsm d.gpm n.gpm adv d.npm

δίκαιοι ἐκλάμψουσιν ὡς ὁ ἥλιος ἐν τῇ βασιλείᾳ τοῦ πατρὸς αὐτῶν. ὁ
righteous will shine like the sun in the kingdom of their Father. their He
1465 1719 6055 3836 2463 1877 3836 993 3836 899 4252 899 3836
a.npm v.fai.3p pl d.nsm n.nsm p.d d.dsf n.dsf d.gsm n.gsm r.gpm.3 d.nsm

NASB

" I WILL OPEN
MY MOUTH IN
PARABLES;
I WILL UTTER
THINGS HID-
DEN SINCE
THE FOUNDA-
TION OF THE
WORLD."

The Tares Explained

36 Then He left the
crowds and went
into the house. And
His disciples came
to Him and said,
"Explain to us the
parable of the tares
of the field." 37 And
He said, "The one
who sows the good
seed is the Son of
Man, 38 and the field
is the world; and *as
for* the good seed,
these are the sons
of the kingdom;
and the tares are
the sons of the
evil *one;* 39 and the
enemy who sowed
them is the devil,
and the harvest is
the end of the age;
and the reapers are
angels. 40 So just as
the tares are gath-
ered up and burned
with fire, so shall
it be at the end of
the age. 41 The Son
of Man will send
forth His angels,
and they will
gather out of His
kingdom all stum-
bling blocks, and
those who commit
lawlessness, 42 and
will throw them
into the furnace of
fire; in that place
there will be weep-
ing and gnashing
of teeth. 43 Then
THE RIGHTEOUS WILL
SHINE FORTH AS THE
SUN in the kingdom
of their Father. He
who has ears, let

[a] 35 Psalm 78:2

[a] [κόσμου] UBS.

NIV

Whoever has ears,
let them hear.

The Parables of the Hidden Treasure and the Pearl

44“The kingdom
of heaven is like
treasure hidden
in a field. When a
man found it, he
hid it again, and
then in his joy
went and sold all
he had and bought
that field.
45“Again, the
kingdom of heaven
is like a merchant
looking for fine
pearls. 46When he
found one of great
value, he went
away and sold ev-
erything he had
and bought it.

The Parable of the Net

47“Once again,
the kingdom of
heaven is like a net
that was let down
into the lake and
caught all kinds
of fish. 48When it
was full, the fish-
ermen pulled it up
on the shore. Then
they sat down and
collected the good
fish in baskets,
but threw the bad
away. 49This is
how it will be at
the end of the age.
The angels will
come and separate
the wicked from
the righteous 50and
throw them into
the blazing fur-
nace, where there
will be weeping
and gnashing of
teeth.
51“Have you un-
derstood all these
things?” Jesus
asked.
“Yes,” they re-
plied.
52He said to them,
“Therefore every
teacher of the law
who has become a
disciple in the

ἔχων ὦτα ἀκουέτω. 44 ὁμοία ἐστὶν ἡ βασιλεία
⌊who has⌋ ears, let him hear! “The kingdom of heaven is like *is* *The* *kingdom*
2400 4044 201 3836 993 3836 4041 1639 3927 1639 3836 993
pt.pa.nsm n.apn v.pam.3s a.nsf v.pai.3s d.nsf n.nsf

τῶν οὐρανῶν θησαυρῷ κεκρυμμένῳ ἐν τῷ ἀγρῷ, ὃν εὑρὼν ἄνθρωπος
of *heaven* treasure hidden in a field that a man found *man* and
3836 4041 2565 3221 1877 3836 69 4005 476 2351 476
d.gpm n.gpm n.dsm pt.rp.dsm p.d d.dsm n.dsm r.asm pt.aa.nsm n.nsm

ἔκρυψεν, καὶ ἀπὸ τῆς χαρᾶς αὐτοῦ ὑπάγει καὶ πωλεῖ πάντα ὅσα ἔχει καὶ
covered up. Then in *{the}* his joy *his* he goes and sells all that he has and
3221 2779 608 3836 899 5915 899 5632 2779 4797 4246 4012 2400 2779
v.aai.3s cj p.g d.gsf n.gsf r.gsm.3 v.pai.3s cj v.pai.3s a.apn r.apn v.pai.3s cj

ἀγοράζει τὸν ἀγρὸν ἐκεῖνον. 45 πάλιν ὁμοία ἐστὶν
buys *{the}* that field. *that* Again, the kingdom of heaven is like *is*
60 3836 1697 69 1697 4099 3836 993 3836 4041 1639 3927 1639
v.pai.3s d.asm n.asm r.asm adv a.nsf v.pai.3s

ἡ βασιλεία τῶν οὐρανῶν ἀνθρώπῳ ἐμπόρῳ ζητοῦντι καλοὺς μαργαρίτας·
the *kingdom* *of* *heaven* a *{person}* merchant ⌊searching for⌋ fine pearls;
3836 993 3836 4041 476 1867 2426 2819 3449
d.nsf n.nsf d.gpm n.gpm n.dsm n.dsm pt.pa.dsm a.apm n.apm

46 εὑρὼν δὲ ἕνα πολύτιμον μαργαρίτην ↱ ἀπελθὼν πέπρακεν
and ⌊when he found⌋ *and* one pearl of great value, *pearl* he went away and sold
1254 2351 1254 1651 3449 4501 3449 4405 599 4405
pt.aa.nsm cj a.asm a.asm n.asm pt.aa.nsm v.rai.3s

πάντα ὅσα εἶχεν καὶ ἠγόρασεν αὐτόν. 47 πάλιν ὁμοία
all that he had and bought it. Again, the kingdom of heaven is like
4246 4012 2400 2779 60 899 4099 3836 993 3836 4041 1639 3927
a.apn r.apn v.iai.3s cj v.aai.3s r.asm.3 adv a.nsf

ἐστὶν ἡ βασιλεία τῶν οὐρανῶν σαγήνῃ βληθείσῃ εἰς τὴν θάλασσαν καὶ
is *the* *kingdom* *of* *heaven* a dragnet that was cast into the sea and caught
1639 3836 993 3836 4041 4880 965 1650 3836 2498 2779 5251
v.pai.3s d.nsf n.nsf d.gpm n.gpm n.dsf pt.ap.dsf p.a d.asf n.asf cj

ἐκ παντὸς γένους συναγαγούσῃ· 48 ἣν ὅτε ἐπληρώθη ἀναβιβάσαντες
fish of every kind; *caught* *{which}* and when it was full, they pulled it up
1666 4246 1169 5251 4005 4021 4444 328
p.g a.gsn n.gsn pt.aa.dsf r.asf cj v.api.3s pt.aa.npm

ἐπὶ τὸν αἰγιαλὸν καὶ ↱ καθίσαντες συνέλεξαν τὰ καλὰ εἰς ἄγγη,
onto the shore; and they sat down and put the good fish into baskets, but
2093 3836 129 2779 5198 2767 5198 3836 2819 1650 35 1254
p.a d.asm n.asm cj pt.aa.npm v.aai.3p d.apn a.apn p.a n.apn

τὰ δὲ σαπρὰ ἔξω ἔβαλον. 49 οὕτως ἔσται ἐν τῇ συντελείᾳ τοῦ
the *but* bad they threw away. *they threw* So ⌊it will be⌋ at the end of the
3836 1254 4911 965 965 2032 965 4048 1639 1877 3836 5333 3836
d.apn cj a.apn adv v.aai.3p adv v.fmi.3s p.d d.dsf n.dsf d.gsm

αἰῶνος· ἐξελεύσονται οἱ ἄγγελοι καὶ ἀφοριοῦσιν τοὺς πονηροὺς ⌊ἐκ
age; the angels will go out *the* *angels* and separate the wicked from
172 3836 34 2002 3836 34 2779 928 3836 4505 1666
n.gsm v.fmi.3p d.npm n.npm cj v.fai.3p d.apm a.apm p.g

μέσου⌋ τῶν δικαίων 50 καὶ βαλοῦσιν αὐτοὺς εἰς τὴν κάμινον τοῦ πυρός·
the righteous and cast them into the fiery furnace, *{the}* *fiery*
3545 3836 1465 2779 965 899 1650 3836 4786 2825 3836 4786
n.gsn d.gpm a.gpm cj v.fai.3p r.apm.3 p.a d.asf n.asf d.gsn n.gsn

ἐκεῖ ἔσται ὁ κλαυθμὸς καὶ ὁ βρυγμὸς τῶν ὀδόντων.
where ⌊there will be⌋ *{the}* weeping and *{the}* gnashing of teeth.
1695 1639 3836 3088 2779 3836 1106 3836 3848
adv v.fmi.3s d.nsm n.nsm cj d.nsm n.nsm d.gpm n.gpm

51 συνήκατε ταῦτα πάντα; λέγουσιν αὐτῷ, ναί. 52 ὁ δὲ
⌊“Have you understood⌋ all these things?” *all* They said to him, “Yes.” And he *And*
5317 4246 4047 4246 3306 899 3721 1254 3836 1254
v.aai.2p r.apn a.apn v.pai.3p r.dsm.3 pl d.nsm cj

εἶπεν αὐτοῖς, ⌊διὰ τοῦτο⌋ πᾶς γραμματεὺς μαθητευθεὶς τῇ
said to them, “Therefore every scribe ⌊who has become a disciple⌋ ⌊in the⌋
3306 899 1328 4047 4246 1208 3411 3836
v.aai.3s r.dpm.3 p.a r.asn a.nsm n.nsm pt.ap.nsm d.dsf

NASB

him hear.

Hidden Treasure

44“The kingdom
of heaven is like a
treasure hidden in
the field, which a
man found and hid
again; and from
joy over it he goes
and sells all that he
has and buys that
field.

A Costly Pearl

45“Again, the
kingdom of heaven
is like a merchant
seeking fine pearls,
46and upon finding
one pearl of great
value, he went and
sold all that he had
and bought it.

A Dragnet

47“Again, the
kingdom of heaven
is like a dragnet
cast into the sea,
and gathering *fish*
of every kind; 48and
when it was filled,
they drew it up on
the beach; and they
sat down and gath-
ered the good *fish*
into containers, but
the bad they threw
away. 49So it will
be at the end of
the age; the angels
will come forth and
take out the wicked
from among the
righteous, 50and
will throw them
into the furnace of
fire; in that place
there will be weep-
ing and gnashing
of teeth.
51“Have you un-
derstood all these
things?” They *said
to Him, “Yes.”
52And Jesus said to
them, “Therefore
every scribe who
has become a dis-
ciple of the

NIV

kingdom of heaven is like the owner of a house who brings out of his storeroom new treasures as well as old."

A Prophet Without Honor

53 When Jesus had finished these parables, he moved on from there.
54 Coming to his hometown, he began teaching the people in their synagogue, and they were amazed. "Where did this man get this wisdom and these miraculous powers?" they asked.
55 "Isn't this the carpenter's son? Isn't his mother's name Mary, and aren't his brothers James, Joseph, Simon and Judas?
56 Aren't all his sisters with us? Where then did this man get all these things?"
57 And they took offense at him.

But Jesus said to them, "A prophet is not without honor except in his own town and in his own home."
58 And he did not do many miracles there because of their lack of faith.

John the Baptist Beheaded

14 At that time Herod the tetrarch heard the reports about Jesus,
2 and he said to his attendants, "This is John the Baptist; he has risen from the dead! That is why

βασιλεία τῶν οὐρανῶν ὅμοιός ἐστιν ἀνθρώπῳ οἰκοδεσπότῃ, ὅστις ἐκβάλλει
kingdom of heaven is like *is* *{person}* the master of a house who brings out
993 3836 4041 1639 3927 1639 476 3867 4015 1675
n.dsf d.gpm n.gpm a.nsm v.pai.3s n.dsm n.dsm r.nsm v.pai.3s

ἐκ τοῦ θησαυροῦ αὐτοῦ καινὰ καὶ παλαιά. 53 καὶ ἐγένετο ὅτε
of *{the}* his treasure *his* things new and old." Now *{it happened that}* when
1666 3836 899 2565 899 2785 2779 4094 2779 1181 4021
p.g d.gsm n.gsm r.gsm.3 a.apn cj a.apn cj v.ami.3s cj

ἐτέλεσεν ὁ Ἰησοῦς τὰς παραβολὰς ταύτας, μετῆρεν ἐκεῖθεν.
Jesus had finished *{the}* *Jesus* *{the}* these parables, *these* ⌞he moved on⌟ from there.
2652 5464 3836 2652 3836 4047 4130 4047 3558 1696
v.aai.3s d.nsm n.nsm d.apf n.apf r.apf v.aai.3s adv

54 καὶ ἐλθὼν εἰς τὴν πατρίδα αὐτοῦ ἐδίδασκεν αὐτοὺς ἐν τῇ
And upon arriving at *{the}* his hometown, *his* he taught them in *{the}* their
2779 2262 1650 3836 899 4258 899 1438 899 1877 3836 899
cj pt.aa.nsm p.a d.asf n.asf r.gsm.3 v.iai.3s r.apm.3 p.d d.dsf

συναγωγῇ αὐτῶν, ὥστε ἐκπλήσσεσθαι αὐτοὺς καὶ λέγειν, πόθεν τούτῳ
synagogue *their* so that they were amazed *they* and said, "Where did this man get
5252 899 6063 899 1742 899 2779 3306 4470 4047
n.dsf r.gpm.3 cj f.pp r.apm.3 cj f.pa cj r.dsm

ἡ σοφία αὕτη καὶ αἱ δυνάμεις; 55 οὐχ οὗτός ἐστιν ὁ τοῦ
such *{the}* wisdom *such* and *{the}* ⌞miraculous powers?⌟ Is not this *Is* the *{the}*
4047 3836 5053 4047 2779 3836 1539 1639 4024 4047 1639 3836 3836
d.nsf n.nsf r.nsf cj d.npf n.npf pl r.nsm v.pai.3s d.nsm d.gsm

τέκτονος υἱός; ➚ οὐχ ἡ μήτηρ αὐτοῦ λέγεται Μαριὰμ καὶ οἱ ἀδελφοὶ
carpenter's son? Is not *{the}* his mother *his* called Mary, and *{the}* his brothers
5454 5626 3306 4024 3836 899 3613 899 3306 3452 2779 3836 899 81
n.gsm n.nsm pl d.nsf n.nsf r.gsm.3 v.ppi.3s n.nsf cj d.npm n.npm

αὐτοῦ Ἰάκωβος καὶ Ἰωσὴφ καὶ Σίμων καὶ Ἰούδας; 56 καὶ αἱ ἀδελφαὶ αὐτοῦ
his James and Joseph and Simon and Judas? And *{the}* his sisters, *his*
899 2610 2779 2737 2779 4981 2779 2683 2779 3836 899 80 899
r.gsm.3 n.nsm cj n.nsm cj n.nsm cj n.nsm cj d.npf n.npf r.gsm.3

οὐχὶ πᾶσαι πρὸς ἡμᾶς εἰσιν; πόθεν οὖν τούτῳ ταῦτα
are they not all with us? *are they* Where then did this man get all these things?"
1639 1639 4049 4246 4639 7005 1639 4470 4036 4047 4246 4047
pl a.npf p.a r.ap.1 v.pai.3p cj cj r.dsm r.npn

πάντα; 57 καὶ ἐσκανδαλίζοντο ἐν αὐτῷ. ὁ δὲ Ἰησοῦς εἶπεν αὐτοῖς,
all And they were deeply offended at him. *{the}* But Jesus said to them, "A
4246 2779 4997 1877 899 3836 1254 2652 3306 899
a.npn cj v.ipi.3p p.d r.dsm.3 d.nsm cj n.nsm v.aai.3s r.dpm.3

οὐκ ἔστιν προφήτης ἄτιμος ⌞εἰ μὴ⌟ ἐν τῇ πατρίδι καὶ ἐν
prophet is not *is* *prophet* ⌞without honor⌟ except in his hometown and in his
4737 1639 4024 1639 4737 872 1623 3590 1877 3836 4258 2779 1877 899
adv v.pai.3s n.nsm a.nsm cj pl p.d d.dsf n.dsf cj p.d

τῇ οἰκίᾳ αὐτοῦ. 58 καὶ ➚ ➚ οὐκ ἐποίησεν ἐκεῖ δυνάμεις
own household." *his* And he did not do many miracles there *miracles*
3836 3864 899 2779 4472 4472 4024 4472 4498 1539 1695 1539
d.dsf n.dsf r.gsm.3 cj adv v.aai.3s adv n.apf

πολλὰς διὰ τὴν ἀπιστίαν αὐτῶν.
many ⌞because of⌟ *{the}* their unbelief. *their*
4498 1328 3836 899 602 899
a.apf p.a d.asf n.asf r.gpm.3

14:1 ἐν ἐκείνῳ τῷ καιρῷ ἤκουσεν Ἡρῴδης ὁ τετραάρχης
About that *{the}* time Herod the tetrarch heard *Herod* *the* *tetrarch*
1877 1697 3836 2789 2476 3836 5490 201 2476 3836 5490
p.d r.dsm d.dsm n.dsm v.aai.3s n.nsm d.nsm n.nsm

τὴν ἀκοὴν Ἰησοῦ, 2 καὶ εἶπεν τοῖς παισὶν αὐτοῦ, οὗτός ἐστιν Ἰωάννης ὁ
the report about Jesus. And he said to his servants, *his* "This is John the
3836 198 2652 2779 3306 3836 899 4090 899 4047 1639 2722 3836
d.asf n.asf n.gsm cj v.aai.3s d.dpm n.dpm r.gsm.3 r.nsm v.pai.3s n.nsm d.nsm

βαπτιστής· αὐτὸς ἠγέρθη ἀπὸ τῶν νεκρῶν καὶ ⌞διὰ τοῦτο⌟ αἱ
Baptist; he has risen from the dead; and that is why *{the}*
969 899 1586 608 3836 3738 2779 1328 4047 3836
n.nsm r.nsm v.api.3s p.g d.gpm a.gpm cj p.a r.asn d.npf

NASB

kingdom of heaven is like a head of a household, who brings out of his treasure things new and old."

Jesus Revisits Nazareth

53 When Jesus had finished these parables, He departed from there.
54 He came to His hometown and *began* teaching them in their synagogue, so that they were astonished, and said, "Where *did* this man *get* this wisdom and *these* miraculous powers?
55 Is not this the carpenter's son? Is not His mother called Mary, and His brothers, James and Joseph and Simon and Judas?
56 And His sisters, are they not all with us? Where then *did* this man *get* all these things?"
57 And they took offense at Him. But Jesus said to them, "A prophet is not without honor except in his hometown and in his *own* household."
58 And He did not do many miracles there because of their unbelief.

John the Baptist Beheaded

14:1 At that time Herod the tetrarch heard the news about Jesus,
2 and said to his servants, "This is John the Baptist; he has risen from the dead, and that is why miraculous

NIV

miraculous pow-
ers are at work in
him."
3Now Herod had
arrested John and
bound him and put
him in prison be-
cause of Herodias,
his brother Philip's
wife, 4for John
had been saying
to him: "It is not
lawful for you to
have her." 5Her-
od wanted to kill
John, but he was
afraid of the peo-
ple, because they
considered John a
prophet.
6On Herod's
birthday the
daughter of Hero-
dias danced for the
guests and pleased
Herod so much
7that he promised
with an oath to
give her what-
ever she asked.
8Prompted by her
mother, she said,
"Give me here on a
platter the head of
John the Baptist."
9The king was
distressed, but be-
cause of his oaths
and his dinner
guests, he ordered
that her request be
granted 10and had
John beheaded in
the prison. 11His
head was brought
in on a platter
and given to the
girl, who carried
it to her mother.
12John's disciples
came

δυνάμεις ἐνεργοῦσιν ἐν αὐτῷ. 3 ὁ γὰρ Ἡρῴδης κρατήσας τὸν Ἰωάννην
⌞miraculous powers⌟ are at work in him." *{the}* For Herod had arrested *{the}* John,
1539 1919 1877 899 3836 1142 2476 3195 3836 2722
n.npf v.pai.3p p.d r.dsm.3 d.nsm cj n.nsm pt.aa.nsm d.asm n.asm

ἔδησεν αὐτὸν[a] καὶ ἐν φυλακῇ ἀπέθετο διὰ Ἡρῳδιάδα τὴν γυναῖκα
bound him, and put him in prison *put him* ⌞because of⌟ Herodias, the wife
1313 899 2779 700 700 1877 5871 700 1328 2478 3836 1222
v.aai.3s r.asm.3 cj p.d n.dsf v.ami.3s p.a n.asf d.asf n.asf

Φιλίππου τοῦ ἀδελφοῦ αὐτοῦ· 4 ἔλεγεν γὰρ ὁ
of his brother Philip; *of* *brother* *his* because John ⌞had been telling⌟ *because* *{the}*
3836 899 81 5805 3836 81 899 1142 2722 3306 1142 3836
n.gsm d.gsm n.gsm r.gsm.3 v.iai.3s cj d.nsm

Ἰωάννης αὐτῷ, ↱ ↱ οὐκ ἔξεστίν σοι ἔχειν αὐτήν. 5 καὶ → θέλων
John him, "It is not lawful ⌞for you⌟ to have her." And though Herod wanted
2722 899 1997 1997 4024 1997 5148 2400 899 2779 2527
n.nsm r.dsm.3 adv v.pai.3s r.ds.2 f.pa r.asf.3 cj pt.pa.nsm

↱ ↱ αὐτὸν ἀποκτεῖναι ἐφοβήθη τὸν ὄχλον, ὅτι ὡς
to put him to death, he feared the people because they considered him ⌞to be⌟ a
650 650 899 650 5828 3836 4063 4022 2400 2400 899 6055
r.asm.3 f.aa v.api.3s d.asm n.asm cj pl

προφήτην αὐτὸν εἶχον. 6 ↱ γενεσίοις δὲ γενομένοις τοῦ
prophet. *him* *they considered* But when Herod's birthday *But* came, *{the}*
4737 899 2400 1254 1181 2476 1160 1254 1181 3836
n.asm r.asm.3 v.iai.3p n.dpn cj pt.am.dpn d.gsm

Ἡρῴδου ὠρχήσατο ἡ θυγάτηρ τῆς Ἡρῳδιάδος ἐν τῷ μέσῳ καὶ ἤρεσεν
Herod's *danced* the daughter of Herodias danced before *{the}* them and pleased
2476 4004 3836 2588 3836 2478 4004 1877 3836 3545 2779 743
n.gsm v.ami.3s d.nsf n.nsf d.gsf n.gsf p.d d.dsn n.dsn cj v.aai.3s

τῷ Ἡρῴδῃ, 7 ὅθεν μεθ᾽ ὅρκου ὡμολόγησεν αὐτῇ δοῦναι
{the} Herod. So he promised with an oath *he promised* to give her *to give*
3836 2476 3854 3933 3933 3552 3992 3933 1443 1443 899 1443
d.dsm n.dsm cj p.g n.gsm v.aai.3s r.dsf.3 f.aa

⌞ὃ ἐὰν⌟ αἰτήσηται. 8 ἡ δὲ προβιβασθεῖσα ὑπὸ τῆς μητρὸς αὐτῆς,
whatever she asked. *{the}* *{and}* Prompted by *{the}* her mother, *her* she
4005 1569 160 3836 1254 4586 5679 3836 899 3613 899 5774
r.asn pl v.ams.3s d.nsf cj pt.ap.nsf p.g d.gsf n.gsf r.gsf.3

δός μοι, φησίν, ↱ ὧδε ἐπὶ πίνακι τὴν κεφαλὴν
said, "Give me *she said* the head of John the Baptist here on a platter." *the* *head*
5774 1443 1609 5774 3836 3051 2722 2722 3836 969 6045 2093 4402 3836 3051
v.aam.2s r.ds.1 v.pai.3s adv p.d n.dsm d.asf n.asf

Ἰωάννου τοῦ βαπτιστοῦ. 9 καὶ → λυπηθεὶς ὁ βασιλεὺς
John *the* *Baptist* And although the king was distressed, *the* *king*
2722 3836 969 2779 3836 995 3382 3836 995
n.gsm d.gsm n.gsm cj pt.ap.nsm d.nsm n.nsm

διὰ τοὺς ὅρκους καὶ τοὺς συνανακειμένους ἐκέλευσεν δοθῆναι,
⌞because of⌟ his oaths and his dinner guests, he commanded it to be given to her.
1328 3836 3992 2779 3836 5263 3027 1443
p.a d.apm n.apm cj d.apm pt.pm.apm v.aai.3s f.ap

10 καὶ ↱ πέμψας → ἀπεκεφάλισεν τὸν[b] Ἰωάννην ἐν τῇ φυλακῇ. 11 καὶ
So he sent and had John beheaded *{the}* *John* in the prison. And
2779 642 4287 2722 642 3836 2722 1877 3836 5871 2779
cj pt.aa.nsm v.aai.3s d.asm n.asm p.d d.dsf n.dsf cj

ἠνέχθη ἡ κεφαλὴ αὐτοῦ ἐπὶ πίνακι καὶ ἐδόθη τῷ κορασίῳ, καὶ
his head was brought *{the}* *head* *his* on a platter and given ⌞to the⌟ girl, and
899 3051 5770 3836 3051 899 2093 4402 2779 1443 3836 3166 2779
v.api.3s d.nsf n.nsf r.gsm.3 p.d n.dsm cj v.api.3s d.dsn n.dsn cj

ἤνεγκεν τῇ μητρὶ αὐτῆς. 12 καὶ προσελθόντες οἱ μαθηταὶ
she brought it to her mother. *her* *{and}* John's disciples came *{the}* *disciples*
5770 3836 899 3613 899 2779 899 3412 4665 3836 3412
v.aai.3s d.dsf n.dsf r.gsf.3 cj pt.aa.npm d.npm n.npm

NASB

powers are at work
in him."
3For when Herod
had John arrested,
he bound him
and put him in
prison because of
Herodias, the wife
of his brother Phil-
ip. 4For John had
been saying to him,
"It is not lawful for
you to have her."
5Although Herod
wanted to put him
to death, he feared
the crowd, because
they regarded John
as a prophet.
6But when
Herod's birthday
came, the daughter
of Herodias danced
before *them* and
pleased Herod, 7so
much that he prom-
ised with an oath to
give her whatever
she asked. 8Having
been prompted by
her mother, she
*said, "Give me
here on a plat-
ter the head of
John the Baptist."
9Although he was
grieved, the king
commanded *it* to
be given because
of his oaths, and
because of his din-
ner guests. 10He
sent and had John
beheaded in the
prison. 11And his
head was brought
on a platter and
given to the girl,
and she brought it
to her mother. 12His
disciples came and

[a] [αὐτὸν] UBS.
[b] [τὸν] UBS.

NIV

and took his body
and buried it. Then
they went and told
Jesus.

Jesus Feeds the Five Thousand

13 When Jesus
heard what had
happened, he
withdrew by boat
privately to a sol-
itary place. Hear-
ing of this, the
crowds followed
him on foot from
the towns. 14 When
Jesus landed and
saw a large crowd,
he had compas-
sion on them and
healed their sick.
15 As evening ap-
proached, the dis-
ciples came to him
and said, "This is a
remote place, and
it's already get-
ting late. Send the
crowds away, so
they can go to the
villages and buy
themselves some
food."
16 Jesus replied,
"They do not need
to go away. You
give them some-
thing to eat."
17 "We have here
only five loaves
of bread and two
fish," they an-
swered.
18 "Bring them
here to me," he
said. 19 And he di-
rected the people
to sit down on the
grass. Taking the
five loaves and the
two fish and look-
ing up to heaven,
he gave thanks and
broke the loaves.
Then he gave them
to the disciples,
and the disciples
gave them to the
people. 20 They all
ate and were satis-
fied, and the disci-
ples picked up

αὐτοῦ ἦραν τὸ πτῶμα καὶ ἔθαψαν αὐτὸ[a] καὶ ↱ ἐλθόντες ἀπήγγειλαν τῷ
John's and took the corpse and buried it; then they went and told *{the}*
899 149 3836 4773 2779 2507 899 2779 550 2262 550 3836
r.gsm.3 v.aai.3p d.asn n.asn cj v.aai.3p r.asn.3 cj pt.aa.npm v.aai.3p d.dsm

Ἰησοῦ. 13 → ἀκούσας δὲ ὁ Ἰησοῦς ἀνεχώρησεν ἐκεῖθεν ἐν
Jesus. Now when Jesus heard about *Now {the} Jesus* John, he left there by
2652 1254 2652 201 1254 3836 2652 432 1696 1877
n.dsm pt.aa.nsm cj d.nsm n.nsm v.aai.3s adv p.d

πλοίῳ εἰς ἔρημον τόπον ⌞κατ' ἰδίαν·⌟ καὶ → ἀκούσαντες οἱ
boat to a deserted place to be alone; but when the crowds heard about *the*
4450 1650 2245 5536 2848 2625 2779 3836 4063 201 3836
n.dsn p.a a.asm n.asm p.a a.asf cj pt.aa.npm d.npm

ὄχλοι ἠκολούθησαν αὐτῷ πεζῇ ἀπὸ τῶν πόλεων. 14 καὶ ἐξελθὼν εἶδεν
crowds it, they followed him on foot from the towns. And ⌞when he came ashore,⌟ he saw
4063 199 899 4270 608 3836 4484 2779 2002 1625
n.npm v.aai.3p r.dsm.3 adv p.g d.gpf n.gpf cj pt.aa.nsm v.aai.3s

πολὺν ὄχλον καὶ ἐσπλαγχνίσθη ἐπ' αὐτοῖς καὶ ἐθεράπευσεν τοὺς ἀρρώστους
a great crowd; and he had compassion on them and healed *{the}* their sick.
4498 4063 2779 5072 2093 899 2779 2543 3836 899 779
a.asm n.asm cj v.api.3s p.d r.dpm.3 cj v.aai.3s d.apm a.apm

αὐτῶν. 15 ↱ ὀψίας δὲ γενομένης προσῆλθον αὐτῷ οἱ μαθηταὶ
their When evening *{and}* came, the disciples approached him, *the disciples*
899 1181 4068 1254 1181 3836 3412 4665 899 3836 3412
r.gpm.3 n.gsf cj pt.am.gsf v.aai.3p r.dsm.3 d.npm n.npm

λέγοντες, ἔρημός ἐστιν ὁ τόπος καὶ ἡ ὥρα ↱ ἤδη παρῆλθεν·
saying, "This is a deserted place *This is {the} place* and the hour is now late;
3306 1639 1639 2245 5536 1639 3836 5536 2779 3836 6052 4216 2453 4216
pt.pa.npm a.nsm v.pai.3s d.nsm n.nsm cj d.nsf n.nsf adv v.aai.3s

ἀπόλυσον τοὺς ὄχλους, ↰ ἵνα ↱ ↱ ἀπελθόντες εἰς τὰς κώμας ἀγοράσωσιν
send the crowds away so they can go into the villages and buy
668 3836 4063 668 2671 60 60 599 1650 3836 3267 60
v.aam.2s d.apm n.apm cj pt.aa.npm p.a d.apf n.apf v.aas.3p

ἑαυτοῖς βρώματα. 16 ὁ δὲ Ἰησοῦς[b] εἶπεν αὐτοῖς, οὐ χρείαν
food for themselves." *food {the}* But Jesus said to them, "They have no need
1109 1571 1109 3836 1254 2652 3306 899 2400 2400 4024 5970
r.dpm.3 n.apn d.nsm cj n.nsm v.aai.3s r.dpm.3 adv n.asf

ἔχουσιν ἀπελθεῖν, δότε αὐτοῖς ὑμεῖς φαγεῖν. 17 οἱ δὲ
They have to go away; you give them *you* something to eat." And they *And*
2400 599 7007 1443 899 7007 2266 1254 3836 1254
v.pai.3p f.aa v.aam.2p r.dpm.3 r.np.2 f.aa d.npm cj

λέγουσιν αὐτῷ, οὐκ ἔχομεν ὧδε ⌞εἰ μὴ⌟ πέντε ἄρτους καὶ δύο ἰχθύας.
said to him, "We have nothing *We have* here but five loaves and two fish."
3306 899 2400 2400 4024 2400 6045 1623 3590 4297 788 2779 1545 2716
v.pai.3p r.dsm.3 adv v.pai.1p adv cj pl a.apm n.apm cj a.apm n.apm

18 ὁ δὲ εἶπεν, φέρετέ μοι ὧδε αὐτούς. 19 καὶ κελεύσας τοὺς
And he *And* said, "Bring them here to me." *here them* Then he ordered the
1254 3836 1254 3306 5770 899 6045 1609 6045 899 2779 3027 3836
d.nsm cj v.aai.3s v.pam.2p r.ds.1 adv r.apm.3 cj pt.aa.nsm d.apm

ὄχλους ἀνακλιθῆναι ἐπὶ τοῦ χόρτου, λαβὼν τοὺς πέντε ἄρτους καὶ τοὺς δύο
crowds to sit down on the grass, and taking the five loaves and the two
4063 369 2093 3836 5965 3284 3836 4297 788 2779 3836 1545
n.apm f.ap p.g d.gsm n.gsm pt.aa.nsm d.apm a.apm n.apm cj d.apm a.apm

ἰχθύας, ↱ ἀναβλέψας εἰς τὸν οὐρανὸν εὐλόγησεν καὶ κλάσας ἔδωκεν
fish, he looked up to *{the}* heaven, said a blessing, and broke the loaves. He gave
2716 2328 329 1650 3836 4041 2328 2779 3089 1443
n.apm pt.aa.nsm p.a d.asm n.asm v.aai.3s cj pt.aa.nsm v.aai.3s

τοῖς μαθηταῖς τοὺς ἄρτους, οἱ δὲ μαθηταὶ τοῖς ὄχλοις.
the loaves to the disciples, *the loaves* and the *and* disciples gave them to the crowds.
3836 788 3836 3412 3836 788 1254 3836 1254 3412 3836 4063
d.dpm n.dpm d.apm n.apm d.npm cj n.npm d.dpm n.dpm

20 καὶ → ἔφαγον πάντες καὶ ἐχορτάσθησαν, καὶ ἦραν τὸ περισσεῦον
And they all ate *all* and were filled; and ⌞they picked up⌟ what remained
2779 4246 2266 4246 2779 5963 2779 149 3836 4355
cj v.aai.3p a.npm cj v.api.3p cj v.aai.3p d.asn pt.pa.asn

[a] αὐτὸ TNIV, NET. αὐτὸ[ν] UBS.
[b] [Ἰησοῦς] UBS, omitted by NET.

NASB

took away the body
and buried it; and
they went and re-
ported to Jesus.

Five Thousand Fed

13 Now when Jesus
heard *about John,*
He withdrew from
there in a boat to a
secluded place by
Himself; and when
the people heard *of*
this, they followed
Him on foot from
the cities. 14 When
He went ashore, He
saw a large crowd,
and felt compas-
sion for them and
healed their sick.
15 When it was
evening, the dis-
ciples came to Him
and said, "This
place is desolate
and the hour is al-
ready late; so send
the crowds away,
that they may go
into the villages
and buy food for
themselves."
16 But Jesus said
to them, "They
do not need to go
away; you give
them *something*
to eat!" 17 They
*said to Him, "We
have here only five
loaves and two
fish." 18 And He
said, "Bring them
here to Me." 19 Or-
dering the people
to sit down on the
grass, He took the
five loaves and
the two fish, and
looking up toward
heaven, He blessed
the food, and
breaking the loaves
He gave them to
the disciples, and
the disciples *gave*
them to the crowds,
20 and they all ate
and were satisfied.
They picked up
what was left

NIV

twelve basketfuls
of broken pieces
that were left over.
21 The number of
those who ate was
about five thou-
sand men, besides
women and chil-
dren.

Jesus Walks on the Water

22 Immediately
Jesus made the
disciples get into
the boat and go
on ahead of him
to the other side,
while he dismissed
the crowd. 23 After
he had dismissed
them, he went up
on a mountainside
by himself to pray.
Later that night,
he was there alone,
24 and the boat was
already a consider-
able distance from
land, buffeted by
the waves because
the wind was
against it.
25 Shortly be-
fore dawn Jesus
went out to them,
walking on the
lake. 26 When the
disciples saw him
walking on the
lake, they were
terrified. "It's a
ghost," they said,
and cried out in
fear.
27 But Jesus im-
mediately said to
them: "Take cour-
age! It is I. Don't
be afraid."
28 "Lord, if it's
you," Peter re-
plied, "tell me to
come to you on the
water."

τῶν κλασμάτων δώδεκα κοφίνους πλήρεις. 21 οἱ
of the broken pieces, twelve baskets full. Not counting women and children, there
3836 3083 1557 3186 4441 6006 6006 1222 2779 4086 3836
d.gpn n.gpn a.apm n.apm a.apm d.npm

δὲ ἐσθίοντες ἦσαν ἄνδρες ὡσεὶ πεντακισχίλιοι
{and} were about five thousand men who had eaten. *were* *men* *about* *five thousand*
1254 1639 6059 4295 4295 467 2266 1639 467 6059 4295
cj pt.pa.npm v.iai.3p n.npm pl a.npm

χωρὶς γυναικῶν καὶ παιδίων. 22 καὶ εὐθέως ἠνάγκασεν τοὺς μαθητὰς
Not counting *women* *and* *children* *{and}* Immediately Jesus made his disciples
6006 1222 2779 4086 2779 2311 337 3836 3412
p.g n.gpf cj n.gpn cj adv v.aai.3s d.apm n.apm

ἐμβῆναι εἰς τὸ πλοῖον καὶ προάγειν αὐτὸν εἰς τὸ πέραν, ⌞ἕως οὗ⌟
get into the boat and ⌞go on ahead of⌟ him to the ⌞opposite shore,⌟ until
1832 1650 3836 4450 2779 4575 899 1650 3836 4305 2401 4005
f.aa p.a d.asn n.asn cj f.pa r.asm.3 p.a d.asn adv p.g r.gsm

ἀπολύσῃ τοὺς ὄχλους. 23 καὶ ἀπολύσας τοὺς ὄχλους ↰ ἀνέβη εἰς τὸ
he had dismissed the crowds. And after sending the crowds away, ⌞he went up⌟ on the
668 3836 4063 2779 668 3836 4063 668 326 1650 3836
v.aas.3s d.apm n.apm cj pt.aa.nsm d.apm n.apm v.aai.3s p.a d.asn

ὄρος κατ᾽ ἰδίαν προσεύξασθαι. ↱ ὀψίας δὲ γενομένης
mountainside by himself to pray; and when evening *and* came, he was there
4001 2848 2625 4667 1254 1181 4068 1254 1181 1639 1639 1695
n.asn p.a a.asf f.am n.gsf cj pt.am.gsf

μόνος ἦν ἐκεῖ. 24 τὸ δὲ πλοῖον ἤδη ⌞σταδίους πολλοὺς⌟ ἀπὸ
alone. *he was* *there* Meanwhile the *Meanwhile* boat, already far from
3668 1639 1695 1254 3836 1254 4450 2453 5084 4498 608
a.nsm v.iai.3s adv d.nsn cj n.nsn adv n.apm a.apm p.g

τῆς γῆς ἀπεῖχεν βασανιζόμενον ὑπὸ τῶν κυμάτων, ἦν γὰρ ἐναντίος
{the} land, was being tossed by the waves, for the wind was *for* against
3836 1178 600 989 5679 3836 3246 1142 3836 449 1639 1142 1885
d.gsf n.gsf v.iai.3s pt.pp.nsn p.g d.gpn n.gpn v.iai.3s cj a.nsm

ὁ ἄνεμος. 25 → τετάρτῃ δὲ φυλακῇ τῆς νυκτὸς ἦλθεν[a] πρὸς αὐτοὺς
it. *the* *wind* And in the fourth *And* watch of the night he came to them,
3836 449 1254 5480 1254 5871 3836 3816 2262 4639 899
d.nsm n.nsm a.dsf cj n.dsf d.gsf n.gsf v.aai.3s p.a r.apm.3

περιπατῶν ἐπὶ τὴν θάλασσαν. 26 ↱ οἱ δὲ μαθηταὶ ἰδόντες αὐτὸν ἐπὶ
walking on the sea. When the *{and}* disciples saw him walking on
4344 2093 3836 2498 1625 3836 1254 3412 1625 899 4344 2093
pt.pa.nsm p.a d.asf n.asf d.npm cj n.npm pt.aa.npm r.asm.3 p.g

τῆς θαλάσσης περιπατοῦντα ἐταράχθησαν λέγοντες ὅτι φάντασμά
the sea, *walking* they were frightened and said, ~ "It is a ghost!"
3836 2498 4344 5429 3306 4022 1639 1639 5753
d.gsf n.gsf pt.pa.asm v.api.3p pt.pa.npm cj n.nsn

ἐστιν, καὶ ἀπὸ τοῦ φόβου ἔκραξαν. 27 εὐθὺς δὲ
It is And they cried out in *{the}* fear. *they cried out* But right away *But* Jesus
1639 2779 3189 3189 3189 608 3836 5832 3189 1254 2318 1254 2652
v.pai.3s cj p.g d.gsm n.gsm v.aai.3p adv cj

ἐλάλησεν [b]ὁ Ἰησοῦς αὐτοῖς λέγων, θαρσεῖτε, ἐγώ εἰμι· ↱ μὴ
spoke *{the}* *Jesus* to them, saying, "Take courage, it is I! *it is* Do not
3281 3836 2652 899 3306 2510 1639 1639 1609 1639 5828 3590
v.aai.3s d.nsm n.nsm r.dpm.3 pt.pa.nsm v.pam.2p r.ns.1 v.pai.1s pl

φοβεῖσθε. 28 ἀποκριθεὶς δὲ αὐτῷ ὁ Πέτρος εἶπεν, κύριε, εἰ
be afraid." And Peter answered *And* him, *{the}* *Peter* saying, "Lord, if it is
5828 1254 4377 646 1254 899 3836 4377 3306 3261 1623 1639 1639
v.ppm.2p pt.ap.nsm cj r.dsm.3 d.nsm n.nsm v.aai.3s n.vsm cj

σὺ εἶ, κέλευσόν με ἐλθεῖν πρός σε ἐπὶ τὰ ὕδατα. 29 ὁ δὲ εἶπεν,
you, *it is* tell me to come to you on the water." And he *And* said,
5148 1639 3027 1609 2262 4639 5148 2093 3836 5623 1254 3836 1254 3306
r.ns.2 v.pai.2s v.aam.2s r.as.1 f.aa p.a r.as.2 p.a d.apn n.apn d.nsm cj v.aai.3s

[a] ἦλθεν UBS, NET. TNIV.
[b] [ὁ Ἰησοῦς] UBS.

NASB

over of the broken
pieces, twelve full
baskets. 21 There
were about five
thousand men who
ate, besides women
and children.

Jesus Walks on the Water

22 Immediately He
made the disciples
get into the boat
and go ahead of
Him to the other
side, while He sent
the crowds away.
23 After He had sent
the crowds away,
He went up on the
mountain by Him-
self to pray; and
when it was eve-
ning, He was there
alone. 24 But the
boat was already [a]a
long distance from
the land, battered
by the waves; for
the wind was con-
trary. 25 And in the
[b]fourth watch of
the night He came
to them, walking
on the sea. 26 When
the disciples saw
Him walking on
the sea, they were
terrified, and said,
"It is a ghost!" And
they cried out in
fear. 27 But immedi-
ately Jesus spoke
to them, saying,
"Take courage, it is
I; do not be afraid."
28 Peter said to
Him, "Lord, if it is
You, command me
to come to You on
the water." 29 And
He said, "Come!"

[a] Lit *many stadia from;* a stadion was about 600 feet or about 182 meters
[b] I.e. 3-6 a.m.

NIV

[29]"Come," he
said.
Then Peter got
down out of the
boat, walked on
the water and
came toward
Jesus. [30]But when
he saw the wind,
he was afraid and,
beginning to sink,
cried out, "Lord,
save me!"
[31]Immediate-
ly Jesus reached
out his hand and
caught him. "You
of little faith," he
said, "why did you
doubt?"
[32]And when they
climbed into the
boat, the wind
died down. [33]Then
those who were in
the boat worshiped
him, saying, "Tru-
ly you are the Son
of God."
[34]When they had
crossed over, they
landed at Gennes-
aret. [35]And when
the men of that
place recognized
Jesus, they sent
word to all the sur-
rounding country.
People brought all
their sick to him
[36]and begged him
to let the sick just
touch the edge of
his cloak, and all
who touched it
were healed.

That Which Defiles

15 Then some
Pharisees
and teachers of the
law came to Jesus
from Jerusalem
and asked, [2]"Why
do your disciples
break the tradition
of the elders? They
don't wash

ἐλθέ. καὶ καταβὰς ἀπὸ τοῦ πλοίου ὁ[a] Πέτρος περιεπάτησεν ἐπὶ τὰ ὕδατα
"Come!" So Peter got out of the boat, *{the}* *Peter* stepped out on the water
2262 2779 4377 2849 608 3836 4450 3836 4377 4344 2093 3836 5623
v.aam.2s cj pt.aa.nsm p.g d.gsn n.gsn d.nsm n.nsm v.aai.3s p.a d.apn n.apn

καὶ ἦλθεν πρὸς τὸν Ἰησοῦν. 30 βλέπων δὲ τὸν ἄνεμον ἰσχυρὸν[b]
and headed toward *{the}* Jesus. But ⌞when he realized⌟ *But* that the wind was blustery,
2779 2262 4639 3836 2652 1254 1063 1254 3836 449 2708
cj v.aai.3s p.a d.asm n.asm pt.pa.nsm cj d.asm n.asm a.asm

ἐφοβήθη, καὶ ἀρξάμενος καταποντίζεσθαι ἔκραξεν λέγων, κύριε, σῶσόν με.
⌞he became afraid;⌟ and starting to sink, he cried out, *{saying}* "Lord, save me!"
5828 2779 806 2931 3189 3306 3261 5392 1609
v.api.3s cj pt.am.nsm f.pp v.aai.3s pt.pa.nsm n.vsm v.aam.2s r.as.1

31 εὐθέως δὲ ὁ Ἰησοῦς ἐκτείνας τὴν χεῖρα ἐπελάβετο αὐτοῦ καὶ λέγει
And immediately *And* *{the}* Jesus reached out his hand, took hold of him, and said
1254 2311 1254 3836 2652 1753 3836 5931 2138 899 2779 3306
adv cj d.nsm n.nsm pt.aa.nsm d.asf n.asf v.ami.3s r.gsm.3 cj v.pai.3s

αὐτῷ, ὀλιγόπιστε, ⌞εἰς τί⌟ ἐδίστασας; 32 καὶ → ἀναβάντων αὐτῶν
to him, "O you of little faith, why did you doubt?" And when they got *they*
899 3899 1650 5515 1491 2779 899 326 899
r.dsm.3 a.vsm p.a r.asn v.aai.2s cj pt.aa.gpm r.gpm.3

εἰς τὸ πλοῖον ἐκόπασεν ὁ ἄνεμος. 33 οἱ δὲ ἐν τῷ πλοίῳ
into the boat, the wind died down. *the* *wind* And those *And* in the boat
1650 3836 4450 3836 449 3156 3836 449 1254 3836 1254 1877 3836 4450
p.a d.asn n.asn v.aai.3s d.nsm n.nsm d.npm cj p.d d.dsn n.dsn

προσεκύνησαν αὐτῷ λέγοντες, ἀληθῶς θεοῦ υἱὸς εἶ. 34 καὶ
worshiped him, saying, "Truly you are the Son of God." *Son* *you are* And
4686 899 3306 242 1639 1639 5626 2536 5626 1639 2779
v.aai.3p r.dsm.3 pt.pa.npm adv n.gsm n.nsm v.pai.2s cj

διαπεράσαντες ἦλθον ἐπὶ τὴν γῆν εἰς Γεννησαρέτ. 35 καὶ →
⌞when they had crossed over,⌟ they came to *{the}* land at Gennesaret. *{and}* When the
1385 2262 2093 3836 1178 1650 1166 2779 3836
pt.aa.npm v.aai.3p p.a d.asf n.asf p.a n.asf cj

ἐπιγνόντες αὐτὸν οἱ ἄνδρες τοῦ τόπου ἐκείνου ἀπέστειλαν
men of that place recognized him, *the* *men* *of* *place* *that* they sent word
467 3836 1697 5536 2105 899 3836 467 3836 5536 1697 690
pt.aa.npm r.asm.3 d.npm n.npm d.gsm n.gsm r.gsm v.aai.3p

εἰς ὅλην τὴν περίχωρον ἐκείνην καὶ προσήνεγκαν αὐτῷ πάντας τοὺς
into all *{the}* that ⌞surrounding area⌟ *that* and brought to him all who were
1650 3910 3836 1697 4369 1697 2779 4712 899 4246 3836 2400
p.a a.asf d.asf a.asf r.asf cj v.aai.3p r.dsm.3 a.apm d.apm

κακῶς ἔχοντας 36 καὶ παρεκάλουν αὐτὸν ἵνα ↱ ↱ μόνον ἅψωνται τοῦ
sick. *were* And they begged him that they might just touch the
2809 2400 2779 4151 899 2671 721 721 3667 721 3836
adv pt.pa.apm cj v.iai.3p r.asm.3 cj adv v.ams.3p d.gsn

κρασπέδου τοῦ ἱματίου αὐτοῦ· καὶ ὅσοι ἥψαντο διεσώθησαν.
fringe of his cloak; *his* and ⌞as many as⌟ touched it were healed.
3192 3836 899 2668 899 2779 4012 721 1407
n.gsn d.gsn n.gsn r.gsm.3 cj r.npm v.ami.3p v.api.3p

15:1 τότε προσέρχονται τῷ Ἰησοῦ ἀπὸ Ἱεροσολύμων
Then Pharisees and scribes came to Jesus from Jerusalem,
5538 5757 2779 1208 4665 3836 2652 608 2642
adv v.pmi.3p d.dsm n.dsm p.g n.gpn

Φαρισαῖοι καὶ γραμματεῖς λέγοντες, 2 ⌞διὰ τί⌟ ↱ οἱ μαθηταί σου
Pharisees *and* *scribes* saying, "Why do *{the}* your disciples *your*
5757 2779 1208 3306 1328 5515 4124 3836 5148 3412 5148
n.npm cj n.npm pt.pa.npm p.a r.asn d.npm n.npm r.gs.2

παραβαίνουσιν τὴν παράδοσιν τῶν πρεσβυτέρων; ↱ ↱ οὐ γὰρ νίπτονται
break the tradition of the elders? For they do not *For* wash
4124 3836 4142 3836 4565 1142 3782 3782 4024 1142 3782
v.pai.3p d.asf n.asf d.gpm a.gpm adv cj v.pmi.3p

[a] [ὁ] UBS.
[b] [ἰσχυρὸν] UBS, omitted by TNIV.

NASB

And Peter got out
of the boat, and
walked on the
water and came
toward Jesus. [30]But
seeing the wind, he
became frightened,
and beginning to
sink, he cried out,
"Lord, save me!"
[31]Immediately
Jesus stretched out
His hand and took
hold of him, and
*said to him, "You
of little faith, why
did you doubt?"
[32]When they got
into the boat, the
wind stopped.
[33]And those who
were in the boat
worshiped Him,
saying, "You are
certainly God's
Son!"
[34]When they had
crossed over, they
came to land at
Gennesaret. [35]And
when the men of
that place recog-
nized Him, they
sent *word* into all
that surrounding
district and brought
to Him all who
were sick; [36]and
they implored Him
that they might just
touch the fringe of
His cloak; and as
many as touched *it*
were cured.

Tradition and Commandment

[15:1]Then some
Pharisees and
scribes *came to Je-
sus from Jerusalem
and said, [2]"Why
do Your disciples
break the tradition
of the elders? For
they do not wash
their

NIV

their hands before
they eat!"
3 Jesus replied,
"And why do you
break the com-
mand of God for
the sake of your
tradition? 4 For
God said, 'Hon-
or your father
and mother'[a] and
'Anyone who
curses their father
or mother is to
be put to death.'[b]
5 But you say that
if anyone declares
that what might
have been used to
help their father or
mother is 'devoted
to God,' 6 they are
not to 'honor their
father or mother'
with it. Thus you
nullify the word of
God for the sake
of your tradition.
7 You hypocrites!
Isaiah was right
when he prophe-
sied about you:

8 "'These people
honor me
with their
lips,
but their hearts
are far from
me.
9 They worship me
in vain;
their teachings
are merely
human
rules.'[c]"

10 Jesus called
the crowd to him
and said, "Listen
and understand.
11 What goes into
someone's mouth
does not defile
them, but what
comes out of their
mouth, that is what
defiles them."
12 Then the disci-
ples came

τὰς χεῖρας αὐτῶν[a] ὅταν ἄρτον ἐσθίωσιν. 3 ὁ δὲ ἀποκριθεὶς
{the} their hands their when they eat bread." they eat But he But answered
3836 899 5931 899 4020 2266 2266 788 2266 1254 3836 1254 646
d.apf n.apf r.gpm.3 cj n.asm v.pas.3p d.nsm cj pt.ap.nsm

εἶπεν αὐτοῖς, ⌊διὰ τί⌋ καὶ ↱ ὑμεῖς παραβαίνετε τὴν ἐντολὴν τοῦ
saying them, saying, "And why And do you break the commandment of
3306 899 3306 2779 1328 5515 2779 4124 7007 4124 3836 1953 3836
v.aai.3s r.dpm.3 p.a r.asn adv r.np.2 v.pai.2p d.asf n.asf d.gsm

θεοῦ διὰ τὴν παράδοσιν ὑμῶν; 4 ὁ γὰρ θεὸς εἶπεν, τίμα τὸν
God ⌊for the sake of⌋ {the} your tradition? your {the} For God said, 'Honor your
2536 1328 3836 7007 4142 7007 3836 1142 2536 3306 5506 3836
n.gsm p.a d.asf n.asf r.gp.2 d.nsm cj n.nsm v.aai.3s v.pam.2s d.asm

πατέρα καὶ τὴν μητέρα, καί, ὁ κακολογῶν πατέρα ἢ μητέρα
father and your mother,' and, 'Whoever speaks evil of his father or mother must be put
4252 2779 3836 3613 2779 3836 2800 4252 2445 3613 5462 5462 5462
n.asm cj d.asf n.asf cj d.nsm pt.pa.nsm n.asm cj n.asf

θανάτῳ τελευτάτω. 5 ὑμεῖς δὲ λέγετε, ⌊ὃς ἂν⌋ εἴπῃ τῷ πατρὶ ἢ τῇ
to death.' must be put But you But say, 'Whoever says ⌊to his⌋ father or his
2505 5462 1254 7007 1254 3306 4005 323 3306 3836 4252 2445 3836
n.dsm v.pam.3s r.np.2 cj v.pai.2p r.nsm pl v.aas.3s d.dsm n.dsm cj d.dsf

μητρί, δῶρον ⌊ὃ ἐὰν⌋
mother, "Whatever benefit you might have received from me is a gift to God," Whatever
3613 4005 6067 6067 6067 6067 6067 1666 1609 1565 4005 1569
n.dsf n.nsn r.asn pl

ἐξ ἐμοῦ ὠφεληθῇς, 6 ↱ ↱ ⌊οὐ μὴ⌋ τιμήσει τὸν πατέρα
from me benefit you might have received he need not honor {the} his father.'
1666 1609 6067 5506 5506 4024 3590 5506 3836 899 4252
p.g r.gs.1 v.aps.2s adv pl v.fai.3s d.asm n.asm

αὐτοῦ·[b] καὶ ἠκυρώσατε τὸν λόγον τοῦ θεοῦ διὰ τὴν παράδοσιν
his So you have nullified the word of God ⌊for the sake of⌋ {the} your tradition.
899 2779 218 3836 3364 3836 2536 1328 3836 7007 4142
r.gsm.3 cj v.aai.2p d.asm n.asm d.gsm n.gsm p.a d.asf n.asf

ὑμῶν. 7 ὑποκριταί, καλῶς → ἐπροφήτευσεν περὶ ὑμῶν Ἠσαΐας λέγων,
your You hypocrites! Well did Isaiah prophesy about you, Isaiah ⌊when he said:⌋
7007 5695 2822 2480 4736 4309 7007 2480 3306
r.gp.2 n.vpm adv v.aai.3s p.g r.gp.2 n.nsm pt.pa.nsm

8 ὁ λαὸς οὗτος τοῖς χείλεσίν με τιμᾷ, ἡ δὲ καρδία
{the} 'This people This honors me ⌊with their⌋ lips, me honors {the} but their hearts
3836 4047 3295 4047 5506 1609 3836 5927 1609 5506 3836 1254 899 2840
d.nsm n.nsm r.nsm d.dpn n.dpn r.as.1 v.pai.3s d.nsf cj n.nsf

αὐτῶν πόρρω ἀπέχει ἀπ' ἐμοῦ· 9 μάτην δὲ σέβονταί με διδάσκοντες
their are far are from me. And in vain And do they worship me, teaching as
899 600 4522 600 608 1609 1254 3472 1254 4936 1609 1438
r.gpm.3 adv v.pai.3s p.g r.gs.1 adv cj v.pmi.3p r.as.1 pt.pa.npm

διδασκαλίας ἐντάλματα ἀνθρώπων. 10 καὶ ↱ προσκαλεσάμενος τὸν ὄχλον
doctrines the commandments of men.'" And he called the crowd
1436 1945 476 2779 3306 4673 3836 4063
n.apf n.apn n.gpm cj pt.am.nsm d.asm n.asm

↤ εἶπεν αὐτοῖς, ἀκούετε καὶ συνίετε· 11 οὐ τὸ εἰσερχόμενον εἰς
to him and said to them, "Hear and understand: It is not what goes into
4673 3306 899 201 2779 5317 4024 3836 1656 1650
v.aai.3s r.dpm.3 v.pam.2p cj v.pam.2p adv d.nsn pt.pm.nsn p.a

τὸ στόμα κοινοῖ τὸν ἄνθρωπον, ἀλλὰ τὸ ἐκπορευόμενον ἐκ τοῦ στόματος
the mouth that defiles a person, but what comes out of the mouth;
3836 5125 3124 3836 476 247 3836 1744 1666 3836 5125
d.asn n.asn v.pai.3s d.asm n.asm cj d.nsn pt.pm.nsn p.g d.gsn n.gsn

τοῦτο κοινοῖ τὸν ἄνθρωπον. 12 τότε προσελθόντες οἱ μαθηταὶ
this defiles a person." Then the disciples came the disciples and
4047 3124 3836 476 5538 3836 3412 4665 3836 3412
r.nsn v.pai.3s d.asm n.asm adv pt.aa.npm d.npm n.npm

NASB

hands when they
eat bread." 3 And
He answered and
said to them, "Why
do you yourselves
transgress the
commandment of
God for the sake of
your tradition? 4 For
God said, 'HONOR
YOUR FATHER AND
MOTHER,' and, 'HE
WHO SPEAKS EVIL OF
FATHER OR MOTHER
IS TO BE PUT TO
DEATH.' 5 But you
say, 'Whoever says
to *his* father or
mother, "Whatever
I have that would
help you has been
given *to God*,"
6 he is not to honor
his father or his
mother[a].' And *by
this* you invali-
dated the word of
God for the sake of
your tradition. 7 You
hypocrites, rightly
did Isaiah prophesy
of you:
8 'THIS PEOPLE
HONORS ME
WITH THEIR
LIPS,
BUT THEIR
HEART IS FAR
AWAY FROM
ME.
9 'BUT IN VAIN DO
THEY WORSHIP
ME,
TEACHING AS
DOCTRINES THE
PRECEPTS OF
MEN.'"
10 After Jesus
called the crowd
to Him, He said to
them, "Hear and
understand. 11 *It is*
not what enters
into the mouth *that*
defiles the man, but
what proceeds out
of the mouth, this
defiles the man."
12 Then the dis-
ciples *came and *

a 4 Exodus 20:12; Deut. 5:16
b 4 Exodus 21:17; Lev. 20:9
c 9 Isaiah 29:13

a [αὐτῶν] UBS, omitted by NET.
b ἢ τὴν μητέρα αὐτοῦ included by TR after αὐτοῦ.

a I.e. by supporting them with it

NIV

to him and asked,
"Do you know that
the Pharisees were
offended when
they heard this?"
13He replied, "Ev-
ery plant that my
heavenly Father
has not planted
will be pulled
up by the roots.
14Leave them; they
are blind guides.[a]
If the blind lead
the blind, both will
fall into a pit."
15Peter said, "Ex-
plain the parable
to us."
16"Are you still so
dull?" Jesus asked
them. 17"Don't you
see that whatever
enters the mouth
goes into the stom-
ach and then out
of the body? 18But
the things that
come out of a per-
son's mouth come
from the heart,
and these defile
them. 19For out of
the heart come evil
thoughts—mur-
der, adultery,
sexual immoral-
ity, theft, false
testimony, slander.
20These are what
defile a person;
but eating with un-
washed hands does
not defile them."

The Faith of a Canaanite Woman

21Leaving that
place, Jesus with-
drew to the region
of Tyre and Sidon.

[a] 14 Some manuscripts *blind guides of the blind*

λέγουσιν αὐτῷ, οἶδας ὅτι οἱ Φαρισαῖοι ἀκούσαντες τὸν
said to him, ⌊"Do you know⌋ that the Pharisees were offended when they heard what
3306 899 3857 4022 3836 5757 4997 4997 201 3836
v.pai.3p r.dsm.3 v.rai.2s cj d.npm n.npm pt.aa.npm d.asm

λόγον ἐσκανδαλίσθησαν; 13 ὁ δὲ ἀποκριθεὶς εἶπεν, πᾶσα φυτεία ἣν
you said?" *were offended* And he *And* answered, saying, "Every plant that my
3364 4997 1254 3836 1254 646 3306 4246 5884 4005 1609
n.asm v.api.3p d.nsm cj pt.ap.nsm v.aai.3s a.nsf n.nsf r.asf

↱ οὐκ ἐφύτευσεν ὁ πατήρ μου ὁ οὐράνιος ἐκριζωθήσεται.
heavenly Father did not plant *{the}* *Father* *my* *{the}* *heavenly* will be rooted up.
4039 4252 5885 4024 5885 3836 4252 1609 3836 4039 1748
adv v.aai.3s d.nsm n.nsm r.gs.1 d.nsm a.nsm v.fpi.3s

14 ἄφετε αὐτούς· ↰ τυφλοί εἰσιν ὁδηγοί[a] τυφλὸς δὲ
Leave them be! They are blind *They are* guides. And if a blind man *And* guides a
918 899 918 1639 1639 5603 1639 3843 1254 1569 5603 1254 3842
v.aam.2p r.apm.3 a.npm v.pai.3p n.npm a.nsm cj

τυφλὸν ἐὰν ὁδηγῇ, ἀμφότεροι εἰς βόθυνον πεσοῦνται. 15
blind man, *if* *guides* both will fall into a pit." *will fall* Then Peter
5603 1569 3842 317 4406 4406 1650 1073 4406 1254 4377
a.asm cj v.pas.3s a.npm p.a n.asm v.fmi.3p

ἀποκριθεὶς δὲ ὁ Πέτρος εἶπεν αὐτῷ, φράσον ἡμῖν τὴν
answered *Then* *{the}* *Peter* him, saying, *him* "Explain this parable to us." *{the}*
646 1254 3836 4377 899 3306 899 5851 4047 4130 7005 3836
pt.ap.nsm cj d.nsm n.nsm v.aai.3s r.dsm.3 v.aam.2s r.dp.1 d.asf

παραβολὴν ταύτην.[b] 16 ὁ δὲ εἶπεν, ἀκμὴν
parable *this* And he *And* said, "Are you without understanding even now?
4130 4047 1254 3836 1254 3306 1639 7007 852 852 2779 197
n.asf r.asf d.nsm cj v.aai.3s adv

καὶ ὑμεῖς ἀσύνετοί ἐστε; 17 ↱ ↱ οὐ νοεῖτε ὅτι πᾶν τὸ
even *you* *without understanding* *Are* Do you not understand that everything that
2779 7007 852 1639 3783 3783 4024 3783 4022 4246 3836
adv r.np.2 a.npm v.pai.2p pl v.pai.2p cj a.nsn d.nsn

εἰσπορευόμενον εἰς τὸ στόμα εἰς τὴν κοιλίαν χωρεῖ καὶ εἰς
goes into the mouth passes through the stomach *passes* and is expelled into
1660 1650 3836 5125 6003 1650 3836 3120 6003 2779 1675 1675 1650
pt.pm.nsn p.a d.asn n.asn p.a d.asf n.asf v.pai.3s cj p.a

ἀφεδρῶνα ἐκβάλλεται; 18 τὰ δὲ ἐκπορευόμενα ἐκ τοῦ στόματος ἐκ
the latrine? *is expelled* But the *But* things that go out of the mouth come from
909 1675 1254 3836 1254 1744 1666 3836 5125 2002 1666
n.asm v.ppi.3s d.npn cj pt.pm.npn p.g d.gsn n.gsn p.g

τῆς καρδίας ἐξέρχεται, κἀκεῖνα κοινοῖ τὸν ἄνθρωπον. 19 ἐκ γὰρ τῆς καρδίας
the heart, *come* and these defile the person. For ⌊out of⌋ *For* the heart
3836 2840 2002 2797 3124 3836 476 1142 1666 1142 3836 2840
d.gsf n.gsf v.pmi.3s cj v.pai.3s d.asm n.asm p.g cj d.gsf n.gsf

ἐξέρχονται διαλογισμοὶ πονηροί, φόνοι, μοιχεῖαι, πορνεῖαι, κλοπαί,
come evil thoughts, *evil* murder, adultery, sexual immorality, theft,
2002 4505 1369 4505 5840 3657 4518 3113
v.pmi.3p n.npm a.npm n.npm n.npf n.npf n.npf

ψευδομαρτυρίαι, βλασφημίαι. 20 ταῦτά ἐστιν τὰ κοινοῦντα τὸν ἄνθρωπον, τὸ
false witness, slander. These are the things that defile a person, *{the}*
6019 1060 4047 1639 3836 3124 3836 476 3836
n.npf n.npf r.npn v.pai.3s d.npn pt.pa.npn d.asm n.asm d.nsn

δὲ ἀνίπτοις χερσὶν φαγεῖν ↱ οὐ κοινοῖ τὸν ἄνθρωπον. 21 καὶ
but to eat with unwashed hands *to eat* does not defile a person." And
1254 2266 2266 481 5931 2266 3124 4024 3124 3836 476 2779
cj a.dpf n.dpf f.aa adv v.pai.3s d.asm n.asm cj

ἐξελθὼν ἐκεῖθεν ὁ Ἰησοῦς ἀνεχώρησεν εἰς τὰ μέρη Τύρου καὶ Σιδῶνος. 22 καὶ
leaving there, *{the}* Jesus withdrew into the region of Tyre and Sidon. And
2002 1696 3836 2652 432 1650 3836 3538 5602 2779 4972 2779
pt.aa.nsm adv d.nsm n.nsm v.aai.3s p.a d.apn n.apn n.gsf cj n.gsf cj

[a] τυφλῶν included by UBS after ὁδηγοί.
[b] [ταύτην] UBS, omitted by TNIV.

NASB

said to Him, "Do
You know that
the Pharisees
were offended
when they heard
this statement?"
13But He answered
and said, "Every
plant which My
heavenly Father
did not plant shall
be uprooted. 14Let
them alone; they
are blind guides [a]of
the blind. And if a
blind man guides
a blind man, both
will fall into a pit."

The Heart of Man

15Peter said to
Him, "Explain the
parable to us." 16Je-
sus said, "Are you
still lacking in un-
derstanding also?
17Do you not under-
stand that every-
thing that goes into
the mouth passes
into the stomach,
and is eliminated?
18But the things
that proceed out of
the mouth come
from the heart, and
those defile the
man. 19For out of
the heart come evil
thoughts, murders,
adulteries, fornica-
tions, thefts, false
witness, slanders.
20These are the
things which defile
the man; but to eat
with unwashed
hands does not de-
file the man."

The Syrophoenician Woman

21Jesus went away
from there, and
withdrew into the
district of Tyre and
Sidon. 22And a

[a] Later mss add *of the blind*

NIV

[22]A Canaanite
woman from that
vicinity came to
him, crying out,
"Lord, Son of Da-
vid, have mercy on
me! My daughter
is demon-pos-
sessed and suffer-
ing terribly."
[23]Jesus did not
answer a word.
So his disciples
came to him and
urged him, "Send
her away, for she
keeps crying out
after us."
[24]He answered,
"I was sent only to
the lost sheep of
Israel."
[25]The woman
came and knelt
before him. "Lord,
help me!" she said.
[26]He replied,
"It is not right to
take the children's
bread and toss it to
the dogs."
[27]"Yes it is,
Lord," she said.
"Even the dogs
eat the crumbs
that fall from their
master's table."
[28]Then Jesus said
to her, "Woman,
you have great
faith! Your request
is granted." And
her daughter was
healed at that mo-
ment.

Jesus Feeds the Four Thousand

[29]Jesus left there
and went along
the Sea of Galilee.
Then he went up
on a mountain-
side and sat down.
[30]Great crowds
came to him,
bringing the

ἰδοὺ γυνὴ Χαναναία ἀπὸ τῶν ὁρίων ἐκείνων ἐξελθοῦσα
{behold} a Canaanite woman *Canaanite* from *{the}* that region *that* came out and
2627 5914 1222 5914 608 3836 1697 3990 1697 2002
j n.nsf a.nsf p.g d.gpn n.gpn r.gpn pt.aa.nsf

ἔκραζεν λέγουσα, ἐλέησόν με, κύριε υἱὸς Δαυίδ· ἡ θυγάτηρ
⌊began to shout,⌋ saying, ⌊"Have mercy on⌋ me, O Lord, Son of David; *{the}* my daughter
3189 3306 1796 1609 3261 5626 1253 3836 1609 2588
v.iai.3s pt.pa.nsf v.aam.2s r.as.1 n.vsm n.nsm n.gsm d.nsf n.nsf

μου ↱ κακῶς δαιμονίζεται. 23 ὁ δὲ οὐκ ἀπεκρίθη αὐτῇ
my is horribly demon-possessed." But he *But* answered her not *answered* *her* a
1609 1227 2809 1227 1254 3836 1254 646 899 4024 646 899
r.gs.1 adv v.ppi.3s d.nsm cj adv v.api.3s r.dsf.3

λόγον. καὶ προσελθόντες οἱ μαθηταὶ αὐτοῦ ἠρώτουν αὐτὸν
word. And his disciples came *{the}* *disciples* *his* and urged him,
3364 2779 899 3412 4665 3836 3412 899 2263 899
n.asm cj pt.aa.npm d.npm n.npm r.gsm.3 v.iai.3p r.asm.3

λέγοντες, ἀπόλυσον αὐτήν, ↰ ὅτι κράζει ὄπισθεν ἡμῶν. 24 ὁ
saying, "Send her away, because ⌊she keeps shouting⌋ after us." But he
3306 668 899 668 4022 3189 3957 7005 1254 3836
pt.pa.npm v.aam.2s r.asf.3 cj v.pai.3s p.g r.gp.1 d.nsm

δὲ ἀποκριθεὶς εἶπεν, ↱ ↱ οὐκ ἀπεστάλην ⌊εἰ μὴ⌋ εἰς τὰ πρόβατα τὰ
But answered, saying, "I was not sent except to the lost sheep *{the}*
1254 646 3306 690 690 4024 690 1623 3590 1650 3836 660 4585 3836
cj pt.ap.nsm v.aai.3s adv v.api.1s cj pl p.a d.apn n.apn d.apn

ἀπολωλότα → οἴκου Ἰσραήλ. 25 ἡ δὲ ἐλθοῦσα προσεκύνει αὐτῷ
lost of the house of Israel." Then she *Then* came and knelt before him,
660 3875 2702 1254 3836 1254 2262 4686 899
pt.ra.apn n.gsm n.gsm d.nsf cj pt.aa.nsf v.iai.3s r.dsm.3

λέγουσα, κύριε, βοήθει μοι. 26 ὁ δὲ ἀποκριθεὶς εἶπεν, οὐκ ἔστιν
saying, "Lord, help me!" And he *And* answered, *{he said}* "It is not *It is*
3306 3261 1070 1609 1254 3836 1254 646 3306 1639 1639 4024 1639
pt.pa.nsf n.vsm v.pam.2s r.ds.1 d.nsm cj pt.ap.nsm v.aai.3s adv v.pai.3s

καλὸν λαβεῖν τὸν ἄρτον τῶν τέκνων καὶ βαλεῖν τοῖς κυναρίοις. 27
right to take *{the}* bread ⌊from the⌋ children and toss it to the dogs." "Yes, Lord,"
2819 3284 3836 788 3836 5451 2779 965 3836 3249 3721 3261
a.nsn f.aa d.asm n.asm d.gpn n.gpn cj f.aa d.dpn n.dpn

ἡ δὲ εἶπεν, ναὶ κύριε, καὶ γὰρ τὰ κυνάρια ἐσθίει ἀπὸ τῶν ψιχίων τῶν
she *{and}* said, *Yes* *Lord* "but even *but* the dogs feed on the crumbs that
3836 1254 3306 3721 3261 1142 2779 1142 3836 3249 2266 608 3836 6033 3836
d.nsf cj v.aai.3s pl n.vsm adv cj d.npn n.npn v.pai.3s p.g d.gpn n.gpn d.gpn

πιπτόντων ἀπὸ τῆς τραπέζης τῶν κυρίων αὐτῶν. 28 τότε ἀποκριθεὶς
fall from *{the}* their masters' table." *{the}* *masters'* *their* Then Jesus answered,
4406 608 3836 899 3261 5544 3836 3261 899 5538 2652 646
pt.pa.gpn p.g d.gsf n.gsf d.gpm n.gpm r.gpm.3 adv pt.ap.nsm

ὁ Ἰησοῦς εἶπεν αὐτῇ, ὦ γύναι, μεγάλη σου ἡ πίστις·
{the} *Jesus* saying to her, "O woman, great is your *{the}* faith! What you desire
3836 2652 3306 899 6043 1222 3489 5148 3836 4411 6055 2527 2527
d.nsm n.nsm v.aai.3s r.dsf.3 j n.vsf a.nsf r.gs.2 d.nsf n.nsf

γενηθήτω σοι ὡς θέλεις. καὶ ἰάθη ἡ θυγάτηρ αὐτῆς ἀπὸ
will be done ⌊for you."⌋ *What you desire* And her daughter was healed *{the}* *daughter* *her* from
1181 5148 6055 2527 2779 899 2588 2615 3836 2588 899 608
v.apm.3s r.ds.2 cj v.pai.2s cj v.api.3s d.nsf n.nsf r.gsf.3 p.g

τῆς ὥρας ἐκείνης. 29 καὶ → μεταβὰς ἐκεῖθεν ὁ Ἰησοῦς ἦλθεν
{the} that hour. *that* *{and}* After Jesus left from there, *{the}* *Jesus* he passed
3836 1697 6052 1697 2779 2652 3553 1696 3836 2652 2262
d.gsf n.gsf r.gsf cj pt.aa.nsm adv d.nsm n.nsm v.aai.3s

παρὰ τὴν θάλασσαν τῆς Γαλιλαίας, καὶ ἀναβὰς εἰς τὸ ὄρος ἐκάθητο
by the Sea of Galilee and went up on the mountain where he sat down.
4123 3836 2498 3836 1133 2779 326 1650 3836 4001 1695 2764
p.a d.asf n.asf d.gsf n.gsf cj pt.aa.nsm p.a d.asn n.asn v.imi.3s

ἐκεῖ. 30 καὶ προσῆλθον αὐτῷ ὄχλοι πολλοὶ ἔχοντες μεθ᾽ ἑαυτῶν
where And great crowds came to him, *crowds* *great* bringing with them
1695 2779 4498 4063 4665 899 4063 4498 2400 3552 1571
adv cj v.aai.3p r.dsm.3 n.npm a.npm pt.pa.npm p.g r.gpm.3

NASB

Canaanite woman
from that region
came out and *be-
gan* to cry out, say-
ing, "Have mercy
on me, Lord, Son
of David; my
daughter is cruelly
demon-possessed."
[23]But He did not
answer her a word.
And His disciples
came and implored
Him, saying, "Send
her away, because
she keeps shouting
at us." [24]But He
answered and said,
"I was sent only to
the lost sheep of
the house of Isra-
el." [25]But she came
and *began* to bow
down before Him,
saying, "Lord, help
me!" [26]And He
answered and said,
"It is not good to
take the children's
bread and throw it
to the dogs." [27]But
she said, "Yes,
Lord; but even the
dogs feed on the
crumbs which fall
from their masters'
table." [28]Then Jesus
said to her, "O
woman, your faith
is great; it shall be
done for you as
you wish." And
her daughter was
healed at once.

Healing Crowds

[29]Departing from
there, Jesus went
along by the Sea of
Galilee, and hav-
ing gone up on the
mountain, He was
sitting there. [30]And
large crowds came
to Him, bringing
with them *those*

NIV

lame, the blind,
the crippled, the
mute and many
others, and laid
them at his feet;
and he healed
them. 31 The people
were amazed when
they saw the mute
speaking, the crip-
pled made well,
the lame walk-
ing and the blind
seeing. And they
praised the God of
Israel.
32 Jesus called his
disciples to him
and said, "I have
compassion for
these people; they
have already been
with me three days
and have nothing
to eat. I do not
want to send them
away hungry, or
they may collapse
on the way."
33 His disciples
answered, "Where
could we get
enough bread in
this remote place
to feed such a
crowd?"
34 "How many
loaves do you
have?" Jesus
asked.
"Seven," they re-
plied, "and a few
small fish."
35 He told the
crowd to sit down
on the ground.
36 Then he took
the seven loaves
and the fish, and
when he had given
thanks, he broke
them and gave
them to the disci-
ples, and they in
turn to the people.
37 They all ate and
were satisfied.
Afterward the dis-
ciples picked up
seven basketfuls of
broken pieces that
were left over.

χωλούς, τυφλούς, κυλλούς, κωφούς, καὶ ἑτέρους πολλοὺς καὶ
⌊those who were lame,⌋ blind, crippled, mute, and many others; *many* and
6000 5603 3245 3273 2779 4498 2283 4498 2779
a.apm a.apm a.apm a.apm cj r.apm a.apm cj

ἔρριψαν αὐτοὺς ↰ παρὰ τοὺς πόδας αὐτοῦ, καὶ ἐθεράπευσεν αὐτούς· 31 ὥστε
they put them down at *{the}* his feet *his* and he healed them. So
4849 899 4849 4123 3836 899 4546 899 2779 2543 899 6063
v.aai.3p r.apm.3 p.a d.apm n.apm r.gsm.3 cj v.aai.3s r.apm.3 cj

τὸν ὄχλον θαυμάσαι βλέποντας κωφοὺς λαλοῦντας, κυλλοὺς ὑγιεῖς καὶ
the crowd was astonished when they saw the mute speaking, the crippled restored, *{and}*
3836 4063 2513 1063 3273 3281 3245 5618 2779
d.asm n.asm f.aa pt.pa.apm a.apm pt.pa.apm a.apm a.apm cj

χωλοὺς περιπατοῦντας καὶ τυφλοὺς βλέποντας· καὶ ἐδόξασαν τὸν θεὸν
the lame walking, and the blind seeing, and they praised the God
6000 4344 2779 5603 1063 2779 1519 3836 2536
a.apm pt.pa.apm cj a.apm pt.pa.apm cj v.aai.3p d.asm n.asm

Ἰσραήλ. 32 ὁ δὲ Ἰησοῦς προσκαλεσάμενος τοὺς μαθητὰς αὐτοῦ[a] ↰
of Israel. *{the}* Then Jesus called *{the}* his disciples *his* to him and
2702 3836 1254 2652 4673 3836 899 3412 899 4673
n.gsm d.nsm cj n.nsm pt.am.nsm d.apm n.apm r.gsm.3

εἶπεν, σπλαγχνίζομαι ἐπὶ τὸν ὄχλον, ὅτι ἤδη
said, "I have compassion on the crowd because they have already been with me three
3306 5072 2093 3836 4063 4022 4693 4693 2453 4693 4693 1609 5552
v.aai.3s v.ppi.1s p.a d.asm n.asm cj adv

ἡμέραι τρεῖς προσμένουσίν μοι καὶ οὐκ ἔχουσιν τί φάγωσιν· καὶ
days *three* *they have been with* *me* and have nothing *have* ~ to eat; and I do
2465 5552 4693 1609 2779 2400 4024 2400 5515 2266 2779 2527 2527
n.npf a.npf v.pai.3p r.ds.1 cj adv v.pai.3p r.asn v.aas.3p cj

ἀπολῦσαι αὐτοὺς ↰ νήστεις οὐ θέλω, μήποτε ἐκλυθῶσιν
not want to send them away hungry, *not* *I do want* lest ⌊they faint from exhaustion⌋
4024 2527 668 899 668 3765 4024 2527 3607 1725
f.aa r.apm.3 a.apm adv v.pai.1s cj v.aps.3p

ἐν τῇ ὁδῷ. 33 καὶ λέγουσιν αὐτῷ οἱ μαθηταί, πόθεν ἡμῖν ἐν
on the way." And the disciples said to him, *{the}* *the disciples* "Where *we* in such
1877 3836 3847 2779 3412 3412 3306 899 3836 3412 4470 7005 1877
p.d d.dsf n.dsf cj v.pai.3p r.dsm.3 d.npm n.npm cj r.dp.1 p.d

ἐρημίᾳ ἄρτοι τοσοῦτοι ὥστε χορτάσαι ὄχλον
a ⌊desolate place⌋ could we find enough bread *enough* to feed so great a crowd?"
2244 7005 5537 788 5537 6063 5963 5537 5537 4063
n.dsf n.npm r.npm cj f.aa n.asm

τοσοῦτον; 34 καὶ λέγει αὐτοῖς ὁ Ἰησοῦς, πόσους ἄρτους ἔχετε;
so great And Jesus said to them, *{the}* *Jesus* "How many loaves ⌊do you have?"⌋ And
5537 2779 2652 3306 899 3836 2652 4531 788 2400 1254
r.asm cj v.pai.3s r.dpm.3 d.nsm n.nsm r.apm n.apm v.pai.2p

οἱ δὲ εἶπαν, ἑπτὰ καὶ ὀλίγα ἰχθύδια. 35 καὶ παραγγείλας τῷ ὄχλῳ ἀναπεσεῖν
they *And* said, "Seven, and a few little fish." And instructing the crowd to sit down
3836 1254 3306 2231 2779 3900 2715 2779 4133 3836 4063 404
d.npm cj v.aai.3p a.apm cj a.apn n.apn cj pt.aa.nsm d.dsm n.dsm f.aa

ἐπὶ τὴν γῆν 36 ἔλαβεν τοὺς ἑπτὰ ἄρτους καὶ τοὺς ἰχθύας καὶ
on the ground, he took the seven loaves and the fish: and
2093 3836 1178 3284 3836 2231 788 2779 3836 2716 2779
p.a d.asf n.asf v.aai.3s d.apm a.apm n.apm cj d.apm n.apm cj

εὐχαριστήσας ἔκλασεν καὶ ἐδίδου τοῖς μαθηταῖς, οἱ
⌊when he had given thanks,⌋ he broke them and began distributing them to the disciples, and the
2373 3089 2779 1443 3836 3412 1254 3836
pt.aa.nsm v.aai.3s cj v.iai.3s d.dpm n.dpm d.npm

δὲ μαθηταὶ τοῖς ὄχλοις. 37 καὶ → ἔφαγον πάντες καὶ ἐχορτάσθησαν. καὶ
and disciples to the crowds. And they all ate *all* and were filled; and they
1254 3412 3836 4063 2779 4246 2266 4246 2779 5963 2779 149
cj n.npm d.dpm n.dpm cj v.aai.3p a.npm cj v.api.3p cj

τὸ περισσεῦον τῶν κλασμάτων ἦραν ἑπτὰ σπυρίδας πλήρεις.
picked up what was left over of the broken pieces, *they picked up* seven large baskets full.
149 149 3836 4355 3836 3083 149 2231 5083 4441
d.asn pt.pa.asn d.gpn n.gpn v.aai.3p a.apf n.apf a.apf

NASB

who were lame,
crippled, blind,
mute, and many
others, and they
laid them down at
His feet; and He
healed them. 31 So
the crowd mar-
veled as they saw
the mute speak-
ing, the crippled
restored, and the
lame walking, and
the blind seeing;
and they glorified
the God of Israel.

Four Thousand Fed

32 And Jesus called
His disciples to
Him, and said, "I
feel compassion
for the people,
because they have
remained with Me
now three days
and have nothing
to eat; and I do not
want to send them
away hungry, for
they might faint
on the way." 33 The
disciples *said
to Him, "Where
would we get so
many loaves in *this*
desolate place to
satisfy such a large
crowd?" 34 And
Jesus *said to them,
"How many loaves
do you have?" And
they said, "Seven,
and a few small
fish." 35 And He
directed the people
to sit down on the
ground; 36 and He
took the seven
loaves and the fish;
and giving thanks,
He broke them and
started giving them
to the disciples,
and the disciples
gave them to the
people. 37 And they
all ate and were
satisfied, and they
picked up what
was left over of
the broken pieces,
seven large baskets
full. 38 And

[a] αὐτοῦ omitted by NET.

NIV

[38]The number of
those who ate was
four thousand
men, besides wom-
en and children.
[39]After Jesus had
sent the crowd
away, he got into
the boat and went
to the vicinity of
Magadan.

The Demand for a Sign

16 The Phar-
isees and
Sadducees came
to Jesus and tested
him by asking him
to show them a
sign from heaven.
[2]He replied,
"When evening
comes, you say,
'It will be fair
weather, for the
sky is red,' [3]and
in the morning,
'Today it will be
stormy, for the sky
is red and over-
cast.' You know
how to interpret
the appearance of
the sky, but you
cannot interpret
the signs of the
times.[a] [4]A wick-
ed and adulterous
generation looks
for a sign, but none
will be given it
except the sign of
Jonah." Jesus then
left them and went
away.

The Yeast of the Pharisees and Sadducees

[5]When they went
across the lake, the
disciples forgot to
take bread. [6]"Be
careful," Jesus said
to them. "Be on
your guard against
the yeast of the
Pharisees and

[a] 2,3 Some early manuscripts do not have *When evening comes . . . of the times.*

---

38 οἱ δὲ ἐσθίοντες ἦσαν
Not counting women and children, there *{and}* were four thousand men who had eaten. *were*
6006 6006 1222 2779 4086 3836 1254 1639 5483 5483 467 2266 1639
d.npm cj pt.pa.npm v.iai.3p

τετρακισχίλιοι ἄνδρες χωρὶς γυναικῶν καὶ παιδίων.[a] 39 Καὶ ἀπολύσας
four thousand *men* *Not counting* *women* *and* *children* And ⌊when he had sent⌋
5483 467 6006 1222 2779 4086 2779 668
a.npm n.npm p.g n.gpf cj n.gpn cj pt.aa.nsm

τοὺς ὄχλους ↰ ἐνέβη εἰς τὸ πλοῖον καὶ ἦλθεν εἰς τὰ ὅρια Μαγαδάν.
the crowds away, he got into the boat and went to the region of Magadan.
3836 4063 668 1832 1650 3836 4450 2779 2262 1650 3836 3990 3400
d.apm n.apm v.aai.3s p.a d.asn n.asn cj v.aai.3s p.a d.apn n.apn n.gsf

16:1 καὶ προσελθόντες οἱ Φαρισαῖοι καὶ
Now when the Pharisees and Sadducees came *the* *Pharisees* *and*
2779 3836 5757 2779 4881 4665 3836 5757 2779
cj pt.aa.npm d.npm n.npm cj

Σαδδουκαῖοι πειράζοντες ἐπηρώτησαν αὐτὸν σημεῖον ἐκ τοῦ
Sadducees to test Jesus, they asked him to show them a sign from *{the}*
4881 4279 2089 899 2109 2109 899 4956 1666 3836
n.npm pt.pa.npm v.aai.3p r.asm.3 n.asn p.g d.gsm

οὐρανοῦ ἐπιδεῖξαι αὐτοῖς. 2 ὁ δὲ ἀποκριθεὶς εἶπεν αὐτοῖς, ↱
heaven. *to show* *them* And he *And* answered them, saying, *them* "When
4041 2109 899 1254 3836 1254 646 899 3306 899 1181
n.gsm f.aa r.dpm.3 d.nsm cj pt.ap.nsm v.aai.3s r.dpm.3

[ὀψίας γενομένης λέγετε, εὐδία, πυρράζει γὰρ ὁ
evening comes, you say, ⌊'The weather will be fair,⌋ for the sky is red'; *for* *the*
4068 1181 3306 2304 1142 3836 4041 4793 1142 3836
n.gsf pt.am.gsf v.pai.2p n.nsf v.pai.3s cj d.nsm

οὐρανός· 3 καὶ πρωΐ· σήμερον χειμών, πυρράζει
sky and ⌊in the morning,⌋ 'It will be stormy today, *stormy* for the sky is red
4041 2779 4745 5930 4958 5930 1142 3836 4041 4793
n.nsm cj adv adv n.nsm v.pai.3s

γὰρ στυγνάζων ὁ οὐρανός.[b] τὸ μὲν πρόσωπον τοῦ
for and threatening.' *the* *sky* You know how to interpret the ~ appearance of the
1142 5145 3836 4041 1182 1182 1359 1359 3836 3525 4725 3836
cj pt.pa.nsm d.nsm n.nsm d.asn pl n.asn d.gsm

οὐρανοῦ γινώσκετε διακρίνειν, τὰ δὲ σημεῖα τῶν
sky, *You know* *to interpret* but you are not able to evaluate the *but* signs of the
4041 1182 1359 1254 1538 1538 4024 1538 3836 1254 4956 3836
n.gsm v.pai.2p f.pa d.apn cj n.apn d.gpm

καιρῶν οὐ δύνασθε;]4 γενεὰ πονηρὰ καὶ μοιχαλὶς
times? *not* *you are able* An evil and adulterous generation *evil* *and* *adulterous* looks for
2789 4024 1538 4505 2779 3655 1155 4505 2779 3655 2118 2118
n.gpm adv v.ppi.2p n.nsf a.nsf cj a.nsf

σημεῖον ἐπιζητεῖ, καὶ σημεῖον οὐ δοθήσεται αὐτῇ ⌊εἰ μὴ⌋ τὸ σημεῖον
a sign, *looks for* but no sign *no* will be given it except the sign
4956 2118 2779 4024 4956 4024 1443 899 1623 3590 3836 4956
n.asn v.pai.3s cj n.nsn adv v.fpi.3s r.dsf.3 cj pl d.nsn n.nsn

Ἰωνᾶ. καὶ ↱ καταλιπὼν αὐτοὺς ἀπῆλθεν. 5 καὶ ἐλθόντες οἱ
of Jonah." Then he left them and went away. *{and}* The disciples arrived *The*
2731 2779 599 2901 899 599 2779 3836 3412 2262 3836
n.gsm cj pt.aa.nsm r.apm.3 v.aai.3s cj pt.aa.npm d.npm

μαθηταὶ εἰς τὸ πέραν ἐπελάθοντο ἄρτους λαβεῖν. 6 ὁ δὲ
disciples at the other side but had forgotten to take any bread. *to take* *{the}* *{and}*
3412 1650 3836 4305 2140 3284 3284 788 3284 3836 1254
n.npm p.a d.asn adv v.ami.3p n.apm f.aa d.nsm cj

Ἰησοῦς εἶπεν αὐτοῖς, ὁρᾶτε καὶ προσέχετε ἀπὸ τῆς ζύμης τῶν Φαρισαίων καὶ
Jesus said to them, ⌊"Watch out,⌋ and beware of the leaven of the Pharisees and
2652 3306 899 3972 2779 4668 608 3836 2434 3836 5757 2779
n.nsm v.aai.3s r.dpm.3 v.pam.2p cj v.pam.2p p.g d.gsf n.gsf d.gpm n.gpm cj

[a] γυναικῶν καὶ παιδίων omitted by NET.
[b] ὑποκριταί included by TR after οὐρανός.

NASB

those who ate were
four thousand men,
besides women and
children.
[39]And sending
away the crowds,
Jesus got into the
boat and came
to the region of
Magadan.

Pharisees Test Jesus

[16:1]The Pharisees
and Sadducees
came up, and
testing Jesus,
they asked Him
to show them a
sign from heaven.
[2]But He replied
to them, "When
it is evening, you
say, '*It will be* fair
weather, for the
sky is red.' [3]And
in the morning,
'*There will be* a
storm today, for
the sky is red and
threatening.' Do
you know how to
discern the appear-
ance of the sky, but
cannot *discern* the
signs of the times?
[4]An evil and adul-
terous generation
seeks after a sign;
and a sign will not
be given it, except
the sign of Jonah."
And He left them
and went away.
[5]And the disciples
came to the other
side *of the sea,* but
they had forgotten
to bring *any* bread.
[6]And Jesus said
to them, "Watch
out and beware of
the leaven of the
Pharisees and Sad-
ducees." [7]They

NIV

Sadducees."
[7]They discussed
this among them-
selves and said,
"It is because we
didn't bring any
bread."
[8]Aware of their
discussion, Jesus
asked, "You of lit-
tle faith, why are
you talking among
yourselves about
having no bread?
[9]Do you still not
understand? Don't
you remember
the five loaves for
the five thousand,
and how many
basketfuls you
gathered? [10]Or the
seven loaves for
the four thousand,
and how many
basketfuls you
gathered? [11]How
is it you don't un-
derstand that I was
not talking to you
about bread? But
be on your guard
against the yeast
of the Pharisees
and Sadducees."
[12]Then they under-
stood that he was
not telling them
to guard against
the yeast used in
bread, but against
the teaching of the
Pharisees and Sad-
ducees.

Peter Declares That Jesus Is the Messiah

[13]When Jesus
came to the region
of Caesarea Phi-
lippi, he asked his
disciples, "Who do
people say the Son
of Man is?"
[14]They replied,
"Some say John
the Baptist; others
say Elijah; and still
others, Jeremiah or
one of the proph-
ets."
[15]"But what about
you?" he asked.
"Who do you say
I am?"
[16]Simon Peter an-
swered, "You are

Σαδδουκαίων. 7 οἱ δὲ διελογίζοντο ἐν ἑαυτοῖς λέγοντες
Sadducees." And they *And* began to discuss this among themselves, saying, "It is
4881 1254 3836 1254 1368 1877 1571 3306
n.gpm d.npm cj v.imi.3p p.d r.dpm.3 pt.pa.npm

ὅτι ἄρτους οὐκ ἐλάβομεν. 8 → γνοὺς δὲ ὁ
because we brought no bread." *no* *we brought* But when Jesus ⌊became aware⌋ *But* *{the}*
4022 3284 3284 4024 788 4024 3284 1254 2652 1182 1254 3836
cj n.apm adv v.aai.1p pt.aa.nsm cj d.nsm

Ἰησοῦς εἶπεν, τί διαλογίζεσθε ἐν ἑαυτοῖς,
Jesus of this, he said, "O you of little faith, why are you discussing among yourselves
2652 3306 3899 3899 3899 3899 5515 1368 1877 1571
n.nsm v.aai.3s r.asn v.pmi.2p p.d r.dpm.2

ὀλιγόπιστοι, ὅτι ἄρτους οὐκ ἔχετε; 9 ↱ ↱ οὔπω νοεῖτε,
you of little faith the fact that you have no bread? *no* *you have* Do you not yet understand?
3899 4022 2400 2400 4024 788 4024 2400 3783 3783 4037 3783
a.vpm cj n.apm adv v.pai.2p adv v.pai.2p

↱ ↱ οὐδὲ μνημονεύετε τοὺς πέντε ἄρτους τῶν πεντακισχιλίων καὶ πόσους
Do you not remember the five loaves for the five thousand, and how many
3648 3648 4028 3648 3836 4297 788 3836 4295 2779 4531
cj v.pai.2p d.apm a.apm n.apm d.gpm a.gpm cj r.apm

κοφίνους ἐλάβετε; 10 οὐδὲ τοὺς ἑπτὰ ἄρτους τῶν τετρακισχιλίων καὶ πόσας
baskets you gathered? Or the seven loaves for the four thousand, and how many
3186 3284 4028 3836 2231 788 3836 5483 2779 4531
n.apm v.aai.2p cj d.apm a.apm n.apm d.gpm a.gpm cj r.apf

σπυρίδας ἐλάβετε; 11 πῶς ↱ ↱ οὐ νοεῖτε ὅτι οὐ
baskets you gathered? How is it that you do not understand that I was not speaking
5083 3284 4802 3783 3783 4024 3783 4022 3306 3306 4024 3306
n.apf v.aai.2p cj adv v.pai.2p cj adv

περὶ ἄρτων εἶπον ὑμῖν; προσέχετε δὲ ἀπὸ τῆς ζύμης τῶν
to you about bread? *I was speaking* *to you* Beware *{and}* of the leaven of the
7007 7007 4309 788 3306 7007 4668 1254 608 3836 2434 3836
p.g n.gpm v.aai.1s r.dp.2 v.pam.2p cj p.g d.gsf n.gsf d.gpm

Φαρισαίων καὶ Σαδδουκαίων. 12 τότε συνῆκαν ὅτι ↱ ↱ οὐκ εἶπεν
Pharisees and Sadducees." Then they understood that he had not told them
5757 2779 4881 5538 5317 4022 3306 3306 4024 3306
n.gpm cj n.gpm adv v.aai.3p cj adv v.aai.3s

προσέχειν ἀπὸ τῆς ζύμης τῶν ἄρτων ἀλλὰ ἀπὸ τῆς διδαχῆς τῶν Φαρισαίων καὶ
to beware of the leaven of bread but of the teaching of the Pharisees and
4668 608 3836 2434 3836 788 247 608 3836 1439 3836 5757 2779
f.pa p.g d.gsf n.gsf d.gpm n.gpm cj p.g d.gsf n.gsf d.gpm n.gpm cj

Σαδδουκαίων. 13 → ἐλθὼν δὲ ὁ Ἰησοῦς εἰς τὰ μέρη Καισαρείας
Sadducees. Now when Jesus came *Now* *{the}* *Jesus* into the region of Caesarea
4881 1254 2652 2262 1254 3836 2652 1650 3836 3538 2791
n.gpm pt.aa.nsm cj d.nsm n.nsm p.a d.apn n.apn n.gsf

τῆς Φιλίππου ἠρώτα τοὺς μαθητὰς αὐτοῦ λέγων, τίνα → λέγουσιν οἱ
{the} Philippi, he asked *{the}* his disciples, *his* *{saying}* "Who do people say *{the}*
3836 5805 2263 3836 899 3412 899 3306 5515 476 3306 3836
d.gsf n.gsm v.iai.3s d.apm n.apm r.gsm.3 pt.pa.nsm r.asm v.pai.3p d.npm

ἄνθρωποι εἶναι τὸν υἱὸν τοῦ ἀνθρώπου; 14 οἱ δὲ εἶπαν, οἱ
people *is* that the Son of Man is?" And they *And* said, "Some
476 1639 3836 5626 3836 476 1639 1254 3836 1254 3306 3836
n.npm f.pa d.asm n.asm d.gsm n.gsm d.npm cj v.aai.3p d.npm

μὲν Ἰωάννην τὸν βαπτιστήν, ἄλλοι δὲ Ἠλίαν, ἕτεροι δὲ Ἰερεμίαν ἢ
~ say John the Baptist, others *{and}* Elijah, and others *and* Jeremiah or
3525 2722 3836 969 257 1254 2460 1254 2283 1254 2635 2445
pl n.asm d.asm n.asm r.npm pl n.asm r.npm pl n.asm cj

ἕνα τῶν προφητῶν. 15 λέγει αὐτοῖς, ὑμεῖς δὲ τίνα με
one of the prophets." He said to them, "But you, *But* who do you say that I
1651 3836 4737 3306 899 1254 7007 1254 5515 3306 3306 3306 1609
a.asm d.gpm n.gpm v.pai.3s r.dpm.3 r.np.2 cj r.asm r.as.1

λέγετε εἶναι; 16 ἀποκριθεὶς δὲ Σίμων Πέτρος εἶπεν, σὺ εἶ
do you say am?" And Simon Peter answered, *And* *Simon* *Peter* saying, "You are
3306 1639 1254 4981 4377 646 1254 4981 4377 3306 5148 1639
v.pai.2p f.pa pt.ap.nsm cj n.nsm n.nsm v.aai.3s r.ns.2 v.pai.2s

NASB

began to discuss
this among them-
selves, saying, "*He
said that* because
we did not bring
any bread." [8]But
Jesus, aware of
this, said, "You
men of little faith,
why do you discuss
among yourselves
that you have no
bread? [9]Do you
not yet understand
or remember the
five loaves of the
five thousand, and
how many baskets
full you picked
up? [10]Or the seven
loaves of the four
thousand, and how
many large baskets
full you picked up?
[11]How is it that you
do not understand
that I did not speak
to you concerning
bread? But beware
of the leaven of
the Pharisees and
Sadducees." [12]Then
they understood
that He did not say
to beware of the
leaven of bread,
but of the teaching
of the Pharisees
and Sadducees.

Peter's Confession of Christ

[13]Now when
Jesus came into
the district of
Caesarea Philippi,
He was asking His
disciples, "Who
do people say that
the Son of Man
is?" [14]And they
said, "Some *say*
John the Baptist;
and others, Elijah;
but still others,
Jeremiah, or one of
the prophets." [15]He
*said to them, "But
who do you say
that I am?" [16]Simon
Peter answered,
"You are

NIV

the Messiah, the
Son of the living
God."
17 Jesus replied,
"Blessed are you,
Simon son of Jo-
nah, for this was
not revealed to you
by flesh and blood,
but by my Father
in heaven. 18 And
I tell you that you
are Peter,[a] and on
this rock I will
build my church,
and the gates of
Hades[b] will not
overcome it. 19 I
will give you the
keys of the king-
dom of heaven;
whatever you bind
on earth will be[c]
bound in heaven,
and whatever you
loose on earth will
be[d] loosed in heav-
en." 20 Then he or-
dered his disciples
not to tell anyone
that he was the
Messiah.

Jesus Predicts His Death

21 From that time
on Jesus began to
explain to his dis-
ciples that he must
go to Jerusalem
and suffer many
things at the hands
of the elders, the
chief priests and
the teachers of the
law, and that he
must be killed and
on the third day be
raised to life.
22 Peter took him
aside and began to
rebuke him. "Nev-
er, Lord!" he said.
"This shall never
happen to you!"
23 Jesus turned
and said to Peter,
"Get behind me,
Satan! You are a
stumbling block
to me; you do not
have in mind the
concerns

[a] 18 The Greek word for *Peter* means *rock.*
[b] 18 That is, the realm of the dead
[c] 19 Or *will have been*
[d] 19 Or *will have been*

ὁ χριστὸς ὁ υἱὸς τοῦ θεοῦ τοῦ ζῶντος. 17 ἀποκριθεὶς δὲ ὁ
the Christ, the Son of the living God." *{the}* *living* And Jesus responded, *And* *{the}*
3836 5986 3836 5626 3836 2409 2536 3836 2409 1254 2652 646 1254 3836
d.nsm n.nsm d.nsm n.nsm d.gsm n.gsm d.gsm pt.pa.gsm pt.ap.nsm cj d.nsm

Ἰησοῦς εἶπεν αὐτῷ, μακάριος εἶ, Σίμων Βαριωνᾶ, ὅτι σὰρξ καὶ αἷμα
Jesus saying to him, "Blessed ⌊are you,⌋ Simon son of Jonah, because flesh and blood did
2652 3306 899 3421 1639 4981 980 4022 4922 2779 135 636
n.nsm v.aai.3s r.dsm.3 a.nsm v.pai.2s n.vsm n.vsm cj n.nsf cj n.nsn

οὐκ ἀπεκάλυψέν σοι ἀλλ᾽ ὁ πατήρ μου ὁ ἐν τοῖς οὐρανοῖς.
not reveal this to you, but *{the}* my Father *my* *{the}* in *{the}* heaven.
4024 636 5148 247 3836 1609 4252 1609 3836 1877 3836 4041
adv v.aai.3s r.ds.2 cj d.nsm n.nsm r.gs.1 d.nsm p.d d.dpm n.dpm

18 κἀγὼ δέ σοι λέγω ὅτι σὺ εἶ Πέτρος, καὶ ἐπὶ ταύτῃ τῇ πέτρᾳ
And I *{and}* say to you, *say* ~ you are Peter, and on this *{the}* rock
2743 1254 3306 5148 3306 4022 5148 1639 4377 2779 2093 4047 3836 4376
crasis cj r.ds.2 v.pai.1s cj r.ns.2 v.pai.2s n.nsm cj p.d r.dsf d.dsf n.dsf

οἰκοδομήσω μου τὴν ἐκκλησίαν καὶ πύλαι ᾅδου οὐ κατισχύσουσιν
I will build my *{the}* church, and the gates of Hades will not overpower
3868 1609 3836 1711 2779 4783 87 2996 4024 2996
v.fai.1s r.gs.1 d.asf n.asf cj n.npf n.gsm adv v.fai.3p

αὐτῆς. 19 δώσω σοι τὰς κλεῖδας τῆς βασιλείας τῶν οὐρανῶν, καὶ ⌊ὃ ἐὰν⌋
it. I will give you the keys of the kingdom of heaven, and whatever
899 1443 5148 3836 3090 3836 993 3836 4041 2779 4005 1569
r.gsf.3 v.fai.1s r.ds.2 d.apf n.apf d.gsf n.gsf d.gpm n.gpm cj r.asn pl

δήσῃς ἐπὶ τῆς γῆς ἔσται δεδεμένον ἐν τοῖς οὐρανοῖς, καὶ ⌊ὃ ἐὰν⌋
you bind on *{the}* earth will have been bound in *{the}* heaven, and whatever
1313 2093 3836 1178 1639 1313 1877 3836 4041 2779 4005 1569
v.aas.2s p.g d.gsf n.gsf v.fmi.3s pt.rp.nsn p.d d.dpm n.dpm cj r.asn pl

λύσῃς ἐπὶ τῆς γῆς ἔσται λελυμένον ἐν τοῖς οὐρανοῖς. 20 τότε διεστείλατο
you loose on *{the}* earth will have been loosed in *{the}* heaven." Then he ordered
3395 2093 3836 1178 1639 3395 1877 3836 4041 5538 1403
v.aas.2s p.g d.gsf n.gsf v.fmi.3s pt.rp.nsn p.d d.dpm n.dpm adv v.ami.3s

τοῖς μαθηταῖς ἵνα μηδενὶ εἴπωσιν ὅτι αὐτός ἐστιν ὁ χριστός. 21 ἀπὸ
his disciples to tell no one *tell* that he was the Messiah From
3836 3412 2671 3306 3594 3306 4022 899 1639 3836 5986 608
d.dpm n.dpm cj a.dsm v.aas.3p cj r.nsm v.pai.3s d.nsm n.nsm p.g

τότε ἤρξατο ὁ Ἰησοῦς δεικνύειν τοῖς μαθηταῖς αὐτοῦ ὅτι δεῖ
⌊that time⌋ Jesus began *{the}* *Jesus* to explain to his disciples *his* that he must
5538 2652 806 3836 2652 1260 3836 899 3412 899 4022 899 1256
adv v.ami.3s d.nsm n.nsm f.pa d.dpm n.dpm r.gsm.3 cj v.pai.3s

αὐτὸν εἰς Ἱεροσόλυμα ἀπελθεῖν καὶ πολλὰ παθεῖν ἀπὸ τῶν
he go to Jerusalem *go* and suffer many things *suffer* from the
899 599 1650 2642 599 2779 4248 4498 4248 608 3836
r.asm.3 p.a n.apn f.aa cj a.apn f.aa p.g d.gpm

πρεσβυτέρων καὶ ἀρχιερέων καὶ γραμματέων καὶ ἀποκτανθῆναι καὶ τῇ τρίτῃ
elders and ruling priests and scribes, and be killed, and ⌊on the⌋ third
4565 2779 797 2779 1208 2779 650 2779 3836 5569
a.gpm cj n.gpm cj n.gpm cj f.ap cj d.dsf a.dsf

ἡμέρᾳ ἐγερθῆναι. 22 καὶ προσλαβόμενος αὐτὸν ὁ Πέτρος ἤρξατο
day be raised. And Peter took him aside *{the}* *Peter* and began
2465 1586 2779 4377 4689 899 4689 3836 4377 806
n.dsf f.ap cj pt.am.nsm r.asm.3 d.nsm n.nsm v.ami.3s

ἐπιτιμᾶν αὐτῷ λέγων, ἵλεώς σοι, κύριε· ⌊οὐ μὴ⌋ ἔσται σοι
to rebuke him, saying, ⌊"Far be it⌋ ⌊from you,⌋ Lord! This must never ⌊happen to⌋ you."
2203 899 3306 2664 5148 3261 4047 1639 4024 3590 1639 5148
f.pa r.dsm.3 pt.pa.nsm a.nsm r.ds.2 n.vsm adv pl v.fmi.3s r.ds.2

τοῦτο. 23 ὁ δὲ στραφεὶς εἶπεν τῷ Πέτρῳ, ὕπαγε ὀπίσω μου, σατανᾶ·
This But Jesus *But* turned and said to Peter, "Get behind me, Satan!
4047 1254 3836 1254 5138 3306 3836 4377 5632 3958 1609 4928
r.nsn d.nsm cj pt.ap.nsm v.aai.3s d.dsm n.dsm v.pam.2s p.g r.gs.1 n.vsm

σκάνδαλον εἶ ἐμοῦ, ὅτι οὐ φρονεῖς τὰ
You are an obstacle *You are* in my way, because you are not thinking the thoughts
1639 1639 4998 1639 1609 4022 5858 5858 4024 5858 3836
n.nsn v.pai.2s r.gs.1 cj adv v.pai.2s d.apn

NASB

the Christ, the Son
of the living God."
17 And Jesus said
to him, "Blessed
are you, Simon
Barjona, because
flesh and blood did
not reveal *this* to
you, but My Father
who is in heaven.
18 I also say to you
that you are Peter,
and upon this rock
I will build My
church; and the
gates of Hades will
not overpower it.
19 I will give you the
keys of the king-
dom of heaven;
and whatever
you bind on earth
shall have been
bound in heaven,
and whatever you
loose on earth shall
have been loosed
in heaven." 20 Then
He warned the
disciples that they
should tell no one
that He was the
Christ.

Jesus Foretells His Death

21 From that time
Jesus began to
show His disciples
that He must go
to Jerusalem, and
suffer many things
from the elders
and chief priests
and scribes, and
be killed, and be
raised up on the
third day. 22 Peter
took Him aside and
began to rebuke
Him, saying, "God
forbid *it,* Lord!
This shall never
happen to You."
23 But He turned
and said to Peter,
"Get behind Me,
Satan! You are a
stumbling block to
Me; for you are not
setting your mind

NIV

of God, but merely
human concerns."
24 Then Jesus said
to his disciples,
"Whoever wants
to be my disciple
must deny them-
selves and take
up their cross and
follow me. 25 For
whoever wants to
save their life[a] will
lose it, but whoev-
er loses their life
for me will find it.
26 What good will
it be for someone
to gain the whole
world, yet forfeit
their soul? Or what
can anyone give in
exchange for their
soul? 27 For the Son
of Man is going
to come in his Fa-
ther's glory with
his angels, and
then he will re-
ward each person
according to what
they have done.
28 "Truly I tell
you, some who are
standing here will
not taste death be-
fore they see the
Son of Man com-
ing in his king-
dom."

The Transfiguration

17 After six
days Jesus
took with him
Peter, James and
John the brother
of James, and led
them up a high
mountain by them-
selves. 2 There he
was transfigured
before them.

τοῦ θεοῦ ἀλλὰ τὰ τῶν ἀνθρώπων. 24 τότε ὁ Ἰησοῦς εἶπεν τοῖς μαθηταῖς
of God but those of men." Then {the} Jesus told {the} his disciples,
3836 2536 247 3836 3836 476 5538 3836 2652 3306 3836 899 3412
d.gsm n.gsm cj d.apn d.gpm n.gpm adv d.nsm n.nsm v.aai.3s d.dpm n.dpm

αὐτοῦ, εἴ τις θέλει ὀπίσω μου ἐλθεῖν, ἀπαρνησάσθω ἑαυτὸν καὶ
his "If anyone resolves to come after me, to come he must deny himself and
899 1623 5516 2527 2262 2262 3958 1609 2262 565 1571 2779
r.gsm.3 cj r.nsm v.pai.3s p.g r.gs.1 f.aa v.amm.3s r.asm.3 cj

ἀράτω τὸν σταυρὸν αὐτοῦ καὶ ἀκολουθείτω μοι. 25 ὃς γὰρ ἐὰν θέλῃ
take up {the} his cross his and follow me. For whoever For ~ resolves
149 3836 899 5089 899 2779 199 1609 1142 4005 1142 1569 2527
v.aam.3s d.asm n.asm r.gsm.3 cj v.pam.3s r.ds.1 r.nsm cj pl v.pas.3s

τὴν ψυχὴν αὐτοῦ σῶσαι ἀπολέσει αὐτήν· ὃς δ᾽ ἂν ἀπολέσῃ
to save {the} his life his to save will lose it; but whoever but ~ loses
5392 5392 3836 899 6034 899 5392 660 899 1254 4005 1254 323 660
d.asf n.asf r.gsm.3 f.aa v.fai.3s r.asf.3 r.nsm cj pl v.aas.3s

τὴν ψυχὴν αὐτοῦ ἕνεκεν ἐμοῦ ↤ εὑρήσει αὐτήν. 26 τί γὰρ
{the} his life his for my sake will find it. For what For
3836 899 6034 899 1914 1609 1914 2351 899 1142 5515 1142
d.asf n.asf r.gsm.3 p.g r.gs.1 v.fai.3s r.asf.3 r.asn cj

ὠφεληθήσεται ἄνθρωπος ἐὰν τὸν κόσμον ὅλον κερδήσῃ
⌞advantage will there be for⌟ a person if he gains the whole world whole he gains
6067 476 1569 3045 3045 3836 3910 3180 3910 3045
v.fpi.3s n.nsm cj d.asm n.asm a.asm v.aas.3s

τὴν δὲ ψυχὴν αὐτοῦ ζημιωθῇ; ἢ τί → δώσει ἄνθρωπος
yet forfeits {the} yet his life? his forfeits Or what will a person give person
1254 2423 3836 1254 899 6034 899 2423 2445 5515 476 1443 476
d.asf cj n.asf r.gsm.3 v.aps.3s cj r.asn v.fai.3s n.nsm

ἀντάλλαγμα τῆς ψυχῆς αὐτοῦ; 27 μέλλει γὰρ ὁ υἱὸς τοῦ ἀνθρώπου
in exchange for {the} his life? his is For the Son of Man is
498 3836 899 6034 899 3516 1142 3836 5626 3836 476 3516
n.asn d.gsf n.gsf r.gsm.3 v.pai.3s cj d.nsm n.nsm d.gsm n.gsm

ἔρχεσθαι ἐν τῇ δόξῃ τοῦ πατρὸς αὐτοῦ μετὰ τῶν ἀγγέλων αὐτοῦ, καὶ τότε
to come in the glory of his Father his with {the} his angels, his and then
2262 1877 3836 1518 3836 899 4252 899 3552 3836 899 34 899 2779 5538
f.pm p.d d.dsf n.dsf d.gsm n.gsm r.gsm.3 p.g d.gpm n.gpm r.gsm.3 cj adv

ἀποδώσει ἑκάστῳ κατὰ τὴν πρᾶξιν αὐτοῦ. 28 ἀμὴν
he will repay each person ⌞according to⌟ {the} his conduct. his I tell you the truth,
625 1667 2848 3836 899 4552 899 3306 3306 7007 297
v.fai.3s r.dsm p.a d.asf n.asf r.gsm.3 pl

λέγω ὑμῖν ὅτι εἰσίν τινες τῶν ὧδε ἑστώτων οἵτινες ↱ ⌞οὐ μὴ⌟
I tell you ~ ⌞there are⌟ some of those standing here standing who will not
3306 7007 4022 1639 5516 3836 2705 6045 2705 4015 1174 4024 3590
v.pai.1s r.dp.2 cj v.pai.3p r.npm d.gpm adv pt.ra.gpm r.npm adv pl

γεύσωνται θανάτου ⌞ἕως ἂν⌟ ἴδωσιν τὸν υἱὸν τοῦ ἀνθρώπου ἐρχόμενον ἐν τῇ
taste death until they see the Son of Man coming in {the} his
1174 2505 2401 323 1625 3836 5626 3836 476 2262 1877 3836 899
v.ams.3p n.gsm cj pl v.aas.3p d.asm n.asm d.gsm n.gsm pt.pm.asm p.d d.dsf

βασιλείᾳ αὐτοῦ.
kingdom. his
993 899
n.dsf r.gsm.3

17:1 καὶ μεθ᾽ ἡμέρας ἓξ παραλαμβάνει ὁ Ἰησοῦς τὸν Πέτρον
{and} Six days later days Six Jesus took {the} Jesus {the} Peter
2779 1971 2465 3552 2465 1971 2652 4161 3836 2652 3836 4377
cj p.a n.apf a.apf v.pai.3s d.nsm n.nsm d.asm n.asm

καὶ Ἰάκωβον καὶ Ἰωάννην τὸν ἀδελφὸν αὐτοῦ καὶ ἀναφέρει αὐτοὺς ↤ εἰς
and James and John {the} his brother, his and led them up {to} a
2779 2610 2779 2722 3836 899 81 899 2779 429 899 429 1650
cj n.asm cj n.asm d.asm n.asm r.gsm.3 cj v.pai.3s r.apm.3 p.a

ὄρος ὑψηλὸν κατ᾽ ἰδίαν. 2 καὶ μετεμορφώθη ἔμπροσθεν αὐτῶν, καὶ
very high mountain very high by themselves. And he was transfigured before them, and
5734 5734 4001 5734 2848 2625 2779 3565 1869 899 2779
n.asn a.asn p.a a.asf cj v.api.3s p.g r.gpm.3 cj

NASB

on God's interests,
but man's."

Discipleship Is Costly

24 Then Jesus said
to His disciples, "If
anyone wishes to
come after Me, he
must deny himself,
and take up his
cross and follow
Me. 25 For whoever
wishes to save his
life will lose it; but
whoever loses his
life for My sake
will find it. 26 For
what will it profit a
man if he gains the
whole world and
forfeits his soul?
Or what will a man
give in exchange
for his soul? 27 For
the Son of Man is
going to come in
the glory of His
Father with His
angels, and WILL
THEN REPAY EVERY
MAN ACCORDING TO
HIS DEEDS.
28 "Truly I say to
you, there are some
of those who are
standing here who
will not taste death
until they see the
Son of Man com-
ing in His king-
dom."

The Transfiguration

17:1 Six days later
Jesus *took with
Him Peter and
James and John his
brother, and *led
them up on a high
mountain by them-
selves. 2 And He
was transfigured
before them;

[a] 25 The Greek word means either *life* or *soul*; also in verse 26.

NIV

His face shone like
the sun, and his
clothes became as
white as the light.
3 Just then there
appeared before
them Moses and
Elijah, talking
with Jesus.
4 Peter said to
Jesus, "Lord, it is
good for us to be
here. If you wish,
I will put up three
shelters — one for
you, one for Mo-
ses and one for
Elijah."
5 While he was
still speaking, a
bright cloud cov-
ered them, and
a voice from the
cloud said, "This
is my Son, whom
I love; with him I
am well pleased.
Listen to him!"
6 When the dis-
ciples heard this,
they fell facedown
to the ground, ter-
rified. 7 But Jesus
came and touched
them. "Get up,"
he said. "Don't be
afraid." 8 When
they looked up,
they saw no one
except Jesus.
9 As they were
coming down the
mountain, Jesus
instructed them,
"Don't tell any-
one what you have
seen, until the Son
of Man has been
raised from the
dead."
10 The disciples
asked him, "Why
then do the

ἔλαμψεν τὸ πρόσωπον αὐτοῦ ὡς ὁ ἥλιος, τὰ δὲ ἱμάτια αὐτοῦ
his face shone {the} face his like the sun, {the} and his clothes his
899 4725 3290 3836 4725 899 6055 3836 2463 3836 1254 899 2668 899
v.aai.3s d.nsn n.nsn r.gsm.3 pl d.nsm n.nsm d.npn cj n.npn r.gsm.3

ἐγένετο λευκὰ ὡς τὸ φῶς. 3 καὶ ἰδοὺ ὤφθη αὐτοῖς Μωϋσῆς καὶ Ἠλίας
became white as {the} light. {and} Suddenly there appeared to them Moses and Elijah,
1181 3328 6055 3836 5890 2779 2627 3972 899 3707 2779 2460
v.ami.3s a.npn pl d.nsn n.nsn cj j v.api.3s r.dpm.3 n.nsm cj n.nsm

συλλαλοῦντες μετ᾽ αὐτοῦ. 4 ἀποκριθεὶς δὲ ὁ Πέτρος εἶπεν
talking with him. And Peter spoke And {the} Peter to Jesus, saying,
5196 3552 899 1254 4377 646 1254 3836 4377 3836 2652 3306
pt.pa.npm p.g r.gsm.3 pt.ap.nsm cj d.nsm n.nsm v.aai.3s

τῷ Ἰησοῦ, κύριε, καλόν ἐστιν ἡμᾶς ὧδε εἶναι· εἰ θέλεις,
to Jesus "Lord, it is good it is that we are here. are If you wish,
3836 2652 3261 1639 1639 2819 1639 7005 1639 6045 1639 1623 2527
d.dsm n.dsm n.vsm a.nsn v.pai.3s r.ap.1 adv f.pa cj v.pai.2s

ποιήσω ὧδε τρεῖς σκηνάς, σοὶ μίαν καὶ Μωϋσεῖ
⌊I will put up⌋ three shelters here three shelters — one ⌊for you,⌋ one {and} one for Moses,
4472 5552 5008 6045 5552 5008 1651 5148 1651 2779 1651 3707
v.fai.1s adv a.apf n.apf r.ds.2 a.asf cj n.dsm

μίαν καὶ Ἠλίᾳ μίαν. 5 ↱ ↱ ἔτι αὐτοῦ λαλοῦντος ἰδοὺ
one and one for Elijah." one While he was still he speaking, {behold} a bright
1651 2779 1651 2460 1651 3281 899 3281 2285 899 3281 2627 5893
a.asf cj n.dsm a.asf adv r.gsm.3 pt.pa.gsm j

νεφέλη φωτεινὴ ἐπεσκίασεν αὐτούς, καὶ ἰδοὺ φωνὴ ἐκ τῆς νεφέλης λέγουσα,
cloud bright overshadowed them and {behold} a voice from the cloud said,
3749 5893 2173 899 2779 2627 5889 1666 3836 3749 3306
n.nsf a.nsf v.aai.3s r.apm.3 cj j n.nsf p.g d.gsf n.gsf pt.pa.nsf

οὗτός ἐστιν ὁ υἱός μου ὁ ἀγαπητός, ἐν ᾧ εὐδόκησα· ἀκούετε
"This is {the} my Son, my the Beloved, in whom I am well pleased; listen to
4047 1639 3836 1609 5626 1609 3836 28 1877 4005 2305 201
r.nsm v.pai.3s d.nsm n.nsm r.gs.1 d.nsm a.nsm p.d r.dsm v.aai.1s v.pam.2p

αὐτοῦ. 6 καὶ → ἀκούσαντες οἱ μαθηταὶ
him!" And when the disciples heard the disciples this, they were overcome with
899 2779 3836 3412 201 3836 3412 5828 5828 5379 5828
r.gsm.3 cj pt.aa.npm d.npm n.npm

ἔπεσαν ἐπὶ πρόσωπον αὐτῶν καὶ ἐφοβήθησαν σφόδρα. 7 καὶ
fear and fell on their faces. their and they were with fear overcome But Jesus
5828 2779 4406 2093 899 4725 899 2779 5828 5379 2779 2652
v.aai.3p p.a n.asn r.gpm.3 cj v.api.3p adv cj

προσῆλθεν ὁ Ἰησοῦς καὶ ἁψάμενος αὐτῶν εἶπεν, ἐγέρθητε καὶ ↱ μὴ φοβεῖσθε.
came over {the} Jesus and touched them, saying, "Rise, and do not be afraid."
4665 3836 2652 2779 721 899 3306 1586 2779 5828 3590 5828
v.aai.3s d.nsm n.nsm cj pt.am.nsm r.gpm.3 v.aai.3s v.apm.2p cj pl v.ppm.2p

8 ἐπάραντες δὲ τοὺς ὀφθαλμοὺς αὐτῶν οὐδένα εἶδον ⌊εἰ
And when they raised And {the} their eyes, their they saw no one they saw except
1254 2048 1254 3836 899 4057 899 1625 1625 4029 1625 1623
pt.aa.npm cj d.apm n.apm r.gpm.3 a.asm v.aai.3p cj

μὴ⌋ αὐτὸν Ἰησοῦν μόνον. 9 καὶ → καταβαινόντων αὐτῶν ἐκ τοῦ ὄρους
Jesus himself Jesus alone. And as they were coming down they from the mountain,
3590 2652 899 2652 3668 2779 899 2849 899 1666 3836 4001
pl r.asm n.asm adv cj pt.pa.gpm r.gpm.3 p.g d.gsn n.gsn

ἐνετείλατο αὐτοῖς ὁ Ἰησοῦς λέγων, μηδενὶ εἴπητε τὸ ὅραμα
Jesus commanded them, {the} Jesus saying, "Tell the vision to no one Tell the vision
2652 1948 899 3836 2652 3306 3306 3836 3969 3594 3306 3836 3969
v.ami.3s r.dpm.3 d.nsm n.nsm pt.pa.nsm a.dsm v.aas.2p d.asn n.asn

⌊ἕως οὗ⌋ ὁ υἱὸς τοῦ ἀνθρώπου ἐκ νεκρῶν ἐγερθῇ.
until the Son of Man has been raised from the dead." has been raised
2401 4005 3836 5626 3836 476 1586 1586 1586 1666 3738 1586
p.g r.gsm d.nsm n.nsm d.gsm n.gsm p.g a.gpm v.aps.3s

10 καὶ ἐπηρώτησαν αὐτὸν οἱ μαθηταὶ λέγοντες, τί οὖν ↱ οἱ
And the disciples asked him, the disciples saying, "Why then do the
2779 3836 3412 2089 899 3836 3412 3306 5515 4036 3306 3836
cj v.aai.3p r.asm.3 d.npm n.npm pt.pa.npm r.asn cj d.npm

NASB

and His face shone
like the sun, and
His garments be-
came as white as
light. 3 And behold,
Moses and Elijah
appeared to them,
talking with Him.
4 Peter said to Jesus,
"Lord, it is good
for us to be here;
if You wish, I will
make three taber-
nacles here, one
for You, and one
for Moses, and one
for Elijah." 5 While
he was still speak-
ing, a bright cloud
overshadowed
them, and behold,
a voice out of the
cloud said, "This is
My beloved Son,
with whom I am
well-pleased; listen
to Him!" 6 When
the disciples heard
this, they fell face
down to the ground
and were terrified.
7 And Jesus came to
them and touched
them and said,
"Get up, and do not
be afraid." 8 And
lifting up their
eyes, they saw no
one except Jesus
Himself alone.
9 As they were
coming down from
the mountain, Jesus
commanded them,
saying, "Tell the
vision to no one
until the Son of
Man has risen from
the dead." 10 And
His disciples asked
Him, "Why then do

NIV

teachers of the
law say that Elijah
must come first?"
11 Jesus replied,
"To be sure, Elijah
comes and will
restore all things.
12 But I tell you,
Elijah has already
come, and they
did not recognize
him, but have done
to him everything
they wished. In the
same way the Son
of Man is going
to suffer at their
hands." 13 Then the
disciples under-
stood that he was
talking to them
about John the
Baptist.

Jesus Heals a Demon-Possessed Boy

14 When they
came to the crowd,
a man approached
Jesus and knelt be-
fore him. 15 "Lord,
have mercy on
my son," he said.
"He has seizures
and is suffering
greatly. He often
falls into the fire
or into the water.
16 I brought him to
your disciples, but
they could not heal
him."
17 "You unbeliev-
ing and perverse
generation," Jesus
replied, "how long
shall I stay with
you? How long
shall I put up with
you? Bring the
boy here to me."
18 Jesus rebuked
the demon, and it
came out of the
boy, and he was
healed at that mo-
ment.
19 Then the disci-
ples came to Jesus
in private and
asked, "Why

γραμματεῖς λέγουσιν ὅτι Ἠλίαν δεῖ ἐλθεῖν πρῶτον; 11 ὁ δὲ ἀποκριθεὶς εἶπεν,
scribes say that Elijah must come first?" He *{and}* answered, saying,
1208 3306 4022 2460 1256 2262 4754 3836 1254 646 3306
n.npm v.pai.3p cj n.asm v.pai.3s f.aa adv d.nsm cj pt.ap.nsm v.aai.3s

Ἠλίας μὲν ἔρχεται καὶ ἀποκαταστήσει πάντα· 12 λέγω δὲ
"To be sure, Elijah *To be sure* does come, and he will restore all things. And I tell *And*
3525 3525 3525 2460 3525 2262 2779 635 4246 1254 3306 1254
n.nsm pl v.pmi.3s cj v.fai.3s a.apn v.pai.1s cj

ὑμῖν ὅτι Ἠλίας ἤδη ἦλθεν, καὶ ↱ ↱ οὐκ ἐπέγνωσαν αὐτὸν ἀλλὰ
you that Elijah has come already, *has come* and they did not recognize him, but
7007 4022 2460 2262 2262 2453 2262 2779 2105 2105 4024 2105 899 247
r.dp.2 cj n.nsm adv v.aai.3s cj adv v.aai.3p r.asm.3 cj

ἐποίησαν ἐν αὐτῷ ὅσα ἠθέλησαν· οὕτως καὶ ὁ υἱὸς τοῦ ἀνθρώπου μέλλει
did to him whatever they wished. So also the Son of Man will
4472 1877 899 4012 2527 4048 2779 3836 5626 3836 476 3516
v.aai.3p p.d r.dsm.3 r.apn v.aai.3p adv adv d.nsm n.nsm d.gsm n.gsm v.pai.3s

πάσχειν ὑπ' αὐτῶν. 13 τότε συνῆκαν οἱ μαθηταὶ ὅτι
suffer at their hands." Then the disciples understood *the disciples* that he had
4248 5679 899 5538 3836 3412 5317 3836 3412 4022 3306 3306
f.pa p.g r.gpm.3 adv v.aai.3p d.npm n.npm cj

περὶ Ἰωάννου τοῦ βαπτιστοῦ εἶπεν αὐτοῖς. 14 καὶ
spoken to them about John the Baptist. *he had spoken to them* *{and}*
3306 899 899 4309 2722 3836 969 3306 899 2779
p.g n.gsm d.gsm n.gsm v.aai.3s r.dpm.3 cj

ἐλθόντων πρὸς τὸν ὄχλον προσῆλθεν αὐτῷ ἄνθρωπος γονυπετῶν αὐτὸν
⌊When they returned⌋ to the crowd, a man approached Jesus, *man* knelt before him,
2262 4639 3836 4063 476 4665 899 476 1206 899
pt.aa.gpm p.a d.asm n.asm v.aai.3s r.dsm.3 n.nsm pt.pa.nsm r.asm.3

15 καὶ λέγων, κύριε, ἐλέησόν μου τὸν υἱόν, ὅτι σεληνιάζεται καὶ
and said, "Lord, ⌊take pity on⌋ my *{the}* son, because he is an epileptic and suffers
2779 3306 3261 1796 1609 3836 5626 4022 4944 2779 4248
cj pt.pa.nsm n.vsm v.aam.2s r.gs.1 d.asm n.asm cj v.ppi.3s cj

κακῶς πάσχει· ↱ πολλάκις γὰρ πίπτει εἰς τὸ πῦρ καὶ πολλάκις εἰς τὸ
terribly; *suffers* for he often *for* falls into the fire and often into the
2809 4248 1142 4406 4490 1142 4406 1650 3836 4786 2779 4490 1650 3836
adv v.pai.3s adv cj v.pai.3s p.a d.asn n.asn cj adv p.a d.asn

ὕδωρ. 16 καὶ προσήνεγκα αὐτὸν τοῖς μαθηταῖς σου, καὶ οὐκ
water. And I brought him to your disciples *your* but they could not
5623 2779 4712 899 3836 5148 3412 5148 2779 1538 1538 4024
n.asn cj v.aai.1s r.asm.3 d.dpm n.dpm r.gs.2 cj adv

ἠδυνήθησαν αὐτὸν θεραπεῦσαι. 17 ἀποκριθεὶς δὲ ὁ Ἰησοῦς εἶπεν, ὦ
they could heal him." *heal* Jesus answered, *{and}* *{the}* *Jesus* saying, "O
1538 2543 899 2543 2652 646 1254 3836 2652 3306 6043
v.api.3p r.asm.3 f.aa pt.ap.nsm cj d.nsm n.nsm v.aai.3s j

γενεὰ ἄπιστος καὶ διεστραμμένη, ⌊ἕως πότε⌋ μεθ'
generation unbelieving and perverse generation, how long am I to be with
1155 603 2779 1406 1155 2401 4537 1639 1639 1639 1639 3552
n.vsf a.vsf cj pt.rp.vsf p.g adv p.g

ὑμῶν ἔσομαι; ⌊ἕως πότε⌋ ἀνέξομαι ὑμῶν; φέρετέ μοι αὐτὸν ὧδε.
you? *am I to be* How long ⌊must I put up with⌋ you? Bring him here to me." *him* *here*
7007 1639 2401 4537 462 7007 5770 899 6045 1609 899 6045
r.gp.2 v.fmi.1s p.g adv v.fmi.1s r.gp.2 v.pam.2p r.ds.1 r.asm.3 adv

18 καὶ ἐπετίμησεν αὐτῷ ὁ Ἰησοῦς καὶ ἐξῆλθεν ἀπ' αὐτοῦ τὸ
Then Jesus rebuked *{him}* the demon *{the}* *Jesus* and it came out of him; *the*
2779 2652 2203 899 3836 1228 3836 2652 2779 2002 608 899 3836
cj v.aai.3s r.dsm.3 d.nsm n.nsm cj v.aai.3s p.g r.gsm.3 d.nsn

δαιμόνιον καὶ ἐθεραπεύθη ὁ παῖς ἀπὸ τῆς ὥρας ἐκείνης. 19 τότε
demon and the boy was healed *the* *boy* from *{the}* that hour. *that* Then the
1228 2779 3836 4090 2543 3836 4090 608 3836 1697 6052 1697 5538 3836
n.nsn cj v.api.3s d.nsm n.nsm p.g d.gsf n.gsf r.gsf adv

προσελθόντες οἱ μαθηταὶ τῷ Ἰησοῦ ⌊κατ' ἰδίαν⌋ εἶπον, ⌊διὰ τί⌋
disciples came *the* *disciples* to Jesus privately and said, "Why
3412 4665 3836 3412 3836 2652 2848 2625 3306 1328 5515
pt.aa.npm d.npm n.npm d.dsm n.dsm p.a a.asf v.aai.3p p.a r.asn

NASB

the scribes say that
Elijah must come
first?" 11 And He
answered and said,
"Elijah is coming
and will restore all
things; 12 but I say
to you that Elijah
already came, and
they did not recog-
nize him, but did to
him whatever they
wished. So also
the Son of Man
is going to suffer
at their hands."
13 Then the disciples
understood that He
had spoken to them
about John the
Baptist.

The Demoniac

14 When they came
to the crowd, a
man came up to
Jesus, falling on
his knees before
Him and saying,
15 "Lord, have
mercy on my son,
for he is a lunatic
and is very ill; for
he often falls into
the fire and often
into the water. 16 I
brought him to
Your disciples, and
they could not cure
him." 17 And Jesus
answered and said,
"You unbelieving
and perverted gen-
eration, how long
shall I be with you?
How long shall I
put up with you?
Bring him here to
Me." 18 And Jesus
rebuked him, and
the demon came
out of him, and the
boy was cured at
once.
19 Then the disci-
ples came to Jesus
privately and said,
"Why could we

NIV

couldn't we drive it out?"
[20]He replied, "Because you have so little faith. Truly I tell you, if you have faith as small as a mustard seed, you can say to this mountain, 'Move from here to there,' and it will move. Nothing will be impossible for you." [21][a]

Jesus Predicts His Death a Second Time

[22]When they came together in Galilee, he said to them, "The Son of Man is going to be delivered into the hands of men. [23]They will kill him, and on the third day he will be raised to life." And the disciples were filled with grief.

The Temple Tax

[24]After Jesus and his disciples arrived in Capernaum, the collectors of the two-drachma temple tax came to Peter and asked, "Doesn't your teacher pay the temple tax?"
[25]"Yes, he does," he replied.
When Peter came into the house, Jesus was the first to speak. "What do you think, Simon?" he asked. "From whom do the kings of the earth collect duty and taxes—from their own children or from others?"
[26]"From others," Peter answered.
"Then the children are exempt," Jesus said to him. [27]"But so that we may not cause offense, go to the

[a] *21* Some manuscripts include here words similar to Mark 9:29.

ἡμεῖς οὐκ ἠδυνήθημεν ἐκβαλεῖν αὐτό; ↰ 20 ὁ δὲ λέγει αὐτοῖς,
could we not *could* cast it out?" He *{and}* said to them,
1538 7005 4024 1538 1675 899 1675 3836 1254 3306 899
r.np.1 adv v.api.1p f.aa r.asn.3 d.nsm cj v.pai.3s r.dpm.3

διὰ τὴν ὀλιγοπιστίαν ὑμῶν· ↰ ἀμὴν γὰρ λέγω ὑμῖν, ἐὰν ἔχητε
⌊"Because of⌋ the poverty of your faith. *the truth* *{for}* I tell you the truth, if you have
1328 3836 3898 7007 3898 297 1142 3306 7007 297 297 1569 2400
p.a d.asf n.asf r.gp.2 pl cj v.pai.1s r.dp.2 cj v.pas.2p

πίστιν ὡς κόκκον σινάπεως, ἐρεῖτε τῷ ὄρει τούτῳ,
faith the ⌊size of⌋ a mustard seed, *mustard* ⌊you can say⌋ to this mountain, *this*
4411 6055 4983 3133 4983 3306 3836 4047 4001 4047
n.asf pl n.asm n.gsn v.fai.2p d.dsn n.dsn r.dsn

μετάβα ἔνθεν ↰ ἐκεῖ, καὶ μεταβήσεται· καὶ οὐδὲν ἀδυνατήσει ὑμῖν.[a]
'Move from here to there,' and it will move; and nothing will be impossible for you."
3553 1925 3553 1695 2779 3553 2779 4029 104 7007
v.aam.2s adv adv cj v.fmi.3s cj a.nsn v.fai.3s r.dp.2

22 → συστρεφομένων δὲ αὐτῶν ἐν τῇ Γαλιλαίᾳ εἶπεν αὐτοῖς ὁ
While they were still together *{and}* *they* in *{the}* Galilee, Jesus said to them, *{the}*
899 5370 1254 899 1877 3836 1133 2652 3306 899 3836
pt.pp.gpm cj r.gpm.3 p.d d.dsf n.dsf v.aai.3s r.dpm.3 d.nsm

Ἰησοῦς, μέλλει ὁ υἱὸς τοῦ ἀνθρώπου παραδίδοσθαι εἰς χεῖρας
Jesus *is about* "The Son of Man is about to be delivered into the hands
2652 3516 3836 5626 3836 476 3516 3516 4140 1650 5931
n.nsm v.pai.3s d.nsm n.nsm d.gsm n.gsm f.pp p.a n.apf

ἀνθρώπων, 23 καὶ ἀποκτενοῦσιν αὐτόν, καὶ τῇ τρίτῃ ἡμέρᾳ ἐγερθήσεται. καὶ
of men, and they will kill him, and ⌊on the⌋ third day he will be raised." And
476 2779 650 899 2779 3836 5569 2465 1586 2779
n.gpm cj v.fai.3p r.asm.3 cj d.dsf a.dsf n.dsf v.fpi.3s cj

→ → ἐλυπήθησαν σφόδρα. 24 → ἐλθόντων δὲ αὐτῶν εἰς
they were greatly distressed. *greatly* And when they arrived *And* *they* at
5379 3382 5379 1254 899 2262 1254 899 1650
v.api.3p adv pt.aa.gpm cj r.gpm.3 p.a

Καφαρναοὺμ προσῆλθον οἱ τὰ δίδραχμα λαμβάνοντες τῷ Πέτρῳ
Capernaum, *came* the collectors of the temple tax *collectors* came to Peter
3019 4665 3836 3284 3836 1440 3284 4665 3836 4377
n.asf v.aai.3p d.npm d.apn n.apn pt.pa.npm d.dsm n.dsm

καὶ εἶπαν, ↱ ὁ διδάσκαλος ὑμῶν οὐ τελεῖ τὰ[b] δίδραχμα; 25
and said, "Does *{the}* your teacher *your* not pay the two-drachma tax?" "Yes,"
2779 3306 5464 3836 7007 1437 7007 4024 5464 3836 1440 3721
cj v.aai.3p d.nsm n.nsm r.gp.2 pl v.pai.3s d.apn n.apn

λέγει, ναί. καὶ ἐλθόντα εἰς τὴν οἰκίαν προέφθασεν αὐτὸν ↰ ὁ
he answered. *Yes* And when he went into the house, Jesus spoke to Peter first, *{the}*
3306 3721 2779 2262 1650 3836 3864 2652 4740 899 4740 3836
v.pai.3s pl cj pt.aa.asm p.a d.asf n.asf v.aai.3s r.asm.3 d.nsm

Ἰησοῦς λέγων, τί ↱ σοι δοκεῖ, Σίμων; ↱ οἱ βασιλεῖς τῆς
Jesus saying, "What do you think, Simon? From whom do *{the}* earthly kings *{the}*
2652 3306 5515 1506 5148 1506 4981 608 5515 3284 3836 1178 995 3836
n.nsm pt.pa.nsm r.nsn r.ds.2 v.pai.3s n.vsm d.npm n.npm d.gsf

γῆς ἀπὸ τίνων λαμβάνουσιν τέλη ἢ κῆνσον; ἀπὸ τῶν υἱῶν αὐτῶν ἢ
earthly *From* *whom* collect tolls or taxes — from *{the}* their sons *their* or
1178 608 5515 3284 5465 2445 3056 608 3836 899 5626 899 2445
n.gsf p.g r.gpm v.pai.3p n.apn cj n.asm p.g d.gpm n.gpm r.gpm.3 cj

ἀπὸ τῶν ἀλλοτρίων; 26 εἰπόντος δέ, ἀπὸ τῶν ἀλλοτρίων, ἔφη
from *{the}* outsiders?" And when he answered, *And* "From *{the}* outsiders," Jesus said
608 3836 259 1254 3306 1254 608 3836 259 2652 5774
p.g d.gpm n.gpm pt.aa.gsm cj p.g d.gpm n.gpm v.iai.3s

αὐτῷ ὁ Ἰησοῦς, ἄρα γε ἐλεύθεροί εἰσιν οἱ υἱοί. 27 ⌊ἵνα δὲ
to him, *{the}* *Jesus* "Then ~ the sons are exempt. *are* *the* *sons* But lest
899 3836 2652 726 1145 3836 5626 1639 1801 1639 3836 5626 2671 1254
r.dsm.3 d.nsm n.nsm cj pl a.npm v.pai.3p d.npm n.npm cj cj

μὴ⌋ σκανδαλίσωμεν αὐτούς, πορευθεὶς εἰς θάλασσαν βάλε ἄγκιστρον καὶ
we offend them, go to the sea, cast in a hook, and take
3590 4997 899 4513 1650 2498 965 45 2779 149
pl v.aas.1p r.apm.3 pt.ap.nsm p.a n.asf v.aam.2s n.asn cj

a 21 τοῦτο δὲ τὸ γένος οὐκ ἐκπορεύεται εἰ μὴ ἐν προσευχῇ καὶ νηστείᾳ. included by TR after ὑμῖν.
b [τὰ] UBS.

NASB

not drive it out?" [20]And He *said to them, "Because of the littleness of your faith; for truly I say to you, if you have faith the size of a mustard seed, you will say to this mountain, 'Move from here to there,' and it will move; and nothing will be impossible to you. [21][[a]But this kind does not go out except by prayer and fasting."]
[22]And while they were gathering together in Galilee, Jesus said to them, "The Son of Man is going to be delivered into the hands of men; [23]and they will kill Him, and He will be raised on the third day." And they were deeply grieved.

The Tribute Money

[24]When they came to Capernaum, those who collected the [b]two-drachma *tax* came to Peter and said, "Does your teacher not pay the two-drachma *tax?*" [25]He *said, "Yes." And when he came into the house, Jesus spoke to him first, saying, "What do you think, Simon? From whom do the kings of the earth collect customs or poll-tax, from their sons or from strangers?" [26]When Peter said, "From strangers," Jesus said to him, "Then the sons are exempt. [27]However, so that we do not offend them, go to the sea and throw in a hook, and take

[a] Early mss do not contain this v
[b] Equivalent to two denarii or two days' wages, paid as a temple tax

NIV

lake and throw out
your line. Take
the first fish you
catch; open its
mouth and you
will find a four-
drachma coin.
Take it and give it
to them for my tax
and yours."

The Greatest in the Kingdom of Heaven

18 At that time
the disciples
came to Jesus and
asked, "Who, then,
is the greatest in
the kingdom of
heaven?"
2He called a little
child to him, and
placed the child
among them. 3And
he said: "Truly I
tell you, unless
you change and
become like little
children, you will
never enter the
kingdom of heav-
en. 4Therefore,
whoever takes the
lowly position of
this child is the
greatest in the
kingdom of heav-
en. 5And whoever
welcomes one such
child in my name
welcomes me.

Causing to Stumble

6"If anyone caus-
es one of these
little ones—those
who believe in
me—to stumble,
it would be better
for them to have
a large millstone
hung around their
neck and to be
drowned in the
depths of the sea.
7Woe to the world
because of the
things that cause
people to stumble!
Such things must
come, but woe to
the person through
whom they

τὸν ἀναβάντα πρῶτον ἰχθὺν ἆρον, καὶ ἀνοίξας τὸ
the first fish that comes up. *first* *fish* *take* *{and}* ⌞When you have opened⌟ *{the}* its
4755 2716 3836 326 4755 2716 149 2779 487 3836 899
d.asm pt.aa.asm a.asm n.asm v.aam.2s cj pt.aa.nsm d.asn

στόμα αὐτοῦ εὑρήσεις στατῆρα· ἐκεῖνον λαβὼν δὸς αὐτοῖς
mouth, *its* you will find a ⌞four drachma coin;⌟ take it *take* and give it to them
5125 899 2351 5088 3284 1697 3284 1443 899
n.asn r.gsm.3 v.fai.2s n.asm r.asm pt.aa.nsm v.aam.2s r.dpm.3

ἀντὶ ἐμοῦ καὶ σοῦ.
for me and you."
505 1609 2779 5148
p.g r.gs.1 cj r.gs.2

18:1 ἐν ἐκείνῃ τῇ ὥρᾳ προσῆλθον οἱ μαθηταὶ τῷ Ἰησοῦ
At that *{the}* time the disciples came *the* *disciples* to Jesus,
1877 1697 3836 6052 3836 3412 4665 3836 3412 3836 2652
p.d r.dsf d.dsf n.dsf v.aai.3p d.npm n.npm d.dsm n.dsm

λέγοντες, τίς ἄρα μείζων ἐστὶν ἐν τῇ βασιλείᾳ τῶν οὐρανῶν; 2 καὶ
saying, "Who then is the greatest *is* in the kingdom of heaven?" *{and}* Jesus
3306 5515 726 1639 3489 1639 1877 3836 993 3836 4041 2779
pt.pa.npm r.nsm cj a.nsm.c v.pai.3s p.d d.dsf n.dsf d.gpm n.gpm cj

προσκαλεσάμενος παιδίον ↰ ↰ ↰ ἔστησεν αὐτὸ ἐν μέσῳ αὐτῶν
invited a child to come to him, and placing him in their midst, *their*
4673 4086 4673 4673 4673 2705 899 1877 899 3545 899
pt.am.nsm n.asn v.aai.3s r.asn.3 p.d n.dsn r.gpm.3

3 καὶ εἶπεν, ἀμὴν λέγω ὑμῖν, ⌞ἐὰν μὴ⌟ στραφῆτε καὶ γένησθε ὡς
{and} said, "I tell you the truth, *I tell* *you* unless you change and become like
2779 3306 3306 3306 7007 297 3306 7007 1569 3590 5138 2779 1181 6055
cj v.aai.3s pl v.pai.1s r.dp.2 cj pl v.aps.2p cj v.ams.2p pl

τὰ παιδία, ↱ ↱ ⌞οὐ μὴ⌟ ⌞εἰσέλθητε εἰς⌟ τὴν βασιλείαν τῶν οὐρανῶν. 4
{the} children, you will never enter the kingdom of heaven! For
3836 4086 1656 1656 4024 3590 1656 1650 3836 993 3836 4041 4036
d.npn n.npn adv pl v.aas.2p p.a d.asf n.asf d.gpm n.gpm

ὅστις οὖν ταπεινώσει ἑαυτὸν ὡς τὸ παιδίον τοῦτο, οὗτός ἐστιν ὁ
whoever *For* humbles himself as *{the}* this child *this* *{this one}* is *{the}*
4015 4036 5427 1571 6055 3836 4047 4086 4047 4047 1639 3836
r.nsm cj v.fai.3s r.asm.3 pl d.nsn n.nsn r.nsn r.nsm v.pai.3s d.nsm

μείζων ἐν τῇ βασιλείᾳ τῶν οὐρανῶν. 5 καὶ ⌞ὃς ἐὰν⌟ δέξηται ἓν παιδίον
greatest in the kingdom of heaven. And whoever welcomes a child
3489 1877 3836 993 3836 4041 2779 4005 1569 1312 1651 4086
a.nsm.c p.d d.dsf n.dsf d.gpm n.gpm cj r.nsm pl v.ams.3s a.asn n.asn

τοιοῦτο ἐπὶ τῷ ὀνόματί μου, ἐμὲ δέχεται. 6 ὃς δ᾽ ἂν
like this in *{the}* my name *my* welcomes me. *welcomes* But whoever *But* ~
5525 2093 3836 1609 3950 1609 1312 1609 1312 1254 4005 1254 323
r.asn p.d d.dsn n.dsn r.gs.1 r.as.1 v.pmi.3s r.nsm cj pl

σκανδαλίσῃ ἕνα τῶν μικρῶν τούτων τῶν πιστευόντων εἰς ἐμέ, ↰ ↰
causes one of these little ones *these* who believe in me to sin,
4997 1651 3836 4047 3625 4047 3836 4409 1650 1609 4997 4997
v.aas.3s a.asm d.gpm a.gpm r.gpm d.gpm pt.pa.gpm p.a r.as.1

συμφέρει αὐτῷ ἵνα → κρεμασθῇ μύλος ὀνικὸς περὶ τὸν
⌞it would be better⌟ for him to have a large millstone hung *millstone* *large* around *{the}*
5237 899 2671 3948 3685 3203 3685 3948 4309 3836
v.pai.3s r.dsm.3 cj v.aps.3s n.nsm a.nsm p.a d.asm

τράχηλον αὐτοῦ καὶ καταποντισθῇ ἐν τῷ πελάγει τῆς θαλάσσης.
his neck *his* and be drowned far out at *{the}* *far out* *{the}* sea.
899 5549 899 2779 2931 4283 4283 1877 3836 4283 3836 2498
n.asm r.gsm.3 cj v.aps.3s p.d d.dsn n.dsn d.gsf n.gsf

7 οὐαὶ τῷ κόσμῳ ἀπὸ τῶν σκανδάλων· ἀνάγκη γὰρ
Woe ⌞to the⌟ world ⌞because of⌟ the ⌞things that cause people to sin!⌟ It is inevitable *{for}* that
4026 3836 3180 608 3836 4998 340 1142
j d.dsm n.dsm p.g d.gpn n.gpn n.nsf cj

ἐλθεῖν τὰ σκάνδαλα, πλὴν οὐαὶ τῷ ἀνθρώπῳ δι᾽ οὗ ⌞τὸ
such things come, *such* *things* but woe ⌞to the⌟ one through whom they
3836 4998 2262 3836 4998 4440 4026 3836 476 1328 4005 3836
f.aa d.apn n.apn cj j d.dsm n.dsm p.g r.gsm d.nsn

NASB

the first fish that
comes up; and
when you open its
mouth, you will
find [a]a shekel. Take
that and give it to
them for you and
Me."

Rank in the Kingdom

18:1At that time
the disciples came
to Jesus and said,
"Who then is great-
est in the kingdom
of heaven?" 2And
He called a child
to Himself and set
him before them,
3and said, "Truly I
say to you, unless
you are converted
and become like
children, you will
not enter the king-
dom of heaven.
4Whoever then
humbles himself
as this child, he is
the greatest in the
kingdom of heav-
en. 5And whoever
receives one such
child in My name
receives Me; 6but
whoever causes
one of these little
ones who believe
in Me to stumble,
it would be better
for him to have a
heavy millstone
hung around his
neck, and to be
drowned in the
depth of the sea.

Stumbling Blocks

7"Woe to the
world because
of *its* stumbling
blocks! For it is
inevitable that
stumbling blocks
come; but woe to
that man through
whom

[a] Lit *standard coin,* which was a shekel

NIV

come! 8If your hand or your foot causes you to stumble, cut it off and throw it away. It is better for you to enter life maimed or crippled than to have two hands or two feet and be thrown into eternal fire. 9And if your eye causes you to stumble, gouge it out and throw it away. It is better for you to enter life with one eye than to have two eyes and be thrown into the fire of hell.

The Parable of the Wandering Sheep

10"See that you do not despise one of these little ones. For I tell you that their angels in heaven always see the face of my Father in heaven. [11][a]

12"What do you think? If a man owns a hundred sheep, and one of them wanders away, will he not leave the ninety-nine on the hills and go to look for the one that wandered off? 13And if he finds it, truly I tell you, he is happier about that one sheep than about the ninety-nine that did not wander off. 14In the same way your Father in heaven is not willing that any of these little ones should perish.

σκάνδαλον⌋ ἔρχεται. 8 εἰ δὲ ἡ χείρ σου ἢ ὁ πούς σου
come! "If {and} {the} your hand your or {the} your foot your
4998 2262 1623 1254 3836 5148 5931 5148 2445 3836 5148 4546 5148
n.nsn v.pmi.3s cj cj d.nsf n.nsf r.gs.2 cj d.nsm n.nsm r.gs.2

σκανδαλίζει σε, ↰ ↰ ἔκκοψον αὐτὸν ↰ καὶ βάλε ⌊ἀπὸ σοῦ·⌋ καλόν
causes you to sin, cut it off and throw it away; it is better
4997 5148 4997 4997 1716 899 1716 2779 965 608 5148 1639 1639 2819
v.pai.3s r.as.2 v.aam.2s r.asm.3 cj v.aam.2s p.g r.gs.2 a.nsn

σοί ἐστιν ⌊εἰσελθεῖν εἰς⌋ τὴν ζωὴν κυλλὸν ἢ χωλὸν ἢ δύο χεῖρας ἢ
⌊for you⌋ it is to enter {the} life crippled or lame than with two hands or
5148 1639 1656 1650 3836 2437 3245 2445 6000 2445 2400 1545 5931 2445
r.ds.2 v.pai.3s f.aa p.a d.asf n.asf a.asm cj a.asm pl a.apf n.apf cj

δύο πόδας ἔχοντα βληθῆναι εἰς τὸ πῦρ τὸ αἰώνιον. 9 καὶ εἰ ὁ
two feet with to be thrown into {the} eternal fire. {the} eternal And if {the} your
1545 4546 2400 965 1650 3836 173 4786 3836 173 2779 1623 3836 5148
a.apm n.apm pt.pa.asm f.ap p.a d.asn n.asn d.asn a.asn cj cj d.nsm

ὀφθαλμός σου σκανδαλίζει σε, ↰ ↰ ἔξελε αὐτὸν ↰ καὶ βάλε ⌊ἀπὸ σοῦ·⌋
eye your causes you to sin, gouge it out and throw it away;
4057 5148 4997 5148 4997 4997 1975 899 1975 2779 965 608 5148
n.nsm r.gs.2 v.pai.3s r.as.2 v.aam.2s r.asm.3 cj v.aam.2s p.g r.gs.2

καλόν σοί ἐστιν ↱ μονόφθαλμον εἰς τὴν ζωὴν εἰσελθεῖν
it is better ⌊for you⌋ it is to enter life with one eye {into} {the} life to enter
1639 1639 2819 5148 1639 1656 1656 2437 2400 3669 1650 3836 2437 1656
a.nsn r.ds.2 v.pai.3s a.asm p.a d.asf n.asf f.aa

ἢ δύο ὀφθαλμοὺς ἔχοντα βληθῆναι εἰς τὴν γέενναν τοῦ πυρός. 10 ὁρᾶτε
than with two eyes with to be thrown into the hell of fire. "See that
2445 2400 1545 4057 2400 965 1650 3836 1147 3836 4786 3972
pl a.apm n.apm pt.pa.asm f.ap p.a d.asf n.asf d.gsn n.gsn v.pam.2p

↱ ↱ μὴ καταφρονήσητε ἑνὸς τῶν μικρῶν τούτων· λέγω γὰρ ὑμῖν ὅτι
you do not despise one of these little ones. these For I tell For you that
2969 2969 3590 2969 1651 3836 4047 3625 4047 1142 3306 1142 7007 4022
cj v.aas.2p a.gsm d.gpm a.gpm r.gpm v.pai.1s cj r.dp.2 cj

οἱ ἄγγελοι αὐτῶν ἐν οὐρανοῖς ⌊διὰ παντὸς⌋ βλέπουσι τὸ πρόσωπον τοῦ
{the} their angels their in heaven always see the face of
3836 899 34 899 1877 4041 1328 4246 1063 3836 4725 3836
d.npm n.npm r.gpm.3 p.d n.dpm p.g a.gsm v.pai.3p d.asn n.asn d.gsm

πατρός μου τοῦ ἐν οὐρανοῖς.[a] 12 τί ↱ ὑμῖν δοκεῖ; ἐὰν γένηταί
my Father my who is in heaven. What do you think? If a man has
1609 4252 1609 3836 1877 4041 5515 1506 7007 1506 1569 5516 476 1181
n.gsm r.gs.1 d.gsm p.d n.dpm r.nsn r.dp.2 v.pai.3s cj v.ams.3s

τινι ἀνθρώπῳ ἑκατὸν πρόβατα καὶ πλανηθῇ ἓν ἐξ αὐτῶν, ↱ ↱
a man a hundred sheep and one of them goes astray, one of them will he
5516 476 1669 4585 2779 1651 1666 899 4414 1651 1666 899 918 918
r.dsm n.dsm a.npn n.npn cj v.aps.3s a.nsn p.g r.gpn.3

οὐχὶ ἀφήσει τὰ ⌊ἐνενήκοντα ἐννέα⌋ ἐπὶ τὰ ὄρη καὶ πορευθεὶς ζητεῖ τὸ
not leave the ninety-nine on the slopes and go ⌊in search of⌋ the
4049 918 3836 1916 1933 2093 3836 4001 2779 4513 2426 3836
pl v.fai.3s d.apn a.apn a.apn p.a d.apn n.apn cj pt.ap.nsm v.pai.3s d.asn

πλανώμενον; 13 καὶ ἐὰν ⌊γένηται εὑρεῖν⌋ αὐτό, ἀμὴν
⌊one that has wandered off?⌋ And if he finds it, I tell you the truth,
4414 2779 1569 1181 2351 899 3306 3306 7007 297
pt.pp.asn cj cj v.ams.3s f.aa r.asn.3 pl

λέγω ὑμῖν ὅτι χαίρει ἐπ᾽ αὐτῷ μᾶλλον ἢ ἐπὶ τοῖς ⌊ἐνενήκοντα ἐννέα⌋ τοῖς
I tell you ~ ⌊he will rejoice⌋ over it more than over the ninety-nine that
3306 7007 4022 5897 2093 899 3437 2445 2093 3836 1916 1933 3836
v.pai.1s r.dp.2 cj v.pai.3s p.d r.dsn.3 adv.c pl p.d d.dpn a.dpn a.dpn d.dpn

↱ μὴ πεπλανημένοις. 14 οὕτως οὐκ ἔστιν θέλημα ἔμπροσθεν
did not go astray. ⌊In the same way,⌋ it is not it is the will {before}
4414 3590 4414 4048 1639 1639 4024 1639 2525 1869
pl pt.rp.dpn adv adv v.pai.3s n.nsn p.g

τοῦ πατρὸς ὑμῶν τοῦ ἐν οὐρανοῖς ἵνα ἀπόληται
of your Father your {the} in heaven that even one of these little ones should perish.
3836 7007 4252 7007 3836 1877 4041 2671 1651 3836 4047 3625 3625 660
d.gsm n.gsm r.gp.2 d.gsm p.d n.dpm cj v.ams.3s

NASB

the stumbling block comes!

8"If your hand or your foot causes you to stumble, cut it off and throw it from you; it is better for you to enter life crippled or lame, than to have two hands or two feet and be cast into the eternal fire. 9If your eye causes you to stumble, pluck it out and throw it from you. It is better for you to enter life with one eye, than to have two eyes and be cast into the fiery hell.

10"See that you do not despise one of these little ones, for I say to you that their angels in heaven continually see the face of My Father who is in heaven. 11[[a]For the Son of Man has come to save that which was lost.]

Ninety-nine Plus One

12"What do you think? If any man has a hundred sheep, and one of them has gone astray, does he not leave the ninety-nine on the mountains and go and search for the one that is straying? 13If it turns out that he finds it, truly I say to you, he rejoices over it more than over the ninety-nine which have not gone astray. 14So it is not *the* will of your Father who is in heaven that one of these little ones perish.

[a] *11* Some manuscripts include here the words of Luke 19:10.

[a] *11* ἦλθε γὰρ ὁ υἱὸς τοῦ ἀνθρώπου σῶσαι τὸ ἀπολωλός. included by TR after οὐρανοῖς.

[a] Early mss do not contain this v

NIV

Dealing With Sin in the Church

15 "If your brother or sister[a] sins,[b] go and point out their fault, just between the two of you. If they listen to you, you have won them over. 16 But if they will not listen, take one or two others along, so that 'every matter may be established by the testimony of two or three witnesses.'[c] 17 If they still refuse to listen, tell it to the church; and if they refuse to listen even to the church, treat them as you would a pagan or a tax collector.

18 "Truly I tell you, whatever you bind on earth will be[d] bound in heaven, and whatever you loose on earth will be[e] loosed in heaven.

19 "Again, truly I tell you that if two of you on earth agree about anything they ask for, it will be done for them by my Father in heaven. 20 For where two or three gather in my name, there am I with them."

The Parable of the Unmerciful Servant

21 Then Peter came to Jesus and asked, "Lord, how many times shall I forgive my brother or sister who sins

[a] 15 The Greek word for *brother or sister* (*adelphos*) refers here to a fellow disciple, whether man or woman; also in verses 21 and 35.
[b] 15 Some manuscripts *sins against you*
[c] 16 Deut. 19:15
[d] 18 Or *will have been*
[e] 18 Or *will have been*

ἓν τῶν μικρῶν τούτων. 15 ἐὰν δὲ ἁμαρτήσῃ[a] ὁ ἀδελφός σου, ὕπαγε
one of little ones these "If *{and}* your brother sins, *{the} brother your* go
1651 3836 3625 4047 1569 1254 5148 81 279 3836 81 5148 5632
a.nsn d.gpn a.gpn r.gpn cj cj v.aas.3s d.nsm n.nsm r.gs.2 v.pam.2s

ἔλεγξον αὐτὸν μεταξὺ σοῦ καὶ αὐτοῦ μόνου. ἐάν σου ἀκούσῃ,
and point out his fault between you and him alone. If he listens to you, *he listens to*
1794 899 1794 3568 5148 2779 899 3668 1569 201 201 201 5148 201
v.aam.2s r.asm.3 p.g r.gs.2 cj r.gsm.3 a.gsm cj r.gs.2 v.aas.3s

ἐκέρδησας τὸν ἀδελφόν σου· 16 ἐὰν δὲ μὴ ἀκούσῃ,
⌊you have won back⌋ *{the}* your brother. *your* But if *But* he does not listen,
3045 3836 5148 81 5148 1254 1569 1254 201 201 3590 201
v.aai.2s d.asm n.asm r.gs.2 cj cj pl v.aas.3s

παράλαβε μετὰ σοῦ ἔτι ἕνα ἢ δύο, ἵνα
take one or two others with you *others one or two* so that every matter may be
4161 1651 2445 1545 2285 3552 5148 2285 1651 2445 1545 2671 4246 4839 2705 2705
v.aam.2s p.g r.gs.2 adv a.asm cj a.apm cj

ἐπὶ στόματος δύο μαρτύρων ἢ τριῶν σταθῇ πᾶν
confirmed on the evidence of two or three witnesses. *or three may be confirmed every*
2705 2093 5125 1545 2445 5552 3459 2445 5552 2705 4246
p.g n.gsn a.gpm n.gpm cj a.gpm v.aps.3s a.nsn

ῥῆμα· 17 ἐὰν δὲ παρακούσῃ αὐτῶν, εἰπὲ τῇ ἐκκλησίᾳ, ἐὰν δὲ
matter If *{and}* ⌊he refuses to listen to⌋ them, tell it ⌊to the⌋ church; and if *and*
4839 1569 1254 4159 899 3306 3836 1711 1254 1569 1254
n.nsn cj cj v.aas.3s r.gpm.3 v.aam.2s d.dsf n.dsf cj cj

καὶ τῆς ἐκκλησίας παρακούσῃ, ἔστω σοι
he refuses to listen even to the church, *he refuses to listen to* you ⌊are to treat him⌋ *you*
4159 4159 4159 4159 2779 4159 3836 1711 4159 5148 1639 5148
adv d.gsf n.gsf v.aas.3s v.pam.3s r.ds.2

ὥσπερ ὁ ἐθνικὸς καὶ ὁ τελώνης. 18 ἀμὴν λέγω ὑμῖν, ⌊ὅσα
as a pagan and a tax collector. "I tell you the truth, *I tell you* whatever
6061 3836 1618 2779 3836 5467 3306 3306 7007 297 3306 7007 4012
pl d.nsm a.nsm cj d.nsm n.nsm pl v.pai.1s r.dp.2 r.apn

ἐὰν⌋ δήσητε ἐπὶ τῆς γῆς ἔσται δεδεμένα ἐν οὐρανῷ, καὶ ⌊ὅσα ἐὰν⌋
you bind on *{the}* earth will ⌊have been bound⌋ in heaven, and whatever
1569 1313 2093 3836 1178 1639 1313 1877 4041 2779 4012 1569
pl v.aas.2p p.g d.gsf n.gsf v.fmi.3s pt.rp.npn p.d n.dsm cj r.apn pl

λύσητε ἐπὶ τῆς γῆς ἔσται λελυμένα ἐν οὐρανῷ. 19 πάλιν
you loose on *{the}* earth will ⌊have been loosed⌋ in heaven. "Again, I tell you
3395 2093 3836 1178 1639 3395 1877 4041 4099 3306 3306 7007
v.aas.2p p.g d.gsf n.gsf v.fmi.3s pt.rp.npn p.d n.dsm adv

ἀμὴν[b] λέγω ὑμῖν ὅτι ἐὰν δύο συμφωνήσωσιν ἐξ ὑμῶν ἐπὶ
the truth, *I tell you {that}* if two of you on earth are in agreement *of you on*
297 3306 7007 4022 1569 1545 1666 7007 2093 1178 5244 1666 7007 2093
pl v.pai.1s r.dp.2 cj cj a.npm v.aas.3p p.g r.gp.2 p.g

τῆς γῆς περὶ ⌊παντὸς πράγματος⌋ ⌊οὗ ἐὰν⌋ αἰτήσωνται, γενήσεται αὐτοῖς
{the} earth about anything whatever you may ask, it will be done for you
3836 1178 4309 4246 4547 4005 1569 160 1181 899
d.gsf n.gsf p.g a.gsn n.gsn r.gsn pl v.ams.3p v.fmi.3s r.dpm.3

παρὰ τοῦ πατρός μου τοῦ ἐν οὐρανοῖς. 20 οὗ γάρ εἰσιν
by *{the}* my Father *my* who is in heaven. For where *For* two or three are
4123 3836 1609 4252 1609 3836 1877 4041 1142 4023 1142 1545 2445 5552 1639
p.g d.gsm n.gsm r.gs.1 d.gsm p.d n.dpm adv cj v.pai.3p

δύο ἢ τρεῖς συνηγμένοι εἰς τὸ ἐμὸν ὄνομα, ἐκεῖ εἰμι ἐν μέσῳ
two or three gathered in *{the}* my name, I am there *I am* in their midst."
1545 2445 5552 5251 1650 3836 1847 3950 1639 1639 1695 1639 1877 899 3545
a.npm cj a.npm pt.rp.npm p.a d.asn r.asn.1 n.asn adv v.pai.1s p.d n.dsn

αὐτῶν. 21 τότε προσελθὼν ὁ Πέτρος εἶπεν αὐτῷ, κύριε, ποσάκις
their Then Peter came to *{the} Peter* Jesus and said, *Jesus* "Lord, how often must
899 5538 4377 4665 3836 4377 899 3306 899 3261 4529 918
r.gpm.3 adv pt.aa.nsm d.nsm n.nsm v.aai.3s r.dsm.3 n.vsm adv

ἁμαρτήσει εἰς ἐμὲ ὁ ἀδελφός μου καὶ ἀφήσω
I forgive my brother when he sins against me? *{the} brother my {and} must I forgive*
918 918 1609 81 279 1650 1609 3836 81 1609 2779 918
v.fai.3s p.a r.as.1 d.nsm n.nsm r.gs.1 cj v.fai.1s

[a] εἰς σὲ included by UBS after ἁμαρτήσῃ.
[b] [ἀμὴν] UBS.

NASB

Discipline and Prayer

15 "If your brother sins[a], go and show him his fault in private; if he listens to you, you have won your brother. 16 But if he does not listen *to you,* take one or two more with you, so that BY THE MOUTH OF TWO OR THREE WITNESSES EVERY FACT MAY BE CONFIRMED. 17 If he refuses to listen to them, tell it to the church; and if he refuses to listen even to the church, let him be to you as a Gentile and a tax collector. 18 Truly I say to you, whatever you bind on earth shall have been bound in heaven; and whatever you loose on earth shall have been loosed in heaven.

19 "Again I say to you, that if two of you agree on earth about anything that they may ask, it shall be done for them by My Father who is in heaven. 20 For where two or three have gathered together in My name, I am there in their midst."

Forgiveness

21 Then Peter came and said to Him, "Lord, how often shall my brother sin against me and I forgive him? Up

[a] Late mss add *against you*

NIV

against me? Up to
seven times?"
22 Jesus answered,
"I tell you, not sev-
en times, but sev-
enty-seven times.[a]
23 "Therefore,
the kingdom of
heaven is like a
king who wanted
to settle accounts
with his servants.
24 As he began the
settlement, a man
who owed him ten
thousand bags of
gold[b] was brought
to him. 25 Since
he was not able to
pay, the master or-
dered that he and
his wife and his
children and all
that he had be sold
to repay the debt.
26 "At this the
servant fell on his
knees before him.
'Be patient with
me,' he begged,
'and I will pay
back everything.'
27 The servant's
master took pity
on him, canceled
the debt and let
him go.
28 "But when that
servant went out,
he found one of
his fellow servants
who owed him
a hundred silver
coins.[c] He grabbed
him and began to
choke him. 'Pay
back what you owe
me!' he demanded.
29 "His fellow
servant fell to his
knees and begged
him, 'Be patient
with me, and I will
pay it back.'
30 "But he refused.

[a] 22 Or *seventy times seven*
[b] 24 Greek *ten thousand talents*; a talent was worth about 20 years of a day laborer's wages.
[c] 28 Greek *a hundred denarii*; a denarius was the usual daily wage of a day laborer (see 20:2).

αὐτῷ; ἕως ἑπτάκις; 22 λέγει αὐτῷ ὁ Ἰησοῦς, ↱ ↱ οὐ λέγω σοι
⌞Up to⌟ seven times?" Jesus said to him, *{the}* *Jesus* "I do not say to you,
899 2401 2232 2652 3306 899 3836 2652 3306 3306 4024 3306 5148
r.dsm.3 p.g adv v.pai.3s r.dsm.3 d.nsm n.nsm adv v.pai.1s r.ds.2

ἕως ἑπτάκις ἀλλὰ ἕως ἑβδομηκοντάκις ἑπτά. 23 ⌞διὰ τοῦτο⌟
up to seven times, but up to seventy times seven. Therefore the kingdom of
2401 2232 247 2401 1574 2231 1328 4047 3836 993 3836
p.g adv cj p.g adv a.apn p.a r.asn

ὡμοιώθη ἡ βασιλεία τῶν οὐρανῶν ἀνθρώπῳ βασιλεῖ, ὃς ἠθέλησεν
heaven is like *the* *kingdom* *of* *heaven* *{person}* a king who decided
4041 3929 3836 993 3836 4041 476 995 4005 2527
v.api.3s d.nsf n.nsf d.gpm n.gpm n.dsm n.dsm r.nsm v.aai.3s

συνᾶραι λόγον μετὰ τῶν δούλων αὐτοῦ. 24 → ἀρξαμένου δὲ αὐτοῦ
to settle accounts with *{the}* his servants. *his* And when he had begun *And* *he*
5256 3364 3552 3836 899 1529 899 1254 899 806 1254 899
f.aa n.asm p.g d.gpm n.gpm r.gsm.3 pt.am.gsm cj r.gsm.3

συναίρειν προσηνέχθη αὐτῷ εἷς ὀφειλέτης
to settle them, a man who owed ten thousand talents was brought to him. *man* *who owed*
5256 1651 4050 4050 3692 3692 5419 4712 899 1651 4050
f.pa v.api.3s r.dsm.3 a.nsm n.nsm

μυρίων ταλάντων. 25 ↱ ↱ μὴ ἔχοντος δὲ αὐτοῦ ἀποδοῦναι
ten thousand *talents* And since he did not have *And* *he* the means to repay
3692 5419 1254 2400 899 2400 3590 2400 1254 899 625
a.gpn n.gpn pl pt.pa.gsm cj r.gsm.3 f.aa

ἐκέλευσεν αὐτὸν ὁ κύριος πραθῆναι καὶ τὴν γυναῖκα
the debt, his master commanded that he *his* *master* be sold ⌞along with⌟ his wife
3836 3261 3027 899 3836 3261 4405 2779 3836 1222
v.aai.3s r.asm.3 d.nsm n.nsm f.ap cj d.asf n.asf

καὶ τὰ τέκνα καὶ ⌞πάντα ὅσα⌟ ἔχει, καὶ ἀποδοθῆναι. 26
and *{the}* children and everything he had, and that payment be made. So the servant
2779 3836 5451 2779 4246 4012 2400 2779 625 4036 3836 1529
cj d.apn n.apn cj a.apn r.apn v.pai.3s cj f.ap

πεσὼν οὖν ὁ δοῦλος προσεκύνει αὐτῷ λέγων, μακροθύμησον ἐπ' ἐμοί,
⌞fell to the ground⌟ *So* *the* *servant* prostate before him, saying, 'Have patience with me,
4406 4036 3836 1529 4686 899 3306 3428 2093 1609
pt.aa.nsm cj d.nsm n.nsm v.iai.3s r.dsm.3 pt.pa.nsm v.aam.2s p.d r.ds.1

καὶ πάντα ἀποδώσω σοι. 27 σπλαγχνισθεὶς δὲ ὁ
and I will repay you everything.' *I will repay* *you* Moved with compassion, *{and}* the
2779 625 625 625 5148 4246 625 5148 5072 1254 3836
cj a.apn v.fai.1s r.ds.2 pt.ap.nsm cj d.nsm

κύριος τοῦ δούλου ἐκείνου ἀπέλυσεν αὐτὸν καὶ τὸ δάνειον ἀφῆκεν
master of that servant *that* released him and forgave him the debt. *forgave*
3261 3836 1697 1529 1697 668 899 2779 918 899 3836 1245 918
n.nsm d.gsm n.gsm r.gsm v.aai.3s r.asm.3 cj d.asn n.asn v.aai.3s

αὐτῷ. 28 ἐξελθὼν δὲ ὁ δοῦλος ἐκεῖνος εὗρεν ἕνα τῶν
him *then went out* But that same servant *same* then went out and found one of
899 2002 1254 3836 1697 1529 1697 2002 2002 2002 2351 1651 3836
r.dsm.3 pt.aa.nsm cj d.nsm n.nsm r.nsm v.aai.3s a.asm d.gpm

συνδούλων αὐτοῦ, ὃς ὤφειλεν αὐτῷ ἑκατὸν δηνάρια, καὶ κρατήσας αὐτὸν
his fellow servants *his* who owed him a hundred denarii; and seizing him by
899 5281 899 4005 4053 899 1669 1324 2779 3195 899
n.gpm r.gsm.3 r.nsm v.iai.3s r.dsm.3 a.apn n.apn cj pt.aa.nsm r.asm.3

ἔπνιγεν λέγων, ἀπόδος ⌞εἴ τι⌟ ὀφείλεις. 29
the throat ⌞began to choke⌟ him, saying, 'Pay back what you owe.' Therefore his fellow
4464 3306 625 1623 5516 4053 4036 899 5281
v.iai.3s pt.pa.nsm v.aam.2s cj r.asn v.pai.2s

πεσὼν οὖν ὁ σύνδουλος αὐτοῦ[a] παρεκάλει αὐτὸν
servant fell to the ground *Therefore* *{the}* *fellow servant* *his* and pleaded with him,
5281 4406 4036 3836 5281 899 4151 899
pt.aa.nsm cj d.nsm n.nsm r.gsm.3 v.iai.3s r.asm.3

λέγων, μακροθύμησον ἐπ' ἐμοί, καὶ ἀποδώσω σοι. 30 ὁ δὲ ⌞οὐκ ἤθελεν⌟
saying 'Have patience with me, and I will repay you.' But he *But* refused.
3306 3428 2093 1609 2779 625 5148 1254 3836 1254 4024 2527
pt.pa.nsm v.aam.2s p.d r.ds.1 cj v.fai.1s r.ds.2 d.nsm cj adv v.iai.3s

[a] εἰς τοὺς πόδας αὐτοῦ included by TR after αὐτοῦ.

NASB

to seven times?"
22 Jesus *said to
him, "I do not
say to you, up to
seven times, but up
to seventy times
seven.
23 "For this reason
the kingdom of
heaven may be
compared to a king
who wished to
settle accounts with
his slaves. 24 When
he had begun to
settle *them,* one
who owed him [a]ten
thousand talents
was brought to
him. 25 But since he
did not have *the
means* to repay, his
lord commanded
him to be sold,
along with his wife
and children and
all that he had,
and repayment
to be made. 26 So
the slave fell *to
the ground* and
prostrated himself
before him, saying,
'Have patience
with me and I will
repay you every-
thing.' 27 And the
lord of that slave
felt compassion
and released him
and forgave him
the debt. 28 But that
slave went out
and found one of
his fellow slaves
who owed him a
hundred [b]denarii;
and he seized him
and *began* to choke
him, saying, 'Pay
back what you
owe.' 29 So his fel-
low slave fell *to the
ground* and *began*
to plead with him,
saying, 'Have pa-
tience with me and
I will repay you.'
30 But he was un-
willing and went

[a] A talent was worth more than fifteen years' wages of a laborer
[b] The denarius was a day's wages

NIV

Instead, he went
off and had the
man thrown into
prison until he
could pay the debt.
31 When the other
servants saw what
had happened,
they were outraged
and went and told
their master ev-
erything that had
happened.
32 "Then the
master called the
servant in. 'You
wicked servant,'
he said, 'I can-
celed all that debt
of yours because
you begged me to.
33 Shouldn't you
have had mercy
on your fellow
servant just as I
had on you?' 34 In
anger his master
handed him over
to the jailers to be
tortured, until he
should pay back all
he owed.
35 "This is how my
heavenly Father
will treat each of
you unless you for-
give your brother
or sister from your
heart."

Divorce

19 When Jesus
had fin-
ished saying these
things, he left Gal-
ilee and went into
the region of Judea
to the other side of
the Jordan. 2 Large
crowds followed
him, and he healed
them there.
3 Some Pharisees
came to him to test
him. They asked,
"Is it lawful for a
man to divorce his

ἀλλὰ ↱ ἀπελθὼν ἔβαλεν αὐτὸν εἰς φυλακὴν ἕως ἀποδῷ τὸ
Instead, he went and threw him in prison until ⌞he should pay back⌟ the
247 965 599 965 899 1650 5871 2401 625 3836
cj pt.aa.nsm v.aai.3s r.asm.3 p.a n.asf cj v.aas.3s d.asn

ὀφειλόμενον. 31 → ἰδόντες οὖν οἱ σύνδουλοι αὐτοῦ τὰ
debt. So when his fellow servants saw *So* *{the}* *fellow servants* *his* what
4053 4036 899 5281 5281 1625 4036 3836 5281 899 3836
pt.pp.asn pt.aa.npm cj d.npm n.npm r.gsm.3 d.apn

γενόμενα ⌞ἐλυπήθησαν σφόδρα⌟ καὶ ἐλθόντες διεσάφησαν τῷ κυρίῳ
had happened, they became indignant and went and told *{the}* their master
1181 3382 5379 2779 2262 1397 3836 1571 3261
pt.am.apn v.api.3p adv cj pt.aa.npm v.aai.3p d.dsm n.dsm

ἑαυτῶν πάντα τὰ γενόμενα. 32 τότε προσκαλεσάμενος αὐτὸν ↰ ὁ
their all that had taken place. Then his master called him in *{the}*
1571 4246 3836 1181 5538 899 3261 4673 899 4673 3836
r.gpm.3 a.apn d.apn pt.am.apn adv pt.am.nsm r.asm.3 d.nsm

κύριος αὐτοῦ λέγει αὐτῷ, → δοῦλε πονηρέ, πᾶσαν τὴν
master *his* and said to him, 'You wicked servant! *wicked* I forgave you all *{the}*
3261 899 3306 899 4505 1529 4505 918 918 5148 4246 3836
n.nsm r.gsm.3 v.pai.3s r.dsm.3 n.vsm a.vsm a.asf d.asf

ὀφειλὴν ἐκείνην ἀφῆκά σοι, ἐπεὶ παρεκάλεσάς με· 33 οὐκ ἔδει
that debt *that* *I forgave* *you* because you pleaded with me. And should not *should*
1697 4051 1697 918 5148 2075 4151 1609 1256 4024 1256
n.asf r.asf v.aai.1s r.ds.2 cj v.aai.2s r.as.1 pl v.iai.3s

καὶ σὲ ἐλεῆσαι τὸν σύνδουλόν σου, ↱ ὡς κἀγὼ
you also *you* ⌞have had mercy on⌟ *{the}* your fellow servant, *your* even as I had mercy
5148 2779 5148 1796 3836 5148 5281 5148 2743 6055 2743 1796 1796
adv r.as.2 f.aa d.asm n.asm r.gs.2 cj crasis

σὲ ἠλέησα; 34 καὶ ὀργισθεὶς ὁ κύριος αὐτοῦ παρέδωκεν αὐτὸν ↰
on you?' *had mercy on* And in anger *{the}* his lord *his* handed him over
1796 5148 1796 2779 3974 3836 899 3261 899 4140 899 4140
r.as.2 v.aai.1s cj pt.ap.nsm d.nsm n.nsm r.gsm.3 v.aai.3s r.asm.3

τοῖς βασανισταῖς ⌞ἕως οὗ⌟ ἀποδῷ πᾶν τὸ ὀφειλόμενον.
to the ⌞prison guards to torture⌟ him until ⌞he should pay back⌟ all *{the}* he owed.
3836 991 2401 4005 625 4246 3836 4053
d.dpm n.dpm p.g r.gsm v.aas.3s a.asn d.asn pt.pp.asn

35 οὕτως καὶ ↱ ὁ πατήρ μου ὁ οὐράνιος ποιήσει ὑμῖν, ⌞ἐὰν μὴ⌟
So also will *{the}* my heavenly Father *my* *{the}* *heavenly* do to you, unless
4048 2779 4472 3836 1609 4039 4252 1609 3836 4039 4472 7007 1569 3590
adv adv d.nsm n.nsm r.gs.1 d.nsm a.nsm v.fai.3s r.dp.2 cj pl

→ ἀφῆτε ἕκαστος τῷ ἀδελφῷ αὐτοῦ ἀπὸ τῶν καρδιῶν ὑμῶν.
you each forgive *each* *{the}* your brother *your* from *{the}* your heart." *your*
1667 918 1667 3836 899 81 899 608 3836 7007 2840 7007
v.aas.2p r.nsm d.dsm n.dsm r.gsm.3 p.g d.gpf n.gpf r.gp.2

19:1 ⌞καὶ ἐγένετο⌟ ὅτε ἐτέλεσεν ὁ Ἰησοῦς τοὺς λόγους τούτους,
Now when Jesus had finished *{the}* *Jesus* *{the}* these sayings, *these*
2779 1181 4021 2652 5464 3836 2652 3836 4047 3364 4047
cj v.ami.3s cj v.aai.3s d.nsm n.nsm d.apm n.apm r.apm

μετῆρεν ἀπὸ τῆς Γαλιλαίας καὶ ἦλθεν εἰς τὰ ὅρια τῆς Ἰουδαίας πέραν τοῦ
he left *{from}* *{the}* Galilee and went to the region of Judea beyond the
3558 608 3836 1133 2779 2262 1650 3836 3990 3836 2677 4305 3836
v.aai.3s p.g d.gsf n.gsf cj v.aai.3s p.a d.apn n.apn d.gsf n.gsf p.g d.gsm

Ἰορδάνου. 2 καὶ ἠκολούθησαν αὐτῷ ὄχλοι πολλοί, καὶ
Jordan River. *{and}* Large crowds followed him, *crowds* *Large* and
2674 2779 4498 4063 199 899 4063 4498 2779
n.gsm cj v.aai.3p r.dsm.3 n.npm a.npm cj

ἐθεράπευσεν αὐτοὺς ἐκεῖ. 3 καὶ προσῆλθον αὐτῷ Φαρισαῖοι
he healed them there. *{and}* Some Pharisees came to him *Pharisees* and
2543 899 1695 2779 5757 4665 899 5757 2779
v.aai.3s r.apm.3 adv cj v.aai.3p r.dsm.3 n.npm

πειράζοντες αὐτὸν καὶ λέγοντες, εἰ ἔξεστιν → ἀνθρώπῳ[a] ἀπολῦσαι τὴν
tested him *and* by asking, *{if}* "Is it lawful for a man to divorce *{the}* his
4279 899 2779 3306 1623 1997 476 668 3836 899
pt.pa.npm r.asm.3 cj pt.pa.npm cj v.pai.3s n.dsm f.aa d.asf

NASB

and threw him in
prison until he
should pay back
what was owed.
31 So when his fel-
low slaves saw
what had hap-
pened, they were
deeply grieved and
came and reported
to their lord all
that had happened.
32 Then summon-
ing him, his lord
*said to him, 'You
wicked slave, I
forgave you all
that debt because
you pleaded with
me. 33 Should you
not also have had
mercy on your fel-
low slave, in the
same way that I
had mercy on you?'
34 And his lord,
moved with anger,
handed him over to
the torturers until
he should repay
all that was owed
him. 35 My heavenly
Father will also do
the same to you, if
each of you does
not forgive his
brother from your
heart."

Concerning Divorce

19:1 When Jesus
had finished these
words, He departed
from Galilee and
came into the
region of Judea
beyond the Jordan;
2 and large crowds
followed Him, and
He healed them
there.
3 *Some* Pharisees
came to Jesus, test-
ing Him and ask-
ing, "Is it lawful
for a man to

[a] ἀνθρώπῳ omitted by NET.

NIV

wife for any and
every reason?”
4“Haven’t you
read,” he replied,
“that at the begin-
ning the Creator
‘made them male
and female,’[a]
5and said, ‘For
this reason a man
will leave his fa-
ther and mother
and be united to
his wife, and the
two will become
one flesh’[b]? 6So
they are no longer
two, but one flesh.
Therefore what
God has joined to-
gether, let no one
separate.”
7“Why then,”
they asked, “did
Moses command
that a man give his
wife a certificate
of divorce and
send her away?”
8Jesus replied,
“Moses permit-
ted you to divorce
your wives be-
cause your hearts
were hard. But it
was not this way
from the begin-
ning. 9I tell you
that anyone who
divorces his wife,
except for sexual
immorality, and
marries another
woman commits
adultery.”
10The disciples
said to him, “If
this is the situation
between a husband
and wife, it is bet-
ter not to marry.”
11Jesus replied,
“Not everyone can
accept this

γυναῖκα αὐτοῦ κατὰ πᾶσαν αἰτίαν; 4ὁ δὲ ἀποκριθεὶς εἶπεν, ↱ ↱ οὐκ
wife *his* for any cause?” He *{and}* answered, saying, “Have you not
1222 899 2848 4246 162 3836 1254 646 3306 336 336 4024
n.asf r.gsm.3 p.a a.asf n.asf d.nsm cj pt.ap.nsm v.aai.3s pl

ἀνέγνωτε ὅτι ὁ κτίσας ἀπ’ ἀρχῆς ἄρσεν καὶ θῆλυ
read that he who created them from the beginning ‘made them male and female?’”
336 4022 3836 3231 608 794 4472 899 781 2779 2559
v.aai.2p cj d.nsm pt.aa.nsm p.g n.gsf a.asn cj a.asn

ἐποίησεν αὐτούς; 5καὶ εἶπεν, ἕνεκα τούτου καταλείψει ἄνθρωπος τὸν
made *them* And he added, “For this reason a man will leave *man* his
4472 899 2779 3306 1914 4047 476 2901 476 3836
v.aai.3s r.apm.3 cj v.aai.3s p.g r.gsn v.fai.3s n.nsm d.asm

πατέρα καὶ τὴν μητέρα καὶ κολληθήσεται τῇ γυναικὶ αὐτοῦ, καὶ
father and *{the}* mother and be joined to his wife, *his* and the two
4252 2779 3836 3613 2779 3140 3836 899 1222 899 2779 3836 1545
n.asm cj d.asf n.asf cj v.fpi.3s d.dsf n.dsf r.gsm.3 cj

ἔσονται οἱ δύο εἰς σάρκα μίαν. 6ὥστε οὐκέτι εἰσὶν δύο
will become *the* *two* *{into}* one flesh.’ *one* So then they are no longer *they are* two,
1639 3836 1545 1650 1651 4922 1651 6063 1639 1639 4033 1639 1545
v.fmi.3p d.npm a.npm p.a n.asf a.asf cj adv v.pai.3p a.npm

ἀλλὰ σὰρξ μία. ὃ οὖν ὁ θεὸς συνέζευξεν ἄνθρωπος
but one flesh. *one* Therefore what *Therefore* *{the}* God has joined together, no one
247 1651 4922 1651 4036 4005 4036 3836 2536 5183 3590 476
cj n.nsf a.nsf r.asn cj d.nsm n.nsm v.aai.3s n.nsm

μὴ χωριζέτω. 7 λέγουσιν αὐτῷ, τί οὖν ↱ Μωϋσῆς ἐνετείλατο
no must separate.” “Why then,” they asked, *{to him}* *Why* *then* “did Moses command that a
3590 6004 5515 4036 3306 899 5515 4036 1948 3707 1948
pl v.pam.3s v.pai.3p r.dsm.3 r.asn cj n.nsm v.ami.3s

δοῦναι βιβλίον ἀποστασίου καὶ ἀπολῦσαι αὐτήν;[a] 8
certificate of divorce be given *certificate* *of divorce* before she be sent away?” *she* Jesus
1046 687 687 1443 1046 687 2779 899 668 899
f.aa n.asn n.gsn cj f.aa r.asf.3

λέγει αὐτοῖς ὅτι Μωϋσῆς πρὸς τὴν
replied to them, ~ “Moses allowed you to divorce your wives ⌞because of⌟ the
3306 899 4022 3707 2205 7007 668 668 7007 1222 4639 3836
v.pai.3s r.dpm.3 cj n.nsm p.a d.asf

σκληροκαρδίαν ὑμῶν ↰ ἐπέτρεψεν ὑμῖν ἀπολῦσαι τὰς γυναῖκας ὑμῶν,
hardness of your hearts; *allowed* *you* *to divorce* *{the}* *wives* *your* but it
5016 7007 5016 2205 7007 668 3836 1222 7007 1254 1181
n.asf r.gp.2 v.aai.3s r.dp.2 f.aa d.apf n.apf r.gp.2

ἀπ’ ἀρχῆς δὲ οὐ γέγονεν οὕτως. 9 λέγω δὲ ὑμῖν
was not that way from the beginning. *but* *not* *it was* *that way* But I say *But* to you,
1181 4024 4048 4048 608 794 1254 4024 1181 4048 1254 3306 1254 7007
p.g n.gsf cj adv v.rai.3s adv v.pai.1s cj r.dp.2

ὅτι ⌞ὃς ἂν⌟ ἀπολύσῃ τὴν γυναῖκα αὐτοῦ μὴ ἐπὶ πορνείᾳ καὶ
{that} whoever divorces *{the}* his wife, *his* except for sexual immorality, and
4022 4005 323 668 3836 899 1222 899 3590 2093 4518 2779
cj r.nsm pl v.aas.3s d.asf n.asf r.gsm.3 pl p.d n.dsf cj

γαμήσῃ ἄλλην μοιχᾶται.[b] 10 λέγουσιν αὐτῷ οἱ μαθηταί[c] εἰ
marries another, commits adultery.” The disciples said to him, *The* *disciples* “If
1138 257 3656 3836 3412 3306 899 3836 3412 1623
v.aas.3s r.asf v.ppi.3s v.pai.3p r.dsm.3 d.npm n.npm cj

οὕτως ἐστὶν ἡ αἰτία τοῦ ἀνθρώπου μετὰ τῆς γυναικός, οὐ
such is the case of a man with his wife, it is better not
4048 1639 3836 162 3836 476 3552 3836 1222 5237 5237 5237 4024
adv v.pai.3s d.nsf n.nsf d.gsm n.gsm p.g d.gsf n.gsf adv

συμφέρει γαμῆσαι. 11ὁ δὲ εἶπεν αὐτοῖς, οὐ πάντες χωροῦσιν τὸν
it is better to marry.” Jesus *{and}* replied to them, “Not everyone can accept *{the}* this
5237 1138 3836 1254 3306 899 4024 4246 6003 3836 4047
v.pai.3s f.aa d.nsm cj v.aai.3s r.dpm.3 adv a.npm v.pai.3p d.asm

NASB

divorce his wife for
any reason at all?”
4And He answered
and said, “Have
you not read that
He who created
them from the be-
ginning MADE THEM
MALE AND FEMALE,
5and said, ‘FOR
THIS REASON A MAN
SHALL LEAVE HIS
FATHER AND MOTHER
AND BE JOINED TO
HIS WIFE, AND THE
TWO SHALL BECOME
ONE FLESH’? 6So
they are no longer
two, but one flesh.
What therefore
God has joined to-
gether, let no man
separate.” 7They
*said to Him, “Why
then did Moses
command to GIVE
HER A CERTIFICATE
OF DIVORCE AND
SEND *her* AWAY?”
8He *said to them,
“Because of your
hardness of heart
Moses permitted
you to divorce your
wives; but from the
beginning it has
not been this way.
9And I say to you,
whoever divorces
his wife, except for
immorality, and
marries another
woman commits
adultery.”
10The disciples
*said to Him, “If
the relationship of
the man with his
wife is like this,
it is better not to
marry.” 11But He
said to them, “Not
all men *can* accept
this statement,

[a] 4 Gen. 1:27
[b] 5 Gen. 2:24

[a] [αὐτήν] UBS, omitted by NET.
[b] καὶ ὁ ἀπολελυμένην γαμήσας μοιχᾶται included by TR after μοιχᾶται.
[c] αὐτοῦ included by UBS after μαθηταί.

NIV

word, but only
those to whom it
has been given.
12For there are eu-
nuchs who were
born that way, and
there are eunuchs
who have been
made eunuchs by
others—and there
are those who
choose to live like
eunuchs for the
sake of the king-
dom of heaven.
The one who can
accept this should
accept it."

The Little Children and Jesus

13Then people
brought little chil-
dren to Jesus for
him to place his
hands on them and
pray for them. But
the disciples re-
buked them.
14Jesus said, "Let
the little children
come to me, and
do not hinder
them, for the king-
dom of heaven
belongs to such
as these." 15When
he had placed his
hands on them,
he went on from
there.

The Rich and the Kingdom of God

16Just then a man
came up to Jesus
and asked, "Teach-
er, what good
thing must I do to
get eternal life?"
17"Why do you
ask me about what
is good?" Jesus
replied. "There is
only One who is
good. If you want
to enter life, keep
the command-
ments."
18"Which ones?"
he inquired.
Jesus replied,
"'You shall not
murder, you shall
not commit adul-
tery, you shall not
steal, you shall not

λόγον τοῦτον[a] ἀλλ᾽ οἷς δέδοται. 12 εἰσὶν γὰρ εὐνοῦχοι
statement, *this* but only ⌊those to whom⌋ it is given. For ⌊there are⌋ *For* eunuchs
3364 4047 247 4005 1443 1142 1639 1142 2336
n.asm r.asm cj r.dpm v.rpi.3s v.pai.3p cj n.npm

οἵτινες ἐκ κοιλίας μητρὸς ἐγεννήθησαν οὕτως, καὶ
who have been that way from their mother's womb, *mother's* *have been* *that way* and
4015 1164 1164 4048 4048 1666 3613 3120 3613 1164 4048 2779
r.npm p.g n.gsf n.gsf v.api.3p adv cj

εἰσὶν εὐνοῦχοι οἵτινες εὐνουχίσθησαν ὑπὸ τῶν ἀνθρώπων, καὶ εἰσὶν
⌊there are⌋ eunuchs who were made eunuchs by *{the}* others, and ⌊there are⌋
1639 2336 4015 2335 5679 3836 476 2779 1639
v.pai.3p n.npm r.npm v.api.3p p.g d.gpm n.gpm cj v.pai.3p

εὐνοῦχοι οἵτινες εὐνούχισαν ἑαυτοὺς ↰ διὰ τὴν βασιλείαν τῶν
eunuchs who made themselves eunuchs ⌊for the sake of⌋ the kingdom of
2336 4015 2335 1571 2335 1328 3836 993 3836
n.npm r.npm v.aai.3p r.apm.3 p.a d.asf n.asf d.gpm

οὐρανῶν. ὁ δυνάμενος χωρεῖν χωρείτω. 13 τότε
heaven. The one who is able to accept this should accept it." Then children
4041 3836 1538 6003 6003 5538 4086
n.gpm d.nsm pt.pp.nsm f.pa v.pam.3s adv

προσηνέχθησαν αὐτῷ παιδία ἵνα τὰς χεῖρας ἐπιθῇ αὐτοῖς
were brought to Jesus *children* so that he might lay his hands *he might lay on* on them
4712 899 4086 2671 2202 2202 2202 3836 5931 2202 2202 899
v.api.3p r.dsm.3 n.npn cj d.apf n.apf v.aas.3s r.dpm.3

καὶ προσεύξηται· οἱ δὲ μαθηταὶ ἐπετίμησαν αὐτοῖς. 14 ὁ
and pray, but the *but* disciples rebuked those who brought them. *{the}*
2779 4667 1254 3836 1254 3412 2203 899 3836
cj v.ams.3s d.npm cj n.npm v.aai.3p r.dpm.3 d.nsm

δὲ Ἰησοῦς εἶπεν, ἄφετε τὰ παιδία καὶ ↱ μὴ κωλύετε αὐτὰ
But Jesus said, "Let the children come to me and do not try to prevent them,
1254 2652 3306 918 3836 4086 2262 4639 1609 2779 3266 3590 3266 899
cj n.nsm v.aai.3s v.aam.2p d.apn n.apn cj pl v.pam.2p r.apn.3

ἐλθεῖν πρός με, τῶν γὰρ τοιούτων ἐστιν ἡ
come *to* *me* *{the}* for the kingdom of heaven belongs ⌊to such as these."⌋ *belongs* *the*
2262 4639 1609 3836 1142 3836 993 3836 4041 1639 5525 1639 3836
f.aa p.a r.as.1 d.gpm cj r.gpm v.pai.3s d.nsf

βασιλεία τῶν οὐρανῶν. 15 καὶ ↱ ἐπιθεὶς τὰς χεῖρας ↰ αὐτοῖς ἐπορεύθη
kingdom *of* *heaven* And he placed his hands on them and went
993 3836 4041 2779 4513 2202 3836 5931 2202 899 4513
n.nsf d.gpm n.gpm cj pt.aa.nsm d.apf n.apf r.dpm.3 v.api.3s

ἐκεῖθεν. 16 καὶ ἰδοὺ εἷς προσελθὼν αὐτῷ εἶπεν, διδάσκαλε, τί
on his way. *{and}* *{behold}* A young man came up to Jesus and asked, "Teacher, what
1696 2779 2627 1651 4665 899 3306 1437 5515
adv cj j a.nsm pt.aa.nsm r.dsm.3 v.aai.3s n.vsm r.asn

ἀγαθὸν ποιήσω ἵνα σχῶ ζωὴν αἰώνιον; 17 ὁ δὲ εἶπεν αὐτῷ,
good thing must I do so that ⌊I may have⌋ eternal life?" *eternal* And Jesus *And* replied to him,
19 4472 2671 2400 173 2437 173 1254 3836 1254 3306 899
a.asn v.aas.1s cj v.aas.1s n.asf a.asf d.nsm cj v.aai.3s r.dsm.3

τί με ἐρωτᾷς περὶ τοῦ ἀγαθοῦ; εἷς ἐστιν ὁ
"Why do you ask me *do you ask* about what is good? There is only one *There is* who is
5515 2263 2263 2263 1609 2263 4309 3836 19 1639 1639 1651 1639 3836
r.asn r.as.1 v.pai.2s p.g d.gsn a.gsn a.nsm v.pai.3s d.nsm

ἀγαθός· εἰ δὲ θέλεις εἰς τὴν ζωὴν εἰσελθεῖν, τήρησον τὰς
good. If *{and}* you want to enter *{into}* *{the}* life, *to enter* keep the
19 1623 1254 2527 1656 1656 1650 3836 2437 1656 5498 3836
a.nsm cj cj v.pai.2s p.a d.asf n.asf f.aa v.aam.2s d.apf

ἐντολάς. 18 λέγει αὐτῷ, ποίας; ὁ δὲ Ἰησοῦς εἶπεν,
commandments." "Which ones?" he inquired. *{of him}* *Which ones* *{the}* And Jesus said,
1953 4481 4481 3306 899 4481 3836 1254 2652 3306
n.apf v.pai.3s r.dsm.3 r.apf d.nsm cj n.nsm v.aai.3s

τὸ ↱ οὐ φονεύσεις, ↱ οὐ μοιχεύσεις, ↱ οὐ κλέψεις, ↱ οὐ
{the} "'Do not murder, Do not commit adultery, Do not steal, Do not
3836 5839 4024 5839 3658 4024 3658 3096 4024 3096 6018 4024
d.asn adv v.fai.2s adv v.fai.2s adv v.fai.2s adv

[a] [τοῦτον] UBS.

NASB

but *only* those to
whom it has been
given. 12For there
are eunuchs who
were born that way
from their mother's
womb; and there
are eunuchs who
were made eunuchs
by men; and there
are *also* eunuchs
who made them-
selves eunuchs
for the sake of the
kingdom of heav-
en. He who is able
to accept *this,* let
him accept *it.*"

Jesus Blesses Little Children

13Then *some* chil-
dren were brought
to Him so that
He might lay His
hands on them and
pray; and the disci-
ples rebuked them.
14But Jesus said,
"Let the children
alone, and do not
hinder them from
coming to Me; for
the kingdom of
heaven belongs
to such as these."
15After laying His
hands on them,
He departed from
there.

The Rich Young Ruler

16And someone
came to Him and
said, "Teacher,
what good thing
shall I do that I
may obtain eternal
life?" 17And He
said to him, "Why
are you asking
Me about what
is good? There
is *only* One who
is good; but if
you wish to enter
into life, keep the
commandments."
18*Then* he *said
to Him, "Which
ones?" And Jesus
said, "YOU SHALL
NOT COMMIT MUR-
DER; YOU SHALL NOT
COMMIT ADULTERY;
YOU SHALL NOT
STEAL; YOU SHALL

NIV

give false testimo-
ny, [19]honor your
father and moth-
er,'[a] and 'love your
neighbor as your-
self.'[b]"
20 "All these I
have kept," the
young man said.
"What do I still
lack?"
21 Jesus answered,
"If you want to
be perfect, go,
sell your posses-
sions and give to
the poor, and you
will have treasure
in heaven. Then
come, follow me."
22 When the
young man heard
this, he went away
sad, because he
had great wealth.
23 Then Jesus said
to his disciples,
"Truly I tell you, it
is hard for some-
one who is rich to
enter the kingdom
of heaven. [24]Again
I tell you, it is eas-
ier for a camel to
go through the eye
of a needle than
for someone who
is rich to enter the
kingdom of God."
25 When the dis-
ciples heard this,
they were greatly
astonished and
asked, "Who then
can be saved?"
26 Jesus looked
at them and said,
"With man this
is impossible,
but with God all
things are possi-
ble."
27 Peter answered
him, "We have
left everything to
follow you! What
then

ψευδομαρτυρήσεις, [19] τίμα τὸν πατέρα καὶ τὴν μητέρα, καὶ ἀγαπήσεις τὸν
give false testimony, Honor your father and {the} mother, and, Love {the} your
6018 5506 3836 4252 2779 3836 3613 2779 26 3836 5148
v.fai.2s v.pam.2s d.asm n.asm cj d.asf n.asf cj v.fai.2s d.asm

πλησίον σου ὡς σεαυτόν. [20] λέγει αὐτῷ ὁ νεανίσκος, πάντα
neighbor your as yourself." The young man said to him, The young man "All
4446 5148 6055 4932 3836 3734 3734 3306 899 3836 3734 4246
adv r.gs.2 cj r.asm.2 v.pai.3s r.dsm.3 d.nsm n.nsm a.apn

ταῦτα ἐφύλαξα· τί ↱ ↱ ἔτι ὑστερῶ; [21] ἔφη αὐτῷ ὁ Ἰησοῦς, εἰ
these I have kept. What do I still lack?" Jesus said to him, {the} Jesus "If
4047 5875 5515 5728 5728 2285 5728 2652 5774 899 3836 2652 1623
r.apn v.aai.1s r.asn adv v.pai.1s v.iai.3s r.dsm.3 d.nsm n.nsm cj

θέλεις τέλειος εἶναι, ὕπαγε πώλησόν σου τὰ ὑπάρχοντα καὶ δὸς
you want to be perfect, to be go and sell your {the} possessions and give
2527 1639 1639 5455 1639 5632 4797 5148 3836 5639 2779 1443
v.pai.2s a.nsm f.pa v.pam.2s v.aam.2s r.gs.2 d.apn pt.pa.apn cj v.aam.2s

τοῖς[a] πτωχοῖς, καὶ ἕξεις θησαυρὸν ἐν οὐρανοῖς, καὶ δεῦρο ἀκολούθει μοι.
to the poor, and ⌞you will have⌟ treasure in heaven; then come, follow me."
3836 4777 2779 2400 2565 1877 4041 2779 1306 199 1609
d.dpm a.dpm cj v.fai.2s n.asm p.d n.dpm cj adv v.pam.2s r.ds.1

[22] → ἀκούσας δὲ ὁ νεανίσκος ⌞τὸν λόγον⌟ ἀπῆλθεν
But when the young man heard But the young man this, he went away
1254 3836 3734 3734 201 1254 3836 3734 3836 3364 599
pt.aa.nsm cj d.nsm n.nsm d.asm n.asm v.aai.3s

λυπούμενος· ἦν γὰρ ἔχων κτήματα πολλά. [23] ὁ δὲ Ἰησοῦς εἶπεν
greatly distressed, {he was} for he had many possessions. many {the} And Jesus said
3382 1639 1142 2400 4498 3228 4498 3836 1254 2652 3306
pt.pp.nsm v.iai.3s cj pt.pa.nsm n.apn a.apn d.nsm cj n.nsm v.aai.3s

τοῖς μαθηταῖς αὐτοῦ, ἀμὴν λέγω ὑμῖν ὅτι ↱
to his disciples, his "I tell you the truth, I tell you {that} only with difficulty will
3836 899 3412 899 3306 3306 7007 297 3306 7007 4022 1552 1552 1656
d.dpm n.dpm r.gsm.3 pl v.pai.1s r.dp.2 cj

πλούσιος δυσκόλως ⌞εἰσελεύσεται εἰς⌟ τὴν βασιλείαν τῶν οὐρανῶν. [24] πάλιν
a rich person with difficulty enter the kingdom of heaven. Again
4454 1552 1656 1650 3836 993 3836 4041 4099
a.nsm adv v.fmi.3s p.a d.asf n.asf d.gpm n.gpm adv

δὲ λέγω ὑμῖν, εὐκοπώτερόν ἐστιν ↰ κάμηλον διὰ
{and} I say to you, it is easier it is for a camel to go through the
1254 3306 7007 1639 1639 2324 1639 2324 2823 1451 1451 1328
cj v.pai.1s r.dp.2 a.nsn.c v.pai.3s n.asf p.g

τρυπήματος → ῥαφίδος διελθεῖν ἢ ↰ πλούσιον ⌞εἰσελθεῖν εἰς⌟ τὴν
eye of a needle to go than for ⌞someone who is rich⌟ to enter the
5585 4827 1451 2445 2324 4454 1656 1650 3836
n.gsn n.gsf f.aa pl a.asm f.aa p.a d.asf

βασιλείαν τοῦ θεοῦ. [25] → ἀκούσαντες δὲ οἱ μαθηταὶ →
kingdom of God." When the disciples heard {and} the disciples this, they
993 3836 2536 3836 3412 201 1254 3836 3412
n.asf d.gsm n.gsm pt.aa.npm cj d.npm n.npm

→ ἐξεπλήσσοντο σφόδρα λέγοντες, τίς ἄρα δύναται σωθῆναι; [26]
were greatly astounded greatly and said, "Who then can be saved?" Jesus
5379 1742 5379 3306 5515 726 1538 5392 2652
v.ipi.3p adv pt.pa.npm r.nsm cj v.ppi.3s f.ap

ἐμβλέψας δὲ ὁ Ἰησοῦς εἶπεν αὐτοῖς, παρὰ ἀνθρώποις τοῦτο
⌞looked straight at⌟ {and} {the} Jesus them and said, them "With man this is
1838 1254 3836 2652 899 3306 899 4123 476 4047 1639
pt.aa.nsm cj d.nsm n.nsm v.aai.3s r.dpm.3 p.d n.dpm r.nsn

ἀδύνατόν ἐστιν, παρὰ δὲ θεῷ πάντα δυνατά. [27] τότε ἀποκριθεὶς ὁ
impossible, is but with but God all things are possible." Then Peter responded, {the}
105 1639 1254 4123 1254 2536 4246 1543 5538 4377 646 3836
a.nsn v.pai.3s p.d cj n.dsm a.npn a.npn adv pt.ap.nsm d.nsm

Πέτρος εἶπεν αὐτῷ, ἰδοὺ ἡμεῖς ἀφήκαμεν πάντα καὶ ἠκολουθήσαμέν σοι· τί ἄρα
Peter saying to him, "See, we have left everything and followed you. What then
4377 3306 899 2627 7005 918 4246 2779 199 5148 5515 726
n.nsm v.aai.3s r.dsm.3 j r.np.1 v.aai.1p a.apn cj v.aai.1p r.ds.2 r.nsn cj

NASB

NOT BEAR FALSE
WITNESS; [19]HONOR
YOUR FATHER AND
MOTHER; and YOU
SHALL LOVE YOUR
NEIGHBOR AS YOUR-
SELF." [20]The young
man *said to Him,
"All these things
I have kept; what
am I still lacking?"
[21]Jesus said to him,
"If you wish to be
complete, go *and*
sell your posses-
sions and give to
the poor, and you
will have treasure
in heaven; and
come, follow Me."
[22]But when the
young man heard
this statement, he
went away griev-
ing; for he was one
who owned much
property.
[23]And Jesus said
to His disciples,
"Truly I say to you,
it is hard for a rich
man to enter the
kingdom of heav-
en. [24]Again I say
to you, it is easier
for a camel to go
through the eye
of a needle, than
for a rich man to
enter the kingdom
of God." [25]When
the disciples heard
this, they were very
astonished and
said, "Then who
can be saved?"
[26]And looking at
them Jesus said to
them, "With people
this is impossible,
but with God all
things are pos-
sible."

The Disciples' Reward

[27]Then Peter said
to Him, "Behold,
we have left every-
thing and followed
You; what then will

[a] 19 Exodus 20:12-16; Deut. 5:16-20
[b] 19 Lev. 19:18

[a] [τοῖς] UBS.

NIV

will there be
for us?"
[28]Jesus said to
them, "Truly I tell
you, at the renewal
of all things, when
the Son of Man
sits on his glorious
throne, you who
have followed me
will also sit on
twelve thrones,
judging the twelve
tribes of Israel.
[29]And everyone
who has left hous-
es or brothers or
sisters or father or
mother or wife[a] or
children or fields
for my sake will
receive a hundred
times as much and
will inherit eternal
life. [30]But many
who are first will
be last, and many
who are last will
be first.

The Parable of the Workers in the Vineyard

20 "For the
kingdom
of heaven is like
a landowner who
went out early in
the morning to
hire workers for
his vineyard. [2]He
agreed to pay them
a denarius[b] for the
day and sent them
into his vineyard.
[3]"About nine in
the morning he
went out and saw
others standing in
the marketplace
doing nothing. [4]He
told them, 'You
also go and work
in my vineyard,
and I will pay you
whatever is right.'
[5]So they went.

[a] 29 Some manuscripts do not have *or wife*.
[b] 2 A denarius was the usual daily wage of a day laborer.

ἔσται ἡμῖν; [28] ὁ δὲ Ἰησοῦς εἶπεν αὐτοῖς, ἀμὴν λέγω ὑμῖν
⌊will there be⌋ for us?" *{the}* *{and}* Jesus said to them, "I tell you the truth *I tell* *you*
1639 7005 3836 1254 2652 3306 899 3306 3306 7007 297 3306 7007
v.fmi.3s r.dp.1 d.nsm cj n.nsm v.aai.3s r.dpm.3 pl v.pai.1s r.dp.2

ὅτι ὑμεῖς
that in the new age, when the Son of Man is seated on his glorious throne, you
4022 1877 3836 4098 4098 4020 3836 5626 3836 476 2767 2767 2093 899 1518 2585 7007
cj r.np.2

οἱ ἀκολουθήσαντές μοι ἐν τῇ παλιγγενεσίᾳ, ὅταν καθίσῃ ὁ υἱὸς τοῦ
who have followed me *in* *the* *new age* *when* *is seated* *the* *Son* *of*
3836 199 1609 1877 3836 4098 4020 2767 3836 5626 3836
d.npm pt.aa.npm r.ds.1 p.d d.dsf n.dsf cj v.aas.3s d.nsm n.nsm d.gsm

ἀνθρώπου ἐπὶ θρόνου δόξης αὐτοῦ, → καθήσεσθε καὶ ὑμεῖς ἐπὶ δώδεκα
Man *on* *throne* *glorious* *his* will also sit *also* *{you}* on twelve
476 2093 2585 1518 899 2779 2764 2779 7007 2093 1557
n.gsm p.g n.gsm n.gsf r.gsm.3 v.fmi.2p adv r.np.2 p.a a.apm

θρόνους κρίνοντες τὰς δώδεκα φυλὰς τοῦ Ἰσραήλ. [29] καὶ πᾶς ὅστις ἀφῆκεν
thrones judging the twelve tribes of Israel. And everyone who has left
2585 3212 3836 1557 5876 3836 2702 2779 4246 4015 918
n.apm pt.pa.npm d.apf a.apf n.apf d.gsm n.gsm cj a.nsm r.nsm v.aai.3s

οἰκίας ἢ ἀδελφοὺς ἢ ἀδελφὰς ἢ πατέρα ἢ μητέρα[a] ἢ τέκνα ἢ ἀγροὺς
houses or brothers or sisters or father or mother or children or lands
3864 2445 81 2445 80 2445 4252 2445 3613 2445 5451 2445 69
n.apf cj n.apm cj n.apf cj n.asm cj n.asf cj n.apn cj n.apm

ἕνεκεν τοῦ ὀνόματός μου, ↰ ἑκατονταπλασίονα λήμψεται καὶ
for *{the}* my name's *my* sake will receive a hundredfold *will receive* and will
1914 3836 1609 3950 1609 1914 3284 3284 1671 3284 2779 3099
p.g d.gsn n.gsn r.gs.1 a.apn v.fmi.3s cj

ζωὴν αἰώνιον κληρονομήσει. [30] πολλοὶ δὲ ἔσονται πρῶτοι
inherit eternal life. *eternal* *will inherit* But many *But* will be first who were
3099 173 2437 173 3099 1254 4498 1254 1639 4755
n.asf a.asf v.fai.3s a.npm cj v.fmi.3p a.npm

ἔσχατοι καὶ ἔσχατοι πρῶτοι.
last, and last who were first.
2274 2779 2274 4755
a.npm cj a.npm a.npm

20:1
ὁμοία γάρ ἐστιν ἡ βασιλεία τῶν οὐρανῶν
"For the kingdom of heaven is like *For* *is* *the* *kingdom* *of* *heaven*
1142 3836 993 3836 4041 1639 3927 1142 1639 3836 993 3836 4041
a.nsf cj v.pai.3s d.nsf n.nsf d.gpm n.gpm

ἀνθρώπῳ οἰκοδεσπότῃ, ὅστις ἐξῆλθεν ⌊ἅμα πρωῒ⌋ μισθώσασθαι
{person} the owner of an estate who went out early in the morning to hire
476 3867 4015 2002 275 4745 3636
n.dsm n.dsm r.nsm v.aai.3s p.d adv f.am

ἐργάτας εἰς τὸν ἀμπελῶνα αὐτοῦ. [2] συμφωνήσας δὲ μετὰ τῶν ἐργατῶν
men to work in *{the}* his vineyard. *his* After having agreed *{and}* with the workers
2239 1650 3836 899 308 899 5244 1254 3552 3836 2239
n.apm p.a d.asm n.asm r.gsm.3 pt.aa.nsm cj p.g d.gpm n.gpm

ἐκ δηναρίου τὴν ἡμέραν ἀπέστειλεν αὐτοὺς εἰς τὸν ἀμπελῶνα αὐτοῦ. [3] καὶ
for a denarius per day, he sent them into *{the}* his vineyard. *his* And
1666 1324 3836 2465 690 899 1650 3836 899 308 899 2779
p.g n.gsn d.asf n.asf v.aai.3s r.apm.3 p.a d.asm n.asm r.gsm.3 cj

ἐξελθὼν περὶ τρίτην ὥραν εἶδεν ἄλλους ἑστῶτας ἐν τῇ ἀγορᾷ
going out about the third hour, he saw others standing in the marketplace
2002 4309 5569 6052 1625 257 2705 1877 3836 59
pt.aa.nsm p.a a.asf n.asf v.aai.3s r.apm pt.ra.apm p.d d.dsf n.dsf

ἀργούς [4] καὶ ἐκείνοις εἶπεν, ὑπάγετε καὶ ὑμεῖς
⌊with nothing to do.⌋ And to them he said, "You go into the vineyard as well, *You*
734 2779 1697 3306 7007 5632 1650 3836 308 2779 7007
a.apm cj r.dpm v.aai.3s v.pam.2p adv r.np.2

εἰς τὸν ἀμπελῶνα, καὶ ⌊ὃ ἐὰν⌋ ᾖ δίκαιον δώσω ὑμῖν. [5] οἱ δὲ
into *the* *vineyard* and whatever is fair I will pay you.' So they *So*
1650 3836 308 2779 4005 1569 1639 1465 1443 7007 1254 3836 1254
p.a d.asm n.asm cj r.nsn pl v.pas.3s a.nsn v.fai.1s r.dp.2 d.npm cj

[a] ἢ γυναῖκα included by TNIV after μητέρα.

NASB

there be for us?"
[28]And Jesus said
to them, "Truly
I say to you, that
you who have fol-
lowed Me, in the
regeneration when
the Son of Man
will sit on His glo-
rious throne, you
also shall sit upon
twelve thrones,
judging the twelve
tribes of Israel.
[29]And everyone
who has left houses
or brothers or
sisters or father or
mother [a]or children
or farms for My
name's sake, will
receive many times
as much, and will
inherit eternal life.
[30]But many *who are*
first will be last;
and *the* last, first.

Laborers in the Vineyard

20:1"For the king-
dom of heaven is
like a landowner
who went out early
in the morning to
hire laborers for his
vineyard. [2]When he
had agreed with the
laborers for a [b]den-
arius for the day,
he sent them into
his vineyard. [3]And
he went out about
the [c]third hour
and saw others
standing idle in the
market place; [4]and
to those he said,
'You also go into
the vineyard, and
whatever is right
I will give you.'
And *so* they went.
[5]Again he went out
about the [d]

[a] One early ms adds *or wife*
[b] The denarius was a day's wages
[c] I.e. 9 a.m.
[d] I.e. noon and 3 p.m.

NIV

"He went out again about noon and about three in the afternoon and did the same thing. [6]About five in the afternoon he went out and found still others standing around. He asked them, 'Why have you been standing here all day long doing nothing?'
[7]"'Because no one has hired us,' they answered.
"He said to them, 'You also go and work in my vineyard.'
[8]"When evening came, the owner of the vineyard said to his foreman, 'Call the workers and pay them their wages, beginning with the last ones hired and going on to the first.'
[9]"The workers who were hired about five in the afternoon came and each received a denarius. [10]So when those came who were hired first, they expected to receive more. But each one of them also received a denarius. [11]When they received it, they began to grumble against the landowner. [12]'These who were hired last worked only one hour,' they said, 'and you have made them equal to us who have borne the burden of the work and the heat of the day.'
[13]"But he answered one of them,

ἀπῆλθον. πάλιν[a] ἐξελθὼν περὶ ἕκτην καὶ ἐνάτην
went off. When he went out again *When he went out* about the sixth hour and the ninth
599 2002 2002 2002 2002 4099 2002 4309 1761 2779 1888
v.aai.3p adv pt.aa.nsm p.a a.asf cj a.asf

ὥραν ἐποίησεν ὡσαύτως. [6] περὶ δὲ τὴν ἑνδεκάτην ἐξελθὼν
hour, he did the same thing. And about *And* the eleventh hour, ⌊when had gone out⌋ and
6052 4472 6058 1254 4309 1254 3836 1895 2002
n.asf v.aai.3s adv p.a cj d.asf a.asf pt.aa.nsm

εὗρεν ἄλλους ἑστῶτας καὶ λέγει αὐτοῖς, τί ὧδε
found others standing around, *{and}* he said to them, 'Why have you been standing here
2351 257 2705 2779 3306 899 5515 2705 2705 2705 2705 6045
v.aai.3s r.apm pt.ra.apm cj v.pai.3s r.dpm.3 r.asn adv

ἑστήκατε ὅλην τὴν ἡμέραν ↰ ἀργοί; [7]λέγουσιν αὐτῷ, ὅτι οὐδεὶς
have you been standing idle all *{the}* day long?' *idle* They said to him, 'Because no one
2705 734 3910 3836 2465 3910 734 3306 899 4022 4029
v.rai.2p a.asf d.asf n.asf a.npm v.pai.3p r.dsm.3 cj a.nsm

ἡμᾶς ἐμισθώσατο. λέγει αὐτοῖς, ὑπάγετε καὶ ὑμεῖς
has hired us.' *has hired* He said to them, 'You go into the vineyard too.' *You*
3636 3636 7005 3636 3306 899 7007 5632 1650 3836 308 2779 7007
r.ap.1 v.ami.3s v.pai.3s r.dpm.3 v.pam.2p adv r.np.2

εἰς τὸν ἀμπελῶνα.[b] [8] ↱ ὀψίας δὲ γενομένης λέγει ὁ κύριος τοῦ
into the vineyard And when evening *And* came, *said* the owner of the
1650 3836 308 1254 1181 4068 1254 1181 3306 3836 3261 3836
p.a d.asm n.asm n.gsf cj pt.am.gsf v.pai.3s d.nsm n.nsm d.gsm

ἀμπελῶνος τῷ ἐπιτρόπῳ αὐτοῦ, κάλεσον τοὺς ἐργάτας καὶ ἀπόδος αὐτοῖς[c]
vineyard said to his foreman, *his* 'Call the workers and pay them
308 3306 3836 899 2207 899 2813 3836 2239 2779 625 899
n.gsm d.dsm n.dsm r.gsm.3 v.aam.2s d.apm n.apm cj v.aam.2s r.dpm.3

τὸν μισθὸν ἀρξάμενος ἀπὸ τῶν ἐσχάτων ἕως τῶν πρώτων. [9]καὶ
their wages, beginning with the last and ⌊going back to⌋ the first.' *{and}* Those
3836 3635 806 608 3836 2274 2401 3836 4755 2779 3836
d.asm n.asm pt.am.nsm p.g d.gpm a.gpm p.g d.gpm a.gpm cj

ἐλθόντες οἱ περὶ τὴν ἑνδεκάτην ὥραν ἔλαβον
hired about the eleventh hour came *Those about the eleventh hour* and each received
4309 3836 1895 6052 2262 3836 4309 3836 1895 6052 324 3284
pt.aa.npm d.npm p.a d.asf a.asf n.asf v.aai.3p

ἀνὰ δηνάριον. [10] καὶ → ἐλθόντες οἱ πρῶτοι
each a denarius. *{and}* When those who were hired first came, *those first*
324 1324 2779 3836 4755 2262 3836 4755
p.a n.asn cj pt.aa.npm d.npm a.npm

ἐνόμισαν ὅτι πλεῖον λήμψονται· καὶ ἔλαβον τὸ[d]
they thought *{that}* they would receive more; *they would receive* but they also each received *{the}*
3787 4022 3284 3284 3284 4498 3284 2779 899 2779 324 3284 3836
v.aai.3p cj a.asn.c v.fmi.3p cj v.aai.3p d.asn

ἀνὰ δηνάριον καὶ αὐτοί. [11] λαβόντες δὲ ἐγόγγυζον κατὰ
each a denarius. *also they* And ⌊when they received⌋ *And* it, ⌊they began to grumble⌋ against
324 1324 2779 899 1254 3284 1254 1197 2848
p.a n.asn adv r.npm pt.aa.npm cj v.iai.3p p.g

τοῦ οἰκοδεσπότου [12] λέγοντες, οὗτοι οἱ ἔσχατοι μίαν ὥραν ἐποίησαν,
the owner of the estate, saying, 'These *{the}* last worked but one hour, *worked*
3836 3867 3306 4047 3836 2274 4472 1651 6052 4472
d.gsm n.gsm pt.pa.npm r.npm d.npm a.npm a.asf n.asf v.aai.3p

καὶ ἴσους ἡμῖν αὐτοὺς ἐποίησας τοῖς βαστάσασι τὸ βάρος
and you have made them equal to us *them* *you have made* who have borne the burden
2779 4472 4472 4472 899 2698 7005 899 4472 3836 1002 3836 983
cj a.apm r.dp.1 r.apm.3 v.aai.2s d.dpm pt.aa.dpm d.asn n.asn

τῆς ἡμέρας καὶ τὸν καύσωνα. [13] ὁ δὲ ἀποκριθεὶς ἑνὶ αὐτῶν εἶπεν,
of the day and the scorching heat.' But he *But* answered one of them, saying,
3836 2465 2779 3836 3014 1254 3836 1254 646 1651 899 3306
d.gsf n.gsf cj d.asm n.asm d.nsm cj pt.ap.nsm a.dsm r.gpm.3 v.aai.3s

NASB

sixth and the ninth hour, and did the same thing. [6]And about the [a]eleventh *hour* he went out and found others standing *around;* and he *said to them, 'Why have you been standing here idle all day long?' [7]They *said to him, 'Because no one hired us.' He *said to them, 'You go into the vineyard too.'
[8]"When evening came, the owner of the vineyard *said to his foreman, 'Call the laborers and pay them their wages, beginning with the last *group* to the first.' [9]When those *hired* about the eleventh hour came, each one received a [b]denarius. [10]When those *hired* first came, they thought that they would receive more; but each of them also received a denarius. [11]When they received it, they grumbled at the landowner, [12]saying, 'These last men have worked *only* one hour, and you have made them equal to us who have borne the burden and the scorching heat of the day.' [13]But he answered and said to one of them,

[a] δὲ included by UBS, NET after πάλιν.
[b] καὶ ὃ ἐὰν ᾖ δίκαιον λήψεσθε included by TR after ἀμπελῶνα.
[c] αὐτοῖς omitted by NET.
[d] [τὸ] UBS, omitted by TNIV.

[a] I.e. 5 p.m.
[b] The denarius was a day's wages

NIV

'I am not being
unfair to you,
friend. Didn't you
agree to work for
a denarius? [14]Take
your pay and go.
I want to give the
one who was hired
last the same as I
gave you. [15]Don't
I have the right
to do what I want
with my own mon-
ey? Or are you en-
vious because I am
generous?'
[16]"So the last will
be first, and the
first will be last."

Jesus Predicts His Death a Third Time

[17]Now Jesus was
going up to Jeru-
salem. On the way,
he took the Twelve
aside and said to
them, [18]"We are
going up to Je-
rusalem, and the
Son of Man will
be delivered over
to the chief priests
and the teachers
of the law. They
will condemn him
to death [19]and will
hand him over to
the Gentiles to
be mocked and
flogged and cruci-
fied. On the third
day he will be
raised to life!"

A Mother's Request

[20]Then the moth-
er of Zebedee's
sons came to Jesus
with her sons and,
kneeling down,
asked a favor of
him.
[21]"What is it you
want?" he asked.
She said, "Grant
that one of these
two sons of mine
may sit at your
right and

ἑταῖρε, ↱ ↱ οὐκ ἀδικῶ σε· ↱ οὐχὶ → δηναρίου
'Friend, I am not ⌊being unfair to⌋ you. Did you not agree with me to work for a denarius?
2279 92 92 4024 92 5148 5244 5244 4049 5244 5244 1609 1324
n.vsm adv v.pai.1s r.as.2 pl n.gsn

συνεφώνησάς μοι; [14] ἆρον τὸ σὸν καὶ ὕπαγε. θέλω δὲ τούτῳ τῷ
you agree with *me* Take what is yours and be gone. I choose *{and}* to give to this *{the}*
5244 1609 149 3836 5050 2779 5632 2527 1254 1443 1443 4047 3836
v.aai.2s r.ds.1 v.aam.2s d.asn r.asn.2 cj v.pam.2s v.pai.1s cj r.dsm d.dsm

ἐσχάτῳ δοῦναι ὡς καὶ σοί· [15] ↱ [a]οὐκ ἔξεστίν μοι
last man *to give* the same as *same* I give to you. Am I not allowed *I* to do
2274 1443 2779 6055 2779 5148 1997 1609 4024 1997 1609 4472 4472
a.dsm f.aa cj cj r.ds.2 pl v.pai.3s r.ds.1

ὃ θέλω ποιῆσαι ἐν τοῖς ἐμοῖς; ἢ ὁ ὀφθαλμός σου πονηρός ἐστιν
what I choose *to do* with what belongs to me? Or *{the}* *{eye}* are you envious *are*
4005 2527 4472 1877 3836 1847 2445 3836 4057 1639 5148 4505 1639
r.asn v.pai.1s f.aa p.d d.dpn r.dpn.1 cj d.nsm n.nsm r.gs.2 a.nsm v.pai.3s

ὅτι ἐγὼ ἀγαθός εἰμι; [16] οὕτως ἔσονται οἱ ἔσχατοι πρῶτοι καὶ
because I am generous?' *am* So the last will be *the* *last* first, and
4022 1609 1639 19 1639 4048 3836 2274 1639 3836 2274 4755 2779
cj r.ns.1 a.nsm v.pai.1s adv v.fmi.3p d.npm a.npm a.npm cj

οἱ πρῶτοι ἔσχατοι.[b] [17] καὶ → ἀναβαίνων ὁ Ἰησοῦς εἰς
the first will be last." *{and}* As Jesus was going up *{the}* *Jesus* to
3836 4755 2274 2779 2652 326 3836 2652 1650
d.npm a.npm a.npm cj pt.pa.nsm d.nsm n.nsm p.a

Ἱεροσόλυμα παρέλαβεν τοὺς δώδεκα[c] ⌊κατ' ἰδίαν⌋ καὶ ἐν τῇ
Jerusalem, he took the twelve disciples aside and said to them on the
2642 4161 3836 1557 2848 2625 2779 3306 899 899 1877 3836
n.apn v.aai.3s d.apm a.apm p.a a.asf cj p.d d.dsf

ὁδῷ εἶπεν αὐτοῖς, [18] ἰδοὺ ἀναβαίνομεν εἰς Ἱεροσόλυμα, καὶ ὁ υἱὸς τοῦ
way, *said* *to them* *{Look}* ⌊"We are going up⌋ to Jerusalem, and the Son of
3847 3306 899 2627 326 1650 2642 2779 3836 5626 3836
n.dsf v.aai.3s r.dpm.3 j v.pai.1p p.a n.apn cj d.nsm n.nsm d.gsm

ἀνθρώπου παραδοθήσεται τοῖς ἀρχιερεῦσιν καὶ γραμματεῦσιν, καὶ
Man will be handed over to the ruling priests and the scribes. *{and}*
476 4140 3836 797 2779 1208 2779
n.gsm v.fpi.3s d.dpm n.dpm cj n.dpm cj

κατακρινοῦσιν αὐτὸν θανάτῳ [19] καὶ παραδώσουσιν αὐτὸν ↰ τοῖς ἔθνεσιν εἰς
They will condemn him to death, *{and}* hand him over to the Gentiles to be
2891 899 2505 2779 4140 899 4140 3836 1620 1650
v.fai.3p r.asm.3 n.dsm cj v.fai.3p r.asm.3 d.dpn n.dpn p.a

τὸ ἐμπαῖξαι καὶ μαστιγῶσαι καὶ σταυρῶσαι, καὶ τῇ τρίτῃ ἡμέρᾳ ἐγερθήσεται.
{the} mocked and flogged and crucified, and ⌊on the⌋ third day he will be raised."
3836 1850 2779 3463 2779 5090 2779 3836 5569 2465 1586
d.asn f.aa cj f.aa cj f.aa cj d.dsf a.dsf n.dsf v.fpi.3s

[20] τότε προσῆλθεν αὐτῷ ἡ μήτηρ τῶν υἱῶν
Then the mother of the sons of Zebedee came to Jesus *the* *mother* *of the* *sons*
5538 3836 3613 3836 3836 5626 2411 2411 4665 899 3836 3613 3836 5626
adv v.aai.3s r.dsm.3 d.nsf n.nsf d.gpm n.gpm

Ζεβεδαίου μετὰ τῶν υἱῶν αὐτῆς προσκυνοῦσα καὶ αἰτοῦσά τι ἀπ'
of Zebedee with *{the}* her sons, *her* and kneeling down *{and}* she asked something from
2411 3552 3836 899 5626 899 4686 2779 160 5516 608
n.gsm p.g d.gpm n.gpm r.gsf.3 pt.pa.nsf cj pt.pa.nsf r.asn p.g

αὐτοῦ. [21] ὁ δὲ εἶπεν αὐτῇ, τί θέλεις; λέγει αὐτῷ, εἰπὲ ἵνα
him. And he *And* said to her, "What ⌊do you wish?"⌋ She said to him, "Grant that
899 1254 3836 1254 3306 899 5515 2527 3306 899 3306 2671
r.gsm.3 d.nsm cj v.aai.3s r.dsf.3 r.asn v.pai.2s v.pai.3s r.dsm.3 v.aam.2s cj

καθίσωσιν οὗτοι οἱ δύο υἱοί μου εἷς ἐκ δεξιῶν σου καὶ εἷς
may sit these *{the}* two sons of mine may sit, one at your right hand *your* and one
2767 4047 3836 1545 5626 1609 2767 2767 1651 1666 5148 1288 5148 2779 1651
v.aas.3p r.npm d.npm a.npm n.npm r.gs.1 a.nsm p.g a.gpf r.gs.2 cj a.nsm

NASB

'Friend, I am doing
you no wrong; did
you not agree with
me for a denarius?
[14]Take what is
yours and go, but I
wish to give to this
last man the same
as to you. [15]Is it not
lawful for me to do
what I wish with
what is my own?
Or is your eye en-
vious because I am
generous?' [16]So the
last shall be first,
and the first last."

Death, Resurrection Foretold

[17]As Jesus was
about to go up
to Jerusalem, He
took the twelve
disciples aside by
themselves, and on
the way He said to
them, [18]"Behold,
we are going up to
Jerusalem; and the
Son of Man will
be delivered to the
chief priests and
scribes, and they
will condemn Him
to death, [19]and will
hand Him over
to the Gentiles to
mock and scourge
and crucify *Him,*
and on the third
day He will be
raised up."

Preferment Asked

[20]Then the mother
of the sons of
Zebedee came
to Jesus with her
sons, bowing
down and making
a request of Him.
[21]And He said to
her, "What do you
wish?" She *said to
Him, "Command
that in Your king-
dom these two sons
of mine may sit
one on Your right
and one on Your

[a] ἢ included by UBS before οὐκ.
[b] πολλοὶ γάρ εἰσιν κλητοί, ὀλίγοι δὲ ἐκλεκτοί included by TR after ἔσχατοι.
[c] μαθητὰς included by UBS after δώδεκα.

NIV

the other at your
left in your king-
dom."
22 "You don't
know what you are
asking," Jesus said
to them. "Can you
drink the cup I am
going to drink?"
"We can," they
answered.
23 Jesus said to
them, "You will
indeed drink from
my cup, but to
sit at my right or
left is not for me
to grant. These
places belong to
those for whom
they have been
prepared by my
Father."
24 When the ten
heard about this,
they were indig-
nant with the two
brothers. 25 Jesus
called them togeth-
er and said, "You
know that the rul-
ers of the Gentiles
lord it over them,
and their high of-
ficials exercise au-
thority over them.
26 Not so with you.
Instead, whoever
wants to become
great among you
must be your ser-
vant, 27 and who-
ever wants to be
first must be your
slave — 28 just as
the Son of Man
did not come to
be served, but to
serve, and to give
his life as a ran-
som for many."

Two Blind Men Receive Sight

29 As Jesus and
his disciples were
leaving Jericho, a
large crowd fol-
lowed him. 30 Two
blind men were
sitting by the road-
side, and when
they heard that

ἐξ εὐωνύμων σου ἐν τῇ βασιλείᾳ σου. 22 ἀποκριθεὶς δὲ ὁ
at your left, *your* in *{the}* your kingdom." *your* Jesus answered, *{and}* *{the}*
1666 5148 2381 5148 1877 3836 5148 993 5148 2652 646 1254 3836
p.g a.gpf r.gs.2 p.d d.dsf n.dsf r.gs.2 pt.ap.nsm cj d.nsm

Ἰησοῦς εἶπεν, ↱ ↱ οὐκ οἴδατε τί αἰτεῖσθε. δύνασθε πιεῖν τὸ ποτήριον
Jesus saying, "You do not realize what you are asking. Are you able to drink the cup
2652 3306 3857 3857 4024 3857 5515 160 1538 4403 3836 4539
n.nsm v.aai.3s adv v.rai.2p r.asn v.pmi.2p v.ppi.2p f.aa d.asn n.asn

ὃ ἐγὼ μέλλω πίνειν;[a] λέγουσιν αὐτῷ, δυνάμεθα. 23 λέγει αὐτοῖς, τὸ μὲν
that I am about to drink?" They said to him, "We are able." He said to them, *{the}* ~ "My
4005 1609 3516 4403 3306 899 1538 3306 899 3836 3525 1609
r.asn r.ns.1 v.pai.1s f.pa v.pai.3p r.dsm.3 v.ppi.1p v.pai.3s r.dpm.3 d.asn pl

ποτήριόν μου πίεσθε,[b] τὸ δὲ καθίσαι ἐκ δεξιῶν μου καὶ ἐξ
cup *My* you will drink, *{the}* but to sit at my right hand *my* and at my
4539 1609 4403 3836 1254 2767 1666 1609 1288 1609 2779 1666
n.asn r.gs.1 v.fmi.2p d.nsn cj f.aa p.g a.gpf r.gs.1 cj p.g

εὐωνύμων οὐκ ἔστιν ἐμὸν[c] δοῦναι, ἀλλ' οἷς ἡτοίμασται
left is not *is* mine to grant, but it is ⌞for those⌟ for whom it has been prepared
2381 1639 4024 1639 1847 1443 247 4005 2286
a.gpf adv v.pai.3s r.nsn.1 f.aa cj r.dpm v.rpi.3s

ὑπὸ τοῦ πατρός μου. 24 καὶ → ἀκούσαντες οἱ δέκα
by *{the}* my Father." *my* *{and}* When the ten heard *the* *ten* this,
5679 3836 1609 4252 1609 2779 3836 1274 201 3836 1274
p.g d.gsm n.gsm r.gs.1 cj pt.aa.npm d.npm a.npm

ἠγανάκτησαν περὶ τῶν δύο ἀδελφῶν. 25 ὁ δὲ Ἰησοῦς προσκαλεσάμενος
they were indignant with the two brothers. *{the}* But Jesus called
24 4309 3836 1545 81 3836 1254 2652 4673
v.aai.3p p.g d.gpm a.gpm n.gpm d.nsm cj n.nsm pt.am.nsm

αὐτοὺς ↰ εἶπεν, οἴδατε ὅτι οἱ ἄρχοντες τῶν ἐθνῶν κατακυριεύουσιν
them to him and said, "You know that the rulers of the nations lord it over
899 4673 3306 3857 4022 3836 807 3836 1620 2894
r.apm.3 v.aai.3s v.rai.2p cj d.npm n.npm d.gpn n.gpn v.pai.3p

αὐτῶν καὶ οἱ μεγάλοι κατεξουσιάζουσιν αὐτῶν. 26 οὐχ οὕτως
them, and their leaders exercise authority over them. It will not be so
899 2779 3836 3489 2980 899 1639 1639 4024 1639 4048
r.gpm.3 cj d.npm a.npm v.pai.3p r.gpm.3 adv adv

ἔσται ἐν ὑμῖν, ἀλλ' ὃς ἐὰν⌟ θέλῃ ἐν ὑμῖν μέγας γενέσθαι
It will be among you. But whoever would be great among you *great* *be*
1639 1877 7007 247 4005 1569 2527 1181 3489 1877 7007 3489 1181
v.fmi.3s p.d r.dp.2 cj r.nsm pl v.pas.3s p.d r.dp.2 a.nsm f.am

ἔσται ὑμῶν διάκονος, 27 καὶ ⌞ὃς ἂν⌟ θέλῃ ἐν ὑμῖν εἶναι πρῶτος
must be your servant, and whoever would be first among you *be* *first*
1639 7007 1356 2779 4005 323 2527 1639 4755 1877 7007 1639 4755
v.fmi.3s r.gp.2 n.nsm cj r.nsm pl v.pas.3s p.d r.dp.2 f.pa a.nsm

ἔσται ὑμῶν δοῦλος· 28 ὥσπερ ὁ υἱὸς τοῦ ἀνθρώπου οὐκ ἦλθεν διακονηθῆναι
must be your servant; just as the Son of Man came not *came* to be served
1639 7007 1529 6061 3836 5626 3836 476 2262 4024 2262 1354
v.fmi.3s r.gp.2 n.nsm cj d.nsm n.nsm d.gsm n.gsm adv v.aai.3s f.ap

ἀλλὰ διακονῆσαι καὶ δοῦναι τὴν ψυχὴν αὐτοῦ λύτρον ἀντὶ πολλῶν. 29 καὶ →
but to serve, and to give *{the}* his life *his* a ransom for many." *{and}* As
247 1354 2779 1443 3836 899 6034 899 3389 505 4498 2779
cj f.aa cj f.aa d.asf n.asf r.gsm.3 n.asn p.g a.gpm cj

ἐκπορευομένων αὐτῶν ἀπὸ Ἰεριχὼ ἠκολούθησεν αὐτῷ ὄχλος πολύς.
they were going out *they* of Jericho, a large crowd followed him. *crowd* *large*
899 1744 899 608 2637 4498 4063 199 899 4063 4498
pt.pm.gpm r.gpm.3 p.g n.gsf v.aai.3s r.dsm.3 n.nsm a.nsm

30 καὶ ἰδοὺ δύο τυφλοὶ καθήμενοι παρὰ τὴν ὁδὸν ἀκούσαντες ὅτι Ἰησοῦς
{and} *{Look}* Two blind men were sitting beside the road, and when they heard that Jesus
2779 2627 1545 5603 2764 4123 3836 3847 201 4022 2652
cj j a.npm a.npm pt.pm.npm p.a d.asf n.asf pt.aa.npm cj n.nsm

NASB

left." 22 But Jesus
answered, "You do
not know what you
are asking. Are you
able to drink the
cup that I am about
to drink?" They
*said to Him, "We
are able." 23 He *said
to them, "My cup
you shall drink; but
to sit on My right
and on *My* left, this
is not Mine to give,
but it is for those
for whom it has
been prepared by
My Father."
24 And hearing
this, the ten be-
came indignant
with the two broth-
ers. 25 But Jesus
called them to
Himself and said,
"You know that the
rulers of the Gen-
tiles lord it over
them, and *their*
great men exercise
authority over
them. 26 It is not this
way among you,
but whoever wish-
es to become great
among you shall be
your servant, 27 and
whoever wishes to
be first among you
shall be your slave;
28 just as the Son of
Man did not come
to be served, but to
serve, and to give
His life a ransom
for many."

Sight for the Blind

29 As they were
leaving Jericho, a
large crowd fol-
lowed Him. 30 And
two blind men
sitting by the road,
hearing that Jesus

[a] καὶ τὸ βάπτισμα ὃ ἐγὼ βαπτίζομαι βαπτισθῆναι; included by TR after πίνειν.
[b] καὶ τὸ βάπτισμα ὃ ἐγὼ βαπτίζομαι βαπτισθήσεσθε included by TR after πίεσθε.
[c] τοῦτο included by UBS after ἐμόν.

NIV

Jesus was going by, they shouted, "Lord, Son of David, have mercy on us!"

31 The crowd rebuked them and told them to be quiet, but they shouted all the louder, "Lord, Son of David, have mercy on us!"

32 Jesus stopped and called them. "What do you want me to do for you?" he asked.

33 "Lord," they answered, "we want our sight."

34 Jesus had compassion on them and touched their eyes. Immediately they received their sight and followed him.

Jesus Comes to Jerusalem as King

21 As they approached Jerusalem and came to Bethphage on the Mount of Olives, Jesus sent two disciples, 2 saying to them, "Go to the village ahead of you, and at once you will find a donkey tied there, with her colt by her. Untie them and bring them to me. 3 If anyone says anything to you, say that the Lord needs them, and he will send them right away."

4 This took place to fulfill what was spoken through the prophet:

παράγει, ἔκραξαν λέγοντες, ἐλέησον ἡμᾶς, κύριε,[a]
˛was passing by˛ ˛they cried out,˛ {saying} "Lord, Son of David, ˛have mercy on˛ us!" *Lord*
4135 3189 3306 3261 5626 1253 1253 1796 7005 3261
v.pai.3s v.aai.3p pt.pa.npm v.aam.2s r.ap.1 n.vsm

υἱὸς Δαυίδ. 31 ὁ δὲ ὄχλος ἐπετίμησεν αὐτοῖς ἵνα σιωπήσωσιν·
Son *of David* The {and} crowd rebuked them and told them to be quiet, but
5626 1253 3836 1254 4063 2203 899 4995 2671 4995 1254
n.nsm n.gsm d.nsm cj n.nsm v.aai.3s r.dpm.3 cj v.aas.3p

οἱ δὲ μεῖζον ἔκραξαν λέγοντες, ἐλέησον
they *but* cried out ˛all the louder,˛ *cried out* {saying} "Lord, Son of David, ˛have mercy on˛
3836 1254 3189 3189 3489 3189 3306 3261 5626 1253 1253 1796
d.npm cj adv.c v.aai.3p pt.pa.npm v.aam.2s

ἡμᾶς, κύριε,[b] υἱὸς Δαυίδ. 32 καὶ στὰς ὁ Ἰησοῦς ἐφώνησεν αὐτοὺς καὶ
us!" *Lord* *Son* *of David* {and} Jesus stopped {the} *Jesus* and called them, {and}
7005 3261 5626 1253 2779 2652 2705 3836 2652 5888 899 2779
r.ap.1 n.vsm n.nsm n.gsm cj pt.aa.nsm d.nsm n.nsm v.aai.3s r.apm.3 cj

εἶπεν, τί θέλετε ποιήσω ὑμῖν; 33 λέγουσιν αὐτῷ, κύριε, ἵνα
saying, "What ˛do you want˛ me to do for you?" They said to him, "Lord, let our eyes
3306 5515 2527 4472 7007 3306 899 3261 2671 7005 4057
v.aai.3s r.asn v.pai.2p v.aas.1s r.dp.2 v.pai.3p r.dsm.3 n.vsm cj

ἀνοιγῶσιν οἱ ὀφθαλμοὶ ἡμῶν. 34 σπλαγχνισθεὶς δὲ ὁ Ἰησοῦς ἥψατο
be opened." {the} *eyes* *our* Moved with compassion, {and} {the} Jesus touched
487 3836 4057 7005 5072 1254 3836 2652 721
v.aps.3p d.npm n.npm r.gp.1 pt.ap.nsm cj d.nsm n.nsm v.ami.3s

τῶν ὀμμάτων αὐτῶν, καὶ εὐθέως ἀνέβλεψαν καὶ ἠκολούθησαν
{the} their eyes. *their* {and} Immediately ˛they received their sight˛ and followed
3836 899 3921 899 2779 2311 329 2779 199
d.gpn n.gpn r.gpm.3 cj adv v.aai.3p cj v.aai.3p

αὐτῷ.
him.
899
r.dsm.3

21:1 καὶ ὅτε ἤγγισαν εἰς Ἱεροσόλυμα καὶ ἦλθον εἰς Βηθφαγὴ εἰς τὸ
Now when ˛they drew near˛ to Jerusalem and came to Bethphage, to the
2779 4021 1581 1650 2642 2779 2262 1650 1036 1650 3836
cj cj v.aai.3p p.a n.apn cj v.aai.3p p.a n.asf p.a d.asn

ὄρος τῶν ἐλαιῶν, τότε Ἰησοῦς ἀπέστειλεν δύο μαθητὰς 2 λέγων αὐτοῖς, πορεύεσθε
Mount of Olives, then Jesus sent two disciples, saying to them, "Go
4001 3836 1777 5538 2652 690 1545 3412 3306 899 4513
n.asn d.gpf n.gpf adv n.nsm v.aai.3s a.apm n.apm pt.pa.nsm r.dpm.3 v.pmm.2p

εἰς τὴν κώμην τὴν κατέναντι ὑμῶν, καὶ εὐθέως εὑρήσετε ὄνον δεδεμένην καὶ
into the village {the} ahead of you, and right away you will find a donkey tethered, and
1650 3836 3267 3836 2978 7007 2779 2311 2351 3952 1313 2779
p.a d.asf n.asf d.asf p.g r.gp.2 cj adv v.fai.2p n.asf pt.rp.asf cj

πῶλον μετ' αὐτῆς· λύσαντες ἀγάγετέ μοι. 3 καὶ ἐάν τις
a colt with her. Untie them and bring them to me. {and} If anyone says
4798 3552 899 3395 72 1609 2779 1569 5516 3306
n.asm p.g r.gsf.3 pt.aa.npm v.aam.2p r.ds.1 cj cj r.nsm

ὑμῖν εἴπῃ τι, ἐρεῖτε ὅτι ὁ κύριος αὐτῶν χρείαν
anything to you, *says* *anything* ˛you are to say,˛ ~ 'The Lord has need of them.' *need*
5516 7007 3306 5516 3306 4022 3836 3261 2400 5970 899 5970
r.dp.2 v.aas.3s r.asn v.fai.2p cj d.nsm n.nsm r.gpm.3 n.asf

ἔχει· εὐθὺς δὲ ἀποστελεῖ αὐτούς. 4 τοῦτο δὲ γέγονεν ἵνα
has *at once* And he will send them at once." This {and} took place ˛in order that˛
2400 2318 1254 690 899 2318 2318 4047 1254 1181 2671
v.pai.3s adv cj v.fai.3s r.apm.3 r.nsn cj v.rai.3s cj

πληρωθῇ τὸ ῥηθὲν διὰ τοῦ προφήτου λέγοντος,
might be fulfilled what ˛had been spoken˛ by the prophet might be fulfilled, saying,
4444 3836 3306 1328 3836 4737 4444 4444 4444 3306
v.aps.3s d.nsn pt.ap.nsn p.g d.gsm n.gsm pt.pa.gsm

NASB

was passing by, cried out, "Lord, have mercy on us, Son of David!" 31 The crowd sternly told them to be quiet, but they cried out all the more, "Lord, Son of David, have mercy on us!" 32 And Jesus stopped and called them, and said, "What do you want Me to do for you?" 33 They *said to Him, "Lord, *we want* our eyes to be opened." 34 Moved with compassion, Jesus touched their eyes; and immediately they regained their sight and followed Him.

The Triumphal Entry

21:1 When they had approached Jerusalem and had come to Bethphage, at the Mount of Olives, then Jesus sent two disciples, 2 saying to them, "Go into the village opposite you, and immediately you will find a donkey tied *there* and a colt with her; untie them and bring them to Me. 3 If anyone says anything to you, you shall say, 'The Lord has need of them,' and immediately he will send them." 4 This took place to fulfill what was spoken through the prophet:

---

[a] [κύριε] UBS.
[b] κύριε omitted by NET.

NIV

⁵“Say to Daughter
Zion,
‘See, your king
comes to
you,
gentle and riding
on a donkey,
and on a colt,
the foal of a
donkey.’ ”[a]

[6]The disciples went
and did as Jesus had
instructed them. [7]They
brought the donkey
and the colt and placed
their cloaks on them for
Jesus to sit on. [8]A very
large crowd spread
their cloaks on the
road, while others cut
branches from the trees
and spread them on
the road. [9]The crowds
that went ahead of him
and those that followed
shouted,

“Hosanna[b] to
the Son of
David!”
“Blessed is he who
comes in the
name of the
Lord!”[c]
“Hosanna[d] in
the highest
heaven!”

[10]When Jesus en-
tered Jerusalem,
the whole city was
stirred and asked,
“Who is this?”
[11]The crowds an-
swered, “This is
Jesus, the prophet
from Nazareth in
Galilee.”

Jesus at the Temple

[12]Jesus entered
the temple courts
and drove out all
who were buying
and selling there.
He overturned the
tables of the money
changers and the
benches of those
selling doves.

[a] 5 Zech. 9:9
[b] 9 A Hebrew expression meaning “Save!” which became an exclamation of praise; also in verse 15
[c] 9 Psalm 118:25,26
[d] 9 A Hebrew expression meaning “Save!” which became an exclamation of praise; also in verse 15

---

⁵εἴπατε τῇ θυγατρὶ Σιών, ἰδοὺ ὁ βασιλεύς σου ἔρχεταί σοι πραῢς
“Say ⌊to the⌋ daughter of Zion, ‘Behold, *{the}* your king *your* is coming to you, humble
3306 3836 2588 4994 2627 3836 5148 995 5148 2262 5148 4558
v.aam.2p d.dsf n.dsf n.gsf j d.nsm n.nsm r.gs.2 v.pmi.3s r.ds.2 a.nsm

καὶ ἐπιβεβηκὼς ἐπὶ ὄνον καὶ ἐπὶ πῶλον υἱὸν → ὑποζυγίου. ⁶
and mounted on a donkey, and on a colt, the foal of a beast of burden.’ ” So the
2779 2094 2093 3952 2779 2093 4798 5626 5689 1254 3836
cj pt.ra.nsm p.a n.asm cj p.a n.asm n.asm n.gsn

πορευθέντες δὲ οἱ μαθηταὶ καὶ ποιήσαντες καθὼς συνέταξεν αὐτοῖς
disciples went *So the disciples* and did as Jesus had instructed them.
3412 4513 1254 3836 3412 2779 4472 2777 2652 5332 899
pt.ap.npm cj d.npm n.npm cj pt.aa.npm cj v.aai.3s r.dpm.3

ὁ Ἰησοῦς ⁷ἤγαγον τὴν ὄνον καὶ τὸν πῶλον καὶ ἐπέθηκαν ἐπ᾽
{the} Jesus They brought the donkey and the colt, and placed their cloaks on
3836 2652 72 3836 3952 2779 3836 4798 2779 2202 3836 2668 2093
d.nsm n.nsm v.aai.3p d.asf n.asf cj d.asm n.asm cj v.aai.3p p.g

αὐτῶν τὰ ἱμάτια, καὶ ἐπεκάθισεν ἐπάνω αὐτῶν. ⁸ὁ δὲ πλεῖστος ὄχλος
them; *their cloaks* and he sat on them. *{the} {and}* A very large crowd
899 3836 2668 2779 2125 2062 899 3836 1254 4498 4063
r.gpm.3 d.apn n.apn cj v.aai.3s p.g r.gpm.3 d.nsm cj a.nsm.s n.nsm

ἔστρωσαν ἑαυτῶν τὰ ἱμάτια ἐν τῇ ὁδῷ, ἄλλοι δὲ ἔκοπτον κλάδους ἀπὸ
spread their *{the}* cloaks on the road, while others *while* cut branches from
5143 1571 3836 2668 1877 3836 3847 1254 257 1254 3164 3080 608
v.aai.3p r.gpm.3 d.apn n.apn p.d d.dsf n.dsf r.npm cj v.iai.3p n.apm p.g

τῶν δένδρων καὶ ἐστρώννυον ἐν τῇ ὁδῷ. ⁹οἱ δὲ ὄχλοι οἱ προάγοντες
{the} trees and spread them on the road. The *{and}* crowds that went before
3836 1285 2779 5143 1877 3836 3847 3836 1254 4063 3836 4575
d.gpn n.gpn cj v.iai.3p p.d d.dsf n.dsf d.npm cj n.npm d.npm pt.pa.npm

αὐτὸν καὶ οἱ ἀκολουθοῦντες ἔκραζον λέγοντες, ὡσαννὰ τῷ υἱῷ Δαυίδ·
him and those that followed were shouting, *{saying}* “Hosanna ⌊to the⌋ Son of David!
899 2779 3836 199 3189 3306 6057 3836 5626 1253
r.asm.3 cj d.npm pt.pa.npm v.iai.3p pt.pa.npm j d.dsm n.dsm n.gsm

εὐλογημένος ὁ ἐρχόμενος ἐν ὀνόματι → κυρίου· ὡσαννὰ ἐν τοῖς
Blessed is he who comes in the name of the Lord! Hosanna in the
2328 3836 2262 1877 3950 3261 6057 1877 3836
pt.rp.nsm d.nsm pt.pm.nsm p.d n.dsn n.gsm j p.d d.dpn

ὑψίστοις. ¹⁰καὶ → εἰσελθόντος αὐτοῦ εἰς Ἱεροσόλυμα
highest!” And when he entered *he {into}* Jerusalem, the whole city
5736 2779 899 1656 899 1650 2642 3836 4246 4484
a.dpn.s cj pt.aa.gsm r.gsm.3 p.a n.apn

ἐσείσθη πᾶσα ἡ πόλις λέγουσα, τίς ἐστιν οὗτος; ¹¹οἱ δὲ ὄχλοι
was in turmoil, *whole the city* asking, “Who is this?” And the *And* crowds
4940 4246 3836 4484 3306 5515 1639 4047 1254 3836 1254 4063
v.api.3s a.nsf d.nsf n.nsf pt.pa.nsf r.nsm v.pai.3s r.nsm d.npm cj n.npm

ἔλεγον, οὗτός ἐστιν ὁ προφήτης Ἰησοῦς ὁ ἀπὸ Ναζαρὲθ τῆς Γαλιλαίας. ¹²καὶ
said, “This is the prophet, Jesus *{the}* from Nazareth of Galilee.” And
3306 4047 1639 3836 4737 2652 3836 608 3714 3836 1133 2779
v.iai.3p r.nsm v.pai.3s d.nsm n.nsm n.nsm d.nsm p.g n.gsf d.gsf n.gsf cj

εἰσῆλθεν Ἰησοῦς εἰς τὸ ἱερὸν καὶ ἐξέβαλεν πάντας τοὺς πωλοῦντας καὶ
Jesus entered *Jesus {into}* the temple and drove out all who were selling and
2652 1656 2652 1650 3836 2639 2779 1675 4246 3836 4797 2779
v.aai.3s n.nsm p.a d.asn n.asn cj v.aai.3s a.apm d.apm pt.pa.apm cj

ἀγοράζοντας ἐν τῷ ἱερῷ, καὶ τὰς τραπέζας τῶν κολλυβιστῶν
buying in the temple, and he overturned the tables of the moneychangers
60 1877 3836 2639 2779 2951 2951 3836 5544 3836 3142
pt.pa.apm p.d d.dsn n.dsn cj d.apf n.apf d.gpm n.gpm

κατέστρεψεν καὶ τὰς καθέδρας τῶν πωλούντων τὰς περιστεράς, ¹³καὶ λέγει
he overturned and the chairs of those who were selling *{the}* doves. And he said
2951 2779 3836 2756 3836 4797 3836 4361 2779 3306
v.aai.3s cj d.apf n.apf d.gpm pt.pa.gpm d.apf n.apf cj v.pai.3s

---

NASB

⁵“ SAY TO THE
DAUGHTER OF
ZION,
‘ BEHOLD YOUR
KING IS COM-
ING TO YOU,
GENTLE, AND
MOUNTED ON A
DONKEY,
EVEN ON A
COLT, THE
FOAL OF A
BEAST OF BUR-
DEN.’ ”
[6]The disciples went
and did just as Je-
sus had instructed
them, [7]and brought
the donkey and the
colt, and laid their
coats on them; and
He sat on the coats.
[8]Most of the crowd
spread their coats
in the road, and
others were cutting
branches from the
trees and spreading
them in the road.
[9]The crowds go-
ing ahead of Him,
and those who
followed, were
shouting,
“ Hosanna to the
Son of David;
BLESSED IS HE
WHO COMES IN
THE NAME OF
THE LORD;
Hosanna in the
highest!”
[10]When He had en-
tered Jerusalem, all
the city was stirred,
saying, “Who is
this?” [11]And the
crowds were say-
ing, “This is the
prophet Jesus,
from Nazareth in
Galilee.”

Cleansing the Temple

[12]And Jesus en-
tered the temple
and drove out all
those who were
buying and sell-
ing in the temple,
and overturned the
tables of the money
changers and the
seats of those who
were selling doves.

NIV

[13]"It is written,"
he said to them,
"'My house will
be called a house
of prayer,'[a] but you
are making it 'a
den of robbers.'[b]"
[14]The blind and
the lame came to
him at the tem-
ple, and he healed
them. [15]But when
the chief priests
and the teachers
of the law saw the
wonderful things
he did and the chil-
dren shouting in
the temple courts,
"Hosanna to the
Son of David,"
they were indig-
nant.
[16]"Do you hear
what these chil-
dren are saying?"
they asked him.
"Yes," replied
Jesus, "have you
never read,

"'From the lips of
children and
infants
you, Lord,
have called
forth your
praise'[c]?"

[17]And he left
them and went
out of the city to
Bethany, where he
spent the night.

Jesus Curses a Fig Tree

[18]Early in the
morning, as Jesus
was on his way
back to the city, he
was hungry. [19]See-
ing a fig tree by
the road, he went
up to it but found
nothing on it ex-
cept leaves. Then
he said to it, "May
you never bear
fruit again!" Im-
mediately the tree
withered.
[20]When the dis-
ciples saw this,
they were amazed.
"How did the fig
tree wither so
quickly?" they
asked.

[a] 13 Isaiah 56:7
[b] 13 Jer. 7:11
[c] 16 Psalm 8:2 (see Septuagint)

αὐτοῖς, γέγραπται, ὁ οἶκός μου οἶκος προσευχῆς
to them, "It stands written, {the} 'My house My will be called a house of prayer,'
899 1211 3836 1609 3875 1609 2813 2813 2813 3875 4666
r.dpm.3 v.rpi.3s d.nsm n.nsm r.gs.1 n.nsm n.gsf

κληθήσεται, ὑμεῖς δὲ αὐτὸν ποιεῖτε σπήλαιον λῃστῶν. [14] καὶ
will be called but you but are making it are making a den of thieves." Then
2813 1254 7007 1254 4472 4472 899 4472 5068 3334 2779
v.fpi.3s r.np.2 cj r.asm.3 v.pai.2p n.asn n.gpm cj

προσῆλθον αὐτῷ τυφλοὶ καὶ χωλοὶ ἐν τῷ ἱερῷ, καὶ
the blind and the lame came to him blind and lame in the temple and
5603 2779 6000 4665 899 5603 2779 6000 1877 3836 2639 2779
v.aai.3p r.dsm.3 a.npm cj a.npm p.d d.dsn n.dsn cj

ἐθεράπευσεν αὐτούς. [15] ἰδόντες δὲ οἱ ἀρχιερεῖς καὶ οἱ γραμματεῖς
he healed them. when saw But when the ruling priests and the scribes saw
2543 899 1625 1254 1625 3836 797 2779 3836 1208 1625
v.aai.3s r.apm.3 pt.aa.npm cj d.npm n.npm cj d.npm n.npm

τὰ θαυμάσια ἃ ἐποίησεν καὶ τοὺς παῖδας τοὺς κράζοντας ἐν τῷ ἱερῷ
the wonderful things that he did, and the children who ⌞were crying out⌟ in the temple,
3836 2514 4005 4472 2779 3836 4090 3836 3189 1877 3836 2639
d.apn n.apn r.apn v.aai.3s cj d.apm n.apm d.apm pt.pa.apm p.d d.dsn n.dsn

καὶ λέγοντας, ὡσαννὰ τῷ υἱῷ Δαυίδ, ἠγανάκτησαν [16] καὶ εἶπαν αὐτῷ,
{and} {saying} "Hosanna ⌞to the⌟ Son of David!" they were indignant, and they said to him,
2779 3306 6057 3836 5626 1253 24 2779 3306 899
cj pt.pa.apm j d.dsm n.dsm n.gsm v.aai.3p cj v.aai.3p r.dsm.3

ἀκούεις τί οὗτοι λέγουσιν; ὁ δὲ Ἰησοῦς λέγει αὐτοῖς, ναί.
⌞"Do you hear⌟ what they are saying?" "Yes," replied {the} {and} Jesus, replied {to them} Yes
201 5515 4047 3306 3721 3306 3836 1254 2652 3306 899 3721
v.pai.2s r.asn r.npm v.pai.3p d.nsm cj n.nsm v.pai.3s r.dpm.3 pl

οὐδέποτε → → ← ἀνέγνωτε ὅτι ἐκ στόματος νηπίων καὶ θηλαζόντων
"but have you never read, ~ ⌞'Out of⌟ the mouth of infants and nursing babies
4030 336 4022 1666 5125 3758 2779 2558
adv v.aai.2p cj p.g n.gsn a.gpm cj pt.pa.gpm

κατηρτίσω αἶνον; [17] καὶ καταλιπὼν αὐτοὺς ἐξῆλθεν ἔξω τῆς πόλεως εἰς
⌞you have brought forth⌟ praise'?" And leaving them, he went out of the city to
2936 142 2779 2901 899 2002 2032 3836 4484 1650
v.ami.2s n.asm cj pt.aa.nsm r.apm.3 v.aai.3s p.g d.gsf n.gsf p.a

Βηθανίαν καὶ ηὐλίσθη ἐκεῖ. [18] πρωῒ δὲ ἐπανάγων εἰς τὴν
Bethany and ⌞spent the night⌟ there. ⌞In the morning,⌟ {and} as he was returning to the
1029 2779 887 1695 4745 1254 2056 1650 3836
n.asf cj v.api.3s adv adv cj pt.pa.nsm p.a d.asf

πόλιν ἐπείνασεν. [19] καὶ ἰδὼν συκῆν μίαν ἐπὶ τῆς ὁδοῦ ἦλθεν ἐπ'
city, he became hungry. And seeing a fig tree a by the road, ⌞he went over⌟ to
4484 4277 2779 1625 1651 5190 1651 2093 3836 3847 2262 2093
n.asf v.aai.3s cj pt.aa.nsm n.asf a.asf p.g d.gsf n.gsf v.aai.3s p.a

αὐτὴν καὶ οὐδὲν εὗρεν ἐν αὐτῇ ⌞εἰ μὴ⌟ φύλλα μόνον, καὶ λέγει αὐτῇ,
it and found nothing found on it except leaves only. And he said to it, "May
899 2779 2351 4029 2351 1877 899 1623 3590 5877 3667 2779 3306 899 1181
r.asf.3 cj a.asn v.aai.3s p.d r.dsf.3 cj pl n.apn adv cj v.pai.3s r.dsf.3

μηκέτι ← ἐκ σοῦ καρπὸς γένηται εἰς τὸν αἰῶνα. καὶ ἐξηράνθη
no fruit ever come from you fruit May come for all time!" And withered away
3600 2843 1181 1666 5148 2843 1181 1650 3836 172 2779 3830
adv p.g r.gs.2 n.nsm v.ams.3s p.a d.asm n.asm cj v.api.3s

παραχρῆμα ἡ συκῆ. [20] καὶ → ἰδόντες οἱ μαθηταὶ
at once the fig tree withered away. {and} When the disciples saw the disciples
4202 3836 5190 3830 3830 2779 3836 3412 1625 3836 3412
adv d.nsf n.nsf cj pt.aa.npm d.npm n.npm

ἐθαύμασαν λέγοντες, πῶς παραχρῆμα
this, they were astonished and said, "How did the fig tree wither away so quickly?"
2513 3306 4802 3830 3836 5190 5190 3830 3830 4202
v.aai.3p pt.pa.npm pl adv

NASB

[13]And He *said to
them, "It is written,
'MY HOUSE SHALL
BE CALLED A HOUSE
OF PRAYER'; but
you are making it a
ROBBERS' DEN."
[14]And *the* blind
and *the* lame
came to Him in
the temple, and
He healed them.
[15]But when the
chief priests and
the scribes saw the
wonderful things
that He had done,
and the children
who were shouting
in the temple, "Ho-
sanna to the Son
of David," they
became indignant
[16]and said to Him,
"Do You hear what
these *children* are
saying?" And Jesus
*said to them, "Yes;
have you never
read, 'OUT OF THE
MOUTH OF INFANTS
AND NURSING BABIES
YOU HAVE PREPARED
PRAISE FOR YOUR-
SELF'?" [17]And He
left them and went
out of the city to
Bethany, and spent
the night there.

The Barren Fig Tree

[18]Now in the
morning, when He
was returning to
the city, He became
hungry. [19]Seeing a
lone fig tree by the
road, He came to
it and found noth-
ing on it except
leaves only; and
He *said to it, "No
longer shall there
ever be *any* fruit
from you." And at
once the fig tree
withered.
[20]Seeing *this,* the
disciples were
amazed and asked,
"How did the fig
tree wither *all* at

NIV

[21]Jesus replied,
"Truly I tell you,
if you have faith
and do not doubt,
not only can you
do what was done
to the fig tree, but
also you can say
to this mountain,
'Go, throw your-
self into the sea,'
and it will be done.
[22]If you believe,
you will receive
whatever you ask
for in prayer."

The Authority of Jesus Questioned

[23]Jesus entered
the temple courts,
and, while he was
teaching, the chief
priests and the el-
ders of the people
came to him. "By
what authority are
you doing these
things?" they
asked. "And who
gave you this au-
thority?"
[24]Jesus replied,
"I will also ask
you one question.
If you answer me,
I will tell you by
what authority I
am doing these
things. [25]John's
baptism—where
did it come from?
Was it from heav-
en, or of human
origin?"
They discussed
it among them-
selves and said,
"If we say, 'From
heaven,' he will
ask, 'Then why
didn't you believe
him?' [26]But if we
say, 'Of human
origin'—we are
afraid of the peo-
ple, for they all
hold that John was
a prophet."
[27]So they an-
swered

ἐξηράνθη ἡ συκῆ; 21 ἀποκριθεὶς δὲ ὁ Ἰησοῦς εἶπεν αὐτοῖς,
did wither away *the* *fig tree* And Jesus answered *And* *{the}* *Jesus* *{said}* them, "I
3830 3836 5190 1254 2652 646 1254 3836 2652 3306 899 3306
v.api.3s d.nsf n.nsf pt.ap.nsm cj d.nsm n.nsm v.aai.3s r.dpm.3

ἀμὴν λέγω ὑμῖν, ἐὰν ἔχητε πίστιν καὶ ↱ μὴ διακριθῆτε, οὐ μόνον
tell you the truth, *I tell* *you* if you have faith and do not doubt, not only
3306 7007 297 3306 7007 1569 2400 4411 2779 1359 3590 1359 4024 3667
pl v.pai.1s r.dp.2 cj v.pas.2p n.asf cj pl v.aps.2p pl adv

τὸ τῆς συκῆς ποιήσετε, ἀλλὰ κἂν τῷ
will you do what was done to the fig tree, *will you do* but ⌊even if⌋ you say to this
4472 4472 4472 3836 3836 5190 4472 247 2829 3306 3306 3836 4047
d.asn d.gsf n.gsf v.fai.2p cj crasis d.dsn

ὄρει τούτῳ εἴπητε, ἄρθητι καὶ βλήθητι εἰς τὴν θάλασσαν, γενήσεται·
mountain, *this* *you say* ⌊'Be lifted up⌋ and thrown into the sea,' it will happen.
4001 4047 3306 149 2779 965 1650 3836 2498 1181
n.dsn r.dsn v.aas.2p v.apm.2s cj v.apm.2s p.a d.asf n.asf v.fmi.3s

22 καὶ ⌊πάντα ὅσα ἂν⌋ αἰτήσητε ἐν τῇ προσευχῇ πιστεύοντες λήμψεσθε.
And whatever you ask in *{the}* prayer, if you believe, you will receive."
2779 4246 4012 323 160 1877 3836 4666 4409 3284
cj a.apn r.apn pl v.aas.2p p.d d.dsf n.dsf pt.pa.npm v.fmi.2p

23 καὶ → ἐλθόντος αὐτοῦ εἰς τὸ ἱερὸν
And when he had entered *he* *{into}* the temple, the ruling priests and the elders of
2779 899 2262 899 1650 3836 2639 3836 797 797 2779 3836 4565 3836
cj pt.aa.gsm r.gsm.3 p.a d.asn n.asn

προσῆλθον αὐτῷ διδάσκοντι οἱ ἀρχιερεῖς καὶ οἱ πρεσβύτεροι
the people approached him ⌊while he was teaching⌋ *the* *ruling priests* *and* *the* *elders*
3836 3295 4665 899 1438 3836 797 2779 3836 4565
v.aai.3p r.dsm.3 pt.pa.dsm d.npm n.npm cj d.npm a.npm

τοῦ λαοῦ λέγοντες, ἐν ποίᾳ ἐξουσίᾳ ταῦτα ποιεῖς; καὶ
of the *people* and said, "By what authority are you doing these things, *are you doing* and
3836 3295 3306 1877 4481 2026 4472 4472 4472 4047 4472 2779
d.gsm n.gsm pt.pa.npm p.d r.dsf n.dsf r.apn v.pai.2s cj

τίς σοι ἔδωκεν τὴν ἐξουσίαν ταύτην; 24 ἀποκριθεὶς δὲ ὁ Ἰησοῦς
who gave you *gave* *{the}* this authority?" *this* Jesus answered *{and}* *{the}* *Jesus*
5515 1443 5148 1443 3836 4047 2026 4047 2652 646 1254 3836 2652
r.nsm r.ds.2 v.aai.3s d.asf n.asf r.asf pt.ap.nsm cj d.nsm n.nsm

εἶπεν αὐτοῖς, ἐρωτήσω ὑμᾶς κἀγὼ λόγον ἕνα, ὃν ἐὰν
them, saying, *them* "I also will ask you *I also* one question, *one* and *{which}* if
899 3306 899 2743 2743 2263 7007 2743 1651 3364 1651 4005 1569
v.aai.3s r.dpm.3 v.fai.1s r.ap.2 crasis n.asm a.asm r.asm cj

εἴπητέ μοι ↰ ↰ κἀγὼ ὑμῖν ἐρῶ ἐν ποίᾳ ἐξουσίᾳ
you give me an answer, then I will tell you *will tell* by what authority I do
3306 1609 3306 3306 2743 3306 3306 7007 3306 1877 4481 2026 4472 4472
v.aas.2p r.ds.1 crasis r.dp.2 v.fai.1s p.d r.dsf n.dsf

ταῦτα ποιῶ· 25 τὸ βάπτισμα τὸ Ἰωάννου πόθεν ἦν; ↰ ἐξ οὐρανοῦ
these things. *I do* The baptism of John, where ⌊did it come⌋ from? From heaven
4047 4472 3836 967 3836 2722 4470 1639 4470 1666 4041
r.apn v.pai.1s d.nsn n.nsn d.nsn n.gsm cj v.iai.3s p.g n.gsm

ἢ ἐξ ἀνθρώπων; οἱ δὲ διελογίζοντο ἐν ἑαυτοῖς λέγοντες, ἐὰν εἴπωμεν,
or from man?" They *{and}* reasoned among themselves, saying, "If we say,
2445 1666 476 3836 1254 1368 1877 1571 3306 1569 3306
cj p.g n.gpm d.npm cj v.imi.3p p.d r.dpm.3 pt.pa.npm cj v.aas.1p

ἐξ οὐρανοῦ, ἐρεῖ ἡμῖν, ⌊διὰ τί⌋ οὖν ↱ ↱ οὐκ ἐπιστεύσατε αὐτῷ;
'From heaven,' ⌊he will say⌋ to us, 'Why then did you not believe him?'
1666 4041 3306 7005 1328 5515 4036 4409 4409 4024 4409 899
p.g n.gsm v.fai.3s r.dp.1 p.a r.asn cj pl v.aai.2p r.dsm.3

26 ἐὰν δὲ εἴπωμεν, ἐξ ἀνθρώπων, φοβούμεθα τὸν ὄχλον, πάντες γὰρ
But if *But* we say, 'From man,' ⌊we are afraid of⌋ the crowd, for they *for*
1254 1569 1254 3306 1666 476 5828 3836 4063 1142 4246 1142
cj cj v.aas.1p p.g n.gpm v.ppi.1p d.asm n.asm a.npm cj

ὡς προφήτην ἔχουσιν τὸν Ἰωάννην. 27 καὶ ↱ ἀποκριθέντες τῷ
hold that John was a prophet." *hold* *{the}* *John* So they answered *{the}*
2400 6055 2722 4737 2400 3836 2722 2779 3306 646 3836
pl n.asm v.pai.3p d.asm n.asm cj pt.ap.npm d.dsm

NASB

once?" [21]And Jesus
answered and said
to them, "Truly I
say to you, if you
have faith and do
not doubt, you will
not only do what
was done to the
fig tree, but even
if you say to this
mountain, 'Be
taken up and cast
into the sea,' it will
happen. [22]And all
things you ask in
prayer, believing,
you will receive."

Authority Challenged

[23]When He en-
tered the temple,
the chief priests
and the elders of
the people came to
Him while He was
teaching, and said,
"By what author-
ity are You doing
these things, and
who gave You this
authority?" [24]Jesus
said to them, "I
will also ask you
one thing, which if
you tell Me, I will
also tell you by
what authority I do
these things. [25]The
baptism of John
was from what
source, from heav-
en or from men?"
And they *began*
reasoning among
themselves, saying,
"If we say, 'From
heaven,' He will
say to us, 'Then
why did you not
believe him?' [26]But
if we say, 'From
men,' we fear the
people; for they all
regard John as a
prophet." [27]And an-
swering Jesus, they
said, "We do

NIV

Jesus, "We don't
know."
Then he said,
"Neither will I tell
you by what au-
thority I am doing
these things.

The Parable of the Two Sons

28"What do you
think? There was a
man who had two
sons. He went to
the first and said,
'Son, go and work
today in the vine-
yard.'
29"'I will not,' he
answered, but lat-
er he changed his
mind and went.
30"Then the fa-
ther went to the
other son and said
the same thing. He
answered, 'I will,
sir,' but he did
not go.
31"Which of the
two did what his
father wanted?"
"The first," they
answered.
Jesus said to
them, "Truly I
tell you, the tax
collectors and the
prostitutes are en-
tering the kingdom
of God ahead of
you. 32For John
came to you to
show you the way
of righteousness,
and you did not be-
lieve him, but the
tax collectors and
the prostitutes did.
And even after you
saw this, you did
not repent and be-
lieve him.

The Parable of the Tenants

33"Listen to an-
other parable:
There was a land-
owner who planted
a vineyard. He put
a wall around it,
dug a winepress
in it and built a
watchtower. Then
he rented the

Ἰησοῦ εἶπαν, ↱ ↱ οὐκ οἴδαμεν. ἔφη αὐτοῖς καὶ αὐτός· οὐδὲ ↱ ἐγὼ
Jesus, saying, "We do not know." And he said to them, {also} he "Neither will I
2652 3306 3857 3857 4024 3857 899 5774 899 2779 899 4028 3306 1609
n.dsm v.aai.3p pl v.rai.1p v.iai.3s r.dpm.3 adv r.nsm cj r.ns.1

λέγω ὑμῖν ἐν ποίᾳ ἐξουσίᾳ ταῦτα ποιῶ. 28 τί δὲ ↱ ὑμῖν δοκεῖ;
tell you by what authority I do these things. I do "What {and} do you think?
3306 7007 1877 4481 2026 4472 4472 4047 4472 5515 1254 1506 7007 1506
v.pai.1s r.dp.2 p.d r.dsf n.dsf r.apn v.pai.1s r.nsn cj r.dp.2 v.pai.3s

ἄνθρωπος εἶχεν τέκνα δύο. καὶ προσελθὼν τῷ πρώτῳ εἶπεν, τέκνον,
A man had two sons, two and he went ⌊to the⌋ first and said, 'Son,
476 2400 1545 5451 1545 2779 4665 3836 4755 3306 5451
n.nsm v.iai.3s n.apn a.apn cj pt.aa.nsm d.dsn a.dsn v.aai.3s n.vsn

ὕπαγε σήμερον ἐργάζου ἐν τῷ ἀμπελῶνι. 29 ὁ δὲ ἀποκριθεὶς
go and work today work in the vineyard.' And he And answered,
5632 2237 4958 2237 1877 3836 308 1254 3836 1254 646
v.pam.2s adv v.pmm.2s p.d d.dsm n.dsm d.nsm cj pt.ap.nsm

εἶπεν, οὐ θέλω, ὕστερον δὲ μεταμεληθεὶς ἀπῆλθεν. 30
saying, 'I will not,' I will but later but ⌊he changed his mind⌋ and went. Then
3306 2527 2527 4024 2527 1254 5731 1254 3564 599 1254
v.aai.3s pl v.pai.1s adv.c cj pt.ap.nsm v.aai.3s

προσελθὼν δὲ τῷ ἑτέρῳ εἶπεν ὡσαύτως. ὁ δὲ
the man went Then ⌊to the⌋ second son and said the same thing. And he And
4665 1254 3836 2283 3306 6058 1254 3836 1254
pt.aa.nsm cj d.dsm r.dsm v.aai.3s adv d.nsm cj

ἀποκριθεὶς εἶπεν, ἐγώ, κύριε, καὶ ↱ ↱ οὐκ ἀπῆλθεν. 31 τίς ἐκ τῶν δύο
answered, saying, 'I will, sir,' but he did not go. Which of the two
646 3306 1609 3261 2779 599 599 4024 599 5515 1666 3836 1545
pt.ap.nsm v.aai.3s r.ns.1 n.vsm cj pl v.aai.3s r.nsm p.g d.gpm a.gpm

ἐποίησεν τὸ θέλημα τοῦ πατρός; λέγουσιν, ὁ πρῶτος. λέγει αὐτοῖς ὁ
did the will of his father?" They said, "The first." Jesus said to them, {the}
4472 3836 2525 3836 4252 3306 3836 4755 2652 3306 899 3836
v.aai.3s d.asn n.asn d.gsm n.gsm v.pai.3p d.nsm a.nsm v.pai.3s r.dpm.3 d.nsm

Ἰησοῦς, ἀμὴν λέγω ὑμῖν ὅτι οἱ τελῶναι καὶ αἱ πόρναι
Jesus "I tell you the truth, I tell you {that} {the} tax collectors and {the} prostitutes
2652 3306 3306 7007 297 3306 7007 4022 3836 5467 2779 3836 4520
n.nsm pl v.pai.1s r.dp.2 cj d.npm n.npm cj d.npf n.npf

προάγουσιν ← ὑμᾶς εἰς τὴν βασιλείαν τοῦ θεοῦ. 32
will enter the kingdom of God before you! {into} the kingdom of God For
4575 3836 993 3836 2536 7007 1650 3836 993 3836 2536 1142
v.pai.3p r.ap.2 p.a d.asf n.asf d.gsm n.gsm

ἦλθεν γὰρ Ἰωάννης πρὸς ὑμᾶς ἐν ὁδῷ δικαιοσύνης, καὶ ↱ ↱ οὐκ
John came For John to show you {in} the way of righteousness, and you did not
2722 2262 1142 2722 4639 7007 1877 3847 1466 2779 4409 4409 4024
v.aai.3s cj n.nsm p.a r.ap.2 p.d n.dsf n.gsf cj pl

ἐπιστεύσατε αὐτῷ, οἱ δὲ τελῶναι καὶ αἱ πόρναι ἐπίστευσαν αὐτῷ· ↱
believe him; {the} but tax collectors and {the} prostitutes did believe. {him} And even
4409 899 3836 1254 5467 2779 3836 4520 4409 899 1254 1625
v.aai.2p r.dsm.3 d.npm cj n.npm cj d.npf n.npf v.aai.3p r.dsm.3

↱ ὑμεῖς δὲ ἰδόντες ↱ ↱ οὐδὲ μετεμελήθητε ὕστερον τοῦ πιστεῦσαι
when you And saw it, you did not change your minds afterward {the} and believe
1625 7007 1254 1625 3564 3564 4028 3564 5731 3836 4409
r.np.2 cj pt.aa.npm adv v.api.2p adv.c d.gsn f.aa

αὐτῷ. 33 ἄλλην παραβολὴν ἀκούσατε. ἄνθρωπος ἦν οἰκοδεσπότης
him. "Listen to another parable: Listen to {a man} ⌊There was⌋ a landowner
899 201 201 257 4130 201 476 1639 3867
r.dsm.3 r.asf n.asf v.aam.2p n.nsm v.iai.3s n.nsm

ὅστις ἐφύτευσεν ἀμπελῶνα καὶ φραγμὸν αὐτῷ περιέθηκεν καὶ
who planted a vineyard. {and} He put a fence around it, He put around {and}
4015 5885 308 2779 4363 4363 5850 4363 899 4363 2779
r.nsm v.aai.3s n.asm cj n.asm r.dsm.3 v.aai.3s cj

ὤρυξεν ἐν αὐτῷ ληνὸν καὶ ᾠκοδόμησεν πύργον καὶ ἐξέδετο αὐτὸν
dug a winepress in it, winepress and built a watchtower. Then he leased it
4002 3332 1877 899 3332 2779 3868 4788 2779 1686 899
v.aai.3s p.d r.dsm.3 n.asf cj v.aai.3s n.asm cj v.ami.3s r.asm.3

NASB

not know." He also
said to them, "Nei-
ther will I tell you
by what authority I
do these things.

Parable of Two Sons

28"But what do
you think? A man
had two sons, and
he came to the first
and said, 'Son, go
work today in the
vineyard.' 29And he
answered, 'I will
not'; but afterward
he regretted it
and went. 30The
man came to the
second and said
the same thing;
and he answered,
'I *will*, sir'; but he
did not go. 31Which
of the two did the
will of his father?"
They *said, "The
first." Jesus *said
to them, "Truly I
say to you that the
tax collectors and
prostitutes will get
into the kingdom
of God before you.
32For John came to
you in the way of
righteousness and
you did not believe
him; but the tax
collectors and
prostitutes did be-
lieve him; and you,
seeing *this,* did not
even feel remorse
afterward so as to
believe him.

Parable of the Landowner

33"Listen to anoth-
er parable. There
was a landowner
who PLANTED A
VINEYARD AND PUT A
WALL AROUND IT AND
DUG A WINE PRESS
IN IT, AND BUILT A
TOWER, and rented

NIV

vineyard to some
farmers and moved
to another place.
34 When the harvest
time approached,
he sent his servants
to the tenants to
collect his fruit.
35 "The tenants
seized his ser-
vants; they beat
one, killed anoth-
er, and stoned a
third. 36 Then he
sent other servants
to them, more than
the first time, and
the tenants treat-
ed them the same
way. 37 Last of all,
he sent his son to
them. 'They will
respect my son,'
he said.
38 "But when the
tenants saw the
son, they said to
each other, 'This
is the heir. Come,
let's kill him and
take his inheri-
tance.' 39 So they
took him and
threw him out of
the vineyard and
killed him.
40 "Therefore,
when the owner of
the vineyard comes,
what will he do to
those tenants?"
41 "He will bring
those wretches to
a wretched end,"
they replied, "and
he will rent the
vineyard to other
tenants, who will
give him his share
of the crop at har-
vest time."
42 Jesus said to
them, "Have you
never read in the
Scriptures:

"'The stone the
builders
rejected
has become the
cornerstone;
the Lord has done
this,

γεωργοῖς καὶ ἀπεδήμησεν. 34 ὅτε δὲ ἤγγισεν ὁ καιρὸς
to tenants and ⌊went away on a journey.⌋ When {and} the harvest time drew near, the time
1177 2779 623 4021 1254 3836 2843 2789 1581 3836 2789
n.dpm cj v.aai.3s cj cj v.aai.3s d.nsm n.nsm

τῶν καρπῶν, ἀπέστειλεν τοὺς δούλους αὐτοῦ πρὸς τοὺς γεωργοὺς λαβεῖν
{the} harvest he sent {the} his servants his to the tenants to collect his
3836 2843 690 3836 899 1529 899 4639 3836 1177 3284 899
d.gpm n.gpm v.aai.3s d.apm n.apm r.gsm.3 p.a d.apm n.apm f.aa

τοὺς καρποὺς αὐτοῦ. 35 καὶ λαβόντες οἱ γεωργοὶ τοὺς
share of the crop. his But the tenants seized the tenants {the} his
3836 2843 899 2779 3836 1177 3284 3836 1177 3836 899
d.apm n.apm r.gsm.3 cj pt.aa.npm d.npm n.npm d.apm

δούλους αὐτοῦ ⌊ὃν μὲν⌋ ἔδειραν, ⌊ὃν δὲ⌋ ἀπέκτειναν, ⌊ὃν δὲ⌋
servants; his one ⌊they severely beat,⌋ another they killed, and still another
1529 899 4005 3525 1296 4005 1254 650 1254 4005 1254
n.apm r.gsm.3 r.asm pl v.aai.3p r.asm pl v.aai.3p r.asm pl

ἐλιθοβόλησαν. 36 πάλιν ἀπέστειλεν ἄλλους δούλους πλείονας τῶν πρώτων,
they stoned. Then he sent other servants, more ⌊than the⌋ first time,
3344 4099 690 257 1529 4498 3836 4755
v.aai.3p adv v.aai.3s r.apm n.apm a.apm.c d.gpm a.gpm

καὶ ἐποίησαν αὐτοῖς ὡσαύτως. 37 ὕστερον δὲ ἀπέστειλεν πρὸς
and they did the same to them. same Finally {and} he sent his son to
2779 4472 6058 899 6058 5731 1254 690 899 5626 4639
cj v.aai.3p r.dpm.3 adv adv.c cj v.aai.3s p.a

αὐτοὺς τὸν υἱὸν αὐτοῦ λέγων, ἐντραπήσονται τὸν υἱόν μου. 38 οἱ
them, {the} son his saying, 'They will respect {the} my son.' my But when the
899 3836 5626 899 3306 1956 3836 1609 5626 1609 1254 1625 3836
r.apm.3 d.asm n.asm r.gsm.3 pt.pa.nsm v.fpi.3p d.asm n.asm r.gs.1 d.npm

δὲ γεωργοὶ ἰδόντες τὸν υἱὸν εἶπον ἐν ἑαυτοῖς, οὗτός ἐστιν ὁ κληρονόμος·
But tenants saw the son, they said to one another, 'This is the heir;
1254 1177 1625 3836 5626 3306 1877 1571 4047 1639 3836 3101
cj n.npm pt.aa.npm d.asm n.asm v.aai.3p p.d r.dpm.3 r.nsm v.pai.3s d.nsm n.nsm

δεῦτε ἀποκτείνωμεν αὐτὸν καὶ σχῶμεν τὴν κληρονομίαν αὐτοῦ. 39 καὶ
⌊come on,⌋ let us kill him and take {the} his inheritance.' his So
1307 650 899 2779 2400 3836 899 3100 899 2779
adv v.aas.1p r.asm.3 cj v.aas.1p d.asf n.asf r.gsm.3 cj

λαβόντες αὐτὸν ἐξέβαλον ἔξω τοῦ ἀμπελῶνος καὶ ἀπέκτειναν. 40
they seized him and threw him out of the vineyard and killed him. Now
3284 899 1675 2032 3836 308 2779 650 4036
pt.aa.npm r.asm.3 v.aai.3p p.g d.gsm n.gsm cj v.aai.3p

ὅταν οὖν ἔλθῃ ὁ κύριος τοῦ ἀμπελῶνος, τί ποιήσει τοῖς γεωργοῖς
when Now returns the owner of the vineyard returns, what will he do to those tenants?"
4020 4036 2262 3836 3261 3836 308 2262 5515 4472 3836 1697 1177
cj cj v.aas.3s d.nsm n.nsm d.gsm n.gsm r.asn v.fai.3s d.dpm n.dpm

ἐκείνοις; 41 λέγουσιν αὐτῷ, κακοὺς κακῶς ἀπολέσει αὐτούς
those They said to him, "He will bring those wretches to a wretched end those
1697 3306 899 660 660 660 899 2805 660 2809 660 899
r.dpm v.pai.3p r.dsm.3 a.apm adv v.fai.3s r.apm.3

καὶ τὸν ἀμπελῶνα ἐκδώσεται ἄλλοις γεωργοῖς, οἵτινες ἀποδώσουσιν αὐτῷ τοὺς
and lease the vineyard lease to other tenants who will give him his
2779 1686 3836 308 1686 257 1177 4015 625 899 3836
cj d.asm n.asm v.fmi.3s r.dpm n.dpm r.npm v.fai.3p r.dsm.3 d.apm

καρποὺς ἐν τοῖς καιροῖς αὐτῶν. 42 λέγει αὐτοῖς ὁ Ἰησοῦς,
share at {the} their harvest." their Jesus said to them, {the} Jesus "Have you
2843 1877 3836 899 2789 899 2652 3306 899 3836 2652 336 336
n.apm p.d d.dpm n.dpm r.gpm.3 v.pai.3s r.dpm.3 d.nsm n.nsm

οὐδέποτε ἀνέγνωτε ἐν ταῖς γραφαῖς, λίθον ὃν ἀπεδοκίμασαν οἱ
never read in the Scriptures: 'A stone that the builders rejected the
4030 336 1877 3836 1210 3345 4005 3836 3868 627 3836
adv v.aai.2p p.d d.dpf n.dpf n.asm r.asm v.aai.3p d.npm

οἰκοδομοῦντες, οὗτος ἐγενήθη εἰς ⌊κεφαλὴν γωνίας·⌋ παρὰ
builders {this} has become {into} the cornerstone; this was {from} the
3868 4047 1181 1650 3051 1224 4047 1181 4123
pt.pa.npm r.nsm v.api.3s p.a n.asf n.gsf p.g

NASB

it out to vine-grow-
ers and went on a
journey. 34 When the
harvest time ap-
proached, he sent
his slaves to the
vine-growers to re-
ceive his produce.
35 The vine-growers
took his slaves and
beat one, and killed
another, and stoned
a third. 36 Again he
sent another group
of slaves larger
than the first; and
they did the same
thing to them. 37 But
afterward he sent
his son to them,
saying, 'They will
respect my son.'
38 But when the
vine-growers saw
the son, they said
among themselves,
'This is the heir;
come, let us kill
him and seize
his inheritance.'
39 They took him,
and threw him out
of the vineyard
and killed him.
40 Therefore when
the owner of the
vineyard comes,
what will he do to
those vine-grow-
ers?" 41 They *said
to Him, "He will
bring those wretch-
es to a wretched
end, and will rent
out the vineyard to
other vine-growers
who will pay him
the proceeds at the
proper seasons."
42 Jesus *said to
them, "Did you
never read in the
Scriptures,

'THE STONE
WHICH THE
BUILDERS RE-
JECTED,
THIS BECAME
THE CHIEF
CORNER *stone;*
THIS CAME
ABOUT FROM
THE LORD,

NIV

and it is
marvelous in
our eyes'[a]?
43 "Therefore I tell
you that the king-
dom of God will be
taken away from
you and given to
a people who will
produce its fruit.
44 Anyone who
falls on this stone
will be broken to
pieces; anyone on
whom it falls will
be crushed."[b]
45 When the chief
priests and the
Pharisees heard
Jesus' parables,
they knew he was
talking about them.
46 They looked for
a way to arrest
him, but they were
afraid of the crowd
because the people
held that he was a
prophet.

The Parable of the Wedding Banquet

22 Jesus spoke
to them
again in parables,
saying: 2 "The king-
dom of heaven is
like a king who
prepared a wedding
banquet for his son.
3 He sent his ser-
vants to those who
had been invited
to the banquet to
tell them to come,
but they refused to
come.
4 "Then he sent
some more servants
and said, 'Tell those
who have been in-
vited that I have
prepared my din-
ner: My oxen and
fattened cattle have
been butchered, and
everything is ready.
Come to the wed-
ding banquet.'
5 "But they paid no
attention and went
off—one to his
field, another to his
business. 6 The rest

κυρίου ἐγένετο αὕτη καὶ ἔστιν θαυμαστὴ ἐν ὀφθαλμοῖς ἡμῶν; 43 ⌊διὰ
Lord's doing, *this* and it is amazing in our eyes'? *our* Therefore
3261 1181 4047 2779 1639 2515 1877 7005 4057 7005 1328
n.gsm v.ami.3s r.nsf cj v.pai.3s a.nsf p.d n.dpm r.gp.1 p.a

τοῦτο⌋ λέγω ὑμῖν ὅτι ἀρθήσεται ἀφ᾽ ὑμῶν ἡ βασιλεία
I tell you that the kingdom of God ⌊will be taken away⌋ from you *the* *kingdom*
4047 3306 7007 4022 3836 993 3836 2536 149 608 7007 3836 993
r.asn v.pai.1s r.dp.2 cj v.fpi.3s p.g r.gp.2 d.nsf n.nsf

τοῦ θεοῦ καὶ δοθήσεται → ἔθνει ποιοῦντι τοὺς καρποὺς αὐτῆς.[a] 45 καὶ
of *God* and given to a people who will produce *{the}* its fruit." *its* *{and}*
3836 2536 2779 1443 1620 4472 3836 899 2843 899 2779
d.gsm n.gsm cj v.fpi.3s n.dsn pt.pa.dsn d.apm n.apm r.gsf.3 cj

ἀκούσαντες οἱ ἀρχιερεῖς καὶ οἱ Φαρισαῖοι τὰς παραβολὰς
When heard When the ruling priests and the Pharisees heard *{the}* his parables,
201 201 3836 797 2779 3836 5757 201 3836 899 4130
pt.aa.npm d.npm n.npm cj d.npm n.npm d.apf n.apf

αὐτοῦ ἔγνωσαν ὅτι περὶ αὐτῶν λέγει, 46 καὶ
his they perceived that he was speaking about them. *he was speaking* And
899 1182 4022 3306 3306 3306 4309 899 3306 2779
r.gsm.3 v.aai.3p cj p.g r.gpm.3 v.pai.3s cj

ζητοῦντες αὐτὸν κρατῆσαι ἐφοβήθησαν τοὺς ὄχλους, ἐπεὶ
⌊although they wanted⌋ to arrest him, *to arrest* ⌊they were afraid of⌋ the crowds because
2426 3195 3195 899 3195 5828 3836 4063 2075
pt.pa.npm r.asm.3 f.aa v.api.3p d.apm n.apm cj

εἰς προφήτην αὐτὸν εἶχον.
they held him to be a prophet. *him* *they held*
2400 2400 899 1650 4737 899 2400
p.a n.asm r.asm.3 v.iai.3p

22:1 καὶ ἀποκριθεὶς ὁ Ἰησοῦς πάλιν εἶπεν ἐν παραβολαῖς
Once *{answering}* again *{the}* Jesus *again* spoke to them in parables,
2779 646 4099 3836 2652 4099 3306 899 899 1877 4130
cj pt.ap.nsm d.nsm n.nsm adv v.aai.3s p.d n.dpf

αὐτοῖς λέγων, 2 ὡμοιώθη ἡ βασιλεία τῶν οὐρανῶν ἀνθρώπῳ βασιλεῖ,
to them saying: *is like* "The kingdom of heaven is like a *{man}* king
899 3306 3929 3836 993 3836 4041 3929 3929 476 995
r.dpm.3 pt.pa.nsm v.api.3s d.nsf n.nsf d.gpm n.gpm n.dsm n.dsm

ὅστις ἐποίησεν γάμους τῷ υἱῷ αὐτοῦ. 3 καὶ ἀπέστειλεν τοὺς δούλους
who prepared a ⌊wedding feast⌋ for his son *his* and sent *{the}* his servants
4015 4472 1141 3836 899 5626 899 2779 690 3836 899 1529
r.nsm v.aai.3s n.apm d.dsm n.dsm r.gsm.3 cj v.aai.3s d.apm n.apm

αὐτοῦ καλέσαι τοὺς κεκλημένους εἰς τοὺς γάμους, καὶ οὐκ ἤθελον
his to call those who had been invited to the feast; but they would not *they would*
899 2813 3836 2813 1650 3836 1141 2779 2527 2527 4024 2527
r.gsm.3 f.aa d.apm pt.rp.apm p.a d.apm n.apm cj pl v.iai.3p

ἐλθεῖν. 4 πάλιν ἀπέστειλεν ἄλλους δούλους λέγων, εἴπατε τοῖς κεκλημένοις,
come. Then he sent other servants, saying, 'Tell those ⌊who have been invited,⌋
2262 4099 690 257 1529 3306 3306 3836 2813
f.aa adv v.aai.3s r.apm n.apm pt.pa.nsm v.aam.2p d.dpm pt.rp.dpm

ἰδοὺ τὸ ἄριστόν μου ἡτοίμακα, οἱ ταῦροί μου καὶ
"See, I have prepared *{the}* my banquet, *my* *I have prepared* *{the}* my oxen *my* and
2627 2286 2286 2286 3836 1609 756 1609 2286 3836 1609 5436 1609 2779
j d.asn n.asn r.gs.1 v.rai.1s d.npm n.npm r.gs.1 cj

τὰ σιτιστὰ τεθυμένα καὶ πάντα ἕτοιμα· δεῦτε εἰς τοὺς
{the} ⌊fattened calves⌋ ⌊have been slaughtered,⌋ and everything is ready. Come to the
3836 4990 2604 2779 4246 2289 1307 1650 3836
d.npn a.npn pt.rp.npn cj a.npn a.npn adv p.a d.apm

γάμους. 5 οἱ δὲ ἀμελήσαντες ἀπῆλθον, ⌊ὃς μὲν⌋ εἰς τὸν
⌊wedding feast."'⌋ But they *But* paid no attention and ⌊went on their way,⌋ one to *{the}*
1141 1254 3836 1254 288 599 4005 3525 1650 3836
n.apm d.npm cj pt.aa.npm v.aai.3p r.nsm pl p.a d.asm

ἴδιον ἀγρόν, ⌊ὃς δὲ⌋ ἐπὶ τὴν ἐμπορίαν αὐτοῦ· 6 οἱ δὲ λοιποὶ
his farm, another to *{the}* his business, *his* while the *while* rest
2625 69 4005 1254 2093 3836 899 1865 899 1254 3836 1254 3370
a.asm n.asm r.nsm pl p.a d.asf n.asf r.gsm.3 d.npm pl a.npm

NASB

AND IT IS MAR-
VELOUS IN OUR
EYES'?
43 Therefore I say to
you, the kingdom
of God will be
taken away from
you and given to a
people, producing
the fruit of it. 44 And
he who falls on
this stone will be
broken to pieces;
but on whomever it
falls, it will scatter
him like dust."
45 When the chief
priests and the
Pharisees heard
His parables, they
understood that
He was speaking
about them. 46 When
they sought to
seize Him, they
feared the people,
because they con-
sidered Him to be a
prophet.

Parable of the Marriage Feast

22:1 Jesus spoke to
them again in para-
bles, saying, 2 "The
kingdom of heaven
may be compared
to a king who gave
a wedding feast for
his son. 3 And he
sent out his slaves
to call those who
had been invited to
the wedding feast,
and they were
unwilling to come.
4 Again he sent out
other slaves say-
ing, 'Tell those
who have been
invited, "Behold, I
have prepared my
dinner; my oxen
and my fattened
livestock are *all*
butchered and ev-
erything is ready;
come to the wed-
ding feast."' 5 But
they paid no atten-
tion and went their
way, one to his
own farm, another
to his business,
6 and the rest

[a] 42 Psalm 118:22,23
[b] 44 Some manuscripts do not have verse 44.

[a] UBS puts v 44 in brackets. It was accidentally omitted. καὶ (and) ὁ (the) πεσὼν (one who falls, 4406) ἐπὶ (on) τὸν (the) λίθον (stone, 3345) τοῦτον (this) συνθλασθήσεται (will be broken to pieces, 5314)· ἐφ᾽ (upon) ὃν (whomever) δ᾽ (and) πέσῃ (it falls) ἂν (~) λικμήσει (it will crush, 3347) αὐτόν (him).

NIV

seized his servants,
mistreated them
and killed them.
7The king was en-
raged. He sent his
army and destroyed
those murderers
and burned their
city.
8"Then he said to
his servants, 'The
wedding banquet
is ready, but those
I invited did not
deserve to come.
9So go to the street
corners and invite
to the banquet
anyone you find.'
10So the servants
went out into the
streets and gath-
ered all the people
they could find,
the bad as well as
the good, and the
wedding hall was
filled with guests.
11"But when the
king came in to
see the guests,
he noticed a man
there who was
not wearing wed-
ding clothes. 12He
asked, 'How did
you get in here
without wedding
clothes, friend?'
The man was
speechless.
13"Then the king
told the attendants,
'Tie him hand and
foot, and throw
him outside, into
the darkness,
where there will
be weeping and
gnashing of teeth.'
14"For many are
invited, but few
are chosen."

Paying the Imperial Tax to Caesar

15Then the Phari-
sees went out

κρατήσαντες τοὺς δούλους αὐτοῦ ὕβρισαν ← καὶ ἀπέκτειναν.
seized {the} his servants, his treated them shamefully, and killed them.
3195 3836 899 1529 899 5614 2779 650
pt.aa.npm d.apm n.apm r.gsm.3 v.aai.3p cj v.aai.3p

7 ὁ δὲ βασιλεὺς ὠργίσθη καὶ ↱ πέμψας τὰ στρατεύματα αὐτοῦ
The {and} king was furious! {and} He sent {the} his troops his and
3836 1254 995 3974 2779 660 4287 3836 899 5128 899
d.nsm cj n.nsm v.api.3s cj pt.aa.nsm d.apn n.apn r.gsm.3

ἀπώλεσεν τοὺς φονεῖς ἐκείνους καὶ τὴν πόλιν αὐτῶν
destroyed {the} those murderers those and burned {the} their city their to the
660 3836 1697 5838 1697 2779 1856 3836 899 4484 899 1856 1856
v.aai.3s d.apm n.apm r.apm cj d.asf n.asf r.gpm.3

ἐνέπρησεν. 8 τότε λέγει τοῖς δούλοις αὐτοῦ, ὁ μὲν γάμος
ground. *burned to the ground* Then he said to his servants, his 'The ~ ⌊wedding feast⌋
1856 1856 5538 3306 3836 899 1529 899 3836 3525 1141
v.aai.3s adv v.pai.3s d.dpm n.dpm r.gsm.3 d.nsm pl n.nsm

ἕτοιμός ἐστιν, οἱ δὲ κεκλημένοι οὐκ ἦσαν ἄξιοι· 9 πορεύεσθε
is ready, is but those but who were invited were not were worthy. Go
1639 2289 1639 1254 3836 1254 2813 1639 4024 1639 545 4513
a.nsm v.pai.3s d.npm cj pt.rp.npm pl v.iai.3p a.npm v.pmm.2p

οὖν ἐπὶ τὰς διεξόδους τῶν ὁδῶν καὶ ⌊ὅσους ἐὰν⌋ εὕρητε
therefore to the busy {the} intersections and invite everyone ⌊you can find⌋
4036 2093 3836 1447 3836 3847 2779 2813 4012 1569 2351
cj p.a d.apf n.apf d.gpf n.gpf cj r.apm pl v.aas.2p

καλέσατε εἰς τοὺς γάμους. 10 καὶ ἐξελθόντες οἱ δοῦλοι ἐκεῖνοι
invite to the ⌊wedding feast.'⌋ So those servants went out {the} servants those
2813 1650 3836 1141 2779 1697 1529 2002 3836 1529 1697
v.aam.2p p.a d.apm n.apm cj pt.aa.npm d.npm n.npm r.npm

εἰς τὰς ὁδοὺς συνήγαγον ⌊πάντας οὓς⌋ εὗρον, πονηρούς ⌊τε καὶ⌋
into the streets and gathered everyone ⌊they could find,⌋ rogues as well as
1650 3836 3847 5251 4246 4005 2351 4505 5445 2779
p.a d.apf n.apf v.aai.3p a.apm r.apm v.aai.3p a.apm cj cj

ἀγαθούς· καὶ ἐπλήσθη ὁ γάμος ἀνακειμένων. 11
⌊honorable men;⌋ and the wedding hall was packed the wedding hall with guests. But
19 2779 3836 1141 1141 4398 3836 1141 367 1254
a.apm cj v.api.3s d.nsm n.nsm pt.pm.gpm

→ εἰσελθὼν δὲ ὁ βασιλεὺς θεάσασθαι τοὺς ἀνακειμένους εἶδεν
when the king came in But the king to see the guests, he noticed a
3836 995 1656 1254 3836 995 2517 3836 367 1625
pt.aa.nsm cj d.nsm n.nsm f.am d.apm pt.pm.apm v.aai.3s

ἐκεῖ ἄνθρωπον ↱ ↱ οὐκ ἐνδεδυμένον ἔνδυμα γάμου, 12 καὶ λέγει
man there man who was not wearing a wedding garment. wedding And he said
476 1695 476 1907 1907 4024 1907 1141 1903 1141 2779 3306
adv n.asm pl pt.rm.asm n.asn n.gsm cj v.pai.3s

αὐτῷ, ἑταῖρε, πῶς εἰσῆλθες ὧδε ⌊μὴ ἔχων⌋ ἔνδυμα γάμου; ὁ
to him, 'Friend, how ⌊did you get in⌋ here without a wedding garment?' wedding And the
899 2279 4802 1656 6045 3590 2400 1141 1903 1141 1254 3836
r.dsm.3 n.vsm cj v.aai.2s adv pl pt.pa.nsm n.asn n.gsm d.nsm

δὲ ἐφιμώθη. 13 τότε ὁ βασιλεὺς εἶπεν τοῖς διακόνοις, δήσαντες αὐτοῦ
And man was speechless. Then the king said to his assistants, 'Bind him
1254 5821 5538 3836 995 3306 3836 1356 1313 899
cj v.api.3s adv d.nsm n.nsm v.aai.3s d.dpm n.dpm pt.aa.npm r.gsm.3

πόδας καὶ χεῖρας ἐκβάλετε αὐτὸν ↰ εἰς τὸ σκότος τὸ ἐξώτερον· ἐκεῖ
foot and hand and throw him out into {the} outer darkness, {the} outer where
4546 2779 5931 1675 899 1675 1650 3836 2035 5030 3836 2035 1695
n.apm cj n.apf v.aam.2p r.asm.3 p.a d.asn n.asn d.asn a.asn.c adv

ἔσται ὁ κλαυθμὸς καὶ ὁ βρυγμὸς τῶν ὀδόντων. 14 πολλοὶ γάρ εἰσιν
⌊there will be⌋ {the} weeping and {the} gnashing of teeth.' For many For are
1639 3836 3088 2779 3836 1106 3836 3848 1142 4498 1142 1639
v.fmi.3s d.nsm n.nsm cj d.nsm n.nsm d.gpm n.gpm a.npm cj v.pai.3p

κλητοί, ὀλίγοι δὲ ἐκλεκτοί. 15 τότε πορευθέντες οἱ Φαρισαῖοι
called, but few but are chosen." Then the Pharisees went out the Pharisees
3105 1254 3900 1254 1723 5538 3836 5757 4513 3836 5757
a.npm a.npm cj a.npm adv pt.ap.npm d.npm n.npm

NASB

seized his slaves
and mistreated
them and killed
them. 7But the king
was enraged, and
he sent his armies
and destroyed
those murderers
and set their city
on fire. 8Then he
*said to his slaves,
'The wedding is
ready, but those
who were invited
were not worthy.
9Go therefore to
the main highways,
and as many as you
find *there,* invite to
the wedding feast.'
10Those slaves went
out into the streets
and gathered
together all they
found, both evil
and good; and the
wedding hall was
filled with dinner
guests.
11"But when the
king came in to
look over the din-
ner guests, he saw
a man there who
was not dressed in
wedding clothes,
12and he *said to
him, 'Friend, how
did you come in
here without wed-
ding clothes?'
And the man was
speechless. 13Then
the king said to
the servants, 'Bind
him hand and foot,
and throw him into
the outer darkness;
in that place there
will be weeping
and gnashing of
teeth.' 14For many
are called, but few
are chosen."

Tribute to Caesar

15Then the Phari-
sees went and

NIV

and laid plans to trap him in his words. 16 They sent their disciples to him along with the Herodians. "Teacher," they said, "we know that you are a man of integrity and that you teach the way of God in accordance with the truth. You aren't swayed by others, because you pay no attention to who they are. 17 Tell us then, what is your opinion? Is it right to pay the imperial tax[a] to Caesar or not?"

18 But Jesus, knowing their evil intent, said, "You hypocrites, why are you trying to trap me? 19 Show me the coin used for paying the tax." They brought him a denarius, 20 and he asked them, "Whose image is this? And whose inscription?"

21 "Caesar's," they replied.

Then he said to them, "So give back to Caesar what is Caesar's, and to God what is God's."

22 When they heard this, they were amazed. So they left him and went away.

Marriage at the Resurrection

23 That same day the Sadducees, who say there is no resurrection, came to him with a question. 24 "Teacher," they said, "Moses told us that if a man dies without having children, his brother must marry the

[a] 17 A special tax levied on subject peoples, not on Roman citizens

---

⌊συμβούλιον ἔλαβον⌋ ὅπως αὐτὸν παγιδεύσωσιν ἐν λόγῳ.
and plotted how they could trap him *they could trap* in ⌊what he said.⌋
5206 3284 3968 4074 4074 4074 899 4074 1877 3364
n.asn v.aai.3p cj r.asm.3 v.aas.3p p.d n.dsm

16 καὶ ἀποστέλλουσιν αὐτῷ τοὺς μαθητὰς αὐτῶν μετὰ τῶν
And they sent their disciples to him *{the}* *disciples* *their* ⌊along with⌋ the
2779 690 899 3412 899 3836 3412 899 3552 3836
cj v.pai.3p r.dsm.3 d.apm n.apm r.gpm.3 p.g d.gpm

Ἡρῳδιανῶν λέγοντες, διδάσκαλε, οἴδαμεν ὅτι ἀληθὴς εἶ καὶ τὴν
Herodians, saying, "Teacher, we know that you are true *you are* and teach the
2477 3306 1437 3857 4022 1639 1639 239 1639 2779 1438 3836
n.gpm pt.pa.npm n.vsm v.rai.1p cj a.nsm v.pai.2s cj d.asf

ὁδὸν τοῦ θεοῦ ἐν ἀληθείᾳ διδάσκεις καὶ οὐ μέλει σοι περὶ οὐδενός·
way of God in truth, *teach* and ~ ⌊show deference⌋ *{you}* to no one, for
3847 3836 2536 1877 237 1438 2779 4024 3508 5148 4309 4029 1142
n.asf d.gsm n.gsm p.d n.dsf v.pai.2s cj pl v.pai.3s r.ds.2 p.g a.gsm

↱ ↱ οὐ γὰρ βλέπεις εἰς ⌊πρόσωπον ἀνθρώπων,⌋ 17 εἰπὲ οὖν ἡμῖν τί
you are not *for* swayed by appearances. So tell *So* us, what
1063 1063 4024 1142 1063 1650 4725 476 4036 3306 4036 7005 5515
pl cj v.pai.2s p.a n.asn n.gpm v.aam.2s cj r.dp.1 r.nsn

↱ σοι δοκεῖ· ἔξεστιν δοῦναι κῆνσον Καίσαρι ἢ οὔ; 18 γνοὺς
do you think? Is it proper to pay a tax to Caesar or not?" But Jesus, perceiving
1506 5148 1506 1997 1443 3056 2790 2445 4024 1254 2652 1182
r.ds.2 v.pai.3s v.pai.3s f.aa n.asm n.dsm cj pl pt.aa.nsm

δὲ ὁ Ἰησοῦς τὴν πονηρίαν αὐτῶν εἶπεν, τί με πειράζετε,
But *{the}* *Jesus* *{the}* their evil intent, *their* said, "Why are you testing me, *are you testing*
1254 3836 2652 3836 899 4504 899 3306 5515 4279 4279 4279 1609 4279
cj d.nsm n.nsm d.asf n.asf r.gpm.3 v.aai.3s r.asn r.as.1 v.pai.2p

ὑποκριταί; 19 ἐπιδείξατέ μοι τὸ νόμισμα τοῦ κήνσου. οἱ δὲ
you hypocrites? Show me the coin used ⌊for the⌋ tax." So they *So*
5695 2109 1609 3836 3790 3836 3056 1254 3836 1254
n.vpm v.aam.2p r.ds.1 d.asn n.asn d.gsm n.gsm d.npm cj

προσήνεγκαν αὐτῷ δηνάριον. 20 καὶ λέγει αὐτοῖς, τίνος ἡ εἰκὼν αὕτη
brought him a denarius. And Jesus said to them, "Whose *{the}* image is this,
4712 899 1324 2779 3306 899 5515 3836 1635 4047
v.aai.3p r.dsm.3 n.asn cj v.pai.3s r.dpm.3 r.gsm d.nsf n.nsf r.nsf

καὶ ↰ ἡ ἐπιγραφή; 21 λέγουσιν αὐτῷ, Καίσαρος. τότε λέγει αὐτοῖς,
and whose *{the}* inscription?" They answered him, "Caesar's." Then he said to them,
2779 5515 3836 2107 3306 899 2790 5538 3306 899
cj d.nsf n.nsf v.pai.3p r.dsm.3 n.gsm adv v.pai.3s r.dpm.3

ἀπόδοτε οὖν τὰ Καίσαρος Καίσαρι καὶ
"Render therefore to Caesar ⌊the things⌋ that are Caesar's, *to Caesar* and to God
625 4036 2790 2790 3836 2790 2790 2779 3836 2536
v.aam.2p cj d.apn n.gsm n.dsm cj

τὰ τοῦ θεοῦ τῷ θεῷ. 22 καὶ ἀκούσαντες ἐθαύμασαν,
⌊the things⌋ that are *{the}* God's." *to* *God* *{and}* When they heard this they were astonished,
3836 3836 2536 3836 2536 2779 201 2513
d.apn d.gsm n.gsm d.dsm n.dsm cj pt.aa.npm v.aai.3p

καὶ ἀφέντες αὐτὸν ἀπῆλθαν. 23 ἐν ἐκείνῃ τῇ ἡμέρᾳ
so they left him and went away. On that *{the}* day the Sadducees who say there
2779 918 899 599 1877 1697 3836 2465 4881 3306 3306 1639
cj pt.aa.npm r.asm.3 v.aai.3p p.d r.dsf d.dsf n.dsf

προσῆλθον αὐτῷ Σαδδουκαῖοι, λέγοντες μὴ εἶναι ἀνάστασιν,
is no resurrection came to him *Sadducees* *who say* *no* *there is* *resurrection*
1639 3590 414 4665 899 4881 3306 3590 1639 414
v.aai.3p r.dsm.3 n.npm pt.pa.npm pl f.pa n.asf

καὶ ἐπηρώτησαν αὐτὸν 24 λέγοντες, διδάσκαλε, Μωϋσῆς εἶπεν, ἐάν τις ἀποθάνῃ
and posed a question. *{him}* They said, "Teacher, Moses said, 'If a man dies
2779 2089 899 3306 1437 3707 3306 1569 5516 633
cj v.aai.3p r.asm.3 pt.pa.npm n.vsm n.nsm v.aai.3s cj r.nsm v.aas.3s

μὴ ἔχων τέκνα, ἐπιγαμβρεύσει ὁ ἀδελφὸς αὐτοῦ τὴν
having no *having* children, his brother must marry *{the}* *brother* *his* *{the}* his
2400 3590 2400 5451 899 81 2102 3836 81 899 3836 899
pl pt.pa.nsm n.apn v.fai.3s d.nsm n.nsm r.gsm.3 d.asf

NASB

plotted together how they might trap Him in what He said. 16 And they *sent their disciples to Him, along with the Herodians, saying, "Teacher, we know that You are truthful and teach the way of God in truth, and defer to no one; for You are not partial to any. 17 Tell us then, what do You think? Is it lawful to give a poll-tax to Caesar, or not?" 18 But Jesus perceived their malice, and said, "Why are you testing Me, you hypocrites? 19 Show Me the coin *used* for the poll-tax." And they brought Him a denarius. 20 And He *said to them, "Whose likeness and inscription is this?" 21 They *said to Him, "Caesar's." Then He *said to them, "Then render to Caesar the things that are Caesar's; and to God the things that are God's." 22 And hearing *this,* they were amazed, and leaving Him, they went away.

Jesus Answers the Sadducees

23 On that day *some* Sadducees (who say there is no resurrection) came to Jesus and questioned Him, 24 asking, "Teacher, Moses said, 'IF A MAN DIES HAVING NO CHILDREN, HIS BROTHER AS NEXT OF KIN SHALL MARRY

NIV

widow and raise
up offspring for
him. 25Now there
were seven broth-
ers among us. The
first one married
and died, and since
he had no chil-
dren, he left his
wife to his brother.
26The same thing
happened to the
second and third
brother, right on
down to the sev-
enth. 27Finally,
the woman died.
28Now then, at
the resurrection,
whose wife will
she be of the sev-
en, since all of
them were married
to her?”
29Jesus replied,
“You are in er-
ror because you
do not know the
Scriptures or the
power of God. 30At
the resurrection
people will neither
marry nor be given
in marriage; they
will be like the
angels in heaven.
31But about the
resurrection of the
dead—have you
not read what God
said to you, 32‘I am
the God of Abra-
ham, the God of
Isaac, and the God
of Jacob’[a]? He is
not the God of the
dead but of the
living.”
33When the
crowds heard this,
they were aston-
ished at his teach-
ing.

The Greatest Commandment

34Hearing that
Jesus had silenced
the Sadducees,
the Pharisees got
together. 35One of
them, an expert in
the law,

[a] 32 Exodus 3:6

γυναῖκα αὐτοῦ καὶ ἀναστήσει σπέρμα τῷ ἀδελφῷ αὐτοῦ. 25 ἦσαν δὲ
widow his and raise up children for his brother.’ his Now there were Now
1222 899 2779 482 5065 3836 899 81 899 1254 1639 1254
n.asf r.gsm.3 cj v.fai.3s n.asn d.dsm n.dsm r.gsm.3 v.iai.3p cj

παρ’ ἡμῖν ἑπτὰ ἀδελφοί· καὶ ὁ πρῶτος γήμας ἐτελεύτησεν, καὶ
seven brothers among us; seven brothers {and} the first one married and died, and
2231 81 4123 7005 2231 81 2779 3836 4755 1138 5462 2779
p.d r.dp.1 a.npm n.npm cj d.nsm a.nsm pt.aa.nsm v.aai.3s cj

↱ μὴ ἔχων σπέρμα ἀφῆκεν τὴν γυναῖκα αὐτοῦ τῷ ἀδελφῷ
since he had no had children, he left {the} his wife his to his brother.
2400 2400 3590 2400 5065 918 3836 899 1222 899 3836 899 81
pl pt.pa.nsm n.asn v.aai.3s d.asf n.asf r.gsm.3 d.dsm n.dsm

αὐτοῦ· 26 ὁμοίως καὶ ὁ δεύτερος καὶ ὁ τρίτος ἕως τῶν ἑπτά.
his So also the second and the third, and so on to the seventh.
899 3931 2779 3836 1311 2779 3836 5569 2401 3836 2231
r.gsm.3 adv adv d.nsm a.nsm cj d.nsm a.nsm p.g d.gpm a.gpm

27 ὕστερον δὲ πάντων ἀπέθανεν ἡ γυνή. 28 ἐν τῇ
Finally, {and} the woman died as well. died the woman Therefore in the
5731 1254 3836 1222 633 4246 633 3836 1222 4036 1877 3836
adv.c cj a.gpn v.aai.3s d.nsf n.nsf p.d d.dsf

ἀναστάσει οὖν τίνος τῶν ἑπτὰ ἔσται γυνή; ↱ πάντες γὰρ ἔσχον
resurrection, Therefore whose wife of the seven ⌊will she be?⌋ wife For they all For had
414 4036 5515 1222 3836 2231 1639 1222 1142 2400 4246 1142 2400
n.dsf cj r.gsm d.gpm a.gpm v.fmi.3s n.nsf a.npm cj v.aai.3p

αὐτήν· 29 ἀποκριθεὶς δὲ ὁ Ἰησοῦς εἶπεν αὐτοῖς,
married her.” Jesus answered {and} {the} Jesus them, saying, them
899 2652 646 1254 3836 2652 899 3306 899
r.asf.3 pt.ap.nsm cj d.nsm n.nsm v.aai.3s r.dpm.3

πλανᾶσθε ↱ μὴ εἰδότες τὰς γραφὰς μηδὲ τὴν δύναμιν τοῦ
“You are mistaken, because you know neither know the Scriptures nor the power of
4414 3857 3857 3590 3857 3836 1210 3593 3836 1539 3836
v.ppi.2p pl pt.ra.npm d.apf n.apf cj d.asf n.asf d.gsm

θεοῦ· 30 ἐν γὰρ τῇ ἀναστάσει ↱ ↱ οὔτε γαμοῦσιν οὔτε γαμίζονται,
God. For in For the resurrection they will neither marry nor be given in marriage,
2536 1142 1877 1142 3836 414 1138 1138 4046 1138 4046 1139
n.gsm p.d cj d.dsf n.dsf cj v.pai.3p cj v.ppi.3p

ἀλλ’ ὡς ἄγγελοι ἐν τῷ οὐρανῷ εἰσιν. 31 περὶ δὲ τῆς
but will be like the angels in {the} heaven. will be But concerning But the
247 1639 1639 6055 34 1877 3836 4041 1639 1254 4309 1254 3836
cj cj n.npm p.d d.dsm n.dsm v.pai.3p p.g cj d.gsf

ἀναστάσεως τῶν νεκρῶν ↱ ↱ οὐκ ἀνέγνωτε τὸ ῥηθὲν ὑμῖν ὑπὸ τοῦ θεοῦ
resurrection of the dead, have you not read what was spoken to you by {the} God:
414 3836 3738 336 336 4024 336 3836 3306 7007 5679 3836 2536
n.gsf d.gpm a.gpm pl v.aai.2p d.asn pt.ap.asn r.dp.2 p.g d.gsm n.gsm

λέγοντος, 32 ἐγώ εἰμι ὁ θεὸς Ἀβραὰμ καὶ ὁ θεὸς Ἰσαὰκ καὶ ὁ θεὸς
{saying} ‘I am the God of Abraham and the God of Isaac and the God
3306 1609 1639 3836 2536 11 2779 3836 2536 2693 2779 3836 2536
pt.pa.gsm r.ns.1 v.pai.1s d.nsm n.nsm n.gsm cj d.nsm n.nsm n.gsm cj d.nsm n.nsm

Ἰακώβ; οὐκ ἔστιν ὁ[a] θεὸς → νεκρῶν ἀλλὰ → ζώντων. 33 καὶ →
of Jacob’? He is not He is the God of the dead but of the living.” And when
2609 1639 1639 4024 1639 3836 2536 3738 247 2409 2779
n.gsm pl v.pai.3s d.nsm n.nsm a.gpm cj pt.pa.gpm cj

ἀκούσαντες οἱ ὄχλοι ἐξεπλήσσοντο ἐπὶ τῇ διδαχῇ αὐτοῦ.
the crowd heard the crowd this, they were astounded at {the} his teaching. his
3836 4063 201 3836 4063 1742 2093 3836 899 1439 899
pt.aa.npm d.npm n.npm v.ipi.3p p.d d.dsf n.dsf r.gsm.3

34 ↱ οἱ δὲ Φαρισαῖοι ἀκούσαντες ὅτι ἐφίμωσεν τοὺς Σαδδουκαίους
Now when the Now Pharisees heard that he had silenced the Sadducees,
1254 201 3836 1254 5757 201 4022 5821 3836 4881
d.npm cj n.npm pt.aa.npm cj v.aai.3s d.apm n.apm

συνήχθησαν ⌊ἐπὶ τὸ αὐτό,⌋ 35 καὶ ἐπηρώτησεν εἷς ἐξ αὐτῶν νομικὸς[b]
they met together and asked one of them, an ⌊expert in the law,⌋
5251 2093 3836 899 2779 2089 1651 1666 899 3788
v.api.3p p.a d.asn r.asn cj v.aai.3s a.nsm p.g r.gpm.3 n.nsm

[a] [ὁ] UBS.
[b] [νομικὸς] UBS.

NASB

HIS WIFE, AND RAISE
UP CHILDREN FOR HIS
BROTHER.’ 25Now
there were seven
brothers with us;
and the first mar-
ried and died, and
having no children
left his wife to his
brother; 26so also
the second, and
the third, down to
the seventh. 27Last
of all, the woman
died. 28In the resur-
rection, therefore,
whose wife of the
seven will she be?
For they all had
married her.”
29But Jesus an-
swered and said
to them, “You
are mistaken, not
understanding
the Scriptures
nor the power of
God. 30For in the
resurrection they
neither marry nor
are given in mar-
riage, but are like
angels in heaven.
31But regarding the
resurrection of the
dead, have you not
read what was spo-
ken to you by God:
32‘I AM THE GOD OF
ABRAHAM, AND THE
GOD OF ISAAC, AND
THE GOD OF JACOB’?
He is not the God
of the dead but of
the living.” 33When
the crowds heard
this, they were
astonished at His
teaching.
34But when the
Pharisees heard
that Jesus had
silenced the Sad-
ducees, they gath-
ered themselves
together. 35One of

NIV

tested him with this question: [36]"Teacher, which is the greatest commandment in the Law?"

[37]Jesus replied: "'Love the Lord your God with all your heart and with all your soul and with all your mind.'[a] [38]This is the first and greatest commandment. [39]And the second is like it: 'Love your neighbor as yourself.'[b] [40]All the Law and the Prophets hang on these two commandments."

Whose Son Is the Messiah?

[41]While the Pharisees were gathered together, Jesus asked them, [42]"What do you think about the Messiah? Whose son is he?"

"The son of David," they replied.

[43]He said to them, "How is it then that David, speaking by the Spirit, calls him 'Lord'? For he says,

[44]"'The Lord said to my Lord:
"Sit at my right hand
until I put your enemies
under your feet."'[c]

[45]If then David calls him 'Lord,' how can he be his son?" [46]No one could say a word in reply, and from that day on no one dared to ask him any more questions.

A Warning Against Hypocrisy

23 Then Jesus said to the crowds and to his disciples:

[a] 37 Deut. 6:5
[b] 39 Lev. 19:18
[c] 44 Psalm 110:1

πειράζων αὐτόν· [36] διδάσκαλε, ποία ἐντολὴ μεγάλη
wanted to test him, and asked, "Teacher, which is the greatest commandment *greatest*
4279 899 2089 1437 4481 3489 1953 3489
pt.pa.nsm r.asm.3 n.vsm r.nsf n.nsf a.nsf

ἐν τῷ νόμῳ; [37] ὁ δὲ ἔφη αὐτῷ, ἀγαπήσεις κύριον τὸν θεόν
in the law?" And he *And* said to him, "'You shall love the Lord *{the}* your God
1877 3836 3795 1254 3836 1254 5774 899 26 3261 3836 5148 2536
p.d d.dsm n.dsm d.nsm cj v.iai.3s r.dsm.3 v.fai.2s n.asm d.asm n.asm

σου ἐν ὅλῃ τῇ καρδίᾳ σου καὶ ἐν ὅλῃ τῇ ψυχῇ σου καὶ ἐν ὅλῃ τῇ
your with all *{the}* your heart, *your* *{and}* with all *{the}* your soul, *your* and with all *{the}*
5148 1877 3910 3836 5148 2840 5148 2779 1877 3910 3836 5148 6034 5148 2779 1877 3910 3836
r.gs.2 p.d a.dsf d.dsf n.dsf r.gs.2 cj p.d a.dsf d.dsf n.dsf r.gs.2 cj p.d a.dsf d.dsf

διανοίᾳ σου· [38] αὕτη ἐστὶν ἡ μεγάλη καὶ πρώτη ἐντολή. [39] δευτέρα
your mind.' *your* This is the greatest and first commandment. And a second
5148 1379 5148 4047 1639 3836 3489 2779 4755 1953 1254 1311
n.dsf r.gs.2 r.nsf v.pai.3s d.nsf a.nsf cj a.nsf n.nsf a.nsf

δὲ ὁμοία αὐτῇ, ἀγαπήσεις τὸν πλησίον σου ὡς σεαυτόν. [40] ἐν ταύταις
And is like it, 'You shall love *{the}* your neighbor *your* as yourself.' On these
1254 3927 899 26 3836 5148 4446 5148 6055 4932 1877 4047
cj a.nsf r.dsf.3 v.fai.2s d.asm adv r.gs.2 cj r.asm.2 p.d r.dpf

ταῖς δυσὶν ἐντολαῖς ὅλος ὁ νόμος κρέμαται καὶ οἱ προφῆται.
{the} two commandments depends the whole *the* Law *depends* and the Prophets."
3836 1545 1953 3203 3836 3910 3836 3795 3203 2779 3836 4737
d.dpf a.dpf n.dpf a.nsm d.nsm n.nsm v.ppi.3s cj d.npm n.npm

[41] → συνηγμένων δὲ τῶν Φαρισαίων ἐπηρώτησεν
Now while the Pharisees were assembled, *Now* *the* *Pharisees* Jesus ⌞put this question to⌟
1254 3836 5757 5251 1254 3836 5757 2652 2089
pt.rp.gpm cj d.gpm n.gpm v.aai.3s

αὐτοὺς ὁ Ἰησοῦς [42] λέγων, τί ↱ ὑμῖν δοκεῖ περὶ τοῦ χριστοῦ; τίνος υἱός
them: *{the}* *Jesus* *{saying}* "What do you think about the Messiah? Whose son
899 3836 2652 3306 5515 1506 7007 1506 4309 3836 5986 5515 5626
r.apm.3 d.nsm n.nsm pt.pa.nsm r.nsn r.dp.2 v.pai.3s p.g d.gsm n.gsm r.gsm n.nsm

ἐστιν; λέγουσιν αὐτῷ, τοῦ Δαυίδ. [43] λέγει αὐτοῖς, πῶς οὖν ↱ Δαυὶδ ἐν
is he?" They said to him, *{the}* "David's." He said to them, "How then does David in the
1639 3306 899 3836 1253 3306 899 4802 4036 2813 1253 1877
v.pai.3s v.pai.3p r.dsm.3 d.gsm n.gsm v.pai.3s r.dpm.3 cj cj n.nsm p.d

πνεύματι καλεῖ αὐτὸν κύριον λέγων, [44] εἶπεν κύριος τῷ κυρίῳ μου,
Spirit call him 'Lord,' saying, 'The Lord said *Lord* to my Lord, *my*
4460 2813 899 3261 3306 3261 3306 3261 3836 1609 3261 1609
n.dsn v.pai.3s r.asm.3 n.asm pt.pa.nsm v.aai.3s n.nsm d.dsm n.dsm r.gs.1

κάθου ἐκ δεξιῶν μου, ⌞ἕως ἂν⌟ θῶ τοὺς ἐχθρούς σου ὑποκάτω τῶν
"Sit at my right hand *my* until I put *{the}* your enemies *your* under *{the}*
2764 1666 1609 1288 1609 2401 323 5502 3836 5148 2398 5148 5691 3836
v.pmm.2s p.g a.gpf r.gs.1 cj pl v.aas.1s d.apm a.apm r.gs.2 p.g d.gpm

ποδῶν σου; [45] εἰ οὖν Δαυὶδ καλεῖ αὐτὸν κύριον, πῶς υἱὸς
your feet"'? *your* If therefore David calls him 'Lord,' how can he be his son?"
5148 4546 5148 1623 4036 1253 2813 899 3261 4802 1639 1639 1639 899 5626
n.gpm r.gs.2 cj cj n.nsm v.pai.3s r.asm.3 n.asm cj n.nsm

αὐτοῦ ἐστιν; [46] καὶ οὐδεὶς ἐδύνατο ἀποκριθῆναι αὐτῷ λόγον οὐδὲ →
his *can he be* And no one was able to answer him a word, nor did anyone
899 1639 2779 4029 1538 646 899 3364 4028 5516
r.gsm.3 v.pai.3s cj a.nsm v.ipi.3s f.ap r.dsm.3 n.asm cj

ἐτόλμησέν τις ἀπ' ἐκείνης τῆς ἡμέρας ἐπερωτῆσαι
dare *anyone* to question him any more from that *{the}* day on. *to question*
5528 5516 2089 2089 899 4033 4033 608 1697 3836 2465 2089
v.aai.3s r.nsm p.g r.gsf d.gsf n.gsf f.aa

αὐτὸν οὐκέτι.
him *any more*
899 4033
r.asm.3 adv

[23:1] τότε ὁ Ἰησοῦς ἐλάλησεν τοῖς ὄχλοις καὶ τοῖς μαθηταῖς αὐτοῦ
Then *{the}* Jesus spoke to the crowds and to his disciples, *his*
5538 3836 2652 3281 3836 4063 2779 3836 899 3412 899
adv d.nsm n.nsm v.aai.3s d.dpm n.dpm cj d.dpm n.dpm r.gsm.3

NASB

them, [a]a lawyer, asked Him *a question,* testing Him, [36]"Teacher, which is the great commandment in the Law?" [37]And He said to him, "'YOU SHALL LOVE THE LORD YOUR GOD WITH ALL YOUR HEART, AND WITH ALL YOUR SOUL, AND WITH ALL YOUR MIND.' [38]This is the great and foremost commandment. [39]The second is like it, 'YOU SHALL LOVE YOUR NEIGHBOR AS YOURSELF.' [40]On these two commandments depend the whole Law and the Prophets."

[41]Now while the Pharisees were gathered together, Jesus asked them a question: [42]"What do you think about the Christ, whose son is He?" They *said to Him, "*The son* of David." [43]He *said to them, "Then how does David in the Spirit call Him 'Lord,' saying,

[44]'THE LORD SAID TO MY LORD,
"SIT AT MY RIGHT HAND,
UNTIL I PUT YOUR ENEMIES BENEATH YOUR FEET"'?

[45]If David then calls Him 'Lord,' how is He his son?" [46]No one was able to answer Him a word, nor did anyone dare from that day on to ask Him another question.

Pharisaism Exposed

[23:1]Then Jesus spoke to the crowds and to His disciples, [2]saying:

[a] I.e. an expert in the Mosaic Law

NIV

2"The teachers
of the law and
the Pharisees sit
in Moses' seat.
3So you must be
careful to do ev-
erything they tell
you. But do not
do what they do,
for they do not
practice what they
preach. 4They tie
up heavy, cumber-
some loads and put
them on other peo-
ple's shoulders, but
they themselves
are not willing
to lift a finger to
move them.
5"Everything
they do is done
for people to see:
They make their
phylacteries[a] wide
and the tassels on
their garments
long; 6they love
the place of honor
at banquets and
the most important
seats in the syna-
gogues; 7they love
to be greeted with
respect in the mar-
ketplaces and to be
called 'Rabbi' by
others.
8"But you are
not to be called
'Rabbi,' for you
have one Teacher,
and you are all
brothers. 9And do
not call anyone on
earth 'father,' for
you have one Fa-
ther, and he is in
heaven. 10Nor are
you to be called in-
structors,

[a] 5 That is, boxes containing Scripture verses, worn on forehead and arm

---

2λέγων, ἐπὶ τῆς Μωϋσέως καθέδρας
saying, "The scribes and the Pharisees now sit on the chair of Moses. *chair*
3306 3836 1208 2779 3836 5757 2767 2093 3836 2756 3707 2756
pt.pa.nsm p.g d.gsf n.gsm n.gsf

ἐκάθισαν οἱ γραμματεῖς καὶ οἱ Φαρισαῖοι. 3πάντα οὖν
sit *The* *scribes* *and* *the* *Pharisees* *{all things}* Therefore put into practice
2767 3836 1208 2779 3836 5757 4246 4036 4472 4472 4472
v.aai.3p d.npm n.npm cj d.npm n.npm a.apn cj

⌞ὅσα ἐὰν⌟ εἴπωσιν ὑμῖν ποιήσατε καὶ τηρεῖτε,
and continue to do whatever they tell you; *put into practice* *and* *continue to do* but do
2779 5498 5498 5498 4012 1569 3306 7007 4472 2779 5498 1254 4472
r.apn pl v.aas.3p r.dp.2 v.aam.2p cj v.pam.2p

κατὰ δὲ τὰ ἔργα αὐτῶν μὴ ποιεῖτε· λέγουσιν γὰρ καὶ ↱ οὐ
not imitate what *but* they *{the}* do, *they* *not* *do imitate* for they teach *for* but do not
3590 4472 2848 1254 899 3836 2240 899 3590 4472 1142 3306 1142 2779 4472 4024
p.a cj d.apn n.apn r.gpm.3 pl v.pam.2p v.pai.3p cj cj pl

ποιοῦσιν. 4 δεσμεύουσιν δὲ φορτία βαρέα [a]καὶ δυσβάστακτα καὶ
practice. For they tie up *For* heavy burdens, *heavy* *{and}* hard to bear, and
4472 1254 1297 1254 987 5845 987 2779 1546 2779
v.pai.3p v.pai.3p cj n.apn a.apn cj a.apn cj

ἐπιτιθέασιν ἐπὶ τοὺς ὤμους τῶν ἀνθρώπων, αὐτοὶ δὲ
lay them on *{the}* people's shoulders, *{the}* *people's* but they themselves *but*
2202 2093 3836 476 6049 3836 476 1254 2527 899 1254
v.pai.3p p.a d.apm n.apm d.gpm n.gpm r.npm cj

τῷ δακτύλῳ αὐτῶν οὐ θέλουσιν κινῆσαι
are not willing to move them with their finger, *their* *not* *they are willing* *to move*
2527 4024 2527 3075 3075 899 3836 899 1235 899 4024 2527 3075
d.dsm n.dsm r.gpm.3 pl v.pai.3p f.aa

αὐτά. 5 πάντα δὲ τὰ ἔργα αὐτῶν ποιοῦσιν πρὸς τὸ θεαθῆναι τοῖς
them They do all *{and}* *{the}* their deeds *their* *They do* to *{the}* be seen by
899 4472 4472 4246 1254 3836 899 2240 899 4472 4639 3836 2517 3836
r.apn.3 a.apn cj d.apn n.apn r.gpm.3 v.pai.3p p.a d.asn f.ap d.dpm

ἀνθρώποις· πλατύνουσιν γὰρ τὰ φυλακτήρια αὐτῶν ↰ καὶ
others: they make *{for}* *{the}* their phylacteries *their* broad and their tassels
476 4425 1142 3836 899 5873 899 4425 2779 3836 3192
n.dpm v.pai.3p cj d.apn n.apn r.gpm.3 cj

μεγαλύνουσιν τὰ κράσπεδα, 6φιλοῦσιν δὲ τὴν πρωτοκλισίαν ἐν τοῖς δείπνοις
long, *their* *tassels* they love *{and}* the place of honor at *{the}* banquets
3486 3836 3192 5797 1254 3836 4752 1877 3836 1270
v.pai.3p d.apn n.apn v.pai.3p cj d.asf n.asf p.d d.dpn n.dpn

καὶ τὰς πρωτοκαθεδρίας ἐν ταῖς συναγωγαῖς 7καὶ τοὺς ἀσπασμοὺς ἐν ταῖς
and the most important seats in the synagogues, and *{the}* greetings in the
2779 3836 4751 1877 3836 5252 2779 3836 833 1877 3836
cj d.apf n.apf p.d d.dpf n.dpf cj d.apm n.apm p.d d.dpf

ἀγοραῖς καὶ καλεῖσθαι ὑπὸ τῶν ἀνθρώπων ῥαββί. 8 ὑμεῖς δὲ ↱ μὴ
marketplaces, and to be called 'Rabbi' by *{the}* others. *Rabbi* But you *But* are not
59 2779 2813 4806 5679 3836 476 4806 1254 7007 1254 2813 3590
n.dpf cj f.pp p.g d.gpm n.gpm n.nsm r.np.2 cj pl

κληθῆτε ῥαββί· εἷς γὰρ ἐστιν ὑμῶν ὁ διδάσκαλος,
to be called 'Rabbi,' for you have but one *for* *have* *you* *{the}* teacher, and you are
2813 4806 1142 7007 1639 1651 1142 1639 7007 3836 1437 1254 7007 1639
v.aps.2p n.nsm a.nsm cj v.pai.3s r.gp.2 d.nsm n.nsm

πάντες δὲ ὑμεῖς ἀδελφοί ἐστε. 9καὶ πατέρα ↱ μὴ καλέσητε ὑμῶν
all *and* *you* brothers. *are* And *father* do not call anyone on earth your
4246 1254 7007 81 1639 2779 4252 2813 3590 2813 2093 1178 7007
a.npm cj r.np.2 n.npm v.pai.2p cj n.asm pl v.aas.2p r.gp.2

ἐπὶ τῆς γῆς, εἷς γὰρ ἐστιν ὑμῶν ὁ πατὴρ ὁ
'father,' *on* *{the}* *earth* for you have but one *for* *have* *you* *{the}* Father, and he is in
4252 2093 3836 1178 1142 7007 1639 1651 1142 1639 7007 3836 4252 3836
p.g d.gsf n.gsf a.nsm cj v.pai.3s r.gp.2 d.nsm n.nsm d.nsm

οὐράνιος. 10μηδὲ κληθῆτε καθηγηταί, ὅτι καθηγητὴς
heaven. Nor ⌞should you be called⌟ 'instructors,' because Christ is your only instructor.
4039 3593 2813 2762 4022 5986 1639 7007 1651 2762
a.nsm cj v.aps.2p n.npm cj n.nsm

[a] [καὶ δυσβάστακτα] UBS.

NASB

"The scribes and
the Pharisees have
seated themselves
in the chair of Mo-
ses; 3therefore all
that they tell you,
do and observe, but
do not do accord-
ing to their deeds;
for they say *things*
and do not do
them. 4They tie up
heavy burdens and
lay them on men's
shoulders, but
they themselves
are unwilling to
move them with *so
much as* a finger.
5But they do all
their deeds to be
noticed by men;
for they broaden
their [a]phylacteries
and lengthen the
tassels *of their gar-
ments.* 6They love
the place of honor
at banquets and the
chief seats in the
synagogues, 7and
respectful greet-
ings in the market
places, and being
called Rabbi by
men. 8But do not
be called Rabbi;
for One is your
Teacher, and you
are all brothers.
9Do not call *any-
one* on earth your
father; for One is
your Father, He
who is in heaven.
10Do not be called
leaders; for One is
your Leader, *that
is,* Christ. 11But the

[a] I.e. small cases containing Scripture texts worn on the left arm and forehead for religious purposes

NIV

for you have one Instructor, the Messiah. [11]The greatest among you will be your servant. [12]For those who exalt themselves will be humbled, and those who humble themselves will be exalted.

Seven Woes on the Teachers of the Law and the Pharisees

[13]"Woe to you, teachers of the law and Pharisees, you hypocrites! You shut the door of the kingdom of heaven in people's faces. You yourselves do not enter, nor will you let those enter who are trying to. [14][a]

[15]"Woe to you, teachers of the law and Pharisees, you hypocrites! You travel over land and sea to win a single convert, and when you have succeeded, you make them twice as much a child of hell as you are.

[16]"Woe to you, blind guides! You say, 'If anyone swears by the temple, it means nothing; but anyone who swears by the gold of the temple is bound by that oath.' [17]You blind fools! Which is greater: the gold, or the temple that makes the gold sacred? [18]You also say, 'If anyone swears by the altar, it means nothing; but anyone who swears by the gift on the altar is bound by that oath.' [19]You blind men! Which is greater: the gift, or the altar that makes the gift sacred?

[a] 14 Some manuscripts include here words similar to Mark 12:40 and Luke 20:47.

ὑμῶν ἐστιν εἷς ὁ Χριστός. [11] ὁ δὲ μείζων ὑμῶν ἔσται ὑμῶν διάκονος.
your is only {the} Christ The {and} greatest ⌊among you⌋ will be your servant.
7007 1639 1651 3836 5986 3836 1254 3489 7007 1639 7007 1356
r.gp.2 v.pai.3s a.nsm d.nsm n.nsm d.nsm cj a.nsm r.gp.2 v.fmi.3s r.gp.2 n.nsm

[12] ὅστις δὲ ὑψώσει ἑαυτὸν ταπεινωθήσεται καὶ ὅστις ταπεινώσει ἑαυτὸν
And whoever And will exalt himself will be humbled, and whoever will humble himself
1254 4015 1254 5738 1571 5427 2779 4015 5427 1571
r.nsm cj v.fai.3s r.asm.3 v.fpi.3s cj r.nsm v.fai.3s r.asm.3

ὑψωθήσεται. [13] οὐαὶ δὲ ὑμῖν, γραμματεῖς καὶ Φαρισαῖοι ὑποκριταί, ὅτι
will be exalted. "But woe But to you, scribes and Pharisees, hypocrites, because
5738 1254 4026 1254 7007 1208 2779 5757 5695 4022
v.fpi.3s j cj r.dp.2 n.vpm cj n.vpm n.vpm cj

κλείετε τὴν βασιλείαν τῶν οὐρανῶν → ἔμπροσθεν τῶν ἀνθρώπων· ὑμεῖς
you shut the kingdom of heaven in men's faces. {the} men's For you
3091 3836 993 3836 4041 476 1869 3836 476 1142 7007
v.pai.2p d.asf n.asf d.gpm n.gpm p.g d.gpm n.gpm r.np.2

γὰρ οὐκ εἰσέρχεσθε οὐδὲ τοὺς εἰσερχομένους ἀφίετε εἰσελθεῖν.[a] [15] οὐαὶ
For neither enter yourselves nor allow those who would enter allow to go in. "Woe
1142 4024 1656 4028 918 3836 1656 918 1656 4026
cj pl v.pmi.2p cj d.apm pt.pm.apm v.pai.2p f.aa j

ὑμῖν, γραμματεῖς καὶ Φαρισαῖοι ὑποκριταί, ὅτι περιάγετε τὴν θάλασσαν καὶ
to you, scribes and Pharisees, hypocrites, because you travel over {the} sea and
7007 1208 2779 5757 5695 4022 4310 3836 2498 2779
r.dp.2 n.vpm cj n.vpm n.vpm cj v.pai.2p d.asf n.asf cj

τὴν ξηρὰν ποιῆσαι ἕνα προσήλυτον, καὶ ὅταν γένηται ποιεῖτε αὐτὸν
{the} land to gain a single convert; and when he becomes one, you make him twice
3836 3831 4472 1651 4670 2779 4020 1181 4472 899 1487
d.asf a.asf f.aa a.asm n.asm cj cj v.ams.3s v.pai.2p r.asm.3

υἱὸν γεέννης διπλότερον ὑμῶν. [16] οὐαὶ ὑμῖν, ὁδηγοὶ
as much a son of hell twice as much as as yourselves. "Woe to you, blind guides
1487 1487 5626 1147 1487 1487 7007 4026 7007 5603 3843
n.asm n.gsf adv.c r.gp.2 j r.dp.2 n.vpm

τυφλοὶ οἱ λέγοντες, ↱ ⌊ὃς ἂν⌋ ὀμόσῃ ἐν τῷ ναῷ, οὐδέν ἐστιν·
blind who say, 'If someone swears by the temple it means nothing; it means
5603 3836 3306 3923 4005 323 3923 1877 3836 3724 1639 1639 4029 1639
a.vpm d.vpm pt.pa.vpm r.nsm pl v.aas.3s p.d d.dsm n.dsm a.nsn v.pai.3s

↱ ὃς δ' ἂν ὀμόσῃ ἐν τῷ χρυσῷ τοῦ ναοῦ, ὀφείλει.
but if someone but ~ swears by the gold of the temple, he is bound by his oath.'
1254 3923 4005 1254 323 3923 1877 3836 5996 3836 3724 4053
r.nsm cj pl v.aas.3s p.d d.dsm n.dsm d.gsm n.gsm v.pai.3s

[17] μωροὶ καὶ τυφλοί, τίς γὰρ μείζων ἐστίν, ὁ χρυσὸς ἢ ὁ ναὸς
You fools and blind men! For which For is greater, is the gold or the temple
3704 2779 5603 1142 5515 1142 1639 3489 1639 3836 5996 2445 3836 3724
a.vpm cj a.vpm r.nsm cj a.nsm.c v.pai.3s d.nsm n.nsm cj d.nsm n.nsm

ὁ → ἁγιάσας τὸν χρυσόν; [18] καί, ↱ ⌊ὃς ἂν⌋ ὀμόσῃ ἐν
that makes the gold sacred? the gold And you say, 'If someone swears by
3836 3836 5996 39 3836 5996 2779 3923 4005 323 3923 1877
d.nsm pt.aa.nsm d.asm n.asm cj r.nsm pl v.aas.3s p.d

τῷ θυσιαστηρίῳ, οὐδέν ἐστιν, ↱ ὃς δ' ἂν ὀμόσῃ ἐν τῷ
the altar it means nothing; it means but if someone but ~ swears by the
3836 2603 1639 1639 4029 1639 1254 3923 4005 1254 323 3923 1877 3836
d.dsn n.dsn a.nsn v.pai.3s r.nsm cj pl v.aas.3s p.d d.dsn

δώρῳ τῷ ἐπάνω αὐτοῦ, ὀφείλει. [19] τυφλοί, τί γὰρ
gift that is on it, he is bound by his oath.' How blind you are! For which For is
1565 3836 2062 899 4053 5603 1142 5515 1142
n.dsn d.dsn p.g r.gsn v.pai.3s a.vpm r.nsn cj

μεῖζον, τὸ δῶρον ἢ τὸ θυσιαστήριον τὸ → ἁγιάζον τὸ δῶρον;
greater, the gift or the altar that makes the gift sacred? the gift
3489 3836 1565 2445 3836 2603 3836 3836 1565 39 3836 1565
a.nsn.c d.nsn n.nsn cj d.nsn n.nsn d.nsn pt.pa.nsn d.asn n.asn

[a] 14 Οὐαὶ ὑμῖν, γραμματεῖς καὶ Φαρισαῖοι, ὑποκριταί, ὅτι κατεσθίετε τὰς οἰκίας τῶν χηρῶν, καὶ προφάσει μακρὰ προσευχόμενοι· διὰ τοῦτο λήψεσθε περισσότερον κρίμα. included by TR after εἰσελθεῖν.

NASB

greatest among you shall be your servant. [12]Whoever exalts himself shall be humbled; and whoever humbles himself shall be exalted.

Eight Woes

[13]"But woe to you, scribes and Pharisees, hypocrites, because you shut off the kingdom of heaven from people; for you do not enter in yourselves, nor do you allow those who are entering to go in. [14][[a]Woe to you, scribes and Pharisees, hypocrites, because you devour widows' houses, and for a pretense you make long prayers; therefore you will receive greater condemnation.]

[15]"Woe to you, scribes and Pharisees, hypocrites, because you travel around on sea and land to make one proselyte; and when he becomes one, you make him twice as much a son of hell as yourselves.

[16]"Woe to you, blind guides, who say, 'Whoever swears by the temple, *that* is nothing; but whoever swears by the gold of the temple is obligated.' [17]You fools and blind men! Which is more important, the gold or the temple that sanctified the gold? [18]And, 'Whoever swears by the altar, *that* is nothing, but whoever swears by the offering on it, he is obligated.' [19]You blind men, which is more important, the offering, or the altar

[a] This v not found in early mss

NIV

20 Therefore, any-
one who swears
by the altar swears
by it and by every-
thing on it. 21 And
anyone who swears
by the temple
swears by it and by
the one who dwells
in it. 22 And any-
one who swears by
heaven swears by
God's throne and
by the one who sits
on it.
23 "Woe to you,
teachers of the
law and Pharisees,
you hypocrites!
You give a tenth
of your spic-
es—mint, dill and
cumin. But you
have neglected
the more impor-
tant matters of the
law—justice, mer-
cy and faithful-
ness. You should
have practiced
the latter, without
neglecting the for-
mer. 24 You blind
guides! You strain
out a gnat but
swallow a camel.
25 "Woe to you,
teachers of the law
and Pharisees, you
hypocrites! You
clean the outside of
the cup and dish,
but inside they are
full of greed and
self-indulgence.
26 Blind Pharisee!
First clean the in-
side of the cup and
dish, and then the
outside also will
be clean.
27 "Woe to you,
teachers of the law
and Pharisees, you
hypocrites! You
are like white-
washed tombs,
which look beauti-
ful on the outside
but on the inside
are full of the
bones of the dead
and everything
unclean. 28 In the
same way,

20 ὁ οὖν ὀμόσας ἐν τῷ θυσιαστηρίῳ ὀμνύει ἐν αὐτῷ καὶ
So the *So* ⌞one who swears⌟ by the altar, swears not only by it but
4036 3836 4036 3923 1877 3836 2603 3923 1877 899 2779
d.nsm cj pt.aa.nsm p.d d.dsn n.dsn v.pai.3s p.d r.dsn.3 cj

ἐν πᾶσι τοῖς ἐπάνω αὐτοῦ· 21 καὶ ὁ ὀμόσας ἐν τῷ ναῷ ὀμνύει
by everything *{the}* on it. And the ⌞one who swears⌟ by the temple, swears not
1877 4246 3836 2062 899 2779 3836 3923 1877 3836 3724 3923
p.d a.dpn d.dpn p.g r.gsn.3 cj d.nsm pt.aa.nsm p.d d.dsm n.dsm v.pai.3s

ἐν αὐτῷ καὶ ἐν τῷ κατοικοῦντι αὐτόν, 22 καὶ ὁ ὀμόσας ἐν τῷ
only by it but by the one who dwells there. And the ⌞one who swears⌟ by *{the}*
1877 899 2779 1877 3836 2997 899 2779 3836 3923 1877 3836
p.d r.dsm.3 cj p.d d.dsm pt.pa.dsm r.asm.3 cj d.nsm pt.aa.nsm p.d d.dsm

οὐρανῷ ὀμνύει ἐν τῷ θρόνῳ τοῦ θεοῦ καὶ ἐν τῷ καθημένῳ ἐπάνω
heaven, swears not only by the throne of God but by the one who sits on
4041 3923 1877 3836 2585 3836 2536 2779 1877 3836 2764 2062
n.dsm v.pai.3s p.d d.dsm n.dsm d.gsm n.gsm cj p.d d.dsm pt.pm.dsm p.g

αὐτοῦ. 23 οὐαὶ ὑμῖν, γραμματεῖς καὶ Φαρισαῖοι ὑποκριταί, ὅτι ἀποδεκατοῦτε
it. "Woe to you, scribes and Pharisees, hypocrites, because you tithe
899 4026 7007 1208 2779 5757 5695 4022 620
r.gsm.3 j r.dp.2 n.vpm cj n.vpm n.vpm cj v.pai.2p

τὸ ἡδύοσμον καὶ τὸ ἄνηθον καὶ τὸ κύμινον καὶ ἀφήκατε τὰ βαρύτερα
{the} mint and *{the}* dill and *{the}* cumin, and have neglected the weightier matters
3836 2455 2779 3836 464 2779 3836 3248 2779 918 3836 987
d.asn n.asn cj d.asn n.asn cj d.asn n.asn cj v.aai.2p d.apn a.apn.c

τοῦ νόμου, τὴν κρίσιν καὶ τὸ ἔλεος καὶ τὴν πίστιν· ταῦτα δὲ [a] ἔδει
of the law: *{the}* justice and *{the}* mercy and *{the}* faithfulness. These *{and}* ⌞you ought⌟
3836 3795 3836 3213 2779 3836 1799 2779 3836 4411 4047 1254 1256
d.gsm n.gsm d.asf n.asf cj d.asn n.asn cj d.asf n.asf r.apn cj v.iai.3s

ποιῆσαι κἀκεῖνα μὴ ἀφιέναι. 24 → ὁδηγοὶ τυφλοί, οἱ
to have done *former* without neglecting the former. You blind guides! *blind* *{the}*
4472 2797 3590 918 2797 5603 3843 5603 3836
f.aa adv pl f.pa n.vpm a.vpm d.vpm

διϋλίζοντες τὸν κώνωπα, τὴν δὲ κάμηλον καταπίνοντες. 25 οὐαὶ
You strain out the gnat but gulp down the *but* camel! *gulp down* "Woe
1494 3836 3270 1254 2927 2927 3836 1254 2823 2927 4026
pt.pa.vpm d.asm n.asm d.asf cj n.asf pt.pa.vpm j

ὑμῖν, γραμματεῖς καὶ Φαρισαῖοι ὑποκριταί, ὅτι καθαρίζετε τὸ ἔξωθεν τοῦ
to you, scribes and Pharisees, hypocrites, because you clean off the outside of the
7007 1208 2779 5757 5695 4022 2751 3836 2033 3836
r.dp.2 n.vpm cj n.vpm n.vpm cj v.pai.2p d.asn p.g d.gsn

ποτηρίου καὶ τῆς παροψίδος, ἔσωθεν δὲ γέμουσιν ἐξ ἁρπαγῆς καὶ
cup and the plate while inside *while* they are full of greed and
4539 2779 3836 4243 1254 2277 1254 1154 1666 771 2779
n.gsn cj d.gsf n.gsf adv cj v.pai.3p p.g n.gsf cj

ἀκρασίας. 26 → φαρισαῖε τυφλέ, καθάρισον πρῶτον τὸ ἐντὸς τοῦ
self-indulgence. You blind Pharisee! *blind* First clean *First* the inside of the
202 5603 5757 5603 4754 2751 4754 3836 1955 3836
n.gsf n.vsm a.vsm v.aam.2s a.asn d.asn p.g d.gsn

ποτηρίου ἵνα γένηται καὶ τὸ ἐκτὸς αὐτοῦ καθαρόν. 27 οὐαὶ
cup, so that its outside may become clean too. *{the}* *outside* *its* *clean* "Woe
4539 2671 899 1760 1181 2754 2779 3836 1760 899 2754 4026
n.gsn cj v.ams.3s adv d.nsn adv r.gsn.3 a.nsn j

ὑμῖν, γραμματεῖς καὶ Φαρισαῖοι ὑποκριταί, ὅτι παρομοιάζετε τάφοις
to you, scribes and Pharisees, hypocrites, because you are like whitewashed tombs
7007 1208 2779 5757 5695 4022 4234 3154 5439
r.dp.2 n.vpm cj n.vpm n.vpm cj v.pai.2p n.dpm

κεκονιαμένοις, οἵτινες ἔξωθεν μὲν φαίνονται ὡραῖοι, ἔσωθεν
whitewashed that look beautiful on the outside ~ *look* *beautiful* but on the inside
3154 4015 5743 6053 2033 3525 5743 6053 1254 2277
pt.rp.dpm r.npm adv pl v.ppi.3p a.npm adv

δὲ γέμουσιν → ὀστέων νεκρῶν καὶ πάσης ἀκαθαρσίας. 28 οὕτως
but are full of dead men's bones *dead men's* and all kinds of filth. So you
1254 1154 3738 3738 4014 3738 2779 4246 174 4048 7007
cj v.pai.3p n.gpn a.gpm cj a.gsf n.gsf adv

NASB

that sanctifies the
offering? 20 There-
fore, whoever
swears by the altar,
swears *both* by the
altar and by every-
thing on it. 21 And
whoever swears by
the temple, swears
both by the temple
and by Him who
dwells within it.
22 And whoever
swears by heaven,
swears *both* by the
throne of God and
by Him who sits
upon it.
23 "Woe to you,
scribes and Phari-
sees, hypocrites!
For you tithe mint
and dill and cum-
min, and have
neglected the
weightier provi-
sions of the law:
justice and mercy
and faithfulness;
but these are the
things you should
have done without
neglecting the oth-
ers. 24 You blind
guides, who strain
out a gnat and
swallow a camel!
25 "Woe to you,
scribes and Phari-
sees, hypocrites!
For you clean the
outside of the cup
and of the dish,
but inside they are
full of robbery and
self-indulgence.
26 You blind Phari-
see, first clean the
inside of the cup
and of the dish,
so that the outside
of it may become
clean also.
27 "Woe to you,
scribes and Phari-
sees, hypocrites!
For you are like
whitewashed
tombs which on
the outside appear
beautiful, but in-
side they are full of
dead men's bones
and all unclean-
ness. 28 So you, too,

[a] [δὲ] UBS, omitted by NET.

NIV

on the outside you
appear to people
as righteous but on
the inside you are
full of hypocrisy
and wickedness.
29 "Woe to you,
teachers of the law
and Pharisees, you
hypocrites! You
build tombs for the
prophets and dec-
orate the graves
of the righteous.
30 And you say, 'If
we had lived in
the days of our an-
cestors, we would
not have taken
part with them in
shedding the blood
of the prophets.'
31 So you testify
against yourselves
that you are the
descendants of
those who mur-
dered the prophets.
32 Go ahead, then,
and complete what
your ancestors
started!
33 "You snakes!
You brood of vi-
pers! How will
you escape being
condemned to
hell? 34 Therefore
I am sending you
prophets and sages
and teachers.
Some of them you
will kill and cruci-
fy; others you will
flog in your syna-
gogues and pursue
from town to town.
35 And so upon you
will come all the
righteous blood
that has been shed
on earth, from the
blood of righteous
Abel to the blood
of Zechariah son
of Berekiah, whom
you murdered
between the tem-
ple and the altar.
36 Truly I tell you,
all this will come
on this generation.

καὶ ὑμεῖς ἔξωθεν μὲν φαίνεσθε τοῖς ἀνθρώποις δίκαιοι, ἔσωθεν δέ ἐστε
also *you* outwardly ~ appear to others as righteous but within *but* you are
2779 7007 2033 3525 5743 3836 476 1465 1254 2277 1254 1639
adv r.np.2 adv pl v.ppi.2p d.dpm n.dpm a.npm cj adv cj v.pai.2p

μεστοὶ ὑποκρίσεως καὶ ἀνομίας. 29 οὐαὶ ὑμῖν, γραμματεῖς καὶ Φαρισαῖοι
full of hypocrisy and lawlessness. "Woe to you, scribes and Pharisees,
3550 5694 2779 490 4026 7007 1208 2779 5757
a.npm n.gsf cj n.gsf j r.dp.2 n.vpm cj n.vpm

ὑποκριταί, ὅτι οἰκοδομεῖτε τοὺς τάφους τῶν προφητῶν καὶ κοσμεῖτε τὰ μνημεῖα
hypocrites, because you build the tombs of the prophets and decorate the graves
5695 4022 3868 3836 5439 3836 4737 2779 3175 3836 3646
n.vpm cj v.pai.2p d.apm n.apm d.gpm n.gpm cj v.pai.2p d.apn n.apn

τῶν δικαίων, 30 καὶ λέγετε, εἰ ἤμεθα ἐν ταῖς ἡμέραις τῶν πατέρων
of the righteous, and you say, 'If ⌊we had lived⌋ in the days of our fathers,
3836 1465 2779 3306 1623 1639 1877 3836 2465 3836 7005 4252
d.gpm a.gpm cj v.pai.2p cj v.imi.1p p.d d.dpf n.dpf d.gpm n.gpm

ἡμῶν, ↱ οὐκ ἂν ἤμεθα αὐτῶν κοινωνοὶ ἐν τῷ
our we would not *would* have taken part with them *taken part with* in shedding the
7005 1639 323 4024 323 1639 3128 3128 3128 899 3128 1877 3836
r.gp.1 pl pl v.imi.1p r.gpm.3 n.npm p.d d.dsn

αἵματι τῶν προφητῶν. 31 ὥστε μαρτυρεῖτε ἑαυτοῖς ὅτι
blood of the prophets.' ⌊By saying this⌋ you testify against yourselves that you are
135 3836 4737 6063 3455 1571 4022 1639 1639
n.dsn d.gpm n.gpm cj v.pai.2p r.dpm.2 cj

υἱοί ἐστε τῶν φονευσάντων τοὺς προφήτας. 32 καὶ ὑμεῖς πληρώσατε
descendants *you are* of those who murdered the prophets. *then* *{you}* Fill up then
5626 1639 3836 5839 3836 4737 2779 7007 4444 2779
n.npm v.pai.2p d.gpm pt.aa.gpm d.apm n.apm cj r.np.2 v.aam.2p

τὸ μέτρον τῶν πατέρων ὑμῶν. 33 ὄφεις, γεννήματα ἐχιδνῶν, πῶς
the measure of your fathers' *your* guilt. You snakes! You brood of vipers! How
3836 3586 3836 7007 4252 7007 4058 1165 2399 4802
d.asn n.asn d.gpm n.gpm r.gp.2 n.vpm n.vpn n.gpf cj

φύγητε ἀπὸ τῆς κρίσεως τῆς γεέννης; 34 ⌊Διὰ τοῦτο⌋ ἰδοὺ
⌊will you escape⌋ from *{the}* ⌊being condemned to⌋ *{the}* hell? Therefore *{behold}*
5771 608 3836 3213 3836 1147 1328 4047 2627
v.aas.2p p.g d.gsf n.gsf d.gsf n.gsf p.a r.asn j

ἐγὼ ἀποστέλλω πρὸς ὑμᾶς προφήτας καὶ σοφοὺς καὶ γραμματεῖς· ἐξ αὐτῶν
I am sending *{to}* you prophets and wise men and scribes, ⌊some of⌋ whom
1609 690 4639 7007 4737 2779 5055 2779 1208 1666 899
r.ns.1 v.pai.1s p.a r.ap.2 n.apm cj a.apm cj n.apm p.g r.gpm.3

ἀποκτενεῖτε καὶ σταυρώσετε καὶ ἐξ αὐτῶν μαστιγώσετε ἐν ταῖς
you will kill and crucify, and ⌊some of⌋ whom you will flog in *{the}* your
650 2779 5090 2779 1666 899 3463 1877 3836 7007
v.fai.2p cj v.fai.2p cj p.g r.gpm.3 v.fai.2p p.d d.dpf

συναγωγαῖς ὑμῶν καὶ διώξετε ἀπὸ πόλεως εἰς πόλιν· 35 ὅπως ἔλθῃ ἐφ'
synagogues *your* and pursue from town to town, so that upon you will come *upon*
5252 7007 2779 1503 608 4484 1650 4484 3968 2093 7007 2262 2093
n.dpf r.gp.2 cj v.fai.2p p.g n.gsf p.a n.asf cj v.aas.3s p.a

ὑμᾶς πᾶν αἷμα δίκαιον ἐκχυννόμενον ἐπὶ τῆς γῆς ἀπὸ τοῦ αἵματος →
you all the righteous blood *righteous* shed on *{the}* earth, from the blood of
7007 4246 1465 135 1465 1773 2093 3836 1178 608 3836 135
r.ap.2 a.nsn n.nsn a.nsn pt.pp.nsn p.g d.gsf n.gsf p.g d.gsn n.gsn

Ἅβελ τοῦ δικαίου ἕως τοῦ αἵματος Ζαχαρίου υἱοῦ Βαραχίου, ὃν
righteous Abel *{the}* *righteous* to the blood of Zechariah son of Barachiah, whom
1465 6 3836 1465 2401 3836 135 2408 5626 974 4005
n.gsm d.gsm a.gsm p.g d.gsn n.gsn n.gsm n.gsm n.gsm r.asm

ἐφονεύσατε μεταξὺ τοῦ ναοῦ καὶ τοῦ θυσιαστηρίου. 36 ἀμὴν
you murdered between the sanctuary and the altar. I tell you the truth,
5839 3568 3836 3724 2779 3836 2603 3306 3306 7007 297
v.aai.2p p.g d.gsm n.gsm cj d.gsn n.gsn pl

λέγω ὑμῖν, ἥξει ταῦτα πάντα ἐπὶ τὴν γενεὰν ταύτην.
I tell *you* all these things ⌊will come⌋ *these things* *all* upon *{the}* this generation. *this*
3306 7007 4246 4047 4047 2457 4047 4246 2093 3836 4047 1155 4047
v.pai.1s r.dp.2 v.fai.3s r.npn a.npn p.a d.asf n.asf r.asf

NASB

outwardly appear
righteous to men,
but inwardly you
are full of hypoc-
risy and lawless-
ness.
29 "Woe to you,
scribes and Phari-
sees, hypocrites!
For you build
the tombs of the
prophets and adorn
the monuments of
the righteous, 30 and
say, 'If we had
been *living* in the
days of our fathers,
we would not have
been partners with
them in *shedding*
the blood of the
prophets.' 31 So
you testify against
yourselves, that
you are sons of
those who mur-
dered the prophets.
32 Fill up, then,
the measure *of*
the guilt of your
fathers. 33 You ser-
pents, you brood
of vipers, how will
you escape the sen-
tence of hell?
34 "Therefore,
behold, I am send-
ing you prophets
and wise men and
scribes; some of
them you will kill
and crucify, and
some of them you
will scourge in
your synagogues,
and persecute from
city to city, 35 so that
upon you may fall
the guilt of all the
righteous blood
shed on earth, from
the blood of righ-
teous Abel to the
blood of Zechariah,
the son of Bere-
chiah, whom you
murdered between
the temple and the
altar. 36 Truly I say
to you, all these
things will come
upon this genera-
tion.

NIV

37 "Jerusalem, Jerusalem, you who kill the prophets and stone those sent to you, how often I have longed to gather your children together, as a hen gathers her chicks under her wings, and you were not willing.
38 Look, your house is left to you desolate.
39 For I tell you, you will not see me again until you say, 'Blessed is he who comes in the name of the Lord.'[a]"

The Destruction of the Temple and Signs of the End Times

24 Jesus left the temple and was walking away when his disciples came up to him to call his attention to its buildings.
2 "Do you see all these things?" he asked. "Truly I tell you, not one stone here will be left on another; every one will be thrown down."
3 As Jesus was sitting on the Mount of Olives, the disciples came to him privately. "Tell us," they said, "when will this happen, and what will be the sign of your coming and of the end of the age?"
4 Jesus answered: "Watch out that no one deceives you.
5 For many will come in my name, claiming, 'I am

37 Ἰερουσαλὴμ Ἰερουσαλήμ, ↱ ἡ ἀποκτείνουσα τοὺς προφήτας καὶ λιθοβολοῦσα
"Jerusalem, O Jerusalem, you who kill the prophets and stone
2647 2647 650 3836 650 3836 4737 2779 3344
n.vsf n.vsf d.vsf pt.pa.vsf d.apm n.apm cj pt.pa.vsf

τοὺς ἀπεσταλμένους πρὸς αὐτήν, ποσάκις ἠθέλησα ἐπισυναγαγεῖν τὰ τέκνα
those who are sent to you! How often have I wanted to gather *{the}* your children
3836 690 4639 899 4529 2527 2190 3836 5148 5451
d.apm pt.rp.apm p.a r.asf.3 adv v.aai.1s f.aa d.apn n.apn

σου, ↰ ⌊ὃν τρόπον⌋ ὄρνις ἐπισυνάγει τὰ νοσσία αὐτῆς ὑπὸ τὰς
your together as a hen gathers *{the}* her chicks *her* under her
5148 2190 4005 5573 3998 2190 3836 899 3800 899 5679 3836
r.gs.2 r.asm n.asm n.nsf v.pai.3s d.apn n.apn r.gsf.3 p.a d.apf

πτέρυγας, καὶ ↱ ↱ οὐκ ἠθελήσατε. 38 ἰδοὺ ἀφίεται ὑμῖν ὁ οἶκος
wings, but you were not willing! Look, your house is left to you *{the}* *house*
4763 2779 2527 2527 4024 2527 2627 7007 3875 918 7007 3836 3875
n.apf cj pl v.aai.2p j v.ppi.3s r.dp.2 d.nsm n.nsm

ὑμῶν ἔρημος. 39 λέγω γὰρ ὑμῖν, ⌊οὐ μὴ⌋ με ἴδητε ἀπ'
your desolate! For I say *For* to you, you will not see me *you will see* from
7007 2245 1142 3306 1142 7007 1625 1625 4024 3590 1625 1609 1625 608
r.gp.2 a.nsm v.pai.1s cj r.dp.2 pl pl r.as.1 v.aas.2p p.g

ἄρτι ⌊ἕως ἂν⌋ εἴπητε, εὐλογημένος ὁ ἐρχόμενος ἐν ὀνόματι → κυρίου.
now until you say, 'Blessed is he who comes in the name of the Lord.'"
785 2401 323 3306 2328 3836 2262 1877 3950 3261
adv cj pl v.aas.2p pt.rp.nsm d.nsm pt.pm.nsm p.d n.dsn n.gsm

24:1 καὶ → ἐξελθὼν ὁ Ἰησοῦς ἀπὸ τοῦ ἱεροῦ ἐπορεύετο,
{and} When Jesus had left *{the}* *Jesus* *{from}* the temple and ⌊was walking away,⌋
2779 2652 2002 3836 2652 608 3836 2639 4513
cj pt.aa.nsm d.nsm n.nsm p.g d.gsn n.gsn v.imi.3s

καὶ προσῆλθον οἱ μαθηταὶ αὐτοῦ ↰ ἐπιδεῖξαι αὐτῷ ↰ ↰ τὰς
{and} his disciples came *{the}* *disciples* *his* up to call his attention to the
2779 899 3412 4665 3836 3412 899 4665 2109 899 2109 2109 3836
cj v.aai.3p d.npm n.npm r.gsm.3 f.aa r.dsm.3 d.apf

οἰκοδομὰς τοῦ ἱεροῦ. 2 ὁ δὲ ἀποκριθεὶς εἶπεν αὐτοῖς, οὐ βλέπετε
buildings of the temple. And he *And* responded to them, saying, *to them* *not* "You see
3869 3836 2639 1254 3836 1254 646 899 899 3306 899 4024 1063
n.apf d.gsn n.gsn d.nsm cj pt.ap.nsm v.aai.3s r.dpm.3 pl v.pai.2p

ταῦτα πάντα; ἀμὴν λέγω ὑμῖν, ⌊οὐ μὴ⌋
all these things, *all* do you not? I tell you the truth, *I tell* *you* not even one
4246 4047 4246 4024 3306 3306 7007 297 3306 7007 4024 3590
r.apn a.apn pl v.pai.1s r.dp.2 pl pl

ἀφεθῇ ὧδε λίθος ἐπὶ λίθον ὃς ↱ οὐ καταλυθήσεται. 3 →
stone ⌊will be left⌋ here *stone* upon another that will not be thrown down." And when he
3345 918 6045 3345 2093 3345 4005 2907 4024 2907 1254 899
v.aps.3s adv n.nsm p.a n.asm r.nsm pl v.fpi.3s

καθημένου δὲ αὐτοῦ ἐπὶ τοῦ ὄρους τῶν ἐλαιῶν προσῆλθον αὐτῷ οἱ
was seated *And* *he* on the Mount of Olives, the disciples came to him *the*
2764 1254 899 2093 3836 4001 3836 1777 3836 3412 4665 899 3836
pt.pm.gsm cj r.gsm.3 p.g d.gsn n.gsn d.gpf n.gpf v.aai.3p r.dsm.3 d.npm

μαθηταὶ ⌊κατ' ἰδίαν⌋ λέγοντες, εἰπὲ ἡμῖν, πότε ↱ ταῦτα ἔσται καὶ
disciples privately, saying, "Tell us, when are these things ⌊to take place,⌋ and
3412 2848 2625 3306 3306 7005 4537 1639 4047 1639 2779
n.npm p.a a.asf pt.pa.npm v.aam.2s r.dp.1 cj r.npn v.fmi.3s cj

τί τὸ σημεῖον τῆς σῆς παρουσίας καὶ συντελείας τοῦ αἰῶνος; 4 Καὶ
what will be the sign of your coming and the consummation of the age?" And
5515 3836 4956 3836 5050 4242 2779 5333 3836 172 2779
r.nsn d.nsn n.nsn d.gsf r.gsf.2 n.gsf cj n.gsf d.gsm n.gsm cj

ἀποκριθεὶς ὁ Ἰησοῦς εἶπεν αὐτοῖς, βλέπετε μή τις ↱ ὑμᾶς
Jesus answered *{the}* *Jesus* them, saying, *them* "Take care that no one leads you
2652 646 3836 2652 899 3306 899 1063 3590 5516 4414 7007
pt.ap.nsm d.nsm n.nsm v.aai.3s r.dpm.3 v.pam.2p cj r.nsm r.ap.2

πλανήσῃ· 5 πολλοὶ γὰρ ἐλεύσονται ἐπὶ τῷ ὀνόματί μου λέγοντες, ἐγώ εἰμι
astray. For many *For* will come in *{the}* my name, *my* saying, 'I am
4414 1142 4498 1142 2262 2093 3836 1609 3950 1609 3306 1609 1639
v.aas.3s a.npm cj v.fmi.3p p.d d.dsn n.dsn r.gs.1 pt.pa.npm r.ns.1 v.pai.1s

NASB

Lament over Jerusalem

37 "Jerusalem, Jerusalem, who kills the prophets and stones those who are sent to her! How often I wanted to gather your children together, the way a hen gathers her chicks under her wings, and you were unwilling.
38 Behold, your house is being left to you desolate!
39 For I say to you, from now on you will not see Me until you say, 'BLESSED IS HE WHO COMES IN THE NAME OF THE LORD!'"

Signs of Christ's Return

24:1 Jesus came out from the temple and was going away when His disciples came up to point out the temple buildings to Him.
2 And He said to them, "Do you not see all these things? Truly I say to you, not one stone here will be left upon another, which will not be torn down."
3 As He was sitting on the Mount of Olives, the disciples came to Him privately, saying, "Tell us, when will these things happen, and what *will be* the sign of Your coming, and of the end of the age?"
4 And Jesus answered and said to them, "See to it that no one misleads you.
5 For many will come in My name, saying,

[a] 39 Psalm 118:26

NIV

the Messiah,' and will deceive many. [6]You will hear of wars and rumors of wars, but see to it that you are not alarmed. Such things must happen, but the end is still to come. [7]Nation will rise against nation, and kingdom against kingdom. There will be famines and earthquakes in various places. [8]All these are the beginning of birth pains.

[9]"Then you will be handed over to be persecuted and put to death, and you will be hated by all nations because of me. [10]At that time many will turn away from the faith and will betray and hate each other, [11]and many false prophets will appear and deceive many people. [12]Because of the increase of wickedness, the love of most will grow cold, [13]but the one who stands firm to the end will be saved. [14]And this gospel of the kingdom will be preached in the whole world as a testimony to all nations, and then the end will come.

[15]"So when you see standing in the holy place 'the abomination that causes desolation,'[a] spoken of through the prophet Daniel—let the reader understand— [16]then let those who are

[a] 15 Daniel 9:27; 11:31; 12:11

ὁ χριστός, καὶ ↱ ↱ ↱ πολλοὺς πλανήσουσιν. 6 μελλήσετε δὲ ἀκούειν
the Christ,' and they will lead many astray. And you will *And* hear
3836 5986 2779 4414 4414 4414 4498 4414 1254 3516 1254 201
d.nsm n.nsm cj a.apm v.fai.3p v.fai.2p cj f.pa

πολέμους καὶ ἀκοὰς πολέμων· ὁρᾶτε ↱ ↱ μὴ θροεῖσθε· δεῖ γὰρ
of wars and rumors of wars. See that you are not alarmed, for this must *for*
4483 2779 198 4483 3972 2583 2583 3590 2583 1142 1256 1142
n.apm cj n.apf n.gpm v.pam.2p pl v.ppm.2p v.pai.3s cj

γενέσθαι, ἀλλ' οὔπω ἐστὶν τὸ τέλος. 7 ἐγερθήσεται γὰρ ἔθνος
take place but the end is not yet. *is* *the* *end* For nation will rise up *For* *nation*
1181 247 3836 5465 1639 4037 1639 3836 5465 1142 1620 1586 1142 1620
f.am cj adv v.pai.3s d.nsn n.nsn v.fpi.3s cj n.nsn

ἐπὶ ἔθνος καὶ βασιλεία ἐπὶ βασιλείαν καὶ ἔσονται λιμοὶ καὶ σεισμοὶ
against nation and kingdom against kingdom, and ⌞there will be⌟ famines and earthquakes
2093 1620 2779 993 2093 993 2779 1639 3350 2779 4939
p.a n.asn cj n.nsf p.a n.asf cj v.fmi.3p n.npf cj n.npm

κατὰ τόπους· 8 πάντα δὲ ταῦτα ἀρχὴ ὠδίνων. 9 τότε
in various places. But all *But* these things are only the beginning of birth pangs. Then
2848 5536 1254 4246 1254 4047 794 6047 5538
p.a n.apm a.npn cj r.npn n.nsf n.gpf adv

παραδώσουσιν ὑμᾶς ↰ εἰς θλῖψιν καὶ ἀποκτενοῦσιν ὑμᾶς, καὶ ἔσεσθε
they will hand you over to be persecuted and will kill you, and ⌞you will be⌟
4140 7007 4140 1650 2568 2779 650 7007 2779 1639
v.fai.3p r.ap.2 p.a n.asf cj v.fai.3p r.ap.2 cj v.fmi.2p

μισούμενοι ὑπὸ πάντων τῶν ἐθνῶν διὰ τὸ ὄνομά μου. 10 καὶ τότε
hated by all *{the}* nations ⌞because of⌟ *{the}* my name. *my* *{and}* ⌞At that time⌟
3631 5679 4246 3836 1620 1328 3836 1609 3950 1609 2779 5538
pt.pp.npm p.g a.gpn d.gpn n.gpn p.a d.asn n.asn r.gs.1 cj adv

σκανδαλισθήσονται πολλοὶ καὶ ἀλλήλους παραδώσουσιν καὶ
many will fall away *many* and will betray one another *will betray* and
4498 4997 4498 2779 4140 4140 253 4140 2779
v.fpi.3p a.npm cj r.apm v.fai.3p cj

μισήσουσιν ἀλλήλους· 11 καὶ πολλοὶ ψευδοπροφῆται ἐγερθήσονται καὶ πλανήσουσιν
hate one another. And many false prophets will arise and lead
3631 253 2779 4498 6021 1586 2779 4414
v.fai.3p r.apm cj a.npm n.npm v.fpi.3p cj v.fai.3p

πολλούς· ↰ 12 καὶ διὰ τὸ πληθυνθῆναι τὴν ἀνομίαν
many astray; and because ~ lawlessness will be increased, *{the}* *lawlessness* the love
4498 4414 2779 1328 3836 490 4437 3836 490 3836 27
a.apm cj p.a d.asn n.asn f.ap d.asf n.asf

ψυγήσεται ἡ ἀγάπη τῶν πολλῶν. 13 ὁ δὲ ὑπομείνας εἰς
of many will grow cold. *the* *love* *of* *many* But the *But* one who endures to
3836 4498 6038 3836 27 3836 4498 1254 3836 1254 5702 1650
v.fpi.3s d.nsf n.nsf d.gpm a.gpm d.nsm cj pt.aa.nsm p.a

τέλος οὗτος σωθήσεται. 14 καὶ κηρυχθήσεται τοῦτο τὸ εὐαγγέλιον τῆς
the end *{this one}* will be saved. And *will be proclaimed* this *{the}* gospel of the
5465 4047 5392 2779 3062 4047 3836 2295 3836
n.asn r.nsm v.fpi.3s cj v.fpi.3s r.nsn d.nsn n.nsn d.gsf

βασιλείας ἐν ὅλῃ τῇ οἰκουμένῃ εἰς μαρτύριον πᾶσιν τοῖς
kingdom will be proclaimed in all the world as a testimony to every *{the}*
993 3062 3062 3062 1877 3910 3836 3876 1650 3457 4246 3836
n.gsf p.d a.dsf d.dsf n.dsf p.a n.asn a.dpn d.dpn

ἔθνεσιν, καὶ τότε ἥξει τὸ τέλος. 15 ὅταν οὖν ἴδητε τὸ
nation, and then the end ⌞will come.⌟ *the* *end* "Therefore when *Therefore* you see the
1620 2779 5538 3836 5465 2457 3836 5465 4036 4020 4036 1625 3836
n.dpn cj adv v.fai.3s d.nsn n.nsn cj cj v.aas.2p d.asn

βδέλυγμα τῆς ἐρημώσεως τὸ ῥηθὲν διὰ Δανιὴλ τοῦ προφήτου
'abomination of desolation' *{the}* ⌞spoken of⌟ by the prophet Daniel, *the* *prophet*
1007 3836 2247 3836 3306 1328 3836 4737 1248 3836 4737
n.asn d.gsf n.gsf d.asn pt.ap.asn p.g n.gsm d.gsm n.gsm

ἑστὸς ἐν τόπῳ ἁγίῳ, ↱ ὁ ἀναγινώσκων νοείτω, 16 τότε οἱ
standing in the holy place *holy* (let the reader understand), then those who are
2705 1877 41 5536 41 3783 3836 336 3783 5538 3836
pt.ra.asn p.d n.dsm a.dsm d.nsm pt.pa.nsm v.pam.3s adv d.npm

NASB

'I am the Christ,' and will mislead many. [6]You will be hearing of wars and rumors of wars. See that you are not frightened, for *those things* must take place, but *that* is not yet the end. [7]For nation will rise against nation, and kingdom against kingdom, and in various places there will be famines and earthquakes. [8]But all these things are *merely* the beginning of birth pangs.

[9]"Then they will deliver you to tribulation, and will kill you, and you will be hated by all nations because of My name. [10]At that time many will fall away and will betray one another and hate one another. [11]Many false prophets will arise and will mislead many. [12]Because lawlessness is increased, most people's love will grow cold. [13]But the one who endures to the end, he will be saved. [14]This gospel of the kingdom shall be preached in the whole world as a testimony to all the nations, and then the end will come.

Perilous Times

[15]"Therefore when you see the ABOMINATION OF DESOLATION which was spoken of through Daniel the prophet, standing in the holy place (let the reader understand), [16]then those who

NIV

in Judea flee to
the mountains.
17 Let no one on the
housetop go down
to take anything
out of the house.
18 Let no one in the
field go back to get
their cloak. 19 How
dreadful it will be
in those days for
pregnant women
and nursing moth-
ers! 20 Pray that
your flight will
not take place in
winter or on the
Sabbath. 21 For
then there will be
great distress, un-
equaled from the
beginning of the
world until now—
and never to be
equaled again.
22 "If those days
had not been cut
short, no one
would survive, but
for the sake of the
elect those days
will be shortened.
23 At that time if
anyone says to
you, 'Look, here is
the Messiah!' or,
'There he is!' do
not believe it. 24 For
false messiahs and
false prophets will
appear and per-
form great signs
and wonders to
deceive, if possi-
ble, even the elect.
25 See, I have told
you ahead of time.
26 "So if anyone
tells you, 'There
he is, out in the
wilderness,' do not
go out; or, 'Here
he is, in the inner
rooms,' do not be-
lieve it. 27 For as

ἐν τῇ Ἰουδαίᾳ φευγέτωσαν εἰς τὰ ὄρη, 17 ὁ ἐπὶ τοῦ δώματος ↱
in {the} Judea must flee to the mountains, the one on the housetop must
1877 3836 2677 5771 1650 3836 4001 3836 2093 3836 1560 2849
p.d d.dsf n.dsf v.pam.3p p.a d.apn n.apn d.nsm p.g d.gsn n.gsn

μὴ καταβάτω ἆραι τὰ ἐκ τῆς οἰκίας αὐτοῦ, 18 καὶ ὁ ἐν τῷ
not go down ⌊to gather up⌋ what is in {the} his house, his and the one in the
3590 2849 149 3836 1666 3836 899 3864 899 2779 3836 1877 3836
pl v.aam.3s f.aa d.apn p.g d.gsf n.gsf r.gsm.3 cj d.nsm p.d d.dsm

ἀγρῷ ↱ μὴ ἐπιστρεψάτω ὀπίσω ἆραι τὸ ἱμάτιον αὐτοῦ. 19 οὐαὶ δὲ
field must not go back ⌊to pick up⌋ {the} his coat. his But woe But
69 2188 3590 2188 3958 149 3836 899 2668 899 1254 4026 1254
n.dsm pl v.aam.3s adv f.aa d.asn n.asn r.gsm.3 j cj

ταῖς ⌊ἐν γαστρὶ⌋ ἐχούσαις καὶ ταῖς
to women who are pregnant women who are and to
3836 2400 2400 2400 1877 1143 2400 2779 3836
d.dpf p.d n.dsf pt.pa.dpf cj d.dpf

θηλαζούσαις ἐν ἐκείναις ταῖς ἡμέραις. 20 προσεύχεσθε δὲ ἵνα
⌊mothers who are nursing babies⌋ in those {the} days! And pray And that
2558 1877 1697 3836 2465 1254 4667 1254 2671
pt.pa.dpf p.d r.dpf d.dpf n.dpf v.pmm.2p cj cj

↱ μὴ γένηται ἡ φυγὴ ὑμῶν χειμῶνος μηδὲ → σαββάτῳ. 21
your flight will not be {the} flight your in winter or on a Sabbath. For then
7007 5870 1181 3590 1181 3836 5870 7007 5930 3593 4879 1142 5538
pl v.ams.3s d.nsf n.nsf r.gp.2 n.gsm cj n.dsn

ἔσται γὰρ τότε θλῖψις μεγάλη οἵα ↱ οὐ γέγονεν ἀπ᾽ ἀρχῆς →
⌊there will be⌋ For then great suffering, great ⌊such as⌋ has not been from the beginning of
1639 1142 5538 3489 2568 3489 3888 1181 4024 1181 608 794
v.fmi.3s cj adv n.nsf a.nsf r.nsf pl v.rai.3s p.g n.gsf

κόσμου ἕως τοῦ νῦν οὐδ᾽ ↱ ⌊οὐ μὴ⌋ γένηται. ↰ 22 καὶ ⌊εἰ μὴ⌋
the world until {the} now, and will never be again. And unless those days
3180 2401 3836 3814 4028 1181 4024 3590 1181 4024 2779 1623 3590 1697 2465
n.gsm p.g d.gsn adv cj pl pl v.ams.3s cj cj pl

ἐκολοβώθησαν αἱ ἡμέραι ἐκεῖναι, οὐκ ἂν ἐσώθη πᾶσα σάρξ·
were shortened, {the} days those no human being would survive. {every} human being But
3143 3836 2465 1697 4024 4922 4922 323 5392 4246 4922 1254
v.api.3p d.npf n.npf r.npf pl pl v.api.3s a.nsf n.nsf

διὰ δὲ τοὺς ἐκλεκτοὺς κολοβωθήσονται αἱ ἡμέραι ἐκεῖναι.
⌊for the sake of⌋ But the elect those days will be shortened. {the} days those
1328 1254 3836 1723 1697 2465 3143 3836 2465 1697
p.a cj d.apm a.apm v.fpi.3p d.npf n.npf r.npf

23 τότε ἐάν τις ὑμῖν εἴπῃ, ἰδοὺ ὧδε ὁ χριστός, ἤ, ὧδε, ↱
Then if anyone says to you, says 'Look, here is the Christ!' or, 'There he is!' Do
5538 1569 5516 3306 7007 3306 2627 6045 3836 5986 2445 6045 4409
adv cj r.nsm r.dp.2 v.aas.3s j adv d.nsm n.nsm cj adv

μὴ πιστεύσητε· 24 ἐγερθήσονται γὰρ ψευδόχριστοι καὶ ψευδοπροφῆται
not believe him. will appear For false messiahs and false prophets will
3590 4409 1586 1142 6023 2779 6021 1586
pl v.aas.2p v.fpi.3p cj n.npm cj n.npm

καὶ δώσουσιν σημεῖα μεγάλα καὶ τέρατα ὥστε πλανῆσαι, εἰ
appear, and they will perform great signs great and wonders so as to lead astray, if that
1586 2779 1443 3489 4956 3489 2779 5469 6063 4414 1623
cj v.fai.3p n.apn a.apn cj n.apn cj f.aa cj

δυνατόν, καὶ τοὺς ἐκλεκτούς. 25 ἰδοὺ προείρηκα ὑμῖν. ↰ ↰
were possible, even the elect. ⌊Mark well,⌋ I have warned you in advance.
1543 2779 3836 1723 2627 4597 7007 4597 4597
a.nsn adv d.apm a.apm j v.rai.1s r.dp.2

26 ἐὰν οὖν εἴπωσιν ὑμῖν, ἰδοὺ ἐν τῇ ἐρήμῳ ἐστίν, ↱ μὴ
So, if So they say to you, 'There he is, out in the wilderness!' he is do not
4036 1569 4036 3306 7007 2627 1639 1639 1877 3836 2245 1639 2002 3590
cj cj v.aas.3p r.dp.2 j p.d d.dsf n.dsf v.pai.3s pl

ἐξέλθητε· ἰδοὺ ἐν τοῖς ταμείοις, ↱ μὴ πιστεύσητε· 27 ὥσπερ γὰρ
go out; or, 'Here he is, in the inner rooms!' do not believe it. For as For
2002 2627 1877 3836 5421 4409 3590 4409 1142 6061 1142
v.aas.2p j p.d d.dpn n.dpn pl v.aas.2p cj cj

NASB

are in Judea must
flee to the moun-
tains. 17 Whoever
is on the housetop
must not go down
to get the things
out that are in his
house. 18 Whoever
is in the field must
not turn back to
get his cloak. 19 But
woe to those who
are pregnant and
to those who are
nursing babies in
those days! 20 But
pray that your
flight will not be
in the winter, or
on a Sabbath. 21 For
then there will be
a great tribula-
tion, such as has
not occurred since
the beginning of
the world until
now, nor ever will.
22 Unless those
days had been
cut short, no life
would have been
saved; but for the
sake of the elect
those days will be
cut short. 23 Then
if anyone says to
you, 'Behold, here
is the Christ,' or
'There *He is,*' do
not believe *him.*
24 For false Christs
and false prophets
will arise and will
show great signs
and wonders, so
as to mislead, if
possible, even the
elect. 25 Behold, I
have told you in
advance. 26 So if
they say to you,
'Behold, He is in
the wilderness,' do
not go out, *or,* 'Be-
hold, He is in the
inner rooms,' do
not believe *them.*
27 For just as the

NIV

lightning that
comes from the
east is visible even
in the west, so will
be the coming of
the Son of Man.
28 Wherever there
is a carcass, there
the vultures will
gather.
29 "Immediately
after the distress of
those days

"'the sun will be
darkened,
and the moon
will not give
its light;
the stars will fall
from the sky,
and the
heavenly
bodies will
be shaken.'[a]

30 "Then will ap-
pear the sign of
the Son of Man
in heaven. And
then all the peo-
ples of the earth[b]
will mourn when
they see the Son
of Man coming on
the clouds of heav-
en, with power
and great glory.[c]
31 And he will send
his angels with a
loud trumpet call,
and they will gath-
er his elect from
the four winds,
from one end of
the heavens to the
other.
32 "Now learn this
lesson from the fig
tree: As soon as
its twigs get ten-
der and its leaves
come out, you
know that summer
is near. 33 Even so,
when you see all
these things, you
know that it[d] is
near, right at the
door. 34 Truly I tell
you, this genera-
tion will certainly
not pass away until

ἡ ἀστραπὴ ἐξέρχεται ἀπὸ ἀνατολῶν καὶ φαίνεται ἕως δυσμῶν, οὕτως ἔσται
the lightning comes from the east and flashes to the west, so will
3836 847 2002 608 424 2779 5743 2401 1553 4048 1639
d.nsf n.nsf v.pmi.3s p.g n.gpf cj v.ppi.3s p.g n.gpf adv v.fmi.3s

ἡ παρουσία τοῦ υἱοῦ τοῦ ἀνθρώπου· ↰ 28 ⌊ὅπου ἐὰν⌋ ᾖ τὸ
the coming of the Son of Man be. Wherever the corpse is, *the*
3836 4242 3836 5626 3836 476 1639 3963 1569 3836 4773 1639 3836
d.nsf n.nsf d.gsm n.gsm d.gsm n.gsm cj pl v.pas.3s d.nsn

πτῶμα, ἐκεῖ συναχθήσονται οἱ ἀετοί. 29 εὐθέως δὲ μετὰ τὴν
corpse there the vultures will gather. *the vultures* "Immediately *{and}* after the
4773 1695 3836 108 5251 3836 108 2311 1254 3552 3836
n.nsn adv v.fpi.3p d.npm n.npm adv cj p.a d.asf

θλῖψιν τῶν ἡμερῶν ἐκείνων ὁ ἥλιος σκοτισθήσεται, καὶ ἡ σελήνη ↱ οὐ
suffering of those days, *those* the sun will be darkened and the moon will not
2568 3836 1697 2465 1697 3836 2463 5029 2779 3836 4943 1443 4024
n.asf d.gpf n.gpf r.gpf d.nsm n.nsm v.fpi.3s cj d.nsf n.nsf pl

δώσει τὸ φέγγος αὐτῆς, καὶ οἱ ἀστέρες πεσοῦνται ἀπὸ τοῦ οὐρανοῦ, καὶ αἱ
give *{the}* its light, *its* and the stars will fall from the sky and the
1443 3836 899 5766 899 2779 3836 843 4406 608 3836 4041 2779 3836
v.fai.3s d.asn n.asn r.gsf.3 cj d.npm n.npm v.fmi.3p p.g d.gsm n.gsm cj d.npf

δυνάμεις τῶν οὐρανῶν σαλευθήσονται. 30 καὶ τότε φανήσεται τὸ σημεῖον τοῦ
powers of the heavens will be shaken. And then *will appear* the sign of the
1539 3836 4041 4888 2779 5538 5743 3836 4956 3836
n.npf d.gpm n.gpm v.fpi.3p cj adv v.fpi.3s d.nsn n.nsn d.gsm

υἱοῦ τοῦ ἀνθρώπου ἐν οὐρανῷ, καὶ τότε κόψονται πᾶσαι αἱ φυλαὶ
Son of Man will appear in the sky, and then *will mourn* all the tribes
5626 3836 476 5743 5743 1877 4041 2779 5538 3164 4246 3836 5876
n.gsm d.gsm n.gsm p.d n.dsm cj adv v.fmi.3p a.npf d.npf n.npf

τῆς γῆς καὶ ὄψονται τὸν υἱὸν τοῦ ἀνθρώπου ἐρχόμενον ἐπὶ τῶν
of the earth will mourn, and ⌊they will see⌋ the Son of Man coming on the
3836 1178 3164 3164 2779 3972 3836 5626 3836 476 2262 2093 3836
d.gsf n.gsf cj v.fmi.3p d.asm n.asm d.gsm n.gsm pt.pm.asm p.g d.gpf

νεφελῶν τοῦ οὐρανοῦ μετὰ δυνάμεως καὶ δόξης πολλῆς· 31 καὶ ἀποστελεῖ τοὺς
clouds of the sky with power and great glory. *great* And he will send *{the}*
3749 3836 4041 3552 1539 2779 4498 1518 4498 2779 690 3836
n.gpf d.gsm n.gsm p.g n.gsf cj n.gsf a.gsf cj v.fai.3s d.apm

ἀγγέλους αὐτοῦ μετὰ σάλπιγγος μεγάλης, καὶ ἐπισυνάξουσιν τοὺς
his angels *his* with a loud trumpet call, *loud* and they will gather *{the}* his
899 34 899 3552 3489 4894 3489 2779 2190 3836 899
n.apm r.gsm.3 p.g n.gsf a.gsf cj v.fai.3p d.apm

ἐκλεκτοὺς αὐτοῦ ἐκ τῶν τεσσάρων ἀνέμων ἀπ' ἄκρων → οὐρανῶν ἕως τῶν[a]
elect *his* from the four winds, from one end of the heavens to the
1723 899 1666 3836 5475 449 608 216 4041 2401 3836
a.apm r.gsm.3 p.g d.gpm a.gpm n.gpm p.g n.gpn n.gpm p.g d.gpn

ἄκρων αὐτῶν. 32 ἀπὸ δὲ τῆς συκῆς μάθετε τὴν παραβολήν·
other. *{their}* "Learn this parable from *{and}* the fig tree: *Learn this parable*
216 899 3443 3836 4130 608 1254 3836 5190 3443 3836 4130
n.gpn r.gpm.3 p.g cj d.gsf n.gsf v.aam.2p d.asf n.asf

⌊ὅταν ἤδη⌋ ὁ κλάδος αὐτῆς γένηται ἁπαλὸς καὶ τὰ φύλλα ἐκφύῃ,
as soon as *{the}* its branch *its* becomes tender and puts out its leaves, *puts out*
4020 2453 3836 899 3080 899 1181 559 2779 1770 1770 3836 5877 1770
cj adv d.nsm n.nsm r.gsf.3 v.ams.3s a.nsm cj d.apn n.apn v.pas.3s

γινώσκετε ὅτι ἐγγὺς τὸ θέρος· 33 οὕτως καὶ ὑμεῖς, ὅταν ἴδητε πάντα
you know that summer is near. *{the} summer* So also, when you *when* see all
1182 4022 2550 1584 3836 2550 4048 2779 4020 7007 4020 1625 4246
v.pai.2p cj adv d.nsn n.nsn adv adv r.np.2 cj v.aas.2p a.apn

ταῦτα, γινώσκετε ὅτι ἐγγύς ἐστιν ἐπὶ θύραις. 34
these things, you know that it is near, *it is* at the very door. I tell you
4047 1182 4022 1639 1639 1584 1639 2093 2598 3306 3306 7007
r.apn v.pai.2p cj adv v.pai.3s p.d n.dpf

ἀμὴν λέγω ὑμῖν ὅτι ↱ ⌊οὐ μὴ⌋ παρέλθῃ ἡ γενεὰ αὕτη ⌊ἕως
the truth, *I tell you {that}* this generation will not pass away *{the} generation this* until
297 3306 7007 4022 4047 1155 4216 4024 3590 4216 3836 1155 4047 2401
pl v.pai.1s r.dp.2 cj pl pl v.aas.3s d.nsf n.nsf r.nsf cj

[a] [τῶν] UBS.

NASB

lightning comes
from the east and
flashes even to the
west, so will the
coming of the Son
of Man be. 28 Wher-
ever the corpse is,
there the vultures
will gather.

The Glorious Return

29 "But imme-
diately after the
tribulation of those
days THE SUN WILL
BE DARKENED, AND
THE MOON WILL NOT
GIVE ITS LIGHT, AND
THE STARS WILL FALL
from the sky, and
the powers of the
heavens will be
shaken. 30 And then
the sign of the Son
of Man will appear
in the sky, and
then all the tribes
of the earth will
mourn, and they
will see the SON
OF MAN COMING ON
THE CLOUDS OF THE
SKY with power and
great glory. 31 And
He will send forth
His angels with A
GREAT TRUMPET and
THEY WILL GATHER
TOGETHER His elect
from the four
winds, from one
end of the sky to
the other.

Parable of the Fig Tree

32 "Now learn the
parable from the
fig tree: when its
branch has already
become tender
and puts forth its
leaves, you know
that summer is
near; 33 so, you
too, when you see
all these things,
recognize that He
is near, *right* at the
door. 34 Truly I say
to you, this genera-
tion will not pass
away until all these

[a] 29 Isaiah 13:10; 34:4
[b] 30 Or *the tribes of the land*
[c] 30 See Daniel 7:13-14.
[d] 33 Or *he*

NIV

all these things
have happened.
35 Heaven and earth
will pass away,
but my words will
never pass away.

The Day and Hour Unknown

36 "But about that
day or hour no one
knows, not even
the angels in heav-
en, nor the Son,[a]
but only the Fa-
ther. 37 As it was in
the days of Noah,
so it will be at the
coming of the Son
of Man. 38 For in
the days before
the flood, people
were eating and
drinking, marry-
ing and giving in
marriage, up to
the day Noah en-
tered the ark; 39 and
they knew nothing
about what would
happen until the
flood came and
took them all
away. That is how
it will be at the
coming of the Son
of Man. 40 Two men
will be in the field;
one will be taken
and the other left.
41 Two women will
be grinding with a
hand mill; one will
be taken and the
other left.
42 "Therefore keep
watch, because
you do not know
on what day your
Lord will come.
43 But understand
this: If the owner
of the house had
known at what
time of night the
thief was coming,
he would have kept
watch and would
not have let his
house be broken
into.

[a] 36 Some manuscripts do not have *nor the Son.*

ἂν⌋ πάντα ταῦτα γένηται. 35 ὁ οὐρανὸς καὶ ἡ γῆ παρελεύσεται, οἱ δὲ
all these things take place. *{the}* Heaven and *{the}* earth will pass away, *{the}* but
323 4246 4047 1181 3836 4041 2779 3836 1178 4216 3836 1254
pl a.npn r.npn v.ams.3s d.nsm n.nsm cj d.nsf n.nsf v.fmi.3s d.npm cj

λόγοι μου ↱ ⌊οὐ μὴ⌋ παρέλθωσιν. 36 περὶ δὲ τῆς ἡμέρας
my words *my* will never pass away. "But concerning *But* *{the}* that day
1609 3364 1609 4216 4024 3590 4216 1254 4309 1254 3836 1697 2465
n.npm r.gs.1 pl pl v.aas.3p p.g cj d.gsf n.gsf

ἐκείνης καὶ ὥρας οὐδεὶς οἶδεν, οὐδὲ οἱ ἄγγελοι τῶν οὐρανῶν οὐδὲ ὁ υἱός,[a]
that and hour, no one knows, neither the angels of heaven nor the Son,
1697 2779 6052 4029 3857 4028 3836 34 3836 4041 4028 3836 5626
r.gsf cj n.gsf a.nsm v.rai.3s adv d.npm n.npm d.gpm n.gpm adv d.nsm n.nsm

⌊εἰ μὴ⌋ ὁ πατὴρ μόνος. 37 ὥσπερ γὰρ αἱ ἡμέραι τοῦ Νῶε, οὕτως ἔσται ἡ
but the Father only. For as were *For* the days of Noah, so will be the
1623 3590 3836 4252 3668 1142 6061 1142 3836 2465 3836 3820 4048 1639 3836
cj pl d.nsm n.nsm a.nsm cj cj d.npf n.npf d.gsm n.gsm adv v.fmi.3s d.nsf

παρουσία τοῦ υἱοῦ τοῦ ἀνθρώπου. 38 ὡς γὰρ ἦσαν ἐν ταῖς ἡμέραις[b] ταῖς
coming of the Son of Man. For as *For* *were* in the days *{the}*
4242 3836 5626 3836 476 1142 6055 1142 1639 1877 3836 2465 3836
n.nsf d.gsm n.gsm d.gsm n.gsm cj cj v.iai.3p p.d d.dpf n.dpf d.dpf

πρὸ τοῦ κατακλυσμοῦ τρώγοντες καὶ πίνοντες, γαμοῦντες καὶ
before the flood people were eating and drinking, marrying and
4574 3836 2886 1639 5592 2779 4403 1138 2779
p.g d.gsm n.gsm pt.pa.npm cj pt.pa.npm pt.pa.npm cj

γαμίζοντες, ἄχρι ἧς ἡμέρας εἰσῆλθεν Νῶε εἰς τὴν κιβωτόν, 39 καὶ
giving in marriage, until the day Noah entered *Noah* *{into}* the ark, and they
1139 948 4005 2465 3820 1656 3820 1650 3836 3066 2779 1182
pt.pa.npm p.g r.gsf n.gsf v.aai.3s n.nsm p.a d.asf n.asf cj

οὐκ ἔγνωσαν ἕως ἦλθεν ὁ κατακλυσμὸς καὶ ἦρεν ἅπαντας, ↰
knew nothing *they knew* until the flood came *the* *flood* and took them all away,
1182 4024 1182 2401 3836 2886 2262 3836 2886 2779 149 570 149
pl v.aai.3p cj v.aai.3s d.nsm n.nsm cj v.aai.3s a.apm

οὕτως ἔσται καὶ[c] ἡ παρουσία τοῦ υἱοῦ τοῦ ἀνθρώπου. ↰ 40 τότε
so will *{also}* the coming of the Son of Man be. ⌊At that time⌋
4048 1639 2779 3836 4242 3836 5626 3836 476 1639 5538
adv v.fmi.3s adv d.nsf n.nsf d.gsm n.gsm d.gsm n.gsm adv

δύο ἔσονται ἐν τῷ ἀγρῷ, εἷς παραλαμβάνεται καὶ εἷς ἀφίεται·
⌊two men⌋ will be in the field; one will be taken and the other left.
1545 1639 1877 3836 69 1651 4161 2779 1651 918
a.npm v.fmi.3p p.d d.dsm n.dsm a.nsm v.ppi.3s cj a.nsm v.ppi.3s

41 δύο ἀλήθουσαι ἐν τῷ μύλῳ, μία παραλαμβάνεται καὶ μία ἀφίεται.
⌊Two women⌋ will be grinding at the mill; one will be taken and the other left.
1545 241 1877 3836 3685 1651 4161 2779 1651 918
a.npf pt.pa.npf p.d d.dsm n.dsm a.nsf v.ppi.3s cj a.nsf v.ppi.3s

42 γρηγορεῖτε οὖν, ὅτι ↱ ↱ οὐκ οἴδατε ποίᾳ ἡμέρᾳ ὁ
Therefore be alert, *Therefore* because you do not know on what day *{the}* your
4036 1213 4036 4022 3857 3857 4024 3857 4481 2465 3836 7007
v.pam.2p cj cj pl v.rai.2p r.dsf n.dsf d.nsm

κύριος ὑμῶν ἔρχεται. 43 ἐκεῖνο δὲ γινώσκετε ὅτι εἰ ᾔδει ὁ
Lord *your* will come. But understand this: *But* *understand* *{that}* if *had known* the
3261 7007 2262 1254 1182 1697 1254 1182 4022 1623 3857 3836
n.nsm r.gp.2 v.pmi.3s r.asn cj v.pam.2p cj cj v.lai.3s d.nsm

οἰκοδεσπότης ποίᾳ φυλακῇ ὁ κλέπτης ἔρχεται, →
owner of the house had known ⌊at what time⌋ of night the thief was coming, he would
3867 3857 3857 4481 5871 3836 3095 2262 323
n.nsm r.dsf n.dsf d.nsm n.nsm v.pmi.3s

ἐγρηγόρησεν ἂν καὶ οὐκ ἂν εἴασεν διορυχθῆναι τὴν
⌊have been on the alert⌋ *would* and would not *would* have allowed his house to be broken into. *{the}*
1213 323 2779 323 4024 323 1572 899 3864 1482 3836
v.aai.3s pl cj pl pl v.aai.3s f.ap d.asf

[a] οὐδὲ ὁ υἱός omitted by NET.
[b] ἐκείναις included by UBS, NET after ἡμέραις.
[c] [καὶ] UBS, omitted by TNIV.

NASB

things take place.
35 Heaven and earth
will pass away, but
My words will not
pass away.
36 "But of that
day and hour no
one knows, not
even the angels
of heaven, nor the
Son, but the Father
alone. 37 For the
coming of the Son
of Man will be just
like the days of
Noah. 38 For as in
those days before
the flood they were
eating and drink-
ing, marrying and
giving in marriage,
until the day that
Noah entered the
ark, 39 and they did
not understand un-
til the flood came
and took them all
away; so will the
coming of the Son
of Man be. 40 Then
there will be two
men in the field;
one will be taken
and one will be
left. 41 Two women
will be grinding at
the mill; one will
be taken and one
will be left.

Be Ready for His Coming

42 "Therefore be on
the alert, for you
do not know which
day your Lord is
coming. 43 But be
sure of this, that
if the head of the
house had known
at what time of the
night the thief was
coming, he would
have been on the
alert and would not
have allowed his
house to be broken

NIV

[44]So you also must
be ready, because
the Son of Man
will come at an
hour when you do
not expect him.
[45]"Who then is
the faithful and
wise servant,
whom the master
has put in charge
of the servants in
his household to
give them their
food at the proper
time? [46]It will be
good for that ser-
vant whose master
finds him doing so
when he returns.
[47]Truly I tell you,
he will put him in
charge of all his
possessions. [48]But
suppose that ser-
vant is wicked and
says to himself,
'My master is stay-
ing away a long
time,' [49]and he
then begins to beat
his fellow servants
and to eat and
drink with drunk-
ards. [50]The master
of that servant
will come on a day
when he does not
expect him and at
an hour he is not
aware of. [51]He will
cut him to pieces
and assign him
a place with the
hypocrites, where
there will be weep-
ing and gnashing
of teeth.

The Parable of the Ten Virgins

25 "At that
time the
kingdom of heaven
will be like

οἰκίαν αὐτοῦ. 44 διὰ τοῦτο καὶ ὑμεῖς γίνεσθε ἕτοιμοι, ὅτι
house his For this reason you also *you* must be ready, because the Son of
3864 899 1328 4047 7007 2779 7007 1181 2289 4022 3836 5626 3836
n.asf r.gsm.3 p.a r.asn adv r.np.2 v.pmm.2p a.npm cj

ᾗ ↱ ↱ οὐ δοκεῖτε ὥρᾳ ὁ υἱὸς τοῦ ἀνθρώπου ἔρχεται.
Man will come at an hour you do not expect. *hour the Son of Man will come*
476 2262 2262 4005 6052 1506 1506 4024 1506 6052 3836 5626 3836 476 2262
r.dsf pl v.pai.2p n.dsf d.nsm n.nsm d.gsm n.gsm v.pmi.3s

45 τίς ἄρα ἐστὶν ὁ πιστὸς δοῦλος καὶ φρόνιμος ὃν
"Who then is the faithful and wise servant *and wise* whom his master
5515 726 1639 3836 4412 2779 5861 1529 2779 5861 4005 3836 3261
r.nsm cj v.pai.3s d.nsm a.nsm n.nsm cj a.nsm r.asm

κατέστησεν ὁ κύριος ἐπὶ τῆς οἰκετείας αὐτοῦ τοῦ δοῦναι αὐτοῖς
has put in charge *his master* of *{the}* his household *his* to give other servants
2770 3836 3261 2093 3836 899 3859 899 3836 1443 899
v.aai.3s d.nsm n.nsm p.g d.gsf n.gsf r.gsm.3 d.gsn f.aa r.dpm.3

τὴν τροφὴν ἐν καιρῷ; 46 μακάριος ὁ δοῦλος ἐκεῖνος ὃν
their food at the proper time? Blessed is *{the}* that servant *that* whom
3836 5575 1877 2789 3421 3836 1697 1529 1697 4005
d.asf n.asf p.d n.dsm a.nsm d.nsm n.nsm r.nsm r.asm

ἐλθὼν ὁ κύριος αὐτοῦ εὑρήσει οὕτως ποιοῦντα·
when he returns {the} his master *his* will find so doing when he returns.
2262 3836 899 3261 899 2351 4048 4472 2262 2262 2262
pt.aa.nsm d.nsm n.nsm r.gsm.3 v.fai.3s adv pt.pa.asm

47 ἀμὴν λέγω ὑμῖν ὅτι ἐπὶ πᾶσιν
I tell you the truth, *I tell you {that}* he will put that servant in charge of all
3306 3306 7007 297 3306 7007 4022 2770 2770 2770 899 899 2770 2770 2093 4246
pl v.pai.1s r.dp.2 cj p.d a.dpn

τοῖς ὑπάρχουσιν αὐτοῦ καταστήσει αὐτόν. 48 ἐὰν δὲ
{the} his possessions. *his he will put in charge that servant* But suppose *But* that servant is
3836 899 5639 899 2770 899 1254 1569 1254 1697 1529
d.dpn pt.pa.dpn r.gsm.3 v.fai.3s r.asm.3 cj cj

εἴπῃ ὁ κακὸς δοῦλος ἐκεῖνος ἐν τῇ καρδίᾳ αὐτοῦ,
wicked and says *{the} wicked servant that* in *{the}* his heart, *his* 'My master
2805 3306 3836 2805 1529 1697 1877 3836 899 2840 899 1609 3261
v.aas.3s d.nsm a.nsm n.nsm r.nsm p.d d.dsf n.dsf r.gsm.3

χρονίζει μου ὁ κύριος, 49 καὶ ἄρξηται τύπτειν τοὺς συνδούλους
⌞is slow to return,'⌟ *My {the} master* and begins to beat *{the}* his fellow servants,
5988 1609 3836 3261 2779 806 5597 3836 899 5281
v.pai.3s r.gs.1 d.nsm n.nsm cj v.ams.3s f.pa d.apm n.apm

αὐτοῦ, ἐσθίῃ δὲ καὶ πίνῃ μετὰ τῶν μεθυόντων, 50 ἥξει ὁ κύριος τοῦ
his and eats *and* and drinks with *{the}* drunkards; *will come* the master of
899 1254 2266 1254 2779 4403 3552 3836 3501 2457 3836 3261 3836
r.gsm.3 v.pas.3s cj cj v.pas.3s p.g d.gpm pt.pa.gpm v.fai.3s d.nsm n.nsm d.gsm

δούλου ἐκείνου ἐν ἡμέρᾳ ᾗ ↱ ↱ οὐ προσδοκᾷ καὶ ἐν
that servant *that* will come on a day when he does not expect and at an
1697 1529 1697 2457 2457 1877 2465 4005 4659 4659 4024 4659 2779 1877
n.gsm r.gsm p.d n.dsf r.dsf pl v.pai.3s cj p.d

ὥρᾳ ᾗ ↱ ↱ οὐ γινώσκει, 51 καὶ διχοτομήσει αὐτὸν ↰ ↰ καὶ
hour that he does not know, and will cut him in pieces and assign him
6052 4005 1182 1182 4024 1182 2779 1497 899 1497 1497 2779 5502 899
n.dsf r.dsf pl v.pai.3s cj v.fai.3s r.asm.3 cj

τὸ μέρος αὐτοῦ μετὰ τῶν ὑποκριτῶν θήσει· ἐκεῖ ἔσται ὁ κλαυθμὸς καὶ
a place *him* with the hypocrites, *assign* where there will be *{the}* weeping and
3836 3538 899 3552 3836 5695 5502 1695 1639 3836 3088 2779
d.asn n.asn r.gsm.3 p.g d.gpm n.gpm v.fai.3s adv v.fmi.3s d.nsm n.nsm cj

ὁ βρυγμὸς τῶν ὀδόντων.
{the} gnashing of teeth.
3836 1106 3836 3848
d.nsm n.nsm d.gpm n.gpm

25:1 τότε ὁμοιωθήσεται ἡ βασιλεία τῶν
⌞"At that time⌟ the kingdom of heaven will be like *the kingdom of*
5538 3836 993 3836 4041 3929 3836 993 3836
adv v.fpi.3s d.nsf n.nsf d.gpm

NASB

into. [44]For this
reason you also
must be ready; for
the Son of Man is
coming at an hour
when you do not
think *He will.*
[45]"Who then is
the faithful and
sensible slave
whom his master
put in charge of
his household to
give them their
food at the proper
time? [46]Blessed is
that slave whom
his master finds
so doing when
he comes. [47]Truly
I say to you that
he will put him
in charge of all
his possessions.
[48]But if that evil
slave says in his
heart, 'My master
is not coming for
a long time,' [49]and
begins to beat his
fellow slaves and
eat and drink with
drunkards; [50]the
master of that slave
will come on a day
when he does not
expect *him* and at
an hour which he
does not know,
[51]and will cut him
in pieces and as-
sign him a place
with the hypo-
crites; in that place
there will be weep-
ing and gnashing
of teeth.

Parable of Ten Virgins

[25:1]"Then the king-
dom of heaven will

NIV

ten virgins who
took their lamps
and went out to
meet the bride-
groom. 2Five of
them were fool-
ish and five were
wise. 3The foolish
ones took their
lamps but did not
take any oil with
them. 4The wise
ones, however,
took oil in jars
along with their
lamps. 5The bride-
groom was a long
time in coming,
and they all be-
came drowsy and
fell asleep.
6"At midnight
the cry rang out:
'Here's the bride-
groom! Come out
to meet him!'
7"Then all the
virgins woke up
and trimmed their
lamps. 8The fool-
ish ones said to
the wise, 'Give us
some of your oil;
our lamps are go-
ing out.'
9" 'No,' they re-
plied, 'there may
not be enough for
both us and you.
Instead, go to
those who sell oil
and buy some for
yourselves.'
10"But while they
were on their way
to buy the oil, the
bridegroom ar-
rived. The virgins
who were ready
went in with him
to the wedding
banquet. And the
door was shut.
11"Later the oth-
ers also came.
'Lord,

οὐρανῶν δέκα παρθένοις, αἵτινες λαβοῦσαι τὰς λαμπάδας ἑαυτῶν ἐξῆλθον
heaven ten virgins who took *{the}* their torches *their* and went out
4041 1274 4221 4015 3284 3836 1571 3286 1571 2002
n.gpm a.dpf n.dpf r.npf pt.aa.npf d.apf n.apf r.gpf.3 v.aai.3p

εἰς ὑπάντησιν τοῦ νυμφίου. 2 πέντε δὲ ἐξ αὐτῶν ἦσαν μωραὶ καὶ πέντε
to meet the bridegroom. Now five *Now* of them were foolish and five were
1650 5637 3836 3812 1254 4297 1254 1666 899 1639 3704 2779 4297
p.a n.asf d.gsm n.gsm a.npf cj p.g r.gpf.3 v.iai.3p a.npf cj a.npf

φρόνιμοι. 3 ↱ αἱ γὰρ μωραὶ λαβοῦσαι τὰς λαμπάδας αὐτῶν ↱ ↱ οὐκ
wise. For when the *For* foolish took *{the}* their torches, *their* they did not
5861 1142 3284 3836 1142 3704 3284 3836 899 3286 899 3284 3284 4024
a.npf d.npf cj a.npf pt.aa.npf d.apf n.apf r.gpf.3 pl

ἔλαβον μεθ᾽ ἑαυτῶν ἔλαιον. 4 αἱ δὲ φρόνιμοι ἔλαβον ἔλαιον ἐν τοῖς
take oil with them. *oil* But the *But* wise took oil in *{the}*
3284 1778 3552 1571 1778 1254 3836 1254 5861 3284 1778 1877 3836
v.aai.3p p.g r.gpf.3 n.asn d.npf cj a.npf v.aai.3p n.asn p.d d.dpn

ἀγγείοις μετὰ τῶν λαμπάδων ἑαυτῶν. 5 →
containers ⸤along with⸥ *{the}* their torches. *their* Now since the bridegroom
31 3552 3836 1571 3286 1571 1254 3836 3812
n.dpn p.g d.gpf n.gpf r.gpf.3

χρονίζοντος δὲ τοῦ νυμφίου → ἐνύσταξαν πᾶσαι καὶ ἐκάθευδον.
was slow in coming, *Now the bridegroom* they all became drowsy *all* and fell asleep.
5988 1254 3836 3812 4246 3818 4246 2779 2761
pt.pa.gsm cj d.gsm n.gsm v.aai.3p a.npf cj v.iai.3p

6 μέσης δὲ νυκτὸς κραυγὴ γέγονεν, ἰδοὺ ὁ νυμφίος, ἐξέρχεσθε
But at *But* midnight there was a shout, *there was* 'Look, the bridegroom! Come out
1254 3545 1254 3816 1181 1181 3199 1181 2627 3836 3812 2002
a.gsf cj n.gsf n.nsf v.rai.3s j d.nsm n.nsm v.pmm.2p

εἰς ἀπάντησιν αὐτοῦ.[a] 7 τότε ἠγέρθησαν πᾶσαι αἱ παρθένοι
to meet him.' Then all those virgins woke up *all* *{the} virgins*
1650 561 899 5538 4246 1697 4221 1586 4246 3836 4221
p.a n.asf r.gsm.3 adv v.api.3p a.npf d.npf n.npf

ἐκεῖναι καὶ ἐκόσμησαν τὰς λαμπάδας ἑαυτῶν. 8 αἱ δὲ μωραὶ ταῖς
those and prepared *{the}* their torches. *their* The *{and}* foolish said to the
1697 2779 3175 3836 1571 3286 1571 3836 1254 3704 3306 3836
r.npf cj v.aai.3p d.apf n.apf r.gpf.3 d.npf cj a.npf d.dpf

φρονίμοις εἶπαν, δότε ἡμῖν ἐκ τοῦ ἐλαίου ὑμῶν, ὅτι αἱ λαμπάδες
wise, *said* 'Give us some of your oil, *your* because *{the}* our torches
5861 3306 1443 7005 1666 3836 7007 1778 7007 4022 3836 7005 3286
a.dpf v.aai.3p v.aam.2p r.dp.1 p.g d.gsn n.gsn r.gp.2 cj d.npf n.npf

ἡμῶν σβέννυνται. 9 ἀπεκρίθησαν δὲ αἱ φρόνιμοι λέγουσαι, μήποτε
our are going out.' But the wise answered, *But the wise* saying, 'Perhaps
7005 4931 1254 3836 5861 646 1254 3836 5861 3306 3607
r.gp.1 v.ppi.3p v.api.3p cj d.npf a.npf pt.pa.npf cj

↱ ↱ ⸤οὐ μὴ⸥ ἀρκέσῃ → ἡμῖν καὶ ὑμῖν· πορεύεσθε μᾶλλον πρὸς τοὺς
there will not be enough for both us and you, so go rather to the
758 758 4024 3590 758 7005 2779 7007 4513 3437 4639 3836
pl pl v.aas.3s r.dp.1 cj r.dp.2 v.pmm.2p adv.c p.a d.apm

πωλοῦντας καὶ ἀγοράσατε ἑαυταῖς. 10 → ἀπερχομένων δὲ
dealers and buy some for yourselves.' And while they were away *And*
4797 2779 60 1571 1254 899 599 1254
pt.pa.apm cj v.aam.2p r.dpf.2 pt.pm.gpf cj

αὐτῶν ἀγοράσαι ἦλθεν ὁ νυμφίος, καὶ αἱ ἕτοιμοι
they buying it, the bridegroom came *the bridegroom* and the virgins ⸤who were ready⸥
899 60 3836 3812 2262 3836 3812 2779 3836 2289
r.gpf.3 f.aa v.aai.3s d.nsm n.nsm cj d.npf a.npf

εἰσῆλθον μετ᾽ αὐτοῦ εἰς τοὺς γάμους καὶ ἐκλείσθη ἡ θύρα.
went in with him to the ⸤wedding feast,⸥ and the door was shut. *the door*
1656 3552 899 1650 3836 1141 2779 3836 2598 3091 3836 2598
v.aai.3p p.g r.gsm.3 p.a d.apm n.apm cj v.api.3s d.nsf n.nsf

11 ὕστερον δὲ ἔρχονται καὶ αἱ λοιπαὶ παρθένοι λέγουσαι, κύριε
Later *{and}* the other virgins came, *{and} the other virgins* saying, 'Sir!
5731 1254 3836 3370 4221 2262 2779 3836 3370 4221 3306 3261
adv.c cj v.pmi.3p cj d.npf a.npf n.npf pt.pa.npf n.vsm

[a] [αὐτοῦ] UBS, omitted by NET.

NASB

be comparable to
ten virgins, who
took their lamps
and went out to
meet the bride-
groom. 2Five of
them were foolish,
and five were pru-
dent. 3For when the
foolish took their
lamps, they took
no oil with them,
4but the prudent
took oil in flasks
along with their
lamps. 5Now while
the bridegroom
was delaying, they
all got drowsy and
began to sleep.
6But at midnight
there was a shout,
'Behold, the bride-
groom! Come out
to meet *him*.' 7Then
all those virgins
rose and trimmed
their lamps. 8The
foolish said to the
prudent, 'Give us
some of your oil,
for our lamps are
going out.' 9But the
prudent answered,
'No, there will not
be enough for us
and you *too;* go
instead to the deal-
ers and buy *some*
for yourselves.'
10And while they
were going away to
make the purchase,
the bridegroom
came, and those
who were ready
went in with him to
the wedding feast;
and the door was
shut. 11Later the
other virgins also
came, saying,

NIV

Lord,' they said,
'open the door
for us!'
[12]"But he replied,
'Truly I tell you, I
don't know you.'
[13]"Therefore keep
watch, because
you do not know
the day or the
hour.

The Parable of the Bags of Gold

[14]"Again, it will
be like a man go-
ing on a journey,
who called his
servants and en-
trusted his wealth
to them. [15]To one
he gave five bags
of gold, to another
two bags, and to
another one bag,[a]
each according to
his ability. Then
he went on his
journey. [16]The man
who had received
five bags of gold
went at once and
put his money to
work and gained
five bags more.
[17]So also, the one
with two bags of
gold gained two
more. [18]But the
man who had re-
ceived one bag
went off, dug a
hole in the ground
and hid his mas-
ter's money.
[19]"After a long
time the master
of those servants
returned and set-
tled accounts with
them. [20]The man
who had received
five bags of gold
brought the other
five. 'Master,' he
said, 'you entrust-
ed me with five
bags of gold. See,
I have gained five
more.'
[21]"His master re-
plied,

[a] 15 Greek *five talents . . . two talents . . . one talent*; also throughout this parable; a talent was worth about 20 years of a day laborer's wage.

κύριε, ἄνοιξον ἡμῖν. 12 ὁ δὲ ἀποκριθεὶς εἶπεν, ἀμὴν
Sir! ⌞Open the door⌟ for us.' But he *But* replied, saying, 'I tell you the truth,
3261 487 7005 1254 3836 1254 646 3306 3306 3306 7007 297
n.vsm v.aam.2s r.dp.1 d.nsm cj pt.ap.nsm v.aai.3s pl

λέγω ὑμῖν, ↱ ↱ οὐκ οἶδα ὑμᾶς. 13 γρηγορεῖτε οὖν, ὅτι
I tell *you* I do not know you!' Therefore stay alert, *Therefore* because you know
3306 7007 3857 3857 4024 3857 7007 4036 1213 4036 4022 3857 3857
v.pai.1s r.dp.2 pl v.rai.1s r.ap.2 v.pam.2p cj cj

οὐκ οἴδατε τὴν ἡμέραν οὐδὲ τὴν ὥραν.[a] 14 ὥσπερ γὰρ
neither *you know* the day nor the hour. "For the kingdom of heaven is like *For* a
4024 3857 3836 2465 4028 3836 6052 1142 6061 1142
pl v.rai.2p d.asf n.asf cj d.asf n.asf cj cj

ἄνθρωπος ἀποδημῶν ἐκάλεσεν τοὺς ἰδίους δούλους καὶ
man ⌞about to leave on a long trip,⌟ who called in *{the}* his servants and
476 623 2813 3836 2625 1529 2779
n.nsm pt.pa.nsm v.aai.3s d.apm a.apm n.apm cj

παρέδωκεν αὐτοῖς τὰ ὑπάρχοντα αὐτοῦ, 15 καὶ ⌞ᾧ μὲν⌟ ἔδωκεν πέντε
entrusted his money to them. *{the}* *money* *his* *{and}* To one he gave five
4140 899 5639 899 3836 5639 899 2779 4005 3525 1443 4297
v.aai.3s r.dpm.3 d.apn pt.pa.apn r.gsm.3 cj r.dsm pl v.aai.3s a.apn

τάλαντα, ⌞ᾧ δὲ⌟ δύο, ⌞ᾧ δὲ⌟ ἕν, ἑκάστῳ κατὰ τὴν ἰδίαν
talents, to another two, to another one — to each ⌞according to⌟ *{the}* his
5419 4005 1254 1545 4005 1254 1651 1667 2848 3836 2625
n.apn r.dsm pl a.apn r.dsm pl a.asn r.dsm p.a d.asf a.asf

δύναμιν, καὶ ἀπεδήμησεν. εὐθέως 16 πορευθεὶς ὁ τὰ
ability. Then ⌞he went on his journey.⌟ *immediately* *went* The one who had received *{the}*
1539 2779 623 2311 4513 3836 3284 3284 3284 3284 3836
n.asf cj v.aai.3s adv pt.ap.nsm d.nsm d.apn

πέντε τάλαντα λαβὼν ἠργάσατο ἐν αὐτοῖς ↰
five talents *one who had received* went immediately and put *{in}* his money to
4297 5419 3284 4513 2311 2237 1877 899 2237
a.apn n.apn pt.aa.nsm v.ami.3s p.d r.dpn.3

↰ καὶ ἐκέρδησεν ἄλλα πέντε· 17 ὡσαύτως ὁ τὰ δύο ἐκέρδησεν
work and gained another five. Likewise the one who had the two gained
2237 2779 3045 257 4297 6058 3836 3836 1545 3045
cj v.aai.3s r.apn a.apn adv d.nsm d.apn a.apn v.aai.3s

ἄλλα δύο. 18 ὁ δὲ τὸ ἓν λαβὼν
another two. But the *But* servant who had received the one *who had received* talent
257 1545 1254 3836 1254 3284 3284 3284 3836 1651 3284
r.apn a.apn d.nsm cj d.asn a.asn pt.aa.nsm

ἀπελθὼν ὤρυξεν γῆν καὶ ἔκρυψεν τὸ ἀργύριον τοῦ
went out and ⌞dug a hole in⌟ the ground and hid his master's *{the}* money. *{the}*
599 4002 1178 2779 3221 899 3261 3836 736 3836
pt.aa.nsm v.aai.3s n.asf cj v.aai.3s d.asn n.asn d.gsm

κυρίου αὐτοῦ. 19 μετὰ δὲ πολὺν χρόνον ἔρχεται ὁ κύριος τῶν
master's *his* Now after *Now* a long time *returned* the master of those
3261 899 1254 3552 1254 4498 5989 2262 3836 3261 3836 1697
n.gsm r.gsm.3 p.a cj a.asm n.asm v.pmi.3s d.nsm n.nsm d.gpm

δούλων ἐκείνων καὶ συναίρει λόγον μετ' αὐτῶν. 20 καὶ προσελθὼν ὁ
servants *those* returned and settled accounts with them. *{and}* *came* The one
1529 1697 2262 2779 5256 3364 3552 899 2779 4665 3836 3284
n.gpm r.gpm cj v.pai.3s n.asm p.g r.gpm.3 cj pt.aa.nsm d.nsm

τὰ πέντε τάλαντα λαβὼν προσήνεγκεν ἄλλα
who had received the five talents *one who had received* came and brought another
3284 3284 3284 3836 4297 5419 3284 4665 4712 257
d.apn a.apn n.apn pt.aa.nsm v.aai.3s r.apn

πέντε τάλαντα λέγων, κύριε, πέντε τάλαντά μοι παρέδωκας· ἴδε
five, *{talents}* saying, 'Master, you entrusted five talents to me; *you entrusted* look, I
4297 5419 3306 3261 4140 4140 4297 5419 1609 4140 2623 3045
a.apn n.apn pt.pa.nsm n.vsm a.apn n.apn r.ds.1 v.aai.2s pl

ἄλλα πέντε τάλαντα ἐκέρδησα. 21 ἔφη αὐτῷ ὁ κύριος
have gained five more.' *five* *{talents}* *I have gained* His master said to him, *{the}* *master*
3045 3045 4297 257 4297 5419 3045 899 3261 5774 899 3836 3261
r.apn a.apn n.apn v.aai.1s v.iai.3s r.dsm.3 d.nsm n.nsm

[a] ἐν ῇ ὁ υἱὸς τοῦ ἀνθρώπου ἔρχεται included by TR after ὥραν.

NASB

'Lord, lord, open
up for us.' [12]But he
answered, 'Truly I
say to you, I do not
know you.' [13]Be on
the alert then, for
you do not know
the day nor the
hour.

Parable of the Talents

[14]"For *it is* just
like a man *about*
to go on a journey,
who called his
own slaves and
entrusted his pos-
sessions to them.
[15]To one he gave
five talents, to an-
other, two, and to
another, one, each
according to his
own ability; and he
went on his jour-
ney. [16]Immediately
the one who had
received the five
talents went and
traded with them,
and gained five
more talents. [17]In
the same manner
the one who *had*
received the two
talents gained two
more. [18]But he who
received the one
talent went away,
and dug *a hole* in
the ground and
hid his master's
money.
[19]"Now after
a long time the
master of those
slaves *came and
*settled accounts
with them. [20]The
one who had re-
ceived the five tal-
ents came up and
brought five more
talents, saying,
'Master, you en-
trusted five talents
to me. See, I have
gained five more
talents.' [21]His mas-
ter said to him,

NIV

'Well done, good
and faithful ser-
vant! You have
been faithful with
a few things; I will
put you in charge
of many things.
Come and share
your master's hap-
piness!'
22"The man with
two bags of gold
also came. 'Mas-
ter,' he said, 'you
entrusted me with
two bags of gold;
see, I have gained
two more.'
23"His master re-
plied, 'Well done,
good and faithful
servant! You have
been faithful with
a few things; I will
put you in charge
of many things.
Come and share
your master's hap-
piness!'
24"Then the man
who had received
one bag of gold
came. 'Master,'
he said, 'I knew
that you are a hard
man, harvesting
where you have
not sown and gath-
ering where you
have not scattered
seed. 25So I was
afraid and went
out and hid your
gold in the ground.
See, here is what
belongs to you.'
26"His master re-
plied, 'You wick-
ed, lazy servant!
So you knew that
I harvest where
I have not sown
and gather where I
have not scattered
seed? 27Well then,
you should have
put my money on
deposit with the
bankers,

αὐτοῦ, εὖ, δοῦλε ἀγαθὲ καὶ πιστέ,
His ⌞'Well done,⌟ good and faithful servant. *good and faithful* You have been trustworthy
899 2292 19 2779 4412 1529 19 2779 4412 1639 1639 1639 4412
r.gsm.3 adv n.vsm a.vsm cj a.vsm

ἐπὶ ὀλίγα ἧς πιστός, ἐπὶ πολλῶν σε
in a few things; *You have been trustworthy* I will put you in charge of many things. *you*
2093 3900 1639 4412 2770 2770 2770 5148 2770 2770 2093 4498 5148
p.a a.apn v.iai.2s a.nsm p.g a.gpn r.as.2

καταστήσω· εἴσελθε εἰς τὴν χαρὰν τοῦ κυρίου σου. 22 προσελθὼν δὲ [a] καὶ
I will put in charge Enter into the joy of your master.' *your came {and} also*
2770 1656 1650 3836 5915 3836 5148 3261 5148 4665 1254 2779
v.fai.1s v.aam.2s p.a d.asf n.asf d.gsm n.gsm r.gs.2 pt.aa.nsm cj adv

ὁ τὰ δύο τάλαντα εἶπεν, κύριε, δύο
The one who had received the two talents also came, saying, "Master, you entrusted two
3836 3836 1545 5419 2779 4665 3306 3261 4140 4140 1545
d.nsm d.apn a.apn n.apn v.aai.3s n.vsm a.apn

τάλαντά μοι παρέδωκας· ἴδε ἄλλα δύο τάλαντα ἐκέρδησα.
talents to me. *you entrusted* Look, I have gained two more.' *two {talents} I have gained*
5419 1609 4140 2623 3045 3045 3045 1545 257 1545 5419 3045
n.apn r.ds.1 v.aai.2s pl r.apn a.apn n.apn v.aai.1s

23 ἔφη αὐτῷ ὁ κύριος αὐτοῦ, εὖ, δοῦλε ἀγαθὲ
His master said to him, *{the} master His* ⌞'Well done,⌟ good and faithful servant. *good*
899 3261 5774 899 3836 3261 899 2292 19 2779 4412 1529 19
v.iai.3s r.dsm.3 d.nsm n.nsm r.gsm.3 adv n.vsm a.vsm

καὶ πιστέ, ἐπὶ ὀλίγα ἧς πιστός,
and faithful You have been trustworthy in a few things; *You have been trustworthy* I will put
2779 4412 1639 1639 1639 4412 2093 3900 1639 4412 2770 2770 2770
cj a.vsm p.a a.apn v.iai.2s a.nsm

ἐπὶ πολλῶν σε καταστήσω· εἴσελθε εἰς τὴν χαρὰν τοῦ
you in charge of many things. *you I will put in charge* Enter into the joy of your
5148 2770 2770 2093 4498 5148 2770 1656 1650 3836 5915 3836 5148
p.g a.gpn r.as.2 v.fai.1s v.aam.2s p.a d.asf n.asf d.gsm

κυρίου σου. 24 προσελθὼν δὲ καὶ ὁ τὸ ἓν τάλαντον
master.' *your came* Then *also* the one who had received the one talent also
3261 5148 4665 1254 2779 3836 3284 3284 3284 3284 3836 1651 5419 2779
n.gsm r.gs.2 pt.aa.nsm cj adv d.nsm d.asn a.asn n.asn

εἰληφὼς εἶπεν, κύριε, ἔγνων σε ὅτι σκληρὸς εἶ
one who had received came, saying, 'Master, I knew *{you}* that you were an unscrupulous *you were*
3284 4665 3306 3261 1182 5148 4022 1639 1639 5017 1639
pt.ra.nsm v.aai.3s n.vsm v.aai.1s r.as.2 cj a.nsm v.pai.2s

ἄνθρωπος, θερίζων ὅπου ↱ ↱ οὐκ ἔσπειρας καὶ συνάγων ὅθεν ↱ ↱ οὐ
man, reaping where you have not sown and gathering where you scattered no
476 2545 3963 5062 5062 4024 5062 2779 5251 3854 1399 1399 4024
n.nsm pt.pa.nsm cj pl v.aai.2s cj pt.pa.nsm cj pl

διεσκόρπισας, 25 καὶ φοβηθεὶς ↱ ἀπελθὼν ἔκρυψα τὸ τάλαντόν σου ἐν
seed; and being afraid, I went off and hid *{the}* your talent *your* in
1399 2779 5828 3221 599 3221 3836 5148 5419 5148 1877
v.aai.2s cj pt.ap.nsm pt.aa.nsm v.aai.1s d.asn n.asn r.gs.2 p.d

τῇ γῇ· ἴδε ἔχεις τὸ σόν. 26 ἀποκριθεὶς δὲ ὁ κύριος
the ground. Look, you have what is yours.' But his master answered *But {the} master*
3836 1178 2623 2400 3836 5050 1254 899 3261 646 1254 3836 3261
d.dsf n.dsf pl v.pai.2s d.asn r.asn.2 pt.ap.nsm cj d.nsm n.nsm

αὐτοῦ εἶπεν αὐτῷ, πονηρὲ δοῦλε καὶ ὀκνηρέ, ᾔδεις ὅτι θερίζω
his him, saying, *him* 'You wicked and lazy servant! *and lazy* You knew that I reap
899 899 3306 899 4505 2779 3891 1529 2779 3891 3857 4022 2545
r.gsm.3 v.aai.3s r.dsm.3 a.vsm n.vsm cj a.vsm v.lai.2s cj v.pai.1s

ὅπου ↱ ↱ οὐκ ἔσπειρα καὶ συνάγω ὅθεν ↱ ↱ οὐ διεσκόρπισα; 27
where I have not sown and gather where I scattered no seed? Then
3963 5062 5062 4024 5062 2779 5251 3854 1399 1399 4024 1399 4036
cj pl v.aai.1s cj v.pai.1s cj pl v.aai.1s

ἔδει σε οὖν βαλεῖν τὰ ἀργύριά μου τοῖς τραπεζίταις, καὶ →
you ought *you Then* ⌞to have deposited⌟ *{the}* my money *my* ⌞with the⌟ bankers, and at
5148 1256 5148 4036 965 3836 1609 736 1609 3836 5545 2779
v.iai.3s r.as.2 cj f.aa d.apn n.apn r.gs.1 d.dpm n.dpm cj

NASB

'Well done, good
and faithful slave.
You were faithful
with a few things,
I will put you in
charge of many
things; enter into
the joy of your
master.'
22"Also the one
who *had received*
the two talents
came up and said,
'Master, you en-
trusted two talents
to me. See, I have
gained two more
talents.' 23His
master said to him,
'Well done, good
and faithful slave.
You were faithful
with a few things,
I will put you in
charge of many
things; enter into
the joy of your
master.'
24"And the one
also who had
received the one
talent came up and
said, 'Master, I
knew you to be a
hard man, reaping
where you did not
sow and gather-
ing where you
scattered no *seed.*
25And I was afraid,
and went away and
hid your talent in
the ground. See,
you have what is
yours.'
26"But his master
answered and
said to him, 'You
wicked, lazy slave,
you knew that I
reap where I did
not sow and gather
where I scattered
no *seed.* 27Then you
ought to have put
my money in the
bank, and on

[a] [δὲ] UBS, omitted by TNIV.

NIV

so that when I re-
turned I would
have received it
back with interest.
28 "'So take the
bag of gold from
him and give it to
the one who has
ten bags. 29 For
whoever has will
be given more,
and they will have
an abundance.
Whoever does not
have, even what
they have will be
taken from them.
30 And throw that
worthless servant
outside, into the
darkness, where
there will be weep-
ing and gnashing
of teeth.'

The Sheep and the Goats

31 "When the Son
of Man comes in
his glory, and all
the angels with
him, he will sit
on his glorious
throne. 32 All the
nations will be
gathered before
him, and he will
separate the people
one from another
as a shepherd sep-
arates the sheep
from the goats.
33 He will put the
sheep on his right
and the goats on
his left.
34 "Then the
King will say to
those on his right,
'Come, you who
are blessed by my
Father; take your
inheritance, the
kingdom prepared
for you since the
creation of the
world. 35 For I was
hungry and you
gave me some-
thing to eat, I was
thirsty and you
gave me some-
thing to drink, I
was a stranger and
you invited me in,
36 I needed clothes
and

ἐλθὼν ἐγὼ ἐκομισάμην ἂν τὸ ἐμὸν σὺν τόκῳ. 28 ἄρατε οὖν
my return I would have recovered *would* what was mine plus interest! So take *So*
2262 1609 323 3152 323 3836 1847 5250 5527 4036 149 4036
pt.aa.nsm r.ns.1 v.ami.1s pl d.asn r.asn.1 p.d n.dsm v.aam.2p cj

← ἀπ᾽ αὐτοῦ τὸ τάλαντον καὶ δότε τῷ ἔχοντι τὰ δέκα
the talent away from him, *the talent* and give it ⌞to the⌟ ⌞one who has⌟ the ten
3836 5419 149 608 899 3836 5419 2779 1443 3836 2400 3836 1274
p.g r.gsm.3 d.asn n.asn cj v.aam.2p d.dsm pt.pa.dsm d.apn a.apn

τάλαντα· 29 τῷ γὰρ ἔχοντι παντὶ → δοθήσεται καὶ
talents. For to *For* everyone who has *everyone* will more be given, and
5419 1142 3836 1142 4246 2400 4246 1443 2779
n.apn d.dsm cj pt.pa.dsm a.dsm v.fpi.3s cj

περισσευθήσεται, τοῦ δὲ μὴ ἔχοντος καὶ ὃ ἔχει
he will have an abundance; but from him *but* who has not, *who has* even what he has
4355 1254 3836 1254 2400 2400 3590 2400 2779 4005 2400
v.fpi.3s d.gsm cj pl pt.pa.gsm adv r.asn v.pai.3s

ἀρθήσεται ἀπ᾽ αὐτοῦ. 30 καὶ τὸν ἀχρεῖον δοῦλον ἐκβάλετε εἰς τὸ
will be taken from him. And throw the worthless servant *throw* into the outer
149 608 899 2779 1675 3836 945 1529 1675 1650 3836 2035
v.fpi.3s p.g r.gsm.3 cj d.asm a.asm n.asm v.aam.2p p.a d.asn

σκότος τὸ ἐξώτερον· ἐκεῖ ἔσται ὁ κλαυθμὸς καὶ ὁ βρυγμὸς τῶν
darkness, *{the} outer* where ⌞there will be⌟ *{the}* weeping and *{the}* gnashing of
5030 3836 2035 1695 1639 3836 3088 2779 3836 1106 3836
n.asn d.asn a.asn.c adv v.fmi.3s d.nsm n.nsm cj d.nsm n.nsm d.gpm

ὀδόντων. 31 ὅταν δὲ ἔλθῃ ὁ υἱὸς τοῦ ἀνθρώπου ἐν τῇ δόξῃ
teeth.' "When *{and} comes* the Son of Man comes in *{the}* his glory,
3848 4020 1254 2262 3836 5626 3836 476 2262 1877 3836 899 1518
n.gpm cj cj v.aas.3s d.nsm n.nsm d.gsm n.gsm p.d d.dsf n.dsf

αὐτοῦ καὶ πάντες οἱ ἄγγελοι μετ᾽ αὐτοῦ, τότε καθίσει ἐπὶ θρόνου
his and all the angels with him, then he will sit on his glorious throne.
899 2779 4246 3836 34 3552 899 5538 2767 2093 899 1518 2585
r.gsm.3 cj a.npm d.npm n.npm p.g r.gsm.3 adv v.fai.3s p.g n.gsm

δόξης αὐτοῦ· 32 καὶ συναχθήσονται ἔμπροσθεν αὐτοῦ πάντα τὰ
glorious his {and} All the nations will be gathered before him, *All the*
1518 899 2779 4246 3836 1620 5251 1869 899 4246 3836
n.gsf r.gsm.3 cj v.fpi.3p p.g r.gsm.3 a.npn d.npn

ἔθνη, καὶ ἀφορίσει αὐτοὺς ἀπ᾽ ἀλλήλων, ὥσπερ ὁ ποιμὴν ἀφορίζει
nations and he will separate the people one from another as a shepherd separates
1620 2779 928 899 608 253 6061 3836 4478 928
n.npn cj v.fai.3s r.apm.3 p.g r.gpm cj d.nsm n.nsm v.pai.3s

τὰ πρόβατα ἀπὸ τῶν ἐρίφων, 33 καὶ στήσει τὰ μὲν πρόβατα ἐκ δεξιῶν
the sheep from the goats; and ⌞he will place⌟ the ~ sheep on his right,
3836 4585 608 3836 2253 2779 2705 3836 3525 4585 1666 899 1288
d.apn n.apn p.g d.gpm n.gpm cj v.fai.3s d.apn pl n.apn p.g a.gpf

αὐτοῦ, τὰ δὲ ἐρίφια ἐξ εὐωνύμων. 34 τότε ἐρεῖ ὁ βασιλεὺς
his and the *and* goats on the left. Then the King ⌞will say⌟ *the King*
899 1254 3836 1254 2252 1666 2381 5538 3836 995 3306 3836 995
r.gsm.3 d.apn cj n.apn p.g a.gpf adv v.fai.3s d.nsm n.nsm

τοῖς ἐκ δεξιῶν αὐτοῦ, δεῦτε οἱ εὐλογημένοι τοῦ πατρός μου,
to those on his right, *his* 'Come, ⌞you who⌟ are blessed by my Father; *my*
3836 1666 899 1288 899 1307 3836 2328 3836 1609 4252 1609
d.dpm p.g a.gpf r.gsm.3 adv d.vpm pt.rp.vpm d.gsm n.gsm r.gs.1

κληρονομήσατε τὴν ἡτοιμασμένην ὑμῖν βασιλείαν ἀπὸ καταβολῆς →
inherit the kingdom prepared for you *kingdom* from the foundation of the
3099 3836 993 2286 7007 993 608 2856
v.aam.2p d.asf pt.rp.asf r.dp.2 n.asf p.g n.gsf

κόσμου. 35 ἐπείνασα γὰρ καὶ ἐδώκατέ μοι φαγεῖν, ἐδίψησα καὶ ἐποτίσατέ
world. For I was hungry *For* and you gave me food, I was thirsty and you gave
3180 1142 4277 1142 2779 1443 1609 2266 1498 2779 4540
n.gsm v.aai.1s cj cj v.aai.2p r.ds.1 f.aa v.aai.1s cj v.aai.2p

με, ← ξένος ἤμην καὶ συνηγάγετέ με, ← 36 γυμνὸς καὶ
me drink, I was a stranger *I was* and you invited me in, I was naked and
1609 4540 1639 1639 3828 1639 2779 5251 1609 5251 1218 2779
r.as.1 n.nsm v.imi.1s cj v.aai.2p r.as.1 a.nsm cj

NASB

my arrival I would
have received my
money back with
interest. 28 Therefore
take away the tal-
ent from him, and
give it to the one
who has the ten
talents.'
29 "For to everyone
who has, *more*
shall be given,
and he will have
an abundance; but
from the one who
does not have,
even what he does
have shall be taken
away. 30 Throw out
the worthless slave
into the outer dark-
ness; in that place
there will be weep-
ing and gnashing
of teeth.

The Judgment

31 "But when the
Son of Man comes
in His glory, and
all the angels with
Him, then He will
sit on His glori-
ous throne. 32 All
the nations will be
gathered before
Him; and He will
separate them from
one another, as the
shepherd separates
the sheep from the
goats; 33 and He will
put the sheep on
His right, and the
goats on the left.
34 "Then the King
will say to those
on His right,
'Come, you who
are blessed of My
Father, inherit the
kingdom prepared
for you from the
foundation of the
world. 35 For I was
hungry, and you
gave Me *something*
to eat; I was thirsty,
and you gave Me
something to drink;
I was a stranger,
and you invited Me
in; 36 naked, and

NIV

you clothed me, I
was sick and you
looked after me, I
was in prison and
you came to vis-
it me.'
37 "Then the righ-
teous will answer
him, 'Lord, when
did we see you
hungry and feed
you, or thirsty and
give you some-
thing to drink?
38 When did we
see you a stranger
and invite you in,
or needing clothes
and clothe you?
39 When did we see
you sick or in pris-
on and go to visit
you?'
40 "The King will
reply, 'Truly I tell
you, whatever
you did for one of
the least of these
brothers and sis-
ters of mine, you
did for me.'
41 "Then he will
say to those on his
left, 'Depart from
me, you who are
cursed, into the
eternal fire pre-
pared for the devil
and his angels.
42 For I was hun-
gry and you gave
me nothing to eat,
I was thirsty and
you gave me noth-
ing to drink, 43 I
was a stranger and
you did not invite
me in, I needed
clothes and you
did not clothe me,
I was sick and in
prison and you did
not look after me.'
44 "They also will
answer, 'Lord,
when did we see
you hungry or
thirsty or a strang-
er or needing
clothes or

περιεβάλετέ με, ἠσθένησα καὶ ἐπεσκέψασθέ με, ἐν φυλακῇ ἤμην καὶ
you clothed me, I was sick and you took care of me, I was in prison *I was* and
4314 1609 820 2779 2170 1609 1639 1639 1877 5871 1639 2779
v.aai.2p r.as.1 v.aai.1s cj v.ami.2p r.as.1 p.d n.dsf v.iai.1s cj

⌊ἤλθατε πρός⌋ με. 37 τότε ἀποκριθήσονται αὐτῷ οἱ δίκαιοι λέγοντες,
you visited me.' Then the righteous will answer him, *the* *righteous* saying,
2262 4639 1609 5538 3836 1465 646 899 3836 1465 3306
v.aai.2p p.a r.as.1 adv v.fpi.3p r.dsm.3 d.npm a.npm pt.pa.npm

κύριε, πότε σε εἴδομεν πεινῶντα καὶ ἐθρέψαμεν, ἢ διψῶντα καὶ
'Lord, when did we see you *did we see* hungry and feed you, or thirsty and
3261 4537 1625 1625 1625 5148 1625 4277 2779 5555 2445 1498 2779
n.vsm cj r.as.2 v.aai.1p pt.pa.asm cj v.aai.1p cj pt.pa.asm cj

ἐποτίσαμεν; 38 πότε δέ σε εἴδομεν ξένον καὶ συνηγάγομεν,
give you drink? And when *And* did we see you *did we see* a stranger and invite
4540 1254 4537 1254 1625 1625 1625 5148 1625 3828 2779 5251
v.aai.1p cj cj r.as.2 v.aai.1p n.asm cj v.aai.1p

← ἢ γυμνὸν καὶ περιεβάλομεν; 39 πότε δέ σε εἴδομεν
you in, or naked and clothe you? And when *And* did we see you *did we see*
2445 1218 2779 4314 1254 4537 1254 1625 1625 1625 5148 1625
cj a.asm cj v.aai.1p cj cj r.as.2 v.aai.1p

ἀσθενοῦντα ἢ ἐν φυλακῇ καὶ ⌊ἤλθομεν πρός⌋ σε; 40 καὶ ↱
sick or in prison and visit you?' And the King will
820 2445 1877 5871 2779 2262 4639 5148 2779 3836 995 3306
pt.pa.asm cj p.d n.dsf cj v.aai.1p p.a r.as.2 cj

ἀποκριθεὶς ὁ βασιλεὺς ἐρεῖ αὐτοῖς, ἀμὴν λέγω ὑμῖν,
answer them, *the* *King* saying, *them* 'I tell you the truth, *I tell* *you*
646 899 3836 995 3306 899 3306 3306 7007 297 3306 7007
pt.ap.nsm d.nsm n.nsm v.fai.3s r.dpm.3 pl v.pai.1s r.dp.2

⌊ἐφ' ὅσον⌋ ἐποιήσατε ἑνὶ τούτων τῶν ἀδελφῶν μου τῶν
insofar as you did it to one of the least of these *{the}* my brothers, *my* *of the*
2093 4012 4472 1651 3836 3836 1788 4047 3836 1609 81 1609 3836
p.a r.asn v.aai.2p a.dsm r.gpm d.gpm n.gpm r.gs.1 d.gpm

ἐλαχίστων, ἐμοὶ ἐποιήσατε. 41 τότε ἐρεῖ καὶ τοῖς ἐξ
least you did it to me.' *you did* "Then ⌊he will say⌋ *{also}* to those on his
1788 4472 4472 1609 4472 5538 3306 2779 3836 1666
a.gpm.s r.ds.1 v.aai.2p adv v.fai.3s adv d.dpm p.g

εὐωνύμων, πορεύεσθε ἀπ' ἐμοῦ οἱ[a] κατηραμένοι εἰς τὸ πῦρ τὸ αἰώνιον
left, 'Depart from me, you cursed ones, to the eternal fire *{the}* *eternal*
2381 4513 608 1609 3836 2933 1650 3836 173 4786 3836 173
a.gpf v.pmm.2p p.g r.gs.1 d.vpm pt.rp.vpm p.a d.asn n.asn d.asn a.asn

τὸ ἡτοιμασμένον τῷ διαβόλῳ καὶ τοῖς ἀγγέλοις αὐτοῦ. 42 ἐπείνασα γὰρ
{the} prepared for the devil and *{the}* his angels. *his* For I was hungry *For*
3836 2286 3836 1333 2779 3836 899 34 899 1142 4277 1142
d.asn pt.rp.asn d.dsm n.dsm cj d.dpm n.dpm r.gsm.3 v.aai.1s cj

καὶ οὐκ ἐδώκατέ μοι φαγεῖν, ἐδίψησα καὶ ↱ ↱ οὐκ
and you gave me no *you gave* *me* food, I was thirsty and you gave me no
2779 1443 1443 1609 4024 1443 1609 2266 1498 2779 4024 4540 1609 4024
cj pl v.aai.2p r.ds.1 f.aa v.aai.1s cj pl

ἐποτίσατέ με, 43 ξένος ἤμην καὶ ↱ ↱ οὐ συνηγάγετέ με, ↰
drink, *me* I was a stranger *I was* and you did not invite me in,
4540 1609 1639 1639 3828 1639 2779 5251 5251 4024 5251 1609 5251
v.aai.2p r.as.1 n.nsm v.imi.1s cj pl v.aai.2p r.as.1

γυμνὸς καὶ ↱ ↱ οὐ περιεβάλετέ με, ἀσθενὴς καὶ ἐν φυλακῇ καὶ ↱ ↱ οὐκ
naked and you did not clothe me, sick and in prison and you did not
1218 2779 4314 4314 4024 4314 1609 822 2779 1877 5871 2779 2170 2170 4024
a.nsm cj pl v.aai.2p r.as.1 a.nsm cj p.d n.dsf cj pl

ἐπεσκέψασθέ με. 44 τότε ἀποκριθήσονται καὶ αὐτοὶ λέγοντες, κύριε, πότε
visit me.' Then they also will answer, *also* *they* saying, 'Lord, when
2170 1609 5538 899 2779 646 2779 899 3306 3261 4537
v.ami.2p r.as.1 adv v.fpi.3p adv r.npm pt.pa.npm n.vsm cj

σε εἴδομεν πεινῶντα ἢ διψῶντα ἢ ξένον ἢ γυμνὸν ἢ
did we see you *did we see* hungry or thirsty or a stranger or naked or
1625 1625 1625 5148 1625 4277 2445 1498 2445 3828 2445 1218 2445
r.as.2 v.aai.1p pt.pa.asm cj pt.pa.asm cj n.asm cj a.asm cj

NASB

you clothed Me;
I was sick, and
you visited Me;
I was in prison,
and you came to
Me.' 37 Then the
righteous will an-
swer Him, 'Lord,
when did we
see You hungry,
and feed You, or
thirsty, and give
You *something* to
drink? 38 And when
did we see You a
stranger, and invite
You in, or naked,
and clothe You?
39 When did we see
You sick, or in
prison, and come
to You?' 40 The King
will answer and
say to them, 'Truly
I say to you, to the
extent that you did
it to one of these
brothers of Mine,
even the least *of*
them, you did it to
Me.'
41 "Then He will
also say to those
on His left, 'Depart
from Me, accursed
ones, into the eter-
nal fire which has
been prepared for
the devil and his
angels; 42 for I was
hungry, and you
gave Me *nothing* to
eat; I was thirsty,
and you gave Me
nothing to drink; 43 I
was a stranger, and
you did not invite
Me in; naked, and
you did not clothe
Me; sick, and in
prison, and you
did not visit Me.'
44 Then they them-
selves also will an-
swer, 'Lord, when
did we see You
hungry, or thirsty,
or a stranger, or na-
ked, or sick, or in

[a] [οἱ] UBS.

NIV

sick or in prison,
and did not help
you?'
45"He will reply,
'Truly I tell you,
whatever you did
not do for one of
the least of these,
you did not do
for me.'
46"Then they will
go away to eternal
punishment, but
the righteous to
eternal life."

The Plot Against Jesus

26 When
Jesus had
finished saying
all these things,
he said to his dis-
ciples, 2"As you
know, the Pass-
over is two days
away—and the
Son of Man will be
handed over to be
crucified."
3Then the chief
priests and the el-
ders of the people
assembled in the
palace of the high
priest, whose name
was Caiaphas,
4and they schemed
to arrest Jesus se-
cretly and kill him.
5"But not during
the festival," they
said, "or there may
be a riot among the
people."

Jesus Anointed at Bethany

6While Jesus was
in Bethany in the
home of Simon the
Leper, 7a woman
came to him with
an alabaster jar
of very expensive
perfume, which
she poured on his
head as he was re-
clining at the table.
8When the disci-
ples saw

ἀσθενῆ ἢ ἐν φυλακῇ καὶ ↱ οὐ διηκονήσαμέν σοι; 45 τότε ἀποκριθήσεται
sick or in prison and did not help you?' Then he will answer
822 2445 1877 5871 2779 1354 4024 1354 5148 5538 646
a.asm cj p.d n.dsf cj pl v.aai.1p r.ds.2 adv v.fpi.3s

αὐτοῖς λέγων, ἀμὴν λέγω ὑμῖν, ⸤ἐφ' ὅσον⸥ ↱ ↱ οὐκ
them, saying, 'I tell you the truth, *I tell* *you* insofar as you did not
899 3306 3306 3306 7007 297 3306 7007 2093 4012 4472 4472 4024
r.dpm.3 pt.pa.nsm pl v.pai.1s r.dp.2 p.a r.asn pl

ἐποιήσατε ἑνὶ τούτων τῶν ἐλαχίστων, οὐδὲ ἐμοὶ
do it to one of the least of these, *of the* *least* you did not do it to me.'
4472 1651 3836 3836 1788 4047 3836 1788 4472 4472 4028 4472 1609
v.aai.2p a.dsm r.gpm d.gpm a.gpm.s cj r.ds.1

ἐποιήσατε. 46 καὶ ἀπελεύσονται οὗτοι εἰς κόλασιν αἰώνιον, οἱ
you did do And these will depart *these* to eternal punishment, *eternal* but the
4472 2779 4047 599 4047 1650 173 3136 173 1254 3836
v.aai.2p cj v.fmi.3p r.npm p.a n.asf a.asf d.npm

δὲ δίκαιοι εἰς ζωὴν αἰώνιον.
but righteous to eternal life." *eternal*
1254 1465 1650 173 2437 173
cj a.npm p.a n.asf a.asf

26:1 καὶ ἐγένετο ὅτε ἐτέλεσεν ὁ Ἰησοῦς πάντας τοὺς
{and} *{it happened that}* When Jesus had finished *{the}* *Jesus* all *{the}* these
2779 1181 4021 2652 5464 3836 2652 4246 3836 4047
cj v.ami.3s cj v.aai.3s d.nsm n.nsm a.apm d.apm

λόγους τούτους, εἶπεν τοῖς μαθηταῖς αὐτοῦ, 2 οἴδατε ὅτι μετὰ δύο ἡμέρας τὸ
sayings, *these* he said to his disciples, *his* "You know that after two days the
3364 4047 3306 3836 899 3412 899 3857 4022 3552 1545 2465 3836
n.apm r.apm v.aai.3s d.dpm n.dpm r.gsm.3 v.rai.2p cj p.a a.apf n.apf d.nsn

πάσχα γίνεται, καὶ ὁ υἱὸς τοῦ ἀνθρώπου παραδίδοται εἰς τὸ
Passover is coming, and the Son of Man ⸤will be handed over⸥ to *{the}*
4247 1181 2779 3836 5626 3836 476 4140 1650 3836
n.nsn v.pmi.3s cj d.nsm n.nsm d.gsm n.gsm v.ppi.3s p.a d.asn

σταυρωθῆναι. 3 τότε συνήχθησαν οἱ ἀρχιερεῖς καὶ οἱ πρεσβύτεροι τοῦ λαοῦ
be crucified." Then *gathered* the ruling priests and the elders of the people
5090 5538 5251 3836 797 2779 3836 4565 3836 3295
f.ap adv v.api.3p d.npm n.npm cj d.npm a.npm d.gsm n.gsm

εἰς τὴν αὐλὴν τοῦ ἀρχιερέως τοῦ λεγομένου Καϊάφα 4 καὶ
gathered in the palace of the high priest, who was called Caiaphas, and
5251 1650 3836 885 3836 797 3836 3306 2780 2779
p.a d.asf n.asf d.gsm n.gsm d.gsm pt.pp.gsm n.gsm cj

συνεβουλεύσαντο ἵνα τὸν Ἰησοῦν δόλῳ κρατήσωσιν καὶ ἀποκτείνωσιν·
they plotted together to seize *{the}* Jesus by stealth *seize* and kill him.
5205 2671 3195 3836 2652 1515 3195 2779 650
v.ami.3p cj d.asm n.asm n.dsm v.aas.3p cj v.aas.3p

5 ἔλεγον δέ, μὴ ἐν τῇ ἑορτῇ, ⸤ἵνα μὴ⸥ θόρυβος γένηται ἐν
But they said, *But* "Not during the feast, lest there be a riot *there be* among
1254 3306 1254 3590 1877 3836 2038 2671 3590 1181 1181 2573 1181 1877
v.iai.3p cj pl p.d d.dsf n.dsf cj pl n.nsm v.ams.3s p.d

τῷ λαῷ. 6 τοῦ δὲ ↱ Ἰησοῦ γενομένου ἐν Βηθανίᾳ ἐν οἰκίᾳ Σίμωνος
the people." *{the}* Now while Jesus was in Bethany, in the house of Simon
3836 3295 3836 1254 1181 2652 1181 1877 1029 1877 3864 4981
d.dsm n.dsm d.gsm cj n.gsm pt.am.gsm p.d n.dsf p.d n.dsf n.gsm

τοῦ λεπροῦ, 7 προσῆλθεν αὐτῷ γυνὴ ἔχουσα ἀλάβαστρον →
the leper, a woman came to him *woman* with an alabaster flask of very expensive
3836 3320 1222 4665 899 1222 2400 223 988 988
d.gsm a.gsm v.aai.3s r.dsm.3 n.nsf pt.pa.nsf n.asn

μύρου βαρυτίμου καὶ κατέχεεν ἐπὶ τῆς κεφαλῆς αὐτοῦ
perfume *very expensive* *{and}* that she poured over *{the}* his head *his*
3693 988 2779 2972 2093 3836 899 3051 899
n.gsn a.gsn cj v.aai.3s p.g d.gsf n.gsf r.gsm.3

ἀνακειμένου. 8 → ἰδόντες δὲ οἱ μαθηταὶ
⸤as he reclined at table.⸥ And when the disciples saw *And* *the* *disciples* it,
367 1254 3836 3412 1625 1254 3836 3412
pt.pm.gsm pt.aa.npm cj d.npm n.npm

NASB

prison, and did not
take care of You?'
45Then He will an-
swer them, 'Truly
I say to you, to the
extent that you did
not do it to one of
the least of these,
you did not do it to
Me.' 46These will
go away into eter-
nal punishment,
but the righteous
into eternal life."

The Plot to Kill Jesus

26:1When Jesus had
finished all these
words, He said
to His disciples,
2"You know that
after two days the
Passover is com-
ing, and the Son
of Man is *to be*
handed over for
crucifixion."
3Then the chief
priests and the
elders of the people
were gathered to-
gether in the court
of the high priest,
named Caiaphas;
4and they plotted
together to seize
Jesus by stealth
and kill Him. 5But
they were saying,
"Not during the
festival, otherwise
a riot might occur
among the people."

The Precious Ointment

6Now when Jesus
was in Bethany, at
the home of Simon
the leper, 7a woman
came to Him with
an alabaster vial
of very costly
perfume, and she
poured it on His
head as He reclined
at the table. 8But
the disciples were

NIV

this, they were
indignant. "Why
this waste?" they
asked. 9"This per-
fume could have
been sold at a high
price and the mon-
ey given to the
poor."
10Aware of this,
Jesus said to them,
"Why are you
bothering this
woman? She has
done a beautiful
thing to me. 11The
poor you will al-
ways have with
you,[a] but you will
not always have
me. 12When she
poured this per-
fume on my body,
she did it to pre-
pare me for burial.
13Truly I tell you,
wherever this gos-
pel is preached
throughout the
world, what she
has done will also
be told, in memory
of her."

Judas Agrees to Betray Jesus

14Then one of the
Twelve—the one
called Judas Iscar-
iot—went to the
chief priests 15and
asked, "What are
you willing to give
me if I deliver
him over to you?"
So they counted
out for him thirty
pieces of silver.
16From then on
Judas watched for
an opportunity to
hand him over.

The Last Supper

17On the first day
of the Festival of
Unleavened Bread,
the disciples came
to Jesus and asked,
"Where do you
want us to make
preparations for
you to eat the
Passover?"

ἠγανάκτησαν λέγοντες, ⌊εἰς τί⌋ ἡ ἀπώλεια αὕτη; 9
they were indignant and said, "Why *{the}* this waste? *this* For this
24 3306 1650 5515 3836 4047 724 4047 1142 4047
v.aai.3p pt.pa.npm p.a r.asn d.nsf n.nsf r.nsf

ἐδύνατο γὰρ τοῦτο πραθῆναι → πολλοῦ καὶ δοθῆναι →
⌊could have been⌋ *For* *this* sold for a high price and the money given to the
1538 1142 4047 4405 4498 2779 1443
v.ipi.3s cj r.asn f.ap a.gsn cj f.ap

πτωχοῖς. 10 γνοὺς δὲ ὁ Ἰησοῦς εἶπεν αὐτοῖς, τί
poor." But aware *But* of this, *{the}* Jesus said to them, "Why are you causing
4777 1254 1182 1254 3836 2652 3306 899 5515 4218 4218 4218
a.dpm pt.aa.nsm cj d.nsm n.nsm v.aai.3s r.dpm.3 r.asn

κόπους παρέχετε τῇ γυναικί; ἔργον γὰρ καλὸν ἠργάσατο
trouble *are you causing* ⌊for the⌋ woman? *thing* For she has done a kind thing *she has done*
3160 4218 3836 1222 2240 1142 2237 2237 2237 2819 2240 2237
n.apm v.pai.2p d.dsf n.dsf n.asn cj a.asn v.ami.3s

εἰς ἐμέ· 11 πάντοτε γὰρ τοὺς πτωχοὺς ἔχετε μεθ᾽ ἑαυτῶν, ἐμὲ δὲ
to me. You will always ~ have the poor *You will have* with you, *me* but
1650 1609 2400 2400 4121 1142 2400 3836 4777 2400 3552 1571 1609 1254
p.a r.as.1 adv cj d.apm a.apm v.pai.2p p.g r.gpm.2 r.as.1 cj

↱ ↱ οὐ πάντοτε ἔχετε· 12 βαλοῦσα γὰρ αὕτη τὸ μύρον τοῦτο ἐπὶ
you will not always have me. For by pouring *For* *she* *{the}* this perfume *this* on
2400 2400 4024 4121 2400 1609 1142 965 1142 4047 3836 4047 3693 4047 2093
pl adv v.pai.2p pt.aa.nsf cj r.nsf d.asn n.asn r.asn p.g

τοῦ σώματός μου πρὸς τὸ ἐνταφιάσαι με ἐποίησεν.
{the} my body, *my* she has prepared me for *{the}* burial. *me* *has prepared*
3836 1609 5393 1609 4047 4472 4472 1609 4639 3836 1946 1609 4472
d.gsn n.gsn r.gs.1 p.a d.asn f.aa r.as.1 v.aai.3s

13 ἀμὴν λέγω ὑμῖν, ⌊ὅπου ἐὰν⌋ κηρυχθῇ τὸ
I tell you the truth, *I tell* *you* wherever this gospel is proclaimed *{the}*
3306 3306 7007 297 3306 7007 3963 1569 4047 2295 3062 3836
pl v.pai.1s r.dp.2 cj pl v.aps.3s d.nsn

εὐαγγέλιον τοῦτο ⌊ἐν ὅλῳ⌋ τῷ κόσμῳ, → λαληθήσεται
gospel *this* throughout the world, what she has done will also be recounted
2295 4047 1877 3910 3836 3180 4005 4047 4472 4472 2779 3281
n.nsn r.nsn p.d a.dsm d.dsm n.dsm v.fpi.3s

καὶ ὃ ἐποίησεν αὕτη εἰς μνημόσυνον αὐτῆς. 14 τότε πορευθεὶς εἷς
also *what* *has done* *she* as her memorial *her* to me." Then *went* one
2779 4005 4472 4047 1650 899 3649 899 5538 4513 1651
cj r.asn v.aai.3s r.nsf p.a n.asn r.gsf.3 adv pt.ap.nsm a.nsm

τῶν δώδεκα, ὁ λεγόμενος Ἰούδας Ἰσκαριώτης, πρὸς τοὺς ἀρχιερεῖς 15
of the twelve, the one named Judas Iscariot, went to the ruling priests and
3836 1557 3836 3306 2683 2697 4513 4639 3836 797
d.gpm a.gpm d.nsm pt.pp.nsm n.nsm n.nsm p.a d.apm n.apm

εἶπεν, τί θέλετέ μοι δοῦναι, κἀγὼ ὑμῖν παραδώσω
asked, "What ⌊are you willing⌋ to give me *to give* if I betray him to you?" *betray*
3306 5515 2527 1443 1443 1609 1443 2743 4140 899 7007 4140
v.aai.3s r.asn v.pai.2p r.ds.1 f.aa crasis r.dp.2 v.fai.1s

αὐτόν; οἱ δὲ ἔστησαν αὐτῷ τριάκοντα ἀργύρια. 16 καὶ ἀπὸ τότε
him And they *And* ⌊agreed to pay⌋ him thirty silver coins. So from ⌊then on⌋
899 1254 3836 1254 2705 899 5558 736 2779 608 5538
r.asm.3 d.npm cj v.aai.3p r.dsm.3 a.apn n.apn cj p.g adv

ἐζήτει εὐκαιρίαν ἵνα αὐτὸν παραδῷ. 17 τῇ δὲ πρώτῃ
⌊he watched for⌋ an opportunity to betray Jesus. *betray* Now ⌊on the⌋ *Now* first day
2426 2321 2671 4140 899 4140 1254 3836 1254 4755
v.iai.3s n.asf cj r.asm.3 v.aas.3s d.dsf cj a.dsf

τῶν ἀζύμων προσῆλθον οἱ μαθηταὶ τῷ Ἰησοῦ λέγοντες,
of ⌊Unleavened Bread⌋ the disciples came *the* *disciples* to Jesus and asked,
3836 109 3836 3412 4665 3836 3412 3836 2652 3306
d.gpn n.gpn v.aai.3p d.npm n.npm d.dsm n.dsm pt.pa.npm

ποῦ θέλεις ἑτοιμάσωμέν σοι φαγεῖν τὸ πάσχα; 18 ὁ δὲ
"Where ⌊do you want⌋ us to make preparations ⌊for you⌋ to eat the Passover?" He *{and}*
4543 2527 2286 5148 2266 3836 4247 3836 1254
cj v.pai.2s v.aas.1p r.ds.2 f.aa d.asn n.asn d.nsm cj

NASB

indignant when
they saw *this,* and
said, "Why this
waste? 9For this
perfume might
have been sold for
a high price and
the money given
to the poor." 10But
Jesus, aware of
this, said to them,
"Why do you
bother the woman?
For she has done a
good deed to Me.
11For you always
have the poor with
you; but you do
not always have
Me. 12For when she
poured this per-
fume on My body,
she did it to pre-
pare Me for burial.
13Truly I say to
you, wherever this
gospel is preached
in the whole world,
what this woman
has done will also
be spoken of in
memory of her."

Judas's Bargain

14Then one of the
twelve, named Ju-
das Iscariot, went
to the chief priests
15and said, "What
are you willing to
give me to betray
Him to you?" And
they weighed out
thirty pieces of sil-
ver to him. 16From
then on he *began*
looking for a good
opportunity to be-
tray Jesus.
17Now on the first
day of Unleavened
Bread the disciples
came to Jesus and
asked, "Where do
You want us to pre-
pare for You to eat
the Passover?"

[a] 11 See Deut. 15:11.

NIV

[18]He replied,
"Go into the city
to a certain man
and tell him, 'The
Teacher says: My
appointed time is
near. I am going
to celebrate the
Passover with my
disciples at your
house.'" [19]So the
disciples did as
Jesus had directed
them and prepared
the Passover.
[20]When evening
came, Jesus was
reclining at the
table with the
Twelve. [21]And
while they were
eating, he said,
"Truly I tell you,
one of you will be-
tray me."
[22]They were very
sad and began to
say to him one
after the other,
"Surely you don't
mean me, Lord?"
[23]Jesus replied,
"The one who has
dipped his hand
into the bowl with
me will betray me.
[24]The Son of Man
will go just as it is
written about him.
But woe to that
man who betrays
the Son of Man! It
would be better for
him if he had not
been born."
[25]Then Judas, the
one who would
betray him, said,
"Surely you don't
mean me, Rabbi?"
Jesus answered,
"You have said
so."
[26]While they
were eating, Jesus
took bread, and
when he had given
thanks, he broke it

εἶπεν, ὑπάγετε εἰς τὴν πόλιν πρὸς τὸν δεῖνα καὶ εἴπατε αὐτῷ, ὁ διδάσκαλος
said, "Go into the city to a ⌊certain man⌋ and say to him, 'The Teacher
3306 5632 1650 3836 4484 4639 3836 1265 2779 3306 899 3836 1437
v.aai.3s v.pam.2p p.a d.asf n.asf p.a d.asm n.asm cj v.aam.2p r.dsm.3 d.nsm n.nsm

λέγει, ὁ καιρός μου ἐγγύς ἐστιν, πρὸς
says, *{the}* "My time *My* is at hand. *is* I will be keeping the Passover at
3306 3836 1609 2789 1609 1639 1584 1639 4472 4472 4472 4472 3836 4247 4639
v.pai.3s d.nsm n.nsm r.gs.1 adv v.pai.3s p.a

σὲ ποιῶ τὸ πάσχα μετὰ τῶν μαθητῶν μου. [19] καὶ
your *I will be keeping* *the* *Passover* house with *{the}* my disciples."'" *my* So the disciples
5148 4472 3836 4247 3552 3836 1609 3412 1609 2779 3836 3412
r.as.2 v.pai.1s d.asn n.asn p.g d.gpm n.gpm r.gs.1 cj

ἐποίησαν οἱ μαθηταὶ ὡς συνέταξεν αὐτοῖς ὁ Ἰησοῦς καὶ
did *the* *disciples* as Jesus had directed them *{the}* *Jesus* and
4472 3836 3412 6055 2652 5332 899 3836 2652 2779
v.aai.3p d.npm n.npm cj v.aai.3s r.dpm.3 d.nsm n.nsm cj

ἡτοίμασαν τὸ πάσχα. [20] ↱ ὀψίας δὲ γενομένης
⌊made preparations for⌋ the Passover. Now when evening *Now* came, Jesus
2286 3836 4247 1254 1181 4068 1254 1181
v.aai.3p d.asn n.asn n.gsf cj pt.am.gsf

ἀνέκειτο μετὰ τῶν δώδεκα. [21] καὶ → ἐσθιόντων αὐτῶν εἶπεν,
⌊was reclining at table⌋ with the twelve. And as they were eating *they* he said, "I tell
367 3552 3836 1557 2779 899 2266 899 3306 3306 3306
v.imi.3s p.g d.gpm a.gpm cj pt.pa.gpm r.gpm.3 v.aai.3s

ἀμὴν λέγω ὑμῖν ὅτι εἷς ἐξ ὑμῶν παραδώσει με. [22] καὶ ↱ →
you the truth, *I tell* *you* *{that}* one of you will betray me." And they were greatly
7007 297 3306 7007 4022 1651 1666 7007 4140 1609 2779 806 5379
pl v.pai.1s r.dp.2 cj a.nsm p.g r.gp.2 v.fai.3s r.as.1 cj

λυπούμενοι σφόδρα ἤρξαντο λέγειν αὐτῷ εἷς ἕκαστος, μήτι ἐγώ εἰμι,
distressed *greatly* and began to say to him one after another, ⌊"Surely not⌋ I, *{am I}*
3382 5379 806 3306 899 1651 1667 3614 1609 1639
pt.pp.npm adv v.ami.3p f.pa r.dsm.3 a.nsm r.nsm pl r.ns.1 v.pai.1s

κύριε; [23] ὁ δὲ ἀποκριθεὶς εἶπεν, ὁ ἐμβάψας
Lord?" Jesus *{and}* answered, saying, "The ⌊one who has dipped⌋ his hand into the bowl
3261 3836 1254 646 3306 3836 1835 3836 5931 1877 3836 5581
n.vsm d.nsm cj pt.ap.nsm v.aai.3s d.nsm pt.aa.nsm

μετ' ἐμοῦ τὴν χεῖρα ἐν τῷ τρυβλίῳ οὗτός με παραδώσει. [24] ὁ μὲν
with me *his* *hand* *into* *the* *bowl* *{he}* will betray me. *will betray* The ~
3552 1609 3836 5931 1877 3836 5581 4047 4140 4140 1609 4140 3836 3525
p.g r.gs.1 d.asf n.asf p.d d.dsn n.dsn r.nsm r.as.1 v.fai.3s d.nsm pl

υἱὸς τοῦ ἀνθρώπου ὑπάγει καθὼς γέγραπται περὶ αὐτοῦ, οὐαὶ δὲ τῷ
Son of Man will depart as it is written of him, but woe *but* to that
5626 3836 476 5632 2777 1211 4309 899 1254 4026 1254 3836 1697
n.nsm d.gsm n.gsm v.pai.3s cj v.rpi.3s p.g r.gsm.3 j cj d.dsm

ἀνθρώπῳ ἐκείνῳ δι' οὗ ὁ υἱὸς τοῦ ἀνθρώπου παραδίδοται·
one *that* by whom the Son of Man is betrayed! It would have been
476 1697 1328 4005 3836 5626 3836 476 4140 1639 1639 1639 1639
n.dsm r.dsm p.g r.gsm d.nsm n.nsm d.gsm n.gsm v.ppi.3s

καλὸν ἦν αὐτῷ εἰ ↱ ↱ οὐκ ἐγεννήθη ὁ ἄνθρωπος
better *It would have been* *{for him}* for that man *{if}* had he not been born." *{the}* *man*
2819 1639 899 1697 476 1623 1164 1164 4024 1164 3836 476
a.nsn v.iai.3s r.dsm.3 cj pl v.api.3s d.nsm n.nsm

ἐκεῖνος. [25] ἀποκριθεὶς δὲ Ἰούδας ὁ παραδιδοὺς αὐτὸν εἶπεν, μήτι ἐγώ
that *{answering}* Then Judas, who would betray him, said, ⌊"Surely not⌋ I,
1697 646 1254 2683 3836 4140 899 3306 3614 1609
r.nsm pt.ap.nsm cj n.nsm d.nsm pt.pa.nsm r.asm.3 v.aai.3s pl r.ns.1

εἰμι, ῥαββί; λέγει αὐτῷ, σὺ εἶπας. [26] → ἐσθιόντων δὲ
{am I} Rabbi?" Jesus answered him, "It is as you have said." And as they were eating, *And*
1639 4806 3306 899 5148 3306 1254 899 2266 1254
v.pai.1s n.vsm v.pai.3s r.dsm.3 r.ns.2 v.aai.2s pt.pa.gpm cj

αὐτῶν λαβὼν ὁ Ἰησοῦς ἄρτον καὶ εὐλογήσας ἔκλασεν καὶ
they Jesus took *{the}* *Jesus* bread; and ⌊when he had given thanks,⌋ he broke it and
899 2652 3284 3836 2652 788 2779 2328 3089 2779
r.gpm.3 pt.aa.nsm d.nsm n.nsm n.asm cj pt.aa.nsm v.aai.3s cj

NASB

[18]And He said,
"Go into the city
to a certain man,
and say to him,
'The Teacher says,
"My time is near;
I *am to* keep the
Passover at your
house with My
disciples."'" [19]The
disciples did as
Jesus had directed
them; and they pre-
pared the Passover.

The Last Passover

[20]Now when eve-
ning came, Jesus
was reclining *at*
the table with the
twelve disciples.
[21]As they were
eating, He said,
"Truly I say to you
that one of you
will betray Me."
[22]Being deeply
grieved, they each
one began to say
to Him, "Surely
not I, Lord?" [23]And
He answered, "He
who dipped his
hand with Me in
the bowl is the one
who will betray
Me. [24]The Son of
Man *is to* go, just
as it is written of
Him; but woe to
that man by whom
the Son of Man is
betrayed! It would
have been good for
that man if he had
not been born."
[25]And Judas, who
was betraying Him,
said, "Surely it
is not I, Rabbi?"
Jesus *said to him,
"You have said *it*
yourself."

The Lord's Supper Instituted

[26]While they were
eating, Jesus took
some bread, and
after a blessing, He
broke *it*

NIV

and gave it to his
disciples, saying,
“Take and eat; this
is my body.”
27 Then he took a
cup, and when he
had given thanks,
he gave it to them,
saying, “Drink
from it, all of you.
28 This is my blood
of the[a] covenant,
which is poured
out for many for
the forgiveness of
sins. 29 I tell you,
I will not drink
from this fruit of
the vine from now
on until that day
when I drink it
new with you in
my Father’s king-
dom.”
30 When they had
sung a hymn, they
went out to the
Mount of Olives.

Jesus Predicts Peter’s Denial

31 Then Jesus told
them, “This very
night you will all
fall away on ac-
count of me, for it
is written:

“‘I will strike the
shepherd,
and the sheep
of the flock
will be
scattered.’[b]

32 But after I have
risen, I will go
ahead of you into
Galilee.”
33 Peter replied,
“Even if all fall
away on account
of you, I never
will.”
34 “Truly I tell
you,” Jesus an-
swered, “this very
night, before the
rooster crows, you
will disown me
three times.”
35 But Peter de-
clared, “Even if

[a] 28 Some manuscripts *the new*
[b] 31 Zech. 13:7

δοὺς τοῖς μαθηταῖς εἶπεν, λάβετε φάγετε, τοῦτό ἐστιν τὸ σῶμά μου. 27 καὶ
gave it to his disciples, saying, “Take, eat; this is {the} my body.” *my* And
1443 3836 3412 3306 3284 2266 4047 1639 3836 1609 5393 1609 2779
pt.aa.nsm d.dpm n.dpm v.aai.3s v.aam.2p v.aam.2p r.nsn v.pai.3s d.nsn n.nsn r.gs.1 cj

λαβὼν ποτήριον καὶ εὐχαριστήσας ἔδωκεν αὐτοῖς λέγων, πίετε ἐξ
he took a cup, and ⌞when he had given thanks,⌟ he gave it to them, saying, “Drink from
3284 4539 2779 2373 1443 899 3306 4403 1666
pt.aa.nsm n.asn cj pt.aa.nsm v.aai.3s r.dpm.3 pt.pa.nsm v.aam.2p p.g

αὐτοῦ πάντες, 28 τοῦτο γάρ ἐστιν τὸ αἷμά μου τῆς διαθήκης τὸ
it, all of you, for this *for* is {the} my blood *my* of the covenant that
899 4246 1142 4047 1142 1639 3836 1609 135 1609 3836 1347 3836
r.gsn.3 a.vpm r.nsn cj v.pai.3s d.nsn n.nsn r.gs.1 d.gsf n.gsf d.nsn

περὶ πολλῶν ἐκχυννόμενον εἰς ἄφεσιν ἁμαρτιῶν. 29 λέγω
is poured out for many *is poured out* for the forgiveness of sins. But I say
1773 1773 1773 4309 4498 1773 1650 912 281 1254 3306
p.g a.gpm pt.pp.nsn p.a n.asf n.gpf v.pai.1s

δὲ ὑμῖν, ↱ ↱ ⌞οὐ μὴ⌟ πίω ⌞ἀπ’ ἄρτι⌟ ἐκ τούτου τοῦ γενήματος τῆς
But to you, I will never drink again of this {the} fruit of the
1254 7007 4403 4403 4024 3590 4403 608 785 1666 4047 3836 1163 3836
cj r.dp.2 pl pl v.aas.1s p.g adv p.g r.gsn d.gsn n.gsn d.gsf

ἀμπέλου ἕως τῆς ἡμέρας ἐκείνης ὅταν αὐτὸ πίνω μεθ’ ὑμῶν καινὸν
vine until {the} that day *that* when *wine* I drink the new wine with you *new*
306 2401 3836 1697 2465 1697 4020 899 4403 2785 899 3552 7007 2785
n.gsf p.g d.gsf n.gsf r.gsf cj r.asn.3 v.pas.1s p.g r.gp.2 a.asn

ἐν τῇ βασιλείᾳ τοῦ πατρός μου. 30 καὶ ὑμνήσαντες ἐξῆλθον
in the kingdom of my Father.” *my* And ⌞when they had sung a hymn,⌟ ⌞they went out⌟
1877 3836 993 3836 1609 4252 1609 2779 5630 2002
p.d d.dsf n.dsf d.gsm n.gsm r.gs.1 cj pt.aa.npm v.aai.3p

εἰς τὸ ὄρος τῶν ἐλαιῶν. 31 τότε λέγει αὐτοῖς ὁ Ἰησοῦς, ↱ πάντες
to the Mount of Olives. Then Jesus said to them, {the} *Jesus* “You will all
1650 3836 4001 3836 1777 5538 2652 3306 899 3836 2652 7007 4997 4246
p.a d.asn n.asn d.gpf n.gpf adv v.pai.3s r.dpm.3 d.nsm n.nsm a.npm

ὑμεῖς σκανδαλισθήσεσθε ἐν ἐμοὶ ἐν τῇ νυκτὶ ταύτῃ,
You fall away ⌞because of⌟ me {on} {the} this very night. *this very* For
7007 4997 1877 1609 1877 3836 4047 4047 3816 4047 1142
r.np.2 v.fpi.2p p.d r.ds.1 p.d d.dsf n.dsf r.dsf

γέγραπται γάρ, πατάξω τὸν ποιμένα, καὶ
it stands written, *For* ‘I will strike the shepherd, and the sheep of the flock
1211 1142 4250 3836 4478 2779 3836 4585 3836 3836 4479
v.rpi.3s cj v.fai.1s d.asm n.asm cj

διασκορπισθήσονται τὰ πρόβατα τῆς ποίμνης. 32 μετὰ δὲ τὸ
will be scattered.’ *the sheep of the flock* But after *But* {the} I
1399 3836 4585 3836 4479 1254 3552 1254 3836 1609
v.fpi.3p d.npn n.npn d.gsf n.gsf p.a cj d.asn

ἐγερθῆναί με προάξω ὑμᾶς εἰς τὴν Γαλιλαίαν. 33 ἀποκριθεὶς
have been raised, *I* ⌞I will go ahead of⌟ you into {the} Galilee.” Peter answered,
1586 1609 4575 7007 1650 3836 1133 4377 646
f.ap r.as.1 v.fai.1s r.ap.2 p.a d.asf n.asf pt.ap.nsm

δὲ ὁ Πέτρος εἶπεν αὐτῷ, εἰ ↱ πάντες σκανδαλισθήσονται ἐν σοί,
{and} {the} *Peter* saying to him, “Though they all fall away ⌞because of⌟ you,
1254 3836 4377 3306 899 1623 4997 4246 4997 1877 5148
cj d.nsm n.nsm v.aai.3s r.dsm.3 cj a.npm v.fpi.3p p.d r.ds.2

ἐγὼ ↱ οὐδέποτε σκανδαλισθήσομαι. 34 ἔφη αὐτῷ ὁ Ἰησοῦς,
I will never fall away.” Jesus said to him, {the} *Jesus* “I tell you
1609 4997 4030 4997 2652 5774 899 3836 2652 3306 3306 5148
r.ns.1 adv v.fpi.1s v.iai.3s r.dsm.3 d.nsm n.nsm

ἀμὴν λέγω σοι ὅτι ἐν ταύτῃ τῇ νυκτὶ πρὶν ἀλέκτορα φωνῆσαι
the truth, *I tell you* {that} {on} this very {the} night, before the rooster crows, you will
297 3306 5148 4022 1877 4047 3836 3816 4570 232 5888 565 565
pl v.pai.1s r.ds.2 cj p.d r.dsf d.dsf n.dsf cj n.asm f.aa

τρὶς ἀπαρνήσῃ με. 35 λέγει αὐτῷ ὁ Πέτρος, κἂν
deny me ⌞three times.”⌟ *you will deny me* Peter said to him, {the} *Peter* ⌞“Even though⌟
565 1609 5565 565 1609 4377 3306 899 3836 4377 2829
adv v.fmi.2s r.as.1 v.pai.3s r.dsm.3 d.nsm n.nsm crasis

NASB

and gave *it* to the
disciples, and said,
“Take, eat; this is
My body.” 27 And
when He had taken
a cup and given
thanks, He gave
it to them, saying,
“Drink from it, all
of you; 28 for this
is My blood of the
covenant, which
is poured out for
many for forgive-
ness of sins. 29 But
I say to you, I will
not drink of this
fruit of the vine
from now on until
that day when I
drink it new with
you in My Father’s
kingdom.”
30 After singing a
hymn, they went
out to the Mount of
Olives.
31 Then Jesus *said
to them, “You
will all fall away
because of Me
this night, for it
is written, ‘I WILL
STRIKE DOWN THE
SHEPHERD, AND THE
SHEEP OF THE FLOCK
SHALL BE SCAT-
TERED.’ 32 But after
I have been raised,
I will go ahead of
you to Galilee.”
33 But Peter said to
Him, “*Even* though
all may fall away
because of You,
I will never fall
away.” 34 Jesus said
to him, “Truly I
say to you that this
very night, before a
rooster crows, you
will deny Me three
times.” 35 Peter *said
to Him, “Even if

NIV

I have to die with
you, I will never
disown you." And
all the other disci-
ples said the same.

Gethsemane

[36]Then Jesus went
with his disciples
to a place called
Gethsemane, and
he said to them,
"Sit here while I
go over there and
pray." [37]He took
Peter and the two
sons of Zebedee
along with him,
and he began to
be sorrowful and
troubled. [38]Then
he said to them,
"My soul is over-
whelmed with
sorrow to the point
of death. Stay here
and keep watch
with me."
[39]Going a little
farther, he fell
with his face to
the ground and
prayed, "My Fa-
ther, if it is possi-
ble, may this cup
be taken from me.
Yet not as I will,
but as you will."
[40]Then he re-
turned to his dis-
ciples and found
them sleeping.
"Couldn't you men
keep watch with
me for one hour?"
he asked Peter.
[41]"Watch and pray
so that you will
not fall into temp-
tation. The spirit
is willing, but the
flesh is weak."
[42]He went away
a second time
and prayed, "My
Father, if it is not
possible for this
cup to be taken
away unless I
drink it, may your
will be done."
[43]When he

δέῃ με συν σοὶ ἀποθανεῖν, ⌊οὐ μή⌋ σε ἀπαρνήσομαι.
I must *I* die with you, *die* I will never deny you!" *I will deny*
1609 1256 1609 633 5250 5148 633 565 565 4024 3590 565 5148 565
v.pas.3s r.as.1 p.d r.ds.2 f.aa pl pl r.as.2 v.fmi.1s

ὁμοίως καὶ πάντες οἱ μαθηταὶ εἶπαν. 36 τότε ἔρχεται μετ' αὐτῶν
the same And all the disciples said the same. Then Jesus went with them
3931 2779 4246 3836 3412 3306 3931 3931 5538 2652 2262 3552 899
adv adv a.npm d.npm n.npm v.aai.3p adv v.pmi.3s p.g r.gpm.3

ὁ Ἰησοῦς εἰς χωρίον λεγόμενον Γεθσημανὶ καὶ λέγει τοῖς μαθηταῖς, καθίσατε
{the} *Jesus* to a place called Gethsemane and he said to his disciples, "Sit
3836 2652 1650 6005 3306 1149 2779 3306 3836 3412 2767
d.nsm n.nsm p.a n.asn pt.pp.asn n.asn cj v.pai.3s d.dpm n.dpm v.aam.2p

αὐτοῦ ⌊ἕως οὗ⌋[a] ↱ ἀπελθὼν ἐκεῖ προσεύξωμαι. 37 καὶ παραλαβὼν τὸν
here while I go over there and pray." And taking with him *{the}*
7000 2401 4005 4667 599 1695 4667 2779 4161 3836
adv p.g r.gsm pt.aa.nsm adv v.ams.1s cj pt.aa.nsm d.asm

Πέτρον καὶ τοὺς δύο υἱοὺς Ζεβεδαίου ἤρξατο λυπεῖσθαι καὶ ἀδημονεῖν. 38 τότε
Peter and the two sons of Zebedee, he began to be sorrowful and troubled. Then
4377 2779 3836 1545 5626 2411 806 3382 2779 86 5538
n.asm cj d.apm a.apm n.apm n.gsm v.ami.3s f.pp cj f.pa adv

λέγει αὐτοῖς, περίλυπός ἐστιν ἡ ψυχή μου ἕως
he said to them, "My soul is ⌊exceedingly sorrowful,⌋ *is* *{the}* *soul* *My* ⌊to the point⌋
3306 899 1609 6034 1639 4337 1639 3836 6034 1609 2401
v.pai.3s r.dpm.3 a.nsf v.pai.3s d.nsf n.nsf r.gs.1 p.g

θανάτου· μείνατε ὧδε καὶ γρηγορεῖτε μετ' ἐμοῦ. 39 καὶ προελθὼν μικρὸν ↰
of death; remain here and keep watch with me." And going a short distance beyond
2505 3531 6045 2779 1213 3552 1609 2779 4601 3625 4601
n.gsm v.aam.2p adv cj v.pam.2p p.g r.gs.1 cj pt.aa.nsm a.asn

ἔπεσεν ἐπὶ πρόσωπον αὐτοῦ προσευχόμενος καὶ λέγων, πάτερ μου, εἰ
them, he fell on his face, *his* praying, *{and}* *{saying}* "My Father, *My* if
4406 2093 899 4725 899 4667 2779 3306 1609 4252 1609 1623
v.aai.3s p.a n.asn r.gsm.3 pt.pm.nsm cj pt.pa.nsm n.vsm r.gs.1 cj

δυνατόν ἐστιν, → παρελθάτω ἀπ' ἐμοῦ τὸ ποτήριον τοῦτο· πλὴν
it be possible, *it be* let this cup pass from me! *{the}* *cup* *this* Yet
1639 1639 1543 1639 4047 4539 4216 608 1609 3836 4539 4047 4440
a.nsn v.pai.3s v.aam.3s p.g r.gs.1 d.nsn n.nsn r.nsn cj

οὐχ ὡς ἐγὼ θέλω ἀλλ' ὡς σύ. 40 καὶ ἔρχεται πρὸς τοὺς μαθητὰς καὶ
not as I will but as you will." Then he went to the disciples and
4024 6055 1609 2527 247 6055 5148 2779 2262 4639 3836 3412 2779
pl cj r.ns.1 v.pai.1s cj cj r.ns.2 cj v.pmi.3s p.a d.apm n.apm cj

εὑρίσκει αὐτοὺς καθεύδοντας, καὶ λέγει τῷ Πέτρῳ, οὕτως οὐκ
found them sleeping. *{and}* He said to Peter, "So, could you men not
2351 899 2761 2779 3306 3836 4377 4048 2710 2710 4024
v.pai.3s r.apm.3 pt.pa.apm cj v.pai.3s d.dsm n.dsm adv pl

ἰσχύσατε μίαν ὥραν γρηγορῆσαι μετ' ἐμοῦ; 41 γρηγορεῖτε καὶ
could you keep watch with me for a single hour? *keep watch* *with* *me* Stay alert and
2710 1213 1213 3552 1609 1651 6052 1213 3552 1609 1213 2779
v.aai.2p a.asf n.asf f.aa p.g r.gs.1 v.pam.2p cj

προσεύχεσθε, ⌊ἵνα μὴ⌋ ⌊εἰσέλθητε εἰς⌋ πειρασμόν· τὸ μὲν πνεῦμα
pray lest you enter a time of trial. The *indeed* spirit indeed is
4667 2671 3590 1656 1650 4280 3836 3525 4460 3525
v.pmm.2p cj pl v.aas.2p p.a n.asm d.nsn pl n.nsn

πρόθυμον ἡ δὲ σὰρξ ἀσθενής. 42 ⌊πάλιν ἐκ δευτέρου⌋ ↱ ἀπελθὼν
willing but the *but* flesh is weak." Once again he went away and
4609 1254 3836 1254 4922 822 4099 1666 1311 4667 599
a.nsn d.nsf cj n.nsf a.nsf adv p.g a.gsn pt.aa.nsm

προσηύξατο λέγων, πάτερ μου, εἰ ⌊οὐ δύναται⌋ τοῦτο παρελθεῖν ⌊ἐὰν
prayed, saying, "My Father, *My* if this cannot *this* pass unless
4667 3306 1609 4252 1609 1623 4047 4024 1538 4047 4216 1569
v.ami.3s pt.pa.nsm n.vsm r.gs.1 cj pl v.ppi.3s r.asn f.aa cj

μὴ⌋ αὐτὸ πίω, → γενηθήτω τὸ θέλημά σου. 43 καὶ ↱
I drink it, *I drink* may your will be done." *{the}* *will* *your* Then he
3590 4403 4403 899 4403 5148 2525 1181 3836 2525 5148 2779 2351
pl r.asn.3 v.aas.1s v.apm.3s d.nsn n.nsn r.gs.2 cj

NASB

I have to die with
You, I will not
deny You." All the
disciples said the
same thing too.

The Garden of Gethsemane

[36]Then Jesus
*came with them
to a place called
Gethsemane, and
*said to His dis-
ciples, "Sit here
while I go over
there and pray."
[37]And He took
with Him Peter
and the two sons
of Zebedee, and
began to be grieved
and distressed.
[38]Then He *said to
them, "My soul is
deeply grieved, to
the point of death;
remain here and
keep watch with
Me."
[39]And He went a
little beyond *them,*
and fell on His face
and prayed, saying,
"My Father, if it
is possible, let this
cup pass from Me;
yet not as I will,
but as You will."
[40]And He *came
to the disciples
and *found them
sleeping, and *said
to Peter, "So, you
men could not
keep watch with
Me for one hour?
[41]Keep watching
and praying that
you may not enter
into temptation; the
spirit is willing, but
the flesh is weak."
[42]He went away
again a second
time and prayed,
saying, "My Fa-
ther, if this cannot
pass away unless I
drink it, Your will
be done." [43]Again

[a] [οὐ] UBS.

NIV

came back, he
again found them
sleeping, because
their eyes were
heavy. [44]So he left
them and went
away once more
and prayed the
third time, saying
the same thing.
[45]Then he re-
turned to the dis-
ciples and said to
them, "Are you
still sleeping and
resting? Look, the
hour has come,
and the Son of
Man is delivered
into the hands of
sinners. [46]Rise! Let
us go! Here comes
my betrayer!"

Jesus Arrested

[47]While he was
still speaking,
Judas, one of the
Twelve, arrived.
With him was a
large crowd armed
with swords and
clubs, sent from
the chief priests
and the elders of
the people. [48]Now
the betrayer had
arranged a signal
with them: "The
one I kiss is the
man; arrest him."
[49]Going at once to
Jesus, Judas said,
"Greetings, Rab-
bi!" and kissed
him.
[50]Jesus replied,
"Do what you
came for, friend."[a]
Then the men
stepped forward,
seized Jesus and
arrested him.
[51]With that, one
of Jesus' compan-
ions reached for
his sword, drew it
out and struck the
servant of the high
priest,

[a] 50 Or *"Why have you come, friend?"*

⌊ἐλθὼν πάλιν⌋ εὗρεν αὐτοὺς καθεύδοντας, ἦσαν γὰρ αὐτῶν οἱ
returned and found them sleeping, for their eyes were *for* *their* *{the}*
2262 4099 2351 899 2761 1142 899 4057 1639 1142 899 3836
pt.aa.nsm adv v.aai.3s r.apm.3 pt.pa.apm v.iai.3p cj r.gpm.3 d.npm

ὀφθαλμοὶ βεβαρημένοι. 44 καὶ ἀφεὶς αὐτοὺς πάλιν ἀπελθὼν
eyes heavy. So he left them again and went away, and for the third
4057 976 2779 918 899 4099 599 1666 5569
n.npm pt.rp.npm cj pt.aa.nsm r.apm.3 adv pt.aa.nsm

προσηύξατο ἐκ τρίτου τὸν αὐτὸν λόγον εἰπὼν πάλιν. 45 τότε
time prayed *for* *third time* again using the same words. *using* *again* Then
5569 4667 1666 5569 4099 3306 3836 899 3364 3306 4099 5538
v.ami.3s p.g a.gsn d.asm r.asm n.asm pt.aa.nsm adv adv

ἔρχεται πρὸς τοὺς μαθητὰς καὶ λέγει αὐτοῖς, → → καθεύδετε τὸ[a] λοιπὸν
he returned to his disciples and said to them, "Are you still sleeping *{the}* *still*
2262 4639 3836 3412 2779 3306 899 3370 2761 3836 3370
v.pmi.3s p.a d.apm n.apm cj v.pai.3s r.dpm.3 psai.2p d.asn adv

καὶ ἀναπαύεσθε· ἰδοὺ ἤγγικεν ἡ ὥρα καὶ ὁ υἱὸς τοῦ ἀνθρώπου
and taking your rest? Look, the hour has come, *the* *hour* and the Son of Man
2779 399 2627 3836 6052 1581 3836 6052 2779 3836 5626 3836 476
cj v.pmm.2p j v.rai.3s d.nsf n.nsf cj d.nsm n.nsm d.gsm n.gsm

παραδίδοται εἰς χεῖρας ἁμαρτωλῶν. 46 ἐγείρεσθε ἄγωμεν· ἰδοὺ
is about to be betrayed into the hands of sinners. Get up, ⌊let us be going.⌋ Look,
4140 1650 5931 283 1586 72 2627
v.ppi.3s p.a n.apf a.gpm v.ppm.2p v.pas.1p j

ἤγγικεν ὁ παραδιδούς με. 47 καὶ ↱ ↱ ἔτι αὐτοῦ λαλοῦντος
here comes *{the}* my betrayer." *my* *{and}* While he was still *he* speaking,
1581 3836 1609 4140 1609 2779 3281 899 3281 2285 899 3281
v.rai.3s d.nsm pt.pa.nsm r.as.1 cj adv r.gsm.3 pt.pa.gsm

ἰδοὺ Ἰούδας εἷς τῶν δώδεκα ἦλθεν καὶ ⌊μετ' αὐτοῦ⌋ ὄχλος
{behold} Judas, one of the twelve, arrived *{and}* accompanied by a large crowd
2627 2683 1651 3836 1557 2262 2779 3552 899 4498 4063
j n.nsm a.nsm d.gpm a.gpm v.aai.3s cj p.g r.gsm.3 n.nsm

πολὺς μετὰ μαχαιρῶν καὶ ξύλων ἀπὸ τῶν ἀρχιερέων καὶ πρεσβυτέρων τοῦ
large *with* *swords* *and* *clubs* from the ruling priests and the elders of the
4498 3552 3479 2779 3833 608 3836 797 2779 4565 3836
a.nsm p.g n.gpf cj n.gpn p.g d.gpm n.gpm cj a.gpm d.gsm

λαοῦ. 48 ὁ δὲ παραδιδοὺς αὐτὸν ἔδωκεν αὐτοῖς
people, armed with swords and clubs. The *{and}* betrayer *{him}* had given them a
3295 3552 3479 2779 3833 3836 1254 4140 899 1443 899
n.gsm d.nsm cj pt.pa.nsm r.asm.3 v.aai.3s r.dpm.3

σημεῖον λέγων, ὃν ἂν φιλήσω αὐτός ἐστιν, κρατήσατε αὐτόν. 49 καὶ
sign, saying, "The one ~ I will kiss, he is the one; seize him." *{and}*
4956 3306 4005 323 5797 899 1639 3195 899 2779
n.asn pt.pa.nsm r.asm pl v.aas.1s r.nsm v.pai.3s v.aam.2p r.asm.3 cj

εὐθέως προσελθὼν τῷ Ἰησοῦ εἶπεν, χαῖρε, ῥαββί, καὶ
⌊Without hesitation⌋ Judas went up to Jesus and said, "Greetings, Rabbi!" and
2311 4665 3836 2652 3306 5897 4806 2779
adv pt.aa.nsm d.dsm n.dsm v.aai.3s v.pam.2s n.vsm cj

κατεφίλησεν αὐτόν. 50 ὁ δὲ Ἰησοῦς εἶπεν αὐτῷ, ἑταῖρε, ⌊ἐφ' ὃ⌋ πάρει.
kissed him. *{the}* *{and}* Jesus said to him, "Comrade, do what you came to
2968 899 3836 1254 2652 3306 899 2279 2093 4005 4205
v.aai.3s r.asm.3 d.nsm cj n.nsm v.aai.3s r.dsm.3 n.vsm p.a r.asn v.pai.2s

τότε ↱ προσελθόντες ἐπέβαλον τὰς χεῖρας ἐπὶ τὸν Ἰησοῦν καὶ ἐκράτησαν
do." Then they came forward, laid *{the}* hands on *{the}* Jesus and took
5538 2095 4665 2095 3836 5931 2093 3836 2652 2779 3195
adv pt.aa.npm v.aai.3p d.apf n.apf p.a d.asm n.asm cj v.aai.3p

αὐτόν. ↰ ↰ 51 καὶ ἰδοὺ εἷς τῶν μετὰ Ἰησοῦ ἐκτείνας τὴν χεῖρα
him into custody. But *{behold}* one of those with Jesus ⌊stretched out⌋ his hand,
899 3195 3195 2779 2627 1651 3836 3552 2652 1753 3836 5931
r.asm.3 cj j a.nsm d.gpm p.g n.gsm pt.aa.nsm d.asf n.asf

ἀπέσπασεν τὴν μάχαιραν αὐτοῦ καὶ πατάξας τὸν δοῦλον τοῦ ἀρχιερέως
drew *{the}* his sword, *his* and struck the slave of the high priest,
685 3836 899 3479 899 2779 4250 3836 1529 3836 797
v.aai.3s d.asf n.asf r.gsm.3 cj pt.aa.nsm d.asm n.asm d.gsm n.gsm

[a] [τὸ] UBS.

NASB

He came and found
them sleeping, for
their eyes were
heavy. [44]And He
left them again,
and went away and
prayed a third time,
saying the same
thing once more.
[45]Then He *came to
the disciples and
*said to them, "Are
you still sleeping
and resting? Be-
hold, the hour is at
hand and the Son
of Man is being
betrayed into the
hands of sinners.
[46]Get up, let us be
going; behold, the
one who betrays
Me is at hand!"

Jesus' Betrayal and Arrest

[47]While He was
still speaking, be-
hold, Judas, one of
the twelve, came
up accompanied by
a large crowd with
swords and clubs,
who came from
the chief priests
and elders of the
people. [48]Now he
who was betraying
Him gave them
a sign, saying,
"Whomever I kiss,
He is the one; seize
Him." [49]Immedi-
ately Judas went
to Jesus and said,
"Hail, Rabbi!"
and kissed Him.
[50]And Jesus said
to him, "Friend,
do what you have
come for." Then
they came and laid
hands on Jesus and
seized Him.
[51]And behold, one
of those who were
with Jesus reached
and drew out his
sword, and struck
the slave of the
high priest and cut

NIV

cutting off his ear.
[52]"Put your sword
back in its place,"
Jesus said to him,
"for all who draw
the sword will die
by the sword. [53]Do
you think I cannot
call on my Father,
and he will at once
put at my disposal
more than twelve
legions of angels?
[54]But how then
would the Scrip-
tures be fulfilled
that say it must
happen in this
way?"
[55]In that hour
Jesus said to the
crowd, "Am I
leading a rebel-
lion, that you have
come out with
swords and clubs
to capture me?
Every day I sat in
the temple courts
teaching, and you
did not arrest me.
[56]But this has all
taken place that
the writings of the
prophets might be
fulfilled." Then
all the disciples
deserted him and
fled.

Jesus Before the Sanhedrin

[57]Those who had
arrested Jesus took
him to Caiaphas
the high priest,
where the teachers
of the law and the
elders had assem-
bled. [58]But Peter
followed him at a
distance, right up
to the courtyard
of the high priest.
He entered and
sat down with the
guards to see the
outcome.
[59]The chief
priests and the
whole Sanhedrin
were looking for

ἀφεῖλεν αὐτοῦ τὸ ὠτίον. 52 τότε λέγει αὐτῷ ὁ Ἰησοῦς, ἀπόστρεψον τὴν
cutting off his {the} ear. Then Jesus said to him, {the} Jesus "Put {the}
904 899 3836 6065 5538 2652 3306 899 3836 2652 695 3836
v.aai.3s r.gsm.3 d.asn n.asn adv v.pai.3s r.dsm.3 d.nsm n.nsm v.aam.2s d.asf

μάχαιράν σου ↰ εἰς τὸν τόπον αὐτῆς· πάντες γὰρ οἱ λαβόντες
your sword your back into {the} its place! its For all For who draw the
5148 3479 5148 695 1650 3836 899 5536 899 1142 4246 1142 3836 3284
n.asf r.gs.2 p.a d.asm n.asm r.gsf.3 a.npm cj d.npm pt.aa.npm

μάχαιραν ἐν μαχαίρῃ ἀπολοῦνται. 53 ἢ δοκεῖς ὅτι ↱ ⌊οὐ
sword will die by the sword. will die Or ⌊do you think⌋ that I cannot
3479 660 660 1877 3479 660 2445 1506 4022 1538 4024
n.asf p.d n.dsf v.fmi.3p cj v.pai.2s cj pl

δύναμαι⌋ παρακαλέσαι τὸν πατέρα μου, καὶ → → παραστήσει μοι
ask of {the} my Father, my and he will immediately place at my
1538 4151 3836 1609 4252 1609 2779 785 4225 1609
v.ppi.1s f.aa d.asm n.asm r.gs.1 cj v.fai.3s r.ds.1

ἄρτι πλείω δώδεκα λεγιῶνας ἀγγέλων; 54 πῶς οὖν →
immediately disposal more than twelve legions of angels? But how then would the
785 4498 1557 3305 34 4802 4036 3836
adv adv.c a.apf n.apf n.gpm cj cj

πληρωθῶσιν αἱ γραφαὶ ὅτι οὕτως δεῖ γενέσθαι;
scriptures be fulfilled the scriptures that say it must happen ⌊in this way?"⌋ it must happen
1210 4444 3836 1210 4022 1256 1256 1181 4048 1256 1181
v.aps.3p d.npf n.npf cj adv v.pai.3s f.am

55 Ἐν ἐκείνῃ τῇ ὥρᾳ εἶπεν ὁ Ἰησοῦς τοῖς ὄχλοις, ὡς ἐπὶ λῃστὴν
At that {the} time Jesus said {the} Jesus to the crowds, as though {to} robber
1877 1697 3836 6052 2652 3306 3836 2652 3836 4063 6055 2093 3334
p.d r.dsf d.dsf n.dsf v.aai.3s d.nsm n.nsm d.dpm n.dpm pl p.a n.asm

ἐξήλθατε μετὰ μαχαιρῶν καὶ ξύλων συλλαβεῖν με;
⌊"Have you come out⌋ with swords and clubs to capture me as though I were a robber?
2002 3552 3479 2779 3833 5197 1609 6055 6055 3334
v.aai.2p p.g n.gpf cj n.gpn f.aa r.as.1

καθ' ἡμέραν ἐν τῷ ἱερῷ ἐκαθεζόμην διδάσκων καὶ ↱ ↱ οὐκ
Every day I sat in the temple I sat teaching, and you did not
2848 2465 2757 2757 1877 3836 2639 2757 1438 2779 3195 3195 4024
p.a n.asf p.d d.dsn n.dsn v.imi.1s pt.pa.nsm cj pl

ἐκρατήσατέ με. 56 τοῦτο δὲ ὅλον γέγονεν ἵνα
arrest me. But all this But all has happened that the writings of the
3195 1609 1254 3910 4047 1254 3910 1181 2671 3836 1210 3836 3836
v.aai.2p r.as.1 r.nsn cj a.nsn v.rai.3s cj

πληρωθῶσιν αἱ γραφαὶ τῶν προφητῶν. τότε οἱ μαθηταὶ πάντες
prophets might be fulfilled." the writings of the prophets Then the disciples all
4737 4444 3836 1210 3836 4737 5538 3836 3412 4246
v.aps.3p d.npf n.npf d.gpm n.gpm adv d.npm n.npm a.npm

ἀφέντες αὐτὸν ἔφυγον. 57 οἱ δὲ κρατήσαντες τὸν Ἰησοῦν
deserted him and ran away. Then the Then ⌊men who had laid hold of⌋ {the} Jesus
918 899 5771 1254 3836 1254 3195 3836 2652
pt.aa.npm r.asm.3 v.aai.3p d.npm cj pt.aa.npm d.asm n.asm

ἀπήγαγον πρὸς Καϊάφαν τὸν ἀρχιερέα, ὅπου οἱ γραμματεῖς καὶ οἱ
took him to Caiaphas, the high priest, where the scribes and the
552 4639 2780 3836 797 3963 3836 1208 2779 3836
v.aai.3p p.a n.asm d.asm n.asm cj d.npm n.npm cj d.npm

πρεσβύτεροι συνήχθησαν. 58 ὁ δὲ Πέτρος ἠκολούθει αὐτῷ ἀπὸ μακρόθεν ἕως
elders were gathered. {the} And Peter followed him at a distance, up to
4565 5251 3836 1254 4377 199 899 608 3427 2401
a.npm v.api.3p d.nsm cj n.nsm v.iai.3s r.dsm.3 p.g adv p.g

τῆς αὐλῆς τοῦ ἀρχιερέως καὶ εἰσελθὼν ἔσω ἐκάθητο μετὰ τῶν ὑπηρετῶν ἰδεῖν
the courtyard of the high priest; then going inside he sat down with the guards to see
3836 885 3836 797 2779 1656 2276 2764 3552 3836 5677 1625
d.gsf n.gsf d.gsm n.gsm cj pt.aa.nsm adv v.imi.3s p.g d.gpm n.gpm f.aa

τὸ τέλος. 59 οἱ δὲ ἀρχιερεῖς καὶ τὸ συνέδριον ὅλον ἐζήτουν
the end. Now the Now ruling priests and the entire Sanhedrin entire ⌊were looking for⌋
3836 5465 1254 3836 1254 797 2779 3836 3910 5284 3910 2426
d.asn n.asn d.npm cj n.npm cj d.nsn n.nsn a.nsn v.iai.3p

NASB

off his ear. [52]Then
Jesus *said to him,
"Put your sword
back into its place;
for all those who
take up the sword
shall perish by the
sword. [53]Or do you
think that I can-
not appeal to My
Father, and He will
at once put at My
disposal more than
twelve [a]legions of
angels? [54]How then
will the Scriptures
be fulfilled, *which
say* that it must
happen this way?"
[55]At that time
Jesus said to the
crowds, "Have
you come out with
swords and clubs
to arrest Me as *you
would* against a
robber? Every day
I used to sit in the
temple teaching
and you did not
seize Me. [56]But
all this has taken
place to fulfill the
Scriptures of the
prophets." Then all
the disciples left
Him and fled.

Jesus before Caiaphas

[57]Those who
had seized Jesus
led Him away to
Caiaphas, the high
priest, where the
scribes and the el-
ders were gathered
together. [58]But Pe-
ter was following
Him at a distance
as far as the court-
yard of the high
priest, and entered
in, and sat down
with the officers to
see the outcome.
[59]Now the chief
priests and the
whole Council kept
trying to obtain

[a] A legion equaled 6,000 troops

NIV

false evidence
against Jesus so
that they could put
him to death. 60 But
they did not find
any, though many
false witnesses
came forward.
Finally two came
forward 61 and
declared, "This
fellow said, 'I am
able to destroy the
temple of God and
rebuild it in three
days.'"
62 Then the high
priest stood up
and said to Jesus,
"Are you not going
to answer? What
is this testimony
that these men are
bringing against
you?" 63 But Jesus
remained silent.
The high priest
said to him, "I
charge you under
oath by the living
God: Tell us if you
are the Messiah,
the Son of God."
64 "You have said
so," Jesus replied.
"But I say to all of
you: From now on
you will see the
Son of Man sitting
at the right hand
of the Mighty One
and coming on the
clouds of heaven."[a]
65 Then the high
priest tore his
clothes and said,
"He has spoken
blasphemy! Why
do we need any
more witnesses?
Look, now you
have heard the
blasphemy. 66 What
do you think?"
"He is worthy of
death," they an-
swered.
67 Then they spit
in his face and
struck him with
their fists. Others
slapped him 68 and
said, "Prophesy to
us, Messiah. Who
hit you?"

[a] 64 See Psalm 110:1; Daniel 7:13.

ψευδομαρτυρίαν κατὰ τοῦ Ἰησοῦ ὅπως ↱ ↱ ↱ αὐτὸν θανατώσωσιν, 60 καὶ
false testimony against *{the}* Jesus so they could put him to death, but
6019 2848 3836 2652 3968 2506 2506 2506 899 2506 2779
n.asf p.g d.gsm n.gsm cj r.asm.3 v.aas.3p cj

οὐχ εὗρον ↱ ↱ πολλῶν προσελθόντων
they found none, *they found* even though many false witnesses came forward.
2351 2351 4024 2351 4665 4665 4498 6020 6020 4665
pl v.aai.3p a.gpm pt.aa.gpm

ψευδομαρτύρων. ὕστερον δὲ προσελθόντες δύο 61 εἶπαν, οὗτος ἔφη,
false witnesses Finally *{and}* two came forward *two* and declared, "This man said,
6020 5731 1254 1545 4665 1545 3306 4047 5774
n.gpm adv.c cj pt.aa.npm a.npm v.aai.3p r.nsm v.iai.3s

δύναμαι καταλῦσαι τὸν ναὸν τοῦ θεοῦ καὶ διὰ τριῶν ἡμερῶν
'I am able to destroy the temple of God and rebuild it in three days.'"
1538 2907 3836 3724 3836 2536 2779 3868 1328 5552 2465
v.ppi.1s f.aa d.asm n.asm d.gsm n.gsm cj p.g a.gpf n.gpf

οἰκοδομῆσαι. 62 καὶ ἀναστὰς ὁ ἀρχιερεὺς εἶπεν αὐτῷ, ↱ ↱
rebuild And the high priest stood up *the* *high priest* and said to him, "Have you
3868 2779 3836 797 797 482 3836 797 3306 899 646 646
f.aa cj pt.aa.nsm d.nsm n.nsm v.aai.3s r.dsm.3

οὐδὲν ἀποκρίνῃ τί οὗτοί σου καταμαρτυροῦσιν; 63 ὁ δὲ Ἰησοῦς
no answer to the charge these men *you* are bringing against you?" *{the}* But Jesus
4029 646 5515 4047 5148 2909 5148 3836 1254 2652
a.asn v.pmi.2s r.asn r.npm r.gs.2 v.pai.3p d.nsm cj n.nsm

ἐσιώπα. καὶ ὁ ἀρχιερεὺς εἶπεν αὐτῷ, ἐξορκίζω σε ↰ ↰ κατὰ τοῦ
⌞remained silent.⌟ Then the high priest said to him, "I put you under oath by the living
4995 2779 3836 797 3306 899 2019 5148 2019 2019 2848 3836 2409
v.iai.3s cj d.nsm n.nsm v.aai.3s r.dsm.3 v.pai.1s r.as.2 p.g d.gsm

θεοῦ τοῦ ζῶντος ἵνα ἡμῖν εἴπῃς εἰ σὺ εἶ ὁ χριστὸς ὁ υἱὸς τοῦ
God, *{the}* *living* *{that}* tell us *tell* if you are the Messiah, the Son of
2536 3836 2409 2671 3306 7005 3306 1623 5148 1639 3836 5986 3836 5626 3836
n.gsm d.gsm pt.pa.gsm cj r.dp.1 v.aas.2s cj r.ns.2 v.pai.2s d.nsm n.nsm d.nsm n.nsm d.gsm

θεοῦ. 64 λέγει αὐτῷ ὁ Ἰησοῦς, σὺ εἶπας. πλὴν λέγω ὑμῖν, ἀπ'
God." Jesus said to him, *{the}* *Jesus* "It is as you have said. Yet I tell you, from
2536 2652 3306 899 3836 2652 5148 3306 4440 3306 7007 608
n.gsm v.pai.3s r.dsm.3 d.nsm n.nsm r.ns.2 v.aai.2s cj v.pai.1s r.dp.2 p.g

ἄρτι ὄψεσθε τὸν υἱὸν τοῦ ἀνθρώπου καθήμενον ἐκ δεξιῶν τῆς
⌞now on⌟ ⌞you will see⌟ the Son of Man sitting at the right hand of The
785 3972 3836 5626 3836 476 2764 1666 1288 3836
adv v.fmi.2p d.asm n.asm d.gsm n.gsm pt.pm.asm p.g a.gpf d.gsf

δυνάμεως καὶ ἐρχόμενον ἐπὶ τῶν νεφελῶν τοῦ οὐρανοῦ. 65 τότε ὁ ἀρχιερεὺς
Power and coming on the clouds of heaven." Then the high priest
1539 2779 2262 2093 3836 3749 3836 4041 5538 3836 797
n.gsf cj pt.pm.asm p.g d.gpf n.gpf d.gsm n.gsm adv d.nsm n.nsm

διέρρηξεν τὰ ἱμάτια αὐτοῦ λέγων, ἐβλασφήμησεν· τί ἔτι χρείαν
tore *{the}* his robes *his* and said, "He has blasphemed! What further need
1396 3836 899 2668 899 3306 1059 5515 2285 5970
v.aai.3s d.apn n.apn r.gsm.3 pt.pa.nsm v.aai.3s r.asn adv n.asf

ἔχομεν μαρτύρων; ἴδε ↱ ↱ νῦν ἠκούσατε τὴν βλασφημίαν· 66 τί ↱ ὑμῖν
do we have of witnesses? *{look}* You have now heard his blasphemy. What is your
2400 3459 2623 201 201 3814 201 3836 1060 5515 1506 7007
v.pai.1p n.gpm pl adv v.aai.2p d.asf n.asf r.nsn r.dp.2

δοκεῖ; οἱ δὲ ἀποκριθέντες εἶπαν, ἔνοχος θανάτου ἐστίν. 67 τότε
verdict?" They *{and}* answered, saying, "He is deserving of death!" *He is* Then
1506 3836 1254 646 3306 1639 1639 1944 2505 1639 5538
v.pai.3s d.npm cj pt.ap.npm v.aai.3p a.nsm n.gsm v.pai.3s adv

ἐνέπτυσαν εἰς τὸ πρόσωπον αὐτοῦ καὶ ἐκολάφισαν αὐτόν, οἱ δὲ
they spat in *{the}* his face *his* and struck him; and some *and*
1870 1650 3836 899 4725 899 2779 3139 899 1254 3836 1254
v.aai.3p p.a d.asn n.asn r.gsm.3 cj v.aai.3p r.asm.3 d.npm cj

ἐράπισαν 68 λέγοντες, προφήτευσον ἡμῖν, χριστέ, τίς ἐστιν ὁ παίσας σε;
slapped him, saying, "Prophesy to us, you messiah! Who is it that struck you?"
4824 3306 4736 7005 5986 5515 1639 3836 4091 5148
v.aai.3p pt.pa.npm v.aam.2s r.dp.1 n.vsm r.nsm v.pai.3s d.nsm pt.aa.nsm r.as.2

NASB

false testimony
against Jesus, so
that they might
put Him to death.
60 They did not find
any, even though
many false wit-
nesses came for-
ward. But later on
two came forward,
61 and said, "This
man stated, 'I am
able to destroy
the temple of God
and to rebuild it in
three days.'" 62 The
high priest stood
up and said to
Him, "Do You not
answer? What is it
that these men are
testifying against
You?" 63 But Jesus
kept silent. And
the high priest said
to Him, "I adjure
You by the living
God, that You tell
us whether You are
the Christ, the Son
of God." 64 Jesus
*said to him, "You
have said it *your-
self;* nevertheless I
tell you, hereafter
you will see THE
SON OF MAN SITTING
AT THE RIGHT HAND
OF POWER, and COM-
ING ON THE CLOUDS
OF HEAVEN."
65 Then the high
priest tore his robes
and said, "He has
blasphemed! What
further need do we
have of witnesses?
Behold, you have
now heard the blas-
phemy; 66 what do
you think?" They
answered, "He de-
serves death!"
67 Then they spat
in His face and
beat Him with their
fists; and others
slapped Him, 68 and
said, "Prophesy
to us, You Christ;
who is the one who
hit You?"

NIV

Peter Disowns Jesus

69Now Peter was
sitting out in the
courtyard, and a
servant girl came
to him. "You also
were with Jesus of
Galilee," she said.
70But he denied it
before them all. "I
don't know what
you're talking
about," he said.
71Then he went
out to the gateway,
where another
servant girl saw
him and said to the
people there, "This
fellow was with
Jesus of Nazareth."
72He denied it
again, with an
oath: "I don't
know the man!"
73After a little
while, those stand-
ing there went up
to Peter and said,
"Surely you are
one of them; your
accent gives you
away."
74Then he began
to call down curs-
es, and he swore
to them, "I don't
know the man!"
Immediately a
rooster crowed.
75Then Peter re-
membered the
word Jesus had
spoken: "Before
the rooster crows,
you will disown
me three times."
And he went out-
side and wept bit-
terly.

Judas Hangs Himself

27 Early in the
morning,
all the chief priests
and the elders of
the people made
their plans how
to have Jesus ex-
ecuted. 2So they
bound him, led
him away

69 Ὁ δὲ Πέτρος ἐκάθητο ἔξω ἐν τῇ αὐλῇ· καὶ προσῆλθεν
{the} Now Peter was sitting outside in the courtyard; and a servant girl came up
3836 1254 4377 2764 2032 1877 3836 885 2779 1651 4087 4087 4665
d.nsm cj n.nsm v.imi.3s adv p.d d.dsf n.dsf cj v.aai.3s

αὐτῷ μία παιδίσκη λέγουσα, καὶ σὺ ἦσθα μετὰ Ἰησοῦ τοῦ Γαλιλαίου.
to him *a* *servant girl* and said, "You too *You* were with Jesus of Galilee."
899 1651 4087 3306 5148 2779 5148 1639 3552 2652 3836 1134
r.dsm.3 a.nsf n.nsf pt.pa.nsf adv r.ns.2 v.iai.2s p.g n.gsm d.gsm a.gsm

70 ὁ δὲ ἠρνήσατο ἔμπροσθεν πάντων λέγων, ↱ ↱ οὐκ οἶδα τί
But he *But* denied it before them all, saying, "I do not know what
1254 3836 1254 766 1869 4246 3306 3857 3857 4024 3857 5515
d.nsm cj v.ami.3s p.g a.gpm pt.pa.nsm pl v.rai.1s r.asn

λέγεις. 71 ἐξελθόντα δὲ εἰς τὸν πυλῶνα
⌊you are talking about."⌋ Then he went out *Then* into the gateway, where another servant girl
3306 1254 2002 1254 1650 3836 4784 257 257
v.pai.2s pt.aa.asm cj p.a d.asm n.asm

εἶδεν αὐτὸν ἄλλη καὶ λέγει τοῖς ἐκεῖ, οὗτος ἦν μετὰ Ἰησοῦ τοῦ
saw him *another girl* and said to those who were there, "This man was with Jesus the
1625 899 257 2779 3306 3836 1695 4047 1639 3552 2652 3836
v.aai.3s r.asm.3 r.nsf cj v.pai.3s d.dpm adv r.nsm v.iai.3s p.g n.gsm d.gsm

Ναζωραίου. 72 καὶ πάλιν ἠρνήσατο μετὰ ὅρκου ὅτι ↱ ↱ οὐκ οἶδα τὸν
Nazarene." But again he denied it with an oath, ~ "I do not know the
3717 2779 4099 766 3552 3992 4022 3857 3857 4024 3857 3836
n.gsm cj adv v.ami.3s p.g n.gsm cj pl v.rai.1s d.asm

ἄνθρωπον. 73 μετὰ μικρὸν δὲ προσελθόντες οἱ
man!" And after a little while *And* those standing around came up *those*
476 1254 3552 3625 1254 3836 2705 2705 4665 3836
n.asm p.a a.asn cj pt.aa.npm d.npm

ἑστῶτες εἶπον τῷ Πέτρῳ, ἀληθῶς καὶ σὺ ἐξ αὐτῶν
standing around to Peter and said, *to* *Peter* "Surely you too *you* are one of them,
2705 3836 4377 3306 3836 4377 242 5148 2779 5148 1639 1666 899
pt.ra.npm v.aai.3p d.dsm n.dsm adv adv r.ns.2 p.g r.gpm.3

εἶ, καὶ γὰρ ἡ → λαλιά σου δῆλόν σε ποιεῖ. 74 τότε ἤρξατο
are *{also}* for the way you talk *you* makes it clear." *{you}* *makes* Then he began
1639 2779 1142 3836 5148 3282 5148 4472 1316 5148 4472 5538 806
v.pai.2s adv cj d.nsf n.nsf r.gs.2 a.asm r.as.2 v.pai.3s adv v.ami.3s

καταθεματίζειν καὶ ὀμνύειν ὅτι ↱ ↱ οὐκ οἶδα τὸν ἄνθρωπον.
⌊to invoke curses on himself⌋ and swear to them, ~ "I do not know that man!"
2874 2779 3923 4022 3857 3857 4024 3857 3836 476
f.pa cj f.pa cj pl v.rai.1s d.asm n.asm

καὶ εὐθέως ἀλέκτωρ ἐφώνησεν. 75 καὶ ἐμνήσθη ὁ Πέτρος τοῦ
And immediately the rooster crowed. Then Peter remembered *{the}* *Peter* *{the}*
2779 2311 232 5888 2779 4377 3630 3836 4377 3836
cj adv n.nsm v.aai.3s cj v.api.3s d.nsm n.nsm d.gsn

ῥήματος Ἰησοῦ εἰρηκότος ὅτι πρὶν ἀλέκτορα φωνῆσαι
what Jesus had said, ~ "Before the rooster crows, you will deny me
4839 2652 3306 4022 4570 232 5888 565 565 565 1609
n.gsn n.gsm pt.ra.gsm cj cj n.asm f.aa

τρὶς ἀπαρνήσῃ με· καὶ ↱ ἐξελθὼν ἔξω ἔκλαυσεν πικρῶς.
⌊three times."⌋ *you will deny* *me* And he went outside and wept bitterly.
5565 565 1609 2779 3081 2002 2032 3081 4396
adv v.fmi.2s r.as.1 cj pt.aa.nsm adv v.aai.3s adv

27:1 πρωΐας δὲ γενομένης συμβούλιον ἔλαβον πάντες οἱ
⌊Early in the morning,⌋ *{and}* *{being}* *plans* *laid* all the
4746 1254 1181 5206 3284 4246 3836
n.gsf cj pt.am.gsf n.asn v.aai.3p a.npm d.npm

ἀρχιερεῖς καὶ οἱ πρεσβύτεροι τοῦ λαοῦ κατὰ τοῦ Ἰησοῦ ὥστε
ruling priests and the elders of the people laid plans against *{the}* Jesus, how
797 2779 3836 4565 3836 3295 3284 5206 2848 3836 2652 6063
n.npm cj d.npm a.npm d.gsm n.gsm p.g d.gsm n.gsm cj

θανατῶσαι αὐτόν· ↰ ↰ 2 καὶ δήσαντες αὐτὸν ἀπήγαγον ← καὶ
they might put him to death. And ⌊when they had bound⌋ him, they led him away and
2506 899 2506 2506 2779 1313 899 552 2779
f.aa r.asm.3 cj pt.aa.npm r.asm.3 v.aai.3p cj

NASB

Peter's Denials

69Now Peter was
sitting outside
in the courtyard,
and a servant-girl
came to him and
said, "You too
were with Jesus
the Galilean." 70But
he denied *it* before
them all, saying, "I
do not know what
you are talking
about." 71When he
had gone out to the
gateway, another
servant-girl saw
him and *said to
those who were
there, "This man
was with Jesus of
Nazareth." 72And
again he denied
it with an oath, "I
do not know the
man." 73A little
later the bystanders
came up and said
to Peter, "Surely
you too are *one*
of them; for even
the way you talk
gives you away."
74Then he began to
curse and swear,
"I do not know the
man!" And im-
mediately a rooster
crowed. 75And Pe-
ter remembered the
word which Jesus
had said, "Before a
rooster crows, you
will deny Me three
times." And he
went out and wept
bitterly.

Judas's Remorse

27:1Now when
morning came, all
the chief priests
and the elders of
the people con-
ferred together
against Jesus to put
Him to death; 2and
they bound Him,
and led Him

NIV

and handed him
over to Pilate the
governor.
3 When Judas,
who had betrayed
him, saw that Jesus
was condemned,
he was seized with
remorse and re-
turned the thirty
pieces of silver to
the chief priests
and the elders. 4 "I
have sinned," he
said, "for I have
betrayed innocent
blood."
"What is that to
us?" they replied.
"That's your re-
sponsibility."
5 So Judas threw
the money into
the temple and
left. Then he went
away and hanged
himself.
6 The chief priests
picked up the coins
and said, "It is
against the law to
put this into the
treasury, since it is
blood money." 7 So
they decided to use
the money to buy
the potter's field as
a burial place for
foreigners. 8 That
is why it has been
called the Field of
Blood to this day.
9 Then what was
spoken by Jeremi-
ah the prophet was
fulfilled: "They
took the thirty
pieces of silver, the
price set on him
by the people of
Israel, 10 and they
used them to buy
the potter's field,
as the Lord com-
manded me."[a]

Jesus Before Pilate

11 Meanwhile
Jesus stood before
the governor, and
the governor asked
him, "Are you the
king of the Jews?"

[a] 10 See Zech. 11:12,13; Jer. 19:1-13; 32:6-9.

παρέδωκαν ← Πιλάτῳ τῷ ἡγεμόνι. 3 τότε → ἰδὼν Ἰούδας
turned him over to Pilate the governor. Then when Judas, his betrayer, saw *Judas*
4140 4397 3836 2450 5538 2683 899 4140 1625 2683
v.aai.3p n.dsm d.dsm n.dsm adv pt.aa.nsm n.nsm

ὁ παραδιδοὺς αὐτὸν ὅτι κατεκρίθη, ↱ μεταμεληθεὶς ἔστρεψεν
{the} betrayer his that Jesus was condemned, he ⌊was filled with remorse⌋ and brought
3836 4140 899 4022 2891 5138 3564 5138
d.nsm pt.pa.nsm r.asm.3 cj v.api.3s pt.ap.nsm v.aai.3s

τὰ τριάκοντα ἀργύρια ↰ τοῖς ἀρχιερεῦσιν καὶ πρεσβυτέροις 4 λέγων,
the thirty silver coins back to the ruling priests and elders, saying,
3836 5558 736 5138 3836 797 2779 4565 3306
d.apn a.apn n.apn d.dpm n.dpm cj a.dpm pt.pa.nsm

ἥμαρτον παραδοὺς αἷμα ἀθῷον. οἱ δὲ εἶπαν, τί πρὸς
"I have sinned; I betrayed innocent blood." *innocent* But they *But* said, "What is that to
279 4140 127 135 127 1254 3836 1254 3306 5515 4639
v.aai.1s pt.aa.nsm n.asn a.asn d.npm cj v.aai.3p r.nsn p.a

ἡμᾶς; ↱ ↱ σὺ ὄψῃ. 5 καὶ ↱ ῥίψας τὰ ἀργύρια εἰς τὸν ναὸν
us? It is your responsibility!" Then he threw the silver coins into the temple and
7005 3972 3972 5148 3972 2779 432 4849 3836 736 1650 3836 3724
r.ap.1 r.ns.2 v.fmi.2s cj pt.aa.nsm d.apn n.apn p.a d.asm n.asm

ἀνεχώρησεν, καὶ ἀπελθὼν ἀπήγξατο. 6 οἱ δὲ ἀρχιερεῖς λαβόντες τὰ
left; and going away, he hanged himself. But the *But* ruling priests, picking up the
432 2779 599 551 1254 3836 1254 797 3284 3836
v.aai.3s cj pt.aa.nsm v.ami.3s d.npm cj n.npm pt.aa.npm d.apn

ἀργύρια εἶπαν, ↱ ↱ οὐκ ἔξεστιν βαλεῖν αὐτὰ εἰς τὸν κορβανᾶν, ἐπεὶ
coins, said, "It is not lawful to put these into the treasury, since it is
736 3306 1997 1997 4024 1997 965 899 1650 3836 3168 2075 1639 1639
n.apn v.aai.3p pl v.pai.3s f.aa r.apn.3 p.a d.asm n.asm cj

τιμὴ αἵματός ἐστιν. 7 συμβούλιον δὲ ↱ λαβόντες
blood money." *blood it is with one another* So they consulted with one another and with
135 5507 135 1639 5206 1254 60 3284 5206 5206 5206 1666
n.nsf n.gsn v.pai.3s n.asn cj pt.aa.npm

ἠγόρασαν ἐξ αὐτῶν τὸν ἀγρὸν τοῦ κεραμέως εἰς ταφὴν
the money bought *with money* the potter's field *{the} potter's* as a ⌊place to bury⌋
899 60 1666 899 3836 3038 69 3836 3038 1650 5438
v.aai.3p p.g r.gpn.3 d.asm n.asm d.gsm n.gsm p.a n.asf

τοῖς ξένοις. 8 διὸ ἐκλήθη ὁ ἀγρὸς ἐκεῖνος ἀγρὸς αἵματος
{the} foreigners. Therefore that field ⌊has been called⌋ *{the} field that* the "Field of Blood"
3836 3828 1475 1697 69 2813 3836 69 1697 69 135
d.dpm n.dpm cj v.api.3s d.nsm n.nsm r.nsm n.nsm n.gsn

ἕως τῆς σήμερον. 9 τότε ἐπληρώθη τὸ ῥηθὲν διὰ Ἰερεμίου
to this very day. Then was fulfilled that ⌊which was spoken⌋ by the prophet Jeremiah,
2401 3836 4958 5538 4444 3836 3306 1328 3836 4737 2635
p.g d.gsf adv adv v.api.3s d.nsn pt.ap.nsn p.g n.gsm

τοῦ προφήτου λέγοντος, καὶ ἔλαβον τὰ τριάκοντα ἀργύρια, τὴν τιμὴν τοῦ
the prophet saying, *{and}* "They took the thirty silver coins, the price of
3836 4737 3306 2779 3284 3836 5558 736 3836 5507 3836
d.gsm n.gsm pt.pa.gsm cj v.aai.3p d.apn a.apn n.apn d.asf n.asf d.gsm

τετιμημένου ὃν ἐτιμήσαντο ἀπὸ → → υἱῶν Ἰσραήλ, 10 καὶ ἔδωκαν
him ⌊on whom⌋ a ⌊price had been set⌋ by some of the sons of Israel, and they gave
5506 4005 5506 608 5626 2702 2779 1443
pt.rp.gsm r.asm v.ami.3p p.g n.gpm n.gsm cj v.aai.3p

αὐτὰ εἰς τὸν ἀγρὸν τοῦ κεραμέως, καθὰ συνέταξέν μοι κύριος.
them for the potter's field *{the} potter's* as the Lord directed me." *Lord*
899 1650 3836 3038 69 3836 3038 2745 3261 5332 1609 3261
r.apn.3 p.a d.asm n.asm d.gsm n.gsm cj v.aai.3s r.ds.1 n.nsm

11 ὁ δὲ Ἰησοῦς ἐστάθη ἔμπροσθεν τοῦ ἡγεμόνος· καὶ ἐπηρώτησεν
{the} Then Jesus stood before the governor; and the governor questioned
3836 1254 2652 2705 1869 3836 2450 2779 3836 2450 2089
d.nsm cj n.nsm v.api.3s p.g d.gsm n.gsm cj v.aai.3s

αὐτὸν ὁ ἡγεμὼν λέγων, σὺ εἶ ὁ βασιλεὺς τῶν Ἰουδαίων; ὁ δὲ
him, *the governor* saying, "Are you *Are* the king of the Jews?" *{the} {and}*
899 3836 2450 3306 1639 5148 1639 3836 995 3836 2681 3836 1254
r.asm.3 d.nsm n.nsm pt.pa.nsm r.ns.2 v.pai.2s d.nsm n.nsm d.gpm a.gpm d.nsm cj

NASB

away and delivered
Him to Pilate the
governor.
3 Then when
Judas, who had
betrayed Him, saw
that He had been
condemned, he
felt remorse and
returned the thirty
pieces of silver to
the chief priests
and elders, 4 saying,
"I have sinned by
betraying innocent
blood." But they
said, "What is that
to us? See *to that*
yourself!" 5 And he
threw the pieces
of silver into the
temple sanctuary
and departed; and
he went away and
hanged himself.
6 The chief priests
took the pieces of
silver and said, "It
is not lawful to
put them into the
temple treasury,
since it is the price
of blood." 7 And
they conferred to-
gether and with the
money bought the
Potter's Field as
a burial place for
strangers. 8 For this
reason that field
has been called the
Field of Blood to
this day. 9 Then that
which was spoken
through Jeremiah
the prophet was
fulfilled: "AND
THEY TOOK THE THIR-
TY PIECES OF SILVER,
THE PRICE OF THE
ONE WHOSE PRICE
HAD BEEN SET by the
sons of Israel; 10 AND
THEY GAVE THEM
FOR THE POTTER'S
FIELD, AS THE LORD
DIRECTED ME."

Jesus before Pilate

11 Now Jesus stood
before the gover-
nor, and the gov-
ernor questioned
Him, saying, "Are
You the King of
the Jews?" And

NIV

"You have said
so," Jesus replied.
12 When he was
accused by the
chief priests and
the elders, he
gave no answer.
13 Then Pilate
asked him, "Don't
you hear the tes-
timony they are
bringing against
you?" 14 But Jesus
made no reply, not
even to a single
charge—to the
great amazement
of the governor.
15 Now it was the
governor's custom
at the festival to
release a prison-
er chosen by the
crowd. 16 At that
time they had a
well-known pris-
oner whose name
was Jesus[a] Barab-
bas. 17 So when the
crowd had gath-
ered, Pilate asked
them, "Which one
do you want me
to release to you:
Jesus Barabbas,
or Jesus who is
called the Messi-
ah?" 18 For he knew
it was out of self-
interest that they
had handed Jesus
over to him.
19 While Pilate
was sitting on the
judge's seat, his
wife sent him this
message: "Don't
have anything to
do with that in-
nocent man, for
I have suffered a
great deal today in
a dream because of
him."
20 But the chief
priests and the el-
ders persuaded the
crowd to

[a] 16 Many manu-
scripts do not have
Jesus; also in verse
17.

Ἰησοῦς ἔφη, σὺ λέγεις. 12 καὶ ἐν τῷ κατηγορεῖσθαι αὐτὸν ὑπὸ τῶν
Jesus said, "You say so." But when {the} he was accused *he* by the
2652 5774 5148 3306 2779 1877 3836 899 2989 899 5679 3836
n.nsm v.iai.3s r.ns.2 v.pai.2s cj p.d d.dsn f.pp r.asm.3 p.g d.gpm

ἀρχιερέων καὶ πρεσβυτέρων ↱ ↱ οὐδὲν ἀπεκρίνατο. 13 τότε λέγει αὐτῷ
ruling priests and elders, he gave no answer. Then Pilate said to him,
797 2779 4565 646 646 4029 646 5538 4397 3306 899
n.gpm cj a.gpm a.asn v.ami.3s adv v.pai.3s r.dsm.3

ὁ Πιλᾶτος, ↱ ↱ οὐκ ἀκούεις πόσα σου καταμαρτυροῦσιν;
{the} Pilate "Do you not hear how many *you* ⌊accusations they are bringing against⌋
3836 4397 201 201 4024 201 4531 5148 2909
d.nsm n.nsm pl v.pai.2s r.apn r.gs.2 v.pai.3p

14 καὶ οὐκ ἀπεκρίθη αὐτῷ πρὸς οὐδὲ ἓν ῥῆμα, ὥστε
you?" But Jesus refused to answer *{him} {to}* even a single charge, so that the governor
5148 2779 4024 646 899 4639 4028 1651 4839 6063 3836 2450
cj pl v.api.3s r.dsm.3 p.a adv a.asn n.asn cj

→ θαυμάζειν τὸν ἡγεμόνα λίαν. 15 κατὰ δὲ ἑορτὴν
was greatly astonished. *the governor greatly* Now at *Now* ⌊festival time⌋ the governor
3336 2513 3836 2450 3336 1254 2848 1254 2038 2450
f.pa d.asm n.asm adv p.a cj n.asf

εἰώθει ὁ ἡγεμὼν ἀπολύειν ἕνα τῷ ὄχλῳ δέσμιον ὃν
was accustomed *{the} governor* to release one prisoner ⌊for the⌋ crowd, *prisoner* whomever
1665 3836 2450 668 1651 1300 3836 4063 1300 4005
v.lai.3s d.nsm n.nsm f.pa a.asm d.dsm n.dsm n.asm r.asm

ἤθελον. 16 εἶχον δὲ τότε δέσμιον
they wanted. At that time ⌊they were holding⌋ *{and} At that time* in custody a notorious prisoner
2527 5538 5538 5538 2400 1254 5538 2168 1300
v.iai.3p v.iai.3p cj adv n.asm

ἐπίσημον λεγόμενον Ἰησοῦν[a] Βαραββᾶν. 17 → συνηγμένων οὖν αὐτῶν
notorious named Jesus Barabbas. So when the crowd had gathered, *So crowd*
2168 3306 2652 972 4036 899 5251 4036 899
a.asm pt.pp.asm n.asm n.asm pt.rp.gpm cj r.gpm.3

εἶπεν αὐτοῖς ὁ Πιλᾶτος, τίνα θέλετε ἀπολύσω ὑμῖν, [b]Ἰησοῦν
Pilate said to them, *{the} Pilate* ⌊"Which one⌋ ⌊do you want⌋ me to release for you: Jesus
4397 3306 899 3836 4397 5515 2527 668 7007 2652
v.aai.3s r.dpm.3 d.nsm n.nsm r.asm v.pai.2p v.aas.1s r.dp.2 n.asm

τὸν Βαραββᾶν ἢ Ἰησοῦν τὸν λεγόμενον χριστόν; 18 ᾔδει γὰρ ὅτι
{the} Barabbas, or Jesus who is called Messiah?" For he knew *For* that it was
3836 972 2445 2652 3836 3306 5986 1142 3857 1142 4022
d.asm n.asm cj n.asm d.asm pt.pp.asm n.asm v.lai.3s cj cj

διὰ φθόνον παρέδωκαν αὐτόν. ↰ 19 → καθημένου δὲ αὐτοῦ
⌊out of⌋ envy that they had handed him over. But while Pilate was sitting *But Pilate*
1328 5784 4140 899 4140 1254 899 2764 1254 899
p.a n.asm v.aai.3p r.asm.3 pt.pm.gsm cj r.gsm.3

ἐπὶ τοῦ βήματος ἀπέστειλεν πρὸς αὐτὸν ἡ γυνὴ αὐτοῦ
on the ⌊judgment seat,⌋ his wife sent *{to}* him *{the} wife his* a message,
2093 3836 1037 899 1222 690 4639 899 3836 1222 899
p.g d.gsn n.gsn v.aai.3s p.a r.asm.3 d.nsf n.nsf r.gsm.3

λέγουσα, μηδὲν σοὶ καὶ τῷ δικαίῳ ἐκείνῳ·
saying, "Have nothing *{to you} {and}* to do with that ⌊innocent man;⌋ *that* for I have
3306 3594 5148 2779 3836 1697 1465 1697 1142 4248 4248
pt.pa.nsf a.nsn r.ds.2 cj d.dsm a.dsm r.dsm

πολλὰ γὰρ ἔπαθον σήμερον κατ᾽ ὄναρ δι᾽ αὐτόν.
suffered many things *for I have suffered* in a dream today *in dream* ⌊on account of⌋ him."
4248 4498 1142 4248 2848 3941 4958 2848 3941 1328 899
a.apn cj v.aai.1s adv p.a n.asn p.a r.asm.3

20 οἱ δὲ ἀρχιερεῖς καὶ οἱ πρεσβύτεροι ἔπεισαν τοὺς ὄχλους ἵνα
But the *But* ruling priests and the elders persuaded the crowds to
1254 3836 1254 797 2779 3836 4565 4275 3836 4063 2671
d.npm cj n.npm cj d.npm a.npm v.aai.3p d.apm n.apm cj

[a] [Ἰησοῦν] UBS.
[b] [Ἰησοῦν τὸν] UBS.

NASB

Jesus said to him,
"*It is as* you say."
12 And while He
was being accused
by the chief priests
and elders, He did
not answer. 13 Then
Pilate *said to Him,
"Do You not hear
how many things
they testify against
You?" 14 And He
did not answer him
with regard to even
a *single* charge, so
the governor was
quite amazed.
15 Now at *the* feast
the governor was
accustomed to re-
lease for the people
any one prisoner
whom they wanted.
16 At that time they
were holding a
notorious prisoner,
called Barabbas.
17 So when the
people gathered
together, Pilate said
to them, "Whom
do you want me
to release for you?
Barabbas, or Je-
sus who is called
Christ?" 18 For he
knew that because
of envy they had
handed Him over.
19 While he was
sitting on the
judgment seat, his
wife sent him *a
message,* saying,
"Have nothing to
do with that righ-
teous Man; for last
night I suffered
greatly in a dream
because of Him."
20 But the chief
priests and the el-
ders persuaded the
crowds to ask

NIV

ask for Barabbas
and to have Jesus
executed.
21 "Which of the
two do you want
me to release to
you?" asked the
governor.
"Barabbas," they
answered.
22 "What shall
I do, then, with
Jesus who is called
the Messiah?" Pi-
late asked.
They all an-
swered, "Crucify
him!"
23 "Why? What
crime has he com-
mitted?" asked
Pilate.
But they shout-
ed all the louder,
"Crucify him!"
24 When Pilate
saw that he was
getting nowhere,
but that instead an
uproar was start-
ing, he took water
and washed his
hands in front of
the crowd. "I am
innocent of this
man's blood," he
said. "It is your re-
sponsibility!"
25 All the people
answered, "His
blood is on us and
on our children!"
26 Then he re-
leased Barabbas to
them. But he had
Jesus flogged, and
handed him over
to be crucified.

The Soldiers Mock Jesus

27 Then the gov-
ernor's soldiers
took Jesus into the
Praetorium and
gathered the whole
company of sol-
diers around him.
28 They stripped
him and put a scar-
let robe on him,
29 and then twisted
together

αἰτήσωνται τὸν Βαραββᾶν, τὸν δὲ ↱ ↱ Ἰησοῦν ἀπολέσωσιν. 21
ask for {the} Barabbas {the} and to have Jesus executed. Once again the
160 3836 972 3836 1254 660 660 2652 660 3836
v.ams.3p d.asm n.asm d.asm cj n.asm v.aas.3p

ἀποκριθεὶς δὲ ὁ ἡγεμὼν εἶπεν αὐτοῖς, τίνα θέλετε
governor asked {and} the governor {said} them, "Which of the two ⌞do you want⌟
2450 646 1254 3836 2450 3306 899 5515 608 3836 1545 2527
pt.ap.nsm cj d.nsm n.nsm v.aai.3s r.dpm.3 r.asm v.pai.2p

ἀπὸ τῶν δύο ἀπολύσω ὑμῖν; οἱ δὲ εἶπαν, τὸν Βαραββᾶν. 22 λέγει
of the two me to release for you?" And they And said, {the} "Barabbas." Pilate said
608 3836 1545 668 7007 1254 3836 1254 3306 3836 972 4397 3306
p.g d.gpm a.gpm v.aas.1s r.dp.2 d.npm cj v.aai.3p d.asm n.asm v.pai.3s

αὐτοῖς ὁ Πιλᾶτος, τί οὖν ποιήσω Ἰησοῦν τὸν λεγόμενον χριστόν;
to them, {the} Pilate "Then what Then ⌞shall I do with⌟ Jesus who is called Messiah?"
899 3836 4397 4036 5515 4036 4472 2652 3836 3306 5986
r.dpm.3 d.nsm n.nsm r.asn cj v.aas.1s n.asm d.asm pt.pp.asm n.asm

λέγουσιν πάντες, σταυρωθήτω. 23 ὁ δὲ ἔφη, τί
With one voice they shouted, one voice "Let him be crucified!" Pilate {and} asked, "But what
4246 4246 3306 4246 5090 3836 1254 5774 1142 5515
v.pai.3p a.npm v.apm.3s d.nsm cj v.iai.3s r.asn

γὰρ κακὸν ἐποίησεν; οἱ δὲ περισσῶς ἔκραζον λέγοντες,
But crime has he committed?" But they But all the louder shouted all the louder, {saying}
1142 2805 4472 1254 3836 1254 4360 3189 4360 4360 4360 3306
cj a.asn v.aai.3s d.npm cj adv v.iai.3p pt.pa.npm

σταυρωθήτω. 24 → ἰδὼν δὲ ὁ Πιλᾶτος ὅτι οὐδὲν
"Crucify him!" So when Pilate saw So {the} Pilate that he was getting nowhere
5090 1254 4397 1625 1254 3836 4397 4022 6067 6067 6067 4029
v.apm.3s pt.aa.nsm cj d.nsm n.nsm cj a.asn

ὠφελεῖ ἀλλὰ μᾶλλον θόρυβος γίνεται, ↱ λαβὼν ὕδωρ ἀπενίψατο τὰς
he was getting but rather that a riot was starting, he took water and washed his
6067 247 3437 2573 1181 672 3284 5623 672 3836
v.pai.3s cj adv.c n.nsm v.pmi.3s pt.aa.nsm n.asn v.ami.3s d.apf

χεῖρας ἀπέναντι τοῦ ὄχλου λέγων, ἀθῷός εἰμι ἀπὸ τοῦ
hands before the crowd, saying, "I am innocent I am of {the} this man's
5931 595 3836 4063 3306 1639 1639 127 1639 608 3836 4047 4047
n.apf p.g d.gsm n.gsm pt.pa.nsm a.nsm v.pai.1s p.g d.gsn

αἵματος[a] τούτου· ↱ ↱ ὑμεῖς ὄψεσθε. 25 καὶ ἀποκριθεὶς πᾶς
blood; this man's it is your responsibility." And all the people answered, all
135 4047 3972 3972 7007 3972 2779 4246 3836 3295 646 4246
n.gsn r.gsm r.np.2 v.fmi.2p cj pt.ap.nsm a.nsm

ὁ λαὸς εἶπεν, τὸ αἷμα αὐτοῦ ἐφ' ἡμᾶς καὶ ἐπὶ τὰ τέκνα
the people saying, "Let {the} his blood his be on us and on {the} our children!"
3836 3295 3306 3836 899 135 899 2093 7005 2779 2093 3836 7005 5451
d.nsm n.nsm v.aai.3s d.nsn n.nsn r.gsm.3 p.a r.ap.1 cj p.a d.apn n.apn

ἡμῶν. 26 τότε ἀπέλυσεν αὐτοῖς τὸν Βαραββᾶν, τὸν δὲ ↱
our Then he released Barabbas for them, {the} Barabbas {the} but he scourged
7005 5538 668 972 899 3836 972 3836 1254 4140 5849
r.gp.1 adv v.aai.3s r.dpm.3 d.asm n.asm d.asm cj

Ἰησοῦν φραγελλώσας παρέδωκεν ← ἵνα σταυρωθῇ. 27 τότε οἱ
Jesus scourged and handed him over to be crucified. Then the governor's
2652 5849 4140 2671 5090 5538 3836 2450
n.asm pt.aa.nsm v.aai.3s cj v.aps.3s adv d.npm

στρατιῶται τοῦ ἡγεμόνος παραλαβόντες τὸν Ἰησοῦν εἰς τὸ πραιτώριον
soldiers {the} governor's took {the} Jesus into the praetorium and
5132 3836 2450 4161 3836 2652 1650 3836 4550
n.npm d.gsm n.gsm pt.aa.npm d.asm n.asm p.a d.asn n.asn

συνήγαγον ἐπ' αὐτὸν ὅλην τὴν σπεῖραν. 28 καὶ ἐκδύσαντες
gathered the entire garrison around him. entire the garrison {and} They stripped
5251 3836 3910 5061 2093 899 3910 3836 5061 2779 4363 1694
v.aai.3p p.a r.asm.3 a.asf d.asf n.asf cj pt.aa.npm

αὐτὸν χλαμύδα κοκκίνην περιέθηκαν αὐτῷ, 29 καὶ πλέξαντες
him and put a scarlet cloak scarlet They put on him; and twisting together
899 4363 3132 5948 3132 4363 899 2779 4428
r.asm.3 n.asf a.asf v.aai.3p r.dsm.3 cj pt.aa.npm

[a] τοῦ δικαίου included by TR after αἵματος.

NASB

for Barabbas and to
put Jesus to death.
21 But the gover-
nor said to them,
"Which of the two
do you want me to
release for you?"
And they said,
"Barabbas." 22 Pi-
late *said to them,
"Then what shall I
do with Jesus who
is called Christ?"
They all *said,
"Crucify Him!"
23 And he said,
"Why, what evil
has He done?" But
they kept shout-
ing all the more,
saying, "Crucify
Him!"
24 When Pilate saw
that he was accom-
plishing nothing,
but rather that a
riot was starting,
he took water and
washed his hands
in front of the
crowd, saying, "I
am innocent of this
Man's blood; see
to that yourselves."
25 And all the people
said, "His blood
shall be on us and
on our children!"
26 Then he released
Barabbas for them;
but after having
Jesus scourged, he
handed Him over
to be crucified.

Jesus Is Mocked

27 Then the soldiers
of the governor
took Jesus into the
Praetorium and
gathered the whole
Roman cohort
around Him. 28 They
stripped Him and
put a scarlet robe
on Him. 29 And after
twisting together

NIV

a crown of thorns
and set it on his
head. They put a
staff in his right
hand. Then they
knelt in front of
him and mocked
him. "Hail, king
of the Jews!"
they said. 30 They
spit on him, and
took the staff and
struck him on the
head again and
again. 31 After they
had mocked him,
they took off the
robe and put his
own clothes on
him. Then they led
him away to cruci-
fy him.

The Crucifixion of Jesus

32 As they were
going out, they met
a man from Cyre-
ne, named Simon,
and they forced
him to carry the
cross. 33 They came
to a place called
Golgotha (which
means "the place
of the skull").
34 There they of-
fered Jesus wine
to drink, mixed
with gall; but af-
ter tasting it, he
refused to drink
it. 35 When they
had crucified him,
they divided up his
clothes by casting
lots. 36 And sitting
down, they kept
watch over him
there. 37 Above his
head they placed
the written charge
against him: THIS IS
JESUS, THE KING OF
THE JEWS.
38 Two rebels were
crucified with
him, one on his
right and one on
his left.

στέφανον ἐξ ἀκανθῶν ἐπέθηκαν ἐπὶ τῆς κεφαλῆς αὐτοῦ καὶ
a crown of thorns, they placed it on *{the}* his head. *his* *{and}* They put a
5109 1666 180 2202 2093 3836 899 3051 899 2779
n.asm p.g n.gpf v.aai.3p p.g d.gsf n.gsf r.gsm.3 cj

κάλαμον ἐν τῇ δεξιᾷ αὐτοῦ, καὶ γονυπετήσαντες ἔμπροσθεν αὐτοῦ
staff in *{the}* his right hand, *his* and kneeling before him
2812 1877 3836 899 1288 899 2779 1206 1869 899
n.asm p.d d.dsf a.dsf r.gsm.3 cj pt.aa.npm p.g r.gsm.3

ἐνέπαιξαν αὐτῷ λέγοντες, χαῖρε, βασιλεῦ τῶν Ἰουδαίων, 30 καὶ ↱ ἐμπτύσαντες
they mocked him, saying, "Hail, king of the Jews!" And they spat
1850 899 3306 5897 995 3836 2681 2779 3284 1870
v.aai.3p r.dsm.3 pt.pa.npm v.pam.2s n.vsm d.gpm a.gpm cj pt.aa.npm

εἰς αὐτὸν ἔλαβον τὸν κάλαμον καὶ ἔτυπτον εἰς τὴν κεφαλὴν αὐτοῦ.
on him, and took the staff and kept beating him over the head. *him*
1650 899 3284 3836 2812 2779 5597 899 1650 3836 3051 899
p.a r.asm.3 v.aai.3p d.asm n.asm cj v.iai.3p p.a d.asf n.asf r.gsm.3

31 καὶ ὅτε ἐνέπαιξαν αὐτῷ, ἐξέδυσαν αὐτὸν ↰ τὴν χλαμύδα καὶ
And when ⌊they finished mocking⌋ him, they stripped him of the cloak and
2779 4021 1850 899 1694 899 1694 3836 5948 2779
cj cj v.aai.3p r.dsm.3 v.aai.3p r.asm.3 d.asf n.asf cj

ἐνέδυσαν αὐτὸν τὰ ἱμάτια αὐτοῦ ↰ ↰ καὶ ἀπήγαγον αὐτὸν ↰ εἰς
put *own* *{the}* his own clothes *his* back on and led him away to
1907 899 3836 899 899 2668 899 1907 1907 2779 552 899 552 1650
v.aai.3p r.asm.3 d.apn n.apn r.gsm.3 cj v.aai.3p r.asm.3 p.a

τὸ σταυρῶσαι. 32 ἐξερχόμενοι δὲ εὗρον ἄνθρωπον
{the} crucify him. ⌊As they were going out,⌋ *{and}* ⌊they came across⌋ a man named
3836 5090 2002 1254 2351 476 3950
d.asn f.aa pt.pm.npm cj v.aai.3p n.asm

Κυρηναῖον ὀνόματι Σίμωνα, τοῦτον ἠγγάρευσαν ἵνα ἄρῃ τὸν σταυρὸν
Simon, from Cyrene. *named* *Simon* This man they conscripted to carry *{the}* his cross.
4981 3254 3950 4981 4047 30 2671 149 3836 899 5089
n.asm n.dsn n.asm r.asm v.aai.3p cj v.aas.3s d.asm n.asm

αὐτοῦ. 33 καὶ ἐλθόντες εἰς τόπον λεγόμενον Γολγοθᾶ, ὅ ἐστιν
his And ⌊when they came⌋ to a place called Golgotha, which *{is}* means
899 2779 2262 1650 5536 3306 1201 4005 1639 3306
r.gsm.3 cj pt.aa.npm p.a n.asm pt.pp.asm n.asf r.nsn v.pai.3s

→ Κρανίου Τόπος λεγόμενος, 34 ἔδωκαν αὐτῷ πιεῖν
"Place of a Skull," *Place* *means* they gave him wine mixed with gall to drink;
5536 3191 5536 3306 1443 899 3885 3624 3552 5958 4403
n.gsn n.nsm pt.pp.nsm v.aai.3p r.dsm.3 f.aa

οἶνον μετὰ χολῆς μεμιγμένον· καὶ γευσάμενος ↱ ⌊οὐκ ἠθέλησεν⌋ πιεῖν.
wine *with* *gall* *mixed* but after tasting it, he refused to drink it.
3885 3552 5958 3624 2779 1174 2527 4024 2527 4403
n.asm p.g n.gsf pt.rp.asm cj pt.am.nsm pl v.aai.3s f.aa

35 σταυρώσαντες δὲ αὐτὸν διεμερίσαντο τὰ ἱμάτια αὐτοῦ ↰
And when they had crucified *And* him, they divided *{the}* his clothes *his* among them
1254 5090 1254 899 1374 3836 899 2668 899 1374
pt.aa.npm cj r.asm.3 v.ami.3p d.apn n.apn r.gsm.3

βάλλοντες κλῆρον,[a] 36 καὶ ↱ καθήμενοι ἐτήρουν αὐτὸν ἐκεῖ. 37 καὶ
by casting lots. Then they sat down and ⌊kept watch over⌋ him there. And
965 3102 2779 5498 2764 5498 899 1695 2779
pt.pa.npm n.asm cj pt.pm.npm v.iai.3p r.asm.3 adv cj

ἐπέθηκαν ἐπάνω τῆς κεφαλῆς αὐτοῦ τὴν αἰτίαν αὐτοῦ
above his head they put *above* *{the}* *head* *his* the charge ⌊against him,⌋
2062 899 3051 2202 2062 3836 3051 899 3836 162 899
v.aai.3p p.g d.gsf n.gsf r.gsm.3 d.asf n.asf r.gsm.3

γεγραμμένην, οὗτός ἐστιν Ἰησοῦς ὁ βασιλεὺς τῶν Ἰουδαίων. 38 τότε
which read, "This is Jesus, the king of the Jews." Then two robbers
1211 4047 1639 2652 3836 995 3836 2681 5538 1545 3334
pt.rp.asf r.nsm v.pai.3s n.nsm d.nsm n.nsm d.gpm a.gpm adv

σταυροῦνται σὺν αὐτῷ δύο λῃσταί, εἷς ἐκ δεξιῶν καὶ εἷς ἐξ εὐωνύμων.
were crucified with him, *two* *robbers* one on his right and one on his left.
5090 5250 899 1545 3334 1651 1666 1288 2779 1651 1666 2381
v.ppi.3p p.d r.dsm.3 a.npm n.npm a.nsm p.g a.gpf cj a.nsm p.g a.gpf

[a] ἵνα πληρωθῇ τὸ ῥηθὲν ὑπὸ τοῦ προφήτου, διεμερίσαντο τὰ ἱμάτιά μου ἑαυτοῖς, καὶ ἐπὶ τὸν ἱματισμόν μου ἔβαλον κλῆρον included by TR after κλῆρον.

NASB

a crown of thorns,
they put it on His
head, and a reed in
His right hand; and
they knelt down
before Him and
mocked Him, say-
ing, "Hail, King of
the Jews!" 30 They
spat on Him, and
took the reed and
began to beat Him
on the head. 31 After
they had mocked
Him, they took the
scarlet robe off
Him and put His
own garments back
on Him, and led
Him away to cru-
cify Him.
32 As they were
coming out, they
found a man of
Cyrene named
Simon, whom they
pressed into service
to bear His cross.

The Crucifixion

33 And when they
came to a place
called Golgotha,
which means Place
of a Skull, 34 they
gave Him wine to
drink mixed with
gall; and after tast-
ing *it,* He was un-
willing to drink.
35 And when they
had crucified Him,
they divided up His
garments among
themselves by cast-
ing lots. 36 And sit-
ting down, they *be-
gan* to keep watch
over Him there.
37 And above His
head they put up
the charge against
Him which read,
"THIS IS JESUS
THE KING OF THE
JEWS."
38 At that time
two robbers *were
crucified with Him,
one on the right
and one on the left.

NIV

39 Those who
passed by hurled
insults at him,
shaking their
heads 40 and say-
ing, "You who are
going to destroy
the temple and
build it in three
days, save your-
self! Come down
from the cross, if
you are the Son
of God!" 41 In the
same way the chief
priests, the teach-
ers of the law and
the elders mocked
him. 42 "He saved
others," they said,
"but he can't save
himself! He's
the king of Isra-
el! Let him come
down now from
the cross, and we
will believe in
him. 43 He trusts
in God. Let God
rescue him now if
he wants him, for
he said, 'I am the
Son of God.'" 44 In
the same way the
rebels who were
crucified with him
also heaped insults
on him.

The Death of Jesus

45 From noon until
three in the af-
ternoon darkness
came over all the
land. 46 About three
in the afternoon
Jesus cried out in
a loud voice, *"Eli,
Eli,*[a] *lema sabach-
thani?"* (which
means "My God,
my God, why
have you forsaken
me?").[b]
47 When some
of those standing
there heard this,
they said, "He's
calling Elijah."
48 Immediately
one of them ran
and

[a] 46 Some manu-
scripts *Eloi, Eloi*
[b] 46 Psalm 22:1

39 οἱ δὲ παραπορευόμενοι ἐβλασφήμουν αὐτὸν κινοῦντες τὰς κεφαλὰς
And those *And* who passed by derided him, wagging *{the}* their heads
1254 3836 1254 4182 1059 899 3075 3836 899 3051
d.npm cj pt.pm.npm v.iai.3p r.asm.3 pt.pa.npm d.apf n.apf

αὐτῶν 40 καὶ λέγοντες, ὁ καταλύων τὸν ναὸν καὶ ἐν τρισὶν
their and saying, ⌞"You who⌟ would destroy the temple and rebuild it in three
899 2779 3306 3836 2907 3836 3724 2779 3868 1877 5552
r.gpm.3 cj pt.pa.npm d.vsm pt.pa.vsm d.asm n.asm cj p.d a.dpf

ἡμέραις οἰκοδομῶν, σῶσον σεαυτόν, εἰ υἱὸς εἶ τοῦ θεοῦ,[a] κατάβηθι
days, *rebuild* save yourself! If you are the Son *you are* of God, come down
2465 3868 5392 4932 1623 1639 1639 5626 1639 3836 2536 2849
n.dpf pt.pa.vsm v.aam.2s r.asm.2 cj n.nsm v.pai.2s d.gsm n.gsm v.aam.2s

ἀπὸ τοῦ σταυροῦ. 41 ὁμοίως καὶ οἱ ἀρχιερεῖς ἐμπαίζοντες μετὰ τῶν
from the cross!" *in the same way* *also* The ruling priests *were mocking* along with the
608 3836 5089 3931 2779 3836 797 1850 3552 3836
p.g d.gsm n.gsm adv adv d.npm n.npm pt.pa.npm p.g d.gpm

γραμματέων καὶ πρεσβυτέρων ἔλεγον,
scribes and the elders were also mocking him in the same way, saying,
1208 2779 4565 1850 2779 1850 3931 3931 3931 3931 3306
n.gpm cj a.gpm v.iai.3p

42 ἄλλους ἔσωσεν, ἑαυτὸν οὐ δύναται σῶσαι·
"He saved others, *He saved* but he is not able to save himself! *not* *he is able* *to save*
5392 5392 257 5392 1538 1538 4024 1538 5392 5392 1571 4024 1538 5392
r.apm v.aai.3s r.asm.3 pl v.ppi.3s f.aa

βασιλεὺς Ἰσραήλ ἐστιν, → → καταβάτω νῦν ἀπὸ τοῦ σταυροῦ καὶ
He is the king of Israel! *He is* Let him now come down *now* from the cross, and
1639 1639 995 2702 1639 3814 2849 3814 608 3836 5089 2779
n.nsm n.gsm v.pai.3s v.aam.3s adv p.g d.gsm n.gsm cj

πιστεύσομεν ἐπ' αὐτόν. 43 πέποιθεν ἐπὶ τὸν θεόν, → ῥυσάσθω νῦν
we will believe in him! ⌞He has put his trust⌟ in *{the}* God; let God rescue him now
4409 2093 899 4275 2093 3836 2536 4861 3814
v.fai.1p p.a r.asm.3 v.rai.3s p.a d.asm n.asm v.amm.3s adv

εἰ θέλει αὐτόν· εἶπεν γὰρ ὅτι θεοῦ εἰμι υἱός. 44 τὸ
if he wants him; for he said, *for* ~ 'I am the Son of God.'" *I am* *Son* *the*
1623 2527 899 1142 3306 1142 4022 1639 1639 5626 2536 1639 5626 3836
cj v.pai.3s r.asm.3 v.aai.3s cj cj n.gsm v.pai.1s n.nsm d.asn

δ' αὐτὸ καὶ οἱ λῃσταὶ οἱ συσταυρωθέντες σὺν αὐτῷ ὠνείδιζον αὐτόν.
And *same* *{also}* the robbers who were crucified with him were taunting him in the
1254 899 2779 3836 3334 3836 5365 5250 899 3943 899 3836
cj r.asn adv d.npm n.npm d.npm pt.ap.npm p.d r.dsm.3 v.iai.3p r.asm.3

45 ἀπὸ δὲ ἕκτης ὥρας σκότος ἐγένετο ἐπὶ πᾶσαν τὴν γῆν
same way. And from *And* the sixth hour there was darkness *there was* over all the land
899 1254 608 1254 1761 6052 1181 1181 5030 1181 2093 4246 3836 1178
p.g cj a.gsf n.gsf n.nsn v.ami.3s p.a a.asf d.asf n.asf

ἕως ὥρας ἐνάτης. 46 περὶ δὲ τὴν ἐνάτην ὥραν ἀνεβόησεν ὁ
until the ninth hour. *ninth* And about *And* the ninth hour Jesus cried out *{the}*
2401 1888 6052 1888 1254 4309 1254 3836 1888 6052 2652 331 3836
p.g n.gsf a.gsf p.a cj d.asf a.asf n.asf v.aai.3s d.nsm

Ἰησοῦς → φωνῇ μεγάλῃ λέγων, ηλι ηλι λεμα σαβαχθανι; τοῦτ' ἔστιν·
Jesus in a loud voice, *loud* saying, "Eli, Eli, lema sabachthani?" — which means, "My
2652 3489 5889 3489 3306 2458 2458 3316 4876 4047 1639 1609
n.nsm n.dsf a.dsf pt.pa.nsm j j j j r.nsn v.pai.3s

θεέ μου θεέ μου, ἱνατί με ἐγκατέλιπες; 47 ↱ τινὲς δὲ τῶν
God, *My* my God, *my* why *me* have you forsaken me?" But when some *But* of
2536 1609 1609 2536 1609 2672 1609 1593 1609 1254 201 5516 1254 3836
n.vsm r.gs.1 n.vsm r.gs.1 cj r.as.1 v.aai.2s r.npm cj d.gpm

ἐκεῖ ἑστηκότων ἀκούσαντες ἔλεγον ὅτι
those standing there *those standing* heard it, they said, ~ "This man is calling for
2705 2705 1695 2705 201 3306 4022 4047 4047 5888 5888 5888
adv pt.ra.gpm pt.aa.npm v.iai.3p cj

Ἠλίαν φωνεῖ οὗτος. 48 καὶ εὐθέως δραμὼν εἷς ἐξ αὐτῶν καὶ
Elijah." *is calling for* *This man* And one of them at once ran *one* *of* *them* and
2460 5888 4047 2779 1651 1666 899 2311 5556 1651 1666 899 2779
n.asm v.pai.3s r.nsm cj adv pt.aa.nsm a.nsm p.g r.gpm.3 cj

[a] καὶ included by UBS after θεοῦ.

NASB

39 And those passing
by were hurling
abuse at Him, wag-
ging their heads
40 and saying, "You
who *are going to*
destroy the temple
and rebuild it in
three days, save
Yourself! If You
are the Son of God,
come down from
the cross." 41 In the
same way the chief
priests also, along
with the scribes
and elders, were
mocking *Him* and
saying, 42 "He saved
others; He cannot
save Himself. He is
the King of Israel;
let Him now come
down from the
cross, and we will
believe in Him.
43 HE TRUSTS IN GOD;
LET GOD RESCUE
Him now, IF HE
DELIGHTS IN HIM;
for He said, 'I am
the Son of God.'"
44 The robbers who
had been crucified
with Him were also
insulting Him with
the same words.
45 Now from the
[a]sixth hour dark-
ness fell upon all
the land until the
[b]ninth hour. 46 About
the ninth hour Je-
sus cried out with a
loud voice, saying,
"ELI, ELI, LAMA
SABACHTHANI?" that
is, "MY GOD, MY
GOD, WHY HAVE
YOU FORSAKEN
ME?" 47 And some
of those who were
standing there,
when they heard
it, *began* saying,
"This man is call-
ing for Elijah."
48 Immediately one
of them ran, and

[a] I.e. 12 noon
[b] I.e. 3 p.m.

NIV

got a sponge. He
filled it with wine
vinegar, put it on a
staff, and offered
it to Jesus to drink.
49The rest said,
"Now leave him
alone. Let's see if
Elijah comes to
save him."
50And when Jesus
had cried out again
in a loud voice, he
gave up his spirit.
51At that moment
the curtain of the
temple was torn
in two from top
to bottom. The
earth shook, the
rocks split 52and
the tombs broke
open. The bodies
of many holy peo-
ple who had died
were raised to life.
53They came out
of the tombs after
Jesus' resurrec-
tion and[a] went into
the holy city and
appeared to many
people.
54When the cen-
turion and those
with him who were
guarding Jesus
saw the earthquake
and all that had
happened, they
were terrified, and
exclaimed, "Surely
he was the Son of
God!"
55Many wom-
en were there,
watching from
a distance. They
had followed Jesus
from Galilee to
care for his needs.
56Among them
were Mary Mag-
dalene, Mary the
mother of James
and Joseph,[b] and
the mother of Zeb-
edee's sons.

The Burial of Jesus

57As evening ap-
proached, there
came a rich man
from

[a] 53 Or *tombs, and after Jesus' resurrection they*
[b] 56 Greek *Joses*, a variant of *Joseph*

λαβὼν σπόγγον πλήσας τε ὄξους καὶ περιθεὶς ← καλάμῳ
got a sponge, filled it ~ with sour wine, {and} put it on a staff, and
3284 5074 4398 5445 3954 2779 4363 2812
pt.aa.nsm n.asm pt.aa.nsm cj n.gsn cj pt.aa.nsm n.dsm

ἐπότιζεν αὐτόν. ↰ ↰ 49 οἱ δὲ λοιποὶ ἔλεγον, ἄφες ἴδωμεν εἰ
gave it to him to drink. But the *But* others said, "Wait, let us see whether
4540 899 4540 4540 1254 3836 1254 3370 3306 918 1625 1623
v.iai.3s r.asm.3 d.npm cj a.npm v.iai.3p v.aam.2s v.aas.1p cj

ἔρχεται Ἠλίας σώσων αὐτόν. 50 ὁ δὲ Ἰησοῦς πάλιν κράξας →
Elijah will come *Elijah* to save him." *{the}* And Jesus cried out again *cried out* in a
2460 2262 2460 5392 899 3836 1254 2652 3189 3189 4099 3189
v.pmi.3s n.nsm pt.fa.nsm r.asm.3 d.nsm cj n.nsm adv pt.aa.nsm

φωνῇ μεγάλῃ ἀφῆκεν τὸ πνεῦμα. 51 καὶ ἰδοὺ τὸ καταπέτασμα τοῦ
loud voice *loud* and gave up his spirit. ⌊Just then⌋ *{behold}* the curtain of the
3489 5889 3489 918 3836 4460 2779 2627 3836 2925 3836
n.dsf a.dsf v.aai.3s d.asn n.asn cj j d.nsn n.nsn d.gsm

ναοῦ ἐσχίσθη ἀπ᾽ ἄνωθεν ἕως κάτω εἰς δύο καὶ ἡ γῆ ἐσείσθη καὶ
temple was torn in two from top to bottom; *in two* and the earth shook, and
3724 5387 1650 1545 608 540 2401 3004 1650 1545 2779 3836 1178 4940 2779
n.gsm v.api.3s p.g adv p.g adv p.a a.apn cj d.nsf n.nsf v.api.3s cj

αἱ πέτραι ἐσχίσθησαν, 52 καὶ τὰ μνημεῖα ἀνεῴχθησαν καὶ πολλὰ σώματα τῶν
the rocks were split; *{and}* the tombs were opened, and many bodies of the
3836 4376 5387 2779 3836 3646 487 2779 4498 5393 3836
d.npf n.npf v.api.3p cj d.npn n.npn v.api.3p cj a.npn n.npn d.gpm

κεκοιμημένων ἁγίων ἠγέρθησαν, 53 καὶ ↱ ἐξελθόντες
saints who had fallen asleep *saints* were raised. *{and}* After his resurrection they came out
41 3121 41 1586 2779 3552 899 1587 1656 2002
pt.rp.gpm a.gpm v.api.3p cj pt.aa.npm

ἐκ τῶν μνημείων μετὰ τὴν ἔγερσιν αὐτοῦ ⌊εἰσῆλθον εἰς⌋ τὴν ἁγίαν πόλιν
of the tombs *After {the} resurrection his* and entered the holy city
1666 3836 3646 3552 3836 1587 899 1656 1650 3836 41 4484
p.g d.gpn n.gpn p.a d.asf n.asf r.gsm.3 v.aai.3p p.a d.asf a.asf n.asf

καὶ ἐνεφανίσθησαν πολλοῖς. 54 ↱ ὁ δὲ ἑκατόνταρχος καὶ οἱ μετ᾽ αὐτοῦ
and appeared to many. When the *{and}* centurion and those with him,
2779 1872 4498 1625 3836 1254 1672 2779 3836 3552 899
cj v.api.3p a.dpm d.nsm cj n.nsm cj d.npm p.g r.gsm.3

τηροῦντες τὸν Ἰησοῦν ἰδόντες τὸν σεισμὸν καὶ τὰ γενόμενα
⌊who were keeping watch over⌋ *{the}* Jesus, saw the earthquake and what was happening,
5498 3836 2652 1625 3836 4939 2779 3836 1181
pt.pa.npm d.asm n.asm pt.aa.npm d.asm n.asm cj d.apn pt.am.apn

⌊ἐφοβήθησαν σφόδρα,⌋ λέγοντες, ἀληθῶς θεοῦ υἱὸς
they were terrified, and said, "Truly this man was the Son of God!" *Son*
5828 5379 3306 242 4047 4047 1639 5626 2536 5626
v.api.3p adv pt.pa.npm adv n.gsm n.nsm

ἦν οὗτος. 55 ἦσαν δὲ ἐκεῖ γυναῖκες πολλαὶ
was this man And looking on from a distance were *And {there}* many women *many*
1639 4047 1254 2555 2555 608 3427 1639 1254 1695 4498 1222 4498
v.iai.3s r.nsm v.iai.3p cj adv n.npf a.npf

ἀπὸ μακρόθεν θεωροῦσαι, αἵτινες ἠκολούθησαν τῷ Ἰησοῦ ἀπὸ τῆς Γαλιλαίας
from distance looking on who had followed *{the}* Jesus from *{the}* Galilee
608 3427 2555 4015 199 3836 2652 608 3836 1133
p.g adv pt.pa.npf r.npf v.aai.3p d.dsm n.dsm p.g d.gsf n.gsf

διακονοῦσαι αὐτῷ· ↰ 56 ἐν αἷς ἦν Μαρία ἡ Μαγδαληνὴ καὶ Μαρία
to care for his needs. Among them were Mary *{the}* Magdalene, *{and}* Mary
1354 899 1354 1877 4005 1639 3451 3836 3402 2779 3451
pt.pa.npf r.dsm.3 p.d r.dpf v.iai.3s n.nsf d.nsf n.nsf cj n.nsf

ἡ τοῦ Ἰακώβου καὶ Ἰωσὴφ μήτηρ καὶ ἡ μήτηρ τῶν υἱῶν
the mother of James and Joseph, *mother* and the mother of Zebedee's sons.
3836 3613 3836 2610 2779 2737 3613 2779 3836 3613 3836 2411 5626
d.nsf d.gsm n.gsm cj n.gsm n.nsf cj d.nsf n.nsf d.gpm n.gpm

Ζεβεδαίου. 57 ὀψίας δὲ γενομένης ἦλθεν ἄνθρωπος πλούσιος ἀπὸ
Zebedee's Toward sunset, *{and} Toward* there came a rich man *rich* from
2411 1181 4068 1254 1181 2262 4454 476 4454 608
n.gsm n.gsf cj pt.am.gsf v.aai.3s n.nsm a.nsm p.g

NASB

taking a sponge,
he filled it with
sour wine and put
it on a reed, and
gave Him a drink.
49But the rest *of*
them said, "Let us
see whether Elijah
will come to save
Him[a]." 50And Jesus
cried out again
with a loud voice,
and yielded up
His spirit. 51And
behold, the veil of
the temple was torn
in two from top to
bottom; and the
earth shook and the
rocks were split.
52The tombs were
opened, and many
bodies of the saints
who had fallen
asleep were raised;
53and coming out of
the tombs after His
resurrection they
entered the holy
city and appeared
to many. 54Now
the centurion, and
those who were
with him keeping
guard over Jesus,
when they saw the
earthquake and the
things that were
happening, became
very frightened
and said, "Truly
this was the Son of
God!"
55Many women
were there looking
on from a distance,
who had followed
Jesus from Galilee
while ministering
to Him. 56Among
them was Mary
Magdalene, and
Mary the mother of
James and Joseph,
and the mother
of the sons of
Zebedee.

Jesus Is Buried

57When it was
evening, there
came a rich man
from Arimathea,

[a] Some early mss read *And another took a spear and pierced His side, and there came out water and blood* (cf John 19:34)

NIV

Arimathea, named
Joseph, who had
himself become a
disciple of Jesus.
58Going to Pilate,
he asked for Jesus'
body, and Pilate
ordered that it
be given to him.
59Joseph took the
body, wrapped it
in a clean linen
cloth, 60and placed
it in his own new
tomb that he had
cut out of the
rock. He rolled a
big stone in front
of the entrance
to the tomb and
went away. 61Mary
Magdalene and the
other Mary were
sitting there oppo-
site the tomb.

The Guard at the Tomb

62The next day,
the one after Prep-
aration Day, the
chief priests and
the Pharisees went
to Pilate. 63"Sir,"
they said, "we re-
member that while
he was still alive
that deceiver said,
'After three days
I will rise again.'
64So give the order
for the tomb to be
made secure until
the third day. Oth-
erwise, his disci-
ples may come and
steal the body and
tell the people that
he has been raised
from the dead.
This last deception
will be worse than
the first."
65"Take a guard,"
Pilate answered.
"Go, make the
tomb

Ἀριμαθαίας, τοὔνομα Ἰωσήφ, ὃς ↱ καὶ αὐτὸς ἐμαθητεύθη τῷ Ἰησοῦ·
Arimathea, named Joseph, who himself was also *himself* a disciple of *{the}* Jesus.
751 5540 2737 4005 899 3411 2779 899 3411 3836 2652
n.gsf crasis.nsn n.nsm r.nsm adv r.nsm v.api.3s d.dsm n.dsm

58 οὗτος προσελθὼν τῷ Πιλάτῳ ᾐτήσατο τὸ σῶμα τοῦ Ἰησοῦ. τότε ὁ
This man approached *{the}* Pilate and asked for the body of Jesus. Then *{the}*
4047 4665 3836 4397 160 3836 5393 3836 2652 5538 3836
r.nsm pt.aa.nsm d.dsm n.dsm v.ami.3s d.asn n.asn d.gsm n.gsm adv d.nsm

Πιλᾶτος ἐκέλευσεν ἀποδοθῆναι. 59 καὶ λαβὼν τὸ σῶμα ὁ
Pilate ordered that it be given to him. And Joseph took the body, *{the}*
4397 3027 625 2779 2737 3284 3836 5393 3836
n.nsm v.aai.3s f.ap cj pt.aa.nsm d.asn n.asn d.nsm

Ἰωσὴφ ἐνετύλιξεν αὐτὸ ἐν[a] σινδόνι καθαρᾷ 60 καὶ ἔθηκεν αὐτὸ[b] ἐν τῷ
Joseph wrapped it in a clean linen shroud, *clean* and laid it in *{the}*
2737 1962 899 1877 2754 4984 2754 2779 5502 899 1877 3836
n.nsm v.aai.3s r.asn.3 p.d n.dsf a.dsf cj v.aai.3s r.asn.3 p.d d.dsn

καινῷ αὐτοῦ μνημείῳ ὃ ἐλατόμησεν ἐν τῇ πέτρᾳ καὶ ↱ προσκυλίσας
his own new *his* tomb, which he had cut in the rock. Then he rolled
899 2785 899 3646 4005 3300 1877 3836 4376 2779 599 4685
a.dsn r.gsm.3 n.dsn r.asn v.aai.3s p.d d.dsf n.dsf cj pt.aa.nsm

λίθον μέγαν ↰ τῇ θύρᾳ τοῦ μνημείου ἀπῆλθεν. 61 ἦν δὲ ἐκεῖ
a large stone *large* against the door of the tomb and went away. *were* *{and}* *there*
3489 3345 3489 4685 3836 2598 3836 3646 599 1639 1254 1695
n.asm a.asm d.dsf n.dsf d.gsn n.gsn v.aai.3s v.iai.3s cj adv

Μαριὰμ ἡ Μαγδαληνὴ καὶ ἡ ἄλλη Μαρία καθήμεναι ἀπέναντι τοῦ
Mary *{the}* Magdalene and the other Mary were there, sitting across from the
3452 3836 3402 2779 3836 257 3451 1639 1695 2764 595 3836
n.nsf d.nsf n.nsf cj d.nsf r.nsf n.nsf pt.pm.npf p.g d.gsm

τάφου. 62 τῇ δὲ ἐπαύριον, ἥτις ἐστὶν μετὰ τὴν παρασκευήν, συνήχθησαν
tomb. ⌞On the⌟ *{and}* following day, that is, after the day of Preparation, *went as a group*
5439 3836 1254 2069 4015 1639 3552 3836 4187 5251
n.gsm d.dsf cj adv r.nsf v.pai.3s p.a d.asf n.asf v.api.3p

οἱ ἀρχιερεῖς καὶ οἱ Φαρισαῖοι πρὸς Πιλᾶτον 63 λέγοντες,
the ruling priests and the Pharisees went as a group to Pilate. They said,
3836 797 2779 3836 5757 5251 5251 5251 5251 4639 4397 3306
d.npm n.npm cj d.npm n.npm p.a n.asm pt.pa.npm

κύριε, ἐμνήσθημεν ὅτι ἐκεῖνος ὁ πλάνος εἶπεν ἔτι
"Sir, we remember that while he was still alive that *{the}* impostor said, *still*
3261 3630 4022 2409 2409 2409 2285 2409 1697 3836 4418 3306 2285
n.vsm v.api.1p cj r.nsm d.nsm n.nsm v.aai.3s adv

ζῶν, μετὰ τρεῖς ἡμέρας ἐγείρομαι. 64 κέλευσον οὖν
while he was alive 'After three days I will be raised.' Therefore order *Therefore* the
2409 3552 5552 2465 1586 4036 3027 4036 3836
pt.pa.nsm p.a a.apf n.apf v.ppi.1s v.aam.2s cj

ἀσφαλισθῆναι τὸν τάφον ἕως τῆς τρίτης ἡμέρας, μήποτε ἐλθόντες
tomb to be made secure *the* *tomb* until the third day, lest his disciples come
5439 856 3836 5439 2401 3836 5569 2465 3607 899 3412 2262
f.ap d.asm n.asm p.g d.gsf a.gsf n.gsf cj pt.aa.npm

οἱ μαθηταὶ αὐτοῦ κλέψωσιν αὐτὸν καὶ εἴπωσιν τῷ λαῷ, ἠγέρθη
{the} *disciples* *his* and steal him and say ⌞to the⌟ people, ⌞'He has been raised⌟
3836 3412 899 3096 899 2779 3306 3836 3295 1586
d.npm n.npm r.gsm.3 v.aas.3p r.asm.3 cj v.aas.3p d.dsm n.dsm v.api.3s

ἀπὸ τῶν νεκρῶν, καὶ ἔσται ἡ ἐσχάτη πλάνη χείρων τῆς πρώτης.
from the dead,' and the last deceit will be *the* *last* *deceit* greater ⌞than the⌟ first."
608 3836 3738 2779 3836 2274 4415 1639 3836 2274 4415 5937 3836 4755
p.g d.gpm a.gpm cj v.fmi.3s d.nsf a.nsf n.nsf a.nsf.c d.gsf a.gsf

65 ἔφη αὐτοῖς ὁ Πιλᾶτος, ἔχετε κουστωδίαν· ὑπάγετε ἀσφαλίσασθε
Pilate said to them, *{the}* *Pilate* "Take a guard of soldiers; go and make it
4397 5774 899 3836 4397 2400 3184 5632 856
v.iai.3s r.dpm.3 d.nsm n.nsm v.pai.2p n.asf v.pam.2p v.amm.2p

[a] [ἐν] UBS.
[b] αὐτὸ omitted by NET.

NASB

named Joseph, who
himself had also
become a disciple
of Jesus. 58This
man went to Pilate
and asked for the
body of Jesus.
Then Pilate ordered
it to be given *to*
him. 59And Joseph
took the body and
wrapped it in a
clean linen cloth,
60and laid it in his
own new tomb,
which he had hewn
out in the rock; and
he rolled a large
stone against the
entrance of the
tomb and went
away. 61And Mary
Magdalene was
there, and the other
Mary, sitting oppo-
site the grave.
62Now on the next
day, the day after
the preparation,
the chief priests
and the Pharisees
gathered together
with Pilate, 63and
said, "Sir, we re-
member that when
He was still alive
that deceiver said,
'After three days I
am to rise again.'
64Therefore, give
orders for the grave
to be made secure
until the third
day, otherwise
His disciples may
come and steal
Him away and say
to the people, 'He
has risen from the
dead,' and the last
deception will be
worse than the
first." 65Pilate said
to them, "You have
a guard; go, make
it *as* secure as you
know how." 66And
they went and
made the grave

NIV

as secure as you
know how." 66So
they went and
made the tomb se-
cure by putting a
seal on the stone
and posting the
guard.

Jesus Has Risen

28 After the
Sabbath, at
dawn on the first
day of the week,
Mary Magdalene
and the other Mary
went to look at the
tomb.
2There was a vi-
olent earthquake,
for an angel of the
Lord came down
from heaven and,
going to the tomb,
rolled back the
stone and sat on it.
3His appearance
was like lightning,
and his clothes
were white as
snow. 4The guards
were so afraid
of him that they
shook and became
like dead men.
5The angel said
to the women, "Do
not be afraid, for I
know that you are
looking for Jesus,
who was crucified.
6He is not here;
he has risen, just
as he said. Come
and see the place
where he lay.
7Then go quickly
and tell his disci-
ples: 'He has risen
from the dead and
is going ahead of
you into Galilee.
There you will see
him.' Now I have
told you."
8So the women
hurried away from
the tomb, afraid
yet filled with joy,
and ran

← ὡς οἴδατε. 66 οἱ δὲ πορευθέντες ἠσφαλίσαντο τὸν τάφον
as secure as you know how." So they *So* went and made the tomb
6055 3857 1254 3836 1254 4513 856 3836 5439
cj v.rai.2p d.npm cj pt.ap.npm v.ami.3p d.asm n.asm

↰ σφραγίσαντες τὸν λίθον μετὰ τῆς κουστωδίας.
secure by sealing the stone *{with}* and setting the guard
856 5381 3836 3345 3552 3836 3184
pt.aa.npm d.asm n.asm p.g d.gsf n.gsf

28:1 ὀψὲ δὲ σαββάτων, τῇ ἐπιφωσκούσῃ εἰς μίαν →
Now after *Now* the Sabbath, toward daybreak of the first day of the
1254 4067 1254 4879 3836 2216 1650 1651
p.g cj n.gpn d.dsf pt.pa.dsf p.a a.asf

σαββάτων ἦλθεν Μαριὰμ ἡ Μαγδαληνὴ καὶ ἡ ἄλλη Μαρία θεωρῆσαι τὸν
week, *went* Mary *{the}* Magdalene and the other Mary went to see the
4879 2262 3452 3836 3402 2779 3836 257 3451 2262 2555 3836
n.gpn v.aai.3s n.nsf d.nsf n.nsf cj d.nsf r.nsf n.nsf f.aa d.asm

τάφον. 2καὶ ἰδοὺ σεισμὸς ἐγένετο μέγας· ἄγγελος γὰρ →
tomb. And behold, there was a great earthquake; *there was great* for an angel *for* of the
5439 2779 2627 1181 1181 3489 4939 1181 3489 1142 34 1142
n.asm cj j n.nsm v.ami.3s a.nsm n.nsm cj

κυρίου καταβὰς ἐξ οὐρανοῦ καὶ προσελθὼν ἀπεκύλισεν τὸν λίθον καὶ
Lord descended from heaven and, going to the tomb, rolled away the stone and
3261 2849 1666 4041 2779 4665 653 3836 3345 2779
n.gsm pt.aa.nsm p.g n.gsm cj pt.aa.nsm v.aai.3s d.asm n.asm cj

ἐκάθητο ἐπάνω αὐτοῦ. 3 ἦν δὲ ἡ εἰδέα αὐτοῦ ὡς ἀστραπὴ
sat on it. His appearance was *{and}* *{the}* *appearance His* like lightning
2764 2062 899 899 1624 1639 1254 3836 1624 899 6055 847
v.imi.3s p.g r.gsm.3 v.iai.3s cj d.nsf n.nsf r.gsm.3 conj n.nsf

καὶ τὸ ἔνδυμα αὐτοῦ λευκὸν ὡς χιών. 4 ἀπὸ δὲ τοῦ φόβου αὐτοῦ
and *{the}* his clothing *his* white as snow. And for *And* *{the}* fear of him the
2779 3836 899 1903 899 3328 6055 5946 1254 608 1254 3836 5832 899 3836
cj d.nsn n.nsn r.gsm.3 a.nsn conj n.nsf p.g cj d.gsm n.gsm r.gsm.3

ἐσείσθησαν οἱ τηροῦντες καὶ ἐγενήθησαν ὡς νεκροί. 5ἀποκριθεὶς δὲ ὁ
guards trembled *the* *guards* and became like dead men. *{answering}* But the
5498 4940 3836 5498 2779 1181 6055 3738 646 1254 3836
v.api.3p d.npm pt.pa.npm cj v.api.3p conj a.npm pt.ap.nsm cj d.nsm

ἄγγελος εἶπεν ταῖς γυναιξίν, ↱ μὴ φοβεῖσθε ὑμεῖς, οἶδα γὰρ ὅτι
angel said to the women, "Do not be afraid, *{you}* for I know *for* that you are
34 3306 3836 1222 5828 3590 5828 7007 1142 3857 1142 4022 2426 2426
n.nsm v.aai.3s d.dpf n.dpf pl v.ppm.2p r.np.2 v.rai.1s cj cj

Ἰησοῦν τὸν ἐσταυρωμένον ζητεῖτε· 6 οὐκ ἔστιν ὧδε,
looking for Jesus, who was crucified. *you are looking for* He is not *He is* here, for
2426 2426 2652 3836 5090 2426 1639 1639 4024 1639 6045 1142
n.asm d.asm pt.rp.asm v.pai.2p adv v.pai.3s adv

ἠγέρθη γὰρ καθὼς εἶπεν, δεῦτε ἴδετε τὸν τόπον ὅπου ἔκειτο. 7καὶ
⌞he has been raised,⌟ *for* just as he said. Come, see the place where he was lying. *{and}*
1586 1142 2777 3306 1307 1625 3836 5536 3963 3023 2779
v.api.3s cj cj v.aai.3s adv v.aam.2p d.asm n.asm pl v.imi.3s cj

ταχὺ πορευθεῖσαι εἴπατε τοῖς μαθηταῖς αὐτοῦ ὅτι ἠγέρθη ἀπὸ
Go quickly *Go* and tell *{the}* his disciples *his* that ⌞he has been raised⌟ from
4513 5444 4513 3306 3836 899 3412 899 4022 1586 608
adv pt.ap.npf v.aam.2p d.dpm n.dpm r.gsm.3 cj v.api.3s p.g

τῶν νεκρῶν, καὶ ἰδοὺ προάγει ὑμᾶς εἰς τὴν Γαλιλαίαν,
the dead and *{behold}* ⌞is going ahead of⌟ you to *{the}* Galilee. You will see him
3836 3738 2779 2627 4575 7007 1650 3836 1133 3972 3972 3972 899
d.gpm a.gpm cj j v.pai.3s r.ap.2 p.a d.asf n.asf

ἐκεῖ αὐτὸν ὄψεσθε· ἰδοὺ εἶπον ὑμῖν. 8καὶ ↱ ἀπελθοῦσαι
there. *him* *You will see* Remember, ⌞I have told⌟ you." So they left the tomb
1695 899 3972 2627 3306 7007 2779 5556 599 3836 3646
adv r.asm.3 v.fmi.2p j v.aai.1s r.dp.2 cj pt.aa.npf

ταχὺ ἀπὸ τοῦ μνημείου μετὰ φόβου καὶ χαρᾶς μεγάλης ἔδραμον
at once, *{from}* *the* *tomb* with fear and great joy, *great* and ran
5444 608 3836 3646 3552 5832 2779 3489 5915 3489 5556
adv p.g d.gsn n.gsn p.g n.gsm cj n.gsf a.gsf v.aai.3p

NASB

secure, and along
with the guard they
set a seal on the
stone.

Jesus Is Risen!

28:1Now after
the Sabbath, as
it began to dawn
toward the first *day*
of the week, Mary
Magdalene and the
other Mary came to
look at the grave.
2And behold, a
severe earthquake
had occurred, for
an angel of the
Lord descended
from heaven and
came and rolled
away the stone and
sat upon it. 3And
his appearance
was like lightning,
and his clothing
as white as snow.
4The guards shook
for fear of him and
became like dead
men. 5The angel
said to the women,
"Do not be afraid;
for I know that
you are looking
for Jesus who has
been crucified. 6He
is not here, for He
has risen, just as
He said. Come, see
the place where
He was lying. 7Go
quickly and tell His
disciples that He
has risen from the
dead; and behold,
He is going ahead
of you into Galilee,
there you will see
Him; behold, I
have told you."
8And they left the
tomb quickly with
fear and great joy
and ran to report

NIV

to tell his disciples. [9]Suddenly Jesus met them. "Greetings," he said. They came to him, clasped his feet and worshiped him. [10]Then Jesus said to them, "Do not be afraid. Go and tell my brothers to go to Galilee; there they will see me."

The Guards' Report

[11]While the women were on their way, some of the guards went into the city and reported to the chief priests everything that had happened. [12]When the chief priests had met with the elders and devised a plan, they gave the soldiers a large sum of money, [13]telling them, "You are to say, 'His disciples came during the night and stole him away while we were asleep.' [14]If this report gets to the governor, we will satisfy him and keep you out of trouble." [15]So the soldiers took the money and did as they were instructed. And this story has been widely circulated among the Jews to this very day.

The Great Commission

[16]Then the eleven disciples went to Galilee, to the mountain where Jesus had told them to go. [17]When they saw him,

ἀπαγγεῖλαι τοῖς μαθηταῖς αὐτοῦ. [9] ⌞καὶ ἰδοὺ⌟ Ἰησοῦς ὑπήντησεν αὐταῖς
to break the news to his disciples. *his* Suddenly Jesus met them
550 3836 899 3412 899 2779 2627 2652 5636 899
f.aa d.dpm n.dpm r.gsm.3 cj j n.nsm v.aai.3s r.dpf.3

λέγων, χαίρετε. αἱ δὲ προσελθοῦσαι ἐκράτησαν αὐτοῦ τοὺς
and said, "Good morning!" And they *And* came to him, took hold of his *{the}*
3306 5897 1254 3836 1254 4665 3195 899 3836
pt.pa.nsm v.pam.2p d.npf cj pt.aa.npf v.aai.3p r.gsm.3 d.apm

πόδας καὶ προσεκύνησαν αὐτῷ. [10] τότε λέγει αὐταῖς ὁ Ἰησοῦς, ↱ μὴ
feet, and worshipped him. Then Jesus said to them, *{the}* *Jesus* "Do not
4546 2779 4686 899 5538 2652 3306 899 3836 2652 5828 3590
n.apm cj v.aai.3p r.dsm.3 adv v.pai.3s r.dpf.3 d.nsm n.nsm pl

φοβεῖσθε· ὑπάγετε ἀπαγγείλατε τοῖς ἀδελφοῖς μου ἵνα ἀπέλθωσιν εἰς τὴν
be afraid. Go, tell *{the}* my brothers *my* to depart for *{the}*
5828 5632 550 3836 1609 81 1609 2671 599 1650 3836
v.ppm.2p v.pam.2p v.aam.2p d.dpm n.dpm r.gs.1 cj v.aas.3p p.a d.asf

Γαλιλαίαν, κἀκεῖ με ↰ ὄψονται. [11] → πορευομένων δὲ
Galilee, and they will see me there." *they will see* While they were on their way, *{and}*
1133 2795 3972 3972 3972 1609 2795 3972 899 4513 1254
n.asf crasis r.as.1 v.fmi.3p pt.pm.gpf cj

αὐτῶν ἰδού τινες τῆς κουστωδίας ἐλθόντες εἰς τὴν πόλιν ἀπήγγειλαν τοῖς
they *{behold}* some of the guard went into the city and reported to the
899 2627 5516 3836 3184 2262 1650 3836 4484 550 3836
r.gpf.3 j r.npm d.gsf n.gsf pt.aa.npm p.a d.asf n.asf v.aai.3p d.dpm

ἀρχιερεῦσιν ἅπαντα τὰ γενόμενα. [12] καὶ → συναχθέντες μετὰ τῶν
ruling priests everything that had taken place. And when the priests had met with the
797 570 3836 1181 2779 5251 3552 3836
n.dpm a.apn d.apn pt.am.apn cj pt.ap.npm p.g d.gpm

πρεσβυτέρων συμβούλιόν τε λαβόντες
elders and worked out a plan, *and* *worked out* they gave a considerable sum of
4565 5445 3284 3284 5206 5445 3284 1443 1443 2653 2653
a.gpm n.asn cj pt.aa.npm

ἀργύρια ἱκανὰ ἔδωκαν τοῖς στρατιώταις [13] λέγοντες, εἴπατε
money *considerable sum* *they gave* to the soldiers and told them, ⌞"You are to say,⌟
736 2653 1443 3836 5132 3306 3306
n.apn a.apn v.aai.3p d.dpm n.dpm pt.pa.npm v.aam.2p

ὅτι οἱ μαθηταὶ αὐτοῦ νυκτὸς ἐλθόντες ἔκλεψαν αὐτὸν ↱
~ *{the}* 'His disciples *His* came by night *came* and stole his body while
4022 3836 899 3412 899 2262 3816 2262 3096 899 3121
cj d.npm n.npm r.gsm.3 n.gsf pt.aa.npm v.aai.3p r.asm.3

ἡμῶν κοιμωμένων. [14] καὶ ἐὰν ἀκουσθῇ τοῦτο ἐπὶ τοῦ ἡγεμόνος,
we were sleeping.' And if *should come ears* this should come to the governor's ears,
7005 3121 2779 1569 201 4047 201 201 2093 3836 2450 201
r.gp.1 pt.pp.gpm cj cj v.aps.3s r.nsn p.g d.gsm n.gsm

ἡμεῖς πείσομεν αὐτὸν[a] καὶ ὑμᾶς ἀμερίμνους ποιήσομεν. [15] οἱ δὲ
we will bribe him and keep you out of trouble." *keep* So they *So*
7005 4275 899 2779 4472 7007 291 4472 1254 3836 1254
r.np.1 v.fai.1p r.asm.3 cj r.ap.2 a.apm v.fai.1p d.npm cj

λαβόντες τὰ ἀργύρια ἐποίησαν ὡς ἐδιδάχθησαν. καὶ
took the money and did as they were directed. And this story
3284 3836 736 4472 6055 1438 2779 4047 3364
pt.aa.npm d.apn n.apn v.aai.3p cj v.api.3p cj

διεφημίσθη ὁ λόγος οὗτος παρὰ Ἰουδαίοις μέχρι τῆς ⌞σήμερον ἡμέρας.⌟[b]
has been circulated *{the}* *story* *this* among Jews to this very day.
1424 3836 3364 4047 4123 2681 3588 3836 4958 2465
v.api.3s d.nsm n.nsm r.nsm p.d a.dpm p.g d.gsf adv n.gsf

[16] οἱ δὲ ἕνδεκα μαθηταὶ ἐπορεύθησαν εἰς τὴν Γαλιλαίαν εἰς τὸ ὄρος
So the *So* eleven disciples went to *{the}* Galilee to the mountain
1254 3836 1254 1894 3412 4513 1650 3836 1133 1650 3836 4001
d.npm cj a.npm n.npm v.api.3p p.a d.asf n.asf p.a d.asn n.asn

οὗ ἐτάξατο αὐτοῖς ὁ Ἰησοῦς, [17] καὶ ἰδόντες αὐτὸν
where Jesus had told them *{the}* *Jesus* to go. And ⌞when they saw⌟ him,
4023 2652 5435 899 3836 2652 2779 1625 899
adv v.ami.3s r.dpm.3 d.nsm n.nsm cj pt.aa.npm r.asm.3

NASB

it to His disciples. [9]And behold, Jesus met them and greeted them. And they came up and took hold of His feet and worshiped Him. [10]Then Jesus *said to them, "Do not be afraid; go and take word to My brethren to leave for Galilee, and there they will see Me."

[11]Now while they were on their way, some of the guard came into the city and reported to the chief priests all that had happened. [12]And when they had assembled with the elders and consulted together, they gave a large sum of money to the soldiers, [13]and said, "You are to say, 'His disciples came by night and stole Him away while we were asleep.' [14]And if this should come to the governor's ears, we will win him over and keep you out of trouble." [15]And they took the money and did as they had been instructed; and this story was widely spread among the Jews, *and is* to this day.

The Great Commission

[16]But the eleven disciples proceeded to Galilee, to the mountain which Jesus had designated. [17]When they saw Him, they

[a] [αὐτὸν] UBS, omitted by NET.
[b] [ἡμέρας] UBS, omitted by NET.

NIV

they worshiped
him; but some
doubted. [18]Then
Jesus came to
them and said, "All
authority in heav-
en and on earth
has been given to
me. [19]Therefore go
and make disci-
ples of all nations,
baptizing them in
the name of the Fa-
ther and of the Son
and of the Holy
Spirit, [20]and teach-
ing them to obey
everything I have
commanded you.
And surely I am
with you always,
to the very end of
the age."

προσεκύνησαν,		οἱ	δὲ	ἐδίστασαν.	[18] καὶ		προσελθὼν	ὁ	Ἰησοῦς	
they worshiped	him, but	some	*but*	hesitated.	And	Jesus	came	*{the}*	*Jesus*	and
4686	1254	3836	1254	1491	2779	2652	4665	3836	2652	
v.aai.3p		d.npm	pl	v.aai.3p	cj		pt.aa.nsm	d.nsm	n.nsm	

ἐλάλησεν	αὐτοῖς	λέγων,	ἐδόθη	μοι	πᾶσα	ἐξουσία	ἐν	οὐρανῷ	καὶ	ἐπὶ	τῆς[a]
spoke	to them,	saying,	*has been given*	*to me*	"All	authority	in	heaven	and	on	*{the}*
3281	899	3306	1443	1609	4246	2026	1877	4041	2779	2093	3836
v.aai.3s	r.dpm.3	pt.pa.nsm	v.api.3s	r.ds.1	a.nsf	n.nsf	p.d	n.dsm	cj	p.g	d.gsf

γῆς.						[19]	πορευθέντες	οὖν		μαθητεύσατε	πάντα
earth	has	been	given	to	me.	Therefore	go	*Therefore*	and	⌊make disciples of⌋	all
1178	1443	1443	1443	1609	1609	4036	4513	4036		3411	4246
n.gsf							pt.ap.npm	cj		v.aam.2p	a.apn

τὰ	ἔθνη,	βαπτίζοντες	αὐτοὺς	εἰς	τὸ	ὄνομα	τοῦ	πατρὸς	καὶ	τοῦ	υἱοῦ	καὶ	τοῦ
{the}	nations,	baptizing	them	in	the	name	of the	Father	and	of the	Son	and	of the
3836	1620	966	899	1650	3836	3950	3836	4252	2779	3836	5626	2779	3836
d.apn	n.apn	pt.pa.npm	r.apm.3	p.a	d.asn	n.asn	d.gsm	n.gsm	cj	d.gsm	n.gsm	cj	d.gsn

ἁγίου	πνεύματος,	[20] διδάσκοντες	αὐτοὺς	τηρεῖν	πάντα	ὅσα	ἐνετειλάμην	ὑμῖν·
Holy	Spirit,	teaching	them	to observe	everything	that	I have commanded	you.
41	4460	1438	899	5498	4246	4012	1948	7007
a.gsn	n.gsn	pt.pa.npm	r.apm.3	f.pa	a.apn	r.apn	v.ami.1s	r.dp.2

καὶ	ἰδοὺ	ἐγὼ		μεθ'	ὑμῶν	εἰμι	πάσας	τὰς	ἡμέρας	ἕως	τῆς	συντελείας	τοῦ
And	remember,	I	am	with	you	*am*	all	the	days,	to	the	end	of the
2779	2627	1609	1639	3552	7007	1639	4246	3836	2465	2401	3836	5333	3836
cj	j	r.ns.1		p.g	r.gp.2	v.pai.1s	a.apf	d.apf	n.apf	p.g	d.gsf	n.gsf	d.gsm

αἰῶνος.
age."
172
n.gsm

NASB

worshiped *Him;*
but some were
doubtful. [18]And
Jesus came up and
spoke to them, say-
ing, "All authority
has been given to
Me in heaven and
on earth. [19]Go
therefore and make
disciples of all the
nations, baptiz-
ing them in the
name of the Father
and the Son and
the Holy Spirit,
[20]teaching them to
observe all that I
commanded you;
and lo, I am with
you always, even
to the end of the
age."

[a] [τῆς] UBS, omitted by TNIV.

Mark

NIV

Mark

John the Baptist Prepares the Way

1 The beginning
of the good
news about Jesus
the Messiah,[a] the
Son of God,[b] [2]as it
is written in Isaiah
the prophet:

"I will send my
messenger
ahead of you,
who will
prepare your
way"[c]—
[3]"a voice of one
calling in the
wilderness,
'Prepare the way
for the Lord,
make straight
paths for
him.'"[d]

[4]And so John the
Baptist appeared
in the wilderness,
preaching a bap-
tism of repentance
for the forgiveness
of sins. [5]The whole
Judean countryside
and all the people of
Jerusalem went out
to him. Confessing
their sins, they were
baptized by him in
the Jordan River.
[6]John wore clothing
made of camel's
hair, with a leath-
er belt around his
waist, and he ate lo-
custs and wild hon-
ey. [7]And this was
his message: "After
me comes the one
more powerful
than I, the straps of
whose sandals I am
not worthy to stoop
down and untie. [8]I

[a] 1 Or *Jesus Christ. Messiah* (Hebrew) and *Christ* (Greek) both mean *Anointed One.*
[b] 1 Some manuscripts do not have *the Son of God.*
[c] 2 Mal. 3:1
[d] 3 Isaiah 40:3

1:1 ἀρχὴ τοῦ εὐαγγελίου Ἰησοῦ Χριστοῦ υἱοῦ θεοῦ.[a] [2]καθὼς
The beginning of the gospel of Jesus Christ, the Son of God. As
794 3836 2295 2652 5986 5626 2536 2777
n.nsf d.gsn n.gsn n.gsm n.gsm n.gsm n.gsm cj

γέγραπται ἐν τῷ Ἠσαΐᾳ τῷ προφήτῃ· ἰδοὺ ἀποστέλλω τὸν ἄγγελόν μου
it is written in *{the}* Isaiah the prophet, "Behold, I am sending *{the}* my messenger *my*
1211 1877 3836 2480 3836 4737 2627 690 3836 1609 34 1609
v.rpi.3s p.d d.dsm n.dsm d.dsm n.dsm j v.pai.1s d.asm n.asm r.gs.1

πρὸ προσώπου σου, ὃς κατασκευάσει τὴν ὁδόν σου· [3] φωνὴ βοῶντος
before your face, *your* who will prepare *{the}* your way, *your* a voice calling out
4574 5148 4725 5148 4005 2941 3836 5148 3847 5148 5889 1066
p.g n.gsn r.gs.2 r.nsm v.fai.3s d.asf n.asf r.gs.2 n.nsf pt.pa.gsm

ἐν τῇ ἐρήμῳ· ἑτοιμάσατε τὴν ὁδὸν → κυρίου, εὐθείας ποιεῖτε τὰς τρίβους
in the wilderness: 'Prepare the way of the Lord, *straight* make *{the}* his paths
1877 3836 2245 2286 3836 3847 3261 2318 4472 3836 899 5561
p.d d.dsf n.dsf v.aam.2p d.asf n.asf n.gsm a.apf v.pam.2p d.apf n.apf

αὐτοῦ, [4]ἐγένετο Ἰωάννης ὁ[b] βαπτίζων ἐν τῇ ἐρήμῳ καὶ
his straight.'" *appeared* John the baptizer appeared in the wilderness and
899 2318 1181 2722 3836 966 1181 1877 3836 2245 2779
r.gsm.3 v.ami.3s n.nsm d.nsm pt.pa.nsm p.d d.dsf n.dsf cj

κηρύσσων βάπτισμα μετανοίας εἰς ἄφεσιν ἁμαρτιῶν. [5]καὶ ἐξεπορεύετο
began preaching a baptism of repentance for the forgiveness of sins. And *were going out*
3062 967 3567 1650 912 281 2779 1744
pt.pa.nsm n.asn n.gsf p.a n.asf n.gpf cj v.imi.3s

πρὸς αὐτὸν πᾶσα ἡ Ἰουδαία χώρα καὶ οἱ Ἱεροσολυμῖται πάντες,
to *him* all the Judean countryside and all *{the}* Jerusalem *all* were
4639 899 4246 3836 2677 6001 2779 4246 3836 2643 4246 1744
p.a r.asm.3 a.nsf d.nsf a.nsf n.nsf cj d.npm n.npm a.npm

καὶ ἐβαπτίζοντο ὑπ' αὐτοῦ ἐν τῷ Ἰορδάνῃ ποταμῷ
going out to him and were being baptized by him in the Jordan river,
1744 1744 4639 899 2779 966 5679 899 1877 3836 2674 4532
cj v.ipi.3p p.g r.gsm.3 p.d d.dsm n.dsm n.dsm

ἐξομολογούμενοι τὰς ἁμαρτίας αὐτῶν. [6]καὶ ἦν ὁ Ἰωάννης
confessing *{the}* their sins. *their* Now John was *{the}* *John*
2018 3836 899 281 899 2779 2722 1639 3836 2722
pt.pm.npm d.apf n.apf r.gpm.3 cj v.iai.3s d.nsm n.nsm

ἐνδεδυμένος τρίχας καμήλου καὶ ζώνην δερματίνην περὶ τὴν ὀσφὺν
clothed with *hair* camel's hair with a leather belt *leather* around *{the}* his waist,
1907 2582 2823 2582 2779 1294 2438 1294 4309 3836 899 4019
pt.rp.nsm n.apf n.gsf cj n.asf a.asf p.a d.asf n.asf

αὐτοῦ καὶ ἐσθίων ἀκρίδας καὶ μέλι ἄγριον. [7]καὶ ἐκήρυσσεν λέγων·
his and he fed on locusts and wild honey. *wild* And he was proclaiming, saying,
899 2779 2266 210 2779 67 3510 67 2779 3062 3306
r.gsm.3 cj pt.pa.nsm n.apf cj n.asn a.asn cj v.iai.3s pt.pa.nsm

ἔρχεται ὁ ἰσχυρότερός μου ὀπίσω μου, οὗ οὐκ εἰμὶ
is coming "The ⌊one who is more powerful⌋ ⌊than I⌋ is coming after me; ⌊of whom⌋ *not* I am
2262 3836 2708 1609 2262 2262 3958 1609 4005 4024 1639
v.pmi.3s d.nsm a.nsm.c r.gs.1 p.g r.gs.1 r.gsm pl v.pai.1s

ἱκανὸς κύψας λῦσαι τὸν ἱμάντα τῶν ὑποδημάτων αὐτοῦ. [8]ἐγὼ
not worthy ⌊to stoop down⌋ and untie the thong of his sandals. *his* I
4024 2653 3252 3395 3836 2666 3836 899 5687 899 1609
a.nsm pt.aa.nsm f.aa d.asm n.asm d.gpn n.gpn r.gsm.3 r.ns.1

[a] [υἱοῦ θεοῦ] UBS, omitted by TNIV.
[b] [ὁ] UBS.

NASB

Preaching of John the Baptist

[1:1]The beginning
of the gospel of Je-
sus Christ, the Son
of God.
[2]As it is written in
Isaiah the prophet:
"BEHOLD, I SEND
MY MESSEN-
GER AHEAD OF
YOU,
WHO WILL
PREPARE YOUR
WAY;
[3] THE VOICE OF
ONE CRYING IN
THE WILDER-
NESS,
'MAKE READY
THE WAY OF
THE LORD,
MAKE HIS
PATHS
STRAIGHT.'"
[4]John the Baptist
appeared in the
wilderness [a]preach-
ing a baptism of
repentance for
the forgiveness of
sins. [5]And all the
country of Judea
was going out to
him, and all the
people of Jerusa-
lem; and they were
being baptized by
him in the Jordan
River, confessing
their sins. [6]John
was clothed with
camel's hair and
wore a leather belt
around his waist,
and his diet was
locusts and wild
honey. [7]And he was
preaching, and say-
ing, "After me One
is coming who is
mightier than I, and
I am not fit to stoop
down and untie the
thong of His san-
dals. [8]I baptized

[a] Or *proclaiming*

NIV

baptize you with[a]
water, but he will
baptize you with[b]
the Holy Spirit."

The Baptism and Testing of Jesus

9 At that time
Jesus came from
Nazareth in Gal-
ilee and was bap-
tized by John in
the Jordan. 10 Just
as Jesus was com-
ing up out of the
water, he saw
heaven being torn
open and the Spirit
descending on him
like a dove. 11 And
a voice came from
heaven: "You are
my Son, whom I
love; with you I am
well pleased."
12 At once the
Spirit sent him out
into the wilder-
ness, 13 and he was
in the wilderness
forty days, being
tempted[c] by Satan.
He was with the
wild animals, and
angels attended
him.

Jesus Announces the Good News

14 After John was
put in prison, Jesus
went into Galilee,
proclaiming the
good news of God.
15 "The time has
come," he said.
"The kingdom
of God has come
near. Repent and
believe the good
news!"

Jesus Calls His First Disciples

16 As Jesus walked
beside the Sea of
Galilee, he saw Si-
mon and his broth-
er Andrew casting
a net into the lake,
for they were fish-
ermen. 17 "Come,
follow me," Jesus
said, "and I will
send you out to

a 8 Or *in*
b 8 Or *in*
c 13 The Greek for *tempted* can also mean *tested*.

ἐβάπτισα	ὑμᾶς	ὕδατι,		αὐτὸς	δὲ	βαπτίσει	ὑμᾶς	ἐν			πνεύματι	ἁγίῳ.
baptize	you	with water,	but	he	*but*	will baptize	you	with	the	Holy	Spirit."	*Holy*
966	7007	5623	1254	899	1254	966	7007	1877		41	4460	41
v.aai.1s	r.ap.2	n.dsn		r.nsm	cj	v.fai.3s	r.ap.2	p.d			n.dsn	a.dsn

9 ⌞καὶ	ἐγένετο⌟	ἐν	ἐκείναις	ταῖς	ἡμέραις	ἦλθεν	Ἰησοῦς	ἀπὸ	Ναζαρὲτ	τῆς
Now		in	those	*{the}*	days	Jesus came	*Jesus*	from	Nazareth	of
2779	1181	1877	1697	3836	2465	2652 2262	2652	608	3715	3836
cj	v.ami.3s	p.d	r.dpf	d.dpf	n.dpf	v.aai.3s	n.nsm	p.g	n.gsf	d.gsf

Γαλιλαίας	καὶ	ἐβαπτίσθη	εἰς	τὸν	Ἰορδάνην	ὑπὸ	Ἰωάννου.	10 καὶ	εὐθὺς
Galilee	and	was baptized	in	the	Jordan	River by	John.	And	just as
1133	2779	966	1650	3836	2674	5679	2722	2779	2318
n.gsf	cj	v.api.3s	p.a	d.asm	n.asm	p.g	n.gsm	cj	adv

ἀναβαίνων	ἐκ	τοῦ	ὕδατος	εἶδεν	σχιζομένους	τοὺς	οὐρανοὺς	καί
⌞he was coming up⌟	⌞out of⌟	the	water,	he saw the heavens	opening up	*the*	*heavens*	and
326	1666	3836	5623	1625 3836 4041	5387	3836	4041	2779
pt.pa.nsm	p.g	d.gsn	n.gsn	v.aai.3s	pt.pp.apm	d.apm	n.apm	cj

τὸ	πνεῦμα	ὡς	περιστερὰν	καταβαῖνον	εἰς	αὐτόν·	11 καὶ	φωνὴ	ἐγένετο	ἐκ
the	Spirit	as	a dove	descending	on	him.	Then a	voice	came	from
3836	4460	6055	4361	2849	1650	899	2779	5889	1181	1666
d.asn	n.asn	pl	n.asf	pt.pa.asn	p.a	r.asm.3	cj	n.nsf	v.ami.3s	p.g

τῶν	οὐρανῶν·	σὺ	εἶ	ὁ	υἱός	μου	ὁ	ἀγαπητός,	ἐν	σοὶ
{the}	heaven,	"You	are	*{the}* my beloved	Son;	*my*	*{the}*	*beloved*	in	you
3836	4041	5148	1639	3836 1609 28	5626	1609	3836	28	1877	5148
d.gpm	n.gpm	r.ns.2	v.pai.2s	d.nsm	n.nsm	r.gs.1	d.nsm	a.nsm	p.d	r.ds.2

εὐδόκησα.	12 καὶ	εὐθὺς	τὸ	πνεῦμα	αὐτὸν	ἐκβάλλει	→	εἰς	τὴν	ἔρημον.
I take delight."	*{and}*	At once	the	Spirit	*him*	drove	him out	into	the	wilderness,
2305	2779	2318	3836	4460	899	1675	899	1650	3836	2245
v.aai.1s	cj	adv	d.nsn	n.nsn	r.asm.3	v.pai.3s		p.a	d.asf	n.asf

13 καὶ	ἦν	ἐν	τῇ	ἐρήμῳ	→	τεσσεράκοντα	ἡμέρας	πειραζόμενος	ὑπὸ	τοῦ
and	⌞he was⌟	in	the	wilderness	for	forty	days,	being tempted	by	*{the}*
2779	1639	1877	3836	2245		5477	2465	4279	5679	3836
cj	v.iai.3s	p.d	d.dsf	n.dsf		a.apf	n.apf	pt.pp.nsm	p.g	d.gsm

σατανᾶ,	καὶ	ἦν	μετὰ	τῶν	θηρίων,	καὶ	οἱ	ἄγγελοι	διηκόνουν	αὐτῷ.
Satan.	*{and}*	⌞He was⌟ there	with	the	wild beasts,	and	the	angels	were ministering	to him.
4928	2779	1639	3552	3836	2563	2779	3836	34	1354	899
n.gsm	cj	v.iai.3s	p.g	d.gpn	n.gpn	cj	d.npm	n.npm	v.iai.3p	r.dsm.3

14	μετὰ	δὲ	τὸ	παραδοθῆναι	τὸν	Ἰωάννην	ἦλθεν	ὁ
Now	after	*Now*	*{the}*	John ⌞had been taken into custody,⌟	*{the}*	*John*	Jesus went	*{the}*
1254	3552	1254	3836	2722 4140	3836	2722	2652 2262	3836
	p.a	cj	d.asn	f.ap	d.asm	n.asm	v.aai.3s	d.nsm

Ἰησοῦς	εἰς	τὴν	Γαλιλαίαν	κηρύσσων	τὸ	εὐαγγέλιον	τοῦ	θεοῦ	15 καὶ	λέγων	ὅτι
Jesus	into	*{the}*	Galilee,	proclaiming	the	gospel	of	God,	and	saying,	~
2652	1650	3836	1133	3062	3836	2295	3836	2536	2779	3306	4022
n.nsm	p.a	d.asf	n.asf	pt.pa.nsm	d.asn	n.asn	d.gsm	n.gsm	cj	pt.pa.nsm	cj

πεπλήρωται	ὁ	καιρὸς	καὶ	ἤγγικεν	ἡ	βασιλεία	τοῦ	θεοῦ·	
"The time is fulfilled	*The*	*time*	and	*is at hand*	the	kingdom	of	God	is at hand;
3836 2789 4444	3836	2789	2779	1581	3836	993	3836	2536	1581 1581 1581
v.rpi.3s	d.nsm	n.nsm	cj	v.rai.3s	d.nsf	n.nsf	d.gsm	n.gsm	

μετανοεῖτε	καὶ	πιστεύετε	ἐν	τῷ	εὐαγγελίῳ.	16 καὶ	→ παράγων	παρὰ	τὴν
repent	and	believe	in	the	gospel."	*{and}*	As Jesus was going	alongside	the
3566	2779	4409	1877	3836	2295	2779	4135	4123	3836
v.pam.2p	cj	v.pam.2p	p.d	d.dsn	n.dsn	cj	pt.pa.nsm	p.a	d.asf

θάλασσαν	τῆς	Γαλιλαίας	εἶδεν	Σίμωνα	καὶ	Ἀνδρέαν	τὸν	ἀδελφὸν	Σίμωνος
Sea	of	Galilee,	he saw	Simon	and	Andrew,	the	brother	of Simon,
2498	3836	1133	1625	4981	2779	436	3836	81	4981
n.asf	d.gsf	n.gsf	v.aai.3s	n.asm	cj	n.asm	d.asm	n.asm	n.gsm

ἀμφιβάλλοντας	ἐν	τῇ	θαλάσσῃ·	ἦσαν	γὰρ	ἁλιεῖς.	17 καὶ	εἶπεν	αὐτοῖς
casting a net	into	the	lake,	for they were	*for*	fishermen.	And Jesus	said	to them,
311	1877	3836	2498	1142 1639	1142	243	2779 2652	3306	899
pt.pa.apm	p.d	d.dsf	n.dsf	v.iai.3p	cj	n.npm	cj	v.aai.3s	r.dpm.3

ὁ	Ἰησοῦς·	δεῦτε	ὀπίσω	μου,	καὶ	ποιήσω	ὑμᾶς	γενέσθαι	ἁλιεῖς	ἀνθρώπων.
{the}	*Jesus*	"Come,	follow	me,	and	I will make	you	become	fishers	of men."
3836	2652	1307	3958	1609	2779	4472	7007	1181	243	476
d.nsm	n.nsm	adv	p.g	r.gs.1	cj	v.fai.1s	r.ap.2	f.am	n.apm	n.gpm

NASB

you [a]with water;
but He will baptize
you with the Holy
Spirit."

The Baptism of Jesus

9 In those days
Jesus came from
Nazareth in Galilee
and was baptized
by John in the Jor-
dan. 10 Immediately
coming up out
of the water, He
saw the heavens
opening, and the
Spirit like a dove
descending upon
Him; 11 and a voice
came out of the
heavens: "You are
My beloved Son,
in You I am well-
pleased."
12 Immediately the
Spirit *impelled
Him *to go* out into
the wilderness.
13 And He was in
the wilderness
forty days being
tempted by Satan;
and He was with
the wild beasts,
and the angels
were ministering
to Him.

Jesus Preaches in Galilee

14 Now after John
had been taken
into custody, Jesus
came into Galilee,
preaching the gos-
pel of God, 15 and
saying, "The time
is fulfilled, and the
kingdom of God
is at hand; repent
and believe in the
gospel."
16 As He was going
along by the Sea of
Galilee, He saw Si-
mon and Andrew,
the brother of Si-
mon, casting a net
in the sea; for they
were fishermen.
17 And Jesus said to
them, "Follow Me,
and I will make
you become fishers
of men."

a The Gr here can be translated *in, with* or *by*

NIV

fish for people."
18At once they left
their nets and fol-
lowed him.
19When he had
gone a little far-
ther, he saw James
son of Zebedee
and his brother
John in a boat, pre-
paring their nets.
20Without delay
he called them,
and they left their
father Zebedee in
the boat with the
hired men and fol-
lowed him.

Jesus Drives Out an Impure Spirit

21They went to
Capernaum, and
when the Sabbath
came, Jesus went
into the synagogue
and began to
teach. 22The peo-
ple were amazed
at his teaching,
because he taught
them as one who
had authority, not
as the teachers of
the law. 23Just then
a man in their syn-
agogue who was
possessed by an
impure spirit cried
out, 24"What do
you want with us,
Jesus of Nazareth?
Have you come to
destroy us? I know
who you are—the
Holy One of God!"
25"Be quiet!"
said Jesus stern-
ly. "Come out of
him!" 26The im-
pure spirit shook
the man violently
and came out of
him with a shriek.
27The people
were all so amazed
that they asked
each other, "What
is this? A new
teaching—and
with authority! He
even gives orders

18 καὶ εὐθὺς ↱ ἀφέντες τὰ δίκτυα ἠκολούθησαν αὐτῷ. 19 καὶ προβὰς
And immediately they left their nets and followed him. And going on a
2779 2318 199 918 3836 1473 199 899 2779 4581
cj adv pt.aa.npm d.apn n.apn v.aai.3p r.dsm.3 cj pt.aa.nsm

ὀλίγον εἶδεν Ἰάκωβον τὸν τοῦ Ζεβεδαίου καὶ Ἰωάννην τὸν ἀδελφὸν
little farther, he saw James the son of Zebedee and John *{the}* his brother,
3900 1625 2610 3836 3836 2411 2779 2722 3836 899 81
adv v.aai.3s n.asm d.asm d.gsm n.gsm cj n.asm d.asm n.asm

αὐτοῦ καὶ αὐτοὺς ↱ ἐν τῷ πλοίῳ καταρτίζοντας τὰ δίκτυα, 20 καὶ
his who also *who* were in their boat mending *{the}* nets. And
899 899 2779 899 2936 1877 3836 4450 2936 3836 1473 2779
r.gsm.3 cj r.apm.3 p.d d.dsn n.dsn pt.pa.apm d.apn n.apn cj

εὐθὺς ἐκάλεσεν αὐτούς. καὶ ἀφέντες τὸν πατέρα αὐτῶν Ζεβεδαῖον ἐν τῷ
immediately he called them, and they left *{the}* their father *their* Zebedee in the
2318 2813 899 2779 918 3836 899 4252 899 2411 1877 3836
adv v.aai.3s r.apm.3 cj pt.aa.npm d.asm n.asm r.gpm.3 n.asm p.d d.dsn

πλοίῳ μετὰ τῶν μισθωτῶν ἀπῆλθον ὀπίσω αὐτοῦ. 21 καὶ εἰσπορεύονται εἰς
boat with the hired men and followed *{after}* him. Then they went to
4450 3552 3836 3638 599 3958 899 2779 1660 1650
n.dsn p.g d.gpm n.gpm v.aai.3p p.g r.gsm.3 cj v.pmi.3p p.a

Καφαρναούμ· καὶ εὐθὺς τοῖς σάββασιν εἰσελθὼν εἰς τὴν συναγωγὴν
Capernaum; and on the next *on the* Sabbath Jesus went into the synagogue
3019 2779 3836 3836 2318 3836 4879 1656 1650 3836 5252
n.asf cj adv d.dpn n.dpn pt.aa.nsm p.a d.asf n.asf

ἐδίδασκεν. 22 καὶ ἐξεπλήσσοντο ἐπὶ τῇ διδαχῇ αὐτοῦ· ἦν γὰρ
and began to teach. And they were astonished at *{the}* his teaching, *his* for ⌊he was⌋ *for*
1438 2779 1742 2093 3836 899 1439 899 1142 1639 1142
v.iai.3s cj v.ipi.3p p.d d.dsf n.dsf r.gsm.3 v.iai.3s cj

διδάσκων αὐτοὺς ὡς ἐξουσίαν ἔχων καὶ οὐχ ὡς οἱ γραμματεῖς.
teaching them as one having authority, *one having* and not as their scribes.
1438 899 6055 2400 2400 2026 2400 2779 4024 6055 3836 1208
pt.pa.nsm r.apm.3 pl n.asf pt.pa.nsm cj pl pl d.npm n.npm

23 καὶ εὐθὺς ἦν ἐν τῇ συναγωγῇ αὐτῶν ἄνθρωπος ἐν
{and} Suddenly ⌊there was⌋ in *{the}* their synagogue *their* a man with an unclean
2779 2318 1639 1877 3836 899 5252 899 476 1877 176
cj adv v.iai.3s p.d d.dsf n.dsf r.gpm.3 n.nsm p.d

πνεύματι ἀκαθάρτῳ καὶ ἀνέκραξεν 24 λέγων· τί ἡμῖν καὶ σοί,
spirit, *unclean* and he cried out, saying, "What *with us* *{and}* do you have to do with
4460 176 2779 371 3306 5515 7005 2779 5148 7005
n.dsn a.dsn cj v.aai.3s pt.pa.nsm r.nsn r.dp.1 cj r.ds.2

Ἰησοῦ Ναζαρηνέ; ἦλθες ἀπολέσαι ἡμᾶς; οἶδά σε τίς εἶ, ὁ
us, Jesus of Nazareth? ⌊Have you come⌋ to destroy us? I know *{you}* who ⌊you are⌋ — the
7005 2652 3716 2262 660 7005 3857 5148 5515 1639 3836
n.vsm n.vsm v.aai.2s f.aa r.ap.1 v.rai.1s r.as.2 r.nsm v.pai.2s d.nsm

ἅγιος τοῦ θεοῦ. 25 καὶ ἐπετίμησεν αὐτῷ ὁ Ἰησοῦς λέγων· φιμώθητι καὶ
Holy One of God!" But Jesus rebuked it, *{the}* *Jesus* saying, "Be quiet and
41 3836 2536 2779 2652 2203 899 3836 2652 3306 5821 2779
a.nsm d.gsm n.gsm cj v.aai.3s r.dsm.3 d.nsm n.nsm pt.pa.nsm v.apm.2s cj

ἔξελθε ἐξ αὐτοῦ. 26 καὶ σπαράξαν αὐτὸν ↰ ↰ τὸ
come out of him!" Then the unclean spirit threw the man into convulsions, *the*
2002 1666 899 2779 3836 176 4460 5057 899 5057 5057 3836
v.aam.2s p.g r.gsm.3 cj pt.aa.nsn r.asm.3 d.nsn

πνεῦμα τὸ ἀκάθαρτον καὶ φωνῆσαν → φωνῇ μεγάλῃ ἐξῆλθεν ἐξ
spirit *{the}* *unclean* *{and}* cried out with a loud voice, *loud* and came out of
4460 3836 176 2779 5888 3489 5889 3489 2002 1666
n.nsn d.nsn a.nsn cj pt.aa.nsn n.dsf a.dsf v.aai.3s p.g

αὐτοῦ. 27 καὶ ἐθαμβήθησαν ἅπαντες ὥστε συζητεῖν πρὸς ἑαυτοὺς
him. *{and}* All the people were amazed, *All* so that they asked among themselves,
899 2779 570 2501 570 6063 5184 4639 1571
r.gsm.3 cj v.api.3p a.npm cj f.pa p.a r.apm.3

λέγοντας· τί ἐστιν τοῦτο; διδαχὴ καινὴ κατ᾽ ἐξουσίαν· καὶ
saying, "What is this? A new teaching *new* with authority! He even gives orders
3306 5515 1639 4047 2785 1439 2785 2848 2026 2199 2779 2199 2199
pt.pa.apm r.nsn v.pai.3s r.nsn n.nsf a.nsf p.a n.asf adv

NASB

18Immediately
they left their nets
and followed Him.
19Going on a little
farther, He saw
James the son of
Zebedee, and John
his brother, who
were also in the
boat mending the
nets. 20Immediately
He called them;
and they left their
father Zebedee in
the boat with the
hired servants, and
went away to fol-
low Him.
21They *went into
Capernaum; and
immediately on
the Sabbath He
entered the syna-
gogue and *began*
to teach. 22They
were amazed at
His teaching; for
He was teaching
them as *one* hav-
ing authority, and
not as the scribes.
23Just then there
was a man in their
synagogue with an
unclean spirit; and
he cried out, 24say-
ing, "What busi-
ness do we have
with each other,
Jesus [a]of Nazareth?
Have You come
to destroy us? I
know who You
are—the Holy One
of God!" 25And
Jesus rebuked him,
saying, "Be quiet,
and come out of
him!" 26Throwing
him into convul-
sions, the unclean
spirit cried out
with a loud voice
and came out of
him. 27They were
all amazed, so
that they debated
among themselves,
saying, "What is
this? A new teach-
ing with authority!
He commands

[a] Lit *the Nazarene*

NIV

to impure spir-
its and they obey
him.” 28News
about him spread
quickly over the
whole region of
Galilee.

Jesus Heals Many

29As soon as they
left the synagogue,
they went with
James and John
to the home of Si-
mon and Andrew.
30Simon’s mother-
in-law was in bed
with a fever, and
they immediately
told Jesus about
her. 31So he went
to her, took her
hand and helped
her up. The fever
left her and she
began to wait on
them.
32That evening
after sunset the
people brought
to Jesus all the
sick and demon-
possessed. 33The
whole town gath-
ered at the door,
34and Jesus healed
many who had
various diseases.
He also drove out
many demons, but
he would not let
the demons speak
because they knew
who he was.

Jesus Prays in a Solitary Place

35Very early
in the morning,
while it was still
dark, Jesus got
up, left the house
and went off to
a solitary place,
where he prayed.
36Simon and his
companions went
to look for him,
37and when they
found him, they
exclaimed: “Ev-
eryone

τοῖς πνεύμασι τοῖς ἀκαθάρτοις ἐπιτάσσει, καὶ ὑπακούουσιν αὐτῷ. 28 καὶ
to unclean spirits {the} unclean He gives orders and they obey him.” And
3836 176 4460 3836 176 2199 2779 5634 899 2779
d.dpn n.dpn d.dpn a.dpn v.pai.3s cj v.pai.3p r.dsm.3 cj

ἐξῆλθεν ἡ ἀκοὴ αὐτοῦ εὐθὺς πανταχοῦ εἰς ὅλην τὴν
his fame spread {the} fame his quickly everywhere throughout all the
899 198 2002 3836 198 899 2318 4116 1650 3910 3836
v.aai.3s d.nsf n.nsf r.gsm.3 adv adv p.a a.asf d.asf

περίχωρον τῆς Γαλιλαίας. 29 καὶ εὐθὺς ἐκ τῆς συναγωγῆς
⌞country round about⌟ {the} Galilee. {and} ⌞As soon as⌟ they went ⌞out of⌟ the synagogue
4369 3836 1133 2779 2318 2002 2002 1666 3836 5252
a.asf d.gsf n.gsf cj adv p.g d.gsf n.gsf

ἐξελθόντες ἦλθον εἰς τὴν οἰκίαν Σίμωνος καὶ Ἀνδρέου μετὰ Ἰακώβου καὶ
they went they went to the house of Simon and Andrew, with James and
2002 2262 1650 3836 3864 4981 2779 436 3552 2610 2779
pt.aa.npm v.aai.3p p.a d.asf n.asf n.gsm cj n.gsm p.g n.gsm cj

Ἰωάννου. 30 ἡ δὲ πενθερὰ Σίμωνος κατέκειτο πυρέσσουσα, καὶ
John. Now the Now mother-in-law of Simon lay sick with a fever, and
2722 1254 3836 1254 4289 4981 2879 4789 2779
n.gsm d.nsf cj n.nsf n.gsm v.imi.3s pt.pa.nsf cj

εὐθὺς λέγουσιν αὐτῷ περὶ αὐτῆς. 31 καὶ ↱ προσελθὼν ἤγειρεν αὐτὴν
⌞without delay⌟ they spoke to Jesus about her. So he came and raised her
2318 3306 899 4309 899 2779 1586 4665 1586 899
adv v.pai.3p r.dsm.3 p.g r.gsf.3 cj pt.aa.nsm v.aai.3s r.asf.3

↰ κρατήσας ← τῆς χειρός· καὶ ἀφῆκεν αὐτὴν ὁ πυρετός, καὶ
up, taking her by the hand. Then the fever left her, the fever and
1586 3195 3836 5931 2779 3836 4790 918 899 3836 4790 2779
pt.aa.nsm d.gsf n.gsf cj v.aai.3s r.asf.3 d.nsm n.nsm cj

διηκόνει αὐτοῖς. 32 ↱ ὀψίας δὲ γενομένης, ὅτε ἔδυ
⌞she began to wait on⌟ them. When evening {and} came, after the sun ⌞had gone down,⌟
1354 899 1181 4068 1254 1181 4021 3836 2463 1544
v.iai.3s r.dpm.3 n.gsf cj pt.am.gsf cj v.aai.3s

ὁ ἥλιος, ἔφερον πρὸς αὐτὸν πάντας τοὺς κακῶς ἔχοντας καὶ
the sun ⌞people were bringing⌟ to him all who were sick were ⌞as well as⌟
3836 2463 5770 4639 899 4246 3836 2400 2809 2400 2779
d.nsm n.nsm v.iai.3p p.a r.asm.3 a.apm d.apm adv pt.pa.apm cj

τοὺς δαιμονιζομένους· 33 καὶ ἦν ὅλη ἡ πόλις ἐπισυνηγμένη πρὸς
the demon-possessed. And the entire city was entire the city gathered together at
3836 1227 2779 3836 3910 4484 1639 3910 3836 4484 2190 4639
d.apm pt.pp.apm cj v.iai.3s a.nsf d.nsf n.nsf pt.rp.nsf p.a

τὴν θύραν. 34 καὶ ἐθεράπευσεν πολλοὺς κακῶς ἔχοντας ποικίλαις νόσοις
the door. So he healed many who were sick who were with various diseases,
3836 2598 2779 2543 4498 2400 2400 2809 2400 4476 3798
d.asf n.asf cj v.aai.3s a.apm adv pt.pa.apm a.dpf n.dpf

καὶ δαιμόνια πολλὰ ἐξέβαλεν καὶ ↱ ↱ οὐκ ἤφιεν
and drove out many demons. many drove out But he would not permit the demons
2779 1675 1675 4498 1228 4498 1675 2779 918 918 4024 918 3836 1228
cj n.apn a.apn v.aai.3s cj pl v.iai.3s

λαλεῖν τὰ δαιμόνια, ὅτι ᾔδεισαν αὐτόν. 35 καὶ πρωῒ
to speak, the demons because they knew him. {and} Very ⌞early in the morning,⌟
3281 3836 1228 4022 3857 899 2779 3336 4745
f.pa d.apn n.apn cj v.lai.3p r.asm.3 cj adv

ἔννυχα λίαν ἀναστὰς ἐξῆλθεν καὶ ἀπῆλθεν εἰς ἔρημον
⌞while it was still dark,⌟ Very Jesus arose, left the house and went out to a deserted
1939 3336 482 2002 2779 599 1650 2245
adv adv pt.aa.nsm v.aai.3s cj v.aai.3s p.a a.asm

τόπον κἀκεῖ προσηύχετο. 36 καὶ κατεδίωξεν αὐτὸν Σίμων καὶ οἱ
place; and there ⌞he spent time in prayer.⌟ And searched for him Simon and those who were
5536 2779 4667 2779 2870 899 4981 2779 3836
n.asm crasis v.imi.3s cj v.aai.3s r.asm.3 n.nsm cj d.npm

μετ᾿ αὐτοῦ, 37 καὶ εὗρον αὐτὸν καὶ λέγουσιν αὐτῷ ὅτι πάντες
with him searched for him, {and} found him, and said to him, ~ “Everyone
3552 899 2870 2870 899 2779 2351 899 2779 3306 899 4022 4246
p.g r.gsm.3 cj v.aai.3p r.asm.3 cj v.pai.3p r.dsm.3 cj a.npm

NASB

even the unclean
spirits, and they
obey Him.” 28Im-
mediately the news
about Him spread
everywhere into
all the surrounding
district of Galilee.

Crowds Healed

29And immediate-
ly after they came
out of the syna-
gogue, they came
into the house of
Simon and An-
drew, with James
and John. 30Now
Simon’s mother-in-
law was lying sick
with a fever; and
immediately they
*spoke to Jesus
about her. 31And
He came to her
and raised her up,
taking her by the
hand, and the fever
left her, and she
[a]waited on them.
32When evening
came, after the sun
had set, they *began*
bringing to Him all
who were ill and
those who were
demon-possessed.
33And the whole
city had gathered at
the door. 34And He
healed many who
were ill with vari-
ous diseases, and
cast out many de-
mons; and He was
not permitting the
demons to speak,
because they knew
who He was.
35In the early
morning, while
it was still dark,
Jesus got up, left
the house, and
went away to a
secluded place,
and was praying
there. 36Simon and
his companions
searched for Him;
37they found Him,
and *said to Him,

[a] Or *served*

NIV

is looking for
you!"
[38]Jesus replied,
"Let us go some-
where else—to the
nearby villages—
so I can preach
there also. That is
why I have come."
[39]So he traveled
throughout Gali-
lee, preaching in
their synagogues
and driving out de-
mons.

Jesus Heals a Man With Leprosy

[40]A man with
leprosy[a] came to
him and begged
him on his knees,
"If you are willing,
you can make me
clean."
[41]Jesus was indig-
nant.[b] He reached
out his hand and
touched the man.
"I am willing," he
said. "Be clean!"
[42]Immediately
the leprosy left
him and he was
cleansed.
[43]Jesus sent him
away at once with
a strong warning:
[44]"See that you
don't tell this to
anyone. But go,
show yourself to
the priest and offer
the sacrifices that
Moses command-
ed for your cleans-
ing, as a testimony
to them." [45]Instead
he went out and
began to talk free-
ly, spreading the
news. As a result,
Jesus could no lon-
ger enter a town
openly but stayed
outside in lone-
ly places. Yet the
people still came
to him from every-
where.

a *40* The Greek word traditionally translated *leprosy* was used for various diseases affecting the skin.
b *41* Many manuscripts *Jesus was filled with compassion*

ζητοῦσίν σε. 38 καὶ λέγει αὐτοῖς· ἄγωμεν ἀλλαχοῦ εἰς τὰς ἐχομένας
⌊is looking for⌋ you." And he said to them, "Let us go elsewhere, into the nearby
2426 5148 2779 3306 899 72 250 1650 3836 2400
v.pai.3p r.as.2 cj v.pai.3s r.dpm.3 v.pas.1p adv p.a d.apf pt.pm.apf

κωμοπόλεις, ἵνα καὶ ἐκεῖ κηρύξω· εἰς τοῦτο γὰρ
towns, so that *also* *there* I may preach there also, *to* *that* because that is what
3268 2671 2779 1695 3062 1695 2779 1650 4047 1142 4047
n.apf cj adv adv v.aas.1s p.a r.asn cj

ἐξῆλθον. 39 καὶ ἦλθεν κηρύσσων εἰς τὰς
I came to do." So he traveled throughout all Galilee, preaching in *{the}* their
2002 1650 2779 2262 1650 3910 1133 3062 1650 3836 899
v.aai.1s cj v.aai.3s pt.pa.nsm p.a d.apf

συναγωγὰς αὐτῶν εἰς ὅλην τὴν Γαλιλαίαν καὶ τὰ δαιμόνια
synagogues *their* *throughout* *all* *{the}* *Galilee* and driving out *{the}* demons.
5252 899 1650 3910 3836 1133 2779 1675 1675 3836 1228
n.apf r.gpm.3 p.a a.asf d.asf n.asf cj d.apn n.apn

ἐκβάλλων. 40 καὶ ἔρχεται πρὸς αὐτὸν λεπρὸς παρακαλῶν αὐτὸν [a]καὶ
driving out And a leper came to him, *leper* ⌊pleading for help from⌋ him, and
1675 2779 3320 2262 4639 899 3320 4151 899 2779
pt.pa.nsm cj v.pmi.3s p.a r.asm.3 a.nsm pt.pa.nsm r.asm.3 cj

γονυπετῶν ← καὶ λέγων αὐτῷ ὅτι ἐὰν θέλῃς δύνασαί ↱ με
falling on his knees *{and}* he exclaimed to him, ~ "If ⌊you are willing,⌋ you can make me
1206 2779 3306 899 4022 1569 2527 1538 2751 1609
pt.pa.nsm cj pt.pa.nsm r.dsm.3 cj cj v.pas.2s v.ppi.2s r.as.1

καθαρίσαι. 41 καὶ σπλαγχνισθεὶς[b] ἐκτείνας τὴν χεῖρα αὐτοῦ
clean!" *{and}* Moved with compassion, Jesus ⌊stretched out⌋ *{the}* his hand *his* and
2751 2779 5072 1753 3836 899 5931 899
f.aa cj pt.ap.nsm pt.aa.nsm d.asf n.asf r.gsm.3

ἥψατο καὶ λέγει αὐτῷ· θέλω, καθαρίσθητι· 42 καὶ εὐθὺς
touched him, *{and}* saying to him, ⌊"I am willing;⌋ be made clean." And at once the leprosy
721 2779 3306 899 2527 2751 2779 2318 3836 3319
v.ami.3s cj v.pai.3s r.dsm.3 v.pai.1s v.apm.2s cj adv

ἀπῆλθεν ἀπ' αὐτοῦ ἡ λέπρα, καὶ ἐκαθαρίσθη. 43 καὶ ἐμβριμησάμενος αὐτῷ
left *{from}* him *the* *leprosy* and he was cleansed. And after sternly warning him,
599 608 899 3836 3319 2779 2751 2779 1839 899
v.aai.3s p.g r.gsm.3 d.nsf n.nsf cj v.api.3s cj pt.am.nsm r.dsm.3

εὐθὺς ἐξέβαλεν αὐτὸν ↰ 44 καὶ λέγει αὐτῷ· ὅρα μηδενὶ μηδὲν
at once Jesus sent him away at once, and said to him, "See that *to anyone* *nothing*
2318 1675 899 1675 2318 2318 2779 3306 899 3972 3594 3594
adv v.aai.3s r.asm.3 cj v.pai.3s r.dsm.3 v.pam.2s a.dsm a.asn

εἴπῃς, ἀλλὰ ὕπαγε σεαυτὸν δεῖξον τῷ ἱερεῖ καὶ προσένεγκε
you say nothing to anyone, but go, show yourself *show* ⌊to the⌋ priest and offer
3306 3594 3594 3594 247 5632 1259 4932 1259 3836 2636 2779 4712
v.aas.2s cj v.pam.2s r.asm.2 v.aam.2s d.dsm n.dsm cj v.aam.2s

περὶ τοῦ καθαρισμοῦ σου ἃ προσέταξεν Μωϋσῆς, εἰς μαρτύριον
for *{the}* your cleansing *your* what Moses commanded, *Moses* as a testimony
4309 3836 5148 2752 5148 4005 3707 4705 3707 1650 3457
p.g d.gsm n.gsm r.gs.2 r.apn v.aai.3s n.nsm p.a n.asn

αὐτοῖς. 45 ὁ δὲ ἐξελθὼν ἤρξατο κηρύσσειν πολλὰ καὶ
to them." However, he *However* went out and began to announce it publicly and
899 1254 3836 1254 2002 806 3062 4498 2779
r.dpm.3 d.nsm cj pt.aa.nsm v.ami.3s f.pa a.apn cj

διαφημίζειν τὸν λόγον, ὥστε μηκέτι αὐτὸν δύνασθαι φανερῶς εἰς
spread abroad the news, so that *no longer* Jesus could no longer openly *{into}* enter a
1424 3836 3364 6063 3600 899 1538 3600 3600 5747 1650 1656
f.pa d.asm n.asm cj adv r.asm.3 f.pp adv p.a

πόλιν εἰσελθεῖν, ἀλλ' ἔξω ἐπ' ἐρήμοις τόποις ἦν· καὶ ἤρχοντο πρὸς
town, *enter* but stayed out in unpopulated areas. *stayed* Yet people kept coming to
4484 1656 247 1639 2032 2093 2245 5536 1639 2779 2262 4639
n.asf f.aa cj adv p.d a.dpm n.dpm v.iai.3s cj v.imi.3p p.a

αὐτὸν πάντοθεν.
him ⌊from every quarter.⌋
899 4119
r.asm.3 adv

a [καὶ γονυπετῶν] UBS.
b σπλαγχνισθεὶς UBS, NET. ὀργίσθεις TNIV.

NASB

"Everyone is look-
ing for You." [38]He
*said to them, "Let
us go somewhere
else to the towns
nearby, so that I
may preach there
also; for that is
what I came for."
[39]And He went into
their synagogues
throughout all
Galilee, preaching
and casting out the
demons.
[40]And a leper
*came to Jesus, be-
seeching Him and
falling on his knees
before Him, and
saying, "If You are
willing, You can
make me clean."
[41]Moved with
compassion, Jesus
stretched out His
hand and touched
him, and *said to
him, "I am willing;
be cleansed." [42]Im-
mediately the lep-
rosy left him and
he was cleansed.
[43]And He sternly
warned him and
immediately sent
him away, [44]and He
*said to him, "See
that you say noth-
ing to anyone; but
go, show yourself
to the priest and of-
fer for your cleans-
ing what Moses
commanded, as
a testimony to
them." [45]But he
went out and began
to proclaim it free-
ly and to spread the
news around, to
such an extent that
Jesus could no lon-
ger publicly enter a
city, but [a]stayed out
in unpopulated ar-
eas; and they were
coming to Him
from everywhere.

a Lit *was*

NIV

Jesus Forgives and Heals a Paralyzed Man

2 A few days
later, when
Jesus again en-
tered Capernaum,
the people heard
that he had come
home. 2 They
gathered in such
large numbers
that there was no
room left, not even
outside the door,
and he preached
the word to them.
3 Some men came,
bringing to him
a paralyzed man,
carried by four of
them. 4 Since they
could not get him
to Jesus because
of the crowd, they
made an opening
in the roof above
Jesus by digging
through it and then
lowered the mat
the man was lying
on. 5 When Jesus
saw their faith, he
said to the para-
lyzed man, "Son,
your sins are for-
given."
6 Now some
teachers of the
law were sitting
there, thinking to
themselves, 7 "Why
does this fellow
talk like that? He's
blaspheming! Who
can forgive sins
but God alone?"
8 Immediately
Jesus knew in his
spirit that this was
what they were
thinking in their
hearts, and he said
to them, "Why are
you thinking these
things? 9 Which
is easier: to say
to this paralyzed
man, 'Your sins
are forgiven,' or
to say,

2:1 καὶ → εἰσελθὼν πάλιν εἰς Καφαρναοὺμ δι᾽ ἡμερῶν
And when, after several days, Jesus had returned {again} to Capernaum after days
2779 1328 2465 1656 4099 1650 3019 1328 2465
cj pt.aa.nsm adv p.a n.asf p.g n.gpf

ἠκούσθη ὅτι ἐν οἴκῳ ἐστίν. 2 καὶ συνήχθησαν πολλοὶ
it was reported that he was at home. he was {and} Many people gathered Many
201 4022 1639 1639 1877 3875 1639 2779 4498 5251 4498
v.api.3s cj p.d n.dsm v.pai.3s cj v.api.3p a.npm

ὥστε ↱ ↱ μηκέτι χωρεῖν μηδὲ τὰ πρὸς τὴν θύραν, καὶ ἐλάλει
so that there was no longer any room, not even {the} at the entrance; and ⌊he began speaking⌋
6063 6003 6003 3600 6003 3593 3836 4639 3836 2598 2779 3281
cj adv f.pa adv d.apn p.a d.asf n.asf cj v.iai.3s

αὐτοῖς τὸν λόγον. 3 καὶ ἔρχονται φέροντες πρὸς αὐτὸν
the word to them. the word And some men came, bringing to him a
3836 3364 899 3836 3364 2779 2262 5770 4639 899
r.dpm.3 d.asm n.asm cj v.pmi.3p pt.pa.npm p.a r.asm.3

παραλυτικὸν αἰρόμενον ὑπὸ τεσσάρων. 4 καὶ ↱ ↱ ↱ μὴ δυνάμενοι
paralytic carried by four of them. {and} When they were not able
4166 149 5679 5475 2779 1538 1538 1538 3590 1538
a.asm pt.pp.asm p.g a.gpm cj pl pt.pp.npm

προσενέγκαι αὐτῷ ↰ διὰ τὸν ὄχλον ἀπεστέγασαν τὴν στέγην ὅπου ἦν,
to carry him in ⌊because of⌋ the crowd, they broke through the roof above Jesus,
4712 899 4712 1328 3836 4063 689 3836 5094 3963 1639
f.aa r.dsm.3 p.a d.asm n.asm v.aai.3p d.asf n.asf cj v.iai.3s

καὶ ἐξορύξαντες χαλῶσι τὸν κράβαττον ὅπου ὁ
and ⌊when they had dug out an opening,⌋ they lowered the mat on which the
2779 2021 5899 3836 3187 3963 3836
cj pt.aa.npm v.pai.3p d.asm n.asm cj d.nsm

παραλυτικὸς κατέκειτο. 5 καὶ → ἰδὼν ὁ Ἰησοῦς τὴν πίστιν αὐτῶν
paralytic was lying. {and} When Jesus saw {the} Jesus {the} their faith, their
4166 2879 2779 2652 1625 3836 2652 3836 899 4411 899
a.nsm v.imi.3s cj pt.aa.nsm d.nsm n.nsm d.asf n.asf r.gpm.3

λέγει τῷ παραλυτικῷ· τέκνον, ἀφίενταί σου αἱ ἁμαρτίαι.
he said ⌊to the⌋ paralytic, "My son, are forgiven your {the} sins are forgiven."
3306 3836 4166 5451 918 5148 3836 281 918 918
v.pai.3s d.dsm a.dsm n.vsn v.ppi.3p r.gs.2 d.npf n.npf

6 ἦσαν δέ τινες τῶν γραμματέων ἐκεῖ καθήμενοι καὶ διαλογιζόμενοι ἐν
were Now some of the scribes there were sitting there, {and} reasoning in
1639 1254 5516 3836 1208 1695 1639 2764 1695 2779 1368 1877
v.iai.3p cj r.npm d.gpm n.gpm adv pt.pm.npm cj pt.pm.npm p.d

ταῖς καρδίαις αὐτῶν· 7 τί ↱ οὗτος οὕτως λαλεῖ; βλασφημεῖ· τίς
{the} their hearts, their "Why does this man speak like that? speak It is blasphemy! Who
3836 899 2840 899 5515 3281 4047 3281 4048 3281 1059 5515
d.dpf n.dpf r.gpm.3 r.asn r.nsm adv v.pai.3s v.pai.3s r.nsm

δύναται ἀφιέναι ἁμαρτίας ⌊εἰ μὴ⌋ εἷς ὁ θεός; 8 καὶ
can forgive sins except the One the God?" And Jesus, knowing
1538 918 281 1623 3590 3836 1651 3836 2536 2779 2652 2105
v.ppi.3s f.pa n.apf cj pl a.nsm d.nsm n.nsm cj

εὐθὺς ἐπιγνοὺς ὁ Ἰησοῦς τῷ πνεύματι αὐτοῦ ὅτι
immediately knowing {the} Jesus in his spirit his that they were reasoning
2318 2105 3836 2652 3836 899 4460 899 4022 1368 1368 1368
adv pt.aa.nsm d.nsm n.nsm d.dsn n.dsn r.gsm.3 cj

οὕτως διαλογίζονται ἐν ἑαυτοῖς λέγει αὐτοῖς· τί
⌊in that way⌋ they were reasoning within themselves, said to them, "Why are you contemplating
4048 1368 1877 1571 3306 899 5515 1368 1368 1368
adv v.pmi.3p p.d r.dpm.3 v.pai.3s r.dpm.3 r.asn

ταῦτα διαλογίζεσθε ἐν ταῖς καρδίαις ὑμῶν; 9 τί ἐστιν εὐκοπώτερον,
these things are you contemplating in {the} your hearts? your Which is easier,
4047 1368 1877 3836 7007 2840 7007 5515 1639 2324
r.apn v.pmi.2p p.d d.dpf n.dpf r.gp.2 r.nsn v.pai.3s a.nsn

εἰπεῖν τῷ παραλυτικῷ· ἀφίενταί σου αἱ ἁμαρτίαι, ἢ εἰπεῖν·
to say ⌊to the⌋ paralytic, are forgiven 'Your {the} sins are forgiven,' or to say,
3306 3836 4166 918 5148 3836 281 918 918 2445 3306
f.aa d.dsm a.dsm v.ppi.3p r.gs.2 d.npf n.npf cj f.aa

NASB

The Paralytic Healed

2:1 When He had
come back to Ca-
pernaum several
days afterward,
it was heard that
He was at home.
2 And many were
gathered together,
so that there was
no longer room,
not even near the
door; and He was
speaking the word
to them. 3 And they
*came, bringing to
Him a paralytic,
carried by four
men. 4 Being unable
to get to Him be-
cause of the crowd,
they removed the
roof above Him;
and when they had
dug an opening,
they let down the
pallet on which the
paralytic was lying.
5 And Jesus seeing
their faith *said
to the paralytic,
"[a]Son, your sins
are forgiven." 6 But
some of the scribes
were sitting there
and reasoning in
their hearts, 7 "Why
does this man
speak that way?
He is blaspheming;
who can forgive
sins but God
alone?" 8 Immedi-
ately Jesus, aware
in His spirit that
they were reason-
ing that way within
themselves, *said
to them, "Why
are you reasoning
about these things
in your hearts?
9 Which is easier, to
say to the paralytic,
'Your sins are for-
given'; or to say,

[a] Lit *child*

NIV

‘Get up, take your
mat and walk’?
10But I want you
to know that the
Son of Man has
authority on earth
to forgive sins.”
So he said to the
man, 11“I tell
you, get up, take
your mat and go
home.” 12He got
up, took his mat
and walked out in
full view of them
all. This amazed
everyone and they
praised God, say-
ing, “We have nev-
er seen anything
like this!”

Jesus Calls Levi and Eats With Sinners

13Once again
Jesus went out
beside the lake. A
large crowd came
to him, and he be-
gan to teach them.
14As he walked
along, he saw Levi
son of Alphaeus
sitting at the tax
collector’s booth.
“Follow me,” Jesus
told him, and Levi
got up and fol-
lowed him.
15While Jesus
was having dinner
at Levi’s house,
many tax collec-
tors and sinners
were eating with
him and his dis-
ciples, for there
were many who
followed him.
16When the teach-
ers of the law who
were Pharisees
saw him eating
with the sinners
and tax collectors,
they asked his dis-
ciples: “Why does
he eat with tax
collectors and sin-
ners?”

ἔγειρε καὶ ἆρον τὸν κράβαττόν σου καὶ περιπάτει; 10 ἵνα δὲ
‘Get up, {and} pick up {the} your mat your and walk’? But so that But
1586 2779 149 3836 5148 3187 5148 2779 4344 1254 2671 1254
v.pam.2s cj v.aam.2s d.asm n.asm r.gs.2 cj v.pam.2s cj cj

εἰδῆτε ὅτι ἐξουσίαν ἔχει ὁ υἱὸς τοῦ ἀνθρώπου
⌞you may know⌟ that authority has the Son of Man has authority on the earth
3857 4022 2026 2400 3836 5626 3836 476 2400 2026 2093 3836 1178
v.ras.2p cj n.asf v.pai.3s d.nsm n.nsm d.gsm n.gsm

ἀφιέναι ἁμαρτίας ἐπὶ τῆς γῆς λέγει τῷ παραλυτικῷ· 11 σοὶ λέγω,
to forgive sins” on the earth — he said ⌞to the⌟ paralytic, “I say to you, I say
918 281 2093 3836 1178 3306 3836 4166 3306 3306 5148 3306
f.pa n.apf p.g d.gsf n.gsf v.pai.3s d.dsm a.dsm r.ds.2 v.pai.1s

ἔγειρε ἆρον τὸν κράβαττόν σου καὶ ὕπαγε εἰς τὸν οἶκόν σου. 12 καὶ
get up, pick up {the} your mat, your and go to {the} your home.” your And
1586 149 3836 5148 3187 5148 2779 5632 1650 3836 5148 3875 5148 2779
v.pam.2s v.aam.2s d.asm n.asm r.gs.2 cj v.pam.2s p.a d.asm n.asm r.gs.2 cj

ἠγέρθη καὶ εὐθὺς ἄρας τὸν κράβαττον ἐξῆλθεν
got up {and} immediately the man got up, ⌞picked up⌟ his mat, and went out
1586 2779 2318 1586 1586 149 3836 3187 2002
v.api.3s cj adv pt.aa.nsm d.asm n.asm v.aai.3s

ἔμπροσθεν → πάντων, ὥστε → ἐξίστασθαι πάντας καὶ δοξάζειν τὸν
in full view of them all, so they were all amazed all and praised {the}
1869 4246 6063 4246 2014 4246 2779 1519 3836
p.g a.gpm cj f.pm a.apm cj f.pa d.asm

θεὸν λέγοντας ὅτι οὕτως ↱ ↱ οὐδέποτε εἴδομεν. 13 καὶ
God, saying, ~ like this! “We have never seen anything like this!” {and} Once
2536 3306 4022 4048 1625 1625 4030 1625 4048 4048 2779 4099
n.asm pt.pa.apm cj adv adv v.aai.1p cj

ἐξῆλθεν πάλιν παρὰ τὴν θάλασσαν· καὶ πᾶς ὁ ὄχλος ἤρχετο
again Jesus went out Once again alongside the lake. {and} A large {the} crowd was coming
4099 2002 4099 4123 3836 2498 2779 4246 3836 4063 2262
v.aai.3s adv p.a d.asf n.asf cj a.nsm d.nsm n.nsm v.imi.3s

πρὸς αὐτόν, καὶ ἐδίδασκεν αὐτούς. 14 καὶ παράγων εἶδεν Λευὶν
to him, and he was teaching them. {and} ⌞As he was walking along,⌟ he saw Levi,
4639 899 2779 1438 899 2779 4135 1625 3322
p.a r.asm.3 cj v.iai.3s r.apm.3 cj pt.pa.nsm v.aai.3s n.asm

τὸν τοῦ Ἁλφαίου καθήμενον ἐπὶ τὸ τελώνιον, καὶ λέγει αὐτῷ· ἀκολούθει μοι.
the son of Alphaeus, sitting at the tax booth, and he said to him, “Follow me.”
3836 3836 271 2764 2093 3836 5468 2779 3306 899 199 1609
d.asm d.gsm n.gsm pt.pm.asm p.a d.asn n.asn cj v.pai.3s r.dsm.3 v.pam.2s r.ds.1

καὶ ἀναστὰς ἠκολούθησεν αὐτῷ. 15 καὶ γίνεται → κατακεῖσθαι
So Levi got up and followed him. And {it happened that} as he reclined at table
2779 482 199 899 2779 1181 899 2879
cj pt.aa.nsm v.aai.3s r.dsm.3 cj v.pmi.3s f.pm

αὐτὸν ἐν τῇ οἰκίᾳ αὐτοῦ, καὶ πολλοὶ τελῶναι καὶ ἁμαρτωλοὶ
he in {the} Levi’s house, Levi’s {and} many tax collectors and sinners
899 1877 3836 899 3864 899 2779 4498 5467 2779 283
r.asm.3 p.d d.dsf n.dsf r.gsm.3 cj a.npm n.npm cj a.npm

συνανέκειντο τῷ Ἰησοῦ καὶ τοῖς μαθηταῖς αὐτοῦ· ἦσαν γὰρ πολλοὶ
were reclining with Jesus and {the} his disciples, his for there were for many
5263 3836 2652 2779 3836 899 3412 899 1142 1639 1142 4498
v.imi.3p d.dsm n.dsm cj d.dpm n.dpm r.gsm.3 v.iai.3p cj a.npm

καὶ ἠκολούθουν αὐτῷ. 16 καὶ οἱ γραμματεῖς τῶν Φαρισαίων ἰδόντες ὅτι
{and} who followed him. And the scribes of the Pharisees, ⌞when they saw⌟ that
2779 199 899 2779 3836 1208 3836 5757 1625 4022
cj v.iai.3p r.dsm.3 cj d.npm n.npm d.gpm n.gpm pt.aa.npm cj

ἐσθίει μετὰ τῶν ἁμαρτωλῶν καὶ τελωνῶν ἔλεγον τοῖς μαθηταῖς αὐτοῦ·
⌞he was eating⌟ with {the} sinners and tax collectors, said to his disciples, his
2266 3552 3836 283 2779 5467 3306 3836 899 3412 899
v.pai.3s p.g d.gpm a.gpm cj n.gpm v.iai.3p d.dpm n.dpm r.gsm.3

ὅτι μετὰ τῶν τελωνῶν καὶ ἁμαρτωλῶν ἐσθίει; 17 καὶ →
~ “Why is he eating with {the} tax collectors and sinners?” is he eating {and} When
4022 2266 2266 2266 3552 3836 5467 2779 283 2266 2779
cj p.g d.gpm n.gpm cj a.gpm v.pai.3s cj

NASB

‘Get up, and pick
up your pallet and
walk’? 10But so that
you may know that
the Son of Man has
authority on earth
to forgive sins”—
He *said to the
paralytic, 11“I say
to you, get up, pick
up your pallet and
go home.” 12And he
got up and immedi-
ately picked up the
pallet and went out
in the sight of ev-
eryone, so that they
were all amazed
and were glorifying
God, saying, “We
have never seen
anything like this.”
13And He went out
again by the sea-
shore; and all the
people were com-
ing to Him, and He
was teaching them.

Levi (Matthew) Called

14As He passed by,
He saw Levi the
son of Alphaeus
sitting in the tax
booth, and He *said
to him, “Follow
Me!” And he got
up and followed
Him.
15And it *happened
that He was reclin-
ing *at the table*
in his house, and
many tax collectors
and sinners were
dining with Jesus
and His disciples;
for there were
many of them, and
they were follow-
ing Him. 16When
the scribes of the
Pharisees saw that
He was eating with
the sinners and tax
collectors, they
said to His dis-
ciples, “Why is He
eating and drinking
with tax collectors
and sinners?” 17And

NIV

17 On hearing
this, Jesus said to
them, "It is not the
healthy who need
a doctor, but the
sick. I have not
come to call the
righteous, but sin-
ners."

Jesus Questioned About Fasting

18 Now John's
disciples and the
Pharisees were
fasting. Some
people came and
asked Jesus, "How
is it that John's
disciples and the
disciples of the
Pharisees are fast-
ing, but yours are
not?"
19 Jesus answered,
"How can the
guests of the bride-
groom fast while
he is with them?
They cannot, so
long as they have
him with them.
20 But the time will
come when the
bridegroom will be
taken from them,
and on that day
they will fast.
21 "No one sews
a patch of un-
shrunk cloth on
an old garment.
Otherwise, the
new piece will
pull away from the
old, making the
tear worse. 22 And
no one pours new
wine into old
wineskins. Other-
wise, the wine will
burst the skins,
and both the wine
and the wineskins
will be ruined. No,
they pour new

ἀκούσας ὁ Ἰησοῦς λέγει αὐτοῖς ὅτι[a]
Jesus heard {the} Jesus this he said to them, ~ "Those who are in good health have
2652 201 3836 2652 3306 899 4022 3836 2710 2710 2710 2710 2710 2400
pt.aa.nsm d.nsm n.nsm v.pai.3s r.dpm.3 cj

οὐ χρείαν ἔχουσιν οἱ ἰσχύοντες → ἰατροῦ ἀλλ᾽ οἱ
no need *have* *Those who are in good health* of a doctor, but those who are
4024 5970 2400 3836 2710 2620 247 3836 2400 2400
pl n.asf v.pai.3p d.npm pt.pa.npm n.gsm cj d.npm

κακῶς ἔχοντες· ↱ ↱ οὐκ ἦλθον καλέσαι δικαίους ἀλλὰ ἁμαρτωλούς.[b]
⌞physically ill.⌟ *who are* I have not come to call the pious, but sinners, to
2809 2400 2262 2262 4024 2262 2813 1465 247 283
adv pt.pa.npm pl v.aai.1s f.aa a.apm cj a.apm

18 καὶ ἦσαν οἱ μαθηταὶ Ἰωάννου καὶ οἱ Φαρισαῖοι
repentance." {and} *were* The disciples of John and of the Pharisees were
2779 1639 3836 3412 2722 2779 3836 5757 1639
cj v.iai.3p d.npm n.npm n.gsm cj d.npm n.npm

νηστεύοντες. καὶ ἔρχονται καὶ λέγουσιν αὐτῷ· ⌞διὰ τί⌟ ↱ οἱ
fasting. {and} Some people came and said to him, "Why do the
3764 2779 2262 2779 3306 899 1328 5515 3764 3836
pt.pa.npm cj v.pmi.3p cj v.pai.3p r.dsm.3 p.a r.asn d.npm

μαθηταὶ Ἰωάννου καὶ οἱ μαθηταὶ τῶν Φαρισαίων νηστεύουσιν, οἱ δὲ σοὶ
disciples of John and the disciples of the Pharisees fast, {the} but your
3412 2722 2779 3836 3412 3836 5757 3764 3836 1254 5050
n.npm n.gsm cj d.npm n.npm d.gpm n.gpm v.pai.3p d.npm cj r.npm.2

μαθηταὶ ↱ οὐ νηστεύουσιν; 19 καὶ εἶπεν αὐτοῖς ὁ Ἰησοῦς· μὴ δύνανται
disciples do not fast?" And Jesus said to them, {the} *Jesus* *No* "Do
3412 3764 4024 3764 2779 2652 3306 899 3836 2652 3590 1538
n.npm pl v.pai.3p cj v.aai.3s r.dpm.3 d.nsm n.nsm pl v.ppi.3p

οἱ υἱοὶ τοῦ νυμφῶνος ⌞ἐν ᾧ⌟ ὁ νυμφίος μετ᾽ αὐτῶν ἐστιν
the friends of the bridegroom fast while the bridegroom is with them? *is*
3836 5626 3836 3813 3764 1877 4005 3836 3812 1639 3552 899 1639
d.npm n.npm d.gsm n.gsm p.d r.dsm d.nsm n.nsm p.g r.gpm.3 v.pai.3s

νηστεύειν; ⌞ὅσον χρόνον⌟ ἔχουσιν τὸν νυμφίον μετ᾽ αὐτῶν οὐ δύνανται
fast No, as long as they have the bridegroom with them, *not* they do
3764 3590 4012 5989 2400 3836 3812 3552 899 4024 1538
f.pa r.asm n.asm v.pai.3p d.asm n.asm p.g r.gpm.3 pl v.ppi.3p

νηστεύειν. 20 ἐλεύσονται δὲ ἡμέραι ὅταν ἀπαρθῇ ἀπ᾽
not fast. But days will come *But* *days* when the bridegroom will be taken from
4024 3764 1254 2465 2262 1254 2465 4020 3836 3812 554 608
f.pa v.fmi.3p cj n.npf cj v.aps.3s p.g

αὐτῶν ὁ νυμφίος, καὶ τότε νηστεύσουσιν ἐν ἐκείνῃ τῇ ἡμέρᾳ. 21 οὐδεὶς
them, *the* *bridegroom* and then they will fast in that {the} day. No one sews a
899 3836 3812 2779 5538 3764 1877 1697 3836 2465 4029 2165
r.gpm.3 d.nsm n.nsm cj adv v.fai.3p p.d r.dsf d.dsf n.dsf a.nsm

ἐπίβλημα → ῥάκους ἀγνάφου ἐπιράπτει ἐπὶ ἱμάτιον παλαιόν· ⌞εἰ
piece of unshrunk cloth *unshrunk* *sews* on an old garment. *old* If he does,
2099 47 4820 47 2165 2093 4094 2668 4094 1623
n.asn n.gsn a.gsn v.pai.3s p.a n.asn a.asn cj

δὲ μή,⌟ αἴρει τὸ πλήρωμα ἀπ᾽ αὐτοῦ τὸ καινὸν τοῦ παλαιοῦ
the patch pulls away *the* *patch* from it, the new ⌞from the⌟ old,
1254 3590 3836 4445 149 3836 4445 608 899 3836 2785 3836 4094
cj pl v.pai.3s d.asn n.asn p.g r.gsn.3 d.nsn a.nsn d.gsn a.gsn

καὶ χεῖρον σχίσμα γίνεται. 22 καὶ οὐδεὶς βάλλει οἶνον νέον εἰς
and the *worse* tear becomes worse. And no one puts new wine *new* into old
2779 5937 5388 1181 5937 2779 4029 965 3742 3885 3742 1650 4094
cj a.nsn.c n.nsn v.pmi.3s cj a.nsm v.pai.3s n.asm a.asm p.a

ἀσκοὺς παλαιούς· ⌞εἰ δὲ μή,⌟ ῥήξει ὁ οἶνος τοὺς ἀσκοὺς καὶ
wineskins. *old* If he does, the wine will burst *the* *wine* the skins and
829 4094 1623 1254 3590 3836 3885 4838 3836 3885 3836 829 2779
n.apm a.apm cj cj pl v.fai.3s d.nsm n.nsm d.apm n.apm cj

ὁ οἶνος ἀπόλλυται καὶ οἱ ἀσκοί· ἀλλὰ οἶνον νέον εἰς
the wine will be wasted ⌞as well as⌟ the skins. But new wine *new* is poured into fresh
3836 3885 660 2779 3836 829 247 3742 3885 3742 1650 2785
d.nsm n.nsm v.pmi.3s cj d.npm n.npm cj n.asm a.asm p.a

[a] [ὅτι] UBS, omitted by TNIV.
[b] εἰς μετάνοιαν included by TR after ἁμαρτωλούς.

NASB

hearing *this,* Jesus
*said to them, "*It is*
not those who are
healthy who need
a physician, but
those who are sick;
I did not come to
call the righteous,
but sinners."
18 John's disciples
and the Pharisees
were fasting; and
they *came and
*said to Him, "Why
do John's disciples
and the disciples
of the Pharisees
fast, but Your dis-
ciples do not fast?"
19 And Jesus said to
them, "While the
bridegroom is with
them, the atten-
dants of the bride-
groom cannot fast,
can they? So long
as they have the
bridegroom with
them, they cannot
fast. 20 But the days
will come when
the bridegroom is
taken away from
them, and then
they will fast in
that day.
21 "No one sews a
patch of unshrunk
cloth on an old gar-
ment; otherwise the
patch pulls away
from it, the new
from the old, and a
worse tear results.
22 No one puts new
wine into old wine-
skins; otherwise
the wine will burst
the skins, and the
wine is lost and the
skins *as well;* but
one puts new wine
into fresh wine

NIV

wine into new
wineskins."

Jesus Is Lord of the Sabbath

[23]One Sabbath
Jesus was going
through the grain-
fields, and as his
disciples walked
along, they began
to pick some heads
of grain. [24]The
Pharisees said to
him, "Look, why
are they doing
what is unlawful
on the Sabbath?"
[25]He answered,
"Have you never
read what David
did when he and
his companions
were hungry and
in need? [26]In the
days of Abiathar
the high priest, he
entered the house
of God and ate the
consecrated bread,
which is lawful
only for priests to
eat. And he also
gave some to his
companions."
[27]Then he said to
them, "The Sab-
bath was made for
man, not man for
the Sabbath. [28]So
the Son of Man is
Lord even of the
Sabbath."

Jesus Heals on the Sabbath

3 Another time
Jesus went into
the synagogue,
and a man with
a shriveled hand
was there. [2]Some
of them were look-
ing for a reason to
accuse Jesus, so
they watched him
closely to see if he
would heal him on
the Sabbath. [3]Jesus
said to the man
with the shriveled
hand, "Stand up in
front of everyone."

ἀσκοὺς καινούς. [23] καὶ ἐγένετο αὐτὸν ἐν τοῖς σαββασιν
wineskins." *fresh* *{and}* ⌞It happened that⌟ *Jesus* on the Sabbath Jesus
829 2785 2779 1181 899 1877 3836 4879 899
n.apm a.apm cj v.ami.3s r.asm.3 p.d d.dpn n.dpn

παραπορεύεσθαι διὰ τῶν σπορίμων, καὶ οἱ μαθηταὶ αὐτοῦ ἤρξαντο
was going through the grainfields, and *{the}* his disciples *his* began to make
4182 1328 3836 5077 2779 3836 899 3412 899 806 4472 4472
f.pm p.g d.gpn n.gpn cj d.npm n.npm r.gsm.3 v.ami.3p

ὁδὸν ποιεῖν τίλλοντες τοὺς στάχυας. [24] καὶ οἱ Φαρισαῖοι ἔλεγον
their way along *to make* plucking *{the}* heads of grain. So the Pharisees said
3847 4472 5504 3836 5092 2779 3836 5757 3306
n.asf f.pa pt.pa.npm d.apm n.apm cj d.npm n.npm v.iai.3p

αὐτῷ· ἴδε τί ποιοῦσιν τοῖς σάββασιν ὃ ↱ οὐκ ἔξεστιν;
to him, "Look, why are they doing *on the Sabbath* what is not lawful on the Sabbath?"
899 2623 5515 4472 3836 4879 4005 1997 4024 1997 3836 3836 4879
r.dsm.3 pl r.asn v.pai.3p d.dpn n.dpn r.nsn pl v.pai.3s

[25] καὶ λέγει αὐτοῖς· ↱ ↱ οὐδέποτε ἀνέγνωτε τί ἐποίησεν Δαυὶδ ὅτε
{and} He said to them, "Have you never read what David did *David* when
2779 3306 899 336 336 4030 336 5515 1253 4472 1253 4021
cj v.pai.3s r.dpm.3 adv v.aai.2p r.asn v.aai.3s n.nsm cj

χρείαν ἔσχεν καὶ ἐπείνασεν αὐτὸς καὶ οἱ μετ᾽ αὐτοῦ, [26] πῶς
in need he was in need and became hungry, he and those who were with him? How
5970 2400 5970 5970 2779 4277 899 2779 3836 3552 899 4802
n.asf v.aai.3s cj v.aai.3s r.nsm cj d.npm p.g r.gsm.3 cj

εἰσῆλθεν εἰς τὸν οἶκον τοῦ θεοῦ ἐπὶ Ἀβιαθὰρ ἀρχιερέως καὶ τοὺς
he went into the house of God when Abiathar was high priest and ate the sacred
1656 1650 3836 3875 3836 2536 2093 8 797 2779 2266 3836 4606
v.aai.3s p.a d.asm n.asm d.gsm n.gsm p.g n.gsm n.gsm cj d.apm

ἄρτους τῆς προθέσεως ἔφαγεν, οὓς ↱ οὐκ ἔξεστιν φαγεῖν ⌞εἰ μὴ⌟ τοὺς ἱερεῖς,
bread, *{the}* *sacred* *ate* which is not lawful to eat, except for the priests,
788 3836 4606 2266 4005 1997 4024 1997 2266 1623 3590 3836 2636
n.apm d.gsf n.gsf v.aai.3s r.apm pl v.pai.3s f.aa cj pl d.apm n.apm

καὶ → ἔδωκεν καὶ τοῖς σὺν αὐτῷ οὖσιν; [27] καὶ ἔλεγεν αὐτοῖς· τὸ
and he also gave *also* it to those who were with him?" *who were* And he said to them, "The
2779 2779 1443 2779 3836 1639 1639 5250 899 1639 2779 3306 899 3836
cj v.aai.3s adv d.dpm p.d r.dsm.3 pt.pa.dpm cj v.iai.3s r.dpm.3 d.nsn

σάββατον διὰ τὸν ἄνθρωπον ἐγένετο καὶ οὐχ ὁ ἄνθρωπος διὰ τὸ
Sabbath was made for *{the}* man, *was made* *{and}* not *{the}* man for the
4879 1181 1181 1328 3836 476 1181 2779 4024 3836 476 1328 3836
n.nsn p.a d.asm n.asm v.ami.3s cj pl d.nsm n.nsm p.a d.asn

σάββατον· [28] ὥστε κύριός ἐστιν ὁ υἱὸς τοῦ ἀνθρώπου καὶ τοῦ
Sabbath. So *lord* *is* the Son of Man is lord even of the
4879 6063 3261 1639 3836 5626 3836 476 1639 3261 2779 3836
n.asn cj n.nsm v.pai.3s d.nsm n.nsm d.gsm n.gsm adv d.gsn

σαββάτου.
Sabbath."
4879
n.gsn

[3:1] καὶ εἰσῆλθεν πάλιν εἰς τὴν συναγωγήν. καὶ ἦν ἐκεῖ ἄνθρωπος
{and} Jesus entered again into a synagogue, and *was* *there* a man with
2779 1656 4099 1650 3836 5252 2779 1639 1695 476 2400
cj v.aai.3s adv p.a d.asf n.asf cj v.iai.3s adv n.nsm

ἐξηραμμένην ἔχων τὴν χεῖρα. [2] καὶ παρετήρουν αὐτὸν ↰
a withered *with* *{the}* hand was there. And they were watching him carefully to see
3830 2400 3836 5931 1639 1695 2779 4190 899 4190
pt.rp.asf pt.pa.nsm d.asf n.asf cj v.iai.3p r.asm.3

εἰ τοῖς σάββασιν θεραπεύσει αὐτόν, ἵνα κατηγορήσωσιν αὐτοῦ.
if he would heal him on the Sabbath, *he would heal* *him* so they could accuse him.
1623 2543 2543 2543 899 3836 4879 2543 899 2671 2989 899
cj d.dpn n.dpn v.fai.3s r.asm.3 cj v.aas.3p r.gsm.3

[3] καὶ λέγει τῷ ἀνθρώπῳ τῷ τὴν ξηρὰν χεῖρα ἔχοντι· ἔγειρε εἰς τὸ
And he said ⌞to the⌟ man who had the withered hand, *had* "Get up and step *{the}*
2779 3306 3836 476 3836 2400 3836 3831 5931 2400 1586 1650 3836
cj v.pai.3s d.dsm n.dsm d.dsm d.asf a.asf n.asf pt.pa.dsm v.pam.2s p.a d.asn

NASB

skins."

Question of the Sabbath

[23]And it happened
that He was pass-
ing through the
grainfields on the
Sabbath, and His
disciples began to
make their way
along while pick-
ing the heads *of*
grain. [24]The Phari-
sees were saying
to Him, "Look,
why are they doing
what is not lawful
on the Sabbath?"
[25]And He *said to
them, "Have you
never read what
David did when he
was in need and he
and his compan-
ions became hun-
gry; [26]how he en-
tered the house of
God in the time of
Abiathar *the* high
priest, and ate the
consecrated bread,
which is not lawful
for *anyone* to eat
except the priests,
and he also gave it
to those who were
with him?" [27]Jesus
said to them, "The
Sabbath was made
for man, and not
man for the Sab-
bath. [28]So the Son
of Man is Lord
even of the Sab-
bath."

Jesus Heals on the Sabbath

[3:1]He entered
again into a syna-
gogue; and a man
was there whose
hand was withered.
[2]They were watch-
ing Him *to see* if
He would heal him
on the Sabbath, so
that they might ac-
cuse Him. [3]He *said
to the man with
the withered hand,
"Get up and come

NIV

[4]Then Jesus
asked them,
"Which is lawful
on the Sabbath: to
do good or to do
evil, to save life or
to kill?" But they
remained silent.
[5]He looked
around at them in
anger and, deep-
ly distressed at
their stubborn
hearts, said to the
man, "Stretch out
your hand." He
stretched it out,
and his hand was
completely re-
stored. [6]Then the
Pharisees went out
and began to plot
with the Herodians
how they might
kill Jesus.

Crowds Follow Jesus

[7]Jesus withdrew
with his disciples
to the lake, and a
large crowd from
Galilee followed.
[8]When they heard
about all he was
doing, many peo-
ple came to him
from Judea, Je-
rusalem, Idumea,
and the regions
across the Jor-
dan and around
Tyre and Sidon.
[9]Because of the
crowd he told his
disciples to have a
small boat ready
for him, to keep
the people from
crowding him.
[10]For he had healed
many, so that those
with diseases were
pushing forward
to touch him.
[11]Whenever the
impure spirits saw
him,

μέσον. [4]καὶ λέγει αὐτοῖς· ἔξεστιν τοῖς σάββασιν ἀγαθὸν ποιῆσαι ἢ
forward." And he said to them, "Is it lawful on the Sabbath to do good *to do* or
3545 2779 3306 899 1997 3836 4879 4472 4472 19 4472 2445
n.asn cj v.pai.3s r.dpm.3 v.pai.3s d.dpn n.dpn a.asn f.aa cj

κακοποιῆσαι, ψυχὴν σῶσαι ἢ ἀποκτεῖναι; οἱ δὲ ἐσιώπων.
to do evil, to save life *to save* or to destroy it?" But they *But* remained silent.
2803 5392 5392 6034 5392 2445 650 1254 3836 1254 4995
f.aa n.asf f.aa cj f.aa d.npm cj v.iai.3p

[5]καὶ περιβλεψάμενος αὐτοὺς μετ᾽ ὀργῆς, συλλυπούμενος ἐπὶ τῇ πωρώσει τῆς
And ⌊after looking around at⌋ them in anger, grieved at the hardness of
2779 4315 899 3552 3973 5200 2093 3836 4801 3836
cj pt.am.nsm r.apm.3 p.g n.gsf pt.pp.nsm p.d d.dsf n.dsf d.gsf

καρδίας αὐτῶν λέγει τῷ ἀνθρώπῳ· ἔκτεινον τὴν χεῖρα. καὶ ἐξέτεινεν
their heart, *their* he said ⌊to the⌋ man, "Stretch out your hand." And ⌊he stretched out⌋
899 2840 899 3306 3836 476 1753 3836 5931 2779 1753
n.gsf r.gpm.3 v.pai.3s d.dsm n.dsm v.aam.2s d.asf n.asf cj v.aai.3s

καὶ ἀπεκατεστάθη ἡ χεὶρ αὐτοῦ. [6]καὶ ἐξελθόντες οἱ
his hand and it was restored. *{the} hand his* So the Pharisees went out *the*
899 5931 2779 635 3836 5931 899 2779 3836 5757 2002 3836
cj v.api.3s d.nsf n.nsf r.gsm.3 cj pt.aa.npm d.npm

Φαρισαῖοι εὐθὺς μετὰ τῶν Ἡρωδιανῶν συμβούλιον ἐδίδουν
Pharisees immediately and began plotting with *{the}* Herodians *plotting* *began*
5757 2318 1443 5206 3552 3836 2477 5206 1443
n.npm adv p.g d.gpm n.gpm n.asn v.iai.3p

κατ᾽ αὐτοῦ ὅπως αὐτὸν ἀπολέσωσιν. [7]καὶ ὁ Ἰησοῦς
against him, ⌊as to how⌋ *him* ⌊they might do away with⌋ him. But *{the}* Jesus withdrew
2848 899 3968 899 660 899 2779 3836 2652 432
p.g r.gsm.3 cj r.asm.3 v.aas.3p cj d.nsm n.nsm

μετὰ τῶν μαθητῶν αὐτοῦ ἀνεχώρησεν πρὸς τὴν θάλασσαν, καὶ
with *{the}* his disciples *his* *withdrew* to the lake, and there followed a
3552 3836 899 3412 899 432 4639 3836 2498 2779 199
p.g d.gpm n.gpm r.gsm.3 v.aai.3s p.a d.asf n.asf cj

πολὺ πλῆθος ἀπὸ τῆς Γαλιλαίας ἠκολούθησεν,[a] καὶ ἀπὸ τῆς Ἰουδαίας [8]καὶ ἀπὸ
large crowd from *{the}* Galilee *followed* and from *{the}* Judea, and from
4498 4436 608 3836 1133 199 2779 608 3836 2677 2779 608
a.nsn n.nsn p.g d.gsf n.gsf v.aai.3s cj p.g d.gsf n.gsf cj p.g

Ἱεροσολύμων καὶ ἀπὸ τῆς Ἰδουμαίας καὶ πέραν τοῦ Ἰορδάνου καὶ περὶ Τύρον
Jerusalem and from *{the}* Idumea and beyond the Jordan and around Tyre
2642 2779 608 3836 2628 2779 4305 3836 2674 2779 4309 5602
n.gpn cj p.g d.gsf n.gsf cj p.g d.gsm n.gsm cj p.a n.asf

καὶ Σιδῶνα πλῆθος πολὺ ἀκούοντες ὅσα
and Sidon a large crowd *large* came to him ⌊when they heard about⌋ the things
2779 4972 4498 4436 4498 2262 4639 899 201 4012
cj n.asf n.nsn a.nsn pt.pa.npm r.apn

ἐποίει ἦλθον πρὸς αὐτόν. [9]καὶ εἶπεν τοῖς μαθηταῖς αὐτοῦ ἵνα
⌊he had done.⌋ *came to him* And he told *{the}* his disciples *his* to make ready a
4472 2262 4639 899 2779 3306 3836 899 3412 899 2671 4674 4674
v.iai.3s v.aai.3p p.a r.asm.3 cj v.aai.3s d.dpm n.dpm r.gsm.3 cj

πλοιάριον προσκαρτερῇ αὐτῷ διὰ τὸν ὄχλον ἵνα ↱ ↱ μὴ θλίβωσιν
small boat *make ready* for him ⌊because of⌋ the crowd, so that they would not crush
4449 4674 899 1328 3836 4063 2671 2567 2567 3590 2567
n.nsn v.pas.3s r.dsm.3 p.a d.asm n.asm cj pl v.pas.3p

αὐτόν· [10]πολλοὺς γὰρ ἐθεράπευσεν, ὥστε
him. *many* For he had healed many, so that all who had diseases
899 4498 1142 2543 4498 6063 4012 4012 2400 3465
r.asm.3 a.apm cj v.aai.3s cj

ἐπιπίπτειν αὐτῷ ἵνα αὐτοῦ ἅψωνται ὅσοι εἶχον
⌊were pressing around⌋ him so they could touch him. *they could touch* *all who* *had*
2158 899 2671 721 721 721 899 721 4012 2400
f.pa r.dsm.3 cj r.gsm.3 v.ams.3p r.npm v.iai.3p

μάστιγας. [11]καὶ τὰ πνεύματα τὰ ἀκάθαρτα, ὅταν αὐτὸν
diseases And the unclean spirits, *{the}* *unclean* whenever they saw him,
3465 2779 3836 176 4460 3836 176 4020 2555 2555 899
n.apf cj d.npn n.npn d.npn a.npn cj r.asm.3

NASB

forward!" [4]And
He *said to them,
"Is it lawful to do
good or to do harm
on the Sabbath,
to save a life or to
kill?" But they kept
silent. [5]After look-
ing around at them
with anger, grieved
at their hardness of
heart, He *said to
the man, "Stretch
out your hand."
And he stretched it
out, and his hand
was restored. [6]The
Pharisees went out
and immediately
began conspiring
with the Herodians
against Him, *as to*
how they might
destroy Him.
[7]Jesus withdrew
to the sea with
His disciples; and
a great multitude
from Galilee fol-
lowed; and *also*
from Judea, [8]and
from Jerusalem,
and from Idumea,
and beyond the
Jordan, and the
vicinity of Tyre and
Sidon, a great num-
ber of people heard
of all that He was
doing and came
to Him. [9]And He
told His disciples
that a boat should
stand ready for
Him because of the
crowd, so that they
would not crowd
Him; [10]for He had
healed many, with
the result that all
those who had af-
flictions pressed
around Him in or-
der to touch Him.
[11]Whenever the un-
clean spirits saw

[a] [ἠκολούθησεν] UBS.

NIV

they fell down before him and cried out, "You are the Son of God." [12]But he gave them strict orders not to tell others about him.

Jesus Appoints the Twelve

[13]Jesus went up on a mountainside and called to him those he wanted, and they came to him. [14]He appointed twelve[a] that they might be with him and that he might send them out to preach [15]and to have authority to drive out demons. [16]These are the twelve he appointed: Simon (to whom he gave the name Peter), [17]James son of Zebedee and his brother John (to them he gave the name Boanerges, which means "sons of thunder"), [18]Andrew, Philip, Bartholomew, Matthew, Thomas, James son of Alphaeus, Thaddaeus, Simon the Zealot [19]and Judas Iscariot, who betrayed him.

Jesus Accused by His Family and by Teachers of the Law

[20]Then Jesus entered a house, and again a crowd gathered, so that he and his disciples were not even able to eat. [21]When his family[b] heard about this,

ἐθεώρουν, προσέπιπτον αὐτῷ καὶ ἔκραζον λέγοντες ὅτι σὺ εἶ ὁ υἱὸς τοῦ
they saw fell down before him and cried out saying, ~ "You are the Son of
2555 4700 899 2779 3189 3306 4022 5148 1639 3836 5626 3836
v.iai.3p v.iai.3p r.dsm.3 cj v.iai.3p pt.pa.npm cj r.ns.2 v.pai.2s d.nsm n.nsm d.gsm

θεοῦ. 12 καὶ πολλὰ ἐπετίμα αὐτοῖς ἵνα μὴ αὐτὸν
God!" But he warned them repeatedly *he warned them* ~ not to make him
2536 2779 2203 2203 899 4498 2203 899 2671 3590 4472 4472 899
n.gsm cj a.apn v.iai.3s r.dpm.3 cj pl r.asm.3

φανερὸν ποιήσωσιν. 13 καὶ ἀναβαίνει εἰς τὸ ὄρος καὶ προσκαλεῖται οὓς
known. *to make* And he went up into the mountain and called those whom
5745 4472 2779 326 1650 3836 4001 2779 4673 4005
a.asm v.aas.3p cj v.pai.3s p.a d.asn n.asn cj v.pmi.3s r.apm

→ ἤθελεν αὐτός, καὶ ἀπῆλθον πρὸς αὐτόν. 14 καὶ ἐποίησεν δώδεκα οὓς
he himself wanted, *himself* and they came to him. And he appointed twelve (whom
899 2527 899 2779 599 4639 899 2779 4472 1557 4005
v.iai.3s r.nsm cj v.aai.3p p.a r.asm.3 cj v.aai.3s a.apm r.apm

καὶ ἀποστόλους ὠνόμασεν[a] ἵνα ὦσιν μετ' αὐτοῦ καὶ ἵνα
he also named apostles) *he named* so that ⌊they might be⌋ with him and so that
3951 2779 3951 693 3951 2671 1639 3552 899 2779 2671
adv n.apm v.aai.3s cj v.pas.3p p.g r.gsm.3 cj cj

ἀποστέλλῃ αὐτοὺς ↰ κηρύσσειν 15 καὶ ἔχειν ἐξουσίαν[b] ἐκβάλλειν τὰ δαιμόνια·
he might send them out to preach and have authority to drive out *{the}* demons.
690 899 690 3062 2779 2400 2026 1675 3836 1228
v.pas.3s r.apm.3 f.pa cj f.pa n.asf f.pa d.apn n.apn

16 [c]καὶ ἐποίησεν τοὺς δώδεκα, καὶ ἐπέθηκεν ὄνομα τῷ Σίμωνι
{and} He appointed the Twelve: *{and}* Peter (the name he gave *name* to Simon);
2779 4472 3836 1557 2779 4377 3950 2202 3950 3836 4981
cj v.aai.3s d.apm a.apm cj v.aai.3s n.asn d.dsm n.dsm

Πέτρον, 17 καὶ Ἰάκωβον τὸν τοῦ Ζεβεδαίου καὶ Ἰωάννην τὸν ἀδελφὸν τοῦ
Peter *{and}* James the son of Zebedee, *{and}* John the brother of
4377 2779 2610 3836 3836 2411 2779 2722 3836 81 3836
n.asm cj n.asm d.asm d.gsm n.gsm cj n.asm d.asm n.asm d.gsm

Ἰακώβου καὶ ἐπέθηκεν αὐτοῖς ὄνομα[d] βοανηργές, ὅ ἐστιν υἱοὶ βροντῆς·
James *{and}* (he gave to them the name Boanerges, that is, Sons of Thunder);
2610 2779 2202 899 3950 1065 4005 1639 5626 1103
n.gsm cj v.aai.3s r.dpm.3 n.asn n.apm r.nsn v.pai.3s n.npm n.gsf

18 καὶ Ἀνδρέαν καὶ Φίλιππον καὶ Βαρθολομαῖον καὶ Μαθθαῖον καὶ Θωμᾶν
{and} Andrew, *{and}* Philip, *{and}* Bartholomew, *{and}* Matthew, *{and}* Thomas,
2779 436 2779 5805 2779 978 2779 3414 2779 2605
cj n.asm cj n.asm cj n.asm cj n.asm cj n.asm

καὶ Ἰάκωβον τὸν τοῦ Ἀλφαίου καὶ Θαδδαῖον καὶ Σίμωνα τὸν Καναναῖον
{and} James the son of Alphaeus, *{and}* Thaddaeus, *{and}* Simon the Canaanite;
2779 2610 3836 3836 271 2779 2497 2779 4981 3836 2831
cj n.asm d.asm d.gsm n.gsm cj n.asm cj n.asm d.asm n.asm

19 καὶ Ἰούδαν Ἰσκαριώθ, ὃς καὶ παρέδωκεν αὐτόν. 20 καὶ ἔρχεται εἰς
and Judas Iscariot, who *{also}* betrayed him. Then Jesus went to his
2779 2683 2696 4005 2779 4140 899 2779 2262 1650
cj n.asm n.asm r.nsm cj v.aai.3s r.asm.3 cj v.pmi.3s p.a

οἶκον· καὶ συνέρχεται πάλιν [e]ὄχλος, ὥστε ↱ μὴ δύνασθαι
house, and again a crowd gathered, *again crowd* so that they were not even able
3875 2779 4099 4063 5302 4099 4063 6063 899 1538 3590 3593 1538
n.asm cj v.pmi.3s adv n.nsm cj pl f.pp

αὐτοὺς μηδὲ ἄρτον φαγεῖν. 21 καὶ → ἀκούσαντες οἱ
they even to eat a meal. *to eat* And when his family heard this *family*
899 3593 2266 2266 788 2266 2779 899 3836 201 3836
r.apm.3 adv n.asm f.aa cj pt.aa.npm d.npm

NASB

Him, they would fall down before Him and shout, "You are the Son of God!" [12]And He earnestly warned them not to tell who He was.

The Twelve Are Chosen

[13]And He *went up on the mountain and *summoned those whom He Himself wanted, and they came to Him. [14]And He appointed twelve, so that they would be with Him and that He *could* send them out to preach, [15]and to have authority to cast out the demons. [16]And He appointed the twelve: Simon (to whom He gave the name Peter), [17]and James, the *son* of Zebedee, and John the brother of James (to them He gave the name Boanerges, which means, "Sons of Thunder"); [18]and Andrew, and Philip, and Bartholomew, and Matthew, and Thomas, and James the son of Alphaeus, and Thaddaeus, and Simon the Zealot; [19]and Judas Iscariot, who betrayed Him.

[20]And He *came [a]home, and the crowd *gathered again, to such an extent that they could not even eat a meal. [21]When His own [b]people heard *of this,* they

[a] *14* Some manuscripts *twelve—designating them apostles—*
[b] *21* Or *his associates*

a [οὓς καὶ ἀποστόλους ὠνόμασεν] UBS, omitted by TNIV.
b θεραπεύειν τὰς νόσους included by TR after ἐξουσίαν.
c [καὶ ἐποίησεν τοὺς δώδεκα] UBS.
d ὄνομα TNIV. ὀνόμα[τα] UBS, NET.
e ὁ included by UBS before ὄχλος.

a Lit *into a house*
b Or *kinsmen*

NIV

they went to take
charge of him, for
they said, "He is
out of his mind."
22 And the teach-
ers of the law who
came down from
Jerusalem said,
"He is possessed
by Beelzebul! By
the prince of de-
mons he is driving
out demons."
23 So Jesus called
them over to him
and began to speak
to them in para-
bles: "How can
Satan drive out
Satan? 24 If a king-
dom is divided
against itself, that
kingdom cannot
stand. 25 If a house
is divided against
itself, that house
cannot stand.
26 And if Satan op-
poses himself and
is divided, he can-
not stand; his end
has come. 27 In fact,
no one can enter a
strong man's house
without first ty-
ing him up. Then
he can plunder
the strong man's
house. 28 Truly I
tell you, people
can be forgiven
all their sins and
every slander they
utter, 29 but who-
ever blasphemes
against the Holy
Spirit will never be
forgiven;

παρ᾽ αὐτοῦ ἐξῆλθον κρατῆσαι αὐτόν· ἔλεγον γὰρ ὅτι
{from} his ⌊they went out⌋ ⌊to take charge of⌋ him, for people were saying, for ~
4123 899 2002 3195 899 1142 3306 1142 4022
p.g r.gsm.3 v.aai.3p f.aa r.asm.3 v.iai.3p cj cj

ἐξέστη. 22 καὶ οἱ γραμματεῖς οἱ ἀπὸ Ἱεροσολύμων
⌊"He is out of his mind."⌋ And the scribes who came down from Jerusalem
2014 2779 3836 1208 3836 2849 2849 608 2642
v.aai.3s cj d.npm n.npm d.npm p.g n.gpn

καταβάντες ἔλεγον ὅτι Βεελζεβοὺλ ἔχει καὶ ὅτι ἐν τῷ
came down were saying, ~ "He has Beelzebul He has in him," and ~ "By the
2849 3306 4022 2400 2400 1015 2400 2779 4022 1877 3836
pt.aa.npm v.iai.3p cj n.asm v.pai.3s cj cj p.d d.dsm

ἄρχοντι τῶν δαιμονίων ἐκβάλλει τὰ δαιμόνια. 23 καὶ ↱ προσκαλεσάμενος
prince of demons he drives out {the} demons." So he called
807 3836 1228 1675 3836 1228 2779 3306 4673
n.dsm d.gpn n.gpn v.pai.3s d.apn n.apn cj pt.am.nsm

αὐτοὺς ↰ ἐν παραβολαῖς ἔλεγεν αὐτοῖς· πῶς δύναται
them together in parables and began speaking to them in parables: "How can
899 4673 1877 4130 3306 899 1877 4130 4802 1538
r.apm.3 p.d n.dpf v.iai.3s r.dpm.3 cj v.ppi.3s

σατανᾶς σατανᾶν ἐκβάλλειν; 24 καὶ ἐὰν βασιλεία ἐφ᾽
Satan drive out Satan? drive out {and} If a kingdom is divided against
4928 1675 1675 4928 1675 2779 1569 993 3532 3532 2093
n.nsm n.asm f.pa cj cj n.nsf p.a

ἑαυτὴν μερισθῇ, ⌊οὐ δύναται⌋ σταθῆναι ἡ βασιλεία ἐκείνη· 25 καὶ
itself, is divided that kingdom cannot stand. {the} kingdom that And
1571 3532 1697 993 4024 1538 2705 3836 993 1697 2779
r.asf.3 v.aps.3s pl v.ppi.3s f.ap d.nsf n.nsf r.nsf cj

ἐὰν οἰκία ἐφ᾽ ἑαυτὴν μερισθῇ, ⌊οὐ δυνήσεται⌋ ἡ οἰκία
if a house is divided against itself, is divided that house cannot {the} house
1569 3864 3532 3532 2093 1571 3532 1697 3864 4024 1538 3836 3864
cj n.nsf p.a r.asf.3 v.aps.3s pl v.fpi.3s d.nsf n.nsf

ἐκείνη σταθῆναι. 26 καὶ εἰ ὁ σατανᾶς ἀνέστη ἐφ᾽ ἑαυτὸν καὶ ἐμερίσθη, ↱
that stand. And if {the} Satan rises against himself and is divided, he
1697 2705 2779 1623 3836 4928 482 2093 1571 2779 3532 1538
r.nsf f.ap cj cj d.nsm n.nsm v.aai.3s p.a r.asm.3 cj v.api.3s

⌊οὐ δύναται⌋ στῆναι ἀλλὰ τέλος ἔχει. 27 ἀλλ᾽ οὐ
cannot stand but is coming to an end. is coming to But ~ no one
4024 1538 2705 247 2400 2400 2400 5465 2400 247 4024 4029 4029
pl v.ppi.3s f.aa cj n.asn v.pai.3s cj pl

δύναται οὐδεὶς εἰς τὴν οἰκίαν τοῦ ἰσχυροῦ εἰσελθὼν τὰ
can no one {into} enter the house of the strong man enter and carry off {the} his
1538 4029 1650 1656 3836 3864 3836 2708 1656 1395 1395 3836 899
v.ppi.3s a.nsm p.a d.asf n.asf d.gsm a.gsm pt.aa.nsm d.apn

σκεύη αὐτοῦ διαρπάσαι, ⌊ἐὰν μὴ⌋ πρῶτον τὸν ἰσχυρὸν δήσῃ,
possessions his carry off unless first he ties up the strong man; he ties up
5007 899 1395 1569 3590 4754 1313 1313 1313 3836 2708 1313
n.apn r.gsm.3 f.aa cj pl adv d.asm a.asm v.aas.3s

καὶ τότε τὴν οἰκίαν αὐτοῦ διαρπάσει. 28 ἀμὴν
{and} then he can rob {the} his house. his he can rob "I tell you the truth,
2779 5538 1395 1395 1395 3836 899 3864 899 1395 3306 3306 7007 297
cj adv d.asf n.asf r.gsm.3 v.fai.3s pl

λέγω ὑμῖν ὅτι πάντα ἀφεθήσεται τοῖς υἱοῖς τῶν ἀνθρώπων τὰ ἁμαρτήματα
I tell you ~ all things will be forgiven the sons of men, {the} all sinful behavior
3306 7007 4022 4246 918 3836 5626 3836 476 3836 280
v.pai.1s r.dp.2 cj a.npn v.fpi.3s d.dpm n.dpm d.gpm n.gpm d.npn n.npn

καὶ αἱ βλασφημίαι ⌊ὅσα ἐὰν⌋ βλασφημήσωσιν· 29 ὃς δ᾽ ἂν
and {the} whatever blasphemies whatever they may utter; but whoever but ~
2779 3836 4012 1060 4012 1569 1059 1254 4005 1254 323
cj d.npf n.npf r.apn pl v.aas.3p r.nsm cj pl

βλασφημήσῃ εἰς τὸ πνεῦμα τὸ ἅγιον, ↱ οὐκ ἔχει ἄφεσιν εἰς τὸν
blasphemes against the Holy Spirit {the} Holy will not have forgiveness for all
1059 1650 3836 41 4460 3836 41 2400 4024 2400 912 1650 3836
v.aas.3s p.a d.asn n.asn d.asn a.asn pl v.pai.3s n.asf p.a d.asm

NASB

went out to take
custody of Him;
for they were say-
ing, "He has lost
His senses." 22 The
scribes who came
down from Jerusa-
lem were saying,
"He is possessed
by Beelzebul,"
and "He casts out
the demons by
the ruler of the
demons." 23 And
He called them to
Himself and began
speaking to them in
parables, "How can
Satan cast out Sa-
tan? 24 If a kingdom
is divided against
itself, that kingdom
cannot stand. 25 If
a house is divided
against itself, that
house will not be
able to stand. 26 If
Satan has risen up
against himself
and is divided, he
cannot stand, but
he is finished! 27 But
no one can enter
the strong man's
house and plunder
his property unless
he first binds the
strong man, and
then he will plun-
der his house.
28 "Truly I say to
you, all sins shall
be forgiven the
sons of men, and
whatever blasphe-
mies they utter;
29 but whoever blas-
phemes against the
Holy Spirit never
has forgiveness,

NIV

they are guilty of
an eternal sin.”
30He said this be-
cause they were
saying, “He has an
impure spirit.”
31Then Jesus’
mother and broth-
ers arrived. Stand-
ing outside, they
sent someone in
to call him. 32A
crowd was sitting
around him, and
they told him,
“Your mother and
brothers are out-
side looking for
you.”
33“Who are my
mother and my
brothers?” he
asked.
34Then he looked
at those seated in a
circle around him
and said, “Here are
my mother and my
brothers! 35Whoev-
er does God’s will
is my brother and
sister and mother.”

The Parable of the Sower

4 Again Jesus
began to teach
by the lake. The
crowd that gath-
ered around him
was so large that
he got into a boat
and sat in it out on
the lake, while all
the people were
along the shore at
the water’s edge.
2He taught them
many things by
parables, and in
his teaching said:
3“Listen!

αἰῶνα, ἀλλὰ ἔνοχός ἐστιν → αἰωνίου ἁμαρτήματος. 30 ὅτι ἔλεγον·
time, but is guilty *is* of an eternal sin” because they were saying, “He has
172 247 1639 1944 1639 173 280 4022 3306 2400 2400
n.asm cj a.nsm v.pai.3s a.gsn n.gsn cj v.iai.3p

πνεῦμα ἀκάθαρτον ἔχει. 31 καὶ ἔρχεται ἡ μήτηρ αὐτοῦ καὶ οἱ
an unclean spirit.” *unclean* *He has* Then *came* {the} his mother *his* and {the} his
176 4460 176 2400 2779 2262 3836 899 3613 899 2779 3836 899
n.asn a.asn v.pai.3s cj v.pmi.3s d.nsf n.nsf r.gsm.3 cj d.npm

ἀδελφοὶ αὐτοῦ καὶ ἔξω στήκοντες ἀπέστειλαν πρὸς αὐτὸν
brothers *his* came, and standing outside *standing* they sent word to him,
81 899 2262 2779 5112 2032 5112 690 4639 899
n.npm r.gsm.3 cj adv pt.pa.npm v.aai.3p p.a r.asm.3

καλοῦντες αὐτόν. 32 καὶ ἐκάθητο περὶ αὐτὸν ὄχλος, καὶ λέγουσιν αὐτῷ·
calling for him. And a crowd was sitting around him, *crowd* and they said to him,
2813 899 2779 4063 2764 4309 899 4063 2779 3306 899
pt.pa.npm r.asm.3 cj v.imi.3s p.a r.asm.3 n.nsm cj v.pai.3p r.dsm.3

ἰδοὺ ἡ μήτηρ σου καὶ οἱ ἀδελφοί σου[a] → ἔξω ζητοῦσίν σε.
“Look, {the} your mother *your* and {the} your brothers *your* are outside looking for you.”
2627 3836 5148 3613 5148 2779 3836 5148 81 5148 2426 2032 2426 5148
j d.nsf n.nsf r.gs.2 cj d.npm n.npm r.gs.2 adv v.pai.3p r.as.2

33 καὶ → ἀποκριθεὶς αὐτοῖς λέγει· τίς ἐστιν ἡ μήτηρ μου καὶ οἱ
And he responded to them, saying, “Who is {the} my mother *my* and who are {the}
2779 3306 646 899 3306 5515 1639 3836 1609 3613 1609 2779 3836
cj pt.ap.nsm r.dpm.3 v.pai.3s r.nsm v.pai.3s d.nsf n.nsf r.gs.1 cj d.npm

ἀδελφοί μου;[b] 34 καὶ περιβλεψάμενος τοὺς περὶ αὐτὸν κύκλῳ
my brothers?” *my* And looking around at those who were sitting around him in a circle,
1609 81 1609 2779 4315 3836 2764 2764 2764 4309 899 3241
n.npm r.gs.1 cj pt.am.nsm d.apm p.a r.asm.3 adv

καθημένους λέγει· ἴδε ἡ μήτηρ μου καὶ οἱ ἀδελφοί μου. 35
who were sitting he said, ⌞“Here is⌟ {the} my mother *my* and {the} my brothers! *my* For
2764 3306 2623 3836 1609 3613 1609 2779 3836 1609 81 1609 1142
pt.pm.apm v.pai.3s pl d.nsf n.nsf r.gs.1 cj d.npm n.npm r.gs.1

ὃς γὰρ[c] ἂν ποιήσῃ τὸ θέλημα τοῦ θεοῦ, οὗτος ἀδελφός μου καὶ
whoever *For* ~ does the will of God, this one is my brother *my* and my
4005 1142 323 4472 3836 2525 3836 2536 4047 1639 1609 81 1609 2779
r.nsm cj pl v.aas.3s d.asn n.asn d.gsm n.gsm r.nsm n.nsm r.gs.1 cj

ἀδελφὴ καὶ μήτηρ ἐστίν.
sister and my mother.” *is*
80 2779 3613 1639
n.nsf cj n.nsf v.pai.3s

4:1 καὶ πάλιν ἤρξατο διδάσκειν παρὰ τὴν θάλασσαν· καὶ
{and} Again Jesus began to teach beside the lake. And a very large crowd
2779 4099 806 1438 4123 3836 2498 2779 4498 4498 4063
cj adv v.ami.3s f.pa p.a d.asf n.asf cj

συνάγεται πρὸς αὐτὸν ὄχλος πλεῖστος, ὥστε αὐτὸν εἰς πλοῖον ἐμβάντα
gathered about him, *crowd* *very large* so that he got into a boat *got* and
5251 4639 899 4063 4498 6063 899 1832 1650 4450 1832
v.ppi.3s p.a r.asm.3 n.nsm a.nsm.s cj r.asm.3 p.a n.asn pt.aa.asm

καθῆσθαι ἐν τῇ θαλάσσῃ, καὶ πᾶς ὁ ὄχλος πρὸς τὴν
sat there out on the lake while all the people were on shore ⌞by the edge of⌟ the
2764 1877 3836 2498 2779 4246 3836 4063 1639 2093 1178 4639 3836
f.pm p.d d.dsf n.dsf cj a.nsm d.nsm n.nsm p.a d.asf

θάλασσαν ἐπὶ τῆς γῆς ἦσαν. 2 καὶ ἐδίδασκεν αὐτοὺς ἐν παραβολαῖς
water. *on* {the} *shore were* And he taught them many things by parables,
2498 2093 3836 1178 1639 2779 1438 899 4498 4498 1877 4130
n.asf p.g d.gsf n.gsf v.iai.3p cj v.iai.3s r.apm.3 p.d n.dpf

πολλὰ καὶ ἔλεγεν αὐτοῖς ἐν τῇ διδαχῇ αὐτοῦ· 3 ἀκούετε.
many things and in his teaching said to them: *in* {the} *teaching* *his* “Listen!
4498 2779 1877 899 1439 3306 899 1877 3836 1439 899 201
a.apn cj v.iai.3s r.dpm.3 p.d d.dsf n.dsf r.gsm.3 v.pam.2p

NASB

but is guilty of an
eternal sin”— 30be-
cause they were
saying, “He has an
unclean spirit.”
31Then His mother
and His brothers
*arrived, and stand-
ing outside they
sent *word* to Him
and called Him. 32A
crowd was sitting
around Him, and
they *said to Him,
“Behold, Your
mother and Your
brothers are outside
looking for You.”
33Answering them,
He *said, “Who
are My mother
and My brothers?”
34Looking about
at those who were
sitting around Him,
He *said, “Behold
My mother and
My brothers! 35For
whoever does the
will of God, he is
My brother and sis-
ter and mother.”

Parable of the Sower and Soils

4:1He began to
teach again by the
sea. And such a
very large crowd
gathered to Him
that He got into
a boat in the sea
and sat down; and
the whole crowd
was by the sea on
the land. 2And He
was teaching them
many things in
parables, and was
saying to them
in His teaching,
3“Listen

[a] καὶ αἱ ἀδελφαί σου included by UBS after σου.
[b] [μου] UBS.
[c] [γὰρ] UBS, omitted by TNIV.

NIV

A farmer went out
to sow his seed.
[4]As he was scat-
tering the seed,
some fell along
the path, and the
birds came and ate
it up. [5]Some fell
on rocky places,
where it did not
have much soil. It
sprang up quickly,
because the soil
was shallow. [6]But
when the sun came
up, the plants were
scorched, and they
withered because
they had no root.
[7]Other seed fell
among thorns,
which grew up and
choked the plants,
so that they did not
bear grain. [8]Still
other seed fell on
good soil. It came
up, grew and pro-
duced a crop, some
multiplying thirty,
some sixty, some a
hundred times."
[9]Then Jesus said,
"Whoever has ears
to hear, let them
hear."
[10]When he was
alone, the Twelve
and the others
around him asked
him about the par-
ables. [11]He told
them, "The secret
of the kingdom
of God has been
given to you. But
to those on the
outside everything
is said in parables
[12]so that,

"'they may be
ever seeing
but never
perceiving,
and ever
hearing
but never
under-
standing;
otherwise they
might
turn and
be orgi–
ven!'[a]"

ἰδοὺ ἐξῆλθεν ὁ σπείρων σπεῖραι. [4]καὶ ἐγένετο ἐν τῷ
{behold} A sower went out {the} sower to sow. And {it happened that} as ~
2627 5062 2002 3836 5062 5062 2779 1181 1877 3836
j v.aai.3s d.nsm pt.pa.nsm f.aa cj v.ami.3s p.d d.dsn

σπείρειν ὃ μὲν ἔπεσεν παρὰ τὴν ὁδόν, καὶ ἦλθεν τὰ πετεινὰ καὶ
he was sowing, some ~ seed fell along the path, and birds came {the} birds and
5062 4005 3525 4406 4123 3836 3847 2779 4374 2262 3836 4374 2779
f.pa r.nsn pl v.aai.3s p.a d.asf n.asf cj v.aai.3s d.npn n.npn cj

κατέφαγεν αὐτό. ↰ [5]καὶ ἄλλο ἔπεσεν ἐπὶ τὸ πετρῶδες ὅπου ↱ ↱ οὐκ
ate it up. {and} Other seed fell on {the} rocky ground where it did not
2983 899 2983 2779 257 4406 2093 3836 4378 3963 2400 2400 4024
v.aai.3s r.asn.3 cj r.nsn v.aai.3s p.a d.asn n.asn cj pl

εἶχεν γῆν πολλήν, καὶ εὐθὺς ἐξανέτειλεν διὰ τὸ
have much soil, much and it sprang up right away it sprang up because {the} it had
2400 4498 1178 4498 2779 1984 1984 1984 2318 1984 1328 3836 2400 2400
v.iai.3s n.asf a.asf cj adv v.aai.3s p.a d.asn

μὴ ἔχειν βάθος γῆς· [6]καὶ ὅτε ἀνέτειλεν ὁ ἥλιος ἐκαυματίσθη
no it had depth of soil. {and} When the sun came up the sun the plant was scorched,
3590 2400 958 1178 2779 4021 3836 2463 422 3836 2463 3009
pl f.pa n.asn n.gsf cj cj v.aai.3s d.nsm n.nsm v.api.3s

καὶ διὰ τὸ ↱ ↱ μὴ ἔχειν ῥίζαν ἐξηράνθη. [7]καὶ ἄλλο ἔπεσεν
and because {the} it did not have a root, ⌞it withered away.⌟ {and} Other seed fell
2779 1328 3836 2400 2400 3590 2400 4844 3830 2779 257 4406
cj p.a d.asn pl f.pa n.asf v.api.3s cj r.nsn v.aai.3s

εἰς τὰς ἀκάνθας, καὶ ἀνέβησαν αἱ ἄκανθαι καὶ συνέπνιξαν αὐτό, καὶ
among the thorns, and the thorns came up the thorns and choked it, and
1650 3836 180 2779 3836 180 326 3836 180 2779 5231 899 2779
p.a d.apf n.apf cj v.aai.3p d.npf n.npf cj v.aai.3p r.asn.3 cj

καρπὸν οὐκ ἔδωκεν. [8]καὶ ἄλλα ἔπεσεν εἰς τὴν γῆν
it did not produce grain. not it did produce But other seed fell into {the} good soil
1443 1443 4024 1443 2843 4024 1443 2779 257 4406 1650 3836 2819 1178
n.asm pl v.aai.3s cj r.npn v.aai.3s p.a d.asf n.asf

τὴν καλὴν καὶ ἐδίδου καρπὸν ἀναβαίνοντα καὶ αὐξανόμενα καὶ ἔφερεν ⌞ἓν
{the} good and produced grain, sprouting, {and} growing, and bearing thirty,
3836 2819 2779 1443 2843 326 2779 889 2779 5770 1651
d.asf a.asf cj v.iai.3s n.asm pt.pa.npn cj pt.pp.npn cj v.iai.3s a.nsn

τριάκοντα⌟ καὶ ⌞ἓν ἑξήκοντα⌟ καὶ ⌞ἓν ἑκατόν.⌟ [9]καὶ ἔλεγεν·
{and} sixty, and even a hundredfold." And he said,
5558 2779 1651 2008 2779 1651 1669 2779 3306
a.apn cj a.nsn a.apn cj a.nsn a.apn cj v.iai.3s

ὃς ἔχει ὦτα ἀκούειν ἀκουέτω. [10]καὶ ὅτε ἐγένετο ⌞κατὰ μόνας,⌟
"Whoever has ears to hear, let him listen!" {and} When he was alone,
4005 2400 4044 201 201 2779 4021 1181 2848 3668
r.nsm v.pai.3s n.apn f.pa v.pam.3s cj cj v.ami.3s p.a a.apf

ἠρώτων αὐτὸν οἱ περὶ αὐτὸν σὺν τοῖς δώδεκα τὰς παραβολάς.
asked about him those around him with the twelve asked him about the parables.
2263 899 3836 4309 899 5250 3836 1557 2263 899 2263 3836 4130
v.iai.3p r.asm.3 d.npm p.a r.asm.3 p.d d.dpm a.dpm d.apf n.apf

[11]καὶ ἔλεγεν αὐτοῖς· ὑμῖν τὸ μυστήριον δέδοται τῆς βασιλείας
And he said to them, "To you has been given the mystery has been given of the kingdom
2779 3306 899 7007 1443 1443 1443 3836 3696 1443 3836 993
cj v.iai.3s r.dpm.3 r.dp.2 d.nsn n.nsn v.rpi.3s d.gsf n.gsf

τοῦ θεοῦ· ἐκείνοις δὲ τοῖς ἔξω ἐν παραβολαῖς τὰ πάντα
of God, but to those but {the} outside, everything is in parables, {the} everything
3836 2536 1254 1697 1254 3836 2032 4246 1181 1877 4130 3836 4246
d.gsm n.gsm r.dpm cj d.dpm adv p.d n.dpf d.npn a.npn

γίνεται, [12]ἵνα βλέποντες βλέπωσιν καὶ μὴ ἴδωσιν, καὶ ἀκούοντες
is so that ⌞'when they look,⌟ they may see yet not perceive, and when they listen,
1181 2671 1063 1063 2779 3590 1625 2779 201
v.pmi.3s cj pt.pa.npm v.pas.3p cj pl v.aas.3p cj pt.pa.npm

ἀκούωσιν καὶ μὴ συνιῶσιν, μήποτε ἐπιστρέψωσιν καὶ ἀφεθῇ αὐτοῖς.
they may hear yet not understand; otherwise they might turn and be forgiven.'" {them}
201 2779 3590 5317 3607 2188 2779 918 899
v.pas.3p cj pl v.pas.3p cj v.aas.3p cj v.aps.3s r.dpm.3

NASB

to this! Behold,
the sower went
out to sow; [4]as he
was sowing, some
seed fell beside the
road, and the birds
came and ate it up.
[5]Other *seed* fell on
the rocky *ground*
where it did not
have much soil;
and immediately it
sprang up because
it had no depth of
soil. [6]And after the
sun had risen, it
was scorched; and
because it had no
root, it withered
away. [7]Other *seed*
fell among the
thorns, and the
thorns came up
and choked it, and
it yielded no crop.
[8]Other *seeds* fell
into the good soil,
and as they grew
up and increased,
they yielded a
crop and produced
thirty, sixty, and
a hundredfold."
[9]And He was say-
ing, "He who has
ears to hear, let him
hear."
[10]As soon as He
was alone, His
followers, along
with the twelve,
began asking Him
about the parables.
[11]And He was say-
ing to them, "To
you has been given
the mystery of the
kingdom of God,
but those who are
outside get every-
thing in parables,
[12]so that WHILE SEE-
ING, THEY MAY SEE
AND NOT PERCEIVE,
AND WHILE HEARING,
THEY MAY HEAR AND
NOT UNDERSTAND,
OTHERWISE THEY
MIGHT RETURN AND
BE FORGIVEN."

[a] 12 Isaiah 6:9,10

NIV

13Then Jesus said
to them, "Don't
you understand
this parable? How
then will you
understand any
parable? 14The
farmer sows the
word. 15Some peo-
ple are like seed
along the path,
where the word is
sown. As soon as
they hear it, Satan
comes and takes
away the word that
was sown in them.
16Others, like seed
sown on rocky
places, hear the
word and at once
receive it with joy.
17But since they
have no root, they
last only a short
time. When trou-
ble or persecution
comes because
of the word, they
quickly fall away.
18Still others, like
seed sown among
thorns, hear the
word; 19but the
worries of this life,
the deceitfulness
of wealth and the
desires for other
things come in and
choke the word,
making it unfruit-
ful. 20Others, like
seed sown on good
soil, hear the word,
accept it, and
produce a crop—
some thirty, some
sixty, some a hun-
dred times what
was sown."

A Lamp on a Stand

21He said to them,

13 καὶ λέγει αὐτοῖς· ↱ ↱ οὐκ οἴδατε τὴν παραβολὴν ταύτην, καὶ πῶς
And he said to them, "Do you not understand {the} this parable? this Then how will
2779 3306 899 3857 3857 4024 3857 3836 4047 4130 4047 2779 4802 1182
cj v.pai.3s r.dpm.3 pl v.rai.2p d.asf n.asf r.asf cj cj

πάσας τὰς παραβολὰς γνώσεσθε; 14 ὁ σπείρων τὸν λόγον
you understand all the parables? will you understand The sower sows the word.
1182 1182 4246 3836 4130 1182 3836 5062 5062 3836 3364
a.apf d.apf n.apf v.fmi.2p d.nsm pt.pa.nsm d.asm n.asm

σπείρει. 15 οὗτοι δέ εἰσιν οἱ παρὰ τὴν ὁδόν· ὅπου σπείρεται ὁ
sows These {and} are ⌊the ones⌋ on the path where the word is sown: the
5062 4047 1254 1639 3836 4123 3836 3847 3963 3836 3364 5062 3836
v.pai.3s r.npm cj v.pai.3p d.npm p.a d.asf n.asf cj v.ppi.3s d.nsm

λόγος καὶ ὅταν ἀκούσωσιν, εὐθὺς ἔρχεται ὁ σατανᾶς καὶ αἴρει
word {and} whenever they hear, Satan immediately comes {the} Satan and ⌊carries off⌋
3364 2779 4020 201 4928 2318 2262 3836 4928 2779 149
n.nsm cj cj v.aas.3p adv v.pmi.3s d.nsm n.nsm cj v.pai.3s

τὸν λόγον τὸν ἐσπαρμένον εἰς αὐτούς. 16 καὶ οὗτοί εἰσιν οἱ ἐπὶ τὰ
the word that was sown in them. {and} These are the ones sown on {the}
3836 3364 3836 5062 1650 899 2779 4047 1639 3836 5062 5062 2093 3836
d.asm n.asm d.asm pt.rp.asm p.a r.apm.3 cj r.npm v.pai.3p d.npm p.a d.apn

πετρώδη σπειρόμενοι, οἳ ὅταν ἀκούσωσιν τὸν λόγον εὐθὺς
rocky ground: ones sown {who} whenever they hear the word, they immediately receive
4378 5062 4005 4020 201 3836 3364 3284 2318 3284
n.apn pt.pp.npm r.npm cj v.aas.3p d.asm n.asm adv

μετὰ χαρᾶς λαμβάνουσιν αὐτόν, 17 καὶ οὐκ ἔχουσιν ῥίζαν ἐν ἑαυτοῖς
it with joy. they receive it But they have no they have root in themselves
899 3552 5915 3284 899 2779 2400 2400 4024 2400 4844 1877 1571
p.g n.gsf v.pai.3p r.asm.3 cj pl v.pai.3p n.asf p.d r.dpm.3

ἀλλὰ ← πρόσκαιροί εἰσιν, εἶτα → γενομένης θλίψεως ἢ διωγμοῦ
and last for only a limited time. last for Then, when comes tribulation or persecution
247 1639 1639 4672 1639 1663 1181 2568 2445 1501
cj a.npm v.pai.3p adv pt.am.gsf n.gsf cj n.gsm

θλίψεως ἢ διωγμοῦ διὰ τὸν λόγον εὐθὺς σκανδαλίζονται.
comes tribulation or persecution ⌊because of⌋ the word, immediately they fall away.
1181 2568 2445 1501 1328 3836 3364 2318 4997
n.gsf cj n.gsm p.a d.asm n.asm adv v.ppi.3p

18 καὶ ἄλλοι εἰσὶν οἱ εἰς τὰς ἀκάνθας σπειρόμενοι· οὗτοί εἰσιν
{and} Others are ⌊the ones⌋ sown among the thorns: sown these are
2779 257 1639 3836 5062 1650 3836 180 5062 4047 1639
cj r.npm v.pai.3p d.npm p.a d.apf n.apf pt.pp.npm r.npm v.pai.3p

οἱ τὸν λόγον ἀκούσαντες, 19 καὶ αἱ μέριμναι τοῦ αἰῶνος καὶ ἡ
⌊the ones⌋ who hear the word, who hear but the cares of the world, {and} the
3836 201 201 3836 3364 201 2779 3836 3533 3836 172 2779 3836
d.npm d.asm n.asm pt.aa.npm cj d.npf n.npf d.gsm n.gsm cj d.nsf

ἀπάτη τοῦ πλούτου καὶ αἱ περὶ τὰ λοιπὰ ἐπιθυμίαι
deceitfulness of wealth, and the desires for {the} many other things desires
573 3836 4458 2779 3836 2123 4309 3836 3370 2123
n.nsf d.gsm n.gsm cj d.npf p.a d.apn a.apn n.npf

εἰσπορευόμεναι συμπνίγουσιν τὸν λόγον καὶ ἄκαρπος γίνεται.
come in and choke the word, and it becomes barren. it becomes
1660 5231 3836 3364 2779 1181 1181 182 1181
pt.pm.npf v.pai.3p d.asm n.asm cj a.nsm v.pmi.3s

20 καὶ ἐκεῖνοί εἰσιν οἱ ἐπὶ τὴν γῆν τὴν καλὴν σπαρέντες, οἵτινες
{and} These are ⌊the ones⌋ sown on {the} good soil: {the} good sown they
2779 1697 1639 3836 5062 2093 3836 2819 1178 3836 2819 5062 4015
cj r.npm v.pai.3p d.npm p.a d.asf n.asf d.asf a.asf pt.ap.npm r.npm

ἀκούουσιν τὸν λόγον καὶ παραδέχονται καὶ καρποφοροῦσιν ⌊ἓν τριάκοντα⌋
hear the word, {and} accept it, and bear fruit — thirty,
201 3836 3364 2779 4138 2779 2844 1651 5558
v.pai.3p d.asm n.asm cj v.pmi.3p cj v.pai.3p a.nsn a.apn

καὶ ⌊ἓν ἑξήκοντα⌋ καὶ ⌊ἓν ἑκατόν.⌋ 21 καὶ ἔλεγεν αὐτοῖς·
{and} sixty and even a hundredfold. And he said to them, "A lamp
2779 1651 2008 2779 1651 1669 2779 3306 899 3394
cj a.nsn a.apn cj a.nsn a.apn cj v.iai.3s r.dpm.3

NASB

Explanation

13And He *said
to them, "Do you
not understand this
parable? How will
you understand
all the parables?
14The sower sows
the word. 15These
are the ones who
are beside the road
where the word is
sown; and when
they hear, immedi-
ately Satan comes
and takes away
the word which
has been sown in
them. 16In a similar
way these are the
ones on whom seed
was sown on the
rocky *places,* who,
when they hear the
word, immediately
receive it with joy;
17and they have
no *firm* root in
themselves, but are
only temporary;
then, when afflic-
tion or persecution
arises because
of the word, im-
mediately they fall
away. 18And others
are the ones on
whom seed was
sown among the
thorns; these are
the ones who have
heard the word,
19but the worries
of the [a]world, and
the deceitfulness
of riches, and the
desires for other
things enter in and
choke the word,
and it becomes
unfruitful. 20And
those are the ones
on whom seed
was sown on the
good soil; and they
hear the word and
accept it and bear
fruit, thirty, sixty,
and a hundred-
fold."
21And He was say-
ing to them, "A

[a] Or *age*

NIV

"Do you bring in
a lamp to put it
under a bowl or
a bed? Instead,
don't you put it
on its stand? 22 For
whatever is hid-
den is meant to
be disclosed, and
whatever is con-
cealed is meant
to be brought out
into the open. 23 If
anyone has ears
to hear, let them
hear."
24 "Consider care-
fully what you
hear," he contin-
ued. "With the
measure you use,
it will be measured
to you—and even
more. 25 Whoever
has will be given
more; whoever
does not have,
even what they
have will be taken
from them."

The Parable of the Growing Seed

26 He also said,
"This is what the
kingdom of God is
like. A man scat-
ters seed on the
ground. 27 Night
and day, wheth-
er he sleeps or
gets up, the seed
sprouts and grows,
though he does not
know how. 28 All
by itself the soil
produces grain—
first the stalk, then
the head, then the
full kernel in the
head. 29 As soon as
the grain is ripe,
he puts the sickle
to it, because the
harvest has come."

The Parable of the Mustard Seed

30 Again he said,
"What shall we
say the kingdom
of God is like, or
what parable shall
we use to describe
it? 31 It is like a
mustard seed,

↱ μήτι ἔρχεται ὁ λύχνος ἵνα ὑπὸ τὸν μόδιον τεθῇ ἢ ὑπὸ τὴν
is not brought {the} lamp to be put under a basket be put or under a
2262 3614 2262 3836 3394 2671 5502 5502 5679 3836 3654 5502 2445 5679 3836
pl v.pmi.3s d.nsm n.nsm cj p.a d.asm n.asm v.aps.3s cj p.a d.asf

κλίνην; ↰ ↰ οὐχ ἵνα ἐπὶ τὴν λυχνίαν τεθῇ; 22 οὐ γάρ
bed, is it? Is it not to be put on a lampstand? be put For nothing For
3109 3614 3614 4024 2671 5502 5502 2093 3836 3393 5502 1142 4024 1142
n.asf pl cj p.a d.asf n.asf v.aps.3s pl cj

ἐστιν κρυπτὸν ⌞ἐὰν μὴ⌟ ἵνα φανερωθῇ, οὐδὲ ἐγένετο ἀπόκρυφον ἀλλ᾽ ἵνα
is hidden except to be disclosed; nor is anything concealed, except to
1639 3220 1569 3590 2671 5746 4028 1181 649 247 2671
v.pai.3s a.nsn cj pl cj v.aps.3s cj v.ami.3s a.nsn cj cj

ἔλθῃ εἰς φανερόν. 23 εἴ τις ἔχει ὦτα ἀκούειν ἀκουέτω. 24 καὶ ἔλεγεν
come to light. If anyone has ears to hear, let him listen!" And he said
2262 1650 5745 1623 5516 2400 4044 201 201 2779 3306
v.aas.3s p.a a.asn cj r.nsm v.pai.3s n.apn f.pa v.pam.3s cj v.iai.3s

αὐτοῖς· βλέπετε τί ἀκούετε. ἐν ᾧ μέτρῳ μετρεῖτε μετρηθήσεται
to them, ⌞"Pay attention to⌟ what you hear. By what measure you measure ⌞it will be measured out⌟
899 1063 5515 201 1877 4005 3586 3582 3582
r.dpm.3 v.pam.2p r.asn v.pai.2p p.d r.dsn n.dsn v.pai.2p v.fpi.3s

ὑμῖν καὶ προστεθήσεται ὑμῖν. 25 ὃς γὰρ ἔχει, δοθήσεται αὐτῷ· καὶ
to you, and more will be added to you. For whoever For has, more will be given to him; and
7007 2779 4707 7007 1142 4005 1142 2400 1443 899 2779
r.dp.2 cj v.fpi.3s r.dp.2 r.nsm cj v.pai.3s v.fpi.3s r.dsm.3 cj

ὃς ↱ οὐκ ἔχει, καὶ ὃ ἔχει ἀρθήσεται ἀπ᾽ αὐτοῦ. 26 καὶ
whoever does not have, even what ⌞he does have⌟ ⌞will be taken away⌟ from him." And
4005 2400 4024 2400 2779 4005 2400 149 608 899 2779
r.nsm pl v.pai.3s adv r.asn v.pai.3s v.fpi.3s p.g r.gsm.3 cj

ἔλεγεν· οὕτως ἐστὶν ἡ βασιλεία τοῦ θεοῦ ὡς ἄνθρωπος βάλῃ τὸν
he said, {this} is "The kingdom of God is like a man who scatters {the}
3306 4048 1639 3836 993 3836 2536 1639 6055 476 965 3836
v.iai.3s adv v.pai.3s d.nsf n.nsf d.gsm n.gsm cj n.nsm v.aas.3s d.asm

σπόρον ἐπὶ τῆς γῆς 27 καὶ καθεύδῃ καὶ ἐγείρηται νύκτα καὶ ἡμέραν, καὶ
seed on the ground. {and} ⌞He goes to bed⌟ and gets up, night and day, and
5078 2093 3836 1178 2779 2761 2779 1586 3816 2779 2465 2779
n.asm p.g d.gsf n.gsf cj v.pas.3s cj v.pps.3s n.asf cj n.asf cj

ὁ σπόρος βλαστᾷ καὶ μηκύνηται ὡς ↱ οὐκ οἶδεν αὐτός. 28
the seed sprouts and grows, how although he does not know how. he The
3836 5078 1056 2779 3602 6055 899 3857 4024 3857 6055 899 3836
d.nsm n.nsm v.pas.3s cj v.pps.3s cj pl v.rai.3s r.nsm

αὐτομάτη ἡ γῆ καρποφορεῖ, πρῶτον χόρτον εἶτα
soil produces a crop all by itself: The soil produces a crop first the stalk, then the
1178 2844 2844 2844 897 3836 1178 2844 4754 5965 1663
a.nsf d.nsf n.nsf v.pai.3s adv n.asm adv

στάχυν εἶτα πλήρης[a] σῖτον ἐν τῷ στάχυϊ. 29 ὅταν δὲ παραδοῖ
head, then the full grain in the head. And when And the grain is ripe,
5092 1663 4441 4992 1877 3836 5092 1254 4020 1254 3836 2843 4140
n.asm adv a.asm n.asm p.d d.dsm n.dsm cj cj v.aas.3s

ὁ καρπός, εὐθὺς ἀποστέλλει τὸ δρέπανον, ὅτι παρέστηκεν ὁ
the grain immediately he sends in the sickle, because the harvest has come." the
3836 2843 2318 690 3836 1535 4022 3836 2546 4225 3836
d.nsm n.nsm adv v.pai.3s d.asn n.asn cj v.rai.3s d.nsm

θερισμός. 30 καὶ ἔλεγεν· πῶς ὁμοιώσωμεν τὴν βασιλείαν τοῦ θεοῦ ἢ ἐν τίνι
harvest Then he said, "To what can we compare the kingdom of God, or for what
2546 2779 3306 4802 3929 3836 993 3836 2536 2445 1877 5515
n.nsm cj v.iai.3s cj v.aas.1p d.asf n.asf d.gsm n.gsm cj p.d r.dsf

αὐτὴν παραβολῇ θῶμεν; 31 ὡς κόκκῳ σινάπεως, ὃς ὅταν
it parable ⌞can we use⌟ for it? It is like a mustard seed mustard that, when
899 4130 5502 1877 899 6055 4983 3133 4983 4005 4020
r.asf.3 n.dsf v.aas.1p pl n.dsm n.gsn r.nsm cj

σπαρῇ ἐπὶ τῆς γῆς, μικρότερον ὂν πάντων τῶν σπερμάτων τῶν ἐπὶ τῆς
it is sown in the ground, is smaller is than all of the seeds {the} on {the}
5062 2093 3836 1178 1639 3625 1639 4246 3836 5065 3836 2093 3836
v.aps.3s p.g d.gsf n.gsf a.nsn.c pt.pa.nsn a.gpn d.gpn n.gpn d.gpn p.g d.gsf

[a] πλήρης TNIV, NET. πλήρη[ς] UBS.

NASB

lamp is not brought
to be put under a
basket, is it, or un-
der a bed? Is it not
brought to be put
on the lampstand?
22 For nothing is
hidden, except to
be revealed; nor
has *anything* been
secret, but that it
would come to
light. 23 If anyone
has ears to hear, let
him hear." 24 And
He was saying to
them, "Take care
what you listen to.
By your standard
of measure it will
be measured to
you; and more will
be given you be-
sides. 25 For whoev-
er has, to him *more*
shall be given; and
whoever does not
have, even what he
has shall be taken
away from him."

Parable of the Seed

26 And He was say-
ing, "The kingdom
of God is like a
man who casts
seed upon the soil;
27 and he goes to
bed at night and
gets up by day, and
the seed sprouts
and grows—how,
he himself does
not know. 28 The
soil produces crops
by itself; first the
blade, then the
head, then the
mature grain in the
head. 29 But when
the crop permits,
he immediately
puts in the sickle,
because the harvest
has come."

Parable of the Mustard Seed

30 And He said,
"How shall we
[a]picture the king-
dom of God, or by
what parable shall
we present it? 31 *It*
is like a mustard
seed, which, when
sown upon the soil,
though it is smaller

[a] Lit *compare*

NIV

which is the small-
est of all seeds on
earth. 32 Yet when
planted, it grows
and becomes the
largest of all gar-
den plants, with
such big branches
that the birds can
perch in its shade."
33 With many sim-
ilar parables Jesus
spoke the word to
them, as much as
they could under-
stand. 34 He did not
say anything to
them without us-
ing a parable. But
when he was alone
with his own disci-
ples, he explained
everything.

Jesus Calms the Storm

35 That day when
evening came, he
said to his disci-
ples, "Let us go
over to the other
side." 36 Leaving
the crowd behind,
they took him
along, just as he
was, in the boat.
There were also
other boats with
him. 37 A furious
squall came up,
and the waves
broke over the
boat, so that it was
nearly swamped.
38 Jesus was in the
stern, sleeping on
a cushion. The dis-
ciples woke him
and said to him,
"Teacher, don't
you care if we
drown?"
39 He got up, re-
buked the wind
and said to the
waves, "Quiet! Be
still!" Then the
wind died down
and it was com-
pletely calm.
40 He said to his
disciples, "Why
are you so afraid?
Do you still have

γῆς, 32 καὶ ὅταν σπαρῇ, ἀναβαίνει καὶ γίνεται μεῖζον πάντων τῶν λαχάνων καὶ
earth. Yet when it is sown, it grows up and becomes larger than all the garden plants and
1178 2779 4020 5062 326 2779 1181 3489 4246 3836 3303 2779
n.gsf cj cj v.aps.3s v.pai.3s cj v.pmi.3s a.nsn.c a.gpn d.gpn n.gpn cj

ποιεῖ κλάδους μεγάλους, ὥστε δύνασθαι ὑπὸ
puts out large branches, *large* so that the birds of the air are able to nest in
4472 3489 3080 3489 6063 3836 4374 3836 3836 4041 1538 2942 2942 5679
v.pai.3s n.apm a.apm cj f.pp p.a

τὴν σκιὰν αὐτοῦ τὰ πετεινὰ τοῦ οὐρανοῦ κατασκηνοῦν. 33 καὶ
{the} its shade." *its* *the* *birds* *of the* *air* *to nest* So with many
3836 899 5014 899 3836 4374 3836 4041 2942 2779 4130 4498
d.asf n.asf r.gsn.3 d.apn n.apn d.gsm n.gsm f.pa cj

τοιαύταις παραβολαῖς πολλαῖς ἐλάλει αὐτοῖς τὸν λόγον καθὼς
parables such as these *with parables* *many* he spoke the word to them, *the* *word* as
4130 5525 4130 4498 3281 3836 3364 899 3836 3364 2777
r.dpf n.dpf a.dpf v.iai.3s r.dpm.3 d.asm n.asm cj

ἠδύναντο ἀκούειν· 34 χωρὶς δὲ παραβολῆς ↱ ↱ οὐκ ἐλάλει αὐτοῖς,
they were able to understand. And without *And* a parable he did not speak to them;
1538 201 1254 6006 1254 4130 3281 3281 4024 3281 899
v.ipi.3p f.pa p.g cj n.gsf pl v.iai.3s r.dpm.3

⌊κατ' ἰδίαν⌋ δὲ τοῖς ἰδίοις μαθηταῖς ἐπέλυεν πάντα. 35 καὶ
but privately *but* to his own disciples ⌊he would explain⌋ everything. *{and}* On
1254 2848 2625 1254 3836 2625 3412 2147 4246 2779 1877
p.a a.asf cj d.dpm a.dpm n.dpm v.iai.3s a.apn cj

λέγει αὐτοῖς ἐν ἐκείνῃ τῇ ἡμέρᾳ ὀψίας
that same day, when evening had come, he said to them, *On* *that* *{the}* *day* *evening*
1697 2465 1181 4068 1181 1181 3306 899 1877 1697 3836 2465 4068
v.pai.3s r.dpm.3 p.d r.dsf d.dsf n.dsf n.gsf

γενομένης· διέλθωμεν εἰς τὸ πέραν. 36 καὶ ἀφέντες τὸν ὄχλον
when had come "Let us go over to the other side." So after leaving the crowd,
1181 1451 1650 3836 4305 2779 918 3836 4063
pt.am.gsf v.aas.1p p.a d.asn adv cj pt.aa.npm d.asm n.asm

παραλαμβάνουσιν αὐτὸν ↰ ὡς ἦν ἐν τῷ πλοίῳ, καὶ ἄλλα πλοῖα
they took him with them, ⌊just as⌋ ⌊he was,⌋ in the boat. And other boats
4161 899 4161 6055 1639 1877 3836 4450 2779 257 4450
v.pai.3p r.asm.3 cj v.iai.3s p.d d.dsn n.dsn cj r.npn n.npn

ἦν μετ' αὐτοῦ. 37 καὶ γίνεται λαῖλαψ μεγάλη ἀνέμου καὶ τὰ
were with him. Now a fierce windstorm arose windstorm *fierce* *{wind}* and the
1639 3552 899 2779 3489 3278 1181 3278 3489 449 2779 3836
v.iai.3s p.g r.gsm.3 cj v.pmi.3s n.nsf a.nsf n.gsm cj d.npn

κύματα ἐπέβαλλεν εἰς τὸ πλοῖον, ὥστε ↱ ἤδη γεμίζεσθαι τὸ πλοῖον.
waves began to break into the boat, so that the boat was now filling. *the* *boat*
3246 2095 1650 3836 4450 6063 3836 4450 1153 2453 1153 3836 4450
n.npn v.iai.3s p.a d.asn n.asn cj adv f.pp d.asn n.asn

38 καὶ αὐτὸς ἦν ἐν τῇ πρύμνῃ ἐπὶ τὸ προσκεφάλαιον καθεύδων. καὶ
But Jesus was in the stern, sleeping on a cushion. *sleeping* *{and}*
2779 899 1639 1877 3836 4744 2761 2093 3836 4676 2761 2779
cj r.nsm v.iai.3s p.d d.dsf n.dsf p.a d.asn n.asn pt.pa.nsm cj

ἐγείρουσιν αὐτὸν καὶ λέγουσιν αὐτῷ· διδάσκαλε, ↱ οὐ μέλει σοι ὅτι
They woke him and said to him, "Teacher, do you not care *you* that
1586 899 2779 3306 899 1437 3508 5148 4024 3508 5148 4022
v.pai.3p r.asm.3 cj v.pai.3p r.dsm.3 n.vsm pl v.pai.3s r.ds.2 cj

ἀπολλύμεθα; 39 καὶ ↱ διεγερθεὶς ἐπετίμησεν τῷ ἀνέμῳ καὶ εἶπεν τῇ
we are perishing?" So he got up and rebuked the wind and said ⌊to the⌋
660 2779 2203 1444 2203 3836 449 2779 3306 3836
v.pmi.1p cj pt.ap.nsm v.aai.3s d.dsm n.dsm cj v.aai.3s d.dsf

θαλάσσῃ· σιώπα, πεφίμωσο. καὶ ἐκόπασεν ὁ ἄνεμος καὶ ἐγένετο
sea, "Be still! Settle down!" Then the wind died down *the* *wind* and there was a great
2498 4995 5821 2779 3836 449 3156 3836 449 2779 1181 3489
n.dsf v.pam.2s v.rpm.2s cj v.aai.3s d.nsm n.nsm cj v.ami.3s

γαλήνη μεγάλη. 40 καὶ εἶπεν αὐτοῖς· τί δειλοί ἐστε; οὔπω
calm. *great* And he said to them, "Why are you so fearful? *are you* Have you still no
1132 3489 2779 3306 899 5515 1639 1639 1264 1639 2400 2400 4037
n.nsf a.nsf cj v.aai.3s r.dpm.3 r.asn a.npm v.pai.2p adv

NASB

than all the seeds
that are upon the
soil, 32 yet when it is
sown, it grows up
and becomes larger
than all the garden
plants and forms
large branches; so
that THE BIRDS OF
THE [a]AIR can NEST
UNDER ITS SHADE."
33 With many such
parables He was
speaking the word
to them, so far as
they were able to
hear it; 34 and He
did not speak to
them without a par-
able; but He was
explaining every-
thing privately to
His own disciples.

Jesus Stills the Sea

35 On that day,
when evening
came, He *said to
them, "Let us go
over to the other
side." 36 Leaving the
crowd, they *took
Him along with
them in the boat,
just as He was; and
other boats were
with Him. 37 And
there *arose a fierce
gale of wind, and
the waves were
breaking over
the boat so much
that the boat was
already filling up.
38 Jesus Himself was
in the stern, asleep
on the cushion;
and they *woke
Him and *said to
Him, "Teacher, do
You not care that
we are perishing?"
39 And He got up
and rebuked the
wind and said to
the sea, "Hush, be
still." And the wind
died down and it
became perfectly
calm. 40 And He
said to them, "Why
are you afraid? Do
you still have

[a] Or *sky*

NIV

no faith?"
[41]They were terrified and asked each other, "Who is this? Even the wind and the waves obey him!"

Jesus Restores a Demon-Possessed Man

5 They went across the lake to the region of the Gerasenes.[a] [2]When Jesus got out of the boat, a man with an impure spirit came from the tombs to meet him. [3]This man lived in the tombs, and no one could bind him anymore, not even with a chain. [4]For he had often been chained hand and foot, but he tore the chains apart and broke the irons on his feet. No one was strong enough to subdue him. [5]Night and day among the tombs and in the hills he would cry out and cut himself with stones.
[6]When he saw Jesus from a distance, he ran and fell on his knees in front of him. [7]He shouted at the top of his voice, "What do you want with me, Jesus, Son of the Most High God? In God's name don't torture me!" [8]For Jesus had said to him,

[a] 1 Some manuscripts *Gadarenes*; other manuscripts *Gergesenes*

ἔχετε πίστιν; [41] καὶ ἐφοβήθησαν φόβον μέγαν καὶ ἔλεγον πρὸς
Have you faith?" And ⌊they were filled with⌋ great fear *great* and said to
2400 4411 2779 5828 3489 5832 3489 2779 3306 4639
v.pai.2p n.asf cj v.api.3p n.asm a.asm cj v.iai.3p p.a

ἀλλήλους· τίς ἄρα οὗτός ἐστιν ὅτι καὶ ὁ ἄνεμος καὶ ἡ θάλασσα
one another, "Who then is this, *is* that even the wind and the sea
253 5515 726 1639 4047 1639 4022 2779 3836 449 2779 3836 2498
r.apm r.nsm cj r.nsm v.pai.3s cj adv d.nsm n.nsm cj d.nsf n.nsf

ὑπακούει αὐτῷ;
obey him?"
5634 899
v.pai.3s r.dsm.3

[5:1] Καὶ ἦλθον εἰς τὸ πέραν τῆς θαλάσσης εἰς τὴν χώραν τῶν
So they went to the other side of the lake to the region of the
2779 2262 1650 3836 4305 3836 2498 1650 3836 6001 3836
cj v.aai.3p p.a d.asn p.g d.gsf n.gsf p.a d.asf n.asf d.gpm

Γερασηνῶν.[a] [2] καὶ ἐξελθόντος αὐτοῦ ἐκ τοῦ πλοίου εὐθὺς ὑπήντησεν
Gerasenes. And just as Jesus got out *Jesus* of the boat, *just as* there met
1170 2779 2318 2318 899 2002 899 1666 3836 4450 2318 5636
a.gpm cj pt.aa.gsm r.gsm.3 p.g d.gsn n.gsn adv v.aai.3s

αὐτῷ ἐκ τῶν μνημείων ἄνθρωπος ἐν πνεύματι ἀκαθάρτῳ, [3] ὃς
him from the tombs a man with an unclean spirit. *unclean* He had
899 1666 3836 3646 476 1877 176 4460 176 4005 2400
r.dsm.3 p.g d.gpn n.gpn n.nsm p.d n.dsn a.dsn r.nsm

τὴν κατοίκησιν εἶχεν ἐν τοῖς μνήμασιν, καὶ
his dwelling *had* among the tombs, and no one could bind him any longer,
3836 2998 2400 1877 3836 3645 2779 4029 4029 1538 1313 899 4033 4033
d.asf n.asf v.iai.3s p.d d.dpn n.dpn cj

οὐδὲ → ἁλύσει οὐκέτι οὐδεὶς ἐδύνατο αὐτὸν δῆσαι [4] διὰ τὸ αὐτὸν
not even with a chain. *any longer* *no one* *could* *him* *bind* For *{the}* he had
4028 268 4033 4029 1538 899 1313 1328 3836 899 1313
adv n.dsf adv a.nsm v.ipi.3s r.asm.3 f.aa p.a d.asn r.asm.3

πολλάκις → πέδαις καὶ ἁλύσεσιν δεδέσθαι καὶ
often been bound with shackles and chains, *had been bound* but the chains
4490 1313 1313 4267 2779 268 1313 2779 3836 268
adv n.dpf cj n.dpf f.rp cj

διεσπάσθαι ὑπ' αὐτοῦ τὰς ἁλύσεις καὶ τὰς πέδας συντετρῖφθαι, καὶ οὐδεὶς
were torn apart by him *the* *chains* and the shackles broken in pieces, and no one
1400 5679 899 3836 268 2779 3836 4267 5341 2779 4029
f.rp p.g r.gsm.3 d.apf n.apf cj d.apf n.apf f.rp cj a.nsm

ἴσχυεν αὐτὸν δαμάσαι· [5] καὶ ⌊διὰ παντὸς⌋ νυκτὸς καὶ
⌊was strong enough⌋ to subdue him. *to subdue* *{and}* Unceasingly, night and
2710 1238 1238 899 1238 2779 1328 4246 3816 2779
v.iai.3s r.asm.3 f.aa cj p.g a.gsm n.gsf cj

ἡμέρας ἐν τοῖς μνήμασιν καὶ ἐν τοῖς ὄρεσιν ἦν κράζων καὶ κατακόπτων
day among the tombs and in the mountains, ⌊he kept⌋ crying out and cutting
2465 1877 3836 3645 2779 1877 3836 4001 1639 3189 2779 2888
n.gsf p.d d.dpn n.dpn cj p.d d.dpn n.dpn v.iai.3s pt.pa.nsm cj pt.pa.nsm

ἑαυτὸν λίθοις. [6] καὶ ἰδὼν τὸν Ἰησοῦν ἀπὸ μακρόθεν ἔδραμεν καὶ
himself with stones. But ⌊when he saw⌋ *{the}* Jesus from a distance, he ran and
1571 3345 2779 1625 3836 2652 608 3427 5556 2779
r.asm.3 n.dpm cj pt.aa.nsm d.asm n.asm p.g adv v.aai.3s cj

προσεκύνησεν αὐτῷ [7] καὶ κράξας → φωνῇ μεγάλῃ λέγει· τί
bowed down before him. *{and}* Crying out in a loud voice, *loud* he exclaimed, "What have
4686 899 2779 3189 3489 5889 3489 3306 5515
v.aai.3s r.dsm.3 cj pt.aa.nsm n.dsf a.dsf v.pai.3s r.nsn

ἐμοὶ καὶ σοί, Ἰησοῦ υἱὲ τοῦ θεοῦ τοῦ ὑψίστου; ⌊ὁρκίζω σε⌋
you to do ⌊with me,⌋ *{and}* *you* Jesus, Son of the *God* *{the}* Most High God? Swear to
5148 1609 2779 5148 2652 5626 3836 2536 3836 5736 2536 3991 5148
r.ds.1 cj r.ds.2 n.vsm n.vsm d.gsm n.gsm d.gsm a.gsm.s v.pai.1s r.as.2

τὸν θεόν, μή με βασανίσῃς. [8] ἔλεγεν γὰρ αὐτῷ·
{the} God that you will not torment me!" *you will torment* (For Jesus had said *For* to him,
3836 2536 989 989 3590 989 1609 989 1142 3306 1142 899
d.asm n.asm pl r.as.1 v.aas.2s v.iai.3s cj r.dsm.3

[a] Γαδαρηνῶν included by TR after Γερασηνῶν.

NASB

no faith?" [41]They became very much afraid and said to one another, "Who then is this, that even the wind and the sea obey Him?"

The Gerasene Demoniac

[5:1]They came to the other side of the sea, into the country of the Gerasenes. [2]When He got out of the boat, immediately a man from the tombs with an unclean spirit met Him, [3]and he had his dwelling among the tombs. And no one was able to bind him anymore, even with a chain; [4]because he had often been bound with shackles and chains, and the chains had been torn apart by him and the shackles broken in pieces, and no one was strong enough to subdue him. [5]Constantly, night and day, he was screaming among the tombs and in the mountains, and gashing himself with stones. [6]Seeing Jesus from a distance, he ran up and bowed down before Him; [7]and shouting with a loud voice, he *said, "What business do we have with each other, Jesus, Son of the Most High God? I implore You by God, do not torment me!" [8]For He had been saying

NIV

"Come out of this
man, you impure
spirit!"
9 Then Jesus
asked him, "What
is your name?"
"My name is Le-
gion," he replied,
"for we are many."
10 And he begged
Jesus again and
again not to send
them out of the
area.
11 A large herd of
pigs was feeding
on the nearby hill-
side. 12 The demons
begged Jesus,
"Send us among
the pigs; allow us
to go into them."
13 He gave them
permission, and
the impure spirits
came out and went
into the pigs. The
herd, about two
thousand in num-
ber, rushed down
the steep bank into
the lake and were
drowned.
14 Those tending
the pigs ran off
and reported this
in the town and
countryside, and
the people went
out to see what had
happened. 15 When
they came to
Jesus, they saw the
man who had been
possessed by the
legion of demons,
sitting there,
dressed and in his
right mind; and
they were afraid.
16 Those who had
seen it told the
people what had
happened to the
demon-possessed
man—and told
about the pigs as
well. 17 Then the
people began

ἔξελθε τὸ → πνεῦμα τὸ ἀκάθαρτον ἐκ τοῦ ἀνθρώπου.
⌞"Come out⌟ of the man, *{the}* you unclean spirit!") *{the}* *unclean* *of* *the* *man*
2002 1666 3836 476 3836 176 4460 3836 176 1666 3836 476
v.aam.2s d.vsn n.vsn d.vsn a.vsn p.g d.gsm n.gsm

9 καὶ ἐπηρώτα αὐτόν· τί ὄνομά σοι; καὶ λέγει αὐτῷ· λεγιὼν
And Jesus asked him, "What is your name?" *your* *{and}* He said to him, "Legion is my
2779 2089 899 5515 5148 3950 5148 2779 3306 899 3305 1609
cj v.iai.3s r.asm.3 r.nsn n.nsn r.ds.2 cj v.pai.3s r.dsm.3 n.nsf

ὄνομά μοι, ὅτι πολλοί ἐσμεν. 10 καὶ παρεκάλει αὐτὸν πολλὰ ἵνα
name, *my* for we are many." *we are* And he kept begging him earnestly not to
3950 1609 4022 1639 1639 4498 1639 2779 4151 899 4498 3590 2671
n.nsn r.ds.1 cj a.npm v.pai.1p cj v.iai.3s r.asm.3 a.apn cj

μὴ αὐτὰ ἀποστείλῃ ἔξω τῆς χώρας. 11 ἦν δὲ
not send them *send* ⌞out of⌟ the region. Now a large herd of pigs was *Now*
3590 690 899 690 2032 3836 6001 1254 3489 36 5956 5956 1639 1254
pl r.apn.3 v.aas.3s p.g d.gsf n.gsf v.iai.3s cj

ἐκεῖ πρὸς τῷ ὄρει ἀγέλη χοίρων μεγάλη βοσκομένη· 12 καὶ
feeding there on the mountainside. *herd* *of pigs* *large* *feeding* And the unclean
1081 1695 4639 3836 4001 36 5956 3489 1081 2779
adv p.d d.dsn n.dsn n.nsf n.gpm a.nsf pt.pp.nsf cj

παρεκάλεσαν αὐτὸν λέγοντες· πέμψον ἡμᾶς εἰς τοὺς χοίρους, ἵνα εἰς
spirits begged him, saying, "Send us to the pigs so *{into}* we can
4151 899 3306 4287 7005 1650 3836 5956 2671 1650 1656 1656
v.aai.3p r.asm.3 pt.pa.npm v.aam.2s r.ap.1 p.a d.apm n.apm cj p.a

αὐτοὺς εἰσέλθωμεν. 13 καὶ ἐπέτρεψεν αὐτοῖς. ← καὶ
enter them." *we can enter* So he gave them permission. Then the unclean spirits
1656 899 1656 2779 2205 899 2205 2779 3836 176 4460
r.apm.3 v.aas.1p cj v.aai.3s r.dpn.3 cj

ἐξελθόντα τὰ πνεύματα τὰ ἀκάθαρτα ⌞εἰσῆλθον εἰς⌟ τοὺς χοίρους, καὶ
came out *the* *spirits* *{the}* *unclean* and entered the pigs. *{and}* The
2002 3836 4460 3836 176 1656 1650 3836 5956 2779 3836
pt.aa.npn d.npn n.npn d.npn a.npn v.aai.3p p.a d.apm n.apm cj

ὥρμησεν ἡ ἀγέλη κατὰ τοῦ κρημνοῦ εἰς τὴν
herd (about two thousand strong) rushed *The* *herd* down the steep bank into the
36 6055 1493 1493 3994 3836 36 2848 3836 3204 1650 3836
v.aai.3s d.nsf n.nsf p.g d.gsm n.gsm p.a d.asf

θάλασσαν, ὡς δισχίλιοι, καὶ ⌞ἐπνίγοντο ἐν τῇ θαλάσσῃ.⌟ 14 καὶ οἱ
sea *about* *two thousand* and was drowned. *{and}* Those
2498 6055 1493 2779 4464 1877 3836 2498 2779 3836
n.asf pl a.npm cj v.ipi.3p p.d d.dsf n.dsf cj d.npm

βόσκοντες αὐτοὺς ἔφυγον καὶ ἀπήγγειλαν εἰς τὴν πόλιν καὶ εἰς τοὺς
tending the pigs fled and reported it in the village and throughout the
1081 899 5771 2779 550 1650 3836 4484 2779 1650 3836
pt.pa.npm r.apm.3 v.aai.3p cj v.aai.3p p.a d.asf n.asf cj p.a d.apm

ἀγρούς· καὶ ἦλθον ἰδεῖν τί ἐστιν τὸ γεγονὸς 15 καὶ ἔρχονται πρὸς τὸν
countryside, and people came to see what had *{the}* happened. *{and}* They came to *{the}*
69 2779 2262 1625 5515 1639 3836 1181 2779 2262 4639 3836
n.apm cj v.aai.3p f.aa r.nsn v.pai.3s d.nsn pt.ra.nsn cj v.pmi.3p p.a d.asm

Ἰησοῦν καὶ θεωροῦσιν τὸν δαιμονιζόμενον
Jesus and saw the ⌞demon-possessed man,⌟ the one who had the legion,
2652 2779 2555 3836 1227 3836 2400 2400 2400 3836 3305
n.asm cj v.pai.3p d.asm pt.pp.asm

καθήμενον ἱματισμένον καὶ σωφρονοῦντα, τὸν ἐσχηκότα τὸν λεγιῶνα, καὶ
sitting, clothed and in his right mind, *the* *one who had* *the* *legion* and
2764 2667 2779 5404 3836 2400 3836 3305 2779
pt.pp.asm pt.rp.asm cj pt.pa.asm d.asm pt.ra.asm d.asm n.asm cj

ἐφοβήθησαν. 16 καὶ διηγήσαντο αὐτοῖς οἱ ἰδόντες πῶς
they were afraid. And those who had seen it described to them *those* *who had seen* what
5828 2779 3836 1625 1625 1625 1455 899 3836 1625 4802
v.api.3p cj v.ami.3p r.dpm.3 d.npm pt.aa.npm cj

ἐγένετο τῷ δαιμονιζομένῳ καὶ περὶ τῶν χοίρων. 17 καὶ ἤρξαντο
had happened ⌞to the⌟ ⌞demon-possessed man,⌟ and all about the pigs. Then they began
1181 3836 1227 2779 4309 3836 5956 2779 806
v.ami.3s d.dsm pt.pp.dsm cj p.g d.gpm n.gpm cj v.ami.3p

NASB

to him, "Come out
of the man, you
unclean spirit!"
9 And He was ask-
ing him, "What
is your name?"
And he *said to
Him, "My name is
Legion; for we are
many." 10 And he
began to implore
Him earnestly not
to send them out of
the country. 11 Now
there was a large
herd of swine feed-
ing nearby on the
mountain. 12 *The*
demons implored
Him, saying, "Send
us into the swine so
that we may enter
them." 13 Jesus gave
them permission.
And coming out,
the unclean spirits
entered the swine;
and the herd rushed
down the steep
bank into the sea,
about two thousand
of them; and they
were drowned in
the sea.
14 Their herdsmen
ran away and re-
ported it in the city
and in the country.
And *the people*
came to see what
it was that had
happened. 15 They
*came to Jesus and
*observed the man
who had been de-
mon-possessed sit-
ting down, clothed
and in his right
mind, the very man
who had had the
"legion"; and they
became frightened.
16 Those who had
seen it described
to them how it had
happened to the
demon-possessed
man, and *all* about
the swine. 17 And

NIV

to plead with Jesus
to leave their re-
gion.
[18] As Jesus was
getting into the
boat, the man who
had been demon-
possessed begged
to go with him.
[19] Jesus did not let
him, but said, "Go
home to your own
people and tell
them how much
the Lord has done
for you, and how
he has had mercy
on you." [20] So the
man went away
and began to tell
in the Decapolis[a]
how much Jesus
had done for him.
And all the people
were amazed.

Jesus Raises a Dead Girl and Heals a Sick Woman

[21] When Jesus
had again crossed
over by boat to
the other side of
the lake, a large
crowd gathered
around him while
he was by the lake.
[22] Then one of the
synagogue lead-
ers, named Jairus,
came, and when he
saw Jesus, he fell
at his feet. [23] He
pleaded earnestly
with him, "My lit-
tle daughter is dy-
ing. Please come
and put your hands
on her so that she
will be healed and
live." [24] So Jesus
went with him.
A large crowd
followed and
pressed around
him. [25] And a wom-
an was there who
had been subject to
bleeding for twelve
years. [26] She had
suffered a great
deal under the care
of many doctors
and had spent

[a] 20 That is, the Ten Cities

παρακαλεῖν αὐτὸν ἀπελθεῖν ἀπὸ τῶν ὁρίων αὐτῶν. [18] καὶ → ἐμβαίνοντος
to implore Jesus to depart from {the} their region. their {and} As he was getting
4151 899 599 608 3836 899 3990 899 2779 899 1832
f.pa r.asm.3 f.aa p.g d.gpn n.gpn r.gpm.3 cj pt.pa.gsm

αὐτοῦ εἰς τὸ πλοῖον παρεκάλει αὐτὸν ὁ
he into the boat, the man who had been demon-possessed kept begging him the
899 1650 3836 4450 3836 1227 1227 1227 1227 1227 4151 899 3836
r.gsm.3 p.a d.asn n.asn v.iai.3s r.asm.3 d.nsm

δαιμονισθεὶς ἵνα μετ᾽ αὐτοῦ ᾖ. [19] καὶ ↱ ↱ οὐκ ἀφῆκεν
man who had been demon-possessed to go with him. go But he did not permit
1227 2671 1639 3552 899 1639 2779 918 918 4024 918
pt.ap.nsm cj p.g r.gsm.3 v.pas.3s cj pl v.aai.3s

αὐτόν, ἀλλὰ λέγει αὐτῷ· ὕπαγε εἰς τὸν οἶκόν σου πρὸς τοὺς σούς
him. Instead, he said to him, "Go to {the} your home, your to {the} your own people,
899 247 3306 899 5632 1650 3836 5148 3875 5148 4639 3836 5050
r.asm.3 cj v.pai.3s r.dsm.3 v.pam.2s p.a d.asm n.asm r.gs.2 p.a d.apm r.apm.2

καὶ ἀπάγγειλον αὐτοῖς ὅσα ὁ κύριός σοι πεποίηκεν καὶ
and tell them ⌊how much⌋ the Lord has done ⌊for you⌋ has done and that
2779 550 899 4012 3836 3261 4472 4472 5148 4472 2779
cj v.aam.2s r.dpm.3 r.apn d.nsm n.nsm r.ds.2 v.rai.3s cj

ἠλέησέν σε. [20] καὶ ἀπῆλθεν καὶ ἤρξατο κηρύσσειν ἐν τῇ
⌊he had mercy on⌋ you. {and} The man left and began to proclaim in the
1796 5148 2779 599 2779 806 3062 1877 3836
v.aai.3s r.as.2 cj v.aai.3s cj v.ami.3s f.pa p.d d.dsf

Δεκαπόλει ὅσα ἐποίησεν αὐτῷ ὁ Ἰησοῦς, καὶ πάντες ἐθαύμαζον.
Decapolis ⌊how much⌋ Jesus had done for him; {the} Jesus and everyone was amazed.
1279 4012 2652 4472 899 3836 2652 2779 4246 2513
n.dsf r.apn v.aai.3s r.dsm.3 d.nsm n.nsm cj a.npm v.iai.3p

[21] καὶ → διαπεράσαντος τοῦ Ἰησοῦ [a]ἐν τῷ πλοίῳ πάλιν εἰς τὸ πέραν
{and} When Jesus had crossed {the} Jesus in a boat again to the other side,
2779 2652 1385 3836 2652 1877 3836 4450 4099 1650 3836 4305
cj pt.aa.gsm d.gsm n.gsm p.d d.dsn n.dsn adv p.a d.asn adv

συνήχθη ὄχλος πολὺς ἐπ᾽ αὐτόν, καὶ ἦν παρὰ τὴν θάλασσαν.
a large crowd gathered crowd large around him, and ⌊he was⌋ by the lake.
4498 4063 5251 4063 4498 2093 899 2779 1639 4123 3836 2498
v.api.3s n.nsm a.nsm p.a r.asm.3 cj v.iai.3s p.a d.asf n.asf

[22] καὶ ἔρχεται εἷς τῶν ἀρχισυναγώγων, ὀνόματι Ἰάϊρος, καὶ
Then came one of the synagogue officials, Jairus by name, Jairus came there. {and}
2779 2262 1651 3836 801 2608 3950 2608 2262 2779
cj v.pmi.3s a.nsm d.gpm n.gpm n.dsn n.nsm cj

ἰδὼν αὐτὸν πίπτει πρὸς τοὺς πόδας αὐτοῦ [23] καὶ παρακαλεῖ αὐτὸν
⌊When he saw⌋ Jesus, he fell at {the} his feet his and begged him
1625 899 4406 4639 3836 899 4546 899 2779 4151 899
pt.aa.nsm r.asm.3 v.pai.3s p.a d.apm n.apm r.gsm.3 cj v.pai.3s r.asm.3

πολλὰ λέγων ὅτι τὸ θυγάτριόν μου ἐσχάτως ἔχει, ἵνα ἐλθὼν
earnestly, saying, ~ {the} "My little daughter My is about to die. is about ~ Come
4498 3306 4022 3836 1609 2589 1609 2400 2400 2275 2400 2671 2262
a.apn pt.pa.nsm cj d.nsn n.nsn r.gs.1 adv v.pai.3s cj pt.aa.nsm

ἐπιθῇς τὰς χεῖρας αὐτῇ ἵνα σωθῇ καὶ ζήσῃ. [24] καὶ ἀπῆλθεν μετ᾽
and place your hands on her so ⌊she will be healed⌋ and live." So Jesus went with
2202 3836 5931 899 2671 5392 2779 2409 2779 599 3552
v.aas.2s d.apf n.apf r.dsf.3 cj v.aps.3s cj v.aas.3s cj v.aai.3s p.g

αὐτοῦ. καὶ ἠκολούθει αὐτῷ ὄχλος πολὺς καὶ συνέθλιβον αὐτόν.
him. {and} A large crowd was following him crowd large and crowding around him.
899 2779 4498 4063 199 899 4063 4498 2779 5315 899
r.gsm.3 cj v.iai.3s r.dsm.3 n.nsm a.nsm cj v.iai.3p r.asm.3

[25] καὶ γυνὴ οὖσα ἐν ῥύσει αἵματος δώδεκα ἔτη [26] καὶ
And a woman was there who had had a discharge of blood for twelve years. {and} She had
2779 1222 1639 1877 4868 135 1557 2291 2779 4248 4248
cj n.nsf pt.pa.nsf p.d n.dsf n.gsn a.apn n.apn cj

πολλὰ παθοῦσα ὑπὸ πολλῶν ἰατρῶν καὶ δαπανήσασα τὰ
suffered a great deal She had suffered under the care of many doctors, and had spent {the}
4248 4498 4248 5679 4498 2620 2779 1251 3836
a.apn pt.aa.nsf p.g a.gpm n.gpm cj pt.aa.nsf d.apn

[a] [ἐν τῷ πλοίῳ] UBS.

NASB

they began to im-
plore Him to leave
their region. [18] As
He was getting into
the boat, the man
who had been de-
mon-possessed was
imploring Him that
he might accompa-
ny Him. [19] And He
did not let him, but
He *said to him,
"Go home to your
people and report
to them [a] what great
things the Lord has
done for you, and
how He had mercy
on you." [20] And he
went away and
began to proclaim
in Decapolis what
great things Jesus
had done for him;
and everyone was
amazed.

Miracles and Healing

[21] When Jesus had
crossed over again
in the boat to the
other side, a large
crowd gathered
around Him; and
so He stayed by the
seashore. [22] One of
the synagogue offi-
cials named Jairus
*came up, and on
seeing Him, *fell
at His feet [23] and
*implored Him ear-
nestly, saying, "My
little daughter is at
the point of death;
please come and
lay Your hands on
her, so that she will
get well and live."
[24] And He went off
with him; and a
large crowd was
following Him and
pressing in on Him.
[25] A woman who
had had a hemor-
rhage for twelve
years, [26] and had
endured much at
the hands of many
physicians, and had
spent all that she

[a] Or *everything that*

NIV

all she had, yet
instead of getting
better she grew
worse. 27 When
she heard about
Jesus, she came up
behind him in the
crowd and touched
his cloak, 28 be-
cause she thought,
"If I just touch his
clothes, I will be
healed." 29 Immedi-
ately her bleeding
stopped and she
felt in her body
that she was freed
from her suffering.
30 At once Jesus
realized that power
had gone out from
him. He turned
around in the
crowd and asked,
"Who touched my
clothes?"
31 "You see the
people crowd-
ing against you,"
his disciples an-
swered, "and yet
you can ask, 'Who
touched me?' "
32 But Jesus kept
looking around
to see who had
done it. 33 Then the
woman, knowing
what had hap-
pened to her, came
and fell at his feet
and, trembling
with fear, told him
the whole truth.
34 He said to her,
"Daughter, your
faith has healed
you. Go in peace
and be freed from
your suffering."
35 While Jesus
was still speaking,
some people came
from the house of
Jairus, the syn-
agogue leader.
"Your daughter is
dead,"

παρ᾽ αὐτῆς πάντα καὶ μηδὲν ὠφεληθεῖσα ἀλλὰ
all she had, *{her}* *all* yet it benefitted her nothing; *it benefitted her* rather she had
4246 4123 899 4246 2779 6067 6067 6067 3594 6067 247 2262 2262
p.g r.gsf.3 a.apn cj a.asn pt.ap.nsf cj

⌊μᾶλλον εἰς τὸ χεῖρον⌋ ἐλθοῦσα, 27 ἀκούσασα περὶ τοῦ Ἰησοῦ,
grown worse. *she had grown* When she heard about *{the}* Jesus,
2262 3437 1650 3836 5937 2262 201 4309 3836 2652
adv.c p.a d.asn a.asn.c pt.aa.nsf pt.aa.nsf p.g d.gsm n.gsm

ἐλθοῦσα ἐν τῷ ὄχλῳ ὄπισθεν ἥψατο τοῦ ἱματίου αὐτοῦ·
⌊she came up⌋ behind him in the crowd *behind* and touched *{the}* his cloak, *his*
2262 3957 1877 3836 4063 3957 721 3836 899 2668 899
pt.aa.nsf p.d d.dsm n.dsm adv v.ami.3s d.gsn n.gsn r.gsm.3

28 ἔλεγεν γὰρ ὅτι ἐὰν → → ἅψωμαι κἂν τῶν ἱματίων αὐτοῦ
for ⌊she had been saying,⌋ *for* ~ "If I can only touch *only* *{the}* his clothes, *his*
1142 3306 1142 4022 1569 2829 721 2829 3836 899 2668 899
v.iai.3s cj cj cj v.ams.1s crasis d.gpn n.gpn r.gsm.3

σωθήσομαι. 29 καὶ εὐθὺς ἐξηράνθη ἡ πηγὴ τοῦ
I will be healed." *{and}* Immediately the flow of her blood ⌊was dried up,⌋ *the* *flow* *of*
5392 2779 2318 3836 4380 3836 899 135 3830 3836 4380 3836
v.fpi.1s cj adv v.api.3s d.nsf n.nsf d.gsn

αἵματος αὐτῆς καὶ ἔγνω τῷ σώματι ὅτι ἴαται ἀπὸ τῆς μάστιγος.
blood *her* and she knew ⌊in her⌋ body that ⌊she was healed⌋ of the affliction.
135 899 2779 1182 3836 5393 4022 2615 608 3836 3465
n.gsn r.gsf.3 cj v.aai.3s d.dsn n.dsn cj v.rpi.3s p.g d.gsf n.gsf

30 καὶ εὐθὺς ὁ Ἰησοῦς ἐπιγνοὺς ἐν ἑαυτῷ τὴν ἐξ
And *immediately* *{the}* Jesus, knowing in himself that *{the}* power had gone out from
2779 2318 3836 2652 2105 1877 1571 3836 1539 2002 2002 2002 1666
cj adv d.nsm n.nsm pt.aa.nsm p.d r.dsm.3 d.asf p.g

αὐτοῦ δύναμιν ἐξελθοῦσαν ἐπιστραφεὶς ἐν τῷ ὄχλῳ ἔλεγεν· τίς
him, immediately *power* *had gone out* turned around in the crowd and said, "Who
899 2318 1539 2002 2188 1877 3836 4063 3306 5515
r.gsm.3 n.asf pt.aa.asf pt.ap.nsm p.d d.dsm n.dsm v.iai.3s r.nsm

μου ἥψατο τῶν ἱματίων; 31 καὶ ἔλεγον αὐτῷ οἱ
touched my clothes?" *touched* *{the}* *clothes* And his disciples said to him, *{the}*
721 1609 2668 721 3836 2668 2779 899 3412 3306 899 3836
r.gs.1 v.ami.3s d.gpn n.gpn cj v.iai.3p r.dsm.3 d.npm

μαθηταὶ αὐτοῦ· βλέπεις τὸν ὄχλον συνθλίβοντά σε καὶ λέγεις· τίς μου
disciples *his* "You see the crowd pressing around you and yet you say, "Who touched me?"
3412 899 1063 3836 4063 5315 5148 2779 3306 5515 721 1609
n.npm r.gsm.3 v.pai.2s d.asm n.asm pt.pa.asm r.as.2 cj v.pai.2s r.nsm r.gs.1

ἥψατο; 32 καὶ περιεβλέπετο ἰδεῖν τὴν τοῦτο ποιήσασαν. 33 ἡ δὲ
touched But he looked around to see the *this* one who had done this. Then the *Then*
721 2779 4315 1625 3836 4047 4472 4047 1254 3836 1254
v.ami.3s cj v.imi.3s f.aa d.asf r.asn pt.aa.asf d.nsf cj

γυνὴ φοβηθεῖσα καὶ τρέμουσα, εἰδυῖα ὃ γέγονεν αὐτῇ, ἦλθεν καὶ
woman, with fear and trembling, knowing what had happened to her, came and
1222 5828 2779 5554 3857 4005 1181 899 2262 2779
n.nsf pt.ap.nsf cj pt.pa.nsf pt.ra.nsf r.nsn v.rai.3s r.dsf.3 v.aai.3s cj

προσέπεσεν αὐτῷ καὶ εἶπεν αὐτῷ πᾶσαν τὴν ἀλήθειαν. 34 ὁ δὲ εἶπεν
fell down before him and told him the whole *the* truth. And he *And* said
4700 899 2779 3306 899 3836 4246 3836 237 1254 3836 1254 3306
v.aai.3s r.dsm.3 cj v.aai.3s r.dsm.3 a.asf d.asf n.asf d.nsm cj v.aai.3s

αὐτῇ· θυγάτηρ, ἡ πίστις σου → → σέσωκέν σε· ὕπαγε εἰς εἰρήνην καὶ
to her, "Daughter, *{the}* your faith *your* has made you well. *you* Go in peace and
899 2588 3836 5148 4411 5148 5148 5392 5148 5632 1650 1645 2779
r.dsf.3 n.vsf d.nsf n.nsf r.gs.2 v.rai.3s r.as.2 v.pam.2s p.a n.asf cj

ἴσθι ὑγιὴς ἀπὸ τῆς μάστιγός σου. 35 ↱ ↱ ἔτι αὐτοῦ λαλοῦντος
be healed of *{the}* your affliction." *your* While he was still *he* speaking, people
1639 5618 608 3836 5148 3465 5148 3281 899 3281 2285 899 3281
v.pam.2s a.nsf p.g d.gsf n.gsf r.gs.2 adv r.gsm.3 pt.pa.gsm

ἔρχονται ἀπὸ τοῦ ἀρχισυναγώγου λέγοντες ὅτι ἡ θυγάτηρ σου ἀπέθανεν·
came from the synagogue official, saying, ~ *{the}* "Your daughter *Your* has died.
2262 608 3836 801 3306 4022 3836 5148 2588 5148 633
v.pmi.3p p.g d.gsm n.gsm pt.pa.npm cj d.nsf n.nsf r.gs.2 v.aai.3s

NASB

had and was not
helped at all, but
rather had grown
worse— 27 after
hearing about
Jesus, she came
up in the crowd
behind *Him* and
touched His cloak.
28 For she thought,
"If I just touch His
garments, I will get
well." 29 Immediate-
ly the flow of her
blood was dried
up; and she felt in
her body that she
was healed of her
affliction. 30 Imme-
diately Jesus, per-
ceiving in Himself
that the power *pro-*
ceeding from Him
had gone forth,
turned around in
the crowd and said,
"Who touched My
garments?" 31 And
His disciples said
to Him, "You see
the crowd press-
ing in on You, and
You say, 'Who
touched Me?' "
32 And He looked
around to see the
woman who had
done this. 33 But the
woman fearing and
trembling, aware of
what had happened
to her, came and
fell down before
Him and told Him
the whole truth.
34 And He said to
her, "Daughter,
your faith has
made you well; go
in peace and be
healed of your af-
fliction."
35 While He was
still speaking,
they *came from
the *house of* the
synagogue official,
saying, "Your
daughter has died;
why

NIV

they said. "Why
bother the teacher
anymore?"
36 Overhearing[a]
what they said,
Jesus told him,
"Don't be afraid;
just believe."
37 He did not let
anyone follow
him except Peter,
James and John the
brother of James.
38 When they came
to the home of the
synagogue lead-
er, Jesus saw a
commotion, with
people crying
and wailing loud-
ly. 39 He went in
and said to them,
"Why all this
commotion and
wailing? The child
is not dead but
asleep." 40 But they
laughed at him.
After he put them
all out, he took the
child's father and
mother and the
disciples who were
with him, and went
in where the child
was. 41 He took her
by the hand and
said to her, *"Tali-
tha koum!"* (which
means "Little girl,
I say to you, get
up!"). 42 Immedi-
ately the girl stood
up and began to
walk around (she
was twelve years
old). At this they
were completely
astonished. 43 He
gave strict orders
not to let anyone
know about this,
and told them to
give her something
to eat.

τί ἔτι σκύλλεις τὸν διδάσκαλον; 36 ὁ δὲ Ἰησοῦς παρακούσας
Why *any longer* trouble the teacher any longer?" *{the}* But Jesus, ignoring
5515 2285 5035 3836 1437 2285 2285 3836 1254 2652 4159
r.asn adv v.pai.2s d.asm n.asm d.nsm cj n.nsm pt.aa.nsm

τὸν λόγον λαλούμενον λέγει τῷ ἀρχισυναγώγῳ· ↱ μὴ φοβοῦ, μόνον πίστευε.
{the} what was said, said ⌞to the⌟ synagogue official, "Do not be afraid; only believe."
3836 3364 3281 3306 3836 801 5828 3590 5828 3667 4409
d.asm n.asm pt.pp.asm v.pai.3s d.dsm n.dsm pl v.ppm.2s adv v.pam.2s

37 καὶ ↱ ↱ οὐκ ἀφῆκεν οὐδένα μετ᾽ αὐτοῦ συνακολουθῆσαι ⌞εἰ μὴ⌟
And he did not permit anyone to follow *{after}* him, *to follow* except
2779 918 918 4024 918 4029 5258 5258 3552 899 5258 1623 3590
cj pl v.aai.3s a.asm p.g r.gsm.3 f.aa cj pl

τὸν Πέτρον καὶ Ἰάκωβον καὶ Ἰωάννην τὸν ἀδελφὸν Ἰακώβου. 38 καὶ ἔρχονται
{the} Peter, *{and}* James, and John the brother of James. *{and}* They came
3836 4377 2779 2610 2779 2722 3836 81 2610 2779 2262
d.asm n.asm cj n.asm cj n.asm d.asm n.asm n.gsm cj v.pmi.3p

εἰς τὸν οἶκον τοῦ ἀρχισυναγώγου, καὶ θεωρεῖ θόρυβον καὶ
to the house of the synagogue official, and Jesus saw a commotion *{and}* with people
1650 3836 3875 3836 801 2779 2555 2573 2779
p.a d.asm n.asm d.gsm n.gsm cj v.pai.3s n.asm cj

κλαίοντας καὶ ἀλαλάζοντας πολλά, 39 καὶ εἰσελθὼν λέγει αὐτοῖς· τί
weeping and wailing loudly. *{and}* Upon entering he said to them, "Why
3081 2779 226 4498 2779 1656 3306 899 5515
pt.pa.apm cj pt.pa.apm a.apn cj pt.aa.nsm v.pai.3s r.dpm.3 r.asn

θορυβεῖσθε καὶ κλαίετε; τὸ παιδίον ↱ οὐκ ἀπέθανεν ἀλλὰ
⌞are you making such a commotion⌟ and weeping? The child has not died, but
2572 2779 3081 3836 4086 633 4024 633 247
v.ppi.2p cj v.pai.2p d.nsn n.nsn pl v.aai.3s cj

καθεύδει. 40 καὶ κατεγέλων αὐτοῦ. ↱ αὐτὸς δὲ ἐκβαλὼν
is sleeping. And ⌞they began to ridicule⌟ him. But when he *But* had put them
2761 2779 2860 899 1254 1675 899 1254 1675
v.pai.3s cj v.iai.3p r.gsm.3 r.nsm cj pt.aa.nsm

πάντας ↰ παραλαμβάνει τὸν πατέρα τοῦ παιδίου καὶ τὴν μητέρα καὶ τοὺς
all out, he took the father of the child and her mother and those who
4246 1675 4161 3836 4252 3836 4086 2779 3836 3613 2779 3836
a.apm v.pai.3s d.asm n.asm d.gsn n.gsn cj d.asf n.asf cj d.apm

μετ᾽ αὐτοῦ καὶ εἰσπορεύεται ὅπου ἦν τὸ παιδίον. 41 καὶ
were with him and went in where the child was. *the child* And
3552 899 2779 1660 3963 3836 4086 1639 3836 4086 2779
p.g r.gsm.3 cj v.pmi.3s cj v.iai.3s d.nsn n.nsn cj

κρατήσας τῆς χειρὸς τοῦ παιδίου λέγει αὐτῇ· ταλιθα κουμ, ὅ ἐστιν
⌞taking hold of⌟ the child's hand *{the} child's* he said to her, "Talitha koum!" which is
3195 3836 4086 5931 3836 4086 3306 899 5420 3182 4005 1639
pt.aa.nsm d.gsf n.gsf d.gsn n.gsn v.pai.3s r.dsf.3 j j r.nsn v.pai.3s

μεθερμηνευόμενον· τὸ κοράσιον, σοὶ λέγω, ἔγειρε. 42 καὶ
translated, *{the}* "Little girl, I say to you, *I say* arise." And the little girl got
3493 3836 3166 3306 3306 5148 3306 1586 2779 3836 3166 3166 482
pt.pp.nsn d.vsn n.vsn r.ds.2 v.pai.1s v.pam.2s cj

εὐθὺς ἀνέστη τὸ κοράσιον καὶ περιεπάτει· ἦν γὰρ ἐτῶν
up at once *got up* *the* *little girl* and began to walk; for ⌞she was⌟ *for* twelve ⌞years old.⌟
482 2318 482 3836 3166 2779 4344 1142 1639 1142 1557 2291
adv v.aai.3s d.nsn n.nsn cj v.iai.3s v.iai.3s cj n.gpn

δώδεκα. καὶ → → ἐξέστησαν εὐθὺς[a] ἐκστάσει μεγάλῃ.
twelve And immediately they were utterly amazed. *immediately* *{amazement}* *utterly*
1557 2779 2318 3489 2014 2318 1749 3489
a.gpn cj v.aai.3p adv n.dsf a.dsf

43 καὶ διεστείλατο αὐτοῖς πολλὰ ἵνα μηδεὶς γνοῖ τοῦτο, καὶ
And Jesus strictly ordered them *strictly* that no one ⌞should know about⌟ this, and
2779 4498 1403 899 4498 2671 3594 1182 4047 2779
cj v.ami.3s r.dpm.3 a.apn cj a.nsm v.aas.3s r.asn cj

εἶπεν δοθῆναι αὐτῇ φαγεῖν.
he told them that something to eat ⌞should be given⌟ to her. *to eat*
3306 2266 2266 1443 899 2266
v.aai.3s f.ap r.dsf.3 f.aa

NASB

trouble the Teacher
anymore?" 36 But
Jesus, overhearing
what was being
spoken, *said to the
synagogue official,
"Do not be afraid
any longer, only
believe." 37 And
He allowed no
one to accompany
Him, except Peter
and James and
John the brother
of James. 38 They
*came to the house
of the synagogue
official; and He
*saw a commotion,
and *people* loudly
weeping and wail-
ing. 39 And entering
in, He *said to
them, "Why make
a commotion and
weep? The child
has not died, but
is asleep." 40 They
began laughing at
Him. But putting
them all out, He
*took along the
child's father and
mother and His
own companions,
and *entered *the
room* where the
child was. 41 Taking
the child by the
hand, He *said to
her, "Talitha kum!"
(which translated
means, "Little girl,
I say to you, get
up!"). 42 Immedi-
ately the girl got up
and *began* to walk,
for she was twelve
years old. And
immediately they
were completely
astounded. 43 And
He gave them strict
orders that no one
should know about
this, and He said
that *something*
should be given her
to eat.

[a] 36 Or *Ignoring*

[a] [εὐθὺς] UBS.

NIV

A Prophet Without Honor

6 Jesus left there and went to his hometown, accompanied by his disciples. [2]When the Sabbath came, he began to teach in the synagogue, and many who heard him were amazed.

"Where did this man get these things?" they asked. "What's this wisdom that has been given him? What are these remarkable miracles he is performing? [3]Isn't this the carpenter? Isn't this Mary's son and the brother of James, Joseph,[a] Judas and Simon? Aren't his sisters here with us?" And they took offense at him.

[4]Jesus said to them, "A prophet is not without honor except in his own town, among his relatives and in his own home." [5]He could not do any miracles there, except lay his hands on a few sick people and heal them. [6]He was amazed at their lack of faith.

Jesus Sends Out the Twelve

Then Jesus went around teaching from village to village. [7]Calling the Twelve to him, he began to send them out two by two and gave them authority over impure spirits.

[a] 3 Greek *Joses*, a variant of *Joseph*

Interlinear

6:1 καὶ ἐξῆλθεν ἐκεῖθεν καὶ ἔρχεται εἰς τὴν πατρίδα αὐτοῦ, καὶ
And Jesus left from there and went to {the} his hometown, *his* and his
2779 2002 1696 2779 2262 1650 3836 899 4258 899 2779 899
cj v.aai.3s adv cj v.pmi.3s p.a d.asf n.asf r.gsm.3 cj

ἀκολουθοῦσιν αὐτῷ οἱ μαθηταὶ αὐτοῦ. 2 καὶ → γενομένου
disciples followed him. {the} *disciples* *his* And when the Sabbath came,
3412 199 899 3836 3412 899 2779 4879 1181
v.pai.3p r.dsm.3 d.npm n.npm r.gsm.3 cj pt.am.gsn

σαββάτου ἤρξατο διδάσκειν ἐν τῇ συναγωγῇ, καὶ πολλοὶ ἀκούοντες
Sabbath he began to teach in the synagogue. And many, when they heard him,
4879 806 1438 1877 3836 5252 2779 4498 201
n.gsn v.ami.3s f.pa p.d d.dsf n.dsf cj a.npm pt.pa.npm

ἐξεπλήσσοντο λέγοντες· πόθεν τούτῳ ταῦτα, καὶ τίς ἡ σοφία ἡ
were astonished, saying, "Where does this man get these things? {and} What {the} wisdom {the}
1742 3306 4470 4047 4047 2779 5515 3836 5053 3836
v.ipi.3p pt.pa.npm cj r.dsm r.npn cj r.nsf d.nsf n.nsf d.nsf

δοθεῖσα τούτῳ, καὶ αἱ δυνάμεις τοιαῦται διὰ τῶν
⌞has been given⌟ to him? {also} How are such {the} mighty works *such* done through {the} his
1443 4047 2779 1181 5525 3836 1539 5525 1181 1328 3836 899
pt.ap.nsf r.dsm adv d.npf n.npf r.npf p.g d.gpf

χειρῶν αὐτοῦ γινόμεναι; 3 οὐχ οὗτός ἐστιν ὁ τέκτων, ὁ υἱὸς τῆς
hands?" *his* *are done* Is this man not *this man* *Is* the carpenter, the son of
5931 899 1181 1639 4047 4047 4024 4047 1639 3836 5454 3836 5626 3836
n.gpf r.gsm.3 pt.pm.npf pl r.nsm v.pai.3s d.nsm n.nsm d.nsm n.nsm d.gsf

Μαρίας καὶ ἀδελφὸς Ἰακώβου καὶ Ἰωσῆτος καὶ Ἰούδα καὶ Σίμωνος; καὶ
Mary and the brother of James, {and} Joses, {and} Judas, and Simon? And are
3451 2779 81 2610 2779 2736 2779 2683 2779 4981 2779 1639
n.gsf cj n.nsm n.gsm cj n.gsm cj n.gsm cj n.gsm cj

οὐκ εἰσὶν αἱ ἀδελφαὶ αὐτοῦ ὧδε πρὸς ἡμᾶς; καὶ ἐσκανδαλίζοντο ἐν
not *are* {the} his sisters *his* here with us?" And they were deeply offended at
4024 1639 3836 899 80 899 6045 4639 7005 2779 4997 1877
pl v.pai.3p d.npf n.npf r.gsm.3 adv p.a r.ap.1 cj v.ipi.3p p.d

αὐτῷ. 4 καὶ ἔλεγεν αὐτοῖς ὁ Ἰησοῦς ὅτι οὐκ ἔστιν προφήτης
him. And Jesus said to them, {the} *Jesus* ~ "A prophet is not *is* *prophet*
899 2779 2652 3306 899 3836 2652 4022 4737 1639 4024 1639 4737
r.dsm.3 cj v.iai.3s r.dpm.3 d.nsm n.nsm cj pl v.pai.3s n.nsm

ἄτιμος ⌞εἰ μὴ⌟ ἐν τῇ πατρίδι αὐτοῦ καὶ ἐν τοῖς συγγενεῦσιν
⌞without honor⌟ except in {the} his hometown, *his* and among {the} his relatives,
872 1623 3590 1877 3836 899 4258 899 2779 1877 3836 899 5150
a.nsm cj pl p.d d.dsf n.dsf r.gsm.3 cj p.d d.dpm n.dpm

αὐτοῦ καὶ ἐν τῇ οἰκίᾳ αὐτοῦ. 5 καὶ ↱ ↱ οὐκ ἐδύνατο ἐκεῖ
his and in {the} his own household." *his* And he was not able *there*
899 2779 1877 3836 899 3864 899 2779 1538 1538 4024 1538 1695
r.gsm.3 cj p.d d.dsf n.dsf r.gsm.3 cj pl v.ipi.3s adv

ποιῆσαι οὐδεμίαν δύναμιν, ⌞εἰ μὴ⌟ ↱ ὀλίγοις
to do any mighty work there, except that he laid his hands on a few
4472 4029 1539 1695 1623 3590 2543 2202 3836 5931 2202 3900
f.aa a.asf n.asf cj pl a.dpm

ἀρρώστοις ἐπιθεὶς τὰς χεῖρας ἐθεράπευσεν. 6 καὶ ἐθαύμαζεν διὰ τὴν
sick people *laid on* *his* *hands* and healed them. And he was amazed at {the} their
779 2202 3836 5931 2543 2779 2513 1328 3836 899
a.dpm pt.aa.nsm d.apf n.apf v.aai.3s cj v.iai.3s p.a d.asf

ἀπιστίαν αὐτῶν. καὶ περιῆγεν τὰς κώμας κύκλῳ διδάσκων. 7 καὶ
lack of faith. *their* And he went around among the villages *among* teaching. And
602 899 2779 4310 3241 3836 3267 3241 1438 2779
n.asf r.gpm.3 cj v.iai.3s d.apf n.apf adv pt.pa.nsm cj

προσκαλεῖται τοὺς δώδεκα καὶ ἤρξατο αὐτοὺς ἀποστέλλειν ← δύο δύο
he called to himself the twelve and began *them* to send them out two by two,
4673 3836 1557 2779 806 899 690 899 1545 1545
v.pmi.3s d.apm a.apm cj v.ami.3s r.apm.3 f.pa a.apm a.apm

καὶ ἐδίδου αὐτοῖς ἐξουσίαν τῶν πνευμάτων τῶν ἀκαθάρτων, 8 καὶ
and gave them authority ⌞over the⌟ unclean spirits. {the} *unclean* {and}
2779 1443 899 2026 3836 176 4460 3836 176 2779
cj v.iai.3s r.dpm.3 n.asf d.gpn n.gpn d.gpn a.gpn cj

NASB

Teaching at Nazareth

6:1 Jesus went out from there and *came into His hometown; and His disciples *followed Him. [2]When the Sabbath came, He began to teach in the synagogue; and the many listeners were astonished, saying, "Where did this man *get* these things, and what is *this* wisdom given to Him, and such miracles as these performed by His hands? [3]Is not this the carpenter, the son of Mary, and brother of James and Joses and Judas and Simon? Are not His sisters here with us?" And they took offense at Him. [4]Jesus said to them, "A prophet is not without honor except in his hometown and among his *own* relatives and in his *own* household." [5]And He could do no miracle there except that He laid His hands on a few sick people and healed them. [6]And He wondered at their unbelief.

And He was going around the villages teaching.

The Twelve Sent Out

[7]And He *summoned the twelve and began to send them out in pairs, and gave them authority over the unclean spirits; [8]and

NIV

8These were his
instructions: "Take
nothing for the
journey except a
staff—no bread,
no bag, no mon-
ey in your belts.
9Wear sandals but
not an extra shirt.
10Whenever you
enter a house, stay
there until you
leave that town.
11And if any place
will not welcome
you or listen to
you, leave that
place and shake
the dust off your
feet as a testimony
against them."
12They went out
and preached that
people should re-
pent. 13They drove
out many demons
and anointed many
sick people with
oil and healed
them.

John the Baptist Beheaded

14King Herod
heard about this,
for Jesus' name
had become well
known. Some were
saying,[a] "John the
Baptist has been
raised from the
dead, and that is
why miraculous
powers are at work
in him."
15Others said,
"He is Elijah."
And still others
claimed, "He is a
prophet, like one
of the prophets of
long ago."
16But when Herod
heard this, he said,
"John, whom I be-
headed,

παρήγγειλεν αὐτοῖς ἵνα μηδὲν αἴρωσιν εἰς ὁδὸν ⌊εἰ μὴ⌋ ῥάβδον
He instructed them to take nothing *take* for their journey except simply a staff
4133 899 2671 149 3594 149 1650 3847 1623 3590 3667 4811
v.aai.3s r.dpm.3 cj a.asn v.pas.3p p.a n.asf cj pl n.asf

μόνον, μὴ ἄρτον, μὴ πήραν, μὴ εἰς τὴν ζώνην χαλκόν, 9 ἀλλὰ
simply — no bread, no bag, no money in their belts *money* — but
3667 3590 788 3590 4385 3590 5910 1650 3836 2438 5910 247
adv pl n.asm pl n.asf pl p.a d.asf n.asf n.asm cj

ὑποδεδεμένους σανδάλια, καὶ ↱ μὴ ἐνδύσησθε δύο χιτῶνας. 10 καὶ
to wear sandals. Then he added, "Do not put on two tunics." And
5686 4908 2779 1907 3590 1907 1545 5945 2779
pt.rm.apm n.apn cj pl v.ams.2p a.apm n.apm cj

ἔλεγεν αὐτοῖς· ⌊ὅπου ἐὰν⌋ ⌊εἰσέλθητε εἰς⌋ οἰκίαν, ἐκεῖ μένετε ἕως ἂν
he said to them, "Whenever you enter a house, stay there *stay* until ~
3306 899 3963 1569 1656 1650 3864 3531 1695 3531 2401 323
v.iai.3s r.dpm.3 cj pl v.aas.2p p.a n.asf adv v.pam.2p cj pl

ἐξέλθητε ἐκεῖθεν. 11 καὶ ὃς ἂν τόπος ↰ ↱ μὴ δέξηται ὑμᾶς μηδὲ ἀκούσωσιν
you leave that area. And any ~ place that does not receive you or listen to
2002 1696 2779 4005 323 5536 4005 1312 3590 1312 7007 3593 201
v.aas.2p adv cj r.nsm pl n.nsm pl v.ams.3s r.ap.2 cj v.aas.3p

ὑμῶν, ἐκπορευόμενοι ἐκεῖθεν ἐκτινάξατε τὸν χοῦν τὸν ὑποκάτω τῶν ποδῶν
you, when you leave there, shake off the dust *{the}* from under *{the}* your feet
7007 1744 1696 1759 3836 5967 3836 5691 3836 7007 4546
r.gp.2 pt.pm.npm adv v.aam.2p d.asm n.asm d.asm p.g d.gpm n.gpm

ὑμῶν εἰς μαρτύριον αὐτοῖς.[a] 12 καὶ ἐξελθόντες ἐκήρυξαν ἵνα
your as a witness against them." So departing, they proclaimed that people
7007 1650 3457 899 2779 2002 3062 2671
r.gp.2 p.a n.asn r.dpm.3 cj pt.aa.npm v.aai.3p cj

μετανοῶσιν, 13 καὶ δαιμόνια πολλὰ ἐξέβαλλον, καὶ ↱ ἤλειφον
should repent, and they drove out many demons. *many* *they drove out* *{and}* They anointed
3566 2779 1675 1675 1675 4498 1228 4498 1675 2779 2543 230
v.pas.3p cj n.apn a.apn v.iai.3p cj v.iai.3p

ἐλαίῳ πολλοὺς ἀρρώστους καὶ ἐθεράπευον. 14 καὶ ἤκουσεν ὁ
with oil many who were sick and healed them. *{and}* King Herod heard about *{the}*
1778 4498 779 2779 2543 2779 995 2476 201 3836
n.dsn a.apm a.apm cj v.iai.3p cj v.aai.3s d.nsm

βασιλεὺς Ἡρῴδης, φανερὸν γὰρ ἐγένετο τὸ ὄνομα
King *Herod* this, for Jesus' name had become well known. *for* *had become* *{the}* *name*
995 2476 1142 899 3950 1181 1181 5745 1142 1181 3836 3950
n.nsm n.nsm a.nsn cj v.ami.3s d.nsn n.nsn

αὐτοῦ, καὶ ἔλεγον[b] ὅτι Ἰωάννης ὁ βαπτίζων ἐγήγερται ἐκ νεκρῶν
Jesus' *{and}* Some were saying, ~ "John the baptizer has been raised from the dead.
899 2779 3306 4022 2722 3836 966 1586 1666 3738
r.gsm.3 cj v.iai.3p cj n.nsm d.nsm pt.pa.nsm v.rpi.3s p.g a.gpm

καὶ διὰ τοῦτο ἐνεργοῦσιν αἱ δυνάμεις ἐν αὐτῷ.
{and} ⌊That is why⌋ *{this}* miraculous powers are at work *{the}* *miraculous powers* in him."
2779 1328 4047 1539 1539 1919 3836 1539 1877 899
cj p.a r.asn v.pai.3p d.npf n.npf p.d r.dsm.3

15 ἄλλοι δὲ ἔλεγον ὅτι Ἠλίας ἐστίν· ἄλλοι δὲ ἔλεγον ὅτι
But others *But* were saying, ~ "He is Elijah." *He is* Still others *Still* were saying, ~
1254 257 1254 3306 4022 1639 1639 2460 1639 1254 257 1254 3306 4022
r.npm cj v.iai.3p cj n.nsm v.pai.3s r.npm cj v.iai.3p cj

προφήτης ὡς εἷς τῶν προφητῶν. 16 → ἀκούσας δὲ
"He is a prophet, like one of the prophets of old." But when Herod heard *But*
4737 6055 1651 3836 4737 1254 2476 201 1254
n.nsm pl a.nsm d.gpm n.gpm pt.aa.nsm cj

ὁ Ἡρῴδης ἔλεγεν· ὃν ἐγὼ ἀπεκεφάλισα Ἰωάννην, οὗτος
{the} *Herod* this, he said, "He is John, the man I beheaded; *John* he
3836 2476 3306 2722 4005 1609 642 2722 4047
d.nsm n.nsm v.iai.3s r.asm r.ns.1 v.aai.1s n.asm r.nsm

NASB

He instructed them
that they should
take nothing for
their journey, ex-
cept a mere staff—
no bread, no bag,
no money in their
belt— 9but *to* wear
sandals; and *He*
added, "Do not put
on two [a]tunics."
10And He said to
them, "Wherever
you enter a house,
stay there until you
leave town. 11Any
place that does not
receive you or lis-
ten to you, as you
go out from there,
shake the dust off
the soles of your
feet for a testimony
against them."
12They went out
and preached that
men should repent.
13And they were
casting out many
demons and were
anointing with oil
many sick people
and healing them.

John's Fate Recalled

14And King Herod
heard *of it,* for His
name had become
well known; and
people were say-
ing, "John the
Baptist has risen
from the dead, and
that is why these
miraculous pow-
ers are at work in
Him." 15But others
were saying, "He is
Elijah." And others
were saying, "*He*
is a prophet, like
one of the prophets
of old." 16But when
Herod heard *of it,*
he kept saying,
"John, whom I be-
headed, has risen!"

[a] 14 Some early manuscripts *He was saying*

[a] ἀμὴν λέγω ὑμῖν, ἀνεκτότερον ἔσται Σοδόμοις ἢ Γομόρροις ἐν ἡμέρᾳ κρίσεως, ἢ τῇ πόλει ἐκείνῃ. included by TR after αὐτοῖς.
[b] ἔλεγεν included by TR after ἔλεγον.

[a] Or *inner garments*

NIV

has been raised
from the dead!"
[17]For Herod him-
self had given or-
ders to have John
arrested, and he
had him bound and
put in prison. He
did this because
of Herodias, his
brother Philip's
wife, whom he
had married. [18]For
John had been say-
ing to Herod, "It
is not lawful for
you to have your
brother's wife."
[19]So Herodias
nursed a grudge
against John and
wanted to kill him.
But she was not
able to, [20]because
Herod feared John
and protected him,
knowing him to
be a righteous and
holy man. When
Herod heard John,
he was greatly
puzzled[a]; yet he
liked to listen to
him.
[21]Finally the
opportune time
came. On his
birthday Herod
gave a banquet for
his high officials
and military com-
manders and the
leading men of
Galilee. [22]When
the daughter of[b]
Herodias came in
and danced, she
pleased Herod and
his dinner guests.
The king said
to the girl, "Ask
me for anything
you want, and I'll
give it to you."
[23]And he promised
her with an oath,
"Whatever you ask
I will give you, up
to half my king-
dom."

[a] 20 Some early manuscripts *he did many things*
[b] 22 Some early manuscripts *When his daughter*

ἠγέρθη. | 17 | αὐτὸς γὰρ ὁ Ἡρῴδης ἀποστείλας
⌞has been raised⌟ from the dead." For it was Herod himself *For {the} Herod* who had sent
1586 1142 2476 899 1142 3836 2476 690
v.api.3s r.nsm cj d.nsm n.nsm pt.aa.nsm

ἐκράτησεν τὸν Ἰωάννην καὶ ἔδησεν αὐτὸν ἐν φυλακῇ διὰ Ἡρῳδιάδα
and arrested *{the}* John and bound him in prison ⌞on account of⌟ Herodias,
3195 3836 2722 2779 1313 899 1877 5871 1328 2478
v.aai.3s d.asm n.asm cj v.aai.3s r.asm.3 p.d n.dsf p.a n.asf

τὴν γυναῖκα Φιλίππου τοῦ ἀδελφοῦ αὐτοῦ, ὅτι αὐτὴν ἐγάμησεν·
the wife of Philip *{the}* his brother, *his* because *her* he had married her.
3836 1222 5805 3836 899 81 899 4022 899 1138 899
d.asf n.asf n.gsm d.gsm n.gsm r.gsm.3 cj r.asf.3 v.aai.3s

18 ἔλεγεν γὰρ ὁ Ἰωάννης τῷ Ἡρῴδῃ ὅτι ↱ ↱ οὐκ ἔξεστίν
For John ⌞had been saying⌟ *For {the} John* to Herod, ~ "It is not lawful
1142 2722 3306 1142 3836 2722 3836 2476 4022 1997 1997 4024 1997
v.iai.3s cj d.nsm n.nsm d.dsm n.dsm cj pl v.pai.3s

σοι ἔχειν τὴν γυναῖκα τοῦ ἀδελφοῦ σου. 19 ἡ δὲ Ἡρῳδιὰς
⌞for you⌟ to have the wife of your brother." *your* *{the}* So Herodias
5148 2400 3836 1222 3836 5148 81 5148 3836 1254 2478
r.ds.2 f.pa d.asf n.asf d.gsm n.gsm r.gs.2 d.nsf cj n.nsf

ἐνεῖχεν αὐτῷ καὶ ἤθελεν αὐτὸν ἀποκτεῖναι, καὶ ↱ ↱ οὐκ
⌞was nursing a grudge against⌟ him and wanted to kill him. *to kill* But she was not
1923 899 2779 2527 650 650 899 650 2779 1538 1538 4024
v.iai.3s r.dsm.3 cj v.iai.3s r.asm.3 f.aa cj pl

ἠδύνατο· 20 ὁ γὰρ Ἡρῴδης ἐφοβεῖτο τὸν Ἰωάννην, εἰδὼς αὐτὸν
able to do it, *{the}* because Herod feared *{the}* John, knowing him to be
1538 3836 1142 2476 5828 3836 2722 3857 899
v.ipi.3s d.nsm cj n.nsm v.ipi.3s d.asm n.asm pt.ra.nsm r.asm.3

ἄνδρα δίκαιον καὶ ἅγιον, καὶ συνετήρει αὐτόν, καὶ ἀκούσας αὐτοῦ ↱
man a just and holy man, and he protected him. *{and}* When he heard him, he
467 1465 2779 41 467 2779 5337 899 2779 201 899 679
n.asm a.asm cj a.asm cj v.iai.3s r.asm.3 cj pt.aa.nsm r.gsm.3

↱ πολλὰ ἠπόρει,[a] καὶ ἡδέως αὐτοῦ ἤκουεν. 21 καὶ
was greatly perplexed, yet he heard him gladly. *him* *he heard* Then an opportune day
679 4498 679 2779 201 201 899 2452 899 201 2779 2322 2465
a.apn v.iai.3s cj adv r.gsm.3 v.iai.3s cj

γενομένης ἡμέρας εὐκαίρου ὅτε Ἡρῴδης τοῖς γενεσίοις αὐτοῦ δεῖπνον
came *day* *opportune* when Herod on his birthday *his* gave a banquet
1181 2465 2322 4021 2476 3836 899 1160 899 4472 1270
pt.am.gsf n.gsf a.gsf cj n.nsm d.dpn n.dpn r.gsm.3 n.asn

ἐποίησεν τοῖς μεγιστᾶσιν αὐτοῦ καὶ τοῖς χιλιάρχοις καὶ τοῖς
gave for his government officials, *his* *{and}* *{the}* military commanders, and *{the}*
4472 3836 899 3491 899 2779 3836 5941 2779 3836
v.aai.3s d.dpm n.dpm r.gsm.3 cj d.dpm n.dpm cj d.dpm

πρώτοις τῆς Γαλιλαίας, 22 καὶ → εἰσελθούσης τῆς θυγατρὸς αὐτοῦ
⌞prominent men⌟ of Galilee. *{and}* When the daughter *{his}*
4755 3836 1133 2779 1656 3836 2588 899
a.dpm d.gsf n.gsf cj pt.aa.gsf d.gsf n.gsf r.gsm.3

Ἡρῳδιάδος καὶ ὀρχησαμένης ἤρεσεν τῷ Ἡρῴδῃ καὶ τοῖς
of Herodias came in and danced, she pleased *{the}* Herod and his
2478 1656 1656 2779 4004 743 3836 2476 2779 3836
n.gsf cj pt.am.gsf v.aai.3s d.dsm n.dsm cj d.dpm

συνανακειμένοις. εἶπεν ὁ βασιλεὺς τῷ κορασίῳ· αἴτησόν με ↰
dinner companions. The king said *The* *king* ⌞to the⌟ young girl, "Ask me for
5263 3836 995 3306 3836 995 3836 3166 160 1609 160
pt.pm.dpm v.aai.3s d.nsm n.nsm d.dsn n.dsn v.aam.2s r.as.1

⌞ὃ ἐὰν⌟ θέλῃς, καὶ δώσω σοι· 23 καὶ ὤμοσεν αὐτῇ πολλὰ[b] ↰ ↰
whatever you wish, and I will give it to you." And he promised her insistently with an
4005 1569 2527 2779 1443 5148 2779 3923 899 4498 3923 3923
r.asn pl v.pas.2s cj v.fai.1s r.ds.2 cj v.aai.3s r.dsf.3 a.apn

↰ ⌞ὅ τι ἐὰν⌟ [c]αἰτήσῃς δώσω σοι ἕως ἡμίσους τῆς βασιλείας
oath, "Whatever you ask for, I will give it to you, up to half of my kingdom."
3923 4005 5516 1569 160 1443 5148 2401 2468 3836 1609 993
r.asn r.asn pl v.aas.2s v.fai.1s r.ds.2 p.g a.gsn d.gsf n.gsf

[a] ἐποίει included by TR after ἠπόρει.
[b] [πολλὰ] UBS, omitted by TNIV, NET.
[c] με included by UBS before αἰτήσῃς.

NASB

[17]For Herod
himself had sent
and had John ar-
rested and bound in
prison on account
of Herodias, the
wife of his brother
Philip, because he
had married her.
[18]For John had been
saying to Herod,
"It is not lawful for
you to have your
brother's wife."
[19]Herodias had a
grudge against him
and wanted to put
him to death and
could not *do so;*
[20]for Herod was
afraid of John,
knowing that he
was a righteous
and holy man, and
he kept him safe.
And when he heard
him, he was very
perplexed; but he
used to enjoy lis-
tening to him. [21]A
strategic day came
when Herod on
his birthday gave
a banquet for his
lords and military
commanders and
the leading men
of Galilee; [22]and
when the daugh-
ter of Herodias
herself came in
and danced, she
pleased Herod and
his dinner guests;
and the king said
to the girl, "Ask
me for whatever
you want and I will
give it to you."
[23]And he swore to
her, "Whatever you
ask of me, I will
give it to you; up
to half of my king-
dom." [24]And

NIV

[24]She went out
and said to her
mother, "What
shall I ask for?"
"The head of
John the Baptist,"
she answered.
[25]At once the girl
hurried in to the
king with the re-
quest: "I want you
to give me right
now the head of
John the Baptist on
a platter."
[26]The king was
greatly distressed,
but because of his
oaths and his din-
ner guests, he did
not want to refuse
her. [27]So he im-
mediately sent an
executioner with
orders to bring
John's head. The
man went, behead-
ed John in the pris-
on, [28]and brought
back his head on a
platter. He present-
ed it to the girl,
and she gave it to
her mother. [29]On
hearing of this,
John's disciples
came and took his
body and laid it in
a tomb.

Jesus Feeds the Five Thousand

[30]The apostles
gathered around
Jesus and reported
to him all they had
done and taught.
[31]Then, because so
many people were
coming and going
that they did not
even have a chance
to eat, he said to
them, "Come with
me by yourselves
to a quiet place
and get some rest."

μου. 24 καὶ ἐξελθοῦσα εἶπεν τῇ μητρὶ αὐτῆς· τί αἰτήσωμαι; ἡ
my So she went out and said to her mother, *her* "What should I ask for?" And her
1609 2779 2002 3306 3836 899 3613 899 5515 160 1254 3836
r.gs.1 cj pt.aa.nsf v.aai.3s d.dsf n.dsf r.gsf.3 r.asn v.ams.1s d.nsf

δὲ εἶπεν· τὴν κεφαλὴν Ἰωάννου τοῦ βαπτίζοντος. 25 καὶ
And mother said, "The head of John the baptizer." And immediately,
1254 3306 3836 3051 2722 3836 966 2779 2318
cj v.aai.3s d.asf n.asf n.gsm d.gsm pt.pa.gsm cj

εἰσελθοῦσα εὐθὺς μετὰ σπουδῆς πρὸς τὸν βασιλέα ᾐτήσατο λέγουσα· θέλω
entering *immediately* with haste to the king, she asked him, saying, "I want
1656 2318 3552 5082 4639 3836 995 160 3306 2527
pt.aa.nsf adv p.g n.gsf p.a d.asm n.asm v.ami.3s pt.pa.nsf v.pai.1s

ἵνα ἐξαυτῆς δῷς ἐπὶ πίνακι μοι τὴν κεφαλὴν Ἰωάννου τοῦ
you to give me right now *you give* *on* *platter* *me* the head of John the
1443 2671 1443 1609 1994 1443 2093 4402 1609 3836 3051 2722 3836
cj adv v.aas.2s p.d n.dsm r.ds.1 d.asf n.asf n.gsm d.gsm

βαπτιστοῦ. 26 καὶ περίλυπος γενόμενος ὁ βασιλεὺς
baptizer on a platter." *{and}* The king became very sad, *became* *The* *king*
969 2093 4402 2779 3836 995 1181 4337 1181 3836 995
n.gsm cj a.nsm pt.am.nsm d.nsm n.nsm

διὰ τοὺς ὅρκους καὶ ↰ ↰ τοὺς ἀνακειμένους ↱
but ⌊because of⌋ what ⌊he had promised with an oath,⌋ and because of his dinner guests, he
1328 3836 3992 2779 1328 1328 3836 367 2527
p.a d.apm n.apm cj d.apm pt.pm.apm

↱ οὐκ ἠθέλησεν ἀθετῆσαι αὐτήν· ↰ 27 καὶ εὐθὺς ἀποστείλας
did not want to refuse her request. So ⌊without delay⌋ the king dispatched
2527 4024 2527 119 899 119 2779 2318 3836 995 690
pl v.aai.3s f.aa r.asf.3 cj adv pt.aa.nsm

ὁ βασιλεὺς σπεκουλάτορα ἐπέταξεν ἐνέγκαι τὴν κεφαλὴν αὐτοῦ.
the *king* the executioner and ordered him to bring *{the}* John's head. *John's*
3836 995 5063 2199 5770 3836 899 3051 899
d.nsm n.nsm n.asm v.aai.3s f.aa d.asf n.asf r.gsm.3

καὶ ↱ ἀπελθὼν ἀπεκεφάλισεν αὐτὸν ἐν τῇ φυλακῇ 28 καὶ ἤνεγκεν τὴν
{and} He went and beheaded John in *{the}* prison, and brought *{the}* his
2779 642 599 642 899 1877 3836 5871 2779 5770 3836 899
cj pt.aa.nsm v.aai.3s r.asm.3 p.d d.dsf n.dsf cj v.aai.3s d.asf

κεφαλὴν αὐτοῦ ἐπὶ πίνακι καὶ ἔδωκεν αὐτὴν τῷ κορασίῳ, καὶ τὸ κοράσιον
head *his* on a platter and gave it ⌊to the⌋ young girl. *{and}* The young girl in
3051 899 2093 4402 2779 1443 899 3836 3166 2779 3836 3166
n.asf r.gsm.3 p.d n.dsm cj v.aai.3s r.asf.3 d.dsn n.dsn cj d.nsn n.nsn

ἔδωκεν αὐτὴν τῇ μητρὶ αὐτῆς. 29 καὶ → ἀκούσαντες οἱ
turn gave it to her mother. *her* *{and}* When John's disciples heard *{the}*
1443 899 3836 899 3613 899 2779 899 3412 201 3836
v.aai.3s r.asf.3 d.dsf n.dsf r.gsf.3 cj pt.aa.npm d.npm

μαθηταὶ αὐτοῦ ἦλθον καὶ ἦραν τὸ πτῶμα αὐτοῦ καὶ ἔθηκαν αὐτὸ ἐν
disciples *John's* of this, they came and took *{the}* his corpse *his* and placed it in
3412 899 2262 2779 149 3836 899 4773 899 2779 5502 899 1877
n.npm r.gsm.3 v.aai.3p cj v.aai.3p d.asn n.asn r.gsm.3 cj v.aai.3p r.asn.3 p.d

μνημείῳ. 30 καὶ συνάγονται οἱ ἀπόστολοι πρὸς τὸν Ἰησοῦν καὶ
a tomb. *{and}* The apostles rejoined *The* *apostles* *{with}* *{the}* Jesus and
3646 2779 3836 693 5251 3836 693 4639 3836 2652 2779
n.dsn cj v.ppi.3p d.npm n.npm p.a d.asm n.asm cj

ἀπήγγειλαν αὐτῷ πάντα ὅσα ἐποίησαν καὶ ὅσα ἐδίδαξαν. 31 καὶ λέγει αὐτοῖς·
reported to him all *{that}* they had done and *{that}* taught. And he said to them,
550 899 4246 4012 4472 2779 4012 1438 2779 3306 899
v.aai.3p r.dsm.3 a.apn r.apn v.aai.3p cj r.apn v.aai.3p cj v.pai.3s r.dpm.3

δεῦτε ⌊ὑμεῖς αὐτοὶ κατ᾽ ἰδίαν⌋ εἰς ἔρημον τόπον καὶ ἀναπαύσασθε
⌊"Come away⌋ by yourselves to some deserted place and rest
1307 7007 899 2848 2625 1650 2245 5536 2779 399
adv r.np.2 r.npm p.a a.asf p.a a.asm n.asm cj v.amm.2p

ὀλίγον. ἦσαν γὰρ οἱ ἐρχόμενοι καὶ οἱ ὑπάγοντες πολλοί, καὶ
a while." For many were *For* *{the}* coming and *{the}* going, *many* and they did
3900 1142 4498 1639 1142 3836 2262 2779 3836 5632 4498 2779 2320 2320
adv v.iai.3p cj d.npm pt.pm.npm cj d.npm pt.pa.npm a.npm cj

NASB

she went out and
said to her mother,
"What shall I ask
for?" And she
said, "The head of
John the Baptist."
[25]Immediately she
came in a hurry to
the king and asked,
saying, "I want
you to give me
at once the head
of John the Bap-
tist on a platter."
[26]And although
the king was very
sorry, *yet* because
of his oaths and
because of his
dinner guests, he
was unwilling to
refuse her. [27]Im-
mediately the king
sent an executioner
and commanded
him to bring *back*
his head. And
he went and had
him beheaded in
the prison, [28]and
brought his head
on a platter, and
gave it to the girl;
and the girl gave
it to her mother.
[29]When his dis-
ciples heard *about*
this, they came
and took away his
body and laid it in
a tomb.
[30]The apostles
*gathered together
with Jesus; and
they reported to
Him all that they
had done and
taught. [31]And He
*said to them,
"Come away by
yourselves to a
secluded place and
rest a while." (For
there were many
people coming and
going, and they did

NIV

32 So they went
away by them-
selves in a boat to
a solitary place.
33 But many who
saw them leaving
recognized them
and ran on foot
from all the towns
and got there
ahead of them.
34 When Jesus
landed and saw a
large crowd, he
had compassion on
them, because they
were like sheep
without a shep-
herd. So he began
teaching them
many things.
35 By this time
it was late in the
day, so his disci-
ples came to him.
"This is a remote
place," they said,
"and it's already
very late. 36 Send
the people away
so that they can go
to the surrounding
countryside and
villages and buy
themselves some-
thing to eat."
37 But he an-
swered, "You give
them something
to eat."
They said to him,
"That would take
more than half a
year's wages[a]! Are
we to go and spend
that much on bread
and give it to them
to eat?"
38 "How many
loaves do you
have?" he asked.
"Go and see."
When they found
out, they said,
"Five—and two
fish."
39 Then Jesus
directed them to
have all the people
sit down in groups
on the green grass.
40 So they sat down

[a] 37 Greek *take two hundred denarii*

οὐδὲ φαγεῖν εὐκαίρουν. 32 καὶ ἀπῆλθον ἐν τῷ πλοίῳ εἰς
not even have a time to eat. *they did have a time* So they left in a boat to a
4028 2320 2320 2320 2266 2320 2779 599 1877 3836 4450 1650
adv f.aa v.iai.3p cj v.aai.3p p.d d.dsn n.dsn p.a

ἔρημον τόπον κατ᾽ ἰδίαν. 33 καὶ εἶδον αὐτοὺς ὑπάγοντας καὶ
deserted place by themselves. *{and}* Many people saw them leaving, *{and}*
2245 5536 2848 2625 2779 4498 4498 1625 899 5632 2779
a.asm n.asm p.a a.asf cj v.aai.3p r.apm.3 pt.pa.apm cj

ἐπέγνωσαν πολλοὶ καὶ πεζῇ ἀπὸ πασῶν τῶν πόλεων
recognized them, *Many people* and hurried together on foot from all the towns
2105 4498 2779 5340 5340 4270 608 4246 3836 4484
v.aai.3p a.npm cj adv p.g a.gpf d.gpf n.gpf

συνέδραμον ἐκεῖ καὶ προῆλθον ← ← αὐτούς. 34 καὶ → ἐξελθὼν
hurried together *there* and arrived there ahead of them. *{and}* When Jesus got out of the
5340 1695 2779 4601 1695 899 2779 2002
v.aai.3p adv cj v.aai.3p r.apm.3 cj pt.aa.nsm

εἶδεν πολὺν ὄχλον καὶ ἐσπλαγχνίσθη ἐπ᾽ αὐτούς, ὅτι ἦσαν ὡς
boat he saw the large crowd, and had compassion on them, because they were like
1625 4498 4063 2779 5072 2093 899 4022 1639 6055
v.aai.3s a.asm n.asm cj v.api.3s p.a r.apm.3 cj v.iai.3p pl

πρόβατα ⌞μὴ ἔχοντα⌟ ποιμένα, καὶ ἤρξατο διδάσκειν αὐτοὺς πολλά.
sheep without a shepherd. And he began to teach them many things.
4585 3590 2400 4478 2779 806 1438 899 4498
n.npn pl pt.pa.npn n.asm cj v.ami.3s f.pa r.apm.3 a.apn

35 καὶ ἤδη ὥρας πολλῆς γενομένης προσελθόντες αὐτῷ οἱ
{and} As the hour grew late, *grew* his disciples came to him *{the}*
2779 2453 6052 1181 4498 1181 899 3412 4665 899 3836
cj adv n.gsf a.gsf pt.am.gsf pt.aa.npm r.dsm.3 d.npm

μαθηταὶ αὐτοῦ ἔλεγον ὅτι ἔρημός ἐστιν ὁ τόπος καὶ
disciples *his* and said, ~ "This is a deserted *This is* *{the}* place and the hour is
3412 899 3306 4022 1639 1639 2245 1639 3836 5536 2779 6052
n.npm r.gsm.3 v.iai.3p cj a.nsm v.pai.3s d.nsm n.nsm cj

ἤδη ὥρα πολλή· 36 ἀπόλυσον αὐτούς, ↰ ἵνα ἀπελθόντες εἰς τοὺς κύκλῳ
already *hour* late. Send them away so they can go into the surrounding
2453 6052 4498 668 899 668 2671 599 1650 3836 3241
adv n.nsf a.nsf v.aam.2s r.apm.3 cj pt.aa.npm p.a d.apm adv

ἀγροὺς καὶ κώμας ἀγοράσωσιν ἑαυτοῖς τί φάγωσιν. 37 ὁ δὲ
hamlets and villages and buy for themselves something to eat. But he *But*
69 2779 3267 60 1571 5515 2266 1254 3836 1254
n.apm cj n.apf v.aas.3p r.dpm.3 r.asn v.aas.3p d.nsm cj

ἀποκριθεὶς εἶπεν αὐτοῖς· δότε αὐτοῖς ὑμεῖς φαγεῖν. καὶ
answered them, saying, *them* "You give them *You* something to eat." And
646 899 3306 899 7007 1443 899 7007 2266 2779
pt.ap.nsm v.aai.3s r.dpm.3 v.aam.2p r.dpm.3 r.np.2 f.aa cj

λέγουσιν αὐτῷ· ↱ ↱ ἀπελθόντες ἀγοράσωμεν δηναρίων
they said to him, "Should we go and buy two hundred denarii
3306 899 60 60 599 60 1357 1357 1324
v.pai.3p r.dsm.3 pt.aa.npm v.aas.1p n.gpn

διακοσίων ἄρτους καὶ δώσομεν αὐτοῖς φαγεῖν; 38 ὁ δὲ λέγει
two hundred worth of bread and give it to them to eat?" And he *And* said
1357 788 2779 1443 899 2266 1254 3836 1254 3306
a.gpn n.apm cj v.fai.1p r.dpm.3 f.aa d.nsm cj v.pai.3s

αὐτοῖς· πόσους ἄρτους ἔχετε; ὑπάγετε ἴδετε. καὶ γνόντες
to them, "How many loaves ⌞do you have?⌟ Go and see." *{and}* ⌞When they found out⌟
899 4531 788 2400 5632 1625 2779 1182
r.dpm.3 r.apm n.apm v.pai.2p v.pam.2p v.aam.2p cj pt.aa.npm

λέγουσιν· πέντε, καὶ δύο ἰχθύας. 39 καὶ ἐπέταξεν αὐτοῖς → →
they said, "Five — and two fish." Then he ordered them to have all the people
3306 4297 2779 1545 2716 2779 2199 899 4246
v.pai.3p a.apm cj a.apm n.apm cj v.aai.3s r.dpm.3

ἀνακλῖναι πάντας ⌞συμπόσια συμπόσια⌟ ἐπὶ τῷ χλωρῷ χόρτῳ. 40 καὶ ἀνέπεσαν
sit down *all* in groups on the green grass. So they sat down
369 4246 5235 5235 2093 3836 5952 5965 2779 404
f.aa a.apm n.apn n.apn p.d d.dsm a.dsm n.dsm cj v.aai.3p

NASB

not even have time
to eat.) 32 They went
away in the boat to
a secluded place by
themselves.

Five Thousand Fed

33 *The people* saw
them going, and
many recognized
them and ran there
together on foot
from all the cities,
and got there ahead
of them. 34 When
Jesus went ashore,
He saw a large
crowd, and He felt
compassion for
them because they
were like sheep
without a shepherd;
and He began to
teach them many
things. 35 When it
was already quite
late, His disciples
came to Him and
said, "This place is
desolate and it is
already quite late;
36 send them away
so that they may go
into the surround-
ing countryside and
villages and buy
themselves some-
thing to eat." 37 But
He answered them,
"You give them
something to eat!"
And they *said to
Him, "Shall we
go and spend two
hundred [a]denarii
on bread and give
them *something*
to eat?" 38 And
He *said to them,
"How many loaves
do you have? Go
look!" And when
they found out,
they *said, "Five,
and two fish."
39 And He com-
manded them all to
sit down by groups
on the green grass.
40 They sat down in

[a] The denarius was equivalent to one day's wage

NIV

in groups of hun-
dreds and fifties.
41 Taking the five
loaves and the two
fish and looking
up to heaven, he
gave thanks and
broke the loaves.
Then he gave them
to his disciples to
distribute to the
people. He also
divided the two
fish among them
all. 42 They all ate
and were satisfied,
43 and the disciples
picked up twelve
basketfuls of bro-
ken pieces of bread
and fish. 44 The
number of the men
who had eaten was
five thousand.

Jesus Walks on the Water

45 Immediately
Jesus made his
disciples get into
the boat and go on
ahead of him to
Bethsaida, while
he dismissed the
crowd. 46 After
leaving them,
he went up on a
mountainside to
pray.
47 Later that night,
the boat was in
the middle of the
lake, and he was
alone on land. 48 He
saw the disciples
straining at the
oars, because the
wind was against
them. Shortly be-
fore dawn he went
out to them, walk-
ing on the lake.
He was about to
pass by them, 49 but
when they saw
him walking on
the lake,

˪πρασιαὶ πρασιαὶ˩ κατὰ ἑκατὸν καὶ κατὰ πεντήκοντα. 41 καὶ λαβὼν τοὺς
in orderly groups of hundreds and {of} fifties. And taking the
4555 4555 2848 1669 2779 2848 4299 2779 3284 3836
n.npf n.npf p.a a.apm cj p.a a.apm cj pt.aa.nsm d.apm

πέντε ἄρτους καὶ τοὺς δύο ἰχθύας ἀναβλέψας εἰς τὸν οὐρανὸν εὐλόγησεν καὶ
five loaves and the two fish, and looking up to {the} heaven, he blessed and
4297 788 2779 3836 1545 2716 329 1650 3836 4041 2328 2779
a.apm n.apm cj d.apm a.apm n.apm pt.aa.nsm p.a d.asm n.asm v.aai.3s cj

κατέκλασεν τοὺς ἄρτους καὶ ἐδίδου τοῖς μαθηταῖς αὐτοῦ[a] ἵνα
broke the loaves and gave them to his disciples his so
2880 3836 788 2779 1443 3836 899 3412 899 2671
v.aai.3s d.apm n.apm cj v.iai.3s d.dpm n.dpm r.gsm.3 cj

παρατιθῶσιν αὐτοῖς, καὶ τοὺς δύο ἰχθύας ἐμέρισεν → πᾶσιν.
they could distribute them. And he divided the two fish he divided among them all.
4192 899 2779 3532 3532 3836 1545 2716 3532 4246
v.pas.3p r.dpm.3 cj d.apm a.apm n.apm v.aai.3s a.dpm

42 καὶ → ἔφαγον πάντες καὶ ἐχορτάσθησαν, 43 καὶ ἦραν κλάσματα
So they all ate all and were filled. Then ˪they picked up˩ broken pieces
2779 4246 2266 4246 2779 5963 2779 149 3083
cj v.aai.3p a.npm cj v.api.3p cj v.aai.3p n.apn

δώδεκα κοφίνων πληρώματα καὶ ἀπὸ τῶν ἰχθύων. 44 καὶ
twelve baskets full of broken pieces and ˪what was left of˩ the fish. And
1557 3186 4445 3083 3083 2779 608 3836 2716 2779
a.gpm n.gpm n.apn cj p.g d.gpm n.gpm cj

ἦσαν οἱ φαγόντες τοὺς ἄρτους[b] πεντακισχίλιοι ἄνδρες. 45 καὶ εὐθὺς
were those who had eaten the loaves were five thousand men. {and} Immediately
1639 3836 2266 3836 788 1639 4295 467 2779 2318
v.iai.3p d.npm pt.aa.npm d.apm n.apm a.npm n.npm cj adv

ἠνάγκασεν τοὺς μαθητὰς αὐτοῦ ἐμβῆναι εἰς τὸ πλοῖον καὶ προάγειν
Jesus made {the} his disciples his get into the boat and ˪go on ahead of˩
337 3836 899 3412 899 1832 1650 3836 4450 2779 4575
v.aai.3s d.apm n.apm r.gsm.3 f.aa p.a d.asn n.asn cj f.pa

εἰς τὸ πέραν πρὸς Βηθσαϊδάν, ἕως αὐτὸς ἀπολύει τὸν ὄχλον. 46 καὶ
him to the other side, toward Bethsaida, while he dispersed the crowd. {and}
1650 3836 4305 4639 1034 2401 899 668 3836 4063 2779
p.a d.asn adv p.a n.asf cj r.nsm v.pai.3s d.asm n.asm cj

ἀποταξάμενος αὐτοῖς ἀπῆλθεν εἰς τὸ ὄρος προσεύξασθαι. 47 καὶ ↱
˪After he had taken leave of˩ them, he went to the mountain to pray. {and} When
698 899 599 1650 3836 4001 4667 2779 1181
pt.am.nsm r.dpm.3 v.aai.3s p.a d.asn n.asn f.am cj

ὀψίας γενομένης ἦν τὸ πλοῖον ἐν μέσῳ τῆς θαλάσσης, καὶ αὐτὸς
evening had come, the boat was the boat in the middle of the lake and he
4068 1181 3836 4450 1639 3836 4450 1877 3545 3836 2498 2779 899
n.gsf pt.am.gsf v.iai.3s d.nsn n.nsn p.d n.dsn d.gsf n.gsf cj r.nsm

μόνος ἐπὶ τῆς γῆς. 48 καὶ ἰδὼν αὐτοὺς βασανιζομένους ἐν τῷ ἐλαύνειν,
was alone on the land. {and} He saw them straining at the oars,
3668 2093 3836 1178 2779 1625 899 989 1877 3836 1785
a.nsm p.g d.gsf n.gsf cj pt.aa.nsm r.apm.3 pt.pp.apm p.d d.dsn f.pa

ἦν γὰρ ὁ ἄνεμος ἐναντίος αὐτοῖς, περὶ τετάρτην φυλακὴν τῆς νυκτὸς
was for the wind was against them. About the fourth watch of the night
1639 1142 3836 449 1639 1885 899 4309 5480 5871 3836 3816
v.iai.3s cj d.nsm n.nsm a.nsm r.dpm.3 p.a a.asf n.asf d.gsf n.gsf

ἔρχεται πρὸς αὐτοὺς περιπατῶν ἐπὶ τῆς θαλάσσης καὶ ἤθελεν παρελθεῖν
he came toward them walking on the lake. {and} He intended to pass by
2262 4639 899 4344 2093 3836 2498 2779 2527 4216
v.pmi.3s p.a r.apm.3 pt.pa.nsm p.g d.gsf n.gsf cj v.iai.3s f.aa

αὐτούς. 49 ↱ οἱ δὲ ἰδόντες αὐτὸν ἐπὶ τῆς θαλάσσης περιπατοῦντα
them, But when they But saw him walking on the lake walking
899 1254 1625 3836 1254 1625 899 4344 2093 3836 2498 4344
r.apm.3 d.npm cj pt.aa.npm r.asm.3 p.g d.gsf n.gsf pt.pa.asm

[a] [αὐτοῦ] UBS, omitted by NET.
[b] [τοὺς ἄρτους] UBS, omitted by TNIV.

NASB

groups of hundreds
and of fifties. 41 And
He took the five
loaves and the two
fish, and looking
up toward heaven,
He blessed *the*
food and broke the
loaves and He kept
giving *them* to the
disciples to set be-
fore them; and He
divided up the two
fish among them
all. 42 They all ate
and were satisfied,
43 and they picked
up twelve full bas-
kets of the broken
pieces, and also
of the fish. 44 There
were five thousand
men who ate the
loaves.

Jesus Walks on the Water

45 Immediately Je-
sus made His dis-
ciples get into the
boat and go ahead
of *Him* to the other
side to Bethsaida,
while He Himself
was sending the
crowd away. 46 Af-
ter bidding them
farewell, He left
for the mountain
to pray.
47 When it was
evening, the boat
was in the middle
of the sea, and He
was alone on the
land. 48 Seeing them
straining at the
oars, for the wind
was against them,
at about the fourth
watch of the night
He *came to them,
walking on the sea;
and He intended to
pass by them. 49 But
when they saw
Him walking on
the sea, they

NIV

they thought he was a ghost. They cried out, [50]because they all saw him and were terrified.

Immediately he spoke to them and said, "Take courage! It is I. Don't be afraid." [51]Then he climbed into the boat with them, and the wind died down. They were completely amazed, [52]for they had not understood about the loaves; their hearts were hardened.

[53]When they had crossed over, they landed at Gennesaret and anchored there. [54]As soon as they got out of the boat, people recognized Jesus. [55]They ran throughout that whole region and carried the sick on mats to wherever they heard he was. [56]And wherever he went—into villages, towns or countryside—they placed the sick in the marketplaces. They begged him to let them touch even the edge of his cloak, and all who touched it were healed.

That Which Defiles

7 The Pharisees and some of the teachers of the law

ἔδοξαν ὅτι φάντασμά ἐστιν, καὶ ἀνέκραξαν· 50 ↱ πάντες γὰρ
they thought that he was a ghost. *he was* And they cried out, for they all *for*
1506 4022 1639 1639 5753 1639 2779 371 1142 1625 4246 1142
v.aai.3p cj n.nsn v.pai.3s cj v.aai.3p a.npm cj

αὐτὸν εἶδον καὶ ἐταράχθησαν. ὁ δὲ εὐθὺς ἐλάλησεν μετ᾽
him saw him and were terrified. But immediately he *But* *immediately* spoke with
899 1625 899 2779 5429 1254 2318 3836 1254 2318 3281 3552
r.asm.3 v.aai.3p cj v.api.3p d.nsm cj adv v.aai.3s p.g

αὐτῶν, καὶ λέγει αὐτοῖς· θαρσεῖτε, ἐγώ εἰμι· ↱ μὴ φοβεῖσθε. 51 καὶ
them and said to them, "Take courage! It is I. *It is* Do not be afraid!" Then
899 2779 3306 899 2510 1639 1639 1609 1639 5828 3590 5828 2779
r.gpm.3 cj v.pai.3s r.dpm.3 v.pam.2p r.ns.1 v.pai.1s pl v.ppm.2p cj

ἀνέβη πρὸς αὐτοὺς εἰς τὸ πλοῖον καὶ ἐκόπασεν ὁ ἄνεμος,
he got into the boat with them, *into* *the* *boat* and the wind died down. *the* *wind*
326 1650 3836 4450 4639 899 1650 3836 4450 2779 3836 449 3156 3836 449
v.aai.3s p.a r.apm.3 p.a d.asn n.asn cj v.aai.3s d.nsm n.nsm

καὶ ↱ ↱ ˻λίαν [a]ἐκ περισσοῦ˼ ἐν ἑαυτοῖς ἐξίσταντο· 52 ↱ ↱
And they were absolutely *{among}* *{themselves}* amazed, for they did
2779 2014 2014 3336 1666 4356 1877 1571 2014 1142 5317 5317
cj adv p.g a.gsn p.d r.dpm.3 v.imi.3p

οὐ γὰρ συνῆκαν ἐπὶ τοῖς ἄρτοις, ἀλλ᾽ ἦν αὐτῶν ἡ καρδία
not *for* understand about the loaves; but their heart was *their* *{the}* *heart*
4024 1142 5317 2093 3836 788 247 899 2840 1639 899 3836 2840
pl cj v.aai.3p p.d d.dpm n.dpm cj v.iai.3s r.gpm.3 d.nsf n.nsf

πεπωρωμένη. 53 καὶ διαπεράσαντες ἐπὶ τὴν γῆν ἦλθον εἰς
hardened. So ˻when they had crossed over,˼ they came to *{the}* land *they came* at
4800 2779 1385 2262 2262 2093 3836 1178 2262 1650
pt.rp.nsf cj pt.aa.npm p.a d.asf n.asf v.aai.3p p.a

Γεννησαρὲτ καὶ προσωρμίσθησαν. 54 καὶ → ἐξελθόντων αὐτῶν ἐκ
Gennesaret *{and}* where they tied up the boat. *{and}* When they got out *they* of
1166 2779 4694 2779 899 2002 899 1666
n.asf cj v.api.3p cj pt.aa.gpm r.gpm.3 p.g

τοῦ πλοίου εὐθὺς ἐπιγνόντες αὐτὸν 55 περιέδραμον ὅλην τὴν
the boat, the people immediately recognized Jesus, ran throughout that whole *{the}*
3836 4450 2318 2105 899 4366 1697 3910 3836
d.gsn n.gsn adv pt.aa.npm r.asm.3 v.aai.3p a.asf d.asf

χώραν ἐκείνην καὶ ἤρξαντο ἐπὶ τοῖς κραβάττοις τοὺς
area, *that* and began to bring those who were ill on their mats *those*
6001 1697 2779 806 4367 4367 3836 2400 2400 2809 2093 3836 3187 3836
n.asf r.asf cj v.ami.3p p.d d.dpm n.dpm d.apm

κακῶς ἔχοντας περιφέρειν ὅπου ἤκουον ὅτι ἐστίν. 56 καὶ ˻ὅπου ἂν˼
ill *who were* *to bring* to wherever they heard *{that}* he was. And wherever
2809 2400 4367 3963 201 4022 1639 2779 3963 323
adv pt.pa.apm f.pa cj v.iai.3p cj v.pai.3s cj cj pl

˻εἰσεπορεύετο εἰς˼ κώμας ἢ εἰς πόλεις ἢ εἰς ἀγρούς,
he entered villages, *{or}* *{into}* towns, or *{into}* rural areas, they would place the
1660 1650 3267 2445 1650 4484 2445 1650 69 5502 5502 5502 3836
v.imi.3s p.a n.apf cj p.a n.apf cj p.a n.apm

ἐν ταῖς ἀγοραῖς ἐτίθεσαν τοὺς ἀσθενοῦντας καὶ παρεκάλουν αὐτὸν ἵνα
sick in the marketplaces *they would place* *the* *sick* and implore him that
820 1877 3836 59 5502 3836 820 2779 4151 899 2671
p.d d.dpf n.dpf v.iai.3p d.apm pt.pa.apm cj v.iai.3p r.asm.3 cj

κἂν τοῦ κρασπέδου τοῦ ἱματίου αὐτοῦ ἅψωνται· καὶ ˻ὅσοι
they might touch just the fringe of his cloak. *his* *they might touch* And as many as
721 721 721 2829 3836 3192 3836 899 2668 899 721 2779 4012
crasis d.gsn n.gsn d.gsn n.gsn r.gsm.3 v.ams.3p cj r.npm

ἂν˼ ἥψαντο αὐτοῦ ἐσῴζοντο.
touched him ˻were made well.˼
323 721 899 5392
pl v.ami.3p r.gsm.3 v.ipi.3p

7:1 καὶ οἱ συνάγονται πρὸς αὐτὸν Φαρισαῖοι καί τινες τῶν γραμματέων
{and} The *gathered* *around* *Jesus* Pharisees and some of the scribes
2779 3836 5251 4639 899 5757 2779 5516 3836 1208
cj d.npm v.ppi.3p p.a r.asm.3 n.npm cj r.npm d.gpm n.gpm

[a] [ἐκ περισσοῦ] UBS.

NASB

supposed that it was a ghost, and cried out; [50]for they all saw Him and were terrified. But immediately He spoke with them and *said to them, "Take courage; it is I, do not be afraid." [51]Then He got into the boat with them, and the wind stopped; and they were utterly astonished, [52]for they had not gained any insight from the *incident of* the loaves, but their heart was hardened.

Healing at Gennesaret

[53]When they had crossed over they came to land at Gennesaret, and moored to the shore. [54]When they got out of the boat, immediately *the people* recognized Him, [55]and ran about that whole country and began to carry here and there on their pallets those who were sick, to the place they heard He was. [56]Wherever He entered villages, or cities, or countryside, they were laying the sick in the market places, and imploring Him that they might just touch the fringe of His cloak; and as many as touched it were being cured.

Followers of Tradition

[7:1]The Pharisees and some of the scribes gathered

NIV

who had come
from Jerusalem
gathered around
Jesus [2]and saw
some of his disci-
ples eating food
with hands that
were defiled, that
is, unwashed.
[3](The Pharisees
and all the Jews do
not eat unless they
give their hands a
ceremonial wash-
ing, holding to the
tradition of the
elders. [4]When they
come from the
marketplace they
do not eat unless
they wash. And
they observe many
other traditions,
such as the wash-
ing of cups, pitch-
ers and kettles.[a])
[5]So the Pharisees
and teachers of the
law asked Jesus,
"Why don't your
disciples live ac-
cording to the tra-
dition of the elders
instead of eating
their food with de-
filed hands?"
[6]He replied,
"Isaiah was right
when he proph-
esied about you
hypocrites; as it is
written:

"'These people
honor me
with their
lips,
but their
hearts are
far from
me.
[7]They worship
me in vain;
their
teachings
are merely
human
rules.'[b]

[8]You have let go of
the commands of

ἐλθόντες ἀπὸ Ἱεροσολύμων. [2]καὶ ἰδόντες τινὰς τῶν
who had come from Jerusalem gathered around Jesus and noticed that some of his
2262 608 2642 5251 4639 899 2779 1625 4022 5516 3836 899
pt.aa.npm p.g n.gpn cj pt.aa.npm r.apm d.gpm

μαθητῶν αὐτοῦ ὅτι κοιναῖς χερσίν, τοῦτ'
disciples *his* *that* were eating the loaves with hands that were defiled, *with hands* that
3412 899 4022 2266 2266 3836 788 5931 5931 3123 5931 4047
n.gpm r.gsm.3 cj a.dpf n.dpf r.nsn

ἔστιν ἀνίπτοις, ἐσθίουσιν τοὺς ἄρτους [3] οἱ γὰρ Φαρισαῖοι καὶ πάντες οἱ
is, unwashed. *were eating* *the* *loaves* (For the *For* Pharisees and all the
1639 481 2266 3836 788 1142 3836 1142 5757 2779 4246 3836
v.pai.3s a.dpf v.pai.3p d.apm n.apm d.npm cj n.npm cj a.npm d.npm

Ἰουδαῖοι ˌἐὰν μὴˌ ↱ πυγμῇ νίψωνται τὰς χεῖρας οὐκ ἐσθίουσιν,
Jews do not eat unless they ceremonially wash their hands, *not* *do eat*
2681 2266 4024 2266 1569 3590 3782 4778 3782 3836 5931 4024 2266
a.npm cj pl n.dsf v.ams.3p d.apf n.apf pl v.pai.3p

κρατοῦντες τὴν παράδοσιν τῶν πρεσβυτέρων, [4]καὶ
thus maintaining the tradition of the elders. *{and}* They do not eat anything
3195 3836 4142 3836 4565 2779 2266 2266 4024 2266
pt.pa.npm d.asf n.asf d.gpm a.gpm cj

ἀπ' ἀγορᾶς ˌἐὰν μὴˌ βαπτίσωνται οὐκ ἐσθίουσιν, καὶ
from the marketplace unless ˌit is purified by washing.ˌ *not* *They do eat* And there are many
608 59 1569 3590 966 4024 2266 2779 1639 1639 4498
p.g n.gsf cj pl v.ams.3p pl v.pai.3p cj

ἄλλα πολλά ἐστιν ἃ παρέλαβον κρατεῖν, βαπτισμοὺς
other *many* *there are* customs that ˌthey have received as traditionˌ to keep, like the washing
257 4498 1639 4005 4161 3195 968
r.npn a.npn v.pai.3s r.apn v.aai.3p f.pa n.apm

ποτηρίων καὶ ξεστῶν καὶ χαλκίων [a]καὶ κλινῶν [5]καὶ ἐπερωτῶσιν αὐτὸν
of cups, *{and}* pots, *{and}* copper bowls, and dining couches.) And *asked* *him*
4539 2779 3829 2779 5908 2779 3109 2779 2089 899
n.gpn cj n.gpm cj n.gpn cj n.gpf cj v.pai.3p r.asm.3

οἱ Φαρισαῖοι καὶ οἱ γραμματεῖς· ˌδιὰ τίˌ ↱ οὐ
the Pharisees and *{the}* scribes asked him, "Why do your disciples not
3836 5757 2779 3836 1208 2089 899 1328 5515 4344 5148 3412 4024
d.npm n.npm cj d.npm n.npm p.a r.asn pl

περιπατοῦσιν οἱ μαθηταί σου κατὰ τὴν παράδοσιν τῶν πρεσβυτέρων, ἀλλὰ
walk *{the}* *disciples* *your* ˌaccording toˌ the tradition of the elders, but
4344 3836 3412 5148 2848 3836 4142 3836 4565 247
v.pai.3p d.npm n.npm r.gs.2 p.a d.asf n.asf d.gpm a.gpm cj

κοιναῖς χερσὶν ἐσθίουσιν τὸν ἄρτον; [6] Ὁ δὲ εἶπεν αὐτοῖς·
eat their bread with defiled hands?" *eat* *their* *bread* And he *And* said to them,
2266 3836 788 3123 5931 2266 3836 788 1254 3836 1254 3306 899
a.dpf n.dpf v.pai.3p d.asm n.asm d.nsm cj v.aai.3s r.dpm.3

καλῶς ἐπροφήτευσεν Ἠσαΐας περὶ ὑμῶν τῶν ὑποκριτῶν, ὡς
"Isaiah prophesied accurately *prophesied* *Isaiah* about you *{the}* hypocrites, as
2480 4736 2822 4736 2480 4309 7007 3836 5695 6055
adv v.aai.3s n.nsm p.g r.gp.2 d.gpm n.gpm cj

γέγραπται ὅτι[b] οὗτος ὁ λαὸς τοῖς χείλεσίν με τιμᾷ, ἡ δὲ
it is written: ~ 'This *{the}* people honors me ˌwith theirˌ lips, *me* *honors* *{the}* but their
1211 4022 4047 3836 3295 5506 1609 3836 5927 1609 5506 3836 1254 899
v.rpi.3s cj r.nsm d.nsm n.nsm d.dpn n.dpn r.as.1 v.pai.3s d.nsf cj

καρδία αὐτῶν πόρρω ἀπέχει ἀπ' ἐμοῦ· [7]μάτην δὲ σέβονταί με
heart *their* is far *is* from me. In vain *{and}* do they worship me,
2840 899 600 4522 600 608 1609 3472 1254 4936 1609
n.nsf r.gpm.3 adv v.pai.3s p.g r.gs.1 adv cj v.pmi.3p r.as.1

διδάσκοντες διδασκαλίας ἐντάλματα ἀνθρώπων. [8]ἀφέντες τὴν ἐντολὴν τοῦ
teaching as doctrines the precepts of men.' Neglecting the command of
1438 1436 1945 476 918 3836 1953 3836
pt.pa.npm n.apf n.apn n.gpm pt.aa.npm d.asf n.asf d.gsm

NASB

around Him when
they had come
from Jerusalem,
[2]and had seen that
some of His dis-
ciples were eating
their bread with
impure hands,
that is, unwashed.
[3](For the Pharisees
and all the Jews
do not eat unless
they carefully
wash their hands,
thus observing the
traditions of the
elders; [4]and *when*
they come from
the market place,
they do not eat un-
less they cleanse
themselves; and
there are many
other things which
they have received
in order to observe,
such as the wash-
ing of cups and
pitchers and copper
pots.) [5]The Phari-
sees and the scribes
*asked Him, "Why
do Your disciples
not walk according
to the tradition of
the elders, but eat
their bread with
impure hands?"
[6]And He said to
them, "Rightly did
Isaiah prophesy of
you hypocrites, as
it is written:
'THIS PEOPLE
HONORS ME
WITH THEIR
LIPS,
BUT THEIR
HEART IS FAR
AWAY FROM
ME.
[7]'BUT IN VAIN DO
THEY WORSHIP
ME,
TEACHING AS
DOCTRINES THE
PRECEPTS OF
MEN.'
[8]Neglecting the
commandment

[a] *4* Some early manuscripts *pitchers, kettles and dining couches*
[b] *6,7* Isaiah 29:13

[a] [καὶ κλινῶν] UBS, omitted by TNIV.
[b] [ὅτι] UBS, omitted by TNIV.

NIV

God and are hold-
ing on to human
traditions."
9 And he contin-
ued, "You have a
fine way of setting
aside the com-
mands of God in
order to observe[a]
your own tradi-
tions! 10 For Moses
said, 'Honor your
father and moth-
er,'[b] and, 'Anyone
who curses their
father or moth-
er is to be put to
death.'[c] 11 But you
say that if anyone
declares that what
might have been
used to help their
father or mother
is Corban (that is,
devoted to God)—
12 then you no
longer let them do
anything for their
father or mother.
13 Thus you nullify
the word of God by
your tradition that
you have handed
down. And you do
many things like
that."
14 Again Jesus
called the crowd
to him and said,
"Listen to me,
everyone, and
understand this.
15 Nothing outside
a person can defile
them by going into
them. Rather, it is
what comes out of
a person that de-
files them." [16][d]
17 After he had
left the crowd and
entered the house,
his disciples asked
him about

[a] 9 Some manuscripts *set up*
[b] 10 Exodus 20:12; Deut. 5:16
[c] 10 Exodus 21:17; Lev. 20:9
[d] 16 Some manuscripts include here the words of 4:23.

θεοῦ κρατεῖτε τὴν παράδοσιν τῶν ἀνθρώπων.[a] 9 καὶ ἔλεγεν αὐτοῖς·
God, you maintain the tradition of men." And he said to them, "You are
2536 3195 3836 4142 3836 476 2779 3306 899 119 119
n.gsm v.pai.2p d.asf n.asf d.gpm n.gpm cj v.iai.3s r.dpm.3

καλῶς ἀθετεῖτε τὴν ἐντολὴν τοῦ θεοῦ, ἵνα τὴν παράδοσιν
clever at setting aside the command of God ⌞in order to⌟ *{the}* establish your own tradition.
2822 119 3836 1953 3836 2536 2671 3836 2705 7007 7007 4142
adv v.pai.2p d.asf n.asf d.gsm n.gsm cj d.asf n.asf

ὑμῶν στήσητε.[b] 10 Μωϋσῆς γὰρ εἶπεν· τίμα τὸν πατέρα σου καὶ τὴν
your own *establish* For Moses *For* said, 'Honor *{the}* your father *your* and *{the}*
7007 2705 1142 3707 1142 3306 5506 3836 5148 4252 5148 2779 3836
r.gp.2 v.aas.2p n.nsm cj v.aai.3s v.pam.2s d.asm n.asm r.gs.2 cj d.asf

μητέρα σου, καί· ὁ κακολογῶν πατέρα ἢ μητέρα θανάτῳ
your mother,' *your* and. 'Whoever speaks evil of father or mother must be put to death.'
5148 3613 5148 2779 3836 2800 4252 2445 3613 5462 5462 5462 2505
n.asf r.gs.2 cj d.nsm pt.pa.nsm n.asm cj n.asf n.dsm

τελευτάτω. 11 ὑμεῖς δὲ λέγετε· ἐὰν εἴπῃ ἄνθρωπος τῷ πατρὶ ἢ τῇ
must be put But you *But* say, 'If a man says *man* ⌞to his⌟ father or *{the}*
5462 1254 7007 1254 3306 1569 476 3306 476 3836 4252 2445 3836
v.pam.3s r.np.2 cj v.pai.2p cj v.aas.3s n.nsm d.dsm n.dsm cj d.dsf

μητρί· κορβᾶν, ὅ ἐστιν δῶρον, ⌞ὃ ἐὰν⌟ ἐξ ἐμοῦ
mother, *Corban* *that* *is* *given* "Whatever help you might have received from me
3613 3167 4005 1639 1565 4005 1569 6067 6067 6067 6067 6067 1666 1609
n.dsf n.nsn r.nsn v.pai.3s n.nsn r.asn pl p.g r.gs.1

ὠφεληθῇς, 12 οὐκέτι ἀφίετε
help you might have received is Corban" (that is, given to God), then you no longer allow
6067 3167 4005 1639 1565 918 4033 918
v.aps.2s adv v.pai.2p

αὐτὸν οὐδὲν ποιῆσαι τῷ πατρὶ ἢ τῇ μητρί, 13 ἀκυροῦντες
him to do anything *to do* for his father or *{the}* mother. Thus you invalidate
899 4472 4472 4029 4472 4252 3836 4252 2445 3836 3613 218
r.asm.3 a.asn f.aa d.dsm n.dsm cj d.dsf n.dsf pt.pa.npm

τὸν λόγον τοῦ θεοῦ τῇ παραδόσει ὑμῶν ᾗ παρεδώκατε· καὶ
the word of God with your tradition *your* that ⌞you have handed down.⌟ And you do
3836 3364 3836 2536 3836 7007 4142 7007 4005 4140 2779 4472 4472
d.asm n.asm d.gsm n.gsm d.dsf n.dsf r.gp.2 r.dsf v.aai.2p cj

παρόμοια τοιαῦτα πολλὰ ποιεῖτε. 14 καὶ προσκαλεσάμενος
many similar things." *many* *you do* *{and}* Calling the crowd to him
4498 4235 5525 4498 4472 2779 4673 3836 4063
a.apn r.apn a.apn v.pai.2p cj pt.am.nsm

πάλιν τὸν ὄχλον ἔλεγεν αὐτοῖς· ἀκούσατέ μου πάντες καὶ σύνετε. 15
again, *the* *crowd* he said to them, "Listen to me, everyone, and understand. There is
4099 3836 4063 3306 899 201 1609 4246 2779 5317 1639 1639
adv d.asm n.asm v.iai.3s r.dpm.3 v.aam.2p r.gs.1 a.npm cj v.aam.2p

οὐδέν ἐστιν ἔξωθεν τοῦ ἀνθρώπου ⌞εἰσπορευόμενον εἰς⌟ αὐτὸν ὃ δύναται
nothing *There is* from outside a man that enters him that is able
4029 1639 2033 3836 476 1660 1650 899 4005 1538
a.nsn v.pai.3s p.g d.gsm n.gsm pt.pm.nsn p.a r.asm.3 r.nsn v.ppi.3s

κοινῶσαι αὐτόν, ἀλλὰ τὰ ἐκ τοῦ ἀνθρώπου ἐκπορευόμενά
to defile him. Rather the things that come out of a man *things that come out*
3124 899 247 3836 1744 1744 1744 1744 1666 3836 476 1744
f.aa r.asm.3 cj d.npn p.g d.gsm n.gsm pt.pm.npn

ἐστιν τὰ κοινοῦντα τὸν ἄνθρωπον.[c] 17 καὶ ὅτε ⌞εἰσῆλθεν εἰς⌟
are the things that defile *{the}* him. And when Jesus entered the
1639 3836 3124 3836 476 2779 4021 1656 1650
v.pai.3s d.npn pt.pa.npn d.asm n.asm cj cj v.aai.3s p.a

οἶκον ἀπὸ τοῦ ὄχλου, ἐπηρώτων αὐτὸν οἱ μαθηταὶ αὐτοῦ
house ⌞away from⌟ the crowd, his disciples asked him *{the}* *disciples* *his* about
3875 608 3836 4063 899 3412 2089 899 3836 3412 899 2089
n.asm p.g d.gsm n.gsm v.iai.3p r.asm.3 d.npm n.npm r.gsm.3

[a] βαπτισμοὺς ξεστῶν καὶ ποτηρίων· καὶ ἄλλα παρόμοια τοιαῦτα πολλὰ ποιεῖτε. included by TR after ἀνθρώπων.
[b] στήσητε UBS, NET. τηρήσητε TNIV.
[c] εἴ τίς ἔχει ὦτα ἀκούειν ἀκουέτω. included by TR after ἄνθρωπον.

NASB

of God, you hold
to the tradition of
men."
9 He was also
saying to them,
"You are experts
at setting aside the
commandment of
God in order to
keep your tradi-
tion. 10 For Moses
said, 'HONOR YOUR
FATHER AND YOUR
MOTHER'; and, 'HE
WHO SPEAKS EVIL OF
FATHER OR MOTHER,
IS TO BE PUT TO
DEATH'; 11 but you
say, 'If a man says
to *his* father or *his*
mother, whatever
I have that would
help you is Corban
(that is to say, [a]giv-
en *to God*),' 12 you
no longer permit
him to do anything
for *his* father or *his*
mother; 13 *thus* in-
validating the word
of God by your
tradition which
you have handed
down; and you do
many things such
as that."

The Heart of Man

14 After He called
the crowd to Him
again, He *began*
saying to them,
"Listen to Me,
all of you, and
understand: 15 there
is nothing outside
the man which can
defile him if it goes
into him; but the
things which pro-
ceed out of the man
are what defile the
man. 16 [[b]If anyone
has ears to hear, let
him hear."]
17 When he had
left the crowd *and*
entered the house,
His disciples ques-
tioned Him about

[a] Or *a gift*, i.e. *an offering*
[b] Early mss do not contain this verse

NIV

this parable. [18]"Are
you so dull?" he
asked. "Don't
you see that noth-
ing that enters a
person from the
outside can de-
file them? [19]For
it doesn't go into
their heart but
into their stom-
ach, and then out
of the body." (In
saying this, Jesus
declared all foods
clean.)
[20]He went on:
"What comes out
of a person is what
defiles them. [21]For
it is from within,
out of a person's
heart, that evil
thoughts come—
sexual immorali-
ty, theft, murder,
[22]adultery, greed,
malice, deceit,
lewdness, envy,
slander, arrogance
and folly. [23]All
these evils come
from inside and
defile a person."

Jesus Honors a Syrophoenician Woman's Faith

[24]Jesus left that
place and went
to the vicinity of
Tyre.[a] He entered
a house and did
not want anyone
to know it; yet he
could not keep
his presence se-
cret. [25]In fact,
as soon as she
heard about him,
a woman whose
little daughter was
possessed by an
impure spirit came
and fell at his feet.
[26]The woman was
a Greek, born in
Syrian Phoenicia.

τὴν παραβολήν. 18 καὶ λέγει αὐτοῖς· οὕτως καὶ ὑμεῖς
the parable. So he said to them, "Are you too so *too* *you*
3836 4130 2779 3306 899 1639 7007 2779 4048 2779 7007
d.asf n.asf cj v.pai.3s r.dpm.3 adv cj r.np.2

ἀσύνετοί ἐστε; ↱ ↱ οὐ νοεῖτε ὅτι πᾶν τὸ
⌊lacking in understanding?⌋ *Are* Do you not know that whatever comes into a man *{the}*
852 1639 3783 3783 4024 3783 4022 4246 1660 1650 476 3836
a.npm v.pai.2p pl v.pai.2p cj a.nsn d.nsn

ἔξωθεν εἰσπορευόμενον εἰς τὸν ἄνθρωπον ↱ οὐ δύναται αὐτὸν
from outside *comes* *into* *{the}* *man* is not able to defile him,
2033 1660 1650 3836 476 1538 4024 1538 3124 3124 899
adv pt.pm.nsn p.a d.asm n.asm pl v.ppi.3s r.asm.3

κοινῶσαι 19 ὅτι ↱ ↱ οὐκ εἰσπορεύεται αὐτοῦ εἰς τὴν καρδίαν ἀλλ᾽ εἰς
to defile because it does not enter his *{into}* *{the}* heart, but *{into}*
3124 4022 1660 1660 4024 1660 899 1650 3836 2840 247 1650
f.aa cj pl v.pmi.3s r.gsm.3 p.a d.asf n.asf cj p.a

τὴν κοιλίαν, καὶ εἰς τὸν ἀφεδρῶνα ἐκπορεύεται, καθαρίζων πάντα τὰ
his stomach, and goes out into the latrine?" *goes out* (Thus he declared all *{the}*
3836 3120 2779 1744 1744 1650 3836 909 1744 2751 4246 3836
d.asf n.asf cj p.a d.asm n.asm v.pmi.3s pt.pa.nsm a.apn d.apn

βρώματα; ↰ 20 ἔλεγεν δὲ ὅτι τὸ ἐκ τοῦ ἀνθρώπου
foods clean.) And he said, *And* ~ "What comes out of a person,
1109 2751 1254 3306 1254 4022 3836 1744 1744 1666 3836 476
n.apn v.iai.3s cj cj d.nsn p.g d.gsm n.gsm

ἐκπορευόμενον, ἐκεῖνο κοινοῖ τὸν ἄνθρωπον. 21 ἔσωθεν γὰρ ἐκ τῆς
comes out that is what defiles *{the}* him. For from within, *For* from the
1744 1697 3124 3836 476 1142 2277 1142 1666 3836
pt.pm.nsn r.nsn v.pai.3s d.asm n.asm adv cj p.g d.gsf

καρδίας τῶν ἀνθρώπων οἱ διαλογισμοὶ οἱ κακοὶ ἐκπορεύονται,
heart of a person, come evil *{the}* plots, *{the}* *evil* *come*
2840 3836 476 1744 2805 3836 1369 3836 2805 1744
n.gsf d.gpm n.gpm d.npm n.npm d.npm a.npm v.pmi.3p

πορνεῖαι, κλοπαί, φόνοι, 22 μοιχεῖαι, πλεονεξίαι, πονηρίαι, δόλος, ἀσέλγεια,
immoralities, thefts, murders, adulteries, greedy actions, wicked deeds, deceit, sensuality,
4518 3113 5840 3657 4432 4504 1515 816
n.npf n.npf n.npm n.npf n.npf n.npf n.nsm n.nsf

ὀφθαλμὸς πονηρός, βλασφημία, ὑπερηφανία, ἀφροσύνη· 23 πάντα ταῦτα τὰ
selfishness, *{evil}* slander, arrogance, ⌊lack of moral sense.⌋ All these *{the}*
4057 4505 1060 5661 932 4246 4047 3836
n.nsm a.nsm n.nsf n.nsf n.nsf a.npn r.npn d.npn

πονηρὰ ↰ ἔσωθεν ἐκπορεύεται καὶ κοινοῖ τὸν ἄνθρωπον. 24 ἐκεῖθεν
evil things come from within *come* and they defile a person." From there
4505 4047 1744 2277 1744 2779 3124 3836 476 1696
a.npn adv v.pmi.3s cj v.pai.3s d.asm n.asm adv

δὲ ἀναστὰς ἀπῆλθεν εἰς τὰ ὅρια Τύρου.[a] καὶ ⌊εἰσελθὼν εἰς⌋ οἰκίαν
{and} Jesus arose and went to the region of Tyre. *{and}* He entered a house
1254 482 599 1650 3836 3990 5602 2779 1656 1650 3864
cj pt.aa.nsm v.aai.3s p.a d.apn n.apn n.gsf cj pt.aa.nsm p.a n.asf

οὐδένα ἤθελεν γνῶναι, καὶ ↱ ↱ οὐκ ἠδυνήθη λαθεῖν·
and wanted no one *wanted* ⌊to know about⌋ it, yet he was not able ⌊to escape attention.⌋
2527 4029 2527 1182 2779 1538 1538 4024 1538 3291
a.asm v.iai.3s f.aa cj pl v.api.3s f.aa

25 ἀλλ᾽ εὐθὺς ἀκούσασα γυνὴ περὶ αὐτοῦ, ἧς εἶχεν τὸ
But immediately after hearing of him, a woman *of* *him* whose daughter had *{the}*
247 2318 201 4309 899 1222 4309 899 4005 2589 2400 3836
cj adv pt.aa.nsf n.nsf p.g r.gsm.3 r.gsf v.iai.3s d.nsn

θυγάτριον αὐτῆς πνεῦμα ἀκάθαρτον, ἐλθοῦσα προσέπεσεν πρὸς τοὺς
daughter *{her}* an unclean spirit *unclean* came and fell at *{the}* his
2589 899 176 4460 176 2262 4700 4639 3836 899
n.nsn r.gsf.3 n.asn a.asn pt.aa.nsf v.aai.3s p.a d.apm

πόδας αὐτοῦ· 26 ἡ δὲ γυνὴ ἦν Ἑλληνίς, Συροφοινίκισσα τῷ γένει· καὶ
feet. *his* The *{and}* woman was a Greek, a Syrophoenician by birth. *{and}*
4546 899 3836 1254 1222 1639 1820 5355 3836 1169 2779
n.apm r.gsm.3 d.nsf cj n.nsf v.iai.3s n.nsf n.nsf d.dsn n.dsn cj

NASB

the parable. [18]And
He *said to them,
"Are you so lack-
ing in understand-
ing also? Do you
not understand that
whatever goes into
the man from out-
side cannot defile
him, [19]because it
does not go into
his heart, but into
his stomach, and
is eliminated?"
(*Thus He* declared
all foods clean.)
[20]And He was say-
ing, "That which
proceeds out of the
man, that is what
defiles the man.
[21]For from within,
out of the heart
of men, proceed
the evil thoughts,
fornications, thefts,
murders, adulter-
ies, [22]deeds of
coveting *and* wick-
edness, *as well as*
deceit, sensuality,
envy, slander, pride
and foolishness.
[23]All these evil
things proceed
from within and
defile the man."

The Syrophoenician Woman

[24]Jesus got up and
went away from
there to the region
of Tyre[a]. And when
He had entered a
house, He wanted
no one to know *of*
it; yet He could
not escape notice.
[25]But after hearing
of Him, a woman
whose little daugh-
ter had an unclean
spirit immediately
came and fell at
His feet. [26]Now
the woman was a
[b]Gentile, of the Sy-
rophoenician race.

[a] 24 Many early manuscripts *Tyre and Sidon*

[a] καὶ Σιδῶνός included by TR after Τύρου.

[a] Two early mss add *and Sidon*
[b] Lit *Greek*

NIV

She begged Jesus to drive the demon out of her daughter.

27 "First let the children eat all they want," he told her, "for it is not right to take the children's bread and toss it to the dogs."

28 "Lord," she replied, "even the dogs under the table eat the children's crumbs."

29 Then he told her, "For such a reply, you may go; the demon has left your daughter."

30 She went home and found her child lying on the bed, and the demon gone.

Jesus Heals a Deaf and Mute Man

31 Then Jesus left the vicinity of Tyre and went through Sidon, down to the Sea of Galilee and into the region of the Decapolis.[a] 32 There some people brought to him a man who was deaf and could hardly talk, and they begged Jesus to place his hand on him.

33 After he took him aside, away from the crowd, Jesus put his fingers into the man's ears. Then he spit and touched the man's tongue. 34 He looked up to heaven and with a deep sigh said to him, *"Ephphatha!"* (which means "Be opened!"). 35 At this, the man's ears were opened,

ἠρώτα αὐτὸν ἵνα τὸ δαιμόνιον ἐκβάλῃ ἐκ τῆς θυγατρὸς αὐτῆς.
She begged Jesus to drive out the demon *drive out* from *{the}* her daughter. *her*
2263 899 2671 1675 1675 3836 1228 1675 1666 3836 899 2588 899
v.iai.3s r.asm.3 cj d.asn n.asn v.aas.3s p.g d.gsf n.gsf r.gsf.3

27 καὶ ἔλεγεν αὐτῇ· ἄφες πρῶτον χορτασθῆναι τὰ τέκνα,
{and} He said to her, "Let the children first be fed, *the children* for it is
2779 3306 899 918 3836 5451 4754 5963 3836 5451 1142 1639 1639
cj v.iai.3s r.dsf.3 v.aam.2s a.asn f.ap d.apn n.apn

οὐ γάρ ἐστιν καλὸν λαβεῖν τὸν ἄρτον τῶν τέκνων καὶ τοῖς
not *for* *it is* right to take the children's bread *{the}* *children's* and throw it to the
4024 1142 1639 2819 3284 3836 5451 788 3836 5451 2779 965 3836
pl cj v.pai.3s a.nsn f.aa d.asm n.asm d.gpn n.gpn cj d.dpn

κυναρίοις βαλεῖν. 28 ἡ δὲ ἀπεκρίθη καὶ λέγει αὐτῷ· κύριε· καὶ τὰ
dogs." *throw* *{the}* But she answered him, *{and}* saying, *him* "Lord, even the
3249 965 3836 1254 646 899 2779 3306 899 3261 2779 3836
n.dpn f.aa d.nsf cj v.api.3s cj v.pai.3s r.dsm.3 n.vsm adv d.npn

κυνάρια ὑποκάτω τῆς τραπέζης ἐσθίουσιν ἀπὸ τῶν ψιχίων τῶν παιδίων.
dogs under the table feed from the children's crumbs." *{the}* *children's*
3249 5691 3836 5544 2266 608 3836 4086 6033 3836 4086
n.npn p.g d.gsf n.gsf v.pai.3p p.g d.gpn n.gpn d.gpn n.gpn

29 καὶ εἶπεν αὐτῇ· διὰ τοῦτον τὸν λόγον ὕπαγε, ἐξελήλυθεν
And he said to her, "Because of this *{the}* reply, you may go; the demon has left
2779 3306 899 1328 4047 3836 3364 5632 3836 1228 2002
cj v.aai.3s r.dsf.3 p.a r.asm d.asm n.asm v.pam.2s v.rai.3s

ἐκ τῆς θυγατρός σου τὸ δαιμόνιον. 30 καὶ ἀπελθοῦσα εἰς τὸν οἶκον
{the} your daughter." *your* *the* *demon* And when she arrived at *{the}* her house
1666 3836 5148 2588 5148 3836 1228 2779 599 1650 3836 899 3875
p.g d.gsf n.gsf r.gs.2 d.nsn n.nsn cj pt.aa.nsf p.a d.asm n.asm

αὐτῆς εὗρεν τὸ παιδίον βεβλημένον ἐπὶ τὴν κλίνην καὶ τὸ δαιμόνιον
her she found the child lying on the bed, *{and}* the demon
899 2351 3836 4086 965 2093 3836 3109 2779 3836 1228
r.gsf.3 v.aai.3s d.asn n.asn pt.rp.asn p.a d.asf n.asf cj d.asn n.asn

ἐξεληλυθός. 31 καὶ πάλιν ἐξελθὼν ἐκ τῶν ὁρίων Τύρου ἦλθεν
having departed. *{and}* Departing again *Departing* from the region of Tyre, Jesus went
2002 2779 2002 4099 2002 1666 3836 3990 5602 2262
pt.ra.asn cj adv pt.aa.nsm p.g d.gpn n.gpn n.gsf v.aai.3s

διὰ Σιδῶνος εἰς τὴν θάλασσαν τῆς Γαλιλαίας ἀνὰ μέσον τῶν ὁρίων →
through Sidon to the Sea of Galilee, in the midst of the region of the
1328 4972 1650 3836 2498 3836 1133 324 3545 3836 3990
p.g n.gsf p.a d.asf n.asf d.gsf n.gsf p.a n.asn d.gpn n.gpn

Δεκαπόλεως. 32 καὶ φέρουσιν αὐτῷ κωφὸν καὶ μογιλάλον καὶ
Decapolis. And they brought to him a deaf man *{and}* who could hardly speak, and
1279 2779 5770 899 3273 2779 3652 2779
n.gsf cj v.pai.3p r.dsm.3 a.asm cj a.asm cj

παρακαλοῦσιν αὐτὸν ἵνα ἐπιθῇ ← αὐτῷ τὴν χεῖρα. 33 καὶ ἀπολαβόμενος
they begged him to lay his hand on him. *his* *hand* *{and}* Taking
4151 899 2671 2202 3836 5931 899 3836 5931 2779 655
v.pai.3p r.asm.3 cj v.aas.3s r.dsm.3 d.asf n.asf cj pt.am.nsm

αὐτὸν ↰ ἀπὸ τοῦ ὄχλου κατ' ἰδίαν ἔβαλεν τοὺς δακτύλους αὐτοῦ
him aside from the crowd privately, Jesus put *{the}* his fingers *his*
899 655 608 3836 4063 2848 2625 965 3836 899 1235 899
r.asm.3 p.g d.gsm n.gsm p.a a.asf v.aai.3s d.apm n.apm r.gsm.3

εἰς τὰ ὦτα αὐτοῦ καὶ πτύσας ἥψατο τῆς γλώσσης αὐτοῦ, 34 καὶ
into the man's ears, *man's* and after spitting, he touched *{the}* his tongue. *his* *{and}*
1650 3836 899 4044 899 2779 4772 721 3836 899 1185 899 2779
p.a d.apn n.apn r.gsm.3 cj pt.aa.nsm v.ami.3s d.gsf n.gsf r.gsm.3 cj

ἀναβλέψας εἰς τὸν οὐρανὸν ἐστέναξεν καὶ λέγει αὐτῷ· εφφαθα, ὅ
Looking up to *{the}* heaven, he gave a deep sigh and said to him, "Ephphatha!" (that
329 1650 3836 4041 5100 2779 3306 899 2395 4005
pt.aa.nsm p.a d.asm n.asm v.aai.3s cj v.pai.3s r.dsm.3 j r.nsn

ἐστιν διανοίχθητι. 35 καὶ εὐθέως[a] ἠνοίγησαν αὐτοῦ αἱ ἀκοαί, καὶ
is, "Be opened"). And immediately the man's ears were opened, *man's* *{the}* *ears* *{and}*
1639 1380 2779 2311 899 198 487 899 3836 198 2779
v.pai.3s v.apm.2s cj adv v.api.3p r.gsm.3 d.npf n.npf cj

NASB

And she kept asking Him to cast the demon out of her daughter. 27 And He was saying to her, "Let the children be satisfied first, for it is not good to take the children's bread and throw it to the dogs." 28 But she answered and *said to Him, "Yes, Lord, *but* even the dogs under the table feed on the children's crumbs." 29 And He said to her, "Because of this answer go; the demon has gone out of your daughter." 30 And going back to her home, she found the child lying on the bed, the demon having left.

31 Again He went out from the region of Tyre, and came through Sidon to the Sea of Galilee, within the region of Decapolis. 32 They *brought to Him one who was deaf and spoke with difficulty, and they *implored Him to lay His hand on him. 33 Jesus took him aside from the crowd, by himself, and put His fingers into his ears, and after spitting, He touched his tongue *with the saliva;* 34 and looking up to heaven with a deep sigh, He *said to him, "Ephphatha!" that is, "Be opened!" 35 And his ears were opened,

[a] 31 That is, the Ten Cities

[a] [εὐθέως] UBS.

NIV

his tongue was
loosened and he
began to speak
plainly.
[36]Jesus com-
manded them not
to tell anyone. But
the more he did
so, the more they
kept talking about
it. [37]People were
overwhelmed with
amazement. "He
has done every-
thing well," they
said. "He even
makes the deaf
hear and the mute
speak."

Jesus Feeds the Four Thousand

8 During those
days another
large crowd gath-
ered. Since they
had nothing to eat,
Jesus called his
disciples to him
and said, [2]"I have
compassion for
these people; they
have already been
with me three days
and have nothing
to eat. [3]If I send
them home hun-
gry, they will col-
lapse on the way,
because some of
them have come a
long distance."
[4]His disciples
answered, "But
where in this re-
mote place can
anyone get enough
bread to feed
them?"
[5]"How many
loaves do you
have?" Jesus
asked.
"Seven," they re-
plied.
[6]He told the
crowd to sit down
on the ground.
When he had taken
the seven loaves

ἐλύθη ὁ δεσμὸς τῆς γλώσσης αὐτοῦ καὶ
that which bound his tongue was loosened, *that* *which bound* *{the}* *tongue* *his* and
3836 1301 1301 899 1185 3395 3836 1301 3836 1185 899 2779
v.api.3s d.nsm n.nsm d.gsf n.gsf r.gsm.3 cj

ἐλάλει ὀρθῶς. [36] καὶ διεστείλατο αὐτοῖς ἵνα μηδενὶ λέγωσιν·
⌊he began to speak⌋ clearly. *{and}* Jesus ordered them to tell no one, *tell* but
3281 3987 2779 1403 899 2671 3306 3594 3306 1254
v.iai.3s adv cj v.ami.3s r.dpm.3 cj a.dsm v.pas.3p

ὅσον δὲ αὐτοῖς διεστέλλετο, αὐτοὶ μᾶλλον περισσότερον
the more *but* he ordered them *he ordered* the more they *{more}* *more*
4012 1254 1403 1403 899 1403 4358 899 3437 4358
r.asn cj r.dpm.3 v.imi.3s r.npm adv.c adv.c

ἐκήρυσσον. [37] καὶ ↱ ↱ ὑπερπερισσῶς ἐξεπλήσσοντο λέγοντες·
spread the news. *{and}* They were absolutely astonished, saying, "He has done
3062 2779 1742 1742 5669 1742 3306 4472 4472 4472
v.iai.3p cj adv v.ipi.3p pt.pa.npm

καλῶς πάντα πεποίηκεν, καὶ τοὺς κωφοὺς ποιεῖ ἀκούειν
all things well. *all things* *He has done* *{also}* He makes the deaf *He makes* to hear
4246 4246 2822 4246 4472 2779 4472 4472 3836 3273 4472 201
adv a.apn v.rai.3s adv d.apm a.apm v.pai.3s f.pa

καὶ τοὺς[a] ἀλάλους λαλεῖν.
and the mute to speak!"
2779 3836 228 3281
cj d.apm a.apm f.pa

[8:1] ἐν ἐκείναις ταῖς ἡμέραις ↱ πάλιν πολλοῦ ὄχλου ὄντος καὶ μὴ
In those *{the}* days, when once again a large crowd had gathered, and not
1877 1697 3836 2465 1639 4099 4498 4063 1639 2779 3590
p.d r.dpf d.dpf n.dpf adv a.gsm n.gsm pt.pa.gsm cj pl

ἐχόντων τί φάγωσιν, προσκαλεσάμενος τοὺς μαθητὰς λέγει αὐτοῖς·
having anything to eat, Jesus called his disciples and said to them,
2400 5515 2266 4673 3836 3412 3306 899
pt.pa.gpm r.asn v.aas.3p pt.am.nsm d.apm n.apm v.pai.3s r.dpm.3

[2] σπλαγχνίζομαι ἐπὶ τὸν ὄχλον, ὅτι ἤδη ἡμέραι τρεῖς προσμένουσίν μοι
"I have compassion on the crowd, because *already* *days* *three* ⌊they have stayed with⌋ me
5072 2093 3836 4063 4022 2453 2465 5552 4693 1609
v.ppi.1s p.a d.asm n.asm cj adv n.npf a.npf v.pai.3p r.ds.1

καὶ ↱ ↱ οὐκ ἔχουσιν τί φάγωσιν· [3] καὶ ἐὰν ἀπολύσω
three days already and they do not have anything to eat. *{and}* If I send
5552 2465 2453 2779 2400 2400 4024 2400 5515 2266 2779 1569 668
cj pl v.pai.3p r.asn v.aas.3p cj cj v.aas.1s

αὐτοὺς νήστεις εἰς οἶκον αὐτῶν, ἐκλυθήσονται ἐν
them to their homes ⌊without food,⌋ *to* *homes* *their* ⌊they will faint from exhaustion⌋ on
899 1650 899 3875 3765 1650 3875 899 1725 1877
r.apm.3 a.apm p.a n.asm r.gpm.3 v.fpi.3p p.d

τῇ ὁδῷ· καί τινες αὐτῶν ἀπὸ μακρόθεν ἥκασιν. [4] καὶ
the way; and some of them have come from a distance." *have come* And his disciples
3836 3847 2779 5516 899 2457 2457 608 3427 2457 2779 899 3412
d.dsf n.dsf cj r.npm r.gpm.3 p.g adv v.rai.3p cj

ἀπεκρίθησαν αὐτῷ οἱ μαθηταὶ αὐτοῦ ὅτι πόθεν
answered him, *{the}* *disciples* *his* ~ ⌊"From what source⌋ can anyone feed
646 899 3836 3412 899 4022 4470 1538 5516 5963
v.api.3p r.dsm.3 d.npm n.npm r.gsm.3 cj cj

τούτους δυνήσεταί τις ὧδε χορτάσαι ἄρτων ἐπ᾽ ἐρημίας;
these people *can* *anyone* with bread here *feed* *with bread* in this desolate place?"
4047 1538 5516 788 788 6045 5963 788 2093 2244
r.apm v.fpi.3s r.nsm adv f.aa n.gpm p.g n.gsf

[5] καὶ ἠρώτα αὐτούς· πόσους ἔχετε ἄρτους; οἱ δὲ εἶπαν· ἑπτά.
And he asked them, "How many loaves ⌊do you have?"⌋ *loaves* They *{and}* said, "Seven."
2779 2263 899 4531 788 2400 788 3836 1254 3306 2231
cj v.iai.3s r.apm.3 r.apm v.pai.2p n.apm d.npm cj v.aai.3p a.apm

[6] καὶ παραγγέλλει τῷ ὄχλῳ ἀναπεσεῖν ἐπὶ τῆς γῆς· καὶ λαβὼν τοὺς ἑπτὰ ἄρτους
So he directed the crowd to sit down on the ground. *{and}* Taking the seven loaves
2779 4133 3836 4063 404 2093 3836 1178 2779 3284 3836 2231 788
cj v.pai.3s d.dsm n.dsm f.aa p.g d.gsf n.gsf cj pt.aa.nsm d.apm a.apm n.apm

[a] [τοὺς] UBS.

NASB

and the impedi-
ment of his tongue
was removed, and
he *began* speaking
plainly. [36]And He
gave them orders
not to tell anyone;
but the more He
ordered them,
the more widely
they continued to
proclaim it. [37]They
were utterly aston-
ished, saying, "He
has done all things
well; He makes
even the deaf to
hear and the mute
to speak."

Four Thousand Fed

[8:1]In those days,
when there was
again a large crowd
and they had noth-
ing to eat, Jesus
called His disciples
and *said to them,
[2]"I feel compas-
sion for the people
because they have
remained with Me
now three days and
have nothing to
eat. [3]If I send them
away hungry to
their homes, they
will faint on the
way; and some of
them have come
from a great dis-
tance." [4]And His
disciples answered
Him, "Where will
anyone be able
to find enough
bread here in *this*
desolate place
to satisfy these
people?" [5]And He
was asking them,
"How many loaves
do you have?" And
they said, "Seven."
[6]And He *di-
rected the people
to sit down on the
ground; and taking
the seven loaves,

NIV

and given thanks,
he broke them and
gave them to his
disciples to distrib-
ute to the people,
and they did so.
7They had a few
small fish as well;
he gave thanks
for them also and
told the disciples
to distribute them.
8The people ate
and were satisfied.
Afterward the dis-
ciples picked up
seven basketfuls
of broken pieces
that were left over.
9About four thou-
sand were present.
After he had sent
them away, 10he
got into the boat
with his disciples
and went to the
region of Dalma-
nutha.
11The Pharisees
came and began
to question Jesus.
To test him, they
asked him for a
sign from heaven.
12He sighed deeply
and said, "Why
does this genera-
tion ask for a sign?
Truly I tell you, no
sign will be given
to it." 13Then he
left them, got back
into the boat and
crossed to the oth-
er side.

The Yeast of the Pharisees and Herod

14The disciples
had forgotten to
bring bread, ex-
cept for one loaf
they had with them
in the boat. 15"Be
careful," Jesus
warned them.
"Watch out for the
yeast of the Phar-
isees and that of
Herod."
16They discussed
this with one an-
other and said, "It
is because we have
no bread."

εὐχαριστήσας ἔκλασεν καὶ ἐδίδου τοῖς μαθηταῖς αὐτοῦ ἵνα
and giving thanks, he broke them and gave them to his disciples *his* to
2373 3089 2779 1443 3836 899 3412 899 2671
pt.aa.nsm v.aai.3s cj v.iai.3s d.dpm n.dpm r.gsm.3 cj

παρατιθῶσιν, καὶ παρέθηκαν τῷ ὄχλῳ. 7 ↱ καὶ εἶχον ἰχθύδια
distribute. So they distributed the bread ⌞to the⌟ crowd. They also had a few small fish.
4192 2779 4192 3836 4063 2400 2779 2400 3900 2715
v.pas.3p cj v.aai.3p d.dsm n.dsm cj v.iai.3p n.apn

ὀλίγα· καὶ εὐλογήσας αὐτὰ εἶπεν καὶ ταῦτα
few *{and}* Blessing these, Jesus told them to distribute these as well. *these*
3900 2779 2328 899 3306 4192 4192 4047 2779 4047
a.apn cj pt.aa.nsm r.apn.3 v.aai.3s adv r.apn

παρατιθέναι. 8 καὶ ἔφαγον καὶ ἐχορτάσθησαν, καὶ ἦραν ↱
to distribute And they ate and were filled. And ⌞they picked up⌟ seven baskets of
4192 2779 2266 2779 5963 2779 149 2231 5083 3083
f.pa cj v.aai.3p cj v.api.3p cj v.aai.3p

περισσεύματα κλασμάτων ἑπτὰ σπυρίδας. 9 ἦσαν δὲ ὡς τετρακισχίλιοι.
leftover pieces. *seven baskets* ⌞There were⌟ *{and}* about four thousand
4354 3083 2231 5083 1639 1254 6055 5483
n.apn n.gpn a.apf n.apf v.iai.3p cj pl a.npm

↰ καὶ ἀπέλυσεν αὐτούς. ↰ ↰ ↰ 10 καὶ εὐθὺς ἐμβὰς εἰς τὸ πλοῖον
present, and he sent them on their way. And immediately he got into the boat
1639 2779 668 899 668 668 668 2779 2318 1832 1650 3836 4450
cj v.aai.3s r.apm.3 cj adv pt.aa.nsm p.a d.asn n.asn

μετὰ τῶν μαθητῶν αὐτοῦ ἦλθεν εἰς τὰ μέρη Δαλμανουθά. 11 καὶ
with *{the}* his disciples *his* and went to the district of Dalmanutha. *{and}* The
3552 3836 899 3412 899 2262 1650 3836 3538 1236 2779 3836
p.g d.gpm n.gpm r.gsm.3 v.aai.3s p.a d.apn n.apn n.gsf cj

ἐξῆλθον οἱ Φαρισαῖοι καὶ ἤρξαντο συζητεῖν αὐτῷ, ζητοῦντες παρ᾽ αὐτοῦ
Pharisees came *The Pharisees* and began to argue with him, seeking from him
5757 2002 3836 5757 2779 806 5184 899 2426 4123 899
v.aai.3p d.npm n.npm cj v.ami.3p f.pa r.dsm.3 pt.pa.npm p.g r.gsm.3

σημεῖον ἀπὸ τοῦ οὐρανοῦ, πειράζοντες αὐτόν. 12 καὶ ἀναστενάξας τῷ
a sign from *{the}* heaven, testing him. *{and}* Sighing deeply in his
4956 608 3836 4041 4279 899 2779 417 3836 899
n.asn p.g d.gsm n.gsm pt.pa.npm r.asm.3 cj pt.aa.nsm d.dsn

πνεύματι αὐτοῦ λέγει· τί ↱ ἡ γενεὰ αὕτη ζητεῖ σημεῖον;
spirit *his* he said, "Why does *{the}* this generation *this* seek a sign? I tell
4460 899 3306 5515 2426 3836 4047 1155 4047 2426 4956 3306 3306
n.dsn r.gsm.3 v.pai.3s r.asn d.nsf n.nsf r.nsf v.pai.3s n.nsn

ἀμὴν λέγω ὑμῖν, εἰ δοθήσεται τῇ γενεᾷ ταύτῃ σημεῖον.
you the truth, *I tell you* no sign will be given to this generation." *this sign*
7007 297 3306 7007 1623 4956 1443 3836 4047 1155 4047 4956
pl v.pai.1s r.dp.2 cj v.fpi.3s d.dsf n.dsf r.dsf n.nsn

13 καὶ ἀφεὶς αὐτοὺς πάλιν ἐμβὰς ἀπῆλθεν εἰς τὸ πέραν.
Then he left them, got into the boat again, *got into* and crossed to the other side.
2779 918 899 1832 1832 4099 1832 599 1650 3836 4305
cj pt.aa.nsm r.apm.3 adv pt.aa.nsm v.aai.3s p.a d.asn adv

14 καὶ ἐπελάθοντο λαβεῖν ἄρτους καὶ ⌞εἰ μὴ⌟ ἕνα ἄρτον
Now the disciples had forgotten to take along ⌞loaves of bread,⌟ *{and}* except for one loaf
2779 2140 3284 788 2779 1623 3590 1651 788
cj v.ami.3p f.aa n.apm cj cj pl a.asm n.asm

οὐκ εἶχον μεθ᾽ ἑαυτῶν ἐν τῷ πλοίῳ. 15 καὶ διεστέλλετο αὐτοῖς λέγων·
~ they had with them in the boat. And Jesus began to admonish them, saying,
4024 2400 3552 1571 1877 3836 4450 2779 1403 899 3306
pl v.iai.3p p.g r.gpm.3 p.d d.dsn n.dsn cj v.imi.3s r.dpm.3 pt.pa.nsm

ὁρᾶτε, βλέπετε ἀπὸ τῆς ζύμης τῶν Φαρισαίων καὶ τῆς ζύμης Ἡρῴδου. 16 καὶ
⌞"Watch out!⌟ Beware of the leaven of the Pharisees and the leaven of Herod!" And
3972 1063 608 3836 2434 3836 5757 2779 3836 2434 2476 2779
v.pam.2p v.pam.2p p.g d.gsf n.gsf d.gpm n.gpm cj d.gsf n.gsf n.gsm cj

διελογίζοντο πρὸς ἀλλήλους ὅτι ἄρτους οὐκ ἔχουσιν.[a]
they kept discussing with one another the fact that they had no bread. *no they had*
1368 4639 253 4022 2400 2400 4024 788 4024 2400
v.imi.3p p.a r.apm cj n.apm pl v.pai.3p

[a] ἔχουσιν UBS, NET. ἔχομεν TNIV.

NASB

He gave thanks
and broke them,
and started giv-
ing them to His
disciples to serve
to them, and they
served them to the
people. 7They also
had a few small
fish; and after He
had blessed them,
He ordered these to
be served as well.
8And they ate and
were satisfied; and
they picked up
seven large baskets
full of what was
left over of the bro-
ken pieces. 9About
four thousand were
there; and He sent
them away. 10And
immediately He
entered the boat
with His disciples
and came to the
district of Dalma-
nutha.
11The Pharisees
came out and
began to argue
with Him, seeking
from Him a sign
from heaven, to
test Him. 12Sigh-
ing deeply in His
spirit, He *said,
"Why does this
generation seek
for a sign? Truly I
say to you, no sign
will be given to
this generation."
13Leaving them, He
again embarked
and went away to
the other side.
14And they had
forgotten to take
bread, and did not
have more than
one loaf in the boat
with them. 15And
He was giving
orders to them,
saying, "Watch
out! Beware of the
leaven of the Phari-
sees and the leaven
of Herod." 16They
began to discuss
with one another
the fact that they
had no bread.

NIV

17 Aware of their
discussion, Jesus
asked them: "Why
are you talking
about having no
bread? Do you still
not see or under-
stand? Are your
hearts hardened?
18 Do you have eyes
but fail to see, and
ears but fail to
hear? And don't
you remember?
19 When I broke the
five loaves for the
five thousand, how
many basketfuls
of pieces did you
pick up?"
"Twelve," they
replied.
20 "And when I
broke the seven
loaves for the four
thousand, how
many basketfuls
of pieces did you
pick up?"
They answered,
"Seven."
21 He said to them,
"Do you still not
understand?"

Jesus Heals a Blind Man at Bethsaida

22 They came
to Bethsaida,
and some people
brought a blind
man and begged
Jesus to touch him.
23 He took the blind
man by the hand
and led him out-
side the village.
When he had spit
on the man's eyes
and put his hands
on him, Jesus
asked, "Do you see
anything?"
24 He looked up
and said, "I see
people; they look
like trees walking
around."
25 Once more
Jesus put his hands
on the man's eyes.
Then his eyes were
opened, his sight
was restored, and
he saw everything
clearly.

17 καὶ γνοὺς λέγει αὐτοῖς· τί διαλογίζεσθε ὅτι
{and} Jesus, aware of this, said to them, "Why are you discussing the fact that you have
2779 1182 3306 899 5515 1368 4022 2400 2400
cj pt.aa.nsm v.pai.3s r.dpm.3 r.asn v.pmi.2p cj

ἄρτους οὐκ ἔχετε; ↱ ↱ οὔπω νοεῖτε οὐδὲ συνίετε;
no bread? *no* *you have* Do you not yet perceive or understand? Do you have
4024 788 4024 2400 3783 3783 4037 3783 4028 5317 2400 2400 2400
n.apm pl v.pai.2p adv v.pai.2p cj v.pai.2p

πεπωρωμένην ἔχετε τὴν καρδίαν ὑμῶν; 18 ὀφθαλμοὺς ἔχοντες ↱ ↱ οὐ
hardened *Do you have* *{the}* hearts? *{your}* Having eyes, *Having* do you not
4800 2400 3836 2840 7007 2400 4057 2400 1063 1063 4024
pt.rp.asf v.pai.2p d.asf n.asf r.gp.2 n.apm pt.pa.npm pl

βλέπετε καὶ ὦτα ἔχοντες ↱ ↱ οὐκ ἀκούετε; καὶ ↱ ↱ οὐ μνημονεύετε,
see? And having ears, *having* do you not hear? And do you not remember?
1063 2779 2400 4044 2400 201 201 4024 201 2779 3648 3648 4024 3648
v.pai.2p cj n.apn pt.pa.npm pl v.pai.2p cj pl v.pai.2p

19 ὅτε τοὺς πέντε ἄρτους ἔκλασα εἰς τοὺς πεντακισχιλίους, πόσους
When I broke the five loaves *I broke* for the five thousand, how many
4021 3089 3089 3836 4297 788 3089 1650 3836 4295 4531
cj d.apm a.apm n.apm v.aai.1s p.a d.apm a.apm r.apm

κοφίνους κλασμάτων πλήρεις ἤρατε; λέγουσιν αὐτῷ· δώδεκα.
baskets full of broken pieces *full* ⌞did you pick up?"⌟ They said to him, "Twelve."
3186 4441 3083 4441 149 3306 899 1557
n.apm n.gpn a.apm v.aai.2p v.pai.3p r.dsm.3 a.apm

20 ὅτε τοὺς ἑπτὰ εἰς τοὺς τετρακισχιλίους, πόσων σπυρίδων
"When I broke the seven loaves for the four thousand, how many baskets
4021 3836 2231 1650 3836 5483 4531 5083
cj d.apm a.apm p.a d.apm a.apm r.gpf n.gpf

πληρώματα κλασμάτων ἤρατε; καὶ λέγουσιν[a] ἑπτά. 21 καὶ ἔλεγεν
full of broken pieces ⌞did you pick up?"⌟ And they said, "Seven." And he said
4445 3083 149 2779 3306 2231 2779 3306
n.apn n.gpn v.aai.2p cj v.pai.3p a.gpf cj v.iai.3s

αὐτοῖς· ↱ ↱ οὔπω συνίετε; 22 Καὶ ἔρχονται εἰς Βηθσαϊδάν. καὶ
to them, "Do you not yet understand?" And they came to Bethsaida. And some people
899 5317 5317 4037 5317 2779 2262 1650 1034 2779
r.dpm.3 adv v.pai.2p cj v.pmi.3p p.a n.asf cj

φέρουσιν αὐτῷ τυφλὸν καὶ παρακαλοῦσιν αὐτὸν ἵνα αὐτοῦ ἅψηται. 23 καὶ
brought to him a blind man and begged him to touch him. *touch* And
5770 899 5603 2779 4151 899 2671 721 899 721 2779
v.pai.3p r.dsm.3 a.asm cj v.pai.3p r.asm.3 cj r.gsm.3 v.ams.3s cj

ἐπιλαβόμενος τῆς χειρὸς τοῦ τυφλοῦ ἐξήνεγκεν αὐτὸν ἔξω τῆς κώμης καὶ
taking the hand of the blind man, he led him outside the village. Then,
2138 3836 5931 3836 5603 1766 899 2032 3836 3267 2779
pt.am.nsm d.gsf n.gsf d.gsm a.gsm v.aai.3s r.asm.3 p.g d.gsf n.gsf cj

πτύσας εἰς τὰ ὄμματα αὐτοῦ, ↰ ↰ ἐπιθεὶς τὰς χεῖρας ↰
after moistening *{on}* the eyes ⌞of the blind man⌟ with saliva and laying his hands on
4772 1650 3836 3921 899 4772 4772 2202 3836 5931 2202
pt.aa.nsm p.a d.apn n.apn r.gsm.3 pt.aa.nsm d.apf n.apf

αὐτῷ ἐπηρώτα αὐτόν· ⌞εἴ τι⌟ βλέπεις; 24 καὶ ἀναβλέψας
him, Jesus asked him, "What do you see?" *{and}* ⌞Upon regaining his sight,⌟
899 2089 899 1623 5516 1063 2779 329
r.dsm.3 v.iai.3s r.asm.3 cj r.asn v.pai.2s cj pt.aa.nsm

ἔλεγεν· βλέπω τοὺς ἀνθρώπους ὅτι ὡς δένδρα ὁρῶ
he said, "I see *{the}* people ~ walking, but I see them as trees." *I see*
3306 1063 3836 476 4022 4344 3972 3972 6055 1285 3972
v.iai.3s v.pai.1s d.apm n.apm cj pl n.apn v.pai.1s

περιπατοῦντας. 25 εἶτα πάλιν ἐπέθηκεν τὰς χεῖρας ἐπὶ τοὺς ὀφθαλμοὺς
walking Then Jesus again put his hands on the man's eyes,
4344 1663 4099 2202 3836 5931 2093 3836 899 4057
pt.pa.apm adv adv v.aai.3s d.apf n.apf p.a d.apm n.apm

αὐτοῦ, καὶ διέβλεψεν καὶ ἀπεκατέστη καὶ ἐνέβλεπεν τηλαυγῶς
man's and he saw clearly. *{and}* His sight was restored and he saw everything distinctly.
899 2779 1332 2779 635 2779 1838 570 5495
r.gsm.3 cj v.aai.3s cj v.aai.3s cj v.iai.3s adv

NASB

17 And Jesus,
aware of this, *said
to them, "Why do
you discuss *the*
fact that you have
no bread? Do you
not yet see or un-
derstand? Do you
have a hardened
heart? 18 HAVING
EYES, DO YOU NOT
SEE? AND HAVING
EARS, DO YOU NOT
HEAR? And do you
not remember,
19 when I broke the
five loaves for the
five thousand, how
many baskets full
of broken pieces
you picked up?"
They *said to Him,
"Twelve." 20 "When
I broke the seven
for the four thou-
sand, how many
large baskets full of
broken pieces did
you pick up?" And
they *said to Him,
"Seven." 21 And
He was saying to
them, "Do you not
yet understand?"
22 And they *came
to Bethsaida. And
they *brought a
blind man to Jesus
and *implored
Him to touch him.
23 Taking the blind
man by the hand,
He brought him out
of the village; and
after spitting on
his eyes and laying
His hands on him,
He asked him, "Do
you see anything?"
24 And he looked
up and said, "I see
men, for I see *them*
like trees, walking
around." 25 Then
again He laid His
hands on his eyes;
and he looked
intently and was
restored, and *began*
to see everything
clearly.

[a] αὐτῷ included by UBS after λέγουσιν.

NIV

26 Jesus sent him
home, saying,
"Don't even go
into[a] the village."

Peter Declares That Jesus Is the Messiah

27 Jesus and his
disciples went
on to the villages
around Caesa-
rea Philippi. On
the way he asked
them, "Who do
people say I am?"
28 They replied,
"Some say John
the Baptist; others
say Elijah; and still
others, one of the
prophets."
29 "But what about
you?" he asked.
"Who do you say
I am?"
Peter answered,
"You are the Mes-
siah."
30 Jesus warned
them not to tell
anyone about him.

Jesus Predicts His Death

31 He then be-
gan to teach them
that the Son of
Man must suffer
many things and
be rejected by the
elders, the chief
priests and the
teachers of the law,
and that he must
be killed and af-
ter three days rise
again. 32 He spoke
plainly about this,
and Peter took him
aside and began to
rebuke him.
33 But when Jesus
turned and looked
at his disciples,
he rebuked Peter.
"Get behind me,
Satan!" he said.
"You do not have
in mind the con-
cerns of God, but
merely human
concerns."

[a] 26 Some manu-
scripts *go and tell
anyone in*

ἅπαντα. 26 καὶ ἀπέστειλεν αὐτὸν εἰς οἶκον αὐτοῦ λέγων· μηδὲ
everything And Jesus sent him to his home, *his* saying, "Do not go back
570 2779 690 899 1650 899 3875 899 3306 1656 3593 1656 1656
a.apn cj v.aai.3s r.asm.3 p.a n.asm r.gsm.3 pt.pa.nsm adv

εἰς τὴν κώμην εἰσέλθῃς.[a] 27 καὶ ἐξῆλθεν ὁ Ἰησοῦς καὶ οἱ μαθηταὶ αὐτοῦ
into the village." *Do go back* And *went on* *{the}* Jesus and *{the}* his disciples *his*
1650 3836 3267 1656 2779 2002 3836 2652 2779 3836 899 3412 899
p.a d.asf n.asf v.aas.2s cj v.aai.3s d.nsm n.nsm cj d.npm n.npm r.gsm.3

εἰς τὰς κώμας Καισαρείας τῆς Φιλίππου· καὶ ἐν τῇ ὁδῷ ἐπηρώτα
went on to the villages of Caesarea *{the}* Philippi. *{and}* On the way he questioned
2002 2002 1650 3836 3267 2791 3836 5805 2779 1877 3836 3847 2089
p.a d.apf n.apf n.gsf d.gsf n.gsm cj p.d d.dsf n.dsf v.iai.3s

τοὺς μαθητὰς αὐτοῦ λέγων αὐτοῖς· τίνα με λέγουσιν οἱ
{the} his disciples, *his* saying to them, "Who do people say I *do say* *{the}*
3836 899 3412 899 3306 899 5515 3306 476 3306 1609 3306 3836
d.apm n.apm r.gsm.3 pt.pa.nsm r.dpm.3 r.asm r.as.1 v.pai.3p d.npm

ἄνθρωποι εἶναι; 28 οἱ δὲ εἶπαν αὐτῷ λέγοντες ὅτι[b] Ἰωάννην τὸν
people am?" So they *So* answered him, saying, ~ "John the
476 1639 1254 3836 1254 3306 899 3306 4022 2722 3836
n.npm f.pa d.npm cj v.aai.3p r.dsm.3 pt.pa.npm cj n.asm d.asm

βαπτιστήν, καὶ ἄλλοι Ἠλίαν, ἄλλοι δὲ ὅτι εἷς τῶν προφητῶν. 29 καὶ αὐτὸς
baptizer; and others, Elijah; but others, *but* ~ one of the prophets." And he
969 2779 257 2460 1254 257 1254 4022 1651 3836 4737 2779 899
n.asm cj r.npm n.asm r.npm cj cj a.nsm d.gpm n.gpm cj r.nsm

ἐπηρώτα αὐτούς· ὑμεῖς δὲ τίνα με λέγετε εἶναι; ἀποκριθεὶς
asked them, "But who do you *But* *who* say I *do say* am?" Peter answered,
2089 899 1254 5515 3306 7007 1254 5515 3306 1609 3306 1639 4377 646
v.iai.3s r.apm.3 r.np.2 cj r.asm r.as.1 v.pai.2p f.pa pt.ap.nsm

ὁ Πέτρος λέγει αὐτῷ· σὺ εἶ ὁ χριστός. 30 καὶ ἐπετίμησεν αὐτοῖς ↱
{the} *Peter* saying to him, "You are the Christ." And he strictly warned them not
3836 4377 3306 899 5148 1639 3836 5986 2779 2203 899 3594
d.nsm n.nsm v.pai.3s r.dsm.3 r.ns.2 v.pai.2s d.nsm n.nsm cj v.aai.3s r.dpm.3

ἵνα μηδενὶ λέγωσιν περὶ αὐτοῦ. 31 καὶ ἤρξατο διδάσκειν αὐτοὺς ὅτι
to tell anyone *tell* about him. Then Jesus began to teach them that
2671 3306 3594 3306 4309 899 2779 806 1438 899 4022
cj a.dsm v.pas.3p p.g r.gsm.3 cj v.ami.3s f.pa r.apm.3 cj

δεῖ τὸν υἱὸν τοῦ ἀνθρώπου πολλὰ παθεῖν καὶ
⌊it was necessary⌋ for the Son of Man to suffer many things *to suffer* and
1256 3836 5626 3836 476 4248 4248 4498 4248 2779
v.pai.3s d.asm n.asm d.gsm n.gsm a.apn f.aa cj

ἀποδοκιμασθῆναι ὑπὸ τῶν πρεσβυτέρων καὶ τῶν ἀρχιερέων καὶ τῶν γραμματέων
be rejected by the elders and the ruling priests and *{the}* scribes,
627 5679 3836 4565 2779 3836 797 2779 3836 1208
f.ap p.g d.gpm a.gpm cj d.gpm n.gpm cj d.gpm n.gpm

καὶ ἀποκτανθῆναι καὶ μετὰ τρεῖς ἡμέρας ἀναστῆναι· 32 καὶ
and be killed and after three days to rise again. And he was speaking
2779 650 2779 3552 5552 2465 482 2779 3281 3281 3281
cj f.ap cj p.a a.apf n.apf f.aa cj

παρρησίᾳ τὸν λόγον ἐλάλει. καὶ προσλαβόμενος ὁ Πέτρος αὐτὸν ↰
openly about this. *he was speaking* So Peter took *{the}* *Peter* him aside
4244 3836 3364 3281 2779 4377 4689 3836 4377 899 4689
n.dsf d.asm n.asm v.iai.3s cj pt.am.nsm d.nsm n.nsm r.asm.3

ἤρξατο ἐπιτιμᾶν αὐτῷ. 33 ὁ δὲ ἐπιστραφεὶς καὶ ἰδὼν τοὺς μαθητὰς
and began to rebuke him. *he* But after turning and ⌊looking at⌋ *{the}* his disciples,
806 2203 899 3836 1254 2188 2779 1625 3836 899 3412
v.ami.3s f.pa r.dsm.3 d.nsm cj pt.ap.nsm cj pt.aa.nsm d.apm n.apm

αὐτοῦ ἐπετίμησεν Πέτρῳ καὶ λέγει· ὕπαγε ὀπίσω μου, σατανᾶ, ὅτι ↱ ↱ οὐ
his he rebuked Peter and said, "Get behind me, Satan! For you are not
899 3836 2203 4377 2779 3306 5632 3958 1609 4928 4022 5858 5858 4024
r.gsm.3 v.aai.3s n.dsm cj v.pai.3s v.pam.2s p.g r.gs.1 n.vsm cj pl

φρονεῖς τὰ τοῦ θεοῦ ἀλλὰ τὰ τῶν ἀνθρώπων. 34 καὶ προσκαλεσάμενος
thinking the thoughts of God, but those of men." *{and}* When he had called
5858 3836 3836 2536 247 3836 3836 476 2779 4673
v.pai.2s d.apn d.gsm n.gsm cj d.apn d.gpm n.gpm cj pt.am.nsm

[a] μηδὲ εἴπῃς τινι ἐν τῇ κώμῃ included by TR after εἰσέλθῃς.
[b] [ὅτι] UBS.

NASB

26 And He sent him
to his home, say-
ing, "Do not even
enter the village."

Peter's Confession of Christ

27 Jesus went out,
along with His
disciples, to the vil-
lages of Caesarea
Philippi; and on the
way He questioned
His disciples, say-
ing to them, "Who
do people say that
I am?" 28 They told
Him, saying, "John
the Baptist; and
others *say* Elijah;
but others, one
of the prophets."
29 And He *continued*
by questioning
them, "But who
do you say that I
am?" Peter *an-
swered and *said to
Him, "You are the
Christ." 30 And He
warned them to tell
no one about Him.
31 And He began to
teach them that the
Son of Man must
suffer many things
and be rejected
by the elders and
the chief priests
and the scribes,
and be killed, and
after three days
rise again. 32 And
He was stating
the matter plainly.
And Peter took
Him aside and
began to rebuke
Him. 33 But turning
around and seeing
His disciples, He
rebuked Peter and
*said, "Get behind
Me, Satan; for you
are not setting your
mind on [a]God's in-
terests, but man's."

[a] Lit *the things of
God*

NIV

The Way of the Cross

[34]Then he called
the crowd to him
along with his dis-
ciples and said:
"Whoever wants
to be my disciple
must deny them-
selves and take up
their cross and fol-
low me. [35]For who-
ever wants to save
their life[a] will lose
it, but whoever los-
es their life for me
and for the gospel
will save it. [36]What
good is it for
someone to gain
the whole world,
yet forfeit their
soul? [37]Or what
can anyone give in
exchange for their
soul? [38]If anyone is
ashamed of me and
my words in this
adulterous and sin-
ful generation, the
Son of Man will be
ashamed of them
when he comes in
his Father's glory
with the holy an-
gels."

9 And he said to
them, "Truly I
tell you, some who
are standing here
will not taste death
before they see
that the kingdom
of God has come
with power."

The Transfiguration

[2]After six days
Jesus took Peter,
James and John
with him and led
them up a high
mountain, where
they were all
alone.

[a] 35 The Greek word means either *life* or *soul*; also in verses 36 and 37.

τὸν ὄχλον σὺν τοῖς μαθηταῖς αὐτοῦ εἶπεν αὐτοῖς· εἴ τις θέλει ὀπίσω
the crowd with *{the}* his disciples, *his* he said to them, "If anyone would come after
3836 4063 5250 3836 899 3412 899 3306 899 1623 5516 2527 199 3958
d.asm n.asm p.d d.dpm n.dpm r.gsm.3 v.aai.3s r.dpm.3 cj r.nsm v.pai.3s p.g

μου ἀκολουθεῖν, ἀπαρνησάσθω ἑαυτὸν καὶ ἀράτω τὸν σταυρὸν αὐτοῦ καὶ
me, *come* he must deny himself, *{and}* take up *{the}* his cross *his* and
1609 199 565 1571 2779 149 3836 899 5089 899 2779
r.gs.1 f.pa v.amm.3s r.asm.3 cj v.aam.3s d.asm n.asm r.gsm.3 cj

ἀκολουθείτω μοι. 35 ὃς γὰρ ἐὰν θέλῃ τὴν ψυχὴν αὐτοῦ
follow me. For whoever *For* ~ wishes to save *{the}* his life *his*
199 1609 1142 4005 1142 1569 2527 5392 5392 3836 899 6034 899
v.pam.3s r.ds.1 r.nsm cj pl v.pas.3s d.asf n.asf r.gsm.3

σῶσαι ἀπολέσει αὐτήν· ὃς δ' ἂν ἀπολέσει τὴν ψυχὴν αὐτοῦ ἕνεκεν
to save will lose it, but whoever *but* ~ will lose *{the}* his life *his* for
5392 660 899 1254 4005 1254 323 660 3836 899 6034 899 1914
f.aa v.fai.3s r.asf.3 r.nsm cj pl v.fai.3s d.asf n.asf r.gsm.3 p.g

ἐμοῦ ← καὶ τοῦ εὐαγγελίου σώσει αὐτήν. 36 τί γὰρ ὠφελεῖ
my sake and that of the gospel will save it. For what *For* does it profit a
1609 1914 2779 3836 2295 5392 899 1142 5515 1142 6067
r.gs.1 cj d.gsn n.gsn v.fai.3s r.asf.3 r.asn cj v.pai.3s

ἄνθρωπον κερδῆσαι τὸν κόσμον ὅλον καὶ ζημιωθῆναι τὴν ψυχὴν αὐτοῦ;
man to gain the whole world, *whole* yet forfeit *{the}* his life? *his*
476 3045 3836 3910 3180 3910 2779 2423 3836 899 6034 899
n.asm f.aa d.asm n.asm a.asm cj f.ap d.asf n.asf r.gsm.3

37 τί γὰρ → δοῖ ἄνθρωπος ἀντάλλαγμα τῆς ψυχῆς αὐτοῦ; 38
Or what *Or* can a man give *man* in exchange for *{the}* his life? *his* For
1142 5515 1142 476 1443 476 498 3836 899 6034 899 1142
r.asn cj v.aas.3s n.nsm n.asn d.gsf n.gsf r.gsm.3

ὃς γὰρ ἐὰν ἐπαισχυνθῇ με καὶ τοὺς ἐμοὺς λόγους ἐν τῇ γενεᾷ ταύτῃ τῇ
whoever *For* ~ is ashamed of me and *{the}* my words in *{the}* *generation* this *{the}*
4005 1142 1569 2049 1609 2779 3836 1847 3364 1877 3836 1155 4047 3836
r.nsm cj pl v.aps.3s r.as.1 cj d.apm r.apm.1 n.apm p.d d.dsf n.dsf r.dsf d.dsf

μοιχαλίδι καὶ ἁμαρτωλῷ, καὶ ὁ υἱὸς τοῦ ἀνθρώπου →
adulterous and sinful generation, *also* the Son of Man will also
3655 2779 283 1155 2779 3836 5626 3836 476 2779
a.dsf cj a.dsf adv d.nsm n.nsm d.gsm n.gsm

ἐπαισχυνθήσεται αὐτόν, ὅταν ἔλθῃ ἐν τῇ δόξῃ τοῦ πατρὸς αὐτοῦ μετὰ τῶν
be ashamed of him when he comes in the glory of his Father *his* with his
2049 899 4020 2262 1877 3836 1518 3836 899 4252 899 3552 3836
v.fpi.3s r.asm.3 cj v.aas.3s p.d d.dsf n.dsf d.gsm n.gsm r.gsm.3 p.g d.gpm

ἀγγέλων τῶν ἁγίων.
holy angels." *{the}* *holy*
41 34 3836 41
n.gpm d.gpm a.gpm

9:1 καὶ ἔλεγεν αὐτοῖς· ἀμὴν λέγω ὑμῖν ὅτι εἰσίν τινες
And he said to them, "I tell you the truth, *I tell* *you* *{that}* ⌊there are⌋ some
2779 3306 899 3306 3306 7007 297 3306 7007 4022 1639 5516
cj v.iai.3s r.dpm.3 pl v.pai.1s r.dp.2 cj v.pai.3p r.npm

ὧδε τῶν ἑστηκότων οἵτινες ↱ ⌊οὐ μὴ⌋ γεύσωνται θανάτου ⌊ἕως ἂν⌋
standing here *{the}* *standing* who will not taste death until
2705 6045 3836 2705 4015 1174 4024 3590 1174 2505 2401 323
adv d.gpm pt.ra.gpm r.npm pl pl v.ams.3p n.gsm cj pl

ἴδωσιν τὴν βασιλείαν τοῦ θεοῦ ἐληλυθυῖαν ἐν δυνάμει. 2 καὶ μετὰ ἡμέρας ἓξ
they see the kingdom of God having come with power." And after six days *six*
1625 3836 993 3836 2536 2262 1877 1539 2779 3552 1971 2465 1971
v.aas.3p d.asf n.asf d.gsm n.gsm pt.ra.asf p.d n.dsf cj p.a n.apf a.apf

παραλαμβάνει ὁ Ἰησοῦς ← τὸν Πέτρον καὶ τὸν Ἰάκωβον καὶ τὸν
Jesus took *{the}* *Jesus* with him *{the}* Peter and *{the}* James and *{the}*
2652 4161 3836 2652 4161 3836 4377 2779 3836 2610 2779 3836
v.pai.3s d.nsm n.nsm d.asm n.asm cj d.asm n.asm cj d.asm

Ἰωάννην καὶ ἀναφέρει αὐτοὺς εἰς ὄρος ὑψηλὸν ⌊κατ' ἰδίαν μόνους.⌋
John, and led them up a high mountain *high* by themselves.
2722 2779 429 899 1650 5734 4001 5734 2848 2625 3668
n.asm cj v.pai.3s r.apm.3 p.a n.asn a.asn p.a a.asf a.apm

NASB

[34]And He sum-
moned the crowd
with His disciples,
and said to them,
"If anyone wishes
to come after Me,
he must deny
himself, and take
up his cross and
follow Me. [35]For
whoever wishes to
save his life will
lose it, but who-
ever loses his life
for My sake and
the gospel's will
save it. [36]For what
does it profit a man
to gain the whole
world, and forfeit
his soul? [37]For what
will a man give in
exchange for his
soul? [38]For who-
ever is ashamed of
Me and My words
in this adulterous
and sinful gen-
eration, the Son of
Man will also be
ashamed of him
when He comes in
the glory of His Fa-
ther with the holy
angels."

The Transfiguration

[9:1]And Jesus was
saying to them,
"Truly I say to you,
there are some
of those who are
standing here who
will not taste death
until they see the
kingdom of God
after it has come
with power."
[2]Six days later, Je-
sus *took with Him
Peter and James
and John, and
*brought them up
on a high mountain
by themselves.

NIV

There he was
transfigured be-
fore them. 3His
clothes became
dazzling white,
whiter than anyone
in the world could
bleach them. 4And
there appeared be-
fore them Elijah
and Moses, who
were talking with
Jesus.
5Peter said to
Jesus, "Rabbi, it is
good for us to be
here. Let us put up
three shelters—
one for you, one
for Moses and one
for Elijah." 6(He
did not know what
to say, they were
so frightened.)
7Then a cloud
appeared and cov-
ered them, and a
voice came from
the cloud: "This
is my Son, whom
I love. Listen to
him!"
8Suddenly,
when they looked
around, they no
longer saw anyone
with them except
Jesus.
9As they were
coming down the
mountain, Jesus
gave them orders
not to tell anyone
what they had
seen until the Son
of Man had risen
from the dead.
10They kept the
matter to them-
selves, discussing
what "rising from
the dead" meant.
11And they asked
him, "Why do the
teachers of the
law say that Elijah
must come first?"
12Jesus replied,
"To be sure, Elijah
does come first,
and

καὶ μετεμορφώθη ἔμπροσθεν αὐτῶν, 3καὶ τὰ ἱμάτια αὐτοῦ ἐγένετο στίλβοντα
And he was transfigured before them, and {the} his clothes his became radiant,
2779 3565 1869 899 2779 3836 899 2668 899 1181 5118
cj v.api.3s p.g r.gpm.3 cj d.npn n.npn r.gsm.3 v.ami.3s pt.pa.npn

λευκὰ λίαν, οἷα γναφεὺς ἐπὶ τῆς γῆς οὐ δύναται οὕτως λευκᾶναι.
intensely white, intensely as no launderer on {the} earth no could {so} bleach
3336 3328 3336 3888 4024 1187 2093 3836 1178 4024 1538 4048 3326
a.npn adv r.apn n.nsm p.g d.gsf n.gsf pl v.ppi.3s adv f.aa

4καὶ ὤφθη αὐτοῖς Ἠλίας σὺν Μωϋσεῖ καὶ ἦσαν συλλαλοῦντες τῷ
them. And Elijah appeared to them Elijah with Moses, and they were talking with {the}
2779 2460 3972 899 2460 5250 3707 2779 1639 5196 3836
cj v.api.3s r.dpm.3 n.nsm p.d n.dsm cj v.iai.3p pt.pa.npm d.dsm

Ἰησοῦ. 5καὶ ἀποκριθεὶς ὁ Πέτρος λέγει τῷ Ἰησοῦ· ῥαββί, καλόν ἐστιν
Jesus. And answering, {the} Peter said to Jesus, "Rabbi, it is good it is
2652 2779 646 3836 4377 3306 3836 2652 4806 1639 1639 2819 1639
n.dsm cj pt.ap.nsm d.nsm n.nsm v.pai.3s d.dsm n.dsm n.vsm a.nsn v.pai.3s

ἡμᾶς ὧδε εἶναι, καὶ ποιήσωμεν τρεῖς σκηνάς, σοὶ μίαν καὶ
that we are here. are {and} Let us make three shelters: one ⌞for you⌟ one and one
7005 1639 6045 1639 2779 4472 5552 5008 1651 5148 1651 2779 1651
r.ap.1 adv f.pa cj v.aas.1p a.apf n.apf r.ds.2 a.asf cj

Μωϋσεῖ μίαν καὶ Ἠλίᾳ μίαν. 6 ↱ ↱ οὐ γὰρ ᾔδει τί
for Moses one and one for Elijah" one — for he did not for know what
3707 1651 2779 1651 2460 1651 1142 3857 3857 4024 1142 3857 5515
n.dsm a.asf cj n.dsm a.asf pl cj v.lai.3s r.asn

ἀποκριθῇ, ἔκφοβοι γὰρ ἐγένοντο. 7καὶ ἐγένετο
he should reply, because they were so frightened. because they were Then a cloud appeared
646 1142 1181 1181 1769 1142 1181 2779 3749 1181
v.aps.3s a.npm cj v.ami.3p cj v.ami.3s

νεφέλη ἐπισκιάζουσα αὐτοῖς, καὶ ἐγένετο φωνὴ ἐκ τῆς νεφέλης· οὗτός ἐστιν
cloud overshadowing them, and a voice came voice out of the cloud, "This is
3749 2173 899 2779 5889 1181 5889 1666 3836 3749 4047 1639
n.nsf pt.pa.nsf r.dpm.3 cj v.ami.3s n.nsf p.g d.gsf n.gsf r.nsm v.pai.3s

ὁ υἱός μου ὁ ἀγαπητός, ἀκούετε αὐτοῦ. 8καὶ ἐξάπινα περιβλεψάμενοι
{the} my Son, my the beloved, listen to him!" And suddenly, looking around, they
3836 1609 5626 1609 3836 28 201 899 2779 1988 4315 1625
d.nsm n.nsm r.gs.1 d.nsm a.nsm v.pam.2p r.gsm.3 cj adv pt.am.npm

οὐκέτι οὐδένα εἶδον ἀλλὰ τὸν Ἰησοῦν μόνον μεθ᾽ ἑαυτῶν. 9καὶ →
no longer saw anyone, they saw but only {the} Jesus only with them. And as they
4033 1625 4029 1625 247 3668 3836 2652 3668 3552 1571 2779 899
adv a.asm v.aai.3p cj d.asm n.asm adv p.g r.gpm.3 cj

καταβαινόντων αὐτῶν ἐκ τοῦ ὄρους διεστείλατο αὐτοῖς ↱ ἵνα μηδενὶ ἃ
were coming down they from the mountain he ordered them not to tell anyone what
2849 899 1666 3836 4001 1403 899 3594 2671 1455 3594 4005
pt.pa.gpm r.gpm.3 p.g d.gsn n.gsn v.ami.3s r.dpm.3 cj a.dsm r.apn

εἶδον διηγήσωνται, ⌞εἰ μὴ ὅταν⌟ ὁ υἱὸς τοῦ ἀνθρώπου ἐκ
⌞they had seen,⌟ tell until the Son of Man should rise from the
1625 1455 1623 3590 4020 3836 5626 3836 476 482 482 1666
v.aai.3p v.ams.3p cj pl cj d.nsm n.nsm d.gsm n.gsm p.g

νεκρῶν ἀναστῇ. 10καὶ τὸν λόγον ἐκράτησαν πρὸς ἑαυτοὺς συζητοῦντες
dead. should rise So they kept this saying they kept to themselves, questioning
3738 482 2779 3195 3195 3836 3364 3195 4639 1571 5184
a.gpm v.aas.3s cj d.asm n.asm v.aai.3p p.a r.apm.3 pt.pa.npm

τί ἐστιν τὸ ἐκ νεκρῶν ἀναστῆναι. 11καὶ
what the "rising of the dead" ⌞could mean.⌟ the of dead rising And
5515 3836 482 1666 3738 1639 3836 1666 3738 482 2779
r.nsn v.pai.3s d.nsn p.g a.gpm f.aa cj

ἐπηρώτων αὐτὸν λέγοντες· ὅτι → λέγουσιν οἱ γραμματεῖς ὅτι Ἠλίαν
they asked him, saying, "Why do the scribes say, the scribes ~ 'Elijah
2089 899 3306 4022 3836 1208 3306 3836 1208 4022 2460
v.iai.3p r.asm.3 pt.pa.npm cj v.pai.3p d.npm n.npm cj n.asm

δεῖ ἐλθεῖν πρῶτον; 12 ὁ δὲ ἔφη αὐτοῖς· Ἠλίας μὲν ἐλθὼν πρῶτον
must come first'?" And he And said to them, "Elijah ~ does come first, and
1256 2262 4754 1254 3836 1254 5774 899 2460 3525 2262 4754
v.pai.3s f.aa a.asn d.nsm cj v.iai.3s r.dpm.3 n.nsm pl pt.aa.nsm a.asn

NASB

And He was trans-
figured before
them; 3and His
garments became
radiant and exceed-
ingly white, as no
launderer on earth
can whiten them.
4Elijah appeared
to them along with
Moses; and they
were talking with
Jesus. 5Peter *said
to Jesus, "Rabbi,
it is good for us
to be here; let us
make three tab-
ernacles, one for
You, and one for
Moses, and one
for Elijah." 6For
he did not know
what to answer; for
they became terri-
fied. 7Then a cloud
formed, overshad-
owing them, and a
voice came out of
the cloud, "This is
My beloved Son,
listen to Him!" 8All
at once they looked
around and saw no
one with them any-
more, except Jesus
alone.
9As they were
coming down from
the mountain, He
gave them orders
not to relate to any-
one what they had
seen, until the Son
of Man rose from
the dead. 10They
seized upon that
statement, discuss-
ing with one anoth-
er what rising from
the dead meant.
11They asked Him,
saying, "*Why is it*
that the scribes say
that Elijah must
come first?" 12And
He said to them,
"Elijah does first
come and

NIV

restores all things.
Why then is it
written that the
Son of Man must
suffer much and
be rejected? 13 But
I tell you, Elijah
has come, and they
have done to him
everything they
wished, just as it
is written about
him."

Jesus Heals a Boy Possessed by an Impure Spirit

14 When they
came to the oth-
er disciples, they
saw a large crowd
around them and
the teachers of the
law arguing with
them. 15 As soon as
all the people saw
Jesus, they were
overwhelmed with
wonder and ran to
greet him.
16 "What are you
arguing with them
about?" he asked.
17 A man in the
crowd answered,
"Teacher, I
brought you my
son, who is pos-
sessed by a spirit
that has robbed
him of speech.
18 Whenever it seiz-
es him, it throws
him to the ground.
He foams at the
mouth, gnashes his
teeth and becomes
rigid. I asked your
disciples to drive
out the spirit, but
they could not."
19 "You unbeliev-
ing generation,"
Jesus replied,
"how long shall
I stay with you?
How long shall I
put up with you?
Bring the boy
to me."
20 So they brought
him. When the
spirit saw Jesus,
it immediately
threw the boy into
a convulsion. He
fell to the ground
and rolled around,
foaming at the
mouth. 21 Jesus
asked the boy's

ἀποκαθιστάνει πάντα· καὶ πῶς γέγραπται ἐπὶ τὸν υἱὸν τοῦ ἀνθρώπου ἵνα
restores all things. Yet how is it written about the Son of Man? That he
635 4246 2779 4802 1211 2093 3836 5626 3836 476 2671 4248
v.pai.3s a.apn cj cj v.rpi.3s p.a d.asm n.asm d.gsm n.gsm cj

πολλὰ πάθη καὶ ἐξουδενηθῇ; 13 ἀλλὰ λέγω ὑμῖν
should suffer many things *he should suffer* and ⌞be treated with contempt?⌟ But I tell you
4248 4248 4498 4248 2779 2022 247 3306 7007
a.apn v.aas.3s cj v.aps.3s cj v.pai.1s r.dp.2

ὅτι καὶ Ἠλίας ἐλήλυθεν, καὶ ἐποίησαν αὐτῷ ὅσα ἤθελον, καθὼς γέγραπται
that *{also}* Elijah has come, and they did to him whatever they pleased, just as it is written
4022 2779 2460 2262 2779 4472 899 4012 2527 2777 1211
cj adv n.nsm v.rai.3s cj v.aai.3p r.dsm.3 r.apn v.iai.3p cj v.rpi.3s

ἐπ᾽ αὐτόν. 14 καὶ ἐλθόντες πρὸς τοὺς μαθητὰς εἶδον ὄχλον πολὺν
about him." And ⌞when they came⌟ to the disciples, they saw a large crowd *large*
2093 899 2779 2262 4639 3836 3412 1625 4498 4063 4498
p.a r.asm.3 cj pt.aa.npm p.a d.apm n.apm v.aai.3p n.asm a.asm

περὶ αὐτοὺς καὶ γραμματεῖς συζητοῦντας πρὸς αὐτούς. 15 καὶ εὐθὺς πᾶς
around them, and scribes arguing with them. And immediately the entire
4309 899 2779 1208 5184 4639 899 2779 2318 3836 4246
p.a r.apm.3 cj n.apm pt.pa.apm p.a r.apm cj adv a.nsm

ὁ ὄχλος ἰδόντες αὐτὸν ἐξεθαμβήθησαν καὶ προστρέχοντες ἠσπάζοντο
the crowd, ⌞when they saw⌟ him, were greatly amazed, and running up to him, they greeted
3836 4063 1625 899 1701 2779 4708 832
d.nsm n.nsm pt.aa.npm r.asm.3 v.api.3p cj pt.pa.npm v.imi.3p

αὐτόν. 16 καὶ ἐπηρώτησεν αὐτούς· τί συζητεῖτε πρὸς αὐτούς; 17 καὶ
him. And he asked them, "What ⌞are you arguing about⌟ with them?" And
899 2779 2089 899 5515 5184 4639 899 2779
r.asm.3 cj v.aai.3s r.apm.3 r.asn v.pai.2p p.a r.apm.3 cj

ἀπεκρίθη αὐτῷ εἷς ἐκ τοῦ ὄχλου· διδάσκαλε, ἤνεγκα τὸν υἱόν
answered *him* one of the crowd answered him, "Teacher, I brought *{the}* my son
646 899 1651 1666 3836 4063 646 899 1437 5770 3836 1609 5626
v.api.3s r.dsm.3 a.nsm p.g d.gsm n.gsm n.vsm v.aai.1s d.asm n.asm

μου πρὸς σέ, ἔχοντα πνεῦμα ἄλαλον· 18 καὶ ⌞ὅπου ἐὰν⌟ αὐτὸν
my to you, who has a mute spirit. *mute* And whenever it seizes him,
1609 4639 5148 2400 228 4460 228 2779 3963 1569 2898 2898 899
r.gs.1 p.a r.as.2 pt.pa.asm n.asn a.asn cj cj pl r.asm.3

καταλάβῃ ῥήσσει αὐτόν, ↰ καὶ ἀφρίζει καὶ τρίζει τοὺς ὀδόντας καὶ
it seizes it throws him down, and ⌞he foams at the mouth⌟ and grinds his teeth and
2898 4841 899 4841 2779 930 2779 5563 3836 3848 2779
v.aas.3s v.pai.3s r.asm.3 cj v.pai.3s cj v.pai.3s d.apm n.apm cj

ξηραίνεται· καὶ εἶπα τοῖς μαθηταῖς σου ἵνα αὐτὸ ἐκβάλωσιν, καὶ
becomes rigid. So I asked *{the}* your disciples *your* to cast it *cast out* out, but
3830 2779 3306 3836 5148 3412 5148 2671 1675 899 1675 1675 2779
v.ppi.3s cj v.aai.1s d.dpm n.dpm r.gs.2 cj r.asn.3 v.aas.3p cj

↱ ↱ οὐκ ἴσχυσαν. 19 ὁ δὲ ἀποκριθεὶς αὐτοῖς λέγει· ὦ
they were not able. Answering them he *{and}* *Answering* *them* said, "O
2710 2710 4024 2710 646 899 3836 1254 646 899 3306 6043
pl v.aai.3p d.nsm cj pt.ap.nsm r.dpm.3 v.pai.3s j

γενεὰ ἄπιστος, ἕως πότε πρὸς ὑμᾶς ἔσομαι; ἕως πότε
unbelieving generation! *unbelieving* How long must I be with you? *must I be* How long
603 1155 603 2401 4537 1639 1639 1639 4639 7007 1639 2401 4537
n.vsf a.vsf p.g adv p.a r.ap.2 v.fmi.1s p.g adv

ἀνέξομαι ὑμῶν; φέρετε αὐτὸν πρός με. 20 καὶ ἤνεγκαν αὐτὸν πρὸς
⌞must I put up with⌟ you? Bring him to me." And they brought the boy to
462 7007 5770 899 4639 1609 2779 5770 899 4639
v.fmi.1s r.gp.2 v.pam.2p r.asm.3 p.a r.as.1 cj v.aai.3p r.asm.3 p.a

αὐτόν. καὶ → ἰδὼν αὐτὸν τὸ πνεῦμα εὐθὺς συνεσπάραξεν αὐτόν,
him. And when the spirit saw him, *the* *spirit* immediately it convulsed him;
899 2779 3836 4460 1625 899 3836 4460 2318 5360 899
r.asm.3 cj pt.aa.nsm r.asm.3 d.nsn n.nsn adv v.aai.3s r.asm.3

καὶ πεσὼν ἐπὶ τῆς γῆς ἐκυλίετο ἀφρίζων. 21 καὶ
and falling on the ground the boy ⌞began to roll about,⌟ ⌞foaming at the mouth.⌟ And Jesus
2779 4406 2093 3836 1178 3244 930 2779
cj pt.aa.nsm p.g d.gsf n.gsf v.imi.3s pt.pa.nsm cj

NASB

restore all things.
And *yet* how is it
written of the Son
of Man that He will
suffer many things
and be treated with
contempt? 13 But
I say to you that
Elijah has indeed
come, and they did
to him whatever
they wished, just
as it is written of
him."

All Things Possible

14 When they came
back to the dis-
ciples, they saw a
large crowd around
them, and *some*
scribes arguing
with them. 15 Imme-
diately, when the
entire crowd saw
Him, they were
amazed and *began*
running up to greet
Him. 16 And He
asked them, "What
are you discuss-
ing with them?"
17 And one of the
crowd answered
Him, "Teacher, I
brought You my
son, possessed
with a spirit which
makes him mute;
18 and whenever it
seizes him, it slams
him *to the ground*
and he foams *at the*
mouth, and grinds
his teeth and stiff-
ens out. I told Your
disciples to cast it
out, and they could
not *do it.*" 19 And
He *answered them
and *said, "O unbe-
lieving generation,
how long shall I
be with you? How
long shall I put up
with you? Bring
him to Me!" 20 They
brought the boy to
Him. When he saw
Him, immediately
the spirit threw him
into a convulsion,
and falling to the
ground, he *began*
rolling around and
foaming *at the*
mouth.

NIV

father, "How long
has he been like
this?"
"From child-
hood," he an-
swered. 22"It has
often thrown him
into fire or water
to kill him. But if
you can do any-
thing, take pity on
us and help us."
23"'If you can'?"
said Jesus. "Every-
thing is possible
for one who be-
lieves."
24Immediately
the boy's father
exclaimed, "I do
believe; help me
overcome my un-
belief!"
25When Jesus
saw that a crowd
was running to the
scene, he rebuked
the impure spir-
it. "You deaf and
mute spirit," he
said, "I command
you, come out of
him and never en-
ter him again."
26The spirit
shrieked, con-
vulsed him vio-
lently and came
out. The boy
looked so much
like a corpse that
many said, "He's
dead." 27But Jesus
took him by the
hand and lifted
him to his feet, and
he stood up.
28After Jesus had
gone indoors, his
disciples asked
him privately,
"Why couldn't we
drive it out?"
29He replied,
"This kind can
come only by
prayer.[a]"

[a] 29 Some manu-
scripts *prayer and
fasting*

ἐπηρώτησεν τὸν πατέρα αὐτοῦ· πόσος χρόνος ἐστὶν ⌞ὡς τοῦτο⌟ γέγονεν
asked *{the}* his father, *his* "How long has this been happening
2089 3836 899 4252 899 4531 5989 1639 6055 4047 1181
v.aai.3s d.asm n.asm r.gsm.3 r.nsm n.nsm v.pai.3s cj r.nsn v.rai.3s

αὐτῷ; ὁ δὲ εἶπεν· ἐκ παιδιόθεν· 22 καὶ πολλάκις καὶ
to him?" *he* And he said, "Since childhood; indeed frequently it has even cast him
899 3836 1254 3836 3306 1666 4085 2779 4490 965 965 2779 965 899
r.dsm.3 d.nsm cj v.aai.3s p.g adv cj adv adv

εἰς πῦρ αὐτὸν ἔβαλεν καὶ εἰς ὕδατα ἵνα ἀπολέσῃ αὐτόν· ἀλλ᾽ εἴ τι
into fire *him* *it has cast* and into water to destroy him. But if *anything*
1650 4786 899 965 2779 1650 5623 2671 660 899 247 1623 5516
p.a n.asn r.asm.3 v.aai.3s cj p.a n.apn cj v.aas.3s r.asm.3 cj cj r.asn

δύνῃ, βοήθησον ἡμῖν σπλαγχνισθεὶς ἐφ᾽
⌞you can do⌟ anything, have compassion on us and help us." *have compassion* *on*
1538 5516 5072 5072 2093 7005 1070 7005 5072 2093
v.ppi.2s v.aam.2s r.dp.1 pt.ap.nsm p.a

ἡμᾶς. 23 ὁ δὲ Ἰησοῦς εἶπεν αὐτῷ· τὸ εἰ δύνῃ, πάντα δυνατὰ τῷ
us *{the}* And Jesus said to him, *{the}* "'If you can'! All things are possible ⌞for the⌟
7005 3836 1254 2652 3306 899 3836 1623 1538 4246 1543 3836
r.ap.1 d.nsm cj n.nsm v.aai.3s r.dsm.3 d.asn cj v.ppi.2s a.npn a.npn d.dsm

πιστεύοντι. 24 εὐθὺς κράξας ὁ πατὴρ τοῦ παιδίου ἔλεγεν·
one who has faith." Immediately *cried out* the father of the boy cried out and said,
4409 2318 3189 3836 4252 3836 4086 3189 3189 3306
pt.pa.dsm adv pt.aa.nsm d.nsm n.nsm d.gsn n.gsn v.iai.3s

πιστεύω· βοήθει μου τῇ ἀπιστίᾳ. 25 → ἰδὼν δὲ ὁ Ἰησοῦς ὅτι
"I believe; help my *{the}* unbelief!" When Jesus saw *{and}* *{the}* *Jesus* that a crowd
4409 1070 1609 3836 602 2652 1625 1254 3836 2652 4022 4063
v.pai.1s v.pam.2s r.gs.1 d.dsf n.dsf pt.aa.nsm cj d.nsm n.nsm cj

ἐπισυντρέχει ὄχλος, ἐπετίμησεν τῷ πνεύματι τῷ ἀκαθάρτῳ λέγων
was quickly gathering, *crowd* he rebuked the unclean spirit, *{the}* *unclean* saying
2192 4063 2203 3836 176 4460 3836 176 3306
v.pai.3s n.nsm v.aai.3s d.dsn n.dsn d.dsn a.dsn pt.pa.nsm

αὐτῷ· τὸ ἄλαλον καὶ κωφὸν πνεῦμα, ἐγὼ ἐπιτάσσω σοι, ἔξελθε ἐξ αὐτοῦ καὶ
to it, *{the}* "Mute and deaf spirit, I command you, come ⌞out of⌟ him and
899 3836 228 2779 3273 4460 1609 2199 5148 2002 1666 899 2779
r.dsn.3 d.vsn a.vsn cj a.vsn n.vsn r.ns.1 v.pai.1s r.ds.2 v.aam.2s p.g r.gsm.3 cj

μηκέτι ⌞εἰσέλθῃς εἰς⌟ αὐτόν. ↰ 26 καὶ κράξας καὶ πολλὰ
never enter him again!" *{and}* ⌞After crying out⌟ and convulsing him violently,
3600 1656 1650 899 3600 2779 3189 2779 5057 4498
adv v.aas.2s p.a r.asm.3 cj pt.aa.nsm cj a.apn

σπαράξας ἐξῆλθεν· καὶ ἐγένετο ὡσεὶ νεκρός, ὥστε τοὺς πολλοὺς
convulsing the spirit came out; and the boy was like a corpse, so that *{the}* many
5057 2002 2779 1181 6059 3738 6063 3836 4498
pt.aa.nsm v.aai.3s cj v.ami.3s pl a.nsm cj d.apm a.apm

λέγειν ὅτι ἀπέθανεν. 27 ὁ δὲ Ἰησοῦς κρατήσας ← τῆς χειρὸς αὐτοῦ
were saying, ~ "He is dead." *{the}* But Jesus, taking him by the hand, *him*
3306 4022 633 3836 1254 2652 3195 899 3836 5931 899
f.pa cj v.aai.3s d.nsm cj n.nsm pt.aa.nsm d.gsf n.gsf r.gsm.3

ἤγειρεν αὐτόν, ↰ καὶ ἀνέστη. 28 καὶ → εἰσελθόντος αὐτοῦ εἰς οἶκον
lifted him up, and ⌞he stood up.⌟ And when he had entered *he* *{into}* the house,
1586 899 1586 2779 482 2779 899 1656 899 1650 3875
v.aai.3s r.asm.3 cj v.aai.3s cj pt.aa.gsm r.gsm.3 p.a n.asm

οἱ μαθηταὶ αὐτοῦ ⌞κατ᾽ ἰδίαν⌟ ἐπηρώτων αὐτόν· ὅτι ↱ ἡμεῖς
{the} his disciples *his* asked him in private, *asked* *him* "Why were we
3836 899 3412 899 2089 899 2848 2625 2089 899 4022 1538 7005
d.npm n.npm r.gsm.3 p.a a.asf v.iai.3p r.asm.3 cj r.np.1

οὐκ ἠδυνήθημεν ἐκβαλεῖν αὐτό; ↰ 29 καὶ εἶπεν αὐτοῖς· τοῦτο τὸ γένος ⌞ἐν
not able to cast it out?" And he said to them, "This *{the}* kind cannot
4024 1538 1675 899 1675 2779 3306 899 4047 3836 1169 1877
pl v.api.1p f.aa r.asn.3 cj v.aai.3s r.dpm.3 r.asn d.asn n.asn p.d

οὐδενὶ δύναται⌟ ἐξελθεῖν ⌞εἰ μὴ⌟ ἐν προσευχῇ.[a] 30 κἀκεῖθεν ἐξελθόντες ↰
come out except by prayer." And leaving there,
4029 1538 2002 1623 3590 1877 4666 2796 2002 2796
a.dsn v.ppi.3s f.aa cj pl p.d n.dsf crasis pt.aa.npm

[a] καὶ νηστείᾳ included by TR after προσευχῇ.

NASB

21And He asked
his father, "How
long has this been
happening to him?"
And he said, "From
childhood. 22It has
often thrown him
both into the fire
and into the water
to destroy him.
But if You can do
anything, take pity
on us and help us!"
23And Jesus said to
him, "'If You can?'
All things are pos-
sible to him who
believes." 24Im-
mediately the boy's
father cried out and
said, "I do believe;
help my unbelief."
25When Jesus saw
that a crowd was
rapidly gather-
ing, He rebuked
the unclean spirit,
saying to it, "You
deaf and mute
spirit, I command
you, come out of
him and do not
enter him again."
26After crying out
and throwing him
into terrible con-
vulsions, it came
out; and *the boy*
became so much
like a corpse that
most *of them* said,
"He is dead!" 27But
Jesus took him by
the hand and raised
him; and he got up.
28When He came
into *the* house, His
disciples *began*
questioning Him
privately, "Why
could we not drive
it out?" 29And He
said to them, "This
kind cannot come
out by anything but
prayer."

NIV

Jesus Predicts His Death a Second Time

30They left that
place and passed
through Galilee.
Jesus did not want
anyone to know
where they were,
31because he was
teaching his dis-
ciples. He said to
them, "The Son
of Man is going to
be delivered into
the hands of men.
They will kill him,
and after three
days he will rise."
32But they did not
understand what
he meant and were
afraid to ask him
about it.
33They came to
Capernaum. When
he was in the
house, he asked
them, "What were
you arguing about
on the road?" 34But
they kept quiet be-
cause on the way
they had argued
about who was the
greatest.
35Sitting down,
Jesus called the
Twelve and said,
"Anyone who
wants to be first
must be the very
last, and the ser-
vant of all."
36He took a lit-
tle child whom
he placed among
them. Taking the
child in his arms,
he said to them,
37"Whoever wel-
comes one of these
little children in
my name wel-
comes me; and
whoever welcomes
me does not wel-
come me but the
one who sent me."

Whoever Is Not Against Us Is for Us

38"Teacher," said
John, "we saw
someone driving
out demons in
your name and we
told him to stop,
because he was

παρεπορεύοντο διὰ τῆς Γαλιλαίας, καὶ ↱ οὐκ ἤθελεν ἵνα τις γνοῖ·
they went on through {the} Galilee. And Jesus did not want ~ anyone to know
4182 1328 3836 1133 2779 2527 4024 2527 2671 5516 1182
v.imi.3p p.g d.gsf n.gsf cj pl v.iai.3s cj r.nsm v.aas.3s

31 ἐδίδασκεν γὰρ τοὺς μαθητὰς αὐτοῦ καὶ ἔλεγεν αὐτοῖς ὅτι ὁ
about it; for he was teaching for {the} his disciples his and saying to them, ~ "The
1142 1438 1142 3836 899 3412 899 2779 3306 899 4022 3836
v.iai.3s cj d.apm n.apm r.gsm.3 cj v.iai.3s r.dpm.3 cj d.nsm

υἱὸς τοῦ ἀνθρώπου παραδίδοται εἰς χεῖρας ἀνθρώπων, καὶ ἀποκτενοῦσιν
Son of Man is going to be delivered into the hands of men, and they will kill
5626 3836 476 4140 1650 5931 476 2779 650
n.nsm d.gsm n.gsm v.ppi.3s p.a n.apf n.gpm cj v.fai.3p

αὐτόν, καὶ ἀποκτανθεὶς μετὰ τρεῖς ἡμέρας ἀναστήσεται. 32 οἱ
him. Then three days after he has been killed, after three days he will rise But they
899 2779 5552 2465 3552 650 3552 5552 2465 482 1254 3836
r.asm.3 cj pt.ap.nsm p.a a.apf n.apf v.fmi.3s d.npm

δὲ ἠγνόουν τὸ ῥῆμα, καὶ ἐφοβοῦντο αὐτὸν ἐπερωτῆσαι. 33 καὶ
But did not understand the saying, and they were afraid to ask him. to ask And
1254 51 3836 4839 2779 5828 2089 2089 899 2089 2779
cj v.iai.3p d.asn n.asn cj v.ipi.3p r.asm.3 f.aa cj

ἦλθον εἰς Καφαρναούμ. καὶ ἐν τῇ οἰκίᾳ γενόμενος ἐπηρώτα
they came to Capernaum; and when he was in the house when he was he asked
2262 1650 3019 2779 1181 1181 1181 1877 3836 3864 1181 2089
v.aai.3p p.a n.asf cj p.d d.dsf n.dsf pt.am.nsm v.iai.3s

αὐτούς· τί ἐν τῇ ὁδῷ διελογίζεσθε; 34 οἱ δὲ
them, "What were you discussing on the way? were you discussing But they But
899 5515 1368 1368 1368 1877 3836 3847 1368 1254 3836 1254
r.apm.3 r.asn p.d d.dsf n.dsf v.imi.2p d.npm cj

ἐσιώπων· πρὸς ἀλλήλους γὰρ διελέχθησαν ἐν τῇ
kept silent, for on the way they had argued among themselves for they had argued on the
4995 1142 1877 3836 3847 1363 1363 1363 4639 253 1142 1363 1877 3836
v.iai.3p p.a r.apm cj v.api.3p p.d d.dsf

ὁδῷ τίς μείζων. 35 καὶ καθίσας ἐφώνησεν τοὺς δώδεκα καὶ λέγει
way about who was the greatest. And sitting down, he called the Twelve and said
3847 5515 3489 2779 2767 5888 3836 1557 2779 3306
n.dsf r.nsm a.nsm.c cj pt.aa.nsm v.aai.3s d.apm a.apm cj v.pai.3s

αὐτοῖς· εἴ τις θέλει πρῶτος εἶναι, ἔσται πάντων ἔσχατος καὶ
to them, "If anyone would be first, be ⌊he must be⌋ last of all last and servant
899 1623 5516 2527 1639 4755 1639 1639 2274 4246 2274 2779 1356
r.dpm.3 cj r.nsm v.pai.3s a.nsm f.pa v.fmi.3s a.gpm a.nsm cj

πάντων διάκονος. 36 καὶ λαβὼν παιδίον ἔστησεν αὐτὸ ἐν μέσῳ αὐτῶν καὶ
of all." servant And taking a child he put him in the midst of them, and
4246 1356 2779 3284 4086 2705 899 1877 3545 899 2779
a.gpm n.nsm cj pt.aa.nsm n.asn v.aai.3s r.asn.3 p.d n.dsn r.gpm.3 cj

ἐναγκαλισάμενος αὐτὸ ↰ ↰ ↰ εἶπεν αὐτοῖς· 37 ⌊ὃς ἂν⌋ ἓν τῶν
taking him in his arms, he said to them, "Whoever receives one of
1878 899 1878 1878 1878 3306 899 4005 323 1312 1651 3836
pt.am.nsm r.asn.3 v.aai.3s r.dpm.3 r.nsm pl a.asn d.gpn

τοιούτων παιδίων δέξηται ἐπὶ τῷ ὀνόματί μου, ἐμὲ δέχεται· καὶ ⌊ὃς
these children receives in {the} my name, my receives me; receives and whoever
5525 4086 1312 2093 3836 1609 3950 1609 1312 1609 1312 2779 4005
r.gpn n.gpn v.ams.3s p.d d.dsn n.dsn r.gs.1 r.as.1 v.pmi.3s cj r.nsm

ἂν⌋ ἐμὲ δέχηται, οὐκ ἐμὲ δέχεται ἀλλὰ τὸν ἀποστείλαντά με.
receives me, receives receives not me receives but the one who sent me."
323 1312 1609 1312 1312 4024 1609 1312 247 3836 690 1609
pl r.as.1 v.pms.3s pl r.as.1 v.pmi.3s cj d.asm pt.aa.asm r.as.1

38 ἔφη αὐτῷ ὁ Ἰωάννης· διδάσκαλε, εἴδομέν τινα ἐν
John said to him, {the} John "Teacher, we saw someone casting out demons in
2722 5774 899 3836 2722 1437 1625 5516 1675 1675 1228 1877
v.iai.3s r.dsm.3 d.nsm n.nsm n.vsm v.aai.1p r.asm p.d

τῷ ὀνόματί σου ἐκβάλλοντα δαιμόνια καὶ ἐκωλύομεν αὐτόν, ὅτι ↱ ↱
{the} your name, your casting out demons and we tried to stop him because he was
3836 5148 3950 5148 1675 1228 2779 3266 899 4022 199 199
d.dsn n.dsn r.gs.2 pt.pa.asm n.apn cj v.iai.1p r.asm.3 cj

NASB

Death and Resurrection Foretold

30From there they
went out and *be-
gan* to go through
Galilee, and He did
not want anyone
to know *about it.*
31For He was teach-
ing His disciples
and telling them,
"The Son of Man
is to be [a]delivered
into the hands of
men, and they
will kill Him; and
when He has been
killed, He will rise
three days later."
32But they did not
understand *this*
statement, and they
were afraid to ask
Him.
33They came to
Capernaum; and
when He was in the
house, He *began*
to question them,
"What were you
discussing on the
way?" 34But they
kept silent, for on
the way they had
discussed with one
another which *of
them was* the great-
est. 35Sitting down,
He called the
twelve and *said to
them, "If anyone
wants to be first,
he shall be last
of all and servant
of all." 36Taking a
child, He set him
before them, and
taking him in His
arms, He said to
them, 37"Whoever
receives one child
like this in My
name receives
Me; and whoever
receives Me does
not receive Me, but
Him who sent Me."

Dire Warnings

38John said to
Him, "Teacher,
we saw someone
casting out demons
in Your name, and
we tried to prevent
him because he

[a] Or *betrayed*

NIV

not one of us."
39"Do not stop
him," Jesus said.
"For no one who
does a miracle in
my name can in
the next moment
say anything bad
about me, 40for
whoever is not
against us is for us.
41Truly I tell you,
anyone who gives
you a cup of water
in my name be-
cause you belong
to the Messiah will
certainly not lose
their reward.

Causing to Stumble

42"If anyone
causes one of these
little ones—those
who believe in
me—to stumble,
it would be better
for them if a large
millstone were
hung around their
neck and they
were thrown into
the sea. 43If your
hand causes you
to stumble, cut it
off. It is better for
you to enter life
maimed than with
two hands to go
into hell, where
the fire never goes
out. [44][a] 45And if
your foot causes
you to stumble, cut
it off. It is better
for you to enter
life crippled than
to have two feet
and be thrown into
hell. [46][b] 47And if
your eye

οὐκ ἠκολούθει ἡμῖν. 39 ὁ δὲ Ἰησοῦς εἶπεν· ↱ μὴ κωλύετε αὐτόν.
not following us." {the} But Jesus said, "Do not stop him, for there is
4024 199 7005 3836 1254 2652 3306 3266 3590 3266 899 1142 1639 1639
pl v.iai.3s r.dp.1 d.nsm cj n.nsm v.aai.3s pl v.pam.2p r.asm.3

οὐδεὶς γάρ ἐστιν ὃς ποιήσει δύναμιν ἐπὶ τῷ ὀνόματί μου καὶ δυνήσεται
no one for there is who will do a mighty work in {the} my name my and be able
4029 1142 1639 4005 4472 1539 2093 3836 1609 3950 1609 2779 1538
a.nsm cj v.pai.3s r.nsm v.fai.3s n.asf p.d d.dsn n.dsn r.gs.1 cj v.fmi.3s

ταχὺ κακολογῆσαί με· 40 ὃς γὰρ οὐκ ἔστιν καθ' ἡμῶν, ὑπὲρ
⌞soon after⌟ to speak evil of me. For whoever For is not is against us is for
5444 2800 1609 1142 4005 1142 1639 4024 1639 2848 7005 1639 5642
adv f.aa r.as.1 r.nsm cj pl v.pai.3s p.g r.gp.1 p.g

ἡμῶν ἐστιν. 41 ὃς γὰρ ἂν →
us. is For I tell you the truth, whoever For ~ gives you a cup of water
7005 1639 1142 3306 3306 7007 297 297 4005 1142 323 7007 4539 5623 5623
r.gp.1 v.pai.3s r.nsm cj pl

ποτίσῃ ὑμᾶς ποτήριον ὕδατος ἐν ὀνόματι ὅτι Χριστοῦ ἐστε,
to drink you cup of water {in} because you bear the name because of Christ you bear
4540 7007 4539 5623 1877 4022 1639 1639 3950 4022 5986 1639
v.aas.3s r.ap.2 n.asn n.gsn p.d n.dsn cj n.gsm v.pai.2p

ἀμὴν λέγω ὑμῖν ὅτι ↱ ⌞οὐ μὴ⌟ ἀπολέσῃ τὸν μισθὸν αὐτοῦ.
the truth I tell you ~ will most certainly not lose {the} his reward. his
297 3306 7007 4022 660 4024 3590 660 3836 899 3635 899
pl v.pai.1s r.dp.2 cj pl pl v.aas.3s d.asm n.asm r.gsm.3

42 καὶ ⌞ὃς ἂν⌟ σκανδαλίσῃ ἕνα τῶν μικρῶν τούτων τῶν πιστευόντων
"And whoever causes one of these little ones these who believe
2779 4005 323 4997 1651 3836 4047 3625 4047 3836 4409
cj r.nsm pl v.aas.3s a.asm d.gpm a.gpm r.gpm d.gpm pt.pa.gpm

[a]εἰς ἐμέ, ↰ ↰ καλόν ἐστιν αὐτῷ μᾶλλον εἰ
in me to sin, it would be better it would be for him {rather} if a large millstone
1650 1609 4997 4997 1639 1639 1639 2819 1639 899 3437 1623 3948 3685
p.a r.as.1 a.nsn v.pai.3s r.dsm.3 adv.c cj

περίκειται μύλος ὀνικὸς περὶ τὸν τράχηλον αὐτοῦ καὶ βέβληται εἰς τὴν
were hung millstone large around {the} his neck his and he were thrown into the
4329 3685 3948 4309 3836 899 5549 899 2779 965 1650 3836
v.pmi.3s n.nsm a.nsm p.a d.asm n.asm r.gsm.3 cj v.rpi.3s p.a d.asf

θάλασσαν. 43 καὶ ἐὰν σκανδαλίζῃ σε ↰ ↰ ἡ χείρ σου, ἀπόκοψον
sea. And if your hand causes you to sin, {the} hand your cut
2498 2779 1569 5148 5931 4997 5148 4997 4997 3836 5931 5148 644
n.asf cj cj v.pas.3s r.as.2 d.nsf n.nsf r.gs.2 v.aam.2s

αὐτήν· ↰ καλόν ἐστίν σε κυλλὸν εἰσελθεῖν εἰς τὴν ζωὴν ἢ
it off; it is better it is for you crippled to enter into {the} life crippled than
899 644 1639 1639 2819 1639 5148 3245 1656 1650 3836 2437 3245 2445
r.asf.3 a.nsn v.pai.3s r.as.2 a.asm f.aa p.a d.asf n.asf pl

τὰς δύο χεῖρας ἔχοντα ἀπελθεῖν εἰς τὴν γέενναν, εἰς τὸ πῦρ
having {the} two hands having to go to {the} hell, to the unquenchable fire.
2400 3836 1545 5931 2400 599 1650 3836 1147 1650 3836 812 4786
d.apf a.apf n.apf pt.pa.asm f.aa p.a d.asf n.asf p.a d.asn n.asn

τὸ ἄσβεστον.[b] 45 καὶ ἐὰν ὁ πούς σου σκανδαλίζῃ σε, ↰ ↰ ἀπόκοψον
{the} unquenchable And if {the} your foot your causes you to sin, cut
3836 812 2779 1569 3836 5148 4546 5148 4997 5148 4997 4997 644
d.asn a.asn cj cj d.nsm n.nsm r.gs.2 v.pas.3s r.as.2 v.aam.2s

αὐτόν· ↰ καλόν ἐστίν σε εἰσελθεῖν εἰς τὴν ζωὴν χωλὸν ἢ
it off; it is better it is for you to enter into {the} life lame than having
899 644 1639 1639 2819 1639 5148 1656 1650 3836 2437 6000 2445 2400
r.asm.3 a.nsn v.pai.3s r.as.2 f.aa p.a d.asf n.asf a.asm pl

τοὺς δύο πόδας ἔχοντα βληθῆναι εἰς τὴν γέενναν.[c] 47 καὶ ἐὰν ὁ ὀφθαλμός
{the} two feet having to be cast into {the} hell. And if {the} your eye
3836 1545 4546 2400 965 1650 3836 1147 2779 1569 3836 5148 4057
d.apm a.apm n.apm pt.pa.asm f.ap p.a d.asf n.asf cj cj d.nsm n.nsm

NASB

was not following
us." 39But Jesus
said, "Do not hin-
der him, for there
is no one who will
perform a miracle
in My name, and
be able soon af-
terward to speak
evil of Me. 40For he
who is not against
us is [a]for us. 41For
whoever gives you
a cup of water to
drink because of
your name as *fol-
lowers* of Christ,
truly I say to you,
he will not lose his
reward.
42"Whoever
causes one of
these little ones
who believe to
stumble, it would
be better for him
if, with a heavy
millstone hung
around his neck, he
had been cast into
the sea. 43If your
hand causes you to
stumble, cut it off;
it is better for you
to enter life crip-
pled, than, having
your two hands, to
go into hell, into
the unquenchable
fire, 44[[b]where THEIR
WORM DOES NOT
DIE, AND THE FIRE IS
NOT QUENCHED.] 45If
your foot causes
you to stumble, cut
it off; it is better
for you to enter life
lame, than, having
your two feet, to
be cast into hell,
46[[c]where THEIR
WORM DOES NOT
DIE, AND THE FIRE IS
NOT QUENCHED.] 47If
your eye

a 44 Some manuscripts include here the words of verse 48.
b 46 Some manuscripts include here the words of verse 48.

a [εἰς ἐμέ] UBS.
b 44ὅπου ὁ σκώληξ αὐτῶν οὐ τελευτᾷ, καὶ τὸ πῦρ οὐ σβέννυται. included by TR after ἄσβεστον.
c 46εἰς τὸ πῦρ τὸ ἄσβεστον, ὅπου ὁ σκώληξ αὐτῶν οὐ τελευτᾷ, καὶ τὸ πῦρ οὐ σβέννυται. included by TR after γέενναν.

a Or *on our side*
b Vv 44 and 46, which are identical to v 48, are not found in the early mss
c See v 44, note

NIV

causes you to
stumble, pluck it
out. It is better for
you to enter the
kingdom of God
with one eye than
to have two eyes
and be thrown into
hell, 48where

"'the worms
that eat
them do not
die,
and the fire
is not
quenched.'[a]

49Everyone will be
salted with fire.
50"Salt is good,
but if it loses its
saltiness, how can
you make it salty
again? Have salt
among yourselves,
and be at peace
with each other."

Divorce

10 Jesus then
left that
place and went
into the region of
Judea and across
the Jordan. Again
crowds of people
came to him, and
as was his custom,
he taught them.
2Some Pharisees
came and tested
him by asking,
"Is it lawful for a
man to divorce his
wife?"
3"What did Mo-
ses command
you?" he replied.
4They said, "Mo-
ses permitted a
man to write a
certificate of di-
vorce and send her
away."
5"It was because
your hearts were
hard that Moses
wrote you this
law," Jesus replied.
6"But at the begin-
ning

[a] 48 Isaiah 66:24

σου σκανδαλίζῃ σε, ↰ ↰ ἔκβαλε αὐτόν· ↰ καλόν σέ ἐστιν
your causes you to sin, throw it away; it is better for you *it is*
5148 4997 5148 4997 4997 1675 899 1675 1639 1639 2819 5148 1639
r.gs.2 v.pas.3s r.as.2 v.aam.2s r.asm.3 a.nsn r.as.2 v.pai.3s

μονόφθαλμον ⌊εἰσελθεῖν εἰς⌋ τὴν βασιλείαν τοῦ θεοῦ ἢ δύο
one eye to enter the kingdom of God having one eye than having two
3669 1656 1650 3836 993 3836 2536 3669 3669 2445 2400 1545
a.asm f.aa p.a d.asf n.asf d.gsm n.gsm pl a.apm

ὀφθαλμοὺς ἔχοντα βληθῆναι εἰς τὴν γέενναν, 48 ὅπου ὁ σκώληξ αὐτῶν ↱
eyes *having* to be cast into *{the}* hell, where *{the}* 'their worm *their* does
4057 2400 965 1650 3836 1147 3963 3836 899 5038 899 5462
n.apm pt.pa.asm f.ap p.a d.asf n.asf cj d.nsm n.nsm r.gpm.3

οὐ τελευτᾷ καὶ τὸ πῦρ ↱ οὐ σβέννυται. 49 πᾶς γὰρ
not die, and the fire is not quenched.' For everyone *For* will be salted
4024 5462 2779 3836 4786 4931 4024 4931 1142 4246 1142 245 245 245
pl v.pai.3s cj d.nsn n.nsn pl v.ppi.3s a.nsm cj

πυρὶ ἁλισθήσεται. 50 καλὸν τὸ ἅλας· ἐὰν δὲ τὸ ἅλας
⌊with fire.⌋ *will be salted* Salt is good, *{the} Salt* but if *but* the salt has become
4786 245 229 2819 3836 229 1254 1569 1254 3836 229 1181 1181
n.dsn v.fpi.3s a.nsn d.nsn n.nsn cj cj d.nsn n.nsn

ἄναλον γένηται, ἐν τίνι ↱ ↱ ↱ αὐτὸ ἀρτύσετε; ἔχετε ἐν ἑαυτοῖς ἅλα
unsalty, *has become* with what will you make it savory? Have salt in yourselves, *salt*
383 1181 1877 5515 789 789 789 899 789 2400 229 1877 1571 229
a.nsn v.ams.3s p.d r.dsn r.asn.3 v.fai.2p v.pam.2p p.d r.dpm.2 n.asn

καὶ εἰρηνεύετε ἐν ἀλλήλοις.
and be at peace with one another."
2779 1644 1877 253
cj v.pam.2p p.d r.dpm

10:1 καὶ ἐκεῖθεν ἀναστὰς ἔρχεται εἰς τὰ ὅρια τῆς Ἰουδαίας καὶ[a]
Then Jesus left that place *left* and went to the region of Judea and
2779 482 1696 482 2262 1650 3836 3990 3836 2677 2779
cj adv pt.aa.nsm v.pmi.3s p.a d.apn n.apn d.gsf n.gsf cj

πέραν τοῦ Ἰορδάνου, καὶ συμπορεύονται πάλιν ὄχλοι πρὸς αὐτόν,
beyond the Jordan, and crowds gathered around him again. *crowds around him*
4305 3836 2674 2779 4063 5233 4639 899 4099 4063 4639 899
p.g d.gsm n.gsm cj v.pmi.3p adv n.npm p.a r.asm.3

καὶ ὡς εἰώθει πάλιν ἐδίδασκεν αὐτούς. 2 καὶ
And again, as ⌊was his custom,⌋ *again* ⌊he began to teach⌋ them. And Pharisees
2779 4099 6055 1665 4099 1438 899 2779 5757
cj cj v.lai.3s adv v.iai.3s r.apm.3 cj

προσελθόντες Φαρισαῖοι ἐπηρώτων αὐτὸν εἰ ἔξεστιν ἀνδρὶ
came up *Pharisees* and asked him if ⌊it was lawful for⌋ a man to divorce
4665 5757 2089 899 1623 1997 467 668 668
pt.aa.npm n.npm v.iai.3p r.asm.3 cj v.pai.3s n.dsm

γυναῖκα ἀπολῦσαι, πειράζοντες αὐτόν. 3 ὁ δὲ ἀποκριθεὶς εἶπεν
his wife, *to divorce* in order to test him. In response he *{and} In response* said
1222 668 4279 899 646 646 3836 1254 646 3306
n.asf f.aa pt.pa.npm r.asm.3 d.nsm cj pt.ap.nsm v.aai.3s

αὐτοῖς· τί ὑμῖν ἐνετείλατο Μωϋσῆς; 4 οἱ δὲ εἶπαν·
to them, "What did Moses command you?" *did command Moses* They *{and}* said, "Moses
899 5515 1948 3707 1948 7007 1948 3707 3836 1254 3306 3707
r.dpm.3 r.asn r.dp.2 v.ami.3s n.nsm d.npm cj v.aai.3p

ἐπέτρεψεν Μωϋσῆς βιβλίον ἀποστασίου γράψαι καὶ ἀπολῦσαι.
permitted *Moses* a man to write a certificate of divorce *to write* and to send her
2205 3707 1211 1211 1046 687 1211 2779 668
v.aai.3s n.nsm n.asn n.gsn f.aa cj f.aa

← 5 ὁ δὲ Ἰησοῦς εἶπεν αὐτοῖς· πρὸς τὴν σκληροκαρδίαν ὑμῶν
away." *{the}* But Jesus said to them, ⌊"Because of⌋ *{the}* your hardness of heart *your*
3836 1254 2652 3306 899 4639 3836 7007 5016 7007
d.nsm cj n.nsm v.aai.3s r.dpm.3 p.a d.asf n.asf r.gp.2

ἔγραψεν ὑμῖν τὴν ἐντολὴν ταύτην. 6 ἀπὸ δὲ ἀρχῆς
he wrote this commandment for you. *{the} commandment this* But from *But* the beginning
1211 4047 1953 7007 3836 1953 4047 1254 608 1254 794
v.aai.3s r.dp.2 d.asf n.asf r.asf p.g cj n.gsf

[a] [καὶ] UBS.

NASB

causes you to
stumble, throw it
out; it is better for
you to enter the
kingdom of God
with one eye, than,
having two eyes,
to be cast into hell,
48where THEIR WORM
DOES NOT DIE, AND
THE FIRE IS NOT
QUENCHED.
49"For everyone
will be salted with
fire. 50Salt is good;
but if the salt
becomes unsalty,
with what will
you make it salty
again? Have salt in
yourselves, and be
at peace with one
another."

Jesus' Teaching about
Divorce

10:1Getting up, He
*went from there
to the region of
Judea and beyond
the Jordan; crowds
*gathered around
Him again, and,
according to His
custom, He once
more *began* to
teach them.
2*Some* Pharisees
came up to Jesus,
testing Him, and
began to question
Him whether it was
lawful for a man
to divorce a wife.
3And He answered
and said to them,
"What did Moses
command you?"
4They said, "Moses
permitted *a man* TO
WRITE A CERTIFICATE
OF DIVORCE AND
SEND *her* AWAY."
5But Jesus said to
them, "Because
of your hardness
of heart he wrote
you this command-
ment. 6But from
the beginning of
creation,

NIV

of creation God
'made them male
and female.'[a] 7 'For
this reason a man
will leave his fa-
ther and mother
and be united to
his wife,[b] 8 and the
two will become
one flesh.'[c] So
they are no longer
two, but one flesh.
9 Therefore what
God has joined to-
gether, let no one
separate."
10 When they were
in the house again,
the disciples asked
Jesus about this.
11 He answered,
"Anyone who di-
vorces his wife
and marries anoth-
er woman commits
adultery against
her. 12 And if she
divorces her hus-
band and marries
another man, she
commits adultery."

The Little Children and Jesus

13 People were
bringing little chil-
dren to Jesus for
him to place his
hands on them,
but the disciples
rebuked them.
14 When Jesus saw
this, he was indig-
nant. He said to
them, "Let the lit-
tle children come
to me, and do
not hinder them,
for the kingdom
of God belongs
to such as these.
15 Truly I tell you,
anyone who will
not receive the
kingdom of God
like a little child
will never enter
it." 16 And he took
the children in his
arms, placed his
hands on them and
blessed them.

a 6 Gen. 1:27
b 7 Some early manuscripts do not have *and be united to his wife.*
c 8 Gen. 2:24

κτίσεως ἄρσεν καὶ θῆλυ ἐποίησεν αὐτούς· 7 ἕνεκεν τούτου καταλείψει
of creation, 'male and female' he made them. 'For this reason a man shall leave
3232 781 2779 2559 4472 899 1914 4047 476 2901
n.gsf a.asn cj a.asn v.aai.3s r.apm.3 p.g r.gsn v.fai.3s

ἄνθρωπος τὸν πατέρα αὐτοῦ καὶ τὴν μητέρα [a]καὶ προσκολληθήσεται πρὸς τὴν
man *{the}* his father *his* and *{the}* mother and be joined to *{the}*
476 3836 899 4252 899 2779 3836 3613 2779 4681 4639 3836
n.nsm d.asm n.asm r.gsm.3 cj d.asf n.asf cj v.fpi.3s p.a d.asf

γυναῖκα αὐτοῦ, 8 καὶ ἔσονται οἱ δύο εἰς σάρκα μίαν· ὥστε
his wife, *his* and the two shall be *the* *two* *{into}* one flesh.' *one* So
899 1222 899 2779 3836 1545 1639 3836 1545 1650 1651 4922 1651 6063
n.asf r.gsm.3 cj v.fmi.3p d.npm a.npm p.a n.asf a.asf cj

οὐκέτι εἰσὶν δύο ἀλλὰ μία σάρξ. 9 ὃ οὖν ὁ θεὸς
no longer are they two, but one flesh. Therefore, what *Therefore* *{the}* God
4033 1639 1545 247 1651 4922 4036 4005 4036 3836 2536
adv v.pai.3p a.npm cj a.nsf n.nsf r.asn cj d.nsm n.nsm

συνέζευξεν ↱ ἄνθρωπος μὴ χωριζέτω. 10 καὶ εἰς τὴν οἰκίαν
has joined together, let not man *not* divide." And in the house the disciples
5183 6004 3590 476 3590 6004 2779 1650 3836 3864 3836 3412
v.aai.3s n.nsm pl v.pam.3s cj p.a d.asf n.asf

πάλιν οἱ μαθηταὶ περὶ τούτου ἐπηρώτων αὐτόν. 11 καὶ
were again *the* *disciples* questioning him about this matter. *were questioning* *him* And
2089 4099 3836 3412 2089 899 4309 4047 2089 899 2779
adv d.npm n.npm p.g r.gsn v.iai.3p r.asm.3 cj

λέγει αὐτοῖς· ⌞ὃς ἂν⌟ ἀπολύσῃ τὴν γυναῖκα αὐτοῦ καὶ γαμήσῃ
he said to them, "Whoever divorces *{the}* his wife *his* and marries
3306 899 4005 323 668 3836 899 1222 899 2779 1138
v.pai.3s r.dpm.3 r.nsm pl v.aas.3s d.asf n.asf r.gsm.3 cj v.aas.3s

ἄλλην μοιχᾶται ἐπ' αὐτήν· 12 καὶ ἐὰν αὐτὴ ἀπολύσασα τὸν
⌞another woman⌟ commits adultery against her. And if she, after divorcing *{the}* her
257 3656 2093 899 2779 1569 899 668 3836 899
r.asf v.ppi.3s p.a r.asf.3 cj cj r.nsf pt.aa.nsf d.asm

ἄνδρα αὐτῆς γαμήσῃ ἄλλον μοιχᾶται. 13 καὶ προσέφερον
husband, *her* marries ⌞another man,⌟ ⌞she commits adultery."⌟ And people were bringing
467 899 1138 257 3656 2779 4712
n.asm r.gsf.3 v.aas.3s r.asm v.ppi.3s cj v.iai.3p

αὐτῷ παιδία ἵνα αὐτῶν ἅψηται· οἱ δὲ μαθηταὶ ἐπετίμησαν
to him children so that *them* ⌞he could touch⌟ them, but his *but* disciples rebuked
899 4086 2671 899 721 899 1254 3836 1254 3412 2203
r.dsm.3 n.apn cj r.gpn.3 v.ams.3s d.npm cj n.npm v.aai.3p

αὐτοῖς. 14 → ἰδὼν δὲ ὁ Ἰησοῦς ἠγανάκτησεν καὶ εἶπεν αὐτοῖς·
them. But when Jesus saw it, *But* *{the}* *Jesus* he was indignant and said to them,
899 1254 2652 1625 1254 3836 2652 24 2779 3306 899
r.dpm.3 pt.aa.nsm cj d.nsm n.nsm v.aai.3s cj v.aai.3s r.dpm.3

ἄφετε τὰ παιδία ἔρχεσθαι πρός με, ↱ μὴ κωλύετε αὐτά, τῶν γὰρ τοιούτων ἐστὶν
"Let the children come to me. Do not prevent them, *{the}* for of such is
918 3836 4086 2262 4639 1609 3266 3590 3266 899 3836 1142 5525 1639
v.aam.2p d.apn n.apn f.pm p.a r.as.1 pl v.pam.2p r.apn.3 d.gpn cj r.gpn v.pai.3s

ἡ βασιλεία τοῦ θεοῦ. 15 ἀμὴν λέγω ὑμῖν, ⌞ὃς ἂν⌟ ↱ μὴ
the kingdom of God. I tell you the truth, *I tell* *you* whoever does not
3836 993 3836 2536 3306 3306 7007 297 3306 7007 4005 323 1312 3590
d.nsf n.nsf d.gsm n.gsm pl v.pai.1s r.dp.2 r.nsm pl pl

δέξηται τὴν βασιλείαν τοῦ θεοῦ ὡς παιδίον, ↱ ⌞οὐ μὴ⌟ ⌞εἰσέλθῃ εἰς⌟ αὐτήν.
receive the kingdom of God as a child will never enter it."
1312 3836 993 3836 2536 6055 4086 1656 4024 3590 1656 1650 899
v.ams.3s d.asf n.asf d.gsm n.gsm pl n.nsn pl pl v.aas.3s p.a r.asf.3

16 καὶ ἐναγκαλισάμενος αὐτὰ ↰ ↰ κατευλόγει τιθεὶς τὰς χεῖρας ἐπ'
And taking them into his arms, he blessed them, laying his hands on
2779 1878 899 1878 1878 2986 5502 3836 5931 2093
cj pt.am.nsm r.apn.3 v.iai.3s pt.pa.nsm d.apf n.apf p.a

αὐτά. 17 καὶ → ἐκπορευομένου αὐτοῦ εἰς ὁδὸν προσδραμὼν εἷς καὶ
them. And as he was going out *he* on the road, a man ran up, *a man* and
899 2779 899 1744 899 1650 3847 1651 1651 4708 1651 2779
r.apn.3 cj pt.pm.gsm r.gsm.3 p.a n.asf pt.aa.nsm a.nsm cj

a [καὶ προσκολληθήσεται πρὸς τὴν γυναῖκα αὐτοῦ] UBS.

NASB

God MADE THEM
MALE AND FEMALE.
7 FOR THIS REASON
A MAN SHALL LEAVE
HIS FATHER AND
MOTHER[a], 8 AND THE
TWO SHALL BECOME
ONE FLESH; so they
are no longer two,
but one flesh.
9 What therefore
God has joined to-
gether, let no man
separate."
10 In the house the
disciples *began*
questioning Him
about this again.
11 And He *said to
them, "Whoever
divorces his wife
and marries anoth-
er woman commits
adultery against
her; 12 and if she
herself divorces her
husband and mar-
ries another man,
she is committing
adultery."

Jesus Blesses Little Children

13 And they were
bringing children
to Him so that He
might touch them;
but the disciples re-
buked them. 14 But
when Jesus saw
this, He was indig-
nant and said to
them, "Permit the
children to come
to Me; do not hin-
der them; for the
kingdom of God
belongs to such as
these. 15 Truly I say
to you, whoever
does not receive
the kingdom of
God like a child
will not enter it *at
all.*" 16 And He took
them in His arms
and *began* blessing
them, laying His
hands on them.

a Many late mss add *and shall cling to his wife*

NIV

The Rich and the
Kingdom of God
17 As Jesus started
on his way, a man
ran up to him and
fell on his knees
before him. "Good
teacher," he asked,
"what must I do
to inherit eternal
life?"
18 "Why do you
call me good?"
Jesus answered.
"No one is good—
except God alone.
19 You know the
commandments:
'You shall not
murder, you shall
not commit adul-
tery, you shall not
steal, you shall
not give false tes-
timony, you shall
not defraud, honor
your father and
mother.'[a]"
20 "Teacher," he
declared, "all these
I have kept since I
was a boy."
21 Jesus looked
at him and loved
him. "One thing
you lack," he said.
"Go, sell every-
thing you have and
give to the poor,
and you will have
treasure in heaven.
Then come, fol-
low me."
22 At this the
man's face fell. He
went away sad, be-
cause he had great
wealth.
23 Jesus looked
around and said
to his disciples,
"How hard it is for
the rich to enter
the kingdom of
God!"
24 The disciples
were amazed at
his words. But
Jesus said again,
"Children, how
hard it is[b] to enter
the kingdom of
God! 25 It is easier
for a camel to go
through

[a] 19 Exodus 20:12-16; Deut. 5:16-20
[b] 24 Some manuscripts *is for those who trust in riches*

γονυπετήσας αὐτὸν ἐπηρώτα αὐτόν· διδάσκαλε ἀγαθέ, τί ποιήσω ἵνα
kneeling before him, asked him, "Good teacher, *Good* what must I do to inherit
1206 899 2089 899 19 1437 19 5515 4472 2671 3099
pt.aa.nsm r.asm.3 v.iai.3s r.asm.3 n.vsm a.vsm r.asn v.aas.1s cj

ζωὴν αἰώνιον κληρονομήσω; 18 ὁ δὲ Ἰησοῦς εἶπεν αὐτῷ· τί
eternal life?" *eternal* *inherit* *{the}* But Jesus said to him, "Why do you call
173 2437 173 3099 3836 1254 2652 3306 899 5515 3306 3306 3306
n.asf a.asf v.aas.1s d.nsm cj n.nsm v.aai.3s r.dsm.3 r.asn

με λέγεις ἀγαθόν; οὐδεὶς ἀγαθὸς ⌞εἰ μὴ⌟ εἷς ὁ θεός. 19 τὰς
me *do you call* good? No one is good except one — *{the}* God. You know the
1609 3306 19 4029 19 1623 3590 1651 3836 2536 3857 3857 3836
r.as.1 v.pai.2s a.asm a.nsm a.nsm cj pl a.nsm d.nsm n.nsm d.apf

ἐντολὰς οἶδας· ➝ μὴ φονεύσῃς, ➝ μὴ μοιχεύσῃς, ➝ μὴ κλέψῃς,
commandments: *You know* 'Do not murder, Do not commit adultery, Do not steal,
1953 3857 5839 3590 5839 3658 3590 3658 3096 3590 3096
n.apf v.rai.2s pl v.aas.2s pl v.aas.2s pl v.aas.2s

➝ μὴ ψευδομαρτυρήσῃς, ➝ μὴ ἀποστερήσῃς, τίμα τὸν πατέρα σου καὶ
Do not bear false witness, Do not defraud, Honor *{the}* your father *your* and
6018 3590 6018 691 3590 691 5506 3836 5148 4252 5148 2779
pl v.aas.2s pl v.aas.2s v.pam.2s d.asm n.asm r.gs.2 cj

τὴν μητέρα. 20 ὁ δὲ ἔφη αὐτῷ· διδάσκαλε, ταῦτα πάντα
{the} mother'." And the man *And* said to him, "Teacher, all these *all*
3836 3613 1254 3836 1254 5774 899 1437 4246 4047 4246
d.asf n.asf d.nsm cj v.iai.3s r.dsm.3 n.vsm r.apn a.apn

ἐφυλαξάμην ἐκ νεότητός μου. 21 ὁ δὲ Ἰησοῦς ἐμβλέψας αὐτῷ ἠγάπησεν
I have kept from my youth." *my* *{the}* But Jesus, looking at him, loved
5875 1666 1609 3744 1609 3836 1254 2652 1063 899 26
v.ami.1s p.g n.gsf r.gs.1 d.nsm cj n.nsm pt.aa.nsm r.dsm.3 v.aai.3s

αὐτὸν καὶ εἶπεν αὐτῷ· ἕν σε ὑστερεῖ· ὕπαγε, ὅσα ἔχεις
him and said to him, "You lack ⌞one thing⌟ *You* *lack* — go, sell whatever you have
899 2779 3306 899 5148 5728 1651 5148 5728 5632 4797 4012 2400
r.asm.3 cj v.aai.3s r.dsm.3 a.nsn r.as.2 v.pai.3s v.pam.2s r.apn v.pai.2s

πώλησον καὶ δὸς τοῖς[a] πτωχοῖς, καὶ ἕξεις θησαυρὸν ἐν οὐρανῷ,
sell and give the money to the poor; then ⌞you will have⌟ treasure in heaven.
4797 2779 1443 3836 4777 2779 2400 2565 1877 4041
v.aam.2s cj v.aam.2s d.dpm a.dpm cj v.fai.2s n.asm p.d n.dsm

καὶ δεῦρο ἀκολούθει μοι. 22 ὁ δὲ στυγνάσας ἐπὶ τῷ λόγῳ ἀπῆλθεν
And come, follow me." *the* *{and}* Disheartened by the saying, the man went away
2779 1306 199 1609 3836 1254 5145 2093 3836 3364 3836 599
cj j v.pam.2s r.ds.1 d.nsm cj pt.aa.nsm p.d d.dsm n.dsm v.aai.3s

λυπούμενος· ἦν γὰρ ↞ ἔχων κτήματα πολλά. 23 καὶ περιβλεψάμενος
grieving; *{he was}* for he had many possessions. *many* And looking around,
3382 1639 1142 1639 2400 4498 3228 4498 2779 4315
pt.pp.nsm v.iai.3s cj pt.pa.nsm n.apn a.apn cj pt.am.nsm

ὁ Ἰησοῦς λέγει τοῖς μαθηταῖς αὐτοῦ· πῶς δυσκόλως οἱ τὰ
{the} Jesus said to his disciples, *his* "How difficult it is for those *{the}* who
3836 2652 3306 3836 899 3412 899 4802 1552 3836 3836 2400
d.nsm n.nsm v.pai.3s d.dpm n.dpm r.gsm.3 pl adv d.npm d.apn

χρήματα ἔχοντες εἰς τὴν βασιλείαν τοῦ θεοῦ εἰσελεύσονται. 24 οἱ
have wealth *who have* to enter *{into}* the kingdom of God. *to enter* The
2400 5975 2400 1656 1656 1650 3836 993 3836 2536 1656 3836
n.apn pt.pa.npm p.a d.asf n.asf d.gsm n.gsm v.fmi.3p d.npm

δὲ μαθηταὶ ἐθαμβοῦντο ἐπὶ τοῖς λόγοις αὐτοῦ. ὁ δὲ Ἰησοῦς
{and} disciples were shocked at *{the}* his words. *his* *{the}* But Jesus responding
1254 3412 2501 2093 3836 899 3364 899 3836 1254 2652 646
cj n.npm v.ipi.3p p.d d.dpm n.dpm r.gsm.3 d.nsm cj n.nsm

πάλιν ἀποκριθεὶς λέγει αὐτοῖς· τέκνα, πῶς δύσκολόν ἐστιν[b] εἰς τὴν
again, *responding* said to them, "Children, how difficult it is to enter *{into}* the
4099 646 3306 899 5451 4802 1551 1639 1656 1656 1650 3836
adv pt.ap.nsm v.pai.3s r.dpm.3 n.vpn pl a.nsn v.pai.3s p.a d.asf

βασιλείαν τοῦ θεοῦ εἰσελθεῖν· 25 εὐκοπώτερόν ἐστιν ➝ κάμηλον
kingdom of God! *to enter* It is easier *It is* for a camel to pass
993 3836 2536 1656 1639 1639 2324 1639 2823 1451 1451
n.asf d.gsm n.gsm f.aa a.nsn.c v.pai.3s n.asf

[a] [τοῖς] UBS.
[b] τοὺς πεποιθότας ἐπὶ τοῖς χρήμασιν included by TR after ἐστιν.

NASB

The Rich Young Ruler
17 As He was set-
ting out on a jour-
ney, a man ran up
to Him and knelt
before Him, and
asked Him, "Good
Teacher, what
shall I do to inherit
eternal life?" 18 And
Jesus said to him,
"Why do you call
Me good? No one
is good except God
alone. 19 You know
the command-
ments, 'DO NOT
MURDER, DO NOT
COMMIT ADULTERY,
DO NOT STEAL, DO
NOT BEAR FALSE
WITNESS, Do not de-
fraud, HONOR YOUR
FATHER AND MOTH-
ER.'" 20 And he said
to Him, "Teacher, I
have kept all these
things from my
youth up." 21 Look-
ing at him, Jesus
felt a love for him
and said to him,
"One thing you
lack: go and sell
all you possess and
give to the poor,
and you will have
treasure in heaven;
and come, follow
Me." 22 But at these
words he was
saddened, and he
went away griev-
ing, for he was one
who owned much
property.
23 And Jesus, look-
ing around, *said
to His disciples,
"How hard it will
be for those who
are wealthy to
enter the kingdom
of God!" 24 The dis-
ciples were amazed
at His words. But
Jesus *answered
again and *said to
them, "Children,
how hard it is to
enter the kingdom
of God! 25 It is easi-
er for a camel to

NIV

the eye of a needle
than for someone
who is rich to en-
ter the kingdom of
God."
26The disciples
were even more
amazed, and said
to each other,
"Who then can be
saved?"
27Jesus looked
at them and said,
"With man this
is impossible, but
not with God; all
things are possible
with God."
28Then Peter
spoke up, "We
have left every-
thing to follow
you!"
29"Truly I tell
you," Jesus re-
plied, "no one who
has left home or
brothers or sisters
or mother or fa-
ther or children or
fields for me and
the gospel 30will
fail to receive a
hundred times as
much in this pres-
ent age: homes,
brothers, sisters,
mothers, children
and fields—along
with persecu-
tions—and in
the age to come
eternal life. 31But
many who are first
will be last, and
the last first."

Jesus Predicts His Death a Third Time

32They were on
their way up to
Jerusalem, with
Jesus leading the
way, and the dis-
ciples were aston-
ished, while those
who followed were
afraid. Again he
took

διὰ τῆς[a] τρυμαλιᾶς τῆς[b] ῥαφίδος διελθεῖν ἢ πλούσιον
through the eye of a needle *to pass* than for ⌞someone who is rich⌟ to enter
1328 3836 5584 3836 4827 1451 2445 4454 1656 1656
p.g d.gsf n.gsf d.gsf n.gsf f.aa pl n.asm

εἰς τὴν βασιλείαν τοῦ θεοῦ εἰσελθεῖν. 26 οἱ δὲ ↱ περισσῶς ἐξεπλήσσοντο
{into} the kingdom of God." *to enter* They *{and}* were even more astonished,
1650 3836 993 3836 2536 1656 3836 1254 1742 4360 1742
p.a d.asf n.asf d.gsm n.gsm f.aa d.npm cj adv v.ipi.3p

λέγοντες πρὸς ἑαυτούς· καὶ τίς δύναται σωθῆναι; 27 ἐμβλέψας αὐτοῖς ὁ
saying to themselves, "Then who is able to be saved?" Looking at them, *{the}*
3306 4639 1571 2779 5515 1538 5392 1838 899 3836
pt.pa.npm p.a r.apm.3 cj r.nsm v.ppi.3s f.ap pt.aa.nsm r.dpm.3 d.nsm

Ἰησοῦς λέγει· παρὰ ἀνθρώποις ἀδύνατον, ἀλλ᾽ οὐ παρὰ θεῷ· πάντα γὰρ
Jesus said, "With man it is impossible, but not with God; for all things *for*
2652 3306 4123 476 105 247 4024 4123 2536 1142 4246 1142
n.nsm v.pai.3s p.d n.dpm a.nsn cj pl p.d n.dsm a.npn cj

δυνατὰ παρὰ τῷ θεῷ. 28 ἤρξατο λέγειν ὁ Πέτρος αὐτῷ· ἰδοὺ ἡμεῖς
are possible with *{the}* God." Peter started to speak *{the}* *Peter* to him, "Well, we
1543 4123 3836 2536 4377 806 3306 3836 4377 899 2627 7005
a.npn p.d d.dsm n.dsm v.ami.3s f.pa d.nsm n.nsm r.dsm.3 j r.np.1

ἀφήκαμεν πάντα καὶ ἠκολουθήκαμέν σοι. 29 ἔφη ὁ Ἰησοῦς·
have left everything and have followed you." Jesus said, *{the}* *Jesus* "I tell you
918 4246 2779 199 5148 2652 5774 3836 2652 3306 3306 7007
v.aai.1p a.apn cj v.rai.1p r.ds.2 v.iai.3s d.nsm n.nsm

ἀμὴν λέγω ὑμῖν, οὐδείς ἐστιν ὃς ἀφῆκεν οἰκίαν ἢ ἀδελφοὺς ἢ
the truth, *I tell* *you* there is no one *there is* who has left home or brothers or
297 3306 7007 1639 1639 4029 1639 4005 918 3864 2445 81 2445
pl v.pai.1s r.dp.2 a.nsm v.pai.3s r.nsm v.aai.3s n.asf cj n.apm cj

ἀδελφὰς ἢ μητέρα ἢ πατέρα[c] ἢ τέκνα ἢ ἀγροὺς ἕνεκεν ἐμοῦ ↰ καὶ
sisters or mother or father or children or fields for my sake and
80 2445 3613 2445 4252 2445 5451 2445 69 1914 1609 1914 2779
n.apf cj n.asf cj n.asm cj n.apn cj n.apm p.g r.gs.1 cj

ἕνεκεν τοῦ εὐαγγελίου, 30 ἐὰν ↱ ↱ μὴ λάβῃ ἑκατονταπλασίονα νῦν ἐν
⌞for the sake of⌟ the gospel, ~ who will not receive one hundredfold now in
1914 3836 2295 1569 3284 3284 3590 3284 1671 3814 1877
p.g d.gsn n.gsn cj pl v.aas.3s a.apn adv p.d

τῷ καιρῷ τούτῳ οἰκίας καὶ ἀδελφοὺς καὶ ἀδελφὰς καὶ μητέρας καὶ
{the} this ⌞present time⌟ *this* — houses and brothers and sisters and mothers and
3836 4047 2789 4047 3864 2779 81 2779 80 2779 3613 2779
d.dsm n.dsm r.dsm n.apf cj n.apm cj n.apf cj n.apf cj

τέκνα καὶ ἀγροὺς μετὰ διωγμῶν, καὶ ἐν τῷ αἰῶνι τῷ ἐρχομένῳ
children and fields, with persecutions — and in the coming age, *{the}* *coming* eternal
5451 2779 69 3552 1501 2779 1877 3836 2262 172 3836 2262 173
n.apn cj n.apm p.g n.gpm cj p.d d.dsm n.dsm d.dsm pt.pm.dsm

ζωὴν αἰώνιον. 31 πολλοὶ δὲ ἔσονται πρῶτοι ἔσχατοι καὶ οἱ[d]
life. *eternal* But many *But* who are first will be *first* last, and the
2437 173 1254 4498 1254 4755 1639 4755 2274 2779 3836
n.asf a.asf a.npm cj v.fmi.3p a.npm a.npm cj d.npm

ἔσχατοι πρῶτοι. 32 ἦσαν δὲ ἐν τῇ ὁδῷ ἀναβαίνοντες εἰς
last will be first." Now they were *Now* on the road, going up to
2274 4755 1254 1639 1254 1877 3836 3847 326 1650
a.npm a.npm v.iai.3p cj p.d d.dsf n.dsf pt.pa.npm p.a

Ἱεροσόλυμα, καὶ ἦν προάγων αὐτοὺς ὁ Ἰησοῦς, καὶ
Jerusalem and Jesus was ⌞going on ahead of⌟ them. *{the}* *Jesus* *{and}*
2642 2779 2652 1639 4575 899 3836 2652 2779
n.apn cj v.iai.3s pt.pa.nsm r.apm.3 d.nsm n.nsm cj

ἐθαμβοῦντο, οἱ δὲ ἀκολουθοῦντες ἐφοβοῦντο. καὶ παραλαβὼν
⌞They were filled with awe,⌟ but those *but* who followed behind were afraid. And taking
2501 1254 3836 1254 199 5828 2779 4161
v.ipi.3p d.npm cj pt.pa.npm v.ipi.3p cj pt.aa.nsm

NASB

go through the eye
of a needle than
for a rich man to
enter the kingdom
of God." 26They
were even more
astonished and said
to Him, "Then who
can be saved?"
27Looking at them,
Jesus *said, "With
people it is impos-
sible, but not with
God; for all things
are possible with
God."
28Peter began to
say to Him, "Be-
hold, we have left
everything and
followed You."
29Jesus said, "Truly
I say to you, there
is no one who has
left house or broth-
ers or sisters or
mother or father or
children or farms,
for My sake and
for the gospel's
sake, 30but that
he will receive a
hundred times as
much now in the
present age, houses
and brothers and
sisters and mothers
and children and
farms, along with
persecutions; and
in the age to come,
eternal life. 31But
many *who are* first
will be last, and the
last, first."

Jesus' Sufferings Foretold

32They were on
the road going up
to Jerusalem, and
Jesus was walking
on ahead of them;
and they were
amazed, and those
who followed were
fearful. And again

---

[a] [τῆς] UBS.
[b] [τῆς] UBS.
[c] ἢ γυναῖκα included by TR after πατέρα.
[d] [οἱ] UBS.

NIV

the Twelve aside
and told them
what was going
to happen to him.
33“We are going
up to Jerusalem,”
he said, “and the
Son of Man will
be delivered over
to the chief priests
and the teachers
of the law. They
will condemn him
to death and will
hand him over to
the Gentiles, 34who
will mock him and
spit on him, flog
him and kill him.
Three days later he
will rise.”

The Request of James and John

35Then James and
John, the sons of
Zebedee, came to
him. “Teacher,”
they said, “we
want you to do for
us whatever we
ask.”
36“What do you
want me to do for
you?” he asked.
37They replied,
“Let one of us sit
at your right and
the other at your
left in your glory.”
38“You don’t
know what you
are asking,” Jesus
said. “Can you
drink the cup I
drink or be bap-
tized with the bap-
tism I am baptized
with?”
39“We can,” they
answered.
Jesus said to
them, “You will
drink the cup I
drink and be bap-
tized with the bap-
tism I am baptized
with, 40but to sit at
my right or

← πάλιν τοὺς δώδεκα ἤρξατο αὐτοῖς λέγειν τὰ
the twelve aside again, *the* *twelve* he began to tell them *to tell* the
3836 1557 4099 3836 1557 806 3306 3306 899 3306 3836
adv d.apm a.apm v.ami.3s r.dpm.3 f.pa d.apn

μέλλοντα αὐτῷ συμβαίνειν 33 ὅτι ἰδοὺ ἀναβαίνομεν εἰς
⌞things that were going⌟ to happen to him: *to happen* ~ “Listen, we are going up to
3516 5201 5201 899 5201 4022 2627 326 1650
pt.pa.apn r.dsm.3 f.pa cj j v.pai.1p p.a

Ἱεροσόλυμα, καὶ ὁ υἱὸς τοῦ ἀνθρώπου παραδοθήσεται τοῖς ἀρχιερεῦσιν καὶ
Jerusalem, and the Son of Man will be handed over to the ruling priests and
2642 2779 3836 5626 3836 476 4140 3836 797 2779
n.apn cj d.nsm n.nsm d.gsm n.gsm v.fpi.3s d.dpm n.dpm cj

τοῖς γραμματεῦσιν, καὶ κατακρινοῦσιν αὐτὸν θανάτῳ καὶ παραδώσουσιν αὐτὸν ↰
the scribes, and they will condemn him to death and hand him over
3836 1208 2779 2891 899 2505 2779 4140 899 4140
d.dpm n.dpm cj v.fai.3p r.asm.3 n.dsm cj v.fai.3p r.asm.3

τοῖς ἔθνεσιν 34 καὶ ἐμπαίξουσιν αὐτῷ καὶ ἐμπτύσουσιν αὐτῷ καὶ μαστιγώσουσιν
to the Gentiles. And they will mock him, and spit on him, and flog
3836 1620 2779 1850 899 2779 1870 899 2779 3463
d.dpm n.dpn cj v.fai.3p r.dsm.3 cj v.fai.3p r.dsm.3 cj v.fai.3p

αὐτὸν καὶ ἀποκτενοῦσιν, καὶ μετὰ τρεῖς ἡμέρας ἀναστήσεται. 35 καὶ
him, and kill him; but after three days he will rise.” Then
899 2779 650 2779 3552 5552 2465 482 2779
r.asm.3 cj v.fai.3p cj p.a a.apf n.apf v.fmi.3s cj

προσπορεύονται αὐτῷ Ἰάκωβος καὶ Ἰωάννης οἱ υἱοὶ Ζεβεδαίου
approached *Jesus* James and John, the sons of Zebedee, approached Jesus and
4702 899 2610 2779 2722 3836 5626 2411 4702 899
v.pmi.3p r.dsm.3 n.nsm cj n.nsm d.npm n.npm n.gsm

λέγοντες αὐτῷ· διδάσκαλε, θέλομεν ἵνα ⌞ὃ ἐὰν⌟ αἰτήσωμέν σε
said to him, “Teacher, we want you to do for us whatever we ask.” *you*
3306 899 1437 2527 5148 2671 4472 7005 7005 4005 1569 160 5148
pt.pa.npm r.dsm.3 n.vsm v.pai.1p cj r.asn pl v.aas.1p r.as.2

ποιήσῃς ἡμῖν. 36 ὁ δὲ εἶπεν αὐτοῖς· τί θέλετέ με[a] ποιήσω ὑμῖν;
do *for us* And he *And* said to them, “What ⌞do you want⌟ me to do for you?”
4472 7005 1254 3836 1254 3306 899 5515 2527 1609 4472 7007
v.aas.2s r.dp.1 d.nsm cj v.aai.3s r.dpm.3 r.asn v.pai.2p r.as.1 v.aas.1s r.dp.2

37 οἱ δὲ εἶπαν αὐτῷ· δὸς ἡμῖν ἵνα εἷς σου ἐκ δεξιῶν
And they *And* said to him, “Give us permission to sit, one on your *on* right
1254 3836 1254 3306 899 1443 7005 2671 2767 1651 1666 5148 1666 1288
d.npm cj v.aai.3p r.dsm.3 v.aam.2s r.dp.1 cj a.nsm r.gs.2 p.g a.gpf

καὶ εἷς ἐξ ἀριστερῶν καθίσωμεν ἐν τῇ δόξῃ σου. 38 ὁ δὲ Ἰησοῦς
and one on your left, *sit* in *{the}* your glory.” *your* *{the}* But Jesus
2779 1651 1666 754 2767 1877 3836 5148 1518 5148 3836 1254 2652
cj a.nsm p.g a.gpf v.aas.1p p.d d.dsf n.dsf r.gs.2 d.nsm cj n.nsm

εἶπεν αὐτοῖς· ↱ ↱ οὐκ οἴδατε τί αἰτεῖσθε. δύνασθε πιεῖν τὸ ποτήριον
said to them, “You do not know what you are asking. Are you able to drink the cup
3306 899 3857 3857 4024 3857 5515 160 1538 4403 3836 4539
v.aai.3s r.dpm.3 pl v.rai.2p r.asn v.pmi.2p v.ppi.2p f.aa d.asn n.asn

ὃ ἐγὼ πίνω ἢ τὸ βάπτισμα ὃ ἐγὼ βαπτίζομαι
that I drink, or to be baptized with the baptism with which I am baptized?”
4005 1609 4403 2445 966 966 966 3836 967 4005 1609 966
r.asn r.ns.1 v.pai.1s cj d.asn n.asn r.asn r.ns.1 v.ppi.1s

βαπτισθῆναι; 39 οἱ δὲ εἶπαν αὐτῷ· δυνάμεθα. ὁ δὲ Ἰησοῦς εἶπεν αὐτοῖς·
to be baptized They *{and}* said to him, “We are able.” *{the}* And Jesus said to them,
966 3836 1254 3306 899 1538 3836 1254 2652 3306 899
f.ap d.npm cj v.aai.3p r.dsm.3 v.ppi.1p d.nsm cj n.nsm v.aai.3s r.dpm.3

τὸ ποτήριον ὃ ἐγὼ πίνω πίεσθε καὶ τὸ βάπτισμα ὃ ἐγὼ
“The cup that I drink ⌞you will drink,⌟ and with the baptism with which I
3836 4539 4005 1609 4403 4403 2779 3836 967 4005 1609
d.asn n.asn r.asn r.ns.1 v.pai.1s v.fmi.2p cj d.asn n.asn r.asn r.ns.1

βαπτίζομαι βαπτισθήσεσθε, 40 τὸ δὲ καθίσαι ἐκ δεξιῶν μου ἢ ἐξ
am baptized, you will be baptized; *{the}* but to sit on my right *my* or on my
966 966 3836 1254 2767 1666 1609 1288 1609 2445 1666
v.ppi.1s v.fpi.2p d.nsn cj f.aa p.g a.gpf r.gs.1 cj p.g

NASB

He took the twelve
aside and began to
tell them what was
going to happen
to Him, 33*saying,*
“Behold, we are
going up to Jeru-
salem, and the Son
of Man will be [a]de-
livered to the chief
priests and the
scribes; and they
will condemn Him
to death and will
hand Him over to
the Gentiles. 34They
will mock Him and
spit on Him, and
scourge Him and
kill *Him,* and three
days later He will
rise again.”
35James and John,
the two sons of
Zebedee, *came up
to Jesus, saying,
“Teacher, we want
You to do for us
whatever we ask
of You.” 36And
He said to them,
“What do you want
Me to do for you?”
37They said to Him,
“Grant that we may
sit, one on Your
right and one on
Your left, in Your
glory.” 38But Jesus
said to them, “You
do not know what
you are asking. Are
you able to drink
the cup that I drink,
or to be baptized
with the baptism
with which I am
baptized?” 39They
said to Him, “We
are able.” And
Jesus said to them,
“The cup that I
drink you shall
drink; and you
shall be baptized
with the baptism
with which I am
baptized. 40But to
sit on My right or

[a] [με] UBS.

[a] Or *betrayed*

NIV

left is not for me to
grant. These plac-
es belong to those
for whom they
have been pre-
pared."
41 When the ten
heard about this,
they became indig-
nant with James
and John. 42 Jesus
called them to-
gether and said,
"You know that
those who are re-
garded as rulers of
the Gentiles lord
it over them, and
their high officials
exercise authority
over them. 43 Not
so with you. In-
stead, whoever
wants to become
great among you
must be your ser-
vant, 44 and whoev-
er wants to be first
must be slave of
all. 45 For even the
Son of Man did not
come to be served,
but to serve, and
to give his life as a
ransom for many."

Blind Bartimaeus Receives His Sight

46 Then they
came to Jericho.
As Jesus and his
disciples, together
with a large crowd,
were leaving the
city, a blind man,
Bartimaeus (which
means "son of
Timaeus"), was
sitting by the
roadside begging.
47 When he heard
that it was Jesus of
Nazareth, he began
to shout, "Jesus,
Son of David, have
mercy on me!"
48 Many rebuked
him and told him
to be quiet, but
he shouted all the
more, "Son of Da-
vid, have mercy
on me!"
49 Jesus stopped
and said, "Call

εὐωνύμων οὐκ ἔστιν ἐμὸν δοῦναι, ἀλλ' οἷς ἡτοίμασται.
left is not *is* mine to give, but it is for those ˻for whom˼ it has been prepared."
2381 1639 4024 1639 1847 1443 247 4005 2286
a.gpf pl v.pai.3s r.nsn.1 f.aa cj r.dpm v.rpi.3s

41 καὶ ἀκούσαντες οἱ δέκα ἤρξαντο ἀγανακτεῖν περὶ Ἰακώβου καὶ Ἰωάννου.
And hearing this, the ten began to be indignant at James and John.
2779 201 3836 1274 806 24 4309 2610 2779 2722
cj pt.aa.npm d.npm a.npm v.ami.3p f.pa p.g n.gsm cj n.gsm

42 καὶ προσκαλεσάμενος αὐτοὺς ← ὁ Ἰησοῦς λέγει αὐτοῖς· οἴδατε ὅτι
And calling them to him, *{the}* Jesus said to them, "You know that
2779 4673 899 4673 3836 2652 3306 899 3857 4022
cj pt.am.nsm r.apm.3 d.nsm n.nsm v.pai.3s r.dpm.3 v.rai.2p cj

οἱ δοκοῦντες ἄρχειν τῶν ἐθνῶν κατακυριεύουσιν ← αὐτῶν καὶ οἱ
those who are supposed ˻to rule over˼ the Gentiles lord it over them, and *{the}*
3836 1506 806 3836 1620 2894 899 2779 3836
d.npm pt.pa.npm f.pa d.gpn n.gpn v.pai.3p r.gpn.3 cj d.npm

μεγάλοι αὐτῶν κατεξουσιάζουσιν αὐτῶν. 43 οὐχ οὕτως δέ
their leaders *their* domineer over them. But it is not to be so *But*
899 3489 899 2980 899 1254 1639 1639 4024 4048 1254
a.npm r.gpn.3 v.pai.3p r.gpn.3 pl adv cj

ἐστιν ἐν ὑμῖν, ἀλλ' ˻ὃς ἂν˼ θέλῃ μέγας γενέσθαι ἐν ὑμῖν ἔσται ὑμῶν
it is among you. But whoever would be great *be* among you must be your
1639 1877 7007 247 4005 323 2527 1181 3489 1181 1877 7007 1639 7007
v.pai.3s p.d r.dp.2 cj r.nsm pl v.pas.3s a.nsm f.am p.d r.dp.2 v.fmi.3s r.gp.2

διάκονος, 44 καὶ ˻ὃς ἂν˼ θέλῃ ἐν ὑμῖν εἶναι πρῶτος ἔσται
servant, and whoever would be first among you *be* *first* must be servant
1356 2779 4005 323 2527 1639 4755 1877 7007 1639 4755 1639 1529
n.nsm cj r.nsm pl v.pas.3s p.d r.dp.2 f.pa a.nsm v.fmi.3s

πάντων δοῦλος· 45 καὶ γὰρ ὁ υἱὸς τοῦ ἀνθρώπου οὐκ ἦλθεν
of all. *servant* For even *For* the Son of Man came not *came*
4246 1529 1142 2779 1142 3836 5626 3836 476 2262 4024 2262
a.gpm n.nsm adv cj d.nsm n.nsm d.gsm n.gsm pl v.aai.3s

διακονηθῆναι ἀλλὰ διακονῆσαι καὶ δοῦναι τὴν ψυχὴν αὐτοῦ λύτρον ἀντὶ
to be served but to serve, and to give *{the}* his life *his* as a ransom for
1354 247 1354 2779 1443 3836 899 6034 899 3389 505
f.ap cj f.aa cj f.aa d.asf n.asf r.gsm.3 n.asn p.g

πολλῶν. 46 καὶ ἔρχονται εἰς Ἰεριχώ. καὶ → ἐκπορευομένου αὐτοῦ ἀπὸ Ἰεριχὼ
many." And they came to Jericho. And as he was going out *he* from Jericho
4498 2779 2262 1650 2637 2779 899 1744 899 608 2637
a.gpm cj v.pmi.3p p.a n.asf cj pt.pm.gsm r.gsm.3 p.g n.dsf

καὶ τῶν μαθητῶν αὐτοῦ καὶ ὄχλου ἱκανοῦ
with *{the}* his disciples *his* and a considerable crowd, *considerable* a blind beggar,
2779 3836 899 3412 899 2779 2653 4063 2653 5603 4645
cj d.gpm n.gpm r.gsm.3 cj n.gsm a.gsm

ὁ υἱὸς Τιμαίου Βαρτιμαῖος, τυφλὸς προσαίτης, ἐκάθητο παρὰ τὴν
Bartimaeus the son of Timaeus, *Bartimaeus* *blind* *beggar* was sitting by the
985 3836 5626 5505 985 5603 4645 2764 4123 3836
d.nsm n.nsm n.gsm n.nsm a.nsm n.nsm v.imi.3s p.a d.asf

ὁδόν. 47 καὶ ἀκούσας ὅτι Ἰησοῦς ὁ Ναζαρηνός ἐστιν ἤρξατο κράζειν
road. And hearing that it was Jesus of Nazareth, *it was* he began to cry out
3847 2779 201 4022 1639 1639 2652 3836 3716 1639 806 3189
n.asf cj pt.aa.nsm cj n.nsm d.nsm n.nsm v.pai.3s v.ami.3s f.pa

καὶ λέγειν· υἱὲ Δαυὶδ Ἰησοῦ, ἐλέησόν με. 48 καὶ ἐπετίμων
and say, "Son of David, Jesus, ˻have mercy on˼ me!" And many ˻were sternly telling˼
2779 3306 5626 1253 2652 1796 1609 2779 4498 2203
cj f.pa n.vsm n.gsm n.vsm v.aam.2s r.as.1 cj v.iai.3p

αὐτῷ πολλοὶ ἵνα σιωπήσῃ· ὁ δὲ πολλῷ μᾶλλον ἔκραζεν· υἱὲ
him *many* to be quiet; *he* but all the more he ˻kept crying out,˼ "Son
899 4498 2671 4995 3836 1254 4498 3437 3836 3189 5626
r.dsm.3 a.npm cj v.aas.3s d.nsm cj a.dsn adv.c v.iai.3s n.vsm

Δαυίδ, ἐλέησόν με. 49 καὶ στὰς ὁ Ἰησοῦς εἶπεν· φωνήσατε
of David, ˻have mercy on˼ me!" And Jesus stopped *{the}* *Jesus* and said, "Call
1253 1796 1609 2779 2652 2705 3836 2652 3306 5888
n.gsm v.aam.2s r.as.1 cj pt.aa.nsm d.nsm n.nsm v.aai.3s v.aam.2p

NASB

on *My* left, this is
not Mine to give;
but it is for those
for whom it has
been prepared."
41 Hearing *this*,
the ten began to
feel indignant with
James and John.
42 Calling them to
Himself, Jesus
*said to them, "You
know that those
who are recog-
nized as rulers of
the Gentiles lord
it over them; and
their great men
exercise authority
over them. 43 But
it is not this way
among you, but
whoever wishes
to become great
among you shall be
your servant; 44 and
whoever wishes to
be first among you
shall be slave of
all. 45 For even the
Son of Man did not
come to be served,
but to serve, and to
give His life a ran-
som for many."

Bartimaeus Receives His Sight

46 Then they *came
to Jericho. And
as He was leav-
ing Jericho with
His disciples and
a large crowd,
a blind beggar
named Bartimaeus,
the son of Timaeus,
was sitting by the
road. 47 When he
heard that it was
Jesus the Nazarene,
he began to cry out
and say, "Jesus,
Son of David, have
mercy on me!"
48 Many were stern-
ly telling him to be
quiet, but he kept
crying out all the
more, "Son of Da-
vid, have mercy on
me!" 49 And Jesus
stopped and said,
"Call him *here*."

NIV

him."
So they called
to the blind man,
"Cheer up! On
your feet! He's
calling you."
50 Throwing his
cloak aside, he
jumped to his feet
and came to Jesus.
51 "What do you
want me to do for
you?" Jesus asked
him.
The blind man
said, "Rabbi, I
want to see."
52 "Go," said
Jesus, "your faith
has healed you."
Immediately he
received his sight
and followed Jesus
along the road.

Jesus Comes to Jerusalem as King

11 As they ap-
proached
Jerusalem and
came to Bethphage
and Bethany at the
Mount of Olives,
Jesus sent two
of his disciples,
2 saying to them,
"Go to the village
ahead of you, and
just as you enter
it, you will find
a colt tied there,
which no one has
ever ridden. Untie
it and bring it here.
3 If anyone asks
you, 'Why are you
doing this?' say,
'The Lord needs
it and will send it
back here short-
ly.'"
4 They went and
found a colt out-
side in the street,
tied at a doorway.
As they untied
it, 5 some people
standing there
asked, "What are
you doing, untying
that colt?" 6 They
answered as Jesus
had told them to,

αὐτόν. καὶ φωνοῦσιν τὸν τυφλὸν λέγοντες αὐτῷ· θάρσει, ἔγειρε, φωνεῖ
him." And they called the blind man, saying to him, "Take courage! Get up! He is calling
899 2779 5888 3836 5603 3306 899 2510 1586 5888
r.asm.3 cj v.pai.3p d.asm a.asm pt.pa.npm r.dsm.3 v.pam.2s v.pam.2s v.pai.3s

σε. 50 ὁ δὲ ἀποβαλὼν τὸ ἱμάτιον αὐτοῦ ἀναπηδήσας ἦλθεν
you." *he* And throwing aside *{the}* his cloak, *his* he ⌞jumped to his feet⌟ and came
5148 3836 1254 610 3836 899 2668 899 3836 403 2262
r.as.2 d.nsm cj pt.aa.nsm d.asn n.asn r.gsm.3 pt.aa.nsm v.aai.3s

πρὸς τὸν Ἰησοῦν. 51 καὶ ἀποκριθεὶς αὐτῷ ὁ Ἰησοῦς εἶπεν· τί σοι
to *{the}* Jesus. And answering him, *{the}* Jesus said, "What *for you*
4639 3836 2652 2779 646 899 3836 2652 3306 5515 5148
p.a d.asm n.asm cj pt.ap.nsm r.dsm.3 d.nsm n.nsm v.aai.3s r.asn r.ds.2

θέλεις ποιήσω; ὁ δὲ τυφλὸς εἶπεν αὐτῷ· ραββουνί, ἵνα
⌞do you want⌟ me to do for you? "And the *And* blind man said to him, "Rabbi, that
2527 4472 5148 5148 1254 3836 1254 5603 3306 899 4808 2671
v.pai.2s v.aas.1s d.nsm cj a.nsm v.aai.3s r.dsm.3 n.vsm cj

ἀναβλέψω. 52 καὶ ὁ Ἰησοῦς εἶπεν αὐτῷ· ὕπαγε, ἡ πίστις σου σέσωκέν
I might see again." And *{the}* Jesus said to him, "Go, *{the}* your faith *your* has healed
329 2779 3836 2652 3306 899 5632 3836 5148 4411 5148 5392
v.aas.1s cj d.nsm n.nsm v.aai.3s r.dsm.3 v.pam.2s d.nsf n.nsf r.gs.2 v.rai.3s

σε. καὶ εὐθὺς ἀνέβλεψεν καὶ ἠκολούθει αὐτῷ ἐν τῇ ὁδῷ.
you." And immediately ⌞he regained his sight⌟ and began following him on the way.
5148 2779 2318 329 2779 199 899 1877 3836 3847
r.as.2 cj adv v.aai.3s cj v.iai.3s r.dsm.3 p.d d.dsf n.dsf

11:1 καὶ ὅτε ἐγγίζουσιν εἰς Ἱεροσόλυμα εἰς Βηθφαγὴ καὶ Βηθανίαν πρὸς τὸ
And when they drew near to Jerusalem, *{to}* Bethphage, and Bethany, at the
2779 4021 1581 1650 2642 1650 1036 2779 1029 4639 3836
cj cj v.pai.3p p.a n.apn p.a n.asf cj n.asf p.a d.asn

ὄρος τῶν ἐλαιῶν, ἀποστέλλει δύο τῶν μαθητῶν αὐτοῦ 2 καὶ λέγει αὐτοῖς·
Mount of Olives, Jesus dispatched two of his disciples *his* and said to them,
4001 3836 1777 690 1545 3836 899 3412 899 2779 3306 899
n.asn d.gpf n.gpf v.pai.3s a.apm d.gpm n.gpm r.gsm.3 cj v.pai.3s r.dpm.3

ὑπάγετε εἰς τὴν κώμην τὴν κατέναντι ὑμῶν, καὶ εὐθὺς ⌞εἰσπορευόμενοι εἰς⌟
"Go into the village *{the}* directly ahead of you, and immediately upon entering
5632 1650 3836 3267 3836 2978 7007 2779 2318 1660 1650
v.pam.2p p.a d.asf n.asf d.asf p.g r.gp.2 cj adv pt.pm.npm p.a

αὐτὴν εὑρήσετε πῶλον δεδεμένον ἐφ᾽ ὃν οὐδεὶς ↱ οὔπω ἀνθρώπων
it you will find a tethered colt *tethered* on which no one has ever *one*
899 2351 1313 4798 1313 2093 4005 4029 476 2767 4037 476
r.asf.3 v.fai.2p n.asm pt.rp.asm p.a r.asm a.nsm adv n.gpm

ἐκάθισεν· λύσατε αὐτὸν καὶ φέρετε. 3 καὶ ἐάν τις ὑμῖν εἴπῃ· τί
sat. Untie it and bring it. *{and}* If anyone says to you, *says* 'Why
2767 3395 899 2779 5770 2779 1569 5516 3306 7007 3306 5515
v.aai.3s v.aam.2p r.asm.3 cj v.pam.2p cj cj r.nsm r.dp.2 v.aas.3s r.asn

ποιεῖτε τοῦτο; εἴπατε· ὁ κύριος αὐτοῦ χρείαν ἔχει, καὶ
⌞are you doing⌟ this?' say, 'The Lord has need of it, *need* *has* and will send it
4472 4047 3306 3836 3261 2400 5970 899 5970 2400 2779 690 690 899
v.pai.2p r.asn v.aam.2p d.nsm n.nsm r.gsm.3 n.asf v.pai.3s cj

εὐθὺς αὐτὸν ἀποστέλλει πάλιν ὧδε. 4 καὶ ἀπῆλθον καὶ
back here ⌞as soon as possible.'"⌟ *it* *will send* *back* *here* So ⌞they went away⌟ and
4099 6045 2318 899 690 4099 6045 2779 599 2779
adv r.asm.3 v.pai.3s adv adv cj v.aai.3p cj

εὗρον πῶλον δεδεμένον πρὸς θύραν ἔξω ἐπὶ τοῦ ἀμφόδου καὶ λύουσιν
found a tethered colt *tethered* at a door outside in the street, and they untied
2351 1313 4798 1313 4639 2598 2032 2093 3836 316 2779 3395
v.aai.3p n.asm pt.rp.asm p.a n.asf adv p.g d.gsn n.gsn cj v.pai.3p

αὐτόν. 5 καί τινες τῶν ἐκεῖ ἑστηκότων ἔλεγον αὐτοῖς· τί ποιεῖτε
it. And some of those standing there *standing* said to them, "What ⌞are you doing,⌟
899 2779 5516 3836 2705 1695 2705 3306 899 5515 4472
r.asm.3 cj r.npm d.gpm adv pt.ra.gpm v.iai.3p r.dpm.3 r.asn v.pai.2p

λύοντες τὸν πῶλον; 6 οἱ δὲ εἶπαν αὐτοῖς καθὼς εἶπεν ὁ Ἰησοῦς,
untying the colt?" And they *And* spoke to them just as Jesus had said, *{the}* *Jesus*
3395 3836 4798 1254 3836 1254 3306 899 2777 2652 3306 3836 2652
pt.pa.npm d.asm n.asm d.npm cj v.aai.3p r.dpm.3 cj v.aai.3s d.nsm n.nsm

NASB

So they *called the
blind man, say-
ing to him, "Take
courage, stand up!
He is calling for
you." 50 Throwing
aside his cloak,
he jumped up and
came to Jesus.
51 And answering
him, Jesus said,
"What do you want
Me to do for you?"
And the blind man
said to Him, "[a]Rab-
boni, *I want* to
regain my sight!"
52 And Jesus said
to him, "Go; your
faith has made you
well." Immediately
he regained his
sight and *began*
following Him on
the road.

The Triumphal Entry

11:1 As they *ap-
proached Jerusa-
lem, at Bethphage
and Bethany, near
the Mount of Ol-
ives, He *sent two
of His disciples,
2 and *said to them,
"Go into the vil-
lage opposite you,
and immediately
as you enter it, you
will find a colt tied
there, on which no
one yet has ever
sat; untie it and
bring it *here.* 3 If
anyone says to you,
'Why are you do-
ing this?' you say,
'The Lord has need
of it'; and immedi-
ately he will send it
back here." 4 They
went away and
found a colt tied at
the door, outside in
the street; and they
*untied it. 5 Some
of the bystanders
were saying to
them, "What are
you doing, untying
the colt?" 6 They
spoke to them just
as Jesus had told
them, and

[a] I.e. My Master

NIV

and the people let
them go. 7 When
they brought the
colt to Jesus and
threw their cloaks
over it, he sat on
it. 8 Many people
spread their cloaks
on the road, while
others spread
branches they had
cut in the fields.
9 Those who went
ahead and those
who followed
shouted,

"Hosanna![a]"

"Blessed is he who comes in the name of the Lord!"[b]

10 "Blessed is the coming kingdom of our father David!"

"Hosanna in the highest heaven!"

11 Jesus entered
Jerusalem and
went into the tem-
ple courts. He
looked around at
everything, but
since it was al-
ready late, he went
out to Bethany
with the Twelve.

Jesus Curses a Fig Tree and Clears the Temple Courts

12 The next day as
they were leaving
Bethany, Jesus was
hungry. 13 Seeing
in the distance a
fig tree in leaf, he
went to find out
if it had any fruit.
When he reached
it, he found noth-
ing but leaves,
because it was not
the season for figs.
14 Then he said to
the tree, "May no
one ever eat fruit
from you again."
And his disciples
heard him say it.
15 On reaching

[a] 9 A Hebrew expression meaning "Save!" which became an exclamation of praise; also in verse 10
[b] 9 Psalm 118:25,26

καὶ ἀφῆκαν αὐτούς. ↰ 7 καὶ φέρουσιν τὸν πῶλον πρὸς τὸν Ἰησοῦν καὶ
and they gave them permission. Then they brought the colt to *{the}* Jesus and
2779 918 899 918 2779 5770 3836 4798 4639 3836 2652 2779
cj v.aai.3p r.apm.3 cj v.pai.3p d.asm n.asm p.a d.asm n.asm cj

ἐπιβάλλουσιν ← αὐτῷ τὰ ἱμάτια αὐτῶν, καὶ ἐκάθισεν ἐπ' αὐτόν. 8 καὶ
threw their cloaks on it, *{the}* *cloaks* *their* and he sat on it. And
2095 899 2668 899 3836 2668 899 2779 2767 2093 899 2779
v.pai.3p r.dsm.3 d.apn n.apn r.gpm.3 cj v.aai.3s p.a r.asm.3 cj

πολλοὶ τὰ ἱμάτια αὐτῶν ἔστρωσαν εἰς τὴν ὁδόν, ἄλλοι δὲ
many spread *{the}* their cloaks *their* *spread* on the road, while others *while* spread
4498 5143 3836 899 2668 899 5143 1650 3836 3847 1254 257 1254
a.npm d.apn n.apn r.gpm.3 v.aai.3p p.a d.asf n.asf r.npm pl

στιβάδας κόψαντες ἐκ τῶν ἀγρῶν. 9 καὶ οἱ προάγοντες καὶ οἱ
tall grass, cutting it from the fields. And those who went before and those
5115 3164 1666 3836 69 2779 3836 4575 2779 3836
n.apf pt.aa.npm p.g d.gpm n.gpm cj d.npm pt.pa.npm cj d.npm

ἀκολουθοῦντες ἔκραζον· ὡσαννά· εὐλογημένος ὁ ἐρχόμενος ἐν
who followed ⌊were crying out,⌋ "Hosanna! Blessed is he who comes in the
199 3189 6057 2328 3836 2262 1877
pt.pa.npm v.iai.3p j pt.rp.nsm d.nsm pt.pm.nsm p.d

ὀνόματι → κυρίου· 10 εὐλογημένη ἡ ἐρχομένη βασιλεία[a] τοῦ πατρὸς ἡμῶν
name of the Lord! Blessed is the coming kingdom of our father *our*
3950 3261 2328 3836 2262 993 3836 7005 4252 7005
n.dsn n.gsm pt.rp.nsf d.nsf pt.pm.nsf n.nsf d.gsm n.gsm r.gp.1

Δαυίδ· ὡσαννὰ ἐν τοῖς ὑψίστοις. 11 καὶ ⌊εἰσῆλθεν εἰς⌋ Ἱεροσόλυμα εἰς
David! Hosanna in the highest!" And he entered Jerusalem and went into
1253 6057 1877 3836 5736 2779 1656 1650 2642 1650
n.gsm j p.d d.dpn a.dpn.s cj v.aai.3s p.a n.apn p.a

τὸ ἱερὸν καὶ περιβλεψάμενος πάντα, ὀψίας ἤδη οὔσης τῆς
the temple. And looking around at everything, the hour already being late, *already* *being* *the*
3836 2639 2779 4315 4246 3836 6052 2453 1639 4068 2453 1639 3836
d.asn n.asn cj pt.am.nsm a.apn n.gsf adv pt.pa.gsf d.gsf

ὥρας, ἐξῆλθεν εἰς Βηθανίαν μετὰ τῶν δώδεκα. 12 καὶ τῇ ἐπαύριον →
hour he went out to Bethany with the twelve. And ⌊on the⌋ next day, when they
6052 2002 1650 1029 3552 3836 1557 2779 3836 2069 899
n.gsf v.aai.3s p.a n.asf p.g d.gpm a.gpm cj d.dsf adv

ἐξελθόντων αὐτῶν ἀπὸ Βηθανίας ἐπείνασεν. 13 καὶ ἰδὼν
had left *they* from Bethany, Jesus became hungry. And seeing at a distance a
2002 899 608 1029 4277 2779 1625 608 3427
pt.aa.gpm r.gpm.3 p.g n.gsf v.aai.3s cj pt.aa.nsm

συκῆν ἀπὸ μακρόθεν ἔχουσαν φύλλα ἦλθεν, εἰ ἄρα τι
fig tree *at* *distance* in leaf, he went to see if *{then}* he could find anything
5190 608 3427 2400 5877 2262 1623 726 2351 2351 2351 5516
n.asf p.g adv pt.pa.asf n.apn v.aai.3s cj cj r.asn

εὑρήσει ἐν αὐτῇ, καὶ ἐλθὼν ἐπ' αὐτὴν οὐδὲν εὗρεν ⌊εἰ μὴ⌋
he could find on it. And ⌊when he came⌋ to it he found nothing *he found* but
2351 1877 899 2779 2262 2093 899 2351 2351 4029 2351 1623 3590
v.fai.3s p.d r.dsf.3 cj pt.aa.nsm p.a r.asf.3 a.asn v.aai.3s cj pl

φύλλα· ὁ γὰρ καιρὸς οὐκ ἦν σύκων. 14 καὶ ἀποκριθεὶς εἶπεν
leaves, *{the}* for it was not the season *not* *it was* for figs. So in response he said
5877 3836 1142 1639 1639 4024 2789 4024 1639 5192 2779 646 3306
n.apn d.nsm cj n.nsm pl v.iai.3s n.gpn cj pt.ap.nsm v.aai.3s

αὐτῇ· μηκέτι εἰς τὸν αἰῶνα ἐκ σοῦ μηδεὶς καρπὸν φάγοι.
to it, "May no one ever *{for}* *{all}* *{time}* eat fruit from you *no one* *fruit* *May eat*
899 2266 3594 3594 3600 1650 3836 172 2266 2843 1666 5148 3594 2843 2266
r.dsf.3 adv p.a d.asm n.asm p.g r.gs.2 a.nsm n.asm v.aao.3s

↰ καὶ ἤκουον οἱ μαθηταὶ αὐτοῦ. 15 καὶ ἔρχονται εἰς
again!" And his disciples were listening. *{the}* *disciples* *his* Then they went into
3600 2779 899 3412 201 3836 3412 899 2779 2262 1650
cj v.iai.3p d.npm n.npm r.gsm.3 cj v.pmi.3p p.a

[a] ἐν ὀνόματι Κυρίου included by TR after βασιλεία.

NASB

they gave them
permission. 7 They
*brought the colt to
Jesus and put their
coats on it; and
He sat on it. 8 And
many spread their
coats in the road,
and others *spread*
leafy branches
which they had
cut from the fields.
9 Those who went
in front and those
who followed were
shouting:

" Hosanna!
BLESSED IS HE WHO COMES IN THE NAME OF THE LORD;
10 Blessed *is* the coming kingdom of our father David;
Hosanna in the highest!"

11 Jesus entered Je-
rusalem *and came*
into the temple;
and after looking
around at every-
thing, He left for
Bethany with the
twelve, since it was
already late.
12 On the next
day, when they
had left Bethany,
He became hun-
gry. 13 Seeing at a
distance a fig tree
in leaf, He went
to see if perhaps
He would find
anything on it; and
when He came to
it, He found noth-
ing but leaves, for
it was not the sea-
son for figs. 14 He
said to it, "May no
one ever eat fruit
from you again!"
And His disciples
were listening.

Jesus Drives Money Changers from the Temple

15 Then they *came

NIV

Jerusalem, Jesus
entered the temple
courts and began
driving out those
who were buying
and selling there.
He overturned
the tables of the
money changers
and the benches
of those selling
doves, 16 and would
not allow anyone
to carry merchan-
dise through the
temple courts.
17 And as he taught
them, he said,
"Is it not written:
'My house will be
called a house of
prayer for all na-
tions'[a]? But you
have made it 'a den
of robbers.'[b]"
18 The chief
priests and the
teachers of the
law heard this and
began looking for
a way to kill him,
for they feared
him, because the
whole crowd was
amazed at his
teaching.
19 When evening
came, Jesus and
his disciples[c] went
out of the city.
20 In the morning,
as they went along,
they saw the fig
tree withered from
the roots. 21 Pe-
ter remembered
and said to Jesus,
"Rabbi, look! The
fig tree you cursed
has withered!"
22 "Have faith in
God," Jesus an-
swered. 23 "Truly[d] I
tell you, if anyone
says to this moun-
tain, 'Go, throw
yourself into the
sea,' and does not
doubt in their heart
but believes

Ἱεροσόλυμα. καὶ ⌞εἰσελθὼν εἰς⌟ τὸ ἱερὸν ἤρξατο ἐκβάλλειν τοὺς πωλοῦντας
Jerusalem. And entering the temple, he began to drive out those who were selling
2642 2779 1656 1650 3836 2639 806 1675 3836 4797
n.apn cj pt.aa.nsm p.a d.asn n.asn v.ami.3s f.pa d.apm pt.pa.apm

καὶ τοὺς ἀγοράζοντας ἐν τῷ ἱερῷ, καὶ τὰς τραπέζας τῶν
and those who were buying in the temple; and he overturned the tables of the
2779 3836 60 1877 3836 2639 2779 2951 2951 3836 5544 3836
cj d.apm pt.pa.apm p.d d.dsn n.dsn cj d.apf n.apf d.gpm

κολλυβιστῶν καὶ τὰς καθέδρας τῶν πωλούντων τὰς περιστερὰς κατέστρεψεν,
moneychangers and the chairs of those who were selling {the} pigeons, *he overturned*
3142 2779 3836 2756 3836 4797 3836 4361 2951
n.gpm cj d.apf n.apf d.gpm pt.pa.gpm d.apf n.apf v.aai.3s

16 καὶ ↱ ↱ οὐκ ἤφιεν ἵνα τις διενέγκῃ σκεῦος διὰ τοῦ ἱεροῦ. 17 καὶ
and he would not allow {that} anyone to carry merchandise through the temple. And
2779 918 918 4024 918 2671 5516 1422 5007 1328 3836 2639 2779
cj pl v.iai.3s cj r.nsm v.aas.3s n.asn p.g d.gsn n.gsn cj

ἐδίδασκεν καὶ ἔλεγεν αὐτοῖς· ↱ ↱ οὐ γέγραπται ὅτι ὁ οἶκός μου
he was teaching and saying to them, "Is it not written, ~ {the} 'My house *My* shall
1438 2779 3306 899 1211 1211 4024 1211 4022 3836 1609 3875 1609 2813
v.iai.3s cj v.iai.3s r.dpm.3 pl v.rpi.3s cj d.nsm n.nsm r.gs.1

οἶκος προσευχῆς κληθήσεται πᾶσιν τοῖς ἔθνεσιν; ὑμεῖς δὲ
be called a house of prayer *shall be called* for all the nations'? But you *But*
2813 2813 3875 4666 2813 4246 3836 1620 1254 7007 1254
n.nsm n.gsf v.fpi.3s a.dpn d.dpn n.dpn r.np.2 cj

πεποιήκατε αὐτὸν σπήλαιον λῃστῶν. 18 καὶ ἤκουσαν οἱ ἀρχιερεῖς καὶ οἱ
have made it 'a hideout for robbers.'" And *heard* the ruling priests and the
4472 899 5068 3334 2779 201 3836 797 2779 3836
v.rai.2p r.asm.3 n.asn n.gpm cj v.aai.3p d.npm n.npm cj d.npm

γραμματεῖς καὶ ἐζήτουν πῶς αὐτὸν ἀπολέσωσιν· ἐφοβοῦντο
scribes heard of this and began seeking how *him* they could destroy him, for they feared
1208 201 2779 2426 4802 899 660 899 1142 5828
n.npm cj v.iai.3p cj r.asm.3 v.aas.3p v.ipi.3p

γὰρ αὐτόν, πᾶς γὰρ ὁ ὄχλος ἐξεπλήσσετο ἐπὶ τῇ διδαχῇ αὐτοῦ.
for him, because all *because* the people were impressed by {the} his teaching. *his*
1142 899 1142 4246 1142 3836 4063 1742 2093 3836 899 1439 899
cj r.asm.3 a.nsm cj d.nsm n.nsm v.ipi.3s p.d d.dsf n.dsf r.gsm.3

19 καὶ ὅταν ὀψὲ ἐγένετο, ἐξεπορεύοντο ἔξω τῆς πόλεως. 20 καὶ παραπορευόμενοι
And when evening came, they went out of the city. And passing by
2779 4020 4067 1181 1744 2032 3836 4484 2779 4182
cj cj adv v.ami.3s v.imi.3p p.g d.gsf n.gsf cj pt.pm.npm

πρωῒ εἶδον τὴν συκῆν ἐξηραμμένην ἐκ ῥιζῶν. 21 καὶ ἀναμνησθεὶς
⌞in the morning,⌟ they saw the fig tree withered ⌞down to⌟ the roots. And thinking back,
4745 1625 3836 5190 3830 1666 4844 2779 389
adv v.aai.3p d.asf n.asf pt.rp.asf p.g n.gpf cj pt.ap.nsm

ὁ Πέτρος λέγει αὐτῷ· ῥαββί, ἴδε ἡ συκῆ ἣν κατηράσω ἐξήρανται. 22 καὶ
{the} Peter said to him, "Rabbi, look! The fig tree that you cursed has withered!" And
3836 4377 3306 899 4806 2623 3836 5190 4005 2933 3830 2779
d.nsm n.nsm v.pai.3s r.dsm.3 n.vsm pl d.nsf n.nsf r.asf v.ami.2s v.rpi.3s cj

ἀποκριθεὶς ὁ Ἰησοῦς λέγει αὐτοῖς· ἔχετε πίστιν θεοῦ. 23 ἀμὴν
answering, {the} Jesus said to them, "Have faith in God." I tell you the truth,
646 3836 2652 3306 899 2400 4411 2536 3306 3306 7007 297
pt.ap.nsm d.nsm n.nsm v.pai.3s r.dpm.3 v.pam.2p n.asf n.gsm pl

λέγω ὑμῖν ὅτι ⌞ὃς ἂν⌟ εἴπῃ τῷ ὄρει τούτῳ· ἄρθητι καὶ βλήθητι
I tell *you* that if anyone says to this mountain, *this* ⌞'Be taken up⌟ and cast
3306 7007 4022 4005 323 3306 3836 4047 4001 4047 149 2779 965
v.pai.1s r.dp.2 cj r.nsm pl v.aas.3s d.dsn n.dsn r.dsn v.apm.2s cj v.apm.2s

εἰς τὴν θάλασσαν, καὶ ↱ μὴ διακριθῇ ἐν τῇ καρδίᾳ αὐτοῦ ἀλλὰ πιστεύῃ
into the sea,' and does not waver in {the} his heart *his* but believes
1650 3836 2498 2779 1359 3590 1359 1877 3836 899 2840 899 247 4409
p.a d.asf n.asf cj pl v.aps.3s p.d d.dsf n.dsf r.gsm.3 cj v.pas.3s

NASB

to Jerusalem. And
He entered the
temple and began
to drive out those
who were buy-
ing and selling in
the temple, and
overturned the
tables of the money
changers and the
seats of those who
were selling doves;
16 and He would
not permit anyone
to carry merchan-
dise through the
temple. 17 And He
began to teach
and say to them,
"Is it not written,
'MY HOUSE SHALL
BE CALLED A HOUSE
OF PRAYER FOR ALL
THE NATIONS'? But
you have made it
a ROBBERS' DEN."
18 The chief priests
and the scribes
heard *this,* and
began seeking how
to destroy Him; for
they were afraid
of Him, for the
whole crowd was
astonished at His
teaching.
19 When evening
came, they would
go out of the city.
20 As they were
passing by in the
morning, they saw
the fig tree with-
ered from the roots
up. 21 Being remind-
ed, Peter *said to
Him, "Rabbi, look,
the fig tree which
You cursed has
withered." 22 And
Jesus *answered
saying to them,
"Have faith in God.
23 Truly I say to
you, whoever says
to this mountain,
'Be taken up and
cast into the sea,'
and does not doubt
in his heart, but be-
lieves that what

[a] *17* Isaiah 56:7
[b] *17* Jer. 7:11
[c] *19* Some early manuscripts *came, Jesus*
[d] *22,23* Some early manuscripts *"If you have faith in God," Jesus answered, 23 "truly*

NIV

that what they say
will happen, it will
be done for them.
24 Therefore I tell
you, whatever you
ask for in prayer,
believe that you
have received
it, and it will be
yours. 25 And when
you stand praying,
if you hold any-
thing against any-
one, forgive them,
so that your Father
in heaven may
forgive you your
sins." [26] a

The Authority of Jesus Questioned

27 They arrived
again in Jerusa-
lem, and while
Jesus was walk-
ing in the temple
courts, the chief
priests, the teach-
ers of the law and
the elders came
to him. 28 "By
what authority are
you doing these
things?" they
asked. "And who
gave you authority
to do this?"
29 Jesus replied,
"I will ask you one
question. Answer
me, and I will
tell you by what
authority I am do-
ing these things.
30 John's baptism —
was it from heav-
en, or of human
origin? Tell me!"
31 They discussed
it among them-
selves and said,
"If we say, 'From
heaven,' he will
ask, 'Then why
didn't you believe
him?' 32 But if we
say, 'Of human
origin' . . ." (They
feared the

ὅτι ὃ λαλεῖ γίνεται, ἔσται αὐτῷ. 24 διὰ τοῦτο λέγω ὑμῖν, ⌊πάντα
that what he says will happen, ⌊it will be done⌋ for him. For this reason I tell you, whatever
4022 4005 3281 1181 1639 899 1328 4047 3306 7007 4246
cj r.asn v.pai.3s v.pmi.3s v.fmi.3s r.dsm.3 p.a r.asn v.pai.1s r.dp.2 a.apn

ὅσα⌋ προσεύχεσθε καὶ αἰτεῖσθε, πιστεύετε ὅτι ἐλάβετε, καὶ ἔσται ὑμῖν.
you pray and ask for, believe that ⌊you have received⌋ it, and ⌊it will be⌋ yours.
4012 4667 2779 160 4409 4022 3284 2779 1639 7007
r.apn v.pmi.2p cj v.pmi.2p v.pam.2p cj v.aai.2p cj v.fmi.3s r.dp.2

25 καὶ ὅταν στήκετε προσευχόμενοι, ἀφίετε εἴ τι ἔχετε κατά
And whenever you stand praying, forgive if you have something *you have* against
2779 4020 5112 4667 918 1623 2400 2400 5516 2400 2848
cj cj v.pai.2p pt.pm.npm v.pam.2p cj r.asn v.pai.2p p.g

τινος, ἵνα καὶ ὁ πατὴρ ὑμῶν ὁ ἐν τοῖς οὐρανοῖς → ἀφῇ ὑμῖν
someone, so that *also* *{the}* your Father *your* *{the}* in *{the}* heaven may also forgive you
5516 2671 2779 3836 7007 4252 7007 3836 1877 3836 4041 2779 918 7007
r.gsm cj adv d.nsm n.nsm r.gp.2 d.nsm p.d d.dpm n.dpm v.aas.3s r.dp.2

τὰ παραπτώματα ὑμῶν.[a] 27 καὶ ἔρχονται πάλιν εἰς Ἱεροσόλυμα. καὶ
{the} your transgressions." *your* And they came again to Jerusalem. And while he
3836 7007 4183 7007 2779 2262 4099 1650 2642 2779 4344 899
d.apn n.apn r.gp.2 cj v.pmi.3p adv p.a n.apn cj

ἐν τῷ ἱερῷ περιπατοῦντος αὐτοῦ ἔρχονται πρὸς αὐτὸν οἱ
was walking about in the temple, *while was walking about* *he* *came* *to* *him* the
4344 4344 4344 1877 3836 2639 4344 899 2262 4639 899 3836
p.d d.dsn n.dsn pt.pa.gsm r.gsm.3 v.pmi.3p p.a r.asm.3 d.npm

ἀρχιερεῖς καὶ οἱ γραμματεῖς καὶ οἱ πρεσβύτεροι 28 καὶ ἔλεγον
ruling priests and the scribes and the elders came to him, and were asking
797 2779 3836 1208 2779 3836 4565 2262 4639 899 2779 3306
n.npm cj d.npm n.npm cj d.npm a.npm cj v.iai.3p

αὐτῷ· ἐν ποίᾳ ἐξουσίᾳ ταῦτα ποιεῖς; ἢ τίς σοι
him, "By what authority are you doing these things?" *are you doing* and "Who gave you
899 1877 4481 2026 4472 4472 4472 4047 4472 2445 5515 1443 5148
r.dsm.3 p.d r.dsf n.dsf r.apn v.pai.2s cj r.nsm r.ds.2

ἔδωκεν τὴν ἐξουσίαν ταύτην ἵνα ταῦτα ποιῇς; 29 ὁ δὲ Ἰησοῦς
gave *{the}* this authority *this* to do these things?" *do* *{the}* But Jesus
1443 3836 4047 2026 4047 2671 4472 4047 4472 3836 1254 2652
v.aai.3s d.asf n.asf r.asf cj r.apn v.pas.2s d.nsm cj n.nsm

εἶπεν αὐτοῖς· ἐπερωτήσω ὑμᾶς ἕνα λόγον, καὶ ἀποκρίθητέ μοι καὶ ἐρῶ ὑμῖν
said to them, "I will ask you one thing; *{and}* answer me, and ⌊I will tell⌋ you
3306 899 2089 7007 1651 3364 2779 646 1609 2779 3306 7007
v.aai.3s r.dpm.3 v.fai.1s r.ap.2 a.asm n.asm cj v.apm.2p r.ds.1 cj v.fai.1s r.dp.2

ἐν ποίᾳ ἐξουσίᾳ ταῦτα ποιῶ· 30 τὸ βάπτισμα τὸ Ἰωάννου
by what authority I do these things. *I do* The baptism of John — was it
1877 4481 2026 4472 4472 4047 4472 3836 967 3836 2722 1639 1639
p.d r.dsf n.dsf r.apn v.pai.1s d.nsn n.nsn d.nsn n.gsm

ἐξ οὐρανοῦ ἦν ἢ ἐξ ἀνθρώπων; ἀποκρίθητέ μοι. 31 καὶ διελογίζοντο πρὸς
from heaven *was it* or from man? Answer me!" So they discussed it among
1666 4041 1639 2445 1666 476 646 1609 2779 1368 4639
p.g n.gsm v.iai.3s cj p.g n.gpm v.apm.2p r.ds.1 cj v.imi.3p p.a

ἑαυτοὺς λέγοντες· ἐὰν εἴπωμεν· ἐξ οὐρανοῦ, ἐρεῖ· ⌊διὰ τί⌋ οὖν[b] ↱ ↱
themselves, saying, "If we say, 'From heaven,' ⌊he will say,⌋ 'Why then did you
1571 3306 1569 3306 1666 4041 3306 1328 5515 4036 4409 4409
r.apm.3 pt.pa.npm cj v.aas.1p p.g n.gsm v.fai.3s p.a r.asn cj

οὐκ ἐπιστεύσατε αὐτῷ; 32 ἀλλὰ εἴπωμεν· ἐξ ἀνθρώπων; ἐφοβοῦντο τὸν
not believe him?' But if we say, 'From man'", – ⌊(they were afraid of⌋ the
4024 4409 899 247 3306 1666 476 5828 3836
pl v.aai.2p r.dsm.3 cj v.aas.1p p.g n.gpm v.ipi.3p d.asm

NASB

he says is going
to happen, it will
be *granted* him.
24 Therefore I say
to you, all things
for which you pray
and ask, believe
that you have re-
ceived them, and
they will be *grant-
ed* you. 25 Whenever
you stand praying,
forgive, if you have
anything against
anyone, so that
your Father who is
in heaven will also
forgive you your
transgressions.
26 [aBut if you do
not forgive, neither
will your Father
who is in heaven
forgive your trans-
gressions."]

Jesus' Authority Questioned

27 They *came
again to Jerusalem.
And as He was
walking in the
temple, the chief
priests and the
scribes and the el-
ders *came to Him,
28 and *began* saying
to Him, "By what
authority are You
doing these things,
or who gave You
this authority to
do these things?"
29 And Jesus said to
them, "I will ask
you one question,
and you answer
Me, and *then* I will
tell you by what
authority I do these
things. 30 Was the
baptism of John
from heaven, or
from men? Answer
Me." 31 They *began*
reasoning among
themselves, saying,
"If we say, 'From
heaven,' He will
say, 'Then why did
you not believe
him?' 32 But shall
we say, 'From
men'?"—they were
afraid of the

a 26 Some manu-
scripts include here
words similar to
Matt. 6:15.

a 26 εἴ δὲ ὑμεῖς οὐκ ἀφίετε, οὐδὲ ὁ πατὴρ ὑμῶν ὁ ἐν τοῖς οὐρανοῖς ἀφήσει τὰ παραπτώματα ὑμῶν. included by TR after ὑμῶν.
b [οὖν] UBS.

a Early mss do not
contain this v

NIV

people, for ev-
eryone held that
John really was a
prophet.)
33 So they an-
swered Jesus, "We
don't know."
Jesus said, "Nei-
ther will I tell you
by what authority
I am doing these
things."

The Parable of the Tenants

12 Jesus then
began to
speak to them in
parables: "A man
planted a vine-
yard. He put a wall
around it, dug a
pit for the wine-
press and built a
watchtower. Then
he rented the vine-
yard to some farm-
ers and moved
to another place.
2 At harvest time
he sent a servant
to the tenants to
collect from them
some of the fruit of
the vineyard. 3 But
they seized him,
beat him and sent
him away empty-
handed. 4 Then he
sent another ser-
vant to them; they
struck this man on
the head and treat-
ed him shameful-
ly. 5 He sent still
another, and that
one they killed. He
sent many others;
some of them they
beat, others they
killed.
6 "He had one
left to send, a son,
whom he loved. He
sent him last of all,
saying, 'They will
respect my son.'
7 "But the tenants
said to one anoth-
er, 'This is the

ὄχλον· ἅπαντες γὰρ εἶχον τὸν Ἰωάννην ὄντως ὅτι προφήτης ἦν.
people, for everyone *for* considered that *{the}* John was truly *that* a prophet). *was*
4063 1142 570 1142 2400 4022 3836 2722 1639 3953 4022 4737 1639
n.asm a.npm cj v.iai.3p d.asm n.asm adv cj n.nsm v.iai.3s

33 καὶ ἀποκριθέντες τῷ Ἰησοῦ λέγουσιν· ↱ ↱ οὐκ οἴδαμεν. καὶ ὁ Ἰησοῦς
So in answer to Jesus, they said, "We do not know." And *{the}* Jesus
2779 646 3836 2652 3306 3857 3857 4024 3857 2779 3836 2652
cj pt.ap.npm d.dsm n.dsm v.pai.3p pl v.rai.1p cj d.nsm n.nsm

λέγει αὐτοῖς· οὐδὲ ↱ ἐγὼ λέγω ὑμῖν ἐν ποίᾳ ἐξουσίᾳ ταῦτα
said to them, "Neither will I tell you by what authority I am doing these things."
3306 899 4028 3306 1609 3306 7007 1877 4481 2026 4472 4472 4472 4047
v.pai.3s r.dpm.3 cj r.ns.1 v.pai.1s r.dp.2 p.d r.dsf n.dsf r.apn

ποιῶ.
I am doing
4472
v.pai.1s

12:1 καὶ ἤρξατο αὐτοῖς ἐν παραβολαῖς λαλεῖν·
And he began to speak to them in parables. *to speak* "A man planted a
2779 806 3281 3281 899 1877 4130 3281 476 5885
cj v.ami.3s r.dpm.3 p.d n.dpf f.pa

ἀμπελῶνα ἄνθρωπος ἐφύτευσεν καὶ περιέθηκεν φραγμὸν ↰ καὶ ὤρυξεν
vineyard *man* *planted* and put a fence around it. *{and}* He dug a
308 476 5885 2779 4363 5850 4363 2779 4002
n.asm n.nsm v.aai.3s cj v.aai.3s n.asm cj v.aai.3s

ὑπολήνιον καὶ ᾠκοδόμησεν πύργον καὶ ἐξέδετο αὐτὸν ↰ γεωργοῖς
pit for the winepress and built a tower; then he leased it out to tenant farmers
5700 2779 3868 4788 2779 1686 899 1686 1177
n.asn cj v.aai.3s n.asm cj v.ami.3s r.asm.3 n.dpm

καὶ ἀπεδήμησεν. 2 καὶ ἀπέστειλεν πρὸς τοὺς γεωργοὺς
and went on a journey. *{and}* At harvest time he sent a servant to the tenant farmers
2779 623 2779 3836 2789 2789 690 1529 4639 3836 1177
cj v.aai.3s cj v.aai.3s p.a d.apm n.apm

τῷ καιρῷ δοῦλον ἵνα παρὰ τῶν γεωργῶν λάβῃ ἀπὸ τῶν καρπῶν
At *harvest time* *servant* to receive from the farmers *receive* a ⌞portion of⌟ the fruit
3836 2789 1529 2671 3284 4123 3836 1177 3284 608 3836 2843
d.dsm n.dsm n.asm cj p.g d.gpm n.gpm v.aas.3s p.g d.gpm n.gpm

τοῦ ἀμπελῶνος· 3 καὶ ↱ λαβόντες αὐτὸν ἔδειραν καὶ ἀπέστειλαν
⌞from the⌟ vineyard. But they took him and beat him and sent him
3836 308 2779 1296 3284 899 1296 2779 690
d.gsm n.gsm cj pt.aa.npm r.asm.3 v.aai.3p cj v.aai.3p

← κενόν. 4 καὶ πάλιν ἀπέστειλεν πρὸς αὐτοὺς ἄλλον δοῦλον· κἀκεῖνον
away empty-handed. And again he sent to them another servant; and that one
3031 2779 4099 690 4639 899 257 1529 2797
a.asm cj adv v.aai.3s p.a r.apm.3 r.asm n.asm cj

ἐκεφαλίωσαν καὶ ἠτίμασαν. 5 καὶ ἄλλον ἀπέστειλεν· κἀκεῖνον
⌞they struck on the head⌟ and treated dishonorably. So he sent another; *he sent* and that one
3052 2779 869 2779 690 690 257 690 2797
v.aai.3p cj v.aai.3p cj r.asm v.aai.3s cj

ἀπέκτειναν, καὶ πολλοὺς ἄλλους, οὓς μὲν δέροντες, οὓς
they killed — and so with many others, beating some ~ *beating* and killing others.
650 2779 4498 257 1296 4005 3525 1296 1254 650 4005
v.aai.3p cj a.apm r.apm r.apm pl pt.pa.npm r.apm

δὲ ἀποκτέννοντες. 6 ἔτι ἕνα εἶχεν υἱὸν ἀγαπητόν·
and *killing* He had still one other, *He had* a beloved son. *beloved*
1254 650 2400 2400 2285 1651 2400 28 5626 28
pl pt.pa.npm adv a.asm v.iai.3s n.asm a.asm

ἀπέστειλεν αὐτὸν ἔσχατον πρὸς αὐτοὺς λέγων ὅτι ἐντραπήσονται τὸν υἱόν
He sent him last to them, saying, ~ 'They will respect *{the}* my son.'
690 899 2274 4639 899 3306 4022 1956 3836 1609 5626
v.aai.3s r.asm.3 a.asm p.a r.apm.3 pt.pa.nsm cj v.fpi.3p d.asm n.asm

μου. 7 ἐκεῖνοι δὲ οἱ γεωργοὶ πρὸς ἑαυτοὺς εἶπαν ὅτι οὗτός ἐστιν ὁ
my But those *But* *{the}* tenants said to themselves, *said* ~ 'This is the
1609 1254 1697 1254 3836 1177 3306 4639 1571 3306 4022 4047 1639 3836
r.gs.1 r.npm cj d.npm n.npm p.a r.apm.3 v.aai.3p cj r.nsm v.pai.3s d.nsm

NASB

people, for every-
one considered
John to have been a
real prophet. 33 An-
swering Jesus, they
*said, "We do not
know." And Jesus
*said to them, "Nor
will I tell you by
what authority I do
these things."

Parable of the Vine-growers

12:1 And He began
to speak to them in
parables: "A man
PLANTED A VINEYARD
AND PUT A WALL
AROUND IT, AND
DUG A VAT UNDER
THE WINE PRESS AND
BUILT A TOWER, and
rented it out to
[a]vine-growers and
went on a journey.
2 At the *harvest*
time he sent a
slave to the vine-
growers, in order
to receive *some*
of the produce of
the vineyard from
the vine-growers.
3 They took him,
and beat him and
sent him away
empty-handed.
4 Again he sent
them another slave,
and they wounded
him in the head,
and treated him
shamefully. 5 And
he sent another,
and that one they
killed; and *so with*
many others, beat-
ing some and kill-
ing others. 6 He had
one more *to send,*
a beloved son; he
sent him last *of all*
to them, saying,
'They will respect
my son.' 7 But those
vine-growers said
to one another,
'This is the

[a] Or *tenant farmers,* also vv 2, 7, 9

NIV

heir. Come, let's kill him, and the inheritance will be ours.' 8So they took him and killed him, and threw him out of the vineyard.

9"What then will the owner of the vineyard do? He will come and kill those tenants and give the vineyard to others. 10Haven't you read this passage of Scripture:

"'The stone the builders rejected
has become the cornerstone;
11the Lord has done this,
and it is marvelous in our eyes'[a]?"

12Then the chief priests, the teachers of the law and the elders looked for a way to arrest him because they knew he had spoken the parable against them. But they were afraid of the crowd; so they left him and went away.

Paying the Imperial Tax to Caesar

13Later they sent some of the Pharisees and Herodians to Jesus to catch him in his words. 14They came to him and said, "Teacher, we know that you are a man of integrity. You aren't swayed by others, because you pay no attention to who they are; but you teach the way of God in accordance with the truth. Is it right to pay the imperial tax[b] to Caesar or not? 15Should we pay or shouldn't we?"

But Jesus knew their hypocrisy.

[a] 11 Psalm 118:22,23
[b] 14 A special tax levied on subject peoples, not on Roman citizens

---

κληρονόμος· δεῦτε ἀποκτείνωμεν αὐτόν, καὶ ἡμῶν ἔσται ἡ
heir; come, let us kill him, and the inheritance will be ours.' *will be* *the*
3101 1307 650 899 2779 3836 3100 1639 1639 7005 1639 3836
n.nsm adv v.aas.1p r.asm.3 cj r.gp.1 v.fmi.3s d.nsf

κληρονομία. 8 καὶ λαβόντες ἀπέκτειναν αὐτὸν καὶ ἐξέβαλον αὐτὸν ἔξω τοῦ
inheritance And taking him, they killed him and threw him ⌞out of⌟ the
3100 2779 3284 650 899 2779 1675 899 2032 3836
n.nsf cj pt.aa.npm v.aai.3p r.asm.3 cj v.aai.3p r.asm.3 p.g d.gsm

ἀμπελῶνος. 9 τί οὖν[a] → ποιήσει ὁ κύριος τοῦ ἀμπελῶνος; ἐλεύσεται
vineyard. What therefore will *do* the owner of the vineyard do? He will come
308 5515 4036 4472 3836 3261 3836 308 4472 2262
n.gsm r.asn cj v.fai.3s d.nsm n.nsm d.gsm n.gsm v.fmi.3s

καὶ ἀπολέσει τοὺς γεωργοὺς καὶ δώσει τὸν ἀμπελῶνα ἄλλοις. 10 οὐδὲ
and destroy the tenants and give the vineyard to others. Have you not even
2779 660 3836 1177 2779 1443 3836 308 257 336 336 4028
cj v.fai.3s d.apm n.apm cj v.fai.3s d.asm n.asm r.dpm adv

τὴν γραφὴν ταύτην ἀνέγνωτε· λίθον ὃν ἀπεδοκίμασαν
read *{the}* this scripture: *this* *Have you read* 'The stone that the builders rejected
336 3836 4047 1210 4047 336 3345 4005 3836 3868 627
d.asf n.asf r.asf v.aai.2p n.asm r.asm v.aai.3p

οἱ οἰκοδομοῦντες, οὗτος ἐγενήθη εἰς ⌞κεφαλὴν γωνίας·⌟ 11
the *builders* *{this one}* has become *{into}* the capstone; this came about
3836 3868 4047 1181 1650 3051 1224 4047 1181 1181
d.npm pt.pa.npm r.nsm v.api.3s p.a n.asf n.gsf

παρὰ κυρίου ἐγένετο αὕτη καὶ ἔστιν θαυμαστὴ ἐν ὀφθαλμοῖς ἡμῶν;
from the Lord, *came about* *this* and it is marvelous in our eyes'?" *our*
4123 3261 1181 4047 2779 1639 2515 1877 7005 4057 7005
p.g n.gsm v.ami.3s r.nsf cj v.pai.3s a.nsf p.d n.dpm r.gp.1

12 Καὶ ἐζήτουν αὐτὸν κρατῆσαι, καὶ ἐφοβήθησαν τὸν ὄχλον,
And ⌞they were seeking⌟ to arrest him, *to arrest* but feared the people, for
2779 2426 3195 3195 899 3195 2779 5828 3836 4063 1142
cj v.iai.3p r.asm.3 f.aa cj v.api.3p d.asm n.asm

ἔγνωσαν γὰρ ὅτι πρὸς αὐτοὺς τὴν παραβολὴν εἶπεν.
they knew *for* that he had spoken the parable against them. *the* *parable* *he had spoken*
1182 1142 4022 3306 3306 3306 3836 4130 4639 899 3836 4130 3306
v.aai.3p cj cj p.a r.apm.3 d.asf n.asf v.aai.3s

καὶ ἀφέντες αὐτὸν ἀπῆλθον. 13 καὶ ἀποστέλλουσιν πρός αὐτόν τινας τῶν
So they left him and went away. And they sent to him some of the
2779 918 899 599 2779 690 4639 899 5516 3836
cj pt.aa.npm r.asm.3 v.aai.3p cj v.pai.3p p.a r.asm.3 r.apm d.gpm

Φαρισαίων καὶ τῶν Ἡρῳδιανῶν ἵνα αὐτὸν ἀγρεύσωσιν → λόγῳ.
Pharisees and some of the Herodians to trap him *trap* with a statement.
5757 2779 3836 2477 2671 65 899 65 3364
n.gpm cj d.gpm n.gpm cj r.asm.3 v.aas.3p n.dsm

14 καὶ ἐλθόντες λέγουσιν αὐτῷ· διδάσκαλε, οἴδαμεν ὅτι ἀληθὴς
{and} ⌞When they came⌟ they said to him, "Teacher, we know that you are truthful
2779 2262 3306 899 1437 3857 4022 1639 1639 239
cj pt.aa.npm v.pai.3p r.dsm.3 n.vsm v.rai.1p cj a.nsm

εἶ καὶ ↱ ↱ οὐ μέλει σοι περὶ οὐδενός· ↱
you are and that the opinion of another is of no concern to you. *opinion* *of another* For you
1639 2779 4309 4029 4029 3508 3508 4024 3508 5148 4309 4029 1142 1063
v.pai.2s cj pl v.pai.3s r.ds.2 p.g a.gsm

↱ οὐ γὰρ βλέπεις εἰς πρόσωπον ἀνθρώπων, ἀλλ' ⌞ἐπ' ἀληθείας⌟ τὴν
do not *For* regard *{into}* the position of men, but you truly teach the
1063 4024 1142 1063 1650 4725 476 247 1438 2093 237 1438 3836
pl cj v.pai.2s p.a n.asn n.gpm cj p.g n.gsf d.asf

ὁδὸν τοῦ θεοῦ διδάσκεις· ἔξεστιν δοῦναι κῆνσον Καίσαρι ἢ οὔ; δῶμεν
way of God. *you teach* Is it lawful to pay tax to Caesar, or not? ⌞Should we pay⌟
3847 3836 2536 1438 1997 1443 3056 2790 2445 4024 1443
n.asf d.gsm n.gsm v.pai.2s v.pai.3s f.aa n.asm n.dsm cj pl v.aas.1p

ἢ ↱ ↱ μὴ δῶμεν; 15 ὁ[b] δὲ εἰδὼς αὐτῶν τὴν ὑπόκρισιν εἶπεν
or should we not pay?" *he* But knowing their *{the}* hypocrisy, he said
2445 1443 1443 3590 1443 3836 1254 3857 899 3836 5694 3836 3306
cj pl v.aas.1p d.nsm cj pt.ra.nsm r.gpm.3 d.asf n.asf v.aai.3s

[a] [οὖν] UBS.
[b] δῶμεν, ἢ μὴ δῶμεν; included by TR before ὁ.

NASB

heir; come, let us kill him, and the inheritance will be ours!' 8They took him, and killed him and threw him out of the vineyard. 9What will the owner of the vineyard do? He will come and destroy the vine-growers, and will give the vineyard to others. 10Have you not even read this Scripture:

'The stone which the builders rejected,
This became the chief corner *stone;*
11This came about from the Lord,
And it is marvelous in our eyes'?"

12And they were seeking to seize Him, and *yet* they feared the people, for they understood that He spoke the parable against them. And *so* they left Him and went away.

Jesus Answers the Pharisees, Sadducees and Scribes

13Then they *sent some of the Pharisees and Herodians to Him in order to trap Him in a statement. 14They *came and *said to Him, "Teacher, we know that You are truthful and defer to no one; for You are not partial to any, but teach the way of God in truth. Is it lawful to pay a poll-tax to Caesar, or not? 15Shall we pay or shall we not pay?" But He, knowing their hypocrisy, said to

NIV

"Why are you try-
ing to trap me?"
he asked. "Bring
me a denarius and
let me look at it."
[16]They brought the
coin, and he asked
them, "Whose im-
age is this? And
whose inscrip-
tion?"
"Caesar's," they
replied.
[17]Then Jesus said
to them, "Give
back to Caesar
what is Caesar's
and to God what is
God's."
And they were
amazed at him.

Marriage at the Resurrection

[18]Then the Sad-
ducees, who say
there is no resur-
rection, came to
him with a ques-
tion. [19]"Teacher,"
they said, "Moses
wrote for us that
if a man's brother
dies and leaves a
wife but no chil-
dren, the man
must marry the
widow and raise
up offspring for
his brother. [20]Now
there were seven
brothers. The first
one married and
died without leav-
ing any children.
[21]The second one
married the wid-
ow, but he also
died, leaving no
child. It was the
same with the
third. [22]In fact,
none of the seven
left any children.
Last of all, the
woman died too.
[23]At the resurrec-
tion[a] whose wife
will she be, since
the seven were
married to her?"
[24]Jesus replied,
"Are you not in er-
ror because

[a] 23 Some manuscripts *resurrection, when people rise from the dead,*

αὐτοῖς· τί με πειράζετε; φέρετέ μοι δηνάριον ἵνα ἴδω.
to them, "Why do you test me? *do you test* Bring me a denarius and let ⌞me look at⌟ it"
899 5515 4279 4279 4279 1609 4279 5770 1609 1324 2671 1625
r.dpm.3 r.asn r.as.1 v.pai.2p v.pam.2p r.ds.1 n.asn cj v.aas.1s

16 οἱ δὲ ἤνεγκαν. καὶ λέγει αὐτοῖς· τίνος ἡ εἰκὼν αὕτη καὶ
So they *So* brought one. And he said to them, "Of whom is *{the}* this likeness *this* and
1254 3836 1254 5770 2779 3306 899 5515 3836 4047 1635 4047 2779
d.npm cj v.aai.3p cj v.pai.3s r.dpm.3 r.gsm d.nsf n.nsf r.nsf cj

ἡ ἐπιγραφή; οἱ δὲ εἶπαν αὐτῷ· Καίσαρος. 17 ὁ δὲ Ἰησοῦς εἶπεν
{the} inscription?" And they *And* said to him, "Caesar." *{the}* *{and}* Jesus said
3836 2107 1254 3836 1254 3306 899 2790 3836 1254 2652 3306
d.nsf n.nsf d.npm cj v.aai.3p r.dsm.3 n.gsm d.nsm cj n.nsm v.aai.3s

αὐτοῖς· τὰ Καίσαρος ἀπόδοτε Καίσαρι καὶ
to them, "Give to Caesar ⌞what belongs to⌟ Caesar, *Give* *to Caesar* but give to God
899 625 2790 2790 3836 2790 625 2790 2779 3836 2536
r.dpm.3 d.apn n.gsm v.aam.2p n.dsm cj

τὰ τοῦ θεοῦ τῷ θεῷ. καὶ ἐξεθαύμαζον ἐπ' αὐτῷ. 18 καὶ
⌞what belongs to⌟ *{the}* God." *to* *God* And they were amazed at him. And the Sadducees,
3836 3836 2536 3836 2536 2779 1703 2093 899 2779 4881
d.apn d.gsm n.gsm d.dsm n.dsm cj v.iai.3p p.d r.dsm.3 cj

ἔρχονται Σαδδουκαῖοι πρὸς αὐτόν, οἵτινες λέγουσιν
who say there is no resurrection, came *Sadducees* to him, *who* *say*
4015 3306 1639 1639 3590 414 2262 4881 4639 899 4015 3306
v.pmi.3p n.npm p.a r.asm.3 r.npm v.pai.3p

ἀνάστασιν μὴ εἶναι, καὶ ἐπηρώτων αὐτὸν λέγοντες· 19 διδάσκαλε, Μωϋσῆς
resurrection *no* *there is* and they were questioning him, saying, "Teacher, Moses
414 3590 1639 2779 2089 899 3306 1437 3707
n.asf pl f.pa cj v.iai.3p r.asm.3 pt.pa.npm n.vsm n.nsm

ἔγραψεν ἡμῖν ὅτι ἐάν τινος ἀδελφὸς ἀποθάνῃ καὶ καταλίπῃ γυναῖκα καὶ μὴ
wrote for us that if someone's brother should die and leave behind a wife, but not
1211 7005 4022 1569 5516 81 633 2779 2901 1222 2779 3590
v.aai.3s r.dp.1 cj cj r.gsm n.nsm v.aas.3s cj v.aas.3s n.asf cj pl

ἀφῇ τέκνον, ἵνα λάβῃ ὁ ἀδελφὸς αὐτοῦ τὴν γυναῖκα καὶ
⌞leave behind⌟ a child, that his brother ⌞should take⌟ *{the}* *brother* *his* the widow and
918 5451 2671 899 81 3284 3836 81 899 3836 1222 2779
v.aas.3s n.asn cj v.aas.3s d.nsm n.nsm r.gsm.3 d.asf n.asf cj

ἐξαναστήσῃ σπέρμα τῷ ἀδελφῷ αὐτοῦ. 20 ἑπτὰ ἀδελφοὶ ἦσαν· καὶ
raise up offspring for his brother. *his* There were seven brothers; *There were* *{and}*
1985 5065 3836 899 81 899 1639 1639 2231 81 1639 2779
v.aas.3s n.asn d.dsm n.dsm r.gsm.3 a.npm n.npm v.iai.3p cj

ὁ πρῶτος ἔλαβεν γυναῖκα καὶ ἀποθνῄσκων οὐκ ἀφῆκεν σπέρμα· 21 καὶ
the first took a wife, and when he died he left no *he left* offspring. Then
3836 4755 3284 1222 2779 633 918 918 4024 918 5065 2779
d.nsm a.nsm v.aai.3s n.asf cj pt.pa.nsm pl v.aai.3s n.asn cj

ὁ δεύτερος ἔλαβεν αὐτὴν καὶ ἀπέθανεν μὴ καταλιπὼν
the second brother took her, and he died, leaving behind no *leaving behind*
3836 1311 3284 899 2779 633 2901 2901 3590 2901
d.nsm a.nsm v.aai.3s r.asf.3 cj v.aai.3s pl pt.aa.nsm

σπέρμα· καὶ ὁ τρίτος ὡσαύτως· 22 καὶ οἱ ἑπτὰ ↱ οὐκ ἀφῆκαν σπέρμα. ἔσχατον
offspring. And the third likewise. And the seven did not leave offspring. Last
5065 2779 3836 5569 6058 2779 3836 2231 918 4024 918 5065 2274
n.asn cj d.nsm a.nsm adv cj d.npm a.npm pl v.aai.3p n.asn adv

πάντων καὶ ἡ γυνὴ ἀπέθανεν. 23 ἐν τῇ ἀναστάσει [a]ὅταν
of all the woman also *the* *woman* died. In the resurrection, when
4246 3836 1222 2779 3836 1222 633 1877 3836 414 4020
a.gpn adv d.nsf n.nsf v.aai.3s p.d d.dsf n.dsf cj

ἀναστῶσιν τίνος αὐτῶν ἔσται γυνή; οἱ γὰρ ἑπτὰ ἔσχον αὐτὴν γυναῖκα.
they rise again, of which of them ⌞will she be⌟ wife? For all *For* seven had her as wife."
482 5515 899 1639 1222 1142 3836 1142 2231 2400 899 1222
v.aas.3p r.gsm r.gpm.3 v.fmi.3s n.nsf d.npm cj a.npm v.aai.3p r.asf.3 n.asf

24 ἔφη αὐτοῖς ὁ Ἰησοῦς· οὐ διὰ τοῦτο πλανᾶσθε
Jesus said to them, *{the}* *Jesus* "Are you not mistaken for this reason, *Are you mistaken*
2652 5774 899 3836 2652 4414 4414 4024 4414 1328 4047 4414
v.iai.3s r.dpm.3 d.nsm n.nsm pl p.a r.asn v.ppi.2p

[a] [ὅταν ἀναστῶσιν] UBS, omitted by TNIV.

NASB

them, "Why are
you testing Me?
Bring Me a [a]den-
arius to look at."
[16]They brought *one.*
And He *said to
them, "Whose like-
ness and inscrip-
tion is this?" And
they said to Him,
"Caesar's." [17]And
Jesus said to them,
"Render to Caesar
the things that are
Caesar's, and to
God the things that
are God's." And
they were amazed
at Him.
[18]*Some* Sadducees
(who say that there
is no resurrection)
*came to Jesus, and
began question-
ing Him, saying,
[19]"Teacher, Moses
wrote for us that
IF A MAN'S BROTHER
DIES and leaves
behind a wife AND
LEAVES NO CHILD,
HIS BROTHER SHOULD
MARRY THE WIFE AND
RAISE UP CHILDREN
TO HIS BROTHER.
[20]There were seven
brothers; and the
first took a wife,
and died leaving
no children. [21]The
second one married
her, and died leav-
ing behind no chil-
dren; and the third
likewise; [22]and
so all seven left
no children. Last
of all the woman
died also. [23]In the
resurrection, [b]when
they rise again,
which one's wife
will she be? For all
seven had married
her." [24]Jesus said to
them, "Is this not
the reason you are
mistaken, that you

[a] The denarius was a day's wages
[b] Early mss do not contain *when they rise again*

NIV

you do not know the Scriptures or the power of God? [25]When the dead rise, they will neither marry nor be given in marriage; they will be like the angels in heaven. [26]Now about the dead rising—have you not read in the Book of Moses, in the account of the burning bush, how God said to him, 'I am the God of Abraham, the God of Isaac, and the God of Jacob'[a]? [27]He is not the God of the dead, but of the living. You are badly mistaken!"

The Greatest Commandment

[28]One of the teachers of the law came and heard them debating. Noticing that Jesus had given them a good answer, he asked him, "Of all the commandments, which is the most important?"

[29]"The most important one," answered Jesus, "is this: 'Hear, O Israel: The Lord our God, the Lord is one.[b] [30]Love the Lord your God with all your heart and with all your soul and with all your mind and with all your strength.'[c] [31]The second is this: 'Love your neighbor as yourself.'[d] There is no commandment greater than these."

[32]"Well said, teacher,"

[a] 26 Exodus 3:6
[b] 29 Or *The Lord our God is one Lord*
[c] 30 Deut. 6:4,5
[d] 31 Lev. 19:18

μὴ εἰδότες τὰς γραφὰς μηδὲ τὴν δύναμιν τοῦ θεοῦ; 25 ὅταν
that you know neither *you know* the scriptures nor the power of God? For when
3857 3857 3590 3857 3836 1210 3593 3836 1539 3836 2536 1142 4020
pl pt.ra.npm d.apf n.apf cj d.asf n.asf d.gsm n.gsm cj

γὰρ ἐκ νεκρῶν ἀναστῶσιν ↱ οὔτε γαμοῦσιν οὔτε
For people rise from the dead, *rise* they neither marry nor
1142 482 1666 3738 482 1138 4046 1138 4046
cj p.g a.gpm v.aas.3p cj v.pai.3p cj

γαμίζονται, ἀλλ᾽ εἰσὶν ὡς ἄγγελοι ἐν τοῖς οὐρανοῖς. 26 περὶ
⌊are they given in marriage,⌋ but they are as angels in *{the}* heaven. But concerning
1139 247 1639 6055 34 1877 3836 4041 1254 4309
v.ppi.3p cj v.pai.3p pl n.npm p.d d.dpm n.dpm p.g

δὲ τῶν νεκρῶν ὅτι ἐγείρονται ↱ ↱ οὐκ ἀνέγνωτε ἐν τῇ βίβλῳ Μωϋσέως
But the dead, that they are raised, have you not read in the book of Moses in
1254 3836 3738 4022 1586 336 336 4024 336 1877 3836 1047 3707
cj d.gpm a.gpm cj v.ppi.3p pl v.aai.2p p.d d.dsf n.dsf n.gsm

ἐπὶ τοῦ βάτου πῶς εἶπεν αὐτῷ ὁ θεὸς λέγων· ἐγὼ ὁ θεὸς
the passage about the bush, how God spoke to him *{the}* *God* saying, 'I am the God
2093 3836 1004 4802 2536 3306 899 3836 2536 3306 1609 3836 2536
p.g d.gsm n.gsm cj v.aai.3s r.dsm.3 d.nsm n.nsm pt.pa.nsm r.ns.1 d.nsm n.nsm

Ἀβραὰμ καὶ ὁ[a] θεὸς Ἰσαὰκ καὶ ὁ[b] θεὸς Ἰακώβ; 27 οὐκ ἔστιν θεὸς →
of Abraham, and the God of Isaac, and the God of Jacob'? He is not *He is* God of
11 2779 3836 2536 2693 2779 3836 2536 2609 1639 1639 4024 1639 2536
n.gsm cj d.nsm n.nsm n.gsm cj d.nsm n.nsm n.gsm pl v.pai.3s n.nsm

νεκρῶν ἀλλὰ → ζώντων· ↱ ↱ πολὺ πλανᾶσθε. 28 καὶ
the dead, but of the living. You are greatly mistaken!" And one of the scribes
3738 247 2409 4414 4414 4498 4414 2779 1651 3836 3836 1208
a.gpm cj pt.pa.gpm adv v.ppi.2p cj

προσελθὼν εἷς τῶν γραμματέων ἀκούσας αὐτῶν συζητούντων, ἰδὼν ὅτι
came up *one* *of the* *scribes* and heard them disputing. Seeing how
4665 1651 3836 1208 201 899 5184 1625 4022
pt.aa.nsm a.nsm d.gpm n.gpm pt.aa.nsm r.gpm.3 pt.pa.gpm pt.aa.nsm cj

καλῶς ἀπεκρίθη αὐτοῖς ἐπηρώτησεν αὐτόν· ποία ἐστὶν
well Jesus had answered them, he put this question to him: "Which commandment is
2822 646 899 2089 899 4481 1953 1639
adv v.api.3s r.dpm.3 v.aai.3s r.asm.3 r.nsf v.pai.3s

ἐντολὴ πρώτη πάντων; 29 ἀπεκρίθη ὁ Ἰησοῦς ὅτι
commandment the most important of all?" Jesus answered, *{the}* *Jesus* ~ "The
1953 4755 4246 2652 646 3836 2652 4022
n.nsf a.nsf a.gpn v.api.3s d.nsm n.nsm cj

πρώτη ἐστίν· ἄκουε, Ἰσραήλ, κύριος ὁ θεὸς ἡμῶν κύριος εἷς
most important is, 'Hear, Israel, the Lord *{the}* our God, *our* the Lord is one;
4755 1639 201 2702 3261 3836 7005 2536 7005 3261 1639 1651
a.nsf v.pai.3s v.pam.2s n.vsm n.nsm d.nsm n.nsm r.gp.1 n.nsm a.nsm

ἐστιν, 30 καὶ ἀγαπήσεις κύριον τὸν θεόν σου ἐξ ὅλης τῆς καρδίας
is and you shall love the Lord *{the}* your God *your* with your whole *{the}* heart,
1639 2779 26 3261 3836 5148 2536 5148 1666 5148 3910 3836 2840
v.pai.3s cj v.fai.2s n.asm d.asm n.asm r.gs.2 p.g a.gsf d.gsf n.gsf

σου καὶ ἐξ ὅλης τῆς ψυχῆς σου καὶ ἐξ ὅλης τῆς διανοίας σου καὶ ἐξ
your and with your whole *{the}* life, *your* and with your whole *{the}* mind, *your* and with
5148 2779 1666 5148 3910 3836 6034 5148 2779 1666 5148 3910 3836 1379 5148 2779 1666
r.gs.2 cj p.g a.gsf d.gsf n.gsf r.gs.2 cj p.g a.gsf d.gsf n.gsf r.gs.2 cj p.g

ὅλης τῆς ἰσχύος σου. 31 δευτέρα αὕτη· ἀγαπήσεις τὸν πλησίον
your whole *{the}* strength.' *your* The second is this: 'You shall love *{the}* your neighbor
5148 3910 3836 2709 5148 1311 4047 26 3836 5148 4446
a.gsf d.gsf n.gsf r.gs.2 a.nsf r.nsf v.fai.2s d.asm adv

σου ὡς σεαυτόν. μείζων τούτων ἄλλη ἐντολὴ
your as yourself.' There is no other commandment greater than these." *other* *commandment*
5148 6055 4932 1639 1639 4024 257 1953 3489 4047 257 1953
r.gs.2 cj r.asm.2 a.nsf.c r.gpf r.nsf n.nsf

οὐκ ἔστιν. 32 καὶ εἶπεν αὐτῷ ὁ γραμματεύς· καλῶς, διδάσκαλε,
no *There is* And the scribe said to him, *the* *scribe* "Well said, teacher.
4024 1639 2779 3836 1208 3306 899 3836 1208 2822 1437
pl v.pai.3s cj v.aai.3s r.dsm.3 d.nsm n.nsm adv n.vsm

[a] [ὁ] UBS.
[b] [ὁ] UBS.

NASB

do not understand the Scriptures or the power of God? [25]For when they rise from the dead, they neither marry nor are given in marriage, but are like angels in heaven. [26]But regarding the fact that the dead rise again, have you not read in the book of Moses, in the *passage* about *the burning* bush, how God spoke to him, saying, 'I AM THE GOD OF ABRAHAM, AND THE GOD OF ISAAC, and the God of Jacob'? [27]He is not the God of the dead, but of the living; you are greatly mistaken."

[28]One of the scribes came and heard them arguing, and recognizing that He had answered them well, asked Him, "What commandment is the foremost of all?" [29]Jesus answered, "The foremost is, 'HEAR, O ISRAEL! THE LORD OUR GOD IS ONE LORD; [30]AND YOU SHALL LOVE THE LORD YOUR GOD WITH ALL YOUR HEART, AND WITH ALL YOUR SOUL, AND WITH ALL YOUR MIND, AND WITH ALL YOUR STRENGTH.' [31]The second is this, 'YOU SHALL LOVE YOUR NEIGHBOR AS YOURSELF.' There is no other commandment greater than these." [32]The scribe said to Him, "Right, Teacher;

NIV

the man replied. "You are right in saying that God is one and there is no other but him. [33]To love him with all your heart, with all your understanding and with all your strength, and to love your neighbor as yourself is more important than all burnt offerings and sacrifices."

[34]When Jesus saw that he had answered wisely, he said to him, "You are not far from the kingdom of God." And from then on no one dared ask him any more questions.

Whose Son Is the Messiah?

[35]While Jesus was teaching in the temple courts, he asked, "Why do the teachers of the law say that the Messiah is the son of David? [36]David himself, speaking by the Holy Spirit, declared:

> " 'The Lord said to my Lord:
> "Sit at my right hand
> until I put your enemies
> under your feet." '[a]

[37]David himself calls him 'Lord.' How then can he be his son?"

The large crowd listened to him with delight.

Warning Against the Teachers of the Law

[38]As he taught, Jesus said, "Watch out for the teachers of the law. They like to walk around in flowing robes and be greeted with respect in the marketplaces, [39]and

[a] 36 Psalm 110:1

⌊ἐπ' ἀληθείας⌋ εἶπες ὅτι εἷς ἐστιν καὶ
You have spoken truthfully; *You have spoken* ~ 'he is one, *he is* and there
3306 3306 3306 2093 237 3306 4022 1639 1639 1651 1639 2779 1639
p.g n.gsf v.aai.2s cj a.nsm v.pai.3s cj

οὐκ ἔστιν ἄλλος πλὴν αὐτοῦ· 33 καὶ τὸ ἀγαπᾶν αὐτὸν ἐξ ὅλης τῆς
is no *there is* other besides him.' And *{the}* 'to love him with the whole *the*
1639 4024 1639 257 4440 899 2779 3836 26 899 1666 3836 3910 3836
pl v.pai.3s r.nsm p.g r.gsm.3 cj d.nsn f.pa r.asm.3 p.g a.gsf d.gsf

καρδίας καὶ ἐξ ὅλης τῆς συνέσεως καὶ ἐξ ὅλης τῆς ἰσχύος καὶ τὸ
heart, and with the whole *the* understanding, and with the whole *the* strength,' and *{the}*
2840 2779 1666 3836 3910 3836 5304 2779 1666 3836 3910 3836 2709 2779 3836
n.gsf cj p.g a.gsf d.gsf n.gsf cj p.g a.gsf d.gsf n.gsf cj d.nsn

ἀγαπᾶν τὸν πλησίον ὡς ἑαυτὸν περισσότερόν ἐστιν πάντων τῶν
'to love one's neighbor as oneself,' is much more *is* than all *{the}*
26 3836 4446 6055 1571 1639 4358 1639 4246 3836
f.pa d.asm adv cj r.asm.3 a.nsn.c v.pai.3s a.gpn d.gpn

ὁλοκαυτωμάτων καὶ θυσιῶν. 34 καὶ ὁ Ἰησοῦς ἰδὼν αὐτὸν[a] ὅτι
whole burnt offerings and sacrifices." And *{the}* Jesus, seeing *{him}* that the scribe had
3906 2779 2602 2779 3836 2652 1625 899 4022 646
n.gpn cj n.gpf cj d.nsm n.nsm pt.aa.nsm r.asm.3 cj

νουνεχῶς ἀπεκρίθη εἶπεν αὐτῷ· οὐ μακρὰν εἶ ἀπὸ τῆς
answered wisely, *had answered* said to him, "You are not far *You are* from the
646 3807 646 3306 899 1639 1639 4024 3426 1639 608 3836
adv v.api.3s v.aai.3s r.dsm.3 pl adv v.pai.2s p.g d.gsf

βασιλείας τοῦ θεοῦ. καὶ οὐδεὶς οὐκέτι ἐτόλμα αὐτὸν
kingdom of God." And no one dared to question him any more. *dared* *him*
993 3836 2536 2779 4029 5528 2089 2089 899 4033 5528 899
n.gsf d.gsm n.gsm cj a.nsm adv v.iai.3s r.asm.3

ἐπερωτῆσαι. 35 καὶ ἀποκριθεὶς ὁ Ἰησοῦς ἔλεγεν
to question *{and}* *{answering}* While *{the}* Jesus was teaching in the temple, he said,
2089 2779 646 1438 3836 2652 1438 1438 1877 3836 2639 3306
f.aa cj pt.ap.nsm d.nsm n.nsm v.iai.3s

διδάσκων ἐν τῷ ἱερῷ· πῶς → λέγουσιν οἱ γραμματεῖς ὅτι
While was teaching *in* *the* *temple* "How can the scribes say *the* *scribes* that
1438 1877 3836 2639 4802 3836 1208 3306 3836 1208 4022
pt.pa.nsm p.d d.dsn n.dsn cj v.pai.3p d.npm n.npm cj

ὁ χριστὸς υἱὸς Δαυίδ ἐστιν; 36 αὐτὸς Δαυὶδ
{the} Christ is the son of David? *is* David himself, *David* by the Holy Spirit,
3836 5986 1639 5626 1253 1639 1253 899 1253 1877 3836 41 4460
d.nsm n.nsm n.nsm n.gsm v.pai.3s r.nsm n.nsm

εἶπεν ἐν τῷ πνεύματι τῷ ἁγίῳ· εἶπεν κύριος τῷ κυρίῳ μου· κάθου
said, *by* *the* *Spirit* *{the}* *Holy'* 'The Lord said *Lord* to my Lord, *my* "Sit
3306 1877 3836 4460 3836 41 3261 3306 3261 3836 1609 3261 1609 2764
v.aai.3s p.d d.dsn n.dsn d.dsn a.dsn v.aai.3s n.nsm d.dsm n.dsm r.gs.1 v.pmm.2s

ἐκ δεξιῶν μου, ⌊ἕως ἂν⌋ θῶ τοὺς ἐχθρούς σου ὑποκάτω τῶν
at my right hand, *my* until I put *{the}* your enemies *your* beneath *{the}* your
1666 1609 1288 1609 2401 323 5502 3836 5148 2398 5148 5691 3836 5148
p.g a.gpf r.gs.1 cj pl v.aas.1s d.apm a.apm r.gs.2 p.g d.gpm

ποδῶν σου. 37 αὐτὸς Δαυὶδ λέγει αὐτὸν κύριον, καὶ πόθεν αὐτοῦ ἐστιν
feet."' *your* David himself *David* calls him 'Lord;' so how *his* ⌊can he be⌋ his
4546 5148 1253 899 1253 3306 899 3261 2779 4470 899 1639 899
n.gpm r.gs.2 r.nsm n.nsm v.pai.3s r.asm.3 n.asm cj cj r.gsm.3 v.pai.3s

υἱός; Καὶ ὁ[b] πολὺς ὄχλος ἤκουεν αὐτοῦ ἡδέως. 38 καὶ ἐν τῇ
son?" And the large crowd ⌊was listening to⌋ him with delight. And in *{the}* his
5626 2779 3836 4498 4063 201 899 2452 2779 1877 3836 899
n.nsm cj d.nsm a.nsm n.nsm v.iai.3s r.gsm.3 adv cj p.d d.dsf

διδαχῇ αὐτοῦ ἔλεγεν· βλέπετε ἀπὸ τῶν γραμματέων τῶν θελόντων
teaching *his* he was saying, "Beware of the scribes, who like to parade
1439 899 3306 1063 608 3836 1208 3836 2527 4344 4344
n.dsf r.gsm.3 v.iai.3s v.pam.2p p.g d.gpm n.gpm d.gpm pt.pa.gpm

ἐν στολαῖς περιπατεῖν καὶ ἀσπασμοὺς ἐν ταῖς ἀγοραῖς 39 καὶ
around in flowing robes, *to parade around* and want greetings in the marketplaces and
4344 1877 5124 4344 2779 833 1877 3836 59 2779
p.d n.dpf f.pa cj n.apm p.d d.dpf n.dpf cj

[a] [αὐτὸν] UBS, omitted by TNIV.
[b] [ὁ] UBS.

NASB

You have truly stated that HE IS ONE, AND THERE IS NO ONE ELSE BESIDES HIM; [33]AND TO LOVE HIM WITH ALL THE HEART AND WITH ALL THE UNDERSTANDING AND WITH ALL THE STRENGTH, AND TO LOVE ONE'S NEIGHBOR AS HIMSELF, is much more than all burnt offerings and sacrifices." [34]When Jesus saw that he had answered intelligently, He said to him, "You are not far from the kingdom of God." After that, no one would venture to ask Him any more questions.

[35]And Jesus *began* to say, as He taught in the temple, "How *is it that* the scribes say that the Christ is the son of David? [36]David himself said in the Holy Spirit,

> [36]'THE LORD SAID TO MY LORD,
> [36]"SIT AT MY RIGHT HAND,
> UNTIL I PUT YOUR ENEMIES BENEATH YOUR FEET." '

[37]David himself calls Him 'Lord'; so in what sense is He his son?" And the large crowd enjoyed listening to Him.

[38]In His teaching He was saying: "Beware of the scribes who like to walk around in long robes, and *like* respectful greetings in the market places, [39]and

NIV

have the most im-
portant seats in
the synagogues
and the places of
honor at banquets.
40They devour
widows' houses
and for a show
make lengthy
prayers. These
men will be pun-
ished most severe-
ly."

The Widow's Offering

41Jesus sat down
opposite the place
where the offer-
ings were put and
watched the crowd
putting their mon-
ey into the temple
treasury. Many
rich people threw
in large amounts.
42But a poor wid-
ow came and put
in two very small
copper coins,
worth only a few
cents.
43Calling his
disciples to him,
Jesus said, "Tru-
ly I tell you, this
poor widow has
put more into the
treasury than all
the others. 44They
all gave out of
their wealth; but
she, out of her pov-
erty, put in every-
thing—all she had
to live on."

The Destruction of the Temple and Signs of the End Times

13 As Jesus
was leaving
the temple, one of
his disciples said
to him, "Look,
Teacher! What
massive stones!
What magnificent
buildings!"
2"Do you see all
these great build-
ings?" replied
Jesus. "Not one
stone here will

πρωτοκαθεδρίας ἐν ταῖς συναγωγαῖς καὶ πρωτοκλισίας ἐν τοῖς δείπνοις,
the front seats in the synagogues, and the places of honor at {the} banquets.
4751 1877 3836 5252 2779 4752 1877 3836 1270
n.apf p.d d.dpf n.dpf cj n.apf p.d d.dpn n.dpn

40 οἱ κατεσθίοντες τὰς οἰκίας τῶν χηρῶν καὶ προφάσει ↱ ↱ μακρὰ
They devour the property of widows and, as a show, offer up long
3836 2983 3836 3864 3836 5939 2779 4733 4667 4667 3431
d.npm pt.pa.npm d.apf n.apf d.gpf n.gpf cj n.dsf adv

προσευχόμενοι· οὗτοι λήμψονται περισσότερον κρίμα. 41 καὶ καθίσας
prayers. ⌊These men⌋ will receive a more severe judgment. And taking a seat
4667 4047 3284 4358 3210 2779 2767
pt.pm.npm r.npm v.fmi.3p a.asn.c n.asn cj pt.aa.nsm

κατέναντι τοῦ γαζοφυλακίου ἐθεώρει πῶς ὁ ὄχλος βάλλει χαλκὸν εἰς
opposite the treasury, he was watching how the people were putting money into
2978 3836 1126 2555 4802 3836 4063 965 5910 1650
p.g d.gsn n.gsn v.iai.3s cj d.nsm n.nsm v.pai.3s n.asm p.a

τὸ γαζοφυλάκιον. καὶ πολλοὶ πλούσιοι ἔβαλλον πολλά· 42 καὶ
the offering box. {and} Many rich people ⌊were putting in⌋ large sums. {and} A poor
3836 1126 2779 4498 4454 965 4498 2779 1651 4777
d.asn n.asn cj a.npm a.npm v.iai.3p a.apn cj

ἐλθοῦσα μία χήρα πτωχὴ ἔβαλεν λεπτὰ δύο, ⌊ὅ ἐστιν⌋
widow approached A widow poor and put in two small coins, two about a
5939 2262 1651 5939 4777 965 1545 3321 1545 4005 1639
pt.aa.nsf a.nsf n.nsf a.nsf v.aai.3s n.apn a.apn r.nsn v.pai.3s

κοδράντης. 43 καὶ προσκαλεσάμενος τοὺς μαθητὰς αὐτοῦ ↰ ↰ εἶπεν
penny. And he called {the} his disciples his to him and said
3119 2779 4673 3836 899 3412 899 4673 4673 3306
n.nsm cj pt.am.nsm d.apm n.apm r.gsm.3 v.aai.3s

αὐτοῖς· ἀμὴν λέγω ὑμῖν ὅτι ἡ χήρα αὕτη ἡ πτωχὴ
to them, "I tell you the truth, I tell you ~ {the} this poor widow this {the} poor has
899 3306 3306 7007 297 3306 7007 4022 3836 4047 4777 5939 4047 3836 4777 965
r.dpm.3 pl v.pai.1s r.dp.2 cj d.nsf n.nsf r.nsf d.nsf a.nsf

πλεῖον πάντων ἔβαλεν τῶν βαλλόντων εἰς τὸ γαζοφυλάκιον·
put in more than all has put in those who are putting large amounts into the offering box.
965 965 4498 4246 965 3836 965 1650 3836 1126
a.asn.c a.gpm v.aai.3s d.gpm pt.pa.gpm p.a d.asn n.asn

44 πάντες γὰρ ἐκ τοῦ περισσεύοντος αὐτοῖς ἔβαλον, αὕτη
For they all For put in from {the} their abundance, their they put in but she
1142 965 4246 1142 965 965 1666 3836 899 4355 899 965 1254 4047
a.npm cj p.g d.gsn pt.pa.gsn r.dpm.3 v.aai.3p r.nsf

δὲ ἐκ τῆς ὑστερήσεως αὐτῆς ⌊πάντα ὅσα⌋ εἶχεν ἔβαλεν ὅλον
but from {the} her need her has put in everything she had has put in — all
1254 1666 3836 899 5730 899 965 965 965 4246 4012 2400 965 3910
cj p.g d.gsf n.gsf r.gsf.3 a.apn r.apn v.iai.3s v.aai.3s a.asm

τὸν βίον αὐτῆς.
{the} she had to live on." she had
3836 899 899 1050 899
d.asm n.asm r.gsf.3

13:1 καὶ → ἐκπορευομένου αὐτοῦ ἐκ τοῦ ἱεροῦ λέγει
And as he went out he of the temple, one of his disciples said
2779 899 1744 899 1666 3836 2639 1651 3836 899 3412 3306
cj pt.pm.gsm r.gsm.3 p.g d.gsn n.gsn v.pai.3s

αὐτῷ εἷς τῶν μαθητῶν αὐτοῦ· διδάσκαλε, ἴδε ποταποὶ λίθοι καὶ ποταπαὶ
to him, one of disciples his "Teacher, look, what ⌊massive stones⌋ and what
899 1651 3836 3412 899 1437 2623 4534 3345 2779 4534
r.dsm.3 a.nsm d.gpm n.gpm r.gsm.3 n.vsm pl r.npm n.npm cj r.npf

οἰκοδομαί. 2 καὶ ὁ Ἰησοῦς εἶπεν αὐτῷ· βλέπεις ταύτας τὰς μεγάλας
⌊magnificent buildings!"⌋ And {the} Jesus said to him, ⌊"Do you see⌋ these {the} great
3869 2779 3836 2652 3306 899 1063 4047 3836 3489
n.npf cj d.nsm n.nsm v.aai.3s r.dsm.3 v.pai.2s r.apf d.apf a.apf

οἰκοδομάς; ⌊οὐ μὴ⌋ ἀφεθῇ ὧδε λίθος ↰ ἐπὶ λίθον ὃς ↱
buildings? Not a single stone ⌊will be left⌋ here single stone resting on another that will
3869 4024 3590 3345 3345 918 6045 3345 918 2093 3345 4005 2907
n.apf pl pl v.aps.3s adv n.nsm p.a n.asm r.nsm

NASB

chief seats in the
synagogues and
places of honor at
banquets, 40who
devour widows'
houses, and for
appearance's sake
offer long prayers;
these will receive
greater condemna-
tion."

The Widow's Mite

41And He sat
down opposite the
treasury, and *began*
observing how the
people were put-
ting money into
the treasury; and
many rich people
were putting in
large sums. 42A
poor widow came
and put in two
small copper coins,
which amount to a
cent. 43Calling His
disciples to Him,
He said to them,
"Truly I say to you,
this poor widow
put in more than all
the contributors to
the treasury; 44for
they all put in out
of their surplus,
but she, out of her
poverty, put in all
she owned, all she
had to live on."

Things to Come

13:1As He was
going out of the
temple, one of His
disciples *said to
Him, "Teacher, be-
hold [a]what wonder-
ful stones and what
wonderful build-
ings!" 2And Jesus
said to him, "Do
you see these great
buildings? Not one
stone will be left
upon another

[a] Lit *how great*

NIV

be left on another;
every one will be
thrown down."
3 As Jesus was sit-
ting on the Mount
of Olives opposite
the temple, Peter,
James, John and
Andrew asked him
privately, 4 "Tell
us, when will these
things happen?
And what will be
the sign that they
are all about to be
fulfilled?"
5 Jesus said to
them: "Watch out
that no one de-
ceives you. 6 Many
will come in my
name, claiming,
'I am he,' and will
deceive many.
7 When you hear of
wars and rumors
of wars, do not
be alarmed. Such
things must hap-
pen, but the end
is still to come.
8 Nation will rise
against nation, and
kingdom against
kingdom. There
will be earth-
quakes in various
places, and fam-
ines. These are the
beginning of birth
pains.
9 "You must be on
your guard. You
will be handed
over to the lo-
cal councils and
flogged in the
synagogues. On
account of me you
will stand before
governors and
kings as witnesses
to them. 10 And the
gospel must first
be preached to all
nations. 11 Whenev-
er you are arrested
and brought to
trial, do not worry
beforehand about
what to say. Just
say whatever is
given you at the

⌞οὐ μὴ⌟ καταλυθῇ. 3 καὶ → καθημένου αὐτοῦ εἰς τὸ ὄρος τῶν ἐλαιῶν
not be thrown down." So while he was sitting *he* on the Mount of Olives
4024 3590 2907 2779 899 2764 899 1650 3836 4001 3836 1777
pl pl v.aps.3s cj pt.pm.gsm r.gsm.3 p.a d.asn n.asn d.gpf n.gpf

κατέναντι τοῦ ἱεροῦ ἐπηρώτα αὐτὸν ⌞κατ' ἰδίαν⌟
opposite the temple, Peter, James, John and Andrew questioned him privately,
2978 3836 2639 4377 2610 2722 2779 436 2089 899 2848 2625
p.g d.gsn n.gsn v.iai.3s r.asm.3 p.a a.asf

Πέτρος καὶ Ἰάκωβος καὶ Ἰωάννης καὶ Ἀνδρέας· 4 εἰπὸν ἡμῖν, πότε ↱ ταῦτα
Peter *{and}* *James* *{and}* *John* *and* *Andrew* "Tell us, when will these things
4377 2779 2610 2779 2722 2779 436 3306 7005 4537 1639 4047
n.nsm cj n.nsm cj n.nsm cj n.nsm v.aam.2s r.dp.1 cj r.npn

ἔσται καὶ τί τὸ σημεῖον ὅταν μέλλῃ ταῦτα
be, and what will be the sign when all these things are about *these things*
1639 2779 5515 3836 4956 4020 4246 4047 4047 3516 4047
v.fmi.3s cj r.nsn d.nsn n.nsn cj v.pas.3s r.npn

συντελεῖσθαι πάντα; 5 ὁ δὲ Ἰησοῦς ἤρξατο λέγειν αὐτοῖς· βλέπετε μή τις
to take place?" *all* *{the}* And Jesus began to speak to them, "Watch out lest someone
5334 4246 3836 1254 2652 806 3306 899 1063 3590 5516
f.pp a.npn d.nsm cj n.nsm v.ami.3s f.pa r.dpm.3 v.pam.2p cj r.nsm

ὑμᾶς πλανήσῃ· 6 πολλοὶ ἐλεύσονται ἐπὶ τῷ ὀνόματί μου λέγοντες ὅτι
mislead you. *mislead* Many will come in *{the}* my name *my* saying, ~
4414 7007 4414 4498 2262 2093 3836 1609 3950 1609 3306 4022
r.ap.2 v.aas.3s a.npm v.fmi.3p p.d d.dsn n.dsn r.gs.1 pt.pa.npm cj

ἐγώ εἰμι, καὶ πολλοὺς πλανήσουσιν. 7 ὅταν δὲ ἀκούσητε
'I am he,' and they will deceive many. *they will deceive* And when *And* you hear
1609 1639 2779 4414 4414 4414 4498 4414 1254 4020 1254 201
r.ns.1 v.pai.1s cj a.apm v.fai.3p cj cj v.aas.2p

πολέμους καὶ ἀκοὰς πολέμων, ↱ μὴ θροεῖσθε· δεῖ γενέσθαι, ἀλλ'
of wars and rumors of wars, do not be alarmed; those things must happen, but the
4483 2779 198 4483 2583 3590 2583 1256 1181 247 3836
n.apm cj n.apf n.gpm pl v.ppm.2p v.pai.3s f.am cj

οὔπω τὸ τέλος. 8 ἐγερθήσεται γὰρ ἔθνος ἐπ' ἔθνος καὶ βασιλεία
end is not yet. *the* *end* For nation will rise *For* *nation* against nation and kingdom
5465 4037 3836 5465 1142 1620 1586 1142 1620 2093 1620 2779 993
adv d.nsn n.nsn v.fpi.3s cj n.nsn p.a n.asn cj n.nsf

ἐπὶ βασιλείαν, ἔσονται σεισμοὶ κατὰ τόπους, ἔσονται λιμοί·
against kingdom. ⌞There will be⌟ earthquakes in various places; ⌞there will be⌟ famines. These are
2093 993 1639 4939 2848 5536 1639 3350 4047
p.a n.asf v.fmi.3p n.npm p.a n.apm v.fmi.3p n.npf

ἀρχὴ ὠδίνων ταῦτα. 9 βλέπετε δὲ ὑμεῖς ἑαυτούς· παραδώσουσιν
the beginning of birth pains. *These* But ⌞watch out for⌟ *But* *{you}* yourselves; they will deliver
794 6047 4047 1254 1063 1254 7007 1571 4140
n.nsf n.gpf r.npn v.pam.2p cj r.np.2 r.apm.2 v.fai.3p

ὑμᾶς ↰ εἰς συνέδρια καὶ εἰς συναγωγὰς δαρήσεσθε καὶ ἐπὶ ἡγεμόνων
you over to local councils, and in synagogues you will be beaten, and before governors
7007 4140 1650 5284 2779 1650 5252 1296 2779 2093 2450
r.ap.2 p.a n.apn cj p.a n.apf v.fpi.2p cj p.g n.gpm

καὶ βασιλέων σταθήσεσθε ἕνεκεν ἐμοῦ ↰ εἰς μαρτύριον αὐτοῖς. 10 καὶ
and kings ⌞you will be made to stand⌟ for my sake, to bear witness to them. *{and}*
2779 995 2705 1914 1609 1914 1650 3457 899 2779
cj n.gpm v.fpi.2p p.g r.gs.1 p.a n.asn r.dpm.3 cj

εἰς πάντα τὰ ἔθνη πρῶτον δεῖ κηρυχθῆναι τὸ
First the gospel must be preached to every *{the}* nation. *First* *must* *be preached* *the*
4754 3836 2295 1256 3062 3062 1650 4246 3836 1620 4754 1256 3062 3836
p.a a.apn d.apn n.apn adv v.pai.3s f.ap d.asn

εὐαγγέλιον. 11 καὶ ὅταν ἄγωσιν ὑμᾶς ↰ ↰ παραδιδόντες, ← ↱ μὴ
gospel And when they bring you to trial and deliver you over, do not
2295 2779 4020 72 7007 72 72 4140 4628 3590
n.asn cj cj v.pas.3p r.ap.2 pt.pa.npm pl

προμεριμνᾶτε τί λαλήσητε, ἀλλ' ⌞ὃ ἐὰν⌟ δοθῇ ὑμῖν ἐν ἐκείνῃ τῇ
⌞worry ahead of time⌟ what you should say, but whatever is given you in that *{the}*
4628 5515 3281 247 4005 1569 1443 7007 1877 1697 3836
v.pam.2p r.asn v.aas.2p cj r.nsn pl v.aps.3s r.dp.2 p.d r.dsf d.dsf

NASB

which will not be
torn down."
3 As He was sitting
on the Mount of
Olives opposite the
temple, Peter and
James and John
and Andrew were
questioning Him
privately, 4 "Tell us,
when will these
things be, and
what *will be* the
sign when all these
things are going
to be fulfilled?"
5 And Jesus began
to say to them,
"See to it that no
one misleads you.
6 Many will come
in My name, say-
ing, 'I am *He!*'
and will mislead
many. 7 When you
hear of wars and
rumors of wars, do
not be frightened;
those things must
take place; but *that*
is not yet the end.
8 For nation will
rise up against na-
tion, and kingdom
against kingdom;
there will be earth-
quakes in various
places; there will
also be famines.
These things are
merely the begin-
ning of birth pangs.
9 "But be on your
guard; for they will
deliver you to *the*
courts, and you
will be flogged in
the synagogues,
and you will stand
before governors
and kings for My
sake, as a testimo-
ny to them. 10 The
gospel must first
be preached to all
the nations. 11 When
they arrest you and
hand you over, do
not worry before-
hand about what
you are to say, but
say whatever is
given you in

NIV

time, for it is not you speaking, but the Holy Spirit.

[12]"Brother will betray brother to death, and a father his child. Children will rebel against their parents and have them put to death. [13]Everyone will hate you because of me, but the one who stands firm to the end will be saved.

[14]"When you see 'the abomination that causes desolation'[a] standing where it[b] does not belong—let the reader understand—then let those who are in Judea flee to the mountains. [15]Let no one on the housetop go down or enter the house to take anything out. [16]Let no one in the field go back to get their cloak. [17]How dreadful it will be in those days for pregnant women and nursing mothers! [18]Pray that this will not take place in winter, [19]because those will be days of distress unequaled from the beginning, when God created the world, until now—and never to be equaled again.

[20]"If the Lord had not cut short those days, no one would survive.

[a] 14 Daniel 9:27; 11:31; 12:11
[b] 14 Or *he*

ὥρᾳ τοῦτο λαλεῖτε· οὐ γάρ ἐστε ὑμεῖς οἱ λαλοῦντες
hour, *{this}* speak; for you are not *for* *are* *you* the ˌones who will be speaking,ˌ
6052 4047 3281 1142 7007 1639 4024 1142 1639 7007 3836 3281
n.dsf r.asn v.pam.2p pl cj v.pai.2p r.np.2 d.npm pt.pa.npm

ἀλλὰ τὸ πνεῦμα τὸ ἅγιον. 12 καὶ παραδώσει ἀδελφὸς ἀδελφὸν εἰς
but the Holy Spirit. *{the}* *Holy* And brother will deliver over *brother* brother to
247 3836 41 4460 3836 41 2779 81 4140 81 81 1650
cj d.nsn n.nsn d.nsn a.nsn cj v.fai.3s n.nsm n.asm p.a

θάνατον καὶ πατὴρ τέκνον, καὶ ἐπαναστήσονται τέκνα ἐπὶ γονεῖς
death, and a father his child; and children will rise up in rebellion *children* against parents
2505 2779 4252 5451 2779 5451 2060 5451 2093 1204
n.asm cj n.nsm n.asn cj v.fmi.3p n.npn p.a n.apm

καὶ → θανατώσουσιν αὐτούς· 13 καὶ ἔσεσθε μισούμενοι ὑπὸ πάντων
and have them put to death. *them* And ˌyou will beˌ hated by all
2779 899 2506 899 2779 1639 3631 5679 4246
cj v.fai.3p r.apm.3 cj v.fmi.2p pt.pp.npm p.g a.gpm

διὰ τὸ ὄνομά μου. ὁ δὲ ὑπομείνας εἰς τέλος οὗτος
ˌon account ofˌ *{the}* my name. *my* But the *But* one who perseveres to the end *{this one}*
1328 3836 1609 3950 1609 1254 3836 1254 5702 1650 5465 4047
p.a d.asn n.asn r.gs.1 d.nsm cj pt.aa.nsm p.a n.asn r.nsm

σωθήσεται. 14 ὅταν δὲ ἴδητε τὸ βδέλυγμα τῆς ἐρημώσεως[a] ἑστηκότα ὅπου ↱
will be saved. "When *{and}* you see the 'abomination of desolation' standing where he
5392 4020 1254 1625 3836 1007 3836 2247 2705 3963 1256
v.fpi.3s cj cj v.aas.2p d.asn n.asn d.gsf n.gsf pt.ra.asn cj

↱ οὐ δεῖ, ↱ ὁ ἀναγινώσκων νοείτω, τότε ↱ οἱ ἐν τῇ
should not be (let the reader understand), then let those who are in *{the}*
1256 4024 1256 336 3836 336 3783 5538 5771 3836 1877 3836
pl v.pai.3s d.nsm pt.pa.nsm v.pam.3s adv d.npm p.d d.dsf

Ἰουδαίᾳ φευγέτωσαν εἰς τὰ ὄρη, 15 ↱ ὁ δὲ[b] ἐπὶ τοῦ δώματος
Judea flee to the mountains. Let ˌthe oneˌ *{and}* who is on the housetop
2677 5771 1650 3836 4001 2849 3836 1254 2093 3836 1560
n.dsf v.pam.3p p.a d.apn n.apn d.nsm cj p.g d.gsn n.gsn

μὴ καταβάτω μηδὲ εἰσελθάτω ἆραί τι ἐκ τῆς οἰκίας αὐτοῦ,
not come down, nor enter his house to remove anything from it; *{the}* *house* *his*
3590 2849 3593 1656 899 3864 149 5516 1666 3836 3864 899
pl v.aam.3s cj v.aam.3s f.aa r.asn p.g d.gsf n.gsf r.gsm.3

16 καὶ ↱ ὁ εἰς τὸν ἀγρὸν μὴ ἐπιστρεψάτω εἰς τὰ ὀπίσω ἆραι τὸ
and let ˌthe oneˌ who is in the field not return *{into}* *{the}* *{back}* to get *{the}*
2779 2188 3836 1650 3836 69 3590 2188 1650 3836 3958 149 3836
cj d.nsm p.a d.asm n.asm pl v.aam.3s p.a d.apn adv f.aa d.asn

ἱμάτιον αὐτοῦ. 17 οὐαὶ δὲ ταῖς ˌἐν γαστρὶˌ
his cloak. *his* But woe *But* to those women who are pregnant
899 2668 899 1254 4026 1254 3836 2400 2400 2400 1877 1143
n.asn r.gsm.3 j cj d.dpf p.d n.dsf

ἐχούσαις καὶ ταῖς θηλαζούσαις ἐν ἐκείναις ταῖς ἡμέραις. 18 προσεύχεσθε
women who are and to those who are nursing in those *{the}* days. And pray
2400 2779 3836 2558 1877 1697 3836 2465 1254 4667
pt.pa.dpf cj d.dpf pt.pa.dpf p.d r.dpf d.dpf n.dpf v.pmm.2p

δὲ ἵνα ↱ ↱ μὴ γένηται χειμῶνος· 19 ἔσονται γὰρ αἱ ἡμέραι
And that it may not happen during winter, because those will be *because* *{the}* days
1254 2671 1181 1181 3590 1181 5930 1142 1697 1639 1142 3836 2465
cj cj pl v.ams.3s n.gsm v.fmi.3p cj d.npf n.npf

ἐκεῖναι → θλῖψις οἵα ↱ οὐ γέγονεν τοιαύτη ἀπ' ἀρχῆς κτίσεως
those of such tribulation as has never happened *such* from the beginning of creation,
1697 5525 2568 3888 1181 4024 1181 5525 608 794 3232
r.npf n.nsf r.nsf pl v.rai.3s r.nsf p.g n.gsf n.gsf

ἣν ἔκτισεν ὁ θεὸς ἕως τοῦ νῦν ˌκαὶ οὐ μὴˌ γένηται. 20 καὶ ˌεἰ μὴˌ
which God created, *{the}* *God* until *{the}* now, nor ever will be. And unless
4005 2536 3231 3836 2536 2401 3836 3814 2779 4024 3590 1181 2779 1623 3590
r.asf v.aai.3s d.nsm n.nsm p.g d.gsm adv cj pl pl v.ams.3s cj cj pl

ἐκολόβωσεν κύριος τὰς ἡμέρας, οὐκ ἂν ἐσώθη ˌπᾶσα σάρξ·ˌ
the Lord had cut short *Lord* the number of days, no one would survive; *one*
3261 3143 3261 3836 2465 4024 4246 323 5392 4246 4922
v.aai.3s n.nsm d.apf n.apf pl pl v.api.3s a.nsf n.nsf

[a] τὸ ῥηθὲν ὑπὸ Δανιὴλ τοῦ προφήτου included by TR after ἐρημώσεως.
[b] [δὲ] UBS, omitted by TNIV.

NASB

that hour; for it is not you who speak, but *it is* the Holy Spirit. [12]Brother will betray brother to death, and a father *his* child; and children will rise up against parents and have them put to death. [13]You will be hated by all because of My name, but the one who endures to the end, he will be saved.

[14]"But when you see the ABOMINATION OF DESOLATION standing where it should not be (let the reader understand), then those who are in Judea must flee to the mountains. [15]The one who is on the housetop must not go down, or go in to get anything out of his house; [16]and the one who is in the field must not turn back to get his coat. [17]But woe to those who are pregnant and to those who are nursing babies in those days! [18]But pray that it may not happen in the winter. [19]For those days will be a *time of* tribulation such as has not occurred since the beginning of the creation which God created until now, and never will. [20]Unless the Lord had shortened *those* days, no life would have been saved;

NIV

But for the sake of
the elect, whom he
has chosen, he has
shortened them.
21 At that time if
anyone says to
you, 'Look, here
is the Messiah!'
or, 'Look, there
he is!' do not be-
lieve it. 22 For false
messiahs and false
prophets will ap-
pear and perform
signs and won-
ders to deceive,
if possible, even
the elect. 23 So be
on your guard; I
have told you ev-
erything ahead of
time.
24 "But in those
days, following
that distress,

"'the sun will be
darkened,
and the moon
will not give
its light;
25 the stars will fall
from the sky,
and the
heavenly
bodies will
be shaken.'[a]

26 "At that time
people will see the
Son of Man com-
ing in clouds with
great power and
glory. 27 And he
will send his an-
gels and gather his
elect from the four
winds, from the
ends of the earth
to the ends of the
heavens.
28 "Now learn this
lesson from the fig
tree: As soon as
its twigs get ten-
der and its leaves
come out, you
know that summer
is near. 29 Even so,
when you see these
things happening,
you know that it[b]
is near, right at the
door. 30 Truly I tell
you, this gener-
ation

[a] 25 Isaiah 13:10; 34:4
[b] 29 Or *he*

ἀλλὰ διὰ τοὺς ἐκλεκτοὺς οὓς ἐξελέξατο ἐκολόβωσεν τὰς ἡμέρας. 21 καὶ
but ⌊on account of⌋ the elect, whom he chose, he cut short the days. And
247 1328 3836 1723 4005 1721 3143 3836 2465 2779
cj p.a d.apm a.apm r.apm v.ami.3s v.aai.3s d.apf n.apf cj

τότε ἐάν τις ὑμῖν εἴπῃ· ἴδε ὧδε ὁ χριστός, ἴδε ἐκεῖ,
then if someone should say to you, *should say* 'Look, here is the Christ!' or 'Look, there he
5538 1569 5516 3306 3306 7007 3306 2623 6045 3836 5986 2623 1695
adv cj r.nsm r.dp.2 v.aas.3s pl adv d.nsm n.nsm pl adv

μὴ πιστεύετε· 22 ἐγερθήσονται γὰρ ψευδόχριστοι καὶ ψευδοπροφῆται
is!' — do not believe it. *will arise* For false christs and false prophets
4409 3590 4409 1586 1142 6023 2779 6021
pl v.pam.2p v.fpi.3p cj n.npm cj n.npm

καὶ δώσουσιν σημεῖα καὶ τέρατα πρὸς τὸ ἀποπλανᾶν, εἰ δυνατόν,
will arise and will offer signs and wonders ⌊in order to⌋ *{the}* deceive, if possible,
1586 1586 2779 1443 4956 2779 5469 4639 3836 675 1623 1543
cj v.fai.3p n.apn cj n.apn p.a d.asn f.pa cj a.nsn

τοὺς ἐκλεκτούς. 23 ὑμεῖς δὲ βλέπετε· προείρηκα ὑμῖν πάντα.
the elect. But you, *But* beware; I have told you all this in advance.
3836 1723 1254 7007 1254 1063 4597 7007 4246 4597 4597
d.apm a.apm r.np.2 cj v.pam.2p v.rai.1s r.dp.2 a.apn

24 ἀλλὰ ἐν ἐκείναις ταῖς ἡμέραις μετὰ τὴν θλῖψιν ἐκείνην ὁ ἥλιος
But in those *{the}* days, after *{the}* that tribulation, *that* the sun
247 1877 1697 3836 2465 3552 3836 1697 2568 1697 3836 2463
cj p.d r.dpf d.dpf n.dpf p.a d.asf n.asf r.asf d.nsm n.nsm

σκοτισθήσεται, καὶ ἡ σελήνη οὐ δώσει τὸ φέγγος αὐτῆς, 25 καὶ οἱ
will be darkened, and the moon will not give *{the}* its light, *its* and the
5029 2779 3836 4943 1443 4024 1443 3836 899 5766 899 2779 3836
v.fpi.3s cj d.nsf n.nsf pl v.fai.3s d.asn n.asn r.gsf.3 cj d.npm

ἀστέρες ἔσονται ἐκ τοῦ οὐρανοῦ πίπτοντες, καὶ αἱ δυνάμεις αἱ ἐν τοῖς
stars will be falling from *{the}* heaven, *falling* and the powers *{the}* in the
843 1639 4406 1666 3836 4041 4406 2779 3836 1539 3836 1877 3836
n.npm v.fmi.3p p.g d.gsm n.gsm pt.pa.npm cj d.npf n.npf d.npf p.d d.dpm

οὐρανοῖς σαλευθήσονται. 26 καὶ τότε ὄψονται τὸν υἱὸν τοῦ ἀνθρώπου
heavens will be shaken. And then ⌊they will see⌋ the Son of Man
4041 4888 2779 5538 3972 3836 5626 3836 476
n.dpm v.fpi.3p cj adv v.fmi.3p d.asm n.asm d.gsm n.gsm

ἐρχόμενον ἐν νεφέλαις μετὰ δυνάμεως πολλῆς καὶ δόξης. 27 καὶ τότε
coming in clouds, with great power *great* and glory. And ⌊at that time⌋
2262 1877 3749 3552 4498 1539 4498 2779 1518 2779 5538
pt.pm.asm p.d n.dpf p.g n.gsf a.gsf cj n.gsf cj adv

ἀποστελεῖ τοὺς ἀγγέλους καὶ ἐπισυνάξει τοὺς ἐκλεκτοὺς αὐτοῦ[a] ἐκ τῶν
he will send his angels, and will gather *{the}* his elect *his* from the
690 3836 34 2779 2190 3836 899 1723 899 1666 3836
v.fai.3s d.apm n.apm cj v.fai.3s d.apm a.apm r.gsm.3 p.g d.gpm

τεσσάρων ἀνέμων ἀπ' ἄκρου γῆς ἕως ἄκρου οὐρανοῦ. 28 ἀπὸ δὲ
four winds, from the ends of the earth to the ends of heaven. "Now from *Now*
5475 449 608 216 1178 2401 216 4041 1254 608 1254
a.gpm n.gpm p.g n.gsn n.gsf p.g n.gsn n.gsm p.g cj

τῆς συκῆς μάθετε τὴν παραβολήν· ⌊ὅταν ἤδη⌋ ὁ κλάδος αὐτῆς
the fig tree learn its parable: As soon as *{the}* its bough *its* becomes
3836 5190 3443 3836 4130 4020 2453 3836 899 3080 899 1181
d.gsf n.gsf v.aam.2p d.asf n.asf cj adv d.nsm n.nsm r.gsf.3

ἁπαλὸς γένηται καὶ ἐκφύῃ τὰ φύλλα, γινώσκετε ὅτι ἐγγὺς τὸ θέρος
tender *becomes* and puts out its leaves, you know that summer is near. *{the}* *summer*
559 1181 2779 1770 3836 5877 1182 4022 2550 1639 1584 3836 2550
a.nsm v.ams.3s cj v.pas.3s d.apn n.apn v.pai.2p cj adv d.nsn n.nsn

ἐστίν· 29 οὕτως καὶ ὑμεῖς, ὅταν ἴδητε ταῦτα γινόμενα, γινώσκετε ὅτι
is So also, when you *when* see these things taking place, you know that he
1639 4048 2779 4020 7007 4020 1625 4047 1181 1182 4022 1639
v.pai.3s adv adv r.np.2 cj v.aas.2p r.apn pt.pm.apn v.pam.2p cj

ἐγγύς ἐστιν ἐπὶ θύραις. 30 ἀμὴν λέγω ὑμῖν ὅτι
is near, *he is* at the gates. I tell you the truth, *I tell* *you* ~ this generation
1639 1584 1639 2093 2598 3306 3306 7007 297 3306 7007 4022 4047 1155
adv v.pai.3s p.d n.dpf pl v.pai.1s r.dp.2 cj

[a] [αὐτοῦ] UBS.

NASB

but for the sake of
the elect, whom
He chose, He
shortened the days.
21 And then if any-
one says to you,
'Behold, here is the
Christ'; or, 'Be-
hold, *He is* there';
do not believe *him;*
22 for false Christs
and false prophets
will arise, and will
show signs and
wonders, in order
to lead astray, if
possible, the elect.
23 But take heed;
behold, I have told
you everything in
advance.

The Return of Christ

24 "But in those
days, after that
tribulation, THE SUN
WILL BE DARKENED
AND THE MOON WILL
NOT GIVE ITS LIGHT,
25 AND THE STARS
WILL BE FALLING
from heaven, and
the powers that are
in the heavens will
be shaken. 26 Then
they will see THE
SON OF MAN COM-
ING IN CLOUDS with
great power and
glory. 27 And then
He will send forth
the angels, and will
gather together His
elect from the four
winds, from the
farthest end of the
earth to the farthest
end of heaven.
28 "Now learn the
parable from the
fig tree: when its
branch has already
become tender
and puts forth its
leaves, you know
that summer is
near. 29 Even so, you
too, when you see
these things hap-
pening, recognize
that He is near,
right at the door.
30 Truly I say to you,
this [a]generation

[a] Or *race*

NIV

will certainly not
pass away until all
these things have
happened. 31 Heav-
en and earth will
pass away, but my
words will never
pass away.

The Day and Hour Unknown

32 "But about that
day or hour no
one knows, not
even the angels
in heaven, nor the
Son, but only the
Father. 33 Be on
guard! Be alert[a]!
You do not know
when that time
will come. 34 It's
like a man going
away: He leaves
his house and puts
his servants in
charge, each with
their assigned
task, and tells the
one at the door to
keep watch.
35 "Therefore keep
watch because you
do not know when
the owner of the
house will come
back—whether in
the evening, or at
midnight, or when
the rooster crows,
or at dawn. 36 If
he comes sudden-
ly, do not let him
find you sleeping.
37 What I say to
you, I say to every-
one: 'Watch!'"

Jesus Anointed at Bethany

14 Now the
Passover
and the Festival of
Unleavened Bread
were only two
days away, and the
chief priests and
the teachers of the
law were scheming
to arrest Jesus se-
cretly and kill him.
2 "But not during
the festival," they
said, "or the peo-
ple may riot."

[a] 33 Some manuscripts *alert and pray*

↱ ⌊οὐ μὴ⌋ παρέλθῃ ἡ γενεὰ αὕτη ⌊μέχρις οὗ⌋ ταῦτα πάντα
will not pass away *{the} generation this* until all these things *all*
4216 4024 3590 4216 3836 1155 4047 3588 4005 4246 4047 4246
pl pl v.aas.3s d.nsf n.nsf r.nsf p.g r.gsm r.npn a.npn

γένηται. 31 ὁ οὐρανὸς καὶ ἡ γῆ παρελεύσονται, οἱ δὲ λόγοι
⌊begin to take place.⌋ *{the}* Heaven and *{the}* earth will pass away, *{the}* but my words
1181 3836 4041 2779 3836 1178 4216 3836 1254 1609 3364
v.ams.3s d.nsm n.nsm cj d.nsf n.nsf v.fmi.3p d.npm cj n.npm

μου ↱ ⌊οὐ μὴ⌋ παρελεύσονται. 32 περὶ δὲ τῆς ἡμέρας ἐκείνης ἢ τῆς
my will never pass away. "But of *But {the}* that day *that* or *{the}*
1609 4216 4024 3590 4216 1254 4309 1254 3836 1697 2465 1697 2445 3836
r.gs.1 pl pl v.fmi.3p p.g cj d.gsf n.gsf r.gsf cj d.gsf

ὥρας οὐδεὶς οἶδεν, οὐδὲ οἱ ἄγγελοι ἐν οὐρανῷ οὐδὲ ὁ υἱός, ⌊εἰ μὴ⌋ ὁ
hour no one knows, neither the angels in heaven, nor the Son, but only the
6052 4029 3857 4028 3836 34 1877 4041 4028 3836 5626 1623 3590 3836
n.gsf a.nsm v.rai.3s adv d.npm n.npm p.d n.dsm cj d.nsm n.nsm cj pl d.nsm

πατήρ. 33 βλέπετε, ἀγρυπνεῖτε·[a] ↱ ↱ οὐκ οἴδατε γὰρ πότε ὁ καιρός
Father. Watch out, be alert, for you do not know *for* when the time
4252 1063 70 1142 3857 3857 4024 3857 1142 4537 3836 2789
n.nsm v.pam.2p v.pam.2p pl v.rai.2p cj cj d.nsm n.nsm

ἐστιν. 34 ὡς ἄνθρωπος ἀπόδημος ἀφεὶς τὴν οἰκίαν αὐτοῦ καὶ
will come. It is like a man ⌊going on a journey.⌋ He left *{the}* his home *his* and
1639 6055 476 624 918 3836 899 3864 899 2779
v.pai.3s cj n.nsm a.nsm pt.aa.nsm d.asf n.asf r.gsm.3 cj

δοὺς τοῖς δούλοις αὐτοῦ τὴν ἐξουσίαν ἑκάστῳ τὸ ἔργον αὐτοῦ
gave authority to his servants, *his {the} authority* to each one *{the}* his work, *his*
1443 2026 3836 899 1529 899 3836 2026 1667 3836 899 2240 899
pt.aa.nsm d.dpm n.dpm r.gsm.3 d.asf n.asf r.dsm d.asn n.asn r.gsm.3

καὶ τῷ θυρωρῷ ἐνετείλατο ἵνα γρηγορῇ. 35 γρηγορεῖτε οὖν·
and he ordered the doorkeeper *he ordered* to stay alert. So stay alert *So* — for
2779 1948 1948 3836 2601 1948 2671 1213 4036 1213 4036 1142
cj d.dsm n.dsm v.ami.3s cj v.pas.3s v.pam.2p cj

↱ ↱ οὐκ οἴδατε γὰρ πότε ὁ κύριος τῆς οἰκίας ἔρχεται, ἢ ὀψὲ
you do not know *for* when the master of the house will return, whether ⌊in the evening,⌋
3857 3857 4024 3857 1142 4537 3836 3261 3836 3864 2262 2445 4067
pl v.rai.2p cj cj d.nsm n.nsm d.gsf n.gsf v.pmi.3s cj adv

ἢ μεσονύκτιον ἢ ἀλεκτοροφωνίας ἢ πρωΐ, 36 μὴ ἐλθὼν ἐξαίφνης
or at midnight, or at cock crowing, or ⌊toward daybreak⌋ — lest coming suddenly
2445 3543 2445 231 2445 4745 3590 2262 1978
cj n.asn cj n.gsf cj adv cj pt.aa.nsm adv

εὕρῃ ὑμᾶς καθεύδοντας. 37 ὃ δὲ ὑμῖν λέγω πᾶσιν
⌊he should find⌋ you sleeping. And what *And* I say to you, *I say* I say to all:
2351 7007 2761 1254 4005 1254 3306 3306 7007 3306 3306 3306 4246
v.aas.3s r.ap.2 pt.pa.apm r.asn cj r.dp.2 v.pai.1s a.dpm

λέγω, γρηγορεῖτε.
I say Stay alert!"
3306 1213
v.pai.1s v.pam.2p

14:1 ἦν δὲ τὸ πάσχα καὶ τὰ ἄζυμα
⌊It was⌋ now two days before the Passover and *{the}* ⌊Festival of Unleavened Bread.⌋
1639 1254 1545 2465 3552 3836 4247 2779 3836 109
v.iai.3s cj d.nsn n.nsn cj d.npn n.npn

μετὰ δύο ἡμέρας. καὶ ἐζήτουν οἱ ἀρχιερεῖς καὶ οἱ γραμματεῖς
before two days And *were seeking* the ruling priests and the scribes were seeking
3552 1545 2465 2779 2426 3836 797 2779 3836 1208 2426 2426
p.a a.apf n.apf cj v.iai.3p d.npm n.npm cj d.npm n.npm

πῶς αὐτὸν ἐν δόλῳ κρατήσαντες ἀποκτείνωσιν· 2
how to seize him by treachery *to seize* and put him to death, but
4802 3195 3195 899 1877 1515 3195 650 1142
cj r.asm.3 p.d n.dsm pt.aa.npm v.pas.3p

ἔλεγον γάρ· μὴ ἐν τῇ ἑορτῇ, μήποτε ἔσται θόρυβος τοῦ
⌊they were saying,⌋ *but* "Not during the festival, lest there be an uproar ⌊among the⌋
3306 1142 3590 1877 3836 2038 3607 1639 2573 3836
v.iai.3p cj pl p.d d.dsf n.dsf cj v.fmi.3s n.nsm d.gsm

[a] καὶ προσεύχεσθε included by TR after ἀγρυπνεῖτε.

NASB

will not pass away
until all these
things take place.
31 Heaven and earth
will pass away, but
My words will not
pass away. 32 But
of that day or hour
no one knows, not
even the angels
in heaven, nor the
Son, but the Father
alone.
33 "Take heed,
keep on the alert;
for you do not
know when the *ap-*
pointed time will
come. 34 *It is* like
a man away on a
journey, *who* upon
leaving his house
and putting his
slaves in charge,
assigning to each
one his task, also
commanded the
doorkeeper to
stay on the alert.
35 Therefore, be on
the alert—for you
do not know when
the master of the
house is coming,
whether in the eve-
ning, at midnight,
or when the rooster
crows, or in the
morning— 36 in case
he should come
suddenly and find
you asleep. 37 What
I say to you I say
to all, 'Be on the
alert!'"

Death Plot and Anointing

14:1 Now the
Passover and Un-
leavened Bread
were two days
away; and the chief
priests and the
scribes were seek-
ing how to seize
Him by stealth and
kill *Him;* 2 for they
were saying, "Not
during the festival,
otherwise there
might be a riot of
the people."

NIV

[3]While he was in
Bethany, reclining
at the table in the
home of Simon
the Leper, a wom-
an came with an
alabaster jar of
very expensive
perfume, made
of pure nard. She
broke the jar and
poured the per-
fume on his head.
[4]Some of those
present were say-
ing indignantly to
one another, "Why
this waste of per-
fume? [5]It could
have been sold
for more than a
year's wages[a] and
the money given
to the poor." And
they rebuked her
harshly.
[6]"Leave her
alone," said Jesus.
"Why are you
bothering her?
She has done a
beautiful thing to
me. [7]The poor you
will always have
with you,[b] and you
can help them any
time you want.
But you will not
always have me.
[8]She did what she
could. She poured
perfume on my
body beforehand
to prepare for my
burial. [9]Truly I tell
you, wherever the
gospel is preached
throughout the
world, what she
has done will also
be told, in memory
of her."
[10]Then Judas Is-
cariot, one of the
Twelve, went to

[a] 5 Greek *than three hundred denarii*
[b] 7 See Deut. 15:11.

λαοῦ. 3 καὶ → ὄντος αὐτοῦ ἐν Βηθανίᾳ ἐν τῇ οἰκίᾳ Σίμωνος τοῦ
people." And while he was *he* in Bethany in the house of Simon the
3295 2779 899 1639 899 1877 1029 1877 3836 3864 4981 3836
n.gsm cj pt.pa.gsm r.gsm.3 p.d n.dsf p.d d.dsf n.dsf n.gsm d.gsm

λεπροῦ, → κατακειμένου αὐτοῦ ἦλθεν γυνὴ ἔχουσα ἀλάβαστρον →
leper, as he reclined at table, *he* there came a woman with an alabaster flask of very
3320 899 2879 899 2262 1222 2400 223 4500
a.gsm pt.pm.gsm r.gsm.3 v.aai.3s n.nsf pt.pa.nsf n.asf

μύρου → νάρδου πιστικῆς πολυτελοῦς, συντρίψασα τὴν ἀλάβαστρον
costly anointment of pure nard; *pure* *very costly* and breaking the flask,
4500 3693 4410 3726 4410 4500 5341 3836 223
n.gsn n.gsf a.gsf n.gsf pt.aa.nsf d.asf n.asf

κατέχεεν ← αὐτοῦ τῆς κεφαλῆς. 4 ἦσαν δέ τινες ἀγανακτοῦντες
she poured it over his *{the}* head. But some were *But* *some* indignant, and
2972 899 3836 3051 1254 5516 1639 1254 5516 24
v.aai.3s r.gsm.3 d.gsf n.gsf v.iai.3p cj r.npm pt.pa.npm

πρὸς ἑαυτούς· εἰς τί ἡ ἀπώλεια αὕτη τοῦ μύρου
began saying to themselves, "For ⌞what purpose⌟ was *{the}* this waste *this* of ointment?
4639 1571 1650 5515 1181 3836 4047 724 4047 3836 3693
p.a r.apm.3 p.a r.asn d.nsf n.nsf r.nsf d.gsn n.gsn

γέγονεν; 5 ἠδύνατο γὰρ τοῦτο τὸ μύρον πραθῆναι ἐπάνω
was For this ointment could *For* *this* *{the}* *ointment* have been sold ⌞for more than⌟
1181 1142 4047 3693 1538 1142 4047 3836 3693 4405 2062
v.rai.3s v.ipi.3s cj r.nsn d.nsn n.nsn f.ap p.g

δηναρίων τριακοσίων καὶ δοθῆναι τοῖς πτωχοῖς· καὶ ἐνεβριμῶντο αὐτῇ.
three hundred denarii *three hundred* and given to the poor." And they rebuked her
5559 5559 1324 5559 2779 1443 3836 4777 2779 1839 899
n.gpn a.gpn cj f.ap d.dpm a.dpm cj v.imi.3p r.dsf.3

↰ 6 ὁ δὲ Ἰησοῦς εἶπεν· ἄφετε αὐτήν· ↰ τί αὐτῇ κόπους
harshly. *{the}* But Jesus said, "Leave her alone. Why are you causing her trouble?
1839 3836 1254 2652 3306 918 899 918 5515 4218 4218 4218 899 3160
d.nsm cj n.nsm v.aai.3s v.aam.2p r.asf.3 r.asn r.dsf.3 n.apm

παρέχετε; καλὸν ἔργον ἠργάσατο ἐν ἐμοί. 7 πάντοτε
are you causing She has done a beautiful thing *She has done* to me. For you will always
4218 2237 2237 2237 2819 2240 2237 1877 1609 1142 2400 2400 4121
v.pai.2p a.asn n.asn v.ami.3s p.d r.ds.1 adv

γὰρ τοὺς πτωχοὺς ἔχετε μεθ' ἑαυτῶν καὶ ὅταν θέλητε δύνασθε
For have the poor *you will have* with you, and whenever you want you can do
1142 2400 3836 4777 2400 3552 1571 2779 4020 2527 1538 4472
cj d.apm a.apm v.pai.2p p.g r.gpm.2 cj cj v.pas.2p v.ppi.2p

αὐτοῖς εὖ ποιῆσαι, ἐμὲ δὲ οὐ πάντοτε
something good for them, *good* *do* but you will not always have me. *but* *not* *always*
2292 899 2292 4472 1254 2400 2400 4024 4121 2400 1609 1254 4024 4121
r.dpm.3 adv f.aa r.as.1 cj pl adv

ἔχετε. 8 ὃ ἔσχεν ἐποίησεν· ⌞προέλαβεν μυρίσαι⌟ τὸ
you will have She has done what she could; *She has done* she has anointed *{the}* my
2400 4472 4472 4472 4005 2400 4472 4624 3690 3836 1609
v.pai.2p r.asn v.aai.3s v.aai.3s v.aai.3s f.aa d.asn

σῶμά μου ↰ εἰς τὸν ἐνταφιασμόν. 9 ἀμὴν δὲ λέγω ὑμῖν,
body *my* beforehand for *{the}* burial. I tell you the truth, *{and}* *I tell* *you*
5393 1609 4624 1650 3836 1947 3306 3306 7007 297 1254 3306 7007
n.asn r.gs.1 p.a d.asm n.asm pl cj v.pai.1s r.dp.2

⌞ὅπου ἐὰν⌟ κηρυχθῇ τὸ εὐαγγέλιον εἰς ὅλον τὸν κόσμον,
wherever the gospel is preached *the* *gospel* in the whole *the* world, what
3963 1569 3836 2295 3062 3836 2295 1650 3836 3910 3836 3180 4005
cj pl v.aps.3s d.nsn n.nsn p.a a.asm d.asm n.asm

↱ καὶ ὃ ἐποίησεν αὕτη λαληθήσεται εἰς μνημόσυνον
this woman has done will also *what has done* *this woman* be told in memory
4047 4047 4472 4472 3281 2779 4005 4472 4047 3281 1650 3649
adv r.asn v.aai.3s r.nsf v.fpi.3s p.a n.asn

αὐτῆς. 10 καὶ Ἰούδας Ἰσκαριὼθ ὁ εἷς τῶν δώδεκα ἀπῆλθεν πρὸς τοὺς
of her." Then Judas Iscariot, *{the}* one of the Twelve, went to the
899 2779 2683 2696 3836 1651 3836 1557 599 4639 3836
r.gsf.3 cj n.nsm n.nsm d.nsm a.nsm d.gpm a.gpm v.aai.3s p.a d.apm

NASB

[3]While He was
in Bethany at the
home of Simon the
leper, and reclining
at the table, there
came a woman
with an alabaster
vial of very costly
perfume of pure
nard; *and* she
broke the vial and
poured it over His
head. [4]But some
were indignantly
remarking to one
another, "Why has
this perfume been
wasted? [5]For this
perfume might
have been sold for
over three hundred
[a]denarii, and *the*
money given to the
poor." And they
were scolding her.
[6]But Jesus said,
"Let her alone;
why do you bother
her? She has done
a good deed to Me.
[7]For you always
have the poor with
you, and whenever
you wish you can
do good to them;
but you do not
always have Me.
[8]She has done what
she could; she has
anointed My body
beforehand for
the burial. [9]Truly I
say to you, wher-
ever the gospel
is preached in
the whole world,
what this woman
has done will also
be spoken of in
memory of her."
[10]Then Judas
Iscariot, who was
one of the twelve,
went off to the

[a] The denarius was equivalent to a day's wages

NIV

the chief priests
to betray Jesus to
them. 11 They were
delighted to hear
this and promised
to give him money.
So he watched for
an opportunity to
hand him over.

The Last Supper

12 On the first
day of the Festi-
val of Unleavened
Bread, when it was
customary to sac-
rifice the Passover
lamb, Jesus' dis-
ciples asked him,
"Where do you
want us to go and
make preparations
for you to eat the
Passover?"
13 So he sent two
of his disciples,
telling them, "Go
into the city, and a
man carrying a jar
of water will meet
you. Follow him.
14 Say to the owner
of the house he en-
ters, 'The Teacher
asks: Where is my
guest room, where
I may eat the Pass-
over with my dis-
ciples?' 15 He will
show you a large
room upstairs, fur-
nished and ready.
Make preparations
for us there."
16 The disciples
left, went into the
city and found
things just as Jesus
had told them. So
they prepared the
Passover.
17 When eve-
ning came, Jesus
arrived with the
Twelve. 18 While
they were reclin-
ing at the table
eating, he said,
"Truly I tell you,

ἀρχιερεῖς ἵνα ↱ ↱ ↱ αὐτὸν παραδοῖ αὐτοῖς. 11 ↱ οἱ δὲ
ruling priests so he might hand Jesus over to them. And when they *And*
797 2671 4140 4140 4140 899 4140 899 1254 201 3836 1254
n.apm cj r.asm.3 v.aas.3s r.dpm.3 d.npm cj

ἀκούσαντες ἐχάρησαν καὶ ἐπηγγείλαντο αὐτῷ ἀργύριον δοῦναι. καὶ
heard it, they were pleased and promised to give him money. *to give* So
201 5897 2779 2040 1443 1443 899 736 1443 2779
pt.aa.npm v.api.3p cj v.ami.3p r.dsm.3 n.asn f.aa cj

ἐζήτει πῶς αὐτὸν εὐκαίρως παραδοῖ.
Judas was seeking how he might hand him over ⌊at a convenient moment.⌋ *he might hand over*
2426 4802 4140 4140 4140 899 4140 2323 4140
v.iai.3s cj r.asm.3 adv v.aas.3s

12 καὶ τῇ πρώτῃ ἡμέρᾳ τῶν ἀζύμων, ὅτε τὸ
And ⌊on the⌋ first day of ⌊Unleavened Bread,⌋ when people were slaughtering the
2779 3836 4755 2465 3836 109 4021 2604 2604 3836
cj d.dsf a.dsf n.dsf d.gpn n.gpn cj d.asn

πάσχα ἔθυον, λέγουσιν αὐτῷ οἱ μαθηταὶ αὐτοῦ· ποῦ
⌊Passover lamb,⌋ *were slaughtering* his disciples said to him, *{the}* *disciples* *his* "Where
4247 2604 899 3412 3306 899 3836 3412 899 4543
n.asn v.iai.3p v.pai.3p r.dsm.3 d.npm n.npm r.gsm.3 cj

θέλεις ↱ ἀπελθόντες ἑτοιμάσωμεν ἵνα φάγῃς τὸ πάσχα; 13 καὶ
⌊do you want⌋ us to go and prepare for you to eat the Passover?" And
2527 2286 599 2286 2671 2266 3836 4247 2779
v.pai.2s pt.aa.npm v.aas.1p cj v.aas.2s d.asn n.asn cj

ἀποστέλλει δύο τῶν μαθητῶν αὐτοῦ καὶ λέγει αὐτοῖς· ὑπάγετε εἰς τὴν πόλιν,
he sent two of his disciples *his* and said to them, "Go into the city
690 1545 3836 899 3412 899 2779 3306 899 5632 1650 3836 4484
v.pai.3s a.apm d.gpm n.gpm r.gsm.3 cj v.pai.3s r.dpm.3 v.pam.2p p.a d.asf n.asf

καὶ ἀπαντήσει ὑμῖν ἄνθρωπος κεράμιον ὕδατος
and a man carrying a pitcher of water will meet you; *man* *pitcher* *of water*
2779 476 1002 3040 5623 5623 560 7007 476 3040 5623
cj v.fai.3s r.dp.2 n.nsm n.asn n.gsn

βαστάζων· ἀκολουθήσατε αὐτῷ 14 καὶ ⌊ὅπου ἐὰν⌋ εἰσέλθῃ εἴπατε τῷ
carrying follow him. And wherever he enters, say ⌊to the⌋
1002 199 899 2779 3963 1569 1656 3306 3836
pt.pa.nsm v.aam.2p r.dsm.3 cj cj pl v.aas.3s v.aam.2p d.dsm

οἰκοδεσπότῃ ὅτι ὁ διδάσκαλος λέγει· ποῦ ἐστιν τὸ κατάλυμά μου
owner of the house, ~ 'The Teacher says, "Where is *{the}* my guest room, *my*
3867 4022 3836 1437 3306 4543 1639 3836 1609 2906 1609
n.dsm cj d.nsm n.nsm v.pai.3s cj v.pai.3s d.nsn n.nsn r.gs.1

ὅπου τὸ πάσχα μετὰ τῶν μαθητῶν μου φάγω; 15 καὶ αὐτὸς
where I may eat the Passover with *{the}* my disciples?"' *my* *I may eat* And he
3963 2266 2266 2266 3836 4247 3552 3836 1609 3412 1609 2266 2779 899
cj d.asn n.asn p.g d.gpm n.gpm r.gs.1 v.aas.1s cj r.nsm

ὑμῖν δείξει ἀνάγαιον μέγα ἐστρωμένον ἕτοιμον· καὶ ἐκεῖ
will show you *will show* a large upper room, *large* furnished and ready; *{and}* there
1259 1259 7007 1259 3489 333 3489 5143 2289 2779 1695
r.dp.2 v.fai.3s n.asn a.asn pt.rp.asn a.asn cj adv

ἑτοιμάσατε ἡμῖν. 16 καὶ ἐξῆλθον οἱ μαθηταὶ καὶ ἦλθον εἰς τὴν
prepare for us." *{and}* The disciples left, *The* *disciples* *{and}* came to the
2286 7005 2779 3836 3412 2002 3836 3412 2779 2262 1650 3836
v.aam.2p r.dp.1 cj v.aai.3p d.npm n.npm cj v.aai.3p p.a d.asf

πόλιν καὶ εὗρον καθὼς εἶπεν αὐτοῖς καὶ ἡτοίμασαν τὸ πάσχα. 17 καὶ
city, and found things just as ⌊he had told⌋ them. So they prepared the Passover. And
4484 2779 2351 2777 3306 899 2779 2286 3836 4247 2779
n.asf cj v.aai.3p cj v.aai.3s r.dpm.3 cj v.aai.3p d.asn n.asn cj

ὀψίας γενομένης ἔρχεται μετὰ τῶν δώδεκα. 18 καὶ →
when it was evening, *when it was* he came with the twelve. And while they
1181 1181 1181 4068 1181 2262 3552 3836 1557 2779 899
n.gsf pt.am.gsf v.pmi.3s p.g d.gpm a.gpm cj

ἀνακειμένων αὐτῶν καὶ ἐσθιόντων ὁ Ἰησοῦς εἶπεν· ἀμὴν
⌊were reclining at table⌋ *they* and eating, *{the}* Jesus said, "I tell you the truth,
367 899 2779 2266 3836 2652 3306 3306 3306 7007 297
pt.pm.gpm r.gpm.3 cj pt.pa.gpm d.nsm n.nsm v.aai.3s pl

NASB

chief priests in or-
der to betray Him
to them. 11 They
were glad when
they heard *this,* and
promised to give
him money. And he
began seeking how
to betray Him at an
opportune time.

The Last Passover

12 On the first day
of Unleavened
Bread, when the
Passover *lamb* was
being sacrificed,
His disciples *said
to Him, "Where
do You want us
to go and prepare
for You to eat the
Passover?" 13 And
He *sent two of His
disciples and *said
to them, "Go into
the city, and a man
will meet you car-
rying a pitcher of
water; follow him;
14 and wherever he
enters, say to the
owner of the house,
'The Teacher
says, "Where is
My guest room in
which I may eat
the Passover with
My disciples?"'
15 And he himself
will show you a
large upper room
furnished *and*
ready; prepare for
us there." 16 The dis-
ciples went out and
came to the city,
and found *it* just as
He had told them;
and they prepared
the Passover.
17 When it was
evening He *came
with the twelve.
18 As they were re-
clining *at the table*
and eating, Jesus
said, "Truly I say
to you that

NIV

one of you will be-
tray me—one who
is eating with me."
19They were sad-
dened, and one by
one they said to
him, "Surely you
don't mean me?"
20"It is one of
the Twelve," he
replied, "one who
dips bread into
the bowl with me.
21The Son of Man
will go just as it is
written about him.
But woe to that
man who betrays
the Son of Man! It
would be better for
him if he had not
been born."
22While they
were eating, Jesus
took bread, and
when he had given
thanks, he broke it
and gave it to his
disciples, saying,
"Take it; this is my
body."
23Then he took a
cup, and when he
had given thanks,
he gave it to them,
and they all drank
from it.
24"This is my
blood of the[a] cov-
enant, which is
poured out for
many," he said
to them. 25"Truly
I tell you, I will
not drink again
from the fruit of
the vine until that
day when I drink
it new in the king-
dom of God."
26When they had
sung a hymn, they
went out to the
Mount of Olives.

Jesus Predicts Peter's Denial

27"You will all
fall away," Jesus
told them, "for it is
written:

"'I will strike
the
shepherd,
and the sheep
will be
scattered.'[b]

[a] 24 Some manuscripts *the new*
[b] 27 Zech. 13:7

λέγω ὑμῖν ὅτι εἷς ἐξ ὑμῶν παραδώσει με ὁ ἐσθίων μετ᾽ ἐμοῦ.
I tell *you* ~ one of you will betray me, one who is eating with me."
3306 7007 4022 1651 1666 7007 4140 1609 3836 2266 3552 1609
v.pai.1s r.dp.2 cj a.nsm p.g r.gp.2 v.fai.3s r.as.1 d.nsm pt.pa.nsm p.g r.gs.1

19 ἤρξαντο λυπεῖσθαι καὶ λέγειν αὐτῷ εἷς κατὰ εἷς· μήτι ἐγώ; 20 ὁ
They began to be grieved and to say to him one after the other, ⌞"Surely not⌟ I?" He
806 3382 2779 3306 899 1651 2848 1651 3614 1609 3836
v.ami.3p f.pp cj f.pa r.dsm.3 a.nsm p.a a.nsm pl r.ns.1 d.nsm

δὲ εἶπεν αὐτοῖς· εἷς τῶν δώδεκα, ὁ ἐμβαπτόμενος
{and} said to them, "It is one of the twelve, one ⌞who is dipping his bread⌟ into the bowl
1254 3306 899 1651 3836 1557 3836 1835 1650 3836 5581
cj v.aai.3s r.dpm.3 a.nsm d.gpm a.gpm d.nsm pt.pm.nsm

μετ᾽ ἐμοῦ εἰς τὸ τρύβλιον. 21 ὅτι ὁ μὲν υἱὸς τοῦ ἀνθρώπου ὑπάγει καθὼς
with me. *into the bowl* For the ~ Son of Man is going as
3552 1609 1650 3836 5581 4022 3836 3525 5626 3836 476 5632 2777
p.g r.gs.1 p.a d.asn n.asn cj d.nsm pl n.nsm d.gsm n.gsm v.pai.3s cj

γέγραπται περὶ αὐτοῦ, οὐαὶ δὲ τῷ ἀνθρώπῳ ἐκείνῳ δι᾽ οὗ ὁ υἱὸς
it is written of him; but woe *but* to that man *that* by whom the Son
1211 4309 899 1254 4026 1254 3836 1697 476 1697 1328 4005 3836 5626
v.rpi.3s p.g r.gsm.3 j cj d.dsm n.dsm r.dsm p.g r.gsm d.nsm n.nsm

τοῦ ἀνθρώπου παραδίδοται· καλὸν αὐτῷ εἰ ↱ οὐκ ἐγεννήθη ὁ
of Man is betrayed — better for him if that man had not been born." *{the}*
3836 476 4140 2819 899 1623 1697 476 1164 4024 1164 3836
d.gsm n.gsm v.ppi.3s a.nsn r.dsm.3 cj pl v.api.3s d.nsm

ἄνθρωπος ἐκεῖνος. 22 καὶ → ἐσθιόντων αὐτῶν λαβὼν ἄρτον
man *that* And while they were eating, *they* he took bread, and
476 1697 2779 899 2266 899 3284 788
n.nsm r.nsm cj pt.pa.gpm r.gpm.3 pt.aa.nsm n.asm

εὐλογήσας ἔκλασεν καὶ ἔδωκεν αὐτοῖς καὶ εἶπεν· λάβετε, τοῦτό ἐστιν τὸ
after giving thanks he broke it and gave it to them and said, "Take; this is *{the}*
2328 3089 2779 1443 899 2779 3306 3284 4047 1639 3836
pt.aa.nsm v.aai.3s cj v.aai.3s r.dpm.3 cj v.aai.3s v.aam.2p r.nsn v.pai.3s d.nsn

σῶμά μου. 23 καὶ λαβὼν ποτήριον εὐχαριστήσας ἔδωκεν
my body." *my* And ⌞when he had taken⌟ the cup and given thanks, he passed it
1609 5393 1609 2779 3284 4539 2373 1443
n.nsn r.gs.1 cj pt.aa.nsm n.asn pt.aa.nsm v.aai.3s

αὐτοῖς, καὶ → ἔπιον ἐξ αὐτοῦ πάντες. 24 καὶ εἶπεν αὐτοῖς· τοῦτό ἐστιν τὸ
to them, and they all drank from it. *all* And he said to them, "This is *{the}*
899 2779 4246 4403 1666 899 4246 2779 3306 899 4047 1639 3836
r.dpm.3 cj v.aai.3p p.g r.gsn.3 a.npm cj v.aai.3s r.dpm.3 r.nsn v.pai.3s d.nsn

αἷμά μου τῆς διαθήκης τὸ ἐκχυννόμενον ὑπὲρ πολλῶν. 25
my blood *my* of the covenant, which is poured out ⌞in behalf of⌟ many. I tell you
1609 135 1609 3836 1347 3836 1773 5642 4498 3306 3306 7007
n.nsn r.gs.1 d.gsf n.gsf d.nsn pt.pp.nsn p.g a.gpm

ἀμὴν λέγω ὑμῖν ὅτι ↱ ↱ ⌞οὐκέτι οὐ μὴ⌟ πίω ἐκ τοῦ γενήματος τῆς
the truth, *I tell* *you* ~ I will not again drink from the fruit of the
297 3306 7007 4022 4403 4403 4033 4024 3590 4403 1666 3836 1163 3836
pl v.pai.1s r.dp.2 cj adv pl pl v.aas.1s p.g d.gsn n.gsn d.gsf

ἀμπέλου ἕως τῆς ἡμέρας ἐκείνης ὅταν αὐτὸ πίνω καινὸν ἐν τῇ
vine until *{the}* that day *that* when I drink it *I drink* new in the
306 2401 3836 1697 2465 1697 4020 4403 4403 899 4403 2785 1877 3836
n.gsf p.g d.gsf n.gsf r.gsf cj r.asn.3 v.pas.1s a.asn p.d d.dsf

βασιλείᾳ τοῦ θεοῦ. 26 καὶ ὑμνήσαντες ἐξῆλθον εἰς τὸ ὄρος τῶν
kingdom of God." Then ⌞after singing a hymn,⌟ ⌞they went out⌟ to the Mount of
993 3836 2536 2779 5630 2002 1650 3836 4001 3836
n.dsf d.gsm n.gsm cj pt.aa.npm v.aai.3p p.a d.asn n.asn d.gpf

ἐλαιῶν. 27 καὶ λέγει αὐτοῖς ὁ Ἰησοῦς ὅτι πάντες σκανδαλισθήσεσθε,
Olives. And Jesus said to them, *{the}* *Jesus* ~ "All of you will fall away,
1777 2779 2652 3306 899 3836 2652 4022 4246 4997
n.gpf cj v.pai.3s r.dpm.3 d.nsm n.nsm cj a.npm v.fpi.2p

ὅτι γέγραπται· πατάξω τὸν ποιμένα, καὶ τὰ πρόβατα διασκορπισθήσονται.
because it is written, 'I will strike the shepherd, and the sheep will be scattered.'
4022 1211 4250 3836 4478 2779 3836 4585 1399
cj v.rpi.3s v.fai.1s d.asm n.asm cj d.npn n.npn v.fpi.3p

NASB

one of you will
betray Me—one
who is eating with
Me." 19They began
to be grieved and
to say to Him one
by one, "Surely not
I?" 20And He said
to them, "*It is* one
of the twelve, one
who dips with Me
in the bowl. 21For
the Son of Man *is*
to go just as it is
written of Him; but
woe to that man by
whom the Son of
Man is betrayed!
It would have been
good for that man
if he had not been
born."

The Lord's Supper

22While they were
eating, He took
some bread, and
after a blessing He
broke *it,* and gave
it to them, and said,
"Take *it;* this is My
body." 23And when
He had taken a cup
and given thanks,
He gave *it* to them,
and they all drank
from it. 24And He
said to them, "This
is My blood of the
covenant, which
is poured out for
many. 25Truly I say
to you, I will never
again drink of the
fruit of the vine un-
til that day when I
drink it new in the
kingdom of God."
26After singing a
hymn, they went
out to the Mount of
Olives.
27And Jesus *said
to them, "You will
all fall away, be-
cause it is written,
'I WILL STRIKE DOWN
THE SHEPHERD, AND
THE SHEEP SHALL BE
SCATTERED.'

NIV

28But after I have
risen, I will go
ahead of you into
Galilee."
29Peter declared,
"Even if all fall
away, I will not."
30"Truly I tell
you," Jesus answered,
"today—yes, tonight—before
the rooster crows twice[a] you
yourself will disown
me three times."
31But Peter insisted
emphatically, "Even if I have to
die with you, I will
never disown you."
And all the others
said the same.

Gethsemane

32They went to
a place called
Gethsemane, and
Jesus said to his
disciples, "Sit here
while I pray." 33He
took Peter, James
and John along
with him, and he
began to be deeply
distressed and
troubled. 34"My
soul is overwhelmed
with sorrow to the point of
death," he said to
them. "Stay here
and keep watch."
35Going a little
farther, he fell to
the ground and
prayed that if
possible the hour
might pass from
him. 36"*Abba*,[b]
Father," he said,
"everything is possible
for you. Take
this cup from me.
Yet not what I will,
but what you will."
37Then he returned
to his disciples
and found
them sleeping.

[a] 30 Some early manuscripts do not have *twice*.
[b] 36 Aramaic for *father*

28 ἀλλὰ μετὰ τὸ ἐγερθῆναί με προάξω ὑμᾶς εἰς τὴν Γαλιλαίαν.
But after *{the}* I am raised up, *I* ⌊I will go on ahead of⌋ you into *{the}* Galilee."
247 3552 3836 1609 1586 1609 4575 7007 1650 3836 1133
cj p.a d.asn f.ap r.as.1 v.fai.1s r.ap.2 p.a d.asf n.asf

29 ὁ δὲ Πέτρος ἔφη αὐτῷ· εἰ καὶ ↱ πάντες σκανδαλισθήσονται, ἀλλ'
{the} *{and}* Peter said to him, "Even though *Even* they all fall away, *{yet}*
3836 1254 4377 5774 899 2779 1623 2779 4997 4246 4997 247
d.nsm cj n.nsm v.iai.3s r.dsm.3 cj adv a.npm v.fpi.3p cj

οὐκ ἐγώ. 30 καὶ λέγει αὐτῷ ὁ Ἰησοῦς· ἀμὴν λέγω
I will not! *I* And Jesus said to him, *{the}* *Jesus* I tell you the truth, *I tell*
1609 4024 1609 2779 2652 3306 899 3836 2652 3306 3306 5148 297 3306
pl r.ns.1 cj v.pai.3s r.dsm.3 d.nsm n.nsm pl v.pai.1s

σοι ὅτι σὺ σήμερον ταύτῃ τῇ νυκτὶ ⌊πρὶν ἢ⌋ δὶς ἀλέκτορα
you ~ *you* today — this very night, before the rooster crows twice *rooster*
5148 4022 5148 4958 4047 3836 3816 4570 2445 232 5888 1489 232
r.ds.2 cj r.ns.2 adv r.dsf d.dsf n.dsf cj pl adv n.asm

φωνῆσαι τρίς με ἀπαρνήσῃ. 31 ὁ δὲ
crows — you will deny me ⌊three times.⌋ *me* *you will deny* But Peter *But* exclaimed
5888 5148 565 565 1609 5565 1609 565 1254 3836 1254 3281
f.aa adv r.as.1 v.fmi.2s d.nsm cj

ἐκπερισσῶς ἐλάλει· ἐὰν δέῃ με συναποθανεῖν σοι, ⌊οὐ μή⌋
vehemently, *exclaimed* ⌊"Even if⌋ I must *I* die with you, I will never deny
1735 3281 1569 1609 1256 1609 5271 5148 565 565 4024 3590 565
adv v.iai.3s cj v.pas.3s r.as.1 f.aa r.ds.2 pl pl

σε ἀπαρνήσομαι. ὡσαύτως δὲ καὶ πάντες ἔλεγον.
you!" *I will deny* And all the others repeated the same thing. *And* *{also}* *all* *repeated*
5148 565 1254 4246 3306 6058 1254 2779 4246 3306
r.as.2 v.fmi.1s adv cj adv a.npm v.iai.3p

32 καὶ ἔρχονται εἰς χωρίον οὗ τὸ ὄνομα Γεθσημανὶ καὶ λέγει τοῖς
And they went to a place that *{the}* was named Gethsemane; and he said to his
2779 2262 1650 6005 4005 3836 3950 1149 2779 3306 3836 899
cj v.pmi.3p p.a n.asn r.gsn d.nsn n.nsn n.nsn cj v.pai.3s d.dpm

μαθηταῖς αὐτοῦ· καθίσατε ὧδε ἕως προσεύξωμαι. 33 καὶ παραλαμβάνει τὸν Πέτρον
disciples, *his* "Sit here while I pray." And he took along *{the}* Peter
3412 899 2767 6045 2401 4667 2779 4161 3836 4377
n.dpm r.gsm.3 v.aam.2p adv cj v.ams.1s cj v.pai.3s d.asm n.asm

καὶ τὸν[a] Ἰάκωβον καὶ τὸν[b] Ἰωάννην μετ' αὐτοῦ καὶ ἤρξατο ἐκθαμβεῖσθαι καὶ
and *{the}* James and *{the}* John with him, and began to be distressed and
2779 3836 2610 2779 3836 2722 3552 899 2779 806 1701 2779
cj d.asm n.asm cj d.asm n.asm p.g r.gsm.3 cj v.ami.3s f.pp cj

ἀδημονεῖν 34 καὶ λέγει αὐτοῖς· περίλυπός ἐστιν ἡ ψυχή
troubled. And he said to them, "My soul is ⌊exceedingly sorrowful,⌋ *is* *{the}* *soul*
86 2779 3306 899 1609 6034 1639 4337 1639 3836 6034
f.pa cj v.pai.3s r.dpm.3 a.nsf v.pai.3s d.nsf n.nsf

μου ἕως θανάτου· μείνατε ὧδε καὶ γρηγορεῖτε. 35 καὶ προελθὼν
My ⌊even to the point⌋ of death; remain here and stay alert." And going on a
1609 2401 2505 3531 6045 2779 1213 2779 4601
r.gs.1 p.g n.gsm v.aam.2p adv cj v.pam.2p cj pt.aa.nsm

μικρὸν ἔπιπτεν ἐπὶ τῆς γῆς καὶ προσηύχετο ἵνα εἰ δυνατόν ἐστιν
little farther, he fell to the ground and prayed that, if it were possible, *it were*
3625 4406 2093 3836 1178 2779 4667 2671 1623 1639 1639 1543 1639
a.asn v.iai.3s p.g d.gsf n.gsf cj v.imi.3s cj cj a.nsn v.pai.3s

παρέλθῃ ← ἀπ' αὐτοῦ ἡ ὥρα, 36 καὶ ἔλεγεν· αββα ὁ πατήρ,
the hour might pass him by. *{from}* *him* *the* *hour* And he said, "Abba, *{the}* Father,
3836 6052 4216 899 608 899 3836 6052 2779 3306 5 3836 4252
v.aas.3s p.g r.gsm.3 d.nsf n.nsf cj v.iai.3s n.vsm d.vsm n.vsm

πάντα δυνατά σοι· παρένεγκε τὸ ποτήριον τοῦτο ἀπ' ἐμοῦ· ἀλλ' οὐ τί
all things are possible for you. Remove *{the}* this cup *this* from me. Yet not what
4246 1543 5148 4195 3836 4047 4539 4047 608 1609 247 4024 5515
a.npn a.npn r.ds.2 v.aam.2s d.asn n.asn r.asn p.g r.gs.1 cj pl r.asn

ἐγὼ θέλω ἀλλὰ τί σύ. 37 καὶ ἔρχεται καὶ εὑρίσκει αὐτοὺς καθεύδοντας,
I will, but what you will." Then he returned and found them sleeping.
1609 2527 247 5515 5148 2779 2262 2779 2351 899 2761
r.ns.1 v.pai.1s cj r.asn r.ns.2 cj v.pmi.3s cj v.pai.3s r.apm.3 pt.pa.apm

[a] [τὸν] UBS.
[b] [τὸν] UBS.

NASB

28But after I have
been raised, I will
go ahead of you
to Galilee." 29But
Peter said to Him,
"*Even* though all
may fall away, yet
I will not." 30And
Jesus *said to him,
"Truly I say to you,
that this very night,
before a rooster
crows twice, you
yourself will deny
Me three times."
31But *Peter* kept
saying insistently,
"*Even* if I have to
die with You, I will
not deny You!"
And they all were
saying the same
thing also.

Jesus in Gethsemane

32They *came to
a place named
Gethsemane; and
He *said to His
disciples, "Sit
here until I have
prayed." 33And He
*took with Him Peter
and James and
John, and began to
be very distressed
and troubled.
34And He *said to
them, "My soul is
deeply grieved to
the point of death;
remain here and
keep watch." 35And
He went a little beyond
them, and fell
to the ground and
began to pray that
if it were possible,
the hour might pass
Him by. 36And He
was saying, "Abba!
Father! All things
are possible for
You; remove this
cup from Me; yet
not what I will, but
what You will."
37And He *came
and *found them

NIV

"Simon," he said
to Peter, "are you
asleep? Couldn't
you keep watch for
one hour? [38]Watch
and pray so that
you will not fall
into temptation.
The spirit is will-
ing, but the flesh is
weak."
[39]Once more he
went away and
prayed the same
thing. [40]When he
came back, he
again found them
sleeping, because
their eyes were
heavy. They did
not know what to
say to him.
[41]Returning the
third time, he said
to them, "Are you
still sleeping and
resting? Enough!
The hour has
come. Look, the
Son of Man is de-
livered into the
hands of sinners.
[42]Rise! Let us go!
Here comes my
betrayer!"

Jesus Arrested

[43]Just as he was
speaking, Judas,
one of the Twelve,
appeared. With
him was a crowd
armed with swords
and clubs, sent
from the chief
priests, the teach-
ers of the law, and
the elders.
[44]Now the betray-
er had arranged a
signal with them:
"The one I kiss
is the man; ar-
rest him and lead
him away under
guard." [45]Going at
once to Jesus, Ju-
das said, "Rabbi!"
and kissed him.

καὶ λέγει τῷ Πέτρῳ· Σίμων, καθεύδεις; ↱ ↱ οὐκ ἴσχυσας
So he said to Peter, "Simon, are you sleeping? Were you not able to stay alert for
2779 3306 3836 4377 4981 2761 2710 2710 4024 2710 1213 1213 1213
cj v.pai.3s d.dsm n.dsm n.vsm v.pai.2s pl v.aai.2s

μίαν ὥραν γρηγορῆσαι; [38] γρηγορεῖτε καὶ προσεύχεσθε, ἵνα ↱ ↱ μὴ ἔλθητε
one hour?" *to stay alert* Stay alert and pray so that you will not come
1651 6052 1213 1213 2779 4667 2671 2262 2262 3590 2262
a.asf n.asf f.aa v.pam.2p cj v.pmm.2p cj pl v.aas.2p

εἰς πειρασμόν· τὸ μὲν πνεῦμα πρόθυμον ἡ δὲ σὰρξ ἀσθενής. [39] καὶ
into temptation; the ~ spirit is willing but the *but* flesh is weak." And
1650 4280 3836 3525 4460 4609 1254 3836 1254 4922 822 2779
p.a n.asm d.nsn pl n.nsn a.nsn d.nsf cj n.nsf a.nsf cj

πάλιν ἀπελθὼν προσηύξατο τὸν αὐτὸν λόγον εἰπών. [40] καὶ πάλιν ἐλθὼν
again, going away, he prayed, saying the same thing. *saying* And again, returning,
4099 599 4667 3306 3836 899 3364 3306 2779 4099 2262
adv pt.aa.nsm v.ami.3s d.asm r.asm n.asm pt.aa.nsm cj adv pt.aa.nsm

εὗρεν αὐτοὺς καθεύδοντας, ἦσαν γὰρ αὐτῶν οἱ ὀφθαλμοὶ
he found them sleeping, for their eyes were *for their {the} eyes*
2351 899 2761 1142 899 4057 1639 1142 899 3836 4057
v.aai.3s r.apm.3 pt.pa.apm v.iai.3p cj r.gpm.3 d.npm n.npm

καταβαρυνόμενοι, καὶ ↱ ↱ οὐκ ᾔδεισαν τί ἀποκριθῶσιν αὐτῷ. [41] καὶ
heavy, and they did not know how they should answer him. And
2852 2779 3857 3857 4024 3857 5515 646 899 2779
pt.pm.npm cj pl v.lai.3p r.asn v.aps.3p r.dsm.3 cj

ἔρχεται τὸ τρίτον καὶ λέγει αὐτοῖς· → → καθεύδετε τὸ λοιπὸν καὶ
he returned *{the}* a third time and said to them, "Are you still sleeping *{the} still* and
2262 3836 5568 2779 3306 899 3370 2761 3836 3370 2779
v.pmi.3s d.asn a.asn cj v.pai.3s r.dpm.3 v.pai.2p d.asn adv cj

ἀναπαύεσθε· ἀπέχει· ἦλθεν ἡ ὥρα, ἰδοὺ
taking your rest? Enough! The hour has come. *The hour* Look, the Son of Man
399 600 3836 6052 2262 3836 6052 2627 3836 5626 3836 476
v.pmi.2p v.pai.3s v.aai.3s d.nsf n.nsf j

παραδίδοται ὁ υἱὸς τοῦ ἀνθρώπου εἰς τὰς χεῖρας τῶν ἁμαρτωλῶν.
is about to be betrayed *the Son of Man* into the hands of sinners.
4140 3836 5626 3836 476 1650 3836 5931 3836 283
v.ppi.3s d.nsm n.nsm d.gsm n.gsm p.a d.apf n.apf d.gpm a.gpm

[42] ἐγείρεσθε ἄγωμεν· ἰδοὺ ὁ παραδιδούς με ἤγγικεν. [43] καὶ
Get up, ⌊let us be on our way;⌋ see, *{the}* my betrayer *my* has arrived. And
1586 72 2627 3836 1609 4140 1609 1581 2779
v.ppm.2p v.pas.1p j d.nsm pt.pa.nsm r.as.1 v.rai.3s cj

εὐθὺς ↱ ↱ ἔτι αὐτοῦ λαλοῦντος παραγίνεται Ἰούδας εἷς τῶν δώδεκα
immediately, while he was still *he* speaking, *appeared* Judas, one of the twelve,
2318 3281 899 3281 2285 899 3281 4134 2683 1651 3836 1557
adv adv r.gsm.3 pt.pa.gsm v.pmi.3s n.nsm a.nsm d.gpm a.gpm

καὶ μετ' αὐτοῦ ὄχλος μετὰ μαχαιρῶν καὶ ξύλων παρὰ τῶν ἀρχιερέων καὶ
appeared, and with him a crowd with swords and clubs, from the ruling priests and
4134 2779 3552 899 4063 3552 3479 2779 3833 4123 3836 797 2779
cj p.g r.gsm.3 n.nsm p.g n.gpf cj n.gpn p.g d.gpm n.gpm cj

τῶν γραμματέων καὶ τῶν πρεσβυτέρων. [44] δεδώκει δὲ ὁ
the scribes and the elders. Now his betrayer had given *Now {the}*
3836 1208 2779 3836 4565 1254 899 4140 1443 1254 3836
d.gpm n.gpm cj d.gpm a.gpm v.lai.3s cj d.nsm

παραδιδοὺς αὐτὸν σύσσημον αὐτοῖς λέγων· ⌊ὃν ἂν⌋ φιλήσω
betrayer his them a sign, *them* saying, "The one I will kiss, it is
4140 899 899 5361 899 3306 4005 323 5797 1639 1639
pt.pa.nsm r.asm.3 n.asn r.dpm.3 pt.pa.nsm r.asm pl v.aas.1s

αὐτός ἐστιν, κρατήσατε αὐτὸν καὶ ἀπάγετε ← ἀσφαλῶς. [45] καὶ →
he. *it is* Seize him and lead him away under guard." And when Judas
899 1639 3195 899 2779 552 857 2779
r.nsm v.pai.3s v.aam.2p r.asm.3 cj v.pam.2p adv cj

ἐλθὼν εὐθὺς προσελθὼν αὐτῷ λέγει· ῥαββί, καὶ κατεφίλησεν αὐτόν·
arrived, immediately he went up to Jesus and said, "Rabbi!" And he kissed him.
2262 2318 4665 899 3306 4806 2779 2968 899
pt.aa.nsm adv pt.aa.nsm r.dsm.3 v.pai.3s n.vsm cj v.aai.3s r.asm.3

NASB

sleeping, and *said
to Peter, "Simon,
are you asleep?
Could you not
keep watch for
one hour? [38]Keep
watching and
praying that you
may not come
into temptation;
the spirit is will-
ing, but the flesh
is weak." [39]Again
He went away and
prayed, saying the
same words. [40]And
again He came
and found them
sleeping, for their
eyes were very
heavy; and they
did not know what
to answer Him.
[41]And He *came
the third time, and
*said to them, "Are
you still sleeping
and resting? It is
enough; the hour
has come; behold,
the Son of Man
is being betrayed
into the hands of
sinners. [42]Get up,
let us be going;
behold, the one
who betrays Me is
at hand!"

Betrayal and Arrest

[43]Immediately
while He was still
speaking, Judas,
one of the twelve,
*came up accom-
panied by a crowd
with swords and
clubs, *who were*
from the chief
priests and the
scribes and the el-
ders. [44]Now he who
was betraying Him
had given them
a signal, saying,
"Whomever I kiss,
He is the one; seize
Him and lead Him
away under guard."
[45]After coming,
Judas immediately
went to Him, say-
ing, "Rabbi!" and
kissed Him.

NIV

[46]The men seized
Jesus and arrested
him. [47]Then one
of those stand-
ing near drew his
sword and struck
the servant of the
high priest, cutting
off his ear.
[48]"Am I leading
a rebellion," said
Jesus, "that you
have come out
with swords and
clubs to capture
me? [49]Every day
I was with you,
teaching in the
temple courts,
and you did not
arrest me. But the
Scriptures must be
fulfilled." [50]Then
everyone deserted
him and fled.
[51]A young man,
wearing nothing
but a linen gar-
ment, was follow-
ing Jesus. When
they seized him,
[52]he fled naked,
leaving his gar-
ment behind.

Jesus Before the Sanhedrin

[53]They took Jesus
to the high priest,
and all the chief
priests, the elders
and the teachers
of the law came
together. [54]Peter
followed him at
a distance, right
into the courtyard
of the high priest.
There he sat with
the guards and
warmed himself at
the fire.
[55]The chief
priests and the
whole Sanhedrin
were looking for
evidence against
Jesus so that they
could put him to
death, but they
did not find any.
[56]Many testified
falsely against
him, but

46 οἱ δὲ ἐπέβαλον τὰς χεῖρας ↰ αὐτῷ καὶ ἐκράτησαν αὐτόν. 47 εἷς
And they *And* laid *{the}* hands on him and seized him. But one
1254 3836 1254 2095 3836 5931 2095 899 2779 3195 899 1254 1651
d.npm cj v.aai.3p d.apf n.apf r.dsm.3 cj v.aai.3p r.asm.3 a.nsm

δέ τις[a] τῶν παρεστηκότων σπασάμενος τὴν μάχαιραν ἔπαισεν τὸν
But *{a certain one}* of those standing by, having drawn his sword, struck the
1254 5516 3836 4225 5060 3836 3479 4091 3836
cj r.nsm d.gpm pt.ra.gpm pt.am.nsm d.asf n.asf v.aai.3s d.asm

δοῦλον τοῦ ἀρχιερέως καὶ ἀφεῖλεν αὐτοῦ τὸ ὠτάριον. 48 καὶ ἀποκριθεὶς ὁ
servant of the high priest and cut off his *{the}* ear. And responding, *{the}*
1529 3836 797 2779 904 899 3836 6064 2779 646 3836
n.asm d.gsm n.gsm cj v.aai.3s r.gsm.3 d.asn n.asn cj pt.ap.nsm d.nsm

Ἰησοῦς εἶπεν αὐτοῖς· ὡς ἐπὶ λῃστὴν ἐξήλθατε μετὰ μαχαιρῶν καὶ ξύλων
Jesus said to them, "As against a robber ⌊have you come out⌋ with swords and clubs
2652 3306 899 6055 2093 3334 2002 3552 3479 2779 3833
n.nsm v.aai.3s r.dpm.3 pl p.a n.asm v.aai.2p p.g n.gpf cj n.gpn

συλλαβεῖν με; 49 ⌊καθ' ἡμέραν⌋ ἤμην πρὸς ὑμᾶς ἐν τῷ ἱερῷ διδάσκων καὶ ↱
to take me? Daily I was with you in the temple, teaching, and you
5197 1609 2848 2465 1639 4639 7007 1877 3836 2639 1438 2779 3195
f.aa r.as.1 p.a n.asf v.imi.1s p.a r.ap.2 p.d d.dsn n.dsn pt.pa.nsm cj

↱ οὐκ ἐκρατήσατέ με· ἀλλ' ἵνα πληρωθῶσιν αἱ γραφαί. 50 καὶ
did not seize me. But the Scriptures must be fulfilled." *the* *Scriptures* And
3195 4024 3195 1609 247 3836 1210 2671 4444 3836 1210 2779
pl v.aai.2p r.as.1 cj cj v.aps.3p d.npf n.npf cj

ἀφέντες αὐτὸν → ἔφυγον πάντες. 51 καὶ νεανίσκος τις συνηκολούθει
leaving him, they all fled. *all* And a certain young man *certain* was following
918 899 4246 5771 4246 2779 5516 3734 5516 5258
pt.aa.npm r.asm.3 v.aai.3p a.npm cj n.nsm r.nsm v.iai.3s

αὐτῷ περιβεβλημένος σινδόνα ἐπὶ γυμνοῦ, καὶ
him, with a linen cloth wrapped *linen cloth* around his naked body; and
899 4984 4984 4314 4984 2093 1218 2779
r.dsm.3 pt.rp.nsm n.asf p.g a.gsn cj

κρατοῦσιν αὐτόν· 52 ὁ δὲ καταλιπὼν τὴν σινδόνα γυμνὸς
⌊they tried to seize⌋ him, *he* but leaving behind the linen cloth, he ran away naked
3195 899 3836 1254 2901 3836 4984 3836 5771 5771 1218
v.pai.3p r.asm.3 d.nsm cj pt.aa.nsm d.asf n.asf a.nsm

ἔφυγεν. 53 καὶ ἀπήγαγον τὸν Ἰησοῦν πρὸς τὸν ἀρχιερέα, καὶ συνέρχονται πάντες
ran away And they led *{the}* Jesus to the high priest; and *came together* all
5771 2779 552 3836 2652 4639 3836 797 2779 5302 4246
v.aai.3s cj v.aai.3p d.asm n.asm p.a d.asm n.asm cj v.pmi.3p a.npm

οἱ ἀρχιερεῖς καὶ οἱ πρεσβύτεροι καὶ οἱ γραμματεῖς. 54 καὶ ὁ
the ruling priests and the elders and the scribes came together. And *{the}*
3836 797 2779 3836 4565 2779 3836 1208 5302 5302 2779 3836
d.npm n.npm cj d.npm a.npm cj d.npm n.npm cj d.nsm

Πέτρος ἀπὸ μακρόθεν ἠκολούθησεν αὐτῷ ⌊ἕως ἔσω⌋ εἰς τὴν αὐλὴν
Peter followed him from a distance, *followed* *him* right into the courtyard
4377 199 899 608 3427 199 899 2401 2276 1650 3836 885
n.nsm p.g adv v.aai.3s r.dsm.3 p.g adv p.a d.asf n.asf

τοῦ ἀρχιερέως καὶ ἦν συγκαθήμενος μετὰ τῶν ὑπηρετῶν καὶ θερμαινόμενος
of the high priest, and ⌊he was⌋ sitting with the officers and warming himself
3836 797 2779 1639 5153 3552 3836 5677 2779 2548
d.gsm n.gsm cj v.iai.3s pt.pm.nsm p.g d.gpm n.gpm cj pt.pm.nsm

πρὸς τὸ φῶς. 55 οἱ δὲ ἀρχιερεῖς καὶ ὅλον τὸ συνέδριον ἐζήτουν
at the fire. Now the *Now* ruling priests and the entire *the* council were seeking
4639 3836 5890 1254 3836 1254 797 2779 3836 3910 3836 5284 2426
p.a d.asn n.asn d.npm cj n.npm cj a.nsn d.nsn n.nsn v.iai.3p

κατὰ τοῦ Ἰησοῦ μαρτυρίαν εἰς τὸ θανατῶσαι αὐτόν, ↰ ↰ καὶ ↱
testimony against *{the}* Jesus *testimony* to *{the}* put him to death, but they
3456 2848 3836 2652 3456 1650 3836 2506 899 2506 2506 2779 2351
p.g d.gsm n.gsm n.asf p.a d.asn f.aa r.asm.3 cj

↱ οὐχ ηὕρισκον· 56 πολλοὶ γὰρ ἐψευδομαρτύρουν κατ' αὐτοῦ, καὶ
were not finding any. For many *For* were giving false testimony against him, but
2351 4024 2351 1142 4498 1142 6018 2848 899 2779
pl v.iai.3p a.npm cj v.iai.3p p.g r.gsm.3 cj

NASB

[46]They laid hands
on Him and seized
Him. [47]But one of
those who stood
by drew his sword,
and struck the slave
of the high priest
and cut off his ear.
[48]And Jesus said
to them, "Have
you come out with
swords and clubs
to arrest Me, as
you would against
a robber? [49]Every
day I was with
you in the temple
teaching, and you
did not seize Me;
but *this has taken
place* to fulfill the
Scriptures." [50]And
they all left Him
and fled.
[51]A young man
was following
Him, wearing
nothing but a linen
sheet over *his* na-
ked *body;* and they
*seized him. [52]But
he pulled free of
the linen sheet and
escaped naked.

Jesus before His Accusers

[53]They led Jesus
away to the high
priest; and all the
chief priests and
the elders and the
scribes *gathered
together. [54]Peter
had followed Him
at a distance, right
into the courtyard
of the high priest;
and he was sitting
with the officers
and warming
himself at the fire.
[55]Now the chief
priests and the
whole [a]Council
kept trying to
obtain testimony
against Jesus to put
Him to death, and
they were not find-
ing any. [56]For many
were giving false
testimony against
Him, but their

[a] [τις] UBS.

[a] Or *Sanhedrin*

NIV

their statements
did not agree.
57 Then some
stood up and gave
this false testimo-
ny against him:
58 "We heard him
say, 'I will destroy
this temple made
with human hands
and in three days
will build anoth-
er, not made with
hands.'" 59 Yet
even then their
testimony did not
agree.
60 Then the high
priest stood up
before them and
asked Jesus, "Are
you not going to
answer? What
is this testimony
that these men are
bringing against
you?" 61 But Jesus
remained silent
and gave no an-
swer.
Again the high
priest asked him,
"Are you the Mes-
siah, the Son of the
Blessed One?"
62 "I am," said
Jesus. "And you
will see the Son
of Man sitting at
the right hand of
the Mighty One
and coming on the
clouds of heaven."
63 The high priest
tore his clothes.
"Why do we need
any more witness-
es?" he asked.
64 "You have heard
the blasphemy.
What do you
think?"
They all con-
demned him as
worthy of death.
65 Then some began
to spit at him; they
blindfolded him,
struck him with
their fists, and
said, "Prophesy!"
And the guards

ἴσαι αἱ μαρτυρίαι οὐκ ἦσαν. 57 καί τινες ἀναστάντες
in agreement their testimonies were not *were* in agreement. And some, standing up,
2698 3836 3456 1639 4024 1639 2698 2698 2779 5516 482
a.npf d.npf n.npf pl v.iai.3p cj r.npm pt.aa.npm

ἐψευδομαρτύρουν κατ᾽ αὐτοῦ λέγοντες 58 ὅτι ἡμεῖς ἠκούσαμεν αὐτοῦ
were giving false testimony against him, saying, ~ "We heard him
6018 2848 899 3306 4022 7005 201 899
v.iai.3p p.g r.gsm.3 pt.pa.npm cj r.np.1 v.aai.1p r.gsm.3

λέγοντος ὅτι ἐγὼ καταλύσω τὸν ναὸν τοῦτον τὸν χειροποίητον καὶ διὰ
saying, ~ 'I will destroy *{the}* this temple *this* *{the}* made with hands, and in
3306 4022 1609 2907 3836 4047 3724 4047 3836 5935 2779 1328
pt.pa.gsm cj r.ns.1 v.fai.1s d.asm n.asm r.asm d.asm a.asm cj p.g

τριῶν ἡμερῶν ἄλλον ἀχειροποίητον οἰκοδομήσω. 59 καὶ οὐδὲ
three days I will build another not made with hands.'" *I will build* Yet not even
5552 2465 3868 3868 3868 257 942 3868 2779 4028
a.gpf n.gpf r.asm a.asm v.fai.1s cj adv

οὕτως ἴση ἦν ἡ μαρτυρία αὐτῶν. 60 καὶ
about this was their testimony in agreement. *was* *{the}* *testimony* *their* Then the high
4048 1639 899 3456 2698 1639 3836 3456 899 2779 3836 797
adv a.nsf v.iai.3s d.nsf n.nsf r.gpm.3 cj

ἀναστὰς ὁ ἀρχιερεὺς εἰς μέσον ἐπηρώτησεν τὸν Ἰησοῦν λέγων· ↱
priest, standing up *the* *high priest* in their midst, asked *{the}* Jesus, saying, "Are
797 482 3836 797 1650 3545 2089 3836 2652 3306 646
pt.aa.nsm d.nsm n.nsm p.a n.asn v.aai.3s d.asm n.asm pt.pa.nsm

↱ οὐκ ἀποκρίνῃ οὐδὲν τί οὗτοί σου καταμαρτυροῦσιν; 61
you not ⌊going to reply to⌋ *{nothing}* what these men *you* are testifying against you?" But
646 4024 646 4029 5515 4047 5148 2909 5148 1254
pl v.pmi.2s a.asn r.asn r.npm r.gs.2 v.pai.3p

ὁ δὲ ἐσιώπα καὶ οὐκ ἀπεκρίνατο οὐδέν. πάλιν ὁ ἀρχιερεὺς ἐπηρώτα
he *But* ⌊remained silent⌋ and *{not}* answered back nothing. Again the high priest questioned
3836 1254 4995 2779 4024 646 4029 4099 3836 797 2089
d.nsm cj v.iai.3s cj pl v.ami.3s a.asn adv d.nsm n.nsm v.iai.3s

αὐτὸν καὶ λέγει αὐτῷ· σὺ εἶ ὁ χριστὸς ὁ υἱὸς τοῦ εὐλογητοῦ;
him and said to him, "Are you *Are* the Christ, the Son of the Blessed?"
899 2779 3306 899 1639 5148 1639 3836 5986 3836 5626 3836 2329
r.asm.3 cj v.pai.3s r.dsm.3 r.ns.2 v.pai.2s d.nsm n.nsm d.nsm n.nsm d.gsm a.gsm

62 ὁ δὲ Ἰησοῦς εἶπεν· ἐγώ εἰμι, καὶ ὄψεσθε τὸν υἱὸν τοῦ ἀνθρώπου
{the} And Jesus said, "I am; and ⌊you will see⌋ the Son of Man sitting
3836 1254 2652 3306 1609 1639 2779 3972 3836 5626 3836 476 2764
d.nsm cj n.nsm v.aai.3s r.ns.1 v.pai.1s cj v.fmi.2p d.asm n.asm d.gsm n.gsm

ἐκ δεξιῶν καθήμενον τῆς δυνάμεως καὶ ἐρχόμενον μετὰ τῶν νεφελῶν τοῦ
at the right hand *sitting* of Power and coming with the clouds of
1666 1288 2764 3836 1539 2779 2262 3552 3836 3749 3836
p.g a.gpf pt.pm.asm d.gsf n.gsf cj pt.pm.asm p.g d.gpf n.gpf d.gsm

οὐρανοῦ. 63 ὁ δὲ ἀρχιερεὺς διαρρήξας τοὺς χιτῶνας αὐτοῦ λέγει· τί ↱
heaven." *{the}* And the high priest, tearing *{the}* his garments, *his* said, "Why do
4041 3836 1254 797 1396 3836 899 5945 899 3306 5515 2400
n.gsm d.nsm cj n.nsm pt.aa.nsm d.apm n.apm r.gsm.3 v.pai.3s r.asn

↱ ἔτι χρείαν ἔχομεν μαρτύρων; 64 ἠκούσατε τῆς βλασφημίας· τί
we still have need *have* of witnesses? You have heard the blasphemy! What appears
2400 2285 2400 5970 2400 3459 201 3836 1060 5515 5743
adv n.asf v.pai.1p n.gpm v.aai.2p d.gsf n.gsf r.nsn

ὑμῖν φαίνεται; οἱ δὲ πάντες κατέκριναν αὐτὸν ἔνοχον εἶναι
to be right to you?" *appears* And they *And* all condemned him as deserving *as*
7007 5743 1254 3836 1254 4246 2891 899 1639 1944 1639
r.dp.2 v.ppi.3s d.npm cj a.npm v.aai.3p r.asm.3 a.asm f.pa

θανάτου. 65 καὶ ἤρξαντό τινες ἐμπτύειν αὐτῷ καὶ περικαλύπτειν αὐτοῦ τὸ
death. And some began *some* to spit on him, and to cover his *{the}*
2505 2779 5516 806 5516 1870 899 2779 4328 899 3836
n.gsm cj v.ami.3p r.npm f.pa r.dsm.3 cj f.pa r.gsm.3 d.asn

πρόσωπον καὶ κολαφίζειν αὐτὸν καὶ λέγειν αὐτῷ· προφήτευσον, καὶ οἱ ὑπηρέται
face, and to strike him, and to say to him, "Prophesy!" Even the officers
4725 2779 3139 899 2779 3306 899 4736 2779 3836 5677
n.asn cj f.pa r.asm.3 cj f.pa r.dsm.3 v.aam.2s cj d.npm n.npm

NASB

testimony was not
consistent. 57 Some
stood up and *be-*
gan to give false
testimony against
Him, saying, 58 "We
heard Him say, 'I
will destroy this
temple made with
hands, and in three
days I will build
another made with-
out hands.'" 59 Not
even in this respect
was their testi-
mony consistent.
60 The high priest
stood up *and came*
forward and ques-
tioned Jesus, say-
ing, "Do You not
answer? What is it
that these men are
testifying against
You?" 61 But He
kept silent and did
not answer. Again
the high priest
was questioning
Him, and saying to
Him, "Are You the
Christ, the Son of
the Blessed *One?*"
62 And Jesus said,
"I am; and you
shall see THE SON
OF MAN SITTING AT
THE RIGHT HAND OF
POWER, and COMING
WITH THE CLOUDS OF
HEAVEN." 63 Tearing
his clothes, the
high priest *said,
"What further need
do we have of wit-
nesses? 64 You have
heard the blas-
phemy; how does
it seem to you?"
And they all con-
demned Him to be
deserving of death.
65 Some began to
spit at Him, and
to blindfold Him,
and to beat Him
with their fists,
and to say to Him,
"Prophesy!" And
the officers

NIV

took him and beat him.

Peter Disowns Jesus

66While Peter was below in the courtyard, one of the servant girls of the high priest came by. 67When she saw Peter warming himself, she looked closely at him.

"You also were with that Nazarene, Jesus," she said.

68But he denied it. "I don't know or understand what you're talking about," he said, and went out into the entryway.[a]

69When the servant girl saw him there, she said again to those standing around, "This fellow is one of them." 70Again he denied it.

After a little while, those standing near said to Peter, "Surely you are one of them, for you are a Galilean."

71He began to call down curses, and he swore to them, "I don't know this man you're talking about."

72Immediately the rooster crowed the second time.[b] Then Peter remembered the word Jesus had spoken to him: "Before the rooster crows twice[c] you will disown me three times." And he broke down and wept.

[a] 68 Some early manuscripts *entryway and the rooster crowed*
[b] 72 Some early manuscripts do not have *the second time.*
[c] 72 Some early manuscripts do not have *twice.*

ῥαπίσμασιν αὐτὸν ἔλαβον. 66 καὶ → ὄντος τοῦ Πέτρου
received him with slaps to the face. *him* *received* And while Peter was *{the}* *Peter*
3284 899 4825 899 3284 2779 4377 1639 3836 4377
n.dpn r.asm.3 v.aai.3p cj pt.pa.gsm d.gsm n.gsm

κάτω ἐν τῇ αὐλῇ ἔρχεται μία τῶν παιδισκῶν τοῦ ἀρχιερέως
below in the courtyard, *came by* one of the maid servants of the high priest came by,
3004 1877 3836 885 2262 1651 3836 4087 3836 797 2262 2262
adv p.d d.dsf n.dsf v.pmi.3s a.nsf d.gpf n.gpf d.gsm n.gsm

67 καὶ ἰδοῦσα τὸν Πέτρον θερμαινόμενον ἐμβλέψασα αὐτῷ λέγει· καὶ
and seeing *{the}* Peter warming himself, she looked closely at him and said, "You also
2779 1625 3836 4377 2548 1838 899 3306 5148 2779
cj pt.aa.nsf d.asm n.asm pt.pm.asm pt.aa.nsf r.dsm.3 v.pai.3s adv

σὺ μετὰ τοῦ Ναζαρηνοῦ ἦσθα τοῦ Ἰησοῦ. 68 ὁ δὲ ἠρνήσατο λέγων·
You were with the Nazarene, *were* *{the}* Jesus." But he *But* denied it, saying,
5148 1639 3552 3836 3716 1639 3836 2652 1254 3836 1254 766 3306
r.ns.2 p.g d.gsm n.gsm v.iai.2s d.gsm n.gsm d.nsm cj v.ami.3s pt.pa.nsm

↱ οὔτε οἶδα οὔτε ἐπίσταμαι σὺ τί λέγεις. καὶ ἐξῆλθεν ἔξω εἰς τὸ
"I neither know nor understand what you *what* are saying." And he went out into the
3857 4046 3857 4046 2179 5515 5148 5515 3306 2779 2002 2032 1650 3836
cj v.rai.1s cj v.ppi.1s r.ns.2 r.asn v.pai.2s cj v.aai.3s adv p.a d.asn

προαύλιον καὶ ἀλέκτωρ ἐφώνησεν.[a] 69 καὶ ἡ παιδίσκη ἰδοῦσα αὐτὸν
exterior court, and a rooster crowed. And the maid servant, seeing him,
4580 2779 232 5888 2779 3836 4087 1625 899
n.asn cj n.nsm v.aai.3s cj d.nsf n.nsf pt.aa.nsf r.asm.3

ἤρξατο πάλιν λέγειν τοῖς παρεστῶσιν ὅτι οὗτος ἐξ αὐτῶν
began again to say to those ⌊who were standing around,⌋ ~ "This man is ⌊one of⌋ them."
806 4099 3306 3836 4225 4022 4047 1639 1666 899
v.ami.3s adv f.pa d.dpm pt.ra.dpm cj r.nsm p.g r.gpm.3

ἐστιν. 70 ὁ δὲ πάλιν ἠρνεῖτο. καὶ μετὰ μικρὸν πάλιν οἱ
is But again he *But* *again* denied it. And after a little while again those
1639 1254 4099 3836 1254 4099 766 2779 3552 3625 4099 3836
v.pai.3s d.nsm cj adv v.imi.3s cj p.a a.asn adv d.npm

παρεστῶτες ἔλεγον τῷ Πέτρῳ· ἀληθῶς ἐξ αὐτῶν εἶ, καὶ
standing around said to Peter, "Surely you are ⌊one of⌋ them, *you are* for you also
4225 3306 3836 4377 242 1639 1639 1666 899 1639 1142 1639 2779
pt.ra.npm v.iai.3p d.dsm n.dsm adv p.g r.gpm.3 v.pai.2s adv

γὰρ Γαλιλαῖος εἶ.[b] 71 ὁ δὲ ἤρξατο ἀναθεματίζειν καὶ
for are a Galilean," *you are* Then Peter *Then* began ⌊to call down curses on himself⌋ and
1142 1639 1134 1639 1254 3836 1254 806 354 2779
cj a.nsm v.pai.2s d.nsm cj v.ami.3s f.pa cj

ὀμνύναι ὅτι ↱ ↱ οὐκ οἶδα τὸν ἄνθρωπον τοῦτον ὃν λέγετε. 72 καὶ
to swear, ~ "I do not know *{the}* this man *this* of whom you speak!" And
3923 4022 3857 3857 4024 3857 3836 4047 476 4047 4005 3306 2779
f.pa cj pl v.rai.1s d.asm n.asm r.asm r.asm v.pai.2p cj

εὐθὺς ⌊ἐκ δευτέρου⌋ ἀλέκτωρ ἐφώνησεν. καὶ
immediately the rooster crowed a second time. *rooster* *crowed* Then Peter
2318 232 5888 1666 1311 232 5888 2779 4377
adv p.g a.gsn n.nsm v.aai.3s cj

ἀνεμνήσθη ὁ Πέτρος τὸ ῥῆμα ὡς εἶπεν αὐτῷ ὁ Ἰησοῦς ὅτι πρὶν
remembered *{the}* *Peter* the word that Jesus had said to him, *{the}* *Jesus* ~ "Before the
389 3836 4377 3836 4839 6055 2652 3306 899 3836 2652 4022 4570
v.api.3s d.nsm n.nsm d.asn n.asn cj v.aai.3s r.dsm.3 d.nsm n.nsm cj cj

ἀλέκτορα φωνῆσαι δὶς τρίς με ἀπαρνήσῃ· καὶ
rooster crows twice, you will deny me ⌊three times."⌋ *me* *you will deny* And
232 5888 1489 565 565 565 1609 5565 1609 565 2779
n.asm f.aa adv adv r.as.1 v.fmi.2s cj

ἐπιβαλὼν ἔκλαιεν.
upon reflection, ⌊he broke into tears.⌋
2095 3081
pt.aa.nsm v.iai.3s

[a] [καὶ ἀλέκτωρ ἐφώνησεν] UBS, omitted by TNIV.
[b] καὶ ἡ λαλιά σου ὁμοιάζει included by TR after εἶ.

NASB

received Him with slaps *in the face.*

Peter's Denials

66As Peter was below in the courtyard, one of the servant-girls of the high priest *came, 67and seeing Peter warming himself, she looked at him and *said, "You also were with Jesus the Nazarene." 68But he denied *it,* saying, "I neither know nor understand what you are talking about." And he went out onto the porch.[a] 69The servant-girl saw him, and began once more to say to the bystanders, "This is *one* of them!" 70But again he denied it. And after a little while the bystanders were again saying to Peter, "Surely you are *one* of them, for you are a Galilean too." 71But he began to curse and swear, "I do not know this man you are talking about!" 72Immediately a rooster crowed a second time. And Peter remembered how Jesus had made the remark to him, "Before a rooster crows twice, you will deny Me three times." And he began to weep.

[a] Later mss add *and a rooster crowed*

NIV

Jesus Before Pilate

15 Very ear-
ly in the
morning, the chief
priests, with the
elders, the teachers
of the law and the
whole Sanhedrin,
made their plans.
So they bound
Jesus, led him
away and handed
him over to Pilate.
2"Are you the
king of the Jews?"
asked Pilate.
"You have said
so," Jesus replied.
3The chief priests
accused him of
many things. 4So
again Pilate asked
him, "Aren't you
going to answer?
See how many
things they are ac-
cusing you of."
5But Jesus still
made no reply, and
Pilate was amazed.
6Now it was the
custom at the fes-
tival to release a
prisoner whom the
people request-
ed. 7A man called
Barabbas was in
prison with the in-
surrectionists who
had committed
murder in the up-
rising. 8The crowd
came up and asked
Pilate to do for
them what he usu-
ally did.
9"Do you want
me to release to
you the king of
the Jews?" asked
Pilate, 10know-
ing it was out of
self-interest that
the chief priests
had handed Jesus
over to him. 11But
the chief priests
stirred up the

15:1 καὶ εὐθὺς πρωῒ συμβούλιον
{and} ⌞As soon as⌟ ⌞it was morning,⌟ the ruling priests, after holding a consultation
2779 2318 4745 3836 797 797 4472 4472 5206
cj adv adv n.asn

ποιήσαντες οἱ ἀρχιερεῖς μετὰ τῶν πρεσβυτέρων καὶ γραμματέων καὶ ὅλον
after holding *the* *ruling priests* with the elders and scribes and the entire
4472 3836 797 3552 3836 4565 2779 1208 2779 3836 3910
pt.aa.npm d.npm n.npm p.g d.gpm a.gpm cj n.gpm cj a.nsn

τὸ συνέδριον, δήσαντες τὸν Ἰησοῦν ἀπήνεγκαν ← καὶ παρέδωκαν ←
the council, bound *{the}* Jesus, led him away, and handed him over
3836 5284 1313 3836 2652 708 2779 4140
d.nsn n.nsn pt.aa.npm d.asm n.asm v.aai.3p cj v.aai.3p

Πιλάτῳ. 2 καὶ ἐπηρώτησεν αὐτὸν ὁ Πιλᾶτος· σὺ εἶ ὁ βασιλεὺς
to Pilate. And Pilate questioned him, *{the}* *Pilate* "Are you *Are* the king
4397 2779 4397 2089 899 3836 4397 1639 5148 1639 3836 995
n.dsm cj v.aai.3s r.asm.3 d.nsm n.nsm r.ns.2 v.pai.2s d.nsm n.nsm

τῶν Ἰουδαίων; ὁ δὲ ἀποκριθεὶς αὐτῷ λέγει· σὺ λέγεις. 3 καὶ
of the Jews?" *he* And answering him, he said, "You say it." And the ruling
3836 2681 3836 1254 646 899 3836 3306 5148 3306 2779 3836 797
d.gpm a.gpm d.nsm cj pt.ap.nsm r.dsm.3 v.pai.3s r.ns.2 v.pai.2s cj

κατηγόρουν αὐτοῦ οἱ ἀρχιερεῖς πολλά.[a] 4 ὁ δὲ Πιλᾶτος
priests accused him *the* *ruling priests* repeatedly. *{the}* Then Pilate questioned him
797 2989 899 3836 797 4498 3836 1254 4397 2089 899
v.iai.3p r.gsm.3 d.npm n.npm a.apn d.nsm cj n.nsm

πάλιν ἐπηρώτα αὐτὸν λέγων· οὐκ ἀποκρίνῃ οὐδέν; ἴδε πόσα σου
again, *questioned* *him* saying, *{not}* "Do you answer nothing? See how many *you*
4099 2089 899 3306 4024 646 4029 2623 4531 5148
adv v.iai.3s r.asm.3 pt.pa.nsm pl v.ppi.2s a.asn pl r.apn r.gs.2

κατηγοροῦσιν. 5 ὁ δὲ Ἰησοῦς οὐκέτι ↱ οὐδὲν
⌞accusations they are bringing against⌟ you." *{the}* But Jesus no longer gave any
2989 5148 3836 1254 2652 4033 646 4029
v.pai.3p d.nsm cj n.nsm adv a.asn

ἀπεκρίθη, ὥστε θαυμάζειν τὸν Πιλᾶτον. 6 κατὰ δὲ ἑορτὴν
reply, so that Pilate was amazed. *{the}* *Pilate* Now at *Now* the feast
646 6063 4397 2513 3836 4397 1254 2848 1254 2038
v.api.3s cj f.pa d.asm n.asm p.a cj n.asf

ἀπέλυεν αὐτοῖς ἕνα δέσμιον ὃν παρῃτοῦντο. 7 ἦν δὲ ὁ λεγόμενος
⌞he used to release⌟ to them one prisoner whom they requested. *there was* *{and}* *man* *called*
668 899 1651 1300 4005 4148 1639 1254 3836 3306
v.iai.3s r.dpm.3 a.asm n.asm r.asm v.imi.3p v.iai.3s cj d.nsm pt.pp.nsm

Βαραββᾶς μετὰ τῶν στασιαστῶν δεδεμένος οἵτινες ἐν τῇ στάσει
Barabbas Among the rebels in prison, who in the insurrection had committed
972 3552 3836 5086 1313 4015 1877 3836 5087 4472 4472
n.nsm p.g d.gpm n.gpm pt.rp.nsm r.npm p.d d.dsf n.dsf

φόνον πεποιήκεισαν. 8 καὶ ἀναβὰς ὁ
murder, *had committed* there was a man called Barabbas. And coming up, the
5840 4472 1639 1639 3836 3306 972 2779 326 3836
n.asm v.lai.3p cj pt.aa.nsm d.nsm

ὄχλος ἤρξατο αἰτεῖσθαι καθὼς ἐποίει αὐτοῖς. 9 ὁ δὲ Πιλᾶτος
crowd began to ask Pilate to do as ⌞he usually did⌟ for them. *{the}* So Pilate
4063 806 160 2777 4472 899 3836 1254 4397
n.nsm v.ami.3s f.pm cj v.iai.3s r.dpm.3 d.nsm cj n.nsm

ἀπεκρίθη αὐτοῖς λέγων· θέλετε ἀπολύσω ὑμῖν τὸν βασιλέα τῶν Ἰουδαίων;
responded to them, saying, ⌞"Do you want⌟ me to release to you the king of the Jews?"
646 899 3306 2527 668 7007 3836 995 3836 2681
v.api.3s r.dpm.3 pt.pa.nsm v.pai.2p v.aas.1s r.dp.2 d.asm n.asm d.gpm a.gpm

10 ἐγίνωσκεν γὰρ ὅτι διὰ φθόνον
For he knew *For* that the ruling priests had handed Jesus over ⌞out of⌟ envy.
1142 1182 1142 4022 3836 797 797 4140 4140 899 4140 1328 5784
v.iai.3s cj cj p.a n.asm

παραδεδώκεισαν αὐτὸν οἱ ἀρχιερεῖς. 11 οἱ δὲ ἀρχιερεῖς ἀνέσεισαν τὸν
had handed over *Jesus* *the* *ruling priests* But the *But* ruling priests stirred up the
4140 899 3836 797 1254 3836 1254 797 411 3836
v.lai.3p r.asm.3 d.npm n.npm d.npm cj n.npm v.aai.3p d.asm

[a] αὐτὸς δὲ οὐδὲν ἀπεκρίνατο included by TR after πολλά.

NASB

Jesus before Pilate

15:1Early in the
morning the chief
priests with the
elders and scribes
and the whole
[a]Council, immedi-
ately held a consul-
tation; and binding
Jesus, they led Him
away and delivered
Him to Pilate.
2Pilate questioned
Him, "Are You the
King of the Jews?"
And He *answered
him, "*It is as* you
say." 3The chief
priests *began* to ac-
cuse Him harshly.
4Then Pilate ques-
tioned Him again,
saying, "Do You
not answer? See
how many charges
they bring against
You!" 5But Jesus
made no further
answer; so Pilate
was amazed.
6Now at *the* feast
he used to release
for them *any* one
prisoner whom
they requested.
7The man named
Barabbas had been
imprisoned with
the insurrectionists
who had commit-
ted murder in the
insurrection. 8The
crowd went up and
began asking him
to do as he had
been accustomed to
do for them. 9Pilate
answered them,
saying, "Do you
want me to release
for you the King of
the Jews?" 10For he
was aware that the
chief priests had
handed Him over
because of envy.
11But the chief
priests stirred up

[a] Or *Sanhedrin*

NIV

crowd to have Pi-
late release Barab-
bas instead.
12 "What shall I
do, then, with the
one you call the
king of the Jews?"
Pilate asked them.
13 "Crucify him!"
they shouted.
14 "Why? What
crime has he com-
mitted?" asked
Pilate.
But they shout-
ed all the louder,
"Crucify him!"
15 Wanting to sat-
isfy the crowd, Pi-
late released Bar-
abbas to them. He
had Jesus flogged,
and handed him
over to be cruci-
fied.

The Soldiers Mock Jesus

16 The soldiers led
Jesus away into
the palace (that is,
the Praetorium)
and called together
the whole com-
pany of soldiers.
17 They put a purple
robe on him, then
twisted together
a crown of thorns
and set it on him.
18 And they began
to call out to him,
"Hail, king of the
Jews!" 19 Again
and again they
struck him on the
head with a staff
and spit on him.
Falling on their
knees, they paid
homage to him.
20 And when they
had mocked him,
they took off the
purple robe and
put his own clothes
on him. Then they
led him out to cru-
cify him.

The Crucifixion of Jesus

21 A certain

ὄχλον ἵνα μᾶλλον τὸν Βαραββᾶν ἀπολύσῃ
crowd so that Pilate would release Barabbas to them instead. *{the} Barabbas would release*
4063 2671 668 668 972 899 899 3437 3836 972 668
n.asm cj adv.c d.asm n.asm v.aas.3s

αὐτοῖς. 12 ὁ δὲ Πιλᾶτος πάλιν ἀποκριθεὶς ἔλεγεν αὐτοῖς· τί οὖν
to them *{the}* And Pilate answering again, *answering* said to them, "What, then,
899 3836 1254 4397 646 4099 646 3306 899 5515 4036
r.dpm.3 d.nsm cj n.nsm adv pt.ap.nsm v.iai.3s r.dpm.3 r.asn cj

θέλετε[a] ποιήσω [b]ὃν λέγετε τὸν βασιλέα τῶν Ἰουδαίων; 13 οἱ
do you want me to do with the man you call the king of the Jews?" But again they
2527 4472 4005 3306 3836 995 3836 2681 1254 4099 3836
v.pai.2p v.aas.1s r.asm v.pai.2p d.asm n.asm d.gpm a.gpm d.npm

δὲ πάλιν ἔκραξαν· σταύρωσον αὐτόν. 14 ὁ δὲ Πιλᾶτος ἔλεγεν αὐτοῖς· τί
But again cried out, "Crucify him!" *{the}* And Pilate said to them, "Why, what
1254 4099 3189 5090 899 3836 1254 4397 3306 899 1142 5515
cj adv v.aai.3p v.aam.2s r.asm.3 d.nsm cj n.nsm v.iai.3s r.dpm.3 r.asn

γὰρ ἐποίησεν κακόν; οἱ δὲ περισσῶς ἔκραξαν· σταύρωσον
Why evil has he done?" *evil* But they *But* cried out all the more, *cried out* "Crucify
1142 2805 4472 2805 1254 3836 1254 3189 3189 4360 3189 5090
cj v.aai.3s a.asn d.npm cj adv v.aai.3p v.aam.2s

αὐτόν. 15 ὁ δὲ Πιλᾶτος βουλόμενος τῷ ὄχλῳ τὸ ⌊ἱκανὸν
him!" *{the}* So Pilate, wishing to satisfy the crowd, *{the} to satisfy*
899 3836 1254 4397 1089 2653 2653 3836 4063 3836 2653
r.asm.3 d.nsm cj n.nsm pt.pm.nsm d.dsm n.dsm d.asn a.asn

ποιῆσαι⌋ ἀπέλυσεν αὐτοῖς τὸν Βαραββᾶν, καὶ παρέδωκεν
released to them *{the}* Barabbas; and having scourged Jesus, he handed him
4472 668 899 3836 972 2779 5849 5849 2652 4140
f.aa v.aai.3s r.dpm.3 d.asm n.asm cj v.aai.3s

← τὸν Ἰησοῦν φραγελλώσας ἵνα σταυρωθῇ. 16 οἱ δὲ στρατιῶται ἀπήγαγον
over *{the} Jesus having scourged* to be crucified. And the *And* soldiers led
3836 2652 5849 2671 5090 1254 3836 1254 5132 552
d.asm n.asm pt.aa.nsm cj v.aps.3s d.npm cj n.npm v.aai.3p

αὐτὸν ↰ ἔσω τῆς αὐλῆς, ὅ ἐστιν πραιτώριον, καὶ συγκαλοῦσιν ὅλην
him away into the palace (that is, the praetorium) and they called together the whole
899 552 2276 3836 885 4005 1639 4550 2779 5157 3836 3910
r.asm.3 p.g d.gsf n.gsf r.nsn v.pai.3s n.nsn cj v.pai.3p a.asf

τὴν σπεῖραν. 17 καὶ ἐνδιδύσκουσιν αὐτὸν ↰ πορφύραν καὶ
the ⌊company of soldiers.⌋ And they clothed him in purple; and twisting some
3836 5061 2779 1898 899 1898 4525 2779 4428
d.asf n.asf cj v.pai.3p r.asm.3 n.asf cj

περιτιθέασιν ← αὐτῷ πλέξαντες ἀκάνθινον στέφανον· 18 καὶ
thorns into a crown, they placed it on him. *twisting thorns crown* Then
181 5109 4363 899 4428 181 5109 2779
v.pai.3p r.dsm.3 pt.aa.npm a.asm n.asm cj

ἤρξαντο ἀσπάζεσθαι αὐτόν· χαῖρε, βασιλεῦ τῶν Ἰουδαίων· 19 καὶ ἔτυπτον
they began to greet him, "Hail, king of the Jews!" And ⌊they kept striking⌋
806 832 899 5897 995 3836 2681 2779 5597
v.ami.3p f.pm r.asm.3 v.pam.2s n.vsm d.gpm a.gpm cj v.iai.3p

αὐτοῦ τὴν κεφαλὴν καλάμῳ καὶ ἐνέπτυον αὐτῷ καὶ τιθέντες τὰ γόνατα
his *{the}* head with a staff and spitting on him; and falling to their knees,
899 3836 3051 2812 2779 1870 899 2779 5502 3836 1205
r.gsm.3 d.asf n.asf n.dsm cj v.iai.3p r.dsm.3 cj pt.pa.npm d.apn n.apn

προσεκύνουν αὐτῷ. 20 καὶ ὅτε ἐνέπαιξαν αὐτῷ, ἐξέδυσαν αὐτὸν
⌊they paid homage to⌋ him. And when ⌊they had finished mocking⌋ him, they stripped him
4686 899 2779 4021 1850 899 1694 899
v.iai.3p r.dsm.3 cj cj v.aai.3p r.dsm.3 v.aai.3p r.asm.3

↰ τὴν πορφύραν καὶ ἐνέδυσαν ← αὐτὸν τὰ ἱμάτια αὐτοῦ. καὶ
of the purple robe and put his own clothes on him. *{the} clothes his own* Then
1694 3836 4525 2779 1907 899 899 2668 899 3836 2668 899 2779
d.asf n.asf cj v.aai.3p r.asm.3 d.apn n.apn r.gsm.3 cj

ἐξάγουσιν αὐτὸν ↰ ἵνα σταυρώσωσιν αὐτόν. 21 καὶ ἀγγαρεύουσιν
they led him out to crucify him. And they conscripted a certain
1974 899 1974 2671 5090 899 2779 30 5516
v.pai.3p r.asm.3 cj v.aas.3p r.asm.3 cj v.pai.3p

NASB

the crowd *to ask*
him to release Ba-
rabbas for them in-
stead. 12 Answering
again, Pilate said to
them, "Then what
shall I do with Him
whom you call the
King of the Jews?"
13 They shouted
back, "Crucify
Him!" 14 But Pi-
late said to them,
"Why, what evil
has He done?" But
they shouted all
the more, "Crucify
Him!" 15 Wishing to
satisfy the crowd,
Pilate released
Barabbas for them,
and after having
Jesus scourged, he
handed Him over
to be crucified.

Jesus Is Mocked

16 The soldiers
took Him away
into the palace
(that is, the Prae-
torium), and they
*called together
the whole *Roman*
[a]cohort. 17 They
*dressed Him up in
purple, and after
twisting a crown
of thorns, they put
it on Him; 18 and
they began to ac-
claim Him, "Hail,
King of the Jews!"
19 They kept beating
His head with a
[b]reed, and spitting
on Him, and kneel-
ing and bowing
before Him. 20 After
they had mocked
Him, they took
the purple robe off
Him and put His
own garments on
Him. And they *led
Him out to crucify
Him.
21 They *pressed

[a] [θέλετε] UBS, omitted by TNIV.
[b] [ὃν λέγετε] UBS.

[a] Or *battalion*
[b] Or *staff* (made of a reed)

NIV

man from Cyre-
ne, Simon, the
father of Alex-
ander and Rufus,
was passing by on
his way in from
the country, and
they forced him
to carry the cross.
22 They brought
Jesus to the place
called Golgotha
(which means
"the place of the
skull"). 23 Then
they offered him
wine mixed with
myrrh, but he did
not take it. 24 And
they crucified him.
Dividing up his
clothes, they cast
lots to see what
each would get.
25 It was nine in
the morning when
they crucified him.
26 The written no-
tice of the charge
against him read:
THE KING OF THE
JEWS.
27 They cruci-
fied two rebels
with him, one
on his right and
one on his left.
[28]a 29 Those who
passed by hurled
insults at him,
shaking their
heads and saying,
"So! You who are
going to destroy
the temple and
build it in three
days, 30 come down
from the cross and
save yourself!"
31 In the same way
the chief priests
and the teachers
of the law mocked
him among them-
selves. "He saved
others," they said,
"but he can't save
himself! 32 Let this
Messiah, this king
of Israel,

[a] 28 Some manuscripts include here words similar to Luke 22:37.

παράγοντά τινα Σίμωνα Κυρηναῖον
passerby, *certain* Simon of Cyrene (the father of Alexander and Rufus),
4135 5516 4981 3254 3836 4252 235 235 2779 4859
pt.pa.asm r.asm n.asm n.asm

ἐρχόμενον ἀπ᾽ ἀγροῦ, τὸν πατέρα Ἀλεξάνδρου καὶ Ῥούφου, ἵνα ἄρῃ
⌞as he was coming in⌟ from the country, *the* *father* *of Alexander* *and* *Rufus* to bear
2262 608 69 3836 4252 235 2779 4859 2671 149
pt.pm.asm p.g n.gsm d.asm n.asm n.gsm cj n.gsm cj v.aas.3s

τὸν σταυρὸν αὐτοῦ. 22 καὶ φέρουσιν αὐτὸν ἐπὶ τὸν Γολγοθᾶν τόπον,
{the} his cross. *his* And they brought him to the place Golgotha, *place*
3836 899 5089 899 2779 5770 899 2093 3836 5536 1201 5536
d.asm n.asm r.gsm.3 cj v.pai.3p r.asm.3 p.a d.asm n.asf n.asm

ὅ ⌞ἐστιν μεθερμηνευόμενον⌟ Κρανίου Τόπος. 23 καὶ ἐδίδουν αὐτῷ
(which means, Place of the Skull). *Place* And they offered him wine
4005 1639 3493 5536 3191 5536 2779 1443 899 3885
r.nsn v.pai.3s pt.pp.nsn n.gsn n.nsm cj v.iai.3p r.dsm.3

ἐσμυρνισμένον οἶνον· ὃς δὲ ↱ οὐκ ἔλαβεν. 24 καὶ σταυροῦσιν αὐτὸν
mixed with myrrh, *wine* but he *but* would not take it. Then they crucified him
5046 3885 1254 4005 1254 3284 4024 3284 2779 5090 899
pt.rp.asm n.asm r.nsm cj pl v.aai.3s cj v.pai.3p r.asm.3

καὶ διαμερίζονται τὰ ἱμάτια αὐτοῦ, βάλλοντες κλῆρον ἐπ᾽ αὐτὰ τίς
and divided *{the}* his clothing, *his* casting lots for them, to see who
2779 1374 3836 899 2668 899 965 3102 2093 899 5515
cj v.pmi.3p d.apn n.apn r.gsm.3 pt.pa.npm n.asm p.a r.apn.3 r.nsm

τί ἄρῃ. 25 ἦν δὲ ὥρα τρίτη καὶ ἐσταύρωσαν αὐτόν.
would take what. *would take* ⌞It was⌟ *{and}* the third hour, *third* and they crucified him.
149 149 5515 149 1639 1254 5569 6052 5569 2779 5090 899
r.asn v.aas.3s v.iai.3s cj n.nsf a.nsf cj v.aai.3p r.asm.3

26 καὶ ἦν ἡ ἐπιγραφὴ τῆς αἰτίας αὐτοῦ ἐπιγεγραμμένη· ὁ
And the inscription giving *the* *inscription* the accusation ⌞against him⌟ read, "The
2779 3836 2107 1639 3836 2107 3836 162 899 2108 3836
cj v.iai.3s d.nsf n.nsf d.gsf n.gsf r.gsm.3 pt.rp.nsf d.nsm

βασιλεὺς τῶν Ἰουδαίων. 27 καὶ σὺν αὐτῷ σταυροῦσιν δύο λῃστάς, ἕνα ἐκ
King of the Jews." And with him they crucified two robbers, one on his
995 3836 2681 2779 5250 899 5090 1545 3334 1651 1666
n.nsm d.gpm a.gpm cj p.d r.dsm.3 v.pai.3p a.apm n.apm a.asm p.g

δεξιῶν καὶ ἕνα ἐξ εὐωνύμων αὐτοῦ.[a] 29 καὶ οἱ παραπορευόμενοι
right and one on his left. *his* And those passing by
1288 2779 1651 1666 899 2381 899 2779 3836 4182
a.gpf cj a.asm p.g a.gpf r.gsm.3 cj d.npm pt.pm.npm

ἐβλασφήμουν αὐτὸν κινοῦντες τὰς κεφαλὰς αὐτῶν καὶ λέγοντες· οὐὰ ὁ
ridiculed him, wagging *{the}* their heads, *their* and saying, "Aha! ⌞You who⌟
1059 899 3075 3836 899 3051 899 2779 3306 4025 3836
v.iai.3p r.asm.3 pt.pa.npm d.apf n.apf r.gpm.3 cj pt.pa.npm j d.vsm

καταλύων τὸν ναὸν καὶ οἰκοδομῶν ἐν τρισὶν ἡμέραις, 30
would destroy the temple and rebuild it in three days, come down from the
2907 3836 3724 2779 3868 1877 5552 2465 2849 2849 608 3836
pt.pa.vsm d.asm n.asm cj pt.pa.vsm p.d a.dpf n.dpf

σῶσον σεαυτὸν καταβὰς ἀπὸ τοῦ σταυροῦ. 31 ὁμοίως καὶ οἱ ἀρχιερεῖς
cross and save yourself." *come down* *from* *the* *cross* So also the ruling priests,
5089 5392 4932 2849 608 3836 5089 3931 2779 3836 797
v.aam.2s r.asm.2 pt.aa.nsm p.g d.gsm n.gsm adv adv d.npm n.npm

ἐμπαίζοντες πρὸς ἀλλήλους μετὰ τῶν γραμματέων ἔλεγον· ἄλλους ἔσωσεν,
mocking among themselves, with the scribes, were saying, "Others he saved;
1850 4639 253 3552 3836 1208 3306 257 5392
pt.pa.npm p.a r.apm p.g d.gpm n.gpm v.iai.3p r.apm v.aai.3s

ἑαυτὸν οὐ δύναται σῶσαι· 32 ↱ ὁ χριστὸς ὁ βασιλεὺς Ἰσραὴλ
himself he can not *he can* save! Let the Christ, the king of Israel
1571 1538 1538 4024 1538 5392 2849 3836 5986 3836 995 2702
r.asm.3 pl v.ppi.3s f.aa d.nsm n.nsm d.nsm n.nsm n.gsm

[a] 28 καὶ ἐπληρώθη ἡ γραφὴ ἡ λέγουσα, καὶ μετὰ ἀνόμων ἐλογίσθη. included by TR after αὐτοῦ.

NASB

into service a pass-
er-by coming from
the country, Simon
of Cyrene (the
father of Alexander
and Rufus), to bear
His cross.

The Crucifixion

22 Then they
*brought Him to
the place Golgotha,
which is translated,
Place of a Skull.
23 They tried to give
Him wine mixed
with myrrh; but
He did not take it.
24 And they *cruci-
fied Him, and
*divided up His
garments among
themselves, cast-
ing lots for them
to decide what
each man should
take. 25 It was the
[a]third hour when
they crucified Him.
26 The inscription of
the charge against
Him read, "THE
KING OF THE
JEWS."
27 They *crucified
two robbers with
Him, one on His
right and one on
His left. 28 [[b]And
the Scripture was
fulfilled which
says, "And He was
numbered with
transgressors."]
29 Those passing by
were hurling abuse
at Him, wagging
their heads, and
saying, "Ha! You
who *are going to*
destroy the temple
and rebuild it in
three days, 30 save
Yourself, and
come down from
the cross!" 31 In the
same way the chief
priests also, along
with the scribes,
were mocking *Him*
among themselves
and saying, "He
saved others;
He cannot save
Himself. 32 Let *this*
Christ, the King
of Israel, now

[a] I.e. 9 a.m.
[b] Early mss do not contain this v

NIV

come down now from the cross, that we may see and believe." Those crucified with him also heaped insults on him.

The Death of Jesus

33 At noon, darkness came over the whole land until three in the afternoon. 34 And at three in the afternoon Jesus cried out in a loud voice, *"Eloi, Eloi, lema sabachthani?"* (which means "My God, my God, why have you forsaken me?").[a]

35 When some of those standing near heard this, they said, "Listen, he's calling Elijah."

36 Someone ran, filled a sponge with wine vinegar, put it on a staff, and offered it to Jesus to drink. "Now leave him alone. Let's see if Elijah comes to take him down," he said.

37 With a loud cry, Jesus breathed his last.

38 The curtain of the temple was torn in two from top to bottom.

39 And when the centurion, who stood there in front of Jesus, saw how he died,[b] he said, "Surely this man was the Son of God!"

40 Some women were watching from a distance. Among them were Mary Magdalene, Mary the mother of James the younger and of Joseph,[c] and Salome. 41 In Galilee these women had followed

a 34 Psalm 22:1
b 39 Some manuscripts *saw that he died with such a cry*
c 40 Greek *Joses,* a variant of *Joseph*; also in verse 47

καταβάτω νῦν ἀπὸ τοῦ σταυροῦ, ἵνα ἴδωμεν καὶ πιστεύσωμεν. καὶ οἱ
come down now from the cross, so that ⌞we may see⌟ and believe." And those
2849 3814 608 3836 5089 2671 1625 2779 4409 2779 3836
v.aam.3s adv p.g d.gsm n.gsm cj v.aas.1p cj v.aas.1p cj d.npm

συνεσταυρωμένοι σὺν αὐτῷ ὠνείδιζον αὐτόν. 33 καὶ → γενομένης
crucified with him were reviling him. And when the sixth hour had come,
5365 5250 899 3943 899 2779 1761 6052 1181
pt.rp.npm p.d r.dsm.3 v.iai.3p r.asm.3 cj pt.am.gsf

ὥρας ἕκτης σκότος ἐγένετο ἐφ᾽ ὅλην τὴν γῆν ἕως ὥρας ἐνάτης. 34 καὶ
hour *sixth* darkness fell over the whole *the* land until the ninth hour. *ninth* And
6052 1761 5030 1181 2093 3836 3910 3836 1178 2401 1888 6052 1888 2779
n.gsf a.gsf n.nsn v.ami.3s p.a a.asf d.asf n.asf p.g n.gsf a.gsf cj

τῇ ἐνάτῃ ὥρᾳ ἐβόησεν ὁ Ἰησοῦς → φωνῇ μεγάλῃ· ελωι ελωι λεμα
⌞at the⌟ ninth hour Jesus cried *{the}* *Jesus* with a loud voice, *loud* "Eloi, Eloi, lema
3836 1888 6052 2652 1066 3836 2652 3489 5889 3489 1830 1830 3316
d.dsf a.dsf n.dsf v.aai.3s d.nsm n.nsm n.dsf a.dsf j j j

σαβαχθανι; ὅ ⌞ἐστιν μεθερμηνευόμενον·⌟ ὁ θεός μου ὁ θεός μου,
sabachthani?" which means, *{the}* "My God, *My* *{the}* my God, *my*
4876 4005 1639 3493 3836 1609 2536 1609 3836 1609 2536 1609
j r.nsn v.pai.3s pt.pp.nsn d.vsm n.vsm r.gs.1 d.vsm n.vsm r.gs.1

⌞εἰς τί⌟ ἐγκατέλιπές με; 35 καί ↱ τινες τῶν παρεστηκότων ἀκούσαντες
why did you forsake me?" And when some of the bystanders heard this,
1650 5515 1593 1609 2779 201 5516 3836 4225 201
p.a r.asn v.aai.2s r.as.1 cj r.npm d.gpm pt.ra.gpm pt.aa.npm

ἔλεγον· ἴδε Ἠλίαν φωνεῖ. 36 δραμὼν δέ τις
they said, "Listen, he is calling Elijah!" *he is calling* Then someone ran, *Then* *someone*
3306 2623 5888 5888 5888 2460 5888 1254 5516 5556 1254 5516
v.iai.3p pl n.asm v.pai.3s pt.aa.nsm cj r.nsm

καὶ [a] γεμίσας σπόγγον ὄξους περιθεὶς → καλάμῳ ἐπότιζεν αὐτόν
{and} filled a sponge ⌞with sour wine,⌟ put it on a staff, and gave it to him
2779 1153 5074 3954 4363 2812 4540 899
cj pt.aa.nsm n.asm n.gsn pt.aa.nsm n.dsm v.iai.3s r.asm.3

↰ ↰ λέγων· ἄφετε ἴδωμεν εἰ ἔρχεται Ἠλίας καθελεῖν αὐτόν. ↰
to drink, saying, "Permit me; let us see if Elijah will come *Elijah* to take him down."
4540 4540 3306 918 1625 1623 2460 2262 2460 2747 899 2747
pt.pa.nsm v.aam.2p v.aas.1p cj v.pmi.3s n.nsm f.aa r.asm.3

37 ὁ δὲ Ἰησοῦς ἀφεὶς φωνὴν μεγάλην ἐξέπνευσεν. 38 καὶ τὸ
{the} And Jesus, uttering a loud cry, *loud* breathed his last. And the
3836 1254 2652 918 3489 5889 3489 1743 2779 3836
d.nsm cj n.nsm pt.aa.nsm n.asf a.asf v.aai.3s cj d.nsn

καταπέτασμα τοῦ ναοῦ ἐσχίσθη εἰς δύο ἀπ᾽ ἄνωθεν ἕως κάτω. 39 ἰδὼν δὲ
veil of the temple was torn in two, from top to bottom. *when saw* And
2925 3836 3724 5387 1650 1545 608 540 2401 3004 1625 1254
n.nsn d.gsm n.gsm v.api.3s p.a a.apn p.g adv p.g adv pt.aa.nsm cj

ὁ κεντυρίων ὁ παρεστηκὼς ἐξ ἐναντίας αὐτοῦ ὅτι οὕτως
when the centurion, who was standing in front of him, saw that ⌞in this way⌟
1625 3836 3035 3836 4225 1666 1885 899 1625 4022 4048
d.nsm n.nsm d.nsm pt.ra.nsm p.g a.gsf r.gsm.3 cj adv

ἐξέπνευσεν εἶπεν· ἀληθῶς οὗτος ὁ ἄνθρωπος υἱὸς θεοῦ ἦν.
he had died, he said, "Truly, this *{the}* man was the son of God!" *was*
1743 3306 242 4047 3836 476 1639 5626 2536 1639
v.aai.3s v.aai.3s adv r.nsm d.nsm n.nsm n.nsm n.gsm v.iai.3s

40 ἦσαν δὲ καὶ γυναῖκες ἀπὸ μακρόθεν θεωροῦσαι, ἐν αἷς
⌞There were⌟ *{and}* also women there, watching from a distance, *watching* among whom
1639 1254 2779 1222 2555 608 3427 2555 1877 4005
v.iai.3p cj adv n.npf p.g adv pt.pa.npf p.d r.dpf

καὶ Μαρία ἡ Μαγδαληνὴ καὶ Μαρία ἡ Ἰακώβου τοῦ μικροῦ καὶ
{also} were Mary *{the}* Magdalene, and Mary the mother of James the younger and
2779 3451 3836 3402 2779 3451 3836 3613 2610 3836 3625 2779
adv n.nsf d.nsf n.nsf cj n.nsf d.nsf n.gsm d.gsm a.gsm cj

Ἰωσῆτος μήτηρ καὶ Σαλώμη, 41 αἳ ὅτε ἦν ἐν τῇ Γαλιλαίᾳ ἠκολούθουν
of Joses, *mother* and Salome, who, when ⌞he was⌟ in *{the}* Galilee, used to follow
2736 3613 2779 4897 4005 4021 1639 1877 3836 1133 199
n.gsm n.nsf cj n.nsf r.npf cj v.iai.3s p.d d.dsf n.dsf v.iai.3p

a [καὶ] UBS, omitted by TNIV.

NASB

come down from the cross, so that we may see and believe!" Those who were crucified with Him were also insulting Him.

33 When the [a]sixth hour came, darkness fell over the whole land until the [b]ninth hour.
34 At the ninth hour Jesus cried out with a loud voice, "ELOI, ELOI, LAMA SABACHTHANI?" which is translated, "MY GOD, MY GOD, WHY HAVE YOU FORSAKEN ME?"
35 When some of the bystanders heard it, they *began* saying, "Behold, He is calling for Elijah."
36 Someone ran and filled a sponge with sour wine, put it on a reed, and gave Him a drink, saying, "Let us see whether Elijah will come to take Him down." 37 And Jesus uttered a loud cry, and breathed His last. 38 And the veil of the temple was torn in two from top to bottom.
39 When the centurion, who was standing right in front of Him, saw the way He breathed His last, he said, "Truly this man was the Son of God!"
40 There were also *some* women looking on from a distance, among whom *were* Mary Magdalene, and Mary the mother of James the Less and Joses, and Salome.
41 When He was in Galilee, they used to follow Him and

a I.e. noon
b I.e. 3 p.m.

NIV

him and cared for his needs. Many other women who had come up with him to Jerusalem were also there.

The Burial of Jesus

[42]It was Preparation Day (that is, the day before the Sabbath). So as evening approached, [43]Joseph of Arimathea, a prominent member of the Council, who was himself waiting for the kingdom of God, went boldly to Pilate and asked for Jesus' body. [44]Pilate was surprised to hear that he was already dead. Summoning the centurion, he asked him if Jesus had already died. [45]When he learned from the centurion that it was so, he gave the body to Joseph. [46]So Joseph bought some linen cloth, took down the body, wrapped it in the linen, and placed it in a tomb cut out of rock. Then he rolled a stone against the entrance of the tomb. [47]Mary Magdalene and Mary the mother of Joseph saw where he was laid.

Jesus Has Risen

16 When the Sabbath was over, Mary Magdalene, Mary the mother of James, and Salome bought spices so that they might go to anoint Jesus' body. [2]Very early on the first day of the week,

αὐτῷ καὶ διηκόνουν αὐτῷ, ↰ καὶ ἄλλαι πολλαὶ αἱ
him and care for his needs; and many other women *many* were there who
899 2779 1354 899 1354 2779 4498 257 4498 3836
r.dsm.3 cj v.iai.3p r.dsm.3 cj r.npf a.npf d.npf

συναναβᾶσαι αὐτῷ εἰς Ἱεροσόλυμα. 42 καὶ ↱ ↱ ἤδη ὀψίας
had come up with him to Jerusalem. And when evening had already *evening*
5262 899 1650 2642 2779 1181 4068 1181 2453 4068
pt.aa.npf r.dsm.3 p.a n.apn cj adv n.gsf

γενομένης, ἐπεὶ ἦν παρασκευὴ ὅ ἐστιν προσάββατον, 43 ἐλθὼν
come, since it was the day of Preparation (that is, the day before the Sabbath), *{going}*
1181 2075 1639 4187 4005 1639 4640 2262
pt.am.gsf cj v.iai.3s n.nsf r.nsn v.pai.3s a.nsn pt.aa.nsm

Ἰωσὴφ ὁ[a] ἀπὸ Ἁριμαθαίας εὐσχήμων βουλευτής, ὃς καὶ αὐτὸς ἦν
Joseph *{the}* of Arimathea, a respected ⌊member of the council,⌋ who also himself was
2737 3836 608 751 2363 1085 4005 2779 899 1639
n.nsm d.nsm p.g n.gsf a.nsm n.nsm r.nsm adv r.nsm v.iai.3s

προσδεχόμενος τὴν βασιλείαν τοῦ θεοῦ, τολμήσας εἰσῆλθεν πρὸς τὸν Πιλᾶτον
expecting the kingdom of God, went boldly *went* to *{the}* Pilate
4657 3836 993 3836 2536 1656 5528 1656 4639 3836 4397
pt.pm.nsm d.asf n.asf d.gsm n.gsm pt.aa.nsm v.aai.3s p.a d.asm n.asm

καὶ ᾐτήσατο τὸ σῶμα τοῦ Ἰησοῦ. 44 ὁ δὲ Πιλᾶτος ἐθαύμασεν εἰ ↱ ↱
and asked for the body of Jesus. *{the}* *{and}* Pilate was surprised that he was
2779 160 3836 5393 3836 2652 3836 1254 4397 2513 1623 2569 2569
cj v.ami.3s d.asn n.asn d.gsm n.gsm d.nsm cj n.nsm v.aai.3s cj

ἤδη τέθνηκεν καὶ προσκαλεσάμενος τὸν κεντυρίωνα ἐπηρώτησεν αὐτὸν εἰ
already dead, so summoning the centurion, he asked him if he
2453 2569 2779 4673 3836 3035 2089 899 1623 633
adv v.rai.3s cj pt.am.nsm d.asm n.asm v.aai.3s r.asm.3 cj

→ πάλαι ἀπέθανεν· 45 καὶ γνοὺς ἀπὸ τοῦ κεντυρίωνος
had been dead for a long time. *he had been dead* And learning from the centurion that he
633 633 633 4093 633 2779 1182 608 3836 3035
adv v.aai.3s cj pt.aa.nsm p.g d.gsm n.gsm

ἐδωρήσατο τὸ πτῶμα τῷ Ἰωσήφ. 46 καὶ ἀγοράσας σινδόνα
was dead, he gave the corpse to Joseph. So he brought a linen shroud, and
1563 3836 4773 3836 2737 2779 60 4984
v.ami.3s d.asn n.asn d.dsm n.dsm cj pt.aa.nsm n.asf

καθελὼν αὐτὸν ↰ ἐνείλησεν ← τῇ σινδόνι καὶ ἔθηκεν αὐτὸν ἐν μνημείῳ
taking him down, he wrapped him in the linen shroud and laid him in a tomb,
2747 899 2747 1912 3836 4984 2779 5502 899 1877 3646
pt.aa.nsm r.asm.3 v.aai.3s d.dsf n.dsf cj v.aai.3s r.asm.3 p.d n.dsn

ὃ ἦν λελατομημένον ἐκ πέτρας καὶ προσεκύλισεν λίθον ἐπὶ τὴν
which ⌊had been⌋ hewn ⌊out of⌋ rock; and he rolled a stone across the
4005 1639 3300 1666 4376 2779 4685 3345 2093 3836
r.nsn v.iai.3s pt.rp.nsn p.g n.gsf cj v.aai.3s n.asm p.a d.asf

θύραν τοῦ μνημείου. 47 ἡ δὲ Μαρία ἡ Μαγδαληνὴ καὶ Μαρία ἡ
entrance of the tomb. *{the}* *{and}* Mary *{the}* Magdalene and Mary the mother
2598 3836 3646 3836 1254 3451 3836 3402 2779 3451 3836
n.asf d.gsn n.gsn d.nsf cj n.nsf d.nsf n.nsf cj n.nsf d.nsf

Ἰωσῆτος ἐθεώρουν ποῦ τέθειται.
of Joses ⌊were watching closely⌋ where he was laid.
2736 2555 4543 5502
n.gsm v.iai.3p cj v.rpi.3s

16:1 καὶ → διαγενομένου τοῦ σαββάτου Μαρία ἡ Μαγδαληνὴ
And when the Sabbath was over, *the Sabbath* Mary *{the}* Magdalene,
2779 3836 4879 1335 3836 4879 3451 3836 3402
cj pt.am.gsn d.gsn n.gsn n.nsf d.nsf n.nsf

καὶ Μαρία ἡ τοῦ[b] Ἰακώβου καὶ Σαλώμη ἠγόρασαν ἀρώματα ἵνα
and Mary the mother of James, and Salome bought spices so that
2779 3451 3836 3836 2610 2779 4897 60 808 2671
cj n.nsf d.nsf d.gsm n.gsm cj n.nsf v.aai.3p n.apn cj

ἐλθοῦσαι ἀλείψωσιν αὐτόν. 2 καὶ λίαν πρωῒ τῇ μιᾷ τῶν σαββάτων
⌊they might go⌋ and anoint him. *{and}* Very early ⌊on the⌋ first day of the week,
2262 230 899 2779 3336 4745 3836 1651 3836 4879
pt.aa.npf v.aas.3p r.asm.3 cj adv adv d.dsf a.dsf d.gpn n.gpn

[a] [ὁ] UBS.
[b] [τοῦ] UBS.

NASB

minister to Him; and *there were* many other women who came up with Him to Jerusalem.

Jesus Is Buried

[42]When evening had already come, because it was the preparation day, that is, the day before the Sabbath, [43]Joseph of Arimathea came, a prominent member of the Council, who himself was waiting for the kingdom of God; and he gathered up courage and went in before Pilate, and asked for the body of Jesus. [44]Pilate wondered if He was dead by this time, and summoning the centurion, he questioned him as to whether He was already dead. [45]And ascertaining this from the centurion, he granted the body to Joseph. [46]Joseph bought a linen cloth, took Him down, wrapped Him in the linen cloth and laid Him in a tomb which had been hewn out in the rock; and he rolled a stone against the entrance of the tomb. [47]Mary Magdalene and Mary the *mother* of Joses were looking on *to see* where He was laid.

The Resurrection

[16:1]When the Sabbath was over, Mary Magdalene, and Mary the *mother* of James, and Salome, bought spices, so that they might come and anoint Him. [2]Very early on the first day of the week,

NIV

just after sunrise,
they were on their
way to the tomb
3and they asked
each other, "Who
will roll the stone
away from the
entrance of the
tomb?"
4But when they
looked up, they
saw that the stone,
which was very
large, had been
rolled away. 5As
they entered the
tomb, they saw
a young man
dressed in a white
robe sitting on the
right side, and they
were alarmed.
6"Don't be
alarmed," he said.
"You are looking
for Jesus the Naz-
arene, who was
crucified. He has
risen! He is not
here. See the place
where they laid
him. 7But go, tell
his disciples and
Peter, 'He is going
ahead of you into
Galilee. There you
will see him, just
as he told you.'"
8Trembling and
bewildered, the
women went out
and fled from the
tomb. They said
nothing to anyone,
because they were
afraid.[a]

[The earliest manuscripts and some other ancient witnesses do not have verses 9–20.]

[a] 8 Some manuscripts have the following ending between verses 8 and 9, and one manuscript has it after verse 8 (omitting verses 9-20): *Then they quickly reported all these instructions to those around Peter. After this, Jesus himself also sent out through them from east to west the sacred and imperishable proclamation of eternal salvation. Amen.*

ἔρχονται ἐπὶ τὸ μνημεῖον ἀνατείλαντος τοῦ ἡλίου. 3καὶ ἔλεγον
they came to the tomb, the sun having risen. *the* *sun* And ⌊they were saying⌋
2262 2093 3836 3646 3836 2463 422 3836 2463 2779 3306
v.pmi.3p p.a d.asn n.asn pt.aa.gsm d.gsm n.gsm cj v.iai.3p

πρὸς ἑαυτάς· τίς ἀποκυλίσει ἡμῖν τὸν λίθον ἐκ τῆς θύρας τοῦ
to themselves, "Who will roll away the stone for us *the* *stone* from the entrance of the
4639 1571 5515 653 3836 3345 7005 3836 3345 1666 3836 2598 3836
p.a r.apf.3 r.nsm v.fai.3s r.dp.1 d.asm n.asm p.g d.gsf n.gsf d.gsn

μνημείου; 4καὶ ἀναβλέψασαι θεωροῦσιν ὅτι ἀποκεκύλισται ὁ λίθος·
tomb?" And looking up, they saw that the stone had been rolled away *the* *stone*
3646 2779 329 2555 4022 3836 3345 653 3836 3345
n.gsn cj pt.aa.npf v.pai.3p cj v.rpi.3s d.nsm n.nsm

ἦν γὰρ μέγας σφόδρα. 5καὶ ⌊εἰσελθοῦσαι εἰς⌋ τὸ μνημεῖον εἶδον
— for it was *for* very large. *very* And entering the tomb, they saw a
1142 1639 1142 5379 3489 5379 2779 1656 1650 3836 3646 1625
v.iai.3s cj a.nsm adv cj pt.aa.npf p.a d.asn n.asn v.aai.3p

νεανίσκον καθήμενον ἐν τοῖς δεξιοῖς περιβεβλημένον στολὴν λευκήν, καὶ
young man sitting on the right, dressed in a white robe, *white* and
3734 2764 1877 3836 1288 4314 3328 5124 3328 2779
n.asm pt.pm.asm p.d d.dpn a.dpn pt.rm.asm n.asf a.asf cj

ἐξεθαμβήθησαν. 6ὁ δὲ λέγει αὐταῖς· ↱ μὴ ἐκθαμβεῖσθε· Ἰησοῦν
they were alarmed. But he *But* said to them, "Do not be alarmed. You seek Jesus
1701 1254 3836 1254 3306 899 1701 3590 1701 2426 2426 2652
v.api.3p d.nsm cj v.pai.3s r.dpf.3 pl v.ppm.2p n.asm

ζητεῖτε τὸν Ναζαρηνὸν τὸν ἐσταυρωμένον· ἠγέρθη, οὐκ ἔστιν
You seek the Nazarene, who was crucified. ⌊He has been raised.⌋ He is not *He is*
2426 3836 3716 3836 5090 1586 1639 1639 4024 1639
v.pai.2p d.asm n.asm d.asm pt.rp.asm v.api.3s pl v.pai.3s

ὧδε· ἴδε ὁ τόπος ὅπου ἔθηκαν αὐτόν. 7ἀλλὰ ὑπάγετε εἴπατε τοῖς
here. Look, there is the place where they laid him. But go, tell *{the}* his
6045 2623 3836 5536 3963 5502 899 247 5632 3306 3836 899
adv pl d.nsm n.nsm cj v.aai.3p r.asm.3 cj v.pam.2p v.aam.2p d.dpm

μαθηταῖς αὐτοῦ καὶ τῷ Πέτρῳ ὅτι προάγει ὑμᾶς εἰς τὴν Γαλιλαίαν·
disciples *his* and *{the}* Peter, ~ ⌊'He is going before⌋ you into *{the}* Galilee.
3412 899 2779 3836 4377 4022 4575 7007 1650 3836 1133
n.dpm r.gsm.3 cj d.dsm n.dsm cj v.pai.3s r.ap.2 p.a d.asf n.asf

ἐκεῖ αὐτὸν ὄψεσθε, καθὼς εἶπεν ὑμῖν. 8καὶ ἐξελθοῦσαι ἔφυγον ἀπὸ
There you will see him, *you will see* just as he told you.'" And going outside, they fled from
1695 3972 3972 3972 899 3972 2777 3306 7007 2779 2002 5771 608
adv r.asm.3 v.fmi.2p cj v.aai.3s r.dp.2 cj pt.aa.npf v.aai.3p p.g

τοῦ μνημείου, εἶχεν γὰρ αὐτὰς τρόμος καὶ
the tomb, for trembling and astonishment ⌊had taken hold of⌋ *for* them. *trembling* *and*
3836 3646 1142 5571 2779 1749 2400 1142 899 5571 2779
d.gsn n.gsn v.iai.3s cj r.apf.3 n.nsm cj

ἔκστασις· καὶ οὐδενὶ οὐδὲν εἶπαν, ἐφοβοῦντο γάρ. 9 →
astonishment And they said nothing to anyone, *nothing they said* for they were afraid. *for* Now when
1749 2779 3306 3306 4029 4029 4029 3306 1142 5828 1142 1254
n.nsf cj a.dsm a.asn v.aai.3p v.imi.3p cj

⟦ἀναστὰς δὲ πρωῒ → πρώτῃ → σαββάτου ἐφάνη πρῶτον Μαρίᾳ
Jesus arose *Now* early on the first day of the week, he appeared first to Mary
482 1254 4745 4755 4879 5743 4754 3451
pt.aa.nsm cj adv a.dsf n.gsn v.api.3s adv n.dsf

τῇ Μαγδαληνῇ, παρ' ἧς ἐκβεβλήκει ἑπτὰ δαιμόνια. 10ἐκείνη πορευθεῖσα
{the} Magdalene, from whom he had cast out seven demons. She went out and
3836 3402 4123 4005 1675 2231 1228 1697 4513
d.dsf n.dsf p.g r.gsf v.lai.3s a.apn n.apn r.nsf pt.ap.nsf

ἀπήγγειλεν τοῖς μετ' αὐτοῦ γενομένοις πενθοῦσι καὶ
reported to those who had been with him, *who had been* ⌊as they were mourning⌋ and
550 3836 1181 1181 1181 3552 899 1181 4291 2779
v.aai.3s d.dpm p.g r.gsm.3 pt.am.dpm pt.pa.dpm cj

κλαίουσιν· 11κἀκεῖνοι ἀκούσαντες ὅτι ζῇ καὶ ἐθεάθη ὑπ' αὐτῆς
weeping. And when they heard that ⌊he was alive⌋ and ⌊had been seen⌋ by her,
3081 2797 201 4022 2409 2779 2517 5679 899
pt.pa.dpm cj pt.aa.npm cj v.pai.3s cj v.api.3s p.g r.gsf.3

NASB

they *came to the
tomb when the sun
had risen. 3They
were saying to one
another, "Who
will roll away the
stone for us from
the entrance of
the tomb?" 4Look-
ing up, they *saw
that the stone had
been rolled away,
although it was
extremely large.
5Entering the tomb,
they saw a young
man sitting at the
right, wearing a
white robe; and
they were amazed.
6And he *said to
them, "Do not be
amazed; you are
looking for Jesus
the Nazarene, who
has been crucified.
He has risen; He is
not here; behold,
here is the place
where they laid
Him. 7But go, tell
His disciples and
Peter, 'He is going
ahead of you to
Galilee; there you
will see Him, just
as He told you.'"
8They went out and
fled from the tomb,
for trembling and
astonishment had
gripped them; and
they said nothing
to anyone, for they
were afraid.
9[[a]Now after He
had risen early
on the first day of
the week, He first
appeared to Mary
Magdalene, from
whom He had cast
out seven demons.
10She went and
reported to those
who had been with
Him, while they
were mourning and
weeping. 11When
they heard that He
was alive and had
been seen by her,

[a] Later mss add vv 9-20

NIV

[9]When Jesus rose
early on the first day
of the week, he ap-
peared first to Mary
Magdalene, out of
whom he had driv-
en seven demons.
[10]She went and told
those who had been
with him and who
were mourning and
weeping. [11]When they
heard that Jesus was
alive and that she
had seen him, they
did not believe it.
[12]Afterward Jesus
appeared in a dif-
ferent form to two of
them while they were
walking in the coun-
try. [13]These returned
and reported it to the
rest; but they did not
believe them either.
[14]Later Jesus ap-
peared to the Eleven
as they were eating;
he rebuked them for
their lack of faith and
their stubborn refus-
al to believe those
who had seen him af-
ter he had risen.
[15]He said to them,
"Go into all the
world and preach
the gospel to all cre-
ation. [16]Whoever
believes and is bap-
tized will be saved,
but whoever does not
believe will be con-
demned. [17]And these
signs will accompany
those who believe:
In my name they will
drive out demons;
they will speak in
new tongues; [18]they
will pick up snakes
with their hands;
and when they drink
deadly poison, it will
not hurt them at all;
they will place their
hands on sick peo-
ple, and they will get
well."
[19]After the Lord
Jesus had spoken to
them, he was taken
up into heaven and

ἠπίστησαν. [12] μετὰ δὲ ταῦτα δυσὶν ἐξ
⌊they refused to believe⌋ it. After {and} this, he appeared in another form to two of
601 3552 1254 4047 5746 5746 1877 2283 3671 1545 1666
v.aai.3p p.a cj r.apn a.dpm p.g

αὐτῶν περιπατοῦσιν ἐφανερώθη ἐν ἑτέρᾳ μορφῇ πορευομένοις εἰς
them ⌊as they were walking along,⌋ he appeared in another form going into the
899 4344 5746 1877 2283 3671 4513 1650
r.gpm.3 pt.pa.dpm v.api.3s p.d r.dsf n.dsf pt.pm.dpm p.a

ἀγρόν· [13] κἀκεῖνοι → ← ἀπελθόντες ἀπήγγειλαν τοῖς λοιποῖς· οὐδὲ ←
country. And when they returned, they reported it to the others; but they refused
69 2797 599 550 3836 3370 4028 4409
n.asm cj pt.aa.npm v.aai.3p d.dpm a.dpm cj

ἐκείνοις ἐπίστευσαν. [14] ὕστερον δὲ [a]
to believe them. they to believe Later {and} he appeared to the eleven themselves
4409 4409 1697 4409 5731 1254 5746 5746 3836 3836 1894 899
r.dpm v.aai.3p adv.c cj

ἀνακειμένοις αὐτοῖς τοῖς ἕνδεκα ἐφανερώθη καὶ ὠνείδισεν τὴν
⌊as they were reclining at table;⌋ themselves to the eleven he appeared and he reproached {the} their
367 899 3836 1894 5746 2779 3943 3836 899
pt.pm.dpm r.dpm d.dpm a.dpm v.api.3s cj v.aai.3s d.asf

ἀπιστίαν αὐτῶν καὶ σκληροκαρδίαν ὅτι τοῖς
unbelief their and hardness of heart, because they had refused to believe those
602 899 2779 5016 4022 4409 4409 4024 4409 4409 3836
n.asf r.gpm.3 cj n.asf cj d.dpm

θεασαμένοις αὐτὸν ἐγηγερμένον οὐκ ἐπίστευσαν. [15] καὶ εἶπεν αὐτοῖς·
who had seen him resurrected. refused they had to believe And he said to them,
2517 899 1586 4024 4409 2779 3306 899
pt.am.dpm r.asm.3 pt.rp.asm pl v.aai.3p cj v.aai.3s r.dpm.3

πορευθέντες εἰς τὸν κόσμον ἅπαντα κηρύξατε τὸ εὐαγγέλιον πάσῃ τῇ
"Go into all the world all and proclaim the gospel to every {the}
4513 1650 570 3836 3180 570 3062 3836 2295 4246 3836
pt.ap.npm p.a d.asm n.asm a.asm v.aam.2p d.asn n.asn a.dsf d.dsf

κτίσει. [16] ὁ πιστεύσας καὶ βαπτισθεὶς σωθήσεται, ὁ δὲ
creature. The one who believes and is baptized will be saved, but the but
3232 3836 4409 2779 966 5392 1254 3836 1254
n.dsf d.nsm pt.aa.nsm cj pt.ap.nsm v.fpi.3s d.nsm cj

ἀπιστήσας κατακριθήσεται. [17] σημεῖα δὲ τοῖς
⌊one who refuses to believe⌋ will be condemned. And these signs And will accompany those
601 2891 1254 4047 4956 1254 4158 4158 3836
pt.aa.nsm v.fpi.3s n.npn cj d.dpm

πιστεύσασιν ταῦτα παρακολουθήσει· ἐν τῷ ὀνόματί μου
who believe: these will accompany in {the} my name my they will cast out
4409 4047 4158 1877 3836 1609 3950 1609 1675 1675 1675 1675
pt.aa.dpm r.npn v.fai.3s p.d d.dsn n.dsn r.gs.1

δαιμόνια ἐκβαλοῦσιν, → γλώσσαις λαλήσουσιν καιναῖς, [18] [b]καὶ
demons; they will cast out they will speak in new tongues; they will speak new {and}
1228 1675 3281 3281 3281 2785 1185 3281 2785 2779
n.apn v.fai.3p n.dpf v.fai.3p a.dpf cj

ἐν ταῖς χερσὶν ὄφεις ἀροῦσιν κἂν θανάσιμόν
with their hands they will pick up snakes; they will pick up ⌊and if⌋ they drink any deadly poison
1877 3836 5931 149 149 149 149 4058 149 2829 4403 4403 5516 2503
p.d d.dpf n.dpf n.apm v.fai.3p crasis a.asn

τι πίωσιν ⌊οὐ μὴ⌋ αὐτοὺς βλάψῃ, ἐπὶ
any they drink it will in no way harm them; it will harm they will lay hands on the
5516 4403 1055 1055 4024 3590 1055 899 1055 2202 2202 2202 5931 2093
r.asn v.aas.3p pl pl r.apm.3 v.aas.3s p.a

ἀρρώστους χεῖρας ἐπιθήσουσιν καὶ ⌊καλῶς ἕξουσιν.⌋ [19] ὁ μὲν οὖν
sick, hands they will lay and they will recover." Then the ~ Then
779 5931 2202 2779 2822 2400 4036 3836 3525 4036
a.apm n.apf v.fai.3p cj adv v.fai.3p d.nsm pl cj

κύριος Ἰησοῦς μετὰ τὸ λαλῆσαι αὐτοῖς ἀνελήμφθη εἰς τὸν οὐρανὸν καὶ
Lord Jesus, after {the} he had spoken to them, was taken up into {the} heaven, and
3261 2652 3552 3836 3281 899 377 1650 3836 4041 2779
n.nsm n.nsm p.a d.asn f.aa r.dpm.3 v.api.3s p.a d.asm n.asm cj

[a] [δὲ] UBS.
[b] [καὶ ἐν ταῖς χερσὶν] UBS.

NASB

they refused to be-
lieve it.
[12]After that, He
appeared in a dif-
ferent form to two
of them while they
were walking along
on their way to the
country. [13]They
went away and
reported it to the
others, but they did
not believe them
either.

The Disciples Commissioned

[14]Afterward He
appeared to the
eleven themselves
as they were reclin-
ing *at the table;*
and He reproached
them for their un-
belief and hardness
of heart, because
they had not be-
lieved those who
had seen Him after
He had risen. [15]And
He said to them,
"Go into all the
world and preach
the gospel to all
creation. [16]He who
has believed and
has been baptized
shall be saved;
but he who has
disbelieved shall
be condemned.
[17]These signs will
accompany those
who have believed:
in My name they
will cast out de-
mons, they will
speak with new
tongues; [18]they will
pick up serpents,
and if they drink
any deadly *poison,*
it will not hurt
them; they will
lay hands on the
sick, and they will
recover."
[19]So then, when
the Lord Jesus had
spoken to them, He
was received up
into heaven and

NIV

he sat at the right
hand of God.
20 Then the disci-
ples went out and
preached every-
where, and the
Lord worked with
them and con-
firmed his word by
the signs that ac-
companied it.

ἐκάθισεν	ἐκ		δεξιῶν	τοῦ	θεοῦ. 20			ἐκεῖνοι	δὲ	ἐξελθόντες
sat down	at	the	right hand	of	God.	And	going out,	they	*And*	*going out*
2767	1666		1288	3836	2536	1254	2002 2002	1697	1254	2002
v.aai.3s	p.g		a.gpf	d.gsm	n.gsm			r.npm	cj	pt.aa.npm

ἐκήρυξαν	πανταχοῦ,	↱	τοῦ	κυρίου	συνεργοῦντος	καὶ		τὸν	λόγον
proclaimed	everywhere,	while	the	Lord	worked alongside	and	confirmed	the	message
3062	4116	5300	3836	3261	5300	2779	1011	3836	3364
v.aai.3p	adv		d.gsm	n.gsm	pt.pa.gsm	cj		d.asm	n.asm

βεβαιοῦντος	διὰ	τῶν	ἐπακολουθούντων	σημείων.
confirmed	through	the	accompanying	signs.
1011	1328	3836	2051	4956
pt.pa.gsm	p.g	d.gpn	pt.pa.gpn	n.gpn

NASB

sat down at the
right hand of God.
20 And they went
out and preached
everywhere, while
the Lord worked
with them, and
confirmed the word
by the signs that
followed.]

[[a] *And they promptly reported all these instructions to Peter and his companions. And after that, Jesus Himself sent out through them from east to west the sacred and imperishable proclamation of eternal salvation.*]

[a] A few late mss and versions contain this paragraph, usually after v 8; a few have it at the end of ch

Luke

NIV

Luke

Introduction

1 Many have
undertaken
to draw up an ac-
count of the things
that have been ful-
filled[a] among us,
²just as they were
handed down to us
by those who from
the first were eye-
witnesses and ser-
vants of the word.
³With this in mind,
since I myself have
carefully investi-
gated everything
from the begin-
ning, I too decided
to write an orderly
account for you,
most excellent
Theophilus, ⁴so
that you may know
the certainty of the
things you have
been taught.

The Birth of John the Baptist Foretold

⁵In the time of
Herod king of
Judea there was
a priest named
Zechariah, who
belonged to the
priestly division
of Abijah; his wife
Elizabeth was also
a descendant of
Aaron. ⁶Both of
them were righ-
teous in the sight
of God, observing
all the Lord's com-
mands and decrees
blamelessly. ⁷But
they were childless
because Elizabeth
was not able to
conceive, and they
were both very

[a] 1 Or *been surely believed*

1:1 ἐπειδήπερ πολλοὶ ἐπεχείρησαν ἀνατάξασθαι διήγησιν περὶ τῶν
Inasmuch as many ⌊have taken it in hand⌋ to compile a narrative concerning the
2077 4498 2217 421 1456 4309 3836
cj a.npm v.aai.3p f.am n.asf p.g d.gpn

πεπληροφορημένων ἐν ἡμῖν πραγμάτων, ²καθὼς παρέδοσαν ἡμῖν οἱ
things that have been accomplished among us, *things* just as *have delivered* *to us* those
4547 4442 1877 7005 4547 2777 4140 7005 3836
pt.rp.gpn p.d r.dp.1 n.gpn cj v.aai.3p r.dp.1 d.npm

ἀπ' ἀρχῆς αὐτόπται καὶ ὑπηρέται γενόμενοι τοῦ λόγου,
who were, from the beginning, eyewitnesses and became ministers *became* of the word,
608 794 898 2779 1181 5677 1181 3836 3364
p.g n.gsf n.npm cj n.npm pt.am.npm d.gsm n.gsm

³ἔδοξε κἀμοὶ → παρηκολουθηκότι
have delivered it to us, ⌊it seemed good⌋ to me also, having carefully investigated
4140 4140 7005 7005 1506 2743 209 4158
v.aai.3s crasis pt.ra.dsm

ἄνωθεν πᾶσιν ἀκριβῶς καθεξῆς
everything ⌊for a long time,⌋ *everything* *carefully* to write down the events ⌊in an orderly sequence⌋
4246 540 4246 209 1211 1211 1211 2759
adv a.dpn adv adv

σοι γράψαι, κράτιστε Θεόφιλε, ⁴ἵνα ἐπιγνῷς περὶ
⌊for you,⌋ *to write down* most excellent Theophilus, so that ⌊you may know⌋ the truth about the
5148 1211 3196 2541 2671 2105 3836 854 4309
r.ds.2 f.aa a.vsm.s n.vsm cj v.aas.2s p.g

ὧν κατηχήθης λόγων τὴν ἀσφάλειαν. ⁵ἐγένετο ἐν ταῖς ἡμέραις
things that ⌊you have been taught.⌋ *things* *the* *truth* There was in the days
3364 4005 2994 3364 3836 854 1181 1877 3836 2465
r.gpm v.api.2s n.gpm d.asf n.asf v.ami.3s p.d d.dpf n.dpf

Ἡρῴδου βασιλέως τῆς Ἰουδαίας ἱερεύς τις → ὀνόματι Ζαχαρίας ἐξ
of Herod, king of Judah, a certain priest *certain* by the name of Zechariah, of
2476 995 3836 2677 5516 2636 5516 3950 2408 1666
n.gsm n.gsm d.gsf n.gsf n.nsm r.nsm n.dsn n.nsm p.g

ἐφημερίας Ἀβιά, καὶ γυνὴ αὐτῷ ἐκ τῶν θυγατέρων Ἀαρὼν καὶ
the priestly division of Abijah; and his wife *his* was from the daughters of Aaron, and
2389 7 2779 899 1222 899 1666 3836 2588 2 2779
n.gsf n.gsm cj n.nsf r.dsm.3 p.g d.gpf n.gpf n.gsm cj

τὸ ὄνομα αὐτῆς Ἐλισάβετ. ⁶ ἦσαν δὲ δίκαιοι ἀμφότεροι
{the} her name *her* was Elizabeth. And they were *And* both righteous *both*
3836 899 3950 899 1810 1254 1639 1254 317 1465 317
d.nsn n.nsn r.gsf.3 n.nsf v.iai.3p cj a.npm a.npm

ἐναντίον τοῦ θεοῦ, πορευόμενοι ἐν πάσαις ταῖς ἐντολαῖς καὶ
before *{the}* God, walking blamelessly in all the commandments and
1883 3836 2536 4513 289 1877 4246 3836 1953 2779
p.g d.gsm n.gsm pt.pm.npm p.d a.dpf d.dpf n.dpf cj

δικαιώμασιν τοῦ κυρίου ἄμεμπτοι. ⁷καὶ ↱ οὐκ ἦν αὐτοῖς τέκνον, καθότι
ordinances of the Lord. *blamelessly* But they did not have *they* a child, because
1468 3836 3261 289 2779 899 1639 4024 1639 899 5451 2776
n.dpn d.gsm n.gsm a.npm cj pl v.iai.3s r.dpm.3 n.nsn cj

ἦν ἡ Ἐλισάβετ στεῖρα, καὶ ἀμφότεροι προβεβηκότες ἐν
Elizabeth was *{the}* *Elizabeth* barren, and both of them were advanced in
1810 1639 3836 1810 5096 2779 317 899 899 1639 4581 1877
v.iai.3s d.nsf n.nsf a.nsf cj a.npm pt.ra.npm p.d

NASB

Introduction

1:1Inasmuch as
many have under-
taken to compile
an account of the
things accom-
plished among us,
²just as they were
handed down to
us by those who
from the beginning
were eyewitnesses
and servants of the
[a]word, ³it seemed
fitting for me as
well, having inves-
tigated everything
carefully from the
beginning, to write
it out for you in
consecutive order,
most excellent
Theophilus; ⁴so
that you may know
the exact truth
about the things
you have been
taught.

Birth of John the Baptist Foretold

⁵In the days of
Herod, king of
Judea, there was
a priest named
Zacharias, of the
division of [b]Abijah;
and he had a wife
[c]from the daughters
of Aaron, and her
name was Eliza-
beth. ⁶They were
both righteous in
the sight of God,
walking blameless-
ly in all the com-
mandments and
requirements of the
Lord. ⁷But they had
no child, because
Elizabeth was bar-
ren, and they were
both advanced in

[a] I.e. gospel
[b] Gr *Abia*
[c] I.e. of priestly de-
scent

NIV

old.
8 Once when
Zechariah's divi-
sion was on duty
and he was serving
as priest before
God, 9 he was cho-
sen by lot, accord-
ing to the custom
of the priesthood,
to go into the tem-
ple of the Lord
and burn incense.
10 And when the
time for the burn-
ing of incense
came, all the as-
sembled worship-
ers were praying
outside.
11 Then an an-
gel of the Lord
appeared to him,
standing at the
right side of the
altar of incense.
12 When Zecha-
riah saw him, he
was startled and
was gripped with
fear. 13 But the an-
gel said to him:
"Do not be afraid,
Zechariah; your
prayer has been
heard. Your wife
Elizabeth will bear
you a son, and you
are to call him
John. 14 He will be
a joy and delight to
you, and many will
rejoice because of
his birth, 15 for he
will be great in the
sight of the Lord.
He is never to take
wine or other fer-
mented drink, and
he will be filled
with the Holy Spir-
it even before he
is born. 16 He will
bring back many
of the people of
Israel to the Lord
their God. 17 And

ταῖς ἡμέραις αὐτῶν ἦσαν. 8 ἐγένετο δὲ ἐν τῷ ἱερατεύειν
{the} years. *of them* *were* Now it happened, *Now* while *{the}* he ⌊was serving as priest⌋
3836 2465 899 1639 1254 1181 1254 1877 3836 899 2634
d.dpf n.dpf r.gpm.3 v.iai.3p v.ami.3s cj p.d d.dsn f.pa

αὐτὸν ἐν τῇ τάξει τῆς ἐφημερίας αὐτοῦ ἔναντι
he before God when *{the}* his priestly division ⌊was on duty,⌋ *{the}* *division* *his* *before*
899 1882 2536 1877 3836 899 2389 5423 3836 2389 899 1882
r.asm.3 p.d d.dsf n.dsf d.gsf n.gsf r.gsm.3 p.g

τοῦ θεοῦ, 9 κατὰ τὸ ἔθος τῆς ἱερατείας ἔλαχε τοῦ
{the} *God* that ⌊according to⌋ the custom of the priesthood, ⌊he was chosen by lot⌋ to
3836 2536 2848 3836 1621 3836 2632 3275 3836
d.gsm n.gsm p.a d.asn n.asn d.gsf n.gsf v.aai.3s d.gsn

θυμιάσαι εἰσελθὼν εἰς τὸν ναὸν τοῦ κυρίου, 10 καὶ πᾶν
burn incense go into the temple of the Lord and burn incense, and the whole
2594 1656 1650 3836 3724 3836 3261 2594 2594 2779 3836 4246
f.aa pt.aa.nsm p.a d.asm n.asm d.gsm n.gsm cj a.nsn

τὸ πλῆθος ἦν τοῦ λαοῦ ↰ προσευχόμενον ἔξω τῇ ὥρᾳ τοῦ
the crowd of people was *of* *people* there, praying outside ⌊at the⌋ hour of
3836 4436 3836 3295 1639 3836 3295 1639 4667 2032 3836 6052 3836
d.nsn n.nsn v.iai.3s d.gsm n.gsm pt.pm.nsn adv d.dsf n.dsf d.gsn

θυμιάματος. 11 ὤφθη δὲ αὐτῷ ἄγγελος κυρίου ἑστὼς
incense. And an angel of the Lord appeared *And* to him, *angel* *of Lord* standing
2592 1254 34 3261 3261 3972 1254 899 34 3261 2705
n.gsn v.api.3s cj r.dsm.3 n.nsm n.gsm pt.ra.nsm

ἐκ δεξιῶν τοῦ θυσιαστηρίου τοῦ θυμιάματος. 12 καὶ ἐταράχθη
at the right side of the altar of incense. *{and}* Zechariah was troubled
1666 1288 3836 2603 3836 2592 2779 2408 5429
p.g a.gpf d.gsn n.gsn d.gsn n.gsn cj v.api.3s

Ζαχαρίας ἰδὼν καὶ φόβος ἐπέπεσεν ἐπ᾽ αὐτόν. 13 εἶπεν δὲ
Zechariah ⌊when he saw⌋ him and fear fell upon him. But the angel said *But*
2408 1625 2779 5832 2158 2093 899 1254 3836 34 3306 1254
n.nsm pt.aa.nsm cj n.nsm v.aai.3s p.a r.asm.3 v.aai.3s cj

πρὸς αὐτὸν ὁ ἄγγελος, ↱ μὴ φοβοῦ, Ζαχαρία, διότι εἰσηκούσθη
to him: *the* *angel* "Do not fear, Zechariah, because your prayer has been heard,
4639 899 3836 34 5828 3590 5828 2408 1484 5148 1255 1653
p.a r.asm.3 d.nsm n.nsm pl v.ppm.2s n.vsm cj v.api.3s

ἡ δέησίς σου, καὶ ἡ γυνή σου Ἐλισάβετ γεννήσει υἱόν σοι καὶ
{the} *prayer* *your* and *{the}* your wife *your* Elizabeth will bear you a son, *you* and
3836 1255 5148 2779 3836 5148 1222 5148 1810 1164 5148 5626 5148 2779
d.nsf n.nsf r.gs.2 cj d.nsf n.nsf r.gs.2 n.nsf v.fai.3s n.asm r.ds.2 cj

καλέσεις τὸ ὄνομα αὐτοῦ Ἰωάννην. 14 καὶ ἔσται χαρά σοι
you will call *{the}* his name *his* John. And for you ⌊there will be⌋ joy *for you*
2813 3836 899 3950 899 2722 2779 5148 5148 1639 5915 5148
v.fai.2s d.asn n.asn r.gsm.3 n.asm cj v.fmi.3s n.nsf r.ds.2

καὶ ἀγαλλίασις καὶ πολλοὶ ἐπὶ τῇ γενέσει αὐτοῦ χαρήσονται.
and gladness, and many will rejoice ⌊because of,⌋ *{the}* his birth, *his* *will rejoice*
2779 21 2779 4498 5897 5897 2093 3836 899 1161 899 5897
cj n.nsf cj a.npm p.d d.dsf n.dsf r.gsm.3 v.fpi.3p

15 ἔσται γὰρ μέγας ἐνώπιον τοῦ[a] κυρίου, καὶ οἶνον καὶ
for ⌊he will be⌋ *for* great before the Lord. And he must not drink wine and
1142 1639 1142 3489 1967 3836 3261 2779 4403 4403 4024 4403 3885 2779
v.fmi.3s cj a.nsm p.g d.gsm n.gsm cj n.asm cj

σίκερα ⌊οὐ μὴ⌋ πίῃ, καὶ πνεύματος ἁγίου
strong drink, *not* *he must drink* and he will be filled with the Holy Spirit, *Holy*
4975 4024 3590 4403 2779 4398 4398 4398 4398 4398 41 4460 41
n.asn pl pl v.aas.3s cj n.gsn a.gsn

πλησθήσεται ἔτι ἐκ κοιλίας μητρὸς αὐτοῦ, 16 καὶ
he will be filled with even from his mother's womb. *mother's* *his* and he will restore
4398 2285 1666 899 3613 3120 3613 899 2779 2188 2188 2188
v.fpi.3s adv p.g n.gsf n.gsf r.gsm.3 cj

πολλοὺς τῶν υἱῶν Ἰσραὴλ ἐπιστρέψει ἐπὶ κύριον τὸν θεὸν αὐτῶν. 17 καὶ
many of the sons of Israel *he will restore* to the Lord *{the}* their God. *their* *{and}*
4498 3836 5626 2702 2188 2093 3261 3836 899 2536 899 2779
a.apm d.gpm n.gpm n.gsm v.fai.3s p.a n.asm d.asm n.asm r.gpm.3 cj

[a] [τοῦ] UBS.

NASB

years.
8 Now it happened
that while he was
performing his
priestly service
before God in the
appointed order of
his division, 9 ac-
cording to the cus-
tom of the priestly
office, he was
chosen by lot to
enter the temple of
the Lord and burn
incense. 10 And the
whole multitude
of the people were
in prayer outside
at the hour of the
incense offering.
11 And an angel of
the Lord appeared
to him, standing
to the right of the
altar of incense.
12 Zacharias was
troubled when he
saw *the angel,* and
fear gripped him.
13 But the angel said
to him, "Do not be
afraid, Zacharias,
for your petition
has been heard, and
your wife Elizabeth
will bear you a son,
and you will give
him the name John.
14 You will have joy
and gladness, and
many will rejoice
at his birth. 15 For
he will be great
in the sight of the
Lord; and he will
drink no wine or
liquor, and he will
be filled with the
Holy Spirit while
yet in his mother's
womb. 16 And he
will turn many of
the sons of Israel
back to the Lord
their God. 17 It is

NIV

he will go on be-
fore the Lord,
in the spirit and
power of Elijah,
to turn the hearts
of the parents to
their children and
the disobedient
to the wisdom of
the righteous—to
make ready a peo-
ple prepared for
the Lord."
[18]Zechariah asked
the angel, "How
can I be sure of
this? I am an old
man and my wife
is well along in
years."
[19]The angel said
to him, "I am Ga-
briel. I stand in the
presence of God,
and I have been
sent to speak to
you and to tell you
this good news.
[20]And now you
will be silent and
not able to speak
until the day this
happens, because
you did not believe
my words, which
will come true at
their appointed
time."
[21]Meanwhile, the
people were wait-
ing for Zechariah
and wondering
why he stayed so
long in the temple.
[22]When he came
out, he could not
speak to them.
They realized he
had seen a vision
in the temple, for
he kept making
signs to them but
remained unable to
speak.
[23]When his time
of service was
completed, he re-
turned

αὐτὸς προελεύσεται ἐνώπιον αὐτοῦ ἐν πνεύματι καὶ δυνάμει Ἠλίου, ἐπιστρέψαι
He will go on before him, in the spirit and power of Elijah, to turn
899 4601 1967 899 1877 4460 2779 1539 2460 2188
r.nsm v.fmi.3s p.g r.gsm.3 p.d n.dsn cj n.dsf n.gsm f.aa

καρδίας πατέρων ἐπὶ τέκνα καὶ ἀπειθεῖς ἐν φρονήσει →
the hearts of fathers toward their children, and the disobedient to the wisdom of the
2840 4252 2093 5451 2779 579 1877 5860
n.apf n.gpm p.a n.apn cj a.apm p.d n.dsf

δικαίων, ἑτοιμάσαι → κυρίῳ λαὸν κατεσκευασμένον. [18] καὶ
righteous, in order to establish for the Lord a people who are prepared for him." But
1465 2286 3261 3295 2941 2779
a.gpm f.aa n.dsm n.asm pt.rp.asm cj

εἶπεν Ζαχαρίας πρὸς τὸν ἄγγελον, ⌞κατὰ τί⌟ γνώσομαι τοῦτο; ἐγὼ
Zechariah said *Zechariah* to the angel, "How ⌞can I be sure of⌟ this? For I
2408 3306 2408 4639 3836 34 2848 5515 1182 4047 1142 1609
v.aai.3s n.nsm p.a d.asm n.asm p.a r.asn v.fmi.1s r.asn r.ns.1

γάρ εἰμι πρεσβύτης καὶ ἡ γυνή μου προβεβηκυῖα ἐν ταῖς ἡμέραις αὐτῆς.
For am an old man and *{the}* my wife *my* is advanced in *{the}* years?" *{her}*
1142 1639 4566 2779 3836 1609 1222 1609 4581 1877 3836 2465 899
cj v.pai.1s n.nsm cj d.nsf n.nsf r.gs.1 pt.ra.nsf p.d d.dpf n.dpf r.gsf.3

[19] καὶ ἀποκριθεὶς ὁ ἄγγελος εἶπεν αὐτῷ, ἐγώ εἰμι Γαβριὴλ ὁ
And the angel answered, *the* *angel* saying to him, "I am Gabriel, who
2779 3836 34 646 3836 34 3306 899 1609 1639 1120 3836
cj pt.ap.nsm d.nsm n.nsm v.aai.3s r.dsm.3 r.ns.1 v.pai.1s n.nsm d.nsm

παρεστηκὼς ἐνώπιον τοῦ θεοῦ καὶ ἀπεστάλην λαλῆσαι πρὸς σὲ καὶ
stands in the presence of God, and I was sent to speak to you, and
4225 1967 3836 2536 2779 690 3281 4639 5148 2779
pt.ra.nsm p.g d.gsm n.gsm cj v.api.1s f.aa p.a r.as.2 cj

εὐαγγελίσασθαί σοι ↰ ↰ ↰ ↰ ταῦτα· [20] καὶ ἰδοὺ ἔσῃ
to tell you the good news of these things. And now ⌞you will be⌟
2294 5148 2294 2294 2294 2294 4047 2779 2627 1639
f.am r.ds.2 r.apn cj j v.fmi.2s

σιωπῶν καὶ μὴ δυνάμενος λαλῆσαι ἄχρι ἧς ἡμέρας ↰ ↰
⌞reduced to silence⌟ and not be able to speak until the day in which these things
4995 2779 3590 1538 3281 948 4005 2465 4005 4005 4047 4047
pt.pa.nsm cj pl pt.pp.nsm f.aa p.g r.gsf n.gsf

γένηται ταῦτα, ⌞ἀνθ' ὧν⌟ ↱ ↱ οὐκ ἐπίστευσας τοῖς λόγοις μου, οἵτινες
happen, *these things* because you did not believe *{the}* my words, *my* which
1181 4047 505 4005 4409 4409 4024 4409 3836 1609 3364 1609 4015
v.ams.3s r.npn p.g r.gpn pl v.aai.2s d.dpm n.dpm r.gs.1 r.npm

πληρωθήσονται εἰς τὸν καιρὸν αὐτῶν. [21] καὶ ἦν ὁ λαὸς
will be fulfilled in *{the}* their time." *their* And the people were *the* *people*
4444 1650 3836 899 2789 899 2779 3836 3295 1639 3836 3295
v.fpi.3p p.a d.asm n.asm r.gpm.3 cj v.iai.3s d.nsm n.nsm

προσδοκῶν τὸν Ζαχαρίαν καὶ ἐθαύμαζον ἐν τῷ χρονίζειν ἐν τῷ
waiting for *{the}* Zechariah, and ⌞they began to wonder⌟ why *{the}* he stayed so long in the
4659 3836 2408 2779 2513 1877 3836 899 5988 1877 3836
pt.pa.nsm d.asm n.asm cj v.iai.3p p.d d.dsn f.pa p.d d.dsm

ναῷ αὐτόν. [22] ἐξελθὼν δὲ ↱ ↱ οὐκ ἐδύνατο λαλῆσαι αὐτοῖς, καὶ
temple. *he* ⌞When he came out,⌟ *{and}* he was not able to speak to them; and
3724 899 2002 1254 1538 1538 4024 1538 3281 899 2779
n.dsm r.asm.3 pt.aa.nsm cj pl v.ipi.3s f.aa r.dpm.3 cj

ἐπέγνωσαν ὅτι ὀπτασίαν ἑώρακεν ἐν τῷ ναῷ· καὶ αὐτὸς ἦν
they realized that he had seen a vision *he had seen* in the temple *{and}* (he kept
2105 4022 3972 3972 3972 3965 3972 1877 3836 3724 2779 899 1639
v.aai.3p cj n.asf v.rai.3s p.d d.dsm n.dsm cj r.nsm v.iai.3s

διανεύων αὐτοῖς καὶ διέμενεν κωφός. [23] καὶ ἐγένετο ὡς
gesturing to them and remained mute). *{and}* *{it happened that}* When the days of his
1377 899 2779 1373 3273 2779 1181 6055 3836 2465 3836 899
pt.pa.nsm r.dpm.3 cj v.iai.3s a.nsm cj v.ami.3s cj

ἐπλήσθησαν αἱ ἡμέραι τῆς λειτουργίας αὐτοῦ, ἀπῆλθεν εἰς τὸν
priestly service were over, *the* *days* *of* *priestly service* *his* he went to *{the}* his
3311 3311 4398 3836 2465 3836 3311 899 599 1650 3836 899
v.api.3p d.npf n.npf d.gsf n.gsf r.gsm.3 v.aai.3s p.a d.asm

NASB

he who will go
as a forerunner
before Him in the
spirit and power
of Elijah, TO TURN
THE HEARTS OF THE
FATHERS BACK TO
THE CHILDREN, and
the disobedient to
the attitude of the
righteous, so as
to make ready a
people prepared for
the Lord."
[18]Zacharias said
to the angel, "How
will I know this *for*
certain? For I am
an old man and my
wife is advanced
in years." [19]The
angel answered
and said to him, "I
am Gabriel, who
stands in the pres-
ence of God, and I
have been sent to
speak to you and to
bring you this good
news. [20]And be-
hold, you shall be
silent and unable to
speak until the day
when these things
take place, because
you did not believe
my words, which
will be fulfilled in
their proper time."
[21]The people were
waiting for Zacha-
rias, and were won-
dering at his delay
in the temple. [22]But
when he came out,
he was unable to
speak to them; and
they realized that
he had seen a vi-
sion in the temple;
and he kept making
signs to them, and
remained mute.
[23]When the days of
his priestly service
were ended, he

NIV

home. [24]After this his wife Elizabeth became pregnant and for five months remained in seclusion. [25]"The Lord has done this for me," she said. "In these days he has shown his favor and taken away my disgrace among the people."

The Birth of Jesus Foretold

[26]In the sixth month of Elizabeth's pregnancy, God sent the angel Gabriel to Nazareth, a town in Galilee, [27]to a virgin pledged to be married to a man named Joseph, a descendant of David. The virgin's name was Mary. [28]The angel went to her and said, "Greetings, you who are highly favored! The Lord is with you."

[29]Mary was greatly troubled at his words and wondered what kind of greeting this might be. [30]But the angel said to her, "Do not be afraid, Mary; you have found favor with God. [31]You will conceive and give birth to a son, and you are to call him Jesus. [32]He will be great and will be called the Son of the Most High. The Lord God will give him the throne of his father David, [33]and he will reign over Jacob's

---

οἶκον αὐτοῦ. [24] μετὰ δὲ ταύτας τὰς ἡμέρας συνέλαβεν
home. *his* After *{and}* these *{the}* days, Elizabeth his wife became pregnant,
3875 899 3552 1254 4047 3836 2465 1810 899 1222 5197
n.asm r.gsm.3 p.a cj r.apf d.apf n.apf v.aai.3s

Ἐλισάβετ ἡ γυνὴ αὐτοῦ καὶ περιέκρυβεν ἑαυτὴν ↰ ↰ μῆνας πέντε
Elizabeth *{the}* *wife* *his* and she kept herself in seclusion for five months, *five*
1810 3836 1222 899 2779 4332 1571 4332 4332 4297 3604 4297
n.nsf d.nsf n.nsf r.gsm.3 cj v.iai.3s r.asf.3 n.apm a.apm

λέγουσα [25] ὅτι οὕτως μοι πεποίηκεν κύριος ἐν ἡμέραις
saying, ~ "Thus the Lord has done ⌊for me⌋ *has done* *Lord* in the days
3306 4022 4048 3261 4472 4472 1609 4472 3261 1877 2465
pt.pa.nsf cj adv r.ds.1 v.rai.3s n.nsm p.d n.dpf

αἷς ἐπεῖδεν ἀφελεῖν ὄνειδός μου ἐν ἀνθρώποις. [26] ἐν δὲ
in which he looked with favor to take away my reproach *my* among people." In *{and}*
4005 2078 904 1609 3945 1609 1877 476 1877 1254
r.dpf v.aai.3s f.aa n.asn r.gs.1 p.d n.dpm p.d cj

τῷ μηνὶ τῷ ἕκτῳ ἀπεστάλη ὁ ἄγγελος Γαβριὴλ ἀπὸ τοῦ
the sixth month *{the}* *sixth* the angel Gabriel was sent *the* *angel* *Gabriel* from *{the}*
3836 1761 3604 3836 1761 3836 34 1120 690 3836 34 1120 608 3836
d.dsm n.dsm d.dsm a.dsm v.api.3s d.nsm n.nsm n.nsm p.g d.gsm

θεοῦ εἰς πόλιν τῆς Γαλιλαίας ᾗ ὄνομα Ναζαρὲθ [27] πρὸς παρθένον
God to a town of Galilee that was called Nazareth, to a virgin
2536 1650 4484 3836 1133 4005 3950 3714 4639 4221
n.gsm p.a n.asf d.gsf n.gsf r.dsf n.nsn n.nsf p.a n.asf

ἐμνηστευμένην → ἀνδρὶ ᾧ ὄνομα Ἰωσὴφ ἐξ οἴκου Δαυὶδ καὶ τὸ
pledged to be married to a man whose name was Joseph, of the house of David, and the
3650 467 4005 3950 2737 1666 3875 1253 2779 3836
pt.rp.asf n.dsm r.dsm n.nsn n.nsm p.g n.gsm n.gsm cj d.nsn

ὄνομα τῆς παρθένου Μαριάμ. [28] καὶ ↱ εἰσελθὼν πρὸς αὐτὴν εἶπεν,
name of the virgin was Mary. And he came to her and said,
3950 3836 4221 3452 2779 3306 1656 4639 899 3306
n.nsn d.gsf n.gsf n.nsf cj pt.aa.nsm p.a r.asf.3 v.aai.3s

χαῖρε, κεχαριτωμένη, ὁ κύριος μετὰ σοῦ.[a] [29] ἡ δὲ
"Greetings, highly favored one, the Lord is with you!" She *{and}* was thoroughly
5897 5923 3836 3261 3552 5148 3836 1254 1410 1410
v.pam.2s pt.rp.vsf d.nsm n.nsm p.g r.gs.2 d.nsf cj

ἐπὶ τῷ λόγῳ διεταράχθη καὶ διελογίζετο ποταπὸς
troubled by what he said, *was thoroughly troubled* and tried to discern ⌊what sort of⌋ greeting this
1410 2093 3836 3364 1410 2779 1368 4534 833 4047
p.d d.dsm n.dsm v.api.3s cj v.imi.3s r.nsm

εἴη ὁ ἀσπασμὸς οὗτος. [30] καὶ εἶπεν ὁ ἄγγελος αὐτῇ, ↱ μὴ
⌊could be.⌋ *{the}* *greeting* *this* And the angel said *the* *angel* to her, "Do not
1639 3836 833 4047 2779 3836 34 3306 3836 34 899 5828 3590
v.pao.3s d.nsm n.nsm r.nsm cj v.aai.3s d.nsm n.nsm r.dsf.3 pl

φοβοῦ, Μαριάμ, εὗρες γὰρ χάριν παρὰ τῷ θεῷ. [31] καὶ ἰδοὺ
be afraid, Mary, for ⌊you have found⌋ *for* favor with *{the}* God. *{and}* Look,
5828 3452 1142 2351 1142 5921 4123 3836 2536 2779 2627
v.ppm.2s n.vsf v.aai.2s cj n.asf p.d d.dsm n.dsm cj j

συλλήμψῃ ἐν γαστρὶ καὶ τέξῃ υἱὸν καὶ καλέσεις τὸ ὄνομα
you will conceive in your womb and ⌊give birth to⌋ a son, and you will call *{the}* his name
5197 1877 1143 2779 5503 5626 2779 2813 3836 899 3950
v.fmi.2s p.d n.dsf cj v.fmi.2s n.asm cj v.fai.2s d.asn n.asn

αὐτοῦ Ἰησοῦν. [32] οὗτος ἔσται μέγας καὶ υἱὸς →
his Jesus. ⌊This very one⌋ will be great, and will be called the Son of the
899 2652 4047 1639 3489 2779 2813 2813 2813 5626
r.gsm.3 n.asm r.nsm v.fmi.3s a.nsm cj n.nsm

ὑψίστου κληθήσεται καὶ δώσει αὐτῷ κύριος ὁ θεὸς τὸν θρόνον
Most High; *will be called* and the Lord God will give him *Lord* *the* *God* the throne
5736 2813 2779 3836 3261 2536 1443 899 3261 3836 2536 3836 2585
a.gsm.s v.fpi.3s cj v.fai.3s r.dsm.3 n.nsm d.nsm n.nsm d.asm n.asm

Δαυὶδ τοῦ πατρὸς αὐτοῦ, [33] καὶ βασιλεύσει ἐπὶ τὸν οἶκον Ἰακὼβ
of his father David. *of* *father* *his* *{and}* He will reign over the house of Jacob
3836 899 4252 1253 3836 4252 899 2779 996 2093 3836 3875 2609
n.gsm d.gsm n.gsm r.gsm.3 cj v.fai.3s p.a d.asm n.asm n.gsm

[a] εὐλογημένη σὺ ἐν γυναιξίν included by TR after σοῦ.

NASB

went back home.

[24]After these days Elizabeth his wife became pregnant, and she kept herself in seclusion for five months, saying, [25]"This is the way the Lord has dealt with me in the days when He looked *with favor* upon *me,* to take away my disgrace among men."

Jesus' Birth Foretold

[26]Now in the sixth month the angel Gabriel was sent from God to a city in Galilee called Nazareth, [27]to a virgin engaged to a man whose name was Joseph, of the descendants of David; and the virgin's name was Mary. [28]And coming in, he said to her, "Greetings, favored one! The Lord *is* with you." [29]But she was very perplexed at *this* statement, and kept pondering what kind of salutation this was. [30]The angel said to her, "Do not be afraid, Mary; for you have found favor with God. [31]And behold, you will conceive in your womb and bear a son, and you shall name Him Jesus. [32]He will be great and will be called the Son of the Most High; and the Lord God will give Him the throne of His father David; [33]and He will reign over the house of Jacob

NIV

descendants for-
ever; his kingdom
will never end.”
34“How will this
be,” Mary asked
the angel, “since I
am a virgin?”
35The angel an-
swered, “The Holy
Spirit will come on
you, and the power
of the Most High
will overshadow
you. So the holy
one to be born will
be called[a] the Son
of God. 36Even
Elizabeth your
relative is going
to have a child in
her old age, and
she who was said
to be unable to
conceive is in her
sixth month. 37For
no word from God
will ever fail.”
38“I am the Lord’s
servant,” Mary an-
swered. “May your
word to me be ful-
filled.” Then the
angel left her.

Mary Visits Elizabeth

39At that time
Mary got ready
and hurried to a
town in the hill
country of Judea,
40where she en-
tered Zechariah’s
home and greeted
Elizabeth. 41When
Elizabeth heard
Mary’s greeting,
the baby leaped
in her womb, and
Elizabeth was
filled with the
Holy Spirit. 42In a
loud voice she ex-
claimed:

εἰς τοὺς αἰῶνας καὶ τῆς βασιλείας αὐτοῦ οὐκ ἔσται τέλος.
for all time, and of his kingdom *his* there will be no *there will be* end.”
1650 3836 172 2779 3836 899 993 899 1639 1639 1639 4024 1639 5465
p.a d.apm n.apm cj d.gsf n.gsf r.gsm.3 pl v.fmi.3s n.nsn

34 εἶπεν δὲ Μαριὰμ πρὸς τὸν ἄγγελον, πῶς → ἔσται τοῦτο, ἐπεὶ
Mary said *{and}* *Mary* to the angel, “How will this be, *this* since I
3452 3306 1254 3452 4639 3836 34 4802 4047 1639 4047 2075 1182
v.aai.3s cj n.nsf p.a d.asm n.asm cj v.fmi.3s r.nsn cj

ἄνδρα οὐ γινώσκω; 35 καὶ
have no sexual relationship with a man?” *no* *I have sexual relationship with* And the angel
1182 4024 1182 1182 1182 467 4024 1182 2779 3836 34
n.asm pl v.pai.1s cj

ἀποκριθεὶς ὁ ἄγγελος εἶπεν αὐτῇ, πνεῦμα ἅγιον ἐπελεύσεται ἐπὶ σὲ
answered, *the* *angel* saying to her, “The Holy Spirit *Holy* will come upon you
646 3836 34 3306 899 41 4460 41 2088 2093 5148
pt.ap.nsn d.nsm n.nsm v.aai.3s r.dsf.3 n.nsn a.nsn v.fmi.3s p.a r.as.2

καὶ δύναμις → ὑψίστου ἐπισκιάσει σοι· διὸ καὶ τὸ γεννώμενον
and the power of the Most High will overshadow you: therefore *{also}* the child to be born will
2779 1539 5736 2173 5148 1475 2779 3836 1164
cj n.nsf a.gsm.s v.fai.3s r.ds.2 cj adv d.nsn pt.pp.nsn

ἅγιον κληθήσεται υἱὸς θεοῦ. 36 καὶ ἰδοὺ Ἐλισάβετ ἡ
be holy; he will be called the Son of God. *{and}* Look, your relative Elizabeth, *{the}*
41 2813 5626 2536 2779 2627 5148 5151 1810 3836
a.nsn v.fpi.3s n.nsm n.gsm cj j n.nsf d.nsf

συγγενίς σου καὶ αὐτὴ συνείληφεν υἱὸν ἐν γήρει αὐτῆς καὶ οὗτος
relative *your* she also *she* has conceived a son in her old age; *her* indeed, this is
5151 5148 899 2779 899 5197 5626 1877 899 1179 899 2779 4047 1639
n.nsf r.gs.2 adv r.nsf v.rai.3s n.asm p.d n.dsn r.gsf.3 cj r.nsm

μὴν ἕκτος ἐστὶν αὐτῇ τῇ καλουμένῃ στείρᾳ· 37 ὅτι οὐκ
the sixth month *sixth* *is* with her who was called barren. For *{not}* nothing
1761 3604 1761 1639 899 3836 2813 5096 4022 4024 4246
n.nsm a.nsm v.pai.3s r.dsf.3 d.dsf pt.pp.dsf a.dsf cj pl

ἀδυνατήσει παρὰ τοῦ θεοῦ ⌞πᾶν ῥῆμα.⌟ 38 εἶπεν δὲ Μαριάμ, ἰδοὺ
will be impossible for *{the}* God.” *nothing* So Mary said, *So* *Mary* “Behold,
104 4123 3836 2536 4246 4839 1254 3452 3306 1254 3452 2627
v.fai.3s p.g d.gsm n.gsm a.nsn n.nsn v.aai.3s cj n.nsf j

ἡ δούλη → κυρίου· γένοιτό μοι κατὰ τὸ ῥῆμά σου. καὶ
the maidservant of the Lord! Let it happen to me ⌞according to⌟ *{the}* your word.” *your* Then
3836 1527 3261 1181 1609 2848 3836 5148 4839 5148 2779
d.nsf n.nsf n.gsm v.amo.3s r.ds.1 p.a d.asn n.asn r.gs.2 cj

ἀπῆλθεν ἀπ’ αὐτῆς ὁ ἄγγελος. 39 ἀναστᾶσα δὲ
the angel departed from her. *the* *angel* In those days Mary arose *{and}*
3836 34 599 608 899 3836 34 1877 4047 2465 3452 482 1254
v.aai.3s p.g r.gsf.3 d.nsm n.nsm pt.aa.nsf cj

Μαριὰμ ἐν ταῖς ἡμέραις ταύταις ἐπορεύθη εἰς τὴν ὀρεινὴν μετὰ σπουδῆς εἰς
Mary *In* *{the}* *days* *those* and went into the hill country with eagerness, to
3452 1877 3836 2465 4047 4513 1650 3836 3978 3552 5082 1650
n.nsf p.d d.dpf n.dpf r.dpf v.api.3s p.a d.asf n.asf p.g n.gsf p.a

πόλιν Ἰούδα, 40 καὶ εἰσῆλθεν εἰς τὸν οἶκον Ζαχαρίου καὶ ἠσπάσατο τὴν
a town in Judah, and she entered into the house of Zechariah. *{and}* She greeted *{the}*
4484 2683 2779 1656 1650 3836 3875 2408 2779 832 3836
n.asf n.gsm cj v.aai.3s p.a d.asm n.asm n.gsm cj v.ami.3s d.asf

Ἐλισάβετ. 41 καὶ ἐγένετο ὡς ἤκουσεν τὸν ἀσπασμὸν τῆς Μαρίας
Elizabeth, and *{it happened that}* when Elizabeth heard the greeting of Mary,
1810 2779 1181 6055 1810 201 3836 833 3836 3451
n.asf cj v.ami.3s cj v.aai.3s d.asm n.asm d.gsf n.gsf

ἡ Ἐλισάβετ, ἐσκίρτησεν τὸ βρέφος ἐν τῇ κοιλίᾳ αὐτῆς, καὶ
{the} *Elizabeth* the baby leaped *the* *baby* in *{the}* her womb. *her* *{and}*
3836 1810 3836 1100 5015 3836 1100 1877 3836 899 3120 899 2779
d.nsf n.nsf v.aai.3s d.nsn n.nsn p.d d.dsf n.dsf r.gsf.3 cj

ἐπλήσθη → πνεύματος ἁγίου ἡ Ἐλισάβετ, 42 καὶ ἀνεφώνησεν
Elizabeth was filled with the Holy Spirit, *Holy* *{the}* *Elizabeth* and exclaimed
1810 4398 41 4460 41 3836 1810 2779 430
v.api.3s n.gsn a.gsn d.nsf n.nsf cj v.aai.3s

NASB

forever, and His
kingdom will have
no end.” 34Mary
said to the angel,
“How can this be,
since I am a vir-
gin?” 35The angel
answered and said
to her, “The Holy
Spirit will come
upon you, and the
power of the Most
High will over-
shadow you; and
for that reason the
holy Child shall be
called the Son of
God. 36And behold,
even your relative
Elizabeth has also
conceived a son in
her old age; and
she who was called
barren is now in
her sixth month.
37For nothing will
be impossible with
God.” 38And Mary
said, “Behold, the
[a]bondslave of the
Lord; may it be
done to me accord-
ing to your word.”
And the angel de-
parted from her.

Mary Visits Elizabeth

39Now at this time
Mary arose and
went in a hurry to
the hill country,
to a city of Judah,
40and entered the
house of Zacha-
rias and greeted
Elizabeth. 41When
Elizabeth heard
Mary’s greeting,
the baby leaped
in her womb; and
Elizabeth was
filled with the Holy
Spirit. 42And she
cried out with

[a] 35 Or *So the child to be born will be called holy,*

[a] I.e. female slave

NIV

"Blessed are you
among women,
and blessed is the
child you will
bear! 43 But why
am I so favored,
that the mother of
my Lord should
come to me? 44 As
soon as the sound
of your greeting
reached my ears,
the baby in my
womb leaped for
joy. 45 Blessed is
she who has be-
lieved that the
Lord would fulfill
his promises to
her!"

Mary's Song

46 And Mary said:

"My soul glorifies
the Lord
47 and my spirit
rejoices in
God my
Savior,
48 for he has been
mindful
of the humble
state of his
servant.
From now on all
generations
will call me
blessed,
49 for the Mighty
One has done
great things
for me—
holy is his
name.
50 His mercy extends
to those who
fear him,
from
generation to
generation.
51 He has performed
mighty deeds
with his arm;
he has scattered
those who
are proud in
their inmost
thoughts.
52 He has brought
down rulers
from their
thrones
but has lifted up
the humble.
53 He has filled the

→ κραυγῇ μεγάλῃ καὶ εἶπεν, εὐλογημένη σὺ ἐν γυναιξὶν καὶ
with a loud cry, *loud* *{and}* saying, "Blessed are you among women, and
3489 3199 3489 2779 3306 2328 5148 1877 1222 2779
n.dsf a.dsf cj v.aai.3s pt.rp.nsf r.ns.2 p.d n.dpf cj

εὐλογημένος ὁ καρπὸς τῆς κοιλίας σου. 43 καὶ πόθεν μοι
blessed is the fruit of your womb! *your* And why should this happen to me
2328 3836 2843 3836 5148 3120 5148 2779 4470 4047 1609
pt.rp.nsm d.nsm n.nsm d.gsf n.gsf r.gs.2 cj pl r.ds.1

τοῦτο ἵνα ἔλθῃ ἡ μήτηρ τοῦ κυρίου μου πρὸς ἐμέ;
this that the mother of my Lord ⌊should come⌋ *the* *mother* *of* *Lord* *my* to me?
4047 2671 3836 3613 3836 1609 3261 2262 3836 3613 3836 3261 1609 4639 1609
r.nsn cj v.aas.3s d.nsf n.nsf d.gsm n.gsm r.gs.1 p.a r.as.1

44 ἰδοὺ γὰρ ὡς ἐγένετο ἡ φωνὴ τοῦ ἀσπασμοῦ σου
For behold, *For* as the sound of your greeting came *the* *sound* *of* *greeting* *your*
1142 2627 1142 6055 3836 5889 3836 5148 833 1181 3836 5889 3836 833 5148
j cj cj v.ami.3s d.nsf n.nsf d.gsm n.gsm r.gs.2

εἰς τὰ ὦτά μου, ἐσκίρτησεν ἐν ἀγαλλιάσει τὸ βρέφος
into *{the}* my ear, *my* the baby in my womb leaped for joy. *the* *baby*
1650 3836 1609 4044 1609 3836 1100 1877 1609 3120 5015 1877 21 3836 1100
p.a d.apn n.apn r.gs.1 v.aai.3s p.d n.dsf d.nsn n.nsn

ἐν τῇ κοιλίᾳ μου. 45 καὶ μακαρία ἡ πιστεύσασα ὅτι ἔσται
in *{the}* *womb* *my* *{and}* Blessed is she who believed that ⌊there would be⌋ a
1877 3836 3120 1609 2779 3421 3836 4409 4022 1639
p.d d.dsf n.dsf r.gs.1 cj a.nsf d.nsf pt.aa.nsf cj v.fmi.3s

τελείωσις τοῖς λελαλημένοις αὐτῇ παρὰ κυρίου. 46 καὶ εἶπεν Μαριάμ,
fulfillment of what was spoken to her from the Lord." And Mary said, *Mary* "My
5459 3836 3281 899 4123 3261 2779 3452 3306 3452 1609
n.nsf d.dpn pt.rp.dpn r.dsf.3 p.g n.gsm cj v.aai.3s n.nsf

μεγαλύνει ἡ ψυχή μου τὸν κύριον, 47 καὶ ἠγαλλίασεν τὸ πνεῦμά
soul magnifies *{the}* *soul* *My* the Lord, and my spirit rejoices *{the}* *spirit*
6034 3486 3836 6034 1609 3836 3261 2779 1609 4460 22 3836 4460
v.pai.3s d.nsf n.nsf r.gs.1 d.asm n.asm cj v.aai.3s d.nsn n.nsn

μου ἐπὶ τῷ θεῷ τῷ σωτῆρί μου, 48 ὅτι ἐπέβλεψεν ἐπὶ τὴν ταπείνωσιν
my because of God *{the}* my Savior, *my* for he has looked on the humble estate
1609 2093 3836 2536 3836 1609 5400 1609 4022 2098 2093 3836 5428
r.gs.1 p.d d.dsm n.dsm d.dsm n.dsm r.gs.1 cj v.aai.3s p.a d.asf n.asf

τῆς δούλης αὐτοῦ. ἰδοὺ γὰρ ἀπὸ τοῦ νῦν μακαριοῦσίν
of his maidservant. *his* For behold, *For* from *{the}* now on all generations will declare
3836 899 1527 899 1142 2627 1142 608 3836 3814 4246 1155 3420
d.gsf n.gsf r.gsm.3 j cj p.g d.gsn adv v.fai.3p

με ↰ πᾶσαι αἱ γενεαί, 49 ὅτι ἐποίησέν μοι
me blessed, *all* *{the}* *generations* because the Almighty has done great things ⌊for me.⌋
1609 3420 4246 3836 1155 4022 3836 1543 4472 3489 3489 1609
r.as.1 a.npf d.npf n.npf cj v.aai.3s r.ds.1

μεγάλα ὁ δυνατός. καὶ ἅγιον τὸ ὄνομα αὐτοῦ, 50 καὶ τὸ ἔλεος
great things *the* *Almighty* *{and}* His name is holy, *{the}* *name* *His* and *{the}* his mercy
3489 3836 1543 2779 899 3950 41 3836 3950 899 2779 3836 899 1799
a.apn d.nsm a.nsm cj a.nsn d.nsn n.nsn r.gsm.3 cj d.nsn n.nsn

αὐτοῦ εἰς γενεὰς καὶ γενεὰς τοῖς φοβουμένοις
his extends to those who fear him, from generation to generation. *to those* *who fear*
899 3836 3836 5828 5828 899 1650 1155 2779 1155 3836 5828
r.gsm.3 p.a n.apf cj n.apf d.dpm pt.pp.dpm

αὐτόν. 51 ἐποίησεν κράτος ἐν βραχίονι αὐτοῦ, διεσκόρπισεν
him "He has displayed might with his arm; *his* he has scattered
899 4472 3197 1877 899 1098 899 1399
r.asm.3 v.aai.3s n.asn p.d n.dsm r.gsm.3 v.aai.3s

ὑπερηφάνους → διανοίᾳ καρδίας αὐτῶν· 52 καθεῖλεν
those who are proud in the thoughts of their hearts. *their* ⌊He has brought down⌋
5662 1379 899 2840 899 2747
a.apm n.dsf n.gsf r.gpm.3 v.aai.3s

δυνάστας ἀπὸ θρόνων καὶ ὕψωσεν ταπεινούς, 53
rulers from their thrones and exalted ⌊those of humble position.⌋ He has filled the
1541 608 2585 2779 5738 5424 1858 1858 1858
n.apm p.g n.gpm cj v.aai.3s a.apm

NASB

a loud voice and
said, "Blessed *are*
you among wom-
en, and blessed *is*
the fruit of your
womb! 43 And how
has it *happened*
to me, that the
mother of my Lord
would come to
me? 44 For behold,
when the sound
of your greeting
reached my ears,
the baby leaped in
my womb for joy.
45 And blessed *is*
she who believed
that there would
be a fulfillment of
what had been spo-
ken to her by the
Lord."

The Magnificat

46 And Mary said:
" My soul exalts
the Lord,
47 And my spirit
has rejoiced
in God my
Savior.
48 " For He has had
regard for the
humble state
of His bond-
slave;
For behold,
from this
time on all
generations
will count me
blessed.
49 " For the Mighty
One has done
great things
for me;
And holy is
His name.
50 " AND HIS MERCY
IS UPON GEN-
ERATION AFTER
GENERATION
TOWARD THOSE
WHO FEAR
HIM.
51 " He has done
mighty deeds
with His arm;
He has scat-
tered *those*
who were
proud in the
thoughts of
their heart.
52 " He has brought
down rulers
from *their*
thrones,
And has ex-

NIV

hungry with
good things
but has sent the
rich away
empty.
54 He has helped
his servant
Israel,
remembering to
be merciful
55 to Abraham and
his descen-
dants
forever,
just as he
promised our
ancestors."

56 Mary stayed
with Elizabeth for
about three months
and then returned
home.

The Birth of John the Baptist

57 When it was
time for Elizabeth
to have her baby,
she gave birth to a
son. 58 Her neigh-
bors and relatives
heard that the
Lord had shown
her great mercy,
and they shared
her joy.
59 On the eighth
day they came to
circumcise the
child, and they
were going to
name him after his
father Zechariah,
60 but his mother
spoke up and said,
"No! He is to be
called John."
61 They said to
her, "There is no
one among your
relatives who has
that name."
62 Then they made
signs to his father,
to find out what he
would like to name
the child. 63 He
asked for a

πεινῶντας ἐνέπλησεν ἀγαθῶν καὶ πλουτοῦντας ἐξαπέστειλεν κενούς.
hungry *He has filled* ⌊with good things,⌋ but the rich he has sent away empty.
4277 1858 19 2779 4456 1990 3031
pt.pa.apm v.aai.3s a.gpn cj pt.pa.apm v.aai.3s a.apm

54 ἀντελάβετο Ἰσραὴλ παιδὸς αὐτοῦ, μνησθῆναι ἐλέους, 55 καθὼς
He has helped his servant Israel, *servant* *his* remembering his mercy, as
514 899 4090 2702 4090 899 3630 1799 2777
v.ami.3s n.gsm n.gsm r.gsm.3 f.ap n.gsn cj

ἐλάλησεν πρὸς τοὺς πατέρας ἡμῶν, τῷ Ἀβραὰμ καὶ τῷ σπέρματι αὐτοῦ
he spoke to *{the}* our fathers, *our* to Abraham and *{the}* his descendants *his*
3281 4639 3836 7005 4252 7005 3836 11 2779 3836 899 5065 899
v.aai.3s p.a d.apm n.apm r.gp.1 d.dsm n.dsm cj d.dsn n.dsn r.gsm.3

εἰς τὸν αἰῶνα. 56 Ἔμεινεν δὲ Μαριὰμ σὺν αὐτῇ ὡς μῆνας τρεῖς, καὶ
for all time." Mary remained *{and}* *Mary* with her about three months *three* and
1650 3836 172 3452 3531 1254 3452 5250 899 6055 5552 3604 5552 2779
p.a d.asm n.asm v.aai.3s cj n.nsf p.d r.dsf.3 pl n.apm a.apm cj

ὑπέστρεψεν εἰς τὸν οἶκον αὐτῆς. 57 Τῇ δὲ Ἐλισάβετ ἐπλήσθη
returned to *{the}* her home. *her* The time arrived for *{and}* Elizabeth *arrived*
5715 1650 3836 899 3875 899 3836 5989 4398 3836 1254 1810 4398
v.aai.3s p.a d.asm n.asm r.gsf.3 d.dsf cj n.dsf v.api.3s

ὁ χρόνος τοῦ τεκεῖν αὐτὴν καὶ ἐγέννησεν υἱόν. 58 καὶ
The *time* to give birth, *{her}* and she bore a son. And her neighbors and relatives
3836 5989 3836 5503 899 2779 1164 5626 2779 899 4341 2779 5150
d.nsm n.nsm d.gsn f.aa r.asf.3 cj v.aai.3s n.asm cj

ἤκουσαν οἱ περίοικοι καὶ οἱ συγγενεῖς αὐτῆς ὅτι ἐμεγάλυνεν
heard *{the}* *neighbors* *and* *{the}* *relatives* *her* that the Lord had greatly displayed
201 3836 4341 2779 3836 5150 899 4022 3261 3486
v.aai.3p d.npm n.npm cj d.npm n.npm r.gsf.3 cj v.iai.3s

κύριος τὸ ἔλεος αὐτοῦ μετ᾽ αὐτῆς καὶ συνέχαιρον αὐτῇ. 59 καὶ
Lord *{the}* his mercy *his* to her, and ⌊they rejoiced with⌋ her. *{and}*
3261 3836 899 1799 899 3552 899 2779 5176 899 2779
n.nsm d.asn n.asn r.gsm.3 p.g r.gsf.3 cj v.iai.3p r.dsf.3 cj

ἐγένετο ἐν τῇ ἡμέρᾳ τῇ ὀγδόῃ ἦλθον περιτεμεῖν τὸ παιδίον καὶ
{it happened that} On the eighth day *{the}* *eighth* they came to circumcise the child, and
1181 1877 3836 3838 2465 3836 3838 2262 4362 3836 4086 2779
v.ami.3s p.d d.dsf n.dsf d.dsf a.dsf v.aai.3p f.aa d.asn n.asn cj

ἐκάλουν αὐτὸ ἐπὶ τῷ ὀνόματι τοῦ πατρὸς αὐτοῦ Ζαχαρίαν. 60 καὶ
⌊they wanted to call⌋ him by the name of his father, *his* Zechariah. But his
2813 899 2093 3836 3950 3836 899 4252 899 2408 2779 899
v.iai.3p r.asn.3 p.d d.dsn n.dsn d.gsm n.gsm r.gsm.3 n.asm cj

ἀποκριθεῖσα ἡ μήτηρ αὐτοῦ εἶπεν, οὐχί, ↱ ↱ ἀλλὰ κληθήσεται Ἰωάννης.
mother responded, *{the}* *mother* *his* saying, "No; he is rather to be called John."
3613 646 3836 3613 899 3306 4049 2813 2813 247 2813 2722
pt.ap.nsf d.nsf n.nsf r.gsm.3 v.aai.3s pl cj v.fpi.3s n.nsm

61 καὶ εἶπαν πρὸς αὐτὴν ὅτι οὐδείς ἐστιν ἐκ τῆς συγγενείας
And they said to her, ~ "There is no one *There is* among *{the}* your relatives
2779 3306 4639 899 4022 1639 1639 4029 1639 1666 3836 5148 5149
cj v.aai.3p p.a r.asf.3 cj a.nsm v.pai.3s p.g d.gsf n.gsf

σου ὃς καλεῖται τῷ ὀνόματι τούτῳ. 62 ἐνένευον δὲ τῷ πατρὶ
your who is called by this name." *this* So they motioned *So* to his father
5148 4005 2813 3836 4047 3950 4047 1254 1935 1254 3836 899 4252
r.gs.2 r.nsm v.ppi.3s d.dsn n.dsn r.dsn v.iai.3p cj d.dsm n.dsm

αὐτοῦ τὸ τί ↱ ἂν θέλοι καλεῖσθαι αὐτό. 63 καὶ ↱ αἰτήσας
his to find out *{the}* what he would like him to be called. *him* *{and}* He asked for a
899 3836 5515 2527 323 2527 899 2813 899 2779 1211 160
r.gsm.3 d.asn r.asn pl v.pao.3s f.pp r.asn.3 cj pt.aa.nsm

NASB

alted those
who were
humble.
53 "HE HAS FILLED
THE HUNGRY
WITH GOOD
THINGS;
And sent away
the rich emp-
ty-handed.
54 "He has given
help to Israel
His servant,
In remem-
brance of His
mercy,
55 As He spoke
to our fathers,
To Abraham
and his de-
scendants
forever."
56 And Mary
stayed with her
about three months,
and *then* returned
to her home.

John Is Born

57 Now the time
had come for
Elizabeth to give
birth, and she gave
birth to a son. 58 Her
neighbors and her
relatives heard
that the Lord had
displayed His great
mercy toward her;
and they were re-
joicing with her.
59 And it happened
that on the eighth
day they came to
circumcise the
child, and they
were going to call
him Zacharias,
after his father.
60 But his mother
answered and said,
"No indeed; but
he shall be called
John." 61 And they
said to her, "There
is no one among
your relatives who
is called by that
name." 62 And they
made signs to his
father, as to what
he wanted him
called. 63 And he
asked for a

NIV

writing tablet, and to everyone's astonishment he wrote, "His name is John." [64]Immediately his mouth was opened and his tongue set free, and he began to speak, praising God. [65]All the neighbors were filled with awe, and throughout the hill country of Judea people were talking about all these things. [66]Everyone who heard this wondered about it, asking, "What then is this child going to be?" For the Lord's hand was with him.

Zechariah's Song

[67]His father Zechariah was filled with the Holy Spirit and prophesied:

68 "Praise be to
the Lord,
the God of
Israel,
because he has
come to his
people and
redeemed
them.
69 He has raised up
a horn[a] of
salvation for
us
in the house of
his servant
David
70 (as he said through
his holy
prophets of
long ago),
71 salvation from our
enemies
and from the
hand of all
who hate
us—
72 to show mercy to
our ancestors
and to
remember
his holy
covenant,
73 the oath he
swore to our
father

[a] 69 *Horn* here symbolizes a strong king.

πινακίδιον ἔγραψεν λέγων, Ἰωάννης ἐστὶν ὄνομα αὐτοῦ. καὶ →
writing tablet and wrote, {saying} "His name is John." *is* *name* *His* And they
4400 1211 3306 899 3950 1639 2722 1639 3950 899 2779
n.asn v.aai.3s pt.pa.nsm n.nsm v.pai.3s n.nsn r.gsm.3 cj

→ ἐθαύμασαν πάντες. 64 ἀνεῴχθη δὲ τὸ στόμα αὐτοῦ
were all astonished. *all* Instantly his mouth was opened {and} {the} *mouth* *his*
4246 2513 4246 4202 899 5125 487 1254 3836 5125 899
v.aai.3p a.npm v.api.3s cj d.nsn n.nsn r.gsm.3

παραχρῆμα καὶ ἡ γλῶσσα αὐτοῦ, ↰ καὶ ἐλάλει εὐλογῶν τὸν
Instantly and {the} his tongue *his* loosed, and ⌞he began to speak,⌟ praising {the}
4202 2779 3836 899 1185 899 487 2779 3281 2328 3836
adv cj d.nsf n.nsf r.gsm.3 cj v.iai.3s pt.pa.nsm d.asm

θεόν. 65 καὶ ἐγένετο ἐπὶ πάντας φόβος τοὺς περιοικοῦντας αὐτούς,
God. {and} {it happened that} Fear came upon all *Fear* who lived around them,
2536 2779 1181 5832 2093 4246 5832 3836 4340 899
n.asm cj v.ami.3s p.a a.apm n.nsm d.apm pt.pa.apm r.apm.3

καὶ ἐν ὅλῃ τῇ ὀρεινῇ τῆς
and all these things were being talked about throughout the whole {the} hill country of
2779 4246 4047 4839 1362 1362 1362 1362 1877 3910 3836 3978 3836
cj p.d a.dsf d.dsf n.dsf d.gsf

Ἰουδαίας διελαλεῖτο πάντα τὰ ῥήματα ταῦτα, 66 καὶ ἔθεντο
Judea. *were being talked about* *all* {the} *things* *these* {and} All who heard took
2677 1362 4246 3836 4839 4047 2779 4246 3836 201 5502
n.gsf v.ipi.3s a.npn d.npn n.npn r.npn cj v.ami.3p

πάντες οἱ ἀκούσαντες ἐν τῇ καρδίᾳ αὐτῶν λέγοντες, τί ἄρα
All *who* *heard* these things to {the} their heart, *their* saying, "What, then,
4246 3836 201 1877 3836 899 2840 899 3306 5515 726
a.npm d.npm pt.aa.npm p.d d.dsf n.dsf r.gpm.3 pt.pa.npm r.nsn cj

↱ τὸ παιδίον τοῦτο ἔσται; καὶ γὰρ χεὶρ → κυρίου ἦν μετ᾽ αὐτοῦ.
will {the} this child *this* be?" {also} For the hand of the Lord was with him.
1639 3836 4047 4086 4047 1639 2779 1142 5931 3261 1639 3552 899
d.nsn n.nsn r.nsn v.fmi.3s adv cj n.nsf n.gsm v.iai.3s p.g r.gsm.3

67 καὶ Ζαχαρίας ὁ πατὴρ αὐτοῦ ἐπλήσθη πνεύματος ἁγίου καὶ
{and} Zechariah, {the} his father, *his* ⌞was filled with⌟ the Holy Spirit *Holy* and
2779 2408 3836 899 4252 899 4398 41 4460 41 2779
cj n.nsm d.nsm n.nsm r.gsm.3 v.api.3s n.gsn a.gsn cj

ἐπροφήτευσεν λέγων, 68 εὐλογητὸς κύριος ὁ θεὸς τοῦ Ἰσραήλ, ὅτι
prophesied, saying, "Blessed be the Lord {the} God of Israel, for
4736 3306 2329 3261 3836 2536 3836 2702 4022
v.aai.3s pt.pa.nsm a.nsm n.nsm d.nsm n.nsm d.gsm n.gsm cj

ἐπεσκέψατο καὶ ἐποίησεν λύτρωσιν τῷ λαῷ αὐτοῦ, 69 καὶ ἤγειρεν
he has visited and brought redemption to his people. *his* For ⌞he has raised up⌟ a
2170 2779 4472 3391 3836 899 3295 899 2779 1586
v.ami.3s cj v.aai.3s n.asf d.dsm n.dsm r.gsm.3 cj v.aai.3s

κέρας σωτηρίας ἡμῖν ἐν οἴκῳ Δαυὶδ παιδὸς αὐτοῦ, 70 καθὼς ἐλάλησεν
horn of salvation for us in the house of David his servant, *his* just as he spoke
3043 5401 7005 1877 3875 1253 899 4090 899 2777 3281
n.asn n.gsf r.dp.1 p.d n.dsm n.gsm n.gsm r.gsm.3 cj v.aai.3s

διὰ στόματος τῶν ἁγίων ἀπ᾽ αἰῶνος προφητῶν αὐτοῦ, 71
through the mouth of his holy prophets from of old, *prophets* *his* that we
1328 5125 3836 899 41 4737 608 172 4737 899
p.g n.gsn d.gpm a.gpm p.g n.gsm n.gpm r.gsm.3

σωτηρίαν ἐξ ἐχθρῶν ἡμῶν καὶ ἐκ χειρὸς πάντων τῶν μισούντων
should be saved from our enemies, *our* and from the hand of all who hate
5401 1666 7005 2398 7005 2779 1666 5931 4246 3836 3631
n.asf p.g a.gpm r.gp.1 cj p.g n.gsf a.gpm d.gpm pt.pa.gpm

ἡμᾶς, 72 ποιῆσαι ἔλεος μετὰ τῶν πατέρων ἡμῶν καὶ
us. He has done this to show the mercy promised to {the} our fathers, *our* and
7005 4472 1799 3552 3836 7005 4252 7005 2779
r.ap.1 f.aa n.asn p.g d.gpm n.gpm r.gp.1 cj

μνησθῆναι διαθήκης ἁγίας αὐτοῦ, 73 ὅρκον ὃν ὤμοσεν πρὸς
to remember his holy covenant, *holy* *his* the oath that he swore to our father
3630 899 41 1347 41 899 3992 4005 3923 4639 7005 4252
f.ap n.gsf a.gsf r.gsm.3 n.asm r.asm v.aai.3s p.a

NASB

tablet and wrote as follows, "His name is John." And they were all astonished. [64]And at once his mouth was opened and his tongue *loosed,* and he *began* to speak in praise of God. [65]Fear came on all those living around them; and all these matters were being talked about in all the hill country of Judea. [66]All who heard them kept them in mind, saying, "What then will this child *turn out to* be?" For the hand of the Lord was certainly with him.

Zacharias's Prophecy

[67]And his father Zacharias was filled with the Holy Spirit, and prophesied, saying:

68 "Blessed *be* the
Lord God of
Israel,
For He has
visited us and
accomplished
redemption for His
people,
69 And has raised
up a horn of
salvation for
us
In the house
of David His
servant—
70 As He spoke
by the mouth
of His holy
prophets from
of old—
71 Salvation FROM
OUR ENEMIES,
And FROM THE
HAND OF ALL
WHO HATE US;
72 To show
mercy toward
our fathers,
And to remember His holy
covenant,
73 The oath
which He
swore to

NIV

Abraham:
74 to rescue us from
the hand of
our enemies,
and to enable us
to serve him
without fear
75 in holiness and
righteous–
ness before
him all our
days.

76 And you, my
child, will
be called a
prophet of
the Most
High;
for you will go
on before
the Lord to
prepare the
way for him,
77 to give his
people the
knowledge of
salvation
through the
forgiveness
of their sins,
78 because of the
tender mercy
of our God,
by which the
rising sun
will come
to us from
heaven
79 to shine on those
living in
darkness
and in the
shadow of
death,
to guide our feet
into the path
of peace."

80 And the child
grew and became
strong in spirit[a];
and he lived in the
wilderness until he
appeared publicly
to Israel.

The Birth of Jesus

2 In those days
Caesar Augus-
tus issued a de-
cree that a census
should be taken of
the entire Roman
world. 2 (This was
the first census
that took place
while[b] Quirinius
was governor of
Syria.)

[a] 80 Or *in the Spirit*
[b] 2 Or *This census took place before*

Ἀβραὰμ τὸν πατέρα ἡμῶν, τοῦ δοῦναι ἡμῖν 74 ἀφόβως ἐκ
Abraham, *{the}* father *our* to grant us *without fear* that we, being rescued from the
11 3836 4252 7005 3836 1443 7005 925 4861 4861 1666
n.asm d.asm n.asm r.gp.1 d.gsn f.aa r.dp.1 adv p.g

χειρὸς ἐχθρῶν ῥυσθέντας λατρεύειν αὐτῷ 75 ἐν ὁσιότητι καὶ
hand of enemies, *being rescued* might serve him without fear, in holiness and
5931 2398 4861 3302 899 925 925 1877 4009 2779
n.gsf a.gpm pt.ap.apm f.pa r.dsm.3 p.d n.dsf cj

δικαιοσύνῃ ἐνώπιον αὐτοῦ πάσαις ταῖς ἡμέραις ἡμῶν. 76 Καὶ σὺ δέ, παιδίον,
righteousness before him all *{the}* our days. *our* And you, *{and}* child,
1466 1967 899 4246 3836 7005 2465 7005 2779 5148 1254 4086
n.dsf p.g r.gsm.3 a.dpf d.dpf n.dpf r.gp.1 cj r.ns.2 cj n.vsn

προφήτης → ὑψίστου κληθήσῃ· προπορεύσῃ γὰρ ἐνώπιον
will be called prophet of the Most High; *will be called* for you will go *for* before the
2813 2813 2813 4737 5736 2813 1142 4638 1142 1967
n.nsm a.gsm.s v.fpi.2s v.fmi.2s cj p.g

κυρίου ἑτοιμάσαι ὁδοὺς αὐτοῦ, 77 τοῦ δοῦναι γνῶσιν σωτηρίας
Lord to prepare his ways, *his* to give his people the knowledge of salvation
3261 2286 899 3847 899 3836 1443 899 3295 1194 5401
n.gsm f.aa n.apf r.gsm.3 d.gsn f.aa n.asf n.gsf

τῷ λαῷ αὐτοῦ ἐν ἀφέσει → ἁμαρτιῶν αὐτῶν, 78 διὰ
{the} people his by the forgiveness of their sins, *their* ⌊because of⌋ the
3836 3295 899 1877 912 899 281 899 1328
d.dsm n.dsm r.gsm.3 p.d n.dsf n.gpf r.gpm.3 p.a

σπλάγχνα ἐλέους → θεοῦ ἡμῶν, ἐν οἷς ἐπισκέψεται
tender mercies of our God, *our* by which the rising sun of heaven will visit
5073 1799 7005 2536 7005 1877 4005 424 424 1666 5737 2170
n.apn n.gsn n.gsm r.gp.1 p.d r.dpn v.fmi.3s

ἡμᾶς ἀνατολὴ ἐξ ὕψους, 79 ἐπιφᾶναι τοῖς ἐν σκότει καὶ σκιᾷ
us, *rising sun of heaven* to shine on those who sit in darkness and the shadow
7005 424 1666 5737 2210 3836 2764 2764 1877 5030 2779 5014
r.ap.1 n.nsf p.g n.gsn f.aa d.dpm p.d n.dsn cj n.dsf

θανάτου καθημένοις, τοῦ κατευθῦναι τοὺς πόδας ἡμῶν εἰς ὁδὸν εἰρήνης.
of death, *who sit* to guide *{the}* our feet *our* into the way of peace."
2505 2764 3836 2985 3836 7005 4546 7005 1650 3847 1645
n.gsm pt.pm.dpm d.gsn f.aa d.apm n.apm r.gp.1 p.a n.asf n.gsf

80 τὸ δὲ παιδίον ηὔξανεν καὶ ἐκραταιοῦτο πνεύματι, καὶ ἦν ἐν ταῖς
And the *And* child grew and became strong in spirit, and ⌊he was⌋ in *{the}*
1254 3836 1254 4086 889 2779 3194 4460 2779 1639 1877 3836
d.nsn cj n.nsn v.iai.3s cj v.ipi.3s n.dsn cj v.iai.3s p.d d.dpf

ἐρήμοις ἕως ἡμέρας → ἀναδείξεως αὐτοῦ πρὸς τὸν Ἰσραήλ.
⌊wilderness areas⌋ until the day of his public appearance *his* to *{the}* Israel.
2245 2401 2465 899 345 899 4639 3836 2702
a.dpf p.g n.gsf n.gsf r.gsm.3 p.a d.asm n.asm

2:1 Ἐγένετο δὲ ἐν ταῖς ἡμέραις ἐκείναις ἐξῆλθεν δόγμα
{it happened that} {and} In *{the}* those days *those* a decree went out *decree*
1181 1254 1877 3836 1697 2465 1697 1504 2002 1504
v.ami.3s cj p.d d.dpf n.dpf r.dpf v.aai.3s n.nsn

παρὰ Καίσαρος Αὐγούστου ἀπογράφεσθαι πᾶσαν τὴν οἰκουμένην.
from Caesar Augustus for all the world to be registered. *all the world*
4123 2790 880 4246 3836 3876 616 4246 3836 3876
p.g n.gsm n.gsm f.pp a.asf d.asf n.asf

2 αὕτη ἀπογραφὴ πρώτη ἐγένετο → ἡγεμονεύοντος τῆς Συρίας Κυρηνίου.
This registration first took place while Quirinius was governing *{the}* Syria. *Quirinius*
4047 615 4755 1181 3256 2448 3836 5353 3256
r.nsf n.nsf a.nsf v.ami.3s pt.pa.gsm d.gsf n.gsf n.gsm

NASB

Abraham our
father,
74 To grant us
that we, being
rescued from
the hand of
our enemies,
Might serve
Him without
fear,
75 In holiness and
righteousness
before Him
all our days.
76 "And you,
child, will
be called the
prophet of the
Most High;
For you will
go on BEFORE
THE LORD TO
PREPARE HIS
WAYS;
77 To give to His
people *the*
knowledge of
salvation
By the forgive-
ness of their
sins,
78 Because of the
tender mercy
of our God,
With which the
Sunrise from
on high will
visit us,
79 TO SHINE UPON
THOSE WHO
SIT IN DARK-
NESS AND THE
SHADOW OF
DEATH,
To guide our
feet into
the way of
peace."
80 And the child
continued to grow
and to become
strong in spirit, and
he lived in the des-
erts until the day of
his public appear-
ance to Israel.

Jesus' Birth in Bethlehem

2:1 Now in those
days a decree went
out from Caesar
Augustus, that a
census be taken of
all [a]the inhabited
earth. 2 This was the
first census taken
while [b]Quirinius

[a] I.e. the Roman empire
[b] Gr *Kyrenios*

NIV

3 And everyone
went to their own
town to register.
4 So Joseph also
went up from the
town of Nazareth
in Galilee to Ju-
dea, to Bethlehem
the town of Da-
vid, because he
belonged to the
house and line of
David. 5 He went
there to register
with Mary, who
was pledged to be
married to him and
was expecting a
child. 6 While they
were there, the
time came for the
baby to be born,
7 and she gave birth
to her firstborn, a
son. She wrapped
him in cloths and
placed him in a
manger, because
there was no guest
room available for
them.
8 And there were
shepherds living
out in the fields
nearby, keeping
watch over their
flocks at night.
9 An angel of the
Lord appeared
to them, and the
glory of the Lord
shone around
them, and they
were terrified.
10 But the angel
said to them, "Do
not be afraid. I
bring you good
news that will
cause great joy
for all the people.
11 Today in the
town of David a
Savior has been
born to you; he is
the Messiah, the
Lord.

3 καὶ ἐπορεύοντο πάντες ἀπογράφεσθαι, ἕκαστος εἰς τὴν ἑαυτοῦ πόλιν.
And everyone went *everyone* to be registered, each to *{the}* his own town.
2779 4246 4513 4246 616 1667 1650 3836 1571 4484
cj v.imi.3p a.npm f.pm r.nsm p.a d.asf r.gsm.3 n.asf

4 ἀνέβη δὲ καὶ Ἰωσὴφ ἀπὸ τῆς Γαλιλαίας ἐκ πόλεως Ναζαρὲθ
So Joseph also went up *So* *also* *Joseph* from *{the}* Galilee, from the town of Nazareth,
1254 2737 2779 326 1254 2779 2737 608 3836 1133 1666 4484 3714
v.aai.3s cj adv n.nsm p.g d.gsf n.gsf p.g n.gsf n.gsf

εἰς τὴν Ἰουδαίαν εἰς πόλιν Δαυὶδ ἥτις καλεῖται Βηθλέεμ, διὰ τὸ
to *{the}* Judea, to the city of David, which is called Bethlehem, because *{the}* he
1650 3836 2677 1650 4484 1253 4015 2813 1033 1328 3836 899
p.a d.asf n.asf p.a n.asf n.gsm r.nsf v.ppi.3s n.nsf p.a d.asn

εἶναι αὐτὸν ἐξ οἴκου καὶ πατριᾶς Δαυίδ, 5 ἀπογράψασθαι σὺν Μαριὰμ τῇ
was *he* of the house and lineage of David, to be registered with Mary, who
1639 899 1666 3875 2779 4255 1253 616 5250 3452 3836
f.pa r.asm.3 p.g n.gsm cj n.gsf n.gsm f.am p.d n.dsf d.dsf

ἐμνηστευμένῃ αὐτῷ, οὔσῃ ἐγκύῳ. 6 ἐγένετο δὲ ἐν τῷ
was pledged in marriage to him, and who was ⌊expecting a child.⌋ *{it happened that}* And while *{the}*
3650 899 1639 1607 1181 1254 1877 3836
pt.rp.dsf r.dsm.3 pt.pa.dsf a.dsf v.ami.3s cj p.d d.dsn

εἶναι αὐτοὺς ἐκεῖ ἐπλήσθησαν αἱ ἡμέραι τοῦ τεκεῖν αὐτήν,
they were *they* there, the days were completed *the* *days* for her to give birth, *her*
899 1639 899 1695 3836 2465 4398 3836 2465 899 3836 5503 899
f.pa r.apm.3 adv v.api.3p d.npf n.npf d.gsn f.aa r.asf.3

7 καὶ ἔτεκεν τὸν υἱὸν αὐτῆς τὸν πρωτότοκον, καὶ ἐσπαργάνωσεν αὐτὸν
and ⌊she gave birth to⌋ a son, her *{the}* firstborn. *{and}* She wrapped him
2779 5503 3836 5626 899 3836 4758 2779 5058 899
cj v.aai.3s d.asm n.asm r.gsf.3 d.asm a.asm cj v.aai.3s r.asm.3

↰ ↰ ↰ καὶ ἀνέκλινεν αὐτὸν ἐν φάτνῃ, διότι οὐκ ἦν
in swaddling cloths and laid him in a manger, because there was no *there was*
5058 5058 5058 2779 369 899 1877 5764 1484 1639 1639 4024 1639
cj v.aai.3s r.asm.3 p.d n.dsf cj pl v.iai.3s

αὐτοῖς τόπος ἐν τῷ καταλύματι. 8 καὶ ποιμένες ἦσαν ἐν
place for them *place* in the inn. *{and}* There were shepherds *There were* in that
5536 899 5536 1877 3836 2906 2779 1639 1639 4478 1639 1877 899
r.dpm.3 n.nsm p.d d.dsn n.dsn cj n.npm v.iai.3p p.d

τῇ χώρᾳ τῇ αὐτῇ ἀγραυλοῦντες καὶ φυλάσσοντες ⌊φυλακὰς τῆς
{the} region *{the}* *that* ⌊who were living out in the fields⌋ and keeping night-watch
3836 6001 3836 899 64 2779 5875 5871 3836
d.dsf n.dsf d.dsf r.dsf pt.pa.npm cj pt.pa.npm n.apf d.gsf

νυκτὸς⌋ ἐπὶ τὴν ποίμνην αὐτῶν. 9 καὶ ἄγγελος → κυρίου
over *{the}* their flock. *their* *{and}* An angel of the Lord
3816 2093 3836 899 4479 899 2779 34 3261
n.gsf p.a d.asf n.asf r.gpm.3 cj n.nsm n.gsm

ἐπέστη αὐτοῖς καὶ δόξα → κυρίου περιέλαμψεν αὐτούς, καὶ → →
⌊suddenly appeared⌋ to them, and the glory of the Lord shone around them, and they were
2392 899 2779 1518 3261 4334 899 2779
v.aai.3s r.dpm.3 cj n.nsf n.gsm v.aai.3s r.apm.3 cj

⌊ἐφοβήθησαν φόβον⌋ μέγαν. 10 καὶ εἶπεν αὐτοῖς ὁ ἄγγελος, ↱
terribly afraid. *terribly* But the angel said to them, *the* *angel* "Do
3489 5828 5832 3489 2779 3836 34 3306 899 3836 34 5828
v.api.3p n.asm a.asm cj v.aai.3s r.dpm.3 d.nsm n.nsm

μὴ φοβεῖσθε, ἰδοὺ γὰρ εὐαγγελίζομαι ὑμῖν ↰ ↰ χαρὰν μεγάλην
not be afraid; for behold, *for* I announce to you good news of a great joy *great*
3590 5828 1142 2627 1142 2294 7007 2294 2294 3489 5915 3489
pl v.ppm.2p j cj v.pmi.1s r.dp.2 n.asf a.asf

ἥτις ἔσται παντὶ τῷ λαῷ, 11 ὅτι ἐτέχθη ὑμῖν
which will be for all the people, because this very day ⌊there has been born⌋ to you,
4015 1639 4246 3836 3295 4022 4958 4958 4958 5503 7007
r.nsf v.fmi.3s a.dsm d.dsm n.dsm cj v.api.3s r.dp.2

σήμερον σωτὴρ ὅς ἐστιν χριστὸς κύριος ἐν πόλει
this very day in the city of David, a savior who is Messiah, the Lord. *in* *city*
4958 1877 4484 1253 1253 5400 4005 1639 5986 3261 1877 4484
adv n.nsm r.nsm v.pai.3s n.nsm n.nsm p.d n.dsf

NASB

was governor of
Syria. 3 And every-
one was on his way
to register for the
census, each to his
own city. 4 Joseph
also went up from
Galilee, from the
city of Nazareth, to
Judea, to the city
of David which is
called Bethlehem,
because he was
of the house and
family of David,
5 in order to register
along with Mary,
who was engaged
to him, and was
with child. 6 While
they were there,
the days were
completed for her
to give birth. 7 And
she gave birth to
her firstborn son;
and she wrapped
Him in cloths, and
laid Him in a man-
ger, because there
was no room for
them in the inn.
8 In the same
region there were
some shepherds
staying out in the
fields and keeping
watch over their
flock by night.
9 And an angel of
the Lord suddenly
stood before them,
and the glory of
the Lord shone
around them; and
they were terribly
frightened. 10 But
the angel said to
them, "Do not be
afraid; for behold,
I bring you good
news of great joy
which will be for
all the people; 11 for
today in the city
of David there has
been born for you
a Savior, who is
[a]Christ the Lord.

[a] I.e. Messiah

NIV

[12]This will be a
sign to you: You
will find a baby
wrapped in cloths
and lying in a
manger."
[13]Suddenly a
great company of
the heavenly host
appeared with the
angel, praising
God and saying,
[14]"Glory to God
in the
highest
heaven,
and on earth
peace to
those on
whom
his favor
rests."
[15]When the an-
gels had left them
and gone into
heaven, the shep-
herds said to one
another, "Let's
go to Bethlehem
and see this thing
that has happened,
which the Lord has
told us about."
[16]So they hur-
ried off and found
Mary and Joseph,
and the baby, who
was lying in the
manger. [17]When
they had seen him,
they spread the
word concerning
what had been told
them about this
child, [18]and all
who heard it were
amazed at what the
shepherds said to
them. [19]But Mary
treasured up all
these things and
pondered them in
her heart. [20]The
shepherds re-
turned, glorifying
and praising God
for all the things
they had heard and
seen, which were
just as they had
been told.
[21]On the eighth
day,

Δαυίδ. [12] καὶ τοῦτο ὑμῖν τὸ[a] σημεῖον, εὑρήσετε βρέφος
of David And this is the sign for you: *the* *sign* you will find a baby
1253 2779 4047 3836 4956 7007 3836 4956 2351 1100
n.gsm cj r.nsn r.dp.2 d.nsn n.nsn v.fai.2p n.asn

ἐσπαργανωμένον καὶ κείμενον ἐν φάτνῃ. [13] καὶ ἐξαίφνης ἐγένετο σὺν
⌊wrapped in swaddling cloths⌋ and lying in a manger." And suddenly there was, with
5058 2779 3023 1877 5764 2779 1978 1181 5250
pt.rp.asn cj pt.pm.asn p.d n.dsf cj adv v.ami.3s p.d

τῷ ἀγγέλῳ πλῆθος → στρατιᾶς οὐρανίου αἰνούντων τὸν θεὸν καὶ
the angel, a multitude of the heavenly host, *heavenly* praising *{the}* God and
3836 34 4436 4039 5131 4039 140 3836 2536 2779
d.dsm n.dsm n.nsn n.gsf a.gsf pt.pa.gpm d.asm n.asm cj

λεγόντων, [14] δόξα ἐν ὑψίστοις θεῷ καὶ ἐπὶ γῆς εἰρήνη
saying, "Glory to God in the highest heaven, *to God* and peace on earth *peace*
3306 1518 2536 2536 1877 5736 2536 2779 1645 2093 1178 1645
pt.pa.gpm n.nsf p.d a.dpn.s n.dsm cj p.g n.gsf n.nsf

ἐν ἀνθρώποις εὐδοκίας. [15] καὶ ἐγένετο ὡς ἀπῆλθον
among those ⌊whom he has favored!"⌋ *{and}* *{it happened that}* When the angels departed
1877 476 2306 2779 1181 6055 3836 34 599
p.d n.dpm n.gsf cj v.ami.3s cj v.aai.3p

ἀπ' αὐτῶν εἰς τὸν οὐρανὸν οἱ ἄγγελοι, οἱ ποιμένες ἐλάλουν πρὸς
from them into *{the}* heaven, *the* *angels* the shepherds began to speak to
608 899 1650 3836 4041 3836 34 3836 4478 3281 4639
p.g r.gpm.3 p.a d.asm n.asm d.npm n.npm d.npm n.npm v.iai.3p p.a

ἀλλήλους, διέλθωμεν δὴ ἕως Βηθλέεμ καὶ ἴδωμεν τὸ ῥῆμα τοῦτο τὸ
one another, "Well, let us go across *Well* to Bethlehem and see *{the}* this thing *this* that
253 1314 1451 1314 2401 1033 2779 1625 3836 4047 4839 4047 3836
r.apm v.aas.1p pl p.g n.gsf cj v.aas.1p d.asn n.asn r.asn d.asn

γεγονὸς ὃ ὁ κύριος ἐγνώρισεν ἡμῖν. [16] καὶ ἦλθαν σπεύσαντες καὶ
⌊has taken place,⌋ which the Lord has made known to us." So they came in haste and
1181 4005 3836 3261 1192 7005 2779 2262 5067 2779
pt.ra.asn r.asn d.nsm n.nsm v.aai.3s r.dp.1 cj v.aai.3p pt.aa.npm cj

ἀνεῦραν τήν τε Μαριὰμ καὶ τὸν Ἰωσὴφ καὶ τὸ βρέφος κείμενον ἐν τῇ φάτνῃ·
found *{the}* ~ Mary and *{the}* Joseph, and the baby lying in the manger.
461 3836 5445 3452 2779 3836 2737 2779 3836 1100 3023 1877 3836 5764
v.aai.3p d.asf cj n.asf cj d.asm n.asm cj d.asn n.asn pt.pm.asn p.d d.dsf n.dsf

[17] ἰδόντες δὲ → → ἐγνώρισαν περὶ τοῦ ῥήματος τοῦ
And ⌊when they had seen⌋ him, *And* they made it known concerning the message that
1254 1625 1254 1192 4309 3836 4839 3836
pt.aa.npm cj v.aai.3p p.g d.gsn n.gsn d.gsn

λαληθέντος αὐτοῖς περὶ τοῦ παιδίου τούτου. [18] καὶ πάντες οἱ ἀκούσαντες
had been spoken to them about *{the}* this child. *this* And all who heard
3281 899 4309 3836 4047 4086 4047 2779 4246 3836 201
pt.ap.gsn r.dpm.3 p.g d.gsn n.gsn r.gsn cj a.npm d.npm pt.aa.npm

ἐθαύμασαν περὶ τῶν λαληθέντων ὑπὸ τῶν ποιμένων πρὸς αὐτούς· [19] ἡ
marveled about what had been told to them by the shepherds. *to* *them* *{the}*
2513 4309 3836 3281 4639 899 5679 3836 4478 4639 899 3836
v.aai.3p p.g d.gpn pt.ap.gpn p.g d.gpm n.gpm p.a r.apm.3 d.nsf

δὲ Μαριὰμ πάντα συνετήρει τὰ ῥήματα ταῦτα
{and} Mary remembered all *remembered* that ⌊had been said,⌋ pondering them
1254 3452 5337 4246 5337 3836 4839 5202 4047
cj n.nsf a.apn v.iai.3s d.apn n.apn r.apn

συμβάλλουσα ἐν τῇ καρδίᾳ αὐτῆς. [20] καὶ ὑπέστρεψαν οἱ
pondering in *{the}* her heart. *her* Then the shepherds returned, *the*
5202 1877 3836 899 2840 899 2779 3836 4478 5715 3836
pt.pa.nsf p.d d.dsf n.dsf r.gsf.3 cj v.aai.3p d.npm

ποιμένες δοξάζοντες καὶ αἰνοῦντες τὸν θεὸν ἐπὶ πᾶσιν οἷς ἤκουσαν καὶ εἶδον
shepherds glorifying and praising *{the}* God for all that they had heard and seen,
4478 1519 2779 140 3836 2536 2093 4246 4005 201 2779 1625
n.npm pt.pa.npm cj pt.pa.npm d.asm n.asm p.d a.dpn r.dpn v.aai.3p cj v.aai.3p

καθὼς ἐλαλήθη πρὸς αὐτούς. [21] καὶ ὅτε ἐπλήσθησαν ἡμέραι ὀκτὼ
just as ⌊it had been told⌋ to them. *{and}* When eight days had gone by *days* *eight*
2777 3281 4639 899 2779 4021 3893 2465 4398 2465 3893
cj v.api.3s p.a r.apm.3 cj cj v.api.3p n.npf a.npf

NASB

[12]This *will be* a
sign for you: you
will find a baby
wrapped in cloths
and lying in a
manger." [13]And
suddenly there
appeared with the
angel a multitude
of the heavenly
host praising God
and saying,
[14]"Glory to God
in the highest,
And on earth
peace among
men [a]with
whom He is
pleased."
[15]When the angels
had gone away
from them into
heaven, the shep-
herds *began* saying
to one another,
"Let us go straight
to Bethlehem then,
and see this thing
that has happened
which the Lord has
made known to
us." [16]So they came
in a hurry and
found their way to
Mary and Joseph,
and the baby as He
lay in the manger.
[17]When they had
seen this, they
made known the
statement which
had been told them
about this Child.
[18]And all who
heard it wondered
at the things which
were told them
by the shepherds.
[19]But Mary trea-
sured all these
things, pondering
them in her heart.
[20]The shepherds
went back, glorify-
ing and praising
God for all that
they had heard and
seen, just as had
been told them.

Jesus Presented at the Temple

[21]And when eight
days had passed,

[a] τὸ omitted by TNIV.

[a] Lit *of good pleasure;* or *of good will*

NIV

when it was time
to circumcise
the child, he was
named Jesus, the
name the angel
had given him
before he was con-
ceived.

Jesus Presented in the Temple

22 When the time
came for the pu-
rification rites
required by the
Law of Moses,
Joseph and Mary
took him to Jeru-
salem to present
him to the Lord
23 (as it is written
in the Law of the
Lord, "Every first-
born male is to be
consecrated to the
Lord"[a]), 24 and to
offer a sacrifice in
keeping with what
is said in the Law
of the Lord: "a pair
of doves or two
young pigeons."[b]
25 Now there was
a man in Jerusa-
lem called Simeon,
who was righteous
and devout. He
was waiting for
the consolation
of Israel, and the
Holy Spirit was on
him. 26 It had been
revealed to him by
the Holy Spirit that
he would not die
before he had seen
the Lord's Messi-
ah. 27 Moved by the
Spirit, he went into
the temple courts.
When the parents
brought in the
child Jesus to do
for him what the
custom of the Law
required, 28 Sime-
on took him in his
arms and praised
God, saying:

τοῦ περιτεμεῖν αὐτὸν καὶ ἐκλήθη τὸ ὄνομα αὐτοῦ Ἰησοῦς,
and it was time to circumcise him, {and} his name was called {the} name his Jesus,
3836 4362 899 2779 899 3950 2813 3836 3950 899 2652
d.gsn f.aa r.asm.3 cj v.api.3s d.nsn n.nsn r.gsm.3 n.nsm

τὸ κληθὲν ὑπὸ τοῦ ἀγγέλου πρὸ τοῦ συλλημφθῆναι αὐτὸν ἐν τῇ
the name he was called by the angel before he {the} was conceived he in the
3836 2813 5679 3836 34 4574 899 3836 5197 899 1877 3836
d.nsn pt.ap.nsn p.g d.gsm n.gsm p.g d.gsn f.ap r.asm.3 p.d d.dsf

κοιλίᾳ. 22 καὶ ὅτε ἐπλήσθησαν αἱ ἡμέραι τοῦ καθαρισμοῦ αὐτῶν
womb. And when the days were completed the days for their purification their
3120 2779 4021 3836 2465 4398 3836 2465 3836 899 2752 899
n.dsf cj cj v.api.3p d.npf n.npf d.gsm n.gsm r.gpm.3

κατὰ τὸν νόμον Μωϋσέως, ἀνήγαγον αὐτὸν ↰ εἰς Ἱεροσόλυμα παραστῆσαι
⌊according to⌋ the law of Moses, they brought him up to Jerusalem to present
2848 3836 3795 3707 343 899 343 1650 2642 4225
p.a d.asm n.asm n.gsm v.aai.3p r.asm.3 p.a n.apn f.aa

τῷ κυρίῳ, 23 καθὼς γέγραπται ἐν νόμῳ → κυρίου ὅτι πᾶν ἄρσεν
⌊to the⌋ Lord (as it is written in the law of the Lord: ~ "Every male
3836 3261 2777 1211 1877 3795 3261 4022 4246 781
d.dsm n.dsm cj v.rpi.3s p.d n.dsm n.gsm cj a.nsn a.nsn

διανοῖγον μήτραν ἅγιον τῷ κυρίῳ κληθήσεται, 24 καὶ τοῦ
who first opens the womb will be called holy ⌊to the⌋ Lord") will be called and to
1380 3616 2813 2813 2813 41 3836 3261 2813 2779 3836
pt.pa.nsn n.asf a.nsn d.dsm n.dsm v.fpi.3s cj d.gsn

δοῦναι θυσίαν κατὰ τὸ εἰρημένον ἐν τῷ νόμῳ → κυρίου, ζεῦγος
offer a sacrifice ⌊according to⌋ what is said in the law of the Lord, "A pair
1443 2602 2848 3836 3306 1877 3836 3795 3261 2414
f.aa n.asf p.a d.asn pt.rp.asn p.d d.dsm n.dsm n.gsm n.asn

τρυγόνων ἢ δύο νοσσοὺς περιστερῶν. 25 καὶ ἰδοὺ ἄνθρωπος ἦν
of turtledoves or two young pigeons." Now ~ there was a man there was
5583 2445 1545 3801 4361 2779 2627 1639 1639 476 1639
n.gpf cj a.apm n.apm n.gpf cj j n.nsm v.iai.3s

ἐν Ἰερουσαλὴμ ᾧ ὄνομα Συμεὼν καὶ ὁ ἄνθρωπος οὗτος δίκαιος
in Jerusalem, whose name was Simeon, and {the} this man this was righteous
1877 2647 4005 3950 5208 2779 3836 4047 476 4047 1465
p.d n.dsf r.dsm n.nsn n.nsm cj d.nsm n.nsm r.nsm a.nsm

καὶ εὐλαβὴς προσδεχόμενος παράκλησιν τοῦ Ἰσραήλ, καὶ πνεῦμα
and devout, ⌊waiting expectantly for⌋ the consolation of Israel, and the Holy Spirit
2779 2327 4657 4155 3836 2702 2779 41 4460
cj a.nsm pt.pm.nsm n.asf d.gsm n.gsm cj n.nsn

ἦν ἅγιον ἐπ' αὐτόν· 26 καὶ ἦν αὐτῷ κεχρηματισμένον ὑπὸ τοῦ
was Holy upon him. And ⌊it had been⌋ revealed to him revealed by the
1639 41 2093 899 2779 1639 5976 899 5976 5679 3836
v.iai.3s a.nsn p.a r.asm.3 cj v.iai.3s r.dsm.3 pt.rp.nsn p.g d.gsn

πνεύματος τοῦ ἁγίου ↱ ↱ μὴ ἰδεῖν θάνατον ⌊πρὶν ἢ[a] ἂν⌋
Holy Spirit {the} Holy that he would not see death before
41 4460 3836 41 1625 1625 3590 1625 2505 4570 2445 323
n.gsn d.gsn a.gsn pl f.aa n.asm cj pl pl

ἴδῃ τὸν χριστὸν κυρίου. 27 καὶ ἦλθεν ἐν τῷ πνεύματι εἰς τὸ
⌊he had seen⌋ the Lord's Christ. Lord's So he came in the Spirit into the
1625 3836 3261 5986 3261 2779 2262 1877 3836 4460 1650 3836
v.aas.3s d.asm n.asm n.gsm cj v.aai.3s p.d d.dsn n.dsn p.a d.asn

ἱερόν· καὶ ἐν τῷ εἰσαγαγεῖν τοὺς γονεῖς τὸ παιδίον Ἰησοῦν τοῦ
temple, and when {the} the parents brought in the child the parents Jesus, to
2639 2779 1877 3836 3836 4086 1652 3836 1204 3836 4086 2652 3836
n.asn cj p.d d.dsn f.aa d.apm n.apm d.asn n.asn n.asm d.gsn

ποιῆσαι αὐτοὺς κατὰ τὸ εἰθισμένον τοῦ νόμου περὶ αὐτοῦ 28 καὶ
do {they} for him ⌊according to⌋ the custom of the Law, for him {and}
4472 899 4309 899 2848 3836 1616 3836 3795 4309 899 2779
f.aa r.apm.3 p.a d.asn pt.rp.asn d.gsm n.gsm p.g r.gsm.3 cj

αὐτὸς ἐδέξατο αὐτὸ εἰς τὰς ἀγκάλας καὶ εὐλόγησεν τὸν θεὸν καὶ εἶπεν, 29 νῦν
he received him in his arms and blessed {the} God and said, "Now,
899 1312 899 1650 3836 44 2779 2328 3836 2536 2779 3306 3814
r.nsm v.ami.3s r.asn.3 p.a d.apf n.apf cj v.aai.3s d.asm n.asm cj v.aai.3s adv

NASB

before His circum-
cision, His name
was *then* called Je-
sus, the name given
by the angel before
He was conceived
in the womb.
22 And when the
days for their puri-
fication according
to the law of Moses
were completed,
they brought Him
up to Jerusalem
to present Him to
the Lord 23 (as it
is written in the
Law of the Lord,
"EVERY *firstborn*
MALE THAT OPENS
THE WOMB SHALL
BE CALLED HOLY TO
THE LORD"), 24 and
to offer a sacrifice
according to what
was said in the
Law of the Lord,
"A PAIR OF TURTLE-
DOVES OR TWO
YOUNG PIGEONS."
25 And there was a
man in Jerusalem
whose name was
Simeon; and this
man was righteous
and devout, look-
ing for the consola-
tion of Israel; and
the Holy Spirit
was upon him.
26 And it had been
revealed to him
by the Holy Spirit
that he would not
see death before he
had seen the Lord's
Christ. 27 And he
came in the Spirit
into the temple;
and when the
parents brought in
the child Jesus, to
carry out for Him
the custom of the
Law, 28 then he took
Him into his arms,
and blessed God,
and said,

[a] 23 Exodus 13:2,12
[b] 24 Lev. 12:8

[a] [ἢ] UBS.

NIV

29"Sovereign Lord,
as you have
promised,
you may now
dismiss[a]
your servant
in peace.
30 For my eyes have
seen your
salvation,
31 which you have
prepared in
the sight of
all nations:
32 a light for
revelation to
the Gentiles,
and the glory of
your people
Israel."

33The child's fa-
ther and mother
marveled at what
was said about
him. 34Then Sim-
eon blessed them
and said to Mary,
his mother: "This
child is destined
to cause the fall-
ing and rising of
many in Israel,
and to be a sign
that will be spoken
against, 35so that
the thoughts of
many hearts will
be revealed. And a
sword will pierce
your own soul
too."
36There was also
a prophet, Anna,
the daughter of
Penuel, of the tribe
of Asher. She was
very old; she had
lived with her hus-
band seven years
after her marriage,
37and then was a
widow until she
was eighty-four.[b]
She never left the
temple but wor-
shiped night and
day, fasting and
praying. 38Com-
ing up to them at
that very moment,
she gave thanks to
God and spoke

[a] 29 Or *promised, / now dismiss*
[b] 37 Or *then had been a widow for eighty-four years.*

ἀπολύεις τὸν δοῦλόν σου, δέσποτα, κατὰ τὸ
Master, you are dismissing *{the}* your servant *your* *Master* in peace, ⌞according to⌟ *{the}* your
1305 668 3836 5148 1529 5148 1305 1877 1645 2848 3836 5148
v.pai.2s d.asm n.asm r.gs.2 n.vsm p.a d.asn

ῥῆμά σου ἐν εἰρήνῃ· 30 ὅτι εἶδον οἱ ὀφθαλμοί μου τὸ
word; *your* *in* *peace* because my eyes have seen *{the}* *eyes* *my* *{the}* your
4839 5148 1877 1645 4022 1609 4057 1625 3836 4057 1609 3836 5148
n.asn r.gs.2 p.d n.dsf cj v.aai.3p d.npm n.npm r.gs.1 d.asn

σωτήριόν σου, 31 ὃ ἡτοίμασας κατὰ πρόσωπον πάντων τῶν λαῶν, 32
salvation, *your* which you have prepared in the presence of all *{the}* peoples, a
5402 5148 4005 2286 2848 4725 4246 3836 3295
n.asn r.gs.2 r.asn v.aai.2s p.a n.asn a.gpm d.gpm n.gpm

φῶς εἰς ἀποκάλυψιν → ἐθνῶν καὶ δόξαν → λαοῦ σου Ἰσραήλ. 33 καὶ
light for revelation to the Gentiles, and for glory for your people *your* Israel." *{and}*
5890 1650 637 1620 2779 1518 5148 3295 5148 2702 2779
n.asn p.a n.asf n.gpn cj n.asf n.gsm r.gs.2 n.gsm cj

ἦν ὁ πατὴρ αὐτοῦ καὶ ἡ μήτηρ θαυμάζοντες ἐπὶ τοῖς
were *{the}* His father *His* and *{the}* mother were amazed at the
1639 3836 899 4252 899 2779 3836 3613 1639 2513 2093 3836
v.iai.3s d.nsm n.nsm r.gsm.3 cj d.nsf n.nsf pt.pa.npm p.d d.dpn

λαλουμένοις περὶ αὐτοῦ. 34 καὶ εὐλόγησεν αὐτοὺς Συμεὼν καὶ
⌞things that were being said⌟ about him. Then Simeon blessed them *Simeon* and
3281 4309 899 2779 5208 2328 899 5208 2779
pt.pp.dpn p.g r.gsm.3 cj v.aai.3s r.apm.3 n.nsm cj

εἶπεν πρὸς Μαριὰμ τὴν μητέρα αὐτοῦ, ἰδοὺ οὗτος κεῖται εἰς
said to Mary *{the}* his mother, *his* ⌞"Take note,⌟ this child is appointed for the
3306 4639 3452 3836 899 3613 899 2627 4047 3023 1650
v.aai.3s p.a n.asf d.asf n.asf r.gsm.3 j r.nsm v.pmi.3s p.a

πτῶσιν καὶ ἀνάστασιν πολλῶν ἐν τῷ Ἰσραὴλ καὶ εἰς σημεῖον ἀντιλεγόμενον
fall and rising of many in *{the}* Israel, and for a sign that will be opposed
4774 2779 414 4498 1877 3836 2702 2779 1650 4956 515
n.asf cj n.asf a.gpm p.d d.dsm n.dsm cj p.a n.asn pt.pp.asn

35 καὶ σοῦ δὲ[a] αὐτῆς τὴν ψυχὴν διελεύσεται ῥομφαία
also (and a sword will pierce your *and* own *{the}* soul *will pierce* *sword* also),
2779 1254 4855 1451 1451 5148 1254 899 3836 6034 1451 4855 2779
adv r.gs.2 cj r.gsf d.asf n.asf v.fmi.3s n.nsf

ὅπως ἂν ἀποκαλυφθῶσιν ἐκ πολλῶν καρδιῶν διαλογισμοί.
that ~ thoughts of many hearts may be revealed." *of* *many* *hearts* *thoughts*
3968 323 1369 1666 4498 2840 636 1666 4498 2840 1369
cj pl v.aps.3p p.g a.gpf n.gpf n.npm

36 καὶ ἦν Ἅννα προφῆτις, θυγάτηρ Φανουήλ, ἐκ φυλῆς
Now ⌞there was⌟ a prophetess, Anna, *prophetess* the daughter of Phanuel, of the tribe
2779 1639 4739 483 4739 2588 5750 1666 5876
cj v.iai.3s n.nsf n.nsf n.nsf n.gsm p.g n.gsf

Ἀσήρ· αὕτη προβεβηκυῖα ἐν ⌞ἡμέραις πολλαῖς,⌟ ζήσασα μετὰ ἀνδρὸς ἔτη
of Asher. She was advanced in years, having lived with her husband seven
818 4047 4581 1877 2465 4498 2409 3552 467 2291
n.gsm r.nsf pt.ra.nsf p.d n.dpf a.dpf pt.aa.nsf p.g n.gsm n.apn

ἑπτὰ ἀπὸ τῆς παρθενίας αὐτῆς 37 καὶ αὐτὴ χήρα ἕως
years from *{the}* her virginity, *her* and then she was a widow until she was eighty-four
2231 608 3836 899 4220 899 2779 899 5939 2401 3837
a.apn p.g d.gsf n.gsf r.gsf.3 cj r.nsf n.nsf p.g

ἐτῶν ⌞ὀγδοήκοντα τεσσάρων,⌟ ἣ ↱ οὐκ ἀφίστατο τοῦ ἱεροῦ
years old. *eighty-four* She did not leave the temple, worshipping night
2291 3837 5475 4005 923 4024 923 3836 2639 3302 3816
n.gpn a.gpn a.gpn r.nsf pl v.imi.3s d.gsn n.gsn

→ νηστείαις καὶ δεήσεσιν λατρεύουσα νύκτα καὶ ἡμέραν. 38 καὶ
and day with fasting and prayer. *worshipping* *night* *and* *day* *{and}*
2779 2465 3763 2779 1255 3302 3816 2779 2465 2779
n.dpf cj n.dpf pt.pa.nsf n.asf cj n.asf cj

αὐτῇ τῇ ὥρᾳ ἐπιστᾶσα ἀνθωμολογεῖτο τῷ θεῷ καὶ ἐλάλει
⌞At that very⌟ *{the}* hour she came up and began to give thanks to God and ⌞continued to speak⌟
899 3836 6052 2392 469 3836 2536 2779 3281
r.dsf d.dsf n.dsf pt.aa.nsf v.imi.3s d.dsm n.dsm cj v.iai.3s

[a] [δὲ] UBS.

NASB

29" Now Lord,
You are re-
leasing Your
bond-servant
to depart in
peace,
According to
Your word;
30 For my eyes
have seen
Your salva-
tion,
31 Which You
have prepared
in the pres-
ence of all
peoples,
32 A LIGHT OF
REVELATION TO
THE GENTILES,
And the glory
of Your peo-
ple Israel."
33And His father
and mother were
amazed at the
things which were
being said about
Him. 34And Simeon
blessed them and
said to Mary His
mother, "Behold,
this *Child* is ap-
pointed for the fall
and rise of many
in Israel, and for
a sign to be op-
posed— 35and a
sword will pierce
even your own
soul—to the end
that thoughts from
many hearts may
be revealed."
36And there was a
prophetess, Anna
the daughter of
Phanuel, of the
tribe of Asher. She
was advanced in
years and had lived
with *her* husband
seven years after
her marriage, 37and
then as a widow to
the age of eighty-
four. She never left
the temple, serv-
ing night and day
with fastings and
prayers. 38At that
very moment she
came up and *began*
giving thanks to
God, and continued

NIV

about the child to
all who were look-
ing forward to the
redemption of Je-
rusalem.
39 When Joseph
and Mary had
done everything
required by the
Law of the Lord,
they returned to
Galilee to their
own town of Naz-
areth. 40 And the
child grew and
became strong;
he was filled with
wisdom, and the
grace of God was
on him.

The Boy Jesus at the Temple

41 Every year
Jesus' parents
went to Jerusalem
for the Festival
of the Passover.
42 When he was
twelve years old,
they went up to the
festival, accord-
ing to the custom.
43 After the festival
was over, while his
parents were re-
turning home, the
boy Jesus stayed
behind in Jeru-
salem, but they
were unaware of
it. 44 Thinking he
was in their com-
pany, they traveled
on for a day. Then
they began look-
ing for him among
their relatives and
friends. 45 When
they did not find
him, they went
back to Jerusalem
to look for him.
46 After three days
they found him in
the temple courts,
sitting among the
teachers, listen-
ing to them and
asking them ques-
tions. 47 Everyone
who heard him
was amazed at
his understanding
and his answers.
48 When his parents
saw

περὶ αὐτοῦ πᾶσιν τοῖς προσδεχομένοις λύτρωσιν Ἰερουσαλήμ. 39 καὶ
of him to all who ⌊were waiting expectantly for⌋ the redemption of Jerusalem. And
4309 899 4246 3836 4657 3391 2647 2779
p.g r.gsm.3 a.dpm d.dpm pt.pm.dpm n.asf n.gsf cj

ὡς ἐτέλεσαν πάντα τὰ κατὰ τὸν νόμον → κυρίου, ἐπέστρεψαν
when they had completed everything *{the}* ⌊according to⌋ the law of the Lord, they returned
6055 5464 4246 3836 2848 3836 3795 3261 2188
cj v.aai.3p a.apn d.apn p.a d.asm n.asm n.gsm v.aai.3p

εἰς τὴν Γαλιλαίαν εἰς πόλιν ἑαυτῶν Ναζαρέθ. 40 τὸ δὲ παιδίον
to *{the}* Galilee, to their own town, *their own* Nazareth. And the *And* child
1650 3836 1133 1650 1571 1571 4484 1571 3714 1254 3836 1254 4086
p.a d.asf n.asf p.a n.asf r.gpm.3 n.asf d.nsn cj n.nsn

ηὔξανεν καὶ ἐκραταιοῦτο πληρούμενον σοφίᾳ, καὶ χάρις θεοῦ ἦν ἐπ᾽
grew and became strong, filled with wisdom; and the favor of God was upon
889 2779 3194 4444 5053 2779 5921 2536 1639 2093
v.iai.3s cj v.ipi.3s pt.pp.nsn n.dsf cj n.nsf n.gsm v.iai.3s p.a

αὐτό. 41 καὶ ἐπορεύοντο οἱ γονεῖς αὐτοῦ κατ᾽ ἔτος εἰς Ἰερουσαλὴμ
him. Now his parents went *{the}* *parents* *his* year by year to Jerusalem
899 2779 899 1204 4513 3836 1204 899 2848 2291 1650 2647
r.asn.3 cj v.imi.3p d.npm n.npm r.gsm.3 p.a n.asn p.a n.asf

τῇ ἑορτῇ τοῦ πάσχα. 42 καὶ ὅτε ἐγένετο ἐτῶν δώδεκα, →
⌊for the⌋ feast of Passover And when he was twelve years *twelve* old, when they
3836 2038 3836 4247 2779 4021 1181 1557 2291 1557 899
d.dsf n.dsf d.gsn n.gsn cj cj v.ami.3s n.gpn a.gpn

ἀναβαινόντων αὐτῶν κατὰ τὸ ἔθος τῆς ἑορτῆς 43 καὶ τελειωσάντων τὰς
went up *they* ⌊according to⌋ the custom of the feast and had completed the
326 899 2848 3836 1621 3836 2038 2779 5457 3836
pt.pa.gpm r.gpm.3 p.a d.asn n.asn d.gsf n.gsf cj pt.aa.gpm d.apf

ἡμέρας, ἐν τῷ ὑποστρέφειν αὐτοὺς ὑπέμεινεν Ἰησοῦς ὁ παῖς
days, as *{the}* they were returning, *they* the boy Jesus stayed behind *Jesus* *the* *boy*
2465 1877 3836 899 5715 899 3836 4090 2652 5702 2652 3836 4090
n.apf p.d d.dsn f.pa r.apm.3 v.aai.3s n.nsm d.nsm n.nsm

ἐν Ἰερουσαλήμ, καὶ ↱ οὐκ ἔγνωσαν οἱ γονεῖς αὐτοῦ.
in Jerusalem, and his parents did not know *{the}* *parents* *his* it.
1877 2647 2779 899 1204 1182 4024 1182 3836 1204 899
p.d n.dsf cj pl v.aai.3p d.npm n.npm r.gsm.3

44 νομίσαντες δὲ αὐτὸν εἶναι ἐν τῇ συνοδίᾳ ἦλθον ἡμέρας ὁδὸν καὶ
Thinking *{and}* him to be in the caravan, they went a day's journey, ⌊but then⌋
3787 1254 899 1639 1877 3836 5322 2262 2465 3847 2779
pt.aa.npm cj r.asm.3 f.pa p.d d.dsf n.dsf v.aai.3p n.gsf n.asf cj

ἀνεζήτουν αὐτὸν ἐν τοῖς συγγενεῦσιν καὶ τοῖς γνωστοῖς, 45 καὶ ↱
⌊began looking for⌋ him among their relatives and *{the}* acquaintances. *{and}* When
349 899 1877 3836 5150 2779 3836 1196 2779 2351
v.iai.3p r.asm.3 p.d d.dpm n.dpm cj d.dpm a.dpm cj

↱ ↱ μὴ εὑρόντες ὑπέστρεψαν εἰς Ἰερουσαλὴμ ἀναζητοῦντες αὐτόν.
they did not find him, they went back to Jerusalem to look for him.
2351 2351 3590 2351 5715 1650 2647 349 899
pl pt.aa.npm v.aai.3p p.a n.asf pt.pa.npm r.asm.3

46 καὶ ἐγένετο μετὰ ἡμέρας τρεῖς εὗρον αὐτὸν ἐν τῷ ἱερῷ
Then *{it happened that}* after three days *three* they found him in the temple,
2779 1181 3552 5552 2465 5552 2351 899 1877 3836 2639
cj v.ami.3s p.a n.apf a.apf v.aai.3p r.asm.3 p.d d.dsn n.dsn

καθεζόμενον ἐν μέσῳ τῶν διδασκάλων καὶ ἀκούοντα αὐτῶν καὶ ἐπερωτῶντα
seated in the midst of the teachers, *{and}* listening to them and asking
2757 1877 3545 3836 1437 2779 201 899 2779 2089
pt.pm.asm p.d n.dsn d.gpm n.gpm cj pt.pa.asm r.gpm.3 cj pt.pa.asm

αὐτούς· ↰ 47 ἐξίσταντο δὲ πάντες οἱ ἀκούοντες
them questions. And all who heard him were amazed *And* *all* *who* *heard*
899 2089 1254 4246 3836 201 899 2014 1254 4246 3836 201
r.apm.3 v.imi.3p cj a.npm d.npm pt.pa.npm

αὐτοῦ ἐπὶ τῇ ↱ συνέσει καὶ ταῖς ἀποκρίσεσιν αὐτοῦ. 48 καὶ ἰδόντες
him at *{the}* his understanding and *{the}* his answers. *his* And ⌊when they saw⌋
899 2093 3836 899 5304 2779 3836 899 647 899 2779 1625
r.gsm.3 p.d d.dsf n.dsf cj d.dpf n.dpf r.gsm.3 cj pt.aa.npm

NASB

to speak of Him
to all those who
were looking for
the redemption of
Jerusalem.

Return to Nazareth

39 When they had
performed every-
thing according
to the Law of the
Lord, they returned
to Galilee, to their
own city of Naza-
reth. 40 The Child
continued to grow
and become strong,
increasing in wis-
dom; and the grace
of God was upon
Him.

Visit to Jerusalem

41 Now His parents
went to Jerusa-
lem every year at
the Feast of the
Passover. 42 And
when He became
twelve, they went
up *there* according
to the custom of
the Feast; 43 and as
they were return-
ing, after spending
the full number of
days, the boy Jesus
stayed behind in
Jerusalem. But
His parents were
unaware of it, 44 but
supposed Him to
be in the caravan,
and went a day's
journey; and they
began looking
for Him among
their relatives and
acquaintances.
45 When they did
not find Him,
they returned to
Jerusalem looking
for Him. 46 Then,
after three days
they found Him in
the temple, sitting
in the midst of
the teachers, both
listening to them
and asking them
questions. 47 And
all who heard Him
were amazed at
His understanding
and His answers.
48 When they saw

NIV

him, they were
astonished. His
mother said to
him, "Son, why
have you treated
us like this? Your
father and I have
been anxiously
searching for you."
[49]"Why were you
searching for me?"
he asked. "Didn't
you know I had to
be in my Father's
house?"[a] [50]But
they did not under-
stand what he was
saying to them.
[51]Then he went
down to Nazareth
with them and was
obedient to them.
But his mother
treasured all these
things in her heart.
[52]And Jesus grew
in wisdom and
stature, and in fa-
vor with God and
man.

John the Baptist Prepares the Way

3 In the fifteenth
year of the
reign of Tiberius
Caesar—when
Pontius Pilate was
governor of Judea,
Herod tetrarch of
Galilee, his broth-
er Philip tetrarch
of Iturea and Trac-
onitis, and Lysani-
as tetrarch of Abi-
lene— [2]during the
high-priesthood of
Annas and Caia-
phas, the word of
God came to John
son of Zechariah
in the wilderness.
[3]He went into all
the country around
the Jordan,

αὐτὸν ἐξεπλάγησαν, καὶ εἶπεν πρὸς αὐτὸν ἡ μήτηρ αὐτοῦ, τέκνον,
him, they were astounded, and his mother said to him, *{the}* *mother* *his* "Child,
899 1742 2779 899 3613 3306 4639 899 3836 3613 899 5451
r.asm.3 v.api.3p cj v.aai.3s p.a r.asm.3 d.nsf n.nsf r.gsm.3 n.vsn

τί ἐποίησας ἡμῖν οὕτως; ἰδοὺ ὁ πατήρ σου κἀγὼ ὀδυνώμενοι
why did you treat us like this? Look, *{the}* your father *you* and I ˌhave been terribly worriedˌ
5515 4472 7005 4048 2627 3836 5148 4252 5148 2743 3849
r.asn v.aai.2s r.dp.1 adv j d.nsm n.nsm r.gs.2 crasis pt.pp.npm

ἐζητοῦμέν σε. [49] καὶ εἶπεν πρὸς αὐτούς, τί ὅτι ἐζητεῖτέ με;
trying to find you." And he said to them, "Why is it that ˌyou were looking forˌ me? Did
2426 5148 2779 3306 4639 899 5515 4022 2426 1609 3857
v.iai.1p r.as.2 cj v.aai.3s p.a r.apm.3 r.asn cj v.iai.2p r.as.1

οὐκ ᾔδειτε ὅτι ἐν τοῖς τοῦ πατρός μου
you not know that I would have to be in *{the}* *{the}* my Father's *my* house?"
3857 4024 3857 4022 1609 1256 1256 1639 1639 1877 3836 3836 1609 4252 1609
pl v.lai.2p cj p.d d.dpn d.gsm n.gsm r.gs.1

δεῖ εἶναί με; [50] καὶ αὐτοὶ οὐ συνῆκαν τὸ ῥῆμα ὃ ἐλάλησεν αὐτοῖς.
would have *to be* *I* But they did not understand the saying that he spoke to them.
1256 1639 1609 2779 899 5317 4024 5317 3836 4839 4005 3281 899
v.pai.3s f.pa r.as.1 cj r.npm pl v.aai.3p d.asn n.asn r.asn v.aai.3s r.dpm.3

[51] καὶ κατέβη μετ' αὐτῶν καὶ ἦλθεν εἰς Ναζαρὲθ καὶ ἦν ὑποτασσόμενος
Then ˌhe went downˌ with them and came to Nazareth and was obedient
2779 2849 3552 899 2779 2262 1650 3714 2779 1639 5718
cj v.aai.3s p.g r.gpm.3 cj v.aai.3s p.a n.asf cj v.iai.3s pt.pp.nsm

αὐτοῖς. καὶ ἡ μήτηρ αὐτοῦ διετήρει πάντα τὰ ῥήματα ἐν τῇ καρδίᾳ
to them. And *{the}* his mother *his* treasured all that was said in *{the}* her heart.
899 2779 3836 899 3613 899 1413 4246 3836 4839 1877 3836 899 2840
r.dpm.3 cj d.nsf n.nsf r.gsm.3 v.iai.3s a.apn d.apn n.apn p.d d.dsf n.dsf

αὐτῆς. [52] καὶ Ἰησοῦς προέκοπτεν [a]ἐν τῇ σοφίᾳ καὶ ἡλικίᾳ καὶ χάριτι
her And Jesus advanced in *{the}* wisdom and in stature, and in favor
899 2779 2652 4621 1877 3836 5053 2779 1877 2461 2779 1877 5921
r.gsf.3 cj n.nsm v.iai.3s p.d d.dsf n.dsf cj n.dsf cj n.dsf

παρὰ θεῷ καὶ ἀνθρώποις.
with God and man.
4123 2536 2779 476
p.d n.dsm cj n.dpm

[3:1] ἐν ἔτει δὲ πεντεκαιδεκάτῳ τῆς ἡγεμονίας Τιβερίου Καίσαρος,
In the fifteenth year *{and}* *fifteenth* of the reign of Tiberius Caesar,
1877 4298 2291 1254 4298 3836 2449 5501 2790
p.d n.dsn cj a.dsn d.gsf n.gsf n.gsm n.gsm

ἡγεμονεύοντος Ποντίου Πιλάτου τῆς Ἰουδαίας, καὶ
when Pontius Pilate was governing *Pontius* *Pilate* *{the}* Judea, and Herod
4508 4397 2448 4508 4397 3836 2677 2779 2476
pt.pa.gsm n.gsm n.gsm d.gsf n.gsf cj

τετρααρχοῦντος τῆς Γαλιλαίας Ἡρῴδου, Φιλίππου δὲ τοῦ ἀδελφοῦ αὐτοῦ
was tetrarch of Galilee *Herod* and Philip *and* *{the}* his brother *his*
5489 3836 1133 2476 1254 5805 1254 3836 899 81 899
pt.pa.gsm d.gsf n.gsf n.gsm n.gsm cj d.gsm n.gsm r.gsm.3

τετρααρχοῦντος τῆς Ἰτουραίας καὶ Τραχωνίτιδος χώρας, καὶ Λυσανίου
tetrarch of the region of Ituraea and Trachonitis, *region* and Lysanias was
5489 3836 6001 2714 2779 5551 6001 2779 3384 5489
pt.pa.gsm d.gsf n.gsf cj n.gsf n.gsf cj n.gsm

τῆς Ἀβιληνῆς τετρααρχοῦντος, [2]ἐπὶ ἀρχιερέως Ἅννα καὶ Καϊάφα,
tetrarch of Abilene, *was tetrarch* when Annas was high priest, *Annas* and Caiaphas,
5489 3836 9 5489 2093 484 797 484 2779 2780
d.gsf n.gsf pt.pa.gsm p.g n.gsm n.gsm cj n.gsm

ἐγένετο ῥῆμα θεοῦ ἐπὶ Ἰωάννην τὸν Ζαχαρίου υἱὸν ἐν τῇ
the word of God came *word* *of God* upon John the son of Zechariah *son* in the
4839 2536 2536 1181 4839 2536 2093 2722 3836 5626 2408 5626 1877 3836
v.ami.3s n.nsn n.gsm p.a n.asm d.asm n.gsm n.asm p.d d.dsf

ἐρήμῳ. [3]καὶ ἦλθεν εἰς πᾶσαν τὴν[b] περίχωρον τοῦ Ἰορδάνου
wilderness. And he went into the region all *the* around the Jordan,
2245 2779 2262 1650 3836 4369 4246 3836 4369 3836 2674
n.dsf cj v.aai.3s p.a a.asf d.asf a.asf d.gsm n.gsm

NASB

Him, they were
astonished; and
His mother said to
Him, "Son, why
have You treated
us this way? Be-
hold, Your father
and I have been
anxiously looking
for You." [49]And
He said to them,
"Why is it that
you were looking
for Me? Did you
not know that I
had to be in My
Father's *house?*"
[50]But they did not
understand the
statement which
He had made to
them. [51]And He
went down with
them and came
to Nazareth, and
He continued in
subjection to them;
and His mother
treasured all *these*
things in her heart.
[52]And Jesus kept
increasing in wis-
dom and stature,
and in favor with
God and men.

John the Baptist Preaches

[3:1]Now in the fif-
teenth year of the
reign of Tiberius
Caesar, when Pon-
tius Pilate was gov-
ernor of Judea, and
Herod was tetrarch
of Galilee, and
his brother Philip
was tetrarch of the
region of Ituraea
and Trachonitis,
and Lysanias was
tetrarch of Abilene,
[2]in the high priest-
hood of Annas
and Caiaphas, the
word of God came
to John, the son of
Zacharias, in the
wilderness. [3]And
he came into all the
district around the
Jordan,

[a] 49 Or *be about my Father's business*

[a] [ἐν τῇ] UBS.
[b] [τὴν] UBS.

NIV

preaching a bap-
tism of repentance
for the forgiveness
of sins. 4As it is
written in the book
of the words of Isa-
iah the prophet:

"A voice of one
calling in the
wilderness,
'Prepare the way
for the Lord,
make straight
paths for
him.
5Every valley shall
be filled in,
every mountain
and hill
made low.
The crooked roads
shall become
straight,
the rough ways
smooth.
6And all people
will see
God's salva–
tion.'"[a]

7John said to the
crowds coming out
to be baptized by
him, "You brood
of vipers! Who
warned you to flee
from the coming
wrath? 8Produce
fruit in keeping
with repentance.
And do not begin
to say to your-
selves, 'We have
Abraham as our
father.' For I tell
you that out of
these stones God
can raise up chil-
dren for Abraham.
9The ax is already
at the root of the
trees, and every
tree that does not
produce good fruit
will be cut down
and thrown into
the fire."
10"What should
we do then?" the
crowd asked.
11John answered,

κηρύσσων βάπτισμα μετανοίας εἰς ἄφεσιν ἁμαρτιῶν, 4ὡς γέγραπται ἐν
proclaiming a baptism of repentance for the forgiveness of sins. As it is written in
3062 967 3567 1650 912 281 6055 1211 1877
pt.pa.nsm n.asn n.gsf p.a n.asf n.gpf cj v.rpi.3s p.d

βίβλῳ → λόγων Ἠσαΐου τοῦ προφήτου, φωνὴ βοῶντος ἐν τῇ
the book of the words of Isaiah the prophet, "The voice ⌊of one calling out⌋ in the
1047 3364 2480 3836 4737 5889 1066 1877 3836
n.dsf n.gpm n.gsm d.gsm n.gsm n.nsf pt.pa.gsm p.d d.dsf

ἐρήμῳ· ἑτοιμάσατε τὴν ὁδὸν → κυρίου, εὐθείας ποιεῖτε τὰς
wilderness: 'Prepare the way for the Lord, make the paths straight *make* *the*
2245 2286 3836 3847 3261 4472 3836 5561 2318 4472 3836
n.dsf v.aam.2p d.asf n.asf n.gsm a.apf v.pam.2p d.apf

τρίβους αὐτοῦ· 5πᾶσα φάραγξ πληρωθήσεται καὶ πᾶν ὄρος καὶ βουνὸς
paths for him. Every ravine will be filled in and every mountain and hill
5561 899 4246 5754 4444 2779 4246 4001 2779 1090
n.apf r.gsm.3 a.nsf n.nsf v.fpi.3s cj a.nsn n.nsn cj n.nsm

ταπεινωθήσεται, καὶ ἔσται τὰ σκολιὰ εἰς εὐθείαν καὶ
will be leveled off; *{and}* the crooked places will become *the* *crooked places* *{into}* straight and
5427 2779 3836 5021 5021 1639 3836 5021 1650 2318 2779
v.fpi.3s cj v.fmi.3s d.npn a.npn p.a a.asf cj

αἱ τραχεῖαι ↰ ↰ εἰς ὁδοὺς λείας· 6καὶ → ὄψεται πᾶσα
the rough places will become *{into}* smooth roads. *smooth* Then will all flesh see *all*
3836 5550 1639 1639 1650 3308 3847 3308 2779 4246 4922 3972 4246
d.npf a.npf p.a n.apf a.apf cj v.fmi.3s a.nsf

σὰρξ τὸ σωτήριον τοῦ θεοῦ. 7 ἔλεγεν οὖν τοῖς ἐκπορευομένοις ὄχλοις
flesh the salvation of God!'" So he said *So* to the crowds that were coming out *crowds*
4922 3836 5402 3836 2536 4036 3306 4036 3836 4063 1744 4063
n.nsf d.asn n.asn d.gsm n.gsm v.iai.3s cj d.dpm pt.pm.dpm n.dpm

βαπτισθῆναι ὑπ' αὐτοῦ, γεννήματα ἐχιδνῶν, τίς ὑπέδειξεν ὑμῖν φυγεῖν ἀπὸ τῆς
to be baptized by him, "You offspring of vipers! Who warned you to flee from the
966 5679 899 1165 2399 5515 5683 7007 5771 608 3836
f.ap p.g r.gsm.3 n.vpn n.gpf r.nsm v.aai.3s r.dp.2 f.aa p.g d.gsf

μελλούσης ὀργῆς; 8ποιήσατε οὖν καρποὺς ἀξίους τῆς μετανοίας καὶ ↱ μὴ
coming wrath? Bear, then, fruits worthy of repentance. *{and}* Do not even
3516 3973 4472 4036 2843 545 3836 3567 2779 806 3590
pt.pa.gsf n.gsf v.aam.2p cj n.apm a.apm d.gsf n.gsf cj pl

ἄρξησθε λέγειν ἐν ἑαυτοῖς, → πατέρα ἔχομεν τὸν Ἀβραάμ.
begin to say to yourselves, 'We have Abraham as our father.' *We have* *{the}* *Abraham* For
806 3306 1877 1571 2400 2400 11 4252 2400 3836 11 1142
v.ams.2p f.pa p.d r.dpm.2 n.asm v.pai.1p d.asm n.asm

λέγω γὰρ ὑμῖν ὅτι δύναται ὁ θεὸς ἐκ τῶν λίθων τούτων ἐγεῖραι
I say *For* to you that God is able, *{the}* *God* ⌊out of⌋ *{the}* these stones, *these* to raise up
3306 1142 7007 4022 2536 1538 3836 2536 1666 3836 4047 3345 4047 1586
v.pai.1s cj r.dp.2 cj v.ppi.3s d.nsm n.nsm p.g d.gpm n.gpm r.gpm f.aa

τέκνα τῷ Ἀβραάμ. 9 ἤδη δὲ καὶ ἡ ἀξίνη πρὸς τὴν ῥίζαν
children to Abraham. Indeed, already *{and}* *Indeed* the axe is laid to the root
5451 3836 11 2779 2453 1254 2779 3836 544 3023 3023 4639 3836 4844
n.apn d.dsm n.dsm adv cj adv d.nsf n.nsf p.a d.asf n.asf

τῶν δένδρων κεῖται· πᾶν οὖν δένδρον ↱ μὴ ποιοῦν καρπὸν
of the trees; *is laid* therefore every *therefore* tree that does not bear good fruit
3836 1285 3023 4036 4246 4036 1285 4472 3590 4472 2819 2843
d.gpn n.gpn v.pmi.3s a.nsn cj n.nsn pl pt.pa.nsn n.asm

καλὸν ἐκκόπτεται καὶ εἰς πῦρ βάλλεται. 10καὶ ἐπηρώτων
good will be cut down and thrown into the fire. *thrown* *{and}* The crowds asked
2819 1716 2779 965 1650 4786 965 2779 3836 4063 2089
a.asm v.ppi.3s cj p.a n.asn v.ppi.3s cj v.iai.3p

αὐτὸν οἱ ὄχλοι λέγοντες, τί οὖν ποιήσωμεν; 11 ↱ ↱ ἀποκριθεὶς δὲ
him *The* *crowds* saying, "What, then, shall we do?" And he would answer, *And*
899 3836 4063 3306 5515 4036 4472 1254 3306 3306 646 1254
r.asm.3 d.npm n.npm pt.pa.npm r.asn cj v.aas.1p pt.ap.nsm cj

NASB

preaching a bap-
tism of repentance
for the forgiveness
of sins; 4as it is
written in the book
of the words of Isa-
iah the prophet,
"THE VOICE OF
ONE CRYING IN
THE WILDER-
NESS,
'MAKE READY
THE WAY OF
THE LORD,
MAKE HIS
PATHS
STRAIGHT.
5'EVERY RAVINE
WILL BE
FILLED,
AND EVERY
MOUNTAIN AND
HILL WILL BE
BROUGHT LOW;
THE CROOKED
WILL BECOME
STRAIGHT,
AND THE
ROUGH ROADS
SMOOTH;
6AND ALL FLESH
WILL SEE THE
SALVATION OF
GOD.'"
7So he *began* say-
ing to the crowds
who were going
out to be baptized
by him, "You
brood of vipers,
who warned you
to flee from the
wrath to come?
8Therefore bear
fruits in keeping
with repentance,
and do not begin to
say to yourselves,
'We have Abraham
for our father,' for
I say to you that
from these stones
God is able to
raise up children to
Abraham. 9Indeed
the axe is already
laid at the root of
the trees; so every
tree that does not
bear good fruit
is cut down and
thrown into the
fire."
10And the crowds
were questioning
him, saying, "Then
what shall we do?"
11And he would
answer and say

[a] 6 Isaiah 40:3-5

NIV

"Anyone who has
two shirts should
share with the one
who has none, and
anyone who has
food should do the
same."
12 Even tax col-
lectors came to be
baptized. "Teach-
er," they asked,
"what should
we do?"
13 "Don't collect
any more than you
are required to," he
told them.
14 Then some sol-
diers asked him,
"And what should
we do?"
He replied,
"Don't extort mon-
ey and don't ac-
cuse people false-
ly—be content
with your pay."
15 The people
were waiting ex-
pectantly and were
all wondering in
their hearts if John
might possibly
be the Messiah.
16 John answered
them all, "I baptize
you with[a] water.
But one who is
more powerful
than I will come,
the straps of whose
sandals I am not
worthy to untie.
He will baptize
you with[b] the Holy
Spirit and fire.
17 His winnowing
fork is in his hand
to clear his thresh-
ing floor and to
gather the wheat
into his barn, but
he will burn up
the chaff with un-
quenchable fire."

ἔλεγεν αὐτοῖς, ὁ ἔχων δύο χιτῶνας μεταδότω τῷ μὴ
saying to them, "He ⌊who has⌋ two tunics, ⌊let him share with⌋ the one who has none;
3306 899 3836 2400 1545 5945 3556 3836 2400 2400 2400 3590
v.iai.3s r.dpm.3 d.nsm pt.pa.nsm a.apm n.apm v.aam.3s d.dsm pl

ἔχοντι, καὶ ὁ ἔχων βρώματα ὁμοίως ποιείτω. 12
one who has and he ⌊who has⌋ food, let him do the same." *let him do* Tax collectors
2400 2779 3836 2400 1109 4472 4472 4472 3931 4472 5467 5467
pt.pa.dsm cj d.nsm pt.pa.nsm n.apn adv v.pam.3s

ἦλθον δὲ καὶ τελῶναι βαπτισθῆναι καὶ εἶπαν πρὸς αὐτόν, διδάσκαλε, τί
also came *{and}* *also* *Tax collectors* to be baptized and they said to him, "Teacher, what
2779 2262 1254 2779 5467 966 2779 3306 4639 899 1437 5515
v.aai.3p cj adv n.npm f.ap cj v.aai.3p p.a r.asm.3 n.vsm r.asn

ποιήσωμεν; 13 ὁ δὲ εἶπεν πρὸς αὐτούς, μηδὲν πλέον παρὰ τὸ
should we do?" And he *And* said to them, "Collect no more than what
4472 1254 3836 1254 3306 4639 899 4556 3594 4498 4123 3836
v.aas.1p d.nsm cj v.aai.3s p.a r.apm.3 a.asn a.asn.c p.a d.asn

διατεταγμένον ὑμῖν πράσσετε. 14 → ἐπηρώτων δὲ αὐτὸν καὶ
has been prescribed for you." *Collect* Soldiers were also questioning *{and}* him, *also*
1411 7007 4556 5129 2779 2089 1254 899 2779
pt.rp.asn r.dp.2 v.pam.2p v.iai.3p cj r.asm.3 adv

στρατευόμενοι λέγοντες, τί ποιήσωμεν καὶ ἡμεῖς; καὶ εἶπεν αὐτοῖς,
Soldiers saying, "And we, what should we do?" *And* *we* *{and}* He said to them,
5129 3306 2779 7005 5515 4472 2779 7005 2779 3306 899
pt.pm.npm pt.pa.npm r.asn v.aas.1p adv r.np.1 cj v.aai.3s r.dpm.3

↱ μηδένα διασείσητε ↰ μηδὲ συκοφαντήσητε ← καὶ
"Do not ⌊extort money from⌋ anyone, or accuse them falsely; and
1398 3594 1398 3594 3593 5193 2779
a.asm v.aas.2p cj v.aas.2p cj

ἀρκεῖσθε τοῖς ὀψωνίοις ὑμῶν. 15 → προσδοκῶντος
⌊be content with⌋ *{the}* your wages." *your* Since the people were filled with anticipation
758 3836 7007 4072 7007 3836 3295 4659
v.ppm.2p d.dpn n.dpn r.gp.2 pt.pa.gsm

δὲ τοῦ λαοῦ καὶ διαλογιζομένων πάντων ἐν ταῖς καρδίαις αὐτῶν περὶ
{and} *the* *people* and all were questioning *all* in *{the}* their hearts *their* about
1254 3836 3295 2779 4246 1368 4246 1877 3836 899 2840 899 4309
cj d.gsm n.gsm cj pt.pm.gpm a.gpm p.d d.dpf n.dpf r.gpm.3 p.g

τοῦ Ἰωάννου, ↱ μήποτε αὐτὸς εἴη ὁ χριστός, 16 ἀπεκρίνατο
{the} John ("Could he perhaps *he* be the Messiah?") John gave an answer to
3836 2722 1639 899 3607 899 1639 3836 5986 2722 646 4246
d.gsm n.gsm cj r.nsm v.pao.3s d.nsm n.nsm v.ami.3s

λέγων πᾶσιν ὁ Ἰωάννης, ἐγὼ μὲν ὕδατι βαπτίζω ὑμᾶς·
all, saying, *to all* *{the}* *John* "I indeed baptize you with water, *baptize* *you* but
4246 3306 4246 3836 2722 1609 3525 966 7007 5623 966 7007 1254
pt.pa.nsm a.dpm d.nsm n.nsm r.ns.1 pl n.dsn v.pai.1s r.ap.2

ἔρχεται δὲ ὁ ἰσχυρότερός μου, οὗ οὐκ εἰμὶ ἱκανὸς λῦσαι
there is coming *but* one who is mightier ⌊than I,⌋ ⌊of whom⌋ I am not *I am* worthy to untie
2262 1254 3836 2708 1609 4005 1639 1639 4024 1639 2653 3395
v.pmi.3s cj d.nsm a.nsm.c r.gs.1 r.gsm pl v.pai.1s a.nsm f.aa

τὸν ἱμάντα τῶν ὑποδημάτων αὐτοῦ· αὐτὸς ὑμᾶς βαπτίσει ἐν
the thong of his sandals. *his* He it is who will baptize you *will baptize* with
3836 2666 3836 899 5687 899 899 966 966 7007 966 1877
d.asm n.asm d.gpn n.gpn r.gsm.3 r.nsm r.ap.2 v.fai.3s p.d

πνεύματι ἁγίῳ καὶ πυρί· 17 οὗ τὸ πτύον ἐν τῇ χειρὶ
the Holy Spirit *Holy* and fire. His *{the}* ⌊winnowing fork⌋ is in *{the}* his hand,
41 4460 41 2779 4786 4005 3836 4768 1877 3836 899 5931
n.dsn a.dsn cj n.dsn r.gsm d.nsn n.nsn p.d d.dsf n.dsf

αὐτοῦ διακαθᾶραι τὴν ἅλωνα αὐτοῦ καὶ συναγαγεῖν τὸν σῖτον εἰς τὴν
his to clear *{the}* his ⌊threshing floor⌋ *his* and to gather the wheat into *{the}*
899 1350 3836 899 272 899 2779 5251 3836 4992 1650 3836
r.gsm.3 f.aa d.asf n.asf r.gsm.3 cj f.aa d.asm n.asm p.a d.asf

ἀποθήκην αὐτοῦ, τὸ δὲ ἄχυρον κατακαύσει → πυρὶ
his granary; *his* but the *but* chaff he will burn with unquenchable fire."
899 630 899 1254 3836 1254 949 2876 812 4786
n.asf r.gsm.3 d.asn cj n.asn v.fai.3s n.dsn

NASB

to them, "The man
who has two tunics
is to share with him
who has none; and
he who has food
is to do likewise."
12 And *some* tax col-
lectors also came
to be baptized,
and they said to
him, "Teacher,
what shall we do?"
13 And he said to
them, "Collect no
more than what
you have been
ordered to." 14 *Some*
soldiers were
questioning him,
saying, "And *what*
about us, what
shall we do?" And
he said to them,
"Do not take mon-
ey from anyone by
force, or accuse
anyone falsely, and
be content with
your wages."
15 Now while the
people were in a
state of expecta-
tion and all were
wondering in their
hearts about John,
as to whether he
was the Christ,
16 John answered
and said to them
all, "As for me, I
baptize you with
water; but One
is coming who is
mightier than I, and
I am not fit to untie
the thong of His
sandals; He will
baptize you with
the Holy Spirit and
fire. 17 His winnow-
ing fork is in His
hand to thoroughly
clear His threshing
floor, and to gather
the wheat into His
barn; but He will
burn up the chaff
with unquenchable
fire."

[a] *16* Or *in*
[b] *16* Or *in*

NIV

18 And with many
other words John
exhorted the peo-
ple and proclaimed
the good news to
them.
19 But when John
rebuked Herod the
tetrarch because
of his marriage
to Herodias, his
brother's wife,
and all the other
evil things he had
done, 20 Herod add-
ed this to them all:
He locked John up
in prison.

The Baptism and Genealogy of Jesus

21 When all the
people were being
baptized, Jesus
was baptized too.
And as he was
praying, heaven
was opened 22 and
the Holy Spirit de-
scended on him in
bodily form like a
dove. And a voice
came from heav-
en: "You are my
Son, whom I love;
with you I am well
pleased."
23 Now Jesus
himself was about
thirty years old
when he began his
ministry. He was
the son, so it was
thought, of Joseph,
the son of Heli,
24 the son of
Matthat,
the son of Levi,
the son of
Melki,
the son of Jan-
nai, the son
of Joseph,
25 the son of Mat-
tathias, the
son of Amos,
the son of Na-
hum, the son
of Esli,
the son of Nag-
gai, 26 the son
of Maath,
the son of Mat-
tathias, the
son of Seme-
in,
the son of Jo-
sek,

ἀσβέστῳ. 18 πολλὰ μὲν οὖν καὶ ἕτερα ↱ παρακαλῶν
unquenchable And with many ~ *{then}* *And* other words he exhorted the people, and
812 2779 4498 3525 4036 2779 2283 2294 4151 3836 3295
a.dsn a.apn pl cj cj r.apn pt.pa.nsm

εὐηγγελίζετο τὸν λαόν. 19 ὁ δὲ Ἡρῴδης ὁ τετραάρχης,
evangelized them. *the* *people* *{the}* But Herod the tetrarch,
2294 3836 3295 3836 1254 2476 3836 5490
v.imi.3s d.asm n.asm d.nsm cj n.nsm d.nsm n.nsm

ἐλεγχόμενος ὑπ' αὐτοῦ περὶ Ἡρῳδιάδος τῆς γυναικὸς τοῦ ἀδελφοῦ
when he was reproved by him concerning Herodias, the wife of his brother,
1794 5679 899 4309 2478 3836 1222 3836 899 81
pt.pp.nsm p.g r.gsm.3 p.g n.gsf d.gsf n.gsf d.gsm n.gsm

αὐτοῦ καὶ περὶ πάντων ὧν ἐποίησεν πονηρῶν ὁ
his and concerning all the evil things which Herod had done, *evil things* *{the}*
899 2779 4309 4246 4505 4505 4005 2476 4472 4505 3836
r.gsm.3 cj p.g a.gpn r.gpn v.aai.3s a.gpn d.nsm

Ἡρῴδης, 20 προσέθηκεν καὶ τοῦτο ἐπὶ πᾶσιν καὶ [a] κατέκλεισεν τὸν
Herod added this also *this* to them all: *{and}* he confined *{the}*
2476 4707 4047 2779 4047 2093 4246 2779 2881 3836
n.nsm v.aai.3s cj r.asn p.d a.dpn cj v.aai.3s d.asm

Ἰωάννην ἐν φυλακῇ. 21 ἐγένετο δὲ ἐν τῷ βαπτισθῆναι
John in prison. *{it happened that}* Now when *{the}* all the people had been baptized,
2722 1877 5871 1181 1254 1877 3836 570 3836 3295 966
n.asm p.d n.dsf v.ami.3s cj p.d d.dsn f.ap

ἅπαντα τὸν λαὸν καὶ ↱ Ἰησοῦ βαπτισθέντος καὶ προσευχομένου
all *the* *people* and when Jesus was baptized and was praying, the heavens
570 3836 3295 2779 966 2652 966 2779 4667 3836 4041
a.asm d.asm n.asm cj n.gsm pt.ap.gsm cj pt.pm.gsm

ἀνεῳχθῆναι τὸν οὐρανὸν 22 καὶ καταβῆναι τὸ πνεῦμα τὸ ἅγιον
were opened, *the* *heavens* and the Holy Spirit descended *the* *Spirit* *{the}* *Holy* on
487 3836 4041 2779 3836 41 4460 2849 3836 4460 3836 41 2093
f.ap d.asm n.asm cj f.aa d.asn n.asn d.asn a.asn

σωματικῷ εἴδει ὡς περιστερὰν ἐπ' αὐτόν, καὶ φωνὴν ἐξ οὐρανοῦ
him in bodily form, like a dove; *on* *him* and a voice came from heaven,
899 5394 1626 6055 4361 2093 899 2779 5889 1181 1666 4041
a.dsn n.dsn pl n.asf p.a r.asm.3 cj n.asf p.g n.gsm

γενέσθαι, σὺ εἶ ὁ υἱός μου ὁ ἀγαπητός, ἐν σοὶ εὐδόκησα.
came "You are *{the}* my Son, *my* the Beloved; with you I am well pleased."
1181 5148 1639 3836 1609 5626 1609 3836 28 1877 5148 2305
f.am r.ns.2 v.pai.2s d.nsm n.nsm r.gs.1 d.nsm a.nsm p.d r.ds.2 v.aai.1s

23 καὶ αὐτὸς ἦν Ἰησοῦς ἀρχόμενος ὡσεὶ ἐτῶν
So Jesus, when he began his ministry, was *Jesus* *when began* about thirty years
2779 2652 806 899 806 1639 2652 806 6059 5558 2291
cj r.nsm v.iai.3s n.nsm pt.pm.nsm pl n.gpn

τριάκοντα, ὢν υἱός, ὡς ἐνομίζετο, Ἰωσὴφ τοῦ Ἡλὶ 24 τοῦ
thirty of age, being the son (as it was thought) of Joseph, the son of Helix, the
5558 1639 5626 6055 3787 2737 3836 2459 3836
a.gpn pt.pa.nsm n.nsm cj v.ipi.3s n.gsm d.gsm n.gsm d.gsm

Μαθθὰτ τοῦ Λευὶ τοῦ Μελχὶ τοῦ Ἰανναὶ τοῦ Ἰωσὴφ
son of Matzot, the son of Levi, the son of Melchi, the son of Jannai, the son of Joseph,
3415 3836 3322 3836 3518 3836 2613 3836 2737
n.gsm d.gsm n.gsm d.gsm n.gsm d.gsm n.gsm d.gsm n.gsm

25 τοῦ Ματταθίου τοῦ Ἀμὼς τοῦ Ναοὺμ τοῦ Ἑσλὶ τοῦ
the son of Mattathias, the son of Amos, the son of Nahum, the son of Esli, the son
3836 3478 3836 322 3836 3725 3836 2268 3836
d.gsm n.gsm d.gsm n.gsm d.gsm n.gsm d.gsm n.gsm d.gsm

Ναγγαὶ 26 τοῦ Μάαθ τοῦ Ματταθίου τοῦ Σεμεῒν τοῦ Ἰωσὴχ
of Naggai, the son of Maath, the son of Mattathias, the son of Semein, the son of Josech,
3710 3836 3399 3836 3478 3836 4946 3836 2738
n.gsm d.gsm n.gsm d.gsm n.gsm d.gsm n.gsm d.gsm n.gsm

NASB

18 So with many
other exhorta-
tions he preached
the gospel to the
people. 19 But when
Herod the tetrarch
was reprimanded
by him because
of Herodias, his
brother's wife,
and because of all
the wicked things
which Herod had
done, 20 Herod also
added this to them
all: he locked John
up in prison.

Jesus Is Baptized

21 Now when all
the people were
baptized, Jesus
was also baptized,
and while He was
praying, heaven
was opened, 22 and
the Holy Spirit
descended upon
Him in bodily form
like a dove, and a
voice came out of
heaven, "You are
My beloved Son,
in You I am well-
pleased."

Genealogy of Jesus

23 When He began
His ministry, Jesus
Himself was about
thirty years of age,
being, as was sup-
posed, the son of
Joseph, the son of
Eli, 24 the son of
Matthat, the son
of Levi, the son of
Melchi, the son of
Jannai, the son of
Joseph, 25 the son of
Mattathias, the son
of Amos, the son
of Nahum, the son
of Hesli, the son of
Naggai, 26 the son of
Maath, the son of
Mattathias, the son
of Semein, the son
of Josech,

[a] [καὶ] UBS, omitted by TNIV.

NIV

the son of
Joda,
27 the son of Joa-
nan, the son
of Rhesa,
the son of Ze-
rubbabel, the
son of Sheal-
tiel,
the son of Neri,
28 the son of
Melki,
the son of Addi,
the son of
Cosam,
the son of El-
madam, the
son of Er,
29 the son of Josh-
ua, the son of
Eliezer,
the son of Jo-
rim, the son
of Matthat,
the son of Levi,
30 the son of
Simeon,
the son of Ju-
dah, the son
of Joseph,
the son of Jo-
nam, the son
of Eliakim,
31 the son of Me-
lea, the son
of Menna,
the son of Mat-
tatha, the son
of Nathan,
the son of Da-
vid, 32 the son
of Jesse,
the son of
Obed, the
son of Boaz,
the son of Sal-
mon,[a] the
son of Nah-
shon,
33 the son of Am-
minadab, the
son of Ram,[b]
the son of Hez-
ron, the son
of Perez,
the son of Ju-
dah, 34 the
son of Jacob,
the son of Isaac,
the son of
Abraham,
the son of Te-
rah, the son

τοῦ	Ἰωδὰ	27 τοῦ	Ἰωανὰν	τοῦ	Ῥησὰ	τοῦ	Ζοροβαβὲλ	τοῦ
the	son of Joda,	the	son of Joanan,	the	son of Rhesa,	the	son of Zerubbabel,	the son
3836	2726	3836	2720	3836	4840	3836	2431	3836
d.gsm	n.gsm	d.gsm	n.gsm	d.gsm	n.gsm	d.gsm	n.gsm	d.gsm

Σαλαθιὴλ	τοῦ	Νηρὶ	28 τοῦ	Μελχὶ	τοῦ	Ἀδδὶ	τοῦ	Κωσὰμ	τοῦ
of Shealtiel,	the	son of Neri,	the	son of Melchi,	the	son of Addi,	the	son of Cosam,	the
4886	3836	3760	3836	3518	3836	79	3836	3272	3836
n.gsm	d.gsm	n.gsm	d.gsm	n.gsm	d.gsm	n.gsm	d.gsm	n.gsm	d.gsm

Ἐλμαδὰμ	τοῦ	Ἢρ	29 τοῦ	Ἰησοῦ	τοῦ	Ἐλιέζερ	τοῦ	Ἰωρὶμ
son of Elmadam,	the	son of Er,	the	son of Joshua,	the	son of Eliezer,	the	son of Jorim,
1825	3836	2474	3836	2652	3836	1808	3836	2733
n.gsm	d.gsm	n.gsm	d.gsm	n.gsm	d.gsm	n.gsm	d.gsm	n.gsm

τοῦ	Μαθθὰτ	τοῦ	Λευὶ	30 τοῦ	Συμεὼν	τοῦ	Ἰούδα	τοῦ
the	son of Matthat,	the	son of Levi,	the	son of Simeon,	the	son of Judah,	the son
3836	3415	3836	3322	3836	5208	3836	2683	3836
d.gsm	n.gsm	d.gsm	n.gsm	d.gsm	n.gsm	d.gsm	n.gsm	d.gsm

Ἰωσὴφ	τοῦ	Ἰωνὰμ	τοῦ	Ἐλιακὶμ	31 τοῦ	Μελεὰ	τοῦ	Μεννὰ
of Joseph,	the	son of Jonam,	the	son of Eliakim,	the	son of Melea,	the	son of Menna,
2737	3836	2729	3836	1806	3836	3507	3836	3527
n.gsm	d.gsm	n.gsm	d.gsm	n.gsm	d.gsm	n.gsm	d.gsm	n.gsm

τοῦ	Ματταθὰ	τοῦ	Ναθὰμ	τοῦ	Δαυὶδ	32 τοῦ	Ἰεσσαὶ	τοῦ
the	son of Mattatha,	the	son of Nathan,	the	son of David,	the	son of Jesse,	the son
3836	3477	3836	3718	3836	1253	3836	2649	3836
d.gsm	n.gsm	d.gsm	n.gsm	d.gsm	n.gsm	d.gsm	n.gsm	d.gsm

Ἰωβὴδ	τοῦ	Βόος	τοῦ	Σαλὰ[a]	τοῦ	Ναασσὼν	33 τοῦ	Ἀμιναδὰβ
of Obed,	the	son of Boaz,	the	son of Sala,	the	son of Nahshon,	the	son of Amminadab,
2725	3836	1078	3836	4885	3836	3709	3836	300
n.gsm	d.gsm	n.gsm	d.gsm	n.gsm	d.gsm	n.gsm	d.gsm	n.gsm

τοῦ	Ἀδμὶν[b]	τοῦ	Ἀρνὶ	τοῦ	Ἑσρὼμ	τοῦ	Φάρες	τοῦ	Ἰούδα
the	son of Admin,	the	son of Arni,	the	son of Hezron,	the	son of Perez,	the	son of Judah,
3836	98	3836	747	3836	2272	3836	5756	3836	2683
d.gsm	n.gsm	d.gsm	n.gsm	d.gsm	n.gsm	d.gsm	n.gsm	d.gsm	n.gsm

34 τοῦ	Ἰακὼβ	τοῦ	Ἰσαὰκ	τοῦ	Ἀβραὰμ	τοῦ	Θάρα	τοῦ
the	son of Jacob,	the	son of Isaac,	the	son of Abraham,	the	son of Terah,	the son
3836	2609	3836	2693	3836	11	3836	2508	3836
d.gsm	n.gsm	d.gsm	n.gsm	d.gsm	n.gsm	d.gsm	n.gsm	d.gsm

NASB

the son of Joda,
27 the son of Joanan,
the son of Rhesa,
the son of Zerub-
babel, the son of
Shealtiel, the son
of Neri, 28 the son
of Melchi, the son
of Addi, the son of
Cosam, the son of
Elmadam, the son
of Er, 29 the son of
Joshua, the son of
Eliezer, the son of
Jorim, the son of
Matthat, the son of
Levi, 30 the son of
Simeon, the son of
Judah, the son of
Joseph, the son of
Jonam, the son of
Eliakim, 31 the son
of Melea, the son
of Menna, the son
of Mattatha, the
son of Nathan, the
son of David, 32 the
son of Jesse, the
son of Obed, the
son of Boaz, the
son of Salmon, the
son of Nahshon,
33 the son of Am-
minadab, the son
of Admin, the son
of Ram, the son of
Hezron, the son of
Perez, the son of
Judah, 34 the son of
Jacob, the son of
Isaac, the son of
Abraham, the son

[a] 32 Some early manuscripts *Sala*
[b] 33 Some manuscripts *Amminadab, the son of Admin, the son of Arni*; other manuscripts vary widely.

[a] Σαλὰ UBS, NET. Σαλμών TNIV.
[b] Ἀδμὶν UBS, NET. Ἀραμ TNIV.

NIV

of Nahor,
35 the son of Se-
rug, the son
of Reu,
the son of Pe-
leg, the son
of Eber,
the son of She-
lah, 36 the son
of Cainan,
the son of Ar-
phaxad, the
son of Shem,
the son of Noah,
the son of
Lamech,
37 the son of Me-
thuselah,
the son of
Enoch,
the son of Jared,
the son of
Mahalalel,
the son of Ke-
nan, 38 the
son of Enosh,
the son of Seth,
the son of
Adam,
the son of God.

Jesus Is Tested in the Wilderness

4 Jesus, full of
the Holy Spir-
it, left the Jordan
and was led by
the Spirit into the
wilderness, 2 where
for forty days he
was tempted[a] by
the devil. He ate
nothing during
those days, and at
the end of them he
was hungry.
3 The devil said
to him, "If you are
the Son of God,
tell this stone to
become bread."
4 Jesus answered,
"It is written:
'Man shall not live
on bread alone.'[b]"
5 The devil led
him up to a high
place and showed
him in an instant
all the kingdoms
of the world. 6 And
he said to him, "I
will give you all
their authority and
splendor;

Ναχὼρ 35 τοῦ Σεροὺχ τοῦ Ῥαγαὺ τοῦ Φάλεκ τοῦ Ἔβερ τοῦ
of Nahor, the son of Serug, the son of Reu, the son of Peleg, the son of Eber, the son
3732 3836 4952 3836 4814 3836 5744 3836 1576 3836
n.gsm d.gsm n.gsm d.gsm n.gsm d.gsm n.gsm d.gsm n.gsm d.gsm

Σαλὰ 36 τοῦ Καϊνὰμ τοῦ Ἀρφαξὰδ τοῦ Σὴμ τοῦ Νῶε
of Shelah, the son of Cainan, the son of Arphaxad, the son of Shem, the son of Noah,
4885 3836 2783 3836 790 3836 4954 3836 3820
n.gsm d.gsm n.gsm d.gsm n.gsm d.gsm n.gsm d.gsm n.gsm

τοῦ Λάμεχ 37 τοῦ Μαθουσαλὰ τοῦ Ἑνὼχ τοῦ Ἰάρετ τοῦ
the son of Lamech, the son of Methuselah, the son of Enoch, the son of Jared, the son
3836 3285 3836 3417 3836 1970 3836 2616 3836
d.gsm n.gsm d.gsm n.gsm d.gsm n.gsm d.gsm n.gsm d.gsm

Μαλελεὴλ τοῦ Καϊνὰμ 38 τοῦ Ἐνὼς τοῦ Σὴθ τοῦ Ἀδὰμ τοῦ
of Mahalalel, the son of Kenan, the son of Enosh, the son of Seth, the son of Adam, the
3435 3836 2783 3836 1968 3836 4953 3836 77 3836
n.gsm d.gsm n.gsm d.gsm n.gsm d.gsm n.gsm d.gsm n.gsm d.gsm

θεοῦ.
son of God.
2536
n.gsm

4:1 Ἰησοῦς δὲ πλήρης → πνεύματος ἁγίου ὑπέστρεψεν ἀπὸ τοῦ
Then Jesus, *Then* full of the Holy Spirit, *Holy* returned from the
1254 2652 1254 4441 41 4460 41 5715 608 3836
n.nsm cj a.nsm n.gsn a.gsn v.aai.3s p.g d.gsm

Ἰορδάνου καὶ ἤγετο ἐν τῷ πνεύματι ἐν τῇ ἐρήμῳ 2 → ἡμέρας
Jordan and was led by the Spirit in the wilderness for forty days,
2674 2779 72 1877 3836 4460 1877 3836 2245 5477 2465
n.gsm cj v.ipi.3s p.d d.dsn n.dsn p.d d.dsf n.dsf n.apf

τεσσεράκοντα πειραζόμενος ὑπὸ τοῦ διαβόλου. καὶ οὐκ ἔφαγεν οὐδὲν ἐν ταῖς
forty being tempted by the devil. And ~ he ate nothing during *{the}* those
5477 4279 5679 3836 1333 2779 4024 2266 4029 1877 3836 1697
a.apf pt.pp.nsm p.g d.gsm n.gsm cj pl v.aai.3s a.asn p.d d.dpf

ἡμέραις ἐκείναις καὶ → συντελεσθεισῶν αὐτῶν ἐπείνασεν. 3 εἶπεν
days, *those* so when they were completed *they* he was hungry. The devil said
2465 1697 2779 899 5334 899 4277 3836 1333 3306
n.dpf r.dpf cj pt.ap.gpf r.gpf.3 v.aai.3s v.aai.3s

δὲ αὐτῷ ὁ διάβολος, εἰ υἱὸς εἶ τοῦ θεοῦ, εἰπὲ τῷ
{and} to him, *The* *devil* "If you are the Son *you are* of God, tell *{the}* this
1254 899 3836 1333 1623 1639 1639 5626 1639 3836 2536 3306 3836 4047
cj r.dsm.3 d.nsm n.nsm cj n.nsm v.pai.2s d.gsm n.gsm v.aam.2s d.dsm

λίθῳ τούτῳ ἵνα γένηται ἄρτος. 4 καὶ ⸤ἀπεκρίθη πρὸς⸥ αὐτὸν ὁ Ἰησοῦς,
stone *this* to become bread." And Jesus answered him, *{the}* *Jesus*
3345 4047 2671 1181 788 2779 2652 646 4639 899 3836 2652
n.dsm r.dsm cj v.ams.3s n.nsm cj v.api.3s p.a r.asm.3 d.nsm n.nsm

γέγραπται ὅτι οὐκ ἐπ' ἄρτῳ μόνῳ ζήσεται ὁ ἄνθρωπος.[a] 5 καὶ
"It is written, ~ 'Man shall not live by bread alone.'" *shall live* *{the}* *Man* Then
1211 4022 476 2409 4024 2409 2093 788 3668 2409 3836 476 2779
v.rpi.3s cj pl p.d n.dsm a.dsm v.fmi.3s d.nsm n.nsm cj

ἀναγαγὼν αὐτὸν[b] ↰ ἔδειξεν αὐτῷ πάσας τὰς βασιλείας τῆς οἰκουμένης ἐν
he led him up and showed him all the kingdoms of the world in a
343 899 343 1259 899 4246 3836 993 3836 3876 1877
pt.aa.nsm r.asm.3 v.aai.3s r.dsm.3 a.apf d.apf n.apf d.gsf n.gsf p.d

στιγμῇ χρόνου 6 καὶ εἶπεν αὐτῷ ὁ διάβολος, σοὶ δώσω τὴν
moment of time. *{and}* The devil said to him, *The* *devil* ⸤"To you⸥ I will give *{the}* all
5117 5989 2779 3836 1333 3306 899 3836 1333 5148 1443 3836 570
n.dsf n.gsm cj v.aai.3s r.dsm.3 d.nsm n.nsm r.ds.2 v.fai.1s d.asf

ἐξουσίαν ταύτην ἅπασαν καὶ τὴν δόξαν αὐτῶν, ὅτι ἐμοὶ
this authority *this* *all* and *{the}* their glory, *their* for to me
4047 2026 4047 570 2779 3836 899 1518 899 4022 1609
n.asf r.asf a.asf cj d.asf n.asf r.gpf.3 cj r.ds.1

NASB

of Terah, the son
of Nahor, 35 the son
of Serug, the son
of Reu, the son of
Peleg, the son of
Heber, the son of
Shelah, 36 the son of
Cainan, the son of
Arphaxad, the son
of Shem, the son
of Noah, the son of
Lamech, 37 the son
of Methuselah, the
son of Enoch, the
son of Jared, the
son of Mahalaleel,
the son of Cainan,
38 the son of Enosh,
the son of Seth, the
son of Adam, the
son of God.

The Temptation of Jesus

4:1 Jesus, full of
the Holy Spirit,
returned from the
Jordan and was led
around by the Spir-
it in the wilderness
2 for forty days,
being tempted by
the devil. And He
ate nothing during
those days, and
when they had
ended, He became
hungry. 3 And the
devil said to Him,
"If You are the Son
of God, tell this
stone to become
bread." 4 And Jesus
answered him, "It
is written, 'MAN
SHALL NOT LIVE ON
BREAD ALONE.'"
5 And he led Him
up and showed
Him all the king-
doms of the world
in a moment of
time. 6 And the
devil said to Him,
"I will give You all
this domain and its
glory; for it has

[a] 2 The Greek for *tempted* can also mean *tested.*
[b] 4 Deut. 8:3

[a] ἀλλ' ἐπὶ παντὶ ῥήματι Θεοῦ included by TR after ἄνθρωπος.
[b] ὁ διάβολος εἰς ὄρος ὑψηλὸν included by TNIV and TR after αὐτὸν.

NIV

it has been given
to me, and I can
give it to anyone
I want to. 7If you
worship me, it will
all be yours."
8Jesus answered,
"It is written:
'Worship the Lord
your God and
serve him only.'[a]"
9The devil led
him to Jerusalem
and had him stand
on the highest
point of the tem-
ple. "If you are the
Son of God," he
said, "throw your-
self down from
here. 10For it is
written:

"'He will
command
his angels
concerning
you
to guard you
carefully;
11they will lift you
up in their
hands,
so that you will
not strike
your foot
against a
stone.'[b]"

12Jesus answered,
"It is said: 'Do not
put the Lord your
God to the test.'[c]"
13When the devil
had finished all
this tempting, he
left him until an
opportune time.

Jesus Rejected at Nazareth

14Jesus returned
to Galilee in the
power of the
Spirit, and news
about him spread
through the whole
countryside. 15He
was teaching in
their synagogues,
and everyone
praised him.
16He went to Naz-
areth, where he
had been brought
up, and on the
Sabbath

παραδέδοται καὶ ᾧ ἐὰν θέλω δίδωμι αὐτήν· 7 σὺ οὖν ἐὰν
⌊it has been handed over,⌋ and to whomever I desire, I give it. If you then *If*
4140 2779 4005 1569 2527 1443 899 1569 5148 4036 1569
v.rpi.3s cj r.dsm pl v.pas.1s v.pai.1s r.asf.3 r.ns.2 cj cj

⌊προσκυνήσῃς ἐνώπιον⌋ ἐμοῦ, ἔσται σοῦ πᾶσα. 8 καὶ
will bow down and worship me, all this will be yours." *all* But Jesus
4686 1967 1609 4246 1639 5148 4246 2779 2652
v.aas.2s p.g r.gs.1 v.fmi.3s r.gs.2 a.nsf cj

ἀποκριθεὶς ὁ Ἰησοῦς εἶπεν αὐτῷ,[a] γέγραπται, κύριον τὸν
answered, *{the}* *Jesus* saying to him, "It is written, 'You shall worship the Lord *{the}* your
646 3836 2652 3306 899 1211 4686 4686 4686 3261 3836 5148
pt.ap.nsm d.nsm n.nsm v.aai.3s r.dsm.3 v.rpi.3s n.asm d.asm

θεόν σου προσκυνήσεις καὶ αὐτῷ μόνῳ λατρεύσεις. 9 ἤγαγεν δὲ αὐτὸν εἰς
God *your* *You shall worship* and him only shall you serve.'" Then he took *Then* him to
2536 5148 4686 2779 899 3668 3302 1254 72 1254 899 1650
n.asm r.gs.2 v.fai.2s cj r.dsm.3 a.dsm v.fai.2s v.aai.3s cj r.asm.3 p.a

Ἰερουσαλὴμ καὶ ἔστησεν ἐπὶ τὸ πτερύγιον τοῦ ἱεροῦ καὶ εἶπεν αὐτῷ, εἰ
Jerusalem and set him on the pinnacle of the temple and said to him, "If you
2647 2779 2705 2093 3836 4762 3836 2639 2779 3306 899 1623 1639
n.asf cj v.aai.3s p.a d.asn n.asn d.gsn n.gsn cj v.aai.3s r.dsm.3 cj

υἱὸς εἶ τοῦ θεοῦ, βάλε σεαυτὸν ἐντεῦθεν κάτω· 10 γέγραπται
are the Son *you are* of God, throw yourself down from here; *down* for it is written,
1639 5626 1639 3836 2536 965 4932 3004 1949 3004 1142 1211
n.nsm v.pai.2s d.gsm n.gsm v.aam.2s r.asm.2 adv adv v.rpi.3s

γὰρ ὅτι τοῖς ἀγγέλοις αὐτοῦ ἐντελεῖται περὶ σοῦ τοῦ διαφυλάξαι
for ~ 'To his angels *his* ⌊he will give orders⌋ concerning you, to protect
1142 4022 3836 899 34 899 1948 4309 5148 3836 1428
cj cj d.dpm n.dpm r.gsm.3 v.fmi.3s p.g r.gs.2 d.gsn f.aa

σε 11 καὶ ὅτι ἐπὶ χειρῶν ἀροῦσίν σε, ↰ μήποτε → → ← προσκόψῃς
you,' and, ~ 'On their hands ⌊they will raise⌋ you up, so that you will not strike
5148 2779 4022 2093 5931 149 5148 149 3607 4684
r.as.2 cj cj p.g n.gpf v.fai.3p r.as.2 cj v.aas.2s

πρὸς λίθον τὸν πόδα σου. 12 καὶ ἀποκριθεὶς εἶπεν αὐτῷ ὁ
your foot against a stone.'" *{the}* *foot* *your* But answering Jesus said to him, *{the}*
5148 4546 4639 3345 3836 4546 5148 2779 646 2652 3306 899 3836
p.a n.asm d.asm n.asm r.gs.2 cj pt.ap.nsm v.aai.3s r.dsm.3 d.nsm

Ἰησοῦς ὅτι εἴρηται, ↱ ↱ οὐκ ἐκπειράσεις κύριον τὸν θεόν σου.
Jesus ~ ⌊"It has been said,⌋ 'You are not to put the Lord *{the}* your God *your*
2652 4022 3306 1733 1733 4024 1733 3261 3836 5148 2536 5148
n.nsm cj v.rpi.3s pl v.fai.2s n.asm d.asm n.asm r.gs.2

↰ ↰ ↰ 13 καὶ συντελέσας πάντα πειρασμὸν ὁ διάβολος
to the test.'" And ⌊when he had completed⌋ ⌊every kind of⌋ temptation, the devil
1733 1733 1733 2779 5334 4246 4280 3836 1333
cj pt.aa.nsm a.asm n.asm d.nsm n.nsm

ἀπέστη ἀπ' αὐτοῦ ἄχρι καιροῦ. 14 καὶ ὑπέστρεψεν ὁ Ἰησοῦς
departed from him until a ⌊more favorable time.⌋ Then Jesus returned *{the}* *Jesus*
923 608 899 948 2789 2779 2652 5715 3836 2652
v.aai.3s p.g r.gsm.3 p.g n.gsm cj v.aai.3s d.nsm n.nsm

ἐν τῇ δυνάμει τοῦ πνεύματος εἰς τὴν Γαλιλαίαν. καὶ φήμη ἐξῆλθεν
in the power of the Spirit to *{the}* Galilee, and a report about him spread
1877 3836 1539 3836 4460 1650 3836 1133 2779 5773 4309 899 2002
p.d d.dsf n.dsf d.gsn n.gsn p.a d.asf n.asf cj n.nsf v.aai.3s

καθ' ὅλης τῆς περιχώρου περὶ αὐτοῦ. 15 καὶ αὐτὸς ἐδίδασκεν ἐν ταῖς
throughout the whole *the* countryside. *about* *him* *{and}* He was teaching in *{the}*
2848 3836 3910 3836 4369 4309 899 2779 899 1438 1877 3836
p.g a.gsf d.gsf a.gsf p.g r.gsm.3 cj r.nsm v.iai.3s p.d d.dpf

συναγωγαῖς αὐτῶν δοξαζόμενος ὑπὸ πάντων. 16 καὶ ἦλθεν εἰς Ναζαρά, οὗ
their synagogues, *their* being praised by everyone. *{and}* He went to Nazareth where
899 5252 899 1519 5679 4246 2779 2262 1650 3711 4023
n.dpf r.gpm.3 pt.pp.nsm p.g a.gpm cj v.aai.3s p.a n.asf adv

ἦν τεθραμμένος, καὶ εἰσῆλθεν κατὰ τὸ εἰωθὸς αὐτῷ ἐν τῇ
⌊he had been⌋ brought up and, *he went* as was *{the}* his custom *his* on the Sabbath
1639 5555 2779 1656 2848 3836 899 1665 899 1877 3836 4879
v.iai.3s pt.rp.nsm cj v.aai.3s p.a d.asn pt.ra.asn r.dsm.3 p.d d.dsf

---

NASB

been handed over
to me, and I give
it to whomever I
wish. 7Therefore if
You worship be-
fore me, it shall all
be Yours." 8Jesus
answered him, "It
is written, 'YOU
SHALL WORSHIP THE
LORD YOUR GOD
AND SERVE HIM
ONLY.'"
9And he led Him
to Jerusalem and
had Him stand on
the pinnacle of the
temple, and said to
Him, "If You are
the Son of God,
throw Yourself
down from here;
10for it is written,
'HE WILL
COMMAND
HIS ANGELS
CONCERNING
YOU TO GUARD
YOU,'
11and,
'ON *their* HANDS
THEY WILL
BEAR YOU UP,
SO THAT YOU
WILL NOT
STRIKE YOUR
FOOT AGAINST
A STONE.'"
12And Jesus an-
swered and said
to him, "It is said,
'YOU SHALL NOT
PUT THE LORD YOUR
GOD TO THE TEST.'"
13When the devil
had finished every
temptation, he left
Him until an op-
portune time.

Jesus' Public Ministry

14And Jesus re-
turned to Galilee
in the power of the
Spirit, and news
about Him spread
through all the sur-
rounding district.
15And He *began*
teaching in their
synagogues and
was praised by all.
16And He came to
Nazareth, where
He had been
brought up; and as
was His custom,

---

[a] 8 Deut. 6:13
[b] 11 Psalm 91:11,12
[c] 12 Deut. 6:16

[a] ὕπαγε ὀπίσω μου, Σατανᾶ included by TR after αὐτῷ.

NIV

day he went into the synagogue, as was his custom. He stood up to read, [17]and the scroll of the prophet Isaiah was handed to him. Unrolling it, he found the place where it is written:

18 "The Spirit of the Lord is on me,
because he has anointed me
to proclaim good news to the poor.
He has sent me to proclaim freedom for the prisoners
and recovery of sight for the blind,
to set the oppressed free,
19 to proclaim the year of the Lord's favor."[a]

[20]Then he rolled up the scroll, gave it back to the attendant and sat down. The eyes of everyone in the synagogue were fastened on him. [21]He began by saying to them, "Today this scripture is fulfilled in your hearing."

[22]All spoke well of him and were amazed at the gracious words that came from his lips. "Isn't this Joseph's son?" they asked.

[23]Jesus said to them, "Surely you will quote this proverb to me: 'Physician, heal yourself!' And you will tell me, 'Do here in your hometown what we have heard that you did in Capernaum.'"

[a] 19 Isaiah 61:1,2 (see Septuagint); Isaiah 58:6

ἡμέρᾳ τῶν σαββάτων εἰς τὴν συναγωγὴν καὶ ἀνέστη ἀναγνῶναι. 17 καὶ
day, *{the}* *Sabbath* he went into the synagogue and stood up to read. And the
2465 3836 4879 1656 1656 1650 3836 5252 2779 482 336 2779
n.dsf d.gpn n.gpn p.a d.asf n.asf cj v.aai.3s f.aa cj

ἐπεδόθη αὐτῷ βιβλίον τοῦ προφήτου Ἠσαΐου καὶ
scroll of the prophet Isaiah was given to him, *scroll* *of the* *prophet* *Isaiah* and
1046 3836 3836 4737 2480 2113 899 1046 3836 4737 2480 2779
v.api.3s r.dsm.3 n.nsn d.gsm n.gsm n.gsm cj

ἀναπτύξας τὸ βιβλίον εὗρεν τὸν τόπον οὗ ἦν γεγραμμένον, 18
⌊when he had unrolled⌋ the scroll, he found the place where it was written, "The
408 3836 1046 2351 3836 5536 4023 1639 1211
pt.aa.nsm d.asn n.asn v.aai.3s d.asm n.asm adv v.iai.3s pt.rp.nsn

πνεῦμα → κυρίου ἐπ' ἐμὲ ⌊οὗ εἵνεκεν⌋ ἔχρισέν με
Spirit of the Lord is upon me, because he has anointed me
4460 3261 2093 1609 4005 1641 5987 1609
n.nsn n.gsm p.a r.as.1 r.gsn p.g v.aai.3s r.as.1

εὐαγγελίσασθαι → πτωχοῖς, ἀπέσταλκέν με,[a] κηρύξαι →
⌊to preach the good news⌋ to the poor. He has sent me to proclaim liberty to the
2294 4777 690 1609 3062 912
f.am a.dpm v.rai.3s r.as.1 f.aa

αἰχμαλώτοις ἄφεσιν καὶ → τυφλοῖς ἀνάβλεψιν, ἀποστεῖλαι
captives *liberty* and recovery of sight to the blind, *recovery of sight* to send the
171 912 2779 330 330 330 5603 330 690
n.dpm n.asf cj a.dpm n.asf f.aa

τεθραυσμένους ↰ ἐν ἀφέσει, 19 κηρύξαι ἐνιαυτὸν → κυρίου
oppressed away in liberty, to proclaim the year acceptable to the Lord."
2575 690 1877 912 3062 1929 1283 3261
pt.rp.apm p.d n.dsf f.aa n.asm n.gsm

δεκτόν. 20 καὶ πτύξας τὸ βιβλίον ἀποδοὺς ← τῷ ὑπηρέτῃ
acceptable *{and}* ⌊When he had rolled⌋ the scroll and given it back ⌊to the⌋ attendant,
1283 2779 4771 3836 1046 625 3836 5677
a.asm cj pt.aa.nsm d.asn n.asn pt.aa.nsm d.dsm n.dsm

ἐκάθισεν· καὶ πάντων οἱ ὀφθαλμοὶ ἐν τῇ συναγωγῇ ἦσαν
he sat down. And the eyes of everyone *the* *eyes* in the synagogue were
2767 2779 3836 4057 4246 3836 4057 1877 3836 5252 1639
v.aai.3s cj a.gpm d.npm n.npm p.d d.dsf n.dsf v.iai.3p

ἀτενίζοντες αὐτῷ. 21 ἤρξατο δὲ ⌊λέγειν πρὸς⌋ αὐτοὺς ὅτι σήμερον
fixed on him. And he set about *And* telling them, ~ "Today this
867 899 1254 806 1254 3306 4639 899 4022 4958 4047
pt.pa.npm r.dsm.3 v.ami.3s cj f.pa p.a r.apm.3 cj adv

πεπλήρωται ἡ γραφὴ αὕτη ἐν τοῖς ὠσὶν ὑμῶν. 22 καὶ ↱ ↱
scripture has been fulfilled *{the}* *scripture* *this* in *{the}* your ears." *your* *{and}* They were
1210 4444 3836 1210 4047 1877 3836 7007 4044 7007 2779 3455 3455
v.rpi.3s d.nsf n.nsf r.nsf p.d d.dpn n.dpn r.gp.2 cj

πάντες ἐμαρτύρουν αὐτῷ καὶ ἐθαύμαζον ἐπὶ τοῖς λόγοις τῆς
all bearing witness to him in that *{and}* they were marveling at the gracious words *{the}*
4246 3455 899 2779 2513 2093 3836 5921 3364 3836
a.npm v.iai.3p r.dsm.3 cj v.iai.3p p.d d.dpm n.dpm d.gsf

χάριτος τοῖς ἐκπορευομένοις ἐκ τοῦ στόματος αὐτοῦ καὶ ἔλεγον, οὐχὶ
gracious that were coming from *{the}* his mouth. *his* Then they said, "Is not this
5921 3836 1744 1666 3836 899 5125 899 2779 3306 1639 4049 4047
n.gsf d.dpm pt.pm.dpm p.g d.gsn n.gsn r.gsm.3 cj v.iai.3p pl

υἱός ἐστιν Ἰωσὴφ οὗτος; 23 καὶ εἶπεν πρὸς αὐτούς, πάντως ἐρεῖτέ
Joseph's son?" *Is* *Joseph's* *this* And he said to them, "No doubt ⌊you will quote⌋
2737 5626 1639 2737 4047 2779 3306 4639 899 4122 3306
n.nsm v.pai.3s n.gsm r.nsm cj v.aai.3s p.a r.apm.3 adv v.fai.2p

μοι τὴν παραβολὴν ταύτην, ἰατρέ, θεράπευσον σεαυτόν· ὅσα
this proverb to me: *{the}* *proverb* *this* 'Physician, heal yourself.' What
4047 4130 1609 3836 4130 4047 2620 2543 4932 4012
r.ds.1 d.asf n.asf r.asf n.vsm v.aam.2s r.asm.2 r.apn

ἠκούσαμεν γενόμενα εἰς τὴν Καφαρναοὺμ ποίησον καὶ ὧδε ἐν τῇ πατρίδι
we have heard happened in *{the}* Capernaum, do also here in *{the}* your hometown."
201 1181 1650 3836 3019 4472 2779 6045 1877 3836 5148 4258
v.aai.1p pt.am.apn p.a d.asf n.asf v.aam.2s adv adv p.d d.dsf n.dsf

[a] ἰάσασθαι τοὺς συντετριμμένους τὴν καρδίαν included by TR after με.

NASB

He entered the synagogue on the Sabbath, and stood up to read. [17]And the book of the prophet Isaiah was handed to Him. And He opened the book and found the place where it was written,

18 "THE SPIRIT OF THE LORD IS UPON ME,
BECAUSE HE ANOINTED ME TO PREACH THE GOSPEL TO THE POOR.
HE HAS SENT ME TO PROCLAIM RELEASE TO THE CAPTIVES,
AND RECOVERY OF SIGHT TO THE BLIND,
TO SET FREE THOSE WHO ARE OPPRESSED,
19 TO PROCLAIM THE FAVORABLE YEAR OF THE LORD."

[20]And He closed the book, gave it back to the attendant and sat down; and the eyes of all in the synagogue were fixed on Him. [21]And He began to say to them, "Today this Scripture has been fulfilled in your hearing." [22]And all were speaking well of Him, and wondering at the gracious words which were falling from His lips; and they were saying, "Is this not Joseph's son?" [23]And He said to them, "No doubt you will quote this proverb to Me, 'Physician, heal yourself! Whatever we heard was done at Capernaum, do here in your hometown as well.'"

NIV

24 “Truly I tell you,” he continued, “no prophet is accepted in his hometown. 25 I assure you that there were many widows in Israel in Elijah’s time, when the sky was shut for three and a half years and there was a severe famine throughout the land. 26 Yet Elijah was not sent to any of them, but to a widow in Zarephath in the region of Sidon. 27 And there were many in Israel with leprosy[a] in the time of Elisha the prophet, yet not one of them was cleansed—only Naaman the Syrian.”

28 All the people in the synagogue were furious when they heard this. 29 They got up, drove him out of the town, and took him to the brow of the hill on which the town was built, in order to throw him off the cliff. 30 But he walked right through the crowd and went on his way.

Jesus Drives Out an Impure Spirit

31 Then he went down to Capernaum, a town in Galilee, and on the Sabbath he taught the people. 32 They were amazed at his teaching, because his words had authority.

33 In the synagogue there was a man

σου. 24 εἶπεν δέ, ἀμὴν λέγω ὑμῖν ὅτι οὐδεὶς προφήτης
your And he said, *And* “I tell you the truth, *I tell* *you* ~ no prophet is
5148 1254 3306 1254 3306 3306 7007 297 3306 7007 4022 4029 4737 1639
r.gs.2 v.aai.3s cj pl v.pai.1s r.dp.2 cj a.nsm n.nsm

δεκτός ἐστιν ἐν τῇ πατρίδι αὐτοῦ. 25 ἐπʼ ἀληθείας δὲ λέγω ὑμῖν,
acceptable *is* in *{the}* his hometown. *his* But in truth *But* I tell you,
1283 1639 1877 3836 899 4258 899 1254 2093 237 1254 3306 7007
a.nsm v.pai.3s p.d d.dsf n.dsf r.gsm.3 p.g n.gsf cj v.pai.1s r.dp.2

πολλαὶ χῆραι ἦσαν ἐν ταῖς ἡμέραις Ἠλίου ἐν τῷ Ἰσραήλ,
there were many widows *there were* in Israel in the days of Elijah, *in* *{the}* *Israel*
1639 1639 4498 5939 1639 1877 2702 1877 3836 2465 2460 1877 3836 2702
a.npf n.npf v.iai.3p p.d d.dpf n.dpf n.gsm p.d d.dsm n.dsm

ὅτε ἐκλείσθη ὁ οὐρανὸς ἐπὶ ἔτη τρία καὶ μῆνας ἕξ, ὡς
when the sky was shut up *the* *sky* for three years *three* and six months, *six* as a
4021 3836 4041 3091 3836 4041 2093 5552 2291 5552 2779 1971 3604 1971 6055
cj v.api.3s d.nsm n.nsm p.a n.apn a.apn cj n.apm a.apm cj

ἐγένετο λιμὸς μέγας ἐπὶ πᾶσαν τὴν γῆν, 26 καὶ πρὸς οὐδεμίαν
great famine spread *famine* *great* throughout the whole *{the}* land; and to none
3489 3350 1181 3350 3489 2093 4246 3836 1178 2779 4639 4029
v.ami.3s n.nsm a.nsm p.a a.asf d.asf n.asf cj p.a a.asf

αὐτῶν → ἐπέμφθη Ἠλίας ⌊εἰ μὴ⌋ εἰς Σάρεπτα τῆς Σιδωνίας
of them was Elijah sent, *Elijah* only to Zarephath, in the territory of Sidon,
899 2460 4287 2460 1623 3590 1650 4919 3836 4973
r.gpf.3 v.api.3s n.nsm cj pl p.a n.apn d.gsf a.gsf

πρὸς γυναῖκα χήραν. 27 καὶ πολλοὶ λεπροὶ ἦσαν ἐν τῷ
to a widow woman. *widow* And there were many lepers *there were* in *{the}*
4639 5939 1222 5939 2779 1639 1639 4498 3320 1639 1877 3836
p.a n.asf n.asf cj a.npm a.npm v.iai.3p p.d d.dsm

Ἰσραὴλ ἐπὶ Ἐλισαίου τοῦ προφήτου, καὶ οὐδεὶς αὐτῶν ἐκαθαρίσθη ⌊εἰ μὴ⌋
Israel in the time of Elisha the prophet, and none of them was cleansed, only
2702 2093 1811 3836 4737 2779 4029 899 2751 1623 3590
n.dsm p.g n.gsm d.gsm n.gsm cj a.nsm r.gpm.3 v.api.3s cj pl

Ναιμὰν ὁ Σύρος. 28 καὶ ἐπλήσθησαν πάντες θυμοῦ
Naaman, the Syrian.” And everyone in the synagogue was filled *everyone* with wrath
3722 3836 5354 2779 4246 1877 3836 5252 4398 4246 2596
n.nsm d.nsm n.nsm cj v.api.3p a.npm n.gsm

ἐν τῇ συναγωγῇ ἀκούοντες ταῦτα 29 καὶ ἀναστάντες ἐξέβαλον αὐτὸν
in *the* *synagogue* when they heard these things. *{and}* They rose up, drove him
1877 3836 5252 201 4047 2779 482 1675 899
p.d d.dsf n.dsf pt.pa.npm r.apn cj pt.aa.npm v.aai.3p r.asm.3

ἔξω τῆς πόλεως καὶ ἤγαγον αὐτὸν ἕως ὀφρύος τοῦ ὄρους ἐφʼ οὗ ἡ
⌊out of⌋ the town, and took him to a cliff of the hill on which *{the}* their
2032 3836 4484 2779 72 899 2401 4059 3836 4001 2093 4005 3836 899
p.g d.gsf n.gsf cj v.aai.3p r.asm.3 p.g n.gsf d.gsn n.gsn p.g r.gsn d.nsf

πόλις ᾠκοδόμητο αὐτῶν ὥστε κατακρημνίσαι αὐτόν· ↵ 30 αὐτὸς δὲ διελθὼν
town was built, *their* so that they could cast him down. But he *But* passed
4484 3868 899 6063 2889 899 2889 1254 899 1254 1451
n.nsf v.lpi.3s r.gpm.3 cj f.aa r.asm.3 r.nsm cj pt.aa.nsm

διὰ μέσου αὐτῶν ἐπορεύετο. 31 καὶ κατῆλθεν εἰς Καφαρναοὺμ
through their midst *their* and ⌊went on his way.⌋ And he went down to Capernaum, a
1328 899 3545 899 4513 2779 2982 1650 3019
p.g n.gsn r.gpm.3 v.imi.3s cj v.aai.3s p.a n.asf

πόλιν τῆς Γαλιλαίας. καὶ ἦν διδάσκων αὐτοὺς ἐν τοῖς σάββασιν· 32 καὶ
city of Galilee. *{and}* ⌊He was⌋ teaching them on the Sabbath; and
4484 3836 1133 2779 1639 1438 899 1877 3836 4879 2779
n.asf d.gsf n.gsf cj v.iai.3s pt.pa.nsm r.apm.3 p.d d.dpn n.dpn cj

ἐξεπλήσσοντο ἐπὶ τῇ διδαχῇ αὐτοῦ, ὅτι ἐν ἐξουσίᾳ
they were astonished at *{the}* his teaching, *his* because his message was with authority.
1742 2093 3836 899 1439 899 4022 899 3364 1639 1877 2026
v.ipi.3p p.d d.dsf n.dsf r.gsm.3 cj p.d n.dsf

ἦν ὁ λόγος αὐτοῦ. 33 καὶ ἐν τῇ συναγωγῇ ἦν ἄνθρωπος ἔχων
was *{the}* *message* *his* Now in the synagogue ⌊there was⌋ a man ⌊who had⌋ the
1639 3836 3364 899 2779 1877 3836 5252 1639 476 2400
v.iai.3s d.nsm n.nsm r.gsm.3 cj p.d d.dsf n.dsf v.iai.3s n.nsm pt.pa.nsm

NASB

24 And He said, “Truly I say to you, no prophet is welcome in his hometown. 25 But I say to you in truth, there were many widows in Israel in the days of Elijah, when the sky was shut up for three years and six months, when a great famine came over all the land; 26 and yet Elijah was sent to none of them, but only to Zarephath, *in the land* of Sidon, to a woman who was a widow. 27 And there were many lepers in Israel in the time of Elisha the prophet; and none of them was cleansed, but only Naaman the Syrian.” 28 And all *the people* in the synagogue were filled with rage as they heard these things; 29 and they got up and drove Him out of the city, and led Him to the brow of the hill on which their city had been built, in order to throw Him down the cliff. 30 But passing through their midst, He went His way.

31 And He came down to Capernaum, a city of Galilee, and He was teaching them on the Sabbath; 32 and they were amazed at His teaching, for His message was with authority. 33 In the synagogue there was a man

[a] 27 The Greek word traditionally translated *leprosy* was used for various diseases affecting the skin.

NIV

possessed by a
demon, an impure
spirit. He cried out
at the top of his
voice, 34 "Go away!
What do you want
with us, Jesus of
Nazareth? Have
you come to de-
stroy us? I know
who you are — the
Holy One of God!"
35 "Be quiet!"
Jesus said stern-
ly. "Come out of
him!" Then the
demon threw the
man down before
them all and came
out without injur-
ing him.
36 All the people
were amazed and
said to each other,
"What words these
are! With author-
ity and power he
gives orders to
impure spirits and
they come out!"
37 And the news
about him spread
throughout the
surrounding area.

Jesus Heals Many

38 Jesus left the
synagogue and
went to the home
of Simon. Now
Simon's mother-in-
law was suffering
from a high fever,
and they asked
Jesus to help her.
39 So he bent over
her and rebuked
the fever, and it
left her. She got up
at once and began
to wait on them.
40 At sunset, the
people brought to
Jesus all who had
various kinds of
sickness, and lay-
ing his hands on
each one,

πνεῦμα → δαιμονίου ἀκαθάρτου καὶ ἀνέκραξεν → φωνῇ μεγάλῃ,
spirit of an unclean demon, *unclean* and he cried out in a loud voice, *loud*
4460 176 1228 176 2779 371 3489 5889 3489
n.asn n.gsn a.gsn cj v.aai.3s n.dsf a.dsf

34 ἔα, τί ἡμῖν καὶ σοί, Ἰησοῦ Ναζαρηνέ; ἦλθες
"Ha! What do you have to do ⌊with us,⌋ *{and}* *you* Jesus of Nazareth? ⌊Have you come⌋
1568 5515 5148 7005 2779 5148 2652 3716 2262
j r.nsn r.dp.1 cj r.ds.2 n.vsm n.vsm v.aai.2s

ἀπολέσαι ἡμᾶς; οἶδά σε τίς εἶ, ὁ ἅγιος τοῦ θεοῦ. 35 καὶ
to destroy us? I know who you *who* are — the Holy One of God!" But Jesus
660 7005 3857 5515 5148 5515 1639 3836 41 3836 2536 2779 2652
f.aa r.ap.1 v.rai.1s r.as.2 r.nsm v.pai.2s d.nsm a.nsm d.gsm n.gsm cj

ἐπετίμησεν αὐτῷ ὁ Ἰησοῦς λέγων, φιμώθητι καὶ ἔξελθε ἀπ' αὐτοῦ. καὶ →
rebuked him, *{the}* *Jesus* saying, "Be quiet, and come out of him!" And when the
2203 899 3836 2652 3306 5821 2779 2002 608 899 2779 3836
v.aai.3s r.dsn.3 d.nsm n.nsm pt.pa.nsm v.apm.2s cj v.aam.2s p.g r.gsm.3 cj

ῥίψαν αὐτὸν τὸ δαιμόνιον ↰ εἰς τὸ μέσον ἐξῆλθεν ἀπ' αὐτοῦ
demon had thrown him *the* *demon* down in their midst, ⌊he came out⌋ of him,
1228 4849 899 3836 1228 4849 1650 3836 3545 2002 608 899
pt.aa.nsn r.asm.3 d.nsn n.nsn p.a d.asn n.asn v.aai.3s p.g r.gsm.3

↱ ↱ μηδὲν βλάψαν αὐτόν. 36 καὶ ἐγένετο θάμβος ἐπὶ
having done him no harm. *him* *{and}* Astonishment came *Astonishment* over them
1055 1055 899 3594 1055 899 2779 2502 1181 2502 2093
a.asn pt.aa.nsn r.asm.3 cj v.ami.3s n.nsn p.a

πάντας καὶ συνελάλουν πρὸς ἀλλήλους λέγοντες, τίς ὁ λόγος οὗτος
all, and they said to one another, *{saying}* "What is *{the}* this teaching? *this*
4246 2779 5196 4639 253 3306 5515 3836 4047 3364 4047
a.apm cj v.iai.3p p.a r.apm pt.pa.npm r.nsm d.nsm n.nsm r.nsm

ὅτι ἐν ἐξουσίᾳ καὶ δυνάμει ἐπιτάσσει τοῖς ἀκαθάρτοις πνεύμασιν καὶ
For with authority and power he commands the unclean spirits and
4022 1877 2026 2779 1539 2199 3836 176 4460 2779
cj p.d n.dsf cj n.dsf v.pai.3s d.dpn a.dpn n.dpn cj

ἐξέρχονται; 37 καὶ ἐξεπορεύετο ἦχος περὶ αὐτοῦ εἰς πάντα τόπον
they come out!" So the news about him went out *news* *about him* into every place
2002 2779 2491 4309 899 1744 2491 4309 899 1650 4246 5536
v.pmi.3p cj v.imi.3s n.nsm p.g r.gsm.3 p.a a.asm n.asm

τῆς περιχώρου. 38 ἀναστὰς δὲ ἀπὸ τῆς συναγωγῆς εἰσῆλθεν εἰς τὴν
in the surrounding region. After leaving *{and}* from the synagogue, Jesus went to *{the}*
3836 4369 482 1254 608 3836 5252 1656 1650 3836
d.gsf a.gsf pt.aa.nsm cj p.g d.gsf n.gsf v.aai.3s p.a d.asf

οἰκίαν Σίμωνος. πενθερὰ δὲ τοῦ Σίμωνος ἦν συνεχομένη
Simon's house. *Simon's* Now Simon's mother-in-law *Now* *{the}* *Simon's* was suffering a
4981 3864 4981 1254 4981 4289 1254 3836 4981 1639 5309
n.asf n.gsm n.nsf cj d.gsm n.gsm v.iai.3s pt.pp.nsf

πυρετῷ μεγάλῳ καὶ ἠρώτησαν αὐτὸν περὶ αὐτῆς. ↰ 39 καὶ
severe fever, *severe* and ⌊they made a request to⌋ him on her behalf. *{and}*
3489 4790 3489 2779 2263 899 4309 899 4309 2779
n.dsm a.dsm cj v.aai.3p r.asm.3 p.g r.gsf.3 cj

ἐπιστὰς ἐπάνω αὐτῆς ἐπετίμησεν τῷ πυρετῷ καὶ ἀφῆκεν αὐτήν· παραχρῆμα δὲ ↱
Standing over her he rebuked the fever, and it left her. Immediately *{and}* she
2392 2062 899 2203 3836 4790 2779 918 899 4202 1254 1354
pt.aa.nsm p.g r.gsf.3 v.aai.3s d.dsm n.dsm cj v.aai.3s r.asf.3 adv cj

ἀναστᾶσα διηκόνει αὐτοῖς. 40 → δύνοντος δὲ τοῦ ἡλίου
got up and ⌊began to wait on⌋ them. As the sun ⌊was going down,⌋ *{and}* *the* *sun*
482 1354 899 3836 2463 1544 1254 3836 2463
pt.aa.nsf v.iai.3s r.dpm.3 pt.pa.gsm cj d.gsm n.gsm

ἅπαντες ὅσοι εἶχον ἀσθενοῦντας → νόσοις ποικίλαις ἤγαγον αὐτοὺς
all ⌊those who⌋ had any sick with various diseases *various* brought them
570 4012 2400 820 4476 3798 4476 72 899
a.npm r.npm v.iai.3p pt.pa.apm n.dpf a.dpf v.aai.3p r.apm.3

πρὸς αὐτόν· ὁ δὲ → ἑνὶ ἑκάστῳ αὐτῶν τὰς χεῖρας
to him. *{the}* *{and}* Placing his hands on each one *each* of them, *his* *hands*
4639 899 3836 1254 2202 3836 5931 1667 1651 1667 899 3836 5931
p.a r.asm.3 d.nsm cj a.dsm r.dsm r.gpm.3 d.apf n.apf

NASB

possessed by the
spirit of an unclean
demon, and he
cried out with a
loud voice, 34 "Let
us alone! What
business do we
have with each
other, Jesus of
Nazareth? Have
You come to de-
stroy us? I know
who You are—the
Holy One of God!"
35 But Jesus rebuked
him, saying, "Be
quiet and come
out of him!" And
when the demon
had thrown him
down in the midst
of the people, he
came out of him
without doing him
any harm. 36 And
amazement came
upon them all, and
they *began* talking
with one another
saying, "What is
this message? For
with authority and
power He com-
mands the unclean
spirits and they
come out." 37 And
the report about
Him was spreading
into every locality
in the surrounding
district.

Many Are Healed

38 Then He got up
and *left* the syna-
gogue, and entered
Simon's home.
Now Simon's
mother-in-law was
suffering from a
high fever, and
they asked Him
to help her. 39 And
standing over her,
He rebuked the
fever, and it left
her; and she imme-
diately got up and
waited on them.
40 While the sun
was setting, all
those who had any
who were sick with
various diseases
brought them to
Him; and laying
His hands on each
one of them,

NIV

he healed them.
[41]Moreover, de-
mons came out
of many people,
shouting, "You are
the Son of God!"
But he rebuked
them and would
not allow them to
speak, because
they knew he was
the Messiah.
[42]At daybreak,
Jesus went out to a
solitary place. The
people were look-
ing for him and
when they came to
where he was, they
tried to keep him
from leaving them.
[43]But he said, "I
must proclaim the
good news of the
kingdom of God
to the other towns
also, because that
is why I was sent."
[44]And he kept on
preaching in the
synagogues of
Judea.

Jesus Calls His First Disciples

5 One day as
Jesus was
standing by the
Lake of Gennes-
aret,[a] the people
were crowding
around him and
listening to the
word of God. [2]He
saw at the water's
edge two boats,
left there by the
fishermen, who
were washing their
nets. [3]He got into
one of the boats,
the one belong-
ing to Simon, and
asked him to put
out a little from
shore. Then he sat
down and taught
the people from
the boat.
[4]When he had
finished speaking,
he said to

[a] *1* That is, the Sea of Galilee

ἐπιτιθεὶς ἐθεράπευεν αὐτούς. 41 ἐξήρχετο δὲ καὶ δαιμόνια ἀπὸ πολλῶν
Placing he healed them. Also, demons came out *{and}* *Also* *demons* from many,
2202 2543 899 2779 1228 2002 1254 2779 1228 608 4498
pt.pa.nsm v.iai.3s r.apm.3 v.imi.3s cj adv n.npn p.g a.gpm

κραυγάζοντα[a] καὶ λέγοντα ὅτι σὺ εἶ ὁ υἱὸς τοῦ θεοῦ. καὶ ἐπιτιμῶν
crying out and saying, ~ "You are the Son of God!" But he rebuked them and
3198 2779 3306 4022 5148 1639 3836 5626 3836 2536 2779 2203
pt.pa.npn cj pt.pa.npn cj r.ns.2 v.pai.2s d.nsm n.nsm d.gsm n.gsm cj pt.pa.nsm

↱ οὐκ εἴα αὐτὰ λαλεῖν, ὅτι ᾔδεισαν τὸν χριστὸν αὐτὸν εἶναι.
did not allow them to speak, because they knew him to be the Christ. *him* *to be*
1572 4024 1572 899 3281 4022 3857 899 1639 1639 3836 5986 899 1639
pl v.iai.3s r.apn.3 f.pa cj v.lai.3p d.asm n.asm r.asm.3 f.pa

42 → γενομένης δὲ ἡμέρας ↱ ἐξελθὼν ἐπορεύθη εἰς ἔρημον τόπον·
When daylight came *{and}* *daylight* he left and went to a deserted place.
2465 1181 1254 2465 4513 2002 4513 1650 2245 5536
pt.am.gsf cj n.gsf pt.aa.nsm v.api.3s p.a a.asm n.asm

καὶ οἱ ὄχλοι ἐπεζήτουν αὐτὸν καὶ ἦλθον ἕως αὐτοῦ καὶ κατεῖχον αὐτὸν
And the crowds ⌞were looking for⌟ him. *{and}* They came to him and tried to keep him
2779 3836 4063 2118 899 2779 2262 2401 899 2779 2988 899
cj d.npm n.npm v.iai.3p r.asm.3 cj v.aai.3p p.g r.gsm.3 cj v.iai.3p r.asm.3

τοῦ μὴ ⌞πορεύεσθαι ἀπ'⌟ αὐτῶν. 43 ὁ δὲ εἶπεν πρὸς αὐτοὺς ὅτι καὶ
{the} from leaving them, but he *but* said to them, ~ *as well* "I
3836 3590 4513 608 899 1254 3836 1254 3306 4639 899 4022 2779 1609
d.gsn pl f.pm p.g r.gpm.3 d.nsm cj v.aai.3s p.a r.apm.3 cj adv

ταῖς ἑτέραις πόλεσιν
must preach the good news of the kingdom of God in the other towns as well;
1256 2294 2294 2294 2294 3836 993 3836 2536 3836 2283 4484 2779 2779
d.dpf r.dpf n.dpf

εὐαγγελίσασθαί με δεῖ τὴν βασιλείαν τοῦ θεοῦ, ὅτι ἐπὶ τοῦτο
preach the good news *I* *must* *the* *kingdom* *of* *God* because for this purpose
2294 1609 1256 3836 993 3836 2536 4022 2093 4047
f.am r.as.1 v.pai.3s d.asf n.asf d.gsm n.gsm cj p.a r.asn

ἀπεστάλην. 44 καὶ ἦν κηρύσσων εἰς τὰς συναγωγὰς τῆς Ἰουδαίας.
I was sent." So ⌞he kept on⌟ preaching in the synagogues of Judea.
690 2779 1639 3062 1650 3836 5252 3836 2677
v.api.1s cj v.iai.3s pt.pa.nsm p.a d.apf n.apf d.gsf n.gsf

5:1 ἐγένετο δὲ ἐν τῷ τὸν ὄχλον ἐπικεῖσθαι αὐτῷ καὶ
⌞It happened that,⌟ *{and}* when ~ the crowd ⌞was pressing around⌟ him and
1181 1254 1877 3836 3836 4063 2130 899 2779
v.ami.3s cj p.d d.dsn d.asm n.asm f.pm r.dsm.3 cj

ἀκούειν τὸν λόγον τοῦ θεοῦ καὶ αὐτὸς ἦν ἑστὼς παρὰ τὴν λίμνην
⌞listening to⌟ the word of God, *{and}* he was standing beside the lake
201 3836 3364 3836 2536 2779 899 1639 2705 4123 3836 3349
f.pa d.asm n.asm d.gsm n.gsm cj r.nsm v.iai.3s pt.ra.nsm p.a d.asf n.asf

Γεννησαρὲτ 2 καὶ εἶδεν δύο πλοῖα ἑστῶτα παρὰ τὴν λίμνην· οἱ δὲ ἁλιεῖς
of Gennesaret and he saw two boats *{standing}* by the lake, but the *but* fishermen
1166 2779 1625 1545 4450 2705 4123 3836 3349 1254 3836 1254 243
n.gsf cj v.aai.3s a.apn n.apn pt.ra.apn p.a d.asf n.asf d.npm cj n.npm

ἀπ' αὐτῶν ἀποβάντες ἔπλυνον τὰ δίκτυα. 3 ἐμβὰς δὲ εἰς
had gotten out of them *had gotten out* and were washing their nets. He got *{and}* into
609 609 609 608 899 609 4459 3836 1473 1832 1254 1650
p.g r.gpn.3 pt.aa.npm v.iai.3p d.apn n.apn pt.aa.nsm cj p.a

ἓν τῶν πλοίων, ὃ ἦν Σίμωνος, ἠρώτησεν αὐτὸν ἀπὸ
one of the boats, which was Simon's, and asked him to put out a little from
1651 3836 4450 4005 1639 4981 2263 899 2056 2056 2056 3900 608
a.asn d.gpn n.gpn r.nsn v.iai.3s n.gsm v.aai.3s r.asm.3 p.g

τῆς γῆς ἐπαναγαγεῖν ὀλίγον· καθίσας δὲ ἐκ τοῦ
the shore. *to put out* *little* Then he sat down *Then* and taught the crowds from the
3836 1178 2056 3900 1254 2767 1254 1438 3836 4063 1666 3836
d.gsf n.gsf f.aa adv pt.aa.nsm cj p.g d.gsn

πλοίου ἐδίδασκεν τοὺς ὄχλους. 4 ὡς δὲ ἐπαύσατο λαλῶν, εἶπεν πρὸς τὸν
boat. *taught* *the* *crowds* When *{and}* he stopped speaking, he said to *{the}*
4450 1438 3836 4063 6055 1254 4264 3281 3306 4639 3836
n.gsn v.iai.3s d.apm n.apm cj cj v.ami.3s pt.pa.nsm v.aai.3s p.a d.asm

[a] κραυγάζοντα UBS, NET. κράζοντα TNIV.

NASB

He was healing
them. [41]Demons
also were coming
out of many, shout-
ing, "You are the
Son of God!" But
rebuking them, He
would not allow
them to speak,
because they knew
Him to be the
Christ.
[42]When day came,
Jesus left and went
to a secluded place;
and the crowds
were searching for
Him, and came to
Him and tried to
keep Him from
going away from
them. [43]But He said
to them, "I must
preach the king-
dom of God to the
other cities also,
for I was sent for
this purpose."
[44]So He kept on
preaching in the
synagogues of
[a]Judea.

The First Disciples

[5:1]Now it hap-
pened that while
the crowd was
pressing around
Him and listening
to the word of God,
He was standing
by the lake of
Gennesaret; [2]and
He saw two boats
lying at the edge
of the lake; but
the fishermen had
gotten out of them
and were washing
their nets. [3]And He
got into one of the
boats, which was
Simon's, and asked
him to put out a
little way from the
land. And He sat
down and *began*
teaching the people
from the boat.
[4]When He had
finished speaking,
He said

[a] I.e. the country of the Jews (including Galilee)

NIV

Simon, "Put out
into deep water,
and let down the
nets for a catch."
5 Simon an-
swered, "Master,
we've worked
hard all night and
haven't caught
anything. But be-
cause you say so,
I will let down the
nets."
6 When they had
done so, they
caught such a large
number of fish that
their nets began
to break. 7 So they
signaled their part-
ners in the other
boat to come and
help them, and
they came and
filled both boats so
full that they be-
gan to sink.
8 When Simon Pe-
ter saw this, he fell
at Jesus' knees and
said, "Go away
from me, Lord; I
am a sinful man!"
9 For he and all his
companions were
astonished at the
catch of fish they
had taken, 10 and
so were James and
John, the sons of
Zebedee, Simon's
partners.
Then Jesus said
to Simon, "Don't
be afraid; from
now on you will
fish for people."
11 So they pulled
their boats up on
shore, left every-
thing and followed
him.

Jesus Heals a Man With Leprosy

12 While Jesus
was in one of the
towns, a man came
along who was
covered with lep-
rosy.[a]

Σίμωνα, ἐπανάγαγε εἰς τὸ βάθος καὶ χαλάσατε τὰ δίκτυα ὑμῶν εἰς
Simon, "Put out into the deep water and lower {the} your nets your for a
4981 2056 1650 3836 958 2779 5899 3836 7007 1473 7007 1650
n.asm v.aam.2s p.a d.asn n.asn cj v.aam.2p d.apn n.apn r.gp.2 p.a

ἄγραν. 5 καὶ ἀποκριθεὶς Σίμων εἶπεν, ἐπιστάτα, ⌞δι᾽ ὅλης⌟ νυκτὸς ↰
catch." But Simon responded, Simon saying, "Master, all night long
62 2779 4981 646 4981 3306 2181 1328 3910 3816 1328
n.asf cj pt.ap.nsm n.nsm v.aai.3s n.vsm p.g a.gsf n.gsf

κοπιάσαντες οὐδὲν ἐλάβομεν· ἐπὶ δὲ τῷ ῥήματί σου
we have toiled and have caught nothing! have caught But at But {the} your word your
3159 3284 3284 4029 3284 1254 2093 1254 3836 5148 4839 5148
pt.aa.npm a.asn v.aai.1p p.d cj d.dsn n.dsn r.gs.2

χαλάσω τὰ δίκτυα. 6 καὶ τοῦτο ποιήσαντες συνέκλεισαν
I will lower the nets." And when they had done this, when they had done they enclosed a
5899 3836 1473 2779 4472 4472 4472 4472 4047 4472 5168
v.fai.1s d.apn n.apn cj r.asn pt.aa.npm v.aai.3p

πλῆθος ἰχθύων πολύ, διερρήσσετο δὲ τὰ δίκτυα αὐτῶν.
large number of fish, large and their nets ⌞were about to break.⌟ and {the} nets their
4498 4436 2716 4498 1254 899 1473 1393 1254 3836 1473 899
n.asn n.gpm a.asn v.ipi.3s cj d.npn n.npn r.gpm.3

7 καὶ κατένευσαν τοῖς μετόχοις ἐν τῷ ἑτέρῳ πλοίῳ τοῦ ἐλθόντας
{and} They signaled to their partners in the other boat {the} to come and
2779 2916 3836 3581 1877 3836 2283 4450 3836 2262
cj v.aai.3p d.dpm n.dpm p.d d.dsn r.dsn n.dsn d.gsn pt.aa.apm

συλλαβέσθαι αὐτοῖς· καὶ ἦλθον καὶ ἔπλησαν ἀμφότερα τὰ πλοῖα ὥστε
help them. And they came and filled both the boats, so that they
5197 899 2779 2262 2779 4398 317 3836 4450 6063 899
f.am r.dpm.3 cj v.aai.3p cj v.aai.3p a.apn d.apn n.apn cj

βυθίζεσθαι αὐτά. 8 → ἰδὼν δὲ Σίμων Πέτρος προσέπεσεν
⌞were about to sink.⌟ they When Simon Peter saw {and} Simon Peter this, he fell
1112 899 4981 4377 1625 1254 4981 4377 4700
f.pp r.apn.3 pt.aa.nsm cj n.nsm n.nsm v.aai.3s

τοῖς γόνασιν Ἰησοῦ λέγων, ἔξελθε ἀπ᾽ ἐμοῦ, ὅτι ἀνὴρ
at the knees of Jesus, saying, "Go away from me, Lord, for I am a sinful man!"
3836 1205 2652 3306 2002 608 1609 3261 4022 1639 1639 283 467
d.dpn n.dpn n.gsm pt.pa.nsm v.aam.2s p.g r.gs.1 cj n.nsm

ἁμαρτωλός εἰμι, κύριε. 9 θάμβος γὰρ περιέσχεν αὐτὸν καὶ πάντας τοὺς
sinful I am Lord For amazement For ⌞had taken hold of⌟ him and all who
283 1639 3261 1142 2502 1142 4321 899 2779 4246 3836
a.nsm v.pai.1s n.vsm n.nsn cj v.aai.3s r.asm.3 cj a.apm d.apm

σὺν αὐτῷ ἐπὶ τῇ ἄγρᾳ τῶν ἰχθύων ὧν συνέλαβον, 10 ὁμοίως δὲ
were with him ⌞because of⌟ the catch of fish that they had taken, and so and
5250 899 2093 3836 62 3836 2716 4005 5197 1254 3931 1254
p.d r.dsm.3 p.d d.dsf n.dsf d.gpm n.gpm r.gpm v.aai.3p adv cj

καὶ Ἰάκωβον καὶ Ἰωάννην υἱοὺς Ζεβεδαίου, οἳ ἦσαν κοινωνοὶ τῷ Σίμωνι.
also were James and John, sons of Zebedee, who were partners with Simon.
2779 2610 2779 2722 5626 2411 4005 1639 3128 3836 4981
adv n.asm cj n.asm n.apm n.gsm d.npm v.iai.3p n.npm d.dsm n.dsm

καὶ εἶπεν πρὸς τὸν Σίμωνα ὁ Ἰησοῦς, ↱ μὴ φοβοῦ· ἀπὸ τοῦ νῦν
But Jesus said to {the} Simon, {the} Jesus "Do not be afraid; from {the} now on you
2779 2652 3306 4639 3836 4981 3836 2652 5828 3590 5828 608 3836 3814 1639
cj v.aai.3s p.a d.asm n.asm d.nsm n.nsm pl v.ppm.2s p.g d.gsm adv

ἀνθρώπους ἔσῃ ζωγρῶν. 11 καὶ καταγαγόντες τὰ πλοῖα ἐπὶ
will be catching men." you will be catching Then they brought the boats to
1639 1639 2436 476 1639 2436 2779 2864 3836 4450 2093
n.apm v.fmi.2s pt.pa.nsm cj pt.aa.npm d.apn n.apn p.a

τὴν γῆν ἀφέντες πάντα ἠκολούθησαν αὐτῷ. 12 καὶ ἐγένετο ἐν τῷ
{the} shore, left everything, and followed him. {and} ⌞It happened that,⌟ when {the}
3836 1178 918 4246 199 899 2779 1181 1877 3836
d.asf n.asf pt.aa.npm a.apn v.aai.3p r.dsm.3 cj v.ami.3s p.d d.dsn

εἶναι αὐτὸν ἐν μιᾷ τῶν πόλεων καὶ ἰδοὺ ἀνὴρ πλήρης λέπρας·
he was he in one of the cities, {and} ⌞there was⌟ a man full of leprosy. And
899 1639 899 1877 1651 3836 4484 2779 2627 467 4441 3319 1254
f.pa r.asm.3 p.d a.dsf d.gpf n.gpf cj j n.nsm a.nsm n.gsf

NASB

to Simon, "Put out
into the deep water
and let down your
nets for a catch."
5 Simon answered
and said, "Master,
we worked hard all
night and caught
nothing, but I will
do as You say
and let down the
nets." 6 When they
had done this,
they enclosed a
great quantity of
fish, and their nets
began to break;
7 so they signaled
to their partners
in the other boat
for them to come
and help them.
And they came and
filled both of the
boats, so that they
began to sink. 8 But
when Simon Peter
saw *that,* he fell
down at Jesus' feet,
saying, "Go away
from me Lord, for
I am a sinful man!"
9 For amazement
had seized him and
all his companions
because of the
catch of fish which
they had taken;
10 and so also *were*
James and John,
sons of Zebedee,
who were partners
with Simon. And
Jesus said to Si-
mon, "Do not fear,
from now on you
will be catching
men." 11 When they
had brought their
boats to land, they
left everything and
followed Him.

The Leper and the Paralytic

12 While He was
in one of the cities,
behold, *there was* a
man covered with
leprosy; and

[a] 12 The Greek word traditionally translated *leprosy* was used for various diseases affecting the skin.

NIV

When he saw
Jesus, he fell with
his face to the
ground and begged
him, "Lord, if
you are willing,
you can make me
clean."
13 Jesus reached
out his hand and
touched the man.
"I am willing," he
said. "Be clean!"
And immediately
the leprosy left
him.
14 Then Jesus or-
dered him, "Don't
tell anyone, but go,
show yourself to
the priest and offer
the sacrifices that
Moses command-
ed for your cleans-
ing, as a testimony
to them."
15 Yet the news
about him spread
all the more, so
that crowds of
people came to
hear him and to
be healed of their
sicknesses. 16 But
Jesus often with-
drew to lonely
places and prayed.

Jesus Forgives and Heals a Paralyzed Man

17 One day Jesus
was teaching, and
Pharisees and
teachers of the
law were sitting
there. They had
come from every
village of Galilee
and from Judea
and Jerusalem.
And the power of
the Lord was with
Jesus to heal the
sick. 18 Some men
came carrying a
paralyzed man on
a mat and tried
to take him into
the house to lay
him before Jesus.
19 When they could
not find a way to
do this because of
the crowd, they
went up on

ἰδὼν δὲ τὸν Ἰησοῦν, πεσὼν ἐπὶ πρόσωπον ἐδεήθη αὐτοῦ λέγων, κύριε,
seeing *And* *{the}* Jesus, he fell on his face and implored him, saying, "Lord,
1625 1254 3836 2652 4406 2093 4725 1289 899 3306 3261
pt.aa.nsm cj d.asm n.asm pt.aa.nsm p.a n.asn v.api.3s r.gsm.3 pt.pa.nsm n.vsm

ἐὰν θέλῃς δύνασαί ↱ με καθαρίσαι. 13 καὶ ἐκτείνας τὴν χεῖρα
if ⌞you are willing,⌟ you can make me clean." And Jesus ⌞stretched out⌟ his hand
1569 2527 1538 2751 1609 2751 2779 1753 3836 5931
cj v.pas.2s v.ppi.2s r.as.1 f.aa cj pt.aa.nsm d.asf n.asf

ἥψατο αὐτοῦ λέγων, θέλω, καθαρίσθητι· καὶ εὐθέως ἡ λέπρα
and touched him, saying, ⌞"I am willing;⌟ become clean." And immediately the leprosy
721 899 3306 2527 2751 2779 2311 3836 3319
v.ami.3s r.gsm.3 pt.pa.nsm v.pai.1s v.apm.2s cj adv d.nsf n.nsf

⌞ἀπῆλθεν ἀπ'⌟ αὐτοῦ. 14 καὶ αὐτὸς παρήγγειλεν αὐτῷ μηδενὶ εἰπεῖν,
left him. Then Jesus ordered the man to tell no one: *to tell*
599 608 899 2779 899 4133 899 3306 3306 3594 3306
v.aai.3s p.g r.gsm.3 cj r.nsm v.aai.3s r.dsm.3 a.dsm f.aa

ἀλλὰ ἀπελθὼν δεῖξον σεαυτὸν τῷ ἱερεῖ καὶ προσένεγκε περὶ τοῦ
"Go, rather, *Go* and show yourself ⌞to the⌟ priest and make an offering for *{the}* your
599 247 599 1259 4932 3836 2636 2779 4712 4309 3836 5148
cj pt.aa.nsm v.aam.2s r.asm.2 d.dsm n.dsm cj v.aam.2s p.g d.gsm

καθαρισμοῦ σου καθὼς προσέταξεν Μωϋσῆς, εἰς μαρτύριον αὐτοῖς. 15
cleansing, *your* just as Moses commanded *Moses* as a testimony to them." Then
2752 5148 2777 3707 4705 3707 1650 3457 899 1254
n.gsm r.gs.2 cj v.aai.3s n.nsm p.a n.asn r.dpm.3

διήρχετο δὲ μᾶλλον ὁ λόγος περὶ αὐτοῦ, καὶ
the word about him spread *Then* even more, *the* *word* *about him* and large crowds
3836 3364 4309 899 1451 1254 3437 3836 3364 4309 899 2779 4498 4063
v.imi.3s cj adv.c d.nsm n.nsm p.g r.gsm.3 cj

συνήρχοντο ὄχλοι πολλοὶ ἀκούειν καὶ θεραπεύεσθαι ἀπὸ τῶν
would come together *crowds* *large* to hear him and to be healed of *{the}* their
5302 4063 4498 201 2779 2543 608 3836 899
v.imi.3p n.npm a.npm f.pa cj f.pp p.g d.gpf

ἀσθενειῶν αὐτῶν· 16 αὐτὸς δὲ ἦν ὑποχωρῶν ἐν ταῖς ἐρήμοις καὶ
diseases. *their* But he *But* would go off to *{the}* ⌞wilderness places⌟ and
819 899 1254 899 1254 1639 5723 1877 3836 2245 2779
n.gpf r.gpm.3 r.nsm cj v.iai.3s pt.pa.nsm p.d d.dpf a.dpf cj

προσευχόμενος. 17 καὶ ἐγένετο ἐν μιᾷ τῶν ἡμερῶν καὶ αὐτὸς ἦν διδάσκων,
pray. *{and}* It happened on one of those days when he was teaching,
4667 2779 1181 1877 1651 3836 2465 2779 899 1639 1438
pt.pm.nsm cj v.ami.3s p.d a.dsf d.gpf n.gpf cj r.nsm v.iai.3s pt.pa.nsm

καὶ ἦσαν καθήμενοι Φαρισαῖοι καὶ νομοδιδάσκαλοι οἳ ἦσαν ἐληλυθότες
and sitting there were *sitting* Pharisees and teachers of the law who had come
2779 2764 1639 2764 5757 2779 3791 4005 1639 2262
cj v.iai.3p pt.pm.npm n.npm cj n.npm r.npm v.iai.3p pt.ra.npm

ἐκ πάσης κώμης τῆς Γαλιλαίας καὶ Ἰουδαίας καὶ ↰ Ἰερουσαλήμ· καὶ δύναμις
from every village of Galilee and Judea and from Jerusalem, and power
1666 4246 3267 3836 1133 2779 2677 2779 1666 2647 2779 1539
p.g a.gsf n.gsf d.gsf n.gsf cj n.gsf cj n.gsf cj n.nsf

→ κυρίου ἦν εἰς τὸ ἰᾶσθαι αὐτόν. 18 καὶ ἰδοὺ ἄνδρες
from the Lord ⌞was there⌟ for him *{the}* to heal, *him* and ⌞there were⌟ men
3261 1639 1650 899 3836 2615 899 2779 2627 467
n.gsm v.iai.3s p.a d.asn f.pm r.asm.3 cj j n.npm

φέροντες ἐπὶ κλίνης ἄνθρωπον ὃς ἦν παραλελυμένος καὶ ἐζήτουν
carrying on a stretcher a man who was paralyzed. *{and}* ⌞They were trying⌟
5770 2093 3109 476 4005 1639 4168 2779 2426
pt.pa.npm p.g n.gsf n.asm r.nsm v.iai.3s pt.rp.nsm cj v.iai.3p

αὐτὸν εἰσενεγκεῖν ← καὶ θεῖναι αὐτὸν[a] ἐνώπιον αὐτοῦ. 19 καὶ μὴ
to bring him *to bring* in and place him before Jesus. But not
1662 1662 899 1662 2779 5502 899 1967 899 2779 3590
r.asm.3 f.aa cj f.aa r.asm.3 p.g r.gsm.3 cj pl

εὑρόντες ποίας εἰσενέγκωσιν αὐτὸν ↰ διὰ τὸν ὄχλον, ἀναβάντες ἐπὶ
finding any way to bring him in ⌞on account of⌟ the crowd, they went up on
2351 4481 1662 899 1662 1328 3836 4063 326 2093
pt.aa.npm r.gsf v.aas.3p r.asm.3 p.a d.asm n.asm pt.aa.npm p.a

[a] [αὐτὸν] UBS.

NASB

when he saw Jesus,
he fell on his face
and implored Him,
saying, "Lord, if
You are willing,
You can make me
clean." 13 And He
stretched out His
hand and touched
him, saying, "I
am willing; be
cleansed." And
immediately the
leprosy left him.
14 And He ordered
him to tell no one,
"But go and show
yourself to the
priest and make an
offering for your
cleansing, just as
Moses command-
ed, as a testimony
to them." 15 But the
news about Him
was spreading even
farther, and large
crowds were gath-
ering to hear *Him*
and to be healed
of their sicknesses.
16 But Jesus Himself
would *often* slip
away to the wilder-
ness and pray.
17 One day He was
teaching; and there
were *some* Phari-
sees and teachers
of the law sitting
there, who had
come from every
village of Galilee
and Judea and
from Jerusalem;
and the power
of the Lord was
present for Him to
perform healing.
18 And *some* men
were carrying on
a bed a man who
was paralyzed; and
they were trying to
bring him in and
to set him down in
front of Him. 19 But
not finding any
way to bring him
in because of the
crowd, they went
up on the

NIV

the roof and low-
ered him on his
mat through the
tiles into the mid-
dle of the crowd,
right in front of
Jesus.
20When Jesus saw
their faith, he said,
"Friend, your sins
are forgiven."
21The Pharisees
and the teachers
of the law began
thinking to them-
selves, "Who is
this fellow who
speaks blasphe-
my? Who can for-
give sins but God
alone?"
22Jesus knew
what they were
thinking and
asked, "Why are
you thinking these
things in your
hearts? 23Which
is easier: to say,
'Your sins are for-
given,' or to say,
'Get up and walk'?
24But I want you
to know that the
Son of Man has
authority on earth
to forgive sins." So
he said to the par-
alyzed man, "I tell
you, get up, take
your mat and go
home." 25Immedi-
ately he stood up
in front of them,
took what he had
been lying on and
went home prais-
ing God. 26Every-
one was amazed
and gave praise to
God. They were
filled with awe
and said, "We have
seen remarkable
things today."

τὸ δῶμα διὰ τῶν κεράμων καθῆκαν αὐτὸν
the roof and lowered him, along with the stretcher, through the tiles *lowered* *him*
3836 1560 2768 899 5250 3836 3110 1328 3836 3041 2768 899
d.asn n.asn p.g d.gpm n.gpm v.aai.3p r.asm.3

σὺν τῷ κλινιδίῳ εἰς τὸ μέσον ἔμπροσθεν τοῦ Ἰησοῦ. 20 καὶ ἰδὼν τὴν
with the stretcher into the midst, in front of *{the}* Jesus. And ⌊when he saw⌋ *{the}* their
5250 3836 3110 1650 3836 3545 1869 3836 2652 2779 1625 3836 899
p.d d.dsn n.dsn p.a d.asn n.asn p.g d.gsm n.gsm cj pt.aa.nsm d.asf

πίστιν αὐτῶν εἶπεν, ἄνθρωπε, ἀφέωνταί σοι αἱ ἁμαρτίαι σου. 21 καὶ
faith, *their* he said, "Man, your sins are forgiven you." *{the}* *sins* *your* And the
4411 899 3306 476 5148 281 918 5148 3836 281 5148 2779 3836
n.asf r.gpm.3 v.aai.3s n.vsm v.rpi.3p r.ds.2 d.npf n.npf r.gs.2 cj

ἤρξαντο διαλογίζεσθαι οἱ γραμματεῖς καὶ οἱ Φαρισαῖοι
scribes and the Pharisees began to ponder, *the* *scribes* *and* *the* *Pharisees*
1208 2779 3836 5757 806 1368 3836 1208 2779 3836 5757
v.ami.3p f.pm d.npm n.npm cj d.npm n.npm

λέγοντες, τίς ἐστιν οὗτος ὃς λαλεῖ βλασφημίας; τίς δύναται ἁμαρτίας
saying, "Who is this who speaks blasphemies? Who is able to forgive sins
3306 5515 1639 4047 4005 3281 1060 5515 1538 918 918 281
pt.pa.npm r.nsm v.pai.3s r.nsm r.nsm v.pai.3s n.apf r.nsm v.ppi.3s n.apf

ἀφεῖναι ⌊εἰ μὴ⌋ μόνος ὁ θεός; 22 ἐπιγνοὺς δὲ ὁ Ἰησοῦς τοὺς
to forgive except God alone?" *{the}* *God* Jesus, perceiving *{and}* *{the}* *Jesus* *{the}* their
918 1623 3590 2536 3668 3836 2536 2652 2105 1254 3836 2652 3836 899
f.aa cj pl a.nsm d.nsm n.nsm pt.aa.nsm cj d.nsm n.nsm d.apm

διαλογισμοὺς αὐτῶν ἀποκριθεὶς εἶπεν πρὸς αὐτούς, τί διαλογίζεσθε ἐν ταῖς
thoughts, *their* answered, saying to them, "Why are you questioning in *{the}*
1369 899 646 3306 4639 899 5515 1368 1877 3836
n.apm r.gpm.3 pt.ap.nsm v.aai.3s p.a r.apm.3 r.asn v.pmi.2p p.d d.dpf

καρδίαις ὑμῶν; 23 τί ἐστιν εὐκοπώτερον, εἰπεῖν, ἀφέωνταί
your hearts? *your* Which is easier, to say, 'Your sins ⌊have been forgiven⌋
7007 2840 7007 5515 1639 2324 3306 5148 281 918
n.dpf r.gp.2 r.nsn v.pai.3s a.nsn.c f.aa v.rpi.3p

σοι αἱ ἁμαρτίαι σου, ἢ εἰπεῖν, ἔγειρε καὶ περιπάτει; 24 ἵνα δὲ
you,' *{the}* *sins* *Your* or to say, 'Get up and walk'? But that *But*
5148 3836 281 5148 2445 3306 1586 2779 4344 1254 2671 1254
r.ds.2 d.npf n.npf r.gs.2 cj f.aa v.pam.2s cj v.pam.2s cj cj

εἰδῆτε ὅτι ὁ υἱὸς τοῦ ἀνθρώπου ἐξουσίαν ἔχει ἐπὶ τῆς γῆς ἀφιέναι
⌊you may know⌋ that the Son of Man has authority *has* on *{the}* earth to forgive
3857 4022 3836 5626 3836 476 2400 2026 2400 2093 3836 1178 918
v.ras.2p cj d.nsm n.nsm d.gsm n.gsm n.asf v.pai.3s p.g d.gsf n.gsf f.pa

ἁμαρτίας εἶπεν τῷ παραλελυμένῳ, σοὶ λέγω, ἔγειρε καὶ
sins" — he said ⌊to the⌋ paralyzed man, "I say to you, *I say* get up, and
281 3306 3836 4168 3306 3306 5148 3306 1586 2779
n.apf v.aai.3s d.dsm pt.rp.dsm r.ds.2 v.pai.1s v.pam.2s cj

ἄρας τὸ κλινίδιόν σου πορεύου εἰς τὸν οἶκόν σου.
⌊when you have picked up⌋ *{the}* your stretcher, *your* go to *{the}* your house." *your*
149 3836 5148 3110 5148 4513 1650 3836 5148 3875 5148
pt.aa.nsm d.asn n.asn r.gs.2 v.pmm.2s p.a d.asm n.asm r.gs.2

25 καὶ παραχρῆμα ἀναστὰς ἐνώπιον αὐτῶν, ἄρας
{and} Immediately, ⌊having stood up⌋ before them and ⌊picked up⌋ what he had been
2779 4202 482 1967 899 149 4005 2879 2879 2879
cj adv pt.aa.nsm p.g r.gpm.3 pt.aa.nsm

ἐφ' ὃ κατέκειτο, ἀπῆλθεν εἰς τὸν οἶκον αὐτοῦ δοξάζων τὸν θεόν.
lying on, *what he had been lying* he went off to *{the}* his house *his* praising *{the}* God.
2879 2093 4005 2879 599 1650 3836 899 3875 899 1519 3836 2536
p.a r.asn v.imi.3s v.aai.3s p.a d.asm n.asm r.gsm.3 pt.pa.nsm d.asm n.asm

26 καὶ ἔκστασις ἔλαβεν ἅπαντας καὶ ἐδόξαζον τὸν θεὸν καὶ
{and} Astonishment gripped them all, and ⌊they began to glorify⌋ *{the}* God. *{and}*
2779 1749 3284 570 2779 1519 3836 2536 2779
cj n.nsf v.aai.3s a.apm cj v.iai.3p d.asm n.asm cj

ἐπλήσθησαν φόβου λέγοντες ὅτι εἴδομεν παράδοξα σήμερον. 27 καὶ
⌊They were filled with⌋ awe, saying, ~ ⌊"We have seen⌋ incredible things today." *{and}*
4398 5832 3306 4022 1625 4141 4958 2779
v.api.3p n.gsm pt.pa.npm cj v.aai.1p a.apn adv cj

NASB

roof and let him
down through
the tiles with his
stretcher, into
the middle *of the*
crowd, in front
of Jesus. 20Seeing
their faith, He said,
"Friend, your sins
are forgiven you."
21The scribes and
the Pharisees began
to reason, say-
ing, "Who is this
man who speaks
blasphemies? Who
can forgive sins,
but God alone?"
22But Jesus, aware
of their reasonings,
answered and said
to them, "Why
are you reasoning
in your hearts?
23Which is easier,
to say, 'Your sins
have been forgiven
you,' or to say,
'Get up and walk'?
24But, so that you
may know that the
Son of Man has au-
thority on earth to
forgive sins,"—He
said to the paralyt-
ic—"I say to you,
get up, and pick
up your stretcher
and go home."
25Immediately he
got up before them,
and picked up
what he had been
lying on, and went
home glorifying
God. 26They were
all struck with
astonishment and
began glorifying
God; and they were
filled with fear,
saying, "We have
seen remarkable
things today."

NIV

Jesus Calls Levi and Eats With Sinners

27 After this, Jesus
went out and saw
a tax collector by
the name of Levi
sitting at his tax
booth. "Follow
me," Jesus said to
him, 28 and Levi
got up, left every-
thing and followed
him.
29 Then Levi held
a great banquet for
Jesus at his house,
and a large crowd
of tax collectors
and others were
eating with them.
30 But the Pharisees
and the teachers
of the law who be-
longed to their sect
complained to his
disciples, "Why do
you eat and drink
with tax collectors
and sinners?"
31 Jesus answered
them, "It is not
the healthy who
need a doctor, but
the sick. 32 I have
not come to call
the righteous, but
sinners to repen-
tance."

Jesus Questioned About Fasting

33 They said to
him, "John's dis-
ciples often fast
and pray, and so
do the disciples of
the Pharisees, but
yours go on eating
and drinking."
34 Jesus answered,
"Can you make
the friends of the
bridegroom fast
while he is with
them? 35 But the
time will come
when the bride-
groom will be tak-
en from them;

μετὰ ταῦτα ἐξῆλθεν καὶ ἐθεάσατο τελώνην ὀνόματι Λευὶν καθήμενον ἐπὶ τὸ
After this he went out and saw a tax collector named Levi, sitting at the
3552 4047 2002 2779 2517 5467 3950 3322 2764 2093 3836
p.a r.apn v.aai.3s cj v.ami.3s n.asm n.dsn n.asm pt.pm.asm p.a d.asn

τελώνιον, καὶ εἶπεν αὐτῷ, ἀκολούθει μοι. 28 καὶ καταλιπὼν πάντα ↱ ἀναστὰς
tax booth. And he said to him, "Follow me." So leaving everything, he got up
5468 2779 3306 899 199 1609 2779 2901 4246 199 482
n.asn cj v.aai.3s r.dsm.3 v.pam.2s r.ds.1 cj pt.aa.nsm a.apn pt.aa.nsm

ἠκολούθει αὐτῷ. 29 καὶ ἐποίησεν δοχὴν μεγάλην Λευὶς αὐτῷ ἐν
and followed him. And Levi made a great banquet *great* *Levi* for him in
199 899 2779 3322 4472 3489 1531 3489 3322 899 1877
v.iai.3s r.dsm.3 cj v.aai.3s n.asf a.asf n.nsm r.dsm.3 p.d

τῇ οἰκίᾳ αὐτοῦ, καὶ ἦν ὄχλος πολὺς τελωνῶν καὶ ἄλλων οἳ
{the} his house, *his* and ⌞there was⌟ a great crowd *great* of tax collectors and others who
3836 899 3864 899 2779 1639 4498 4063 4498 5467 2779 257 4005
d.dsf n.dsf r.gsm.3 cj v.iai.3s n.nsm a.nsm n.gpm cj r.gpm r.npm

ἦσαν μετ᾽ αὐτῶν κατακείμενοι. 30 καὶ
were reclining at table with them. *reclining at table* And the Pharisees and their scribes
1639 2879 2879 2879 3552 899 2879 2779 3836 5757 2779 899 1208
v.iai.3p p.g r.gpm.3 pt.pm.npm cj

ἐγόγγυζον οἱ Φαρισαῖοι καὶ οἱ γραμματεῖς αὐτῶν πρὸς τοὺς μαθητὰς
were grumbling *the* *Pharisees* *and* *{the}* *scribes* *their* at *{the}* his disciples,
1197 3836 5757 2779 3836 1208 899 4639 3836 899 3412
v.iai.3p d.npm n.npm cj d.npm n.npm r.gpm.3 p.a d.apm n.apm

αὐτοῦ λέγοντες, ⌞διὰ τί⌟ μετὰ τῶν τελωνῶν καὶ
his saying, "Why do you eat and drink with the tax collectors and
899 3306 1328 5515 2266 2266 2266 2779 4403 3552 3836 5467 2779
r.gsm.3 pt.pa.npm p.a r.asn p.g d.gpm n.gpm cj

ἁμαρτωλῶν ἐσθίετε καὶ πίνετε; 31 καὶ ἀποκριθεὶς ὁ Ἰησοῦς εἶπεν πρὸς αὐτούς,
sinners?" *do you eat* *and* *drink* *{and}* In response *{the}* Jesus said to them,
283 2266 2779 4403 2779 646 3836 2652 3306 4639 899
a.gpm v.pai.2p cj v.pai.2p cj pt.ap.nsm d.nsm n.nsm v.aai.3s p.a r.apm.3

οὐ χρείαν ἔχουσιν οἱ ὑγιαίνοντες → ἰατροῦ ἀλλὰ
"Those who are healthy have no need *have* *Those who are healthy* of a doctor, but
3836 5617 5617 5617 2400 4024 5970 2400 3836 5617 2620 247
pl n.asf v.pai.3p d.npm pt.pa.npm n.gsm cj

οἱ κακῶς ἔχοντες· 32 ↱ ↱ οὐκ ἐλήλυθα καλέσαι δικαίους ἀλλὰ
those ⌞who are sick⌟ do; I have not come to call righteous people, but
3836 2809 2400 2262 2262 4024 2262 2813 1465 247
d.npm adv pt.pa.npm pl v.rai.1s f.aa a.apm cj

ἁμαρτωλοὺς εἰς μετάνοιαν. 33 οἱ δὲ εἶπαν πρὸς αὐτόν, οἱ μαθηταὶ
sinners, to repentance." And they *And* said to him, "The disciples
283 1650 3567 1254 3836 1254 3306 4639 899 3836 3412
a.apm p.a n.asf d.npm cj v.aai.3p p.a r.asm.3 d.npm n.npm

Ἰωάννου νηστεύουσιν πυκνὰ καὶ δεήσεις ποιοῦνται ὁμοίως καὶ οἱ
of John often fast *often* and offer prayers, *offer* so also do the
2722 4781 3764 4781 2779 4472 1255 4472 3931 2779 3836
n.gsm v.pai.3p adv cj n.apf v.pmi.3p adv adv d.npm

τῶν Φαρισαίων, οἱ δὲ σοὶ ἐσθίουσιν καὶ πίνουσιν. 34 ὁ δὲ
disciples of the Pharisees, *{the}* but yours ⌞continue to eat⌟ and drink." *{the}* So
3836 5757 3836 1254 5050 2266 2779 4403 3836 1254
d.gpm n.gpm d.npm cj r.npm.2 v.pai.3p cj v.pai.3p d.nsm cj

Ἰησοῦς εἶπεν πρὸς αὐτούς, ↱ ⌞μὴ δύνασθε⌟ τοὺς υἱοὺς
Jesus said to them, "Certainly you cannot make the wedding guests
2652 3306 4639 899 1538 3590 1538 4472 3836 3813 5626
n.nsm v.aai.3s p.a r.apm.3 pl v.ppi.2p d.apm n.apm

τοῦ νυμφῶνος ⌞ἐν ᾧ⌟ ὁ νυμφίος μετ᾽ αὐτῶν ἐστιν ποιῆσαι νηστεῦσαι;
{the} *wedding* fast while the bridegroom is with them? *is* *make* *fast*
3836 3813 3764 1877 4005 3836 3812 1639 3552 899 1639 4472 3764
d.gsm n.gsm p.d r.dsm d.nsm n.nsm p.g r.gpm.3 v.pai.3s f.aa f.aa

35 ἐλεύσονται δὲ ἡμέραι, καὶ ὅταν ἀπαρθῇ ἀπ᾽ αὐτῶν
The days will come *{and}* *days* *{and}* when the bridegroom is taken away from them,
2465 2262 1254 2465 2779 4020 3836 3812 554 608 899
v.fmi.3p cj n.npf cj cj v.aps.3s p.g r.gpm.3

NASB

Call of Levi (Matthew)

27 After that He
went out and no-
ticed a tax collector
named Levi sitting
in the tax booth,
and He said to
him, "Follow Me."
28 And he left every-
thing behind, and
got up and *began*
to follow Him.
29 And Levi gave
a big reception for
Him in his house;
and there was a
great crowd of tax
collectors and other
people who were
reclining *at the*
table with them.
30 The Pharisees and
their scribes *began*
grumbling at His
disciples, saying,
"Why do you eat
and drink with the
tax collectors and
sinners?" 31 And
Jesus answered and
said to them, "*It*
is not those who
are well who need
a physician, but
those who are sick.
32 I have not come
to call the righ-
teous but sinners to
repentance."
33 And they said
to Him, "The
disciples of John
often fast and offer
prayers, the *dis-*
ciples of the Phari-
sees also do the
same, but Yours eat
and drink." 34 And
Jesus said to them,
"You cannot make
the attendants of
the bridegroom
fast while the
bridegroom is with
them, can you?
35 But *the* days will
come; and when
the bridegroom is
taken away from

NIV

in those days they
will fast."
36He told them
this parable: "No
one tears a piece
out of a new gar-
ment to patch an
old one. Other-
wise, they will
have torn the new
garment, and the
patch from the
new will not match
the old. 37And no
one pours new
wine into old
wineskins. Other-
wise, the new
wine will burst
the skins; the wine
will run out and
the wineskins will
be ruined. 38No,
new wine must be
poured into new
wineskins. 39And
no one after drink-
ing old wine wants
the new, for they
say, 'The old is
better.'"

Jesus Is Lord of the Sabbath

6 One Sabbath
Jesus was go-
ing through the
grainfields, and
his disciples began
to pick some heads
of grain, rub them
in their hands and
eat the kernels.
2Some of the Phar-
isees asked, "Why
are you doing what
is unlawful on the
Sabbath?"
3Jesus answered
them, "Have you
never read what
David did

ὁ νυμφίος, τότε νηστεύσουσιν ἐν ἐκείναις ταῖς ἡμέραις. 36 → ἔλεγεν
the bridegroom and then they will fast in those {the} days." He also told
3836 3812 5538 3764 1877 1697 3836 2465 2779 3306
d.nsm n.nsm adv v.fai.3p p.d r.dpf d.dpf n.dpf v.iai.3s

δὲ καὶ παραβολὴν πρὸς αὐτοὺς ὅτι οὐδεὶς ἐπίβλημα ἀπὸ ἱματίου
{and} also a parable to them: ~ "No one tears a patch from a new garment
1254 2779 4130 4639 899 4022 4029 5387 2099 608 2785 2668
cj adv n.asf p.a r.apm.3 cj a.nsm n.asn p.g n.gsn

καινοῦ σχίσας ἐπιβάλλει ἐπὶ ἱμάτιον παλαιόν· ˻εἰ δὲ μή γε,˼
new tears and sews it on an old garment. old If he does,
2785 5387 2095 2093 4094 2668 4094 1623 1254 3590 1145
a.gsn pt.aa.nsm v.pai.3s p.a n.asn a.asn cj cj pl pl

καὶ τὸ καινὸν σχίσει καὶ τῷ
he both tears the new, he tears and the patch from the new will not match the
5387 2779 5387 3836 2785 5387 2779 3836 2099 608 3836 2785 5244 4024 5244 3836
cj d.asn a.asn v.fai.3s cj d.dsn

παλαιῷ οὐ συμφωνήσει τὸ ἐπίβλημα τὸ ἀπὸ τοῦ καινοῦ. 37 καὶ οὐδεὶς βάλλει
old. not will match the patch {the} from the new And no one puts
4094 4024 5244 3836 2099 3836 608 3836 2785 2779 4029 965
a.dsn pl v.fai.3s d.nsn n.nsn d.nsn p.g d.gsn a.gsn cj a.nsm v.pai.3s

οἶνον νέον εἰς ἀσκοὺς παλαιούς· ˻εἰ δὲ μή γε,˼
new wine new into old wineskins. old If he does, the new wine
3742 3885 3742 1650 4094 829 4094 1623 1254 3590 1145 3836 3742 3885
n.asm a.asm p.a n.apm a.apm cj cj pl pl

ῥήξει ὁ οἶνος ὁ νέος τοὺς ἀσκοὺς καὶ αὐτὸς ἐκχυθήσεται καὶ οἱ ἀσκοὶ
will burst the wine {the} new the skins and it will be spilled, and the skins
4838 3836 3885 3836 3742 3836 829 2779 899 1773 2779 3836 829
v.fai.3s d.nsm n.nsm d.nsm a.nsm d.apm n.apm cj r.nsm v.fpi.3s cj d.npm n.npm

ἀπολοῦνται· 38 ἀλλὰ οἶνον νέον εἰς ἀσκοὺς καινοὺς
will be destroyed. Rather, new wine new is to be put into new wineskins new
660 247 3742 3885 3742 1064 1064 1064 1064 1650 2785 829 2785
v.fmi.3p cj n.asm a.asm p.a n.apm a.apm

βλητέον.[a] 39 καὶ[b] οὐδεὶς πιὼν παλαιὸν θέλει νέον· λέγει γάρ, ὁ
is to be put And no one drinking the old desires the new; for he says, for 'The
1064 2779 4029 4403 4094 2527 3742 1142 3306 1142 3836
a.nsn cj a.nsm pt.aa.nsm a.asm v.pai.3s a.asm v.pai.3s cj d.nsm

παλαιὸς χρηστός ἐστιν.
old is good.'" is
4094 1639 5982 1639
a.nsm a.nsm v.pai.3s

6:1 ἐγένετο δὲ ἐν σαββάτῳ → διαπορεύεσθαι αὐτὸν διὰ
{it happened that} {and} One Sabbath, as Jesus was going Jesus through
1181 1254 1877 4879 899 1388 899 1328
v.ami.3s cj p.d n.dsn f.pm r.asm.3 p.g

σπορίμων, καὶ ἔτιλλον οἱ μαθηταὶ αὐτοῦ καὶ ἤσθιον τοὺς
grainfields, {and} his disciples ˻began to pick˼ {the} disciples his and eat some
5077 2779 899 3412 5504 3836 3412 899 2779 2266 3836
n.gpn cj v.iai.3p d.npm n.npm r.gsm.3 cj v.iai.3p d.apm

στάχυας ψώχοντες ταῖς χερσίν. 2 τινὲς δὲ τῶν Φαρισαίων
heads of grain, rub them in their hands, and eat them. Some {and} of the Pharisees
5092 6041 3836 5931 2779 2266 5516 1254 3836 5757
n.apm pt.pa.npm d.dpf n.dpf r.npm cj d.gpm n.gpm

εἶπαν, τί ποιεῖτε ὃ ↱ οὐκ ἔξεστιν τοῖς σάββασιν; 3 καὶ ἀποκριθεὶς πρὸς
asked, "Why do you do what is not lawful on the Sabbath?" {and} In answer to
3306 5515 4472 4005 1997 4024 1997 3836 4879 2779 646 4639
v.aai.3p r.asn v.pai.2p r.nsn pl v.pai.3s d.dpn n.dpn cj pt.ap.nsm p.a

αὐτοὺς εἶπεν ὁ Ἰησοῦς, ↱ ↱ οὐδὲ τοῦτο ἀνέγνωτε ὃ ἐποίησεν
them Jesus said, {the} Jesus "Have you not {this} read what David did
899 2652 3306 3836 2652 336 336 4028 4047 336 4005 1253 4472
r.apm.3 v.aai.3s d.nsm n.nsm adv r.asn v.aai.2p r.asn v.aai.3s

NASB

them, then they
will fast in those
days." 36And He
was also telling
them a parable:
"No one tears a
piece of cloth from
a new garment and
puts it on an old
garment; otherwise
he will both tear
the new, and the
piece from the new
will not match the
old. 37And no one
puts new wine into
old wineskins;
otherwise the new
wine will burst the
skins and it will
be spilled out, and
the skins will be
ruined. 38But new
wine must be put
into fresh wine-
skins. 39And no
one, after drinking
old *wine* wishes for
new; for he says,
'The old is good
enough.'"

Jesus Is Lord of the Sabbath

6:1Now it hap-
pened that He was
passing through
some grainfields
on a Sabbath; and
His disciples were
picking the heads
of grain, rubbing
them in their
hands, and eating
the grain. 2But
some of the Phari-
sees said, "Why do
you do what is not
lawful on the Sab-
bath?" 3And Jesus
answering them
said, "Have you
not even read what
David did when he

[a] καὶ ἀμφότεροι συντηροῦνται included by TR after βλητέον.
[b] [καὶ] UBS, omitted by NET.

NIV

when he and his
companions were
hungry? 4 He en-
tered the house of
God, and taking
the consecrated
bread, he ate what
is lawful only
for priests to eat.
And he also gave
some to his com-
panions." 5 Then
Jesus said to them,
"The Son of Man
is Lord of the Sab-
bath."
6 On another Sab-
bath he went into
the synagogue and
was teaching, and
a man was there
whose right hand
was shriveled.
7 The Pharisees and
the teachers of the
law were looking
for a reason to
accuse Jesus, so
they watched him
closely to see if
he would heal on
the Sabbath. 8 But
Jesus knew what
they were think-
ing and said to
the man with the
shriveled hand,
"Get up and stand
in front of every-
one." So he got up
and stood there.
9 Then Jesus said
to them, "I ask
you, which is law-
ful on the Sabbath:
to do good or to do
evil, to save life or
to destroy it?"
10 He looked
around at them all,
and then said to
the man, "Stretch
out your hand."
He did so, and his
hand was com-
pletely restored.
11 But the Pharisees
and the teachers of
the law

Δαυὶδ ὅτε ἐπείνασεν αὐτὸς καὶ οἱ μετ᾽ αὐτοῦ ὄντες,[a] 4 ὡς[b] ⌞εἰσῆλθεν
David when he was hungry, he and those who were with him? *who were* how he entered
1253 4021 4277 899 2779 3836 1639 1639 3552 899 1639 6055 1656
n.nsm cj v.aai.3s r.nsm cj d.npm p.g r.gsm.3 pt.pa.npm cj v.aai.3s

εἰς⌟ τὸν οἶκον τοῦ θεοῦ καὶ τοὺς ἄρτους τῆς προθέσεως λαβὼν ἔφαγεν καὶ
the house of God, and taking the Bread of the Presence, *taking* he ate it and
1650 3836 3875 3836 2536 2779 3284 3836 788 3836 4606 3284 2266 2779
p.a d.asm n.asm d.gsm n.gsm cj d.apm n.apm d.gsf n.gsf pt.aa.nsm v.aai.3s cj

ἔδωκεν τοῖς μετ᾽ αὐτοῦ, οὓς ↱ οὐκ ἔξεστιν
gave some to those with him — which is not lawful for any but the priests
1443 3836 3552 899 4005 1997 4024 1997 3668 3668 1623 3836 2636
v.aai.3s d.dpm p.g r.gsm.3 r.apm pl v.pai.3s

φαγεῖν ⌞εἰ μὴ⌟ μόνους τοὺς ἱερεῖς; 5 καὶ ἔλεγεν αὐτοῖς,
to eat?" *but* *for any* *the* *priests* Then he said to them, "The Son of Man is
2266 1623 3590 3668 3836 2636 2779 3306 899 3836 5626 3836 476 1639
f.aa cj pl a.apm d.apm n.apm cj v.iai.3s r.dpm.3

κύριός ἐστιν τοῦ σαββάτου ὁ υἱὸς τοῦ ἀνθρώπου. 6 ἐγένετο δὲ ἐν ἑτέρῳ
Lord *is* of the Sabbath." *The* *Son* *of* *Man* It happened *{and}* on another
3261 1639 3836 4879 3836 5626 3836 476 1181 1254 1877 2283
n.nsm v.pai.3s d.gsn n.gsn d.nsm n.nsm d.gsm n.gsm v.ami.3s cj p.d r.dsn

σαββάτῳ ↰ εἰσελθεῖν αὐτὸν εἰς τὴν συναγωγὴν καὶ διδάσκειν. καὶ
Sabbath that he went *he* into the synagogue and began to teach. *{and}* A man
4879 1181 899 1656 899 1650 3836 5252 2779 1438 2779 476
n.dsn f.aa r.asm.3 p.a d.asf n.asf cj f.pa cj

ἦν ἄνθρωπος ἐκεῖ καὶ ἡ χεὶρ αὐτοῦ ἡ δεξιὰ ἦν ξηρά. 7
was *man* there *{and}* *{the}* whose right hand *whose* *{the}* *right* was withered. So
1639 476 1695 2779 3836 899 1288 5931 899 3836 1288 1639 3831 1254
v.iai.3s n.nsm adv cj d.nsf n.nsf r.gsm.3 d.nsf a.nsf v.iai.3s a.nsf

παρετηροῦντο δὲ αὐτὸν ↰ ↰ ↰ οἱ
the scribes and the Pharisees were watching *So* him carefully to see *the*
3836 1208 2779 3836 5757 4190 1254 899 4190 4190 4190 3836
v.imi.3p cj r.asm.3 d.npm

γραμματεῖς καὶ οἱ Φαρισαῖοι εἰ ἐν τῷ σαββάτῳ θεραπεύει, ἵνα
scribes *and* *the* *Pharisees* whether he healed on the Sabbath, *he healed* so that
1208 2779 3836 5757 1623 2543 2543 1877 3836 4879 2543 2671
n.npm cj d.npm n.npm cj p.d d.dsn n.dsn v.pai.3s cj

εὕρωσιν κατηγορεῖν αὐτοῦ. 8 αὐτὸς δὲ ᾔδει τοὺς διαλογισμοὺς
⌞they could find⌟ a reason to accuse him. But he *But* knew *{the}* their thoughts,
2351 2989 899 1254 899 1254 3857 3836 899 1369
v.aas.3p f.pa r.gsm.3 r.nsm cj v.lai.3s d.apm n.apm

αὐτῶν, εἶπεν δὲ τῷ ἀνδρὶ τῷ ξηρὰν ἔχοντι τὴν χεῖρα, ἔγειρε καὶ
their so he said *so* ⌞to the⌟ man with the withered *with* *{the}* hand, "Get up and
899 1254 3306 1254 3836 467 2400 3836 3831 2400 3836 5931 1586 2779
r.gpm.3 v.aai.3s cj d.dsm n.dsm d.dsm a.asf pt.pa.dsm d.asf n.asf v.pam.2s cj

στῆθι εἰς τὸ μέσον· καὶ ↱ ἀναστὰς ἔστη. 9 εἶπεν δὲ
stand here in *{the}* front." So he got up and ⌞came forward.⌟ Then Jesus said *Then*
2705 1650 3836 3545 2779 2705 482 2705 1254 2652 3306 1254
v.aam.2s p.a d.asn n.asn cj pt.aa.nsm v.aai.3s v.aai.3s cj

ὁ Ἰησοῦς πρὸς αὐτούς, ἐπερωτῶ ὑμᾶς εἰ ἔξεστιν τῷ σαββάτῳ
{the} *Jesus* to them, "I ask you whether it is lawful ⌞on the⌟ Sabbath
3836 2652 4639 899 2089 7007 1623 1997 3836 4879
d.nsm n.nsm p.a r.apm.3 v.pai.1s r.ap.2 cj v.pai.3s d.dsn n.dsn

ἀγαθοποιῆσαι ἢ κακοποιῆσαι, ψυχὴν σῶσαι ἢ ἀπολέσαι; 10 καὶ
to do good or to do harm, to save life *to save* or to destroy it?" *{and}*
16 2445 2803 5392 5392 6034 5392 2445 660 2779
f.aa cj f.aa n.asf f.aa cj f.aa cj

περιβλεψάμενος πάντας αὐτοὺς εἶπεν → αὐτῷ, ἔκτεινον τὴν χεῖρά
After looking around at them all, *them* he said to the man, "Stretch out *{the}* your hand."
4315 899 4246 899 3306 899 1753 3836 5148 5931
pt.am.nsm a.apm r.apm.3 v.aai.3s r.dsm.3 v.aam.2s d.asf n.asf

σου. ὁ δὲ ἐποίησεν καὶ ἀπεκατεστάθη ἡ χεὶρ αὐτοῦ. 11 αὐτοὶ
your He *{and}* did it, and his hand was restored. *{the}* *hand* *his* But they
5148 3836 1254 4472 2779 899 5931 635 3836 5931 899 1254 899
r.gs.2 d.nsm cj v.aai.3s cj v.api.3s d.nsf n.nsf r.gsm.3 cj r.npm

NASB

was hungry, he and
those who were
with him, 4 how he
entered the house
of God, and took
and ate the [a]conse-
crated bread which
is not lawful for
any to eat except
the priests alone,
and gave it to his
companions?"
5 And He was say-
ing to them, "The
Son of Man is Lord
of the Sabbath."
6 On another Sab-
bath He entered
the synagogue and
was teaching; and
there was a man
there whose right
hand was withered.
7 The scribes and
the Pharisees were
watching Him
closely *to see* if He
healed on the Sab-
bath, so that they
might find *reason*
to accuse Him.
8 But He knew what
they were think-
ing, and He said
to the man with
the withered hand,
"Get up and come
forward!" And he
got up and came
forward. 9 And Je-
sus said to them, "I
ask you, is it law-
ful to do good or
to do harm on the
Sabbath, to save a
life or to destroy
it?" 10 After looking
around at them all,
He said to him,
"Stretch out your
hand!" And he did
so; and his hand
was restored. 11 But
they themselves

[a] [ὄντες] UBS, omitted by TNIV.
[b] [ὡς] UBS, omitted by TNIV.

[a] Or *showbread;* lit *loaves of presentation*

NIV

were furious and
began to discuss
with one another
what they might do
to Jesus.

The Twelve Apostles

[12]One of those
days Jesus went
out to a mountain-
side to pray, and
spent the night
praying to God.
[13]When morning
came, he called
his disciples to
him and chose
twelve of them,
whom he also des-
ignated apostles:
[14]Simon (whom he
named Peter), his
brother Andrew,
James, John, Phil-
ip, Bartholomew,
[15]Matthew, Thom-
as, James son of
Alphaeus, Simon
who was called the
Zealot, [16]Judas son
of James, and Ju-
das Iscariot, who
became a traitor.

Blessings and Woes

[17]He went down
with them and
stood on a lev-
el place. A large
crowd of his disci-
ples was there and
a great number of
people from all
over Judea, from
Jerusalem, and
from the coast-
al region around
Tyre and Sidon,
[18]who had come
to hear him and to
be healed of their
diseases. Those
troubled by impure
spirits were cured,
[19]and the people all
tried to touch him,
because power was
coming from him
and healing them

δὲ ἐπλήσθησαν ἀνοίας καὶ διελάλουν πρὸς ἀλλήλους τί ἂν
But were filled with ⌊senseless anger⌋ and began discussing with one another what ~
1254 4398 486 2779 1362 4639 253 5515 323
cj v.api.3p n.gsf cj v.iai.3p p.a r.apm r.asn pl

ποιήσαιεν τῷ Ἰησοῦ. 12 ἐγένετο δὲ ἐν ταῖς ἡμέραις ταύταις ↰
⌊they might do⌋ to Jesus. It happened *{and}* in *{the}* those days *those* that Jesus
4472 3836 2652 1181 1254 1877 3836 4047 2465 4047 1181 899
v.aao.3p d.dsm n.dsm v.ami.3s cj p.d d.dpf n.dpf r.dpf

ἐξελθεῖν αὐτὸν εἰς τὸ ὄρος προσεύξασθαι, καὶ ⌊ἦν
went out *Jesus* to the mountain to pray, and spent the whole night
2002 899 1650 3836 4001 4667 2779 1639
f.aa r.asm.3 p.a d.asn n.asn f.am cj v.iai.3s

διανυκτερεύων⌋ ἐν τῇ προσευχῇ τοῦ θεοῦ. 13 καὶ ὅτε ἐγένετο ἡμέρα,
in *{the}* prayer to God. *{and}* When day came, *day*
1381 1877 3836 4666 3836 2536 2779 4021 2465 1181 2465
pt.pa.nsm p.d d.dsf n.dsf d.gsm n.gsm cj cj v.ami.3s n.nsf

προσεφώνησεν τοὺς μαθητὰς αὐτοῦ, καὶ ἐκλεξάμενος ἀπ᾽ αὐτῶν δώδεκα, οὓς
he gathered *{the}* his disciples *his* and chose from them twelve, whom
4715 3836 899 3412 899 2779 1721 608 899 1557 4005
v.aai.3s d.apm n.apm r.gsm.3 cj pt.am.nsm p.g r.gpm.3 a.apm r.apm

καὶ ἀποστόλους ὠνόμασεν· 14 Σίμωνα ὃν καὶ ὠνόμασεν Πέτρον, καὶ
{also} he called apostles: *he called* Simon (whom *{also}* he called Peter), and
2779 3951 3951 693 3951 4981 4005 2779 3951 4377 2779
adv n.apm v.aai.3s n.asm r.asm adv v.aai.3s n.asm cj

Ἀνδρέαν τὸν ἀδελφὸν αὐτοῦ, καὶ Ἰάκωβον καὶ Ἰωάννην καὶ Φίλιππον καὶ
Andrew *{the}* his brother, *his* and James, and John, and Philip, and
436 3836 899 81 899 2779 2610 2779 2722 2779 5805 2779
n.asm d.asm n.asm r.gsm.3 cj n.asm cj n.asm cj n.asm cj

Βαρθολομαῖον 15 καὶ Μαθθαῖον καὶ Θωμᾶν καὶ Ἰάκωβον Ἁλφαίου καὶ Σίμωνα
Bartholomew, and Matthew, and Thomas, and James son of Alphaeus, and Simon
978 2779 3414 2779 2605 2779 2610 271 2779 4981
n.asm cj n.asm cj n.asm cj n.asm n.gsm cj n.asm

τὸν καλούμενον ζηλωτὴν 16 καὶ Ἰούδαν Ἰακώβου καὶ Ἰούδαν Ἰσκαριώθ, ὃς
who was called a Zealot, and Judas son of James, and Judas Iscariot, who
3836 2813 2421 2779 2683 2610 2779 2683 2696 4005
d.asm pt.pp.asm n.asm cj n.asm n.gsm cj n.asm n.asm r.nsm

ἐγένετο προδότης. 17 καὶ καταβὰς μετ᾽ αὐτῶν ἔστη
became a traitor. Then, coming down with them from the mountain, ⌊he took his stand⌋
1181 4595 2779 2849 3552 899 2705
v.ami.3s n.nsm cj pt.aa.nsm p.g r.gpm.3 v.aai.3s

ἐπὶ τόπου πεδινοῦ, καὶ ὄχλος πολὺς ➝ μαθητῶν αὐτοῦ,
on a level place. *level* *{and}* A large crowd *large* of his disciples *his* was there
2093 4268 5536 4268 2779 4498 4063 4498 899 3412 899
p.g n.gsm a.gsm cj n.nsm a.nsm n.gpm r.gsm.3

καὶ πλῆθος πολὺ τοῦ λαοῦ ἀπὸ πάσης τῆς Ἰουδαίας καὶ Ἰερουσαλὴμ
⌊along with⌋ a great number *great* of people from all over Judea and Jerusalem
2779 4498 4436 4498 3836 3295 608 4246 3836 2677 2779 2647
cj n.nsn a.nsn d.gsm n.gsm p.g a.gsf d.gsf n.gsf cj n.gsf

καὶ ↰ τῆς παραλίου Τύρου καὶ Σιδῶνος, 18 οἳ ἦλθον ἀκοῦσαι αὐτοῦ
and from the coastal region of Tyre and Sidon. They had come to hear him speak
2779 608 3836 4163 5602 2779 4972 4005 2262 201 899
cj d.gsf n.gsf n.gsf cj n.gsf r.npm v.aai.3p f.aa r.gsm.3

καὶ ἰαθῆναι ἀπὸ τῶν νόσων αὐτῶν· καὶ οἱ ἐνοχλούμενοι ἀπὸ
and to be healed of *{the}* their diseases; *their* and those who were troubled with unclean
2779 2615 608 3836 899 3798 899 2779 3836 1943 608 176
cj f.ap p.g d.gpf n.gpf r.gpm.3 cj d.npm pt.pp.npm p.g

πνευμάτων ἀκαθάρτων ἐθεραπεύοντο, 19 καὶ πᾶς ὁ ὄχλος ἐζήτουν ἅπτεσθαι
spirits *unclean* were healed. And all the crowd was trying to touch
4460 176 2543 2779 4246 3836 4063 2426 721
n.gpn a.gpn v.ipi.3p cj a.nsm d.nsm n.nsm v.iai.3p f.pm

αὐτοῦ, ὅτι δύναμις παρ᾽ αὐτοῦ ἐξήρχετο καὶ ἰᾶτο
him, because power was coming out from him *was coming out* and healing them
899 4022 1539 2002 2002 2002 4123 899 2002 2779 2615
r.gsm.3 cj n.nsf p.g r.gsm.3 v.imi.3s cj v.imi.3s

NASB

were filled with
rage, and discussed
together what they
might do to Jesus.

Choosing the Twelve

[12]It was at this
time that He went
off to the mountain
to pray, and He
spent the whole
night in prayer to
God. [13]And when
day came, He
called His disciples
to Him and chose
twelve of them,
whom He also
named as apostles:
[14]Simon, whom He
also named Peter,
and Andrew his
brother; and James
and John; and Phil-
ip and Bartholom-
ew; [15]and Matthew
and Thomas; James
the son of Alpha-
eus, and Simon
who was called the
Zealot; [16]Judas *the*
son of James, and
Judas Iscariot, who
became a traitor.
[17]Jesus came
down with them
and stood on a lev-
el place; and *there*
was a large crowd
of His disciples,
and a great throng
of people from all
Judea and Jerusa-
lem and the coastal
region of Tyre and
Sidon, [18]who had
come to hear Him
and to be healed of
their diseases; and
those who were
troubled with un-
clean spirits were
being cured. [19]And
all the people were
trying to touch
Him, for power
was coming from
Him and healing
them all.

NIV

all.
20 Looking at his
disciples, he said:

"Blessed are you
who are
poor,
for yours is the
kingdom of
God.
21 Blessed are you
who hunger
now,
for you will be
satisfied.
Blessed are you
who weep
now,
for you will
laugh.
22 Blessed are you
when people
hate you,
when they
exclude you
and insult
you
and reject your
name as evil,
because of
the Son of
Man.

23 "Rejoice in that
day and leap for
joy, because great
is your reward in
heaven. For that
is how their an-
cestors treated the
prophets.
24 "But woe to you
who are rich,
for you have
already
received your
comfort.
25 Woe to you who
are well fed
now,
for you will go
hungry.
Woe to you who
laugh now,
for you will
mourn and
weep.
26 Woe to you when
everyone
speaks well
of you,
for that is
how their
ancestors
treated
the false
prophets.

Love for Enemies

27 "But to you
who are listening
I say: Love your
enemies, do good
to those who hate
you, 28 bless those
who curse you,
pray for those who
mistreat

πάντας. 20 καὶ αὐτὸς ˌἐπάρας τοὺς ὀφθαλμοὺς αὐτοῦˌ εἰς τοὺς μαθητὰς
all. Then, *he* looking up at *{the}* his disciples,
4246 2779 899 2048 3836 4057 899 1650 3836 899 3412
a.apm cj r.nsm pt.aa.nsm d.apm n.apm r.gsm.3 p.a d.apm n.apm

αὐτοῦ ἔλεγεν, μακάριοι οἱ πτωχοί, ὅτι ὑμετέρα ἐστὶν ἡ βασιλεία τοῦ
his he said: "Blessed are you poor, for yours is the kingdom of
899 899 3306 3421 3836 4777 4022 5629 1639 3836 993 3836
r.gsm.3 v.iai.3s a.npm d.vpm a.vpm cj r.nsf.2 v.pai.3s d.nsf n.nsf d.gsm

θεοῦ. 21 μακάριοι οἱ πεινῶντες νῦν, ὅτι χορτασθήσεσθε. μακάριοι οἱ
God. Blessed are you who hunger now, for you will be satisfied. "Blessed are you
2536 3421 3836 4277 3814 4022 5963 3421 3836
n.gsm a.npm d.vpm pt.pa.vpm adv cj v.fpi.2p a.npm d.vpm

κλαίοντες νῦν, ὅτι γελάσετε. 22 μακάριοί ἐστε ὅταν μισήσωσιν ὑμᾶς οἱ
who weep now, for you will laugh. Blessed are you when people hate you, *{the}*
3081 3814 4022 1151 3421 1639 4020 476 3631 7007 3836
pt.pa.vpm adv cj v.fai.2p a.npm v.pai.2p cj v.aas.3p r.ap.2 d.npm

ἄνθρωποι καὶ ὅταν ἀφορίσωσιν ὑμᾶς καὶ ὀνειδίσωσιν καὶ ἐκβάλωσιν τὸ
people and when they exclude you and insult you and reject *{the}* your
476 2779 4020 928 7007 2779 3943 2779 1675 3836 7007
n.npm cj cj v.aas.3p r.ap.2 cj v.aas.3p cj v.aas.3p d.asn

ὄνομα ὑμῶν ὡς πονηρὸν ἕνεκα τοῦ υἱοῦ τοῦ ἀνθρώπου· 23 χάρητε ἐν
name *your* as evil ˌon account ofˌ the Son of Man! Rejoice in
3950 7007 6055 4505 1914 3836 5626 3836 476 5897 1877
n.asn r.gp.2 pl a.asn p.g d.gsm n.gsm d.gsm n.gsm v.apm.2p p.d

ἐκείνῃ τῇ ἡμέρᾳ καὶ σκιρτήσατε, ἰδοὺ γὰρ ὁ μισθὸς ὑμῶν πολὺς ἐν
that *{the}* day, and leap for joy, for behold, *for* *{the}* your reward *your* is great in
1697 3836 2465 2779 5015 1142 2627 1142 3836 7007 3635 7007 4498 1877
r.dsf d.dsf n.dsf cj v.aam.2p j cj d.nsm n.nsm r.gp.2 a.nsm p.d

τῷ οὐρανῷ· κατὰ τὰ αὐτὰ ↰ γὰρ ἐποίουν τοῖς
{the} heaven. For their fathers treated the prophets in the same way. *For* *treated* *the*
3836 4041 1142 899 4252 4472 3836 4737 2848 3836 899 2848 1142 4472 3836
d.dsm n.dsm p.a d.apn r.apn cj v.iai.3p d.dpm

προφήταις οἱ πατέρες αὐτῶν. 24 πλὴν οὐαὶ ὑμῖν τοῖς πλουσίοις, ὅτι
prophets *{the}* *fathers* *their* "But, woe to you who are rich, for
4737 3836 4252 899 4440 4026 7007 3836 4454 4022
n.dpm d.npm n.npm r.gpm.3 cj j r.dp.2 d.dpm a.dpm cj

ἀπέχετε τὴν παράκλησιν ὑμῶν. 25 οὐαὶ ὑμῖν, οἱ ἐμπεπλησμένοι νῦν,
ˌyou have receivedˌ *{the}* your consolation. *your* Woe to you who have had your fill now,
600 3836 7007 4155 7007 4026 7007 3836 1858 3814
v.pai.2p d.asf n.asf r.gp.2 j r.dp.2 d.vpm pt.rp.vpm adv

ὅτι πεινάσετε. οὐαί, οἱ γελῶντες νῦν, ὅτι πενθήσετε καὶ κλαύσετε.
for you will be hungry. Woe to you who laugh now, for you will mourn and weep.
4022 4277 4026 3836 1151 3814 4022 4291 2779 3081
cj v.fai.2p j d.vpm pt.pa.vpm adv cj v.fai.2p cj v.fai.2p

26 οὐαὶ ὅταν ὑμᾶς καλῶς εἴπωσιν πάντες οἱ
Woe to you when all people speak well of you, *well* *speak of* *all* *{the}*
4026 4020 4246 476 3306 2822 3306 7007 2822 3306 4246 3836
j cj r.ap.2 adv v.aas.3p a.npm d.npm

ἄνθρωποι, κατὰ τὰ αὐτὰ ↰ γὰρ ἐποίουν
people for their fathers treated the false prophets in the same way. *For* *treated*
476 1142 899 4252 4472 3836 6021 6021 2848 3836 899 2848 1142 4472
n.npm p.a d.apn r.apn cj v.iai.3p

τοῖς ψευδοπροφήταις οἱ πατέρες αὐτῶν. 27 ἀλλὰ ὑμῖν λέγω τοῖς
the *false prophets* *{the}* *fathers* *their* "But I say to you *I say* who
3836 6021 3836 4252 899 247 3306 3306 7007 3306 3836
d.dpm n.dpm d.npm n.npm r.gpm.3 cj r.dp.2 v.pai.1s d.dpm

ἀκούουσιν, ἀγαπᾶτε τοὺς ἐχθροὺς ὑμῶν, καλῶς ποιεῖτε τοῖς μισοῦσιν
are listening to me: Love *{the}* your enemies; *your* do good *do* to those who hate
201 26 3836 7007 2398 7007 4472 2822 4472 3836 3631
pt.pa.dpm v.pam.2p d.apm a.apm r.gp.2 adv v.pam.2p d.dpm pt.pa.dpm

ὑμᾶς, 28 εὐλογεῖτε τοὺς καταρωμένους ὑμᾶς, προσεύχεσθε περὶ τῶν ἐπηρεαζόντων
you, bless those who curse you; pray for those who threaten
7007 2328 3836 2933 7007 4667 4309 3836 2092
r.ap.2 v.pam.2p d.apm pt.pm.apm r.ap.2 v.pmm.2p p.g d.gpm pt.pa.gpm

NASB

The Beatitudes

20 And turning His
gaze toward His
disciples, He *began*
to say, "Blessed *are*
you *who are* poor,
for yours is the
kingdom of God.
21 Blessed *are* you
who hunger now,
for you shall be
satisfied. Blessed
are you who weep
now, for you shall
laugh. 22 Blessed are
you when men hate
you, and ostracize
you, and insult
you, and scorn
your name as evil,
for the sake of the
Son of Man. 23 Be
glad in that day
and leap *for joy,*
for behold, your
reward is great in
heaven. For in the
same way their
fathers used to treat
the prophets. 24 But
woe to you who
are rich, for you
are receiving your
comfort in full.
25 Woe to you who
are well-fed now,
for you shall be
hungry. Woe *to you*
who laugh now, for
you shall mourn
and weep. 26 Woe *to*
you when all men
speak well of you,
for their fathers
used to treat the
false prophets in
the same way.
27 "But I say to
you who hear, love
your enemies, do
good to those who
hate you, 28 bless
those who curse
you, pray for those
who mistreat you.

NIV

you. 29 If some-
one slaps you on
one cheek, turn
to them the other
also. If someone
takes your coat, do
not withhold your
shirt from them.
30 Give to everyone
who asks you, and
if anyone takes
what belongs to
you, do not de-
mand it back. 31 Do
to others as you
would have them
do to you.
32 "If you love
those who love
you, what credit is
that to you? Even
sinners love those
who love them.
33 And if you do
good to those who
are good to you,
what credit is that
to you? Even sin-
ners do that. 34 And
if you lend to those
from whom you
expect repayment,
what credit is that
to you? Even sin-
ners lend to sin-
ners, expecting to
be repaid in full.
35 But love your en-
emies, do good to
them, and lend to
them without ex-
pecting to get any-
thing back. Then
your reward will
be great, and you
will be children of
the Most High, be-
cause he is kind to
the ungrateful and
wicked. 36 Be mer-
ciful, just as your
Father is merciful.

Judging Others

37 "Do not judge,
and you will not be
judged. Do

ὑμᾶς. 29 τῷ τύπτοντί σε ἐπὶ τὴν σιαγόνα πάρεχε καὶ τὴν ἄλλην,
you. ⌞To the⌟ one who strikes you on the cheek, offer the other also; *the other*
7007 3836 5597 5148 2093 3836 4965 4218 3836 257 2779 3836 257
r.ap.2 d.dsm pt.pa.dsm r.as.2 p.a d.asf n.asf v.pam.2s adv d.asf r.asf

καὶ ἀπὸ τοῦ αἴροντός σου τὸ ἱμάτιον καὶ τὸν χιτῶνα μὴ
and from the one who takes your *{the}* coat, do not withhold even your shirt. *not*
2779 608 3836 149 5148 3836 2668 3266 3590 3266 2779 3836 5945 3590
cj p.g d.gsm pt.pa.gsm r.gs.2 d.asn n.asn adv d.asm n.asm pl

κωλύσῃς. 30 παντὶ αἰτοῦντί σε δίδου, καὶ ἀπὸ τοῦ αἴροντος τὰ
do withhold To all who ask of you, give, and from the ⌞one who takes away⌟ what
3266 4246 160 5148 1443 2779 608 3836 149 3836
v.aas.2s a.dsm pt.pa.dsm r.as.2 v.pam.2s cj p.g d.gsm pt.pa.gsm d.apn

σὰ ↱ μὴ ἀπαίτει. ← 31 καὶ καθὼς θέλετε ἵνα ποιῶσιν ὑμῖν
⌞belongs to you,⌟ do not demand it back. "And as you wish that others would do to you,
5050 555 3590 555 2779 2777 2527 2671 476 4472 7007
r.ap.2 pl v.pam.2s cj cj v.pai.2p cj v.pas.3p r.dp.2

οἱ ἄνθρωποι ποιεῖτε αὐτοῖς ὁμοίως. 32 καὶ εἰ ἀγαπᾶτε τοὺς ἀγαπῶντας ὑμᾶς,
{the} *others* do so to them. *so* And if you love those who love you,
3836 476 4472 3931 899 3931 2779 1623 26 3836 26 7007
d.npm n.npm v.pam.2p r.dpm.3 adv cj cj v.pai.2p d.apm pt.pa.apm r.ap.2

ποία ὑμῖν χάρις ἐστίν; καὶ γὰρ οἱ ἁμαρτωλοὶ τοὺς
what credit is it to you? *credit* *is it* For even *For* *{the}* sinners love those
4481 5921 1639 1639 7007 5921 1639 1142 2779 1142 3836 283 26 3836
r.nsf r.dp.2 n.nsf v.pai.3s adv cj d.npm a.npm d.apm

ἀγαπῶντας αὐτοὺς ἀγαπῶσιν. 33 καὶ[a] γὰρ[b] ἐὰν ἀγαθοποιῆτε τοὺς ἀγαθοποιοῦντας
who love them. *love* And *{for}* if you do good to those who love
26 899 26 2779 1142 1569 16 3836 16
pt.pa.apm r.apm.3 v.pai.3p adv cj cj v.pas.2p d.apm pt.pa.apm

ὑμᾶς, ποία ὑμῖν χάρις ἐστιν; καὶ οἱ ἁμαρτωλοὶ τὸ αὐτὸ
you, what credit is that to you? *credit* *is that* Even *{the}* sinners do the same.
7007 4481 5921 1639 1639 7007 5921 1639 2779 3836 283 4472 3836 899
r.ap.2 r.nsf r.dp.2 n.nsf v.pai.3s adv d.npm a.npm d.asn r.asn

ποιοῦσιν. 34 καὶ ἐὰν δανίσητε παρ᾽ ὧν ἐλπίζετε λαβεῖν, ποία
do And if you lend to those from whom you hope to receive, what credit is that
4472 2779 1569 1244 4123 4005 1827 3284 4481 5921 1639 1639
v.pai.3p cj cj v.aas.2p p.g r.gpm v.pai.2p f.aa r.nsf

ὑμῖν χάρις ἐστίν;[c] καὶ ἁμαρτωλοὶ ἁμαρτωλοῖς δανίζουσιν ἵνα ἀπολάβωσιν
to you? *credit* *is that* Even sinners lend to sinners *lend* that they may receive
7007 5921 1639 2779 283 1244 283 1244 2671 655
r.dp.2 n.nsf v.pai.3s adv a.npm a.dpm v.pai.3p cj v.aas.3p

τὰ ἴσα. 35 πλὴν ἀγαπᾶτε τοὺς ἐχθροὺς ὑμῶν καὶ ἀγαθοποιεῖτε καὶ δανίζετε
{the} in return. But love *{the}* your enemies, *your* and do good, and lend,
3836 2698 4440 26 3836 7007 2398 7007 2779 16 2779 1244
d.apn a.apn cj v.pam.2p d.apm a.apm r.gp.2 cj v.pam.2p cj v.pam.2p

↱ μηδὲν ἀπελπίζοντες· καὶ ἔσται ὁ μισθὸς ὑμῶν πολύς, καὶ
expecting nothing in return. Then your reward will be *{the}* *reward* *your* great, and
594 3594 594 2779 7007 3635 1639 3836 3635 7007 4498 2779
a.asn pt.pa.npm cj v.fmi.3s d.nsm n.nsm r.gp.2 a.nsm cj

ἔσεσθε υἱοὶ → ὑψίστου, ὅτι αὐτὸς χρηστός ἐστιν ἐπὶ τοὺς ἀχαρίστους
⌞you will be⌟ sons of the Most High, for he is kind *is* to the ungrateful
1639 5626 5736 4022 899 1639 5982 1639 2093 3836 940
v.fmi.2p n.npm a.gsm.s cj r.nsm a.nsm v.pai.3s p.a d.apm a.apm

καὶ πονηρούς. 36 γίνεσθε οἰκτίρμονες καθὼς καὶ[d] ὁ πατὴρ ὑμῶν
and evil. "Be compassionate, just as *{also}* *{the}* your Father *your* is
2779 4505 1181 3881 2777 2779 3836 7007 4252 7007 1639
cj a.apm v.pmm.2p a.npm cj adv d.nsm n.nsm r.gp.2

οἰκτίρμων ἐστίν. 37 καὶ ↱ μὴ κρίνετε, καὶ ↱ ↱ ⌞οὐ μὴ⌟ κριθῆτε· καὶ ↱
compassionate. *is* *{and}* Do not judge, and you will not be judged; *{and}* do
3881 1639 2779 3212 3590 3212 2779 3212 3212 4024 3590 3212 2779 2868
a.nsm v.pai.3s cj pl v.pam.2p cj pl pl v.aps.2p cj

NASB

29 Whoever hits you
on the cheek, offer
him the other also;
and whoever takes
away your coat,
do not withhold
your shirt from him
either. 30 Give to ev-
eryone who asks of
you, and whoever
takes away what
is yours, do not
demand it back.
31 Treat others the
same way you want
them to treat you.
32 If you love those
who love you,
what credit is *that*
to you? For even
sinners love those
who love them.
33 If you do good to
those who do good
to you, what credit
is *that* to you? For
even sinners do
the same. 34 If you
lend to those from
whom you expect
to receive, what
credit is *that* to
you? Even sinners
lend to sinners in
order to receive
back the same
amount. 35 But love
your enemies, and
do good, and lend,
expecting noth-
ing in return; and
your reward will
be great, and you
will be sons of the
Most High; for He
Himself is kind to
ungrateful and evil
men. 36 Be merciful,
just as your Father
is merciful.
37 "Do not judge,
and you will not be
judged; and do

[a] καὶ omitted by TNIV, NET.
[b] [γὰρ] UBS.
[c] [ἐστίν] UBS.
[d] [καὶ] UBS, omitted by TNIV.

NIV

not condemn,
and you will not
be condemned.
Forgive, and you
will be forgiven.
38 Give, and it will
be given to you.
A good measure,
pressed down,
shaken together
and running over,
will be poured into
your lap. For with
the measure you
use, it will be mea-
sured to you."
39 He also told
them this parable:
"Can the blind
lead the blind?
Will they not
both fall into a
pit? 40 The student
is not above the
teacher, but every-
one who is fully
trained will be like
their teacher.
41 "Why do you
look at the speck
of sawdust in your
brother's eye and
pay no attention
to the plank in
your own eye?
42 How can you say
to your brother,
'Brother, let me
take the speck out
of your eye,' when
you yourself fail
to see the plank in
your own eye? You
hypocrite, first
take the plank out
of your eye, and
then you will see
clearly to remove
the speck from
your brother's eye.

A Tree and Its Fruit

43 "No good tree
bears bad fruit,
nor does a bad tree
bear good fruit.

μὴ καταδικάζετε, καὶ ↱ ↱ ⌞οὐ μὴ⌟ καταδικασθῆτε. ἀπολύετε, καὶ
not condemn, and you will not be condemned; forgive, and
3590 2868 2779 2868 2868 4024 3590 2868 668 2779
pl v.pam.2p cj pl pl v.aps.2p v.pam.2p cj

ἀπολυθήσεσθε· 38 δίδοτε, καὶ δοθήσεται ὑμῖν· μέτρον καλὸν *good*
you will be forgiven; give, and it will be given to you — good measure,
668 1443 2779 1443 7007 2819 3586 2819
v.fpi.2p v.pam.2p cj v.fpi.3s r.dp.2 n.asn a.asn

πεπιεσμένον σεσαλευμένον ὑπερεκχυννόμενον δώσουσιν εἰς τὸν κόλπον
pressed down, shaken together, running over, will be poured into *{the}* your lap.
4390 4888 5658 1443 1650 3836 7007 3146
pt.rp.asn pt.rp.asn pt.pp.asn v.fai.3p p.a d.asm n.asm

ὑμῶν· ᾧ γὰρ μέτρῳ μετρεῖτε ἀντιμετρηθήσεται ὑμῖν.
your For ⌞by what⌟ *For* measure you measure, ⌞it will be measured in return⌟ to you."
7007 1142 4005 1142 3586 3582 520 7007
r.gp.2 r.dsn cj n.dsn v.pai.2p v.fpi.3s r.dp.2

39 εἶπεν δὲ καὶ παραβολὴν αὐτοῖς· μήτι δύναται τυφλὸς
He spoke *{and}* to them also a parable: *to them* *{not}* "Can a blind man lead a
3306 1254 899 899 2779 4130 899 3614 1538 5603 3842
v.aai.3s cj adv n.asf r.dpm.3 pl v.ppi.3s a.nsm

τυφλὸν ὁδηγεῖν; οὐχὶ ἀμφότεροι εἰς βόθυνον ἐμπεσοῦνται; 40
blind man? *lead* Won't they both fall into a ditch? *they fall* A student
5603 3842 4049 1860 317 1860 1650 1073 1860 3412
a.asm f.pa pl a.npm p.a n.asm v.fmi.3p

οὐκ ἔστιν μαθητὴς ὑπὲρ τὸν διδάσκαλον· κατηρτισμένος δὲ
is not *is* *student* above his teacher, but everyone when fully prepared *but*
1639 4024 1639 3412 5642 3836 1437 1254 4246 2936 1254
pl v.pai.3s n.nsm p.a d.asm n.asm pt.rp.nsm cj

πᾶς ἔσται ὡς ὁ διδάσκαλος αὐτοῦ. 41 τί δὲ βλέπεις τὸ κάρφος
everyone will be like *{the}* his teacher. *his* "Why *{and}* ⌞do you look at⌟ the speck
4246 1639 6055 3836 899 1437 899 5515 1254 1063 3836 2847
a.nsm v.fmi.3s pl d.nsm n.nsm r.gsm.3 r.asn cj v.pai.2s d.asn n.asn

τὸ ἐν τῷ ὀφθαλμῷ τοῦ ἀδελφοῦ σου, τὴν δὲ δοκὸν τὴν
{the} in the eye of your brother, *your* but do not notice the *but* beam *{the}*
3836 1877 3836 4057 3836 5148 81 5148 1254 2917 4024 2917 3836 1254 1512 3836
d.asn p.d d.dsm n.dsm d.gsm n.gsm r.gs.2 d.asf cj n.asf d.asf

ἐν τῷ ἰδίῳ ὀφθαλμῷ οὐ κατανοεῖς; 42 πῶς δύνασαι λέγειν τῷ ἀδελφῷ
in *{the}* ⌞your own⌟ eye? *not* *do notice* How can you say to your brother,
1877 3836 2625 4057 4024 2917 4802 1538 3306 3836 5148 81
p.d d.dsm a.dsm n.dsm pl v.pai.2s cj v.ppi.2s f.pa d.dsm n.dsm

σου, ἀδελφέ, ἄφες ἐκβάλω τὸ κάρφος τὸ ἐν τῷ ὀφθαλμῷ σου,
your 'Brother, let me take out the speck that is in *{the}* your eye,' *your* when you
5148 81 918 1675 3836 2847 3836 1877 3836 5148 4057 5148
r.gs.2 n.vsm v.aam.2s v.aas.1s d.asn n.asn d.asn p.d d.dsm n.dsm r.gs.2

αὐτὸς τὴν ἐν τῷ ὀφθαλμῷ σου δοκὸν οὐ βλέπων;
yourself don't see the log that is in *{the}* your own eye? *your own* *log* *dont* *see*
899 4024 1063 3836 1512 1877 3836 5148 5148 4057 5148 1512 4024 1063
r.nsm d.asf p.d d.dsm n.dsm r.gs.2 n.asf pl pt.pa.nsm

ὑποκριτά, ἔκβαλε πρῶτον τὴν δοκὸν ἐκ τοῦ ὀφθαλμοῦ σου, καὶ
You hypocrite! First take *First* the log out of your own eye, *your own* and
5695 4754 1675 4754 3836 1512 1666 3836 5148 5148 4057 5148 2779
n.vsm v.aam.2s adv d.asf n.asf p.g d.gsm n.gsm r.gs.2 cj

τότε διαβλέψεις τὸ κάρφος τὸ ἐν τῷ ὀφθαλμῷ
then ⌞you will see clearly⌟ to take out the speck that is in your brother's *{the}* eye.
5538 1332 1675 1675 1675 3836 2847 3836 1877 5148 81 3836 4057
adv v.fai.2s d.asn n.asn d.asn p.d d.dsm n.dsm

τοῦ ἀδελφοῦ σου ἐκβαλεῖν. 43 οὐ γάρ ἐστιν δένδρον καλὸν
{the} *brother's* *your* *to take out* "For it is not *For* *it is* a good tree *good*
3836 81 5148 1675 1142 1639 1639 4024 1142 1639 2819 1285 2819
d.gsm n.gsm r.gs.2 f.aa pl cj v.pai.3s n.nsn a.nsn

ποιοῦν καρπὸν σαπρόν, οὐδὲ πάλιν δένδρον σαπρὸν ποιοῦν καρπὸν
that bears bad fruit, *bad* nor again, a bad tree *bad* that bears good fruit,
4472 4911 2843 4911 4028 4099 4911 1285 4911 4472 2819 2843
pt.pa.nsn n.asm a.asm cj adv n.nsn a.nsn pt.pa.nsn n.asm

NASB

not condemn,
and you will not
be condemned;
pardon, and you
will be pardoned.
38 Give, and it will
be given to you.
They will pour into
your lap a good
measure—pressed
down, shaken
together, *and* run-
ning over. For by
your standard of
measure it will be
measured to you in
return."
39 And He also
spoke a parable
to them: "A blind
man cannot guide
a blind man, can
he? Will they not
both fall into a pit?
40 A pupil is not
above his teacher;
but everyone, after
he has been fully
trained, will be
like his teacher.
41 Why do you look
at the speck that is
in your brother's
eye, but do not
notice the log that
is in your own
eye? 42 Or how can
you say to your
brother, 'Brother,
let me take out the
speck that is in
your eye,' when
you yourself do not
see the log that is
in your own eye?
You hypocrite, first
take the log out of
your own eye, and
then you will see
clearly to take out
the speck that is
in your brother's
eye. 43 For there is
no good tree which
produces bad fruit,
nor, on the other
hand, a bad tree
which produces
good fruit.

NIV

[44]Each tree is rec-
ognized by its own
fruit. People do
not pick figs from
thornbushes, or
grapes from bri-
ers. [45]A good man
brings good things
out of the good
stored up in his
heart, and an evil
man brings evil
things out of the
evil stored up in
his heart. For the
mouth speaks what
the heart is full of.

The Wise and Foolish Builders

[46]"Why do you
call me, 'Lord,
Lord,' and do not
do what I say?
[47]As for every-
one who comes to
me and hears my
words and puts
them into practice,
I will show you
what they are like.
[48]They are like a
man building a
house, who dug
down deep and
laid the foundation
on rock. When a
flood came, the
torrent struck that
house but could
not shake it, be-
cause it was well
built. [49]But the
one who hears my
words and does
not put them into
practice is like
a man who built
a house on the
ground without a
foundation. The
moment the torrent
struck that house,
it collapsed and its
destruction was
complete."

καλόν. 44 ἕκαστον γὰρ δένδρον ἐκ τοῦ ἰδίου καρποῦ γινώσκεται·
good for each *for* tree is known by *{the}* its own fruit. *is known*
2819 1142 1667 1142 1285 1182 1182 1666 3836 2625 2843 1182
a.asm r.nsn cj n.nsn p.g d.gsm a.gsm n.gsm v.ppi.3s

οὐ γὰρ ἐξ ἀκανθῶν συλλέγουσιν σῦκα οὐδὲ
For they do not *For* gather figs from thornbushes, *they do gather* *figs* nor do they pick
1142 5198 5198 4024 1142 5198 5192 1666 180 5198 5192 4028 5582 5582 5582
pl cj p.g n.gpf v.pai.3p n.apn cj

ἐκ βάτου σταφυλὴν τρυγῶσιν. 45 ὁ ἀγαθὸς ἄνθρωπος ἐκ τοῦ
grapes from brambles. *grapes* *do they pick* The good person ˪out of˩ the
5091 1666 1004 5091 5582 3836 19 476 1666 3836
p.g n.gsf n.asf v.pai.3p d.nsm a.nsm n.nsm p.g d.gsm

ἀγαθοῦ θησαυροῦ τῆς καρδίας προφέρει τὸ ἀγαθόν, καὶ ὁ πονηρὸς ἐκ τοῦ
good treasure of his heart produces *{the}* good, and the evil person ˪out of˩ his
19 2565 3836 2840 4734 3836 19 2779 3836 4505 1666 3836
a.gsm n.gsm d.gsf n.gsf v.pai.3s d.asn a.asn cj d.nsm a.nsm p.g d.gsm

πονηροῦ προφέρει τὸ πονηρόν· ἐκ γὰρ περισσεύματος →
evil treasure produces *{the}* evil, for ˪out of˩ *for* the abundance of the
4505 4734 3836 4505 1142 1666 1142 4354
a.gsm v.pai.3s d.asn a.asn p.g cj n.gsn

καρδίας λαλεῖ τὸ στόμα αὐτοῦ. 46 τί δέ με καλεῖτε,
heart his mouth speaks. *{the}* *mouth* *his* "Why *{and}* do you call me, *do you call*
2840 899 5125 3281 3836 5125 899 5515 1254 2813 2813 2813 1609 2813
n.gsf v.pai.3s d.nsn n.nsn r.gsm.3 r.asn cj r.as.1 v.pai.2p

κύριε κύριε, καὶ → οὐ ποιεῖτε ἃ λέγω; 47 Πᾶς ὁ ἐρχόμενος πρός με καὶ
'Lord, Lord,' and do not do what I say? Everyone who comes to me and
3261 3261 2779 4472 4024 4472 4005 3306 4246 3836 2262 4639 1609 2779
n.vsm n.vsm cj pl v.pai.2p r.apn v.pai.1s a.nsm d.nsm pt.pm.nsm p.a r.as.1 cj

ἀκούων μου τῶν λόγων καὶ ποιῶν αὐτούς, ὑποδείξω ὑμῖν τίνι ἐστὶν ὅμοιος·
hears my *{the}* words and does them — I will show you whom he is like:
201 1609 3836 3364 2779 4472 899 5683 7007 5515 1639 3927
pt.pa.nsm r.gs.1 d.gpm n.gpm cj pt.pa.nsm r.apm.3 v.fai.1s r.dp.2 r.dsm v.pai.3s a.nsm

48 ὅμοιός ἐστιν ἀνθρώπῳ οἰκοδομοῦντι οἰκίαν ὃς ἔσκαψεν καὶ
he is like *he is* a man building a house, who dug *{and}*
1639 1639 3927 1639 476 3868 3864 4005 4999 2779
a.nsm v.pai.3s n.dsm pt.pa.dsm n.asf r.nsm v.aai.3s cj

ἐβάθυνεν καὶ ἔθηκεν θεμέλιον ἐπὶ τὴν πέτραν· → πλημμύρης δὲ γενομένης
deep and laid the foundation on *{the}* bedrock; when a flood *{and}* arose,
959 2779 5502 2529 2093 3836 4376 1181 4439 1254 1181
v.aai.3s cj v.aai.3s n.asm p.a d.asf n.asf n.gsf cj pt.am.gsf

προσέρηξεν ὁ ποταμὸς τῇ οἰκίᾳ ἐκείνῃ, καὶ οὐκ ἴσχυσεν
the river broke against *the* *river* *{the}* that house *that* but could not *could*
3836 4532 4704 3836 4532 3836 1697 3864 1697 2779 2710 4024 2710
v.aai.3s d.nsm n.nsm d.dsf n.dsf r.dsf cj pl v.aai.3s

σαλεῦσαι αὐτὴν διὰ τὸ → → καλῶς οἰκοδομῆσθαι αὐτήν. 49 ὁ δὲ
shake it, because *{the}* it had been well built. *it* But the *But*
4888 899 1328 3836 899 3868 3868 2822 3868 899 1254 3836 1254
f.aa r.asf.3 p.a d.asn adv f.rp r.asf.3 d.nsm cj

ἀκούσας καὶ μὴ ποιήσας ὅμοιός ἐστιν ἀνθρώπῳ οἰκοδομήσαντι
one who hears and does not do them is like *is* a man building a
201 2779 3590 4472 1639 3927 1639 476 3868
pt.aa.nsm cj pl pt.aa.nsm a.nsm v.pai.3s n.dsm pt.aa.dsm

οἰκίαν ἐπὶ τὴν γῆν χωρὶς θεμελίου, ᾗ προσέρηξεν ὁ ποταμός,
house on the ground without a foundation; when the river burst against *the* *river* it,
3864 2093 3836 1178 6006 2529 4005 3836 4532 4704 3836 4532
n.asf p.a d.asf n.asf p.g n.gsm r.dsf v.aai.3s d.nsm n.nsm

καὶ εὐθὺς συνέπεσεν καὶ ἐγένετο τὸ ῥῆγμα τῆς οἰκίας
{and} immediately it fell, and the ruin of that house was *the* *ruin* *of* *house*
2779 2318 5229 2779 3836 4837 3836 1697 3864 1181 3836 4837 3836 3864
cj adv v.aai.3s cj v.ami.3s d.nsn n.nsn d.gsf n.gsf

ἐκείνης μέγα.
that great."
1697 3489
r.gsf a.nsn

NASB

[44]For each tree is
known by its own
fruit. For men do
not gather figs from
thorns, nor do they
pick grapes from
a briar bush. [45]The
good man out of
the good treasure
of his heart brings
forth what is good;
and the evil *man*
out of the evil *trea-
sure* brings forth
what is evil; for his
mouth speaks from
that which fills his
heart.

Builders and Foundations

[46]"Why do you
call Me, 'Lord,
Lord,' and do not
do what I say?
[47]Everyone who
comes to Me and
hears My words
and acts on them,
I will show you
whom he is like:
[48]he is like a man
building a house,
who dug deep and
laid a foundation
on the rock; and
when a flood oc-
curred, the torrent
burst against that
house and could
not shake it, be-
cause it had been
well built. [49]But
the one who has
heard and has not
acted *accordingly,*
is like a man who
built a house on
the ground without
any foundation;
and the torrent
burst against it and
immediately it col-
lapsed, and the ruin
of that house was
great."

NIV

The Faith of the Centurion

7 When Jesus
had finished
saying all this to
the people who
were listening, he
entered Caperna-
um. 2There a cen-
turion's servant,
whom his master
valued highly, was
sick and about to
die. 3The centuri-
on heard of Jesus
and sent some el-
ders of the Jews to
him, asking him
to come and heal
his servant. 4When
they came to Jesus,
they pleaded ear-
nestly with him,
"This man de-
serves to have you
do this, 5because
he loves our nation
and has built our
synagogue." 6So
Jesus went with
them.
He was not far
from the house
when the centu-
rion sent friends
to say to him:
"Lord, don't trou-
ble yourself, for
I do not deserve
to have you come
under my roof.
7That is why I did
not even consider
myself worthy to
come to you. But
say the word, and
my servant will
be healed. 8For I
myself am a man
under authority,
with soldiers un-
der me. I tell this
one, 'Go,' and he
goes; and that one,
'Come,' and

7:1 ἐπειδὴ ἐπλήρωσεν πάντα τὰ ῥήματα αὐτοῦ εἰς τὰς ἀκοὰς τοῦ
After he had finished speaking all *{the}* his sayings *his* in the ears of the
2076 4444 4246 3836 899 4839 899 1650 3836 198 3836
cj v.aai.3s a.apn d.apn n.apn r.gsm.3 p.a d.apf n.apf d.gsm

λαοῦ, ⌊εἰσῆλθεν εἰς⌋ Καφαρναούμ. 2 → ἑκατοντάρχου δέ τινος
people, he entered Capernaum. The servant of a certain centurion *{and}* *certain*
3295 1656 1650 3019 1529 5516 1672 1254 5516
n.gsm v.aai.3s p.a n.asf n.gsm cj r.gsm

δοῦλος κακῶς ἔχων ἤμελλεν τελευτᾶν, ὃς
servant who was highly valued by him was sick *was* and about to die. *who*
1529 4005 1639 1952 1952 899 899 2400 2809 2400 3516 5462 4005
n.nsm adv pt.pa.nsm v.iai.3s f.pa r.nsm

ἦν αὐτῷ ἔντιμος. 3 → ἀκούσας δὲ περὶ τοῦ Ἰησοῦ ἀπέστειλεν
was *by him* *highly valued* When the centurion heard *{and}* about *{the}* Jesus, he sent
1639 899 1952 201 1254 4309 3836 2652 690
v.iai.3s r.dsm.3 a.nsm pt.aa.nsm cj p.g d.gsm n.gsm v.aai.3s

πρὸς αὐτὸν πρεσβυτέρους τῶν Ἰουδαίων ἐρωτῶν αὐτὸν ὅπως ἐλθὼν διασώσῃ
to him elders of the Jews, asking him to come and heal
4639 899 4565 3836 2681 2263 899 3968 2262 1407
p.a r.asm.3 a.apm d.gpm a.gpm pt.pa.nsm r.asm.3 cj pt.aa.nsm v.aas.3s

τὸν δοῦλον αὐτοῦ. 4 ↱ οἱ δὲ παραγενόμενοι πρὸς τὸν Ἰησοῦν
{the} his servant. *his* And when they *And* came to *{the}* Jesus,
3836 899 1529 899 1254 4134 3836 1254 4134 4639 3836 2652
d.asm n.asm r.gsm.3 d.npm cj pt.am.npm p.a d.asm n.asm

παρεκάλουν αὐτὸν σπουδαίως λέγοντες ὅτι ἄξιός ἐστιν ᾧ
they pleaded with him earnestly, saying, ~ "He is worthy *He is* that
4151 899 5081 3306 4022 1639 1639 545 1639 4005
v.iai.3p r.asm.3 adv pt.pa.npm cj a.nsm v.pai.3s r.dsm

παρέξῃ τοῦτο· 5 ἀγαπᾷ γὰρ τὸ ἔθνος ἡμῶν καὶ τὴν
⌊you should grant⌋ this, for he loves *for* *{the}* our nation *our* and he built the
4218 4047 1142 26 1142 3836 7005 1620 7005 2779 899 3868 3836
v.fmi.2s r.asn v.pai.3s cj d.asn n.asn r.gp.1 cj d.asf

συναγωγὴν αὐτὸς ᾠκοδόμησεν ἡμῖν. 6 ὁ δὲ Ἰησοῦς ἐπορεύετο σὺν αὐτοῖς.
synagogue *he* *built* for us." *{the}* So Jesus went with them. And
5252 899 3868 7005 3836 1254 2652 4513 5250 899 1254
n.asf r.nsm v.aai.3s r.dp.1 d.nsm cj n.nsm v.imi.3s p.d r.dpm.3

ἤδη δὲ αὐτοῦ οὐ μακρὰν ἀπέχοντος ἀπὸ τῆς οἰκίας ἔπεμψεν
when *And* he was not far *was* from the house, the centurion sent
2453 1254 899 600 4024 3426 600 608 3836 3864 3836 1672 4287
adv cj r.gsm.3 pl adv pt.pa.gsm p.g d.gsf n.gsf v.aai.3s

φίλους ὁ ἑκατοντάρχης λέγων αὐτῷ, κύριε, ↱ μὴ σκύλλου,
friends, *the* *centurion* saying to him, "Lord, do not trouble yourself, for I am
5813 3836 1672 3306 899 3261 5035 3590 5035 1142 1639 1639
n.apm d.nsm n.nsm pt.pa.nsm r.dsm.3 n.vsm pl v.ppm.2s

οὐ γὰρ ἱκανός εἰμι ἵνα ὑπὸ τὴν στέγην μου εἰσέλθῃς·
not *for* worthy *I am* that you should come under *{the}* my roof. *my* *you should come*
4024 1142 2653 1639 2671 1656 1656 1656 5679 3836 1609 5094 1609 1656
pl cj a.nsm v.pai.1s cj p.a d.asf n.asf r.gs.1 v.aas.2s

7 διὸ ↱ ↱ οὐδὲ ↱ ἐμαυτὸν ἠξίωσα πρὸς σὲ ἐλθεῖν· ἀλλὰ
⌊For that reason⌋ I did not consider myself worthy to come to you. *to come* But
1475 546 546 4028 546 1831 546 2262 2262 4639 5148 2262 247
cj adv r.asm.1 v.aai.1s p.a r.as.2 f.aa cj

εἰπὲ λόγῳ, καὶ → ἰαθήτω ὁ παῖς μου. 8 καὶ γὰρ ἐγὼ
speak the word and let my servant be healed. *{the}* *servant* *my* For I too *For* *I*
3306 3364 2779 1609 4090 2615 3836 4090 1609 1142 1609 2779 1142 1609
v.aam.2s n.dsm cj v.apm.3s d.nsm n.nsm r.gs.1 adv cj r.ns.1

ἄνθρωπός εἰμι ὑπὸ ἐξουσίαν τασσόμενος ἔχων ὑπ᾽ ἐμαυτὸν
am a man *am* set under authority, *set* having soldiers under me:
1639 476 1639 5435 5679 2026 5435 2400 5132 5679 1831
n.nsm v.pai.1s p.a n.asf pt.pp.nsm pt.pa.nsm p.a r.asm.1

στρατιώτας, καὶ λέγω τούτῳ, πορεύθητι, καὶ πορεύεται, καὶ ἄλλῳ, ἔρχου, καὶ
soldiers and I say to this one, 'Go,' and he goes; and to another, 'Come,' and
5132 2779 3306 4047 4513 2779 4513 2779 257 2262 2779
n.apm cj v.pai.1s r.dsm v.apm.2s cj v.pmi.3s cj r.dsm v.pmm.2s cj

NASB

Jesus Heals a Centurion's Servant

7:1When He had
completed all His
discourse in the
hearing of the
people, He went to
Capernaum.
2And a centurion's
slave, who was
highly regarded
by him, was sick
and about to die.
3When he heard
about Jesus, he
sent some Jew-
ish elders asking
Him to come and
save the life of his
slave. 4When they
came to Jesus, they
earnestly implored
Him, saying, "He
is worthy for You
to grant this to
him; 5for he loves
our nation and it
was he who built
us our synagogue."
6Now Jesus *started*
on His way with
them; and when
He was not far
from the house,
the centurion sent
friends, saying to
Him, "Lord, do not
trouble Yourself
further, for I am
not worthy for You
to come under my
roof; 7for this rea-
son I did not even
consider myself
worthy to come to
You, but *just* say
the word, and my
servant will be
healed. 8For I also
am a man placed
under authority,
with soldiers under
me; and I say to
this one, 'Go!' and
he goes, and to an-
other, 'Come!' and

NIV

he comes. I say
to my servant,
'Do this,' and he
does it."
9 When Jesus
heard this, he was
amazed at him,
and turning to the
crowd following
him, he said, "I
tell you, I have not
found such great
faith even in Isra-
el." 10 Then the men
who had been sent
returned to the
house and found
the servant well.

Jesus Raises a Widow's Son

11 Soon afterward,
Jesus went to a
town called Nain,
and his disciples
and a large crowd
went along with
him. 12 As he ap-
proached the town
gate, a dead person
was being carried
out—the only son
of his mother, and
she was a widow.
And a large crowd
from the town was
with her. 13 When
the Lord saw her,
his heart went out
to her and he said,
"Don't cry."
14 Then he went
up and touched the
bier they were car-
rying him on, and
the bearers stood
still. He said,
"Young man, I say
to you, get up!"
15 The dead man
sat up and began
to talk, and Jesus
gave him back to
his mother.
16 They were all
filled with awe and
praised God. "A
great prophet has
appeared among
us," they said.
"God has come to
help his

ἔρχεται, καὶ τῷ δούλῳ μου, ποίησον τοῦτο, καὶ ποιεῖ. 9 → ἀκούσας
he comes; and to my servant, *my* 'Do this,' and he does it." When Jesus heard
2262 2779 3836 1609 1529 1609 4472 4047 2779 4472 2652 201
v.pmi.3s cj d.dsm n.dsm r.gs.1 v.aam.2s r.asn cj v.pai.3s pt.aa.nsm

δὲ ταῦτα ὁ Ἰησοῦς ἐθαύμασεν αὐτὸν καὶ στραφεὶς τῷ
{and} these things, *{the}* *Jesus* he admired him. *{and}* Turning ⌊to the⌋ crowd
1254 4047 3836 2652 2513 899 2779 5138 3836 4063
cj r.apn d.nsm n.nsm v.aai.3s r.asm.3 cj pt.ap.nsm d.dsm

ἀκολουθοῦντι αὐτῷ ὄχλῳ εἶπεν, λέγω ὑμῖν, οὐδὲ ἐν τῷ Ἰσραὴλ
that was following him, *crowd* he said, "I tell you, not even in *{the}* Israel have I found
199 899 4063 3306 3306 7007 4028 1877 3836 2702 2351 2351 2351
pt.pa.dsm r.dsm.3 n.dsm v.aai.3s v.pai.1s r.dp.2 adv p.d d.dsm n.dsm

τοσαύτην πίστιν εὗρον. 10 καὶ ὑποστρέψαντες εἰς τὸν οἶκον οἱ
such faith." *have I found* *{and}* Returning to the house, those
5537 4411 2351 2779 5715 1650 3836 3875 3836
r.asf n.asf v.aai.1s cj pt.aa.npm p.a d.asm n.asm d.npm

πεμφθέντες εὗρον τὸν δοῦλον ὑγιαίνοντα. 11 καὶ ἐγένετο ⌊ἐν τῷ
⌊who had been sent⌋ found the servant in good health. *{and}* It happened soon afterward
4287 2351 3836 1529 5617 2779 1181 1877 3836
pt.ap.npm v.aai.3p d.asm n.asm pt.pa.asm cj v.ami.3s p.d d.dsm

ἑξῆς⌋ ← ἐπορεύθη εἰς πόλιν καλουμένην Ναῒν καὶ
that Jesus went to a town called Nain, and his disciples and a large
2009 1181 4513 1650 4484 2813 3723 2779 899 3412 2779 4498
adv v.api.3s p.a n.asf pt.pp.asf n.asf cj

συνεπορεύοντο αὐτῷ οἱ μαθηταὶ αὐτοῦ καὶ ὄχλος πολύς. 12 ὡς δὲ
crowd went with him. *{the}* *disciples* *his* *and* *crowd* *large* As *{and}* Jesus
4063 5233 899 3836 3412 899 2779 4063 4498 6055 1254
v.imi.3p r.dsm.3 d.npm n.npm r.gsm.3 cj n.nsm a.nsm cj cj

ἤγγισεν τῇ πύλῃ τῆς πόλεως, καὶ ἰδοὺ ἐξεκομίζετο
approached the gate of the town, *{and}* ~ a man who had died ⌊was being carried out⌋
1581 3836 4783 3836 4484 2779 2627 2569 2569 2569 2569 1714
v.aai.3s d.dsf n.dsf d.gsf n.gsf cj j v.ipi.3s

τεθνηκὼς μονογενὴς υἱὸς τῇ μητρὶ αὐτοῦ καὶ αὐτὴ ἦν χήρα,
man who had died — the only son of his mother *his* *{and}* (she was a widow).
2569 3666 5626 3836 899 3613 899 2779 899 1639 5939
pt.ra.nsm a.nsm n.nsm d.dsf n.dsf r.gsm.3 cj r.nsf v.iai.3s n.nsf

καὶ ὄχλος τῆς πόλεως ἱκανὸς ἦν σὺν αὐτῇ. 13 καὶ ἰδὼν αὐτὴν ὁ
{and} A large crowd ⌊from the⌋ town *large* was with her. *{and}* Seeing her, the
2779 2653 4063 3836 4484 2653 1639 5250 899 2779 1625 899 3836
cj n.nsm d.gsf n.gsf a.nsm v.iai.3s p.d r.dsf.3 cj pt.aa.nsm r.asf.3 d.nsm

κύριος ἐσπλαγχνίσθη ἐπ' αὐτῇ καὶ εἶπεν αὐτῇ, ↱ μὴ κλαῖε. 14 καὶ ↱
Lord had compassion on her and said to her, "Do not weep." *{and}* He
3261 5072 2093 899 2779 3306 899 3081 3590 3081 2779 721
n.nsm v.api.3s p.d r.dsf.3 cj v.aai.3s r.dsf.3 pl v.pam.2s cj

προσελθὼν ἥψατο τῆς σοροῦ, οἱ δὲ βαστάζοντες ἔστησαν, καὶ εἶπεν,
went up and touched the coffin, and those *and* who carried it stopped. And he said,
4665 721 3836 5049 1254 3836 1254 1002 2705 2779 3306
pt.aa.nsm v.ami.3s d.gsf n.gsf d.npm cj pt.pa.npm v.aai.3p cj v.aai.3s

νεανίσκε, σοὶ λέγω, ἐγέρθητι. 15 καὶ ἀνεκάθισεν ὁ
"Young man, I say to you, *I say* get up!" *{and}* The dead man sat up *The*
3734 3306 3306 5148 3306 1586 2779 3836 3738 3738 361 3836
n.vsm r.ds.2 v.pai.1s v.apm.2s cj v.aai.3s d.nsm

νεκρὸς καὶ ἤρξατο λαλεῖν, καὶ ἔδωκεν αὐτὸν ← τῇ μητρὶ αὐτοῦ.
dead man and began to speak, and Jesus gave him back to his mother. *his*
3738 2779 806 3281 2779 1443 899 1443 3836 899 3613 899
a.nsm cj v.ami.3s f.pa cj v.aai.3s r.asm.3 d.dsf n.dsf r.gsm.3

16 ἔλαβεν δὲ φόβος πάντας καὶ ἐδόξαζον τὸν θεὸν λέγοντες ὅτι
Fear gripped *{and}* *Fear* them all, and they glorified *{the}* God, saying, ~ "A great
5832 3284 1254 5832 4246 2779 1519 3836 2536 3306 4022 3489
v.aai.3s cj n.nsm a.apm cj v.iai.3p d.asm n.asm pt.pa.npm cj

προφήτης μέγας ἠγέρθη ἐν ἡμῖν καὶ ὅτι ἐπεσκέψατο ὁ θεὸς τὸν
prophet *great* has arisen among us!" and, ~ "God has come to help *{the}* *God* *{the}* his
4737 3489 1586 1877 7005 2779 4022 2536 2170 3836 2536 3836 899
n.nsm a.nsm v.api.3s p.d r.dp.1 cj cj v.ami.3s d.nsm n.nsm d.asm

NASB

he comes, and
to my slave, 'Do
this!' and he does
it." 9 Now when Je-
sus heard this, He
marveled at him,
and turned and
said to the crowd
that was follow-
ing Him, "I say to
you, not even in
Israel have I found
such great faith."
10 When those who
had been sent
returned to the
house, they found
the slave in good
health.
11 Soon afterwards
He went to a city
called Nain; and
His disciples were
going along with
Him, accompanied
by a large crowd.
12 Now as He ap-
proached the gate
of the city, a dead
man was being car-
ried out, the only
son of his mother,
and she was a
widow; and a size-
able crowd from
the city was with
her. 13 When the
Lord saw her, He
felt compassion for
her, and said to her,
"Do not weep."
14 And He came
up and touched
the coffin; and the
bearers came to a
halt. And He said,
"Young man, I
say to you, arise!"
15 The dead man sat
up and began to
speak. And *Jesus*
gave him back to
his mother. 16 Fear
gripped them all,
and they *began*
glorifying God,
saying, "A great
prophet has arisen
among us!" and,
"God has visited

NIV

people." [17]This
news about Jesus
spread throughout
Judea and the sur-
rounding country.

Jesus and John the Baptist

[18]John's disciples
told him about all
these things. Call-
ing two of them,
[19]he sent them to
the Lord to ask,
"Are you the one
who is to come, or
should we expect
someone else?"
[20]When the men
came to Jesus,
they said, "John
the Baptist sent us
to you to ask, 'Are
you the one who is
to come, or should
we expect some-
one else?'"
[21]At that very
time Jesus cured
many who had
diseases, sick-
nesses and evil
spirits, and gave
sight to many who
were blind. [22]So
he replied to the
messengers, "Go
back and report
to John what you
have seen and
heard: The blind
receive sight, the
lame walk, those
who have leprosy[a]
are cleansed, the
deaf hear, the dead
are raised, and
the good news is
proclaimed to the
poor. [23]Blessed is
anyone who does
not stumble on ac-
count of me."
[24]After John's
messengers left,
Jesus began to
speak to the crowd
about John: "What
did you go out

[a] 22 The Greek word traditionally translated *leprosy* was used for various diseases affecting the skin.

λαὸν αὐτοῦ. [17] καὶ ἐξῆλθεν ὁ λόγος οὗτος ⌞ἐν ὅλῃ⌟
people!" *his* *{and}* This report about Jesus spread *{the}* *report* *This* throughout
3295 899 2779 4047 3364 4309 899 2002 3836 3364 4047 1877 3910
n.asm r.gsm.3 cj v.aai.3s d.nsm n.nsm r.nsm p.d a.dsf

τῇ Ἰουδαίᾳ περὶ αὐτοῦ καὶ πάσῃ τῇ περιχώρῳ. [18] καὶ
{the} Judea *about Jesus* and all the ⌞surrounding area.⌟ *{and}* The disciples of John
3836 2677 4309 899 2779 4246 3836 4369 2779 3836 3412 2722 2722
d.dsf n.dsf p.g r.gsm.3 cj a.dsf d.dsf a.dsf cj

ἀπήγγειλαν Ἰωάννῃ οἱ μαθηταὶ αὐτοῦ περὶ πάντων τούτων. καὶ
told *of John* *The* *disciples* him about all these things. *{and}*
550 2722 3836 3412 899 4309 4246 4047 2779
v.aai.3p n.dsm d.npm n.npm r.gsm.3 p.g a.gpn r.gpn cj

προσκαλεσάμενος ⌞δύο τινὰς⌟ τῶν μαθητῶν αὐτοῦ ὁ Ἰωάννης [19] ἔπεμψεν
Calling two of his disciples, *his* *{the}* John sent
4673 1545 5516 3836 899 3412 899 3836 2722 4287
pt.am.nsm a.apm r.apm d.gpm n.gpm r.gsm.3 d.nsm n.nsm v.aai.3s

πρὸς τὸν κύριον[a] λέγων, σὺ εἶ ὁ ἐρχόμενος ἢ
them to the Lord, saying, "Are you *Are* the ⌞one who was to come,⌟ or should we
4639 3836 3261 3306 1639 5148 1639 3836 2262 2445 4659 4659
p.a d.asm n.asm pt.pa.nsm r.ns.2 v.pai.2s d.nsm pt.pm.nsm cj

ἄλλον προσδοκῶμεν; [20] παραγενόμενοι δὲ πρὸς αὐτὸν οἱ
expect ⌞someone else?"⌟ *should we expect* The men went *{and}* to Jesus *The*
4659 257 4659 3836 467 4134 1254 4639 899 3836
r.asm v.pai.1p pt.am.npm cj p.a r.asm.3 d.npm

ἄνδρες εἶπαν, Ἰωάννης ὁ βαπτιστὴς ἀπέστειλεν ἡμᾶς πρὸς σὲ λέγων, σὺ
men and said, "John the Baptist has sent us to you to ask, 'Are you
467 3306 2722 3836 969 690 7005 4639 5148 3306 1639 5148
n.npm v.aai.3p n.nsm d.nsm n.nsm v.aai.3s r.ap.1 p.a r.as.2 pt.pa.nsm r.ns.2

εἶ ὁ ἐρχόμενος ἢ ἄλλον προσδοκῶμεν;
Are the ⌞one who is to come,⌟ or should we expect ⌞someone else?'"⌟ *should we expect*
1639 3836 2262 2445 4659 4659 4659 257 4659
v.pai.2s d.nsm pt.pm.nsm cj r.asm v.pai.1p

[21] ἐν ἐκείνῃ τῇ ὥρᾳ ἐθεράπευσεν πολλοὺς ἀπὸ νόσων καὶ μαστίγων καὶ
In that *{the}* hour he healed many people of diseases, *{and}* sicknesses and evil
1877 1697 3836 6052 2543 4498 608 3798 2779 3465 2779 4505
p.d r.dsf d.dsf n.dsf v.aai.3s a.apm p.g n.gpf cj n.gpf cj

πνευμάτων πονηρῶν καὶ → τυφλοῖς πολλοῖς ἐχαρίσατο βλέπειν.
spirits; *evil* and to many who were blind *many* ⌞he gave the ability⌟ to see.
4460 4505 2779 4498 5603 4498 5919 1063
n.gpn a.gpn cj a.dpm a.dpm v.ami.3s f.pa

[22] καὶ ἀποκριθεὶς εἶπεν αὐτοῖς, πορευθέντες ἀπαγγείλατε Ἰωάννῃ ἃ
Then he answered, saying to them, "Go and tell John what
2779 646 3306 899 4513 550 2722 4005
cj pt.ap.nsm v.aai.3s r.dpm.3 pt.ap.npm v.aam.2p n.dsm r.apn

εἴδετε καὶ ἠκούσατε· τυφλοὶ ἀναβλέπουσιν, χωλοὶ περιπατοῦσιν, λεπροὶ
⌞you have seen⌟ and heard: the blind see, the lame walk, lepers
1625 2779 201 5603 329 6000 4344 3320
v.aai.2p cj v.aai.2p a.npm v.pai.3p a.npm v.pai.3p a.npm

καθαρίζονται καὶ κωφοὶ ἀκούουσιν, νεκροὶ ἐγείρονται, πτωχοὶ
are cleansed, and the deaf hear, the dead are raised, the poor
2751 2779 3273 201 3738 1586 4777
v.ppi.3p cj a.npm v.pai.3p a.npm v.ppi.3p a.npm

εὐαγγελίζονται· [23] καὶ μακάριός ἐστιν ⌞ὃς ἐὰν⌟ ↱ μὴ
have good news brought to them. And blessed is whoever is not
2294 2779 3421 1639 4005 1569 4997 3590
v.ppi.3p cj a.nsm v.pai.3s r.nsm pl pl

σκανδαλισθῇ ἐν ἐμοί. [24] → ἀπελθόντων δὲ τῶν ἀγγέλων
offended by me." When John's messengers left, *{and}* *{the}* *messengers*
4997 1877 1609 2722 34 599 1254 3836 34
v.aps.3s p.d r.ds.1 pt.aa.gpm cj d.gpm n.gpm

Ἰωάννου ἤρξατο λέγειν πρὸς τοὺς ὄχλους περὶ Ἰωάννου, τί ἐξήλθατε
John's Jesus began to speak to the crowds about John: "What ⌞did you go out⌟
2722 806 3306 4639 3836 4063 4309 2722 5515 2002
n.gsm v.ami.3s f.pa p.a d.apm n.apm p.g n.gsm r.asn v.aai.2p

[a] κύριον UBS, TNIV. Ἰησοῦν NET.

NASB

His people!" [17]This
report concerning
Him went out all
over Judea and in
all the surrounding
district.

A Deputation from John

[18]The disciples of
John reported to
him about all these
things. [19]Sum-
moning two of his
disciples, John sent
them to the Lord,
saying, "Are You
the Expected One,
or do we look for
someone else?"
[20]When the men
came to Him, they
said, "John the
Baptist has sent us
to You, to ask, 'Are
You the Expected
One, or do we
look for someone
else?'" [21]At that
very time He cured
many *people* of
diseases and afflic-
tions and evil spir-
its; and He gave
sight to many *who*
were blind. [22]And
He answered and
said to them, "Go
and report to John
what you have
seen and heard:
the BLIND RECEIVE
SIGHT, *the* lame
walk, *the* lepers
are cleansed, and
the deaf hear, *the*
dead are raised up,
the POOR HAVE THE
GOSPEL PREACHED
TO THEM. [23]Blessed
is he who does
not take offense at
Me."
[24]When the mes-
sengers of John
had left, He began
to speak to the
crowds about John,
"What did you go

NIV

into the wilder-
ness to see? A
reed swayed by
the wind? 25 If not,
what did you go
out to see? A man
dressed in fine
clothes? No, those
who wear expen-
sive clothes and
indulge in luxury
are in palaces.
26 But what did you
go out to see? A
prophet? Yes, I tell
you, and more than
a prophet. 27 This
is the one about
whom it is written:

"'I will send my
messenger
ahead of you,
who will
prepare your
way before
you.'[a]

28 I tell you, among
those born of
women there is no
one greater than
John; yet the one
who is least in the
kingdom of God is
greater than he."
29 (All the peo-
ple, even the tax
collectors, when
they heard Jesus'
words, acknowl-
edged that God's
way was right,
because they had
been baptized by
John. 30 But the
Pharisees and the
experts in the law
rejected God's
purpose for them-
selves, because
they had not been
baptized by John.)
31 Jesus went on
to say, "To what,
then, can I com-
pare the people of
this generation?
What are they
like? 32 They are
like children sit-
ting in the market-
place

[a] 27 Mal. 3:1

εἰς τὴν ἔρημον θεάσασθαι; κάλαμον ὑπὸ ἀνέμου σαλευόμενον;
into the wilderness to look at? A reed being shaken by the wind? *being shaken*
1650 3836 2245 2517 2812 4888 4888 5679 449 4888
p.a d.asf n.asf f.am n.asm p.g n.gsm pt.pp.asm

25 ἀλλὰ τί ἐξήλθατε ἰδεῖν; ἄνθρωπον ἐν μαλακοῖς ἱματίοις
But what ⌞did you go out⌟ to see? A man dressed in luxurious clothing?
247 5515 2002 1625 476 314 1877 3434 2668
cj r.asn v.aai.2p f.aa n.asm p.d a.dpn n.dpn

ἠμφιεσμένον; ἰδοὺ οἱ ἐν ἱματισμῷ ἐνδόξῳ καὶ τρυφῇ
dressed ~ Those who wear expensive clothing *expensive* and live in luxury
314 2627 3836 1877 1902 2669 1902 2779 5639 5588
pt.rp.asm j d.npm p.d n.dsm a.dsm cj n.dsf

ὑπάρχοντες ἐν τοῖς βασιλείοις εἰσίν. 26 ἀλλὰ τί ἐξήλθατε ἰδεῖν;
live are found in *{the}* royal palaces. *are* But what ⌞did you go out⌟ to see? A
5639 1639 1877 3836 994 1639 247 5515 2002 1625
pt.pa.npm p.d d.dpn a.dpn v.pai.3p cj r.asn v.aai.2p f.aa

προφήτην; ναὶ λέγω ὑμῖν, καὶ περισσότερον → προφήτου. 27 οὗτός
prophet? Yes, I tell you, and one who is more than a prophet. This
4737 3721 3306 7007 2779 4358 4737 4047
n.asm pl v.pai.1s r.dp.2 cj adv.c n.gsm r.nsm

ἐστιν περὶ οὗ γέγραπται, ἰδοὺ ἀποστέλλω τὸν ἄγγελόν μου ⌞πρὸ
is he of whom it is written, 'Behold, I am sending *{the}* my messenger *my* ahead of
1639 4309 4005 1211 2627 690 3836 1609 34 1609 4574
v.pai.3s p.g r.gsm v.rpi.3s j v.pai.1s d.asm n.asm r.gs.1 p.g

προσώπου⌟ σου, ὃς κατασκευάσει τὴν ὁδόν σου ἔμπροσθέν σου. 28 λέγω ὑμῖν,
you, who will prepare *{the}* your way *your* before you.' I tell you,
4725 5148 4005 2941 3836 5148 3847 5148 1869 5148 3306 7007
n.gsn r.gs.2 r.nsm v.fai.3s d.asf n.asf r.gs.2 p.g r.gs.2 v.pai.1s r.dp.2

μείζων ἐν γεννητοῖς γυναικῶν
among those born of women there is no one greater *among those born* *of women*
1877 1168 1168 1222 1222 1639 1639 4029 4029 3489 1877 1168 1222
a.nsm.c p.d n.dpm n.gpf

Ἰωάννου οὐδείς ἐστιν· ὁ δὲ μικρότερος ἐν τῇ βασιλείᾳ τοῦ θεοῦ
than John. *no one* *there is* Yet the *Yet* one who is least in the kingdom of God is
2722 4029 1639 1254 3836 1254 3625 1877 3836 993 3836 2536 1639
n.gsm a.nsm v.pai.3s d.nsm cj a.nsm.c p.d d.dsf n.dsf d.gsm n.gsm

μείζων αὐτοῦ ἐστιν. 29 καὶ ↱ πᾶς ὁ λαὸς
greater than he." *is* *{and}* When all the people including the tax collectors (those
3489 899 1639 2779 201 4246 3836 3295 2779 3836 5467 5467 966
a.nsm.c r.gsm.3 v.pai.3s cj a.nsm d.nsm n.nsm

ἀκούσας καὶ οἱ τελῶναι
who had been baptized with the baptism of John) heard this, *including* *the* *tax collectors*
966 966 966 966 3836 967 2722 2722 201 2779 3836 5467
pt.aa.nsm cj d.npm n.npm

ἐδικαίωσαν τὸν θεὸν ↰ βαπτισθέντες τὸ βάπτισμα Ἰωάννου· 30
they declared *{the}* God just; *those who had been baptized* *the* *baptism* *of John* but
1467 3836 2536 1467 966 3836 967 2722 1254
v.aai.3p d.asm n.asm pt.ap.npm d.asn n.asn n.gsm

οἱ δὲ Φαρισαῖοι καὶ οἱ νομικοὶ
the *but* Pharisees and the lawyers (those who had not been baptized by John) rejected
3836 1254 5757 2779 3836 3788 966 966 966 3590 966 966 5679 899 119
d.npm cj n.npm cj d.npm n.npm

τὴν βουλὴν τοῦ θεοῦ ἠθέτησαν εἰς ἑαυτοὺς μὴ βαπτισθέντες ὑπ' αὐτοῦ.
the purpose of God *rejected* for themselves. *not* *those who had been baptized* *by* *John*
3836 1087 3836 2536 119 1650 1571 3590 966 5679 899
d.asf n.asf d.gsm n.gsm v.aai.3p p.a r.apm.3 pl pt.ap.npm p.g r.gsm.3

31 τίνι οὖν ὁμοιώσω τοὺς ἀνθρώπους τῆς γενεᾶς ταύτης καὶ τίνι
⌞"To what⌟ then shall I compare the people of this generation? *this* *{and}* What
5515 4036 3929 3836 476 3836 4047 1155 4047 2779 5515
r.dsn cj v.fai.1s d.apm n.apm d.gsf n.gsf r.gsf cj r.dsn

εἰσὶν ὅμοιοι; 32 ὅμοιοί εἰσιν παιδίοις τοῖς ἐν ἀγορᾷ
are they like? They are like *They are* children *{the}* sitting in the marketplace
1639 3927 1639 1639 3927 1639 4086 3836 2764 1877 59
v.pai.3p a.npm a.npm v.pai.3p n.dpn d.dpn p.d n.dsf

NASB

out into the wil-
derness to see? A
reed shaken by the
wind? 25 But what
did you go out to
see? A man dressed
in soft clothing?
Those who are
splendidly clothed
and live in luxury
are *found* in royal
palaces! 26 But what
did you go out to
see? A prophet?
Yes, I say to you,
and one who is
more than a proph-
et. 27 This is the one
about whom it is
written,

'Behold, I send
My messen-
ger ahead of
You,
Who will
prepare Your
way before
You.'

28 I say to you,
among those born
of women there
is no one greater
than John; yet he
who is least in the
kingdom of God is
greater than he."
29 When all the peo-
ple and the tax col-
lectors heard *this,*
they acknowledged
God's justice, hav-
ing been baptized
with the baptism
of John. 30 But the
Pharisees and the
[a]lawyers rejected
God's purpose for
themselves, not
having been bap-
tized by John.
31 "To what then
shall I compare the
men of this genera-
tion, and what are
they like? 32 They
are like children
who sit in the mar-
ket place and

[a] I.e. experts in the Mosaic Law

NIV

and calling out to
each other:

"'We played the
pipe for you,
and you did not
dance;
we sang a dirge,
and you did not
cry.'

33 For John the
Baptist came nei-
ther eating bread
nor drinking wine,
and you say, 'He
has a demon.'
34 The Son of Man
came eating and
drinking, and
you say, 'Here is
a glutton and a
drunkard, a friend
of tax collectors
and sinners.' 35 But
wisdom is proved
right by all her
children."

Jesus Anointed by a Sinful Woman

36 When one of
the Pharisees in-
vited Jesus to have
dinner with him,
he went to the
Pharisee's house
and reclined at the
table. 37 A woman
in that town who
lived a sinful life
learned that Jesus
was eating at the
Pharisee's house,
so she came there
with an alabaster
jar of perfume.
38 As she stood
behind him at his
feet weeping, she
began to wet his
feet with her tears.
Then she wiped
them with her hair,
kissed them and
poured perfume on
them.
39 When the Phar-
isee who had invit-
ed him saw this, he
said to himself, "If

καθημένοις καὶ προσφωνοῦσιν ἀλλήλοις ἃ λέγει, ηὐλήσαμεν ὑμῖν
sitting and calling to one another, they are saying, ⌊'We played the flute⌋ for you,
2764 2779 4715 253 4005 3306 884 7007
pt.pm.dpn cj pt.pa.dpn r.dpn r.npn v.pai.3s v.aai.1p r.dp.2

καὶ ↱ ↱ οὐκ ὠρχήσασθε, ἐθρηνήσαμεν καὶ ↱ ↱ οὐκ ἐκλαύσατε.
but you did not dance; we wailed in mourning, but you did not weep.'
2779 4004 4004 4024 4004 2577 2779 3081 3081 4024 3081
cj pl v.ami.2p v.aai.1p cj pl v.aai.2p

33 ἐλήλυθεν γὰρ Ἰωάννης ὁ βαπτιστὴς μὴ ἐσθίων ἄρτον μήτε
For John the Baptist has come *For John the Baptist* neither eating bread nor
1142 2722 3836 969 2262 1142 2722 3836 969 3590 2266 788 3612
v.rai.3s cj n.nsm d.nsm n.nsm pl pt.pa.nsm n.asm cj

πίνων οἶνον, καὶ λέγετε, δαιμόνιον ἔχει. 34 ἐλήλυθεν
drinking wine, and you say, 'He has a demon.' *He has* The Son of Man has come
4403 3885 2779 3306 2400 2400 1228 2400 3836 5626 3836 476 2262
pt.pa.nsm n.asm cj v.pai.2p n.asn v.pai.3s v.rai.3s

ὁ υἱὸς τοῦ ἀνθρώπου ἐσθίων καὶ πίνων, καὶ λέγετε, ἰδοὺ ἄνθρωπος
The Son of Man both eating and drinking, and you say, 'Look! A man, a
3836 5626 3836 476 2266 2779 4403 2779 3306 2627 476
d.nsm n.nsm d.gsm n.gsm pt.pa.nsm cj pt.pa.nsm cj v.pai.2p j n.nsm

φάγος καὶ οἰνοπότης, φίλος τελωνῶν καὶ ἁμαρτωλῶν. 35 καὶ
glutton and a drunkard, a friend of tax collectors and sinners!' Nevertheless, wisdom
5741 2779 3884 5813 5467 2779 283 2779 5053
n.nsm cj n.nsm n.nsm n.gpm cj a.gpm cj

ἐδικαιώθη ἡ σοφία ἀπὸ πάντων τῶν τέκνων αὐτῆς. 36
is proved right *{the} wisdom* by all *{the}* her children." *her* Now one of the
1467 3836 5053 608 4246 3836 899 5451 899 1254 5516 3836 3836
v.api.3s d.nsf n.nsf p.g a.gpn d.gpn n.gpn r.gsf.3

ἠρώτα δέ τις αὐτὸν τῶν Φαρισαίων ἵνα φάγῃ μετʼ αὐτοῦ, καὶ ↱
Pharisees asked *Now one* him *of the Pharisees* to eat with him, so he
5757 2263 1254 5516 899 3836 5757 2671 2266 3552 899 2779 2884
v.iai.3s cj r.nsm r.asm.3 d.gpm n.gpm cj v.aas.3s p.g r.gsm.3 cj

εἰσελθὼν εἰς τὸν οἶκον τοῦ Φαρισαίου κατεκλίθη. 37 καὶ ἰδοὺ
went into the house of the Pharisee and ⌊took his place at table.⌋ Now ~ there
1656 1650 3836 3875 3836 5757 2884 2779 2627 1639
pt.aa.nsm p.a d.asm n.asm d.gsm n.gsm v.api.3s cj j

γυνὴ ἥτις ἦν ἐν τῇ πόλει → ἁμαρτωλός, καὶ ἐπιγνοῦσα ὅτι
was a woman known *there was* in the city as a sinner, and when she learned that
1639 1222 4015 1639 1877 3836 4484 283 2779 2105 4022
n.nsf r.nsf v.iai.3s p.d d.dsf n.dsf a.nsf cj pt.aa.nsf cj

κατάκειται ἐν τῇ οἰκίᾳ τοῦ Φαρισαίου, κομίσασα ἀλάβαστρον
Jesus ⌊was reclining at table⌋ in the house of the Pharisee, she brought an alabaster jar
2879 1877 3836 3864 3836 5757 3152 223
v.pmi.3s p.d d.dsf n.dsf d.gsm n.gsm pt.aa.nsf n.asn

μύρου 38 καὶ στᾶσα ὀπίσω παρὰ τοὺς πόδας αὐτοῦ κλαίουσα
of perfume, and standing behind him at *{the}* his feet, *his* weeping, she began
3693 2779 2705 3958 4123 3836 899 4546 899 3081 806 806
n.gsn cj pt.aa.nsf adv p.a d.apm n.apm r.gsm.3 pt.pa.nsf

τοῖς δάκρυσιν ἤρξατο βρέχειν τοὺς πόδας αὐτοῦ καὶ
to bathe his feet ⌊with her⌋ tears. *she began to bathe {the} feet his {and}* She kept
1101 1101 899 4546 3836 1232 806 1101 3836 4546 899 2779 1726 1726
d.dpn n.dpn v.ami.3s f.pa d.apm n.apm r.gsm.3 cj

ταῖς θριξὶν τῆς κεφαλῆς αὐτῆς ἐξέμασσεν καὶ κατεφίλει τοὺς
wiping his feet ⌊with the⌋ hair of her head, *her She kept wiping* and kissing them
1726 899 4546 3836 2582 3836 899 3051 899 1726 2779 2968 3836
d.dpf n.dpf d.gsf n.gsf r.gsf.3 v.iai.3s cj v.iai.3s d.apm

πόδας αὐτοῦ καὶ ἤλειφεν τῷ μύρῳ. ↰ 39 →
feet his and pouring the perfume on them. When the Pharisee who had invited him
4546 899 2779 230 3836 3693 230 3836 5757 3836 2813 2813 899
n.apm r.gsm.3 cj v.iai.3s d.dsn n.dsn

ἰδὼν δὲ ὁ Φαρισαῖος ὁ καλέσας αὐτὸν εἶπεν ἐν ἑαυτῷ λέγων,
saw *{and}* this, *the Pharisee who had invited him* he said to himself, *{saying}* "If
1625 1254 3836 5757 3836 2813 899 3306 1877 1571 3306 1623
pt.aa.nsm cj d.nsm n.nsm d.nsm pt.aa.nsm r.asm.3 v.aai.3s p.d r.dsm.3 pt.pa.nsm

NASB

call to one another,
and they say, 'We
played the flute for
you, and you did
not dance; we sang
a dirge, and you
did not weep.' 33 For
John the Baptist
has come eating no
bread and drinking
no wine, and you
say, 'He has a de-
mon!' 34 The Son of
Man has come eat-
ing and drinking,
and you say, 'Be-
hold, a gluttonous
man and a drunk-
ard, a friend of tax
collectors and sin-
ners!' 35 Yet wisdom
is vindicated by all
her children."
36 Now one of
the Pharisees was
requesting Him
to dine with him,
and He entered the
Pharisee's house
and reclined *at the*
table. 37 And there
was a woman in
the city who was a
sinner; and when
she learned that He
was reclining *at the*
table in the Phari-
see's house, she
brought an alabas-
ter vial of perfume,
38 and standing
behind *Him* at His
feet, weeping, she
began to wet His
feet with her tears,
and kept wiping
them with the hair
of her head, and
kissing His feet
and anointing them
with the perfume.
39 Now when the
Pharisee who had
invited Him saw
this, he said to
himself, "If this

NIV

this man were a
prophet, he would
know who is
touching him and
what kind of wom-
an she is—that
she is a sinner."
40 Jesus answered
him, "Simon, I
have something to
tell you."
"Tell me, teach-
er," he said.
41 "Two people
owed money to
a certain money-
lender. One owed
him five hundred
denarii,[a] and the
other fifty. 42 Nei-
ther of them had
the money to pay
him back, so he
forgave the debts
of both. Now
which of them will
love him more?"
43 Simon replied,
"I suppose the one
who had the bigger
debt forgiven."
"You have judged
correctly," Jesus
said.
44 Then he turned
toward the wom-
an and said to
Simon, "Do you
see this woman?
I came into your
house. You did not
give me any water
for my feet, but
she wet my feet
with her tears and
wiped them with
her hair. 45 You did
not give me a kiss,
but this woman,
from the time I
entered, has not
stopped kissing
my feet. 46 You did
not put oil on

[a] 41 A denarius was the usual daily wage of a day laborer (see Matt. 20:2)

οὗτος εἰ ἦν προφήτης, → ἐγίνωσκεν ἂν τίς καὶ ποταπὴ ἡ
this man If were a prophet, he would know would who and ⌊what kind of⌋ {the}
4047 1623 1639 4737 323 1182 323 5515 2779 4534 3836
r.nsm cj v.iai.3s n.nsm v.iai.3s pl r.nsf cj r.nsf d.nsf

γυνὴ ἥτις ἅπτεται αὐτοῦ, ὅτι ἁμαρτωλός ἐστιν. 40 καὶ
woman this is who is touching him — that she is a sinner." she is And Jesus,
1222 4015 721 899 4022 1639 1639 283 1639 2779 2652
n.nsf r.nsf v.pmi.3s r.gsm.3 cj a.nsf v.pai.3s cj

ἀποκριθεὶς ὁ Ἰησοῦς εἶπεν πρὸς αὐτόν, Σίμων, ἔχω σοί
answering, {the} Jesus said to him, "Simon, I have something to say to you."
646 3836 2652 3306 4639 899 4981 2400 5516 3306 3306 5148
pt.ap.nsm d.nsm n.nsm v.aai.3s p.a r.asm.3 n.vsm v.pai.1s r.ds.2

τι εἰπεῖν. ὁ δέ, διδάσκαλε, εἰπέ, φησίν. 41 δύο
something to say And he And said, "Teacher, say it." said "There were two
5516 3306 1254 3836 1254 5774 1437 3306 5774 1639 1639 1545
r.asn f.aa d.nsm cj n.vsm v.aam.2s v.pai.3s a.npm

χρεοφειλέται ἦσαν → δανιστῇ τινι· ὁ εἷς ὤφειλεν
debtors There were to a certain moneylender. certain The one owed five hundred
5971 1639 5516 1250 5516 3836 1651 4053 4296 4296
n.npm v.iai.3p n.dsm r.dsm d.nsm a.nsm v.iai.3s

δηνάρια πεντακόσια, ὁ δὲ ἕτερος πεντήκοντα. 42 ↱ ⌊μὴ
denarii, five hundred and the and other fifty. When they were unable
1324 4296 1254 3836 1254 2283 4299 2400 899 3590
n.apn a.apn d.nsm pl r.nsm a.apn pl

ἐχόντων⌋ αὐτῶν ἀποδοῦναι ἀμφοτέροις ἐχαρίσατο.
they to pay, he cancelled the debt of both. he cancelled the debt Now
2400 899 625 5919 5919 5919 5919 317 5919 4036
pt.pa.gpm r.gpm.3 f.aa a.dpm v.ami.3s

τίς οὖν αὐτῶν πλεῖον ἀγαπήσει αὐτόν; 43 ἀποκριθεὶς Σίμων
which Now of them will love him more?" will love him Simon answered, Simon
5515 4036 899 26 26 899 4498 26 899 4981 646 4981
r.nsm cj r.gpm.3 adv.c v.fai.3s r.asm.3 pt.ap.nsm n.nsm

εἶπεν, ὑπολαμβάνω ὅτι ᾧ τὸ πλεῖον
saying, "I suppose {that} it would be ⌊the one for whom⌋ he cancelled the greater debt."
3306 5696 4022 4005 5919 5919 3836 4498 5919
v.aai.3s v.pai.1s cj r.dsm d.asn a.asn.c

ἐχαρίσατο. ὁ δὲ εἶπεν αὐτῷ, ὀρθῶς ἔκρινας.
he cancelled debt And he And said to him, "You have judged correctly." You have judged
5919 1254 3836 1254 3306 899 3212 3212 3212 3987 3212
v.ami.3s d.nsm cj v.aai.3s r.dsm.3 adv v.aai.2s

44 καὶ στραφεὶς πρὸς τὴν γυναῖκα τῷ Σίμωνι ἔφη, βλέπεις ταύτην τὴν
Then turning toward the woman, he said to Simon, he said "You see this {the}
2779 5138 4639 3836 1222 5774 5774 3836 4981 5774 1063 4047 3836
cj pt.ap.nsm p.a d.asf n.asf d.dsm n.dsm v.iai.3s v.pai.2s r.asf d.asf

γυναῖκα; εἰσῆλθόν σου εἰς τὴν οἰκίαν, ὕδωρ μοι ἐπὶ
woman? I came into your into {the} house; you did not provide water for my for
1222 1656 1650 5148 1650 3836 3864 1443 1443 4024 1443 5623 2093 1609 2093
n.asf v.aai.1s r.gs.2 p.a d.asf n.asf n.asn r.ds.1 p.a

πόδας οὐκ ἔδωκας· αὕτη δὲ τοῖς δάκρυσιν ἔβρεξέν
feet, not you did provide but she but has bathed my feet ⌊with her⌋ tears has bathed
4546 4024 1443 1254 4047 1254 1101 1101 1609 4546 3836 1232 1101
n.apm pl v.aai.2s r.nsf cj d.dpn n.dpn v.aai.3s

μου τοὺς πόδας καὶ ταῖς θριξὶν αὐτῆς ἐξέμαξεν. 45
my {the} feet and wiped them with her hair. her wiped You did not give
1609 3836 4546 2779 1726 3836 899 2582 899 1726 1443 1443 4024 1443
r.gs.1 d.apm n.apm cj d.dpf n.dpf r.gsf.3 v.aai.3s

φίλημά μοι οὐκ ἔδωκας· αὕτη δὲ ἀφʼ ἧς
me a kiss, me not You did give but from the time I came in she but from time
1609 5799 1609 4024 1443 1254 608 4005 1656 1656 1656 4047 1254 608 4005
n.asn r.ds.1 pl v.aai.2s r.nsf cj p.g r.gsf

εἰσῆλθον ↱ οὐ διέλιπεν καταφιλοῦσά μου τοὺς πόδας. 46
I came in has not stopped kissing my {the} feet. You did not anoint my
1656 1364 4024 1364 2968 1609 3836 4546 230 230 4024 230 1609
v.aai.1s pl v.aai.3s pt.pa.nsf r.gs.1 d.apm n.apm

NASB

man were a proph-
et He would know
who and what
sort of person this
woman is who is
touching Him, that
she is a sinner."

Parable of Two Debtors

40 And Jesus
answered him,
"Simon, I have
something to say
to you." And he
replied, "Say it,
Teacher." 41 "A
moneylender had
two debtors: one
owed five hundred
[a]denarii, and the
other fifty. 42 When
they were unable to
repay, he gracious-
ly forgave them
both. So which of
them will love him
more?" 43 Simon
answered and said,
"I suppose the one
whom he forgave
more." And He
said to him, "You
have judged cor-
rectly." 44 Turning
toward the woman,
He said to Simon,
"Do you see this
woman? I entered
your house; you
gave Me no water
for My feet, but
she has wet My
feet with her tears
and wiped them
with her hair. 45 You
gave Me no kiss;
but she, since the
time I came in, has
not ceased to kiss
My feet. 46 You did
not anoint My

[a] The denarius was equivalent to a day's wages

NIV

my head, but she
has poured per-
fume on my feet.
47 Therefore, I tell
you, her many sins
have been forgiv-
en—as her great
love has shown.
But whoever has
been forgiven little
loves little."
48 Then Jesus said
to her, "Your sins
are forgiven."
49 The other
guests began to
say among them-
selves, "Who is
this who even for-
gives sins?"
50 Jesus said to
the woman, "Your
faith has saved
you; go in peace."

The Parable of the Sower

8 After this,
Jesus traveled
about from one
town and village to
another, proclaim-
ing the good news
of the kingdom of
God. The Twelve
were with him,
2 and also some
women who had
been cured of evil
spirits and diseas-
es: Mary (called
Magdalene) from
whom seven de-
mons had come
out; 3 Joanna the
wife of Chuza,
the manager of
Herod's house-
hold; Susanna;
and many others.
These women were
helping to support
them out of their
own means.
4 While a large
crowd was gath-
ering and people
were

ἐλαίῳ τὴν κεφαλήν μου οὐκ ἤλειψας· αὕτη δὲ μύρῳ
head with oil, *{the}* *head* *my* *not* *You did anoint* but she *but* has poured perfume
3051 1778 3836 3051 1609 4024 230 1254 4047 1254 230 230 3693
n.dsn d.asf n.asf r.gs.1 pl v.aai.2s r.nsf cj n.dsn

ἤλειψεν τοὺς πόδας μου. 47 ⌊οὗ χάριν⌋ λέγω σοι,
has poured on on *{the}* my feet. *my* Therefore ⌊I can tell⌋ you, "Her sins, which
230 3836 1609 4546 1609 4005 5920 3306 5148 899 281 3836
v.aai.3s d.apm n.apm r.gs.1 r.gsn p.g v.pai.1s r.ds.2

ἀφέωνται αἱ ἁμαρτίαι αὐτῆς αἱ πολλαί, ὅτι ἠγάπησεν πολύ·
were many, ⌊have been forgiven,⌋ *{the}* *sins* *Her* *which* *many* for she loved much.
4498 918 3836 281 899 3836 4498 4022 26 4498
v.rpi.3p d.npf n.npf r.gsf.3 d.npf a.npf cj v.aai.3s adv

ᾧ δὲ ὀλίγον ἀφίεται, ὀλίγον ἀγαπᾷ. 48 εἶπεν δὲ αὐτῇ,
But ⌊the one to whom⌋ *But* little is forgiven loves little.'" *loves* He said *{and}* to her,
1254 4005 1254 3900 918 26 3900 26 3306 1254 899
r.dsm cj a.nsn v.ppi.3s adv v.pai.3s v.aai.3s cj r.dsf.3

ἀφέωνται σου αἱ ἁμαρτίαι. 49 καὶ
"Your sins ⌊have been forgiven."⌋ *Your* *{the}* *sins* Then those reclining at table with him
5148 281 918 5148 3836 281 2779 3836 5263 5263 5263 5263
v.rpi.3p r.gs.2 d.npf n.npf cj

ἤρξαντο οἱ συνανακείμενοι λέγειν ἐν ἑαυτοῖς, τίς οὗτός ἐστιν ὃς καὶ
began *those* *reclining at table with* to say to themselves, "Who is this, *is* who even
806 3836 5263 3306 1877 1571 5515 1639 4047 1639 4005 2779
v.ami.3p d.npm pt.pm.npm f.pa p.d r.dpm.3 r.nsm r.nsm v.pai.3s r.nsm adv

ἁμαρτίας ἀφίησιν; 50 εἶπεν δὲ πρὸς τὴν γυναῖκα, ἡ πίστις σου
forgives sins?" *forgives* He said *{and}* to the woman, *{the}* "Your faith *Your*
918 281 918 3306 1254 4639 3836 1222 3836 5148 4411 5148
n.apf v.pai.3s v.aai.3s cj p.a d.asf n.asf d.nsf n.nsf r.gs.2

σέσωκέν σε· πορεύου εἰς εἰρήνην.
has saved you; go in peace."
5392 5148 4513 1650 1645
v.rai.3s r.as.2 v.pmm.2s p.a n.asf

8:1 καὶ ἐγένετο ⌊ἐν τῷ καθεξῆς καὶ⌋ αὐτὸς διώδευεν
{and} ⌊It happened that⌋ soon afterward Jesus ⌊began to travel around⌋
2779 1181 1877 3836 2759 2779 899 1476
cj v.ami.3s p.d d.dsm adv cj r.nsm v.iai.3s

κατὰ πόλιν καὶ κώμην κηρύσσων καὶ εὐαγγελιζόμενος τὴν
from one town and village to another, proclaiming and ⌊bringing the good news of⌋ the
2848 4484 2779 3267 3062 2779 2294 3836
p.a n.asf cj n.asf pt.pa.nsm cj pt.pm.nsm d.asf

βασιλείαν τοῦ θεοῦ καὶ οἱ δώδεκα σὺν αὐτῷ, 2 καὶ
kingdom of God. *{and}* The twelve disciples were with him, ⌊as well as⌋ certain
993 3836 2536 2779 3836 1557 5250 899 2779 5516
n.asf d.gsm n.gsm cj d.npm a.npm p.d r.dsm.3 cj

γυναῖκές τινες αἳ ἦσαν τεθεραπευμέναι ἀπὸ πνευμάτων πονηρῶν καὶ
women *certain* who had been healed from evil spirits *evil* and
1222 5516 4005 1639 2543 608 4505 4460 4505 2779
n.npf r.npf r.npf v.iai.3p pt.rp.npf p.g n.gpn a.gpn cj

ἀσθενειῶν, Μαρία ἡ καλουμένη Μαγδαληνή, ἀφ᾽ ἧς δαιμόνια ἑπτὰ
diseases (Mary who is called Magdalene, from whom seven demons *seven*
819 3451 3836 2813 3402 608 4005 2231 1228 2231
n.gpf n.nsf d.nsf pt.pp.nsf n.nsf p.g r.gsf n.npn a.npn

ἐξεληλύθει, 3 καὶ Ἰωάννα γυνὴ Χουζᾶ ἐπιτρόπου Ἡρῴδου καὶ Σουσάννα
had gone out, and Joanna, wife of Chuza, Herod's steward, *Herod's* and Susanna)
2002 2779 2721 1222 5966 2476 2207 2476 2779 5052
v.lai.3s cj n.nsf n.nsf n.gsm n.gsm n.gsm cj n.nsf

καὶ ἕτεραι πολλαί, αἵτινες διηκόνουν αὐτοῖς ↰ ἐκ τῶν
and many other women *many* who cared for their needs ⌊out of⌋ *{the}* their own
2779 4498 2283 4498 4015 1354 899 1354 1666 3836 899 899
cj r.npf a.npf r.npf v.iai.3p r.dpm.3 p.g d.gpn

ὑπαρχόντων αὐταῖς. 4 → συνιόντος δὲ ὄχλου πολλοῦ καὶ τῶν
resources. *their own* As a large crowd was gathering *{and}* *crowd* *large* and people were
5639 899 4498 4063 5290 1254 4063 4498 2779 3836 2164
pt.pa.gpn r.dpf.3 pt.pa.gsm cj n.gsm a.gsm cj d.gpm

NASB

head with oil, but
she anointed My
feet with perfume.
47 For this reason
I say to you, her
sins, which are
many, have been
forgiven, for she
loved much; but
he who is for-
given little, loves
little." 48 Then He
said to her, "Your
sins have been
forgiven." 49 Those
who were reclin-
ing *at the table*
with Him began to
say to themselves,
"Who is this *man*
who even forgives
sins?" 50 And He
said to the woman,
"Your faith has
saved you; go in
peace."

Ministering Women

8:1 Soon after-
wards, He *began*
going around from
one city and vil-
lage to another,
proclaiming and
preaching the king-
dom of God. The
twelve were with
Him, 2 and *also*
some women who
had been healed
of evil spirits and
sicknesses: Mary
who was called
Magdalene, from
whom seven de-
mons had gone
out, 3 and Joanna
the wife of Chuza,
Herod's steward,
and Susanna, and
many others who
were contributing
to their support
out of their private
means.

Parable of the Sower

4 When a large
crowd was coming
together, and

NIV

coming to Jesus
from town after
town, he told this
parable: [5]"A farm-
er went out to sow
his seed. As he
was scattering the
seed, some fell
along the path; it
was trampled on,
and the birds ate it
up. [6]Some fell on
rocky ground, and
when it came up,
the plants withered
because they had
no moisture. [7]Oth-
er seed fell among
thorns, which
grew up with it
and choked the
plants. [8]Still other
seed fell on good
soil. It came up
and yielded a crop,
a hundred times
more than was
sown."
When he said
this, he called out,
"Whoever has ears
to hear, let them
hear."
[9]His disciples
asked him what
this parable meant.
[10]He said, "The
knowledge of
the secrets of the
kingdom of God
has been given to
you, but to others I
speak in parables,
so that,

"'though seeing,
they may not
see;
though hearing,
they may not
understand.'[a]

[11]"This is the
meaning of the
parable: The seed
is the word of God.
[12]Those along the
path are the ones
who hear, and then
the devil comes
and takes away the
word from their
hearts,

κατὰ πόλιν ↰ ↰ ἐπιπορευομένων πρὸς αὐτὸν εἶπεν διὰ
coming to Jesus from one town after another, *were coming* *to* *Jesus* he spoke using a
2164 4639 899 2848 4484 2848 2848 2164 4639 899 3306 1328
p.a n.asf pt.pm.gpm p.a r.asm.3 v.aai.3s p.g

παραβολῆς· [5] ἐξῆλθεν ὁ σπείρων τοῦ σπεῖραι τὸν σπόρον αὐτοῦ. καὶ
parable. "A sower went out *{the}* *sower* to sow *{the}* his seed. *his* And
4130 5062 2002 3836 5062 3836 5062 3836 899 5078 899 2779
n.gsf v.aai.3s d.nsm pt.pa.nsm d.gsn f.aa d.asm n.asm r.gsm.3 cj

ἐν τῷ σπείρειν αὐτὸν ὃ μὲν ἔπεσεν παρὰ τὴν ὁδὸν καὶ κατεπατήθη,
as *{the}* he sowed, *he* some ~ fell along the path and was trampled underfoot,
1877 3836 899 5062 899 4005 3525 4406 4123 3836 3847 2779 2922
p.d d.dsn f.pa r.asm.3 r.nsn pl v.aai.3s p.a d.asf n.asf cj v.api.3s

καὶ τὰ πετεινὰ τοῦ οὐρανοῦ κατέφαγεν αὐτό. [6] καὶ ἕτερον κατέπεσεν ἐπὶ τὴν
and the birds of heaven devoured it. *{and}* Other seed fell on *{the}*
2779 3836 4374 3836 4041 2983 899 2779 2283 2928 2093 3836
cj d.npn n.npn d.gsm n.gsm v.aai.3s r.asn.3 cj r.nsn v.aai.3s p.a d.asf

πέτραν, καὶ φυὲν ἐξηράνθη διὰ τὸ μὴ ἔχειν ἰκμάδα.
rock, and ⌊when it came up,⌋ ⌊it withered away,⌋ because *{the}* it had no *it had* moisture.
4376 2779 5886 3830 1328 3836 2400 2400 3590 2400 2657
n.asf cj pt.ap.nsn v.api.3s p.a d.asn pl f.pa n.asf

[7] καὶ ἕτερον ἔπεσεν ἐν μέσῳ τῶν ἀκανθῶν, καὶ → συμφυεῖσαι
{and} Other seed fell in the middle of thorns, and when the thorns came up with
2779 2283 4406 1877 3545 3836 180 2779 3836 180 5243
cj r.nsn v.aai.3s p.d n.dsn d.gpf n.gpf cj pt.ap.npf

αἱ ἄκανθαι ἀπέπνιξαν αὐτό. [8] καὶ ἕτερον ἔπεσεν εἰς τὴν γῆν τὴν
it, *the* *thorns* they choked it. *{and}* Other seed fell into *{the}* good soil, *{the}*
3836 180 678 899 2779 2283 4406 1650 3836 19 1178 3836
d.npf n.npf v.aai.3p r.asn.3 cj r.nsn v.aai.3s p.a d.asf n.asf d.asf

ἀγαθὴν καὶ φυὲν ἐποίησεν καρπὸν ἑκατονταπλασίονα.
good and ⌊when it came up,⌋ it produced fruit a hundredfold." As he was
19 2779 5886 4472 2843 1671 3306 3306 3306
a.asf cj pt.ap.nsn v.aai.3s n.asm a.asm

ταῦτα λέγων ἐφώνει, ↱ ὁ ἔχων ὦτα ἀκούειν
saying these things *As he was saying* ⌊he began to call out,⌋ "Let the ⌊one who has⌋ ears to hear,
3306 4047 3306 5888 201 3836 2400 4044 201
r.apn pt.pa.nsm v.iai.3s d.nsm pt.pa.nsm n.apn f.pa

ἀκουέτω. [9] ἐπηρώτων δὲ αὐτὸν οἱ μαθηταὶ αὐτοῦ τίς
hear." Now his disciples were questioning *Now* him *{the}* *disciples* *his* as to what
201 1254 899 3412 2089 1254 899 3836 3412 899 5515
v.pam.3s v.iai.3p cj r.asm.3 d.npm n.npm r.gsm.3 r.nsf

αὕτη εἴη ἡ παραβολή. [10] ὁ δὲ εἶπεν, ὑμῖν δέδοται γνῶναι
this parable meant. *{the}* *parable* He *{and}* said, "To you ⌊it has been given⌋ to know
4047 4130 1639 3836 4130 3836 1254 3306 7007 1443 1182
r.nsf v.pao.3s d.nsf n.nsf d.nsm cj v.aai.3s r.dp.2 v.rpi.3s f.aa

τὰ μυστήρια τῆς βασιλείας τοῦ θεοῦ, τοῖς δὲ λοιποῖς ἐν
the secrets of the kingdom of God, but to the *but* rest I speak in
3836 3696 3836 993 3836 2536 1254 3836 1254 3370 1877
d.apn n.apn d.gsf n.gsf d.gsm n.gsm d.dpm cj a.dpm p.d

παραβολαῖς, ἵνα βλέποντες ↱ ↱ μὴ βλέπωσιν καὶ ἀκούοντες ↱ ↱ μὴ
parables, so that seeing they may not see, and hearing they may not
4130 2671 1063 1063 1063 3590 1063 2779 201 5317 5317 3590
n.dpf cj pt.pa.npm pl v.pas.3p cj pt.pa.npm pl

συνιῶσιν. [11] ἔστιν δὲ αὕτη ἡ παραβολή· ὁ σπόρος ἐστὶν
understand. "Now this is *Now* *this* what the parable means: The seed is
5317 1254 4047 1639 1254 4047 3836 4130 3836 5078 1639
v.pas.3p v.pai.3s cj r.nsf d.nsf n.nsf d.nsm n.nsm v.pai.3s

ὁ λόγος τοῦ θεοῦ. [12] οἱ δὲ παρὰ τὴν ὁδόν εἰσιν οἱ ἀκούσαντες, εἶτα
the word of God. Those *{and}* along the path are the ones who hear — then
3836 3364 3836 2536 3836 1254 4123 3836 3847 1639 3836 201 1663
d.nsm n.nsm d.gsm n.gsm d.npm cj p.a d.asf n.asf v.pai.3p d.npm pt.aa.npm adv

ἔρχεται ὁ διάβολος καὶ αἴρει τὸν λόγον ἀπὸ τῆς καρδίας
the devil comes *the* *devil* and ⌊takes away⌋ the word from *{the}* their heart,
3836 1333 2262 3836 1333 2779 149 3836 3364 608 3836 899 2840
v.pmi.3s d.nsm n.nsm cj v.pai.3s d.asm n.asm p.g d.gsf n.gsf

NASB

those from the
various cities were
journeying to Him,
He spoke by way
of a parable: [5]"The
sower went out to
sow his seed; and
as he sowed, some
fell beside the road,
and it was trampled
under foot and the
birds of the air ate
it up. [6]Other *seed*
fell on rocky *soil*,
and as soon as it
grew up, it with-
ered away, because
it had no moisture.
[7]Other *seed* fell
among the thorns;
and the thorns
grew up with it and
choked it out. [8]Oth-
er *seed* fell into the
good soil, and grew
up, and produced
a crop a hundred
times as great."
As He said these
things, He would
call out, "He who
has ears to hear, let
him hear."
[9]His disciples
began questioning
Him as to what
this parable meant.
[10]And He said, "To
you it has been
granted to know
the mysteries of the
kingdom of God,
but to the rest *it is*
in parables, so that
SEEING THEY MAY
NOT SEE, AND HEAR-
ING THEY MAY NOT
UNDERSTAND.
[11]"Now the para-
ble is this: the seed
is the word of God.
[12]Those beside the
road are those who
have heard; then
the devil comes
and takes away the
word from their

[a] *10* Isaiah 6:9

NIV

so that they may
not believe and be
saved. [13]Those on
the rocky ground
are the ones who
receive the word
with joy when they
hear it, but they
have no root. They
believe for a while,
but in the time of
testing they fall
away. [14]The seed
that fell among
thorns stands for
those who hear,
but as they go on
their way they are
choked by life's
worries, riches and
pleasures, and they
do not mature.
[15]But the seed on
good soil stands
for those with a
noble and good
heart, who hear
the word, retain it,
and by persevering
produce a crop.

A Lamp on a Stand

[16]"No one lights
a lamp and hides
it in a clay jar or
puts it under a bed.
Instead, they put it
on a stand, so that
those who come
in can see the
light. [17]For there
is nothing hid-
den that will not
be disclosed, and
nothing concealed
that will not be
known or brought
out into the open.
[18]Therefore con-
sider carefully
how you listen.
Whoever has will
be given more;
whoever does not
have, even what
they think they
have will be taken
from them."

Jesus' Mother and Brothers

[19]Now Jesus'
mother and

αὐτῶν, ἵνα ↱ ↱ μὴ πιστεύσαντες σωθῶσιν. 13 οἱ δὲ ἐπὶ τῆς
their so that they may not believe and be saved. Those *{and}* that fall on *{the}*
899 2671 5392 4409 3590 4409 5392 3836 1254 2093 3836
r.gpm.3 cj pl pt.aa.npm v.aps.3p d.npm cj p.g d.gsf

πέτρας οἳ ὅταν ἀκούσωσιν μετὰ χαρᾶς δέχονται τὸν
rock are ⌊the ones who,⌋ when they hear the word, receive it with joy; *receive* *the*
4376 4005 4020 201 3836 3364 1312 3552 5915 1312 3836
n.gsf r.npm cj v.aas.3p p.g n.gsf v.pmi.3p d.asm

λόγον, καὶ οὗτοι ῥίζαν οὐκ ἔχουσιν, οἳ πρὸς καιρὸν
word but they have no root *no* *have* — they believe for a while
3364 2779 4047 2400 4024 4844 4024 2400 4005 4409 4639 2789
n.asm cj r.npm n.asf pl v.pai.3p r.npm p.a n.asm

πιστεύουσιν καὶ ἐν καιρῷ πειρασμοῦ ἀφίστανται. 14 τὸ δὲ εἰς
believe but in a time of testing they fall away. As for what *As for* fell among
4409 2779 1877 2789 4280 923 1254 1254 3836 1254 4406 1650
v.pai.3p cj p.d n.dsm n.gsm v.pmi.3p d.nsn pl p.a

τὰς ἀκάνθας πεσόν, οὗτοί εἰσιν οἱ ἀκούσαντες, καὶ
the thorns *fell* — these are the ones who hear, but as they go on their way
3836 180 4406 4047 1639 3836 201 2779 4513 4513 4513 4513 4513 4513
d.apf n.apf pt.aa.nsn r.npm v.pai.3p d.npm pt.aa.npm cj

ὑπὸ μεριμνῶν καὶ πλούτου καὶ ἡδονῶν τοῦ βίου
they are choked by the cares and riches and pleasures of life,
5231 5231 5231 5679 3533 2779 4458 2779 2454 3836 1050
p.g n.gpf cj n.gsm cj n.gpf d.gsm n.gsm

πορευόμενοι συμπνίγονται καὶ ↱ ↱ οὐ τελεσφοροῦσιν. 15
as they go on their way *they are choked* and they do not bring fruit to maturity. But as for
4513 5231 2779 5461 5461 4024 5461 1254 1254 1254
pt.pm.npm v.ppi.3p cj pl v.pai.3p

τὸ δὲ ἐν τῇ καλῇ γῇ, οὗτοί εἰσιν οἵτινες ἐν
that *But as for* in the good soil — these are ⌊the ones who,⌋ having heard with an honest
3836 1254 1877 3836 2819 1178 4047 1639 4015 201 201 1877 2819
d.nsn pl p.d d.dsf a.dsf n.dsf r.npm v.pai.3p r.npm p.d

καρδίᾳ καλῇ καὶ ἀγαθῇ ἀκούσαντες τὸν λόγον κατέχουσιν
and good heart, *honest* *and* *good* *having heard* hold firmly onto the word *hold firmly onto*
2779 19 2840 2819 2779 19 201 2988 2988 2988 3836 3364 2988
n.dsf a.dsf cj a.dsf pt.aa.npm d.asm n.asm v.pai.3p

καὶ καρποφοροῦσιν ἐν ὑπομονῇ. 16 οὐδεὶς δὲ λύχνον
and bear fruit through patient endurance. "No one *{and}* after lighting a lamp
2779 2844 1877 5705 4029 1254 721 721 3394
cj v.pai.3p p.d n.dsf a.nsm cj n.asm

ἅψας καλύπτει αὐτὸν → σκεύει ἢ ὑποκάτω κλίνης τίθησιν, ἀλλ᾽
after lighting covers it with a container or puts it under a bed, *puts* but
721 2821 899 5007 2445 5502 5691 3109 5502 247
pt.aa.nsm v.pai.3s r.asm.3 n.dsn cj p.g n.gsf v.pai.3s cj

ἐπὶ λυχνίας τίθησιν, ἵνα οἱ εἰσπορευόμενοι βλέπωσιν τὸ φῶς. 17
places it on a lampstand, *places* so that those who come in may see the light. For
5502 2093 3393 5502 2671 3836 1660 1063 3836 5890 1142
p.g n.gsf v.pai.3s cj d.npm pt.pm.npm v.pas.3p d.asn n.asn

οὐ γάρ ἐστιν κρυπτὸν ὃ οὐ φανερὸν γενήσεται οὐδὲ ἀπόκρυφον ὃ
nothing *For* is hidden that will not be disclosed, *will be* nor secret that
4024 1142 1639 3220 4005 1181 4024 1181 5745 1181 4028 649 4005
pl cj v.pai.3s a.nsn r.nsn pl a.nsn v.fmi.3s cj a.nsn r.nsn

↱ ⌊οὐ μὴ⌋ γνωσθῇ καὶ εἰς φανερὸν ἔλθῃ. 18 βλέπετε οὖν πῶς ἀκούετε·
will not be known and come to light. *come* "Take care, then, how you hear! For
1182 4024 3590 1182 2779 2262 1650 5745 2262 1063 4036 4802 201 1142
pl pl v.aps.3s cj p.a a.asn v.aas.3s v.pam.2p cj cj v.pai.2p

⌊ὃς ἂν⌋ γὰρ ἔχῃ, δοθήσεται αὐτῷ· καὶ ὃς ἂν ↱ μὴ ἔχῃ,
whoever *For* has — more will be given to him; and whoever does not have —
4005 323 1142 2400 1443 899 2779 4005 323 2400 3590 2400
r.nsm pl cj v.pas.3s v.fpi.3s r.dsm.3 cj r.nsm pl pl v.pas.3s

καὶ ὃ δοκεῖ ἔχειν ἀρθήσεται ἀπ᾽ αὐτοῦ. 19
even what he seems to have ⌊will be taken away⌋ from him." The mother of Jesus and his
2779 4005 1506 2400 149 608 899 3836 3613 2779 899
adv r.asn v.pai.3s f.pa v.fpi.3s p.g r.gsm.3

NASB

heart, so that they
will not believe
and be saved.
[13]Those on the
rocky *soil are* those
who, when they
hear, receive the
word with joy; and
these have no *firm*
root; they believe
for a while, and in
time of temptation
fall away. [14]The
seed which fell
among the thorns,
these are the ones
who have heard,
and as they go on
their way they are
choked with wor-
ries and riches and
pleasures of *this*
life, and bring no
fruit to maturity.
[15]But the *seed* in
the good soil, these
are the ones who
have heard the
word in an honest
and good heart,
and hold it fast,
and bear fruit with
perseverance.

Parable of the Lamp

[16]"Now no one
after lighting a
lamp covers it over
with a container, or
puts it under a bed;
but he puts it on a
lampstand, so that
those who come in
may see the light.
[17]For nothing is
hidden that will not
become evident,
nor *anything* secret
that will not be
known and come to
light. [18]So take care
how you listen; for
whoever has, to
him *more* shall be
given; and whoever
does not have, even
what he thinks he
has shall be taken
away from him."
[19]And His mother

NIV

brothers came to
see him, but they
were not able to
get near him be-
cause of the crowd.
20 Someone told
him, "Your mother
and brothers are
standing outside,
wanting to see
you."
21 He replied, "My
mother and broth-
ers are those who
hear God's word
and put it into
practice."

Jesus Calms the Storm

22 One day Jesus
said to his disci-
ples, "Let us go
over to the other
side of the lake."
So they got into a
boat and set out.
23 As they sailed,
he fell asleep. A
squall came down
on the lake, so that
the boat was be-
ing swamped, and
they were in great
danger.
24 The disciples
went and woke
him, saying, "Mas-
ter, Master, we're
going to drown!"
He got up and
rebuked the wind
and the raging
waters; the storm
subsided, and
all was calm.
25 "Where is your
faith?" he asked
his disciples.
In fear and
amazement they
asked one another,
"Who is this? He
commands even
the winds and the
water, and

παρεγένετο δὲ πρὸς αὐτὸν ἡ μήτηρ καὶ οἱ ἀδελφοὶ αὐτοῦ καὶ ↱ ↱
brothers came *{and}* to him, *The* *mother* *and* *{the}* *brothers* *his* but they were
81 4134 1254 4639 899 3836 3613 2779 3836 81 899 2779 1538 1538
v.ami.3s cj p.a r.asm.3 d.nsf n.nsf cj d.npm n.npm r.gsm.3 cj

οὐκ ἠδύναντο συντυχεῖν αὐτῷ διὰ τὸν ὄχλον. 20 ἀπηγγέλη δὲ αὐτῷ, ἡ
not able to get near him ⌊because of⌋ the crowd. It was reported *{and}* to him, *{the}*
4024 1538 5344 899 1328 3836 4063 550 1254 899 3836
pl v.ipi.3p f.aa r.dsm.3 p.a d.asm n.asm v.api.3s cj r.dsm.3 d.nsf

μήτηρ σου καὶ οἱ ἀδελφοί σου ἑστήκασιν ἔξω ἰδεῖν θέλοντές
"Your mother *Your* and *{the}* your brothers *your* are standing outside, wanting to see *wanting*
5148 3613 5148 2779 3836 5148 81 5148 2705 2032 2527 1625 2527
n.nsf r.gs.2 cj d.npm n.npm r.gs.2 v.rai.3p adv f.aa pt.pa.npm

σε. 21 ὁ δὲ ἀποκριθεὶς εἶπεν πρὸς αὐτούς,
you." In response he *{and}* *In response* said to them, "Those who hear and do
5148 646 646 3836 1254 646 3306 4639 899 4047 3836 201 2779 4472
r.as.2 d.nsm cj pt.ap.nsm v.aai.3s p.a r.apm.3

μήτηρ μου καὶ ἀδελφοί μου οὗτοί εἰσιν οἱ τὸν
the word of God are my mother *my* and my brothers." *my* *Those* *are* *who* *the*
3836 3364 3836 2536 1639 1609 3613 1609 2779 1609 81 1609 4047 1639 3836 3836
n.nsf r.gs.1 cj n.npm r.gs.1 r.npm v.pai.3p d.npm d.asm

λόγον τοῦ θεοῦ ἀκούοντες καὶ ποιοῦντες. 22 ἐγένετο δὲ ἐν μιᾷ τῶν ἡμερῶν
word *of* *God* *hear* *and* *do* It happened *{and}* in one of those days
3364 3836 2536 201 2779 4472 1181 1254 1877 1651 3836 2465
n.asm d.gsm n.gsm pt.pa.npm cj pt.pa.npm v.ami.3s cj p.d a.dsf d.gpf n.gpf

καὶ ↰ αὐτὸς ἐνέβη εἰς πλοῖον καὶ οἱ μαθηταὶ αὐτοῦ καὶ
{and} that he and his disciples got into a boat, *and* *{the}* *disciples* *his* and
2779 1181 899 2779 899 3412 1832 1650 4450 2779 3836 3412 899 2779
cj r.nsm v.aai.3s p.a n.asn cj d.npm n.npm r.gsm.3 cj

εἶπεν πρὸς αὐτούς, διέλθωμεν εἰς τὸ πέραν τῆς λίμνης, καὶ
he said to them, "Let us go across to the other side of the lake." So
3306 4639 899 1451 1650 3836 4305 3836 3349 2779
v.aai.3s p.a r.apm.3 v.aas.1p p.a d.asn p.g d.gsf n.gsf cj

ἀνήχθησαν. 23 → πλεόντων δὲ αὐτῶν ἀφύπνωσεν. καὶ
⌊they put out from shore.⌋ As they ⌊were sailing along,⌋ *{and}* *they* he fell asleep, and a
343 899 4434 1254 899 934 2779
v.api.3p pt.pa.gpm cj r.gpm.3 v.aai.3s cj

κατέβη ⌊λαῖλαψ ἀνέμου⌋ εἰς τὴν λίμνην καὶ συνεπληροῦντο καὶ
windstorm swept down *windstorm* on the lake and they were being swamped and
3278 2849 3278 449 1650 3836 3349 2779 5230 2779
v.aai.3s n.nsf n.gsm p.a d.asf n.asf cj v.ipi.3p cj

ἐκινδύνευον. 24 ↱ προσελθόντες δὲ διήγειραν αὐτὸν ↰ λέγοντες,
were in danger. They went *{and}* to Jesus and woke him up, saying,
3073 1444 4665 1254 1444 899 1444 3306
v.iai.3p pt.aa.npm cj v.aai.3p r.asm.3 pt.pa.npm

ἐπιστάτα ἐπιστάτα, ἀπολλύμεθα. ὁ δὲ
"Master, Master, ⌊we are about to perish!"⌋ Having been awakened he *{and}*
2181 2181 660 1444 1444 1444 3836 1254
n.vsm n.vsm v.pmi.1p d.nsm cj

διεγερθεὶς ἐπετίμησεν τῷ ἀνέμῳ καὶ τῷ κλύδωνι τοῦ ὕδατος· καὶ
Having been awakened rebuked the wind and the raging of the water, and
1444 2203 3836 449 2779 3836 3114 3836 5623 2779
pt.ap.nsm v.aai.3s d.dsm n.dsm cj d.dsm n.dsm d.gsn n.gsn cj

ἐπαύσαντο καὶ ἐγένετο γαλήνη. 25 εἶπεν δὲ αὐτοῖς, ποῦ ἡ πίστις
they stopped, and there was a calm. He said *{and}* to them, "Where is *{the}* your faith?"
4264 2779 1181 1132 3306 1254 899 4543 3836 7007 4411
v.ami.3p cj v.ami.3s n.nsf v.aai.3s cj r.dpm.3 cj d.nsf n.nsf

ὑμῶν; ↱ φοβηθέντες δὲ ἐθαύμασαν λέγοντες πρὸς ἀλλήλους, τίς ἄρα
your They were afraid *{and}* and amazed, saying to one another, "Who, then, is
7007 2513 5828 1254 2513 3306 4639 253 5515 726 1639
r.gp.2 pt.ap.npm cj v.aai.3p pt.pa.npm p.a r.apm r.nsm cj

οὗτός ἐστιν ὅτι καὶ τοῖς ἀνέμοις ἐπιτάσσει καὶ τῷ ὕδατι, καὶ
this *is* that he commands even the winds *he commands* and the water and
4047 1639 4022 2199 2199 2779 3836 449 2199 2779 3836 5623 2779
r.nsm v.pai.3s cj adv d.dpm n.dpm v.pai.3s cj d.dsn n.dsn cj

NASB

and brothers came
to Him, and they
were unable to get
to Him because of
the crowd. 20 And
it was reported to
Him, "Your mother
and Your brothers
are standing out-
side, wishing to see
You." 21 But He an-
swered and said to
them, "My mother
and My brothers
are these who hear
the word of God
and do it."

Jesus Stills the Sea

22 Now on one of
those days Jesus
and His disciples
got into a boat, and
He said to them,
"Let us go over
to the other side
of the lake." So
they launched out.
23 But as they were
sailing along He
fell asleep; and a
fierce gale of wind
descended on the
lake, and they *be-*
gan to be swamped
and to be in danger.
24 They came to Je-
sus and woke Him
up, saying, "Mas-
ter, Master, we are
perishing!" And He
got up and rebuked
the wind and the
surging waves, and
they stopped, and
it became calm.
25 And He said to
them, "Where is
your faith?" They
were fearful and
amazed, saying to
one another, "Who
then is this, that He
commands even
the winds and the

NIV

they obey him."

Jesus Restores a Demon-Possessed Man

[26]They sailed
to the region of
the Gerasenes,[a]
which is across the
lake from Gali-
lee. [27]When Jesus
stepped ashore,
he was met by a
demon-possessed
man from the
town. For a long
time this man had
not worn clothes
or lived in a house,
but had lived in
the tombs. [28]When
he saw Jesus, he
cried out and fell
at his feet, shout-
ing at the top of
his voice, "What
do you want with
me, Jesus, Son
of the Most High
God? I beg you,
don't torture me!"
[29]For Jesus had
commanded the
impure spirit to
come out of the
man. Many times
it had seized him,
and though he was
chained hand and
foot and kept un-
der guard, he had
broken his chains
and had been
driven by the de-
mon into solitary
places.
[30]Jesus asked
him, "What is your
name?"
"Legion," he
replied, because
many demons had
gone into him.
[31]And they begged
Jesus repeatedly
not to order them
to go into the
Abyss.
[32]A large herd of
pigs was feeding
there on the hill-
side. The demons
begged Jesus to let
them go into the
pigs,

[a] 26 Some manuscripts *Gadarenes*; other manuscripts *Gergesenes*; also in verse 37

ὑπακούουσιν αὐτῷ; 26 Καὶ κατέπλευσαν εἰς τὴν χώραν τῶν Γερασηνῶν,[a] ἥτις
they obey him?" Then they came to land in the region of the Gerasenes, which
5634 899 2779 2929 1650 3836 6001 3836 1170 4015
v.pai.3p r.dsm.3 cj v.aai.3p p.a d.asf n.asf d.gpm a.gpm r.nsf

ἐστὶν ἀντιπέρα τῆς Γαλιλαίας. 27 → ἐξελθόντι δὲ αὐτῷ ἐπὶ τὴν γῆν
is ⌊across the lake⌋ from Galilee. When he stepped out *{and}* *he* on the land,
1639 527 3836 1133 899 2002 1254 899 2093 3836 1178
v.pai.3s p.g d.gsf n.gsf pt.aa.dsm cj r.dsm.3 p.a d.asf n.asf

ὑπήντησεν ἀνήρ τις ἐκ τῆς πόλεως ἔχων
a man from the town met *man* *a* *from* *the* *town* him, ⌊who was possessed by⌋
5516 467 1666 3836 4484 5636 467 5516 1666 3836 4484 2400
v.aai.3s n.nsm r.nsm p.g d.gsf n.gsf pt.pa.nsm

δαιμόνια καὶ → χρόνῳ ἱκανῷ ↱ οὐκ ἐνεδύσατο ἱμάτιον καὶ ἐν
demons, and for a long time *long* had not worn clothes or had not lived in
1228 2779 2653 5989 2653 1907 4024 1907 2668 2779 3531 4024 3531 1877
n.apn cj n.dsm a.dsm pl v.ami.3s n.asn cj p.d

οἰκίᾳ οὐκ ἔμενεν ἀλλ᾽ ἐν τοῖς μνήμασιν. 28 ἰδὼν δὲ τὸν Ἰησοῦν ↱
a house *not* *had lived* but among the tombs. ⌊When he saw⌋ *{and}* *{the}* Jesus, he
3864 4024 3531 247 1877 3836 3645 1625 1254 3836 2652 4700
n.dsf pl v.iai.3s cj p.d d.dpn n.dpn pt.aa.nsm cj d.asm n.asm

ἀνακράξας προσέπεσεν αὐτῷ καὶ → φωνῇ μεγάλῃ εἶπεν, τί ἐμοὶ
cried out and fell prostrate before him and in a loud voice *loud* said, "What have I
371 4700 899 2779 3489 5889 3489 3306 5515 1609
pt.aa.nsm v.aai.3s r.dsm.3 cj n.dsf a.dsf v.aai.3s r.nsn r.ds.1

καὶ σοί, Ἰησοῦ υἱὲ τοῦ θεοῦ τοῦ ὑψίστου; δέομαί σου,
{and} to do ⌊with you,⌋ Jesus, Son of the Most High God? *{the}* *Most High* I beg you, do
2779 5148 2652 5626 3836 5736 5736 2536 3836 5736 1289 5148 989
cj r.ds.2 n.vsm n.vsm d.gsm n.gsm d.gsm a.gsm.s v.pmi.1s r.gs.2

μή με βασανίσῃς. 29 παρήγγειλεν[b] γὰρ τῷ πνεύματι τῷ
not torment me!?" *do torment* For Jesus had commanded *For* the unclean spirit *{the}*
3590 989 1609 989 1142 4133 1142 3836 176 4460 3836
pl r.as.1 v.aas.2s v.aai.3s cj d.dsn n.dsn d.dsn

ἀκαθάρτῳ ἐξελθεῖν ἀπὸ τοῦ ἀνθρώπου. πολλοῖς γὰρ χρόνοις συνηρπάκει αὐτὸν
unclean to come out of the man; for many *for* times it had seized him
176 2002 608 3836 476 1142 4498 1142 5989 5275 899
a.dsn f.aa p.g d.gsm n.gsm a.dpm cj n.dpm v.lai.3s r.asm.3

καὶ ἐδεσμεύετο ἁλύσεσιν καὶ πέδαις φυλασσόμενος καὶ
and ⌊he was kept under guard⌋ and bound with chains and shackles, *bound* yet
2779 1297 5875 268 2779 4267 5875 2779
cj v.ipi.3s n.dpf cj n.dpf pt.pp.nsm cj

διαρρήσσων τὰ δεσμὰ ἠλαύνετο ὑπὸ τοῦ δαιμονίου εἰς τὰς ἐρήμους. 30
he would break his bonds and be driven by the demon into the desert. Jesus
1393 3836 1301 1785 5679 3836 1228 1650 3836 2245 2652
pt.pa.nsm d.apn n.apn v.ipi.3s p.g d.gsn n.gsn p.a d.apf a.apf

ἐπηρώτησεν δὲ αὐτὸν ὁ Ἰησοῦς, τί σοι ὄνομά ἐστιν; ὁ δὲ εἶπεν,
asked *{and}* him, *{the}* *Jesus* "What is your name?" *is* And he *And* said,
2089 1254 899 3836 2652 5515 1639 5148 3950 1639 1254 3836 1254 3306
v.aai.3s cj r.asm.3 d.nsm n.nsm r.nsn r.ds.2 n.nsn v.pai.3s d.nsm cj v.aai.3s

λεγιών, ὅτι εἰσῆλθεν δαιμόνια πολλὰ εἰς αὐτόν. 31 καὶ παρεκάλουν
"Legion." (For many demons had entered *demons* *many* into him.) And they begged
3305 4022 4498 1228 1656 1228 4498 1650 899 2779 4151
n.nsf cj v.aai.3s n.npn a.npn p.a r.asm.3 cj v.iai.3p

αὐτὸν ἵνα μὴ ἐπιτάξῃ αὐτοῖς εἰς τὴν ἄβυσσον ἀπελθεῖν. 32
him not to *not* order them to go away into the abyss. *to go away* A large
899 3590 2671 3590 2199 899 599 599 599 1650 3836 12 599 2653
r.asm.3 cj pl v.aas.3s r.dpn.3 p.a d.asf n.asf f.aa

ἦν δὲ ἐκεῖ ἀγέλη χοίρων ἱκανῶν βοσκομένη ἐν τῷ ὄρει·
herd of pigs was *{and}* grazing there *herd* *of pigs* *large* *grazing* on the hillside;
36 5956 5956 1639 1254 1081 1695 36 5956 2653 1081 1877 3836 4001
v.iai.3s cj adv n.nsf n.gpm a.gpm pt.pp.nsf p.d d.dsn n.dsn

καὶ παρεκάλεσαν αὐτὸν ἵνα ἐπιτρέψῃ αὐτοῖς εἰς ἐκείνους
and the demons begged Jesus to permit them to go into them,
2779 4151 899 2671 2205 899 1656 1656 1650 1697
cj v.aai.3p r.asm.3 cj v.aas.3s r.dpn.3 p.a r.apm

[a] Γαδαρηνῶν included by TR after Γερασηνῶν.
[b] παρήγγειλεν UBS, TNIV. παρήγγελλεν NET.

NASB

water, and they
obey Him?"

The Demoniac Cured

[26]Then they sailed
to the country of
the Gerasenes,
which is opposite
Galilee. [27]And
when He came out
onto the land, He
was met by a man
from the city who
was possessed with
demons; and who
had not put on any
clothing for a long
time, and was not
living in a house,
but in the tombs.
[28]Seeing Jesus,
he cried out and
fell before Him,
and said in a loud
voice, "What busi-
ness do we have
with each other,
Jesus, Son of the
Most High God?
I beg You, do not
torment me." [29]For
He had command-
ed the unclean spir-
it to come out of
the man. For it had
seized him many
times; and he was
bound with chains
and shackles and
kept under guard,
and *yet* he would
break his bonds
and be driven by
the demon into
the desert. [30]And
Jesus asked him,
"What is your
name?" And he
said, "Legion";
for many demons
had entered him.
[31]They were im-
ploring Him not to
command them to
go away into the
abyss.
[32]Now there was
a herd of many
swine feeding there
on the mountain;
and *the demons*
implored Him to
permit them to en-
ter the swine.

NIV

and he gave
them permission.
33 When the de-
mons came out of
the man, they went
into the pigs, and
the herd rushed
down the steep
bank into the lake
and was drowned.
34 When those
tending the pigs
saw what had hap-
pened, they ran off
and reported this
in the town and
countryside, 35 and
the people went
out to see what had
happened. When
they came to
Jesus, they found
the man from
whom the demons
had gone out, sit-
ting at Jesus' feet,
dressed and in his
right mind; and
they were afraid.
36 Those who had
seen it told the
people how the
demon-possessed
man had been
cured. 37 Then all
the people of the
region of the Ger-
asenes asked Jesus
to leave them,
because they were
overcome with
fear. So he got into
the boat and left.
38 The man from
whom the de-
mons had gone out
begged to go with
him, but Jesus sent
him away, saying,
39 "Return home
and tell how much
God has done for
you."

εἰσελθεῖν· καὶ ἐπέτρεψεν αὐτοῖς. ↰ 33 ἐξελθόντα δὲ τὰ
to go and he gave them permission. The demons came out *{and}* *The*
1656 2779 2205 899 2205 3836 1228 2002 1254 3836
f.aa cj v.aai.3s r.dpn.3 pt.aa.npn cj d.npn

δαιμόνια ἀπὸ τοῦ ἀνθρώπου εἰσῆλθον εἰς τοὺς χοίρους, καὶ ὥρμησεν
demons of the man and went into the pigs, and the herd rushed
1228 608 3836 476 1656 1650 3836 5956 2779 3836 36 3994
n.npn p.g d.gsm n.gsm v.aai.3p p.a d.apm n.apm cj v.aai.3s

ἡ ἀγέλη κατὰ τοῦ κρημνοῦ εἰς τὴν λίμνην καὶ ἀπεπνίγη. 34 →
the *herd* down the steep bank into the lake and drowned. When the herdsmen
3836 36 2848 3836 3204 1650 3836 3349 2779 678 3836 1081
d.nsf n.nsf p.g d.gsm n.gsm p.a d.asf n.asf cj v.api.3s

ἰδόντες δὲ οἱ βόσκοντες τὸ γεγονὸς ἔφυγον καὶ ἀπήγγειλαν εἰς τὴν
saw *{and}* *the* *herdsmen* what had happened, they fled and reported it in the
1625 1254 3836 1081 3836 1181 5771 2779 550 1650 3836
pt.aa.npm cj d.npm pt.pa.npm d.asn pt.ra.asn v.aai.3p cj v.aai.3p p.a d.asf

πόλιν καὶ εἰς τοὺς ἀγρούς. 35 ἐξῆλθον δὲ ἰδεῖν τὸ γεγονὸς καὶ
town and in the countryside. Then people went out *Then* to see what happened, and
4484 2779 1650 3836 69 1254 2002 1254 1625 3836 1181 2779
n.asf cj p.a d.apm n.apm v.aai.3p cj f.aa d.asn pt.ra.asn cj

ἦλθον πρὸς τὸν Ἰησοῦν καὶ εὗρον
they came to *{the}* Jesus and found the man from whom the demons had come out,
2262 4639 3836 2652 2779 2351 3836 476 608 4005 3836 1228 2002 2002 2002
v.aai.3p p.a d.asm n.asm cj v.aai.3p

καθήμενον τὸν ἄνθρωπον ἀφ' οὗ τὰ δαιμόνια ἐξῆλθεν
sitting *the* *man* *from* *whom* *the* *demons* *had come out* at the feet of Jesus,
2764 3836 476 608 4005 3836 1228 2002 4123 3836 4546 3836 2652
pt.pm.asm d.asm n.asm p.g r.gsm d.npn n.npn v.aai.3s

ἱματισμένον καὶ σωφρονοῦντα παρὰ τοὺς πόδας τοῦ Ἰησοῦ, καὶ ἐφοβήθησαν.
dressed and in his right mind; *at* *the* *feet* *of* *Jesus* and they were afraid.
2667 2779 5404 4123 3836 4546 3836 2652 2779 5828
pt.rp.asm cj pt.pa.asm p.a d.apm n.apm d.gsm n.gsm cj v.api.3p

36 ἀπήγγειλαν δὲ αὐτοῖς οἱ ἰδόντες πῶς
Those who had seen it told *{and}* them *Those who had seen* how the
3836 1625 1625 1625 550 1254 899 3836 1625 4802 3836
v.aai.3p cj r.dpm.3 d.npm pt.aa.npm cj

ἐσώθη ὁ δαιμονισθείς. 37 καὶ
demon-possessed man ⌊had been healed.⌋ *the* *demon-possessed man* Then all the people of
1227 1227 5392 3836 1227 2779 570 3836 4436 3836
v.api.3s d.nsm pt.ap.nsm cj

ἠρώτησεν αὐτὸν ἅπαν τὸ πλῆθος τῆς
the surrounding region of the Gerasenes asked Jesus *all* *the* *people* *of the*
3836 4369 4369 3836 3836 1170 2263 899 570 3836 4436 3836
v.aai.3s r.asm.3 a.nsn d.nsn n.nsn d.gsf

περιχώρου τῶν Γερασηνῶν[a] ἀπελθεῖν ἀπ' αὐτῶν, ὅτι
surrounding region *of the* *Gerasenes* to go away from them, because they were seized with a
4369 3836 1170 599 608 899 4022 5309 5309 5309 5309
a.gsf d.gpm a.gpm f.aa p.g r.gpm.3 cj

φόβῳ μεγάλῳ συνείχοντο· αὐτὸς δὲ ἐμβὰς εἰς πλοῖον
great fear. *great* *they were seized with* So he *So* got into a boat and
3489 5832 3489 5309 1254 899 1254 1832 1650 4450
n.dsm a.dsm v.ipi.3p r.nsm cj pt.aa.nsm p.a n.asn

ὑπέστρεψεν. 38 ἐδεῖτο δὲ αὐτοῦ ὁ ἀνὴρ ἀφ' οὗ ἐξεληλύθει τὰ
returned. *begged* But *{of him}* the man from whom the demons had gone out *the*
5715 1289 1254 899 3836 467 608 4005 3836 1228 2002 3836
v.aai.3s v.imi.3s cj r.gsm.3 d.nsm n.nsm p.g r.gsm v.lai.3s d.npn

δαιμόνια εἶναι σὺν αὐτῷ· ἀπέλυσεν δὲ αὐτὸν ↰ λέγων,
demons begged to go with him, but Jesus sent *but* him away, saying,
1228 1289 1639 5250 899 1254 668 1254 899 668 3306
n.npn f.pa p.d r.dsm.3 v.aai.3s cj r.asm.3 pt.pa.nsm

39 ὑπόστρεφε εἰς τὸν οἶκόν σου καὶ διηγοῦ ὅσα σοι
"Return to *{the}* your house *your* and declare ⌊how much⌋ God has done ⌊for you."⌋
5715 1650 3836 5148 3875 5148 2779 1455 4012 2536 4472 4472 5148
v.pam.2s p.a d.asm n.asm r.gs.2 cj v.pmm.2s r.apn r.ds.2

NASB

And He gave them
permission. 33 And
the demons came
out of the man and
entered the swine;
and the herd rushed
down the steep
bank into the lake
and was drowned.
34 When the herds-
men saw what had
happened, they ran
away and reported
it in the city and
out in the country.
35 *The people* went
out to see what
had happened; and
they came to Jesus,
and found the man
from whom the
demons had gone
out, sitting down
at the feet of Jesus,
clothed and in his
right mind; and
they became fright-
ened. 36 Those who
had seen it reported
to them how the
man who was de-
mon-possessed had
been made well.
37 And all the people
of the country of
the Gerasenes and
the surrounding
district asked Him
to leave them, for
they were gripped
with great fear;
and He got into a
boat and returned.
38 But the man from
whom the demons
had gone out was
begging Him that
he might accom-
pany Him; but He
sent him away,
saying, 39 "Return
to your house and
describe what great
things God has
done for you."

[a] Γαδαρηνῶν included by TR after Γερασηνῶν.

NIV

So the man went
away and told all
over town how
much Jesus had
done for him.

Jesus Raises a Dead Girl and Heals a Sick Woman

[40]Now when
Jesus returned, a
crowd welcomed
him, for they were
all expecting him.
[41]Then a man
named Jairus, a
synagogue leader,
came and fell at
Jesus' feet, plead-
ing with him to
come to his house
[42]because his only
daughter, a girl of
about twelve, was
dying.
As Jesus was
on his way, the
crowds almost
crushed him.
[43]And a woman
was there who
had been subject
to bleeding for
twelve years,[a] but
no one could heal
her. [44]She came up
behind him and
touched the edge
of his cloak, and
immediately her
bleeding stopped.
[45]"Who touched
me?" Jesus asked.
When they all
denied it, Peter
said, "Master, the
people are crowd-
ing and pressing
against you."
[46]But Jesus said,
"Someone touched
me;

[a] 43 Many manuscripts *years, and she had spent all she had on doctors*

ἐποίησεν ὁ θεός. καὶ ἀπῆλθεν καθ᾽ ὅλην τὴν πόλιν κηρύσσων ὅσα
has done *{the}* *God* And he went about the whole *the* city proclaiming what Jesus
4472 3836 2536 2779 599 2848 3836 3910 3836 4484 3062 4012 2652
v.aai.3s d.nsm n.nsm cj v.aai.3s p.a a.asf d.asf n.asf pt.pa.nsm r.apn

ἐποίησεν αὐτῷ ὁ Ἰησοῦς. [40] ἐν δὲ τῷ ὑποστρέφειν τὸν Ἰησοῦν
had done for him. *{the}* *Jesus* As *{and}* *{the}* Jesus was returning *{the}* *Jesus* the
4472 899 3836 2652 1877 1254 3836 2652 5715 3836 2652 3836
v.aai.3s r.dsm.3 d.nsm n.nsm p.d cj d.dsn f.pa d.asm n.asm

ἀπεδέξατο αὐτὸν ὁ ὄχλος· ἦσαν γὰρ πάντες προσδοκῶντες αὐτόν.
crowd welcomed him, *the* *crowd* for they were *for* all waiting for him.
4063 622 899 3836 4063 1142 1639 1142 4246 4659 899
v.ami.3s r.asm.3 d.nsm n.nsm v.iai.3p cj a.npm pt.pa.npm r.asm.3

[41] καὶ ἰδοὺ ἦλθεν ἀνὴρ ᾧ ὄνομα Ἰάϊρος καὶ οὗτος ἄρχων
⌞Just then⌟ ~ there came a man named Jairus. *{and}* This man was a ruler
2779 2627 2262 467 4005 3950 2608 2779 4047 5639 807
cj j v.aai.3s n.nsm r.dsm n.nsn n.nsm cj r.nsm n.nsm

τῆς συναγωγῆς ὑπῆρχεν, καὶ ↱ πεσὼν παρὰ τοὺς πόδας τοῦ[a] Ἰησοῦ
of the synagogue, *was* and he fell at the feet of Jesus and
3836 5252 5639 2779 4151 4406 4123 3836 4546 3836 2652
d.gsf n.gsf v.iai.3s cj pt.aa.nsm p.a d.apm n.apm d.gsm n.gsm

παρεκάλει αὐτὸν εἰσελθεῖν εἰς τὸν οἶκον αὐτοῦ, [42] ὅτι
implored him to come into *{the}* his house, *his* because he had an only
4151 899 1656 1650 3836 899 3875 899 4022 899 1639 3666
v.iai.3s r.asm.3 f.aa p.a d.asm n.asm r.gsm.3 cj

θυγάτηρ μονογενὴς ἦν αὐτῷ ὡς ἐτῶν δώδεκα καὶ αὐτὴ ἀπέθνῃσκεν.
daughter, *only* *had* *he* about twelve years *twelve* old, and she was dying.
2588 3666 1639 899 6055 1557 2291 1557 2779 899 633
n.nsf a.nsf v.iai.3s r.dsm.3 pl n.gpn a.gpn cj r.nsf v.iai.3s

ἐν δὲ τῷ ὑπάγειν αὐτὸν οἱ ὄχλοι συνέπνιγον αὐτόν. [43] καὶ
As *{and}* *{the}* he went, *he* the crowds ⌞were pressing in on⌟ him. Now there
1877 1254 3836 899 5632 899 3836 4063 5231 899 2779 1639
p.d cj d.dsn f.pa r.asm.3 d.npm n.npm v.iai.3p r.asm.3 cj

γυνὴ οὖσα ἐν ῥύσει αἵματος ἀπὸ ἐτῶν δώδεκα,
was a woman *there was* ⌞who had⌟ suffered a flow of blood for twelve years, *twelve* but
1639 1222 1639 1877 4868 135 608 1557 2291 1557
n.nsf pt.pa.nsf p.d n.dsf n.gsn p.g n.gpn a.gpn

ἥτις[b] ↱ οὐκ ἴσχυσεν ἀπ᾽ οὐδενὸς θεραπευθῆναι, [44] ↱ προσελθοῦσα
she was not able to be healed by anyone. *to be healed* She came up
4015 2710 4024 2710 2543 2543 2543 608 4029 2543 721 4665
r.nsf pl v.aai.3s p.g a.gsm f.ap pt.aa.nsf

ὄπισθεν ἥψατο τοῦ κρασπέδου τοῦ ἱματίου αὐτοῦ καὶ παραχρῆμα
behind him and touched the edge of his cloak *his* and at once her flow
3957 721 3836 3192 3836 899 2668 899 2779 4202 899 4868
adv v.ami.3s d.gsn n.gsn d.gsn n.gsn r.gsm.3 cj adv

ἔστη ἡ ῥύσις τοῦ αἵματος αὐτῆς. [45] καὶ εἶπεν ὁ Ἰησοῦς, τίς
of blood stopped. *{the}* *flow* *of* *blood* *her* And Jesus said, *{the}* *Jesus* "Who
3836 135 2705 3836 4868 3836 135 899 2779 2652 3306 3836 2652 5515
v.aai.3s d.nsf n.nsf d.gsn n.gsn r.gsf.3 cj v.aai.3s d.nsm n.nsm r.nsm

ὁ ἁψάμενός μου; → ἀρνουμένων δὲ πάντων εἶπεν ὁ
was it who touched me?" As everyone denied it, *{and}* *everyone* Peter said, *{the}*
3836 721 1609 4246 766 1254 4246 4377 3306 3836
d.nsm pt.am.nsm r.gs.1 pt.pm.gpm cj a.gpm v.aai.3s d.nsm

Πέτρος, ἐπιστάτα, οἱ ὄχλοι συνέχουσίν σε καὶ
Peter "Master, the crowds ⌞are pressing in on all sides⌟ and crowding you." *and*
4377 2181 3836 4063 5309 2779 632 5148 2779
n.nsm n.vsm d.npm n.npm v.pai.3p r.as.2 cj

ἀποθλίβουσιν.[c] [46] ὁ δὲ Ἰησοῦς εἶπεν, ἥψατό μού τις, ἐγὼ γὰρ
crowding *{the}* But Jesus said, "Someone touched me, *Someone* for I *for*
632 3836 1254 2652 3306 5516 721 1609 5516 1142 1609 1142
v.pai.3p d.nsm cj n.nsm v.aai.3s v.ami.3s r.gs.1 r.nsm r.ns.1 cj

[a] [τοῦ] UBS.
[b] ἥτις omitted by TNIV, NET. ἰατροῖς προσαναλώσασα ὅλον τὸν βίον included by UBS, TR after ἥτις.
[c] καὶ λέγεις, Τίς ὁ ἁψάμενός μου; included by TR after ἀποθλίβουσιν.

NASB

So he went away,
proclaiming
throughout the
whole city what
great things Jesus
had done for him.

Miracles of Healing

[40]And as Jesus re-
turned, the people
welcomed Him, for
they had all been
waiting for Him.
[41]And there came a
man named Jairus,
and he was an of-
ficial of the syna-
gogue; and he fell
at Jesus' feet, and
began to implore
Him to come to his
house; [42]for he had
an only daughter,
about twelve years
old, and she was
dying. But as He
went, the crowds
were pressing
against Him.
[43]And a woman
who had a hemor-
rhage for twelve
years, and could
not be healed by
anyone, [44]came
up behind Him
and touched the
fringe of His cloak,
and immediately
her hemorrhage
stopped. [45]And
Jesus said, "Who
is the one who
touched Me?" And
while they were all
denying it, Peter
said, "Master, the
people are crowd-
ing and pressing in
on You." [46]But Je-
sus said, "Someone
did touch Me,

NIV

I know that pow-
er has gone out
from me."
47 Then the wom-
an, seeing that
she could not go
unnoticed, came
trembling and fell
at his feet. In the
presence of all
the people, she
told why she had
touched him and
how she had been
instantly healed.
48 Then he said to
her, "Daughter,
your faith has
healed you. Go in
peace."
49 While Jesus
was still speaking,
someone came
from the house of
Jairus, the syn-
agogue leader.
"Your daughter
is dead," he said.
"Don't bother the
teacher anymore."
50 Hearing this,
Jesus said to Ja-
irus, "Don't be
afraid; just believe,
and she will be
healed."
51 When he ar-
rived at the house
of Jairus, he did
not let anyone go
in with him except
Peter, John and
James, and the
child's father and
mother. 52 Mean-
while, all the peo-
ple were wailing
and mourning for
her. "Stop wail-
ing," Jesus said.
"She is not dead
but asleep."
53 They laughed
at him, knowing
that she was dead.
54 But he took her
by the hand and
said, "My child,
get up!" 55 Her spir-
it returned, and at
once she stood up.

ἔγνων δύναμιν ἐξεληλυθυῖαν ἀπ᾽ ἐμοῦ. 47 ἰδοῦσα δὲ
˻was aware of˼ power going out from me." Seeing *{and}* that she had not
1182 1539 2002 608 1609 1625 1254 4022 3291 3291 4024
v.aai.1s n.asf pt.ra.asf p.g r.gs.1 pt.aa.nsf cj

ἡ γυνὴ ὅτι οὐκ ἔλαθεν, τρέμουσα ἦλθεν
escaped notice, the woman *that* *not* *she had escaped notice* *trembling* ˻stepped forward,˼ trembling,
3291 3291 3836 1222 4022 4024 3291 5554 2262 5554
d.nsf n.nsf cj pl v.aai.3s pt.pa.nsf v.aai.3s

καὶ προσπεσοῦσα αὐτῷ ˻δι᾽ ἣν
and fell down before him. She declared in the presence of all the people why
2779 4700 899 550 550 1967 1967 1967 1967 4246 3836 3295 1328 4005
cj pt.aa.nsf r.dsm.3 p.a r.asf

αἰτίαν˼ ἥψατο αὐτοῦ ἀπήγγειλεν ἐνώπιον παντὸς τοῦ λαοῦ καὶ ὡς
˻she had touched˼ him *She declared* *in the presence of* *all* *the* *people* and how
162 721 899 550 1967 4246 3836 3295 2779 6055
n.asf v.ami.3s r.gsm.3 v.aai.3s p.g a.gsm d.gsm n.gsm cj cj

ἰάθη παραχρῆμα. 48 ὁ δὲ εἶπεν αὐτῇ, θυγάτηρ, ἡ πίστις
˻she had been healed˼ at once. Then Jesus *The* said to her, "Daughter, *{the}* your faith
2615 4202 1254 3836 1254 3306 899 2588 3836 5148 4411
v.api.3s adv d.nsm cj v.aai.3s r.dsf.3 n.vsf d.nsf n.nsf

σου σέσωκέν σε· ↰ πορεύου εἰς εἰρήνην. 49 ↱ ↱ ἔτι αὐτοῦ λαλοῦντος
your has made you well; go in peace." While he was still *he* speaking,
5148 5392 5148 5392 4513 1650 1645 3281 899 3281 2285 899 3281
r.gs.2 v.rai.3s r.as.2 v.pmm.2s p.a n.asf adv r.gsm.3 pt.pa.gsm

ἔρχεταί τις παρὰ τοῦ ἀρχισυναγώγου λέγων ὅτι
someone came *someone* from the house of the synagogue-ruler, saying, ~ "Your daughter
5516 2262 5516 4123 3836 801 3306 4022 5148 2588
v.pmi.3s r.nsm p.g d.gsm n.gsm pt.pa.nsm cj

τέθνηκεν ἡ θυγάτηρ σου· ↱ μηκέτι σκύλλε τὸν διδάσκαλον. ↰ ↰ 50 ὁ
is dead; *{the}* *daughter* *Your* do not bother the Teacher any longer." *{the}*
2569 3836 2588 5148 5035 3600 5035 3836 1437 3600 3600 3836
v.rai.3s d.nsf n.nsf r.gs.2 adv v.pam.2s d.asm n.asm d.nsm

δὲ ↱ Ἰησοῦς ἀκούσας ἀπεκρίθη αὐτῷ, ↱ μὴ φοβοῦ, μόνον πίστευσον,
{and} When Jesus heard this, he said to him, "Do not be afraid, only believe,
1254 201 2652 201 646 899 5828 3590 5828 3667 4409
cj n.nsm pt.aa.nsm v.api.3s r.dsm.3 pl v.ppm.2s adv v.aam.2s

καὶ σωθήσεται. 51 ἐλθὼν δὲ εἰς τὴν οἰκίαν ↱ ↱ οὐκ ἀφῆκεν
and she will get better." ˻When he went˼ *{and}* into the house he did not allow anyone
2779 5392 2262 1254 1650 3836 3864 918 918 4024 918 5516
cj v.fpi.3s pt.aa.nsm cj p.a d.asf n.asf pl v.aai.3s

εἰσελθεῖν τινα σὺν αὐτῷ ˻εἰ μὴ˼ Πέτρον καὶ Ἰωάννην καὶ Ἰάκωβον καὶ τὸν
to go in *anyone* with him except Peter and John and James, and the
1656 5516 5250 899 1623 3590 4377 2779 2722 2779 2610 2779 3836
f.aa r.asm p.d r.dsm.3 cj pl n.asm cj n.asm cj n.asm cj d.asm

πατέρα τῆς παιδὸς καὶ τὴν μητέρα. 52 ἔκλαιον δὲ πάντες καὶ
father of the child and her mother. And all the people were weeping *And* *all* and
4252 3836 4090 2779 3836 3613 1254 4246 3081 1254 4246 2779
n.asm d.gsf n.gsf cj d.asf n.asf v.iai.3p cj a.npm cj

ἐκόπτοντο αὐτήν. ὁ δὲ εἶπεν, μὴ κλαίετε, ↱ ↱ οὐ γὰρ ἀπέθανεν ἀλλὰ
mourning for her. He *{and}* said, "Stop weeping, for she did not *for* die; but
3164 899 3836 1254 3306 3590 3081 1142 633 633 4024 1142 633 247
v.imi.3p r.asf.3 d.nsm cj v.aai.3s pl v.pam.2p pl cj v.aai.3s cj

καθεύδει. 53 καὶ κατεγέλων αὐτοῦ εἰδότες ὅτι ἀπέθανεν. 54
is sleeping." And ˻they laughed at˼ him, knowing that she had died. But taking her by
2761 2779 2860 899 3857 4022 633 1254 3195 899 3195
v.pai.3s cj v.iai.3p r.gsm.3 pt.ra.npm cj v.aai.3s

αὐτὸς δὲ[a] κρατήσας τῆς χειρὸς αὐτῆς ἐφώνησεν λέγων, ἡ παῖς, ἔγειρε.
the hand, he *But* *taking by* *the* *hand* *her* called out, saying, *{the}* "Child, arise!"
3836 5931 899 1254 3195 3836 5931 899 5888 3306 3836 4090 1586
r.nsm cj pt.aa.nsm d.gsf n.gsf r.gsf.3 v.aai.3s pt.pa.nsm d.vsf n.vsf v.pam.2s

55 καὶ ἐπέστρεψεν τὸ πνεῦμα αὐτῆς καὶ ἀνέστη παραχρῆμα καὶ
And her spirit returned, *{the}* *spirit* *her* and ˻she got up˼ at once. *{and}*
2779 899 4460 2188 3836 4460 899 2779 482 4202 2779
cj v.aai.3s d.nsn n.nsn r.gsf.3 cj v.aai.3s adv cj

NASB

for I was aware
that power had
gone out of Me."
47 When the woman
saw that she had
not escaped no-
tice, she came
trembling and fell
down before Him,
and declared in
the presence of
all the people the
reason why she
had touched Him,
and how she had
been immedi-
ately healed. 48 And
He said to her,
"Daughter, your
faith has made you
well; go in peace."
49 While He was
still speaking,
someone *came
from *the house
of* the synagogue
official, saying,
"Your daughter has
died; do not trouble
the Teacher any-
more." 50 But when
Jesus heard *this,*
He answered him,
"Do not be afraid
any longer; only
believe, and she
will be made well."
51 When He came to
the house, He did
not allow anyone
to enter with Him,
except Peter and
John and James,
and the girl's fa-
ther and mother.
52 Now they were
all weeping and
lamenting for her;
but He said, "Stop
weeping, for she
has not died, but is
asleep." 53 And they
began laughing
at Him, knowing
that she had died.
54 He, however, took
her by the hand
and called, saying,
"Child, arise!"
55 And her spirit re-
turned, and she got
up immediately;

[a] ἐκβαλὼν ἔξω πάντας, καί included by TR after δὲ.

NIV

Then Jesus told
them to give her
something to eat.
56 Her parents were
astonished, but he
ordered them not
to tell anyone what
had happened.

Jesus Sends Out the Twelve

9 When Jesus
had called the
Twelve together,
he gave them pow-
er and authority
to drive out all de-
mons and to cure
diseases, 2 and he
sent them out to
proclaim the king-
dom of God and to
heal the sick. 3 He
told them: "Take
nothing for the
journey—no staff,
no bag, no bread,
no money, no extra
shirt. 4 Whatever
house you enter,
stay there until
you leave that
town. 5 If people do
not welcome you,
leave their town
and shake the dust
off your feet as a
testimony against
them." 6 So they set
out and went from
village to village,
proclaiming the
good news and
healing people ev-
erywhere.
7 Now Herod the
tetrarch heard
about all that was
going on. And he
was perplexed be-
cause some were
saying that John

διέταξεν αὐτῇ δοθῆναι φαγεῖν. 56 καὶ
He commanded that something be given her *be given* to eat. *{and}* Her parents
1411 1443 1443 899 1443 2266 2779 899 1204
v.aai.3s r.dsf.3 f.ap f.aa cj

ἐξέστησαν οἱ γονεῖς αὐτῆς· ὁ δὲ παρήγγειλεν αὐτοῖς μηδενὶ
were astonished; *{the}* *parents* *Her* but he *but* ordered them to tell no one
2014 3836 1204 899 1254 3836 1254 4133 899 3306 3306 3594
v.aai.3p d.npm n.npm r.gsf.3 d.nsm cj v.aai.3s r.dpm.3 a.dsm

εἰπεῖν τὸ γεγονός.
to tell what had happened.
3306 3836 1181
f.aa d.asn pt.ra.asn

9:1 ↱ συγκαλεσάμενος δὲ τοὺς δώδεκα ἔδωκεν αὐτοῖς δύναμιν καὶ
And he called together *And* the twelve and gave them power and
1254 1443 5157 1254 3836 1557 1443 899 1539 2779
pt.am.nsm cj d.apm a.apm v.aai.3s r.dpm.3 n.asf cj

ἐξουσίαν ἐπὶ πάντα τὰ δαιμόνια καὶ νόσους θεραπεύειν 2 καὶ ἀπέστειλεν
authority over all *{the}* demons, and to cure diseases. *to cure* Then he sent
2026 2093 4246 3836 1228 2779 2543 2543 3798 2543 2779 690
n.asf p.a a.apn d.apn n.apn cj n.apf f.pa cj v.aai.3s

αὐτοὺς ↰ κηρύσσειν τὴν βασιλείαν τοῦ θεοῦ καὶ ἰᾶσθαι [a]τοὺς ἀσθενεῖς, 3 καὶ
them out to proclaim the kingdom of God and to heal the sick. *{and}*
899 690 3062 3836 993 3836 2536 2779 2615 3836 822 2779
r.apm.3 f.pa d.asf n.asf d.gsm n.gsm cj f.pm d.apm a.apm cj

εἶπεν πρὸς αὐτούς, μηδὲν αἴρετε εἰς τὴν ὁδόν, μήτε ῥάβδον μήτε πήραν
He said to them, "Take nothing *Take* on the journey — no staff, nor bag,
3306 4639 899 149 3594 149 1650 3836 3847 3612 4811 3612 4385
v.aai.3s p.a r.apm.3 a.asn v.pam.2p p.a d.asf n.asf cj n.asf cj n.asf

μήτε ἄρτον μήτε ἀργύριον μήτε ἀνὰ[b] δύο χιτῶνας ἔχειν. 4 καὶ εἰς
nor bread, nor money. No one is to have two tunics. *to have* And *{into}*
3612 788 3612 736 3612 324 2400 2400 1545 5945 2400 2779 1650
cj n.asm cj n.asn cj p.a a.apm n.apm f.pa cj p.a

⌊ἣν ἂν⌋ οἰκίαν εἰσέλθητε, ἐκεῖ μένετε καὶ ἐκεῖθεν ἐξέρχεσθε. 5 καὶ ⌊ὅσοι
whatever house you enter, stay there, *stay* and from there go out. And wherever
4005 323 3864 1656 3531 1695 3531 2779 1696 2002 2779 4012
r.asf pl n.asf v.aas.2p adv v.pam.2p cj adv v.pmm.2p cj r.npm

ἂν⌋ ↱ ↱ μὴ δέχωνται ὑμᾶς, ἐξερχόμενοι ἀπὸ τῆς πόλεως ἐκείνης
they do not receive you, leave from *{the}* that town *that* and shake
323 1312 1312 3590 1312 7007 2002 608 3836 1697 4484 1697 701
pl pl v.pms.3p r.ap.2 pt.pm.npm p.g d.gsf n.gsf r.gsf

τὸν κονιορτὸν ἀπὸ τῶν ποδῶν ὑμῶν ἀποτινάσσετε εἰς μαρτύριον
off the dust from *{the}* your feet *your* *shake off* as an act that testifies
701 3836 3155 608 3836 7007 4546 7007 701 1650 3457
d.asm n.asm p.g d.gpm n.gpm r.gp.2 v.pam.2p p.a n.asn

ἐπ᾽ αὐτούς. 6 ↱ ἐξερχόμενοι δὲ διήρχοντο κατὰ τὰς κώμας
against them." So they set out *So* and traveled throughout the villages,
2093 899 1254 1451 2002 1254 1451 2848 3836 3267
p.a r.apm.3 pt.pm.npm cj v.imi.3p p.a d.apf n.apf

εὐαγγελιζόμενοι καὶ θεραπεύοντες πανταχοῦ. 7 ἤκουσεν
⌊preaching the good news⌋ and healing everywhere. Now Herod the tetrarch heard about
2294 2779 2543 4116 1254 2476 3836 5490 201
pt.pm.npm cj pt.pa.npm adv v.aai.3s

δὲ Ἡρῴδης ὁ τετραάρχης τὰ γινόμενα πάντα καὶ
Now *Herod* *the* *tetrarch* everything that was happening, *everything* and
1254 2476 3836 5490 4246 3836 1181 4246 2779
cj n.nsm d.nsm n.nsm d.apn pt.pm.apn a.apn cj

διηπόρει διὰ τὸ λέγεσθαι ὑπό τινων ὅτι Ἰωάννης
⌊he was thoroughly perplexed⌋ because *{the}* ⌊it was being said⌋ by some that John
1389 1328 3836 3306 5679 5516 4022 2722
v.iai.3s p.a d.asn f.pp p.g r.gpm cj n.nsm

[a] [τοὺς ἀσθενεῖς] UBS, omitted by TNIV.
[b] [ἀνὰ] UBS, omitted by TNIV.

NASB

and He gave orders
for *something* to
be given her to eat.
56 Her parents were
amazed; but He
instructed them to
tell no one what
had happened.

Ministry of the Twelve

9:1 And He called
the twelve to-
gether, and gave
them power and
authority over all
the demons and
to heal diseases.
2 And He sent them
out to proclaim the
kingdom of God
and to perform
healing. 3 And He
said to them, "Take
nothing for *your*
journey, neither a
staff, nor a bag, nor
bread, nor money;
and do not *even*
have two tunics
apiece. 4 Whatever
house you enter,
stay there until
you leave that
city. 5 And as for
those who do not
receive you, as you
go out from that
city, shake the dust
off your feet as a
testimony against
them." 6 Departing,
they *began* going
throughout the
villages, preach-
ing the gospel and
healing every-
where.
7 Now Herod the
tetrarch heard of
all that was hap-
pening; and he was
greatly perplexed,
because it was said
by some that John

NIV

had been raised
from the dead,
8 others that Elijah
had appeared, and
still others that
one of the prophets
of long ago had
come back to life.
9 But Herod said,
"I beheaded John.
Who, then, is this
I hear such things
about?" And he
tried to see him.

Jesus Feeds the Five Thousand

10 When the apos-
tles returned, they
reported to Jesus
what they had
done. Then he took
them with him and
they withdrew by
themselves to a
town called Beth-
saida, 11 but the
crowds learned
about it and fol-
lowed him. He
welcomed them
and spoke to them
about the kingdom
of God, and healed
those who needed
healing.
12 Late in the af-
ternoon the Twelve
came to him and
said, "Send the
crowd away so
they can go to
the surrounding
villages and coun-
tryside and find
food and lodging,
because we are
in a remote place
here."
13 He replied,
"You give them
something to eat."
They answered,
"We have only five
loaves of bread
and two fish—un-
less we go and buy
food for all this
crowd." 14 (About
five thousand men
were there.)
But he said

ἠγέρθη ἐκ νεκρῶν, 8 ὑπό τινων δὲ ὅτι Ἠλίας ἐφάνη, ↰
⌞had been raised⌟ from the dead, by some *{and}* that Elijah had appeared, and by
1586 1666 3738 5679 5516 1254 4022 2460 5743 1254 5679
v.api.3s p.g a.gpm p.g r.gpm pl cj n.nsm v.api.3s

ἄλλων δὲ ὅτι προφήτης τις τῶν ἀρχαίων ἀνέστη.
others *and* that a certain one of the ancient prophets *certain one of the ancient* had risen.
257 1254 4022 5516 5516 3836 3836 792 4737 5516 3836 792 482
r.gpm pl cj n.nsm r.nsm d.gpm a.gpm v.aai.3s

9 εἶπεν δὲ Ἡρῴδης, Ἰωάννην ἐγὼ ἀπεκεφάλισα· τίς δέ ἐστιν οὗτος
Herod said, *{and} Herod* "John I beheaded, but who *but* is this
2476 3306 1254 2476 2722 1609 642 1254 5515 1254 1639 4047
v.aai.3s pl n.nsm n.asm r.ns.1 v.aai.1s r.nsm cj v.pai.3s r.nsm

περὶ οὗ ἀκούω τοιαῦτα; καὶ ἐζήτει ἰδεῖν αὐτόν. 10 καὶ →
about whom I hear such things?" So ⌞he was trying⌟ to see him. *{and}* When the apostles
4309 4005 201 5525 2779 2426 1625 899 2779 3836 693
p.g r.gsm v.pai.1s r.apn cj v.iai.3s f.aa r.asm.3 cj

ὑποστρέψαντες οἱ ἀπόστολοι διηγήσαντο αὐτῷ ὅσα ἐποίησαν. καὶ παραλαβὼν
returned *the apostles* they recounted to Jesus all they had done; and he took
5715 3836 693 1455 899 4012 4472 2779 4161
pt.aa.npm d.npm n.npm v.ami.3p r.dsm.3 r.apn v.aai.3p cj pt.aa.nsm

αὐτοὺς ὑπεχώρησεν ⌞κατ' ἰδίαν⌟ εἰς πόλιν καλουμένην Βηθσαϊδά. 11 ↱
them and withdrew privately to a town called Bethsaida. When
899 5723 2848 2625 1650 4484 2813 1034 1182
r.apm.3 v.aai.3s p.a a.asf p.a n.asf pt.pp.asf n.asf

οἱ δὲ ὄχλοι γνόντες ἠκολούθησαν αὐτῷ· καὶ ↱ ἀποδεξάμενος αὐτοὺς
the *{and}* crowds ⌞found out about⌟ it, they followed him. So he welcomed them,
3836 1254 4063 1182 199 899 2779 3281 622 899
d.npm cj n.npm pt.aa.npm v.aai.3p r.dsm.3 cj pt.am.nsm r.apm.3

ἐλάλει αὐτοῖς περὶ τῆς βασιλείας τοῦ θεοῦ, καὶ τοὺς χρείαν
and spoke to them about the kingdom of God and cured those who had need
3281 899 4309 3836 993 3836 2536 2779 2615 3836 2400 2400 5970
v.iai.3s r.dpm.3 p.g d.gsf n.gsf d.gsm n.gsm cj d.apm n.asf

ἔχοντας θεραπείας ἰᾶτο. 12 ἡ δὲ ἡμέρα ἤρξατο κλίνειν·
who had of healing. *cured* Now the *Now* day began to wear away, so the twelve
2400 2542 2615 1254 3836 1254 2465 806 3111 1254 3836 1557
pt.pa.apm n.gsf v.imi.3s d.nsf cj n.nsf v.ami.3s f.pa

προσελθόντες δὲ οἱ δώδεκα εἶπαν αὐτῷ, ἀπόλυσον τὸν ὄχλον, ↰ ἵνα ↱
came *so the twelve* and said to him, "Send the crowd away so that they
4665 1254 3836 1557 3306 899 668 3836 4063 668 2671 2907
pt.aa.npm cj d.npm a.npm v.aai.3p r.dsm.3 v.aam.2s d.asm n.asm cj

↱ πορευθέντες εἰς τὰς κύκλῳ κώμας καὶ ἀγροὺς καταλύσωσιν καὶ
may go into the surrounding villages and countryside and secure lodging and
2907 4513 1650 3836 3241 3267 2779 69 2907 2779
pt.ap.npm p.a d.apf adv n.apf cj n.apm v.aas.3p cj

εὕρωσιν ἐπισιτισμόν, ὅτι ὧδε ἐν ἐρήμῳ τόπῳ ἐσμέν.
get provisions, for we are in a desolate place here." *in desolate place we are*
2351 2169 4022 1639 1639 1877 2245 5536 6045 1877 2245 5536 1639
v.aas.3p n.asm cj adv p.d a.dsm n.dsm v.pai.1p

13 εἶπεν δὲ πρὸς αὐτούς, δότε αὐτοῖς ὑμεῖς φαγεῖν. οἱ δὲ
But he said *But* to them, "You give them *You* something to eat." They *{and}*
1254 3306 1254 4639 899 7007 1443 899 7007 2266 3836 1254
v.aai.3s cj p.a r.apm.3 v.aam.2p r.dpm.3 r.np.2 f.aa d.npm cj

εἶπαν, οὐκ εἰσὶν ἡμῖν πλεῖον ἢ ἄρτοι πέντε καὶ ἰχθύες δύο, ⌞εἰ
said, "We have no *have We* more than five loaves *five* and two fish, *two* unless
3306 7005 1639 4024 1639 7005 4498 2445 4297 788 4297 2779 1545 2716 1545 1623
v.aai.3p pl v.pai.3p r.dp.1 adv.c pl n.npm a.npm cj n.npm a.npm cj

μήτι⌟ πορευθέντες ἡμεῖς ἀγοράσωμεν εἰς πάντα τὸν λαὸν τοῦτον
we go *we* and buy food for all *{the}* these people." *these*
3614 7005 4513 7005 60 1109 1650 4246 3836 4047 3295 4047
pl pt.ap.npm r.np.1 v.aas.1p p.a a.asm d.asm n.asm r.asm

βρώματα. 14 ἦσαν γὰρ ὡσεὶ ἄνδρες πεντακισχίλιοι. εἶπεν δὲ
food For there were *For* about five thousand men. *five thousand* He said *{and}*
1109 1142 1639 1142 6059 4295 4295 467 4295 3306 1254
n.apn v.iai.3p cj pl n.npm a.npm v.aai.3s cj

NASB

had risen from the
dead, 8 and by some
that Elijah had ap-
peared, and by oth-
ers that one of the
prophets of old had
risen again. 9 Herod
said, "I myself had
John beheaded; but
who is this man
about whom I hear
such things?" And
he kept trying to
see Him.
10 When the apos-
tles returned, they
gave an account to
Him of all that they
had done. Taking
them with Him, He
withdrew by Him-
self to a city called
Bethsaida. 11 But
the crowds were
aware of this and
followed Him; and
welcoming them,
He *began* speaking
to them about the
kingdom of God
and curing those
who had need of
healing.

Five Thousand Fed

12 Now the day
was ending, and
the twelve came
and said to Him,
"Send the crowd
away, that they
may go into the
surrounding villag-
es and countryside
and find lodging
and get something
to eat; for here
we are in a deso-
late place." 13 But
He said to them,
"You give them
something to eat!"
And they said,
"We have no more
than five loaves
and two fish, un-
less perhaps we go
and buy food for
all these people."
14 (For there were
about five thousand
men.) And He said

NIV

to his disciples, "Have them sit down in groups of about fifty each." [15]The disciples did so, and everyone sat down. [16]Taking the five loaves and the two fish and looking up to heaven, he gave thanks and broke them. Then he gave them to the disciples to distribute to the people. [17]They all ate and were satisfied, and the disciples picked up twelve basketfuls of broken pieces that were left over.

Peter Declares That Jesus Is the Messiah

[18]Once when Jesus was praying in private and his disciples were with him, he asked them, "Who do the crowds say I am?"

[19]They replied, "Some say John the Baptist; others say Elijah; and still others, that one of the prophets of long ago has come back to life."

[20]"But what about you?" he asked. "Who do you say I am?"

Peter answered, "God's Messiah."

Jesus Predicts His Death

[21]Jesus strictly warned them not to tell this to anyone. [22]And he said, "The Son of Man must suffer many things and be rejected by the elders, the chief priests and the teachers of the law,

πρὸς τοὺς μαθητὰς αὐτοῦ, → κατακλίνατε αὐτοὺς κλισίας ὡσεὶ[a]
to {the} his disciples, his "Have them sit down them in groups of about fifty
4639 3836 899 3412 899 899 2884 899 3112 6059 4299
p.a d.apm n.apm r.gsm.3 v.aam.2p r.apm.3 n.apf pl

ἀνὰ πεντήκοντα. 15 καὶ ἐποίησαν οὕτως καὶ → κατέκλιναν ἅπαντας.
each." fifty And they did so, and had them all sit down. all
324 4299 2779 4472 4048 2779 570 2884 570
p.a a.apm cj v.aai.3p adv cj v.aai.3p a.apm

16 λαβὼν δὲ τοὺς πέντε ἄρτους καὶ τοὺς δύο ἰχθύας ↱ ἀναβλέψας εἰς τὸν
Taking {and} the five loaves and the two fish, he looked up to {the}
3284 1254 3836 4297 788 2779 3836 1545 2716 2328 329 1650 3836
pt.aa.nsm cj d.apm a.apm n.apm cj d.apm a.apm n.apm pt.aa.nsm p.a d.asm

οὐρανὸν εὐλόγησεν αὐτοὺς καὶ κατέκλασεν καὶ ἐδίδου τοῖς
heaven and said a blessing and broke them; and broke then he gave them to the
4041 2328 2779 2880 899 2779 2880 2779 1443 3836
n.asm v.aai.3s r.apm.3 cj v.aai.3s cj v.iai.3s d.dpm

μαθηταῖς παραθεῖναι τῷ ὄχλῳ. 17 καὶ ἔφαγον καὶ ἐχορτάσθησαν πάντες,
disciples to distribute ⌊to the⌋ crowd. {and} They ate and all were satisfied. all
3412 4192 3836 4063 2779 2266 2779 4246 5963 4246
n.dpm f.aa d.dsm n.dsm cj v.aai.3p cj v.api.3p a.npm

καὶ ἤρθη τὸ περισσεῦσαν αὐτοῖς
{and} What was left over ⌊was gathered up⌋ What was left over by them, twelve baskets
2779 3836 4355 4355 4355 149 3836 4355 899 1557 3186
cj v.api.3s d.nsn pt.aa.nsn r.dpm.3

κλασμάτων κόφινοι δώδεκα. 18 καὶ ἐγένετο ἐν τῷ εἶναι αὐτὸν
of broken pieces. baskets twelve Now ⌊it happened that⌋ as {the} he was he
3083 3186 1557 2779 1181 1877 3836 899 1639 899
n.gpn n.npm a.npm cj v.ami.3s p.d d.dsn f.pa r.asm.3

προσευχόμενον κατὰ μόνας συνῆσαν αὐτῷ οἱ μαθηταί, καὶ
praying by himself, the disciples were near him. the disciples {and}
4667 2848 3668 3836 3412 5289 899 3836 3412 2779
pt.pm.asm p.a a.apf v.iai.3p r.dsm.3 d.npm n.npm cj

ἐπηρώτησεν αὐτοὺς λέγων, τίνα με λέγουσιν οἱ ὄχλοι
He asked them, saying, "Who do the crowds say that I do say the crowds
2089 899 3306 5515 3306 3836 4063 3306 1609 3306 3836 4063
v.aai.3s r.apm.3 pt.pa.nsm r.asm r.as.1 v.pai.3p d.npm n.npm

εἶναι; 19 οἱ δὲ ἀποκριθέντες εἶπαν, Ἰωάννην τὸν βαπτιστήν, ἄλλοι δὲ
am?" They {and} replied, saying, "John the Baptist; others {and} say,
1639 3836 1254 646 3306 2722 3836 969 257 1254
f.pa d.npm cj pt.ap.npm v.aai.3p n.asm d.asm n.asm r.npm pl

Ἠλίαν, ἄλλοι δὲ ὅτι προφήτης τις τῶν ἀρχαίων ἀνέστη. 20
Elijah; still others still that prophets one of the ancient prophets has risen." Then
2460 1254 257 1254 4022 4737 5516 3836 792 4737 482 1254
n.asm r.npm pl cj n.nsm r.nsm d.gpm a.gpm v.aai.3s

εἶπεν δὲ αὐτοῖς, ὑμεῖς δὲ τίνα με λέγετε εἶναι;
he said Then to them, "Now you, Now who do you say that I do you say am?" And
3306 1254 899 1254 7007 1254 5515 3306 3306 3306 1609 3306 1639 1254
v.aai.3s cj r.dpm.3 r.np.2 cj r.asm r.as.1 v.pai.2p f.pa

Πέτρος δὲ ⌊ἀποκριθεὶς εἶπεν,⌋ τὸν χριστὸν τοῦ θεοῦ. 21
Peter And replied, "The Christ of God." Then, with a warning,
4377 1254 646 3306 3836 5986 3836 2536 1254 2203 2203 2203
n.nsm cj pt.ap.nsm v.aai.3s d.asm n.asm d.gsm n.gsm

ὁ δὲ ἐπιτιμήσας αὐτοῖς παρήγγειλεν μηδενὶ λέγειν τοῦτο
he Then with a warning commanded them commanded to tell no one to tell this,
3836 1254 2203 4133 899 4133 3306 3306 3594 3306 4047
d.nsm cj pt.aa.nsm r.dpm.3 v.aai.3s a.dsm f.pa r.asn

22 εἰπὼν ὅτι δεῖ τὸν υἱὸν τοῦ ἀνθρώπου πολλὰ παθεῖν
saying, ~ ⌊"It is necessary⌋ for the Son of Man to suffer many things to suffer
3306 4022 1256 3836 5626 3836 476 4248 4248 4498 4248
pt.aa.nsm cj v.pai.3s d.asm n.asm d.gsm n.gsm a.apn f.aa

καὶ ἀποδοκιμασθῆναι ἀπὸ τῶν πρεσβυτέρων καὶ ἀρχιερέων καὶ γραμματέων καὶ
and to be rejected by the elders and chief priests and scribes, and
2779 627 608 3836 4565 2779 797 2779 1208 2779
cj f.ap p.g d.gpm a.gpm cj n.gpm cj n.gpm cj

NASB

to His disciples, "Have them sit down *to eat* in groups of about fifty each." [15]They did so, and had them all sit down. [16]Then He took the five loaves and the two fish, and looking up to heaven, He blessed them, and broke *them,* and kept giving *them* to the disciples to set before the people. [17]And they all ate and were satisfied; and the broken pieces which they had left over were picked up, twelve baskets *full.*

[18]And it happened that while He was praying alone, the disciples were with Him, and He questioned them, saying, "Who do the people say that I am?" [19]They answered and said, "John the Baptist, and others *say* Elijah; but others, that one of the prophets of old has risen again." [20]And He said to them, "But who do you say that I am?" And Peter answered and said, "The Christ of God." [21]But He warned them and instructed *them* not to tell this to anyone, [22]saying, "The Son of Man must suffer many things and be rejected by the elders and chief priests and scribes,

[a] [ὡσεὶ] UBS, omitted by TNIV.

NIV

and he must be
killed and on the
third day be raised
to life."
[23]Then he said to
them all: "Who-
ever wants to be
my disciple must
deny themselves
and take up their
cross daily and
follow me. [24]For
whoever wants to
save their life will
lose it, but whoev-
er loses their life
for me will save
it. [25]What good
is it for someone
to gain the whole
world, and yet lose
or forfeit their very
self? [26]Whoever
is ashamed of me
and my words, the
Son of Man will be
ashamed of them
when he comes in
his glory and in
the glory of the
Father and of the
holy angels.
[27]"Truly I tell
you, some who are
standing here will
not taste death be-
fore they see the
kingdom of God."

The Transfiguration

[28]About eight
days after Jesus
said this, he took
Peter, John and
James with him
and went up onto a
mountain to pray.
[29]As he was pray-
ing, the appear-
ance of his face
changed, and his
clothes became as
bright as a flash of
lightning.

ἀποκτανθῆναι καὶ τῇ τρίτῃ ἡμέρᾳ ἐγερθῆναι. 23 ἔλεγεν δὲ πρὸς πάντας,
to be killed, and ⌊on the⌋ third day to be raised." Then he said *Then* to all,
650 2779 3836 5569 2465 1586 1254 3306 1254 4639 4246
f.ap cj d.dsf a.dsf n.dsf f.ap v.iai.3s cj p.a a.apm

εἴ τις θέλει ὀπίσω μου ἔρχεσθαι, ἀρνησάσθω ἑαυτὸν καὶ
"If someone wants to come after me, *to come* let him deny himself, and
1623 5516 2527 2262 2262 3958 1609 2262 766 1571 2779
cj r.nsm v.pai.3s p.g r.gs.1 f.pm v.amm.3s r.asm.3 cj

ἀράτω τὸν σταυρὸν αὐτοῦ ⌊καθʼ ἡμέραν⌋ καὶ ἀκολουθείτω μοι. 24
⌊let him take up⌋ *{the}* his cross *his* daily, and let him follow me. For
149 3836 899 5089 899 2848 2465 2779 199 1609 1142
v.aam.3s d.asm n.asm r.gsm.3 p.a n.asf cj v.pam.3s r.ds.1

ὃς γὰρ ἂν θέλῃ τὴν ψυχὴν αὐτοῦ σῶσαι ἀπολέσει αὐτήν·
whoever *For* ~ wants to save *{the}* his life *his* *to save* will lose it, but
4005 1142 323 2527 5392 5392 3836 899 6034 899 5392 660 899 1254
r.nsm cj pl v.pas.3s d.asf n.asf r.gsm.3 f.aa v.fai.3s r.asf.3

ὃς δʼ ἂν ἀπολέσῃ τὴν ψυχὴν αὐτοῦ ἕνεκεν ἐμοῦ ↰ οὗτος σώσει
whoever *but* ~ loses *{the}* his life *his* for my sake, this person will save
4005 1254 323 660 3836 899 6034 899 1914 1609 1914 4047 5392
r.nsm cj pl v.aas.3s d.asf n.asf r.gsm.3 p.g r.gs.1 r.nsm v.fai.3s

αὐτήν. 25 τί γὰρ ὠφελεῖται ἄνθρωπος κερδήσας τὸν κόσμον
it. For what *For* ⌊good will it do⌋ a person who has gained the whole world
899 1142 5515 1142 6067 476 3045 3836 3910 3180
r.asf.3 r.asn cj v.ppi.3s n.nsm pt.aa.nsm d.asm n.asm

ὅλον ἑαυτὸν δὲ ἀπολέσας ἢ ζημιωθείς; 26 ὃς
whole but has lost or forfeited ⌊his very self?⌋ *but* *has lost* *or* *forfeited* For whoever
3910 1254 660 660 2445 2423 1571 1254 660 2445 2423 1142 4005
a.asm r.asm.3 cj pt.aa.nsm cj pt.ap.nsm r.nsm

γὰρ ἂν ἐπαισχυνθῇ με καὶ ↰ τοὺς ἐμοὺς λόγους, ↱ τοῦτον ↱ ὁ υἱὸς τοῦ
For ~ is ashamed of me and of *{the}* my words, of this one will the Son of
1142 323 2049 1609 2779 2049 3836 1847 3364 2049 4047 2049 3836 5626 3836
cj pl v.aps.3s r.as.1 cj d.apm r.apm.1 n.apm r.asm d.nsm n.nsm d.gsm

ἀνθρώπου ἐπαισχυνθήσεται, ὅταν ἔλθῃ ἐν τῇ δόξῃ αὐτοῦ καὶ ↰ τοῦ
Man be ashamed when he comes in *the* his glory *his* and the glory of the
476 2049 4020 2262 1877 3836 899 1518 899 2779 3836 1518 3836
n.gsm v.fpi.3s cj v.aas.3s p.d d.dsf n.dsf r.gsm.3 cj d.gsm

πατρὸς καὶ τῶν ἁγίων ἀγγέλων. 27 λέγω δὲ ὑμῖν ἀληθῶς, εἰσίν τινες
Father and of the holy angels. But I tell *But* you most certainly: ⌊There are⌋ some
4252 2779 3836 41 34 1254 3306 1254 7007 242 1639 5516
n.gsm cj d.gpm a.gpm n.gpm v.pai.1s cj r.dp.2 adv v.pai.3p r.npm

τῶν αὐτοῦ ἑστηκότων οἳ ↱ ⌊οὐ μὴ⌋ γεύσωνται θανάτου ⌊ἕως ἂν⌋
of those *here* standing here who will certainly not taste death before
3836 7000 2705 7000 4005 1174 4024 3590 1174 2505 2401 323
d.gpm adv pt.ra.gpm r.npm pl pl v.ams.3p n.gsm cj pl

ἴδωσιν τὴν βασιλείαν τοῦ θεοῦ. 28 ἐγένετο
they see the kingdom of God." About eight days after these sayings, ⌊it happened that⌋
1625 3836 993 3836 2536 6059 3893 2465 3552 4047 3364 1181
v.aas.3p d.asf n.asf d.gsm n.gsm v.ami.3s

δὲ μετὰ τοὺς λόγους τούτους ὡσεὶ ἡμέραι ὀκτὼ
{and} *after* *{the}* *sayings* *these* *About* *days* *eight* he went up on the mountain to
1254 3552 3836 3364 4047 6059 2465 3893 326 326 326 1650 3836 4001 4667
cj p.a d.apm n.apm r.apm pl n.npf a.npf

καὶ [a] παραλαβὼν Πέτρον καὶ Ἰωάννην καὶ Ἰάκωβον ἀνέβη εἰς τὸ ὄρος
pray, *{and}* taking along Peter and John and James. *he went up* *on* *the* *mountain*
4667 2779 4161 4377 2779 2722 2779 2610 326 1650 3836 4001
cj pt.aa.nsm n.asm cj n.asm cj n.asm v.aai.3s p.a d.asn n.asn

προσεύξασθαι. 29 καὶ ἐγένετο ἐν τῷ προσεύχεσθαι αὐτὸν τὸ εἶδος
to pray *{and}* *{it happened that}* As *{the}* he was praying, *he* the appearance
4667 2779 1181 1877 3836 899 4667 899 3836 1626
f.am cj v.ami.3s p.d d.dsn f.pm r.asm.3 d.nsn n.nsn

τοῦ προσώπου αὐτοῦ ἕτερον καὶ ὁ ἱματισμὸς αὐτοῦ
of his face *his* was changed, and *{the}* his clothing *his* turned a dazzling
3836 899 4725 899 2283 2779 3836 899 2669 899 1993 1993 1993
d.gsn n.gsn r.gsm.3 r.nsn cj d.nsm n.nsm r.gsm.3

NASB

and be killed and
be raised up on the
third day."
[23]And He was
saying to *them*
all, "If anyone
wishes to come
after Me, he must
deny himself, and
take up his cross
daily and follow
Me. [24]For whoever
wishes to save his
life will lose it, but
whoever loses his
life for My sake, he
is the one who will
save it. [25]For what
is a man profited if
he gains the whole
world, and loses or
forfeits himself?
[26]For whoever is
ashamed of Me
and My words, the
Son of Man will
be ashamed of him
when He comes in
His glory, and *the*
glory of the Father
and of the holy
angels. [27]But I say
to you truthfully,
there are some of
those standing here
who will not taste
death until they
see the kingdom of
God."

The Transfiguration

[28]Some eight days
after these sayings,
He took along
Peter and John and
James, and went up
on the mountain to
pray. [29]And while
He was praying,
the appearance of
His face became
different, and His
clothing *became*

[a] [καὶ] UBS, omitted by TNIV.

NIV

[30]Two men, Moses
and Elijah, ap-
peared in glorious
splendor, talking
with Jesus. [31]They
spoke about his de-
parture,[a] which he
was about to bring
to fulfillment at
Jerusalem. [32]Peter
and his compan-
ions were very
sleepy, but when
they became fully
awake, they saw
his glory and the
two men standing
with him. [33]As the
men were leaving
Jesus, Peter said to
him, "Master, it is
good for us to be
here. Let us put up
three shelters—
one for you, one
for Moses and one
for Elijah." (He did
not know what he
was saying.)
[34]While he was
speaking, a cloud
appeared and cov-
ered them, and
they were afraid
as they entered
the cloud. [35]A
voice came from
the cloud, saying,
"This is my Son,
whom I have cho-
sen; listen to him."
[36]When the voice
had spoken, they
found that Jesus
was alone. The
disciples kept this
to themselves and
did not tell anyone
at that time what
they had seen.

Jesus Heals a Demon-Possessed Boy

[37]The next day,
when they came
down from the
mountain,

[a] 31 Greek *exodus*

λευκὸς ἐξαστράπτων. 30 καὶ ἰδοὺ ἄνδρες δύο συνελάλουν αὐτῷ, οἵτινες ἦσαν
white, *turned a dazzling* and ~ two men *two* were talking with him; they were
3328 1993 2779 2627 1545 467 1545 5196 899 4015 1639
a.nsm pt.pa.nsm cj j n.npm a.npm v.iai.3p r.dsm.3 r.npm v.iai.3p

Μωϋσῆς καὶ Ἠλίας, 31 οἳ ὀφθέντες ἐν δόξῃ ἔλεγον τὴν
Moses and Elijah, who had appeared with ⌊glorious splendor⌋ and ⌊were speaking of⌋ *{the}*
3707 2779 2460 4005 3972 1877 1518 3306 3836
n.nsm cj n.nsm r.npm pt.ap.npm p.d n.dsf v.iai.3p d.asf

ἔξοδον αὐτοῦ, ἣν ἤμελλεν πληροῦν ἐν Ἰερουσαλήμ. 32 ὁ δὲ
his departure, *his* which he was soon to accomplish at Jerusalem. *{the}* *{and}*
899 2016 899 4005 3516 4444 1877 2647 3836 1254
n.asf r.gsm.3 r.asf v.iai.3s f.pa p.d n.dsf d.nsm cj

Πέτρος καὶ οἱ σὺν αὐτῷ ἦσαν βεβαρημένοι ὕπνῳ· ↱
Peter and those who were with him were weighed down with sleep, but they
4377 2779 3836 5250 899 1639 976 5678 1254 1625
n.nsm cj d.npm p.d r.dsm.3 v.iai.3p pt.rp.npm n.dsm

διαγρηγορήσαντες δὲ εἶδον τὴν δόξαν αὐτοῦ καὶ τοὺς δύο ἄνδρας τοὺς
kept awake *but* and saw *{the}* his glory *his* and the two men who
1340 1254 1625 3836 899 1518 899 2779 3836 1545 467 3836
pt.aa.npm cj v.aai.3p d.asf n.asf r.gsm.3 cj d.apm a.apm n.apm d.apm

συνεστῶτας αὐτῷ. 33 καὶ ἐγένετο ἐν τῷ διαχωρίζεσθαι
⌊were standing with⌋ him. *{and}* *{it happened that}* As *{the}* the men were about to leave
5319 899 2779 1181 1877 3836 899 1431
pt.ra.apm r.dsm.3 cj v.ami.3s p.d d.dsn f.pm

αὐτοὺς ἀπ' αὐτοῦ εἶπεν ὁ Πέτρος πρὸς τὸν Ἰησοῦν, ἐπιστάτα,
men *{from}* him, Peter said *{the}* *Peter* to *{the}* Jesus, "Master, it is
899 608 899 4377 3306 3836 4377 4639 3836 2652 2181 1639 1639
r.apm.3 p.g r.gsm.3 v.aai.3s d.nsm n.nsm p.a d.asm n.asm n.vsm

καλόν ἐστιν ἡμᾶς ὧδε εἶναι, καὶ ποιήσωμεν σκηνὰς τρεῖς, μίαν σοὶ
good *it is* for us to be here. *to be* *{and}* Let us make three shelters, *three* one ⌊for you⌋
2819 1639 7005 1639 1639 6045 1639 2779 4472 5552 5008 5552 1651 5148
a.nsn v.pai.3s r.ap.1 adv f.pa cj v.aas.1p n.apf a.apf a.asf r.ds.2

καὶ μίαν Μωϋσεῖ καὶ μίαν Ἠλίᾳ, μὴ εἰδὼς ὃ λέγει. 34
and one for Moses and one for Elijah" — not knowing what ⌊he was saying.⌋ While he
2779 1651 3707 2779 1651 2460 3590 3857 4005 3306 3306 899
cj a.asf n.dsm cj a.asf n.dsm pl pt.ra.nsm r.asn v.pai.3s

ταῦτα δὲ αὐτοῦ λέγοντος ἐγένετο νεφέλη καὶ ἐπεσκίαζεν
was saying these things, *{and}* *he* *While was saying* a cloud came *cloud* and enveloped
3306 3306 4047 1254 899 3306 3749 1181 3749 2779 2173
r.apn cj r.gsm.3 pt.pa.gsm v.ami.3s n.nsf cj v.iai.3s

αὐτούς· ἐφοβήθησαν δὲ ἐν τῷ εἰσελθεῖν αὐτοὺς εἰς τὴν νεφέλην.
them; and they were afraid *and* as *{the}* they entered *they* *{into}* the cloud.
899 1254 5828 1254 1877 3836 899 1656 899 1650 3836 3749
r.apm.3 v.api.3p cj p.d d.dsn f.aa r.apm.3 p.a d.asf n.asf

35 καὶ φωνὴ ἐγένετο ἐκ τῆς νεφέλης λέγουσα, οὗτός ἐστιν ὁ υἱός μου
Then a voice came ⌊out of⌋ the cloud, saying, "This is *{the}* my Son, *my*
2779 5889 1181 1666 3836 3749 3306 4047 1639 3836 1609 5626 1609
cj n.nsf v.ami.3s p.g d.gsf n.gsf pt.pa.nsf r.nsm v.pai.3s d.nsm n.nsm r.gs.1

ὁ ἐκλελεγμένος, αὐτοῦ ἀκούετε. 36 καὶ ἐν τῷ γενέσθαι τὴν
the Chosen One; listen to him!" *listen to* And when *{the}* the voice had spoken, *the*
3836 1721 201 201 899 201 2779 1877 3836 3836 5889 1181 3836
d.nsm pt.rp.nsm r.gsm.3 v.pam.2p cj p.d d.dsn f.am d.asf

φωνὴν εὑρέθη Ἰησοῦς μόνος. καὶ αὐτοὶ ἐσίγησαν καὶ οὐδενὶ
voice Jesus was found *Jesus* to be alone. And they kept silent and told no one
5889 2652 2351 2652 3668 2779 899 4967 2779 550 4029
n.asf v.api.3s n.nsm a.nsm cj r.npm v.aai.3p cj a.dsm

ἀπήγγειλαν ἐν ἐκείναις ταῖς ἡμέραις οὐδὲν ὧν ἑώρακαν. 37
told in those *{the}* days anything of what they had seen. Now on the next
550 1877 1697 3836 2465 4029 4005 3972 1254 3836 3836 2009
v.aai.3p p.d r.dpf d.dpf n.dpf a.asn r.gpn v.rai.3p

ἐγένετο δὲ τῇ ἑξῆς ἡμέρᾳ → κατελθόντων αὐτῶν ἀπὸ τοῦ
day, ⌊it so happened that⌋ *Now* *on the* *next* *day* when they had come down *they* from the
2465 1181 1254 3836 2009 2465 899 2982 899 608 3836
v.ami.3s cj d.dsf adv n.dsf pt.aa.gpm r.gpm.3 p.g d.gsn

NASB

white *and* gleam-
ing. [30]And behold,
two men were talk-
ing with Him; and
they were Moses
and Elijah, [31]who,
appearing in glory,
were speaking
of His departure
which He was
about to accom-
plish at Jerusalem.
[32]Now Peter and
his companions
had been overcome
with sleep; but
when they were
fully awake, they
saw His glory
and the two men
standing with Him.
[33]And as these
were leaving Him,
Peter said to Jesus,
"Master, it is good
for us to be here;
let us make three
tabernacles: one
for You, and one
for Moses, and one
for Elijah"—not
realizing what he
was saying. [34]While
he was saying this,
a cloud formed
and *began* to over-
shadow them; and
they were afraid
as they entered
the cloud. [35]Then a
voice came out of
the cloud, saying,
"This is My Son,
My Chosen One;
listen to Him!"
[36]And when the
voice had spoken,
Jesus was found
alone. And they
kept silent, and
reported to no one
in those days any
of the things which
they had seen.
[37]On the next day,
when they came
down from the

NIV

a large crowd met
him. 38 A man in
the crowd called
out, "Teacher, I
beg you to look
at my son, for he
is my only child.
39 A spirit seizes
him and he sud-
denly screams; it
throws him into
convulsions so that
he foams at the
mouth. It scarcely
ever leaves him
and is destroying
him. 40 I begged
your disciples to
drive it out, but
they could not."
41 "You unbeliev-
ing and perverse
generation," Jesus
replied, "how long
shall I stay with
you and put up
with you? Bring
your son here."
42 Even while the
boy was coming,
the demon threw
him to the ground
in a convulsion.
But Jesus rebuked
the impure spir-
it, healed the boy
and gave him
back to his father.
43 And they were
all amazed at the
greatness of God.

Jesus Predicts His Death a Second Time

While everyone
was marveling at
all that Jesus did,
he said to his dis-
ciples, 44 "Listen
carefully to what
I am about to tell
you: The Son of
Man is going to
be delivered into
the hands of men."
45 But they did not
understand

ὄρους συνήντησεν αὐτῷ ὄχλος πολύς. 38 καὶ ἰδοὺ ἀνὴρ ἀπὸ τοῦ
mountain, a large crowd met him. *crowd* *large* *{and}* Suddenly a man from the
4001 4498 4063 5267 899 4063 4498 2779 2627 467 608 3836
n.gsn v.aai.3s r.dsm.3 n.nsm a.nsm cj j n.nsm p.g d.gsm

ὄχλου ἐβόησεν λέγων, διδάσκαλε, δέομαί σου ἐπιβλέψαι ἐπὶ τὸν υἱόν μου,
crowd cried out, saying, "Teacher, I beg you ⌊to look with pity⌋ on *{the}* my son, *my*
4063 1066 3306 1437 1289 5148 2098 2093 3836 1609 5626 1609
n.gsm v.aai.3s pt.pa.nsm n.vsm v.pmi.1s r.gs.2 f.aa p.a d.asm n.asm r.gs.1

ὅτι μονογενής μοί ἐστιν, 39 καὶ ἰδοὺ πνεῦμα λαμβάνει αὐτὸν
because he is my only child; *my* *he is* and *{behold}* a spirit seizes him,
4022 1639 1639 1609 3666 1609 1639 2779 2627 4460 3284 899
cj a.nsm r.ds.1 v.pai.3s cj j n.nsn v.pai.3s r.asm.3

καὶ ↱ ἐξαίφνης κράζει καὶ σπαράσσει αὐτὸν ↰ ↰ μετὰ
and he suddenly cries out; and it throws him into convulsions and causes him to
2779 3189 1978 3189 2779 5057 899 5057 5057 3552
cj adv v.pai.3s cj v.pai.3s r.asm.3 p.g

ἀφροῦ καὶ μόγις ἀποχωρεῖ ἀπ' αὐτοῦ συντρῖβον αὐτόν·
foam at the mouth; and with difficulty it departs from him, bruising him as it leaves.
931 2779 3653 713 608 899 5341 899
n.gsm cj adv v.pai.3s p.g r.gsm.3 pt.pa.nsn r.asm.3

40 καὶ ἐδεήθην τῶν μαθητῶν σου ἵνα ἐκβάλωσιν αὐτό, ↰ καὶ οὐκ
And I begged *{the}* your disciples *your* to cast it out, but they could not."
2779 1289 3836 5148 3412 5148 2671 1675 899 1675 2779 1538 1538 4024
cj v.api.1s d.gpm n.gpm r.gs.2 cj v.aas.3p r.asn.3 cj pl

ἠδυνήθησαν. 41 ἀποκριθεὶς δὲ ὁ Ἰησοῦς εἶπεν, ὦ γενεὰ
they could In answer *{and}* *{the}* Jesus said, "O faithless and perverse generation,
1538 646 1254 3836 2652 3306 6043 603 2779 1406 1155
v.api.3p pt.ap.nsm cj d.nsm n.nsm v.aai.3s j n.vsf

ἄπιστος καὶ διεστραμμένη, ἕως πότε ἔσομαι πρὸς ὑμᾶς καὶ ἀνέξομαι ὑμῶν;
faithless *and* *perverse* how long ⌊am I to be⌋ with you and put up with you?
603 2779 1406 2401 4537 1639 4639 7007 2779 462 7007
a.vsf cj pt.rp.vsf p.g adv v.fmi.1s p.a r.ap.2 cj v.fmi.1s r.gp.2

προσάγαγε ὧδε τὸν υἱόν σου. 42 ἔτι δὲ προσερχομένου αὐτοῦ
Bring your son here." *{the}* *son* *your* While *{and}* he was on his way, *he* the
4642 5148 5626 6045 3836 5626 5148 2285 1254 899 4665 899 3836
v.aam.2s adv d.asm n.asm r.gs.2 adv cj pt.pm.gsm r.gsm.3

ἔρρηξεν αὐτὸν ↰ τὸ δαιμόνιον καὶ συνεσπάραξεν· ἐπετίμησεν
demon threw him down *the* *demon* and convulsed him. But Jesus rebuked
1228 4838 899 4838 3836 1228 2779 5360 1254 2652 2203
v.aai.3s r.asm.3 d.nsn n.nsn cj v.aai.3s v.aai.3s

δὲ ὁ Ἰησοῦς τῷ πνεύματι τῷ ἀκαθάρτῳ καὶ ἰάσατο τὸν παῖδα καὶ
But *{the}* *Jesus* the unclean spirit, *{the}* *unclean* *{and}* healed the child, and
1254 3836 2652 3836 176 4460 3836 176 2779 2615 3836 4090 2779
cj d.nsm n.nsm d.dsn n.dsn d.dsn a.dsn cj v.ami.3s d.asm n.asm cj

ἀπέδωκεν αὐτὸν ↰ τῷ πατρὶ αὐτοῦ. 43 ἐξεπλήσσοντο δὲ πάντες ἐπὶ
gave him back to his father. *his* And all were astonished *And* *all* at
625 899 625 3836 899 4252 899 1254 4246 1742 1254 4246 2093
v.aai.3s r.asm.3 d.dsm n.dsm r.gsm.3 v.ipi.3p cj a.npm p.d

τῇ μεγαλειότητι τοῦ θεοῦ. ↱ ↱ ↱ πάντων δὲ θαυμαζόντων ἐπὶ πᾶσιν
the majesty of God. While they were all *{and}* still marveling at everything
3836 3484 3836 2536 2513 2513 2513 4246 1254 2513 2093 4246
d.dsf n.dsf d.gsm n.gsm a.gpm cj pt.pa.gpm p.d a.dpn

οἷς ἐποίει εἶπεν πρὸς τοὺς μαθητὰς αὐτοῦ, 44 → θέσθε ὑμεῖς
he was doing, Jesus said to *{the}* his disciples, *his* "Let these words sink *{you}*
4005 4472 3306 4639 3836 899 3412 899 4047 3364 5502 7007
r.dpn v.iai.3s v.aai.3s p.a d.apm n.apm r.gsm.3 v.amm.2p r.np.2

εἰς τὰ ὦτα ὑμῶν τοὺς λόγους τούτους· ὁ γὰρ υἱὸς τοῦ ἀνθρώπου
into *{the}* your ears: *your* *{the}* *words* *these* For the *For* Son of Man
1650 3836 7007 4044 7007 3836 3364 4047 1142 3836 1142 5626 3836 476
p.a d.apn n.apn r.gp.2 d.apm n.apm r.apm d.nsm cj n.nsm d.gsm n.gsm

μέλλει παραδίδοσθαι εἰς χεῖρας ἀνθρώπων. 45 οἱ δὲ ἠγνόουν τὸ
is about to be betrayed into the hands of men." But they *But* did not understand *{the}*
3516 4140 1650 5931 476 1254 3836 1254 51 3836
v.pai.3s f.pp p.a n.apf n.gpm d.npm cj v.iai.3p d.asn

NASB

mountain, a large
crowd met Him.
38 And a man from
the crowd shouted,
saying, "Teacher,
I beg You to look
at my son, for he
is my only *boy,*
39 and a spirit seizes
him, and he sud-
denly screams,
and it throws him
into a convulsion
with foaming *at*
the mouth; and
only with difficulty
does it leave him,
mauling him *as it*
leaves. 40 I begged
Your disciples to
cast it out, and they
could not." 41 And
Jesus answered
and said, "You un-
believing and per-
verted generation,
how long shall I be
with you and put
up with you? Bring
your son here."
42 While he was still
approaching, the
demon slammed
him *to the ground*
and threw him
into a convulsion.
But Jesus rebuked
the unclean spirit,
and healed the
boy and gave him
back to his father.
43 And they were
all amazed at the
greatness of God.
But while every-
one was marveling
at all that He was
doing, He said
to His disciples,
44 "Let these words
sink into your
ears; for the Son
of Man is going to
be delivered into
the hands of men."
45 But they did not
understand

NIV

what this meant. It
was hidden from
them, so that they
did not grasp it,
and they were
afraid to ask him
about it.
46 An argument
started among
the disciples as
to which of them
would be the great-
est. 47 Jesus, know-
ing their thoughts,
took a little child
and had him stand
beside him. 48 Then
he said to them,
"Whoever wel-
comes this little
child in my name
welcomes me; and
whoever welcomes
me welcomes the
one who sent me.
For it is the one
who is least among
you all who is the
greatest."
49 "Master," said
John, "we saw
someone driving
out demons in
your name and we
tried to stop him,
because he is not
one of us."
50 "Do not stop
him," Jesus said,
"for whoever is not
against you is for
you."

Samaritan Opposition

51 As the time ap-
proached for him
to be taken up to
heaven, Jesus res-
olutely set out for
Jerusalem. 52 And
he sent messengers
on ahead, who
went into a Samar-
itan village

ῥῆμα τοῦτο καὶ ἦν παρακεκαλυμμένον ἀπ᾿ αὐτῶν ἵνα ↱ ↱ μὴ
this saying. *this* *{and}* ⌊It was⌋ concealed from them, so that they might not
4047 4839 4047 2779 1639 4152 608 899 2671 150 150 3590
n.asn r.asn cj v.iai.3s pt.rp.nsn p.g r.gpm.3 cj pl

αἴσθωνται αὐτό, καὶ ἐφοβοῦντο ἐρωτῆσαι αὐτὸν περὶ τοῦ ῥήματος τούτου.
understand it; and they were afraid to ask him about *{the}* this saying. *this*
150 899 2779 5828 2263 899 4309 3836 4047 4839 4047
v.ams.3p r.asn.3 cj v.ipi.3p f.aa r.asm.3 p.g d.gsn n.gsn r.gsn

46 εἰσῆλθεν δὲ διαλογισμὸς ἐν αὐτοῖς, τὸ ⌊τίς ἂν⌋
An argument arose *{and}* *argument* among them *{the}* as to which of them
1369 1656 1254 1369 1877 899 3836 5515 323 899 899
v.aai.3s cj n.nsm p.d r.dpm.3 d.nsn r.nsm pl

εἴη μείζων αὐτῶν. 47 ὁ δὲ Ἰησοῦς εἰδὼς τὸν διαλογισμὸν τῆς
⌊might be⌋ the greatest. *of them* *{the}* But Jesus, ⌊aware of⌋ the reasoning of their
1639 3489 899 3836 1254 2652 3857 3836 1369 3836 899
v.pao.3s a.nsm.c r.gpm.3 d.nsm cj n.nsm pt.ra.nsm d.asm n.asm d.gsf

καρδίας αὐτῶν, ἐπιλαβόμενος παιδίον → ἔστησεν αὐτὸ παρ᾿ ἑαυτῷ 48 καὶ
heart, *their* took a child, had him stand *him* at his side, and
2840 899 2138 4086 899 2705 899 4123 1571 2779
n.gsf r.gpm.3 pt.am.nsm n.asn v.aai.3s r.asn.3 p.d r.dsm.3 cj

εἶπεν αὐτοῖς, ⌊ὃς ἐὰν⌋ δέξηται τοῦτο τὸ παιδίον ἐπὶ τῷ ὀνόματί μου,
said to them, "Whoever receives this *{the}* child in *{the}* my name *my*
3306 899 4005 1569 1312 4047 3836 4086 2093 3836 1609 3950 1609
v.aai.3s r.dpm.3 r.nsm pl v.ams.3s r.asn d.asn n.asn p.d d.dsn n.dsn r.gs.1

ἐμὲ δέχεται· καὶ ⌊ὃς ἂν⌋ ἐμὲ δέξηται, δέχεται τὸν ἀποστείλαντά
receives me, *receives* and whoever receives me *receives* receives him who sent
1312 1609 1312 2779 4005 323 1312 1609 1312 1312 3836 690
r.as.1 v.pmi.3s cj r.nsm pl r.as.1 v.ams.3s v.pmi.3s d.asm pt.aa.asm

με· ὁ γὰρ μικρότερος ἐν πᾶσιν ὑμῖν ὑπάρχων οὗτός ἐστιν
me. So the *So* one who is least among you all, *you* this is the one who *this* is
1609 1142 3836 1142 3625 1877 7007 4246 7007 4047 5639 4047 1639
r.as.1 d.nsm cj a.nsm.c p.d a.dpm r.dp.2 pt.pa.nsm r.nsm v.pai.3s

μέγας. 49 ἀποκριθεὶς δὲ Ἰωάννης εἶπεν, ἐπιστάτα, εἴδομέν τινα
great." Answering, *{and}* John said, "Master, we saw someone casting out
3489 646 1254 2722 3306 2181 1625 5516 1675 1675
a.nsm pt.ap.nsm cj n.nsm v.aai.3s n.vsm v.aai.1p r.asm

ἐν τῷ ὀνόματί σου ἐκβάλλοντα δαιμόνια καὶ ἐκωλύομεν αὐτόν,
demons in *{the}* your name, *your* *casting out* *demons* and we tried to stop him,
1228 1877 3836 5148 3950 5148 1675 1228 2779 3266 899
p.d d.dsn n.dsn r.gs.2 pt.pa.asm n.apn cj v.iai.1p r.asm.3

ὅτι ↱ ↱ οὐκ ἀκολουθεῖ μεθ᾿ ἡμῶν. 50 εἶπεν δὲ πρὸς αὐτὸν ὁ
because he does not follow you with us." Jesus said *{and}* to him, *{the}*
4022 199 199 4024 199 3552 7005 2652 3306 1254 4639 899 3836
cj pl v.pai.3s p.g r.gp.1 v.aai.3s cj p.a r.asm.3 d.nsm

Ἰησοῦς, ↱ μὴ κωλύετε· ὃς γὰρ οὐκ ἔστιν καθ᾿ ὑμῶν,
Jesus "Do not try to stop him, for the one who *for* is not *is* against you is
2652 3266 3590 3266 1142 4005 1142 1639 4024 1639 2848 7007 1639
n.nsm pl v.pam.2p r.nsm cj pl v.pai.3s p.g r.gp.2

ὑπὲρ ὑμῶν ἐστιν. 51 ἐγένετο δὲ ἐν τῷ
for you." *is* *{it happened that}* Now when ~ the days of his ascension
5642 7007 1639 1181 1254 1877 3836 3836 2465 3836 899 378
p.g r.gp.2 v.pai.3s v.ami.3s cj p.d d.dsn

συμπληροῦσθαι τὰς ἡμέρας τῆς ἀναλήμψεως αὐτοῦ καὶ αὐτὸς τὸ πρόσωπον
drew near, *the* *days* *of* *ascension* *his* *{and}* Jesus set his face
5230 3836 2465 3836 378 899 2779 899 5114 3836 4725
f.pp d.apf n.apf d.gsf n.gsf r.gsm.3 cj r.nsm d.asn n.asn

ἐστήρισεν τοῦ πορεύεσθαι εἰς Ἰερουσαλήμ. 52 καὶ ἀπέστειλεν ἀγγέλους πρὸ
set to go to Jerusalem. *{and}* He sent messengers before his
5114 3836 4513 1650 2647 2779 690 34 4574 899
v.aai.3s d.gsn f.pm p.a n.asf cj v.aai.3s n.apm p.g

προσώπου αὐτοῦ. καὶ πορευθέντες ⌊εἰσῆλθον εἰς⌋ κώμην → Σαμαριτῶν ὡς
face. *his* *{and}* Having set off, they entered a village of the Samaritans, ⌊in order⌋
4725 899 2779 4513 1656 1650 3267 4901 6055
n.gsn r.gsm.3 cj pt.ap.npm v.aai.3p p.a n.asf n.gpm cj

NASB

this statement, and
it was concealed
from them so that
they would not
perceive it; and
they were afraid to
ask Him about this
statement.

The Test of Greatness

46 An argument
started among them
as to which of
them might be the
greatest. 47 But Je-
sus, knowing what
they were thinking
in their heart, took
a child and stood
him by His side,
48 and said to them,
"Whoever receives
this child in My
name receives Me,
and whoever re-
ceives Me receives
Him who sent Me;
for the one who is
least among all of
you, this is the one
who is great."
49 John answered
and said, "Master,
we saw someone
casting out demons
in Your name; and
we tried to prevent
him because he
does not follow
along with us."
50 But Jesus said
to him, "Do not
hinder *him;* for he
who is not against
you is for you."
51 When the days
were approaching
for His ascension,
He was determined
to go to Jerusalem;
52 and He sent mes-
sengers on ahead

NIV

to get things ready
for him; 53 but the
people there did
not welcome him,
because he was
heading for Jeru-
salem. 54 When the
disciples James
and John saw this,
they asked, "Lord,
do you want us
to call fire down
from heaven to
destroy them[a]?"
55 But Jesus turned
and rebuked them.
56 Then he and his
disciples went to
another village.

The Cost of Following Jesus

57 As they were
walking along the
road, a man said
to him, "I will fol-
low you wherever
you go."
58 Jesus replied,
"Foxes have dens
and birds have
nests, but the Son
of Man has no
place to lay his
head."
59 He said to an-
other man, "Fol-
low me."
But he replied,
"Lord, first let me
go and bury my
father."
60 Jesus said to
him, "Let the dead
bury their own
dead, but you go
and proclaim the
kingdom of God."
61 Still another
said, "I will follow
you, Lord; but first
let me go back and
say goodbye to my
family."
62 Jesus replied,

[a] 54 Some manu-
scripts *them, just as
Elijah did*

ἑτοιμάσαι αὐτῷ· 53 καὶ ↱ ↱ οὐκ ἐδέξαντο αὐτόν, ὅτι τὸ πρόσωπον
to prepare for him. But they did not receive him, because {the} his face
2286 899 2779 1312 1312 4024 1312 899 4022 3836 899 4725
f.aa r.dsm.3 cj pl v.ami.3p r.asm.3 cj d.nsn n.nsn

αὐτοῦ ἦν πορευόμενον εἰς Ἰερουσαλήμ. 54 ἰδόντες δὲ οἱ μαθηταὶ
his was set toward Jerusalem. Seeing {and} this, his disciples
899 1639 4513 1650 2647 1625 1254 3836 3412
r.gsm.3 v.iai.3s pt.pm.nsn p.a n.asf pt.aa.npm cj d.npm n.npm

Ἰάκωβος καὶ Ἰωάννης εἶπαν, κύριε, θέλεις εἴπωμεν πῦρ καταβῆναι ἀπὸ τοῦ
James and John said, "Lord, ⌞do you want⌟ us to tell fire to come down from {the}
2610 2779 2722 3306 3261 2527 3306 4786 2849 608 3836
n.nsm cj n.nsm v.aai.3p n.vsm v.pai.2s v.aas.1p n.asn f.aa p.g d.gsm

οὐρανοῦ καὶ ἀναλῶσαι αὐτούς;[a] 55 ↱ στραφεὶς δὲ ἐπετίμησεν αὐτοῖς.[b]
heaven and consume them?" But he turned {But} and rebuked them,
4041 2779 384 899 1254 2203 5138 1254 2203 899
n.gsm cj f.aa r.apm.3 pt.ap.nsm cj v.aai.3s r.dpm.3

56 [c]καὶ ἐπορεύθησαν εἰς ἑτέραν κώμην. 57 καὶ → πορευομένων αὐτῶν ἐν τῇ
and they moved on to another village. {and} As they were going they along the
2779 4513 1650 2283 3267 2779 899 4513 899 1877 3836
cj v.api.3p p.a r.asf n.asf cj pt.pm.gpm r.gpm.3 p.d d.dsf

ὁδῷ εἶπέν τις πρὸς αὐτόν, ἀκολουθήσω σοι ⌞ὅπου ἐὰν⌟ ἀπέρχῃ.
road, someone said {someone} to him, "I will follow you wherever you are heading."
3847 5516 3306 5516 4639 899 199 5148 3963 1569 599
n.dsf v.aai.3s r.nsm p.a r.asm.3 v.fai.1s r.ds.2 cj pl v.pms.2s

58 καὶ εἶπεν αὐτῷ ὁ Ἰησοῦς, αἱ ἀλώπεκες φωλεοὺς ἔχουσιν καὶ τὰ
{and} Jesus said to him, {the} Jesus {the} "Foxes have holes, have and {the}
2779 2652 3306 899 3836 2652 3836 273 2400 5887 2400 2779 3836
cj v.aai.3s r.dsm.3 d.nsm n.nsm d.npf n.npf n.apm v.pai.3p cj d.npn

πετεινὰ τοῦ οὐρανοῦ κατασκηνώσεις, ὁ δὲ υἱὸς τοῦ ἀνθρώπου οὐκ
birds of the air have nests, but the but Son of Man has no
4374 3836 4041 2943 1254 3836 1254 5626 3836 476 2400 4024
n.npn d.gsm n.gsm n.apf d.nsm cj n.nsm d.gsm n.gsm pl

ἔχει ποῦ τὴν κεφαλὴν κλίνῃ. 59 εἶπεν δὲ πρὸς ἕτερον, ἀκολούθει
has place to lay his head." to lay He said {and} to ⌞another person,⌟ "Follow
2400 4543 3111 3111 3836 3051 3111 3306 1254 4639 2283 199
v.pai.3s cj d.asf n.asf v.pas.3s v.aai.3s cj p.a r.asm v.pam.2s

μοι. ὁ δὲ εἶπεν, κύριε,[d] ἐπίτρεψόν μοι ἀπελθόντι πρῶτον θάψαι
me." But that But one said, "Lord, let me first go first and bury
1609 1254 3836 1254 3306 3261 2205 1609 4754 599 4754 2507
r.ds.1 d.nsm cj v.aai.3s n.vsm v.aam.2s r.ds.1 pt.aa.dsm adv f.aa

τὸν πατέρα μου. 60 εἶπεν δὲ αὐτῷ, ἄφες τοὺς νεκροὺς θάψαι τοὺς
{the} my father." my Jesus said {and} to him, "Leave the dead to bury their
3836 1609 4252 1609 3306 1254 899 918 3836 3738 2507 3836
d.asm n.asm r.gs.1 v.aai.3s cj r.dsm.3 v.aam.2s d.apm a.apm f.aa d.apm

ἑαυτῶν νεκρούς, σὺ δὲ ἀπελθὼν διάγγελλε τὴν βασιλείαν τοῦ θεοῦ.
own dead. But you But go and proclaim the kingdom of God."
1571 3738 1254 5148 1254 599 1334 3836 993 3836 2536
r.gpm.3 a.apm r.ns.2 cj pt.aa.nsm v.pam.2s d.asf n.asf d.gsm n.gsm

61 εἶπεν δὲ καὶ ἕτερος, ἀκολουθήσω σοι, κύριε· πρῶτον δὲ
Yet another said, {and} Yet another "I will follow you, Lord, but first but
2779 2283 3306 1254 2779 2283 199 5148 3261 1254 4754 1254
v.aai.3s cj adv r.nsm v.fai.1s r.ds.2 n.vsm adv cj

ἐπίτρεψόν μοι ἀποτάξασθαι τοῖς εἰς τὸν οἶκόν μου. 62 εἶπεν δὲ [e]πρὸς
allow me to say good-bye to those at {the} my home." my Jesus said {and} to
2205 1609 698 3836 1650 3836 1609 3875 1609 2652 3306 1254 4639
v.aam.2s r.ds.1 f.am d.dpm p.a d.asm n.asm r.gs.1 v.aai.3s cj p.a

[a] ὡς καὶ Ἠλίας ἐποίησε included by TR after αὐτούς.
[b] καὶ εἶπεν, Οὐκ οἴδατε οἵου πνεύματός ἐστε ὑμεῖς· ὁ γὰρ υἱὸς τοῦ ἀνθρώπου οὐκ ἦλθε ψυχὰς ἀνθρώπων ἀπολέσαι, ἀλλὰ σῶσαι. included by TR after αὐτοῖς.
[c] ὁ γὰρ υἱὸς τοῦ ἀνθρώπου οὐκ ἦλθε ψυχὰς ἀνθρώπων ἀπολέσαι, ἀλλὰ σῶσαι. included by TR before καὶ.
[d] [κύριε] UBS.
[e] [πρὸς αὐτὸν] UBS, omitted by TNIV.

NASB

of Him, and they
went and entered a
village of the Sa-
maritans to make
arrangements for
Him. 53 But they did
not receive Him,
because He was
traveling toward
Jerusalem. 54 When
His disciples James
and John saw *this,*
they said, "Lord,
do You want us
to command fire
to come down
from heaven and
consume them?"
55 But He turned and
rebuked them, [and
said, "You do not
know what kind
of spirit you are
of; 56 for the Son of
Man did not come
to destroy men's
lives, but to save
them."] And they
went on to another
village.

Exacting Discipleship

57 As they were go-
ing along the road,
someone said to
Him, "I will follow
You wherever You
go." 58 And Jesus
said to him, "The
foxes have holes
and the birds of
the air *have* nests,
but the Son of Man
has nowhere to lay
His head." 59 And
He said to another,
"Follow Me." But
he said, "Lord,
permit me first to
go and bury my
father." 60 But He
said to him, "Allow
the dead to bury
their own dead; but
as for you, go and
proclaim every-
where the kingdom
of God." 61 Another
also said, "I will
follow You, Lord;
but first permit me
to say good-bye
to those at home."
62 But Jesus said to

NIV

"No one who puts
a hand to the plow
and looks back is
fit for service in
the kingdom of
God."

Jesus Sends Out the Seventy-Two

10 After this
the Lord
appointed sev-
enty-two[a] others
and sent them two
by two ahead of
him to every town
and place where
he was about to
go. 2He told them,
"The harvest is
plentiful, but the
workers are few.
Ask the Lord of
the harvest, there-
fore, to send out
workers into his
harvest field. 3Go!
I am sending you
out like lambs
among wolves.
4Do not take a
purse or bag or
sandals; and do not
greet anyone on
the road.
5"When you en-
ter a house, first
say, 'Peace to this
house.' 6If some-
one who promotes
peace is there,
your peace will
rest on them; if
not, it will return
to you. 7Stay there,
eating and drink-
ing whatever they
give you, for the
worker deserves
his wages. Do not
move around from

αὐτὸν[a] ὁ Ἰησοῦς, οὐδεὶς ἐπιβαλὼν τὴν χεῖρα ἐπ' ἄροτρον καὶ βλέπων ⌊εἰς
him, *{the}* *Jesus* "No one who puts his hand to the plow and looks back
899 3836 2652 4029 2095 3836 5931 2093 770 2779 1063 1650
r.asm.3 d.nsm n.nsm a.nsm pt.aa.nsm d.asf n.asf p.a n.asn cj pt.pa.nsm p.a

τὰ ὀπίσω⌋ εὔθετός ἐστιν τῇ βασιλείᾳ τοῦ θεοῦ.
is fit *is* ⌊for the⌋ kingdom of God."
3836 3958 1639 2310 1639 3836 993 3836 2536
d.apn adv a.nsm v.pai.3s d.dsf n.dsf d.gsm n.gsm

10:1 μετὰ δὲ ταῦτα ἀνέδειξεν ὁ κύριος ἑτέρους
After *{and}* this the Lord appointed *the* *Lord* seventy-two others
3552 1254 4047 3836 3261 344 3836 3261 1573 2283
p.a cj r.apn v.aai.3s d.nsm n.nsm r.apm

⌊ἑβδομήκοντα δύο⌋[b] καὶ ἀπέστειλεν αὐτοὺς ἀνὰ δύο δύο[c]
seventy-two and sent them on ahead of him, two by two, *two*
1573 1545 2779 690 899 4574 4725 899 899 1545 324 1545 1545
a.apm a.apm cj v.aai.3s r.apm.3 p.a a.apm a.apm

πρὸ προσώπου αὐτοῦ εἰς πᾶσαν πόλιν καὶ τόπον οὗ → ἤμελλεν αὐτὸς
on *ahead* *of him* into every town and place where he himself was about *himself*
4574 4725 899 1650 4246 4484 2779 5536 4023 899 3516 899
p.g n.gsn r.gsm.3 p.a a.asf n.asf cj n.asm adv v.iai.3s r.nsm

ἔρχεσθαι. 2 ἔλεγεν δὲ πρὸς αὐτούς, ὁ μὲν θερισμὸς πολύς, οἱ δὲ
to go. And he said *And* to them, "The ~ harvest is plentiful, but the *but*
2262 1254 3306 1254 4639 899 3836 3525 2546 4498 1254 3836 1254
f.pm v.iai.3s cj p.a r.apm.3 d.nsm pl n.nsm a.nsm d.npm cj

ἐργάται ὀλίγοι· δεήθητε οὖν τοῦ κυρίου τοῦ θερισμοῦ ὅπως
workers are few. Therefore ask *Therefore* the Lord of the harvest to send out
2239 3900 4036 1289 4036 3836 3261 3836 2546 3968 1675 1675
n.npm a.npm v.apm.2p cj d.gsm n.gsm d.gsm n.gsm cj

ἐργάτας ἐκβάλῃ εἰς τὸν θερισμὸν αὐτοῦ. 3 ὑπάγετε· ἰδοὺ ἀποστέλλω ὑμᾶς
workers *send out* into *{the}* his harvest. *his* Go then. ~ I am sending you
2239 1675 1650 3836 899 2546 899 5632 2627 690 7007
n.apm v.aas.3s p.a d.asm n.asm r.gsm.3 v.pam.2p j v.pai.1s r.ap.2

ὡς ἄρνας ἐν μέσῳ λύκων. 4 μὴ βαστάζετε βαλλάντιον, μὴ πήραν, μὴ
as lambs into the midst of wolves. Carry no *Carry* moneybag, no knapsack, no
6055 748 1877 3545 3380 1002 3590 1002 964 3590 4385 3590
pl n.apm p.d n.dsn n.gpm pl v.pam.2p n.asn pl n.asf pl

ὑποδήματα, καὶ μηδένα κατὰ τὴν ὁδὸν ἀσπάσησθε. 5 εἰς ἣν δ' ἂν
sandals; and greet no one along the way. *greet* In whichever *{and}* ~ house
5687 2779 832 3594 2848 3836 3847 832 1650 4005 1254 323 3864
n.apn cj a.asm p.a d.asf n.asf v.ams.2p p.a r.asf cj pl

εἰσέλθητε οἰκίαν, πρῶτον λέγετε, εἰρήνη τῷ οἴκῳ τούτῳ. 6 καὶ ἐὰν
you enter, *house* first say, 'Peace be to this house!' *this* And if there is
1656 3864 4754 3306 1645 3836 4047 3875 4047 2779 1569 1639 1639
v.aas.2p n.asf adv v.pam.2p n.nsf d.dsm n.dsm r.dsm cj cj

ἐκεῖ ᾖ υἱὸς εἰρήνης, ἐπαναπαήσεται ἐπ' αὐτὸν ἡ
a son of peace there, *there is* *son* *of peace* your peace will rest upon him; *{the}*
5626 1645 1645 1695 1639 5626 1645 7007 1645 2058 2093 899 3836
adv v.pas.3s n.nsm n.gsf v.fpi.3s p.a r.asm.3 d.nsf

εἰρήνη ὑμῶν· εἰ δὲ μή γε, ἐφ' ὑμᾶς ἀνακάμψει. 7 ἐν
peace *your* but if *but* not, ~ it will return to you. *it will return* Remain in
1645 7007 1254 1623 1254 3590 1145 366 366 366 2093 7007 366 3531 1877
n.nsf r.gp.2 cj cj pl pl p.a r.ap.2 v.fai.3s p.d

αὐτῇ δὲ τῇ οἰκίᾳ μένετε ἐσθίοντες καὶ πίνοντες τὰ ⌊παρ' αὐτῶν⌋·
that *{and}* *{the}* house, *Remain* eating and drinking what they provide, for the
899 1254 3836 3864 3531 2266 2779 4403 3836 4123 899 1142 3836
r.dsf cj d.dsf n.dsf v.pam.2p pt.pa.npm cj pt.pa.npm d.apn p.g r.gpm.3

ἄξιος γὰρ ὁ ἐργάτης τοῦ μισθοῦ αὐτοῦ. ↱ μὴ μεταβαίνετε ἐξ
worker is worthy *for* *the* *worker* of his wages. *his* Do not move around from
2239 545 1142 3836 2239 3836 899 3635 899 3553 3590 3553 1666
a.nsm cj d.nsm n.nsm d.gsm n.gsm r.gsm.3 pl v.pam.2p p.g

NASB

him, "No one, after
putting his hand
to the plow and
looking back, is fit
for the kingdom of
God."

The Seventy Sent Out

10:1Now after this
the Lord appointed
seventy others,
and sent them in
pairs ahead of Him
to every city and
place where He
Himself was go-
ing to come. 2And
He was saying to
them, "The harvest
is plentiful, but the
laborers are few;
therefore beseech
the Lord of the
harvest to send
out laborers into
His harvest. 3Go;
behold, I send you
out as lambs in the
midst of wolves.
4Carry no money
belt, no bag, no
shoes; and greet
no one on the way.
5Whatever house
you enter, first say,
'Peace *be* to this
house.' 6If a man of
peace is there, your
peace will rest on
him; but if not, it
will return to you.
7Stay in that house,
eating and drinking
what they give

[a] 1 Some manu-
scripts *seventy*; also
in verse 17

[a] αὐτὸν omitted by TNIV.
[b] [δύο] UBS, omitted by TR.
[c] [δύο] UBS, omitted by TR.

NIV

house to house.
[8]“When you en-
ter a town and are
welcomed, eat
what is offered to
you. [9]Heal the sick
who are there and
tell them, ‘The
kingdom of God
has come near to
you.’ [10]But when
you enter a town
and are not wel-
comed, go into its
streets and say,
[11]‘Even the dust
of your town we
wipe from our feet
as a warning to
you. Yet be sure of
this: The kingdom
of God has come
near.’ [12]I tell you, it
will be more bear-
able on that day
for Sodom than for
that town.
[13]“Woe to you,
Chorazin! Woe to
you, Bethsaida!
For if the miracles
that were per-
formed in you had
been performed
in Tyre and Sidon,
they would have
repented long ago,
sitting in sackcloth
and ashes. [14]But
it will be more
bearable for Tyre
and Sidon at the
judgment than for
you. [15]And you,
Capernaum, will
you be lifted to the
heavens? No, you
will go down to
Hades.[a]
[16]“Whoever lis-
tens to you listens
to me;

οἰκίας εἰς οἰκίαν. [8]καὶ εἰς ⌞ἣν ἄν⌟ πόλιν εἰσέρχησθε καὶ δέχωνται ὑμᾶς,
house to house. {and} “In whichever town you enter, and they receive you,
3864 1650 3864 2779 1650 4005 323 4484 1656 2779 1312 7007
n.gsf p.a n.asf cj p.a r.asf pl n.asf v.pms.2p cj v.pms.3p r.ap.2

ἐσθίετε τὰ παρατιθέμενα ὑμῖν [9]καὶ θεραπεύετε τοὺς ἐν αὐτῇ ἀσθενεῖς καὶ
eat what is placed before you, and heal the sick in it *sick* and
2266 3836 4192 7007 2779 2543 3836 822 1877 899 822 2779
v.pam.2p d.apn pt.pp.apn r.dp.2 cj v.pam.2p d.apm p.d r.dsf.3 a.apm cj

λέγετε αὐτοῖς, ἤγγικεν ἐφ᾽ ὑμᾶς ἡ βασιλεία τοῦ θεοῦ.
say to them, ‘The kingdom of God ⌞has come near⌟ to you.’ *The kingdom of God*
3306 899 3836 993 3836 2536 1581 2093 7007 3836 993 3836 2536
v.pam.2p r.dpm.3 v.rai.3s p.a r.ap.2 d.nsf n.nsf d.gsm n.gsm

[10]εἰς ἣν δ᾽ ἂν πόλιν εἰσέλθητε καὶ ↱ ↱ μὴ δέχωνται ὑμᾶς, ἐξελθόντες
In whichever {and} ~ town you enter, and they do not receive you, go out
1650 4005 1254 323 4484 1656 2779 1312 1312 3590 1312 7007 2002
p.a r.asf cj pl n.asf v.aas.2p cj pl v.pms.3p r.ap.2 pt.aa.npm

εἰς τὰς πλατείας αὐτῆς εἴπατε, [11]καὶ τὸν κονιορτὸν τὸν
into {the} its streets *its* and say, ‘Even the dust of your town that
1650 3836 899 4426 899 3306 2779 3836 3155 1666 7007 4484 3836
p.a d.apf n.apf r.gsf.3 v.aam.2p cj d.asm n.asm d.asm

κολληθέντα ἡμῖν ἐκ τῆς πόλεως ὑμῶν εἰς τοὺς πόδας ἀπομασσόμεθα
clings to our *of* {the} *town* *your* *to* {the} feet we wipe off
3140 1650 7005 1666 3836 4484 7007 1650 3836 4546 669
pt.ap.asm r.dp.1 p.g d.gsf n.gsf r.gp.2 p.a d.apm n.apm v.pmi.1p

ὑμῖν· πλὴν τοῦτο γινώσκετε ὅτι ἤγγικεν ἡ
⌞against you.⌟ But know this: *know* ~ the kingdom of God ⌞has come near.’⌟ *the*
7007 4440 1182 4047 1182 4022 3836 993 3836 2536 1581 3836
r.dp.2 cj r.asn v.pam.2p cj v.rai.3s d.nsf

βασιλεία τοῦ θεοῦ. [12]λέγω ὑμῖν ὅτι Σοδόμοις ἐν τῇ
kingdom of God I tell you, {that} it will be more bearable for Sodom on {the}
993 3836 2536 3306 7007 4022 1639 1639 1639 445 445 5047 1877 3836
n.nsf d.gsm n.gsm v.pai.1s r.dp.2 cj n.dpn p.d d.dsf

ἡμέρᾳ ἐκείνῃ ἀνεκτότερον ἔσται ἢ τῇ πόλει ἐκείνῃ. [13]οὐαί σοι,
that day *that* *more bearable* *it will be* than for that town. *that* Woe to you,
1697 2465 1697 445 1639 2445 3836 1697 4484 1697 4026 5148
n.dsf r.dsf a.nsn.c v.fmi.3s pl d.dsf n.dsf r.dsf j r.ds.2

Χοραζίν, οὐαί σοι, Βηθσαϊδά· ὅτι εἰ
Chorazin! Woe to you, Bethsaida! For if the mighty works that were done in you had
5960 4026 5148 1034 4022 1623 3836 1539 1539 3836 1181 1181 1877 7007 1181
n.vsf j r.ds.2 n.vsf cj cj

ἐν Τύρῳ καὶ Σιδῶνι ἐγενήθησαν αἱ δυνάμεις αἱ γενόμεναι ἐν ὑμῖν,
been done in Tyre and Sidon, *had been done the mighty works that were done in you*
1181 1181 1877 5602 2779 4972 1181 3836 1539 3836 1181 1877 7007
p.d n.dsf cj n.dsf v.api.3p d.npf n.npf d.npf pt.am.npf p.d r.dp.2

πάλαι ἂν ἐν σάκκῳ καὶ σποδῷ καθήμενοι
long ago they would have repented, sitting in sackcloth and ashes. *sitting*
4093 3566 323 3566 3566 2764 1877 4884 2779 5075 2764
adv pl p.d n.dsm cj n.dsf pt.pm.npm

μετενόησαν. [14]πλὴν Τύρῳ καὶ Σιδῶνι ἀνεκτότερον
they have repented But it will be more tolerable for Tyre and Sidon *more tolerable*
3566 4440 1639 1639 1639 445 445 5602 2779 4972 445
v.aai.3p cj n.dsf cj n.dsf a.nsn.c

ἔσται ἐν τῇ κρίσει ἢ ὑμῖν. [15]καὶ σύ, Καφαρναούμ,
it will be in the judgment than for you! And you, Capernaum! Will you be exalted to
1639 1877 3836 3213 2445 7007 2779 5148 3019 5738 5738 5738 5738 2401
v.fmi.3s p.d d.dsf n.dsf pl r.dp.2 cj r.ns.2 n.vsf

μὴ ἕως οὐρανοῦ ὑψωθήσῃ; ἕως τοῦ ᾅδου
heaven? No. *to heaven Will you be exalted* You will go down to {the} Hades.
4041 3590 2401 4041 5738 2849 2849 2849 2849 2401 3836 87
pl p.g n.gsm v.fpi.2s p.g d.gsm n.gsm

καταβήσῃ. [16]ὁ ἀκούων ὑμῶν ἐμοῦ ἀκούει, καὶ ὁ
You will go down “The ⌞one who listens to⌟ you listens to me, *listens to* and the
2849 3836 201 7007 201 201 1609 201 2779 3836
v.fmi.2s d.nsm pt.pa.nsm r.gp.2 r.gs.1 v.pai.3s cj d.nsm

NASB

you; for the laborer
is worthy of his
wages. Do not
keep moving from
house to house.
[8]Whatever city you
enter and they re-
ceive you, eat what
is set before you;
[9]and heal those in
it who are sick,
and say to them,
‘The kingdom of
God has come
near to you.’ [10]But
whatever city you
enter and they do
not receive you, go
out into its streets
and say, [11]‘Even the
dust of your city
which clings to our
feet we wipe off *in*
protest against you;
yet be sure of this,
that the kingdom
of God has come
near.’ [12]I say to you,
it will be more tol-
erable in that day
for Sodom than for
that city.
[13]“Woe to you,
Chorazin! Woe to
you, Bethsaida!
For if the miracles
had been per-
formed in Tyre
and Sidon which
occurred in you,
they would have
repented long ago,
sitting in sackcloth
and ashes. [14]But it
will be more toler-
able for Tyre and
Sidon in the judg-
ment than for you.
[15]And you, Caper-
naum, will not be
exalted to heaven,
will you? You will
be brought down to
Hades!

[a] *15* That is, the
realm of the dead

NIV

whoever rejects
you rejects me; but
whoever rejects
me rejects him
who sent me."
[17]The seven-
ty-two returned
with joy and said,
"Lord, even the
demons submit to
us in your name."
[18]He replied, "I
saw Satan fall like
lightning from
heaven. [19]I have
given you author-
ity to trample on
snakes and scor-
pions and to over-
come all the power
of the enemy;
nothing will harm
you. [20]However,
do not rejoice that
the spirits submit
to you, but rejoice
that your names
are written in
heaven."
[21]At that time
Jesus, full of joy
through the Holy
Spirit, said, "I
praise you, Father,
Lord of heaven and
earth, because you
have hidden these
things from the
wise and learned,
and revealed them
to little children.
Yes, Father, for
this is what you
were pleased to do.
[22]"All things have
been committed to
me by my Father.
No one knows who
the Son is except
the Father, and no
one knows who the
Father is except
the Son and those
to whom the Son
chooses

ἀθετῶν ὑμᾶς ἐμὲ ἀθετεῖ· ὁ δὲ ἐμὲ ἀθετῶν
⌞one who rejects⌟ you rejects me, *rejects* and the *and* one who rejects me *one who rejects*
119 7007 119 1609 119 1254 3836 1254 119 119 119 1609 119
pt.pa.nsm r.ap.2 r.as.1 v.pai.3s d.nsm cj r.as.1 pt.pa.nsm

ἀθετεῖ τὸν ἀποστείλαντά με. 17 ὑπέστρεψαν δὲ οἱ
rejects the one who sent me." The seventy-two returned {and} *The*
119 3836 690 1609 3836 1573 5715 1254 3836
v.pai.3s d.asm pt.aa.asm r.as.1 v.aai.3p cj d.npm

⌞ἑβδομήκοντα δύο⌟[a] μετὰ χαρᾶς λέγοντες, κύριε, καὶ τὰ δαιμόνια ὑποτάσσεται
seventy-two with joy, saying, "Lord, even the demons are subject
1573 1545 3552 5915 3306 3261 2779 3836 1228 5718
a.npm a.npm p.g n.gsf pt.pa.npm n.vsm adv d.npn n.npn v.ppi.3s

ἡμῖν ἐν τῷ ὀνόματί σου. 18 εἶπεν δὲ αὐτοῖς, ἐθεώρουν τὸν σατανᾶν
to us in {the} your name!" *your* He said {and} to them, "I saw {the} Satan as
7005 1877 3836 5148 3950 5148 3306 1254 899 2555 3836 4928 4406
r.dp.1 p.d d.dsn n.dsn r.gs.2 v.aai.3s cj r.dpm.3 v.iai.1s d.asm n.asm

ὡς ἀστραπὴν ἐκ τοῦ οὐρανοῦ πεσόντα. 19 ἰδοὺ δέδωκα ὑμῖν
he fell, like a bolt of lightening from the sky. *as he fell* ~ I have given you
4406 4406 6055 847 1666 3836 4041 4406 2627 1443 7007
pl n.asf p.g d.gsm n.gsm pt.aa.asm j v.rai.1s r.dp.2

τὴν ἐξουσίαν τοῦ πατεῖν ἐπάνω ὄφεων καὶ σκορπίων, καὶ ↰ ἐπὶ πᾶσαν τὴν
{the} authority to tread on serpents and scorpions, and authority over all the
3836 2026 3836 4251 2062 4058 2779 5026 2779 2026 2093 4246 3836
d.asf n.asf d.gsn f.pa p.g n.gpm cj n.gpm cj p.a a.asf d.asf

δύναμιν τοῦ ἐχθροῦ, καὶ οὐδὲν ὑμᾶς ⌞οὐ μὴ⌟ ἀδικήσῃ. 20 πλὴν
power of the enemy; {and} nothing may hurt you at all. *may hurt* However, do
1539 3836 2398 2779 4029 92 92 7007 4024 3590 92 4440 5897
n.asf d.gsm a.gsm cj a.nsn r.ap.2 pl pl v.aas.3s cj

ἐν τούτῳ μὴ χαίρετε ὅτι τὰ πνεύματα ὑμῖν ὑποτάσσεται,
not rejoice in this, *not* *do rejoice* that the spirits are subject to you, *are subject*
3590 5897 1877 4047 3590 5897 4022 3836 4460 5718 5718 7007 5718
p.d r.dsn pl v.pam.2p cj d.npn n.npn r.dp.2 v.ppi.3s

χαίρετε δὲ ὅτι τὰ ὀνόματα ὑμῶν ἐγγέγραπται ἐν τοῖς οὐρανοῖς.
but rejoice *but* that {the} your names *your* have been recorded in {the} heaven."
1254 5897 1254 4022 3836 7007 3950 7007 1582 1877 3836 4041
v.pam.2p cj cj d.npn n.npn r.gp.2 v.rpi.3s p.d d.dpm n.dpm

21 ἐν αὐτῇ τῇ ὥρᾳ ἠγαλλιάσατο ἐν[b] τῷ πνεύματι τῷ ἁγίῳ καὶ
At this {the} time Jesus ⌞was filled with joy⌟ by the Holy Spirit, {the} *Holy* and
1877 899 3836 6052 22 1877 3836 41 4460 3836 41 2779
p.d r.dsf d.dsf n.dsf v.ami.3s p.d d.dsn n.dsn d.dsn a.dsn cj

εἶπεν, ἐξομολογοῦμαί σοι, πάτερ, κύριε τοῦ οὐρανοῦ καὶ τῆς γῆς, ὅτι ἀπέκρυψας
said, "I thank you, Father, Lord of heaven and {the} earth, that you have hidden
3306 2018 5148 4252 3261 3836 4041 2779 3836 1178 4022 648
v.aai.3s v.pmi.1s r.ds.2 n.vsm n.vsm d.gsm n.gsm cj d.gsf n.gsf cj v.aai.2s

ταῦτα ἀπὸ σοφῶν καὶ συνετῶν καὶ ἀπεκάλυψας αὐτὰ νηπίοις· ναί
these things from the wise and understanding and revealed them to little children; yes,
4047 608 5055 2779 5305 2779 636 899 3758 3721
r.apn p.g a.gpm cj a.gpm cj v.aai.2s r.apn.3 a.dpm pl

ὁ πατήρ, ὅτι οὕτως εὐδοκία ἐγένετο → ἔμπροσθέν σου. 22 πάντα
{the} Father, for such was well-pleasing *was* in your sight. *your* All things have
3836 4252 4022 4048 1181 2306 1181 5148 1869 5148 4246 4140
d.vsm n.vsm cj adv n.nsf v.ami.3s p.g r.gs.2 a.npn

μοι παρεδόθη ὑπὸ τοῦ πατρός μου, καὶ οὐδεὶς γινώσκει
been handed over to me *have been handed over* by {the} my Father, *my* and no one knows
4140 4140 4140 1609 4140 5679 3836 1609 4252 1609 2779 4029 1182
r.ds.1 v.api.3s p.g d.gsm n.gsm r.gs.1 cj a.nsm v.pai.3s

τίς ἐστιν ὁ υἱὸς ⌞εἰ μὴ⌟ ὁ πατήρ, καὶ τίς ἐστιν ὁ
who the Son is *the* *Son* except the Father, or who the Father is *the*
5515 3836 5626 1639 3836 5626 1623 3590 3836 4252 2779 5515 3836 4252 1639 3836
r.nsm v.pai.3s d.nsm n.nsm cj pl d.nsm n.nsm cj r.nsm v.pai.3s d.nsm

πατὴρ ⌞εἰ μὴ⌟ ὁ υἱὸς καὶ ⌞ᾧ ἐὰν⌟ βούληται ὁ υἱὸς
Father except the Son and anyone to whom the Son decides *the* *Son*
4252 1623 3590 3836 5626 2779 4005 1569 3836 5626 1089 3836 5626
n.nsm cj pl d.nsm n.nsm cj r.dsm pl v.pms.3s d.nsm n.nsm

[a] [δύο] UBS.
[b] [ἐν] UBS, omitted by TNIV.

NASB

[16]"The one who
listens to you lis-
tens to Me, and the
one who rejects
you rejects Me;
and he who rejects
Me rejects the One
who sent Me."

The Happy Results

[17]The seventy
returned with joy,
saying, "Lord,
even the demons
are subject to us in
Your name." [18]And
He said to them,
"I was watching
Satan fall from
heaven like light-
ning. [19]Behold, I
have given you
authority to tread
on serpents and
scorpions, and over
all the power of the
enemy, and noth-
ing will injure you.
[20]Nevertheless do
not rejoice in this,
that the spirits are
subject to you, but
rejoice that your
names are recorded
in heaven."
[21]At that very time
He rejoiced greatly
in the Holy Spirit,
and said, "I praise
You, O Father,
Lord of heaven
and earth, that You
have hidden these
things from *the*
wise and intelligent
and have revealed
them to infants.
Yes, Father, for
this way was well-
pleasing in Your
sight. [22]All things
have been handed
over to Me by My
Father, and no one
knows who the Son
is except the Fa-
ther, and who the
Father is except

NIV

to reveal him."
23 Then he turned
to his disciples
and said privately,
"Blessed are the
eyes that see what
you see. 24 For I
tell you that many
prophets and kings
wanted to see what
you see but did not
see it, and to hear
what you hear but
did not hear it."

The Parable of the Good Samaritan

25 On one occa-
sion an expert in
the law stood up to
test Jesus. "Teach-
er," he asked,
"what must I do
to inherit eternal
life?"
26 "What is writ-
ten in the Law?"
he replied. "How
do you read it?"
27 He answered,
" 'Love the Lord
your God with
all your heart and
with all your soul
and with all your
strength and with
all your mind'[a];
and, 'Love your
neighbor as your-
self.'[b]"
28 "You have an-
swered correctly,"
Jesus replied. "Do
this and you will
live."
29 But he wanted
to justify himself,
so he asked Jesus,
"And who is my
neighbor?"
30 In reply Jesus
said: "A man
was going down
from Jerusalem
to Jericho, when
he was attacked
by robbers. They
stripped him of his
clothes, beat him
and went away,
leaving him half
dead. 31 A priest
happened

[a] 27 Deut. 6:5
[b] 27 Lev. 19:18

ἀποκαλύψαι. 23 καὶ στραφεὶς πρὸς τοὺς μαθητὰς ⌊κατ᾽
to reveal him." {and} Having turned to the disciples, he said to them privately,
636 2779 5138 4639 3836 3412 3306 3306 2848
f.aa cj pt.ap.nsm p.a d.apm n.apm p.a

ἰδίαν⌋ εἶπεν, μακάριοι οἱ ὀφθαλμοὶ οἱ βλέποντες ἃ βλέπετε. 24 λέγω
he said "Fortunate are the eyes that see what you see! For I tell
2625 3306 3421 3836 4057 3836 1063 4005 1063 1142 3306
a.asf v.aai.3s a.npm d.npm n.npm d.npm pt.pa.npm r.apn v.pai.2p v.pai.1s

γὰρ ὑμῖν ὅτι πολλοὶ προφῆται καὶ βασιλεῖς ἠθέλησαν ἰδεῖν ἃ ὑμεῖς βλέπετε καὶ
For you that many prophets and kings desired to see what you see, but
1142 7007 4022 4498 4737 2779 995 2527 1625 4005 7007 1063 2779
cj r.dp.2 cj a.npm n.npm cj n.npm v.aai.3p f.aa r.apn r.np.2 v.pai.2p cj

↱ οὐκ εἶδαν, καὶ ἀκοῦσαι ἃ ἀκούετε καὶ ↱ οὐκ ἤκουσαν. 25 ⌊καὶ ἰδού⌋
did not see it, and to hear what you hear, but did not hear it." Once
1625 4024 1625 2779 201 4005 201 2779 201 4024 201 2779 2627
pl v.aai.3p cj f.aa r.apn v.pai.2p cj pl v.aai.3p cj j

νομικός τις ἀνέστη ἐκπειράζων αὐτὸν ↰ ↰ ↰ λέγων, διδάσκαλε, τί →
a lawyer a stood up to put him to the test, saying, "Teacher, what must
5516 3788 5516 482 1733 899 1733 1733 1733 3306 1437 5515
n.nsm r.nsm v.aai.3s pt.pa.nsm r.asm.3 pt.pa.nsm n.vsm r.asn

ποιήσας ζωὴν αἰώνιον κληρονομήσω; 26 ὁ δὲ εἶπεν πρὸς
I do to inherit eternal life?" eternal I to inherit He {and} said to
3099 4472 3099 3099 173 2437 173 3099 3836 1254 3306 4639
pt.aa.nsm n.asf a.asf v.fai.1s d.nsm cj v.aai.3s p.a

αὐτόν, ἐν τῷ νόμῳ τί γέγραπται; πῶς ἀναγινώσκεις; 27
him, "What is written in the Law? What is written How do you read it?" In
899 5515 1211 1211 1877 3836 3795 5515 1211 4802 336 646
r.asm.3 p.d d.dsm n.dsm r.nsn v.rpi.3s cj v.pai.2s

ὁ δὲ ἀποκριθεὶς εἶπεν, ἀγαπήσεις κύριον τὸν θεόν σου ἐξ
answer he {and} In answer said, "You shall love the Lord {the} your God your with
646 3836 1254 646 3306 26 3261 3836 5148 2536 5148 1666
d.nsm cj pt.ap.nsm v.aai.3s v.fai.2s n.asm d.asm n.asm r.gs.2 p.g

ὅλης τῆς[a] καρδίας σου καὶ ἐν ὅλῃ τῇ ψυχῇ σου καὶ ἐν ὅλῃ τῇ
all {the} your heart, our and with all {the} your life, your and with all {the} your
3910 3836 5148 2840 5148 2779 1877 3910 3836 5148 6034 5148 2779 1877 3910 3836 5148
a.gsf d.gsf n.gsf r.gs.2 cj p.d a.dsf d.dsf n.dsf r.gs.2 cj p.d a.dsf d.dsf

ἰσχύϊ σου καὶ ἐν ὅλῃ τῇ διανοίᾳ σου, καὶ τὸν πλησίον σου ὡς
strength, your and with all {the} your mind, your and {the} your neighbor your as
2709 5148 2779 1877 3910 3836 5148 1379 5148 2779 3836 5148 4446 5148 6055
n.dsf r.gs.2 cj p.d a.dsf d.dsf n.dsf r.gs.2 cj d.asm adv r.gs.2 cj

σεαυτόν. 28 εἶπεν δὲ αὐτῷ, ὀρθῶς ἀπεκρίθης·
yourself." Jesus said {and} to him, "You have answered correctly; You have answered do
4932 3306 1254 899 646 646 646 3987 646 4472
r.asm.2 v.aai.3s cj r.dsm.3 adv v.api.2s

τοῦτο ποίει καὶ ζήσῃ. 29 ὁ δὲ θέλων δικαιῶσαι ἑαυτὸν εἶπεν πρὸς
this, do and ⌊you will live."⌋ But he, But wishing to justify himself, said to
4047 4472 2779 2409 1254 3836 1254 2527 1467 1571 3306 4639
r.asn v.pam.2s cj v.fmi.2s d.nsm cj pt.pa.nsm f.aa r.asm.3 v.aai.3s p.a

τὸν Ἰησοῦν, καὶ τίς ἐστίν μου πλησίον; 30 Ὑπολαβὼν ὁ Ἰησοῦς εἶπεν,
{the} Jesus, "And who is my neighbor?" Jesus continued, {the} Jesus saying,
3836 2652 2779 5515 1639 1609 4446 2652 5696 3836 2652 3306
d.asm n.asm cj r.nsm v.pai.3s r.gs.1 adv pt.aa.nsm d.nsm n.nsm v.aai.3s

ἄνθρωπός τις κατέβαινεν ἀπὸ Ἰερουσαλὴμ εἰς Ἰεριχὼ καὶ
"A man A was going down from Jerusalem to Jericho, and he fell among
5516 476 5516 2849 608 2647 1650 2637 2779 4346 4346 4346
n.nsm r.nsm v.iai.3s p.g n.gsf p.a n.asf cj

λῃσταῖς περιέπεσεν, οἳ καὶ ἐκδύσαντες αὐτὸν ↰ ↰ καὶ ⌊πληγὰς
robbers. he fell among they {also} After stripping him of his clothes and beating
3334 4346 4005 2779 1694 899 1694 1694 2779 4435
n.dpm v.aai.3s r.npm adv pt.aa.npm r.asm.3 cj n.apf

ἐπιθέντες⌋ ἀπῆλθον ἀφέντες ἡμιθανῆ. 31 κατὰ συγκυρίαν δὲ
him, they went off, leaving him half dead. Now by chance Now a
2202 4005 599 918 2467 1254 2848 5175 1254 5516
pt.aa.npm v.aai.3p pt.aa.npm a.asm p.a n.asf cj

[a] [τῆς] UBS, omitted by TNIV.

NASB

the Son, and any-
one to whom the
Son wills to reveal
Him."
23 Turning to the
disciples, He said
privately, "Blessed
are the eyes which
see the things you
see, 24 for I say to
you, that many
prophets and kings
wished to see the
things which you
see, and did not see
them, and to hear
the things which
you hear, and did
not hear *them.*"
25 And a lawyer
stood up and put
Him to the test,
saying, "Teacher,
what shall I do
to inherit eternal
life?" 26 And He
said to him, "What
is written in the
Law? How does
it read to you?"
27 And he answered,
"YOU SHALL LOVE
THE LORD YOUR
GOD WITH ALL YOUR
HEART, AND WITH
ALL YOUR SOUL,
AND WITH ALL YOUR
STRENGTH, AND WITH
ALL YOUR MIND;
AND YOUR NEIGH-
BOR AS YOURSELF."
28 And He said to
him, "You have
answered correctly;
DO THIS AND YOU
WILL LIVE." 29 But
wishing to justify
himself, he said to
Jesus, "And who is
my neighbor?"

The Good Samaritan

30 Jesus replied
and said, "A man
was going down
from Jerusalem to
Jericho, and fell
among robbers,
and they stripped
him and beat him,

NIV

to be going down
the same road, and
when he saw the
man, he passed by
on the other side.
32 So too, a Levite,
when he came to
the place and saw
him, passed by
on the other side.
33 But a Samaritan,
as he traveled,
came where the
man was; and
when he saw him,
he took pity on
him. 34 He went
to him and ban-
daged his wounds,
pouring on oil
and wine. Then
he put the man on
his own donkey,
brought him to an
inn and took care
of him. 35 The next
day he took out
two denarii[a] and
gave them to the
innkeeper. 'Look
after him,' he said,
'and when I return,
I will reimburse
you for any extra
expense you may
have.'
36 "Which of these
three do you think
was a neighbor to
the man who fell
into the hands of
robbers?"
37 The expert in
the law replied,
"The one who had
mercy on him."
Jesus told him,
"Go and do like-
wise."

At the Home of Martha and Mary

38 As Jesus and his
disciples were on
their way, he came
to a village where
a woman named
Martha opened her
home to him. 39 She
had a sister called
Mary, who sat at
the Lord's feet

[a] 35 A denarius was the usual daily wage of a day laborer (see Matt. 20:2).

ἱερεύς τις κατέβαινεν ἐν τῇ ὁδῷ ἐκείνῃ καὶ ἰδὼν αὐτὸν
priest *a* was going down by *{the}* that way *that* and, ˻when he saw˼ him,
2636 5516 2849 1877 3836 1697 3847 1697 2779 1625 899
n.nsm r.nsm v.iai.3s p.d d.dsf n.dsf r.dsf cj pt.aa.nsm r.asm.3

ἀντιπαρῆλθεν· 32 ὁμοίως δὲ καὶ Λευίτης γενόμενος[a]
˻he passed by on the other side.˼ So *{and}* too a Levite, *{being}* when he came
524 3931 1254 2779 3324 1181 2262 2262 2262
v.aai.3s adv cj adv n.nsm pt.am.nsm

κατὰ τὸν τόπον ἐλθὼν καὶ ἰδὼν ἀντιπαρῆλθεν. 33
to the place *when he came* and saw him, ˻passed by on the other side.˼ But a
2848 3836 5536 2262 2779 1625 524 1254 5516
p.a d.asm n.asm pt.aa.nsm cj pt.aa.nsm v.aai.3s

Σαμαρίτης δέ τις ὁδεύων ἦλθεν κατ᾽ αὐτὸν καὶ ἰδὼν
Samaritan *But a* ˻who was traveling˼ came to where he was, and ˻when he saw˼ him,
4901 1254 5516 3841 2262 2848 899 2779 1625
n.nsm cj r.nsm pt.pa.nsm v.aai.3s p.a r.asm.3 cj pt.aa.nsm

ἐσπλαγχνίσθη, 34 καὶ ↱ προσελθὼν κατέδησεν τὰ
was moved with compassion for him. *{and}* He went to him and bound up *{the}* his
5072 2779 2866 4665 2866 3836 899
v.api.3s cj pt.aa.nsm v.aai.3s d.apn

τραύματα αὐτοῦ ἐπιχέων ἔλαιον καὶ οἶνον, ↱ ἐπιβιβάσας δὲ αὐτὸν ἐπὶ τὸ
wounds, *his* pouring on oil and wine. Then he set *Then* him on his
5546 899 2219 1778 2779 3885 1254 72 2097 1254 899 2093 3836
n.apn r.gsm.3 pt.pa.nsm n.asn cj n.asm pt.aa.nsm cj r.asm.3 p.a d.asn

ἴδιον κτῆνος ἤγαγεν αὐτὸν εἰς πανδοχεῖον καὶ ἐπεμελήθη αὐτοῦ. 35 καὶ ἐπὶ
own animal and brought him to an inn and took care of him. *{and}* *{on}*
2625 3229 72 899 1650 4106 2779 2150 899 2779 2093
a.asn n.asn v.aai.3s r.asm.3 p.a n.asn cj v.api.3s r.gsm.3 cj p.a

τὴν αὔριον ↱ ἐκβαλὼν ἔδωκεν δύο δηνάρια τῷ πανδοχεῖ
The next day he took out two denarii and gave *two denarii* them ˻to the˼ innkeeper,
3836 892 1443 1675 1545 1324 1443 1545 1324 3836 4107
d.asf adv pt.aa.nsm v.aai.3s a.apn n.apn d.dsm n.dsm

καὶ εἶπεν, ἐπιμελήθητι αὐτοῦ, καὶ ˻ὅ τι ἂν˼ προσδαπανήσῃς ἐγὼ
{and} saying, 'Take care of him, and whatever more you spend, I will repay
2779 3306 2150 899 2779 4005 5516 323 4655 1609 625 625
cj v.aai.3s v.apm.2s r.gsm.3 cj r.asn r.asn pl v.aas.2s r.ns.1

ἐν τῷ ἐπανέρχεσθαί με ἀποδώσω σοι. 36 τίς τούτων τῶν τριῶν
to you when *{the}* I come back.' *I* *will repay* *to you* Which of these *{the}* three,
5148 5148 1877 3836 1609 2059 1609 625 5148 5515 4047 3836 5552
p.d d.dsn f.pm r.as.1 v.fai.1s r.ds.2 r.nsm r.gpm d.gpm a.gpm

πλησίον δοκεῖ σοι γεγονέναι τοῦ ἐμπεσόντος εἰς τοὺς
do you think, became a neighbor *do think* *you* *became* to the man who fell among the
1506 5148 1506 1181 4446 1506 5148 1181 3836 1860 1650 3836
adv v.pai.3s r.ds.2 f.ra d.gsm pt.aa.gsm p.a d.apm

λῃστάς; 37 ὁ δὲ εἶπεν, ὁ ποιήσας τὸ ἔλεος μετ᾽ αὐτοῦ. εἶπεν
robbers?" He *{and}* said, "The one who showed *{the}* mercy to him." And Jesus said
3334 3836 1254 3306 3836 4472 3836 1799 3552 899 1254 2652 3306
n.apm d.nsm cj v.aai.3s d.nsm pt.aa.nsm d.asn n.asn p.g r.gsm.3 v.aai.3s

δὲ αὐτῷ ὁ Ἰησοῦς, πορεύου καὶ σὺ ποίει ὁμοίως. 38 ἐν δὲ τῷ
And to him, *{the}* *Jesus* "Go, and you do the same." Now as *Now* *{the}* they
1254 899 3836 2652 4513 2779 5148 4472 3931 1254 1877 1254 3836 899
cj r.dsm.3 d.nsm n.nsm v.pmm.2s cj r.ns.2 v.pam.2s adv p.d cj d.dsn

πορεύεσθαι αὐτοὺς αὐτὸς ˻εἰσῆλθεν εἰς˼ κώμην τινά·
˻continued on their way,˼ *they* Jesus entered a certain village, *certain* and a
4513 899 899 1656 1650 5516 3267 5516 1254 5516
f.pm r.apm.3 r.nsm v.aai.3s p.a n.asf r.asf

γυνὴ δέ τις ὀνόματι Μάρθα ὑπεδέξατο αὐτόν. ↰ ↰ ↰ 39 καὶ τῇδε ἦν
woman *and* *a* named Martha welcomed him as a guest. *{and}* She had a
1222 1254 5516 3950 3450 5685 899 5685 5685 5685 2779 3840 1639
n.nsf cj r.nsf n.dsn n.nsf v.ami.3s r.asm.3 cj r.dsf v.iai.3s

ἀδελφὴ καλουμένη Μαριάμ, ἣ[b] καὶ παρακαθεσθεῖσα πρὸς τοὺς πόδας τοῦ
sister called Mary, who, *{also}* ˻after she had seated herself˼ at the feet of the
80 2813 3452 4005 2779 4149 4639 3836 4546 3836
n.nsf pt.pp.nsf n.nsf r.nsf adv pt.ap.nsf p.a d.apm n.apm d.gsm

[a] [γενόμενος] UBS, omitted by TNIV.
[b] [ἣ] UBS.

NASB

and went away
leaving him half
dead. 31 And by
chance a priest
was going down
on that road, and
when he saw him,
he passed by on
the other side.
32 Likewise a Levite
also, when he came
to the place and
saw him, passed by
on the other side.
33 But a Samaritan,
who was on a
journey, came upon
him; and when he
saw him, he felt
compassion, 34 and
came to him and
bandaged up his
wounds, pouring
oil and wine on
them; and he put
him on his own
beast, and brought
him to an inn and
took care of him.
35 On the next day
he took out two
[a]denarii and gave
them to the inn-
keeper and said,
'Take care of him;
and whatever more
you spend, when I
return I will repay
you.' 36 Which of
these three do you
think proved to
be a neighbor to
the man who fell
into the robbers'
hands?" 37 And
he said, "The one
who showed mercy
toward him." Then
Jesus said to him,
"Go and do the
same."

Martha and Mary

38 Now as they
were traveling
along, He entered
a village; and a
woman named
Martha welcomed
Him into her home.
39 She had a sister

[a] The denarius was equivalent to a day's wages

NIV

listening to what
he said. [40]But Mar-
tha was distracted
by all the prepa-
rations that had to
be made. She came
to him and asked,
"Lord, don't you
care that my sister
has left me to do
the work by my-
self? Tell her to
help me!"
[41]"Martha, Mar-
tha," the Lord an-
swered, "you are
worried and upset
about many things,
[42]but few things
are needed—or
indeed only one.[a]
Mary has chosen
what is better, and
it will not be taken
away from her."

Jesus' Teaching on Prayer

11 One day
Jesus was
praying in a cer-
tain place. When
he finished, one of
his disciples said
to him, "Lord,
teach us to pray,
just as John taught
his disciples."
[2]He said to them,
"When you pray,
say:

> "'Father,[b]
> hallowed be your name,
> your kingdom come.[c]
> [3]Give us each day our daily bread.
> [4]Forgive us our sins,
> for we also forgive everyone who sins against us.[d]

[a] 42 Some manuscripts *but only one thing is needed*
[b] 2 Some manuscripts *Our Father in heaven*
[c] 2 Some manuscripts *come. May your will be done on earth as it is in heaven.*
[d] 4 Greek *everyone who is indebted to us*

κυρίου ἤκουεν τὸν λόγον αὐτοῦ. 40 ἡ δὲ Μάρθα περιεσπᾶτο περὶ
Lord, ⌊was listening to⌋ *{the}* his teaching. *his* *{the}* But Martha was distracted by a
3261 201 3836 899 3364 899 3836 1254 3450 4352 4309
n.gsm v.iai.3s d.asm n.asm r.gsm.3 d.nsf cj n.nsf v.ipi.3s p.a

πολλὴν διακονίαν· ἐπιστᾶσα δὲ εἶπεν, κύριε, ↱ οὐ μέλει σοι ὅτι ἡ
lot of preparation. ⌊She burst in and⌋ *{and}* said, "Lord, do you not care *you* that *{the}*
4498 1355 2392 1254 3306 3261 3508 5148 4024 3508 5148 4022 3836
a.asf n.asf pt.aa.nsf cj v.aai.3s n.vsm pl v.pai.3s r.ds.2 cj d.nsf

ἀδελφή μου μόνην με κατέλιπεν διακονεῖν;
my sister *my* has left me to do all the work by myself? *me* *has left* *to do the work*
1609 80 1609 2901 2901 1609 1354 1354 1354 1354 3668 1609 2901 1354
n.nsf r.gs.1 a.asf r.as.1 v.aai.3s f.pa

εἰπὲ οὖν αὐτῇ ἵνα μοι συναντιλάβηται. 41 ἀποκριθεὶς δὲ
Tell her then *her* to help me." *help* But in answer *But* the Lord
3306 899 4036 899 2671 5269 1609 5269 1254 646 1254 3836 3261
v.aam.2s cj r.dsf.3 cj r.ds.1 v.ams.3s pt.ap.nsm cj

εἶπεν αὐτῇ ὁ κύριος, Μάρθα Μάρθα, μεριμνᾷς καὶ θορυβάζῃ περὶ πολλά,
said to her, *the* *Lord* "Martha, Martha, you are worried and troubled about many things,
3306 899 3836 3261 3450 3450 3534 2779 2571 4309 4498
v.aai.3s r.dsf.3 d.nsm n.nsm n.vsf n.vsf v.pai.2s cj v.ppi.2s p.a a.apn

42 ἑνὸς[a] δέ ἐστιν χρεία· Μαριὰμ γὰρ τὴν ἀγαθὴν
but only one thing *but* is necessary. Mary *{for}* has chosen the most important
1254 1651 1254 1639 5970 3452 1142 1721 1721 3836 19
a.gsn cj v.pai.3s n.nsf n.nsf cj d.asf a.asf

μερίδα ἐξελέξατο ἥτις ↱ οὐκ ἀφαιρεθήσεται αὐτῆς.
thing, *has chosen* which will not be taken away from her."
3535 1721 4015 904 4024 904 899
n.asf v.ami.3s r.nsf pl v.fpi.3s r.gsf.3

11:1 καὶ ἐγένετο ἐν τῷ εἶναι αὐτὸν ἐν τόπῳ
{and} *{it happened that}* *{when}* *{the}* Jesus was praying *Jesus* in a certain place,
2779 1181 1877 3836 899 1639 4667 899 1877 5516 5536
cj v.ami.3s p.d d.dsn f.pa r.asm.3 p.d n.dsm

τινὶ προσευχόμενον, ὡς ἐπαύσατο, εἶπέν τις τῶν
certain *praying* and when he finished one of his disciples said *one* *of*
5516 4667 6055 4264 5516 3836 899 3412 3306 5516 3836
r.dsm pt.pm.asm cj v.ami.3s v.aai.3s r.nsm d.gpm

μαθητῶν αὐτοῦ πρὸς αὐτόν, κύριε, δίδαξον ἡμᾶς προσεύχεσθαι, καθὼς καὶ Ἰωάννης
disciples *his* to him, "Lord, teach us to pray, just as *{also}* John
3412 899 4639 899 3261 1438 7005 4667 2777 2779 2722
n.gpm r.gsm.3 p.a r.asm.3 n.vsm v.aam.2s r.ap.1 f.pm cj adv n.nsm

ἐδίδαξεν τοὺς μαθητὰς αὐτοῦ. 2 εἶπεν δὲ αὐτοῖς, ὅταν προσεύχησθε λέγετε,
taught *{the}* his disciples." *his* He said *{and}* to them, "When you pray, say:
1438 3836 899 3412 899 3306 1254 899 4020 4667 3306
v.aai.3s d.apm n.apm r.gsm.3 v.aai.3s cj r.dpm.3 cj v.pms.2p v.pam.2p

Πάτερ,[b] → ἁγιασθήτω τὸ ὄνομά σου· → ἐλθέτω ἡ
'Father, may your name be held in honor; *{the}* *name* *your* may your reign begin. *{the}*
4252 5148 3950 39 3836 3950 5148 5148 993 2262 3836
n.vsm v.apm.3s d.nsn n.nsn r.gs.2 v.aam.3s d.nsf

βασιλεία σου·[c] 3 τὸν ἄρτον ἡμῶν τὸν ἐπιούσιον δίδου
reign *your* Give us each day *{the}* our daily bread; *our* *{the}* *daily* *Give*
993 5148 1443 7005 2848 2465 3836 7005 2157 788 7005 3836 2157 1443
n.nsf r.gs.2 d.asm n.asm r.gp.1 d.asm a.asm v.pam.2s

ἡμῖν τὸ καθ' ἡμέραν· 4 καὶ ἄφες ἡμῖν τὰς ἁμαρτίας ἡμῶν, καὶ γὰρ ↱
us *{the}* *each* *day* and forgive us *{the}* our sins, *our* *{also}* for we
7005 3836 2848 2465 2779 918 7005 3836 7005 281 7005 2779 1142 918
r.dp.1 d.asn p.a n.asf cj v.aam.2s r.dp.1 d.apf n.apf r.gp.1 adv cj

αὐτοὶ ἀφίομεν παντὶ ὀφείλοντι ἡμῖν· καὶ ↱ μὴ εἰσενέγκῃς ἡμᾶς εἰς
ourselves forgive everyone indebted to us. And do not bring us into a
899 918 4246 4053 7005 2779 1662 3590 1662 7005 1650
r.npm v.pai.1p a.dsm pt.pa.dsm r.dp.1 cj pl v.aas.2s r.ap.1 p.a

[a] ἑνὸς UBS, NET. ὀλίγων TNIV.
[b] ἡμῶν ὁ ἐν τοῖς οὐρανοῖς included by TR after Πάτερ.
[c] γενηθήτω τὸ θέλημά σου, ὡς ἐν οὐρανῷ, καὶ ἐπὶ τῆς γῆς included by TR after σου.

NASB

called Mary, who
was seated at the
Lord's feet, listen-
ing to His word.
[40]But Martha was
distracted with all
her preparations;
and she came up
to Him and said,
"Lord, do You not
care that my sister
has left me to do
all the serving
alone? Then tell
her to help me."
[41]But the Lord
answered and said
to her, "Martha,
Martha, you are
worried and both-
ered about so many
things; [42]but *only*
one thing is neces-
sary, for Mary has
chosen the good
part, which shall
not be taken away
from her."

Instruction about Prayer

[11:1]It happened that
while Jesus was
praying in a certain
place, after He had
finished, one of His
disciples said to
Him, "Lord, teach
us to pray just as
John also taught
his disciples." [2]And
He said to them,
"When you pray,
say:

> '[a]Father, hallowed be Your name.
> Your kingdom come.
> [3]'Give us each day our daily bread.
> [4]'And forgive us our sins,
> For we ourselves also

[a] Later mss add phrases from Matt 6:9-13 to make the two passages closely similar

NIV

And lead us not
into tempta-
tion.[a]'"
[5]Then Jesus said
to them, "Suppose
you have a friend,
and you go to him
at midnight and
say, 'Friend, lend
me three loaves of
bread; [6]a friend of
mine on a journey
has come to me,
and I have no food
to offer him.' [7]And
suppose the one
inside answers,
'Don't bother me.
The door is al-
ready locked, and
my children and I
are in bed. I can't
get up and give
you anything.'
[8]I tell you, even
though he will
not get up and
give you the bread
because of friend-
ship, yet because
of your shameless
audacity[b] he will
surely get up and
give you as much
as you need.
[9]"So I say to you:
Ask and it will be
given to you; seek
and you will find;
knock and the door
will be opened
to you. [10]For ev-
eryone who asks
receives; the one
who seeks finds;
and to the one who
knocks, the door
will be opened.
[11]"Which of you
fathers, if your
son asks for[c] a
fish, will give him
a snake instead?
[12]Or if he asks
for an egg, will
give him a scorpi-
on? [13]If you then,
though you are
evil,

[a] 4 Some manuscripts *temptation, but deliver us from the evil one*
[b] 8 Or *yet to preserve his good name*
[c] 11 Some manuscripts *for bread, will give him a stone? Or if he asks for*

πειρασμόν.[a] [5]καὶ εἶπεν πρὸς αὐτούς, τίς ἐξ ὑμῶν ἕξει φίλον καὶ
time of trial.'" {and} He said to them, ⌊"Suppose one⌋ of you has a friend, and
4280 2779 3306 4639 899 5515 1666 7007 2400 5813 2779
n.asm cj v.aai.3s p.a r.apm.3 r.nsm p.g r.gp.2 v.fai.3s n.asm cj

πορεύσεται πρὸς αὐτὸν μεσονυκτίου καὶ εἴπῃ αὐτῷ, φίλε, χρῆσόν μοι τρεῖς
you go to him at midnight and say to him, 'Friend, lend me three
4513 4639 899 3543 2779 3306 899 5813 3079 1609 5552
v.fmi.3s p.a r.asm.3 n.gsn cj v.aas.3s r.dsm.3 n.vsm v.aam.2s r.ds.1 a.apm

ἄρτους, [6]ἐπειδὴ φίλος μου παρεγένετο ἐξ ὁδοῦ πρός με καὶ
⌊loaves of bread,⌋ since a friend of mine has come to me from a journey *to me* and
788 2076 5813 1609 4134 4639 1609 1666 3847 4639 1609 2779
n.apm cj n.nsm r.gs.1 v.ami.3s p.g n.gsf p.a r.as.1 cj

→ → οὐκ ἔχω ὃ παραθήσω αὐτῷ· [7]κἀκεῖνος ἔσωθεν ἀποκριθεὶς εἴπῃ,
I do not have anything to set before him'; and he from inside answers, saying,
2400 2400 4024 2400 4005 4192 899 2797 2277 646 3306
pl v.pai.1s r.asn v.fai.1s r.dsm.3 crasis adv pt.ap.nsm v.aas.3s

μή μοι κόπους πάρεχε· ἤδη ἡ θύρα κέκλεισται καὶ τὰ παιδία
'Do not cause me trouble; *Do cause* already the door has been locked and {the} my children
4218 3590 4218 1609 3160 4218 2453 3836 2598 3091 2779 3836 1609 4086
pl r.ds.1 n.apm v.pam.2s adv d.nsf n.nsf v.rpi.3s cj d.npn n.npn

μου μετ' ἐμοῦ εἰς τὴν κοίτην εἰσίν· ⌊οὐ δύναμαι⌋ ἀναστὰς δοῦναί σοι.
my are with me in {the} bed. *are* I cannot get up and give you
1609 1639 3552 1609 1650 3836 3130 1639 4024 1538 482 1443 5148
r.gs.1 p.g r.gs.1 p.a d.asf n.asf v.pai.3p pl v.ppi.1s pt.aa.nsm f.aa r.ds.2

[8]λέγω ὑμῖν, εἰ καὶ → → οὐ δώσει αὐτῷ ἀναστὰς
anything.' I say to you, even though *even* he will not get up and give him *get up*
3306 7007 2779 1623 2779 1443 1443 4024 482 482 1443 899 482
v.pai.1s r.dp.2 cj adv pl v.fai.3s r.dsm.3 pt.aa.nsm

διὰ τὸ εἶναι φίλον αὐτοῦ, διά γε τὴν
anything because {the} he is his friend, *his* yet ⌊because of⌋ *yet* the
1328 3836 1639 899 5813 899 1145 1328 1145 3836
p.a d.asn f.pa n.asm r.gsm.3 p.a pl d.asf

ἀναίδειαν αὐτοῦ ἐγερθεὶς δώσει αὐτῷ ὅσων χρῄζει.
⌊prospect of being put to shame⌋ he will get up and give him ⌊as much as⌋ he needs.
357 899 1586 1443 899 4012 5974
n.asf r.gsm.3 pt.ap.nsm v.fai.3s r.dsm.3 r.gpn v.pai.3s

[9]κἀγὼ ὑμῖν ← λέγω, αἰτεῖτε καὶ δοθήσεται ὑμῖν, ζητεῖτε καὶ εὑρήσετε,
"So to you I say, ask and it will be given to you; seek and you will find;
2743 7007 2743 3306 160 2779 1443 7007 2426 2779 2351
crasis r.dp.2 v.pai.1s v.pam.2p cj v.fpi.3s r.dp.2 v.pam.2p cj v.fai.2p

κρούετε καὶ ἀνοιγήσεται ὑμῖν· [10]πᾶς γὰρ ὁ αἰτῶν λαμβάνει καὶ
knock and it will be opened for you. For everyone *For* who asks receives, and
3218 2779 487 7007 1142 4246 1142 3836 160 3284 2779
v.pam.2p cj v.fpi.3s r.dp.2 a.nsm cj d.nsm pt.pa.nsm v.pai.3s cj

ὁ ζητῶν εὑρίσκει καὶ → τῷ κρούοντι ἀνοιγήσεται.[b] [11]τίνα
everyone who seeks finds, and for everyone who knocks it will be opened. What
3836 2426 2351 2779 3836 3218 487 5515
d.nsm pt.pa.nsm v.pai.3s cj d.dsm pt.pa.dsm v.fpi.3s r.asm

δὲ ἐξ ὑμῶν τὸν πατέρα → αἰτήσει ὁ υἱὸς[c] ἰχθύν, καὶ
{and} father among you, {the} *father* should his son ask for *his son* a fish, {and}
1254 4252 1666 7007 3836 4252 3836 5626 160 3836 5626 2716 2779
cj p.g r.gp.2 d.asm n.asm v.fai.3s d.nsm n.nsm n.asm cj

ἀντὶ ἰχθύος ὄφιν αὐτῷ ἐπιδώσει; [12]ἢ καὶ αἰτήσει
will ⌊instead of⌋ a fish, give him a snake? *him will give* Or {also} ⌊should he ask for⌋ an
2113 505 2716 2113 899 4058 899 2113 2445 2779 160
p.g n.gsm n.asm r.dsm.3 v.fai.3s cj adv v.fai.3s

ᾠόν, ἐπιδώσει αὐτῷ σκορπίον; [13]εἰ οὖν ὑμεῖς πονηροὶ ὑπάρχοντες
egg, will give him a scorpion? If you then, *you* who are evil, *who are*
6051 2113 899 5026 1623 7007 4036 7007 5639 5639 4505 5639
n.asn v.fai.3s r.dsm.3 n.asm cj cj r.np.2 a.npm pt.pa.npm

[a] ἀλλὰ ῥῦσαι ἡμᾶς ἀπὸ τοῦ πονηροῦ included by TR after πειρασμόν.
[b] ἀνοιγήσεται TNIV, NET. ἀνοιγ[ήσ]εται UBS.
[c] ἄρτον, μὴ λίθον ἐπιδώσει included by TR after υἱὸς.

NASB

forgive ev-
eryone who
is indebted to
us.
And lead
us not into
temptation.'"
[5]Then He said to
them, "Suppose
one of you has a
friend, and goes
to him at midnight
and says to him,
'Friend, lend me
three loaves; [6]for a
friend of mine has
come to me from
a journey, and I
have nothing to
set before him';
[7]and from inside he
answers and says,
'Do not bother
me; the door has
already been shut
and my children
and I are in bed; I
cannot get up and
give you *anything*.'
[8]I tell you, even
though he will
not get up and
give him *anything*
because he is his
friend, yet because
of his persistence
he will get up and
give him as much
as he needs.
[9]"So I say to you,
ask, and it will be
given to you; seek,
and you will find;
knock, and it will
be opened to you.
[10]For everyone
who asks, receives;
and he who seeks,
finds; and to him
who knocks, it will
be opened. [11]Now
suppose one of you
fathers is asked by
his son for a fish;
he will not give
him a snake instead
of a fish, will he?
[12]Or *if* he is asked

NIV

know how to
give good gifts
to your children,
how much more
will your Father
in heaven give
the Holy Spirit
to those who ask
him!"

Jesus and Beelzebul

14 Jesus was driv-
ing out a demon
that was mute.
When the de-
mon left, the man
who had been
mute spoke, and
the crowd was
amazed. 15 But
some of them said,
"By Beelzebul, the
prince of demons,
he is driving out
demons." 16 Others
tested him by ask-
ing for a sign from
heaven.
17 Jesus knew
their thoughts
and said to them:
"Any kingdom
divided against
itself will be ru-
ined, and a house
divided against
itself will fall. 18 If
Satan is divided
against himself,
how can his king-
dom stand? I say
this because you
claim that I drive
out demons by Be-
elzebul. 19 Now if I
drive out demons
by Beelzebul, by
whom do your fol-
lowers drive them
out? So then, they
will be your

οἴδατε δόματα ἀγαθὰ διδόναι τοῖς τέκνοις ὑμῶν, πόσῳ μᾶλλον
know how to give good gifts *good* *to give* to your children, *your* how much more
3857 1443 1443 19 1517 19 1443 3836 7007 5451 7007 4531 3437
v.rai.2p n.apn a.apn f.pa d.dpn n.dpn r.gp.2 r.dsn adv.c

↱ ὁ πατὴρ ὁ [a] ⸤ἐξ οὐρανοῦ⸥ δώσει πνεῦμα ἅγιον τοῖς
will your heavenly Father *{the}* *heavenly* give the Holy Spirit *Holy* to those
1443 3836 1666 4252 3836 1666 4041 1443 41 4460 41 3836
d.nsm n.nsm d.nsm p.g n.gsm v.fai.3s n.asn a.asn d.dpm

αἰτοῦσιν αὐτόν. 14 καὶ ἦν ἐκβάλλων δαιμόνιον [b] καὶ αὐτὸ ἦν
who ask him!" ⸤One day⸥ Jesus was casting out a demon *{and}* that was
160 899 2779 1639 1675 1228 2779 899 1639
pt.pa.dpm r.asm.3 cj v.iai.3s pt.pa.nsm n.asn cj r.nsn v.iai.3s

κωφόν· ἐγένετο δὲ ↱ τοῦ δαιμονίου ἐξελθόντος
mute. *{it happened that}* *{and}* When the demon came out, the speechless man
3273 1181 1254 2002 3836 1228 2002 3836 3273 3273
a.nsn v.ami.3s cj d.gsn n.gsn pt.aa.gsn

ἐλάλησεν ὁ κωφὸς καὶ ἐθαύμασαν οἱ ὄχλοι. 15 τινὲς δὲ
spoke *the* *speechless man* and the people were amazed. *the* *people* But some *But*
3281 3836 3273 2779 3836 4063 2513 3836 4063 1254 5516 1254
v.aai.3s d.nsm a.nsm cj v.aai.3p d.npm n.npm r.npm cj

ἐξ αὐτῶν εἶπον, ἐν Βεελζεβοὺλ τῷ ἄρχοντι τῶν δαιμονίων ἐκβάλλει τὰ
of them said, "By Beelzebul, the prince of demons, he casts out *{the}*
1666 899 3306 1877 1015 3836 807 3836 1228 1675 3836
p.g r.gpm.3 v.aai.3p p.d n.dsm d.dsm n.dsm d.gpn n.gpn v.pai.3s d.apn

δαιμόνια· 16 ἕτεροι δὲ πειράζοντες σημεῖον ἐξ
demons!" Others, *{and}* to test him, kept demanding from him a sign from
1228 2283 1254 4279 2426 2426 4123 899 4956 1666
n.apn r.npm cj pt.pa.npm n.asn p.g

οὐρανοῦ ἐζήτουν παρ᾽ αὐτοῦ. 17 αὐτὸς δὲ εἰδὼς αὐτῶν τὰ διανοήματα
heaven. *kept demanding* *from* *him* But he, *But* knowing their *{the}* thoughts,
4041 2426 4123 899 1254 899 1254 3857 899 3836 1378
n.gsm v.iai.3p p.g r.gsm.3 r.nsm cj pt.ra.nsm r.gpm.3 d.apn n.apn

εἶπεν αὐτοῖς, πᾶσα βασιλεία ἐφ᾽ ἑαυτὴν διαμερισθεῖσα ἐρημοῦται καὶ
said to them, "Every kingdom divided against itself *divided* is laid waste, and a
3306 899 4246 993 1374 2093 1571 1374 2246 2779
v.aai.3s r.dpm.3 a.nsf n.nsf p.a r.asf.3 pt.ap.nsf v.ppi.3s cj

οἶκος ἐπὶ οἶκον πίπτει. 18 εἰ δὲ καὶ ὁ σατανᾶς
house divided against a house falls. And if *And* Satan also *{the}* *Satan* has been
3875 2093 3875 4406 1254 1623 1254 4928 2779 3836 4928 1374 1374
n.nsm p.a n.asm v.pai.3s cj cj adv d.nsm n.nsm

ἐφ᾽ ἑαυτὸν διεμερίσθη, πῶς → σταθήσεται ἡ βασιλεία
divided against himself, *has been divided* how will his kingdom stand? *{the}* *kingdom*
1374 2093 1571 1374 4802 899 993 2705 3836 993
p.a r.asm.3 v.api.3s cj v.fpi.3s d.nsf n.nsf

αὐτοῦ; ὅτι λέγετε ἐν Βεελζεβοὺλ ἐκβάλλειν με τὰ δαιμόνια. 19 εἰ
his For you say that by Beelzebul I cast out *I* *{the}* demons. And if
899 4022 3306 1877 1015 1609 1675 1609 3836 1228 1254 1623
r.gsm.3 cj v.pai.2p p.d n.dsm f.pa r.as.1 d.apn n.apn cj

δὲ ἐγὼ ἐν Βεελζεβοὺλ ἐκβάλλω τὰ δαιμόνια, ↱ οἱ
And by Beelzebul I *by* *Beelzebul* cast out *{the}* demons, by whom do *{the}* your
1254 1877 1015 1609 1877 1015 1675 3836 1228 1877 5515 1675 3836 7007
cj r.ns.1 p.d n.dsm v.pai.1s d.apn n.apn d.npm

υἱοὶ ὑμῶν ἐν τίνι ἐκβάλλουσιν; ← ⸤διὰ τοῦτο⸥ αὐτοὶ ὑμῶν
sons *your* *by* *whom* cast them out? Therefore they will be your
5626 7007 1877 5515 1675 1328 4047 899 1639 1639 7007
n.npm r.gp.2 p.d r.dsm v.pai.3p p.a r.asn r.npm r.gp.2

[a] [ὁ] UBS.
[b] [καὶ αὐτὸ ἦν] UBS, omitted by TNIV.

NASB

for an egg, he will
not give him a
scorpion, will he?
13 If you then, being
evil, know how to
give good gifts to
your children, how
much more will
your heavenly Fa-
ther give the Holy
Spirit to those who
ask Him?"

Pharisees' Blasphemy

14 And He was
casting out a de-
mon, and it was
mute; when the
demon had gone
out, the mute
man spoke; and
the crowds were
amazed. 15 But some
of them said, "He
casts out demons
by Beelzebul, the
ruler of the de-
mons." 16 Others,
to test *Him*, were
demanding of Him
a sign from heaven.
17 But He knew
their thoughts and
said to them, "Any
kingdom divided
against itself is
laid waste; and
a house *divided*
against itself falls.
18 If Satan also is
divided against
himself, how will
his kingdom stand?
For you say that I
cast out demons by
Beelzebul. 19 And if
I by Beelzebul cast
out demons, by
whom do your sons
cast them out? So
they will be your

NIV

judges. [20]But if I
drive out demons
by the finger of
God, then the
kingdom of God
has come upon
you.
[21]"When a
strong man, fully
armed, guards his
own house, his
possessions are
safe. [22]But when
someone stron-
ger attacks and
overpowers him,
he takes away the
armor in which
the man trusted
and divides up his
plunder.
[23]"Whoever is not
with me is against
me, and whoever
does not gather
with me scatters.
[24]"When an im-
pure spirit comes
out of a person,
it goes through
arid places seek-
ing rest and does
not find it. Then
it says, 'I will re-
turn to the house
I left.' [25]When it
arrives, it finds the
house swept clean
and put in order.
[26]Then it goes and
takes seven other
spirits more wick-
ed than itself, and
they go in and
live there. And
the final condi-
tion of that person
is worse than the
first."
[27]As Jesus was
saying these
things, a woman
in the crowd called
out, "Blessed is the
mother

κριταὶ ἔσονται. 20 εἰ δὲ ἐν δακτύλῳ θεοῦ ἐγὼ[a] ἐκβάλλω τὰ
judges. *will be* But if *But* I by the finger of God *I* cast out *{the}*
3216 1639 1254 1623 1254 1609 1877 1235 2536 1609 1675 3836
n.npm v.fmi.3p cj cj p.d n.dsm n.gsm r.ns.1 v.pai.1s d.apn

δαιμόνια, ἄρα ἔφθασεν ἐφ' ὑμᾶς ἡ βασιλεία τοῦ θεοῦ.
demons, then the kingdom of God has come upon you. *the kingdom of God*
1228 726 3836 993 3836 2536 5777 2093 7007 3836 993 3836 2536
n.apn cj v.aai.3s p.a r.ap.2 d.nsf n.nsf d.gsm n.gsm

21 ὅταν ὁ ἰσχυρὸς καθωπλισμένος φυλάσσῃ τὴν ἑαυτοῦ αὐλήν,
"When the strong man, fully armed, guards his own palace, his goods are
4020 3836 2708 2774 5875 3836 1571 885 899 5639 1639
cj d.nsm a.nsm pt.rm.nsm v.pas.3s d.asf r.gsm.3 n.asf

˻ἐν εἰρήνῃ˼ ἐστὶν τὰ ὑπάρχοντα αὐτοῦ· 22 ἐπὰν δὲ ἰσχυρότερος αὐτοῦ
secured; *are {the} goods his* but when *but* one stronger than he
1877 1645 1639 3836 5639 899 1254 2054 1254 2708 899
p.d n.dsf v.pai.3s d.npn pt.pa.npn r.gsm.3 cj cj a.nsm.c r.gsm.3

ἐπελθὼν νικήσῃ αὐτόν, τὴν πανοπλίαν αὐτοῦ αἴρει
attacks him and overpowers him, he takes away *{the}* his armor *his he takes away*
2088 3771 899 149 149 149 3836 899 4110 899 149
pt.aa.nsm v.aas.3s r.asm.3 d.asf n.asf r.gsm.3 v.pai.3s

ἐφ' ᾗ ἐπεποίθει καὶ τὰ σκῦλα αὐτοῦ διαδίδωσιν.
in which ˻he has placed his trust˼ and divides up *{the}* his spoil. *his divides up*
2093 4005 4275 2779 1344 1344 3836 899 5036 899 1344
p.d r.dsf v.lai.3s cj d.apn n.apn r.gsm.3 v.pai.3s

23 ὁ μὴ ὢν μετ' ἐμοῦ κατ' ἐμοῦ ἐστιν, καὶ ὁ ↱ ↱
"The one who is not *one who is* with me is against me; *is* and the one who
3836 1639 1639 1639 3590 1639 3552 1609 1639 2848 1609 1639 2779 3836 5251 5251
d.nsm pl pt.pa.nsm p.g r.gs.1 p.g r.gs.1 v.pai.3s cj d.nsm

↱ μὴ συνάγων μετ' ἐμοῦ σκορπίζει. 24 ὅταν τὸ ἀκάθαρτον πνεῦμα ἐξέλθῃ ἀπὸ
does not gather with me scatters. "When the unclean spirit departs from
5251 3590 5251 3552 1609 5025 4020 3836 176 4460 2002 608
pl pt.pa.nsm p.g r.gs.1 v.pai.3s cj d.nsn a.nsn n.nsn v.aas.3s p.g

τοῦ ἀνθρώπου, διέρχεται δι' ἀνύδρων τόπων ζητοῦν ἀνάπαυσιν καὶ μὴ
a person, it travels through waterless places seeking rest, and not
3836 476 1451 1328 536 5536 2426 398 2779 3590
d.gsm n.gsm v.pmi.3s p.g n.gpm n.gpm pt.pa.nsn n.asf cj pl

εὑρίσκον· τότε[b] λέγει, ὑποστρέψω εἰς τὸν οἶκόν μου ὅθεν ἐξῆλθον·
finding one; then it says, 'I will return to *{the}* my house *my* ˻from which˼ I departed.'
2351 5538 3306 5715 1650 3836 1609 3875 1609 3854 2002
pt.pa.nsn adv v.pai.3s v.fai.1s p.a d.asm n.asm r.gs.1 cj v.aai.1s

25 καὶ → ἐλθὸν εὑρίσκει σεσαρωμένον καὶ κεκοσμημένον.
{and} When the spirit returns, it finds the house swept and put in order.
2779 2262 2351 4924 2779 3175
cj pt.aa.nsn v.pai.3s pt.rp.asm cj pt.rp.asm

26 τότε πορεύεται καὶ παραλαμβάνει ἕτερα πνεύματα πονηρότερα ἑαυτοῦ ἑπτὰ
Then it goes and takes along seven other spirits more evil than itself, *seven*
5538 4513 2779 4161 2231 2283 4460 4505 1571 2231
adv v.pmi.3s cj v.pai.3s r.apn n.apn a.apn.c r.gsn.3 a.apn

καὶ εἰσελθόντα κατοικεῖ ἐκεῖ· καὶ γίνεται
and after going in ˻they settle down to live˼ there. So the last state of that person has become
2779 1656 2997 1695 2779 3836 2274 3836 1697 476 1181
cj pt.aa.npn v.pai.3s adv cj v.pmi.3s

τὰ ἔσχατα τοῦ ἀνθρώπου ἐκείνου χείρονα τῶν πρώτων. 27 ἐγένετο δὲ
the last of person that worse than the first." *{it happened that} {and}*
3836 2274 3836 476 1697 5937 3836 4755 1181 1254
d.npn a.npn d.gsm n.gsm r.gsm a.npn.c d.gpn a.gpn v.ami.3s cj

ἐν τῷ λέγειν αὐτὸν ταῦτα ἐπάρασά τις
While *{the}* he was saying *he* these things, a woman in the crowd raised *a* her
1877 3836 899 3306 899 4047 5516 1222 1666 3836 4063 2048 5516
p.d d.dsn f.pa r.asm.3 r.apn pt.aa.nsf r.nsf

φωνὴν γυνὴ ἐκ τοῦ ὄχλου εἶπεν αὐτῷ, μακαρία ἡ κοιλία ἡ βαστάσασά
voice *woman in the crowd* and said to him, "Blessed is the womb that carried
5889 1222 1666 3836 4063 3306 899 3421 3836 3120 3836 1002
n.asf n.nsf p.g d.gsm n.gsm v.aai.3s r.dsm.3 a.nsf d.nsf n.nsf d.nsf pt.aa.nsf

[a] [ἐγὼ] UBS.
[b] [τότε] UBS, omitted by NET.

NASB

judges. [20]But if I
cast out demons by
the finger of God,
then the kingdom
of God has come
upon you. [21]When
a strong *man,* fully
armed, guards his
own house, his
possessions are
undisturbed. [22]But
when someone
stronger than he
attacks him and
overpowers him,
he takes away from
him all his armor
on which he had
relied and distrib-
utes his plunder.
[23]He who is not
with Me is against
Me; and he who
does not gather
with Me, scatters.
[24]"When the un-
clean spirit goes
out of a man, it
passes through wa-
terless places seek-
ing rest, and not
finding any, it says,
'I will return to my
house from which I
came.' [25]And when
it comes, it finds
it swept and put
in order. [26]Then
it goes and takes
along seven other
spirits more evil
than itself, and
they go in and live
there; and the last
state of that man
becomes worse
than the first."
[27]While Jesus was
saying these things,
one of the women
in the crowd raised
her voice and said
to Him, "Blessed is
the womb that bore
You and the

NIV

who gave you birth
and nursed you."
28 He replied,
"Blessed rather are
those who hear the
word of God and
obey it."

The Sign of Jonah

29 As the crowds
increased, Jesus
said, "This is a
wicked genera-
tion. It asks for a
sign, but none will
be given it except
the sign of Jonah.
30 For as Jonah was
a sign to the Nine-
vites, so also will
the Son of Man be
to this generation.
31 The Queen of the
South will rise at
the judgment with
the people of this
generation and
condemn them, for
she came from the
ends of the earth to
listen to Solomon's
wisdom; and now
something greater
than Solomon is
here. 32 The men of
Nineveh will stand
up at the judgment
with this genera-
tion and condemn
it, for they repent-
ed at the preaching
of Jonah; and now
something greater
than Jonah is here.

The Lamp of the Body

33 "No one lights
a lamp and puts it
in a place where it
will be hidden, or
under a bowl. In-
stead they put it on
its stand, so that
those who come in
may see the light.
34 Your eye is the
lamp of your body.
When your eyes
are healthy,[a]

[a] *34* The Greek for *healthy* here implies *generous.*

σε καὶ μαστοὶ οὓς ἐθήλασας. 28 αὐτὸς δὲ εἶπεν, μενοῦν μακάριοι
you, and the breasts that nursed you!" But he *But* said, ⌊"On the contrary,⌋ blessed
5148 2779 3466 4005 2558 1254 899 1254 3306 3528 3421
r.as.2 cj n.npm r.apm v.aai.2s r.nsm cj v.aai.3s pl a.npm

↰ οἱ ἀκούοντες τὸν λόγον τοῦ θεοῦ καὶ φυλάσσοντες. 29 ↱ τῶν δὲ
rather are those who hear the word of God and keep it!" As the *{and}*
3528 3836 201 3836 3364 3836 2536 2779 5875 2044 3836 1254
d.npm pt.pa.npm d.asm n.asm d.gsm n.gsm cj pt.pa.npm d.gpm cj

ὄχλων ἐπαθροιζομένων ἤρξατο λέγειν, ἡ γενεὰ αὕτη
crowds were getting larger, Jesus began to say, *{the}* "This generation *This* is an evil
4063 2044 806 3306 3836 4047 1155 4047 1639 4505
n.gpm pt.pp.gpm v.ami.3s f.pa d.nsf n.nsf r.nsf

γενεὰ πονηρά ἐστιν· σημεῖον ζητεῖ, καὶ σημεῖον οὐ
generation; *evil* *is* it looks for a sign, *it looks for* but no sign *no*
1155 4505 1639 2426 2426 2426 4956 2426 2779 4024 4956 4024
n.nsf a.nsf v.pai.3s n.asn v.pai.3s cj n.nsn pl

δοθήσεται αὐτῇ ⌊εἰ μὴ⌋ τὸ σημεῖον Ἰωνᾶ. 30 καθὼς γὰρ ἐγένετο
will be given to it except the sign of Jonah. For as *For* Jonah became
1443 899 1623 3590 3836 4956 2731 1142 2777 1142 2731 1181
v.fpi.3s r.dsf.3 cj pl d.nsn n.nsn n.gsm cj cj v.ami.3s

Ἰωνᾶς τοῖς Νινευίταις σημεῖον, οὕτως ἔσται καὶ ὁ
Jonah a sign to the people of Nineveh, *sign* so the Son of Man will be *{also}* *the*
2731 4956 3836 3780 4956 4048 3836 5626 3836 476 1639 2779 3836
n.nsm d.dpm n.dpm n.nsn adv v.fmi.3s adv d.nsm

υἱὸς τοῦ ἀνθρώπου τῇ γενεᾷ ταύτῃ. 31 βασίλισσα → νότου
Son *of* *Man* a sign to this generation. *this* The queen of the South
5626 3836 476 3836 4047 1155 4047 999 3803
n.nsm d.gsm n.gsm d.dsf n.dsf r.dsf n.nsf n.gsm

ἐγερθήσεται ἐν τῇ κρίσει μετὰ τῶν ἀνδρῶν τῆς γενεᾶς ταύτης καὶ
will rise in the judgment with the men of this generation *this* and
1586 1877 3836 3213 3552 3836 467 3836 4047 1155 4047 2779
v.fpi.3s p.d d.dsf n.dsf p.g d.gpm n.gpm d.gsf n.gsf r.gsf cj

κατακρινεῖ αὐτούς, ὅτι ἦλθεν ἐκ τῶν περάτων τῆς γῆς ἀκοῦσαι τὴν σοφίαν
will condemn them, because she came from the ends of the earth to hear the wisdom
2891 899 4022 2262 1666 3836 4306 3836 1178 201 3836 5053
v.fai.3s r.apm.3 cj v.aai.3s p.g d.gpn n.gpn d.gsf n.gsf f.aa d.asf n.asf

Σολομῶνος, καὶ ἰδοὺ πλεῖον Σολομῶνος ὧδε. 32 ἄνδρες
of Solomon, and behold, something ⌊greater than⌋ Solomon is here. The men
5048 2779 2627 4498 5048 6045 467
n.gsm cj j a.nsn.c n.gsm adv n.npm

Νινευῖται ἀναστήσονται ἐν τῇ κρίσει μετὰ τῆς γενεᾶς ταύτης καὶ
of Nineveh will rise up in the judgment with *{the}* this generation *this* and
3780 482 1877 3836 3213 3552 3836 4047 1155 4047 2779
n.npm v.fmi.3p p.d d.dsf n.dsf p.g d.gsf n.gsf r.gsf cj

κατακρινοῦσιν αὐτήν· ὅτι μετενόησαν εἰς τὸ κήρυγμα Ἰωνᾶ, καὶ ἰδοὺ
condemn it, because they repented at the preaching of Jonah, and behold,
2891 899 4022 3566 1650 3836 3060 2731 2779 2627
v.fai.3p r.asf.3 cj v.aai.3p p.a d.asn n.asn n.gsm cj j

πλεῖον Ἰωνᾶ ὧδε. 33 οὐδεὶς λύχνον ἅψας εἰς
something ⌊greater than⌋ Jonah is here. "No one lights a lamp *lights* and puts it in a
4498 2731 6045 4029 721 3394 721 5502 1650
a.nsn.c n.gsm adv a.nsm n.asm pt.aa.nsm p.a

κρύπτην τίθησιν [a]οὐδὲ ὑπὸ τὸν μόδιον ἀλλ᾽ ἐπὶ τὴν λυχνίαν, ἵνα οἱ
vault *puts* or under a basket, but on a lampstand, so that those
3219 5502 4028 5679 3836 3654 247 2093 3836 3393 2671 3836
n.asf v.pai.3s cj p.a d.asm n.asm cj p.a d.asf n.asf cj d.npm

εἰσπορευόμενοι τὸ φῶς βλέπωσιν. 34 ὁ λύχνος τοῦ
who come in can see the light. *can see* Your eye is the lamp of the
1660 1063 1063 3836 5890 1063 5148 4057 1639 3836 3394 3836
pt.pm.npm d.asn n.asn v.pas.3p d.nsm n.nsm d.gsn

σώματός ἐστιν ὁ ὀφθαλμός σου. ὅταν ὁ ὀφθαλμός σου ἁπλοῦς ᾖ,
body. *is* *{the}* *eye* *Your* When *{the}* your eye *your* is sound, *is*
5393 1639 3836 4057 5148 4020 3836 5148 4057 5148 1639 606 1639
n.gsn v.pai.3s d.nsm n.nsm r.gs.2 cj d.nsm n.nsm r.gs.2 a.nsm v.pas.3s

[a] [οὐδὲ ὑπὸ τὸν μόδιον] UBS.

NASB

breasts at which
You nursed." 28 But
He said, "On the
contrary, blessed
are those who hear
the word of God
and observe it."

The Sign of Jonah

29 As the crowds
were increasing,
He began to say,
"This generation is
a wicked genera-
tion; it seeks for a
sign, and *yet* no
sign will be given
to it but the sign
of Jonah. 30 For just
as Jonah became
a sign to the Nin-
evites, so will the
Son of Man be to
this generation.
31 The Queen of the
South will rise up
with the men of
this generation at
the judgment and
condemn them,
because she came
from the ends of
the earth to hear
the wisdom of Sol-
omon; and behold,
something greater
than Solomon is
here. 32 The men
of Nineveh will
stand up with this
generation at the
judgment and con-
demn it, because
they repented at the
preaching of Jonah;
and behold, some-
thing greater than
Jonah is here.
33 "No one, after
lighting a lamp,
puts it away in a
cellar nor under a
basket, but on the
lampstand, so that
those who enter
may see the light.
34 The eye is the
lamp of your body;
when your eye is

NIV

your whole body also is full of light. But when they are unhealthy,[a] your body also is full of darkness. 35 See to it, then, that the light within you is not darkness. 36 Therefore, if your whole body is full of light, and no part of it dark, it will be just as full of light as when a lamp shines its light on you."

Woes on the Pharisees and the Experts in the Law

37 When Jesus had finished speaking, a Pharisee invited him to eat with him; so he went in and reclined at the table. 38 But the Pharisee was surprised when he noticed that Jesus did not first wash before the meal.

39 Then the Lord said to him, "Now then, you Pharisees clean the outside of the cup and dish, but inside you are full of greed and wickedness. 40 You foolish people! Did not the one who made the outside make the inside also? 41 But now as for what is inside you—be generous to the poor, and everything will be clean for you.

42 "Woe to you Pharisees, because you give God a tenth of your mint, rue and all other kinds of garden herbs, but you neglect justice and the love of God. You should have practiced the latter without leaving the

[a] 34 The Greek for *unhealthy* here implies *stingy.*

καὶ ὅλον τὸ σῶμά σου φωτεινόν ἐστιν· ἐπὰν δὲ πονηρὸς
then your whole *{the}* body *your* is full of light, *is* but when *but* it is diseased,
2779 5148 3910 3836 5393 5148 1639 5893 1639 1254 2054 1254 1639 1639 4505
adv a.nsn d.nsn n.nsn r.gs.2 a.nsn v.pai.3s cj cj a.nsm

ᾖ, καὶ τὸ σῶμά σου σκοτεινόν. 35 σκόπει οὖν
it is then *{the}* your body *your* is full of darkness. Therefore consider *Therefore* whether the
1639 2779 3836 5148 5393 5148 5027 4036 5023 4036 3836
v.pas.3s adv d.nsn n.nsn r.gs.2 a.nsn v.pam.2s cj

μὴ τὸ φῶς τὸ ἐν σοὶ σκότος ἐστίν. 36 εἰ οὖν τὸ
'light' that is in you is not *the light that in you* darkness. *is* If then *{the}*
5890 3836 1877 5148 1639 3590 3836 5890 3836 1877 5148 5030 1639 1623 4036 3836
cj d.nsn n.nsn d.nsn p.d r.ds.2 n.nsn v.pai.3s cj cj d.nsn

σῶμά σου ὅλον φωτεινόν, μὴ ἔχον μέρος τι σκοτεινόν,
your whole body *your whole* is full of light, having no *having* part of it dark,
5148 3910 5393 5148 3910 5893 2400 3590 2400 3538 5516 5027
n.nsn r.gs.2 a.nsn a.nsn pl pt.pa.nsn n.asn r.asn a.asn

ἔσται φωτεινὸν ὅλον ὡς ὅταν ὁ λύχνος τῇ ἀστραπῇ
⌊it will be⌋ wholly bright, *wholly* as when a lamp gives you light ⌊with its⌋ rays."
1639 3910 5893 3910 6055 4020 3836 3394 5894 5148 5894 3836 847
v.fmi.3s a.nsn a.nsn cj cj d.nsm n.nsm d.dsf n.dsf

φωτίζῃ σε. 37 ἐν δὲ τῷ λαλῆσαι ἐρωτᾷ αὐτὸν Φαρισαῖος
gives light you When *{and} {the}* Jesus finished speaking, a Pharisee asked him *Pharisee*
5894 5148 1877 1254 3836 3281 5757 2263 899 5757
v.pas.3s r.as.2 p.d cj d.dsn f.aa v.pai.3s r.asm.3 n.nsm

ὅπως ἀριστήσῃ παρ' αὐτῷ· ➝ εἰσελθὼν δὲ ἀνέπεσεν. 38 ὁ δὲ
to have a meal with him, so he went in *so* and ⌊reclined at table.⌋ The *{and}*
3968 753 4123 899 1254 404 1656 1254 404 3836 1254
cj v.aas.3s p.d r.dsm.3 pt.aa.nsm cj v.aai.3s d.nsm cj

Φαρισαῖος ἰδὼν ἐθαύμασεν ὅτι οὐ πρῶτον
Pharisee was surprised ⌊when he observed⌋ *was surprised* that Jesus did not wash first,
5757 2513 2513 1625 2513 4022 966 4024 966 4754
n.nsm pt.aa.nsm v.aai.3s cj pl adv

ἐβαπτίσθη πρὸ τοῦ ἀρίστου. 39 εἶπεν δὲ ὁ κύριος πρὸς αὐτόν, νῦν
did wash before the meal. The Lord said *{and} The Lord* to him, "Now
966 4574 3836 756 3836 3261 3306 1254 3836 3261 4639 899 3814
v.api.3s p.g d.gsn n.gsn v.aai.3s cj d.nsm n.nsm p.a r.asm.3 adv

ὑμεῖς οἱ Φαρισαῖοι τὸ ἔξωθεν τοῦ ποτηρίου καὶ τοῦ πίνακος καθαρίζετε,
you *{the}* Pharisees cleanse the outside of the cup and of the dish; *cleanse*
7007 3836 5757 2751 3836 2033 3836 4539 2779 3836 4402 2751
r.np.2 d.npm n.npm d.asn p.g d.gsn n.gsn cj d.gsm n.gsm v.pai.2p

τὸ δὲ ἔσωθεν ὑμῶν γέμει ἁρπαγῆς καὶ πονηρίας. 40 ἄφρονες, ➝ οὐχ ὁ
but the *but* inside of you is full of greed and wickedness. Fools! Did not he
1254 3836 1254 2277 7007 1154 771 2779 4504 933 4472 4024 3836
d.nsn cj adv r.gp.2 v.pai.3s n.gsf cj n.gsf a.vpm pl d.nsm

ποιήσας τὸ ἔξωθεν καὶ τὸ ἔσωθεν ἐποίησεν; 41 πλὴν
who made the outside make the inside also? *the inside make* Rather,
4472 3836 2033 4472 3836 2277 2779 3836 2277 4472 4440
pt.aa.nsm d.asn adv adv d.asn adv v.aai.3s cj

τὰ ἐνόντα δότε ἐλεημοσύνην, καὶ ἰδοὺ πάντα
⌊in connection with what⌋ is inside, ⌊you should give⌋ alms, and then everything will be
3836 1913 1443 1797 2779 2627 4246 1639 1639
d.apn pt.pa.apn v.aam.2p n.asf cj j a.npn

καθαρὰ ὑμῖν ἐστιν. 42 ἀλλὰ οὐαὶ ὑμῖν τοῖς Φαρισαίοις, ὅτι ἀποδεκατοῦτε τὸ
clean for you. *will be* But woe to you *{the}* Pharisees! For you tithe *{the}*
2754 7007 1639 247 4026 7007 3836 5757 4022 620 3836
a.npn r.dp.2 v.pai.3s cj j r.dp.2 d.dpm n.dpm cj v.pai.2p d.asn

ἡδύοσμον καὶ τὸ πήγανον καὶ πᾶν λάχανον καὶ παρέρχεσθε τὴν κρίσιν
mint and *{the}* rue and ⌊every kind⌋ of garden herb, yet disregard *{the}* justice
2455 2779 3836 4379 2779 4246 3303 2779 4216 3836 3213
n.asn cj d.asn n.asn cj a.asn n.asn cj v.pmi.2p d.asf n.asf

καὶ τὴν ἀγάπην τοῦ θεοῦ· ταῦτα δὲ ἔδει ποιῆσαι
and the love of God. These *{and}* ⌊you should have⌋ done, without neglecting the
2779 3836 27 3836 2536 4047 1254 1256 4472 3590 4223
cj d.asf n.asf d.gsm n.gsm r.apn cj v.iai.3s f.aa

NASB

clear, your whole body also is full of light; but when it is bad, your body also is full of darkness. 35 Then watch out that the light in you is not darkness. 36 If therefore your whole body is full of light, with no dark part in it, it will be wholly illumined, as when the lamp illumines you with its rays."

Woes upon the Pharisees

37 Now when He had spoken, a Pharisee *asked Him to have lunch with him; and He went in, and reclined *at the table.* 38 When the Pharisee saw it, he was surprised that He had not first ceremonially washed before the meal. 39 But the Lord said to him, "Now you Pharisees clean the outside of the cup and of the platter; but inside of you, you are full of robbery and wickedness. 40 You foolish ones, did not He who made the outside make the inside also? 41 But give that which is within as charity, and then all things are clean for you.

42 "But woe to you Pharisees! For you pay tithe of mint and rue and every *kind of* garden herb, and *yet* disregard justice and the love of God; but these are the things you should have done without

NIV

former undone.
43 "Woe to you
Pharisees, because
you love the most
important seats in
the synagogues
and respectful
greetings in the
marketplaces.
44 "Woe to you,
because you are
like unmarked
graves, which
people walk over
without know-
ing it."
45 One of the ex-
perts in the law
answered him,
"Teacher, when
you say these
things, you insult
us also."
46 Jesus replied,
"And you experts
in the law, woe to
you, because you
load people down
with burdens they
can hardly carry,
and you your-
selves will not lift
one finger to help
them.
47 "Woe to you,
because you build
tombs for the
prophets, and it
was your ances-
tors who killed
them. 48 So you
testify that you
approve of what
your ancestors
did; they killed the
prophets, and you
build their tombs.
49 Because of this,
God in his wisdom
said, 'I will send
them prophets and
apostles, some of
whom they will
kill and others
they will perse-
cute.' 50 Therefore
this generation
will be held re-
sponsible for the
blood of all the
prophets that has
been shed since
the beginning of
the world,

κἀκεῖνα μὴ παρεῖναι. 43 οὐαὶ ὑμῖν τοῖς Φαρισαίοις, ὅτι ἀγαπᾶτε τὴν
others. *without* *neglecting* Woe to you *{the}* Pharisees! For you love the
2797 3590 4223 4026 7007 3836 5757 4022 26 3836
cj pl f.aa j r.dp.2 d.dpm n.dpm cj v.pai.2p d.asf

πρωτοκαθεδρίαν ἐν ταῖς συναγωγαῖς καὶ τοὺς ἀσπασμοὺς ἐν ταῖς ἀγοραῖς.
seat of honor in the synagogues and *{the}* greetings in the marketplaces.
4751 1877 3836 5252 2779 3836 833 1877 3836 59
n.asf p.d d.dpf n.dpf cj d.apm n.apm p.d d.dpf n.dpf

44 οὐαὶ ὑμῖν,[a] ὅτι ἐστὲ ὡς τὰ μνημεῖα τὰ ἄδηλα, καὶ οἱ ἄνθρωποι
Woe to you! For you are like *{the}* unmarked tombs; *{the}* *unmarked* *{and}* *{the}* people
4026 7007 4022 1639 6055 3836 83 3646 3836 83 2779 3836 476
j r.dp.2 cj v.pai.2p pl d.npn n.npn d.npn a.npn cj d.npm n.npm

οἱ[b] περιπατοῦντες ἐπάνω οὐκ οἴδασιν. 45 ἀποκριθεὶς
{the} walk over them without realizing it." One of the lawyers responded
3836 4344 2062 4024 3857 5516 3836 3836 3788 646
d.npm pt.pa.npm adv pl v.rai.3p pt.ap.nsm

δέ τις τῶν νομικῶν λέγει αὐτῷ, διδάσκαλε, ταῦτα λέγων
{and} *One* *of the* *lawyers* and said to him, "Teacher, in saying these things *in saying* you
1254 5516 3836 3788 3306 899 1437 3306 3306 4047 3306 5614
cj r.nsm d.gpm n.gpm v.pai.3s r.dsm.3 n.vsm r.apn pt.pa.nsm

καὶ ἡμᾶς ὑβρίζεις. 46 ὁ δὲ εἶπεν, καὶ ὑμῖν τοῖς νομικοῖς
insult us as well." *us* *you insult* Jesus *{and}* replied, *also!* "Woe to you *{the}* lawyers
5614 7005 2779 7005 5614 3836 1254 3306 2779 4026 7007 3836 3788
adv r.ap.1 v.pai.2s d.nsm cj v.aai.3s adv r.dp.2 d.dpm n.dpm

οὐαί, ὅτι φορτίζετε τοὺς ἀνθρώπους ↰ ↰ φορτία δυσβάστακτα, καὶ
Woe also! For you load *{the}* people down with burdens hard to bear, yet you
4026 2779 4022 5844 3836 476 5844 5844 5845 1546 2779 4718
j cj v.pai.2p d.apm n.apm n.apn a.apn cj

αὐτοὶ ἑνὶ τῶν δακτύλων ὑμῶν οὐ
yourselves will not touch the burdens ⌊with one⌋ of your fingers. *your* *not*
899 4718 4024 4718 3836 5845 1651 3836 7007 1235 7007 4024
r.npm a.dsm d.gpm n.gpm r.gp.2 pl

προσψαύετε τοῖς φορτίοις. 47 οὐαὶ ὑμῖν, ὅτι οἰκοδομεῖτε τὰ μνημεῖα τῶν
you will touch *the* *burdens* Woe to you! For you build *{the}* memorials to the
4718 3836 5845 4026 7007 4022 3868 3836 3646 3836
v.pai.2p d.dpn n.dpn j r.dp.2 cj v.pai.2p d.apn n.apn d.gpm

προφητῶν, οἱ δὲ πατέρες ὑμῶν ἀπέκτειναν αὐτούς. 48 ἄρα μάρτυρές
prophets, *{the}* but your fathers *your* killed them. So you are witnesses:
4737 3836 1254 7007 4252 7007 650 899 726 1639 1639 3459
n.gpm d.npm cj n.npm r.gp.2 v.aai.3p r.apm.3 cj n.npm

ἐστε καὶ συνευδοκεῖτε τοῖς ἔργοις τῶν πατέρων ὑμῶν, ὅτι αὐτοὶ μὲν
you are *{and}* you approve of the deeds of your fathers, *your* because while they *while*
1639 2779 5306 3836 2240 3836 7007 4252 7007 4022 3525 899 3525
v.pai.2p cj v.pai.2p d.dpn n.dpn d.gpm n.gpm r.gp.2 cj r.npm pl

ἀπέκτειναν αὐτούς, ὑμεῖς δὲ οἰκοδομεῖτε.[c] 49 διὰ τοῦτο
killed them, you *{and}* build the memorials. Indeed, for this reason
650 899 7007 1254 3868 2779 1328 4047
v.aai.3p r.apm.3 r.np.2 cj v.pai.2p p.a r.asn

καὶ ἡ σοφία τοῦ θεοῦ εἶπεν, ἀποστελῶ εἰς αὐτοὺς προφήτας καὶ ἀποστόλους,
Indeed the Wisdom of God said, 'I will send to them prophets and apostles,
2779 3836 5053 3836 2536 3306 690 1650 899 4737 2779 693
adv d.nsf n.nsf d.gsm n.gsm v.aai.3s v.fai.1s p.a r.apm.3 n.apm cj n.apm

καὶ ἐξ αὐτῶν ἀποκτενοῦσιν καὶ διώξουσιν, 50 ἵνα ἐκζητηθῇ τὸ αἷμα
{and} some of whom they will kill and persecute,' so that *may be charged* the blood
2779 1666 899 650 2779 1503 2671 1699 3836 135
cj p.g r.gpm.3 v.fai.3p cj v.fai.3p cj v.aps.3s d.nsn n.nsn

πάντων τῶν προφητῶν τὸ ἐκκεχυμένον ἀπὸ καταβολῆς → κόσμου
of all the prophets, *{the}* shed since the foundation of the world, may be
4246 3836 4737 3836 1773 608 2856 3180 1699 1699
a.gpm d.gpm n.gpm d.nsn pt.rp.nsn p.g n.gsf n.gsm 1699

[a] γραμματεῖς καὶ Φαρισαῖοι, ὑποκριταὶ included by TR after ὑμῖν.
[b] [οἱ] UBS, omitted by TNIV.
[c] αὐτῶν τὰ μνημεῖα included by TR after οἰκοδομεῖτε.

NASB

neglecting the oth-
ers. 43 Woe to you
Pharisees! For you
love the chief seats
in the synagogues
and the respectful
greetings in the
market places.
44 Woe to you! For
you are like con-
cealed tombs, and
the people who
walk over *them* are
unaware *of it*."
45 One of the [a]law-
yers *said to Him
in reply, "Teacher,
when You say
this, You insult
us too." 46 But He
said, "Woe to you
lawyers as well!
For you weigh men
down with burdens
hard to bear, while
you yourselves
will not even
touch the burdens
with one of your
fingers. 47 Woe to
you! For you build
the tombs of the
prophets, and *it*
was your fathers
who killed them.
48 So you are wit-
nesses and approve
the deeds of your
fathers; because
it was they who
killed them, and
you build *their*
tombs. 49 For this
reason also the
wisdom of God
said, 'I will send to
them prophets and
apostles, and *some*
of them they will
kill and *some* they
will persecute, 50 so
that the blood of all
the prophets, shed
since the founda-
tion of the world,
may be charged

[a] I.e. experts in the Mosaic Law

NIV

[51]from the blood of
Abel to the blood
of Zechariah, who
was killed between
the altar and the
sanctuary. Yes, I
tell you, this gen-
eration will be
held responsible
for it all.
[52]"Woe to you
experts in the law,
because you have
taken away the key
to knowledge. You
yourselves have
not entered, and
you have hindered
those who were
entering."
[53]When Jesus
went outside, the
Pharisees and the
teachers of the law
began to oppose
him fiercely and to
besiege him with
questions, [54]wait-
ing to catch him
in something he
might say.

Warnings and Encouragements

12 Meanwhile,
when a
crowd of many
thousands had
gathered, so that
they were tram-
pling on one an-
other, Jesus began
to speak first to
his disciples, say-
ing: "Be[a] on your
guard against the
yeast of the Phari-
sees, which is hy-
pocrisy. [2]There is
nothing concealed
that will not be
disclosed, or hid-
den that will not
be made known.
[3]What you have
said in the dark
will be heard in
the daylight, and
what you have
whispered in the
ear in the inner
rooms

[a] 1 Or *speak to his disciples, saying: "First of all, be*

ἀπὸ τῆς γενεᾶς ταύτης, 51 ἀπὸ αἵματος Ἅβελ ἕως αἵματος
charged against {the} this generation, *this* from the blood of Abel to the blood
1699 608 3836 4047 1155 4047 608 135 6 2401 135
p.g d.gsf n.gsf r.gsf p.g n.gsn n.gsm p.g n.gsn

Ζαχαρίου τοῦ ἀπολομένου μεταξὺ τοῦ θυσιαστηρίου καὶ τοῦ οἴκου· ναὶ λέγω
of Zechariah, who perished between the altar and the sanctuary. Yes, I tell
2408 3836 660 3568 3836 2603 2779 3836 3875 3721 3306
n.gsm d.gsm pt.am.gsm p.g d.gsn n.gsn cj d.gsm n.gsm pl v.pai.1s

ὑμῖν, ἐκζητηθήσεται ἀπὸ τῆς γενεᾶς ταύτης. 52 οὐαὶ ὑμῖν τοῖς νομικοῖς,
you, it will be charged against {the} this generation. *this* Woe to you {the} lawyers!
7007 1699 608 3836 4047 1155 4047 4026 7007 3836 3788
r.dp.2 v.fpi.3s p.g d.gsf n.gsf r.gsf j r.dp.2 d.dpm n.dpm

ὅτι ἤρατε τὴν κλεῖδα τῆς γνώσεως· αὐτοὶ οὐκ
For ⌞you have taken away⌟ the key of knowledge. You did not enter yourselves, *not*
4022 149 3836 3090 3836 1194 1656 1656 4024 1656 899 4024
cj v.aai.2p d.asf n.asf d.gsf n.gsf r.npm pl

εἰσήλθατε καὶ τοὺς εἰσερχομένους ἐκωλύσατε. 53
You did enter and have hindered those who wanted to enter." *have hindered* When he went out
1656 2779 3266 3266 3836 1656 3266 2002 899 2002 2002
v.aai.2p cj d.apm pt.pm.apm v.aai.2p

κἀκεῖθεν ἐξελθόντος αὐτοῦ ἤρξαντο οἱ γραμματεῖς
from there, *When went out he* the scribes and the Pharisees began *the scribes*
2796 2002 899 3836 1208 2779 3836 5757 806 3836 1208
crasis pt.aa.gsm r.gsm.3 v.ami.3p d.npm n.npm

καὶ οἱ Φαρισαῖοι ↱ ↱ δεινῶς ἐνέχειν καὶ ἀποστοματίζειν αὐτὸν ↰ περὶ
and the Pharisees to be terribly hostile, and to question him sharply about
2779 3836 5757 1923 1923 1267 1923 2779 694 899 694 4309
cj d.npm n.npm adv f.pa cj f.pa r.asm.3 p.g

πλειόνων, 54 ἐνεδρεύοντες αὐτὸν θηρεῦσαί τι ἐκ τοῦ στόματος
many things, plotting against him, to catch him in something from {the} his mouth.
4498 1910 899 2561 5516 1666 3836 899 5125
a.gpn.c pt.pa.npm r.asm.3 f.aa r.asn p.g d.gsn n.gsn

αὐτοῦ.
his
899
r.gsm.3

12:1 ἐν οἷς → ἐπισυναχθεισῶν τῶν
In the meantime, when many thousands of the crowd had gathered {the}
1877 4005 3689 3689 3836 3836 4063 2190 3836
p.d r.dpn pt.ap.gpf d.gpf

μυριάδων τοῦ ὄχλου, ὥστε καταπατεῖν ἀλλήλους, ἤρξατο λέγειν πρὸς
many thousands of the crowd so that they were trampling one another, Jesus began to say (to
3689 3836 4063 6063 2922 253 806 3306 4639
n.gpf d.gsm n.gsm cj f.pa r.apm v.ami.3s f.pa p.a

τοὺς μαθητὰς αὐτοῦ πρῶτον, ⌞προσέχετε ἑαυτοῖς⌟ ἀπὸ τῆς ζύμης,
{the} his disciples *his* first), "Beware of the yeast of the
3836 899 3412 899 4754 4668 1571 608 3836 2434 3836 3836
d.apm n.apm r.gsm.3 adv v.pam.2p r.dpm.2 p.g d.gsf n.gsf

ἥτις ἐστὶν ὑπόκρισις, τῶν Φαρισαίων. 2 οὐδὲν δὲ
Pharisees, which is hypocrisy. *of the Pharisees* Nothing {and} is
5757 4015 1639 5694 3836 5757 4029 1254 1639
r.nsf v.pai.3s n.nsf d.gpm n.gpm a.nsn cj

συγκεκαλυμμένον ἐστὶν ὃ ↱ οὐκ ἀποκαλυφθήσεται καὶ κρυπτὸν ὃ ↱ οὐ
covered up *is* that will not be revealed, or hidden that will not
5158 1639 4005 636 4024 636 2779 3220 4005 1182 4024
pt.rp.nsn v.pai.3s r.nsn pl v.fpi.3s cj a.nsn r.nsn pl

γνωσθήσεται. 3 ⌞ἀνθ' ὧν⌟ ὅσα ἐν τῇ σκοτίᾳ εἴπατε
be known. {therefore} All that you said in the darkness *you said* will be heard
1182 505 4005 4012 3306 3306 1877 3836 5028 3306 201 201 201
v.fpi.3s p.g r.gpn r.apn p.d d.dsf n.dsf v.aai.2p

ἐν τῷ φωτὶ ἀκουσθήσεται, καὶ ὃ πρὸς τὸ οὖς ἐλαλήσατε ἐν τοῖς ταμείοις
in the light, *will be heard* and what {in} {the} {ear} you said in {the} private rooms
1877 3836 5890 201 2779 4005 4639 3836 4044 3281 1877 3836 5421
p.d d.dsn n.dsn v.fpi.3s cj r.asn p.a d.asn n.asn v.aai.2p p.d d.dpn n.dpn

NASB

against this gen-
eration, [51]from
the blood of Abel
to the blood of
Zechariah, who
was killed between
the altar and the
house *of God;* yes,
I tell you, it shall
be charged against
this generation.'
[52]Woe to you law-
yers! For you have
taken away the
key of knowledge;
you yourselves did
not enter, and you
hindered those who
were entering."
[53]When He left
there, the scribes
and the Pharisees
began to be very
hostile and to ques-
tion Him closely
on many subjects,
[54]plotting against
Him to catch *Him*
in something He
might say.

God Knows and Cares

[12:1]Under these cir-
cumstances, after
so many thousands
of people had gath-
ered together that
they were stepping
on one another, He
began saying to
His disciples first
of all, "Beware of
the leaven of the
Pharisees, which
is hypocrisy. [2]But
there is nothing
covered up that
will not be re-
vealed, and hidden
that will not be
known. [3]Accord-
ingly, whatever
you have said in
the dark will be
heard in the light,
and what you have
whispered in the
inner rooms will be

NIV

will be proclaimed
from the roofs.
[4]"I tell you, my
friends, do not
be afraid of those
who kill the body
and after that can
do no more. [5]But
I will show you
whom you should
fear: Fear him
who, after your
body has been
killed, has au-
thority to throw
you into hell. Yes,
I tell you, fear
him. [6]Are not five
sparrows sold for
two pennies? Yet
not one of them is
forgotten by God.
[7]Indeed, the very
hairs of your head
are all numbered.
Don't be afraid;
you are worth
more than many
sparrows.
[8]"I tell you,
whoever publicly
acknowledges me
before others, the
Son of Man will
also acknowledge
before the angels
of God. [9]But who-
ever disowns me
before others will
be disowned be-
fore the angels of
God. [10]And every-
one who speaks a
word against the
Son of Man will
be forgiven, but
anyone who blas-
phemes against the
Holy Spirit will
not be forgiven.
[11]"When you are
brought before
synagogues, rulers
and authorities, do
not worry about
how you will de-
fend yourselves or
what you will say,
[12]for the Holy

κηρυχθήσεται ἐπὶ τῶν δωμάτων. [4]λέγω δὲ ὑμῖν τοῖς φίλοις μου, ↱ μὴ
will be proclaimed on the housetops. "I tell {and} you, {the} my friends, *my* do not
3062 2093 3836 1560 3306 1254 7007 3836 1609 5813 1609 5828 3590
v.fpi.3s p.g d.gpn n.gpn v.pai.1s cj r.dp.2 d.dpm n.dpm r.gs.1 pl

φοβηθῆτε ἀπὸ τῶν ἀποκτεινόντων τὸ σῶμα καὶ μετὰ ταῦτα μὴ ἐχόντων
fear {from} those who can kill the body, and after that have nothing *have*
5828 608 3836 650 3836 5393 2779 3552 4047 2400 3590 2400
v.aps.2p p.g d.gpm pt.pa.gpm d.asn n.asn cj p.a r.apn pl pt.pa.gpm

περισσότερόν τι ποιῆσαι. [5]ὑποδείξω δὲ ὑμῖν τίνα φοβηθῆτε· φοβήθητε
more that they can do. I will show {and} you whom ⌞you should fear:⌟ Fear
4358 5516 4472 5683 1254 7007 5515 5828 5828
a.asn.c r.asn f.aa v.fai.1s cj r.dp.2 r.asm v.aps.2p v.apm.2p

τὸν ↱ ↱ μετὰ τὸ ἀποκτεῖναι ἔχοντα ἐξουσίαν ἐμβαλεῖν εἰς τὴν γέενναν.
the one who, after {the} he kills, has authority to throw you into {the} Gehenna.
3836 2026 2400 3552 3836 650 2400 2026 1833 1650 3836 1147
d.asm p.a d.asn f.aa pt.pa.asm n.asf f.aa p.a d.asf n.asf

ναὶ λέγω ὑμῖν, τοῦτον φοβήθητε. [6]↱ οὐχὶ πέντε στρουθία πωλοῦνται →
Yes, I tell you, fear this one! *fear* "Are not five sparrows sold for two
3721 3306 7007 5828 4047 5828 4797 4049 4297 5141 4797 1545
pl v.pai.1s r.dp.2 r.asm v.apm.2p pl a.npn n.npn v.ppi.3p

ἀσσαρίων δύο; καὶ ἓν ἐξ αὐτῶν οὐκ ἔστιν ἐπιλελησμένον ἐνώπιον τοῦ θεοῦ.
pennies? *two* And not one of them *not* is forgotten before {the} God.
837 1545 2779 4024 1651 1666 899 4024 1639 2140 1967 3836 2536
n.gpn a.gpn cj a.nsn p.g r.gpn.3 pl v.pai.3s pt.rp.nsn p.g d.gsm n.gsm

[7]ἀλλὰ καὶ αἱ τρίχες τῆς κεφαλῆς ὑμῶν ↱ πᾶσαι ἠρίθμηνται. ↱ μὴ
In fact, even the hairs of your head *your* are all numbered. Do not
247 2779 3836 2582 3836 7007 3051 7007 749 4246 749 5828 3590
cj adv d.npf n.npf d.gsf n.gsf r.gp.2 a.npf v.rpi.3p pl

φοβεῖσθε· πολλῶν στρουθίων διαφέρετε. [8]λέγω δὲ ὑμῖν,
fear; you are worth more than many sparrows. *you are worth more* "I say {and} to you,
5828 1422 1422 1422 1422 4498 5141 1422 3306 1254 7007
v.ppm.2p a.gpn n.gpn v.pai.2p v.pai.1s cj r.dp.2

πᾶς ὃς ἂν ⌞ὁμολογήσῃ ἐν⌟ ἐμοὶ ἔμπροσθεν τῶν ἀνθρώπων,
everyone who ~ acknowledges me before {the} men, the Son of Man
4246 4005 323 3933 1877 1609 1869 3836 476 3836 5626 3836 476
a.nsm r.nsm pl v.aas.3s p.d r.ds.1 p.g d.gpm n.gpm

καὶ ὁ υἱὸς τοῦ ἀνθρώπου ⌞ὁμολογήσει ἐν⌟ αὐτῷ ἔμπροσθεν τῶν ἀγγέλων
will also *the* *Son* *of* *Man* acknowledge him before the angels
2779 3836 5626 3836 476 3933 1877 899 1869 3836 34
adv d.nsm n.nsm d.gsm n.gsm v.fai.3s p.d r.dsm.3 p.g d.gpm n.gpm

τοῦ θεοῦ· [9]ὁ δὲ ἀρνησάμενός με ἐνώπιον τῶν ἀνθρώπων ἀπαρνηθήσεται
of God; but the *but* one who denies me before {the} men will be denied
3836 2536 1254 3836 1254 766 1609 1967 3836 476 565
d.gsm n.gsm d.nsm cj pt.am.nsm r.as.1 p.g d.gpm n.gpm v.fpi.3s

ἐνώπιον τῶν ἀγγέλων τοῦ θεοῦ. [10]καὶ πᾶς ὃς ἐρεῖ λόγον εἰς τὸν υἱὸν
before the angels of God. And everyone who speaks a word against the Son
1967 3836 34 3836 2536 2779 4246 4005 3306 3364 1650 3836 5626
p.g d.gpm n.gpm d.gsm n.gsm cj a.nsm r.nsm v.fai.3s n.asm p.a d.asm n.asm

τοῦ ἀνθρώπου, ἀφεθήσεται αὐτῷ· τῷ δὲ εἰς τὸ ἅγιον
of Man will be forgiven, {him} but the *but* one who blasphemes against the Holy
3836 476 918 899 1254 3836 1254 1059 1059 1059 1650 3836 41
d.gsm n.gsm v.fpi.3s r.dsm.3 d.dsm cj p.a d.asn a.asn

πνεῦμα βλασφημήσαντι ↱ οὐκ ἀφεθήσεται. [11]ὅταν δὲ εἰσφέρωσιν ὑμᾶς ἐπὶ τὰς
Spirit *one who blasphemes* will not be forgiven. When {and} they bring you before the
4460 1059 918 4024 918 4020 1254 1662 7007 2093 3836
n.asn pt.aa.dsm pl v.fpi.3s cj cj v.pas.3p r.ap.2 p.a d.apf

συναγωγὰς καὶ τὰς ἀρχὰς καὶ τὰς ἐξουσίας, ↱ μὴ μεριμνήσητε πῶς ἢ τί
synagogues, {and} the rulers, and the authorities, do not worry: How or what
5252 2779 3836 794 2779 3836 2026 3534 3590 3534 4802 2445 5515
n.apf cj d.apf n.apf cj d.apf n.apf pl v.aas.2p cj cj r.asn

ἀπολογήσησθε ἢ τί εἴπητε, [12]τὸ γὰρ ἅγιον
⌞words should you use in your defense?⌟ or, What ⌞should you say?⌟ For the *for* Holy
664 2445 5515 3306 1142 3836 1142 41
v.ams.2p cj r.asn v.aas.2p d.nsn cj a.nsn

NASB

proclaimed upon
the housetops.
[4]"I say to you, My
friends, do not be
afraid of those who
kill the body and
after that have no
more that they can
do. [5]But I will warn
you whom to fear:
fear the One who,
after He has killed,
has authority to
cast into hell; yes, I
tell you, fear Him!
[6]Are not five spar-
rows sold for two
cents? *Yet* not one
of them is forgotten
before God. [7]In-
deed, the very hairs
of your head are all
numbered. Do not
fear; you are more
valuable than many
sparrows.
[8]"And I say to
you, everyone who
confesses Me be-
fore men, the Son
of Man will con-
fess him also be-
fore the angels of
God; [9]but he who
denies Me before
men will be denied
before the angels
of God. [10]And ev-
eryone who speaks
a word against the
Son of Man, it will
be forgiven him;
but he who blas-
phemes against the
Holy Spirit, it will
not be forgiven
him. [11]When they
bring you before
the synagogues and
the rulers and the
authorities, do not
worry about how
or what you are to
speak in your de-
fense, or what you
are to say; [12]for the
Holy Spirit will

NIV

Spirit will teach
you at that time
what you should
say."

The Parable of the Rich Fool

13 Someone in the
crowd said to him,
"Teacher, tell my
brother to divide
the inheritance
with me."
14 Jesus replied,
"Man, who ap-
pointed me a
judge or an arbiter
between you?"
15 Then he said to
them, "Watch out!
Be on your guard
against all kinds
of greed; life does
not consist in an
abundance of pos-
sessions."
16 And he told
them this parable:
"The ground of a
certain rich man
yielded an abun-
dant harvest. 17 He
thought to himself,
'What shall I do?
I have no place to
store my crops.'
18 "Then he said,
'This is what I'll
do. I will tear
down my barns
and build bigger
ones, and there I
will store my sur-
plus grain. 19 And
I'll say to myself,
"You have plenty
of grain laid up
for many years.
Take life easy; eat,
drink and be mer-
ry." '
20 "But God said
to him, 'You fool!
This very night
your life will be
demanded from
you. Then who
will get what you
have prepared for
yourself?'
21 "This is how

πνεῦμα διδάξει ὑμᾶς ἐν αὐτῇ τῇ ὥρᾳ ἃ δεῖ εἰπεῖν. 13
Spirit will teach you in that very hour what ⌊it is necessary⌋ to say." Someone from
4460 1438 7007 1877 899 3836 6052 4005 1256 3306 5516 1666
n.nsn v.fai.3s r.ap.2 p.d r.dsf d.dsf n.dsf r.apn v.pai.3s f.aa

εἶπεν δέ τις ἐκ τοῦ ὄχλου αὐτῷ, διδάσκαλε, εἰπὲ τῷ
the crowd said *{and}* *Someone* *from* *the* *crowd* to him, "Teacher, tell *{the}* my
3836 4063 3306 1254 5516 1666 3836 4063 899 1437 3306 3836 1609
v.aai.3s cj r.nsm p.g d.gsm n.gsm r.dsm.3 n.vsm v.aam.2s d.dsm

ἀδελφῷ μου μερίσασθαι μετʼ ἐμοῦ τὴν κληρονομίαν. 14 ὁ
brother *my* to divide the family inheritance with me." *the* *inheritance* But he
81 1609 3532 3836 3100 3552 1609 3836 3100 1254 3836
n.dsm r.gs.1 f.am p.g r.gs.1 d.asf n.asf d.nsm

δὲ εἶπεν αὐτῷ, ἄνθρωπε, τίς με κατέστησεν κριτὴν ἢ μεριστὴν ἐφʼ
But said to him, "Friend, who appointed me *appointed* a judge or arbitrator between
1254 3306 899 476 5515 2770 1609 2770 3216 2445 3537 2093
cj v.aai.3s r.dsm.3 n.vsm r.nsm r.as.1 v.aai.3s n.asm cj n.asm p.a

ὑμᾶς; 15 εἶπεν δὲ πρὸς αὐτούς, ὁρᾶτε καὶ φυλάσσεσθε ἀπὸ πάσης
you two?" And he said *And* to them, ⌊"Watch out⌋ and be on guard against all types
7007 1254 3306 1254 4639 899 3972 2779 5875 608 4246
r.ap.2 v.aai.3s cj p.a r.apm.3 v.pam.2p cj v.pmm.2p p.g a.gsf

πλεονεξίας, ὅτι οὐκ ἐν τῷ ⌊περισσεύειν τινὶ⌋ ἡ ζωὴ
of greed, because one's life does not consist in the abundance *{the}* *life*
4432 4022 899 2437 1639 4024 1639 1877 3836 4355 5516 3836 2437
n.gsf cj pl p.d d.dsn f.pa r.dsm d.nsf n.nsf

αὐτοῦ ἐστιν ἐκ τῶν ὑπαρχόντων αὐτῷ. 16 εἶπεν δὲ παραβολὴν πρὸς
one's *does consist* of *{the}* his possessions." *his* Then he told *Then* a parable to
899 1639 1666 3836 899 5639 899 1254 3306 1254 4130 4639
r.gsm.3 v.pai.3s p.g d.gpn pt.pa.gpn r.dsm.3 v.aai.3s cj n.asf p.a

αὐτοὺς λέγων, → ἀνθρώπου τινὸς πλουσίου εὐφόρησεν
them, saying: "The land of a certain rich man *certain rich* ⌊produced a good crop.⌋
899 3306 3836 6001 5516 4454 476 5516 4454 2369
r.apm.3 pt.pa.nsm n.gsm r.gsm a.gsm v.aai.3s

ἡ χώρα. 17 καὶ διελογίζετο ἐν ἑαυτῷ λέγων, τί ποιήσω, ὅτι οὐκ
The *land* And he thought to himself, saying, 'What shall I do, for I have no
3836 6001 2779 1368 1877 1571 3306 5515 4472 4022 2400 2400 4024
d.nsf n.nsf cj v.imi.3s p.d r.dsm.3 pt.pa.nsm r.asn v.aas.1s cj pl

ἔχω ποῦ συνάξω τοὺς καρπούς μου; 18 καὶ εἶπεν, τοῦτο ποιήσω,
I have place to store *{the}* my crops?' *my* Then he said, 'This is what I will do:
2400 4543 5251 3836 1609 2843 1609 2779 3306 4047 4472
v.pai.1s cj v.aas.1s d.apm n.apm r.gs.1 cj v.aai.3s r.asn v.fai.1s

καθελῶ μου τὰς ἀποθήκας καὶ μείζονας οἰκοδομήσω καὶ
⌊I will tear down⌋ my *{the}* barns and I will build bigger ones; *I will build* and
2747 1609 3836 630 2779 3868 3868 3868 3489 3868 2779
v.fai.1s r.gs.1 d.apf n.apf cj a.apf.c v.fai.1s cj

συνάξω ἐκεῖ πάντα τὸν → σῖτον καὶ τὰ ἀγαθά μου 19 καὶ ἐρῶ τῇ
I will store there all *{the}* my grain and *{the}* my goods. *my* Then ⌊I will say⌋ to
5251 1695 4246 3836 1609 4992 2779 3836 1609 19 1609 2779 3306 3836
v.fai.1s adv a.asm d.asm n.asm cj d.apn a.apn r.gs.1 cj v.fai.1s d.dsf

ψυχῇ μου, ψυχή, ἔχεις πολλὰ ἀγαθὰ κείμενα εἰς ἔτη πολλά·
my soul, *my* "Soul, you have many good things laid up for many years; *many*
1609 6034 1609 6034 2400 4498 19 3023 1650 4498 2291 4498
n.dsf r.gs.1 n.vsf v.pai.2s a.apn a.apn pt.pm.apn p.a n.apn a.apn

ἀναπαύου, φάγε, πίε, εὐφραίνου. 20 εἶπεν δὲ αὐτῷ ὁ θεός, ἄφρων,
take your rest, eat, drink, be merry."' But God said *But* to him, *{the}* *God* 'You fool!
399 2266 4403 2370 1254 2536 3306 1254 899 3836 2536 933
v.pmm.2s v.aam.2s v.aam.2s v.ppm.2s v.aai.3s cj r.dsm.3 d.nsm n.nsm a.vsm

ταύτῃ τῇ νυκτὶ τὴν ψυχήν σου ἀπαιτοῦσιν ἀπὸ σοῦ· ἃ δὲ
This very night *{the}* your soul *your* will be demanded of you. And what *And*
4047 3836 3816 3836 5148 6034 5148 555 608 5148 1254 4005 1254
r.dsf d.dsf n.dsf d.asf n.asf r.gs.2 v.pai.3p p.g r.gs.2 r.apn cj

ἡτοίμασας, τίνι ἔσται; 21 οὕτως ὁ
⌊you have prepared for yourself,⌋ whose will it be?' So it is with the
2286 5515 1639 4048 3836
v.aai.2s r.dsm v.fmi.3s adv d.nsm

NASB

teach you in that
very hour what you
ought to say."

Covetousness Denounced

13 Someone in
the crowd said to
Him, "Teacher,
tell my brother to
divide the *family*
inheritance with
me." 14 But He said
to him, "Man, who
appointed Me a
judge or arbitrator
over you?" 15 Then
He said to them,
"Beware, and be
on your guard
against every form
of greed; for not
even when one has
an abundance does
his life consist of
his possessions."
16 And He told them
a parable, saying,
"The land of a
rich man was very
productive. 17 And
he began reasoning
to himself, say-
ing, 'What shall
I do, since I have
no place to store
my crops?' 18 Then
he said, 'This is
what I will do: I
will tear down my
barns and build
larger ones, and
there I will store
all my grain and
my goods. 19 And I
will say to my soul,
"Soul, you have
many goods laid
up for many years
to come; take your
ease, eat, drink *and*
be merry." ' 20 But
God said to him,
'You fool! This
very night your
soul is required of
you; and *now* who
will own what you
have prepared?'
21 So is the man who

NIV

it will be with
whoever stores up
things for them-
selves but is not
rich toward God."

Do Not Worry

[22]Then Jesus
said to his disci-
ples: "Therefore
I tell you, do not
worry about your
life, what you will
eat; or about your
body, what you
will wear. [23]For
life is more than
food, and the body
more than clothes.
[24]Consider the ra-
vens: They do not
sow or reap, they
have no storeroom
or barn; yet God
feeds them. And
how much more
valuable you are
than birds! [25]Who
of you by wor-
rying can add a
single hour to your
life[a]? [26]Since you
cannot do this very
little thing, why do
you worry about
the rest?
[27]"Consider how
the wild flowers
grow. They do not
labor or spin. Yet
I tell you, not even
Solomon in all
his splendor was
dressed like one of
these. [28]If that is
how God clothes
the grass of the
field, which is here
today, and tomor-
row is thrown into
the fire, how much
more will he clothe
you—you of lit-
tle faith! [29]And do
not set your heart
on what you will
eat or drink; do
not worry about it.
[30]For the

[a] 25 Or *single cubit to your height*

θησαυρίζων ἑαυτῷ καὶ μὴ εἰς θεὸν πλουτῶν. [22] εἶπεν
⌊one who stores up treasures⌋ for himself, but is not rich toward God." *is rich* He said
2564 1571 2779 4456 3590 4456 1650 2536 4456 3306
pt.pa.nsm r.dsm.3 cj pl p.a n.asm pt.pa.nsm v.aai.3s

δὲ πρὸς τοὺς μαθητὰς αὐτοῦ,[a] ⌊διὰ τοῦτο⌋ λέγω ὑμῖν, ↱ μὴ μεριμνᾶτε
{and} to *{the}* his disciples, *his* "Therefore I tell you, do not be anxious
1254 4639 3836 899 3412 899 1328 4047 3306 7007 3534 3590 3534
cj p.a d.apm n.apm r.gsm.3 p.a r.asn v.pai.1s r.dp.2 pl v.pam.2p

τῇ ψυχῇ τί φάγητε, μηδὲ τῷ σώματι τί ἐνδύσησθε. [23] ἡ γὰρ
⌊about your⌋ life, what ⌊you will eat,⌋ nor ⌊about your⌋ body, what you will wear. *{the}* For
3836 6034 5515 2266 3593 3836 5393 5515 1907 3836 1142
d.dsf n.dsf r.asn v.aas.2p cj d.dsn n.dsn r.asn v.ams.2p d.nsf cj

ψυχὴ πλεῖόν ἐστιν τῆς τροφῆς καὶ τὸ σῶμα ↰ τοῦ ἐνδύματος.
life is more *is* than food, and the body more than clothing.
6034 1639 4498 1639 3836 5575 2779 3836 5393 4498 3836 1903
n.nsf a.nsn.c v.pai.3s d.gsf n.gsf cj d.nsn n.nsn d.gsn n.gsn

[24] κατανοήσατε τοὺς κόρακας ὅτι ↱ ↱ οὐ σπείρουσιν οὐδὲ θερίζουσιν,
Consider the ravens: for they do not sow, neither do they reap;
2917 3836 3165 4022 5062 5062 4024 5062 4028 2545
v.aam.2p d.apm n.apm cj pl v.pai.3p cj v.pai.3p

οἷς οὐκ ἔστιν ταμεῖον οὐδὲ ἀποθήκη, καὶ ὁ θεὸς τρέφει αὐτούς·
⌊for them⌋ there is neither *there is* storehouse nor granary, yet *{the}* God feeds them.
4005 1639 1639 4024 1639 5421 4028 630 2779 3836 2536 5555 899
r.dpm pl v.pai.3s n.nsn cj n.nsf cj d.nsm n.nsm v.pai.3s r.apm.3

πόσῳ μᾶλλον ὑμεῖς διαφέρετε τῶν πετεινῶν. [25] τίς δὲ ἐξ
⌊Of how much⌋ more value are you *value are* ⌊than the⌋ birds! And which *And* of
4531 3437 1422 1422 7007 1422 3836 4374 1254 5515 1254 1666
r.dpn adv.c r.np.2 v.pai.2p d.gpn n.gpn r.nsm cj p.g

ὑμῶν μεριμνῶν δύναται ἐπὶ τὴν ἡλικίαν αὐτοῦ προσθεῖναι
you by worrying can add a single hour to *{the}* his span of life? *his* *add*
7007 3534 1538 4707 4388 4388 2093 3836 899 2461 899 4707
r.gp.2 pt.pa.nsm v.ppi.3s p.a d.asf n.asf r.gsm.3 f.aa

πῆχυν; [26] εἰ οὖν οὐδὲ → ἐλάχιστον
single hour If then, you are unable to accomplish such an ⌊insignificant thing,⌋
4388 1623 4036 1538 1538 4028 1538 1538 1788
n.asm cj cj adv a.asn.s

δύνασθε, τί περὶ τῶν λοιπῶν μεριμνᾶτε; [27] κατανοήσατε
you are to accomplish why do you worry about *{the}* other things? *do you worry* Consider
1538 5515 3534 3534 3534 4309 3836 3370 3534 2917
v.ppi.2p r.asn p.g d.gpn a.gpn v.pai.2p v.aam.2p

τὰ κρίνα πῶς αὐξάνει· ↱ οὐ κοπιᾷ οὐδὲ νήθει· λέγω δὲ ὑμῖν, οὐδὲ
the lilies, how they grow. They neither toil nor spin, yet I tell *yet* you, not even
3836 3211 4802 889 3159 4024 3159 4028 3756 1254 3306 1254 7007 4028
d.apn n.apn cj v.pai.3s pl v.pai.3s cj v.pai.3s v.pai.1s cj r.dp.2 adv

Σολομὼν ἐν πάσῃ τῇ δόξῃ αὐτοῦ περιεβάλετο ὡς ἓν τούτων. [28] εἰ δὲ
Solomon in all *{the}* his glory *his* clothed himself like one of these. If *{and}*
5048 1877 4246 3836 899 1518 899 4314 6055 1651 4047 1623 1254
n.nsm p.d a.dsf d.dsf n.dsf r.gsm.3 v.ami.3s pl a.nsn r.gpn cj cj

ἐν ἀγρῷ τὸν χόρτον ὄντα σήμερον καὶ αὔριον
God so clothes the grass in the field, *the* *grass* ⌊which is alive⌋ today and tomorrow
2536 4048 313 3836 5965 1877 69 3836 5965 1639 4958 2779 892
p.d n.dsm d.asm n.asm pt.pa.asm adv cj adv

εἰς κλίβανον βαλλόμενον ὁ θεὸς οὕτως ἀμφιέζει, πόσῳ μᾶλλον
is thrown into the oven, *is thrown* *{the}* *God* *so* *clothes* how much more will
965 965 1650 3106 965 3836 2536 4048 313 4531 3437
p.a n.asm pt.pp.asm d.nsm n.nsm adv v.pai.3s r.dpn adv.c

ὑμᾶς, ὀλιγόπιστοι. [29] καὶ ὑμεῖς ↱ μὴ ζητεῖτε
he clothe you, ⌊you people of little faith!⌋ And you, do not ⌊have as an overriding concern⌋
7007 3899 2779 7007 2426 3590 2426
r.ap.2 a.vpm cj r.np.2 pl v.pam.2p

τί φάγητε καὶ τί πίητε καὶ ↱ μὴ μετεωρίζεσθε· [30]
what to eat and what to drink; *{and}* do not ⌊let such things bother you.⌋ For all the
5515 2266 2779 5515 4403 2779 3577 3590 3577 1142 4246 3836
r.asn v.aas.2p cj r.asn v.aas.2p cj pl v.ppm.2p

[a] [αὐτοῦ] UBS.

NASB

stores up treasure
for himself, and
is not rich toward
God."
[22]And He said to
His disciples, "For
this reason I say to
you, do not worry
about *your* life, *as*
to what you will
eat; nor for your
body, *as to* what
you will put on.
[23]For life is more
than food, and the
body more than
clothing. [24]Consider
the ravens, for they
neither sow nor
reap; they have
no storeroom nor
barn, and *yet* God
feeds them; how
much more valu-
able you are than
the birds! [25]And
which of you by
worrying can add
a *single* [a]hour to
his [b]life's span? [26]If
then you cannot do
even a very little
thing, why do you
worry about other
matters? [27]Consider
the lilies, how they
grow: they neither
toil nor spin; but I
tell you, not even
Solomon in all
his glory clothed
himself like one
of these. [28]But if
God so clothes the
grass in the field,
which is *alive*
today and tomor-
row is thrown into
the furnace, how
much more *will He*
clothe you? You
men of little faith!
[29]And do not seek
what you will eat
and what you will
drink, and do not
keep worrying.
[30]For all these

[a] Lit *cubit* (approx 18 in.)
[b] Or *height*

NIV

pagan world runs
after all such
things, and your
Father knows that
you need them.
31 But seek his
kingdom, and
these things will
be given to you as
well.
32 "Do not be
afraid, little flock,
for your Father has
been pleased to
give you the king-
dom. 33 Sell your
possessions and
give to the poor.
Provide purses for
yourselves that
will not wear out,
a treasure in heav-
en that will never
fail, where no thief
comes near and
no moth destroys.
34 For where your
treasure is, there
your heart will be
also.

Watchfulness

35 "Be dressed
ready for service
and keep your
lamps burning,
36 like servants
waiting for their
master to return
from a wedding
banquet, so that
when he comes
and knocks they
can immediate-
ly open the door
for him. 37 It will
be good for those
servants whose
master finds them
watching when he
comes. Truly I tell
you, he will dress
himself to serve,
will have them
recline at the ta-
ble and will come
and wait on them.
38 It will be good
for those servants
whose master
finds them ready,
even if he comes
in the middle of

↱ ταῦτα γὰρ πάντα τὰ ἔθνη τοῦ κόσμου
nations of the world have these things *For all the nations of the world*
1620 3836 3836 3180 2118 4047 1142 4246 3836 1620 3836 3180
r.apn cj a.apn d.npn n.npn d.gsm n.gsm

ἐπιζητοῦσιν, ὑμῶν δὲ ὁ πατὴρ οἶδεν ὅτι χρῄζετε τούτων.
⌊as their overriding concern,⌋ and your *and {the}* Father knows full well that you need them.
2118 1254 7007 1254 3836 4252 3857 4022 5974 4047
v.pai.3p r.gp.2 cj d.nsm n.nsm v.rai.3s cj v.pai.2p r.gpn

31 πλὴν ζητεῖτε τὴν βασιλείαν αὐτοῦ, ↰ ↰ ↰ ↰ καὶ ταῦτα
Instead, have *{the}* his kingdom *his* as your overriding concern, and these things
4440 2426 3836 899 993 899 2426 2426 2426 2426 2779 4047
cj v.pam.2p d.asf n.asf r.gsm.3 cj r.npn

προστεθήσεται ὑμῖν. ↰ ↰ 32 ↱ μὴ φοβοῦ, τὸ μικρὸν ποίμνιον, ὅτι
will be given to you in addition. Do not be afraid, *{the}* little flock, because
4707 7007 4707 4707 5828 3590 5828 3836 3625 4480 4022
v.fpi.3s r.dp.2 pl v.ppm.2s d.vsn a.vsn n.vsn cj

εὐδόκησεν ὁ πατὴρ ὑμῶν δοῦναι ὑμῖν τὴν βασιλείαν.
your Father ⌊has determined in his pleasure⌋ *{the} Father your* to give you the kingdom.
7007 4252 2305 3836 4252 7007 1443 7007 3836 993
v.aai.3s d.nsm n.nsm r.gp.2 f.aa r.dp.2 d.asf n.asf

33 πωλήσατε τὰ ὑπάρχοντα ὑμῶν καὶ δότε ἐλεημοσύνην· ποιήσατε ἑαυτοῖς
Sell *{the}* your possessions *your* and give alms. Make for yourselves
4797 3836 7007 5639 7007 2779 1443 1797 4472 1571
v.aam.2p d.apn pt.pa.apn r.gp.2 cj v.aam.2p n.asf v.aam.2p r.dpm.2

βαλλάντια ↱ μὴ παλαιούμενα, θησαυρὸν ἀνέκλειπτον ἐν τοῖς οὐρανοῖς,
moneybags that do not wear out, a treasure unfailing in *{the}* heaven,
964 4096 3590 4096 2565 444 1877 3836 4041
n.apn pl pt.pp.apn n.asm a.asm p.d d.dpm n.dpm

ὅπου κλέπτης οὐκ ἐγγίζει οὐδὲ σὴς διαφθείρει· 34 ὅπου γάρ
where no thief *no* comes near and no moth destroys. For where *For* your treasure
3963 4024 3095 4024 1581 4028 4962 1425 1142 3963 1142 7007 2565
cj n.nsm pl v.pai.3s cj n.nsm v.pai.3s cj cj

ἐστιν ὁ θησαυρὸς ὑμῶν, ἐκεῖ καὶ ἡ καρδία ὑμῶν ἔσται.
is, *{the} treasure your* there will your heart be as well. *{the} heart your will be*
1639 3836 2565 7007 1695 1639 7007 2840 1639 2779 3836 2840 7007 1639
v.pai.3s d.nsm n.nsm r.gp.2 adv adv d.nsf n.nsf r.gp.2 v.fmi.3s

35 → ἔστωσαν ὑμῶν αἱ ὀσφύες περιεζωσμέναι καὶ οἱ λύχνοι
"Let your waists be *your {the} waists* girded and your lamps
7007 4019 1639 7007 3836 4019 4322 2779 3836 3394
v.pam.3p r.gp.2 d.npf n.npf pt.rp.npf cj d.npm n.npm

καιόμενοι· 36 καὶ ὑμεῖς ὅμοιοι ἀνθρώποις προσδεχομένοις τὸν κύριον ἑαυτῶν
burning; and *{you}* be like men waiting for *{the}* their master *their*
2794 2779 7007 3927 476 4657 3836 1571 3261 1571
pt.pp.npm cj r.np.2 a.npm n.dpm pt.pm.dpm d.asm n.asm r.gpm.3

πότε ἀναλύσῃ ἐκ τῶν γάμων, ἵνα ἐλθόντος καὶ κρούσαντος
to come home from the wedding, so that when he comes and knocks, they will open the
4537 386 1666 3836 1141 2671 2262 2779 3218 487 487 487
cj v.aas.3s p.g d.gpm n.gpm cj pt.aa.gsm cj pt.aa.gsm

εὐθέως ἀνοίξωσιν αὐτῷ. 37 μακάριοι οἱ δοῦλοι ἐκεῖνοι,
door for him immediately. *they will open for him* Fortunate are *{the}* those servants *those*
899 899 2311 487 899 3421 3836 1697 1529 1697
adv v.aas.3p r.dsm.3 a.npm d.npm n.npm r.npm

οὓς ἐλθὼν ὁ κύριος εὑρήσει γρηγοροῦντας· ἀμὴν
whom the master finds awake ⌊when he comes.⌋ *the master finds awake* Truly
4005 3836 3261 2351 1213 2262 3836 3261 2351 1213 297
r.apm pt.aa.nsm d.nsm n.nsm v.fai.3s pt.pa.apm pl

λέγω ὑμῖν ὅτι περιζώσεται καὶ → ἀνακλινεῖ αὐτοὺς καὶ
I say to you, *{that}* ⌊he will dress himself for service,⌋ *{and}* have them recline at table, *them* and
3306 7007 4022 4322 2779 899 369 899 2779
v.pai.1s r.dp.2 cj v.fmi.3s cj v.fai.3s r.apm.3 cj

παρελθὼν διακονήσει αὐτοῖς. 38 κἂν ἐν τῇ δευτέρᾳ κἂν ἐν τῇ
will come and serve them. If he comes in the second or in the
4216 1354 899 2829 2262 2262 1877 3836 1311 2829 1877 3836
pt.aa.nsm v.fai.3s r.dpm.3 crasis p.d d.dsf n.dsf crasis p.d d.dsf

NASB

things the na-
tions of the world
eagerly seek; but
your Father knows
that you need these
things. 31 But seek
His kingdom, and
these things will
be added to you.
32 Do not be afraid,
little flock, for your
Father has chosen
gladly to give you
the kingdom.
33 "Sell your pos-
sessions and give
to charity; make
yourselves money
belts which do
not wear out, an
unfailing treasure
in heaven, where
no thief comes near
nor moth destroys.
34 For where your
treasure is, there
your heart will be
also.

Be in Readiness

35 "Be dressed
in readiness, and
keep your lamps
lit. 36 Be like men
who are waiting
for their master
when he returns
from the wedding
feast, so that they
may immediately
open *the door* to
him when he
comes and knocks.
37 Blessed are those
slaves whom the
master will find
on the alert when
he comes; truly I
say to you, that he
will gird himself
to serve, and have
them recline *at
the table,* and will
come up and wait
on them. 38 Whether
he comes in the
[a] second watch, or
even in the [b] third,

[a] I.e. 9 p.m. to midnight
[b] I.e. midnight to 3 a.m.

NIV

the night or toward
daybreak. [39]But
understand this: If
the owner of the
house had known
at what hour the
thief was coming,
he would not have
let his house be
broken into. [40]You
also must be ready,
because the Son
of Man will come
at an hour when
you do not expect
him."
[41]Peter asked,
"Lord, are you
telling this parable
to us, or to every-
one?"
[42]The Lord an-
swered, "Who
then is the faithful
and wise manager,
whom the master
puts in charge of
his servants to
give them their
food allowance at
the proper time?
[43]It will be good
for that servant
whom the mas-
ter finds doing so
when he returns.
[44]Truly I tell you,
he will put him in
charge of all his
possessions. [45]But
suppose the ser-
vant says to him-
self, 'My master is
taking a long time
in coming,' and he
then begins to beat
the other servants,
both men and
women, and to eat
and drink and get
drunk. [46]The mas-
ter of that servant
will come

τρίτῃ φυλακῇ ἔλθῃ καὶ εὕρῃ οὕτως, μακάριοί εἰσιν ἐκεῖνοι.
third watch *he comes* and finds it so, those ones are fortunate. *are* *those ones*
5569 5871 2262 2779 2351 4048 1697 1697 1639 3421 1639 1697
a.dsf n.dsf v.aas.3s cj v.aas.3s adv a.npm v.pai.3p r.npm

39 τοῦτο δὲ γινώσκετε ὅτι εἰ ᾔδει ὁ
"Know this: *{and}* *Know* that if the master of the house ˌhad knownˌ *the*
1182 4047 1254 1182 4022 1623 3836 3867 3867 3867 3867 3857 3836
r.asn cj v.pam.2p cj cj v.lai.3s d.nsm

οἰκοδεσπότης ποίᾳ ὥρᾳ ὁ κλέπτης ἔρχεται, οὐκ ἂν ἀφῆκεν
master of the house at what hour the thief would come, he would not *would* have allowed his
3867 4481 6052 3836 3095 2262 918 323 4024 323 918 899
n.nsm r.dsf n.dsf d.nsm n.nsm v.pmi.3s pl pl v.aai.3s

διορυχθῆναι τὸν οἶκον αὐτοῦ. 40 καὶ ὑμεῖς γίνεσθε ἕτοιμοι, ὅτι
house be broken into. *{the}* *house* *his* So you too must be ready, for the Son
3875 1482 3836 3875 899 2779 7007 2779 1181 2289 4022 3836 5626
f.ap d.asm n.asm r.gsm.3 cj r.np.2 v.pmm.2p a.npm cj

ᾗ ὥρᾳ οὐ δοκεῖτε ὁ υἱὸς τοῦ
of Man is coming at an hour when you do not expect him." *the* *Son* *of*
3836 476 2262 2262 4005 6052 1506 1506 4024 1506 3836 5626 3836
r.dsf n.dsf pl v.pai.2p d.nsm n.nsm d.gsm

ἀνθρώπου ἔρχεται. 41 εἶπεν δὲ ὁ Πέτρος, κύριε,
Man *is coming* Then Peter said, *Then* *{the}* *Peter* "Lord, are you telling this
476 2262 1254 4377 3306 1254 3836 4377 3261 3306 3306 3306 4047
n.gsm v.pmi.3s v.aai.3s cj d.nsm n.nsm n.vsm

πρὸς ἡμᾶς τὴν παραβολὴν ταύτην λέγεις ἢ καὶ πρὸς πάντας; 42 καὶ
parable to us *{the}* *parable* *this* *are you telling* or *{also}* to everyone?" And
4130 4639 7005 3836 4130 4047 3306 2445 2779 4639 4246 2779
p.a r.ap.1 d.asf n.asf r.asf v.pai.2s cj adv p.a a.apm cj

εἶπεν ὁ κύριος, τίς ἄρα ἐστὶν ὁ πιστὸς οἰκονόμος ὁ
the Lord said, *the* *Lord* "Who, then, is the faithful and wise steward, *{the}*
3836 3261 3306 3836 3261 5515 726 1639 3836 4412 5861 3874 3836
v.aai.3s d.nsm n.nsm r.nsm cj v.pai.3s d.nsm a.nsm n.nsm d.nsm

φρόνιμος, ὃν καταστήσει ὁ κύριος ἐπὶ τῆς θεραπείας αὐτοῦ
wise whom the master will put in charge *the* *master* of *{the}* his servants, *his*
5861 4005 3836 3261 2770 3836 3261 2093 3836 899 2542 899
a.nsm r.asm v.fai.3s d.nsm n.nsm p.g d.gsf n.gsf r.gsm.3

τοῦ διδόναι ἐν καιρῷ τὸ[a] σιτομέτριον; 43 μακάριος ὁ
to give the food ration at the ˌproper time?ˌ *the* *food ration* Fortunate is *{the}*
3836 1443 3836 4991 4991 1877 2789 3836 4991 3421 3836
d.gsn f.pa p.d n.dsm d.asn n.asn a.nsm d.nsm

δοῦλος ἐκεῖνος, ὃν ἐλθὼν ὁ κύριος αὐτοῦ εὑρήσει
that servant *that* whom his master, ˌwhen he comes,ˌ *{the}* *master* *his* will find
1697 1529 1697 4005 899 3261 2262 3836 3261 899 2351
n.nsm r.nsm r.asm pt.aa.nsm d.nsm n.nsm r.gsm.3 v.fai.3s

ποιοῦντα οὕτως. 44 ἀληθῶς λέγω ὑμῖν ὅτι
doing so. I tell you the truth, *I tell* *you* *{that}* he will put him in charge
4472 4048 3306 3306 7007 242 3306 7007 4022 2770 2770 2770 899 2770 2770
pt.pa.asm adv adv v.pai.1s r.dp.2 cj

ἐπὶ πᾶσιν τοῖς ὑπάρχουσιν αὐτοῦ καταστήσει αὐτόν. 45 ἐὰν δὲ
of all *{the}* his possessions. *his* *he will put in charge* *him* But if *But* that
2093 4246 3836 899 5639 899 2770 899 1254 1569 1254 1697
p.d a.dpn d.dpn pt.pa.dpn r.gsm.3 v.fai.3s r.asm.3 cj cj

εἴπῃ ὁ δοῦλος ἐκεῖνος ἐν τῇ καρδίᾳ αὐτοῦ, χρονίζει ὁ
servant says *{the}* *servant* *that* in *{the}* his heart, *his* 'My master is delayed *{the}*
1529 3306 3836 1529 1697 1877 3836 899 2840 899 1609 3261 5988 3836
v.aas.3s d.nsm n.nsm r.nsm p.d d.dsf n.dsf r.gsm.3 v.pai.3s d.nsm

κύριός μου ἔρχεσθαι, καὶ ἄρξηται τύπτειν τοὺς παῖδας καὶ τὰς παιδίσκας,
master *My* in coming,' and begins to beat the male and *{the}* female servants, and
3261 1609 2262 2779 806 5597 3836 4090 2779 3836 4087 5445
n.nsm r.gs.1 f.pm cj v.ams.3s f.pa d.apm n.apm cj d.apf n.apf

ἐσθίειν τε καὶ πίνειν καὶ μεθύσκεσθαι, 46 ἥξει
to eat *and* and drink and get drunk; then the master of that servant ˌwill comeˌ
2266 5445 2779 4403 2779 3499 3836 3261 3836 1697 1529 2457
f.pa cj cj f.pa cj f.pp v.fai.3s

[a] [τὸ] UBS.

NASB

and finds *them* so,
blessed are those
slaves.
[39]"But be sure
of this, that if the
head of the house
had known at what
hour the thief was
coming, he would
not have allowed
his house to be
broken into. [40]You
too, be ready; for
the Son of Man is
coming at an hour
that you do not
expect."
[41]Peter said,
"Lord, are You
addressing this
parable to us, or to
everyone *else* as
well?" [42]And the
Lord said, "Who
then is the faith-
ful and sensible
steward, whom
his master will
put in charge of
his servants, to
give them their ra-
tions at the proper
time? [43]Blessed is
that slave whom
his master finds
so doing when he
comes. [44]Truly I
say to you that he
will put him in
charge of all his
possessions. [45]But
if that slave says
in his heart, 'My
master will be a
long time in com-
ing,' and begins
to beat the slaves,
both men and
women, and to eat
and drink and get
drunk; [46]the master
of that slave will
come on a day

NIV

on a day when he
does not expect
him and at an hour
he is not aware of.
He will cut him to
pieces and assign
him a place with
the unbelievers.
47"The servant
who knows the
master's will
and does not get
ready or does not
do what the mas-
ter wants will be
beaten with many
blows. 48But the
one who does not
know and does
things deserving
punishment will
be beaten with
few blows. From
everyone who
has been given
much, much will
be demanded; and
from the one who
has been entrust-
ed with much,
much more will be
asked.

Not Peace but Division

49"I have come to
bring fire on the
earth, and how I
wish it were al-
ready kindled!
50But I have a
baptism to under-
go, and what con-
straint I am under
until it is complet-
ed! 51Do you think
I came to bring
peace on earth?
No, I tell you, but
division. 52From
now on there will
be five in one
family divided
against each other,
three against two
and two against
three. 53They will
be divided, father
against son and
son against father,
mother against
daughter and
daughter against
mother, mother-in-
law against daugh-
ter-in-law and

ὁ κύριος τοῦ δούλου ἐκείνου ἐν ἡμέρᾳ ᾗ ↱ ↱ οὐ προσδοκᾷ καὶ
the master of servant that on a day when he does not expect him and
3836 3261 3836 1529 1697 1877 2465 4005 4659 4659 4024 4659 2779
d.nsm n.nsm d.gsm n.gsm r.gsm p.d n.dsf r.dsf pl v.pai.3s cj

ἐν ὥρᾳ ᾗ ↱ ↱ οὐ γινώσκει, καὶ διχοτομήσει αὐτὸν ↰ ↰ καὶ
at an hour that he does not know about, and he will cut him in pieces and will
1877 6052 4005 1182 1182 4024 1182 2779 1497 899 1497 1497 2779 5502
p.d n.dsf r.dsf pl v.pai.3s cj v.fai.3s r.asm.3 cj

τὸ μέρος αὐτοῦ μετὰ τῶν ἀπίστων θήσει. 47 ἐκεῖνος δὲ ὁ
assign him *{the}* his place *his* with the unfaithful. *will assign* "And that *And {the}*
5502 3836 899 3538 899 3552 3836 603 5502 1254 1697 1254 3836
d.asn n.asn r.gsm.3 p.g d.gpm a.gpm v.fai.3s r.nsm cj d.nsm

δοῦλος ὁ γνοὺς τὸ θέλημα τοῦ κυρίου αὐτοῦ καὶ ↱ μὴ
servant who knew *{the}* his master's will *{the} master's his* but did not
1529 3836 1182 3836 899 3261 2525 3836 3261 899 2779 2286 3590
n.nsm d.nsm pt.aa.nsm d.asn n.asn d.gsm n.gsm r.gsm.3 cj pl

ἑτοιμάσας ἢ ποιήσας πρὸς τὸ θέλημα αὐτοῦ δαρήσεται πολλάς·
get ready or act ⌊in accord with⌋ *{the}* his will, *his* ⌊will be beaten with⌋ many
2286 2445 4472 4639 3836 899 2525 899 1296 4498
pt.aa.nsm cj pt.aa.nsm p.a d.asn n.asn r.gsm.3 v.fpi.3s a.apf

↰ 48 ὁ δὲ ↱ ↱ ↱ μὴ γνούς, ποιήσας δὲ ἄξια πληγῶν
blows. But the *But* one who did not know, and did *and* ⌊things worthy⌋ of blows,
1296 1254 3836 1254 1182 1182 1182 3590 1182 1254 4472 1254 545 4435
d.nsm cj pl pt.aa.nsm pt.aa.nsm cj a.apn n.gpf

δαρήσεται ὀλίγας. ↰ παντὶ δὲ ᾧ ἐδόθη πολύ, πολὺ
⌊will be beaten with⌋ few blows. Everyone *{and}* ⌊to whom⌋ much was given, *much* much
1296 3900 1296 4246 1254 4005 4498 1443 4498 4498
v.fpi.3s a.apf a.dsm cj r.dsm v.api.3s a.nsn a.nsn

ζητηθήσεται παρ' αὐτοῦ, καὶ ᾧ παρέθεντο πολύ,
will be required from him, and ⌊to whom⌋ much ⌊was handed over,⌋ *much* they will ask
2426 4123 899 2779 4005 4498 4192 4498 160 160 160
v.fpi.3s p.g r.gsm.3 cj r.dsm v.ami.3p a.asn

περισσότερον αἰτήσουσιν αὐτόν. 49 πῦρ ἦλθον βαλεῖν ἐπὶ τὴν
more *they will ask* of him. "I came to cast fire *I came to cast* on the
4358 160 899 2262 2262 965 965 4786 2262 965 2093 3836
a.asn.c v.fai.3p r.asm.3 n.asn v.aai.1s f.aa p.a d.asf

γῆν, καὶ τί θέλω εἰ ↱ ↱ ἤδη ἀνήφθη. 50 βάπτισμα δὲ
earth, and would that *would* ~ it were already kindled! I have a baptism *{and}*
1178 2779 2527 5515 2527 1623 409 409 2453 409 2400 2400 967 1254
n.asf cj r.asn v.pai.1s cj adv v.api.3s n.asn cj

ἔχω βαπτισθῆναι, καὶ πῶς συνέχομαι ⌊ἕως ὅτου⌋ τελεσθῇ. 51 δοκεῖτε
I have to be baptized with, and how ⌊distressed I am⌋ until it is completed! Do you think
2400 966 2779 4802 5309 2401 4015 5464 1506
v.pai.1s f.ap cj pl v.ppi.1s p.g r.gsn v.aps.3s v.pai.2p

ὅτι εἰρήνην παρεγενόμην δοῦναι ἐν τῇ γῇ; οὐχί, λέγω ὑμῖν,
that I came to give peace *I came to give* in the earth? No, I tell you,
4022 4134 4134 1443 1443 1645 4134 1443 1877 3836 1178 4049 3306 7007
cj n.asf v.ami.1s f.aa p.d d.dsf n.dsf pl v.pai.1s r.dp.2

ἀλλ' ἢ διαμερισμόν. 52 ἔσονται γὰρ ἀπὸ τοῦ νῦν πέντε ἐν
but rather division! For from now on ⌊there will be⌋ *For from {the} now* five in
247 2445 1375 1142 608 3814 1639 1142 608 3836 3814 4297 1877
cj pl n.asm v.fmi.3p cj p.g d.gsm adv a.npm p.d

ἑνὶ οἴκῳ διαμεμερισμένοι, τρεῖς ἐπὶ δυσὶν καὶ δύο ἐπὶ τρισίν, 53
one household divided, three against two and two against three; father
1651 3875 1374 5552 2093 1545 2779 1545 2093 5552 4252
a.dsm n.dsm pt.rp.npm a.npm p.d a.dpm cj a.npm p.d a.dpm

διαμερισθήσονται πατὴρ ἐπὶ υἱῷ καὶ υἱὸς ἐπὶ πατρί, μήτηρ ἐπὶ τὴν θυγατέρα
will be divided *father* against son and son against father, mother against *{the}* daughter
1374 4252 2093 5626 2779 5626 2093 4252 3613 2093 3836 2588
v.fpi.3p n.nsm p.d n.dsm cj n.nsm p.d n.dsm n.nsf p.a d.asf n.asf

καὶ θυγάτηρ ἐπὶ τὴν μητέρα, πενθερὰ ἐπὶ τὴν νύμφην αὐτῆς καὶ
and daughter against *{the}* mother, mother-in-law against *{the}* her daughter-in-law *her* and
2779 2588 2093 3836 3613 4289 2093 3836 899 3811 899 2779
cj n.nsf p.a d.asf n.asf n.nsf p.a d.asf n.asf r.gsf.3 cj

NASB

when he does not
expect *him* and at
an hour he does
not know, and will
cut him in pieces,
and assign him
a place with the
unbelievers. 47And
that slave who
knew his master's
will and did not get
ready or act in ac-
cord with his will,
will receive many
lashes, 48but the one
who did not know
it, and committed
deeds worthy of
a flogging, will
receive but few.
From everyone
who has been
given much, much
will be required;
and to whom they
entrusted much, of
him they will ask
all the more.

Christ Divides Men

49"I have come
to cast fire upon
the earth; and how
I wish it were
already kindled!
50But I have a bap-
tism to undergo,
and how distressed
I am until it is ac-
complished! 51Do
you suppose that
I came to grant
peace on earth? I
tell you, no, but
rather division;
52for from now
on five *members*
in one household
will be divided,
three against two
and two against
three. 53They will
be divided, father
against son and
son against father,
mother against
daughter and
daughter against
mother, mother-in-
law against daugh-
ter-in-law and

NIV

daughter-in-law
against mother-in-
law."

Interpreting the Times

[54]He said to the
crowd: "When
you see a cloud
rising in the west,
immediately you
say, 'It's going to
rain,' and it does.
[55]And when the
south wind blows,
you say, 'It's going
to be hot,' and it
is. [56]Hypocrites!
You know how to
interpret the ap-
pearance of the
earth and the sky.
How is it that you
don't know how to
interpret this pres-
ent time?
[57]"Why don't
you judge for
yourselves what
is right? [58]As you
are going with
your adversary to
the magistrate, try
hard to be recon-
ciled on the way,
or your adversary
may drag you off
to the judge, and
the judge turn
you over to the
officer, and the
officer throw you
into prison. [59]I tell
you, you will not
get out until you
have paid the last
penny."

Repent or Perish

13 Now there
were some
present at that
time who told
Jesus about the
Galileans whose
blood Pilate had
mixed with their
sacrifices. [2]Jesus
answered, "Do you
think that these

νύμφη ἐπὶ τὴν πενθεράν. [54] → ἔλεγεν δὲ καὶ τοῖς ὄχλοις, ὅταν
daughter-in-law against *{the}* mother-in-law." He also said *{and}* *also* to the crowds, "When
3811 2093 3836 4289 2779 3306 1254 2779 3836 4063 4020
n.nsf p.a d.asf n.asf v.iai.3s cj adv d.dpm n.dpm cj

ἴδητε [a]νεφέλην ἀνατέλλουσαν ἐπὶ δυσμῶν, εὐθέως λέγετε ὅτι
you see a cloud rising in the west, you say at once, *you say* ~ 'A
1625 3749 422 2093 1553 3306 3306 2311 3306 4022
v.aas.2p n.asf pt.pa.asf p.g n.gpf adv v.pai.2p cj

ὄμβρος ἔρχεται, καὶ γίνεται οὕτως· [55] καὶ ὅταν νότον πνέοντα,
rainstorm is coming,' and so it happens. *so* And when there is a ⌊south wind⌋ blowing,
3915 2262 2779 4048 1181 4048 2779 4020 3803 4463
n.nsm v.pmi.3s cj v.pmi.3s adv cj cj n.asm pt.pa.asm

λέγετε ὅτι καύσων ἔσται, καὶ γίνεται. [56] ὑποκριταί,
you say, ~ 'There will be hot weather,' *There will be* and it happens. Hypocrites! You know
3306 4022 1639 1639 1639 3014 1639 2779 1181 5695 3857 3857
v.pai.2p cj n.nsm v.fmi.3s cj v.pmi.3s n.vpm

τὸ πρόσωπον τῆς γῆς καὶ τοῦ οὐρανοῦ οἴδατε δοκιμάζειν,
how to interpret the appearance of the earth and the sky. *You know how* *to interpret*
3857 1507 1507 3836 4725 3836 1178 2779 3836 4041 3857 1507
d.asn n.asn d.gsf n.gsf cj d.gsm n.gsm v.rai.2p f.pa

τὸν καιρὸν δὲ τοῦτον πῶς
How is it that you do not know how to interpret *{the}* this ⌊present time?⌋ *{and}* *this* *How*
4802 3857 3857 4024 3857 3857 1507 1507 3836 4047 2789 1254 4047 4802
d.asm n.asm cj r.asm cj

οὐκ οἴδατε δοκιμάζειν; [57] Τί δὲ καὶ ἀφ᾽ ἑαυτῶν
not *you do know how* *to interpret* "Why, *{and}* indeed, do you not judge for yourselves
4024 3857 1507 5515 1254 2779 3212 3212 4024 3212 608 1571
pl v.rai.2p f.pa r.asn cj adv p.g r.gpm.2

οὐ κρίνετε τὸ δίκαιον; [58] ὡς γὰρ ← ὑπάγεις μετὰ τοῦ ἀντιδίκου σου
not *do you judge* what is right? So *{for}* when you go with *{the}* your opponent *your*
4024 3212 3836 1465 6055 1142 6055 5632 3552 3836 5148 508 5148
pl v.pai.2p d.asn a.asn cj cj v.pai.2s p.g d.gsm n.gsm r.gs.2

ἐπ᾽ ἄρχοντα, ἐν τῇ ὁδῷ δὸς
before the magistrate, make an effort to receive a settlement from him on the way; *make*
2093 807 1443 2238 557 557 557 557 608 899 1877 3836 3847 1443
p.a n.asm p.d d.dsf n.dsf v.aam.2s

ἐργασίαν ἀπηλλάχθαι ἀπ᾽ αὐτοῦ, μήποτε κατασύρῃ σε ← πρὸς τὸν κριτήν,
effort *to receive a settlement* *from* *him* otherwise he will drag you off to the judge,
2238 557 608 899 3607 2955 5148 2955 4639 3836 3216
n.asf f.rp p.g r.gsm.3 cj v.pas.3s r.as.2 p.a d.asm n.asm

καὶ ὁ κριτὴς ↱ ↱ σε παραδώσει τῷ πράκτορι, καὶ ὁ πράκτωρ
and the judge will hand you over ⌊to the⌋ bailiff, and the bailiff will throw
2779 3836 3216 4140 4140 5148 4140 3836 4551 2779 3836 4551 965 965
cj d.nsm n.nsm r.as.2 v.fai.3s d.dsm n.dsm cj d.nsm n.nsm

σε βαλεῖ εἰς φυλακήν. [59] λέγω σοι, ↱ ↱ ⌊οὐ μὴ⌋ ἐξέλθῃς ἐκεῖθεν,
you *will throw* into prison. I say to you, you will certainly not get out of there
5148 965 1650 5871 3306 5148 2002 2002 4024 3590 2002 1696
r.as.2 v.fai.3s p.a n.asf v.pai.1s r.ds.2 pl pl v.aas.2s adv

ἕως καὶ τὸ ἔσχατον λεπτὸν ἀποδῷς.
until *{also}* you have paid the last penny." *you have paid*
2401 2779 625 625 625 3836 2274 3321 625
cj adv d.asn a.asn n.asn v.aas.2s

13:1 → → παρῆσαν δέ τινες ἐν αὐτῷ τῷ καιρῷ
At that very time there were some present *{and}* *some* *At* *that very* *{the}* *time*
1877 899 899 2789 5516 4205 1254 5516 1877 899 3836 2789
v.iai.3p cj r.npm p.d r.dsm d.dsm n.dsm

ἀπαγγέλλοντες αὐτῷ περὶ τῶν Γαλιλαίων ὧν τὸ αἷμα Πιλᾶτος ἔμιξεν μετὰ
who told him about the Galileans whose *{the}* blood Pilate had mingled with
550 899 4309 3836 1134 4005 3836 135 4397 3624 3552
pt.pa.npm r.dsm.3 p.g d.gpm a.gpm r.gpm d.asn n.asn n.nsm v.aai.3s p.g

τῶν θυσιῶν αὐτῶν. [2] καὶ ἀποκριθεὶς εἶπεν αὐτοῖς, δοκεῖτε ὅτι οἱ
{the} their sacrifices. *their* *{and}* In response he said to them, ⌊"Do you think⌋ that *{the}*
3836 899 2602 899 2779 646 3306 899 1506 4022 3836
d.gpf n.gpf r.gpm.3 cj pt.ap.nsm v.aai.3s r.dpm.3 v.pai.2p cj d.npm

[a] τὴν included by UBS before νεφέλην.

NASB

daughter-in-law
against mother-in-
law."
[54]And He was
also saying to the
crowds, "When
you see a cloud
rising in the west,
immediately you
say, 'A shower is
coming,' and so
it turns out. [55]And
when *you see* a
south wind blow-
ing, you say, 'It
will be a hot day,'
and it turns out *that*
way. [56]You hypo-
crites! You know
how to analyze the
appearance of the
earth and the sky,
but why do you not
analyze this present
time?
[57]"And why do
you not even on
your own initia-
tive judge what is
right? [58]For while
you are going with
your opponent to
appear before the
magistrate, on *your*
way *there* make an
effort to settle with
him, so that he may
not drag you before
the judge, and the
judge turn you over
to the officer, and
the officer throw
you into prison.
[59]I say to you, you
will not get out
of there until you
have paid the very
last cent."

Call to Repent

[13:1]Now on the
same occasion
there were some
present who re-
ported to Him
about the Galileans
whose blood Pilate
had mixed with
their sacrifices.
[2]And Jesus said to
them, "Do you sup-
pose that these

NIV

Galileans were
worse sinners than
all the other Gali-
leans because they
suffered this way?
[3]I tell you, no! But
unless you repent,
you too will all
perish. [4]Or those
eighteen who died
when the tower
in Siloam fell on
them—do you
think they were
more guilty than
all the others liv-
ing in Jerusalem?
[5]I tell you, no! But
unless you repent,
you too will all
perish."
[6]Then he told
this parable: "A
man had a fig tree
growing in his
vineyard, and he
went to look for
fruit on it but did
not find any. [7]So
he said to the man
who took care of
the vineyard, 'For
three years now
I've been coming
to look for fruit on
this fig tree and
haven't found any.
Cut it down! Why
should it use up
the soil?'
[8]"'Sir,' the man
replied, 'leave it
alone for one more
year, and I'll dig
around it and fer-
tilize it. [9]If it bears
fruit next year,
fine! If not, then
cut it down.'"

Jesus Heals a Crippled Woman on the Sabbath

[10]On a Sabbath
Jesus was teaching
in one of the syn-
agogues, [11]and a
woman was there

Γαλιλαῖοι οὗτοι ἁμαρτωλοὶ παρὰ πάντας τοὺς Γαλιλαίους
these Galileans *these* were worse sinners than all the other Galileans,
4047 1134 4047 1181 283 4123 4246 3836 1134
a.npm r.npm a.npm p.a a.apm d.apm a.apm

ἐγένοντο, ὅτι ταῦτα πεπόνθασιν; [3]οὐχί, λέγω ὑμῖν, ἀλλ᾽ ˻ἐὰν
were because they suffered these things? *they suffered* No, I tell you; but unless
1181 4022 4248 4248 4047 4248 4049 3306 7007 247 1569
v.ami.3p cj r.apn v.rai.3p pl v.pai.1s r.dp.2 cj cj

μὴ˼ μετανοῆτε πάντες ὁμοίως ἀπολεῖσθε. [4]ἢ ἐκεῖνοι οἱ
you repent, you will all perish as they did. *you will perish* Or those *{the}*
3590 3566 660 660 4246 660 3931 660 2445 1697 3836
pl v.pas.2p a.npm adv v.fmi.2p cj r.npm d.npm

δεκαοκτὼ ἐφ᾽ οὓς ἔπεσεν ὁ πύργος ἐν τῷ Σιλωὰμ καὶ
eighteen on whom the tower in Siloam fell *the tower in {the} Siloam* and
1277 2093 4005 3836 4788 1877 4978 4406 3836 4788 1877 3836 4978 2779
a.npm p.a r.apm v.aai.3s d.nsm n.nsm p.d d.dsm n.dsm cj

ἀπέκτεινεν αὐτούς, δοκεῖτε ὅτι αὐτοὶ ὀφειλέται ἐγένοντο παρὰ
killed them — do you think that they were worse offenders *were* than
650 899 1506 4022 899 1181 4050 1181 4123
v.aai.3s r.apm.3 v.pai.2p cj r.npm n.npm v.ami.3p p.a

πάντας τοὺς ἀνθρώπους τοὺς κατοικοῦντας Ἰερουσαλήμ; [5]οὐχί, λέγω ὑμῖν, ἀλλ᾽
all the others *{the}* living in Jerusalem? No, I tell you; but
4246 3836 476 3836 2997 2647 4049 3306 7007 247
a.apm d.apm n.apm d.apm pt.pa.apm n.asf pl v.pai.1s r.dp.2 cj

˻ἐὰν μὴ˼ μετανοῆτε πάντες ὡσαύτως ἀπολεῖσθε. [6] ἔλεγεν
unless you repent, you will all perish just as they did." *you will perish* Then he told
1569 3590 3566 660 660 4246 660 6058 660 1254 3306
cj pl v.pas.2p a.npm adv v.fmi.2p v.iai.3s

δὲ ταύτην τὴν παραβολήν· συκῆν εἶχέν τις πεφυτευμένην ἐν τῷ
Then this *{the}* parable: "A man had a fig tree *had A man* planted in *{the}*
1254 4047 3836 4130 5516 5516 2400 5190 2400 5516 5885 1877 3836
cj r.asf d.asf n.asf n.asf v.iai.3s r.nsm pt.rp.asf p.d d.dsm

ἀμπελῶνι αὐτοῦ, καὶ ἦλθεν ζητῶν καρπὸν ἐν αὐτῇ καὶ οὐχ εὗρεν.
his vineyard, *his* and he came ˻looking for˼ fruit on it and found none. *found*
899 308 899 2779 2262 2426 2843 1877 899 2779 2351 4024 2351
n.dsm r.gsm.3 cj v.aai.3s pt.pa.nsm n.asm p.d r.dsf.3 cj pl v.aai.3s

[7] εἶπεν δὲ πρὸς τὸν ἀμπελουργόν, ἰδοὺ τρία ἔτη ˻ἀφ᾽ οὗ˼ ἔρχομαι
And he said *And* to the vineyard worker, 'Look, for three years now, I have come
1254 3306 1254 4639 3836 307 2627 5552 2291 608 4005 2262
v.aai.3s cj p.a d.asm n.asm j a.npn n.npn p.g r.gsm v.pmi.1s

ζητῶν καρπὸν ἐν τῇ συκῇ ταύτῃ καὶ οὐχ εὑρίσκω· ἔκκοψον
˻looking for˼ fruit on *{the}* this fig tree, *this* and I find none. *I find* Remove
2426 2843 1877 3836 4047 5190 4047 2779 2351 2351 4024 2351 1716
pt.pa.nsm n.asm p.d d.dsf n.dsf r.dsf cj pl v.pai.1s v.aam.2s

[a]αὐτήν, ἱνατί καὶ τὴν γῆν καταργεῖ; [8] ὁ δὲ
it. Why *{also}* should it use up the soil?' *should it use up* And he *And*
899 2672 2779 2934 2934 2934 2934 3836 1178 2934 1254 3836 1254
r.asf.3 cj adv d.asf n.asf v.pai.3s d.nsm cj

ἀποκριθεὶς λέγει αὐτῷ, κύριε, ἄφες αὐτὴν ↰ καὶ τοῦτο τὸ ἔτος, ˻ἕως
answered, saying to him, 'Sir, leave it alone this year also, *this {the} year* until
646 3306 899 3261 918 899 918 4047 2291 2779 4047 3836 2291 2401
pt.ap.nsm v.pai.3s r.dsm.3 n.vsm v.aam.2s r.asf.3 adv r.asn d.asn n.asn p.g

ὅτου˼ σκάψω περὶ αὐτὴν καὶ βάλω κόπρια, [9]κἂν μὲν ποιήσῃ καρπὸν ˻εἰς τὸ
I dig around it and put on manure. Perhaps ~ it will bear fruit next
4015 4999 4309 899 2779 965 3162 2829 3525 4472 2843 1650 3836
r.gsn v.aas.1s p.a r.asf.3 cj v.aas.1s n.apn crasis pl v.aas.3s n.asm p.a d.asn

μέλλον·˼ εἰ δὲ μή γε, ἐκκόψεις αὐτήν. [10] ἦν δὲ
year; but if *but* not, ~ you may remove it.'" Now ˻he was˼ *Now*
3516 1254 1623 1254 3590 1145 1716 899 1254 1639 1254
pt.pa.asn cj cj pl pl v.fai.2s r.asf.3 v.iai.3s cj

διδάσκων ἐν μιᾷ τῶν συναγωγῶν ἐν τοῖς σάββασιν. [11]καὶ ἰδοὺ γυνὴ
teaching in one of the synagogues on the Sabbath, and ˻there was˼ a woman there
1438 1877 1651 3836 5252 1877 3836 4879 2779 2627 1222
pt.pa.nsm p.d a.dsf d.gpf n.gpf p.d d.dpn n.dpn cj j n.nsf

NASB

Galileans were
greater sinners
than all *other*
Galileans because
they suffered this
fate? [3]I tell you,
no, but unless you
repent, you will
all likewise perish.
[4]Or do you suppose
that those eighteen
on whom the tower
in Siloam fell and
killed them were
worse culprits than
all the men who
live in Jerusalem?
[5]I tell you, no, but
unless you repent,
you will all like-
wise perish."
[6]And He *began*
telling this parable:
"A man had a fig
tree which had
been planted in
his vineyard; and
he came looking
for fruit on it and
did not find any.
[7]And he said to the
vineyard-keeper,
'Behold, for three
years I have come
looking for fruit on
this fig tree without
finding any. Cut it
down! Why does
it even use up the
ground?' [8]And
he answered and
said to him, 'Let it
alone, sir, for this
year too, until I dig
around it and put
in fertilizer; [9]and if
it bears fruit next
year, *fine;* but if
not, cut it down.'"

Healing on the Sabbath

[10]And He was
teaching in one of
the synagogues on
the Sabbath. [11]And
there was a woman

[a] οὖν included by UBS before αὐτήν.

NIV

who had been crip-
pled by a spirit for
eighteen years.
She was bent over
and could not
straighten up at all.
12 When Jesus saw
her, he called her
forward and said
to her, "Woman,
you are set free
from your infirmi-
ty." 13 Then he put
his hands on her,
and immediately
she straightened
up and praised
God.
14 Indignant be-
cause Jesus had
healed on the
Sabbath, the syn-
agogue leader
said to the people,
"There are six
days for work.
So come and be
healed on those
days, not on the
Sabbath."
15 The Lord an-
swered him,
"You hypocrites!
Doesn't each of
you on the Sabbath
untie your ox or
donkey from the
stall and lead it
out to give it wa-
ter? 16 Then should
not this woman, a
daughter of Abra-
ham, whom Satan
has kept bound
for eighteen long
years, be set free
on the Sabbath day
from what bound
her?"
17 When he said
this, all his oppo-
nents were humil-
iated, but the peo-
ple were delighted
with all the won-
derful things

πνεῦμα ἔχουσα ἀσθενείας ἔτη δεκαοκτὼ καὶ ἦν
who had had a spirit *who had had* of weakness for eighteen years. *for eighteen* *{and}* ⌊She was⌋
2400 2400 2400 4460 2400 819 1277 1277 2291 1277 2779 1639
n.asn pt.pa.nsf n.gsf n.apn a.apn cj v.iai.3s

συγκύπτουσα καὶ μὴ δυναμένη ἀνακύψαι εἰς τὸ παντελές. 12 ἰδὼν δὲ
bent over and not able ⌊to straighten up⌋ at *{the}* all. Seeing *{and}*
5174 2779 3590 1538 376 1650 3836 4117 1625 1254
pt.pa.nsf cj pl pt.pp.nsf f.aa p.a d.asn a.asn pt.aa.nsm cj

αὐτὴν ὁ Ἰησοῦς προσεφώνησεν καὶ εἶπεν αὐτῇ, γύναι, ἀπολέλυσαι τῆς
her, *{the}* Jesus called out and said to her, "Woman ⌊you are released from⌋ *{the}*
899 3836 2652 4715 2779 3306 899 1222 668 3836
r.asf.3 d.nsm n.nsm v.aai.3s cj v.aai.3s r.dsf.3 n.vsf v.rpi.2s d.gsf

ἀσθενείας σου, 13 καὶ ἐπέθηκεν αὐτῇ τὰς χεῖρας· καὶ παραχρῆμα
your weakness." *your* *{and}* He placed his hands on her, *his* *hands* and immediately
5148 819 5148 2779 2202 3836 5931 899 3836 5931 2779 4202
n.gsf r.gs.2 cj v.aai.3s r.dsf.3 d.apf n.apf cj adv

ἀνωρθώθη καὶ ἐδόξαζεν τὸν θεόν. 14 ἀποκριθεὶς δὲ ὁ
⌊she was made erect again⌋ and began to praise *{the}* God. *{answering}* *{and}* *the*
494 2779 1519 3836 2536 646 1254 3836
v.api.3s cj v.iai.3s d.asm n.asm pt.ap.nsm cj d.nsm

ἀρχισυνάγωγος, ἀγανακτῶν ὅτι τῷ σαββάτῳ ἐθεράπευσεν
ruler of the synagogue Indignant because Jesus had healed ⌊on the⌋ Sabbath, *had healed*
801 24 4022 2652 2543 2543 3836 4879 2543
n.nsm pt.pa.nsm cj d.dsn n.dsn v.aai.3s

ὁ Ἰησοῦς, ἔλεγεν τῷ ὄχλῳ ὅτι ἓξ ἡμέραι
{the} *Jesus* the ruler of the synagogue said ⌊to the⌋ crowd, ~ "There are six days
3836 2652 3836 801 801 801 801 3306 3836 4063 4022 1639 1639 1971 2465
d.nsm n.nsm v.iai.3s d.dsm n.dsm cj a.npf n.npf

εἰσὶν ἐν αἷς ↱ δεῖ ἐργάζεσθαι· ἐν αὐταῖς οὖν ἐρχόμενοι
There are in which work ought to be done. Come on those days *{therefore}* *Come*
1639 1877 4005 2237 1256 2237 2262 1877 899 4036 2262
v.pai.3p p.d r.dpf v.pai.3s f.pm p.d r.dpf.3 cj pt.pm.npm

θεραπεύεσθε καὶ μὴ τῇ ἡμέρᾳ τοῦ σαββάτου. 15
and be healed, and not ⌊on the⌋ Sabbath day." *{the}* *Sabbath* Then the Lord
2543 2779 3590 3836 4879 2465 3836 4879 1254 3836 3261
v.ppm.2p cj pl d.dsf n.dsf d.gsn n.gsn

ἀπεκρίθη δὲ αὐτῷ ὁ κύριος καὶ εἶπεν, ὑποκριταί, ↱ ἕκαστος ὑμῶν
answered *Then* him, *the* *Lord* *{and}* saying, "You hypocrites! Does not each of you
646 1254 899 3836 3261 2779 3306 5695 3395 4024 1667 7007
v.api.3s cj r.dsm.3 d.nsm n.nsm cj v.aai.3s n.vpm r.nsm r.gp.2

τῷ σαββάτῳ οὐ λύει τὸν βοῦν αὐτοῦ ἢ τὸν ὄνον ἀπὸ τῆς φάτνης καὶ
⌊on the⌋ Sabbath *not* untie *{the}* his ox *his* or his donkey from the manger *{and}*
3836 4879 4024 3395 3836 899 1091 899 2445 3836 3952 608 3836 5764 2779
d.dsn n.dsn pl v.pai.3s d.asm n.asm r.gsm.3 cj d.asm n.asm p.g d.gsf n.gsf cj

ἀπαγαγὼν ← ποτίζει; 16 ταύτην δὲ θυγατέρα Ἀβραὰμ
to lead it away and to water it? And ought not this woman, *And* a daughter of Abraham
552 4540 1254 1256 4024 4047 1254 2588 11
pt.aa.nsm v.pai.3s r.asf cj n.asf n.gsm

οὖσαν, ἣν ἔδησεν ὁ σατανᾶς ἰδοὺ → ⌊δέκα καὶ ὀκτὼ⌋ ἔτη, οὐκ ἔδει
{being} whom Satan bound *{the}* *Satan* ~ for eighteen years, *not* *ought*
1639 4005 4928 1313 3836 4928 2627 1274 2779 3893 2291 4024 1256
pt.pa.asf r.asf v.aai.3s d.nsm n.nsm j a.apn cj a.npn n.npn pl v.iai.3s

λυθῆναι ἀπὸ τοῦ δεσμοῦ τούτου τῇ ἡμέρᾳ τοῦ σαββάτου; 17 καὶ
be released from *{the}* this bondage *this* ⌊on the⌋ day of the Sabbath?" *{and}* As he
3395 608 3836 4047 1301 4047 3836 2465 3836 4879 2779 3306 899
f.ap p.g d.gsm n.gsm r.gsm d.dsf n.dsf d.gsn n.gsn cj

ταῦτα λέγοντος αὐτοῦ κατῃσχύνοντο πάντες οἱ
said these things, *As said* *he* all his adversaries were put to shame, *all* *{the}*
3306 4047 3306 899 4246 899 512 2875 4246 3836
r.apn pt.pa.gsm r.gsm.3 v.ipi.3p a.npm d.npm

ἀντικείμενοι αὐτῷ, καὶ πᾶς ὁ ὄχλος ἔχαιρεν ἐπὶ πᾶσιν τοῖς ἐνδόξοις τοῖς
adversaries *his* while all the people rejoiced at all the glorious things that
512 899 2779 4246 3836 4063 5897 2093 4246 3836 1902 3836
pt.pm.npm r.dsm.3 cj a.nsm d.nsm n.nsm v.iai.3s p.d a.dpn d.dpn a.dpn d.dpn

NASB

who for eighteen
years had had a
sickness caused by
a spirit; and she
was bent double,
and could not
straighten up at all.
12 When Jesus saw
her, He called her
over and said to
her, "Woman, you
are freed from your
sickness." 13 And
He laid His hands
on her; and im-
mediately she was
made erect again
and *began* glorify-
ing God. 14 But the
synagogue official,
indignant because
Jesus had healed
on the Sabbath,
began saying to the
crowd in response,
"There are six days
in which work
should be done; so
come during them
and get healed, and
not on the Sab-
bath day." 15 But
the Lord answered
him and said, "You
hypocrites, does
not each of you
on the Sabbath
untie his ox or
his donkey from
the stall and lead
him away to water
him? 16 And this
woman, a daughter
of Abraham as she
is, whom Satan has
bound for eighteen
long years, should
she not have been
released from this
bond on the Sab-
bath day?" 17 As He
said this, all His
opponents were be-
ing humiliated; and
the entire crowd
was rejoicing over
all the glorious

NIV

he was doing.

The Parables of the Mustard Seed and the Yeast

[18]Then Jesus
asked, "What is
the kingdom of
God like? What
shall I compare
it to? [19]It is like
a mustard seed,
which a man took
and planted in his
garden. It grew
and became a
tree, and the birds
perched in its
branches."
[20]Again he asked,
"What shall I com-
pare the kingdom
of God to? [21]It is
like yeast that a
woman took and
mixed into about
sixty pounds[a]
of flour until it
worked all through
the dough."

The Narrow Door

[22]Then Jesus
went through the
towns and vil-
lages, teaching
as he made his
way to Jerusalem.
[23]Someone asked
him, "Lord, are
only a few peo-
ple going to be
saved?"
He said to them,
[24]"Make every
effort to enter
through the nar-
row door, because
many, I tell you,
will try to enter
and will not be
able to. [25]Once
the owner of the
house gets up and
closes the door,
you will stand
outside knock-
ing and pleading,
'Sir, open the door
for us.'
"But he will an-
swer, 'I don't know
you or where you
come from.'
[26]"Then you will
say, 'We ate and
drank with you,

[a] 21 Or about 27 kilograms

γινομένοις ὑπ᾽ αὐτοῦ. 18 ἔλεγεν οὖν, τίνι ὁμοία
were done by him. Then he said, *Then* "What is the kingdom of God like,
1181 5679 899 4036 3306 4036 5515 1639 3836 993 3836 2536 3927
pt.pm.dpn p.g r.gsm.3 v.iai.3s cj r.dsn a.nsf

ἐστὶν ἡ βασιλεία τοῦ θεοῦ καὶ τίνι ὁμοιώσω αὐτήν; 19 ὁμοία ἐστὶν
is *the* *kingdom* *of* *God* and to what shall I compare it? It is like *It is*
1639 3836 993 3836 2536 2779 5515 3929 899 1639 1639 3927 1639
v.pai.3s d.nsf n.nsf d.gsm n.gsm cj r.dsn v.fai.1s r.asf.3 a.nsf v.pai.3s

κόκκῳ σινάπεως, ὃν λαβὼν ἄνθρωπος ἔβαλεν εἰς κῆπον
a mustard seed *mustard* that a man took *man* and threw into his garden.
4983 3133 4983 4005 476 3284 476 965 1650 1571 3057
n.dsm n.gsn r.asm pt.aa.nsm n.nsm v.aai.3s p.a n.asm

ἑαυτοῦ, καὶ ηὔξησεν καὶ ἐγένετο εἰς δένδρον, καὶ τὰ πετεινὰ τοῦ οὐρανοῦ
his *{and}* It grew and became a tree, and the birds of the sky
1571 2779 889 2779 1181 1650 1285 2779 3836 4374 3836 4041
r.gsm.3 cj v.aai.3s cj v.ami.3s p.a n.asn cj d.npn n.npn d.gsm n.gsm

κατεσκήνωσεν ἐν τοῖς κλάδοις αὐτοῦ. 20 καὶ πάλιν εἶπεν, τίνι
made nests in *{the}* its branches." *its* And again he said, "To what
2942 1877 3836 899 3080 899 2779 4099 3306 5515
v.aai.3s p.d d.dpm n.dpm r.gsn.3 cj adv v.aai.3s r.dsn

ὁμοιώσω τὴν βασιλείαν τοῦ θεοῦ; 21 ὁμοία ἐστὶν ζύμῃ, ἣν
shall I compare the kingdom of God? It is like *It is* leaven that a woman
3929 3836 993 3836 2536 1639 1639 3927 1639 2434 4005 1222
v.fai.1s d.asf n.asf d.gsm n.gsm a.nsf v.pai.3s n.dsf r.asf

λαβοῦσα γυνὴ ἐνέκρυψεν[a] εἰς ἀλεύρου σάτα τρία ἕως οὗ →
took *woman* and hid in three measures of flour, *measures* *three* until it
3284 1222 1606 1650 5552 4929 236 4929 5552 2401 4005
pt.aa.nsf n.nsf v.aai.3s p.a n.gsn n.apn a.apn p.g r.gsm

→ ἐζυμώθη ὅλον. 22 καὶ διεπορεύετο κατὰ πόλεις καὶ κώμας
was all leavened." *all* Then Jesus went through town after town and village after
3910 2435 3910 2779 1388 2848 4484 2779 3267
v.api.3s a.nsn cj v.imi.3s p.a n.apf cj n.apf

διδάσκων καὶ πορείαν ποιούμενος εἰς Ἱεροσόλυμα. 23
village, teaching as he made his way *he made* to Jerusalem. Someone
1438 2779 4472 4472 4512 4472 1650 2642 5516
pt.pa.nsm cj n.asf pt.pm.nsm p.a n.apn

εἶπεν δέ τις αὐτῷ, κύριε, εἰ ὀλίγοι οἱ σῳζόμενοι;
said *{and}* *Someone* to him, "Lord, ~ will those who are saved be few?" *those* *who are saved*
3306 1254 5516 899 3261 1623 3836 5392 5392 5392 3900 3836 5392
v.aai.3s cj r.nsm r.dsm.3 n.vsm cj a.npm d.npm pt.pp.npm

ὁ δὲ εἶπεν πρὸς αὐτούς, 24 ἀγωνίζεσθε εἰσελθεῖν διὰ τῆς στενῆς θύρας,
And he *And* said to them, "Do your best to go in through the narrow door;
1254 3836 1254 3306 4639 899 76 1656 1328 3836 5101 2598
d.nsm cj v.aai.3s p.a r.apm.3 v.pmm.2p f.aa p.g d.gsf a.gsf n.gsf

ὅτι πολλοί, λέγω ὑμῖν, ζητήσουσιν εἰσελθεῖν καὶ οὐκ ἰσχύσουσιν. 25 ἀφ᾽ οὗ ἂν
for many, I tell you, will try to go in and not be able. "Once
4022 4498 3306 7007 2426 1656 2779 4024 2710 608 4005 323
cj a.npm v.pai.1s r.dp.2 v.fai.3p f.aa cj pl v.fai.3p p.g r.gsm pl

ἐγερθῇ ὁ οἰκοδεσπότης καὶ ἀποκλείσῃ τὴν θύραν καὶ
the owner of the house has risen *the* *owner of the house* and shut the door, and
3836 3867 3867 3867 3867 1586 3836 3867 2779 643 3836 2598 2779
v.aps.3s d.nsm n.nsm cj v.aas.3s d.asf n.asf cj

ἄρξησθε ἔξω ἑστάναι καὶ κρούειν τὴν θύραν λέγοντες, κύριε, ἄνοιξον
you are left standing outside, *standing* *{and}* knocking at the door, saying, 'Sir, open
806 2705 2032 2705 2779 3218 3836 2598 3306 3261 487
v.ams.2p adv f.ra cj f.pa d.asf n.asf pt.pa.npm n.vsm v.aam.2s

ἡμῖν, καὶ ἀποκριθεὶς ἐρεῖ ὑμῖν, → → οὐκ οἶδα ὑμᾶς πόθεν ἐστέ.
the door for us!' then he will respond to you, 'I do not know you or where you are
7005 2779 646 3306 7007 3857 3857 4024 3857 7007 4470 1639
r.dp.1 cj pt.ap.nsm v.fai.3s r.dp.2 pl v.rai.1s r.ap.2 cj v.pai.2p

← 26 τότε ἄρξεσθε λέγειν, ἐφάγομεν → ἐνώπιόν σου καὶ ἐπίομεν καὶ
from.' Then you will say, 'We ate and drank in your presence, *your* *and* *drank* and
4470 5538 806 3306 2266 2779 4403 5148 1967 5148 2779 4403 2779
adv v.fmi.2p f.pa v.aai.1p p.g r.gs.2 cj v.aai.1p cj

[a] ἐνέκρυψεν TNIV, NET. [ἐν]έκρυψεν UBS.

NASB

things being done
by Him.

Parables of Mustard Seed and Leaven

[18]So He was say-
ing, "What is the
kingdom of God
like, and to what
shall I compare it?
[19]It is like a mus-
tard seed, which
a man took and
threw into his own
garden; and it grew
and became a tree,
and THE BIRDS OF
THE AIR NESTED IN
ITS BRANCHES."
[20]And again He
said, "To what
shall I compare the
kingdom of God?
[21]It is like leaven,
which a woman
took and hid in
three pecks of flour
until it was all
leavened."

Teaching in the Villages

[22]And He was
passing through
from one city and
village to another,
teaching, and pro-
ceeding on His
way to Jerusalem.
[23]And someone
said to Him, "Lord,
are there *just* a
few who are be-
ing saved?" And
He said to them,
[24]"Strive to enter
through the narrow
door; for many, I
tell you, will seek
to enter and will
not be able. [25]Once
the head of the
house gets up and
shuts the door, and
you begin to stand
outside and knock
on the door, saying,
'Lord, open up to
us!' then He will
answer and say
to you, 'I do not
know where you
are from.' [26]Then
you will begin to
say, 'We ate and
drank in Your pres-
ence,

NIV

and you taught in
our streets.'
[27]"But he will re-
ply, 'I don't know
you or where you
come from. Away
from me, all you
evildoers!'
[28]"There will be
weeping there, and
gnashing of teeth,
when you see
Abraham, Isaac
and Jacob and all
the prophets in the
kingdom of God,
but you yourselves
thrown out. [29]Peo-
ple will come from
east and west and
north and south,
and will take their
places at the feast
in the kingdom
of God. [30]Indeed
there are those
who are last who
will be first, and
first who will be
last."

Jesus' Sorrow for Jerusalem

[31]At that time
some Pharisees
came to Jesus
and said to him,
"Leave this place
and go somewhere
else. Herod wants
to kill you."
[32]He replied, "Go
tell that fox, 'I will
keep on driving
out demons and
healing people to-
day and tomorrow,
and on the third
day I will reach
my goal.' [33]In any
case, I must press
on today and to-
morrow and the
next day—for
surely no prophet
can die outside Je-
rusalem!
[34]"Jerusalem, Je-
rusalem, you who
kill the prophets
and stone those
sent to you, how
often I have longed

ἐν ταῖς πλατείαις ἡμῶν ἐδίδαξας· [27] καὶ ἐρεῖ λέγων ὑμῖν,
you taught in {the} our streets.' *our* *you taught* And ⌊he will speak,⌋ saying to you,
1438 1438 1877 3836 7005 4426 7005 1438 2779 3306 3306 7007
p.d d.dpf n.dpf r.gp.1 v.aai.2s cj v.fai.3s pt.pa.nsm r.dp.2

↱ ↱ οὐκ οἶδα ὑμᾶς[a] πόθεν ἐστέ· ↰ ἀπόστητε ἀπ' ἐμοῦ πάντες ἐργάται
'I do not know you or where you are from. Depart from me, all you workers
3857 3857 4024 3857 7007 4470 1639 4470 923 608 1609 4246 2239
pl v.rai.1s r.ap.2 cj v.pai.2p v.aam.2p p.g r.gs.1 a.vpm n.vpm

ἀδικίας. [28] ἐκεῖ ἔσται ὁ κλαυθμὸς καὶ ὁ βρυγμὸς τῶν ὀδόντων,
of unrighteousness!' *there* ⌊There will be⌋ {the} weeping and {the} gnashing of teeth
94 1695 1639 3836 3088 2779 3836 1106 3836 3848
n.gsf adv v.fmi.3s d.nsm n.nsm cj d.nsm n.nsm d.gpm n.gpm

ὅταν ὄψησθε Ἀβραὰμ καὶ Ἰσαὰκ καὶ Ἰακὼβ καὶ πάντας τοὺς προφήτας ἐν
there, when you see Abraham and Isaac, and Jacob, and all the prophets in
1695 4020 3972 11 2779 2693 2779 2609 2779 4246 3836 4737 1877
cj v.ams.2p n.asm cj n.asm cj n.asm cj a.apm d.apm n.apm p.d

τῇ βασιλείᾳ τοῦ θεοῦ, ὑμᾶς δὲ ἐκβαλλομένους ἔξω. [29] καὶ
the kingdom of God, but you yourselves {and} cast outside. "Then
3836 993 3836 2536 1254 7007 1254 1675 2032 2779
d.dsf n.dsf d.gsm n.gsm r.ap.2 cj pt.pp.apm adv cj

ἥξουσιν ἀπὸ ἀνατολῶν καὶ δυσμῶν καὶ ἀπὸ βορρᾶ καὶ νότου καὶ
⌊they will come⌋ from east and west, and from north and south, and
2457 608 424 2779 1553 2779 608 1080 2779 3803 2779
v.fai.3p p.g n.gpf cj n.gpf cj p.g n.gsm cj n.gsm cj

ἀνακλιθήσονται ἐν τῇ βασιλείᾳ τοῦ θεοῦ. [30] καὶ ἰδοὺ εἰσὶν ἔσχατοι
recline at table in the kingdom of God. But take note, some who are last
369 1877 3836 993 3836 2536 2779 2627 4005 1639 2274
v.fpi.3p p.d d.dsf n.dsf d.gsm n.gsm cj j v.pai.3p a.npm

οἳ ἔσονται πρῶτοι καὶ εἰσὶν πρῶτοι οἳ ἔσονται ἔσχατοι. [31] ἐν αὐτῇ τῇ
who will be first, and some are first who will be last." In that very {the}
4005 1639 4755 2779 1639 4755 4005 1639 2274 1877 899 3836
r.npm v.fmi.3p a.npm cj v.pai.3p a.npm r.npm v.fmi.3p a.npm p.d r.dsf d.dsf

ὥρᾳ προσῆλθάν τινες Φαρισαῖοι λέγοντες αὐτῷ, ἔξελθε καὶ πορεύου
hour some Pharisees came, *some* *Pharisees* saying to him, "Leave and get away
6052 5516 5757 4665 5516 5757 3306 899 2002 2779 4513
n.dsf v.aai.3p r.npm n.npm pt.pa.npm r.dsm.3 v.aam.2s cj v.pmm.2s

ἐντεῦθεν, ὅτι Ἡρῴδης θέλει σε ἀποκτεῖναι. [32] καὶ εἶπεν αὐτοῖς,
from here, for Herod wants to kill you." *to kill* And he said to them,
1949 4022 2476 2527 650 650 5148 650 2779 3306 899
adv cj n.nsm v.pai.3s r.as.2 f.aa cj v.aai.3s r.dpm.3

πορευθέντες εἴπατε τῇ ἀλώπεκι ταύτῃ, ἰδοὺ ἐκβάλλω δαιμόνια καὶ
"Go and tell {the} that fox, *that* 'Behold, ⌊I am casting out⌋ demons and
4513 3306 3836 4047 273 4047 2627 1675 1228 2779
pt.ap.npm v.aam.2p d.dsf n.dsf r.dsf j v.pai.1s n.apn cj

ἰάσεις ἀποτελῶ σήμερον καὶ αὔριον καὶ τῇ τρίτῃ τελειοῦμαι.
performing cures *performing* today and tomorrow, and the third day ⌊I complete my task.'⌋
699 2617 699 4958 2779 892 2779 3836 5569 5457
n.apf v.pai.1s adv cj adv cj d.dsf a.dsf v.ppi.1s

[33] πλὴν δεῖ με σήμερον καὶ αὔριον καὶ τῇ
Nevertheless I must *I* continue on my way today and tomorrow and the
4440 1609 1256 1609 4513 4513 4513 4513 4958 2779 892 2779 3836
cj v.pai.3s r.as.1 adv cj adv cj d.dsf

ἐχομένῃ πορεύεσθαι, ὅτι ↱ ↱ οὐκ ἐνδέχεται προφήτην ἀπολέσθαι
next day; *continue on my way* because it is not possible for a prophet to die
2400 4513 4022 1896 1896 4024 1896 4737 660
pt.pm.dsf f.pm cj pl v.pmi.3s n.asm f.am

ἔξω Ἰερουσαλήμ. [34] Ἰερουσαλὴμ Ἰερουσαλήμ, ἡ ἀποκτείνουσα τοὺς
⌊outside of⌋ Jerusalem." "O Jerusalem, Jerusalem, the city that kills the
2032 2647 2647 2647 3836 650 3836
p.g n.gsf n.vsf n.vsf d.vsf pt.pa.vsf d.apm

προφήτας καὶ λιθοβολοῦσα τοὺς ἀπεσταλμένους πρὸς αὐτήν, ποσάκις ἠθέλησα
prophets and stones those who have been sent to it! How often I wanted
4737 2779 3344 3836 690 4639 899 4529 2527
n.apm cj pt.pa.vsf d.apm pt.rp.apm p.a r.asf.3 adv v.aai.1s

NASB

and You taught in
our streets'; [27]and
He will say, 'I
tell you, I do not
know where you
are from; DEPART
FROM ME, ALL YOU
EVILDOERS.' [28]In
that place there
will be weeping
and gnashing of
teeth when you see
Abraham and Isaac
and Jacob and all
the prophets in the
kingdom of God,
but yourselves
being thrown out.
[29]And they will
come from east
and west and from
north and south,
and will recline
at the table in the
kingdom of God.
[30]And behold, *some*
are last who will
be first and *some*
are first who will
be last."
[31]Just at that time
some Pharisees
approached, say-
ing to Him, "Go
away, leave here,
for Herod wants
to kill You." [32]And
He said to them,
"Go and tell that
fox, 'Behold, I cast
out demons and
perform cures to-
day and tomorrow,
and the third *day*
I reach My goal.'
[33]Nevertheless I
must journey on to-
day and tomorrow
and the next *day;*
for it cannot be that
a prophet would
perish outside of
Jerusalem. [34]O
Jerusalem, Jerusa-
lem, *the city* that
kills the prophets
and stones those
sent to her! How
often I wanted to

[a] [ὑμᾶς] UBS.

NIV

to gather your
children together,
as a hen gathers
her chicks under
her wings, and
you were not will-
ing. [35]Look, your
house is left to
you desolate. I tell
you, you will not
see me again until
you say, 'Blessed
is he who comes
in the name of the
Lord.'[a]"

Jesus at a Pharisee's House

14 One Sab-
bath, when
Jesus went to eat
in the house of a
prominent Phari-
see, he was being
carefully watched.
[2]There in front of
him was a man
suffering from ab-
normal swelling
of his body. [3]Jesus
asked the Phari-
sees and experts
in the law, "Is it
lawful to heal on
the Sabbath or
not?" [4]But they
remained silent.
So taking hold of
the man, he healed
him and sent him
on his way.
[5]Then he asked
them, "If one of
you has a child[b] or
an ox that falls into
a well on the Sab-
bath day, will you
not immediately
pull it out?" [6]And
they had nothing
to say.
[7]When he no-
ticed how the
guests picked the
places of honor at
the table, he told
them this parable:
[8]"When someone
invites you to a
wedding feast,

ἐπισυνάξαι τὰ τέκνα σου ↰ ⌊ὃν τρόπον⌋ ὄρνις τὴν ἑαυτῆς
to gather {the} your children your together as a hen gathers {the} her
2190 3836 5148 5451 5148 2190 4005 5573 3998 3836 1571
f.aa d.apn n.apn r.gs.2 r.asm n.asm n.nsf d.asf r.gsf.3

νοσσιὰν ὑπὸ τὰς πτέρυγας, καὶ ↱ ↱ οὐκ ἠθελήσατε. [35] ἰδοὺ
brood under her wings, and you did not want it! Behold, your house
3799 5679 3836 4763 2779 2527 2527 4024 2527 2627 7007 3875
n.asf p.a d.apf n.apf cj pl v.aai.2p j

ἀφίεται ὑμῖν ὁ οἶκος ὑμῶν. λέγω δὲ[a] ὑμῖν, ↱ ↱ ⌊οὐ μὴ⌋ ἴδητέ
is left to you {the} house your desolate. And I tell And you, you will not see
918 7007 3836 3875 7007 1254 3306 1254 7007 1625 1625 4024 3590 1625
v.ppi.3s r.dp.2 d.nsm n.nsm r.gp.2 v.pai.1s cj r.dp.2 pl pl v.aas.2p

με ἕως[b] εἴπητε, εὐλογημένος ὁ ἐρχόμενος ἐν ὀνόματι → κυρίου.
me until you say, 'Blessed is the one who comes in the name of the Lord!'"
1609 2401 3306 2328 3836 2262 1877 3950 3261
r.as.1 cj v.aas.2p pt.rp.nsm d.nsm pt.pm.nsm p.d n.dsn n.gsm

[14:1] καὶ ἐγένετο ἐν τῷ ἐλθεῖν αὐτὸν εἰς οἶκόν → τινος τῶν
{and} {it happened that} When ~ Jesus went Jesus into the house of a certain {the}
2779 1181 1877 3836 899 2262 899 1650 3875 5516 3836
cj v.ami.3s p.d d.dsn f.aa r.asm.3 p.a n.asm r.gsm d.gpm

ἀρχόντων τῶν[c] Φαρισαίων → σαββάτῳ φαγεῖν ἄρτον καὶ αὐτοὶ ἦσαν
ruler of the Pharisees on the Sabbath to eat bread and they were
807 3836 5757 4879 2266 788 2779 899 1639
n.gpm d.gpm n.gpm n.dsn f.aa n.asm cj r.npm v.iai.3p

παρατηρούμενοι αὐτόν. ↰ [2]καὶ ἰδοὺ ἄνθρωπός τις
watching him closely, {and} ~ it happened that a certain man certain
4190 899 4190 2779 2627 5516 476 5516
pt.pm.npm r.asm.3 cj j n.nsm r.nsm

ἦν ὑδρωπικὸς ἔμπροσθεν αὐτοῦ. [3]καὶ ἀποκριθεὶς ὁ
was ⌊suffering from dropsy⌋ was right there in front of him. {and} In response {the}
1639 5622 1639 1869 899 2779 646 3836
v.iai.3s a.nsm p.g r.gsm.3 cj pt.ap.nsm d.nsm

Ἰησοῦς εἶπεν πρὸς τοὺς νομικοὺς καὶ Φαρισαίους λέγων, ἔξεστιν τῷ σαββάτῳ
Jesus spoke to the lawyers and Pharisees, saying, "Is it lawful ⌊on the⌋ Sabbath
2652 3306 4639 3836 3788 2779 5757 3306 1997 3836 4879
n.nsm v.aai.3s p.a d.apm n.apm cj n.apm pt.pa.nsm v.pai.3s d.dsn n.dsn

θεραπεῦσαι ἢ οὔ; [4] οἱ δὲ ἡσύχασαν. καὶ ↱ ἐπιλαβόμενος
to heal, or not?" But they But remained silent. So he took hold of the man,
2543 2445 4024 1254 3836 1254 2483 2779 2615 2138
f.aa cj pl d.npm cj v.aai.3p cj pt.am.nsm

ἰάσατο αὐτὸν καὶ ἀπέλυσεν. ← [5]καὶ πρὸς αὐτοὺς εἶπεν, τίνος ὑμῶν
healed him, and sent him away. And to them, he said, "Which of you, when
2615 899 2779 668 2779 4639 899 3306 5515 7007
v.ami.3s r.asm.3 cj v.aai.3s cj p.a r.apm.3 v.aai.3s r.gsm r.gp.2

υἱὸς ἢ βοῦς εἰς φρέαρ πεσεῖται, καὶ ↱ οὐκ εὐθέως
his son or his ox has fallen into a well, has fallen {and} does not immediately
5626 2445 1091 4406 4406 1650 5853 4406 2779 413 4024 2311
n.nsm cj n.nsm p.a n.asn v.fmi.3s cj pl adv

ἀνασπάσει αὐτὸν ↰ ἐν ἡμέρᾳ τοῦ σαββάτου; [6]καὶ ↱ ↱ οὐκ
pull it up, even on the Sabbath day?" the Sabbath And they were not
413 899 413 1877 3836 4879 2465 3836 4879 2779 2710 2710 4024
v.fai.3s r.asm.3 p.d n.dsf d.gsn n.gsn cj pl

ἴσχυσαν ἀνταποκριθῆναι πρὸς ταῦτα. [7]ἔλεγεν δὲ πρὸς τοὺς
able to give an answer to this. ⌊He began speaking⌋ {and} a parable to those
2710 503 4639 4047 3306 1254 4130 4639 3836
v.aai.3p f.ap p.a r.apn v.iai.3s cj p.a d.apm

κεκλημένους παραβολήν, ἐπέχων πῶς τὰς
who had been invited parable ⌊when he noticed⌋ how they were seeking out the
2813 4130 2091 4802 1721 1721 1721 1721 3836
pt.rp.apm n.asf pt.pa.nsm cj d.apf

NASB

gather your chil-
dren together, just
as a hen *gathers*
her brood under
her wings, and you
would not *have*
it! [35]Behold, your
house is left to you
desolate; and I say
to you, you will not
see Me until *the*
time comes when
you say, 'BLESSED
IS HE WHO COMES
IN THE NAME OF THE
LORD!'"

Jesus Heals on the Sabbath

[14:1]It happened
that when He went
into the house of
one of the leaders
of the Pharisees on
the Sabbath to eat
bread, they were
watching Him
closely. [2]And there
in front of Him was
a man suffering
from dropsy. [3]And
Jesus answered and
spoke to the law-
yers and Pharisees,
saying, "Is it lawful
to heal on the Sab-
bath, or not?" [4]But
they kept silent.
And He took hold
of him and healed
him, and sent him
away. [5]And He said
to them, "Which
one of you will
have a son or an ox
fall into a well, and
will not immedi-
ately pull him out
on a Sabbath day?"
[6]And they could
make no reply to
this.

Parable of the Guests

[7]And He *began*
speaking a par-
able to the invited
guests when He
noticed how they
had been picking

[a] 35 Psalm 118:26
[b] 5 Some manu-
scripts *donkey*

[a] [δὲ] UBS.
[b] [ἥξει ὅτε] included by UBS after ἕως. Omitted by TNIV, NET, TR.
[c] [τῶν] UBS.

NIV

do not take the
place of honor,
for a person more
distinguished than
you may have been
invited. 9 If so, the
host who invited
both of you will
come and say to
you, 'Give this
person your seat.'
Then, humiliat-
ed, you will have
to take the least
important place.
10 But when you
are invited, take
the lowest place,
so that when your
host comes, he
will say to you,
'Friend, move up
to a better place.'
Then you will be
honored in the
presence of all the
other guests. 11 For
all those who exalt
themselves will
be humbled, and
those who humble
themselves will be
exalted."
12 Then Jesus
said to his host,
"When you give a
luncheon or din-
ner, do not invite
your friends, your
brothers or sisters,
your relatives, or
your rich neigh-
bors; if you do,
they may invite
you back and so
you will be repaid.
13 But when you
give a banquet,
invite the poor,
the crippled, the
lame, the blind,
14 and you will be
blessed. Although
they cannot

πρωτοκλισίας ἐξελέγοντο, λέγων πρὸς αὐτούς, 8 ὅταν κληθῇς ὑπό τινος
places of honor. *they were seeking out* He said to them, "When you are invited by someone
4752 1721 3306 4639 899 4020 2813 5679 5516
n.apf v.imi.3p pt.pa.nsm p.a r.apm.3 cj v.aps.2s p.g r.gsm

εἰς γάμους, μὴ κατακλιθῇς εἰς τὴν πρωτοκλισίαν, μήποτε ↱
to a ⌊wedding feast,⌋ do not take a seat in a place of honor, lest someone more
1650 1141 3590 2884 1650 3836 4752 3607 5148
p.a n.apm pl v.aps.2s p.a d.asf n.asf cj

ἐντιμότερός σου ᾖ κεκλημένος ὑπ' αὐτοῦ, 9 καὶ ἐλθὼν ὁ
distinguished ⌊than you⌋ ⌊may have been⌋ invited by your host, and *{after coming}* the
1952 5148 1639 2813 5679 899 2779 2262 3836
a.nsm.c r.gs.2 v.pas.3s pt.rp.nsm p.g r.gsm.3 cj pt.aa.nsm d.nsm

σὲ καὶ αὐτὸν καλέσας ἐρεῖ σοι, δὸς
one who invited both you and him *one who invited* ⌊will say⌋ to you, 'Give your place
2813 2813 2813 5148 2779 899 2813 3306 5148 1443 5536
r.as.2 cj r.asm.3 pt.aa.nsm v.fai.3s r.ds.2 v.aam.2s

τούτῳ τόπον, καὶ τότε ἄρξῃ μετὰ αἰσχύνης τὸν
⌊to this person,'⌋ *place* and then with shame ⌊you will proceed⌋ *with shame* to take the
4047 5536 2779 5538 3552 158 806 3552 158 2988 2988 3836
r.dsm n.asm cj adv v.fmi.2s p.g n.gsf d.asm

ἔσχατον τόπον κατέχειν. 10 ἀλλ' ὅταν κληθῇς, πορευθεὶς ἀνάπεσε εἰς
least important place. *to take* Rather, when you are invited, go and recline in
2274 5536 2988 247 4020 2813 4513 404 1650
a.asm n.asm f.pa cj cj v.aps.2s pt.ap.nsm v.aam.2s p.a

τὸν ἔσχατον τόπον, ἵνα ὅταν ἔλθῃ ὁ κεκληκώς
the least important place so that when the one who invited you comes *the* *one who invited*
3836 2274 5536 2671 4020 3836 2813 2813 2813 5148 2262 3836 2813
d.asm a.asm n.asm cj cj v.aas.3s d.nsm pt.ra.nsm

σε ἐρεῖ σοι, φίλε, προσανάβηθι ἀνώτερον· τότε ἔσται σοι δόξα
you ⌊he may say⌋ to you, 'Friend, move up higher!' Then you will have *you* glory
5148 3306 5148 5813 4646 542 5538 5148 1639 5148 1518
r.as.2 v.fai.3s r.ds.2 n.vsm v.aam.2s adv.c adv v.fmi.3s r.ds.2 n.nsf

ἐνώπιον πάντων τῶν συνανακειμένων σοι. 11 ὅτι πᾶς ὁ ὑψῶν
in the presence of all who are reclining at table ⌊with you.⌋ For everyone who exalts
1967 4246 3836 5263 5148 4022 4246 3836 5738
p.g a.gpm d.gpm pt.pm.gpm r.ds.2 cj a.nsm d.nsm pt.pa.nsm

ἑαυτὸν ταπεινωθήσεται, καὶ ὁ ταπεινῶν ἑαυτὸν ὑψωθήσεται. 12 →
himself will be humbled, and the one who humbles himself will be exalted." Then he also
1571 5427 2779 3836 5427 1571 5738 1254 2779
r.asm.3 v.fpi.3s cj d.nsm pt.pa.nsm r.asm.3 v.fpi.3s

ἔλεγεν δὲ καὶ τῷ κεκληκότι αὐτόν, ὅταν ποιῇς ἄριστον ἢ
said *Then* *also* ⌊to the⌋ ⌊one who had invited⌋ him, "When you give a luncheon or a
3306 1254 2779 3836 2813 899 4020 4472 756 2445
v.iai.3s cj adv d.dsm pt.ra.dsm r.asm.3 cj v.pas.2s n.asn cj

δεῖπνον, μὴ φώνει τοὺς φίλους σου μηδὲ τοὺς ἀδελφούς σου μηδὲ τοὺς
dinner do not invite *{the}* your friends, *your* or *{the}* your brothers, *your* or *{the}*
1270 3590 5888 3836 5148 5813 5148 3593 3836 5148 81 5148 3593 3836
n.asn pl v.pam.2s d.apm n.apm r.gs.2 cj d.apm n.apm r.gs.2 cj d.apm

συγγενεῖς σου μηδὲ γείτονας πλουσίους, μήποτε καὶ αὐτοὶ
your relatives, *your* or rich neighbors, *rich* in case they also *they*
5148 5150 5148 3593 4454 1150 4454 3607 899 2779 899
n.apm r.gs.2 cj n.apm a.apm cj adv r.npm

ἀντικαλέσωσίν σε ↰ ↰ καὶ γένηται ἀνταπόδομά σοι. 13 ἀλλ' ὅταν
invite you in return, and ⌊there would be⌋ a repayment to you. But when you
511 5148 511 511 2779 1181 501 5148 247 4020 4472
v.aas.3p r.as.2 cj v.ams.3s n.nsn r.ds.2 cj cj

δοχὴν ποιῇς, κάλει πτωχούς, ἀναπείρους, χωλούς, τυφλούς·
give a feast, *you give* invite the poor, the crippled, the lame, the blind.
4472 1531 4472 2813 4777 401 6000 5603
n.asf v.pas.2s v.pam.2s a.apm n.apm a.apm a.apm

14 καὶ μακάριος ἔσῃ, ὅτι ↱ ↱ οὐκ ἔχουσιν
Then you will be blessed, *you will be* because they do not have a way
2779 1639 1639 1639 3421 1639 4022 2400 2400 4024 2400
cj a.nsm v.fmi.2s cj pl v.pai.3p

NASB

out the places of
honor *at the table,*
saying to them,
8 "When you are
invited by some-
one to a wedding
feast, do not take
the place of honor,
for someone more
distinguished than
you may have been
invited by him,
9 and he who invited
you both will come
and say to you,
'Give *your* place to
this man,' and then
in disgrace you
proceed to occupy
the last place. 10 But
when you are invit-
ed, go and recline
at the last place, so
that when the one
who has invited
you comes, he may
say to you, 'Friend,
move up higher';
then you will have
honor in the sight
of all who are at
the table with you.
11 For everyone who
exalts himself will
be humbled, and
he who humbles
himself will be
exalted."
12 And He also
went on to say
to the one who
had invited Him,
"When you give a
luncheon or a din-
ner, do not invite
your friends or
your brothers or
your relatives or
rich neighbors,
otherwise they may
also invite you in
return and *that* will
be your repayment.
13 But when you
give a reception,
invite *the* poor, *the*
crippled, *the* lame,
the blind, 14 and you
will be blessed,
since they do not
have *the means* to

NIV

repay you, you
will be repaid at
the resurrection of
the righteous."

The Parable of the Great Banquet

15 When one of
those at the table
with him heard
this, he said to
Jesus, "Blessed is
the one who will
eat at the feast in
the kingdom of
God."
16 Jesus replied:
"A certain man
was preparing
a great banquet
and invited many
guests. 17 At the
time of the banquet
he sent his servant
to tell those who
had been invited,
'Come, for ev-
erything is now
ready.'
18 "But they all
alike began to
make excuses. The
first said, 'I have
just bought a field,
and I must go and
see it. Please ex-
cuse me.'
19 "Another said,
'I have just bought
five yoke of oxen,
and I'm on my way
to try them out.
Please excuse me.'
20 "Still another
said, 'I just got
married, so I can't
come.'
21 "The servant
came back and re-
ported this to his
master. Then the
owner of the house
became angry
and ordered his
servant, 'Go out
quickly into the
streets and alleys
of the town and
bring in the poor,
the crippled, the

ἀνταποδοῦναί σοι, ↰ ἀνταποδοθήσεται γάρ σοι ἐν τῇ ἀναστάσει
to pay you back, for there will be a repayment *for* ⌊for you⌋ at the resurrection
500 5148 500 1142 500 1142 5148 1877 3836 414
f.aa r.ds.2 v.fpi.3s cj r.ds.2 p.d d.dsf n.dsf

τῶν δικαίων. 15 → ἀκούσας δέ τις
of the righteous." When one of those reclining at table with him heard *{and}* *one*
3836 1465 5516 3836 5263 5263 5263 5263 5263 201 1254 5516
d.gpm a.gpm pt.aa.nsm cj r.nsm

τῶν συνανακειμένων ταῦτα εἶπεν αὐτῷ, μακάριος ὅστις
of *those reclining at table with* him say these things, he said to him, "Blessed is the person who
3836 5263 4047 3306 899 3421 4015
d.gpm pt.pm.gpm r.apn v.aai.3s r.dsm.3 a.nsm r.nsm

φάγεται ἄρτον[a] ἐν τῇ βασιλείᾳ τοῦ θεοῦ. 16 ὁ δὲ εἶπεν αὐτῷ,
will eat bread in the kingdom of God!" But he *But* said to him, "A
2266 788 1877 3836 993 3836 2536 1254 3836 1254 3306 899 5516
v.fmi.3s n.asm p.d d.dsf n.dsf d.gsm n.gsm d.nsm cj v.aai.3s r.dsm.3

ἄνθρωπός τις ἐποίει δεῖπνον μέγα, καὶ ἐκάλεσεν πολλοὺς 17 καὶ
man *A* once gave a great banquet *great* and invited many guests. And
476 5516 4472 3489 1270 3489 2779 2813 4498 2779
n.nsm r.nsm v.iai.3s n.asn a.asn cj v.aai.3s a.apm cj

ἀπέστειλεν τὸν δοῦλον αὐτοῦ τῇ ὥρᾳ τοῦ δείπνου εἰπεῖν τοῖς
he sent *{the}* his servant *his* ⌊at the⌋ hour of the banquet to say to those
690 3836 899 1529 899 3836 6052 3836 1270 3306 3836
v.aai.3s d.asm n.asm r.gsm.3 d.dsf n.dsf d.gsn n.gsn f.aa d.dpm

κεκλημένοις, ἔρχεσθε, ὅτι ἤδη ἕτοιμά ἐστιν. 18 καὶ
who had been invited, 'Come, for everything is now ready.' *is* But one after another
2813 2262 4022 1639 2453 2289 1639 2779 1651 608
pt.rp.dpm v.pmm.2p cj adv a.npn v.pai.3s cj

→ ἤρξαντο ἀπὸ μιᾶς πάντες παραιτεῖσθαι. ὁ πρῶτος εἶπεν αὐτῷ,
they all began *after* *one* *all* to make excuses. The first said to him, 'I bought a
4246 806 608 1651 4246 4148 3836 4755 3306 899 60 60
v.ami.3p p.g a.gsf a.npm f.pm d.nsm a.nsm v.aai.3s r.dsm.3

ἀγρὸν ἠγόρασα καὶ ⌊ἔχω ἀνάγκην⌋ ἐξελθὼν ἰδεῖν αὐτόν· ἐρωτῶ σε, ἔχε με
field, *I bought* and I must go out to see it. I ask you, have me
69 60 2779 2400 340 2002 1625 899 2263 5148 2400 1609
n.asm v.aai.1s cj v.pai.1s n.asf pt.aa.nsm f.aa r.asm.3 v.pai.1s r.as.2 v.pam.2s r.as.1

παρῃτημένον. 19 καὶ ἕτερος εἶπεν, ζεύγη βοῶν ἠγόρασα πέντε
excused.' And another said, 'I have bought five yoke of oxen, *I have bought* *five*
4148 2779 2283 3306 60 60 60 4297 2414 1091 60 4297
pt.rp.asm cj r.nsm v.aai.3s n.apn n.gpm v.aai.1s a.apn

καὶ πορεύομαι δοκιμάσαι αὐτά· ↰ ἐρωτῶ σε, ἔχε με παρῃτημένον. 20 καὶ
and I am going to try them out. I ask you, have me excused.' And
2779 4513 1507 899 1507 2263 5148 2400 1609 4148 2779
cj v.pmi.1s f.aa r.apn.3 v.pai.1s r.as.2 v.pam.2s r.as.1 pt.rp.asm cj

ἕτερος εἶπεν, γυναῖκα ἔγημα καὶ διὰ τοῦτο ↱ ↱ οὐ
another said, 'I have married a wife, *I have married* and ⌊because of⌋ this I am not
2283 3306 1138 1138 1138 1222 1138 2779 1328 4047 1538 1538 4024
r.nsm v.aai.3s n.asf v.aai.1s cj p.a r.asn pl

δύναμαι ἐλθεῖν. 21 καὶ παραγενόμενος ὁ δοῦλος ἀπήγγειλεν
able to come.' So the servant came *the* *servant* and reported these
1538 2262 2779 3836 1529 4134 3836 1529 550 4047
v.ppi.1s f.aa cj pt.am.nsm d.nsm n.nsm v.aai.3s

τῷ κυρίῳ αὐτοῦ ταῦτα. τότε ὀργισθεὶς ὁ
things to his master. *his* *these things* Then the master of the house was angry *the*
4047 3836 899 3261 899 4047 5538 3836 3867 3867 3867 3867 3974 3836
d.dsm n.dsm r.gsm.3 r.apn adv pt.ap.nsm d.nsm

οἰκοδεσπότης εἶπεν τῷ δούλῳ αὐτοῦ, ἔξελθε ταχέως εἰς τὰς πλατείας καὶ
master of the house and said to his servant, *his* 'Go out quickly into the streets and
3867 3306 3836 899 1529 899 2002 5441 1650 3836 4426 2779
n.nsm v.aai.3s d.dsm n.dsm r.gsm.3 v.aam.2s adv p.a d.apf n.apf cj

ῥύμας τῆς πόλεως καὶ τοὺς πτωχοὺς καὶ ἀναπείρους καὶ
alleys of the city, and bring in here the poor, *{and}* the crippled, *{and}* the
4860 3836 4484 2779 1652 1652 6045 3836 4777 2779 401 2779
n.apf d.gsf n.gsf cj d.apm a.apm cj n.apm cj

NASB

repay you; for you
will be repaid at
the resurrection of
the righteous."
15 When one of
those who were
reclining *at the*
table with Him
heard this, he said
to Him, "Blessed is
everyone who will
eat bread in the
kingdom of God!"

Parable of the Dinner

16 But He said to
him, "A man was
giving a big din-
ner, and he invited
many; 17 and at the
dinner hour he
sent his slave to
say to those who
had been invited,
'Come; for every-
thing is ready now.'
18 But they all alike
began to make
excuses. The first
one said to him,
'I have bought a
piece of land and I
need to go out and
look at it; please
consider me ex-
cused.' 19 Another
one said, 'I have
bought five yoke
of oxen, and I am
going to try them
out; please con-
sider me excused.'
20 Another one said,
'I have married a
wife, and for that
reason I cannot
come.' 21 And the
slave came *back*
and reported this
to his master. Then
the head of the
household became
angry and said to
his slave, 'Go out
at once into the
streets and lanes of
the city and bring
in here the poor
and crippled and

[a] ἄρτον UBS, NET. ἄριστον TNIV.

NIV

blind and the
lame.'
[22]"'Sir,' the ser-
vant said, 'what
you ordered has
been done, but
there is still room.'
[23]"Then the mas-
ter told his servant,
'Go out to the
roads and country
lanes and compel
them to come in,
so that my house
will be full. [24]I
tell you, not one
of those who were
invited will get a
taste of my ban-
quet.'"

The Cost of Being a Disciple

[25]Large crowds
were traveling
with Jesus, and
turning to them he
said: [26]"If anyone
comes to me and
does not hate fa-
ther and mother,
wife and children,
brothers and sis-
ters—yes, even
their own life—
such a person can-
not be my disciple.
[27]And whoever
does not car-
ry their cross and
follow me cannot
be my disciple.
[28]"Suppose one of
you wants to build
a tower. Won't you
first sit down and
estimate the cost
to see if you have
enough money to
complete it? [29]For
if you lay the foun-
dation and are not
able to finish it,
everyone who sees
it will ridicule you,
[30]saying, 'This
person began to
build and wasn't
able to finish.'
[31]"Or suppose a

τυφλοὺς καὶ χωλοὺς εἰσάγαγε ὧδε. 22 καὶ εἶπεν ὁ δοῦλος, κύριε,
blind, and the lame.' *bring in* *here* *{and}* The slave said, *The* *slave* 'Sir, what
5603 2779 6000 1652 6045 2779 3836 1529 3306 3836 1529 3261 4005
a.apm cj a.apm v.aam.2s adv cj v.aai.3s d.nsm n.nsm n.vsm

γέγονεν ὃ ἐπέταξας, καὶ ἔτι τόπος ἐστίν. 23 καὶ
you ordered ⌊has been done,⌋ *what* *you ordered* and still there is room.' *there is* *{and}* The
2199 2199 1181 4005 2199 2779 2285 1639 1639 5536 1639 2779 3836
v.rai.3s r.asn v.aai.2s cj adv n.nsm v.pai.3s cj

εἶπεν ὁ κύριος πρὸς τὸν δοῦλον, ἔξελθε εἰς τὰς ὁδοὺς καὶ φραγμοὺς καὶ
master said *The* *master* to the servant, 'Go out to the highways and hedgerows and
3261 3306 3836 3261 4639 3836 1529 2002 1650 3836 3847 2779 5850 2779
v.aai.3s d.nsm n.nsm p.a d.asm n.asm v.aam.2s p.a d.apf n.apf cj n.apm cj

ἀνάγκασον εἰσελθεῖν, ἵνα γεμισθῇ μου ὁ οἶκος· 24 λέγω
urge people to come in, so that my house may be filled. *my* *{the}* *house* For I say
337 1656 2671 1609 3875 1153 1609 3836 3875 1142 3306
v.aam.2s f.aa cj v.aps.3s r.gs.1 d.nsm n.nsm v.pai.1s

γὰρ ὑμῖν ὅτι οὐδεὶς τῶν ἀνδρῶν ἐκείνων τῶν κεκλημένων γεύσεταί μου τοῦ
For to you that none of those men *those* who were invited will taste my *{the}*
1142 7007 4022 4029 3836 1697 467 1697 3836 2813 1174 1609 3836
cj r.dp.2 cj a.nsm d.gpm n.gpm r.gpm d.gpm pt.rp.gpm v.fmi.3s r.gs.1 d.gsn

δείπνου. 25 συνεπορεύοντο δὲ αὐτῷ ὄχλοι πολλοί, καὶ ↱
banquet.'" Great crowds of people were traveling with *{and}* him, *crowds* *Great* and he
1270 4498 4063 5233 1254 899 4063 4498 2779 3306
n.gsn v.imi.3p cj r.dsm.3 n.npm a.npm cj

στραφεὶς εἶπεν πρὸς αὐτούς, 26 εἴ τις ἔρχεται πρός με καὶ ↱ οὐ μισεῖ
turned and said to them, "If anyone comes to me and does not hate
5138 3306 4639 899 1623 5516 2262 4639 1609 2779 3631 4024 3631
pt.ap.nsm v.aai.3s p.a r.apm.3 cj r.nsm v.pmi.3s p.a r.as.1 cj pl v.pai.3s

τὸν πατέρα ἑαυτοῦ καὶ τὴν μητέρα καὶ τὴν γυναῖκα καὶ τὰ τέκνα καὶ
{the} his own father *his own* and *{the}* mother, and *{the}* wife and *{the}* children, and
3836 1571 1571 4252 1571 2779 3836 3613 2779 3836 1222 2779 3836 5451 2779
d.asm n.asm r.gsm.3 cj d.asf n.asf cj d.asf n.asf cj d.apn n.apn cj

τοὺς ἀδελφοὺς καὶ τὰς ἀδελφὰς ἔτι τε καὶ τὴν ψυχὴν ἑαυτοῦ,
{the} brothers and *{the}* sisters, and even *and* *{also}* *{the}* his own life, *his own*
3836 81 2779 3836 80 5445 2285 5445 2779 3836 1571 1571 6034 1571
d.apm n.apm cj d.apf n.apf adv cj adv d.asf n.asf r.gsm.3

⌊οὐ δύναται⌋ εἶναί μου μαθητής. 27 ὅστις ↱ οὐ βαστάζει τὸν
he cannot be my disciple. Whoever does not carry *{the}* his own
4024 1538 1639 1609 3412 4015 1002 4024 1002 3836 1571 1571
pl v.ppi.3s f.pa r.gs.1 n.nsm r.nsm pl v.pai.3s d.asm

σταυρὸν ἑαυτοῦ καὶ ἔρχεται ὀπίσω μου, ⌊οὐ δύναται⌋ εἶναί μου μαθητής. 28
cross *his own* and come after me cannot be my disciple. "For
5089 1571 2779 2262 3958 1609 4024 1538 1639 1609 3412 1142
n.asm r.gsm.3 cj v.pmi.3s p.g r.gs.1 pl v.ppi.3s f.pa r.gs.1 n.nsm

τίς γὰρ ἐξ ὑμῶν θέλων πύργον οἰκοδομῆσαι ↱ οὐχὶ πρῶτον καθίσας
which *For* of you, wanting to build a tower, *to build* does not first sit down
5515 1142 1666 7007 2527 3868 3868 4788 3868 2767 4049 4754 2767
r.nsm cj p.g r.gp.2 pt.pa.nsm n.asm f.aa pl adv pt.aa.nsm

ψηφίζει τὴν δαπάνην, εἰ ἔχει εἰς ἀπαρτισμόν; 29 ⌊ἵνα
and calculate the cost, whether he has enough to bring it to completion; otherwise,
6028 3836 1252 1623 2400 1650 568 2671
v.pai.3s d.asf n.asf cj v.pai.3s p.a n.asm cj

μήποτε⌋ → θέντος αὐτοῦ θεμέλιον καὶ ↱ μὴ ἰσχύοντος ἐκτελέσαι
when he has laid *he* the foundation and is not able to complete the
3607 899 5502 899 2529 2779 2710 3590 2710 1754
pl pt.aa.gsm r.gsm.3 n.asm cj pl pt.pa.gsm f.aa

πάντες οἱ θεωροῦντες ἄρξωνται αὐτῷ ἐμπαίζειν 30 λέγοντες ὅτι
tower, all who see it will begin to ridicule him, *to ridicule* saying, ~
4246 3836 2555 806 1850 1850 899 1850 3306 4022
a.npm d.npm pt.pa.npm v.ams.3p r.dsm.3 f.pa pt.pa.npm cj

οὗτος ὁ ἄνθρωπος ἤρξατο οἰκοδομεῖν καὶ ↱ οὐκ ἴσχυσεν ἐκτελέσαι. 31 ἢ τίς
'This *{the}* man began to build and was not able to complete.' Or what
4047 3836 476 806 3868 2779 2710 4024 2710 1754 2445 5515
r.nsm d.nsm n.nsm v.ami.3s f.pa cj pl v.aai.3s f.aa cj r.nsm

NASB

blind and lame.'
[22]And the slave
said, 'Master, what
you commanded
has been done,
and still there is
room.' [23]And the
master said to the
slave, 'Go out into
the highways and
along the hedges,
and compel *them*
to come in, so that
my house may be
filled. [24]For I tell
you, none of those
men who were in-
vited shall taste of
my dinner.'"

Discipleship Tested

[25]Now large
crowds were going
along with Him;
and He turned and
said to them, [26]"If
anyone comes
to Me, and does
not [a]hate his own
father and mother
and wife and chil-
dren and brothers
and sisters, yes,
and even his own
life, he cannot
be My disciple.
[27]Whoever does
not carry his own
cross and come
after Me cannot be
My disciple. [28]For
which one of you,
when he wants to
build a tower, does
not first sit down
and calculate the
cost to see if he has
enough to complete
it? [29]Otherwise,
when he has laid a
foundation and is
not able to finish,
all who observe it
begin to ridicule
him, [30]saying, 'This
man began to build
and was not able to
finish.' [31]Or what

[a] I.e. by comparison of his love for Me

NIV

king is about to
go to war against
another king.
Won't he first sit
down and consider
whether he is able
with ten thousand
men to oppose
the one coming
against him with
twenty thousand?
32 If he is not able,
he will send a
delegation while
the other is still a
long way off and
will ask for terms
of peace. 33 In the
same way, those
of you who do not
give up everything
you have cannot be
my disciples.
34 "Salt is good,
but if it loses its
saltiness, how can
it be made salty
again? 35 It is fit
neither for the soil
nor for the manure
pile; it is thrown
out.
"Whoever has
ears to hear, let
them hear."

The Parable of the Lost Sheep

15 Now the
tax collec-
tors and sinners
were all gathering
around to hear
Jesus. 2 But the
Pharisees and the
teachers of the law
muttered, "This
man welcomes sin-
ners and eats with
them."
3 Then Jesus told
them this parable:
4 "Suppose one of
you has a hundred
sheep and loses
one of them.

βασιλεὺς πορευόμενος ἑτέρῳ βασιλεῖ συμβαλεῖν εἰς πόλεμον ↱ οὐχὶ
king, going out to encounter another king *to encounter* in war, will not
995 4513 5202 5202 2283 995 5202 1650 4483 2767 4049
n.nsm pt.pm.nsm r.dsm n.dsm f.aa p.a n.asm pl

καθίσας πρῶτον βουλεύσεται εἰ δυνατός ἐστιν ἐν δέκα
sit down first and deliberate whether he is able *he is* with ten
2767 4754 1086 1623 1639 1639 1543 1639 1877 1274
pt.aa.nsm adv v.fmi.3s cj a.nsm v.pai.3s p.d a.dpf

χιλιάσιν ὑπαντῆσαι τῷ μετὰ εἴκοσι χιλιάδων ἐρχομένῳ
⌞thousand troops⌟ to oppose the one coming against him with twenty thousand? *one coming*
5942 5636 3836 2262 2262 2093 899 3552 1633 5942 2262
n.dpf f.aa d.dsm p.g a.gpf n.gpf pt.pm.dsm

ἐπ᾽ αὐτόν; 32 εἰ δὲ μή γε, ἔτι αὐτοῦ πόρρω ὄντος
against him And if *And* not, ~ while he is yet *he* a ⌞great way off,⌟ *while is*
2093 899 1254 1623 1254 3590 1145 1639 899 1639 2285 899 4522 1639
p.a r.asm.3 cj cj pl pl adv r.gsm.3 adv pt.pa.gsm

πρεσβείαν ἀποστείλας ἐρωτᾷ τὰ πρὸς εἰρήνην. 33 οὕτως
he will send a delegation *he will send* and ask for terms of peace. ⌞In the same way,⌟
690 690 690 4561 690 2263 3836 4639 1645 4048
n.asf pt.aa.nsm v.pai.3s d.apn p.a n.asf adv

οὖν πᾶς ἐξ ὑμῶν ὃς ↱ οὐκ ἀποτάσσεται πᾶσιν τοῖς ἑαυτοῦ ὑπάρχουσιν
therefore, everyone of you who does not renounce all *{the}* his possessions
4036 4246 1666 7007 4005 698 4024 698 4246 3836 1571 5639
cj a.nsm p.g r.gp.2 r.nsm pl v.pmi.3s a.dpn d.dpn r.gsm.3 pt.pa.dpn

⌞οὐ δύναται⌟ εἶναί μου μαθητής. 34 καλὸν οὖν τὸ ἅλας· ἐὰν δὲ
cannot be my disciple. "Salt, then, is good; *then* *{the}* *Salt* but if *but*
4024 1538 1639 1609 3412 229 4036 2819 4036 3836 229 1254 1569 1254
pl v.ppi.3s f.pa r.gs.1 n.nsm a.nsn cj d.nsn n.nsn cj cj

καὶ τὸ ἅλας μωρανθῇ, ἐν τίνι ἀρτυθήσεται; 35 οὔτε εἰς γῆν οὔτε
{also} *{the}* salt ⌞has become insipid,⌟ with what shall it be seasoned? Neither for soil or
2779 3836 229 3701 1877 5515 789 4046 1650 1178 4046
adv d.nsn n.nsn v.aps.3s p.d r.dsn v.fpi.3s cj p.a n.asf cj

εἰς κοπρίαν εὔθετόν ἐστιν, ἔξω βάλλουσιν αὐτό.
for the dung-heap is it of any use; *is it* they throw it away. *they throw* *it*
1650 3161 1639 1639 2310 1639 965 965 899 2032 965 899
p.a n.asf a.nsn v.pai.3s adv v.pai.3p r.asn.3

ὁ ἔχων ὦτα ἀκούειν ἀκουέτω.
The ⌞one who has⌟ ears to hear, let him hear."
3836 2400 4044 201 201
d.nsm pt.pa.nsm n.apn f.pa v.pam.3s

15:1 ἦσαν δὲ αὐτῷ
Now all the tax collectors and the sinners used to *Now* come near him
1254 4246 3836 5467 5467 2779 3836 283 1639 1254 1581 1581 899
v.iai.3p cj r.dsm.3

ἐγγίζοντες πάντες οἱ τελῶναι καὶ οἱ ἁμαρτωλοὶ ἀκούειν αὐτοῦ. 2 καὶ
come near *all* *the* *tax collectors* *and* *the* *sinners* to listen to him. And the
1581 4246 3836 5467 2779 3836 283 201 899 2779 3836
pt.pa.npm a.npm d.npm n.npm cj d.npm a.npm f.pa r.gsm.3 cj

διεγόγγυζον οἵ τε Φαρισαῖοι καὶ οἱ γραμματεῖς
Pharisees and the scribes were grumbling, *the* ~ *Pharisees* *and* *the* *scribes*
5757 2779 3836 1208 1339 3836 5445 5757 2779 3836 1208
v.iai.3p d.npm cj n.npm cj d.npm n.npm

λέγοντες ὅτι οὗτος ἁμαρτωλοὺς προσδέχεται καὶ συνεσθίει αὐτοῖς.
saying, ~ "This fellow welcomes sinners *welcomes* and eats with them!"
3306 4022 4047 4657 283 4657 2779 5303 899
pt.pa.npm cj r.nsm a.apm v.pmi.3s cj v.pai.3s r.dpm.3

3 εἶπεν δὲ πρὸς αὐτοὺς τὴν παραβολὴν ταύτην λέγων, 4 τίς ἄνθρωπος
So he told *So* *{to}* them *{the}* this parable. *this* *{saying}* "Which man
1254 3306 1254 4639 899 3836 4047 4130 4047 3306 5515 476
v.aai.3s cj p.a r.apm.3 d.asf n.asf r.asf pt.pa.nsm r.nsm n.nsm

ἐξ ὑμῶν ἔχων ἑκατὸν πρόβατα καὶ ἀπολέσας ἐξ αὐτῶν ἓν ↱
among you, ⌞who has⌟ a hundred sheep, *{and}* should he lose one of them, *one* would
1666 7007 2400 1669 4585 2779 660 1651 1666 899 1651 2901
p.g r.gp.2 pt.pa.nsm a.apn n.apn cj pt.aa.nsm p.g r.gpn.3 a.asn

NASB

king, when he
sets out to meet
another king in
battle, will not
first sit down and
consider whether
he is strong enough
with ten thousand
men to encounter
the one coming
against him with
twenty thousand?
32 Or else, while
the other is still far
away, he sends a
delegation and asks
for terms of peace.
33 So then, none of
you can be My dis-
ciple who does not
give up all his own
possessions.
34 "Therefore, salt
is good; but if even
salt has become
tasteless, with what
will it be seasoned?
35 It is useless either
for the soil or for
the manure pile; it
is thrown out. He
who has ears to
hear, let him hear."

The Lost Sheep

15:1 Now all the tax
collectors and the
sinners were com-
ing near Him to lis-
ten to Him. 2 Both
the Pharisees and
the scribes *began*
to grumble, saying,
"This man receives
sinners and eats
with them."
3 So He told them
this parable, say-
ing, 4 "What man
among you, if
he has a hundred
sheep and has lost
one of them,

NIV

Doesn't he leave
the ninety-nine in
the open country
and go after the
lost sheep until
he finds it? [5]And
when he finds it,
he joyfully puts it
on his shoulders
[6]and goes home.
Then he calls his
friends and neigh-
bors together and
says, 'Rejoice with
me; I have found
my lost sheep.' [7]I
tell you that in the
same way there
will be more re-
joicing in heaven
over one sinner
who repents than
over ninety-nine
righteous persons
who do not need to
repent.

The Parable of the Lost Coin

[8]"Or suppose a
woman has ten
silver coins[a] and
loses one. Doesn't
she light a lamp,
sweep the house
and search careful-
ly until she finds
it? [9]And when she
finds it, she calls
her friends and
neighbors together
and says, 'Rejoice
with me; I have
found my lost
coin.' [10]In the same
way, I tell you,
there is rejoicing
in the presence of
the angels of God
over one sinner
who repents."

The Parable of the Lost Son

[11]Jesus continued:
"There was a man
who had two sons.
[12]The younger one
said to his father,
'Father, give me
my share of the
estate.' So he di-
vided his property
between them.
[13]"Not long after
that,

[a] 8 Greek *ten drachmas,* each worth about a day's wages

οὐ καταλείπει τὰ ⌞ἐνενήκοντα ἐννέα⌟ ἐν τῇ ἐρήμῳ καὶ πορεύεται ἐπὶ τὸ
not leave the ninety-nine in the open pasture and go after the
4024 2901 3836 1916 1933 1877 3836 2245 2779 4513 2093 3836
pl v.pai.3s d.apn a.apn a.apn p.d d.dsf n.dsf cj v.pmi.3s p.a d.asn

ἀπολωλὸς ἕως εὕρῃ αὐτό; [5]καὶ εὑρὼν ἐπιτίθησιν ἐπὶ τοὺς
one that is lost until he finds it? And ⌞when he finds⌟ it, ⌞would he not place⌟ it on *{the}* his
660 2401 2351 899 2779 2351 2202 2093 3836 899
pt.ra.asn cj v.aas.3s r.asn.3 cj pt.aa.nsm v.pai.3s p.a d.apm

ὤμους αὐτοῦ χαίρων [6]καὶ ἐλθὼν εἰς τὸν οἶκον → → συγκαλεῖ
shoulders, *his* rejoicing? And ⌞when he returns⌟ to his house, would he not call together
6049 899 5897 2779 2262 1650 3836 3875 5157
n.apm r.gsm.3 pt.pa.nsm cj pt.aa.nsm p.a d.asm n.asm v.pai.3s

τοὺς φίλους καὶ τοὺς γείτονας λέγων αὐτοῖς, συγχάρητέ μοι, ὅτι εὗρον
his friends and his neighbors, and say to them, 'Rejoice with me, for ⌞I have found⌟
3836 5813 2779 3836 1150 3306 899 5176 1609 4022 2351
d.apm n.apm cj d.apm n.apm pt.pa.nsm r.dpm.3 v.apm.2p r.ds.1 cj v.aai.1s

τὸ πρόβατόν μου τὸ ἀπολωλός. [7]λέγω ὑμῖν ὅτι οὕτως
{the} my sheep *my* that was lost'? I tell you, ~ ⌞in the same way⌟ there will be
3836 1609 4585 1609 3836 660 3306 7007 4022 4048 1639 1639 1639
d.asn n.asn r.gs.1 d.asn pt.ra.asn v.pai.1s r.dp.2 cj adv

χαρὰ ἐν τῷ οὐρανῷ ἔσται ἐπὶ ἑνὶ ἁμαρτωλῷ μετανοοῦντι ἢ ἐπὶ
more joy in *{the}* heaven *there will be* over one sinner who repents than over
5915 1877 3836 4041 1639 2093 1651 283 3566 2445 2093
n.nsf p.d d.dsm n.dsm v.fmi.3s p.d a.dsm a.dsm pt.pa.dsm pl p.d

⌞ἐνενήκοντα ἐννέα⌟ δικαίοις οἵτινες οὐ χρείαν ἔχουσιν μετανοίας.
ninety-nine righteous people who have no need *have* of repentance.
1916 1933 1465 4015 2400 4024 5970 2400 3567
a.dpm a.dpm a.dpm r.npm pl n.asf v.pai.3p n.gsf

[8]ἢ τίς γυνὴ δραχμὰς ἔχουσα δέκα ἐὰν ἀπολέσῃ δραχμὴν
"Or what woman, who has ten silver coins, *who has* *ten* should she lose one coin,
2445 5515 1222 2400 2400 1274 1534 2400 1274 1569 660 1651 1534
cj r.nsf n.nsf n.apf pt.pa.nsf a.apf cj v.aas.3s n.asf

μίαν, ↱ οὐχὶ ἅπτει λύχνον καὶ σαροῖ τὴν οἰκίαν καὶ ζητεῖ ἐπιμελῶς ⌞ἕως οὗ⌟
one would not light a lamp, *{and}* sweep the house, and search diligently until
1651 721 4049 721 3394 2779 4924 3836 3864 2779 2426 2151 2401 4005
a.asf pl v.pai.3s n.asm cj v.pai.3s d.asf n.asf cj v.pai.3s adv p.g r.gsm

εὕρῃ; [9]καὶ εὑροῦσα → → συγκαλεῖ τὰς φίλας καὶ γείτονας
she finds it? And ⌞when she finds⌟ it, would she not call together her friends and neighbors,
2351 2779 2351 5157 3836 5813 2779 1150
v.aas.3s cj pt.aa.nsf v.pai.3s d.apf n.apf cj n.apf

λέγουσα, συγχάρητέ μοι, ὅτι εὗρον τὴν δραχμὴν ἣν ἀπώλεσα. [10]οὕτως,
saying, 'Rejoice with me, for ⌞I have found⌟ the coin that I had lost'? Just so,
3306 5176 1609 4022 2351 3836 1534 4005 660 4048
pt.pa.nsf v.apm.2p r.ds.1 cj v.aai.1s d.asf n.asf r.asf v.aai.1s adv

λέγω ὑμῖν, γίνεται χαρὰ ἐνώπιον τῶν ἀγγέλων τοῦ θεοῦ ἐπὶ ἑνὶ ἁμαρτωλῷ
I tell you, there is joy before the angels of God over one sinner
3306 7007 1181 5915 1967 3836 34 3836 2536 2093 1651 283
v.pai.1s r.dp.2 v.pmi.3s n.nsf p.g d.gpm n.gpm d.gsm n.gsm p.d a.dsm a.dsm

μετανοοῦντι. [11]εἶπεν δέ, ἄνθρωπός τις εἶχεν δύο υἱούς. [12]καὶ
who repents." Then he said, *Then* "A certain man *certain* had two sons. *{and}*
3566 1254 3306 1254 5516 476 5516 2400 1545 5626 2779
pt.pa.dsm v.aai.3s cj n.nsm r.nsm v.iai.3s a.apm n.apm cj

εἶπεν ὁ νεώτερος αὐτῶν τῷ πατρί, πάτερ, δός μοι τὸ
The younger of them said *The* *younger* *of them* ⌞to the⌟ father, 'Father, give me the
3836 3742 899 899 3306 3836 3742 899 3836 4252 4252 1443 1609 3836
v.aai.3s d.nsm a.nsm.c r.gpm.3 d.dsm n.dsm n.vsm v.aam.2s r.ds.1 d.asn

ἐπιβάλλον μέρος τῆς οὐσίας. ὁ δὲ διεῖλεν
share of the property ⌞that will belong to me.'⌟ *share* *of the* *property* So he *So* divided
3538 3836 3836 4045 2095 3538 3836 4045 1254 3836 1254 1349
pt.pa.asn n.asn d.gsf n.gsf d.nsm cj v.aai.3s

← αὐτοῖς τὸν βίον. [13]καὶ μετ᾽ οὐ πολλὰς ἡμέρας
the estate between them. *the* *estate* *{and}* Not many days later, *Not* *many* *days* the
3836 1050 899 3836 1050 2779 4024 4498 2465 3552 4024 4498 2465 3836
r.dpm.3 d.asm n.asm cj p.a pl a.apf n.apf

NASB

does not leave the
ninety-nine in the
open pasture and
go after the one
which is lost until
he finds it? [5]When
he has found it,
he lays it on his
shoulders, rejoic-
ing. [6]And when
he comes home,
he calls together
his friends and his
neighbors, saying
to them, 'Rejoice
with me, for I have
found my sheep
which was lost!' [7]I
tell you that in the
same way, there
will be *more* joy in
heaven over one
sinner who repents
than over ninety-
nine righteous
persons who need
no repentance.

The Lost Coin

[8]"Or what woman,
if she has ten silver
coins and loses
one coin, does not
light a lamp and
sweep the house
and search care-
fully until she finds
it? [9]When she has
found it, she calls
together her friends
and neighbors,
saying, 'Rejoice
with me, for I have
found the coin
which I had lost!'
[10]In the same way,
I tell you, there is
joy in the presence
of the angels of
God over one sin-
ner who repents."

The Prodigal Son

[11]And He said, "A
man had two sons.
[12]The younger of
them said to his
father, 'Father, give
me the share of the
estate that falls to
me.' So he divided
his wealth between
them. [13]And not
many days later,

NIV

the younger son
got together all
he had, set off for
a distant country
and there squan-
dered his wealth in
wild living. 14 Af-
ter he had spent
everything, there
was a severe fam-
ine in that whole
country, and he be-
gan to be in need.
15 So he went and
hired himself out
to a citizen of that
country, who sent
him to his fields
to feed pigs. 16 He
longed to fill his
stomach with the
pods that the pigs
were eating, but no
one gave him any-
thing.
17 "When he came
to his senses, he
said, 'How many
of my father's
hired servants
have food to spare,
and here I am
starving to death!
18 I will set out
and go back to my
father and say to
him: Father, I have
sinned against
heaven and against
you. 19 I am no lon-
ger worthy to be
called your son;
make me like one
of your hired ser-
vants.' 20 So he got
up and went to his
father.
"But while he
was still a long
way off, his father
saw him and was
filled with com-
passion for him;
he ran to his son,
threw his arms
around him and
kissed him.
21 "The son said
to him,

συναγαγὼν πάντα ὁ νεώτερος υἱὸς ἀπεδήμησεν εἰς
younger son gathered up everything *the* *younger* *son* and left for a journey to a distant
3742 5626 5251 4246 3836 3742 5626 623 1650 3431
pt.aa.nsm a.apn d.nsm a.nsm.c n.nsm v.aai.3s p.a

χώραν μακρὰν καὶ ἐκεῖ διεσκόρπισεν τὴν οὐσίαν αὐτοῦ ζῶν ἀσώτως.
country, *distant* and there he squandered *{the}* his property *his* by living recklessly.
6001 3431 2779 1695 1399 3836 899 4045 899 2409 862
n.asf a.asf cj adv v.aai.3s d.asf n.asf r.gsm.3 pt.pa.nsm adv

14 → δαπανήσαντος δὲ αὐτοῦ πάντα ἐγένετο λιμὸς ἰσχυρὰ κατὰ
When he had spent *{and}* *he* everything, there was a severe famine *severe* in
899 1251 1254 899 4246 1181 2708 3350 2708 2848
pt.aa.gsm cj r.gsm.3 a.apn v.ami.3s n.nsf a.nsf p.a

τὴν χώραν ἐκείνην, καὶ αὐτὸς ἤρξατο ὑστερεῖσθαι. 15 καὶ ↱ πορευθεὶς
{the} that country, *that* and he began to be in need. So he went and
3836 1697 6001 1697 2779 899 806 5728 2779 3140 4513
d.asf n.asf r.asf cj r.nsm v.ami.3s f.pp cj pt.ap.nsm

ἐκολλήθη ἑνὶ τῶν πολιτῶν τῆς χώρας ἐκείνης, καὶ ἔπεμψεν αὐτὸν εἰς
˻hired himself out˼ to one of the citizens of that country, *that* and he sent him into
3140 1651 3836 4489 3836 1697 6001 1697 2779 4287 899 1650
v.api.3s a.dsm d.gpm n.gpm d.gsf n.gsf r.gsf cj v.aai.3s r.asm.3 p.a

τοὺς ἀγροὺς αὐτοῦ βόσκειν χοίρους, 16 καὶ ἐπεθύμει χορτασθῆναι[a] ἐκ τῶν
{the} his fields *his* to feed pigs. *{and}* He longed to be fed with the
3836 899 69 899 1081 5956 2779 2121 5963 1666 3836
d.apm n.apm r.gsm.3 f.pa n.apm cj v.iai.3s f.ap p.g d.gpn

κερατίων ὧν ἤσθιον οἱ χοῖροι, καὶ οὐδεὶς ἐδίδου αὐτῷ.
pods that the pigs were eating, *the* *pigs* but no one would give him anything.
3044 4005 3836 5956 2266 3836 5956 2779 4029 1443 899
n.gpn r.gpn v.iai.3p d.npm n.npm cj a.nsm v.iai.3s r.dsm.3

17 εἰς ἑαυτὸν δὲ ἐλθὼν ἔφη, πόσοι μίσθιοι τοῦ
"Coming to himself, *{and}* *Coming* he said, 'How many of my father's hired servants *of*
2262 1650 1571 1254 2262 5774 4531 3836 1609 4252 3634 3836
p.a r.asm.3 cj pt.aa.nsm v.iai.3s r.npm n.npm d.gsm

πατρός μου περισσεύονται ἄρτων, ἐγὼ δὲ λιμῷ ὧδε
father's *my* have more than enough bread, but here I *but* am, dying ˻from hunger!˼ *here*
4252 1609 4355 788 1254 6045 1609 1254 660 660 3350 6045
n.gsm r.gs.1 v.pmi.3p n.gpm r.ns.1 cj n.dsf adv

ἀπόλλυμαι. 18 ↱ ↱ ἀναστὰς πορεύσομαι πρὸς τὸν πατέρα μου
am dying I will leave this place and go to *{the}* my father, *my*
660 4513 4513 482 4513 4639 3836 1609 4252 1609
v.pmi.1s pt.aa.nsm v.fmi.1s p.a d.asm n.asm r.gs.1

καὶ ἐρῶ αὐτῷ, πάτερ, ἥμαρτον εἰς τὸν οὐρανὸν καὶ ἐνώπιόν σου, 19
and ˻I will say˼ to him, 'Father, I have sinned against *{the}* heaven and before you; I
2779 3306 899 4252 279 1650 3836 4041 2779 1967 5148 1639
cj v.fai.1s r.dsm.3 n.vsm v.aai.1s p.a d.asm n.asm cj p.g r.gs.2

οὐκέτι εἰμὶ ἄξιος κληθῆναι υἱός σου· ποίησόν με ↰ ὡς ἕνα τῶν
am no longer *I am* worthy to be called your son. *your* Take me on as one of your
1639 4033 1639 545 2813 5148 5626 5148 4472 1609 4472 6055 1651 3836 5148
adv v.pai.1s a.nsm f.ap n.nsm r.gs.2 v.aam.2s r.as.1 pl a.asm d.gpm

μισθίων σου. 20 καὶ ↱ ἀναστὰς ἦλθεν πρὸς τὸν πατέρα
hired servants.' *your* So he left that place and went to *{the}* his father.
3634 5148 2779 2262 482 2262 4639 3836 1571 4252
n.gpm r.gs.2 cj pt.aa.nsm v.aai.3s p.a d.asm n.asm

ἑαυτοῦ. ἔτι δὲ αὐτοῦ μακρὰν ἀπέχοντος εἶδεν
his While he was still *{and}* *he* a long way *While was from* from home, his father saw
1571 600 899 600 2285 1254 899 3426 600 600 899 4252 1625
r.gsm.3 adv cj r.gsm.3 adv pt.pa.gsm v.aai.3s

αὐτὸν ὁ πατὴρ αὐτοῦ καὶ ἐσπλαγχνίσθη καὶ ↱ δραμὼν ἐπέπεσεν
him *{the}* *father* *his* and was filled with compassion; *{and}* he ran and fell
899 3836 4252 899 2779 5072 2779 2158 5556 2158
r.asm.3 d.nsm n.nsm r.gsm.3 cj v.api.3s cj pt.aa.nsm v.aai.3s

ἐπὶ τὸν τράχηλον αὐτοῦ καὶ κατεφίλησεν αὐτόν. 21 εἶπεν δὲ ὁ
upon *{the}* his neck *his* and kissed him. And the son said *And* *the*
2093 3836 899 5549 899 2779 2968 899 1254 3836 5626 3306 1254 3836
p.a d.asm n.asm r.gsm.3 cj v.aai.3s r.asm.3 v.aai.3s cj d.nsm

NASB

the younger son
gathered every-
thing together and
went on a journey
into a distant
country, and there
he squandered his
estate with loose
living. 14 Now when
he had spent ev-
erything, a severe
famine occurred
in that country,
and he began to be
impoverished. 15 So
he went and hired
himself out to one
of the citizens of
that country, and
he sent him into
his fields to feed
swine. 16 And he
would have gladly
filled his stomach
with the pods that
the swine were
eating, and no one
was giving *any-
thing* to him. 17 But
when he came to
his senses, he said,
'How many of my
father's hired men
have more than
enough bread, but I
am dying here with
hunger! 18 I will get
up and go to my
father, and will say
to him, "Father, I
have sinned against
heaven, and in your
sight; 19 I am no
longer worthy to
be called your son;
make me as one of
your hired men."'
20 So he got up and
came to his father.
But while he was
still a long way off,
his father saw him
and felt compas-
sion *for him,* and
ran and embraced
him and kissed
him. 21 And the son
said to him,

[a] χορτασθῆναι UBS, NET. χορτασθῆναι TNIV.

NIV

'Father, I have
sinned against
heaven and against
you. I am no lon-
ger worthy to be
called your son.'
22 "But the fa-
ther said to his
servants, 'Quick!
Bring the best robe
and put it on him.
Put a ring on his
finger and sandals
on his feet. 23 Bring
the fattened calf
and kill it. Let's
have a feast and
celebrate. 24 For
this son of mine
was dead and is
alive again; he was
lost and is found.'
So they began to
celebrate.
25 "Meanwhile,
the older son was
in the field. When
he came near the
house, he heard
music and danc-
ing. 26 So he called
one of the servants
and asked him
what was going on.
27 'Your brother has
come,' he replied,
'and your father
has killed the fat-
tened calf because
he has him back
safe and sound.'
28 "The older
brother became
angry and refused
to go in. So his fa-
ther went out and
pleaded with him.
29 But he answered
his father, 'Look!
All these years
I've been slaving
for you and

υἱός αὐτῷ, πάτερ, ἥμαρτον εἰς τὸν οὐρανὸν καὶ ἐνώπιόν σου, οὐκέτι
son to him, 'Father, I have sinned against *{the}* heaven and before you. I am no longer
5626 899 4252 279 1650 3836 4041 2779 1967 5148 1639 1639 4033
n.nsm r.dsm.3 n.vsm v.aai.1s p.a d.asm n.asm cj p.g r.gs.2 adv

εἰμὶ ἄξιος κληθῆναι υἱός σου. 22 εἶπεν δὲ ὁ πατὴρ πρὸς
I am worthy to be called your son.' *your* But the father said *But the father* to
1639 545 2813 5148 5626 5148 1254 3836 4252 3306 1254 3836 4252 4639
v.pai.1s a.nsm f.ap n.nsm r.gs.2 v.aai.3s cj d.nsm n.nsm p.a

τοὺς δούλους αὐτοῦ, ταχὺ ἐξενέγκατε στολὴν τὴν πρώτην καὶ
{the} his servants, *his* 'Quickly bring out a robe — the best one — and
3836 899 1529 899 5444 1766 5124 3836 4755 2779
d.apm n.apm r.gsm.3 adv v.aam.2p n.asf d.asf a.asf cj

ἐνδύσατε ← αὐτόν, καὶ δότε δακτύλιον εἰς τὴν χεῖρα αὐτοῦ καὶ
put it on him, and give him a ring for *{the}* his finger, *his* and
1907 899 2779 1443 1234 1650 3836 899 5931 899 2779
v.aam.2p r.asm.3 cj v.aam.2p n.asm p.a d.asf n.asf r.gsm.3 cj

ὑποδήματα εἰς τοὺς πόδας, 23 καὶ φέρετε τὸν μόσχον τὸν σιτευτόν,
sandals for his feet. *{and}* Bring the fattened calf *{the} fattened* and
5687 1650 3836 4546 2779 5770 3836 4988 3675 3836 4988
n.apn p.a d.apm n.apm cj v.pam.2p d.asm n.asm d.asm a.asm

θύσατε, καὶ ↱ ↱ φαγόντες εὐφρανθῶμεν, 24 ὅτι οὗτος ὁ υἱός
⌊make the kill!⌋ *{and}* Let us eat and celebrate; for this, *{the}* my son,
2604 2779 2370 2370 2266 2370 4022 4047 3836 1609 5626
v.aam.2p cj pt.aa.npm v.aps.1p cj r.nsm d.nsm n.nsm

μου νεκρὸς ἦν καὶ ἀνέζησεν, ἦν ἀπολωλὼς καὶ
my was dead, *was* and ⌊has come back to life again;⌋ ⌊he was⌋ lost, and
1609 1639 3738 1639 2779 348 1639 660 2779
r.gs.1 a.nsm v.iai.3s cj v.aai.3s v.iai.3s pt.ra.nsm cj

εὑρέθη. καὶ ἤρξαντο εὐφραίνεσθαι. 25 ἦν δὲ
⌊has been found.'⌋ So they began to celebrate. "Meanwhile his older son was *Meanwhile*
2351 2779 806 2370 1254 899 4565 5626 1639 1254
v.api.3s cj v.ami.3p f.pp v.iai.3s cj

ὁ υἱὸς αὐτοῦ ὁ πρεσβύτερος ἐν ἀγρῷ· καὶ ὡς ↱ ἐρχόμενος ἤγγισεν
{the} son his {the} older in the field, and as he came and drew near
3836 5626 899 3836 4565 1877 69 2779 6055 1581 2262 1581
d.nsm n.nsm r.gsm.3 d.nsm a.nsm p.d n.dsm cj cj pt.pm.nsm v.aai.3s

τῇ οἰκίᾳ, ἤκουσεν συμφωνίας καὶ χορῶν, 26 καὶ προσκαλεσάμενος ἕνα τῶν
⌊to the⌋ house, he heard music and dancing. So calling one of his
3836 3864 201 5246 2779 5962 2779 4673 1651 3836
d.dsf n.dsf v.aai.3s n.gsf cj n.gpm cj pt.am.nsm a.asm d.gpm

παίδων ἐπυνθάνετο τί ⌊ἂν εἴη⌋ ταῦτα. 27 ὁ δὲ εἶπεν αὐτῷ
servants, he asked what this might be. *this* The *{and}* servant said to him,
4090 4785 5515 4047 323 1639 4047 3836 1254 3306 899
n.gpm v.imi.3s r.nsn pl v.pao.3s r.npn d.nsm cj v.aai.3s r.dsm.3

ὅτι ὁ ἀδελφός σου ἥκει, καὶ ἔθυσεν ὁ πατήρ σου τὸν
~ *{the}* 'Your brother *You* has come, and your father has killed *{the} father your* the
4022 3836 5148 81 5148 2457 2779 5148 4252 2604 3836 4252 5148 3836
cj d.nsm n.nsm r.gs.2 v.rai.3s cj v.aai.3s d.nsm n.nsm r.gs.2 d.asm

μόσχον τὸν σιτευτόν, ὅτι ὑγιαίνοντα αὐτὸν
fattened calf, *{the} fattened* because he received him back safe and sound.' *him*
4988 3675 3836 4988 4022 655 655 899 655 5617 899
n.asm d.asm a.asm cj pt.pa.asm r.asm.3

ἀπέλαβεν. 28 ὠργίσθη δὲ καὶ ⌊οὐκ ἤθελεν⌋ εἰσελθεῖν, ὁ
he received back But the older son became angry *But* and refused to go in. *{the}*
655 1254 3974 1254 2779 4024 2527 1656 3836
v.aai.3s v.api.3s cj cj pl v.iai.3s f.aa d.nsm

δὲ πατὴρ αὐτοῦ ἐξελθὼν παρεκάλει αὐτόν. 29 ὁ δὲ
{and} His father *His* came out and ⌊began to appeal to⌋ him, but he *but*
1254 899 4252 899 2002 4151 899 1254 3836 1254
cj n.nsm r.gsm.3 pt.aa.nsm v.iai.3s r.asm.3 d.nsm cj

⌊ἀποκριθεὶς εἶπεν⌋ τῷ πατρὶ αὐτοῦ, ἰδοὺ τοσαῦτα ἔτη δουλεύω σοι καὶ
answered *{the}* his father, *his* 'Look, these many years I have served you, and
646 3306 3836 899 4252 899 2627 5537 2291 1526 5148 2779
pt.ap.nsm v.aai.3s d.dsm n.dsm r.gsm.3 j r.apn n.apn v.pai.1s r.ds.2 cj

NASB

'Father, I have
sinned against
heaven and in your
sight; I am no lon-
ger worthy to be
called your son.'
22 But the father
said to his slaves,
'Quickly bring out
the best robe and
put it on him, and
put a ring on his
hand and sandals
on his feet; 23 and
bring the fattened
calf, kill it, and let
us eat and cele-
brate; 24 for this son
of mine was dead
and has come to
life again; he was
lost and has been
found.' And they
began to celebrate.
25 "Now his older
son was in the
field, and when
he came and ap-
proached the
house, he heard
music and danc-
ing. 26 And he
summoned one of
the servants and
began inquiring
what these things
could be. 27 And he
said to him, 'Your
brother has come,
and your father has
killed the fattened
calf because he has
received him back
safe and sound.'
28 But he became
angry and was not
willing to go in;
and his father came
out and *began*
pleading with him.
29 But he answered
and said to his fa-
ther, 'Look! For so
many years I have
been serving you

NIV

never disobeyed
your orders. Yet
you never gave
me even a young
goat so I could
celebrate with
my friends. 30But
when this son of
yours who has
squandered your
property with
prostitutes comes
home, you kill the
fattened calf for
him!'
31"'My son,' the
father said, 'you
are always with
me, and every-
thing I have is
yours. 32But we
had to celebrate
and be glad, be-
cause this brother
of yours was dead
and is alive again;
he was lost and is
found.'"

The Parable of the Shrewd Manager

16 Jesus told
his disci-
ples: "There was
a rich man whose
manager was ac-
cused of wasting
his possessions.
2So he called him
in and asked him,
'What is this I hear
about you? Give
an account of your
management, be-
cause you cannot
be manager any
longer.'
3"The manager
said to himself,
'What shall I do
now? My master
is taking away my
job. I'm not strong
enough to dig, and
I'm ashamed to
beg—

οὐδέποτε ἐντολήν σου παρῆλθον, καὶ ἐμοὶ οὐδέποτε
I never disregarded a command of yours, *I disregarded* yet you never gave me *never*
4216 4030 4216 1953 5148 4216 2779 1443 4030 1443 1609 4030
adv n.asf r.gs.2 v.aai.1s cj r.ds.1 adv

ἔδωκας ἔριφον ἵνα μετὰ τῶν φίλων μου εὐφρανθῶ·
you gave a young goat, that I might celebrate with *{the}* my friends. *my* *I might celebrate*
1443 2253 2671 2370 2370 2370 3552 3836 1609 5813 1609 2370
v.aai.2s n.asm cj p.g d.gpm n.gpm r.gs.1 v.aps.1s

30 ὅτε δὲ ὁ υἱός σου οὗτος ὁ καταφαγών σου τὸν βίον
But when *But* *{the}* this son of yours *this* came, who has consumed your *{the}* estate
1254 4021 1254 3836 4047 5626 5148 4047 2262 3836 2983 5148 3836 1050
cj cj d.nsm n.nsm r.gs.2 r.nsm d.nsm pt.aa.nsm r.gs.2 d.asm n.asm

μετὰ πορνῶν ἦλθεν, ἔθυσας αὐτῷ τὸν σιτευτὸν μόσχον. 31
with prostitutes, *came* you killed the fattened calf for him!' *the* *fattened* *calf* Then
3552 4520 2262 2604 3836 4988 3675 899 3836 4988 3675 1254
p.g n.gpf v.aai.3s v.aai.2s r.dsm.3 d.asm a.asm n.asm

ὁ δὲ εἶπεν αὐτῷ, τέκνον, σὺ πάντοτε μετ' ἐμοῦ εἶ, καὶ πάντα
the *Then* father said to him, 'Son, you are always with me, *are* and everything
3836 1254 3306 899 5451 5148 1639 4121 3552 1609 1639 2779 4246
d.nsm cj v.aai.3s r.dsm.3 n.vsn r.ns.2 adv p.g r.gs.1 v.pai.2s cj a.npn

τὰ ἐμὰ σά ἐστιν· 32 εὐφρανθῆναι δὲ καὶ χαρῆναι ἔδει, ὅτι
{the} I have is yours. *is* We had to celebrate *{and}* and rejoice, *We had* because
3836 1847 1639 5050 1639 1256 1256 2370 1254 2779 5897 1256 4022
d.npn r.npn.1 r.npn.2 v.pai.3s f.ap cj cj f.ap v.iai.3s cj

ὁ ἀδελφός σου οὗτος νεκρὸς ἦν καὶ ἔζησεν, καὶ ↱
{the} this brother of yours, *this* was dead *was* and ⌞has come alive;⌟ *{and}* he
3836 4047 81 5148 4047 1639 3738 1639 2779 2409 2779 2351
d.nsm n.nsm r.gs.2 r.nsm a.nsm v.iai.3s cj v.aai.3s cj

ἀπολωλὼς καὶ εὑρέθη.
was lost and ⌞has been found.'"⌟
660 2779 2351
pt.ra.nsm cj v.api.3s

16:1 ἔλεγεν δὲ καὶ πρὸς τοὺς μαθητάς,
Then Jesus also said *Then* *also* to his disciples, "There was a rich
1254 2779 3306 1254 2779 4639 3836 3412 1639 1639 5516 4454
v.iai.3s cj adv p.a d.apm n.apm

ἄνθρωπός τις ἦν πλούσιος ὃς εἶχεν οἰκονόμον, καὶ
man *a* *There was* *rich* who had a manager, and charges were brought to
476 5516 1639 4454 4005 2400 3874 2779 1330 1330 1330 899
n.nsm r.nsm v.iai.3s a.nsm r.nsm v.iai.3s n.asm cj

οὗτος διεβλήθη αὐτῷ ὡς διασκορπίζων τὰ ὑπάρχοντα αὐτοῦ.
him that this man *charges were brought* *to him* *that* was wasting *{the}* his assets. *his*
899 6055 4047 1330 899 6055 1399 3836 899 5639 899
r.nsm v.api.3s r.dsm.3 pl pt.pa.nsm d.apn pt.pa.apn r.gsm.3

2 καὶ ↱ φωνήσας αὐτὸν εἶπεν αὐτῷ, τί τοῦτο ἀκούω περὶ σοῦ; ἀπόδος
So he called him in and said to him, 'What is this I hear about you? Hand over
2779 3306 5888 899 3306 899 5515 4047 201 4309 5148 625
cj pt.aa.nsm r.asm.3 v.aai.3s r.dsm.3 r.nsn r.nsn v.pai.1s p.g r.gs.2 v.aam.2s

τὸν λόγον τῆς οἰκονομίας σου, ↱ οὐ γὰρ δύνῃ
the account of your stewardship, *your* because you cannot *because* be my manager
3836 3364 3836 5148 3873 5148 1142 1538 4024 1142 1538 3872
d.asm n.asm d.gsf n.gsf r.gs.2 pl cj v.ppi.2s

ἔτι οἰκονομεῖν. 3 εἶπεν δὲ ἐν ἑαυτῷ ὁ οἰκονόμος, τί
⌞any longer.'⌟ *manager* And the manager said *And* to himself, *the* *manager* 'What
2285 3872 1254 3836 3874 3306 1254 1877 1571 3836 3874 5515
adv f.pa v.aai.3s cj p.d r.dsm.3 d.nsm n.nsm r.asn

ποιήσω, ὅτι ὁ κύριός μου ἀφαιρεῖται τὴν οἰκονομίαν ↰ ἀπ' ἐμοῦ;
shall I do, since *{the}* my master *my* is taking the management away from me? I
4472 4022 3836 1609 3261 1609 904 3836 3873 904 608 1609 2710
v.aas.1s cj d.nsm n.nsm r.gs.1 v.pmi.3s d.asf n.asf p.g r.gs.1

σκάπτειν οὐκ ἰσχύω, ἐπαιτεῖν
am not strong enough to dig, *not* *I am strong enough* and I am ashamed to beg.
2710 4024 2710 2710 4999 4024 2710 159 159 159 2050
f.pa pl v.pai.1s f.pa

NASB

and I have never
neglected a com-
mand of yours;
and *yet* you have
never given me a
young goat, so that
I might celebrate
with my friends;
30but when this son
of yours came,
who has devoured
your wealth with
prostitutes, you
killed the fattened
calf for him.' 31And
he said to him,
'Son, you have
always been with
me, and all that is
mine is yours. 32But
we had to celebrate
and rejoice, for this
brother of yours
was dead and *has*
begun to live, and
was lost and has
been found.'"

The Unrighteous Steward

16:1Now He was
also saying to the
disciples, "There
was a rich man
who had a man-
ager, and this *man-*
ager was reported
to him as squander-
ing his possessions.
2And he called him
and said to him,
'What is this I hear
about you? Give an
accounting of your
management, for
you can no longer
be manager.' 3The
manager said to
himself, 'What
shall I do, since my
master is taking the
management away
from me? I am not
strong enough to
dig; I am ashamed
to beg.

NIV

4I know what I'll
do so that, when I
lose my job here,
people will wel-
come me into their
houses.'
5"So he called
in each one of his
master's debtors.
He asked the first,
'How much do you
owe my master?'
6" 'Nine hundred
gallons[a] of olive
oil,' he replied.
"The manager
told him, 'Take
your bill, sit down
quickly, and make
it four hundred and
fifty.'
7"Then he asked
the second, 'And
how much do you
owe?'
" 'A thousand
bushels[b] of wheat,'
he replied.
"He told him,
'Take your bill and
make it eight hun-
dred.'
8"The master
commended the
dishonest manag-
er because he had
acted shrewdly.
For the people
of this world are
more shrewd in
dealing with their
own kind than are
the people of the
light. 9I tell you,
use worldly wealth
to gain friends for
yourselves, so that
when it is gone,
you will be wel-
comed into eternal
dwellings.
10"Whoever can
be trusted with
very little can also
be trusted with
much, and who-
ever is dishonest
with very little
will also be dis-
honest with much.
11So if you have
not been trustwor-
thy in handling
worldly wealth,

[a] 6 Or about 3,000 liters
[b] 7 Or about 30 tons

αἰσχύνομαι. 4ἔγνων τί ποιήσω, ἵνα ὅταν μετασταθῶ ἐκ τῆς οἰκονομίας
I am ashamed I know what to do, so that when I am removed from *{the}* management, people
159 1182 5515 4472 2671 4020 3496 1666 3836 3873
v.pmi.1s v.aai.1s r.asn v.aas.1s cj cj v.aps.1s p.g d.gsf n.gsf

δέξωνταί με εἰς τοὺς οἴκους αὐτῶν. 5καὶ προσκαλεσάμενος ἕνα
will welcome me into *{the}* their homes.' *their* *{and}* Calling each one
1312 1609 1650 3836 899 3875 899 2779 4673 1667 1651
v.ams.3p r.as.1 p.a d.apm n.apm r.gpm.3 cj pt.am.nsm a.asm

ἕκαστον τῶν χρεοφειλετῶν τοῦ κυρίου ἑαυτοῦ ἔλεγεν τῷ πρώτῳ,
each of his master's debtors, *{the}* *master's* *his* he said ⌞to the⌟ first,
1667 3836 1571 3261 5971 3836 3261 1571 3306 3836 4755
r.asm d.gpm n.gpm d.gsm n.gsm r.gsm.3 v.iai.3s d.dsm a.dsm

πόσον ὀφείλεις τῷ κυρίῳ μου; 6ὁ δὲ εἶπεν, ἑκατὸν βάτους
'How much do you owe *{the}* my master?' *my* He *{and}* said, 'A hundred measures
4531 4053 3836 1609 3261 1609 3836 1254 3306 1669 1003
r.asn v.pai.2s d.dsm n.dsm r.gs.1 d.nsm cj v.aai.3s a.apm n.apm

ἐλαίου. ὁ δὲ εἶπεν αὐτῷ, δέξαι σου τὰ γράμματα καὶ καθίσας ταχέως
of oil.' So he *So* told him, 'Take your *{the}* contract, *{and}* sit down quickly, and
1778 1254 3836 1254 3306 899 1312 5148 3836 1207 2779 2767 5441
n.gsn d.nsm cj v.aai.3s r.dsm.3 v.amm.2s r.gs.2 d.apn n.apn cj pt.aa.nsm adv

γράψον πεντήκοντα. 7ἔπειτα ἑτέρῳ εἶπεν, ↱ σὺ δὲ
write fifty.' Then he said to another, *he said* 'And how much do you *And*
1211 4299 2083 3306 3306 2283 3306 1254 4531 4531 4053 5148 1254
v.aam.2s a.apm adv r.dsm v.aai.3s r.ns.2 cj

πόσον ὀφείλεις; ὁ δὲ εἶπεν, ἑκατὸν κόρους σίτου. λέγει αὐτῷ, δέξαι
how much owe?' He *{and}* answered, 'A hundred measures of wheat.' He said to him, 'Take
4531 4053 3836 1254 3306 1669 3174 4992 3306 899 1312
r.asn v.pai.2s d.nsm cj v.aai.3s a.apm n.apm n.gsm v.pai.3s r.dsm.3 v.amm.2s

σου τὰ γράμματα καὶ γράψον ὀγδοήκοντα. 8καὶ ἐπῄνεσεν ὁ κύριος
your *{the}* contract, and write eighty.' *{and}* The master commended *The* *master*
5148 3836 1207 2779 1211 3837 2779 3836 3261 2046 3836 3261
r.gs.2 d.apn n.apn cj v.aam.2s a.apm cj v.aai.3s d.nsm n.nsm

τὸν οἰκονόμον τῆς ἀδικίας ὅτι φρονίμως ἐποίησεν· ὅτι οἱ
the dishonest manager *{the}* *dishonest* because he acted shrewdly. *he acted* For the
3836 94 3874 3836 94 4022 4472 4472 5862 4472 4022 3836
d.asm n.asm d.gsf n.gsf cj adv v.aai.3s cj d.npm

υἱοὶ τοῦ αἰῶνος τούτου φρονιμώτεροι ὑπὲρ
sons of this world *this* are ⌞more shrewd in dealing⌟ with their own generation than
5626 3836 4047 172 4047 1639 5861 1650 1571 1571 1155 5642
n.npm d.gsm n.gsm r.gsm a.npm.c p.a

τοὺς υἱοὺς τοῦ φωτὸς εἰς τὴν γενεὰν τὴν ἑαυτῶν εἰσιν. 9καὶ ἐγὼ ὑμῖν
the sons of light. *with* *{the}* *generation* *{the}* *their own* *are* And I say to you,
3836 5626 3836 5890 1650 3836 1155 3836 1571 1639 2779 1609 3306 7007
d.apm n.apm d.gsn n.gsn p.a d.asf n.asf d.asf r.gpm.3 v.pai.3p cj r.ns.1 r.dp.2

λέγω, ἑαυτοῖς ποιήσατε φίλους ἐκ τοῦ μαμωνᾶ τῆς
say make friends for yourselves *make* *friends* ⌞by means of⌟ the wealth of
3306 4472 5813 1571 4472 5813 1666 3836 3440 3836
v.pai.1s r.dpm.2 v.aam.2p n.apm p.g d.gsm n.gsm d.gsf

ἀδικίας, ἵνα ὅταν ἐκλίπῃ δέξωνται ὑμᾶς εἰς τὰς αἰωνίους σκηνάς.
unrighteousness, so that when it fails they may receive you into the eternal homes.
94 2671 4020 1722 1312 7007 1650 3836 173 5008
n.gsf cj cj v.aas.3s v.ams.3p r.ap.2 p.a d.apf a.apf n.apf

10ὁ πιστὸς ἐν ἐλαχίστῳ καὶ ἐν πολλῷ
"The one who is faithful in the smallest thing is also faithful in ⌞something great;⌟
3836 4412 1877 1788 1639 2779 4412 1877 4498
d.nsm a.nsm p.d a.dsn.s adv p.d a.dsn

πιστός ἐστιν, καὶ ὁ ἐν ἐλαχίστῳ ἄδικος καὶ
faithful *is* and the one who is dishonest in the smallest thing *dishonest* is also dishonest
4412 1639 2779 3836 96 1877 1788 96 1639 2779 96
a.nsm v.pai.3s cj d.nsm p.d a.dsn.s a.nsm adv

ἐν πολλῷ ἄδικός ἐστιν. 11 εἰ οὖν ἐν τῷ ἀδίκῳ μαμωνᾷ
in ⌞something great.⌟ *dishonest* *is* Therefore if *Therefore* in *{the}* unrighteous wealth
1877 4498 96 1639 4036 1623 4036 1877 3836 96 3440
p.d a.dsn a.nsm v.pai.3s cj cj p.d d.dsm a.dsm n.dsm

NASB

4I know what
I shall do, so
that when I am
removed from
the management
people will wel-
come me into their
homes.' 5And he
summoned each
one of his master's
debtors, and he
began saying to the
first, 'How much
do you owe my
master?' 6And he
said, 'A hundred
measures of oil.'
And he said to
him, 'Take your
bill, and sit down
quickly and write
fifty.' 7Then he said
to another, 'And
how much do you
owe?' And he said,
'A hundred mea-
sures of wheat.'
He *said to him,
'Take your bill, and
write eighty.' 8And
his master praised
the unrighteous
manager because
he had acted
shrewdly; for the
sons of this age
are more shrewd
in relation to their
own kind than the
sons of light. 9And
I say to you, make
friends for your-
selves by means
of the [a]wealth of
unrighteousness, so
that when it fails,
they will receive
you into the eternal
dwellings.
10"He who is
faithful in a very
little thing is faith-
ful also in much;
and he who is
unrighteous in a
very little thing is
unrighteous also in
much. 11Therefore
if you have not

[a] Gr *mamonas,* for Aram *mamon* (mammon); i.e. wealth, etc., personified as an object of worship

NIV

who will trust you
with true riches?
12And if you have
not been trustwor-
thy with someone
else's property,
who will give you
property of your
own?
13"No one can
serve two masters.
Either you will
hate the one and
love the other, or
you will be devot-
ed to the one and
despise the other.
You cannot serve
both God and
money."
14The Pharisees,
who loved money,
heard all this and
were sneering at
Jesus. 15He said to
them, "You are the
ones who justify
yourselves in the
eyes of others, but
God knows your
hearts. What peo-
ple value highly is
detestable in God's
sight.

Additional Teachings

16"The Law and
the Prophets were
proclaimed until
John. Since that
time, the good
news of the king-
dom of God is be-
ing preached, and
everyone is forcing
their way into it.
17It is easier for
heaven and earth
to disappear than
for the least stroke
of a pen to drop
out of the Law.
18"Anyone who
divorces his wife
and marries anoth-
er woman commits
adultery,

πιστοὶ οὐκ ἐγένεσθε, τὸ
you have not been faithful, *not* *you have been* who will entrust to you ⌊that which⌋ is
1181 1181 4024 1181 4412 4024 1181 5515 4409 4409 7007 7007 3836
a.npm pl v.ami.2p d.asn

ἀληθινὸν τίς ὑμῖν πιστεύσει; 12 καὶ εἰ ἐν τῷ
of true value? *who* *to you* *will entrust* And if you have not been faithful in what belongs
240 5515 7007 4409 2779 1623 1181 1181 4024 1181 4412 1877 3836
a.asn r.nsm r.dp.2 v.fai.3s cj cj p.d d.dsn

ἀλλοτρίῳ πιστοὶ οὐκ ἐγένεσθε, τὸ ὑμέτερον τίς ὑμῖν
to another, *faithful* *not* *you have been* who will give you what ⌊is to be your own?⌋ *who* *you*
259 4412 4024 1181 5515 1443 1443 7007 3836 5629 5515 7007
a.dsn a.npm pl v.ami.2p d.asn r.asn.2 r.nsm r.dp.2

δώσει; 13 Οὐδεὶς οἰκέτης δύναται δυσὶ κυρίοις δουλεύειν· ἢ γὰρ
will give "No servant is able to serve two masters. *to serve* For either *For* he
1443 4029 3860 1538 1526 1526 1545 3261 1526 1142 2445 1142 3631
v.fai.3s a.nsm n.nsm v.ppi.3s a.dpm n.dpm f.pa cj cj

τὸν ἕνα μισήσει καὶ τὸν ἕτερον ἀγαπήσει, ἢ
will hate the one *he will hate* and love the other, *love* or he will be devoted to
3631 3631 3836 1651 3631 2779 26 3836 2283 26 2445 504 504 504 504 504
d.asm a.asm v.fai.3s cj d.asm r.asm v.fai.3s cj

ἑνὸς ἀνθέξεται καὶ τοῦ ἑτέρου καταφρονήσει. ⌊οὐ δύνασθε⌋
the one *he will be devoted to* and despise the other. *despise* You cannot
1651 504 2779 2969 3836 2283 2969 4024 1538
a.gsm v.fmi.3s cj d.gsm r.gsm v.fai.3s pl v.ppi.2p

θεῷ δουλεύειν καὶ μαμωνᾷ. 14 ἤκουον
serve God *serve* and money." The Pharisees (who were lovers of money) heard
1526 2536 1526 2779 3440 3836 5757 5639 5639 5795 5795 5795 201
n.dsm f.pa cj n.dsm v.iai.3p

δὲ ταῦτα πάντα οἱ Φαρισαῖοι φιλάργυροι ὑπάρχοντες καὶ
{and} all these things, *all* *The* *Pharisees* *lovers of money* *who were* and
1254 4246 4047 4246 3836 5757 5795 5639 2779
cj r.apn a.apn d.npm n.npm a.npm pt.pa.npm cj

ἐξεμυκτήριζον αὐτόν. 15 καὶ εἶπεν αὐτοῖς, ὑμεῖς ἐστε οἱ δικαιοῦντες ἑαυτοὺς
they ridiculed him. And he said to them, "You are those who justify yourselves
1727 899 2779 3306 899 7007 1639 3836 1467 1571
v.iai.3p r.asm.3 cj v.aai.3s r.dpm.3 r.np.2 v.pai.2p d.npm pt.pa.npm r.apm.2

ἐνώπιον τῶν ἀνθρώπων, ὁ δὲ θεὸς γινώσκει τὰς καρδίας ὑμῶν· ὅτι τὸ
before *{the}* men, *{the}* but God knows *{the}* your hearts. *your* For what is
1967 3836 476 3836 1254 2536 1182 3836 7007 2840 7007 4022 3836
p.g d.gpm n.gpm d.nsm cj n.nsm v.pai.3s d.apf n.apf r.gp.2 cj d.nsn

ἐν ἀνθρώποις ὑψηλὸν βδέλυγμα ἐνώπιον τοῦ θεοῦ. 16 ὁ νόμος καὶ
exalted among men *exalted* is an abomination before *{the}* God. "The Law and
5734 1877 476 5734 1007 1967 3836 2536 3836 3795 2779
p.d n.dpm a.nsn n.nsn p.g d.gsm n.gsm d.nsm n.nsm cj

οἱ προφῆται μέχρι Ἰωάννου· ἀπὸ τότε ↱ ↱ ἡ βασιλεία τοῦ θεοῦ
the Prophets were until John; since then the good news of the kingdom of God
3836 4737 3588 2722 608 5538 2294 2294 3836 993 3836 2536
d.npm n.npm p.g n.gsm p.g adv d.nsf n.nsf d.gsm n.gsm

εὐαγγελίζεται καὶ πᾶς εἰς αὐτὴν βιάζεται. 17
is preached, and everyone takes vigorous steps to enter it. *takes vigorous steps* It is
2294 2779 4246 1041 1041 1041 1650 899 1041 1639 1639
v.ppi.3s cj a.nsm p.a r.asf.3 v.pmi.3s

εὐκοπώτερον δέ ἐστιν τὸν οὐρανὸν καὶ τὴν γῆν παρελθεῖν ἢ
easier *{and}* *It is* *{the}* for heaven and *{the}* earth to pass away than for the smallest
2324 1254 1639 3836 4041 2779 3836 1178 4216 2445 3037
a.nsn.c cj v.pai.3s d.asm n.asm cj d.asf n.asf f.aa pl

τοῦ νόμου μίαν κεραίαν πεσεῖν. 18 πᾶς
part of a single letter in the law *single* *smallest part of a letter* ⌊to lose its force.⌋ Anyone
3037 3037 3037 1651 3037 3836 3795 1651 3037 4406 4246
d.gsm n.gsm a.asf n.asf f.aa a.nsm

ὁ ἀπολύων τὴν γυναῖκα αὐτοῦ καὶ γαμῶν ἑτέραν μοιχεύει, καὶ
who divorces *{the}* his wife *his* and marries ⌊another woman⌋ commits adultery, and
3836 668 3836 899 1222 899 2779 1138 2283 3658 2779
d.nsm pt.pa.nsm d.asf n.asf r.gsm.3 cj pt.pa.nsm r.asf v.pai.3s cj

NASB

been faithful in the
use of unrighteous
wealth, who will
entrust the true
riches to you?
12And if you have
not been faithful
in *the use of* that
which is another's,
who will give you
that which is your
own? 13No servant
can serve two mas-
ters; for either he
will hate the one
and love the other,
or else he will be
devoted to one and
despise the other.
You cannot serve
God and wealth."
14Now the Phari-
sees, who were
lovers of money,
were listening to
all these things and
were scoffing at
Him. 15And He said
to them, "You are
those who justify
yourselves in the
sight of men, but
God knows your
hearts; for that
which is highly es-
teemed among men
is detestable in the
sight of God.
16"The Law and
the Prophets *were*
proclaimed until
John; since that
time the gospel
of the kingdom
of God has been
preached, and
everyone is forc-
ing his way into it.
17But it is easier for
heaven and earth
to pass away than
for one stroke of
a letter of the Law
to fail.
18"Everyone
who divorces his
wife and marries
another commits
adultery, and he

NIV

and the man who
marries a divorced
woman commits
adultery.

The Rich Man and Lazarus

[19]"There was a
rich man who was
dressed in purple
and fine linen and
lived in luxury
every day. [20]At
his gate was laid
a beggar named
Lazarus, covered
with sores [21]and
longing to eat what
fell from the rich
man's table. Even
the dogs came and
licked his sores.
[22]"The time came
when the beggar
died and the an-
gels carried him
to Abraham's side.
The rich man also
died and was bur-
ied. [23]In Hades,
where he was in
torment, he looked
up and saw Abra-
ham far away,
with Lazarus by
his side. [24]So he
called to him,
'Father Abraham,
have pity on me
and send Lazarus
to dip the tip of his
finger in water and
cool my tongue,
because I am in
agony in this fire.'
[25]"But Abraham
replied, 'Son, re-
member that in
your lifetime you
received your good
things, while Laz-
arus received

ὁ ἀπολελυμένην ἀπὸ ἀνδρὸς γαμῶν μοιχεύει.
the one who marries a woman divorced from her husband *one who marries* commits adultery.
3836 1138 1138 1138 668 608 467 1138 3658
d.nsm pt.rp.asf p.g n.gsm pt.pa.nsm v.pai.3s

19 ἄνθρωπος δέ τις ἦν πλούσιος, καὶ ἐνεδιδύσκετο πορφύραν καὶ
A certain man *{and}* *certain* was rich, and ˪he was dressed in˩ purple and
5516 476 1254 5516 1639 4454 2779 1898 4525 2779
n.nsm cj r.nsm v.iai.3s a.nsm cj v.imi.3s n.asf cj

βύσσον εὐφραινόμενος καθ᾿ ἡμέραν λαμπρῶς. 20 πτωχὸς δέ
fine linen and he made merry every day ˪in a luxurious manner.˩ And a poor man *And*
1116 2370 2848 2465 3289 1254 5516 4777 1254
n.asf pt.pp.nsm p.a n.asf adv a.nsm cj

τις → ὀνόματι Λάζαρος ἐβέβλητο πρὸς τὸν πυλῶνα
a by the name of Lazarus, who was covered with sores, was laid at the gate,
5516 3950 3276 1815 1815 1815 1815 1815 965 4639 3836 4784
r.nsm n.dsn n.nsm v.lpi.3s p.a d.asm n.asm

αὐτοῦ εἱλκωμένος 21 καὶ ἐπιθυμῶν χορτασθῆναι ἀπὸ τῶν πιπτόντων
{his} *who was covered with sores* *{and}* who longed to eat *{from}* what fell
899 1815 2779 2121 5963 608 3836 4406
r.gsm.3 pt.rp.nsm cj pt.pa.nsm f.ap p.g d.gpn pt.pa.gpn

ἀπὸ τῆς τραπέζης τοῦ πλουσίου· ἀλλὰ καὶ οἱ κύνες ἐρχόμενοι
from the rich man's table. *{the}* *rich man's* But instead, the dogs used to come and
608 3836 4454 4454 5544 3836 4454 247 2779 3836 3264 2262
p.g d.gsf n.gsf d.gsm a.gsm cj adv d.npm n.npm pt.pm.npm

ἐπέλειχον τὰ ἕλκη αὐτοῦ. 22 ἐγένετο δὲ ἀποθανεῖν τὸν
lick *{the}* his sores. *his* *{it happened that}* *{and}* The poor man died *The*
2143 3836 899 1814 899 1181 1254 3836 4777 4777 633 3836
v.iai.3p d.apn n.apn r.gsm.3 v.ami.3s cj f.aa d.asm

πτωχὸν καὶ ἀπενεχθῆναι αὐτὸν ὑπὸ τῶν ἀγγέλων εἰς τὸν κόλπον
poor man and he was carried *he* by the angels to *{the}* Abraham's side.
4777 2779 899 708 899 5679 3836 34 1650 3836 11 3146
a.asm cj f.ap r.asm.3 p.g d.gpm n.gpm p.a d.asm n.asm

Ἀβραάμ· ἀπέθανεν δὲ καὶ ὁ πλούσιος καὶ ἐτάφη. 23 καὶ
Abraham's The rich man also died *{and}* *also* *The* *rich man* and was buried, And
11 3836 4454 4454 2779 633 1254 2779 3836 4454 2779 2507 2779
n.gsm v.aai.3s cj adv d.nsm a.nsm cj v.api.3s cj

ἐν τῷ ᾅδῃ ἐπάρας τοὺς ὀφθαλμοὺς αὐτοῦ, ὑπάρχων ἐν
being in torment in *{the}* Hades, he lifted *{the}* his eyes *his* *being* *in*
5639 1877 992 1877 3836 87 2048 3836 899 4057 899 5639 1877
p.d d.dsm n.dsm pt.aa.nsm d.apm n.apm r.gsm.3 pt.pa.nsm p.d

βασάνοις, ὁρᾷ Ἀβραὰμ ἀπὸ μακρόθεν καὶ Λάζαρον ἐν τοῖς κόλποις
torment and saw Abraham from afar and Lazarus at *{the}* his side.
992 3972 11 608 3427 2779 3276 1877 3836 899 3146
n.dpf v.pai.3s n.asm p.g adv cj n.asm p.d d.dpm n.dpm

αὐτοῦ. 24 καὶ αὐτὸς φωνήσας εἶπεν, πάτερ Ἀβραάμ, ἐλέησόν με
his And calling out he *calling out* said, 'Father Abraham, ˪have mercy on˩ me,
899 2779 5888 5888 899 5888 3306 4252 11 1796 1609
r.gsm.3 cj r.nsm pt.aa.nsm v.aai.3s n.vsm n.vsm v.aam.2s r.as.1

καὶ πέμψον Λάζαρον ἵνα βάψῃ τὸ ἄκρον τοῦ δακτύλου αὐτοῦ ὕδατος καὶ
and send Lazarus to dip the tip of his finger *his* in water and
2779 4287 3276 2671 970 3836 216 3836 899 1235 899 5623 2779
cj v.aam.2s n.asm cj v.aas.3s d.asn n.asn d.gsm n.gsm r.gsm.3 n.gsn cj

καταψύξῃ τὴν γλῶσσάν μου, ὅτι ὀδυνῶμαι ἐν τῇ φλογὶ ταύτῃ.
cool *{the}* my tongue, *my* for I am in anguish in *{the}* this flame.' *this*
2976 3836 1609 1185 1609 4022 3849 1877 3836 4047 5825 4047
v.aas.3s d.asf n.asf r.gs.1 cj v.ppi.1s p.d d.dsf n.dsf r.dsf

25 εἶπεν δὲ Ἀβραάμ, τέκνον, μνήσθητι ὅτι ἀπέλαβες τὰ
But Abraham said, *But* *Abraham* 'Child, remember that you received *{the}* your
1254 11 3306 1254 11 5451 3630 4022 655 3836 5148
v.aai.3s cj n.nsm n.vsn v.apm.2s cj v.aai.2s d.apn

ἀγαθά σου ἐν τῇ ζωῇ σου, καὶ Λάζαρος ὁμοίως τὰ
good things *your* during *{the}* your lifetime, *your* and Lazarus correspondingly received *{the}*
19 5148 1877 3836 5148 2437 5148 2779 3276 3931 3836
a.apn r.gs.2 p.d d.dsf n.dsf r.gs.2 cj n.nsm adv d.apn

NASB

who marries one
who is divorced
from a husband
commits adultery.

The Rich Man and Lazarus

[19]"Now there was
a rich man, and he
habitually dressed
in purple and fine
linen, joyously
living in splendor
every day. [20]And a
poor man named
Lazarus was laid at
his gate, covered
with sores, [21]and
longing to be fed
with the *crumbs*
which were falling
from the rich man's
table; besides, even
the dogs were com-
ing and licking his
sores. [22]Now the
poor man died and
was carried away
by the angels to
Abraham's bosom;
and the rich man
also died and was
buried. [23]In Hades
he lifted up his
eyes, being in tor-
ment, and [a]saw
Abraham far away
and Lazarus in his
bosom. [24]And he
cried out and said,
'Father Abraham,
have mercy on me,
and send Lazarus
so that he may dip
the tip of his finger
in water and cool
off my tongue, for I
am in agony in this
flame.' [25]But Abra-
ham said, 'Child,
remember that dur-
ing your life you
received your good
things, and like-
wise Lazarus

NIV

bad things, but
now he is com-
forted here and
you are in agony.
26 And besides all
this, between us
and you a great
chasm has been
set in place, so that
those who want
to go from here to
you cannot, nor
can anyone cross
over from there
to us.'
27 "He answered,
'Then I beg you,
father, send Laza-
rus to my family,
28 for I have five
brothers. Let him
warn them, so that
they will not also
come to this place
of torment.'
29 "Abraham re-
plied, 'They have
Moses and the
Prophets; let them
listen to them.'
30 " 'No, father
Abraham,' he said,
'but if someone
from the dead goes
to them, they will
repent.'
31 "He said to
him, 'If they do
not listen to Moses
and the Prophets,
they will not be
convinced even
if someone rises
from the dead.' "

Sin, Faith, Duty

17 Jesus said
to his disci-
ples: "Things that
cause people to
stumble are bound
to come, but woe
to anyone through
whom they come.
2 It would be bet-
ter for them to be
thrown into the sea
with a millstone
tied around their
neck than to cause
one of these little
ones

κακά· νῦν δὲ ὧδε παρακαλεῖται, σὺ δὲ ὀδυνᾶσαι.
bad things; but now *but* he is comforted here, *he is comforted* and you *and* are in anguish.
2805 1254 3814 1254 4151 4151 4151 6045 4151 1254 5148 1254 3849
a.apn adv cj adv v.ppi.3s r.ns.2 cj v.ppi.2s

26 καὶ ἐν πᾶσι τούτοις μεταξὺ ἡμῶν καὶ ὑμῶν χάσμα μέγα
{and} Besides all this, between us and you a great chasm *great*
2779 1877 4246 4047 3568 7005 2779 7007 3489 5926 3489
cj p.d a.dpn r.dpn p.g r.gp.1 cj r.gp.2 n.nsn a.nsn

ἐστήρικται, ὅπως οἱ θέλοντες διαβῆναι ἔνθεν πρὸς ὑμᾶς μὴ
⌞has been put in place,⌟ so that those wishing to cross over from here to you are not
5114 3968 3836 2527 1329 1925 4639 7007 1538 3590
v.rpi.3s cj d.npm pt.pa.npm f.aa adv p.a r.ap.2 pl

δύνωνται, μηδὲ ἐκεῖθεν πρὸς ἡμᾶς διαπερῶσιν. 27
able, and no one can cross from there to us.' *can cross* So the rich man
1538 3593 1385 1385 1696 4639 7005 1385 1254
v.pps.3p cj adv p.a r.ap.1 v.pas.3p

εἶπεν δέ, ἐρωτῶ σε οὖν, πάτερ, ἵνα πέμψῃς αὐτὸν εἰς τὸν οἶκον τοῦ
said, *So* 'Then I beg you, *Then* father, to send Lazarus to the house of my
3306 1254 4036 2263 5148 4036 4252 2671 4287 899 1650 3836 3875 3836 1609
v.aai.3s cj v.pai.1s r.as.2 cj n.vsm cj v.aas.2s r.asm.3 p.a d.asm n.asm d.gsm

πατρός μου, 28 ἔχω γὰρ πέντε ἀδελφούς, ὅπως διαμαρτύρηται αὐτοῖς, ἵνα
father *my* (for I have *for* five brothers), that he might warn them so that they
4252 1609 1142 2400 1142 4297 81 3968 1371 899 2671 899
n.gsm r.gs.1 v.pai.1s cj a.apm n.apm cj v.pms.3s r.dpm.3 cj

μὴ καὶ αὐτοὶ ἔλθωσιν εἰς τὸν τόπον τοῦτον τῆς βασάνου.
might not come as well *they* *might come* into *{the}* this place *this* of torment.'
2262 3590 2262 2779 899 2262 1650 3836 4047 5536 4047 3836 992
pl adv r.npm v.aas.3p p.a d.asm n.asm r.asm d.gsf n.gsf

29 λέγει δὲ Ἀβραάμ, ἔχουσι Μωϋσέα καὶ τοὺς προφήτας·
But Abraham said, *But* *Abraham* 'They have Moses and the Prophets;
1254 11 3306 1254 11 2400 3707 2779 3836 4737
v.pai.3s cj n.nsm v.pai.3p n.asm cj d.apm n.apm

ἀκουσάτωσαν αὐτῶν. 30 ὁ δὲ εἶπεν, οὐχί, πάτερ Ἀβραάμ, ἀλλ' ἐάν
let them listen to them.' Then the *Then* rich man said, 'No, father Abraham; but if
201 899 1254 3836 1254 3306 4049 4252 11 247 1569
v.aam.3p r.gpm.3 d.nsm cj v.aai.3s pl n.vsm n.vsm cj cj

τις ἀπὸ νεκρῶν πορευθῇ πρὸς αὐτοὺς μετανοήσουσιν. 31 εἶπεν δὲ αὐτῷ,
someone from the dead goes to them, they will repent.' He said *{and}* to him,
5516 608 3738 4513 4639 899 3566 3306 1254 899
r.nsm p.g a.gpm v.aps.3s p.a r.apm.3 v.fai.3p v.aai.3s cj r.dsm.3

εἰ Μωϋσέως καὶ τῶν προφητῶν οὐκ ἀκούουσιν, οὐδ'
'If they do not listen to Moses and the Prophets, *not* *they do listen to* neither will
1623 201 201 4024 201 201 3707 2779 3836 4737 4024 201 4028 4275
cj n.gsm cj d.gpm n.gpm pl v.pai.3p adv

ἐάν τις ἐκ νεκρῶν ἀναστῇ πεισθήσονται.
they be persuaded should someone rise from the dead.'" *rise* *will they be persuaded*
4275 4275 4275 1569 5516 482 1666 3738 482 4275
cj r.nsm p.g a.gpm v.aas.3s v.fpi.3p

17:1 εἶπεν δὲ πρὸς τοὺς μαθητὰς αὐτοῦ, ἀνένδεκτόν ἐστιν τοῦ
And he said *And* to *{the}* his disciples, *his* "It is inevitable *It is* that
1254 3306 1254 4639 3836 899 3412 899 1639 1639 450 1639 3836
v.aai.3s cj p.a d.apm n.apm r.gsm.3 a.nsn v.pai.3s d.gsn

τὰ σκάνδαλα μὴ ἐλθεῖν, πλὴν οὐαὶ δι' οὗ ἔρχεται·
occasions for stumbling ~ will come, but woe to the one through whom they come!
3836 4998 3590 2262 4440 4026 1328 4005 2262
d.apn n.apn pl f.aa cj j p.g r.gsm v.pmi.3s

2 λυσιτελεῖ αὐτῷ εἰ ⌞λίθος μυλικὸς⌟ περίκειται περὶ τὸν τράχηλον αὐτοῦ
It is better for him if a millstone is hung around *{the}* his neck *his*
3387 899 1623 3345 3683 4329 4309 3836 899 5549 899
v.pai.3s r.dsm.3 cj n.nsm a.nsm v.pmi.3s p.a d.asm n.asm r.gsm.3

καὶ ἔρριπται εἰς τὴν θάλασσαν ἢ ἵνα σκανδαλίσῃ τῶν μικρῶν τούτων
and he is cast into the sea than that he should cause one of these little ones *these*
2779 4849 1650 3836 2498 2445 2671 4997 1651 3836 4047 3625 4047
cj v.rpi.3s p.a d.asf n.asf pl cj v.aas.3s d.gpm a.gpm r.gpm

NASB

bad things; but
now he is being
comforted here,
and you are in ag-
ony. 26 And besides
all this, between
us and you there
is a great chasm
fixed, so that those
who wish to come
over from here
to you will not
be able, and *that*
none may cross
over from there to
us.' 27 And he said,
'Then I beg you,
father, that you
send him to my
father's house—
28 for I have five
brothers—in order
that he may warn
them, so that they
will not also come
to this place of tor-
ment.' 29 But Abra-
ham *said, 'They
have Moses and
the Prophets; let
them hear them.'
30 But he said, 'No,
father Abraham,
but if someone
goes to them from
the dead, they will
repent!' 31 But he
said to him, 'If
they do not listen
to Moses and the
Prophets, they will
not be persuaded
even if someone
rises from the
dead.' "

Instructions

17:1 He said to
His disciples, "It
is inevitable that
stumbling blocks
come, but woe to
him through whom
they come! 2 It
would be better for
him if a millstone
were hung around
his neck and he
were thrown into
the sea, than that
he would cause one
of these little

NIV

to stumble. 3So
watch yourselves.
"If your broth-
er or sister[a] sins
against you, re-
buke them; and if
they repent, for-
give them. 4Even
if they sin against
you seven times
in a day and seven
times come back
to you saying 'I
repent,' you must
forgive them."
5The apostles
said to the Lord,
"Increase our
faith!"
6He replied, "If
you have faith as
small as a mustard
seed, you can say
to this mulberry
tree, 'Be uprooted
and planted in the
sea,' and it will
obey you.
7"Suppose one of
you has a servant
plowing or looking
after the sheep.
Will he say to the
servant when he
comes in from the
field, 'Come along
now and sit down
to eat'? 8Won't he
rather say, 'Pre-
pare my supper,
get yourself ready
and wait on me
while I eat and
drink; after that
you may eat and
drink'? 9Will he
thank the servant
because he did
what he was told to
do? 10So you also,
when you have
done everything
you were told to
do, should say,
'We are unwor-
thy servants; we
have only done our
duty.'"

Jesus Heals Ten Men With Leprosy

11Now on his way
to Jerusalem, Jesus
traveled along the
border between

[a] 3 The Greek word for *brother or sister* (*adelphos*) refers here to a fellow disciple, whether man or woman.

ἕνα. ↰ ↰ 3→ → προσέχετε ἑαυτοῖς. ἐὰν ἁμάρτῃ ὁ ἀδελφός
one to stumble. "Be on your guard! *your* If your brother sins, *{the}* *brother*
1651 4997 4997 1571 4668 1571 1569 5148 81 279 3836 81
a.asm v.pam.2p r.dpm.2 cj v.aas.3s d.nsm n.nsm

σου ἐπιτίμησον αὐτῷ, καὶ ἐὰν μετανοήσῃ ἄφες αὐτῷ. 4καὶ ἐὰν
your rebuke him, and if he repents, forgive him. And if he sins against you
5148 2203 899 2779 1569 3566 918 899 2779 1569 279 279 1650 5148
r.gs.2 v.aam.2s r.dsm.3 cj cj v.aas.3s v.aam.2s r.dsm.3 cj cj

ἑπτάκις τῆς ἡμέρας ἁμαρτήσῃ εἰς σὲ καὶ ἑπτάκις ἐπιστρέψῃ πρὸς σὲ
seven times in a day, *he sins* *against you* and seven times returns to you
2232 3836 2465 279 1650 5148 2779 2232 2188 4639 5148
adv d.gsf n.gsf v.aas.3s p.a r.as.2 cj adv v.aas.3s p.a r.as.2

λέγων, μετανοῶ, ἀφήσεις αὐτῷ. 5καὶ εἶπαν οἱ ἀπόστολοι
saying, 'I repent,' ⌊you must forgive⌋ him." *{and}* The apostles said *The* *apostles*
3306 3566 918 899 2779 3836 693 3306 3836 693
pt.pa.nsm v.pai.1s v.fai.2s r.dsm.3 cj v.aai.3p d.npm n.npm

τῷ κυρίῳ, πρόσθες ἡμῖν πίστιν. 6 εἶπεν δὲ ὁ κύριος, εἰ ἔχετε
⌊to the⌋ Lord, "Increase our faith!" And the Lord said, *And* *the* *Lord* "If you had
3836 3261 4707 7005 4411 1254 3836 3261 3306 1254 3836 3261 1623 2400
d.dsm n.dsm v.aam.2s r.dp.1 n.asf v.aai.3s cj d.nsm n.nsm cj v.pai.2p

πίστιν ὡς κόκκον σινάπεως, → ἐλέγετε ἂν τῇ συκαμίνῳ ταύτῃ,[a]
faith like a grain ⌊of mustard seed,⌋ you could say *could* to this sycamore, *this*
4411 6055 3133 4983 323 3306 323 3836 4047 5189 4047
n.asf pl n.asm n.gsn v.iai.2p pl d.dsf n.dsf r.dsf

ἐκριζώθητι καὶ φυτεύθητι ἐν τῇ θαλάσσῃ· καὶ → ὑπήκουσεν ἂν ὑμῖν.
'Be uprooted and planted in the sea,' and it would obey *would* you.
1748 2779 5885 1877 3836 2498 2779 323 5634 323 7007
v.apm.2s cj v.apm.2s p.d d.dsf n.dsf cj v.aai.3s pl r.dp.2

7τίς δὲ ἐξ ὑμῶν δοῦλον ἔχων ἀροτριῶντα ἢ ποιμαίνοντα, ὃς
⌊Which one⌋ *{and}* of you, having a servant *having* plowing or tending sheep, who,
5515 1254 1666 7007 2400 1529 2400 769 2445 4477 4005
r.nsm cj p.g r.gp.2 n.asm pt.pa.nsm pt.pa.asm cj pt.pa.asm r.nsm

εἰσελθόντι ἐκ τοῦ ἀγροῦ ἐρεῖ αὐτῷ, εὐθέως παρελθὼν
⌊when he comes in⌋ from the field, ⌊will say⌋ to him, 'Come here at once *Come here* and
1656 1666 3836 69 3306 899 4216 4216 2311 4216
pt.aa.dsm p.g d.gsm n.gsm v.fai.3s r.dsm.3 adv pt.aa.nsm

ἀνάπεσε, 8↱ ↱ ἀλλ᾽ οὐχὶ ἐρεῖ αὐτῷ, ἑτοίμασον τί δειπνήσω καὶ
recline at dinner'? Will he not, rather, *not* say to him, 'Prepare what I am to eat, then
404 3306 3306 4049 247 4049 3306 899 2286 5515 1268 2779
v.aam.2s cj pl v.fai.3s r.dsm.3 v.aam.2s r.asn v.aas.1s cj

περιζωσάμενος διακόνει μοι ἕως φάγω καὶ πίω, καὶ μετὰ ταῦτα φάγεσαι
change clothes and wait on me while I eat and drink, and after this you may eat
4322 1354 1609 2401 2266 2779 4403 2779 3552 4047 5148 2266
pt.am.nsm v.pam.2s r.ds.1 cj v.aas.1s cj v.aas.1s cj p.a r.apn v.fmi.2s

καὶ πίεσαι σύ; 9μὴ ἔχει χάριν τῷ δούλῳ ὅτι ἐποίησεν τὰ
and drink'? *you* *{not}* ⌊Does he express⌋ thanks ⌊to the⌋ servant because he did the things
2779 4403 5148 3590 2400 5921 3836 1529 4022 4472 3836
cj v.fmi.2s r.ns.2 pl v.pai.3s n.asf d.dsm n.dsm cj v.aai.3s d.apn

διαταχθέντα; 10οὕτως καὶ ὑμεῖς, ὅταν ποιήσητε πάντα τὰ
that were commanded? So *{also}* it is with you. When you have done all that
1411 4048 2779 7007 4020 4472 4246 3836
pt.ap.apn adv adv r.np.2 cj v.aas.2p a.apn d.apn

διαταχθέντα ὑμῖν, λέγετε ὅτι δοῦλοι ἀχρεῖοί ἐσμεν,
was commanded, *{to you}* say, ~ 'We are unworthy servants; *unworthy* *We are* we have
1411 7007 3306 4022 1639 1639 945 1529 945 1639 4472 4472
pt.ap.apn r.dp.2 v.pam.2p cj n.npm a.npm v.pai.1p

ὃ ὠφείλομεν ποιῆσαι πεποιήκαμεν. 11καὶ ἐγένετο ἐν τῷ
done no more than we were obliged to do.'" *we have done* *{and}* *{it happened that}* As *{the}*
4472 4005 4053 4472 4472 2779 1181 1877 3836
r.asn v.iai.1p f.aa v.rai.1p cj v.ami.3s p.d d.dsn

πορεύεσθαι εἰς Ἰερουσαλὴμ καὶ αὐτὸς διήρχετο διὰ μέσον
Jesus was on his way to Jerusalem, *{and}* he passed through the region between
4513 1650 2647 2779 899 1451 1328 3545
f.pm p.a n.asf cj r.nsm v.imi.3s p.a n.asn

[a] [ταύτῃ] UBS.

NASB

ones to stumble.
3Be on your guard!
If your brother
sins, rebuke him;
and if he repents,
forgive him. 4And
if he sins against
you seven times a
day, and returns to
you seven times,
saying, 'I repent,'
forgive him."
5The apostles
said to the Lord,
"Increase our
faith!" 6And the
Lord said, "If you
had faith like a
mustard seed, you
would say to this
mulberry tree, 'Be
uprooted and be
planted in the sea';
and it would obey
you.
7"Which of you,
having a slave
plowing or tending
sheep, will say to
him when he has
come in from the
field, 'Come im-
mediately and sit
down to eat'? 8But
will he not say
to him, 'Prepare
something for me
to eat, and *properly*
clothe yourself and
serve me while I
eat and drink; and
afterward you may
eat and drink'?
9He does not thank
the slave because
he did the things
which were com-
manded, does he?
10So you too, when
you do all the
things which are
commanded you,
say, 'We are un-
worthy slaves; we
have done *only* that
which we ought to
have done.'"

Ten Lepers Cleansed

11While He was
on the way to Je-
rusalem, He was
passing between

NIV

Samaria and Gal-
ilee. [12]As he was
going into a vil-
lage, ten men who
had leprosy[a] met
him. They stood
at a distance [13]and
called out in a
loud voice, "Jesus,
Master, have pity
on us!"
[14]When he saw
them, he said, "Go,
show yourselves to
the priests." And
as they went, they
were cleansed.
[15]One of them,
when he saw he
was healed, came
back, praising God
in a loud voice.
[16]He threw himself
at Jesus' feet and
thanked him—and
he was a Samar-
itan.
[17]Jesus asked,
"Were not all ten
cleansed? Where
are the other nine?
[18]Has no one re-
turned to give
praise to God ex-
cept this foreign-
er?" [19]Then he said
to him, "Rise and
go; your faith has
made you well."

The Coming of the Kingdom of God

[20]Once, on be-
ing asked by the
Pharisees when
the kingdom of
God would come,
Jesus replied, "The
coming of the
kingdom of God is
not something that
can be observed,
[21]nor will people
say, 'Here it is,' or
'There it is,' be-
cause the kingdom
of God is

[a] 12 The Greek word traditionally translated *leprosy* was used for various diseases affecting the skin.

Σαμαρείας καὶ Γαλιλαίας. 12 καὶ → εἰσερχομένου αὐτοῦ εἴς τινα κώμην
Samaria and Galilee. {and} As he entered *he* {into} a certain village,
4899 2779 1133 2779 899 1656 899 1650 5516 3267
n.gsf cj n.gsf cj pt.pm.gsm r.gsm.3 p.a r.asf n.asf

ἀπήντησαν αὐτῷ[a] δέκα λεπροὶ ἄνδρες, οἳ ἔστησαν
ten men with leprosy met him, *ten* *leprosy* *men* who ⌊normally stood⌋
1274 467 3320 560 899 1274 3320 467 4005 2705
v.aai.3p r.dsm.3 a.npm a.npm n.npm r.npm v.aai.3p

πόρρωθεν 13 καὶ αὐτοὶ ἦραν φωνὴν λέγοντες, Ἰησοῦ ἐπιστάτα, ἐλέησον
at a distance. {and} They raised their voices, saying, "Jesus, Master, ⌊have mercy on⌋
4523 2779 899 149 5889 3306 2652 2181 1796
adv cj r.npm v.aai.3p n.asf pt.pa.npm n.vsm n.vsm v.aam.2s

ἡμᾶς. 14 καὶ ἰδὼν εἶπεν αὐτοῖς, πορευθέντες ἐπιδείξατε ἑαυτοὺς
us!" {and} ⌊When he saw⌋ them, he said to them, "Go and show yourselves
7005 2779 1625 3306 899 4513 2109 1571
r.ap.1 cj pt.aa.nsm v.aai.3s r.dpm.3 pt.ap.npm v.aam.2p r.apm.2

τοῖς ἱερεῦσιν. καὶ ἐγένετο ἐν τῷ ὑπάγειν αὐτοὺς ἐκαθαρίσθησαν.
to the priests." And {it happened that} as {the} they went *they* they were made clean.
3836 2636 2779 1181 1877 3836 899 5632 899 2751
d.dpm n.dpm cj v.ami.3s p.d d.dsn f.pa r.apm.3 v.api.3p

15 εἷς δὲ ἐξ αὐτῶν, ἰδὼν ὅτι ἰάθη, ὑπέστρεψεν
Then one *Then* of them, ⌊when he saw⌋ that ⌊he had been healed,⌋ returned, praising
1254 1651 1254 1666 899 1625 4022 2615 5715 1519
a.nsm cj p.g r.gpm.3 pt.aa.nsm cj v.api.3s v.aai.3s

μετὰ φωνῆς μεγάλης δοξάζων τὸν θεόν, 16 καὶ ἔπεσεν ἐπὶ πρόσωπον
God in a loud voice, *loud* *praising* {the} *God* and fell on his face
2536 3552 3489 5889 3489 1519 3836 2536 2779 4406 2093 4725
p.g n.gsf a.gsf pt.pa.nsm d.asm n.asm cj v.aai.3s p.a n.asn

παρὰ τοὺς πόδας αὐτοῦ εὐχαριστῶν αὐτῷ· ↵ καὶ αὐτὸς ἦν
at {the} Jesus' feet, *Jesus'* giving him thanks — and he was a
4123 3836 899 4546 899 2373 899 2373 2779 899 1639
p.a d.apm n.apm r.gsm.3 pt.pa.nsm r.dsm.3 cj r.nsm v.iai.3s

Σαμαρίτης. 17 ἀποκριθεὶς δὲ ὁ Ἰησοῦς εἶπεν, ↱ οὐχὶ οἱ δέκα
Samaritan. Then Jesus responded, *Then* {the} *Jesus* saying, "Were not {the} ten
4901 1254 2652 646 1254 3836 2652 3306 2751 4049 3836 1274
n.nsm pt.ap.nsm cj d.nsm n.nsm v.aai.3s pl d.npm a.npm

ἐκαθαρίσθησαν; οἱ δὲ ἐννέα ποῦ; 18 ↱ ↱ οὐχ εὑρέθησαν
made clean? The {and} other nine, where are they? Were they not found,
2751 3836 1254 1933 4543 2351 2351 4024 2351
v.api.3p d.npm cj a.npm cj pl v.api.3p

ὑποστρέψαντες δοῦναι δόξαν τῷ θεῷ ⌊εἰ μή⌋ ὁ ἀλλογενὴς οὗτος;
so as to return and give praise to God, except {the} this foreigner?" *this*
5715 1443 1518 3836 2536 1623 3590 3836 4047 254 4047
pt.aa.npm f.aa n.asf d.dsm n.dsm cj pl d.nsm n.nsm r.nsm

19 καὶ εἶπεν → αὐτῷ, ἀναστὰς πορεύου· ἡ πίστις σου σέσωκέν σε.
Then he said to the man, "Get up and go; {the} your faith *your* has made you
2779 3306 899 482 4513 3836 5148 4411 5148 5392 5148
cj v.aai.3s r.dsm.3 pt.aa.nsm v.pmm.2s d.nsf n.nsf r.gs.2 v.rai.3s r.as.2

↵ 20 ἐπερωτηθεὶς δὲ ὑπὸ τῶν Φαρισαίων πότε
well." Having been asked {and} by the Pharisees when the kingdom of God
5392 2089 1254 5679 3836 5757 4537 3836 993 3836 2536
pt.ap.nsm cj p.g d.gpm n.gpm cj

ἔρχεται ἡ βασιλεία τοῦ θεοῦ ἀπεκρίθη αὐτοῖς καὶ εἶπεν,
would come, *the* *kingdom* *of* *God* he answered them, {and} saying, "The kingdom of
2262 3836 993 3836 2536 646 899 2779 3306 3836 993 3836
v.pmi.3s d.nsf n.nsf d.gsm n.gsm v.api.3s r.dpm.3 cj v.aai.3s

↱ οὐκ ἔρχεται ἡ βασιλεία τοῦ θεοῦ μετὰ παρατηρήσεως, 21 οὐδὲ ἐροῦσιν,
God will not come *The* *kingdom* *of* *God* with observation. Nor will they say,
2536 2262 4024 2262 3836 993 3836 2536 3552 4191 4028 3306
pl v.pmi.3s d.nsf n.nsf d.gsm n.gsm p.g n.gsf cj v.fai.3p

ἰδοὺ ὧδε ἤ, ἐκεῖ, ἰδοὺ γάρ ἡ βασιλεία τοῦ θεοῦ
'Look, here it is!' or, 'There it is!' For behold, *For* the kingdom of God is
2627 6045 2445 1695 1142 2627 1142 3836 993 3836 2536 1639
j adv cj adv j cj d.nsf n.nsf d.gsm n.gsm

[a] [αὐτῷ] UBS.

NASB

Samaria and
Galilee. [12]As He
entered a village,
ten leprous men
who stood at a
distance met Him;
[13]and they raised
their voices, say-
ing, "Jesus, Master,
have mercy on
us!" [14]When He
saw them, He said
to them, "Go and
show yourselves to
the priests." And
as they were going,
they were cleansed.
[15]Now one of them,
when he saw that
he had been healed,
turned back, glo-
rifying God with
a loud voice, [16]and
he fell on his face
at His feet, giving
thanks to Him. And
he was a Samari-
tan. [17]Then Jesus
answered and said,
"Were there not ten
cleansed? But the
nine—where are
they? [18]Was no one
found who returned
to give glory to
God, except this
foreigner?" [19]And
He said to him,
"Stand up and go;
your faith [a]has
made you well."
[20]Now having
been questioned by
the Pharisees as to
when the kingdom
of God was com-
ing, He answered
them and said,
"The kingdom of
God is not coming
with signs to be
observed; [21]nor will
they say, 'Look,
here *it is!*' or,
'There *it is!*' For
behold, the king-
dom of God is in

[a] Lit *has saved you*

NIV

in your midst."[a]
22 Then he said to
his disciples, "The
time is coming
when you will long
to see one of the
days of the Son of
Man, but you will
not see it. 23 Peo-
ple will tell you,
'There he is!' or
'Here he is!' Do
not go running off
after them. 24 For
the Son of Man in
his day[b] will be
like the lightning,
which flashes and
lights up the sky
from one end to
the other. 25 But
first he must suffer
many things and
be rejected by this
generation.
26 "Just as it was
in the days of
Noah, so also will
it be in the days of
the Son of Man.
27 People were
eating, drinking,
marrying and
being given in
marriage up to the
day Noah entered
the ark. Then the
flood came and
destroyed them all.
28 "It was the
same in the days of
Lot. People were
eating and drink-
ing, buying and
selling, planting
and building. 29 But
the day Lot left
Sodom, fire and
sulfur rained down
from heaven and
destroyed them all.
30 "It will be just
like this

[a] 21 Or *is within you*
[b] 24 Some manuscripts do not have *in his day.*

ἐντὸς ὑμῶν ἐστιν. 22 εἶπεν δὲ πρὸς τοὺς μαθητάς, ἐλεύσονται
⌊in the midst⌋ of you." *is* And he said *And* to the disciples, "Days are coming
1955 7007 1639 1254 3306 1254 4639 3836 3412 2465 2262
p.g r.gp.2 v.pai.3s v.aai.3s cj p.a d.apm n.apm v.fmi.3p

ἡμέραι ὅτε ἐπιθυμήσετε μίαν τῶν ἡμερῶν τοῦ υἱοῦ τοῦ ἀνθρώπου ἰδεῖν
Days when you will desire to see one of the days of the Son of Man, *to see*
2465 4021 2121 1625 1625 1651 3836 2465 3836 5626 3836 476 1625
n.npf cj v.fai.2p a.asf d.gpf n.gpf d.gsm n.gsm d.gsm n.gsm f.aa

καὶ ↱ ↱ οὐκ ὄψεσθε. 23 καὶ ἐροῦσιν ὑμῖν, ἰδοὺ ἐκεῖ, ἤ,[a] ἰδοὺ ὧδε· ↱
and you will not see it. And ⌊they will say⌋ to you, 'Look, there!' or, 'Look, here!' Do
2779 3972 3972 4024 3972 2779 3306 7007 2627 1695 2445 2627 6045 599
cj pl v.fmi.2p cj v.fai.3p r.dp.2 j adv cj j adv

μὴ ἀπέλθητε μηδὲ διώξητε. 24 ὥσπερ γὰρ ἡ ἀστραπὴ ἀστράπτουσα
not go out or pursue them. For just as *For* the lightning, when it flashes, lights
3590 599 3593 1503 1142 6061 1142 3836 847 848 3290
pl v.aas.2p cj v.aas.2p cj cj d.nsf n.nsf pt.pa.nsf

ἐκ τῆς ὑπὸ τὸν οὐρανὸν εἰς τὴν ⌊ὑπ' οὐρανὸν⌋ λάμπει, οὕτως ἔσται ὁ
up from one end of heaven to the other, *lights up* so will be the
3290 1666 3836 5679 3836 4041 1650 3836 5679 4041 3290 4048 1639 3836
p.g d.gsf p.a d.asm n.asm p.a d.asf p.a n.asm v.pai.3s adv v.fmi.3s d.nsm

υἱὸς τοῦ ἀνθρώπου [b]ἐν τῇ ἡμέρᾳ αὐτοῦ. 25 πρῶτον δὲ δεῖ αὐτὸν
Son of Man in *{the}* his day. *his* But first *But* he must *he*
5626 3836 476 1877 3836 899 2465 899 1254 4754 1254 899 1256 899
n.nsm d.gsm n.gsm p.d d.dsf n.dsf r.gsm.3 adv cj v.pai.3s r.asm.3

πολλὰ παθεῖν καὶ ἀποδοκιμασθῆναι ἀπὸ τῆς γενεᾶς ταύτης. 26 καὶ
suffer many things *suffer* and be rejected by *{the}* this generation. *this* And
4248 4498 4248 2779 627 608 3836 4047 1155 4047 2779
a.apn f.aa cj f.ap p.g d.gsf n.gsf r.gsf cj

καθὼς ἐγένετο ἐν ταῖς ἡμέραις Νῶε, οὕτως ἔσται καὶ ἐν ταῖς ἡμέραις
just as it was in the days of Noah, so also ⌊will it be⌋ *also* in the days
2777 1181 1877 3836 2465 3820 4048 2779 1639 2779 1877 3836 2465
cj v.ami.3s p.d d.dpf n.dpf n.gsm adv v.fmi.3s adv p.d d.dpf n.dpf

τοῦ υἱοῦ τοῦ ἀνθρώπου· 27 ἤσθιον, ἔπινον, ἐγάμουν,
of the Son of Man. ⌊They were eating,⌋ ⌊they were drinking,⌋ ⌊they were marrying,⌋
3836 5626 3836 476 2266 4403 1138
d.gsm n.gsm d.gsm n.gsm v.iai.3p v.iai.3p v.iai.3p

ἐγαμίζοντο, ἄχρι ἧς ἡμέρας εἰσῆλθεν Νῶε εἰς
⌊they were being given in marriage,⌋ until the day ⌊in which⌋ *day* Noah went *Noah* into
1139 948 2465 4005 2465 3820 1656 3820 1650
v.ipi.3p p.g r.gsf n.gsf v.aai.3s n.nsm p.a

τὴν κιβωτὸν καὶ ἦλθεν ὁ κατακλυσμὸς καὶ ἀπώλεσεν πάντας.
the ark and the flood came *the* *flood* and destroyed them all.
3836 3066 2779 3836 2886 2262 3836 2886 2779 660 4246
d.asf n.asf cj v.aai.3s d.nsm n.nsm cj v.aai.3s a.apm

28 ὁμοίως καθὼς ἐγένετο ἐν ταῖς ἡμέραις Λώτ· ἤσθιον, ἔπινον,
Likewise, just as it was in the days of Lot: ⌊they were eating,⌋ ⌊they were drinking,⌋
3931 2777 1181 1877 3836 2465 3397 2266 4403
adv cj v.ami.3s p.d d.dpf n.dpf n.gsm v.iai.3p v.iai.3p

ἠγόραζον, ἐπώλουν, ἐφύτευον, ᾠκοδόμουν· 29 →
they were buying, they were selling, they were planting, they were building; but on the day
60 4797 5885 3868 1254 2465
v.iai.3p v.iai.3p v.iai.3p v.iai.3p

ᾗ δὲ ἡμέρᾳ ἐξῆλθεν Λὼτ ἀπὸ Σοδόμων, ἔβρεξεν πῦρ καὶ
⌊in which⌋ *but* *day* Lot went out *Lot* of Sodom, fire and sulfur rained down *fire* *and*
4005 1254 2465 3397 2002 3397 608 5047 4786 2779 2520 1101 4786 2779
r.dsf cj n.dsf v.aai.3s n.nsm p.g n.gpn v.aai.3s n.asn cj

θεῖον ἀπ' οὐρανοῦ καὶ ἀπώλεσεν πάντας. 30 ⌊κατὰ τὰ αὐτὰ⌋
sulfur from heaven and destroyed them all. It will be just like this
2520 608 4041 2779 660 4246 1639 1639 1639 2848 3836 899
n.asn p.g n.gsm cj v.aai.3s a.apm p.a d.apn r.apn

[a] [ἤ] UBS.
[b] [ἐν τῇ ἡμέρᾳ αὐτοῦ] UBS.

NASB

your midst."

Second Coming Foretold

22 And He said to
the disciples, "The
days will come
when you will long
to see one of the
days of the Son of
Man, and you will
not see it. 23 They
will say to you,
'Look there! Look
here!' Do not go
away, and do not
run after *them.*
24 For just like the
lightning, when it
flashes out of one
part of the sky,
shines to the other
part of the sky,
so will the Son of
Man be in His day.
25 But first He must
suffer many things
and be rejected by
this generation.
26 And just as it
happened in the
days of Noah, so it
will be also in the
days of the Son of
Man: 27 they were
eating, they were
drinking, they were
marrying, they
were being given
in marriage, until
the day that Noah
entered the ark, and
the flood came and
destroyed them all.
28 It was the same
as happened in the
days of Lot: they
were eating, they
were drinking, they
were buying, they
were selling, they
were planting, they
were building; 29 but
on the day that
Lot went out from
Sodom it rained
fire and brimstone
from heaven and
destroyed them all.
30 It will be just

NIV

on the day the Son
of Man is revealed.
31 On that day no
one who is on the
housetop, with
possessions inside,
should go down
to get them. Like-
wise, no one in
the field should go
back for anything.
32 Remember Lot's
wife! 33 Whoever
tries to keep their
life will lose it,
and whoever los-
es their life will
preserve it. 34 I tell
you, on that night
two people will
be in one bed;
one will be taken
and the other left.
35 Two women will
be grinding grain
together; one will
be taken and the
other left." [36][a]
37 "Where, Lord?"
they asked.
He replied,
"Where there is a
dead body, there
the vultures will
gather."

The Parable of the Persistent Widow

18 Then Jesus
told his dis-
ciples a parable
to show them that
they should always
pray and not give
up. 2 He said: "In a
certain town there
was a judge who
neither feared God
nor cared what
people thought.
3 And there was
a widow in that
town who kept
coming to him

[a] 36 Some manu-
scripts include here
words similar to
Matt. 24:40.

ἔσται ἡ ἡμέρᾳ ὁ υἱὸς τοῦ ἀνθρώπου ἀποκαλύπτεται. 31 ἐν ἐκείνῃ τῇ
It will be on the day the Son of Man is revealed. "On that *{the}*
1639 4005 2465 3836 5626 3836 476 636 1877 1697 3836
v.fmi.3s r.dsf n.dsf d.nsm n.nsm d.gsm n.gsm v.ppi.3s p.d r.dsf d.dsf

ἡμέρᾳ ὃς ἔσται ἐπὶ τοῦ δώματος καὶ τὰ σκεύη αὐτοῦ ἐν τῇ
day the one who is on the housetop, and *{the}* his belongings *his* are in the
2465 4005 1639 2093 3836 1560 2779 3836 899 5007 899 1877 3836
n.dsf r.nsm v.fmi.3s p.g d.gsn n.gsn cj d.npn n.npn r.gsm.3 p.d d.dsf

οἰκίᾳ, ↱ μὴ καταβάτω ἆραι αὐτά, καὶ ὁ ἐν ἀγρῷ ὁμοίως
house, must not go down to get them, and likewise the one who is in the field *likewise*
3864 2849 3590 2849 149 899 2779 3931 3836 1877 69 3931
n.dsf pl v.aam.3s f.aa r.apn.3 cj d.nsm p.d n.dsm adv

↱ μὴ ἐπιστρεψάτω ⌞εἰς τὰ ὀπίσω.⌟ 32 μνημονεύετε τῆς γυναικὸς Λώτ.
must not turn back. Remember *{the}* Lot's wife. *Lot's*
2188 3590 2188 1650 3836 3958 3648 3836 3397 1222 3397
pl v.aam.3s p.a d.apn adv v.pam.2p d.gsf n.gsf n.gsm

33 ⌞ὃς ἐὰν⌟ ζητήσῃ ↱ ↱ τὴν ψυχὴν αὐτοῦ περιποιήσασθαι ἀπολέσει
Whoever tries to retain *{the}* his life *his* for himself will lose
4005 1569 2426 4347 4347 3836 899 6034 899 4347 660
r.nsm pl v.aas.3s d.asf n.asf r.gsm.3 f.am v.fai.3s

αὐτήν, ὃς δ᾽ ἂν ἀπολέσῃ ζῳογονήσει αὐτήν. 34 λέγω ὑμῖν, ταύτῃ
it, and whoever *and* ~ loses his life will preserve it. I tell you, on that
899 1254 4005 1254 323 660 2441 899 3306 7007 4047
r.asf.3 r.nsm cj pl v.aas.3s v.fai.3s r.asf.3 v.pai.1s r.dp.2 r.dsf

τῇ νυκτὶ ἔσονται δύο ἐπὶ κλίνης μιᾶς, ὁ εἷς παραλημφθήσεται καὶ
{the} night ⌞there will be⌟ two in one bed; *one* *{the}* one will be taken and
3836 3816 1639 1545 2093 1651 3109 1651 3836 1651 4161 2779
d.dsf n.dsf v.fmi.3p a.npm p.g n.gsf a.gsf d.nsm a.nsm v.fpi.3s cj

ὁ ἕτερος ἀφεθήσεται· 35 ἔσονται δύο ἀλήθουσαι ἐπὶ τὸ αὐτό,
the other left behind. ⌞There will be⌟ ⌞two women⌟ grinding at the mill together;
3836 2283 918 1639 1545 241 2093 3836 899
d.nsm r.nsm v.fpi.3s v.fmi.3p a.npf pt.pa.npf p.a d.asn r.asn

ἡ μία παραλημφθήσεται, ἡ δὲ ἑτέρα ἀφεθήσεται.[a] 37 καὶ
{the} one will be taken and the *and* other left behind." Then the disciples said
3836 1651 4161 1254 3836 1254 2283 918 2779 3306
d.nsf a.nsf v.fpi.3s d.nsf cj r.nsf v.fpi.3s cj

ἀποκριθέντες λέγουσιν αὐτῷ, ποῦ, κύριε; ὁ δὲ εἶπεν αὐτοῖς, ὅπου
to him in response, *say* *to him* "Where, Lord?" And he *And* said to them, "Where
899 899 646 3306 899 4543 3261 1254 3836 1254 3306 899 3963
pt.ap.npm v.pai.3p r.dsm.3 cj n.vsm d.nsm cj v.aai.3s r.dpm.3 cj

τὸ σῶμα, ἐκεῖ καὶ οἱ ἀετοὶ ἐπισυναχθήσονται.
the corpse is, there also the vultures will be gathered."
3836 5393 1695 2779 3836 108 2190
d.nsn n.nsn adv adv d.npm n.npm v.fpi.3p

18:1 ἔλεγεν δὲ παραβολὴν αὐτοῖς πρὸς τὸ δεῖν
Then Jesus told *Then* them a parable *them* to the effect that they should
1254 3306 1254 899 4130 899 4639 3836 899 1256
v.iai.3s cj n.asf r.dpm.3 p.a d.asn f.pa

πάντοτε προσεύχεσθαι αὐτοὺς καὶ μὴ ἐγκακεῖν, 2 λέγων,
continue to pray at all times *should continue to pray* *they* and never give up. He said,
4667 4667 4667 4121 4667 899 2779 3590 1591 3306
adv f.pm r.apm.3 cj pl f.pa pt.pa.nsm

κριτής τις ἦν ἔν τινι πόλει τὸν θεὸν
"There was a certain judge *certain* *There was* in a certain city who neither feared *{the}* God
1639 1639 5516 3216 5516 1639 1877 5516 4484 5828 3590 5828 3836 2536
n.nsm r.nsm v.iai.3s p.d r.dsf n.dsf d.asm n.asm

μὴ φοβούμενος καὶ ἄνθρωπον μὴ ἐντρεπόμενος. 3
neither *who feared* *{and}* nor had any regard for people. *nor* *had regard for* There
3590 5828 2779 3590 1956 1956 1956 476 3590 1956 1639
pl pt.pp.nsm cj n.asm pl pt.pp.nsm

χήρα δὲ ἦν ἐν τῇ πόλει ἐκείνῃ καὶ ἤρχετο πρὸς αὐτὸν
was a widow *{and}* *There was* in *{the}* that city, *that* and ⌞she kept coming⌟ to him,
1639 5939 1254 1639 1877 3836 1697 4484 1697 2779 2262 4639 899
n.nsf cj v.iai.3s p.d d.dsf n.dsf r.dsf cj v.imi.3s p.a r.asm.3

[a] 36 δύο ἔσονται ἐν τῷ ἀγρῷ· ὁ εἷς παραληφθήσεται, καὶ ὁ ἕτερος ἀφεθήσεται. included by TR after ἀφεθήσεται.

NASB

the same on the
day that the Son of
Man is revealed.
31 On that day, the
one who is on
the housetop and
whose goods are
in the house must
not go down to
take them out; and
likewise the one
who is in the field
must not turn back.
32 Remember Lot's
wife. 33 Whoever
seeks to keep his
life will lose it, and
whoever loses *his*
life will preserve it.
34 I tell you, on that
night there will be
two in one bed; one
will be taken and
the other will be
left. 35 There will be
two women grind-
ing at the same
place; one will be
taken and the other
will be left. 36 [[a]Two
men will be in
the field; one will
be taken and the
other will be left."]
37 And answering
they *said to Him,
"Where, Lord?"
And He said to
them, "Where the
body *is,* there also
the vultures will be
gathered."

Parables on Prayer

18:1 Now He was
telling them a par-
able to show that
at all times they
ought to pray and
not to lose heart,
2 saying, "In a
certain city there
was a judge who
did not fear God
and did not respect
man. 3 There was a
widow in that city,
and she kept com-
ing to him,

[a] Early mss do not
contain this v

NIV

with the plea,
'Grant me justice
against my adver-
sary.'
4"For some time
he refused. But
finally he said to
himself, 'Even
though I don't
fear God or care
what people think,
5yet because this
widow keeps both-
ering me, I will
see that she gets
justice, so that she
won't eventually
come and attack
me!'"
6And the Lord
said, "Listen to
what the unjust
judge says. 7And
will not God bring
about justice for
his chosen ones,
who cry out to him
day and night?
Will he keep put-
ting them off? 8I
tell you, he will
see that they get
justice, and quick-
ly. However, when
the Son of Man
comes, will he
find faith on the
earth?"

The Parable of the Pharisee and the Tax Collector

9To some who
were confident of
their own righ-
teousness and
looked down on
everyone else,
Jesus told this
parable: 10"Two
men went up to the
temple to pray, one
a Pharisee and the
other a tax collec-
tor. 11The Pharisee
stood by himself
and prayed: 'God,
I thank you that I
am not like other
people—robbers,
evildoers, adulter-
ers—or even

λέγουσα, ἐκδίκησόν με ἀπὸ τοῦ ἀντιδίκου μου. 4 καὶ ↱ οὐκ ἤθελεν ἐπὶ
saying, 'Vindicate me against {the} my adversary.' my {and} He didn't want to for a
3306 1688 1609 608 3836 1609 508 1609 2779 2527 4024 2527 2093
pt.pa.nsf v.aam.2s r.as.1 p.g d.gsm n.gsm r.gs.1 cj pl v.iai.3s p.a

χρόνον. μετὰ δὲ ταῦτα εἶπεν ἐν ἑαυτῷ, εἰ καὶ τὸν θεὸν
time. But later But on he said to himself, 'Though {also} I neither fear {the} God
5989 1254 3552 1254 4047 3306 1877 1571 1623 2779 5828 4024 5828 3836 2536
n.asm p.a cj r.apn v.aai.3s p.d r.dsm.3 cj adv d.asm n.asm

οὐ φοβοῦμαι οὐδὲ ἄνθρωπον ἐντρέπομαι, 5 διά γε τὸ
neither I fear nor have regard for people, have regard for yet because yet {the} this
4024 5828 4028 1956 1956 1956 476 1956 1145 1328 1145 3836 4047
pl v.ppi.1s cj n.asm v.ppi.1s p.a pl d.asn

παρέχειν μοι κόπον τὴν χήραν ταύτην ἐκδικήσω αὐτήν, ἵνα
widow keeps bothering me, bothering {the} widow this I will vindicate her, so that
5939 4218 3160 1609 3160 3836 5939 4047 1688 899 2671
f.pa r.ds.1 n.asm d.asf n.asf r.asf v.fai.1s r.asf.3 cj

↱ ↱ μὴ ⌞εἰς τέλος⌟ ἐρχομένη ὑπωπιάζῃ με. ↰ 6
by her coming she will not ultimately by her coming wear me out.'" And
2262 2262 2262 5724 5724 3590 1650 5465 2262 5724 1609 5724 1254
pl p.a n.asn pt.pm.nsf v.pas.3s r.as.1

εἶπεν δὲ ὁ κύριος, ἀκούσατε τί ὁ κριτὴς τῆς ἀδικίας
the Lord said, And the Lord "Hear what the unrighteous judge {the} unrighteous
3836 3261 3306 1254 3836 3261 201 5515 3836 94 3216 3836 94
v.aai.3s cj d.nsm n.nsm v.aam.2p r.asn d.nsm n.nsm d.gsf n.gsf

λέγει. 7 ↱ ↱ ὁ δὲ θεὸς ⌞οὐ μὴ⌟ ⌞ποιήσῃ τὴν ἐκδίκησιν⌟ τῶν
says. Will not {the} {and} God certainly vindicate {the} his
3306 4472 4024 3836 1254 2536 4024 3590 4472 3836 1689 3836 899
v.pai.3s d.nsm cj n.nsm pl pl v.aas.3s d.asf n.asf d.gpm

ἐκλεκτῶν αὐτοῦ τῶν βοώντων αὐτῷ ἡμέρας καὶ νυκτός, καὶ μακροθυμεῖ ἐπ' αὐτοῖς;
elect, his who cry to him day and night, and have patience with them?
1723 899 3836 1066 899 2465 2779 3816 2779 3428 2093 899
a.gpm r.gsm.3 d.gpm pt.pa.gpm r.dsm.3 n.gsf cj n.gsf cj v.pai.3s p.d r.dpm.3

8 λέγω ὑμῖν ὅτι ⌞ποιήσει τὴν ἐκδίκησιν⌟ αὐτῶν ⌞ἐν τάχει.⌟ πλὴν ↱
I tell you, ~ he will vindicate them without delay; but will
3306 7007 4022 4472 3836 1689 899 1877 5443 4440 2351
v.pai.1s r.dp.2 cj v.fai.3s d.asf n.asf r.gpm.3 p.d n.dsn cj

ὁ υἱὸς τοῦ ἀνθρώπου ἐλθὼν ἆρα εὑρήσει τὴν πίστιν ἐπὶ τῆς γῆς;
the Son of Man, ⌞when he comes,⌟ {then} find {the} faith on {the} earth?"
3836 5626 3836 476 2262 727 2351 3836 4411 2093 3836 1178
d.nsm n.nsm d.gsm n.gsm pt.aa.nsm pl v.fai.3s d.asf n.asf p.g d.gsf n.gsf

9 → Εἶπεν δὲ καὶ πρός τινας τοὺς πεποιθότας ἐφ' ἑαυτοῖς
He also told also {also} this parable to some who were confident in themselves,
1254 3306 1254 2779 4047 4130 4639 5516 3836 4275 2093 1571
v.aai.3s cj adv p.a r.apm d.apm pt.ra.apm p.d r.dpm.3

ὅτι εἰσὶν δίκαιοι καὶ ἐξουθενοῦντας τοὺς λοιποὺς ↰ ↰ τὴν
because they were righteous, and treated {the} others with contempt. {the}
4022 1639 1465 2779 2024 3836 3370 2024 2024 3836
cj v.pai.3p a.npm cj pt.pa.apm d.apm a.apm d.asf

παραβολὴν ταύτην· 10 ἄνθρωποι δύο ἀνέβησαν εἰς τὸ ἱερὸν προσεύξασθαι,
parable this "Two men Two went up into the temple to pray,
4130 4047 1545 476 1545 326 1650 3836 2639 4667
n.asf r.asf n.npm a.npm v.aai.3p p.a d.asn n.asn f.am

ὁ εἷς Φαρισαῖος καὶ ὁ ἕτερος τελώνης. 11 ὁ Φαρισαῖος σταθεὶς
the one a Pharisee and the other a tax collector. The Pharisee stood and
3836 1651 5757 2779 3836 2283 5467 3836 5757 2705
d.nsm a.nsm n.nsm cj d.nsm r.nsm n.nsm d.nsm n.nsm pt.ap.nsm

πρὸς ἑαυτὸν ταῦτα προσηύχετο· ὁ θεός, εὐχαριστῶ σοι ὅτι
prayed like this to himself: his prayed {the} 'God, I thank you that I am
4667 4047 4639 1571 4047 4667 3836 2536 2373 5148 4022 1639 1639
p.a r.asm.3 r.apn v.imi.3s d.vsm n.vsm v.pai.1s r.ds.2 cj

οὐκ εἰμὶ ὥσπερ οἱ λοιποὶ τῶν ἀνθρώπων, ἅρπαγες, ἄδικοι, μοιχοί, ἢ καὶ
not I am like the rest of mankind — swindlers, rogues, adulterers, or even
4024 1639 6061 3836 3370 3836 476 774 96 3659 2445 2779
pl v.pai.1s pl d.npm a.npm d.gpm n.gpm a.npm a.npm n.npm cj adv

NASB

saying, 'Give me
legal protection
from my oppo-
nent.' 4For a while
he was unwilling;
but afterward he
said to himself,
'Even though I
do not fear God
nor respect man,
5yet because this
widow bothers
me, I will give
her legal protec-
tion, otherwise by
continually coming
she will wear me
out.'" 6And the
Lord said, "Hear
what the unrigh-
teous judge *said;
7now, will not God
bring about justice
for His elect who
cry to Him day
and night, and
will He delay long
over them? 8I tell
you that He will
bring about justice
for them quickly.
However, when the
Son of Man comes,
will He find faith
on the earth?"

The Pharisee and the Publican

9And He also
told this parable to
some people who
trusted in them-
selves that they
were righteous, and
viewed others with
contempt: 10"Two
men went up into
the temple to pray,
one a Pharisee
and the other a tax
collector. 11The
Pharisee stood and
was praying this
to himself: 'God,
I thank You that I
am not like other
people: swindlers,
unjust, adulterers,

NIV

like this tax collec-
tor. 12I fast twice
a week and give a
tenth of all I get.'
13"But the tax
collector stood at a
distance. He would
not even look up
to heaven, but beat
his breast and said,
'God, have mercy
on me, a sinner.'
14"I tell you that
this man, rather
than the other,
went home justi-
fied before God.
For all those who
exalt themselves
will be humbled,
and those who
humble themselves
will be exalted."

The Little Children and Jesus

15People were
also bringing ba-
bies to Jesus for
him to place his
hands on them.
When the disci-
ples saw this, they
rebuked them.
16But Jesus called
the children to
him and said, "Let
the little chil-
dren come to me,
and do not hin-
der them, for the
kingdom of God
belongs to such as
these. 17Truly I tell
you, anyone who
will not receive the
kingdom of God
like a little child
will never enter it."

The Rich and the Kingdom of God

18A certain ruler
asked him, "Good
teacher, what must
I do to inherit eter-
nal life?"
19"Why do you
call me good?"
Jesus answered.
"No one is good —
except

ὡς οὗτος ὁ τελώνης· 12 νηστεύω δὶς τοῦ σαββάτου, ἀποδεκατῶ πάντα ὅσα
like this *{the}* tax collector. I fast twice a week; I tithe all that
6055 4047 3836 5467 3764 1489 3836 4879 620 4246 4012
pl r.nsm d.nsm n.nsm v.pai.1s adv d.gsn n.gsn v.pai.1s a.apn r.apn

κτῶμαι. 13 ὁ δὲ τελώνης μακρόθεν ἑστὼς οὐκ
I get.' The *however* tax collector, however, standing at a distance, *standing* would not
3227 3836 1254 5467 1254 2705 3427 2705 2527 4024
v.pmi.1s d.nsm cj n.nsm adv pt.ra.nsm pl

ἤθελεν οὐδὲ τοὺς ὀφθαλμοὺς ἐπᾶραι εἰς τὸν οὐρανόν, ἀλλ᾽ ἔτυπτεν τὸ
would even raise his eyes *raise* to *{the}* heaven, but kept beating *{the}* his
2527 4028 2048 3836 4057 2048 1650 3836 4041 247 5597 3836 899
v.iai.3s adv d.apm n.apm f.aa p.a d.asm n.asm cj v.iai.3s d.asn

στῆθος αὐτοῦ λέγων, ὁ θεός, ἱλάσθητί μοι τῷ ἁμαρτωλῷ. 14 λέγω ὑμῖν,
breast, *his* saying, *{the}* 'God, be merciful to me, a sinner!' I tell you, this
5111 899 3306 3836 2536 2661 1609 3836 283 3306 7007 4047
n.asn r.gsm.3 pt.pa.nsm d.vsm n.vsm v.apm.2s r.ds.1 d.dsm a.dsm v.pai.1s r.dp.2

κατέβη οὗτος δεδικαιωμένος εἰς τὸν οἶκον
man went down *this man* to his house upright in the sight of God, *to* *{the}* *house*
4047 2849 4047 1650 899 3875 1467 1650 3836 3875
v.aai.3s r.nsm pt.rp.nsm p.a d.asm n.asm

αὐτοῦ παρ᾽ ἐκεῖνον· ὅτι πᾶς ὁ ὑψῶν ἑαυτὸν ταπεινωθήσεται,
his ⌊rather than⌋ the other. For everyone who exalts himself will be humbled, and
899 4123 1697 4022 4246 3836 5738 1571 5427 1254
r.gsm.3 p.a r.asm cj a.nsm d.nsm pt.pa.nsm r.asm.3 v.fpi.3s

ὁ δὲ ταπεινῶν ἑαυτὸν ὑψωθήσεται. 15 προσέφερον δὲ αὐτῷ
the *and* one who humbles himself will be exalted." Now people ⌊were bringing to⌋ *Now* him
3836 1254 5427 1571 5738 1254 4712 1254 899
d.nsm cj pt.pa.nsm r.asm.3 v.fpi.3s v.iai.3p cj r.dsm.3

καὶ τὰ βρέφη ἵνα αὐτῶν ἅπτηται· →
even *{the}* little ones so he would touch them. *he would touch* However, when the disciples
2779 3836 1100 2671 721 721 721 899 721 1254 3836 3412
adv d.apn n.apn cj r.gpn.3 v.pms.3s

ἰδόντες δὲ οἱ μαθηταὶ ἐπετίμων αὐτοῖς. 16 ὁ δὲ Ἰησοῦς
saw *However* *the* *disciples* it, ⌊they began to rebuke⌋ them. *{the}* But Jesus
1625 1254 3836 3412 2203 899 3836 1254 2652
pt.aa.npm cj d.npm n.npm v.iai.3p r.dpm.3 d.nsm cj n.nsm

προσεκαλέσατο αὐτὰ ↰ λέγων, ἄφετε τὰ παιδία ἔρχεσθαι πρός με καὶ ↱
called them to him, saying, "Let the children come to me, and do
4673 899 4673 3306 918 3836 4086 2262 4639 1609 2779 3266
v.ami.3s r.apn.3 pt.pa.nsm v.aam.2p d.apn n.apn f.pm p.a r.as.1 cj

μὴ κωλύετε αὐτά, τῶν γὰρ τοιούτων ἐστὶν ἡ βασιλεία
not stop them, for it is to *for* such as these *it is that belongs* that the kingdom
3590 3266 899 1142 1639 1639 3836 1142 5525 1639 1639 3836 993
pl v.pam.2p r.apn.3 d.gpn cj r.gpn v.pai.3s d.nsf n.nsf

τοῦ θεοῦ. 17 ἀμὴν λέγω ὑμῖν, ⌊ὃς ἂν⌋ ↱ μὴ δέξηται
of God belongs. I tell you the truth, *I tell* *you* whoever does not receive
3836 2536 1639 3306 3306 7007 297 3306 7007 4005 323 1312 3590 1312
d.gsm n.gsm pl v.pai.1s r.dp.2 r.nsm pl pl v.ams.3s

τὴν βασιλείαν τοῦ θεοῦ ὡς παιδίον, ↱ ⌊οὐ μὴ⌋ ⌊εἰσέλθῃ εἰς⌋ αὐτήν.
the kingdom of God like a child shall certainly never enter it."
3836 993 3836 2536 6055 4086 1656 4024 3590 1656 1650 899
d.asf n.asf d.gsm n.gsm pl n.nsn pl pl v.aas.3s p.a r.asf.3

18 καὶ ἐπηρώτησέν τις αὐτὸν ἄρχων λέγων, διδάσκαλε ἀγαθέ,
Now a certain ruler asked *certain* him, *ruler* saying, "Good Teacher, *Good*
2779 5516 807 2089 5516 899 807 3306 19 1437 19
cj v.aai.3s r.nsm r.asm.3 n.nsm pt.pa.nsm n.vsm a.vsm

τί ποιήσας ζωὴν αἰώνιον κληρονομήσω; 19 εἶπεν δὲ
what must I do to inherit eternal life?" *eternal* *to inherit* And Jesus said *And*
5515 4472 3099 3099 173 2437 173 3099 1254 2652 3306 1254
r.asn pt.aa.nsm n.asf a.asf v.fai.1s v.aai.3s cj

αὐτῷ ὁ Ἰησοῦς, τί με λέγεις ἀγαθόν; οὐδεὶς ἀγαθὸς ⌊εἰ
to him, *{the}* *Jesus* "Why do you call me *do you call* good? No one is good except
899 3836 2652 5515 3306 3306 3306 1609 3306 19 4029 19 1623
r.dsm.3 d.nsm n.nsm r.asn r.as.1 v.pai.2s a.asm a.nsm a.nsm cj

NASB

or even like this
tax collector. 12I
fast twice a week;
I pay tithes of all
that I get.' 13But
the tax collector,
standing some
distance away, was
even unwilling to
lift up his eyes to
heaven, but was
beating his breast,
saying, 'God, be
merciful to me,
the sinner!' 14I tell
you, this man went
to his house justi-
fied rather than the
other; for everyone
who exalts himself
will be humbled,
but he who hum-
bles himself will be
exalted."
15And they were
bringing even their
babies to Him so
that He would
touch them, but
when the disciples
saw it, they *began*
rebuking them.
16But Jesus called
for them, say-
ing, "Permit the
children to come
to Me, and do
not hinder them,
for the kingdom
of God belongs
to such as these.
17Truly I say to you,
whoever does not
receive the king-
dom of God like a
child will not enter
it *at all.*"

The Rich Young Ruler

18A ruler ques-
tioned Him, saying,
"Good Teacher,
what shall I do
to inherit eternal
life?" 19And Jesus
said to him, "Why
do you call Me
good? No one is
good except God

NIV

God alone. [20]You
know the com-
mandments: 'You
shall not commit
adultery, you shall
not murder, you
shall not steal, you
shall not give false
testimony, honor
your father and
mother.'[a]"
[21]"All these I
have kept since
I was a boy," he
said.
[22]When Jesus
heard this, he said
to him, "You still
lack one thing. Sell
everything you
have and give to
the poor, and you
will have treasure
in heaven. Then
come, follow me."
[23]When he heard
this, he became
very sad, be-
cause he was very
wealthy. [24]Jesus
looked at him
and said, "How
hard it is for the
rich to enter the
kingdom of God!
[25]Indeed, it is eas-
ier for a camel to
go through the eye
of a needle than
for someone who
is rich to enter the
kingdom of God."
[26]Those who
heard this asked,
"Who then can be
saved?"
[27]Jesus replied,
"What is impos-
sible with man
is possible with
God."
[28]Peter said

μὴ εἷς ὁ θεός. [20] τὰς ἐντολὰς οἶδας· ↱ ↱ μὴ
one — {the} God. You know the commandments: *You know* 'You shall not
3590 1651 3836 2536 3857 3857 3836 1953 3857 3658 3658 3590
pl a.nsm d.nsm n.nsm d.apf n.apf v.rai.2s pl

μοιχεύσῃς, ↱ ↱ μὴ φονεύσῃς, ↱ ↱ μὴ κλέψῃς, ↱ ↱ μὴ
commit adultery; You shall not murder; You shall not steal; You shall not
3658 5839 5839 3590 5839 3096 3096 3590 3096 6018 6018 3590
v.aas.2s pl v.aas.2s pl v.aas.2s pl

ψευδομαρτυρήσῃς, τίμα τὸν πατέρα σου καὶ τὴν μητέρα. [21] ὁ δὲ
bear false witness; Honor {the} your father *your* and {the} mother.' The {and} man
6018 5506 3836 5148 4252 5148 2779 3836 3613 3836 1254
v.aas.2s v.pam.2s d.asm n.asm r.gs.2 cj d.asf n.asf d.nsm cj

εἶπεν, ταῦτα πάντα ἐφύλαξα ἐκ νεότητος. [22] ἀκούσας δὲ ὁ
replied, "All these *All* I have kept since my youth." Upon hearing this, {and} {the}
3306 4246 4047 4246 5875 1666 3744 201 1254 3836
v.aai.3s r.apn a.apn v.aai.1s p.g n.gsf pt.aa.nsm cj d.nsm

Ἰησοῦς εἶπεν αὐτῷ, ἔτι ἕν σοι λείπει· πάντα ὅσα ἔχεις
Jesus said to him, "One thing you still *One* *you* lack: sell all that you have
2652 3306 899 1651 5148 2285 1651 5148 3309 4797 4246 4012 2400
n.nsm v.aai.3s r.dsm.3 adv a.nsn r.ds.2 v.pai.3s a.apn r.apn v.pai.2s

πώλησον καὶ διάδος → πτωχοῖς, καὶ ἕξεις θησαυρὸν ἐν τοῖς[a]
Sell and distribute the proceeds to the poor, and ⌞you will have⌟ treasure in {the}
4797 2779 1344 4777 2779 2400 2565 1877 3836
v.aam.2s cj v.aam.2s a.dpm cj v.fai.2s n.asm p.d d.dpm

οὐρανοῖς, καὶ δεῦρο ἀκολούθει μοι. [23] ↱ ὁ δὲ ἀκούσας ταῦτα
heaven. Then come, follow me." But when he *But* heard this, he became
4041 2779 1306 199 1609 1254 201 3836 1254 201 4047 1181 1181
n.dpm cj j v.pam.2s r.ds.1 d.nsm cj pt.aa.nsm r.apn

περίλυπος ἐγενήθη· ἦν γὰρ πλούσιος σφόδρα. [24] ἰδὼν δὲ
very sad, *he became* for ⌞he was⌟ *for* extremely wealthy. *extremely* Jesus ⌞looked at⌟ {and}
4337 1181 1142 1639 1142 5379 4454 5379 2652 1625 1254
a.nsm v.api.3s v.iai.3s cj a.nsm adv pt.aa.nsm cj

αὐτὸν ὁ Ἰησοῦς [b]περίλυπον γενόμενον εἶπεν, πῶς δυσκόλως
him, {the} *Jesus* becoming very sad, *becoming* and said, "How difficult it is for
899 3836 2652 1181 4337 1181 3306 4802 1552
r.asm.3 d.nsm n.nsm a.asm pt.am.asm v.aai.3s pl adv

οἱ τὰ χρήματα ἔχοντες εἰς τὴν βασιλείαν τοῦ θεοῦ
those who have {the} wealth *who have* to enter {into} the kingdom of God!
3836 2400 2400 3836 5975 2400 1660 1660 1650 3836 993 3836 2536
d.npm d.apn n.apn pt.pa.npm p.a d.asf n.asf d.gsm n.gsm

εἰσπορεύονται· [25] εὐκοπώτερον γάρ ἐστιν κάμηλον
to enter In fact, it is easier *In fact* *it is* for a camel to go
1660 1142 1142 1639 1639 2324 1142 1639 2823 1656 1656
v.pmi.3p a.nsn.c cj v.pai.3s n.asm

διὰ τρήματος → βελόνης εἰσελθεῖν ἢ πλούσιον εἰς τὴν
through the eye of a needle *to go* than for a rich man to enter {into} the
1328 5557 1017 1656 2445 4454 1656 1656 1650 3836
p.g n.gsn n.gsf f.aa pl a.asm p.a d.asf

βασιλείαν τοῦ θεοῦ εἰσελθεῖν. [26] εἶπαν δὲ οἱ ἀκούσαντες,
kingdom of God!" *to enter* Those who heard it said, {and} *Those* *who heard*
993 3836 2536 1656 3836 201 201 3306 1254 3836 201
n.asf d.gsm n.gsm f.aa v.aai.3p cj d.npm pt.aa.npm

καὶ τίς δύναται σωθῆναι; [27] ὁ δὲ εἶπεν, τὰ ἀδύνατα παρὰ
"Who, then, *Who* can be saved?" Jesus {and} said, "What is impossible for
5515 2779 5515 1538 5392 3836 1254 3306 3836 105 4123
cj r.nsm v.ppi.3s f.ap d.nsm cj v.aai.3s d.npn a.npn p.d

ἀνθρώποις δυνατὰ παρὰ τῷ θεῷ ἐστιν. [28] εἶπεν δὲ ὁ Πέτρος,
mortal beings is possible for {the} God." *is* Then Peter said, *Then* {the} *Peter*
476 1639 1543 4123 3836 2536 1639 1254 4377 3306 1254 3836 4377
n.dpm a.npn p.d d.dsm n.dsm v.pai.3s v.aai.3s cj d.nsm n.nsm

NASB

alone. [20]You know
the command-
ments, 'DO NOT
COMMIT ADULTERY,
DO NOT MURDER,
DO NOT STEAL, DO
NOT BEAR FALSE
WITNESS, HONOR
YOUR FATHER AND
MOTHER.'" [21]And
he said, "All these
things I have kept
from *my* youth."
[22]When Jesus heard
this, He said to
him, "One thing
you still lack; sell
all that you possess
and distribute it to
the poor, and you
shall have treasure
in heaven; and
come, follow Me."
[23]But when he had
heard these things,
he became very
sad, for he was ex-
tremely rich. [24]And
Jesus looked at him
and said, "How
hard it is for those
who are wealthy to
enter the kingdom
of God! [25]For it is
easier for a camel
to go through the
eye of a needle
than for a rich
man to enter the
kingdom of God."
[26]They who heard
it said, "Then who
can be saved?"
[27]But He said, "The
things that are
impossible with
people are possible
with God."
[28]Peter said,

[a] 20 Exodus 20:12-16; Deut. 5:16-20

[a] [τοῖς] UBS.
[b] [περίλυπον γενόμενον] UBS, omitted by TNIV.

NIV

to him, "We have
left all we had to
follow you!"
29"Truly I tell
you," Jesus said to
them, "no one who
has left home or
wife or brothers or
sisters or parents
or children for the
sake of the king-
dom of God 30will
fail to receive
many times as
much in this age,
and in the age to
come eternal life."

Jesus Predicts His Death a Third Time

31Jesus took the
Twelve aside and
told them, "We are
going up to Jeru-
salem, and every-
thing that is writ-
ten by the prophets
about the Son of
Man will be ful-
filled. 32He will be
delivered over to
the Gentiles. They
will mock him,
insult him and spit
on him; 33they will
flog him and kill
him. On the third
day he will rise
again."
34The disciples
did not under-
stand any of this.
Its meaning was
hidden from them,
and they did not
know what he was
talking about.

A Blind Beggar Receives His Sight

35As Jesus ap-
proached Jericho,
a blind man was
sitting by the
roadside begging.
36When he heard
the crowd going
by, he asked what
was happening.
37They told him,
"Jesus of Nazareth
is passing by."
38He called out,
"Jesus, Son of
David,

ἰδοὺ ἡμεῖς ἀφέντες τὰ ἴδια ἠκολουθήσαμέν σοι. 29 ὁ δὲ εἶπεν
"Look, we have left what was ours and followed you." Then Jesus *Then* said
2627 7005 918 3836 2625 199 5148 1254 3836 1254 3306
j r.np.1 pt.aa.npm d.apn a.apn v.aai.1p r.ds.2 d.nsm cj v.aai.3s

αὐτοῖς, ἀμὴν λέγω ὑμῖν ὅτι οὐδείς ἐστιν ὃς ἀφῆκεν
to them, "I tell you the truth, *I tell* *you* ~ there is no one *there is* who has left
899 3306 3306 7007 297 3306 7007 4022 1639 1639 4029 1639 4005 918
r.dpm.3 pl v.pai.1s r.dp.2 cj a.nsm v.pai.3s r.nsm v.aai.3s

οἰκίαν ἢ γυναῖκα ἢ ἀδελφοὺς ἢ γονεῖς ἢ τέκνα ἕνεκεν τῆς
home or wife or siblings or parents or children, ⌊for the sake of⌋ the
3864 2445 1222 2445 81 2445 1204 2445 5451 1914 3836
n.asf cj n.asf cj n.apm cj n.apm cj n.apn p.g d.gsf

βασιλείας τοῦ θεοῦ, 30 ὃς ↱ ⌊οὐχὶ μὴ⌋ ἀπολάβη[a] πολλαπλασίονα ἐν τῷ
kingdom of God who will not receive many times as much in *{the}* this
993 3836 2536 4005 655 4049 3590 655 4491 1877 3836 4047
n.gsf d.gsm n.gsm r.nsm pl pl v.aas.3s a.apn p.d d.dsm

καιρῷ τούτῳ καὶ ἐν τῷ αἰῶνι τῷ ἐρχομένῳ ζωὴν αἰώνιον. 31 παραλαβὼν
age *this* and, in the age to come, eternal life." *eternal* Taking
2789 4047 2779 1877 3836 172 3836 2262 173 2437 173 4161
n.dsm r.dsm cj p.d d.dsm n.dsm d.dsm pt.pm.dsm n.asf a.asf pt.aa.nsm

δὲ τοὺς δώδεκα ↰ εἶπεν πρὸς αὐτούς, ἰδοὺ ἀναβαίνομεν εἰς Ἰερουσαλήμ, καὶ
{and} the twelve aside, he said to them, "See, we are going up to Jerusalem, and
1254 3836 1557 4161 3306 4639 899 2627 326 1650 2647 2779
cj d.apm a.apm v.aai.3s p.a r.apm.3 j v.pai.1p p.a n.asf cj

τελεσθήσεται πάντα τὰ γεγραμμένα διὰ τῶν προφητῶν τῷ υἱῷ τοῦ
will be carried out everything *{the}* written by the prophets regarding the Son of
5464 4246 3836 1211 1328 3836 4737 3836 5626 3836
v.fpi.3s a.npn d.npn pt.rp.npn p.g d.gpm n.gpm d.dsm n.dsm d.gsm

ἀνθρώπου· 32 παραδοθήσεται γὰρ τοῖς ἔθνεσιν καὶ
Man will be carried out. For ⌊he will be handed over⌋ *For* to the Gentiles and
476 5464 5464 5464 5464 1142 4140 1142 3836 1620 2779
n.gsm v.fpi.3s cj d.dpn n.dpn cj

ἐμπαιχθήσεται καὶ ὑβρισθήσεται καὶ ἐμπτυσθήσεται 33 καὶ μαστιγώσαντες
will be ridiculed and ill-treated and spat on. Then after scourging him,
1850 2779 5614 2779 1870 2779 3463
v.fpi.3s cj v.fpi.3s cj v.fpi.3s cj pt.aa.npm

ἀποκτενοῦσιν αὐτόν, καὶ τῇ ἡμέρᾳ τῇ τρίτῃ ἀναστήσεται. 34 καὶ
they will kill him, but ⌊on the⌋ third day *{the}* *third* he will arise again." But the
650 899 2779 3836 5569 2465 3836 5569 482 2779
v.fai.3p r.asm.3 cj d.dsf n.dsf d.dsf a.dsf v.fmi.3s cj

αὐτοὶ οὐδὲν τούτων συνῆκαν καὶ ἦν τὸ ῥῆμα
twelve understood none ⌊of these things;⌋ *understood* in fact, what he said was *what* *said*
899 5317 4029 4047 5317 2779 3836 4047 4839 1639 3836 4839
r.npm a.asn r.gpn v.aai.3p cj v.iai.3s d.nsn n.nsn

τοῦτο κεκρυμμένον ἀπ᾽ αὐτῶν καὶ ↱ ↱ οὐκ ἐγίνωσκον τὰ λεγόμενα.
he kept hidden from them and they did not grasp what was being said.
4047 3221 608 899 2779 1182 1182 4024 1182 3836 3306
r.nsn pt.rp.nsn p.g r.gpm.3 cj pl v.iai.3p d.apn pt.pp.apn

35 ἐγένετο δὲ ἐν τῷ ἐγγίζειν αὐτὸν εἰς Ἰεριχὼ ↱ τυφλός
{it happened that} *{and}* As ~ Jesus drew near *Jesus* to Jericho, there was a blind man
1181 1254 1877 3836 899 1581 899 1650 2637 2764 5516 5603
v.ami.3s cj p.d d.dsn f.pa r.asm.3 p.a n.asf a.nsm

τις ἐκάθητο παρὰ τὴν ὁδὸν ἐπαιτῶν. 36 ἀκούσας δὲ ὄχλου
a sitting by the roadside, asking for alms. When he heard *{and}* a crowd
5516 2764 4123 3836 3847 2050 201 1254 4063
r.nsm v.imi.3s p.a d.asf n.asf pt.pa.nsm pt.aa.nsm cj n.gsm

διαπορευομένου ἐπυνθάνετο τί εἴη τοῦτο. 37 ἀπήγγειλαν δὲ αὐτῷ ὅτι
going by, he inquired what this ⌊might be.⌋ *this* They told *{and}* him that
1388 4785 5515 4047 1639 4047 550 1254 899 4022
pt.pm.gsm v.imi.3s r.nsn v.pao.3s r.nsn v.aai.3p cj r.dsm.3 cj

Ἰησοῦς ὁ Ναζωραῖος παρέρχεται. 38 καὶ ἐβόησεν λέγων, Ἰησοῦ υἱὲ Δαυίδ,
Jesus of Nazareth was passing by. So ⌊he called out,⌋ saying, "Jesus, Son of David,
2652 3836 3717 4216 2779 1066 3306 2652 5626 1253
n.nsm d.nsm n.nsm v.pmi.3s cj v.aai.3s pt.pa.nsm n.vsm n.vsm n.gsm

[a] ἀπολάβῃ omitted by UBS.

NASB

"Behold, we have
left our own *homes*
and followed You."
29And He said to
them, "Truly I say
to you, there is no
one who has left
house or wife or
brothers or parents
or children, for the
sake of the king-
dom of God, 30who
will not receive
many times as
much at this time
and in the age to
come, eternal life."
31Then He took
the twelve aside
and said to them,
"Behold, we are
going up to Je-
rusalem, and all
things which are
written through the
prophets about the
Son of Man will
be accomplished.
32For He will be
handed over to
the Gentiles, and
will be mocked
and mistreated and
spit upon, 33and
after they have
scourged Him, they
will kill Him; and
the third day He
will rise again."
34But the disciples
understood none of
these things, and
the meaning of this
statement was hid-
den from them, and
they did not com-
prehend the things
that were said.

Bartimaeus Receives Sight

35As Jesus was ap-
proaching Jericho,
a blind man was
sitting by the road
begging. 36Now
hearing a crowd
going by, he *began*
to inquire what this
was. 37They told
him that Jesus of
Nazareth was pass-
ing by. 38And he
called out, saying,
"Jesus, Son of

NIV

have mercy
on me!”
[39]Those who led
the way rebuked
him and told him
to be quiet, but
he shouted all the
more, “Son of Da-
vid, have mercy
on me!”
[40]Jesus stopped
and ordered the
man to be brought
to him. When
he came near,
Jesus asked him,
[41]“What do you
want me to do for
you?”
“Lord, I want to
see,” he replied.
[42]Jesus said to
him, “Receive
your sight; your
faith has healed
you.” [43]Immediate-
ly he received his
sight and followed
Jesus, praising
God. When all the
people saw it, they
also praised God.

Zacchaeus the Tax Collector

19 Jesus en-
tered Jeri-
cho and was pass-
ing through. [2]A
man was there by
the name of Zac-
chaeus; he was a
chief tax collector
and was wealthy.
[3]He wanted to see
who Jesus was, but
because he was
short he could not
see over the crowd.
[4]So he ran ahead
and climbed a
sycamore-fig tree
to see him, since
Jesus was coming
that way.
[5]When Jesus
reached the spot,
he looked up and
said to him,

ἐλέησόν με. [39] καὶ οἱ προάγοντες ἐπετίμων αὐτῷ ἵνα
˪have mercy on˩ me!” {and} Those ˪who were leading the way˩ began to rebuke him that
1796 1609 2779 3836 4575 2203 899 2671
v.aam.2s r.as.1 cj d.npm pt.pa.npm v.iai.3p r.dsm.3 cj

σιγήσῃ, αὐτὸς δὲ πολλῷ μᾶλλον ἔκραζεν, υἱὲ Δαυίδ,
˪he should be quiet;˩ but he but cried out all the more, cried out “Son of David,
4967 1254 899 1254 3189 3189 4498 3437 3189 5626 1253
v.aas.3s r.nsm cj a.dsn adv.c v.iai.3s n.vsm n.gsm

ἐλέησόν με. [40] σταθεὶς δὲ ὁ Ἰησοῦς ἐκέλευσεν αὐτὸν
˪have mercy on˩ me!” Jesus stopped {and} {the} Jesus and ordered the beggar
1796 1609 2652 2705 1254 3836 2652 3027 899
v.aam.2s r.as.1 pt.ap.nsm cj d.nsm n.nsm v.aai.3s r.asm.3

ἀχθῆναι πρὸς αὐτόν. → ἐγγίσαντος δὲ αὐτοῦ ἐπηρώτησεν
to be brought to him. When the man had come near, {and} man Jesus asked
72 4639 899 899 1581 1254 899 2089
f.ap p.a r.asm.3 pt.aa.gsm cj r.gsm.3 v.aai.3s

αὐτόν, [41] τί σοι θέλεις ποιήσω; ὁ δὲ εἶπεν, κύριε, ἵνα
him, “What for you ˪do you want˩ me to do for you?” He {and} said, “Lord, that
899 5515 5148 2527 4472 5148 5148 3836 1254 3306 3261 2671
r.asm.3 r.asn r.ds.2 v.pai.2s v.aas.1s d.nsm cj v.aai.3s n.vsm cj

ἀναβλέψω. [42] καὶ ὁ Ἰησοῦς εἶπεν αὐτῷ, ἀνάβλεψον· ἡ πίστις σου
I might see again.” {and} {the} Jesus said to him, “See again! {the} Your faith Your
329 2779 3836 2652 3306 899 329 3836 5148 4411 5148
v.aas.1s cj d.nsm n.nsm v.aai.3s r.dsm.3 v.aam.2s d.nsf n.nsf r.gs.2

σέσωκέν σε. [43] καὶ παραχρῆμα ἀνέβλεψεν καὶ ἠκολούθει αὐτῷ
has saved you.” And immediately ˪he could see again,˩ and began to follow Jesus,
5392 5148 2779 4202 329 2779 199 899
v.rai.3s r.as.2 cj adv v.aai.3s cj v.iai.3s r.dsm.3

δοξάζων τὸν θεόν. καὶ πᾶς ὁ λαὸς ἰδὼν ἔδωκεν αἶνον τῷ
˪giving glory to˩ {the} God. And all the people, ˪when they saw˩ this, gave praise to
1519 3836 2536 2779 4246 3836 3295 1625 1443 142 3836
pt.pa.nsm d.asm n.asm cj a.nsm d.nsm n.nsm pt.aa.nsm v.aai.3s n.asm d.dsm

θεῷ.
God.
2536
n.dsm

[19:1] καὶ εἰσελθὼν διήρχετο τὴν Ἰεριχώ. [2] καὶ
{and} Jesus entered Jericho and ˪was passing through.˩ {the} Jericho {and}
2779 1656 2637 1451 3836 2637 2779
cj pt.aa.nsm v.imi.3s d.asf n.asf cj

ἰδοὺ ἀνὴρ → ὀνόματι καλούμενος Ζακχαῖος, καὶ αὐτὸς ἦν
˪There was˩ a man called by the name called of Zacchaeus; {and} he was a
2627 467 2813 3950 2813 2405 2779 899 1639
j n.nsm n.dsn pt.pp.nsm n.nsm cj r.nsm v.iai.3s

ἀρχιτελώνης καὶ αὐτὸς πλούσιος· [3] καὶ ἐζήτει ἰδεῖν τὸν Ἰησοῦν
chief tax collector and he was wealthy. {and} ˪He was trying˩ to see {the} Jesus —
803 2779 899 4454 2779 2426 1625 3836 2652
n.nsm cj r.nsm a.nsm cj v.iai.3s f.aa d.asm n.asm

τίς ἐστιν καὶ ↱ οὐκ ἠδύνατο ἀπὸ τοῦ ὄχλου, ὅτι
who he was — but was not able to ˪on account of˩ the crowd, because he was short
5515 1639 2779 1538 4024 1538 608 3836 4063 4022 1639 1639 3625
r.nsm v.pai.3s cj pl v.ipi.3s p.g d.gsm n.gsm cj

τῇ ἡλικίᾳ μικρὸς ἦν. [4] καὶ ↱ προδραμὼν ˪εἰς τὸ ἔμπροσθεν˩ ἀνέβη
in stature. short he was So he ran on ahead and ˪climbed up˩
3836 2461 3625 1639 2779 326 4731 1650 3836 1869 326
d.dsf n.dsf a.nsm v.iai.3s cj pt.aa.nsm p.a d.asn adv v.aai.3s

ἐπὶ συκομορέαν ἵνα ἴδῃ αὐτὸν ὅτι ἐκείνης ἤμελλεν διέρχεσθαι.
into a sycamore-fig tree to see him, for that way he was about to pass that way.
2093 5191 2671 1625 899 4022 1697 3516 1451 1697 1697
p.a n.asf cj v.aas.3s r.asm.3 cj r.gsf v.iai.3s f.pm

[5] καὶ ὡς ἦλθεν ἐπὶ τὸν τόπον, ἀναβλέψας ὁ Ἰησοῦς εἶπεν πρὸς αὐτόν,
{and} As he came to that spot, Jesus looked up {the} Jesus and said to him,
2779 6055 2262 2093 3836 5536 2652 329 3836 2652 3306 4639 899
cj cj v.aai.3s p.a d.asm n.asm pt.aa.nsm d.nsm n.nsm v.aai.3s p.a r.asm.3

NASB

David, have mercy
on me!” [39]Those
who led the way
were sternly telling
him to be quiet;
but he kept crying
out all the more,
“Son of David,
have mercy on
me!” [40]And Je-
sus stopped and
commanded that
he be brought to
Him; and when
he came near, He
questioned him,
[41]“What do you
want Me to do for
you?” And he said,
“Lord, *I want* to
regain my sight!”
[42]And Jesus said
to him, “Receive
your sight; your
faith has made you
well.” [43]Immedi-
ately he regained
his sight and *began*
following Him,
glorifying God;
and when all the
people saw it, they
gave praise to God.

Zaccheus Converted

[19:1]He entered
Jericho and was
passing through.
[2]And there was a
man called by the
name of Zaccheus;
he was a chief tax
collector and he
was rich. [3]Zacch-
eus was trying to
see who Jesus was,
and was unable be-
cause of the crowd,
for he was small
in stature. [4]So he
ran on ahead and
climbed up into a
sycamore tree in
order to see Him,
for He was about
to pass through that
way. [5]When Jesus
came to the place,
He looked up and
said to him,

NIV

“Zacchaeus, come
down immediate-
ly. I must stay at
your house today.”
[6]So he came down
at once and wel-
comed him gladly.
[7]All the people
saw this and be-
gan to mutter, “He
has gone to be the
guest of a sinner.”
[8]But Zacchae-
us stood up and
said to the Lord,
“Look, Lord! Here
and now I give half
of my possessions
to the poor, and if I
have cheated any-
body out of any-
thing, I will pay
back four times the
amount.”
[9]Jesus said to
him, “Today sal-
vation has come
to this house, be-
cause this man,
too, is a son of
Abraham. [10]For the
Son of Man came
to seek and to save
the lost.”

The Parable of the Ten Minas

[11]While they were
listening to this,
he went on to tell
them a parable, be-
cause he was near
Jerusalem and the
people thought
that the kingdom
of God was going
to appear at once.
[12]He said: “A man
of noble birth went
to a distant coun-
try to have himself
appointed king and
then to return. [13]So
he called ten of his
servants and gave
them ten minas.[a]

[a] 13 A mina was about three months’ wages.

Ζακχαῖε, σπεύσας κατάβηθι, σήμερον γὰρ ἐν τῷ οἴκῳ
“Zacchaeus, hurry and climb down, for today *for* I must stay at *{the}* your house.”
2405 5067 2849 1142 4958 1142 1609 1256 3531 1877 3836 5148 3875
n.vsm pt.aa.nsm v.aam.2s adv cj p.d d.dsm n.dsm

σου δεῖ με μεῖναι. 6 καὶ ↱ σπεύσας κατέβη καὶ ὑπεδέξατο αὐτὸν
your must I stay So he hurried and ⌞climbed down⌟ and welcomed him,
5148 1256 1609 3531 2779 2849 5067 2849 2779 5685 899
r.gs.2 v.pai.3s r.as.1 f.aa cj pt.aa.nsm v.aai.3s cj v.ami.3s r.asm.3

χαίρων. 7 καὶ ἰδόντες πάντες διεγόγγυζον λέγοντες ὅτι
rejoicing. And everyone, ⌞when they saw⌟ *everyone* this, began to grumble, saying, ~ “He
5897 2779 4246 1625 4246 1339 3306 4022 1656
pt.pa.nsm cj pt.aa.npm a.npm v.iai.3p pt.pa.npm cj

παρὰ ἁμαρτωλῷ ἀνδρὶ εἰσῆλθεν καταλῦσαι. 8 → ↱
went in to lodge with a sinful man.” *He went in to lodge* Zacchaeus, as he
1656 1656 2907 2907 4123 283 467 1656 2907 2405 3306
p.d a.dsm n.dsm v.aai.3s f.aa

σταθεὶς δὲ Ζακχαῖος εἶπεν πρὸς τὸν κύριον, ἰδοὺ τὰ ἡμίσιά → μου
stood *{and} Zacchaeus* there, said to the Lord, “Look, *{the}* half of what I
2705 1254 2405 3306 4639 3836 3261 2627 3836 2468 3836 1609
pt.ap.nsm cj n.nsm v.aai.3s p.a d.asm n.asm j d.apn a.apn r.gs.1

τῶν ὑπαρχόντων, κύριε, τοῖς πτωχοῖς δίδωμι, καὶ εἴ
what own, Lord, I will give to the poor, *I will give* and if I have
3836 5639 3261 1443 1443 1443 3836 4777 1443 2779 1623 5193 5193
d.gpn pt.pa.gpn n.vsm d.dpm a.dpm v.pai.1s cj cj

τινός τι ἐσυκοφάντησα ἀποδίδωμι τετραπλοῦν. 9 εἶπεν δὲ
defrauded anyone of anything, *I have defrauded of* I will repay fourfold.” Jesus said *{and}*
5193 5516 5193 5516 5193 625 5487 2652 3306 1254
r.gsm r.asn v.aai.1s v.pai.1s adv v.aai.3s cj

πρὸς αὐτὸν ὁ Ἰησοῦς ὅτι σήμερον σωτηρία τῷ οἴκῳ τούτῳ
to him, *{the} Jesus* ~ “Today salvation has come to this house, *this*
4639 899 3836 2652 4022 4958 5401 1181 1181 3836 4047 3875 4047
p.a r.asm.3 d.nsm n.nsm cj adv n.nsf d.dsm n.dsm r.dsm

ἐγένετο, καθότι καὶ αὐτὸς υἱὸς Ἀβραάμ ἐστιν· 10
has come since he too *he* is a son of Abraham. *is* For the Son of Man
1181 2776 899 2779 899 1639 5626 11 1639 1142 3836 5626 3836 476
v.ami.3s cj adv r.nsm n.nsm n.gsm v.pai.3s

ἦλθεν γὰρ ὁ υἱὸς τοῦ ἀνθρώπου ζητῆσαι καὶ σῶσαι τὸ ἀπολωλός. 11 →
came *For the Son of Man* to seek and to save the lost.” As they
2262 1142 3836 5626 3836 476 2426 2779 5392 3836 660 899
v.aai.3s cj d.nsm n.nsm d.gsm n.gsm f.aa cj f.aa d.asn pt.ra.asn

ἀκουόντων δὲ αὐτῶν ταῦτα ↱ προσθεὶς εἶπεν παραβολὴν διὰ τὸ
⌞were listening to⌟ *{and} they* this, he went on to tell a parable, because *{the}* he
201 1254 899 4047 3306 4707 3306 4130 1328 3836 899
pt.pa.gpm cj r.gpm.3 r.apn pt.aa.nsm v.aai.3s n.asf p.a d.asn

ἐγγὺς εἶναι Ἰερουσαλὴμ αὐτὸν καὶ δοκεῖν αὐτοὺς ὅτι
was near *was* Jerusalem, *he* and they supposed *they* that the kingdom of God
1639 1584 1639 2647 899 2779 899 1506 899 4022 3836 993 3836 2536
p.g f.pa n.gsf r.asm.3 cj f.pa r.apm.3 cj

παραχρῆμα μέλλει ἡ βασιλεία τοῦ θεοῦ ἀναφαίνεσθαι.
was going to appear at once. *was going the kingdom of God to appear*
3516 3516 428 428 4202 3516 3836 993 3836 2536 428
adv v.pai.3s d.nsf n.nsf d.gsm n.gsm f.pp

12 εἶπεν οὖν, ἄνθρωπός τις εὐγενὴς ἐπορεύθη εἰς
So he said, *So* “A certain man *certain* ⌞of noble birth⌟ went to a distant
4036 3306 4036 5516 476 5516 2302 4513 1650 3431
v.aai.3s cj n.nsm r.nsm a.nsm v.api.3s p.a

χώραν μακρὰν λαβεῖν ἑαυτῷ βασιλείαν καὶ ὑποστρέψαι. 13
country *distant* to acquire royal power for himself *royal power* and then to return. So,
6001 3431 3284 993 993 1571 993 2779 5715 1254
n.asf a.asf f.aa r.dsm.3 n.asf cj f.aa

καλέσας δὲ δέκα → δούλους ἑαυτοῦ ἔδωκεν αὐτοῖς δέκα μνᾶς καὶ εἶπεν πρὸς
calling *So* ten of his servants, *his* he gave them ten minas, and said to
2813 1254 1274 1571 1529 1571 1443 899 1274 3641 2779 3306 4639
pt.aa.nsm cj a.apm n.apm r.gsm.3 v.aai.3s r.dpm.3 a.apf n.apf cj v.aai.3s p.a

---

NASB

“Zaccheus, hurry
and come down,
for today I must
stay at your
house.” [6]And he
hurried and came
down and received
Him gladly. [7]When
they saw it, they all
began to grumble,
saying, “He has
gone to be the
guest of a man who
is a sinner.” [8]Zac-
cheus stopped and
said to the Lord,
“Behold, Lord, half
of my possessions
I will give to the
poor, and if I have
defrauded anyone
of anything, I will
give back four
times as much.”
[9]And Jesus said to
him, “Today salva-
tion has come to
this house, because
he, too, is a son of
Abraham. [10]For the
Son of Man has
come to seek and
to save that which
was lost.”

Parable of Money Usage

[11]While they were
listening to these
things, Jesus went
on to tell a parable,
because He was
near Jerusalem,
and they supposed
that the kingdom of
God was going to
appear immediate-
ly. [12]So He said, “A
nobleman went to
a distant country to
receive a kingdom
for himself, and
then return. [13]And
he called ten of his
slaves, and gave
them ten [a]minas
and said to them,

[a] A mina is equal to about 100 days’ wages

NIV

'Put this mon-
ey to work,' he
said, 'until I come
back.'
14 "But his sub-
jects hated him
and sent a dele-
gation after him
to say, 'We don't
want this man to
be our king.'
15 "He was made
king, however, and
returned home.
Then he sent for
the servants to
whom he had giv-
en the money, in
order to find out
what they had
gained with it.
16 "The first one
came and said,
'Sir, your mina has
earned ten more.'
17 " 'Well done,
my good servant!'
his master replied.
'Because you have
been trustworthy
in a very small
matter, take charge
of ten cities.'
18 "The second
came and said,
'Sir, your mina has
earned five more.'
19 "His master
answered, 'You
take charge of five
cities.'
20 "Then another
servant came and
said, 'Sir, here is
your mina; I have
kept it laid away in
a piece of cloth. 21 I
was afraid of you,
because you are
a hard man. You
take out what you
did not put in and
reap what you did
not sow.'
22 "His master re-
plied, 'I will judge
you by your own
words, you wick-
ed servant! You
knew, did you, that
I am

αὐτούς, πραγματεύσασθε ⌞ἐν ᾧ⌟ ἔρχομαι. 14 οἱ δὲ πολῖται αὐτοῦ ἐμίσουν
them, 'Conduct business until I return.' {the} But his citizens *his* hated
899 4549 1877 4005 2262 3836 1254 899 4489 899 3631
r.apm.3 v.amm.2p p.d r.dsm v.pmi.1s d.npm cj n.npm r.gsm.3 v.iai.3p

αὐτὸν καὶ ἀπέστειλαν πρεσβείαν ὀπίσω αὐτοῦ λέγοντες, ↱ ↱ οὐ θέλομεν
him and sent a delegation after him, saying, 'We do not want
899 2779 690 4561 3958 899 3306 2527 2527 4024 2527
r.asm.3 cj v.aai.3p n.asf p.g r.gsm.3 pt.pa.npm pl v.pai.1p

τοῦτον βασιλεῦσαι ἐφ' ἡμᾶς. 15 καὶ ἐγένετο ἐν τῷ ἐπανελθεῖν
this person to rule over us.' {and} {it happened that} When {the} he returned,
4047 996 2093 7005 2779 1181 1877 3836 899 2059
r.asm f.aa p.a r.ap.1 cj v.ami.3s p.d d.dsn f.aa

αὐτὸν λαβόντα τὴν βασιλείαν καὶ εἶπεν
he having acquired {the} royal power, {and} he ordered these servants to whom he had
899 3284 3836 993 2779 3306 4047 1529 4005 4005 1443 1443
r.asm.3 pt.aa.asm d.asf n.asf cj v.aai.3s

φωνηθῆναι αὐτῷ τοὺς δούλους τούτους οἷς δεδώκει τὸ
given the money to be called to him, {the} *servants* *these* *to whom* *he had given* *the*
1443 3836 736 5888 899 3836 1529 4047 4005 1443 3836
f.ap r.dsm.3 d.apm n.apm r.apm r.dpm v.lai.3s d.asn

ἀργύριον, ἵνα γνοῖ τί διεπραγματεύσαντο. 16
money that ⌞he might know⌟ what ⌞they had gained by doing business.⌟ The first
736 2671 1182 5515 1390 3836 4755
n.asn cj v.aas.3s r.asn v.ami.3p

παρεγένετο δὲ ὁ πρῶτος λέγων, κύριε, ἡ μνᾶ σου δέκα
came before {and} *The* *first* him, saying, 'Master, {the} your mina *your* has gained ten
4134 1254 3836 4755 3306 3261 3836 5148 3641 5148 4664 4664 1274
v.ami.3s cj d.nsm a.nsm pt.pa.nsm n.vsm d.nsf n.nsf r.gs.2 a.apf

προσηργάσατο μνᾶς. 17 καὶ εἶπεν αὐτῷ, εὖγε, ἀγαθὲ δοῦλε, ὅτι
has gained minas.' And he said to him, ⌞'Well done,⌟ good servant! Because you have
4664 3641 2779 3306 899 2301 19 1529 4022 1181 1181
v.ami.3s n.apf cj v.aai.3s r.dsm.3 adv a.vsm n.vsm cj

ἐν ἐλαχίστῳ πιστὸς ἐγένου, ἴσθι ἐξουσίαν
been trustworthy in a ⌞very small matter,⌟ *trustworthy* *you have been* ⌞you will⌟ have authority
1181 4412 1877 1788 4412 1181 1639 2400 2026
p.d a.dsn.s a.nsm v.ami.2s v.pam.2s n.asf

ἔχων ἐπάνω δέκα πόλεων. 18 καὶ ἦλθεν ὁ δεύτερος λέγων, ἡ
have over ten cities.' And the second came, *the* *second* saying, {the} 'Your
2400 2062 1274 4484 2779 3836 1311 2262 3836 1311 3306 3836 5148
pt.pa.nsm p.g a.gpf n.gpf cj v.aai.3s d.nsm a.nsm pt.pa.nsm d.nsf

μνᾶ σου, κύριε, ἐποίησεν πέντε μνᾶς. 19 εἶπεν δὲ καὶ τούτῳ,
mina, *Your* Master, has gained five minas.' So he said *So* to this one as well, *to this one*
3641 5148 3261 4472 4297 3641 1254 3306 1254 4047 4047 4047 2779 4047
n.nsf r.gs.2 n.vsm v.aai.3s a.apf n.apf v.aai.3s cj adv r.dsm

καὶ σὺ ἐπάνω γίνου πέντε πόλεων. 20 καὶ ὁ ἕτερος ἦλθεν λέγων, κύριε,
'And you, rule over *rule* five cities.' Then the other came, saying, 'Master,
2779 5148 1181 2062 1181 4297 4484 2779 3836 2283 2262 3306 3261
adv r.ns.2 p.g v.pmm.2s a.gpf n.gpf cj d.nsm r.nsm v.aai.3s pt.pa.nsm n.vsm

ἰδοὺ ἡ μνᾶ σου ἣν εἶχον ἀποκειμένην ἐν σουδαρίῳ· 21 ἐφοβούμην
look, {the} your mina *your* that I kept laid away in a piece of cloth, for ⌞I was afraid of⌟
2627 3836 5148 3641 5148 4005 2400 641 1877 5051 1142 5828
j d.nsf n.nsf r.gs.2 r.asf v.iai.1s pt.pm.asf p.d n.dsn v.ipi.1s

γάρ σε, ὅτι ἄνθρωπος αὐστηρὸς εἶ, αἴρεις ὃ ↱
for you, because you are an exacting man: *exacting* *you are* ⌞you take up⌟ what you
1142 5148 4022 1639 1639 893 476 893 1639 149 4005 5502
cj r.as.2 cj n.nsm a.nsm v.pai.2s v.pai.2s r.asn

↱ οὐκ ἔθηκας καὶ θερίζεις ὃ ↱ ↱ οὐκ ἔσπειρας. 22 λέγει αὐτῷ, ἐκ τοῦ
did not lay down, and reap what you did not sow.' He said to him, 'Out of
5502 4024 5502 2779 2545 4005 5062 5062 4024 5062 3306 899 1666 3836
pl v.aai.2s cj v.pai.2s r.asn pl v.aai.2s v.pai.3s r.dsm.3 p.g d.gsn

στόματός σου κρινῶ σε, πονηρὲ δοῦλε. ᾔδεις ὅτι ἐγὼ
your own mouth *your own* I will judge you, wicked servant. You knew, did you, that I am
5148 5148 5125 5148 3212 5148 4505 1529 3857 4022 1609 1639
n.gsn r.gs.2 v.fai.1s r.as.2 a.vsm n.vsm v.lai.2s cj r.ns.1

NASB

'Do business *with*
this until I come
back.' 14 But his citi-
zens hated him and
sent a delegation
after him, saying,
'We do not want
this man to reign
over us.' 15 When
he returned, after
receiving the king-
dom, he ordered
that these slaves,
to whom he had
given the money,
be called to him so
that he might know
what business they
had done. 16 The
first appeared, say-
ing, 'Master, your
mina has made ten
minas more.' 17 And
he said to him,
'Well done, good
slave, because you
have been faith-
ful in a very little
thing, you are to be
in authority over
ten cities.' 18 The
second came, say-
ing, 'Your mina,
master, has made
five minas.' 19 And
he said to him also,
'And you are to be
over five cities.'
20 Another came,
saying, 'Master,
here is your mina,
which I kept put
away in a hand-
kerchief; 21 for I
was afraid of you,
because you are an
exacting man; you
take up what you
did not lay down
and reap what you
did not sow.' 22 He
*said to him, 'By
your own words I
will judge you, you
worthless slave.
Did you know that

NIV

a hard man, taking
out what I did not
put in, and reap-
ing what I did not
sow? [23] Why then
didn't you put my
money on depos-
it, so that when I
came back, I could
have collected it
with interest?'
[24] "Then he said
to those standing
by, 'Take his mina
away from him
and give it to the
one who has ten
minas.'
[25] " 'Sir,' they
said, 'he already
has ten!'
[26] "He replied,
'I tell you that
to everyone who
has, more will be
given, but as for
the one who has
nothing, even what
they have will be
taken away. [27] But
those enemies of
mine who did not
want me to be king
over them—bring
them here and
kill them in front
of me.' "

Jesus Comes to Jerusalem as King

[28] After Jesus had
said this, he went
on ahead, going up
to Jerusalem. [29] As
he approached
Bethphage and
Bethany at the hill
called the Mount
of Olives, he sent
two of his disci-
ples, saying to
them, [30] "Go to the
village ahead of
you, and as you
enter it, you will
find a colt tied
there, which no
one has ever rid-
den. Untie it and
bring it here. [31] If
anyone asks you,
'Why are you un-
tying it?' say, 'The
Lord needs it.' "

ἄνθρωπος αὐστηρός εἰμι, αἴρων ὃ ↱ ↱ οὐκ ἔθηκα καὶ θερίζων
an exacting man, *exacting* *am* ⌊taking up⌋ what I did not lay down and reaping
893 476 893 1639 149 4005 5502 5502 4024 5502 2779 2545
n.nsm a.nsm v.pai.1s pt.pa.nsm r.asn pl v.aai.1s cj pt.pa.nsm

ὃ ↱ ↱ οὐκ ἔσπειρα; [23] καὶ ⌊διὰ τί⌋ ↱ ↱ οὐκ ἔδωκάς μου τὸ
what I did not sow? Why then *Why* did you not put my *{the}*
4005 5062 5062 4024 5062 1328 2779 1328 5515 1443 1443 4024 1443 1609 3836
r.asn pl v.aai.1s cj p.a r.asn pl v.aai.2s r.gs.1 d.asn

ἀργύριον ἐπὶ τράπεζαν; κἀγὼ ἐλθὼν σὺν
money in the bank? Then ⌊when I returned⌋ I could have collected it with
736 2093 5544 2743 2262 4556 323 4556 4556 899 5250
n.asn p.a n.asf crasis pt.aa.nsm p.d

τόκῳ ἂν αὐτὸ ἔπραξα. [24] καὶ τοῖς παρεστῶσιν εἶπεν, ἄρατε ἀπ'
interest.' *could* *it* *I have collected* Then he said to his attendants, *he said* 'Take from
5527 323 899 4556 2779 3306 3306 3836 4225 3306 149 608
n.dsm pl r.asn.3 v.aai.1s cj d.dpm pt.ra.dpm v.aai.3s v.aam.2p p.g

αὐτοῦ τὴν μνᾶν καὶ δότε τῷ τὰς δέκα μνᾶς ἔχοντι [25] καὶ
him the mina and give it ⌊to the⌋ one who has the ten minas.' *one who has* And
899 3836 3641 2779 1443 3836 2400 2400 2400 3836 1274 3641 2400 2779
r.gsm.3 d.asf n.asf cj v.aam.2p d.dsm d.apf a.apf n.apf pt.pa.dsm cj

εἶπαν αὐτῷ, κύριε, ἔχει δέκα μνᾶς [26] λέγω ὑμῖν ὅτι παντὶ τῷ ἔχοντι
they said to him, 'Master, he has ten minas!' I tell you that to everyone who has,
3306 899 3261 2400 1274 3641 3306 7007 4022 4246 3836 2400
v.aai.3p r.dsm.3 n.vsm v.pai.3s a.apf n.apf v.pai.1s r.dp.2 cj a.dsm d.dsm pt.pa.dsm

δοθήσεται, ἀπὸ δὲ τοῦ ↱ ↱ ↱ μὴ ἔχοντος καὶ ὃ ἔχει
more will be given; but from *but* the one who does not have, even what he has
1443 1254 608 1254 3836 2400 2400 2400 3590 2400 2779 4005 2400
v.fpi.3s p.g cj d.gsm pl pt.pa.gsm adv r.asn v.pai.3s

ἀρθήσεται. [27] πλὴν τοὺς ἐχθρούς μου τούτους τοὺς ↱ μὴ
⌊will be taken away.⌋ But as for *{the}* these enemies of mine *these* who did not
149 4440 3836 4047 2398 1609 4047 3836 2527 3590
v.fpi.3s cj d.apm a.apm r.gs.1 r.apm d.apm pl

θελήσαντάς με βασιλεῦσαι ἐπ' αὐτοὺς ἀγάγετε ὧδε καὶ κατασφάξατε αὐτοὺς
want me to reign over them, bring them here and slaughter them
2527 1609 996 2093 899 72 6045 2779 2956 899
pt.aa.apm r.as.1 f.aa p.a r.apm.3 v.aam.2p adv cj v.aam.2p r.apm.3

ἔμπροσθέν μου. [28] καὶ εἰπὼν ταῦτα ἐπορεύετο ἔμπροσθεν ἀναβαίνων εἰς
before me." *{and}* ⌊Having said⌋ these things, he went on ahead, going up to
1869 1609 2779 3306 4047 4513 1869 326 1650
p.g r.gs.1 cj pt.aa.nsm r.apn v.imi.3s adv pt.pa.nsm p.a

Ἱεροσόλυμα. [29] καὶ ἐγένετο ὡς ἤγγισεν εἰς Βηθφαγὴ καὶ Βηθανίαν[a]
Jerusalem. *{and}* ⌊It happened that⌋ as ⌊he came near⌋ *{to}* Bethphage and Bethany
2642 2779 1181 6055 1581 1650 1036 2779 1029
n.apn cj v.ami.3s cj v.aai.3s p.a n.asf cj n.asf

πρὸς τὸ ὄρος τὸ καλούμενον Ἐλαιῶν, ἀπέστειλεν δύο τῶν μαθητῶν
to the hill *{the}* called "The Mount of Olives," he sent two of his disciples,
4639 3836 4001 3836 2813 1777 690 1545 3836 3412
p.a d.asn n.asn d.asn pt.pp.asn n.gpf v.aai.3s a.apm d.gpm n.gpm

[30] λέγων, ὑπάγετε εἰς τὴν κατέναντι κώμην, ⌊ἐν ᾗ⌋ εἰσπορευόμενοι
saying, "Go into the village ahead of *village* you, where, as you enter,
3306 5632 1650 3836 3267 2978 3267 1877 4005 1660
pt.pa.nsm v.pam.2p p.a d.asf adv n.asf p.d r.dsf pt.pm.npm

εὑρήσετε πῶλον δεδεμένον, ἐφ' ὃν οὐδεὶς ↱ πώποτε ἀνθρώπων ἐκάθισεν,
you will find a colt tied, on which no one has ever yet *one* sat.
2351 4798 1313 2093 4005 4029 476 2767 4799 476 2767
v.fai.2p n.asm pt.rp.asm p.a r.asm a.nsm adv n.gpm v.aai.3s

καὶ λύσαντες αὐτὸν ἀγάγετε. [31] καὶ ἐάν τις ὑμᾶς ἐρωτᾷ, ⌊διὰ
{and} Untie it and bring it here. *{and}* If someone asks you *asks* why
2779 3395 899 72 2779 1569 5516 2263 7007 2263 1328
cj pt.aa.npm r.asm.3 v.aam.2p cj cj r.nsm r.ap.2 v.pas.3s p.a

τί⌋ λύετε; οὕτως ἐρεῖτε, ὅτι ὁ κύριος αὐτοῦ
⌊are you untying⌋ it, you shall say this: *you shall say* ~ 'The Lord has need of it.'"
5515 3395 3306 3306 3306 4048 3306 4022 3836 3261 2400 5970 899
r.asn v.pai.2p adv v.fai.2p cj d.nsm n.nsm r.gsm.3

NASB

I am an exacting
man, taking up
what I did not lay
down and reap-
ing what I did not
sow? [23] Then why
did you not put
my money in the
bank, and having
come, I would have
collected it with
interest?' [24] Then he
said to the bystand-
ers, 'Take the mina
away from him
and give it to the
one who has the
ten minas.' [25] And
they said to him,
'Master, he has ten
minas *already.*'
[26] I tell you that
to everyone who
has, more shall be
given, but from the
one who does not
have, even what he
does have shall be
taken away. [27] But
these enemies of
mine, who did not
want me to reign
over them, bring
them here and slay
them in my pres-
ence."

Triumphal Entry

[28] After He had
said these things,
He was going on
ahead, going up to
Jerusalem.
[29] When He ap-
proached Beth-
phage and Bethany,
near the mount that
is called Olivet,
He sent two of the
disciples, [30] saying,
"Go into the vil-
lage ahead of *you;*
there, as you enter,
you will find a colt
tied on which no
one yet has ever
sat; untie it and
bring it *here.* [31] If
anyone asks you,
'Why are you unty-
ing it?' you shall
say, 'The Lord has
need of it.' "

[a] Βηθανίαν TNIV, NET. Βηθανία[ν] UBS.

NIV

[32]Those who were
sent ahead went
and found it just as
he had told them.
[33]As they were
untying the colt,
its owners asked
them, "Why are
you untying the
colt?"
[34]They re-
plied, "The Lord
needs it."
[35]They brought
it to Jesus, threw
their cloaks on
the colt and put
Jesus on it. [36]As he
went along, people
spread their cloaks
on the road.
[37]When he came
near the place
where the road
goes down the
Mount of Olives,
the whole crowd
of disciples began
joyfully to praise
God in loud voices
for all the miracles
they had seen:

[38]"Blessed is the
king who
comes in the
name of the
Lord!"[a]

"Peace in heaven
and glory in
the highest!"

[39]Some of the
Pharisees in the
crowd said to
Jesus, "Teacher,
rebuke your disci-
ples!"
[40]"I tell you," he
replied, "if they
keep quiet, the
stones will cry
out."
[41]As he ap-
proached Jerusa-
lem and saw the
city, he wept over
it [42]and said, "If
you, even you, had
only known on
this day

χρείαν ἔχει. 32 ἀπελθόντες δὲ οἱ ἀπεσταλμένοι
need *has* Those who were sent away left *{and}* *Those who were sent away* and
5970 2400 3836 690 690 690 690 599 1254 3836 690
n.asf v.pai.3s pt.aa.npm cj d.npm pt.rp.npm

εὗρον καθὼς εἶπεν αὐτοῖς. 33 → λυόντων δὲ αὐτῶν τὸν
found everything just as ˻he has described˼ it to them. As they were untying *{and}* *they* the
2351 2777 3306 899 899 3395 1254 899 3836
v.aai.3p cj v.aai.3s r.dpm.3 pt.pa.gpm cj r.gpm.3 d.asm

πῶλον εἶπαν οἱ κύριοι αὐτοῦ πρὸς αὐτούς, τί λύετε τὸν
colt, its owners said *{the}* *owners* *its* to them, "Why ˻are you untying˼ the
4798 899 3261 3306 3836 3261 899 4639 899 5515 3395 3836
n.asm v.aai.3p d.npm n.npm r.gsm.3 p.a r.apm.3 r.asn v.pai.2p d.asm

πῶλον; 34 οἱ δὲ εἶπαν, ὅτι ὁ κύριος αὐτοῦ χρείαν ἔχει.
colt?" And they *And* said, "Because the Lord has need of it." *need* *has*
4798 1254 3836 1254 3306 4022 3836 3261 2400 5970 899 5970 2400
n.asm d.npm cj v.aai.3p cj d.nsm n.nsm r.gsm.3 n.asf v.pai.3s

35 καὶ ἤγαγον αὐτὸν πρὸς τὸν Ἰησοῦν καὶ ἐπιρίψαντες αὐτῶν τὰ ἱμάτια ἐπὶ
Then they brought it to *{the}* Jesus, and throwing their *{the}* cloaks onto
2779 72 899 4639 3836 2652 2779 2166 899 3836 2668 2093
cj v.aai.3p r.asm.3 p.a d.asm n.asm cj pt.aa.npm r.gpm.3 d.apn n.apn p.a

τὸν πῶλον ἐπεβίβασαν τὸν Ἰησοῦν. ↰ 36 → πορευομένου δὲ αὐτοῦ
the colt, they put *{the}* Jesus on it. And as he rode along, *And* *he*
3836 4798 2097 3836 2652 2097 1254 899 4513 1254 899
d.asm n.asm v.aai.3p d.asm n.asm pt.pm.gsm cj r.gsm.3

ὑπεστρώννυον τὰ ἱμάτια αὐτῶν ἐν τῇ ὁδῷ. 37 → → ἐγγίζοντος
they spread *{the}* their cloaks *their* on the road. As he was already approaching
5716 3836 899 2668 899 1877 3836 3847 899 2453 1581
v.iai.3p d.apn n.apn r.gpm.3 p.d d.dsf n.dsf pt.pa.gsm

δὲ αὐτοῦ ἤδη πρὸς τῇ καταβάσει τοῦ ὄρους τῶν ἐλαιῶν
{and} *he* *already* to the descent of the Mount of Olives, the whole crowd of
1254 899 2453 4639 3836 2853 3836 4001 3836 1777 3836 570 4436 3836
cj r.gsm.3 adv p.d d.dsf n.dsf d.gsn n.gsn d.gpf n.gpf

ἤρξαντο ἅπαν τὸ πλῆθος τῶν μαθητῶν χαίροντες αἰνεῖν τὸν θεὸν →
disciples began *whole* *the* *crowd* *of* *disciples* to rejoice and praise *{the}* God with a
3412 806 570 3836 4436 3836 3412 5897 140 3836 2536
v.ami.3p a.nsn d.nsn n.nsn d.gpm n.gpm pt.pa.npm f.pa d.asm n.asm

φωνῇ μεγάλῃ περὶ πασῶν ὧν εἶδον δυνάμεων,
loud voice *loud* for all the mighty works that ˻they had seen,˼ *mighty works*
3489 5889 3489 4309 4246 1539 1539 4005 1625 1539
n.dsf a.dsf p.g a.gpf r.gpf v.aai.3p n.gpf

38 λέγοντες, εὐλογημένος ὁ ἐρχόμενος, ὁ βασιλεὺς ἐν
saying, "Blessed is the coming one, the king, the one who comes in the
3306 2328 3836 2262 3836 995 1877
pt.pa.npm pt.rp.nsm d.nsm pt.pm.nsm d.nsm n.nsm p.d

ὀνόματι → κυρίου· ἐν οὐρανῷ εἰρήνη καὶ δόξα ἐν ὑψίστοις. 39 καί
name of the Lord! Peace in heaven *Peace* and glory in the highest!" And
3950 3261 1645 1877 4041 1645 2779 1518 1877 5736 2779
n.dsn n.gsm p.d n.dsm n.nsf cj n.nsf p.d a.dpm.s cj

τινες τῶν Φαρισαίων ἀπὸ τοῦ ὄχλου εἶπαν πρὸς αὐτόν, διδάσκαλε, ἐπιτίμησον τοῖς
some of the Pharisees in the crowd said to him, "Teacher, rebuke *{the}*
5516 3836 5757 608 3836 4063 3306 4639 899 1437 2203 3836
r.npm d.gpm n.gpm p.g d.gsm n.gsm v.aai.3p p.a r.asm.3 n.vsm v.aam.2s d.dpm

μαθηταῖς σου. 40 καὶ ˻ἀποκριθεὶς εἶπεν,˼ λέγω ὑμῖν, ἐὰν οὗτοι σιωπήσουσιν,
your disciples." *your* *{and}* He answered, "I tell you, if these are silent,
5148 3412 5148 2779 646 3306 3306 7007 1569 4047 4995
n.dpm r.gs.2 cj pt.ap.nsm v.aai.3s v.pai.1s r.dp.2 cj r.npm v.fai.3p

οἱ λίθοι κράξουσιν. 41 καὶ ὡς ἤγγισεν ἰδὼν τὴν πόλιν ἔκλαυσεν ἐπ'
the stones will cry out." *{and}* As Jesus drew near and saw the city, he wept over
3836 3345 3189 2779 6055 1581 1625 3836 4484 3081 2093
d.npm n.npm v.fai.3p cj cj v.aai.3s pt.aa.nsm d.asf n.asf v.aai.3s p.a

αὐτὴν 42 λέγων ὅτι εἰ → ἔγνως ἐν τῇ ἡμέρᾳ ταύτῃ καὶ
it, saying, ~ "Would that you, even you, had known on *{the}* this day *this* *even*
899 3306 4022 1623 2779 5148 1182 1877 3836 4047 2465 4047 2779
r.asf.3 pt.pa.nsm cj cj v.aai.2s p.d d.dsf n.dsf r.dsf adv

NASB

[32]So those who
were sent went
away and found it
just as He had told
them. [33]As they
were untying the
colt, its owners
said to them, "Why
are you untying the
colt?" [34]They said,
"The Lord has
need of it." [35]They
brought it to Jesus,
and they threw
their coats on the
colt and put Jesus
on it. [36]As He was
going, they were
spreading their
coats on the road.
[37]As soon as He
was approaching,
near the descent
of the Mount of
Olives, the whole
crowd of the dis-
ciples began to
praise God joyfully
with a loud voice
for all the miracles
which they had
seen, [38]shouting:

"BLESSED IS THE
KING WHO
COMES IN THE
NAME OF THE
LORD;
Peace in
heaven and
glory in the
highest!"

[39]Some of the
Pharisees in the
crowd said to Him,
"Teacher, rebuke
Your disciples."
[40]But Jesus an-
swered, "I tell you,
if these become
silent, the stones
will cry out!"
[41]When He ap-
proached *Jerusa-
lem,* He saw the
city and wept over
it, [42]saying, "If you
had known in this
day, even you,

---

[a] 38 Psalm 118:26

NIV

what would bring you peace—but now it is hidden from your eyes. [43]The days will come upon you when your enemies will build an embankment against you and encircle you and hem you in on every side. [44]They will dash you to the ground, you and the children within your walls. They will not leave one stone on another, because you did not recognize the time of God's coming to you."

Jesus at the Temple

[45]When Jesus entered the temple courts, he began to drive out those who were selling. [46]"It is written," he said to them, " 'My house will be a house of prayer'[a]; but you have made it 'a den of robbers.'[b]"

[47]Every day he was teaching at the temple. But the chief priests, the teachers of the law and the leaders among the people were trying to kill him. [48]Yet they could not find any way to do it, because all the people hung on his words.

The Authority of Jesus Questioned

20 One day as Jesus was teaching the people in the temple courts and proclaiming the good news, the chief priests and the teachers of the law, together with the elders, came up to him.

σὺ τὰ πρὸς εἰρήνην· νῦν δὲ ἐκρύβη ἀπὸ ὀφθαλμῶν
you the things that make for peace! But now *But* ⌊they are hidden⌋ from your eyes.
5148 3836 4639 1645 1254 3814 1254 3221 608 5148 4057
r.ns.2 d.apn p.a n.asf adv cj v.api.3s p.g n.gpm

σου. 43 ὅτι ἥξουσιν ἡμέραι ἐπὶ σὲ καὶ παρεμβαλοῦσιν οἱ
your For the days will come *days* upon you when your enemies will build *{the}*
5148 4022 2465 2457 2465 2093 5148 2779 5148 2398 4212 3836
r.gs.2 cj v.fai.3p n.npf p.a r.as.2 cj v.fai.3p d.npm

ἐχθροί σου χάρακά ↰ σοι καὶ περικυκλώσουσίν σε καὶ συνέξουσίν σε
enemies your an embankment against you and surround you and close in on you
2398 5148 5918 4212 5148 2779 4333 5148 2779 5309 5148
a.npm r.gs.2 n.asm r.ds.2 cj v.fai.3p r.as.2 cj v.fai.3p r.as.2

πάντοθεν, 44 καὶ ἐδαφιοῦσίν σε καὶ τὰ τέκνα σου ἐν σοί,
⌊from every side.⌋ And ⌊they will tear down⌋ both you and *{the}* your children *your* within you,
4119 2779 1610 5148 2779 3836 5148 5451 5148 1877 5148
adv cj v.fai.3p r.as.2 cj d.apn n.apn r.gs.2 p.d r.ds.2

καὶ ↱ ↱ οὐκ ἀφήσουσιν λίθον ἐπὶ λίθον ἐν σοί, ⌊ἀνθ᾽ ὧν⌋ ↱ ↱ οὐκ
and they will not leave stone upon stone in you, because you did not
2779 918 918 4024 918 3345 2093 3345 1877 5148 505 4005 1182 1182 4024
cj pl v.fai.3p n.asm p.a n.asm p.d r.ds.2 p.g r.gpn pl

ἔγνως τὸν καιρὸν τῆς ἐπισκοπῆς σου. 45 καὶ ⌊εἰσελθὼν εἰς⌋ τὸ ἱερὸν
recognize the time of your visitation." *your* *{and}* Having entered the temple,
1182 3836 2789 3836 5148 2175 5148 2779 1656 1650 3836 2639
v.aai.2s d.asm n.asm d.gsf n.gsf r.gs.2 cj pt.aa.nsm p.a d.asn n.asn

ἤρξατο ἐκβάλλειν τοὺς πωλοῦντας[a] 46 λέγων αὐτοῖς, γέγραπται, καὶ
Jesus began to drive out those who were selling things, saying to them, "It is written, *{and}*
806 1675 3836 4797 3306 899 1211 2779
v.ami.3s f.pa d.apm pt.pa.apm pt.pa.nsm r.dpm.3 v.rpi.3s cj

ἔσται ὁ οἶκός μου οἶκος προσευχῆς, ὑμεῖς δὲ αὐτὸν
'My house shall be *{the} house My* a house of prayer,' but you *but* have made it
1609 3875 1639 3836 3875 1609 3875 4666 1254 7007 1254 4472 4472 899
v.fmi.3s d.nsm n.nsm r.gs.1 n.nsm n.gsf r.np.2 cj r.asm.3

ἐποιήσατε σπήλαιον λῃστῶν. 47 καὶ ἦν διδάσκων τὸ ⌊καθ᾽ ἡμέραν⌋ ἐν
have made a den of robbers." *{and}* ⌊He began⌋ to teach *{the}* daily in
4472 5068 3334 2779 1639 1438 3836 2848 2465 1877
v.aai.2p n.asn n.gpm cj v.iai.3s pt.pa.nsm d.asn p.a n.asf p.d

τῷ ἱερῷ. οἱ δὲ ἀρχιερεῖς καὶ οἱ γραμματεῖς
the temple. The *{and}* chief priests and the scribes and the leading men among the
3836 2639 3836 1254 797 2779 3836 1208 2779 3836 4755 4755 3836 3836
d.dsn n.dsn d.npm cj n.npm cj d.npm n.npm

ἐζήτουν αὐτὸν ἀπολέσαι καὶ οἱ πρῶτοι τοῦ λαοῦ, 48 καὶ
people were trying to destroy him, *to destroy and the leading men among the people* but
3295 2426 660 660 899 660 2779 3836 4755 3836 3295 2779
v.iai.3p r.asm.3 f.aa cj d.npm a.npm d.gsm n.gsm cj

↱ ↱ οὐχ εὕρισκον ⌊τὸ τί⌋ ποιήσωσιν, ὁ λαὸς γὰρ ἅπας
they could not find what they might do, because all the people *because all*
2351 2351 4024 2351 3836 5515 4472 1142 570 3836 3295 1142 570
pl v.iai.3p d.asn r.asn v.aas.3p d.nsm n.nsm cj a.nsm

ἐξεκρέματο αὐτοῦ ἀκούων.
⌊were hanging on⌋ his words.
1717 899 201
v.imi.3s r.gsm.3 pt.pa.nsm

20:1 καὶ ἐγένετο ἐν μιᾷ τῶν ἡμερῶν → διδάσκοντος αὐτοῦ τὸν
{and} {it happened that} {on} One *{the}* day, as Jesus was teaching *Jesus* the
2779 1181 1877 1651 3836 2465 899 1438 899 3836
cj v.ami.3s p.d a.dsf d.gpf n.gpf pt.pa.gsm r.gsm.3 d.asm

λαὸν ἐν τῷ ἱερῷ καὶ εὐαγγελιζομένου ἐπέστησαν οἱ ἀρχιερεῖς καὶ οἱ
people in the temple and preaching the gospel, *came up* the chief priests and the
3295 1877 3836 2639 2779 2294 2392 3836 797 2779 3836
n.asm p.d d.dsn n.dsn cj pt.pm.gsm v.aai.3p d.npm n.npm cj d.npm

γραμματεῖς σὺν τοῖς πρεσβυτέροις 2 καὶ εἶπαν λέγοντες πρὸς
scribes, ⌊along with⌋ the elders, came up and spoke to him, saying, *to*
1208 5250 3836 4565 2392 2392 2779 3306 4639 899 3306 4639
n.npm p.d d.dpm a.dpm cj v.aai.3p pt.pa.npm p.a

NASB

the things which make for peace! But now they have been hidden from your eyes. [43]For the days will come upon you when your enemies will throw up a barricade against you, and surround you and hem you in on every side, [44]and they will level you to the ground and your children within you, and they will not leave in you one stone upon another, because you did not recognize the time of your visitation."

Traders Driven from the Temple

[45]Jesus entered the temple and began to drive out those who were selling, [46]saying to them, "It is written, 'AND MY HOUSE SHALL BE A HOUSE OF PRAYER,' but you have made it a ROBBERS' DEN."

[47]And He was teaching daily in the temple; but the chief priests and the scribes and the leading men among the people were trying to destroy Him, [48]and they could not find anything that they might do, for all the people were hanging on to every word He said.

Jesus' Authority Questioned

[20:1]On one of the days while He was teaching the people in the temple and preaching the gospel, the chief priests and the scribes with the elders confronted *Him,* [2]and they spoke, saying to

---

[a] 46 Isaiah 56:7
[b] 46 Jer. 7:11

[a] ἐν αὐτῷ καὶ ἀγοράζοντας included by TR after πωλοῦντας.

NIV

[2]"Tell us by what
authority you
are doing these
things," they said.
"Who gave you
this authority?"
[3]He replied, "I
will also ask you a
question. Tell me:
[4]John's baptism—
was it from heav-
en, or of human
origin?"
[5]They discussed
it among them-
selves and said,
"If we say, 'From
heaven,' he will
ask, 'Why didn't
you believe him?'
[6]But if we say, 'Of
human origin,' all
the people will
stone us, because
they are persuad-
ed that John was a
prophet."
[7]So they an-
swered, "We don't
know where it was
from."
[8]Jesus said, "Nei-
ther will I tell you
by what authority
I am doing these
things."

The Parable of the Tenants

[9]He went on to
tell the people this
parable: "A man
planted a vineyard,
rented it to some
farmers and went
away for a long
time. [10]At harvest
time he sent a ser-
vant to the tenants
so they would
give him some
of the fruit of the
vineyard. But the
tenants beat him
and sent him away
empty-handed.
[11]He sent another
servant, but that
one

αὐτόν, εἰπὸν ἡμῖν ἐν ποίᾳ ἐξουσίᾳ ταῦτα ποιεῖς, ἢ τίς
him "Tell us by what authority you are doing these things; *you are doing* or who
899 3306 7005 1877 4481 2026 4472 4472 4472 4047 4472 2445 5515
r.asm.3 v.aam.2s r.dp.1 p.d r.dsf n.dsf r.apn v.pai.2s cj r.nsm

ἐστιν ὁ δούς σοι τὴν ἐξουσίαν ταύτην; [3] ↱ ἀποκριθεὶς δὲ εἶπεν πρὸς
it is who gave you *{the}* this authority?" *this* He answered, *{and}* saying to
1639 3836 1443 5148 3836 4047 2026 4047 3306 646 1254 3306 4639
v.pai.3s d.nsm pt.aa.nsm r.ds.2 d.asf n.asf r.asf pt.ap.nsm cj v.aai.3s p.a

αὐτούς, → ἐρωτήσω ὑμᾶς κἀγὼ λόγον, καὶ εἴπατέ μοι, ↰
them, "I will also ask you *I also* a question, and ⌊you must give⌋ me the answer:
899 2743 2743 2263 7007 2743 3364 2779 3306 1609 3306
r.apm.3 v.fai.1s r.ap.2 crasis n.asm cj v.aam.2p r.ds.1

[4] τὸ βάπτισμα Ἰωάννου ἐξ οὐρανοῦ ἦν ἢ ἐξ
The baptism of John, was it authorized from heaven *was it* or did it come from
3836 967 2722 1639 1639 1666 4041 1639 2445 1666
d.nsn n.nsn n.gsm p.g n.gsm v.iai.3s cj p.g

ἀνθρώπων; [5] οἱ δὲ συνελογίσαντο πρὸς ἑαυτοὺς λέγοντες ὅτι ἐὰν εἴπωμεν,
men?" They *{and}* reasoned among themselves, saying, ~ "If we say,
476 3836 1254 5199 4639 1571 3306 4022 1569 3306
n.gpm d.npm cj v.ami.3p p.a r.apm.3 pt.pa.npm cj cj v.aas.1p

ἐξ οὐρανοῦ, ἐρεῖ, ⌊διὰ τί⌋ ↱ ↱ οὐκ ἐπιστεύσατε αὐτῷ; [6] ἐὰν
'From heaven,' then ⌊he will say,⌋ 'Why did you not believe him?' But if
1666 4041 3306 1328 5515 4409 4409 4024 4409 899 1254 1569
p.g n.gsm v.fai.3s p.a r.asn pl v.aai.2p r.dsm.3 cj

δὲ εἴπωμεν, ἐξ ἀνθρώπων, ὁ λαὸς ἅπας καταλιθάσει ἡμᾶς, ↰ ↰
But we say, 'From men,' all the people *all* will stone us to death,
1254 3306 1666 476 570 3836 3295 570 2902 7005 2902 2902
cj v.aas.1p p.g n.gpm d.nsm n.nsm a.nsm v.fai.3s r.ap.1

πεπεισμένος γάρ ἐστιν Ἰωάννην προφήτην εἶναι. [7] καὶ
because they are convinced *because they are* that John was a prophet." *was* So
1142 1639 1639 4275 1142 1639 2722 1639 4737 1639 2779
pt.rp.nsm cj v.pai.3s n.asm n.asm f.pa cj

ἀπεκρίθησαν ↱ ↱ μὴ εἰδέναι πόθεν. ← [8] καὶ ὁ Ἰησοῦς εἶπεν
they replied that they did not know where it was from. Then *{the}* Jesus said
646 3857 3857 3590 3857 4470 2779 3836 2652 3306
v.api.3p pl f.ra pl cj d.nsm n.nsm v.aai.3s

αὐτοῖς, οὐδὲ ↱ ἐγὼ λέγω ὑμῖν ἐν ποίᾳ ἐξουσίᾳ ταῦτα ποιῶ.
to them, "Neither will I tell you by what authority I do these things." *I do*
899 4028 3306 1609 3306 7007 1877 4481 2026 4472 4472 4047 4472
r.dpm.3 cj r.ns.1 v.pai.1s r.dp.2 p.d r.dsf n.dsf r.apn v.pai.1s

[9] ἤρξατο δὲ πρὸς τὸν λαὸν λέγειν τὴν παραβολὴν ταύτην,
Then he began *Then* to tell *{to}* the people *to tell* *{the}* this parable: *this* "A
1254 806 1254 3306 3306 4639 3836 3295 3306 3836 4047 4130 4047
v.ami.3s cj p.a d.asm n.asm f.pa d.asf n.asf r.asf

ἄνθρωπός[a] ἐφύτευσεν ἀμπελῶνα καὶ ἐξέδετο αὐτὸν γεωργοῖς καὶ ἀπεδήμησεν →
man planted a vineyard and leased it to tenants; then he went away for
476 5885 308 2779 1686 899 1177 2779 623
n.nsm v.aai.3s n.asm cj v.ami.3s r.asm.3 n.dpm cj v.aai.3s

χρόνους ἱκανούς. [10] καὶ → καιρῷ ἀπέστειλεν πρὸς
quite some time. *quite some* *{and}* When the season came, he sent a servant to
2653 2653 5989 2653 2779 2789 690 1529 4639
n.apm a.apm cj n.dsm v.aai.3s p.a

τοὺς γεωργοὺς δοῦλον ἵνα ἀπὸ τοῦ καρποῦ τοῦ
the tenants *servant* so that they might give him his share of the produce of the
3836 1177 1529 2671 1443 1443 1443 899 608 3836 2843 3836
d.apm n.apm n.asm cj p.g d.gsm n.gsm d.gsm

ἀμπελῶνος δώσουσιν αὐτῷ· οἱ δὲ γεωργοὶ ἐξαπέστειλαν αὐτὸν
vineyard; *they might give* *him* but the *but* tenants beat him and sent him
308 1443 899 1254 3836 1254 1177 1296 1990 899
n.gsm v.fai.3p r.dsm.3 d.npm cj n.npm v.aai.3p r.asm.3

↰ δείραντες κενόν. [11] καὶ ⌊προσέθετο ἕτερον πέμψαι⌋ δοῦλον· οἱ δὲ
away *beat* empty-handed. So he sent another servant; but they *but*
1990 1296 3031 2779 4707 2283 4287 1529 1254 3836 1254
pt.aa.npm a.asm cj v.ami.3s r.asm f.aa n.asm d.npm cj

[a] τις included by UBS after ἄνθρωπός.

NASB

Him, "Tell us by
what authority You
are doing these
things, or who is
the one who gave
You this author-
ity?" [3]Jesus an-
swered and said to
them, "I will also
ask you a question,
and you tell Me:
[4]Was the baptism
of John from heav-
en or from men?"
[5]They reasoned
among themselves,
saying, "If we say,
'From heaven,' He
will say, 'Why did
you not believe
him?' [6]But if we
say, 'From men,'
all the people will
stone us to death,
for they are con-
vinced that John
was a prophet." [7]So
they answered that
they did not know
where *it came*
from. [8]And Jesus
said to them, "Nor
will I tell you by
what authority I do
these things."

Parable of the Vine-growers

[9]And He began to
tell the people this
parable: "A man
planted a vineyard
and rented it out
to vine-growers,
and went on a
journey for a long
time. [10]At the
harvest time he
sent a slave to the
vine-growers, so
that they would
give him *some*
of the produce of
the vineyard; but
the vine-growers
beat him and sent
him away empty-
handed. [11]And he
proceeded to send
another slave; and

NIV

also they beat and
treated shameful-
ly and sent away
empty-handed.
12 He sent still a
third, and they
wounded him and
threw him out.
13 "Then the own-
er of the vineyard
said, 'What shall I
do? I will send my
son, whom I love;
perhaps they will
respect him.'
14 "But when the
tenants saw him,
they talked the
matter over. 'This
is the heir,' they
said. 'Let's kill
him, and the in-
heritance will be
ours.' 15 So they
threw him out of
the vineyard and
killed him.
"What then will
the owner of the
vineyard do to
them? 16 He will
come and kill
those tenants and
give the vineyard
to others."
When the people
heard this, they
said, "God forbid!"
17 Jesus looked
directly at them
and asked, "Then
what is the mean-
ing of that which is
written:

"'The stone the
builders
rejected
has become
the cornerstone'[a]?

18 Everyone who
falls on that stone
will be broken to
pieces; anyone on
whom it falls will
be crushed."
19 The teachers
of the law and
the chief priests
looked for a way to
arrest him

κἀκεῖνον δείραντες καὶ ἀτιμάσαντες ← ἐξαπέστειλαν ←
beat that one *beat* as well, treated him shamefully, and sent him away
1296 2797 1296 2779 869 1990
adv pt.aa.npm cj pt.aa.npm v.aai.3p

κενόν. 12 καὶ ⌊προσέθετο τρίτον πέμψαι·⌋ οἱ δὲ καὶ
empty-handed. So he sent a third; but they *but* wounded this one too,
3031 2779 4707 5569 4287 1254 3836 1254 5547 4047 4047 2779
a.asm cj v.ami.3s a.asm f.aa d.npm cj adv

τοῦτον τραυματίσαντες ἐξέβαλον. ← 13 εἶπεν
this one wounded and threw him out. Then the owner of the vineyard said,
4047 5547 1675 1254 3836 3261 3836 3836 308 3306
r.asm pt.aa.npm v.aai.3p v.aai.3s

δὲ ὁ κύριος τοῦ ἀμπελῶνος, τί ποιήσω; πέμψω τὸν υἱόν μου τὸν
Then the owner of the vineyard 'What shall I do? I will send *{the}* my son, *my* whom
1254 3836 3261 3836 308 5515 4472 4287 3836 1609 5626 1609 3836
cj d.nsm n.nsm d.gsm n.gsm r.asn v.aas.1s v.fai.1s d.asm n.asm r.gs.1 d.asm

ἀγαπητόν· ἴσως τοῦτον ἐντραπήσονται. 14 → ἰδόντες
I love; perhaps they will respect him.' *they will respect* When the tenants saw
28 2711 1956 1956 1956 4047 1956 3836 1177 1625
a.asm adv r.asm v.fpi.3p pt.aa.npm

δὲ αὐτὸν οἱ γεωργοὶ διελογίζοντο πρὸς ἀλλήλους λέγοντες, οὗτός ἐστιν ὁ
{and} him, *the tenants* they reasoned among themselves, saying, 'This is the
1254 899 3836 1177 1368 4639 253 3306 4047 1639 3836
cj r.asm.3 d.npm n.npm v.imi.3p p.a r.apm pt.pa.npm r.nsm v.pai.3s d.nsm

κληρονόμος· ἀποκτείνωμεν αὐτόν, ἵνα ἡμῶν γένηται ἡ
heir. Let us kill him, so that the inheritance may be ours.' *may be the*
3101 650 899 2671 3836 3100 1181 1181 7005 1181 3836
n.nsm v.aas.1p r.asm.3 cj r.gp.1 v.ams.3s d.nsf

κληρονομία. 15 καὶ ↱ ἐκβαλόντες αὐτὸν ἔξω τοῦ ἀμπελῶνος ἀπέκτειναν.
inheritance And they threw him ⌊out of⌋ the vineyard and killed him.
3100 2779 650 1675 899 2032 3836 308 650
n.nsf cj pt.aa.npm r.asm.3 p.g d.gsm n.gsm v.aai.3p

τί οὖν → ποιήσει αὐτοῖς ὁ κύριος τοῦ ἀμπελῶνος;
What then will the owner of the vineyard do to them? *the owner of the vineyard*
5515 4036 3836 3261 3836 3836 308 4472 899 3836 3261 3836 308
r.asn cj v.fai.3s r.dpm.3 d.nsm n.nsm d.gsm n.gsm

16 ἐλεύσεται καὶ ἀπολέσει τοὺς γεωργοὺς τούτους καὶ δώσει τὸν ἀμπελῶνα
He will come and destroy *{the}* those tenants *those* and give the vineyard
2262 2779 660 3836 4047 1177 4047 2779 1443 3836 308
v.fmi.3s cj v.fai.3s d.apm n.apm r.apm cj v.fai.3s d.asm n.asm

ἄλλοις. ἀκούσαντες δὲ εἶπαν, ⌊μὴ γένοιτο.⌋ 17
to others." When they heard *{and}* this, they said, "Surely not!" But looking straight
257 201 1254 3306 3590 1181 1254 1838 1838
r.dpm pt.aa.npm cj v.aai.3p pl v.amo.3s

ὁ δὲ ἐμβλέψας αὐτοῖς εἶπεν, τί οὖν ἐστιν τὸ γεγραμμένον
at them he *But looking straight at them* said, "What then is this that is written:
1838 899 3836 1254 1838 899 3306 5515 4036 1639 4047 3836 1211
d.nsm cj pt.aa.nsm r.dpm.3 v.aai.3s r.nsn cj v.pai.3s d.nsn pt.rp.nsn

τοῦτο, λίθον ὃν ἀπεδοκίμασαν οἱ οἰκοδομοῦντες, οὗτος
this "The stone that the builders rejected *the builders* — this one
4047 3345 4005 3836 3868 627 3836 3868 4047
r.nsn n.asm r.asm v.aai.3p d.npm pt.pa.npm r.nsm

⌊ἐγενήθη εἰς⌋ κεφαλὴν → γωνίας; 18 πᾶς ὁ πεσὼν ἐπ' ἐκεῖνον τὸν
became the head of the corner'? Everyone who falls on that *{the}*
1181 1650 3051 1224 4246 3836 4406 2093 1697 3836
v.api.3s p.a n.asf n.gsf a.nsm d.nsm pt.aa.nsm p.a r.asm d.asm

λίθον συνθλασθήσεται· ἐφ' ὃν δ' ἂν πέσῃ, λικμήσει αὐτόν.
stone will be broken into pieces, and on whomever *and* ~ it falls, it will crush him."
3345 5314 1254 2093 4005 1254 323 4406 3347 899
n.asm v.fpi.3s p.a r.asm cj pl v.aas.3s v.fai.3s r.asm.3

19 καὶ ἐζήτησαν οἱ γραμματεῖς καὶ οἱ ἀρχιερεῖς ἐπιβαλεῖν ἐπ' αὐτὸν
{and} tried The scribes and the chief priests tried to lay hands on him
2779 2426 3836 1208 2779 3836 797 2426 2095 5931 2093 899
cj v.aai.3p d.npm n.npm cj d.npm n.npm f.aa p.a r.asm.3

NASB

they beat him also
and treated him
shamefully and
sent him away
empty-handed.
12 And he proceeded
to send a third; and
this one also they
wounded and cast
out. 13 The owner of
the vineyard said,
'What shall I do?
I will send my be-
loved son; perhaps
they will respect
him.' 14 But when
the vine-growers
saw him, they
reasoned with one
another, saying,
'This is the heir; let
us kill him so that
the inheritance will
be ours.' 15 So they
threw him out of
the vineyard and
killed him. What,
then, will the
owner of the vine-
yard do to them?
16 He will come and
destroy these vine-
growers and will
give the vineyard
to others." When
they heard it, they
said, "May it never
be!" 17 But Jesus
looked at them and
said, "What then is
this that is written:

'THE STONE
WHICH THE
BUILDERS RE-
JECTED,
THIS BECAME
THE CHIEF
CORNER
stone'?

18 Everyone who
falls on that stone
will be broken
to pieces; but on
whomever it falls,
it will scatter him
like dust."

Tribute to Caesar

19 The scribes and
the chief priests
tried to lay hands

[a] 17 Psalm 118:22

NIV

immediately, be-
cause they knew
he had spoken this
parable against
them. But they
were afraid of the
people.

Paying Taxes to Caesar

20 Keeping a close
watch on him,
they sent spies,
who pretended to
be sincere. They
hoped to catch
Jesus in something
he said, so that
they might hand
him over to the
power and author-
ity of the gover-
nor. 21 So the spies
questioned him:
"Teacher, we know
that you speak and
teach what is right,
and that you do not
show partiality but
teach the way of
God in accordance
with the truth. 22 Is
it right for us to
pay taxes to Cae-
sar or not?"
23 He saw through
their duplicity
and said to them,
24 "Show me a de-
narius. Whose im-
age and inscription
are on it?"
"Caesar's," they
replied.
25 He said to them,
"Then give back
to Caesar what
is Caesar's, and
to God what is
God's."
26 They were un-
able to trap him in
what he had said
there in public.
And astonished by
his answer, they
became silent.

The Resurrection and Marriage

27 Some of the
Sadducees, who
say there is no
resurrection,

τὰς χεῖρας ἐν αὐτῇ τῇ ὥρᾳ,
{the} hands at that very {the} hour, for they perceived that he had spoken this parable
3836 5931 1877 899 3836 6052 1142 1182 1182 4022 3306 3306 3306 4047 4130
d.apf n.apf p.d r.dsf d.dsf n.dsf

καὶ ἐφοβήθησαν τὸν λαόν, ἔγνωσαν γὰρ ὅτι πρὸς αὐτοὺς εἶπεν
against them, but they feared the people. *they perceived* *for* *that* *against* *them* *he had spoken*
4639 899 2779 5828 3836 3295 1182 1142 4022 4639 899 3306
cj v.api.3p d.asm n.asm v.aai.3p cj cj p.a r.apm.3 v.aai.3s

τὴν παραβολὴν ταύτην. 20 καὶ ↱ παρατηρήσαντες ← ἀπέστειλαν
{the} *parable* *this* So they watched him closely and sent
3836 4130 4047 2779 690 4190 690
d.asf n.asf r.asf cj pt.aa.npm v.aai.3p

ἐγκαθέτους ὑποκρινομένους ἑαυτοὺς δικαίους εἶναι, ἵνα ἐπιλάβωνται
spies who pretended to be *who* righteous *to be* so they could catch
1588 1571 5693 1639 1639 1571 1465 1639 2671 2138
n.apm pt.pm.apm r.apm.3 a.apm f.pa cj v.ams.3p

← αὐτοῦ λόγου, ὥστε παραδοῦναι αὐτὸν τῇ ἀρχῇ καὶ τῇ
him in his word, and ⌊in this way⌋ deliver him ⌊to the⌋ jurisdiction and *{the}*
899 3364 6063 4140 899 3836 794 2779 3836
r.gsm.3 n.gsm cj f.aa r.asm.3 d.dsf n.dsf cj d.dsf

ἐξουσίᾳ τοῦ ἡγεμόνος. 21 καὶ ἐπηρώτησαν αὐτὸν λέγοντες, διδάσκαλε, οἴδαμεν
authority of the governor. *{and}* They questioned him, saying, "Teacher, we know
2026 3836 2450 2779 2089 899 3306 1437 3857
n.dsf d.gsm n.gsm cj v.aai.3p r.asm.3 pt.pa.npm n.vsm v.rai.1p

ὅτι ὀρθῶς λέγεις καὶ διδάσκεις καὶ οὐ λαμβάνεις
that you speak and teach truthfully *you speak* *and* *teach* and show no *show*
4022 3306 3306 2779 1438 3987 3306 2779 1438 2779 3284 4024 3284
cj adv v.pai.2s cj v.pai.2s cj pl v.pai.2s

πρόσωπον, ἀλλ' ⌊ἐπ' ἀληθείας⌋ τὴν ὁδὸν τοῦ θεοῦ διδάσκεις· 22 ἔξεστιν
partiality, but truly teach the way of God. *teach* ⌊Is it lawful for⌋
4725 247 2093 237 1438 3836 3847 3836 2536 1438 1997
n.asn cj p.g n.gsf d.asf n.asf d.gsm n.gsm v.pai.2s v.pai.3s

ἡμᾶς Καίσαρι φόρον δοῦναι ἢ οὔ; 23 ↱ κατανοήσας δὲ
us to give tribute to Caesar, *tribute* *to give* or not?" But he realized *But*
7005 1443 1443 5843 2790 5843 1443 2445 4024 1254 3306 2917 1254
r.ap.1 n.dsm n.asm f.aa cj pl pt.aa.nsm cj

αὐτῶν τὴν πανουργίαν εἶπεν πρὸς αὐτούς, 24 δείξατέ μοι δηνάριον· τίνος
their *{the}* duplicity, and said to them, "Show me a denarius. Whose
899 3836 4111 3306 4639 899 1259 1609 1324 5515
r.gpm.3 d.asf n.asf v.aai.3s p.a r.apm.3 v.aam.2p r.ds.1 n.asn r.gsm

ἔχει εἰκόνα καὶ ἐπιγραφήν; οἱ δὲ εἶπαν, Καίσαρος.
image and inscription ⌊does it have?"⌋ *image* *and* *inscription* They *{and}* said, "Caesar's."
1635 2779 2107 2400 1635 2779 2107 3836 1254 3306 2790
v.pai.3s n.asf cj n.asf d.npm cj v.aai.3p n.gsm

25 ὁ δὲ εἶπεν πρὸς αὐτούς, τοίνυν ἀπόδοτε τὰ
He *{and}* said to them, "Then give to Caesar the things that are
3836 1254 3306 4639 899 5523 625 2790 2790 3836
d.nsm cj v.aai.3s p.a r.apm.3 cj v.aam.2p d.apn

Καίσαρος Καίσαρι καὶ τὰ τοῦ θεοῦ τῷ θεῷ. 26 καὶ
Caesar's, *to Caesar* and to God the things that are *{the}* God's." *to* *God* And
2790 2790 2779 3836 2536 3836 3836 2536 3836 2536 2779
n.gsm n.dsm cj d.apn d.gsm n.gsm d.dsm n.dsm cj

⌊οὐκ ἴσχυσαν⌋ ἐπιλαβέσθαι αὐτοῦ ↰ ῥήματος ἐναντίον τοῦ λαοῦ
they were unable to trap him in what he said in the presence of the people,
4024 2710 2138 899 2138 4839 1883 3836 3295
pl v.aai.3p f.am r.gsm.3 n.gsn p.g d.gsm n.gsm

καὶ θαυμάσαντες ἐπὶ τῇ ἀποκρίσει αὐτοῦ ἐσίγησαν.
but, marveling at *{the}* his answer, *his* ⌊they were reduced to silence.⌋
2779 2513 2093 3836 899 647 899 4967
cj pt.aa.npm p.d d.dsf n.dsf r.gsm.3 v.aai.3p

27 προσελθόντες δέ τινες τῶν Σαδδουκαίων, οἱ λέγοντες[a] ἀνάστασιν
came up Now some *{the}* Sadducees (who deny there is a resurrection)
4665 1254 5516 3836 4881 3836 3306 1639 1639 414
pt.aa.npm cj r.npm d.gpm n.gpm d.npm pt.pa.npm n.asf

[a] λέγοντες TNIV, NET. [ἀντι]λέγοντες UBS.

NASB

on Him that very
hour, and they
feared the people;
for they understood
that He spoke this
parable against
them. 20 So they
watched Him, and
sent spies who
pretended to be
righteous, in order
that they might
catch Him in some
statement, so that
they *could* deliver
Him to the rule and
the authority of the
governor. 21 They
questioned Him,
saying, "Teacher,
we know that You
speak and teach
correctly, and You
are not partial to
any, but teach the
way of God in
truth. 22 Is it lawful
for us to pay taxes
to Caesar, or not?"
23 But He detected
their trickery and
said to them,
24 "Show Me a [a]den-
arius. Whose like-
ness and inscrip-
tion does it have?"
They said, "Cae-
sar's." 25 And He
said to them, "Then
render to Caesar
the things that are
Caesar's, and to
God the things that
are God's." 26 And
they were unable
to catch Him in a
saying in the pres-
ence of the people;
and being amazed
at His answer, they
became silent.

Is There a Resurrection?

27 Now there came
to Him some of the
Sadducees (who
say that there is no
resurrection),

[a] The denarius was a day's wages

NIV

came to Jesus
with a question.
[28]“Teacher,” they
said, “Moses wrote
for us that if a
man’s brother dies
and leaves a wife
but no children,
the man must mar-
ry the widow and
raise up offspring
for his brother.
[29]Now there were
seven brothers.
The first one mar-
ried a woman and
died childless.
[30]The second [31]and
then the third mar-
ried her, and in the
same way the sev-
en died, leaving no
children. [32]Finally,
the woman died
too. [33]Now then,
at the resurrection
whose wife will
she be, since the
seven were mar-
ried to her?”
[34]Jesus replied,
“The people of this
age marry and are
given in marriage.
[35]But those who
are considered
worthy of taking
part in the age to
come and in the
resurrection from
the dead will nei-
ther marry nor be
given in marriage,
[36]and they can no
longer die; for they
are like the angels.
They are God’s
children, since
they are children
of the resurrec-
tion. [37]But in the
account of the
burning bush, even
Moses showed that
the dead rise, for
he calls the Lord
‘the God of Abra-
ham, and the God
of Isaac, and the
God of Jacob.’[a]
[38]He is not

μὴ εἶναι, ἐπηρώτησαν αὐτὸν 28 λέγοντες, διδάσκαλε, Μωϋσῆς ἔγραψεν
{not} there is came up and questioned him, saying, “Teacher, Moses wrote
3590 1639 4665 4665 2089 899 3306 1437 3707 1211
pl f.pa v.aai.3p r.asm.3 pt.pa.npm n.vsm n.nsm v.aai.3s

ἡμῖν, ἐάν τινος ἀδελφὸς ἀποθάνῃ ἔχων γυναῖκα, καὶ οὗτος ἄτεκνος
for us that if someone’s brother dies, having a wife, but {this one} is childless,
7005 1569 5516 81 633 2400 1222 2779 4047 1639 866
r.dp.1 cj r.gsm n.nsm v.aas.3s pt.pa.nsm n.asf cj r.nsm a.nsm

ᾖ, ἵνα λάβῃ ὁ ἀδελφὸς αὐτοῦ τὴν γυναῖκα καὶ ἐξαναστήσῃ
is then his brother ⌊must take⌋ {the} brother his the widow and raise up
1639 2671 899 81 3284 3836 81 899 3836 1222 2779 1985
v.pas.3s cj v.aas.3s d.nsm n.nsm r.gsm.3 d.asf n.asf cj v.aas.3s

σπέρμα τῷ ἀδελφῷ αὐτοῦ. 29 ἑπτὰ οὖν ἀδελφοὶ ἦσαν· καὶ ὁ
offspring for his brother. his Now there were seven Now brothers. there were {and} The
5065 3836 899 81 899 4036 1639 1639 2231 4036 81 1639 2779 3836
n.asn d.dsm n.dsm r.gsm.3 a.npm cj n.npm v.iai.3p cj d.nsm

πρῶτος λαβὼν γυναῖκα ἀπέθανεν ἄτεκνος· 30 καὶ[a] ὁ δεύτερος[b] 31 καὶ ὁ
first, ⌊having taken⌋ a wife, died childless. Both the second and the
4755 3284 1222 633 866 2779 3836 1311 2779 3836
a.nsm pt.aa.nsm n.asf v.aai.3s a.nsm cj d.nsm a.nsm cj d.nsm

τρίτος ἔλαβεν αὐτήν, ὡσαύτως δὲ καὶ οἱ ἑπτὰ οὐ κατέλιπον τέκνα
third took her, and likewise and also the seven: they left no they left children
5569 3284 899 1254 6058 1254 2779 3836 2231 2901 2901 4024 2901 5451
a.nsm v.aai.3s r.asf.3 adv cj adv d.npm a.npm pl v.aai.3p n.apn

καὶ ἀπέθανον. 32 ὕστερον καὶ ἡ γυνὴ ἀπέθανεν. 33 ἡ γυνὴ οὖν
and died. Later on the woman also the woman died. So the woman So
2779 633 5731 3836 1222 2779 3836 1222 633 4036 3836 1222 4036
cj v.aai.3p adv.c adv d.nsf n.nsf v.aai.3s d.nsf n.nsf cj

ἐν τῇ ἀναστάσει τίνος αὐτῶν γίνεται γυνή; οἱ γὰρ ἑπτὰ ἔσχον
— in the resurrection — of which of them ⌊will she be⌋ wife? For all For seven had
1877 3836 414 5515 899 1181 1222 1142 3836 1142 2231 2400
p.d d.dsf n.dsf r.gsm r.gpm.3 v.pmi.3s n.nsf d.npm cj a.npm v.aai.3p

αὐτὴν γυναῖκα. 34 καὶ εἶπεν αὐτοῖς ὁ Ἰησοῦς, οἱ υἱοὶ τοῦ αἰῶνος
her as wife.” And Jesus said to them, {the} Jesus “The sons of this age
899 1222 2779 2652 3306 899 3836 2652 3836 5626 3836 4047 172
r.asf.3 n.asf cj v.aai.3s r.dpm.3 d.nsm n.nsm d.npm n.npm d.gsm n.gsm

τούτου γαμοῦσιν καὶ γαμίσκονται, 35 οἱ δὲ καταξιωθέντες
this marry and are given in marriage, but those but ⌊who are considered worthy⌋ to
4047 1138 2779 1140 1254 3836 1254 2921 5593
r.gsm v.pai.3p cj v.ppi.3p d.npm cj pt.ap.npm

τοῦ αἰῶνος ἐκείνου τυχεῖν καὶ τῆς ἀναστάσεως τῆς ἐκ νεκρῶν
attain to {the} that age that to attain and to the resurrection {the} from the dead
5593 3836 1697 172 1697 5593 2779 3836 414 3836 1666 3738
d.gsm n.gsm r.gsm f.aa cj d.gsf n.gsf d.gsf p.g a.gpm

οὔτε γαμοῦσιν οὔτε γαμίζονται· 36 οὐδὲ γὰρ
neither marry nor are given in marriage. In fact, they can no In fact longer
4046 1138 4046 1139 1142 1142 1538 1538 4028 1142 2285
cj v.pai.3p cj v.ppi.3p cj cj

ἀποθανεῖν ἔτι δύνανται, ἰσάγγελοι γάρ εἰσιν καὶ υἱοί εἰσιν
die, longer they can since they are like angels since they are and are sons are
633 2285 1538 1142 1639 1639 2694 1142 1639 2779 1639 5626 1639
f.aa adv v.ppi.3p a.npm cj v.pai.3p cj n.npm v.pai.3p

θεοῦ τῆς ἀναστάσεως υἱοὶ ὄντες. 37 ὅτι δὲ ἐγείρονται
of God, being sons of the resurrection. sons being But that But the dead are raised,
2536 1639 5626 3836 414 5626 1639 1254 4022 1254 3836 3738 1586
n.gsm d.gsf n.gsf n.npm pt.pa.npm cj cj v.ppi.3p

οἱ νεκροί, καὶ Μωϋσῆς ἐμήνυσεν ἐπὶ τῆς βάτου, ὡς λέγει
the dead even Moses made known, in the passage about the bush, for he calls the
3836 3738 2779 3707 3606 2093 3836 1004 6055 3306
d.npm a.npm adv n.nsm v.aai.3s p.g d.gsf n.gsf cj v.pai.3s

κύριον τὸν θεὸν Ἀβραὰμ καὶ θεὸν Ἰσαὰκ καὶ θεὸν Ἰακώβ. 38
Lord, ‘the God of Abraham and the God of Isaac and the God of Jacob.’ He is not
3261 3836 2536 11 2779 2536 2693 2779 2536 2609 1639 1639 4024
n.asm d.asm n.asm n.gsm cj n.asm n.gsm cj n.asm n.gsm

NASB

[28]and they ques-
tioned Him, saying,
“Teacher, Moses
wrote for us that
IF A MAN’S BROTHER
DIES, having a wife,
AND HE IS CHILDLESS,
HIS BROTHER SHOULD
MARRY THE WIFE AND
RAISE UP CHILDREN
TO HIS BROTHER.
[29]Now there were
seven brothers; and
the first took a wife
and died childless;
[30]and the second
[31]and the third mar-
ried her; and in the
same way all seven
died, leaving no
children. [32]Finally
the woman died
also. [33]In the resur-
rection therefore,
which one’s wife
will she be? For all
seven had married
her.”
[34]Jesus said to
them, “The sons of
this age marry and
are given in mar-
riage, [35]but those
who are considered
worthy to attain
to that age and the
resurrection from
the dead, neither
marry nor are
given in marriage;
[36]for they cannot
even die anymore,
because they are
like angels, and
are sons of God,
being sons of the
resurrection. [37]But
that the dead are
raised, even Moses
showed, in the
passage about
the burning bush,
where he calls the
Lord THE GOD OF
ABRAHAM, AND THE
GOD OF ISAAC, AND
THE GOD OF JACOB.
[38]Now He

[a] 37 Exodus 3:6

[a] ἔλαβεν included by TR after καὶ.
[b] τὴν γυναῖκα, καὶ οὗτος ἀπέθανεν ἄτεκνος included by TR after δεύτερος.

NIV

the God of the
dead, but of the
living, for to him
all are alive."
39 Some of the
teachers of the
law responded,
"Well said, teach-
er!" 40 And no one
dared to ask him
any more ques-
tions.

Whose Son Is the Messiah?

41 Then Jesus said
to them, "Why
is it said that the
Messiah is the son
of David? 42 David
himself declares
in the Book of
Psalms:

"'The Lord said to
my Lord:
"Sit at my right
hand
43 until I make your
enemies
a footstool for
your feet."'[a]

44 David calls him
'Lord.' How then
can he be his son?"

Warning Against the Teachers of the Law

45 While all the
people were lis-
tening, Jesus said
to his disciples,
46 "Beware of the
teachers of the law.
They like to walk
around in flowing
robes and love to
be greeted with
respect in the mar-
ketplaces and have
the most important
seats in the syn-
agogues and the
places of honor at
banquets. 47 They
devour widows'
houses and for
a show make
lengthy prayers.
These men will be
punished most se-
verely."

The Widow's Offering

21 As Jesus
looked up,
he saw the rich
putting their gifts
into the temple
treasury. 2 He also

[a] 43 Psalm 110:1

θεὸς δὲ οὐκ ἔστιν → νεκρῶν ἀλλὰ → ζώντων, ↱ ↱ πάντες γὰρ
God {and} not He is of the dead, but of the living! For to him they are all For
2536 1254 4024 1639 3738 247 2409 1142 899 899 2409 2409 4246 1142
n.nsm cj pl v.pai.3s a.gpm cj pt.pa.gpm a.npm cj

αὐτῷ ζῶσιν. 39 ἀποκριθέντες δέ τινες τῶν γραμματέων εἶπαν, διδάσκαλε,
to him alive." In response {and} some of the scribes said, "Teacher, you have
899 2409 646 1254 5516 3836 1208 3306 1437 3306 3306
r.dsm.3 v.pai.3p pt.ap.npm cj r.npm d.gpm n.gpm v.aai.3p n.vsm

καλῶς εἶπας. 40 οὐκέτι γὰρ ἐτόλμων ἐπερωτᾶν αὐτὸν ↰
spoken well!" you have spoken For no longer For did they dare to question him about
3306 2822 3306 1142 4033 1142 5528 2089 899 2089
adv v.aai.2s adv cj v.iai.3p f.pa r.asm.3

οὐδέν. 41 εἶπεν δὲ πρὸς αὐτούς, πῶς λέγουσιν τὸν χριστὸν εἶναι
anything. Then he said Then to them, "How can they say that the Messiah is to be a
4029 1254 3306 1254 4639 899 4802 3306 3836 5986 1639
a.asn v.aai.3s cj p.a r.apm.3 cj v.pai.3p d.asm n.asm f.pa

Δαυὶδ υἱόν; 42 αὐτὸς γὰρ Δαυὶδ λέγει ἐν βίβλῳ ψαλμῶν,
son of David? son For David himself For David says in the book of Psalms, 'The
5626 1253 5626 1142 1253 899 1142 1253 3306 1877 1047 6011
n.gsm n.asm r.nsm cj n.nsm v.pai.3s p.d n.dsf n.gpm

εἶπεν κύριος τῷ κυρίῳ μου, κάθου ἐκ δεξιῶν μου, 43 ⌞ἕως ἂν⌟
Lord said Lord to my Lord, my "Sit at my right hand, my until
3261 3306 3261 3836 1609 3261 1609 2764 1666 1609 1288 1609 2401 323
v.aai.3s n.nsm d.dsm n.dsm r.gs.1 v.pmm.2s p.g a.gpf r.gs.1 cj pl

θῶ τοὺς ἐχθρούς σου ὑποπόδιον τῶν ποδῶν σου. 44 Δαυὶδ οὖν
I make {the} your enemies your a footstool for your feet."' your David thus calls him
5502 3836 5148 2398 5148 5711 3836 5148 4546 5148 1253 4036 2813 899
v.aas.1s d.apm a.apm r.gs.2 n.asn d.gpm n.gpm r.gs.2 n.nsm cj

κύριον αὐτὸν καλεῖ, καὶ πῶς αὐτοῦ υἱός ἐστιν; 45 →
'Lord.' him calls So how could he be his son?" could he be As all the people
3261 899 2813 2779 4802 1639 1639 1639 899 5626 1639 4246 3836 3295
n.asm r.asm.3 v.pai.3s cj cj r.gsm.3 n.nsm v.pai.3s

Ἀκούοντος δὲ παντὸς τοῦ λαοῦ εἶπεν τοῖς μαθηταῖς αὐτοῦ,[a] 46 προσέχετε
were listening, {and} all the people he said to his disciples, his "Beware
201 1254 4246 3836 3295 3306 3836 899 3412 899 4668
pt.pa.gsm cj a.gsm d.gsm n.gsm v.aai.3s d.dpm n.dpm r.gsm.3 v.pam.2p

ἀπὸ τῶν γραμματέων τῶν θελόντων περιπατεῖν ἐν στολαῖς καὶ φιλούντων
of those scribes, who like to walk around in flowing robes, and love
608 3836 1208 3836 2527 4344 1877 5124 2779 5797
p.g d.gpm n.gpm d.gpm pt.pa.gpm f.pa p.d n.dpf cj pt.pa.gpm

ἀσπασμοὺς ἐν ταῖς ἀγοραῖς καὶ πρωτοκαθεδρίας ἐν ταῖς συναγωγαῖς καὶ
greetings in the marketplaces and the most important seats in the synagogues and the
833 1877 3836 59 2779 4751 1877 3836 5252 2779
n.apm p.d d.dpf n.dpf cj n.apf p.d d.dpf n.dpf cj

πρωτοκλισίας ἐν τοῖς δείπνοις, 47 οἳ κατεσθίουσιν τὰς οἰκίας τῶν χηρῶν καὶ
places of honor at {the} feasts, who devour the houses of widows and
4752 1877 3836 1270 4005 2983 3836 3864 3836 5939 2779
n.apf p.d d.dpn n.dpn r.npm v.pai.3p d.apf n.apf d.gpf n.gpf cj

προφάσει ↱ μακρὰ προσεύχονται· οὗτοι λήμψονται περισσότερον
⌞for the sake of appearance⌟ make lengthy prayers. These will receive the greater
4733 4667 3431 4667 4047 3284 4358
n.dsf adv v.pmi.3p r.npm v.fmi.3p a.asn.c

κρίμα.
condemnation."
3210
n.asn

21:1 ἀναβλέψας δὲ εἶδεν τοὺς βάλλοντας εἰς τὸ
Looking up, {and} Jesus saw {the} rich people putting their gifts into the
329 1254 1625 3836 4454 4454 965 899 1565 1650 3836
pt.aa.nsm cj v.aai.3s d.apm pt.pa.apm p.a d.asn

γαζοφυλάκιον τὰ δῶρα αὐτῶν πλουσίους. 2 εἶδεν δέ τινα χήραν πενιχρὰν
offering box, {the} gifts their rich people and he saw and a poor widow poor
1126 3836 1565 899 4454 1254 1625 1254 5516 4293 5939 4293
n.asn d.apn n.apn r.gpm.3 a.apm v.aai.3s cj r.asf n.asf a.asf

[a] [αὐτοῦ] UBS.

NASB

is not the God of
the dead but of the
living; for all live
to Him." 39 Some
of the scribes an-
swered and said,
"Teacher, You have
spoken well." 40 For
they did not have
courage to question
Him any longer
about anything.
41 Then He said to
them, "How *is it*
that they say [a]the
Christ is David's
son? 42 For David
himself says in the
book of Psalms,
'THE LORD SAID
TO MY LORD,
"SIT AT MY
RIGHT HAND,
43 UNTIL I MAKE
YOUR ENEMIES
A FOOTSTOOL
FOR YOUR
FEET."'
44 Therefore David
calls Him 'Lord,'
and how is He his
son?"
45 And while all
the people were
listening, He said
to the disciples,
46 "Beware of the
scribes, who like
to walk around in
long robes, and
love respectful
greetings in the
market places, and
chief seats in the
synagogues and
places of honor at
banquets, 47 who
devour widows'
houses, and for
appearance's sake
offer long prayers.
These will receive
greater condemna-
tion."

The Widow's Gift

21:1 And He looked
up and saw the rich
putting their gifts
into the treasury.
2 And He saw a
poor widow

[a] I.e. the Messiah

NIV

saw a poor wid-
ow put in two
very small copper
coins. 3 "Truly I
tell you," he said,
"this poor widow
has put in more
than all the others.
4 All these people
gave their gifts out
of their wealth; but
she out of her pov-
erty put in all she
had to live on."

The Destruction of the Temple and Signs of the End Times

5 Some of his
disciples were
remarking about
how the temple
was adorned with
beautiful stones
and with gifts ded-
icated to God. But
Jesus said, 6 "As for
what you see here,
the time will come
when not one stone
will be left on an-
other; every one
of them will be
thrown down."
7 "Teacher," they
asked, "when will
these things hap-
pen? And what
will be the sign
that they are about
to take place?"
8 He replied:
"Watch out that
you are not de-
ceived. For many
will come in my
name, claiming, 'I
am he,' and, 'The
time is near.' Do
not follow them.
9 When you hear
of wars and up-
risings, do not be
frightened. These
things must hap-
pen first, but the
end will not come
right away."
10 Then he said to
them: "Nation will
rise against na-
tion, and kingdom
against kingdom.
11 There will be
great earthquakes,
famines

βάλλουσαν ἐκεῖ λεπτὰ δύο, 3 καὶ εἶπεν, ἀληθῶς λέγω ὑμῖν
put in two small coins. *two* And he said, "I tell you the truth, *I tell* *you*
965 1695 1545 3321 1545 2779 3306 3306 3306 7007 242 3306 7007
pt.pa.asf adv n.apn a.apn cj v.aai.3s adv v.pai.1s r.dp.2

ὅτι ἡ χήρα αὕτη ἡ πτωχὴ πλεῖον πάντων ἔβαλεν·
that *{the}* this poor widow *this* *{the}* *poor* has put in more than all the rest. *has put*
4022 3836 4047 4777 5939 4047 3836 4777 965 965 4498 4246 965
cj d.nsf n.nsf r.nsf d.nsf a.nsf a.asn.c a.gpm v.aai.3s

4 πάντες γὰρ οὗτοι ἐκ τοῦ περισσεύοντος αὐτοῖς ἔβαλον εἰς τὰ δῶρα,
For they all, *For* *they* out of their excess, *their* put in their gifts,
1142 4047 4246 1142 4047 1666 3836 899 4355 899 965 1650 3836 1565
a.npm cj r.npm p.g d.gsn pt.pa.gsn r.dpm.3 v.aai.3p p.a d.apn n.apn

αὕτη δὲ ἐκ τοῦ ὑστερήματος αὐτῆς πάντα τὸν
but she, *but* out of her need, *her* put in everything that she had *{the}*
1254 4047 1254 1666 3836 899 5729 899 965 965 4246 4005 2400 2400 3836
r.nsf cj p.g d.gsn n.gsn r.gsf.3 a.asm d.asm

βίον ὃν εἶχεν ἔβαλεν. 5 καί ↱ τινων λεγόντων περὶ τοῦ ἱεροῦ ὅτι
⌞to live on."⌟ *that* *she had* *put in* And while some were speaking of the temple, how it
1050 4005 2400 965 2779 3306 5516 3306 4309 3836 2639 4022 3175
n.asm r.asm v.iai.3s v.aai.3s cj r.gpm pt.pa.gpm p.g d.gsn n.gsn cj

→ λίθοις καλοῖς καὶ ἀναθήμασιν κεκόσμηται εἶπεν,
was adorned with beautiful stones *beautiful* and ⌞gifts dedicated to God,⌟ *it was adorned* Jesus said,
3175 3175 2819 3345 2819 2779 356 3175 3306
n.dpm a.dpm cj n.dpn v.rpi.3s v.aai.3s

6 ταῦτα ἃ θεωρεῖτε ἐλεύσονται ἡμέραι ἐν αἷς ↱ ↱ οὐκ
⌞"These things⌟ that you see — days will come *days* in which there will not
4047 4005 2555 2465 2262 2465 1877 4005 918 918 4024
r.apn r.apn v.pai.2p v.fmi.3p n.npf p.d r.dpf pl

ἀφεθήσεται λίθος ἐπὶ λίθῳ ὃς ↱ οὐ καταλυθήσεται. 7 ἐπηρώτησαν δὲ
be left stone upon stone that will not be thrown down." And they asked *And*
918 3345 2093 3345 4005 2907 4024 2907 1254 2089 1254
v.fpi.3s n.nsm p.d n.dsm r.nsm pl v.fpi.3s v.aai.3p cj

αὐτὸν λέγοντες, διδάσκαλε, πότε οὖν ↱ ταῦτα ἔσται καὶ τί τὸ σημεῖον
him, saying, "Teacher, when *{then}* will these things be, and what is the sign
899 3306 1437 4537 4036 1639 4047 1639 2779 5515 3836 4956
r.asm.3 pt.pa.npm n.vsm cj cj r.npn v.fmi.3s cj r.nsn d.nsn n.nsn

ὅταν μέλλῃ ταῦτα γίνεσθαι; 8 ὁ δὲ εἶπεν, βλέπετε ↱
when these things are about *these things* to happen?" And he *And* said, "See that you
4020 4047 4047 3516 4047 1181 1254 3836 1254 3306 1063 4414
cj v.pas.3s r.npn f.pm d.nsm cj v.aai.3s v.pam.2p

↱ μὴ πλανηθῆτε· πολλοὶ γὰρ ἐλεύσονται ἐπὶ τῷ ὀνόματί μου λέγοντες,
are not led astray! For many *For* will come in *{the}* my name, *my* saying,
4414 3590 4414 1142 4498 1142 2262 2093 3836 1609 3950 1609 3306
cj v.aps.2p a.npm cj v.fmi.3p p.d d.dsn n.dsn r.gs.1 pt.pa.npm

ἐγώ εἰμι, καί, ὁ καιρὸς ἤγγικεν. ↱ μὴ πορευθῆτε ὀπίσω αὐτῶν. 9 ὅταν
'I am he!' and, 'The time is at hand!' Do not go after them. When
1609 1639 2779 3836 2789 1581 4513 3590 4513 3958 899 4020
r.ns.1 v.pai.1s cj d.nsm n.nsm v.rai.3s cj v.aps.2p p.g r.gpm.3 cj

δὲ ἀκούσητε πολέμους καὶ ἀκαταστασίας, ↱ μὴ πτοηθῆτε· δεῖ
{and} you hear of wars and rebellions, do not be terrified, for these things must
1254 201 4483 2779 189 4765 3590 4765 1142 4047 4047 1256
cj v.aas.2p n.apm cj n.apf pl v.aps.2p v.pai.3s

γὰρ ταῦτα γενέσθαι πρῶτον, ἀλλ' οὐκ εὐθέως τὸ τέλος.
for *these things* take place first, but the end will not follow immediately." *the* *end*
1142 4047 1181 4754 247 3836 5465 4024 2311 3836 5465
cj r.apn f.am adv cj pl adv d.nsn n.nsn

10 τότε ἔλεγεν αὐτοῖς, ἐγερθήσεται ἔθνος ἐπ' ἔθνος καὶ βασιλεία ἐπὶ
Then he said to them, "Nation will rise *Nation* against nation, and kingdom against
5538 3306 899 1620 1586 1620 2093 1620 2779 993 2093
adv v.iai.3s r.dpm.3 v.fpi.3s n.nsn p.a n.asn cj n.nsf p.a

βασιλείαν, 11 σεισμοί τε μεγάλοι καὶ κατὰ τόπους λιμοὶ
kingdom; there will be great earthquakes, ~ *great* and in various places famines
993 1639 1639 1639 3489 4939 5445 3489 2779 2848 5536 3350
n.asf n.npm cj a.npm cj p.a n.apm n.npm

NASB

putting in two
small copper coins.
3 And He said,
"Truly I say to you,
this poor widow
put in more than
all *of them;* 4 for
they all out of their
surplus put into the
offering; but she
out of her poverty
put in all that she
had to live on."
5 And while some
were talking about
the temple, that it
was adorned with
beautiful stones
and votive gifts,
He said, 6 "*As for*
these things which
you are looking at,
the days will come
in which there will
not be left one
stone upon another
which will not be
torn down."
7 They questioned
Him, saying,
"Teacher, when
therefore will these
things happen?
And what *will be*
the sign when these
things are about to
take place?" 8 And
He said, "See to
it that you are not
misled; for many
will come in My
name, saying, 'I
am *He,*' and, 'The
time is near.' Do
not go after them.
9 When you hear of
wars and distur-
bances, do not be
terrified; for these
things must take
place first, but the
end *does* not *follow*
immediately."

Things to Come

10 Then He con-
tinued by saying
to them, "Nation
will rise against na-
tion and kingdom
against kingdom,
11 and there will be
great earthquakes,
and in various
places plagues and

NIV

and pestilences in
various places, and
fearful events and
great signs from
heaven.
12 “But before
all this, they will
seize you and per-
secute you. They
will hand you over
to synagogues and
put you in pris-
on, and you will
be brought before
kings and gover-
nors, and all on ac-
count of my name.
13 And so you will
bear testimony to
me. 14 But make up
your mind not to
worry beforehand
how you will de-
fend yourselves.
15 For I will give
you words and
wisdom that none
of your adversar-
ies will be able to
resist or contra-
dict. 16 You will be
betrayed even by
parents, brothers
and sisters, rela-
tives and friends,
and they will put
some of you to
death. 17 Everyone
will hate you be-
cause of me. 18 But
not a hair of your
head will perish.
19 Stand firm, and
you will win life.
20 “When you see
Jerusalem being
surrounded by
armies, you will
know that its des-
olation is near.
21 Then let those
who are in Judea
flee to the moun-
tains, let those in
the city get out,
and let those in the
country not enter
the city.

καὶ λοιμοὶ ἔσονται, φόβητρά τε καὶ ἀπ᾽ οὐρανοῦ
and plagues. *there will be* There will be dreadful portents ~ and great signs from heaven.
2779 3369 1639 1639 1639 1639 5831 5445 2779 3489 4956 608 4041
cj n.npm v.fmi.3p n.npn cj cj p.g n.gsm

σημεῖα μεγάλα ἔσται. 12 πρὸ δὲ τούτων πάντων ἐπιβαλοῦσιν
signs *great* *There will be* But before *But* all these things, *all* they will lay their
4956 3489 1639 1254 4574 1254 4246 4047 4246 2095 899
n.npn a.npn v.fmi.3s p.g cj r.gpn a.gpn v.fai.3p

ἐφ᾽ ὑμᾶς τὰς χεῖρας αὐτῶν καὶ διώξουσιν, παραδιδόντες ← εἰς τὰς
hands on you *{the}* *hands* *their* and persecute you, handing you over to the
5931 2093 7007 3836 5931 899 2779 1503 4140 1650 3836
p.a r.ap.2 d.apf n.apf r.gpm.3 cj v.fai.3p pt.pa.npm p.a d.apf

συναγωγὰς καὶ φυλακάς, ἀπαγομένους ἐπὶ βασιλεῖς καὶ ἡγεμόνας ἕνεκεν
synagogues and prisons, bringing you before kings and governors ⌊for the sake of⌋
5252 2779 5871 552 2093 995 2779 2450 1914
n.apf cj n.apf pt.pp.apm p.a n.apm cj n.apm p.g

τοῦ ὀνόματός μου· 13 ἀποβήσεται ὑμῖν εἰς μαρτύριον.
{the} my name. *my* ⌊This will result in⌋ an opportunity for you for witness.
3836 1609 3950 1609 609 7007 1650 3457
d.gsn n.gsn r.gs.1 v.fmi.3s r.dp.2 p.a n.asn

14 θέτε οὖν ἐν ταῖς καρδίαις ὑμῶν μὴ προμελετᾶν
So determine *So* in *{the}* your hearts *your* not to rehearse beforehand how
4036 5502 4036 1877 3836 7007 2840 7007 3590 4627
v.aam.2p cj p.d d.dpf n.dpf r.gp.2 pl f.pa

ἀπολογηθῆναι· 15 ἐγὼ γὰρ δώσω ὑμῖν στόμα καὶ σοφίαν ᾗ
to defend yourself, For I *for* am the one who will give you a mouth and wisdom, which
664 1142 1609 1142 1443 7007 5125 2779 5053 4005
f.ap r.ns.1 cj v.fai.1s r.dp.2 n.asn cj n.asf r.dsf

οὐ δυνήσονται ἀντιστῆναι ἢ ἀντειπεῖν ἅπαντες οἱ ἀντικείμενοι
none of your adversaries will be able to resist or contradict. *{all}* *{the}* *adversaries*
4024 7007 512 1538 468 2445 515 570 3836 512
pl v.fpi.3p f.aa cj f.aa a.npm d.npm pt.pm.npm

ὑμῖν. 16 παραδοθήσεσθε δὲ καὶ ὑπὸ γονέων καὶ ἀδελφῶν καὶ συγγενῶν καὶ
your ⌊You will be handed over⌋ *{and}* even by parents and brothers and relatives and
7007 4140 1254 2779 5679 1204 2779 81 2779 5150 2779
r.dp.2 v.fpi.2p cj adv p.g n.gpm cj n.gpm cj n.gpm cj

φίλων, καὶ θανατώσουσιν ἐξ ὑμῶν, 17 καὶ ἔσεσθε μισούμενοι
friends, and some of you they will put to death. *of* *you* *{and}* ⌊You will be⌋ hated
5813 2779 1666 7007 2506 1666 7007 2779 1639 3631
n.gpm cj v.fai.3p p.g r.gp.2 cj v.fmi.2p pt.pp.npm

ὑπὸ πάντων διὰ τὸ ὄνομά μου. 18 καὶ θρὶξ ἐκ τῆς κεφαλῆς
by all ⌊because of⌋ *{the}* my name. *my* Yet not a hair of *{the}* your head
5679 4246 1328 3836 1609 3950 1609 2779 4024 2582 1666 3836 7007 3051
p.g a.gpm p.a d.asn n.asn r.gs.1 cj n.nsf p.g d.gsf n.gsf

ὑμῶν ⌊οὐ μὴ⌋ ἀπόληται. 19 ἐν τῇ ὑπομονῇ ὑμῶν κτήσασθε τὰς ψυχὰς
your *not* will perish. By *{the}* your endurance *your* you will gain *{the}* your lives.
7007 4024 3590 660 1877 3836 7007 5705 7007 3227 3836 7007 6034
r.gp.2 pl pl v.ams.3s p.d d.dsf n.dsf r.gp.2 v.amm.2p d.apf n.apf

ὑμῶν. 20 ὅταν δὲ ἴδητε κυκλουμένην ὑπὸ στρατοπέδων Ἰερουσαλήμ,
your “But when *But* you see Jerusalem surrounded by armies, *Jerusalem*
7007 1254 4020 1254 1625 2647 3240 5679 5136 2647
r.gp.2 cj cj v.aas.2p pt.pp.asf p.g n.gpn n.asf

τότε γνῶτε ὅτι ἤγγικεν ἡ ἐρήμωσις αὐτῆς. 21 τότε οἱ
then know that its desolation ⌊has drawn near.⌋ *{the}* *desolation* *its* Then those who are
5538 1182 4022 899 2247 1581 3836 2247 899 5538 3836
adv v.aam.2p cj v.rai.3s d.nsf n.nsf r.gsf.3 adv d.npm

ἐν τῇ Ἰουδαίᾳ φευγέτωσαν εἰς τὰ ὄρη καὶ οἱ ἐν μέσῳ → αὐτῆς
in *{the}* Judea must flee to the mountains, and those in the midst of the city
1877 3836 2677 5771 1650 3836 4001 2779 3836 1877 3545 899
p.d d.dsf n.dsf v.pam.3p p.a d.apn n.apn cj d.npm p.d n.dsn r.gsf.3

ἐκχωρείτωσαν καὶ οἱ ἐν ταῖς χώραις ↱ μὴ ⌊εἰσερχέσθωσαν εἰς⌋ αὐτήν,
must evacuate, and those in the country must not enter it,
1774 2779 3836 1877 3836 6001 1656 3590 1656 1650 899
v.pam.3p cj d.npm p.d d.dpf n.dpf pl v.pmm.3p p.a r.asf.3

NASB

famines; and there
will be terrors and
great signs from
heaven.
12 “But before all
these things, they
will lay their hands
on you and will
persecute you,
delivering you to
the synagogues and
prisons, bringing
you before kings
and governors for
My name’s sake.
13 It will lead to an
opportunity for
your testimony.
14 So make up your
minds not to pre-
pare beforehand to
defend yourselves;
15 for I will give you
utterance and wis-
dom which none
of your opponents
will be able to re-
sist or refute. 16 But
you will be be-
trayed even by par-
ents and brothers
and relatives and
friends, and they
will put *some* of
you to death, 17 and
you will be hated
by all because of
My name. 18 Yet not
a hair of your head
will perish. 19 By
your endurance
you will gain your
lives.
20 “But when you
see Jerusalem sur-
rounded by armies,
then recognize that
her desolation is
near. 21 Then those
who are in Judea
must flee to the
mountains, and
those who are in
the midst of the
city must leave,
and those who are
in the country must
not enter the city;

NIV

22 For this is the
time of punish-
ment in fulfillment
of all that has been
written. 23 How
dreadful it will be
in those days for
pregnant women
and nursing moth-
ers! There will be
great distress in
the land and wrath
against this people.
24 They will fall
by the sword and
will be taken as
prisoners to all the
nations. Jerusalem
will be trampled
on by the Gentiles
until the times of
the Gentiles are
fulfilled.
25 "There will be
signs in the sun,
moon and stars.
On the earth, na-
tions will be in
anguish and per-
plexity at the roar-
ing and tossing of
the sea. 26 People
will faint from ter-
ror, apprehensive
of what is coming
on the world, for
the heavenly bod-
ies will be shaken.
27 At that time they
will see the Son of
Man coming in a
cloud with power
and great glo-
ry. 28 When these
things begin to
take place, stand
up and lift up your
heads, because
your redemption is
drawing near."
29 He told them
this parable:
"Look at the fig
tree and all the
trees. 30 When they
sprout leaves, you
can see for your-
selves and

22 ὅτι ἡμέραι ἐκδικήσεως αὗταί εἰσιν τοῦ
for these are days of vengeance, *these* *are* so that everything that has been written
4022 4047 1639 2465 1689 4047 1639 3836 4246 3836 1211 1211 1211
cj n.npf n.gsf r.npf v.pai.3p d.gsn

πλησθῆναι πάντα τὰ γεγραμμένα. 23 οὐαὶ ταῖς ⌞ἐν γαστρὶ⌟
may be fulfilled. *everything* *that* *has been written* Woe to those who are pregnant
4398 4246 3836 1211 4026 3836 2400 2400 1877 1143
f.ap a.apn d.apn pt.rp.apn j d.dpf p.d n.dsf

ἐχούσαις καὶ ταῖς θηλαζούσαις ἐν ἐκείναις ταῖς ἡμέραις· ἔσται
who are and to those ⌞who are nursing infants⌟ in those *{the}* days! For ⌞there will be⌟
2400 2779 3836 2558 1877 1697 3836 2465 1142 1639
pt.pa.dpf cj d.dpf pt.pa.dpf p.d r.dpf d.dpf n.dpf v.fmi.3s

γὰρ ἀνάγκη μεγάλη ἐπὶ τῆς γῆς καὶ ὀργὴ τῷ λαῷ τούτῳ, 24 καὶ
For great distress *great* on the earth and wrath against this people. *this* *{and}*
1142 3489 340 3489 2093 3836 1178 2779 3973 3836 4047 3295 4047 2779
cj n.nsf a.nsf p.g d.gsf n.gsf cj n.nsf d.dsm n.dsm r.dsm cj

πεσοῦνται → στόματι → μαχαίρης καὶ αἰχμαλωτισθήσονται εἰς τὰ
They will fall by the edge of the sword and be led captive to *{the}* all
4406 5125 3479 2779 170 1650 3836 4246
v.fmi.3p n.dsn n.gsf cj v.fpi.3p p.a d.apn

ἔθνη πάντα, καὶ Ἰερουσαλὴμ ἔσται πατουμένη ὑπὸ ἐθνῶν, ⌞ἄχρι οὗ⌟
nations, *all* and Jerusalem will be trampled underfoot by the Gentiles, until the
1620 4246 2779 2647 1639 4251 5679 1620 948 4005
n.apn a.apn cj n.nsf v.fmi.3s pt.pp.nsf p.g n.gpn p.g r.gsm

πληρωθῶσιν καιροὶ ἐθνῶν. 25 καὶ ἔσονται σημεῖα ἐν
times of the Gentiles are fulfilled. *times* *of Gentiles* *{and}* ⌞"There will be⌟ signs in the
2789 1620 1620 4444 2789 1620 2779 1639 4956 1877
v.aps.3p n.npm n.gpn cj v.fmi.3p n.npn p.d

ἡλίῳ καὶ σελήνῃ καὶ ἄστροις, καὶ ἐπὶ τῆς γῆς συνοχὴ ἐθνῶν ἐν ἀπορίᾳ
sun and moon and stars; and on the earth distress ⌞among nations⌟ *{by}* confused by
2463 2779 4943 2779 849 2779 2093 3836 1178 5330 1620 1877 680
n.dsm cj n.dsf cj n.dpn cj p.g d.gsf n.gsf n.nsf n.gpn p.d n.dsf

ἤχους → θαλάσσης καὶ σάλου, 26 ἀποψυχόντων ἀνθρώπων
the roaring and surging of the sea; *and* *surging* people fainting *people*
2492 2779 4893 2498 2779 4893 476 715 476
n.gsn n.gsf cj n.gsm pt.pa.gpm n.gpm

ἀπὸ φόβου καὶ προσδοκίας τῶν ἐπερχομένων τῇ οἰκουμένῃ, αἱ γὰρ
with fear and foreboding of what is coming ⌞on the⌟ world. For the *For*
608 5832 2779 4660 3836 2088 3836 3876 1142 3836 1142
p.g n.gsm cj n.gsf d.gpn pt.pm.gpn d.dsf n.dsf d.npf cj

δυνάμεις τῶν οὐρανῶν σαλευθήσονται. 27 καὶ τότε ὄψονται τὸν υἱὸν τοῦ
powers of the heavens will be shaken. And then ⌞they will see⌟ the Son of
1539 3836 4041 4888 2779 5538 3972 3836 5626 3836
n.npf d.gpm n.gpm v.fpi.3p cj adv v.fmi.3p d.asm n.asm d.gsm

ἀνθρώπου ἐρχόμενον ἐν νεφέλῃ μετὰ δυνάμεως καὶ δόξης πολλῆς. 28 →
Man coming on a cloud with power and great glory. *great* Now when
476 2262 1877 3749 3552 1539 2779 4498 1518 4498 1254
n.gsm pt.pm.asm p.d n.dsf p.g n.gsf cj n.gsf a.gsf

ἀρχομένων δὲ τούτων γίνεσθαι ἀνακύψατε καὶ ἐπάρατε τὰς
these things begin *Now* *these things* to happen, ⌞straighten yourselves up⌟ and raise *{the}*
4047 4047 806 1254 4047 1181 376 2779 2048 3836
pt.pm.gpn cj r.gpn f.pm v.aam.2p cj v.aam.2p d.apf

κεφαλὰς ὑμῶν, διότι ἐγγίζει ἡ ἀπολύτρωσις ὑμῶν.
your heads, *your* because your deliverance ⌞is drawing near."⌟ *{the}* *deliverance* *your*
7007 3051 7007 1484 7007 667 1581 3836 667 7007
n.apf r.gp.2 cj v.pai.3s d.nsf n.nsf r.gp.2

29 καὶ εἶπεν παραβολὴν αὐτοῖς· ἴδετε τὴν συκῆν καὶ πάντα τὰ δένδρα·
And he told them a parable: *them* ⌞"Look at⌟ the fig tree, and all the trees.
2779 3306 899 4130 899 1625 3836 5190 2779 4246 3836 1285
cj v.aai.3s n.asf r.dpm.3 v.aam.2p d.asf n.asf cj a.apn d.apn n.apn

30 ὅταν → → προβάλωσιν ἤδη, βλέποντες ἀφ᾽ ἑαυτῶν
When they have already put forth *already* their leaves, you see for yourselves and
4020 2453 4582 2453 1063 608 1571
cj v.aas.3p adv pt.pa.npm p.g r.gpm.2

NASB

22 because these are
days of vengeance,
so that all things
which are written
will be fulfilled.
23 Woe to those who
are pregnant and to
those who are nurs-
ing babies in those
days; for there will
be great distress
upon the land and
wrath to this peo-
ple; 24 and they will
fall by the edge
of the sword, and
will be led captive
into all the nations;
and Jerusalem will
be trampled under
foot by the Gen-
tiles until the times
of the Gentiles are
fulfilled.

The Return of Christ

25 "There will be
signs in sun and
moon and stars,
and on the earth
dismay among na-
tions, in perplexity
at the roaring of the
sea and the waves,
26 men fainting from
fear and the expec-
tation of the things
which are coming
upon the world;
for the powers of
the heavens will be
shaken. 27 Then they
will see THE SON OF
MAN COMING IN A
CLOUD with power
and great glory.
28 But when these
things begin to take
place, straighten
up and lift up your
heads, because
your redemption is
drawing near."
29 Then He told
them a parable:
"Behold the fig
tree and all the
trees; 30 as soon
as they put forth
leaves, you see it
and know for your-
selves that

NIV

know that summer
is near. 31 Even so,
when you see these
things happening,
you know that the
kingdom of God
is near.
32 "Truly I tell
you, this genera-
tion will certainly
not pass away until
all these things
have happened.
33 Heaven and earth
will pass away,
but my words will
never pass away.
34 "Be careful, or
your hearts will
be weighed down
with carousing,
drunkenness and
the anxieties of
life, and that day
will close on you
suddenly like a
trap. 35 For it will
come on all those
who live on the
face of the whole
earth. 36 Be always
on the watch, and
pray that you may
be able to escape
all that is about to
happen, and that
you may be able
to stand before the
Son of Man."
37 Each day Jesus
was teaching at the
temple, and each
evening he went
out to spend the
night on the hill
called the Mount
of Olives, 38 and all
the people came
early in the morn-
ing to hear him at
the temple.

Judas Agrees to Betray Jesus

22 Now the
Festival of
Unleavened Bread,
called the

γινώσκετε ὅτι ἤδη ἐγγὺς τὸ θέρος ἐστίν· 31 οὕτως καὶ ὑμεῖς, ὅταν
know that summer is already near. {the} summer is So also you, when
1182 4022 2550 1639 2453 1584 3836 2550 1639 4048 2779 7007 4020
v.pai.2p cj adv adv d.nsn n.nsn v.pai.3s adv adv r.np.2 cj

ἴδητε ταῦτα γινόμενα, γινώσκετε ὅτι ἐγγύς ἐστιν ἡ
you see these things happening, will know that the kingdom of God is near. is the
1625 4047 1181 1182 4022 3836 993 3836 2536 1639 1584 1639 3836
v.aas.2p r.apn pt.pm.apn v.pam.2p cj adv v.pai.3s d.nsf

βασιλεία τοῦ θεοῦ. 32 ἀμὴν λέγω ὑμῖν ὅτι
kingdom of God I tell you the truth, I tell you that this generation will
993 3836 2536 3306 3306 7007 297 3306 7007 4022 4047 1155 4216
n.nsf d.gsm n.gsm pl v.pai.1s r.dp.2 cj

˻οὐ μὴ˼ παρέλθῃ ἡ γενεὰ αὕτη ˻ἕως ἂν˼ πάντα γένηται.
by no means ˻have passed away˼ {the} generation this before all things have happened.
4024 3590 4216 3836 1155 4047 2401 323 4246 1181
pl pl v.aas.3s d.nsf n.nsf r.nsf cj pl a.npn v.ams.3s

33 ὁ οὐρανὸς καὶ ἡ γῆ παρελεύσονται, οἱ δὲ λόγοι μου ˻οὐ μὴ˼
{the} Heaven and {the} earth will pass away, {the} but my words my will not
3836 4041 2779 3836 1178 4216 3836 1254 1609 3364 1609 4216 4024 3590
d.nsm n.nsm cj d.nsf n.nsf v.fmi.3p d.npm cj n.npm r.gs.1 pl pl

παρελεύσονται. 34 προσέχετε δὲ ἑαυτοῖς μήποτε βαρηθῶσιν ὑμῶν
pass away. "But watch But yourselves lest your minds be dulled your
4216 1254 4668 1254 1571 3607 7007 2840 976 7007
v.fmi.3p v.pam.2p cj r.dpm.2 cj v.aps.3p r.gp.2

αἱ καρδίαι ἐν κραιπάλῃ καὶ μέθῃ καὶ μερίμναις βιωτικαῖς καὶ
{the} minds by dissipation and drunkenness and the anxieties of this life, and that day
3836 2840 1877 3190 2779 3494 2779 3533 1053 2779 1697 2465
d.npf n.npf p.d n.dsf cj n.dsf cj n.dpf a.dpf cj

ἐπιστῇ ἐφ' ὑμᾶς αἰφνίδιος ἡ ἡμέρα ἐκείνη 35 ὡς παγίς· ἐπεισελεύσεται
close down upon you suddenly, {the} day that like a trap. For it will come
2392 2093 7007 167 3836 2465 1697 6055 4075 1142 2082
v.aas.3s p.a r.ap.2 a.nsf d.nsf n.nsf r.nsf pl n.nsf v.fmi.3s

γὰρ ἐπὶ πάντας τοὺς καθημένους ἐπὶ πρόσωπον πάσης τῆς γῆς.
For upon all those who live on the face of the whole the earth.
1142 2093 4246 3836 2764 2093 4725 3836 4246 3836 1178
cj p.a a.apm d.apm pt.pm.apm p.a n.asn a.gsf d.gsf n.gsf

36 ἀγρυπνεῖτε δὲ ἐν παντὶ καιρῷ δεόμενοι ἵνα κατισχύσητε ἐκφυγεῖν
Be alert {and} at all times, praying that ˻you may have strength˼ to escape all
70 1254 1877 4246 2789 1289 2671 2996 1767 4246
v.pam.2p cj p.d a.dsm n.dsm pt.pm.npm cj v.aas.2p f.aa

ταῦτα πάντα τὰ μέλλοντα γίνεσθαι καὶ σταθῆναι ἔμπροσθεν τοῦ υἱοῦ τοῦ
these things all that will take place, and to stand before the Son of
4047 4246 3836 3516 1181 2779 2705 1869 3836 5626 3836
r.apn a.apn d.apn pt.pa.apn f.pm cj f.ap p.g d.gsm n.gsm d.gsm

ἀνθρώπου. 37 ἦν δὲ τὰς ἡμέρας ἐν τῷ ἱερῷ διδάσκων,
Man." During the day ˻he was˼ {and} the day in the temple teaching, but
476 2465 3836 2465 1639 1254 3836 2465 1877 3836 2639 1438 1254
n.gsm v.iai.3s cj d.apf n.apf p.d d.dsn n.dsn pt.pa.nsm

τὰς δὲ νύκτας ἐξερχόμενος ηὐλίζετο εἰς τὸ ὄρος τὸ καλούμενον
at but night he went out and stayed on the hill {the} called "The
3836 1254 3816 887 2002 887 1650 3836 4001 3836 2813
d.apf cj n.apf pt.pm.nsm v.imi.3s p.a d.asn n.asn d.asn pt.pp.asn

Ἐλαιῶν· 38 καὶ πᾶς ὁ λαὸς ὤρθριζεν πρὸς αὐτὸν ἐν τῷ ἱερῷ
Mount of Olives." And all the people came to him in the temple at dawn
1777 2779 4246 3836 3295 3983 4639 899 1877 3836 2639 3983 3983
n.gpf cj a.nsm d.nsm n.nsm v.iai.3s p.a r.asm.3 p.d d.dsn n.dsn

ἀκούειν αὐτοῦ.
to listen to him.
201 899
f.pa r.gsm.3

22:1 ἤγγιζεν δὲ ἡ ἑορτὴ τῶν ἀζύμων ἡ λεγομένη
was drawing near Now the Festival of ˻Unleavened Bread,˼ which is called the
1581 1254 3836 2038 3836 109 3836 3306
v.iai.3s cj d.nsf n.nsf d.gpn n.gpn d.nsf pt.pp.nsf

NASB

summer is now
near. 31 So you also,
when you see these
things happening,
recognize that the
kingdom of God
is near. 32 Truly I
say to you, this
generation will not
pass away until all
things take place.
33 Heaven and earth
will pass away, but
My words will not
pass away.
34 "Be on guard,
so that your
hearts will not be
weighted down
with dissipation
and drunkenness
and the worries
of life, and that
day will not come
on you suddenly
like a trap; 35 for it
will come upon all
those who dwell
on the face of all
the earth. 36 But
keep on the alert at
all times, praying
that you may have
strength to escape
all these things that
are about to take
place, and to stand
before the Son of
Man."
37 Now during the
day He was teach-
ing in the temple,
but at evening He
would go out and
spend the night
on the mount that
is called Olivet.
38 And all the people
would get up early
in the morning *to
come* to Him in the
temple to listen to
Him.

Preparing the Passover

22:1 Now the Feast
of Unleavened
Bread, which is

NIV

Passover, was ap-
proaching, 2and
the chief priests
and the teachers
of the law were
looking for some
way to get rid of
Jesus, for they
were afraid of the
people. 3Then Sa-
tan entered Judas,
called Iscariot,
one of the Twelve.
4And Judas went
to the chief priests
and the officers of
the temple guard
and discussed with
them how he might
betray Jesus.
5They were de-
lighted and agreed
to give him money.
6He consented, and
watched for an op-
portunity to hand
Jesus over to them
when no crowd
was present.

The Last Supper

7Then came the
day of Unleavened
Bread on which
the Passover lamb
had to be sacri-
ficed. 8Jesus sent
Peter and John,
saying, "Go and
make preparations
for us to eat the
Passover."
9"Where do you
want us to prepare
for it?" they asked.
10He replied, "As
you enter the city,
a man carrying a
jar of water will
meet you. Fol-
low him to the
house that he en-
ters, 11and say to
the owner of the
house, 'The Teach-
er asks: Where is
the guest room,
where I may eat
the Passover with

πάσχα. 2καὶ ἐζήτουν οἱ
Passover, was drawing near. {and} The chief priests and the scribes ⌊were looking for⌋ The
4247 1581 1581 1581 2779 3836 797 797 2779 3836 1208 2426 3836
n.nsn cj v.iai.3p d.npm

ἀρχιερεῖς καὶ οἱ γραμματεῖς τὸ πῶς ἀνέλωσιν αὐτόν, ↰ ↰
chief priests and the scribes a way how ⌊they might put⌋ Jesus to death, for
797 2779 3836 1208 3836 4802 359 899 359 359 1142
n.npm cj d.npm n.npm d.asn cj v.aas.3p r.asm.3

ἐφοβοῦντο γὰρ τὸν λαόν. 3 εἰσῆλθεν δὲ σατανᾶς εἰς Ἰούδαν τὸν
⌊they were afraid of⌋ for the people. Then Satan entered Then Satan into Judas, the
5828 1142 3836 3295 1254 4928 1656 1254 4928 1650 2683 3836
v.ipi.3p cj d.asm n.asm v.aai.3s cj n.nsm p.a n.asm d.asm

καλούμενον Ἰσκαριώτην, ὄντα ἐκ τοῦ ἀριθμοῦ τῶν δώδεκα· 4καὶ ↱
one called Iscariot, ⌊who was⌋ of the number of the twelve. {and} He
2813 2697 1639 1666 3836 750 3836 1557 2779 5196
pt.pp.asm n.asm pt.pa.asm p.g d.gsm n.gsm d.gpm a.gpm cj

ἀπελθὼν συνελάλησεν τοῖς ἀρχιερεῦσιν καὶ στρατηγοῖς τὸ πῶς
went and conferred with the chief priests and officers about how he might deliver
599 5196 3836 797 2779 5130 3836 4802 4140 4140 4140
pt.aa.nsm v.aai.3s d.dpm n.dpm cj n.dpm d.asn cj

αὐτοῖς παραδῷ αὐτόν. 5καὶ ἐχάρησαν καὶ συνέθεντο
up Jesus to them. he might deliver up Jesus {and} ⌊They were delighted⌋ and decided to
4140 899 899 4140 899 2779 5897 2779 5338 1443
r.dpm.3 v.aas.3s r.asm.3 cj v.api.3p cj v.ami.3p

αὐτῷ ἀργύριον δοῦναι. 6καὶ ἐξωμολόγησεν, καὶ ἐζήτει εὐκαιρίαν
give him money. to give {and} He agreed and ⌊began looking for⌋ an opportunity
1443 899 736 1443 2779 2018 2779 2426 2321
r.dsm.3 n.asn f.aa cj v.aai.3s cj v.iai.3s n.asf

τοῦ παραδοῦναι αὐτὸν ↰ ἄτερ → ὄχλου αὐτοῖς. 7 ἦλθεν δὲ
to deliver him up to them ⌊in the absence⌋ of a crowd. to them Then came Then
3836 4140 899 4140 899 899 868 4063 899 1254 2262 1254
d.gsn f.aa r.asm.3 p.g n.gsm r.dpm.3 v.aai.3s cj

ἡ ἡμέρα τῶν ἀζύμων, ἐν[a] ᾗ ἔδει θύεσθαι τὸ
the day of ⌊Unleavened Bread,⌋ in which the Passover lamb had to be sacrificed. the
3836 2465 3836 109 1877 4005 3836 4247 4247 1256 2604 3836
d.nsf n.nsf d.gpn n.gpn p.d r.dsf v.iai.3s f.pp d.asn

πάσχα· 8καὶ ἀπέστειλεν Πέτρον καὶ Ἰωάννην εἰπών, πορευθέντες
Passover lamb So Jesus sent Peter and John, saying, "Go and
4247 2779 690 4377 2779 2722 3306 4513
n.asn cj v.aai.3s n.asm cj n.asm pt.aa.nsm pt.ap.npm

ἑτοιμάσατε ἡμῖν τὸ πάσχα ἵνα φάγωμεν. 9οἱ δὲ εἶπαν
prepare the Passover for us, the Passover that we may eat it together." They {and} said
2286 3836 4247 7005 3836 4247 2671 2266 3836 1254 3306
v.aam.2p r.dp.1 d.asn n.asn cj v.aas.1p d.npm cj v.aai.3p

αὐτῷ, ποῦ θέλεις ἑτοιμάσωμεν; 10ὁ δὲ εἶπεν αὐτοῖς, ἰδοὺ →
to him, "Where ⌊do you want⌋ us to prepare it?" He {and} said to them, "Look, when you
899 4543 2527 2286 3836 1254 3306 899 2627 7007
r.dsm.3 cj v.pai.2s v.aas.1p d.nsm cj v.aai.3s r.dpm.3 j

εἰσελθόντων ὑμῶν εἰς τὴν πόλιν συναντήσει ὑμῖν
have entered you {into} the city, a man carrying a jar of water will meet you.
1656 7007 1650 3836 4484 476 1002 3040 5623 5623 5267 7007
pt.aa.gpm r.gp.2 p.a d.asf n.asf v.fai.3s r.dp.2

ἄνθρωπος κεράμιον ὕδατος βαστάζων· ἀκολουθήσατε αὐτῷ εἰς τὴν οἰκίαν εἰς ἣν
man jar of water carrying Follow him into the house into which
476 3040 5623 1002 199 899 1650 3836 3864 1650 4005
n.nsm n.asn n.gsn pt.pa.nsm v.aam.2p r.dsm.3 p.a d.asf n.asf p.a r.asf

εἰσπορεύεται, 11καὶ ἐρεῖτε τῷ οἰκοδεσπότῃ τῆς οἰκίας, λέγει σοι
he enters, and say ⌊to the⌋ master of the house, 'The Teacher says to you,
1660 2779 3306 3836 3867 3836 3864 3836 1437 3306 5148
v.pmi.3s cj v.fai.2p d.dsm n.dsm d.gsf n.gsf v.pai.3s r.ds.2

ὁ διδάσκαλος, ποῦ ἐστιν τὸ κατάλυμα ὅπου τὸ πάσχα μετὰ
The Teacher "Where is the guest room, where I may eat the Passover with
3836 1437 4543 1639 3836 2906 3963 2266 2266 2266 3836 4247 3552
d.nsm n.nsm cj v.pai.3s d.nsn n.nsn cj d.asn n.asn p.g

NASB

called the Passover,
was approaching.
2The chief priests
and the scribes
were seeking how
they might put Him
to death; for they
were afraid of the
people.
3And Satan en-
tered into Judas
who was called
Iscariot, belonging
to the number of
the twelve. 4And
he went away and
discussed with the
chief priests and
officers how he
might betray Him
to them. 5They
were glad and
agreed to give him
money. 6So he con-
sented, and *began*
seeking a good op-
portunity to betray
Him to them apart
from the crowd.
7Then came the
first day of Un-
leavened Bread on
which the Passover
lamb had to be
sacrificed. 8And Je-
sus sent Peter and
John, saying, "Go
and prepare the
Passover for us, so
that we may eat it."
9They said to Him,
"Where do You
want us to prepare
it?" 10And He said
to them, "When
you have entered
the city, a man will
meet you carrying
a pitcher of water;
follow him into
the house that he
enters. 11And you
shall say to the
owner of the house,
'The Teacher says
to you, "Where is
the guest room in
which I may eat the
Passover with

[a] [ἐν] UBS, omitted by TNIV.

NIV

my disciples?'
12He will show
you a large room
upstairs, all fur-
nished. Make
preparations
there."
13They left and
found things just
as Jesus had told
them. So they pre-
pared the Passover.
14When the hour
came, Jesus and
his apostles re-
clined at the table.
15And he said to
them, "I have ea-
gerly desired to eat
this Passover with
you before I suffer.
16For I tell you,
I will not eat it
again until it finds
fulfillment in the
kingdom of God."
17After taking
the cup, he gave
thanks and said,
"Take this and di-
vide it among you.
18For I tell you
I will not drink
again from the
fruit of the vine
until the kingdom
of God comes."
19And he took
bread, gave thanks
and broke it, and
gave it to them,
saying, "This is
my body given
for you; do this
in remembrance
of me."
20In the same
way, after the sup-
per he took the
cup, saying, "This
cup is the new cov-
enant in my blood,
which is poured
out for you.[a] 21But
the hand of

τῶν μαθητῶν μου φάγω; 12 κἀκεῖνος ὑμῖν δείξει
{the} my disciples?'" *my* *I may eat* He will show you *will show* a large
3836 1609 3412 1609 2266 2797 1259 1259 7007 1259 3489
d.gpm n.gpm r.gs.1 v.aas.1s crasis r.dp.2 v.fai.3s

ἀνάγαιον μέγα ἐστρωμένον· ἐκεῖ ἑτοιμάσατε. 13
room upstairs, *large* already furnished. Make preparations for us there." *Make preparations* So
333 3489 5143 2286 2286 1695 2286 1254
n.asn a.asn pt.rp.asn adv v.aam.2p

→ ἀπελθόντες δὲ εὗρον καθὼς εἰρήκει αὐτοῖς καὶ ἡτοίμασαν τὸ
they went *So* and found everything as he had said to them; and they prepared the
2351 599 1254 2351 2777 3306 899 2779 2286 3836
pt.aa.npm cj v.aai.3p cj v.lai.3s r.dpm.3 cj v.aai.3p d.asn

πάσχα. 14 καὶ ὅτε ἐγένετο ἡ ὥρα, ἀνέπεσεν καὶ οἱ
⌞Passover meal.⌟ And when the hour came, *the* *hour* Jesus ⌞reclined at table⌟ and the
4247 2779 4021 3836 6052 1181 3836 6052 404 2779 3836
n.asn cj cj v.ami.3s d.nsf n.nsf v.aai.3s cj d.npm

ἀπόστολοι σὺν αὐτῷ. 15 καὶ εἶπεν πρὸς αὐτούς, → ἐπιθυμίᾳ
apostles were with him. *{and}* He said to them, "With great desire
693 5250 899 2779 3306 4639 899 2123
n.npm p.d r.dsm.3 cj v.aai.3s p.a r.apm.3 n.dsf

ἐπεθύμησα τοῦτο τὸ πάσχα φαγεῖν μεθ' ὑμῶν πρὸ τοῦ με παθεῖν·
I desired to eat this *{the}* Passover *to eat* with you before *{the}* I suffer!
2121 2266 2266 4047 3836 4247 2266 3552 7007 4574 3836 1609 4248
v.aai.1s r.asn d.asn n.asn f.aa p.g r.gp.2 p.g d.gsn r.as.1 f.aa

16 λέγω γὰρ ὑμῖν ὅτι → → ⌞οὐ μὴ⌟ φάγω αὐτὸ ἕως ὅτου
For I say *For* to you that I will certainly not eat it again until it
1142 3306 1142 7007 4022 2266 2266 4024 3590 2266 899 2401 4015
v.pai.1s cj r.dp.2 cj pl pl v.aas.1s r.asn.3 p.g r.gsn

πληρωθῇ ἐν τῇ βασιλείᾳ τοῦ θεοῦ. 17 καὶ δεξάμενος ποτήριον
is fulfilled in the kingdom of God." Then he took a cup, and
4444 1877 3836 993 3836 2536 2779 1312 4539
v.aps.3s p.d d.dsf n.dsf d.gsm n.gsm cj pt.am.nsm n.asn

εὐχαριστήσας εἶπεν, λάβετε τοῦτο καὶ διαμερίσατε εἰς ἑαυτούς· 18
⌞after he had given thanks⌟ he said, "Take this and divide it among yourselves. For
2373 3306 3284 4047 2779 1374 1650 1571 1142
pt.aa.nsm v.aai.3s v.aam.2p r.asn cj v.aam.2p p.a r.apm.2

λέγω γὰρ ὑμῖν, ὅτι[a] → → ⌞οὐ μὴ⌟ πίω ἀπὸ τοῦ νῦν ἀπὸ τοῦ
I say *For* to you that from now on I shall certainly not drink *from* *{the}* *now* of the
3306 1142 7007 4022 608 3814 4403 4403 4024 3590 4403 608 3836 3814 608 3836
v.pai.1s cj r.dp.2 cj pl pl v.aas.1s p.g d.gsn adv p.g d.gsn

γενήματος τῆς ἀμπέλου ⌞ἕως οὗ⌟ ἡ βασιλεία τοῦ θεοῦ ἔλθῃ. 19 καὶ λαβὼν
fruit of the vine until the kingdom of God comes." Then taking
1163 3836 306 2401 4005 3836 993 3836 2536 2262 2779 3284
n.gsn d.gsf n.gsf p.g r.gsm d.nsf n.nsf d.gsm n.gsm v.aas.3s cj pt.aa.nsm

ἄρτον εὐχαριστήσας ἔκλασεν καὶ ἔδωκεν αὐτοῖς λέγων, τοῦτό ἐστιν τὸ
bread and giving thanks he broke it and gave it to them, saying, "This is *{the}* my
788 2373 3089 2779 1443 899 3306 4047 1639 3836 1609
n.asm pt.aa.nsm v.aai.3s cj v.aai.3s r.dpm.3 pt.pa.nsm r.nsn v.pai.3s d.nsn

σῶμά μου τὸ ὑπὲρ ὑμῶν διδόμενον· τοῦτο ποιεῖτε εἰς τὴν
body, *my* which is given for you; *is given* do this *do* in *{the}*
5393 1609 3836 1443 1443 5642 7007 1443 4472 4047 4472 1650 3836
n.nsn r.gs.1 d.nsn p.g r.gp.2 pt.pp.nsn r.asn v.pam.2p p.a d.asf

ἐμὴν ἀνάμνησιν. 20 καὶ τὸ ποτήριον ὡσαύτως μετὰ
remembrance of me." *remembrance* And he did the same with the cup *same* after
390 1847 390 2779 6058 3836 4539 6058 3552
r.asf.1 n.asf cj d.asn n.asn adv p.a

τὸ δειπνῆσαι, λέγων, τοῦτο τὸ ποτήριον ἡ καινὴ διαθήκη ἐν τῷ
{the} they had eaten, saying, "This *{the}* cup is the new covenant in *{the}* my
3836 1268 3306 4047 3836 4539 3836 2785 1347 1877 3836 1609
d.asn f.aa pt.pa.nsm r.nsn d.nsn n.nsn d.nsf a.nsf n.nsf p.d d.dsn

αἵματί μου τὸ → ὑπὲρ ὑμῶν ἐκχυννόμενον. 21 πλὴν ἰδοὺ ἡ χεὶρ τοῦ
blood, *my* which on your behalf *your* is being poured out. "But see, the hand of the
135 1609 3836 7007 5642 7007 1773 4440 2627 3836 5931 3836
n.dsn r.gs.1 d.nsn p.g r.gp.2 pt.pp.nsn cj j d.nsf n.nsf d.gsm

NASB

My disciples?"'
12And he will show
you a large, fur-
nished upper room;
prepare it there."
13And they left and
found *everything*
just as He had told
them; and they pre-
pared the Passover.

The Lord's Supper

14When the hour
had come, He re-
clined *at the table,*
and the apostles
with Him. 15And
He said to them,
"I have earnestly
desired to eat this
Passover with you
before I suffer; 16for
I say to you, I shall
never again eat it
until it is fulfilled
in the kingdom of
God." 17And when
He had taken a cup
and given thanks,
He said, "Take this
and share it among
yourselves; 18for I
say to you, I will
not drink of the
fruit of the vine
from now on until
the kingdom of
God comes." 19And
when He had taken
some bread *and*
given thanks, He
broke it and gave
it to them, saying,
"This is My body
which is given
for you; do this in
remembrance of
Me." 20And in the
same way *He took*
the cup after they
had eaten, saying,
"This cup which
is poured out for
you is the new cov-
enant in My blood.
21But behold, the
hand of the one

[a] 19,20 Some manuscripts do not have *given for you . . . poured out for you.*

[a] [ὅτι] UBS, omitted by TNIV.

NIV

him who is going
to betray me is
with mine on the
table. 22 The Son of
Man will go as it
has been decreed.
But woe to that
man who betrays
him!" 23 They be-
gan to question
among themselves
which of them
it might be who
would do this.
24 A dispute also
arose among them
as to which of
them was consid-
ered to be greatest.
25 Jesus said to
them, "The kings
of the Gentiles lord
it over them; and
those who exer-
cise authority over
them call them-
selves Benefactors.
26 But you are not
to be like that. In-
stead, the greatest
among you should
be like the youn-
gest, and the one
who rules like the
one who serves.
27 For who is great-
er, the one who is
at the table or the
one who serves? Is
it not the one who
is at the table? But
I am among you
as one who serves.
28 You are those
who have stood by
me in my trials.
29 And I confer on
you a kingdom,
just as my Father
conferred one on
me, 30 so that you
may eat and drink
at my table in my
kingdom and sit on
thrones, judging
the twelve tribes of

παραδιδόντος με μετ᾽ ἐμοῦ ἐπὶ τῆς τραπέζης. 22 ὅτι ὁ υἱὸς μὲν τοῦ
one who will betray me is with me on the table. For the Son ~ of
4140 1609 3552 1609 2093 3836 5544 4022 3836 5626 3525 3836
pt.pa.gsm r.as.1 p.g r.gs.1 p.g d.gsf n.gsf cj d.nsm n.nsm pl d.gsm

ἀνθρώπου κατὰ τὸ ὡρισμένον πορεύεται, πλὴν οὐαὶ τῷ
Man goes ⌞according to⌟ what has been determined, *goes* but woe to that
476 4513 2848 3836 3988 4513 4440 4026 3836 1697
n.gsm p.a d.asn pt.rp.asn v.pmi.3s cj j d.dsm

ἀνθρώπῳ ἐκείνῳ δι᾽ οὗ παραδίδοται. 23 καὶ αὐτοὶ ἤρξαντο συζητεῖν πρὸς
man *that* by whom he is betrayed." And they began to question among
476 1697 1328 4005 4140 2779 899 806 5184 4639
n.dsm r.dsm p.g r.gsm v.ppi.3s cj r.npm v.ami.3p f.pa p.a

ἑαυτοὺς τὸ τίς ἄρα εἴη ἐξ αὐτῶν ὁ τοῦτο
one another, *{the}* which of them *{then}* ⌞it might be⌟ *of* *them* who would do this.
1571 3836 5515 1666 899 726 1639 1666 899 3836 3516 4556 4047
r.apm.3 d.asn r.nsm cj v.pao.3s p.g r.gpm.3 d.nsm r.asn

μέλλων πράσσειν. 24 ἐγένετο δὲ καὶ φιλονεικία ἐν αὐτοῖς, τὸ
would *do* A dispute also arose *{and}* *also* *dispute* among them ⌞as to⌟
3516 4556 5808 2779 1181 1254 2779 5808 1877 899 3836
pt.pa.nsm f.pa v.ami.3s cj adv n.nsf p.d r.dpm.3 d.nsn

τίς αὐτῶν δοκεῖ εἶναι μείζων. 25 ὁ δὲ εἶπεν αὐτοῖς, οἱ βασιλεῖς τῶν
which of them seemed to be the greatest. So Jesus *So* said to them, "The kings of the
5515 899 1506 1639 3489 1254 3836 1254 3306 899 3836 995 3836
r.nsm r.gpm.3 v.pai.3s f.pa a.nsm.c d.nsm cj v.aai.3s r.dpm.3 d.npm n.npm d.gpn

ἐθνῶν κυριεύουσιν αὐτῶν καὶ οἱ ἐξουσιάζοντες αὐτῶν
nations exercise lordship over them and those in authority over them call themselves
1620 3259 899 2779 3836 2027 899 2813 2813
n.gpn v.pai.3p r.gpn.3 cj d.npm pt.pa.npm r.gpn.3

εὐεργέται καλοῦνται. 26 ὑμεῖς δὲ οὐχ οὕτως, ἀλλ᾽ ↱ ὁ
'benefactors.' *call themselves* But with you *But* it must not be so! Rather, let the
2309 2813 1254 7007 1254 4024 4048 247 1181 3836
n.npm v.ppi.3p r.np.2 cj pl adv cj d.nsm

μείζων ἐν ὑμῖν γινέσθω ὡς ὁ νεώτερος καὶ ὁ ἡγούμενος ὡς ὁ
greatest among you become like the youngest, and the leader like the
3489 1877 7007 1181 6055 3836 3742 2779 3836 2451 6055 3836
a.nsm.c p.d r.dp.2 v.pmm.3s pl d.nsm a.nsm.c cj d.nsm pt.pm.nsm pl d.nsm

διακονῶν. 27 τίς γὰρ μείζων, ὁ ἀνακείμενος ἢ ὁ
one who serves. For who *For* is the greater, the ⌞one who reclines at table⌟ or the
1354 1142 5515 1142 3489 3836 367 2445 3836
pt.pa.nsm r.nsm cj a.nsm.c d.nsm pt.pm.nsm cj d.nsm

διακονῶν; οὐχὶ ὁ ἀνακείμενος; ἐγὼ δὲ ἐν
one who serves? Is it not the ⌞one who reclines at table?⌟ But in your midst I *But* *in*
1354 4049 3836 367 1254 1877 7007 3545 1609 1254 1877
pt.pa.nsm pl d.nsm pt.pm.nsm r.ns.1 cj p.d

μέσῳ ὑμῶν εἰμι ὡς ὁ διακονῶν. 28 ὑμεῖς δέ ἐστε οἱ διαμεμενηκότες
midst *your* am like the one who serves. You *{and}* are the ones who have stayed
3545 7007 1639 6055 3836 1354 7007 1254 1639 3836 1373
n.dsn r.gp.2 v.pai.1s pl d.nsm pt.pa.nsm r.np.2 cj v.pai.2p d.npm pt.ra.npm

μετ᾽ ἐμοῦ ἐν τοῖς πειρασμοῖς μου· 29
with me in *{the}* my trials. *my* Just as my Father conferred on me kingly
3552 1609 1877 3836 1609 4280 1609 2777 2777 1609 4252 1416 1609 1609 993
p.g r.gs.1 p.d d.dpm n.dpm r.gs.1

κἀγὼ → ← διατίθεμαι ὑμῖν καθὼς διέθετό μοι ὁ πατήρ μου
authority, so also do I confer it on you, *Just as* *conferred* *on me* *{the}* *Father* *my*
993 2743 1416 7007 2777 1416 1609 3836 4252 1609
crasis v.pmi.1s r.dp.2 cj v.ami.3s r.ds.1 d.nsm n.nsm r.gs.1

βασιλείαν, 30 ἵνα ἔσθητε καὶ πίνητε ἐπὶ τῆς τραπέζης μου ἐν τῇ
kingly authority that ⌞you may eat⌟ and drink at *{the}* my table *my* in *{the}* my
993 2671 2266 2779 4403 2093 3836 1609 5544 1609 1877 3836 1609
n.asf cj v.pas.2p cj v.pas.2p p.g d.gsf n.gsf r.gs.1 p.d d.dsf

βασιλείᾳ μου, καὶ καθήσεσθε ἐπὶ θρόνων τὰς δώδεκα φυλὰς κρίνοντες τοῦ
kingdom *my* and sit on thrones judging the twelve tribes *judging* of
993 1609 2779 2764 2093 2585 3212 3836 1557 5876 3212 3836
n.dsf r.gs.1 cj v.fmi.2p p.g n.gpm d.apf a.apf n.apf pt.pa.npm d.gsm

NASB

betraying Me is
with Mine on the
table. 22 For indeed,
the Son of Man is
going as it has been
determined; but
woe to that man
by whom He is be-
trayed!" 23 And they
began to discuss
among themselves
which one of them
it might be who
was going to do
this thing.

Who Is Greatest

24 And there arose
also a dispute
among them *as to*
which one of them
was regarded to be
greatest. 25 And He
said to them, "The
kings of the Gen-
tiles lord it over
them; and those
who have author-
ity over them are
called 'Benefac-
tors.' 26 But *it is* not
this way with you,
but the one who is
the greatest among
you must become
like the youngest,
and the leader like
the servant. 27 For
who is greater, the
one who reclines *at*
the table or the one
who serves? Is it
not the one who re-
clines *at the table?*
But I am among
you as the one who
serves.
28 "You are those
who have stood by
Me in My trials;
29 and just as My
Father has granted
Me a kingdom, I
grant you 30 that you
may eat and drink
at My table in My
kingdom, and you
will sit on thrones
judging the twelve
tribes of Israel.

NIV

Israel.
31 "Simon, Simon,
Satan has asked
to sift all of you
as wheat. 32 But I
have prayed for
you, Simon, that
your faith may not
fail. And when you
have turned back,
strengthen your
brothers."
33 But he replied,
"Lord, I am ready
to go with you
to prison and to
death."
34 Jesus answered,
"I tell you, Peter,
before the rooster
crows today, you
will deny three
times that you
know me."
35 Then Jesus
asked them,
"When I sent you
without purse, bag
or sandals, did you
lack anything?"
"Nothing," they
answered.
36 He said to them,
"But now if you
have a purse, take
it, and also a bag;
and if you don't
have a sword, sell
your cloak and
buy one. 37 It is
written: 'And he
was numbered
with the trans-
gressors'[a]; and I
tell you that this
must be fulfilled
in me. Yes, what is
written about me
is reaching its ful-
fillment."
38 The disciples
said, "See, Lord,
here are two
swords."
"That's enough!"
he replied.

Jesus Prays on the Mount of Olives

39 Jesus went out

Ἰσραήλ. 31 Σίμων Σίμων, ἰδοὺ ὁ σατανᾶς ἐξῃτήσατο
Israel. Simon, Simon! Pay attention! *{the}* Satan ⌞has demanded permission to have⌟ all of
2702 4981 4981 2627 3836 4928 1977
n.gsm n.vsm n.vsm j d.nsm n.nsm v.ami.3s

ὑμᾶς ↰ ↰ τοῦ σινιάσαι ὡς τὸν σῖτον· 32 ἐγὼ δὲ ἐδεήθην περὶ
you for himself, to sift you like *{the}* wheat, but I *but* have prayed for
7007 1977 1977 3836 4985 6055 3836 4992 1254 1609 1254 1289 4309
r.ap.2 d.gsn f.aa pl d.asm n.asm r.ns.1 cj v.api.1s p.g

σοῦ ἵνα ↱ μὴ ἐκλίπῃ ἡ πίστις σου· καὶ σύ ποτε ἐπιστρέψας
you that your faith may not fail. *{the} faith your* And when you *when* have returned,
5148 2671 5148 4411 1722 3590 1722 3836 4411 5148 2779 4537 5148 4537 2188
r.gs.2 cj pl v.aas.3s d.nsf n.nsf r.gs.2 cj r.ns.2 adv pt.aa.nsm

στήρισον τοὺς ἀδελφούς σου. 33 ὁ δὲ εἶπεν αὐτῷ, κύριε,
strengthen *{the}* your brothers." *your* Peter *{and}* said to him, "Lord, I am ready to
5114 3836 5148 81 5148 3836 1254 3306 899 3261 1639 1639 2289 4513
v.aam.2s d.apm n.apm r.gs.2 d.nsm cj v.aai.3s r.dsm.3 n.vsm

μετὰ σοῦ ἕτοιμός εἰμι καὶ εἰς φυλακὴν καὶ εἰς θάνατον πορεύεσθαι. 34 ὁ
go with you *ready I am* both to prison and to death." *to go* Jesus
4513 3552 5148 2289 1639 2779 1650 5871 2779 1650 2505 4513 3836
p.g r.gs.2 a.nsm v.pai.1s cj p.a n.asf cj p.a n.asm f.pm d.nsm

δὲ εἶπεν, λέγω σοι, Πέτρε, ↱ οὐ φωνήσει σήμερον ἀλέκτωρ ἕως
{and} said, "I tell you, Peter, a rooster will not crow this day *rooster* before you
1254 3306 3306 5148 4377 232 5888 4024 5888 4958 232 2401 565
cj v.aai.3s v.pai.1s r.ds.2 n.vsm pl v.fai.3s adv n.nsm cj

τρίς με ἀπαρνήσῃ εἰδέναι. 35 καὶ εἶπεν αὐτοῖς,
have denied ⌞three times⌟ that you know me." *you have denied you know* And he said to them,
565 565 5565 3857 3857 1609 565 3857 2779 3306 899
adv r.as.1 v.ams.2s f.ra cj v.aai.3s r.dpm.3

ὅτε ἀπέστειλα ὑμᾶς ↰ ἄτερ βαλλαντίου καὶ πήρας καὶ ὑποδημάτων, μή
"When I sent you out without moneybag or knapsack or sandals, *{not}* did
4021 690 7007 690 868 964 2779 4385 2779 5687 3590 5728
cj v.aai.1s r.ap.2 p.g n.gsn cj n.gsf cj n.gpn pl

τινος ὑστερήσατε; οἱ δὲ εἶπαν, οὐθενός. 36 εἶπεν δὲ αὐτοῖς,
you lack anything?" *did you lack* They *{and}* replied, "Nothing." He said *{and}* to them,
5728 5728 5516 5728 3836 1254 3306 4032 3306 1254 899
r.gsn v.aai.2p d.npm cj v.aai.3p a.gsn v.aai.3s cj r.dpm.3

ἀλλὰ νῦν ↱ ὁ ἔχων βαλλάντιον ἀράτω, ὁμοίως καὶ πήραν, καὶ
"But now let the ⌞one who has⌟ a moneybag take it, and likewise *{also}* a knapsack. And
247 3814 149 3836 2400 964 149 3931 2779 4385 2779
cj adv d.nsm pt.pa.nsm n.asn v.aam.3s adv adv n.asf cj

ὁ μὴ ἔχων πωλησάτω τὸ ἱμάτιον αὐτοῦ καὶ
the one who has no *one who has* sword, let him sell *{the}* his cloak *his* and
3836 2400 2400 2400 3590 2400 3479 4797 3836 899 2668 899 2779
d.nsm pl pt.pa.nsm v.aam.3s d.asn n.asn r.gsm.3 cj

ἀγορασάτω μάχαιραν. 37 λέγω γὰρ ὑμῖν ὅτι
buy one. *sword* For I tell *For* you that there must be fulfilled in me
60 3479 1142 3306 1142 7007 4022 1256 1256 5464 5464 1877 1609
v.aam.3s n.asf v.pai.1s cj r.dp.2 cj

τοῦτο τὸ γεγραμμένον δεῖ τελεσθῆναι ἐν ἐμοί, τό· καὶ μετὰ
this that stands written: *there must be fulfilled in me {the}* 'And he was numbered with
4047 3836 1211 1256 5464 1877 1609 3836 2779 3357 3357 3357 3552
r.asn d.asn pt.rp.asn v.pai.3s f.ap p.d r.ds.1 d.asn cj p.g

ἀνόμων ἐλογίσθη· καὶ γὰρ τὸ περὶ ἐμοῦ τέλος
the lawless.' *he was numbered* And indeed, *And* that which concerns me has its fulfillment."
491 3357 1142 2779 1142 3836 4309 1609 2400 5465
a.gpm v.api.3s adv cj d.nsn p.g r.gs.1 n.asn

ἔχει. 38 οἱ δὲ εἶπαν, κύριε, ἰδοὺ μάχαιραι ὧδε δύο. ὁ
has So they *So* said, "Lord, look! Here are two swords." *Here two* Then he
2400 1254 3836 1254 3306 3261 2627 6045 1545 3479 6045 1545 1254 3836
v.pai.3s d.npm cj v.aai.3p n.vsm j n.npf adv a.npf d.nsm

δὲ εἶπεν αὐτοῖς, ἱκανόν ἐστιν. 39 καὶ ἐξελθὼν ἐπορεύθη κατὰ
Then told them, "It is enough." *It is* Then Jesus went out and made his way, as
1254 3306 899 1639 1639 2653 1639 2779 2002 4513 2848
cj v.aai.3s r.dpm.3 a.nsn v.pai.3s cj pt.aa.nsm v.api.3s p.a

NASB

31 "Simon, Simon,
behold, Satan has
demanded *permis-*
sion to sift you like
wheat; 32 but I have
prayed for you,
that your faith may
not fail; and you,
when once you
have turned again,
strengthen your
brothers." 33 But
he said to Him,
"Lord, with You
I am ready to go
both to prison and
to death!" 34 And He
said, "I say to you,
Peter, the rooster
will not crow today
until you have
denied three times
that you know
Me."
35 And He said to
them, "When I sent
you out without
money belt and bag
and sandals, you
did not lack any-
thing, did you?"
They said, "*No,*
nothing." 36 And
He said to them,
"But now, whoever
has a money belt
is to take it along,
likewise also a bag,
and whoever has
no sword is to sell
his coat and buy
one. 37 For I tell you
that this which is
written must be
fulfilled in Me,
'AND HE WAS NUM-
BERED WITH TRANS-
GRESSORS'; for that
which refers to Me
has *its* fulfillment."
38 They said, "Lord,
look, here are two
swords." And He
said to them, "It is
enough."

The Garden of Gethsemane

39 And He came
out and proceeded

[a] 37 Isaiah 53:12

NIV

as usual to the
Mount of Olives,
and his disciples
followed him. 40On
reaching the place,
he said to them,
"Pray that you
will not fall into
temptation." 41He
withdrew about a
stone's throw be-
yond them, knelt
down and prayed,
42"Father, if you
are willing, take
this cup from
me; yet not my
will, but yours be
done." 43An angel
from heaven ap-
peared to him and
strengthened him.
44And being in an-
guish, he prayed
more earnestly,
and his sweat
was like drops of
blood falling to the
ground.[a]
45When he rose
from prayer and
went back to the
disciples, he found
them asleep, ex-
hausted from sor-
row. 46"Why are
you sleeping?" he
asked them. "Get
up and pray so that
you will not fall
into temptation."

Jesus Arrested

47While he was
still speaking a
crowd came up,
and the man who
was called Judas,
one of the Twelve,
was leading them.
He approached
Jesus to kiss him,
48but Jesus asked
him, "Judas, are
you betraying the
Son of Man with a
kiss?"
49When Jesus'
followers saw

[a] 43,44 Many early manuscripts do not have verses 43 and 44.

τὸ ἔθος εἰς τὸ ὄρος τῶν ἐλαιῶν, ἠκολούθησαν δὲ αὐτῷ
was his custom, to the Mount of Olives; and the disciples followed *and* him.
3836 1621 1650 3836 4001 3836 1777 1254 3836 3412 199 1254 899
d.asn n.asn p.a d.asn n.asn d.gpf n.gpf v.aai.3p cj r.dsm.3

καὶ οἱ μαθηταί. 40 γενόμενος δὲ ἐπὶ τοῦ τόπου εἶπεν αὐτοῖς, προσεύχεσθε
{also} the disciples When he arrived *{and}* at the place, he said to them, "Pray
2779 3836 3412 1181 1254 2093 3836 5536 3306 899 4667
adv d.npm n.npm pt.am.nsm cj p.g d.gsm n.gsm v.aai.3s r.dpm.3 v.pmm.2p

↱ ↱ μὴ ⌊εἰσελθεῖν εἰς⌋ πειρασμόν. 41 καὶ αὐτὸς ἀπεσπάσθη ἀπ'
that you may not enter a time of trial." Then he withdrew from
1656 1656 3590 1656 1650 4280 2779 899 685 608
pl f.aa p.a n.asm cj r.nsm v.api.3s p.g

αὐτῶν ὡσεὶ λίθου βολὴν καὶ ⌊θεὶς τὰ γόνατα⌋ προσηύχετο 42 λέγων,
them about a stone's throw, *and* knelt down and began to pray, saying,
899 6059 3345 1074 2779 5502 3836 1205 2779 4667 3306
r.gpm.3 pl n.gsm n.asf cj pt.aa.nsm d.apn n.apn v.imi.3s pt.pa.nsm

πάτερ, εἰ βούλει παρένεγκε τοῦτο τὸ ποτήριον ↰ ἀπ' ἐμοῦ· πλὴν μὴ
"Father, if ⌊you are willing,⌋ take this *{the}* cup away from me. Yet, not
4252 1623 1089 4195 4047 3836 4539 4195 608 1609 4440 3590
n.vsm cj v.pmi.2s v.aam.2s r.asn d.asn n.asn p.g r.gs.1 cj pl

τὸ θέλημά μου ἀλλὰ τὸ σὸν γινέσθω. 43 [ὤφθη δὲ αὐτῷ
{the} my will, *my* but *{the}* yours be done." And there appeared to him an
3836 1609 2525 1609 247 3836 5050 1181 1254 3972 1254 899
d.nsn n.nsn r.gs.1 cj d.nsn r.nsn.2 v.pmm.3s v.api.3s cj r.dsm.3

ἄγγελος ἀπ' οὐρανοῦ ἐνισχύων αὐτόν. 44 καὶ γενόμενος ἐν ἀγωνίᾳ
angel from heaven, strengthening him. And being in agony he prayed
34 608 4041 1932 899 2779 1181 1877 75 4667 4667
n.nsm p.g n.gsm pt.pa.nsm r.asm.3 cj pt.am.nsm p.d n.dsf

ἐκτενέστερον προσηύχετο· καὶ ἐγένετο ὁ ἱδρὼς αὐτοῦ ὡσεὶ θρόμβοι
more earnestly; and his *{the}* sweat became like great drops
1757 4667 2779 1181 899 3836 2629 899 1181 6059 2584
adv.c v.imi.3s cj v.ami.3s d.nsm n.nsm r.gsm.3 pl n.npm

αἵματος καταβαίνοντες ἐπὶ τὴν γῆν.] 45 καὶ ἀναστὰς ἀπὸ τῆς προσευχῆς ↱
of blood falling down to the ground. *{and}* ⌊When he rose⌋ from *{the}* prayer, he
135 2849 2093 3836 1178 2779 482 608 3836 4666 2351
n.gsn pt.pa.gsn p.a d.asf n.asf cj pt.aa.nsm p.g d.gsf n.gsf

ἐλθὼν πρὸς τοὺς μαθητὰς εὗρεν κοιμωμένους αὐτοὺς ἀπὸ τῆς λύπης,
went back to the disciples and found them sleeping *them* from *{the}* grief.
2262 4639 3836 3412 2351 899 3121 899 608 3836 3383
pt.aa.nsm p.a d.apm n.apm v.aai.3s pt.pp.apm r.apm.3 p.g d.gsf n.gsf

46 καὶ εἶπεν αὐτοῖς, τί καθεύδετε; ἀναστάντες προσεύχεσθε, ἵνα ↱ ↱
{and} He said to them, "Why are you sleeping? Rise and pray that you may
2779 3306 899 5515 2761 482 4667 2671 1656 1656
cj v.aai.3s r.dpm.3 r.asn v.pai.2p pt.aa.npm v.pmm.2p cj

μὴ ⌊εἰσέλθητε εἰς⌋ πειρασμόν. 47 ↱ ↱ ἔτι αὐτοῦ λαλοῦντος
not enter a time of trial." While he was still *he* speaking,
3590 1656 1650 4280 3281 899 3281 2285 899 3281
pl v.aas.2p p.a n.asm adv r.gsm.3 pt.pa.gsm

ἰδοὺ ὄχλος, καὶ ὁ λεγόμενος Ἰούδας εἷς τῶν δώδεκα
⌊there came⌋ a crowd, and the one called Judas, one of the twelve,
2627 4063 2779 3836 3306 2683 1651 3836 1557
j n.nsm cj d.nsm pt.pp.nsm n.nsm a.nsm d.gpm a.gpm

προήρχετο αὐτοὺς καὶ ἤγγισεν τῷ Ἰησοῦ φιλῆσαι αὐτόν. 48
⌊was coming on ahead of⌋ them. *{and}* ⌊He went up⌋ to Jesus to kiss him, but
4601 899 2779 1581 3836 2652 5797 899 1254
v.imi.3s r.apm.3 cj v.aai.3s d.dsm n.dsm f.aa r.asm.3

Ἰησοῦς δὲ εἶπεν αὐτῷ, Ἰούδα, → φιλήματι τὸν υἱὸν
Jesus *But* said to him, "Judas, is it with a kiss that you intend to betray the Son
2652 1254 3306 899 2683 5799 4140 4140 4140 4140 3836 5626
n.nsm cj v.aai.3s r.dsm.3 n.vsm n.dsn d.asm n.asm

τοῦ ἀνθρώπου παραδίδως; 49 → ἰδόντες δὲ οἱ
of Man?" *you intend to betray* When those who were around him saw *{and} those*
3836 476 4140 3836 4309 899 1625 1254 3836
d.gsm n.gsm v.pai.2s pt.aa.npm cj d.npm

NASB

as was His custom
to the Mount of
Olives; and the
disciples also fol-
lowed Him. 40When
He arrived at the
place, He said to
them, "Pray that
you may not enter
into temptation."
41And He withdrew
from them about
a stone's throw,
and He knelt down
and *began* to pray,
42saying, "Father,
if You are willing,
remove this cup
from Me; yet not
My will, but Yours
be done." 43Now an
angel from heaven
appeared to Him,
strengthening Him.
44And being in ago-
ny He was praying
very fervently; and
His sweat became
like drops of blood,
falling down upon
the ground. 45When
He rose from
prayer, He came to
the disciples and
found them sleep-
ing from sorrow,
46and said to them,
"Why are you
sleeping? Get up
and pray that you
may not enter into
temptation."

Jesus Betrayed by Judas

47While He was
still speaking,
behold, a crowd
came, and the one
called Judas, one
of the twelve, was
preceding them;
and he approached
Jesus to kiss Him.
48But Jesus said to
him, "Judas, are
you betraying the
Son of Man with
a kiss?" 49When
those who were
around Him saw

NIV

what was going to
happen, they said,
“Lord, should we
strike with our
swords?” [50]And
one of them struck
the servant of the
high priest, cutting
off his right ear.
[51]But Jesus an-
swered, “No more
of this!” And he
touched the man’s
ear and healed
him.
[52]Then Jesus said
to the chief priests,
the officers of the
temple guard, and
the elders, who
had come for him,
“Am I leading a
rebellion, that you
have come with
swords and clubs?
[53]Every day I was
with you in the
temple courts, and
you did not lay a
hand on me. But
this is your hour—
when darkness
reigns.”

Peter Disowns Jesus

[54]Then seizing
him, they led him
away and took him
into the house of
the high priest.
Peter followed at
a distance. [55]And
when some there
had kindled a fire
in the middle of
the courtyard and
had sat down to-
gether, Peter sat
down with them.
[56]A servant girl
saw him seated
there in the fire-
light. She looked
closely at him and
said, “This man
was with him.”
[57]But he denied it.
“Woman, I don’t
know him,” he
said.
[58]A little later

περὶ αὐτὸν τὸ ἐσόμενον εἶπαν, κύριε, εἰ πατάξομεν ἐν μαχαίρῃ;
around him what ⌞was about to happen,⌟ they said, “Lord, shall we strike with the sword?”
4309 899 3836 1639 3306 3261 1623 4250 1877 3479
p.a r.asm.3 d.asn pt.fm.asn v.aai.3p n.vsm cj v.fai.1p p.d n.dsf

50 καὶ ἐπάταξεν εἷς τις ἐξ αὐτῶν τοῦ
And a certain one of them struck *one certain of them* the servant of the
2779 5516 1651 1666 899 4250 1651 5516 1666 899 3836 1529 3836
cj v.aai.3s a.nsm r.nsm p.g r.gpm.3 d.gsm

ἀρχιερέως τὸν δοῦλον καὶ ἀφεῖλεν τὸ οὖς αὐτοῦ τὸ δεξιόν.
high priest *the servant* and cut off *{the}* his right ear. *his {the} right*
797 3836 1529 2779 904 3836 899 1288 4044 899 3836 1288
n.gsm d.asm n.asm cj v.aai.3s d.asn n.asn r.gsm.3 d.asn a.asn

51 ἀποκριθεὶς δὲ ὁ Ἰησοῦς εἶπεν, ἐᾶτε ἕως τούτου· καὶ ἁψάμενος τοῦ
In response *{and} {the}* Jesus said, “Stop! ⌞No more⌟ of this.” And touching the
646 1254 3836 2652 3306 1572 2401 4047 2779 721 3836
pt.ap.nsm cj d.nsm n.nsm v.aai.3s v.pam.2p p.g r.gsn cj pt.am.nsm d.gsn

ὠτίου ἰάσατο αὐτόν. 52 εἶπεν δὲ Ἰησοῦς πρὸς τοὺς παραγενομένους
ear, he healed it. Then Jesus said *Then Jesus* to those who had come out
6065 2615 899 1254 2652 3306 1254 2652 4639 3836 4134
n.gsn v.ami.3s r.asm.3 v.aai.3s cj n.nsm p.a d.apm pt.am.apm

ἐπ’ αὐτὸν ἀρχιερεῖς καὶ στρατηγοὺς τοῦ ἱεροῦ καὶ πρεσβυτέρους·
against him — the chief priests and officers of the temple and elders, “Why
2093 899 797 2779 5130 3836 2639 2779 4565
p.a r.asm.3 n.apm cj n.apm d.gsn n.gsn cj a.apm

ὡς ἐπὶ λῃστὴν ἐξήλθατε μετὰ μαχαιρῶν καὶ ξύλων;
did you come out as against a robber, *did you come out* with swords and clubs?
2002 2002 2002 2002 6055 2093 3334 2002 3552 3479 2779 3833
pl p.a n.asm v.aai.2p p.g n.gpf cj n.gpn

53 ↱ καθ’ ἡμέραν → ὄντος μου μεθ’ ὑμῶν ἐν τῷ ἱερῷ ↱ ↱ οὐκ
Day after day, when I was *I* with you in the temple, you did not
2465 2848 2465 1609 1639 1609 3552 7007 1877 3836 2639 1753 1753 4024
p.a n.asf pt.pa.gsm r.gs.1 p.g r.gp.2 p.d d.dsn n.dsn pl

ἐξετείνατε τὰς χεῖρας ἐπ’ ἐμέ, ἀλλ’ αὕτη ἐστὶν ὑμῶν ἡ ὥρα καὶ ἡ
stretch out your hands against me. But this is your *{the}* hour, and the hour for the
1753 3836 5931 2093 1609 247 4047 1639 7007 3836 6052 2779 3836
v.aai.2p d.apf n.apf p.a r.as.1 cj r.nsf v.pai.3s r.gp.2 d.nsf n.nsf cj d.nsf

ἐξουσία τοῦ σκότους. 54 ↱ συλλαβόντες δὲ αὐτὸν ἤγαγον ← καὶ
power of darkness. Then they seized *Then* him and led him away, and
2026 3836 5030 1254 72 5197 1254 899 72 2779
n.nsf d.gsn n.gsn pt.aa.npm cj r.asm.3 v.aai.3p cj

εἰσήγαγον εἰς τὴν οἰκίαν τοῦ ἀρχιερέως· ὁ δὲ Πέτρος ἠκολούθει
brought him into the house of the high priest. *{the} {and}* Peter was following
1652 1650 3836 3864 3836 797 3836 1254 4377 199
v.aai.3p p.a d.asf n.asf d.gsm n.gsm d.nsm cj n.nsm v.iai.3s

μακρόθεν. 55 περιαψάντων δὲ πῦρ ἐν μέσῳ τῆς αὐλῆς καὶ
at a distance. Some people had kindled *{and}* a fire in the middle of the courtyard and
3427 4312 1254 4786 1877 3545 3836 885 2779
adv pt.aa.gpm cj n.asn p.d n.dsn d.gsf n.gsf cj

συγκαθισάντων ἐκάθητο ὁ Πέτρος μέσος αὐτῶν. 56 ἰδοῦσα δὲ αὐτὸν
sat down together. Peter sat down *{the} Peter* among them. Seeing *{and}* him sitting
5154 4377 2764 3836 4377 3545 899 1625 1254 899 2764
pt.aa.gpm v.imi.3s d.nsm n.nsm a.nsm r.gpm.3 pt.aa.nsf cj r.asm.3

παιδίσκη τις καθήμενον πρὸς τὸ φῶς καὶ ἀτενίσασα αὐτῷ
at the fire, a certain servant girl *certain sitting at the fire {and}* looked at him
4639 3836 5890 5516 4087 5516 2764 4639 3836 5890 2779 867 899
n.nsf r.nsf pt.pm.asm p.a d.asn n.asn cj pt.aa.nsf r.dsm.3

↰ εἶπεν, καὶ οὗτος σὺν αὐτῷ ἦν. 57 ὁ δὲ ἠρνήσατο
intently and said, “This man also *This man* was with him.” *was* But he *But* denied
867 3306 4047 4047 2779 4047 1639 5250 899 1639 1254 3836 1254 766
v.aai.3s adv r.nsm p.d r.dsm.3 v.iai.3s d.nsm cj v.ami.3s

λέγων, ↱ ↱ οὐκ οἶδα αὐτόν, γύναι. 58 καὶ μετὰ βραχὺ
it, saying, “Woman, I do not know him!” *Woman* *{and}* After a little while
3306 1222 3857 3857 4024 3857 899 1222 2779 3552 1099
pt.pa.nsm pl v.rai.1s r.asm.3 n.vsf cj p.a a.asn

NASB

what was going
to happen, they
said, “Lord, shall
we strike with the
sword?” [50]And one
of them struck the
slave of the high
priest and cut off
his right ear. [51]But
Jesus answered
and said, “Stop!
No more of this.”
And He touched
his ear and healed
him. [52]Then Jesus
said to the chief
priests and officers
of the temple and
elders who had
come against Him,
“Have you come
out with swords
and clubs as you
would against a
robber? [53]While I
was with you daily
in the temple, you
did not lay hands
on Me; but this
hour and the power
of darkness are
yours.”

Jesus’ Arrest

[54]Having arrested
Him, they led Him
away and brought
Him to the house
of the high priest;
but Peter was
following at a dis-
tance. [55]After they
had kindled a fire
in the middle of the
courtyard and had
sat down together,
Peter was sitting
among them. [56]And
a servant-girl, see-
ing him as he sat
in the firelight and
looking intently at
him, said, “This
man was with
Him too.” [57]But he
denied *it,* saying,
“Woman, I do not
know Him.” [58]A
little later,

NIV

someone else saw
him and said, "You
also are one of
them."
"Man, I am not!"
Peter replied.
59 About an hour
later another as-
serted, "Certainly
this fellow was
with him, for he is
a Galilean."
60 Peter replied,
"Man, I don't
know what you're
talking about!"
Just as he was
speaking, the
rooster crowed.
61 The Lord turned
and looked straight
at Peter. Then Pe-
ter remembered
the word the Lord
had spoken to him:
"Before the roost-
er crows today,
you will disown
me three times."
62 And he went
outside and wept
bitterly.

The Guards Mock Jesus

63 The men who
were guarding
Jesus began mock-
ing and beating
him. 64 They blind-
folded him and de-
manded, "Prophe-
sy! Who hit you?"
65 And they said
many other insult-
ing things to him.

Jesus Before Pilate and Herod

66 At daybreak
the council of
the elders of the
people, both the
chief priests and
the teachers of the
law, met together,
and Jesus was led
before them. 67 "If
you are the Mes-
siah," they said,
"tell us."
Jesus answered,
"If I tell you,

ἕτερος ἰδὼν αὐτὸν ἔφη, καὶ σὺ ἐξ αὐτῶν εἶ. ὁ δὲ
⌞someone else⌟ noticed him and said, "You also *You* are one of them." *are* *{the}* But
2283 1625 899 5774 5148 2779 5148 1639 1666 899 1639 3836 1254
r.nsm pt.aa.nsm r.asm.3 v.iai.3s adv r.ns.2 p.g r.gpm.3 v.pai.2s d.nsm cj

Πέτρος ἔφη, ἄνθρωπε, οὐκ εἰμί. 59 καὶ → διαστάσης ὡσεὶ
Peter said, "Man, I am not!" *I am* Then after about an hour had passed *about*
4377 5774 476 1639 1639 4024 1639 2779 6059 1651 6052 1460 6059
n.nsm v.iai.3s n.vsm pl v.pai.1s cj pt.aa.gsf pl

ὥρας μιᾶς ἄλλος τις διϊσχυρίζετο λέγων, ⌞ἐπ' ἀληθείας⌟
hour *an* a certain other *certain* person kept insisting, saying, "Surely this person
6052 1651 5516 257 5516 1462 3306 2093 237 4047 4047
n.gsf a.gsf r.nsm r.nsm v.imi.3s pt.pa.nsm p.g n.gsf

καὶ οὗτος μετ' αὐτοῦ ἦν, καὶ γὰρ Γαλιλαῖός ἐστιν. 60
also *this person* was with him, *was* for he too *for* is a Galilean." *he is* But
2779 4047 1639 3552 899 1639 1142 1639 2779 1142 1639 1134 1639 1254
adv r.nsm p.g r.gsm.3 v.iai.3s adv cj a.nsm v.pai.3s

εἶπεν δὲ ὁ Πέτρος, ἄνθρωπε, ↱ ↱ οὐκ οἶδα ὃ λέγεις.
Peter said, *But* *{the}* *Peter* "Man, I do not know what ⌞you are talking about."⌟
4377 3306 1254 3836 4377 476 3857 3857 4024 3857 4005 3306
v.aai.3s cj d.nsm n.nsm n.vsm pl v.rai.1s r.asn v.pai.2s

καὶ παραχρῆμα ↱ ↱ ἔτι λαλοῦντος αὐτοῦ ἐφώνησεν ἀλέκτωρ.
And immediately, while he was still speaking, *he* the rooster crowed. *rooster*
2779 4202 3281 899 3281 2285 3281 899 232 5888 232
cj adv adv pt.pa.gsm r.gsm.3 v.aai.3s n.nsm

61 καὶ στραφεὶς ὁ κύριος ἐνέβλεψεν τῷ Πέτρῳ, καὶ ὑπεμνήσθη
Then the Lord turned *the* *Lord* and looked at Peter, and Peter remembered
2779 3836 3261 5138 3836 3261 1838 3836 4377 2779 4377 5703
cj pt.ap.nsm d.nsm n.nsm v.aai.3s d.dsm n.dsm cj v.api.3s

ὁ Πέτρος τοῦ ῥήματος τοῦ κυρίου ὡς εἶπεν αὐτῷ ὅτι πρὶν ἀλέκτορα
{the} *Peter* the word of the Lord that ⌞he had said⌟ to him, ~ "Before the rooster
3836 4377 3836 4839 3836 3261 6055 3306 899 4022 4570 232
d.nsm n.nsm d.gsn n.gsn d.gsm n.gsm cj v.aai.3s r.dsm.3 cj cj n.asm

φωνῆσαι σήμερον ἀπαρνήσῃ με τρίς. 62 καὶ ↱ ἐξελθὼν ἔξω ἔκλαυσεν
crows today, you will deny me ⌞three times."⌟ And he went out and wept
5888 4958 565 1609 5565 2779 3081 2002 2032 3081
f.aa adv v.fmi.2s r.as.1 adv cj pt.aa.nsm adv v.aai.3s

πικρῶς. 63 καὶ οἱ ἄνδρες οἱ συνέχοντες αὐτὸν ↰ ↰ ἐνέπαιζον αὐτῷ
bitterly. Now the men who were holding Jesus in custody began to mock him and
4396 2779 3836 467 3836 5309 899 5309 5309 1850 899
adv cj d.npm n.npm d.npm pt.pa.npm r.asm.3 v.iai.3p r.dsm.3

δέροντες, 64 καὶ περικαλύψαντες αὐτὸν ⌞ἐπηρώτων[a] λέγοντες,⌟ προφήτευσον,
beat him, and blindfolding him they kept asking, "Tell
1296 2779 4328 899 2089 3306 4736
pt.pa.npm cj pt.aa.npm r.asm.3 v.iai.3p pt.pa.npm v.aam.2s

τίς ἐστιν ὁ παίσας σε; 65 καὶ ἕτερα πολλὰ
us, who is it that struck you?" *{and}* They also said to him many other *many*
5515 1639 3836 4091 5148 2779 3306 3306 1650 899 4498 2283 4498
r.nsm v.pai.3s d.nsm pt.aa.nsm r.as.2 cj r.apn a.apn

βλασφημοῦντες ἔλεγον εἰς αὐτόν. 66 καὶ ὡς ἐγένετο ἡμέρα, συνήχθη τὸ
blasphemous things. *They said* *to* *him* And when day came, *day* *was assembled* the
1059 3306 1650 899 2779 6055 2465 1181 2465 5251 3836
pt.pa.npm v.iai.3p p.a r.asm.3 cj cj v.ami.3s n.nsf v.api.3s d.nsn

πρεσβυτέριον τοῦ λαοῦ, ἀρχιερεῖς τε καὶ γραμματεῖς, καὶ →
council of elders of the people was assembled, both chief priests *both* and scribes, and they
4564 3836 3295 5251 5251 5445 797 5445 2779 1208 2779
n.nsn d.gsm n.gsm n.npm cj cj n.npm cj

→ ἀπήγαγον αὐτὸν εἰς τὸ συνέδριον αὐτῶν 67 λέγοντες, εἰ σὺ
had Jesus brought *Jesus* into *{the}* their council chamber *their* and said, "If you
899 552 899 1650 3836 899 5284 899 3306 1623 5148
v.aai.3p r.asm.3 p.a d.asn n.asn r.gpm.3 pt.pa.npm cj r.ns.2

εἶ ὁ χριστός, εἰπὸν ἡμῖν. εἶπεν δὲ αὐτοῖς, ἐὰν ὑμῖν εἴπω, ↱
are the Messiah, tell us." But he said *But* to them, "If I tell you, *I tell* you
1639 3836 5986 3306 7005 1254 3306 1254 899 1569 3306 3306 7007 3306 4409
v.pai.2s d.nsm n.nsm v.aam.2s r.dp.1 v.aai.3s cj r.dpm.3 cj r.dp.2 v.aas.1s

NASB

another saw him
and said, "You are
one of them too!"
But Peter said,
"Man, I am not!"
59 After about an
hour had passed,
another man *began*
to insist, saying,
"Certainly this man
also was with Him,
for he is a Galilean
too." 60 But Peter
said, "Man, I do
not know what you
are talking about."
Immediately,
while he was still
speaking, a rooster
crowed. 61 The Lord
turned and looked
at Peter. And Peter
remembered the
word of the Lord,
how He had told
him, "Before a
rooster crows to-
day, you will deny
Me three times."
62 And he went out
and wept bitterly.
63 Now the men
who were holding
Jesus in custody
were mocking Him
and beating Him,
64 and they blind-
folded Him and
were asking Him,
saying, "Prophesy,
who is the one who
hit You?" 65 And
they were saying
many other things
against Him, blas-
pheming.

Jesus before the Sanhedrin

66 When it was day,
the [a]Council of
elders of the people
assembled, both
chief priests and
scribes, and they
led Him away to
their council *cham-
ber,* saying, 67 "If
You are the Christ,
tell us." But He
said to them, "If I
tell you, you

[a] αὐτοῦ τὸ πρόσωπον, καί included by TR after ἐπηρώτων.

[a] Or *Sanhedrin*

NIV

you will not be-
lieve me, 68 and if
I asked you, you
would not answer.
69 But from now
on, the Son of Man
will be seated at
the right hand of
the mighty God."
70 They all asked,
"Are you then the
Son of God?"
He replied, "You
say that I am."
71 Then they said,
"Why do we need
any more testimo-
ny? We have heard
it from his own
lips."
23 Then the
whole as-
sembly rose and
led him off to Pi-
late. 2 And they be-
gan to accuse him,
saying, "We have
found this man
subverting our na-
tion. He opposes
payment of taxes
to Caesar and
claims to be Mes-
siah, a king."
3 So Pilate asked
Jesus, "Are you the
king of the Jews?"
"You have said
so," Jesus replied.
4 Then Pilate an-
nounced to the
chief priests and
the crowd, "I find
no basis for a
charge against this
man."
5 But they insist-
ed, "He stirs up
the people all over
Judea by his teach-
ing. He started in

↱ ⌞οὐ μὴ⌟ πιστεύσητε· 68 ἐὰν δὲ ἐρωτήσω, ↱ ↱ ⌞οὐ μὴ⌟
will not believe, and if *and* I question you, you will not
4409 4024 3590 4409 1254 1569 1254 2263 646 646 4024 3590
pl pl v.aas.2p cj cj v.aas.1s pl pl

ἀποκριθῆτε.[a] 69 ἀπὸ τοῦ νῦν δὲ ἔσται ὁ υἱὸς τοῦ
answer. But from *{the}* now on *But* the Son of Man shall be *the* *Son* *of*
646 1254 608 3836 3814 1254 3836 5626 3836 476 1639 3836 5626 3836
v.aps.2p p.g d.gsn adv cj v.fmi.3s d.nsm n.nsm d.gsm

ἀνθρώπου καθήμενος ἐκ δεξιῶν τῆς δυνάμεως τοῦ θεοῦ. 70 → εἶπαν
Man seated at the right hand of the power of God." They all said,
476 2764 1666 1288 3836 1539 3836 2536 4246 3306
n.gsm pt.pm.nsm p.g a.gpf d.gsf n.gsf d.gsm n.gsm v.aai.3p

δὲ πάντες, σὺ οὖν εἶ ὁ υἱὸς τοῦ θεοῦ; ὁ δὲ πρὸς αὐτούς
{and} *all* "Are you, then, *Are* the Son of God?" And he *And* said to them,
1254 4246 1639 5148 4036 1639 3836 5626 3836 2536 1254 3836 1254 5774 4639 899
cj a.npm r.ns.2 cj v.pai.2s d.nsm n.nsm d.gsm n.gsm d.nsm cj p.a r.apm.3

ἔφη, ὑμεῖς λέγετε ὅτι ἐγώ εἰμι. 71 οἱ δὲ εἶπαν, τί ἔτι ἔχομεν
said "You say that I am." Then they *Then* said, "What further need do we have
5774 7007 3306 4022 1609 1639 1254 3836 1254 3306 5515 2285 5970 2400
v.iai.3s r.np.2 v.pai.2p cj r.ns.1 v.pai.1s d.npm cj v.aai.3p r.asn adv v.pai.1p

→ μαρτυρίας χρείαν; αὐτοὶ γὰρ ἠκούσαμεν ἀπὸ τοῦ
of a witness? *need* For we have heard it ourselves *For* *We have heard* from *{the}* his own
3456 5970 1142 201 201 201 899 1142 201 608 3836 899 899
n.gsf n.asf r.npm cj v.aai.1p p.g d.gsn

στόματος αὐτοῦ.
lips." *his own*
5125 899
n.gsn r.gsm.3

23:1 καὶ ἀναστὰν ἅπαν τὸ πλῆθος αὐτῶν ἤγαγον
Then the whole assembly of them rose up *whole* *the* *assembly* *of them* and brought
2779 3836 570 4436 899 899 482 570 3836 4436 899 72
cj pt.aa.nsn a.nsn d.nsn n.nsn r.gpm.3 v.aai.3p

αὐτὸν ἐπὶ τὸν Πιλᾶτον. 2 ἤρξαντο δὲ κατηγορεῖν αὐτοῦ λέγοντες,
Jesus before *{the}* Pilate. And they began *And* to accuse him, saying, "We found
899 2093 3836 4397 1254 806 1254 2989 899 3306 2351 2351
r.asm.3 p.a d.asm n.asm v.ami.3p cj f.pa r.gsm.3 pt.pa.npm

τοῦτον εὕραμεν διαστρέφοντα τὸ ἔθνος ἡμῶν καὶ κωλύοντα
this man *We found* trying to mislead *{the}* our nation, *our* *{and}* opposing the payment of
4047 2351 1406 3836 7005 1620 7005 2779 3266 1443
r.asm v.aai.1p pt.pa.asm d.asn n.asn r.gp.1 cj pt.pa.asm

φόρους Καίσαρι διδόναι καὶ λέγοντα ἑαυτὸν χριστὸν βασιλέα εἶναι. 3 ὁ
taxes to Caesar, *payment* and claiming himself to be Christ, a king." *to be* *{the}*
5843 2790 1443 2779 3306 1571 1639 1639 5986 995 1639 3836
n.apm n.dsm f.pa cj pt.pa.asm r.asm.3 n.asm n.asm f.pa d.nsm

δὲ Πιλᾶτος ἠρώτησεν αὐτὸν λέγων, σὺ εἶ ὁ βασιλεὺς τῶν Ἰουδαίων;
So Pilate asked Jesus, saying, "Are you *Are* the king of the Jews?"
1254 4397 2263 899 3306 1639 5148 1639 3836 995 3836 2681
cj n.nsm v.aai.3s r.asm.3 pt.pa.nsm r.ns.2 v.pai.2s d.nsm n.nsm d.gpm a.gpm

ὁ δὲ ἀποκριθεὶς αὐτῷ ἔφη, σὺ λέγεις. 4 ὁ δὲ
In response Jesus *{and}* *In response* *to him* said to him, "You say so." *{the}* Then
646 646 3836 1254 646 899 5774 899 899 5148 3306 3836 1254
d.nsm cj pt.ap.nsm r.dsm.3 v.iai.3s r.ns.2 v.pai.2s d.nsm cj

Πιλᾶτος εἶπεν πρὸς τοὺς ἀρχιερεῖς καὶ τοὺς ὄχλους, οὐδὲν εὑρίσκω
Pilate said to the chief priests and the crowds, "I find no basis *I find* for a
4397 3306 4639 3836 797 2779 3836 4063 2351 2351 4029 2351
n.nsm v.aai.3s p.a d.apm n.apm cj d.apm n.apm a.asn v.pai.1s

αἴτιον ἐν τῷ ἀνθρώπῳ τούτῳ. 5 οἱ δὲ ἐπίσχυον λέγοντες ὅτι
charge against *{the}* this man." *this* But they *But* kept insisting, saying, ~
165 1877 3836 4047 476 4047 1254 3836 1254 2196 3306 4022
n.asn p.d d.dsm n.dsm r.dsm d.npm cj v.iai.3p pt.pa.npm cj

ἀνασείει τὸν λαὸν διδάσκων καθ' ὅλης τῆς Ἰουδαίας, καὶ ἀρξάμενος ἀπὸ
"He stirs up the people, teaching throughout all *{the}* Judea, *{and}* starting from
411 3836 3295 1438 2848 3910 3836 2677 2779 806 608
v.pai.3s d.asm n.asm pt.pa.nsm p.g a.gsf d.gsf n.gsf cj pt.am.nsm p.g

NASB

will not believe;
68 and if I ask a
question, you will
not answer. 69 But
from now on THE
SON OF MAN WILL
BE SEATED AT THE
RIGHT HAND of the
power OF GOD."
70 And they all said,
"Are You the Son
of God, then?" And
He said to them,
"Yes, I am." 71 Then
they said, "What
further need do we
have of testimony?
For we have heard
it ourselves from
His own mouth."

Jesus before Pilate

23:1 Then the whole
body of them got
up and brought
Him before Pilate.
2 And they began
to accuse Him,
saying, "We found
this man mislead-
ing our nation and
forbidding to pay
taxes to Caesar,
and saying that He
Himself is Christ,
a King." 3 So Pilate
asked Him, saying,
"Are You the King
of the Jews?" And
He answered him
and said, "*It is as*
you say." 4 Then
Pilate said to the
chief priests and
the crowds, "I find
no guilt in this
man." 5 But they
kept on insisting,
saying, "He stirs up
the people, teach-
ing all over Judea,
starting from

[a] μοι ἢ ἀπολύσητε included by TR after ἀποκριθῆτε.

NIV

Galilee and has
come all the way
here."
[6]On hearing this,
Pilate asked if the
man was a Gal-
ilean. [7]When he
learned that Jesus
was under Herod's
jurisdiction, he
sent him to Herod,
who was also in
Jerusalem at that
time.
[8]When Herod
saw Jesus, he was
greatly pleased,
because for a long
time he had been
wanting to see
him. From what he
had heard about
him, he hoped to
see him perform a
sign of some sort.
[9]He plied him with
many questions,
but Jesus gave him
no answer. [10]The
chief priests and
the teachers of the
law were standing
there, vehement-
ly accusing him.
[11]Then Herod and
his soldiers ridi-
culed and mocked
him. Dressing
him in an elegant
robe, they sent
him back to Pilate.
[12]That day Herod
and Pilate became
friends — before
this they had been
enemies.
[13]Pilate called
together the chief
priests, the rulers
and the people,

τῆς Γαλιλαίας ἕως ὧδε. 6 ↱ Πιλᾶτος δὲ ἀκούσας ἐπηρώτησεν
{the} Galilee ⌊even to⌋ this place." Now when Pilate *Now* heard this, he asked
3836 1133 2401 6045 1254 201 4397 1254 201 2089
d.gsf n.gsf p.g adv n.nsm cj pt.aa.nsm v.aai.3s

εἰ ὁ ἄνθρωπος Γαλιλαῖός ἐστιν, 7 καὶ ἐπιγνοὺς ὅτι ἐκ τῆς
whether the man was a Galilean. *was* *{and}* Learning that he was from *{the}*
1623 3836 476 1639 1134 1639 2779 2105 4022 1639 1639 1666 3836
cj d.nsm n.nsm a.nsm v.pai.3s cj pt.aa.nsm cj p.g d.gsf

ἐξουσίας Ἡρῴδου ἐστὶν ἀνέπεμψεν αὐτὸν ↰ πρὸς Ἡρῴδην, ὄντα καὶ
Herod's jurisdiction, *Herod's* *he was* he sent him off to Herod, who was also
2476 2026 2476 1639 402 899 402 4639 2476 899 1639 2779
n.gsf n.gsm v.pai.3s v.aai.3s r.asm.3 p.a n.asm pt.pa.asm adv

αὐτὸν ἐν Ἱεροσολύμοις ἐν ταύταις ταῖς ἡμέραις. 8 ὁ δὲ
who in Jerusalem during those *{the}* days. Upon seeing Jesus, *{the}* *{and}*
899 1877 2642 1877 4047 3836 2465 1625 1625 2652 3836 1254
r.asm.3 p.d n.dpn p.d r.dpf d.dpf n.dpf d.nsm cj

Ἡρῴδης ἰδὼν τὸν Ἰησοῦν ➝ ἐχάρη λίαν, ἦν γὰρ ἐξ ἱκανῶν
Herod *Upon seeing* *{the}* *Jesus* was very glad, *very* *he had been* since for a long
2476 1625 3836 2652 3336 5897 3336 1639 1142 1666 2653
n.nsm pt.aa.nsm d.asm n.asm v.api.3s adv v.iai.3s cj p.g a.gpm

χρόνων θέλων ἰδεῖν αὐτὸν διὰ τὸ ἀκούειν περὶ αὐτοῦ καὶ
time he had been wanting to see him, ⌊because of⌋ what he had heard about him, and
5989 1639 1639 1639 2527 1625 899 1328 3836 201 4309 899 2779
n.gpm pt.pa.nsm f.aa r.asm.3 p.a d.asn f.pa p.g r.gsm.3 cj

ἤλπιζέν τι σημεῖον ἰδεῖν ὑπ' αὐτοῦ γινόμενον. 9
he was hoping to see some ⌊miraculous sign⌋ *to see* done by him. *done* So Herod
1827 1625 1625 5516 4956 1625 1181 5679 899 1181 1254
v.iai.3s r.asn n.asn f.aa p.g r.gsm.3 pt.pm.asn

ἐπηρώτα δὲ αὐτὸν ἐν λόγοις ἱκανοῖς, αὐτὸς δὲ ↱ οὐδὲν
questioned *So* him with many words; *many* but Jesus *but* gave him no
2089 1254 899 1877 2653 3364 2653 1254 899 1254 646 899 4029
v.iai.3s cj r.asm.3 p.d n.dpm a.dpm r.nsm cj a.asn

ἀπεκρίνατο αὐτῷ. 10 εἱστήκεισαν δὲ οἱ
answer, *him* even though the chief priests and the scribes stood by, *{and}* *the*
646 899 3836 797 797 2779 3836 1208 2705 1254 3836
v.ami.3s r.dsm.3 v.lai.3p cj d.npm

ἀρχιερεῖς καὶ οἱ γραμματεῖς εὐτόνως κατηγοροῦντες αὐτοῦ. 11 ➝
chief priests *and* *the* *scribes* vehemently accusing him. Then, when Herod,
797 2779 3836 1208 2364 2989 899 1254 2476
n.npm cj d.npm n.npm adv pt.pa.npm r.gsm.3

ἐξουθενήσας ← ← δὲ αὐτὸν καὶ [a] ὁ Ἡρῴδης
along with his soldiers, had treated him with contempt *Then* *him* *{also}* *{the}* *Herod*
5250 5250 899 5128 2024 899 1254 899 2779 3836 2476
pt.aa.nsm cj r.asm.3 adv d.nsm n.nsm

σὺν τοῖς στρατεύμασιν αὐτοῦ καὶ ἐμπαίξας περιβαλὼν ἐσθῆτα
along with *{the}* *soldiers* *his* and ridiculed him, they put an elegant robe
5250 3836 5128 899 2779 1850 4314 3287 2264
p.d d.dpn n.dpn r.gsm.3 cj pt.aa.nsm pt.aa.nsm n.asf

λαμπρὰν ↰ ἀνέπεμψεν αὐτὸν ↰ τῷ Πιλάτῳ. 12
elegant on him, and sent him back to Pilate. And Herod and Pilate
3287 4314 402 899 402 3836 4397 1254 2476 2779 4397
a.asf v.aai.3s r.asm.3 d.dsm n.dsm

ἐγένοντο δὲ φίλοι ὅ τε Ἡρῴδης καὶ ὁ Πιλᾶτος ἐν αὐτῇ τῇ
became *And* friends *{the}* ~ *Herod* *and* *{the}* *Pilate* with each other that very *{the}*
1181 1254 5813 3836 5445 2476 2779 3836 4397 3552 253 253 1877 899 3836
v.ami.3p cj n.npm d.nsm cj n.nsm cj d.nsm n.nsm p.d r.dsf d.dsf

ἡμέρᾳ μετ' ἀλλήλων· προϋπῆρχον γὰρ ⌊ἐν ἔχθρᾳ⌋ ὄντες
day, *with* *each other* for before this *for* they had been hostile *they had been*
2465 3552 253 1142 4732 1142 1639 1639 1639 1877 2397 1639
n.dsf p.g r.gpm v.iai.3p cj p.d n.dsf pt.pa.npm

πρὸς αὐτούς. 13 Πιλᾶτος δὲ συγκαλεσάμενος τοὺς ἀρχιερεῖς καὶ τοὺς ἄρχοντας
toward each other. Pilate then called together the chief priests, *{and}* the rulers,
4639 899 4397 1254 5157 3836 797 2779 3836 807
p.a r.apm.3 n.nsm cj pt.am.nsm d.apm n.apm cj d.apm n.apm

[a] [καὶ] UBS, omitted by TNIV.

NASB

Galilee even as far
as this place."
[6]When Pilate
heard it, he asked
whether the
man was a Gali-
lean. [7]And when he
learned that He be-
longed to Herod's
jurisdiction, he sent
Him to Herod, who
himself also was in
Jerusalem at that
time.

Jesus before Herod

[8]Now Herod was
very glad when
he saw Jesus; for
he had wanted to
see Him for a long
time, because he
had been hearing
about Him and was
hoping to see some
sign performed
by Him. [9]And he
questioned Him at
some length; but
He answered him
nothing. [10]And the
chief priests and
the scribes were
standing there,
accusing Him
vehemently. [11]And
Herod with his sol-
diers, after treating
Him with contempt
and mocking Him,
dressed Him in
a gorgeous robe
and sent Him back
to Pilate. [12]Now
Herod and Pilate
became friends
with one another
that very day; for
before they had
been enemies with
each other.

Pilate Seeks Jesus' Release

[13]Pilate sum-
moned the chief
priests and the

NIV

[14]and said to them,
"You brought me
this man as one
who was inciting
the people to rebel-
lion. I have exam-
ined him in your
presence and have
found no basis
for your charges
against him. [15]Nei-
ther has Herod, for
he sent him back
to us; as you can
see, he has done
nothing to deserve
death. [16]Therefore,
I will punish him
and then release
him." [17][a]
[18]But the whole
crowd shouted,
"Away with this
man! Release
Barabbas to us!"
[19](Barabbas had
been thrown into
prison for an in-
surrection in the
city, and for mur-
der.)
[20]Wanting to re-
lease Jesus, Pilate
appealed to them
again. [21]But they
kept shouting,
"Crucify him!
Crucify him!"
[22]For the third
time he spoke
to them: "Why?
What crime has
this man commit-
ted? I have found
in him no grounds
for the death pen-
alty. Therefore
I will have him
punished and then
release him."
[23]But with loud
shouts they insis-
tently demanded
that he be cru-
cified, and their
shouts prevailed.

[a] 17 Some manuscripts include here words similar to Matt. 27:15 and Mark 15:6.

καὶ τὸν λαὸν 14 εἶπεν πρὸς αὐτούς, προσηνέγκατέ μοι τὸν ἄνθρωπον
and the people, and said to them, "You brought me {the} this man
2779 3836 3295 3306 4639 899 4712 1609 3836 4047 476
cj d.asm n.asm v.aai.3s p.a r.apm.3 v.aai.2p r.ds.1 d.asm n.asm

τοῦτον ὡς ἀποστρέφοντα τὸν λαόν, καὶ ἰδοὺ
this as ⌊one who was trying to mislead⌋ the people. And indeed, having examined him in
4047 6055 695 3836 3295 2779 2627 373 373 1967
r.asm pl pt.pa.asm d.asm n.asm cj j

ἐγὼ ἐνώπιον ὑμῶν ἀνακρίνας οὐθὲν εὗρον
your presence, I *in presence your having examined* found no basis *found* for your charges
7007 1967 1609 1967 7007 373 2351 4032 165 2351 4005 2989 2989
r.ns.1 p.g r.gp.2 pt.aa.nsm a.asn v.aai.1s

ἐν τῷ ἀνθρώπῳ τούτῳ αἴτιον ὧν κατηγορεῖτε κατ' αὐτοῦ.
against {the} this man. *this basis for your charges {against} {him}*
1877 3836 4047 476 4047 165 4005 2989 2848 899
p.d d.dsm n.dsm r.dsm n.asn r.gpn v.pai.2p p.g r.gsm.3

15 ἀλλ' οὐδὲ Ἡρῴδης, ἀνέπεμψεν γὰρ αὐτὸν ↰ πρὸς ἡμᾶς, καὶ
⌊For that matter,⌋ neither did Herod, for he sent *for* him back to us. *{and}*
247 4028 2476 1142 402 1142 899 402 4639 7005 2779
cj cj n.nsm v.aai.3s cj r.asm.3 p.a r.ap.1 cj

ἰδοὺ οὐδὲν ἄξιον θανάτου ἐστὶν πεπραγμένον αὐτῷ· 16 ↱ ↱ →
Look, nothing deserving death has been done by him. So I will have him
2627 4029 545 2505 1639 4556 899 4036 668 668 899
j a.nsn a.nsn n.gsm v.pai.3s pt.rp.nsn r.dsm.3

παιδεύσας οὖν αὐτὸν ἀπολύσω.[a] 18 ἀνέκραγον δὲ παμπληθεὶ
flogged *So him* and release him." But they cried out *But* together,
4084 4036 899 668 1254 371 1254 4101
pt.aa.nsm cj r.asm.3 v.fai.1s v.aai.3p cj adv

λέγοντες, αἶρε τοῦτον, ↰ ἀπόλυσον δὲ ἡμῖν τὸν Βαραββᾶν· 19 ὅστις ἦν
saying, "Take this man away! Release *{and}* for us *{the}* Barabbas!" who was
3306 149 4047 149 668 1254 7005 3836 972 4015 1639
pt.pa.npm v.pam.2s r.asm v.aam.2s cj r.dp.1 d.asm n.asm r.nsm v.iai.3s

διὰ στάσιν τινὰ γενομένην ἐν τῇ πόλει καὶ
thrown into prison ⌊because of⌋ a certain riot *certain* that had occurred in the city and for
965 1877 5871 1328 5516 5087 5516 1181 1877 3836 4484 2779
p.a n.asf r.asf pt.am.asf p.d d.dsf n.dsf cj

φόνον βληθεὶς ἐν τῇ φυλακῇ. 20 πάλιν δὲ ὁ Πιλᾶτος
murder. *thrown into {the} prison* Once again *{and} {the}* Pilate, wanting to release
5840 965 1877 3836 5871 4099 1254 3836 4397 2527 668 668
n.asm pt.ap.nsm p.d d.dsf n.dsf adv cj d.nsm n.nsm

προσεφώνησεν αὐτοῖς θέλων ἀπολῦσαι τὸν Ἰησοῦν. 21 οἱ δὲ
Jesus, called out to them, *wanting to release {the} Jesus* but they *but*
2652 4715 899 2527 668 3836 2652 1254 3836 1254
v.aai.3s r.dpm.3 pt.pa.nsm f.aa d.asm n.asm d.npm cj

ἐπεφώνουν λέγοντες, σταύρου σταύρου αὐτόν. 22 ὁ δὲ τρίτον εἶπεν
kept shouting, saying, "Crucify, crucify him!" A third time he *{and} third time* spoke
2215 3306 5090 5090 899 5568 5568 3836 1254 5568 3306
v.iai.3p pt.pa.npm v.pam.2s v.pam.2s r.asm.3 d.nsm cj adv v.aai.3s

πρὸς αὐτούς, τί γὰρ κακὸν ἐποίησεν οὗτος; ↰ οὐδὲν
to them, "What ~ evil did this man do? I have found in him no
4639 899 5515 1142 2805 4472 4047 4472 2351 2351 2351 1877 899 4029
p.a r.apm.3 r.asn cj a.asn v.aai.3s r.nsm a.asn

αἴτιον θανάτου εὗρον ἐν αὐτῷ· → → παιδεύσας οὖν
guilt ⌊deserving death.⌋ *I have found in him* I will therefore punish *therefore* and release
165 2505 2351 1877 899 4036 4084 4036 668
n.asn n.gsm v.aai.1s p.d r.dsm.3 pt.aa.nsm cj

αὐτὸν ἀπολύσω. 23 οἱ δὲ ἐπέκειντο → φωναῖς μεγάλαις
him." *release* But they *But* were insistent, demanding with loud cries *loud*
899 668 1254 3836 1254 2130 160 3489 5889 3489
r.asm.3 v.fai.1s d.npm cj v.imi.3p n.dpf a.dpf

αἰτούμενοι αὐτὸν σταυρωθῆναι, καὶ κατίσχυον αἱ φωναὶ αὐτῶν.[b]
demanding that he should be crucified, and their cries prevailed. *{the} cries their*
160 899 5090 2779 899 5889 2996 3836 5889 899
pt.pm.npm r.asm.3 f.ap cj v.iai.3p d.npf n.npf r.gpm.3

[a] 17 ἀνάγκην δὲ εἶχεν ἀπολύειν αὐτοῖς κατὰ ἑορτὴν ἕνα. included by TR after ἀπολύσω.
[b] καὶ τῶν ἀρχιερέων included by TR after αὐτῶν.

NASB

rulers and the
people, [14]and said
to them, "You
brought this man
to me as one who
incites the people
to rebellion, and
behold, having
examined Him
before you, I have
found no guilt in
this man regarding
the charges which
you make against
Him. [15]No, nor has
Herod, for he sent
Him back to us;
and behold, noth-
ing deserving death
has been done by
Him. [16]Therefore
I will punish Him
and release Him."
[17][[a]Now he was
obliged to release
to them at the feast
one prisoner.]
[18]But they cried
out all together,
saying, "Away
with this man, and
release for us Ba-
rabbas!" [19](He was
one who had been
thrown into prison
for an insurrection
made in the city,
and for murder.)
[20]Pilate, wanting
to release Jesus,
addressed them
again, [21]but they
kept on calling
out, saying, "Cru-
cify, crucify Him!"
[22]And he said to
them the third
time, "Why, what
evil has this man
done? I have found
in Him no guilt
demanding death;
therefore I will
punish Him and
release Him." [23]But
they were insistent,
with loud voices
asking that He be
crucified. And their
voices *began* to
prevail.

[a] Early mss do not contain this v

NIV

24 So Pilate decid-
ed to grant their
demand. 25 He
released the man
who had been
thrown into prison
for insurrection
and murder, the
one they asked for,
and surrendered
Jesus to their will.

The Crucifixion of Jesus

26 As the soldiers
led him away, they
seized Simon from
Cyrene, who was
on his way in from
the country, and
put the cross on
him and made him
carry it behind
Jesus. 27 A large
number of people
followed him, in-
cluding women
who mourned and
wailed for him.
28 Jesus turned
and said to them,
"Daughters of Je-
rusalem, do not
weep for me; weep
for yourselves and
for your children.
29 For the time will
come when you
will say, 'Blessed
are the childless
women, the wombs
that never bore
and the breasts
that never nursed!'
30 Then

"'they will
say to the
mountains,
"Fall on
us!"
and to the
hills,
"Cover
us!"'[a]

31 For if people do
these things when
the tree is green,
what will happen
when it is dry?"
32 Two other men,
both criminals,
were also led out
with him to be
executed. 33 When
they came to the
place

24 καὶ Πιλᾶτος ἐπέκρινεν γενέσθαι τὸ αἴτημα αὐτῶν·
So Pilate decided that their demand ⌊should be granted.⌋ {the} demand their
2779 4397 2137 899 161 1181 3836 161 899
cj n.nsm v.aai.3s f.am d.asn n.asn r.gpm.3

25 ἀπέλυσεν δὲ τὸν διὰ στάσιν καὶ φόνον
He released {and} the man who had been thrown into prison for insurrection and murder,
668 1254 3836 965 965 965 965 965 1650 5871 1328 5087 2779 5840
v.aai.3s cj d.asm p.a n.asf cj n.asm

βεβλημένον εἰς φυλακὴν ὃν ᾐτοῦντο, τὸν δὲ
man who had been thrown into prison for whom they asked, but he handed over {the} but
965 1650 5871 160 4005 160 1254 4140 4140 4140 3836 1254
pt.rp.asm p.a n.asf r.asm v.imi.3p d.asm cj

Ἰησοῦν παρέδωκεν τῷ θελήματι αὐτῶν. 26 καὶ ὡς ἀπήγαγον αὐτόν,
Jesus he handed over to their will. their {and} As they led him away,
2652 4140 3836 899 2525 899 2779 6055 552 899 552
n.asm v.aai.3s d.dsn n.dsn r.gpm.3 cj cj v.aai.3p r.asm.3

ἐπιλαβόμενοι Σίμωνά τινα Κυρηναῖον ἐρχόμενον ἀπ'
they took hold of a certain Simon certain of Cyrene, ⌊who was coming in⌋ from the
2202 2138 5516 4981 5516 3254 2262 608
pt.am.npm n.asm r.asm n.asm pt.pm.asm p.g

ἀγροῦ ἐπέθηκαν αὐτῷ τὸν σταυρὸν φέρειν ὄπισθεν τοῦ Ἰησοῦ.
countryside, and put the cross on him the cross to carry it behind {the} Jesus.
69 2202 3836 5089 899 3836 5089 5770 3957 3836 2652
n.gsm v.aai.3p r.dsm.3 d.asm n.asm f.pa p.g d.gsm n.gsm

27 ἠκολούθει δὲ αὐτῷ πολὺ πλῆθος τοῦ λαοῦ καὶ
And there followed And him a great crowd of the people, and among them were
1254 199 1254 899 4498 4436 3836 3295 2779
v.iai.3s cj r.dsm.3 a.nsn n.nsn d.gsm n.gsm cj

γυναικῶν αἳ ἐκόπτοντο καὶ ἐθρήνουν αὐτόν. 28 στραφεὶς δὲ πρὸς αὐτὰς ὁ[a]
women who were mourning and wailing for him. Turning {and} to them, {the}
1222 4005 3164 2779 2577 899 5138 1254 4639 899 3836
n.gpf r.npf v.imi.3p cj v.iai.3p r.asm.3 pt.ap.nsm cj p.a r.apf.3 d.nsm

Ἰησοῦς εἶπεν, θυγατέρες Ἰερουσαλήμ, μὴ κλαίετε ἐπ' ἐμέ· πλὴν ἐφ'
Jesus said, "Daughters of Jerusalem, do not weep for me, but weep for
2652 3306 2588 2647 3081 3590 3081 2093 1609 4440 3081 2093
n.nsm v.aai.3s n.vpf n.gsf pl v.pam.2p p.a r.as.1 cj p.a

ἑαυτὰς κλαίετε καὶ ἐπὶ τὰ τέκνα ὑμῶν, 29 ὅτι ἰδοὺ
yourselves weep and for {the} your children. your For ~ the days are surely
1571 3081 2779 2093 3836 7007 5451 7007 4022 2627 2465
r.apf.2 v.pam.2p cj p.a d.apn n.apn r.gp.2 cj j

ἔρχονται ἡμέραι ⌊ἐν αἷς⌋ ἐροῦσιν, μακάριαι αἱ στεῖραι καὶ αἱ κοιλίαι αἳ
coming days when they will say, 'Blessed are the barren and the wombs that
2262 2465 1877 4005 3306 3421 3836 5096 2779 3836 3120 4005
v.pmi.3p n.npf p.d r.dpf v.fai.3p a.npf d.npf n.npf cj d.npf n.npf r.npf

οὐκ ἐγέννησαν καὶ μαστοὶ οἳ οὐκ ἔθρεψαν. 30 τότε ἄρξονται λέγειν τοῖς
never gave birth and the breasts that never nursed!' Then they will begin to say to the
4024 1164 2779 3466 4005 4024 5555 5538 806 3306 3836
pl v.aai.3p cj n.npm r.npm pl v.aai.3p adv v.fmi.3p f.pa d.dpn

ὄρεσιν, πέσετε ἐφ' ἡμᾶς, καὶ τοῖς βουνοῖς, καλύψατε ἡμᾶς· 31 ὅτι εἰ
mountains, 'Fall on us!' and to the hills, 'Cover us!' For if they do
4001 4406 2093 7005 2779 3836 1090 2821 7005 4022 1623 4472 4472
n.dpn v.aam.2p p.a r.ap.1 cj d.dpm n.dpm v.aam.2p r.ap.1 cj cj

ἐν τῷ ὑγρῷ ξύλῳ ταῦτα ποιοῦσιν, ἐν τῷ
these things when the wood is green, wood these things they do what will happen when {the} it
4047 4047 1877 3836 3833 5619 3833 4047 4472 5515 1181 1181 1877 3836
p.d d.dsn a.dsn n.dsn r.apn v.pai.3p p.d d.dsn

ξηρῷ τί γένηται; 32 Ἤγοντο δὲ καὶ ἕτεροι κακοῦργοι
is dry?" what will happen And they also led away And also two others, who were criminals,
3831 5515 1181 1254 2779 72 1254 2779 1545 2283 2806
a.dsn r.nsn v.ams.3s v.ipi.3p cj adv r.npm n.npm

δύο σὺν αὐτῷ ἀναιρεθῆναι. 33 καὶ ὅτε ἦλθον ἐπὶ τὸν τόπον
two to be put to death with him. to be put to death And when they came to the place
1545 359 359 359 359 359 5250 899 359 2779 4021 2262 2093 3836 5536
a.npm p.d r.dsm.3 f.ap cj cj v.aai.3p p.a d.asm n.asm

NASB

24 And Pilate pro-
nounced sentence
that their demand
be granted. 25 And
he released the
man they were
asking for who had
been thrown into
prison for insurrec-
tion and murder,
but he delivered
Jesus to their will.

Simon Bears the Cross

26 When they led
Him away, they
seized a man,
Simon of Cyrene,
coming in from the
country, and placed
on him the cross to
carry behind Jesus.
27 And following
Him was a large
crowd of the peo-
ple, and of women
who were mourn-
ing and lamenting
Him. 28 But Jesus
turning to them
said, "Daughters
of Jerusalem, stop
weeping for Me,
but weep for your-
selves and for your
children. 29 For be-
hold, the days are
coming when they
will say, 'Blessed
are the barren, and
the wombs that
never bore, and the
breasts that never
nursed.' 30 Then
they will begin TO
SAY TO THE MOUN-
TAINS, 'FALL ON US,'
AND TO THE HILLS,
'COVER US.' 31 For
if they do these
things when the
tree is green, what
will happen when
it is dry?"
32 Two others also,
who were crimi-
nals, were being
led away to be put
to death with Him.

The Crucifixion

33 When they came
to the place called

[a] 30 Hosea 10:8

[a] [ὁ] UBS, omitted by TNIV.

NIV

called the Skull,
they crucified
him there, along
with the crimi-
nals—one on his
right, the other on
his left. [34]Jesus
said, "Father, for-
give them, for they
do not know what
they are doing."[a]
And they divided
up his clothes by
casting lots.
[35]The people
stood watching,
and the rulers even
sneered at him.
They said, "He
saved others; let
him save himself
if he is God's Mes-
siah, the Chosen
One."
[36]The soldiers
also came up and
mocked him. They
offered him wine
vinegar [37]and said,
"If you are the
king of the Jews,
save yourself."
[38]There was a
written notice
above him, which
read: THIS IS THE
KING OF THE JEWS.
[39]One of the
criminals who
hung there hurled
insults at him:
"Aren't you the
Messiah? Save
yourself and us!"
[40]But the other
criminal rebuked
him. "Don't you
fear God," he said,
"since you are
under the same
sentence? [41]We are
punished justly,
for we are getting
what our deeds
deserve. But this
man has done
nothing wrong."
[42]Then he said,
"Jesus, remember

[a] 34 Some early manuscripts do not have this sentence.

τὸν καλούμενον Κρανίον, ἐκεῖ ἐσταύρωσαν αὐτὸν καὶ τοὺς κακούργους, ὃν
{the} called "The Skull," there they crucified him and the criminals — one
3836 2813 3191 1695 5090 899 2779 3836 2806 4005
d.asm pt.pp.asm n.asn adv v.aai.3p r.asm.3 cj d.apm n.apm r.asm

μὲν ἐκ δεξιῶν ὃν δὲ ἐξ ἀριστερῶν. [34] ⟦ὁ δὲ Ἰησοῦς ἔλεγεν,
~ on his right and one *and* on his left. *{the}* And Jesus was saying,
3525 1666 1288 1254 4005 1254 1666 754 3836 1254 2652 3306
pl p.g a.gpf r.asm pl p.g a.gpf d.nsm cj n.nsm v.iai.3s

πάτερ, ἄφες αὐτοῖς, ↱ ↱ οὐ γὰρ οἴδασιν τί ποιοῦσιν.⟧
"Father, forgive them; for they do not *for* know what they are doing." Then
4252 918 899 1142 3857 3857 4024 1142 3857 5515 4472 1254
n.vsm v.aam.2s r.dpm.3 pl cj v.rai.3p r.asn v.pai.3p

διαμεριζόμενοι δὲ τὰ ἱμάτια αὐτοῦ ἔβαλον κλήρους. [35] καὶ
⌞in order to divide up⌟ *Then* *{the}* his clothing *his* they cast lots. *{and}* The people
1374 1254 3836 899 2668 899 965 3102 2779 3836 3295
pt.pm.npm cj d.apn n.apn r.gsm.3 v.aai.3p n.apm cj

εἱστήκει ὁ λαὸς θεωρῶν. ἐξεμυκτήριζον δὲ καὶ οἱ ἄρχοντες
stood by, *The* *people* watching. The rulers even scoffed *{and}* *even* *The* *rulers* at
2705 3836 3295 2555 3836 807 2779 1727 1254 2779 3836 807
v.lai.3s d.nsm n.nsm pt.pa.nsm v.iai.3p cj adv d.npm n.npm

λέγοντες, ἄλλους ἔσωσεν, σωσάτω ἑαυτόν, εἰ οὗτός ἐστιν ὁ
him, saying, "He saved others; *He saved* let him save himself, if he is the
3306 5392 5392 257 5392 5392 1571 1623 4047 1639 3836
pt.pa.npm r.apm v.aai.3s v.aam.3s r.asm.3 cj r.nsm v.pai.3s d.nsm

χριστὸς τοῦ θεοῦ ὁ ἐκλεκτός. [36] ἐνέπαιξαν δὲ αὐτῷ καὶ οἱ
Christ of God, the Chosen One!" The soldiers, also, mocked *{and}* him, *also* *The*
5986 3836 2536 3836 1723 3836 5132 2779 1850 1254 899 2779 3836
n.nsm d.gsm n.gsm d.nsm a.nsm v.aai.3p cj r.dsm.3 adv d.npm

στρατιῶται προσερχόμενοι, ὄξος προσφέροντες αὐτῷ [37] καὶ
soldiers coming up and offering him ⌞sour wine⌟ *offering* *him* and
5132 4665 4712 899 3954 4712 899 2779
n.npm pt.pm.npm n.asn pt.pa.npm r.dsm.3 cj

λέγοντες, εἰ σὺ εἶ ὁ βασιλεὺς τῶν Ἰουδαίων, σῶσον σεαυτόν. [38]
saying, "If you are the king of the Jews, save yourself!" In fact,
3306 1623 5148 1639 3836 995 3836 2681 5392 4932 2779 2779
pt.pa.npm cj r.ns.2 v.pai.2s d.nsm n.nsm d.gpm a.gpm v.aam.2s r.asm.2

ἦν δὲ καὶ ἐπιγραφὴ ἐπ' αὐτῷ·[a] ὁ βασιλεὺς τῶν Ἰουδαίων
⌞there was⌟ *{and}* *In fact* an inscription above him, "This is the King of the Jews."
1639 1254 2779 2107 2093 899 4047 3836 995 3836 2681
v.iai.3s cj adv n.nsf p.d r.dsm.3 d.nsm n.nsm d.gpm a.gpm

οὗτος. [39] εἷς δὲ τῶν κρεμασθέντων κακούργων ἐβλασφήμει αὐτὸν
This One *{and}* of the criminals hanging there *criminals* kept deriding him,
4047 1651 1254 3836 2806 3203 2806 1059 899
r.nsm a.nsm cj d.gpm pt.ap.gpm n.gpm v.iai.3s r.asm.3

λέγων, οὐχὶ σὺ εἶ ὁ χριστός; σῶσον σεαυτὸν καὶ ἡμᾶς. [40]
saying, "Are you not *you* *Are* the Messiah? Save yourself and us!" But the
3306 1639 5148 4049 5148 1639 3836 5986 5392 4932 2779 7005 1254 3836
pt.pa.nsm pl r.ns.2 v.pai.2s d.nsm n.nsm v.aam.2s r.asm.2 cj r.ap.1

ἀποκριθεὶς δὲ ὁ ἕτερος → ἐπιτιμῶν αὐτῷ ἔφη, ↱ οὐδὲ
other responded *But* *the* *other* to him with a rebuke, *to him* saying, "Do you not
2283 646 1254 3836 2283 899 899 2203 899 5774 5828 5148 4028
pt.ap.nsm cj d.nsm r.nsm pt.pa.nsm r.dsm.3 v.iai.3s adv

φοβῇ σὺ τὸν θεόν, ὅτι ἐν τῷ αὐτῷ κρίματι εἶ; [41] καὶ ἡμεῖς μὲν
fear *you* *{the}* God, since you are under the same sentence? *you are* And we indeed
5828 5148 3836 2536 4022 1639 1639 1877 3836 899 3210 1639 2779 7005 3525
v.ppi.2s r.ns.2 d.asm n.asm cj p.d d.dsn r.dsn n.dsn v.pai.2s cj r.np.1 pl

δικαίως, ἄξια γὰρ ὧν ἐπράξαμεν ἀπολαμβάνομεν·
justly. For we are receiving ⌞what we deserve⌟ *For* ⌞for what⌟ we did; *we are receiving*
1469 1142 655 655 655 545 1142 4005 4556 655
adv a.apn cj r.gpn v.aai.1p v.pai.1p

οὗτος δὲ οὐδὲν ἄτοπον ἔπραξεν. [42] καὶ ἔλεγεν, Ἰησοῦ, μνήσθητί
but this man *but* has done nothing improper." *has done* Then he said, "Jesus, remember
1254 4047 1254 4556 4556 4029 876 4556 2779 3306 2652 3630
r.nsm cj a.asn a.asn v.aai.3s cj v.iai.3s n.vsm v.apm.2s

[a] γράμμασιν Ἑλληνικοῖς καὶ Ῥωμαϊκοῖς καὶ Ἑβραϊκοῖς included by TR after αὐτῷ.

NASB

The Skull, there
they crucified Him
and the criminals,
one on the right
and the other on
the left. [34]But Jesus
was saying, "Fa-
ther, forgive them;
for they do not
know what they are
doing." And they
cast lots, dividing
up His garments
among themselves.
[35]And the people
stood by, looking
on. And even the
rulers were sneer-
ing at Him, saying,
"He saved oth-
ers; let Him save
Himself if this is
the Christ of God,
His Chosen One."
[36]The soldiers also
mocked Him,
coming up to Him,
offering Him sour
wine, [37]and saying,
"If You are the
King of the Jews,
save Yourself!"
[38]Now there was
also an inscription
above Him, "THIS
IS THE KING OF
THE JEWS."
[39]One of the
criminals who were
hanged *there* was
hurling abuse at
Him, saying, "Are
You not the Christ?
Save Yourself and
us!" [40]But the other
answered, and
rebuking him said,
"Do you not even
fear God, since you
are under the same
sentence of con-
demnation? [41]And
we indeed *are suf-*
fering justly, for we
are receiving what
we deserve for our
deeds; but this man
has done nothing
wrong." [42]And he
was saying, "Jesus,
remember me

NIV

me when you come
into your king-
dom.[a]"
43 Jesus answered
him, "Truly I tell
you, today you
will be with me in
paradise."

The Death of Jesus

44 It was now
about noon, and
darkness came
over the whole
land until three in
the afternoon, 45 for
the sun stopped
shining. And the
curtain of the tem-
ple was torn in
two. 46 Jesus called
out with a loud
voice, "Father, into
your hands I com-
mit my spirit."[b]
When he had said
this, he breathed
his last.
47 The centurion,
seeing what had
happened, praised
God and said,
"Surely this was
a righteous man."
48 When all the
people who had
gathered to wit-
ness this sight saw
what took place,
they beat their
breasts and went
away. 49 But all
those who knew
him, including the
women who had
followed him from
Galilee, stood at a
distance, watching
these things.

The Burial of Jesus

50 Now there was
a man named Jo-
seph, a member
of the Council, a
good and upright
man, 51 who had

[a] 42 Some manuscripts *come with your kingly power*
[b] 46 Psalm 31:5

μου ὅταν ἔλθῃς εἰς[a] τὴν βασιλείαν σου. 43 καὶ εἶπεν αὐτῷ,
me when you come in *{the}* your kingdom." *your* And Jesus said to him,
1609 4020 2262 1650 3836 5148 993 5148 2779 3306 899
r.gs.1 cj v.aas.2s p.a d.asf n.asf r.gs.2 cj v.aai.3s r.dsm.3

ἀμὴν σοι λέγω, σήμερον μετ᾽ ἐμοῦ ἔσῃ ἐν τῷ
⌊"In solemn truth⌋ I tell you: *I tell* today you will be with me *you will be* in *{the}*
297 3306 3306 5148 3306 4958 1639 1639 1639 3552 1609 1639 1877 3836
pl r.ds.2 v.pai.1s adv p.g r.gs.1 v.fmi.2s p.d d.dsm

παραδείσῳ. 44 καὶ ἦν ἤδη ὡσεὶ ὥρα ἕκτη καὶ σκότος ⌊ἐγένετο
paradise." *{and}* ⌊It was⌋ already only about the sixth hour *sixth* but darkness covered
4137 2779 1639 2453 6059 1761 6052 1761 2779 5030 1181
n.dsm cj v.iai.3s adv pl n.nsf a.nsf cj n.nsn v.ami.3s

ἐφ᾽⌋ ὅλην τὴν γῆν ἕως ὥρας ἐνάτης 45 ↱ τοῦ ἡλίου
the whole *{the}* land until the ninth hour, *ninth* because the light of the sun
2093 3910 3836 1178 2401 1888 6052 1888 1722 3836 2463
p.a a.asf d.asf n.asf p.g n.gsf a.gsf d.gsm n.gsm

ἐκλιπόντος, ἐσχίσθη δὲ τὸ καταπέτασμα τοῦ ναοῦ
had been eclipsed. The curtain of the temple was torn *{and}* *The* *curtain* *of the* *temple*
1722 3836 2925 3836 3836 3724 5387 1254 3836 2925 3836 3724
pt.aa.gsm v.api.3s cj d.nsn n.nsn d.gsm n.gsm

→ μέσον. 46 καὶ φωνήσας → φωνῇ μεγάλῃ ὁ Ἰησοῦς εἶπεν, πάτερ,
down the middle. Then Jesus, crying out in a loud voice, *loud* *{the}* *Jesus* said, "Father,
3545 2779 2652 5888 3489 5889 3489 3836 2652 3306 4252
adv cj pt.aa.nsm n.dsf a.dsf d.nsm n.nsm v.aai.3s n.vsm

εἰς χεῖράς σου παρατίθεμαι τὸ πνεῦμά μου. τοῦτο δὲ
into your hands *your* I commit *{the}* my spirit!" *my* Having said this, *{and}*
1650 5148 5931 5148 4192 3836 1609 4460 1609 3306 3306 4047 1254
p.a n.apf r.gs.2 v.pmi.1s d.asn n.asn r.gs.1 r.asn cj

εἰπὼν ἐξέπνευσεν. 47 → ἰδὼν δὲ ὁ ἑκατοντάρχης
Having said ⌊he breathed his last.⌋ Now when the centurion saw *Now* *the* *centurion*
3306 1743 1254 3836 1672 1625 1254 3836 1672
pt.aa.nsm v.aai.3s pt.aa.nsm cj d.nsm n.nsm

τὸ γενόμενον ἐδόξαζεν τὸν θεὸν λέγων, ὄντως ὁ ἄνθρωπος οὗτος
what had happened, he praised *{the}* God, saying, "Truly *{the}* this man *this* was
3836 1181 1519 3836 2536 3306 3953 3836 4047 476 4047 1639
d.asn pt.am.asn v.iai.3s d.asm n.asm pt.pa.nsm adv d.nsm n.nsm r.nsm

δίκαιος ἦν. 48 καὶ ↱ πάντες οἱ συμπαραγενόμενοι ὄχλοι ἐπὶ τὴν
righteous!" *was* And when all the crowds who had gathered *crowds* for *{the}* this
1465 1639 2779 2555 4246 3836 4063 5219 4063 2093 3836 4047
a.nsm v.iai.3s cj a.npm d.npm pt.am.npm n.npm p.a d.asf

θεωρίαν ταύτην, θεωρήσαντες τὰ γενόμενα, τύπτοντες τὰ
spectacle *this* saw what had happened, they returned home, beating their
2556 4047 2555 3836 1181 5715 5715 5597 3836
n.asf r.asf pt.aa.npm d.apn pt.am.apn pt.pa.npm d.apn

στήθη ὑπέστρεφον. 49 εἱστήκεισαν δὲ πάντες οἱ γνωστοὶ αὐτῷ ἀπὸ μακρόθεν
breasts. *they returned* *were standing* And all who knew Jesus, *at* *distance*
5111 5715 2705 1254 4246 3836 1196 899 608 3427
n.apn v.iai.3p v.lai.3p cj a.npm d.npm a.npm r.dsm.3 p.g adv

καὶ γυναῖκες αἱ συνακολουθοῦσαι αὐτῷ ἀπὸ τῆς Γαλιλαίας
including the women who had followed him from *{the}* Galilee, were standing at
2779 1222 3836 5258 899 608 3836 1133 2705 2705 608
cj n.npf d.npf pt.pa.npf r.dsm.3 p.g d.gsf n.gsf

ὁρῶσαι ταῦτα. 50 καὶ ἰδοὺ ἀνὴρ ὀνόματι Ἰωσὴφ
a distance, watching these things. Now ⌊there was⌋ a man named Joseph, a member of the
3427 3972 4047 2779 2627 467 3950 2737 5639
pt.pa.npf r.apn cj j n.nsm n.dsn n.nsm

βουλευτὴς ὑπάρχων καὶ[b] ἀνὴρ ἀγαθὸς καὶ δίκαιος 51 οὗτος
Council, *member* *{and}* a good and righteous man. *good* *and* *righteous* (He had
1085 5639 2779 19 2779 1465 467 19 2779 1465 4047 1639
n.nsm pt.pa.nsm cj n.nsm a.nsm cj a.nsm r.nsm

[a] εἰς τὴν βασιλείαν NET.
[b] [καὶ] UBS, omitted by TNIV.

NASB

when You come in
Your kingdom!"
43 And He said to
him, "Truly I say
to you, today you
shall be with Me in
Paradise."
44 It was now about
[a]the sixth hour,
and darkness fell
over the whole
land until [b]the ninth
hour, 45 because the
sun was obscured;
and the veil of the
temple was torn in
two. 46 And Jesus,
crying out with a
loud voice, said,
"Father, INTO YOUR
HANDS I COMMIT MY
SPIRIT." Having said
this, He breathed
His last. 47 Now
when the centurion
saw what had hap-
pened, he *began*
praising God,
saying, "Certainly
this man was inno-
cent." 48 And all the
crowds who came
together for this
spectacle, when
they observed what
had happened,
began to return,
beating their
breasts. 49 And all
His acquaintances
and the women
who accompanied
Him from Galilee
were standing at
a distance, seeing
these things.

Jesus Is Buried

50 And a man
named Joseph, who
was a member of
the Council, a good
and righteous man

[a] I.e. noon
[b] I.e. 3 p.m.

NIV

not consented to
their decision and
action. He came
from the Judean
town of Arima-
thea, and he him-
self was waiting
for the kingdom
of God. [52]Going
to Pilate, he asked
for Jesus' body.
[53]Then he took it
down, wrapped it
in linen cloth and
placed it in a tomb
cut in the rock, one
in which no one
had yet been laid.
[54]It was Prepara-
tion Day, and the
Sabbath was about
to begin.
[55]The women
who had come
with Jesus from
Galilee followed
Joseph and saw the
tomb and how his
body was laid in it.
[56]Then they went
home and prepared
spices and per-
fumes. But they
rested on the Sab-
bath in obedience
to the command-
ment.

Jesus Has Risen

24 On the first
day of the
week, very early
in the morning,
the women took
the spices they
had prepared and
went to the tomb.
[2]They found the
stone rolled away
from the tomb,
[3]but when they
entered, they did
not find the body
of the Lord Jesus.
[4]While they were
wondering about
this, suddenly two
men in clothes that
gleamed like light-
ning stood beside

οὐκ ἦν συγκατατεθειμένος τῇ βουλῇ καὶ τῇ πράξει αὐτῶν ἀπὸ
not *had* agreed with their decision or *{the}* their action.) *their* He was from the
4024 1639 5163 3836 1087 2779 3836 899 4552 899 608 3836
pl v.iai.3s pt.rp.nsm d.dsf n.dsf cj d.dsf n.dsf r.gpm.3 p.g

Ἁριμαθαίας πόλεως τῶν Ἰουδαίων, ὃς προσεδέχετο τὴν
Jewish town of Arimathea, *town* *the* *Jewish* and he ˪was waiting expectantly for˩ the
2681 4484 751 4484 3836 2681 4005 4657 3836
n.gsf n.gsf d.gpm a.gpm r.nsm v.imi.3s d.asf

βασιλείαν τοῦ θεοῦ, [52] οὗτος προσελθὼν τῷ Πιλάτῳ ᾐτήσατο τὸ σῶμα τοῦ
kingdom of God. This man went to Pilate and asked for the body of
993 3836 2536 4047 4665 3836 4397 160 3836 5393 3836
n.asf d.gsm n.gsm r.nsm pt.aa.nsm d.dsm n.dsm v.ami.3s d.asn n.asn d.gsm

Ἰησοῦ [53] καὶ καθελὼν ← ἐνετύλιξεν αὐτὸ ↰ σινδόνι καὶ ἔθηκεν αὐτὸν[a]
Jesus; then taking it down, he wrapped it in a linen cloth, and laid him
2652 2779 2747 1962 899 1962 4984 2779 5502 899
n.gsm cj pt.aa.nsm v.aai.3s r.asn.3 n.dsf cj v.aai.3s r.asm.3

ἐν μνήματι λαξευτῷ οὗ οὐκ → ἦν οὐδεὶς οὔπω κείμενος.
in a tomb cut in stone, where *{not}* no one had yet been *no one* *yet* laid.
1877 3645 3292 4023 4024 4029 4029 4037 1639 4029 4037 3023
p.d n.dsn a.dsn adv pl v.iai.3s a.nsm adv pt.pm.nsm

[54] καὶ ἡμέρα ἦν παρασκευῆς καὶ σάββατον ἐπέφωσκεν.
{and} It was the day *It was* of preparation and the Sabbath ˪was about to begin.˩
2779 1639 1639 2465 1639 4187 2779 4879 2216
cj n.nsf v.iai.3s n.gsf cj n.nsn v.iai.3s

[55] κατακολουθήσασαι δὲ αἱ
The women who had come with him from Galilee followed along behind *{and}* *The*
3836 1222 4015 1639 5302 5302 899 1666 1133 2887 1254 3836
pt.aa.npf cj d.npf

γυναῖκες, αἵτινες ἦσαν συνεληλυθυῖαι ἐκ τῆς Γαλιλαίας αὐτῷ, ἐθεάσαντο τὸ
women *who* *had* *come with* *from* *{the}* *Galilee* *him* and saw the
1222 4015 1639 5302 1666 3836 1133 899 2517 3836
n.npf r.npf v.iai.3p pt.ra.npf p.g d.gsf n.gsf r.dsm.3 v.ami.3p d.asn

μνημεῖον καὶ ὡς ἐτέθη τὸ σῶμα αὐτοῦ, [56] ↱ ὑποστρέψασαι
tomb, and how his body was laid in it *{the}* *body* *his* Then they returned
3646 2779 6055 899 5393 5502 3836 5393 899 1254 2286 5715
n.asn cj cj v.api.3s d.nsn n.nsn r.gsm.3 pt.aa.npf

δὲ ἡτοίμασαν ἀρώματα καὶ μύρα. καὶ ↱ τὸ μὲν σάββατον ἡσύχασαν
Then and prepared anointing spices and perfumes. *{and}* On the ~ Sabbath they rested
1254 2286 808 2779 3693 2779 4879 3836 3525 4879 2483
cj v.aai.3p n.apn cj n.apn cj d.asn pl n.asn v.aai.3p

κατὰ τὴν ἐντολήν.
˪according to˩ the commandment.
2848 3836 1953
p.a d.asf n.asf

24:1 τῇ δὲ μιᾷ τῶν σαββάτων → ὄρθρου βαθέως
But ˪on the˩ *But* first day of the week, at early dawn, *early* the women came
1254 3836 1254 1651 3836 4879 960 3986 960 2262
d.dsf cj a.dsf d.gpn n.gpn n.gsm a.gsm

ἐπὶ τὸ μνῆμα ἦλθον φέρουσαι ἃ ἡτοίμασαν ἀρώματα.
to the tomb, *came* bringing the anointing spices that they had prepared. *anointing spices*
2093 3836 3645 2262 5770 808 808 4005 2286 808
p.a d.asn n.asn v.aai.3p pt.pa.npf r.apn v.aai.3p n.apn

[2] εὗρον δὲ τὸν λίθον ἀποκεκυλισμένον ἀπὸ τοῦ μνημείου, [3] εἰσελθοῦσαι
They found *{and}* the stone rolled away from the tomb, and going inside
2351 1254 3836 3345 653 608 3836 3646 1254 1656
v.aai.3p cj d.asm n.asm pt.rp.asm p.g d.gsn n.gsn pt.aa.npf

δὲ ↱ ↱ οὐχ εὗρον τὸ σῶμα τοῦ κυρίου Ἰησοῦ. [4] καὶ ἐγένετο ἐν
and they did not find the body of the Lord Jesus. *{and}* ˪It happened that,˩ while
1254 2351 2351 4024 2351 3836 5393 3836 3261 2652 2779 1181 1877
cj pl v.aai.3p d.asn n.asn d.gsm n.gsm n.gsm cj v.ami.3s p.d

τῷ ἀπορεῖσθαι αὐτὰς περὶ τούτου καὶ ἰδοὺ ἄνδρες δύο ἐπέστησαν
{the} they were wondering *they* about this, *{and}* suddenly two men *two* stood beside
3836 899 679 899 4309 4047 2779 2627 1545 467 1545 2392
d.dsn f.pm r.apf.3 p.g r.gsn cj j n.npm a.npm v.aai.3p

[a] αὐτὸν omitted by TNIV.

NASB

[51](he had not con-
sented to their plan
and action), *a man*
from Arimathea,
a city of the Jews,
who was waiting
for the kingdom
of God; [52]this man
went to Pilate and
asked for the body
of Jesus. [53]And
he took it down
and wrapped it in
a linen cloth, and
laid Him in a tomb
cut into the rock,
where no one had
ever lain. [54]It was
the preparation day,
and the Sabbath
was about to begin.
[55]Now the women
who had come
with Him out of
Galilee followed,
and saw the tomb
and how His body
was laid. [56]Then
they returned and
prepared spices and
perfumes.
And on the Sab-
bath they rested
according to the
commandment.

The Resurrection

[24:1]But on the first
day of the week,
at early dawn,
they came to the
tomb bringing
the spices which
they had prepared.
[2]And they found
the stone rolled
away from the
tomb, [3]but when
they entered, they
did not find the
body of the Lord
Jesus. [4]While they
were perplexed
about this, behold,
two men suddenly
stood near

NIV

them. 5In their
fright the wom-
en bowed down
with their faces
to the ground, but
the men said to
them, “Why do
you look for the
living among the
dead? 6He is not
here; he has risen!
Remember how
he told you, while
he was still with
you in Galilee:
7‘The Son of Man
must be delivered
over to the hands
of sinners, be cru-
cified and on the
third day be raised
again.’ ” 8Then
they remembered
his words.
9When they came
back from the
tomb, they told all
these things to the
Eleven and to all
the others. 10It was
Mary Magdalene,
Joanna, Mary the
mother of James,
and the others with
them who told
this to the apos-
tles. 11But they
did not believe
the women, be-
cause their words
seemed to them
like nonsense.
12Peter, however,
got up and ran to
the tomb. Bending
over, he saw the
strips of linen ly-
ing by themselves,
and he went away,
wondering to him-
self what had hap-
pened.

On the Road to Emmaus

13Now that same
day two of them
were going to a
village called Em-
maus, about seven
miles[a] from Jeru-
salem. 14They were
talking with each
other about every-
thing that had hap-
pened. 15As

[a] 13 Or about 11 kilometers

αὐταῖς ἐν ἐσθῆτι ἀστραπτούσῃ. 5 ἐμφόβων δὲ
them dressed in dazzling attire. *dazzling* The women were frightened *{and}*
899 1877 848 2264 848 899 1181 1873 1254
r.dpf.3 p.d n.dsf pt.pa.dsf a.gpf cj

γενομένων αὐτῶν καὶ κλινουσῶν τὰ πρόσωπα εἰς τὴν γῆν εἶπαν πρὸς
were *women* and bowed their faces to the ground, but the men said to
1181 899 2779 3111 3836 4725 1650 3836 1178 3306 4639
pt.am.gpf r.gpf.3 cj pt.pa.gpf d.apn n.apn p.a d.asf n.asf v.aai.3p p.a

αὐτάς, τί ζητεῖτε τὸν ζῶντα μετὰ τῶν νεκρῶν; 6 οὐκ ἔστιν ὧδε,
them, “Why ⌊do you look for⌋ the living among the dead? He is not *He is* here,
899 5515 2426 3836 2409 3552 3836 3738 1639 1639 4024 1639 6045
r.apf.3 r.asn v.pai.2p d.asm pt.pa.asm p.g d.gpm a.gpm pl v.pai.3s adv

ἀλλὰ ἠγέρθη. μνήσθητε ὡς ἐλάλησεν ὑμῖν ἔτι ὢν
but ⌊he has been raised.⌋ Remember how he spoke to you, while he was still *while he was*
247 1586 3630 6055 3281 7007 1639 1639 1639 2285 1639
cj v.api.3s v.apm.2p cj v.aai.3s r.dp.2 adv pt.pa.nsm

ἐν τῇ Γαλιλαίᾳ 7 λέγων τὸν υἱὸν τοῦ ἀνθρώπου ὅτι
in *{the}* Galilee, saying that it was necessary for the Son of Man *that*
1877 3836 1133 3306 4022 1256 1256 1256 3836 5626 3836 476 4022
p.d d.dsf n.dsf pt.pa.nsm d.asm n.asm d.gsm n.gsm cj

δεῖ παραδοθῆναι εἰς χεῖρας → ἀνθρώπων ἁμαρτωλῶν καὶ
it was necessary to be delivered into the hands of sinful men *sinful* and
1256 4140 1650 5931 283 476 283 2779
v.pai.3s f.ap p.a n.apf n.gpm a.gpm cj

σταυρωθῆναι καὶ τῇ τρίτῃ ἡμέρᾳ ἀναστῆναι. 8 καὶ ἐμνήσθησαν τῶν
to be crucified and ⌊on the⌋ third day to rise again.” Then they remembered *{the}* his
5090 2779 3836 5569 2465 482 2779 3630 3836 899
f.ap cj d.dsf a.dsf n.dsf f.aa cj v.api.3p d.gpn

ῥημάτων αὐτοῦ. 9 καὶ ὑποστρέψασαι ἀπὸ τοῦ μνημείου ἀπήγγειλαν ταῦτα
words. *his* And returning from the tomb, they told all these things
4839 899 2779 5715 608 3836 3646 550 4246 4047
n.gpn r.gsm.3 cj pt.aa.npf p.g d.gsn n.gsn v.aai.3p r.apn

πάντα τοῖς ἕνδεκα καὶ πᾶσιν τοῖς λοιποῖς. 10 ἦσαν δὲ ἡ Μαγδαληνὴ
all to the eleven and to all the others. It was *{and}* *{the}* Mary Magdalene
4246 3836 1894 2779 4246 3836 3370 1639 1254 3836 3451 3402
a.apn d.dpm a.dpm cj a.dpm d.dpm a.dpm v.iai.3p cj d.nsf n.nsf

Μαρία καὶ Ἰωάννα καὶ Μαρία ἡ Ἰακώβου καὶ αἱ λοιπαὶ σὺν αὐταῖς.
Mary and Joanna and Mary the mother of James and the other women with them.
3451 2779 2721 2779 3451 3836 2610 2779 3836 3370 5250 899
n.nsf cj n.nsf cj n.nsf d.nsf n.gsm cj d.npf a.npf p.d r.dpf.3

ἔλεγον πρὸς τοὺς ἀποστόλους ταῦτα, 11 καὶ
⌊They kept telling⌋ these things to the apostles, *these things* but these words
3306 4047 4047 4639 3836 693 4047 2779 4047 4839
v.iai.3p p.a d.apm n.apm r.apn cj

ἐφάνησαν ἐνώπιον αὐτῶν ὡσεὶ λῆρος τὰ ῥήματα ταῦτα, καὶ
seemed like nonsense to them, *like* *nonsense* *{the}* *words* *these* and
5743 6059 3333 1967 899 6059 3333 3836 4839 4047 2779
v.api.3p p.g r.gpm.3 pl n.nsm d.npn n.npn r.npn cj

ἠπίστουν αὐταῖς. 13 καὶ ἰδοὺ δύο ἐξ αὐτῶν ἐν αὐτῇ
⌊they did not believe⌋ them. Now ~ on that same day two of them *on* *same*
601 899 2779 2627 1877 3836 899 2465 1545 1666 899 1877 899
v.iai.3p r.dpf.3 cj j a.npm p.g r.gpm.3 p.d r.dsf

τῇ ἡμέρᾳ ἦσαν πορευόμενοι εἰς κώμην ἀπέχουσαν ⌊σταδίους ἑξήκοντα⌋ ἀπὸ
that *day* were on their way to a village about seven miles from
3836 2465 1639 4513 1650 3267 600 5084 2008 608
d.dsf n.dsf v.iai.3p pt.pm.npm p.a n.asf pt.pa.asf n.apm a.apm p.g

Ἰερουσαλήμ, ᾗ ὄνομα Ἐμμαοῦς, 14 καὶ αὐτοὶ ὡμίλουν πρὸς ἀλλήλους
Jerusalem, Emmaus by name. *Emmaus* And they were talking with one another
2647 1843 4005 3950 1843 2779 899 3917 4639 253
n.gsf r.dsf n.nsn n.nsf cj r.npm v.iai.3p p.a r.apm

περὶ πάντων τῶν συμβεβηκότων τούτων. 15 καὶ ἐγένετο ἐν τῷ
about all these things that had taken place. *these things* *{and}* *it happened that* While ~
4309 4246 4047 4047 3836 5201 4047 2779 1181 1877 3836
p.g a.gpn d.gpn pt.ra.gpn r.gpn cj v.ami.3s p.d d.dsn

NASB

them in dazzling
clothing; 5and as
the women were
terrified and bowed
their faces to the
ground, *the men*
said to them, “Why
do you seek the
living One among
the dead? 6He is
not here, but He
has risen. Remem-
ber how He spoke
to you while He
was still in Galilee,
7saying that the
Son of Man must
be delivered into
the hands of sinful
men, and be cruci-
fied, and the third
day rise again.”
8And they remem-
bered His words,
9and returned
from the tomb and
reported all these
things to the eleven
and to all the rest.
10Now they were
Mary Magdalene
and Joanna and
Mary the *mother*
of James; also the
other women with
them were telling
these things to
the apostles. 11But
these words ap-
peared to them as
nonsense, and they
would not believe
them. 12But Peter
got up and ran to
the tomb; stooping
and looking in,
he *saw the linen
wrappings only;
and he went away
to his home, mar-
veling at what had
happened.

The Road to Emmaus

13And behold, two
of them were go-
ing that very day
to a village named
Emmaus, which
was [a]about seven
miles from Jeru-
salem. 14And they
were talking with
each other about
all these things
which had taken
place. 15While

[a] Lit *60 stadia;* one stadion was about 600 ft

NIV

they talked and
discussed these
things with each
other, Jesus him-
self came up and
walked along with
them; 16but they
were kept from
recognizing him.
17He asked them,
"What are you dis-
cussing together as
you walk along?"
They stood
still, their faces
downcast. 18One
of them, named
Cleopas, asked
him, "Are you the
only one visiting
Jerusalem who
does not know the
things that have
happened there in
these days?"
19"What things?"
he asked.
"About Jesus of
Nazareth," they
replied. "He was a
prophet, powerful
in word and deed
before God and all
the people. 20The
chief priests and
our rulers hand-
ed him over to be
sentenced to death,
and they crucified
him; 21but we had
hoped that he was
the one who was
going to redeem
Israel. And what
is more, it is the
third day since all
this took place.
22In addition, some
of our women
amazed us. They
went to the tomb
early this morning
23but didn't find
his body.

ὁμιλεῖν αὐτοὺς καὶ συζητεῖν καὶ αὐτὸς
they were talking *they* and debating these things, *and* it happened that Jesus himself
899 3917 899 2779 5184 2779 1181 1181 1181 2652 899
f.pa r.apm.3 cj f.pa cj r.nsm

Ἰησοῦς ἐγγίσας συνεπορεύετο αὐτοῖς, 16 οἱ δὲ ὀφθαλμοὶ αὐτῶν
Jesus drew near and walked along with them, *{the}* but their eyes *their*
2652 1581 2779 5233 899 3836 1254 899 4057 899
n.nsm pt.aa.nsm v.imi.3s r.dpm.3 d.npm cj n.npm r.gpm.3

ἐκρατοῦντο τοῦ μὴ ἐπιγνῶναι αὐτόν. 17 εἶπεν δὲ πρὸς αὐτούς, τίνες οἱ
were kept from ~ *{not}* recognizing him. He said *{and}* to them, "What are *{the}*
3195 3836 3590 2105 899 3306 1254 4639 899 5515 3836
v.ipi.3p d.gsn pl f.aa r.asm.3 v.aai.3s cj p.a r.apm.3 r.npm d.npm

λόγοι οὗτοι οὓς ἀντιβάλλετε πρὸς ἀλλήλους περιπατοῦντες; καὶ
these matters *these* that you are discussing with each other as you walk along?" *{and}*
4047 3364 4047 4005 506 4639 253 4344 2779
n.npm r.npm r.apm v.pai.2p p.a r.apm pt.pa.npm cj

ἐστάθησαν σκυθρωποί. 18 ἀποκριθεὶς δὲ εἷς
⌞They came to a stop,⌟ looking sad. Then one of them, named Cleopas, answered, *Then* *one*
2705 5034 1254 1651 3950 3093 646 1254 1651
v.api.3p a.npm pt.ap.nsm cj a.nsm

ὀνόματι Κλεοπᾶς εἶπεν πρὸς αὐτόν, ↱ σὺ μόνος παροικεῖς Ἰερουσαλὴμ καὶ
named *Cleopas* saying to him, "Are you the only visitor to Jerusalem *{and}*
3950 3093 3306 4639 899 4228 5148 3668 4228 2647 2779
n.dsn n.nsm v.aai.3s p.a r.asm.3 r.ns.2 a.nsm v.pai.2s n.asf cj

↱ ↱ οὐκ ἔγνως τὰ γενόμενα ⌞ἐν αὐτῇ⌟ ἐν ταῖς ἡμέραις
who does not know the things that have happened there in *{the}* these days?"
1182 1182 4024 1182 3836 1181 1877 899 1877 3836 4047 2465
pl v.aai.2s d.apn pt.am.apn p.d r.dsf.3 p.d d.dpf n.dpf

ταύταις; 19 καὶ εἶπεν αὐτοῖς, ποῖα; οἱ δὲ εἶπαν αὐτῷ, τὰ περὶ
these And he said to them, ⌞"What things?"⌟ They *{and}* answered him, "The things about
4047 2779 3306 899 4481 3836 1254 3306 899 3836 4309
r.dpf cj v.aai.3s r.dpm.3 r.apn d.npm cj v.aai.3p r.dsm.3 d.apn p.g

Ἰησοῦ τοῦ Ναζαρηνοῦ, ὃς ἐγένετο ἀνὴρ προφήτης δυνατὸς ἐν ἔργῳ καὶ
Jesus of Nazareth, a man who was *man* a prophet mighty in deed and
2652 3836 3716 467 4005 1181 467 4737 1543 1877 2240 2779
n.gsm d.gsm n.gsm r.nsm v.ami.3s n.nsm n.nsm a.nsm p.d n.dsn cj

λόγῳ ἐναντίον τοῦ θεοῦ καὶ παντὸς τοῦ λαοῦ, 20 ὅπως τε
word before *{the}* God and all the people, that ~ our chief priests and rulers
3364 1883 3836 2536 2779 4246 3836 3295 3968 5445 7005 797 797 2779 807
n.dsm p.g d.gsm n.gsm cj a.gsm d.gsm n.gsm cj cj

παρέδωκαν αὐτὸν ↰ οἱ ἀρχιερεῖς καὶ οἱ ἄρχοντες ἡμῶν εἰς κρίμα
delivered him up *{the}* *chief priests* *and* *{the}* *rulers* *our* to be condemned
4140 899 4140 3836 797 2779 3836 807 7005 1650 3210
v.aai.3p r.asm.3 d.npm n.npm cj d.npm n.npm r.gp.1 p.a n.asn

θανάτου καὶ ἐσταύρωσαν αὐτόν. 21 ἡμεῖς δὲ ἠλπίζομεν ὅτι αὐτός ἐστιν ὁ
to death and crucified him. But we *But* had hoped that he was the
2505 2779 5090 899 1254 7005 1254 1827 4022 899 1639 3836
n.gsm cj v.aai.3p r.asm.3 r.np.1 cj v.iai.1p cj r.nsm v.pai.3s d.nsm

μέλλων λυτροῦσθαι τὸν Ἰσραήλ· ἀλλά ⌞γε καὶ⌟ σὺν πᾶσιν τούτοις
⌞one who was going⌟ to redeem *{the}* Israel. *but* Indeed, besides all this,
3516 3390 3836 2702 247 1145 2779 5250 4246 4047
pt.pa.nsm f.pm d.asm n.asm cj pl adv p.d a.dpn r.dpn

τρίτην ταύτην ἡμέραν ἄγει ⌞ἀφ' οὗ⌟ ταῦτα ἐγένετο.
but it is now the third *now* day *it is* since these things happened.
247 72 72 4047 5569 4047 2465 72 608 4005 4047 1181
a.asf r.asf n.asf v.pai.3s p.g r.gsm r.npn v.ami.3s

22 ⌞ἀλλὰ καὶ⌟ γυναῖκές τινες ἐξ ἡμῶν ἐξέστησαν ἡμᾶς, γενόμεναι
Moreover, some women *some* of our group astonished us: going to
247 2779 5516 1222 5516 1666 7005 2014 7005 1181 2093
cj adv n.npf r.npf p.g r.gp.1 v.aai.3p r.ap.1 pt.am.npf

ὀρθριναὶ ἐπὶ τὸ μνημεῖον, 23 καὶ μὴ εὑροῦσαι τὸ σῶμα
the tomb ⌞early in the morning⌟ *to* *the* *tomb* and not finding *{the}* his body,
3836 3646 3984 2093 3836 3646 2779 3590 2351 3836 899 5393
a.npf p.a d.asn n.asn cj pl pt.aa.npf d.asn n.asn

NASB

they were talking
and discussing,
Jesus Himself
approached and
began traveling
with them. 16But
their eyes were
prevented from
recognizing Him.
17And He said to
them, "What are
these words that
you are exchanging
with one another
as you are walk-
ing?" And they
stood still, looking
sad. 18One *of them,*
named Cleopas,
answered and said
to Him, "Are You
the only one visit-
ing Jerusalem and
unaware of the
things which have
happened here in
these days?" 19And
He said to them,
"What things?"
And they said to
Him, "The things
about Jesus the
Nazarene, who was
a prophet mighty
in deed and word
in the sight of God
and all the people,
20and how the chief
priests and our rul-
ers delivered Him
to the sentence of
death, and crucified
Him. 21But we were
hoping that it was
He who was going
to redeem Israel.
Indeed, besides all
this, it is the third
day since these
things happened.
22But also some
women among us
amazed us. When
they were at the
tomb early in the
morning, 23and did
not find His body,

NIV

They came and
told us that they
had seen a vision
of angels, who
said he was alive.
24 Then some of our
companions went
to the tomb and
found it just as the
women had said,
but they did not
see Jesus."
25 He said to them,
"How foolish you
are, and how slow
to believe all that
the prophets have
spoken! 26 Did not
the Messiah have
to suffer these
things and then
enter his glory?"
27 And beginning
with Moses and all
the Prophets, he
explained to them
what was said in
all the Scriptures
concerning him-
self.
28 As they ap-
proached the vil-
lage to which they
were going, Jesus
continued on as
if he were going
farther. 29 But they
urged him strong-
ly, "Stay with us,
for it is nearly
evening; the day
is almost over." So
he went in to stay
with them.
30 When he
was at the table
with them, he
took bread, gave
thanks, broke it
and began to give
it to them. 31 Then
their eyes were
opened and they
recognized him,
and he

αὐτοῦ ἦλθον λέγουσαι καὶ ὀπτασίαν ἀγγέλων ἑωρακέναι,
his they came back saying that they had even seen a vision of angels *they had seen*
899 2262 3306 3972 3972 2779 3972 3965 34 3972
r.gsm.3 v.aai.3p pt.pa.npf adv n.asf n.gpm f.ra

οἳ λέγουσιν αὐτὸν ζῆν. 24 καὶ ἀπῆλθόν
who said that he ⌞was alive.⌟ Then some of those who were with us went
4005 3306 899 2409 2779 5516 3836 3836 5250 7005 599
r.npm v.pai.3p r.asm.3 f.pa cj v.aai.3p

τινες τῶν σὺν ἡμῖν ἐπὶ τὸ μνημεῖον καὶ εὗρον οὕτως καθὼς καὶ αἱ γυναῖκες
some of those with us to the tomb, and found it just as *{also}* the women
5516 3836 5250 7005 2093 3836 3646 2779 2351 4048 2777 2779 3836 1222
r.npm d.gpm p.d r.dp.1 p.a d.asn n.asn cj v.aai.3p adv cj adv d.npf n.npf

εἶπον, αὐτὸν δὲ ↱ ↱ οὐκ εἶδον. 25 καὶ αὐτὸς εἶπεν πρὸς αὐτούς, ὦ
had said, but him *but* they did not see." So he said to them, "You
3306 1254 899 1254 1625 1625 4024 1625 2779 899 3306 4639 899 6043
v.aai.3p r.asm.3 cj pl v.aai.3p cj r.nsm v.aai.3s p.a r.apm.3 j

ἀνόητοι καὶ βραδεῖς τῇ καρδίᾳ τοῦ πιστεύειν ἐπὶ πᾶσιν οἷς
foolish people, *{and}* slow of heart to believe in all that the prophets
485 2779 1096 3836 2840 3836 4409 2093 4246 4005 3836 4737
a.vpm cj a.vpm d.dsf n.dsf d.gsn f.pa p.d a.dpn r.dpn

ἐλάλησαν οἱ προφῆται· 26 οὐχὶ
have spoken! *the prophets* Was it not necessary for the Messiah to suffer
3281 3836 4737 1256 1256 4049 1256 3836 5986 4248 4248
v.aai.3p d.npm n.npm pl

ταῦτα ἔδει παθεῖν τὸν χριστὸν καὶ εἰσελθεῖν εἰς τὴν δόξαν αὐτοῦ;
these things *Was it necessary to suffer the Messiah* and enter into *{the}* his glory?" *his*
4047 1256 4248 3836 5986 2779 1656 1650 3836 899 1518 899
r.apn v.iai.3s f.aa d.asm n.asm cj f.aa p.a d.asf n.asf r.gsm.3

27 καὶ ἀρξάμενος ἀπὸ Μωϋσέως καὶ ἀπὸ πάντων τῶν προφητῶν διερμήνευσεν
Then, beginning with Moses and *{from}* all the Prophets, he interpreted
2779 806 608 3707 2779 608 4246 3836 4737 1450
cj pt.am.nsm p.g n.gsm cj p.g a.gpm d.gpm n.gpm v.aai.3s

αὐτοῖς ἐν πάσαις ταῖς γραφαῖς τὰ περὶ ἑαυτοῦ.
to them the things written about himself in all the Scriptures. *the about himself*
899 3836 4309 1571 1877 4246 3836 1210 3836 4309 1571
r.dpm.3 p.d a.dpf d.dpf n.dpf d.apn p.g r.gsm.3

28 καὶ ἤγγισαν εἰς τὴν κώμην οὗ ἐπορεύοντο, καὶ αὐτὸς
When ⌞they drew near⌟ to the village ⌞to which⌟ they were going, *{and}* he
2779 1581 1650 3836 3267 4023 4513 2779 899
cj v.aai.3p p.a d.asf n.asf adv v.imi.3p cj r.nsm

προσεποιήσατο πορρώτερον πορεύεσθαι. 29 καὶ παρεβιάσαντο αὐτὸν
made as though he was going farther, *he was going* but they urged him
4701 4513 4513 4513 4522 4513 2779 4128 899
v.ami.3s adv.c f.pm cj v.ami.3p r.asm.3

↰ λέγοντες, μεῖνον μεθ᾽ ἡμῶν, ὅτι πρὸς ἑσπέραν ἐστὶν καὶ →
strongly, saying, "Stay with us, for it is toward evening *it is* and the day is
4128 3306 3531 3552 7005 4022 1639 1639 4639 2270 1639 2779 3836 2465
pt.pa.npm v.aam.2s p.g r.gp.1 cj p.a n.asf v.pai.3s cj

→ κέκλικεν ἤδη ἡ ἡμέρα. καὶ εἰσῆλθεν τοῦ μεῖναι σὺν αὐτοῖς. 30 καὶ
already far spent." *already the day* So he went in to stay with them. *{and}*
2453 3111 2453 3836 2465 2779 1656 3836 3531 5250 899 2779
v.rai.3s adv d.nsf n.nsf cj v.aai.3s d.gsn f.aa p.d r.dpm.3 cj

ἐγένετο ἐν τῷ κατακλιθῆναι αὐτὸν μετ᾽ αὐτῶν ↱ λαβὼν τὸν
{it happened that} When ~ he ⌞was reclining at the table⌟ *he* with them, he took the
1181 1877 3836 899 2884 899 3552 899 2328 3284 3836
v.ami.3s p.d d.dsn f.ap r.asm.3 p.g r.gpm.3 pt.aa.nsm d.asm

ἄρτον εὐλόγησεν καὶ κλάσας ἐπεδίδου αὐτοῖς, 31 αὐτῶν
bread, blessed and broke it, and gave it to them. At this point their
788 2328 2779 3089 2113 899 1254 1254 1254 899
n.asm v.aai.3s cj pt.aa.nsm v.iai.3s r.dpm.3 r.gpm.3

δὲ διηνοίχθησαν οἱ ὀφθαλμοὶ καὶ ἐπέγνωσαν αὐτόν· καὶ αὐτὸς
At this point eyes were opened, *{the} eyes* and they recognized him. Then he
1254 4057 1380 3836 4057 2779 2105 899 2779 899
cj v.api.3p d.npm n.npm cj v.aai.3p r.asm.3 cj r.nsm

NASB

they came, saying
that they had also
seen a vision of
angels who said
that He was alive.
24 Some of those
who were with us
went to the tomb
and found it just
exactly as the
women also had
said; but Him they
did not see." 25 And
He said to them,
"O foolish men
and slow of heart
to believe in all
that the prophets
have spoken! 26 Was
it not necessary
for the Christ to
suffer these things
and to enter into
His glory?" 27 Then
beginning with
Moses and with all
the prophets, He
explained to them
the things concern-
ing Himself in all
the Scriptures.
28 And they ap-
proached the vil-
lage where they
were going, and
He acted as though
He were going
farther. 29 But they
urged Him, saying,
"Stay with us, for
it is *getting* toward
evening, and the
day is now nearly
over." So He went
in to stay with
them. 30 When He
had reclined *at the
table* with them,
He took the bread
and blessed *it,* and
breaking *it,* He
began giving *it* to
them. 31 Then their
eyes were opened
and they recog-
nized Him;

NIV

disappeared from their sight. 32 They asked each other, "Were not our hearts burning within us while he talked with us on the road and opened the Scriptures to us?"

33 They got up and returned at once to Jerusalem. There they found the Eleven and those with them, assembled together 34 and saying, "It is true! The Lord has risen and has appeared to Simon." 35 Then the two told what had happened on the way, and how Jesus was recognized by them when he broke the bread.

Jesus Appears to the Disciples

36 While they were still talking about this, Jesus himself stood among them and said to them, "Peace be with you."

37 They were startled and frightened, thinking they saw a ghost. 38 He said to them, "Why are you troubled, and why do doubts rise in your minds? 39 Look at my hands and my feet. It is I myself! Touch me and see; a ghost does not have flesh and bones, as you see I have."

40 When he had said this, he showed them his hands and feet. 41 And while they still did not believe it because of joy and amazement,

⌞ἄφαντος ἐγένετο⌟ ἀπ' αὐτῶν. ↰ 32 καὶ εἶπαν πρὸς ἀλλήλους, οὐχὶ ἡ
vanished from their sight. {and} They said to each other, "Were not {the}
908 1181 608 899 908 2779 3306 4639 253 1639 4049 3836
a.nsm v.ami.3s p.g r.gpm.3 cj v.aai.3p p.a r.apm pl d.nsf

καρδία ἡμῶν καιομένη ἦν [a]ἐν ἡμῖν ὡς ἐλάλει ἡμῖν ἐν τῇ ὁδῷ, ὡς
our hearts our burning Were within us as he spoke to us on the road, as
7005 2840 7005 2794 1639 1877 7005 6055 3281 7005 1877 3836 3847 6055
n.nsf r.gp.1 pt.pp.nsf v.iai.3s p.d r.dp.1 cj v.iai.3s r.dp.1 p.d d.dsf n.dsf cj

διήνοιγεν ἡμῖν τὰς γραφάς; 33 Καὶ ἀναστάντες αὐτῇ τῇ ὥρᾳ ὑπέστρεψαν
he opened to us the Scriptures?" So they got up that very that hour and returned
1380 7005 3836 1210 2779 482 3836 899 3836 6052 5715
v.iai.3s r.dp.1 d.apf n.apf cj pt.aa.npm r.dsf d.dsf n.dsf v.aai.3p

εἰς Ἰερουσαλὴμ καὶ εὗρον ἠθροισμένους
to Jerusalem, {and} where they found the eleven and those with them gathered together,
1650 2647 2779 2351 3836 1894 2779 3836 5250 899 125
p.a n.asf cj v.aai.3p pt.rp.apm

τοὺς ἕνδεκα καὶ τοὺς σὺν αὐτοῖς, 34 λέγοντας ὅτι ↱ ὄντως ἠγέρθη ὁ
the eleven and those with them saying, ~ "The Lord has indeed been raised The
3836 1894 2779 3836 5250 899 3306 4022 3836 3261 1586 3953 1586 3836
d.apm a.apm cj d.apm p.d r.dpm.3 pt.pa.apm cj adv v.api.3s d.nsm

κύριος καὶ ὤφθη Σίμωνι. 35 καὶ αὐτοὶ ἐξηγοῦντο τὰ ἐν τῇ
Lord and has appeared to Simon!" Then the two explained what had happened on the
3261 2779 3972 4981 2779 899 2007 3836 1877 3836
n.nsm cj v.api.3s n.dsm cj r.npm v.imi.3p d.apn p.d d.dsf

ὁδῷ καὶ ὡς ἐγνώσθη αὐτοῖς ἐν τῇ κλάσει τοῦ ἄρτου. 36
road, and how Jesus ⌞had been made known⌟ to them in the breaking of the bread. While
3847 2779 6055 1182 899 1877 3836 3082 3836 788 3281
n.dsf cj cj v.api.3s r.dpm.3 p.d d.dsf n.dsf d.gsm n.gsm

ταῦτα δὲ αὐτῶν λαλούντων αὐτὸς ἔστη ἐν μέσῳ
they were saying these things, {and} they While were saying Jesus himself stood in their midst
899 3281 3281 4047 1254 899 3281 899 2705 1877 899 3545
r.apn cj r.gpm.3 pt.pa.gpm r.nsm v.aai.3s p.d n.dsn

αὐτῶν καὶ λέγει αὐτοῖς, εἰρήνη ὑμῖν. 37 πτοηθέντες δὲ καὶ ἔμφοβοι
their and said to them, "Peace to you." But they were startled But and frightened,
899 2779 3306 899 1645 7007 1254 1181 1181 4765 1254 2779 1873
r.gpm.3 cj v.pai.3s r.dpm.3 n.nsf r.dp.2 pt.ap.npm cj cj a.npm

γενόμενοι ἐδόκουν πνεῦμα θεωρεῖν. 38 καὶ εἶπεν αὐτοῖς,
they were and thought they were seeing a ghost. they were seeing And he said to them,
1181 1506 2555 2555 2555 4460 2555 2779 3306 899
pt.am.npm v.iai.3p n.asn f.pa cj v.aai.3s r.dpm.3

τί τεταραγμένοι ἐστὲ καὶ ⌞διὰ τί⌟ ↱ διαλογισμοὶ ἀναβαίνουσιν ἐν
"Why are you so troubled are you and why are doubts arising in
5515 1639 1639 5429 1639 2779 1328 5515 326 1369 326 1877
r.asn pt.rp.npm v.pai.2p cj p.a r.asn n.npm v.pai.3p p.d

τῇ καρδίᾳ ὑμῶν; 39 ἴδετε τὰς χεῖράς μου καὶ τοὺς πόδας μου ὅτι
{the} your hearts? your ⌞Look at⌟ {the} my hands my and {the} my feet, my that
3836 7007 2840 7007 1625 3836 1609 5931 1609 2779 3836 1609 4546 1609 4022
d.dsf n.dsf r.gp.2 v.aam.2p d.apf n.apf r.gs.1 cj d.apm n.apm r.gs.1 cj

ἐγώ εἰμι αὐτός· ψηλαφήσατέ με καὶ ἴδετε, ὅτι πνεῦμα
it is I it is myself. Touch me and see, for a ghost does not have
1639 1639 1609 1639 899 6027 1609 2779 1625 4022 4460 2400 4024 2400
r.ns.1 v.pai.1s r.nsm v.aam.2p r.as.1 cj v.aam.2p cj n.nsn

σάρκα καὶ ὀστέα οὐκ ἔχει καθὼς ἐμὲ θεωρεῖτε ἔχοντα. 41 ↱
flesh and bones not does have as you see that I you see have." While they
4922 2779 4014 4024 2400 2777 2555 2555 1609 2555 2400 601 899
n.asf cj n.apn pl v.pai.3s cj r.as.1 v.pai.2p pt.pa.asm

ἔτι δὲ ἀπιστούντων αὐτῶν ἀπὸ τῆς χαρᾶς καὶ θαυμαζόντων εἶπεν
still {and} could not believe they it for {the} joy and ⌞were continuing to marvel,⌟ he said
2285 1254 601 899 608 3836 5915 2779 2513 3306
adv cj pt.pa.gpm r.gpm.3 p.g d.gsf n.gsf cj pt.pa.gpm v.aai.3s

NASB

and He vanished from their sight. 32 They said to one another, "Were not our hearts burning within us while He was speaking to us on the road, while He was explaining the Scriptures to us?" 33 And they got up that very hour and returned to Jerusalem, and found gathered together the eleven and those who were with them, 34 saying, "The Lord has really risen and has appeared to Simon." 35 They *began* to relate their experiences on the road and how He was recognized by them in the breaking of the bread.

Other Appearances

36 While they were telling these things, He Himself stood in their midst and *said to them, "Peace be to you." 37 But they were startled and frightened and thought that they were seeing a spirit. 38 And He said to them, "Why are you troubled, and why do doubts arise in your hearts? 39 See My hands and My feet, that it is I Myself; touch Me and see, for a spirit does not have flesh and bones as you see that I have." 40 And when He had said this, He showed them His hands and His feet. 41 While they still could not believe *it* because of their joy and amazement, He said to them,

[a] [ἐν ἡμῖν] UBS, omitted by NET.

NIV

he asked them,
"Do you have any-
thing here to eat?"
[42]They gave him
a piece of broiled
fish, [43]and he took
it and ate it in their
presence.
[44]He said to them,
"This is what I
told you while I
was still with you:
Everything must
be fulfilled that is
written about me
in the Law of Mo-
ses, the Prophets
and the Psalms."
[45]Then he opened
their minds so they
could understand
the Scriptures.
[46]He told them,
"This is what is
written: The Mes-
siah will suffer
and rise from the
dead on the third
day, [47]and repen-
tance for the for-
giveness of sins
will be preached in
his name to all na-
tions, beginning at
Jerusalem. [48]You
are witnesses of
these things. [49]I
am going to send
you what my Fa-
ther has promised;
but stay in the city
until you have
been clothed with
power from on
high."

The Ascension of Jesus

[50]When he had
led them out to the
vicinity of Betha-
ny, he lifted up his
hands and blessed
them. [51]While he
was blessing them,
he left them and

αὐτοῖς, ἔχετέ τι βρώσιμον ἐνθάδε; 42 οἱ δὲ ἐπέδωκαν αὐτῷ
to them, ⌊"Have you⌋ anything to eat here?" They {and} gave him a piece of
899 2400 5516 1110 1924 3836 1254 2113 899 3538 3966
r.dpm.3 v.pai.2p r.asn n.asn adv d.npm cj v.aai.3p r.dsm.3

ἰχθύος ὀπτοῦ μέρος·[a] 43 καὶ λαβὼν ἐνώπιον αὐτῶν ↰
broiled fish, of broiled piece and he took it and ate in their presence.
3966 2716 3966 3538 2779 2266 3284 2266 1967 899 1967
n.gsm a.gsm n.asn cj pt.aa.nsm p.g r.gpm.3

ἔφαγεν. 44 εἶπεν δὲ πρὸς αὐτούς, οὗτοι οἱ λόγοι μου οὓς ἐλάλησα
he ate Then he said Then to them, "These are {the} my words my which I spoke
2266 1254 3306 1254 4639 899 4047 3836 1609 3364 1609 4005 3281
v.aai.3s v.aai.3s cj p.a r.apm.3 r.npm d.npm n.npm r.gs.1 r.apm v.aai.1s

πρὸς ὑμᾶς ἔτι ὢν σὺν ὑμῖν, ὅτι δεῖ πληρωθῆναι πάντα τὰ
to you while I was still while I was with you, that must be fulfilled everything {the}
4639 7007 1639 1639 1639 2285 1639 5250 7007 4022 1256 4444 4246 3836
p.a r.ap.2 adv pt.pa.nsm p.d r.dp.2 cj v.pai.3s f.ap a.apn d.apn

γεγραμμένα ἐν τῷ νόμῳ Μωϋσέως καὶ τοῖς προφήταις καὶ ψαλμοῖς περὶ ἐμοῦ.
written in the law of Moses and the prophets and psalms about me
1211 1877 3836 3795 3707 2779 3836 4737 2779 6011 4309 1609
pt.rp.apn p.d d.dsm n.dsm n.gsm cj d.dpm n.dpm cj n.dpm p.g r.gs.1

45 τότε διήνοιξεν αὐτῶν τὸν νοῦν τοῦ συνιέναι τὰς
must be fulfilled." Then he opened their {the} minds so ⌊they could understand⌋ the
1256 4444 4444 5538 1380 899 3836 3808 3836 5317 3836
adv v.aai.3s r.gpm.3 d.asm n.asm d.gsn f.pa d.apf

γραφάς· 46 καὶ εἶπεν αὐτοῖς ὅτι οὕτως γέγραπται παθεῖν τὸν
scriptures, and said to them, ~ "Thus it is written, that the Messiah is to suffer the
1210 2779 3306 899 4022 4048 1211 3836 5986 4248 3836
n.apf cj v.aai.3s r.dpm.3 cj adv v.rpi.3s f.aa d.asm

χριστὸν καὶ ἀναστῆναι ἐκ νεκρῶν τῇ τρίτῃ ἡμέρᾳ, 47 καὶ
Messiah and to rise from the dead ⌊on the⌋ third day, and that repentance and
5986 2779 482 1666 3738 3836 5569 2465 2779 3567
n.asm cj f.aa p.g a.gpm d.dsf a.dsf n.dsf cj

κηρυχθῆναι ἐπὶ τῷ ὀνόματι αὐτοῦ μετάνοιαν εἰς
forgiveness of sins is to be proclaimed in {the} his name his repentance {for}
912 281 281 3062 2093 3836 899 3950 899 3567 1650
f.ap p.d d.dsn n.dsn r.gsm.3 n.asf p.a

ἄφεσιν ἁμαρτιῶν εἰς πάντα τὰ ἔθνη. ἀρξάμενοι ἀπὸ Ἰερουσαλὴμ 48 ὑμεῖς
forgiveness of sins to all the nations, beginning from Jerusalem. You are
912 281 1650 4246 3836 1620 806 608 2647 7007
n.asf n.gpf p.a a.apn d.apn n.apn pt.am.npm p.g n.gsf r.np.2

μάρτυρες τούτων. 49 καὶ ἰδοὺ[b] ἐγὼ ἀποστέλλω τὴν ἐπαγγελίαν τοῦ πατρός
witnesses of these things. And behold, I am sending the promise of my Father
3459 4047 2779 2627 1609 690 3836 2039 3836 1609 4252
n.npm r.gpn cj j r.ns.1 v.pai.1s d.asf n.asf d.gsm n.gsm

μου ἐφ' ὑμᾶς· ὑμεῖς δὲ καθίσατε ἐν τῇ πόλει ⌊ἕως οὗ⌋ ἐνδύσησθε
my upon you, {you} but stay in the city until ⌊you have been clothed⌋ with
1609 2093 7007 7007 1254 2767 1877 3836 4484 2401 4005 1907 1539
r.gs.1 p.a r.ap.2 r.np.2 cj v.aam.2p p.d d.dsf n.dsf p.g r.gsm v.ams.2p

ἐξ ὕψους δύναμιν. 50 ἐξήγαγεν δὲ αὐτοὺς ἔξω[c] ἕως πρὸς
power from on high." with power Then he led Then them out ⌊as far as⌋ {to}
1539 1666 5737 1539 1254 1974 1254 899 2032 2401 4639
p.g n.gsn n.asf v.aai.3s cj r.apm.3 adv p.g p.a

Βηθανίαν, καὶ ἐπάρας τὰς χεῖρας αὐτοῦ εὐλόγησεν αὐτούς. 51 καὶ
Bethany, and lifting up {the} his hands his he blessed them. {and}
1029 2779 2048 3836 899 5931 899 2328 899 2779
n.asf cj pt.aa.nsm d.apf n.apf r.gsm.3 v.aai.3s r.apm.3 cj

ἐγένετο ἐν τῷ εὐλογεῖν αὐτὸν αὐτοὺς διέστη ἀπ' αὐτῶν καὶ
{it happened that} While {the} he was blessing he them, he departed from them and
1181 1877 3836 899 2328 899 899 1460 608 899 2779
v.ami.3s p.d d.dsn f.pa r.asm.3 r.apm.3 v.aai.3s p.g r.gpm.3 cj

NASB

"Have you any-
thing here to eat?"
[42]They gave Him a
piece of a broiled
fish; [43]and He took
it and ate *it* before
them.
[44]Now He said to
them, "These are
My words which I
spoke to you while
I was still with
you, that all things
which are written
about Me in the
Law of Moses
and the Prophets
and the Psalms
must be fulfilled."
[45]Then He opened
their minds to
understand the
Scriptures, [46]and
He said to them,
"Thus it is writ-
ten, that the Christ
would suffer and
rise again from the
dead the third day,
[47]and that repen-
tance for forgive-
ness of sins would
be proclaimed in
His name to all the
nations, beginning
from Jerusalem.
[48]You are witnesses
of these things.
[49]And behold, I
am sending forth
the promise of My
Father upon you;
but you are to stay
in the city until you
are clothed with
power from on
high."

The Ascension

[50]And He led
them out as far as
Bethany, and He
lifted up His hands
and blessed them.
[51]While He was
blessing them, He
parted from them

[a] καὶ ἀπὸ μελισσίου κηρίου included by TR after μέρος.
[b] [ἰδοὺ] UBS, omitted by TNIV.
[c] [ἔξω] UBS, omitted by TNIV.

NIV

was taken up into
heaven. [52]Then
they worshiped
him and returned
to Jerusalem with
great joy. [53]And
they stayed contin-
ually at the temple,
praising God.

ἀνεφέρετο	εἰς	τὸν	οὐρανόν.	52 καὶ	αὐτοὶ	προσκυνήσαντες	αὐτὸν		ὑπέστρεψαν
⌞was carried up⌟	into	*{the}*	heaven.	And	they	worshiped	him	and	returned
429	1650	3836	4041	2779	899	4686	899		5715
v.ipi.3s	p.a	d.asm	n.asm	cj	r.npm	pt.aa.npm	r.asm.3		v.aai.3p

εἰς	Ἰερουσαλὴμ	μετὰ		χαρᾶς	μεγάλης	53 καὶ	ἦσαν	⌞διὰ	παντὸς⌟	ἐν	τῷ
to	Jerusalem	with	great	joy,	*great*	and	they were	continually		in	the
1650	2647	3552	3489	5915	3489	2779	1639	1328	4246	1877	3836
p.a	n.asf	p.g		n.gsf	a.gsf	cj	v.iai.3p	p.g	a.gsm	p.d	d.dsn

ἱερῷ	εὐλογοῦντες	τὸν	θεόν.
temple	blessing	*{the}*	God.
2639	2328	3836	2536
n.dsn	pt.pa.npm	d.asm	n.asm

NASB

and was carried up
into heaven. [52]And
they, after worship-
ing Him, returned
to Jerusalem with
great joy, [53]and
were continually in
the temple praising
God.

John

NIV

The Word Became Flesh

1 In the begin-
ning was the
Word, and the
Word was with
God, and the
Word was God.
2He was with God
in the beginning.
3Through him all
things were made;
without him noth-
ing was made that
has been made.
4In him was life,
and that life was
the light of all
mankind. 5The
light shines in the
darkness, and the
darkness has not
overcome[a] it.
6There was a man
sent from God
whose name was
John. 7He came as
a witness to tes-
tify concerning
that light, so that
through him all
might believe. 8He
himself was not
the light; he came
only as a witness
to the light.
9The true light
that gives light
to everyone was
coming into the
world. 10He was
in the world, and
though the world
was made through
him, the world
did not recognize
him. 11He came to
that which was his
own, but his own
did not receive
him. 12Yet to all
who did receive
him, to those who
believed in his
name, he gave the
right

[a] 5 Or *understood*

1:1 ἐν ἀρχῇ ἦν ὁ λόγος, καὶ ὁ λόγος ἦν πρὸς τὸν θεόν, καὶ

In the beginning was the Word, and the Word was with *{the}* God, and

1877 794 1639 3836 3364 2779 3836 3364 1639 4639 3836 2536 2779

p.d n.dsf v.iai.3s d.nsm n.nsm cj d.nsm n.nsm v.iai.3s p.a d.asm n.asm cj

θεὸς ἦν ὁ λόγος. 2οὗτος ἦν ἐν ἀρχῇ πρὸς τὸν θεόν.

the Word was God. *was the Word* He was in the beginning with *{the}* God.

3836 3364 1639 2536 1639 3836 3364 4047 1639 1877 794 4639 3836 2536

n.nsm v.iai.3s d.nsm n.nsm r.nsm v.iai.3s p.d n.dsf p.a d.asm n.asm

3πάντα δι᾽ αὐτοῦ ἐγένετο, καὶ χωρὶς αὐτοῦ

All things were created by him, *were created* and apart from him not a single thing

4246 1181 1181 1328 899 1181 2779 6006 899 4028 1651 1651

a.npn p.g r.gsm.3 v.ami.3s cj p.g r.gsm.3

ἐγένετο οὐδὲ ἕν. ὃ γέγονεν 4ἐν αὐτῷ ζωὴ ἦν, καὶ ἡ ζωὴ

was created *not single thing* that ⌞has been created.⌟ In him was life, *was* and that life

1181 4028 1651 4005 1181 1877 899 1639 2437 1639 2779 3836 2437

v.ami.3s adv a.nsn r.nsn v.rai.3s p.d r.dsm.3 n.nsf v.iai.3s cj d.nsf n.nsf

ἦν τὸ φῶς τῶν ἀνθρώπων· 5καὶ τὸ φῶς ἐν τῇ σκοτίᾳ φαίνει, καὶ

was the light of men. *{and}* The light shines on in the darkness, *shines on* and

1639 3836 5890 3836 476 2779 3836 5890 5743 5743 1877 3836 5028 5743 2779

v.iai.3s d.nsn n.nsn d.gpm n.gpm cj d.nsn n.nsn p.d d.dsf n.dsf v.pai.3s cj

ἡ σκοτία αὐτὸ οὐ κατέλαβεν. 6ἐγένετο

the darkness has not understood it. *not has understood* ⌞There came on the scene⌟ a

3836 5028 2898 4024 2898 899 4024 2898 1181

d.nsf n.nsf r.asn.3 pl v.aai.3s v.ami.3s

ἄνθρωπος, ἀπεσταλμένος παρὰ θεοῦ, ὄνομα αὐτῷ Ἰωάννης· 7οὗτος ἦλθεν

man sent from God, whose name *whose* was John. He came

476 690 4123 2536 899 3950 899 2722 4047 2262

n.nsm pt.rp.nsm p.g n.gsm n.nsn r.dsm.3 n.nsm r.nsm v.aai.3s

εἰς μαρτυρίαν ἵνα μαρτυρήσῃ περὶ τοῦ φωτός, ἵνα πάντες πιστεύσωσιν δι᾽

as a witness to bear testimony about the light so that everyone might believe through

1650 3456 2671 3455 4309 3836 5890 2671 4246 4409 1328

p.a n.asf cj v.aas.3s p.g d.gsn n.gsn cj a.npm v.aas.3p p.g

αὐτοῦ. 8 οὐκ ἦν ἐκεῖνος τὸ φῶς, ἀλλ᾽ ἵνα μαρτυρήσῃ περὶ τοῦ

him. He was not *was He* the light, but came to bear testimony about the

899 1697 1639 4024 1639 1697 3836 5890 247 2671 3455 4309 3836

r.gsm.3 pl v.iai.3s r.nsm d.nsn n.nsn cj cj v.aas.3s p.g d.gsn

φωτός. 9ἦν τὸ φῶς τὸ ἀληθινόν, ὃ φωτίζει ⌞πάντα ἄνθρωπον,⌟

light. *was* The true light, *{the} true* which enlightens everyone, was

5890 1639 3836 240 5890 3836 240 4005 5894 4246 476 1639

n.gsn v.iai.3s d.nsn n.nsn d.nsn a.nsn r.nsn v.pai.3s a.asm n.asm

ἐρχόμενον εἰς τὸν κόσμον. 10 ἐν τῷ κόσμῳ ἦν, καὶ ὁ κόσμος

coming into the world. He was in the world, *He was* and the world was

2262 1650 3836 3180 1639 1639 1877 3836 3180 1639 2779 3836 3180 1181

pt.pm.asm p.a d.asm n.asm p.d d.dsm n.dsm v.iai.3s cj d.nsm n.nsm

δι᾽ αὐτοῦ ἐγένετο, καὶ ὁ κόσμος αὐτὸν οὐκ ἔγνω. 11

created by him, *was created* but the world did not know him. *not did know* He

1181 1328 899 1181 2779 3836 3180 1182 4024 1182 899 4024 1182 2262

p.g r.gsm.3 v.ami.3s cj d.nsm n.nsm r.asm.3 pl v.aai.3s

εἰς τὰ ἴδια ἦλθεν, καὶ οἱ ἴδιοι αὐτὸν οὐ

came to ⌞that which⌟ was his own, *He came* but his ⌞own people⌟ did not accept him. *not*

2262 1650 3836 2625 2262 2779 3836 2625 4161 4024 4161 899 4024

p.a d.apn a.apn v.aai.3s cj d.npm a.npm r.asm.3 pl

παρέλαβον. 12 ὅσοι δὲ ἔλαβον αὐτόν, ἔδωκεν αὐτοῖς ἐξουσίαν

did accept But ⌞as many as⌟ *But* did accept him, to them he gave *to them* the right

4161 1254 4012 1254 3284 899 899 899 1443 899 2026

v.aai.3p r.npm cj v.aai.3p r.asm.3 v.aai.3s r.dpm.3 n.asf

NASB

The Deity of Jesus Christ

1:1In the beginning
was the Word, and
the Word was with
God, and the Word
was God. 2He was
in the beginning
with God. 3All
things came into
being through Him,
and apart from
Him nothing came
into being that has
come into being.
4In Him was life,
and the life was the
Light of men. 5The
Light shines in the
darkness, and the
darkness did not
[a]comprehend it.

The Witness John

6There [b]came a
man sent from
God, whose name
was John. 7He
came as a witness,
to testify about
the Light, so that
all might believe
through him. 8He
was not the Light,
but *he came* to
testify about the
Light.
9There was the
true Light [c]which,
coming into the
world, enlightens
every man. 10He
was in the world,
and the world was
made through Him,
and the world did
not know Him.
11He came to His
[d]own, and those
who were His own
did not receive
Him. 12But as many
as received Him, to
them He gave the

[a] Or *overpower*
[b] Or *came into being*
[c] Or *which enlightens every person coming into the world*
[d] Or *own things, possessions, domain*

NIV

to become children
of God— 13chil-
dren born not of
natural descent, nor
of human decision
or a husband's will,
but born of God.
14The Word be-
came flesh and
made his dwelling
among us. We
have seen his glo-
ry, the glory of the
one and only Son,
who came from
the Father, full of
grace and truth.
15(John testified
concerning him.
He cried out, say-
ing, "This is the
one I spoke about
when I said, 'He
who comes after
me has surpassed
me because he was
before me.'") 16Out
of his fullness we
have all received
grace in place of
grace already giv-
en. 17For the law
was given through
Moses; grace and
truth came through
Jesus Christ. 18No
one has ever seen
God, but the one
and only Son, who
is himself God
and[a] is in closest
relationship with
the Father, has
made him known.

John the Baptist Denies Being the Messiah

19Now this was
John's testimony
when the Jewish
leaders[b] in Jeru-
salem sent priests
and Levites to ask
him who he was.
20He did not fail
to confess, but
confessed freely,

[a] 18 Some manuscripts *but the only Son, who*
[b] 19 The Greek term traditionally translated *the Jews* (*hoi Ioudaioi*) refers here and elsewhere in John's Gospel to those Jewish leaders who opposed Jesus; also in 5:10, 15, 16; 7:1, 11, 13; 9:22; 18:14, 28, 36; 19:7, 12, 31, 38; 20:19.

τέκνα θεοῦ γενέσθαι, τοῖς πιστεύουσιν εἰς τὸ ὄνομα αὐτοῦ,
to become children of God, *to become* to those who believe in *{the}* his name, *his*
1181 1181 5451 2536 1181 3836 4409 1650 3836 899 3950 899
n.apn n.gsm f.am d.dpm pt.pa.dpm p.a d.asn n.asn r.gsm.3

13 οἳ οὐκ ἐξ αἱμάτων οὐδὲ ἐκ θελήματος σαρκὸς οὐδὲ ἐκ
who were born, not from human stock or from a physical impulse *physical* or by a
4005 1164 1164 4024 1666 135 4028 1666 4922 2525 4922 4028 1666
r.npm pl p.g n.gpn cj p.g n.gsn n.gsf cj p.g

θελήματος ἀνδρὸς ἀλλ᾽ ἐκ θεοῦ ἐγεννήθησαν. 14 καὶ ὁ λόγος
husband's decision, *husband's* but by God. *were born* And the Word became
467 2525 467 247 1666 2536 1164 2779 3836 3364 1181
n.gsn n.gsm cj p.g n.gsm v.api.3p cj d.nsm n.nsm

σὰρξ ἐγένετο καὶ ἐσκήνωσεν ἐν ἡμῖν, καὶ ἐθεασάμεθα τὴν δόξαν αὐτοῦ, δόξαν
flesh *became* and dwelt among us, and we gazed on *{the}* his glory, *his* glory
4922 1181 2779 5012 1877 7005 2779 2517 3836 899 1518 899 1518
n.nsf v.ami.3s cj v.aai.3s p.d r.dp.1 cj v.ami.1p d.asf n.asf r.gsm.3 n.asf

ὡς → μονογενοῦς παρὰ πατρός, πλήρης → χάριτος καὶ ἀληθείας. 15 Ἰωάννης
as of the only Son from the Father, full of grace and truth. John
6055 3666 4123 4252 4441 5921 2779 237 2722
pl a.gsm p.g n.gsm a.gsm n.gsf cj n.gsf n.nsm

μαρτυρεῖ περὶ αὐτοῦ καὶ κέκραγεν λέγων, οὗτος ἦν ὃν εἶπον, ὁ
testified about him and cried out, saying, "This ⌊is he⌋ ⌊of whom⌋ I said, 'He who
3455 4309 899 2779 3189 3306 4047 1639 4005 3306 3836 2262
v.pai.3s p.g r.gsm.3 cj v.rai.3s pt.pa.nsm r.nsm v.iai.3s r.asm v.aai.1s d.nsm

ὀπίσω μου ἐρχόμενος ἔμπροσθέν μου γέγονεν, ὅτι πρῶτός
comes after me *who comes* is greater ⌊than I,⌋ *is* because he existed before
2262 3958 1609 2262 1181 1869 1609 1181 4022 1639 1639 4755
p.g r.gs.1 pt.pm.nsm p.g r.gs.1 v.rai.3s cj a.nsm

μου ἦν. 16 ὅτι ἐκ τοῦ πληρώματος αὐτοῦ ἡμεῖς ↱ πάντες ἐλάβομεν καὶ
me.'" *he existed* For from *{the}* his fulness *his* we have all received *{and}*
1609 1639 4022 1666 3836 899 4445 899 7005 3284 4246 3284 2779
r.gs.1 v.iai.3s cj p.g d.gsn n.gsn r.gsm.3 r.np.1 a.npm v.aai.1p cj

χάριν ἀντὶ χάριτος· 17 ὅτι ὁ νόμος διὰ Μωϋσέως ἐδόθη,
⌊one gracious gift⌋ after another. For the law was given through Moses; *was given*
5921 505 5921 4022 3836 3795 1443 1443 1328 3707 1443
n.asf p.g n.gsf cj d.nsm n.nsm p.g n.gsm v.api.3s

ἡ χάρις καὶ ἡ ἀλήθεια διὰ Ἰησοῦ Χριστοῦ ἐγένετο. 18
{the} grace and *{the}* truth came through Jesus Christ. *came* No one has ever
3836 5921 2779 3836 237 1181 1328 2652 5986 1181 4029 4029 3972 4799
d.nsf n.nsf cj d.nsf n.nsf p.g n.gsm n.gsm v.ami.3s

θεὸν οὐδεὶς ἑώρακεν πώποτε· μονογενὴς θεὸς[a] ὁ ὢν εἰς τὸν
seen God. *No one* *has seen* *ever* The only Son, himself God, the ⌊one who is⌋ in the
3972 2536 4029 3972 4799 3666 2536 3836 1639 1650 3836
n.asm a.nsm v.rai.3s adv a.nsm n.nsm d.nsm pt.pa.nsm p.a d.asm

κόλπον τοῦ πατρὸς ἐκεῖνος → → ἐξηγήσατο. 19 καὶ αὕτη ἐστὶν ἡ μαρτυρία
bosom of the Father, he has made him known. And this is the testimony
3146 3836 4252 1697 2007 2779 4047 1639 3836 3456
n.asm d.gsm n.gsm r.nsm v.ami.3s cj r.nsf v.pai.3s d.nsf n.nsf

τοῦ Ἰωάννου, ὅτε ἀπέστειλαν [b]πρὸς αὐτὸν οἱ
of John, when the Jews sent priests and Levites to him *the*
3836 2722 4021 3836 2681 690 2636 2779 3324 4639 899 3836
d.gsm n.gsm cj v.aai.3p p.a r.asm.3 d.npm

Ἰουδαῖοι ἐξ Ἱεροσολύμων ἱερεῖς καὶ Λευίτας ἵνα ἐρωτήσωσιν αὐτόν·
Jews from Jerusalem *priests* *and* *Levites* to ask him, "Who are
2681 1666 2642 2636 2779 3324 2671 2263 899 5515 1639
a.npm p.g n.gpn n.apm cj n.apm cj v.aas.3p r.asm.3

σὺ τίς εἶ; 20 καὶ ὡμολόγησεν καὶ ↱ οὐκ ἠρνήσατο, καὶ ὡμολόγησεν ὅτι ἐγώ
you?" *Who* *are* *{and}* He confessed and did not deny, but confessed, ~ "I
5148 5515 1639 2779 3933 2779 766 4024 766 2779 3933 4022 1609
r.ns.2 r.nsm v.pai.2s cj v.aai.3s cj pl v.ami.3s cj v.aai.3s cj r.ns.1

NASB

right to become
children of God,
even to those who
believe in His
name, 13who were
born, not of blood
nor of the will of
the flesh nor of the
will of man, but of
God.

The Word Made Flesh

14And the Word
became flesh, and
dwelt among us,
and we saw His
glory, glory as of
the only begotten
from the Father,
full of grace and
truth. 15John *testi-
fied about Him and
cried out, saying,
"This was He of
whom I said, 'He
who comes after
me has a higher
rank than I, for
He existed before
me.'" 16For of His
fullness we have
all received, and
grace upon grace.
17For the Law was
given through
Moses; grace and
truth were real-
ized through Jesus
Christ. 18No one
has seen God at
any time; the only
begotten God who
is in the bosom of
the Father, He has
explained *Him*.

The Testimony of John

19This is the tes-
timony of John,
when the Jews sent
to him priests and
Levites from Jeru-
salem to ask him,
"Who are you?"
20And he confessed
and did not deny,
but confessed, "I

[a] μονογενὴς υἱός included by TR after θεὸς.
[b] [πρὸς αὐτὸν] UBS, omitted by NET.

NIV

"I am not the Mes-
siah."
21 They asked
him, "Then who
are you? Are you
Elijah?"
He said, "I am
not."
"Are you the
Prophet?"
He an-
swered, "No."
22 Finally they
said, "Who are
you? Give us an
answer to take
back to those who
sent us. What do
you say about
yourself?"
23 John replied in
the words of Isa-
iah the prophet,
"I am the voice of
one calling in the
wilderness, 'Make
straight the way
for the Lord.' "[a]
24 Now the Phari-
sees who had been
sent 25 questioned
him, "Why then do
you baptize if you
are not the Messi-
ah, nor Elijah, nor
the Prophet?"
26 "I baptize with[b]
water," John re-
plied, "but among
you stands one you
do not know. 27 He
is the one who
comes after me,
the straps of whose
sandals I am not
worthy to untie."
28 This all hap-
pened at Bethany
on the other side of
the Jordan, where
John was baptiz-
ing.

John Testifies About Jesus

29 The next day
John saw Jesus
coming toward
him and said,
"Look, the Lamb
of God, who takes
away the sin

[a] 23 Isaiah 40:3
[b] 26 Or *in*; also in verses 31 and 33 (twice)

οὐκ εἰμὶ ὁ χριστός. 21 καὶ ἠρώτησαν αὐτόν, τί οὖν; σὺ
am not *am* the Christ." So they asked him, "Then who *Then* are you? Are you
1639 4024 1639 3836 5986 2779 2263 899 4036 5515 4036 5148 1639 1639
pl v.pai.1s d.nsm n.nsm cj v.aai.3p r.asm.3 r.nsn cj r.ns.2

Ἠλίας εἶ; καὶ λέγει, οὐκ εἰμί. ὁ προφήτης εἶ σύ; καὶ
Elijah?" *Are you* And he said, "I am not." *I am* "Are you the Prophet?" *Are* *you* And
2460 1639 2779 3306 1639 1639 4024 1639 1639 5148 3836 4737 1639 5148 2779
n.nsm v.pai.2s cj v.pai.3s pl v.pai.1s d.nsm n.nsm v.pai.2s r.ns.2 cj

ἀπεκρίθη, οὔ. 22 εἶπαν οὖν αὐτῷ, τίς εἶ; ἵνα
he replied, "No." Then they said *Then* to him, "Who ⌊are you?⌋ Tell us so we can give an
646 4024 4036 3306 4036 899 5515 1639 2671 1443 1443 1443
v.api.3s pl v.aai.3p cj r.dsm.3 r.nsm v.pai.2s cj

ἀπόκρισιν δῶμεν τοῖς πέμψασιν ἡμᾶς· τί λέγεις περὶ σεαυτοῦ; 23 ἔφη,
answer *we can give* to those who sent us. What ⌊do you say⌋ about yourself?" He said,
647 1443 3836 4287 7005 5515 3306 4309 4932 5774
n.asf v.aas.1p d.dpm pt.aa.dpm r.ap.1 r.asn v.pai.2s p.g r.gsm.2 v.iai.3s

ἐγὼ φωνὴ βοῶντος ἐν τῇ ἐρήμῳ, εὐθύνατε τὴν ὁδὸν →
"I am the voice ⌊of one crying out⌋ in the wilderness, 'Make straight the way for the
1609 5889 1066 1877 3836 2245 2316 3836 3847
r.ns.1 n.nsf pt.pa.gsm p.d d.dsf n.dsf v.aam.2p d.asf n.asf

κυρίου, καθὼς εἶπεν Ἠσαΐας ὁ προφήτης. 24 καὶ → →
Lord,' as Isaiah the prophet said." *Isaiah* *the* *prophet* Now those who had
3261 2777 2480 3836 4737 3306 2480 3836 4737 2779 1639
n.gsm cj v.aai.3s n.nsm d.nsm n.nsm cj

ἀπεσταλμένοι ἦσαν ἐκ τῶν Φαρισαίων. 25 καὶ ἠρώτησαν αὐτὸν
been sent out *had been* ⌊included some⌋ *{the}* Pharisees. So they asked him,
1639 690 1639 1666 3836 5757 2779 2263 899
pt.rp.npm v.iai.3p p.g d.gpm n.gpm cj v.aai.3p r.asm.3

καὶ εἶπαν αὐτῷ, τί οὖν βαπτίζεις εἰ σὺ οὐκ εἶ ὁ χριστὸς
{and} saying, *{to him}* "Why then are you baptizing, if you are not *are* the Christ,
2779 3306 899 5515 4036 966 1623 5148 1639 4024 1639 3836 5986
cj v.aai.3p r.dsm.3 r.asn cj v.pai.2s cj r.ns.2 pl v.pai.2s d.nsm n.nsm

οὐδὲ Ἠλίας οὐδὲ ὁ προφήτης; 26 ἀπεκρίθη αὐτοῖς ὁ Ἰωάννης λέγων, ἐγὼ
nor Elijah, nor the Prophet?" John answered them, *{the}* *John* saying, "I
4028 2460 4028 3836 4737 2722 646 899 3836 2722 3306 1609
cj n.nsm cj d.nsm n.nsm v.api.3s r.dpm.3 d.nsm n.nsm pt.pa.nsm r.ns.1

βαπτίζω ἐν ὕδατι· μέσος ὑμῶν ἕστηκεν ὃν ὑμεῖς ↱ οὐκ
baptize with water, but there stands among you *there stands* ⌊one whom⌋ you do not
966 1877 5623 5112 5112 3545 7007 5112 4005 7007 3857 4024
v.pai.1s p.d n.dsn a.nsm r.gp.2 v.rai.3s r.asm r.np.2 pl

οἴδατε, 27 ὁ ὀπίσω μου ἐρχόμενος, οὗ οὐκ εἰμὶ ἐγὼ[a]
know, the one coming after me; *one coming* *{of whom}* I am not *am* *I*
3857 3836 2262 2262 3958 1609 2262 4005 1609 1639 4024 1639 1609
v.rai.2p d.nsm p.g r.gs.1 pt.pm.nsm r.gsm pl v.pai.1s r.ns.1

ἄξιος ἵνα λύσω αὐτοῦ τὸν ἱμάντα τοῦ ὑποδήματος. 28 ταῦτα
worthy to untie the thong of his *the* *thong* *of* sandals." This took
545 2671 3395 3836 2666 3836 899 3836 2666 3836 5687 4047 1181
a.nsm cj v.aas.1s r.gsm.3 d.asm n.asm d.gsn n.gsn r.npn

ἐν Βηθανίᾳ ἐγένετο → πέραν τοῦ Ἰορδάνου, ὅπου ἦν ὁ
place in Bethany *took place* on the far side of the Jordan where John was *{the}*
1181 1877 1029 1181 4305 3836 2674 3963 2722 1639 3836
p.d n.dsf v.ami.3s p.g d.gsm n.gsm cj v.iai.3s d.nsm

Ἰωάννης βαπτίζων. 29 τῇ ἐπαύριον βλέπει τὸν Ἰησοῦν ἐρχόμενον πρὸς
John baptizing. ⌊On the⌋ following day John saw *{the}* Jesus coming toward
2722 966 3836 2069 1063 3836 2652 2262 4639
n.nsm pt.pa.nsm d.dsf adv v.pai.3s d.asm n.asm pt.pm.asm p.a

αὐτὸν καὶ λέγει, ἴδε ὁ ἀμνὸς τοῦ θεοῦ ὁ αἴρων τὴν ἁμαρτίαν
him and said, "Behold, the Lamb of God, the ⌊one who takes away⌋ the sin
899 2779 3306 2623 3836 303 3836 2536 3836 149 3836 281
r.asm.3 cj v.pai.3s pl d.nsm n.nsm d.gsm n.gsm d.nsm pt.pa.nsm d.asf n.asf

[a] [ἐγὼ] UBS.

NASB

am not the Christ."
21 They asked him,
"What then? Are
you Elijah?" And
he *said, "I am
not." "Are you the
Prophet?" And he
answered, "No."
22 Then they said to
him, "Who are you,
so that we may
give an answer to
those who sent us?
What do you say
about yourself?"
23 He said, "I am A
VOICE OF ONE CRYING
IN THE WILDERNESS,
'MAKE STRAIGHT
THE WAY OF THE
LORD,' as Isaiah the
prophet said."
24 Now they had
been sent from the
Pharisees. 25 They
asked him, and said
to him, "Why then
are you baptizing,
if you are not the
Christ, nor Elijah,
nor the Prophet?"
26 John answered
them saying, "I
baptize [a]in water,
but among you
stands One whom
you do not know.
27 *It is* He who
comes after me,
the thong of whose
sandal I am not
worthy to untie."
28 These things took
place in Bethany
beyond the Jordan,
where John was
baptizing.
29 The next day he
*saw Jesus coming
to him and *said,
"Behold, the Lamb
of God who takes
away the sin of the

[a] The Gr here can be translated *in, with* or *by*

NIV

of the world!
30 This is the one I
meant when I said,
‘A man who comes
after me has sur-
passed me because
he was before me.’
31 I myself did not
know him, but the
reason I came bap-
tizing with water
was that he might
be revealed to Is-
rael.”
32 Then John gave
this testimony:
“I saw the Spirit
come down from
heaven as a dove
and remain on
him. 33 And I my-
self did not know
him, but the one
who sent me to
baptize with water
told me, ‘The man
on whom you see
the Spirit come
down and remain
is the one who
will baptize with
the Holy Spirit.’
34 I have seen and
I testify that this
is God’s Chosen
One.”[a]

John’s Disciples Follow Jesus

35 The next day
John was there
again with two
of his disciples.
36 When he saw
Jesus passing by,
he said, “Look, the
Lamb of God!”
37 When the two
disciples heard
him say this, they
followed Jesus.
38 Turning around,
Jesus saw them
following and
asked, “What do
you want?”
They said,
“Rabbi” (which
means “Teacher”),

[a] 34 See Isaiah 42:1; many manuscripts *is the Son of God.*

τοῦ κόσμου. 30 οὗτός ἐστιν ὑπὲρ οὗ ἐγὼ εἶπον, ὀπίσω μου ἔρχεται ἀνὴρ ὃς
of the world! This is he of whom I said, ‘After me comes a man who
3836 3180 4047 1639 5642 4005 1609 3306 3958 1609 2262 467 4005
d.gsm n.gsm r.nsm v.pai.3s p.g r.gsm r.ns.1 v.aai.1s p.g r.gs.1 v.pmi.3s n.nsm r.nsm

ἔμπροσθέν μου γέγονεν, ὅτι πρῶτός μου ἦν. 31 κἀγὼ ↱
is greater ⌊than I,⌋ *is* because he existed before me.’ *he existed* I myself did
1181 1869 1609 1181 4022 1639 1639 4755 1609 1639 2743 3857
p.g r.gs.1 v.rai.3s cj a.nsm r.gs.1 v.iai.3s crasis

οὐκ ᾔδειν αὐτόν, ἀλλ’ ἵνα
not know him; but I came baptizing with water for this reason, that
4024 3857 899 247 1609 2262 966 1877 5623 1328 4047 4047 2671
adv v.lai.1s r.asm.3 cj cj

φανερωθῇ τῷ Ἰσραὴλ διὰ τοῦτο ἦλθον ἐγὼ ἐν ὕδατι βαπτίζων. 32 καὶ
⌊he might be revealed⌋ to Israel.” *for this reason came I with water baptizing* Then
5746 3836 2702 1328 4047 2262 1609 1877 5623 966 2779
v.aps.3s d.dsm n.dsm p.a r.asn v.aai.1s r.ns.1 p.d n.dsn pt.pa.nsm cj

ἐμαρτύρησεν Ἰωάννης λέγων ὅτι τεθέαμαι τὸ πνεῦμα καταβαῖνον ὡς
John testified, *John* saying, ~ “I saw the Spirit coming down as a
2722 3455 2722 3306 4022 2517 3836 4460 2849 6055
v.aai.3s n.nsm pt.pa.nsm cj v.rmi.1s d.asn n.asn pt.pa.asn pl

περιστερὰν ἐξ οὐρανοῦ καὶ ἔμεινεν ἐπ’ αὐτόν. 33 κἀγὼ ↱ οὐκ ᾔδειν αὐτόν,
dove from heaven, and it remained on him. I myself did not know him,
4361 1666 4041 2779 3531 2093 899 2743 3857 4024 3857 899
n.asf p.g n.gsm cj v.aai.3s p.a r.asm.3 crasis adv v.lai.1s r.asm.3

ἀλλ’ ὁ πέμψας με βαπτίζειν ἐν ὕδατι ἐκεῖνός μοι εἶπεν, ἐφ’
but the ⌊one who sent⌋ me to baptize with water *{that one}* said to me, *said* ‘The one on
247 3836 4287 1609 966 1877 5623 1697 3306 1609 3306 2093
cj d.nsm pt.aa.nsm r.as.1 f.pa p.d n.dsn r.nsm r.ds.1 v.aai.3s p.a

ὃν ἂν ἴδῃς τὸ πνεῦμα καταβαῖνον καὶ μένον ἐπ’ αὐτόν, οὗτός
whom ~ you see the Spirit descending and remaining on him, it is he
4005 323 1625 3836 4460 2849 2779 3531 2093 899 1639 1639 4047
r.asm pl v.aas.2s d.asn n.asn pt.pa.asn cj pt.pa.asn p.a r.asm.3 r.nsm

ἐστιν ὁ βαπτίζων ἐν πνεύματι ἁγίῳ. 34 κἀγὼ ἑώρακα καὶ
it is who will baptize with the Holy Spirit.’ *Holy* I myself saw it, and
1639 3836 966 1877 41 4460 41 2743 3972 2779
v.pai.3s d.nsm pt.pa.nsm p.d n.dsn a.dsn crasis v.rai.1s cj

μεμαρτύρηκα ὅτι οὗτός ἐστιν ὁ ἐκλεκτὸς[a] τοῦ θεοῦ. 35 τῇ
I bear witness that this man is the Son of God.” Again, ⌊on the⌋
3455 4022 4047 1639 3836 1723 3836 2536 4099 3836
v.rai.1s cj r.nsm v.pai.3s d.nsm n.nsm d.gsm n.gsm d.dsf

ἐπαύριον πάλιν εἱστήκει ὁ Ἰωάννης καὶ ἐκ τῶν μαθητῶν
following day, *Again* John was standing *{the}* *John* there with two of *{the}* his disciples.
2069 4099 2722 2705 3836 2722 2779 1545 1666 3836 899 3412
adv adv v.lai.3s d.nsm n.nsm cj p.g d.gpm n.gpm

αὐτοῦ δύο 36 καὶ ἐμβλέψας τῷ Ἰησοῦ περιπατοῦντι λέγει, ἴδε
his *two* *{and}* ⌊Looking intently at⌋ *{the}* Jesus as he walked about, John said, “Behold,
899 1545 2779 1838 3836 2652 4344 3306 2623
r.gsm.3 a.npm cj pt.aa.nsm d.dsm n.dsm pt.pa.dsm v.pai.3s pl

ὁ ἀμνὸς τοῦ θεοῦ. 37 καὶ ἤκουσαν οἱ δύο μαθηταὶ αὐτοῦ
the Lamb of God!” *{and}* The two disciples heard *The two disciples* him
3836 303 3836 2536 2779 3836 1545 3412 201 3836 1545 3412 899
d.nsm n.nsm d.gsm n.gsm cj v.aai.3p d.npm a.npm n.npm r.gsm.3

λαλοῦντος καὶ ἠκολούθησαν τῷ Ἰησοῦ. 38 → στραφεὶς δὲ ὁ
say this, and they followed *{the}* Jesus. When Jesus turned around *{and}* *{the}*
3281 2779 199 3836 2652 2652 5138 1254 3836
pt.pa.gsm cj v.aai.3p d.dsm n.dsm pt.ap.nsm cj d.nsm

Ἰησοῦς καὶ θεασάμενος αὐτοὺς ἀκολουθοῦντας λέγει αὐτοῖς, τί ζητεῖτε;
Jesus and saw them following him, he said to them, “What do you want?”
2652 2779 2517 899 199 3306 899 5515 2426
n.nsm cj pt.am.nsm r.apm.3 pt.pa.apm v.pai.3s r.dpm.3 r.asn v.pai.2p

οἱ δὲ εἶπαν αὐτῷ, ῥαββί, ὃ λέγεται μεθερμηνευόμενον διδάσκαλε,
They *{and}* said to him, “Rabbi” (which translated means *translated* “Teacher”),
3836 1254 3306 899 4806 4005 3493 3306 3493 1437
d.npm cj v.aai.3p r.dsm.3 n.vsm r.nsn v.ppi.3s pt.pp.nsn n.vsm

[a] ἐκλεκτὸς TNIV, NET. υἱός UBS.

NASB

world! 30 This is He
on behalf of whom
I said, ‘After me
comes a Man who
has a higher rank
than I, for He ex-
isted before me.’ 31 I
did not recognize
Him, but so that
He might be mani-
fested to Israel,
I came baptizing
[a]in water.” 32 John
testified saying, “I
have seen the Spirit
descending as a
dove out of heaven,
and He remained
upon Him. 33 I did
not recognize Him,
but He who sent
me to baptize [b]in
water said to me,
‘He upon whom
you see the Spirit
descending and re-
maining upon Him,
this is the One
who baptizes in
the Holy Spirit.’ 34 I
myself have seen,
and have testified
that this is the Son
of God.”

Jesus’ Public Ministry, First Converts

35 Again the next
day John was
standing with two
of his disciples,
36 and he looked
at Jesus as He
walked, and *said,
“Behold, the Lamb
of God!” 37 The two
disciples heard him
speak, and they
followed Jesus.
38 And Jesus turned
and saw them fol-
lowing, and *said
to them, “What
do you seek?”
They said to Him,
“Rabbi (which
translated means
Teacher), where

[a] The Gr here can be translated *in, with* or *by*

[b] The Gr here can be translated *in, with* or *by*

NIV

"where are you
staying?"
39"Come," he
replied, "and you
will see."
So they went and
saw where he was
staying, and they
spent that day with
him. It was about
four in the after-
noon.
40Andrew, Simon
Peter's brother,
was one of the two
who heard what
John had said and
who had followed
Jesus. 41The first
thing Andrew did
was to find his
brother Simon
and tell him, "We
have found the
Messiah" (that is,
the Christ). 42And
he brought him to
Jesus.
Jesus looked at
him and said, "You
are Simon son of
John. You will be
called Cephas"
(which, when
translated, is Pe-
ter[a]).

Jesus Calls Philip and Nathanael

43The next day
Jesus decided to
leave for Galilee.
Finding Philip, he
said to him, "Fol-
low me."
44Philip, like
Andrew and Pe-
ter, was from the
town of Bethsaida.
45Philip found Na-
thanael and told
him, "We have
found the one Mo-
ses wrote about in
the Law, and about
whom the prophets
also wrote—Jesus
of Nazareth, the
son of Joseph."
46"Nazareth! Can
anything good
come from there?"
Nathanael asked.

[a] 42 *Cephas* (Aramaic) and *Peter* (Greek) both mean *rock.*

ποῦ μένεις; 39 λέγει αὐτοῖς, ἔρχεσθε καὶ ὄψεσθε. ἦλθαν οὖν
"where ⌞are you staying?"⌟ He said to them, "Come and ⌞you will see."⌟ So they went *So*
4543 3531 3306 899 2262 2779 3972 4036 2262 4036
cj v.pai.2s v.pai.3s r.dpm.3 v.pmm.2p cj v.fmi.2p v.aai.3p cj

καὶ εἶδαν ποῦ μένει καὶ παρ' αὐτῷ ἔμειναν τὴν
and saw where ⌞he was staying,⌟ and they remained with him *they remained* *{the}* that
2779 1625 4543 3531 2779 3531 3531 4123 899 3531 3836 1697
cj v.aai.3p cj v.pai.3s cj p.d r.dsm.3 v.aai.3p d.asf

ἡμέραν ἐκείνην· ὥρα ἦν ὡς δεκάτη. 40 ἦν Ἀνδρέας
day, *that* for it was about the tenth hour. *it was* *about* *tenth* *was* Andrew,
2465 1697 1639 1639 6055 1281 6052 1639 6055 1281 1639 436
n.asf r.asf n.nsf v.iai.3s pl a.nsf v.iai.3s n.nsm

ὁ ἀδελφὸς Σίμωνος Πέτρου εἷς ἐκ τῶν δύο τῶν ἀκουσάντων παρὰ
the brother of Simon Peter, was one of the two disciples who heard *{from}*
3836 81 4981 4377 1639 1651 1666 3836 1545 3836 201 4123
d.nsm n.nsm n.gsm n.gsm a.nsm p.g d.gpm a.gpm d.gpm pt.aa.gpm p.g

Ἰωάννου καὶ ἀκολουθησάντων αὐτῷ· 41 εὑρίσκει οὗτος
John and followed Jesus. The first thing he ⌞did was to find⌟ *he*
2722 2779 199 899 4754 4754 4047 2351 4047
n.gsm cj pt.aa.gpm r.dsm.3 v.pai.3s r.nsm

πρῶτον τὸν ἀδελφὸν τὸν ἴδιον Σίμωνα καὶ λέγει αὐτῷ, εὑρήκαμεν τὸν
first thing *{the}* his own brother *{the}* *his own* Simon and say to him, "We have found the
4754 3836 2625 2625 81 3836 2625 4981 2779 3306 899 2351 3836
adv d.asm n.asm d.asm a.asm n.asm cj v.pai.3s r.dsm.3 v.rai.1p d.asm

Μεσσίαν, ὅ ἐστιν μεθερμηνευόμενον χριστός. 42 ἤγαγεν αὐτὸν πρὸς τὸν
Messiah!" (which is translated "Christ"). He brought him to *{the}*
3549 4005 1639 3493 5986 72 899 4639 3836
n.asm r.nsn v.pai.3s pt.pp.nsn n.nsm v.aai.3s r.asm.3 p.a d.asm

Ἰησοῦν. ἐμβλέψας αὐτῷ ὁ Ἰησοῦς ↰ εἶπεν, σὺ εἶ Σίμων ὁ
Jesus. Jesus looked at him *{the}* *Jesus* intently and said, "You are Simon, the
2652 2652 1838 899 3836 2652 1838 3306 5148 1639 4981 3836
n.asm pt.aa.nsm r.dsm.3 d.nsm n.nsm v.aai.3s r.ns.2 v.pai.2s n.nsm d.nsm

υἱὸς Ἰωάννου, σὺ κληθήσῃ Κηφᾶς, ὃ ἑρμηνεύεται Πέτρος. 43 τῇ ἐπαύριον
son of John; you will be called Cephas" (which is translated "Peter"). The following day
5626 2722 5148 2813 3064 4005 2257 4377 3836 2069
n.nsm n.gsm r.ns.2 v.fpi.2s n.nsm r.nsn v.ppi.3s n.nsm d.dsf adv

ἠθέλησεν ἐξελθεῖν εἰς τὴν Γαλιλαίαν καὶ εὑρίσκει Φίλιππον. καὶ λέγει
Jesus decided to go to *{the}* Galilee, and he met Philip. And Jesus said
2527 2002 1650 3836 1133 2779 2351 5805 2779 2652 3306
v.aai.3s f.aa p.a d.asf n.asf cj v.pai.3s n.asm cj v.pai.3s

αὐτῷ ὁ Ἰησοῦς, ἀκολούθει μοι. 44 ἦν δὲ ὁ Φίλιππος ἀπὸ
to him, *{the}* *Jesus* "Follow me." Now Philip was *Now* *{the}* *Philip* from
899 3836 2652 199 1609 1254 5805 1639 1254 3836 5805 608
r.dsm.3 d.nsm n.nsm v.pam.2s r.ds.1 v.iai.3s cj d.nsm n.nsm p.g

Βηθσαϊδά, ἐκ τῆς πόλεως Ἀνδρέου καὶ Πέτρου. 45 εὑρίσκει Φίλιππος τὸν
Bethsaida, *{from}* the town of Andrew and Peter. Philip found *Philip* *{the}*
1034 1666 3836 4484 436 2779 4377 5805 2351 5805 3836
n.gsf p.g d.gsf n.gsf n.gsm cj n.gsm v.pai.3s n.nsm d.asm

Ναθαναὴλ καὶ λέγει αὐτῷ, ὃν ἔγραψεν Μωϋσῆς ἐν
Nathanael and told him, "We have found the one of whom Moses wrote *Moses* in
3720 2779 3306 899 2351 2351 2351 4005 3707 1211 3707 1877
n.asm cj v.pai.3s r.dsm.3 r.asm v.aai.3s n.nsm p.d

τῷ νόμῳ καὶ ↰ οἱ προφῆται ↰ εὑρήκαμεν, Ἰησοῦν υἱὸν τοῦ
the law, and of whom the prophets wrote *We have found* — Jesus, the son of
3836 3795 2779 4005 3836 4737 1211 2351 2652 5626 3836
d.dsm n.dsm cj d.npm n.npm v.rai.1p n.asm n.asm d.gsm

Ἰωσὴφ τὸν ἀπὸ Ναζαρέτ. 46 καὶ εἶπεν αὐτῷ Ναθαναήλ,
Joseph, a man from Nazareth." And Nathanael said to him, *Nathanael* "Can anything good
2737 3836 608 3715 2779 3720 3306 899 3720 1538 5516 19
n.gsm d.asm p.g n.gsf cj v.aai.3s r.dsm.3 n.nsm

ἐκ Ναζαρὲτ δύναταί τι ἀγαθὸν εἶναι; λέγει αὐτῷ ὁ[a] Φίλιππος,
come ⌞out of⌟ Nazareth?" *Can* *anything* *good* *come* Philip said to him, *{the}* *Philip*
1639 1666 3715 1538 5516 19 1639 5805 3306 899 3836 5805
p.g n.gsf v.ppi.3s r.asn a.asn f.pa v.pai.3s r.dsm.3 d.nsm n.nsm

[a] [ὁ] UBS.

NASB

are You staying?"
39He *said to them,
"Come, and you
will see." So they
came and saw
where He was
staying; and they
stayed with Him
that day, for it was
about the [a]tenth
hour. 40One of the
two who heard
John *speak* and
followed Him, was
Andrew, Simon
Peter's brother.
41He *found first
his own brother
Simon and *said
to him, "We have
found the Messiah"
(which translated
means Christ). 42He
brought him to Je-
sus. Jesus looked at
him and said, "You
are Simon the son
of John; you shall
be called Cephas"
(which is translated
Peter).
43The next day
He purposed to go
into Galilee, and
He *found Philip.
And Jesus *said to
him, "Follow Me."
44Now Philip was
from Bethsaida, of
the city of Andrew
and Peter. 45Philip
*found Nathanael
and *said to him,
"We have found
Him of whom Mo-
ses in the Law and
also the Prophets
wrote—Jesus of
Nazareth, the son
of Joseph." 46Na-
thanael said to him,
"Can any good
thing come out of
Nazareth?" Philip
*said to him,

[a] Perhaps 10 a.m. (Roman time)

NIV

"Come and see,"
said Philip.
47 When Jesus
saw Nathanael ap-
proaching, he said
of him, "Here tru-
ly is an Israelite in
whom there is no
deceit."
48 "How do you
know me?" Na-
thanael asked.
Jesus answered,
"I saw you while
you were still un-
der the fig tree be-
fore Philip called
you."
49 Then Nathanael
declared, "Rabbi,
you are the Son of
God; you are the
king of Israel."
50 Jesus said,
"You believe[a] be-
cause I told you
I saw you under
the fig tree. You
will see greater
things than that."
51 He then added,
"Very truly I tell
you,[b] you[c] will see
'heaven open, and
the angels of God
ascending and de-
scending on'[d] the
Son of Man."

Jesus Changes Water Into Wine

2 On the third
day a wedding
took place at Cana
in Galilee. Jesus'
mother was there,
2 and Jesus and his
disciples had also
been invited to the
wedding. 3 When
the wine was gone,
Jesus' mother said
to him, "They have
no more wine."

ἔρχου καὶ ἴδε. 47 εἶδεν ὁ Ἰησοῦς τὸν Ναθαναὴλ ἐρχόμενον πρὸς αὐτὸν
"Come and see." Jesus saw {the} Jesus {the} Nathanael coming toward him
2262 2779 2623 2652 1625 3836 2652 3836 3720 2262 4639 899
v.pmm.2s cj v.aam.2s v.aai.3s d.nsm n.nsm d.asm n.asm pt.pm.asm p.a r.asm.3

καὶ λέγει περὶ αὐτοῦ, ἴδε ἀληθῶς Ἰσραηλίτης ἐν ᾧ
and said of him, "Here is a true Israelite, one in whom there is no
2779 3306 4309 899 2623 242 2703 1877 4005 1639 1639 4024
cj v.pai.3s p.g r.gsm.3 pl adv n.nsm p.d r.dsm

δόλος οὐκ ἔστιν. 48 λέγει αὐτῷ Ναθαναήλ, πόθεν με
deceit!" no there is Nathanael asked him, Nathanael "How did you get to know me?"
1515 4024 1639 3720 3306 899 3720 4470 1182 1182 1182 1182 1182 1609
n.nsm pl v.pai.3s v.pai.3s r.dsm.3 n.nsm cj r.as.1

γινώσκεις; ἀπεκρίθη Ἰησοῦς καὶ εἶπεν αὐτῷ, πρὸ τοῦ
did you get to know Jesus answered Jesus him, {and} saying, him "Before {the} Philip called
1182 2652 646 2652 899 2779 3306 899 4574 3836 5805 5888
v.pai.2s v.api.3s n.nsm cj v.aai.3s r.dsm.3 p.g d.gsn

σε Φίλιππον φωνῆσαι ὄντα ὑπὸ τὴν συκῆν εἶδόν σε. 49
you, Philip called ⌊while you were⌋ still under the fig tree, I saw you." Nathanael
5148 5805 5888 1639 5679 3836 5190 1625 5148 3720
r.as.2 n.asm f.aa pt.pa.asm p.a d.asf n.asf v.aai.1s r.as.2

ἀπεκρίθη αὐτῷ Ναθαναήλ, ῥαββί, σὺ εἶ ὁ υἱὸς τοῦ θεοῦ, σὺ
declared to him, Nathanael "Rabbi, you are the Son of God! You are the
646 899 3720 4806 5148 1639 3836 5626 3836 2536 5148 1639
v.api.3s r.dsm.3 n.nsm n.vsm r.ns.2 v.pai.2s d.nsm n.nsm d.gsm n.gsm r.ns.2

βασιλεὺς εἶ τοῦ Ἰσραήλ. 50 ἀπεκρίθη Ἰησοῦς καὶ εἶπεν αὐτῷ, ὅτι
king are of Israel!" Jesus responded, Jesus {and} saying to him, "Is it because
995 1639 3836 2702 2652 646 2652 2779 3306 899 4022
n.nsm v.pai.2s d.gsm n.gsm v.api.3s n.nsm cj v.aai.3s r.dsm.3 cj

εἶπόν σοι ὅτι εἶδόν σε ὑποκάτω τῆς συκῆς, πιστεύεις;
I told you that I saw you under the fig tree that you believe? You will see
3306 5148 4022 1625 5148 5691 3836 5190 4409 3972 3972 3972
v.aai.1s r.ds.2 cj v.aai.1s r.as.2 p.g d.gsf n.gsf v.pai.2s

μείζω τούτων ὄψῃ. 51 καὶ λέγει αὐτῷ, ἀμὴν ἀμὴν
⌊greater things⌋ than that." You will see Then he said to him, "I tell you the solemn truth:
3489 4047 3972 2779 3306 899 3306 3306 7007 297 297
a.apn.c r.gpn v.fmi.2s cj v.pai.3s r.dsm.3 pl pl

λέγω ὑμῖν, ὄψεσθε τὸν οὐρανὸν ἀνεῳγότα καὶ τοὺς ἀγγέλους τοῦ θεοῦ
I tell you ⌊you will see⌋ {the} heaven standing open and the angels of God
3306 7007 3972 3836 4041 487 2779 3836 34 3836 2536
v.pai.1s r.dp.2 v.fmi.2p d.asm n.asm pt.ra.asm cj d.apm n.apm d.gsm n.gsm

ἀναβαίνοντας καὶ καταβαίνοντας ἐπὶ τὸν υἱὸν τοῦ ἀνθρώπου.
ascending and descending on the Son of Man."
326 2779 2849 2093 3836 5626 3836 476
pt.pa.apm cj pt.pa.apm p.a d.asm n.asm d.gsm n.gsm

2:1 καὶ τῇ ἡμέρᾳ τῇ τρίτῃ γάμος ἐγένετο ἐν Κανὰ τῆς
Now ⌊on the⌋ third day {the} third there was a wedding there was at Cana in
2779 3836 5569 2465 3836 5569 1181 1181 1141 1181 1877 2830 3836
cj d.dsf n.dsf d.dsf a.dsf n.nsm v.ami.3s p.d n.dsf d.gsf

Γαλιλαίας, καὶ ἦν ἡ μήτηρ τοῦ Ἰησοῦ ἐκεῖ· 2
Galilee, and the mother of Jesus was the mother of Jesus there. Jesus and his
1133 2779 3836 3613 3836 2652 1639 3836 3613 3836 2652 1695 2652 2779 899
n.gsf cj v.iai.3s d.nsf n.nsf d.gsm n.gsm adv

→ ἐκλήθη δὲ καὶ ὁ Ἰησοῦς καὶ οἱ μαθηταὶ αὐτοῦ εἰς τὸν
disciples were also invited {and} also {the} Jesus and {the} disciples his to the
3412 2779 2813 1254 2779 3836 2652 2779 3836 3412 899 1650 3836
v.api.3s cj adv d.nsm n.nsm cj d.npm n.npm r.gsm.3 p.a d.asm

γάμον. 3 καὶ → ὑστερήσαντος οἴνου λέγει ἡ μήτηρ τοῦ
wedding. {and} When the wine ran out, wine Jesus' mother said {the} mother {the}
1141 2779 3885 5728 3885 2652 3613 3306 3836 3613 3836
n.asm cj pt.aa.gsm n.gsm v.pai.3s d.nsf n.nsf d.gsm

Ἰησοῦ πρὸς αὐτόν, οἶνον οὐκ ἔχουσιν. 4 καὶ[a] λέγει αὐτῇ
Jesus' to him, "They have no more wine." no They have And Jesus said to her,
2652 4639 899 2400 2400 4024 3885 4024 2400 2779 2652 3306 899
n.gsm p.a r.asm.3 n.asm pl v.pai.3p cj v.pai.3s r.dsf.3

NASB

"Come and see."
47 Jesus saw Na-
thanael coming to
Him, and *said of
him, "Behold, an
Israelite indeed, in
whom there is no
deceit!" 48 Natha-
nael *said to Him,
"How do You
know me?" Jesus
answered and said
to him, "Before
Philip called you,
when you were
under the fig tree,
I saw you." 49 Na-
thanael answered
Him, "Rabbi, You
are the Son of God;
You are the King
of Israel." 50 Jesus
answered and said
to him, "Because
I said to you that
I saw you under
the fig tree, do you
believe? You will
see greater things
than these." 51 And
He *said to him,
"Truly, truly, I say
to you, you will see
the heavens opened
and the angels of
God ascending and
descending on the
Son of Man."

Miracle at Cana

2:1 On the third
day there was a
wedding in Cana
of Galilee, and
the mother of
Jesus was there;
2 and both Jesus
and His disciples
were invited to the
wedding. 3 When
the wine ran out,
the mother of Je-
sus *said to Him,
"They have no
wine." 4 And Jesus
*said to her,

[a] 50 Or *Do you believe . . . ?*
[b] 51 The Greek is plural.
[c] 51 The Greek is plural.
[d] 51 Gen. 28:12

[a] [καὶ] UBS, omitted by TNIV.

NIV

4"Woman,[a] why
do you involve
me?" Jesus replied.
"My hour has not
yet come."
5His mother said
to the servants,
"Do whatever he
tells you."
6Nearby stood six
stone water jars,
the kind used by
the Jews for cere-
monial washing,
each holding from
twenty to thirty
gallons.[b]
7Jesus said to the
servants, "Fill the
jars with water";
so they filled them
to the brim.
8Then he told
them, "Now draw
some out and take
it to the master of
the banquet."
They did so, 9and
the master of the
banquet tasted
the water that had
been turned into
wine. He did not
realize where it
had come from,
though the ser-
vants who had
drawn the water
knew. Then he
called the bride-
groom aside 10and
said, "Every-
one brings out
the choice wine
first and then the
cheaper wine after
the guests have
had too much to
drink; but you
have saved the best
till now."
11What Jesus did
here in Cana of
Galilee was the
first of the signs
through which he
revealed his glory;
and his disciples
believed in him.
12After this he
went down to Ca-
pernaum with

[a] 4 The Greek for *Woman* does not denote any disrespect.
[b] 6 Or from about 75 to about 115 liters

ὁ Ἰησοῦς, τί ἐμοὶ καὶ σοί, γύναι; ↱ οὔπω ἥκει ἡ
{the} *Jesus* "Woman, what is that to me and to you? *Woman* My hour has not yet come." *{the}*
3836 2652 1222 5515 1609 2779 5148 1222 1609 6052 2457 4037 2457 3836
d.nsm n.nsm r.nsn r.ds.1 cj r.ds.2 n.vsf adv v.rai.3s d.nsf

ὥρα μου. 5 λέγει ἡ μήτηρ αὐτοῦ τοῖς διακόνοις, ⌞ὅ τι ἄν⌟
hour *My* His mother said *{the}* *mother* *His* to the servants, "Do whatever
6052 1609 899 3613 3306 3836 3613 899 3836 1356 4472 4005 5516 323
n.nsf r.gs.1 v.pai.3s d.nsf n.nsf r.gsm.3 d.dpm n.dpm r.asn r.asn pl

λέγῃ ὑμῖν ποιήσατε. 6 ἦσαν δὲ ἐκεῖ λίθιναι ὑδρίαι ἓξ
he tells you." *Do* Now standing nearby were *Now* *nearby* six stone water jars, *six*
3306 7007 4472 1254 3023 1695 1639 1254 1695 1971 3343 5620 1971
v.pas.3s r.dp.2 v.aam.2p v.iai.3p cj adv a.npf n.npf a.npf

κατὰ τὸν καθαρισμὸν τῶν Ἰουδαίων κείμεναι, χωροῦσαι ἀνὰ
⌞according to⌟ the purification requirements of the Jews, *standing* each holding *each*
2848 3836 2752 3836 2681 3023 324 6003 324
p.a d.asm n.asm d.gpm a.gpm pt.pm.npf pt.pa.npf p.a

μετρητὰς δύο ἢ τρεῖς. 7 λέγει → αὐτοῖς ὁ Ἰησοῦς,
from twenty to thirty gallons. *twenty* *to* *thirty* Jesus said to the servants, *{the}* *Jesus*
1545 2445 5552 3583 1545 2445 5552 2652 3306 899 3836 2652
n.apm a.apm cj a.apm v.pai.3s r.dpm.3 d.nsm n.nsm

γεμίσατε τὰς ὑδρίας ὕδατος. καὶ ἐγέμισαν αὐτὰς ↰ ἕως ἄνω. 8 καὶ λέγει
"Fill the jars with water." So they filled them up to the brim. Then he told
1153 3836 5620 5623 2779 1153 899 1153 2401 539 2779 3306
v.aam.2p d.apf n.apf n.gsn cj v.aai.3p r.apf.3 p.g adv cj v.pai.3s

αὐτοῖς, ἀντλήσατε ← νῦν καὶ φέρετε τῷ ἀρχιτρικλίνῳ· οἱ
them, "Now draw some out *Now* and take it ⌞to the⌟ master of the feast." So they
899 3814 533 3814 2779 5770 3836 804 1254 3836
r.dpm.3 v.aam.2p adv cj v.pam.2p d.dsm n.dsm d.npm

δὲ ἤνεγκαν. 9 ὡς δὲ ἐγεύσατο ὁ
So took him some, and when *and* the master of the feast tasted *the*
1254 5770 1254 6055 1254 3836 804 804 804 804 1174 3836
cj v.aai.3p cj cj v.ami.3s d.nsm

ἀρχιτρίκλινος τὸ ὕδωρ οἶνον γεγενημένον καὶ οὐκ ᾔδει πόθεν
master of the feast the water that had become wine, *that had become* *{and}* not knowing where
804 3836 5623 1181 1181 1181 3885 1181 2779 4024 3857 4470
n.nsm d.asn n.asn n.asn pt.rp.asn cj pl v.lai.3s cj

ἐστίν, ↰ οἱ δὲ διάκονοι ᾔδεισαν οἱ
it came from (though the *though* servants who had drawn the water knew), *who*
1639 4470 1254 3836 1254 1356 3836 533 533 3836 5623 3857 3836
v.pai.3s d.npm cj n.npm v.lai.3p d.npm

ἠντληκότες τὸ ὕδωρ, φωνεῖ τὸν νυμφίον ὁ ἀρχιτρίκλινος 10 καὶ λέγει αὐτῷ,
had drawn *the* *water* he called the bridegroom *{the}* *he* and said to him,
533 3836 5623 804 5888 3836 3812 3836 804 2779 3306 899
pt.ra.npm d.asn n.asn v.pai.3s d.asm n.asm d.nsm n.nsm cj v.pai.3s r.dsm.3

⌞πᾶς ἄνθρωπος⌟ πρῶτον τὸν καλὸν οἶνον τίθησιν καὶ
"Everyone serves the choice wine first, *the* *choice* *wine* *serves* and then
4246 476 5502 3836 2819 3885 4754 3836 2819 3885 5502 2779
a.nsm n.nsm adv d.asm a.asm n.asm v.pai.3s cj

ὅταν μεθυσθῶσιν τὸν ἐλάσσω· σὺ τετήρηκας τὸν καλὸν οἶνον
when the guests are a bit tipsy, ⌞that which⌟ is inferior. But you have kept the good wine
4020 3499 3836 1781 5148 5498 3836 2819 3885
cj v.aps.3p d.asm a.asm.c r.ns.2 v.rai.2s d.asm a.asm n.asm

ἕως ἄρτι. 11 ταύτην ἐποίησεν ἀρχὴν τῶν σημείων ὁ Ἰησοῦς ἐν Κανὰ
until now." Jesus did this, *did* the first of his signs, *{the}* *Jesus* at Cana
2401 785 2652 4472 4047 4472 794 3836 4956 3836 2652 1877 2830
p.g adv r.asf v.aai.3s n.asf d.gpn n.gpn d.nsm n.nsm p.d n.dsf

τῆς Γαλιλαίας καὶ ἐφανέρωσεν τὴν δόξαν αὐτοῦ, καὶ ἐπίστευσαν εἰς
in Galilee, and revealed *{the}* his glory; *his* and his disciples believed in
3836 1133 2779 5746 3836 899 1518 899 2779 899 3412 4409 1650
d.gsf n.gsf cj v.aai.3s d.asf n.asf r.gsm.3 cj v.aai.3p p.a

αὐτὸν οἱ μαθηταὶ αὐτοῦ. 12 μετὰ τοῦτο κατέβη εἰς Καφαρναοὺμ αὐτὸς καὶ
him. *{the}* *disciples* *his* After this he went down to Capernaum *he* with
899 3836 3412 899 3552 4047 899 2849 1650 3019 899 2779
r.asm.3 d.npm n.npm r.gsm.3 p.a r.asn v.aai.3s p.a n.asf r.nsm cj

NASB

"Woman, what
does that have to
do with us? My
hour has not yet
come." 5His mother
*said to the ser-
vants, "Whatever
He says to you,
do it." 6Now there
were six stone wa-
terpots set there for
the Jewish custom
of purification,
containing twenty
or thirty gallons
each. 7Jesus *said to
them, "Fill the wa-
terpots with water."
So they filled them
up to the brim.
8And He *said to
them, "Draw *some*
out now and take it
to the [a]headwaiter."
So they took it *to
him.* 9When the
headwaiter tasted
the water which
had become wine,
and did not know
where it came from
(but the servants
who had drawn the
water knew), the
headwaiter *called
the bridegroom,
10and *said to him,
"Every man serves
the good wine
first, and when *the
people* have drunk
freely, *then he
serves* the poorer
wine; but you have
kept the good wine
until now." 11This
beginning of *His*
signs Jesus did in
Cana of Galilee,
and manifested
His glory, and His
disciples believed
in Him.
12After this He
went down to Ca-
pernaum, He and

[a] Or *steward*

NIV

his mother and
brothers and his
disciples. There
they stayed for a
few days.

Jesus Clears the Temple Courts

13 When it was al-
most time for the
Jewish Passover,
Jesus went up to
Jerusalem. 14 In the
temple courts he
found people sell-
ing cattle, sheep
and doves, and
others sitting at
tables exchanging
money. 15 So he
made a whip out of
cords, and drove
all from the tem-
ple courts, both
sheep and cattle;
he scattered the
coins of the money
changers and over-
turned their tables.
16 To those who
sold doves he said,
"Get these out of
here! Stop turning
my Father's house
into a market!"
17 His disciples re-
membered that it
is written: "Zeal
for your house will
consume me."[a]
18 The Jews then
responded to him,
"What sign can
you show us to
prove your author-
ity to do all this?"
19 Jesus answered
them, "Destroy
this temple, and I
will raise it again
in three days."
20 They replied,
"It has taken forty-
six years to build

ἡ μήτηρ αὐτοῦ καὶ οἱ ἀδελφοὶ[a] καὶ οἱ μαθηταὶ αὐτοῦ καὶ
{the} his mother *his* and his brothers and {the} his disciples, *his* but they stayed
3836 899 3613 899 2779 3836 81 2779 3836 899 3412 899 2779 3531 3531
d.nsf n.nsf r.gsm.3 cj d.npm n.npm cj d.npm n.npm r.gsm.3 cj

ἐκεῖ ἔμειναν ⌊οὐ πολλὰς⌋ ἡμέρας. 13 καὶ ἐγγὺς ἦν
there *they stayed* only a few days. Now the Jewish Passover was at hand, *was*
1695 3531 4024 4498 2465 2779 3836 2681 4247 1639 1584 1639
adv v.aai.3p pl a.apf n.apf cj adv v.iai.3s

τὸ πάσχα τῶν Ἰουδαίων, καὶ ἀνέβη εἰς Ἱεροσόλυμα ὁ Ἰησοῦς. 14 καὶ
the Passover {the} Jewish so Jesus went up to Jerusalem. *{the} Jesus* *{and}*
3836 4247 3836 2681 2779 2652 326 1650 2642 3836 2652 2779
d.nsn n.nsn d.gpm a.gpm cj v.aai.3s p.a n.apn d.nsm n.nsm cj

εὗρεν ἐν τῷ ἱερῷ τοὺς πωλοῦντας βόας καὶ πρόβατα καὶ
In the temple he found *In the temple* people selling cattle and sheep and
1877 3836 2639 2351 1877 3836 2639 3836 4797 1091 2779 4585 2779
v.aai.3s p.d d.dsn n.dsn d.apm pt.pa.apm n.apm cj n.apn cj

περιστερὰς καὶ τοὺς κερματιστὰς καθημένους, 15 καὶ ποιήσας φραγέλλιον
doves, and the money changers seated at their tables. So he made a whip
4361 2779 3836 3048 2764 2779 4472 5848
n.apf cj d.apm n.apm pt.pm.apm cj pt.aa.nsm n.asn

ἐκ σχοινίων πάντας ἐξέβαλεν ἐκ τοῦ ἱεροῦ τά τε
⌊out of⌋ cords and drove them all *drove* ⌊out of⌋ the temple, including the *including*
1666 5389 1675 4246 1675 1666 3836 2639 5445 3836 5445
p.g n.gpn a.apm v.aai.3s p.g d.gsn n.gsn d.apn cj

πρόβατα καὶ τοὺς βόας, καὶ τῶν κολλυβιστῶν ἐξέχεεν τὸ
sheep and the cattle. *{and}* He scattered the coins of the money changers *He scattered the*
4585 2779 3836 1091 2779 1772 1772 3836 3047 3836 3142 1772 3836
n.apn cj d.apm n.apm cj d.gpm n.gpm v.aai.3s d.asn

κέρμα καὶ τὰς τραπέζας ἀνέτρεψεν, 16 καὶ τοῖς τὰς
coins and overturned their tables. *overturned* *{and}* To those who were selling *{the}*
3047 2779 426 3836 5544 426 2779 3836 4797 4797 4797 3836
n.asn cj d.apf n.apf v.aai.3s cj d.dpm d.apf

περιστερὰς πωλοῦσιν εἶπεν, ἄρατε ταῦτα ἐντεῦθεν, ↱ μὴ ποιεῖτε τὸν
doves *who were selling* he said, "Take those out of here! Do not make *{the}* my
4361 4797 3306 149 4047 1949 4472 3590 4472 3836 1609
n.apf pt.pa.dpm v.aai.3s v.aam.2p r.apn adv pl v.pam.2p d.asm

οἶκον τοῦ πατρός μου ⌊οἶκον ἐμπορίου.⌋ 17 ἐμνήσθησαν
Father's house *{the} Father's my* a marketplace!" His disciples remembered
4252 3875 3836 4252 1609 3875 1866 899 3412 3630
n.asm d.gsm n.gsm r.gs.1 n.asm n.gsn v.api.3p

οἱ μαθηταὶ αὐτοῦ ὅτι γεγραμμένον ἐστίν, ὁ ζῆλος τοῦ οἴκου
{the} disciples His that it stands written, *it stands {the}* "Zeal for your house
3836 3412 899 4022 1639 1639 1211 1639 3836 2419 3836 5148 3875
d.npm n.npm r.gsm.3 cj pt.rp.nsn v.pai.3s d.nsm n.nsm d.gsm n.gsm

σου καταφάγεταί με. 18 ἀπεκρίθησαν οὖν οἱ Ἰουδαῖοι καὶ
your will consume me." The Jews therefore replied, *therefore The Jews* *{and}*
5148 2983 1609 3836 2681 4036 646 4036 3836 2681 2779
r.gs.2 v.fmi.3s r.as.1 v.api.3p cj d.npm a.npm cj

εἶπαν αὐτῷ, τί σημεῖον δεικνύεις ἡμῖν ὅτι ταῦτα
saying to him, "What sign can you show us to prove your authority to do all this?"
3306 899 5515 4956 1260 7005 4022 4472 4472 4472 4472 4047
v.aai.3p r.dsm.3 r.asn n.asn v.pai.2s r.dp.1 cj r.apn

ποιεῖς; 19 ἀπεκρίθη Ἰησοῦς καὶ εἶπεν αὐτοῖς, λύσατε τὸν
your authority to do Jesus answered *Jesus* *{and}* them, saying, *them* "Destroy *{the}* this
4472 2652 646 2652 2779 899 3306 899 3395 3836 4047
v.pai.2s v.api.3s n.nsm cj v.aai.3s r.dpm.3 v.aam.2p d.asm

ναὸν τοῦτον καὶ ἐν τρισὶν ἡμέραις ἐγερῶ αὐτόν. 20 εἶπαν οὖν
temple *this* and in three days I will restore it." Then the Jews said, *Then*
3724 4047 2779 1877 5552 2465 1586 899 4036 3836 2681 3306 4036
n.asm r.asm cj p.d a.dpf n.dpf v.fai.1s r.asm.3 v.aai.3p cj

οἱ Ἰουδαῖοι, ⌊τεσσεράκοντα καὶ ἓξ⌋
the Jews "This temple has been under construction for forty-six
3836 2681 4047 3724 3868 3868 3868 3868 5477 2779 1971
d.npm a.npm a.dpn cj a.dpn

NASB

His mother and *His*
brothers and His
disciples; and they
stayed there a few
days.

First Passover—Cleansing the Temple

13 The Passover of
the Jews was near,
and Jesus went
up to Jerusalem.
14 And He found in
the temple those
who were selling
oxen and sheep
and doves, and
the money chang-
ers seated *at their*
tables. 15 And He
made a scourge of
cords, and drove
them all out of the
temple, with the
sheep and the oxen;
and He poured out
the coins of the
money changers
and overturned
their tables; 16 and
to those who were
selling the doves
He said, "Take
these things away;
stop making My
Father's house a
place of business."
17 His disciples
remembered that it
was written, "ZEAL
FOR YOUR HOUSE
WILL CONSUME ME."
18 The Jews then
said to Him, "What
sign do You show
us as your author-
ity for doing these
things?" 19 Jesus an-
swered them, "De-
stroy this temple,
and in three days
I will raise it up."
20 The Jews then
said, "It took forty-
six years to build

[a] 17 Psalm 69:9

[a] αὐτοῦ included by UBS after ἀδελφοὶ.

NIV

this temple, and
you are going to
raise it in three
days?" [21]But the
temple he had
spoken of was his
body. [22]After he
was raised from
the dead, his disci-
ples recalled what
he had said. Then
they believed the
scripture and the
words that Jesus
had spoken.
[23]Now while he
was in Jerusalem
at the Passover
Festival, many
people saw the
signs he was
performing and
believed in his
name.[a] [24]But Jesus
would not entrust
himself to them,
for he knew all
people. [25]He did
not need any testi-
mony about man-
kind, for he knew
what was in each
person.

Jesus Teaches Nicodemus

3 Now there
was a Phari-
see, a man named
Nicodemus who
was a member of
the Jewish ruling
council. [2]He came
to Jesus at night
and said, "Rabbi,
we know that you
are a teacher who
has come from
God. For no one
could perform the
signs you are do-
ing if God were
not with him."
[3]Jesus replied,

ἔτεσιν οἰκοδομήθη ὁ ναὸς οὗτος, καὶ σὺ ἐν τρισὶν
years, *has been under construction* *{the}* *temple* *This* and you can restore it in three
2291 3868 3836 3724 4047 2779 5148 1586 1586 899 1877 5552
n.dpn v.api.3s d.nsm n.nsm r.nsm cj r.ns.2 p.d a.dpf

ἡμέραις ἐγερεῖς αὐτόν; 21 ἐκεῖνος δὲ ἔλεγεν περὶ τοῦ ναοῦ τοῦ
days?" *can restore* *it* But he *But* was speaking about the temple of his
2465 1586 899 1254 1697 1254 3306 4309 3836 3724 3836 899
n.dpf v.fai.2s r.asm.3 r.nsm cj v.iai.3s p.g d.gsm n.gsm d.gsn

σώματος αὐτοῦ. 22 ὅτε οὖν ἠγέρθη ἐκ νεκρῶν,
body. *his* Therefore, when *Therefore* he had risen from the dead, his disciples
5393 899 4036 4021 4036 1586 1666 3738 899 3412
n.gsn r.gsm.3 cj cj v.api.3s p.g a.gpm

ἐμνήσθησαν οἱ μαθηταὶ αὐτοῦ ὅτι τοῦτο ἔλεγεν, καὶ ἐπίστευσαν
remembered *{the}* *disciples* *his* that he had said this, *he had said* and they believed
3630 3836 3412 899 4022 3306 3306 3306 4047 3306 2779 4409
v.api.3p d.npm n.npm r.gsm.3 cj r.asn v.iai.3s cj v.aai.3p

τῇ γραφῇ καὶ τῷ λόγῳ ὃν εἶπεν ὁ Ἰησοῦς. 23 ὡς δὲ
the scripture and the words that Jesus had spoken. *{the}* *Jesus* Now while *Now* Jesus
3836 1210 2779 3836 3364 4005 2652 3306 3836 2652 1254 6055 1254
d.dsf n.dsf cj d.dsm n.dsm r.asm v.aai.3s d.nsm n.nsm cj cj

ἦν ἐν τοῖς Ἱεροσολύμοις ἐν τῷ πάσχα ἐν τῇ ἑορτῇ, πολλοὶ
was in *{the}* Jerusalem during the festival of Passover, *{at}* *{the}* *festival* many people
1639 1877 3836 2642 1877 3836 2038 4247 1877 3836 2038 4498
v.iai.3s p.d d.dpn n.dpn p.d d.dsn n.dsn p.d d.dsf n.dsf a.npm

ἐπίστευσαν εἰς τὸ ὄνομα αὐτοῦ θεωροῦντες αὐτοῦ τὰ σημεῖα ἃ
put their trust in *{the}* his name, *his* for they saw his *{the}* ⌊miraculous signs⌋ that
4409 1650 3836 899 3950 899 2555 899 3836 4956 4005
v.aai.3p p.a d.asn n.asn r.gsm.3 pt.pa.npm r.gsm.3 d.apn n.apn r.apn

ἐποίει· 24 αὐτὸς δὲ Ἰησοῦς ↱ οὐκ ἐπίστευεν αὐτὸν
⌊he was performing.⌋ But as for Jesus, he *But* *Jesus* did not entrust himself
4472 1254 2652 899 1254 2652 4409 4024 4409 899
v.iai.3s r.nsm cj n.nsm pl v.iai.3s r.asm.3

αὐτοῖς διὰ τὸ αὐτὸν γινώσκειν πάντας 25 καὶ ὅτι οὐ χρείαν εἶχεν
to them, because *{the}* he knew all men, and because he had no need *he had*
899 1328 3836 899 1182 4246 2779 4022 2400 2400 4024 5970 2400
r.dpm.3 p.a d.asn r.asm.3 f.pa a.apm cj cj pl n.asf v.iai.3s

ἵνα τις μαρτυρήσῃ περὶ τοῦ ἀνθρώπου· ↱ αὐτὸς γὰρ ἐγίνωσκεν
that anyone should give evidence concerning *{the}* man, for he himself *for* knew
2671 5516 3455 4309 3836 476 1142 1182 899 1142 1182
cj r.nsm v.aas.3s p.g d.gsm n.gsm r.nsm cj v.iai.3s

τί ἦν ἐν τῷ ἀνθρώπῳ.
what was in *{the}* man.
5515 1639 1877 3836 476
r.nsn v.iai.3s p.d d.dsm n.dsm

3:1 ἦν δὲ ἄνθρωπος ἐκ τῶν Φαρισαίων, Νικόδημος ⌊ὄνομα
Now ⌊there was⌋ *Now* a man of the Pharisees named Nicodemus, *named*
1254 1639 1254 476 1666 3836 5757 3950 3773 3950
v.iai.3s cj n.nsm p.g d.gpm n.gpm n.nsm n.nsn

αὐτῷ,⌋ ἄρχων τῶν Ἰουδαίων· 2 οὗτος ἦλθεν πρὸς αὐτὸν νυκτὸς καὶ εἶπεν αὐτῷ,
a ruler of the Jews. This man came to Jesus by night and said to him,
899 807 3836 2681 4047 2262 4639 899 3816 2779 3306 899
r.dsm.3 n.nsm d.gpm a.gpm r.nsm v.aai.3s p.a r.asm.3 n.gsf cj v.aai.3s r.dsm.3

ῥαββί, οἴδαμεν ὅτι ἀπὸ θεοῦ ἐλήλυθας διδάσκαλος·
"Rabbi, we know that you are a teacher come from God, *you are come* *teacher* for
4806 3857 4022 2262 2262 1437 2262 608 2536 2262 1437 1142
n.vsm v.rai.1p cj p.g n.gsm v.rai.2s n.nsm

οὐδεὶς γὰρ δύναται ταῦτα τὰ σημεῖα ποιεῖν ἃ σὺ ποιεῖς,
no one *for* is able to perform these *{the}* ⌊miraculous signs⌋ *to perform* that you are doing
4029 1142 1538 4472 4472 4047 3836 4956 4472 4005 5148 4472
a.nsm cj v.ppi.3s r.apn d.apn n.apn f.pa r.apn r.ns.2 v.pai.2s

⌊ἐὰν μὴ⌋ ᾖ ὁ θεὸς μετ' αὐτοῦ. 3 ἀπεκρίθη Ἰησοῦς καὶ εἶπεν
unless God is *{the}* *God* with him." Jesus answered *Jesus* him, *{and}* saying,
1569 3590 2536 1639 3836 2536 3552 899 2652 646 2652 899 2779 3306
cj pl v.pas.3s d.nsm n.nsm p.g r.gsm.3 v.api.3s n.nsm cj v.aai.3s

NASB

this temple, and
will You raise it
up in three days?"
[21]But He was
speaking of the
temple of His body.
[22]So when He was
raised from the
dead, His disciples
remembered that
He said this; and
they believed the
Scripture and the
word which Jesus
had spoken.
[23]Now when He
was in Jerusalem at
the Passover, dur-
ing the feast, many
believed in His
name, observing
His signs which He
was doing. [24]But
Jesus, on His part,
was not entrusting
Himself to them,
for He knew all
men, [25]and because
He did not need
anyone to testify
concerning man,
for He Himself
knew what was in
man.

The New Birth

[3:1]Now there
was a man of the
Pharisees, named
Nicodemus, a ruler
of the Jews; [2]this
man came to Jesus
by night and said
to Him, "Rabbi,
we know that You
have come from
God *as* a teacher;
for no one can do
these signs that
You do unless God
is with him." [3]Jesus
answered and said

[a] 23 Or *in him*

NIV

"Very truly I tell
you, no one can
see the kingdom
of God unless they
are born again.[a]"
4"How can some-
one be born when
they are old?"
Nicodemus asked.
"Surely they can-
not enter a second
time into their
mother's womb to
be born!"
5Jesus answered,
"Very truly I tell
you, no one can
enter the kingdom
of God unless they
are born of wa-
ter and the Spirit.
6Flesh gives birth
to flesh, but the
Spirit[b] gives birth
to spirit. 7You
should not be sur-
prised at my say-
ing, 'You[c] must be
born again.' 8The
wind blows wher-
ever it pleases.
You hear its sound,
but you cannot tell
where it comes
from or where it is
going. So it is with
everyone born of
the Spirit."[d]
9"How can this
be?" Nicodemus
asked.
10"You are Is-
rael's teacher,"
said Jesus, "and
do you not under-
stand these things?
11Very truly I tell
you, we speak of
what we know, and
we testify to what
we have seen, but
still you people do

αὐτῷ, ἀμὴν ἀμὴν λέγω σοι, ⌊ἐὰν μή⌋ τις γεννηθῇ ἄνωθεν,
him "I tell you the solemn truth, *I tell* *you* unless a person is born again
899 3306 3306 5148 297 297 3306 5148 1569 3590 5516 1164 540
r.dsm.3 pl pl v.pai.1s r.ds.2 cj pl r.nsm v.aps.3s adv

⌊οὐ δύναται⌋ ἰδεῖν τὴν βασιλείαν τοῦ θεοῦ. 4 λέγει πρὸς αὐτὸν ὁ[a]
he cannot see the kingdom of God." Nicodemus said to him, *{the}*
4024 1538 1625 3836 993 3836 2536 3773 3306 4639 899 3836
pl v.ppi.3s f.aa d.asf n.asf d.gsm n.gsm v.pai.3s p.a r.asm.3 d.nsm

Νικόδημος, πῶς δύναται ἄνθρωπος γεννηθῆναι γέρων ὤν;
Nicodemus "How can a man be born when he is old? *when he is*
3773 4802 1538 476 1164 1639 1639 1639 1173 1639
n.nsm cj v.ppi.3s n.nsm f.ap n.nsm pt.pa.nsm

⌊μὴ δύναται⌋ εἰς τὴν κοιλίαν τῆς μητρὸς αὐτοῦ
He cannot enter into *{the}* his mother's womb *{the}* *mother's* *his* and be born a
3590 1538 1656 1650 3836 899 3613 3120 3836 3613 899 2779 1164 1164
pl v.ppi.3s p.a d.asf n.asf d.gsf n.gsf r.gsm.3

δεύτερον εἰσελθεῖν καὶ γεννηθῆναι; 5 ἀπεκρίθη Ἰησοῦς,
second time, *enter* *and* *be born* can he?" Jesus answered, *Jesus* "I tell you
1311 1656 2779 1164 3590 3590 2652 646 2652 3306 3306 5148
adv f.aa cj f.ap v.api.3s n.nsm

ἀμὴν ἀμὴν λέγω σοι, ⌊ἐὰν μή⌋ τις γεννηθῇ ἐξ ὕδατος καὶ πνεύματος,
the solemn truth, *I tell* *you* unless one is born of water and Spirit,
297 297 3306 5148 1569 3590 5516 1164 1666 5623 2779 4460
pl pl v.pai.1s r.ds.2 cj pl r.nsm v.aps.3s p.g n.gsn cj n.gsn

⌊οὐ δύναται⌋ ⌊εἰσελθεῖν εἰς⌋ τὴν βασιλείαν τοῦ θεοῦ. 6 τὸ γεγεννημένον ἐκ
he cannot enter the kingdom of God. What is born of
4024 1538 1656 1650 3836 993 3836 2536 3836 1164 1666
pl v.ppi.3s f.aa p.a d.asf n.asf d.gsm n.gsm d.nsn pt.rp.nsn p.g

τῆς σαρκὸς σάρξ ἐστιν, καὶ τὸ γεγεννημένον ἐκ τοῦ πνεύματος πνεῦμά
the flesh is flesh, *is* and what is born of the Spirit is spirit.
3836 4922 1639 4922 1639 2779 3836 1164 1666 3836 4460 1639 4460
d.gsf n.gsf n.nsf v.pai.3s cj d.nsn pt.rp.nsn p.g d.gsn n.gsn n.nsn

ἐστιν. 7 μὴ θαυμάσῃς ὅτι εἶπόν σοι, δεῖ ὑμᾶς γεννηθῆναι ἄνωθεν.
is Do not be astonished that I said to you, 'You must *You* be born again.'
1639 2513 3590 2513 4022 3306 5148 7007 1256 7007 1164 540
v.pai.3s pl v.aas.2s cj v.aai.1s r.ds.2 v.pai.3s r.ap.2 f.ap adv

8 τὸ πνεῦμα ὅπου θέλει πνεῖ καὶ τὴν φωνὴν αὐτοῦ ἀκούεις,
The wind blows wherever it chooses, *blows* and you hear *{the}* its sound, *its* *you hear*
3836 4460 4463 3963 2527 4463 2779 201 201 3836 899 5889 899 201
d.nsn n.nsn cj v.pai.3s v.pai.3s cj d.asf n.asf r.gsn.3 v.pai.2s

ἀλλ' οὐκ οἶδας πόθεν ἔρχεται καὶ ποῦ ὑπάγει· οὕτως ἐστὶν πᾶς
but do not know where it is coming from or where it is going. So it is with everyone
247 3857 4024 3857 4470 2262 4470 2779 4543 5632 4048 1639 4246
cj pl v.rai.2s cj v.pmi.3s cj cj v.pai.3s adv v.pai.3s a.nsm

ὁ γεγεννημένος ἐκ τοῦ πνεύματος. 9 ἀπεκρίθη Νικόδημος καὶ εἶπεν
{the} born of the Spirit." Nicodemus replied, *Nicodemus* *{and}* saying
3836 1164 1666 3836 4460 3773 646 3773 2779 3306
d.nsm pt.rp.nsm p.g d.gsn n.gsn v.api.3s n.nsm cj v.aai.3s

αὐτῷ, πῶς δύναται ταῦτα γενέσθαι; 10 ἀπεκρίθη Ἰησοῦς καὶ εἶπεν αὐτῷ,
to him, "How can these things be?" Jesus answered, *Jesus* *{and}* saying to him,
899 4802 1538 4047 1181 2652 646 2652 2779 3306 899
r.dsm.3 cj v.ppi.3s r.apn f.am v.api.3s n.nsm cj v.aai.3s r.dsm.3

σὺ εἶ ὁ διδάσκαλος τοῦ Ἰσραὴλ καὶ ταῦτα
"Are you *Are* the teacher of Israel and you do not understand these things?"
1639 5148 1639 3836 1437 3836 2702 2779 1182 1182 4024 1182 4047
r.ns.2 v.pai.2s d.nsm n.nsm d.gsm n.gsm cj r.apn

οὐ γινώσκεις; 11 ἀμὴν ἀμὴν λέγω σοι ὅτι ὃ
not *you do understand* "I tell you the solemn truth, *I tell* *you* ~ we speak about what
4024 1182 3306 3306 5148 297 297 3306 5148 4022 3281 3281 3281 4005
pl v.pai.2s pl pl v.pai.1s r.ds.2 cj r.asn

οἴδαμεν λαλοῦμεν καὶ ὃ ἑωράκαμεν μαρτυροῦμεν, καὶ
we know *we speak about* and testify about what we have seen, *testify about* but you people do
3857 3281 2779 3455 3455 4005 3972 3455 2779 3284 3284
v.rai.1p v.pai.1p cj r.asn v.rai.1p v.pai.1p cj

NASB

to him, "Truly,
truly, I say to you,
unless one is born
again he cannot
see the kingdom of
God."
4Nicodemus *said
to Him, "How
can a man be born
when he is old?
He cannot enter a
second time into
his mother's womb
and be born, can
he?" 5Jesus an-
swered, "Truly,
truly, I say to you,
unless one is born
of water and the
Spirit he cannot
enter into the king-
dom of God. 6That
which is born of
the flesh is flesh,
and that which is
born of the Spirit
is spirit. 7Do not be
amazed that I said
to you, 'You must
be born again.'
8The wind blows
where it wishes
and you hear the
sound of it, but do
not know where
it comes from and
where it is going;
so is everyone
who is born of the
Spirit."
9Nicodemus said
to Him, "How can
these things be?"
10Jesus answered
and said to him,
"Are you the
teacher of Israel
and do not under-
stand these things?
11Truly, truly, I say
to you, we speak of
what we know and
testify of what we
have seen, and you

[a] 3 The Greek for *again* also means *from above*; also in verse 7.
[b] 6 Or *but spirit*
[c] 7 The Greek is plural.
[d] 8 The Greek for *Spirit* is the same as that for *wind*.

[a] [ὁ] UBS.

NIV

not accept our tes-
timony. 12 I have
spoken to you of
earthly things and
you do not believe;
how then will you
believe if I speak
of heavenly things?
13 No one has ever
gone into heav-
en except the one
who came from
heaven — the Son
of Man.[a] 14 Just
as Moses lifted
up the snake in
the wilderness, so
the Son of Man
must be lifted up,[b]
15 that everyone
who believes may
have eternal life in
him."[c]
16 For God so
loved the world
that he gave his
one and only Son,
that whoever be-
lieves in him shall
not perish but
have eternal life.
17 For God did not
send his Son into
the world to con-
demn the world,
but to save the
world through
him. 18 Whoever
believes in him is
not condemned,
but whoever does
not believe stands
condemned al-
ready because they
have not believed
in the name of
God's one and
only Son. 19 This is
the verdict: Light
has come into the
world, but people
loved darkness in-
stead of

τὴν μαρτυρίαν ἡμῶν οὐ λαμβάνετε. 12 εἰ
not accept {the} our testimony. our not you do accept If I have told you about
4024 3284 3836 7005 3456 7005 4024 3284 1623 3306 3306 3306 7007 3306
d.asf n.asf r.gp.1 pl v.pai.2p cj

τὰ ἐπίγεια εἶπον ὑμῖν καὶ ↱ ↱ οὐ πιστεύετε, πῶς
{the} earthly things I have told about you and you do not believe, how will you believe
3836 2103 3306 7007 2779 4409 4409 4024 4409 4802 4409 4409 4409
d.apn a.apn v.aai.1s r.dp.2 cj pl v.pai.2p cj

ἐὰν εἴπω ὑμῖν ↰ τὰ ἐπουράνια πιστεύσετε; 13 καὶ οὐδεὶς ἀναβέβηκεν εἰς
if I tell you about {the} heavenly things? will you believe {and} No one has gone up to
1569 3306 7007 3306 3836 2230 4409 2779 4029 326 1650
cj v.aas.1s r.dp.2 d.apn a.apn v.fai.2p cj a.nsm v.rai.3s p.a

τὸν οὐρανὸν ⌞εἰ μὴ⌟ ὁ ἐκ τοῦ οὐρανοῦ καταβάς,
{the} heaven except the one who came down ⌞out of⌟ {the} heaven, one who came down
3836 4041 1623 3590 3836 2849 2849 2849 2849 1666 3836 4041 2849
d.asm n.asm cj pl d.nsm p.g d.gsm n.gsm pt.aa.nsm

ὁ υἱὸς τοῦ ἀνθρώπου.[a] 14 καὶ καθὼς Μωϋσῆς ὕψωσεν τὸν ὄφιν ἐν τῇ
the Son of Man. And just as Moses lifted up the serpent in the
3836 5626 3836 476 2779 2777 3707 5738 3836 4058 1877 3836
d.nsm n.nsm d.gsm n.gsm cj cj n.nsm v.aai.3s d.asm n.asm p.d d.dsf

ἐρήμῳ, οὕτως ὑψωθῆναι δεῖ τὸν υἱὸν τοῦ ἀνθρώπου,
wilderness, so must the Son of Man be lifted up, must the Son of Man
2245 4048 1256 3836 5626 3836 476 5738 1256 3836 5626 3836 476
n.dsf adv f.ap v.pai.3s d.asm n.asm d.gsm n.gsm

15 ἵνα πᾶς ὁ πιστεύων ἐν αὐτῷ[b] ἔχῃ ζωὴν αἰώνιον. 16
so that everyone who believes in him ⌞may have⌟ eternal life. eternal "For
2671 4246 3836 4409 1877 899 2400 173 2437 173 1142
cj a.nsm d.nsm pt.pa.nsm p.d r.dsm.3 v.pas.3s n.asf a.asf

οὕτως γὰρ ἠγάπησεν ὁ θεὸς τὸν κόσμον, ὥστε τὸν
this is how For God loved {the} God the world: {that} he gave his one and only
4048 1142 2536 26 3836 2536 3836 3180 6063 1443 1443 3836 3666 3666 3666
adv cj v.aai.3s d.nsm n.nsm d.asm n.asm cj d.asm

υἱὸν τὸν μονογενῆ ἔδωκεν, ἵνα πᾶς ὁ πιστεύων εἰς αὐτὸν ↱ μὴ
Son {the} one and only he gave that everyone who believes in him should not
5626 3836 3666 1443 2671 4246 3836 4409 1650 899 660 3590
n.asm d.asm a.asm v.aai.3s cj a.nsm d.nsm pt.pa.nsm p.a r.asm.3 pl

ἀπόληται ἀλλ᾽ ἔχῃ ζωὴν αἰώνιον. 17 ↱ οὐ γὰρ ἀπέστειλεν ὁ
perish but have eternal life. eternal For God did not For send {the}
660 247 2400 173 2437 173 1142 2536 690 4024 1142 690 3836
v.ams.3s cj v.pas.3s n.asf a.asf pl cj v.aai.3s d.nsm

θεὸς τὸν υἱὸν εἰς τὸν κόσμον ἵνα κρίνῃ τὸν κόσμον, ἀλλ᾽ ἵνα
God his Son into the world to condemn the world, but so that the world
2536 3836 5626 1650 3836 3180 2671 3212 3836 3180 247 2671 3836 3180
n.nsm d.asm n.asm p.a d.asm n.asm cj v.aas.3s d.asm n.asm cj cj

σωθῇ ὁ κόσμος δι᾽ αὐτοῦ. 18 ὁ πιστεύων εἰς αὐτὸν ↱ οὐ
⌞might be saved⌟ the world through him. The one who believes in him is not
5392 3836 3180 1328 899 3836 4409 1650 899 3212 4024
v.aps.3s d.nsm n.nsm p.g r.gsm.3 d.nsm pt.pa.nsm p.a r.asm.3 pl

κρίνεται· ὁ δὲ ↱ ↱ ↱ μὴ πιστεύων ἤδη κέκριται,
condemned, but the but one who does not believe is condemned already, is condemned
3212 1254 3836 1254 4409 4409 4409 3590 4409 3212 3212 2453 3212
v.ppi.3s d.nsm cj pl pt.pa.nsm adv v.rpi.3s

ὅτι ↱ ↱ μὴ πεπίστευκεν εἰς τὸ ὄνομα τοῦ μονογενοῦς υἱοῦ τοῦ
because he has not believed in the name of God's one and only Son. {the}
4022 4409 4409 3590 4409 1650 3836 3950 3836 2536 3666 5626 3836
cj pl v.rai.3s p.a d.asn n.asn d.gsm a.gsm n.gsm d.gsm

θεοῦ. 19 αὕτη δέ ἐστιν ἡ κρίσις ὅτι τὸ φῶς
God's And the basis for judging is this, And is the basis for judging that {the} light
2536 1254 3836 3213 3213 3213 1639 4047 1254 1639 3836 3213 4022 3836 5890
n.gsm r.nsf cj v.pai.3s d.nsf n.nsf cj d.nsn n.nsn

ἐλήλυθεν εἰς τὸν κόσμον καὶ ἠγάπησαν οἱ ἄνθρωποι μᾶλλον
has come into the world and people love {the} people darkness rather than
2262 1650 3836 3180 2779 476 26 3836 476 5030 3437 2445
v.rai.3s p.a d.asm n.asm cj v.aai.3p d.npm n.npm adv.c

NASB

do not accept our
testimony. 12 If I
told you earthly
things and you do
not believe, how
will you believe if
I tell you heavenly
things? 13 No one
has ascended into
heaven, but He
who descended
from heaven: the
Son of Man. 14 As
Moses lifted up
the serpent in the
wilderness, even
so must the Son of
Man be lifted up;
15 so that whoever
[a]believes will in
Him have eternal
life.
16 "For God so
loved the world,
that He gave His
only begotten Son,
that whoever be-
lieves in Him shall
not perish, but
have eternal life.
17 For God did not
send the Son into
the world to judge
the world, but that
the world might
be saved through
Him. 18 He who
believes in Him is
not judged; he who
does not believe
has been judged
already, because
he has not believed
in the name of the
only begotten Son
of God. 19 This is
the judgment, that
the Light has come
into the world,
and men loved the
darkness rather

[a] 13 Some manuscripts *Man, who is in heaven*
[b] 14 The Greek for *lifted up* also means *exalted.*
[c] 15 Some interpreters end the quotation with verse 21.

[a] ὁ ὢν ἐν τῷ οὐρανῷ included by TR after ἀνθρώπου.
[b] μὴ ἀπόληται, ἀλλ᾽ included by TR after αὐτῷ.

[a] Or *believes in Him will have eternal life*

NIV

light because their
deeds were evil.
20 Everyone who
does evil hates the
light, and will not
come into the light
for fear that their
deeds will be ex-
posed. 21 But who-
ever lives by the
truth comes into
the light, so that it
may be seen plain-
ly that what they
have done has been
done in the sight
of God.

John Testifies Again About Jesus

22 After this, Jesus
and his disciples
went out into the
Judean country-
side, where he
spent some time
with them, and
baptized. 23 Now
John also was
baptizing at Ae-
non near Salim,
because there was
plenty of water,
and people were
coming and being
baptized. 24 (This
was before John
was put in prison.)
25 An argument de-
veloped between
some of John's dis-
ciples and a certain
Jew over the mat-
ter of ceremonial
washing. 26 They
came to John and
said to him, "Rab-
bi, that man who
was with you on
the other side of
the Jordan—the
one you testified
about—look, he
is baptizing, and
everyone is going
to him."
27 To this John
replied, "A person
can receive only
what is

τὸ σκότος ἢ τὸ φῶς· ἦν γὰρ αὐτῶν πονηρὰ τὰ ἔργα.
{the} darkness than {the} light, because their deeds are because their evil. {the} deeds
3836 5030 2445 3836 5890 1142 899 2240 1639 1142 899 4505 3836 2240
d.asn n.asn pl d.asn n.asn v.iai.3s cj r.gpm.3 a.npn d.npn n.npn

20 πᾶς γὰρ ὁ φαῦλα πράσσων μισεῖ τὸ φῶς καὶ ↱ οὐκ
For everyone For who practices wickedness practices hates the light and does not
1142 4246 1142 3836 4556 5765 4556 3631 3836 5890 2779 2262 4024
a.nsm cj d.nsm a.apn pt.pa.nsm v.pai.3s d.asn n.asn cj pl

ἔρχεται πρὸς τὸ φῶς, ⌊ἵνα μὴ⌋ ἐλεγχθῇ τὰ ἔργα αὐτοῦ· 21
come to the light for fear that his deeds will be exposed. {the} deeds his But
2262 4639 3836 5890 2671 3590 899 2240 1794 3836 2240 899 1254
v.pmi.3s p.a d.asn n.asn cj pl v.aps.3s d.npn n.npn r.gsm.3

ὁ δὲ ποιῶν τὴν ἀλήθειαν ἔρχεται πρὸς τὸ φῶς, ἵνα
the But ⌊one who does⌋ the truth comes to the light, so that his deeds
3836 1254 4472 3836 237 2262 4639 3836 5890 2671 899 2240
d.nsm cj pt.pa.nsm d.asf n.asf v.pmi.3s p.a d.asn n.asn cj

φανερωθῇ αὐτοῦ τὰ ἔργα ὅτι ἐν θεῷ ἐστιν
⌊may be clearly seen,⌋ his {the} deeds that they have been done in God." they have been
5746 899 3836 2240 4022 1639 1639 1639 2237 1877 2536 1639
v.aps.3s r.gsm.3 d.npn n.npn cj p.d n.dsm v.pai.3s

εἰργασμένα. 22 μετὰ ταῦτα ἦλθεν ὁ Ἰησοῦς καὶ οἱ μαθηταὶ
done After this Jesus and his disciples went {the} Jesus and {the} disciples
2237 3552 4047 2652 2779 899 3412 2262 3836 2652 2779 3836 3412
pt.rp.npn p.a r.apn v.aai.3s d.nsm n.nsm cj d.npm n.npm

αὐτοῦ εἰς τὴν Ἰουδαίαν γῆν καὶ ↱ ↱ ἐκεῖ διέτριβεν μετ᾽ αὐτῶν
his into the Judean countryside, and he was there with them for a time with them
899 1650 3836 2681 1178 2779 1417 1417 1695 3552 899 1417 3552 899
r.gsm.3 p.a d.asf a.asf n.asf cj adv v.iai.3s p.g r.gpm.3

καὶ ἐβάπτιζεν. 23 ἦν δὲ καὶ ὁ Ἰωάννης βαπτίζων ἐν Αἰνὼν
and was baptizing. Now John also was Now also {the} John baptizing at Aenon
2779 966 1254 2722 2779 1639 1254 2779 3836 2722 966 1877 143
cj v.iai.3s v.iai.3s cj adv d.nsm n.nsm pt.pa.nsm p.d n.dsf

ἐγγὺς τοῦ Σαλείμ, ὅτι ὕδατα πολλὰ ἦν ἐκεῖ, καὶ
near {the} Salim, because there were many springs many there were there, and people
1584 3836 4890 4022 1639 1639 4498 5623 4498 1639 1695 2779
p.g d.gsn n.gsn cj n.npn a.npn v.iai.3s adv cj

παρεγίνοντο καὶ ἐβαπτίζοντο· 24 οὔπω γὰρ ἦν βεβλημένος εἰς τὴν
kept coming {and} to be baptized. (John had not yet {for} had been thrown into {the}
4134 2779 966 2722 1639 4037 1142 1639 965 1650 3836
v.imi.3p cj v.ipi.3p adv cj v.iai.3s pt.rp.nsm p.a d.asf

φυλακὴν ὁ Ἰωάννης. 25 ἐγένετο οὖν ζήτησις
prison.) {the} John Now an argument about ritual cleansing arose Now argument
5871 3836 2722 4036 2428 4309 2752 2752 1181 4036 2428
n.asf d.nsm n.nsm v.ami.3s cj n.nsf

ἐκ τῶν μαθητῶν Ἰωάννου μετὰ Ἰουδαίου[a] περὶ καθαρισμοῦ.
between some of John's disciples John's and between a certain Jew. about ritual cleansing
3552 1666 3836 2722 3412 2722 3552 2681 4309 2752
p.g d.gpm n.gpm n.gsm p.g a.gsm p.g n.gsm

26 καὶ ἦλθον πρὸς τὸν Ἰωάννην καὶ εἶπαν αὐτῷ, ῥαββί, ὃς ἦν μετὰ
So they came to {the} John and said to him, "Rabbi, that man who was with
2779 2262 4639 3836 2722 2779 3306 899 4806 4005 1639 3552
cj v.aai.3p p.a d.asm n.asm cj v.aai.3p r.dsm.3 n.vsm r.nsm v.iai.3s p.g

σοῦ πέραν τοῦ Ἰορδάνου, ᾧ σὺ μεμαρτύρηκας, ἴδε οὗτος
you ⌊on the far side⌋ of the Jordan, the one ⌊to whom⌋ you bore witness — well, he
5148 4305 3836 2674 4005 5148 3455 2623 4047
r.gs.2 p.g d.gsm n.gsm r.dsm r.ns.2 v.rai.2s pl r.nsm

βαπτίζει καὶ πάντες ἔρχονται πρὸς αὐτόν. 27 ἀπεκρίθη Ἰωάννης καὶ εἶπεν,
is baptizing, and everyone is going to him!" John responded, John {and} saying,
966 2779 4246 2262 4639 899 2722 646 2722 2779 3306
v.pai.3s cj a.npm v.pmi.3p p.a r.asm.3 v.api.3s n.nsm cj v.aai.3s

⌊οὐ δύναται⌋ ἄνθρωπος λαμβάνειν ⌊οὐδὲ ἕν⌋ ⌊ἐὰν μὴ⌋ ᾖ
"A man cannot man receive anything unless ⌊it has been⌋
476 4024 1538 476 3284 4028 1651 1569 3590 1639
pl v.ppi.3s n.nsm f.pa adv a.asn cj pl v.pas.3s

NASB

than the Light, for
their deeds were
evil. 20 For everyone
who does evil hates
the Light, and
does not come to
the Light for fear
that his deeds will
be exposed. 21 But
he who practices
the truth comes to
the Light, so that
his deeds may be
manifested as hav-
ing been wrought
in God."

John's Last Testimony

22 After these
things Jesus and
His disciples came
into the land of
Judea, and there He
was spending time
with them and bap-
tizing. 23 John also
was baptizing in
Aenon near Salim,
because there was
much water there;
and *people* were
coming and were
being baptized—
24 for John had not
yet been thrown
into prison.
25 Therefore there
arose a discus-
sion on the part of
John's disciples
with a Jew about
purification. 26 And
they came to John
and said to him,
"Rabbi, He who
was with you be-
yond the Jordan,
to whom you have
testified, behold,
He is baptizing
and all are coming
to Him." 27 John
answered and said,
"A man can receive
nothing unless it
has been given

[a] Ἰουδαίου UBS, TNIV, NET. Ἰουδαίων TR.

NIV

given them from
heaven. 28 You
yourselves can tes-
tify that I said, 'I
am not the Messiah
but am sent ahead
of him.' 29 The
bride belongs to
the bridegroom.
The friend who
attends the bride-
groom waits and
listens for him, and
is full of joy when
he hears the bride-
groom's voice.
That joy is mine,
and it is now com-
plete. 30 He must
become greater;
I must become
less."[a]
31 The one who
comes from above
is above all; the
one who is from
the earth belongs
to the earth, and
speaks as one from
the earth. The
one who comes
from heaven is
above all. 32 He
testifies to what
he has seen and
heard, but no one
accepts his testi-
mony. 33 Whoever
has accepted it has
certified that God
is truthful. 34 For
the one whom God
has sent speaks
the words of God,
for God[b] gives
the Spirit without
limit. 35 The Father
loves the Son and
has placed every-
thing in his hands.
36 Whoever be-
lieves in the Son

[a] 30 Some interpreters end the quotation with verse 36.
[b] 34 Greek *he*

δεδομένον αὐτῷ ἐκ τοῦ οὐρανοῦ. 28 αὐτοὶ ὑμεῖς ↱ μοι μαρτυρεῖτε ὅτι
given to him from *{the}* heaven. You yourselves *You* bear me witness that
1443 899 1666 3836 4041 7007 899 7007 3455 1609 3455 4022
pt.rp.nsn r.dsm.3 p.g d.gsm n.gsm r.npm r.np.2 r.ds.1 v.pai.2p cj

εἶπον ὅτι[a] οὐκ εἰμὶ ἐγὼ ὁ Χριστός, ἀλλ᾽ ὅτι
I said, ~ 'I am not *am* *I* the Christ,' but rather, ~ 'I am the
3306 4022 1609 1639 4024 1639 1609 3836 5986 247 4022 1639 1639
v.aai.1s cj pl v.pai.1s r.ns.1 d.nsm n.nsm cj cj

ἀπεσταλμένος εἰμὶ ἔμπροσθεν ἐκείνου. 29 ὁ ἔχων τὴν
one sent *I am* ahead of him.' It is the bridegroom ⌊who has⌋ the
690 1639 1869 1697 1639 1639 3836 3812 2400 3836
pt.rp.nsm v.pai.1s p.g r.gsm d.nsm pt.pa.nsm d.asf

νύμφην νυμφίος ἐστίν· ὁ δὲ φίλος τοῦ νυμφίου ὁ ἑστηκὼς καὶ
bride; *bridegroom* *It is* but the *but* friend of the bridegroom, who stands by and
3811 3812 1639 1254 3836 1254 5813 3836 3812 3836 2705 2779
n.asf n.nsm v.pai.3s d.nsm cj n.nsm d.gsm n.gsm d.nsm pt.ra.nsm cj

ἀκούων αὐτοῦ ⌊χαρᾷ χαίρει⌋ διὰ τὴν φωνὴν τοῦ
listens for him, rejoices greatly when he hears the bridegroom's voice. *{the}*
201 899 5915 5897 1328 3836 3812 5889 3836
pt.pa.nsm r.gsm.3 n.dsf v.pai.3s p.a d.asf n.asf d.gsm

νυμφίου. αὕτη οὖν ἡ χαρὰ ἡ ἐμὴ πεπλήρωται. 30 ἐκεῖνον
bridegroom's Therefore this *Therefore* *{the}* joy *{the}* of mine is now complete. He
3812 4036 4047 4036 3836 5915 3836 1847 4444 1697
n.gsm r.nsf cj d.nsf n.nsf d.nsf r.nsf.1 v.rpi.3s r.asm

δεῖ αὐξάνειν, ἐμὲ δὲ ↰ ἐλαττοῦσθαι. 31 ὁ ἄνωθεν
must increase, but I *but* must decrease." He who comes from above
1256 889 1254 1609 1254 1256 1783 3836 2262 2262 540
v.pai.3s f.pa r.as.1 cj f.pp d.nsm adv

ἐρχόμενος ἐπάνω πάντων ἐστίν· ὁ ὢν ἐκ τῆς γῆς ἐκ τῆς γῆς
who comes is superior to all. *is* He ⌊who is⌋ of the earth belongs to the earth
2262 1639 2062 4246 1639 3836 1639 1666 3836 1178 1639 1666 3836 1178
pt.pm.nsm p.g a.gpn v.pai.3s d.nsm pt.pa.nsm p.g d.gsf n.gsf p.g d.gsf n.gsf

ἐστιν καὶ ἐκ τῆς γῆς λαλεῖ. ὁ ἐκ τοῦ οὐρανοῦ
belongs and speaks in an ⌊earthly way.⌋ *speaks* He who comes from *{the}* heaven
1639 2779 3281 1666 3836 1178 3281 3836 2262 2262 1666 3836 4041
v.pai.3s cj p.g d.gsf n.gsf v.pai.3s d.nsm p.g d.gsm n.gsm

ἐρχόμενος [b]ἐπάνω πάντων ἐστίν· 32 ὃ ἑώρακεν καὶ
who comes is superior to all. *is* He bears witness to what he has seen and
2262 1639 2062 4246 1639 3455 3455 3455 3455 4005 3972 2779
pt.pm.nsm p.g a.gpn v.pai.3s r.asn v.rai.3s cj

ἤκουσεν τοῦτο μαρτυρεῖ, καὶ τὴν μαρτυρίαν αὐτοῦ οὐδεὶς
heard, *{this}* *He bears witness to* yet no one accepts *{the}* his testimony. *his* *no one*
201 4047 3455 2779 4029 4029 3284 3836 899 3456 899 4029
v.aai.3s r.asn v.pai.3s cj d.asf n.asf r.gsm.3 a.nsm

λαμβάνει. 33 ὁ λαβὼν αὐτοῦ τὴν μαρτυρίαν ἐσφράγισεν
accepts The ⌊one who has accepted⌋ his *{the}* testimony has thereby acknowledged
3284 3836 3284 899 3836 3456 5381
v.pai.3s d.nsm pt.aa.nsm r.gsm.3 d.asf n.asf v.aai.3s

ὅτι ὁ θεὸς ἀληθής ἐστιν. 34 ὃν γὰρ ἀπέστειλεν ὁ θεὸς
that *{the}* God is truthful. *is* For the one whom *For* God has sent *{the}* *God*
4022 3836 2536 1639 239 1639 1142 4005 1142 2536 690 3836 2536
cj d.nsm n.nsm a.nsm v.pai.3s r.asm cj v.aai.3s d.nsm n.nsm

τὰ ῥήματα τοῦ θεοῦ λαλεῖ, οὐ γὰρ ἐκ
speaks the words of God, *speaks* for God does not *for* give the Spirit in a
3281 3836 4839 3836 2536 3281 1142 1443 4024 1142 1443 3836 4460 1666
d.apn n.apn d.gsm n.gsm v.pai.3s pl cj p.g

μέτρου δίδωσιν τὸ πνεῦμα. 35 ὁ πατὴρ ἀγαπᾷ τὸν υἱὸν καὶ
⌊limited measure.⌋ *does give* *the* *Spirit* The Father loves the Son and has placed
3586 1443 3836 4460 3836 4252 26 3836 5626 2779 1443 1443
n.gsn v.pai.3s d.asn n.asn d.nsm n.nsm v.pai.3s d.asm n.asm cj

πάντα δέδωκεν ἐν τῇ χειρὶ αὐτοῦ. 36 ὁ πιστεύων εἰς τὸν υἱὸν
everything *has placed* in *{the}* his hands. *his* The one who believes in the Son
4246 1443 1877 3836 899 5931 899 3836 4409 1650 3836 5626
a.apn v.rai.3s p.d d.dsf n.dsf r.gsm.3 d.nsm pt.pa.nsm p.a d.asm n.asm

[a] [ὅτι] UBS, omitted by TNIV.
[b] [ἐπάνω πάντων ἐστίν] UBS.

NASB

him from heaven.
28 You yourselves
are my witnesses
that I said, 'I am
not the Christ,' but,
'I have been sent
ahead of Him.' 29 He
who has the bride
is the bridegroom;
but the friend of
the bridegroom,
who stands and
hears him, rejoices
greatly because of
the bridegroom's
voice. So this joy
of mine has been
made full. 30 He
must increase, but I
must decrease.
31 "He who comes
from above is
above all, he who
is of the earth is
from the earth and
speaks of the earth.
He who comes
from heaven is
above all. 32 What
He has seen and
heard, of that He
testifies; and no
one receives His
testimony. 33 He
who has received
His testimony
has set his seal
to *this,* that God
is true. 34 For He
whom God has
sent speaks the
words of God; for
He gives the Spirit
without measure.
35 The Father loves
the Son and has
given all things
into His hand. 36 He
who believes in

NIV

has eternal life, but
whoever rejects
the Son will not
see life, for God's
wrath remains on
them.

Jesus Talks With a Samaritan Woman

4 Now Jesus
learned that
the Pharisees had
heard that he was
gaining and bap-
tizing more disci-
ples than John—
2although in fact it
was not Jesus who
baptized, but his
disciples. 3So he
left Judea and went
back once more to
Galilee.
4Now he had to
go through Samar-
ia. 5So he came to
a town in Samaria
called Sychar, near
the plot of ground
Jacob had given
to his son Joseph.
6Jacob's well was
there, and Jesus,
tired as he was
from the journey,
sat down by the
well. It was about
noon.
7When a Samar-
itan woman came
to draw water,
Jesus said to her,
"Will you give me
a drink?" 8(His
disciples had gone
into the town to
buy food.)
9The Samari-
tan woman said
to him, "You are
a Jew and I am a
Samaritan woman.
How can you ask
me for a drink?"
(For Jews

ἔχει ζωὴν αἰώνιον· ὁ δὲ ἀπειθῶν τῷ υἱῷ ↱ οὐκ ὄψεται
has eternal life; *eternal* but the *but* one who disobeys the Son will not see
2400 173 2437 173 1254 3836 1254 578 3836 5626 3972 4024 3972
v.pai.3s n.asf a.asf d.nsm cj pt.pa.nsm d.dsm n.dsm pl v.fmi.3s

ζωήν, ἀλλ᾽ ἡ ὀργὴ τοῦ θεοῦ μένει ἐπ᾽ αὐτόν.
life, but the wrath of God remains on him.
2437 247 3836 3973 3836 2536 3531 2093 899
n.asf cj d.nsf n.nsf d.gsm n.gsm v.pai.3s p.a r.asm.3

4:1 ὡς οὖν ἔγνω ὁ Ἰησοῦς ὅτι ἤκουσαν οἱ
Now when *Now* Jesus learned *{the}* *Jesus* that the Pharisees had heard *the*
4036 6055 4036 2652 1182 3836 2652 4022 3836 5757 201 3836
cj cj v.aai.3s d.nsm n.nsm cj v.aai.3p d.npm

Φαρισαῖοι ὅτι Ἰησοῦς πλείονας μαθητὰς ποιεῖ καὶ
Pharisees that Jesus was making and baptizing more disciples *was making* *and*
5757 4022 2652 4472 4472 2779 966 4498 3412 4472 2779
n.npm cj n.nsm a.apm.c n.apm v.pai.3s cj

βαπτίζει ἢ Ἰωάννης 2 καίτοιγε Ἰησοῦς αὐτὸς ↱ οὐκ ἐβάπτιζεν ἀλλ᾽ οἱ
baptizing than John — although Jesus himself was not baptizing, but *{the}* his
966 2445 2722 2793 2652 899 966 4024 966 247 3836 899
v.pai.3s pl n.nsm cj n.nsm r.nsm pl v.iai.3s cj d.npm

μαθηταὶ αὐτοῦ 3 ἀφῆκεν τὴν Ἰουδαίαν καὶ ἀπῆλθεν πάλιν εἰς τὴν
disciples *his* were — he left *{the}* Judea and departed again for *{the}*
3412 899 918 3836 2677 2779 599 4099 1650 3836
n.npm r.gsm.3 v.aai.3s d.asf n.asf cj v.aai.3s adv p.a d.asf

Γαλιλαίαν. 4 ἔδει δὲ αὐτὸν διέρχεσθαι διὰ τῆς Σαμαρείας.
Galilee. Now ⌊it was necessary⌋ *Now* that he pass through *{the}* Samaria.
1133 1254 1256 1254 899 1451 1328 3836 4899
n.asf v.iai.3s cj r.asm.3 f.pm p.g d.gsf n.gsf

5 ἔρχεται οὖν εἰς πόλιν τῆς Σαμαρείας λεγομένην Συχὰρ πλησίον τοῦ
So he came *So* to a town in Samaria called Sychar, near the
4036 2262 4036 1650 4484 3836 4899 3306 5373 4446 3836
v.pmi.3s cj p.a n.asf d.gsf n.gsf pt.pp.asf n.asf p.g d.gsn

χωρίου ὃ ἔδωκεν Ἰακὼβ τῷ[a] Ἰωσὴφ τῷ υἱῷ αὐτοῦ· 6
plot of ground that Jacob had given *Jacob* to his son Joseph. *{the}* *son* *his* Jacob's
6005 4005 2609 1443 2609 3836 899 5626 2737 3836 5626 899 2609
n.gsn r.asn v.aai.3s n.nsm d.dsm n.dsm d.dsm n.dsm r.gsm.3

ἦν δὲ ἐκεῖ πηγὴ τοῦ Ἰακώβ. ὁ οὖν Ἰησοῦς κεκοπιακὼς ἐκ τῆς
well was *{and}* there. *well* *{the}* *Jacob's* *{the}* So Jesus, weary from his
4380 1639 1254 1695 4380 3836 2609 3836 4036 2652 3159 1666 3836
v.iai.3s cj adv n.nsf d.gsm n.gsm d.nsm cj n.nsm pt.ra.nsm p.g d.gsf

ὁδοιπορίας ἐκαθέζετο οὕτως ἐπὶ τῇ πηγῇ· ὥρα ἦν ὡς ἕκτη.
journey, sat down *{thus}* by the well. It was about the sixth hour. *It was* *about* *sixth*
3845 2757 4048 2093 3836 4380 1639 1639 6055 1761 6052 1639 6055 1761
n.gsf v.imi.3s adv p.d d.dsf n.dsf n.nsf v.iai.3s pl a.nsf

7 ἔρχεται γυνὴ ἐκ τῆς Σαμαρείας ἀντλῆσαι ὕδωρ. λέγει αὐτῇ ὁ Ἰησοῦς,
There came a woman of *{the}* Samaria to draw water. Jesus said to her, *{the}* *Jesus*
2262 1222 1666 3836 4899 533 5623 2652 3306 899 3836 2652
v.pmi.3s n.nsf p.g d.gsf n.gsf f.aa n.asn v.pai.3s r.dsf.3 d.nsm n.nsm

δός μοι πεῖν· 8 οἱ γὰρ μαθηταὶ αὐτοῦ ἀπεληλύθεισαν εἰς τὴν πόλιν ἵνα
"Give me a drink." *{the}* (For his disciples *his* had gone off to the town to
1443 1609 4403 3836 1142 899 3412 899 599 1650 3836 4484 2671
v.aam.2s r.ds.1 f.aa d.npm cj n.npm r.gsm.3 v.lai.3p p.a d.asf n.asf cj

τροφὰς ἀγοράσωσιν. 9 λέγει οὖν αὐτῷ ἡ γυνὴ ἡ
buy food.) *buy* The Samaritan woman said *{then}* to him, *The* *woman* *{the}*
60 5575 60 3836 4902 1222 3306 4036 899 3836 1222 3836
n.apf v.aas.3p v.pai.3s cj r.dsm.3 d.nsf n.nsf d.nsf

Σαμαρῖτις, πῶς σὺ Ἰουδαῖος ὢν παρ᾽ ἐμοῦ
Samaritan "How is it that you, being a Jew, *being* are asking for a drink from me,
4902 4802 5148 1639 2681 1639 160 160 160 4403 4123 1609
n.nsf cj r.ns.2 a.nsm pt.pa.nsm p.g r.gs.1

πεῖν αἰτεῖς γυναικὸς Σαμαρίτιδος οὔσης; ↱ οὐ γὰρ
drink *are asking for* a woman who is from Samaria?" *who is* (For Jews use nothing *For*
4403 160 1222 1639 1639 4902 1639 1142 2681 5178 4024 1142
f.aa v.pai.2s n.gsf n.gsf pt.pa.gsf pl cj

[a] [τῷ] UBS.

NASB

the Son has eternal
life; but he who
does not obey the
Son will not see
life, but the wrath
of God abides on
him."

Jesus Goes to Galilee

4:1Therefore when
the Lord knew that
the Pharisees had
heard that Jesus
was making and
baptizing more
disciples than John
2(although Jesus
Himself was not
baptizing, but His
disciples were),
3He left Judea and
went away again
into Galilee. 4And
He had to pass
through Samaria.
5So He *came to
a city of Samaria
called Sychar,
near the parcel of
ground that Jacob
gave to his son Jo-
seph; 6and Jacob's
well was there.
So Jesus, being
wearied from His
journey, was sitting
thus by the well.
It was about [a]the
sixth hour.

The Woman of Samaria

7There *came a
woman of Samaria
to draw water.
Jesus *said to her,
"Give Me a drink."
8For His disciples
had gone away
into the city to buy
food. 9Therefore
the Samaritan
woman *said to
Him, "How is it
that You, being a
Jew, ask me for a
drink since I am a
Samaritan wom-
an?" (For Jews
have no dealings

[a] Perhaps 6 p.m. Roman time or noon Jewish time

NIV

do not associate
with Samaritans.[a])
10 Jesus answered
her, "If you knew
the gift of God and
who it is that asks
you for a drink,
you would have
asked him and he
would have given
you living water."
11 "Sir," the wom-
an said, "you have
nothing to draw
with and the well
is deep. Where can
you get this living
water? 12 Are you
greater than our
father Jacob, who
gave us the well
and drank from
it himself, as did
also his sons and
his livestock?"
13 Jesus answered,
"Everyone who
drinks this wa-
ter will be thirsty
again, 14 but who-
ever drinks the
water I give them
will never thirst.
Indeed, the water
I give them will
become in them
a spring of water
welling up to eter-
nal life."
15 The woman
said to him, "Sir,
give me this water
so that I won't get
thirsty and have to
keep coming here
to draw water."
16 He told her,
"Go, call your
husband and come
back."
17 "I have no hus-
band," she replied.
Jesus said to her,
"You are right
when you say you
have

[a] 9 Or *do not use dishes Samaritans have used*

συγχρῶνται Ἰουδαῖοι Σαμαρίταις. 10 ἀπεκρίθη Ἰησοῦς καὶ εἶπεν αὐτῇ,
in common *Jews* with Samaritans.) Jesus answered *Jesus* *{and}* *saying* her,
5178 2681 4901 2652 646 2652 2779 3306 899
v.pmi.3p a.npm n.dpm v.api.3s n.nsm cj v.aai.3s r.dsf.3

εἰ ᾔδεις τὴν δωρεὰν τοῦ θεοῦ καὶ τίς ἐστιν ὁ λέγων σοι,
saying, "If ⌊you had known⌋ the gift of God and who it was that said to you,
3306 1623 3857 3836 1561 3836 2536 2779 5515 1639 3836 3306 5148
cj v.lai.2s d.asf n.asf d.gsm n.gsm cj r.nsm v.pai.3s d.nsm pt.pa.nsm r.ds.2

δός μοι πεῖν, σὺ ἂν ᾔτησας αὐτὸν καὶ → ἔδωκεν ἄν σοι
'Give me a drink,' you would have asked him, and he would have given *would* you living
1443 1609 4403 5148 323 160 899 2779 323 1443 323 5148 2409
v.aam.2s r.ds.1 f.aa r.ns.2 pl v.aai.2s r.asm.3 cj v.aai.3s pl r.ds.2

ὕδωρ ζῶν. 11 λέγει αὐτῷ [a]ἡ γυνή, κύριε, οὔτε ἄντλημα
water." *living* The woman said to him, *The* *woman* "Sir, you have no bucket
5623 2409 3836 1222 3306 899 3836 1222 3261 2400 2400 4046 534
n.asn pt.pa.asn v.pai.3s r.dsm.3 d.nsf n.nsf n.vsm cj n.asn

ἔχεις καὶ τὸ φρέαρ ἐστὶν βαθύ· πόθεν οὖν ἔχεις τὸ ὕδωρ τὸ
you have and the well is deep. How then ⌊are you going to draw⌋ the living water? *{the}*
2400 2779 3836 5853 1639 960 4470 4036 2400 3836 2409 5623 3836
v.pai.2s cj d.nsn n.nsn v.pai.3s a.nsm cj cj v.pai.2s d.asn n.asn d.asn

ζῶν; 12 → μὴ σὺ μείζων εἶ τοῦ πατρὸς ἡμῶν Ἰακώβ, ↰ ↰
living Surely you are not *you* greater *are* than our father *our* Jacob, are you,
2409 5148 1639 3590 5148 3489 1639 3836 7005 4252 7005 2609 3590 3590
pt.pa.asn pl r.ns.2 a.nsm.c v.pai.2s d.gsm n.gsm r.gp.1 n.gsm

ὃς ἔδωκεν ἡμῖν τὸ φρέαρ καὶ αὐτὸς ἐξ αὐτοῦ ἔπιεν καὶ οἱ
who gave us the well and drank from it himself, *from* *it* *drank* as did *{the}* his
4005 1443 7005 3836 5853 2779 4403 1666 899 899 1666 899 4403 2779 3836 899
r.nsm v.aai.3s r.dp.1 d.asn n.asn cj r.nsm p.g r.gsn.3 v.aai.3s cj d.npm

υἱοὶ αὐτοῦ καὶ τὰ θρέμματα αὐτοῦ; 13 ἀπεκρίθη Ἰησοῦς καὶ εἶπεν αὐτῇ,
sons *his* and *{the}* his flocks?" *his* Jesus replied, *Jesus* and said to her,
5626 899 2779 3836 899 2576 899 2652 646 2652 2779 3306 899
n.npm r.gsm.3 cj d.npn n.npn r.gsm.3 v.api.3s n.nsm cj v.aai.3s r.dsf.3

πᾶς ὁ πίνων ἐκ τοῦ ὕδατος τούτου διψήσει πάλιν· 14 ὃς
"Everyone who drinks of *{the}* this water *this* will be thirsty again, but whoever
4246 3836 4403 1666 3836 4047 5623 4047 1498 4099 1254 4005
a.nsm d.nsm pt.pa.nsm p.g d.gsn n.gsn r.gsn v.fai.3s adv r.nsm

δ' ἂν πίῃ ἐκ τοῦ ὕδατος οὗ ἐγὼ δώσω αὐτῷ, ↱ ⌊οὐ μὴ⌋ διψήσει εἰς τὸν
but ~ drinks of the water that I will give him will never be thirsty for all
1254 323 4403 1666 3836 5623 4005 1609 1443 899 1498 4024 3590 1498 1650 3836
cj pl v.aas.3s p.g d.gsn n.gsn r.gsn r.ns.1 v.fai.1s r.dsm.3 pl pl v.fai.3s p.a d.asm

αἰῶνα, ἀλλὰ τὸ ὕδωρ ὃ δώσω αὐτῷ γενήσεται ἐν αὐτῷ πηγὴ ὕδατος
time, but the water that I will give him will become in him a fountain of water
172 247 3836 5623 4005 1443 899 1181 1877 899 4380 5623
n.asm cj d.nsn n.nsn r.asn v.fai.1s r.dsm.3 v.fmi.3s p.d r.dsm.3 n.nsf n.gsn

ἁλλομένου εἰς ζωὴν αἰώνιον. 15 λέγει πρὸς αὐτὸν ἡ γυνή, κύριε,
gushing up to eternal life." *eternal* The woman said to him, *The* *woman* "Sir,
256 1650 173 2437 173 3836 1222 3306 4639 899 3836 1222 3261
pt.pm.gsn p.a n.asf a.asf v.pai.3s p.a r.asm.3 d.nsf n.nsf n.vsm

δός μοι τοῦτο τὸ ὕδωρ, ἵνα ↱ ↱ μὴ διψῶ μηδὲ διέρχωμαι
give me this *{the}* water, so that I will not be thirsty or ⌊have to keep coming⌋
1443 1609 4047 3836 5623 2671 1498 1498 3590 1498 3593 1451
v.aam.2s r.ds.1 r.asn d.asn n.asn cj pl v.pas.1s cj v.pms.1s

ἐνθάδε ἀντλεῖν. 16 λέγει αὐτῇ, ὕπαγε φώνησον τὸν ἄνδρα σου καὶ
here to draw water." Jesus said to her, "Go, call *{the}* your husband, *your* and
1924 533 3306 899 5632 5888 3836 5148 467 5148 2779
adv f.pa v.pai.3s r.dsf.3 v.pam.2s v.aam.2s d.asm n.asm r.gs.2 cj

ἐλθὲ ἐνθάδε. 17 ἀπεκρίθη ἡ γυνὴ καὶ εἶπεν αὐτῷ, ↱ ↱ οὐκ
come back here." The woman replied *The* *woman* and said to him, "I do not
2262 1924 3836 1222 646 3836 1222 2779 3306 899 2400 2400 4024
v.aam.2s adv v.api.3s d.nsf n.nsf cj v.aai.3s r.dsm.3 pl

ἔχω ἄνδρα. λέγει αὐτῇ ὁ Ἰησοῦς, ↱ ↱ καλῶς εἶπας ὅτι
have a husband." Jesus said to her, *{the}* *Jesus* "You are right in saying, ~ 'I do
2400 467 2652 3306 899 3836 2652 3306 3306 2822 3306 4022 2400 2400
v.pai.1s n.asm v.pai.3s r.dsf.3 d.nsm n.nsm adv v.aai.2s cj

[a] [ἡ γυνή] UBS, omitted by NET.

NASB

with Samaritans.)
10 Jesus answered
and said to her, "If
you knew the gift
of God, and who it
is who says to you,
'Give Me a drink,'
you would have
asked Him, and He
would have given
you living water."
11 She *said to Him,
"Sir, You have
nothing to draw
with and the well
is deep; where then
do You get that
living water? 12 You
are not greater than
our father Jacob,
are You, who gave
us the well, and
drank of it himself
and his sons and
his cattle?" 13 Jesus
answered and said
to her, "Everyone
who drinks of
this water will
thirst again; 14 but
whoever drinks
of the water that I
will give him shall
never thirst; but the
water that I will
give him will be-
come in him a well
of water springing
up to eternal life."
15 The woman
*said to Him, "Sir,
give me this water,
so I will not be
thirsty nor come
all the way here to
draw." 16 He *said
to her, "Go, call
your husband and
come here." 17 The
woman answered
and said, "I have
no husband." Jesus
*said to her, "You
have correctly said,

NIV

no husband. 18The
fact is, you have
had five husbands,
and the man you
now have is not
your husband.
What you have just
said is quite true."
19"Sir," the wom-
an said, "I can
see that you are a
prophet. 20Our an-
cestors worshiped
on this mountain,
but you Jews claim
that the place
where we must
worship is in Jeru-
salem."
21"Woman,"
Jesus replied, "be-
lieve me, a time
is coming when
you will worship
the Father neither
on this mountain
nor in Jerusalem.
22You Samaritans
worship what you
do not know; we
worship what we
do know, for sal-
vation is from the
Jews. 23Yet a time
is coming and has
now come when
the true worship-
ers will worship
the Father in the
Spirit and in truth,
for they are the
kind of worshipers
the Father seeks.
24God is spirit,
and his worshipers
must worship in
the Spirit and in
truth."
25The woman
said, "I know that
Messiah" (called
Christ) "is coming.
When he comes,
he will explain ev-
erything to us."

ἄνδρα οὐκ ἔχω· 18 πέντε γὰρ ἄνδρας ἔσχες καὶ
not have a husband,' *not* *I do have* for you have had five *for* husbands, *you have had* and
4024 2400 467 4024 2400 1142 2400 2400 2400 4297 1142 467 2400 2779
n.asm pl v.pai.1s a.apm cj n.apm v.aai.2s cj

↱ νῦν ὃν ἔχεις οὐκ ἔστιν σου ἀνήρ· τοῦτο ἀληθὲς
the man you now *man* have is not *is* your husband. You have spoken the truth."
4005 2400 3814 4005 2400 1639 4024 1639 5148 467 3306 3306 3306 4047 239
adv r.asm v.pai.2s pl v.pai.3s r.gs.2 n.nsm r.asn a.asn

εἴρηκας. 19 λέγει αὐτῷ ἡ γυνή, κύριε, θεωρῶ ὅτι
You have spoken The woman said to him, *The* *woman* "Sir, I can see that you are a
3306 3836 1222 3306 899 3836 1222 3261 2555 4022 5148 1639
v.rai.2s v.pai.3s r.dsm.3 d.nsf n.nsf n.vsm v.pai.1s cj

προφήτης εἶ σύ. 20 οἱ πατέρες ἡμῶν ἐν τῷ ὄρει τούτῳ
prophet. *are* *you* *{the}* Our fathers *Our* worshiped on *{the}* this mountain, *this*
4737 1639 5148 3836 7005 4252 7005 4686 1877 3836 4047 4001 4047
n.nsm v.pai.2s r.ns.2 d.npm n.npm r.gp.1 p.d d.dsn n.dsn r.dsn

προσεκύνησαν· καὶ ὑμεῖς λέγετε ὅτι ἐν
worshiped but you Jews say that the place where people should worship is in
4686 2779 7007 3306 4022 3836 5536 3963 1256 4686 1639 1877
v.aai.3p cj r.np.2 v.pai.2p cj p.d

Ἱεροσολύμοις ἐστὶν ὁ τόπος ὅπου προσκυνεῖν δεῖ. 21 λέγει αὐτῇ ὁ
Jerusalem." *is* *the* *place* *where* *worship* *should* Jesus said to her, *{the}*
2642 1639 3836 5536 3963 4686 1256 2652 3306 899 3836
n.dpn v.pai.3s d.nsm n.nsm cj f.pa v.pai.3s v.pai.3s r.dsf.3 d.nsm

Ἰησοῦς, πίστευέ μοι, γύναι, ὅτι ἔρχεται ὥρα ὅτε
Jesus "Believe me, woman, ~ the hour is coming *hour* when you will worship the Father
2652 4409 1609 1222 4022 6052 2262 6052 4021 4686 4686 4686 3836 4252
n.nsm v.pam.2s r.ds.1 n.vsf cj v.pmi.3s n.nsf cj

οὔτε ἐν τῷ ὄρει τούτῳ οὔτε ἐν Ἱεροσολύμοις προσκυνήσετε τῷ πατρί.
neither on *{the}* this mountain *this* nor in Jerusalem. *you will worship* *the* *Father*
4046 1877 3836 4047 4001 4047 4046 1877 2642 4686 3836 4252
cj p.d d.dsn n.dsn r.dsn cj p.d n.dpn v.fai.2p d.dsm n.dsm

22 ὑμεῖς προσκυνεῖτε ὃ ↱ ↱ οὐκ οἴδατε· ἡμεῖς προσκυνοῦμεν ὃ
You Samaritans worship what you do not know; we worship what
7007 4686 4005 3857 3857 4024 3857 7005 4686 4005
r.np.2 v.pai.2p r.asn pl v.rai.2p r.np.1 v.pai.1p r.asn

οἴδαμεν, ὅτι ἡ σωτηρία ἐκ τῶν Ἰουδαίων ἐστίν. 23 ἀλλὰ
we know, because *{the}* salvation is from the Jews. *is* But the hour
3857 4022 3836 5401 1639 1666 3836 2681 1639 247 6052
v.rai.1p cj d.nsf n.nsf p.g d.gpm a.gpm v.pai.3s cj

ἔρχεται ὥρα καὶ νῦν ἐστιν, ὅτε οἱ ἀληθινοὶ προσκυνηταὶ
is coming, *hour* and is ⌊here already,⌋ *is* when *{the}* true worshipers
2262 6052 2779 1639 3814 1639 4021 3836 240 4687
v.pmi.3s n.nsf cj adv v.pai.3s cj d.npm a.npm n.npm

προσκυνήσουσιν τῷ πατρὶ ἐν πνεύματι καὶ ↰ ἀληθείᾳ· καὶ γὰρ ὁ
will worship the Father in spirit and in truth; for indeed *for* the
4686 3836 4252 1877 4460 2779 1877 237 1142 2779 1142 3836
v.fai.3p d.dsm n.dsm p.d n.dsn cj n.dsf adv cj d.nsm

πατὴρ τοιούτους ζητεῖ τοὺς → → προσκυνοῦντας αὐτόν. 24
Father is seeking just such people *is seeking* *{the}* to be his worshipers. *his* God is
4252 2426 2426 5525 2426 3836 899 4686 899 2536
n.nsm r.apm v.pai.3s d.apm pt.pa.apm r.asm.3

πνεῦμα ὁ θεός, καὶ τοὺς προσκυνοῦντας αὐτὸν ἐν πνεύματι καὶ ↰
spirit, *{the}* *God* and those who worship him must worship in spirit and in
4460 3836 2536 2779 3836 4686 899 1256 4686 1877 4460 2779 1877
n.nsn d.nsm n.nsm cj d.apm pt.pa.apm r.asm.3 p.d n.dsn cj

ἀληθείᾳ δεῖ προσκυνεῖν. 25 λέγει αὐτῷ ἡ γυνή, οἶδα ὅτι Μεσσίας
truth." *must* *worship* The woman said to him, *The* *woman* "I know that Messiah
237 1256 4686 3836 1222 3306 899 3836 1222 3857 4022 3549
n.dsf v.pai.3s f.pa v.pai.3s r.dsm.3 d.nsf n.nsf v.rai.1s cj n.nsm

ἔρχεται ὁ λεγόμενος χριστός· ὅταν ἔλθῃ ἐκεῖνος, ἀναγγελεῖ ἡμῖν
is coming (the one called Christ). When he comes, he will explain everything to us."
2262 3836 3306 5986 4020 2262 1697 334 570 7005
v.pmi.3s d.nsm pt.pp.nsm n.nsm cj v.aas.3s r.nsm v.fai.3s r.dp.1

NASB

'I have no hus-
band'; 18for you
have had five hus-
bands, and the one
whom you now
have is not your
husband; this you
have said truly."
19The woman *said
to Him, "Sir, I
perceive that You
are a prophet. 20Our
fathers worshiped
in this mountain,
and you *people* say
that in Jerusalem
is the place where
men ought to wor-
ship." 21Jesus *said
to her, "Woman,
believe Me, an
hour is coming
when neither in
this mountain
nor in Jerusalem
will you worship
the Father. 22You
worship what you
do not know; we
worship what we
know, for salvation
is from the Jews.
23But an hour is
coming, and now
is, when the true
worshipers will
worship the Father
in spirit and truth;
for such people the
Father seeks to be
His worshipers.
24God is spirit, and
those who worship
Him must worship
in spirit and truth."
25The woman *said
to Him, "I know
that Messiah is
coming (He who
is called Christ);
when that One
comes, He will
declare all things
to us."

NIV

[26]Then Jesus de-
clared, "I, the one
speaking to you—
I am he."

The Disciples Rejoin Jesus

[27]Just then his
disciples returned
and were surprised
to find him talk-
ing with a woman.
But no one asked,
"What do you
want?" or "Why
are you talking
with her?"
[28]Then, leaving
her water jar, the
woman went back
to the town and
said to the people,
[29]"Come, see a
man who told me
everything I ever
did. Could this
be the Messiah?"
[30]They came out of
the town and made
their way toward
him.
[31]Meanwhile his
disciples urged
him, "Rabbi, eat
something."
[32]But he said
to them, "I have
food to eat that
you know nothing
about."
[33]Then his disci-
ples said to each
other, "Could
someone have
brought him
food?"
[34]"My food,"
said Jesus, "is to
do the will of him
who sent me and
to finish his work.
[35]Don't you have
a saying, 'It's still
four months un-
til harvest'? I tell
you, open your
eyes and look at
the fields! They
are

ἅπαντα. 26 λέγει αὐτῇ ὁ Ἰησοῦς, ἐγώ εἰμι,
everything Jesus said to her, {the} Jesus "I, the one speaking to you, am he."
570 2652 3306 899 3836 2652 1609 3836 3281 3281 5148 5148 1639
a.apn v.pai.3s r.dsf.3 d.nsm n.nsm r.ns.1 v.pai.1s

ὁ λαλῶν σοι. 27 καὶ ἐπὶ τούτῳ ἦλθαν οἱ μαθηταὶ αὐτοῦ
the one speaking to you {and} Just then his disciples came back. {the} disciples his
3836 3281 5148 2779 2093 4047 899 3412 2262 3836 3412 899
d.nsm pt.pa.nsm r.ds.2 cj p.d r.dsn v.aai.3p d.npm n.npm r.gsm.3

καὶ ἐθαύμαζον ὅτι μετὰ γυναικὸς ἐλάλει·
{and} They were astonished that he was talking with a woman; he was talking however,
2779 2513 4022 3281 3281 3281 3552 1222 3281 3530
cj v.iai.3p cj p.g n.gsf v.iai.3s

οὐδεὶς μέντοι εἶπεν, τί ζητεῖς ἤ τί λαλεῖς μετ᾽
no one however said to her, "What ⌊do you want?⌋ or to him, "Why ⌊are you talking⌋ with
4029 3530 3306 5515 2426 2445 5515 3281 3552
a.nsm cj v.aai.3s r.asn v.pai.2s cj r.asn v.pai.2s p.g

αὐτῆς; 28 ἀφῆκεν οὖν τὴν ὑδρίαν αὐτῆς ἡ γυνὴ καὶ ἀπῆλθεν
her?" Then the woman left Then {the} her water jar her the woman and went off
899 4036 3836 1222 918 4036 3836 899 5620 899 3836 1222 2779 599
r.gsf.3 v.aai.3s cj d.asf n.asf r.gsf.3 d.nsf n.nsf cj v.aai.3s

εἰς τὴν πόλιν καὶ λέγει τοῖς ἀνθρώποις, 29 δεῦτε ἴδετε ἄνθρωπον
to the town. {and} She told the people there, "Come and see a man
1650 3836 4484 2779 3306 3836 476 1307 1625 476
p.a d.asf n.asf cj v.pai.3s d.dpm n.dpm adv v.aam.2p n.asm

ὃς εἶπέν μοι πάντα ↱ ↱ ὅσα ἐποίησα, μήτι οὗτός ἐστιν ὁ χριστός;
who told me everything I have ever done! Could this man be the Messiah?"
4005 3306 1609 4246 4472 4472 4012 4472 3614 4047 1639 3836 5986
r.nsm v.aai.3s r.ds.1 a.apn r.apn v.aai.1s pl r.nsm v.pai.3s d.nsm n.nsm

30 ἐξῆλθον ἐκ τῆς πόλεως καὶ ἤρχοντο πρὸς αὐτόν. 31 ἐν τῷ
So ⌊they went out⌋ of the town and ⌊made their way⌋ to Jesus. In the
2002 1666 3836 4484 2779 2262 4639 899 1877 3836
v.aai.3p p.g d.gsf n.gsf cj v.imi.3p p.a r.asm.3 p.d d.dsn

μεταξὺ ἠρώτων αὐτὸν οἱ μαθηταὶ λέγοντες, ῥαββί,
meantime the disciples kept urging Jesus, the disciples saying, "Rabbi,
3568 3836 3412 2263 899 3836 3412 3306 4806
adv v.iai.3p r.asm.3 d.npm n.npm pt.pa.npm n.vsm

φάγε. 32 ὁ δὲ εἶπεν αὐτοῖς, ἐγὼ βρῶσιν ἔχω φαγεῖν ↱
⌊take something to eat."⌋ But he But said to them, "I have food have to eat of
2266 1254 3836 1254 3306 899 1609 2400 1111 2400 2266 3857
v.aam.2s d.nsm cj v.aai.3s r.dpm.3 r.ns.1 n.asf v.pai.1s f.aa

ἣν ὑμεῖς οὐκ οἴδατε. 33 ἔλεγον οὖν οἱ μαθηταὶ
which you know nothing." know Then the disciples ⌊began to say⌋ Then the disciples
4005 7007 3857 4024 3857 4036 3836 3412 3306 4036 3836 3412
r.asf r.np.2 pl v.rai.2p v.iai.3p cj d.npm n.npm

πρὸς ἀλλήλους, μή τις ἤνεγκεν αὐτῷ φαγεῖν; ↰ ↰ 34 λέγει
to one another, "No one has brought him something to eat, have they?" Jesus said
4639 253 3590 5516 5770 899 2266 3590 3590 2652 3306
p.a r.apm pl r.nsm v.aai.3s r.dsm.3 f.aa v.pai.3s

αὐτοῖς ὁ Ἰησοῦς, ἐμὸν βρῶμά ἐστιν ἵνα ποιήσω τὸ θέλημα τοῦ πέμψαντός με
to them, {the} Jesus "My food is to do the will of him who sent me
899 3836 2652 1847 1109 1639 2671 4472 3836 2525 3836 4287 1609
r.dpm.3 d.nsm n.nsm r.nsn.1 n.nsn v.pai.3s cj v.aas.1s d.asn n.asn d.gsm pt.aa.gsm r.as.1

καὶ τελειώσω αὐτοῦ τὸ ἔργον. 35 οὐχ ὑμεῖς λέγετε
and to accomplish the work he the work gave me to do. Do you not you say,
2779 5457 3836 2240 899 3836 2240 7007 4024 7007 3306
cj v.aas.1s r.gsm.3 d.asn n.asn pl r.np.2 v.pai.2p

ὅτι ἔτι τετράμηνός ἐστιν καὶ ὁ θερισμὸς ἔρχεται; ἰδοὺ
~ 'There are still four months There are and then comes the harvest'? comes Look,
4022 1639 1639 2285 5485 1639 2779 2262 3836 2546 2262 2627
cj adv n.nsf v.pai.3s cj d.nsm n.nsm v.pmi.3s j

λέγω ὑμῖν, ἐπάρατε τοὺς ὀφθαλμοὺς ὑμῶν καὶ θεάσασθε τὰς χώρας ὅτι
I tell you, lift up {the} your eyes your and look at the fields; ~ they are
3306 7007 2048 3836 7007 4057 7007 2779 2517 3836 6001 4022 1639 1639
v.pai.1s r.dp.2 v.aam.2p d.apm n.apm r.gp.2 cj v.amm.2p d.apf n.apf cj

NASB

[26]Jesus *said to her,
"I who speak to
you am *He.*"
[27]At this point His
disciples came, and
they were amazed
that He had been
speaking with a
woman, yet no one
said, "What do You
seek?" or, "Why
do You speak with
her?" [28]So the
woman left her
waterpot, and went
into the city and
*said to the men,
[29]"Come, see a man
who told me all the
things that I *have*
done; this is not
the Christ, is it?"
[30]They went out of
the city, and were
coming to Him.
[31]Meanwhile the
disciples were
urging Him, say-
ing, "Rabbi, eat."
[32]But He said to
them, "I have food
to eat that you do
not know about."
[33]So the disciples
were saying to
one another, "No
one brought Him
anything to eat, did
he?" [34]Jesus *said
to them, "My food
is to do the will of
Him who sent Me
and to accomplish
His work. [35]Do you
not say, 'There are
yet four months,
and *then* comes the
harvest'? Behold,
I say to you, lift up
your eyes and look
on the fields, that

NIV

ripe for harvest.
36Even now the
one who reaps
draws a wage and
harvests a crop for
eternal life, so that
the sower and the
reaper may be glad
together. 37Thus
the saying 'One
sows and another
reaps' is true. 38I
sent you to reap
what you have not
worked for. Others
have done the hard
work, and you have
reaped the benefits
of their labor."

Many Samaritans Believe

39Many of the
Samaritans from
that town believed
in him because of
the woman's testi-
mony, "He told me
everything I ever
did." 40So when
the Samaritans
came to him, they
urged him to stay
with them, and he
stayed two days.
41And because of
his words many
more became be-
lievers.
42They said to the
woman, "We no
longer believe just
because of what
you said; now we
have heard for
ourselves, and we
know that this man
really is the Savior
of the world."

Jesus Heals an Official's Son

43After the two
days he left for
Galilee. 44(Now
Jesus himself had
pointed out that
a prophet has no
honor

λευκαί εἰσιν πρὸς θερισμόν. ἤδη 36 ὁ θερίζων μισθὸν
white, *they are* ready for harvest. *already* The reaper is already receiving wages
3328 1639 4639 2546 2453 3836 2545 3284 2453 3284 3635
a.npf v.pai.3p p.a n.asm adv d.nsm pt.pa.nsm n.asm

λαμβάνει καὶ συνάγει καρπὸν εἰς ζωὴν αἰώνιον, ἵνα ὁ σπείρων
is receiving and gathering a crop for eternal life, *eternal* so that the sower and the
3284 2779 5251 2843 1650 173 2437 173 2671 3836 5062 2779 3836
v.pai.3s cj v.pai.3s n.asm p.a n.asf a.asf cj d.nsm pt.pa.nsm

ὁμοῦ χαίρῃ καὶ ὁ θερίζων. 37 ἐν γὰρ τούτῳ ὁ λόγος
reaper may rejoice together. *may rejoice and the reaper* For in *For* this the saying
2545 5897 5897 3938 5897 2779 3836 2545 1142 1877 1142 4047 3836 3364
adv v.pas.3s cj d.nsm pt.pa.nsm p.d cj r.dsn d.nsm n.nsm

ἐστὶν ἀληθινὸς ὅτι ἄλλος ἐστὶν ὁ σπείρων καὶ ἄλλος ὁ θερίζων. 38 ἐγὼ
is true, ~ 'One *{is} {the}* sows and another *{the}* reaps.' I
1639 240 4022 257 1639 3836 5062 2779 257 3836 2545 1609
v.pai.3s a.nsm cj r.nsm v.pai.3s d.nsm pt.pa.nsm cj r.nsm d.nsm pt.pa.nsm r.ns.1

ἀπέστειλα ὑμᾶς θερίζειν ὃ ↱ οὐχ ὑμεῖς κεκοπιάκατε· ἄλλοι
sent you to reap a crop for which you did not *you* labor. Others
690 7007 2545 4005 7007 3159 4024 7007 3159 257
v.aai.1s r.ap.2 f.pa r.asn pl r.np.2 v.rai.2p r.npm

κεκοπιάκασιν καὶ ὑμεῖς εἰς τὸν κόπον αὐτῶν
⌊have done the hard work,⌋ and you have reaped the benefits of *{the}* their labor." *their*
3159 2779 7007 1656 1656 1656 1656 1650 3836 899 3160 899
v.rai.3p cj r.np.2 p.a d.asm n.asm r.gpm.3

εἰσεληλύθατε. 39 ἐκ δὲ τῆς πόλεως ἐκείνης
have reaped the benefits Many of the Samaritans from *{and} {the}* that town *that*
1656 4498 3836 3836 4901 1666 1254 3836 1697 4484 1697
v.rai.2p p.g cj d.gsf n.gsf r.gsf

πολλοὶ ἐπίστευσαν εἰς αὐτὸν τῶν Σαμαριτῶν διὰ τὸν λόγον τῆς
Many believed in him *of the Samaritans* ⌊because of⌋ what the woman had said *the*
4498 4409 1650 899 3836 4901 1328 3836 3836 1222 3364 3836
a.npm v.aai.3p p.a r.asm.3 d.gpm n.gpm p.a d.asm n.asm d.gsf

γυναικὸς μαρτυρούσης ὅτι εἶπέν μοι πάντα ἃ ἐποίησα. 40 ὡς οὖν
woman when she testified, ~ "He told me everything that I ever did." When therefore
1222 3455 4022 3306 1609 4246 4005 4472 6055 4036
n.gsf pt.pa.gsf cj v.aai.3s r.ds.1 a.apn r.apn v.aai.1s cj cj

ἦλθον πρὸς αὐτὸν οἱ Σαμαρῖται, ἠρώτων αὐτὸν μεῖναι παρ' αὐτοῖς·
the Samaritans came to him, *the Samaritans* they urged him to stay with them.
3836 4901 2262 4639 899 3836 4901 2263 899 3531 4123 899
v.aai.3p p.a r.asm.3 d.npm n.npm v.iai.3p r.asm.3 f.aa p.d r.dpm.3

καὶ ἔμεινεν ἐκεῖ ↱ δύο ἡμέρας. 41 καὶ πολλῷ πλείους ἐπίστευσαν διὰ τὸν
{and} He stayed there for two days. and many more believed ⌊because of⌋ what
2779 3531 1695 2465 1545 2465 2779 4498 4498 4409 1328 3836
cj v.aai.3s adv a.apf n.apf cj a.dsn a.npm.c v.aai.3p p.a d.asm

λόγον αὐτοῦ, 42 τῇ τε γυναικὶ ἔλεγον ὅτι οὐκέτι
they heard from him. They said ⌊to the⌋ ~ woman, *They said* ~ "No longer is it
3364 899 3306 3306 3836 5445 1222 3306 4022 4033
n.asm r.gsm.3 d.dsf cj n.dsf v.iai.3p cj adv

διὰ τὴν σὴν λαλιὰν πιστεύομεν, αὐτοὶ γὰρ
⌊because of⌋ what you said that we believe, for we have heard him for ourselves, *for*
1328 3836 5050 3282 4409 1142 201 201 201 899 1142
p.a d.asf r.asf.2 n.asf v.pai.1p r.npm cj

ἀκηκόαμεν καὶ οἴδαμεν ὅτι οὗτός ἐστιν ἀληθῶς ὁ σωτὴρ τοῦ κόσμου.
we have heard and we know that this man truly is *truly* the Savior of the world."
201 2779 3857 4022 4047 242 1639 242 3836 5400 3836 3180
v.rai.1p cj v.rai.1p cj r.nsm v.pai.3s adv d.nsm n.nsm d.gsm n.gsm

43 μετὰ δὲ τὰς δύο ἡμέρας ἐξῆλθεν ἐκεῖθεν εἰς τὴν
Two days later *{and} {the} Two days* Jesus left from there and went to *{the}*
1545 2465 3552 1254 3836 1545 2465 2002 1696 1650 3836
p.a cj d.apf a.apf n.apf v.aai.3s adv p.a d.asf

Γαλιλαίαν· 44 αὐτὸς γὰρ Ἰησοῦς ἐμαρτύρησεν ὅτι προφήτης
Galilee (for Jesus himself *for Jesus* had testified that a prophet has no honor
1133 1142 2652 899 1142 2652 3455 4022 4737 2400 4024 5507
n.asf r.nsm cj n.nsm v.aai.3s cj n.nsm

NASB

they are white for
harvest. 36Already
he who reaps is
receiving wages
and is gathering
fruit for life eter-
nal; so that he who
sows and he who
reaps may rejoice
together. 37For in
this *case* the saying
is true, 'One sows
and another reaps.'
38I sent you to reap
that for which you
have not labored;
others have labored
and you have
entered into their
labor."

The Samaritans

39From that city
many of the Sa-
maritans believed
in Him because
of the word of
the woman who
testified, "He told
me all the things
that I *have* done."
40So when the Sa-
maritans came to
Jesus, they were
asking Him to stay
with them; and He
stayed there two
days. 41Many more
believed because
of His word; 42and
they were saying to
the woman, "It is
no longer because
of what you said
that we believe,
for we have heard
for ourselves and
know that this One
is indeed the Sav-
ior of the world."
43After the two
days He went forth
from there into
Galilee. 44For Jesus
Himself testified
that a prophet has
no honor in his

NIV

in his own coun-
try.) 45 When he
arrived in Galilee,
the Galileans wel-
comed him. They
had seen all that he
had done in Jeru-
salem at the Pass-
over Festival, for
they also had been
there.
46 Once more he
visited Cana in
Galilee, where he
had turned the wa-
ter into wine. And
there was a cer-
tain royal official
whose son lay sick
at Capernaum.
47 When this man
heard that Jesus
had arrived in Gal-
ilee from Judea,
he went to him
and begged him to
come and heal his
son, who was close
to death.
48 "Unless you
people see signs
and wonders,"
Jesus told him,
"you will never
believe."
49 The royal of-
ficial said, "Sir,
come down before
my child dies."
50 "Go," Jesus re-
plied, "your son
will live."
The man took
Jesus at his word
and departed.
51 While he was
still on the way,
his servants met
him with the news
that his boy was
living. 52 When he
inquired as to the
time when

ἐν τῇ ἰδίᾳ πατρίδι τιμὴν οὐκ ἔχει. 45 ὅτε οὖν ἦλθεν εἰς τὴν Γαλιλαίαν,
in {the} his own country). honor no has When {then} he arrived in {the} Galilee,
1877 3836 2625 4258 5507 4024 2400 4021 4036 2262 1650 3836 1133
p.d d.dsf a.dsf n.dsf n.asf pl v.pai.3s cj cj v.aai.3s p.a d.asf n.asf

ἐδέξαντο αὐτὸν οἱ Γαλιλαῖοι πάντα ἑωρακότες ὅσα
the Galileans welcomed him, the Galileans having seen all having seen that
3836 1134 1312 899 3836 1134 3972 3972 4246 3972 4012
v.ami.3p r.asm.3 d.npm a.npm a.apn pt.ra.npm r.apn

ἐποίησεν ἐν Ἱεροσολύμοις ἐν τῇ ἑορτῇ, καὶ αὐτοὶ γὰρ ἦλθον εἰς
he had done in Jerusalem during the feast (for they too they for had gone to
4472 1877 2642 1877 3836 2038 1142 899 2779 899 1142 2262 1650
v.aai.3s p.d n.dpn p.d d.dsf n.dsf adv r.npm cj v.aai.3p p.a

τὴν ἑορτήν. 46 ἦλθεν οὖν πάλιν εἰς τὴν Κανὰ τῆς Γαλιλαίας, ὅπου
the feast). So Jesus came So again to {the} Cana in Galilee where
3836 2038 4036 2262 4036 4099 1650 3836 2830 3836 1133 3963
d.asf n.asf v.aai.3s cj adv p.a d.asf n.asf d.gsf n.gsf cj

ἐποίησεν τὸ ὕδωρ οἶνον. καὶ ἦν τις
he had made the water wine. Now in Capernaum ⌊there was⌋ a certain
4472 3836 5623 3885 2779 1877 3019 1639 5516
v.aai.3s d.asn n.asn n.asm cj v.iai.3s r.nsm

βασιλικὸς οὗ ὁ υἱὸς ἠσθένει ἐν Καφαρναούμ. 47 ↱ οὗτος
⌊officer in the royal service⌋ whose {the} son was ill. in Capernaum When this man
997 4005 3836 5626 820 1877 3019 201 4047
a.nsm r.gsm d.nsm n.nsm v.iai.3s p.d n.dsf r.nsm

ἀκούσας ὅτι Ἰησοῦς ἥκει ἐκ τῆς Ἰουδαίας εἰς τὴν Γαλιλαίαν
heard that Jesus had arrived in Galilee from {the} Judea, in {the} Galilee
201 4022 2652 2457 1650 1133 1666 3836 2677 1650 3836 1133
pt.aa.nsm cj n.nsm v.rai.3s p.g d.gsf n.gsf p.a d.asf n.asf

ἀπῆλθεν πρὸς αὐτὸν καὶ ἠρώτα ἵνα καταβῇ καὶ ἰάσηται αὐτοῦ τὸν υἱόν,
he went to him and begged him to come down and heal his {the} son; for
599 4639 899 2779 2263 2671 2849 2779 2615 899 3836 5626 1142
v.aai.3s p.a r.asm.3 cj v.iai.3s cj v.aas.3s cj v.ams.3s r.gsm.3 d.asm n.asm

ἤμελλεν γὰρ ἀποθνῄσκειν. 48 εἶπεν οὖν ὁ Ἰησοῦς πρὸς
⌊he was at the point⌋ for of death. Jesus therefore said therefore {the} Jesus to
3516 1142 633 2652 4036 3306 4036 3836 2652 4639
v.iai.3s cj f.pa v.aai.3s cj d.nsm n.nsm p.a

αὐτόν, ⌊ἐὰν μὴ⌋ σημεῖα καὶ τέρατα ἴδητε, ↱ ↱ ⌊οὐ μὴ⌋
him, "Unless you people see signs and wonders, you see you will never
899 1569 3590 1625 1625 4956 2779 5469 1625 4409 4409 4024 3590
r.asm.3 cj pl n.apn cj n.apn v.aas.2p pl pl

πιστεύσητε. 49 λέγει πρὸς αὐτὸν ὁ βασιλικός, κύριε, κατάβηθι πρὶν
believe!" The officer said to him, The officer "Sir, come down before
4409 3836 997 3306 4639 899 3836 997 3261 2849 4570
v.aas.2p v.pai.3s p.a r.asm.3 d.nsm a.nsm n.vsm v.aam.2s cj

ἀποθανεῖν τὸ παιδίον μου. 50 λέγει αὐτῷ ὁ Ἰησοῦς, πορεύου,
my little boy dies." {the} little boy my Jesus replied to him, {the} Jesus "Go,
1609 4086 4086 633 3836 4086 1609 2652 3306 899 3836 2652 4513
f.aa d.asn n.asn r.gs.1 v.pai.3s r.dsm.3 d.nsm n.nsm v.pmm.2s

ὁ υἱός σου ζῇ. ἐπίστευσεν ὁ ἄνθρωπος τῷ λόγῳ ὃν
{the} your son your lives." The man believed The man the word that Jesus
3836 5148 5626 5148 2409 3836 476 4409 3836 476 3836 3364 4005 2652
d.nsm n.nsm r.gs.2 v.pai.3s v.aai.3s d.nsm n.nsm d.dsm n.dsm r.asm

εἶπεν αὐτῷ ὁ Ἰησοῦς καὶ ἐπορεύετο. 51 ↱ ↱ ἤδη δὲ αὐτοῦ
spoke to him, {the} Jesus and he set off for home. While he was still {and} he
3306 899 3836 2652 2779 4513 2849 899 2849 2453 1254 899
v.aai.3s r.dsm.3 d.nsm n.nsm cj v.imi.3s adv cj r.gsm.3

καταβαίνοντος οἱ δοῦλοι αὐτοῦ ὑπήντησαν αὐτῷ λέγοντες ὅτι ὁ
on his way down {the} his servants his met him and told him that {the} his
2849 3836 899 1529 899 5636 899 3306 4022 3836 899
pt.pa.gsm d.npm n.npm r.gsm.3 v.aai.3p r.dsm.3 pt.pa.npm cj d.nsm

παῖς αὐτοῦ ζῇ. 52 ἐπύθετο οὖν τὴν ὥραν παρ᾿ αὐτῶν ⌊ἐν ᾗ⌋
son his ⌊was living.⌋ So he asked So them what time {from} them it was when
4090 899 2409 4036 4785 4036 899 3836 6052 4123 899 1877 4005
n.nsm r.gsm.3 v.pai.3s v.ami.3s cj d.asf n.asf p.g r.gpm.3 p.d r.dsf

NASB

own country. 45 So
when He came to
Galilee, the Galile-
ans received Him,
having seen all the
things that He did
in Jerusalem at
the feast; for they
themselves also
went to the feast.

Healing a Nobleman's Son

46 Therefore He
came again to Cana
of Galilee where
He had made the
water wine. And
there was a royal
official whose son
was sick at Caper-
naum. 47 When he
heard that Jesus
had come out of
Judea into Galilee,
he went to Him and
was imploring *Him*
to come down and
heal his son; for he
was at the point of
death. 48 So Jesus
said to him, "Un-
less you *people* see
signs and wonders,
you *simply* will
not believe." 49 The
royal official *said
to Him, "Sir, come
down before my
child dies." 50 Jesus
*said to him, "Go;
your son lives."
The man believed
the word that Jesus
spoke to him and
started off. 51 As
he was now going
down, *his* slaves
met him, saying
that his son was
living. 52 So he in-
quired of them the
hour when he

NIV

his son got better,
they said to him,
"Yesterday, at one
in the afternoon,
the fever left him."
[53]Then the father
realized that this
was the exact time
at which Jesus had
said to him, "Your
son will live." So
he and his whole
household be-
lieved.
[54]This was the
second sign Jesus
performed after
coming from Ju-
dea to Galilee.

The Healing at the Pool

5 Some time
later, Jesus
went up to Jerusa-
lem for one of the
Jewish festivals.
[2]Now there is in
Jerusalem near the
Sheep Gate a pool,
which in Aramaic
is called Bethes-
da[a] and which is
surrounded by
five covered col-
onnades. [3]Here a
great number of
disabled people
used to lie—the
blind, the lame, the
paralyzed. [4][b] [5]One
who was there had
been an invalid for
thirty-eight years.
[6]When Jesus saw
him lying there
and learned that
he had been in
this condition for
a long time, he
asked him, "Do
you want to get

[a] 2 Some manuscripts *Bethzatha*; other manuscripts *Bethsaida*
[b] 3,4 Some manuscripts include here, wholly or in part, *paralyzed—and they waited for the moving of the waters. [4]From time to time an angel of the Lord would come down and stir up the waters. The first one into the pool after each such disturbance would be cured of whatever disease they had.*

κομψότερον ἔσχεν· εἶπαν οὖν αὐτῷ ὅτι ἐχθὲς → ὥραν
his son got better, *got* and they said *and* to him, ~ "Yesterday at the seventh hour
2400 3153 2400 4036 3306 4036 899 4022 2396 1575 6052
adv.c v.aai.3s v.aai.3p cj r.dsm.3 cj adv n.asf

ἑβδόμην ἀφῆκεν αὐτὸν ὁ πυρετός. 53 ἔγνω οὖν ὁ
seventh the fever left him." *the* *fever* Then the father realized *Then* *the*
1575 3836 4790 918 899 3836 4790 4036 3836 4252 1182 4036 3836
a.asf v.aai.3s r.asm.3 d.nsm n.nsm v.aai.3s cj d.nsm

πατὴρ ὅτι ἐν[a] ἐκείνῃ τῇ ὥρᾳ ἐν ᾗ εἶπεν αὐτῷ ὁ Ἰησοῦς, ὁ
father that it was at that very hour when Jesus had said to him, *{the}* *Jesus* *{the}*
4252 4022 1877 1697 3836 6052 1877 4005 2652 3306 899 3836 2652 3836
n.nsm cj p.d r.dsf d.dsf n.dsf p.d r.dsf v.aai.3s r.dsm.3 d.nsm n.nsm d.nsm

υἱός σου ζῇ, καὶ ἐπίστευσεν αὐτὸς καὶ ἡ οἰκία
"Your son *Your* lives," and he became a believer, *he* as did *{the}* his entire household.
5148 5626 5148 2409 2779 899 4409 899 2779 3836 899 3910 3864
n.nsm r.gs.2 v.pai.3s cj v.aai.3s r.nsm cj d.nsf n.nsf

αὐτοῦ ὅλη. 54 τοῦτο δὲ[b] πάλιν δεύτερον σημεῖον ἐποίησεν ὁ
his *entire* Now this *Now* *{again}* was the second sign that Jesus performed *{the}*
899 3910 1254 4047 1254 4099 1311 4956 2652 4472 3836
r.gsm.3 a.nsf r.asn cj adv a.asn n.asn v.aai.3s d.nsm

Ἰησοῦς ἐλθὼν ἐκ τῆς Ἰουδαίας εἰς τὴν Γαλιλαίαν.
Jesus after coming from *{the}* Judea into *{the}* Galilee.
2652 2262 1666 3836 2677 1650 3836 1133
n.nsm pt.aa.nsm p.g d.gsf n.gsf p.a d.asf n.asf

5:1 μετὰ ταῦτα ἦν ἑορτὴ τῶν Ἰουδαίων καὶ ἀνέβη Ἰησοῦς εἰς
After this ⌊there was⌋ a festival of the Jews, and Jesus went up *Jesus* to
3552 4047 1639 2038 3836 2681 2779 2652 326 2652 1650
p.a r.apn v.iai.3s n.nsf d.gpm a.gpm cj v.aai.3s n.nsm p.a

Ἱεροσόλυμα. 2 ἔστιν δὲ ἐν τοῖς Ἱεροσολύμοις ἐπὶ τῇ προβατικῇ
Jerusalem. *there is* Now in *{the}* Jerusalem by the Sheep Gate there is a
2642 1639 1254 1877 3836 2642 2093 3836 4583 1639 1639
n.apn v.pai.3s cj p.d d.dpn n.dpn p.d d.dsf a.dsf

κολυμβήθρα ἡ ἐπιλεγομένη Ἑβραϊστὶ Βηθζαθὰ[c] πέντε
pool, in Hebrew *{the}* called *in Hebrew* Bethesda, having five
3148 1580 1580 3836 2141 1580 1032 2400 4297
n.nsf d.nsf pt.pp.nsf adv n.nsf a.apf

στοάς ἔχουσα. 3 ἐν ταύταις κατέκειτο πλῆθος τῶν ἀσθενούντων,
⌊covered colonnades.⌋ *having* In these lay a number of disabled people —
5119 2400 1877 4047 2879 4436 3836 820
n.apf pt.pa.nsf p.d r.dpf v.imi.3s n.nsn d.gpm pt.pa.gpm

τυφλῶν, χωλῶν, ξηρῶν.[d] 5 ἦν δέ τις ἄνθρωπος ἐκεῖ
blind, lame, and paralyzed. One man ⌊who was⌋ *{and}* *One* *man* there had been an
5603 6000 3831 5516 476 1639 1254 5516 476 1695 2400 2400
a.gpm a.gpm a.gpm v.iai.3s cj r.nsm n.nsm adv

→ ⌊τριάκοντα καὶ[e] ὀκτὼ⌋ ἔτη ἔχων ἐν τῇ ἀσθενείᾳ αὐτοῦ· 6
invalid for thirty-eight years. *had been* *{in}* *{the}* *invalid* *{his}* When Jesus
819 5558 2779 3893 2291 2400 1877 3836 819 899 1625 2652
a.apn cj a.apn n.apn pt.pa.nsm p.d d.dsf n.dsf r.gsm.3

τοῦτον ἰδὼν ὁ Ἰησοῦς κατακείμενον καὶ γνοὺς ὅτι
saw him *When saw* *{the}* *Jesus* lying there and learned that he had been in
1625 4047 1625 3836 2652 2879 2779 1182 4022 2400 2400
r.asm pt.aa.nsm d.nsm n.nsm pt.pm.asm cj pt.aa.nsm cj

→ πολὺν ἤδη χρόνον ἔχει, λέγει αὐτῷ, θέλεις
that condition for a long time already, *time* *he had* he said to him, ⌊"Do you want⌋ to be
4498 5989 2453 5989 2400 3306 899 2527 1181 1181
a.asm adv n.asm v.pai.3s v.pai.3s r.dsm.3 v.pai.2s

[a] [ἐν] UBS, omitted by TNIV.
[b] [δὲ] UBS.
[c] Βηθζαθὰ UBS, NET. Βηθεζεσδά TNIV.
[d] ἐκδεχομένων τὴν τοῦ ὕδατος κίνησιν. [4] ἄγγελος γὰρ κατὰ καιρὸν κατέβαινεν ἐν τῇ κολυμβήθρᾳ, καὶ ἐτάρασσε τὸ ὕδωρ· ὁ οὖν πρῶτος ἐμβὰς μετὰ τὴν ταραχὴν τοῦ ὕδατος, ὑγιὴς ἐγίνετο, ᾧ δήποτε κατείχετο νοσήματι included by TR after ξηρῶν.
[e] [καὶ] UBS, omitted by TNIV.

NASB

began to get better.
Then they said to
him, "Yesterday at
the [a]seventh hour
the fever left him."
[53]So the father
knew that *it was* at
that hour in which
Jesus said to him,
"Your son lives";
and he himself
believed and his
whole household.
[54]This is again a
second sign that
Jesus performed
when He had come
out of Judea into
Galilee.

The Healing at Bethesda

[5:1]After these
things there was a
feast of the Jews,
and Jesus went up
to Jerusalem.
[2]Now there is in
Jerusalem by the
sheep *gate* a pool,
which is called in
Hebrew Bethesda,
having five porti-
coes. [3]In these lay a
multitude of those
who were sick,
blind, lame, and
withered, [[b]waiting
for the moving of
the waters; [4]for an
angel of the Lord
went down at cer-
tain seasons into
the pool and stirred
up the water; who-
ever then first, after
the stirring up of
the water, stepped
in was made well
from whatever dis-
ease with which he
was afflicted.] [5]A
man was there who
had been ill for
thirty-eight years.
[6]When Jesus saw
him lying *there,*
and knew that he
had already been
a long time *in that
condition,* He *said
to him, "Do you

[a] Perhaps 7 p.m. Roman time or 1 p.m. Jewish time
[b] Early mss do not contain the remainder of v 3, nor v 4

NIV

well?"
7"Sir," the invalid
replied, "I have no
one to help me into
the pool when the
water is stirred.
While I am trying
to get in, someone
else goes down
ahead of me."
8Then Jesus said
to him, "Get up!
Pick up your mat
and walk." 9At
once the man was
cured; he picked
up his mat and
walked.
The day on which
this took place
was a Sabbath,
10and so the Jewish
leaders said to the
man who had been
healed, "It is the
Sabbath; the law
forbids you to car-
ry your mat."
11But he replied,
"The man who
made me well
said to me, 'Pick
up your mat and
walk.'"
12So they asked
him, "Who is this
fellow who told
you to pick it up
and walk?"
13The man who
was healed had
no idea who it
was, for Jesus had
slipped away into
the crowd that was
there.
14Later Jesus
found him at the
temple and said to
him, "See, you are
well again. Stop
sinning or some-
thing worse may
happen to you."
15The man

ὑγιὴς γενέσθαι; 7 ἀπεκρίθη αὐτῷ ὁ ἀσθενῶν, κύριε,
healed?" *to be* The sick man answered him, *The* *sick man* "Sir, I have no
5618 1181 3836 820 820 646 899 3836 820 3261 2400 2400 4024
a.nsm f.am v.api.3s r.dsm.3 d.nsm pt.pa.nsm n.vsm

ἄνθρωπον οὐκ ἔχω ἵνα ὅταν ταραχθῇ τὸ ὕδωρ
one *no* *I have* to put me into the pool when the water is stirred up, *the* *water*
476 4024 2400 2671 965 1609 1650 3836 3148 4020 3836 5623 5429 3836 5623
n.asm pl v.pai.1s cj cj v.aps.3s d.nsn n.nsn

βάλῃ με εἰς τὴν κολυμβήθραν· ⸤ἐν ᾧ⸥ δὲ ἔρχομαι ἐγώ,
put *me* *into* *the* *pool* but while *but* I ⸤am on my way⸥ *I*
965 1609 1650 3836 3148 1254 1877 4005 1254 1609 2262 1609
v.aas.3s r.as.1 p.a d.asf n.asf p.d r.dsm cj v.pmi.1s r.ns.1

ἄλλος πρὸ ἐμοῦ καταβαίνει. 8 λέγει αὐτῷ ὁ Ἰησοῦς,
⸤someone else⸥ steps down ⸤ahead of⸥ me." *steps down* Jesus said to him, *{the}* *Jesus*
257 2849 2849 4574 1609 2849 2652 3306 899 3836 2652
r.nsm p.g r.gs.1 v.pai.3s v.pai.3s r.dsm.3 d.nsm n.nsm

ἔγειρε ἆρον τὸν κράβαττόν σου καὶ περιπάτει. 9 καὶ εὐθέως
"Get up, pick up *{the}* your mat *your* and walk." And immediately the man
1586 149 3836 5148 3187 5148 2779 4344 2779 2311 3836 476
v.pam.2s v.aam.2s d.asm n.asm r.gs.2 cj v.pam.2s cj adv

ἐγένετο ὑγιὴς ὁ ἄνθρωπος καὶ ἦρεν τὸν κράβαττον αὐτοῦ καὶ
was healed, *the* *man* and ⸤he picked up⸥ *{the}* his mat *his* and
1181 5618 3836 476 2779 149 3836 899 3187 899 2779
v.ami.3s a.nsm d.nsm n.nsm cj v.aai.3s d.asm n.asm r.gsm.3 cj

περιεπάτει. ἦν δὲ σάββατον ἐν ἐκείνῃ τῇ ἡμέρᾳ. 10
started walking. Now that day was *Now* a Sabbath. *{on}* *that* *{the}* *day* So the
4344 1254 1697 2465 1639 1254 4879 1877 1697 3836 2465 4036 3836
v.iai.3s v.iai.3s cj n.nsn p.d r.dsf d.dsf n.dsf

ἔλεγον οὖν οἱ Ἰουδαῖοι τῷ τεθεραπευμένῳ, σάββατόν
Jews said *So* *the* *Jews* ⸤to the⸥ ⸤man who had been healed,⸥ "It is the Sabbath,
2681 3306 4036 3836 2681 3836 2543 1639 1639 4879
v.iai.3p cj d.npm a.npm d.dsm pt.rp.dsm n.nsn

ἐστιν, καὶ ↱ ↱ οὐκ ἔξεστίν σοι ἆραι τὸν κράβαττόν σου. 11 ὁ
It is and it is not lawful ⸤for you⸥ to carry *{the}* your mat. *your* But he
1639 2779 1997 1997 4024 1997 5148 149 3836 5148 3187 5148 1254 3836
v.pai.3s cj pl v.pai.3s r.ds.2 f.aa d.asm n.asm r.gs.2 d.nsm

δὲ ἀπεκρίθη αὐτοῖς, ὁ ποιήσας με ὑγιῆ ἐκεῖνός μοι εἶπεν, ἆρον
But answered them, "The man who made me well *man* said to me, *said* ⸤'Pick up⸥
1254 646 899 3836 1697 4472 1609 5618 1697 3306 1609 3306 149
cj v.api.3s r.dpm.3 d.nsm pt.aa.nsm r.as.1 a.asm r.nsm r.ds.1 v.aai.3s v.aam.2s

τὸν κράβαττόν σου καὶ περιπάτει. 12 ἠρώτησαν αὐτόν, τίς ἐστιν ὁ
{the} your mat *your* and walk.'" They questioned him, "Who is the
3836 5148 3187 5148 2779 4344 2263 899 5515 1639 3836
d.asm n.asm r.gs.2 cj v.pam.2s v.aai.3p r.asm.3 r.nsm v.pai.3s d.nsm

ἄνθρωπος ὁ εἰπών σοι, ἆρον καὶ περιπάτει; 13 ὁ δὲ
man who said to you, ⸤'Pick up⸥ your mat and walk'?" However, the *However*
476 3836 3306 5148 149 2779 4344 1254 3836 1254
n.nsm d.nsm pt.aa.nsm r.ds.2 v.aam.2s cj v.pam.2s d.nsm cj

ἰαθεὶς ↱ οὐκ ᾔδει τίς ἐστιν, ὁ γὰρ Ἰησοῦς ἐξένευσεν
⸤man who had been healed⸥ did not know who it was, *{the}* for Jesus ⸤had slipped away,⸥ there
2615 3857 4024 3857 5515 1639 3836 1142 2652 1728 1639
pt.ap.nsm pl v.lai.3s r.nsm v.pai.3s d.nsm cj n.nsm v.aai.3s

ὄχλου ὄντος ἐν τῷ τόπῳ. 14 μετὰ ταῦτα εὑρίσκει αὐτὸν ὁ
being a crowd *there being* in that place. Later on Jesus found him *{the}*
1639 4063 1639 1877 3836 5536 3552 4047 2652 2351 899 3836
n.gsm pt.pa.gsm p.d d.dsm n.dsm p.a r.apn v.pai.3s r.asm.3 d.nsm

Ἰησοῦς ἐν τῷ ἱερῷ καὶ εἶπεν αὐτῷ, ἴδε ὑγιὴς γέγονας, →
Jesus in the temple and said to him, "See, you have been healed! *you have been* Do not sin
2652 1877 3836 2639 2779 3306 899 2623 1181 1181 1181 5618 1181 279 279
n.nsm p.d d.dsn n.dsn cj v.aai.3s r.dsm.3 pl a.nsm v.rai.2s

μηκέτι ἁμάρτανε, ἵνα μὴ χεῖρόν σοί τι γένηται. 15
any longer, *Do sin* so that nothing worse happens to you." *{thing}* *happens* The man
3600 279 2671 3590 5937 1181 5148 5516 1181 3836 476
adv v.pam.2s cj pl a.nsn.c r.ds.2 r.nsn v.ams.3s

NASB

wish to get well?"
7The sick man an-
swered Him, "Sir, I
have no man to put
me into the pool
when the water
is stirred up, but
while I am coming,
another steps down
before me." 8Jesus
*said to him, "Get
up, pick up your
pallet and walk."
9Immediately the
man became well,
and picked up his
pallet and *began* to
walk.
Now it was the
Sabbath on that
day. 10So the Jews
were saying to
the man who was
cured, "It is the
Sabbath, and it is
not permissible for
you to carry your
pallet." 11But he
answered them,
"He who made
me well was the
one who said to
me, 'Pick up your
pallet and walk.'"
12They asked him,
"Who is the man
who said to you,
'Pick up *your pal-
let* and walk'?"
13But the man who
was healed did
not know who it
was, for Jesus had
slipped away while
there was a crowd
in *that* place.
14Afterward Jesus
*found him in the
temple and said to
him, "Behold, you
have become well;
do not sin any-
more, so that noth-
ing worse happens
to you." 15The

NIV

went away and told
the Jewish leaders
that it was Jesus
who had made him
well.

The Authority of the Son

16 So, because
Jesus was doing
these things on the
Sabbath, the Jew-
ish leaders began
to persecute him.
17 In his defense
Jesus said to them,
"My Father is al-
ways at his work to
this very day, and
I too am working."
18 For this reason
they tried all the
more to kill him;
not only was he
breaking the Sab-
bath, but he was
even calling God
his own Father,
making himself
equal with God.
19 Jesus gave them
this answer: "Very
truly I tell you, the
Son can do noth-
ing by himself; he
can do only what
he sees his Father
doing, because
whatever the Fa-
ther does the Son
also does. 20 For
the Father loves
the Son and shows
him all he does.
Yes, and he will
show him even
greater works than
these, so that you
will be amazed.
21 For just as the
Father raises the
dead and gives
them life, even
so the Son gives
life to whom he is
pleased to give it.
22 Moreover, the
Father judges no
one, but has en-
trusted

ἀπῆλθεν ὁ ἄνθρωπος καὶ ἀνήγγειλεν τοῖς Ἰουδαίοις ὅτι Ἰησοῦς ἐστιν
went away *The* *man* and told the Jews that it was Jesus *it was*
599 3836 476 2779 334 3836 2681 4022 1639 1639 2652 1639
v.aai.3s d.nsm n.nsm cj v.aai.3s d.dpm a.dpm cj n.nsm v.pai.3s

ὁ ποιήσας αὐτὸν ὑγιῆ. 16 καὶ ⌊διὰ τοῦτο⌋ ἐδίωκον οἱ
who had made him well. And this is why the Jews were persecuting *the*
3836 4472 899 5618 2779 1328 4047 3836 2681 1503 3836
d.nsm pt.aa.nsm r.asm.3 a.asm cj p.a r.asn v.iai.3p d.npm

Ἰουδαῖοι[a] τὸν Ἰησοῦν, ὅτι ταῦτα ἐποίει ἐν σαββάτῳ.
Jews *{the}* Jesus, because he was doing these things *he was doing* on the Sabbath.
2681 3836 2652 4022 4472 4472 4472 4047 4472 1877 4879
a.npm d.asm n.asm cj r.apn v.iai.3s p.d n.dsn

17 ὁ δὲ [b]ἀπεκρίνατο αὐτοῖς, ὁ πατήρ μου ἕως ἄρτι
But Jesus *but* answered them, *{the}* "My Father *My* has been working until now,
1254 3836 1254 646 899 3836 1609 4252 1609 2237 2237 2237 2401 785
d.nsm cj v.ami.3s r.dpm.3 d.nsm n.nsm r.gs.1 p.g adv

ἐργάζεται κἀγὼ ἐργάζομαι· 18 ⌊διὰ τοῦτο⌋ οὖν
has been working and I also am working." This was why *{then}* the Jews were seeking
2237 2743 2237 1328 4047 4036 3836 2681 2426 2426
v.pmi.3s crasis v.pmi.1s p.a r.asn cj

μᾶλλον ἐζήτουν αὐτὸν οἱ Ἰουδαῖοι ἀποκτεῖναι, ὅτι ↱ οὐ μόνον
all the more *were seeking* to kill him, *the* *Jews* *to kill* because he not only
3437 2426 650 650 899 3836 2681 650 4022 3395 4024 3667
adv.c v.iai.3p r.asm.3 d.npm a.npm f.aa cj pl adv

ἔλυεν τὸ σάββατον, ἀλλὰ καὶ πατέρα ἴδιον
⌊used to break⌋ the Sabbath, but he also was calling God his own Father, *his own*
3395 3836 4879 247 3306 2779 3306 3306 2536 2625 2625 4252 2625
v.iai.3s d.asn n.asn cj adv n.asm a.asm

ἔλεγεν τὸν θεὸν ἴσον ἑαυτὸν ποιῶν τῷ θεῷ. 19 ἀπεκρίνατο
he was calling *{the}* *God* thus making himself equal *himself* *making* with God. Answering,
3306 3836 2536 4472 1571 2698 1571 4472 3836 2536 646
v.iai.3s d.asm n.asm a.asm r.asm.3 pt.pa.nsm d.dsm n.dsm v.ami.3s

οὖν ὁ Ἰησοῦς καὶ ἔλεγεν αὐτοῖς, ἀμὴν ἀμὴν λέγω ὑμῖν, οὐ
then, *{the}* Jesus *{and}* said to them, "I tell you the solemn truth, *I tell* *you* ~
4036 3836 2652 2779 3306 899 3306 3306 7007 297 297 3306 7007 4024
cj d.nsm n.nsm cj v.iai.3s r.dpm.3 pl pl v.pai.1s r.dp.2 pl

δύναται ὁ υἱὸς ποιεῖν ἀφ᾽ ἑαυτοῦ οὐδὲν ⌊ἐὰν μή⌋ τι βλέπῃ
the Son can *the* *Son* do nothing on his own, *nothing* but only what he sees
3836 5626 1538 3836 5626 4472 4029 608 1571 4029 1569 3590 5516 1063
v.ppi.3s d.nsm n.nsm f.pa p.g r.gsm.3 a.asn cj pl r.asn v.pas.3s

τὸν πατέρα ποιοῦντα· ἃ γὰρ ἂν ἐκεῖνος ποιῇ, ταῦτα καὶ ὁ
the Father doing; for whatever *for* ~ the Father does, *{these things}* *{also}* the
3836 4252 4472 1142 4005 1142 323 1697 4472 4047 2779 3836
d.asm n.asm pt.pa.asm r.apn cj pl r.nsm v.pas.3s r.apn adv d.nsm

υἱὸς ὁμοίως ποιεῖ. 20 ὁ γὰρ πατὴρ φιλεῖ τὸν υἱὸν καὶ
Son is doing likewise. *is doing* For the *For* Father loves the Son and shows him
5626 4472 4472 3931 4472 1142 3836 1142 4252 5797 3836 5626 2779 1259 899
n.nsm adv v.pai.3s d.nsm cj n.nsm v.pai.3s d.asm n.asm cj

πάντα δείκνυσιν αὐτῷ ἃ αὐτὸς ποιεῖ, καὶ μείζονα
everything *shows* *him* that he is doing; and he will show him greater works
4246 1259 899 4005 899 4472 2779 1259 1259 1259 899 3489 2240
a.apn v.pai.3s r.dsm.3 r.apn r.nsm v.pai.3s cj a.apn.c

τούτων δείξει αὐτῷ ἔργα, ἵνα ὑμεῖς θαυμάζητε. 21 ὥσπερ γὰρ ὁ πατὴρ
than these, *he will show* *him* *works* and you will be amazed. For as *For* the Father
4047 1259 899 2240 2671 7007 2513 1142 6061 1142 3836 4252
r.gpn v.fai.3s r.dsm.3 n.apn cj r.np.2 v.pas.2p cj cj d.nsm n.nsm

ἐγείρει τοὺς νεκροὺς καὶ → ζῳοποιεῖ, οὕτως καὶ ὁ υἱὸς οὓς
raises the dead and gives them life, so also the Son gives life to those
1586 3836 3738 2779 2443 4048 2779 3836 5626 2443 2443 2443 4005
v.pai.3s d.apm a.apm cj v.pai.3s adv adv d.nsm n.nsm r.apm

θέλει ζῳοποιεῖ. 22 ⌊οὐδὲ γὰρ⌋ ὁ πατὴρ κρίνει οὐδένα, ἀλλὰ
he chooses. *gives life to* Furthermore, the Father judges no one, but has given
2527 2443 4028 1142 3836 4252 3212 4029 247 1443 1443
v.pai.3s v.pai.3s adv cj d.nsm n.nsm v.pai.3s a.asm cj

NASB

man went away,
and told the Jews
that it was Jesus
who had made him
well. 16 For this rea-
son the Jews were
persecuting Jesus,
because He was
doing these things
on the Sabbath.
17 But He answered
them, "My Father
is working until
now, and I Myself
am working."

Jesus' Equality with God

18 For this reason
therefore the Jews
were seeking all
the more to kill
Him, because
He not only was
breaking the Sab-
bath, but also was
calling God His
own Father, mak-
ing Himself equal
with God.
19 Therefore Jesus
answered and was
saying to them,
"Truly, truly, I say
to you, the Son can
do nothing of Him-
self, unless *it is*
something He sees
the Father doing;
for whatever the
Father does, these
things the Son also
does in like man-
ner. 20 For the Fa-
ther loves the Son,
and shows Him
all things that He
Himself is doing;
and *the Father* will
show Him greater
works than these,
so that you will
marvel. 21 For just
as the Father raises
the dead and gives
them life, even so
the Son also gives
life to whom He
wishes. 22 For not
even the Father
judges anyone, but
He has given all

[a] καὶ ἐζήτουν αὐτὸν ἀποκτεῖναι included by TR after Ἰουδαῖοι.
[b] Ἰησοῦς included by UBS before ἀπεκρίνατο.

NIV

all judgment to the
Son, [23]that all may
honor the Son just
as they honor the
Father. Whoever
does not honor the
Son does not hon-
or the Father, who
sent him.
[24]"Very truly I
tell you, whoever
hears my word and
believes him who
sent me has eter-
nal life and will
not be judged but
has crossed over
from death to life.
[25]Very truly I tell
you, a time is com-
ing and has now
come when the
dead will hear the
voice of the Son
of God and those
who hear will live.
[26]For as the Father
has life in himself,
so he has granted
the Son also to
have life in him-
self. [27]And he has
given him authori-
ty to judge because
he is the Son of
Man.
[28]"Do not be
amazed at this, for
a time is coming
when all who are
in their graves
will hear his voice
[29]and come out—
those who have
done what is good
will rise to live,
and those who
have done what is
evil will rise to be
condemned. [30]By
myself I can do
nothing; I judge
only as I hear,
and my

τὴν κρίσιν πᾶσαν δέδωκεν τῷ υἱῷ, 23 ἵνα πάντες τιμῶσι τὸν υἱὸν
{the} all judgment *all* *has given* ⌊to the⌋ Son, so that everyone should honor the Son
3836 4246 3213 4246 1443 3836 5626 2671 4246 5506 3836 5626
d.asf n.asf a.asf v.rai.3s d.dsm n.dsm cj a.npm v.pas.3p d.asm n.asm

καθὼς τιμῶσι τὸν πατέρα. ὁ ↱ ↱ ↱ μὴ τιμῶν τὸν υἱὸν ↱ οὐ τιμᾷ
just as they honor the Father. The one who does not honor the Son does not honor
2777 5506 3836 4252 3836 5506 5506 5506 3590 5506 3836 5626 5506 4024 5506
cj v.pai.3p d.asm n.asm d.nsm pl pt.pa.nsm d.asm n.asm pl v.pai.3s

τὸν πατέρα τὸν πέμψαντα αὐτόν. 24 ἀμὴν ἀμὴν λέγω ὑμῖν ὅτι
the Father who sent him. I tell you the solemn truth, *I tell* *you* ~
3836 4252 3836 4287 899 3306 3306 7007 297 297 3306 7007 4022
d.asm n.asm d.asm pt.aa.asm r.asm.3 pl pl v.pai.1s r.dp.2 cj

ὁ τὸν λόγον μου ἀκούων καὶ πιστεύων τῷ πέμψαντί με
the one who hears *{the}* my message *my* *one who hears* and believes the one who sent me
3836 201 201 201 3836 1609 3364 1609 201 2779 4409 3836 4287 1609
d.nsm d.asm n.asm r.gs.1 pt.pa.nsm cj pt.pa.nsm d.dsm pt.aa.dsm r.as.1

ἔχει ζωὴν αἰώνιον καὶ εἰς κρίσιν οὐκ ἔρχεται, ἀλλὰ
has eternal life *eternal* and will not come into judgment, *not* *will come* but
2400 173 2437 173 2779 2262 4024 2262 1650 3213 4024 2262 247
v.pai.3s n.asf a.asf cj p.a n.asf pl v.pmi.3s cj

μεταβέβηκεν ἐκ τοῦ θανάτου εἰς τὴν ζωήν. 25 ἀμὴν ἀμὴν λέγω
has passed from *{the}* death to *{the}* life. "I tell you the solemn truth, *I tell*
3553 1666 3836 2505 1650 3836 2437 3306 3306 7007 297 297 3306
v.rai.3s p.g d.gsm n.gsm p.a d.asf n.asf pl pl v.pai.1s

ὑμῖν ὅτι ἔρχεται ὥρα καὶ νῦν ἐστιν ὅτε οἱ νεκροὶ ἀκούσουσιν
you ~ the hour is coming *hour* and is now *is* here, when the dead will hear
7007 4022 6052 2262 6052 2779 1639 3814 1639 4021 3836 3738 201
r.dp.2 cj v.pmi.3s n.nsf cj adv v.pai.3s cj d.npm a.npm v.fai.3p

τῆς φωνῆς τοῦ υἱοῦ τοῦ θεοῦ καὶ οἱ ἀκούσαντες ζήσουσιν. 26 ὥσπερ γὰρ
the voice of the Son of God, and those who hear will live. For as *For*
3836 5889 3836 5626 3836 2536 2779 3836 201 2409 1142 6061 1142
d.gsf n.gsf d.gsm n.gsm d.gsm n.gsm cj d.npm pt.aa.npm v.fai.3p cj cj

ὁ πατὴρ ἔχει ζωὴν ἐν ἑαυτῷ, οὕτως καὶ τῷ υἱῷ ἔδωκεν
the Father has life in himself, so also has he granted the Son *has he granted*
3836 4252 2400 2437 1877 1571 4048 2779 1443 1443 1443 3836 5626 1443
d.nsm n.nsm v.pai.3s n.asf p.d r.dsm.3 adv adv d.dsm n.dsm v.aai.3s

ζωὴν ἔχειν ἐν ἑαυτῷ. 27 καὶ ἐξουσίαν ἔδωκεν αὐτῷ
to have life *to have* in himself; and he has given him authority *he has given* *him*
2400 2400 2437 2400 1877 1571 2779 1443 1443 1443 899 2026 1443 899
n.asf f.pa p.d r.dsm.3 cj n.asf v.aai.3s r.dsm.3

κρίσιν ποιεῖν, ὅτι υἱὸς ἀνθρώπου ἐστίν. 28 ↱ μὴ
to execute judgment *to execute* because he is the Son of Man. *he is* Do not
4472 4472 3213 4472 4022 1639 1639 5626 476 1639 2513 3590
n.asf f.pa cj n.nsm n.gsm v.pai.3s pl

θαυμάζετε τοῦτο, ὅτι ἔρχεται ὥρα ἐν ᾗ πάντες οἱ ἐν τοῖς
be amazed at this, because the hour is coming *hour* in which all who are in their
2513 4047 4022 6052 2262 6052 1877 4005 4246 3836 1877 3836
v.pam.2p r.asn cj v.pmi.3s n.nsf p.d r.dsf a.npm d.npm p.d d.dpn

μνημείοις ἀκούσουσιν τῆς φωνῆς αὐτοῦ 29 καὶ ἐκπορεύσονται οἱ
graves will hear *{the}* his voice *his* and will come out — those who have
3646 201 3836 899 5889 899 2779 1744 3836 4472 4472
n.dpn v.fai.3p d.gsf n.gsf r.gsm.3 cj v.fmi.3p d.npm

τὰ ἀγαθὰ ποιήσαντες εἰς ἀνάστασιν ζωῆς, οἱ δὲ
done *{the}* good, *who have done* to a resurrection unto life, and those *and* who have practiced
4472 3836 19 4472 1650 414 2437 1254 3836 1254 4556 4556 4556
d.apn a.apn pt.aa.npm p.a n.asf n.gsf d.npm cj

τὰ φαῦλα πράξαντες εἰς ἀνάστασιν κρίσεως. 30 οὐ δύναμαι
{the} evil, *who have practiced* to a resurrection unto condemnation. ~ I can
3836 5765 4556 1650 414 3213 4024 1609 1538
d.apn a.apn pt.aa.npm p.a n.asf n.gsf pl v.ppi.1s

ἐγὼ ποιεῖν ἀπ᾽ ἐμαυτοῦ οὐδέν· καθὼς ἀκούω κρίνω, καὶ ἡ
I do nothing on my own; *nothing* I judge only as I hear, *I judge* and *{the}* my
1609 4472 4029 608 1831 4029 3212 3212 2777 201 3212 2779 3836 1847
r.ns.1 f.pa p.g r.gsm.1 a.asn cj v.pai.1s v.pai.1s cj d.nsf

NASB

judgment to the
Son, [23]so that all
will honor the Son
even as they honor
the Father. He who
does not honor the
Son does not honor
the Father who sent
Him.
[24]"Truly, truly, I
say to you, he who
hears My word,
and believes Him
who sent Me, has
eternal life, and
does not come into
judgment, but has
passed out of death
into life.

Two Resurrections

[25]Truly, truly, I say
to you, an hour
is coming and
now is, when the
dead will hear the
voice of the Son
of God, and those
who hear will live.
[26]For just as the
Father has life in
Himself, even so
He gave to the Son
also to have life in
Himself; [27]and He
gave Him authority
to execute judg-
ment, because He
is *the* Son of Man.
[28]Do not marvel at
this; for an hour is
coming, in which
all who are in the
tombs will hear His
voice, [29]and will
come forth; those
who did the good
deeds to a resurrec-
tion of life, those
who committed
the evil *deeds* to
a resurrection of
judgment.
[30]"I can do noth-
ing on My own
initiative. As I hear,
I judge; and My

NIV

judgment is just,
for I seek not to
please myself but
him who sent me.

Testimonies About Jesus

[31]"If I testify
about myself, my
testimony is not
true. [32]There is an-
other who testifies
in my favor, and I
know that his tes-
timony about me
is true.
[33]"You have sent
to John and he has
testified to the
truth. [34]Not that
I accept human
testimony; but I
mention it that
you may be saved.
[35]John was a lamp
that burned and
gave light, and you
chose for a time to
enjoy his light.
[36]"I have testimo-
ny weightier than
that of John. For
the works that the
Father has given
me to finish—the
very works that I
am doing—testify
that the Father has
sent me. [37]And the
Father who sent
me has himself
testified concern-
ing me. You have
never heard his
voice nor seen his
form, [38]nor does
his word dwell in
you, for you do not
believe the one he
sent. [39]You study[a]
the

κρίσις ἡ ἐμὴ δικαία ἐστίν, ὅτι οὐ ζητῶ τὸ θέλημα
judgment *{the}* *my* is just *is* because I seek not *I seek* *{the}* my own will
3213 3836 1847 1639 1465 1639 4022 2426 2426 4024 2426 3836 1847 1847 2525
n.nsf d.nsf r.nsf.1 a.nsf v.pai.3s cj pl v.pai.1s d.asn n.asn

τὸ ἐμὸν ἀλλὰ τὸ θέλημα τοῦ πέμψαντός με. 31 ἐὰν ἐγὼ μαρτυρῶ περὶ
{the} *my own* but the will of him who sent me. "If I bear witness about
3836 1847 247 3836 2525 3836 4287 1609 1569 1609 3455 4309
d.asn r.asn.1 cj d.asn n.asn d.gsm pt.aa.gsm r.as.1 cj r.ns.1 v.pas.1s p.g

ἐμαυτοῦ, ἡ μαρτυρία μου οὐκ ἔστιν ἀληθής· 32 ἄλλος
myself, *{the}* my testimony *my* is not *is* deemed true. There is another
1831 3836 1609 3456 1609 1639 4024 1639 239 1639 1639 257
r.gsm.1 d.nsf n.nsf r.gs.1 pl v.pai.3s a.nsf r.nsm

ἐστὶν ὁ μαρτυρῶν περὶ ἐμοῦ, καὶ οἶδα ὅτι
There is who bears witness about me, and I know that the witness that he bears about me
1639 3836 3455 4309 1609 2779 3857 4022 3836 3456 4005 3455 3455 4309 1609
v.pai.3s d.nsm pt.pa.nsm p.g r.gs.1 cj v.rai.1s cj

ἀληθής ἐστιν ἡ μαρτυρία ἣν μαρτυρεῖ περὶ ἐμοῦ. 33 ὑμεῖς ἀπεστάλκατε
is true. *is* *the* *witness* *which* *he bears* *about* *me* You have sent messengers
1639 239 1639 3836 3456 4005 3455 4309 1609 7007 690
a.nsf v.pai.3s d.nsf n.nsf r.asf v.pai.3s p.g r.gs.1 r.np.2 v.rai.2p

πρὸς Ἰωάννην, καὶ μεμαρτύρηκεν τῇ ἀληθείᾳ· 34 ἐγὼ δὲ οὐ
to John, and he has borne witness ⌊to the⌋ truth. (Not that I *{and}* *Not* accept
4639 2722 2779 3455 3836 237 4024 1609 1254 4024 3284
p.a n.asm cj v.rai.3s d.dsf n.dsf r.ns.1 cj pl

παρὰ ἀνθρώπου τὴν μαρτυρίαν λαμβάνω, ἀλλὰ ταῦτα λέγω ἵνα ὑμεῖς
such human *{the}* testimony, *accept* but I say these things *I say* so that you
4123 476 3836 3456 3284 247 3306 3306 4047 3306 2671 7007
p.g n.gsm d.asf n.asf v.pai.1s cj r.apn v.pai.1s cj r.np.2

σωθῆτε. 35 ἐκεῖνος ἦν ὁ λύχνος ὁ καιόμενος καὶ φαίνων, ὑμεῖς
may be saved.) He was a lamp that was burning and giving light, and you
5392 1697 1639 3836 3394 3836 2794 2779 5743 1254 7007
v.aps.2p r.nsm v.iai.3s d.nsm n.nsm d.nsm pt.pp.nsm cj pt.pa.nsm r.np.2

δὲ ἠθελήσατε ἀγαλλιαθῆναι πρὸς ὥραν ἐν τῷ φωτὶ αὐτοῦ. 36
and were willing for a time to rejoice *for* *time* in *{the}* his light. *his* But
1254 2527 4639 6052 22 4639 6052 1877 3836 899 5890 899 1254
cj v.aai.2p f.ap p.a n.asf p.d d.dsn n.dsn r.gsm.3

ἐγὼ δὲ ἔχω τὴν μαρτυρίαν μείζω τοῦ Ἰωάννου· τὰ γὰρ ἔργα ἃ
I *But* have a witness greater ⌊than that⌋ of John; for the *for* works that the
1609 1254 2400 3836 3456 3489 3836 2722 1142 3836 1142 2240 4005 3836
r.ns.1 cj v.pai.1s d.asf n.asf a.asf.c d.gsm n.gsm d.npn cj n.npn r.apn

δέδωκέν μοι ὁ πατὴρ ἵνα τελειώσω αὐτά, αὐτὰ τὰ ἔργα ἃ
Father has given me *the* *Father* to complete, *{them}* the very *the* works that
4252 1443 1609 3836 4252 2671 5457 899 3836 899 3836 2240 4005
v.rai.3s r.ds.1 d.nsm n.nsm cj v.aas.1s r.apn.3 r.npn d.npn n.npn r.apn

ποιῶ μαρτυρεῖ περὶ ἐμοῦ ὅτι ὁ πατὴρ με ἀπέσταλκεν. 37 καὶ ὁ
I am doing, bear witness about me that the Father has sent me. *has sent* And the
4472 3455 4309 1609 4022 3836 4252 690 690 1609 690 2779 3836
v.pai.1s v.pai.3s p.g r.gs.1 cj d.nsm n.nsm r.as.1 v.rai.3s cj d.nsm

πέμψας με πατὴρ ↱ ἐκεῖνος μεμαρτύρηκεν περὶ ἐμοῦ. οὔτε φωνὴν αὐτοῦ
Father who sent me *Father* has himself borne witness about me. ~ His voice *His*
4252 4287 1609 4252 3455 1697 3455 4309 1609 4046 899 5889 899
pt.aa.nsm r.as.1 n.nsm r.nsm v.rai.3s p.g r.gs.1 cj n.asf r.gsm.3

↱ ↱ πώποτε ἀκηκόατε ↱ ↱ οὔτε εἶδος αὐτοῦ ἑωράκατε, 38 καὶ τὸν
you have never heard, his form you have never *form* *his* seen, and *{the}*
201 201 4799 201 899 1626 3972 3972 4046 1626 899 3972 2779 3836
adv v.rai.2p cj n.asn r.gsm.3 v.rai.2p cj d.asm

λόγον αὐτοῦ ↱ ↱ οὐκ ἔχετε ἐν ὑμῖν μένοντα, ὅτι
his word *his* you do not have residing in you, *residing* because you do not
899 3364 899 2400 2400 4024 2400 3531 1877 7007 3531 4022 7007 4409 4024
n.asm r.gsm.3 pl v.pai.2p p.d r.dp.2 pt.pa.asm cj

ὃν ἀπέστειλεν ἐκεῖνος, τούτῳ ὑμεῖς οὐ πιστεύετε. 39 ἐραυνᾶτε τὰς
believe the one whom he sent. *one* *the* *you* *not* *do believe* "You study the
4409 4047 1697 4005 690 1697 4047 7007 4024 4409 2236 3836
r.asm v.aai.3s r.nsm r.dsm r.np.2 pl v.pai.2p v.pai.2p d.apf

NASB

judgment is just,
because I do not
seek My own will,
but the will of Him
who sent Me.
[31]"If I *alone* tes-
tify about Myself,
My testimony is
not true. [32]There
is another who
testifies of Me, and
I know that the
testimony which
He gives about Me
is true.

Witness of John

[33]You have sent
to John, and he
has testified to the
truth. [34]But the
testimony which
I receive is not
from man, but I say
these things so that
you may be saved.
[35]He was the lamp
that was burning
and was shining
and you were will-
ing to rejoice for a
while in his light.

Witness of Works

[36]But the testimony
which I have is
greater than *the*
testimony of John;
for the works
which the Father
has given Me to
accomplish—the
very works that I
do—testify about
Me, that the Father
has sent Me.

Witness of the Father

[37]And the Father
who sent Me, He
has testified of Me.
You have neither
heard His voice at
any time nor seen
His form. [38]You do
not have His word
abiding in you, for
you do not believe
Him whom He
sent.

Witness of the Scripture

[39a]You search the

[a] 39 Or [39]*Study*

[a] Or (a command) *Search the Scriptures!*

NIV

Scriptures dili-
gently because you
think that in them
you have eternal
life. These are the
very Scriptures that
testify about me,
40 yet you refuse to
come to me to have
life.
41 "I do not ac-
cept glory from
human beings,
42 but I know you. I
know that you do
not have the love
of God in your
hearts. 43 I have
come in my Fa-
ther's name, and
you do not accept
me; but if someone
else comes in his
own name, you
will accept him.
44 How can you
believe since you
accept glory from
one another but do
not seek the glory
that comes from
the only God[a]?
45 "But do not
think I will accuse
you before the Fa-
ther. Your accuser
is Moses, on whom
your hopes are set.
46 If you believed
Moses, you would
believe me, for he
wrote about me.
47 But since you do
not believe what he
wrote, how are you
going to believe
what I say?"

Jesus Feeds the Five Thousand

6 Some time af-
ter this, Jesus
crossed to the far
shore of the Sea of
Galilee (that is, the
Sea of Tiberias),
2 and a great crowd
of people followed
him

[a] 44 Some early manuscripts *the Only One*

γραφάς, ὅτι ὑμεῖς δοκεῖτε ἐν αὐταῖς ζωὴν αἰώνιον
Scriptures because you think that by them you will have eternal life; *eternal*
1210 4022 7007 1506 1877 899 2400 2400 2400 173 2437 173
n.apf cj r.np.2 v.pai.2p p.d r.dpf.3 n.asf a.asf

ἔχειν· καὶ ἐκεῖναί εἰσιν αἱ μαρτυροῦσαι περὶ ἐμοῦ· 40 καὶ ⸂οὐ
you will have and it is they *it is* that bear witness about me, but you refuse
2400 2779 1639 1639 1697 1639 3836 3455 4309 1609 2779 4024
f.pa cj r.npf v.pai.3p d.npf pt.pa.npf p.g r.gs.1 cj pl

θέλετε⸃ ἐλθεῖν πρός με ἵνα ζωὴν ἔχητε. 41
to come to me that you may have life. *you may have* I do not accept
2527 2262 4639 1609 2671 2400 2400 2400 2437 2400 3284 3284 4024 3284
v.pai.2p f.aa p.a r.as.1 cj n.asf v.pas.2p

δόξαν παρὰ ἀνθρώπων οὐ λαμβάνω, 42 ἀλλὰ ἔγνωκα ὑμᾶς ὅτι
praise from people, *not* *I do accept* but I know you — I know that you do
1518 4123 476 4024 3284 247 1182 7007 4022 2400 2400
n.asf p.g n.gpm pl v.pai.1s cj v.rai.1s r.ap.2 cj

τὴν ἀγάπην τοῦ θεοῦ οὐκ ἔχετε ἐν ἑαυτοῖς. 43 ἐγὼ ἐλήλυθα ἐν τῷ
not have the love of God *not* *you do have* in you. I have come in the
4024 2400 3836 27 3836 2536 4024 2400 1877 1571 1609 2262 1877 3836
d.asf n.asf d.gsm n.gsm pl v.pai.2p p.d r.dpm.2 r.ns.1 v.rai.1s p.d d.dsn

ὀνόματι τοῦ πατρός μου, καὶ ↱ ↱ οὐ λαμβάνετέ με· ἐὰν ἄλλος ἔλθῃ
name of my Father *my* and you do not accept me. If ⸤someone else⸥ comes
3950 3836 1609 4252 1609 2779 3284 3284 4024 3284 1609 1569 257 2262
n.dsn d.gsm n.gsm r.gs.1 cj pl v.pai.2p r.as.1 cj r.nsm v.aas.3s

ἐν τῷ ὀνόματι τῷ ἰδίῳ, ἐκεῖνον λήμψεσθε. 44 πῶς δύνασθε ὑμεῖς
in *{the}* his own name, *{the}* *his own* him you will accept. How can you
1877 3836 2625 2625 3950 3836 2625 1697 3284 4802 1538 7007
p.d d.dsn n.dsn d.dsn a.dsn r.asm v.fmi.2p cj v.ppi.2p r.np.2

πιστεῦσαι δόξαν παρὰ ἀλλήλων λαμβάνοντες, καὶ τὴν
believe, when you accept praise from one another *when you accept* but do not seek the
4409 3284 3284 3284 1518 4123 253 3284 2779 2426 4024 2426 3836
f.aa n.asf p.g r.gpm pt.pa.npm cj d.asf

δόξαν τὴν παρὰ τοῦ μόνου θεοῦ οὐ ζητεῖτε; 45 ↱ Μὴ δοκεῖτε ὅτι ἐγὼ
praise that comes from the only God? *not* *do seek* Do not think that I
1518 3836 4123 3836 3668 2536 4024 2426 1506 3590 1506 4022 1609
n.asf d.asf p.g d.gsm a.gsm n.gsm pl v.pai.2p pl v.pam.2p cj r.ns.1

κατηγορήσω ὑμῶν πρὸς τὸν πατέρα· ἔστιν ὁ κατηγορῶν
will accuse you before the Father; the one who accuses you is *the* *one who accuses*
2989 7007 4639 3836 4252 3836 2989 2989 2989 7007 1639 3836 2989
v.fai.1s r.gp.2 p.a d.asm n.asm v.pai.3s d.nsm pt.pa.nsm

ὑμῶν Μωϋσῆς, εἰς ὃν ὑμεῖς ἠλπίκατε. 46 εἰ γὰρ ἐπιστεύετε Μωϋσεῖ, ➝
you Moses, on whom you ⸤have set your hope.⸥ If *{for}* you believed Moses, you
7007 3707 1650 4005 7007 1827 1623 1142 4409 3707
r.gp.2 n.nsm p.a r.asm r.np.2 v.rai.2p cj cj v.iai.2p n.dsm

ἐπιστεύετε ἂν ἐμοί· περὶ γὰρ ἐμοῦ ἐκεῖνος ἔγραψεν. 47 εἰ
would believe *would* me, for he wrote about *for* me. *he* *wrote* But if
323 4409 323 1609 1142 1697 1211 4309 1142 1609 1697 1211 1254 1623
v.iai.2p pl r.ds.1 p.g cj r.gs.1 r.nsm v.aai.3s cj

δὲ τοῖς ἐκείνου γράμμασιν οὐ πιστεύετε, πῶς
But you do not believe *{the}* his writings, *not* *you do believe* how will you believe
1254 4409 4409 4024 4409 3836 1697 1207 4024 4409 4802 4409 4409 4409
cj d.dpn r.gsm n.dpn pl v.pai.2p cj

τοῖς ἐμοῖς ῥήμασιν πιστεύσετε;
{the} my words?" *will you believe*
3836 1847 4839 4409
d.dpn r.dpn.1 n.dpn v.fai.2p

6:1 Μετὰ ταῦτα ἀπῆλθεν ὁ Ἰησοῦς πέραν τῆς θαλάσσης τῆς
After this Jesus went to *{the}* *Jesus* the other side of the Sea of
3552 4047 2652 599 3836 2652 4305 3836 2498 3836
p.a r.apn v.aai.3s d.nsm n.nsm p.g d.gsf n.gsf d.gsf

Γαλιλαίας τῆς Τιβεριάδος. 2 ἠκολούθει δὲ αὐτῷ
Galilee (also called the Sea of Tiberias). A large crowd was following *{and}* him
1133 3836 5500 4498 4063 199 1254 899
n.gsf d.gsf n.gsf v.iai.3s cj r.dsm.3

NASB

Scriptures because
you think that in
them you have
eternal life; it is
these that testify
about Me; 40 and
you are unwilling
to come to Me
so that you may
have life. 41 I do
not receive glory
from men; 42 but
I know you, that
you do not have
the love of God
in yourselves. 43 I
have come in My
Father's name, and
you do not receive
Me; if another
comes in his own
name, you will
receive him. 44 How
can you believe,
when you receive
glory from one
another and you
do not seek the
glory that is from
the *one and* only
God? 45 Do not
think that I will
accuse you before
the Father; the one
who accuses you
is Moses, in whom
you have set your
hope. 46 For if you
believed Moses,
you would believe
Me, for he wrote
about Me. 47 But if
you do not believe
his writings, how
will you believe
My words?"

Five Thousand Fed

6:1 After these
things Jesus went
away to the other
side of the Sea
of Galilee (or
Tiberias). 2 A large
crowd followed
Him, because

NIV

because they saw
the signs he had
performed by heal-
ing the sick. [3]Then
Jesus went up on
a mountainside
and sat down with
his disciples. [4]The
Jewish Passover
Festival was near.
[5]When Jesus
looked up and saw
a great crowd com-
ing toward him,
he said to Philip,
"Where shall we
buy bread for these
people to eat?" [6]He
asked this only to
test him, for he al-
ready had in mind
what he was going
to do.
[7]Philip answered
him, "It would
take more than
half a year's wag-
es[a] to buy enough
bread for each one
to have a bite!"
[8]Another of his
disciples, Andrew,
Simon Peter's
brother, spoke up,
[9]"Here is a boy
with five small
barley loaves and
two small fish,
but how far will
they go among so
many?"
[10]Jesus said,
"Have the people
sit down." There
was plenty of grass
in that place, and
they sat down
(about five thou-
sand men were
there). [11]Jesus then
took the loaves,
gave thanks, and
distributed

ὄχλος πολύς, ὅτι ἐθεώρουν τὰ σημεῖα ἃ ἐποίει ἐπὶ τῶν
crowd *large* because they saw the ⌊miraculous signs⌋ that ⌊he was performing⌋ on those
4063 4498 4022 2555 3836 4956 4005 4472 2093 3836
n.nsm a.nsm cj v.iai.3p d.apn n.apn r.apn v.iai.3s p.g d.gpm

ἀσθενούντων. 3 ἀνῆλθεν δὲ εἰς τὸ ὄρος Ἰησοῦς καὶ
who were sick. Jesus went up *{and}* on the mountainside, *Jesus* and he sat down
820 2652 456 1254 1650 3836 4001 2652 2779 2764 2764 2764
pt.pa.gpm v.aai.3s cj p.a d.asn n.asn n.nsm cj

ἐκεῖ ἐκάθητο μετὰ τῶν μαθητῶν αὐτοῦ. 4
there *he sat down* with *{the}* his disciples. *his* (Now the Passover, the great festival of
1695 2764 3552 3836 899 3412 899 1254 3836 4247 3836 2038 3836
adv v.imi.3s p.g d.gpm n.gpm r.gsm.3

ἦν δὲ ἐγγὺς τὸ πάσχα, ἡ ἑορτὴ τῶν Ἰουδαίων. 5→ ἐπάρας
the Jews, was *Now* at hand.) *the* *Passover* *the* *festival* *of the* *Jews* When Jesus lifted up
3836 2681 1639 1254 1584 3836 4247 3836 2038 3836 2681 2652 2048
v.iai.3s cj adv d.nsn n.nsn d.nsf n.nsf d.gpm a.gpm pt.aa.nsm

οὖν τοὺς ὀφθαλμοὺς ὁ Ἰησοῦς καὶ θεασάμενος ὅτι πολὺς ὄχλος ἔρχεται
{then} his eyes *{the}* *Jesus* and saw that a large crowd was coming
4036 3836 4057 3836 2652 2779 2517 4022 4498 4063 2262
cj d.apm n.apm d.nsm n.nsm cj pt.am.nsm cj a.nsm n.nsm v.pmi.3s

πρὸς αὐτὸν λέγει πρὸς Φίλιππον, πόθεν ἀγοράσωμεν ἄρτους ἵνα
toward him, he said to Philip, "Where can we buy bread so that these people
4639 899 3306 4639 5805 4470 60 788 2671 4047 4047
p.a r.asm.3 v.pai.3s p.a n.asm cj v.aas.1p n.apm cj

φάγωσιν οὗτοι; 6 τοῦτο δὲ ἔλεγεν πειράζων αὐτόν· ↱ αὐτὸς
may eat?" *these people* He said this *{and}* *He said* to test him, because he himself
2266 4047 3306 3306 4047 1254 3306 4279 899 1142 3857 899
v.aas.3p r.npm r.asn cj v.iai.3s pt.pa.nsm r.asm.3 r.nsm

γὰρ ᾔδει τί ἔμελλεν ποιεῖν. 7 ἀπεκρίθη αὐτῷ ὁ[a] Φίλιππος,
because knew what he was about to do. Philip answered him, *{the}* *Philip*
1142 3857 5515 3516 4472 5805 646 899 3836 5805
cj v.lai.3s r.asn v.iai.3s f.pa v.api.3s r.dsm.3 d.nsm n.nsm

διακοσίων δηναρίων ↰ ἄρτοι ↱ οὐκ ἀρκοῦσιν αὐτοῖς ἵνα ἕκαστος
"Two hundred denarii worth of bread is not enough for them, that each one may
1357 1324 1357 788 758 4024 758 899 2671 1667 3284
a.gpn n.gpn n.npm pl v.pai.3p r.dpm.3 cj r.nsm

βραχύ τι[b] λάβῃ. 8 λέγει αὐτῷ εἷς ἐκ τῶν μαθητῶν αὐτοῦ,
receive a little." *a* *may receive* *said* *to him* One of *{the}* his disciples, *his*
3284 5516 1099 5516 3284 3306 899 1651 1666 3836 899 3412 899
a.asn r.asn v.aas.3s v.pai.3s r.dsm.3 a.nsm p.g d.gpm n.gpm r.gsm.3

Ἀνδρέας ὁ ἀδελφὸς Σίμωνος Πέτρου, 9 ἔστιν
Andrew, *{the}* Simon Peter's brother, *Simon* *Peter's* said to him, ⌊"There is⌋ a
436 3836 4981 4377 81 4981 4377 3306 899 899 1639
n.nsm d.nsm n.nsm n.gsm n.gsm v.pai.3s

παιδάριον ὧδε ὃς ἔχει πέντε ἄρτους κριθίνους καὶ δύο ὀψάρια· ἀλλὰ
little boy here who has five barley loaves *barley* and two fish, but what
4081 6045 4005 2400 4297 3209 788 3209 2779 1545 4066 247 5515
n.nsn adv r.nsm v.pai.3s a.apm n.apm a.apm cj a.apn n.apn cj

ταῦτα τί ἐστιν εἰς τοσούτους; 10 εἶπεν ὁ Ἰησοῦς, ποιήσατε τοὺς
are they *what* *are* for so many?" Jesus said, *{the}* *Jesus* "Have the
1639 4047 5515 1639 1650 5537 2652 3306 3836 2652 4472 3836
r.npn r.nsn v.pai.3s p.a r.apm v.aai.3s d.nsm n.nsm v.aam.2p d.apm

ἀνθρώπους ἀναπεσεῖν. ἦν δὲ χόρτος πολὺς ἐν τῷ τόπῳ.
people sit down." ⌊(There was⌋ *{and}* plenty of grass *plenty* in that place.) So the
476 404 1639 1254 4498 5965 4498 1877 3836 5536 4036 3836
n.apm f.aa v.iai.3s cj n.nsm a.nsm p.d d.dsm n.dsm

ἀνέπεσαν οὖν οἱ ἄνδρες τὸν ἀριθμὸν ὡς πεντακισχίλιοι.
men sat down, *So* *the* *men* about five thousand *{the}* in number. *about* *five thousand*
467 404 4036 3836 467 6055 4295 4295 3836 750 6055 4295
v.aai.3p cj d.npm n.npm d.asm n.asm pl a.npm

11 ἔλαβεν οὖν τοὺς ἄρτους ὁ Ἰησοῦς καὶ εὐχαριστήσας διέδωκεν
Then Jesus took *Then* the loaves, *{the}* *Jesus* and ⌊after he had given thanks,⌋ distributed
4036 2652 3284 4036 3836 788 3836 2652 2779 2373 1344
v.aai.3s cj d.apm n.apm d.nsm n.nsm cj pt.aa.nsm v.aai.3s

NASB

they saw the signs
which He was per-
forming on those
who were sick.
[3]Then Jesus went
up on the moun-
tain, and there He
sat down with His
disciples. [4]Now the
Passover, the feast
of the Jews, was
near. [5]Therefore
Jesus, lifting up
His eyes and
seeing that a large
crowd was coming
to Him, *said to
Philip, "Where are
we to buy bread,
so that these may
eat?" [6]This He was
saying to test him,
for He Himself
knew what He was
intending to do.
[7]Philip answered
Him, "Two hun-
dred [a]denarii worth
of bread is not
sufficient for them,
for everyone to re-
ceive a little." [8]One
of His disciples,
Andrew, Simon Pe-
ter's brother, *said
to Him, [9]"There is
a lad here who has
five barley loaves
and two fish, but
what are these for
so many people?"
[10]Jesus said, "Have
the people sit
down." Now there
was much grass in
the place. So the
men sat down, in
number about five
thousand. [11]Jesus
then took the
loaves, and having
given thanks, He
distributed to those

[a] 7 Greek *take two hundred denarii*

[a] [ὁ] UBS, omitted by TNIV.
[b] [τι] UBS.

[a] The denarius was equivalent to a day's wages

NIV

to those who were
seated as much as
they wanted. He
did the same with
the fish.
12 When they had
all had enough to
eat, he said to his
disciples, "Gather
the pieces that are
left over. Let noth-
ing be wasted."
13 So they gathered
them and filled
twelve baskets
with the pieces
of the five barley
loaves left over
by those who had
eaten.
14 After the peo-
ple saw the sign
Jesus performed,
they began to say,
"Surely this is the
Prophet who is
to come into the
world." 15 Jesus,
knowing that they
intended to come
and make him king
by force, withdrew
again to a moun-
tain by himself.

Jesus Walks on the Water

16 When evening
came, his disciples
went down to the
lake, 17 where they
got into a boat and
set off across the
lake for Caperna-
um. By now it was
dark, and Jesus
had not yet joined
them. 18 A strong
wind was blow-
ing and the wa-
ters grew rough.
19 When they had
rowed about three
or four miles,[a]
they saw Jesus
approaching the
boat, walking on

[a] 19 Or about 5 or 6 kilometers

τοῖς[a] ἀνακειμένοις ὁμοίως καὶ ἐκ τῶν ὀψαρίων
them to those ⌊who were sitting down;⌋ and he did the same _and_ with the fish,
3836 367 2779 3931 2779 1666 3836 4066
d.dpm pt.pm.dpm adv adv p.g d.gpn n.gpn

ὅσον ἤθελον. 12 ὡς δὲ ἐνεπλήσθησαν, λέγει τοῖς
⌊as much as⌋ they wanted. And when _And_ the people had eaten their fill, he said to his
4012 2527 1254 6055 1254 1858 3306 3836 899
r.asn v.iai.3p cj cj v.api.3p v.pai.3s d.dpm

μαθηταῖς αὐτοῦ, συναγάγετε τὰ περισσεύσαντα κλάσματα, ἵνα ⌊μὴ τι⌋
disciples, _his_ "Gather up the leftover pieces, so that nothing
3412 899 5251 3836 4355 3083 2671 3590 5516
n.dpm r.gsm.3 v.aam.2p d.apn pt.aa.apn n.apn cj pl r.nsn

ἀπόληται. 13 συνήγαγον ← οὖν καὶ ἐγέμισαν δώδεκα κοφίνους
will go to waste." So they gathered them up _So_ and filled twelve baskets
660 4036 5251 4036 2779 1153 1557 3186
v.ams.3s v.aai.3p cj cj v.aai.3p a.apm n.apm

κλασμάτων ἐκ τῶν πέντε ἄρτων τῶν κριθίνων ἃ ἐπερίσσευσαν τοῖς
with broken pieces of the five barley loaves _{the}_ _barley_ that were left over by those
3083 1666 3836 4297 3209 788 3836 3209 4005 4355 3836
n.gpn p.g d.gpm a.gpm n.gpm d.gpm a.gpm r.npn v.aai.3p d.dpm

βεβρωκόσιν. 14 ↱ οἱ οὖν ἄνθρωποι ἰδόντες ὃ
who had eaten. So when the _So_ people saw the miraculous sign that Jesus
1048 4036 1625 3836 4036 476 1625 4956 4956 4005
pt.ra.dpm d.npm cj n.npm pt.aa.npm r.asn

ἐποίησεν σημεῖον ἔλεγον ὅτι οὗτός ἐστιν ἀληθῶς ὁ προφήτης
had performed, _miraculous sign_ ⌊they began to say,⌋ ~ "This is truly the prophet
4472 4956 3306 4022 4047 1639 242 3836 4737
v.aai.3s n.asn v.iai.3p cj r.nsm v.pai.3s adv d.nsm n.nsm

ὁ ἐρχόμενος εἰς τὸν κόσμον. 15 ↱ Ἰησοῦς οὖν γνοὺς ὅτι
who was to come into the world." Therefore when Jesus _Therefore_ realized that
3836 2262 1650 3836 3180 4036 1182 2652 4036 1182 4022
d.nsm pt.pm.nsm p.a d.asm n.asm n.nsm cj pt.aa.nsm cj

μέλλουσιν ἔρχεσθαι καὶ ἁρπάζειν αὐτὸν ↰ ↰ ἵνα ποιήσωσιν βασιλέα,
they were about to come and take him by force to make him king, he
3516 2262 2779 773 899 773 773 2671 4472 995 899
v.pai.3p f.pm cj f.pa r.asm.3 cj v.aas.3p n.asm

ἀνεχώρησεν πάλιν εἰς τὸ ὄρος αὐτὸς μόνος. 16 ὡς δὲ ὀψία ἐγένετο
withdrew again up the mountainside _he_ alone. Now when _Now_ evening had come,
432 4099 1650 3836 4001 899 3668 1254 6055 1254 4068 1181
v.aai.3s adv p.a d.asn n.asn r.nsm a.nsm cj cj n.nsf v.ami.3s

κατέβησαν οἱ μαθηταὶ αὐτοῦ ἐπὶ τὴν θάλασσαν 17 καὶ ἐμβάντες εἰς
his disciples went down _{the}_ _disciples_ _his_ to the lake, _{and}_ got into
899 3412 2849 3836 3412 899 2093 3836 2498 2779 1832 1650
v.aai.3p d.npm n.npm r.gsm.3 p.a d.asf n.asf cj pt.aa.npm p.a

πλοῖον ἤρχοντο πέραν τῆς θαλάσσης εἰς Καφαρναούμ. καὶ
a boat and started across the sea to Capernaum. _{and}_ It had by then
4450 2262 4305 3836 2498 1650 3019 2779 1181 1181 2453 2453
n.asn v.imi.3p p.g d.gsf n.gsf p.a n.asf cj

σκοτία ἤδη ἐγεγόνει καὶ ↱ οὔπω ἐληλύθει πρὸς αὐτοὺς ὁ
become dark, _by then_ _It had become_ and Jesus had not yet come to them. _{the}_
1181 5028 2453 1181 2779 2652 2262 4037 2262 4639 899 3836
n.nsf adv v.lai.3s cj adv v.lai.3s p.a r.apm.3 d.nsm

Ἰησοῦς, 18 ἡ τε θάλασσα ↱ ἀνέμου μεγάλου
Jesus The ~ sea was getting rough because a strong wind _strong_
2652 3836 5445 2498 1444 1444 1444 4463 3489 449 3489
n.nsm d.nsf cj n.nsf n.gsm a.gsm

πνέοντος διεγείρετο. 19 ἐληλακότες οὖν ὡς ⌊σταδίους
⌊had started to blow.⌋ _was getting rough_ ⌊When they had rowed⌋ _{then}_ about three or four miles,
4463 1444 1785 4036 6055 5084
pt.pa.gsm v.ipi.3s pt.ra.npm cj pl n.apm

εἴκοσι πέντε ἢ τριάκοντα⌋ θεωροῦσιν τὸν Ἰησοῦν περιπατοῦντα ἐπὶ τῆς
they saw _{the}_ Jesus walking on the
1633 4297 2445 5558 2555 3836 2652 4344 2093 3836
a.apm a.apm cj a.apm v.pai.3p d.asm n.asm pt.pa.asm p.g d.gsf

[a] μαθηταῖς, οἱ δὲ μαθηταί included by TR after τοῖς.

NASB

who were seated;
likewise also of
the fish as much
as they wanted.
12 When they were
filled, He *said
to His disciples,
"Gather up the
leftover fragments
so that nothing will
be lost." 13 So they
gathered them up,
and filled twelve
baskets with
fragments from
the five barley
loaves which were
left over by those
who had eaten.
14 Therefore when
the people saw the
sign which He had
performed, they
said, "This is truly
the Prophet who
is to come into the
world."

Jesus Walks on the Water

15 So Jesus, per-
ceiving that they
were intending
to come and take
Him by force to
make Him king,
withdrew again to
the mountain by
Himself alone.
16 Now when eve-
ning came, His dis-
ciples went down
to the sea, 17 and
after getting into a
boat, they _started_
_to_ cross the sea to
Capernaum. It had
already become
dark, and Jesus
had not yet come
to them. 18 The sea
began to be stirred
up because a strong
wind was blowing.
19 Then, when they
had rowed about
three or four miles,
they *saw Jesus
walking on the sea

NIV

the water; and they
were frightened.
[20]But he said to
them, "It is I; don't
be afraid." [21]Then
they were willing
to take him into
the boat, and im-
mediately the boat
reached the shore
where they were
heading.
[22]The next day
the crowd that
had stayed on the
opposite shore of
the lake realized
that only one boat
had been there,
and that Jesus
had not entered it
with his disciples,
but that they had
gone away alone.
[23]Then some boats
from Tiberias
landed near the
place where the
people had eaten
the bread after the
Lord had given
thanks. [24]Once the
crowd realized that
neither Jesus nor
his disciples were
there, they got into
the boats and went
to Capernaum in
search of Jesus.

Jesus the Bread of Life

[25]When they
found him on the
other side of the
lake, they asked
him, "Rabbi, when
did you get here?"
[26]Jesus answered,
"Very truly I tell
you, you are look-
ing for me, not be-
cause you saw the
signs I performed
but because you
ate the loaves and
had your fill. [27]Do
not

θαλάσσης καὶ ἐγγὺς τοῦ πλοίου γινόμενον, καὶ ἐφοβήθησαν. 20 ὁ
lake and coming near the boat, *coming* and they were terrified. But he
2498 2779 1181 1584 3836 4450 1181 2779 5828 1254 3836
n.gsf cj p.g d.gsn n.gsn pt.pm.asm cj v.api.3p d.nsm

δὲ λέγει αὐτοῖς, ἐγώ εἰμι· ↱ μὴ φοβεῖσθε. 21 ἤθελον οὖν
But said to them, "It is I; *It is* do not be afraid." Then ⌊they were glad⌋ *Then*
1254 3306 899 1639 1639 1609 1639 5828 3590 5828 4036 2527 4036
cj v.pai.3s r.dpm.3 r.ns.1 v.pai.1s pl v.ppm.2p v.iai.3p cj

λαβεῖν αὐτὸν εἰς τὸ πλοῖον, καὶ εὐθέως ἐγένετο τὸ πλοῖον ἐπὶ τῆς γῆς
to take him into the boat, and at once the boat reached *the boat {on}* the shore
3284 899 1650 3836 4450 2779 2311 3836 4450 1181 3836 4450 2093 3836 1178
f.aa r.asm.3 p.a d.asn n.asn cj adv v.ami.3s d.nsn n.nsn p.g d.gsf n.gsf

εἰς ἣν ὑπῆγον. 22 τῇ ἐπαύριον ὁ ὄχλος ὁ ἑστηκὼς
toward which ⌊they were going.⌋ ⌊On the⌋ next day the crowd *{the}* ⌊was standing on⌋ the
1650 4005 5632 3836 2069 3836 4063 3836 2705
p.a r.asf v.iai.3p d.dsf adv d.nsm n.nsm d.nsm pt.ra.nsm

πέραν τῆς θαλάσσης εἶδον ὅτι πλοιάριον ἄλλο οὐκ ἦν ἐκεῖ
other side of the lake. ⌊They knew⌋ that only one boat *{other} {not}* ⌊had been⌋ there,
4305 3836 2498 1625 4022 1623 1651 4449 257 4024 1639 1695
p.g d.gsf n.gsf v.aai.3p cj n.nsn r.nsn pl v.iai.3s adv

⌊εἰ μὴ⌋ ἓν καὶ ὅτι ↱ οὐ συνεισῆλθεν ← τοῖς μαθηταῖς
only one and that Jesus had not gotten into the boat with *{the}* his disciples,
1623 3590 1651 2779 4022 2652 5291 4024 5291 1650 3836 4450 3836 899 3412
cj pl a.nsn cj cj pl v.aai.3s d.dpm n.dpm

αὐτοῦ ὁ Ἰησοῦς εἰς τὸ πλοῖον ἀλλὰ μόνοι οἱ μαθηταὶ
his {the} Jesus into the boat but that the disciples had left without *the disciples*
899 3836 2652 1650 3836 4450 247 3836 3412 599 599 3668 3836 3412
r.gsm.3 d.nsm n.nsm p.a d.asn n.asn cj a.npm d.npm n.npm

αὐτοῦ ἀπῆλθον· 23 ἄλλα ἦλθεν πλοιά[a] ἐκ
him. *had left* However, other boats from Tiberias had come ashore *boats from*
899 599 257 4450 1666 5500 2262 4450 1666
r.gsm.3 v.aai.3p r.npn v.aai.3s n.npn p.g

Τιβεριάδος ἐγγὺς τοῦ τόπου ὅπου ἔφαγον τὸν ἄρτον →
Tiberias near the place where ⌊they had eaten⌋ the bread after the Lord
5500 1584 3836 5536 3963 2266 3836 788 3836 3261
n.gsf p.g d.gsm n.gsm cj v.aai.3p d.asm n.asm

εὐχαριστήσαντος τοῦ κυρίου. 24 ὅτε οὖν εἶδεν ὁ ὄχλος ὅτι
had given thanks. *the Lord* So when *So* the crowd realized *the crowd* that
2373 3836 3261 4036 4021 4036 3836 4063 1625 3836 4063 4022
pt.aa.gsm d.gsm n.gsm cj cj v.aai.3s d.nsm n.nsm cj

Ἰησοῦς οὐκ ἔστιν ἐκεῖ οὐδὲ οἱ μαθηταὶ αὐτοῦ, ἐνέβησαν αὐτοὶ εἰς
Jesus was not *was* there, nor *{the}* his disciples, *his* they got *they* into
2652 1639 4024 1639 1695 4028 3836 899 3412 899 899 1832 899 1650
n.nsm pl v.pai.3s adv cj d.npm n.npm r.gsm.3 v.aai.3p r.npm p.a

τὰ πλοιάρια καὶ ἦλθον εἰς Καφαρναοὺμ ζητοῦντες τὸν Ἰησοῦν. 25 καὶ
the boats and went to Capernaum looking for *{the}* Jesus. And
3836 4449 2779 2262 1650 3019 2426 3836 2652 2779
d.apn n.apn cj v.aai.3p p.a n.asf pt.pa.npm d.asm n.asm cj

εὑρόντες αὐτὸν πέραν τῆς θαλάσσης εἶπον αὐτῷ, ῥαββί, πότε
⌊when they found⌋ him on the other side of the lake, they said to him, "Rabbi, when did
2351 899 4305 3836 2498 3306 899 4806 4537 1181
pt.aa.npm r.asm.3 p.g d.gsf n.gsf v.aai.3p r.dsm.3 n.vsm cj

ὧδε γέγονας; 26 Ἀπεκρίθη αὐτοῖς ὁ Ἰησοῦς καὶ εἶπεν,
you come here?" *did you come* Jesus responded to them, *{the} Jesus {and}* saying, "I tell
1181 1181 6045 1181 2652 646 899 3836 2652 2779 3306 3306 3306
adv v.rai.2s v.api.3s r.dpm.3 d.nsm n.nsm cj v.aai.3s

ἀμὴν ἀμὴν λέγω ὑμῖν, → → ζητεῖτέ ← με οὐχ ὅτι εἴδετε
you the solemn truth, *I tell you* you are not looking for me *not* because you saw
7007 297 297 3306 7007 4024 2426 1609 4024 4022 1625
pl pl v.pai.1s r.dp.2 v.pai.2p r.as.1 pl cj v.aai.2p

σημεῖα, ἀλλ᾽ ὅτι ἐφάγετε ἐκ τῶν ἄρτων καὶ ἐχορτάσθητε. 27 →
⌊miraculous signs,⌋ but because you ate *{from}* the loaves and had all you wanted. Do not
4956 247 4022 2266 1666 3836 788 2779 5963 3590
n.apn cj cj v.aai.2p p.g d.gpm n.gpm cj v.api.2p

NASB

and drawing near
to the boat; and
they were fright-
ened. [20]But He
*said to them, "It is
I; do not be afraid."
[21]So they were
willing to receive
Him into the boat,
and immediately
the boat was at the
land to which they
were going.
[22]The next day
the crowd that
stood on the other
side of the sea saw
that there was no
other small boat
there, except one,
and that Jesus had
not entered with
His disciples into
the boat, but *that*
His disciples had
gone away alone.
[23]There came other
small boats from
Tiberias near to
the place where
they ate the bread
after the Lord had
given thanks. [24]So
when the crowd
saw that Jesus was
not there, nor His
disciples, they
themselves got into
the small boats,
and came to Ca-
pernaum seeking
Jesus. [25]When they
found Him on the
other side of the
sea, they said to
Him, "Rabbi, when
did You get here?"

Words to the People

[26]Jesus answered
them and said,
"Truly, truly, I say
to you, you seek
Me, not because
you saw signs, but
because you ate
of the loaves and
were filled. [27]Do

[a] πλοιά UBS, NET. πλοι[άρι]α TNIV.

NIV

work for food that
spoils, but for food
that endures to
eternal life, which
the Son of Man
will give you. For
on him God the Fa-
ther has placed his
seal of approval."
28 Then they asked
him, "What must
we do to do the
works God re-
quires?"
29 Jesus answered,
"The work of God
is this: to believe
in the one he has
sent."
30 So they asked
him, "What sign
then will you give
that we may see it
and believe you?
What will you do?
31 Our ancestors ate
the manna in the
wilderness; as it is
written: 'He gave
them bread from
heaven to eat.'[a]"
32 Jesus said to
them, "Very tru-
ly I tell you, it is
not Moses who
has given you the
bread from heav-
en, but it is my
Father who gives
you the true bread
from heaven. 33 For
the bread of God
is the bread that
comes down from
heaven and gives
life to the world."
34 "Sir," they said,
"always give us
this bread."
35 Then Jesus de-
clared, "I am the
bread of life. Who-
ever comes to me
will never

ἐργάζεσθε μὴ τὴν βρῶσιν τὴν ἀπολλυμένην ἀλλὰ ↰ τὴν βρῶσιν τὴν μένουσαν εἰς
work for *not* the food that perishes, but for the food that lasts for
2237 3590 3836 1111 3836 660 247 2237 3836 1111 3836 3531 1650
v.pmm.2p pl d.asf n.asf d.asf pt.pm.asf cj d.asf n.asf d.asf pt.pa.asf p.a

ζωὴν αἰώνιον, ἣν ὁ υἱὸς τοῦ ἀνθρώπου ὑμῖν δώσει· ↱
eternal life, *eternal* which the Son of Man will give you; *will give* for on
173 2437 173 4005 3836 5626 3836 476 1443 1443 7007 1443 1142 5381
n.asf a.asf r.asf d.nsm n.nsm d.gsm n.gsm r.dp.2 v.fai.3s

τοῦτον γὰρ ὁ πατὴρ ἐσφράγισεν ὁ θεός. 28 εἶπον οὖν πρὸς
him *for* God the Father has set his seal." *{the}* *God* Therefore they said *Therefore* to
4047 1142 2536 3836 4252 5381 3836 2536 4036 3306 4036 4639
r.asm cj d.nsm n.nsm v.aai.3s d.nsm n.nsm v.aai.3p cj p.a

αὐτόν, τί ποιῶμεν ἵνα ἐργαζώμεθα τὰ ἔργα τοῦ θεοῦ; 29
him, "What must we do to carry out the works *{the}* God requires?" Jesus
899 5515 4472 2671 2237 3836 2240 3836 2536 2652
r.asm.3 r.asn v.pas.1p cj v.pms.1p d.apn n.apn d.gsm n.gsm

ἀπεκρίθη ὁ[a] Ἰησοῦς καὶ εἶπεν αὐτοῖς, τοῦτό ἐστιν τὸ ἔργον τοῦ θεοῦ,
answered, *{the}* *Jesus* *{and}* saying to them, "This is the work that God requires,
646 3836 2652 2779 3306 899 4047 1639 3836 2240 3836 2536
v.api.3s d.nsm n.nsm cj v.aai.3s r.dpm.3 r.nsn v.pai.3s d.nsn n.nsn d.gsm n.gsm

ἵνα πιστεύητε εἰς ὃν ἀπέστειλεν ἐκεῖνος. 30 εἶπον οὖν αὐτῷ,
that you believe in ⌊him whom⌋ he has sent." *he* Then they said *Then* to him, "So
2671 4409 1650 4005 1697 690 1697 4036 3306 4036 899 4036
cj v.pas.2p p.a r.asm v.aai.3s r.nsm v.aai.3p cj r.dsm.3

τί οὖν → ποιεῖς σὺ σημεῖον, ἵνα ἴδωμεν καὶ
what *So* miraculous sign will you perform *you* *miraculous sign* that ⌊we may see⌋ it and
5515 4036 4956 4956 5148 4472 5148 4956 2671 1625 2779
r.asn cj v.pai.2s r.ns.2 n.asn cj v.aas.1p cj

πιστεύσωμέν σοι; τί ἐργάζῃ; 31 οἱ πατέρες ἡμῶν τὸ μάννα ἔφαγον
believe in you? What ⌊will you do?⌋ *{the}* Our fathers *Our* ate *{the}* manna *ate*
4409 5148 5515 2237 3836 7005 4252 7005 2266 3836 3445 2266
v.aas.1p r.ds.2 r.asn v.pmi.2s d.npm n.npm r.gp.1 d.asn n.asn v.aai.3p

ἐν τῇ ἐρήμῳ, καθώς ἐστιν γεγραμμένον, ἄρτον ἐκ τοῦ οὐρανοῦ
in the wilderness; as it is written, 'He gave them bread from *{the}* heaven
1877 3836 2245 2777 1639 1211 1443 1443 899 788 1666 3836 4041
p.d d.dsf n.dsf cj v.pai.3s pt.rp.nsn n.asm p.g d.gsm n.gsm

ἔδωκεν αὐτοῖς φαγεῖν. 32 εἶπεν οὖν αὐτοῖς ὁ Ἰησοῦς, ἀμὴν
He gave *them* to eat.'" Jesus said *{then}* to them, *{the}* *Jesus* "I tell you the solemn
1443 899 2266 2652 3306 4036 899 3836 2652 3306 3306 7007 297
v.aai.3s r.dpm.3 f.aa v.aai.3s cj r.dpm.3 d.nsm n.nsm pl

ἀμὴν λέγω ὑμῖν, οὐ Μωϋσῆς δέδωκεν ὑμῖν τὸν ἄρτον ἐκ τοῦ οὐρανοῦ,
truth, *I tell* *you* it was not Moses who gave you the bread from *{the}* heaven,
297 3306 7007 4024 3707 1443 7007 3836 788 1666 3836 4041
pl v.pai.1s r.dp.2 pl n.nsm v.rai.3s r.dp.2 d.asm n.asm p.g d.gsm n.gsm

ἀλλ' ὁ πατήρ μου δίδωσιν ὑμῖν τὸν ἄρτον ἐκ τοῦ οὐρανοῦ τὸν
but it is *{the}* my Father *my* who gives you the true bread from *{the}* heaven. *{the}*
247 3836 1609 4252 1609 1443 7007 3836 240 788 1666 3836 4041 3836
cj d.nsm n.nsm r.gs.1 v.pai.3s r.dp.2 d.asm n.asm p.g d.gsm n.gsm d.asm

ἀληθινόν· 33 ὁ γὰρ ἄρτος τοῦ θεοῦ ἐστιν ὁ καταβαίνων ἐκ τοῦ
true For the *For* bread of God is that which comes down from *{the}*
240 1142 3836 1142 788 3836 2536 1639 3836 2849 1666 3836
a.asm d.nsm cj n.nsm d.gsm n.gsm v.pai.3s d.nsm pt.pa.nsm p.g d.gsm

οὐρανοῦ καὶ ζωὴν διδοὺς τῷ κόσμῳ. 34 εἶπον οὖν πρὸς αὐτόν, κύριε,
heaven and gives life *gives* ⌊to the⌋ world." So they said *So* to him, "Sir,
4041 2779 1443 2437 1443 3836 3180 4036 3306 4036 4639 899 3261
n.gsm cj n.asf pt.pa.nsm d.dsm n.dsm v.aai.3p cj p.a r.asm.3 n.vsm

πάντοτε δὸς ἡμῖν τὸν ἄρτον τοῦτον. 35 εἶπεν αὐτοῖς
give us this bread ⌊from now on!"⌋ *give* *us* *{the}* *bread* *this* Jesus said to them,
1443 7005 4047 788 4121 1443 7005 3836 788 4047 2652 3306 899
adv v.aam.2s r.dp.1 d.asm n.asm r.asm v.aai.3s r.dpm.3

ὁ Ἰησοῦς, ἐγώ εἰμι ὁ ἄρτος τῆς ζωῆς· ὁ ἐρχόμενος πρὸς ἐμὲ ↱ ⌊οὐ
{the} *Jesus* "I am the bread of life; the one who comes to me will never
3836 2652 1609 1639 3836 788 3836 2437 3836 2262 4639 1609 4277 4024
d.nsm n.nsm r.ns.1 v.pai.1s d.nsm n.nsm d.gsf n.gsf d.nsm pt.pm.nsm p.a r.as.1 pl

NASB

not work for
the food which
perishes, but for
the food which
endures to eternal
life, which the
Son of Man will
give to you, for on
Him the Father,
God, has set His
seal." 28 Therefore
they said to Him,
"What shall we
do, so that we may
work the works
of God?" 29 Jesus
answered and said
to them, "This is
the work of God,
that you believe
in Him whom He
has sent." 30 So
they said to Him,
"What then do
You do for a sign,
so that we may
see, and believe
You? What work
do You perform?
31 Our fathers ate
the manna in the
wilderness; as it is
written, 'HE GAVE
THEM BREAD OUT OF
HEAVEN TO EAT.'"
32 Jesus then said
to them, "Truly,
truly, I say to you,
it is not Moses who
has given you the
bread out of heav-
en, but it is My
Father who gives
you the true bread
out of heaven.
33 For the bread of
God is [a]that which
comes down out of
heaven, and gives
life to the world."
34 Then they said
to Him, "Lord,
always give us this
bread."
35 Jesus said to
them, "I am the
bread of life; he
who comes to Me
will not hunger,

[a] 31 Exodus 16:4; Neh. 9:15; Psalm 78:24,25

[a] [ὁ] UBS, omitted by TNIV.

[a] Or *He who comes*

NIV

go hungry, and
whoever believes
in me will never be
thirsty. 36 But as I
told you, you have
seen me and still
you do not believe.
37 All those the Fa-
ther gives me will
come to me, and
whoever comes
to me I will never
drive away. 38 For
I have come down
from heaven not to
do my will but to
do the will of him
who sent me. 39 And
this is the will of
him who sent me,
that I shall lose
none of all those he
has given me, but
raise them up at
the last day. 40 For
my Father's will is
that everyone who
looks to the Son
and believes in him
shall have eternal
life, and I will raise
them up at the last
day."
41 At this the Jews
there began to
grumble about him
because he said, "I
am the bread that
came down from
heaven." 42 They
said, "Is this not
Jesus, the son of
Joseph, whose fa-
ther and mother
we know? How
can he now say, 'I
came down from
heaven'?"
43 "Stop

μὴ⌋ πεινάσῃ, καὶ ὁ πιστεύων εἰς ἐμὲ ↱ ⌊οὐ μὴ⌋ διψήσει πώποτε.
go hungry, and the one who believes in me will never be thirsty again.
3590 4277 2779 3836 4409 1650 1609 1498 4024 3590 1498 4799
pl v.aas.3s cj d.nsm pt.pa.nsm p.a r.as.1 pl pl v.fai.3s adv

36 ἀλλ᾽ εἶπον ὑμῖν ὅτι καὶ ἑωράκατέ με[a] καὶ ↱ ↱ ↱ οὐ πιστεύετε.
But as I told you, {that} {and} you have seen me and still you do not believe.
247 3306 7007 4022 2779 3972 1609 2779 4409 4409 4409 4024 4409
cj v.aai.1s r.dp.2 cj cj v.rai.2p r.as.1 cj pl v.pai.2p

37 πᾶν ὃ δίδωσίν μοι ὁ πατὴρ πρὸς ἐμὲ ἥξει, καὶ τὸν
All that the Father gives me *the Father* will come to me, *will come* and anyone
4246 4005 3836 4252 1443 1609 3836 4252 2457 2457 4639 1609 2457 2779 3836
a.nsn r.asn v.pai.3s r.ds.1 d.nsm n.nsm p.a r.as.1 v.fai.3s cj d.asm

ἐρχόμενον πρὸς ἐμὲ ↱ ↱ ⌊οὐ μὴ⌋ ἐκβάλω ἔξω, 38 ὅτι καταβέβηκα ἀπὸ τοῦ
who comes to me I will never turn away. For I have come down from {the}
2262 4639 1609 1675 1675 4024 3590 1675 2032 4022 2849 608 3836
pt.pm.asm p.a r.as.1 pl pl v.aas.1s adv cj v.rai.1s p.g d.gsm

οὐρανοῦ οὐχ ἵνα ποιῶ τὸ θέλημα τὸ ἐμὸν ἀλλὰ τὸ θέλημα τοῦ
heaven, not to do {the} my own will {the} *my own* but to do the will of
4041 4024 2671 4472 3836 1847 1847 2525 3836 1847 247 3836 2525 3836
n.gsm pl cj v.pas.1s d.asn n.asn d.asn r.asn.1 cj d.asn n.asn d.gsm

πέμψαντός με. 39 τοῦτο δέ ἐστιν τὸ θέλημα τοῦ πέμψαντός με, ἵνα πᾶν
him who sent me. And this *And* is the will of the one who sent me: that of all
4287 1609 1254 4047 1254 1639 3836 2525 3836 4287 1609 2671 4246
pt.aa.gsm r.as.1 r.nsn cj v.pai.3s d.nsn n.nsn d.gsm pt.aa.gsm r.as.1 cj a.asn

ὃ δέδωκέν μοι μὴ ἀπολέσω ἐξ αὐτοῦ, ἀλλὰ ἀναστήσω αὐτὸ
that he has given me I should lose none *I should lose* {from} {them} but raise them
4005 1443 1609 660 660 660 3590 660 1666 899 247 482 899
r.asn v.rai.3s r.ds.1 pl v.aas.1s p.g r.gsn.3 cj v.fai.1s r.asn.3

↰ ἐν[b] τῇ ἐσχάτῃ ἡμέρᾳ. 40 τοῦτο γάρ ἐστιν τὸ θέλημα τοῦ πατρός μου,
up on the last day. For this *For* is the will of my Father, *my*
482 1877 3836 2274 2465 1142 4047 1142 1639 3836 2525 3836 1609 4252 1609
p.d d.dsf a.dsf n.dsf r.nsn cj v.pai.3s d.nsn n.nsn d.gsm n.gsm r.gs.1

ἵνα πᾶς ὁ θεωρῶν τὸν υἱὸν καὶ πιστεύων εἰς αὐτὸν ἔχῃ
that everyone who considers the Son and comes to believe in him ⌊should have⌋ eternal
2671 4246 3836 2555 3836 5626 2779 4409 1650 899 2400 173
cj a.nsm d.nsm pt.pa.nsm d.asm n.asm cj pt.pa.nsm p.a r.asm.3 v.pas.3s

ζωὴν αἰώνιον, καὶ ἀναστήσω αὐτὸν ↰ ἐγὼ ἐν[c] τῇ[d] ἐσχάτῃ ἡμέρᾳ. 41
life, *eternal* and I will raise him up *I* on the last day." Then the
2437 173 2779 1609 482 899 482 1609 1877 3836 2274 2465 4036 3836
n.asf a.asf cj v.fai.1s r.asm.3 r.ns.1 p.d d.dsf a.dsf n.dsf

ἐγόγγυζον οὖν οἱ Ἰουδαῖοι περὶ αὐτοῦ ὅτι εἶπεν, ἐγώ εἰμι ὁ
Jews began to grumble *Then the* *Jews* about him because he said, "I am the
2681 1197 4036 3836 2681 4309 899 4022 3306 1609 1639 3836
v.iai.3p cj d.npm a.npm p.g r.gsm.3 cj v.aai.3s r.ns.1 v.pai.1s d.nsm

ἄρτος ὁ καταβὰς ἐκ τοῦ οὐρανοῦ, 42 καὶ ἔλεγον, οὐχ οὗτός
bread that came down from {the} heaven." And ⌊they were saying,⌋ "Is this not *this*
788 3836 2849 1666 3836 4041 2779 3306 1639 4047 4024 4047
n.nsm d.nsm pt.aa.nsm p.g d.gsm n.gsm cj v.iai.3p pl r.nsm

ἐστιν Ἰησοῦς ὁ υἱὸς Ἰωσήφ, οὗ ἡμεῖς οἴδαμεν τὸν πατέρα καὶ
Is Jesus, the son of Joseph, whose father and mother we know? {the} *father* *and*
1639 2652 3836 5626 2737 4005 4252 2779 3613 7005 3857 3836 4252 2779
v.pai.3s n.nsm d.nsm n.nsm n.gsm r.gsm r.np.1 v.rai.1p d.asm n.asm cj

τὴν μητέρα; πῶς ↱ ↱ νῦν λέγει ὅτι ἐκ τοῦ οὐρανοῦ
{the} *mother* How can he now say, ~ 'I have come down from {the} heaven'?"
3836 3613 4802 3306 3306 3814 3306 4022 2849 2849 2849 2849 1666 3836 4041
d.asf n.asf cj adv v.pai.3s cj p.g d.gsm n.gsm

καταβέβηκα; 43 ἀπεκρίθη Ἰησοῦς καὶ εἶπεν αὐτοῖς, ↱ μὴ
I have come down Jesus answered *Jesus* {and} them, saying, *them* "Do not
2849 2652 646 2652 2779 899 3306 899 1197 3590
v.rai.1s v.api.3s n.nsm cj v.aai.3s r.dpm.3 pl

NASB

and he who
believes in Me will
never thirst. 36 But I
said to you that you
have seen Me, and
yet do not believe.
37 All that the Father
gives Me will
come to Me, and
the one who comes
to Me I will cer-
tainly not cast out.
38 For I have come
down from heaven,
not to do My own
will, but the will of
Him who sent Me.
39 This is the will of
Him who sent Me,
that of all that He
has given Me I lose
nothing, but raise it
up on the last day.
40 For this is the will
of My Father, that
everyone who be-
holds the Son and
believes in Him
will have eternal
life, and I Myself
will raise him up
on the last day."

Words to the Jews

41 Therefore the
Jews were grum-
bling about Him,
because He said,
"I am the bread
that came down
out of heaven."
42 They were saying,
"Is not this Jesus,
the son of Joseph,
whose father and
mother we know?
How does He
now say, 'I have
come down out of
heaven'?" 43 Jesus
answered and said
to them, "Do not

[a] [με] UBS.
[b] [ἐν] UBS, omitted by TNIV.
[c] [ἐν] UBS.
[d] τῇ omitted by TNIV.

NIV

grumbling among
yourselves," Jesus
answered. 44 "No
one can come to
me unless the Fa-
ther who sent me
draws them, and I
will raise them up
at the last day. 45 It
is written in the
Prophets: 'They
will all be taught
by God.'[a] Every-
one who has heard
the Father and
learned from him
comes to me. 46 No
one has seen the
Father except the
one who is from
God; only he has
seen the Father.
47 Very truly I tell
you, the one who
believes has eter-
nal life. 48 I am
the bread of life.
49 Your ancestors
ate the manna in
the wilderness, yet
they died. 50 But
here is the bread
that comes down
from heaven,
which anyone may
eat and not die. 51 I
am the living bread
that came down
from heaven. Who-
ever eats this bread
will live forever.
This bread is my
flesh, which I will
give for the life of
the world."
52 Then the Jews
began to argue
sharply among
themselves, "How
can this man give
us his flesh to
eat?"
53 Jesus said to
them, "Very truly I
tell you,

γογγύζετε μετ᾽ ἀλλήλων. 44 οὐδεὶς δύναται ἐλθεῖν πρός με ⌊ἐὰν μὴ⌋ ὁ
keep grumbling among yourselves. No one can come to me unless the
1197 3552 253 4029 1538 2262 4639 1609 1569 3590 3836
v.pam.2p p.g r.gpm a.nsm v.ppi.3s f.aa p.a r.as.1 cj pl d.nsm

πατὴρ ὁ πέμψας με ἑλκύσῃ αὐτόν, κἀγὼ ἀναστήσω αὐτὸν ↰ ἐν τῇ ἐσχάτῃ
Father who sent me draws him; and I will raise him up on the last
4252 3836 4287 1609 1816 899 2743 482 899 482 1877 3836 2274
n.nsm d.nsm pt.aa.nsm r.as.1 v.aas.3s r.asm.3 crasis v.fai.1s r.asm.3 p.d d.dsf a.dsf

ἡμέρᾳ. 45 ἔστιν γεγραμμένον ἐν τοῖς προφήταις, καὶ → → ἔσονται πάντες
day. It stands written in the prophets, 'And they will all be *all*
2465 1639 1211 1877 3836 4737 2779 4246 1639 4246
n.dsf v.pai.3s pt.rp.nsn p.d d.dpm n.dpm cj v.fmi.3p a.npm

διδακτοὶ θεοῦ· πᾶς ὁ ἀκούσας παρὰ τοῦ πατρὸς καὶ μαθὼν ἔρχεται
taught by God.' Everyone who has heard *from* the Father and learned from him comes
1435 2536 4246 3836 201 4123 3836 4252 2779 3443 4123 2262
a.npm n.gsm a.nsm d.nsm pt.aa.nsm p.g d.gsm n.gsm cj pt.aa.nsm v.pmi.3s

πρὸς ἐμέ. 46 οὐχ ὅτι τὸν πατέρα ἑώρακέν τις ⌊εἰ μὴ⌋ ὁ
to me. Not that anyone has seen the Father, *has seen* *anyone* except the
4639 1609 4024 4022 5516 3972 3972 3836 4252 3972 5516 1623 3590 3836
p.a r.as.1 pl cj d.asm n.asm v.rai.3s r.nsm cj pl d.nsm

ὢν παρὰ τοῦ θεοῦ, οὗτος ἑώρακεν τὸν πατέρα. 47 ἀμὴν
⌊one who is⌋ from {the} God; he has seen the Father. I tell you the solemn
1639 4123 3836 2536 4047 3972 3836 4252 3306 3306 7007 297
pt.pa.nsm p.g d.gsm n.gsm r.nsm v.rai.3s d.asm n.asm pl

ἀμὴν λέγω ὑμῖν, ὁ πιστεύων ἔχει ζωὴν αἰώνιον. 48 ἐγώ εἰμι ὁ
truth, *I tell* *you* the one who believes has eternal life. *eternal* I am the
297 3306 7007 3836 4409 2400 173 2437 173 1609 1639 3836
pl v.pai.1s r.dp.2 d.nsm pt.pa.nsm v.pai.3s n.asf a.asf r.ns.1 v.pai.1s d.nsm

ἄρτος τῆς ζωῆς. 49 οἱ πατέρες ὑμῶν ἔφαγον ἐν τῇ ἐρήμῳ τὸ
bread of life. {the} Your fathers *Your* ate manna in the wilderness, {the}
788 3836 2437 3836 7007 4252 7007 2266 3445 1877 3836 2245 3836
n.nsm d.gsf n.gsf d.npm n.npm r.gp.2 v.aai.3p p.d d.dsf n.dsf d.asn

μάννα καὶ ἀπέθανον· 50 οὗτός ἐστιν ὁ ἄρτος ὁ ἐκ τοῦ
manna and they died. But here is the bread that comes down from {the}
3445 2779 633 4047 1639 3836 788 3836 2849 2849 1666 3836
n.asn cj v.aai.3p r.nsm v.pai.3s d.nsm n.nsm d.nsm p.g d.gsm

οὐρανοῦ καταβαίνων, ἵνα τις ἐξ αὐτοῦ φάγῃ καὶ μὴ ἀποθάνῃ.
heaven, *comes down* so that one may eat of it *may eat* and not die.
4041 2849 2671 5516 2266 2266 1666 899 2266 2779 3590 633
n.gsm pt.pa.nsm cj r.nsm p.g r.gsm.3 v.aas.3s cj pl v.aas.3s

51 ἐγώ εἰμι ὁ ἄρτος ὁ ζῶν ὁ ἐκ τοῦ οὐρανοῦ καταβάς·
I am the living bread {the} *living* that came down from {the} heaven. *came down*
1609 1639 3836 2409 788 3836 2409 3836 2849 2849 1666 3836 4041 2849
r.ns.1 v.pai.1s d.nsm n.nsm d.nsm pt.pa.nsm d.nsm p.g d.gsm n.gsm pt.aa.nsm

ἐάν τις φάγῃ ἐκ τούτου τοῦ ἄρτου ζήσει εἰς τὸν αἰῶνα, καὶ ὁ
If anyone eats of this {the} bread, ⌊he will live⌋ for all time {and} and the
1569 5516 2266 1666 4047 3836 788 2409 1650 3836 172 2779 1254 3836
cj r.nsm v.aas.3s p.g r.gsm d.gsm n.gsm v.fai.3s p.a d.asm n.asm cj d.nsm

ἄρτος δὲ ὃν ἐγὼ δώσω ἡ σάρξ μού ἐστιν ὑπὲρ τῆς
bread *and* that I will give is {the} my flesh *my* *is* — given ⌊on behalf of⌋ the life
788 1254 4005 1609 1443 1639 3836 1609 4922 1609 1639 5642 3836 2437
n.nsm cj r.asm r.ns.1 v.fai.1s d.nsf n.nsf r.gs.1 v.pai.3s p.g d.gsf

τοῦ κόσμου ζωῆς. 52 ἐμάχοντο οὖν πρὸς ἀλλήλους οἱ Ἰουδαῖοι
of the world." *life* Then the Jews began to argue *Then* with one another, *the* *Jews*
3836 3180 2437 4036 3836 2681 3481 4036 4639 253 3836 2681
d.gsm n.gsm n.gsf v.imi.3p cj p.a r.apm d.npm a.npm

λέγοντες, πῶς δύναται οὗτος ἡμῖν δοῦναι τὴν σάρκα αὐτοῦ[a] φαγεῖν;
saying, "How can this man give us *give* {the} his flesh *his* to eat?"
3306 4802 1538 4047 1443 7005 1443 3836 899 4922 899 2266
pt.pa.npm cj v.ppi.3s r.nsm r.dp.1 f.aa d.asf n.asf r.gsm.3 f.aa

53 εἶπεν οὖν αὐτοῖς ὁ Ἰησοῦς, ἀμὴν ἀμὴν λέγω
Jesus therefore said *therefore* to them, {the} *Jesus* "I tell you the solemn truth, *I tell*
2652 4036 3306 4036 899 3836 2652 3306 3306 7007 297 297 3306
v.aai.3s cj r.dpm.3 d.nsm n.nsm pl pl v.pai.1s

NASB

grumble among
yourselves. 44 No
one can come to
Me unless the
Father who sent
Me draws him; and
I will raise him up
on the last day. 45 It
is written in the
prophets, 'AND
THEY SHALL ALL BE
TAUGHT OF GOD.'
Everyone who has
heard and learned
from the Father,
comes to Me. 46 Not
that anyone has
seen the Father,
except the One
who is from God;
He has seen the
Father. 47 Truly,
truly, I say to you,
he who believes
has eternal life. 48 I
am the bread of
life. 49 Your fathers
ate the manna in
the wilderness, and
they died. 50 This
is the bread which
comes down out
of heaven, so that
one may eat of it
and not die. 51 I am
the living bread
that came down
out of heaven; if
anyone eats of this
bread, he will live
forever; and the
bread also which
I will give for the
life of the world is
My flesh."
52 Then the Jews
began to argue
with one another,
saying, "How can
this man give us
His flesh to eat?"
53 So Jesus said to
them, "Truly, truly,
I say to you, unless

[a] 45 Isaiah 54:13

[a] [αὐτοῦ] UBS.

NIV

unless you eat the
flesh of the Son of
Man and drink his
blood, you have no
life in you. 54 Who-
ever eats my flesh
and drinks my
blood has eternal
life, and I will raise
them up at the last
day. 55 For my flesh
is real food and my
blood is real drink.
56 Whoever eats my
flesh and drinks
my blood remains
in me, and I in
them. 57 Just as the
living Father sent
me and I live be-
cause of the Father,
so the one who
feeds on me will
live because of me.
58 This is the bread
that came down
from heaven. Your
ancestors ate man-
na and died, but
whoever feeds on
this bread will live
forever." 59 He said
this while teaching
in the synagogue in
Capernaum.

Many Disciples Desert Jesus

60 On hearing it,
many of his dis-
ciples said, "This
is a hard teaching.
Who can ac-
cept it?"
61 Aware that his
disciples were
grumbling about
this, Jesus said to
them, "Does this
offend you? 62 Then
what if

ὑμῖν, ˻ἐὰν μὴ˼ φάγητε τὴν σάρκα τοῦ υἱοῦ τοῦ ἀνθρώπου καὶ πίητε αὐτοῦ τὸ
you unless you eat the flesh of the Son of Man and drink his *{the}*
7007 1569 3590 2266 3836 4922 3836 5626 3836 476 2779 4403 899 3836
r.dp.2 cj pl v.aas.2p d.asf n.asf d.gsm n.gsm d.gsm n.gsm cj v.aas.2p r.gsm.3 d.asn

αἷμα, οὐκ ἔχετε ζωὴν ἐν ἑαυτοῖς. 54 ὁ τρώγων μου
blood, you will have no *you will have* life in you. The ˻one who feeds on˼ my
135 2400 2400 2400 4024 2400 2437 1877 1571 3836 5592 1609
n.asn pl v.pai.2p n.asf p.d r.dpm.2 d.nsm pt.pa.nsm r.gs.1

τὴν σάρκα καὶ πίνων μου τὸ αἷμα ἔχει ζωὴν αἰώνιον, κἀγὼ ἀναστήσω
{the} flesh and drinks my *{the}* blood has eternal life, *eternal* and I will raise
3836 4922 2779 4403 1609 3836 135 2400 173 2437 173 2743 482
d.asf n.asf cj pt.pa.nsm r.gs.1 d.asn n.asn v.pai.3s n.asf a.asf crasis v.fai.1s

αὐτὸν ↰ τῇ ἐσχάτῃ ἡμέρᾳ. 55 ἡ γὰρ σάρξ μου ἀληθής ἐστιν βρῶσις,
him up ˻on the˼ last day; *{the}* for my flesh *my* is real *is* food
899 482 3836 2274 2465 3836 1142 1609 4922 1609 1639 239 1639 1111
r.asm.3 d.dsf a.dsf n.dsf d.nsf cj n.nsf r.gs.1 a.nsf v.pai.3s n.nsf

καὶ τὸ αἷμά μου ἀληθής ἐστιν πόσις. 56 ὁ τρώγων μου τὴν σάρκα
and *{the}* my blood *my* is real *is* drink. The ˻one who eats˼ my *{the}* flesh
2779 3836 1609 135 1609 1639 239 1639 4530 3836 5592 1609 3836 4922
cj d.nsn n.nsn r.gs.1 a.nsf v.pai.3s n.nsf d.nsm pt.pa.nsm r.gs.1 d.asf n.asf

καὶ πίνων μου τὸ αἷμα ἐν ἐμοὶ μένει κἀγὼ ἐν αὐτῷ. 57 καθὼς
and drinks my *{the}* blood dwells in me, *dwells* and I in him. As the living
2779 4403 1609 3836 135 3531 1877 1609 3531 2743 1877 899 2777 3836 2409
cj pt.pa.nsm r.gs.1 d.asn n.asn p.d r.ds.1 v.pai.3s crasis p.d r.dsm.3 cj

ἀπέστειλέν με ὁ ζῶν πατὴρ κἀγὼ ζῶ διὰ τὸν πατέρα, καὶ ὁ
Father sent me, *the living Father* and I live ˻because of˼ the Father, so the
4252 690 1609 3836 2409 4252 2743 2409 1328 3836 4252 2779 3836
v.aai.3s r.as.1 d.nsm pt.pa.nsm n.nsm crasis v.pai.1s p.a d.asm n.asm cj d.nsm

τρώγων με κἀκεῖνος ζήσει δι' ἐμέ. 58 οὗτός ἐστιν ὁ ἄρτος
˻one who feeds on˼ me *{also that one}* will live ˻because of˼ me. This is the bread
5592 1609 2797 2409 1328 1609 4047 1639 3836 788
pt.pa.nsm r.as.1 crasis v.fai.3s p.a r.as.1 r.nsm v.pai.3s d.nsm n.nsm

ὁ ἐξ οὐρανοῦ καταβάς, οὐ καθὼς ἔφαγον
that came down from heaven; *came down* it is not like that which your fathers ate
3836 2849 2849 1666 4041 2849 4024 2777 3836 4252 2266
d.nsm p.g n.gsm pt.aa.nsm pl cj v.aai.3p

οἱ πατέρες καὶ ἀπέθανον· ὁ τρώγων τοῦτον τὸν ἄρτον ζήσει εἰς τὸν
your fathers and died. The ˻one who feeds on˼ this *{the}* bread will live for all
3836 4252 2779 633 3836 5592 4047 3836 788 2409 1650 3836
d.npm n.npm cj v.aai.3p d.nsm pt.pa.nsm r.asm d.asm n.asm v.fai.3s p.a d.asm

αἰῶνα. 59 ταῦτα εἶπεν ἐν συναγωγῇ
time." Jesus said these things *said* when he was teaching in the synagogue
172 3306 4047 3306 1438 1438 1438 1438 1877 5252
n.asm r.apn v.aai.3s p.d n.dsf

διδάσκων ἐν Καφαρναούμ. 60 ↱ πολλοὶ οὖν
when he was teaching in Capernaum. Therefore, when a number *Therefore* of his
1438 1877 3019 4036 201 4498 4036 1666 899
pt.pa.nsm p.d n.dsf a.npm cj

ἀκούσαντες ἐκ τῶν μαθητῶν αὐτοῦ εἶπαν, σκληρός
disciples heard *of {the} disciples his* it, they said, "This teaching is difficult;
3412 201 1666 3836 3412 899 3306 4047 3364 1639 5017
pt.aa.npm p.g d.gpm n.gpm r.gsm.3 v.aai.3p a.nsm

ἐστιν ὁ λόγος οὗτος· τίς δύναται αὐτοῦ ἀκούειν; 61 εἰδὼς
is {the} teaching This who can understand it?" *understand* But Jesus, aware
1639 3836 3364 4047 5515 1538 201 899 201 1254 2652 3857
v.pai.3s d.nsm n.nsm r.nsm r.nsm v.ppi.3s r.gsm.3 f.pa pt.ra.nsm

δὲ ὁ Ἰησοῦς ἐν ἑαυτῷ ὅτι γογγύζουσιν περὶ τούτου οἱ μαθηταὶ
But {the} Jesus {in} {himself} that his disciples were grumbling about it, *{the} disciples*
1254 3836 2652 1877 1571 4022 899 3412 1197 4309 4047 3836 3412
cj d.nsm n.nsm p.d r.dsm.3 cj v.pai.3p p.g r.gsn d.npm n.npm

αὐτοῦ εἶπεν αὐτοῖς, τοῦτο ὑμᾶς σκανδαλίζει; 62 ἐὰν οὖν
his said to them, "Does this offend you? *Does offend* Then what if *Then*
899 3306 899 4997 4047 4997 7007 4997 4036 1569 4036
r.gsm.3 v.aai.3s r.dpm.3 r.nsn r.ap.2 v.pai.3s cj cj

NASB

you eat the flesh of
the Son of Man and
drink His blood,
you have no life
in yourselves. 54 He
who eats My flesh
and drinks My
blood has eternal
life, and I will raise
him up on the last
day. 55 For My flesh
is true food, and
My blood is true
drink. 56 He who
eats My flesh and
drinks My blood
abides in Me, and I
in him. 57 As the liv-
ing Father sent Me,
and I live because
of the Father, so
he who eats Me,
he also will live
because of Me.
58 This is the bread
which came down
out of heaven; not
as the fathers ate
and died; he who
eats this bread will
live forever."

Words to the Disciples

59 These things He
said in the syna-
gogue as He taught
in Capernaum.
60 Therefore many
of His disciples,
when they heard
this said, "This is
a difficult state-
ment; who can
listen to it?" 61 But
Jesus, conscious
that His disciples
grumbled at this,
said to them, "Does
this cause you to
stumble? 62 *What*

NIV

you see the Son of Man ascend to where he was before! 63 The Spirit gives life; the flesh counts for nothing. The words I have spoken to you—they are full of the Spirit[a] and life. 64 Yet there are some of you who do not believe." For Jesus had known from the beginning which of them did not believe and who would betray him. 65 He went on to say, "This is why I told you that no one can come to me unless the Father has enabled them."

66 From this time many of his disciples turned back and no longer followed him.

67 "You do not want to leave too, do you?" Jesus asked the Twelve.

68 Simon Peter answered him, "Lord, to whom shall we go? You have the words of eternal life. 69 We have come to believe and to know that you are the Holy One of God."

70 Then Jesus replied, "Have I not chosen you, the Twelve? Yet one of you is a devil!" 71 (He meant Judas, the son of Simon Iscariot, who, though one of the Twelve, was later to betray him.)

θεωρῆτε τὸν υἱὸν τοῦ ἀνθρώπου ἀναβαίνοντα ὅπου ἦν τὸ πρότερον;
⌊you were to see⌋ the Son of Man ascending to where ⌊he was⌋ *{the}* before?
2555 3836 5626 3836 476 326 3963 1639 3836 4728
v.pas.2p d.asm n.asm d.gsm n.gsm pt.pa.asm cj v.iai.3s d.asn adv.c

63 τὸ πνεῦμά ἐστιν τὸ ζῳοποιοῦν, ἡ σὰρξ ⌊οὐκ ὠφελεῖ οὐδέν·⌋ τὰ
It is the Spirit *It is* who gives life; the flesh is useless. The
1639 1639 3836 4460 1639 3836 2443 3836 4922 4024 6067 4029 3836
d.nsn n.nsn v.pai.3s d.nsn pt.pa.nsn d.nsf n.nsf pl v.pai.3s a.asn d.npn

ῥήματα ἃ ἐγὼ λελάληκα ὑμῖν πνεῦμά ἐστιν καὶ ζωή ἐστιν. 64 ἀλλ᾽ εἰσὶν
words that I have spoken to you are spirit *are* and life. *{are}* But ⌊there are⌋
4839 4005 1609 3281 7007 1639 4460 1639 2779 2437 1639 247 1639
n.npn r.apn r.ns.1 v.rai.1s r.dp.2 n.nsn v.pai.3s cj n.nsf v.pai.3s cj v.pai.3p

ἐξ ὑμῶν τινες οἳ ↱ οὐ πιστεύουσιν. ᾔδει γὰρ
some among you *some* who do not believe." For from the beginning Jesus knew *For*
5516 1666 7007 5516 4005 4409 4024 4409 1142 1666 794 2652 3857 1142
p.g r.gp.2 r.npm r.npm pl v.pai.3p v.lai.3s cj

ἐξ ἀρχῆς ὁ Ἰησοῦς τίνες εἰσὶν οἱ ↱ μὴ πιστεύοντες καὶ τίς ἐστιν ὁ
from beginning {the} Jesus those *{are}* who would not believe, and who it was who
1666 794 3836 2652 5515 1639 3836 4409 3590 4409 2779 5515 1639 3836
p.g n.gsf d.nsm n.nsm r.npm v.pai.3p d.npm pl pt.pa.npm cj r.nsm v.pai.3s d.nsm

παραδώσων αὐτόν. 65 καὶ ἔλεγεν, διὰ τοῦτο εἴρηκα ὑμῖν ὅτι οὐδεὶς δύναται
would betray him. And he said, "For this reason I have said to you, ~ 'No one can
4140 899 2779 3306 1328 4047 3306 7007 4022 4029 1538
pt.fa.nsm r.asm.3 cj v.iai.3s p.a r.asn v.rai.1s r.dp.2 cj a.nsm v.ppi.3s

ἐλθεῖν πρός με ⌊ἐὰν μὴ⌋ ᾖ δεδομένον αὐτῷ ἐκ τοῦ πατρός. 66 ἐκ τούτου
come to me unless ⌊it is⌋ granted to him by the Father.'" From this
2262 4639 1609 1569 3590 1639 1443 899 1666 3836 4252 1666 4047
f.aa p.a r.as.1 cj pl v.pas.3s pt.rp.nsn r.dsm.3 p.g d.gsm n.gsm p.g r.gsn

πολλοὶ ἐκ[a] τῶν μαθητῶν αὐτοῦ ἀπῆλθον ⌊εἰς τὰ ὀπίσω⌋ καὶ οὐκέτι
time, many of *{the}* his disciples *his* turned back and no longer
4498 1666 3836 899 3412 899 599 1650 3836 3958 2779 4033
a.npm p.g d.gpm n.gpm r.gsm.3 v.aai.3p p.a d.apn adv cj adv

μετ᾽ αὐτοῦ περιεπάτουν. 67 εἶπεν οὖν ὁ Ἰησοῦς τοῖς
associated with him. *associated* Jesus therefore said *Jesus {the} therefore* to the
4344 3552 899 4344 4036 2652 3306 4036 3836 2652 3836
p.g r.gsm.3 v.iai.3p v.aai.3s cj d.nsm n.nsm d.dpm

δώδεκα, ↱ μὴ καὶ ὑμεῖς θέλετε ὑπάγειν; ↰ ↰
twelve, "You do not *like the others You* want to leave me like the others, do you?"
1557 7007 2527 3590 2779 7007 2527 5632 2779 2779 2779 3590 3590
a.dpm pl adv r.np.2 v.pai.2p f.pa

68 ἀπεκρίθη αὐτῷ Σίμων Πέτρος, κύριε, πρὸς τίνα ἀπελευσόμεθα;
Simon Peter answered him, *Simon Peter* "Lord, to whom would we go? You have
4981 4377 646 899 4981 4377 3261 4639 5515 599 2400 2400
v.api.3s r.dsm.3 n.nsm n.nsm n.vsm p.a r.asm v.fmi.1p

ῥήματα → ζωῆς αἰωνίου ἔχεις, 69 καὶ ἡμεῖς πεπιστεύκαμεν καὶ
the words of eternal life, *eternal You have* and we have come to believe and
4839 173 2437 173 2400 2779 7005 4409 2779
n.apn n.gsf a.gsf v.pai.2s cj r.np.1 v.rai.1p cj

ἐγνώκαμεν ὅτι σὺ εἶ ὁ ἅγιος τοῦ θεοῦ.[b] 70 ἀπεκρίθη αὐτοῖς ὁ
to know that you are the Holy One of God." Jesus answered them, *{the}*
1182 4022 5148 1639 3836 41 3836 2536 2652 646 899 3836
v.rai.1p cj r.ns.2 v.pai.2s d.nsm a.nsm d.gsm n.gsm v.api.3s r.dpm.3 d.nsm

Ἰησοῦς, οὐκ ἐγὼ ὑμᾶς τοὺς δώδεκα ἐξελεξάμην; καὶ ἐξ ὑμῶν
Jesus "Did I not *I* choose you, the twelve? *Did choose* Yet one of you
2652 1721 1609 4024 1609 1721 7007 3836 1557 1721 2779 1651 1666 7007
n.nsm pl r.ns.1 r.ap.2 d.apm a.apm v.ami.1s cj p.g r.gp.2

εἷς διάβολός ἐστιν. 71 ἔλεγεν δὲ τὸν Ἰούδαν Σίμωνος
one is a devil." *is* ⌊(He was speaking⌋ *{and}* of *{the}* Judas, son of Simon
1651 1639 1333 1639 3306 1254 3836 2683 4981
a.nsm n.nsm v.pai.3s v.iai.3s cj d.asm n.asm n.gsm

Ἰσκαριώτου· οὗτος γὰρ ἔμελλεν παραδιδόναι αὐτόν, εἷς
Iscariot, for he, *for* one of the twelve, was going to betray him.) *one*
2697 1142 4047 1142 1651 1666 3836 1557 3516 4140 899 1651
n.gsm r.nsm cj v.iai.3s f.pa r.asm.3 a.nsm

NASB

then if you see the Son of Man ascending to where He was before? 63 It is the Spirit who gives life; the flesh profits nothing; the words that I have spoken to you are spirit and are life. 64 But there are some of you who do not believe." For Jesus knew from the beginning who they were who did not believe, and who it was that would betray Him. 65 And He was saying, "For this reason I have said to you, that no one can come to Me unless it has been granted him from the Father."

Peter's Confession of Faith

66 As a result of this many of His disciples withdrew and were not walking with Him anymore. 67 So Jesus said to the twelve, "You do not want to go away also, do you?" 68 Simon Peter answered Him, "Lord, to whom shall we go? You have words of eternal life. 69 We have believed and have come to know that You are the Holy One of God." 70 Jesus answered them, "Did I Myself not choose you, the twelve, and *yet* one of you is a devil?" 71 Now He meant Judas *the son* of Simon Iscariot, for he, one of the twelve, was going to betray Him.

[a] 63 Or *are Spirit;* or *are spirit*

[a] [ἐκ] UBS.
[b] Χριστὸς ὁ υἱὸς τοῦ Θεοῦ τοῦ ζῶντος included by TR after θεοῦ.

NIV

Jesus Goes to the Festival of Tabernacles

7 After this, Jesus went around in Galilee. He did not want[a] to go about in Judea because the Jewish leaders there were looking for a way to kill him. 2 But when the Jewish Festival of Tabernacles was near, 3 Jesus' brothers said to him, "Leave Galilee and go to Judea, so that your disciples there may see the works you do. 4 No one who wants to become a public figure acts in secret. Since you are doing these things, show yourself to the world." 5 For even his own brothers did not believe in him.

6 Therefore Jesus told them, "My time is not yet here; for you any time will do. 7 The world cannot hate you, but it hates me because I testify that its works are evil. 8 You go to the festival. I am not[b] going up to this festival, because my time has not yet fully come."

[a] 1 Some manuscripts *not have authority*
[b] 8 Some manuscripts *not yet*

ἐκ τῶν δώδεκα.
of the Twelve
1666 3836 1557
p.g d.gpm a.gsm

7:1 καὶ μετὰ ταῦτα περιεπάτει ὁ Ἰησοῦς ἐν τῇ Γαλιλαίᾳ·
{and} After this Jesus traveled about *{the} Jesus* in *{the}* Galilee; he chose
2779 3552 4047 2652 4344 3836 2652 1877 3836 1133 2527 2527
cj p.a r.apn v.iai.3s d.nsm n.nsm p.d d.dsf n.dsf

οὐ γὰρ ἤθελεν ἐν τῇ Ἰουδαίᾳ περιπατεῖν, ὅτι ἐζήτουν
not *{for} he chose* to remain in *{the}* Judea, *to remain* because the Jews were seeking
4024 1142 2527 4344 4344 1877 3836 2677 4344 4022 3836 2681 2426
pl cj v.iai.3s p.d d.dsf n.dsf f.pa cj v.iai.3p

αὐτὸν οἱ Ἰουδαῖοι ἀποκτεῖναι. 2 ἦν
to kill him. *the Jews to kill* Now the Jewish festival of Tabernacles was
650 650 899 3836 2681 650 1254 3836 2681 2038 5009 1639
r.asm.3 d.npm a.npm f.aa v.iai.3s

δὲ ἐγγὺς ἡ ἑορτὴ τῶν Ἰουδαίων ἡ σκηνοπηγία. 3 εἶπον οὖν
Now near. *the festival {the} Jewish {the} Tabernacles* So his brothers said *So*
1254 1584 3836 2038 3836 2681 3836 5009 4036 899 81 3306 4036
cj adv d.nsf n.nsf d.gpm a.gpm d.nsf n.nsf v.aai.3p cj

πρὸς αὐτὸν οἱ ἀδελφοὶ αὐτοῦ, μετάβηθι ἐντεῦθεν καὶ ὕπαγε εἰς τὴν
to him, *{the} brothers his* ⌞"You should leave⌟ here and go to *{the}*
4639 899 3836 81 899 3553 1949 2779 5632 1650 3836
p.a r.asm.3 d.npm n.npm r.gsm.3 v.aam.2s adv cj v.pam.2s p.a d.asf

Ἰουδαίαν, ἵνα καὶ οἱ μαθηταί σου θεωρήσουσιν σοῦ
Judea so that your disciples also *{the} disciples your* may observe the works *{your}*
2677 2671 5148 3412 2779 3836 3412 5148 2555 3836 2240 5148
n.asf cj adv d.npm n.npm r.gs.2 v.fai.3p r.gs.2

τὰ ἔργα ἃ ποιεῖς· 4 οὐδεὶς γάρ τι ἐν κρυπτῷ ποιεῖ καὶ
the works that ⌞you are doing.⌟ For no one *For {anything}* acts in secret *acts* if he
3836 2240 4005 4472 1142 4029 1142 5516 4472 1877 3220 4472 2779 899
d.apn n.apn r.apn v.pai.2s a.nsm cj r.asn p.d a.dsn v.pai.3s cj

ζητεῖ αὐτὸς ⌞ἐν παρρησίᾳ εἶναι.⌟ εἰ ταῦτα
desires *he* public recognition. If you are doing these things,
2426 899 1877 4244 1639 1623 4472 4472 4472 4047
v.pai.3s r.nsm p.d n.dsf f.pa cj r.apn

ποιεῖς, φανέρωσον σεαυτὸν τῷ κόσμῳ. 5 οὐδὲ γὰρ οἱ
you are doing show yourself ⌞to the⌟ world." (You see, not even *You see {the}* his
4472 5746 4932 3836 3180 1142 1142 4028 1142 3836 899
v.pai.2s v.aam.2s r.asm.2 d.dsm n.dsm adv cj d.npm

ἀδελφοὶ αὐτοῦ ἐπίστευον εἰς αὐτόν. 6 λέγει οὖν αὐτοῖς ὁ Ἰησοῦς,
brothers *his* had confidence in him.) So Jesus said *So* to them, *{the} Jesus*
81 899 4409 1650 899 4036 2652 3306 4036 899 3836 2652
n.npm r.gsm.3 v.iai.3p p.a r.asm.3 v.pai.3s cj r.dpm.3 d.nsm n.nsm

ὁ καιρὸς ὁ ἐμὸς ↱ οὔπω πάρεστιν, ὁ δὲ καιρὸς ὁ ὑμέτερος
{the} "My time *{the} My* has not yet come, *{the}* but your time *{the} your*
3836 1847 2789 3836 1847 4205 4037 4205 3836 1254 5629 2789 3836 5629
d.nsm n.nsm d.nsm r.nsm.1 adv v.pai.3s d.nsm cj n.nsm d.nsm r.nsm.2

πάντοτέ ἐστιν ἕτοιμος. 7 ⌞οὐ δύναται⌟ ὁ κόσμος μισεῖν ὑμᾶς,
is always *is* here. The world cannot *The world* hate you, but
1639 4121 1639 2289 3836 3180 4024 1538 3836 3180 3631 7007 1254
adv v.pai.3s a.nsm pl v.ppi.3s d.nsm n.nsm f.pa r.ap.2

ἐμὲ δὲ μισεῖ, ὅτι ἐγὼ μαρτυρῶ περὶ αὐτοῦ ὅτι τὰ ἔργα
it hates me *but it hates* because I ⌞am bearing witness⌟ against it that *{the}* its works
3631 3631 1609 1254 3631 4022 1609 3455 4309 899 4022 3836 899 2240
r.as.1 cj v.pai.3s cj r.ns.1 v.pai.1s p.g r.gsm.3 cj d.npn n.npn

αὐτοῦ πονηρά ἐστιν. 8 ὑμεῖς ἀνάβητε εἰς τὴν ἑορτήν· ἐγὼ ↱ οὐκ
its are evil. *are yourselves* You go up to the festival yourselves; I am not
899 1639 4505 1639 7007 326 1650 3836 2038 7007 1609 326 4024
r.gsm.3 a.npn v.pai.3s r.np.2 v.aam.2p p.a d.asf n.asf r.ns.1 pl

ἀναβαίνω εἰς τὴν ἑορτὴν ταύτην, ὅτι ὁ ἐμὸς καιρὸς ↱ οὔπω πεπλήρωται.
going up to *{the}* this festival, *this* for *{the}* my time has not yet fully come."
326 1650 3836 4047 2038 4047 4022 3836 1847 2789 4444 4037 4444
v.pai.1s p.a d.asf n.asf r.asf cj d.nsm r.nsm.1 n.nsm adv v.rpi.3s

---

NASB

Jesus Teaches at the Feast

7:1 After these things Jesus was walking in Galilee, for He was unwilling to walk in Judea because the Jews were seeking to kill Him. 2 Now the feast of the Jews, the Feast of Booths, was near. 3 Therefore His brothers said to Him, "Leave here and go into Judea, so that Your disciples also may see Your works which You are doing. 4 For no one does anything in secret when he himself seeks to be *known* publicly. If You do these things, show Yourself to the world." 5 For not even His brothers were believing in Him. 6 So Jesus *said to them, "My time is not yet here, but your time is always opportune. 7 The world cannot hate you, but it hates Me because I testify of it, that its deeds are evil. 8 Go up to the feast yourselves; I do not go up to this feast because My time has not yet fully come."

NIV

9 After he had said
this, he stayed in
Galilee.
10 However, after
his brothers had
left for the festi-
val, he went also,
not publicly, but
in secret. 11 Now
at the festival the
Jewish leaders
were watching for
Jesus and asking,
"Where is he?"
12 Among the
crowds there was
widespread whis-
pering about him.
Some said, "He is
a good man."
Others replied,
"No, he deceives
the people." 13 But
no one would say
anything publicly
about him for fear
of the leaders.

Jesus Teaches at the Festival

14 Not until half-
way through the
festival did Jesus
go up to the temple
courts and begin
to teach. 15 The
Jews there were
amazed and asked,
"How did this man
get such learning
without having
been taught?"
16 Jesus answered,
"My teaching is
not my own. It
comes from the
one who sent me.
17 Anyone who
chooses to do the
will of God will
find out whether
my teaching comes
from God or
whether I speak on
my own. 18 Whoev-
er speaks

9 ταῦτα δὲ εἰπὼν αὐτὸς ἔμεινεν ἐν τῇ Γαλιλαίᾳ. 10
Having said this, *{and}* *Having said* he stayed behind in *{the}* Galilee. However,
3306 3306 4047 1254 3306 899 3531 1877 3836 1133 1254
r.apn cj pt.aa.nsm r.nsm v.aai.3s p.d d.dsf n.dsf

ὡς δὲ ἀνέβησαν οἱ ἀδελφοὶ αὐτοῦ εἰς τὴν ἑορτήν, τότε
when *However* his brothers had gone up *{the}* *brothers* *his* to the festival, then Jesus
6055 1254 899 81 326 3836 81 899 1650 3836 2038 5538
cj cj v.aai.3p d.npm n.npm r.gsm.3 p.a d.asf n.asf adv

καὶ αὐτὸς ἀνέβη οὐ φανερῶς ἀλλὰ ὡς[a] ἐν κρυπτῷ. 11 οἱ οὖν
himself also *himself* went up, not openly, but ⌊as it were,⌋ in private. The *{then}*
899 2779 899 326 4024 5747 247 6055 1877 3220 3836 4036
adv r.nsm v.aai.3s pl adv cj pl p.d a.dsn d.npm cj

Ἰουδαῖοι ἐζήτουν αὐτὸν ἐν τῇ ἑορτῇ καὶ ἔλεγον, ποῦ ἐστιν ἐκεῖνος;
Jews ⌊were looking for⌋ him at the festival, and saying, "Where is that man?"
2681 2426 899 1877 3836 2038 2779 3306 4543 1639 1697
a.npm v.iai.3p r.asm.3 p.d d.dsf n.dsf cj v.iai.3p cj v.pai.3s r.nsm

12 καὶ γογγυσμὸς περὶ αὐτοῦ ἦν πολὺς ἐν τοῖς
And there was a lot of secret discussion about him *there was* *a lot* among the
2779 1639 1639 4498 4498 1198 4309 899 1639 4498 1877 3836
cj n.nsm p.g r.gsm.3 v.iai.3s a.nsm p.d d.dpm

ὄχλοις· οἱ μὲν ἔλεγον ὅτι ἀγαθός ἐστιν, ἄλλοι δὲ[b] ἔλεγον,
crowds; some ~ were saying, ~ "He is a good man," *He is* but others *but* were saying,
4063 3836 3525 3306 4022 1639 1639 19 1639 1254 257 1254 3306
n.dpm d.npm pl v.iai.3p cj a.nsm v.pai.3s r.npm pl v.iai.3p

οὔ, ἀλλὰ → → → πλανᾷ τὸν ὄχλον. 13 οὐδεὶς μέντοι
"No, ⌊to the contrary,⌋ he is leading people astray." *{the}* *people* No one, however, was speaking
4024 247 4063 4414 3836 4063 4029 3530 3281 3281
pl cj v.pai.3s d.asm n.asm a.nsm cj

παρρησίᾳ ἐλάλει περὶ αὐτοῦ διὰ τὸν φόβον τῶν Ἰουδαίων. 14 ἤδη δὲ
openly *was speaking* about him for *{the}* fear of the Jews. About *{and}*
4244 3281 4309 899 1328 3836 5832 3836 2681 2453 1254
n.dsf v.iai.3s p.g r.gsm.3 p.a d.asm n.asm d.gpm a.gpm adv cj

τῆς ἑορτῆς μεσούσης ἀνέβη Ἰησοῦς εἰς τὸ ἱερὸν καὶ
halfway through the festival *halfway through* Jesus went up *Jesus* to the temple and
3548 3548 3836 2038 3548 2652 326 2652 1650 3836 2639 2779
d.gsf n.gsf pt.pa.gsf v.aai.3s n.nsm p.a d.asn n.asn cj

ἐδίδασκεν. 15 ἐθαύμαζον οὖν οἱ Ἰουδαῖοι λέγοντες, πῶς
began to teach. The Jews were astonished, *{then}* *The* *Jews* and they asked, "How does
1438 3836 2681 2513 4036 3836 2681 3306 4802 3857
v.iai.3s v.iai.3p cj d.npm a.npm pt.pa.npm cj

οὗτος γράμματα οἶδεν ↱ μὴ μεμαθηκώς; 16 ἀπεκρίθη
this man know the sacred letters, *does know* having never studied?" Jesus answered,
4047 3857 1207 3857 3443 3590 3443 2652 646
r.nsm n.apn v.rai.3s pl pt.ra.nsm v.api.3s

οὖν αὐτοῖς ὁ[c] Ἰησοῦς καὶ εἶπεν, ἡ ἐμὴ διδαχὴ οὐκ ἔστιν ἐμὴ ἀλλὰ
{then} them, *{the}* *Jesus* *{and}* saying, *{the}* "My teaching is not *is* mine, but it
4036 899 3836 2652 2779 3306 3836 1847 1439 1639 4024 1639 1847 247
cj r.dpm.3 d.nsm n.nsm cj v.aai.3s d.nsf r.nsf.1 n.nsf pl v.pai.3s r.nsf.1 cj

τοῦ πέμψαντός με· 17 ἐάν τις θέλῃ τὸ θέλημα
comes from the one who sent me. If anyone is willing to do God's *{the}* will,
3836 4287 1609 1569 5516 2527 4472 4472 899 3836 2525
d.gsm pt.aa.gsm r.as.1 cj r.nsm v.pas.3s d.asn n.asn

αὐτοῦ ποιεῖν, γνώσεται περὶ τῆς διδαχῆς πότερον ἐκ τοῦ θεοῦ ἐστιν
God's *to do* he will know about the teaching, whether it comes from *{the}* God *it comes*
899 4472 1182 4309 3836 1439 4538 1639 1639 1666 3836 2536 1639
r.gsm.3 f.pa v.fmi.3s p.g d.gsf n.gsf cj p.g d.gsm n.gsm v.pai.3s

ἢ ἐγὼ ἀπ᾽ ἐμαυτοῦ λαλῶ. 18 ὁ
or whether I am speaking on my own authority. *am speaking* The one who speaks
2445 1609 3281 3281 608 1831 3281 3836 3281 3281 3281
cj r.ns.1 p.g r.gsm.1 v.pai.1s d.nsm

[a] [ὡς] UBS.
[b] [δὲ] UBS.
[c] [ὁ] UBS.

NASB

9 Having said these
things to them, He
stayed in Galilee.
10 But when His
brothers had gone
up to the feast,
then He Himself
also went up, not
publicly, but as if,
in secret. 11 So the
Jews were seeking
Him at the feast
and were saying,
"Where is He?"
12 There was much
grumbling among
the crowds con-
cerning Him; some
were saying, "He
is a good man";
others were say-
ing, "No, on the
contrary, He leads
the people astray."
13 Yet no one was
speaking openly of
Him for fear of the
Jews.
14 But when it was
now the midst of
the feast Jesus
went up into the
temple, and *began
to* teach. 15 The
Jews then were
astonished, saying,
"How has this man
become learned,
having never been
educated?" 16 So
Jesus answered
them and said, "My
teaching is not
Mine, but His who
sent Me. 17 If any-
one is willing to
do His will, he will
know of the teach-
ing, whether it is of
God or *whether* I
speak from Myself.
18 He who speaks

NIV

on their own does
so to gain personal
glory, but he who
seeks the glory
of the one who
sent him is a man
of truth; there is
nothing false about
him. 19 Has not Mo-
ses given you the
law? Yet not one of
you keeps the law.
Why are you trying
to kill me?"
20 "You are de-
mon-possessed,"
the crowd an-
swered. "Who is
trying to kill you?"
21 Jesus said to
them, "I did one
miracle, and you
are all amazed.
22 Yet, because Mo-
ses gave you cir-
cumcision (though
actually it did not
come from Moses,
but from the pa-
triarchs), you cir-
cumcise a boy on
the Sabbath. 23 Now
if a boy can be cir-
cumcised on the
Sabbath so that the
law of Moses may
not be broken, why
are you angry with
me for healing a
man's whole body
on the Sabbath?
24 Stop judging by
mere appearances,
but instead judge
correctly."

Division Over Who Jesus Is

25 At that point
some of the peo-
ple of Jerusalem
began to ask,
"Isn't this the man
they are trying to
kill? 26 Here he is,
speaking publicly,
and they are not
saying a word to
him.

ἀφ᾽ ἑαυτοῦ λαλῶν τὴν δόξαν τὴν ἰδίαν ζητεῖ· ὁ
on his own authority *one who speaks* seeks *{the}* his own honor; *{the}* *his own* *seeks* but the
608 1571 3281 2426 3836 2625 2625 1518 3836 2625 2426 1254 3836
p.g r.gsm.3 pt.pa.nsm d.asf n.asf d.asf a.asf v.pai.3s d.nsm

δὲ ζητῶν τὴν δόξαν τοῦ πέμψαντος αὐτὸν οὗτος ἀληθής ἐστιν καὶ
but ⌊one who seeks⌋ the honor of the one who sent him *{this one}* is truthful, *is* and
1254 2426 3836 1518 3836 4287 899 4047 1639 239 1639 2779
cj pt.pa.nsm d.asf n.asf d.gsm pt.aa.gsm r.asm.3 r.nsm a.nsm v.pai.3s cj

ἀδικία ἐν αὐτῷ οὐκ ἔστιν. 19 ↱ οὐ Μωϋσῆς δέδωκεν
in him there is nothing false. *in* *him* *nothing* *there is* "Has not Moses given
1877 899 1639 1639 4024 94 1877 899 4024 1639 1443 4024 3707 1443
n.nsf p.d r.dsm.3 pl v.pai.3s pl n.nsm v.rai.3s

ὑμῖν τὸν νόμον; καὶ οὐδεὶς ἐξ ὑμῶν ποιεῖ τὸν νόμον. τί
you the law? Yet not one of you keeps the law. Why are you trying to kill
7007 3836 3795 2779 4029 1666 7007 4472 3836 3795 5515 2426 2426 2426 650 650
r.dp.2 d.asm n.asm cj a.nsm p.g r.gp.2 v.pai.3s d.asm n.asm r.asn

με ζητεῖτε ἀποκτεῖναι; 20 ἀπεκρίθη ὁ ὄχλος, δαιμόνιον
me?" *are you trying* *to kill* The crowd answered, *The* *crowd* "You have a demon!
1609 2426 650 3836 4063 646 3836 4063 2400 2400 1228
r.as.1 v.pai.2p f.aa v.api.3s d.nsm n.nsm n.asn

ἔχεις· τίς σε ζητεῖ ἀποκτεῖναι; 21 ἀπεκρίθη Ἰησοῦς καὶ
You have Who is trying to kill you?" *is trying* *to kill* Jesus answered, *Jesus* *{and}*
2400 5515 2426 2426 650 650 5148 2426 650 2652 646 2652 2779
v.pai.2s r.nsm r.as.2 v.pai.3s f.aa v.api.3s n.nsm cj

εἶπεν αὐτοῖς, ἓν ἔργον ἐποίησα καὶ ↱ ↱ πάντες θαυμάζετε.
saying to them, "I performed one work, *I performed* and you are all astonished.
3306 899 4472 4472 1651 2240 4472 2779 2513 2513 4246 2513
v.aai.3s r.dpm.3 a.asn n.asn v.aai.1s cj a.npm v.pai.2p

22 διὰ τοῦτο Μωϋσῆς δέδωκεν ὑμῖν τὴν περιτομήν οὐχ ὅτι ἐκ τοῦ
For this reason Moses gave you *{the}* circumcision — not that it is from *{the}*
1328 4047 3707 1443 7007 3836 4364 4024 4022 1639 1639 1666 3836
p.a r.asn n.nsm v.rai.3s r.dp.2 d.asf n.asf pl cj p.g d.gsm

Μωϋσέως ἐστὶν ἀλλ᾽ ἐκ τῶν πατέρων καὶ ἐν σαββάτῳ
Moses, *it is* but from the patriarchs — and you circumcise a man on the Sabbath.
3707 1639 247 1666 3836 4252 2779 4362 4362 476 1877 4879
n.gsm v.pai.3s cj p.g d.gpm n.gpm cj p.d n.dsn

περιτέμνετε ἄνθρωπον. 23 εἰ περιτομὴν λαμβάνει ἄνθρωπος ἐν
you circumcise *man* If a man receives circumcision *receives* *man* on the
4362 476 1623 476 3284 4364 3284 476 1877
v.pai.2p n.asm cj n.asf v.pai.3s n.nsm p.d

σαββάτῳ ἵνα ↱ μὴ λυθῇ ὁ νόμος Μωϋσέως,
Sabbath so that the law of Moses may not be broken, *the* *law* *of Moses* why are
4879 2671 3836 3795 3707 3707 3395 3590 3395 3836 3795 3707 5957
n.dsn cj pl v.aps.3s d.nsm n.nsm n.gsm

ἐμοὶ χολᾶτε ὅτι ὅλον ἄνθρωπον ὑγιῆ ἐποίησα ἐν
you angry ⌊with me⌋ *are you angry* because I made an entire man well *I made* on the
5957 5957 1609 5957 4022 4472 4472 3910 476 5618 4472 1877
r.ds.1 v.pai.2p cj a.asm n.asm a.asm v.aai.1s p.d

σαββάτῳ; 24 ↱ μὴ κρίνετε κατ᾽ ὄψιν, ἀλλὰ τὴν δικαίαν κρίσιν
Sabbath? Do not judge ⌊according to⌋ appearance, but judge with proper judgment."
4879 3212 3590 3212 2848 4071 247 3212 3836 1465 3213
n.dsn pl v.pam.2p p.a n.asf cj d.asf a.asf n.asf

κρίνετε. 25 ἔλεγον οὖν τινες ἐκ τῶν
judge Then some of the people of Jerusalem ⌊began to say,⌋ *Then* *some* *of* *the*
3212 4036 5516 1666 3836 2643 2643 2643 3306 4036 5516 1666 3836
v.pam.2p v.iai.3p cj r.npm p.g d.gpm

Ἱεροσολυμιτῶν, οὐχ οὗτός ἐστιν ὃν ζητοῦσιν ἀποκτεῖναι; 26 καὶ
people of Jerusalem "Is not this *Is* the man whom they are trying to kill? And
2643 1639 4024 4047 1639 4005 2426 650 2779
n.gpm pl r.nsm v.pai.3s r.asm v.pai.3p f.aa cj

ἴδε παρρησίᾳ λαλεῖ καὶ οὐδὲν αὐτῷ
look, he is speaking boldly *he is speaking* and they are saying nothing to him.
2623 3281 3281 3281 4244 3281 2779 3306 3306 3306 4029 899
pl n.dsf v.pai.3s cj a.asn r.dsm.3

NASB

from himself seeks
his own glory; but
He who is seeking
the glory of the
One who sent Him,
He is true, and
there is no unrigh-
teousness in Him.
19 "Did not Moses
give you the Law,
and *yet* none of
you carries out the
Law? Why do you
seek to kill Me?"
20 The crowd an-
swered, "You have
a demon! Who
seeks to kill You?"
21 Jesus answered
them, "I did one
deed, and you
all marvel. 22 For
this reason Moses
has given you
circumcision (not
because it is from
Moses, but from
the fathers), and
on *the* Sabbath you
circumcise a man.
23 If a man receives
circumcision on *the*
Sabbath so that the
Law of Moses will
not be broken, are
you angry with Me
because I made an
entire man well on
the Sabbath? 24 Do
not judge accord-
ing to appearance,
but judge with
righteous judg-
ment."
25 So some of the
people of Jerusa-
lem were saying,
"Is this not the
man whom they
are seeking to
kill? 26 Look, He is
speaking publicly,
and they are saying
nothing to Him.

NIV

Have the authori-
ties really conclud-
ed that he is the
Messiah? [27]But we
know where this
man is from; when
the Messiah comes,
no one will know
where he is from."
[28]Then Jesus,
still teaching in
the temple courts,
cried out, "Yes,
you know me, and
you know where I
am from. I am not
here on my own
authority, but he
who sent me is
true. You do not
know him, [29]but I
know him because
I am from him and
he sent me."
[30]At this they
tried to seize him,
but no one laid
a hand on him,
because his hour
had not yet come.
[31]Still, many in the
crowd believed in
him. They said,
"When the Mes-
siah comes, will
he perform more
signs than this
man?"
[32]The Pharisees
heard the crowd
whispering such
things about him.
Then the chief
priests and the
Pharisees sent
temple guards to
arrest him.
[33]Jesus said, "I
am with you for
only a short time,
and then

λέγουσιν. μήποτε ἀληθῶς ἔγνωσαν οἱ ἄρχοντες ὅτι οὗτός
they are saying Is it possible that our rulers know for sure *know* *our* *rulers* that this man
3306 3607 3836 807 1182 242 1182 3836 807 4022 4047
v.pai.3p pl adv v.aai.3p d.npm n.npm cj r.nsm

ἐστιν ὁ χριστός; 27 ἀλλὰ ↱ τοῦτον οἴδαμεν πόθεν ἐστίν·
is the Christ? Yet we know where this man *we know* is from; *is* when
1639 3836 5986 247 3857 3857 4470 4047 3857 1639 4470 1639 4020
v.pai.3s d.nsm n.nsm cj r.asm v.rai.1p cj v.pai.3s

ὁ δὲ χριστὸς ὅταν ἔρχηται οὐδεὶς γινώσκει πόθεν ἐστίν. ↰ 28 ἔκραξεν οὖν
the *{and}* Christ *when* appears, no one will know where he is from." *cried out* Then
3836 1254 5986 4020 2262 4029 1182 4470 1639 4470 3189 4036
d.nsm cj n.nsm cj v.pms.3s a.nsm v.pai.3s cj v.pai.3s v.aai.3s cj

ἐν τῷ ἱερῷ διδάσκων ὁ Ἰησοῦς καὶ
Jesus, as he was teaching in the temple, *as he was teaching* *{the}* *Jesus* cried out, *{and}*
2652 1438 1438 1438 1438 1877 3836 2639 1438 3836 2652 3189 3189 2779
p.d d.dsn n.dsn pt.pa.nsm d.nsm n.nsm cj

λέγων, κἀμὲ οἴδατε καὶ οἴδατε πόθεν εἰμί· ↰ καὶ
saying, "You know me, *You know* and you know where I am from? *{and}* I have not
3306 3857 3857 2743 3857 2779 3857 4470 1639 4470 2779 2262 2262 4024
pt.pa.nsm crasis v.rai.2p cj v.rai.2p cj v.pai.1s cj

ἀπ᾽ ἐμαυτοῦ οὐκ ἐλήλυθα, ἀλλ᾽ ἔστιν ἀληθινὸς ὁ
come on my own. *not* *I have come* But the one who sent me is true, *the*
2262 608 1831 4024 2262 247 3836 4287 4287 4287 1609 1639 240 3836
p.g r.gsm.1 pl v.rai.1s cj v.pai.3s a.nsm d.nsm

πέμψας με, ὃν ὑμεῖς ↱ οὐκ οἴδατε· 29 ἐγὼ οἶδα αὐτόν, ὅτι
one who sent *me* and him you do not know; but I know him, because I am
4287 1609 4005 7007 3857 4024 3857 1609 3857 899 4022 1639 1639
pt.aa.nsm r.as.1 r.asm r.np.2 pl v.rai.2p r.ns.1 v.rai.1s r.asm.3 cj

παρ᾽ αὐτοῦ εἰμι κἀκεῖνός με ἀπέστειλεν. 30 ἐζήτουν οὖν
from him *I am* and he it is who sent me." *who sent* So ⌊they were anxious⌋ *So*
4123 899 1639 2797 690 690 1609 690 4036 2426 4036
p.g r.gsm.3 v.pai.1s crasis r.as.1 v.aai.3s v.iai.3p cj

αὐτὸν πιάσαι, καὶ οὐδεὶς ἐπέβαλεν ἐπ᾽ αὐτὸν τὴν χεῖρα, ὅτι
to arrest him, *to arrest* but no one laid a hand on him, *{the}* *hand* because his
4389 4389 899 4389 2779 4029 2095 5931 2093 899 3836 5931 4022 899
r.asm.3 f.aa cj a.nsm v.aai.3s p.a r.asm.3 d.asf n.asf cj

↱ οὔπω ἐληλύθει ἡ ὥρα αὐτοῦ. 31 ἐκ τοῦ ὄχλου δὲ πολλοὶ
hour had not yet come. *{the}* *hour* *his* Yet many of the crowd *Yet* *many*
6052 2262 4037 2262 3836 6052 899 1254 4498 1666 3836 4063 1254 4498
adv v.lai.3s d.nsf n.nsf r.gsm.3 p.g d.gsm n.gsm cj a.npm

ἐπίστευσαν εἰς αὐτὸν καὶ ἔλεγον, ὁ χριστὸς ὅταν ἔλθῃ μὴ
believed in him, *{and}* saying, "When the Christ *When* comes, he will not
4409 1650 899 2779 3306 4020 3836 5986 4020 2262 4472 4472 3590
v.aai.3p p.a r.asm.3 cj v.iai.3p d.nsm n.nsm cj v.aas.3s pl

πλείονα σημεῖα ποιήσει ὧν οὗτος ἐποίησεν; ↰ ↰ 32
perform more ⌊miraculous signs⌋ *he will perform* than this man has, will he?" The
4472 4498 4956 4472 4005 4047 4472 3590 3590 3836
a.apn.c n.apn v.fai.3s r.gpn r.nsm v.aai.3s

ἤκουσαν οἱ Φαρισαῖοι τοῦ ὄχλου γογγύζοντος περὶ αὐτοῦ
Pharisees heard *The* *Pharisees* the crowd secretly discussing these things about Jesus,
5757 201 3836 5757 3836 4063 1197 4047 4047 4309 899
v.aai.3p d.npm n.npm d.gsm n.gsm pt.pa.gsm p.g r.gsm.3

ταῦτα, καὶ ἀπέστειλαν οἱ ἀρχιερεῖς καὶ οἱ
these things so the chief priests and Pharisees sent *the* *chief priests* *and* *{the}*
4047 2779 3836 797 797 2779 5757 690 3836 797 2779 3836
r.apn cj v.aai.3p d.npm n.npm cj d.npm

Φαρισαῖοι ὑπηρέτας ἵνα πιάσωσιν αὐτόν. 33 εἶπεν οὖν ὁ Ἰησοῦς,
Pharisees temple guards to arrest him. Then Jesus said, *Then* *{the}* *Jesus* "I
5757 5677 2671 4389 899 4036 2652 3306 4036 3836 2652 1639
n.npm n.apm cj v.aas.3p r.asm.3 v.aai.3s cj d.nsm n.nsm

ἔτι χρόνον μικρὸν μεθ᾽ ὑμῶν εἰμι καὶ
will be with you for a little while longer, *while* *little* *with* *you* *I will be* and then
1639 1639 3552 7007 3625 5989 2285 5989 3625 3552 7007 1639 2779
adv n.asm a.asm p.g r.gp.2 v.pai.1s cj

NASB

The rulers do not
really know that
this is the Christ,
do they? [27]How-
ever, we know
where this man is
from; but when-
ever the Christ
may come, no one
knows where He is
from." [28]Then Jesus
cried out in the
temple, teaching
and saying, "You
both know Me
and know where
I am from; and I
have not come of
Myself, but He
who sent Me is
true, whom you do
not know. [29]I know
Him, because I am
from Him, and He
sent Me." [30]So they
were seeking to
seize Him; and no
man laid his hand
on Him, because
His hour had not
yet come. [31]But
many of the crowd
believed in Him;
and they were
saying, "When the
Christ comes, He
will not perform
more signs than
those which this
man has, will He?"
[32]The Pharisees
heard the crowd
muttering these
things about Him,
and the chief
priests and the
Pharisees sent of-
ficers to seize Him.
[33]Therefore Jesus
said, "For a little
while longer I am
with you, then I go

NIV

I am going to the one who sent me. [34]You will look for me, but you will not find me; and where I am, you cannot come."
[35]The Jews said to one another, "Where does this man intend to go that we cannot find him? Will he go where our people live scattered among the Greeks, and teach the Greeks? [36]What did he mean when he said, 'You will look for me, but you will not find me,' and 'Where I am, you cannot come'?"
[37]On the last and greatest day of the festival, Jesus stood and said in a loud voice, "Let anyone who is thirsty come to me and drink. [38]Whoever believes in me, as Scripture has said, rivers of living water will flow from within them."[a] [39]By this he meant the Spirit, whom those who believed in him were later to receive. Up to that time the Spirit had not been given, since Jesus had not yet been glorified.
[40]On hearing his words, some of the people said, "Surely this man is the Prophet."
[41]Others said, "He is the Messiah."

[a] 37,38 Or *me. And let anyone drink [38]who believes in me." As Scripture has said, "Out of him* (or *them*) *will flow rivers of living water."*

ὑπάγω πρὸς τὸν πέμψαντά με. [34] ζητήσετέ με καὶ ↱ ↱ οὐχ
⌊I am going back⌋ to the one who sent me. ⌊You will look for⌋ me, but you will not
5632 4639 3836 4287 1609 2426 1609 2779 2351 2351 4024
v.pai.1s p.a d.asm pt.aa.asm r.as.1 v.fai.2p r.as.1 cj pl

εὑρήσετέ με,[a] καὶ ὅπου εἰμὶ ἐγὼ ὑμεῖς ⌊οὐ δύνασθε⌋ ἐλθεῖν. [35]
find me; and where I am, *I* you cannot go." Then the Jews
2351 1609 2779 3963 1609 1639 1609 7007 4024 1538 2262 4036 3836 2681
v.fai.2p r.as.1 cj cj v.pai.1s r.ns.1 r.np.2 pl v.ppi.2p f.aa

εἶπον οὖν οἱ Ἰουδαῖοι πρὸς ἑαυτούς, ποῦ ↱ οὗτος μέλλει πορεύεσθαι ὅτι
said *Then the Jews* to one another, "Where is this man about to go that
3306 4036 3836 2681 4639 1571 4543 3516 4047 3516 4513 4022
v.aai.3p cj d.npm a.npm p.a r.apm.3 cj r.nsm v.pai.3s f.pm cj

ἡμεῖς ↱ οὐχ εὑρήσομεν αὐτόν; → μὴ εἰς τὴν
we will not find him? Surely he is not going to go to our
7005 2351 4024 2351 899 3516 3516 3590 3516 4513 4513 1650 3836
r.np.1 pl v.fai.1p r.asm.3 pl p.a d.asf

διασπορὰν τῶν Ἑλλήνων μέλλει πορεύεσθαι καὶ διδάσκειν τοὺς Ἕλληνας;
people dispersed ⌊among the⌋ Greeks *he is going to go* and teach the Greeks,
1402 3836 1818 3516 4513 2779 1438 3836 1818
n.asf d.gpm n.gpm v.pai.3s f.pm cj f.pa d.apm n.apm

↰ ↰ [36] τίς ἐστιν ὁ λόγος οὗτος ὃν εἶπεν, ζητήσετέ
is he? What ⌊can it mean,⌋ *{the}* this saying *this* ⌊of his:⌋ *{he said}* ⌊'You will look for⌋
3590 3590 5515 1639 3836 4047 3364 4047 4005 3306 2426
r.nsm v.pai.3s d.nsm n.nsm r.nsm r.asm v.aai.3s v.fai.2p

με καὶ ↱ ↱ οὐχ εὑρήσετέ με,[b] καὶ ὅπου εἰμὶ ἐγὼ ὑμεῖς ⌊οὐ δύνασθε⌋
me but you will not find me,' and 'Where I am *I* you cannot
1609 2779 2351 2351 4024 2351 1609 2779 3963 1609 1639 1609 7007 4024 1538
r.as.1 cj pl v.fai.2p r.as.1 cj cj v.pai.1s r.ns.1 r.np.2 pl v.ppi.2p

ἐλθεῖν; [37] Ἐν δὲ τῇ ἐσχάτῃ ἡμέρᾳ τῇ μεγάλῃ τῆς ἑορτῆς
go'?" On *{and}* the last day of the festival, the great day, *of the festival*
2262 1877 1254 3836 2274 2465 3836 3836 2038 3836 3489 3836 2038
f.aa p.d cj d.dsf a.dsf n.dsf d.dsf a.dsf d.gsf n.gsf

εἱστήκει ὁ Ἰησοῦς καὶ ἔκραξεν λέγων, ἐάν τις διψᾷ ἐρχέσθω πρός
Jesus stood *{the} Jesus* and cried out, saying, "If anyone is thirsty, let him come to
2652 2705 3836 2652 2779 3189 3306 1569 5516 1498 2262 4639
v.lai.3s d.nsm n.nsm cj v.aai.3s pt.pa.nsm cj r.nsm v.pas.3s v.pmm.3s p.a

με καὶ πινέτω. [38] ὁ πιστεύων εἰς ἐμέ, καθὼς εἶπεν ἡ γραφή,
me and drink. The one who believes in me, as the scripture says, *the scripture*
1609 2779 4403 3836 4409 1650 1609 2777 3836 1210 3306 3836 1210
r.as.1 cj v.pam.3s d.nsm pt.pa.nsm p.a r.as.1 cj v.aai.3s d.nsf n.nsf

ποταμοὶ ἐκ τῆς κοιλίας αὐτοῦ ῥεύσουσιν → ὕδατος
"Out of his heart will flow rivers *Out of heart his will flow* of living water.'"
1666 3836 899 3120 4835 4835 4532 1666 3836 3120 899 4835 2409 5623
n.npm p.g d.gsf n.gsf r.gsm.3 v.fai.3p n.gsn

ζῶντος. [39] τοῦτο δὲ εἶπεν περὶ τοῦ πνεύματος ὃ
living Now he said this *Now he said* about the Spirit, which those who believed
2409 1254 3306 3306 4047 1254 3306 4309 3836 4460 4005 3836 4409 4409
pt.pa.gsn r.asn cj v.aai.3s p.g d.gsn n.gsn r.asn

ἔμελλον λαμβάνειν οἱ πιστεύσαντες εἰς αὐτόν· ↱ οὔπω γὰρ
in him were to receive; *those who believed in him* for the Spirit was not yet *for*
1650 899 3516 3284 3836 4409 1650 899 1142 4460 1639 4037 1142
v.iai.3p f.pa d.npm pt.aa.npm p.a r.asm.3 adv cj

ἦν πνεῦμα, ὅτι Ἰησοῦς ↱ οὐδέπω ἐδοξάσθη. [40]
present, *Spirit* because Jesus had not yet been glorified. After hearing these words,
1639 4460 4022 2652 1519 4031 1519 201 201 4047 3364
v.iai.3s n.nsn cj n.nsm adv v.api.3s

ἐκ τοῦ ὄχλου οὖν ἀκούσαντες τῶν λόγων τούτων ἔλεγον, οὗτός
⌊some of⌋ the crowd *{then} After hearing {the} words these* ⌊began to say,⌋ "This man really
1666 3836 4063 4036 201 3836 3364 4047 3306 4047 242
p.g d.gsm n.gsm cj pt.aa.npm d.gpm n.gpm r.gpm v.iai.3p r.nsm

ἐστιν ἀληθῶς ὁ προφήτης· [41] ἄλλοι ἔλεγον, οὗτός ἐστιν ὁ χριστός,
is *really* the prophet." Others were saying, "This man is the Christ." But
1639 242 3836 4737 257 3306 4047 1639 3836 5986 1254
v.pai.3s adv d.nsm n.nsm r.npm v.iai.3p r.nsm v.pai.3s d.nsm n.nsm

[a] [με] UBS.
[b] [με] UBS.

NASB

to Him who sent Me. [34]You will seek Me, and will not find Me; and where I am, you cannot come." [35]The Jews then said to one another, "Where does this man intend to go that we will not find Him? He is not intending to go to the Dispersion among the Greeks, and teach the Greeks, is He? [36]What is this statement that He said, 'You will seek Me, and will not find Me; and where I am, you cannot come'?"
[37]Now on the last day, the great *day* of the feast, Jesus stood and cried out, saying, "If anyone is thirsty, let him come to Me and drink. [38]He who believes in Me, as the Scripture said, 'From his innermost being will flow rivers of living water.'" [39]But this He spoke of the Spirit, whom those who believed in Him were to receive; for the Spirit was not yet *given,* because Jesus was not yet glorified.

Division of People over Jesus

[40]*Some* of the people therefore, when they heard these words, were saying, "This certainly is the Prophet." [41]Others were saying, "This is the Christ." Still

NIV

Still others
asked, "How
can the Messiah
come from Gal-
ilee? [42]Does not
Scripture say that
the Messiah will
come from David's
descendants and
from Bethlehem,
the town where
David lived?"
[43]Thus the peo-
ple were divided
because of Jesus.
[44]Some wanted to
seize him, but no
one laid a hand on
him.

Unbelief of the Jewish Leaders

[45]Finally the tem-
ple guards went
back to the chief
priests and the
Pharisees, who
asked them, "Why
didn't you bring
him in?"
[46]"No one ever
spoke the way this
man does," the
guards replied.
[47]"You mean he
has deceived you
also?" the Phar-
isees retorted.
[48]"Have any of the
rulers or of the
Pharisees believed
in him? [49]No!
But this mob that
knows nothing of
the law—there is
a curse on them."
[50]Nicodemus,
who had gone to
Jesus earlier and
who was one of
their own number,
asked, [51]"Does our
law condemn a
man without first
hearing him to
find out what

οἱ δὲ ἔλεγον, → μὴ γὰρ ἐκ τῆς Γαλιλαίας ὁ
others *But* were saying, "Surely the Christ does not *{for}* come from *{the}* Galilee, *the*
3836 1254 3306 3836 5986 2262 3590 1142 2262 1666 3836 1133 3836
d.npm pl v.iai.3p pl cj p.g d.gsf n.gsf d.nsm

χριστὸς ἔρχεται; ↰ ↰ 42 ↱ οὐχ ἡ γραφὴ εἶπεν ὅτι ἐκ
Christ does come does he? Has not the scripture said that the Christ will be *{from}*
5986 2262 3590 3590 3306 4024 3836 1210 3306 4022 3836 5986 1666
n.nsm v.pmi.3s pl d.nsf n.nsf v.aai.3s cj p.g

τοῦ σπέρματος Δαυὶδ καὶ ἀπὸ Βηθλέεμ τῆς κώμης ὅπου ἦν Δαυὶδ
a descendant of David and come from Bethlehem, the village where David was *David*
3836 5065 1253 2779 2262 608 1033 3836 3267 3963 1253 1639 1253
d.gsn n.gsn n.gsm cj p.g n.gsf d.gsf n.gsf cj v.iai.3s n.nsm

ἔρχεται ὁ χριστός; 43 σχίσμα οὖν ἐγένετο ἐν τῷ ὄχλῳ
born?" *come the Christ* So there was a division *So there was* among the people
2262 3836 5986 4036 1181 1181 5388 4036 1181 1877 3836 4063
v.pmi.3s d.nsm n.nsm n.nsn cj v.ami.3s p.d d.dsm n.dsm

δι' αὐτόν· 44 τινὲς δὲ ἤθελον ἐξ αὐτῶν πιάσαι αὐτόν, ἀλλ' οὐδεὶς
⌞because of⌟ him. Some *{and}* of them wanted *of them* to arrest him, but no one
1328 899 5516 1254 1666 899 2527 1666 899 4389 899 247 4029
p.a r.asm.3 r.npm cj v.iai.3p p.g r.gpm.3 f.aa r.asm.3 cj a.nsm

ἐπέβαλεν ἐπ' αὐτὸν τὰς χεῖρας. 45 ἦλθον οὖν οἱ
laid a hand on him. *{the} hand* Then the temple guards went back *Then the*
2095 5931 2093 899 3836 5931 4036 3836 5677 5677 2262 4036 3836
v.aai.3s p.a r.asm.3 d.apf n.apf v.aai.3p cj d.npm

ὑπηρέται πρὸς τοὺς ἀρχιερεῖς καὶ Φαρισαίους, καὶ εἶπον αὐτοῖς ἐκεῖνοι,
temple guards to the chief priests and Pharisees, *{and}* who said to them, *who*
5677 4639 3836 797 2779 5757 2779 1697 3306 899 1697
n.npm p.a d.apm n.apm cj n.apm cj v.aai.3p r.dpm.3 r.npm

⌞διὰ τί⌟ ↱ ↱ οὐκ ἠγάγετε αὐτόν; 46 ἀπεκρίθησαν οἱ ὑπηρέται,
"Why did you not bring him?" The guards answered, *The guards*
1328 5515 72 72 4024 72 899 3836 5677 646 3836 5677
p.a r.asn pl v.aai.2p r.asm.3 v.api.3p d.npm n.npm

οὐδέποτε → ἐλάλησεν οὕτως ἄνθρωπος. 47 ἀπεκρίθησαν οὖν
"Never has a man spoken like this man!" The Pharisees responded *{then}*
4030 3281 4048 476 3836 5757 646 4036
adv v.aai.3s adv n.nsm v.api.3p cj

αὐτοῖς οἱ Φαρισαῖοι, → μὴ καὶ ὑμεῖς πεπλάνησθε;
to them, *The Pharisees* "Surely you have not been deceived as well, *you have been deceived*
899 3836 5757 7007 4414 3590 4414 4414 2779 7007 4414
r.dpm.3 d.npm n.npm pl adv r.np.2 v.rpi.2p

↰ ↰ 48 ⌞μή τις⌟ ἐκ τῶν ἀρχόντων ἐπίστευσεν εἰς αὐτὸν
have you? None of the rulers or the Pharisees have believed in him,
3590 3590 3590 5516 1666 3836 807 2445 3836 5757 4409 1650 899
pl r.nsm p.g d.gpm n.gpm v.aai.3s p.a r.asm.3

ἢ ἐκ τῶν Φαρισαίων; ↰ ↰ 49 ἀλλὰ ὁ ὄχλος οὗτος ὁ ↱ μὴ
or {from} the Pharisees have they? As for *{the}* this mob *this* that does not
2445 1666 3836 5757 3590 3590 247 3836 4047 4063 4047 3836 1182 3590
cj p.g d.gpm n.gpm cj d.nsm n.nsm r.nsm d.nsm pl

γινώσκων τὸν νόμον ἐπάρατοί εἰσιν. 50 λέγει Νικόδημος πρὸς
know the law — they are accursed!" *they are* *put this question* Nicodemus *to*
1182 3836 3795 1639 1639 2063 1639 3306 3773 4639
pt.pa.nsm d.asm n.asm a.npm v.pai.3p v.pai.3s n.nsm p.a

αὐτούς, ὁ → → ἐλθὼν πρὸς αὐτὸν τὸ [a] πρότερον, εἷς ὢν ἐξ
them (he who had earlier come to Jesus), *{the} earlier* being one *being* of
899 3836 4728 2262 4639 899 3836 4728 1639 1651 1639 1666
r.apm.3 d.nsm pt.aa.nsm p.a r.asm.3 d.asn adv a.nsm pt.pa.nsm p.g

αὐτῶν· 51 → ↱ μὴ ὁ νόμος ἡμῶν
their number, put this question to them: "Surely our law does not *{the} law our*
899 3306 3306 3306 4639 899 7005 3795 3212 3590 3836 3795 7005
r.gpm.3 pl d.nsm n.nsm r.gp.1

κρίνει τὸν ἄνθρωπον ⌞ἐὰν μὴ⌟ → ἀκούσῃ πρῶτον παρ' αὐτοῦ καὶ γνῷ τί
judge a man unless it first hears *first* from him and ⌞finds out⌟ what
3212 3836 476 1569 3590 4754 201 4754 4123 899 2779 1182 5515
v.pai.3s d.asm n.asm cj pl v.aas.3s a.asn p.g r.gsm.3 cj v.aas.3s r.asn

[a] [τὸ] UBS, omitted by TNIV.

NASB

others were saying,
"Surely the Christ
is not going to
come from Galilee,
is He? [42]Has not the
Scripture said that
the Christ comes
from the descen-
dants of David, and
from Bethlehem,
the village where
David was?" [43]So a
division occurred
in the crowd
because of Him.
[44]Some of them
wanted to seize
Him, but no one
laid hands on Him.
[45]The officers
then came to the
chief priests and
Pharisees, and
they said to them,
"Why did you not
bring Him?" [46]The
officers answered,
"Never has a man
spoken the way
this man speaks."
[47]The Pharisees
then answered
them, "You have
not also been led
astray, have you?
[48]No one of the
rulers or Pharisees
has believed in
Him, has he? [49]But
this crowd which
does not know the
Law is accursed."
[50]Nicodemus (he
who came to Him
before, being one
of them) *said to
them, [51]"Our Law
does not judge a
man unless it first
hears from him and
knows what he is

NIV

he has been doing?"
52 They replied, "Are you from Galilee, too? Look into it, and you will find that a prophet does not come out of Galilee."

[The earliest manuscripts and many other ancient witnesses do not have John 7:53—8:11. A few manuscripts include these verses, wholly or in part, after John 7:36, John 21:25, Luke 21:38 or Luke 24:53.]

53 Then they all went home,

8 *1 but Jesus went to the Mount of Olives.*
2 At dawn he appeared again in the temple courts, where all the people gathered around him, and he sat down to teach them. 3 The teachers of the law and the Pharisees brought in a woman caught in adultery. They made her stand before the group 4 and said to Jesus, "Teacher, this woman was caught in the act of adultery. 5 In the Law Moses commanded us to stone such women. Now what do you say?" 6 They were using this question as a trap, in order to have a basis for accusing him.
But Jesus bent down and started to write on the ground with his finger.
7 When they kept on questioning him, he straightened up and said to them, "Let any one of you who is without sin be the

ποιεῖ; ↰ ↰ 52 ἀπεκρίθησαν καὶ εἶπαν αὐτῷ, μὴ καὶ
he is doing, does it?" They replied {and} saying to him, saying, "You too are not too
4472 3590 3590 646 2779 3306 899 3306 5148 2779 1639 3590 2779
v.pai.3s v.api.3p cj v.aai.3p r.dsm.3 pl adv

σὺ ἐκ τῆς Γαλιλαίας εἶ; ↰ ↰ ἐραύνησον καὶ ἴδε ὅτι
You from {the} Galilee, are are you? Search and ⌊you will see⌋ that no prophet
5148 1666 3836 1133 1639 3590 3590 2236 2779 2623 4022 4024 4737
r.ns.2 p.g d.gsf n.gsf v.pai.2s v.aam.2s cj v.aam.2s cj

ἐκ τῆς Γαλιλαίας προφήτης οὐκ ἐγείρεται. 53 ⟦καὶ ἐπορεύθησαν
will arise from {the} Galilee." prophet no will arise Then each one went
1586 1586 1666 3836 1133 4737 4024 1586 2779 1667 1667 4513
p.g d.gsf n.gsf n.nsm pl v.ppi.3s cj v.api.3p

ἕκαστος εἰς τὸν οἶκον αὐτοῦ,
each one to {the} his own house, his own
1667 1650 3836 899 899 3875 899
r.nsm p.a d.asm n.asm r.gsm.3

8:1 Ἰησοῦς δὲ ἐπορεύθη εἰς τὸ ὄρος τῶν ἐλαιῶν. 2 ὄρθρου
but Jesus but went to the Mount of Olives. ⌊Early in the morning⌋
1254 2652 1254 4513 1650 3836 4001 3836 1777 3986
n.nsm cj v.api.3s p.a d.asn n.asn d.gpf n.gpf n.gsm

δὲ πάλιν παρεγένετο εἰς τὸ ἱερὸν καὶ πᾶς ὁ λαὸς ἤρχετο πρὸς
{and} he came again he came to the temple. {and} All the people were coming to
1254 4134 4134 4099 4134 1650 3836 2639 2779 4246 3836 3295 2262 4639
cj adv v.ami.3s p.a d.asn n.asn cj a.nsm d.nsm n.nsm v.imi.3s p.a

αὐτόν, καὶ ↱ καθίσας ἐδίδασκεν αὐτούς. 3
him, and he sat down and began to teach them. The scribes and the Pharisees
899 2779 1438 2767 1438 899 3836 1208 2779 3836 5757
r.asm.3 cj pt.aa.nsm v.iai.3s r.apm.3

ἄγουσιν δὲ οἱ γραμματεῖς καὶ οἱ Φαρισαῖοι γυναῖκα ἐπὶ
brought {and} The scribes and the Pharisees a woman who had been caught in
72 1254 3836 1208 2779 3836 5757 1222 2898 2898 2898 2898 2093
v.pai.3p cj d.npm n.npm cj d.npm n.npm n.asf p.d

μοιχείᾳ κατειλημμένην καὶ στήσαντες αὐτὴν ↰ ⌊ἐν μέσῳ⌋ 4 λέγουσιν
adultery, who had been caught and making her stand before them, they said
3657 2898 2779 2705 899 2705 1877 3545 3306
n.dsf pt.rp.asf cj pt.aa.npm r.asf.3 p.d n.dsn v.pai.3p

αὐτῷ, διδάσκαλε, αὕτη ἡ γυνὴ κατείληπται ἐπ᾽ αὐτοφώρῳ
to Jesus, "Teacher, this {the} woman was caught in the very act of
899 1437 4047 3836 1222 2898 2093 900
r.dsm.3 n.vsm r.nsf d.nsf n.nsf v.rpi.3s p.d a.dsn

μοιχευομένη· 5 ἐν δὲ τῷ νόμῳ ἡμῖν Μωϋσῆς ἐνετείλατο
committing adultery. Moses commanded us in {and} the law us Moses commanded
3658 3707 1948 7005 1877 1254 3836 3795 7005 3707 1948
pt.pp.nsf p.d cj d.dsm n.dsm r.dp.1 n.nsm v.ami.3s

τὰς τοιαύτας λιθάζειν. σὺ οὖν τί λέγεις; 6
to stone to death {the} such women. to stone But you, But what ⌊do you say?"⌋ (They said
3342 3342 3836 5525 3342 4036 5148 4036 5515 3306 3306 3306
d.apf r.apf f.pa r.ns.2 cj r.asn v.pai.2s

τοῦτο δὲ ἔλεγον → πειράζοντες αὐτόν, ἵνα ἔχωσιν
this {and} They said as a trap, {him} so ⌊they could have⌋ some basis for
4047 1254 3306 4279 899 2671 2400
r.asn cj v.iai.3p pt.pa.npm r.asm.3 cj v.pas.3p

κατηγορεῖν αὐτοῦ. ὁ δὲ Ἰησοῦς κάτω κύψας
accusing him.) {the} {and} Jesus bent down bent and started writing on the ground
2989 899 3836 1254 2652 3252 3004 3252 2863 2863 1650 3836 1178
f.pa r.gsm.3 d.nsm cj n.nsm adv pt.aa.nsm

τῷ δακτύλῳ κατέγραφεν εἰς τὴν γῆν. 7 ὡς δὲ ἐπέμενον ἐρωτῶντες αὐτόν,
⌊with his⌋ finger. started writing on the ground When {and} they kept on questioning him,
3836 1235 2863 1650 3836 1178 6055 1254 2152 2263 899
d.dsm n.dsm v.iai.3s p.a d.asf n.asf cj cj v.iai.3p pt.pa.npm r.asm.3

ἀνέκυψεν καὶ εἶπεν αὐτοῖς, ὁ → ἀναμάρτητος ὑμῶν
⌊he straightened up⌋ and said to them, "The man among you without sin, among you let him
376 2779 3306 899 3836 7007 7007 387 7007 965 965
v.aai.3s cj v.aai.3s r.dpm.3 d.nsm a.nsm r.gp.2

NASB

doing, does it?"
52 They answered him, "You are not also from Galilee, are you? Search, and see that no prophet arises out of Galilee."
53 [[a]Everyone went to his home.

The Adulterous Woman

8:1 But Jesus went to the Mount of Olives. 2 Early in the morning He came again into the temple, and all the people were coming to Him; and He sat down and *began* to teach them. 3 The scribes and the Pharisees *brought a woman caught in adultery, and having set her in the center *of the court,* 4 they *said to Him, "Teacher, this woman has been caught in adultery, in the very act. 5 Now in the Law Moses commanded us to stone such women; what then do You say?" 6 They were saying this, testing Him, so that they might have grounds for accusing Him. But Jesus stooped down and with His finger wrote on the ground. 7 But when they persisted in asking Him, He straightened up, and said to them, "He who is without sin among you, let

[a] Later mss add the story of the adulterous woman, numbering it as John 7:53-8:11

NIV

first to throw a
stone at her." 8 Again
he stooped down and
wrote on the ground.
9 At this, those who
heard began to go
away one at a time,
the older ones first,
until only Jesus was
left, with the woman
still standing there.
10 Jesus straightened
up and asked her,
"Woman, where are
they? Has no one
condemned you?"
11 "No one, sir,"
she said.
"Then neither do I
condemn you," Jesus
declared. "Go now
and leave your life
of sin."

Dispute Over Jesus' Testimony

12 When Jesus
spoke again to the
people, he said,
"I am the light of
the world. Who-
ever follows me
will never walk in
darkness, but will
have the light of
life."
13 The Pharisees
challenged him,
"Here you are,
appearing as your
own witness; your
testimony is not
valid."
14 Jesus answered,
"Even if I testify
on my own behalf,
my testimony is
valid, for I know
where I came from
and where I am
going. But you
have no idea where
I come from or
where I am going.
15 You judge

πρῶτος ἐπ᾽ αὐτὴν βαλέτω λίθον. 8 καὶ πάλιν ↱
be the first to throw a stone at her." *let him throw* *stone* *{and}* Once again he
4755 965 3345 2093 899 965 3345 2779 4099 1211
a.nsm p.a r.asf.3 v.aam.3s n.asm cj adv

κατακύψας ἔγραφεν εἰς τὴν γῆν. 9 οἱ δὲ ἀκούσαντες[a]
bent down and wrote on the ground. At this, those *At this* who had heard
2893 1211 1650 3836 1178 1254 1254 3836 1254 201
pt.aa.nsm v.iai.3s p.a d.asf n.asf d.npm cj pt.aa.npm

ἐξήρχοντο εἷς καθ᾽ εἷς ἀρξάμενοι ἀπὸ τῶν πρεσβυτέρων καὶ
began to leave one by one, starting with the oldest; and Jesus alone
2002 1651 2848 1651 806 608 3836 4565 2779 3668
v.imi.3p a.nsm p.a a.nsm pt.am.npm p.g d.gpm a.gpm cj

κατελείφθη μόνος καὶ ἡ γυνὴ ⌊ἐν μέσῳ⌋ οὖσα. 10
was left, *alone* with the woman standing before him. *standing* Jesus
2901 3668 2779 3836 1222 1639 1877 3545 1639 2652
v.api.3s a.nsm cj d.nsf n.nsf p.d n.dsn pt.pa.nsf

ἀνακύψας δὲ ὁ Ἰησοῦς[b] εἶπεν αὐτῇ, γύναι, ποῦ εἰσιν; οὐδείς
⌊straightened up⌋ *{and}* *{the}* *Jesus* and said to her, "Woman, where are they? Did no one
376 1254 3836 2652 3306 899 1222 4543 1639 2891 4029
pt.aa.nsm cj d.nsm n.nsm v.aai.3s r.dsf.3 n.vsf cj v.pai.3p a.nsm

σε κατέκρινεν; 11 ἡ δὲ εἶπεν, οὐδείς, κύριε. εἶπεν δὲ ὁ
condemn you?" *Did condemn* She *{and}* said, "No one, Lord." Then Jesus said, *Then* *{the}*
2891 5148 2891 3836 1254 3306 4029 3261 1254 2652 3306 1254 3836
r.as.2 v.aai.3s d.nsf cj v.aai.3s a.nsm n.vsm v.aai.3s cj d.nsm

Ἰησοῦς, οὐδὲ ἐγώ σε κατακρίνω· πορεύου, καὶ[c] ἀπὸ τοῦ νῦν
Jesus "Neither do I condemn you; *do condemn* go, and from *{the}* now on sin
2652 4028 2891 1609 2891 5148 2891 4513 2779 608 3836 3814 279
n.nsm cj r.ns.1 r.as.2 v.pai.1s v.pmm.2s cj p.g d.gsn adv

μηκέτι ἁμάρτανε.]] 12 πάλιν οὖν αὐτοῖς ἐλάλησεν ὁ Ἰησοῦς λέγων,
no more." *sin* Again *{then}* Jesus spoke to them, *spoke* *{the}* *Jesus* saying,
3600 279 4099 4036 2652 3281 899 3281 3836 2652 3306
adv v.pam.2s adv cj r.dpm.3 v.aai.3s d.nsm n.nsm pt.pa.nsm

ἐγώ εἰμι τὸ φῶς τοῦ κόσμου· ὁ ἀκολουθῶν ἐμοὶ ↱ ⌊οὐ μὴ⌋ περιπατήσῃ
"I am the light of the world. The one who follows me will never walk
1609 1639 3836 5890 3836 3180 3836 199 1609 4344 4024 3590 4344
r.ns.1 v.pai.1s d.nsn n.nsn d.gsm n.gsm d.nsm pt.pa.nsm r.ds.1 pl pl v.aas.3s

ἐν τῇ σκοτίᾳ, ἀλλ᾽ ἕξει τὸ φῶς τῆς ζωῆς. 13 εἶπον
in *{the}* darkness, but ⌊will have⌋ the light of life." Therefore the Pharisees said
1877 3836 5028 247 2400 3836 5890 3836 2437 4036 3836 5757 3306
p.d d.dsf n.dsf cj v.fai.3s d.asn n.asn d.gsf n.gsf v.aai.3p

οὖν αὐτῷ οἱ Φαρισαῖοι, σὺ περὶ σεαυτοῦ μαρτυρεῖς·
Therefore to him, *the* *Pharisees* "You are bearing witness about yourself; *are bearing witness*
4036 899 3836 5757 5148 3455 3455 3455 4309 4932 3455
cj r.dsm.3 d.npm n.npm r.ns.2 p.g r.gsm.2 v.pai.2s

ἡ μαρτυρία σου οὐκ ἔστιν ἀληθής. 14 ἀπεκρίθη Ἰησοῦς καὶ
{the} your testimony *your* is not *is* valid." Jesus answered *Jesus* them, *{and}*
3836 5148 3456 5148 1639 4024 1639 239 2652 646 2652 899 2779
d.nsf n.nsf r.gs.2 pl v.pai.3s a.nsf v.api.3s n.nsm cj

εἶπεν αὐτοῖς, κἂν ἐγὼ μαρτυρῶ περὶ ἐμαυτοῦ, ἀληθής
saying, *them* ⌊"Even if⌋ I ⌊am bearing witness⌋ about myself, my testimony is valid,
3306 899 2829 1609 3455 4309 1831 1609 3456 1639 239
v.aai.3s r.dpm.3 crasis r.ns.1 v.pas.1s p.g r.gsm.1 a.nsf

ἐστιν ἡ μαρτυρία μου, ὅτι οἶδα πόθεν ἦλθον ↰ καὶ ποῦ ὑπάγω· ὑμεῖς
is *{the}* *testimony* *my* because I know where I came from and where I am going. You,
1639 3836 3456 1609 4022 3857 4470 2262 4470 2779 4543 5632 7007
v.pai.3s d.nsf n.nsf r.gs.1 cj v.rai.1s cj v.aai.1s cj cj v.pai.1s r.np.2

δὲ ↱ οὐκ οἴδατε πόθεν ἔρχομαι ↰ ἢ ποῦ ὑπάγω. 15 ὑμεῖς
⌊on the other hand,⌋ do not know where I come from or where I am going. You judge
1254 3857 4024 3857 4470 2262 4470 2445 4543 5632 7007 3212
cj pl v.rai.2p cj v.pmi.1s cj cj v.pai.1s r.np.2

[a] καὶ ὑπὸ τῆς συνειδήσεως ἐλεγχόμενοι included by TR after ἀκούσαντες.
[b] καὶ μηδένα θεασάμενος πλὴν τῆς γυναικός included by TR after Ἰησοῦς.
[c] [καὶ] UBS.

NASB

him *be the* first
to throw a stone
at her." 8 Again
He stooped down
and wrote on the
ground. 9 When
they heard it,
they *began* to go
out one by one,
beginning with the
older ones, and He
was left alone, and
the woman, where
she was, in the
center *of the court.*
10 Straightening up,
Jesus said to her,
"Woman, where
are they? Did
no one condemn
you?" 11 She said,
"No one, Lord."
And Jesus said, "I
do not condemn
you, either. Go.
From now on sin
no more."]

Jesus Is the Light of the World

12 Then Jesus again
spoke to them,
saying, "I am the
Light of the world;
he who follows Me
will not walk in the
darkness, but will
have the Light of
life." 13 So the Phar-
isees said to Him,
"You are testifying
about Yourself;
Your testimony is
not true." 14 Jesus
answered and said
to them, "Even if I
testify about My-
self, My testimony
is true, for I know
where I came from
and where I am
going; but you do
not know where
I come from or
where I am going.
15 You judge

NIV

by human stan-
dards; I pass judg-
ment on no one.
16But if I do judge,
my decisions are
true, because I am
not alone. I stand
with the Father,
who sent me. 17In
your own Law it
is written that the
testimony of two
witnesses is true.
18I am one who
testifies for myself;
my other witness
is the Father, who
sent me."
19Then they asked
him, "Where is
your father?"
"You do not
know me or my
Father," Jesus
replied. "If you
knew me, you
would know my
Father also." 20He
spoke these words
while teaching in
the temple courts
near the place
where the offer-
ings were put. Yet
no one seized him,
because his hour
had not yet come.

Dispute Over Who Jesus Is

21Once more
Jesus said to them,
"I am going away,
and you will look
for me, and you
will die in your
sin. Where I go,
you cannot come."
22This made the
Jews ask, "Will
he kill himself? Is
that why he says,
'Where I go, you
cannot come'?"
23But he contin-
ued, "You are from
below;

κατὰ τὴν σάρκα κρίνετε, ἐγὼ οὐ κρίνω οὐδένα. 16 καὶ ἐὰν
⌊according to⌋ {the} ⌊human standards;⌋ judge I {not} judge no one. But even if
2848 3836 4922 3212 1609 4024 3212 4029 1254 2779 1569
p.a d.asf n.asf v.pai.2p r.ns.1 pl v.pai.1s a.asm adv cj

κρίνω δὲ ἐγώ, ἡ κρίσις ἡ ἐμὴ ἀληθινή ἐστιν, ὅτι
I do judge, But I {the} my judgment {the} my is trustworthy, is because it
1609 3212 1254 1609 3836 1847 3213 3836 1847 1639 240 1639 4022 1639
v.pas.1s cj r.ns.1 d.nsf n.nsf d.nsf r.nsf.1 a.nsf v.pai.3s cj

μόνος οὐκ εἰμί, ἀλλ᾽ ἐγὼ καὶ ὁ πέμψας με πατήρ.
is not I alone not it is I who judge, but I and the Father who sent me. Father
1639 4024 1639 3668 4024 1639 247 1609 2779 3836 4252 4287 1609 4252
a.nsm pl v.pai.1s cj r.ns.1 cj d.nsm pt.aa.nsm r.as.1 n.nsm

17 καὶ ἐν τῷ νόμῳ δὲ τῷ ὑμετέρῳ γέγραπται ὅτι ↱
{also} In {the} your own law {and} {the} your own it is written that the testimony of
2779 1877 3836 5629 5629 3795 1254 3836 5629 1211 4022 3836 3456 476
adv p.d d.dsm n.dsm cj d.dsm r.dsm.2 v.rpi.3s cj

δύο ἀνθρώπων ἡ μαρτυρία ἀληθής ἐστιν. 18 ἐγώ εἰμι ὁ μαρτυρῶν
two men the testimony is conclusive. is I am one who bears witness
1545 476 3836 3456 1639 239 1639 1609 1639 3836 3455
a.gpm n.gpm d.nsf n.nsf a.nsf v.pai.3s r.ns.1 v.pai.1s d.nsm pt.pa.nsm

περὶ ἐμαυτοῦ καὶ μαρτυρεῖ περὶ ἐμοῦ ὁ πέμψας με
about myself, and the Father who sent me also bears witness about me." the who sent me
4309 1831 2779 3836 4252 4287 4287 1609 3455 4309 1609 3836 4287 1609
p.g r.gsm.1 cj v.pai.3s p.g r.gs.1 d.nsm pt.aa.nsm r.as.1

πατήρ. 19 ἔλεγον οὖν αὐτῷ, ποῦ ἐστιν ὁ πατήρ σου;
Father Then ⌊they began asking⌋ Then him, "Where is {the} your father?" your Jesus
4252 4036 3306 4036 899 4543 1639 3836 5148 4252 5148 2652
n.nsm v.iai.3p cj r.dsm.3 cj v.pai.3s d.nsm n.nsm r.gs.2

ἀπεκρίθη Ἰησοῦς, οὔτε ἐμὲ οἴδατε οὔτε τὸν πατέρα μου· εἰ
replied, Jesus "You know neither me You know nor {the} my Father. my If you
646 2652 3857 3857 4046 1609 3857 4046 3836 1609 4252 1609 1623 3857
v.api.3s n.nsm cj r.as.1 v.rai.2p cj d.asm n.asm r.gs.1 cj

ἐμὲ ᾔδειτε, καὶ τὸν πατέρα μου ἂν ᾔδειτε.
knew me you knew you would know my Father also." {the} Father my would you know
3857 1609 3857 3857 323 3857 1609 4252 2779 3836 4252 1609 323 3857
r.as.1 v.lai.2p adv d.asm n.asm r.gs.1 pl v.lai.2p

20 ταῦτα τὰ ῥήματα ἐλάλησεν ἐν τῷ γαζοφυλακίῳ διδάσκων ἐν
Jesus spoke these {the} words spoke near the treasury as he was teaching in
3281 4047 3836 4839 3281 1877 3836 1126 1438 1877
r.apn d.apn n.apn v.aai.3s p.d d.dsn n.dsn pt.pa.nsm p.d

τῷ ἱερῷ· καὶ οὐδεὶς ἐπίασεν αὐτόν, ὅτι ↱ οὔπω ἐληλύθει ἡ ὥρα
the temple. {and} No one seized him because his hour had not yet come. {the} hour
3836 2639 2779 4029 4389 899 4022 899 6052 2262 4037 2262 3836 6052
d.dsn n.dsn cj a.nsm v.aai.3s r.asm.3 cj adv v.lai.3s d.nsf n.nsf

αὐτοῦ. 21 εἶπεν οὖν πάλιν αὐτοῖς, ἐγὼ ὑπάγω καὶ
his Then he said Then to them again, to them "I ⌊am going away,⌋ and
899 4036 3306 4036 899 899 4099 899 1609 5632 2779
r.gsm.3 v.aai.3s cj adv r.dpm.3 r.ns.1 v.pai.1s cj

ζητήσετέ με, καὶ ἐν τῇ ἁμαρτίᾳ ὑμῶν ἀποθανεῖσθε· ὅπου ἐγὼ
⌊you will search for⌋ me but will die in {the} your sin. your will die Where I
2426 1609 2779 633 633 1877 3836 7007 281 7007 633 3963 1609
v.fai.2p r.as.1 cj p.d d.dsf n.dsf r.gp.2 v.fmi.2p cj r.ns.1

ὑπάγω ὑμεῖς ⌊οὐ δύνασθε⌋ ἐλθεῖν. 22 ἔλεγον οὖν οἱ Ἰουδαῖοι,
am going, you cannot come." So the Jews said, So the Jews
5632 7007 4024 1538 2262 4036 3836 2681 3306 4036 3836 2681
v.pai.1s r.np.2 pl v.ppi.2p f.aa v.iai.3p cj d.npm a.npm

→ ↱ ↱ μήτι ἀποκτενεῖ ἑαυτόν, ↰ ↰ ὅτι λέγει, ὅπου ἐγὼ ὑπάγω
"Surely he is not going to kill himself, is he, because he said, 'Where I am going,
650 650 3614 650 1571 3614 3614 4022 3306 3963 1609 5632
pl v.fai.3s r.asm.3 cj v.pai.3s cj r.ns.1 v.pai.1s

ὑμεῖς ⌊οὐ δύνασθε⌋ ἐλθεῖν; 23 καὶ ἔλεγεν αὐτοῖς, ὑμεῖς ἐκ τῶν κάτω ἐστέ,
you cannot come'?" {and} He said to them, "You are from {the} below; are
7007 4024 1538 2262 2779 3306 899 7007 1639 1666 3836 3004 1639
r.np.2 pl v.ppi.2p f.aa cj v.iai.3s r.dpm.3 r.np.2 p.g d.gpn adv v.pai.2p

NASB

according to the
flesh; I am not
judging anyone.
16But even if I do
judge, My judg-
ment is true; for I
am not alone *in it,*
but I and the Father
who sent Me.
17Even in your law
it has been written
that the testimony
of two men is true.
18I am He who tes-
tifies about Myself,
and the Father who
sent Me testifies
about Me." 19So
they were saying
to Him, "Where
is Your Father?"
Jesus answered,
"You know neither
Me nor My Father;
if you knew Me,
you would know
My Father also."
20These words He
spoke in the trea-
sury, as He taught
in the temple; and
no one seized Him,
because His hour
had not yet come.
21Then He said
again to them, "I
go away, and you
will seek Me, and
will die in your sin;
where I am going,
you cannot come."
22So the Jews were
saying, "Surely He
will not kill Him-
self, will He, since
He says, 'Where I
am going, you can-
not come'?" 23And
He was saying to
them, "You are
from below, I am

NIV

I am from above. You are of this world; I am not of this world. 24 I told you that you would die in your sins; if you do not believe that I am he, you will indeed die in your sins."

25 "Who are you?" they asked.

"Just what I have been telling you from the beginning," Jesus replied. 26 "I have much to say in judgment of you. But he who sent me is trustworthy, and what I have heard from him I tell the world."

27 They did not understand that he was telling them about his Father. 28 So Jesus said, "When you have lifted up[a] the Son of Man, then you will know that I am he and that I do nothing on my own but speak just what the Father has taught me. 29 The one who sent me is with me; he has not left me alone, for I always do what pleases him." 30 Even as he spoke, many believed in him.

Dispute Over Whose Children Jesus' Opponents Are

31 To the Jews who had believed him, Jesus said,

ἐγώ ἐκ τῶν ἄνω εἰμί· ὑμεῖς ἐκ τούτου τοῦ κόσμου ἐστέ, ἐγὼ οὐκ
I am from {the} above. am You are of this {the} world; are I am not
1609 1639 1666 3836 539 1639 7007 1639 1666 4047 3836 3180 1639 1609 1639 4024
r.ns.1 p.g d.gpn adv v.pai.1s r.np.2 p.g r.gsm d.gsm n.gsm v.pai.2p r.ns.1 pl

εἰμὶ ἐκ τοῦ κόσμου τούτου. 24 εἶπον οὖν ὑμῖν ὅτι
am of {the} this world. this This is why I said This is why to you that
1639 1666 3836 4047 3180 4047 4036 4036 4036 3306 4036 7007 4022
v.pai.1s p.g d.gsm n.gsm r.gsm v.aai.1s cj r.dp.2 cj

ἀποθανεῖσθε ἐν ταῖς ἁμαρτίαις ὑμῶν· ἐὰν γὰρ ↱ ↱ μὴ πιστεύσητε ὅτι
you would die in {the} your sins, your for if for you do not believe that
633 1877 3836 7007 281 7007 1142 1569 1142 4409 4409 3590 4409 4022
v.fmi.2p p.d d.dpf n.dpf r.gp.2 cj cj pl v.aas.2p cj

ἐγώ εἰμι, ἀποθανεῖσθε ἐν ταῖς ἁμαρτίαις ὑμῶν. 25 ἔλεγον οὖν αὐτῷ,
I am he, you will die in {the} your sins." your So they said So to him,
1609 1639 633 1877 3836 7007 281 7007 4036 3306 4036 899
r.ns.1 v.pai.1s v.fmi.2p p.d d.dpf n.dpf r.gp.2 v.iai.3p cj r.dsm.3

σύ τίς εἶ; εἶπεν αὐτοῖς ὁ Ἰησοῦς,
"Who are you?" Who are Jesus said to them, {the} Jesus "Just what I have been
5515 1639 5148 5515 1639 2652 3306 899 3836 2652 4005 5516 3281 3281 3281
r.ns.2 r.nsm v.pai.2s v.aai.3s r.dpm.3 d.nsm n.nsm

τὴν ἀρχὴν ὅ τι καὶ λαλῶ ὑμῖν; 26 πολλὰ
telling you from the beginning. Just what {also} I have been telling you I have many things
3281 7007 3836 794 4005 5516 2779 3281 7007 2400 2400 4498
d.asf n.asf r.asn r.asn adv v.pai.1s r.dp.2 a.apn

ἔχω περὶ ὑμῶν λαλεῖν καὶ κρίνειν, ἀλλ᾽ ὁ πέμψας με
I have to say about you to say {and} ⌊by way of judgment;⌋ but the ⌊one who sent⌋ me
2400 3281 3281 4309 7007 3281 2779 3212 247 3836 4287 1609
v.pai.1s p.g r.gp.2 f.pa cj f.pa cj d.nsm pt.aa.nsm r.as.1

ἀληθής ἐστιν, κἀγὼ ἃ ἤκουσα παρ᾽ αὐτοῦ
is truthful, is and I say to the world only that which I have heard from him."
1639 239 1639 2743 3281 1650 3836 3180 4047 4005 201 4123 899
a.nsm v.pai.3s crasis r.apn v.aai.1s p.g r.gsm.3

ταῦτα λαλῶ εἰς τὸν κόσμον. 27 ↱ ↱ οὐκ ἔγνωσαν ὅτι
that say to the world They did not understand that he was speaking to them
4047 3281 1650 3836 3180 1182 1182 4024 1182 4022 3306 3306 3306 899 899
r.apn v.pai.1s p.a d.asm n.asm pl v.aai.3p cj

τὸν πατέρα αὐτοῖς ἔλεγεν. 28 εἶπεν οὖν αὐτοῖς[a] ὁ Ἰησοῦς,
about the Father. to them he was speaking So Jesus said So to them, {the} Jesus
3836 4252 899 3306 4036 2652 3306 4036 899 3836 2652
d.asm n.asm r.dpm.3 v.iai.3s v.aai.3s cj r.dpm.3 d.nsm n.nsm

ὅταν ὑψώσητε τὸν υἱὸν τοῦ ἀνθρώπου, τότε γνώσεσθε ὅτι ἐγώ εἰμι, καὶ
"When you lift up the Son of Man, then you will know that I am he. {and}
4020 5738 3836 5626 3836 476 5538 1182 4022 1609 1639 2779
cj v.aas.2p d.asm n.asm d.gsm n.gsm adv v.fmi.2p cj r.ns.1 v.pai.1s cj

ἀπ᾽ ἐμαυτοῦ ποιῶ οὐδέν, ἀλλὰ καθὼς
I do nothing on my own, I do nothing but speak only those things the Father
4472 4472 4029 608 1831 4472 4029 247 3281 2777 4047 4047 3836 4252
p.g r.gsm.1 v.pai.1s a.asn cj cj

ἐδίδαξέν με ὁ πατὴρ ταῦτα λαλῶ. 29 καὶ ὁ πέμψας με μετ᾽ ἐμοῦ
has taught me. the Father those things speak And the ⌊one who sent⌋ me is with me;
1438 1609 3836 4252 4047 3281 2779 3836 4287 1609 1639 3552 1609
v.aai.3s r.as.1 d.nsm n.nsm r.apn v.pai.1s cj d.nsm pt.aa.nsm r.as.1 p.g r.gs.1

ἐστιν· ↱ ↱ οὐκ ἀφῆκέν με μόνον, ὅτι ἐγὼ τὰ ἀρεστὰ αὐτῷ ποιῶ
is he has not left me alone, for I always do what is pleasing to him." do
1639 918 918 4024 918 1609 3668 4022 1609 4121 4472 3836 744 899 4472
v.pai.3s pl v.aai.3s r.as.1 a.asm cj r.ns.1 d.apn a.apn r.dsm.3 v.pai.1s

πάντοτε. 30 ταῦτα αὐτοῦ λαλοῦντος πολλοὶ ἐπίστευσαν εἰς
always As he was saying these things, he As was saying many came to believe in
4121 3281 899 3281 3281 4047 899 3281 4498 4409 1650
adv r.apn r.gsm.3 pt.pa.gsm a.npm v.aai.3p p.a

αὐτόν. 31 ἔλεγεν οὖν ὁ Ἰησοῦς πρὸς τοὺς πεπιστευκότας
him. Jesus therefore said therefore {the} Jesus to the Jews ⌊who had put their trust⌋
899 2652 4036 3306 4036 3836 2652 4639 3836 2681 4409
r.asm.3 v.iai.3s cj d.nsm n.nsm p.a d.apm pt.ra.apm

NASB

from above; you are of this world, I am not of this world. 24 Therefore I said to you that you will die in your sins; for unless you believe that I am *He,* you will die in your sins." 25 So they were saying to Him, "Who are You?" Jesus said to them, "What have I been saying to you *from* the beginning? 26 I have many things to speak and to judge concerning you, but He who sent Me is true; and the things which I heard from Him, these I speak to the world." 27 They did not realize that He had been speaking to them about the Father. 28 So Jesus said, "When you lift up the Son of Man, then you will know that I am *He,* and I do nothing on My own initiative, but I speak these things as the Father taught Me. 29 And He who sent Me is with Me; He has not left Me alone, for I always do the things that are pleasing to Him." 30 As He spoke these things, many came to believe in Him.

The Truth Will Make You Free

31 So Jesus was saying to those Jews who had believed Him, "If

[a] 28 The Greek for *lifted up* also means *exalted.*

[a] [αὐτοῖς] UBS.

NIV

"If you hold to my
teaching, you are
really my disciples.
32 Then you will
know the truth, and
the truth will set
you free."
33 They answered
him, "We are
Abraham's descen-
dants and have
never been slaves
of anyone. How
can you say that
we shall be set
free?"
34 Jesus replied,
"Very truly I tell
you, everyone who
sins is a slave to
sin. 35 Now a slave
has no permanent
place in the family,
but a son belongs
to it forever. 36 So
if the Son sets you
free, you will be
free indeed. 37 I
know that you are
Abraham's descen-
dants. Yet you are
looking for a way
to kill me, because
you have no room
for my word. 38 I
am telling you
what I have seen in
the Father's pres-
ence, and you are
doing what you
have heard from
your father.[a]"
39 "Abraham is
our father," they
answered.
"If you were
Abraham's chil-
dren," said Jesus,
"then you would[b]
do what Abraham
did. 40 As it is, you
are looking for a
way to kill me, a

αὐτῷ Ἰουδαίους, ἐὰν ὑμεῖς μείνητε ἐν τῷ λόγῳ τῷ ἐμῷ, ἀληθῶς
in him, Jews "If you continue in {the} my word, {the} my you are truly
899 2681 1569 7007 3531 1877 3836 1847 3364 3836 1847 1639 1639 242
r.dsm.3 a.apm cj r.np.2 v.aas.2p p.d d.dsm n.dsm d.dsm r.dsm.1 adv

μαθηταί μού ἐστε 32 καὶ γνώσεσθε τὴν ἀλήθειαν, καὶ ἡ ἀλήθεια
my disciples, my you are and ⌞you will come to know⌟ the truth, and the truth
1609 3412 1609 1639 2779 1182 3836 237 2779 3836 237
n.npm r.gs.1 v.pai.2p cj v.fmi.2p d.asf n.asf cj d.nsf n.nsf

→ → ἐλευθερώσει ὑμᾶς. 33 ἀπεκρίθησαν πρὸς αὐτόν, σπέρμα
will set you free." you They replied to him, "We are descendants
7007 1802 7007 646 4639 899 1639 1639 5065
v.fai.3s r.ap.2 v.api.3p p.a r.asm.3 n.nsn

Ἀβραάμ ἐσμεν καὶ οὐδενὶ δεδουλεύκαμεν πώποτε· πῶς ↱
of Abraham We are and have never been slaves to anyone! have been slaves never How can
11 1639 2779 1526 4799 1526 1526 4029 1526 4799 4802 3306
n.gsm v.pai.1p cj a.dsm v.rai.1p adv cj

σὺ λέγεις ὅτι ἐλεύθεροι γενήσεσθε; 34 ἀπεκρίθη αὐτοῖς ὁ
you say, ~ 'You will become free'?" You will become Jesus answered them, {the}
5148 3306 4022 1181 1181 1181 1801 1181 2652 646 899 3836
r.ns.2 v.pai.2s cj a.npm v.fmi.2p v.api.3s r.dpm.3 d.nsm

Ἰησοῦς, ἀμὴν ἀμὴν λέγω ὑμῖν ὅτι πᾶς ὁ ποιῶν τὴν
Jesus "I tell you the solemn truth, I tell you ~ everyone who commits {the}
2652 3306 3306 7007 297 297 3306 7007 4022 4246 3836 4472 3836
n.nsm pl pl v.pai.1s r.dp.2 cj a.nsm d.nsm pt.pa.nsm d.asf

ἁμαρτίαν δοῦλός ἐστιν τῆς ἁμαρτίας. 35 ὁ δὲ δοῦλος ↱ οὐ μένει ἐν
sin is a slave is to sin. A {and} slave does not remain in
281 1639 1529 1639 3836 281 3836 1254 1529 3531 4024 3531 1877
n.asf n.nsm v.pai.3s d.gsf n.gsf d.nsm cj n.nsm pl v.pai.3s p.d

τῇ οἰκίᾳ εἰς τὸν αἰῶνα, ὁ υἱὸς μένει εἰς τὸν αἰῶνα. 36 ἐὰν οὖν ὁ
the house for all time, but a son remains for all time. If therefore the
3836 3864 1650 3836 172 3836 5626 3531 1650 3836 172 1569 4036 3836
d.dsf n.dsf p.a d.asm n.asm d.nsm n.nsm v.pai.3s p.a d.asm n.asm cj cj d.nsm

υἱὸς ↱ ὑμᾶς ἐλευθερώσῃ, ὄντως ἐλεύθεροι ἔσεσθε. 37 οἶδα ὅτι
Son sets you free, you will be free indeed. free you will be I know that
5626 1802 7007 1802 1639 1639 1639 1801 3953 1801 1639 3857 4022
n.nsm r.ap.2 v.aas.3s adv a.npm v.fmi.2p v.rai.1s cj

σπέρμα Ἀβραάμ ἐστε· ἀλλὰ ζητεῖτέ με
you are Abraham's descendants; Abraham's you are but ⌞you are intent on⌟ killing me,
1639 1639 11 5065 11 1639 247 2426 650 1609
n.nsn n.gsm v.pai.2p cj v.pai.2p r.as.1

ἀποκτεῖναι, ὅτι ὁ λόγος ὁ ἐμὸς ↱ οὐ χωρεῖ ἐν ὑμῖν. 38
killing because {the} my teaching {the} my makes no headway in you. I
650 4022 3836 1847 3364 3836 1847 6003 4024 6003 1877 7007 3281
f.aa cj d.nsm n.nsm d.nsm r.nsm.1 pl v.pai.3s p.d r.dp.2

ἃ ἐγὼ ἑώρακα παρὰ τῷ πατρὶ λαλῶ· καὶ ὑμεῖς οὖν
speak about the things I have seen while with my Father, I speak about but you {then} do
3281 3281 4005 1609 3972 4123 3836 4252 3281 2779 7007 4036 4472
r.apn r.ns.1 v.rai.1s p.d d.dsm n.dsm v.pai.1s cj r.np.2 cj

ἃ ἠκούσατε παρὰ τοῦ πατρὸς ποιεῖτε. 39 ἀπεκρίθησαν καὶ εἶπαν αὐτῷ,
⌞that which⌟ you have heard from your father." do They answered {and} saying him,
4005 201 4123 3836 4252 4472 646 2779 3306 899
r.apn v.aai.2p p.g d.gsm n.gsm v.pai.2p v.api.3p cj v.aai.3p r.dsm.3

ὁ πατὴρ ἡμῶν Ἀβραάμ ἐστιν. λέγει αὐτοῖς ὁ Ἰησοῦς, εἰ
saying, {the} "Our father Our is Abraham!" is Jesus said to them, {the} Jesus "If
3306 3836 7005 4252 7005 1639 11 1639 2652 3306 899 3836 2652 1623
d.nsm n.nsm r.gp.1 n.nsm v.pai.3s v.pai.3s r.dpm.3 d.nsm n.nsm cj

τέκνα τοῦ Ἀβραάμ ἐστε,[a] τὰ ἔργα
you were really Abraham's children, {the} Abraham's you were you would be doing the deeds
1639 1639 11 5451 3836 11 1639 4472 4472 4472 4472 3836 2240
n.npn d.gsm n.gsm v.pai.2p d.apn n.apn

τοῦ Ἀβραὰμ ἐποιεῖτε· 40 νῦν δὲ ζητεῖτέ με ἀποκτεῖναι
of Abraham. you would be doing But now But ⌞you are intent on⌟ killing me, killing a
3836 11 4472 1254 3814 1254 2426 650 1609 650
d.gsm n.gsm v.iai.2p adv cj v.pai.2p r.as.1 f.aa

NASB

you continue in
My word, then you
are truly disciples
of Mine; 32 and
you will know
the truth, and the
truth will make
you free." 33 They
answered Him,
"We are Abraham's
descendants and
have never yet
been enslaved to
anyone; how is
it that You say,
'You will become
free'?"
34 Jesus answered
them, "Truly, truly,
I say to you, every-
one who commits
sin is the slave of
sin. 35 The slave
does not remain in
the house forever;
the son does re-
main forever. 36 So
if the Son makes
you free, you will
be free indeed. 37 I
know that you are
Abraham's descen-
dants; yet you seek
to kill Me, because
My word has no
place in you. 38 I
speak the things
which I have seen
with My Father;
therefore you also
do the things which
you heard from
your father."
39 They answered
and said to Him,
"Abraham is our
father." Jesus *said
to them, "If you are
Abraham's chil-
dren, do the deeds
of Abraham. 40 But
as it is, you are
seeking to kill Me,

a 38 Or presence. Therefore do what you have heard from the Father.
b 39 Some early manuscripts "If you are Abraham's children," said Jesus, "then

a ἐστε UBS, NET. ἦτε TNIV.

NIV

man who has told
you the truth that
I heard from God.
Abraham did not
do such things.
41 You are doing the
works of your own
father."
"We are not ille-
gitimate children,"
they protested.
"The only Father
we have is God
himself."
42 Jesus said to
them, "If God
were your Father,
you would love
me, for I have
come here from
God. I have not
come on my own;
God sent me.
43 Why is my lan-
guage not clear to
you? Because you
are unable to hear
what I say. 44 You
belong to your fa-
ther, the devil, and
you want to carry
out your father's
desires. He was
a murderer from
the beginning,
not holding to the
truth, for there is
no truth in him.
When he lies, he
speaks his native
language, for he is
a liar and the fa-
ther of lies. 45 Yet
because I tell the
truth, you do not
believe me! 46 Can
any of you prove
me guilty of sin? If
I am telling

ἄνθρωπον ὃς τὴν ἀλήθειαν ὑμῖν λελάληκα ἣν ἤκουσα παρὰ τοῦ
man who has told you the truth *you* *has told* that I heard from *{the}*
476 4005 3281 3281 7007 3836 237 7007 3281 4005 201 4123 3836
n.asm r.nsm d.asf n.asf r.dp.2 v.rai.1s r.asf v.aai.1s p.g d.gsm

θεοῦ· τοῦτο Ἀβραὰμ οὐκ ἐποίησεν. 41 ὑμεῖς ποιεῖτε τὰ ἔργα τοῦ
God. This is not what Abraham *not* did! You are doing the deeds of your
2536 4047 4024 11 4024 4472 7007 4472 3836 2240 3836 7007
n.gsm r.asn n.nsm pl v.aai.3s r.np.2 v.pai.2p d.apn n.apn d.gsm

πατρὸς ὑμῶν. εἶπαν [a]αὐτῷ, ἡμεῖς ἐκ πορνείας οὐ
father." *your* They said to him, "We have not been born ⌞as a result of⌟ fornication; *not*
4252 7007 3306 899 7005 1164 4024 1164 1164 1666 4518 4024
n.gsm r.gp.2 v.aai.3p r.dsm.3 r.np.1 p.g n.gsf pl

γεγεννήμεθα, ἕνα πατέρα ἔχομεν τὸν θεόν. 42 εἶπεν αὐτοῖς
have been born we have only one father, *we have* *{the}* God himself." Jesus said to them,
1164 2400 2400 1651 4252 2400 3836 2536 2652 3306 899
v.rpi.1p a.asm n.asm v.pai.1p d.asm n.asm v.aai.3s r.dpm.3

ὁ Ἰησοῦς, εἰ ὁ θεὸς πατὴρ ὑμῶν ἦν → ἠγαπᾶτε ἂν ἐμέ,
{the} *Jesus* "If *{the}* God were your Father, *your* *were* you would love *would* me,
3836 2652 1623 3836 2536 1639 7007 4252 7007 1639 323 26 323 1609
d.nsm n.nsm cj d.nsm n.nsm n.nsm r.gp.2 v.iai.3s v.iai.2p pl r.as.1

ἐγὼ γὰρ ἐκ τοῦ θεοῦ ἐξῆλθον καὶ ἥκω· οὐδὲ γὰρ
for I *for* came from *{the}* God *came* and now ⌞I am here.⌟ I have not *{for}* come
1142 1609 1142 2002 1666 3836 2536 2002 2779 2457 2262 2262 4028 1142 2262
r.ns.1 cj p.g d.gsm n.gsm v.aai.1s cj v.rai.1s adv cj

ἀπ᾽ ἐμαυτοῦ ἐλήλυθα, ἀλλ᾽ ἐκεῖνός με ἀπέστειλεν. 43 ⌞διὰ τί⌟
on my own, *I have come* but he sent me. *sent* Why do you not
608 1831 2262 247 1697 690 1609 690 1328 5515 1182 1182 4024
p.g r.gsm.1 v.rai.1s cj r.nsm r.as.1 v.aai.3s p.a r.asn

τὴν → λαλιὰν τὴν ἐμὴν οὐ γινώσκετε; ὅτι ⌞οὐ
understand the way I speak? *{the}* *I* *not* *do you understand* It is because you are unable
1182 3836 1847 3282 3836 1847 4024 1182 4022 4024
d.asf n.asf d.asf r.asf.1 pl v.pai.2p cj pl

δύνασθε⌟ ἀκούειν τὸν λόγον τὸν ἐμόν. 44 ὑμεῖς ἐκ τοῦ πατρὸς τοῦ
to grasp *{the}* my message. *{the}* *my* You belong to your father the
1538 201 3836 1847 3364 3836 1847 7007 1639 1666 3836 4252 3836
v.ppi.2p f.pa d.asm n.asm d.asm r.asm.1 r.np.2 p.g d.gsm n.gsm d.gsm

διαβόλου ἐστὲ καὶ τὰς ἐπιθυμίας τοῦ πατρὸς ὑμῶν
devil, *belong* and your will is to carry out the desires of your father. *your*
1333 1639 2779 2527 2527 2527 4472 4472 4472 3836 2123 3836 7007 4252 7007
n.gsm v.pai.2p cj d.apf n.apf d.gsm n.gsm r.gp.2

θέλετε ποιεῖν. ἐκεῖνος ἀνθρωποκτόνος ἦν ἀπ᾽ ἀρχῆς καὶ
your will is *to carry out* He was a murderer *was* from the beginning and never did
2527 4472 1697 1639 475 1639 608 794 2779 4024 5112
v.pai.2p f.pa r.nsm n.nsm v.iai.3s p.g n.gsf cj

ἐν τῇ ἀληθείᾳ οὐκ ἔστηκεν, ὅτι οὐκ ἔστιν ἀλήθεια ἐν αὐτῷ.
stand in the truth, *never* *did stand* because there is no *there is* truth in him.
5112 1877 3836 237 4024 5112 4022 1639 1639 4024 1639 237 1877 899
p.d d.dsf n.dsf pl v.iai.3s cj pl v.pai.3s n.nsf p.d r.dsm.3

ὅταν ⌞λαλῇ τὸ ψεῦδος,⌟ ἐκ τῶν ἰδίων
When he lies, he is giving expression to *{the}* his own nature,
4020 3281 3836 6022 3281 3281 3281 3281 1666 3836 2625
cj v.pas.3s d.asn n.asn p.g d.gpn a.gpn

λαλεῖ, ὅτι ψεύστης ἐστὶν καὶ ὁ πατὴρ αὐτοῦ. 45
he is giving expression for he is a liar *he is* and the father of lies. Yet because
3281 4022 1639 1639 6026 1639 2779 3836 4252 899 1254 4022
v.pai.3s cj n.nsm v.pai.3s cj d.nsm n.nsm r.gsn.3

ἐγὼ δὲ ὅτι τὴν ἀλήθειαν λέγω, ↱ ↱ οὐ πιστεύετέ μοι.
I *Yet* *because* am speaking the truth, *am speaking* you do not believe me.
1609 1254 4022 3306 3306 3836 237 3306 4409 4409 4024 4409 1609
r.ns.1 cj cj d.asf n.asf v.pai.1s pl v.pai.2p r.ds.1

46 τίς ἐξ ὑμῶν → → ἐλέγχει με περὶ ἁμαρτίας; εἰ
Who among you can prove me guilty *me* of any sin? If I am speaking
5515 1666 7007 1609 1794 1609 4309 281 1623 3306 3306 3306
r.nsm p.g r.gp.2 v.pai.3s r.as.1 p.g n.gsf cj

NASB

a man who has
told you the truth,
which I heard from
God; this Abraham
did not do. 41 You
are doing the deeds
of your father."
They said to Him,
"We were not born
of fornication; we
have one Father:
God." 42 Jesus said
to them, "If God
were your Father,
you would love
Me, for I proceed-
ed forth and have
come from God,
for I have not even
come on My own
initiative, but He
sent Me. 43 Why do
you not understand
what I am saying?
It is because you
cannot hear My
word. 44 You are
of *your* father the
devil, and you want
to do the desires of
your father. He was
a murderer from
the beginning, and
does not stand in
the truth because
there is no truth
in him. Whenever
he speaks a lie, he
speaks from his
own *nature,* for
he is a liar and the
father of lies. 45 But
because I speak
the truth, you do
not believe Me.
46 Which one of you
convicts Me of sin?
If I speak truth,

[a] οὖν included by UBS before αὐτῷ.

NIV

the truth, why
don't you believe
me? 47 Whoever be-
longs to God hears
what God says.
The reason you do
not hear is that you
do not belong to
God."

Jesus' Claims About Himself

48 The Jews an-
swered him,
"Aren't we right
in saying that you
are a Samaritan
and demon-pos-
sessed?"
49 "I am not pos-
sessed by a de-
mon," said Jesus,
"but I honor my
Father and you dis-
honor me. 50 I am
not seeking glory
for myself; but
there is one who
seeks it, and he is
the judge. 51 Very
truly I tell you,
whoever obeys my
word will never
see death."
52 At this they
exclaimed, "Now
we know that you
are demon-pos-
sessed! Abraham
died and so did the
prophets, yet you
say that whoever
obeys your word
will never taste
death. 53 Are you
greater than our
father Abraham?
He died, and so did
the prophets. Who
do you think you
are?"
54 Jesus replied,
"If I glorify my-
self, my glory
means nothing.
My Father,

ἀλήθειαν λέγω, ⌊διὰ τί⌋ ὑμεῖς οὐ πιστεύετέ μοι; 47 ὁ ὢν
the truth, *I am speaking* why don't you *dont* believe me? Whoever belongs
237 3306 1328 5515 4024 7007 4024 4409 1609 3836 1639
n.asf v.pai.1s p.a r.asn r.np.2 pl v.pai.2p r.ds.1 d.nsm pt.pa.nsm

ἐκ τοῦ θεοῦ τὰ ῥήματα τοῦ θεοῦ ἀκούει· ⌊διὰ τοῦτο⌋ ὑμεῖς ↱
to *{the}* God listens to the words of God. *listens to* The reason why you do
1666 3836 2536 201 201 3836 4839 3836 2536 201 1328 4047 7007 201
p.g d.gsm n.gsm d.apn n.apn d.gsm n.gsm v.pai.3s p.a r.asn r.np.2

οὐκ ἀκούετε, ὅτι ἐκ τοῦ θεοῦ οὐκ ἐστέ. 48
not listen is that you do not belong to *{the}* God." *not* *you do belong* The Jews
4024 201 4022 1639 1639 4024 1639 1666 3836 2536 4024 1639 3836 2681
pl v.pai.2p cj p.g d.gsm n.gsm pl v.pai.2p

ἀπεκρίθησαν οἱ Ἰουδαῖοι καὶ εἶπαν αὐτῷ, οὐ καλῶς λέγομεν ἡμεῖς
answered *The* *Jews* *{and}* him, saying, *him* "Are we not correct in saying *we*
646 3836 2681 2779 899 3306 899 7005 4024 2822 3306 7005
v.api.3p d.npm a.npm cj v.aai.3p r.dsm.3 pl adv v.pai.1p r.np.1

ὅτι Σαμαρίτης εἶ σὺ καὶ δαιμόνιον ἔχεις; 49 ἀπεκρίθη
that you are a Samaritan *are* *you* and have a demon?" *have* Jesus answered,
4022 5148 1639 4901 1639 5148 2779 2400 1228 2400 2652 646
cj n.nsm v.pai.2s r.ns.2 cj n.asn v.pai.2s v.api.3s

Ἰησοῦς, ἐγὼ δαιμόνιον οὐκ ἔχω, ἀλλὰ τιμῶ τὸν πατέρα μου,
Jesus "I do not have a demon; *not* *do have* but I honor *{the}* my Father, *my*
2652 1609 2400 4024 2400 1228 4024 2400 247 5506 3836 1609 4252 1609
n.nsm r.ns.1 n.asn pl v.pai.1s cj v.pai.1s d.asm n.asm r.gs.1

καὶ ὑμεῖς ἀτιμάζετέ με. 50 ἐγὼ δὲ ↱ οὐ ζητῶ τὴν δόξαν μου· ἔστιν ὁ
and you dishonor me. I *{and}* am not seeking *{the}* glory for myself; there is one
2779 7007 869 1609 1609 1254 2426 4024 2426 3836 1518 1609 1639 3836
cj r.np.2 v.pai.2p r.as.1 r.ns.1 cj pl v.pai.1s d.asf n.asf r.gs.1 v.pai.3s d.nsm

ζητῶν καὶ κρίνων. 51 ἀμὴν ἀμὴν λέγω ὑμῖν, ἐάν
who seeks it and ⌊he is the one who judges.⌋ I tell you the solemn truth, *I tell* *you* if
2426 2779 3212 3306 3306 7007 297 297 3306 7007 1569
pt.pa.nsm cj pt.pa.nsm pl pl v.pai.1s r.dp.2 cj

τις τὸν ἐμὸν λόγον τηρήσῃ, θάνατον ↱ ↱ ⌊οὐ μὴ⌋ θεωρήσῃ εἰς
anyone keeps *{the}* my word, *keeps* *death* he will never see death." *{for}*
5516 5498 3836 1847 3364 5498 2505 2555 2555 4024 3590 2555 2505 1650
r.nsm d.asm r.asm.1 n.asm v.aas.3s n.asm pl pl v.aas.3s p.a

τὸν αἰῶνα. 52 εἶπον οὖν[a] αὐτῷ οἱ Ἰουδαῖοι, νῦν ἐγνώκαμεν
{all} *{time}* The Jews therefore said *therefore* to him, *The* *Jews* "Now we know
3836 172 3836 2681 4036 3306 4036 899 3836 2681 3814 1182
d.asm n.asm v.aai.3p cj r.dsm.3 d.npm a.npm adv v.rai.1p

ὅτι δαιμόνιον ἔχεις. Ἀβραὰμ ἀπέθανεν καὶ οἱ προφῆται, καὶ
that you have a demon! *you have* Abraham died, and so did the prophets, yet
4022 2400 2400 1228 2400 11 633 2779 3836 4737 2779
cj n.asn v.pai.2s n.nsm v.aai.3s cj d.npm n.npm cj

σὺ λέγεις, ἐάν τις τὸν λόγον μου τηρήσῃ, ↱ ↱ ⌊οὐ μὴ⌋ γεύσηται
you say, 'If anyone keeps *{the}* my word, *my* *keeps* he will never taste
5148 3306 1569 5516 5498 3836 1609 3364 1609 5498 1174 1174 4024 3590 1174
r.ns.2 v.pai.2s cj r.nsm d.asm n.asm r.gs.1 v.aas.3s pl pl v.ams.3s

θανάτου εἰς τὸν αἰῶνα. 53 → μὴ σὺ μείζων εἶ τοῦ πατρὸς
death.' *{for}* *{all}* *{time.}* Surely you are not *you* greater *are* than our father
2505 1650 3836 172 5148 1639 3590 5148 3489 1639 3836 7005 4252
n.gsm p.a d.asm n.asm pl r.ns.2 a.nsm.c v.pai.2s d.gsm n.gsm

ἡμῶν Ἀβραάμ, ↰ ↰ ὅστις ἀπέθανεν; καὶ οἱ προφῆται ἀπέθανον. τίνα
our Abraham, are you? He died as did the prophets. *did* Who are
7005 11 3590 3590 4015 633 2779 633 3836 4737 633 5515 4472
r.gp.1 n.gsm r.nsm v.aai.3s cj d.npm n.npm v.aai.3p r.asm

σεαυτὸν ποιεῖς; 54 ἀπεκρίθη Ἰησοῦς, ἐὰν ἐγὼ δοξάσω
you making yourself *are you making* out to be?" Jesus replied, *Jesus* "If I glorify
4472 4472 4932 4472 2652 646 2652 1569 1609 1519
r.asm.2 v.pai.2s v.api.3s n.nsm cj r.ns.1 v.aas.1s

ἐμαυτόν, ἡ δόξα μου οὐδέν ἐστιν· ἔστιν ὁ πατήρ μου
myself, *{the}* my glory *my* amounts to nothing. *amounts to* It is *{the}* my Father *my*
1831 3836 1609 1518 1609 1639 1639 4029 1639 1639 3836 1609 4252 1609
r.asm.1 d.nsf n.nsf r.gs.1 a.nsn v.pai.3s v.pai.3s d.nsm n.nsm r.gs.1

NASB

why do you not be-
lieve Me? 47 He who
is of God hears
the words of God;
for this reason you
do not hear *them,*
because you are
not of God."
48 The Jews an-
swered and said
to Him, "Do we
not say rightly
that You are a Sa-
maritan and have
a demon?" 49 Jesus
answered, "I do not
have a demon; but
I honor My Father,
and you dishonor
Me. 50 But I do not
seek My glory;
there is One who
seeks and judges.
51 Truly, truly, I say
to you, if anyone
keeps My word
he will never see
death." 52 The Jews
said to Him, "Now
we know that You
have a demon.
Abraham died, and
the prophets *also;*
and You say, 'If
anyone keeps My
word, he will never
taste of death.'
53 Surely You are
not greater than
our father Abra-
ham, who died?
The prophets died
too; whom do You
make Yourself out
to be?" 54 Jesus
answered, "If I
glorify Myself, My
glory is nothing; it
is My Father who

---

[a] [οὖν] UBS, omitted by NET.

NIV

whom you claim as your God, is the one who glorifies me. [55]Though you do not know him, I know him. If I said I did not, I would be a liar like you, but I do know him and obey his word. [56]Your father Abraham rejoiced at the thought of seeing my day; he saw it and was glad."

[57]"You are not yet fifty years old," they said to him, "and you have seen Abraham!"

[58]"Very truly I tell you," Jesus answered, "before Abraham was born, I am!" [59]At this, they picked up stones to stone him, but Jesus hid himself, slipping away from the temple grounds.

Jesus Heals a Man Born Blind

9 As he went along, he saw a man blind from birth. [2]His disciples asked him, "Rabbi, who sinned, this man or his parents, that he was born blind?"

[3]"Neither this man nor his parents sinned," said Jesus, "but this happened so that the works of God might be displayed in him. [4]As long as it is day, we must do the works of him who sent me. Night is coming,

ὁ δοξάζων με, ὃν ὑμεῖς λέγετε ὅτι θεὸς ἡμῶν ἐστιν, 55 καὶ ↱
who glorifies me, of whom you say, ~ 'He is our God.' *our* *He is* And you
3836 1519 1609 4005 7007 3306 4022 1639 1639 7005 2536 7005 1639 2779 1182
d.nsm pt.pa.nsm r.as.1 r.asm r.np.2 v.pai.2p cj n.nsm r.gp.1 v.pai.3s cj

↱ οὐκ ἐγνώκατε αὐτόν, ἐγὼ δὲ οἶδα αὐτόν. κἂν εἴπω ὅτι ↱ ↱
have not known him, but I *but* know him. If ⌊I were to say⌋ that I did
1182 4024 1182 899 1254 1609 1254 3857 899 2829 3306 4022 3857 3857
pl v.rai.2p r.asm.3 r.ns.1 cj v.rai.1s r.asm.3 crasis v.aas.1s cj

οὐκ οἶδα αὐτόν, ἔσομαι ὅμοιος ὑμῖν ψεύστης· ἀλλὰ οἶδα αὐτὸν καὶ
not know him, ⌊I would be⌋ like you, a liar; but I do know him, and I keep
4024 3857 899 1639 3927 7007 6026 247 3857 899 2779 5498 5498
pl v.rai.1s r.asm.3 v.fmi.1s a.nsm r.dp.2 n.nsm cj v.rai.1s r.asm.3 cj

τὸν λόγον αὐτοῦ τηρῶ. 56 Ἀβραὰμ ὁ πατὴρ ὑμῶν ἠγαλλιάσατο ἵνα ἴδῃ
{the} his word. *his* *I keep* Abraham *{the}* your father *your* rejoiced to see
3836 899 3364 899 5498 11 3836 7007 4252 7007 22 2671 1625
d.asm n.asm r.gsm.3 v.pai.1s n.nsm d.nsm n.nsm r.gp.2 v.ami.3s cj v.aas.3s

τὴν ἡμέραν τὴν ἐμήν, καὶ εἶδεν καὶ ἐχάρη. 57 εἶπον οὖν οἱ
{the} my day; *{the}* *my* *{and}* he saw it and was glad. So the Jews said *So* *the*
3836 1847 2465 3836 1847 2779 1625 2779 5897 4036 3836 2681 3306 4036 3836
d.asf n.asf d.asf r.asf.1 cj v.aai.3s cj v.api.3s v.aai.3p cj d.npm

Ἰουδαῖοι πρὸς αὐτόν, πεντήκοντα ἔτη οὔπω ἔχεις καὶ
Jews to him, "You are not yet fifty ⌊years old,⌋ *not yet* *You are* and you
2681 4639 899 2400 2400 4037 4037 4299 2291 4037 2400 2779 3972
a.npm p.a r.asm.3 a.apn n.apn adv v.pai.2s cj

Ἀβραὰμ ἑώρακας; 58 εἶπεν αὐτοῖς Ἰησοῦς, ἀμὴν
have seen Abraham?" *you have seen* Jesus said to them, *Jesus* "I tell you the solemn
3972 3972 11 3972 2652 3306 899 2652 3306 3306 7007 297
n.asm v.rai.2s v.aai.3s r.dpm.3 n.nsm pl

ἀμὴν λέγω ὑμῖν, πρὶν Ἀβραὰμ γενέσθαι ἐγὼ εἰμί. 59 ἦραν οὖν
truth, *I tell* *you* before Abraham came to be, I am!" Then ⌊they picked up⌋ *Then*
297 3306 7007 4570 11 1181 1609 1639 4036 149 4036
pl v.pai.1s r.dp.2 cj n.asm f.am r.ns.1 v.pai.1s v.aai.3p cj

λίθους ἵνα βάλωσιν ἐπ' αὐτόν. Ἰησοῦς δὲ ἐκρύβη καὶ ἐξῆλθεν ἐκ τοῦ
stones to throw at him; but Jesus *but* hid himself and went out of the
3345 2671 965 2093 899 1254 2652 1254 3221 2779 2002 1666 3836
n.apm cj v.aas.3p p.a r.asm.3 n.nsm cj v.api.3s cj v.aai.3s p.g d.gsn

ἱεροῦ.[a]
temple.
2639
n.gsn

9:1 καὶ παράγων εἶδεν ἄνθρωπον τυφλὸν ἐκ γενετῆς. 2 καὶ
{and} ⌊As he went on his way,⌋ Jesus saw a man blind from birth. And
2779 4135 1625 476 5603 1666 1162 2779
cj pt.pa.nsm v.aai.3s n.asm a.asm p.g n.gsf cj

ἠρώτησαν αὐτὸν οἱ μαθηταὶ αὐτοῦ λέγοντες, ῥαββί, τίς ἥμαρτεν,
his disciples questioned him, *{the}* *disciples* *his* saying, "Rabbi, who sinned,
899 3412 2263 899 3836 3412 899 3306 4806 5515 279
v.aai.3p r.asm.3 d.npm n.npm r.gsm.3 pt.pa.npm n.vsm r.nsm v.aai.3s

οὗτος ἢ οἱ γονεῖς αὐτοῦ, ἵνα τυφλὸς γεννηθῇ; 3 ἀπεκρίθη
this man or *{the}* his parents, *his* that he was born blind?" *he was born* Jesus answered,
4047 2445 3836 899 1204 899 2671 1164 1164 1164 5603 1164 2652 646
r.nsm cj d.npm n.npm r.gsm.3 cj a.nsm v.aps.3s v.api.3s

Ἰησοῦς, οὔτε οὗτος ἥμαρτεν οὔτε οἱ γονεῖς αὐτοῦ, ἀλλ'
Jesus "It is not that this man sinned, or *{the}* his parents; *his* but it happened
2652 4046 4047 279 4046 3836 899 1204 899 247
n.nsm cj r.nsm v.aai.3s cj d.npm n.npm r.gsm.3 cj

ἵνα φανερωθῇ τὰ ἔργα τοῦ θεοῦ ἐν αὐτῷ. 4 ἡμᾶς δεῖ
so that the works of God might be displayed *the* *works* *of* *God* in him. We must
2671 3836 2240 3836 2536 5746 3836 2240 3836 2536 1877 899 7005 1256
cj v.aps.3s d.npn n.npn d.gsm n.gsm p.d r.dsm.3 r.ap.1 v.pai.3s

ἐργάζεσθαι τὰ ἔργα τοῦ πέμψαντός με ἕως ἡμέρα ἐστίν· ἔρχεται
do the works of him who sent me while it is day; *it is* night is coming
2237 3836 2240 3836 4287 1609 2401 1639 1639 2465 1639 3816 2262
f.pm d.apn n.apn d.gsm pt.aa.gsm r.as.1 cj n.nsf v.pai.3s v.pmi.3s

NASB

glorifies Me, of whom you say, 'He is our God'; [55]and you have not come to know Him, but I know Him; and if I say that I do not know Him, I will be a liar like you, but I do know Him and keep His word. [56]Your father Abraham rejoiced to see My day, and he saw *it* and was glad." [57]So the Jews said to Him, "You are not yet fifty years old, and have You seen Abraham?" [58]Jesus said to them, "Truly, truly, I say to you, before Abraham was born, I am." [59]Therefore they picked up stones to throw at Him, but Jesus hid Himself and went out of the temple.

Healing the Man Born Blind

[9:1]As He passed by, He saw a man blind from birth. [2]And His disciples asked Him, "Rabbi, who sinned, this man or his parents, that he would be born blind?" [3]Jesus answered, "*It was* neither *that* this man sinned, nor his parents; but *it was* so that the works of God might be displayed in him. [4]We must work the works of Him who sent Me as long as it is day; night is

[a] διελθὼν διὰ μέσου αὐτῶν· καὶ παρῆγεν οὕτως included by TR after ἱεροῦ.

NIV

when no one can work. 5While I am in the world, I am the light of the world."
6After saying this, he spit on the ground, made some mud with the saliva, and put it on the man's eyes. 7"Go," he told him, "wash in the Pool of Siloam" (this word means "Sent"). So the man went and washed, and came home seeing.
8His neighbors and those who had formerly seen him begging asked, "Isn't this the same man who used to sit and beg?"
9Some claimed that he was.
Others said, "No, he only looks like him."
But he himself insisted, "I am the man."
10"How then were your eyes opened?" they asked.
11He replied, "The man they call Jesus made some mud and put it on my eyes. He told me to go to Siloam and wash. So I went and washed, and then I could see."
12"Where is this man?" they asked him.
"I don't know," he said.

The Pharisees Investigate the Healing

13They brought to the Pharisees the man who had been blind. 14Now the day on which Jesus had made the mud

---

νὺξ ὅτε οὐδεὶς δύναται ἐργάζεσθαι. 5ὅταν ἐν τῷ κόσμῳ ὦ,
night when no one can work. ⌊As long as⌋ I am in the world, *I am* I
3816 4021 4029 1538 2237 4020 1639 1639 1877 3836 3180 1639 1639
n.nsf cj a.nsm v.ppi.3s f.pm cj p.d d.dsm n.dsm v.pas.1s

φῶς εἰμι τοῦ κόσμου. 6 ταῦτα εἰπὼν ἔπτυσεν χαμαὶ
am the light *I am* of the world." After saying this, *After saying* he spat ⌊on the ground⌋
1639 5890 1639 3836 3180 3306 3306 4047 3306 4772 5912
n.nsn v.pai.1s d.gsm n.gsm r.apn pt.aa.nsm v.aai.3s adv

καὶ ἐποίησεν πηλὸν ἐκ τοῦ πτύσματος καὶ ἐπέχρισεν αὐτοῦ τὸν
and made mud with his saliva; then he daubed the mud on the man's *the*
2779 4472 4384 1666 3836 4770 2779 2222 3836 4384 2093 3836 899 3836
cj v.aai.3s n.asm p.g d.gsn n.gsn cj v.aai.3s r.gsm.3 d.asm

πηλὸν ἐπὶ τοὺς ὀφθαλμοὺς 7καὶ εἶπεν αὐτῷ, ὕπαγε νίψαι εἰς τὴν κολυμβήθραν
mud *on* *the* eyes and said to him, "Go, wash in the pool
4384 2093 3836 4057 2779 3306 899 5632 3782 1650 3836 3148
n.asm p.a d.apm n.apm cj v.aai.3s r.dsm.3 v.pam.2s v.amm.2s p.a d.asf n.asf

τοῦ Σιλωάμ (ὃ ἑρμηνεύεται ἀπεσταλμένος). ἀπῆλθεν οὖν καὶ ἐνίψατο καὶ
of Siloam" (which means "Sent"). So he went away *So* and washed, and
3836 4978 4005 2257 690 4036 599 4036 2779 3782 2779
d.gsm n.gsm r.nsn v.ppi.3s pt.rp.nsm v.aai.3s cj cj v.ami.3s cj

ἦλθεν βλέπων. 8 οἱ οὖν γείτονες καὶ οἱ θεωροῦντες αὐτὸν
came back able to see. Then the *Then* neighbors and those ⌊who were used to seeing⌋ him
2262 1063 4036 3836 4036 1150 2779 3836 2555 899
v.aai.3s pt.pa.nsm d.npm cj n.npm cj d.npm pt.pa.npm r.asm.3

τὸ πρότερον ὅτι προσαίτης ἦν ἔλεγον, οὐχ οὗτός ἐστιν ὁ
{the} previously as a beggar *{he was}* said, "Is not this *Is* the
3836 4728 4022 4645 1639 3306 1639 4024 4047 1639 3836
d.asn adv.c cj n.nsm v.iai.3s v.iai.3p pl r.nsm v.pai.3s d.nsm

καθήμενος καὶ προσαιτῶν; 9ἄλλοι ἔλεγον ὅτι οὗτός ἐστιν, ἄλλοι
⌊man who used to sit⌋ and beg?" Some said, ~ "He is the one." *He is* Others
2764 2779 4644 257 3306 4022 1639 1639 4047 1639 257
pt.pm.nsm cj pt.pa.nsm r.npm v.iai.3p cj r.nsm v.pai.3s r.npm

ἔλεγον, οὐχί, ἀλλὰ ὅμοιος αὐτῷ ἐστιν. ↱ ἐκεῖνος ἔλεγεν ὅτι ἐγώ
said, "No, but he looks like him." *he looks* But he himself kept saying, ~ "I
3306 4049 247 1639 1639 3927 899 1639 3306 1697 3306 4022 1609
v.iai.3p pl cj a.nsm r.dsm.3 v.pai.3s r.nsm v.iai.3s cj r.ns.1

εἰμι. 10 ἔλεγον οὖν αὐτῷ, πῶς οὖν[a] → ἠνεῴχθησάν σου
am the man." So they asked *So* him, "How then were your eyes opened?" *your*
1639 4036 3306 4036 899 4802 4036 5148 4057 487 5148
v.pai.1s v.iai.3p cj r.dsm.3 cj cj v.api.3p r.gs.2

οἱ ὀφθαλμοί; 11 ἀπεκρίθη ἐκεῖνος, ὁ ἄνθρωπος ὁ λεγόμενος Ἰησοῦς
{the} *eyes* He answered, *He* "The man *{the}* called Jesus made
3836 4057 1697 646 1697 3836 476 3836 3306 2652 4472
d.npm n.npm v.api.3s r.nsm d.nsm n.nsm d.nsm pt.pp.nsm n.nsm

πηλὸν ἐποίησεν καὶ ἐπέχρισέν ← μου τοὺς ὀφθαλμοὺς καὶ εἶπέν μοι ὅτι ὕπαγε
mud, *made* *{and}* daubed it on my *{the}* eyes, and said to me, ~ 'Go
4384 4472 2779 2222 1609 3836 4057 2779 3306 1609 4022 5632
n.asm v.aai.3s cj v.aai.3s r.gs.1 d.apm n.apm cj v.aai.3s r.ds.1 cj v.pam.2s

εἰς τὸν Σιλωὰμ καὶ νίψαι· ἀπελθὼν οὖν καὶ νιψάμενος
to *{the}* Siloam and wash.' So I went there *So* and washed, and
1650 3836 4978 2779 3782 4036 599 4036 2779 3782
p.a d.asm n.asm cj v.amm.2s pt.aa.nsm cj cj pt.am.nsm

ἀνέβλεψα. 12καὶ εἶπαν αὐτῷ, ποῦ ἐστιν ἐκεῖνος; λέγει, ↱ ↱ οὐκ
⌊I was able to see."⌋ *{and}* They said to him, "Where is that man?" He replied, "I do not
329 2779 3306 899 4543 1639 1697 3306 3857 3857 4024
v.aai.1s cj v.aai.3p r.dsm.3 cj v.pai.3s r.nsm v.pai.3s pl

οἶδα. 13 ἄγουσιν αὐτὸν πρὸς τοὺς Φαρισαίους τόν ποτε
know." They brought to the Pharisees the man *to* *the* *Pharisees* who had been
3857 72 4639 3836 5757 899 4639 3836 5757 3836 4537
v.rai.1s v.pai.3p r.asm.3 p.a d.apm n.apm d.asm adv

τυφλόν. 14 ἦν δὲ σάββατον ⌊ἐν ᾗ⌋ ἡμέρᾳ τὸν πηλὸν
blind. Now it was *Now* a Sabbath day when *day* Jesus made the mud
5603 1254 1639 1254 4879 2465 1877 4005 2465 2652 4472 3836 4384
a.asm v.iai.3s cj n.nsn p.d r.dsf n.dsf d.asm n.asm

[a] [οὖν] UBS.

NASB

coming when no one can work.
5While I am in the world, I am the Light of the world." 6When He had said this, He spat on the ground, and made clay of the spittle, and applied the clay to his eyes, 7and said to him, "Go, wash in the pool of Siloam" (which is translated, Sent). So he went away and washed, and came *back* seeing.
8Therefore the neighbors, and those who previously saw him as a beggar, were saying, "Is not this the one who used to sit and beg?" 9Others were saying, "This is he," *still* others were saying, "No, but he is like him." He kept saying, "I am the one." 10So they were saying to him, "How then were your eyes opened?" 11He answered, "The man who is called Jesus made clay, and anointed my eyes, and said to me, 'Go to Siloam and wash'; so I went away and washed, and I received sight." 12They said to him, "Where is He?" He *said, "I do not know."

Controversy over the Man

13They *brought to the Pharisees the man who was formerly blind. 14Now it was a Sabbath on the day when Jesus made the clay

NIV

and opened the
man's eyes was a
Sabbath. [15]There-
fore the Pharisees
also asked him how
he had received his
sight. "He put mud
on my eyes," the
man replied, "and
I washed, and now
I see."
[16]Some of the
Pharisees said,
"This man is not
from God, for he
does not keep the
Sabbath."
But others asked,
"How can a sin-
ner perform such
signs?" So they
were divided.
[17]Then they
turned again to
the blind man,
"What have you to
say about him? It
was your eyes he
opened."
The man replied,
"He is a prophet."
[18]They still did
not believe that
he had been blind
and had received
his sight until they
sent for the man's
parents. [19]"Is this
your son?" they
asked. "Is this the
one you say was
born blind? How is
it that now he can
see?"
[20]"We know he
is our son," the
parents answered,
"and we know he
was born blind.
[21]But how he can
see now,

ἐποίησεν ὁ Ἰησοῦς καὶ ἀνέῳξεν αὐτοῦ τοὺς ὀφθαλμούς. [15] πάλιν οὖν
made *{the}* *Jesus* and opened his *{the}* eyes. *{again}* Then the Pharisees
4472 3836 2652 2779 487 899 3836 4057 4099 4036 3836 5757
v.aai.3s d.nsm n.nsm cj v.aai.3s r.gsm.3 d.apm n.apm adv cj

ἠρώτων αὐτὸν καὶ οἱ Φαρισαῖοι πῶς ἀνέβλεψεν. ὁ δὲ εἶπεν
also asked him *also* *the* *Pharisees* how ⌊he had received his sight.⌋ And he *And* said
2779 2263 899 2779 3836 5757 4802 329 1254 3836 1254 3306
v.iai.3p r.asm.3 adv d.npm n.npm cj v.aai.3s d.nsm cj v.aai.3s

αὐτοῖς, πηλὸν ἐπέθηκέν μου ἐπὶ τοὺς ὀφθαλμοὺς καὶ ἐνιψάμην καὶ
to them, "He daubed mud *He daubed* on my *on* *{the}* eyes, and I washed, and
899 2202 2202 4384 2202 2093 1609 2093 3836 4057 2779 3782 2779
r.dpm.3 n.asm v.aai.3s r.gs.1 p.a d.apm n.apm cj v.ami.1s cj

βλέπω. [16] ἔλεγον οὖν ἐκ τῶν Φαρισαίων τινές,
now I see." Then some of the Pharisees said, *Then* *of* *the* *Pharisees* *some* "This
1063 4036 5516 1666 3836 5757 3306 4036 1666 3836 5757 5516 4047
v.pai.1s v.iai.3p cj p.g d.gpm n.gpm r.npm

οὐκ ἔστιν οὗτος παρὰ θεοῦ ὁ ἄνθρωπος, ὅτι τὸ
man is not *is* *This* from God *{the}* *man* because he does not keep the
476 1639 4024 1639 4047 4123 2536 3836 476 4022 5498 5498 4024 5498 3836
pl v.pai.3s r.nsm p.g n.gsm d.nsm n.nsm cj d.asn

σάββατον οὐ τηρεῖ. ἄλλοι δὲ[a] ἔλεγον, πῶς δύναται ἄνθρωπος
Sabbath." *not* *he does keep* But others *But* said, "How can a sinful man
4879 4024 5498 1254 257 1254 3306 4802 1538 283 476
n.asn pl v.pai.3s r.npm cj v.iai.3p cj v.ppi.3s n.nsm

ἁμαρτωλὸς τοιαῦτα σημεῖα ποιεῖν; καὶ σχίσμα
sinful perform miraculous signs like this?" *miraculous signs* *perform* And there was a division
283 4472 4956 4956 5525 4956 4472 2779 1639 1639 5388
a.nsm r.apn n.apn f.pa cj n.nsn

ἦν ἐν αὐτοῖς. [17] λέγουσιν οὖν τῷ τυφλῷ πάλιν, τί ↱ σὺ
there was among them. So they spoke *So* again ⌊to the⌋ blind man, *again* "What do you
1639 1877 899 4036 3306 4036 4099 3836 5603 4099 5515 3306 5148
v.iai.3s p.d r.dpm.3 v.pai.3p cj d.dsm a.dsm adv r.asn r.ns.2

λέγεις περὶ αὐτοῦ, ὅτι ἠνέῳξέν σου τοὺς ὀφθαλμούς; ὁ
say about him, since it was your eyes that he opened?" *your* *{the}* *eyes* The man
3306 4309 899 4022 5148 4057 487 5148 3836 4057 3836
v.pai.2s p.g r.gsm.3 cj v.aai.3s r.gs.2 d.apm n.apm d.nsm

δὲ εἶπεν ὅτι προφήτης ἐστίν. [18] ↱ οὐκ ἐπίστευσαν οὖν
{and} replied, ~ "He is a prophet." *He is* The Jews did not believe *{then}*
1254 3306 4022 1639 1639 4737 1639 3836 2681 4409 4024 4409 4036
cj v.aai.3s cj n.nsm v.pai.3s pl v.aai.3p cj

οἱ Ἰουδαῖοι περὶ αὐτοῦ ὅτι ἦν τυφλὸς καὶ ἀνέβλεψεν
The *Jews* the report about him, that ⌊he had been⌋ blind and ⌊had received his sight,⌋
3836 2681 4309 899 4022 1639 5603 2779 329
d.npm a.npm p.g r.gsm.3 cj v.iai.3s a.nsm cj v.aai.3s

⌊ἕως ὅτου⌋ ἐφώνησαν τοὺς γονεῖς → αὐτοῦ τοῦ ἀναβλέψαντος [19] καὶ
until they called the parents of the man who ⌊had received his sight⌋ and
2401 4015 5888 3836 1204 899 3836 329 2779
p.g r.gsn v.aai.3p d.apm n.apm r.gsm.3 d.gsm pt.aa.gsm cj

ἠρώτησαν αὐτοὺς λέγοντες, οὗτός ἐστιν ὁ υἱὸς ὑμῶν, ὃν ὑμεῖς λέγετε
asked them, saying, "Is this *Is* *{the}* your son, *your* who you say
2263 899 3306 1639 4047 1639 3836 7007 5626 7007 4005 7007 3306
v.aai.3p r.apm.3 pt.pa.npm r.nsm v.pai.3s d.nsm n.nsm r.gp.2 r.asm r.np.2 v.pai.2p

ὅτι τυφλὸς ἐγεννήθη; πῶς οὖν → → βλέπει ἄρτι; [20]
~ was born blind? *was born* How then does he now see?" *now* His parents
4022 1164 1164 5603 1164 4802 4036 785 1063 785 899 1204
cj a.nsm v.api.3s cj cj v.pai.3s adv

ἀπεκρίθησαν οὖν οἱ γονεῖς αὐτοῦ καὶ εἶπαν, οἴδαμεν ὅτι οὗτός ἐστιν ὁ
answered, *{then}* *{the}* *parents* *His* *{and}* saying, "We know that this is *{the}* our
646 4036 3836 1204 899 2779 3306 3857 4022 4047 1639 3836 7005
v.api.3p cj d.npm n.npm r.gsm.3 cj v.aai.3p v.rai.1p cj r.nsm v.pai.3s d.nsm

υἱὸς ἡμῶν καὶ ὅτι τυφλὸς ἐγεννήθη· [21] πῶς δὲ ↱ νῦν
son *our* and that he was born blind; *he was born* but how *but* it is that he now
5626 7005 2779 4022 1164 1164 1164 5603 1164 1254 4802 1254 1063 3814
n.nsm r.gp.1 cj cj a.nsm v.api.3s cj cj adv

[a] [δὲ] UBS.

NASB

and opened his
eyes. [15]Then the
Pharisees also were
asking him again
how he received
his sight. And he
said to them, "He
applied clay to
my eyes, and I
washed, and I see."
[16]Therefore some of
the Pharisees were
saying, "This man
is not from God,
because He does
not keep the Sab-
bath." But others
were saying, "How
can a man who is
a sinner perform
such signs?" And
there was a divi-
sion among them.
[17]So they *said
to the blind man
again, "What do
you say about Him,
since He opened
your eyes?" And
he said, "He is a
prophet."
[18]The Jews then
did not believe *it*
of him, that he had
been blind and
had received sight,
until they called
the parents of the
very one who had
received his sight,
[19]and questioned
them, saying, "Is
this your son, who
you say was born
blind? Then how
does he now see?"
[20]His parents an-
swered them and
said, "We know
that this is our son,
and that he was
born blind; [21]but
how he now sees,

NIV

or who opened
his eyes, we don't
know. Ask him. He
is of age; he will
speak for himself."
22 His parents said
this because they
were afraid of the
Jewish leaders,
who already had
decided that any-
one who acknowl-
edged that Jesus
was the Messiah
would be put out
of the synagogue.
23 That was why his
parents said, "He is
of age; ask him."
24 A second time
they summoned
the man who had
been blind. "Give
glory to God by
telling the truth,"
they said. "We
know this man is a
sinner."
25 He replied,
"Whether he is
a sinner or not, I
don't know. One
thing I do know. I
was blind but now
I see!"
26 Then they asked
him, "What did he
do to you? How
did he open your
eyes?"
27 He answered, "I
have told you al-
ready and you did
not listen. Why do
you want to hear
it again? Do you
want to become
his disciples too?"
28 Then they
hurled insults at
him and said, "You
are this fellow's
disciple!

βλέπει ↱ ↱ οὐκ οἴδαμεν, ἢ τίς ἤνοιξεν αὐτοῦ τοὺς ὀφθαλμοὺς
sees we do not know, nor do we know who opened his {the} eyes.
1063 3857 3857 4024 3857 2445 3857 7005 3857 5515 487 899 3836 4057
v.pai.3s pl v.rai.1p cj r.nsm v.aai.3s r.gsm.3 d.apm n.apm

ἡμεῖς οὐκ οἴδαμεν· αὐτὸν ἐρωτήσατε, ἡλικίαν ἔχει, αὐτὸς
we {not} do know Ask him, Ask he is an adult. he is He will speak
7005 4024 3857 2263 899 2263 2400 2400 2461 2400 899 3281 3281
r.np.1 pl v.rai.1p r.asm.3 v.aam.2p n.asf v.pai.3s r.nsm

περὶ ἑαυτοῦ λαλήσει. 22 ταῦτα εἶπαν οἱ γονεῖς αὐτοῦ ὅτι
for himself." will speak His parents said this said {the} parents His because
4309 1571 3281 899 1204 3306 4047 3306 3836 1204 899 4022
p.g r.gsm.3 v.fai.3s r.apn v.aai.3p d.npm n.npm r.gsm.3 cj

ἐφοβοῦντο τοὺς Ἰουδαίους· ↱ ἤδη γὰρ συνετέθειντο οἱ
⌊they were afraid of⌋ the Jews; for the Jews had already for agreed the
5828 3836 2681 1142 3836 2681 5338 2453 1142 5338 3836
v.ipi.3p d.apm a.apm adv cj v.lmi.3p d.npm

Ἰουδαῖοι ἵνα ἐάν τις αὐτὸν ὁμολογήσῃ χριστόν,
Jews that if anyone should confess Jesus should confess to be the Christ, he was to
2681 2671 1569 5516 3933 3933 899 3933 5986 1181 1181 1181
a.npm cj cj r.nsm r.asm.3 v.aas.3s n.asm

ἀποσυνάγωγος γένηται. 23 διὰ τοῦτο οἱ γονεῖς αὐτοῦ εἶπαν ὅτι
be put out of the synagogue. he was to be For this reason {the} his parents his said, ~
1181 697 1181 1328 4047 3836 899 1204 899 3306 4022
a.nsm v.ams.3s p.a r.asn d.npm n.npm r.gsm.3 v.aai.3p cj

ἡλικίαν ἔχει, αὐτὸν ἐπερωτήσατε. 24
"He is an adult, He is ask him." ask So for the second time
2400 2400 2461 2400 2089 899 2089 4036 1666 1311 1311
n.asf v.pai.3s r.asm.3 v.aam.2p

ἐφώνησαν οὖν τὸν ἄνθρωπον ἐκ δευτέρου ὃς ἦν τυφλὸς καὶ εἶπαν αὐτῷ,
they called So the man for second time who ⌊had been⌋ blind and said to him,
5888 4036 3836 476 1666 1311 4005 1639 5603 2779 3306 899
v.aai.3p cj d.asm n.asm p.g a.gsn r.nsm v.iai.3s a.nsm cj v.aai.3p r.dsm.3

δὸς δόξαν τῷ θεῷ· ἡμεῖς οἴδαμεν ὅτι οὗτος ὁ ἄνθρωπος ἁμαρτωλός
"Give the glory to God! We know that this {the} man is a sinner."
1443 1518 3836 2536 7005 3857 4022 4047 3836 476 1639 283
v.aam.2s n.asf d.dsm n.dsm r.np.1 v.rai.1p cj r.nsm d.nsm n.nsm a.nsm

ἐστιν. 25 ἀπεκρίθη οὖν ἐκεῖνος, εἰ ἁμαρτωλός ἐστιν ↱
is He replied, {then} He "Whether or not he is a sinner, he is I
1639 1697 646 4036 1697 1623 1639 1639 283 1639 3857
v.pai.3s v.api.3s cj r.nsm cj a.nsm v.pai.3s

↱ οὐκ οἶδα· ἓν οἶδα ὅτι τυφλὸς
do not know. ⌊One thing⌋ I do know: ~ whereas I used to be blind,
3857 4024 3857 1651 3857 4022 1639 1639 1639 1639 1639 5603
pl v.rai.1s a.asn v.rai.1s cj a.nsm

ὢν ↱ ἄρτι βλέπω. 26 εἶπον οὖν αὐτῷ, τί ἐποίησέν
whereas I used to be I now see." Therefore they said Therefore to him, "What did he do
1639 1063 785 1063 4036 3306 4036 899 5515 4472
pt.pa.nsm adv v.pai.1s v.aai.3p cj r.dsm.3 r.asn v.aai.3s

σοι; πῶς ἤνοιξέν σου τοὺς ὀφθαλμούς; 27 ἀπεκρίθη αὐτοῖς, εἶπον ὑμῖν ἤδη
to you? How did he open your {the} eyes?" He answered them, "I told you already
5148 4802 487 5148 3836 4057 646 899 3306 7007 2453
r.ds.2 cj v.aai.3s r.gs.2 d.apm n.apm v.api.3s r.dpm.3 v.aai.1s r.dp.2 adv

καὶ ↱ ↱ οὐκ ἠκούσατε· τί πάλιν θέλετε ἀκούειν;
and you did not listen. Why do you want to hear it again? do you want to hear You
2779 201 201 4024 201 5515 2527 2527 2527 201 201 4099 2527 201 7007
cj pl v.aai.2p r.asn adv v.pai.2p f.pa

μὴ καὶ ὑμεῖς θέλετε αὐτοῦ μαθηταὶ γενέσθαι; ↰
do not want to become his disciples too, You do want his disciples to become do
2527 3590 2527 1181 1181 899 3412 2779 7007 2527 899 3412 1181 3590
pl adv r.np.2 v.pai.2p r.gsm.3 n.npm f.am

↰ 28 καὶ ἐλοιδόρησαν αὐτὸν καὶ εἶπον, σὺ μαθητὴς εἶ ἐκείνου,
you?" Then they scoffed at him, {and} saying, "You are a disciple are of that man! But
3590 2779 3366 899 2779 3306 5148 1639 3412 1639 1697 1254
cj v.aai.3p r.asm.3 cj v.aai.3p r.ns.2 n.nsm v.pai.2s r.gsm

NASB

we do not know;
or who opened his
eyes, we do not
know. Ask him; he
is of age, he will
speak for himself."
22 His parents said
this because they
were afraid of the
Jews; for the Jews
had already agreed
that if anyone
confessed Him to
be Christ, he was
to be put out of the
synagogue. 23 For
this reason his
parents said, "He is
of age; ask him."
24 So a second time
they called the
man who had been
blind, and said to
him, "Give glory to
God; we know that
this man is a sin-
ner." 25 He then an-
swered, "Whether
He is a sinner, I
do not know; one
thing I do know,
that though I was
blind, now I see."
26 So they said to
him, "What did
He do to you?
How did He open
your eyes?" 27 He
answered them, "I
told you already
and you did not
listen; why do you
want to hear *it*
again? You do not
want to become
His disciples too,
do you?" 28 They re-
viled him and said,
"You are His dis-
ciple, but we are

NIV

We are disciples of Moses! 29 We know that God spoke to Moses, but as for this fellow, we don't even know where he comes from."

30 The man answered, "Now that is remarkable! You don't know where he comes from, yet he opened my eyes. 31 We know that God does not listen to sinners. He listens to the godly person who does his will. 32 Nobody has ever heard of opening the eyes of a man born blind. 33 If this man were not from God, he could do nothing."

34 To this they replied, "You were steeped in sin at birth; how dare you lecture us!" And they threw him out.

Spiritual Blindness

35 Jesus heard that they had thrown him out, and when he found him, he said, "Do you believe in the Son of Man?"

36 "Who is he, sir?" the man asked. "Tell me so that I may believe in him."

37 Jesus said, "You have now seen him; in fact, he is the one speaking with you."

38 Then the man said, "Lord, I believe," and

ἡμεῖς δὲ τοῦ Μωϋσέως ἐσμὲν μαθηταί· 29 ἡμεῖς οἴδαμεν ὅτι
we *But* are disciples of Moses! *are* *disciples* We know that God has
7005 1254 1639 3412 3836 3707 1639 3412 7005 3857 4022 2536 3281
r.np.1 cj d.gsm n.gsm v.pai.1p n.npm r.np.1 v.rai.1p cj

Μωϋσεῖ λελάληκεν ὁ θεός, τοῦτον δὲ ↱ ↱ οὐκ
spoken to Moses, *has spoken* *{the}* *God* but as for this fellow, *but* we do not even
3281 3707 3281 3836 2536 1254 4047 1254 3857 3857 4024
n.dsm v.rai.3s d.nsm n.nsm r.asm cj pl

οἴδαμεν πόθεν ἐστίν. ↰ 30 ἀπεκρίθη ὁ ἄνθρωπος καὶ
know where he comes from." The man responded *The* *man* *{and}* to them,
3857 4470 1639 4470 3836 476 646 3836 476 2779 899 899
v.rai.1p cj v.pai.3s v.api.3s d.nsm n.nsm cj

εἶπεν αὐτοῖς, ἐν τούτῳ γὰρ τὸ θαυμαστόν ἐστιν, ὅτι ὑμεῖς ↱ οὐκ οἴδατε
saying, *to them* *{in}* "This *{for}* is an amazing thing, *is* that you do not know
3306 899 1877 4047 1142 1639 3836 2515 1639 4022 7007 3857 4024 3857
v.aai.3s r.dpm.3 p.d r.dsn cj d.nsn a.nsn v.pai.3s cj r.np.2 pl v.rai.2p

πόθεν ἐστίν, ↰ καὶ ἤνοιξέν μου τοὺς ὀφθαλμούς. 31 οἴδαμεν ὅτι
where he comes from, ⌞and yet⌟ he opened my *{the}* eyes! We know that God does
4470 1639 4470 2779 487 1609 3836 4057 3857 4022 2536 201
cj v.pai.3s cj v.aai.3s r.gs.1 d.apm n.apm v.rai.1p cj

ἁμαρτωλῶν ὁ θεὸς οὐκ ἀκούει, ἀλλ᾽ ἐάν τις θεοσεβὴς ᾖ
not listen to sinners, *{the}* *God* *not* *does listen* but if anyone is devout *is*
4024 201 283 3836 2536 4024 201 247 1569 5516 1639 2538 1639
a.gpm d.nsm n.nsm pl v.pai.3s cj cj r.nsm a.nsm v.pas.3s

καὶ τὸ θέλημα αὐτοῦ ποιῇ τούτου ἀκούει. 32 ἐκ τοῦ
and does *{the}* his will, *his* *does* God listens to him. *listens to* Not since *{the}*
2779 4472 3836 899 2525 899 4472 201 201 4047 201 4024 1666 3836
cj d.asn n.asn r.gsm.3 v.pas.3s r.gsm v.pai.3s p.g d.gsm

αἰῶνος οὐκ ἠκούσθη ὅτι ἠνέῳξέν τις ὀφθαλμοὺς → →
time began *Not* ⌞has it been heard⌟ that anyone opened *anyone* the eyes of a man born
172 4024 201 4022 5516 487 5516 4057 1164
n.gsm pl v.api.3s cj v.aai.3s r.nsm n.apm

τυφλοῦ γεγεννημένου· 33 εἰ μὴ ἦν οὗτος παρὰ θεοῦ, οὐκ ἠδύνατο
blind. *born* If this man were not *were* *this man* from God, *{not}* he could
5603 1164 1623 4047 4047 1639 3590 1639 4047 4123 2536 4024 1538
a.gsm pt.rp.gsm cj pl v.iai.3s r.nsm p.g n.gsm pl v.ipi.3s

ποιεῖν οὐδέν. 34 ἀπεκρίθησαν καὶ εἶπαν αὐτῷ, ἐν
do nothing." They replied *{and}* to him, saying, *to him* "You were born completely in
4472 4029 646 2779 899 899 3306 899 5148 1164 1164 3910 1877
f.pa a.asn v.api.3p cj v.aai.3p r.dsm.3 p.d

ἁμαρτίαις σὺ ἐγεννήθης ὅλος καὶ ↱ σὺ διδάσκεις ἡμᾶς; καὶ ἐξέβαλον αὐτὸν
sin, *You* *were born* *completely* and would you lecture us?" So they threw him
281 5148 1164 3910 2779 1438 5148 1438 7005 2779 1675 899
n.dpf r.ns.2 v.api.2s a.nsm cj r.ns.2 v.pai.2s r.ap.1 cj v.aai.3p r.asm.3

ἔξω. 35 ἤκουσεν Ἰησοῦς ὅτι ἐξέβαλον αὐτὸν ἔξω καὶ εὑρὼν αὐτὸν
out. Jesus heard *Jesus* that they had thrown him out, and ⌞when he found⌟ him,
2032 2652 201 2652 4022 1675 899 2032 2779 2351 899
adv v.aai.3s n.nsm cj v.aai.3p r.asm.3 adv cj pt.aa.nsm r.asm.3

εἶπεν, ↱ σὺ πιστεύεις εἰς τὸν υἱὸν τοῦ ἀνθρώπου; 36 ἀπεκρίθη ἐκεῖνος
he said, "Do you believe in the Son of Man?" The man replied, *man*
3306 4409 5148 4409 1650 3836 5626 3836 476 1697 646 1697
v.aai.3s r.ns.2 v.pai.2s p.a d.asm n.asm d.gsm n.gsm v.api.3s r.nsm

καὶ εἶπεν, καὶ τίς ἐστιν, κύριε, ἵνα πιστεύσω εἰς αὐτόν; 37 εἶπεν
{and} saying, "And who is he, sir? Tell me, so that I may believe in him." Jesus said
2779 3306 2779 5515 1639 3261 2671 4409 1650 899 2652 3306
cj v.aai.3s cj r.nsm v.pai.3s n.vsm cj v.aas.1s p.a r.asm.3 v.aai.3s

αὐτῷ ὁ Ἰησοῦς, καὶ ἑώρακας αὐτὸν καὶ ὁ λαλῶν μετὰ
to him, *{the}* *Jesus* *{and}* ⌞"You have seen⌟ him; in fact, he is the one speaking with
899 3836 2652 2779 3972 899 2779 1697 1639 3836 3281 3552
r.dsm.3 d.nsm n.nsm cj v.rai.2s r.asm.3 cj d.nsm pt.pa.nsm p.g

σοῦ ἐκεῖνός ἐστιν. 38 ὁ δὲ ἔφη, πιστεύω, κύριε· καὶ
you." *he* *is* Then the *Then* man said, "I believe, Lord," and
5148 1697 1639 1254 3836 1254 5774 4409 3261 2779
r.gs.2 r.nsm v.pai.3s d.nsm cj v.iai.3s v.pai.1s n.vsm cj

NASB

disciples of Moses. 29 We know that God has spoken to Moses, but as for this man, we do not know where He is from." 30 The man answered and said to them, "Well, here is an amazing thing, that you do not know where He is from, and *yet* He opened my eyes. 31 We know that God does not hear sinners; but if anyone is God-fearing and does His will, He hears him. 32 Since the beginning of time it has never been heard that anyone opened the eyes of a person born blind. 33 If this man were not from God, He could do nothing." 34 They answered him, "You were born entirely in sins, and are you teaching us?" So they put him out.

Jesus Affirms His Deity

35 Jesus heard that they had put him out, and finding him, He said, "Do you believe in the Son of Man?" 36 He answered, "Who is He, Lord, that I may believe in Him?" 37 Jesus said to him, "You have both seen Him, and He is the one who is talking with you." 38 And he said, "Lord, I believe." And he

NIV

he worshiped him.
39 Jesus said,[a]
"For judgment I
have come into
this world, so that
the blind will see
and those who
see will become
blind."
40 Some Pharisees
who were with him
heard him say this
and asked, "What?
Are we blind too?"
41 Jesus said, "If
you were blind,
you would not be
guilty of sin; but
now that you claim
you can see, your
guilt remains.

The Good Shepherd and His Sheep

10 "Very truly
I tell you
Pharisees, anyone
who does not en-
ter the sheep pen
by the gate, but
climbs in by some
other way, is a
thief and a robber.
2 The one who en-
ters by the gate is
the shepherd of the
sheep. 3 The gate-
keeper opens the
gate for him, and
the sheep listen to
his voice. He calls
his own sheep by
name and leads
them out. 4 When
he has brought
out all his own,
he goes on ahead
of them, and his
sheep follow him
because they know

[a] 38,39 Some early manuscripts do not have *Then the man said . . . 39 Jesus said.*

προσεκύνησεν αὐτῷ. 39 καὶ εἶπεν ὁ Ἰησοῦς,[a] εἰς κρίμα ἐγὼ
⌊he bowed in reverence before⌋ him. *{and}* Jesus said, *{the}* *Jesus* "For judgment I
4686 899 2779 2652 3306 3836 2652 1650 3210 1609
v.aai.3s r.dsm.3 cj v.aai.3s d.nsm n.nsm p.a n.asn r.ns.1

εἰς τὸν κόσμον τοῦτον ἦλθον, ἵνα οἱ ➝ μὴ βλέποντες
came into *{the}* this world, *this* *came* so that those who cannot see
2262 1650 3836 4047 3180 4047 2262 2671 3836 1063 3590 1063
p.a d.asm n.asm r.asm v.aai.1s cj d.npm pl pt.pa.npm

βλέπωσιν καὶ ↰ οἱ βλέποντες τυφλοὶ γένωνται.
⌊may receive their sight,⌋ and that those ⌊who think they see⌋ may become blind." *may become*
1063 2779 2671 3836 1063 1181 1181 5603 1181
v.pas.3p cj d.npm pt.pa.npm a.npm v.ams.3p

40 ἤκουσαν ἐκ τῶν Φαρισαίων ταῦτα οἱ
Some of the Pharisees who were near him heard *of* *the* *Pharisees* this, *Some*
3836 1666 3836 5757 1639 1639 3552 899 201 1666 3836 5757 4047 3836
v.aai.3p p.g d.gpm n.gpm r.apn d.npm

μετ' αὐτοῦ ὄντες καὶ εἶπον αὐτῷ, ➝ μὴ καὶ ἡμεῖς ἐσμεν; τυφλοί
near *him* *who were* and said to him, "Surely we are not *too* *we* *are* blind too,
3552 899 1639 2779 3306 899 7005 1639 3590 2779 7005 1639 5603 2779
p.g r.gsm.3 pt.pa.npm cj v.aai.3p r.dsm.3 pl adv r.np.1 v.pai.1p a.npm

↰ ↰ 41 εἶπεν αὐτοῖς ὁ Ἰησοῦς, εἰ τυφλοὶ ἦτε, ➝
are we?" Jesus said to them, *{the}* *Jesus* "If you were blind, *you were* you would
3590 3590 2652 3306 899 3836 2652 1623 1639 1639 5603 1639 2400 323
v.aai.3s r.dpm.3 d.nsm n.nsm cj a.npm v.iai.2p

οὐκ ἂν εἴχετε ἁμαρτίαν· νῦν δὲ λέγετε ὅτι βλέπομεν, ἡ
not *would* ⌊be guilty of⌋ sin; but now *but* ⌊you are saying,⌋ ~ 'We can see,' so *{the}*
4024 323 2400 281 1254 3814 1254 3306 4022 1063 3836
pl pl v.iai.2p n.asf adv cj v.pai.2p cj v.pai.1p d.nsf

ἁμαρτία ὑμῶν μένει.
your guilt *your* remains.
7007 281 7007 3531
n.nsf r.gp.2 v.pai.3s

10:1 ἀμὴν ἀμὴν λέγω ὑμῖν, ὁ ➝ ➝ ➝ μὴ εἰσερχόμενος
"I tell you the solemn truth, *I tell* *you* the one who does not enter
3306 3306 7007 297 297 3306 7007 3836 1656 1656 1656 3590 1656
pl pl v.pai.1s r.dp.2 d.nsm pl pt.pm.nsm

διὰ τῆς θύρας εἰς τὴν ⌊αὐλὴν τῶν προβάτων⌋ ἀλλὰ ἀναβαίνων
the sheepfold through the gate, *{into}* *the* *sheepfold* but climbs in
3836 885 1328 3836 2598 1650 3836 885 3836 4585 247 326
p.g d.gsf n.gsf p.a d.asf n.asf d.gpn n.gpn cj pt.pa.nsm

ἀλλαχόθεν ἐκεῖνος κλέπτης ἐστὶν καὶ λῃστής· 2 ὁ δὲ
⌊by some other way,⌋ *{that one}* is a thief *is* and a robber. But the *But*
249 1697 1639 3095 1639 2779 3334 1254 3836 1254
adv r.nsm n.nsm v.pai.3s cj n.nsm d.nsm cj

εἰσερχόμενος διὰ τῆς θύρας ποιμήν ἐστιν τῶν προβάτων. 3
one who enters by the gate is the shepherd *is* of the sheep. The watchman
1656 1328 3836 2598 1639 4478 1639 3836 4585 3836 2601
pt.pm.nsm p.g d.gsf n.gsf n.nsm v.pai.3s d.gpn n.gpn

➝ τούτῳ ὁ θυρωρὸς ἀνοίγει καὶ τὰ πρόβατα τῆς φωνῆς
allows him *The* *watchman* to enter, and the sheep pay attention to *{the}* his voice;
487 4047 3836 2601 487 2779 3836 4585 201 201 201 3836 899 5889
r.dsm d.nsm n.nsm v.pai.3s cj d.npn n.npn d.gsf n.gsf

αὐτοῦ ἀκούει καὶ τὰ ἴδια πρόβατα φωνεῖ κατ' ὄνομα καὶ ἐξάγει
his *pay attention to* *{and}* he calls *{the}* his own sheep *he calls* by name and leads
899 201 2779 5888 5888 3836 2625 4585 5888 2848 3950 2779 1974
r.gsm.3 v.pai.3s cj d.apn a.apn n.apn v.pai.3s p.a n.asn cj v.pai.3s

αὐτά. ↰ 4 ὅταν τὰ ἴδια πάντα ἐκβάλῃ,
them out. When he has brought out all *{the}* his own, *all* *he has brought out* he walks
899 1974 4020 1675 1675 1675 1675 4246 3836 2625 4246 1675 4513 4513
r.apn.3 cj d.apn a.apn a.apn v.aas.3s

ἔμπροσθεν αὐτῶν πορεύεται καὶ τὰ πρόβατα αὐτῷ ἀκολουθεῖ, ὅτι οἴδασιν
on ahead of them, *he walks* and the sheep follow him *follow* because they know
1869 899 4513 2779 3836 4585 199 899 199 4022 3857
p.g r.gpn.3 v.pmi.3s cj d.npn n.npn r.dsm.3 v.pai.3s cj v.rai.3p

[a] ὁ δὲ ἔφη, πιστεύω, κύριε· και προσεκύνησεν αὐτῷ. 39 καὶ εἶπεν ὁ Ἰησοῦς omitted by NET, but left bracketed in the text.

NASB

worshiped Him.
39 And Jesus said,
"For judgment
I came into this
world, so that
those who do not
see may see, and
that those who
see may become
blind." 40 Those of
the Pharisees who
were with Him
heard these things
and said to Him,
"We are not blind
too, are we?" 41 Je-
sus said to them,
"If you were blind,
you would have no
sin; but since you
say, 'We see,' your
sin remains.

Parable of the Good Shepherd

10:1 "Truly, truly, I
say to you, he who
does not enter by
the door into the
fold of the sheep,
but climbs up some
other way, he is
a thief and a rob-
ber. 2 But he who
enters by the door
is a shepherd of the
sheep. 3 To him the
doorkeeper opens,
and the sheep hear
his voice, and he
calls his own sheep
by name and leads
them out. 4 When
he puts forth all his
own, he goes ahead
of them, and the
sheep follow him
because they know

NIV

his voice. 5But they
will never follow
a stranger; in fact,
they will run away
from him because
they do not recog-
nize a stranger's
voice." 6Jesus
used this figure
of speech, but the
Pharisees did not
understand what he
was telling them.
7Therefore Jesus
said again, "Very
truly I tell you, I
am the gate for the
sheep. 8All who
have come before
me are thieves
and robbers, but
the sheep have not
listened to them.
9I am the gate;
whoever enters
through me will be
saved.[a] They will
come in and go
out, and find pas-
ture. 10The thief
comes only to steal
and kill and de-
stroy; I have come
that they may have
life, and have it to
the full.
11"I am the good
shepherd. The
good shepherd lays
down his life for
the sheep. 12The
hired hand is not
the shepherd and
does not own the
sheep. So when he
sees the wolf com-
ing, he abandons
the sheep and runs
away. Then the
wolf attacks the
flock and scatters
it. 13The man runs
away because he
is a hired hand and
cares nothing

τὴν φωνὴν αὐτοῦ· 5 ἀλλοτρίῳ δὲ ⌞οὐ μὴ⌟
{the} his voice. *his* They will never follow a stranger, *{and}* *never*
3836 899 5889 899 199 199 4024 199 259 1254 4024 3590
d.asf n.asf r.gsm.3 n.dsm cj pl pl

ἀκολουθήσουσιν, ἀλλὰ φεύξονται ἀπ' αὐτοῦ, ὅτι ↱ ↱ οὐκ οἴδασιν
They will follow but will run away from him, because they do not know the voice
199 247 5771 608 899 4022 3857 3857 4024 3857 3836 5889
v.fai.3p cj v.fmi.3p p.g r.gsm.3 cj pl v.rai.3p

τῶν ἀλλοτρίων τὴν φωνήν. 6 ταύτην τὴν παροιμίαν εἶπεν αὐτοῖς
of strangers." *the* *voice* Jesus told them this *{the}* figurative story, *told* *them*
3836 259 3836 5889 2652 3306 899 4047 3836 4231 3306 899
d.gpm n.gpm d.asf n.asf r.asf d.asf n.asf v.aai.3s r.dpm.3

ὁ Ἰησοῦς, ἐκεῖνοι δὲ ↱ οὐκ ἔγνωσαν τίνα ἦν ἃ ἐλάλει αὐτοῖς.
{the} *Jesus* but they *but* did not understand what *{it was}* *{that}* ⌞he was saying⌟ to them.
3836 2652 1254 1697 1254 1182 4024 1182 5515 1639 4005 3281 899
d.nsm n.nsm r.npm cj pl v.aai.3p r.npn v.iai.3s r.apn v.iai.3s r.dpm.3

7 εἶπεν οὖν πάλιν ὁ Ἰησοῦς, ⌞ἀμὴν ἀμὴν⌟ λέγω
So Jesus said *So* once again, *{the}* *Jesus* "I tell you the solemn truth, *I tell*
4036 2652 3306 4036 4099 3836 2652 3306 3306 7007 297 297 3306
v.aai.3s cj adv d.nsm n.nsm pl pl v.pai.1s

ὑμῖν ὅτι ἐγώ εἰμι ἡ θύρα τῶν προβάτων. 8 πάντες ὅσοι ἦλθον [a]πρὸ ἐμοῦ
you ~ I am the gate for the sheep. All who came before me were
7007 4022 1609 1639 3836 2598 3836 4585 4246 4012 2262 4574 1609 1639
r.dp.2 cj r.ns.1 v.pai.1s d.nsf n.nsf d.gpn n.gpn a.npm r.npm v.aai.3p p.g r.gs.1

κλέπται εἰσὶν καὶ λῃσταί, ἀλλ' ↱ οὐκ ἤκουσαν αὐτῶν τὰ πρόβατα.
thieves *were* and robbers, but the sheep did not listen to them. *the* *sheep*
3095 1639 2779 3334 247 3836 4585 201 4024 201 899 3836 4585
n.npm v.pai.3p cj n.npm cj pl v.aai.3p r.gpm.3 d.npn n.npn

9 ἐγώ εἰμι ἡ θύρα· δι' ἐμοῦ ἐάν τις εἰσέλθῃ σωθήσεται
I am the gate. If anyone enters through me, *If* *anyone* *enters* he will be saved;
1609 1639 3836 2598 1569 5516 1656 1328 1609 1569 5516 1656 5392
r.ns.1 v.pai.1s d.nsf n.nsf p.g r.gs.1 cj r.nsm v.aas.3s v.fpi.3s

καὶ εἰσελεύσεται καὶ ἐξελεύσεται καὶ νομὴν εὑρήσει. 10 ὁ κλέπτης οὐκ
{and} he will come in and go out and find pasture. *find* The thief *{not}*
2779 1656 2779 2002 2779 2351 3786 2351 3836 3095 4024
cj v.fmi.3s cj v.fmi.3s cj n.asf v.fai.3s d.nsm n.nsm pl

ἔρχεται ⌞εἰ μὴ⌟ ἵνα κλέψῃ καὶ θύσῃ καὶ ἀπολέσῃ· ἐγὼ ἦλθον ἵνα
comes only to steal and slaughter and destroy; I have come that they may
2262 1623 3590 2671 3096 2779 2604 2779 660 1609 2262 2671 2400 2400
v.pmi.3s cj pl cj v.aas.3s cj v.aas.3s cj v.aas.3s r.ns.1 v.aai.1s cj

ζωὴν ἔχωσιν καὶ περισσὸν ἔχωσιν. 11 ἐγώ εἰμι ὁ ποιμὴν
have life, *they may have* and have it abundantly. *have* "I am the good shepherd;
2400 2437 2400 2779 2400 4356 2400 1609 1639 3836 2819 4478
n.asf v.pas.3p cj adv v.pas.3p r.ns.1 v.pai.1s d.nsm n.nsm

ὁ καλός. ὁ ποιμὴν ὁ καλὸς τὴν ψυχὴν αὐτοῦ τίθησιν
{the} *good* the good shepherd *{the}* *good* lays down *{the}* his life *his* *lays down*
3836 2819 3836 2819 4478 3836 2819 5502 5502 3836 899 6034 899 5502
d.nsm a.nsm d.nsm n.nsm d.nsm a.nsm d.asf n.asf r.gsm.3 v.pai.3s

ὑπὲρ τῶν προβάτων· 12 ὁ μισθωτὸς καὶ οὐκ ὢν ποιμήν, οὗ
for the sheep. The hired hand, since he is not *he is* a shepherd *{of whom}*
5642 3836 4585 3836 3638 2779 1639 1639 4024 1639 4478 4005
p.g d.gpn n.gpn d.nsm n.nsm cj pl pt.pa.nsm n.nsm r.gsm

↱ οὐκ ἔστιν τὰ πρόβατα ἴδια, θεωρεῖ τὸν λύκον ἐρχόμενον καὶ
and the sheep do not belong *the* *sheep* to him, sees a wolf coming and
3836 4585 1639 4024 1639 3836 4585 2625 2555 3836 3380 2262 2779
pl v.pai.3s d.npn n.npn a.npn v.pai.3s d.asm n.asm pt.pm.asm cj

ἀφίησιν τὰ πρόβατα καὶ φεύγει καὶ ὁ λύκος ἁρπάζει αὐτὰ καὶ σκορπίζει
abandons the sheep and runs away — and the wolf attacks the flock and scatters
918 3836 4585 2779 5771 2779 3836 3380 773 899 2779 5025
v.pai.3s d.apn n.apn cj v.pai.3s cj d.nsm n.nsm v.pai.3s r.apn.3 cj v.pai.3s

13 ὅτι μισθωτός ἐστιν καὶ ↱ οὐ μέλει
them. He does this because he is simply a hired hand *he is* and has no real concern
4022 1639 1639 3638 1639 2779 3508 4024 3508
cj n.nsm v.pai.3s cj pl v.pai.3s

NASB

his voice. 5A
stranger they sim-
ply will not follow,
but will flee from
him, because they
do not know the
voice of strang-
ers." 6This figure of
speech Jesus spoke
to them, but they
did not understand
what those things
were which He
had been saying to
them.
7So Jesus said to
them again, "Truly,
truly, I say to you,
I am the door of
the sheep. 8All who
came before Me
are thieves and
robbers, but the
sheep did not hear
them. 9I am the
door; if anyone en-
ters through Me, he
will be saved, and
will go in and out
and find pasture.
10The thief comes
only to steal and
kill and destroy; I
came that they may
have life, and have
it abundantly.
11"I am the good
shepherd; the good
shepherd lays
down His life for
the sheep. 12He who
is a hired hand,
and not a shepherd,
who is not the
owner of the sheep,
sees the wolf com-
ing, and leaves
the sheep and
flees, and the wolf
snatches them and
scatters *them*. 13*He*
flees because he is
a hired hand and is
not concerned

[a] 9 Or *kept safe*

[a] [πρὸ ἐμοῦ] UBS.

NIV

for the sheep.
14“I am the good
shepherd; I know
my sheep and my
sheep know me—
15just as the Father
knows me and I
know the Father—
and I lay down my
life for the sheep.
16I have other
sheep that are not
of this sheep pen.
I must bring them
also. They too
will listen to my
voice, and there
shall be one flock
and one shepherd.
17The reason my
Father loves me
is that I lay down
my life—only to
take it up again.
18No one takes
it from me, but I
lay it down of my
own accord. I have
authority to lay it
down and author-
ity to take it up
again. This com-
mand I received
from my Father.”
19The Jews who
heard these words
were again di-
vided. 20Many of
them said, “He is
demon-possessed
and raving mad.
Why listen to
him?”
21But others said,
“These are not the
sayings of a man
possessed by a de-
mon. Can a demon
open the eyes of
the blind?”

αὐτῷ περὶ τῶν προβάτων. 14 ἐγώ εἰμι ὁ ποιμὴν ὁ καλὸς καὶ γινώσκω
{to him} for the sheep. I am the good shepherd. {the} good {and} I know
899 4309 3836 4585 1609 1639 3836 2819 4478 3836 2819 2779 1182
r.dsm.3 p.g d.gpn n.gpn r.ns.1 v.pai.1s d.nsm n.nsm d.nsm a.nsm cj v.pai.1s

τὰ ἐμὰ καὶ γινώσκουσί με τὰ ἐμά, 15 καθὼς γινώσκει με
{the} ⌊my own⌋ and they know me, {the} they just as the Father knows me
3836 1847 2779 1847 1182 1609 3836 1847 2777 3836 4252 1182 1609
d.apn r.apn.1 cj v.pai.3p r.as.1 d.npn r.npn.1 cj v.pai.3s r.as.1

ὁ πατὴρ κἀγὼ γινώσκω τὸν πατέρα, καὶ τὴν ψυχήν μου
the Father and I know the Father; and I lay down {the} my life my
3836 4252 2743 1182 3836 4252 2779 5502 5502 5502 3836 1609 6034 1609
d.nsm n.nsm crasis v.pai.1s d.asm n.asm cj d.asf n.asf r.gs.1

τίθημι ὑπὲρ τῶν προβάτων. 16 καὶ ἄλλα πρόβατα ἔχω ἃ οὐκ
I lay down for my sheep. {and} I have other sheep I have which are not
5502 5642 3836 4585 2779 2400 2400 257 4585 2400 4005 1639 4024
v.pai.1s p.g d.gpn n.gpn cj r.apn n.apn v.pai.1s r.npn pl

ἔστιν ἐκ τῆς αὐλῆς ταύτης· κἀκεῖνα δεῖ με ἀγαγεῖν καὶ
are of {the} this fold. this These too I must I bring. {and} They will listen
1639 1666 3836 4047 885 4047 2797 1609 1256 1609 72 2779 201 201 201
v.pai.3s p.g d.gsf n.gsf r.gsf adv v.pai.3s r.as.1 f.aa cj

τῆς φωνῆς μου ἀκούσουσιν, καὶ γενήσονται μία ποίμνη, εἷς ποιμήν.
to {the} my voice, my They will listen to and there will be one flock, with one shepherd.
201 3836 1609 5889 1609 201 2779 1181 1651 4479 1651 4478
d.gsf n.gsf r.gs.1 v.fai.3p cj v.fmi.3p a.nsf n.nsf a.nsm n.nsm

17 ⌊διὰ τοῦτό⌋ με ὁ πατὴρ ἀγαπᾷ ὅτι ἐγὼ τίθημι τὴν
Therefore the Father loves me, the Father loves because I lay down {the} my
1328 4047 3836 4252 26 1609 3836 4252 26 4022 1609 5502 3836 1609
p.a r.asn r.as.1 d.nsm n.nsm v.pai.3s cj r.ns.1 v.pai.1s d.asf

ψυχήν μου, ἵνα πάλιν λάβω αὐτήν. 18 οὐδεὶς αἴρει
life my ⌊in order that⌋ I may take it back again. I may take it No one takes
6034 1609 2671 3284 3284 3284 899 4099 3284 899 4029 149
n.asf r.gs.1 cj adv v.aas.1s r.asf.3 a.nsm v.pai.3s

αὐτὴν ↰ ἀπ᾽ ἐμοῦ, ἀλλ᾽ ἐγὼ τίθημι αὐτὴν ↰ ἀπ᾽ ἐμαυτοῦ.
it away from me, but I lay it down of my own free will. I have the
899 149 608 1609 247 1609 5502 899 5502 608 1831 2400 2400
r.asf.3 p.g r.gs.1 cj r.ns.1 v.pai.1s r.asf.3 p.g r.gsm.1

ἐξουσίαν ἔχω θεῖναι αὐτήν, ↰ καὶ ἐξουσίαν ἔχω
power I have to lay it down, and I have the power I have to take it back
2026 2400 5502 899 5502 2779 2400 2400 2026 2400 3284 3284 899
n.asf v.pai.1s f.aa r.asf.3 cj n.asf v.pai.1s

πάλιν λαβεῖν αὐτήν· ταύτην τὴν ἐντολὴν ἔλαβον παρὰ τοῦ πατρός μου.
again. to take it This {the} command I received from {the} my Father.” my
4099 3284 899 4047 3836 1953 3284 4123 3836 1609 4252 1609
adv f.aa r.asf.3 r.asf d.asf n.asf v.aai.1s p.g d.gsm n.gsm r.gs.1

19 σχίσμα πάλιν ἐγένετο ἐν τοῖς Ἰουδαίοις διὰ τοὺς
Once again there was a division again there was among the Jews ⌊because of⌋ {the}
4099 1181 1181 5388 4099 1181 1877 3836 2681 1328 3836
n.nsn adv v.ami.3s p.d d.dpm a.dpm p.a d.apm

λόγους τούτους. 20 ἔλεγον δὲ πολλοὶ ἐξ αὐτῶν,
these words. these Many of them were saying, {and} Many of them
4047 3364 4047 4498 1666 899 3306 1254 4498 1666 899
n.apm r.apm v.iai.3p cj a.npm p.g r.gpm.3

⌊δαιμόνιον ἔχει⌋ καὶ μαίνεται· τί αὐτοῦ
“He is demon-possessed and out of control. Why are you listening to him?”
1228 2400 2779 3419 5515 201 201 201 201 899
n.asn v.pai.3s cj v.pmi.3s r.asn r.gsm.3

ἀκούετε; 21 ἄλλοι ἔλεγον, ταῦτα τὰ ῥήματα οὐκ ἔστιν →
are you listening to Others were saying, “These are not the words not are of a
201 257 3306 4047 1639 4024 3836 4839 4024 1639
v.pai.2p r.npm v.iai.3p r.npn d.npn n.npn pl v.pai.3s

δαιμονιζομένου· μὴ δαιμόνιον δύναται → τυφλῶν
⌊man possessed by a demon.⌋ {not} Can a demon Can open the eyes of the blind?”
1227 3590 1538 1228 1538 487 4057 5603
pt.pp.gsm pl n.nsn v.ppi.3s a.gpm

NASB

about the sheep.
14I am the good
shepherd, and I
know My own and
My own know
Me, 15even as the
Father knows Me
and I know the
Father; and I lay
down My life for
the sheep. 16I have
other sheep, which
are not of this fold;
I must bring them
also, and they will
hear My voice; and
they will become
one flock *with* one
shepherd. 17For this
reason the Father
loves Me, because
I lay down My life
so that I may take
it again. 18No one
has taken it away
from Me, but I lay
it down on My own
initiative. I have
authority to lay it
down, and I have
authority to take
it up again. This
commandment I
received from My
Father.”
19A division
occurred again
among the Jews
because of these
words. 20Many of
them were saying,
“He has a demon
and is insane.
Why do you listen
to Him?” 21Oth-
ers were saying,
“These are not
the sayings of one
demon-possessed.
A demon cannot
open the eyes of
the blind, can he?”

NIV

Further Conflict Over Jesus' Claims

22 Then came the Festival of Dedication[a] at Jerusalem. It was winter, 23 and Jesus was in the temple courts walking in Solomon's Colonnade. 24 The Jews who were there gathered around him, saying, "How long will you keep us in suspense? If you are the Messiah, tell us plainly."

25 Jesus answered, "I did tell you, but you do not believe. The works I do in my Father's name testify about me, 26 but you do not believe because you are not my sheep. 27 My sheep listen to my voice; I know them, and they follow me. 28 I give them eternal life, and they shall never perish; no one will snatch them out of my hand. 29 My Father, who has given them to me, is greater than all[b]; no one can snatch them out of my Father's hand. 30 I and the Father are one."

31 Again his Jewish

ὀφθαλμοὺς ἀνοῖξαι; 22 Ἐγένετο τότε
eyes open At that time the festival of Dedication ⌊was taking place⌋ *At that time*
4057 487 5538 5538 5538 3836 1589 1589 1589 1181 5538
n.apm f.aa v.ami.3s adv

τὰ ἐγκαίνια ἐν τοῖς Ἱεροσολύμοις, χειμὼν ἦν, 23 καὶ
the festival of Dedication in *{the}* Jerusalem. It was winter, *It was* and Jesus
3836 1589 1877 3836 2642 1639 1639 5930 1639 2779 2652
d.npn n.npn p.d d.dpn n.dpn n.nsm v.iai.3s cj

περιεπάτει ὁ Ἰησοῦς ἐν τῷ ἱερῷ ἐν τῇ στοᾷ τοῦ
was walking *{the} Jesus* in the ⌊temple area,⌋ in *{the}* Solomon's Portico. *{the}*
4344 3836 2652 1877 3836 2639 1877 3836 5048 5119 3836
v.iai.3s d.nsm n.nsm p.d d.dsn n.dsn p.d d.dsf n.dsf d.gsm

Σολομῶνος. 24 ἐκύκλωσαν οὖν αὐτὸν οἱ Ἰουδαῖοι καὶ ἔλεγον αὐτῷ,
Solomon's The Jews surrounded *{then}* him *The Jews* and asked, *{to him}*
5048 3836 2681 3240 4036 899 3836 2681 2779 3306 899
n.gsm v.aai.3p cj r.asm.3 d.npm a.npm cj v.iai.3p r.dsm.3

⌊ἕως πότε⌋ τὴν ψυχὴν ἡμῶν αἴρεις; εἰ
"How much longer will you provoke us to *{the}* anger? *us will you provoke to* If
2401 4537 149 149 149 7005 149 3836 6034 7005 149 1623
p.g adv d.asf n.asf r.gp.1 v.pai.2s cj

σὺ εἶ ὁ χριστός, εἰπὲ ἡμῖν παρρησίᾳ. 25 ἀπεκρίθη αὐτοῖς ὁ Ἰησοῦς,
you are the Christ, tell us plainly." Jesus answered them, *{the} Jesus*
5148 1639 3836 5986 3306 7005 4244 2652 646 899 3836 2652
r.ns.2 v.pai.2s d.nsm n.nsm v.aam.2s r.dp.1 n.dsf v.api.3s r.dpm.3 d.nsm n.nsm

εἶπον ὑμῖν καὶ ↱ ↱ οὐ πιστεύετε· τὰ ἔργα ἃ ἐγὼ ποιῶ ἐν τῷ
⌊"I did tell⌋ you, yet you do not believe. The works that I am doing in *{the}* my
3306 7007 2779 4409 4409 4024 4409 3836 2240 4005 1609 4472 1877 3836 1609
v.aai.1s r.dp.2 cj pl v.pai.2p d.npn n.npn r.apn r.ns.1 v.pai.1s p.d d.dsn

ὀνόματι τοῦ πατρός μου ταῦτα μαρτυρεῖ → περὶ ἐμοῦ· 26 ἀλλὰ ὑμεῖς
Father's name *{the} Father's my {these}* speak on my behalf. *my* But you
4252 3950 3836 4252 1609 4047 3455 1609 4309 1609 247 7007
n.dsn d.gsm n.gsm r.gs.1 r.npn v.pai.3s p.g r.gs.1 cj r.np.2

↱ οὐ πιστεύετε, ὅτι οὐκ ἐστὲ ἐκ τῶν προβάτων τῶν ἐμῶν.
do not believe because you are not *you are* part of my flock. *{the} my*
4409 4024 4409 4022 1639 1639 4024 1639 1666 3836 1847 4585 3836 1847
pl v.pai.2p cj pl v.pai.2p p.g d.gpn n.gpn d.gpn r.gpn.1

27 τὰ πρόβατα τὰ ἐμὰ τῆς φωνῆς μου ἀκούουσιν, κἀγὼ
{the} My sheep *{the} My* listen to *{the}* my voice, *my listen to* and I
3836 1847 4585 3836 1847 201 201 3836 1609 5889 1609 201 2743
d.npn n.npn d.npn r.npn.1 d.gsf n.gsf r.gs.1 v.pai.3p crasis

γινώσκω αὐτὰ καὶ ἀκολουθοῦσίν μοι, 28 κἀγὼ δίδωμι αὐτοῖς ζωὴν αἰώνιον
know them. *{and}* They follow me, and I give them eternal life. *eternal*
1182 899 2779 199 1609 2743 1443 899 173 2437 173
v.pai.1s r.apn.3 cj v.pai.3p r.ds.1 crasis v.pai.1s r.dpn.3 n.asf a.asf

καὶ ↱ ↱ ⌊οὐ μὴ⌋ ἀπόλωνται εἰς τὸν αἰῶνα καὶ οὐχ → ἁρπάσει τις
{and} They will never perish, *{for} {all} {time}* and no one will ever snatch *one*
2779 660 660 4024 3590 660 1650 3836 172 2779 4024 5516 773 5516
cj pl pl v.ams.3p p.a d.asm n.asm cj pl v.fai.3s r.nsm

αὐτὰ ἐκ τῆς χειρός μου. 29 ὁ πατήρ μου ὃ[a] δέδωκέν μοι
them ⌊out of⌋ *{the}* my hand. *my* *{the}* My Father, *My* who has given them to me, is
899 1666 3836 1609 5931 1609 3836 1609 4252 1609 4005 1443 1609 1639
r.apn.3 p.g d.gsf n.gsf r.gs.1 d.nsm n.nsm r.gs.1 r.asn v.rai.3s r.ds.1

πάντων μεῖζόν[b] ἐστιν, καὶ οὐδεὶς δύναται ἁρπάζειν ἐκ τῆς
more powerful than all, *more powerful is* and no one can snatch them ⌊out of⌋ my
3489 3489 4246 3489 1639 2779 4029 1538 773 1666 3836
a.gpm a.nsm.c v.pai.3s cj a.nsm v.ppi.3s f.pa p.g d.gsf

χειρὸς τοῦ πατρός. 30 ἐγὼ καὶ ὁ πατὴρ ἕν ἐσμεν. 31
Father's hand. *{the} Father's* I and the Father are one." *are* The Jews again
4252 5931 3836 4252 1609 2779 3836 4252 1639 1651 1639 3836 2681 4099
n.gsf d.gsm n.gsm r.ns.1 cj d.nsm n.nsm a.nsn v.pai.1p

NASB

Jesus Asserts His Deity

22 At that time the Feast of the Dedication took place at Jerusalem; 23 it was winter, and Jesus was walking in the temple in the portico of Solomon. 24 The Jews then gathered around Him, and were saying to Him, "How long will You keep us in suspense? If You are the Christ, tell us plainly." 25 Jesus answered them, "I told you, and you do not believe; the works that I do in My Father's name, these testify of Me. 26 But you do not believe because you are not of My sheep. 27 My sheep hear My voice, and I know them, and they follow Me; 28 and I give eternal life to them, and they will never perish; and no one will snatch them out of My hand. 29 [a]My Father, who has given *them* to Me, is greater than all; and no one is able to snatch *them* out of the Father's hand. 30 I and the Father are one."

31 The Jews picked

[a] 22 That is, Hanukkah
[b] 29 Many early manuscripts *What my Father has given me is greater than all*

[a] ὅ UBS, NET. ὅς TNIV.
[b] μεῖζόν omitted by TNIV.

[a] One early ms reads *What My Father has given Me is greater than all*

NIV

opponents picked up stones to stone him, [32]but Jesus said to them, "I have shown you many good works from the Father. For which of these do you stone me?"

[33]"We are not stoning you for any good work," they replied, "but for blasphemy, because you, a mere man, claim to be God."

[34]Jesus answered them, "Is it not written in your Law, 'I have said you are "gods"'[a]? [35]If he called them 'gods,' to whom the word of God came—and Scripture cannot be set aside— [36]what about the one whom the Father set apart as his very own and sent into the world? Why then do you accuse me of blasphemy because I said, 'I am God's Son'? [37]Do not believe me unless I do the works of my Father. [38]But if I do them, even though you do not believe me, believe the works, that you may know and understand that the Father is in me, and I in the Father." [39]Again they tried to seize him, but he escaped their grasp.

[a] 34 Psalm 82:6

ἐβάστασαν πάλιν λίθους οἱ Ἰουδαῖοι ἵνα λιθάσωσιν αὐτόν. 32 ἀπεκρίθη
brought *again* stones *The* *Jews* to stone him. Jesus said
1002 4099 3345 3836 2681 2671 3342 899 2652 646
v.aai.3p adv n.apm d.npm a.npm cj v.aas.3p r.asm.3 v.api.3s

αὐτοῖς ὁ Ἰησοῦς, πολλὰ ἔργα καλὰ ἔδειξα ὑμῖν ἐκ
to them, *{the}* *Jesus* "I have shown you many noble works *noble* *I have shown* *you* from
899 3836 2652 1259 1259 1259 7007 4498 2819 2240 2819 1259 7007 1666
r.dpm.3 d.nsm n.nsm a.apn n.apn a.apn v.aai.1s r.dp.2 p.g

τοῦ πατρός· διὰ ποῖον αὐτῶν ἔργον ἐμὲ
the Father; for which one of them *one* do you intend to stone me?"
3836 4252 1328 4481 2240 899 2240 3342 3342 3342 3342 3342 1609
d.gsm n.gsm p.a r.asn r.gpn.3 n.asn r.as.1

λιθάζετε; 33 ἀπεκρίθησαν αὐτῷ οἱ Ἰουδαῖοι, περὶ
do you intend to stone The Jews answered him, *The* *Jews* "It is not for a
3342 3836 2681 646 899 3836 2681 4024 4309
v.pai.2p v.api.3p r.dsm.3 d.npm a.npm p.g

καλοῦ ἔργου οὐ λιθάζομέν σε ἀλλὰ περὶ βλασφημίας, καὶ ὅτι
noble work *not* that ⌊we intend to stone⌋ you but for blasphemy; *{and}* it is because
2819 2240 4024 3342 5148 247 4309 1060 2779 4022
a.gsn n.gsn pl v.pai.1p r.as.2 cj p.g n.gsf cj cj

σὺ ἄνθρωπος ὢν ποιεῖς σεαυτὸν θεόν. 34 ἀπεκρίθη αὐτοῖς ὁ[a]
you, a mere man, *{being}* are making yourself God." Jesus answered them, *{the}*
5148 476 1639 4472 4932 2536 2652 646 899 3836
r.ns.2 n.nsm pt.pa.nsm v.pai.2s r.asm.2 n.asm v.api.3s r.dpm.3 d.nsm

Ἰησοῦς, οὐκ ἔστιν γεγραμμένον ἐν τῷ νόμῳ ὑμῶν ὅτι ἐγὼ εἶπα,
Jesus "Is it not *Is it* written in *{the}* your law, *your* ~ 'I said, you
2652 1639 1639 4024 1639 1211 1877 3836 7007 3795 7007 4022 1609 3306 1639
n.nsm pl v.pai.3s pt.rp.nsn p.d d.dsm n.dsm r.gp.2 cj r.ns.1 v.aai.1s

θεοί ἐστε; 35 εἰ ἐκείνους εἶπεν θεοὺς πρὸς οὓς ὁ λόγος
are gods'? *you are* If the scripture called them *called* 'gods' to whom the word
1639 2536 1639 1623 3306 1697 3306 2536 4639 4005 3836 3364
n.npm v.pai.2p cj r.apm v.aai.3s n.apm p.a r.apm d.nsm n.nsm

τοῦ θεοῦ ἐγένετο, καὶ ⌊οὐ δύναται⌋ λυθῆναι ἡ γραφή, 36
of God came — and scripture cannot be annulled *{the}* *scripture* — do
3836 2536 1181 2779 1210 4024 1538 3395 3836 1210 3306
d.gsm n.gsm v.ami.3s cj pl v.ppi.3s f.ap d.nsf n.nsf

→ ὃν ὁ πατὴρ ἡγίασεν καὶ ἀπέστειλεν εἰς τὸν κόσμον
you say regarding the one whom the Father consecrated and sent into the world,
7007 3306 4005 3836 4252 39 2779 690 1650 3836 3180
r.asm d.nsm n.nsm v.aai.3s cj v.aai.3s p.a d.asm n.asm

ὑμεῖς λέγετε ὅτι βλασφημεῖς, ὅτι εἶπον, υἱὸς τοῦ θεοῦ εἰμι;
you *do say* ~ 'You are blaspheming,' because I said, 'I am the Son of God'? *I am*
7007 3306 4022 1059 4022 3306 1639 1639 5626 3836 2536 1639
r.np.2 v.pai.2p cj v.pai.2s cj v.aai.1s n.nsm d.gsm n.gsm v.pai.1s

37 εἰ ↱ ↱ οὐ ποιῶ τὰ ἔργα τοῦ πατρός μου, ↱ μὴ πιστεύετέ μοι·
If I am not doing the works of my Father, *my* then do not believe me;
1623 4472 4472 4024 4472 3836 2240 3836 1609 4252 1609 4409 3590 4409 1609
cj pl v.pai.1s d.apn n.apn d.gsm n.gsm r.gs.1 pl v.pam.2p r.ds.1

38 εἰ δὲ ποιῶ, κἂν ἐμοὶ μὴ πιστεύητε,
but if *but* I am doing them, ⌊even if⌋ you do not believe me, *not* *you do believe* believe
1254 1623 1254 4472 2829 4409 4409 3590 4409 1609 3590 4409 4409
cj cj v.pai.1s crasis r.ds.1 pl v.pas.2p

τοῖς ἔργοις πιστεύετε, ἵνα γνῶτε καὶ γινώσκητε ὅτι ἐν
the works, *believe* that ⌊you may come to know⌋ and be certain that the Father is in
3836 2240 4409 2671 1182 2779 1182 4022 3836 4252 1877
d.dpn n.dpn v.pam.2p cj v.aas.2p cj v.pas.2p cj p.d

ἐμοὶ ὁ πατὴρ κἀγὼ ← ἐν τῷ πατρί. 39 ἐζήτουν οὖν[b]
me *the* *Father* and that I am in the Father." So once again they tried *So* to
1609 3836 4252 2743 1877 3836 4252 4036 4099 2426 4036 4389
r.ds.1 d.nsm n.nsm crasis p.d d.dsm n.dsm v.iai.3p cj

αὐτὸν πάλιν πιάσαι, καὶ ἐξῆλθεν ἐκ τῆς χειρὸς αὐτῶν. 40 καὶ
arrest him, *again* *to arrest* but he escaped ⌊out of⌋ *{the}* their grasp. *their* *{and}*
4389 899 4099 4389 2779 2002 1666 3836 899 5931 899 2779
r.asm.3 adv f.aa cj v.aai.3s p.g d.gsf n.gsf r.gpm.3 cj

[a] [ὁ] UBS.
[b] [οὖν] UBS, omitted by TNIV.

NASB

up stones again to stone Him. [32]Jesus answered them, "I showed you many good works from the Father; for which of them are you stoning Me?" [33]The Jews answered Him, "For a good work we do not stone You, but for blasphemy; and because You, being a man, make Yourself out *to be* God." [34]Jesus answered them, "Has it not been written in your Law, 'I SAID, YOU ARE GODS'? [35]If he called them gods, to whom the word of God came (and the Scripture cannot be broken), [36]do you say of Him, whom the Father sanctified and sent into the world, 'You are blaspheming,' because I said, 'I am the Son of God'? [37]If I do not do the works of My Father, do not believe Me; [38]but if I do them, though you do not believe Me, believe the works, so that you may know and understand that the Father is in Me, and I in the Father." [39]Therefore they were seeking again to seize Him, and He eluded their grasp.

NIV

40Then Jesus
went back across
the Jordan to the
place where John
had been baptizing
in the early days.
There he stayed,
41and many people
came to him. They
said, "Though
John never per-
formed a sign,
all that John said
about this man was
true." 42And in that
place many be-
lieved in Jesus.

The Death of Lazarus

11 Now a man
named Laz-
arus was sick. He
was from Bethany,
the village of Mary
and her sister Mar-
tha. 2(This Mary,
whose brother
Lazarus now lay
sick, was the same
one who poured
perfume on the
Lord and wiped
his feet with her
hair.) 3So the sis-
ters sent word to
Jesus, "Lord, the
one you love is
sick."
4When he heard
this, Jesus said,
"This sickness will
not end in death.
No, it is for God's
glory so that God's
Son may be glo-
rified through it."
5Now Jesus loved
Martha and her
sister and Laza-
rus. 6So when he
heard that Lazarus
was sick, he stayed
where he was two
more days, 7and
then he said to his
disciples, "Let us
go back to Judea."

ἀπῆλθεν πάλιν πέραν τοῦ Ἰορδάνου εἰς τὸν τόπον ὅπου ἦν Ἰωάννης
He went away again across the Jordan to the place where John ˪had been˩ *John*
599 4099 4305 3836 2674 1650 3836 5536 3963 2722 1639 2722
v.aai.3s adv p.g d.gsm n.gsm p.a d.asm n.asm cj v.iai.3s n.nsm

τὸ πρῶτον βαπτίζων καὶ ἔμεινεν ἐκεῖ. 41 καὶ πολλοὶ
baptizing at an *{the}* earlier time, *baptizing* and there he remained. *there* *{and}* Many people
966 3836 4754 966 2779 1695 3531 1695 2779 4498
d.asn adv pt.pa.nsm cj v.aai.3s adv cj a.npm

ἦλθον πρὸς αὐτὸν καὶ ἔλεγον ὅτι Ἰωάννης μὲν σημεῖον
came to him and were saying, ~ "John ~ performed no ˪miraculous sign,˩
2262 4639 899 2779 3306 4022 2722 3525 4472 4029 4956
v.aai.3p p.g r.asm.3 cj v.iai.3p cj n.nsm pl n.asn

ἐποίησεν οὐδέν, πάντα δὲ ὅσα εἶπεν Ἰωάννης περὶ τούτου
performed *no* but everything *but* *{as much as}* he said *he* about this man was
4472 4029 1254 4246 1254 4012 2722 3306 2722 4309 4047 1639
v.aai.3s a.asn cj a.npn cj r.apn v.aai.3s n.nsm p.g r.gsm

ἀληθῆ ἦν. 42 καὶ πολλοὶ ἐπίστευσαν εἰς αὐτὸν ἐκεῖ.
true!" *was* And many in that place came to believe in Jesus. *in that place*
239 1639 2779 4498 1695 1695 1695 4409 1650 899 1695
a.npn v.iai.3s cj a.npm v.aai.3p p.a r.asm.3 adv

11:1 ἦν δέ τις ἀσθενῶν, Λάζαρος ἀπὸ Βηθανίας, ἐκ τῆς
Now ˪there was˩ *Now* a ˪certain man˩ who was ill, Lazareth of Bethany, *{from}* the
1254 1639 1254 5516 820 3276 608 1029 1666 3836
v.iai.3s cj r.nsm pt.pa.nsm n.nsm p.g n.gsf p.g d.gsf

κώμης Μαρίας καὶ Μάρθας τῆς ἀδελφῆς αὐτῆς. 2 ἦν δὲ Μαριὰμ
village of Mary and her sister Martha. *{the}* *sister* *her* ˪It was˩ *{and}* this Mary
3267 3451 2779 899 80 3450 3836 80 899 1639 1254 3452
n.gsf n.gsf cj n.gsf d.gsf n.gsf r.gsf.3 v.iai.3s cj n.nsf

ἡ ἀλείψασα τὸν κύριον μύρῳ καὶ ἐκμάξασα τοὺς πόδας αὐτοῦ ταῖς
who anointed the Lord with ointment and wiped *{the}* his feet *his* with her
3836 230 3836 3261 3693 2779 1726 3836 899 4546 899 3836 899
d.nsf pt.aa.nsf d.asm n.asm n.dsn cj pt.aa.nsf d.apm n.apm r.gsm.3 d.dpf

θριξὶν αὐτῆς, ἧς ὁ ἀδελφὸς Λάζαρος ἠσθένει. 3 ἀπέστειλαν
hair, *her* whose *{the}* brother Lazarus was ill. So the sisters sent word
2582 899 4005 3836 81 3276 820 4036 3836 80 690
n.dpf r.gsf.3 r.gsf d.nsm n.nsm n.nsm v.iai.3s v.aai.3p

οὖν αἱ ἀδελφαὶ πρὸς αὐτὸν λέγουσαι, κύριε, ἴδε ὃν φιλεῖς ἀσθενεῖ. 4
So *the* *sisters* to him, saying, "Lord, ~ the one you love is ill." But
4036 3836 80 4639 899 3306 3261 2623 4005 5797 820 1254
cj d.npf n.npf p.a r.asm.3 pt.pa.npf n.vsm pl r.asm v.pai.2s v.pai.3s

→ ἀκούσας δὲ ὁ Ἰησοῦς εἶπεν, αὕτη ἡ ἀσθένεια ↱ οὐκ ἔστιν
when Jesus heard *But* *{the}* *Jesus* this, he said, "This *{the}* illness will not lead
2652 201 1254 3836 2652 3306 4047 3836 819 1639 4024 1639
pt.aa.nsm cj d.nsm n.nsm v.aai.3s r.nsf d.nsf n.nsf pl v.pai.3s

πρὸς θάνατον ἀλλʼ ὑπὲρ τῆς δόξης τοῦ θεοῦ, ἵνα δοξασθῇ
to death, but is for the glory of God, that the Son of God may be glorified
4639 2505 247 5642 3836 1518 3836 2536 2671 3836 5626 3836 2536 1519
p.a n.asm cj p.g d.gsf n.gsf d.gsm n.gsm cj v.aps.3s

ὁ υἱὸς τοῦ θεοῦ διʼ αὐτῆς. 5 ἠγάπα δὲ ὁ Ἰησοῦς τὴν Μάρθαν
the *Son* *of* *God* through it." Now Jesus loved *Now* *{the}* *Jesus* *{the}* Martha
3836 5626 3836 2536 1328 899 1254 2652 26 1254 3836 2652 3836 3450
d.nsm n.nsm d.gsm n.gsm p.g r.gsf.3 v.iai.3s cj d.nsm n.nsm d.asf n.asf

καὶ τὴν ἀδελφὴν αὐτῆς καὶ τὸν Λάζαρον. 6 ὡς οὖν ἤκουσεν ὅτι
and *{the}* her sister *her* and *{the}* Lazarus. So when *So* he heard that Lazarus
2779 3836 899 80 899 2779 3836 3276 4036 6055 4036 201 4022
cj d.asf n.asf r.gsf.3 cj d.asm n.asm cj cj v.aai.3s cj

ἀσθενεῖ, τότε μὲν ἔμεινεν ˪ἐν ᾧ˩ ἦν τόπῳ δύο ἡμέρας,
was ill, *{then}* ~ he stayed in the place where ˪he was˩ *in place* for two more days.
820 5538 3525 3531 5536 5536 1877 4005 1639 5536 1545 2465
v.pai.3s adv pl v.aai.3s p.d r.dsm v.iai.3s n.dsm a.apf n.apf

7 ἔπειτα μετὰ τοῦτο λέγει τοῖς μαθηταῖς, ἄγωμεν εἰς τὴν Ἰουδαίαν πάλιν. 8
Then after this he said to the disciples, "Let us go to *{the}* Judea again." The
2083 3552 4047 3306 3836 3412 72 1650 3836 2677 4099 3836
adv p.a r.asn v.pai.3s d.dpm n.dpm v.pas.1p p.a d.asf n.asf adv

NASB

40And He went
away again beyond
the Jordan to the
place where John
was first baptizing,
and He was staying
there. 41Many came
to Him and were
saying, "While
John performed
no sign, yet ev-
erything John said
about this man
was true." 42Many
believed in Him
there.

The Death and Resurrection of Lazarus

11:1Now a certain
man was sick, La-
zarus of Bethany,
the village of Mary
and her sister
Martha. 2It was the
Mary who anointed
the Lord with oint-
ment, and wiped
His feet with her
hair, whose brother
Lazarus was sick.
3So the sisters sent
word to Him, say-
ing, "Lord, behold,
he whom You love
is sick." 4But when
Jesus heard *this,*
He said, "This
sickness is not to
end in death, but
for the glory of
God, so that the
Son of God may
be glorified by it."
5Now Jesus loved
Martha and her
sister and Lazarus.
6So when He heard
that he was sick,
He then stayed two
days *longer* in the
place where He
was. 7Then after
this He *said to the
disciples, "Let us
go to Judea again."

NIV

[8]"But Rabbi,"
they said, "a short
while ago the Jews
there tried to stone
you, and yet you
are going back?"
[9]Jesus answered,
"Are there not
twelve hours of
daylight? Anyone
who walks in the
daytime will not
stumble, for they
see by this world's
light. [10]It is when
a person walks
at night that they
stumble, for they
have no light."
[11]After he had
said this, he went
on to tell them,
"Our friend Laz-
arus has fallen
asleep; but I am
going there to
wake him up."
[12]His disciples re-
plied, "Lord, if he
sleeps, he will get
better." [13]Jesus had
been speaking of
his death, but his
disciples thought
he meant natural
sleep.
[14]So then he
told them plainly,
"Lazarus is dead,
[15]and for your sake
I am glad I was not
there, so that you
may believe. But
let us go to him."
[16]Then Thomas
(also known as
Didymus[a]) said to
the rest of the dis-
ciples, "Let us also
go, that we may
die with him."

Jesus Comforts the Sisters of Lazarus

[17]On his arrival,
Jesus found that

[a] 16 *Thomas* (Aramaic) and *Didymus* (Greek) both mean *twin*.

λέγουσιν αὐτῷ οἱ μαθηταί, ῥαββί, νῦν ἐζήτουν
disciples said to him, *The disciples* "Rabbi, ⌊just recently⌋ the Jews were trying to stone
3412 3306 899 3836 3412 4806 3814 3836 2681 2426 3342 3342
v.pai.3p r.dsm.3 d.npm n.npm n.vsm adv v.iai.3p

σε λιθάσαι οἱ Ἰουδαῖοι, καὶ πάλιν ὑπάγεις ἐκεῖ;
you, *to stone the Jews* and are you going back there again?" *are you going back there*
5148 3342 3836 2681 2779 5632 5632 5632 5632 1695 4099 5632 1695
r.as.2 f.aa d.npm a.npm cj adv v.pai.2s adv

9 ἀπεκρίθη Ἰησοῦς, οὐχὶ δώδεκα ὧραί εἰσιν τῆς ἡμέρας; ἐάν
Jesus answered, *Jesus* "Are there not twelve hours *Are there* in a day? If a
2652 646 2652 1639 1639 4049 1557 6052 1639 3836 2465 1569
v.api.3s n.nsm pl a.npf n.npf v.pai.3p d.gsf n.gsf cj

τις περιπατῇ ἐν τῇ ἡμέρᾳ, ↱ ↱ οὐ προσκόπτει, ὅτι τὸ φῶς
person walks during the day, he will not stumble, because he sees the light
5516 4344 1877 3836 2465 4684 4684 4024 4684 4022 1063 1063 3836 5890
r.nsm v.pas.3s p.d d.dsf n.dsf pl v.pai.3s cj d.asn n.asn

τοῦ κόσμου τούτου βλέπει· 10 ἐὰν δέ τις περιπατῇ ἐν τῇ νυκτί,
of this world. *this he sees* But if *But* someone walks during the night,
3836 4047 3180 4047 1063 1254 1569 1254 5516 4344 1877 3836 3816
d.gsm n.gsm r.gsm v.pai.3s cj cj r.nsm v.pas.3s p.d d.dsf n.dsf

προσκόπτει, ὅτι τὸ φῶς οὐκ ἔστιν ἐν αὐτῷ. 11 ταῦτα εἶπεν, καὶ μετὰ
he will stumble, because the light is not *is* in him." These things he said, and after
4684 4022 3836 5890 1639 4024 1639 1877 899 4047 3306 2779 3552
v.pai.3s cj d.nsn n.nsn pl v.pai.3s p.d r.dsm.3 r.apn v.aai.3s cj p.a

τοῦτο λέγει αὐτοῖς, Λάζαρος ὁ φίλος ἡμῶν κεκοίμηται· ἀλλὰ
that he told them, "Our friend Lazarus *{the} friend Our* has fallen asleep, but
4047 3306 899 7005 5813 3276 3836 5813 7005 3121 247
r.asn v.pai.3s r.dpm.3 n.nsm d.nsm n.nsm r.gp.1 v.rpi.3s cj

πορεύομαι ἵνα ἐξυπνίσω αὐτόν. ↰ ↰ 12 εἶπαν οὖν
I am going there to wake him from sleep." The disciples therefore said *therefore*
4513 2671 2030 899 2030 2030 3836 3412 4036 3306 4036
v.pmi.1s cj v.aas.1s r.asm.3 v.aai.3p cj

οἱ μαθηταὶ αὐτῷ, κύριε, εἰ κεκοίμηται σωθήσεται. 13
The disciples to him, "Lord, if ⌊he has fallen asleep,⌋ he will recover." Jesus, however,
3836 3412 899 3261 1623 3121 5392 2652 1254
d.npm n.npm r.dsm.3 n.vsm cj v.rpi.3s v.fpi.3s

εἰρήκει δὲ ὁ Ἰησοῦς περὶ τοῦ θανάτου αὐτοῦ, ἐκεῖνοι δὲ
⌊had been speaking⌋ *however {the} Jesus* of *{the}* his death, *his* but they *but*
3306 1254 3836 2652 4309 3836 899 2505 899 1254 1697 1254
v.lai.3s cj d.nsm n.nsm p.g d.gsm n.gsm r.gsm.3 r.npm cj

ἔδοξαν ὅτι περὶ τῆς κοιμήσεως τοῦ ὕπνου λέγει.
thought that he was speaking about *{the}* sleep in the sense of slumber. *he was speaking*
1506 4022 3306 3306 3306 4309 3836 3122 3836 5678 3306
v.aai.3p cj p.g d.gsf n.gsf d.gsm n.gsm v.pai.3s

14 ⌊τότε οὖν⌋ εἶπεν αὐτοῖς ὁ Ἰησοῦς παρρησίᾳ, Λάζαρος ἀπέθανεν, 15 καὶ
Then Jesus told them *{the} Jesus* plainly, "Lazarus has died, and
5538 4036 2652 3306 899 3836 2652 4244 3276 633 2779
adv cj v.aai.3s r.dpm.3 d.nsm n.nsm n.dsf n.nsm v.aai.3s cj

χαίρω δι' ὑμᾶς ἵνα πιστεύσητε, ὅτι
for your sake that you might believe, I am glad *for sake your that you might believe* that I
1328 7007 1328 2671 4409 4409 4409 5897 1328 7007 2671 4409 4022 1639
v.pai.1s p.a r.ap.2 cj v.aas.2p cj

οὐκ ἤμην ἐκεῖ· ἀλλὰ ἄγωμεν πρὸς αὐτόν. 16 εἶπεν οὖν
was not *I was* there. But let us go to him." So Thomas (called the Twin) said *So*
1639 4024 1639 1695 247 72 4639 899 4036 2605 3306 1441 3306 4036
pl v.iai.1s adv cj v.pas.1p p.a r.asm.3 v.aai.3s cj

Θωμᾶς ὁ λεγόμενος Δίδυμος τοῖς συμμαθηταῖς, → → ἄγωμεν καὶ ἡμεῖς
Thomas {the} called Twin to his fellow disciples, "Let us also go, *also* that we
2605 3836 3306 1441 3836 5209 2779 72 2779 2671 7005
n.nsm d.nsm pt.pp.nsm n.nsm d.dpm n.dpm v.pas.1p adv r.np.1

ἵνα ἀποθάνωμεν μετ' αὐτοῦ. 17 → ἐλθὼν οὖν ὁ Ἰησοῦς εὗρεν
that may die with him." Now when Jesus arrived, *Now {the} Jesus* he found that
2671 633 3552 899 4036 2652 2262 4036 3836 2652 2351
cj v.aas.1p p.g r.gsm.3 pt.aa.nsm cj d.nsm n.nsm v.aai.3s

NASB

[8]The disciples *said
to Him, "Rabbi, the
Jews were just now
seeking to stone
You, and are You
going there again?"
[9]Jesus answered,
"Are there not
twelve hours in
the day? If anyone
walks in the day, he
does not stumble,
because he sees the
light of this world.
[10]But if anyone
walks in the night,
he stumbles,
because the light is
not in him." [11]This
He said, and after
that He *said to
them, "Our friend
Lazarus has fallen
asleep; but I go, so
that I may awaken
him out of sleep."
[12]The disciples then
said to Him, "Lord,
if he has fallen
asleep, he will
recover." [13]Now
Jesus had spoken
of his death, but
they thought that
He was speaking
of literal sleep. [14]So
Jesus then said to
them plainly, "La-
zarus is dead, [15]and
I am glad for your
sakes that I was
not there, so that
you may believe;
but let us go to
him." [16]Therefore
Thomas, who is
called Didymus,
said to *his* fellow
disciples, "Let us
also go, so that
we may die with
Him."
[17]So when Jesus
came, He found

NIV

Lazarus had al-
ready been in the
tomb for four days.
18 Now Bethany
was less than two
miles[a] from Jeru-
salem, 19 and many
Jews had come to
Martha and Mary
to comfort them
in the loss of their
brother. 20 When
Martha heard that
Jesus was com-
ing, she went out
to meet him, but
Mary stayed at
home.
21 "Lord," Martha
said to Jesus, "if
you had been here,
my brother would
not have died.
22 But I know that
even now God will
give you whatever
you ask."
23 Jesus said to
her, "Your brother
will rise again."
24 Martha an-
swered, "I know
he will rise again
in the resurrection
at the last day."
25 Jesus said to
her, "I am the res-
urrection and the
life. The one who
believes in me will
live, even though
they die; 26 and
whoever lives by
believing in me
will never die. Do
you believe this?"
27 "Yes, Lord,"
she replied, "I be-
lieve that you are
the Messiah, the
Son of God, who
is to come into the
world."
28 After she had
said this,

αὐτὸν τέσσαρας ἤδη ἡμέρας ἔχοντα ἐν τῷ μνημείῳ.
Lazarus had already been in the tomb for four *already* days. *had been* *in* *the* *tomb*
899 2400 2453 2400 1877 3836 3646 5475 2453 2465 2400 1877 3836 3646
r.asm.3 a.apf adv n.apf pt.pa.asm p.d d.dsn n.dsn

18 ἦν δὲ ἡ Βηθανία ἐγγὺς τῶν Ἱεροσολύμων ὡς ἀπὸ
Bethany was *{and}* *{the}* *Bethany* near *{the}* Jerusalem, about two miles away,
1029 1639 1254 3836 1029 1584 3836 2642 6055 5084 5084 608
v.iai.3s cj d.nsf n.nsf p.g d.gpn n.gpn pl p.g

⌞σταδίων δεκαπέντε.⌟ 19 πολλοὶ δὲ ἐκ τῶν Ἰουδαίων ἐληλύθεισαν πρὸς τὴν
two miles and many *and* of the Jews had come to *{the}*
5084 1278 1254 4498 1254 1666 3836 2681 2262 4639 3836
n.gpm a.gpm a.npm cj p.g d.gpm a.gpm v.lai.3p p.a d.asf

Μάρθαν καὶ Μαριὰμ ἵνα παραμυθήσωνται αὐτὰς περὶ τοῦ ἀδελφοῦ. 20 ἡ
Martha and Mary to console them ⌞in regard to⌟ their brother. *{the}*
3450 2779 3452 2671 4170 899 4309 3836 81 3836
n.asf cj n.asf cj v.ams.3p r.apf.3 p.g d.gsm n.gsm d.nsf

οὖν Μάρθα ὡς ἤκουσεν ὅτι Ἰησοῦς ἔρχεται ὑπήντησεν αὐτῷ·
So when Martha *when* heard that Jesus was coming, ⌞she went out to meet⌟ him, but
4036 6055 3450 6055 201 4022 2652 2262 5636 899 1254
cj n.nsf cj v.aai.3s cj n.nsm v.pmi.3s v.aai.3s r.dsm.3

Μαριὰμ δὲ ἐν τῷ οἴκῳ ἐκαθέζετο. 21 εἶπεν οὖν ἡ Μάρθα
Mary *but* remained in the house. *remained* Martha then said *then* *{the}* *Martha*
3452 1254 2757 1877 3836 3875 2757 3450 4036 3306 4036 3836 3450
n.nsf cj p.d d.dsm n.dsm v.imi.3s v.aai.3s cj d.nsf n.nsf

πρὸς τὸν Ἰησοῦν, κύριε, εἰ ἦς ὧδε οὐκ ἂν ἀπέθανεν
to *{the}* Jesus, "Lord, if ⌞you had been⌟ here, my brother would not *would* have died.
4639 3836 2652 3261 1623 1639 6045 1609 81 323 4024 323 633
p.a d.asm n.asm n.vsm cj v.iai.2s adv pl pl v.aai.3s

ὁ ἀδελφός μου· 22 ἀλλὰ[a] καὶ νῦν οἶδα ὅτι ⌞ὅσα ἂν⌟
{the} *brother* *my* But even now I know that God will give you whatever
3836 81 1609 247 2779 3814 3857 4022 2536 1443 1443 5148 4012 323
d.nsm n.nsm r.gs.1 cj adv adv v.rai.1s cj r.apn pl

αἰτήσῃ τὸν θεὸν δώσει σοι ὁ θεός. 23 λέγει αὐτῇ ὁ Ἰησοῦς,
⌞you ask of⌟ *{the}* him." *will give* *you* *{the}* *God* Jesus said to her, *{the}* *Jesus* "Your
160 3836 2536 1443 5148 3836 2536 2652 3306 899 3836 2652 5148
v.ams.2s d.asm n.asm v.fai.3s r.ds.2 d.nsm n.nsm v.pai.3s r.dsf.3 d.nsm n.nsm

ἀναστήσεται ὁ ἀδελφός σου. 24 λέγει αὐτῷ ἡ Μάρθα, οἶδα ὅτι
brother will rise again." *{the}* *brother* *Your* Martha said to him, *{the}* *Martha* "I know that
81 482 3836 81 5148 3450 3306 899 3836 3450 3857 4022
v.fmi.3s d.nsm n.nsm r.gs.2 v.pai.3s r.dsm.3 d.nsf n.nsf v.rai.1s cj

ἀναστήσεται ἐν τῇ ἀναστάσει ἐν τῇ ἐσχάτῃ ἡμέρᾳ. 25 εἶπεν αὐτῇ ὁ
he will rise again in the resurrection at the last day." Jesus said to her, *{the}*
482 1877 3836 414 1877 3836 2274 2465 2652 3306 899 3836
v.fmi.3s p.d d.dsf n.dsf p.d d.dsf a.dsf n.dsf v.aai.3s r.dsf d.nsm

Ἰησοῦς, ἐγώ εἰμι ἡ ἀνάστασις καὶ ἡ ζωή· ὁ πιστεύων εἰς ἐμὲ
Jesus "I am the resurrection and the life. The one who believes in me,
2652 1609 1639 3836 414 2779 3836 2437 3836 4409 1650 1609
n.nsm r.ns.1 v.pai.1s d.nsf n.nsf cj d.nsf n.nsf d.nsm pt.pa.nsm p.a r.as.1

κἂν ἀποθάνῃ ζήσεται, 26 καὶ πᾶς ὁ ζῶν καὶ πιστεύων εἰς ἐμὲ
⌞even though⌟ he die, yet will he live, and everyone who lives and believes in me
2829 633 2409 2779 4246 3836 2409 2779 4409 1650 1609
crasis v.aas.3s v.fmi.3s cj a.nsm d.nsm pt.pa.nsm cj pt.pa.nsm p.a r.as.1

↱ ⌞οὐ μὴ⌟ ἀποθάνῃ εἰς τὸν αἰῶνα. πιστεύεις τοῦτο; 27 λέγει αὐτῷ, ναὶ
will never die. *{for}* *{all}* *{time}* Do you believe this?" She said to him, "Yes,
633 4024 3590 633 1650 3836 172 4409 4047 3306 899 3721
pl pl v.aas.3s p.a d.asm n.asm v.pai.2s r.asn v.pai.3s r.dsm.3 pl

κύριε, ἐγὼ πεπίστευκα ὅτι σὺ εἶ ὁ χριστὸς ὁ υἱὸς τοῦ θεοῦ ὁ
Lord; I firmly believe that you are the Christ, the Son of God, the one who
3261 1609 4409 4022 5148 1639 3836 5986 3836 5626 3836 2536 3836 2262 2262
n.vsm r.ns.1 v.rai.1s cj r.ns.2 v.pai.2s d.nsm n.nsm d.nsm n.nsm d.gsm n.gsm d.nsm

εἰς τὸν κόσμον ἐρχόμενος. 28 καὶ τοῦτο
was to come into the world." *one who was to come* And when she had said this,
2262 2262 2262 1650 3836 3180 2262 2779 3306 3306 3306 3306 4047
p.a d.asm n.asm pt.pm.nsm cj r.asn

NASB

that he had already
been in the tomb
four days. 18 Now
Bethany was near
Jerusalem, about
two miles off;
19 and many of the
Jews had come to
Martha and Mary,
to console them
concerning *their*
brother. 20 Martha
therefore, when she
heard that Jesus
was coming, went
to meet Him, but
Mary stayed at the
house. 21 Martha
then said to Jesus,
"Lord, if You had
been here, my
brother would not
have died. 22 Even
now I know that
whatever You ask
of God, God will
give You." 23 Jesus
*said to her, "Your
brother will rise
again." 24 Martha
*said to Him, "I
know that he will
rise again in the
resurrection on the
last day." 25 Jesus
said to her, "I am
the resurrection
and the life; he
who believes in
Me will live even
if he dies, 26 and
everyone who lives
and believes in Me
will never die. Do
you believe this?"
27 She *said to Him,
"Yes, Lord; I have
believed that You
are the Christ, the
Son of God, *even*
He who comes into
the world."
28 When she had
said this, she went

[a] 18 Or about 3 kilometers

[a] [ἀλλὰ] UBS.

NIV

she went back and
called her sister
Mary aside. "The
Teacher is here,"
she said, "and is
asking for you."
29 When Mary
heard this, she got
up quickly and
went to him. 30 Now
Jesus had not yet
entered the vil-
lage, but was still
at the place where
Martha had met
him. 31 When the
Jews who had been
with Mary in the
house, comforting
her, noticed how
quickly she got
up and went out,
they followed her,
supposing she was
going to the tomb
to mourn there.
32 When Mary
reached the place
where Jesus was
and saw him, she
fell at his feet and
said, "Lord, if you
had been here, my
brother would not
have died."
33 When Jesus saw
her weeping, and
the Jews who had
come along with
her also weeping,
he was deeply
moved in spir-
it and troubled.
34 "Where have
you laid him?" he
asked.
"Come and see,
Lord," they re-
plied.
35 Jesus wept.
36 Then the Jews
said, "See how he
loved him!"
37 But some of
them said, "Could
not he who opened
the eyes of the
blind man

εἰποῦσα ἀπῆλθεν καὶ ἐφώνησεν ← Μαριὰμ τὴν ἀδελφὴν
when she had said she went back and spoke privately to her sister Mary, *{the} sister*
3306 599 2779 5888 3277 899 80 3452 3836 80
pt.aa.nsf v.aai.3s cj v.aai.3s n.asf d.asf n.asf

αὐτῆς λάθρα εἰποῦσα, ὁ διδάσκαλος πάρεστιν καὶ φωνεῖ σε. 29
her privately saying, "The Teacher is here and ⌊is asking for⌋ you." So when
899 3277 3306 3836 1437 4205 2779 5888 5148 1254 6055
r.gsf.3 adv pt.aa.nsf d.nsm n.nsm v.pai.3s cj v.pai.3s r.as.2

ἐκείνη δὲ ὡς ἤκουσεν ἠγέρθη ταχὺ καὶ ἤρχετο πρὸς αὐτόν. 30
Mary heard this, *So when heard* ⌊she got up⌋ quickly and went to him. Now
201 1697 1254 6055 201 1586 5444 2779 2262 4639 899 1254
r.nsf cj cj v.aai.3s v.api.3s adv cj v.imi.3s p.a r.asm.3

↱ οὔπω δὲ ἐληλύθει ὁ Ἰησοῦς εἰς τὴν κώμην, ἀλλ' ἦν ἔτι ἐν τῷ
Jesus had not yet *Now* entered *{the} Jesus {into}* the village, but was still in the
2652 2262 4037 1254 2262 3836 2652 1650 3836 3267 247 1639 2285 1877 3836
adv cj v.lai.3s d.nsm n.nsm p.a d.asf n.asf cj v.iai.3s adv p.d d.dsm

τόπῳ ὅπου ὑπήντησεν αὐτῷ ἡ Μάρθα. 31 ↱ οἱ οὖν Ἰουδαῖοι οἱ
place where Martha had met him. *{the} Martha* When the *{then}* Jews, who
5536 3963 3450 5636 899 3836 3450 1625 3836 4036 2681 3836
n.dsm cj v.aai.3s r.dsm.3 d.nsf n.nsf d.npm cj a.npm d.npm

ὄντες μετ' αὐτῆς ἐν τῇ οἰκίᾳ καὶ παραμυθούμενοι αὐτήν, ἰδόντες τὴν Μαριὰμ
were with Mary in the house *{and}* consoling her saw *{the} {Mary}*
1639 3552 899 1877 3836 3864 2779 4170 899 1625 3836 3452
pt.pa.npm p.g r.gsf.3 p.d d.dsf n.dsf cj pt.pm.npm r.asf.3 pt.aa.npm d.asf n.asf

ὅτι ταχέως ἀνέστη καὶ ἐξῆλθεν, ἠκολούθησαν αὐτῇ δόξαντες
that she had gotten up quickly *she had gotten up* and gone out, they followed her, assuming
4022 482 482 482 482 5441 482 2779 2002 199 899 1506
cj adv v.aai.3s cj v.aai.3s v.aai.3p r.dsf.3 pt.aa.npm

ὅτι ὑπάγει εἰς τὸ μνημεῖον ἵνα κλαύσῃ ἐκεῖ. 32 ἡ οὖν Μαριὰμ
that ⌊she was going⌋ to the tomb to weep there. *{the} {then}* When Mary
4022 5632 1650 3836 3646 2671 3081 1695 3836 4036 6055 3452
cj v.pai.3s p.a d.asn n.asn cj v.aas.3s adv d.nsf cj n.nsf

ὡς ἦλθεν ὅπου ἦν Ἰησοῦς ἰδοῦσα αὐτὸν ἔπεσεν αὐτοῦ πρὸς τοὺς
When came to where Jesus was *Jesus* and saw him, she fell at his *at {the}*
6055 2262 3963 2652 1639 2652 1625 899 4406 4639 899 4639 3836
cj v.aai.3s cj v.iai.3s n.nsm pt.aa.nsf r.asm.3 v.aai.3s r.gsm.3 p.a d.apm

πόδας λέγουσα αὐτῷ, κύριε, εἰ ἦς ὧδε οὐκ ἄν μου
feet, saying to him, "Lord, if ⌊you had been⌋ here, my brother would not *would my*
4546 3306 899 3261 1623 1639 6045 1609 81 323 4024 323 1609
n.apm pt.pa.nsf r.dsm.3 n.vsm cj v.iai.2s adv pl pl r.gs.1

ἀπέθανεν ὁ ἀδελφός. 33 Ἰησοῦς οὖν ὡς εἶδεν αὐτὴν κλαίουσαν καὶ τοὺς
have died." *{the} brother* When Jesus *{then} When* saw her weeping, and the
633 3836 81 6055 2652 4036 6055 1625 899 3081 2779 3836
v.aai.3s d.nsm n.nsm n.nsm cj cj v.aai.3s r.asf.3 pt.pa.asf cj d.apm

συνελθόντας αὐτῇ Ἰουδαίους κλαίοντας, ἐνεβριμήσατο τῷ
Jews ⌊who had come with⌋ her *Jews* weeping, he was deeply moved in his *{the}*
2681 5302 899 2681 3081 1839 1571 3836
pt.aa.apm r.dsf.3 a.apm pt.pa.apm v.ami.3s d.dsn

πνεύματι καὶ ἐτάραξεν ἑαυτὸν 34 καὶ εἶπεν, ποῦ τεθείκατε αὐτόν;
spirit and greatly distressed. *his {and}* He asked, "Where have you laid him?"
4460 2779 5429 1571 2779 3306 4543 5502 899
n.dsn cj v.aai.3s r.asm.3 cj v.aai.3s cj v.rai.2p r.asm.3

λέγουσιν αὐτῷ, κύριε, ἔρχου καὶ ἴδε. 35 ἐδάκρυσεν ὁ Ἰησοῦς.
They replied, *{to him}* "Lord, come and see." Jesus burst into tears. *{the} Jesus*
3306 899 3261 2262 2779 2623 2652 1233 3836 2652
v.pai.3p r.dsm.3 n.vsm v.pmm.2s cj v.aam.2s v.aai.3s d.nsm n.nsm

36 ἔλεγον οὖν οἱ Ἰουδαῖοι, ἴδε πῶς ἐφίλει αὐτόν. 37 τινὲς
So the Jews kept saying, *So the Jews* "See how he loved him!" But some
4036 3836 2681 3306 4036 3836 2681 2623 4802 5797 899 1254 5516
v.iai.3p cj d.npm a.npm pl pl v.iai.3s r.asm.3 r.npm

δὲ ἐξ αὐτῶν εἶπαν, ↱ οὐκ
But of them said, "Was not this man, who could open the eyes of the blind man,
1254 1666 899 3306 1538 4024 4047 4047 3836 487 487 3836 4057 3836 3836 5603 5603
cj p.g r.gpm.3 v.aai.3p pl

NASB

away and called
Mary her sister,
saying secretly,
"The Teacher is
here and is calling
for you." 29 And
when she heard it,
she *got up quickly
and was coming to
Him.
30 Now Jesus had
not yet come into
the village, but was
still in the place
where Martha met
Him. 31 Then the
Jews who were
with her in the
house, and consol-
ing her, when they
saw that Mary got
up quickly and
went out, they
followed her, sup-
posing that she was
going to the tomb
to weep there.
32 Therefore, when
Mary came where
Jesus was, she saw
Him, and fell at
His feet, saying to
Him, "Lord, if You
had been here, my
brother would not
have died." 33 When
Jesus therefore
saw her weeping,
and the Jews who
came with her
also weeping, He
was deeply moved
in spirit and was
troubled, 34 and
said, "Where have
you laid him?"
They *said to Him,
"Lord, come and
see." 35 Jesus wept.
36 So the Jews were
saying, "See how
He loved him!"
37 But some of them
said, "Could not
this man, who
opened the eyes of
the blind man, have

NIV

have kept this man
from dying?"

Jesus Raises Lazarus From the Dead

38 Jesus, once
more deeply
moved, came to
the tomb. It was a
cave with a stone
laid across the
entrance. 39 "Take
away the stone,"
he said.
"But, Lord," said
Martha, the sister
of the dead man,
"by this time there
is a bad odor, for
he has been there
four days."
40 Then Jesus said,
"Did I not tell you
that if you believe,
you will see the
glory of God?"
41 So they took
away the stone.
Then Jesus looked
up and said, "Fa-
ther, I thank you
that you have
heard me. 42 I knew
that you always
hear me, but I said
this for the ben-
efit of the people
standing here, that
they may believe
that you sent me."
43 When he had
said this, Jesus
called in a loud
voice, "Lazarus,
come out!" 44 The
dead man came
out, his hands and
feet wrapped with
strips of linen, and
a cloth around his
face.
Jesus said to
them, "Take off
the grave clothes
and let him go."

The Plot to Kill Jesus

45 Therefore many
of the Jews

ἐδύνατο οὗτος ὁ ἀνοίξας τοὺς ὀφθαλμοὺς τοῦ τυφλοῦ ποιῆσαι ἵνα
able *this man* *who* *could open* *the* *eyes* *of the* *blind man* to do something so that
1538 4047 3836 487 3836 4057 3836 5603 4472 2671
v.ipi.3s r.nsm d.nsm pt.aa.nsm d.apm n.apm d.gsm a.gsm f.aa cj

καὶ οὗτος ↱ μὴ ἀποθάνῃ; 38 Ἰησοῦς οὖν πάλιν ⌊ἐμβριμώμενος ἐν
{also} Lazarus would not have died?" Then Jesus, *Then* once more deeply moved,
2779 4047 633 3590 633 4036 2652 4036 4099 1839 1877
adv r.nsm pl v.aas.3s n.nsm cj adv pt.pm.nsm p.d

ἑαυτῷ⌋ ἔρχεται εἰς τὸ μνημεῖον· ἦν δὲ σπήλαιον καὶ λίθος ἐπέκειτο ἐπ'
came to the tomb. ⌊It was⌋ *{and}* a cave, and a stone was lying across
1571 2262 1650 3836 3646 1639 1254 5068 2779 3345 2130 2093
r.dsm.3 v.pmi.3s p.a d.asn n.asn v.iai.3s cj n.nsn cj n.nsm v.imi.3s p.d

αὐτῷ. 39 λέγει ὁ Ἰησοῦς, ἄρατε τὸν λίθον.
it. Jesus said, *{the}* *Jesus* ⌊"Take away⌋ the stone." Martha, the sister of the
899 2652 3306 3836 2652 149 3836 3345 3450 3836 80 3836 3836
r.dsn.3 v.pai.3s d.nsm n.nsm v.aam.2p d.asm n.asm

λέγει αὐτῷ ἡ ἀδελφὴ τοῦ τετελευτηκότος Μάρθα· κύριε, ἤδη
dead man, said to him, *the* *sister* *of the* *dead man* *Martha* "Lord, by now the body
5462 5462 3306 899 3836 80 3836 5462 3450 3261 2453
v.pai.3s r.dsm.3 d.nsf n.nsf d.gsm pt.ra.gsm n.nsf n.vsm adv

ὄζει, τεταρταῖος γάρ ἐστιν. 40 λέγει αὐτῇ
will smell because it has been buried for four days." *because* *it has been* Jesus said to her,
3853 1142 1639 1639 1639 5479 1142 1639 2652 3306 899
v.pai.3s a.nsm cj v.pai.3s v.pai.3s r.dsf.3

ὁ Ἰησοῦς, ↱ ↱ οὐκ εἶπόν σοι ὅτι ἐὰν πιστεύσῃς ὄψῃ τὴν
{the} *Jesus* "Did I not say to you that if you would believe ⌊you would see⌋ the
3836 2652 3306 3306 4024 3306 5148 4022 1569 4409 3972 3836
d.nsm n.nsm pl v.aai.1s r.ds.2 cj cj v.aas.2s v.fmi.2s d.asf

δόξαν τοῦ θεοῦ; 41 ἦραν οὖν τὸν λίθον.[a] ὁ δὲ Ἰησοῦς ἦρεν
glory of God?" So ⌊they took away⌋ *So* the stone. *{the}* Then Jesus lifted up
1518 3836 2536 4036 149 4036 3836 3345 3836 1254 2652 149 539
n.asf d.gsm n.gsm v.aai.3p cj d.asm n.asm d.nsm cj n.nsm v.aai.3s

τοὺς ὀφθαλμοὺς ἄνω καὶ εἶπεν, πάτερ, εὐχαριστῶ σοι ὅτι ἤκουσάς μου. 42 ἐγὼ
his eyes *up* and said, "Father, I thank you that you have heard me. I
3836 4057 539 2779 3306 4252 2373 5148 4022 201 1609 1609
d.apm n.apm adv cj v.aai.3s n.vsm v.pai.1s r.ds.2 cj v.aai.2s r.gs.1 r.ns.1

δὲ ᾔδειν ὅτι πάντοτέ μου ἀκούεις, ἀλλὰ διὰ τὸν
{and} know that you always hear me, *you hear* but I said this ⌊for the sake of⌋ the
1254 3857 4022 201 4121 201 1609 201 247 3306 3306 1328 3836
cj v.lai.1s cj adv r.gs.1 v.pai.2s cj p.a d.asm

ὄχλον τὸν περιεστῶτα εἶπον, ἵνα πιστεύσωσιν ὅτι σύ με ἀπέστειλας.
crowd *{the}* standing here, *I said* that they may believe that you sent me." *sent*
4063 3836 4325 3306 2671 4409 4022 5148 690 1609 690
n.asm d.asm pt.ra.asm v.aai.1s cj v.aas.3p cj r.ns.2 r.as.1 v.aai.2s

43 καὶ ταῦτα εἰπὼν → φωνῇ μεγάλῃ
{and} When he had said this, *When he had said* he called out in a loud voice, *loud*
2779 3306 3306 3306 3306 4047 3306 3198 3198 3198 3489 5889 3489
cj r.apn pt.aa.nsm n.dsf a.dsf

ἐκραύγασεν, Λάζαρε, δεῦρο ἔξω. 44 ἐξῆλθεν ὁ τεθνηκὼς
he called out "Lazarus, come out! The dead man came out, *The* *dead man* his feet and
3198 3276 1306 2032 3836 2569 2569 2002 3836 2569 3836 4546 2779
v.aai.3s n.vsm j adv v.aai.3s d.nsm pt.ra.nsm

δεδεμένος τοὺς πόδας καὶ τὰς χεῖρας κειρίαις καὶ ἡ ὄψις
his hands bound *his* *feet* *and* *his* *hands* ⌊with strips of cloth,⌋ and *{the}* his face
3836 5931 1313 3836 4546 2779 3836 5931 3024 2779 3836 899 4071
pt.rp.nsm d.apm n.apm cj d.apf n.apf n.dpf cj d.nsf n.nsf

αὐτοῦ → σουδαρίῳ περιεδέδετο. λέγει αὐτοῖς ὁ Ἰησοῦς, λύσατε
his wrapped in a cloth. *wrapped* Jesus said to them, *{the}* *Jesus* "Unwrap
899 4317 5051 4317 2652 3306 899 3836 2652 3395
r.gsm.3 n.dsn v.lpi.3s v.pai.3s r.dpm.3 d.nsm n.nsm v.aam.2p

αὐτὸν καὶ ἄφετε αὐτὸν ὑπάγειν. 45 πολλοὶ οὖν ἐκ τῶν Ἰουδαίων
him, and let him go." Therefore many *Therefore* of the Jews
899 2779 918 899 5632 4036 4498 4036 1666 3836 2681
r.asm.3 cj v.aam.2p r.asm.3 f.pa a.npm cj p.g d.gpm a.gpm

[a] οὐ ἦν ὁ τεθνηκὼς κείμενος included by TR after λίθον.

NASB

kept this man also
from dying?"
38 So Jesus, again
being deeply
moved within,
*came to the tomb.
Now it was a cave,
and a stone was ly-
ing against it. 39 Je-
sus *said, "Remove
the stone." Martha,
the sister of the
deceased, *said to
Him, "Lord, by
this time there will
be a stench, for
he has been *dead*
four days." 40 Jesus
*said to her, "Did
I not say to you
that if you believe,
you will see the
glory of God?" 41 So
they removed the
stone. Then Jesus
raised His eyes,
and said, "Father,
I thank You that
You have heard
Me. 42 I knew that
You always hear
Me; but because of
the people standing
around I said it,
so that they may
believe that You
sent Me." 43 When
He had said these
things, He cried
out with a loud
voice, "Lazarus,
come forth." 44 The
man who had died
came forth, bound
hand and foot with
wrappings, and his
face was wrapped
around with a
cloth. Jesus *said
to them, "Unbind
him, and let him
go."
45 Therefore many
of the Jews who

NIV

who had come to
visit Mary, and had
seen what Jesus
did, believed in
him. 46 But some of
them went to the
Pharisees and told
them what Jesus
had done. 47 Then
the chief priests
and the Pharisees
called a meeting of
the Sanhedrin.
"What are we
accomplishing?"
they asked. "Here
is this man per-
forming many
signs. 48 If we let
him go on like
this, everyone will
believe in him, and
then the Romans
will come and take
away both our
temple and our na-
tion."
49 Then one of
them, named Cai-
aphas, who was
high priest that
year, spoke up,
"You know noth-
ing at all! 50 You
do not realize that
it is better for you
that one man die
for the people than
that the whole na-
tion perish."
51 He did not say
this on his own,
but as high priest
that year he proph-
esied that Jesus
would die for the
Jewish nation,
52 and not only for
that nation but also
for the scattered
children of God, to
bring them togeth-
er and make them
one. 53 So from that
day on they plotted
to take his life.
54 Therefore Jesus

οἱ ἐλθόντες πρὸς τὴν Μαριὰμ καὶ θεασάμενοι ἃ ἐποίησεν ἐπίστευσαν εἰς
who had come with {the} Mary and seen what he had done, believed in
3836 2262 4639 3836 3452 2779 2517 4005 4472 4409 1650
d.npm pt.aa.npm p.a d.asf n.asf cj pt.am.npm r.apn v.aai.3s v.aai.3p p.a

αὐτόν· 46 τινὲς δὲ ἐξ αὐτῶν ἀπῆλθον πρὸς τοὺς Φαρισαίους καὶ
him. Some of them, however, of them went to the Pharisees and
899 5516 1666 899 1254 1666 899 599 4639 3836 5757 2779
r.asm.3 r.npm cj p.g r.gpm.3 v.aai.3p p.a d.apm n.apm cj

εἶπαν αὐτοῖς ἃ ἐποίησεν Ἰησοῦς. 47 συνήγαγον οὖν οἱ ἀρχιερεῖς καὶ
told them what Jesus had done. Jesus gathered together So the chief priests and
3306 899 4005 2652 4472 2652 5251 4036 3836 797 2779
v.aai.3p r.dpm.3 r.apn v.aai.3s n.nsm v.aai.3p cj d.npm n.npm cj

οἱ Φαρισαῖοι συνέδριον καὶ ἔλεγον, τί ποιοῦμεν ὅτι
the Pharisees gathered the Council together and said, "What ⌞are we going to do?⌟ For
3836 5757 5251 5284 5251 2779 3306 5515 4472 4022
d.npm n.npm n.asn cj v.iai.3p r.asn v.pai.1p cj

οὗτος ὁ ἄνθρωπος πολλὰ ποιεῖ σημεῖα; 48 ἐὰν ἀφῶμεν αὐτὸν
this {the} man is performing many is performing signs. If we let him
4047 3836 476 4472 4472 4498 4472 4956 1569 918 899
r.nsm d.nsm n.nsm a.apn v.pai.3s n.apn cj v.aas.1p r.asm.3

↰ ↰ οὕτως, πάντες πιστεύσουσιν εἰς αὐτόν, καὶ ἐλεύσονται οἱ
go on like this, everyone will believe in him, and the Romans will come the
918 918 4048 4246 4409 1650 899 2779 3836 4871 2262 3836
adv a.npm v.fai.3p p.a r.asm.3 cj v.fmi.3p d.npm

Ῥωμαῖοι καὶ ἀροῦσιν ἡμῶν καὶ τὸν τόπον καὶ τὸ ↰ ἔθνος. 49 εἷς
Romans and destroy both our both {the} holy place and {the} our nation." But one
4871 2779 149 2779 7005 2779 3836 5536 2779 3836 7005 1620 1254 1651
n.npm cj v.fai.3p r.gp.1 cj d.asm n.asm cj d.asn n.asn a.nsm

δέ τις ἐξ αὐτῶν Καϊάφας, ἀρχιερεὺς ὢν τοῦ ἐνιαυτοῦ
But {a certain} of them, Caiaphas, who was high priest who was {the} that year,
1254 5516 1666 899 2780 1639 1639 797 1639 3836 1697 1929
cj r.nsm p.g r.gpm.3 n.nsm n.nsm pt.pa.nsm d.gsm n.gsm

ἐκείνου, εἶπεν αὐτοῖς, ὑμεῖς οὐκ οἴδατε οὐδέν, 50 οὐδὲ → → ← λογίζεσθε
that said to them, "You know nothing know at all. Or do you not realize
1697 3306 899 7007 3857 4024 3857 4029 4028 3357
r.gsm v.aai.3s r.dpm.3 r.np.2 pl v.rai.2p a.asn cj v.pmi.2p

ὅτι → → συμφέρει ὑμῖν ἵνα εἷς ἄνθρωπος ἀποθάνῃ ὑπὲρ τοῦ λαοῦ καὶ
that it is to your advantage to your that one man should die for the people and
4022 7007 7007 5237 7007 2671 1651 476 633 5642 3836 3295 2779
cj v.pai.3s r.dp.2 cj a.nsm n.nsm v.aas.3s p.g d.gsm n.gsm cj

↰ ↱ μὴ ὅλον τὸ ἔθνος ἀπόληται. 51 τοῦτο
that the whole nation should not whole the nation perish?" He did not say this
2671 3836 3910 1620 660 3590 3910 3836 1620 660 3306 3306 4024 3306 4047
pl a.nsn d.nsn n.nsn v.ams.3s r.asn

δὲ ἀφ' ἑαυτοῦ οὐκ εἶπεν, ἀλλὰ ἀρχιερεὺς ὢν τοῦ ἐνιαυτοῦ ἐκείνου
{and} on his own, not He did say but being high priest being {the} that year that
1254 608 1571 4024 3306 247 1639 797 1639 3836 1697 1929 1697
cj p.g r.gsm.3 pl v.aai.3s cj n.nsm pt.pa.nsm d.gsm n.gsm r.gsm

ἐπροφήτευσεν ὅτι ἔμελλεν Ἰησοῦς ἀποθνῄσκειν ὑπὲρ τοῦ ἔθνους, 52 καὶ οὐχ
he was prophesying that Jesus was about Jesus to die for the nation, and not
4736 4022 2652 3516 2652 633 5642 3836 1620 2779 4024
v.aai.3s cj v.iai.3s n.nsm f.pa p.g d.gsn n.gsn cj pl

ὑπὲρ τοῦ ἔθνους μόνον ἀλλ' ἵνα καὶ τὰ τέκνα τοῦ
only for the nation, only but that {also} he should gather into one the children of
3667 5642 3836 1620 3667 247 2671 2779 5251 5251 5251 1650 1651 3836 5451 3836
p.g d.gsn n.gsn adv cj cj adv d.apn n.apn d.gsm

θεοῦ τὰ διεσκορπισμένα συναγάγῃ εἰς ἕν. 53 ἀπ' ἐκείνης οὖν τῆς
God who were scattered abroad. he should gather into one So from that So {the}
2536 3836 1399 5251 1650 1651 4036 608 1697 4036 3836
n.gsm d.apn pt.rp.apn v.aas.3s p.a a.asn p.g r.gsf cj d.gsf

ἡμέρας ἐβουλεύσαντο ἵνα → ἀποκτείνωσιν αὐτόν. 54 ὁ οὖν Ἰησοῦς
day on they planned to put him to death. him {the} therefore Jesus
2465 1086 2671 899 650 899 3836 4036 2652
n.gsf v.ami.3p cj v.aas.3p r.asm.3 d.nsm cj n.nsm

NASB

came to Mary, and
saw what He had
done, believed in
Him. 46 But some of
them went to the
Pharisees and told
them the things
which Jesus had
done.

Conspiracy to Kill Jesus

47 Therefore the
chief priests and
the Pharisees con-
vened a council,
and were saying,
"What are we
doing? For this
man is perform-
ing many signs.
48 If we let Him *go*
on like this, all
men will believe
in Him, and the
Romans will come
and take away both
our place and our
nation." 49 But one
of them, Caiaphas,
who was high
priest that year,
said to them, "You
know nothing at
all, 50 nor do you
take into account
that it is expedient
for you that one
man die for the
people, and that
the whole nation
not perish." 51 Now
he did not say this
on his own initia-
tive, but being high
priest that year,
he prophesied that
Jesus was going to
die for the nation,
52 and not for the
nation only, but
in order that He
might also gather
together into one
the children of God
who are scattered
abroad. 53 So from
that day on they
planned together to
kill Him.
54 Therefore Jesus

NIV

no longer moved
about publicly
among the people
of Judea. Instead
he withdrew to
a region near the
wilderness, to
a village called
Ephraim, where he
stayed with his dis-
ciples.
55 When it was al-
most time for the
Jewish Passover,
many went up
from the country
to Jerusalem for
their ceremonial
cleansing before
the Passover.
56 They kept look-
ing for Jesus, and
as they stood in
the temple courts
they asked one
another, "What do
you think? Isn't he
coming to the fes-
tival at all?" 57 But
the chief priests
and the Pharisees
had given orders
that anyone who
found out where
Jesus was should
report it so that
they might arrest
him.

Jesus Anointed at Bethany

12 Six days
before the
Passover, Jesus
came to Bethany,
where Lazarus
lived, whom Jesus
had raised from
the dead. 2 Here a
dinner was given
in Jesus' honor.
Martha served,
while Lazarus was
among those re-
clining at the table
with him. 3 Then
Mary took about a
pint[a] of pure nard,
an expensive per-
fume; she poured
it on Jesus' feet
and wiped his feet
with her hair.

[a] 3 Or about 0.5 liter

οὐκέτι παρρησίᾳ περιεπάτει ἐν τοῖς Ἰουδαίοις, ἀλλὰ
therefore no longer walked about openly *walked about* among the Jews, but
4036 4033 4344 4344 4244 4344 1877 3836 2681 247
adv n.dsf v.iai.3s p.d d.dpm a.dpm cj

ἀπῆλθεν ἐκεῖθεν εἰς τὴν χώραν ἐγγὺς τῆς ἐρήμου, εἰς Ἐφραὶμ
went from there to the region near the wilderness, to a town called Ephraim,
599 1696 1650 3836 6001 1584 3836 2245 1650 4484 3306 2394
v.aai.3s adv p.a d.asf n.asf p.g d.gsf n.gsf p.a n.asm

λεγομένην πόλιν, → κἀκεῖ ἔμεινεν μετὰ τῶν μαθητῶν. 55
called *town* and he stayed there *he stayed* with his disciples. Now the Passover
3306 4484 3531 3531 2795 3531 3552 3836 3412 1254 3836 4247
pt.pp.asf n.asf crasis v.aai.3s p.g d.gpm n.gpm

ἦν δὲ ἐγγὺς τὸ πάσχα τῶν Ἰουδαίων, καὶ ἀνέβησαν πολλοὶ
of the Jews was *Now* near, *the* *Passover* *of the* *Jews* and many went up *many*
3836 3836 2681 1639 1254 1584 3836 4247 3836 2681 2779 4498 326 4498
v.iai.3s cj adv d.nsn n.nsn d.gpm a.gpm cj v.aai.3p a.npm

εἰς Ἱεροσόλυμα ἐκ τῆς χώρας πρὸ τοῦ πάσχα ἵνα ἁγνίσωσιν ἑαυτούς.
to Jerusalem from the country ⌞prior to⌟ the Passover to purify themselves.
1650 2642 1666 3836 6001 4574 3836 4247 2671 49 1571
p.a n.apn p.g d.gsf n.gsf p.g d.gsn n.gsn cj v.aas.3p r.apm.3

56 ἐζήτουν οὖν τὸν Ἰησοῦν καὶ ἔλεγον μετ᾽ ἀλλήλων
⌞They were looking for⌟ *{then}* *{the}* Jesus and were talking with one another as they were
2426 4036 3836 2652 2779 3306 3552 253 2705 2705 2705
v.iai.3p cj d.asm n.asm cj v.iai.3p p.g r.gpm

ἐν τῷ ἱερῷ ἑστηκότες, τί → δοκεῖ ὑμῖν; ὅτι → ↱ ↱
standing in the temple, *as they were standing* "What do you think? *you* ~ Surely he will
2705 1877 3836 2639 2705 5515 7007 1506 7007 4022 2262 2262
p.d d.dsn n.dsn pt.ra.npm r.asn v.pai.3s r.dp.2 cj

⌞οὐ μὴ⌟ ἔλθῃ εἰς τὴν ἑορτήν; 57 δεδώκεισαν δὲ οἱ ἀρχιερεῖς καὶ οἱ
not come to the festival, will he?" *had given* Now the chief priests and the
4024 3590 2262 1650 3836 2038 1443 1254 3836 797 2779 3836
pl pl v.aas.3s p.a d.asf n.asf v.lai.3p cj d.npm n.npm cj d.npm

Φαρισαῖοι ἐντολὰς ἵνα ἐάν τις γνῷ ποῦ ἐστιν
Pharisees had given orders that if anyone knew where Jesus was
5757 1443 1443 1953 2671 1569 5516 1182 4543 1639
n.npm n.apf cj cj r.nsm v.aas.3s cj v.pai.3s

μηνύσῃ, ὅπως πιάσωσιν αὐτόν.
⌞he should let them know,⌟ so ⌞they might arrest⌟ him.
3606 3968 4389 899
v.aas.3s cj v.aas.3p r.asm.3

12:1 ὁ οὖν Ἰησοῦς πρὸ ἓξ ἡμερῶν τοῦ πάσχα ἦλθεν εἰς
{the} *{then}* *Jesus* Six days before *Six* *days* the Passover, Jesus came to
3836 4036 2652 1971 2465 4574 1971 2465 3836 4247 2652 2262 1650
d.nsm cj n.nsm p.g a.gpf n.gpf d.gsn n.gsn v.aai.3s p.a

Βηθανίαν, ὅπου ἦν Λάζαρος, ὃν ἤγειρεν ἐκ νεκρῶν Ἰησοῦς.
Bethany, where Lazarus was, *Lazarus* whom he had raised from the dead. *he*
1029 3963 3276 1639 3276 4005 2652 1586 1666 3738 2652
n.asf cj v.iai.3s n.nsm r.asm v.aai.3s p.g a.gpm n.nsm

2 ἐποίησαν οὖν αὐτῷ δεῖπνον ἐκεῖ, καὶ ἡ Μάρθα διηκόνει, ὁ δὲ
So they made *So* a dinner for him *dinner* there. *{and}* *{the}* Martha was serving, *{the}* and
4036 4472 4036 1270 899 1270 1695 2779 3836 3450 1354 3836 1254
v.aai.3p cj r.dsm.3 n.asn adv cj d.nsf n.nsf v.iai.3s d.nsm cj

Λάζαρος εἷς ἦν ἐκ τῶν ἀνακειμένων σὺν αὐτῷ. 3 ἡ οὖν Μαριὰμ
Lazarus was one *was* of those ⌞reclining at the table⌟ with him. *{the}* *{then}* Mary
3276 1639 1651 1639 1666 3836 367 5250 899 3836 4036 3452
n.nsm a.nsm v.iai.3s p.g d.gpm pt.pm.gpm p.d r.dsm.3 d.nsf cj n.nsf

λαβοῦσα λίτραν → μύρου → → νάρδου πιστικῆς πολυτίμου
took ⌞more than a pint⌟ of expensive perfume made of pure nard *pure* *expensive*
3284 3354 4501 3693 4410 3726 4410 4501
pt.aa.nsf n.asf n.gsn n.gsf a.gsf n.gsf

ἤλειψεν τοὺς πόδας τοῦ Ἰησοῦ καὶ ἐξέμαξεν ταῖς θριξὶν αὐτῆς τοὺς
and anointed the feet of Jesus and dried them with her hair. *her* *{the}*
230 3836 4546 3836 2652 2779 1726 3836 899 2582 899 3836
v.aai.3s d.apm n.apm d.gsm n.gsm cj v.aai.3s d.dpf n.dpf r.gsf.3 d.apm

NASB

no longer con-
tinued to walk
publicly among
the Jews, but went
away from there
to the country near
the wilderness,
into a city called
Ephraim; and there
He stayed with the
disciples.
55 Now the Pass-
over of the Jews
was near, and
many went up to
Jerusalem out of
the country before
the Passover to
purify themselves.
56 So they were
seeking for Jesus,
and were saying to
one another as they
stood in the temple,
"What do you
think; that He will
not come to the
feast at all?" 57 Now
the chief priests
and the Pharisees
had given orders
that if anyone
knew where He
was, he was to re-
port it so that they
might seize Him.

Mary Anoints Jesus

12:1 Jesus, therefore,
six days before the
Passover, came to
Bethany where La-
zarus was, whom
Jesus had raised
from the dead. 2 So
they made Him a
supper there, and
Martha was serv-
ing; but Lazarus
was one of those
reclining *at the*
table with Him.
3 Mary then took
a pound of very
costly perfume
of pure nard, and
anointed the feet
of Jesus and wiped
His feet with her
hair; and the

NIV

And the house was
filled with the fra-
grance of the per-
fume.
4 But one of his
disciples, Judas
Iscariot, who was
later to betray him,
objected, 5 "Why
wasn't this per-
fume sold and the
money given to the
poor? It was worth
a year's wages.[a]"
6 He did not say
this because he
cared about the
poor but because
he was a thief; as
keeper of the mon-
ey bag, he used
to help himself
to what was put
into it.
7 "Leave her
alone," Jesus re-
plied. "It was
intended that she
should save this
perfume for the
day of my burial.
8 You will always
have the poor
among you,[b] but
you will not al-
ways have me."
9 Meanwhile a
large crowd of
Jews found out
that Jesus was
there and came,
not only because
of him but also
to see Lazarus,
whom he had
raised from the
dead. 10 So the
chief priests made
plans to kill Laz-
arus as well, 11 for
on account of him
many of the Jews
were going over to
Jesus

πόδας αὐτοῦ· ἡ δὲ οἰκία ἐπληρώθη ἐκ τῆς ὀσμῆς τοῦ μύρου. 4 λέγει δὲ
{feet} *{of him}* The *{and}* house was filled with the fragrance of the perfume. *said* But
4546 899 3836 1254 3864 4444 1666 3836 4011 3836 3693 3306 1254
n.apm r.gsm.3 d.nsf cj n.nsf v.api.3s p.g d.gsf n.gsf d.gsn n.gsn v.pai.3s cj

Ἰούδας ὁ Ἰσκαριώτης εἷς ἐκ[a] τῶν μαθητῶν αὐτοῦ, ὁ μέλλων
Judas *{the}* Iscariot, one of *{the}* his disciples *his* (the ⌞one who would⌟ betray
2683 3836 2697 1651 1666 3836 899 3412 899 3836 3516 4140
n.nsm d.nsm n.nsm a.nsm p.g d.gpm n.gpm r.gsm.3 d.nsm pt.pa.nsm

αὐτὸν παραδιδόναι, 5 ⌞διὰ τί⌟ ➝ τοῦτο τὸ μύρον οὐκ ἐπράθη
him) *betray* said, "Why was not this *{the}* perfume *not* sold for
899 4140 3306 1328 5515 4405 4024 4047 3836 3693 4024 4405
r.asm.3 f.pa p.a r.asn r.nsn d.nsn n.nsn pl v.api.3s

τριακοσίων δηναρίων καὶ ἐδόθη → πτωχοῖς; 6 εἶπεν δὲ τοῦτο οὐχ
three hundred denarii and the money given to the poor?" He said *{and}* this, not
5559 1324 2779 1443 4777 3306 1254 4047 4024
a.gpn n.gpn cj v.api.3s a.dpm v.aai.3s cj r.asn pl

ὅτι περὶ τῶν πτωχῶν ἔμελεν αὐτῷ, ἀλλ᾽ ὅτι
because he was concerned about the poor, *he was concerned he* but because he was a
4022 899 3508 3508 4309 3836 4777 3508 899 247 4022 1639 1639
cj p.g d.gpm a.gpm v.iai.3s r.dsm.3 cj cj

κλέπτης ἦν καὶ τὸ γλωσσόκομον ἔχων
thief, *he was* and as keeper of the money box, *as keeper of* he used to help himself
3095 1639 2779 2400 2400 2400 3836 1186 2400 1002 1002 1002 1002 1002
n.nsm v.iai.3s cj d.asn n.asn pt.pa.nsm

τὰ βαλλόμενα ἐβάσταζεν. 7 εἶπεν οὖν ὁ
to what was put into it. *he used to help himself to* Jesus therefore said, *therefore* *{the}*
1002 3836 965 1002 2652 4036 3306 4036 3836
d.apn pt.pp.apn v.iai.3s v.aai.3s cj d.nsm

Ἰησοῦς, ἄφες αὐτήν, ↰ ἵνα εἰς τὴν ἡμέραν τοῦ
Jesus "Leave her alone. ~ She had to keep this perfume for the day of
2652 918 899 918 2671 5498 5498 5498 5498 899 899 1650 3836 2465 3836
n.nsm v.aam.2s r.asf.3 cj p.a d.asf n.asf d.gsm

ἐνταφιασμοῦ μου τηρήσῃ αὐτό· 8 τοὺς πτωχοὺς
my burial. *my* *She had to keep* *this perfume* For you will always have the poor
1609 1947 1609 5498 899 1142 2400 2400 4121 2400 3836 4777
n.gsm r.gs.1 v.aas.3s r.asn.3 d.apm a.apm

γὰρ πάντοτε ἔχετε μεθ᾽ ἑαυτῶν, ἐμὲ δὲ οὐ
For *always* *you will have* with you, but you will not always have me." *but* *not*
1142 4121 2400 3552 1571 1254 2400 2400 4024 4121 2400 1609 1254 4024
cj adv v.pai.2p p.g r.gpm.2 r.as.1 cj pl

πάντοτε ἔχετε. 9 → ἔγνω οὖν [b]ὄχλος πολὺς ἐκ
always *you will have* When a large crowd of the Jews learned *{then}* *crowd* *large* *of*
4121 2400 4498 4063 1666 3836 2681 1182 4036 4063 4498 1666
adv v.pai.2p v.aai.3s cj n.nsm a.nsm p.g

τῶν Ἰουδαίων ὅτι ἐκεῖ ἐστιν καὶ ἦλθον οὐ διὰ τὸν
the *Jews* that Jesus was there, *was* *{and}* they came, not only ⌞on account of⌟ *{the}*
3836 2681 4022 1639 1695 1639 2779 2262 4024 3667 1328 3836
d.gpm a.gpm cj adv v.pai.3s cj v.aai.3p pl p.a d.asm

Ἰησοῦν μόνον, ἀλλ᾽ ἵνα καὶ τὸν Λάζαρον ἴδωσιν ὃν
Jesus *only* but also that *also* they might see *{the}* Lazarus *they might see* whom
2652 3667 247 2779 2671 2779 1625 1625 1625 3836 3276 1625 4005
n.asm adv cj cj adv d.asm n.asm v.aas.3p r.asm

ἤγειρεν ἐκ νεκρῶν. 10 ἐβουλεύσαντο δὲ οἱ ἀρχιερεῖς
he had raised from the dead. So the chief priests made plans *So* *the* *chief priests*
1586 1666 3738 1254 3836 797 797 1086 1254 3836 797
v.aai.3s p.g a.gpm v.ami.3p cj d.npm n.npm

ἵνα καὶ τὸν Λάζαρον ἀποκτείνωσιν, 11 ὅτι
to put Lazarus to death as well, *{the}* *Lazarus* *put to death* because on account of
2671 650 3276 650 650 2779 3836 3276 650 4022 1328 1328 1328
cj adv d.asm n.asm v.aas.3p cj

πολλοὶ δι᾽ αὐτὸν ὑπῆγον τῶν Ἰουδαίων
him many *on account of* *him* of the Jews ⌞were going over⌟ *of the* *Jews* to Jesus
899 4498 1328 899 3836 3836 2681 5632 3836 2681 1650 2652
a.npm p.a r.asm.3 v.iai.3p d.gpm a.gpm

NASB

house was filled
with the fragrance
of the perfume.
4 But Judas
Iscariot, one of
His disciples, who
was intending to
betray Him, *said,
5 "Why was this
perfume not sold
for [a]three hundred
denarii and given
to poor *people?*"
6 Now he said this,
not because he
was concerned
about the poor, but
because he was
a thief, and as he
had the money
box, he used to
pilfer what was put
into it. 7 Therefore
Jesus said, "Let her
alone, so that she
may keep [b]it for the
day of My burial.
8 For you always
have the poor with
you, but you do not
always have Me."
9 The large crowd
of the Jews then
learned that He
was there; and
they came, not for
Jesus' sake only,
but that they might
also see Lazarus,
whom He raised
from the dead.
10 But the chief
priests planned
to put Lazarus to
death also; 11 be-
cause on account
of him many of the
Jews were going

[a] 5 Greek *three hundred denarii*
[b] 8 See Deut. 15:11.

[a] [ἐκ] UBS, omitted by TNIV.
[b] ὁ included by UBS before ὄχλος.

[a] Equivalent to 11 months' wages
[b] I.e. the custom of preparing the body for burial

NIV

and believing in
him.

Jesus Comes to Jerusalem as King

[12]The next day
the great crowd
that had come for
the festival heard
that Jesus was on
his way to Jerusa-
lem. [13]They took
palm branches and
went out to meet
him, shouting,

"Hosanna![a]"

"Blessed is he who
comes in the
name of the
Lord!"[b]

"Blessed is the
king of
Israel!"

[14]Jesus found a
young donkey and
sat on it, as it is
written:

[15]"Do not be afraid,
Daughter
Zion;
see, your king
is coming,
seated on a
donkey's
colt."[c]

[16]At first his
disciples did not
understand all this.
Only after Jesus
was glorified did
they realize that
these things had
been written about
him and that these
things had been
done to him.
[17]Now the crowd
that was with him
when he called
Lazarus from the
tomb and raised
him from the
dead continued to
spread the word.
[18]Many people,
because they had
heard that he had
performed this
sign, went out to
meet him. [19]So the

[a] 13 A Hebrew expression meaning "Save!" which became an exclamation of praise

[b] 13 Psalm 118:25,26

[c] 15 Zech. 9:9

καὶ ἐπίστευον εἰς τὸν Ἰησοῦν. 12 τῇ ἐπαύριον ὁ ὄχλος πολὺς
and ⌊putting their faith⌋ in him. *to* *{the}* *Jesus* The next day the large crowd *large*
2779 4409 1650 3836 2652 3836 2069 3836 4498 4063 4498
cj v.iai.3p p.a d.asm n.asm d.dsf adv d.nsm n.nsm a.nsm

ὁ ἐλθὼν εἰς τὴν ἑορτήν, ἀκούσαντες ὅτι ἔρχεται ὁ Ἰησοῦς εἰς
that had come to the festival, on hearing that Jesus was coming *{the}* *Jesus* to
3836 2262 1650 3836 2038 201 4022 2652 2262 3836 2652 1650
d.nsm pt.aa.nsm p.a d.asf n.asf pt.aa.npm cj v.pmi.3s d.nsm n.nsm p.a

Ἱεροσόλυμα 13 ἔλαβον τὰ βαΐα τῶν φοινίκων καὶ ἐξῆλθον εἰς ὑπάντησιν αὐτῷ
Jerusalem, took *{the}* branches of palm trees and went out to meet him.
2642 3284 3836 961 3836 5836 2779 2002 1650 5637 899
n.apn v.aai.3p d.apn n.apn d.gpm n.gpm cj v.aai.3p p.a n.asf r.dsm.3

καὶ ἐκραύγαζον, ὡσαννά· εὐλογημένος ὁ
{and} ⌊They began to cry out,⌋ "Hosanna! Blessed in the name of the Lord is the
2779 3198 6057 2328 1877 3950 3261 3836
cj v.iai.3p n.asn pt.rp.nsm d.nsm

ἐρχόμενος ἐν ὀνόματι κυρίου, καὶ[a] ὁ βασιλεὺς τοῦ Ἰσραήλ. 14 εὑρὼν
coming one, *in* *name* *Lord* even the king of Israel!" And Jesus found
2262 1877 3950 3261 2779 3836 995 3836 2702 1254 2652 2351
pt.pm.nsm p.d n.dsn n.gsm cj d.nsm n.nsm d.gsm n.gsm pt.aa.nsm

δὲ ὁ Ἰησοῦς ὀνάριον ἐκάθισεν ἐπ᾽ αὐτό, καθώς ἐστιν γεγραμμένον,
And *{the}* *Jesus* a young donkey and sat on it; as it is written,
1254 3836 2652 3942 2767 2093 899 2777 1639 1211
cj d.nsm n.nsm n.asn v.aai.3s p.a r.asn.3 cj v.pai.3s pt.rp.nsn

15 ↱ μὴ φοβοῦ, θυγάτηρ Σιών· ἰδοὺ ὁ βασιλεύς σου ἔρχεται, καθήμενος
"Do not be afraid, daughter of Zion; behold, *{the}* your king *your* is coming, seated
5828 3590 5828 2588 4994 2627 3836 5148 995 5148 2262 2764
pl v.ppm.2s n.vsf n.gsf j d.nsm n.nsm r.gs.2 v.pmi.3s pt.pm.nsm

ἐπὶ πῶλον ὄνου. 16 ταῦτα οὐκ
on a donkey's colt!" *donkey's* His disciples did not understand these things *not*
2093 3952 4798 3952 899 3412 1182 4024 1182 4047 4024
p.a n.asm n.gsf r.apn pl

ἔγνωσαν αὐτοῦ οἱ μαθηταὶ τὸ πρῶτον, ἀλλ᾽ ὅτε ἐδοξάσθη Ἰησοῦς τότε
did understand *His* *{the}* *disciples* *{the}* at first, but when Jesus was glorified, *Jesus* then
1182 899 3836 3412 3836 4754 247 4021 2652 1519 2652 5538
v.aai.3p r.gsm.3 d.npm n.npm d.asn adv cj cj v.api.3s n.nsm adv

ἐμνήσθησαν ὅτι ταῦτα ἦν ἐπ᾽ αὐτῷ γεγραμμένα καὶ ↰
they remembered that these things ⌊had been⌋ written about him, *written* and that they had
3630 4022 4047 1639 1211 2093 899 1211 2779 4022 4472 4472
v.api.3p cj r.npn v.iai.3s p.d r.dsm.3 pt.rp.npn cj

ταῦτα ἐποίησαν αὐτῷ. 17 ἐμαρτύρει οὖν ὁ ὄχλος ὁ
done these things *they had done* to him. *continued to bear witness* *{then}* The crowd that
4472 4047 4472 899 3455 4036 3836 4063 3836
r.apn v.aai.3p r.dsm.3 v.iai.3s cj d.nsm n.nsm d.nsm

ὢν μετ᾽ αὐτοῦ ὅτε τὸν Λάζαρον ἐφώνησεν ἐκ τοῦ μνημείου καὶ
⌊had been⌋ with him when he called *{the}* Lazarus *he called* ⌊out of⌋ the tomb and
1639 3552 899 4021 5888 5888 3836 3276 5888 1666 3836 3646 2779
pt.pa.nsm p.g r.gsm.3 cj d.asm n.asm v.aai.3s p.g d.gsn n.gsn cj

ἤγειρεν αὐτὸν ἐκ νεκρῶν. 18 διὰ τοῦτο[b]
raised him from the dead continued to bear witness. For this reason the crowd
1586 899 1666 3738 3455 3455 3455 3455 1328 4047 3836 4063
v.aai.3s r.asm.3 p.g a.gpm p.a r.asn

ὑπήντησεν αὐτῷ ὁ ὄχλος, ὅτι ἤκουσαν τοῦτο αὐτὸν
went to meet him, *the* *crowd* that is, because they heard he had performed this *he*
5636 899 3836 4063 4022 201 899 4472 4472 4047 899
v.aai.3s r.dsm.3 d.nsm n.nsm cj v.aai.3p r.asn r.asm.3

πεποιηκέναι τὸ σημεῖον. 19 οἱ οὖν Φαρισαῖοι εἶπαν πρὸς ἑαυτούς,
had performed *{the}* sign. The Pharisees therefore *Pharisees* said to one another,
4472 3836 4956 3836 5757 4036 5757 3306 4639 1571
f.ra d.asn n.asn d.npm cj n.npm v.aai.3p p.a r.apm.3

[a] [καὶ] UBS.

[b] καὶ included by UBS after τοῦτο.

NASB

away and were
believing in Jesus.

Jesus Enters Jerusalem

[12]On the next day
the large crowd
who had come to
the feast, when
they heard that
Jesus was coming
to Jerusalem, [13]took
the branches of
the palm trees and
went out to meet
Him, and *began* to
shout, "Hosanna!
BLESSED IS HE WHO
COMES IN THE NAME
OF THE LORD, even
the King of Israel."
[14]Jesus, finding a
young donkey, sat
on it; as it is writ-
ten, [15]"FEAR NOT,
DAUGHTER OF ZION;
BEHOLD, YOUR KING
IS COMING, SEATED
ON A DONKEY'S
COLT." [16]These
things His disciples
did not understand
at the first; but
when Jesus was
glorified, then they
remembered that
these things were
written of Him,
and that they had
done these things
to Him. [17]So the
people, who were
with Him when He
called Lazarus out
of the tomb and
raised him from the
dead, continued to
testify *about Him.*
[18]For this reason
also the people
went and met Him,
because they heard
that He had per-
formed this sign.
[19]So the Pharisees
said to one another,

NIV

Pharisees said to
one another, "See,
this is getting us
nowhere. Look
how the whole
world has gone af-
ter him!"

Jesus Predicts His Death

20 Now there
were some Greeks
among those who
went up to wor-
ship at the festival.
21 They came to
Philip, who was
from Bethsaida in
Galilee, with a re-
quest. "Sir," they
said, "we would
like to see Jesus."
22 Philip went to
tell Andrew; An-
drew and Philip in
turn told Jesus.
23 Jesus replied,
"The hour has
come for the Son
of Man to be glo-
rified. 24 Very
truly I tell you,
unless a kernel of
wheat falls to the
ground and dies,
it remains only a
single seed. But if
it dies, it produc-
es many seeds.
25 Anyone who
loves their life
will lose it, while
anyone who hates
their life in this
world will keep
it for eternal life.
26 Whoever serves
me must follow
me; and where I
am, my servant
also will be. My
Father will hon-
or the one who
serves me.
27 "Now my soul
is troubled, and
what shall I say?

θεωρεῖτε ὅτι οὐκ ὠφελεῖτε οὐδέν· ἴδε ὁ κόσμος ὀπίσω αὐτοῦ
"You see, *{that}* *{not}* you are accomplishing nothing. Look, the world has gone after him!"
2555 4022 4024 6067 4029 2623 3836 3180 599 599 3958 899
v.pai.2p cj pl v.pai.2p a.asn pl d.nsm n.nsm p.g r.gsm.3

ἀπῆλθεν. 20 ἦσαν δὲ Ἕλληνές τινες ἐκ τῶν ἀναβαινόντων ἵνα
has gone Now there were *Now* some Greeks *some* among those who went up to
599 1254 1639 1254 5516 1818 5516 1666 3836 326 2671
v.aai.3s v.iai.3p cj n.npm r.npm p.g d.gpm pt.pa.gpm cj

προσκυνήσωσιν ἐν τῇ ἑορτῇ· 21 οὗτοι οὖν προσῆλθον Φιλίππῳ τῷ ἀπὸ
worship at the festival. So these *So* came to Philip, who was from
4686 1877 3836 2038 4036 4047 4036 4665 5805 3836 608
v.aas.3p p.d d.dsf n.dsf r.npm cj v.aai.3p n.dsm d.dsm p.g

Βηθσαϊδὰ τῆς Γαλιλαίας καὶ ἠρώτων αὐτὸν λέγοντες, κύριε, θέλομεν
Bethsaida in Galilee, and asked him, saying, "Sir, ⌞we would like⌟ to see
1034 3836 1133 2779 2263 899 3306 3261 2527 1625 1625
n.gsf d.gsf n.gsf cj v.iai.3p r.asm.3 pt.pa.npm n.vsm v.pai.1p

τὸν Ἰησοῦν ἰδεῖν. 22 ἔρχεται ὁ Φίλιππος καὶ λέγει τῷ Ἀνδρέᾳ,
{the} Jesus." *to see* Philip went *{the}* *Philip* and told *{the}* Andrew; Andrew and
3836 2652 1625 5805 2262 3836 5805 2779 3306 3836 436 436 2779
d.asm n.asm f.aa v.pmi.3s d.nsm n.nsm cj v.pai.3s d.dsm n.dsm

ἔρχεται Ἀνδρέας καὶ Φίλιππος καὶ λέγουσιν τῷ Ἰησοῦ. 23 ὁ δὲ Ἰησοῦς
Philip went *Andrew* *and* *Philip* and told *{the}* Jesus. *{the}* And Jesus
5805 2262 436 2779 5805 2779 3306 3836 2652 3836 1254 2652
v.pmi.3s n.nsm cj n.nsm cj v.pai.3p d.dsm n.dsm d.nsm cj n.nsm

ἀποκρίνεται αὐτοῖς λέγων, ἐλήλυθεν ἡ ὥρα ἵνα
answered them, saying, "The hour has come *The* *hour* for the Son of Man
646 899 3306 3836 6052 2262 3836 6052 2671 3836 5626 3836 476
v.pmi.3s r.dpm.3 pt.pa.nsm v.rai.3s d.nsf n.nsf cj

δοξασθῇ ὁ υἱὸς τοῦ ἀνθρώπου. 24 ⌞ἀμὴν ἀμὴν⌟ λέγω
to be glorified. *the* *Son* *of* *Man* I tell you the solemn truth, *I tell*
1519 3836 5626 3836 476 3306 3306 7007 297 297 3306
v.aps.3s d.nsm n.nsm d.gsm n.gsm pl pl v.pai.1s

ὑμῖν, ⌞ἐὰν μὴ⌟ ὁ κόκκος τοῦ σίτου πεσὼν εἰς τὴν γῆν ἀποθάνῃ, αὐτὸς
you unless a kernel of wheat falls into the ground and dies, it
7007 1569 3590 3836 3133 3836 4992 4406 1650 3836 1178 633 899
r.dp.2 cj pl d.nsm n.nsm d.gsm n.gsm pt.aa.nsm p.a d.asf n.asf v.aas.3s r.nsm

μόνος μένει· ἐὰν δὲ ἀποθάνῃ, πολὺν καρπὸν
remains a single kernel; *remains* but if *but* it dies it produces a great harvest.
3531 3668 3531 1254 1569 1254 633 5770 5770 4498 2843
a.nsm v.pai.3s cj cj v.aas.3s a.asm n.asm

φέρει. 25 ὁ φιλῶν τὴν ψυχὴν αὐτοῦ ἀπολλύει αὐτήν, καὶ ὁ
it produces The ⌞one who loves⌟ *{the}* his life *his* loses it, and the
5770 3836 5797 3836 899 6034 899 660 899 2779 3836
v.pai.3s d.nsm pt.pa.nsm d.asf n.asf r.gsm.3 v.pai.3s r.asf.3 cj d.nsm

μισῶν τὴν ψυχὴν αὐτοῦ ἐν τῷ κόσμῳ τούτῳ εἰς
⌞one who hates⌟ *{the}* his life *his* in *{the}* this world *this* preserves it for eternal
3631 3836 899 6034 899 1877 3836 4047 3180 4047 5875 899 1650 173
pt.pa.nsm d.asf n.asf r.gsm.3 p.d d.dsm n.dsm r.dsm p.a

ζωὴν αἰώνιον φυλάξει αὐτήν. 26 ἐὰν ἐμοί τις διακονῇ,
life. *eternal* *preserves* *it* If anyone would serve me, *anyone* *would serve* he must
2437 173 5875 899 1569 5516 1354 1354 1609 5516 1354 199 199
n.asf a.asf v.fai.3s r.asf.3 cj r.ds.1 r.nsm v.pas.3s

ἐμοὶ ἀκολουθείτω, καὶ ὅπου εἰμὶ ἐγὼ ἐκεῖ καὶ ὁ
follow me; *he must follow* and where I am, *I* my servant will be there also. *{the}*
199 1609 199 2779 3963 1609 1639 1609 1847 1356 1639 1639 1695 2779 3836
r.ds.1 v.pam.3s cj cj v.pai.1s r.ns.1 adv adv d.nsm

διάκονος ὁ ἐμὸς ἔσται· ἐάν τις ἐμοὶ διακονῇ τιμήσει
servant *{the}* *my* *will be* If anyone would serve me, *would serve* the Father will honor
1356 3836 1847 1639 1569 5516 1354 1354 1609 1354 3836 4252 5506
n.nsm d.nsm r.nsm.1 v.fmi.3s cj r.nsm r.ds.1 v.pas.3s v.fai.3s

αὐτὸν ὁ πατήρ. 27 νῦν ↱ ἡ ψυχή μου τετάρακται, καὶ τί εἴπω;
him. *the* *Father* "Now is *{the}* my heart *my* deeply troubled. And what ⌞am I to say?⌟
899 3836 4252 3814 5429 3836 1609 6034 1609 5429 2779 5515 3306
r.asm.3 d.nsm n.nsm adv d.nsf n.nsf r.gs.1 v.rpi.3s cj r.asn v.aas.1s

NASB

"You see that you
are not doing any
good; look, the
world has gone
after Him."

Greeks Seek Jesus

20 Now there
were some Greeks
among those who
were going up
to worship at the
feast; 21 these then
came to Philip,
who was from
Bethsaida of Gali-
lee, and *began to*
ask him, saying,
"Sir, we wish to
see Jesus." 22 Philip
*came and *told
Andrew; Andrew
and Philip *came
and *told Jesus.
23 And Jesus *an-
swered them, say-
ing, "The hour has
come for the Son
of Man to be glori-
fied. 24 Truly, truly,
I say to you, unless
a grain of wheat
falls into the earth
and dies, it remains
alone; but if it dies,
it bears much fruit.
25 He who loves his
life loses it, and
he who hates his
life in this world
will keep it to life
eternal. 26 If anyone
serves Me, he must
follow Me; and
where I am, there
My servant will
be also; if anyone
serves Me, the
Father will honor
him.

Jesus Foretells His Death

27 "Now My
soul has become
troubled; and what
shall I say, 'Father,

NIV

'Father, save me
from this hour'?
No, it was for this
very reason I came
to this hour. [28]Fa-
ther, glorify your
name!"
Then a voice
came from heaven,
"I have glorified
it, and will glori-
fy it again." [29]The
crowd that was
there and heard it
said it had thun-
dered; others said
an angel had spo-
ken to him.
[30]Jesus said,
"This voice was
for your benefit,
not mine. [31]Now
is the time for
judgment on this
world; now the
prince of this
world will be driv-
en out. [32]And I,
when I am lifted
up[a] from the earth,
will draw all peo-
ple to myself."
[33]He said this to
show the kind of
death he was going
to die.
[34]The crowd
spoke up, "We
have heard from
the Law that the
Messiah will re-
main forever, so
how can you say,
'The Son of Man
must be lifted up'?
Who is this 'Son
of Man'?"
[35]Then Jesus told
them, "You are
going to have the
light just a little
while longer. Walk
while you have
the light, before
darkness overtakes
you.

[a] 32 The Greek for *lifted up* also means *exalted.*

πάτερ, σῶσόν με ἐκ τῆς ὥρας ταύτης; ἀλλὰ διὰ τοῦτο ἦλθον
'Father, deliver me from *{the}* this hour'? *this* But for ⌞this very purpose⌟ ⌞I have come⌟
4252 5392 1609 1666 3836 4047 6052 4047 247 1328 4047 2262
n.vsm v.aam.2s r.as.1 p.g d.gsf n.gsf r.gsf cj p.a r.asn v.aai.1s

εἰς τὴν ὥραν ταύτην. 28 πάτερ, δόξασόν σου τὸ ὄνομα. ἦλθεν οὖν
to *{the}* this hour! *this* Father, glorify your *{the}* name." Then a voice came *Then*
1650 3836 4047 6052 4047 4252 1519 5148 3836 3950 4036 5889 2262 4036
p.a d.asf n.asf r.asf n.vsm v.aam.2s r.gs.2 d.asn n.asn v.aai.3s cj

φωνὴ ἐκ τοῦ οὐρανοῦ· καὶ ἐδόξασα καὶ πάλιν δοξάσω.
voice from *{the}* heaven: *{and}* "I have glorified it, and I will glorify it again." *I will glorify*
5889 1666 3836 4041 2779 1519 2779 1519 1519 1519 4099 1519
n.nsf p.g d.gsm n.gsm cj v.aai.1s cj adv v.fai.1s

29 ὁ οὖν ὄχλος ὁ ἑστὼς καὶ ἀκούσας ἔλεγεν
The *{then}* crowd that was standing there and had heard the voice said that it was
3836 4036 4063 3836 2705 2779 201 3306 1181 1181
d.nsm cj n.nsm d.nsm pt.ra.nsm cj pt.aa.nsm v.iai.3s

βροντὴν γεγονέναι, ἄλλοι ἔλεγον, ἄγγελος αὐτῷ λελάληκεν. 30
thunder; *it was* others said, "An angel has spoken to him." *has spoken* Jesus
1103 1181 257 3306 34 3281 3281 899 3281 2652
n.asf f.ra r.npm v.iai.3p n.nsm r.dsm.3 v.rai.3s

ἀπεκρίθη Ἰησοῦς καὶ εἶπεν, οὐ δι᾽ ἐμὲ ↰ ἡ φωνὴ αὕτη
answered, *Jesus* *{and}* saying, "This voice was not for my benefit, *{the}* *voice* *This*
646 2652 2779 3306 4047 5889 1181 4024 1328 1609 1328 3836 5889 4047
v.api.3s n.nsm cj v.aai.3s pl p.a r.as.1 d.nsf n.nsf r.nsf

γέγονεν ἀλλὰ δι᾽ ὑμᾶς. 31 νῦν κρίσις ἐστὶν τοῦ κόσμου τούτου, νῦν
was but for yours. "Now is the judgment *is* of this world; *this* now
1181 247 1328 7007 3814 1639 3213 1639 3836 4047 3180 4047 3814
v.rai.3s cj p.a r.ap.2 adv n.nsf v.pai.3s d.gsm n.gsm r.gsm adv

↱ ὁ ἄρχων τοῦ κόσμου τούτου ἐκβληθήσεται ἔξω· 32 κἀγὼ ἐὰν
will the ruler of this world *this* be driven out. And I, when
1675 3836 807 3836 4047 3180 4047 1675 2032 2743 1569
d.nsm n.nsm d.gsm n.gsm r.gsm v.fpi.3s adv crasis cj

ὑψωθῶ ἐκ τῆς γῆς, πάντας ἑλκύσω πρὸς ἐμαυτόν. 33 τοῦτο
⌞I am lifted up⌟ from the earth, will draw all people *will draw* to myself." He said this
5738 1666 3836 1178 1816 1816 4246 1816 4639 1831 3306 3306 4047
v.aps.1s p.g d.gsf n.gsf a.apm v.fai.1s p.a r.asm.1 r.asn

δὲ ἔλεγεν σημαίνων ποίῳ θανάτῳ ἤμελλεν ἀποθνῄσκειν. 34
{and} *He said* to signify the kind of death he was going to die. The crowd
1254 3306 4955 4481 2505 3516 633 3836 4063
cj v.iai.3s pt.pa.nsm r.dsm n.dsm v.iai.3s f.pa

ἀπεκρίθη οὖν αὐτῷ ὁ ὄχλος, ἡμεῖς ἠκούσαμεν ἐκ τοῦ νόμου ὅτι ὁ χριστὸς
responded, *{then}* *{to him}* *The* *crowd* "We have heard from the law that the Christ
646 4036 899 3836 4063 7005 201 1666 3836 3795 4022 3836 5986
v.api.3s cj r.dsm.3 d.nsm n.nsm r.np.1 v.aai.1p p.g d.gsm n.gsm cj d.nsm n.nsm

μένει εἰς τὸν αἰῶνα, καὶ πῶς λέγεις σὺ ὅτι
is to remain for all time; so how is it that you are saying *you* that the Son of Man
3531 1650 3836 172 2779 4802 5148 3306 5148 4022 3836 5626 3836 476
v.pai.3s p.a d.asm n.asm cj cj v.pai.2s r.ns.2 cj

δεῖ ὑψωθῆναι τὸν υἱὸν τοῦ ἀνθρώπου; τίς ἐστιν οὗτος ὁ υἱὸς τοῦ
must be lifted up? *the* *Son* *of* *Man* Who is this *{the}* Son of
1256 5738 3836 5626 3836 476 5515 1639 4047 3836 5626 3836
v.pai.3s f.ap d.asm n.asm d.gsm n.gsm r.nsm v.pai.3s r.nsm d.nsm n.nsm d.gsm

ἀνθρώπου; 35 εἶπεν οὖν αὐτοῖς ὁ Ἰησοῦς, ↱
Man?" Then Jesus said *Then* to them, *{the}* *Jesus* "The light will be with you for
476 4036 2652 3306 4036 899 3836 2652 3836 5890 1639 1639 1877 7007 5989
n.gsm v.aai.3s cj r.dpm.3 d.nsm n.nsm

ἔτι μικρὸν χρόνον τὸ φῶς ἐν ὑμῖν ἐστιν. περιπατεῖτε ὡς τὸ φῶς
yet a little while. *The* *light* *with* *you* *will be* Keep walking while you have the light,
2285 3625 5989 3836 5890 1877 7007 1639 4344 6055 2400 2400 3836 5890
adv a.asm n.asm d.nsn n.nsn p.d r.dp.2 v.pai.3s v.pam.2p cj d.asn n.asn

ἔχετε, ἵνα μὴ σκοτία ὑμᾶς καταλάβῃ· καὶ ὁ
you have so that the darkness will not *darkness* overtake you. *will overtake* *{and}* The
2400 2671 5028 2898 3590 5028 2898 7007 2898 2779 3836
v.pai.2p cj pl n.nsf r.ap.2 v.aas.3s cj d.nsm

NASB

save Me from
this hour'? But
for this purpose I
came to this hour.
[28]Father, glorify
Your name." Then
a voice came out
of heaven: "I have
both glorified it,
and will glorify
it again." [29]So the
crowd *of people*
who stood by
and heard it were
saying that it had
thundered; others
were saying, "An
angel has spoken
to Him." [30]Jesus
answered and said,
"This voice has not
come for My sake,
but for your sakes.
[31]Now judgment is
upon this world;
now the ruler of
this world will be
cast out. [32]And I,
if I am lifted up
from the earth, will
draw all men to
Myself." [33]But He
was saying this to
indicate the kind
of death by which
He was to die.
[34]The crowd then
answered Him,
"We have heard
out of the Law that
the Christ is to
remain forever; and
how can You say,
'The Son of Man
must be lifted up'?
Who is this Son of
Man?" [35]So Jesus
said to them, "For
a little while longer
the Light is among
you. Walk while
you have the Light,
so that darkness
will not overtake

NIV

Whoever walks in
the dark does not
know where they
are going. [36]Be-
lieve in the light
while you have
the light, so that
you may become
children of light."
When he had fin-
ished speaking,
Jesus left and hid
himself from them.

Belief and Unbelief Among the Jews

[37]Even after Jesus
had performed so
many signs in their
presence, they still
would not believe
in him. [38]This
was to fulfill the
word of Isaiah the
prophet:

"Lord, who has
believed our
message
and to whom
has the
arm of the
Lord been
revealed?"[a]

[39]For this reason
they could not be-
lieve, because, as
Isaiah says else-
where:

[40]"He has blinded
their eyes
and hardened
their hearts,
so they can neither
see with their
eyes,
nor understand
with their
hearts,
nor turn—and
I would heal
them."[b]

[41]Isaiah said this
because he saw
Jesus' glory and
spoke about him.
[42]Yet at the same
time many even
among the leaders
believed in him.
But because of
the Pharisees they
would not openly
acknowledge their
faith for fear they
would be put out
of the synagogue;

[a] 38 Isaiah 53:1
[b] 40 Isaiah 6:10

περιπατῶν ἐν τῇ σκοτίᾳ ↱ οὐκ οἶδεν ποῦ ὑπάγει. [36] ὡς τὸ
one who walks in the darkness does not know where he is going. While you have the
4344 1877 3836 5028 3857 4024 3857 4543 5632 6055 2400 2400 3836
pt.pa.nsm p.d d.dsf n.dsf pl v.rai.3s cj v.pai.3s cj d.asn

φῶς ἔχετε, πιστεύετε εἰς τὸ φῶς, ἵνα υἱοὶ φωτὸς γένησθε.
light, *you have* believe in the light, so that you may become sons of light." *you may become*
5890 2400 4409 1650 3836 5890 2671 1181 1181 1181 5626 5890 1181
n.asn v.pai.2p v.pam.2p p.a d.asn n.asn cj n.npm n.gsn v.ams.2p

ταῦτα ἐλάλησεν Ἰησοῦς, καὶ ↱ ἀπελθὼν ἐκρύβη ἀπ'
When Jesus said these things, *said* *Jesus* *{and}* he went away and hid himself from
2652 3281 4047 3281 2652 2779 3221 599 3221 608
r.apn v.aai.3s n.nsm cj pt.aa.nsm v.api.3s p.g

αὐτῶν. [37] τοσαῦτα δὲ αὐτοῦ σημεῖα πεποιηκότος →
them. Though he had done such great *{and}* *he* signs *Though had done* in their
899 4472 899 4472 4472 5537 1254 899 4956 4472 899
r.gpm.3 r.apn cj r.gsm.3 n.apn pt.ra.gsm

ἔμπροσθεν αὐτῶν ⌊οὐκ ἐπίστευον⌋ εἰς αὐτόν, [38] ἵνα ὁ
presence, *their* they continued in their unbelief toward him, that the
1869 899 4024 4409 1650 899 2671 3836
p.g r.gpm.3 pl v.iai.3p p.a r.asm.3 cj d.nsm

λόγος Ἠσαΐου τοῦ προφήτου πληρωθῇ ὃν εἶπεν, κύριε,
word spoken by the prophet Isaiah *the* *prophet* might be fulfilled: *{that}* *spoken* "Lord,
3364 3306 3836 4737 2480 3836 4737 4444 4005 3306 3261
n.nsm n.gsm d.gsm n.gsm v.aps.3s r.asm v.aai.3s n.vsm

τίς ἐπίστευσεν τῇ ἀκοῇ ἡμῶν; καὶ ↱ ὁ βραχίων → κυρίου
who has believed what they heard from us, and to whom has the arm of the Lord
5515 4409 3836 198 7005 2779 5515 5515 636 3836 1098 3261
r.nsm v.aai.3s d.dsf n.dsf r.gp.1 cj d.nsm n.nsm n.gsm

τίνι ἀπεκαλύφθη; [39] ⌊διὰ τοῦτο⌋ οὐκ ἠδύναντο πιστεύειν,
to whom been revealed?" The reason why they could not *they could* believe was
5515 636 1328 4047 1538 1538 4024 1538 4409
r.dsm v.api.3s p.a r.asn pl v.ipi.3p f.pa

ὅτι πάλιν εἶπεν Ἠσαΐας, [40] τετύφλωκεν αὐτῶν τοὺς ὀφθαλμοὺς καὶ
that in another place Isaiah said, *Isaiah* "He has blinded their *{the}* eyes and
4022 4099 2480 3306 2480 5604 899 3836 4057 2779
cj adv v.aai.3s n.nsm v.rai.3s r.gpm.3 d.apm n.apm cj

ἐπώρωσεν αὐτῶν τὴν καρδίαν, ⌊ἵνα μὴ⌋ ἴδωσιν τοῖς ὀφθαλμοῖς καὶ
hardened their *{the}* heart, lest ⌊they should see⌋ ⌊with their⌋ eyes, and
4800 899 3836 2840 2671 3590 1625 3836 4057 2779
v.aai.3s r.gpm.3 d.asf n.asf cj pl v.aas.3p d.dpm n.dpm cj

νοήσωσιν τῇ καρδίᾳ καὶ στραφῶσιν, καὶ ἰάσομαι αὐτούς. [41]
perceive ⌊with their⌋ heart, and turn, and I would heal them." Isaiah said
3783 3836 2840 2779 5138 2779 2615 899 2480 3306
v.aas.3p d.dsf n.dsf cj v.aps.3p cj v.fmi.1s r.apm.3

ταῦτα εἶπεν Ἠσαΐας ὅτι εἶδεν τὴν δόξαν αὐτοῦ, καὶ ἐλάλησεν περὶ
these things *said* *Isaiah* because he saw *{the}* Christ's glory *Christ's* and spoke of
4047 3306 2480 4022 1625 3836 899 1518 899 2779 3281 4309
r.apn v.aai.3s n.nsm cj v.aai.3s d.asf n.asf r.gsm.3 cj v.aai.3s p.g

αὐτοῦ. [42] ⌊ὅμως μέντοι⌋ καὶ ἐκ τῶν ἀρχόντων πολλοὶ ἐπίστευσαν εἰς
him. Nevertheless, many even of the authorities *many* believed in
899 3940 3530 4498 2779 1666 3836 807 4498 4409 1650
r.gsm.3 adv cj adv p.g d.gpm n.gpm a.npm v.aai.3p p.a

αὐτόν, ἀλλὰ διὰ τοὺς Φαρισαίους ↱ ↱ οὐχ ὡμολόγουν ← ⌊ἵνα μὴ⌋
him, but ⌊for fear of⌋ the Pharisees they would not confess it openly, lest
899 247 1328 3836 5757 3933 3933 4024 3933 2671 3590
r.asm.3 cj p.a d.apm n.apm pl v.iai.3p cj pl

ἀποσυνάγωγοι γένωνται· [43] ἠγάπησαν γὰρ τὴν δόξαν τῶν
they be ⌊expelled from the synagogue.⌋ *they be* For they loved *For* the praise of
1181 1181 697 1181 1142 26 1142 3836 1518 3836
a.npm v.ams.3p v.aai.3p cj d.asf n.asf d.gpm

NASB

you; he who walks
in the darkness
does not know
where he goes.
[36]While you have
the Light, believe
in the Light, so that
you may become
sons of Light."
These things
Jesus spoke, and
He went away and
hid Himself from
them. [37]But though
He had performed
so many signs be-
fore them, *yet* they
were not believ-
ing in Him. [38]*This*
was to fulfill the
word of Isaiah the
prophet which he
spoke: "LORD, WHO
HAS BELIEVED OUR
REPORT? AND TO
WHOM HAS THE ARM
OF THE LORD BEEN
REVEALED?" [39]For
this reason they
could not believe,
for Isaiah said
again, [40]"HE HAS
BLINDED THEIR EYES
AND HE HARDENED
THEIR HEART, SO
THAT THEY WOULD
NOT SEE WITH THEIR
EYES AND PERCEIVE
WITH THEIR HEART,
AND BE CONVERTED
AND I HEAL THEM."
[41]These things Isa-
iah said because he
saw His glory, and
he spoke of Him.
[42]Nevertheless
many even of the
rulers believed in
Him, but because
of the Pharisees
they were not
confessing *Him*,
for fear that they
would be put out
of the synagogue;
[43]for they loved the
approval of men

NIV

[43]for they loved
human praise more
than praise from
God.
[44]Then Jesus
cried out, "Who-
ever believes in me
does not believe
in me only, but in
the one who sent
me. [45]The one
who looks at me
is seeing the one
who sent me. [46]I
have come into the
world as a light,
so that no one
who believes in
me should stay in
darkness.
[47]"If anyone hears
my words but does
not keep them, I do
not judge that per-
son. For I did not
come to judge the
world, but to save
the world. [48]There
is a judge for the
one who rejects me
and does not ac-
cept my words; the
very words I have
spoken will con-
demn them at the
last day. [49]For I did
not speak on my
own, but the Fa-
ther who sent me
commanded me to
say all that I have
spoken. [50]I know
that his command
leads to eternal
life. So whatever I
say is just what the
Father has told me
to say."

Jesus Washes His Disciples' Feet

13 It was just
before the
Passover Festival.
Jesus knew that
the hour had come
for him to leave
this world and
go to

ἀνθρώπων μᾶλλον ἤπερ τὴν δόξαν τοῦ θεοῦ. 44 Ἰησοῦς δὲ ἔκραξεν καὶ εἶπεν,
men more than the praise of God. Then Jesus *Then* cried out, *{and}* saying,
476 3437 2472 3836 1518 3836 2536 1254 2652 1254 3189 2779 3306
n.gpm adv.c pl d.asf n.asf d.gsm n.gsm n.nsm cj v.aai.3s cj v.aai.3s

ὁ πιστεύων εἰς ἐμὲ οὐ πιστεύει εἰς ἐμὲ ἀλλὰ εἰς τὸν
"The one who believes in me believes not *believes* only in me but in the
3836 4409 1650 1609 4409 4024 4409 1650 1609 247 1650 3836
d.nsm pt.pa.nsm p.a r.as.1 pl v.pai.3s p.a r.as.1 cj p.a d.asm

πέμψαντά με, 45 καὶ ὁ θεωρῶν ἐμὲ θεωρεῖ τὸν πέμψαντά με. 46 ἐγὼ
one who sent me. And the ⌊one who sees⌋ me sees the one who sent me. I have
4287 1609 2779 3836 2555 1609 2555 3836 4287 1609 1609 2262
pt.aa.asm r.as.1 cj d.nsm pt.pa.nsm r.as.1 v.pai.3s d.asm pt.aa.asm r.as.1 r.ns.1

φῶς εἰς τὸν κόσμον ἐλήλυθα, ἵνα πᾶς ὁ πιστεύων
come into the world as light, *into the world have come* so that everyone who believes
2262 1650 3836 3180 5890 1650 3836 3180 2262 2671 4246 3836 4409
n.nsn p.a d.asm n.asm v.rai.1s cj a.nsm d.nsm pt.pa.nsm

εἰς ἐμὲ ἐν τῇ σκοτίᾳ μὴ μείνῃ. 47 καὶ ἐάν τίς
in me should not remain in *{the}* darkness. *not should remain* *{and}* If anyone hears
1650 1609 3531 3590 3531 1877 3836 5028 3590 3531 2779 1569 5516 201
p.a r.as.1 p.d d.dsf n.dsf pl v.aas.3s cj cj r.nsm

μου ἀκούσῃ τῶν ῥημάτων καὶ ↱ μὴ φυλάξῃ, ἐγὼ ↱ οὐ ↱ ↱ ↱
my *hears* *{the}* words and does not keep them, I am not the one who
1609 201 3836 4839 2779 5875 3590 5875 1609 3212 4024 3212 3212 3212
r.gs.1 v.aas.3s d.gpn n.gpn cj pl v.aas.3s r.ns.1 pl

κρίνω αὐτόν· ↱ ↱ οὐ γὰρ ἦλθον ἵνα κρίνω τὸν κόσμον, ἀλλ' ἵνα σώσω
will judge him; for I did not *for* come to judge the world but to save
3212 899 1142 2262 2262 4024 1142 2262 2671 3212 3836 3180 247 2671 5392
v.pai.1s r.asm.3 pl cj v.aai.1s cj v.pas.1s d.asm n.asm cj cj v.aas.1s

τὸν κόσμον. 48 ὁ ἀθετῶν ἐμὲ καὶ ↱ μὴ λαμβάνων τὰ ῥήματά μου
the world. The ⌊one who rejects⌋ me and does not receive *{the}* my sayings *my*
3836 3180 3836 119 1609 2779 3284 3590 3284 3836 1609 4839 1609
d.asm n.asm d.nsm pt.pa.nsm r.as.1 cj pl pt.pa.nsm d.apn n.apn r.gs.1

ἔχει τὸν κρίνοντα αὐτόν· ὁ λόγος ὃν ἐλάλησα ἐκεῖνος κρινεῖ αὐτὸν ἐν
has a judge; *{him}* the word that I have spoken *{that one}* will judge him at
2400 3836 3212 899 3836 3364 4005 3281 1697 3212 899 1877
v.pai.3s d.asm pt.pa.asm r.asm.3 d.nsm n.nsm r.asm v.aai.1s r.nsm v.fai.3s r.asm.3 p.d

τῇ ἐσχάτῃ ἡμέρᾳ. 49 ὅτι ἐγὼ ἐξ ἐμαυτοῦ οὐκ ἐλάλησα,
the last day. For I have not spoken on my own authority, *not have spoken*
3836 2274 2465 4022 1609 3281 4024 3281 1666 1831 4024 3281
d.dsf a.dsf n.dsf cj r.ns.1 p.g r.gsm.1 pl v.aai.1s

ἀλλ' ὁ πέμψας με πατὴρ αὐτός μοι ⌊ἐντολὴν δέδωκεν⌋
but the Father who sent me *Father* has himself commanded me *has commanded*
247 3836 4252 4287 1609 4252 1953 899 1953 1609 1953 1443
cj d.nsm pt.aa.nsm r.as.1 n.nsm r.nsm r.ds.1 n.asf v.rai.3s

τί εἴπω καὶ τί λαλήσω. 50 καὶ οἶδα ὅτι ἡ ἐντολὴ αὐτοῦ ζωὴ
what to say and what to speak. And I know that *{the}* his command *his* is eternal life.
5515 3306 2779 5515 3281 2779 3857 4022 3836 899 1953 899 1639 173 2437
r.asn v.aas.1s cj r.asn v.aas.1s cj v.rai.1s cj d.nsf n.nsf r.gsm.3 n.nsf

αἰώνιός ἐστιν. ἃ οὖν ἐγὼ λαλῶ, καθὼς εἴρηκέν
eternal is So whatever *So* I say, I speak just as *has told* the Father has
173 1639 4036 4005 4036 1609 3281 3281 3281 2777 3306 3836 4252 3306
a.nsf v.pai.3s r.apn cj r.ns.1 v.pai.1s cj v.rai.3s

μοι ὁ πατήρ, οὕτως λαλῶ.
told me." *the Father {in this way} I speak*
3306 1609 3836 4252 4048 3281
r.ds.1 d.nsm n.nsm adv v.pai.1s

13:1
πρὸ δὲ τῆς ἑορτῆς τοῦ πάσχα εἰδὼς ὁ Ἰησοῦς
It was just before *{and}* the festival of Passover, and Jesus, knowing *{the} Jesus*
4574 1254 3836 2038 3836 4247 2652 3857 3836 2652
p.g cj d.gsf n.gsf d.gsn n.gsn pt.ra.nsm d.nsm n.nsm

ὅτι ἦλθεν αὐτοῦ ἡ ὥρα ἵνα μεταβῇ ἐκ τοῦ κόσμου τούτου πρὸς
that his hour had come *his {the} hour* to depart from *{the}* this world *this* to
4022 899 6052 2262 899 3836 6052 2671 3553 1666 3836 4047 3180 4047 4639
cj v.aai.3s r.gsm.3 d.nsf n.nsf cj v.aas.3s p.g d.gsm n.gsm r.gsm p.a

NASB

rather than the ap-
proval of God.
[44]And Jesus cried
out and said, "He
who believes in
Me, does not be-
lieve in Me but in
Him who sent Me.
[45]He who sees Me
sees the One who
sent Me. [46]I have
come *as* Light
into the world, so
that everyone who
believes in Me
will not remain
in darkness. [47]If
anyone hears My
sayings and does
not keep them, I
do not judge him;
for I did not come
to judge the world,
but to save the
world. [48]He who
rejects Me and
does not receive
My sayings, has
one who judges
him; the word I
spoke is what will
judge him at the
last day. [49]For I
did not speak on
My own initia-
tive, but the Father
Himself who sent
Me has given Me
a commandment
as to what to say
and what to speak.
[50]I know that His
commandment is
eternal life; there-
fore the things I
speak, I speak just
as the Father has
told Me."

The Lord's Supper

[13:1]Now before the
Feast of the Pass-
over, Jesus know-
ing that His hour
had come that He
would depart out of
this world to

NIV

the Father. Having
loved his own who
were in the world,
he loved them to
the end.
2 The evening
meal was in prog-
ress, and the
devil had already
prompted Judas,
the son of Simon
Iscariot, to betray
Jesus. 3 Jesus knew
that the Father had
put all things un-
der his power, and
that he had come
from God and was
returning to God;
4 so he got up from
the meal, took off
his outer clothing,
and wrapped a
towel around his
waist. 5 After that,
he poured water
into a basin and
began to wash his
disciples' feet,
drying them with
the towel that was
wrapped around
him.
6 He came to Si-
mon Peter, who
said to him, "Lord,
are you going to
wash my feet?"
7 Jesus replied,
"You do not real-
ize now what I am
doing, but later
you will under-
stand."
8 "No," said Peter,
"you shall never
wash my feet."
Jesus answered,
"Unless I wash
you, you have no
part with me."
9 "Then, Lord,"
Simon Peter re-
plied, "not just my
feet but my hands
and my head as
well!"
10 Jesus answered,

τὸν πατέρα, ἀγαπήσας τοὺς ἰδίους τοὺς ἐν τῷ κόσμῳ εἰς
the Father, ⌞showed his love to⌟ {the} his own who were in the world, loving them to
3836 4252 26 3836 2625 3836 1877 3836 3180 26 899 1650
d.asm n.asm pt.aa.nsm d.apm a.apm d.apm p.d d.dsm n.dsm p.a

τέλος ἠγάπησεν αὐτούς. 2 καὶ δείπνου γινομένου, τοῦ διαβόλου ↱ ἤδη
the very end. *loving* *them* *{and}* *evening meal* *During* The devil had already
5465 26 899 2779 1270 1181 3836 1333 965 2453
n.asn v.aai.3s r.apm.3 cj n.gsn pt.pm.gsn d.gsm n.gsm adv

βεβληκότος εἰς τὴν καρδίαν ἵνα παραδοῖ αὐτὸν Ἰούδας
put into the heart of Judas Iscariot, Simon's son, to betray Jesus. *of Judas*
965 1650 3836 2840 2683 2683 2697 4981 2671 4140 899 2683
pt.ra.gsm p.a d.asf n.asf cj v.aas.3s r.asm.3 n.gsm

Σίμωνος Ἰσκαριώτου, 3 εἰδὼς ὅτι
Simon's *Iscariot* During the evening meal Jesus, knowing that the Father had given
4981 2697 1181 1270 1270 3857 4022 3836 4252 1443 1443
n.gsm n.gsm pt.ra.nsm cj

πάντα ἔδωκεν αὐτῷ ὁ πατὴρ εἰς τὰς χεῖρας καὶ ὅτι ἀπὸ θεοῦ
all things *had given* *{to him}* *the* *Father* into his hands, and that he had come from God
4246 1443 899 3836 4252 1650 3836 5931 2779 4022 2002 2002 2002 608 2536
a.apn v.aai.3s r.dsm.3 d.nsm n.nsm p.a d.apf n.apf cj cj p.g n.gsm

ἐξῆλθεν καὶ πρὸς τὸν θεὸν ὑπάγει, 4 ἐγείρεται ἐκ τοῦ δείπνου
he had come and was returning to *{the}* God, *was returning* got up from the table,
2002 2779 5632 5632 4639 3836 2536 5632 1586 1666 3836 1270
v.aai.3s cj p.a d.asm n.asm v.pai.3s v.ppi.3s p.g d.gsn n.gsn

καὶ τίθησιν τὰ ἱμάτια καὶ λαβὼν λέντιον διέζωσεν ← ἑαυτόν·
{and} laid aside his outer garments, and taking a towel, tied it around his waist.
2779 5502 3836 2668 2779 3284 3317 1346 1571
cj v.pai.3s d.apn n.apn cj pt.aa.nsm n.asn v.aai.3s r.asm.3

5 εἶτα βάλλει ὕδωρ εἰς τὸν νιπτῆρα καὶ ἤρξατο νίπτειν τοὺς πόδας τῶν
Then he poured water into a basin and began to wash the disciples' feet *{the}*
1663 965 5623 1650 3836 3781 2779 806 3782 3836 3412 4546 3836
adv v.pai.3s n.asn p.a d.asm n.asm cj v.ami.3s f.pa d.apm n.apm d.gpm

μαθητῶν καὶ ἐκμάσσειν τῷ λεντίῳ ᾧ ἦν διεζωσμένος.
disciples' and to dry them ⌞with the⌟ towel *{that}* *{he had}* tied around his waist.
3412 2779 1726 3836 3317 4005 1639 1346
n.gpm cj f.pa d.dsn n.dsn r.dsn v.iai.3s pt.rp.nsm

6 ἔρχεται οὖν πρὸς Σίμωνα Πέτρον· λέγει αὐτῷ, κύριε, σύ μου
He came *{then}* to Simon Peter, who said to him, "Lord, are you going to wash my
2262 4036 4639 4981 4377 3306 899 3261 3782 5148 3782 3782 3782 1609
v.pmi.3s cj p.a n.asm n.asm v.pai.3s r.dsm.3 n.vsm r.ns.2 r.gs.1

νίπτεις τοὺς πόδας; 7 ἀπεκρίθη Ἰησοῦς καὶ εἶπεν αὐτῷ, ὃ ἐγὼ
are going to wash *{the}* feet?" Jesus answered *Jesus* *{and}* him, saying, *him* "What I
3782 3836 4546 2652 646 2652 2779 899 3306 899 4005 1609
v.pai.2s d.apm n.apm v.api.3s n.nsm cj v.aai.3s r.dsm.3 r.asn r.ns.1

ποιῶ σὺ ↱ οὐκ οἶδας ἄρτι, γνώσῃ δὲ ⌞μετὰ ταῦτα.⌟
am doing you do not understand now, but ⌞you will come to understand⌟ *but* later."
4472 5148 3857 4024 3857 785 1254 1182 1254 3552 4047
v.pai.1s r.ns.2 pl v.rai.2s adv v.fmi.2s cj p.a r.apn

8 λέγει αὐτῷ Πέτρος, ↱ ↱ ⌞οὐ μὴ⌟ νίψῃς μου τοὺς πόδας εἰς τὸν αἰῶνα.
Peter said to him, *Peter* "You will never wash my *{the}* feet!" *{for}* *{all}* *{time}*
4377 3306 899 4377 3782 3782 4024 3590 3782 1609 3836 4546 1650 3836 172
v.pai.3s r.dsm.3 n.nsm pl pl v.aas.2s r.gs.1 d.apm n.apm p.a d.asm n.asm

ἀπεκρίθη Ἰησοῦς αὐτῷ, ἐὰν ↱ ↱ μὴ νίψω σε, οὐκ ἔχεις μέρος
Jesus replied, *Jesus* *{to him}* "If I do not wash you, you have no *you have* share
2652 646 2652 899 1569 3782 3782 3590 3782 5148 2400 2400 4024 2400 3538
v.api.3s n.nsm r.dsm.3 cj pl v.aas.1s r.as.2 pl v.pai.2s n.asn

μετ' ἐμοῦ. 9 λέγει αὐτῷ Σίμων Πέτρος, κύριε, μὴ τοὺς
with me." Simon Peter exclaimed, *{to him}* *Simon* *Peter* "Lord, then wash not only *{the}*
3552 1609 4981 4377 3306 899 4981 4377 3261 3590 3667 3836
p.g r.gs.1 v.pai.3s r.dsm.3 n.nsm n.nsm n.vsm pl d.apm

πόδας μου μόνον ἀλλὰ καὶ τὰς χεῖρας καὶ τὴν κεφαλήν. 10 λέγει αὐτῷ
my feet *my* *only* but also my hands and my head!" Jesus said to him,
1609 4546 1609 3667 247 2779 3836 5931 2779 3836 3051 2652 3306 899
n.apm r.gs.1 adv cj adv d.apf n.apf cj d.asf n.asf v.pai.3s r.dsm.3

NASB

the Father, having
loved His own who
were in the world,
He loved them to
the end. 2 During
supper, the devil
having already put
into the heart of
Judas Iscariot, *the*
son of Simon, to
betray Him, 3 *Jesus,*
knowing that the
Father had given
all things into His
hands, and that He
had come forth
from God and was
going back to God,
4 *got up from sup-
per, and *laid aside
His garments; and
taking a towel, He
girded Himself.

Jesus Washes the Disciples' Feet

5 Then He *poured
water into the ba-
sin, and began to
wash the disciples'
feet and to wipe
them with the
towel with which
He was girded. 6 So
He *came to Simon
Peter. He *said
to Him, "Lord,
do You wash my
feet?" 7 Jesus an-
swered and said to
him, "What I do
you do not realize
now, but you will
understand here-
after." 8 Peter *said
to Him, "Never
shall You wash
my feet!" Jesus
answered him, "If
I do not wash you,
you have no part
with Me." 9 Simon
Peter *said to Him,
"Lord, *then wash*
not only my feet,
but also my hands
and my head." 10 Je-
sus *said to him,

NIV

"Those who have
had a bath need
only to wash their
feet; their whole
body is clean. And
you are clean,
though not every
one of you." 11 For
he knew who was
going to betray
him, and that was
why he said not ev-
ery one was clean.
12 When he had
finished washing
their feet, he put
on his clothes and
returned to his
place. "Do you
understand what
I have done for
you?" he asked
them. 13 "You call
me 'Teacher' and
'Lord,' and right-
ly so, for that is
what I am. 14 Now
that I, your Lord
and Teacher, have
washed your feet,
you also should
wash one another's
feet. 15 I have set
you an example
that you should do
as I have done for
you. 16 Very truly I
tell you, no servant
is greater than his
master, nor is a
messenger greater
than the one who
sent him. 17 Now
that you know
these things, you
will be blessed if
you do them.

Jesus Predicts His Betrayal

18 "I am not refer-
ring to all of you; I
know those I have
chosen. But this is
to fulfill this pas-
sage of Scripture:
'He who shared
my bread has
turned[a] against

[a] 18 Greek *has lifted up his heel*

ὁ Ἰησοῦς, ὁ λελουμένος οὐκ ἔχει χρείαν ⸤εἰ μὴ⸥ τοὺς
{the} *Jesus* "The one who has bathed has no *has* need to wash, except for his
3836 2652 3836 3374 2400 4024 2400 5970 3782 3782 1623 3590 3836
d.nsm n.nsm d.nsm pt.rp.nsm pl v.pai.3s n.asf cj pl d.apm

πόδας νίψασθαι, ἀλλ᾽ ἔστιν καθαρὸς ὅλος· καὶ ὑμεῖς καθαροί ἐστε,
feet, *to wash* but is clean all over. And you men are clean, *are*
4546 3782 247 1639 2754 3910 2779 7007 1639 2754 1639
n.apm f.am cj v.pai.3s a.nsm a.nsm cj r.np.2 a.npm v.pai.2p

ἀλλ᾽ οὐχὶ πάντες. 11 ᾔδει γὰρ τὸν παραδιδόντα αὐτόν· ⸤διὰ
but not all of you." For he knew *For* who was about to betray him; that was why
247 4049 4246 1142 3857 1142 3836 4140 899 1328
cj pl a.npm v.lai.3s cj d.asm pt.pa.asm r.asm.3 p.a

τοῦτο⸥ εἶπεν ὅτι οὐχὶ πάντες καθαροί ἐστε. 12 ὅτε οὖν
he said, ~ "Not all of you are clean." *you are* So when *So* Jesus
4047 3306 4022 4049 4246 1639 1639 2754 1639 4036 4021 4036
r.asn v.aai.3s cj pl a.npm a.npm v.pai.2p cj cj

ἔνιψεν τοὺς πόδας αὐτῶν καὶ[a] ἔλαβεν τὰ ἱμάτια αὐτοῦ καὶ
had washed *{the}* their feet *their* and put on *{the}* his outer garments, *his* *{and}*
3782 3836 899 4546 899 2779 3284 3836 899 2668 899 2779
v.aai.3s d.apm n.apm r.gpm.3 cj v.aai.3s d.apn n.apn r.gsm.3 cj

ἀνέπεσεν πάλιν, εἶπεν αὐτοῖς, γινώσκετε τί πεποίηκα
⸤he sat down at the table⸥ again and said to them, "Do you understand what ⸤I have just done⸥
404 4099 3306 899 1182 5515 4472
v.aai.3s adv v.aai.3s r.dpm.3 v.pai.2p r.asn v.rai.1s

ὑμῖν; 13 ὑμεῖς φωνεῖτέ με· ὁ διδάσκαλος, καί· ὁ κύριος, καὶ καλῶς
for you? You call me *{the}* 'Teacher!' and *{the}* 'Master!' and you speak rightly,
7007 7007 5888 1609 3836 1437 2779 3836 3261 2779 3306 3306 2822
r.dp.2 r.np.2 v.pai.2p r.as.1 d.nsm n.nsm cj d.nsm n.nsm cj adv

λέγετε, εἰμὶ γάρ. 14 εἰ οὖν ἐγὼ ἔνιψα
you speak for so I am. *for* If I, then, *I* your Master and Teacher, have washed
3306 1142 1639 1142 1623 1609 4036 1609 3836 3261 2779 1437 3782
v.pai.2p v.pai.1s cj cj cj r.ns.1 v.aai.1s

ὑμῶν τοὺς πόδας ὁ κύριος καὶ ὁ διδάσκαλος, καὶ ὑμεῖς ὀφείλετε
your *{the}* feet, *your* *Master* *and* *{the}* *Teacher* you also *you* ought to wash
7007 3836 4546 3836 3261 2779 3836 1437 7007 2779 7007 4053 3782 3782
r.gp.2 d.apm n.apm d.nsm n.nsm cj d.nsm n.nsm adv r.np.2 v.pai.2p

ἀλλήλων νίπτειν τοὺς πόδας· 15 ὑπόδειγμα γὰρ ἔδωκα
one another's *to wash* *{the}* feet. For I have given you an example, *For* *I have given*
253 3782 3836 4546 1142 1443 1443 1443 7007 5682 1142 1443
r.gpm f.pa d.apm n.apm n.asn cj v.aai.1s

ὑμῖν ἵνα καθὼς ἐγὼ ἐποίησα ὑμῖν καὶ ὑμεῖς ποιῆτε. 16
you that just as I have done to you, you also *you* are to do. I tell you the
7007 2671 2777 1609 4472 7007 7007 2779 7007 4472 3306 3306 7007
r.dp.2 cj cj r.ns.1 v.aai.1s r.dp.2 adv r.np.2 v.pas.2p

⸤ἀμὴν ἀμὴν⸥ λέγω ὑμῖν, οὐκ ἔστιν δοῦλος μείζων τοῦ κυρίου
solemn truth, *I tell* *you* the servant is not *is* *servant* greater than his master,
297 297 3306 7007 1529 1639 4024 1639 1529 3489 3836 899 3261
pl pl v.pai.1s r.dp.2 pl v.pai.3s n.nsm a.nsm.c d.gsm n.gsm

αὐτοῦ οὐδὲ ἀπόστολος μείζων τοῦ πέμψαντος αὐτόν. 17 εἰ
his nor is the one who is sent greater ⸤than the⸥ one who sent him. If you know
899 4028 693 3489 3836 4287 899 1623 3857 3857
r.gsm.3 cj n.nsm a.nsm.c d.gsm pt.aa.gsm r.asm.3 cj

ταῦτα οἴδατε, μακάριοί ἐστε ἐὰν → → ποιῆτε αὐτά. 18 οὐ
these things, *you know* blessed are you if you put them into practice. *them* I am not
4047 3857 3421 1639 1569 899 4472 899 3306 3306 4024
r.apn v.rai.2p a.npm v.pai.2p cj v.pas.2p r.apn pl

περὶ πάντων ὑμῶν λέγω, ἐγὼ οἶδα τίνας ἐξελεξάμην· ἀλλ᾽ ἵνα ἡ
speaking about all of you; *I am speaking* I know whom I have chosen. But *{that}* the
3306 4309 4246 7007 3306 1609 3857 5515 1721 247 2671 3836
p.g a.gpm r.gp.2 v.pai.1s r.ns.1 v.rai.1s r.apm v.ami.1s cj cj d.nsf

γραφὴ πληρωθῇ, ὁ τρώγων μου τὸν ἄρτον ἐπῆρεν ἐπ᾽
Scripture must be fulfilled, 'The ⸤one who eats⸥ my *{the}* bread ⸤has lifted up⸥ his heel against
1210 4444 3836 5592 1609 3836 788 2048 899 4761 2093
n.nsf v.aps.3s d.nsm pt.pa.nsm r.gs.1 d.asm n.asm v.aai.3s p.a

[a] [καὶ] UBS.

NASB

"He who has
bathed needs only
to wash his feet,
but is completely
clean; and you are
clean, but not all
of you." 11 For He
knew the one who
was betraying Him;
for this reason He
said, "Not all of
you are clean."
12 So when He had
washed their feet,
and taken His gar-
ments and reclined
at the table again,
He said to them,
"Do you know
what I have done
to you? 13 You call
Me Teacher and
Lord; and you
are right, for *so*
I am. 14 If I then,
the Lord and the
Teacher, washed
your feet, you also
ought to wash one
another's feet.
15 For I gave you
an example that
you also should
do as I did to you.
16 Truly, truly, I say
to you, a slave is
not greater than his
master, nor *is* one
who is sent greater
than the one who
sent him. 17 If you
know these things,
you are blessed if
you do them. 18 I
do not speak of all
of you. I know the
ones I have chosen;
but *it is* that the
Scripture may be
fulfilled, 'HE WHO
EATS MY BREAD HAS
LIFTED UP HIS HEEL
AGAINST ME.'

NIV

me.'[a]
[19]"I am telling
you now before it
happens, so that
when it does hap-
pen you will be-
lieve that I am who
I am. [20]Very truly
I tell you, whoev-
er accepts anyone
I send accepts
me; and whoever
accepts me ac-
cepts the one who
sent me."
[21]After he had
said this, Jesus
was troubled in
spirit and testi-
fied, "Very truly
I tell you, one of
you is going to be-
tray me."
[22]His disciples
stared at one an-
other, at a loss to
know which of
them he meant.
[23]One of them,
the disciple whom
Jesus loved, was
reclining next to
him. [24]Simon Peter
motioned to this
disciple and said,
"Ask him which
one he means."
[25]Leaning back
against Jesus, he
asked him, "Lord,
who is it?"
[26]Jesus answered,
"It is the one
to whom I will
give this piece of
bread when I have
dipped it in the
dish." Then, dip-
ping the piece of
bread, he

ἐμὲ τὴν πτέρναν αὐτοῦ. 19 ˻ἀπ᾽ ἄρτι˼ λέγω ὑμῖν πρὸ
me.' {the} heel his I am telling you this now, I am telling you before
1609 3836 4761 899 3306 3306 3306 7007 608 785 3306 7007 4574
r.as.1 d.asf n.asf r.gsm.3 p.g adv v.pai.1s r.dp.2 p.g

τοῦ γενέσθαι, ἵνα πιστεύσητε ὅταν γένηται ὅτι
~ it takes place, so that when it does take place you will believe when it does take place that
3836 1181 2671 4020 1181 1181 1181 1181 4409 4020 1181 4022
d.gsn f.am cj v.aas.2p cj v.ams.3s cj

ἐγώ εἰμι. 20 ˻ἀμὴν ἀμὴν˼ λέγω ὑμῖν, ὁ λαμβάνων ἄν
I am he. I tell you the solemn truth, I tell you whoever receives ~
1609 1639 3306 3306 7007 297 297 3306 7007 3836 3284 323
r.ns.1 v.pai.1s pl pl v.pai.1s r.dp.2 d.nsm pt.pa.nsm pl

τινα πέμψω ἐμὲ λαμβάνει, ὁ δὲ ἐμὲ λαμβάνων
one whom I send receives me, receives and whoever and receives me receives
5516 4287 3284 1609 3284 1254 3836 1254 3284 1609 3284
r.asm v.aas.1s r.as.1 v.pai.3s d.nsm cj r.as.1 pt.pa.nsm

λαμβάνει τὸν πέμψαντά με. 21 ταῦτα εἰπὼν ὁ[a] Ἰησοῦς
receives the one who sent me." After saying these things, After saying {the} Jesus
3284 3836 4287 1609 3306 3306 4047 3306 3836 2652
v.pai.3s d.asm pt.aa.asm r.as.1 r.apn pt.aa.nsm d.nsm n.nsm

ἐταράχθη τῷ πνεύματι καὶ ἐμαρτύρησεν καὶ εἶπεν, ˻ἀμὴν
became troubled in spirit, and testified, {and} saying, "I tell you the solemn truth,
5429 3836 4460 2779 3455 2779 3306 3306 3306 7007 297
v.api.3s d.dsn n.dsn cj v.aai.3s cj v.aai.3s pl

ἀμὴν˼ λέγω ὑμῖν ὅτι εἷς ἐξ ὑμῶν παραδώσει με. 22 ἔβλεπον εἰς
I tell you ~ one of you will betray me." The disciples ˻began to look˼ at
297 3306 7007 4022 1651 1666 7007 4140 1609 3836 3412 1063 1650
pl v.pai.1s r.dp.2 cj a.nsm p.g r.gp.2 v.fai.3s r.as.1 v.iai.3p p.a

ἀλλήλους οἱ μαθηταὶ ἀπορούμενοι περὶ τίνος λέγει. 23 ἦν
one another, The disciples at a loss to know about whom ˻he was speaking.˼ was
253 3836 3412 679 4309 5515 3306 1639
r.apm d.npm n.npm pt.pm.npm p.g r.gsm v.pai.3s v.iai.3s

ἀνακείμενος εἷς ἐκ τῶν μαθητῶν αὐτοῦ
reclining at table One of {the} his disciples his — the one Jesus loved — was reclining
367 1651 1666 3836 899 3412 899 4005 2652 26 1639 367
pt.pm.nsm a.nsm p.g d.gpm n.gpm r.gsm.3

˻ἐν τῷ κόλπῳ˼ τοῦ Ἰησοῦ, ὃν ἠγάπα ὁ Ἰησοῦς. 24
at table close beside {the} Jesus. one loved {the} Jesus So Simon
367 367 1877 3836 3146 3836 2652 4005 26 3836 2652 4036 4981
p.d d.dsm n.dsm d.gsm n.gsm r.asm v.iai.3s d.nsm n.nsm

νεύει οὖν τούτῳ Σίμων Πέτρος πυθέσθαι τίς ἂν εἴη περὶ οὗ
Peter motioned So to him Simon Peter to ask Jesus who ~ it was of whom
4377 3748 4036 4047 4981 4377 4785 5515 323 1639 4309 4005
v.pai.3s cj r.dsm n.nsm n.nsm f.am r.nsm pl v.pao.3s p.g r.gsm

λέγει. 25 ἀναπεσὼν οὖν ἐκεῖνος οὕτως ἐπὶ τὸ στῆθος τοῦ
˻he had spoken.˼ So that disciple, leaning back So that {thus} against the chest of
3306 4036 1697 404 4036 1697 4048 2093 3836 5111 3836
v.pai.3s pt.aa.nsm cj r.nsm adv p.a d.asn n.asn d.gsm

Ἰησοῦ λέγει αὐτῷ, κύριε, τίς ἐστιν; 26 ἀποκρίνεται ὁ[b] Ἰησοῦς,
Jesus, said to him, "Lord, who is it?" Jesus replied, {the} Jesus "It is the
2652 3306 899 3261 5515 1639 2652 646 3836 2652 1639 1639
n.gsm v.pai.3s r.dsm.3 n.vsm r.nsm v.pai.3s v.pmi.3s d.nsm n.nsm

ἐκεῖνός ἐστιν ᾧ ἐγὼ βάψω
one It is ˻to whom˼ I will give this morsel of bread after I have dipped it in the
1697 1639 4005 1443 1443 1443 3836 6040 6040 6040 1609 970
r.nsm v.pai.3s r.dsm r.ns.1 v.fai.1s

τὸ ψωμίον καὶ δώσω αὐτῷ. ➝ βάψας οὖν τὸ ψωμίον[c]
dish." this morsel of bread {and} I will give {to him} Then he dipped Then the morsel and
3836 6040 2779 1443 899 4036 1443 970 4036 3836 6040
d.asn n.asn cj v.fai.1s r.dsm.3 pt.aa.nsm cj d.asn n.asn

NASB

[19]From now on
I am telling you
before *it* comes to
pass, so that when
it does occur, you
may believe that
I am *He.* [20]Truly,
truly, I say to you,
he who receives
whomever I send
receives Me; and
he who receives
Me receives Him
who sent Me."

Jesus Predicts His Betrayal

[21]When Jesus
had said this, He
became troubled in
spirit, and testified
and said, "Truly,
truly, I say to you,
that one of you will
betray Me." [22]The
disciples *began*
looking at one
another, at a loss
to know of which
one He was speak-
ing. [23]There was
reclining on Jesus'
bosom one of His
disciples, whom
Jesus loved. [24]So
Simon Peter *ges-
tured to him, and
*said to him, "Tell
us who it is of
whom He is speak-
ing." [25]He, leaning
back thus on Jesus'
bosom, *said to
Him, "Lord, who
is it?" [26]Jesus then
*answered, "That is
the one for whom I
shall dip the morsel
and give it to him."
So when He had
dipped the morsel,

[a] 18 Psalm 41:9

[a] [ὁ] UBS, omitted by TNIV.
[b] [ὁ] UBS, omitted by TNIV.
[c] λαμβάνει καὶ included by UBS after ψωμίον.

NIV

gave it to Judas,
the son of Simon
Iscariot. [27]As soon
as Judas took the
bread, Satan en-
tered into him.
So Jesus told
him, "What you
are about to do,
do quickly." [28]But
no one at the meal
understood why
Jesus said this to
him. [29]Since Ju-
das had charge of
the money, some
thought Jesus was
telling him to buy
what was needed
for the festival, or
to give something
to the poor. [30]As
soon as Judas had
taken the bread, he
went out. And it
was night.

Jesus Predicts Peter's Denial

[31]When he was
gone, Jesus said,
"Now the Son of
Man is glorified
and God is glori-
fied in him. [32]If
God is glorified
in him,[a] God will
glorify the Son
in himself, and
will glorify him at
once.
[33]"My children,
I will be with you
only a little lon-
ger. You will look
for me, and just
as I told the Jews,
so I tell you now:
Where I am going,
you cannot come.
[34]"A new com-
mand I give you:
Love one another.
As I have loved
you, so you must
love one another.

δίδωσιν Ἰούδᾳ Σίμωνος Ἰσκαριώτου. [27] καὶ μετὰ τὸ
gave it to Judas Iscariot, Simon's son. *Iscariot* *{and}* After Judas had taken the
1443 2683 2697 4981 2697 2779 3552 3836
v.pai.3s n.dsm n.gsm n.gsm cj p.a d.asn

ψωμίον τότε εἰσῆλθεν εἰς ἐκεῖνον ὁ σατανᾶς. λέγει οὖν αὐτῷ
⌞morsel of bread,⌟ *{then}* Satan entered into him. *{the}* *Satan* Jesus said *{then}* to him,
6040 5538 4928 1656 1650 1697 3836 4928 2652 3306 4036 899
n.asn adv v.aai.3s p.a r.asm d.nsm n.nsm v.pai.3s cj r.dsm.3

ὁ Ἰησοῦς, ὃ ποιεῖς ποίησον τάχιον. [28] τοῦτο δὲ[a] οὐδεὶς
{the} *Jesus* "What ⌞you are going to do,⌟ do quickly." *this* Now none of those
3836 2652 4005 4472 4472 5441 4047 1254 4029 3836 367
d.nsm n.nsm r.asn v.pai.2s v.aam.2s adv.c r.asn cj a.nsm

ἔγνω τῶν ἀνακειμένων ⌞πρὸς τί⌟ εἶπεν αὐτῷ. [29] τινὲς γὰρ
reclining at table knew *of* *those reclining at table* why he said this to him. Some *{for}*
367 367 367 1182 3836 367 4639 5515 3306 4047 899 5516 1142
v.aai.3s d.gpm pt.pm.gpm p.a r.asn v.aai.3s r.dsm.3 r.npm cj

ἐδόκουν, ἐπεὶ τὸ γλωσσόκομον εἶχεν Ἰούδας, ὅτι
of them thought, since Judas used to keep the money box, *used to keep* *Judas* that Jesus
1506 2075 2683 2400 2400 2400 3836 1186 2400 2683 4022 2652
v.iai.3p cj d.asn n.asn v.iai.3s n.nsm cj

λέγει αὐτῷ ὁ[b] Ἰησοῦς, ἀγόρασον ὧν ⌞χρείαν ἔχομεν⌟ εἰς τὴν ἑορτήν, ἢ
had said to him, *{the}* *Jesus* "Buy what we need for the festival," or that
3306 899 3836 2652 60 4005 5970 2400 1650 3836 2038 2445 2671
v.pai.3s r.dsm.3 d.nsm n.nsm v.aam.2s r.gpn n.asf v.pai.1p p.a d.asf n.asf cj

τοῖς πτωχοῖς ἵνα τι δῷ. [30] λαβὼν οὖν
he should give something to the poor. *that* *something* *he should give* So after taking *So*
1443 1443 1443 5516 3836 4777 2671 5516 1443 4036 3284 4036
d.dpm a.dpm cj r.asn v.aas.3s pt.aa.nsm cj

τὸ ψωμίον ἐκεῖνος ἐξῆλθεν εὐθύς. ἦν δὲ νύξ. [31] ὅτε οὖν
the ⌞morsel of bread,⌟ Judas went out at once; and it was *and* night. When *{then}*
3836 6040 1697 2002 2318 1254 1639 1254 3816 4021 4036
d.asn n.asn r.nsm v.aai.3s adv v.iai.3s cj n.nsf cj cj

ἐξῆλθεν, λέγει Ἰησοῦς, νῦν → ἐδοξάσθη ὁ υἱὸς τοῦ
⌞he had gone out,⌟ Jesus said, *Jesus* "Now is the Son of Man glorified, *the* *Son* *of*
2002 2652 3306 2652 3814 3836 5626 3836 476 1519 3836 5626 3836
v.aai.3s v.pai.3s n.nsm adv v.api.3s d.nsm n.nsm d.gsm

ἀνθρώπου καὶ ὁ θεὸς ἐδοξάσθη ἐν αὐτῷ· [32] [c]εἰ ὁ θεὸς ἐδοξάσθη ἐν αὐτῷ,
Man and *{the}* God is glorified in him. If *{the}* God is glorified in him,
476 2779 3836 2536 1519 1877 899 1623 3836 2536 1519 1877 899
n.gsm cj d.nsm n.nsm v.api.3s p.d r.dsm.3 cj d.nsm n.nsm v.api.3s p.d r.dsm.3

καὶ ὁ θεὸς → δοξάσει αὐτὸν ἐν αὐτῷ, καὶ εὐθὺς
also *{the}* God will also glorify him in himself, and he will glorify him at once.
2779 3836 2536 2779 1519 899 1877 899 2779 1519 1519 1519 899 2318
adv d.nsm n.nsm v.fai.3s r.asm.3 p.d r.dsm.3 cj adv

δοξάσει αὐτόν. [33] τεκνία, ἔτι μικρὸν μεθ' ὑμῶν εἰμι·
he will glorify *him* Little children, I am with you only a little longer. *with* *you* *I am*
1519 899 5448 1639 1639 3552 7007 2285 3625 3552 7007 1639
v.fai.3s r.asm.3 n.vpn adv a.asn p.g r.gp.2 v.pai.1s

ζητήσετέ με, καὶ καθὼς εἶπον τοῖς Ἰουδαίοις ὅτι ὅπου ἐγὼ ὑπάγω ὑμεῖς
⌞You will look for⌟ me; and just as I told the Jews, ~ 'Where I am going, you
2426 1609 2779 2777 3306 3836 2681 4022 3963 1609 5632 7007
v.fai.2p r.as.1 cj cj v.aai.1s d.dpm a.dpm cj cj r.ns.1 v.pai.1s r.np.2

⌞οὐ δύνασθε⌟ ἐλθεῖν, καὶ ὑμῖν λέγω ἄρτι. [34]
cannot come,' so now I say to you also. *to you* *I say* *now* A new
4024 1538 2262 785 3306 3306 7007 7007 2779 7007 3306 785 2785
pl v.ppi.2p f.aa adv r.dp.2 v.pai.1s adv

ἐντολὴν καινὴν δίδωμι ὑμῖν, ἵνα ἀγαπᾶτε ἀλλήλους, καθὼς ἠγάπησα ὑμᾶς
commandment *new* I give to you: *{that}* Love one another. Just as I have loved you,
1953 2785 1443 7007 2671 26 253 2777 26 7007
n.asf a.asf v.pai.1s r.dp.2 cj v.pas.2p r.apm cj v.aai.1s r.ap.2

NASB

He *took and *gave
it to Judas, *the son*
of Simon Iscariot.
[27]After the morsel,
Satan then entered
into him. Therefore
Jesus *said to him,
"What you do, do
quickly." [28]Now no
one of those reclin-
ing *at the table*
knew for what pur-
pose He had said
this to him. [29]For
some were suppos-
ing, because Judas
had the money
box, that Jesus
was saying to him,
"Buy the things
we have need of
for the feast"; or
else, that he should
give something
to the poor. [30]So
after receiving the
morsel he went out
immediately; and it
was night.
[31]Therefore when
he had gone out,
Jesus *said, "Now
is the Son of Man
glorified, and God
is glorified in Him;
[32]if God is glori-
fied in Him, God
will also glorify
Him in Himself,
and will glorify
Him immediately.
[33]Little children,
I am with you a
little while longer.
You will seek Me;
and as I said to the
Jews, now I also
say to you, 'Where
I am going, you
cannot come.' [34]A
new command-
ment I give to you,
that you love one
another, even as I
have loved you,

[a] 32 Many early manuscripts do not have *If God is glorified in him.*

[a] [δὲ] UBS.
[b] [ὁ] UBS, omitted by TNIV.
[c] [εἰ ὁ θεὸς ἐδοξάσθη ἐν αὐτῷ] UBS.

NIV

[35]By this everyone
will know that you
are my disciples,
if you love one an-
other."
[36]Simon Peter
asked him, "Lord,
where are you go-
ing?"
Jesus replied,
"Where I am go-
ing, you cannot
follow now, but
you will follow
later."
[37]Peter asked,
"Lord, why can't I
follow you now? I
will lay down my
life for you."
[38]Then Jesus an-
swered, "Will you
really lay down
your life for me?
Very truly I tell
you, before the
rooster crows, you
will disown me
three times!

Jesus Comforts His Disciples

14 "Do not let
your hearts
be troubled. You
believe in God[a];
believe also in
me. [2]My Father's
house has many
rooms; if that were
not so, would I
have told you that
I am going there
to prepare a place
for you? [3]And if
I go and prepare
a place for you,
I will come back
and take you to be
with me that you
also may be where
I am. [4]You know
the way to the
place where I am
going."

Jesus the Way to the Father

[5]Thomas said to
him,

[a] 1 Or *Believe in God*

ἵνα καὶ ὑμεῖς ἀγαπᾶτε ἀλλήλους. 35 ἐν τούτῳ γνώσονται πάντες
{that} you also *you* must love one another. By this all people will know *all people*
2671 7007 2779 7007 26 253 1877 4047 4246 4246 1182 4246
cj adv r.np.2 v.pas.2p r.apm p.d r.dsn v.fmi.3p a.npm

ὅτι ἐμοὶ μαθηταί ἐστε, ἐὰν ἀγάπην ἔχητε ἐν ἀλλήλοις.
that you are my disciples, *you are* if you have love *you have* for one another."
4022 1639 1639 1847 3412 1639 1569 2400 2400 27 2400 1877 253
cj a.npm n.npm v.pai.2p cj n.asf v.pas.2p p.d r.dpm

36 λέγει αὐτῷ Σίμων Πέτρος, κύριε, ποῦ ὑπάγεις; ἀπεκρίθη[a]
Simon Peter said to him, *Simon Peter* "Lord, where are you going?" Jesus answered,
4981 4377 3306 899 4981 4377 3261 4543 5632 2652 646
v.pai.3s r.dsm.3 n.nsm n.nsm n.vsm cj v.pai.2s v.api.3s

Ἰησοῦς, ὅπου ὑπάγω ↱ ⌞οὐ δύνασαί⌟ μοι νῦν ἀκολουθῆσαι,
Jesus "Where I am going you cannot follow me now, *follow* but
2652 3963 5632 1538 4024 1538 199 1609 3814 199 1254
n.nsm cj v.pai.1s pl v.ppi.2s r.ds.1 adv f.aa

ἀκολουθήσεις δὲ ὕστερον. 37 λέγει αὐτῷ ὁ Πέτρος, κύριε, ⌞διὰ τί⌟
you will follow *but* later." Peter said to him, *{the} Peter* "Lord, why can
199 1254 5731 4377 3306 899 3836 4377 3261 1328 5515 1538
v.fai.2s cj adv.c v.pai.3s r.dsm.3 d.nsm n.nsm n.vsm p.a r.asn

οὐ δύναμαί σοι ἀκολουθῆσαι ἄρτι; τὴν ψυχήν
I not *can I* follow you *follow* now? I will lay down *{the}* my life
1538 4024 1538 199 5148 199 785 5502 5502 5502 5502 3836 1609 6034
pl v.ppi.1s r.ds.2 f.aa adv d.asf n.asf

μου ὑπὲρ σοῦ θήσω. 38 ἀποκρίνεται Ἰησοῦς, τὴν
my for you." *I will lay down* Jesus replied, *Jesus* "Will you lay down *{the}* your
1609 5642 5148 5502 2652 646 2652 5502 5502 5502 5502 3836 5148
r.gs.1 p.g r.gs.2 v.fai.1s v.pmi.3s n.nsm d.asf

ψυχήν σου ὑπὲρ ἐμοῦ θήσεις; ⌞ἀμὴν ἀμὴν⌟ λέγω σοι,
life *your* for me? *Will you lay down* I tell you the solemn truth, *I tell you* the
6034 5148 5642 1609 5502 3306 3306 5148 297 297 3306 5148
n.asf r.gs.2 p.g r.gs.1 v.fai.2s pl pl v.pai.1s r.ds.2

↱ ⌞οὐ μὴ⌟ ἀλέκτωρ φωνήσῃ ⌞ἕως οὗ⌟ ἀρνήσῃ με τρίς.
rooster will not *rooster* crow before you deny me ⌞three times.⌟
232 5888 4024 3590 232 5888 2401 4005 766 1609 5565
pl pl n.nsm v.aas.3s p.g r.gsm v.ams.2s r.as.1 adv

14:1 ↱ μὴ → ταρασσέσθω ὑμῶν ἡ καρδία· πιστεύετε εἰς τὸν θεὸν
"Do not let your heart be troubled. *your {the} heart* You trust in *{the}* God;
5429 3590 7007 2840 5429 7007 3836 2840 4409 1650 3836 2536
pl v.ppm.3s r.gp.2 d.nsf n.nsf v.pai.2p p.a d.asm n.asm

καὶ εἰς ἐμὲ πιστεύετε. 2 ἐν τῇ οἰκίᾳ τοῦ πατρός μου
trust also in me. *trust* In *{the}* my Father's house *{the} Father's my* there are
4409 2779 1650 1609 4409 1877 3836 1609 4252 3864 3836 4252 1609 1639 1639
adv p.a r.as.1 v.pam.2p p.d d.dsf n.dsf d.gsm n.gsm r.gs.1

μοναὶ πολλαί εἰσιν· εἰ δὲ μή, εἶπον
many ⌞dwelling places;⌟ *many there are* if *{and}* that were not the case, would ⌞I have told⌟
4498 3665 4498 1639 1623 1254 3590 323 3306
n.npf a.npf v.pai.3p cj cj pl v.aai.1s

ἂν ὑμῖν ὅτι πορεύομαι ἑτοιμάσαι τόπον ὑμῖν; 3 καὶ ἐὰν πορευθῶ καὶ
would you that I am going there to prepare a place for you? And if I go and
323 7007 4022 4513 2286 5536 7007 2779 1569 4513 2779
pl r.dp.2 cj v.pmi.1s f.aa n.asm r.dp.2 cj cj v.aps.1s cj

ἑτοιμάσω τόπον ὑμῖν, πάλιν ἔρχομαι καὶ παραλήμψομαι ὑμᾶς
prepare a place for you, I will come again *I will come* and take you to be
2286 5536 7007 2262 2262 2262 4099 2262 2779 4161 7007
v.aas.1s n.asm r.dp.2 adv v.pmi.1s cj v.fmi.1s r.ap.2

πρὸς ἐμαυτόν, ἵνα ὅπου εἰμὶ ἐγὼ καὶ ὑμεῖς ἦτε. 4 καὶ
with me, so that where I am, *I* there you may be also. *you may be* And
4639 1831 2671 3963 1609 1639 1609 7007 1639 1639 2779 7007 1639 2779
p.a r.asm.1 cj cj v.pai.1s r.ns.1 adv r.np.2 v.pas.2p cj

ὅπου ἐγὼ[b] ὑπάγω οἴδατε τὴν ὁδόν. 5 λέγει αὐτῷ
you know the way to where I am going." *you know the way* Thomas said to him,
3857 3857 3836 3847 3963 1609 5632 3857 3836 3847 2605 3306 899
cj r.ns.1 v.pai.1s v.rai.2p d.asf n.asf v.pai.3s r.dsm.3

NASB

that you also love
one another. [35]By
this all men will
know that you are
My disciples, if
you have love for
one another."
[36]Simon Peter
*said to Him,
"Lord, where are
You going?" Jesus
answered, "Where
I go, you cannot
follow Me now;
but you will follow
later." [37]Peter *said
to Him, "Lord,
why can I not fol-
low You right now?
I will lay down
my life for You."
[38]Jesus *answered,
"Will you lay down
your life for Me?
Truly, truly, I say
to you, a rooster
will not crow until
you deny Me three
times.

Jesus Comforts His Disciples

14:1 "Do not let
your heart be
troubled; [a]believe
in God, believe
also in Me. [2]In My
Father's house are
many dwelling
places; if it were
not so, I would
have told you; for
I go to prepare a
place for you. [3]If
I go and prepare
a place for you, I
will come again
and receive you to
Myself, that where
I am, *there* you
may be also. [4]And
you know the way
where I am going."
[5]Thomas *said to

[a] αὐτῷ included by UBS after ἀπεκρίθη.
[b] [ἐγὼ] UBS.

[a] Or *you believe in God*

NIV

"Lord, we don't
know where you
are going, so how
can we know the
way?"
[6]Jesus answered,
"I am the way and
the truth and the
life. No one comes
to the Father ex-
cept through me.
[7]If you really
know me, you will
know[a] my Father
as well. From now
on, you do know
him and have seen
him."
[8]Philip said,
"Lord, show us
the Father and that
will be enough
for us."
[9]Jesus answered:
"Don't you know
me, Philip, even
after I have been
among you such a
long time? Anyone
who has seen me
has seen the Fa-
ther. How can you
say, 'Show us the
Father'? [10]Don't
you believe that I
am in the Father,
and that the Fa-
ther is in me? The
words I say to you
I do not speak on
my own authority.
Rather, it is the
Father, living in
me, who is doing
his work. [11]Believe
me when I say that
I am in the Father
and the Father is
in me; or at least
believe on the evi-
dence of the works
themselves. [12]Very
truly I tell you,
whoever believes
in me will do
the works I have
been doing, and
they will do even
greater things than
these, because I
am going to the
Father. [13]And I
will do whatever
you ask

[a] 7 Some manuscripts *If you really knew me, you would know*

Θωμᾶς, κύριε, ↱ ↱ οὐκ οἴδαμεν ποῦ ὑπάγεις· πῶς δυνάμεθα τὴν
Thomas "Lord, we do not know where you are going, so how can we know the
2605 3261 3857 3857 4024 3857 4543 5632 4802 1538 3857 3836
n.nsm n.vsm pl v.rai.1p cj v.pai.2s cj v.ppi.1p d.asf

ὁδὸν εἰδέναι; [6] λέγει αὐτῷ ὁ[a] Ἰησοῦς, ἐγώ εἰμι ἡ ὁδὸς καὶ ἡ ἀλήθεια
way?" *know* Jesus said to him, *{the}* *Jesus* "I am the way, and the truth,
3847 3857 2652 3306 899 3836 2652 1609 1639 3836 3847 2779 3836 237
n.asf f.ra v.pai.3s r.dsm.3 d.nsm n.nsm r.ns.1 v.pai.1s d.nsf n.nsf cj d.nsf n.nsf

καὶ ἡ ζωή· οὐδεὶς ἔρχεται πρὸς τὸν πατέρα ˌεἰ μὴˌ δι' ἐμοῦ. [7]εἰ
and the life. No one comes to the Father except through me. If
2779 3836 2437 4029 2262 4639 3836 4252 1623 3590 1328 1609 1623
cj d.nsf n.nsf a.nsm v.pmi.3s p.a d.asm n.asm cj pl p.g r.gs.1 cj

ἐγνώκατέ με, καὶ τὸν πατέρα μου γνώσεσθε.[b] καὶ ἀπ'
you have known me, you will know my Father also; *{the}* *Father* *my* *you will know* and from
1182 1609 1182 1182 1182 1609 4252 2779 3836 4252 1609 1182 2779 608
v.rai.2p r.as.1 adv d.asm n.asm r.gs.1 v.fmi.2p cj p.g

ἄρτι γινώσκετε αὐτὸν καὶ ἑωράκατε αὐτόν. [8] λέγει αὐτῷ Φίλιππος, κύριε,
ˌnow onˌ you do know him and have seen him." Philip said to him, *Philip* "Lord,
785 1182 899 2779 3972 899 5805 3306 899 5805 3261
adv v.pai.2p r.asm.3 cj v.rai.2p r.asm.3 v.pai.3s r.dsm.3 n.nsm n.vsm

δεῖξον ἡμῖν τὸν πατέρα, καὶ ἀρκεῖ ἡμῖν. [9] λέγει αὐτῷ ὁ Ἰησοῦς,
show us the Father, and ˌthat will be enoughˌ for us." Jesus said to him, *{the}* *Jesus*
1259 7005 3836 4252 2779 758 7005 2652 3306 899 3836 2652
v.aam.2s r.dp.1 d.asm n.asm cj v.pai.3s r.dp.1 v.pai.3s r.dsm.3 d.nsm n.nsm

τοσούτῳ χρόνῳ μεθ' ὑμῶν εἰμι καὶ ↱ ↱ οὐκ
"Have I been so long a time with you, *Have I been* Philip, and you still do not
1639 1639 1639 5537 5989 3552 7007 1639 5805 2779 1182 1182 4024
r.dsm n.dsm p.g r.gp.2 v.pai.1s cj pl

ἔγνωκάς με, Φίλιππε; ὁ ἑωρακὼς ἐμὲ ἑώρακεν τὸν πατέρα· πῶς ↱ σὺ
know me? *Philip* The ˌone who has seenˌ me has seen the Father! How can you
1182 1609 5805 3836 3972 1609 3972 3836 4252 4802 3306 5148
v.rai.2s r.as.1 n.vsm d.nsm pt.ra.nsm r.as.1 v.rai.3s d.asm n.asm cj r.ns.2

λέγεις, δεῖξον ἡμῖν τὸν πατέρα; [10] ↱ ↱ οὐ πιστεύεις ὅτι ἐγὼ ἐν τῷ πατρὶ
say, 'Show us the Father'? Do you not believe that I am in the Father
3306 1259 7005 3836 4252 4409 4409 4024 4409 4022 1609 1877 3836 4252
v.pai.2s v.aam.2s r.dp.1 d.asm n.asm pl v.pai.2s cj r.ns.1 p.d d.dsm n.dsm

καὶ ὁ πατὴρ ἐν ἐμοί ἐστιν; τὰ ῥήματα ἃ ἐγὼ λέγω ὑμῖν
and the Father is in me? *is* The words that I say to you I do not
2779 3836 4252 1639 1877 1609 1639 3836 4839 4005 1609 3306 7007 3281 3281 4024
cj d.nsm n.nsm p.d r.ds.1 v.pai.3s d.apn n.apn r.apn r.ns.1 v.pai.1s r.dp.2

ἀπ' ἐμαυτοῦ οὐ λαλῶ, ὁ δὲ πατὴρ ἐν ἐμοὶ μένων
speak on my own authority, *not* *I do speak* but the *but* Father residing in me *residing*
3281 608 1831 4024 3281 1254 3836 1254 4252 3531 1877 1609 3531
p.g r.gsm.1 pl v.pai.1s d.nsm cj n.nsm p.d r.ds.1 pt.pa.nsm

ποιεῖ τὰ ἔργα αὐτοῦ. [11] πιστεύετέ μοι ὅτι ἐγὼ ἐν τῷ πατρὶ καὶ ὁ
is doing *{the}* his works. *his* Believe me that I am in the Father and the
4472 3836 899 2240 899 4409 1609 4022 1609 1877 3836 4252 2779 3836
v.pai.3s d.apn n.apn r.gsm.3 v.pam.2p r.ds.1 cj r.ns.1 p.d d.dsm n.dsm cj d.nsm

πατὴρ ἐν ἐμοί· ˌεἰ δὲ μή,ˌ διὰ τὰ ἔργα αὐτὰ πιστεύετε.
Father is in me, or else believe me ˌbecause ofˌ the works themselves. *believe*
4252 1877 1609 1623 1254 3590 4409 1328 3836 2240 899 4409
n.nsm p.d r.ds.1 cj cj pl p.a d.apn n.apn r.apn v.pam.2p

[12] ˌἀμὴν ἀμὴνˌ λέγω ὑμῖν, ὁ πιστεύων εἰς ἐμὲ
I tell you the solemn truth, *I tell* *you* the one who believes in me will do
3306 3306 7007 297 297 3306 7007 3836 4409 1650 1609 4472 4472
pl pl v.pai.1s r.dp.2 d.nsm pt.pa.nsm p.a r.as.1

τὰ ἔργα ἃ ἐγὼ ποιῶ κἀκεῖνος ποιήσει καὶ μείζονα τούτων ποιήσει,
the works that I do; *{also that one}* *will do* in fact, greater works than these will he do,
3836 2240 4005 1609 4472 2797 4472 2779 3489 4047 4472
d.apn n.apn r.apn r.ns.1 v.pai.1s crasis v.fai.3s cj a.apn.c r.gpn v.fai.3s

ὅτι ἐγὼ πρὸς τὸν πατέρα πορεύομαι· [13] καὶ ˌὅ τι ἂνˌ αἰτήσητε
because I am going to the Father. *am going* And whatever you ask
4022 1609 4513 4513 4639 3836 4252 4513 2779 4005 5516 323 160
cj r.ns.1 p.a d.asm n.asm v.pmi.1s cj r.asn r.asn pl v.aas.2p

[a] [ὁ] UBS, omitted by TNIV.
[b] ἐγνώκειτε ἂν included by TR after γνώσεσθε.

NASB

Him, "Lord, we do
not know where
You are going, how
do we know the
way?" [6]Jesus *said
to him, "I am the
way, and the truth,
and the life; no one
comes to the Father
but through Me.

Oneness with the Father

[7]If you had known
Me, you would
have known My
Father also; from
now on you know
Him, and have seen
Him."
[8]Philip *said to
Him, "Lord, show
us the Father, and
it is enough for
us." [9]Jesus *said to
him, "Have I been
so long with you,
and *yet* you have
not come to know
Me, Philip? He
who has seen Me
has seen the Fa-
ther; how *can* you
say, 'Show us the
Father'? [10]Do you
not believe that I
am in the Father,
and the Father is
in Me? The words
that I say to you
I do not speak on
My own initiative,
but the Father abid-
ing in Me does His
works. [11]Believe
Me that I am in
the Father and the
Father is in Me;
otherwise believe
because of the
works themselves.
[12]Truly, truly, I say
to you, he who
believes in Me, the
works that I do, he
will do also; and
greater *works* than
these he will do;
because I go to the
Father. [13]Whatever

NIV

in my name, so
that the Father may
be glorified in the
Son. 14 You may ask
me for anything
in my name, and I
will do it.

Jesus Promises the Holy Spirit

15 "If you love
me, keep my com-
mands. 16 And I
will ask the Father,
and he will give
you another advo-
cate to help you
and be with you
forever— 17 the
Spirit of truth. The
world cannot ac-
cept him, because
it neither sees him
nor knows him.
But you know him,
for he lives with
you and will be[a]
in you. 18 I will not
leave you as or-
phans; I will come
to you. 19 Before
long, the world
will not see me
anymore, but you
will see me. Be-
cause I live, you
also will live. 20 On
that day you will
realize that I am in
my Father, and you
are in me, and I am
in you. 21 Whoever
has my commands
and keeps them
is the one who
loves me. The one
who loves me will
be loved by my
Father, and I too
will love them and
show myself to
them."
22 Then Judas (not
Judas Iscariot)
said, "But, Lord,
why do you intend
to show yourself
to us

ἐν τῷ ὀνόματί μου τοῦτο ποιήσω, ἵνα δοξασθῇ ὁ πατὴρ
in {the} my name *my* {this} I will do, so that the Father may be glorified *the* *Father*
1877 3836 1609 3950 1609 4047 4472 2671 3836 4252 1519 3836 4252
p.d d.dsn n.dsn r.gs.1 r.asn v.fai.1s cj v.aps.3s d.nsm n.nsm

ἐν τῷ υἱῷ. 14 ἐάν τι αἰτήσητέ με ἐν τῷ ὀνόματί μου ἐγὼ
in the Son. If you ask me anything *you ask* *me* in {the} my name, *my* I
1877 3836 5626 1569 160 160 1609 5516 160 1609 1877 3836 1609 3950 1609 1609
p.d d.dsm n.dsm cj r.asn v.aas.2p r.as.1 p.d d.dsn n.dsn r.gs.1 r.ns.1

ποιήσω. 15 ἐὰν ἀγαπᾶτέ με, τὰς ἐντολὰς τὰς ἐμὰς
will do it. "If you love me, you will keep {the} my commandments. {the} *my*
4472 1569 26 1609 5498 5498 5498 3836 1847 1953 3836 1847
v.fai.1s cj v.pas.2p r.as.1 d.apf n.apf d.apf r.apf.1

τηρήσετε· 16 κἀγὼ ἐρωτήσω τὸν πατέρα καὶ ἄλλον παράκλητον
you will keep And I will ask the Father, and he will give you another Paraclete,
5498 2743 2263 3836 4252 2779 1443 1443 1443 7007 257 4156
v.fai.2p crasis v.fai.1s d.asm n.asm cj r.asm n.asm

δώσει ὑμῖν, ἵνα μεθ᾽ ὑμῶν εἰς τὸν αἰῶνα ᾖ, 17 τὸ πνεῦμα τῆς ἀληθείας,
he will give *you* to be with you for all time, *be* the Spirit of truth,
1443 7007 2671 1639 3552 7007 1650 3836 172 1639 3836 4460 3836 237
v.fai.3s r.dp.2 cj p.g r.gp.2 p.a d.asm n.asm v.pas.3s d.asn n.asn d.gsf n.gsf

ὃ ὁ κόσμος ⌞οὐ δύναται⌟ λαβεῖν, ὅτι ↱ οὐ θεωρεῖ αὐτὸ οὐδὲ
whom the world cannot receive, because it neither sees him nor
4005 3836 3180 4024 1538 3284 4022 2555 4024 2555 899 4028
r.asn d.nsm n.nsm pl v.ppi.3s f.aa cj pl v.pai.3s r.asn.3 cj

γινώσκει· ὑμεῖς γινώσκετε αὐτό, ὅτι παρ᾽ ὑμῖν μένει καὶ
knows him; but you will know him, for he will dwell with you *he will dwell* and
1182 7007 1182 899 4022 3531 3531 3531 4123 7007 3531 2779
v.pai.3s r.np.2 v.pai.2p r.asn.3 cj p.d r.dp.2 v.pai.3s cj

ἐν ὑμῖν ἔσται. 18 ↱ ↱ οὐκ ἀφήσω ὑμᾶς ὀρφανούς, ἔρχομαι πρὸς
will be in you. *will be* I will not abandon you as orphans, ⌞I will come back⌟ to
1639 1639 1877 7007 1639 918 918 4024 918 7007 4003 2262 4639
p.d r.dp.2 v.fmi.3s pl v.fai.1s r.ap.2 a.apm v.pmi.1s p.a

ὑμᾶς. 19 ἔτι μικρὸν καὶ ὁ κόσμος με οὐκέτι θεωρεῖ, ὑμεῖς
you. In a little while {and} the world will see me no longer, *will see* but you
7007 2285 3625 2779 3836 3180 2555 2555 1609 4033 2555 1254 7007
r.ap.2 adv a.asn cj d.nsm n.nsm r.as.1 adv v.pai.3s r.np.2

δὲ θεωρεῖτέ με, ὅτι ἐγὼ ζῶ καὶ ὑμεῖς ζήσετε. 20 ἐν ἐκείνῃ τῇ ἡμέρᾳ
but will see me; because I live, you too *you* will live. On that {the} day
1254 2555 1609 4022 1609 2409 7007 2779 7007 2409 1877 1697 3836 2465
cj v.pai.2p r.as.1 cj r.ns.1 v.pai.1s cj r.np.2 v.fai.2p p.d r.dsf d.dsf n.dsf

γνώσεσθε ὑμεῖς ὅτι ἐγὼ ἐν τῷ πατρί μου καὶ ὑμεῖς ἐν ἐμοί
you will know *you* that I am in {the} my Father, *my* and that you are in me,
7007 1182 7007 4022 1609 1877 3836 1609 4252 1609 2779 7007 1877 1609
v.fmi.2p r.np.2 cj r.ns.1 p.d d.dsm n.dsm r.gs.1 cj r.np.2 p.d r.ds.1

κἀγὼ ← ἐν ὑμῖν. 21 ὁ ἔχων τὰς ἐντολάς μου καὶ τηρῶν
and that I am in you. The ⌞one who has⌟ {the} my commandments *my* and keeps
2743 1877 7007 3836 2400 3836 1609 1953 1609 2779 5498
crasis p.d r.dp.2 d.nsm pt.pa.nsm d.apf n.apf r.gs.1 cj pt.pa.nsm

αὐτὰς ἐκεῖνός ἐστιν ὁ ἀγαπῶν με· ὁ δὲ ἀγαπῶν με
them {that one} is the ⌞one who loves⌟ me. And the *And* ⌞one who loves⌟ me
899 1697 1639 3836 26 1609 1254 3836 1254 26 1609
r.apf.3 r.nsm v.pai.3s d.nsm pt.pa.nsm r.as.1 d.nsm cj pt.pa.nsm r.as.1

ἀγαπηθήσεται ὑπὸ τοῦ πατρός μου, κἀγὼ ἀγαπήσω αὐτὸν καὶ ἐμφανίσω
will be loved by {the} my Father, *my* and I will love him and reveal myself
26 5679 3836 1609 4252 1609 2743 26 899 2779 1872 1831
v.fpi.3s p.g d.gsm n.gsm r.gs.1 crasis v.fai.1s r.asm.3 cj v.fai.1s

αὐτῷ ἐμαυτόν. 22 λέγει αὐτῷ Ἰούδας, οὐχ ὁ Ἰσκαριώτης,
to him." *myself* Judas (not Iscariot) said to him, *Judas* *not* {the} *Iscariot*
899 1831 2683 4024 2697 3306 899 2683 4024 3836 2697
r.dsm.3 r.asm.1 v.pai.3s r.dsm.3 n.nsm pl d.nsm n.nsm

κύριε,[a] τί γέγονεν ὅτι ἡμῖν μέλλεις
"Lord, what has happened that you are going to reveal yourself to us, *you are going*
3261 5515 1181 4022 3516 3516 3516 1872 1872 4932 7005 3516
n.vsm r.nsn v.rai.3s cj r.dp.1 v.pai.2s

NASB

you ask in My
name, that will
I do, so that the
Father may be
glorified in the
Son. 14 If you ask
Me anything in My
name, I will do *it.*
15 "If you love Me,
you will keep My
commandments.

Role of the Spirit

16 I will ask the
Father, and He will
give you another
Helper, that He
may be with you
forever; 17 *that is*
the Spirit of truth,
whom the world
cannot receive,
because it does not
see Him or know
Him, *but* you know
Him because He
abides with you
and will be in you.
18 "I will not leave
you as orphans; I
will come to you.
19 After a little while
the world will no
longer see Me, but
you *will* see Me;
because I live, you
will live also. 20 In
that day you will
know that I am in
My Father, and
you in Me, and I
in you. 21 He who
has My command-
ments and keeps
them is the one
who loves Me;
and he who loves
Me will be loved
by My Father, and
I will love him
and will disclose
Myself to him."
22 Judas (not Iscar-
iot) *said to Him,
"Lord, what then
has happened that
You are going to
disclose Yourself

[a] 17 Some early manuscripts *and is*

[a] καὶ included by UBS after κύριε.

NIV

and not to the
world?"
23 Jesus replied,
"Anyone who
loves me will obey
my teaching. My
Father will love
them, and we will
come to them and
make our home
with them. 24 Any-
one who does not
love me will not
obey my teaching.
These words you
hear are not my
own; they belong
to the Father who
sent me.
25 "All this I have
spoken while still
with you. 26 But
the Advocate, the
Holy Spirit, whom
the Father will
send in my name,
will teach you all
things and will re-
mind you of every-
thing I have said
to you. 27 Peace I
leave with you; my
peace I give you. I
do not give to you
as the world gives.
Do not let your
hearts be trou-
bled and do not be
afraid.
28 "You heard me
say, 'I am going
away and I am
coming back to
you.' If you loved
me, you would be
glad that I am go-
ing to the Father,
for the Father is
greater than I. 29 I
have told you now
before it happens,
so that when it
does happen you
will believe. 30 I
will not say much
more to you,

ἐμφανίζειν σεαυτὸν καὶ οὐχὶ τῷ κόσμῳ; 23 ἀπεκρίθη Ἰησοῦς καὶ εἶπεν
to reveal *yourself* and not ⌊to the⌋ world?" Jesus answered *Jesus* *{and}* him, saying,
1872 4932 2779 4049 3836 3180 2652 646 2652 2779 899 3306
f.pa r.asm.2 cj pl d.dsm n.dsm v.api.3s n.nsm cj v.aai.3s

αὐτῷ, ἐάν τις ἀγαπᾷ με τὸν λόγον μου τηρήσει, καὶ ὁ
him "If anyone loves me, he will keep *{the}* my word, *my* *he will keep* and *{the}* my
899 1569 5516 26 1609 5498 5498 5498 3836 1609 3364 1609 5498 2779 3836 1609
r.dsm.3 cj r.nsm v.pas.3s r.as.1 d.asm n.asm r.gs.1 v.fai.3s cj d.nsm

πατήρ μου ἀγαπήσει αὐτὸν καὶ πρὸς αὐτὸν ἐλευσόμεθα καὶ
Father *my* will love him, and we will come to him *we will come* and make our
4252 1609 26 899 2779 2262 2262 2262 4639 899 2262 2779 4472 4472
n.nsm r.gs.1 v.fai.3s r.asm.3 cj p.a r.asm.3 v.fmi.1p cj

μονὴν παρ᾿ αὐτῷ ποιησόμεθα. 24 ὁ ↱ ↱ ↱ μὴ ἀγαπῶν με
⌊dwelling place⌋ with him. *make our* The one who does not love me does not
3665 4123 899 4472 3836 26 26 26 3590 26 1609 5498 4024
n.asf p.d r.dsm.3 v.fmi.1p d.nsm pl pt.pa.nsm r.as.1

τοὺς λόγους μου οὐ τηρεῖ· καὶ ὁ λόγος ὃν ἀκούετε οὐκ
keep *{the}* my words; *my* *not* *does keep* and the word that you are hearing is not
5498 3836 1609 3364 1609 4024 5498 2779 3836 3364 4005 201 1639 4024
d.apm n.apm r.gs.1 pl v.pai.3s cj d.nsm n.nsm r.asm v.pai.2p pl

ἔστιν ἐμὸς ἀλλὰ τοῦ πέμψαντός με πατρός. 25 ταῦτα λελάληκα
is mine, but the Father's who sent me. *Father's* ⌊"These things⌋ I have spoken
1639 1847 247 3836 4252 4287 1609 4252 4047 3281
v.pai.3s r.nsm.1 cj d.gsm pt.aa.gsm r.as.1 n.gsm r.apn v.rai.1s

ὑμῖν παρ᾿ ὑμῖν μένων· 26 ὁ δὲ παράκλητος, τὸ
to you while I am still with you. *while I am still* But the *But* Paraclete, the Holy
7007 3531 3531 3531 3531 4123 7007 3531 1254 3836 1254 4156 3836 41
r.dp.2 p.d r.dp.2 pt.pa.nsm d.nsm cj n.nsm d.nsn

πνεῦμα τὸ ἅγιον, ὃ πέμψει ὁ πατὴρ ἐν τῷ ὀνόματί μου,
Spirit, *{the}* *Holy* whom the Father will send *the* *Father* in *{the}* my name, *my*
4460 3836 41 4005 3836 4252 4287 3836 4252 1877 3836 1609 3950 1609
n.nsn d.nsn a.nsn r.asn v.fai.3s d.nsm n.nsm p.d d.dsn n.dsn r.gs.1

ἐκεῖνος ὑμᾶς διδάξει πάντα καὶ → ὑπομνήσει ὑμᾶς
{that one} will instruct you *will instruct* regarding all things, and cause you to remember *you*
1697 1438 1438 7007 1438 4246 2779 7007 5703 7007
r.nsm r.ap.2 v.fai.3s a.apn cj v.fai.3s r.ap.2

πάντα ἃ εἶπον ὑμῖν ἐγώ.[a] 27 εἰρήνην ἀφίημι ὑμῖν, εἰρήνην τὴν
everything that I have told you. *I* Peace I leave with you; my peace *{the}*
4246 4005 1609 3306 7007 1609 1645 918 7007 1847 1645 3836
a.apn r.apn v.aai.1s r.dp.2 r.ns.1 n.asf v.pai.1s r.dp.2 n.asf d.asf

ἐμὴν δίδωμι ὑμῖν· οὐ καθὼς ὁ κόσμος δίδωσιν ἐγὼ δίδωμι
my I give to you. I give to you not as the world gives. *I* *give*
1847 1443 7007 1609 1443 7007 7007 4024 2777 3836 3180 1443 1609 1443
r.asf.1 v.pai.1s r.dp.2 pl cj d.nsm n.nsm v.pai.3s r.ns.1 v.pai.1s

ὑμῖν. ↱ μὴ → ταρασσέσθω ὑμῶν ἡ καρδία μηδὲ → δειλιάτω.
to you Do not let your heart be troubled, *your* *{the}* *heart* neither let it be afraid.
7007 5429 3590 7007 2840 5429 7007 3836 2840 3593 1262
r.dp.2 pl v.ppm.3s r.gp.2 d.nsf n.nsf cj v.pam.3s

28 ἠκούσατε ὅτι ἐγὼ εἶπον ὑμῖν, ὑπάγω καὶ ἔρχομαι πρὸς ὑμᾶς. εἰ
You heard ~ me say to you, ⌊'I am going away,⌋ and ⌊I will come back⌋ to you.' If
201 4022 1609 3306 7007 5632 2779 2262 4639 7007 1623
v.aai.2p cj r.ns.1 v.aai.1s r.dp.2 v.pai.1s cj v.pmi.1s p.a r.ap.2 cj

ἠγαπᾶτέ με → ἐχάρητε ἂν ὅτι πορεύομαι πρὸς τὸν πατέρα, ὅτι
you loved me, you would have rejoiced, *would* because I am going to the Father, for
26 1609 323 5897 323 4022 4513 4639 3836 4252 4022
v.iai.2p r.as.1 v.api.2p pl cj v.pmi.1s p.a d.asm n.asm cj

ὁ πατὴρ μείζων μού ἐστιν. 29 καὶ νῦν εἴρηκα ὑμῖν πρὶν γενέσθαι, ἵνα
the Father is greater ⌊than I.⌋ *is* And now I have told you before it happens, that
3836 4252 1639 3489 1609 1639 2779 3814 3306 7007 4570 1181 2671
d.nsm n.nsm a.nsm.c r.gs.1 v.pai.3s cj adv v.rai.1s r.dp.2 cj f.am cj

ὅταν γένηται πιστεύσητε. 30 → οὐκέτι πολλὰ
when it does happen you may believe. I will not speak with you much longer, *much*
4020 1181 4409 3281 3281 3281 3552 7007 4498 4033 4498
cj v.ams.3s v.aas.2p adv a.apn

NASB

to us and not to
the world?" 23 Jesus
answered and said
to him, "If anyone
loves Me, he will
keep My word;
and My Father
will love him, and
We will come to
him and make Our
abode with him.
24 He who does not
love Me does not
keep My words;
and the word
which you hear is
not Mine, but the
Father's who sent
Me.
25 "These things
I have spoken to
you while abiding
with you. 26 But the
Helper, the Holy
Spirit, whom the
Father will send
in My name, He
will teach you all
things, and bring
to your remem-
brance all that I
said to you. 27 Peace
I leave with you;
My peace I give
to you; not as the
world gives do I
give to you. Do
not let your heart
be troubled, nor let
it be fearful. 28 You
heard that I said to
you, 'I go away,
and I will come to
you.' If you loved
Me, you would
have rejoiced be-
cause I go to the
Father, for the Fa-
ther is greater than
I. 29 Now I have
told you before it
happens, so that
when it happens,
you may believe.
30 I will not speak
much more

[a] [ἐγώ] UBS, omitted by TNIV.

NIV

for the prince of
this world is com-
ing. He has no hold
over me, [31]but he
comes so that the
world may learn
that I love the Fa-
ther and do exactly
what my Father has
commanded me.
"Come now; let
us leave.

The Vine and the Branches

15 "I am the
true vine,
and my Father
is the gardener.
[2]He cuts off ev-
ery branch in me
that bears no fruit,
while every branch
that does bear fruit
he prunes[a] so that
it will be even
more fruitful. [3]You
are already clean
because of the
word I have spo-
ken to you. [4]Re-
main in me, as I
also remain in you.
No branch can
bear fruit by itself;
it must remain in
the vine. Neither
can you bear fruit
unless you remain
in me.
[5]"I am the
vine; you are the
branches. If you
remain in me and
I in you, you will
bear much fruit;
apart from me you
can do nothing.
[6]If you do not re-
main in me, you
are like a branch
that is thrown
away and withers;
such branches are
picked up, thrown
into the fire and
burned. [7]If you
remain in me and
my words remain
in you,

[a] 2 The Greek for *he prunes* also means *he cleans.*

λαλήσω μεθ᾽ ὑμῶν, ἔρχεται γὰρ ὁ τοῦ κόσμου
I will speak *with* *you* for the ruler of this world is coming. *for* *the* *of this* *world*
3281 3552 7007 1142 3836 807 3836 3836 3180 2262 1142 3836 3836 3180
v.fai.1s p.g r.gp.2 v.pmi.3s cj d.nsm d.gsm n.gsm

ἄρχων· καὶ ἐν ἐμοὶ οὐκ ἔχει οὐδέν, 31 ἀλλ᾽ ἵνα
ruler *{and}* He has no claim on me, *{not}* *He has* *no claim* but so the world
807 2779 2400 2400 4029 4029 1877 1609 4024 2400 4029 247 2671 3836 3180
n.nsm cj p.d r.ds.1 pl v.pai.3s a.asn cj cj

γνῷ ὁ κόσμος ὅτι ἀγαπῶ τὸν πατέρα, καὶ καθὼς
⸤may know⸥ *the* *world* that I love the Father, *{and}* I do exactly as the Father
1182 3836 3180 4022 26 3836 4252 2779 4472 4472 4048 2777 3836 4252
v.aas.3s d.nsm n.nsm cj v.pai.1s d.asm n.asm cj cj

ἐνετείλατό μοι ὁ πατήρ, οὕτως ποιῶ. ἐγείρεσθε, ἄγωμεν ἐντεῦθεν.
commanded me. *the* *Father* *exactly* *I do* Rise up, let us go from this place!
1948 1609 3836 4252 4048 4472 1586 72 1949
v.ami.3s r.ds.1 d.nsm n.nsm adv v.pai.1s v.ppm.2p v.pas.1p adv

15:1 ἐγώ εἰμι ἡ ἄμπελος ἡ ἀληθινὴ καὶ ὁ πατήρ μου ὁ
"I am the true vine, *{the}* *true* and *{the}* my Father *my* is the
1609 1639 3836 240 306 3836 240 2779 3836 1609 4252 1609 1639 3836
r.ns.1 v.pai.1s d.nsf n.nsf d.nsf a.nsf cj d.nsm n.nsm r.gs.1 d.nsm

γεωργός ἐστιν. 2 πᾶν κλῆμα ἐν ἐμοὶ μὴ φέρον καρπὸν αἴρει αὐτό,
vine-grower. *is* Every branch in me that bears no *bears* fruit ⸤he cuts off,⸥ *{it}*
1177 1639 4246 3097 1877 1609 5770 3590 5770 2843 149 899
n.nsm v.pai.3s a.asn n.asn p.d r.ds.1 pl pt.pa.asn n.asm v.pai.3s r.asn.3

καὶ πᾶν τὸ καρπὸν φέρον καθαίρει αὐτὸ ἵνα
but every branch that does bear *{the}* fruit *does bear* he prunes, *{it}* so that it may bear
2779 4246 5770 5770 3836 2843 5770 2748 899 2671 5770 5770 5770
cj a.asn d.asn n.asm pt.pa.asn v.pai.3s r.asn.3 cj

καρπὸν πλείονα φέρῃ. 3 ἤδη ὑμεῖς καθαροί ἐστε διὰ τὸν
more fruit. *more* *it may bear* ⸤By this time⸥ you are clean *are* ⸤because of⸥ the
4498 2843 4498 5770 2453 7007 1639 2754 1639 1328 3836
n.asm a.asm.c v.pas.3s adv r.np.2 a.npm v.pai.2p p.a d.asm

λόγον ὃν λελάληκα ὑμῖν· 4 μείνατε ἐν ἐμοί, κἀγὼ ἐν ὑμῖν. καθὼς τὸ
message that I have spoken to you. Abide in me and I will abide in you. Just as the
3364 4005 3281 7007 3531 1877 1609 2743 1877 7007 2777 3836
n.asm r.asm v.rai.1s r.dp.2 v.aam.2p p.d r.ds.1 crasis p.d r.dp.2 cj d.nsn

κλῆμα ↱ οὐ δύναται καρπὸν φέρειν ἀφ᾽ ἑαυτοῦ ⸤ἐὰν μὴ⸥ μένῃ ἐν τῇ
branch is not able to bear fruit *to bear* by itself, unless it abides in the
3097 1538 4024 1538 5770 5770 2843 5770 608 1571 1569 3590 3531 1877 3836
n.nsn pl v.ppi.3s n.asm f.pa p.g r.gsn.3 cj pl v.pas.3s p.d d.dsf

ἀμπέλῳ, οὕτως οὐδὲ ὑμεῖς ⸤ἐὰν μὴ⸥ ἐν ἐμοὶ μένητε. 5 ἐγώ εἰμι ἡ
vine, so neither can you unless you abide in me. *you abide* I am the
306 4048 4028 7007 1569 3590 3531 3531 1877 1609 3531 1609 1639 3836
n.dsf adv cj r.np.2 cj pl p.d r.ds.1 v.pas.2p r.ns.1 v.pai.1s d.nsf

ἄμπελος, ὑμεῖς τὰ κλήματα. ὁ μένων ἐν ἐμοὶ κἀγὼ ἐν αὐτῷ οὗτος
vine; you are the branches. The ⸤one who abides⸥ in me and I in him *{this one}*
306 7007 3836 3097 3836 3531 1877 1609 2743 1877 899 4047
n.nsf r.np.2 d.npn n.npn d.nsm pt.pa.nsm p.d r.ds.1 crasis p.d r.dsm.3 r.nsm

φέρει καρπὸν πολύν, ὅτι χωρὶς ἐμοῦ οὐ δύνασθε ποιεῖν οὐδέν. 6 ἐὰν
bears much fruit, *much* for apart from me *{not}* you can do nothing. If
5770 4498 2843 4498 4022 6006 1609 4024 1538 4472 4029 1569
v.pai.3s n.asm a.asm cj p.g r.gs.1 pl v.ppi.2p f.pa a.asn cj

↱ μή τις μένῃ ἐν ἐμοί, ἐβλήθη ἔξω ὡς τὸ
anyone does not *anyone* abide in me, he is like a branch that is thrown away *like* *{the}*
5516 3531 3590 5516 3531 1877 1609 6055 3097 965 2032 6055 3836
pl r.nsm v.pas.3s p.d r.ds.1 v.api.3s adv pl d.nsn

κλῆμα καὶ ἐξηράνθη καὶ συνάγουσιν αὐτὰ καὶ εἰς τὸ πῦρ
branch and withers; *{and}* men gather them and throw them into the fire,
3097 2779 3830 2779 5251 899 2779 965 1650 3836 4786
n.nsn cj v.api.3s cj v.pai.3p r.apn.3 cj p.a d.asn n.asn

βάλλουσιν καὶ καίεται. 7 ἐὰν μείνητε ἐν ἐμοὶ καὶ τὰ ῥήματά μου
throw and they are burned. If you abide in me and *{the}* my words *my* abide
965 2779 2794 1569 3531 1877 1609 2779 3836 1609 4839 1609 3531
v.pai.3p cj v.ppi.3s cj v.aas.2p p.d r.ds.1 cj d.npn n.npn r.gs.1

NASB

with you, for the
ruler of the world
is coming, and he
has nothing in Me;
[31]but so that the
world may know
that I love the
Father, I do exactly
as the Father com-
manded Me. Get
up, let us go from
here.

Jesus Is the Vine—Followers Are Branches

15:1 "I am the true
vine, and My
Father is the vine-
dresser. [2]Every
branch in Me that
does not bear fruit,
He takes away;
and every *branch*
that bears fruit, He
[a]prunes it so that
it may bear more
fruit. [3]You are
already clean be-
cause of the word
which I have spo-
ken to you. [4]Abide
in Me, and I in
you. As the branch
cannot bear fruit
of itself unless it
abides in the vine,
so neither *can* you
unless you abide in
Me. [5]I am the vine,
you are the branch-
es; he who abides
in Me and I in him,
he bears much
fruit, for apart from
Me you can do
nothing. [6]If anyone
does not abide in
Me, he is thrown
away as a branch
and dries up; and
they gather them,
and cast them into
the fire and they
are burned. [7]If you
abide in Me, and
My words abide in

[a] Lit *cleans;* used to describe pruning

NIV

ask whatever you wish, and it will be done for you. [8]This is to my Father's glory, that you bear much fruit, showing yourselves to be my disciples.

[9]"As the Father has loved me, so have I loved you. Now remain in my love. [10]If you keep my commands, you will remain in my love, just as I have kept my Father's commands and remain in his love. [11]I have told you this so that my joy may be in you and that your joy may be complete. [12]My command is this: Love each other as I have loved you. [13]Greater love has no one than this: to lay down one's life for one's friends. [14]You are my friends if you do what I command. [15]I no longer call you servants, because a servant does not know his master's business. Instead, I have called you friends, for everything that I learned from my Father I have made known to you. [16]You did not choose me, but I chose you and appointed you so that

ἐν ὑμῖν μείνῃ, ⌞ὃ ἐὰν⌟ θέλητε αἰτήσασθε, καὶ γενήσεται ὑμῖν. 8
in you, *abide* ask whatever you wish *ask* and it will be done for you. My
1877 7007 3531 160 4005 1569 2527 160 2779 1181 7007 1609
p.d r.dp.2 v.aas.3s r.asn pl v.pas.2p v.amm.2p cj v.fmi.3s r.dp.2

ἐν τούτῳ ἐδοξάσθη ὁ πατήρ μου, ἵνα καρπὸν
Father is glorified in this, *is glorified* *{the}* *Father* *My* that you bear much fruit
4252 1519 1519 1877 4047 1519 3836 4252 1609 2671 5770 5770 4498 2843
p.d r.dsn v.api.3s d.nsm n.nsm r.gs.1 cj n.asm

πολὺν φέρητε καὶ γένησθε ἐμοὶ μαθηταί. 9 καθὼς ἠγάπησέν με ὁ
much *you bear* and become my disciples. As the Father has loved me, *the*
4498 5770 2779 1181 1847 3412 2777 3836 4252 26 1609 3836
a.asm v.pas.2p cj v.ams.2p a.dsm n.npm cj v.aai.3s r.as.1 d.nsm

πατήρ, → κἀγὼ ὑμᾶς ἠγάπησα· μείνατε ἐν τῇ ἀγάπῃ τῇ ἐμῇ.
Father I have also loved you; *have loved* abide in *{the}* my love. *{the}* *my*
4252 26 2743 26 7007 26 3531 1877 3836 1847 27 3836 1847
n.nsm crasis r.ap.2 v.aai.1s v.aam.2p p.d d.dsf n.dsf d.dsf r.dsf.1

10 ἐὰν τὰς ἐντολάς μου τηρήσητε, μενεῖτε ἐν τῇ
If you keep *{the}* my commandments, *my* *you keep* ⌞you will abide⌟ in *{the}* my
1569 5498 5498 3836 1609 1953 1609 5498 3531 1877 3836 1609
cj d.apf n.apf r.gs.1 v.aas.2p v.fai.2p p.d d.dsf

ἀγάπῃ μου, καθὼς ἐγὼ τὰς ἐντολὰς τοῦ πατρός μου
love, *my* just as I have kept *{the}* my Father's commandments *{the}* *Father's* *my*
27 1609 2777 1609 5498 5498 3836 1609 4252 1953 3836 4252 1609
n.dsf r.gs.1 cj r.ns.1 d.apf n.apf d.gsm n.gsm r.gs.1

τετήρηκα καὶ μένω αὐτοῦ ἐν τῇ ἀγάπῃ. 11 ταῦτα λελάληκα ὑμῖν ἵνα
have kept and abide in his *in* *{the}* love. These things I have spoken to you, that
5498 2779 3531 1877 899 1877 3836 27 4047 3281 7007 2671
v.rai.1s cj v.pai.1s r.gsm.3 p.d d.dsf n.dsf r.apn v.rai.1s r.dp.2 cj

ἡ χαρὰ ἡ ἐμὴ ἐν ὑμῖν ᾖ καὶ ἡ χαρὰ ὑμῶν
{the} my joy *{the}* *my* may be in you *may be* and that *{the}* your joy *your*
3836 1847 5915 3836 1847 1639 1639 1877 7007 1639 2779 3836 7007 5915 7007
d.nsf n.nsf d.nsf r.nsf.1 p.d r.dp.2 v.pas.3s cj d.nsf n.nsf r.gp.2

πληρωθῇ. 12 αὕτη ἐστὶν ἡ ἐντολὴ ἡ ἐμή, ἵνα ἀγαπᾶτε
may be complete. "This is *{the}* my commandment: *{the}* *my* *{that}* Love
4444 4047 1639 3836 1847 1953 3836 1847 2671 26
v.aps.3s r.nsf v.pai.3s d.nsf n.nsf d.nsf r.nsf.1 cj v.pas.2p

ἀλλήλους καθὼς ἠγάπησα ὑμᾶς. 13 μείζονα ταύτης ἀγάπην οὐδεὶς
one another, as I have loved you. Greater love has no one than this, *love* *no one*
253 2777 26 7007 3489 27 2400 4029 4029 4047 27 4029
r.apm cj v.aai.1s r.ap.2 a.asf.c r.gsf n.asf a.nsm

ἔχει, ἵνα τις τὴν ψυχὴν αὐτοῦ θῇ ὑπὲρ τῶν φίλων
has that a person lays down *{the}* his life *his* *lays down* for *{the}* his friends.
2400 2671 5516 5502 5502 3836 899 6034 899 5502 5642 3836 899 5813
v.pai.3s cj r.nsm d.asf n.asf r.gsm.3 v.aas.3s p.g d.gpm n.gpm

αὐτοῦ. 14 ὑμεῖς φίλοι μού ἐστε ἐὰν ποιῆτε ἃ ἐγὼ ἐντέλλομαι ὑμῖν.
his You are my friends *my* *are* if you do the things I command you.
899 7007 1639 1609 5813 1609 1639 1569 4472 4005 1609 1948 7007
r.gsm.3 r.np.2 n.npm r.gs.1 v.pai.2p cj v.pas.2p r.apn r.ns.1 v.pmi.1s r.dp.2

15 οὐκέτι λέγω ὑμᾶς δούλους, ὅτι ὁ δοῦλος ↱ οὐκ οἶδεν τί
No longer do I call you servants, for a servant does not know what his master
4033 3306 7007 1529 4022 3836 1529 3857 4024 3857 5515 899 3261
adv v.pai.1s r.ap.2 n.apm cj d.nsm n.nsm pl v.rai.3s r.asn

ποιεῖ αὐτοῦ ὁ κύριος· ὑμᾶς δὲ εἴρηκα φίλους, ὅτι
is doing; *his* *{the}* *master* but I have called you *but* *I have called* friends, because
4472 899 3836 3261 1254 3306 3306 3306 7007 1254 3306 5813 4022
v.pai.3s r.gsm.3 d.nsm n.nsm r.ap.2 cj v.rai.1s n.apm cj

πάντα ἃ ἤκουσα παρὰ τοῦ πατρός μου ἐγνώρισα ὑμῖν. 16
all that I have heard from *{the}* my Father *my* ⌞I have made known⌟ to you. You did
4246 4005 201 4123 3836 1609 4252 1609 1192 7007 7007 1721
a.apn r.apn v.aai.1s p.g d.gsm n.gsm r.gs.1 v.aai.1s r.dp.2

οὐχ ὑμεῖς με ἐξελέξασθε, ἀλλ᾽ ἐγὼ ἐξελεξάμην ὑμᾶς καὶ ἔθηκα ὑμᾶς ἵνα
not *You* choose me, *did choose* but I chose you and appointed you that
4024 7007 1721 1609 1721 247 1609 1721 7007 2779 5502 7007 2671
pl r.np.2 r.as.1 v.ami.2p cj r.ns.1 v.ami.1s r.ap.2 cj v.aai.1s r.ap.2 cj

NASB

you, ask whatever you wish, and it will be done for you. [8]My Father is glorified by this, that you bear much fruit, and *so* prove to be My disciples. [9]Just as the Father has loved Me, I have also loved you; abide in My love. [10]If you keep My commandments, you will abide in My love; just as I have kept My Father's commandments and abide in His love. [11]These things I have spoken to you so that My joy may be in you, and *that* your joy may be made full.

Disciples' Relation to Each Other

[12]"This is My commandment, that you love one another, just as I have loved you. [13]Greater love has no one than this, that one lay down his life for his friends. [14]You are My friends if you do what I command you. [15]No longer do I call you slaves, for the slave does not know what his master is doing; but I have called you friends, for all things that I have heard from My Father I have made known to you. [16]You did not choose Me but I chose you, and appointed you that

NIV

you might go and
bear fruit — fruit
that will last — and
so that whatev-
er you ask in my
name the Father
will give you.
17 This is my com-
mand: Love each
other.

The World Hates the Disciples

18 "If the world
hates you, keep in
mind that it hated
me first. 19 If you
belonged to the
world, it would
love you as its
own. As it is, you
do not belong to
the world, but I
have chosen you
out of the world.
That is why the
world hates you.
20 Remember what
I told you: 'A ser-
vant is not greater
than his master.'[a]
If they persecuted
me, they will per-
secute you also.
If they obeyed
my teaching, they
will obey yours
also. 21 They will
treat you this way
because of my
name, for they do
not know the one
who sent me. 22 If I
had not come and
spoken to them,
they would not be
guilty of sin; but
now they have no
excuse for their
sin. 23 Whoever
hates me hates my
Father as well.

ὑμεῖς ὑπάγητε καὶ καρπὸν φέρητε καὶ ὁ καρπὸς ὑμῶν μένῃ,
you should go and bear fruit *bear* and that *{the}* your fruit *your* ⸤should remain,⸥
7007 5632 2779 5770 2843 5770 2779 3836 7007 2843 7007 3531
r.np.2 v.pas.2p cj n.asm v.pas.2p cj d.nsm n.nsm r.gp.2 v.pas.3s

ἵνα ⸤ὅ τι ἂν⸥ αἰτήσητε τὸν πατέρα ἐν τῷ
so that the Father may give you whatever you ask *the* *Father* in *{the}* my
2671 3836 4252 1443 1443 7007 4005 5516 323 160 3836 4252 1877 3836 1609
cj r.asn r.asn pl v.aas.2p d.asm n.asm p.d d.dsn

ὀνόματί μου δῷ ὑμῖν. 17 ταῦτα ἐντέλλομαι ὑμῖν, ἵνα ἀγαπᾶτε
name. *my* *may give* *you* These things I command you, so that you may love
3950 1609 1443 7007 4047 1948 7007 2671 26
n.dsn r.gs.1 v.aas.3s r.dp.2 r.apn v.pmi.1s r.dp.2 cj v.pas.2p

ἀλλήλους. 18 εἰ ὁ κόσμος ὑμᾶς μισεῖ, γινώσκετε ὅτι ἐμὲ
one another. "If the world hates you, *hates* be aware that it has hated me
253 1623 3836 3180 3631 7007 3631 1182 4022 3631 3631 3631 1609
r.apm cj d.nsm n.nsm r.ap.2 v.pai.3s v.pai.2p cj r.as.1

πρῶτον ὑμῶν μεμίσηκεν. 19 εἰ ἐκ τοῦ κόσμου ἦτε, ὁ
before it hated you. *it has hated* If you belonged to the world, *you belonged* the
4754 7007 3631 1623 1639 1639 1666 3836 3180 1639 3836
adv r.gp.2 v.rai.3s cj p.g d.gsm n.gsm v.iai.2p d.nsm

κόσμος ἂν τὸ ἴδιον ἐφίλει· ὅτι δὲ ἐκ
world would love you as *{the}* its own; *love you* but because *but* you do not belong to
3180 323 5797 5797 3836 2625 5797 1254 4022 1254 1639 1639 4024 1639 1666
n.nsm pl d.asn a.asn v.iai.3s cj cj p.g

τοῦ κόσμου οὐκ ἐστέ, ἀλλ᾽ ἐγὼ ἐξελεξάμην ὑμᾶς ἐκ τοῦ κόσμου, διὰ
the world, *not* *you do belong* but I chose you ⸤out of⸥ the world, for
3836 3180 4024 1639 247 1609 1721 7007 1666 3836 3180 1328
d.gsm n.gsm pl v.pai.2p cj r.ns.1 v.ami.1s r.ap.2 p.g d.gsm n.gsm p.a

τοῦτο μισεῖ ὑμᾶς ὁ κόσμος. 20 μνημονεύετε τοῦ λόγου οὗ ἐγὼ
this reason the world hates you. *the* *world* Remember the saying that I
4047 3836 3180 3631 7007 3836 3180 3648 3836 3364 4005 1609
r.asn v.pai.3s r.ap.2 d.nsm n.nsm v.pam.2p d.gsm n.gsm r.gsm r.ns.1

εἶπον ὑμῖν, οὐκ ἔστιν δοῦλος μείζων τοῦ κυρίου αὐτοῦ. εἰ
told you, 'The servant is not *is* *servant* greater than his master.' *his* If they
3306 7007 1529 1639 4024 1639 1529 3489 3836 899 3261 899 1623 1503
v.aai.1s r.dp.2 pl v.pai.3s n.nsm a.nsm.c d.gsm n.gsm r.gsm.3 cj

ἐμὲ ἐδίωξαν, καὶ ὑμᾶς διώξουσιν· εἰ
have persecuted me, *they have persecuted* they will also persecute you; *they will persecute* if they
1503 1503 1609 1503 1503 1503 2779 1503 7007 1503 1623 5498
r.as.1 v.aai.3p adv r.ap.2 v.fai.3p cj

τὸν λόγον μου ἐτήρησαν, καὶ τὸν ὑμέτερον
have kept *{the}* my word, *my* *they have kept* they will keep yours as well. *{the}* *yours*
5498 5498 3836 1609 3364 1609 5498 5498 5498 5498 5629 2779 3836 5629
d.asm n.asm r.gs.1 v.aai.3p adv d.asm r.asm.2

τηρήσουσιν. 21 ἀλλὰ ταῦτα πάντα ποιήσουσιν εἰς ὑμᾶς διὰ τὸ
they will keep But all these things *all* they will do to you ⸤on account of⸥ *{the}*
5498 247 4246 4047 4246 4472 1650 7007 1328 3836
v.fai.3p cj r.apn a.apn v.fai.3p p.a r.ap.2 p.a d.asn

ὄνομά μου, ὅτι ↱ ↱ οὐκ οἴδασιν τὸν πέμψαντά με. 22 εἰ ↱ ↱ μὴ
my name, *my* because they do not know the one who sent me. If I had not
1609 3950 1609 4022 3857 3857 4024 3857 3836 4287 1609 1623 2262 2262 3590
n.asn r.gs.1 cj pl v.rai.3p d.asm pt.aa.asm r.as.1 cj pl

ἦλθον καὶ ἐλάλησα αὐτοῖς, ἁμαρτίαν οὐκ
come and spoken to them, they would not be guilty of sin; *not*
2262 2779 3281 899 2400 2400 4024 2400 2400 2400 281 4024
v.aai.1s cj v.aai.1s r.dpm.3 n.asf pl

εἴχοσαν· νῦν δὲ πρόφασιν οὐκ ἔχουσιν περὶ τῆς
they would be guilty of but now *but* they have no excuse *no* *they have* for *{the}* their
2400 1254 3814 1254 2400 2400 4024 4733 4024 2400 4309 3836 899
v.iai.3p adv cj n.asf pl v.pai.3p p.g d.gsf

ἁμαρτίας αὐτῶν. 23 ὁ ἐμὲ μισῶν καὶ τὸν
sin. *their* The one who hates me *one who hates* hates my Father also. *{the}*
281 899 3836 3631 3631 3631 1609 3631 3631 1609 4252 2779 3836
n.gsf r.gpm.3 d.nsm r.as.1 pt.pa.nsm adv d.asm

NASB

you would go and
bear fruit, and *that*
your fruit would
remain, so that
whatever you ask
of the Father in
My name He may
give to you. 17 This
I command you,
that you love one
another.

Disciples' Relation to the World

18 "If the world
hates you, you
know that it has
hated Me before *it*
hated you. 19 If you
were of the world,
the world would
love its own; but
because you are
not of the world,
but I chose you
out of the world,
because of this the
world hates you.
20 Remember the
word that I said
to you, 'A slave is
not greater than his
master.' If they per-
secuted Me, they
will also persecute
you; if they kept
My word, they
will keep yours
also. 21 But all these
things they will
do to you for My
name's sake, be-
cause they do not
know the One who
sent Me. 22 If I had
not come and spo-
ken to them, they
would not have
sin, but now they
have no excuse for
their sin. 23 He who
hates Me hates My
Father also.

a 20 John 13:16

NIV

[24] If I had not done
among them the
works no one else
did, they would not
be guilty of sin.
As it is, they have
seen, and yet they
have hated both
me and my Father.
[25] But this is to ful-
fill what is written
in their Law: 'They
hated me without
reason.'[a]

The Work of the Holy Spirit

[26] "When the
Advocate comes,
whom I will send
to you from the Fa-
ther—the Spirit of
truth who goes out
from the Father—
he will testify
about me. [27] And
you also must tes-
tify, for you have
been with me from
the beginning.

16 "All this I
have told
you so that you
will not fall away.
[2] They will put you
out of the syna-
gogue; in fact, the
time is coming
when anyone who
kills you will think
they are offering
a service to God.
[3] They will do such
things because
they have not
known the Father
or me. [4] I have told
you this, so that
when their time
comes you will
remember that I
warned you about
them. I did not tell
you this from the
beginning

[a] *25* Psalms 35:19; 69:4

πατέρα μου μισεῖ. [24] εἰ τὰ ἔργα μὴ ἐποίησα ἐν
Father *my* *hates* If I had not done among them the works *not* *I had done* *among*
4252 1609 3631 1623 4472 4472 3590 4472 1877 899 3836 2240 3590 4472 1877
n.asm r.gs.1 v.pai.3s cj d.apn n.apn pl v.aai.1s p.d

αὐτοῖς ἃ οὐδεὶς ἄλλος ἐποίησεν, ἁμαρτίαν οὐκ
them that no one else had done, they would not be guilty of sin; *not*
899 4005 4029 257 4472 2400 2400 4024 2400 2400 2400 281 4024
r.dpm.3 r.apn a.nsm r.nsm v.aai.3s n.asf pl

εἴχοσαν· νῦν δὲ καὶ ἑωράκασιν καὶ μεμισήκασιν καὶ ἐμὲ
they would be guilty of but now *but* *{and}* they have seen the works and have hated both me
2400 1254 3814 1254 2779 3972 2779 3631 2779 1609
v.iai.3p adv cj cj v.rai.3p cj v.rai.3p cj r.as.1

καὶ τὸν πατέρα μου. [25] ἀλλ' ἵνα
and *{the}* my Father. *my* However, *{that}* the word that is written in their law
2779 3836 1609 4252 1609 247 2671 3836 3364 3836 1211 1211 1877 899 3795
cj d.asm n.asm r.gs.1 cj cj

πληρωθῇ ὁ λόγος ὁ ἐν τῷ νόμῳ αὐτῶν γεγραμμένος ὅτι ἐμίσησάν με
had to be fulfilled: *the* *word* *that* *in* *{the}* *law* *their* *is written* ~ 'They hated me
4444 3836 3364 3836 1877 3836 3795 899 1211 4022 3631 1609
v.aps.3s d.nsm n.nsm d.nsm p.d d.dsm n.dsm r.gpm.3 pt.rp.nsm cj v.aai.3p r.as.1

δωρεάν. [26] ὅταν ἔλθῃ ὁ παράκλητος ὃν ἐγὼ πέμψω
⌊without a cause.'⌋ "But when the Paraclete comes, *the* *Paraclete* whom I will send
1562 4020 3836 4156 2262 3836 4156 4005 1609 4287
adv cj v.aas.3s d.nsm n.nsm r.asm r.ns.1 v.fai.1s

ὑμῖν παρὰ τοῦ πατρός, τὸ πνεῦμα τῆς ἀληθείας ὃ παρὰ τοῦ πατρὸς
to you from the Father, the Spirit of truth who comes forth from the Father,
7007 4123 3836 4252 3836 4460 3836 237 4005 1744 1744 4123 3836 4252
r.dp.2 p.g d.gsm n.gsm d.nsn n.nsn d.gsf n.gsf r.nsn p.g d.gsm n.gsm

ἐκπορεύεται, ἐκεῖνος μαρτυρήσει περὶ ἐμοῦ· [27] καὶ ὑμεῖς δὲ
comes forth he will bear witness about me. And you also *you* *And*
1744 1697 3455 4309 1609 1254 7007 2779 7007 1254
v.pmi.3s r.nsm v.fai.3s p.g r.gs.1 adv r.np.2 cj

μαρτυρεῖτε, ὅτι ἀπ' ἀρχῆς μετ' ἐμοῦ ἐστε.
are to bear witness because you have been with me from the beginning. *with* *me* *you have been*
3455 4022 1639 1639 1639 3552 1609 608 794 3552 1609 1639
v.pai.2p cj p.g n.gsf p.g r.gs.1 v.pai.2p

[16:1] ταῦτα λελάληκα ὑμῖν ἵνα ↱ ↱ μὴ
"I have told you these things *I have told* *you* so that you will not
3281 3281 3281 7007 4047 3281 7007 2671 4997 4997 3590
r.apn v.rai.1s r.dp.2 cj pl

σκανδαλισθῆτε. [2] ἀποσυναγώγους ποιήσουσιν ὑμᾶς· ἀλλ'
fall away. They will put you out of the synagogues; *They will put* *you* indeed, the
4997 4472 4472 4472 7007 697 4472 7007 247
v.aps.2p a.apm v.fai.3p r.ap.2 cj

ἔρχεται ὥρα ἵνα πᾶς ὁ ἀποκτείνας ὑμᾶς δόξῃ
hour is coming *hour* when anyone who kills you will think he is offering a
6052 2262 6052 2671 4246 3836 650 7007 1506 4712 4712 4712
v.pmi.3s n.nsf cj a.nsm d.nsm pt.aa.nsm r.ap.2 v.aas.3s

λατρείαν προσφέρειν τῷ θεῷ. [3] καὶ ταῦτα ποιήσουσιν ὅτι ↱ ↱ οὐκ
service *he is offering* to God. And these things they will do because they have not
3301 4712 3836 2536 2779 4047 4472 4022 1182 1182 4024
n.asf f.pa d.dsm n.dsm cj r.apn v.fai.3p cj pl

ἔγνωσαν τὸν πατέρα οὐδὲ ἐμέ. [4] ἀλλὰ ταῦτα λελάληκα ὑμῖν ἵνα
known the Father nor me. But I have said these things *I have said* to you so that
1182 3836 4252 4028 1609 247 3281 3281 3281 4047 3281 7007 2671
v.aai.3p d.asm n.asm cj r.as.1 cj r.apn v.rai.1s r.dp.2 cj

ὅταν ἔλθῃ ἡ ὥρα αὐτῶν μνημονεύητε αὐτῶν
when their hour comes *{the}* *hour* *their* you will remember that I told you about them.
4020 899 6052 2262 3836 6052 899 3648 4022 1609 3306 7007 3306 899
cj v.aas.3s d.nsf n.nsf r.gpn.3 v.pas.2p r.gpn.3

ὅτι ἐγὼ εἶπον ὑμῖν. ταῦτα δὲ ὑμῖν ἐξ ἀρχῆς οὐκ
that *I* *told about* *you* "I did not tell you these things *{and}* *you* at the start *not*
4022 1609 3306 7007 3306 3306 4024 3306 7007 4047 1254 7007 1666 794 4024
cj r.ns.1 v.aai.1s r.dp.2 r.apn cj r.dp.2 p.g n.gsf pl

NASB

[24] If I had not done
among them the
works which no
one else did, they
would not have sin;
but now they have
both seen and hated
Me and My Father
as well. [25] But *they
have done this* to
fulfill the word that
is written in their
Law, 'THEY HATED
ME WITHOUT A
CAUSE.'
[26] "When the Help-
er comes, whom
I will send to you
from the Father,
that is the Spirit of
truth who proceeds
from the Father, He
will testify about
Me, [27] and you
will testify also,
because you have
been with Me from
the beginning.

Jesus' Warning

[16:1] "These things
I have spoken to
you so that you
may be kept from
stumbling. [2] They
will make you
outcasts from the
synagogue, but an
hour is coming for
everyone who kills
you to think that he
is offering service
to God. [3] These
things they will
do because they
have not known the
Father or Me. [4] But
these things I have
spoken to you, so
that when their
hour comes, you
may remember that
I told you of them.
These things I did
not say to you at
the beginning,

NIV

because I was with
you, 5but now I
am going to him
who sent me. None
of you asks me,
'Where are you go-
ing?' 6Rather, you
are filled with grief
because I have said
these things. 7But
very truly I tell
you, it is for your
good that I am
going away. Un-
less I go away, the
Advocate will not
come to you; but
if I go, I will send
him to you. 8When
he comes, he will
prove the world
to be in the wrong
about sin and righ-
teousness and judg-
ment: 9about sin,
because people do
not believe in me;
10about righteous-
ness, because I am
going to the Father,
where you can see
me no longer; 11and
about judgment,
because the prince
of this world now
stands condemned.
12"I have much
more to say to you,
more than you can
now bear. 13But
when he, the Spirit
of truth, comes,
he will guide you
into all the truth.
He will not speak
on his own; he will
speak only what he
hears, and he will
tell you what is yet
to come. 14He will

εἶπον, ὅτι μεθ᾽ ὑμῶν ἤμην. 5 νῦν δὲ ὑπάγω πρὸς τὸν
I did tell because I was with you. *I was* But now *But* ⌊I am going away⌋ to the
3306 4022 1639 1639 3552 7007 1639 1254 3814 1254 5632 4639 3836
v.aai.1s cj p.g r.gp.2 v.imi.1s adv cj v.pai.1s p.a d.asm

πέμψαντά με, καὶ οὐδεὶς ἐξ ὑμῶν ἐρωτᾷ με, ποῦ ὑπάγεις; 6ἀλλ᾽ ὅτι
one who sent me, and none of you asks me, 'Where are you going?' But because
4287 1609 2779 4029 1666 7007 2263 1609 4543 5632 247 4022
pt.aa.asm r.as.1 cj a.nsm p.g r.gp.2 v.pai.3s r.as.1 cj v.pai.2s cj cj

ταῦτα λελάληκα ὑμῖν ἡ λύπη πεπλήρωκεν ὑμῶν τὴν
I have told you these things, *I have told* *you* *{the}* sorrow has filled your *{the}*
3281 3281 3281 7007 4047 3281 7007 3836 3383 4444 7007 3836
r.apn v.rai.1s r.dp.2 d.nsf n.nsf v.rai.3s r.gp.2 d.asf

καρδίαν. 7ἀλλ᾽ ἐγὼ τὴν ἀλήθειαν λέγω ὑμῖν, → → →
heart. Nevertheless I am telling you the truth; *am telling* *you* it is to your
2840 247 1609 3306 3306 7007 3836 237 3306 7007 7007
n.asf cj r.ns.1 d.asf n.asf v.pai.1s r.dp.2

συμφέρει ὑμῖν ἵνα ἐγὼ ἀπέλθω. ἐὰν γὰρ ↱ ↱ μὴ ἀπέλθω, ὁ
advantage *your* that I ⌊am going away.⌋ For if *For* I do not go away, the
5237 7007 2671 1609 599 1142 1569 1142 599 599 3590 599 3836
v.pai.3s r.dp.2 cj r.ns.1 v.aas.1s cj cj pl v.aas.1s d.nsm

παράκλητος ↱ οὐκ ἐλεύσεται πρὸς ὑμᾶς· ἐὰν δὲ πορευθῶ, πέμψω αὐτὸν
Paraclete will not come to you; but if *but* I go away, I will send him
4156 2262 4024 2262 4639 7007 1254 1569 1254 4513 4287 899
n.nsm pl v.fmi.3s p.a r.ap.2 cj cj v.aps.1s v.fai.1s r.asm.3

πρὸς ὑμᾶς. 8καὶ ἐλθὼν ἐκεῖνος ἐλέγξει τὸν κόσμον περὶ
to you. And he, ⌊when he comes,⌋ *he* will convict the world ⌊in regard to⌋
4639 7007 2779 1697 2262 1697 1794 3836 3180 4309
p.a r.ap.2 cj pt.aa.nsm r.nsm v.fai.3s d.asm n.asm p.g

ἁμαρτίας καὶ περὶ δικαιοσύνης καὶ περὶ κρίσεως· 9περὶ
sin and *{in regard to}* righteousness and *{in regard to}* judgment: ⌊in regard to⌋
281 2779 4309 1466 2779 4309 3213 4309
n.gsf cj p.g n.gsf cj p.g n.gsf p.g

ἁμαρτίας μέν, ὅτι ↱ ↱ οὐ πιστεύουσιν εἰς ἐμέ· 10περὶ δικαιοσύνης
sin, ~ because they do not believe in me; ⌊in regard to⌋ righteousness,
281 3525 4022 4409 4409 4024 4409 1650 1609 4309 1466
n.gsf pl cj pl v.pai.3p p.a r.as.1 p.g n.gsf

δέ, ὅτι πρὸς τὸν πατέρα ὑπάγω καὶ
{and} because I am going away to the Father, *I am going away* and you will see me
1254 4022 5632 5632 5632 5632 4639 3836 4252 5632 2779 2555 2555 2555 1609
cj cj p.a d.asm n.asm v.pai.1s cj

οὐκέτι θεωρεῖτέ με· 11περὶ δὲ κρίσεως, ὅτι ὁ ἄρχων τοῦ
no longer; *you will see* *me* ⌊in regard to⌋ *{and}* judgment, because the ruler of this
4033 2555 1609 4309 1254 3213 4022 3836 807 3836 4047
adv v.pai.2p r.as.1 p.g cj n.gsf cj d.nsm n.nsm d.gsm

κόσμου τούτου κέκριται. 12 ἔτι πολλὰ ἔχω
world *this* has been condemned. "I have many more *many* *I have* things to say
3180 4047 3212 2400 2400 4498 2285 4498 2400 3306 3306
n.gsm r.gsm v.rpi.3s adv a.apn v.pai.1s

ὑμῖν λέγειν, ἀλλ᾽ ⌊οὐ δύνασθε⌋ βαστάζειν ἄρτι· 13 ὅταν δὲ
to you, *to say* but you cannot bear them now. But when *But* he, the
7007 3306 247 4024 1538 1002 785 1254 4020 1254 1697 3836
r.dp.2 f.pa cj pl v.ppi.2p f.pa adv cj cj

ἔλθῃ ἐκεῖνος, τὸ πνεῦμα τῆς ἀληθείας, ὁδηγήσει ὑμᾶς ἐν τῇ
Spirit of truth, comes, *he* *the* *Spirit* *of* *truth* he will guide you into *{the}* all
4460 3836 237 2262 1697 3836 4460 3836 237 3842 7007 1877 3836 4246
v.aas.3s r.nsm d.nsn n.nsn d.gsf n.gsf v.fai.3s r.ap.2 p.d d.dsf

ἀληθείᾳ πάσῃ· ↱ ↱ οὐ γὰρ λαλήσει ἀφ᾽ ἑαυτοῦ, ἀλλ᾽ ὅσα
truth, *all* for he will not *for* speak on his own, but will speak ⌊only what⌋
237 4246 1142 3281 3281 4024 1142 3281 608 1571 247 3281 3281 4012
n.dsf a.dsf pl cj v.fai.3s p.g r.gsm.3 cj r.apn

ἀκούσει λαλήσει καὶ τὰ ἐρχόμενα ἀναγγελεῖ ὑμῖν. 14ἐκεῖνος
he hears, *will speak* and he will tell you things yet to come. *he will tell* *you* He will
201 3281 2779 334 334 334 7007 3836 2262 334 7007 1697 1519
v.fai.3s v.fai.3s cj d.apn pt.pm.apn v.fai.3s r.dp.2 r.nsm

NASB

because I was with
you.

The Holy Spirit Promised

5"But now I am
going to Him who
sent Me; and none
of you asks Me,
'Where are You go-
ing?' 6But because
I have said these
things to you, sor-
row has filled your
heart. 7But I tell
you the truth, it is
to your advantage
that I go away; for
if I do not go away,
the Helper will
not come to you;
but if I go, I will
send Him to you.
8And He, when He
comes, will convict
the world concern-
ing sin and righ-
teousness and judg-
ment; 9concerning
sin, because they
do not believe in
Me; 10and concern-
ing righteousness,
because I go to
the Father and you
no longer see Me;
11and concerning
judgment, because
the ruler of this
world has been
judged.
12"I have many
more things to say
to you, but you
cannot bear *them*
now. 13But when
He, the Spirit of
truth, comes, He
will guide you into
all the truth; for
He will not speak
on His own initia-
tive, but whatever
He hears, He will
speak; and He will
disclose to you
what is to come.
14He will glorify

NIV

glorify me because
it is from me that
he will receive
what he will make
known to you.
[15]All that belongs
to the Father is
mine. That is why I
said the Spirit will
receive from me
what he will make
known to you."

The Disciples' Grief Will Turn to Joy

[16]Jesus went on
to say, "In a little
while you will see
me no more, and
then after a little
while you will
see me."
[17]At this, some
of his disciples
said to one anoth-
er, "What does he
mean by saying,
'In a little while
you will see me
no more, and then
after a little while
you will see me,'
and 'Because I am
going to the Fa-
ther'?" [18]They kept
asking, "What
does he mean by
'a little while'? We
don't understand
what he is saying."
[19]Jesus saw that
they wanted to ask
him about this, so
he said to them,
"Are you asking
one another what I
meant when I said,
'In a little while
you will see me
no more, and then
after a little while
you will see me'?
[20]Very truly I tell
you, you will weep
and mourn while
the world rejoices.
You will grieve,
but your grief will
turn to joy. [21]A
woman

ἐμὲ δοξάσει, ὅτι ⌞ἐκ τοῦ ἐμοῦ⌟ λήμψεται καὶ
glorify me, *will glorify* for he will receive what is mine *he will receive* and
1519 1609 1519 4022 3284 3284 3284 1666 3836 1847 3284 2779
r.as.1 v.fai.3s cj p.g d.gsn r.gsn.1 v.fmi.3s cj

ἀναγγελεῖ ὑμῖν. [15] πάντα ὅσα ἔχει ὁ πατὴρ ἐμά ἐστιν· ⌞διὰ
tell it to you. All that the Father has *the Father* is mine; *is* that is why
334 7007 4246 4012 3836 4252 2400 3836 4252 1639 1847 1639 1328
v.fai.3s r.dp.2 a.npn r.apn v.pai.3s d.nsm n.nsm r.npn.1 v.pai.3s p.a

τοῦτο⌟ εἶπον ὅτι ⌞ἐκ τοῦ ἐμοῦ⌟ λαμβάνει καὶ ἀναγγελεῖ ὑμῖν.
I said that he will take what is mine *he will take* and declare it to you.
4047 3306 4022 3284 3284 3284 1666 3836 1847 3284 2779 334 7007
r.asn v.aai.1s cj p.g d.gsn r.gsn.1 v.pai.3s cj v.fai.3s r.dp.2

[16] μικρὸν καὶ ➝ ➝ οὐκέτι θεωρεῖτέ με, καὶ πάλιν μικρὸν καὶ
"A little while and you will no longer see me, and again a little while and
3625 2779 2555 2555 4033 2555 1609 2779 4099 3625 2779
a.asn cj adv v.pai.2p r.as.1 cj adv a.asn cj

ὄψεσθέ με.[a] [17] εἶπαν οὖν ἐκ τῶν μαθητῶν
⌞you will see⌟ me." Some of his disciples therefore said *therefore Some of disciples*
3972 1609 1666 3836 899 3412 4036 3306 4036 1666 3836 3412
v.fmi.2p r.as.1 v.aai.3p cj p.g d.gpm n.gpm

αὐτοῦ πρὸς ἀλλήλους· τί ἐστιν τοῦτο ὃ λέγει ἡμῖν, μικρὸν καὶ ➝
his to one another, "What is this that ⌞he is saying⌟ to us, 'A little while and you
899 4639 253 5515 1639 4047 4005 3306 7005 3625 2779 2555
r.gsm.3 p.a r.apm r.nsn v.pai.3s r.nsn r.asn v.pai.3s r.dp.1 a.asn cj

➝ οὐ θεωρεῖτέ με, καὶ πάλιν μικρὸν καὶ ὄψεσθέ με; καί· ὅτι
will not see me, and again a little while and ⌞you will see⌟ me' and, 'Because
2555 4024 2555 1609 2779 4099 3625 2779 3972 1609 2779 4022
pl v.pai.2p r.as.1 cj adv a.asn cj v.fmi.2p r.as.1 cj cj

ὑπάγω πρὸς τὸν πατέρα; [18] ἔλεγον οὖν, τί ἐστιν τοῦτο
I am going to the Father'?" So ⌞they kept saying,⌟ *So* "What is this 'little while'
5632 4639 3836 4252 4036 3306 4036 5515 1639 4047 3625 3625
v.pai.1s p.a d.asm n.asm v.iai.3p cj r.nsn v.pai.3s r.nsn

[b]ὃ λέγει τὸ μικρόν; ➝ ➝ οὐκ οἴδαμεν τί λαλεῖ.
⌞of which⌟ he speaks? *{the} little while* We do not understand what ⌞he is talking about."⌟
4005 3306 3836 3625 3857 3857 4024 3857 5515 3281
r.asn v.pai.3s d.nsn a.asn pl v.rai.1p r.nsn v.pai.3s

[19] ἔγνω ὁ[c] Ἰησοῦς ὅτι ἤθελον αὐτὸν ἐρωτᾶν, καὶ εἶπεν
Jesus knew *{the} Jesus* that they wanted to question him, *to question* so he said
2652 1182 3836 2652 4022 2527 2263 2263 899 2263 2779 3306
v.aai.3s d.nsm n.nsm cj v.iai.3p r.asm.3 f.pa cj v.aai.3s

αὐτοῖς, περὶ τούτου ζητεῖτε μετ' ἀλλήλων
to them, "Are you deliberating with one another about this *Are you deliberating with one another*
899 2426 2426 2426 3552 253 253 4309 4047 2426 3552 253
r.dpm.3 p.g r.gsn v.pai.2p p.g r.gpm

ὅτι εἶπον, μικρὸν καὶ ➝ ➝ οὐ θεωρεῖτέ με, καὶ πάλιν μικρὸν καὶ
— that I said, 'A little while and you will not see me, and again a little while and
4022 3306 3625 2779 2555 2555 4024 2555 1609 2779 4099 3625 2779
cj v.aai.1s a.asn cj pl v.pai.2p r.as.1 cj adv a.asn cj

ὄψεσθέ με; [20] ⌞ἀμὴν ἀμὴν⌟ λέγω ὑμῖν ὅτι κλαύσετε
⌞you will see⌟ me'? I tell you the solemn truth, *I tell you* ~ you will weep
3972 1609 3306 3306 7007 297 297 3306 7007 4022 7007 3081
v.fmi.2p r.as.1 pl pl v.pai.1s r.dp.2 cj v.fai.2p

καὶ θρηνήσετε ὑμεῖς, ὁ δὲ κόσμος χαρήσεται· ὑμεῖς λυπηθήσεσθε, ἀλλ' ἡ
and wail, *you* and the *and* world will rejoice; you will be sorrowful, but *{the}*
2779 2577 7007 1254 3836 1254 3180 5897 7007 3382 247 3836
cj v.fai.2p r.np.2 d.nsm cj n.nsm v.fpi.3s r.np.2 v.fpi.2p cj d.nsf

λύπη ὑμῶν εἰς χαρὰν γενήσεται. [21] ἡ γυνὴ ὅταν
your sorrow *your* will be turned into joy. *will be* When a woman *When*
7007 3383 7007 1181 1181 1650 5915 1181 4020 3836 1222 4020
n.nsf r.gp.2 p.a n.asf v.fmi.3s d.nsf n.nsf cj

NASB

Me, for He will
take of Mine and
will disclose *it* to
you. [15]All things
that the Father has
are Mine; therefore
I said that He takes
of Mine and will
disclose *it* to you.

Jesus' Death and Resurrection Foretold

[16]"A little while,
and you will no
longer see Me; and
again a little while,
and you will see
Me." [17]*Some* of
His disciples then
said to one another,
"What is this thing
He is telling us,
'A little while, and
you will not see
Me; and again a lit-
tle while, and you
will see Me'; and,
'because I go to
the Father'?" [18]So
they were saying,
"What is this that
He says, 'A little
while'? We do not
know what He is
talking about." [19]Je-
sus knew that they
wished to ques-
tion Him, and He
said to them, "Are
you deliberating
together about this,
that I said, 'A little
while, and you
will not see Me,
and again a little
while, and you will
see Me'? [20]Truly,
truly, I say to you,
that you will weep
and lament, but the
world will rejoice;
you will grieve,
but your grief will
be turned into
joy. [21]Whenever a
woman is in labor

[a] ὅτι ἐγὼ ὑπάγω πρὸς τὸν πατέρα included by TR after με.
[b] [ὃ λέγει] UBS.
[c] [ὁ] UBS, omitted by TNIV.

NIV

giving birth to a
child has pain be-
cause her time has
come; but when
her baby is born
she forgets the
anguish because
of her joy that a
child is born into
the world. 22 So
with you: Now is
your time of grief,
but I will see you
again and you will
rejoice, and no
one will take away
your joy. 23 In that
day you will no
longer ask me any-
thing. Very truly I
tell you, my Father
will give you what-
ever you ask in my
name. 24 Until now
you have not asked
for anything in my
name. Ask and you
will receive, and
your joy will be
complete.
25 "Though I have
been speaking fig-
uratively, a time
is coming when I
will no longer use
this kind of lan-
guage but will tell
you plainly about
my Father. 26 In
that day you will
ask in my name.
I am not saying
that I will ask the
Father on your be-
half. 27 No, the Fa-
ther himself loves
you because you
have loved me and
have believed that
I came from God.

τίκτη λύπην ἔχει, ὅτι ἦλθεν ἡ ὥρα αὐτῆς· ὅταν
⌞is giving birth,⌟ she has sorrow *she has* because her hour has come; *{the}* *hour* *her* but when
5503 2400 2400 3383 2400 4022 899 6052 2262 3836 6052 899 1254 4020
v.pas.3s n.asf v.pai.3s cj v.aai.3s d.nsf n.nsf r.gsf.3 cj

δὲ γεννήσῃ τὸ παιδίον, ↱ οὐκέτι μνημονεύει τῆς θλίψεως διὰ
but the baby is born, *the* *baby* she no longer remembers the anguish, ⌞because of⌟
1254 3836 4086 1164 3836 4086 3648 4033 3648 3836 2568 1328
cj v.aas.3s d.asn n.asn adv v.pai.3s d.gsf n.gsf p.a

τὴν χαρὰν ὅτι ἐγεννήθη ἄνθρωπος εἰς τὸν κόσμον. 22 καὶ
the joy that a child has been born *child* into the world. *{and}* So for now
3836 5915 4022 476 1164 476 1650 3836 3180 2779 4036 3814
d.asf n.asf cj v.api.3s n.nsm p.a d.asm n.asm cj

ὑμεῖς οὖν νῦν μὲν λύπην ἔχετε· πάλιν δὲ ὄψομαι ὑμᾶς,
you *So* *now* ~ have sorrow; *have* but I will see you again, *but* *I will see* *you*
7007 4036 3814 3525 2400 3383 2400 1254 3972 3972 3972 7007 4099 1254 3972 7007
r.np.2 cj adv pl n.asf v.pai.2p adv cj v.fmi.1s r.ap.2

καὶ χαρήσεται ὑμῶν ἡ καρδία, καὶ τὴν χαρὰν ὑμῶν
and your heart will rejoice, *your* *{the}* *heart* and no one will take *{the}* your joy *your*
2779 7007 2840 5897 7007 3836 2840 2779 4029 4029 149 149 3836 7007 5915 7007
cj v.fpi.3s r.gp.2 d.nsf n.nsf cj d.asf n.asf r.gp.2

οὐδεὶς αἴρει ἀφ᾽ ὑμῶν. 23 καὶ ἐν ἐκείνῃ τῇ ἡμέρᾳ ἐμὲ οὐκ
no one *will take* from you. *{and}* On that *{the}* day you will question me *{not}*
4029 149 608 7007 2779 1877 1697 3836 2465 2263 2263 2263 1609 4024
a.nsm v.pai.3s p.g r.gp.2 cj p.d r.dsf d.dsf n.dsf r.as.1 pl

ἐρωτήσετε οὐδέν. ⌞ἀμὴν ἀμὴν⌟ λέγω ὑμῖν, ⌞ἄν
you will question about about nothing. I tell you the solemn truth: *I tell* *you* whatever
2263 2263 4029 3306 3306 7007 297 297 3306 7007 323
v.fai.2p a.asn pl pl v.pai.1s r.dp.2 cj

τι⌟ αἰτήσητε τὸν πατέρα ἐν τῷ ὀνόματί μου δώσει ὑμῖν. 24 ἕως ἄρτι
you ask of the Father in *{the}* my name *my* ⌞he will give⌟ to you. ⌞Up till⌟ now
5516 160 3836 4252 1877 3836 1609 3950 1609 1443 7007 2401 785
r.asn v.aas.2p d.asm n.asm p.d d.dsn n.dsn r.gs.1 v.fai.3s r.dp.2 p.g adv

οὐκ ᾐτήσατε οὐδὲν ἐν τῷ ὀνόματί μου· αἰτεῖτε καὶ λήμψεσθε,
{not} ⌞you have asked for⌟ nothing in *{the}* my name. *my* Ask, and you will receive,
4024 160 4029 1877 3836 1609 3950 1609 160 2779 3284
pl v.aai.2p a.asn p.d d.dsn n.dsn r.gs.1 v.pam.2p cj v.fmi.2p

ἵνα ἡ χαρὰ ὑμῶν ᾖ πεπληρωμένη. 25 ταῦτα ἐν
that *{the}* your joy *your* ⌞may be⌟ complete. "I have told you these things using
2671 3836 7007 5915 7007 1639 4444 3281 3281 3281 7007 4047 1877
cj d.nsf n.nsf r.gp.2 v.pas.3s pt.rp.nsf r.apn p.d

παροιμίαις λελάληκα ὑμῖν· ἔρχεται ὥρα ὅτε οὐκέτι
veiled language. *I have told* *you* The hour is coming *hour* when I will no longer speak to
4231 3281 7007 6052 2262 6052 4021 3281 3281 4033 3281 7007
n.dpf v.rai.1s r.dp.2 v.pmi.3s n.nsf cj adv

ἐν παροιμίαις λαλήσω ὑμῖν, ἀλλὰ παρρησίᾳ περὶ τοῦ πατρὸς
you in veiled language *I will speak* *to you* but will tell you plainly about the Father.
7007 1877 4231 3281 7007 247 550 550 7007 4244 4309 3836 4252
p.d n.dpf v.fai.1s r.dp.2 cj n.dsf p.g d.gsm n.gsm

ἀπαγγελῶ ὑμῖν. 26 ἐν ἐκείνῃ τῇ ἡμέρᾳ ἐν τῷ ὀνόματί μου
will tell *you* In that *{the}* day you will ask in *{the}* my name. *my*
550 7007 1877 1697 3836 2465 160 160 160 1877 3836 1609 3950 1609
v.fai.1s r.dp.2 p.d r.dsf d.dsf n.dsf p.d d.dsn n.dsn r.gs.1

αἰτήσεσθε, καὶ ↱ ↱ οὐ λέγω ὑμῖν ὅτι ἐγὼ ἐρωτήσω τὸν πατέρα →
you will ask *{and}* I am not saying to you that I ⌞will intercede with⌟ the Father on
160 2779 3306 3306 4024 3306 7007 4022 1609 2263 3836 4252
v.fmi.2p cj pl v.pai.1s r.dp.2 cj r.ns.1 v.fai.1s d.asm n.asm

περὶ ὑμῶν· 27 αὐτὸς γὰρ ὁ πατὴρ φιλεῖ ὑμᾶς, ὅτι ὑμεῖς
your behalf; *your* for the Father himself *for* *the* *Father* loves you, because you
7007 4309 7007 1142 3836 4252 899 1142 3836 4252 5797 7007 4022 7007
p.g r.gp.2 r.nsm cj d.nsm n.nsm v.pai.3s r.ap.2 cj r.np.2

ἐμὲ πεφιλήκατε καὶ πεπιστεύκατε ὅτι ἐγὼ παρὰ τοῦ [a] θεοῦ
have loved me *have loved* and have come to believe that I came forth from *{the}* God.
5797 5797 1609 5797 2779 4409 4022 1609 2002 2002 4123 3836 2536
r.as.1 v.rai.2p cj v.rai.2p cj r.ns.1 p.g d.gsm n.gsm

[a] [τοῦ] UBS.

NASB

she has pain, be-
cause her hour has
come; but when
she gives birth to
the child, she no
longer remem-
bers the anguish
because of the joy
that a child has
been born into the
world. 22 Therefore
you too have grief
now; but I will
see you again, and
your heart will
rejoice, and no one
will take your joy
away from you.

Prayer Promises

23 In that day you
will not question
Me about anything.
Truly, truly, I say
to you, if you ask
the Father for any-
thing in My name,
He will give it to
you. 24 Until now
you have asked
for nothing in My
name; ask and you
will receive, so that
your joy may be
made full.
25 "These things I
have spoken to you
in figurative lan-
guage; an hour is
coming when I will
no longer speak to
you in figurative
language, but will
tell you plainly of
the Father. 26 In that
day you will ask in
My name, and I do
not say to you that
I will request of
the Father on your
behalf; 27 for the Fa-
ther Himself loves
you, because you
have loved Me and
have believed that
I came forth from
the Father.

NIV

28 I came from the
Father and entered
the world; now
I am leaving the
world and going
back to the Father."
29 Then Jesus' dis-
ciples said, "Now
you are speaking
clearly and without
figures of speech.
30 Now we can see
that you know all
things and that you
do not even need
to have anyone
ask you questions.
This makes us
believe that you
came from God."
31 "Do you now
believe?" Jesus re-
plied. 32 "A time is
coming and in fact
has come when
you will be scat-
tered, each to your
own home. You
will leave me all
alone. Yet I am not
alone, for my Fa-
ther is with me.
33 "I have told
you these things,
so that in me you
may have peace.
In this world you
will have trouble.
But take heart! I
have overcome the
world."

Jesus Prays to Be Glorified

17 After Jesus
said this,
he looked toward
heaven and prayed:

"Father, the
hour has come.
Glorify your Son,
that your Son
may glorify you.
2 For you grant-
ed him authority
over all people
that he might give
eternal life to all

ἐξῆλθον. 28 ἐξῆλθον παρὰ τοῦ πατρὸς καὶ ἐλήλυθα εἰς τὸν κόσμον· πάλιν
came forth I came forth from the Father and have entered into the world; now
2002 2002 4123 3836 4252 2779 2262 1650 3836 3180 4099
v.aai.1s v.aai.1s p.g d.gsm n.gsm cj v.rai.1s p.a d.asm n.asm adv

ἀφίημι τὸν κόσμον καὶ πορεύομαι πρὸς τὸν πατέρα. 29 λέγουσιν
I am leaving the world and going back to the Father." His disciples said,
918 3836 3180 2779 4513 4639 3836 4252 899 3412 3306
v.pai.1s d.asm n.asm cj v.pmi.1s p.a d.asm n.asm v.pai.3p

οἱ μαθηταὶ αὐτοῦ, ἴδε νῦν ⌊ἐν παρρησίᾳ⌋ λαλεῖς καὶ
{the} disciples His "Ah, now you are speaking plainly *you are speaking* and
3836 3412 899 2623 3814 3281 3281 3281 1877 4244 3281 2779
d.npm n.npm r.gsm.3 pl adv p.d n.dsf v.pai.2s cj

παροιμίαν οὐδεμίαν λέγεις. 30 νῦν οἴδαμεν ὅτι οἶδας πάντα καὶ
not using veiled language! *not* *using* Now we know that you know all things and
4029 3306 4231 4029 3306 3814 3857 4022 3857 4246 2779
n.asf a.asf v.pai.2s adv v.rai.1p cj v.rai.2s a.apn cj

οὐ χρείαν ἔχεις ἵνα τίς σε ἐρωτᾷ· ⌊ἐν τούτῳ⌋
have no need *have* for anyone to question you. *to question* This is why
2400 4024 5970 2400 2671 5516 2263 2263 5148 2263 1877 4047
pl n.asf v.pai.2s cj r.nsm r.as.2 v.pas.3s p.d r.dsn

πιστεύομεν ὅτι ἀπὸ θεοῦ ἐξῆλθες. 31 ἀπεκρίθη
we believe that you have come forth from God." *you have come forth* Jesus answered
4409 4022 2002 2002 2002 2002 608 2536 2002 2652 646
v.pai.1p cj p.g n.gsm v.aai.2s v.api.3s

αὐτοῖς Ἰησοῦς, ↱ ↱ ἄρτι πιστεύετε; 32 ἰδοὺ ἔρχεται ὥρα καὶ
them, *Jesus* "Do you now believe? Behold, the hour is coming, *hour* indeed
899 2652 4409 4409 785 4409 2627 6052 2262 6052 2779
r.dpm.3 n.nsm adv v.pai.2p j v.pmi.3s n.nsf cj

ἐλήλυθεν ἵνα σκορπισθῆτε ἕκαστος εἰς τὰ ἴδια → κἀμὲ
it has come, when you will be scattered, each to *{the}* his own place, and you will leave me
2262 2671 5025 1667 1650 3836 2625 918 918 918 2743
v.rai.3s cj v.aps.2p r.nsm p.a d.apn a.apn crasis

μόνον ἀφῆτε· καὶ οὐκ εἰμὶ μόνος, ὅτι ὁ πατὴρ μετ᾽ ἐμοῦ
alone. *you will leave* And yet I am not *I am* alone, because the Father is with me.
3668 918 2779 1639 1639 4024 1639 3668 4022 3836 4252 1639 3552 1609
a.asm v.aas.2p cj pl v.pai.1s a.nsm cj d.nsm n.nsm p.g r.gs.1

ἐστιν. 33 ταῦτα λελάληκα ὑμῖν ἵνα ἐν ἐμοὶ
is I have told you these things *I have told* *you* so that in me you may have
1639 3281 3281 3281 7007 4047 3281 7007 2671 1877 1609 2400 2400 2400
v.pai.3s r.apn v.rai.1s r.dp.2 cj p.d r.ds.1

εἰρήνην ἔχητε. ἐν τῷ κόσμῳ θλῖψιν ἔχετε· ἀλλὰ
peace. *you may have* In the world you will have tribulation, *you will have* but
1645 2400 1877 3836 3180 2400 2400 2400 2568 2400 247
n.asf v.pas.2p p.d d.dsm n.dsm n.asf v.pai.2p cj

θαρσεῖτε, ἐγὼ νενίκηκα τὸν κόσμον.
take courage, I have conquered the world."
2510 1609 3771 3836 3180
v.pam.2p r.ns.1 v.rai.1s d.asm n.asm

17:1 ταῦτα ἐλάλησεν Ἰησοῦς καὶ ↱
When Jesus had finished saying these things, *had finished saying* *Jesus* *{and}* he
2652 3281 3281 3281 4047 3281 2652 2779 3306
r.apn v.aai.3s n.nsm cj

ἐπάρας τοὺς ὀφθαλμοὺς αὐτοῦ εἰς τὸν οὐρανὸν εἶπεν, πάτερ,
lifted up *{the}* his eyes *his* to *{the}* heaven and said, "Father, the hour
2048 3836 899 4057 899 1650 3836 4041 3306 4252 3836 6052
pt.aa.nsm d.apm n.apm r.gsm.3 p.a d.asm n.asm v.aai.3s n.vsm

ἐλήλυθεν ἡ ὥρα· δόξασόν σου τὸν υἱόν, ἵνα ὁ υἱὸς δοξάσῃ σέ, 2 καθὼς
has come; *the* *hour* glorify your *{the}* Son so that your Son may glorify you, since
2262 3836 6052 1519 5148 3836 5626 2671 3836 5626 1519 5148 2777
v.rai.3s d.nsf n.nsf v.aam.2s r.gs.2 d.asm n.asm cj d.nsm n.nsm v.aas.3s r.as.2 cj

ἔδωκας αὐτῷ ἐξουσίαν πάσης σαρκός, ἵνα ↱ πᾶν
⌊you have given⌋ him authority over all flesh, that he should give eternal life to all
1443 899 2026 4246 4922 2671 1443 1443 1443 173 2437 899 4246
v.aai.2s r.dsm.3 n.asf a.gsf n.gsf cj a.asn

NASB

28 I came forth from
the Father and
have come into the
world; I am leaving
the world again
and going to the
Father."
29 His disciples
*said, "Lo, now
You are speaking
plainly and are
not using a figure
of speech. 30 Now
we know that You
know all things,
and have no need
for anyone to ques-
tion You; by this
we believe that You
came from God."
31 Jesus answered
them, "Do you now
believe? 32 Behold,
an hour is coming,
and has *already*
come, for you to
be scattered, each
to his own *home*,
and to leave Me
alone; and *yet* I am
not alone, because
the Father is with
Me. 33 These things
I have spoken to
you, so that in
Me you may have
peace. In the world
you have tribula-
tion, but take cour-
age; I have over-
come the world."

The High Priestly Prayer

17:1 Jesus spoke
these things; and
lifting up His eyes
to heaven, He said,
"Father, the hour
has come; glorify
Your Son, that the
Son may glorify
You, 2 even as You
gave Him authority
over all flesh, that
to all whom You
have given Him,
He may give

NIV

those you have
given him. 3Now
this is eternal
life: that they
know you, the
only true God,
and Jesus Christ,
whom you have
sent. 4I have
brought you glory
on earth by fin-
ishing the work
you gave me to
do. 5And now, Fa-
ther, glorify me
in your presence
with the glory
I had with you
before the world
began.

Jesus Prays for His Disciples

6"I have re-
vealed you[a] to
those whom you
gave me out of
the world. They
were yours; you
gave them to me
and they have
obeyed your
word. 7Now they
know that every-
thing you have
given me comes
from you. 8For
I gave them the
words you gave
me and they ac-
cepted them.
They knew with
certainty that I
came from you,
and they believed
that you sent me.
9I pray for them.
I am not praying
for the world,
but for those
you have given
me, for they are
yours. 10All I
have is yours, and
all you have is
mine. And glory
has come to me
through them. 11I
will remain in the
world no longer,
but they are still
in the world, and
I am coming to
you.

[a] 6 Greek *your name*

ὃ δέδωκας αὐτῷ δώσῃ αὐτοῖς ζωὴν αἰώνιον. 3 αὕτη δέ ἐστιν
those ⌞you have given⌟ to him. *he should give* *{to them}* *life* *eternal* And this *And* is
4005 1443 899 1443 899 2437 173 1254 4047 1254 1639
r.asn v.rai.2s r.dsm.3 v.aas.3s r.dpm.3 n.asf a.asf r.nsf cj v.pai.3s

ἡ αἰώνιος ζωὴ ἵνα γινώσκωσιν σὲ τὸν μόνον ἀληθινὸν θεὸν καὶ ὃν
{the} eternal life, that they know you, the only true God, and Jesus Christ whom
3836 173 2437 2671 1182 5148 3836 3668 240 2536 2779 2652 5986 4005
d.nsf a.nsf n.nsf cj v.pas.3p r.as.2 d.asm a.nsm a.asm n.asm cj r.asm

ἀπέστειλας Ἰησοῦν Χριστόν. 4 ἐγώ σε ἐδόξασα ἐπὶ τῆς γῆς
you sent. *Jesus* *Christ* I glorified you *glorified* on *{the}* earth, having
690 2652 5986 1609 1519 5148 1519 2093 3836 1178 5457
v.aai.2s n.asm n.asm r.ns.1 r.as.2 v.aai.1s p.g d.gsf n.gsf

τὸ ἔργον τελειώσας ὃ δέδωκάς μοι ἵνα ποιήσω· 5 καὶ νῦν
completed the task *having completed* that you gave me to do; and now, Father,
5457 3836 2240 5457 4005 1443 1609 2671 4472 2779 3814 4252
d.asn n.asn pt.aa.nsm r.asn v.rai.2s r.ds.1 cj v.aas.1s cj adv

δόξασόν με σύ, πάτερ, παρὰ σεαυτῷ τῇ δόξῃ ᾗ εἶχον πρὸ τοῦ
glorify me *{you}* *Father* at your side ⌞with the⌟ glory that I had with you before *{the}*
1519 1609 5148 4252 4123 4932 3836 1518 4005 2400 4123 5148 4574 3836
v.aam.2s r.as.1 r.ns.2 n.vsm p.d r.dsm.2 d.dsf n.dsf r.dsf v.iai.1s p.g d.gsn

τὸν κόσμον εἶναι παρὰ σοί. 6 → → → ἐφανέρωσά σου τὸ ὄνομα τοῖς
the world began. *with* *you* "I have made your name known *your* *{the}* *name* to the
3836 3180 1639 4123 5148 5148 3950 5746 5148 3836 3950 3836
d.asm n.asm f.pa p.d r.ds.2 v.aai.1s r.gs.2 d.asn n.asn d.dpm

ἀνθρώποις οὓς ἔδωκάς μοι ἐκ τοῦ κόσμου. σοὶ ἦσαν →
men whom you gave me ⌞out of⌟ the world. They were yours, *They were* and you
476 4005 1443 1609 1666 3836 3180 1639 1639 5050 1639 1443
n.dpm r.apm v.aai.2s r.ds.1 p.g d.gsm n.gsm r.ds.2 v.iai.3p

κἀμοὶ αὐτοὺς ἔδωκας καὶ τὸν λόγον σου τετήρηκαν.
gave them to me, *them* *you gave* and they have kept *{the}* your word. *your* *they have kept*
1443 899 2743 899 1443 2779 5498 5498 5498 3836 5148 3364 5148 5498
crasis r.apm.3 v.aai.2s cj d.asm n.asm r.gs.2 v.rai.3p

7 νῦν ἔγνωκαν ὅτι πάντα ὅσα δέδωκάς μοι παρὰ σοῦ εἰσιν·
Now ⌞they have come to know⌟ that everything that ⌞you have given⌟ me is from you; *is*
3814 1182 4022 4246 4012 1443 1609 1639 4123 5148 1639
adv v.rai.3p cj a.npn r.apn v.rai.2s r.ds.1 p.g r.gs.2 v.pai.3p

8 ὅτι τὰ ῥήματα ἃ ἔδωκάς μοι δέδωκα αὐτοῖς, καὶ αὐτοὶ ἔλαβον
for the words that you gave to me I have given to them, and they have received them,
4022 3836 4839 4005 1443 1609 1443 899 2779 899 3284
cj d.apn n.apn r.apn v.aai.2s r.ds.1 v.rai.1s r.dpm.3 cj r.npm v.aai.3p

καὶ ἔγνωσαν ἀληθῶς ὅτι παρὰ σοῦ ἐξῆλθον, καὶ ἐπίστευσαν
and come to know in truth that I came forth from you, *I came forth* and they have believed
2779 1182 242 4022 2002 2002 2002 4123 5148 2002 2779 4409
cj v.aai.3p adv cj p.g r.gs.2 v.aai.1s cj v.aai.3p

ὅτι σύ με ἀπέστειλας. 9 ἐγὼ περὶ αὐτῶν ἐρωτῶ, οὐ
that you sent me. *sent* I am praying for them; *am praying* I am not
4022 5148 690 1609 690 1609 2263 2263 4309 899 2263 2263 2263 4024
cj r.ns.2 r.as.1 v.aai.2s r.ns.1 p.g r.gpm.3 v.pai.1s pl

περὶ τοῦ κόσμου ἐρωτῶ ἀλλὰ περὶ ὧν δέδωκάς μοι, ὅτι
praying for the world, *I am praying* but for ⌞those whom⌟ ⌞you have given⌟ to me, for
2263 4309 3836 3180 2263 247 4309 4005 1443 1609 4022
p.g d.gsm n.gsm v.pai.1s cj p.g r.gpm v.rai.2s r.ds.1 cj

σοί εἰσιν, 10 καὶ τὰ ἐμὰ πάντα σά ἐστιν καὶ τὰ σὰ
they are yours; *they are* and all *{the}* mine *all* are yours, *are* and *{the}* yours are
1639 1639 5148 1639 2779 4246 3836 1847 4246 1639 5050 1639 2779 3836 5050
r.ds.2 v.pai.3p cj d.npn r.npn.1 a.npn r.npn.2 v.pai.3s cj d.npn r.npn.2

ἐμά, καὶ δεδόξασμαι ἐν αὐτοῖς. 11 καὶ οὐκέτι εἰμὶ ἐν τῷ
mine, and I have been glorified in them. *{and}* I am no longer *I am* in the
1847 2779 1519 1877 899 2779 1639 1639 4033 1639 1877 3836
r.npn.1 cj v.rpi.1s p.d r.dpm.3 cj adv v.pai.1s p.d d.dsm

κόσμῳ, καὶ αὐτοὶ ἐν τῷ κόσμῳ εἰσίν, κἀγὼ πρὸς σὲ
world, but they are in the world, *are* and I am on my way to you.
3180 2779 899 1639 1877 3836 3180 1639 2743 2262 2262 2262 2262 4639 5148
n.dsm cj r.npm p.d d.dsm n.dsm v.pai.3p crasis p.a r.as.2

NASB

eternal life. 3This
is eternal life, that
they may know
You, the only
true God, and
Jesus Christ whom
You have sent. 4I
glorified You on
the earth, having
accomplished the
work which You
have given Me to
do. 5Now, Father,
glorify Me together
with Yourself, with
the glory which
I had with You
before the world
was.
6"I have manifest-
ed Your name to
the men whom You
gave Me out of the
world; they were
Yours and You
gave them to Me,
and they have kept
Your word. 7Now
they have come
to know that ev-
erything You have
given Me is from
You; 8for the words
which You gave
Me I have given
to them; and they
received *them* and
truly understood
that I came forth
from You, and they
believed that You
sent Me. 9I ask on
their behalf; I do
not ask on behalf
of the world, but of
those whom You
have given Me;
for they are Yours;
10and all things
that are Mine are
Yours, and Yours
are Mine; and I
have been glori-
fied in them. 11I am
no longer in the
world; and *yet* they
themselves are in
the world, and I
come to You. Holy

NIV

Holy Father,
protect them by
the power of[a]
your name, the
name you gave
me, so that they
may be one as we
are one. 12 While
I was with them,
I protected them
and kept them
safe by[b] that
name you gave
me. None has
been lost except
the one doomed
to destruction
so that Scripture
would be ful-
filled.
13 "I am coming
to you now, but I
say these things
while I am still in
the world, so that
they may have
the full measure
of my joy within
them. 14 I have
given them your
word and the
world has hated
them, for they are
not of the world
any more than I
am of the world.
15 My prayer is
not that you take
them out of the
world but that
you protect them
from the evil
one. 16 They are
not of the world,
even as I am not
of it. 17 Sancti-
fy them by[c] the
truth; your word
is truth. 18 As you
sent me into the
world, I have sent
them into the
world. 19 For them
I sanctify myself,
that they too may
be truly sancti-
fied.

Jesus Prays for All Believers

20 "My prayer
is not for them
alone. I pray also
for those who
will believe

[a] 11 Or *Father, keep them faithful to*
[b] 12 Or *kept them faithful to*
[c] 17 Or *them to live in accordance with*

ἔρχομαι. πάτερ ἅγιε, τήρησον αὐτοὺς ἐν τῷ ὀνόματί σου ᾧ
am on my way Holy Father, Holy keep them in {the} your name, your the name that
2262 41 4252 41 5498 899 1877 3836 5148 3950 5148 4005
v.pmi.1s n.vsm a.vsm v.aam.2s r.apm.3 p.d d.dsn n.dsn r.gs.2 r.dsn

δέδωκάς μοι, ἵνα ὦσιν ἓν καθὼς ἡμεῖς. 12 ὅτε ἤμην μετ᾽
⌞you have given⌟ me, so that ⌞they may be⌟ one, just as we are one. While I was with
1443 1609 2671 1639 1651 2777 7005 4021 1639 3552
v.rai.2s r.ds.1 cj v.pas.3p a.nsn cj r.np.1 cj v.imi.1s p.g

αὐτῶν ἐγὼ ἐτήρουν αὐτοὺς ἐν τῷ ὀνόματί σου ᾧ δέδωκάς μοι, καὶ
them, I protected them in {the} your name, your which ⌞you have given⌟ me. {and}
899 1609 5498 899 1877 3836 5148 3950 5148 4005 1443 1609 2779
r.gpm.3 r.ns.1 v.iai.1s r.apm.3 p.d d.dsn n.dsn r.gs.2 r.dsn v.rai.2s r.ds.1 cj

ἐφύλαξα, καὶ οὐδεὶς ἐξ αὐτῶν ἀπώλετο ⌞εἰ μή⌟ ὁ υἱὸς τῆς ἀπωλείας,
I guarded them, and not one of them has been lost except the son of destruction,
5875 2779 4029 1666 899 660 1623 3590 3836 5626 3836 724
v.aai.1s cj a.nsm p.g r.gpm.3 v.ami.3s cj pl d.nsm n.nsm d.gsf n.gsf

ἵνα ἡ γραφὴ πληρωθῇ. 13 νῦν δὲ πρὸς σὲ
that the scripture might be fulfilled. But now But I am on my way to you,
2671 3836 1210 4444 1254 3814 1254 2262 2262 2262 2262 2262 4639 5148
cj d.nsf n.nsf v.aps.3s adv cj p.a r.as.2

ἔρχομαι καὶ ταῦτα λαλῶ ἐν τῷ κόσμῳ ἵνα
I am on my way and I am saying these things I am saying while still in the world that
2262 2779 3281 3281 3281 4047 3281 1877 3836 3180 2671
v.pmi.1s cj r.apn v.pai.1s p.d d.dsm n.dsm cj

ἔχωσιν τὴν χαρὰν τὴν ἐμὴν πεπληρωμένην ἐν ἑαυτοῖς. 14 ἐγὼ δέδωκα
⌞they may have⌟ {the} my joy {the} my made complete in themselves. I have given
2400 3836 1847 5915 3836 1847 4444 1877 1571 1609 1443
v.pas.3p d.asf n.asf d.asf r.asf.1 pt.rp.asf p.d r.dpm.3 r.ns.1 v.rai.1s

αὐτοῖς τὸν λόγον σου καὶ ὁ κόσμος ἐμίσησεν αὐτούς, ὅτι ↱ ↱ οὐκ
them {the} your word, your and the world has hated them because they do not
899 3836 5148 3364 5148 2779 3836 3180 3631 899 4022 1639 1639 4024
r.dpm.3 d.asm n.asm r.gs.2 cj d.nsm n.nsm v.aai.3s r.apm.3 cj pl

εἰσὶν ἐκ τοῦ κόσμου καθὼς ἐγὼ ↱ οὐκ εἰμὶ ἐκ τοῦ κόσμου. 15 ↱ ↱ οὐκ
belong to the world, just as I do not belong to the world. I am not
1639 1666 3836 3180 2777 1609 1639 4024 1639 1666 3836 3180 2263 2263 4024
v.pai.3p p.g d.gsm n.gsm cj r.ns.1 pl v.pai.1s p.g d.gsm n.gsm pl

ἐρωτῶ ἵνα ἄρῃς αὐτοὺς ἐκ τοῦ κόσμου, ἀλλ᾽ ἵνα τηρήσῃς αὐτοὺς ἐκ τοῦ
asking that you take them ⌞out of⌟ the world, but that you protect them from the
2263 2671 149 899 1666 3836 3180 247 2671 5498 899 1666 3836
v.pai.1s cj v.aas.2s r.apm.3 p.g d.gsm n.gsm cj cj v.aas.2s r.apm.3 p.g d.gsm

πονηροῦ. 16 ἐκ τοῦ κόσμου οὐκ εἰσὶν καθὼς ἐγὼ ↱
evil one. They do not belong to the world, not They do belong just as I do
4505 1639 1639 4024 1639 1666 3836 3180 4024 1639 2777 1609 1639
a.gsm p.g d.gsm n.gsm pl v.pai.3p cj r.ns.1

οὐκ εἰμὶ ἐκ τοῦ κόσμου. 17 ἁγίασον αὐτοὺς ἐν τῇ ἀληθείᾳ· ὁ λόγος
not belong to the world. Consecrate them by the truth; {the} your word
4024 1639 1666 3836 3180 39 899 1877 3836 237 3836 5050 3364
pl v.pai.1s p.g d.gsm n.gsm v.aam.2s r.apm.3 p.d d.dsf n.dsf d.nsm n.nsm

ὁ σὸς ἀλήθειά ἐστιν. 18 καθὼς ἐμὲ ἀπέστειλας εἰς τὸν κόσμον,
{the} your is truth. is As you sent me you sent into the world,
3836 5050 1639 237 1639 2777 690 690 1609 690 1650 3836 3180
d.nsm r.nsm.2 n.nsf v.pai.3s cj r.as.1 v.aai.2s p.a d.asm n.asm

κἀγὼ ἀπέστειλα αὐτοὺς εἰς τὸν κόσμον· 19 καὶ ὑπὲρ αὐτῶν ↰ ἐγὼ ἁγιάζω
I also have sent them into the world. And for their sake I consecrate
2743 690 899 1650 3836 3180 2779 5642 899 5642 1609 39
crasis v.aai.1s r.apm.3 p.a d.asm n.asm cj p.g r.gpm.3 r.ns.1 v.pai.1s

ἐμαυτόν, ἵνα ὦσιν καὶ αὐτοὶ ἡγιασμένοι ἐν ἀληθείᾳ. 20 οὐ
myself, that they also may be also they consecrated by the truth. "It is not only
1831 2671 899 2779 1639 2779 899 39 1877 237 4024 3667
r.asm.1 cj v.pas.3p adv r.npm pt.rp.npm p.d n.dsf pl

περὶ τούτων δὲ ἐρωτῶ μόνον, ἀλλὰ καὶ περὶ τῶν πιστευόντων
for these {and} that I am interceding, only but also for those ⌞who will come to believe⌟
4309 4047 1254 2263 3667 247 2779 4309 3836 4409
p.g r.gpm cj v.pai.1s adv cj adv p.g d.gpm pt.pa.gpm

NASB

Father, keep them
in Your name, *the
name* which You
have given Me,
that they may be
one even as We
are. 12 While I was
with them, I was
keeping them in
Your name which
You have given
Me; and I guarded
them and not one
of them perished
but the son of per-
dition, so that the
Scripture would be
fulfilled.

The Disciples in the World

13 But now I come
to You; and these
things I speak in
the world so that
they may have
My joy made full
in themselves. 14 I
have given them
Your word; and the
world has hated
them, because
they are not of the
world, even as I am
not of the world.
15 I do not ask You
to take them out of
the world, but to
keep them from the
evil *one.* 16 They are
not of the world,
even as I am not of
the world. 17 Sanc-
tify them in the
truth; Your word
is truth. 18 As You
sent Me into the
world, I also have
sent them into the
world. 19 For their
sakes I sanctify
Myself, that they
themselves also
may be sanctified
in truth.
20 "I do not ask
on behalf of these
alone, but for those
also who believe in

NIV

in me through
their message,
21 that all of them
may be one, Fa-
ther, just as you
are in me and I
am in you. May
they also be in us
so that the world
may believe that
you have sent me.
22 I have given
them the glory
that you gave
me, that they
may be one as we
are one— 23 I in
them and you in
me—so that they
may be brought
to complete unity.
Then the world
will know that
you sent me and
have loved them
even as you have
loved me.
24 "Father, I want
those you have
given me to be
with me where I
am, and to see my
glory, the glory
you have given
me because you
loved me before
the creation of
the world.
25 "Righteous Fa-
ther, though the
world does not
know you, I know
you, and they
know that you
have sent me. 26 I
have made you[a]
known to them,
and will contin-
ue to make you
known in order
that the love you
have for me may
be in them and
that I myself may
be in them."

Jesus Arrested

18 When he
had finished
praying, Jesus left
with his disciples
and crossed the
Kidron Valley. On
the other side there
was a

[a] 26 Greek *your name*

διὰ τοῦ λόγου αὐτῶν εἰς ἐμέ, 21 ἵνα πάντες ἓν
in me through {the} their word, their in me that they may all be one,
1650 1609 1328 3836 899 3364 899 1650 1609 2671 1639 1639 4246 1639 1651
p.g d.gsm n.gsm r.gpm.3 p.a r.as.1 cj a.npm a.nsn

ὦσιν, καθὼς σύ, πάτερ, ἐν ἐμοὶ κἀγὼ ἐν σοί, ἵνα καὶ αὐτοὶ
they may be just as you, Father, are in me and I am in you, that they also they may
1639 2777 5148 4252 1877 1609 2743 1877 5148 2671 899 2779 899 1639
v.pas.3p cj r.ns.2 n.vsm p.d r.ds.1 crasis p.d r.ds.2 cj adv r.npm

ἐν ἡμῖν ὦσιν, ἵνα ὁ κόσμος πιστεύῃ ὅτι σύ με ἀπέστειλας.
be in us, may be so that the world may believe that you have sent me. have sent
1639 1877 7005 1639 2671 3836 3180 4409 4022 5148 690 690 1609 690
p.d r.dp.1 v.pas.3p cj d.nsm n.nsm v.pas.3s cj r.ns.2 r.as.1 v.aai.2s

22 κἀγὼ τὴν δόξαν ἣν δέδωκάς μοι ↰ δέδωκα αὐτοῖς, ἵνα ὦσιν
And the glory that ⌊you have given⌋ me I have given them, so that ⌊they may be⌋
2743 3836 1518 4005 1443 1609 2743 1443 899 2671 1639
crasis d.asf n.asf r.asf v.rai.2s r.ds.1 v.rai.1s r.dpm.3 cj v.pas.3p

ἓν καθὼς ἡμεῖς ἕν· 23 ἐγὼ ἐν αὐτοῖς καὶ σὺ ἐν ἐμοί, ἵνα ὦσιν
one just as we are one, I in them and you in me, that ⌊they may be⌋
1651 2777 7005 1651 1609 1877 899 2779 5148 1877 1609 2671 1639
a.nsn cj r.np.1 a.nsn r.ns.1 p.d r.dpm.3 cj r.ns.2 p.d r.ds.1 cj v.pas.3p

τετελειωμένοι εἰς ἕν, ἵνα γινώσκῃ ὁ κόσμος ὅτι σύ με
completely {into} one, so that the world may know the world that you sent me,
5457 1650 1651 2671 3836 3180 1182 3836 3180 4022 5148 690 1609
pt.rp.npm p.a a.asn cj v.pas.3s d.nsm n.nsm cj r.ns.2 r.as.1

ἀπέστειλας καὶ ἠγάπησας αὐτοὺς καθὼς ἐμὲ ἠγάπησας. 24 πάτερ,
sent and that you love them even as you love me. you love Father, I
690 2779 26 899 2777 26 26 1609 26 4252 2527
v.aai.2s cj v.aai.2s r.apm.3 cj r.as.1 v.aai.2s n.vsm

ὃ δέδωκάς μοι, θέλω ἵνα ὅπου
desire that those also, whom ⌊you have given⌋ me, I desire that may be with me where I
2527 2671 2797 2797 4005 1443 1609 2527 2671 1639 1639 3552 1609 3963 1609
r.asn v.rai.2s r.ds.1 v.pai.1s cj cj

εἰμὶ ἐγὼ κἀκεῖνοι ὦσιν μετ' ἐμοῦ, ἵνα θεωρῶσιν τὴν δόξαν τὴν ἐμήν, ἣν
am, I those also may be with me so they may see {the} my glory {the} my that
1639 1609 2797 1639 3552 1609 2671 2555 3836 1847 1518 3836 1847 4005
v.pai.1s r.ns.1 adv v.pas.3p p.g r.gs.1 cj v.pas.3p d.asf n.asf d.asf r.asf.1 r.asf

δέδωκάς μοι ὅτι ἠγάπησάς με πρὸ καταβολῆς → κόσμου.
⌊you have given⌋ me because you loved me before the creation of the world.
1443 1609 4022 26 1609 4574 2856 3180
v.rai.2s r.ds.1 cj v.aai.2s r.as.1 p.g n.gsf n.gsm

25 πάτερ δίκαιε, καὶ ὁ κόσμος σε οὐκ ἔγνω, ἐγὼ
Righteous Father, Righteous although the world does not know you, not does know I
1465 4252 1465 2779 3836 3180 1182 4024 1182 5148 4024 1182 1609
n.vsm a.vsm adv d.nsm n.nsm r.as.2 pl v.aai.3s r.ns.1

δέ σε ἔγνων, καὶ οὗτοι ἔγνωσαν ὅτι σύ με ἀπέστειλας· 26 καὶ
{and} know you, know and these men know that you sent me. sent {and}
1254 1182 5148 1182 2779 4047 1182 4022 5148 690 1609 690 2779
cj r.as.2 v.aai.1s cj r.npm v.aai.3p cj r.ns.2 r.as.1 v.aai.2s cj

ἐγνώρισα αὐτοῖς τὸ ὄνομά σου καὶ γνωρίσω, ἵνα
⌊I have made known⌋ to them {the} your name, your and ⌊I will continue to make it known,⌋ so that
1192 899 3836 5148 3950 5148 2779 1192 2671
v.aai.1s r.dpm.3 d.asn n.asn r.gs.2 cj v.fai.1s cj

ἡ ἀγάπη ἣν ἠγάπησάς με ἐν αὐτοῖς ᾖ κἀγὼ ἐν αὐτοῖς.
the love ⌊with which⌋ you have loved me may be in them, may be and I in them."
3836 27 4005 26 1609 1639 1639 1877 899 1639 2743 1877 899
d.nsf n.nsf r.asf v.aai.2s r.as.1 p.d r.dpm.3 v.pas.3s crasis p.d r.dpm.3

18:1 ταῦτα εἰπὼν Ἰησοῦς ἐξῆλθεν σὺν τοῖς
When Jesus had spoken these words, When had spoken Jesus he went out with {the} his
3306 2652 3306 3306 4047 3306 2652 2002 5250 3836 899
r.apn pt.aa.nsm n.nsm v.aai.3s p.d d.dpm

μαθηταῖς αὐτοῦ πέραν τοῦ χειμάρρου τοῦ Κεδρὼν ὅπου ἦν
disciples his across the Kidron valley, {the} Kidron where ⌊there was⌋ an olive
3412 899 4305 3836 3022 5929 3836 3022 3963 1639
n.dpm r.gsm.3 p.g d.gsm n.gsm d.gsm n.gsm cj v.iai.3s

NASB

Me through their
word; 21 that they
may all be one;
even as You, Fa-
ther, *are* in Me and
I in You, that they
also may be in Us,
so that the world
may believe that
You sent Me.

Their Future Glory

22 The glory which
You have given
Me I have given
to them, that they
may be one, just
as We are one; 23 I
in them and You
in Me, that they
may be perfected
in unity, so that the
world may know
that You sent Me,
and loved them,
even as You have
loved Me. 24 Father,
I desire that they
also, whom You
have given Me,
be with Me where
I am, so that they
may see My glory
which You have
given Me, for You
loved Me before
the foundation of
the world.
25 "O righteous
Father, although
the world has not
known You, yet I
have known You;
and these have
known that You
sent Me; 26 and I
have made Your
name known to
them, and will
make it known,
so that the love
with which You
loved Me may be
in them, and I in
them."

Judas Betrays Jesus

18:1 When Jesus
had spoken these
words, He went
forth with His dis-
ciples over the ra-
vine of the Kidron,
where there was a
garden, in which

NIV

garden, and he and
his disciples went
into it.
[2]Now Judas, who
betrayed him,
knew the place,
because Jesus had
often met there
with his disciples.
[3]So Judas came to
the garden, guid-
ing a detachment
of soldiers and
some officials
from the chief
priests and the
Pharisees. They
were carrying
torches, lanterns
and weapons.
[4]Jesus, knowing
all that was going
to happen to him,
went out and asked
them, "Who is it
you want?"
[5]"Jesus of Naza-
reth," they replied.
"I am he," Jesus
said. (And Judas
the traitor was
standing there
with them.) [6]When
Jesus said, "I am
he," they drew
back and fell to the
ground.
[7]Again he asked
them, "Who is it
you want?"
"Jesus of Naza-
reth," they said.
[8]Jesus answered,
"I told you that I
am he. If you are
looking for me,
then let these men
go." [9]This hap-
pened so that the
words he had spo-
ken would be ful-
filled: "I have not
lost one of those
you gave me."[a]
[10]Then Simon
Peter, who had a
sword, drew it and
struck the high
priest's servant,

κῆπος, εἰς ὃν εἰσῆλθεν αὐτὸς καὶ οἱ μαθηταὶ αὐτοῦ. 2
grove, into which he entered *he* with *{the}* his disciples. *his* Now Judas, who
3057 1650 4005 899 1656 899 2779 3836 899 3412 899 1254 2683 3836
n.nsm p.a r.asm v.aai.3s r.nsm cj d.npm n.npm r.gsm.3

ᾔδει δὲ καὶ Ἰούδας ὁ παραδιδοὺς αὐτὸν τὸν τόπον, ὅτι
betrayed him, also knew *Now also Judas who betrayed him* the place, because
4140 899 2779 3857 1254 2779 2683 3836 4140 899 3836 5536 4022
v.lai.3s cj adv n.nsm d.nsm pt.pa.nsm r.asm.3 d.asm n.asm cj

πολλάκις συνήχθη Ἰησοῦς ἐκεῖ μετὰ τῶν μαθητῶν αὐτοῦ. 3 ὁ οὖν Ἰούδας
Jesus often met *Jesus* there with *{the}* his disciples. *his* *{the}* So Judas,
2652 4490 5251 2652 1695 3552 3836 899 3412 899 3836 4036 2683
adv v.api.3s n.nsm adv p.g d.gpm n.gpm r.gsm.3 d.nsm cj n.nsm

λαβὼν τὴν σπεῖραν καὶ ἐκ τῶν ἀρχιερέων καὶ ἐκ
⌊having procured⌋ a ⌊detachment of soldiers⌋ and some officers from the chief priests and
3284 3836 5061 2779 5677 1666 3836 797 2779 1666
pt.aa.nsm d.asf n.asf cj p.g d.gpm n.gpm cj p.g

τῶν Φαρισαίων ὑπηρέτας ἔρχεται ἐκεῖ μετὰ φανῶν καὶ λαμπάδων καὶ ὅπλων.
{the} Pharisees, *officers* went there with lanterns and torches and weapons.
3836 5757 5677 2262 1695 3552 5749 2779 3286 2779 3960
d.gpm n.gpm n.apm v.pmi.3s adv p.g n.gpm cj n.gpf cj n.gpn

4 Ἰησοῦς οὖν εἰδὼς πάντα τὰ ἐρχόμενα ἐπ' αὐτὸν ἐξῆλθεν
Then Jesus, *Then* knowing everything that ⌊was going to happen⌋ to him, stepped forward
4036 2652 4036 3857 4246 3836 2262 2093 899 2002
n.nsm cj pt.ra.nsm a.apn d.apn pt.pm.apn p.a r.asm.3 v.aai.3s

καὶ λέγει αὐτοῖς, τίνα ζητεῖτε; 5 ἀπεκρίθησαν αὐτῷ, Ἰησοῦν τὸν
and said to them, "Who is it that ⌊you are looking for?"⌋ They answered him, "Jesus the
2779 3306 899 5515 2426 646 899 2652 3836
cj v.pai.3s r.dpm.3 r.asm v.pai.2p v.api.3p r.dsm.3 n.asm d.asm

Ναζωραῖον. λέγει αὐτοῖς, ἐγώ εἰμι. εἱστήκει δὲ
Nazarene." He said to them, "I am he." Now Judas, who betrayed him, was standing *Now*
3717 3306 899 1609 1639 1254 2683 3836 4140 899 2705 1254
n.asm v.pai.3s r.dpm.3 r.ns.1 v.pai.1s v.lai.3s cj

καὶ Ἰούδας ὁ παραδιδοὺς αὐτὸν μετ' αὐτῶν. 6 ὡς οὖν εἶπεν αὐτοῖς, ἐγώ
{also} Judas who betrayed him with them. When *{then}* Jesus said to them, "I
2779 2683 3836 4140 899 3552 899 6055 4036 3306 899 1609
adv n.nsm d.nsm pt.pa.nsm r.asm.3 p.g r.gpm.3 cj cj v.aai.3s r.dpm.3 r.ns.1

εἰμι, → ἀπῆλθον ⌊εἰς τὰ ὀπίσω⌋ καὶ ἔπεσαν χαμαί. 7
am he," they all drew back and fell to the ground. Then Jesus asked
1639 599 1650 3836 3958 2779 4406 5912 4036 2089
v.pai.1s v.aai.3p p.a d.apn adv cj v.aai.3p adv

πάλιν οὖν ἐπηρώτησεν αὐτούς, τίνα ζητεῖτε; οἱ δὲ
them again, *Then asked them* "Who is it that ⌊you are looking for?"⌋ And they *And*
899 4099 4036 2089 899 5515 2426 1254 3836 1254
adv cj v.aai.3s r.apm.3 r.asm v.pai.2p d.npm cj

εἶπαν, Ἰησοῦν τὸν Ναζωραῖον. 8 ἀπεκρίθη Ἰησοῦς, εἶπον ὑμῖν ὅτι ἐγώ εἰμι.
said, "Jesus the Nazarene." Jesus replied, *Jesus* "I told you that I am he.
3306 2652 3836 3717 2652 646 2652 3306 7007 4022 1609 1639
v.aai.3p n.asm d.asm n.asm v.api.3s n.nsm v.aai.1s r.dp.2 cj r.ns.1 v.pai.1s

εἰ οὖν ἐμὲ ζητεῖτε, ἄφετε τούτους ὑπάγειν· 9
So if *So* you are looking for me, *you are looking for* let these men go." This
4036 1623 4036 2426 2426 2426 2426 1609 2426 918 4047 5632
cj cj r.as.1 v.pai.2p v.aam.2p r.apm f.pa

ἵνα πληρωθῇ ὁ λόγος ὃν εἶπεν ὅτι
was to fulfill the word that ⌊he had spoken,⌋ ~ "I have not lost a single one of
2671 4444 3836 3364 4005 3306 4022 660 660 4024 660 4029 4029 1666
cj v.aps.3s d.nsm n.nsm r.asm v.aai.3s cj

οὓς δέδωκάς μοι οὐκ ἀπώλεσα ἐξ αὐτῶν οὐδένα. 10 Σίμων οὖν
those whom ⌊you have given⌋ me." *not I have lost of those single one* Then Simon *Then*
899 4005 1443 1609 4024 660 1666 899 4029 4036 4981 4036
r.apm v.rai.2s r.ds.1 pl v.aai.1s p.g r.gpm.3 a.asm n.nsm cj

Πέτρος ἔχων μάχαιραν εἵλκυσεν αὐτὴν καὶ ἔπαισεν τὸν τοῦ ἀρχιερέως
Peter, ⌊who had⌋ a sword, drew it and struck the servant of the high priest,
4377 2400 3479 1816 899 2779 4091 3836 1529 3836 797
n.nsm pt.pa.nsm n.asf v.aai.3s r.asf.3 cj v.aai.3s d.asm d.gsm n.gsm

NASB

He entered with
His disciples. [2]Now
Judas also, who
was betraying Him,
knew the place, for
Jesus had often met
there with His dis-
ciples. [3]Judas then,
having received
the *Roman* cohort
and officers from
the chief priests
and the Pharisees,
*came there with
lanterns and torch-
es and weapons.
[4]So Jesus, knowing
all the things that
were coming upon
Him, went forth
and *said to them,
"Whom do you
seek?" [5]They an-
swered Him, "Je-
sus the Nazarene."
He *said to them,
"I am *He.*" And
Judas also, who
was betraying Him,
was standing with
them. [6]So when
He said to them, "I
am *He,*" they drew
back and fell to the
ground. [7]Therefore
He again asked
them, "Whom do
you seek?" And
they said, "Jesus
the Nazarene."
[8]Jesus answered,
"I told you that I
am *He;* so if you
seek Me, let these
go their way," [9]to
fulfill the word
which He spoke,
"Of those whom
You have given
Me I lost not one."
[10]Simon Peter then,
having a sword,
drew it and struck
the high priest's

[a] 9 John 6:39

NIV

cutting off his right
ear. (The servant's
name was Mal-
chus.)
11 Jesus com-
manded Peter,
"Put your sword
away! Shall I not
drink the cup the
Father has giv-
en me?"
12 Then the de-
tachment of sol-
diers with its com-
mander and the
Jewish officials ar-
rested Jesus. They
bound him 13 and
brought him first
to Annas, who was
the father-in-law
of Caiaphas, the
high priest that
year. 14 Caiaphas
was the one who
had advised the
Jewish leaders that
it would be good if
one man died for
the people.

Peter's First Denial

15 Simon Peter and
another disciple
were following
Jesus. Because
this disciple was
known to the high
priest, he went
with Jesus into
the high priest's
courtyard, 16 but
Peter had to wait
outside at the door.
The other disciple,
who was known
to the high priest,
came back, spoke
to the servant girl
on duty there and
brought Peter in.
17 "You aren't one
of this

δοῦλον καὶ ἀπέκοψεν αὐτοῦ τὸ ὠτάριον τὸ δεξιόν· ἦν
servant {and} cutting off his {the} right ear. {the} right The servant's name was
1529 2779 644 899 3836 1288 6064 3836 1288 3836 1529 3950 1639
n.asm cj v.aai.3s r.gsm.3 d.asn n.asn d.asn a.asn v.iai.3s

δὲ ὄνομα τῷ δούλῳ Μάλχος. 11 εἶπεν οὖν ὁ Ἰησοῦς τῷ
{and} name The servant's Malchus. Jesus therefore said therefore {the} Jesus to
1254 3950 3836 1529 3438 2652 4036 3306 4036 3836 2652 3836
cj n.nsn d.dsm n.dsm n.nsm v.aai.3s cj d.nsm n.nsm d.dsm

Πέτρῳ, βάλε τὴν μάχαιραν εἰς τὴν θήκην· τὸ ποτήριον
Peter, "Put your sword back into its sheath. Am I not to drink the cup
4377 965 3836 3479 1650 3836 2557 4403 4403 4024 4403 4403 3836 4539
n.dsm v.aam.2s d.asf n.asf p.a d.asf n.asf d.asn n.asn

ὃ δέδωκέν μοι ὁ πατὴρ ⌞οὐ μὴ⌟ πίω αὐτό; 12 Ἡ οὖν
which the Father has given me?" the Father not Am I to drink {it} So the So
4005 3836 4252 1443 1609 3836 4252 4024 3590 4403 899 4036 3836 4036
r.asn v.rai.3s r.ds.1 d.nsm n.nsm pl pl v.aas.1s r.asn.3 d.nsf cj

σπεῖρα καὶ ὁ χιλίαρχος καὶ οἱ ὑπηρέται τῶν Ἰουδαίων
⌞detachment of soldiers,⌟ {and} their captain, and the officers of the Jews
5061 2779 3836 5941 2779 3836 5677 3836 2681
n.nsf cj d.nsm n.nsm cj d.npm n.npm d.gpm a.gpm

συνέλαβον τὸν Ἰησοῦν καὶ ἔδησαν αὐτὸν 13 καὶ ἤγαγον πρὸς Ἄνναν
arrested {the} Jesus and bound him. {and} They took him first to Annas,
5197 3836 2652 2779 1313 899 2779 72 4754 4639 484
v.aai.3p d.asm n.asm cj v.aai.3p r.asm.3 cj v.aai.3p p.a n.asm

πρῶτον· ἦν γὰρ πενθερὸς τοῦ Καϊάφα, ὃς ἦν ἀρχιερεὺς τοῦ
first for ⌞he was⌟ for the father-in-law of Caiaphas, who was high priest {the} that
4754 1142 1639 1142 4290 3836 2780 4005 1639 797 3836 1697
adv v.iai.3s cj n.nsm d.gsm n.gsm r.nsm v.iai.3s n.nsm d.gsm

ἐνιαυτοῦ ἐκείνου· 14 ἦν δὲ Καϊάφας ὁ συμβουλεύσας τοῖς
year. that Caiaphas was {and} Caiaphas the man who had advised the
1929 1697 2780 1639 1254 2780 3836 5205 3836
n.gsm r.gsm v.iai.3s cj n.nsm d.nsm pt.aa.nsm d.dpm

Ἰουδαίοις ὅτι συμφέρει ἕνα ἄνθρωπον ἀποθανεῖν ὑπὲρ τοῦ λαοῦ.
Jews that ⌞it was to their advantage⌟ that one man die for the people.
2681 4022 5237 1651 476 633 5642 3836 3295
a.dpm cj v.pai.3s a.asm n.asm f.aa p.g d.gsm n.gsm

15 ἠκολούθει δὲ τῷ Ἰησοῦ Σίμων Πέτρος καὶ ἄλλος μαθητής.
Simon Peter was following {and} {the} Jesus Simon Peter ⌞along with⌟ another disciple.
4981 4377 199 1254 3836 2652 4981 4377 2779 257 3412
v.iai.3s cj d.dsm n.dsm n.nsm n.nsm cj r.nsm n.nsm

ὁ δὲ μαθητὴς ἐκεῖνος ἦν γνωστὸς τῷ ἀρχιερεῖ καὶ συνεισῆλθεν τῷ
{the} Since that disciple that was known ⌞to the⌟ high priest, {and} he went with {the}
3836 1254 1697 3412 1697 1639 1196 3836 797 2779 5291 3836
d.nsm cj n.nsm r.nsm v.iai.3s a.nsm d.dsm n.dsm cj v.aai.3s d.dsm

Ἰησοῦ εἰς τὴν αὐλὴν τοῦ ἀρχιερέως, 16 ὁ δὲ Πέτρος εἱστήκει πρὸς τῇ
Jesus into the courtyard of the high priest, {the} but Peter remained outside at the
2652 1650 3836 885 3836 797 3836 1254 4377 2705 2032 4639 3836
n.dsm p.a d.asf n.asf d.gsm n.gsm d.nsm cj n.nsm v.lai.3s p.d d.dsf

θύρᾳ ἔξω. ἐξῆλθεν οὖν ὁ μαθητὴς ὁ ἄλλος ὁ → γνωστὸς τοῦ
door. outside went out So the other disciple, {the} other the one who was known to the
2598 2032 2002 4036 3836 257 3412 3836 257 3836 1196 3836
n.dsf adv v.aai.3s cj d.nsm n.nsm d.nsm r.nsm d.nsm a.nsm d.gsm

ἀρχιερέως καὶ εἶπεν τῇ θυρωρῷ καὶ εἰσήγαγεν
high priest, went out and spoke ⌞to the⌟ ⌞servant girl who kept watch at the door,⌟ and brought
797 2002 2002 2779 3306 3836 2601 2779 1652
n.gsm cj v.aai.3s d.dsf n.dsf cj v.aai.3s

← τὸν Πέτρον. 17 λέγει οὖν τῷ
Peter in. {the} Peter The servant girl who kept watch at the door said {then} to
4377 3836 4377 3836 4087 4087 3836 2601 2601 2601 2601 2601 3306 4036 3836
d.asm n.asm v.pai.3s cj d.dsm

Πέτρῳ ἡ παιδίσκη ἡ θυρωρός, μὴ καὶ σὺ ἐκ τῶν
Peter, The servant girl who kept watch at the door "You are not {also} You ⌞one of⌟ {the} that
4377 3836 4087 3836 2601 5148 1639 3590 2779 5148 1666 3836 4047
n.dsm d.nsf n.nsf d.nsf n.nsf pl adv r.ns.2 p.g d.gpm

NASB

slave, and cut off
his right ear; and
the slave's name
was Malchus. 11 So
Jesus said to Peter,
"Put the sword into
the sheath; the cup
which the Father
has given Me, shall
I not drink it?"

Jesus before the Priests

12 So the *Roman*
cohort and the
commander and
the officers of the
Jews, arrested
Jesus and bound
Him, 13 and led Him
to Annas first; for
he was father-in-
law of Caiaphas,
who was high
priest that year.
14 Now Caiaphas
was the one who
had advised the
Jews that it was
expedient for one
man to die on be-
half of the people.
15 Simon Peter was
following Jesus,
and *so was* an-
other disciple. Now
that disciple was
known to the high
priest, and entered
with Jesus into the
court of the high
priest, 16 but Peter
was standing at the
door outside. So
the other disciple,
who was known
to the high priest,
went out and spoke
to the doorkeeper,
and brought Pe-
ter in. 17 Then the
slave-girl who kept
the door *said to
Peter, "You are not
also *one* of this

NIV

man's disciples
too, are you?" she
asked Peter.
He replied, "I am
not."
[18] It was cold, and
the servants and
officials stood
around a fire they
had made to keep
warm. Peter also
was standing with
them, warming
himself.

The High Priest Questions Jesus

[19] Meanwhile, the
high priest ques-
tioned Jesus about
his disciples and
his teaching.
[20] "I have spo-
ken openly to
the world," Jesus
replied. "I al-
ways taught in
synagogues or at
the temple, where
all the Jews come
together. I said
nothing in secret.
[21] Why question
me? Ask those
who heard me.
Surely they know
what I said."
[22] When Jesus
said this, one of
the officials near-
by slapped him
in the face. "Is
this the way you
answer the high
priest?" he de-
manded.
[23] "If I said some-
thing wrong,"
Jesus replied,
"testify as to what
is wrong. But if I
spoke the truth,
why did you strike
me?" [24] Then
Annas sent him
bound to Caiaphas
the high priest.

Peter's Second and Third Denials

[25] Meanwhile, Si-
mon Peter was still
standing

μαθητῶν εἶ τοῦ ἀνθρώπου τούτου; ↰ ↰ λέγει ἐκεῖνος,
man's disciples, *are* *{the}* *man's* *that* are you?" He answered, *He* "I am
476 3412 1639 3836 476 4047 3590 3590 1697 3306 1697 1639 1639
n.gpm v.pai.2s d.gsm n.gsm r.gsm v.pai.3s r.nsm

οὐκ εἰμί. [18] εἱστήκεισαν δὲ οἱ δοῦλοι καὶ οἱ ὑπηρέται
not." *I am* *were standing there* *{and}* The servants and *{the}* officers had made a
4024 1639 2705 1254 3836 1529 2779 3836 5677 4472 4472
pl v.pai.1s v.lai.3p cj d.npm n.npm cj d.npm n.npm

ἀνθρακιὰν πεποιηκότες, ὅτι ψῦχος ἦν, καὶ
charcoal fire, *had made* because it was cold, *it was* and were standing there and
471 4472 4022 1639 1639 6036 1639 2779 2705 2705 2705
n.asf pt.ra.npm cj n.nsn v.iai.3s cj

ἐθερμαίνοντο· ἦν δὲ καὶ ὁ Πέτρος μετ' αὐτῶν ἑστὼς
warming themselves, and Peter also was *and* *also* *{the}* *Peter* standing with them *standing*
2548 1254 4377 2779 1639 1254 2779 3836 4377 2705 3552 899 2705
v.imi.3p v.iai.3s cj adv d.nsm n.nsm p.g r.gpm.3 pt.ra.nsm

καὶ θερμαινόμενος. [19] ὁ οὖν ἀρχιερεὺς ἠρώτησεν τὸν Ἰησοῦν περὶ
and warming himself. Meanwhile the *Meanwhile* high priest questioned *{the}* Jesus about
2779 2548 4036 3836 4036 797 2263 3836 2652 4309
cj pt.pm.nsm d.nsm cj n.nsm v.aai.3s d.asm n.asm p.g

τῶν μαθητῶν αὐτοῦ καὶ περὶ τῆς διδαχῆς αὐτοῦ. [20] ἀπεκρίθη αὐτῷ
{the} his disciples *his* and about *{the}* his teaching. *his* Jesus answered him,
3836 899 3412 899 2779 4309 3836 899 1439 899 2652 646 899
d.gpm n.gpm r.gsm.3 cj p.g d.gsf n.gsf r.gsm.3 v.api.3s r.dsm.3

Ἰησοῦς, ἐγὼ παρρησίᾳ λελάληκα τῷ κόσμῳ, ἐγὼ ↱ πάντοτε ἐδίδαξα
Jesus "I have spoken openly *have spoken* ⌞to the⌟ world. I have always taught
2652 1609 3281 3281 4244 3281 3836 3180 1609 1438 4121 1438
n.nsm r.ns.1 n.dsf v.rai.1s d.dsm n.dsm r.ns.1 adv v.aai.1s

ἐν συναγωγῇ καὶ ἐν τῷ ἱερῷ, ὅπου πάντες οἱ Ἰουδαῖοι συνέρχονται, καὶ
in the synagogue and in the temple, where all *{the}* Jews come together. *{and}*
1877 5252 2779 1877 3836 2639 3963 4246 3836 2681 5302 2779
p.d n.dsf cj p.d d.dsn n.dsn cj a.npm d.npm a.npm v.pmi.3p cj

ἐν κρυπτῷ ἐλάλησα οὐδέν. [21] τί με
I have said nothing in secret. *I have said* *nothing* Why do you question me?
3281 3281 3281 4029 1877 3220 3281 4029 5515 2263 2263 2263 1609
p.d a.dsn v.aai.1s a.asn r.asn r.as.1

ἐρωτᾷς; ἐρώτησον τοὺς ἀκηκοότας τί ἐλάλησα αὐτοῖς· ἴδε οὗτοι
do you question Question those who have heard as to what I said to them; ~ they
2263 2263 3836 201 5515 3281 899 2623 4047
v.pai.2s v.aam.2s d.apm pt.ra.apm r.asn v.aai.1s r.dpm.3 pl r.npm

οἴδασιν ἃ εἶπον ἐγώ. [22] ταῦτα δὲ αὐτοῦ εἰπόντος εἷς
know what I said." *I* When he said this, *{and}* *he* *When said* one of the
3857 4005 1609 3306 1609 3306 899 3306 4047 1254 899 3306 1651 3836 3836
v.rai.3p r.apn v.aai.1s r.ns.1 r.apn cj r.gsm.3 pt.aa.gsm a.nsm

παρεστηκὼς τῶν ὑπηρετῶν ἔδωκεν ῥάπισμα τῷ Ἰησοῦ εἰπών,
officers standing there *of the* *officers* gave Jesus a ⌞slap in the face,⌟ *{the}* *Jesus* saying,
5677 4225 3836 5677 1443 2652 4825 3836 2652 3306
pt.ra.nsm d.gpm n.gpm v.aai.3s n.asn d.dsm n.dsm pt.aa.nsm

οὕτως ἀποκρίνῃ τῷ ἀρχιερεῖ; [23] ἀπεκρίθη αὐτῷ Ἰησοῦς, εἰ
⌞"Is that how⌟ you answer the high priest?" Jesus replied, *{to him}* *Jesus* "If I spoke
4048 646 3836 797 2652 646 899 2652 1623 3281 3281
adv v.pmi.2s d.dsm n.dsm v.api.3s r.dsm.3 n.nsm cj

κακῶς ἐλάλησα, μαρτύρησον περὶ τοῦ κακοῦ· εἰ δὲ καλῶς, τί
incorrectly, *I spoke* testify about the error; but if *but* I spoke correctly, why
2809 3281 3455 4309 3836 2805 1254 1623 1254 2822 5515
adv v.aai.1s v.aam.2s p.g d.gsn a.gsn cj cj adv r.asn

με δέρεις; [24] ἀπέστειλεν οὖν αὐτὸν ὁ Ἄννας δεδεμένον
do you hit me?" *do you hit* Then Annas sent *Then* him *{the}* *Annas* bound
1296 1296 1296 1609 1296 4036 484 690 4036 899 3836 484 1313
r.as.1 v.pai.2s v.aai.3s cj r.asm.3 d.nsm n.nsm pt.rp.asm

πρὸς Καϊάφαν τὸν ἀρχιερέα. [25] ἦν δὲ Σίμων Πέτρος ἑστὼς
to Caiaphas the high priest. Now Simon Peter was *Now* *Simon* *Peter* still standing
4639 2780 3836 797 1254 4981 4377 1639 1254 4981 4377 2705
p.a n.asm d.asm n.asm v.iai.3s cj n.nsm n.nsm pt.ra.nsm

NASB

man's disciples, are
you?" He *said, "I
am not." [18] Now the
slaves and the offi-
cers were standing
there, having made
a charcoal fire, for
it was cold and
they were warming
themselves; and
Peter was also with
them, standing and
warming himself.
[19] The high priest
then questioned
Jesus about His
disciples, and
about His teaching.
[20] Jesus answered
him, "I have spo-
ken openly to the
world; I always
taught in syna-
gogues and in the
temple, where all
the Jews come to-
gether; and I spoke
nothing in secret.
[21] Why do you ques-
tion Me? Question
those who have
heard what I spoke
to them; they
know what I said."
[22] When He had
said this, one of
the officers stand-
ing nearby struck
Jesus, saying, "Is
that the way You
answer the high
priest?" [23] Jesus
answered him,
"If I have spoken
wrongly, testify of
the wrong; but if
rightly, why do you
strike Me?" [24] So
Annas sent Him
bound to Caiaphas
the high priest.

Peter's Denial of Jesus

[25] Now Simon Pe-
ter was standing

NIV

there warming
himself. So they
asked him, "You
aren't one of his
disciples too, are
you?"
He denied it, say-
ing, "I am not."
26 One of the high
priest's servants,
a relative of the
man whose ear
Peter had cut off,
challenged him,
"Didn't I see you
with him in the
garden?" 27 Again
Peter denied it,
and at that moment
a rooster began to
crow.

Jesus Before Pilate

28 Then the Jewish
leaders took Jesus
from Caiaphas to
the palace of the
Roman governor.
By now it was ear-
ly morning, and to
avoid ceremonial
uncleanness they
did not enter the
palace, because
they wanted to
be able to eat the
Passover. 29 So Pi-
late came out to
them and asked,
"What charges
are you bringing
against this man?"
30 "If he were not
a criminal," they
replied, "we would
not have handed
him over to you."
31 Pilate said,
"Take him your-
selves and judge
him by your own
law."
"But we have no
right to execute
anyone," they ob-
jected. 32 This took
place to fulfill
what Jesus had
said about the kind
of death

καὶ θερμαινόμενος. εἶπον οὖν αὐτῷ, μὴ καὶ σὺ ἐκ τῶν
and warming himself, so they said *so* to him, "Are you not *{also}* *You* ⌊one of⌋ *{the}* his
2779 2548 4036 3306 4036 899 1639 5148 3590 2779 5148 1666 3836 899
cj pt.pm.nsm v.aai.3p cj r.dsm.3 pl adv r.ns.2 p.g d.gpm

μαθητῶν αὐτοῦ εἶ; ἠρνήσατο ἐκεῖνος καὶ εἶπεν, οὐκ
disciples?" *his* *are* Peter denied *Peter* it and said, "I am not!"
3412 899 1639 1697 766 1697 2779 3306 1639 1639 4024
n.gpm r.gsm.3 v.pai.2s v.ami.3s r.nsm cj v.aai.3s pl

εἰμί. 26 λέγει εἷς ἐκ τῶν δούλων τοῦ ἀρχιερέως, συγγενὴς ὢν
I am *said* One of the servants of the high priest, a relative *{being}* of the man
1639 3306 1651 1666 3836 1529 3836 797 5150 1639
v.pai.1s v.pai.3s a.nsm p.g d.gpm n.gpm d.gsm n.gsm n.nsm pt.pa.nsm

οὗ ἀπέκοψεν Πέτρος τὸ ὠτίον· οὐκ ἐγώ σε εἶδον ἐν τῷ
whose ear Peter had cut off, *Peter* *{the}* *ear* said, *not* "I saw you *saw* in the
4005 6065 4377 644 4377 3836 6065 3306 4024 1609 1625 5148 1625 1877 3836
r.gsm v.aai.3s n.nsm d.asn n.asn pl r.ns.1 r.as.2 v.aai.1s p.d d.dsm

κήπῳ μετ᾽ αὐτοῦ; 27 πάλιν οὖν ἠρνήσατο Πέτρος, καὶ
garden with him, did I not?" Then Peter denied it again, *Then* *denied* *Peter* and
3057 3552 899 4024 4036 4377 766 4099 4036 766 4377 2779
n.dsm p.g r.gsm.3 adv cj v.ami.3s n.nsm cj

εὐθέως ἀλέκτωρ ἐφώνησεν. 28 ἄγουσιν οὖν τὸν Ἰησοῦν ἀπὸ τοῦ Καϊάφα
immediately a rooster began to crow. Then they took *Then* *{the}* Jesus from *{the}* Caiaphas
2311 232 5888 4036 72 4036 3836 2652 608 3836 2780
adv n.nsm v.aai.3s v.pai.3p cj d.asm n.asm p.g d.gsm n.gsm

εἰς τὸ πραιτώριον· ἦν δὲ πρωΐ· καὶ αὐτοὶ ↱ οὐκ εἰσῆλθον εἰς τὸ
to the governor's headquarters. ⌊It was⌋ *{and}* early, and they did not go into the
1650 3836 4550 1639 1254 4745 2779 899 1656 4024 1656 1650 3836
p.a d.asn n.asn v.iai.3s cj adv cj r.npm pl v.aai.3p p.a d.asn

πραιτώριον, ἵνα ↱ ↱ μὴ μιανθῶσιν ἀλλὰ φάγωσιν τὸ πάσχα.
governor's headquarters so that they would not be defiled, but could eat the ⌊Passover meal.⌋
4550 2671 3620 3620 3590 3620 247 2266 3836 4247
n.asn cj pl v.aps.3p cj v.aas.3p d.asn n.asn

29 ἐξῆλθεν οὖν ὁ Πιλᾶτος ἔξω πρὸς αὐτοὺς καὶ φησίν· τίνα
So Pilate came *So* *{the}* *Pilate* outside to them and said, "What
4036 4397 2002 4036 3836 4397 2032 4639 899 2779 5774 5515
v.aai.3s cj d.nsm n.nsm adv p.a r.apm.3 cj v.pai.3s r.asf

κατηγορίαν φέρετε κατὰ[a] τοῦ ἀνθρώπου τούτου; 30 ἀπεκρίθησαν καὶ
accusation ⌊are you bringing⌋ against *{the}* this man?" *this* They replied *{and}*
2990 5770 2848 3836 4047 476 4047 646 2779
n.asf v.pai.2p p.g d.gsm n.gsm r.gsm v.api.3p cj

εἶπαν αὐτῷ, εἰ μὴ ἦν οὗτος κακὸν ποιῶν,
to him, saying, *to him* "If this man were not *were* *this man* doing ⌊something wrong,⌋ *doing*
899 899 3306 899 1623 4047 4047 1639 3590 1639 4047 4472 2805 4472
v.aai.3p r.dsm.3 cj pl v.iai.3s r.nsm a.asn pt.pa.nsm

οὐκ ἄν σοι παρεδώκαμεν αὐτόν. 31
we would not *would* have handed him over to you." *we have handed over* *him* Then Pilate
4140 323 4024 323 4140 4140 899 4140 5148 4140 899 4036 4397
pl pl r.ds.2 v.aai.1p r.asm.3

εἶπεν οὖν αὐτοῖς ὁ Πιλᾶτος, λάβετε αὐτὸν ὑμεῖς καὶ κατὰ τὸν
said *Then* to them, *{the}* *Pilate* "Take him yourselves and judge him ⌊according to⌋ *{the}*
3306 4036 899 3836 4397 3284 899 7007 2779 3212 899 2848 3836
v.aai.3s cj r.dpm.3 d.nsm n.nsm v.aam.2p r.asm.3 r.np.2 cj p.a d.asm

νόμον ὑμῶν κρίνατε αὐτόν. εἶπον αὐτῷ οἱ Ἰουδαῖοι,
your law." *your* *judge* *him* The Jews said to him, *The* *Jews* "It is not
7007 3795 7007 3212 899 3836 2681 3306 899 3836 2681 1997 1997 4024
n.asm r.gp.2 v.aam.2p r.asm.3 v.aai.3p r.dsm.3 d.npm a.npm

ἡμῖν οὐκ ἔξεστιν → → ἀποκτεῖναι οὐδένα· 32 ἵνα ὁ
lawful for us *not* *It is lawful* to put any one to death." *any one* This was to fulfill the
1997 7005 4024 1997 4029 4029 650 4029 2671 4444 3836
r.dp.1 pl v.pai.3s f.aa a.asm cj d.nsm

λόγος τοῦ Ἰησοῦ πληρωθῇ ὃν εἶπεν σημαίνων ποίῳ θανάτῳ
word that *{the}* Jesus *fulfill* *that* had spoken indicating ⌊what kind of⌋ death
3364 4005 3836 2652 4444 4005 3306 4955 4481 2505
n.nsm d.gsm n.gsm v.aps.3s r.asm v.aai.3s pt.pa.nsm r.dsm n.dsm

[a] [κατὰ] UBS.

NASB

and warming him-
self. So they said
to him, "You are
not also *one* of His
disciples, are you?"
He denied *it,* and
said, "I am not."
26 One of the slaves
of the high priest,
being a relative of
the one whose ear
Peter cut off, *said,
"Did I not see you
in the garden with
Him?" 27 Peter then
denied *it* again,
and immediately a
rooster crowed.

Jesus before Pilate

28 Then they *led
Jesus from Ca-
iaphas into the
[a]Praetorium, and it
was early; and they
themselves did
not enter into the
Praetorium so that
they would not be
defiled, but might
eat the Passover.
29 Therefore Pilate
went out to them
and *said, "What
accusation do you
bring against this
Man?" 30 They an-
swered and said to
him, "If this Man
were not an evil-
doer, we would not
have delivered Him
to you." 31 So Pilate
said to them, "Take
Him yourselves,
and judge Him
according to your
law." The Jews
said to him, "We
are not permitted
to put anyone to
death," 32 to fulfill
the word of Jesus
which He spoke,
signifying by what
kind of death He

[a] I.e. governor's official residence

NIV

he was going to
die.
33 Pilate then went
back inside the
palace, summoned
Jesus and asked
him, "Are you the
king of the Jews?"
34 "Is that your
own idea," Jesus
asked, "or did
others talk to you
about me?"
35 "Am I a Jew?"
Pilate replied.
"Your own people
and chief priests
handed you over to
me. What is it you
have done?"
36 Jesus said, "My
kingdom is not
of this world. If it
were, my servants
would fight to pre-
vent my arrest by
the Jewish leaders.
But now my king-
dom is from anoth-
er place."
37 "You are a king,
then!" said Pilate.
Jesus answered,
"You say that I am
a king. In fact, the
reason I was born
and came into the
world is to testify
to the truth. Ev-
eryone on the side
of truth listens
to me."
38 "What is
truth?" retorted
Pilate. With this he
went out

ἤμελλεν ἀποθνῄσκειν. 33 εἰσῆλθεν οὖν πάλιν εἰς τὸ
he was going to die. Then Pilate entered *Then* his headquarters again, *{into}* *his*
3516 633 4036 4397 1656 4036 3836 4550 4099 1650 3836
v.iai.3s f.pa v.aai.3s cj adv p.a d.asn

πραιτώριον ὁ Πιλᾶτος καὶ ἐφώνησεν τὸν Ἰησοῦν καὶ εἶπεν αὐτῷ, σὺ εἶ
headquarters *{the}* *Pilate* *{and}* summoned *{the}* Jesus and said to him, "Are you *Are*
4550 3836 4397 2779 5888 3836 2652 2779 3306 899 1639 5148 1639
n.asn d.nsm n.nsm cj v.aai.3s d.asm n.asm cj v.aai.3s r.dsm.3 r.ns.2 v.pai.2s

ὁ βασιλεὺς τῶν Ἰουδαίων; 34 ἀπεκρίθη Ἰησοῦς, ἀπὸ
the king of the Jews?" Jesus responded, *Jesus* "Are you saying this of
3836 995 3836 2681 2652 646 2652 3306 5148 3306 4047 608
d.nsm n.nsm d.gpm a.gpm v.api.3s n.nsm p.g

σεαυτοῦ σὺ τοῦτο λέγεις ἢ ἄλλοι εἶπόν σοι περὶ ἐμοῦ; 35
your own accord, *you* *this* *Are saying* or did others tell you about me?" Pilate
4932 5148 4047 3306 2445 257 3306 5148 4309 1609 4397
r.gsm.2 r.ns.2 r.asn v.pai.2s cj r.npm v.aai.3p r.ds.2 p.g r.gs.1

ἀπεκρίθη ὁ Πιλᾶτος, μήτι ἐγὼ Ἰουδαῖός εἰμι; ↰ ↰ τὸ
answered, *{the}* *Pilate* "I am not *I* a Jew, *am* am I? *{the}* Your own
646 3836 4397 1609 1639 3614 1609 2681 1639 3614 3614 3836 5050 5050
v.api.3s d.nsm n.nsm pl r.ns.1 a.nsm v.pai.1s d.nsn

ἔθνος τὸ σὸν καὶ οἱ ἀρχιερεῖς παρέδωκάν σε ↰ ἐμοί· τί ἐποίησας;
people *{the}* *Your own* and the chief priests handed you over to me. What have you done?"
1620 3836 5050 2779 3836 797 4140 5148 4140 1609 5515 4472
n.nsn d.nsn r.nsn.2 cj d.npm n.npm v.aai.3p r.as.2 r.ds.1 r.asn v.aai.2s

36 ἀπεκρίθη Ἰησοῦς, ἡ βασιλεία ἡ ἐμὴ οὐκ ἔστιν ἐκ τοῦ
Jesus answered, *Jesus* *{the}* "My kingdom *{the}* *My* is not *is* of *{the}* this
2652 646 2652 3836 1847 993 3836 1847 1639 4024 1639 1666 3836 4047
v.api.3s n.nsm d.nsf n.nsf d.nsf r.nsf.1 pl v.pai.3s p.g d.gsm

κόσμου τούτου· εἰ ἐκ τοῦ κόσμου τούτου ἦν ἡ
world; *this* if my kingdom were of *{the}* this world, *this* *were* *{the}*
3180 4047 1623 1847 993 1639 1666 3836 4047 3180 4047 1639 3836
n.gsm r.gsm cj p.g d.gsm n.gsm r.gsm v.iai.3s d.nsf

βασιλεία ἡ ἐμή, οἱ ὑπηρέται οἱ ἐμοὶ ἠγωνίζοντο ἄν[a] ἵνα μὴ
kingdom *{the}* *my* *{the}* my subjects *{the}* *my* would be fighting *would* to prevent
993 3836 1847 3836 1847 5677 3836 1847 323 76 323 2671 3590
n.nsf d.nsf r.nsf.1 d.npm n.npm d.npm r.npm.1 v.imi.3p pl cj pl

παραδοθῶ τοῖς Ἰουδαίοις· νῦν δὲ ἡ βασιλεία ἡ ἐμὴ
⌊me from being handed over⌋ to the Jews; but ⌊as it is,⌋ *but* *{the}* my kingdom *{the}* *my*
4140 3836 2681 1254 3814 1254 3836 1847 993 3836 1847
v.aps.1s d.dpm a.dpm adv cj d.nsf n.nsf d.nsf r.nsf.1

οὐκ ἔστιν ἐντεῦθεν. 37 εἶπεν οὖν αὐτῷ ὁ Πιλᾶτος, οὐκοῦν
is not *is* from here." Therefore Pilate said *Therefore* to him, *{the}* *Pilate* "So
1639 4024 1639 1949 4036 4397 3306 4036 899 3836 4397 4034
pl v.pai.3s adv v.aai.3s cj r.dsm.3 d.nsm n.nsm cj

βασιλεὺς εἶ σύ; ↰ ἀπεκρίθη ὁ Ἰησοῦς, σὺ λέγεις ὅτι
you are a king, *are* *you* then?" Jesus answered, *{the}* *Jesus* "You say that I
5148 1639 995 1639 5148 4034 2652 646 3836 2652 5148 3306 4022 1639
n.nsm v.pai.2s r.ns.2 v.api.3s d.nsm n.nsm r.ns.2 v.pai.2s cj

βασιλεύς εἰμι. ἐγὼ εἰς τοῦτο γεγέννημαι καὶ εἰς
am a king! *I am* The reason for which I *for* *reason which* was born and *{for}*
1639 995 1639 4047 1650 4047 1609 1650 4047 1164 2779 1650
n.nsm v.pai.1s r.ns.1 p.a r.asn v.rpi.1s cj p.a

τοῦτο ἐλήλυθα εἰς τὸν κόσμον, ἵνα μαρτυρήσω τῇ ἀληθείᾳ·
{this reason} have come into the world, is that ⌊I should bear witness⌋ ⌊to the⌋ truth.
4047 2262 1650 3836 3180 2671 3455 3836 237
r.asn v.rai.1s p.a d.asm n.asm cj v.aas.1s d.dsf n.dsf

πᾶς ὁ ὢν ἐκ τῆς ἀληθείας ἀκούει μου τῆς φωνῆς. 38 λέγει αὐτῷ
Everyone who is of the truth listens to my *{the}* voice." Pilate said to him,
4246 3836 1639 1666 3836 237 201 1609 3836 5889 4397 3306 899
a.nsm d.nsm pt.pa.nsm p.g d.gsf n.gsf v.pai.3s r.gs.1 d.gsf n.gsf v.pai.3s r.dsm.3

ὁ Πιλᾶτος, τί ἐστιν ἀλήθεια; Καὶ τοῦτο εἰπὼν
{the} *Pilate* "What is truth?" And having said this *having said* he went out
3836 4397 5515 1639 237 2779 3306 3306 4047 3306 2002 2002 2002
d.nsm n.nsm r.nsn v.pai.3s n.nsf cj r.asn pt.aa.nsm

[a] [ἂν] UBS.

NASB

was about to die.
33 Therefore Pilate
entered again into
the Praetorium,
and summoned
Jesus and said to
Him, "Are You the
King of the Jews?"
34 Jesus answered,
"Are you saying
this on your own
initiative, or did
others tell you
about Me?" 35 Pi-
late answered, "I
am not a Jew, am
I? Your own na-
tion and the chief
priests delivered
You to me; what
have You done?"
36 Jesus answered,
"My kingdom is
not of this world.
If My kingdom
were of this world,
then My servants
would be fighting
so that I would not
be handed over to
the Jews; but as it
is, My kingdom is
not [a]of this realm."
37 Therefore Pilate
said to Him, "So
You are a king?"
Jesus answered,
"You say *correctly*
that I am a king.
For this I have
been born, and for
this I have come
into the world, to
testify to the truth.
Everyone who is
of the truth hears
My voice." 38 Pi-
late *said to Him,
"What is truth?"
And when he had
said this, he went

[a] Lit *from here*

NIV

again to the Jews
gathered there and
said, "I find no
basis for a charge
against him. 39 But
it is your custom
for me to release to
you one prisoner
at the time of the
Passover. Do you
want me to release
'the king of the
Jews'?"
40 They shouted
back, "No, not
him! Give us Bar-
abbas!" Now Bar-
abbas had taken
part in an uprising.

Jesus Sentenced to Be Crucified

19 Then Pi-
late took
Jesus and had him
flogged. 2 The
soldiers twisted
together a crown
of thorns and put it
on his head. They
clothed him in a
purple robe 3 and
went up to him
again and again,
saying, "Hail, king
of the Jews!" And
they slapped him
in the face.
4 Once more Pi-
late came out and
said to the Jews
gathered there,
"Look, I am bring-
ing him out to you
to let you know
that I find no ba-
sis for a charge
against him."
5 When Jesus came
out wearing the
crown of thorns
and the purple
robe, Pilate said to
them, "Here is the
man!"
6 As soon as the
chief priests and
their officials saw
him,

πάλιν ἐξῆλθεν πρὸς τοὺς Ἰουδαίους καὶ λέγει αὐτοῖς, ἐγὼ οὐδεμίαν εὑρίσκω
again *he went out* to the Jews and said to them, "I find no basis *find*
4099 2002 4639 3836 2681 2779 3306 899 1609 2351 4029 2351
adv v.aai.3s p.a d.apm a.apm cj v.pai.3s r.dpm.3 r.ns.1 a.asf v.pai.1s

ἐν αὐτῷ αἰτίαν. 39 ἔστιν δὲ συνήθεια ὑμῖν ἵνα
for an accusation against him. *accusation* But you have *But* a custom *you* that I
162 1877 899 162 1254 7007 1639 1254 5311 7007 2671 668
p.d r.dsm.3 n.asf v.pai.3s cj n.nsf r.dp.2 cj

ἕνα ἀπολύσω ὑμῖν ἐν τῷ πάσχα· βούλεσθε οὖν
should release someone *I should release* for you at the Passover. So do you want *So*
668 668 1651 668 7007 1877 3836 4247 4036 1089 4036
a.asm v.aas.1s r.dp.2 p.d d.dsn n.dsn v.pmi.2p cj

ἀπολύσω ὑμῖν τὸν βασιλέα τῶν Ἰουδαίων; 40 ἐκραύγασαν οὖν πάλιν λέγοντες,
me to release for you the king of the Jews?" They shouted *{then}* back, saying,
668 7007 3836 995 3836 2681 3198 4036 4099 3306
v.aas.1s r.dp.2 d.asm n.asm d.gpm a.gpm v.aai.3p cj adv pt.pa.npm

μὴ τοῦτον ἀλλὰ τὸν Βαραββᾶν. ἦν δὲ ὁ Βαραββᾶς
"Not that man, but *{the}* Barabbas!" Now Barabbas was *Now* *{the}* *Barabbas* a
3590 4047 247 3836 972 1254 972 1639 1254 3836 972
pl r.asm cj d.asm n.asm v.iai.3s cj d.nsm n.nsm

λῃστής.
revolutionary.
3334
n.nsm

19:1 τότε οὖν ἔλαβεν ὁ Πιλᾶτος τὸν Ἰησοῦν καὶ ἐμαστίγωσεν. 2 καὶ
Then Pilate took *{the}* *Pilate* *{the}* Jesus and had him flogged. And
5538 4036 4397 3284 3836 4397 3836 2652 2779 3463 2779
adv cj v.aai.3s d.nsm n.nsm d.asm n.asm cj v.aai.3s cj

οἱ στρατιῶται πλέξαντες ← στέφανον ἐξ ἀκανθῶν ἐπέθηκαν ←
the soldiers twisted some thorns into a crown *some thorns* and placed it on
3836 5132 4428 1666 180 5109 1666 180 2202
d.npm n.npm pt.aa.npm n.asm p.g n.gpf v.aai.3p

αὐτοῦ τῇ κεφαλῇ καὶ ἱμάτιον πορφυροῦν περιέβαλον
his *{the}* head, and they threw a purple robe *purple* *they threw around* around
899 3836 3051 2779 4314 4314 4528 2668 4528 4314 4314
r.gsm.3 d.dsf n.dsf cj n.asn a.asn v.aai.3p

αὐτὸν 3 καὶ ἤρχοντο πρὸς αὐτὸν καὶ ἔλεγον, χαῖρε ὁ βασιλεὺς τῶν
him. Then ⌞they kept coming up⌟ to him, *{and}* saying, "Hail, *{the}* king of the
899 2779 2262 4639 899 2779 3306 5897 3836 995 3836
r.asm.3 cj v.imi.3p p.a r.asm.3 cj v.iai.3p v.pam.2s d.vsm n.vsm d.gpm

Ἰουδαίων· καὶ ⌞ἐδίδοσαν αὐτῷ ῥαπίσματα.⌟ 4 καὶ ἐξῆλθεν
Jews!" and slapping him in the face. *{and}* Once more Pilate went
2681 2779 1443 899 4825 2779 4099 4099 4397 2002
a.gpm cj v.iai.3p r.dsm.3 n.apn cj v.aai.3s

πάλιν ἔξω ὁ Πιλᾶτος καὶ λέγει αὐτοῖς, ἴδε ἄγω ὑμῖν
out *Once more* *out* *{the}* *Pilate* and said to them, "Look, ⌞I am bringing⌟ him out to you
2032 4099 2032 3836 4397 2779 3306 899 2623 72 899 2032 7007
adv adv d.nsm n.nsm cj v.pai.3s r.dpm.3 pl v.pai.1s r.dp.2

αὐτὸν ἔξω, ἵνα γνῶτε ὅτι οὐδεμίαν αἰτίαν εὑρίσκω ἐν
him *out* that ⌞you may know⌟ that I find no basis for an accusation *I find* against
899 2032 2671 1182 4022 2351 2351 4029 162 2351 1877
r.asm.3 adv cj v.aas.2p cj a.asf n.asf v.pai.1s p.d

αὐτῷ. 5 ἐξῆλθεν οὖν ὁ Ἰησοῦς ἔξω, φορῶν τὸν ἀκάνθινον
him." So Jesus came *So* *{the}* *Jesus* out, wearing the crown of thorns
899 4036 2652 2002 4036 3836 2652 2032 5841 3836 5109 181
r.dsm.3 v.aai.3s cj d.nsm n.nsm adv pt.pa.nsm d.asm a.asm

στέφανον καὶ τὸ πορφυροῦν ἱμάτιον. καὶ λέγει αὐτοῖς, ἰδοὺ ὁ ἄνθρωπος.
crown and the purple robe; and Pilate said to them, "Look, the man!"
5109 2779 3836 4528 2668 2779 3306 899 2627 3836 476
n.asm cj d.asn a.asn n.asn cj v.pai.3s r.dpm.3 j d.nsm n.nsm

6 ὅτε οὖν εἶδον αὐτὸν οἱ ἀρχιερεῖς καὶ οἱ
When *{then}* the chief priests and the officers saw him, *the* *chief priests* *and* *the*
4021 4036 3836 797 797 2779 3836 5677 1625 899 3836 797 2779 3836
cj cj v.aai.3p r.asm.3 d.npm n.npm cj d.npm

NASB

out again to the
Jews and *said to
them, "I find no
guilt in Him. 39 But
you have a custom
that I release some-
one for you at the
Passover; do you
wish then that I
release for you the
King of the Jews?"
40 So they cried
out again, saying,
"Not this Man, but
Barabbas." Now
Barabbas was a
robber.

The Crown of Thorns

19:1 Pilate then took
Jesus and scourged
Him. 2 And the
soldiers twisted
together a crown
of thorns and put
it on His head, and
put a purple robe
on Him; 3 and they
began to come up
to Him and say,
"Hail, King of the
Jews!" and to give
Him slaps *in the
face.* 4 Pilate came
out again and *said
to them, "Behold,
I am bringing Him
out to you so that
you may know that
I find no guilt in
Him." 5 Jesus then
came out, wearing
the crown of thorns
and the purple
robe. *Pilate* *said to
them, "Behold, the
Man!" 6 So when
the chief priests
and the officers
saw Him, they

NIV

they shouted, "Cru-
cify! Crucify!"
But Pilate an-
swered, "You take
him and crucify
him. As for me, I
find no basis for
a charge against
him."
7The Jewish lead-
ers insisted, "We
have a law, and ac-
cording to that law
he must die, be-
cause he claimed
to be the Son of
God."
8When Pilate
heard this, he was
even more afraid,
9and he went back
inside the palace.
"Where do you
come from?" he
asked Jesus, but
Jesus gave him no
answer. 10"Do you
refuse to speak to
me?" Pilate said.
"Don't you realize
I have power either
to free you or to
crucify you?"
11Jesus answered,
"You would have
no power over me
if it were not given
to you from above.
Therefore the
one who handed
me over to you is
guilty of a greater
sin."
12From then on,
Pilate tried to set
Jesus free, but
the Jewish lead-
ers kept shouting,
"If you let this
man go, you are
no friend of Cae-
sar. Anyone who
claims to

ὑπηρέται ἐκραύγασαν λέγοντες, σταύρωσον σταύρωσον. λέγει αὐτοῖς
officers they cried out, saying, "Crucify him! Crucify him!" Pilate said to them,
5677 3198 3306 5090 5090 4397 3306 899
n.npm v.aai.3p pt.pa.npm v.aam.2s v.aam.2s v.pai.3s r.dpm.3

ὁ Πιλᾶτος, λάβετε αὐτὸν ὑμεῖς καὶ σταυρώσατε· ἐγὼ γὰρ
{the} Pilate "Take him yourselves and crucify him; for I *for* find
3836 4397 3284 899 7007 2779 5090 1142 1609 1142 2351
d.nsm n.nsm v.aam.2p r.asm.3 r.np.2 cj v.aam.2p r.ns.1 cj

οὐχ εὑρίσκω ἐν αὐτῷ αἰτίαν. 7 ἀπεκρίθησαν αὐτῷ
⌊no basis for⌋ *find* an accusation against him." *accusation* The Jews answered him,
4024 2351 162 1877 899 162 3836 2681 646 899
pl v.pai.1s p.d r.dsm.3 n.asf v.api.3p r.dsm.3

οἱ Ἰουδαῖοι, ἡμεῖς νόμον ἔχομεν καὶ κατὰ τὸν νόμον ὀφείλει
The Jews "We have a law, *have* and ⌊according to⌋ our law he ought
3836 2681 7005 2400 3795 2400 2779 2848 3836 3795 4053
d.npm a.npm r.np.1 n.asm v.pai.1p cj p.a d.asm n.asm v.pai.3s

ἀποθανεῖν, ὅτι υἱὸν θεοῦ ἑαυτὸν ἐποίησεν.
to die, because he claimed himself to be the Son of God." *himself he claimed to be*
633 4022 4472 4472 1571 4472 4472 5626 2536 1571 4472
f.aa cj n.asm n.gsm r.asm.3 v.aai.3s

8 ὅτε οὖν ἤκουσεν ὁ Πιλᾶτος τοῦτον τὸν λόγον, ↱ ↱ μᾶλλον
Now when *Now* Pilate heard *{the} Pilate* this *{the}* statement, he became even more
4036 4021 4036 4397 201 3836 4397 4047 3836 3364 5828 5828 3437
cj cj v.aai.3s d.nsm n.nsm r.asm d.asm n.asm adv.c

ἐφοβήθη, 9 καὶ εἰσῆλθεν εἰς τὸ πραιτώριον πάλιν καὶ λέγει τῷ Ἰησοῦ,
afraid. *{and}* He went back into his headquarters *back* and said to Jesus,
5828 2779 1656 4099 1650 3836 4550 4099 2779 3306 3836 2652
v.api.3s cj v.aai.3s p.a d.asn n.asn adv cj v.pai.3s d.dsm n.dsm

πόθεν εἶ σύ; ↰ ὁ δὲ Ἰησοῦς ἀπόκρισιν οὐκ ἔδωκεν αὐτῷ.
"Where are you from?" *{the}* But Jesus *answer no* gave him no answer.
4470 1639 5148 4470 3836 1254 2652 647 4024 1443 899 4024 647
cj v.pai.2s r.ns.2 d.nsm cj n.nsm n.asf pl v.aai.3s r.dsm.3

10 λέγει οὖν αὐτῷ ὁ Πιλᾶτος, ἐμοὶ οὐ
So Pilate said *So* to him, *{the} Pilate* "Are you not going to talk to me? *not*
4036 4397 3306 4036 899 3836 4397 3281 3281 4024 3281 3281 3281 1609 4024
v.pai.3s cj r.dsm.3 d.nsm n.nsm r.ds.1 pl

λαλεῖς; οὐκ οἶδας ὅτι ἐξουσίαν ἔχω
Are you going to talk You know, do you not, *You know* that I have the authority *I have*
3281 3857 3857 4024 3857 4022 2400 2400 2026 2400
v.pai.2s pl v.rai.2s cj n.asf v.pai.1s

ἀπολῦσαί σε καὶ ἐξουσίαν ἔχω σταυρῶσαί σε; 11 ἀπεκρίθη[a]
to release you and I have the authority *I have* to crucify you?" Jesus said,
668 5148 2779 2400 2400 2026 2400 5090 5148 2652 646
f.aa r.as.2 cj n.asf v.pai.1s f.aa r.as.2 v.api.3s

Ἰησοῦς, οὐκ εἶχες ἐξουσίαν κατ᾽ ἐμοῦ οὐδεμίαν ⌊εἰ μὴ⌋
Jesus "You would have no *You would have* authority over me at all unless
2652 2400 2400 2400 4024 2400 2026 2848 1609 4029 1623 3590
n.nsm pl v.iai.2s n.asf p.g r.gs.1 a.asf cj pl

ἦν δεδομένον σοι ἄνωθεν· ⌊διὰ τοῦτο⌋ ὁ παραδούς μέ ↰
⌊it had been⌋ given you from above. That is why the man who handed me over
1639 1443 5148 540 1328 4047 3836 4140 1609 4140
v.iai.3s pt.rp.nsn r.ds.2 adv p.a r.asn d.nsm pt.aa.nsm r.as.1

σοι μείζονα ἁμαρτίαν ἔχει. 12 ἐκ τούτου ὁ Πιλᾶτος ἐζήτει ἀπολῦσαι
to you has a greater sin." *has* From that point on *{the}* Pilate tried to release
5148 2400 3489 281 2400 1666 4047 3836 4397 2426 668
r.ds.2 a.asf.c n.asf v.pai.3s p.g r.gsn d.nsm n.nsm v.iai.3s f.aa

αὐτόν· οἱ δὲ Ἰουδαῖοι ἐκραύγασαν λέγοντες, ἐὰν τοῦτον
him, but the *but* Jews kept shouting out, saying, "If you release this man,
899 1254 3836 1254 2681 3198 3306 1569 668 668 4047
r.asm.3 d.npm cj a.npm v.aai.3p pt.pa.npm cj r.asm

ἀπολύσῃς, οὐκ εἶ φίλος τοῦ Καίσαρος· πᾶς ὁ
you release you are no *you are* 'Friend of Caesar.' Anyone who claims himself to
668 1639 1639 4024 1639 5813 3836 2790 4246 3836 4472 1571 4472
v.aas.2s pl v.pai.2s n.nsm d.gsm n.gsm a.nsm d.nsm

NASB

cried out saying,
"Crucify, crucify!"
Pilate *said to
them, "Take Him
yourselves and
crucify Him, for
I find no guilt in
Him." 7The Jews
answered him, "We
have a law, and by
that law He ought
to die because He
made Himself out
to be the Son of
God."
8Therefore when
Pilate heard this
statement, he was
even more afraid;
9and he entered into
the [a]Praetorium
again and *said
to Jesus, "Where
are You from?"
But Jesus gave
him no answer.
10So Pilate *said to
Him, "You do not
speak to me? Do
You not know that
I have authority to
release You, and
I have authority
to crucify You?"
11Jesus answered,
"You would have
no authority over
Me, unless it had
been given you
from above; for
this reason he who
delivered Me to
you has *the* greater
sin." 12As a result
of this Pilate made
efforts to release
Him, but the Jews
cried out saying,
"If you release this
Man, you are no
friend of Caesar;
everyone who
makes himself

[a] αὐτῷ included by UBS after ἀπεκρίθη.

[a] I.e. governor's official residence

NIV

be a king opposes
Caesar."
[13]When Pilate
heard this, he
brought Jesus out
and sat down on
the judge's seat at
a place known as
the Stone Pave-
ment (which in
Aramaic is Gab-
batha). [14]It was the
day of Preparation
of the Passover; it
was about noon.
"Here is your
king," Pilate said
to the Jews.
[15]But they shout-
ed, "Take him
away! Take him
away! Crucify
him!"
"Shall I crucify
your king?" Pilate
asked.
"We have no king
but Caesar," the
chief priests an-
swered.
[16]Finally Pilate
handed him over
to them to be cru-
cified.

The Crucifixion of Jesus

So the soldiers
took charge of
Jesus. [17]Carrying
his own cross, he
went out to the
place of the Skull
(which in Aramaic
is called Golgo-
tha). [18]There they
crucified him, and
with him two oth-
ers—one on each
side and Jesus in
the middle.
[19]Pilate had a no-
tice prepared and
fastened to the
cross. It read: JESUS
OF NAZARETH, THE
KING OF THE JEWS.
[20]Many of the Jews
read this sign,

βασιλέα ἑαυτὸν ποιῶν ἀντιλέγει τῷ Καίσαρι. 13 ὁ οὖν Πιλᾶτος
be a king *himself* *claims to be* opposes *{the}* Caesar." *{the}* *{then}* *Pilate*
4472 995 1571 4472 515 3836 2790 3836 4036 4397
n.asm r.asm.3 pt.pa.nsm v.pai.3s d.dsm n.dsm d.nsm cj n.nsm

ἀκούσας τῶν λόγων τούτων ἤγαγεν ἔξω τὸν Ἰησοῦν καὶ ἐκάθισεν
On hearing *{the}* these words, *these* Pilate brought Jesus out *{the}* *Jesus* and sat down
201 3836 4047 3364 4047 4397 72 2652 2032 3836 2652 2779 2767
pt.aa.nsm d.gpm n.gpm r.gpm v.aai.3s adv d.asm n.asm cj v.aai.3s

ἐπὶ βήματος εἰς τόπον λεγόμενον Λιθόστρωτον, Ἑβραϊστὶ δὲ
on the judge's bench in the place called "Stone Pavement," or in Hebrew, *or*
2093 1037 1650 5536 3306 3346 1254 1580 1254
p.g n.gsn p.a n.asm pt.pp.asm n.asn adv cj

Γαββαθα. 14 ἦν δὲ παρασκευὴ τοῦ πάσχα, ὥρα ἦν ὡς ἕκτη.
"Gabbatha." Now it was *Now* the day of Preparation ⌊for the⌋ Passover, *{hour}* *{was}* about noon.
1119 1254 1639 1254 4187 3836 4247 6052 1639 6055 1761
n.asn v.iai.3s cj n.nsf d.gsn n.gsn n.nsf v.iai.3s pl a.nsf

καὶ λέγει τοῖς Ἰουδαίοις, ἴδε ὁ βασιλεὺς ὑμῶν. 15 ἐκραύγασαν
{and} Pilate said to the Jews, "Here is *{the}* your king!" *your* But they shouted,
2779 3306 3836 2681 2623 3836 7007 995 7007 4036 3198
cj v.pai.3s d.dpm a.dpm pl d.nsm n.nsm r.gp.2 v.aai.3p

οὖν ἐκεῖνοι, ἆρον ἆρον, σταύρωσον αὐτόν. λέγει αὐτοῖς ὁ
But "Away with him! *Away* Away with him! Crucify him!" Pilate said to them, *{the}*
4036 149 1697 149 149 5090 899 4397 3306 899 3836
cj r.npm v.aam.2s v.aam.2s v.aam.2s r.asm.3 v.pai.3s r.dpm.3 d.nsm

Πιλᾶτος, τὸν βασιλέα ὑμῶν σταυρώσω;
Pilate "Shall I crucify *{the}* your king?" *your* *Shall I crucify* The chief priests
4397 5090 5090 5090 3836 7007 995 7007 5090 3836 797 797
n.nsm d.asm n.asm r.gp.2 v.aas.1s

ἀπεκρίθησαν οἱ ἀρχιερεῖς, οὐκ ἔχομεν βασιλέα ⌊εἰ μὴ⌋ Καίσαρα.
answered, *The* *chief priests* "We have no *We have* king but Caesar!"
646 3836 797 2400 2400 4024 2400 995 1623 3590 2790
v.api.3p d.npm n.npm pl v.pai.1p n.asm cj pl n.asm

16 ⌊τότε οὖν⌋ παρέδωκεν αὐτὸν ↰ → αὐτοῖς ἵνα σταυρωθῇ.
Then Pilate handed him over to the soldiers to be crucified. So
5538 4036 4140 899 4140 899 2671 5090 4036
adv cj v.aai.3s r.asm.3 r.dpm.3 cj v.aps.3s

παρέλαβον οὖν τὸν Ἰησοῦν, 17 καὶ βαστάζων ἑαυτῷ τὸν
⌊they took charge of⌋ *So* *{the}* Jesus, *{and}* who, carrying the cross by himself, *{the}*
4161 4036 3836 2652 2779 1002 5089 5089 1571 3836
v.aai.3p cj d.asm n.asm cj pt.pa.nsm r.dsm.3 d.asm

σταυρὸν ἐξῆλθεν εἰς τὸν λεγόμενον → Κρανίου Τόπον, ὃ λέγεται
the cross went out to what was called "The Place of the Skull," *Place* which is called
5089 2002 1650 3836 3306 5536 3191 5536 4005 3306
n.asm v.aai.3s p.a d.asm pt.pp.asm n.gsn n.asm r.nsn v.ppi.3s

Ἑβραϊστὶ Γολγοθα, 18 ὅπου αὐτὸν ἐσταύρωσαν, καὶ μετ' αὐτοῦ
in Hebrew, "Golgotha." There they crucified him, *they crucified* and with him two
1580 1201 3963 5090 5090 899 5090 2779 3552 899 1545
adv n.nsf cj r.asm.3 v.aai.3p cj p.g r.gsm.3

ἄλλους δύο ⌊ἐντεῦθεν καὶ ἐντεῦθεν,⌋ μέσον δὲ τὸν Ἰησοῦν.
others, *two* one on either side with Jesus between *{and}* *{the}* *Jesus* them.
257 1545 1949 2779 1949 2652 3545 1254 3836 2652
r.apm a.apm adv cj adv adv cj d.asm n.asm

19 ἔγραψεν δὲ καὶ τίτλον ὁ Πιλᾶτος καὶ ἔθηκεν ἐπὶ τοῦ
And Pilate wrote *And* *{also}* an inscription *{the}* *Pilate* and fastened it to the
1254 4397 1211 1254 2779 5518 3836 4397 2779 5502 2093 3836
v.aai.3s cj adv n.asm d.nsm n.nsm cj v.aai.3s p.g d.gsm

σταυροῦ· ⌊ἦν δὲ γεγραμμένον,⌋ Ἰησοῦς ὁ Ναζωραῖος ὁ βασιλεὺς τῶν
cross. It read, "Jesus of Nazareth, the King of the
5089 1639 1254 1211 2652 3836 3717 3836 995 3836
n.gsm v.iai.3s cj pt.rp.nsn n.nsm d.nsm n.nsm d.nsm n.nsm d.gpm

Ἰουδαίων. 20 τοῦτον οὖν τὸν τίτλον πολλοὶ ἀνέγνωσαν
Jews." Many of the Jews read this *{then}* *{the}* inscription, *Many* *read*
2681 4498 3836 3836 2681 336 4047 4036 3836 5518 4498 336
a.gpm r.asm cj d.asm n.asm a.npm v.aai.3p

NASB

out *to be* a king op-
poses Caesar."
[13]Therefore when
Pilate heard these
words, he brought
Jesus out, and
sat down on the
judgment seat at
a place called The
Pavement, but in
Hebrew, Gabbatha.
[14]Now it was the
day of preparation
for the Passover;
it was about the
[a]sixth hour. And he
*said to the Jews,
"Behold, your
King!" [15]So they
cried out, "Away
with *Him,* away
with *Him,* crucify
Him!" Pilate *said
to them, "Shall
I crucify your
King?" The chief
priests answered,
"We have no king
but Caesar."

The Crucifixion

[16]So he then handed
Him over to them
to be crucified.
[17]They took Jesus,
therefore, and He
went out, bearing
His own cross, to
the place called the
Place of a Skull,
which is called in
Hebrew, Golgotha.
[18]There they cruci-
fied Him, and with
Him two other
men, one on either
side, and Jesus in
between. [19]Pilate
also wrote an in-
scription and put it
on the cross. It was
written, "JESUS
THE NAZARENE,
THE KING OF THE
JEWS." [20]Therefore
many of the Jews
read this inscrip-
tion, for the place

[a] Perhaps 6 a.m.

NIV

for the place where
Jesus was cruci-
fied was near the
city, and the sign
was written in Ar-
amaic, Latin and
Greek. 21 The chief
priests of the Jews
protested to Pilate,
"Do not write 'The
King of the Jews,'
but that this man
claimed to be king
of the Jews."
22 Pilate an-
swered, "What
I have written, I
have written."
23 When the sol-
diers crucified
Jesus, they took
his clothes, di-
viding them into
four shares, one
for each of them,
with the undergar-
ment remaining.
This garment was
seamless, woven
in one piece from
top to bottom.
24 "Let's not tear
it," they said to
one another. "Let's
decide by lot who
will get it."
This happened
that the scripture
might be fulfilled
that said,

"They divided
my clothes
among
them
and cast lots
for my
garment."[a]

So this is what the
soldiers did.
25 Near the cross
of Jesus stood his
mother, his moth-
er's sister, Mary
the wife of Clopas,
and Mary Magda-
lene. 26 When Jesus
saw his mother
there, and

[a] 24 Psalm 22:18

τῶν Ἰουδαίων, ὅτι ἐγγὺς ἦν ὁ τόπος τῆς
of the Jews for the place where Jesus was crucified was near *was* *the* *place* the
3836 2681 4022 3836 5536 3963 2652 5090 5090 1639 1584 1639 3836 5536 3836
d.gpm a.gpm cj p.g v.iai.3s d.nsm n.nsm d.gsf

πόλεως ὅπου ἐσταυρώθη ὁ Ἰησοῦς· καὶ ἦν γεγραμμένον Ἑβραϊστί, Ῥωμαϊστί,
city, *where* *was crucified* *{the}* *Jesus* and it was written in Hebrew, in Latin,
4484 3963 5090 3836 2652 2779 1639 1211 1580 4872
n.gsf cj v.api.3s d.nsm n.nsm cj v.iai.3s pt.rp.nsn adv adv

Ἑλληνιστί. 21 ἔλεγον οὖν τῷ Πιλάτῳ οἱ
and in Greek. Then the chief priests of the Jews said *Then* to Pilate, *the*
1822 4036 3836 797 797 3836 3836 2681 3306 4036 3836 4397 3836
adv v.iai.3p cj d.dsm n.dsm d.npm

ἀρχιερεῖς τῶν Ἰουδαίων, ↱ μὴ γράφε, ὁ βασιλεὺς τῶν Ἰουδαίων, ἀλλ' ὅτι
chief priests *of the* *Jews* "Do not write, 'The King of the Jews,' but rather, ~
797 3836 2681 1211 3590 1211 3836 995 3836 2681 247 4022
n.npm d.gpm a.gpm pl v.pam.2s d.nsm n.nsm d.gpm a.gpm cj cj

ἐκεῖνος εἶπεν, βασιλεύς εἰμι τῶν Ἰουδαίων. 22 ἀπεκρίθη ὁ
'This man said, I am King *I am* of the Jews.'" Pilate answered, *{the}*
1697 3306 1639 1639 995 1639 3836 2681 4397 646 3836
r.nsm v.aai.3s n.nsm v.pai.1s d.gpm a.gpm v.api.3s d.nsm

Πιλᾶτος, ὃ γέγραφα, γέγραφα. 23 οἱ οὖν στρατιῶται, ὅτε
Pilate "What I have written I have written." When the *{then}* soldiers *When*
4397 4005 1211 1211 4021 3836 4036 5132 4021
n.nsm r.asn v.rai.1s v.rai.1s d.npm cj n.npm cj

ἐσταύρωσαν τὸν Ἰησοῦν, ἔλαβον τὰ ἱμάτια αὐτοῦ καὶ ἐποίησαν ←
crucified *{the}* Jesus, they took *{the}* his garments *his* and separated them into
5090 3836 2652 3284 3836 899 2668 899 2779 4472
v.aai.3p d.asm n.asm v.aai.3p d.apn n.apn r.gsm.3 cj v.aai.3p

τέσσαρα μέρη, ἑκάστῳ στρατιώτῃ μέρος, καὶ τὸν χιτῶνα.
four shares, one share for each soldier. *one share* They also took his tunic, which
5475 3538 3538 3538 1667 5132 3538 2779 3836 5945 5945
a.apn n.apn r.dsm n.dsm n.asn cj d.asm n.asm

ἦν δὲ ὁ χιτὼν ἄραφος, ἐκ τῶν ἄνωθεν ὑφαντὸς δι'
was *{and}* *{the}* *which* seamless, woven from *{the}* top to bottom *woven* as a
1639 1254 3836 5945 731 5733 1666 3836 540 5733 1328
v.iai.3s cj d.nsm n.nsm a.nsm p.g d.gpn adv a.nsm p.g

ὅλου. 24 εἶπαν οὖν πρὸς ἀλλήλους, ↱ ↱ μὴ σχίσωμεν αὐτόν, ἀλλὰ
⌊single piece.⌋ So they said *so* to one another, "Let us not tear it, but
3910 4036 3306 4036 4639 253 5387 5387 3590 5387 899 247
a.gsm v.aai.3p cj p.a r.apm pl v.aas.1p r.asm.3 cj

λάχωμεν περὶ αὐτοῦ τίνος ἔσται· ἵνα ἡ γραφὴ πληρωθῇ [a]ἡ
cast lots for it to see who will get it" — that the Scripture might be fulfilled that
3275 4309 899 5515 1639 2671 3836 1210 4444 3836
v.aas.1p p.g r.gsm.3 r.gsm v.fmi.3s cj d.nsf n.nsf v.aps.3s d.nsf

λέγουσα, διεμερίσαντο τὰ ἱμάτιά μου ↰ ἑαυτοῖς καὶ ἐπὶ τὸν
says, "They divided *{the}* my garments *my* among themselves, and for *{the}* my
3306 1374 3836 1609 2668 1609 1374 1571 2779 2093 3836 1609
pt.pa.nsf v.ami.3p d.apn n.apn r.gs.1 r.dpm.3 cj p.a d.asm

ἱματισμόν μου ἔβαλον κλῆρον. οἱ μὲν οὖν στρατιῶται ταῦτα
clothing *my* they cast lots." So the ~ *So* soldiers did these things.
2669 1609 965 3102 4036 3836 3525 4036 5132 4472 4047
n.asm r.gs.1 v.aai.3p n.asm d.npm pl cj n.npm r.apn

ἐποίησαν. 25 εἱστήκεισαν δὲ παρὰ τῷ σταυρῷ τοῦ Ἰησοῦ ἡ
did Now standing *Now* beside *{the}* Jesus' cross *{the}* *Jesus'* were *{the}* his
4472 1254 2705 1254 4123 3836 2652 5089 3836 2652 3836 899
v.aai.3p v.lai.3p cj p.d d.dsm n.dsm d.gsm n.gsm d.nsf

μήτηρ αὐτοῦ καὶ ἡ ἀδελφὴ τῆς μητρὸς αὐτοῦ, Μαρία ἡ τοῦ
mother, *his* and *{the}* his mother's sister, *{the}* *mother's* *his* Mary the wife of
3613 899 2779 3836 899 3613 80 3836 3613 899 3451 3836 3836
n.nsf r.gsm.3 cj d.nsf n.nsf d.gsf n.gsf r.gsm.3 n.nsf d.nsf d.gsm

Κλωπᾶ καὶ Μαρία ἡ Μαγδαληνή. 26 Ἰησοῦς οὖν ἰδὼν τὴν μητέρα καὶ
Clopas, and Mary *{the}* Magdalene. When Jesus *When* saw his mother and
3116 2779 3451 3836 3402 4036 2652 4036 1625 3836 3613 2779
n.gsm cj n.nsf d.nsf n.nsf n.nsm cj pt.aa.nsm d.asf n.asf cj

[a] [ἡ λέγουσα] UBS.

NASB

where Jesus was
crucified was near
the city; and it was
written in Hebrew,
Latin *and* in Greek.
21 So the chief
priests of the Jews
were saying to Pi-
late, "Do not write,
'The King of the
Jews'; but that He
said, 'I am King of
the Jews.'" 22 Pilate
answered, "What I
have written I have
written."
23 Then the sol-
diers, when they
had crucified Jesus,
took His outer gar-
ments and made
four parts, a part
to every soldier
and *also* the [a]tunic;
now the tunic was
seamless, woven in
one piece. 24 So they
said to one another,
"Let us not tear it,
but cast lots for it,
to decide whose
it shall be"; *this
was* to fulfill the
Scripture: "THEY
DIVIDED MY OUTER
GARMENTS AMONG
THEM, AND FOR MY
CLOTHING THEY CAST
LOTS." 25 Therefore
the soldiers did
these things.
But standing by
the cross of Jesus
were His mother,
and His mother's
sister, Mary the
wife of Clopas, and
Mary Magdalene.
26 When Jesus then
saw His mother,

[a] Gr *khiton,* the gar-
ment worn next to the
skin

NIV

the disciple whom
he loved standing
nearby, he said
to her, “Woman,[a]
here is your son,”
27 and to the disci-
ple, “Here is your
mother.” From that
time on, this dis-
ciple took her into
his home.

The Death of Jesus

28 Later, knowing
that everything
had now been
finished, and so
that Scripture
would be fulfilled,
Jesus said, “I am
thirsty.” 29 A jar
of wine vinegar
was there, so they
soaked a sponge in
it, put the sponge
on a stalk of the
hyssop plant, and
lifted it to Jesus’
lips. 30 When he
had received the
drink, Jesus said,
“It is finished.”
With that, he
bowed his head
and gave up his
spirit.
31 Now it was the
day of Preparation,
and the next day
was to be a special
Sabbath. Because
the Jewish lead-
ers did not want
the bodies left on
the crosses during
the Sabbath, they
asked Pilate to
have the legs bro-
ken and the bodies
taken down. 32 The
soldiers therefore
came and broke
the legs of the
first man who had
been crucified
with Jesus, and
then those of the
other. 33 But when
they came to Jesus
and found that he
was already dead,
they did

[a] 26 The Greek for *Woman* does not denote any disrespect.

τὸν μαθητὴν παρεστῶτα ὃν ἠγάπα, λέγει τῇ μητρί· γύναι,
the disciple whom he loved standing there, *whom he loved* he said ⌞to his⌟ mother, “Woman,
3836 3412 4005 26 26 4225 4005 26 3306 3836 3613 1222
d.asm n.asm pt.ra.asm r.asm v.iai.3s v.pai.3s d.dsf n.dsf n.vsf

ἴδε ὁ υἱός σου. 27 εἶτα λέγει τῷ μαθητῇ, ἴδε ἡ μήτηρ σου.
look, *{the}* your son!” *your* Then he said ⌞to his⌟ disciple, “Look, *{the}* your mother!” *your*
2623 3836 5148 5626 5148 1663 3306 3836 3412 2623 3836 5148 3613 5148
pl d.nsm n.nsm r.gs.2 adv v.pai.3s d.dsm n.dsm pl d.nsf n.nsf r.gs.2

καὶ ἀπ’ ἐκείνης τῆς ὥρας ἔλαβεν ὁ μαθητὴς αὐτὴν εἰς τὰ ἴδια.
And from that *{the}* hour the disciple took *the* *disciple* her into *{the}* his own
2779 608 1697 3836 6052 3836 3412 3284 3836 3412 899 1650 3836 2625
cj p.g r.gsf d.gsf n.gsf v.aai.3s d.nsm n.nsm r.asf.3 p.a d.apn a.apn

28 μετὰ τοῦτο εἰδὼς ὁ Ἰησοῦς ὅτι ↱ ἤδη πάντα τετέλεσται,
home. After this Jesus, knowing *{the}* *Jesus* that all was now *all* accomplished,
3552 4047 2652 3857 3836 2652 4022 4246 5464 2453 4246 5464
p.a r.asn pt.ra.nsm d.nsm n.nsm cj adv a.npn v.rpi.3s

ἵνα τελειωθῇ ἡ γραφή, λέγει, διψῶ. 29 σκεῦος
so that the Scripture would be fulfilled, *the* *Scripture* said, “I am thirsty.” A jar full of
2671 3836 1210 5457 3836 1210 3306 1498 5007 3550
cj v.aps.3s d.nsf n.nsf v.pai.3s v.pai.1s n.nsn

ἔκειτο ὄξους μεστόν· ↱ σπόγγον οὖν μεστὸν τοῦ
sour wine was there, *sour wine* *full* so they attached a sponge *so* ⌞soaked in⌟ the
3954 3954 3023 3954 3550 4036 4712 4363 5074 4036 3550 3836
v.imi.3s n.gsn a.nsn n.asm cj a.asm d.gsn

ὄξους → ὑσσώπῳ περιθέντες προσήνεγκαν αὐτοῦ τῷ στόματι.
sour wine to a stalk of hyssop *attached* and held it to his *to* mouth.
3954 5727 4363 4712 3836 899 3836 5125
n.gsn n.dsf pt.aa.npm v.aai.3p r.gsm.3 d.dsn n.dsn

30 ὅτε οὖν ἔλαβεν τὸ ὄξος ὁ[a] Ἰησοῦς εἶπεν, τετέλεσται, καὶ ↱
When *{then}* he had taken the ⌞sour wine,⌟ *{the}* Jesus said, “It is accomplished!” And he
4021 4036 3284 3836 3954 3836 2652 3306 5464 2779 4140
cj cj v.aai.3s d.asn n.asn d.nsm n.nsm v.aai.3s v.rpi.3s cj

κλίνας τὴν κεφαλὴν παρέδωκεν τὸ πνεῦμα. 31 οἱ οὖν Ἰουδαῖοι, ἐπεὶ
bowed his head and handed over his spirit. *the* Then, *Jews* since it was
3111 3836 3051 4140 3836 4460 3836 4036 2681 2075 1639 1639
pt.aa.nsm d.asf n.asf v.aai.3s d.asn n.asn d.npm cj a.npm cj

παρασκευὴ ἦν, ἵνα ↱ μὴ μείνῃ ἐπὶ τοῦ σταυροῦ τὰ
the day of Preparation, *it was* so that the bodies would not remain on the cross *the*
4187 1639 2671 3836 5393 3531 3590 3531 2093 3836 5089 3836
n.nsf v.iai.3s cj pl v.aas.3s p.g d.gsm n.gsm d.npn

σώματα ἐν τῷ σαββάτῳ, ἦν γὰρ μεγάλη ἡ ἡμέρα ἐκείνου τοῦ
bodies on the Sabbath (for that Sabbath was *for* a high *{the}* day), *that* *{the}*
5393 1877 3836 4879 1142 1697 4879 1639 1142 3489 3836 2465 1697 3836
n.npn p.d d.dsn n.dsn v.iai.3s cj a.nsf d.nsf n.nsf r.gsn d.gsn

σαββάτου, ἠρώτησαν τὸν Πιλᾶτον ἵνα →
Sabbath the Jews asked *{the}* Pilate to have the legs of the crucified men
4879 3836 2681 2263 3836 4397 2671 3836 5003 899 899 899
n.gsn v.aai.3p d.asm n.asm cj

κατεαγῶσιν αὐτῶν τὰ σκέλη καὶ ἀρθῶσιν. 32
broken *of crucified men* *the* *legs* and their bodies taken down. So the soldiers
2862 899 3836 5003 2779 149 4036 3836 5132
v.aps.3p r.gpm.3 d.apn n.apn cj v.aps.3p

ἦλθον οὖν οἱ στρατιῶται καὶ τοῦ μὲν πρώτου κατέαξαν τὰ σκέλη
came *So* *the* *soldiers* and broke the legs of the ~ first man, *broke* *the* *legs*
2262 4036 3836 5132 2779 2862 3836 5003 3836 3525 4755 2862 3836 5003
v.aai.3p cj d.npm n.npm cj d.gsm pl a.gsm v.aai.3p d.apn n.apn

καὶ τοῦ ἄλλου τοῦ συσταυρωθέντος αὐτῷ· 33 ἐπὶ δὲ
then those of the other one who had been crucified with him. But when they came to *But*
2779 3836 257 3836 5365 899 1254 2262 2262 2262 2093 1254
cj d.gsm r.gsm d.gsm pt.ap.gsm r.dsm.3 p.a cj

τὸν Ἰησοῦν ἐλθόντες, ὡς εἶδον ↱ ἤδη αὐτὸν τεθνηκότα, ↱ ↱
{the} Jesus *when they came* *{as}* and saw that he was already *he* dead, they did
3836 2652 2262 6055 1625 899 2569 2453 899 2569 2862 2862
d.asm n.asm pt.aa.npm cj v.aai.3p adv r.asm.3 pt.ra.asm

[a] [ὁ] UBS.

NASB

and the disciple
whom He loved
standing nearby,
He *said to His
mother, “Woman,
behold, your son!”
27 Then He *said
to the disciple,
“Behold, your
mother!” From that
hour the disciple
took her into his
own *household.*
28 After this, Jesus,
knowing that all
things had already
been accom-
plished, to fulfill
the Scripture, *said,
“I am thirsty.” 29 A
jar full of sour
wine was standing
there; so they put a
sponge full of the
sour wine upon *a
branch of* hyssop
and brought it up to
His mouth. 30 There-
fore when Jesus
had received the
sour wine, He said,
“It is finished!”
And He bowed His
head and gave up
His spirit.

Care of the Body of Jesus

31 Then the Jews,
because it was the
day of preparation,
so that the bodies
would not remain
on the cross on the
Sabbath (for that
Sabbath was a high
day), asked Pilate
that their legs
might be broken,
and *that* they might
be taken away. 32 So
the soldiers came,
and broke the legs
of the first man and
of the other who
was crucified with
Him; 33 but coming
to Jesus, when they
saw that He was al-
ready dead, they

NIV

not break his legs.
34 Instead, one of
the soldiers pierced
Jesus' side with
a spear, bringing
a sudden flow of
blood and water.
35 The man who
saw it has given
testimony, and
his testimony is
true. He knows
that he tells the
truth, and he tes-
tifies so that you
also may believe.
36 These things hap-
pened so that the
scripture would
be fulfilled: "Not
one of his bones
will be broken,"[a]
37 and, as anoth-
er scripture says,
"They will look on
the one they have
pierced."[b]

The Burial of Jesus

38 Later, Joseph of
Arimathea asked
Pilate for the body
of Jesus. Now Jo-
seph was a disciple
of Jesus, but se-
cretly because he
feared the Jewish
leaders. With Pi-
late's permission,
he came and took
the body away.
39 He was accom-
panied by Nicode-
mus, the man who
earlier had visited
Jesus at night. Nic-
odemus brought a
mixture of myrrh
and aloes, about
seventy-five
pounds.[c] 40 Tak-
ing Jesus' body,
the two of them
wrapped it, with
the spices, in strips
of linen. This was
in accordance
with Jewish burial
customs. 41 At the
place where Jesus
was crucified,
there was a gar-
den, and

[a] 36 Exodus 12:46; Num. 9:12; Psalm 34:20
[b] 37 Zech. 12:10
[c] 39 Or about 34 kilograms

οὐ κατέαξαν αὐτοῦ τὰ σκέλη, 34 ἀλλ᾽ εἷς τῶν στρατιωτῶν λόγχῃ
not break his {the} legs. Instead, one of the soldiers *with spear* pierced
4024 2862 899 3836 5003 247 1651 3836 5132 3365 3817
pl v.aai.3p r.gsm.3 d.apn n.apn cj a.nsm d.gpm n.gpm n.dsf

αὐτοῦ τὴν πλευρὰν ἔνυξεν, καὶ ἐξῆλθεν
his {the} side with a spear, *pierced* and immediately blood and water came out.
899 3836 4433 3365 3365 3817 2779 2318 135 2779 5623 2002
r.gsm.3 d.asf n.asf v.aai.3s cj v.aai.3s

εὐθὺς αἷμα καὶ ὕδωρ. 35 καὶ ὁ ἑωρακὼς μεμαρτύρηκεν,
immediately blood and water {and} (The man who saw this has borne witness to it so that
2318 135 2779 5623 2779 3836 3972 3455 2671 2671
adv n.nsn cj n.nsn cj d.nsm pt.ra.nsm v.rai.3s

καὶ ἀληθινὴ αὐτοῦ ἐστιν ἡ μαρτυρία, καὶ
you too may believe. {and} His witness is true, *His is* {the} *witness* and
7007 2779 4409 4409 2779 899 3456 1639 240 899 1639 3836 3456 2779
cj a.nsf r.gsm.3 v.pai.3s d.nsf n.nsf cj

ἐκεῖνος οἶδεν ὅτι ἀληθῆ λέγει, ἵνα καὶ ὑμεῖς πιστεύσητε.[a]
he knows that he is telling the truth.) *he is telling so that too you may believe*
1697 3857 4022 3306 3306 3306 239 3306 2671 2779 7007 4409
r.nsm v.rai.3s cj a.apn v.pai.3s cj adv r.np.2 v.aas.2p

36 ἐγένετο γὰρ ταῦτα ἵνα ἡ γραφὴ πληρωθῇ· ὀστοῦν
These things took place {for} *These things* so that the Scripture would be fulfilled, "Not a bone
4047 4047 1181 1142 4047 2671 3836 1210 4444 4024 4014
v.ami.3s cj r.npn cj d.nsf n.nsf v.aps.3s n.nsn

οὐ συντριβήσεται αὐτοῦ. 37 καὶ πάλιν ἑτέρα γραφὴ λέγει,
Not of his body will be broken." *of his* And yet another Scripture says,
4024 899 899 5341 899 2779 4099 2283 1210 3306
pl v.fpi.3s r.gsm.3 cj adv r.nsf n.nsf v.pai.3s

ὄψονται εἰς ὃν ἐξεκέντησαν. 38 μετὰ δὲ ταῦτα ἠρώτησεν τὸν Πιλᾶτον
⌊"They will look⌋ on him whom they pierced." After {and} this *asked* {the} *Pilate*
3972 1650 4005 1708 3552 1254 4047 2263 3836 4397
v.fmi.3p p.a r.asm v.aai.3p p.a cj r.apn v.aai.3s d.asm n.asm

Ἰωσὴφ ὁ[b] ἀπὸ Ἀριμαθαίας, ὢν μαθητὴς τοῦ Ἰησοῦ· → κεκρυμμένος
Joseph {the} of Arimathea, {being} a disciple of Jesus (though a secret one
2737 3836 608 751 1639 3412 3836 2652 3221
n.nsm d.nsm p.g n.gsf pt.pa.nsm n.nsm d.gsm n.gsm pt.rp.nsm

δὲ διὰ τὸν φόβον τῶν Ἰουδαίων, ἵνα ἄρῃ τὸ σῶμα τοῦ
{and} ⌊due to⌋ his fear of the Jews) asked Pilate if ⌊he could remove⌋ the body of
1254 1328 3836 5832 3836 2681 2263 4397 2671 149 3836 5393 3836
cj p.a d.asm n.asm d.gpm a.gpm cj v.aas.3s d.asn n.asn d.gsm

Ἰησοῦ· καὶ → ἐπέτρεψεν ὁ Πιλᾶτος. ἦλθεν οὖν καὶ ἦρεν τὸ
Jesus. {and} Pilate gave him permission, {the} *Pilate* so he came *so* and removed the
2652 2779 4397 2205 3836 4397 4036 2262 4036 2779 149 3836
n.gsm cj v.aai.3s d.nsm n.nsm v.aai.3s cj cj v.aai.3s d.asn

σῶμα αὐτοῦ. 39 ἦλθεν δὲ καὶ Νικόδημος, ὁ ἐλθὼν πρὸς αὐτὸν νυκτὸς
body. *came* {and} *also* Nicodemus, who earlier had come to Jesus at night,
5393 899 2262 1254 2779 3773 3836 4754 2262 4639 899 3816
n.asn r.gsm.3 v.aai.3s cj adv n.nsm d.nsm pt.aa.nsm p.a r.asm.3 n.gsf

τὸ πρῶτον, φέρων μίγμα σμύρνης καὶ ἀλόης ὡς ⌊λίτρας
{the} *earlier* also came, bringing a mixture of myrrh and aloes, about seventy-five pounds.
3836 4754 2779 2262 5770 3623 5043 2779 264 6055 3354
d.asn adv pt.pa.nsm n.asn n.gsf cj n.gsf pl n.apf

ἑκατόν.⌋ 40 ἔλαβον οὖν τὸ σῶμα τοῦ Ἰησοῦ καὶ ἔδησαν αὐτὸ ὀθονίοις
So they took *So* the body of Jesus and wrapped it ⌊in strips of linen⌋
1669 4036 3284 4036 3836 5393 3836 2652 2779 1313 899 3856
a.apf v.aai.3p cj d.asn n.asn d.gsm n.gsm cj v.aai.3p r.asn.3 n.dpn

μετὰ τῶν ἀρωμάτων, καθὼς ἔθος ἐστὶν τοῖς Ἰουδαίοις
with the spices, ⌊in accordance with⌋ the Jewish custom {it is} {the} *Jewish*
3552 3836 808 2777 2681 1621 1639 3836 2681
p.g d.gpn n.gpn cj n.nsn v.pai.3s d.dpm a.dpm

ἐνταφιάζειν. 41 ἦν δὲ ἐν τῷ τόπῳ ὅπου ἐσταυρώθη κῆπος, καὶ
for burial. *there was* Now in the place where he was crucified there was a garden, and
1946 1639 1254 1877 3836 5536 3963 5090 1639 1639 3057 2779
f.pa v.iai.3s cj p.d d.dsm n.dsm cj v.api.3s n.nsm cj

[a] πιστεύ[σ]ητε UBS. πιστεύσητε NET. πιστεύητε TNIV.
[b] [ὁ] UBS.

NASB

did not break His
legs. 34 But one of
the soldiers pierced
His side with a
spear, and imme-
diately blood and
water came out.
35 And he who has
seen has testified,
and his testimony
is true; and he
knows that he is
telling the truth,
so that you also
may believe. 36 For
these things came
to pass to fulfill the
Scripture, "NOT A
BONE OF HIM SHALL
BE BROKEN." 37 And
again another
Scripture says,
"THEY SHALL LOOK
ON HIM WHOM THEY
PIERCED."
38 After these
things Joseph of
Arimathea, being
a disciple of Jesus,
but a secret *one* for
fear of the Jews,
asked Pilate that he
might take away
the body of Jesus;
and Pilate granted
permission. So
he came and took
away His body.
39 Nicodemus, who
had first come to
Him by night, also
came, bringing a
mixture of myrrh
and aloes, about
a hundred pounds
weight. 40 So they
took the body of
Jesus and bound it
in linen wrappings
with the spices, as
is the burial custom
of the Jews. 41 Now
in the place where
He was crucified
there was a garden,

NIV

in the garden a new
tomb, in which no
one had ever been
laid. 42 Because it
was the Jewish day
of Preparation and
since the tomb was
nearby, they laid
Jesus there.

The Empty Tomb

20 Early on
the first day
of the week, while
it was still dark,
Mary Magdalene
went to the tomb
and saw that the
stone had been
removed from the
entrance. 2 So she
came running to
Simon Peter and
the other disci-
ple, the one Jesus
loved, and said,
"They have taken
the Lord out of the
tomb, and we don't
know where they
have put him!"
3 So Peter and
the other disci-
ple started for
the tomb. 4 Both
were running, but
the other disciple
outran Peter and
reached the tomb
first. 5 He bent over
and looked in at
the strips of linen
lying there but did
not go in. 6 Then
Simon Peter came
along behind him
and went straight
into the tomb. He
saw the strips of
linen lying there,
7 as well as the
cloth that had been
wrapped around
Jesus' head. The
cloth was still ly-
ing in its place,

ἐν τῷ κήπῳ μνημεῖον καινὸν ἐν ᾧ ↱ οὐδέπω οὐδεὶς ἦν
in the garden was a new tomb *new* in which no one had ever yet *no one* been
1877 3836 3057 2785 3646 2785 1877 4005 4029 4029 1639 4031 4029 1639
p.d d.dsm n.dsm n.nsn a.nsn p.d r.dsn adv a.nsm v.iai.3s

τεθειμένος· 42 ἐκεῖ οὖν διὰ τὴν παρασκευὴν τῶν Ἰουδαίων, ὅτι
laid. *there* So because it was the Jewish day of Preparation *{the}* *Jewish* *{that}*
5502 1695 4036 1328 3836 2681 4187 3836 2681 4022
pt.rp.nsm adv cj p.a d.asf n.asf d.gpm a.gpm cj

ἐγγὺς ἦν τὸ μνημεῖον, ἔθηκαν τὸν Ἰησοῦν.
and the tomb was nearby, *was* *the* *tomb* they laid *{the}* Jesus there.
3836 3646 1639 1584 1639 3836 3646 5502 3836 2652 1695
adv v.iai.3s d.nsn n.nsn v.aai.3p d.asm n.asm

20:1 τῇ δὲ μιᾷ τῶν σαββάτων Μαρία ἡ Μαγδαληνὴ ἔρχεται
Now ⌊on the⌋ *Now* first day of the week Mary *{the}* Magdalene came
1254 3836 1254 1651 3836 4879 3451 3836 3402 2262
d.dsf cj a.dsf d.gpn n.gpn n.nsf d.nsf n.nsf v.pmi.3s

πρωῒ σκοτίας ἔτι οὔσης εἰς τὸ μνημεῖον καὶ
early to the tomb, while it was still dark, *still* *while it was* *to* *the* *tomb* and
4745 1650 3836 3646 1639 1639 1639 2285 5028 2285 1639 1650 3836 3646 2779
adv n.gsf adv pt.pa.gsf p.a d.asn n.asn cj

βλέπει τὸν λίθον ἠρμένον ἐκ τοῦ μνημείου. 2 τρέχει οὖν καὶ
she saw the stone removed from the tomb. So ⌊she went running⌋ *So* *{and}*
1063 3836 3345 149 1666 3836 3646 4036 5556 4036 2779
v.pai.3s d.asm n.asm pt.rp.asm p.g d.gsn n.gsn v.pai.3s cj cj

ἔρχεται πρὸς Σίμωνα Πέτρον καὶ πρὸς τὸν ἄλλον μαθητὴν ὃν ἐφίλει
{she came} to Simon Peter and *{to}* the other disciple, the one whom Jesus loved,
2262 4639 4981 4377 2779 4639 3836 257 3412 4005 2652 5797
v.pmi.3s p.a n.asm n.asm cj p.a d.asm r.asm n.asm r.asm v.iai.3s

ὁ Ἰησοῦς καὶ λέγει αὐτοῖς, ἦραν τὸν κύριον ἐκ τοῦ μνημείου καὶ
{the} *Jesus* and said to them, ⌊"They have taken⌋ our Master ⌊out of⌋ the tomb, and
3836 2652 2779 3306 899 149 3836 3261 1666 3836 3646 2779
d.nsm n.nsm cj v.pai.3s r.dpm.3 v.aai.3p d.asm n.asm p.g d.gsn n.gsn cj

↱ ↱ οὐκ οἴδαμεν ποῦ ἔθηκαν αὐτόν. 3 ἐξῆλθεν οὖν ὁ Πέτρος καὶ ὁ
we do not know where ⌊they have put⌋ him!" *set out* So *{the}* Peter and the
3857 3857 4024 3857 4543 5502 899 2002 4036 3836 4377 2779 3836
pl v.rai.1p cj v.aai.3p r.asm.3 v.aai.3s cj d.nsm n.nsm cj d.nsm

ἄλλος μαθητὴς καὶ ἤρχοντο εἰς τὸ μνημεῖον. 4 ἔτρεχον δὲ
other disciple set out *{and}* to go to the tomb. The two were running *{and}*
257 3412 2002 2002 2779 2262 1650 3836 3646 3836 1545 5556 1254
r.nsm n.nsm cj v.imi.3p p.a d.asn n.asn v.iai.3p cj

οἱ δύο ὁμοῦ· καὶ ὁ ἄλλος μαθητὴς προέδραμεν τάχιον τοῦ Πέτρου καὶ
The *two* together, but the other disciple ran ahead more quickly than Peter and
3836 1545 3938 2779 3836 257 3412 4731 5441 3836 4377 2779
d.npm a.npm adv cj d.nsm r.nsm n.nsm v.aai.3s adv.c d.gsm n.gsm cj

ἦλθεν πρῶτος εἰς τὸ μνημεῖον, 5 καὶ παρακύψας βλέπει
arrived first at the tomb. *{and}* ⌊When he stooped down to look in,⌋ he saw the linen
2262 4755 1650 3836 3646 2779 4160 1063 3836 3856
v.aai.3s a.nsm p.a d.asn n.asn cj pt.aa.nsm v.pai.3s

κείμενα τὰ ὀθόνια, ↱ ↱ οὐ μέντοι εἰσῆλθεν. 6 ἔρχεται οὖν
wrappings lying there *the* *linen wrappings* but he did not *but* go in. *arrived* Then
3856 3023 3836 3856 3530 1656 1656 4024 3530 1656 2262 4036
pt.pm.apn d.apn n.apn pl cj v.aai.3s v.pmi.3s cj

καὶ Σίμων Πέτρος ἀκολουθῶν αὐτῷ καὶ εἰσῆλθεν εἰς τὸ
also Simon Peter, ⌊who had been behind⌋ him, also arrived, and he went right into the
2779 4981 4377 199 899 2779 2262 2779 1656 1650 3836
adv n.nsm n.nsm pt.pa.nsm r.dsm.3 cj v.aai.3s p.a d.asn

μνημεῖον, καὶ θεωρεῖ τὰ ὀθόνια κείμενα, 7 καὶ τὸ σουδάριον, ὃ ἦν
tomb. *{and}* He saw the linen wrappings lying there, and the face cloth that ⌊had been⌋
3646 2779 2555 3836 3856 3023 2779 3836 5051 4005 1639
n.asn cj v.pai.3s d.apn n.apn pt.pm.apn cj d.asn n.asn r.nsn v.iai.3s

ἐπὶ τῆς κεφαλῆς αὐτοῦ, οὐ μετὰ τῶν ὀθονίων κείμενον
on *{the}* Jesus' head; *Jesus'* it was not lying with the linen wrappings *it was lying*
2093 3836 899 3051 899 3023 3023 4024 3023 3552 3836 3856 3023
p.g d.gsf n.gsf r.gsm.3 pl p.g d.gpn n.gpn pt.pm.asn

NASB

and in the garden
a new tomb in
which no one
had yet been laid.
42 Therefore because
of the Jewish day
of preparation,
since the tomb was
nearby, they laid
Jesus there.

The Empty Tomb

20:1 Now on the first
day of the week
Mary Magdalene
*came early to the
tomb, while it *was
still dark, and *saw
the stone *already*
taken away from
the tomb. 2 So she
*ran and *came to
Simon Peter and to
the other disciple
whom Jesus loved,
and *said to them,
"They have taken
away the Lord
out of the tomb,
and we do not
know where they
have laid Him."
3 So Peter and the
other disciple
went forth, and
they were going
to the tomb. 4 The
two were running
together; and the
other disciple ran
ahead faster than
Peter and came
to the tomb first;
5 and stooping and
looking in, he *saw
the linen wrap-
pings lying *there;*
but he did not go
in. 6 And so Simon
Peter also *came,
following him,
and entered the
tomb; and he *saw
the linen wrap-
pings lying *there,*
7 and the face-cloth
which had been on
His head, not ly-
ing with the linen
wrappings, but

NIV

separate from the
linen. 8 Finally the
other disciple, who
had reached the
tomb first, also
went inside. He
saw and believed.
9 (They still did not
understand from
Scripture that Jesus
had to rise from the
dead.) 10 Then the
disciples went back
to where they were
staying.

Jesus Appears to Mary Magdalene

11 Now Mary
stood outside the
tomb crying. As
she wept, she bent
over to look into
the tomb 12 and
saw two angels
in white, seated
where Jesus' body
had been, one at
the head and the
other at the foot.
13 They asked her,
"Woman, why are
you crying?"
"They have taken
my Lord away,"
she said, "and I
don't know where
they have put
him." 14 At this, she
turned around and
saw Jesus standing
there, but she did
not realize that it
was Jesus.
15 He asked her,
"Woman, why are
you crying? Who
is it you are look-
ing for?"
Thinking he
was the gardener,
she said, "Sir, if
you have carried
him away, tell me
where you have
put him, and I will

ἀλλὰ χωρὶς ἐντετυλιγμένον εἰς ἕνα τόπον. 8 ⌞τότε οὖν⌟
but rolled up in one place by itself. *rolled up* *in* *one* *place* Then
247 1962 1962 1650 1651 5536 6006 1962 1650 1651 5536 5538 4036
cj adv pt.rp.asn p.a a.asm n.asm adv cj

εἰσῆλθεν καὶ ὁ ἄλλος μαθητὴς
the other disciple, the one who had arrived first, also went *also* *the* *other* *disciple*
3836 257 3412 3836 2262 2262 2262 2262 4755 2779 1656 2779 3836 257 3412
v.aai.3s adv d.nsm r.nsm n.nsm

ὁ ἐλθὼν πρῶτος εἰς τὸ μνημεῖον καὶ εἶδεν καὶ ἐπίστευσεν· 9 ↱ →
the *one who had arrived* *first* into the tomb, and he saw and believed. (They still
3836 2262 4755 1650 3836 3646 2779 1625 2779 4409 3857
d.nsm pt.aa.nsm a.nsm p.a d.asn n.asn cj v.aai.3s cj v.aai.3s

↱ οὐδέπω γὰρ ᾔδεισαν τὴν γραφὴν ὅτι δεῖ αὐτὸν ἐκ νεκρῶν
did not *{for}* understand the Scripture that Jesus must *Jesus* rise from the dead.)
3857 4031 1142 3857 3836 1210 4022 899 1256 899 482 1666 3738
adv cj v.lai.3p d.asf n.asf cj v.pai.3s r.asm.3 p.g a.gpm

ἀναστῆναι. 10 ἀπῆλθον οὖν πάλιν πρὸς αὐτοὺς οἱ μαθηταί.
rise So the disciples returned *So* *{again}* to their homes. *the* *disciples*
482 4036 3836 3412 599 4036 4099 4639 899 3836 3412
f.aa v.aai.3p cj adv p.a r.apm.3 d.npm n.npm

11 Μαρία δὲ εἱστήκει πρὸς τῷ μνημείῳ ἔξω κλαίουσα. ὡς
But Mary *But* stood weeping outside *{at}* the tomb. *outside* *weeping* As
1254 3451 1254 2705 3081 2032 4639 3836 3646 2032 3081 6055
n.nsf cj v.lai.3s p.d d.dsn n.dsn adv pt.pa.nsf cj

οὖν ἔκλαιεν, παρέκυψεν εἰς τὸ μνημεῖον 12 καὶ θεωρεῖ δύο
{then} she was weeping ⌞she stooped down to look⌟ into the tomb. *{and}* She saw two
4036 3081 4160 1650 3836 3646 2779 2555 1545
cj v.iai.3s v.aai.3s p.a d.asn n.asn cj v.pai.3s a.apm

ἀγγέλους ἐν λευκοῖς καθεζομένους, ἕνα πρὸς τῇ κεφαλῇ καὶ ἕνα πρὸς τοῖς
angels in white sitting there, one at the head and the other at the
34 1877 3328 2757 1651 4639 3836 3051 2779 1651 4639 3836
n.apm p.d a.dpn pt.pm.apm a.asm p.d d.dsf n.dsf cj a.asm p.d d.dpm

ποσίν, ὅπου ἔκειτο τὸ σῶμα τοῦ Ἰησοῦ.
feet of the place where the body of Jesus ⌞had been lying.⌟ *the* *body* *of* *Jesus*
4546 3963 3836 5393 3836 2652 3023 3836 5393 3836 2652
n.dpm cj v.imi.3s d.nsn n.nsn d.gsm n.gsm

13 καὶ λέγουσιν αὐτῇ ἐκεῖνοι, γύναι, τί κλαίεις; λέγει αὐτοῖς ὅτι
{and} They said to her, *They* "Woman, why are you weeping?" She said to them, ~
2779 1697 3306 899 1697 1222 5515 3081 3306 899 4022
cj v.pai.3p r.dsf.3 r.npm n.vsf r.asn v.pai.2s v.pai.3s r.dpm.3 cj

ἦραν τὸν κύριόν μου, καὶ ↱ ↱ οὐκ οἶδα ποῦ ἔθηκαν
⌞"They have taken away⌟ *{the}* my Master, *my* and I do not know where ⌞they have put⌟
149 3836 1609 3261 1609 2779 3857 3857 4024 3857 4543 5502
v.aai.3p d.asm n.asm r.gs.1 cj pl v.rai.1s cj v.aai.3p

αὐτόν. 14 ταῦτα εἰποῦσα ἐστράφη ⌞εἰς τὰ ὀπίσω⌟ καὶ θεωρεῖ τὸν
him." Having said this, *Having said* she turned around and saw *{the}*
899 3306 3306 4047 3306 5138 1650 3836 3958 2779 2555 3836
r.asm.3 r.apn pt.aa.nsf v.api.3s p.a d.apn adv cj v.pai.3s d.asm

Ἰησοῦν ἑστῶτα καὶ ↱ ↱ οὐκ ᾔδει ὅτι Ἰησοῦς ἐστιν. 15 λέγει
Jesus ⌞standing there,⌟ but she did not know that it was Jesus. *it was* Jesus said
2652 2705 2779 3857 3857 4024 3857 4022 1639 1639 2652 1639 2652 3306
n.asm pt.ra.asm cj pl v.lai.3s cj n.nsm v.pai.3s v.pai.3s

αὐτῇ Ἰησοῦς, γύναι, τί κλαίεις; τίνα ζητεῖς; ἐκείνη
to her, *Jesus* "Woman, why are you weeping? Who is it that ⌞you are looking for?"⌟ *she*
899 2652 1222 5515 3081 5515 2426 1697
r.dsf.3 n.nsm n.vsf r.asn v.pai.2s r.asm v.pai.2s r.nsf

δοκοῦσα ὅτι ὁ κηπουρός ἐστιν λέγει αὐτῷ, κύριε, εἰ σὺ
Thinking that he was the gardener, *he was* she said to him, "Sir, if you
1506 4022 1639 1639 3836 3058 1639 1697 3306 899 3261 1623 5148
pt.pa.nsf cj d.nsm n.nsm v.pai.3s v.pai.3s r.dsm.3 n.vsm cj r.ns.2

ἐβάστασας αὐτόν, ↰ εἰπέ μοι ποῦ ἔθηκας αὐτόν, κἀγὼ
⌞are the one who carried⌟ him away, tell me where ⌞you have put⌟ him, and I will take
1002 899 1002 3306 1609 4543 5502 899 2743 149 149
v.aai.2s r.asm.3 v.aam.2s r.ds.1 cj v.aai.2s r.asm.3 crasis

NASB

rolled up in a place
by itself. 8 So the
other disciple who
had first come to
the tomb then also
entered, and he
saw and believed.
9 For as yet they
did not understand
the Scripture, that
He must rise again
from the dead. 10 So
the disciples went
away again to their
own homes.
11 But Mary was
standing outside
the tomb weep-
ing; and so, as she
wept, she stooped
and looked into
the tomb; 12 and she
*saw two angels in
white sitting, one
at the head and one
at the feet, where
the body of Jesus
had been lying.
13 And they *said to
her, "Woman, why
are you weeping?"
She *said to them,
"Because they
have taken away
my Lord, and I do
not know where
they have laid
Him." 14 When she
had said this, she
turned around and
*saw Jesus standing
there, and did not
know that it was
Jesus. 15 Jesus *said
to her, "Woman,
why are you weep-
ing? Whom are
you seeking?" Sup-
posing Him to be
the gardener, she
*said to Him, "Sir,
if you have carried
Him away, tell me
where you have
laid Him, and I will
take Him away."

NIV

get him."
[16]Jesus said to
her, "Mary."
She turned to-
ward him and
cried out in Ara-
maic, "Rabboni!"
(which means
"Teacher").
[17]Jesus said, "Do
not hold on to me,
for I have not yet
ascended to the
Father. Go instead
to my brothers and
tell them, 'I am
ascending to my
Father and your
Father, to my God
and your God.'"
[18]Mary Magda-
lene went to the
disciples with the
news: "I have seen
the Lord!" And
she told them that
he had said these
things to her.

Jesus Appears to His Disciples

[19]On the evening
of that first day of
the week, when
the disciples were
together, with the
doors locked for
fear of the Jew-
ish leaders, Jesus
came and stood
among them and
said, "Peace be
with you!" [20]Af-
ter he said this, he
showed them his
hands and side.
The disciples were
overjoyed when
they saw the Lord.
[21]Again Jesus
said, "Peace be
with you! As the
Father has sent me,
I am sending you."
[22]And with that he
breathed on them
and said, "Receive
the Holy Spirit.
[23]If you forgive

αὐτὸν ἀρῶ. 16 λέγει αὐτῇ Ἰησοῦς, Μαριάμ. στραφεῖσα ἐκείνη
him away." *will take away* Jesus said to her, *Jesus* "Mary!" She turned *She*
899 149 149 2652 3306 899 2652 3452 1697 5138 1697
r.asm.3 v.fai.1s v.pai.3s r.dsf.3 n.nsm n.vsf pt.ap.nsf r.nsf

λέγει αὐτῷ Ἑβραϊστί, ραββουνι (ὃ λέγεται διδάσκαλε). 17 λέγει αὐτῇ
and said to him in Hebrew, "Rabbouni!" (which means "Teacher"). Jesus said to her,
3306 899 1580 4808 4005 3306 1437 2652 3306 899
v.pai.3s r.dsm.3 adv n.vsm r.nsn v.ppi.3s n.vsm v.pai.3s r.dsf.3

Ἰησοῦς, μή μου ἅπτου, ↱ ↱ οὔπω γὰρ ἀναβέβηκα πρὸς
Jesus "Do not hold on to me, *Do hold on to* for I have not yet *for* ascended to
2652 721 3590 721 721 721 1609 721 1142 326 326 4037 1142 326 4639
n.nsm pl r.gs.1 v.pmm.2s adv cj v.rai.1s p.a

τὸν πατέρα· πορεύου δὲ πρὸς τοὺς ἀδελφούς μου καὶ εἰπὲ αὐτοῖς,
the Father. But go *But* to *{the}* my brothers *my* and say to them,
3836 4252 1254 4513 1254 4639 3836 1609 81 1609 2779 3306 899
d.asm n.asm v.pmm.2s cj p.a d.apm n.apm r.gs.1 cj v.aam.2s r.dpm.3

ἀναβαίνω πρὸς τὸν πατέρα μου καὶ πατέρα ὑμῶν καὶ ↰ θεόν μου
'I am ascending to *{the}* my Father *my* and your Father, *your* *{and}* to my God *my*
326 4639 3836 1609 4252 1609 2779 7007 4252 7007 2779 4639 1609 2536 1609
v.pai.1s p.a d.asm n.asm r.gs.1 cj n.asm r.gp.2 cj n.asm r.gs.1

καὶ θεὸν ὑμῶν. 18 ἔρχεται Μαριὰμ ἡ Μαγδαληνὴ
and your God.'" *your* Mary Magdalene went *Mary* *{the}* *Magdalene* and
2779 7007 2536 7007 3452 3402 2262 3452 3836 3402
cj n.asm r.gp.2 v.pmi.3s n.nsf d.nsf n.nsf

ἀγγέλλουσα τοῖς μαθηταῖς ὅτι ἑώρακα τὸν κύριον, καὶ
reported to the disciples, ~ "I have seen the Master!" and she told them that he had
33 3836 3412 4022 3972 3836 3261 2779 3306 3306
pt.pa.nsf d.dpm n.dpm cj v.rai.1s d.asm n.asm cj

ταῦτα εἶπεν αὐτῇ. 19 οὔσης οὖν ὀψίας τῇ ἡμέρᾳ ἐκείνῃ τῇ
said these things *he had said* to her. On *{then}* the evening *{the}* of that day, *that* the
3306 4047 3306 899 1639 4036 4068 3836 1697 2465 1697 3836
r.apn v.aai.3s r.dsf.3 pt.pa.gsf cj n.gsf d.dsf n.dsf r.dsf d.dsf

μιᾷ → σαββάτων καὶ ↱ τῶν θυρῶν κεκλεισμένων ὅπου ἦσαν
first day of the week, *{and}* when the doors were locked where the disciples were
1651 4879 2779 3091 3836 2598 3091 3963 3836 3412 1639
a.dsf n.gpn cj d.gpf n.gpf pt.rp.gpf cj v.iai.3p

οἱ μαθηταὶ διὰ τὸν φόβον τῶν Ἰουδαίων, ἦλθεν ὁ Ἰησοῦς καὶ ἔστη εἰς
the *disciples* for *{the}* fear of the Jews, Jesus came *{the}* *Jesus* and stood in
3836 3412 1328 3836 5832 3836 2681 2652 2262 3836 2652 2779 2705 1650
d.npm n.npm p.a d.asm n.asm d.gpm a.gpm v.aai.3s d.nsm n.nsm cj v.aai.3s p.a

τὸ μέσον καὶ λέγει αὐτοῖς, εἰρήνη ὑμῖν. 20 καὶ τοῦτο εἰπὼν
their midst and said to them, "Peace be with you." *{and}* Having said this, *Having said*
3836 3545 2779 3306 899 1645 7007 2779 3306 3306 4047 3306
d.asn n.asn cj v.pai.3s r.dpm.3 n.nsf r.dp.2 cj r.asn pt.aa.nsm

ἔδειξεν τὰς χεῖρας καὶ τὴν πλευρὰν αὐτοῖς. ἐχάρησαν
he showed them his hands and his side. *them* Then the disciples ˻were filled with joy˼
1259 899 3836 5931 2779 3836 4433 899 4036 3836 3412 5897
v.aai.3s d.apf n.apf cj d.asf n.asf r.dpm.3 v.api.3p

οὖν οἱ μαθηταὶ ἰδόντες τὸν κύριον. 21 εἶπεν οὖν αὐτοῖς [a]ὁ
Then *the* *disciples* ˻when they saw˼ the Lord. So Jesus said *So* to them *{the}*
4036 3836 3412 1625 3836 3261 4036 2652 3306 4036 899 3836
cj d.npm n.npm pt.aa.npm d.asm n.asm v.aai.3s cj r.dpm.3 d.nsm

Ἰησοῦς πάλιν, εἰρήνη ὑμῖν· καθὼς ἀπέσταλκέν με ὁ πατήρ, κἀγὼ
Jesus again, "Peace be with you. As the Father has sent me, *the* *Father* I also
2652 4099 1645 7007 2777 3836 4252 690 1609 3836 4252 2743
n.nsm adv n.nsf r.dp.2 cj v.rai.3s r.as.1 d.nsm n.nsm crasis

πέμπω ὑμᾶς. 22 καὶ τοῦτο εἰπὼν ἐνεφύσησεν καὶ λέγει
am sending you." *{and}* Having said this, *Having said* he breathed on them and said,
4287 7007 2779 3306 3306 4047 3306 1874 899 2779 3306
v.pai.1s r.ap.2 cj r.asn pt.aa.nsm v.aai.3s cj v.pai.3s

αὐτοῖς, λάβετε πνεῦμα ἅγιον· 23 ˻ἄν τινων˼ ἀφῆτε τὰς
them "Receive the Holy Spirit. *Holy* Whoever's sins you forgive, *{the}*
899 3284 41 4460 41 323 5516 281 918 3836
r.dpm.3 v.aam.2p n.asn a.asn cj r.gpm v.aas.2p d.apf

NASB

[16]Jesus *said to
her, "Mary!" She
turned and *said to
Him in Hebrew,
"Rabboni!" (which
means, Teacher).
[17]Jesus *said to her,
"Stop clinging to
Me, for I have not
yet ascended to the
Father; but go to
My brethren and
say to them, 'I as-
cend to My Father
and your Father,
and My God and
your God.'" [18]Mary
Magdalene *came,
announcing to the
disciples, "I have
seen the Lord," and
that He had said
these things to her.

Jesus among His Disciples

[19]So when it was
evening on that
day, the first *day*
of the week, and
when the doors
were shut where
the disciples were,
for fear of the
Jews, Jesus came
and stood in their
midst and *said to
them, "Peace *be*
with you." [20]And
when He had said
this, He showed
them both His
hands and His side.
The disciples then
rejoiced when they
saw the Lord. [21]So
Jesus said to them
again, "Peace *be*
with you; as the
Father has sent Me,
I also send you."
[22]And when He
had said this, He
breathed on them
and *said to them,
"Receive the Holy
Spirit. [23]If you for-
give the sins of

[a] [ὁ Ἰησοῦς] UBS.

NIV

anyone's sins, their
sins are forgiven; if
you do not forgive
them, they are not
forgiven."

Jesus Appears to Thomas

24 Now Thomas
(also known as
Didymus[a]), one
of the Twelve, was
not with the dis-
ciples when Jesus
came. 25 So the
other disciples told
him, "We have
seen the Lord!"
But he said to
them, "Unless I
see the nail marks
in his hands and
put my finger
where the nails
were, and put my
hand into his side,
I will not believe."
26 A week later his
disciples were in
the house again,
and Thomas was
with them. Though
the doors were
locked, Jesus came
and stood among
them and said,
"Peace be with
you!" 27 Then he
said to Thomas,
"Put your fin-
ger here; see my
hands. Reach out
your hand and put
it into my side.
Stop doubting and
believe."
28 Thomas said
to him, "My Lord
and my God!"
29 Then Jesus told
him, "Because
you have seen me,
you have believed;
blessed are those
who have not seen
and yet have be-
lieved."

The Purpose of John's Gospel

30 Jesus performed
many

[a] 24 *Thomas* (Aramaic) and *Didymus* (Greek) both mean *twin.*

ἁμαρτίας ἀφέωνται αὐτοῖς, ⌊ἄν τινων⌋ κρατῆτε
sins they stand forgiven; *they* whoever's sins ⌊you pronounce unforgiven,⌋
281 899 918 899 323 5516 3195
n.apf v.rpi.3p r.dpm.3 cj r.gpm v.pas.2p

κεκράτηνται. 24 Θωμᾶς δὲ εἷς ἐκ τῶν δώδεκα, ὁ
they remain unforgiven. But Thomas *But* (called the Twin), one of the twelve, *{the}*
3195 1254 2605 1254 3306 1441 1651 1666 3836 1557 3836
v.rpi.3p n.nsm cj a.nsm p.g d.gpm a.gpm d.nsm

λεγόμενος Δίδυμος, οὐκ ἦν μετ᾽ αὐτῶν ὅτε ἦλθεν Ἰησοῦς. 25
called *Twin* was not *was* with them when Jesus came. *Jesus* So the
3306 1441 1639 4024 1639 3552 899 4021 2652 2262 2652 4036 3836
pt.pp.nsm n.nsm pl v.iai.3s p.g r.gpm.3 cj v.aai.3s n.nsm

ἔλεγον οὖν αὐτῷ οἱ ἄλλοι μαθηταί, ἑωράκαμεν τὸν κύριον.
other disciples kept saying *So* to him, *the* *other* *disciples* "We have seen the Master!" But
257 3412 3306 4036 899 3836 257 3412 3972 3836 3261 1254
v.iai.3p cj r.dsm.3 d.npm r.npm n.npm v.rai.1p d.asm n.asm

ὁ δὲ εἶπεν αὐτοῖς, ⌊ἐὰν μὴ⌋ ἴδω ἐν ταῖς χερσὶν αὐτοῦ τὸν τύπον τῶν
he *But* said to them, "Unless I see in *{the}* his hands *his* the mark of the
3836 1254 3306 899 1569 3590 1625 1877 3836 899 5931 899 3836 5596 3836
d.nsm cj v.aai.3s r.dpm.3 cj pl v.aas.1s p.d d.dpf n.dpf r.gsm.3 d.asm n.asm d.gpm

ἥλων καὶ βάλω τὸν δάκτυλόν μου εἰς τὸν τύπον τῶν ἥλων καὶ βάλω
nails, and put *{the}* my finger *my* into the ⌊wound left by⌋ the nails, and put
2464 2779 965 3836 1609 1235 1609 1650 3836 5596 3836 2464 2779 965
n.gpm cj v.aas.1s d.asm n.asm r.gs.1 p.a d.asm n.asm d.gpm n.gpm cj v.aas.1s

μου τὴν χεῖρα εἰς τὴν πλευρὰν αὐτοῦ, ↱ ↱ ⌊οὐ μὴ⌋ πιστεύσω. 26 καὶ
my *{the}* hand into *{the}* his side, *his* I will never believe!" *{and}*
1609 3836 5931 1650 3836 899 4433 899 4409 4409 4024 3590 4409 2779
r.gs.1 d.asf n.asf p.a d.asf n.asf r.gsm.3 pl pl v.aas.1s cj

μεθ᾽ ἡμέρας ὀκτὼ πάλιν ἦσαν ἔσω οἱ
Eight days later *days* *Eight* his disciples were in the house again, *were* *in* *{the}*
3893 2465 3552 2465 3893 899 3412 1639 2276 4099 1639 2276 3836
p.a n.apf a.apf adv v.iai.3p adv d.npm

μαθηταὶ αὐτοῦ καὶ Θωμᾶς μετ᾽ αὐτῶν. ἔρχεται
disciples *his* and Thomas was with them. Although the doors were locked, Jesus came
3412 899 2779 2605 3552 899 3091 3836 2598 3091 3091 2652 2262
n.npm r.gsm.3 cj n.nsm p.g r.gpm.3 v.pmi.3s

ὁ Ἰησοῦς τῶν θυρῶν κεκλεισμένων καὶ ἔστη εἰς τὸ μέσον καὶ εἶπεν, εἰρήνη
{the} *Jesus* *the* *doors* *Although were locked* and stood in their midst and said, "Peace
3836 2652 3836 2598 3091 2779 2705 1650 3836 3545 2779 3306 1645
d.nsm n.nsm d.gpf n.gpf pt.rp.gpf cj v.aai.3s p.a d.asn n.asn cj v.aai.3s n.nsf

ὑμῖν. 27 εἶτα λέγει τῷ Θωμᾷ, φέρε τὸν δάκτυλόν σου ὧδε καὶ
be with you." Then he said to Thomas, "Put *{the}* your finger *your* here, and
7007 1663 3306 3836 2605 5770 3836 5148 1235 5148 6045 2779
r.dp.2 adv v.pai.3s d.dsm n.dsm v.pam.2s d.asm n.asm r.gs.2 adv cj

ἴδε τὰς χεῖράς μου καὶ φέρε τὴν χεῖρά σου καὶ βάλε εἰς τὴν
examine *{the}* my hands; *my* and ⌊reach out⌋ *{the}* your hand, *your* and put it into *{the}*
2623 3836 1609 5931 1609 2779 5770 3836 5148 5931 5148 2779 965 1650 3836
v.aam.2s d.apf n.apf r.gs.1 cj v.pam.2s d.asf n.asf r.gs.2 cj v.aam.2s p.a d.asf

πλευράν μου, καὶ ↱ μὴ γίνου ἄπιστος ἀλλὰ πιστός. 28 ἀπεκρίθη
my side. *my* *{and}* Do not ⌊continue in⌋ unbelief, but believe." Thomas replied
1609 4433 1609 2779 1181 3590 1181 603 247 4412 2605 646
n.asf r.gs.1 cj pl v.pmm.2s a.nsm cj a.nsm v.api.3s

Θωμᾶς καὶ εἶπεν αὐτῷ, ὁ κύριός μου καὶ ὁ θεός μου.
Thomas *{and}* to him, saying, *to him* *{the}* "My Lord, *My* and *{the}* my God!" *my*
2605 2779 899 899 3306 899 3836 1609 3261 1609 2779 3836 1609 2536 1609
n.nsm cj v.aai.3s r.dsm.3 d.vsm n.vsm r.gs.1 cj d.vsm n.vsm r.gs.1

29 λέγει αὐτῷ ὁ Ἰησοῦς, ὅτι ἑώρακάς με πεπίστευκας;
Jesus said to him, *{the}* *Jesus* "You believe because you have seen me. *You believe*
2652 3306 899 3836 2652 4409 4409 4022 3972 1609 4409
v.pai.3s r.dsm.3 d.nsm n.nsm cj v.rai.2s r.as.1 v.rai.2s

μακάριοι οἱ ↱ ↱ μὴ ἰδόντες καὶ πιστεύσαντες. 30 πολλὰ
Blessed are those who have not seen me, yet believe." Now Jesus did many
3421 3836 1625 1625 3590 1625 2779 4409 4036 2652 4472 4498
a.npm d.npm pl pt.aa.npm cj pt.aa.npm a.apn

NASB

any, *their sins*
have been forgiven
them; if you retain
the *sins* of any,
they have been
retained."
24 But Thomas,
one of the twelve,
called Didymus,
was not with them
when Jesus came.
25 So the other dis-
ciples were saying
to him, "We have
seen the Lord!"
But he said to
them, "Unless I see
in His hands the
imprint of the nails,
and put my finger
into the place of
the nails, and put
my hand into His
side, I will not be-
lieve."
26 After eight days
His disciples were
again inside, and
Thomas with them.
Jesus *came, the
doors having been
shut, and stood
in their midst and
said, "Peace *be*
with you." 27 Then
He *said to Thom-
as, "Reach here
with your finger,
and see My hands;
and reach here
your hand and put
it into My side; and
do not be unbeliev-
ing, but believing."
28 Thomas answered
and said to Him,
"My Lord and my
God!" 29 Jesus *said
to him, "Because
you have seen Me,
have you believed?
Blessed *are* they
who did not see,
and *yet* believed."

Why This Gospel Was Written

30 Therefore many
other signs Jesus

NIV

other signs in the presence of his disciples, which are not recorded in this book. [31] But these are written that you may believe[a] that Jesus is the Messiah, the Son of God, and that by believing you may have life in his name.

Jesus and the Miraculous Catch of Fish

21 Afterward Jesus appeared again to his disciples, by the Sea of Galilee.[b] It happened this way: [2] Simon Peter, Thomas (also known as Didymus[c]), Nathanael from Cana in Galilee, the sons of Zebedee, and two other disciples were together. [3] "I'm going out to fish," Simon Peter told them, and they said, "We'll go with you." So they went out and got into the boat, but that night they caught nothing.

[4] Early in the morning, Jesus stood on the shore, but the disciples did not realize that it was Jesus.

[5] He called out to them, "Friends, haven't you any fish?"

"No," they answered.

[a] 31 Or *may continue to believe*
[b] 1 Greek *Tiberias*
[c] 2 *Thomas* (Aramaic) and *Didymus* (Greek) both mean *twin.*

μὲν οὖν καὶ ἄλλα σημεῖα ἐποίησεν ὁ Ἰησοῦς ἐνώπιον τῶν μαθητῶν
~ Now {also} other signs did {the} Jesus in the presence of his disciples,
3525 4036 2779 257 4956 4472 3836 2652 1967 3836 899 3412
pl cj adv r.apn n.apn v.aai.3s d.nsm n.nsm p.g d.gpm n.gpm

αὐτοῦ,[a] ἃ οὐκ ἔστιν γεγραμμένα ἐν τῷ βιβλίῳ τούτῳ· 31 ταῦτα
his which are not are recorded in {the} this book; this but these
899 4005 1639 4024 1639 1211 1877 3836 4047 1046 4047 1254 4047
r.gsm.3 r.npn pl v.pai.3s pt.rp.npn p.d d.dsn n.dsn r.dsn r.npn

δὲ γέγραπται ἵνα πιστεύητε[b] ὅτι Ἰησοῦς ἐστιν ὁ χριστὸς ὁ υἱὸς τοῦ
but are recorded so that you may believe that Jesus is the Christ, the Son of
1254 1211 2671 4409 4022 2652 1639 3836 5986 3836 5626 3836
cj v.rpi.3s cj v.pas.2p cj n.nsm v.pai.3s d.nsm n.nsm d.nsm n.nsm d.gsm

θεοῦ, καὶ ἵνα πιστεύοντες ζωὴν ἔχητε ἐν τῷ ὀνόματι αὐτοῦ.
God, and that by believing you may have life you may have in {the} his name. his
2536 2779 2671 4409 2400 2400 2400 2437 2400 1877 3836 899 3950 899
n.gsm cj cj pt.pa.npm n.asf v.pas.2p p.d d.dsn n.dsn r.gsm.3

21:1 μετὰ ταῦτα ἐφανέρωσεν ἑαυτὸν πάλιν ὁ Ἰησοῦς τοῖς μαθηταῖς
After this Jesus again revealed himself again {the} Jesus to his disciples
3552 4047 2652 4099 5746 1571 4099 3836 2652 3836 3412
p.a r.apn v.aai.3s r.asm.3 adv d.nsm n.nsm d.dpm n.dpm

ἐπὶ τῆς θαλάσσης τῆς Τιβεριάδος· ἐφανέρωσεν δὲ οὕτως. 2
by the Sea of Tiberias, and he revealed himself and in this way. Gathered
2093 3836 2498 3836 5500 1254 5746 1254 4048
p.g d.gsf n.gsf d.gsf n.gsf v.aai.3s cj adv

→ ἦσαν ὁμοῦ Σίμων Πέτρος καὶ Θωμᾶς ὁ λεγόμενος Δίδυμος καὶ
there together were together Simon Peter, {and} Thomas {the} (called the Twin), {and}
3938 1639 3938 4981 4377 2779 2605 3836 3306 1441 2779
v.iai.3p adv n.nsm n.nsm cj n.nsm d.nsm pt.pp.nsm n.nsm cj

Ναθαναὴλ ὁ ἀπὸ Κανὰ τῆς Γαλιλαίας καὶ οἱ τοῦ Ζεβεδαίου καὶ
Nathanael {the} of Cana in Galilee, {and} the sons of Zebedee, and two
3720 3836 608 2830 3836 1133 2779 3836 3836 2411 2779 1545
n.nsm d.nsm p.g n.gsf d.gsf n.gsf cj d.npm d.gsm n.gsm cj

ἄλλοι ἐκ τῶν μαθητῶν αὐτοῦ δύο. 3 λέγει αὐτοῖς Σίμων Πέτρος,
more of {the} his disciples. his two Simon Peter said to them, Simon Peter
257 1666 3836 899 3412 899 1545 4981 4377 3306 899 4981 4377
r.npm p.g d.gpm n.gpm r.gsm.3 a.npm v.pai.3s r.dpm.3 n.nsm n.nsm

ὑπάγω ἁλιεύειν. λέγουσιν αὐτῷ, ἐρχόμεθα καὶ ἡμεῖς σὺν σοί.
"I am going fishing." They said to him, "We will go {also} We with you." So
5632 244 3306 899 7005 2262 2779 7005 5250 5148
v.pai.1s f.pa v.pai.3p r.dsm.3 v.pmi.1p adv r.np.1 p.d r.ds.2

ἐξῆλθον καὶ ἐνέβησαν εἰς τὸ πλοῖον, καὶ ἐν ἐκείνῃ τῇ νυκτὶ ἐπίασαν
⌊they went out⌋ and got into the boat, but {on} that {the} night they caught
2002 2779 1832 1650 3836 4450 2779 1877 1697 3836 3816 4389
v.aai.3p cj v.aai.3p p.a d.asn n.asn cj p.d r.dsf d.dsf n.dsf v.aai.3p

οὐδέν. 4 ↱ πρωΐας δὲ ⌊ἤδη γενομένης⌋ ἔστη Ἰησοῦς εἰς τὸν
nothing. Now when morning Now had dawned, ⌊there stood⌋ Jesus on the
4029 1254 1181 4746 1254 2453 1181 2705 2652 1650 3836
a.asn n.gsf cj adv pt.am.gsf v.aai.3s n.nsm p.a d.asm

αἰγιαλόν, ↱ οὐ μέντοι ᾔδεισαν οἱ μαθηταὶ ὅτι Ἰησοῦς
shore, but the disciples did not but realize the disciples that it was Jesus.
129 3530 3836 3412 3857 4024 3530 3857 3836 3412 4022 1639 1639 2652
n.asm pl cj v.lai.3p d.npm n.npm cj n.nsm

ἐστιν. 5 λέγει οὖν αὐτοῖς ὁ[c] Ἰησοῦς, παιδία, μή τι
it was So Jesus called So to them, {the} Jesus "Boys, you have not caught any
1639 4036 2652 3306 4036 899 3836 2652 4086 2400 2400 3590 5516
v.pai.3s v.pai.3s cj r.dpm.3 d.nsm n.nsm n.vpn pl r.asn

προσφάγιον ἔχετε; ↰ ↰ ἀπεκρίθησαν αὐτῷ, οὔ. 6 ὁ δὲ εἶπεν αὐτοῖς,
fish, you have have you?" They called back to him, "No." He {and} said to them,
4709 2400 3590 3590 646 899 4024 3836 1254 3306 899
n.asn v.pai.2p v.api.3p r.dsm.3 pl d.nsm cj v.aai.3s r.dpm.3

[a] [αὐτοῦ] UBS, omitted by TNIV, NET.
[b] πιστεύητε TNIV, NET. πιστεύ[σ]ητε UBS.
[c] [ὁ] UBS, omitted by TNIV.

NASB

also performed in the presence of the disciples, which are not written in this book; [31] but these have been written so that you may believe that Jesus is the Christ, the Son of God; and that believing you may have life in His name.

Jesus Appears at the Sea of Galilee

[21:1] After these things Jesus manifested Himself again to the disciples at the Sea of Tiberias, and He manifested *Himself* in this way. [2] Simon Peter, and Thomas called Didymus, and Nathanael of Cana in Galilee, and the *sons* of Zebedee, and two others of His disciples were together. [3] Simon Peter *said to them, "I am going fishing." They *said to him, "We will also come with you." They went out and got into the boat; and that night they caught nothing.

[4] But when the day was now breaking, Jesus stood on the beach; yet the disciples did not know that it was Jesus. [5] So Jesus *said to them, "Children, you do not have any fish, do you?" They answered Him, "No." [6] And He said to them,

NIV

[6]He said, "Throw
your net on the
right side of the
boat and you will
find some." When
they did, they were
unable to haul the
net in because of
the large number
of fish.
[7]Then the disci-
ple whom Jesus
loved said to Peter,
"It is the Lord!" As
soon as Simon Pe-
ter heard him say,
"It is the Lord," he
wrapped his outer
garment around
him (for he had
taken it off) and
jumped into the
water. [8]The other
disciples followed
in the boat, tow-
ing the net full of
fish, for they were
not far from shore,
about a hundred
yards.[a] [9]When
they landed, they
saw a fire of burn-
ing coals there
with fish on it, and
some bread.
[10]Jesus said to
them, "Bring some
of the fish you
have just caught."
[11]So Simon Pe-
ter climbed back
into the boat and
dragged the net
ashore. It was full
of large fish, 153,
but even with so
many the net was
not torn. [12]Jesus
said to them,
"Come and have
breakfast." None
of the disciples
dared

βάλετε εἰς τὰ δεξιὰ μέρη τοῦ πλοίου τὸ δίκτυον, καὶ εὑρήσετε.
"Cast your net to the right side of the boat *your net* and you will catch some."
965 3836 1473 1650 3836 1288 3538 3836 4450 3836 1473 2779 2351
v.aam.2p p.a d.apn a.apn n.apn d.gsn n.gsn d.asn n.asn cj v.fai.2p

ἔβαλον οὖν, καὶ → οὐκέτι αὐτὸ ἑλκύσαι
So they cast *So* it there, and then they were not able to haul in the net, *to haul in*
4036 965 4036 2779 2710 2710 4033 2710 1816 1816 1816 899 1816
v.aai.3p cj cj adv r.asn.3 f.aa

ἴσχυον ἀπὸ τοῦ πλήθους τῶν ἰχθύων. 7 λέγει οὖν ὁ μαθητὴς
they were able ⌞because of⌟ the large number of fish. *said* Then *{the}* that disciple
2710 608 3836 4436 3836 2716 3306 4036 3836 1697 3412
v.iai.3p p.g d.gsn n.gsn d.gpm n.gpm v.pai.3s cj d.nsm n.nsm

ἐκεῖνος ὃν ἠγάπα ὁ Ἰησοῦς τῷ Πέτρῳ· ὁ κύριός ἐστιν.
that whom Jesus loved *{the}* *Jesus* said to Peter, "It is the Lord!" *It is*
1697 4005 2652 26 3836 2652 3306 3836 4377 1639 1639 3836 3261 1639
r.nsm r.asm v.iai.3s d.nsm n.nsm d.dsm n.dsm d.nsm n.nsm v.pai.3s

↱ Σίμων οὖν Πέτρος ἀκούσας ὅτι ὁ κύριός ἐστιν τὸν
When Simon *{then}* Peter heard that it was the Lord, *it was* he tucked in his
201 4981 4036 4377 201 4022 1639 1639 3836 3261 1639 1346 1346 1346 3836
n.nsm cj n.nsm pt.aa.nsm cj d.nsm n.nsm v.pai.3s d.asm

ἐπενδύτην διεζώσατο, ἦν γὰρ γυμνός, καὶ ἔβαλεν
outer garment *he tucked in* (for ⌞he was⌟ *for* ⌞wearing nothing underneath),⌟ and jumped
2087 1346 1142 1639 1142 1218 2779 965
n.asm v.ami.3s v.iai.3s cj a.nsm cj v.aai.3s

ἑαυτὸν⌟ εἰς τὴν θάλασσαν. 8 οἱ δὲ ἄλλοι μαθηταὶ τῷ πλοιαρίῳ
into the sea. But the *But* other disciples came ⌞with the⌟ boat,
1571 1650 3836 2498 1254 3836 1254 257 3412 2262 3836 4449
r.asm.3 p.a d.asf n.asf d.npm cj r.npm n.npm d.dsn n.dsn

ἦλθον, οὐ γὰρ ἦσαν μακρὰν ἀπὸ τῆς
came pulling the net full of fish, for they were not *for* *they were* far from *{the}*
2262 5359 3836 1473 3836 2716 1142 1639 1639 4024 1142 1639 3426 608 3836
v.aai.3p pl cj v.iai.3p adv p.g d.gsf

γῆς ἀλλὰ ⌞ὡς ἀπὸ⌟ ⌞πηχῶν διακοσίων,⌟ σύροντες τὸ δίκτυον τῶν
land, *{but}* no more than a hundred yards. *pulling* *the* *net* *of*
1178 247 6055 608 4388 1357 5359 3836 1473 3836
n.gsf cj pl p.g n.gpm a.gpm pt.pa.npm d.asn n.asn d.gpm

ἰχθύων. 9 ὡς οὖν ἀπέβησαν ⌞εἰς τὴν γῆν⌟ βλέπουσιν ἀνθρακιὰν κειμένην
fish When *{then}* they had come ashore, they saw a charcoal fire ready
2716 6055 4036 609 1650 3836 1178 1063 471 3023
n.gpm cj cj v.aai.3p p.a d.asf n.asf v.pai.3p n.asf pt.pm.asf

καὶ ὀψάριον ἐπικείμενον καὶ ἄρτον. 10 λέγει αὐτοῖς ὁ Ἰησοῦς, ἐνέγκατε
with fish lying on it, and bread. Jesus said to them, *{the}* *Jesus* "Bring
2779 4066 2130 2779 788 2652 3306 899 3836 2652 5770
cj n.asn pt.pm.asn cj n.asm v.pai.3s r.dpm.3 d.nsm n.nsm v.aam.2p

ἀπὸ τῶν ὀψαρίων ὧν → → ἐπιάσατε νῦν. 11 ἀνέβη
⌞some of⌟ the fish that you have just caught." *just* So Simon Peter went aboard
608 3836 4066 4005 3814 4389 3814 4036 4981 4377 326
p.g d.gpn n.gpn r.gpn v.aai.2p adv v.aai.3s

οὖν Σίμων Πέτρος καὶ εἵλκυσεν τὸ δίκτυον. ⌞εἰς τὴν γῆν⌟ μεστὸν ἰχθύων
So *Simon* *Peter* and dragged the net ashore, full of large fish,
4036 4981 4377 2779 1816 3836 1473 1650 3836 1178 3550 3489 2716
cj n.nsm n.nsm cj v.aai.3s d.asn n.asn p.a d.asf n.asf a.asn n.gpm

μεγάλων ἑκατὸν ⌞πεντήκοντα τριῶν·⌟ καὶ τοσούτων
large one hundred and fifty-three of them; and although there were so many,
3489 1669 4299 5552 2779 1639 1639 1639 5537
a.gpm a.gpm a.gpm a.gpm cj r.gpm

ὄντων ↱ οὐκ ἐσχίσθη τὸ δίκτυον. 12 λέγει αὐτοῖς ὁ
although there were the net was not torn. *the* *net* Jesus said to them, *{the}*
1639 3836 1473 5387 4024 5387 3836 1473 2652 3306 899 3836
pt.pa.gpm pl v.api.3s d.nsn n.nsn v.pai.3s r.dpm.3 d.nsm

Ἰησοῦς, δεῦτε ἀριστήσατε. οὐδεὶς δὲ ἐτόλμα τῶν
Jesus "Come and have breakfast." Now none *Now* of the disciples ventured *of the*
2652 1307 753 1254 4029 1254 3836 3836 3412 5528 3836
n.nsm adv v.aam.2p a.nsm cj v.iai.3s d.gpm

NASB

"Cast the net on
the right-hand side
of the boat and you
will find *a catch*."
So they cast, and
then they were
not able to haul it
in because of the
great number of
fish. [7]Therefore
that disciple whom
Jesus loved *said
to Peter, "It is the
Lord." So when
Simon Peter heard
that it was the
Lord, he put his
outer garment
on (for he was
stripped *for work*),
and threw himself
into the sea. [8]But
the other disciples
came in the little
boat, for they were
not far from the
land, but about
one hundred yards
away, dragging the
net *full* of fish.
[9]So when they got
out on the land,
they *saw a char-
coal fire *already*
laid and fish placed
on it, and bread.
[10]Jesus *said to
them, "Bring some
of the fish which
you have now
caught." [11]Simon
Peter went up and
drew the net to
land, full of large
fish, a hundred and
fifty-three; and al-
though there were
so many, the net
was not torn.

Jesus Provides

[12]Jesus *said to
them, "Come *and*
have breakfast."
None of the dis-
ciples ventured

[a] 8 Or about 90 meters

NIV

ask him, "Who are
you?" They knew
it was the Lord.
13 Jesus came, took
the bread and gave
it to them, and did
the same with the
fish. 14 This was
now the third time
Jesus appeared to
his disciples after
he was raised from
the dead.

Jesus Reinstates Peter

15 When they had
finished eating,
Jesus said to Si-
mon Peter, "Simon
son of John, do
you love me more
than these?"
"Yes, Lord," he
said, "you know
that I love you."
Jesus said, "Feed
my lambs."
16 Again Jesus
said, "Simon son
of John, do you
love me?"
He answered,
"Yes, Lord, you
know that I love
you."
Jesus said, "Take
care of my sheep."
17 The third time
he said to him,
"Simon son of
John, do you
love me?"
Peter was hurt
because Jesus
asked him the
third time, "Do
you love me?" He
said, "Lord, you
know all things;
you know that I
love you."
Jesus said, "Feed
my sheep. 18 Very
truly I tell you,
when you were
younger you
dressed yourself
and went where
you wanted; but
when you are old
you will stretch
out your hands,
and someone else
will dress you

μαθητῶν ἐξετάσαι αὐτόν, σὺ τίς εἶ; εἰδότες ὅτι ὁ
disciples to ask him, "Who are you?" *Who are* ⌞for they knew⌟ *{that}* it was the
3412 2004 899 5515 1639 5148 5515 1639 3857 4022 1639 1639 3836
n.gpm f.aa r.asm.3 r.ns.2 r.nsm v.pai.2s pt.ra.npm cj d.nsm

κύριός ἐστιν. 13 ἔρχεται Ἰησοῦς καὶ λαμβάνει τὸν ἄρτον καὶ δίδωσιν αὐτοῖς,
Lord. *it was* Jesus came *Jesus* and took the bread and gave it to them,
3261 1639 2652 2262 2652 2779 3284 3836 788 2779 1443 899
n.nsm v.pai.3s v.pmi.3s n.nsm cj v.pai.3s d.asm n.asm cj v.pai.3s r.dpm.3

καὶ τὸ ὀψάριον ὁμοίως. 14 τοῦτο ἤδη τρίτον ἐφανερώθη Ἰησοῦς
and the fish as well. This was now the third time that Jesus was revealed *Jesus*
2779 3836 4066 3931 4047 2453 5568 2652 5746 2652
cj d.asn n.asn adv r.asn adv adv v.api.3s n.nsm

τοῖς μαθηταῖς ἐγερθεὶς ἐκ νεκρῶν. 15 ὅτε οὖν
to his disciples ⌞after he had been raised⌟ from the dead. When *{then}*
3836 3412 1586 1666 3738 4021 4036
d.dpm n.dpm pt.ap.nsm p.g a.gpm cj cj

ἠρίστησαν λέγει τῷ Σίμωνι Πέτρῳ ὁ Ἰησοῦς, Σίμων
⌞they had finished breakfast,⌟ Jesus said to Simon Peter, *{the}* *Jesus* "Simon, son
753 2652 3306 3836 4981 4377 3836 2652 4981
v.aai.3p v.pai.3s d.dsm n.dsm n.dsm d.nsm n.nsm n.vsm

Ἰωάννου, ἀγαπᾷς με πλέον τούτων; λέγει αὐτῷ, ναὶ κύριε, σὺ
of John, do you love me more than these others do?" He said to him, "Yes, Lord, you
2722 26 1609 4498 4047 3306 899 3721 3261 5148
n.gsm v.pai.2s r.as.1 adv.c r.gpm v.pai.3s r.dsm.3 pl n.vsm r.ns.2

οἶδας ὅτι φιλῶ σε. λέγει αὐτῷ, βόσκε τὰ ἀρνία μου. 16 λέγει
know that I love you." Jesus said to him, ⌞"Take care of⌟ *{the}* my lambs." *my* He said
3857 4022 5797 5148 3306 899 1081 3836 1609 768 1609 3306
v.rai.2s cj v.pai.1s r.as.2 v.pai.3s r.dsm.3 v.pam.2s d.apn n.apn r.gs.1 v.pai.3s

αὐτῷ πάλιν δεύτερον, Σίμων Ἰωάννου, ἀγαπᾷς με; λέγει αὐτῷ, ναὶ
to him again, a second time, "Simon, son of John, do you love me?" He said to him, "Yes,
899 4099 1311 4981 2722 26 1609 3306 899 3721
r.dsm.3 adv adv n.vsm n.gsm v.pai.2s r.as.1 v.pai.3s r.dsm.3 pl

κύριε, σὺ οἶδας ὅτι φιλῶ σε. λέγει αὐτῷ, ποίμαινε τὰ πρόβατά μου.
Lord, you know that I love you." Jesus said to him, "Look after *{the}* my sheep." *my*
3261 5148 3857 4022 5797 5148 3306 899 4477 3836 1609 4585 1609
n.vsm r.ns.2 v.rai.2s cj v.pai.1s r.as.2 v.pai.3s r.dsm.3 v.pam.2s d.apn n.apn r.gs.1

17 λέγει αὐτῷ τὸ τρίτον, Σίμων Ἰωάννου, φιλεῖς με;
He said to him the third time, "Simon, son of John, ⌞do you love⌟ me?" Peter was distressed ἐλυπήθη
3306 899 3836 5568 4981 2722 5797 1609 4377 3382
v.pai.3s r.dsm.3 d.asn adv n.vsm n.gsm v.pai.2s r.as.1 v.api.3s

ὁ Πέτρος ὅτι εἶπεν αὐτῷ τὸ τρίτον, φιλεῖς με; καὶ λέγει
{the} *Peter* that Jesus had asked him ⌞for the⌟ third time, ⌞"Do you love⌟ me?" *{and}* He said
3836 4377 4022 3306 899 3836 5568 5797 1609 2779 3306
d.nsm n.nsm cj v.aai.3s r.dsm.3 d.asn adv v.pai.2s r.as.1 cj v.pai.3s

αὐτῷ, κύριε, πάντα σὺ οἶδας, σὺ γινώσκεις ὅτι φιλῶ σε. λέγει
to him, "Lord, you know everything; *you know* you know that I love you." Jesus said
899 3261 5148 3857 4246 5148 3857 5148 1182 4022 5797 5148 2652 3306
r.dsm.3 n.vsm a.apn r.ns.2 v.rai.2s r.ns.2 v.pai.2s cj v.pai.1s r.as.2 v.pai.3s

αὐτῷ [a] ὁ Ἰησοῦς, βόσκε τὰ πρόβατά μου. 18
to him, *{the}* *Jesus* ⌞"Take care of⌟ *{the}* my sheep. *my* I tell you the
899 3836 2652 1081 3836 1609 4585 1609 3306 3306 5148
r.dsm.3 d.nsm n.nsm v.pam.2s d.apn n.apn r.gs.1

⌞ἀμὴν ἀμὴν⌟ λέγω σοι, ὅτε ἦς νεώτερος, ἐζώννυες ←
solemn truth, *I tell* *you* when ⌞you were⌟ young, ⌞you used to fasten on⌟ your clothes
297 297 3306 5148 4021 1639 3742 2439 4932
pl pl v.pai.1s r.ds.2 cj v.iai.2s a.nsm.c v.iai.2s

σεαυτὸν καὶ περιεπάτεις ὅπου ἤθελες· ὅταν δὲ γηράσῃς,
your and go wherever you wanted, but when *but* you grow old,
4932 2779 4344 3963 2527 1254 4020 1254 1180
r.asm.2 cj v.iai.2s cj v.iai.2s cj cj v.aas.2s

ἐκτενεῖς τὰς χεῖράς σου, καὶ ἄλλος σε → → → ζώσει
⌞you will stretch out⌟ *{the}* your hands, *your* and ⌞someone else⌟ *your* will fasten on your clothes
1753 3836 5148 5931 5148 2779 257 5148 5148 2439
v.fai.2s d.apf n.apf r.gs.2 cj r.nsm r.as.2 v.fai.3s

NASB

to question Him,
"Who are You?"
knowing that it was
the Lord. 13 Jesus
*came and *took
the bread and *gave
it to them, and the
fish likewise. 14 This
is now the third
time that Jesus was
manifested to the
disciples, after He
was raised from the
dead.

The Love Motivation

15 So when they
had finished break-
fast, Jesus *said to
Simon Peter, "Si-
mon, *son* of John,
do you love Me
more than these?"
He *said to Him,
"Yes, Lord; You
know that I love
You." He *said to
him, "Tend My
lambs." 16 He *said
to him again a
second time, "Si-
mon, *son* of John,
do you love Me?"
He *said to Him,
"Yes, Lord; You
know that I love
You." He *said to
him, "Shepherd
My sheep." 17 He
*said to him the
third time, "Simon,
son of John, do
you love Me?"
Peter was grieved
because He said
to him the third
time, "Do you love
Me?" And he said
to Him, "Lord, You
know all things;
You know that I
love You." Jesus
*said to him, "Tend
My sheep.

Our Times Are in His Hand

18 Truly, truly, I
say to you, when
you were younger,
you used to gird
yourself and walk
wherever you
wished; but when
you grow old, you
will stretch out
your hands and
someone else will
gird you, and

[a] [ὁ Ἰησοῦς] UBS, omitted by NET.

NIV

and lead you where
you do not want to
go." [19]Jesus said
this to indicate the
kind of death by
which Peter would
glorify God. Then
he said to him,
"Follow me!"
[20]Peter turned
and saw that the
disciple whom
Jesus loved was
following them.
(This was the one
who had leaned
back against Jesus
at the supper and
had said, "Lord,
who is going to
betray you?")
[21]When Peter saw
him, he asked,
"Lord, what about
him?"
[22]Jesus answered,
"If I want him to
remain alive until
I return, what is
that to you? You
must follow me."
[23]Because of this,
the rumor spread
among the be-
lievers that this
disciple would
not die. But Jesus
did not say that
he would not die;
he only said, "If
I want him to re-
main alive until I
return, what is that
to you?"
[24]This is the dis-
ciple who testifies
to these things and
who wrote them
down. We know
that his testimony
is true.
[25]Jesus did many
other things as
well. If

καὶ οἴσει ὅπου ↱ ↱ οὐ θέλεις. 19 τοῦτο δὲ εἶπεν
and take you where you do not want to go." Now he said this *Now he said*
2779 5770 3963 2527 2527 4024 2527 1254 3306 3306 4047 1254 3306
cj v.fai.3s cj pl v.pai.2s r.asn cj v.aai.3s

σημαίνων ποίῳ θανάτῳ δοξάσει τὸν θεόν. καὶ τοῦτο
to indicate ⌞by what kind of⌟ death Peter would glorify *{the}* God. And after saying this
4955 4481 2505 1519 3836 2536 2779 3306 3306 4047
pt.pa.nsm r.dsm n.dsm v.fai.3s d.asm n.asm cj r.asn

εἰπὼν λέγει αὐτῷ, ἀκολούθει μοι. 20 ἐπιστραφεὶς ὁ Πέτρος βλέπει
after saying he told him, "Follow me!" Peter turned *{the}* *Peter* and saw
3306 3306 899 199 1609 4377 2188 3836 4377 1063
pt.aa.nsm v.pai.3s r.dsm.3 v.pam.2s r.ds.1 pt.ap.nsm d.nsm n.nsm v.pai.3s

τὸν μαθητὴν ὃν ἠγάπα ὁ Ἰησοῦς ἀκολουθοῦντα, ὃς
following them the disciple whom Jesus loved, *{the}* *Jesus* *following* the one who
199 3836 3412 4005 2652 26 3836 2652 199 4005
d.asm n.asm r.asm v.iai.3s d.nsm n.nsm pt.pa.asm r.nsm

καὶ ἀνέπεσεν ἐν τῷ δείπνῳ ἐπὶ τὸ ⌞στῆθος αὐτοῦ⌟ καὶ
{also} at the supper ⌞had leaned back⌟ *at* *the* *supper* against *{the}* Jesus and
2779 1877 3836 1270 404 1877 3836 1270 2093 3836 5111 899 2779
adv v.aai.3s p.d d.dsn n.dsn p.a d.asn n.asn r.gsm.3 cj

εἶπεν, κύριε, τίς ἐστιν ὁ παραδιδούς σε; 21 τοῦτον οὖν
said, "Master, who is it that will betray you?" So when Peter saw him, *So*
3306 3261 5515 1639 3836 4140 5148 4036 1625 4377 1625 4047 4036
v.aai.3s n.vsm r.nsm v.pai.3s d.nsm pt.pa.nsm r.as.2 r.asm cj

ἰδὼν ὁ Πέτρος λέγει τῷ Ἰησοῦ, κύριε, οὗτος δὲ τί;
when saw *{the}* *Peter* he said to Jesus, "Lord, and what about him?" *and* *what about*
1625 3836 4377 3306 3836 2652 3261 1254 5515 5515 4047 1254 5515
pt.aa.nsm d.nsm n.nsm v.pai.3s d.dsm n.dsm n.vsm r.nsm cj r.asn

22 λέγει αὐτῷ ὁ Ἰησοῦς, ἐὰν αὐτὸν θέλω μένειν
Jesus replied, *{to him}* *{the}* *Jesus* "If I should want him *I should want* to remain alive
2652 3306 899 3836 2652 1569 2527 2527 2527 899 2527 3531
v.pai.3s r.dsm.3 d.nsm n.nsm cj r.asm.3 v.pas.1s f.pa

ἕως ἔρχομαι, τί πρὸς σέ; σύ μοι ἀκολούθει.
until I come back, ⌞what concern⌟ is that to you? You are to follow me!" *follow*
2401 2262 5515 4639 5148 5148 199 1609 199
cj v.pmi.1s r.nsn p.a r.as.2 r.ns.2 r.ds.1 v.pam.2s

23 ἐξῆλθεν οὖν οὗτος ὁ λόγος εἰς τοὺς ἀδελφοὺς ὅτι ὁ
So this word spread *So* *this* *{the}* *word* among the believers that *{the}* this
4036 4047 3364 2002 4036 4047 3836 3364 1650 3836 81 4022 3836 1697
v.aai.3s cj r.nsm d.nsm n.nsm p.a d.apm n.apm cj d.nsm

μαθητὴς ἐκεῖνος ↱ οὐκ ἀποθνῄσκει· ↱ οὐκ εἶπεν δὲ αὐτῷ ὁ
disciple *this* would not die. But Jesus did not say *But* to him *{the}*
3412 1697 633 4024 633 1254 2652 3306 4024 3306 1254 899 3836
n.nsm r.nsm pl v.pai.3s pl v.aai.3s cj r.dsm.3 d.nsm

Ἰησοῦς ὅτι ↱ ↱ οὐκ ἀποθνῄσκει ἀλλ᾽· ἐὰν αὐτὸν θέλω
Jesus that he would not die, but rather, "If I should want him *I should want*
2652 4022 633 633 4024 633 247 1569 2527 2527 2527 899 2527
n.nsm cj pl v.pai.3s cj cj r.asm.3 v.pas.1s

μένειν ἕως ἔρχομαι [a]τί πρὸς σέ; 24 Οὗτός ἐστιν ὁ
to remain alive until I come back, ⌞what concern⌟ is that to you?" This is the
3531 2401 2262 5515 4639 5148 4047 1639 3836
f.pa cj v.pmi.1s r.nsn p.a r.as.2 r.nsm v.pai.3s d.nsm

μαθητὴς ὁ μαρτυρῶν περὶ τούτων καὶ ὁ γράψας ταῦτα, καὶ οἴδαμεν
disciple who is bearing witness about these things and who wrote these things, and we know
3412 3836 3455 4309 4047 2779 3836 1211 4047 2779 3857
n.nsm d.nsm pt.pa.nsm p.g r.gpn cj d.nsm pt.aa.nsm r.apn cj v.rai.1p

ὅτι ἀληθὴς αὐτοῦ ἡ μαρτυρία ἐστίν. 25 ἔστιν δὲ καὶ
that his witness is true. *his* *{the}* *witness* *is* Now there are *Now* *as well* many
4022 899 3456 1639 239 899 3836 3456 1639 1254 1639 1254 2779 4498
cj a.nsf r.gsm.3 d.nsf n.nsf v.pai.3s v.pai.3s cj adv

ἄλλα πολλὰ ἃ ἐποίησεν ὁ Ἰησοῦς, ἅτινα ἐὰν
⌞other things⌟ *many* which Jesus did *{the}* *Jesus* as well; *{which}* if
257 4498 4005 2652 4472 3836 2652 2779 2779 4015 1569
r.npn a.npn r.apn v.aai.3s d.nsm n.nsm r.npn cj

NASB

bring you where
you do not wish to
go." [19]Now this He
said, signifying by
what kind of death
he would glorify
God. And when He
had spoken this,
He *said to him,
"Follow Me!"
[20]Peter, turning
around, *saw the
disciple whom Je-
sus loved following
them; the one who
also had leaned
back on His bosom
at the supper and
said, "Lord, who
is the one who
betrays You?"
[21]So Peter seeing
him *said to Jesus,
"Lord, and what
about this man?"
[22]Jesus *said to
him, "If I want him
to remain until I
come, what *is that*
to you? You follow
Me!" [23]Therefore
this saying went
out among the
brethren that that
disciple would not
die; yet Jesus did
not say to him that
he would not die,
but *only,* "If I want
him to remain until
I come, what *is*
that to you?"
[24]This is the
disciple who is
testifying to these
things and wrote
these things, and
we know that his
testimony is true.
[25]And there are
also many other
things which Jesus
did, which if they

[a] [τί πρὸς σέ] UBS.

NIV

every one of them were written down, I suppose that even the whole world would not have room for the books that would be written.

γράφηται καθ᾽ ἕν, οὐδ᾽ αὐτὸν οἶμαι
⌊they were written down⌋ one after the other, I imagine that not even the world itself *I imagine*
1211 2848 1651 3887 3887 4028 3836 3180 899 3887
v.pps.3s p.a a.asn adv r.asm v.pmi.1s

τὸν κόσμον χωρῆσαι τὰ γραφόμενα βιβλία.
the *world* could contain the books that would be written. *books*
3836 3180 6003 1046 3836 1211 1046
d.asm n.asm f.aa d.apn pt.pp.apn n.apn

NASB

*were written in detail, I suppose that even the world itself *would not contain the books that *would be written.

Acts

NIV

Jesus Taken Up Into Heaven

1 In my former
book, The-
ophilus, I wrote
about all that Jesus
began to do and
to teach [2]until the
day he was taken
up to heaven, after
giving instructions
through the Holy
Spirit to the apos-
tles he had chosen.
[3]After his suffer-
ing, he presented
himself to them
and gave many
convincing proofs
that he was alive.
He appeared to
them over a period
of forty days and
spoke about the
kingdom of God.
[4]On one occasion,
while he was eat-
ing with them,
he gave them this
command: "Do
not leave Jerusa-
lem, but wait for
the gift my Father
promised, which
you have heard
me speak about.
[5]For John baptized
with[a] water, but
in a few days you
will be baptized
with[b] the Holy
Spirit."
[6]Then they gath-
ered around him
and asked him,
"Lord, are you at
this time going to
restore the king-
dom to Israel?"
[7]He said to them:
"It is not for you
to know the times
or dates the Father
has set by his own
authority.

1:1 τὸν μὲν πρῶτον λόγον ἐποιησάμην περὶ πάντων, ὦ
I wrote the ~ first book, *I wrote* Theophilus, about everything *{O}*
4472 4472 3836 3525 4755 3364 4472 2541 4309 4246 6043
d.asm pl a.asm n.asm v.ami.1s p.g a.gpn j

Θεόφιλε, ὧν ἤρξατο ὁ Ἰησοῦς ποιεῖν τε καὶ διδάσκειν, [2]ἄχρι ἧς ἡμέρας
Theophilus that Jesus began *{the}* *Jesus* to do ~ and to teach, until the day
2541 4005 2652 806 3836 2652 4472 5445 2779 1438 948 4005 2465
n.vsm r.gpn v.ami.3s d.nsm n.nsm f.pa cj cj f.pa p.g r.gsf n.gsf

↰ ἐντειλάμενος τοῖς ἀποστόλοις διὰ πνεύματος
when, having given commands through the Holy Spirit to the apostles *through* *Spirit*
4005 1948 1328 41 4460 3836 693 1328 4460
pt.am.nsm d.dpm n.dpm p.g n.gsn

ἁγίου οὓς ἐξελέξατο ἀνελήμφθη. [3]οἷς καὶ παρέστησεν ἑαυτὸν ζῶντα
Holy *{whom}* he had chosen, ⌞he was taken up;⌟ to whom also he presented himself alive
41 4005 1721 377 4005 2779 4225 1571 2409
a.gsn r.apm v.ami.3s v.api.3s r.dpm adv v.aai.3s r.asm.3 pt.pa.asm

μετὰ τὸ παθεῖν αὐτὸν ἐν πολλοῖς τεκμηρίοις, δι᾽ ← ←
after *{the}* his passion *his* by many proofs, being seen by them over a period of
3552 3836 899 4248 899 1877 4498 5447 3964 3964 899 899 1328
p.a d.asn f.aa r.asm.3 p.d a.dpn n.dpn p.g

ἡμερῶν τεσσεράκοντα ὀπτανόμενος αὐτοῖς καὶ λέγων τὰ περὶ τῆς
forty days *forty* *being seen* *by them* and telling them what concerns the
5477 2465 5477 3964 899 2779 3306 3836 4309 3836
n.gpf a.gpf pt.pm.nsm r.dpm.3 cj pt.pa.nsm d.apn p.g d.gsf

βασιλείας τοῦ θεοῦ· [4]καὶ συναλιζόμενος παρήγγειλεν αὐτοῖς
kingdom of God. *{and}* While he was with them, he ordered them not to depart
993 3836 2536 2779 5259 4133 899 3590 6004 6004
n.gsf d.gsm n.gsm cj pt.pm.nsm v.aai.3s r.dpm.3

ἀπὸ Ἱεροσολύμων μὴ χωρίζεσθαι ἀλλὰ περιμένειν τὴν ἐπαγγελίαν τοῦ πατρὸς
from Jerusalem, *not* *to depart* but to await the promise of the Father,
608 2642 3590 6004 247 4338 3836 2039 3836 4252
p.g n.gpn pl f.pp cj f.pa d.asf n.asf d.gsm n.gsm

ἣν ἠκούσατέ μου, [5]ὅτι Ἰωάννης μὲν ἐβάπτισεν ὕδατι, ὑμεῖς
which, he said, "you heard ⌞from me;⌟ for John ~ baptized with water, but you
4005 201 1609 4022 2722 3525 966 5623 1254 7007
r.asf v.aai.2p r.gs.1 cj n.nsm pl v.aai.3s n.dsn r.np.2

δὲ ἐν πνεύματι βαπτισθήσεσθε ἁγίῳ οὐ μετὰ
but will be baptized with the Holy Spirit *will be baptized* *Holy* not many days from
1254 966 966 966 1877 41 4460 966 41 4024 4498 2465 3552
cj p.d n.dsn v.fpi.2p a.dsn pl p.a

πολλὰς ταύτας ἡμέρας. [6] ↱ οἱ μὲν οὖν συνελθόντες ἠρώτων αὐτὸν
many now." *days* So when they ~ *So* had come together, they asked him,
4498 4047 2465 4036 5302 3836 3525 4036 5302 2263 899
a.apf r.apf n.apf d.npm pl cj pt.aa.npm v.iai.3p r.asm.3

λέγοντες, κύριε, εἰ ἐν τῷ χρόνῳ τούτῳ ἀποκαθιστάνεις τὴν βασιλείαν
saying, "Lord, *{if}* *{at}* is this the time *this* when you will restore the kingdom
3306 3261 1623 1877 4047 3836 5989 4047 635 3836 993
pt.pa.npm n.vsm cj p.d d.dsm n.dsm r.dsm v.pai.2s d.asf n.asf

τῷ Ἰσραήλ; [7]εἶπεν δὲ πρὸς αὐτούς, οὐχ ὑμῶν ἐστιν γνῶναι
to Israel?" But he said *But* to them, "It is not for you *It is* to know the
3836 2702 1254 3306 1254 4639 899 1639 1639 4024 7007 1639 1182
d.dsm n.dsm v.aai.3s cj p.a r.apm.3 pl r.gp.2 v.pai.3s f.aa

χρόνους ἢ καιροὺς οὓς ὁ πατὴρ ἔθετο ἐν τῇ ἰδίᾳ ἐξουσίᾳ, [8]ἀλλὰ
times or seasons that the Father has set by *{the}* his own authority. But
5989 2445 2789 4005 3836 4252 5502 1877 3836 2625 2026 247
n.apm cj n.apm r.apm d.nsm n.nsm v.ami.3s p.d d.dsf a.dsf n.dsf cj

NASB

Introduction

[1:1]The first ac-
count I composed,
Theophilus, about
all that Jesus began
to do and teach,
[2]until the day when
He was taken up
to heaven, after He
had by the Holy
Spirit given orders
to the apostles
whom He had
chosen. [3]To these
He also presented
Himself alive after
His suffering, by
many convincing
proofs, appearing
to them over *a pe-
riod of* forty days
and speaking of the
things concerning
the kingdom of
God. [4]Gathering
them together,
He commanded
them not to leave
Jerusalem, but to
wait for what the
Father had prom-
ised, "Which," *He
said,* "you heard
of from Me; [5]for
John baptized with
water, but you will
be baptized with
the Holy Spirit not
many days from
now."
[6]So when they had
come together, they
were asking Him,
saying, "Lord, is it
at this time You are
restoring the king-
dom to Israel?"
[7]He said to them,
"It is not for you
to know times or
epochs which the
Father has fixed by
His own authority;

[a] 5 Or *in*
[b] 5 Or *in*

NIV

8But you will re-
ceive power when
the Holy Spirit
comes on you; and
you will be my
witnesses in Jeru-
salem, and in all
Judea and Samar-
ia, and to the ends
of the earth."
9After he said
this, he was tak-
en up before their
very eyes, and
a cloud hid him
from their sight.
10They were look-
ing intently up
into the sky as he
was going, when
suddenly two men
dressed in white
stood beside them.
11"Men of Gal-
ilee," they said,
"why do you stand
here looking into
the sky? This same
Jesus, who has
been taken from
you into heaven,
will come back in
the same way you
have seen him go
into heaven."

Matthias Chosen to Replace Judas

12Then the apos-
tles returned to
Jerusalem from
the hill called
the Mount of Ol-
ives, a Sabbath
day's walk[a] from
the city. 13When
they arrived, they
went upstairs to
the room where
they were stay-
ing. Those present
were Peter, John,
James and An-
drew; Philip and
Thomas, Bartholo-
mew and Matthew;
James son of Al-
phaeus and Simon
the Zealot, and Ju-
das son of James.
14They all joined
together constantly
in prayer,

[a] 12 That is, about 5/8 mile or about 1 kilometer

λήμψεσθε δύναμιν → ἐπελθόντος τοῦ ἁγίου πνεύματος ἐφ' ὑμᾶς
you will receive power when the Holy Spirit has come *the Holy Spirit* upon you,
3284 1539 3836 41 4460 2088 3836 41 4460 2093 7007
v.fmi.2p n.asf pt.aa.gsn d.gsn a.gsn n.gsn p.a r.ap.2

καὶ ἔσεσθέ μου μάρτυρες ἔν τε Ἰερουσαλὴμ καὶ ἐν[a] πάσῃ τῇ Ἰουδαίᾳ
and ⌊you will be⌋ my witnesses both in *both* Jerusalem and in all *{the}* Judea
2779 1639 1609 3459 5445 1877 5445 2647 2779 1877 4246 3836 2677
cj v.fmi.2p r.gs.1 n.npm p.d cj n.dsf cj p.d a.dsf d.dsf n.dsf

καὶ Σαμαρείᾳ καὶ ἕως ἐσχάτου τῆς γῆς. 9 καὶ ταῦτα
and Samaria, and to the end of the earth." And when he had said these words,
2779 4899 2779 2401 2274 3836 1178 2779 3306 3306 3306 3306 4047
cj n.dsf cj p.g a.gsn d.gsf n.gsf cj r.apn

εἰπὼν → βλεπόντων αὐτῶν ἐπήρθη καὶ νεφέλη ὑπέλαβεν
when he had said while they were watching, *they* ⌊he was lifted up⌋ and a cloud took
3306 899 1063 899 2048 2779 3749 5696
pt.aa.nsm pt.pa.gpm r.gpm.3 v.api.3s cj n.nsf v.aai.3s

αὐτὸν ← ἀπὸ τῶν ὀφθαλμῶν αὐτῶν. 10 καὶ ὡς ἀτενίζοντες ἦσαν
him away from *{the}* their eyes. *their* And while they were gazing *they were*
899 5696 608 3836 899 4057 899 2779 6055 1639 1639 867 1639
r.asm.3 p.g d.gpm n.gpm r.gpm.3 cj cj pt.pa.npm v.iai.3p

εἰς τὸν οὐρανὸν → πορευομένου αὐτοῦ, καὶ ἰδοὺ ἄνδρες δύο
into the sky, as he was going, *he* *{and}* behold, two men *two*
1650 3836 4041 899 4513 899 2779 2627 1545 467 1545
p.a d.asm n.asm pt.pm.gsm r.gsm.3 cj j n.npm a.npm

παρειστήκεισαν αὐτοῖς ἐν ἐσθήσεσι λευκαῖς, 11 οἳ καὶ εἶπαν, ἄνδρες
stood by them in white robes, *white* *{who}* and said, "Men
4225 899 1877 3328 2264 3328 4005 2779 3306 467
v.lai.3p r.dpm.3 p.d n.dpf a.dpf r.npm adv v.aai.3p n.vpm

Γαλιλαῖοι, τί ἑστήκατε ἐμβλέποντες[b] εἰς τὸν οὐρανόν; οὗτος ὁ Ἰησοῦς ὁ
of Galilee, why do you stand looking up into the sky? This *{the}* Jesus, who
1134 5515 2705 1838 1650 3836 4041 4047 3836 2652 3836
a.vpm r.asn v.rai.2p pt.pa.npm p.a d.asm n.asm r.nsm d.nsm n.nsm d.nsm

ἀναλημφθεὶς ἀφ' ὑμῶν εἰς τὸν οὐρανὸν οὕτως ἐλεύσεται ὃν
was taken up from you into *{the}* heaven, will come in the same way *will come* as
377 608 7007 1650 3836 4041 2262 2262 4048 5573 2262 4005
pt.ap.nsm p.g r.gp.2 p.a d.asm n.asm adv v.fmi.3s r.asm

τρόπον ἐθεάσασθε αὐτὸν πορευόμενον εἰς τὸν οὐρανόν. 12 τότε ὑπέστρεψαν εἰς
way you saw him going into *{the}* heaven." Then they returned to
5573 2517 899 4513 1650 3836 4041 5538 5715 1650
n.asm v.ami.2p r.asm.3 pt.pm.asm p.a d.asm n.asm adv v.aai.3p p.a

Ἰερουσαλὴμ ἀπὸ ὄρους τοῦ καλουμένου Ἐλαιῶνος, ὅ ἐστιν ἐγγὺς
Jerusalem from a hill *{the}* called "The Mount of Olives," which is near
2647 608 4001 3836 2813 1779 4005 1639 1584
n.asf p.g n.gsn d.gsn pt.pp.gsn n.gsm r.nsn v.pai.3s p.g

Ἰερουσαλὴμ σαββάτου ⌊ἔχον ὁδόν.⌋ 13 καὶ ὅτε εἰσῆλθον,
Jerusalem, a Sabbath day's walk away. And when they had entered the city, they
2647 4879 2400 3847 2779 4021 1656 326
n.gsf n.gsn pt.pa.nsn n.asf cj cj v.aai.3p

εἰς τὸ ὑπερῷον ἀνέβησαν οὗ ἦσαν καταμένοντες, ὅ τε Πέτρος
went up to the upper room, *they went up* where they were lodging; *{the}* ~ Peter
326 326 1650 3836 5673 326 4023 1639 2910 3836 5445 4377
p.a d.asn n.asn v.aai.3p adv v.iai.3p pt.pa.npm d.nsm cj n.nsm

καὶ Ἰωάννης καὶ Ἰάκωβος καὶ Ἀνδρέας, Φίλιππος καὶ Θωμᾶς, Βαρθολομαῖος καὶ
and John and James and Andrew, Philip and Thomas, Bartholomew and
2779 2722 2779 2610 2779 436 5805 2779 2605 978 2779
cj n.nsm cj n.nsm cj n.nsm n.nsm cj n.nsm n.nsm cj

Μαθθαῖος, Ἰάκωβος Ἁλφαίου καὶ Σίμων ὁ ζηλωτὴς καὶ Ἰούδας
Matthew, James the son of Alphaeus and Simon the Zealot and Judas the son
3414 2610 271 2779 4981 3836 2421 2779 2683
n.nsm n.nsm n.gsm cj n.nsm d.nsm n.nsm cj n.nsm

Ἰακώβου. 14 οὗτοι πάντες ἦσαν προσκαρτεροῦντες → ὁμοθυμαδὸν τῇ προσευχῇ
of James. These all were devoting themselves with a single purpose to prayer,
2610 4047 4246 1639 4674 3924 3836 4666
n.gsm r.npm a.npm v.iai.3p pt.pa.npm adv d.dsf n.dsf

[a] [ἐν] UBS.
[b] ἐμβλέποντες UBS, NET. βλέποντες TNIV.

NASB

8but you will re-
ceive power when
the Holy Spirit has
come upon you;
and you shall be
My witnesses both
in Jerusalem, and
in all Judea and
Samaria, and even
to the remotest part
of the earth."

The Ascension

9And after He had
said these things,
He was lifted up
while they were
looking on, and a
cloud received Him
out of their sight.
10And as they were
gazing intently
into the sky while
He was going,
behold, two men
in white clothing
stood beside them.
11They also said,
"Men of Galilee,
why do you stand
looking into the
sky? This Jesus,
who has been taken
up from you into
heaven, will come
in just the same
way as you have
watched Him go
into heaven."

The Upper Room

12Then they re-
turned to Jerusalem
from the mount
called Olivet,
which is near
Jerusalem, a Sab-
bath day's journey
away. 13When they
had entered *the*
city, they went up
to the upper room
where they were
staying; that is,
Peter and John and
James and Andrew,
Philip and Thomas,
Bartholomew and
Matthew, James
the son of Alpha-
eus, and Simon the
Zealot, and Judas
the son of James.
14These all with one
mind were continu-
ally devoting them-
selves to prayer,

NIV

along with the
women and Mary
the mother of
Jesus, and with his
brothers.
[15]In those days
Peter stood up
among the be-
lievers (a group
numbering about
a hundred and
twenty) [16]and said,
"Brothers and sis-
ters,[a] the Scripture
had to be fulfilled
in which the Holy
Spirit spoke long
ago through Da-
vid concerning
Judas, who served
as guide for those
who arrested
Jesus. [17]He was
one of our number
and shared in our
ministry."
[18](With the pay-
ment he received
for his wickedness,
Judas bought a
field; there he fell
headlong, his body
burst open and
all his intestines
spilled out. [19]Ev-
eryone in Jerusa-
lem heard about
this, so they called
that field in their
language Akelda-
ma, that is, Field of
Blood.)
[20]"For," said Pe-
ter, "it is written
in the Book of
Psalms:

"'May his
place be
deserted;
let there be
no one to
dwell in
it,'[b]

and,

"'May another
take his place
of leadership.'[c]

[21]Therefore it

[a] *16* The Greek word for *brothers and sisters* (*adelphoi*) refers here to believers, both men and women, as part of God's family; also in 6:3; 11:29; 12:17; 16:40; 18:18, 27; 21:7, 17; 28:14, 15.
[b] *20* Psalm 69:25
[c] *20* Psalm 109:8

σὺν γυναιξὶν καὶ Μαριὰμ τῇ μητρὶ τοῦ Ἰησοῦ καὶ τοῖς ἀδελφοῖς αὐτοῦ.
with the women and Mary, the mother of Jesus, and with his brothers. *his*
5250 1222 2779 3452 3836 3613 3836 2652 2779 3836 899 81 899
p.d n.dpf cj n.dsf d.dsf n.dsf d.gsm n.gsm cj d.dpm n.dpm r.gsm.3

15 καὶ ἐν ταῖς ἡμέραις ταύταις ἀναστὰς Πέτρος ἐν μέσῳ τῶν ἀδελφῶν
And in *{the}* those days *those* Peter stood up *Peter* in the midst of the brothers
2779 1877 3836 4047 2465 4047 4377 482 4377 1877 3545 3836 81
cj p.d d.dpf n.dpf r.dpf pt.aa.nsm n.nsm p.d n.dsn d.gpm n.gpm

εἶπεν, ἦν τε ὄχλος ὀνομάτων ⌞ἐπὶ τὸ
said *{it was}* ~ (a crowd of people, about a hundred and twenty, had gathered together),
3306 1639 5445 4063 3950 6059 1669 1633 2093 3836
v.aai.3s v.iai.3s cj n.nsm n.gpn p.a d.asn

αὐτὸ⌟ ὡσεὶ ἑκατὸν εἴκοσι, 16 ⌞ἄνδρες ἀδελφοί,⌟ ἔδει
about *hundred* *twenty* and said, "My brothers, ⌞it was necessary⌟ for the
899 6059 1669 1633 3306 467 81 1256 3836
r.asn pl a.npm a.npm n.vpm n.vpm v.iai.3s

πληρωθῆναι τὴν γραφὴν ἣν προεῖπεν τὸ πνεῦμα τὸ
Scripture to be fulfilled, *the* *Scripture* which the Holy Spirit spoke beforehand *{the}* *Spirit* *{the}*
1210 4444 3836 1210 4005 41 4460 4597 3836 4460 3836
f.ap d.asf n.asf r.asf v.aai.3s d.nsn n.nsn d.nsn

ἅγιον διὰ στόματος Δαυὶδ περὶ Ἰούδα τοῦ γενομένου ὁδηγοῦ τοῖς
Holy by the mouth of David concerning Judas, who became guide to those
41 1328 5125 1253 4309 2683 3836 1181 3843 3836
a.nsn p.g n.gsn n.gsm p.g n.gsm d.gsm pt.am.gsm n.gsm d.dpm

συλλαβοῦσιν Ἰησοῦν, 17 ὅτι κατηριθμημένος ἦν ἐν ἡμῖν καὶ ἔλαχεν
who arrested Jesus. For he was numbered *he was* among us and received
5197 2652 4022 1639 1639 2935 1639 1877 7005 2779 3275
pt.aa.dpm n.asm cj pt.rp.nsm v.iai.3s p.d r.dp.1 cj v.aai.3s

τὸν κλῆρον τῆς διακονίας ταύτης. 18 οὗτος μὲν οὖν ἐκτήσατο
his allotted share of this ministry." *this* (Now this man ~ *Now* bought a
3836 3102 3836 4047 1355 4047 4036 4047 3525 4036 3227
d.asm n.asm d.gsf n.gsf r.gsf r.nsm pl cj v.ami.3s

χωρίον ἐκ μισθοῦ τῆς ἀδικίας καὶ πρηνὴς γενόμενος ἐλάκησεν
field with the reward of his unjust deed, and falling headfirst *falling* he burst open in the
6005 1666 3635 3836 94 2779 1181 4568 1181 3279
n.asn p.g n.gsm d.gsf n.gsf cj a.nsm pt.am.nsm v.aai.3s

μέσος καὶ ἐξεχύθη πάντα τὰ σπλάγχνα αὐτοῦ· 19 καὶ
middle and all his intestines gushed out. *all* *{the}* *intestines* *his* And it became
3545 2779 4246 899 5073 1773 4246 3836 5073 899 2779 1181 1181
a.nsm cj v.api.3s a.npn d.npn n.npn r.gsm.3 cj

γνωστὸν ἐγένετο πᾶσι τοῖς κατοικοῦσιν Ἰερουσαλήμ, ὥστε κληθῆναι τὸ
known *it became* to all the inhabitants of Jerusalem, so that the field was called *the*
1196 1181 4246 3836 2997 2647 6063 3836 6005 2813 3836
a.nsn v.ami.3s a.dpm d.dpm pt.pa.dpm n.asf cj f.ap d.asn

χωρίον ἐκεῖνο τῇ ἰδίᾳ διαλέκτῳ αὐτῶν Ἀκελδαμάχ, τοῦτ᾽ ἔστιν χωρίον
field *{that}* in their own language *their* Akeldama, that is, "Field
6005 1697 3836 899 2625 1365 899 192 4047 1639 6005
n.asn r.asn d.dsf a.dsf n.dsf r.gpm.3 n.asn r.nsn v.pai.3s n.asn

αἵματος. 20 γέγραπται γὰρ ἐν βίβλῳ ψαλμῶν, → γενηθήτω ἡ
of Blood.") "For it is written *For* in the Book of Psalms, 'Let his house become *{the}*
135 1142 1211 1142 1877 1047 6011 899 2068 1181 3836
n.gsn v.rpi.3s cj p.d n.dsf n.gpm v.apm.3s d.nsf

ἔπαυλις αὐτοῦ ἔρημος καὶ μὴ ἔστω ὁ κατοικῶν ἐν αὐτῇ, καί,
house *his* deserted, and let there be no *let there be* *{the}* one living in it'; and
2068 899 2245 2779 1639 1639 1639 3590 1639 3836 2997 1877 899 2779
n.nsf r.gsm.3 a.nsf cj pl v.pam.3s d.nsm pt.pa.nsm p.d r.dsf.3 cj

τὴν ἐπισκοπὴν αὐτοῦ λαβέτω ἕτερος. 21 δεῖ
'Let another take over *{the}* his responsibilities.' *his* *Let take over* *another* ⌞It is necessary,⌟
3284 2283 3284 3284 3836 899 2175 899 3284 2283 1256
d.asf n.asf r.gsm.3 v.aam.3s r.nsm v.pai.3s

οὖν τῶν συνελθόντων ἡμῖν ἀνδρῶν ἐν παντὶ χρόνῳ ᾧ
therefore, that of the men who have accompanied us *men* during all the time ⌞in which⌟
4036 3836 467 5302 7005 467 1877 4246 5989 4005
cj d.gpm pt.aa.gpm r.dp.1 n.gpm p.d a.dsm n.dsm r.dsm

NASB

along with *the*
women, and Mary
the mother of
Jesus, and with His
brothers.
[15]At this time Pe-
ter stood up in the
midst of the breth-
ren (a gathering of
about one hundred
and twenty per-
sons was there
together), and said,
[16]"Brethren, the
Scripture had to be
fulfilled, which the
Holy Spirit fore-
told by the mouth
of David concern-
ing Judas, who
became a guide to
those who arrested
Jesus. [17]For he was
counted among
us and received
his share in this
ministry." [18](Now
this man acquired a
field with the price
of his wickedness,
and falling head-
long, he burst open
in the middle and
all his intestines
gushed out. [19]And
it became known to
all who were living
in Jerusalem; so
that in their own
language that field
was called Hakel-
dama, that is, Field
of Blood.) [20]"For
it is written in the
book of Psalms,

'LET HIS HOME-
STEAD BE
MADE DESO-
LATE,
AND LET NO
ONE DWELL
IN IT';
and,
[20]'LET ANOTHER
MAN TAKE HIS
OFFICE.'

[21]Therefore it is
necessary that of
the men who have
accompanied us all
the time that the

NIV

is necessary to
choose one of the
men who have
been with us the
whole time the
Lord Jesus was
living among us,
22 beginning from
John's baptism
to the time when
Jesus was taken up
from us. For one of
these must become
a witness with us
of his resurrec-
tion."
23 So they nom-
inated two men:
Joseph called
Barsabbas (also
known as Jus-
tus) and Matthi-
as. 24 Then they
prayed, "Lord, you
know everyone's
heart. Show us
which of these two
you have chosen
25 to take over this
apostolic minis-
try, which Judas
left to go where he
belongs." 26 Then
they cast lots, and
the lot fell to Mat-
thias; so he was
added to the eleven
apostles.

The Holy Spirit Comes at Pentecost

2 When the day
of Pentecost
came, they were
all together in one
place. 2 Suddenly
a sound like the
blowing of a vi-
olent wind came
from heaven and
filled the whole
house where they
were sitting. 3 They
saw what seemed
to be tongues of
fire that separated
and came to rest
on each of them.
4 All of them were
filled with the
Holy Spirit and

εἰσῆλθεν καὶ ἐξῆλθεν ἐφ᾽ ἡμᾶς ὁ κύριος Ἰησοῦς, 22 ἀρξάμενος
the Lord Jesus came in and went out among us, *the Lord Jesus* beginning
3836 3261 2652 1656 2779 2002 2093 7005 3836 3261 2652 806
v.aai.3s cj v.aai.3s p.a r.ap.1 d.nsm n.nsm n.nsm pt.am.nsm

ἀπὸ τοῦ βαπτίσματος Ἰωάννου ἕως τῆς ἡμέρας ἧς ἀνελήμφθη ἀφ᾽ ἡμῶν,
from the baptism of John until the day ⌞on which⌟ ⌞he was taken up⌟ from us —
608 3836 967 2722 2401 3836 2465 4005 377 608 7005
p.g d.gsn n.gsn n.gsm p.g d.gsf n.gsf r.gsf v.api.3s p.g r.gp.1

μάρτυρα τῆς ἀναστάσεως αὐτοῦ σὺν ἡμῖν
that one of these become with us a witness of his resurrection." *his with us*
1651 4047 4047 1181 5250 7005 3459 3836 899 414 899 5250 7005
n.asm d.gsf n.gsf r.gsm.3 p.d r.dp.1

γενέσθαι ἕνα τούτων. 23 καὶ ἔστησαν δύο, Ἰωσὴφ τὸν καλούμενον Βαρσαββᾶν
become one of these So they proposed two, Joseph *{the}* called Barsabbas
1181 1651 4047 2779 2705 1545 2737 3836 2813 984
f.am a.asm r.gpm cj v.aai.3p a.apm n.asm d.asm pt.pp.asm n.asm

ὃς ἐπεκλήθη Ἰοῦστος, καὶ Μαθθίαν. 24 καὶ ↱ προσευξάμενοι εἶπαν, σὺ
(who was called Justus), and Matthias. And they prayed and said, "You,
4005 2126 2688 2779 3416 2779 3306 4667 3306 5148
r.nsm v.api.3s n.nsm cj n.asm cj pt.am.npm v.aai.3p r.ns.2

κύριε καρδιογνῶστα πάντων, ἀνάδειξον ὃν
Lord, the ⌞one who knows the hearts⌟ of all, show which one of these two
3261 2841 4246 344 4005 1651 1666 4047 1545
n.vsm n.vsm a.gpm v.aam.2s r.asm

ἐξελέξω ἐκ τούτων τῶν δύο ἕνα 25 λαβεῖν τὸν τόπον τῆς διακονίας
⌞you have chosen⌟ *of these {the} two one* to take the place of this ministry
1721 1666 4047 3836 1545 1651 3284 3836 5536 3836 4047 1355
v.ami.2s p.g r.gpm d.gpm a.gpm a.asm f.aa d.asm n.asm d.gsf n.gsf

ταύτης καὶ ἀποστολῆς ἀφ᾽ ἧς παρέβη Ἰούδας πορευθῆναι εἰς
this and apostleship, from which Judas turned aside *Judas* to go to his own
4047 2779 692 608 4005 2683 4124 2683 4513 1650 2625 2625
r.gsf cj n.gsf p.g r.gsf v.aai.3s n.nsm f.ap p.a

τὸν τόπον τὸν ἴδιον. 26 καὶ ἔδωκαν κλήρους αὐτοῖς καὶ ἔπεσεν ὁ
{the} place." *{the} his own* And they cast lots for them, and the lot fell *the*
3836 5536 3836 2625 2779 1443 3102 899 2779 3836 3102 4406 3836
d.asm n.asm d.asm a.asm cj v.aai.3p n.apm r.dpm.3 cj v.aai.3s d.nsm

κλῆρος ἐπὶ Μαθθίαν καὶ συγκατεψηφίσθη μετὰ τῶν ἕνδεκα ἀποστόλων.
lot on Matthias, and he was counted with the eleven apostles.
3102 2093 3416 2779 5164 3552 3836 1894 693
n.nsm p.a n.asm cj v.api.3s p.g d.gpm a.gpm n.gpm

2:1 καὶ ἐν τῷ συμπληροῦσθαι τὴν ἡμέραν τῆς
{and} When *{the}* the day of Pentecost arrived, *the day of*
2779 1877 3836 3836 2465 3836 4300 5230 3836 2465 3836
cj p.d d.dsn f.pp d.asf n.asf d.gsf

πεντηκοστῆς ἦσαν πάντες ὁμοῦ ἐπὶ τὸ αὐτό. 2 καὶ
Pentecost they were all together in the same place. And suddenly from heaven
4300 1639 4246 3938 2093 3836 899 2779 924 1666 4041
n.gsf v.iai.3p a.npm adv p.a d.asn r.asn cj

ἐγένετο ἄφνω ἐκ τοῦ οὐρανοῦ ἦχος ὥσπερ φερομένης πνοῆς βιαίας
there came *suddenly from {the} heaven* a sound like a violent blast of wind, *violent*
1181 924 1666 3836 4041 2491 6061 1042 5770 4466 1042
v.ami.3s adv p.g d.gsm n.gsm n.nsm pl pt.pm.gsf n.gsf a.gsf

καὶ ἐπλήρωσεν ὅλον τὸν οἶκον οὗ ἦσαν καθήμενοι 3 καὶ ὤφθησαν
and it filled the whole *the* house where they were sitting. And there appeared
2779 4444 3836 3910 3836 3875 4023 1639 2764 2779 3972
cj v.aai.3s a.asm d.asm n.asm adv v.iai.3p pt.pm.npm cj v.api.3p

αὐτοῖς διαμεριζόμεναι γλῶσσαι ὡσεὶ πυρὸς καὶ ἐκάθισεν ἐφ᾽ ἕνα
to them tongues spreading out *tongues* like fire, and one came to rest on each one
899 1185 1374 1185 6059 4786 2779 2767 2093 1667 1651
r.dpm.3 pt.pp.npf n.npf pl n.gsn cj v.aai.3s p.a a.asm

ἕκαστον αὐτῶν, 4 καὶ → → ἐπλήσθησαν πάντες πνεύματος ἁγίου καὶ
each of them. And they were all filled with *all* the Holy Spirit, *Holy* and
1667 899 2779 4246 4398 4246 41 4460 41 2779
r.asm r.gpm.3 cj v.api.3p a.npm n.gsn a.gsn cj

NASB

Lord Jesus went
in and out among
us— 22 beginning
with the baptism of
John until the day
that He was taken
up from us—one
of these *must*
become a witness
with us of His
resurrection." 23 So
they put forward
two men, Joseph
called Barsabbas
(who was also
called Justus), and
Matthias. 24 And
they prayed and
said, "You, Lord,
who know the
hearts of all men,
show which one of
these two You have
chosen 25 to occupy
this ministry and
apostleship from
which Judas turned
aside to go to his
own place." 26 And
they drew lots
for them, and the
lot fell to Mat-
thias; and he was
added to the eleven
apostles.

The Day of Pentecost

2:1 When the day
of Pentecost had
come, they were
all together in one
place. 2 And sud-
denly there came
from heaven a
noise like a violent
rushing wind, and
it filled the whole
house where they
were sitting. 3 And
there appeared to
them tongues as
of fire distributing
themselves, and
they rested on each
one of them. 4 And
they were all filled
with the Holy Spir-
it and began to

NIV

began to speak in
other tongues[a] as
the Spirit enabled
them.
5 Now there were
staying in Jerusa-
lem God-fearing
Jews from every
nation under heav-
en. 6 When they
heard this sound,
a crowd came
together in bewil-
derment, because
each one heard
their own language
being spoken.
7 Utterly amazed,
they asked: "Aren't
all these who are
speaking Galile-
ans? 8 Then how is
it that each of us
hears them in our
native language?
9 Parthians, Medes
and Elamites;
residents of Mes-
opotamia, Judea
and Cappadocia,
Pontus and Asia,[b]
10 Phrygia and
Pamphylia, Egypt
and the parts of
Libya near Cyre-
ne; visitors from
Rome 11 (both Jews
and converts to
Judaism); Cretans
and Arabs—we
hear them declar-
ing the wonders
of God in our
own tongues!"
12 Amazed and
perplexed, they
asked one another,
"What does this
mean?"
13 Some, however,
made fun of them
and said, "They
have had too much
wine."

Peter Addresses the Crowd

14 Then Peter
stood up

[a] 4 Or *languages*; also in verse 11
[b] 9 That is, the Roman province by that name

ἤρξαντο λαλεῖν ἑτέραις γλώσσαις καθὼς τὸ πνεῦμα ἐδίδου ἀποφθέγγεσθαι
they began to speak with other tongues as the Spirit gave them utterance.
806 3281 2283 1185 2777 3836 4460 1443 899 710
v.ami.3p f.pa r.dpf n.dpf cj d.nsn n.nsn v.iai.3s f.pm

αὐτοῖς. 5 ἦσαν δὲ εἰς Ἰερουσαλὴμ κατοικοῦντες Ἰουδαῖοι,
them Now there were *But* living in Jerusalem *living* Jews, devout
899 1254 1639 1254 2997 1650 2647 2997 2681 2327
r.dpm.3 v.iai.3p cj p.a n.asf pt.pa.npm a.npm

ἄνδρες εὐλαβεῖς ἀπὸ παντὸς ἔθνους τῶν ὑπὸ τὸν οὐρανόν. 6 →
men *devout* from every nation *{the}* under *{the}* heaven. But when this sound
467 2327 608 4246 1620 3836 5679 3836 4041 1254 4047 5889
n.npm a.npm p.g a.gsn n.gsn d.gpn p.a d.asm n.asm

γενομένης δὲ τῆς φωνῆς ταύτης συνῆλθεν τὸ πλῆθος καὶ
was heard *But* *{the}* *sound* *this* the crowd gathered, *the* *crowd* and
1181 1254 3836 5889 4047 3836 4436 5302 3836 4436 2779
pt.am.gsf cj d.gsf n.gsf r.gsf v.aai.3s d.nsn n.nsn cj

συνεχύθη, ὅτι ἤκουον εἷς ἕκαστος τῇ ἰδίᾳ
they were perplexed, because each one was hearing *one* *each* them speak in his own
5177 4022 1667 1651 201 1651 1667 899 3281 3836 2625
v.api.3s cj v.iai.3p a.nsm r.nsm d.dsf a.dsf

διαλέκτῳ λαλούντων αὐτῶν. 7 ἐξίσταντο δὲ καὶ ἐθαύμαζον λέγοντες,
language. *speak* *them* And they were amazed *And* and wondered, saying, "Are
1365 3281 899 1254 2014 1254 2779 2513 3306 1639
n.dsf pt.pa.gpm r.gpm.3 v.imi.3p cj cj v.iai.3p pt.pa.npm

οὐχ ἰδοὺ ἅπαντες οὗτοί εἰσιν οἱ λαλοῦντες Γαλιλαῖοι; 8 καὶ πῶς ↱ ἡμεῖς
not ~ all these *Are* who are speaking Galileans? And how do we
4024 2627 570 4047 1639 3836 3281 1134 2779 4802 201 7005
pl j a.npm r.npm v.pai.3p d.npm pt.pa.npm a.npm cj cj r.np.1

ἀκούομεν ἕκαστος τῇ ἰδίᾳ διαλέκτῳ ἡμῶν ἐν ᾗ ἐγεννήθημεν;
hear, each of us in his own language *of us* to which he was born?
201 1667 7005 7005 3836 2625 1365 7005 1877 4005 1164
v.pai.1p r.nsm d.dsf a.dsf n.dsf r.gp.1 p.d r.dsf v.api.1p

9 Πάρθοι καὶ Μῆδοι καὶ Ἐλαμῖται καὶ οἱ κατοικοῦντες τὴν Μεσοποταμίαν,
Parthians and Medes and Elamites and *{the}* residents of Mesopotamia,
4222 2779 3597 2779 1780 2779 3836 2997 3836 3544
n.npm cj n.npm cj n.npm cj d.npm pt.pa.npm d.asf n.asf

Ἰουδαίαν τε καὶ Καππαδοκίαν, Πόντον καὶ τὴν Ἀσίαν, 10 Φρυγίαν τε καὶ
Judea ~ and Cappadocia, Pontus and *{the}* Asia, Phrygia ~ and
2677 5445 2779 2838 4509 2779 3836 823 5867 5445 2779
n.asf cj cj n.asf n.asm cj d.asf n.asf n.asf cj cj

Παμφυλίαν, Αἴγυπτον καὶ τὰ μέρη τῆς Λιβύης τῆς κατὰ Κυρήνην, καὶ οἱ
Pamphylia, Egypt and the parts of Libya *{the}* near Cyrene, and *{the}*
4103 131 2779 3836 3538 3836 3340 3836 2848 3255 2779 3836
n.asf n.asf cj d.apn n.apn d.gsf n.gsf d.gsf p.a n.asf cj d.npm

ἐπιδημοῦντες Ῥωμαῖοι,[a] 11 Ἰουδαῖοί τε καὶ προσήλυτοι, Κρῆτες καὶ Ἄραβες,
visitors from Rome, Jews ~ and proselytes, Cretans and Arabians —
2111 4871 2681 5445 2779 4670 3205 2779 732
pt.pa.npm n.npm a.npm cj cj n.npm n.npm cj n.npm

ἀκούομεν λαλούντων αὐτῶν ταῖς ἡμετέραις γλώσσαις τὰ μεγαλεῖα τοῦ θεοῦ.
we hear them telling *them* in our own tongues the mighty works of God."
201 899 3281 899 3836 2466 1185 3836 3483 3836 2536
v.pai.1p pt.pa.gpm r.gpm.3 d.dpf r.dpf.1 n.dpf d.apn n.apn d.gsm n.gsm

12 ἐξίσταντο δὲ πάντες καὶ διηπόρουν, ἄλλος πρὸς ἄλλον
And all were amazed *And* *all* and perplexed, saying to one *to* another,
1254 4246 2014 1254 4246 2779 1389 3306 4639 257 4639 257
v.imi.3p cj a.npm cj v.iai.3p r.nsm p.a r.asm

λέγοντες, τί θέλει τοῦτο εἶναι; 13 ἕτεροι δὲ διαχλευάζοντες ἔλεγον ὅτι
saying "What does this mean?" But others *But* mocking said, ~
3306 5515 2527 4047 1639 1254 2283 1254 1430 3306 4022
pt.pa.npm r.asn v.pai.3s r.asn f.pa r.npm cj pt.pa.npm v.iai.3p cj

γλεύκους μεμεστωμένοι εἰσίν. 14 → σταθεὶς δὲ
"They are filled with new wine." *filled with* *They are* But Peter, taking his stand *But*
1639 1639 3551 3551 1183 3551 1639 1254 4377 2705 1254
n.gsn pt.rp.npm v.pai.3p pt.ap.nsm cj

[a] Ἰουδαῖοί τε καὶ προσήλυτοι included by TR after Ῥωμαῖοι.

NASB

speak with other
tongues, as the
Spirit was giving
them utterance.
5 Now there were
Jews living in Jeru-
salem, devout men
from every nation
under heaven.
6 And when this
sound occurred,
the crowd came
together, and were
bewildered because
each one of them
was hearing them
speak in his own
language. 7 They
were amazed and
astonished, say-
ing, "Why, are not
all these who are
speaking Galile-
ans? 8 And how is it
that we each hear
them in our own
language to which
we were born?
9 Parthians and
Medes and Elam-
ites, and residents
of Mesopotamia,
Judea and Cappa-
docia, Pontus and
Asia, 10 Phrygia and
Pamphylia, Egypt
and the districts
of Libya around
Cyrene, and visi-
tors from Rome,
both Jews and
[a]proselytes, 11 Cre-
tans and Arabs—
we hear them in
our *own* tongues
speaking of the
mighty deeds of
God." 12 And they
all continued in
amazement and
great perplexity,
saying to one an-
other, "What does
this mean?" 13 But
others were mock-
ing and saying,
"They are full of
sweet wine."

Peter's Sermon

14 But Peter, taking
his stand with the

[a] I.e. Gentile converts to Judaism

NIV

with the Eleven,
raised his voice
and addressed the
crowd: "Fellow
Jews and all of
you who live in
Jerusalem, let me
explain this to you;
listen carefully to
what I say. [15]These
people are not
drunk, as you sup-
pose. It's only nine
in the morning!
[16]No, this is what
was spoken by the
prophet Joel:

[17]" 'In the last
days, God
says,
I will pour
out my
Spirit on all
people.
Your sons and
daughters
will
prophesy,
your young
men will
see visions,
your old men
will dream
dreams.
[18]Even on my
servants,
both
men and
women,
I will pour out
my Spirit in
those days,
and they will
prophesy.
[19]I will show
wonders in
the heavens
above
and signs on
the earth
below,
blood and fire
and billows
of smoke.
[20]The sun will be
turned to
darkness
and the moon
to blood
before the
coming
of the
great and
glorious
day of the
Lord.

ὁ Πέτρος σὺν τοῖς ἕνδεκα ἐπῆρεν τὴν φωνὴν αὐτοῦ καὶ ἀπεφθέγξατο αὐτοῖς,
{the} Peter with the eleven, lifted up {the} his voice his and addressed them,
3836 4377 5250 3836 1894 2048 3836 899 5889 899 2779 710 899
d.nsm n.nsm p.d d.dpm a.dpm v.aai.3s d.asf n.asf r.gsm.3 cj v.ami.3s r.dpm.3

ἄνδρες Ἰουδαῖοι καὶ οἱ κατοικοῦντες Ἰερουσαλὴμ πάντες, τοῦτο
"Men of Judea and all you who live in Jerusalem, all let this be
467 2681 2779 4246 3836 2997 2647 4246 1639 4047 1639
n.vpm a.vpm cj d.vpm pt.pa.vpm n.asf a.vpm r.nsn

ὑμῖν γνωστὸν ἔστω καὶ ἐνωτίσασθε τὰ ῥήματά μου. 15
known to you, known let be and give ear to {the} my words. my For these men
1196 7007 1196 1639 2779 1969 3836 1609 4839 1609 1142 4047 4047
r.dp.2 a.nsn v.pam.3s cj v.amm.2p d.apn n.apn r.gs.1

→ οὐ γὰρ ὡς ὑμεῖς ὑπολαμβάνετε οὗτοι μεθύουσιν, ἔστιν γὰρ
are not, For as you suppose, these men drunk, since it is since only the third
3501 4024 1142 6055 7007 5696 4047 3501 1142 1639 1142 5569
pl cj cj r.np.2 v.pai.2p r.npm v.pai.3p v.pai.3s cj

ὥρα τρίτη τῆς ἡμέρας, 16 ἀλλὰ τοῦτό ἐστιν τὸ εἰρημένον διὰ τοῦ προφήτου
hour third of the day. But this is what ⌊was spoken of⌋ through the prophet
6052 5569 3836 2465 247 4047 1639 3836 3306 1328 3836 4737
n.nsf a.nsf d.gsf n.gsf cj r.nsn v.pai.3s d.nsn pt.rp.nsn p.g d.gsm n.gsm

Ἰωήλ, 17 καὶ ἔσται ἐν ταῖς ἐσχάταις ἡμέραις, λέγει ὁ θεός, ἐκχεῶ
Joel: 'And ⌊it will be⌋ in the last days,' declares {the} God, 'that ⌊I will pour out⌋
2727 2779 1639 1877 3836 2274 2465 3306 3836 2536 1772
n.gsm cj v.fmi.3s p.d d.dpf a.dpf n.dpf v.pai.3s d.nsm n.nsm v.fai.1s

ἀπὸ τοῦ πνεύματός μου ἐπὶ πᾶσαν σάρκα, καὶ
{from} {the} my Spirit my on all flesh, and your sons and your daughters
608 3836 1609 4460 1609 2093 4246 4922 2779 7007 5626 2779 7007 2588
p.g d.gsn n.gsn r.gs.1 p.a a.asf n.asf cj

προφητεύσουσιν οἱ υἱοὶ ὑμῶν καὶ αἱ θυγατέρες ὑμῶν καὶ οἱ νεανίσκοι
will prophesy, {the} sons your and {the} daughters your and {the} your young men
4736 3836 5626 7007 2779 3836 2588 7007 2779 3836 7007 3734
v.fai.3p d.npm n.npm r.gp.2 cj d.npf n.npf r.gp.2 cj d.npm n.npm

ὑμῶν ὁράσεις ὄψονται καὶ οἱ πρεσβύτεροι ὑμῶν ἐνυπνίοις
your will see visions, will see and {the} your old men your will dream dreams.
7007 3972 3972 3970 3972 2779 3836 7007 4565 7007 1965 1965 1966
r.gp.2 n.apf v.fmi.3p cj d.npm a.npm r.gp.2 n.dpn

ἐνυπνιασθήσονται· 18 καί γε ἐπὶ τοὺς δούλους μου καὶ ἐπὶ τὰς
will dream Even ~ on {the} my male servants my and on {the} my
1965 2779 1145 2093 3836 1609 1529 1609 2779 2093 3836 1609
v.fpi.3p cj pl p.a d.apm n.apm r.gs.1 cj p.a d.apf

δούλας μου ἐν ταῖς ἡμέραις ἐκείναις ἐκχεῶ ἀπὸ τοῦ
female servants my in {the} those days those ⌊I will pour out⌋ {from} {the} my
1527 1609 1877 3836 1697 2465 1697 1772 608 3836 1609
n.apf r.gs.1 p.d d.dpf n.dpf r.dpf v.fai.1s p.g d.gsn

πνεύματός μου, καὶ προφητεύσουσιν. 19 καὶ δώσω τέρατα ἐν τῷ οὐρανῷ ἄνω
Spirit, my and they will prophesy. And I will show wonders in the heavens above
4460 1609 2779 4736 2779 1443 5469 1877 3836 4041 539
n.gsn r.gs.1 cj v.fai.3p cj v.fai.1s n.apn p.d d.dsm n.dsm adv

καὶ σημεῖα ἐπὶ τῆς γῆς κάτω, αἷμα καὶ πῦρ καὶ ἀτμίδα καπνοῦ. 20 ὁ
and signs on the earth below, blood, and fire, and smoky vapor. smoky The
2779 4956 2093 3836 1178 3004 135 2779 4786 2779 2837 874 2837 3836
cj n.apn p.g d.gsf n.gsf adv n.asn cj n.asn cj n.asf n.gsm d.nsm

ἥλιος μεταστραφήσεται εἰς σκότος καὶ ἡ σελήνη εἰς αἷμα, πρὶν ἐλθεῖν
sun will be turned into darkness and the moon into blood, before the coming of the
2463 3570 1650 5030 2779 3836 4943 1650 135 4570 2262 3836
n.nsm v.fpi.3s p.a n.asn cj d.nsf n.nsf p.a n.asn cj f.aa

ἡμέραν → κυρίου τὴν μεγάλην καὶ ἐπιφανῆ. 21 καὶ ἔσται
great and glorious day of the Lord. the great and glorious And ⌊it shall be⌋ that
3489 2779 2212 2465 3261 3836 3489 2779 2212 2779 1639
n.asf n.gsm d.asf a.asf cj a.asf cj v.fmi.3s

NASB

eleven, raised his
voice and declared
to them: "Men of
Judea and all you
who live in Jeru-
salem, let this be
known to you and
give heed to my
words. [15]For these
men are not drunk,
as you suppose, for
it is *only* the [a]third
hour of the day;
[16]but this is what
was spoken of
through the prophet
Joel:
[17]' AND IT SHALL
BE IN THE LAST
DAYS,' God
says,
' THAT I WILL
POUR FORTH OF
MY SPIRIT ON
ALL MANKIND;
AND YOUR SONS
AND YOUR
DAUGHTERS
SHALL PROPH-
ESY,
AND YOUR
YOUNG MEN
SHALL SEE VI-
SIONS,
AND YOUR
OLD MEN
SHALL DREAM
DREAMS;
[18]EVEN ON MY
BONDSLAVES,
BOTH MEN AND
WOMEN,
I WILL IN THOSE
DAYS POUR
FORTH OF MY
SPIRIT
And they shall
prophesy.
[19]' AND I WILL
GRANT WON-
DERS IN THE
SKY ABOVE
AND SIGNS ON
THE EARTH
BELOW,
BLOOD, AND
FIRE, AND VA-
POR OF SMOKE.
[20]' THE SUN WILL
BE TURNED
INTO DARKNESS
AND THE MOON
INTO BLOOD,
BEFORE THE
GREAT AND
GLORIOUS DAY
OF THE LORD
SHALL COME.
[21]' AND IT SHALL

[a] I.e. 9 a.m.

NIV

[21]And everyone
who calls
on the name
of the Lord
will be
saved.’[a]

[22]“Fellow Is-
raelites, listen
to this: Jesus of
Nazareth was a
man accredited
by God to you by
miracles, wonders
and signs, which
God did among
you through him,
as you yourselves
know. [23]This man
was handed over
to you by God’s
deliberate plan and
foreknowledge;
and you, with the
help of wicked
men,[b] put him to
death by nailing
him to the cross.
[24]But God raised
him from the dead,
freeing him from
the agony of death,
because it was im-
possible for death
to keep its hold on
him. [25]David said
about him:

“ ‘I saw the Lord
always
before me.
Because he is
at my right
hand,
I will not be
shaken.
[26]Therefore my
heart is
glad and
my tongue
rejoices;
my body also
will rest in
hope,
[27]because you
will not
abandon
me to the
realm of
the dead,
you will not
let your
holy one
see decay.

[a] 21 Joel 2:28-32
[b] 23 Or *of those not having the law* (that is, Gentiles)

πᾶς ὃς ἂν ἐπικαλέσηται τὸ ὄνομα → κυρίου σωθήσεται. [22] ἄνδρες
everyone who calls upon the name of the Lord will be saved.’ “Men
4246 4005 323 2126 3836 3950 3261 5392 467
a.nsm r.nsm pl v.ams.3s d.asn n.asn n.gsm v.fpi.3s n.vpm

Ἰσραηλῖται, ἀκούσατε τοὺς λόγους τούτους· Ἰησοῦν τὸν Ναζωραῖον, ἄνδρα
of Israel, hear *{the}* these words: *these* Jesus of Nazareth, a man
2703 201 3836 4047 3364 4047 2652 3836 3717 467
n.vpm v.aam.2p d.apm n.apm r.apm n.asm d.asm n.asm n.asm

ἀποδεδειγμένον ἀπὸ τοῦ θεοῦ εἰς ὑμᾶς → δυνάμεσι καὶ τέρασι καὶ
attested to you by *{the}* God *to* *you* with mighty works and wonders and
617 1650 7007 608 3836 2536 1650 7007 1539 2779 5469 2779
pt.rp.asm p.g d.gsm n.gsm p.a r.ap.2 n.dpf cj n.dpn cj

σημείοις οἷς ἐποίησεν δι’ αὐτοῦ ὁ θεὸς ἐν μέσῳ ὑμῶν καθὼς ↱
signs that God did through him *{the}* *God* in your midst, *your* as you
4956 4005 2536 4472 1328 899 3836 2536 1877 7007 3545 7007 2777 3857
n.dpn r.dpn v.aai.3s p.g r.gsm.3 d.nsm n.nsm p.d n.dsn r.gp.2 cj

αὐτοὶ οἴδατε, [23] τοῦτον τῇ ὡρισμένῃ βουλῇ καὶ
yourselves know — this Jesus, delivered up ⌞according to the⌟ determined purpose and
899 3857 4047 1692 1692 3836 3988 1087 2779
r.npm v.rai.2p r.asm d.dsf pt.rp.dsf n.dsf cj

προγνώσει τοῦ θεοῦ ἔκδοτον διὰ χειρὸς ἀνόμων
foreknowledge of God, *delivered up* you, at the hands ⌞of those outside the law,⌟ executed
4590 3836 2536 1692 359 1328 5931 491 359
n.dsf d.gsm n.gsm a.asm p.g n.gsf a.gpm

προσπήξαντες ← ← ← ἀνείλατε, [24] ὃν ὁ θεὸς ἀνέστησεν λύσας τὰς
by nailing him to a cross; *you executed* whom *{the}* God raised up, loosing the
4699 359 4005 3836 2536 482 3395 3836
pt.aa.npm v.aai.2p r.asm d.nsm n.nsm v.aai.3s pt.aa.nsm d.apf

ὠδῖνας τοῦ θανάτου, καθότι οὐκ ἦν δυνατὸν κρατεῖσθαι αὐτὸν
pangs of death, as it was not *it was* possible for him to be held *him*
6047 3836 2505 2776 1639 1639 4024 1639 1543 899 3195 899
n.apf d.gsm n.gsm cj pl v.iai.3s a.nsn f.pp r.asm.3

ὑπ’ αὐτοῦ. [25] Δαυὶδ γὰρ λέγει εἰς αὐτόν, προορώμην τὸν κύριον ἐνώπιόν
by it. For David *For* says regarding him, ‘I foresaw the Lord before
5679 899 1142 1253 1142 3306 1650 899 4632 3836 3261 1967
p.g r.gsm.3 n.nsm cj v.pai.3s p.a r.asm.3 v.imi.1s d.asm n.asm p.g

μου ⌞διὰ παντός,⌟ ὅτι ἐκ δεξιῶν μού ἐστιν ἵνα ↱ ↱ μὴ
me always, for he is at my right hand *my* *he is* that I may not
1609 1328 4246 4022 1639 1639 1666 1609 1288 1609 1639 2671 4888 4888 3590
r.gs.1 p.g a.gsm cj p.g a.gpf r.gs.1 v.pai.3s cj pl

σαλευθῶ. [26] διὰ τοῦτο ηὐφράνθη ἡ καρδία μου καὶ
be shaken; ⌞on account of⌟ this my heart rejoiced, *{the}* *heart* *my* and my tongue
4888 1328 4047 1609 2840 2370 3836 2840 1609 2779 1609 1185
v.aps.1s p.a r.asn v.api.3s d.nsf n.nsf r.gs.1 cj

ἠγαλλιάσατο ἡ γλῶσσά μου, ⌞ἔτι δὲ⌟ καὶ ἡ σάρξ μου
was glad; *{the}* *tongue* *my* moreover my flesh also *{the}* *flesh* *my*
22 3836 1185 1609 2285 1254 1609 4922 2779 3836 4922 1609
v.ami.3s d.nsf n.nsf r.gs.1 adv cj adv d.nsf n.nsf r.gs.1

κατασκηνώσει ἐπ’ ἐλπίδι, [27] ὅτι ↱ ↱ οὐκ ἐγκαταλείψεις τὴν ψυχήν μου
will dwell in hope. For you will not abandon *{the}* my soul *my*
2942 2093 1828 4022 1593 1593 4024 1593 3836 1609 6034 1609
v.fai.3s p.d n.dsf cj pl v.fai.2s d.asf n.asf r.gs.1

εἰς ᾅδην οὐδὲ δώσεις τὸν ὅσιόν σου ἰδεῖν διαφθοράν.
to Hades, or allow *{the}* your Holy One *your* to see corruption.
1650 87 4028 1443 3836 5148 4008 5148 1625 1426
p.a n.asm cj v.fai.2s d.asm a.asm r.gs.2 f.aa n.asf

[28] ἐγνώρισάς μοι ὁδοὺς ζωῆς, → → → πληρώσεις με
⌞You have made known⌟ to me the paths of life; you will make me full *me*
1192 1609 3847 2437 1609 4444 1609
v.aai.2s r.ds.1 n.apf n.gsf v.fai.2s r.as.1

εὐφροσύνης μετὰ τοῦ προσώπου σου. [29] ⌞ἄνδρες ἀδελφοί,⌟ ἐξὸν εἰπεῖν
of joy with *{the}* your presence.’ *your* My brothers, I can speak to
2372 3552 3836 5148 4725 5148 467 81 1997 3306 4639
n.gsf p.g d.gsn n.gsn r.gs.2 n.vpm n.vpm pt.pa.nsn f.aa

NASB

BE THAT EV-
ERYONE WHO
CALLS ON THE
NAME OF THE
LORD WILL BE
SAVED.’
[22]“Men of Is-
rael, listen to these
words: Jesus the
Nazarene, a man
attested to you by
God with miracles
and wonders and
signs which God
performed through
Him in your
midst, just as you
yourselves know—
[23]this *Man,* deliv-
ered over by the
predetermined plan
and foreknowledge
of God, you nailed
to a cross by the
hands of godless
men and put *Him*
to death. [24]But God
raised Him up
again, putting an
end to the agony of
death, since it was
impossible for Him
to be held in its
power. [25]For David
says of Him,
‘I SAW THE LORD
ALWAYS IN MY
PRESENCE;
FOR HE IS AT
MY RIGHT
HAND, SO THAT
I WILL NOT BE
SHAKEN.
[26]‘THEREFORE MY
HEART WAS
GLAD AND MY
TONGUE EX-
ULTED;
MOREOVER MY
FLESH ALSO
WILL LIVE IN
HOPE;
[27]BECAUSE YOU
WILL NOT
ABANDON MY
SOUL TO HA-
DES,
NOR ALLOW
YOUR HOLY
ONE TO UN-
DERGO DECAY.
[28]‘YOU HAVE MADE
KNOWN TO ME
THE WAYS OF
LIFE;
YOU WILL MAKE
ME FULL OF
GLADNESS
WITH YOUR
PRESENCE.’
[29]“Brethren, I may

NIV

[28]You have made
known
to me the
paths of
life;
you will fill
me with
joy in your
presence.'[a]
[29]"Fellow Isra-
elites, I can tell
you confidently
that the patriarch
David died and
was buried, and
his tomb is here to
this day. [30]But he
was a prophet and
knew that God had
promised him on
oath that he would
place one of his
descendants on
his throne. [31]See-
ing what was to
come, he spoke of
the resurrection of
the Messiah, that
he was not aban-
doned to the realm
of the dead, nor
did his body see
decay. [32]God has
raised this Jesus
to life, and we are
all witnesses of it.
[33]Exalted to the
right hand of God,
he has received
from the Father
the promised Holy
Spirit and has
poured out what
you now see and
hear. [34]For David
did not ascend to
heaven, and yet he
said,
"'The Lord said
to my Lord:
"Sit at my
right hand
[35]until I make
your
enemies
a footstool
for your
feet."'[b]
[36]"Therefore let
all Israel be as-
sured of this:

[a] 28 Psalm 16:8-11 (see Septuagint)
[b] 35 Psalm 110:1

⌊μετὰ παρρησίας⌋ πρὸς ὑμᾶς περὶ τοῦ πατριάρχου Δαυὶδ ὅτι ↱ ↱ καὶ
you confidently *to* *you* about the patriarch David, that he is both
7007 3552 4244 4639 7007 4309 3836 4256 1253 4022 5462 5462 2779
p.g n.gsf p.a r.ap.2 p.g d.gsm n.gsm n.gsm cj cj

ἐτελεύτησεν καὶ ἐτάφη, καὶ τὸ μνῆμα αὐτοῦ ἔστιν ἐν ἡμῖν ἄχρι τῆς
dead and buried and *{the}* his tomb *his* is with us to *{the}* this
5462 2779 2507 2779 3836 899 3645 899 1639 1877 7005 948 3836 4047
v.aai.3s cj v.api.3s cj d.nsn n.nsn r.gsm.3 v.pai.3s p.d r.dp.1 p.g d.gsf

ἡμέρας ταύτης. [30] προφήτης οὖν ὑπάρχων καὶ εἰδὼς ὅτι
day. *this* Therefore being a prophet, *Therefore* *being* and knowing that God
2465 4047 4036 5639 4737 4036 5639 2779 3857 4022 2536
n.gsf r.gsf n.nsm cj pt.pa.nsm cj pt.ra.nsm cj

↱ ὅρκῳ ὤμοσεν αὐτῷ ὁ θεὸς
promised him with an oath *promised* *him* *{the}* *God* that he would place
3923 899 3992 3923 899 3836 2536 2767 2767 2767
n.dsm v.aai.3s r.dsm.3 d.nsm n.nsm

⌊ἐκ καρποῦ τῆς ὀσφύος αὐτοῦ⌋[a] καθίσαι ἐπὶ τὸν θρόνον
one of his descendants *he would place* on *{the}* his throne,
1666 2843 3836 4019 899 2767 2093 3836 899 2585
p.g n.gsm d.gsf n.gsf r.gsm.3 f.aa p.a d.asm n.asm

αὐτοῦ, [31] ↱ προϊδὼν ἐλάλησεν περὶ τῆς ἀναστάσεως τοῦ Χριστοῦ ὅτι ↱
his he foresaw and spoke about the resurrection of the Christ, that he
899 3281 4632 3281 4309 3836 414 3836 5986 4022 1593
r.gsm.3 pt.aa.nsm v.aai.3s p.g d.gsf n.gsf d.gsm n.gsm cj

↱ οὔτε ἐγκατελείφθη εἰς ᾅδην οὔτε ↱ ἡ σὰρξ αὐτοῦ εἶδεν διαφθοράν.
was not abandoned to Hades, nor did *{the}* his flesh *his* see corruption.
1593 4046 1593 1650 87 4046 1625 3836 899 4922 899 1625 1426
cj v.api.3s p.a n.asm cj d.nsf n.nsf r.gsm.3 v.aai.3s n.asf

[32] τοῦτον τὸν Ἰησοῦν ἀνέστησεν ὁ θεός, οὗ πάντες ἡμεῖς ἐσμεν
This *{the}* Jesus God raised up, *{the}* *God* ⌊of which⌋ we all *we* are
4047 3836 2652 2536 482 3836 2536 4005 7005 4246 7005 1639
r.asm d.asm n.asm v.aai.3s d.nsm n.nsm r.gsm a.npm r.np.1 v.pai.1p

μάρτυρες· [33] τῇ δεξιᾷ οὖν τοῦ θεοῦ ὑψωθείς,
witnesses. So then, exalted ⌊at the⌋ right hand *So then* of God, *exalted* and having
3459 4036 4036 5738 3836 1288 4036 3836 2536 5738 3284
n.npm d.dsf a.dsf cj d.gsm n.gsm pt.ap.nsm

τήν τε ἐπαγγελίαν τοῦ πνεύματος τοῦ ἁγίου
received from the Father the ~ promise of the Holy Spirit, *{the}* *Holy*
3284 4123 3836 4252 3836 5445 2039 3836 41 4460 3836 41
d.asf cj n.asf d.gsn n.gsn d.gsn a.gsn

λαβὼν παρὰ τοῦ πατρός, ἐξέχεεν τοῦτο ὃ ὑμεῖς ↱ καὶ[b] βλέπετε
having received *from* *the* *Father* ⌊he has poured out⌋ this that you are both seeing
3284 4123 3836 4252 1772 4047 4005 7007 1063 2779 1063
pt.aa.nsm p.g d.gsm n.gsm v.aai.3s r.asn r.asn r.np.2 cj v.pai.2p

καὶ ἀκούετε. [34] ↱ οὐ γὰρ Δαυὶδ ἀνέβη εἰς τοὺς οὐρανούς, ↱
and hearing. For David did not *For* *David* ascend into the heavens, but he himself
2779 201 1142 1253 326 4024 1142 1253 326 1650 3836 4041 1254 899
cj v.pai.2p pl cj n.nsm v.aai.3s p.a d.apm n.apm

λέγει δὲ αὐτός, εἶπεν ὁ[c] κύριος τῷ κυρίῳ μου, κάθου ἐκ
says, *but* *himself* 'The Lord said *The* *Lord* to my Lord, *my* Sit at my
3306 1254 899 3836 3261 3306 3836 3261 3836 1609 3261 1609 2764 1666 1609
v.pai.3s cj r.nsm v.aai.3s d.nsm n.nsm d.dsm n.dsm r.gs.1 v.pmm.2s p.g

δεξιῶν μου, [35] ⌊ἕως ἂν⌋ θῶ τοὺς ἐχθρούς σου ὑποπόδιον τῶν ποδῶν
right hand, *my* until I make *{the}* your enemies *your* a footstool for your feet.'
1288 1609 2401 323 5502 3836 5148 2398 5148 5711 3836 5148 4546
a.gpf r.gs.1 cj pl v.aas.1s d.apm a.apm r.gs.2 n.asn d.gpm n.gpm

σου. [36] ἀσφαλῶς οὖν γινωσκέτω πᾶς οἶκος
your So let the entire house of Israel know for certain *So* *let know* *entire* *house*
5148 4036 1182 4246 3875 2702 2702 1182 857 4036 1182 4246 3875
r.gs.2 adv cj v.pam.3s a.nsm n.nsm

[a] τὸ κατὰ σάρκα ἀναστήσειν τὸν Χριστόν included by TR after αὐτοῦ.
[b] [καὶ] UBS.
[c] [ὁ] UBS, omitted by TNIV.

NASB

confidently say to
you regarding the
patriarch David
that he both died
and was buried,
and his tomb is
with us to this day.
[30]And so, because
he was a prophet
and knew that GOD
HAD SWORN TO HIM
WITH AN OATH TO
SEAT *ONE* OF HIS
DESCENDANTS ON HIS
THRONE, [31]he looked
ahead and spoke
of the resurrection
of [a]the Christ, that
HE WAS NEITHER
ABANDONED TO
HADES, NOR DID His
flesh SUFFER DECAY.
[32]This Jesus God
raised up again, to
which we are all
witnesses. [33]There-
fore having been
exalted to the right
hand of God, and
having received
from the Father
the promise of the
Holy Spirit, He has
poured forth this
which you both
see and hear. [34]For
it was not David
who ascended into
heaven, but he
himself says:
'THE LORD SAID
TO MY LORD,
"SIT AT MY
RIGHT HAND,
[35]UNTIL I MAKE
YOUR ENEMIES
A FOOTSTOOL
FOR YOUR
FEET."'
[36]Therefore let all
the house of Israel
know for certain

[a] I.e. the Messiah

NIV

God has made this
Jesus, whom you
crucified, both
Lord and Mes-
siah."
37 When the peo-
ple heard this, they
were cut to the
heart and said to
Peter and the other
apostles, "Broth-
ers, what shall
we do?"
38 Peter replied,
"Repent and be
baptized, every
one of you, in the
name of Jesus
Christ for the for-
giveness of your
sins. And you will
receive the gift of
the Holy Spirit.
39 The promise is
for you and your
children and for
all who are far
off—for all whom
the Lord our God
will call."
40 With many
other words he
warned them;
and he pleaded
with them, "Save
yourselves from
this corrupt gen-
eration." 41 Those
who accepted his
message were bap-
tized, and about
three thousand
were added to their
number that day.

The Fellowship of the Believers

42 They devoted
themselves to the
apostles' teaching
and to fellowship,
to the breaking
of bread and to
prayer. 43 Everyone
was filled with
awe at the many
wonders and signs
performed by the
apostles.

Ἰσραὴλ ὅτι καὶ κύριον αὐτὸν καὶ χριστὸν ἐποίησεν ὁ θεός,
of Israel that God has made him both Lord *him* and Christ, *has made* *{the}* *God*
2702 4022 2536 4472 4472 899 2779 3261 899 2779 5986 4472 3836 2536
n.gsm cj cj n.asm r.asm.3 cj n.asm v.aai.3s d.nsm n.nsm

τοῦτον τὸν Ἰησοῦν ὃν ὑμεῖς ἐσταυρώσατε. 37 ἀκούσαντες δὲ
this *{the}* Jesus whom you crucified." Now when they heard *Now* this
4047 3836 2652 4005 7007 5090 1254 201 1254
r.asm d.asm n.asm r.asm r.np.2 v.aai.2p pt.aa.npm cj

κατενύγησαν τὴν καρδίαν εἶπόν τε πρὸς τὸν Πέτρον καὶ τοὺς λοιποὺς
they were cut to the heart, and they said *and* to *{the}* Peter and the other
2920 3836 2840 5445 3306 5445 4639 3836 4377 2779 3836 3370
v.api.3p d.asf n.asf v.aai.3p cj p.a d.asm n.asm cj d.apm a.apm

ἀποστόλους, τί ποιήσωμεν, ⸂ἄνδρες ἀδελφοί;⸃ 38 Πέτρος δὲ
apostles, "My brothers, what shall we do?" *My brothers* And Peter *And* said
693 467 467 5515 4472 467 81 1254 4377 1254
n.apm r.asn v.aas.1p n.vpm n.vpm n.nsm cj

πρὸς αὐτούς, μετανοήσατε,[a] καὶ → βαπτισθήτω ἕκαστος ὑμῶν ἐπὶ
to them, "Repent and let every one of you be baptized *every one* *of you* in
4639 899 3566 2779 1667 1667 7007 7007 966 1667 7007 2093
p.a r.apm.3 v.aam.2p cj v.apm.3s r.nsm r.gp.2 p.d

τῷ ὀνόματι Ἰησοῦ Χριστοῦ εἰς ἄφεσιν τῶν ἁμαρτιῶν ὑμῶν καὶ
the name of Jesus Christ for the forgiveness of your sins, *your* and
3836 3950 2652 5986 1650 912 3836 7007 281 7007 2779
d.dsn n.dsn n.gsm n.gsm p.a n.asf d.gpf n.gpf r.gp.2 cj

λήμψεσθε τὴν δωρεὰν τοῦ ἁγίου πνεύματος. 39 ὑμῖν γάρ
you will receive the gift of the Holy Spirit. For the promise is for you *For*
3284 3836 1561 3836 41 4460 1142 3836 2039 1639 7007 1142
v.fmi.2p d.asf n.asf d.gsn a.gsn n.gsn r.dp.2 cj

ἐστιν ἡ ἐπαγγελία καὶ τοῖς τέκνοις ὑμῶν καὶ πᾶσιν τοῖς εἰς μακράν,
is *the* *promise* and for your children *your* and for all who are *{to}* far away —
1639 3836 2039 2779 3836 7007 5451 7007 2779 4246 3836 1650 3426
v.pai.3s d.nsf n.nsf cj d.dpn n.dpn r.gp.2 cj a.dpm d.dpm p.a adv

⸂ὅσους ἂν⸃ προσκαλέσηται κύριος ὁ θεὸς ἡμῶν. 40 →
as many as the Lord our God will call to himself." *Lord* *the* *God* *our* And with
4012 323 3836 3261 7005 2536 4673 3261 3836 2536 7005 5445
r.apm pl v.ams.3s n.nsm d.nsm n.nsm r.gp.1

ἑτέροις τε λόγοις πλείοσιν → → διεμαρτύρατο καὶ παρεκάλει αὐτοὺς
many other *And* words *many* he gave them warning and pleaded with them,
4498 2283 5445 3364 4498 1371 2779 4151 899
r.dpm cj n.dpm a.dpm.c v.ami.3s cj v.iai.3s r.apm.3

λέγων, σώθητε ἀπὸ τῆς γενεᾶς τῆς σκολιᾶς ταύτης. 41 οἱ μὲν
saying, "Escape from *{the}* this corrupt generation." *{the}* *corrupt* *this* So those ~
3306 5392 608 3836 4047 5021 1155 3836 5021 4047 4036 3836 3525
pt.pa.nsm v.apm.2p p.g d.gsf n.gsf d.gsf a.gsf r.gsf d.npm pl

οὖν ἀποδεξάμενοι τὸν λόγον αὐτοῦ ἐβαπτίσθησαν καὶ προσετέθησαν ἐν τῇ
So who received *{the}* his word *his* were baptized, and there were added on *{the}*
4036 622 3836 899 3364 899 966 2779 4707 1877 3836
cj pt.am.npm d.asm n.asm r.gsm.3 v.api.3p cj v.api.3p p.d d.dsf

ἡμέρᾳ ἐκείνῃ ψυχαὶ ὡσεὶ τρισχίλιαι. 42 ἦσαν δὲ
that day *that* about three thousand souls. *about* *three thousand* And they were *And*
1697 2465 1697 6059 5567 5567 6034 6059 5567 1254 1639 1254
n.dsf r.dsf n.npf pl a.npf v.iai.3p cj

προσκαρτεροῦντες τῇ διδαχῇ τῶν ἀποστόλων καὶ τῇ κοινωνίᾳ, τῇ κλάσει
devoting themselves ⸂to the⸃ teaching of the apostles, *{and}* ⸂to the⸃ fellowship, ⸂to the⸃ breaking
4674 3836 1439 3836 693 2779 3836 3126 3836 3082
pt.pa.npm d.dsf n.dsf d.gpm n.gpm cj d.dsf n.dsf d.dsf n.dsf

τοῦ ἄρτου καὶ ταῖς προσευχαῖς. 43 ἐγίνετο δὲ πάσῃ ψυχῇ φόβος, πολλά
of bread, and to prayers. Fear came upon *{and}* every soul, *Fear* and many
3836 788 2779 3836 4666 5832 1181 1254 4246 6034 5832 5445 4498
d.gsm n.gsm cj d.dpf n.dpf v.imi.3s cj a.dsf n.dsf n.nsm a.npn

τε τέρατα καὶ σημεῖα διὰ τῶν ἀποστόλων ἐγίνετο. 44
and wonders and signs were being done through the apostles. *were being done* And
5445 5469 2779 4956 1181 1181 1181 1328 3836 693 1181 1254
cj n.npn cj n.npn p.g d.gpm n.gpm v.imi.3s

[a] φησίν included by UBS after μετανοήσατε.

NASB

that God has made
Him both Lord and
Christ—this Jesus
whom you cruci-
fied."

The Ingathering

37 Now when they
heard *this,* they
were pierced to the
heart, and said to
Peter and the rest
of the apostles,
"Brethren, what
shall we do?" 38 Pe-
ter *said* to them,
"Repent, and each
of you be baptized
in the name of
Jesus Christ for
the forgiveness of
your sins; and you
will receive the gift
of the Holy Spirit.
39 For the promise
is for you and your
children and for all
who are far off, as
many as the Lord
our God will call
to Himself." 40 And
with many other
words he solemnly
testified and kept
on exhorting them,
saying, "Be saved
from this perverse
generation!" 41 So
then, those who
had received his
word were bap-
tized; and that
day there were
added about three
thousand [a]souls.
42 They were con-
tinually devoting
themselves to the
apostles' teaching
and to fellowship,
to the breaking
of bread and to
prayer.
43 Everyone kept
feeling a sense of
awe; and many
wonders and signs
were taking place
through the apos-
tles. 44 And all

[a] I.e. persons

NIV

44 All the believers
were together and
had everything in
common. 45 They
sold property and
possessions to give
to anyone who had
need. 46 Every day
they continued to
meet together in
the temple courts.
They broke bread
in their homes and
ate together with
glad and sincere
hearts, 47 praising
God and enjoying
the favor of all the
people. And the
Lord added to their
number daily those
who were being
saved.

Peter Heals a Lame Beggar

3 One day Pe-
ter and John
were going up to
the temple at the
time of prayer—at
three in the af-
ternoon. 2 Now a
man who was lame
from birth was be-
ing carried to the
temple gate called
Beautiful, where
he was put every
day to beg from
those going into
the temple courts.
3 When he saw Pe-
ter and John about
to enter, he asked
them for mon-
ey. 4 Peter looked
straight at him, as
did John. Then Pe-
ter said, "Look at
us!" 5 So the man
gave them his at-
tention, expecting
to get something
from them.

πάντες δὲ οἱ πιστεύοντες ἦσαν ⌞ἐπὶ τὸ αὐτὸ⌟ καὶ εἶχον ἅπαντα κοινὰ
all *And* who believed were together, and had all things in common;
4246 1254 3836 4409 1639 2093 3836 899 2779 2400 570 3123
a.npm cj d.npm pt.pa.npm v.iai.3p p.a d.asn r.asn cj v.iai.3p a.apn a.apn

45 καὶ τὰ κτήματα καὶ τὰς ὑπάρξεις ἐπίπρασκον καὶ διεμέριζον
and they were selling their possessions and *{the}* belongings *they were selling* and distributing
2779 4405 4405 4405 3836 3228 2779 3836 5638 4405 2779 1374
cj d.apn n.apn cj d.apf n.apf v.iai.3p cj v.iai.3p

αὐτὰ πᾶσιν καθότι ⌞ἂν τις⌟ χρείαν εἶχεν· 46 καθ᾽ ἡμέραν τε
the proceeds to all, as anyone had need. *had* And every day, *And*
899 4246 2776 323 5516 2400 5970 2400 5445 2848 2465 5445
r.apn.3 a.dpm cj pl r.nsm n.asf v.iai.3s p.a n.asf cj

προσκαρτεροῦντες ὁμοθυμαδὸν ἐν τῷ ἱερῷ, κλῶντές τε κατ᾽
they continued to gather together in the temple, breaking ~ bread from house to
4674 3924 1877 3836 2639 3089 5445 788 2848
pt.pa.npm adv p.d d.dsn n.dsn pt.pa.npm cj p.a

οἶκον ἄρτον, μετελάμβανον τροφῆς ἐν ἀγαλλιάσει καὶ ἀφελότητι καρδίας
house, *bread* sharing their food with joy and simplicity of heart,
3875 788 3561 5575 1877 21 2779 911 2840
n.asm n.asm v.iai.3p n.gsf p.d n.dsf cj n.dsf n.gsf

47 αἰνοῦντες τὸν θεὸν καὶ ἔχοντες χάριν πρὸς ὅλον τὸν λαόν. ὁ δὲ κύριος
praising *{the}* God, and finding favor with all the people. And the *And* Lord
140 3836 2536 2779 2400 5921 4639 3910 3836 3295 1254 3836 1254 3261
pt.pa.npm d.asm n.asm cj pt.pa.npm n.asf p.a a.asm d.asm n.asm d.nsm cj n.nsm

προσετίθει τοὺς σῳζομένους καθ᾽ ἡμέραν ἐπὶ τὸ
was adding to their number day by day those ⌞who were being saved.⌟ *by* *day* *to* *their*
4707 2093 3836 899 2848 2465 3836 5392 2848 2465 2093 3836
v.iai.3s d.apm pt.pp.apm p.a n.asf p.a d.asn

αὐτό.
number
899
r.asn

3:1 Πέτρος δὲ καὶ Ἰωάννης ἀνέβαινον εἰς τὸ ἱερὸν ἐπὶ τὴν ὥραν τῆς
Now Peter *Now* and John ⌞were going up⌟ to the temple at the hour of
1254 4377 1254 2779 2722 326 1650 3836 2639 2093 3836 6052 3836
n.nsm cj cj n.nsm v.iai.3p p.a d.asn n.asn p.a d.asf n.asf d.gsf

προσευχῆς τὴν ἐνάτην. 2 καί τις ἀνὴρ χωλὸς ἐκ κοιλίας → μητρὸς
prayer, the ninth hour. And a man lame from the womb of his mother
4666 3836 1888 2779 5516 467 6000 1666 3120 899 3613
n.gsf d.asf a.asf cj r.nsm n.nsm a.nsm p.g n.gsf n.gsf

αὐτοῦ ὑπάρχων ἐβαστάζετο, ὃν ἐτίθουν ⌞καθ᾽ ἡμέραν⌟ πρὸς τὴν θύραν τοῦ ἱεροῦ
his was being carried, whom they laid daily at the gate of the temple
899 5639 1002 4005 5502 2848 2465 4639 3836 2598 3836 2639
r.gsm.3 pt.pa.nsm v.ipi.3s r.asm v.iai.3p p.a n.asf p.a d.asf n.asf d.gsn n.gsn

τὴν λεγομένην Ὡραίαν τοῦ αἰτεῖν ἐλεημοσύνην παρὰ τῶν εἰσπορευομένων
{the} called the "Beautiful Gate" to ask alms from those entering
3836 3306 6053 3836 160 1797 4123 3836 1660
d.asf pt.pp.asf a.asf d.gsn f.pa n.asf p.g d.gpm pt.pm.gpm

εἰς τὸ ἱερόν· 3 ↱ ὃς ἰδὼν Πέτρον καὶ Ἰωάννην μέλλοντας εἰσιέναι εἰς τὸ
into the temple. When he saw Peter and John about to go into the
1650 3836 2639 1625 4005 1625 4377 2779 2722 3516 1655 1650 3836
p.a d.asn n.asn r.nsm pt.aa.nsm n.asm cj n.asm pt.pa.apm f.pa p.a d.asn

ἱερόν, ἠρώτα ἐλεημοσύνην λαβεῖν. 4 ἀτενίσας δὲ Πέτρος
temple, he asked to receive alms. *to receive* But Peter, looking directly *But* *Peter*
2639 2263 3284 3284 1797 3284 1254 4377 867 1254 4377
n.asn v.iai.3s n.asf f.aa pt.aa.nsm cj n.nsm

εἰς αὐτὸν σὺν τῷ Ἰωάννῃ εἶπεν, βλέψον εἰς ἡμᾶς. 5 ὁ δὲ
at him, as did *{the}* John, said, "Look at us." So the *So* lame man
1650 899 5250 3836 2722 3306 1063 1650 7005 1254 3836 1254
p.a r.asm.3 p.d d.dsm n.dsm v.aai.3s v.aam.2s p.a r.ap.1 d.nsm cj

ἐπεῖχεν αὐτοῖς ↰ προσδοκῶν τι παρ᾽ αὐτῶν λαβεῖν. 6
gave them his attention, expecting to receive something from them. *to receive* But
2091 899 2091 4659 3284 3284 5516 4123 899 3284 1254
v.iai.3s r.dpm.3 pt.pa.nsm r.asn p.g r.gpm.3 f.aa

NASB

those who had
believed [a]were
together and
had all things in
common; 45 and
they *began* selling
their property and
possessions and
were sharing them
with all, as anyone
might have need.
46 Day by day con-
tinuing with one
mind in the temple,
and breaking bread
from house to
house, they were
taking their meals
together with glad-
ness and sincerity
of heart, 47 praising
God and having
favor with all the
people. And the
Lord was adding to
their number day
by day those who
were being saved.

Healing the Lame Beggar

3:1 Now Peter and
John were going
up to the temple
at the [b]ninth *hour,*
the hour of prayer.
2 And a man who
had been lame
from his mother's
womb was be-
ing carried along,
whom they used
to set down every
day at the gate of
the temple which
is called Beauti-
ful, in order to beg
[c]alms of those who
were entering the
temple. 3 When he
saw Peter and John
about to go into the
temple, he *began*
asking to receive
alms. 4 But Peter,
along with John,
fixed his gaze
on him and said,
"Look at us!" 5 And
he *began* to give
them his atten-
tion, expecting to
receive something
from them. 6 But

[a] One early ms does not contain *were* and *and*
[b] I.e. 3 p.m.
[c] Or *a gift of charity*

NIV

[6]Then Peter said,
"Silver or gold I do
not have, but what
I do have I give
you. In the name
of Jesus Christ of
Nazareth, walk."
[7]Taking him by
the right hand, he
helped him up, and
instantly the man's
feet and ankles be-
came strong. [8]He
jumped to his feet
and began to walk.
Then he went with
them into the tem-
ple courts, walk-
ing and jumping,
and praising God.
[9]When all the
people saw him
walking and prais-
ing God, [10]they
recognized him as
the same man who
used to sit begging
at the temple gate
called Beautiful,
and they were
filled with wonder
and amazement at
what had happened
to him.

Peter Speaks to the Onlookers

[11]While the man
held on to Peter
and John, all the
people were as-
tonished and came
running to them
in the place called
Solomon's Col-
onnade. [12]When
Peter saw this, he
said to them: "Fel-
low Israelites, why
does this surprise
you? Why do you
stare at us as if by
our own power or
godliness we had
made this

εἶπεν δὲ Πέτρος, ἀργύριον καὶ χρυσίον ↱ οὐχ ὑπάρχει μοι, ὃ δὲ
Peter said, *But* *Peter* "Silver and gold is not possessed by me, but what *but*
4377 3306 1254 4377 736 2779 5992 5639 4024 5639 1609 1254 4005 1254
v.aai.3s cj n.nsm n.nsn cj n.nsn pl v.pai.3s r.ds.1 r.asn cj

ἔχω τοῦτό σοι δίδωμι· ἐν τῷ ὀνόματι Ἰησοῦ Χριστοῦ τοῦ
⌞I do have⌟ *{this}* I give to you. *I give* In the name of Jesus Christ of
2400 4047 1443 1443 5148 1443 1877 3836 3950 2652 5986 3836
v.pai.1s r.asn r.ds.2 v.pai.1s p.d d.dsn n.dsn n.gsm n.gsm d.gsm

Ναζωραίου [a]ἔγειρε καὶ[b] περιπάτει. [7]καὶ πιάσας αὐτὸν τῆς δεξιᾶς χειρὸς
Nazareth, stand up and walk!" Then taking him ⌞by the⌟ right hand, Peter
3717 1586 2779 4344 2779 4389 899 3836 1288 5931
n.gsm v.pam.2s cj v.pam.2s cj pt.aa.nsm r.asm.3 d.gsf a.gsf n.gsf

ἤγειρεν αὐτόν· ↰ παραχρῆμα δὲ ἐστερεώθησαν αἱ βάσεις
raised him up, and immediately *and* his feet and ankles were made strong; *{the}* *feet*
1586 899 1586 1254 4202 1254 899 1000 2779 5383 5105 3836 1000
v.aai.3s r.asm.3 adv cj v.api.3p d.npf n.npf

αὐτοῦ καὶ τὰ σφυδρά, [8]καὶ ἐξαλλόμενος ἔστη καὶ περιεπάτει καὶ εἰσῆλθεν σὺν
his *and* *{the}* *ankles* and jumping up, he stood and began to walk and entered with
899 2779 3836 5383 2779 1982 2705 2779 4344 2779 1656 5250
r.gsm.3 cj d.npn n.npn cj pt.pm.nsm v.aai.3s cj v.iai.3s cj v.aai.3s p.d

αὐτοῖς εἰς τὸ ἱερὸν περιπατῶν καὶ ἁλλόμενος καὶ αἰνῶν τὸν θεόν. [9]καὶ
them into the temple, walking and jumping and praising *{the}* God. And all
899 1650 3836 2639 4344 2779 256 2779 140 3836 2536 2779 4246
r.dpm.3 p.a d.asn n.asn pt.pa.nsm cj pt.pm.nsm cj pt.pa.nsm d.asm n.asm cj

εἶδεν πᾶς ὁ λαὸς αὐτὸν περιπατοῦντα καὶ αἰνοῦντα τὸν θεόν, [10]
the people saw *all* *the* *people* him walking and praising *{the}* God, and
3836 3295 1625 4246 3836 3295 899 4344 2779 140 3836 2536 1254
v.aai.3s a.nsm d.nsm n.nsm r.asm.3 pt.pa.asm cj pt.pa.asm d.asm n.asm

ἐπεγίνωσκον δὲ αὐτὸν ὅτι αὐτὸς ἦν ὁ πρὸς
recognized *and* him — that he was the one who used to sit and ask for
2105 1254 899 4022 899 1639 3836 2764 2764 2764 2764 2764 4639
v.iai.3p cj r.asm.3 cj r.nsm v.iai.3s d.nsm p.a

τὴν ἐλεημοσύνην καθήμενος ἐπὶ τῇ ὡραίᾳ πύλῃ τοῦ ἱεροῦ καὶ
{the} alms *one who used to sit* at the Beautiful Gate of the temple. And
3836 1797 2764 2093 3836 6053 4783 3836 2639 2779
d.asf n.asf pt.pm.nsm p.d d.dsf a.dsf n.dsf d.gsn n.gsn cj

ἐπλήσθησαν θάμβους καὶ ἐκστάσεως ἐπὶ τῷ συμβεβηκότι αὐτῷ. [11] →
⌞they were filled with⌟ awe and amazement at what had happened to him. While he
4398 2502 2779 1749 2093 3836 5201 899 899
v.api.3p n.gsn cj n.gsf p.d d.dsn pt.ra.dsn r.dsm.3

κρατοῦντος δὲ αὐτοῦ τὸν Πέτρον καὶ τὸν Ἰωάννην συνέδραμεν
clung to *{and}* *he* *{the}* Peter and *{the}* John, all the people ran together
3195 1254 899 3836 4377 2779 3836 2722 4246 3836 3295 5340
pt.pa.gsm cj r.gsm.3 d.asm n.asm cj d.asm n.asm v.aai.3s

πᾶς ὁ λαὸς πρὸς αὐτοὺς ἐπὶ τῇ στοᾷ τῇ καλουμένῃ Σολομῶντος
all *the* *people* to them in the ⌞covered walkway⌟ *{the}* called Solomon's
4246 3836 3295 4639 899 2093 3836 5119 3836 2813 5048
a.nsm d.nsm n.nsm p.a r.apm.3 p.d d.dsf n.dsf d.dsf pt.pp.dsf n.gsm

ἔκθαμβοι. [12] → ἰδὼν δὲ ὁ Πέτρος ἀπεκρίνατο πρὸς
Portico, utterly astounded. When Peter saw *{and}* *{the}* *Peter* this, he replied to
1702 4377 1625 1254 3836 4377 646 4639
n.npm pt.aa.nsm cj d.nsm n.nsm v.ami.3s p.a

τὸν λαόν, ἄνδρες Ἰσραηλῖται, τί θαυμάζετε ἐπὶ τούτῳ ἢ ἡμῖν
the people, "Men of Israel, why are you amazed at this, or why do you stare at us,
3836 3295 467 2703 5515 2513 2093 4047 2445 5515 867 867 867 7005
d.asm n.asm n.vpm n.vpm r.asn v.pai.2p p.d r.dsn cj r.dp.1

τί ἀτενίζετε ὡς ἰδίᾳ δυνάμει ἢ εὐσεβείᾳ πεποιηκόσιν τοῦ
why *do you stare* ⌞as though⌟ ⌞by our own⌟ power or piety we had made him *{the}*
5515 867 6055 2625 1539 2445 2354 4472 899 3836
r.asn v.pai.2p pl a.dsf n.dsf cj n.dsf pt.ra.dpm d.gsn

NASB

Peter said, "I do
not possess silver
and gold, but what
I do have I give to
you: In the name
of Jesus Christ the
Nazarene—walk!"
[7]And seizing him
by the right hand,
he raised him
up; and immedi-
ately his feet and
his ankles were
strengthened. [8]With
a leap he stood
upright and *began*
to walk; and he
entered the temple
with them, walking
and leaping and
praising God. [9]And
all the people saw
him walking and
praising God; [10]and
they were taking
note of him as
being the one who
used to sit at the
Beautiful Gate of
the temple to *beg*
alms, and they
were filled with
wonder and amaze-
ment at what had
happened to him.

Peter's Second Sermon

[11]While he was
clinging to Peter
and John, all the
people ran together
to them at the so-
called portico of
Solomon, full of
amazement. [12]But
when Peter saw
this, he replied to
the people, "Men
of Israel, why are
you amazed at this,
or why do you gaze
at us, as if by our
own power or piety
we had made him

[a] [ἔγειρε καὶ] UBS, omitted by TNIV.
[b] καὶ omitted in TNIV.

NIV

man walk? 13The
God of Abraham,
Isaac and Jacob,
the God of our fa-
thers, has glorified
his servant Jesus.
You handed him
over to be killed,
and you disowned
him before Pilate,
though he had de-
cided to let him go.
14You disowned
the Holy and Righ-
teous One and
asked that a mur-
derer be released
to you. 15You
killed the author of
life, but God raised
him from the dead.
We are witnesses
of this. 16By faith
in the name of
Jesus, this man
whom you see and
know was made
strong. It is Jesus'
name and the faith
that comes through
him that has com-
pletely healed him,
as you can all see.
17"Now, fellow
Israelites, I know
that you acted
in ignorance, as
did your leaders.
18But this is how
God fulfilled what
he had foretold
through all the
prophets, saying
that his Messiah
would suffer. 19Re-
pent, then, and
turn to God, so
that your sins may
be wiped out, that
times of refreshing
may come from
the Lord, 20and
that he may send
the Messiah, who
has been appoint-
ed for you—even
Jesus. 21Heaven
must

περιπατεῖν αὐτόν; 13 ὁ θεὸς Ἀβραὰμ καὶ[a] Ἰσαὰκ καὶ[b] Ἰακώβ, ὁ θεὸς τῶν
walk? *him* The God of Abraham, *{and}* Isaac, and Jacob — the God of
4344 899 3836 2536 11 2779 2693 2779 2609 3836 2536 3836
f.pa r.asm.3 d.nsm n.nsm n.gsm cj n.gsm cj n.gsm d.nsm n.nsm d.gpm

πατέρων ἡμῶν, ἐδόξασεν τὸν παῖδα αὐτοῦ Ἰησοῦν ὃν ὑμεῖς μὲν
our fathers *our* — glorified *{the}* his servant *his* Jesus, whom you ~
7005 4252 7005 1519 3836 899 4090 899 2652 4005 7007 3525
n.gpm r.gp.1 v.aai.3s d.asm n.asm r.gsm.3 n.asm r.asm r.np.2 pl

παρεδώκατε καὶ ἠρνήσασθε κατὰ πρόσωπον Πιλάτου, → κρίναντος ἐκείνου
delivered over and disowned in the presence of Pilate, when he had decided *he*
4140 2779 766 2848 4725 4397 1697 3212 1697
v.aai.2p cj v.ami.2p p.a n.asn n.gsm pt.aa.gsm r.gsm

ἀπολύειν· 14 ὑμεῖς δὲ τὸν ἅγιον καὶ δίκαιον ἠρνήσασθε καὶ
to release him. But you *But* denied the Holy and ⌞Righteous One,⌟ *denied* and
668 1254 7007 1254 766 3836 41 2779 1465 766 2779
f.pa r.np.2 cj d.asm a.asm cj a.asm v.ami.2p cj

ᾐτήσασθε ἄνδρα φονέα χαρισθῆναι ὑμῖν, 15 τὸν δὲ
asked that a man who was a murderer be released to you, and you killed the *and*
160 467 5838 5919 7007 1254 650 650 3836 1254
v.ami.2p n.asm n.asm f.ap r.dp.2 d.asm cj

ἀρχηγὸν τῆς ζωῆς ἀπεκτείνατε ὃν ὁ θεὸς ἤγειρεν ἐκ νεκρῶν, οὗ ἡμεῖς
Originator of life, *you killed* whom *{the}* God raised from the dead, ⌞of which⌟ we
795 3836 2437 650 4005 3836 2536 1586 1666 3738 4005 7005
n.asm d.gsf n.gsf v.aai.2p r.asm d.nsm n.nsm v.aai.3s p.g a.gpm r.gsm r.np.1

μάρτυρές ἐσμεν. 16 καὶ ἐπὶ τῇ πίστει τοῦ ὀνόματος αὐτοῦ
are witnesses. *are* And ⌞on the basis of⌟ *{the}* faith in *{the}* his name *his* —
1639 3459 1639 2779 2093 3836 4411 3836 899 3950 899
n.npm v.pai.1p cj p.d d.dsf n.dsf d.gsn n.gsn r.gsm.3

τοῦτον ὃν θεωρεῖτε καὶ οἴδατε, ἐστερέωσεν τὸ
his name itself has made this man strong, whom you see and know. *has made strong* *his*
3836 3950 899 5105 5105 4047 5105 4005 2555 2779 3857 5105 3836
r.asm r.asm v.pai.2p cj v.rai.2p v.aai.3s d.nsn

ὄνομα αὐτοῦ, καὶ ἡ πίστις ἡ δι᾽ αὐτοῦ ἔδωκεν αὐτῷ τὴν ὁλοκληρίαν
name *itself* *{and}* The faith that is through Jesus has given him *{the}* this wholeness
3950 899 2779 3836 4411 3836 1328 899 1443 899 3836 4047 3907
n.nsn r.gsm.3 cj d.nsf n.nsf d.nsf p.g r.gsm.3 v.aai.3s r.dsm.3 d.asf n.asf

ταύτην ἀπέναντι πάντων ὑμῶν. 17 καὶ νῦν, ἀδελφοί, οἶδα ὅτι κατὰ
this before all of you. And now, brothers, I know that you acted in
4047 595 4246 7007 2779 3814 81 3857 4022 4556 4556 2848
r.asf p.g a.gpm r.gp.2 cj adv n.vpm v.rai.1s cj p.a

ἄγνοιαν ἐπράξατε ὥσπερ καὶ οἱ ἄρχοντες ὑμῶν· 18
ignorance, *you acted* as did your rulers as well. *{the}* *rulers* *your* But the things
53 4556 6061 7007 807 2779 3836 807 7007 1254 4005
n.asf v.aai.2p pl adv d.npm n.npm r.gp.2

ὁ δὲ θεός, ἃ προκατήγγειλεν διὰ στόματος πάντων τῶν προφητῶν
{the} *But* God *things* foretold through the mouth of all the prophets, that
3836 1254 2536 4005 4615 1328 5125 4246 3836 4737
d.nsm cj n.nsm r.apn v.aai.3s p.g n.gsn a.gpm d.gpm n.gpm

παθεῖν τὸν χριστὸν αὐτοῦ, ἐπλήρωσεν οὕτως. 19 μετανοήσατε
his Christ would suffer, *{the}* *Christ* *his* he has fulfilled in this way. Repent
899 5986 4248 3836 5986 899 4444 4048 3566
f.aa d.asm n.asm r.gsm.3 v.aai.3s adv v.aam.2p

οὖν καὶ ἐπιστρέψατε εἰς τὸ ἐξαλειφθῆναι ὑμῶν τὰς ἁμαρτίας, 20 ὅπως ἂν
therefore, and turn again, for the blotting out of your *{the}* sins, that
4036 2779 2188 1650 3836 1981 7007 3836 281 3968 323
cj cj v.aam.2p p.a d.asn f.ap r.gp.2 d.apf n.apf cj pl

ἔλθωσιν καιροὶ ἀναψύξεως ἀπὸ προσώπου τοῦ κυρίου καὶ ἀποστείλῃ
⌞there may come⌟ times of refreshing from the presence of the Lord, and that he may send
2262 2789 433 608 4725 3836 3261 2779 690
v.aas.3p n.npm n.gsf p.g n.gsn d.gsm n.gsm cj v.aas.3s

τὸν προκεχειρισμένον ὑμῖν χριστὸν Ἰησοῦν, 21 ὃν δεῖ
the Messiah appointed for you, *Messiah* that is, Jesus, whom heaven must
3836 5986 4741 7007 5986 2652 4005 4041 1256
d.asm pt.rm.asm r.dp.2 n.asm n.asm r.asm v.pai.3s

[a] ὁ θεὸς included by UBS after καὶ.
[b] ὁ θεὸς included by UBS after καὶ.

NASB

walk? 13The God
of Abraham, Isaac
and Jacob, the God
of our fathers, has
glorified His ser-
vant Jesus, *the one*
whom you deliv-
ered and disowned
in the presence of
Pilate, when he had
decided to release
Him. 14But you
disowned the Holy
and Righteous
One and asked for
a murderer to be
granted to you,
15but put to death
the Prince of life,
the one whom
God raised from
the dead, *a fact*
to which we are
witnesses. 16And
on the basis of
faith in His name,
it is the name of
Jesus which has
strengthened this
man whom you
see and know; and
the faith which
comes through
Him has given him
this perfect health
in the presence of
you all.
17"And now,
brethren, I know
that you acted in
ignorance, just as
your rulers did
also. 18But the
things which God
announced before-
hand by the mouth
of all the prophets,
that His Christ
would suffer, He
has thus fulfilled.
19Therefore repent
and return, so that
your sins may be
wiped away, in or-
der that times of re-
freshing may come
from the presence
of the Lord; 20and
that He may send
Jesus, the Christ
appointed for you,
21whom heaven

NIV

receive him until
the time comes
for God to restore
everything, as he
promised long ago
through his holy
prophets. 22 For
Moses said, 'The
Lord your God
will raise up for
you a prophet like
me from among
your own people;
you must listen
to everything he
tells you. 23 Any-
one who does not
listen to him will
be completely cut
off from their peo-
ple.'[a]
24 "Indeed, begin-
ning with Samuel,
all the prophets
who have spo-
ken have foretold
these days. 25 And
you are heirs of
the prophets and
of the covenant
God made with
your fathers. He
said to Abraham,
'Through your off-
spring all peoples
on earth will be
blessed.'[b] 26 When
God raised up his
servant, he sent
him first to you to
bless you by turn-
ing each of you
from your wicked
ways."

Peter and John Before the Sanhedrin

4 The priests
and the cap-
tain of the temple
guard and the Sad-
ducees came up
to Peter and John
while they were
speaking to the
people.

[a] 23 Deut. 18:15,18,19
[b] 25 Gen. 22:18; 26:4

οὐρανὸν μὲν δέξασθαι ἄχρι χρόνων ἀποκαταστάσεως πάντων ὧν
heaven ~ receive until the time of restoration of all things, which God
4041 3525 1312 948 5989 640 4246 4005 2536
n.asm pl f.am p.g n.gpm n.gsf a.gpn r.gpn

ἐλάλησεν ὁ θεὸς διὰ στόματος τῶν ἁγίων ⌞ἀπ᾽ αἰῶνος⌟ αὐτοῦ
spoke *{the} God* by the mouth of his holy prophets long ago. *his*
3281 3836 2536 1328 5125 3836 899 41 4737 608 172 899
v.aai.3s d.nsm n.nsm p.g n.gsn d.gpm a.gpm p.g n.gsm r.gsm.3

προφητῶν. 22 Μωϋσῆς μὲν εἶπεν ὅτι προφήτην ὑμῖν ἀναστήσει
prophets Moses ~ said, ~ *prophet* *for you* 'The Lord your God will raise up
4737 3707 3525 3306 4022 4737 7007 3836 3261 7007 2536 482
n.gpm n.nsm pl v.aai.3s cj n.asm r.dp.2 v.fai.3s

κύριος ὁ θεὸς ὑμῶν ἐκ τῶν ἀδελφῶν ὑμῶν ὡς
for you a prophet *Lord The God your* ⌞from among⌟ *{the}* your brothers, *your* as he
7007 7007 4737 3261 3836 2536 7007 1666 3836 7007 81 7007 6055
n.nsm d.nsm n.nsm r.gp.2 p.g d.gpm n.gpm r.gp.2 pl

ἐμέ· αὐτοῦ ἀκούσεσθε κατὰ πάντα ⌞ὅσα ἂν⌟ λαλήσῃ πρὸς
raised me. You must obey him *You must obey* in all things whatsoever he speaks to
1609 201 201 201 899 201 2848 4246 4012 323 3281 4639
r.as.1 r.gsm.3 v.fmi.2p p.a a.apn r.apn pl v.aas.3s p.a

ὑμᾶς. 23 ἔσται δὲ πᾶσα ψυχὴ ⌞ἥτις ἐὰν⌟ ↱ μὴ ἀκούσῃ τοῦ
you. And ⌞it will be⌟ *And* that every soul who does not obey *{the}* that
7007 1254 1639 1254 4246 6034 4015 1569 201 3590 201 3836 1697
r.ap.2 v.fmi.3s cj a.nsf n.nsf r.nsf pl pl v.aas.3s d.gsm

προφήτου ἐκείνου ἐξολεθρευθήσεται ἐκ τοῦ λαοῦ. 24 καὶ πάντες δὲ οἱ
prophet *that* will be destroyed ⌞from among⌟ the people.' And all *{and}* the
4737 1697 2017 1666 3836 3295 2779 4246 1254 3836
n.gsm r.gsm v.fpi.3s p.g d.gsm n.gsm cj a.npm cj d.npm

προφῆται ἀπὸ Σαμουὴλ καὶ τῶν καθεξῆς ὅσοι ἐλάλησαν καὶ
prophets from Samuel and those ⌞who came after⌟ him, ⌞as many as⌟ have spoken, also
4737 608 4905 2779 3836 2759 4012 3281 2779
n.npm p.g n.gsm cj d.gpm adv r.npm v.aai.3p adv

κατήγγειλαν τὰς ἡμέρας ταύτας. 25 ὑμεῖς ἐστε οἱ υἱοὶ τῶν προφητῶν καὶ
announced *{the}* these days. *these* You are the sons of the prophets and
2859 3836 4047 2465 4047 7007 1639 3836 5626 3836 4737 2779
v.aai.3p d.apf n.apf r.apf r.np.2 v.pai.2p d.npm n.npm d.gpm n.gpm cj

τῆς διαθήκης ἧς διέθετο ὁ θεὸς πρὸς τοὺς πατέρας ὑμῶν λέγων πρὸς
of the covenant which God made *{the} God* with *{the}* your fathers, *your* saying to
3836 1347 4005 2536 1416 3836 2536 4639 3836 7007 4252 7007 3306 4639
d.gsf n.gsf r.gsf v.ami.3s d.nsm n.nsm p.a d.apm n.apm r.gp.2 pt.pa.nsm p.a

Ἀβραάμ, καὶ ἐν τῷ σπέρματί σου →
Abraham, 'And in *{the}* your offspring *your* shall all the families of the earth
11 2779 1877 3836 5148 5065 5148 4246 3836 4255 3836 3836 1178
n.asm cj p.d d.dsn n.dsn r.gs.2

ἐνευλογηθήσονται[a] πᾶσαι αἱ πατριαὶ τῆς γῆς. 26
be blessed.' *all the families of the earth* God, having raised up his servant,
1922 4246 3836 4255 3836 1178 2536 482 482 482 899 4090
v.fpi.3p a.npf d.npf n.npf d.gsf n.gsf

ὑμῖν πρῶτον ἀναστήσας ὁ θεὸς τὸν παῖδα αὐτοῦ ἀπέστειλεν αὐτὸν
sent him to you first, *having raised up {the} God {the} servant his sent him*
690 899 7007 4754 482 3836 2536 3836 4090 899 690 899
r.dp.2 adv pt.aa.nsm d.nsm n.nsm d.asm n.asm r.gsm.3 v.aai.3s r.asm.3

εὐλογοῦντα ὑμᾶς ἐν τῷ ἀποστρέφειν ἕκαστον ἀπὸ τῶν πονηριῶν
to bless you by *{the}* turning each one of you from *{the}* your wicked ways."
2328 7007 1877 3836 695 1667 608 3836 7007 4504
pt.pa.asm r.ap.2 p.d d.dsn f.pa r.asm p.g d.gpf n.gpf

ὑμῶν.
your
7007
r.gp.2

4:1 → λαλούντων δὲ αὐτῶν πρὸς τὸν λαὸν ἐπέστησαν αὐτοῖς οἱ
And as they were speaking *And they* to the people, *moved in on them* the
1254 899 3281 1254 899 4639 3836 3295 2392 899 3836
pt.pa.gpm cj r.gpm.3 p.a d.asm n.asm v.aai.3p r.dpm.3 d.npm

[a] ἐνευλογηθήσονται TNIV, NET. [ἐν]ευλογηθήσονται UBS.

NASB

must receive
until *the* period
of restoration of
all things about
which God spoke
by the mouth of
His holy prophets
from ancient time.
22 Moses said, 'THE
LORD GOD WILL
RAISE UP FOR YOU
A PROPHET LIKE ME
FROM YOUR BRETH-
REN; TO HIM YOU
SHALL GIVE HEED
to everything He
says to you. 23 And
it will be that every
soul that does not
heed that prophet
shall be utterly
destroyed from
among the people.'
24 And likewise,
all the prophets
who have spoken,
from Samuel and
his successors
onward, also
announced these
days. 25 It is you
who are the sons
of the prophets and
of the covenant
which God made
with your fathers,
saying to Abraham,
'AND IN YOUR SEED
ALL THE FAMILIES OF
THE EARTH SHALL BE
BLESSED.' 26 For you
first, God raised
up His Servant and
sent Him to bless
you by turning
every one *of you*
from your wicked
ways."

Peter and John Arrested

4:1 As they were
speaking to the
people, the priests

NIV

²They were greatly
disturbed because
the apostles were
teaching the peo-
ple, proclaiming
in Jesus the res-
urrection of the
dead. ³They seized
Peter and John and,
because it was eve-
ning, they put them
in jail until the next
day. ⁴But many
who heard the mes-
sage believed; so
the number of men
who believed grew
to about five thou-
sand.
⁵The next day the
rulers, the elders
and the teachers
of the law met in
Jerusalem. ⁶An-
nas the high priest
was there, and so
were Caiaphas,
John, Alexander
and others of the
high priest's fami-
ly. ⁷They had Peter
and John brought
before them and
began to question
them: "By what
power or what
name did you do
this?"
⁸Then Peter,
filled with the
Holy Spirit, said
to them: "Rulers
and elders of the
people! ⁹If we
are being called
to account to-
day for an act of
kindness shown
to a man who was
lame and are be-
ing asked how he
was healed, ¹⁰then
know this, you
and all the people
of Israel: It is by
the name of Jesus
Christ of Nazareth,
whom

ἱερεῖς καὶ ὁ στρατηγὸς τοῦ ἱεροῦ καὶ οἱ Σαδδουκαῖοι,
priests and the captain of the temple and the Sadducees moved in on them,
2636 2779 3836 5130 3836 2639 2779 3836 4881 2392 2392 2392 899
n.npm cj d.nsm n.nsm d.gsn n.gsn cj d.npm n.npm

²διαπονούμενοι διὰ τὸ διδάσκειν αὐτοὺς τὸν λαὸν καὶ καταγγέλλειν ἐν
greatly annoyed because *{the}* they were teaching *they* the people and announcing in
1387 1328 3836 899 1438 899 3836 3295 2779 2859 1877
pt.pm.npm p.a d.asn f.pa r.apm.3 d.asm n.asm cj f.pa p.d

τῷ Ἰησοῦ τὴν ἀνάστασιν τὴν ἐκ νεκρῶν, ³καὶ ἐπέβαλον ← αὐτοῖς τὰς
{the} Jesus the resurrection *{the}* from the dead. So they laid hands on them *{the}*
3836 2652 3836 414 3836 1666 3738 2779 2095 5931 899 3836
d.dsm n.dsm d.asf n.asf d.asf p.g a.gpm cj v.aai.3p r.dpm.3 d.apf

χεῖρας καὶ ἔθεντο εἰς τήρησιν εἰς τὴν αὔριον, ἦν γὰρ ἑσπέρα
hands and put them in custody until the next day, since it was *since* already evening.
5931 2779 5502 1650 5499 1650 3836 892 1142 1639 1142 2453 2270
n.apf cj v.ami.3p p.a n.asf p.a d.asf adv v.iai.3s cj n.nsf

ἤδη. ⁴ πολλοὶ δὲ τῶν ἀκουσάντων τὸν λόγον ἐπίστευσαν καὶ
already And many *And* of ⌊those who had heard⌋ the word believed, and the
2453 1254 4498 1254 3836 201 3836 3364 4409 2779 3836
adv a.npm cj d.gpm pt.aa.gpm d.asm n.asm v.aai.3p cj

ἐγενήθη ὁ[a] ἀριθμὸς τῶν ἀνδρῶν ὡς[b] χιλιάδες πέντε.
number of the men came to *the* *number* *of the* *men* about five thousand. *five*
750 3836 3836 467 1181 3836 750 3836 467 6055 4297 5942 4297
v.api.3s d.nsm n.nsm d.gpm n.gpm pl n.npf a.npf

⁵ἐγένετο δὲ ἐπὶ τὴν αὔριον συναχθῆναι αὐτῶν τοὺς ἄρχοντας καὶ
{it happened that} *{and}* On the next day *were gathered together* their *{the}* rulers and
1181 1254 2093 3836 892 5251 899 3836 807 2779
v.ami.3s cj p.a d.asf adv f.ap r.gpm.3 d.apm n.apm cj

τοὺς πρεσβυτέρους καὶ τοὺς γραμματεῖς ἐν Ἰερουσαλήμ, ⁶καὶ
{the} elders and *{the}* scribes were gathered together in Jerusalem, both
3836 4565 2779 3836 1208 5251 5251 5251 1877 2647 2779
d.apm a.apm cj d.apm n.apm p.d n.dsf cj

Ἅννας ὁ ἀρχιερεὺς καὶ Καϊάφας καὶ Ἰωάννης καὶ Ἀλέξανδρος καὶ ὅσοι
Annas the high priest and Caiaphas and John and Alexander, and ⌊as many as⌋
484 3836 797 2779 2780 2779 2722 2779 235 2779 4012
n.nsm d.nsm n.nsm cj n.nsm cj n.nsm cj n.nsm cj r.npm

ἦσαν ἐκ γένους ἀρχιερατικοῦ, ⁷καὶ στήσαντες αὐτοὺς ἐν τῷ μέσῳ
were of the high-priestly family. *high-priestly* And having set them in the midst,
1639 1666 796 1169 796 2779 2705 899 1877 3836 3545
v.iai.3p p.g n.gsn a.gsn cj pt.aa.npm r.apm.3 p.d d.dsn n.dsn

ἐπυνθάνοντο, ἐν ποίᾳ δυνάμει ἢ ἐν ποίῳ ὀνόματι → ἐποιήσατε τοῦτο
they began to inquire, "By what power or by what name did you do this?"
4785 1877 4481 1539 2445 1877 4481 3950 7007 4472 4047
v.imi.3p p.d r.dsf n.dsf cj p.d r.dsn n.dsn v.aai.2p r.asn

ὑμεῖς; ⁸Τότε Πέτρος πλησθεὶς → πνεύματος ἁγίου εἶπεν πρὸς αὐτούς,
you Then Peter, filled with the Holy Spirit, *Holy* said to them,
7007 5538 4377 4398 41 4460 41 3306 4639 899
r.np.2 adv n.nsm pt.ap.nsm n.gsn a.gsn v.aai.3s p.a r.apm.3

ἄρχοντες τοῦ λαοῦ καὶ πρεσβύτεροι, ⁹εἰ ἡμεῖς σήμερον
"Rulers of the people and elders, if we are being examined today
807 3836 3295 2779 4565 1623 7005 373 373 373 4958
n.vpm d.gsm n.gsm cj a.vpm cj r.np.1 adv

ἀνακρινόμεθα ἐπὶ εὐεργεσίᾳ → ἀνθρώπου ἀσθενοῦς ἐν τίνι
are being examined about a good deed done to a sick man, *sick* by what means
373 2093 2307 822 476 822 1877 5515
v.ppi.1p p.d n.dsf n.gsm a.gsm p.d r.dsn

οὗτος σέσωται, ¹⁰ γνωστὸν ἔστω πᾶσιν ὑμῖν καὶ παντὶ
this man has been healed, let it be known *let it be* to you all *to you* and to all
4047 5392 1639 1639 1639 1196 1639 7007 7007 4246 7007 2779 4246
r.nsm v.rpi.3s a.nsn v.pam.3s a.dpm r.dp.2 cj a.dsm

τῷ λαῷ Ἰσραὴλ ὅτι ἐν τῷ ὀνόματι Ἰησοῦ Χριστοῦ τοῦ Ναζωραίου ὃν ὑμεῖς
the people of Israel that by the name of Jesus Christ of Nazareth, whom you
3836 3295 2702 4022 1877 3836 3950 2652 5986 3836 3717 4005 7007
d.dsm n.dsm n.gsm cj p.d d.dsn n.dsn n.gsm n.gsm d.gsm n.gsm r.asm r.np.2

[a] [ὁ] UBS, omitted by TNIV.
[b] [ὡς] UBS.

NASB

and the captain of
the temple *guard*
and the Sadducees
came up to them,
²being greatly
disturbed because
they were teaching
the people and
proclaiming in
Jesus the resur-
rection from the
dead. ³And they
laid hands on them
and put them in jail
until the next day,
for it was already
evening. ⁴But many
of those who had
heard the message
believed; and the
number of the men
came to be about
five thousand.
⁵On the next day,
their rulers and
elders and scribes
were gathered
together in Jeru-
salem; ⁶and Annas
the high priest *was*
there, and Caia-
phas and John and
Alexander, and all
who were of high-
priestly descent.
⁷When they had
placed them in the
center, they *began*
to inquire, "By
what power, or in
what name, have
you done this?"
⁸Then Peter, filled
with the Holy
Spirit, said to them,
"Rulers and elders
of the people, ⁹if
we are on trial
today for a ben-
efit done to a sick
man, as to how
this man has been
made well, ¹⁰let it
be known to all of
you and to all the
people of Israel,
that by the name
of Jesus Christ the
Nazarene, whom

NIV

you crucified but
whom God raised
from the dead, that
this man stands
before you healed.
11 Jesus is

“ ‘the stone you
builders
rejected,
which has
become the
cornerstone.’[a]

12 Salvation is
found in no one
else, for there is no
other name under
heaven given to
mankind by which
we must be saved.”
13 When they saw
the courage of Pe-
ter and John and
realized that they
were unschooled,
ordinary men, they
were astonished
and they took note
that these men had
been with Jesus.
14 But since they
could see the man
who had been
healed standing
there with them,
there was nothing
they could say.
15 So they ordered
them to withdraw
from the San-
hedrin and then
conferred together.
16 “What are we
going to do with
these men?” they
asked. “Everyone
living in Jerusa-
lem knows they
have performed a
notable sign, and
we cannot deny it.
17 But to stop this
thing from spread-
ing any further
among the people,
we must warn
them to speak no
longer to anyone in
this name.”

[a] 11 Psalm 118:22

ἐσταυρώσατε, ὃν ὁ θεὸς ἤγειρεν ἐκ νεκρῶν, ἐν τούτῳ οὗτος παρέστηκεν
crucified, whom {the} God raised from the dead, by him this man is standing
5090 4005 3836 2536 1586 1666 3738 1877 4047 4047 4225
v.aai.2p r.asm d.nsm n.nsm v.aai.3s p.g a.gpm p.d r.dsn r.nsm v.rai.3s

ἐνώπιον ὑμῶν ὑγιής. 11 οὗτός ἐστιν ὁ λίθος, ὁ ἐξουθενηθεὶς ὑφ᾽ ὑμῶν τῶν
before you healthy. This is the stone that was rejected by you, the
1967 7007 5618 4047 1639 3836 3345 3836 2024 5679 7007 3836
p.g r.gp.2 a.nsm r.nsm v.pai.3s d.nsm n.nsm d.nsm pt.ap.nsm p.g r.gp.2 d.gpm

οἰκοδόμων, ὁ γενόμενος εἰς κεφαλὴν γωνίας. 12 καὶ οὐκ ἔστιν ἐν
builders, that has become {for} the chief cornerstone. And {not} salvation is in
3871 3836 1181 1650 3051 1224 2779 4024 5401 1639 1877
n.gpm d.nsm pt.am.nsm p.a n.asf n.gsf cj pl v.pai.3s p.d

ἄλλῳ οὐδενὶ ἡ σωτηρία, οὐδὲ γὰρ ὄνομά ἐστιν ἕτερον
no one else, no one {the} salvation for there is no for other name there is other
4029 4029 257 4029 3836 5401 1142 1639 1639 4028 1142 2283 3950 1639 2283
r.dsm a.dsm d.nsf n.nsf adv cj n.nsn v.pai.3s r.nsn

ὑπὸ τὸν οὐρανὸν τὸ δεδομένον ἐν ἀνθρώποις ἐν ᾧ δεῖ σωθῆναι
under {the} heaven {the} given among men by which we must be saved.”
5679 3836 4041 3836 1443 1877 476 1877 4005 7005 1256 5392
p.a d.asm n.asm d.nsn pt.rp.nsn p.d n.dpm p.d r.dsn v.pai.3s f.ap

ἡμᾶς. 13 θεωροῦντες δὲ τὴν τοῦ Πέτρου παρρησίαν καὶ Ἰωάννου καὶ
we Seeing {and} the boldness of Peter boldness and John, and
7005 2555 1254 3836 4244 3836 4377 4244 2779 2722 2779
r.ap.1 pt.pa.npm cj d.asf d.gsm n.gsm n.asf cj n.gsm cj

καταλαβόμενοι ὅτι ἄνθρωποι ἀγράμματοί εἰσιν καὶ
coming to find that they were uneducated and common men, uneducated they were and
2898 4022 1639 1639 63 2779 2626 476 63 1639 2779
pt.am.npm cj n.npm a.npm v.pai.3p cj

ἰδιῶται, ἐθαύμαζον ἐπεγίνωσκόν τε αὐτοὺς ὅτι σὺν τῷ
common they were astonished and recognized and they that they had been with {the}
2626 2513 5445 2105 5445 899 4022 899 1639 1639 5250 3836
n.npm v.iai.3p v.iai.3p cj r.apm.3 cj p.d d.dsm

Ἰησοῦ ἦσαν, 14 τόν τε ἄνθρωπον βλέποντες
Jesus. had been But seeing the But man seeing who had been healed standing
2652 1639 5445 1063 3836 5445 476 1063 3836 2543 2543 2543 2705
n.dsm v.iai.3p d.asm cj n.asm pt.pa.npm

σὺν αὐτοῖς ἑστῶτα τὸν τεθεραπευμένον οὐδὲν εἶχον ἀντειπεῖν.
with them, standing who had been healed they had nothing they had to say in opposition.
5250 899 2705 3836 2543 2400 2400 4029 2400 515
p.d r.dpm.3 pt.ra.asm d.asm pt.rp.asm a.asn v.iai.3p f.aa

15 κελεύσαντες δὲ αὐτοὺς ἔξω τοῦ συνεδρίου ἀπελθεῖν συνέβαλλον
But commanding But them to go outside the council, to go they discussed the
1254 3027 1254 899 599 599 2032 3836 5284 599 5202
pt.aa.npm cj r.apm.3 p.g d.gsn n.gsn f.aa v.iai.3p

πρὸς ἀλλήλους 16 λέγοντες, τί ποιήσωμεν τοῖς ἀνθρώποις τούτοις;
matter with one another, saying, “What shall we do with these men? these For
4639 253 3306 5515 4472 3836 4047 476 4047 1142
p.a r.apm pt.pa.npm r.asn v.aas.1p d.dpm n.dpm r.dpm

ὅτι μὲν γὰρ γνωστὸν σημεῖον γέγονεν δι᾽ αὐτῶν πᾶσιν τοῖς
that ~ For a notable sign ⌊has been done⌋ through them is evident to all who
4022 3525 1142 1196 4956 1181 1328 899 5745 4246 3836
cj pl cj a.nsn n.nsn v.rai.3s p.g r.gpm.3 a.dpm d.dpm

κατοικοῦσιν Ἰερουσαλὴμ φανερὸν καὶ ↱ ↱ ⌊οὐ δυνάμεθα⌋ ἀρνεῖσθαι·
live in Jerusalem, evident and we are unable to deny it.
2997 2647 5745 2779 1538 1538 4024 1538 766
pt.pa.dpm n.asf a.nsn cj pl v.ppi.1p f.pm

17 ἀλλ᾽ ἵνα μὴ ⌊ἐπὶ πλεῖον⌋ διανεμηθῇ εἰς τὸν λαὸν
But that it may spread no further it may spread among the people,
247 2671 1376 1376 1376 3590 2093 4498 1376 1650 3836 3295
cj cj pl p.a adv.c v.aps.3s p.a d.asm n.asm

ἀπειλησώμεθα αὐτοῖς μηκέτι λαλεῖν ἐπὶ τῷ ὀνόματι τούτῳ μηδενὶ
let us warn them no longer to speak in {the} this name this to anyone
580 899 3600 3281 2093 3836 4047 3950 4047 3594
v.ams.1p r.dpm.3 adv f.pa p.d d.dsn n.dsn r.dsn a.dsm

NASB

you crucified,
whom God raised
from the dead—by
this *name* this
man stands here
before you in good
health. 11 He is the
STONE WHICH WAS
REJECTED by you,
THE BUILDERS, *but*
WHICH BECAME THE
CHIEF CORNER *stone*.
12 And there is
salvation in no one
else; for there is no
other name under
heaven that has
been given among
men by which we
must be saved.”

Threat and Release

13 Now as they
observed the con-
fidence of Peter
and John and un-
derstood that they
were uneducated
and untrained men,
they were amazed,
and *began* to rec-
ognize them as
having been with
Jesus. 14 And seeing
the man who had
been healed stand-
ing with them, they
had nothing to say
in reply. 15 But when
they had ordered
them to leave the
Council, they *be-
gan* to confer with
one another, 16 say-
ing, “What shall
we do with these
men? For the fact
that a noteworthy
miracle has taken
place through them
is apparent to all
who live in Jerusa-
lem, and we can-
not deny it. 17 But
so that it will not
spread any further
among the people,
let us warn them
to speak no longer
to any man in this
name.”

NIV

18Then they called
them in again
and command-
ed them not to
speak or teach at
all in the name of
Jesus. 19But Peter
and John replied,
"Which is right
in God's eyes: to
listen to you, or to
him? You be the
judges! 20As for
us, we cannot help
speaking about
what we have seen
and heard."
21After further
threats they let
them go. They
could not decide
how to punish
them, because all
the people were
praising God for
what had hap-
pened. 22For the
man who was mi-
raculously healed
was over forty
years old.

The Believers Pray

23On their re-
lease, Peter and
John went back
to their own peo-
ple and reported
all that the chief
priests and the
elders had said to
them. 24When they
heard this, they
raised their voices
together in prayer
to God. "Sovereign
Lord," they said,
"you made the
heavens and the
earth and the sea,
and everything in
them. 25You spoke
by the Holy Spirit
through the mouth
of your servant,
our father David:

ἀνθρώπων. 18 καὶ ↱ καλέσαντες αὐτοὺς παρήγγειλαν τὸ καθόλου μὴ
among men." So they called them and ordered {the} at all them not
476 2779 4133 2813 899 4133 3836 2773 3590
n.gpm cj pt.aa.npm r.apm.3 v.aai.3p d.asn adv pl

φθέγγεσθαι μηδὲ διδάσκειν ἐπὶ τῷ ὀνόματι τοῦ Ἰησοῦ. 19 ὁ δὲ Πέτρος
to speak or teach at all in the name of Jesus. {the} But Peter
5779 3593 1438 2773 2773 2093 3836 3950 3836 2652 3836 1254 4377
f.pm cj f.pa p.d d.dsn n.dsn d.gsm n.gsm d.nsm cj n.nsm

καὶ Ἰωάννης ἀποκριθέντες εἶπον πρὸς αὐτούς, εἰ δίκαιόν ἐστιν
and John said in answer said to them, "Whether it is right it is
2779 2722 3306 646 3306 4639 899 1623 1639 1639 1465 1639
cj n.nsm pt.ap.npm v.aai.3p p.a r.apm.3 cj a.nsn v.pai.3s

ἐνώπιον τοῦ θεοῦ ὑμῶν ἀκούειν μᾶλλον ἢ τοῦ θεοῦ, κρίνατε,
before {the} God to obey you to obey rather than {the} God, ⌞you must judge,⌟
1967 3836 2536 201 201 7007 201 3437 2445 3836 2536 3212
p.g d.gsm n.gsm r.gp.2 f.pa adv.c pl d.gsm n.gsm v.aam.2p

20 ⌞οὐ δυνάμεθα⌟ γὰρ ἡμεῖς ἃ εἴδαμεν καὶ
for we cannot for we help speaking of the things ⌞we have seen⌟ and
1142 7005 4024 1538 1142 7005 3590 3281 4005 1625 2779
pl v.ppi.1p cj r.np.1 r.apn v.aai.1p cj

ἠκούσαμεν μὴ λαλεῖν. 21 ↱ οἱ δὲ προσαπειλησάμενοι ← → →
heard." help speaking And when they And had threatened them further, they let
201 3590 3281 1254 4653 3836 1254 4653
v.aai.1p pl f.pa d.npm cj pt.am.npm

ἀπέλυσαν αὐτούς, ↱ ↱ ↱ μηδὲν εὑρίσκοντες τὸ πῶς κολάσωνται
them go, them for they could not find {the} how to punish
899 668 899 2351 2351 2351 3594 2351 3836 4802 3134
v.aai.3p r.apm.3 a.asn pt.pa.npm d.asn cj v.ams.3p

αὐτούς, διὰ τὸν λαόν, ὅτι ↱ πάντες ἐδόξαζον τὸν θεὸν ἐπὶ τῷ
them ⌞on account of⌟ the people, since they all were praising {the} God for what
899 1328 3836 3295 4022 1519 4246 1519 3836 2536 2093 3836
r.apm.3 p.a d.asm n.asm cj a.npm v.iai.3p d.asm n.asm p.d d.dsn

γεγονότι· 22 ἐτῶν γὰρ ἦν πλειόνων τεσσεράκοντα ὁ
had happened. years For the man was over forty years old the
1181 2291 1142 3836 476 1639 4498 5477 2291 3836
pt.ra.dsn n.gpn cj v.iai.3s a.gpn.c a.gpn d.nsm

ἄνθρωπος ἐφ' ὃν γεγόνει τὸ σημεῖον τοῦτο τῆς
man on whom this sign of healing ⌞had been performed.⌟ {the} sign this of
476 2093 4005 4047 4956 3836 2617 1181 3836 4956 4047 3836
n.nsm p.a r.asm v.lai.3s d.nsn n.nsn r.nsn d.gsf

ἰάσεως. 23 ἀπολυθέντες δὲ ἦλθον πρὸς τοὺς ἰδίους καὶ
healing ⌞After they were released,⌟ {and} they went to {the} their friends and
2617 668 1254 2262 4639 3836 2625 2779
n.gsf pt.ap.npm cj v.aai.3p p.a d.apm a.apm cj

ἀπήγγειλαν ὅσα πρὸς αὐτοὺς οἱ ἀρχιερεῖς καὶ οἱ πρεσβύτεροι εἶπαν.
reported all to them that the chief priests and the elders had said to
550 4012 4639 899 3836 797 2779 3836 4565 3306 4639
v.aai.3p r.apn p.a r.apm.3 d.npm n.npm cj d.npm a.npm v.aai.3p

24 ↱ οἱ δὲ ἀκούσαντες ὁμοθυμαδὸν ἦραν φωνὴν πρὸς
them. When they {and} heard this, together they lifted their voices together to
899 201 3836 1254 201 3924 149 5889 3924 4639
d.npm cj pt.aa.npm adv v.aai.3p n.asf p.a

τὸν θεὸν καὶ εἶπαν, δέσποτα, σὺ ὁ ποιήσας τὸν οὐρανὸν καὶ τὴν γῆν
{the} God and said, ⌞"Sovereign Lord,⌟ you who made the heaven and the earth
3836 2536 2779 3306 1305 5148 3836 4472 3836 4041 2779 3836 1178
d.asm n.asm cj v.aai.3p n.vsm r.ns.2 d.nsm pt.aa.nsm d.asm n.asm cj d.asf n.asf

καὶ τὴν θάλασσαν καὶ πάντα τὰ ἐν αὐτοῖς, 25 ὁ τοῦ
and the sea, and everything that is in them, who through the mouth of our
2779 3836 2498 2779 4246 3836 1877 899 3836 5125 3836 7005
cj d.asf n.asf cj a.apn d.apn p.d r.dpm.3 d.nsm d.gsm

πατρὸς ἡμῶν διὰ πνεύματος ἁγίου στόματος Δαυὶδ παιδός
father our David, your servant, by the Holy Spirit Holy mouth David servant
4252 7005 1253 5148 4090 1328 41 4460 41 5125 1253 4090
n.gsm r.gp.1 p.g n.gsn a.gsn n.gsn n.gsm n.gsm

NASB

18And when they
had summoned
them, they com-
manded them not
to speak or teach at
all in the name of
Jesus. 19But Peter
and John answered
and said to them,
"Whether it is
right in the sight
of God to give
heed to you rather
than to God, you
be the judge; 20for
we cannot stop
speaking about
what we have seen
and heard." 21When
they had threatened
them further, they
let them go (find-
ing no basis on
which to punish
them) on account
of the people,
because they were
all glorifying
God for what had
happened; 22for the
man was more than
forty years old on
whom this miracle
of healing had been
performed.
23When they had
been released, they
went to their own
companions and
reported all that
the chief priests
and the elders had
said to them. 24And
when they heard
this, they lifted
their voices to God
with one accord
and said, "O Lord,
it is You who MADE
THE HEAVEN AND
THE EARTH AND THE
SEA, AND ALL THAT
IS IN THEM, 25who
by the Holy Spirit,
through the mouth
of our father David
Your servant, said,

NIV

"'Why do the
nations
rage
and the
peoples
plot in
vain?
[26] The kings of the
earth rise
up
and the rulers
band
together
against the Lord
and against
his
anointed
one.'[a] [b]
[27] Indeed Herod
and Pontius Pilate
met together with
the Gentiles and
the people of Israel
in this city to con-
spire against your
holy servant Jesus,
whom you anoint-
ed. [28] They did
what your power
and will had de-
cided beforehand
should happen.
[29] Now, Lord, con-
sider their threats
and enable your
servants to speak
your word with
great boldness.
[30] Stretch out your
hand to heal and
perform signs and
wonders through
the name of your
holy servant
Jesus."
[31] After they
prayed, the place
where they were
meeting was shak-
en. And they were
all filled with the
Holy Spirit and
spoke the word of
God boldly.

The Believers Share Their Possessions

[32] All the believ-
ers were one in
heart and mind.
No one claimed
that any of their
possessions was
their own, but they
shared everything
they had.

[a] 26 That is, Messiah or Christ
[b] 26 Psalm 2:1,2

σου εἰπών, ἱνατί → ἐφρύαξαν ἔθνη καὶ λαοὶ ἐμελέτησαν
your did say, 'Why did the Gentiles rage, *Gentiles* and the peoples devise
5148 3306 2672 1620 5865 1620 2779 3295 3509
r.gs.2 pt.aa.nsm cj v.aai.3p n.npn cj n.npm v.aai.3p

κενά; [26] παρέστησαν οἱ βασιλεῖς τῆς γῆς καὶ
vain schemes? The kings of the earth took their stand, *The kings of the earth* and
3031 3836 995 3836 3836 1178 4225 3836 995 3836 1178 2779
a.apn v.aai.3p d.npm n.npm d.gsf n.gsf cj

οἱ ἄρχοντες συνήχθησαν ⸤ἐπὶ τὸ αὐτὸ⸥ κατὰ τοῦ κυρίου καὶ κατὰ τοῦ
the rulers gathered together against the Lord and against *{the}* his
3836 807 5251 2093 3836 899 2848 3836 3261 2779 2848 3836 899
d.npm n.npm v.api.3p p.a d.asn r.asn p.g d.gsm n.gsm cj p.g d.gsm

χριστοῦ αὐτοῦ. [27] συνήχθησαν γὰρ ⸤ἐπ' ἀληθείας⸥ ἐν τῇ
Messiah.' *his* For truly ⸤there were gathered together⸥ *For truly* in *{the}*
5986 899 1142 2093 5251 1142 2093 237 1877 3836
n.gsm r.gsm.3 v.api.3p cj p.g n.gsf p.d d.dsf

πόλει ταύτῃ ἐπὶ τὸν ἅγιον παῖδά σου Ἰησοῦν ὃν ἔχρισας,
this city *this* against *{the}* your holy servant *your* Jesus, whom you anointed, both
4047 4484 4047 2093 3836 5148 41 4090 5148 2652 4005 5987 5445
n.dsf r.dsf p.a d.asm a.asm n.asm r.gs.2 n.asm r.asm v.aai.2s

Ἡρῴδης τε καὶ Πόντιος Πιλᾶτος σὺν ἔθνεσιν καὶ λαοῖς Ἰσραήλ,
Herod *both* and Pontius Pilate, ⸤along with⸥ the Gentiles and the peoples of Israel,
2476 5445 2779 4508 4397 5250 1620 2779 3295 2702
n.nsm cj cj n.nsm n.nsm p.d n.dpn cj n.dpm n.gsm

[28] ποιῆσαι ὅσα ἡ χείρ σου καὶ ἡ βουλή σου[a] προώρισεν
to do whatever *{the}* your hand *your* and *{the}* your plan *your* had predetermined
4472 4012 3836 5148 5931 5148 2779 3836 5148 1087 5148 4633
f.aa r.apn d.nsf n.nsf r.gs.2 cj d.nsf n.nsf r.gs.2 v.aai.3s

γενέσθαι. [29] καὶ τὰ νῦν, κύριε, ἔπιδε ἐπὶ τὰς ἀπειλὰς αὐτῶν καὶ δὸς τοῖς
to be. And *{the}* now, Lord, look upon *{the}* their threats *their* and grant to
1181 2779 3836 3814 3261 2078 2093 3836 899 581 899 2779 1443 3836
f.am cj d.apn adv n.vsm v.aam.2s p.a d.apf n.apf r.gpm.3 cj v.aam.2s d.dpm

δούλοις σου μετὰ παρρησίας πάσης λαλεῖν τὸν λόγον σου, [30] ἐν τῷ
your servants *your* with all boldness *all* to speak *{the}* your word, *your* while *{the}*
5148 1529 5148 3552 4246 4244 4246 3281 3836 5148 3364 5148 1877 3836
n.dpm r.gs.2 p.g n.gsf a.gsf f.pa d.asm n.asm r.gs.2 p.d d.dsn

τὴν χεῖρά σου[b] ἐκτείνειν σε εἰς ἴασιν καὶ σημεῖα καὶ τέρατα
you stretch out *{the}* your hand *your stretch out you* to heal, and signs and wonders
5148 1753 1753 3836 5148 5931 5148 1753 5148 1650 2617 2779 4956 2779 5469
d.asf n.asf r.gs.2 f.pa r.as.2 p.a n.asf cj n.apn cj n.apn

γίνεσθαι διὰ τοῦ ὀνόματος τοῦ ἁγίου παιδός σου Ἰησοῦ. [31] καὶ →
are done through the name of your holy servant *your* Jesus." And when they
1181 1328 3836 3950 3836 5148 41 4090 5148 2652 2779 899
f.pp p.g d.gsn n.gsn d.gsm a.gsm n.gsm r.gs.2 n.gsm cj

δεηθέντων αὐτῶν ἐσαλεύθη ὁ τόπος ἐν ᾧ ἦσαν συνηγμένοι,
had prayed, *they was shaken* the place in which they were gathered together was shaken,
1289 899 4888 3836 5536 1877 4005 1639 5251 4888 4888
pt.ap.gpm r.gpm.3 v.api.3s d.nsm n.nsm p.d r.dsm v.iai.3p pt.rp.npm

καὶ → → ἐπλήσθησαν ἅπαντες τοῦ ἁγίου πνεύματος καὶ ἐλάλουν τὸν
and they were all filled with *all* the Holy Spirit and began to speak the
2779 570 4398 570 3836 41 4460 2779 3281 3836
cj v.api.3p a.npm d.gsn a.gsn n.gsn cj v.iai.3p d.asm

λόγον τοῦ θεοῦ μετὰ παρρησίας. [32] τοῦ δὲ πλήθους τῶν πιστευσάντων
word of God with boldness. Now the *Now* whole group of those who believed
3364 3836 2536 3552 4244 1254 3836 1254 4436 3836 4409
n.asm d.gsm n.gsm p.g n.gsf d.gsn cj n.gsn d.gpm pt.aa.gpm

ἦν καρδία καὶ ψυχὴ μία, καὶ οὐδὲ εἷς τι τῶν ὑπαρχόντων
were of one heart and soul, *one* and not even one said that anything that belonged
1639 1651 2840 2779 6034 1651 2779 4028 1651 3306 5516 3836 5639
v.iai.3s n.nsf cj n.nsf a.nsf cj adv a.nsm r.asn d.gpn pt.pa.gpn

αὐτῷ ἔλεγεν ἴδιον εἶναι ἀλλ' ἦν αὐτοῖς ἅπαντα
to him *said* was his own, *was* but everything was common property for them. *everything*
899 3306 1639 2625 1639 247 570 1639 3123 3123 899 570
r.dsm.3 v.iai.3s a.asn f.pa cj v.iai.3s r.dpm.3 a.npn

[a] [σου] UBS, omitted by TNIV.
[b] [σου] UBS.

NASB

' WHY DID THE [a]GENTILES RAGE,
AND THE PEOPLES DEVISE FUTILE THINGS?
[26] ' THE KINGS OF THE EARTH TOOK THEIR STAND,
AND THE RULERS WERE GATHERED TOGETHER
AGAINST THE LORD AND AGAINST HIS CHRIST.'
[27] For truly in
this city there
were gathered
together against
Your holy servant
Jesus, whom You
anointed, both
Herod and Pontius
Pilate, along with
the Gentiles and
the peoples of
Israel, [28] to do what-
ever Your hand and
Your purpose pre-
destined to occur.
[29] And now, Lord,
take note of their
threats, and grant
that Your bond-
servants may speak
Your word with all
confidence, [30] while
You extend Your
hand to heal, and
signs and wonders
take place through
the name of Your
holy servant Je-
sus." [31] And when
they had prayed,
the place where
they had gathered
together was
shaken, and they
were all filled with
the Holy Spirit and
began to speak the
word of God with
boldness.

Sharing among Believers

[32] And the con-
gregation of those
who believed were
of one heart and
soul; and not one
of them claimed
that anything be-
longing to him was
his own, but all

[a] Or *nations*

NIV

33 With great power
the apostles con-
tinued to testify
to the resurrection
of the Lord Jesus.
And God's grace
was so powerfully
at work in them all
34 that there were
no needy persons
among them. For
from time to time
those who owned
land or houses sold
them, brought the
money from the
sales 35 and put it at
the apostles' feet,
and it was distrib-
uted to anyone
who had need.
36 Joseph, a Le-
vite from Cyprus,
whom the apostles
called Barnabas
(which means
"son of encourage-
ment"), 37 sold a
field he owned and
brought the money
and put it at the
apostles' feet.

Ananias and Sapphira

5 Now a man
named Anani-
as, together with
his wife Sapphira,
also sold a piece of
property. 2 With his
wife's full knowl-
edge he kept back
part of the money
for himself, but
brought the rest
and put it at the
apostles' feet.
3 Then Peter said,
"Ananias, how is
it that Satan has so
filled your heart
that you have lied
to the Holy Spirit
and have kept for
yourself some of

κοινά. 33 καὶ → δυνάμει μεγάλη ἀπεδίδουν τὸ
common property And with great power great the apostles ⌊continued to give⌋ the
3123 2779 3489 1539 3489 3836 693 625 3836
a.npn cj n.dsf a.dsf v.iai.3p d.asn

μαρτύριον οἱ ἀπόστολοι τῆς ἀναστάσεως τοῦ κυρίου Ἰησοῦ, χάρις τε
testimony the apostles of the resurrection of the Lord Jesus, and great grace and
3457 3836 693 3836 414 3836 3261 2652 5445 3489 5921 5445
n.asn d.npm n.npm d.gsf n.gsf d.gsm n.gsm n.gsm n.nsf cj

μεγάλη ἦν ἐπὶ πάντας αὐτούς. 34 οὐδὲ γάρ ἐνδεής τις
great was upon them all. them For there was not For a needy person
3489 1639 2093 899 4246 899 1142 1639 1639 4028 1142 1890 5516
a.nsf v.iai.3s p.a a.apm r.apm.3 adv cj a.nsm r.nsm

ἦν ἐν αὐτοῖς, ὅσοι γὰρ κτήτορες χωρίων ἢ οἰκιῶν ὑπῆρχον,
there was among them, for ⌊as many as⌋ for were owners of land or houses were
1639 1877 899 1142 4012 1142 5639 3230 6005 2445 3864 5639
v.iai.3s p.d r.dpm.3 r.npm cj n.npm n.gpn cj n.gpf v.iai.3p

πωλοῦντες ἔφερον τὰς τιμὰς τῶν πιπρασκομένων 35 καὶ ἐτίθουν παρὰ
sold them and brought the proceeds from what was sold and placed it at
4797 5770 3836 5507 3836 4405 2779 5502 4123
pt.pa.npm v.iai.3p d.apf n.apf d.gpn pt.pp.gpn cj v.iai.3p p.a

τοὺς πόδας τῶν ἀποστόλων, διεδίδετο δὲ ἑκάστῳ ⌊καθότι ἄν⌋
the apostles' feet; {the} apostles' and they distributed and to each according as
3836 693 4546 3836 693 1254 1344 1254 1667 2776 323
d.apm n.apm d.gpm n.gpm v.ipi.3s cj r.dsm cj pl

τις χρείαν εἶχεν. 36 Ἰωσὴφ δὲ ὁ ἐπικληθεὶς Βαρναβᾶς ἀπὸ τῶν
anyone had need. had And Joseph, And who was surnamed Barnabas by the
5516 2400 5970 2400 1254 2737 1254 3836 2126 982 608 3836
r.nsm n.asf v.iai.3s n.nsm cj d.nsm pt.ap.nsm n.nsm p.g d.gpm

ἀποστόλων, ⌊ὅ ἐστιν⌋ μεθερμηνευόμενον υἱὸς παρακλήσεως,
apostles (when translated means, when translated "Son of Encouragement"), a
693 3493 3493 4005 1639 3493 5626 4155
n.gpm r.nsn v.pai.3s pt.pp.nsn n.nsm n.gsf

Λευίτης, Κύπριος τῷ γένει, 37 ὑπάρχοντος αὐτῷ ἀγροῦ πωλήσας
Levite, a Cypriot by race, sold a field that belonged to him field sold and
3324 3250 3836 1169 4797 69 5639 899 69 4797
n.nsm n.nsm d.dsn n.dsn pt.pa.gsm r.dsm.3 n.gsm pt.aa.nsm

ἤνεγκεν τὸ χρῆμα καὶ ἔθηκεν πρὸς τοὺς πόδας τῶν ἀποστόλων.
brought the money and placed it at the apostles' feet. {the} apostles'
5770 3836 5975 2779 5502 4639 3836 693 4546 3836 693
v.aai.3s d.asn n.asn cj v.aai.3s p.a d.apm n.apm d.gpm n.gpm

5:1 ἀνὴρ δέ τις Ἁνανίας ὀνόματι σὺν Σαπφίρῃ τῇ γυναικὶ
Now a man Now a named Ananias, named with Sapphira {the} his wife,
1254 5516 467 1254 5516 3950 393 3950 5250 4912 3836 899 1222
n.nsm cj r.nsm n.nsm n.dsn p.d n.dsf d.dsf n.dsf

αὐτοῦ ἐπώλησεν κτῆμα 2 καὶ ἐνοσφίσατο ἀπὸ τῆς τιμῆς,
his sold a ⌊piece of property,⌋ and ⌊kept back for himself⌋ ⌊some of⌋ the proceeds, with
899 4797 3228 2779 3802 608 3836 5507 2779
r.gsm.3 v.aai.3s n.asn cj v.ami.3s p.g d.gsf n.gsf

συνειδυίης καὶ τῆς γυναικός, καὶ ἐνέγκας μέρος τι
his wife's knowledge, with his wife's and brought only part of it and placed it
3836 1222 5323 2779 3836 1222 2779 5770 3538 5516 5502
pt.ra.gsf adv d.gsf n.gsf cj pt.aa.nsm n.asn r.asn

παρὰ τοὺς πόδας τῶν ἀποστόλων ἔθηκεν. 3 εἶπεν δὲ ὁ Πέτρος,
at the apostles' feet. {the} apostles' placed But Peter said, But {the} Peter
4123 3836 693 4546 3836 693 5502 1254 4377 3306 1254 3836 4377
p.a d.apm n.apm d.gpm n.gpm v.aai.3s v.aai.3s cj d.nsm n.nsm

Ἁνανία, ⌊διὰ τί⌋ → ἐπλήρωσεν ὁ σατανᾶς τὴν καρδίαν σου,
"Ananias, why did Satan fill {the} Satan {the} your heart your
393 1328 5515 4928 4444 3836 4928 3836 5148 2840 5148
n.vsm p.a r.asn v.aai.3s d.nsm n.nsm d.asf n.asf r.gs.2

ψεύσασθαί σε τὸ πνεῦμα τὸ ἅγιον καὶ νοσφίσασθαι ἀπὸ τῆς
to lie to {you} the Holy Spirit {the} Holy and ⌊to keep back for yourself⌋ ⌊part of⌋ the
6017 5148 3836 41 4460 3836 41 2779 3802 608 3836
f.am r.as.2 d.asn n.asn d.asn a.asn cj f.am p.g d.gsf

NASB

things were com-
mon property to
them. 33 And with
great power the
apostles were giv-
ing testimony to
the resurrection
of the Lord Jesus,
and abundant grace
was upon them
all. 34 For there was
not a needy person
among them, for all
who were owners
of land or houses
would sell them
and bring the pro-
ceeds of the sales
35 and lay them at
the apostles' feet,
and they would be
distributed to each
as any had need.
36 Now Joseph, a
Levite of Cyprian
birth, who was also
called Barnabas by
the apostles (which
translated means
Son of Encourage-
ment), 37 and who
owned a tract of
land, sold it and
brought the money
and laid it at the
apostles' feet.

Fate of Ananias and Sapphira

5:1 But a man
named Ananias,
with his wife Sap-
phira, sold a piece
of property, 2 and
kept back *some* of
the price for him-
self, with his wife's
full knowledge,
and bringing a por-
tion of it, he laid
it at the apostles'
feet. 3 But Peter
said, "Ananias,
why has Satan
filled your heart
to lie to the Holy
Spirit and to keep
back *some* of the

NIV

the money you
received for the
land? 4 Didn't it be-
long to you before
it was sold? And
after it was sold,
wasn't the money
at your disposal?
What made you
think of doing
such a thing? You
have not lied just
to human beings
but to God."
5 When Ananias
heard this, he fell
down and died.
And great fear
seized all who
heard what had
happened. 6 Then
some young men
came forward,
wrapped up his
body, and carried
him out and buried
him.
7 About three
hours later his
wife came in, not
knowing what had
happened. 8 Peter
asked her, "Tell
me, is this the
price you and An-
anias got for the
land?"
"Yes," she said,
"that is the price."
9 Peter said to her,
"How could you
conspire to test the
Spirit of the Lord?
Listen! The feet of
the men who bur-
ied your husband
are at the door, and
they will carry you
out also."
10 At that moment
she fell down at
his feet and died.
Then the young
men came in and,
finding her dead,
carried her out
and buried her be-
side her husband.
11 Great fear

τιμῆς τοῦ χωρίου; 4 οὐχὶ μένον
proceeds of the field? While it remained unsold, did it not *While it remained* remain
5507 3836 6005 3531 3531 3531 3531 3531 4049 3531 3531
n.gsf d.gsn n.gsn pl pt.pa.nsn

σοὶ ἔμενεν καὶ πραθὲν ἐν τῇ σῇ ἐξουσίᾳ ὑπῆρχεν; τί
yours? *did it remain* And ⌊after it was sold,⌋ was it not under *{the}* your control? *was it* Why
5148 3531 2779 4405 5639 5639 1877 3836 5050 2026 5639 5515
r.ds.2 v.iai.3s cj pt.ap.nsn p.d d.dsf r.dsf.2 n.dsf v.iai.3s r.asn

ὅτι ἔθου ἐν τῇ καρδίᾳ σου τὸ πρᾶγμα τοῦτο; ↱
is it that ⌊you have contrived⌋ this affair in *{the}* your heart? *your* *{the}* *affair* *this* You
4022 5502 4047 4547 1877 3836 5148 2840 5148 3836 4547 4047 6017
cj v.ami.2s p.d d.dsf n.dsf r.gs.2 d.asn n.asn r.asn

↱ οὐκ ἐψεύσω ἀνθρώποις ἀλλὰ τῷ θεῷ. 5 → ἀκούων δὲ ὁ
have not lied to men but to God!" When Ananias heard *{and}* *{the}*
6017 4024 6017 476 247 3836 2536 393 201 1254 3836
pl v.ami.2s n.dpm cj d.dsm n.dsm pt.pa.nsm cj d.nsm

Ἀνανίας τοὺς λόγους τούτους ↱ πεσὼν ἐξέψυξεν, καὶ
Ananias *{the}* these words, *these* he fell down and ⌊breathed his last.⌋ *{and}* Great fear
393 3836 4047 3364 4047 1775 4406 1775 2779 3489 5832
n.nsm d.apm n.apm r.apm pt.aa.nsm v.aai.3s cj

ἐγένετο φόβος μέγας ἐπὶ πάντας τοὺς ἀκούοντας. 6 ἀναστάντες
gripped *fear* *Great* *{on}* all who heard about it. So the young men came forward,
1181 5832 3489 2093 4246 3836 201 1254 3836 3742 3742 482
v.ami.3s n.nsm a.nsm p.a a.apm d.apm pt.pa.apm pt.aa.npm

δὲ οἱ νεώτεροι συνέστειλαν αὐτὸν ↰ καὶ ἐξενέγκαντες ← ἔθαψαν.
So *the* *young men* wrapped him up, then carried him out and buried him.
1254 3836 3742 5366 899 5366 2779 1766 2507
cj d.npm a.npm.c v.aai.3p r.asm.3 cj pt.aa.npm v.aai.3p

7 ⌊ἐγένετο δὲ⌋ ὡς ὡρῶν τριῶν διάστημα καὶ ἡ γυνὴ αὐτοῦ
After an interval of about three hours *three* *interval* *{and}* *{the}* his wife *his*
1181 1254 1404 6055 5552 6052 5552 1404 2779 3836 899 1222 899
v.ami.3s cj pl n.gpf a.gpf n.nsn cj d.nsf n.nsf r.gsm.3

⌊μὴ εἰδυῖα⌋ τὸ γεγονὸς εἰσῆλθεν. 8 ἀπεκρίθη δὲ πρὸς
came in, unaware of what had happened. *came in* And Peter addressed *And* *{to}*
1656 1656 3590 3857 3836 1181 1656 1254 4377 646 1254 4639
pl pt.ra.nsf d.asn pt.ra.asn v.aai.3s v.api.3s cj p.a

αὐτὴν Πέτρος, εἰπέ μοι, εἰ τοσούτου τὸ χωρίον ἀπέδοσθε; ἡ
her, *Peter* "Tell me whether for so much you sold the land" *you sold* And she
899 4377 3306 1609 1623 5537 625 625 3836 6005 625 1254 3836
r.asf.3 n.nsm v.aam.2s r.ds.1 cj r.gsn d.asn n.asn v.ami.2p d.nsf

δὲ εἶπεν, ναί, τοσούτου. 9 ὁ δὲ Πέτρος πρὸς αὐτήν, τί ὅτι
And said, "Yes, for so much." *{the}* And Peter said to her, "Why is it that you
1254 3306 3721 5537 3836 1254 4377 4639 899 5515 4022 7007
cj v.aai.3s pl r.gsn d.nsm cj n.nsm p.a r.asf.3 r.asn cj

συνεφωνήθη ὑμῖν πειράσαι τὸ πνεῦμα → κυρίου; ἰδοὺ οἱ πόδες τῶν
agreed together *you* to test the Spirit of the Lord? Look! The feet of those
5244 7007 4279 3836 4460 3261 2627 3836 4546 3836
v.api.3s r.dp.2 f.aa d.asn n.asn n.gsm j d.npm n.npm d.gpm

θαψάντων τὸν ἄνδρα σου ἐπὶ τῇ θύρᾳ καὶ ἐξοίσουσίν σε. ↰ 10
who buried *{the}* your husband *your* are at the door, and they will carry you out." And
2507 3836 5148 467 5148 2093 3836 2598 2779 1766 5148 1766 1254
pt.aa.gpm d.asm n.asm r.gs.2 p.d d.dsf n.dsf cj v.fai.3p r.as.2

ἔπεσεν δὲ παραχρῆμα πρὸς τοὺς πόδας αὐτοῦ καὶ ἐξέψυξεν· →
⌊she fell down⌋ *And* immediately at *{the}* his feet *his* and ⌊breathed her last.⌋ When
4406 1254 4202 4639 3836 899 4546 899 2779 1775
v.aai.3s cj adv p.a d.apm n.apm r.gsm.3 cj v.aai.3s

εἰσελθόντες δὲ οἱ νεανίσκοι εὗρον αὐτὴν νεκρὰν καὶ ↱
the young men came in *{and}* *the* *young men* and found her dead, *{and}* they
3836 3734 3734 1656 1254 3836 3734 2351 899 3738 2779 2507
pt.aa.npm cj d.npm n.npm v.aai.3p r.asf.3 a.asf cj

ἐξενέγκαντες ← ἔθαψαν πρὸς τὸν ἄνδρα αὐτῆς, 11 καὶ
carried her out and buried her beside *{the}* her husband. *her* *{and}* Great fear
1766 2507 4639 3836 899 467 899 2779 3489 5832
pt.aa.npm v.aai.3p p.a d.asm n.asm r.gsf.3 cj

NASB

price of the land?
4 While it remained
unsold, did it not
remain your own?
And after it was
sold, was it not
under your control?
Why is it that you
have conceived
this deed in your
heart? You have
not lied to men
but to God." 5 And
as he heard these
words, Ananias fell
down and breathed
his last; and great
fear came over all
who heard of it.
6 The young men
got up and covered
him up, and after
carrying him out,
they buried him.
7 Now there
elapsed an interval
of about three
hours, and his
wife came in, not
knowing what had
happened. 8 And
Peter responded
to her, "Tell me
whether you sold
the land for such
and such a price?"
And she said, "Yes,
that was the price."
9 Then Peter *said* to
her, "Why is it that
you have agreed
together to put the
Spirit of the Lord
to the test? Behold,
the feet of those
who have buried
your husband are
at the door, and
they will carry you
out *as well.*" 10 And
immediately she
fell at his feet and
breathed her last,
and the young men
came in and found
her dead, and they
carried her out and
buried her beside
her husband. 11 And
great fear came

NIV

seized the whole
church and all who
heard about these
events.

The Apostles Heal Many

12The apostles
performed many
signs and wonders
among the peo-
ple. And all the
believers used to
meet together in
Solomon's Col-
onnade. 13No one
else dared join
them, even though
they were highly
regarded by the
people. 14Never-
theless, more and
more men and
women believed
in the Lord and
were added to
their number. 15As
a result, people
brought the sick
into the streets
and laid them on
beds and mats so
that at least Peter's
shadow might fall
on some of them
as he passed by.
16Crowds gath-
ered also from
the towns around
Jerusalem, bring-
ing their sick and
those tormented by
impure spirits, and
all of them were
healed.

The Apostles Persecuted

17Then the high
priest and all his
associates, who
were members of
the party of the
Sadducees, were
filled with jealou-
sy. 18They arrested
the apostles and
put them in the
public jail. 19But
during the night an
angel of the Lord
opened the doors
of the jail and

ἐγένετο φόβος μέγας ἐφ᾽ ὅλην τὴν ἐκκλησίαν καὶ ἐπὶ πάντας τοὺς ἀκούοντας
gripped *fear* *Great* *{on}* the entire *the* church, and *{on}* all who heard about
1181 5832 3489 2093 3836 3910 3836 1711 2779 2093 4246 3836 201
v.ami.3s n.nsm a.nsm p.a a.asf d.asf n.asf cj p.a a.apm d.apm pt.pa.apm

ταῦτα. 12 διὰ δὲ τῶν χειρῶν τῶν ἀποστόλων
these things. By *{and}* the hands of the apostles many signs and wonders
4047 1328 1254 3836 5931 3836 693 4498 4956 2779 5469
r.apn p.g cj d.gpf n.gpf d.gpm n.gpm

ἐγίνετο σημεῖα καὶ τέρατα πολλὰ ἐν τῷ λαῷ. καὶ ἦσαν
⌞were being done⌟ *signs* *and* *wonders* *many* among the people. And they were all
1181 4956 2779 5469 4498 1877 3836 3295 2779 1639 570
v.imi.3s n.npn cj n.npn a.npn p.d d.dsm n.dsm cj v.iai.3p

ὁμοθυμαδὸν ἅπαντες ἐν τῇ στοᾷ Σολομῶντος, 13 τῶν δὲ λοιπῶν
together *all* in *{the}* Solomon's Portico. *Solomon's* But of the *But* others
3924 570 1877 3836 5048 5119 5048 1254 3836 1254 3370
adv a.npm p.d d.dsf n.dsf n.gsm d.gpm cj a.gpm

οὐδεὶς ἐτόλμα κολλᾶσθαι αὐτοῖς, ἀλλ᾽ ἐμεγάλυνεν αὐτοὺς ↰ ↰
no one dared to join them; however, the people held them in high
4029 5528 3140 899 247 3836 3295 3486 899 3486 3486
a.nsm v.iai.3s f.pp r.dpm.3 cj v.iai.3s r.apm.3

↰ ὁ λαός. 14 μᾶλλον δὲ προσετίθεντο πιστεύοντες τῷ
regard, *the* *people* and ⌞more than ever⌟ *and* believers were added *believers* ⌞to the⌟
3486 3836 3295 1254 3437 1254 4409 4707 4409 3836
d.nsm n.nsm adv.c cj v.ipi.3p pt.pa.npm d.dsm

κυρίῳ, πλήθη ἀνδρῶν τε καὶ γυναικῶν, 15 ὥστε καὶ
Lord, multitudes both of men *both* and women, so that they carried out the sick even
3261 4436 5445 467 5445 2779 1222 6063 1766 1766 1766 3836 822 2779
n.dsm n.npn n.gpm cj cj n.gpf cj adv

εἰς τὰς πλατείας ἐκφέρειν τοὺς ἀσθενεῖς καὶ τιθέναι ἐπὶ κλιναρίων καὶ
into the streets, *they carried out* *the* *sick* and laid them on cots and
1650 3836 4426 1766 3836 822 2779 5502 2093 3108 2779
p.a d.apf n.apf f.pa d.apm a.apm cj f.pa p.g n.gpn cj

κραβάττων, ἵνα → ἐρχομένου Πέτρου κἂν ἡ σκιὰ ἐπισκιάσῃ τινὶ αὐτῶν.
mats, so that as Peter came by *Peter* at least his shadow might fall on some of them.
3187 2671 4377 2262 4377 2829 3836 5014 2173 5516 899
n.gpm cj pt.pm.gsm n.gsm crasis d.nsf n.nsf v.aas.3s r.dsm r.gpm.3

16 συνήρχετο δὲ καὶ τὸ πλῆθος τῶν πέριξ πόλεων
came *{and}* *also* A great number of people ⌞from the⌟ towns around *towns*
5302 1254 2779 3836 4436 3836 4484 4339 4484
v.imi.3s cj adv d.nsn n.nsn d.gpf adv n.gpf

Ἰερουσαλὴμ φέροντες ἀσθενεῖς καὶ ὀχλουμένους ὑπὸ πνευμάτων
Jerusalem also came, bringing the sick and those tormented by evil spirits,
2647 2779 5302 5770 822 2779 4061 5679 176 4460
n.gsf pt.pa.npm a.apm cj pt.pp.apm p.g n.gpn

ἀκαθάρτων, οἵτινες ἐθεραπεύοντο ἅπαντες. 17 ἀναστὰς
evil and they were healed, all of them. Then the high priest stood up
176 4015 2543 570 1254 3836 797 797 482
a.gpn r.npm v.ipi.3p a.npm pt.aa.nsm

δὲ ὁ ἀρχιερεὺς καὶ πάντες οἱ σὺν αὐτῷ, ἡ οὖσα αἵρεσις τῶν
Then *the* *high priest* and all who were with him (that is, the party of the
1254 3836 797 2779 4246 3836 5250 899 3836 1639 146 3836
cj d.nsm n.nsm cj a.npm d.npm p.d r.dsm.3 d.nsf pt.pa.nsf n.nsf d.gpm

Σαδδουκαίων, ἐπλήσθησαν ζήλου 18 καὶ ἐπέβαλον τὰς χεῖρας ἐπὶ τοὺς
Sadducees), and ⌞they were filled with⌟ indignation, and they laid *{the}* hands on the
4881 4398 2419 2779 2095 3836 5931 2093 3836
n.gpm v.api.3p n.gsm cj v.aai.3p d.apf n.apf p.a d.apm

ἀποστόλους καὶ ἔθεντο αὐτοὺς ἐν τηρήσει δημοσίᾳ. 19 ἄγγελος δὲ
apostles and put them in the public jail. *public* But an angel *But*
693 2779 5502 899 1877 1323 5499 1323 1254 34 1254
n.apm cj v.ami.3p r.apm.3 p.d n.dsf a.dsf n.nsm cj

→ κυρίου διὰ νυκτὸς ἀνοίξας τὰς θύρας τῆς φυλακῆς ἐξαγαγών τε
of the Lord during the night opened the doors of the prison and brought *and*
3261 1328 3816 487 3836 2598 3836 5871 5445 1974 5445
n.gsm p.g n.gsf pt.aa.nsm d.apf n.apf d.gsf n.gsf pt.aa.nsm cj

NASB

over the whole
church, and over
all who heard of
these things.
12At the hands of
the apostles many
signs and wonders
were taking place
among the people;
and they were all
with one accord in
Solomon's portico.
13But none of the
rest dared to as-
sociate with them;
however, the peo-
ple held them in
high esteem. 14And
all the more believ-
ers in the Lord,
multitudes of men
and women, were
constantly added
to *their number,*
15to such an extent
that they even car-
ried the sick out
into the streets and
laid them on cots
and pallets, so that
when Peter came
by at least his shad-
ow might fall on
any one of them.
16Also the people
from the cities in
the vicinity of Jeru-
salem were coming
together, bringing
people who were
sick [a]or afflicted
with unclean spir-
its, and they were
all being healed.

Imprisonment and Release

17But the high
priest rose up,
along with all his
associates (that is
the sect of the Sad-
ducees), and they
were filled with
jealousy. 18They
laid hands on the
apostles and put
them in a public
jail. 19But during
the night an angel
of the Lord opened
the gates of the
prison, and taking

[a] Lit *and*

NIV

brought them out.
[20]"Go, stand in the
temple courts," he
said, "and tell the
people all about
this new life."
[21]At daybreak
they entered the
temple courts, as
they had been told,
and began to teach
the people.
When the high
priest and his asso-
ciates arrived, they
called together the
Sanhedrin—the
full assembly of
the elders of Is-
rael—and sent
to the jail for the
apostles. [22]But on
arriving at the jail,
the officers did not
find them there. So
they went back and
reported, [23]"We
found the jail se-
curely locked,
with the guards
standing at the
doors; but when
we opened them,
we found no one
inside." [24]On hear-
ing this report, the
captain of the tem-
ple guard and the
chief priests were
at a loss, won-
dering what this
might lead to.
[25]Then someone
came and said,
"Look! The men
you put in jail
are standing in
the temple courts
teaching the peo-
ple." [26]At that, the
captain went with
his officers and
brought the apos-
tles. They did not
use force, because
they feared that
the people would
stone them.

αὐτοὺς ↰ εἶπεν, [20] πορεύεσθε καὶ σταθέντες λαλεῖτε ἐν
them out and said, "Go and stand in the temple and speak *in*
899 1974 3306 4513 2779 2705 1877 3836 2639 3281 1877
r.apm.3 v.aai.3s v.pmm.2p cj pt.ap.npm v.pam.2p p.d

τῷ ἱερῷ τῷ λαῷ πάντα τὰ ῥήματα τῆς ζωῆς ταύτης. [21] ἀκούσαντες
the temple ⌊to the⌋ people all the words of this life." *this* And when they heard
3836 2639 3836 3295 4246 3836 4839 3836 4047 2437 4047 1254 201
d.dsn n.dsn d.dsm n.dsm a.apn d.apn n.apn d.gsf n.gsf r.gsf pt.aa.npm

δὲ εἰσῆλθον ὑπὸ τὸν ὄρθρον εἰς τὸ ἱερὸν καὶ ἐδίδασκον.
And this, they entered the temple at *{the}* daybreak *{into}* *the* *temple* and began to teach. But
1254 1656 3836 2639 5679 3836 3986 1650 3836 2639 2779 1438 1254
cj v.aai.3p p.a d.asm n.asm p.a d.asn n.asn cj v.iai.3p

→ παραγενόμενος δὲ ὁ ἀρχιερεὺς καὶ οἱ σὺν αὐτῷ
when the high priest came, *But the high priest* and those who were with him,
3836 797 797 4134 1254 3836 797 2779 3836 5250 899
pt.am.nsm cj d.nsm n.nsm cj d.npm p.d r.dsm.3

συνεκάλεσαν τὸ συνέδριον καὶ πᾶσαν τὴν γερουσίαν τῶν υἱῶν Ἰσραὴλ καὶ
they called together the council and all the elders of the sons of Israel and
5157 3836 5284 2779 4246 3836 1172 3836 5626 2702 2779
v.aai.3p d.asn n.asn cj a.asf d.asf n.asf d.gpm n.gpm n.gsm cj

ἀπέστειλαν εἰς τὸ δεσμωτήριον → → ἀχθῆναι αὐτούς. [22] ↱ οἱ
they sent to the prison to have them brought before them. But when the
690 1650 3836 1303 72 899 1254 4134 3836
v.aai.3p p.a d.asn n.asn f.ap r.apm.3 d.npm

δὲ παραγενόμενοι ὑπηρέται ↱ ↱ οὐχ εὗρον αὐτοὺς ἐν τῇ φυλακῇ,
But officers came, *officers* they did not find them in the prison, so
1254 5677 4134 5677 2351 2351 4024 2351 899 1877 3836 5871 1254
cj pt.am.npm n.npm pl v.aai.3p r.apm.3 p.d d.dsf n.dsf

↱ ἀναστρέψαντες δὲ ἀπήγγειλαν [23] λέγοντες ὅτι τὸ δεσμωτήριον
they returned *so* and reported, saying, ~ "We found the prison
550 418 1254 550 3306 4022 2351 2351 3836 1303
pt.aa.npm cj v.aai.3p pt.pa.npm cj d.asn n.asn

εὕρομεν κεκλεισμένον ἐν πάσῃ ἀσφαλείᾳ καὶ τοὺς φύλακας ἑστῶτας ἐπὶ τῶν
We found locked with every security and the guards standing at the
2351 3091 1877 4246 854 2779 3836 5874 2705 2093 3836
v.aai.1p pt.rp.asn p.d a.dsf n.dsf cj d.apm n.apm pt.ra.apm p.g d.gpf

θυρῶν, ἀνοίξαντες δὲ ἔσω οὐδένα εὕρομεν. [24] ὡς
doors, but when we opened it *but* we found no one inside." *no one* *we found* On
2598 1254 487 1254 2351 2351 4029 4029 2276 4029 2351 6055
n.gpf pt.aa.npm cj adv a.asm v.aai.1p cj

δὲ ἤκουσαν τοὺς λόγους τούτους ὅ τε στρατηγὸς τοῦ ἱεροῦ καὶ
{and} hearing *{the}* these words, *these* both the *both* captain of the temple and
1254 201 3836 4047 3364 4047 5445 3836 5445 5130 3836 2639 2779
cj v.aai.3p d.apm n.apm r.apm d.nsm cj n.nsm d.gsn n.gsn cj

οἱ ἀρχιερεῖς, διηπόρουν περὶ αὐτῶν τί ἂν γένοιτο τοῦτο. [25]
the chief priests were perplexed about them, wondering what ~ this could be. *this* And
3836 797 1389 4309 899 5515 323 4047 1181 4047 1254
d.npm n.npm v.iai.3p p.g r.gpm.3 r.nsn pl v.amo.3s r.nsn

παραγενόμενος δέ τις ἀπήγγειλεν αὐτοῖς ὅτι ἰδοὺ οἱ ἄνδρες
someone came *And someone* and reported to them, ~ "Look! The men
5516 4134 1254 5516 550 899 4022 2627 3836 467
pt.am.nsm cj r.nsm v.aai.3s r.dpm.3 cj j d.npm n.npm

οὓς ἔθεσθε ἐν τῇ φυλακῇ εἰσὶν ἐν τῷ ἱερῷ ἑστῶτες καὶ διδάσκοντες
whom you put in the prison are standing in the temple *standing* and teaching
4005 5502 1877 3836 5871 1639 2705 1877 3836 2639 2705 2779 1438
r.apm v.ami.2p p.d d.dsf n.dsf v.pai.3p p.d d.dsn n.dsn pt.ra.npm cj pt.pa.npm

τὸν λαόν. [26] τότε ἀπελθὼν ὁ στρατηγὸς σὺν τοῖς ὑπηρέταις
the people." Then the captain went *the* *captain* with the officers and
3836 3295 5538 3836 5130 599 3836 5130 5250 3836 5677
d.asm n.asm adv pt.aa.nsm d.nsm n.nsm p.d d.dpm n.dpm

ἦγεν αὐτοὺς οὐ μετὰ βίας, ἐφοβοῦντο γὰρ τὸν λαὸν μὴ λιθασθῶσιν.
brought them, but not with force, for they feared *for* the people, lest they be stoned.
72 899 4024 3552 1040 1142 5828 1142 3836 3295 3590 3342
v.iai.3s r.apm.3 pl p.g n.gsf v.imi.3p cj d.asm n.asm cj v.aps.3p

NASB

them out he said,
[20]"Go, stand and
speak to the people
in the temple the
whole message of
this Life." [21]Upon
hearing *this,* they
entered into the
temple about day-
break and *began* to
teach.
Now when the
high priest and his
associates came,
they called the
Council together,
even all the Sen-
ate of the sons of
Israel, and sent
orders to the prison
house for them to
be brought. [22]But
the officers who
came did not find
them in the prison;
and they returned
and reported back,
[23]saying, "We
found the prison
house locked quite
securely and the
guards standing at
the doors; but when
we had opened
up, we found no
one inside." [24]Now
when the captain
of the temple
guard and the chief
priests heard these
words, they were
greatly perplexed
about them as
to what would
come of this. [25]But
someone came and
reported to them,
"The men whom
you put in prison
are standing in the
temple and teach-
ing the people!"
[26]Then the captain
went along with
the officers and
proceeded to bring
them *back* without
violence (for they
were afraid of the
people, that they
might be stoned).

NIV

27 The apostles
were brought in
and made to ap-
pear before the
Sanhedrin to be
questioned by the
high priest. 28 "We
gave you strict or-
ders not to teach
in this name," he
said. "Yet you have
filled Jerusalem
with your teaching
and are deter-
mined to make
us guilty of this
man's blood."
29 Peter and the
other apostles re-
plied: "We must
obey God rather
than human be-
ings! 30 The God
of our ancestors
raised Jesus from
the dead—whom
you killed by
hanging him on a
cross. 31 God ex-
alted him to his
own right hand as
Prince and Savior
that he might bring
Israel to repen-
tance and forgive
their sins. 32 We are
witnesses of these
things, and so is
the Holy Spirit,
whom God has
given to those who
obey him."
33 When they
heard this, they
were furious and
wanted to put them
to death. 34 But a
Pharisee named
Gamaliel, a teach-
er of the law, who
was honored by all
the people, stood
up in the Sanhe-
drin and ordered
that the men be
put outside for a
little while. 35 Then
he addressed the
Sanhedrin: "Men
of Israel, consider
carefully what you
intend to do

27 ↱ ἀγαγόντες δὲ αὐτοὺς → ἔστησαν ἐν τῷ συνεδρίῳ. καὶ
And they brought *And* them and had them stand before the council. *{and}* The
1254 2705 72 1254 899 2705 1877 3836 5284 2779 3836
pt.aa.npm cj r.apm.3 v.aai.3p p.d d.dsn n.dsn cj

ἐπηρώτησεν αὐτοὺς ὁ ἀρχιερεὺς 28 λέγων,[a] παραγγελίᾳ
high priest questioned them, *The* *high priest* saying, "We gave you a strict order
797 797 2089 899 3836 797 3306 4133 4133 7007 4132
v.aai.3s r.apm.3 d.nsm n.nsm pt.pa.nsm n.dsf

παρηγγείλαμεν ὑμῖν ↱ μὴ διδάσκειν ἐπὶ τῷ ὀνόματι τούτῳ, καὶ ἰδοὺ
Did we give *you* to stop teaching in *{the}* this name. *this* Yet ~
4133 7007 1438 3590 1438 2093 3836 4047 3950 4047 2779 2627
v.aai.1p r.dp.2 pl f.pa p.d d.dsn n.dsn r.dsn cj j

πεπληρώκατε τὴν Ἰερουσαλὴμ τῆς διδαχῆς ὑμῶν καὶ βούλεσθε ἐπαγαγεῖν ἐφ᾽
you have filled *{the}* Jerusalem with your teaching, *your* and you intend to bring on
4444 3836 2647 3836 7007 1439 7007 2779 1089 2042 2093
v.rai.2p d.asf n.asf d.gsf n.gsf r.gp.2 cj v.pmi.2p f.aa p.a

ἡμᾶς τὸ αἷμα τοῦ ἀνθρώπου τούτου. 29 ἀποκριθεὶς δὲ Πέτρος καὶ οἱ
us the blood of this man." *this* But in response, *But* Peter and the
7005 3836 135 3836 4047 476 4047 1254 646 1254 4377 2779 3836
r.ap.1 d.asn n.asn d.gsm n.gsm r.gsm pt.ap.nsm cj n.nsm cj d.npm

ἀπόστολοι εἶπαν, πειθαρχεῖν δεῖ θεῷ μᾶλλον ἢ
other apostles said, "It is necessary to obey *It is necessary* God rather than
693 3306 1256 1256 1256 4272 1256 2536 3437 2445
n.npm v.aai.3p f.pa v.pai.3s n.dsm adv.c pl

ἀνθρώποις. 30 ὁ θεὸς τῶν πατέρων ἡμῶν ἤγειρεν Ἰησοῦν ὃν ὑμεῖς
men." The God of our fathers *our* raised Jesus, whom you
476 3836 2536 3836 7005 4252 7005 1586 2652 4005 7007
n.dpm d.nsm n.nsm d.gpm n.gpm r.gp.1 v.aai.3s n.asm r.asm r.np.2

διεχειρίσασθε κρεμάσαντες ἐπὶ ξύλου· 31 τοῦτον ὁ θεὸς
killed by hanging him on a tree. God exalted this Jesus *{the}* *God* to
1429 3203 2093 3833 2536 5738 4047 3836 2536 3836
v.ami.2p pt.aa.npm p.g n.gsn r.asm d.nsm n.nsm

ἀρχηγὸν καὶ σωτῆρα ὕψωσεν τῇ δεξιᾷ αὐτοῦ τοῦ[b] δοῦναι
his own right hand as Leader and Savior, *exalted* *to* *right hand his* so as to provide
899 1288 1288 795 2779 5400 5738 3836 1288 899 3836 1443
n.asm cj n.asm v.aai.3s d.dsf a.dsf r.gsm.3 d.gsn f.aa

μετάνοιαν τῷ Ἰσραὴλ καὶ ἄφεσιν ἁμαρτιῶν. 32 καὶ ἡμεῖς ἐσμεν μάρτυρες τῶν
repentance for Israel and the remission of sins. And we are witnesses of
3567 3836 2702 2779 912 281 2779 7005 1639 3459 3836
n.asf d.dsm n.dsm cj n.asf n.gpf cj r.np.1 v.pai.1p n.npm d.gpn

ῥημάτων τούτων καὶ τὸ πνεῦμα τὸ ἅγιον ὃ ἔδωκεν ὁ
these events, *these* and so is the Holy Spirit, *{the}* *Holy* whom God has given *{the}*
4047 4839 4047 2779 3836 41 4460 3836 41 4005 2536 1443 3836
n.gpn r.gpn cj d.nsn n.nsn d.nsn a.nsn r.asn v.aai.3s d.nsm

θεὸς τοῖς πειθαρχοῦσιν αὐτῷ. 33 ↱ οἱ δὲ ἀκούσαντες
God to those who obey him." Now when they *Now* heard this,
2536 3836 4272 899 1254 201 3836 1254 201
n.nsm d.dpm pt.pa.dpm r.dsm.3 d.npm cj pt.aa.npm

διεπρίοντο καὶ ἐβούλοντο ἀνελεῖν αὐτούς. 34 ἀναστὰς δέ τις ἐν τῷ
they were enraged and wanted to kill them. But ⌊there stood up⌋ *But* one in the
1391 2779 1089 359 899 1254 482 1254 5516 1877 3836
v.ipi.3p cj v.imi.3p f.aa r.apm.3 pt.aa.nsm cj r.nsm p.d d.dsn

συνεδρίῳ Φαρισαῖος ὀνόματι Γαμαλιήλ, νομοδιδάσκαλος τίμιος παντὶ τῷ
council, a Pharisee named Gamaliel, a teacher of the law, respected by all the
5284 5757 3950 1137 3791 5508 4246 3836
n.dsn n.nsm n.dsn n.nsm n.nsm a.nsm a.dsm d.dsm

λαῷ, ἐκέλευσεν ἔξω → βραχὺ τοὺς ἀνθρώπους
people, and he ordered them to put the men outside for a short time. *the* *men*
3295 3027 4472 4472 3836 476 2032 1099 3836 476
n.dsm v.aai.3s adv adv d.apm n.apm

ποιῆσαι 35 εἶπέν τε πρὸς αὐτούς, ἄνδρες Ἰσραηλῖται, προσέχετε ἑαυτοῖς
to put And he said *And* to them, "Men of Israel, take heed to yourselves
4472 5445 3306 5445 4639 899 467 2703 4668 1571
f.aa v.aai.3s cj p.a r.apm.3 n.vpm n.vpm v.pam.2p r.dpm.3

[a] οὐ included by UBS after λέγων.
[b] [τοῦ] UBS.

NASB

27 When they had
brought them, they
stood them before
the Council. The
high priest ques-
tioned them, 28 say-
ing, "We gave you
strict orders not to
continue teaching
in this name, and
yet, you have filled
Jerusalem with
your teaching and
intend to bring this
man's blood upon
us." 29 But Peter
and the apostles
answered, "We
must obey God
rather than men.
30 The God of our
fathers raised up
Jesus, whom you
had put to death
by hanging Him
on a cross. 31 He is
the one whom God
exalted to His right
hand as a Prince
and a Savior, to
grant repentance to
Israel, and forgive-
ness of sins. 32 And
we are witnesses
[a]of these things;
and *so is* the Holy
Spirit, whom God
has given to those
who obey Him."

Gamaliel's Counsel

33 But when they
heard this, they
were cut to the
quick and intended
to kill them. 34 But
a Pharisee named
Gamaliel, a teacher
of the Law, re-
spected by all the
people, stood up
in the Council and
gave orders to put
the men outside for
a short time. 35 And
he said to them,
"Men of Israel,
take care what

[a] One early ms adds *in Him*

NIV

to these men.
36 Some time ago
Theudas appeared,
claiming to be
somebody, and
about four hundred
men rallied to him.
He was killed, all
his followers were
dispersed, and it
all came to noth-
ing. 37 After him,
Judas the Galilean
appeared in the
days of the census
and led a band of
people in revolt.
He too was killed,
and all his follow-
ers were scattered.
38 Therefore, in
the present case I
advise you: Leave
these men alone!
Let them go! For
if their purpose
or activity is of
human origin, it
will fail. 39 But if it
is from God, you
will not be able to
stop these men;
you will only find
yourselves fight-
ing against God."
40 His speech per-
suaded them. They
called the apostles
in and had them
flogged. Then they
ordered them not
to speak in the
name of Jesus, and
let them go.
41 The apostles
left the Sanhedrin,
rejoicing because
they had been
counted worthy of
suffering disgrace
for the Name.
42 Day after day, in
the temple courts

ἐπὶ τοῖς ἀνθρώποις τούτοις τί μέλλετε πράσσειν. 36 πρὸ γὰρ τούτων
about {the} these men, these what you intend to do. For before For these
2093 3836 4047 476 4047 5515 3516 4556 1142 4574 1142 4047
p.d d.dpm n.dpm r.dpm r.asn v.pai.2p f.pa p.g cj r.gpf

τῶν ἡμερῶν ἀνέστη Θευδᾶς λέγων → εἶναί τινα ἑαυτόν,
{the} days ⌊there rose up⌋ Theudas, saying that he himself was someone, himself and a
3836 2465 482 2554 3306 1571 1639 5516 1571
d.gpf n.gpf v.aai.3s n.nsm pt.pa.nsm f.pa r.asm r.asm.3

ᾧ προσεκλίθη ἀνδρῶν ἀριθμὸς ὡς
number of men, about four hundred, joined him. joined of men number about
750 467 467 6055 5484 5484 4679 4005 4679 467 750 6055
r.dsm v.api.3s n.gpm n.nsm pl

τετρακοσίων· ὃς ἀνῃρέθη, καὶ πάντες ὅσοι ἐπείθοντο αὐτῷ διελύθησαν καὶ
four hundred He was killed, and all, ⌊as many as⌋ followed him, were dispersed, and
5484 4005 359 2779 4246 4012 4275 899 1370 2779
a.gpm r.nsm v.api.3s cj a.npm r.npm v.ipi.3p r.dsm.3 v.api.3p cj

ἐγένοντο εἰς οὐδέν. 37 μετὰ τοῦτον ἀνέστη Ἰούδας ὁ Γαλιλαῖος ἐν
the movement came to nothing. After him rose up Judas the Galilean, in
1181 1650 4029 3552 4047 482 2683 3836 1134 1877
v.ami.3p p.a a.asn p.a r.asm v.aai.3s n.nsm d.nsm a.nsm p.d

ταῖς ἡμέραις τῆς ἀπογραφῆς καὶ ἀπέστησεν λαὸν ὀπίσω αὐτοῦ·
the days of the census and mislead people, so that they followed him.
3836 2465 3836 615 2779 923 3295 3958 899
d.dpf n.dpf d.gsf n.gsf cj v.aai.3s n.asm p.g r.gsm.3

κἀκεῖνος ἀπώλετο καὶ πάντες ὅσοι ἐπείθοντο αὐτῷ διεσκορπίσθησαν. 38 καὶ
He too perished, and all, ⌊as many as⌋ followed him, were scattered. So
2797 660 2779 4246 4012 4275 899 1399 2779
crasis v.ami.3s cj a.npm r.npm v.ipi.3p r.dsm.3 v.api.3p cj

τὰ νῦν λέγω ὑμῖν, ἀπόστητε ἀπὸ τῶν ἀνθρώπων τούτων καὶ ἄφετε
⌊in the⌋ present case I tell you, keep away from {the} these men these and leave
3836 3814 3306 7007 923 608 3836 4047 476 4047 2779 918
d.apn adv v.pai.1s r.dp.2 v.aam.2p p.g d.gpm n.gpm r.gpm cj v.aam.2p

αὐτούς, ↰ ὅτι ἐὰν ᾖ ἐξ ἀνθρώπων ἡ βουλὴ
them alone, for if this plan or this undertaking be of men, {the} plan
899 918 4022 1569 4047 1087 2445 4047 2240 1639 1666 476 3836 1087
r.apm.3 cj cj v.pas.3s p.g n.gpm d.nsf n.nsf

αὕτη ἢ τὸ ἔργον τοῦτο, καταλυθήσεται, 39 εἰ δὲ ἐκ θεοῦ
this or {the} undertaking this it will fail; but if but it is of God,
4047 2445 3836 2240 4047 2907 1254 1623 1254 1639 1639 1666 2536
r.nsf cj d.nsn n.nsn r.nsn v.fpi.3s cj cj p.g n.gsm

ἐστιν, ↱ ↱ οὐ δυνήσεσθε καταλῦσαι αὐτούς, μήποτε καὶ
it is you will not be able to stop them; lest you be found also
1639 1538 1538 4024 1538 2907 899 3607 2351 2351 2351 2779
v.pai.3s pl v.fmi.2p f.aa r.apm.3 cj adv

θεομάχοι εὑρεθῆτε. ἐπείσθησαν δὲ αὐτῷ 40 καὶ προσκαλεσάμενοι τοὺς
opposing God!" you be found They were persuaded {and} by him, so summoning the
2534 2351 4275 1254 899 2779 4673 3836
a.npm v.aps.2p v.api.3p cj r.dsm.3 cj pt.am.npm d.apm

ἀποστόλους ↱ δείραντες παρήγγειλαν μὴ λαλεῖν ἐπὶ τῷ ὀνόματι
apostles, they beat them and ordered them not to speak in the name
693 4133 1296 4133 3590 3281 2093 3836 3950
n.apm pt.aa.npm v.aai.3p pl f.pa p.d d.dsn n.dsn

τοῦ Ἰησοῦ καὶ ἀπέλυσαν. 41 οἱ μὲν οὖν ἐπορεύοντο χαίροντες ἀπὸ
of Jesus, and they released them. So then they So then went rejoicing from
3836 2652 2779 668 3525 4036 3836 3525 4036 4513 5897 608
d.gsm n.gsm cj v.aai.3p d.npm pl cj v.imi.3p pt.pa.npm p.g

προσώπου τοῦ συνεδρίου, ὅτι κατηξιώθησαν
the presence of the council, because ⌊they had been considered worthy⌋ to suffer indignity
4725 3836 5284 4022 2921 869 869 869
n.gsn d.gsn n.gsn cj v.api.3p

ὑπὲρ τοῦ ὀνόματος ἀτιμασθῆναι, 42 πᾶσάν τε ἡμέραν ἐν τῷ ἱερῷ
⌊on behalf of⌋ the name. to suffer indignity And every And day, both in the temple
5642 3836 3950 869 5445 4246 5445 2465 1877 3836 2639
p.g d.gsn n.gsn f.ap a.asf cj n.asf p.d d.dsn n.dsn

NASB

you propose to do
with these men.
36 For some time
ago Theudas rose
up, claiming to
be somebody, and
a group of about
four hundred men
joined up with
him. But he was
killed, and all who
followed him were
dispersed and came
to nothing. 37 After
this man, Judas
of Galilee rose up
in the days of the
census and drew
away *some* people
after him; he too
perished, and all
those who followed
him were scattered.
38 So in the present
case, I say to you,
stay away from
these men and let
them alone, for if
this plan or action
is of men, it will be
overthrown; 39 but
if it is of God, you
will not be able to
overthrow them; or
else you may even
be found fighting
against God."
40 They took his
advice; and after
calling the apostles
in, they flogged
them and ordered
them not to speak
in the name of
Jesus, and *then*
released them.
41 So they went on
their way from the
presence of the
Council, rejoicing
that they had been
considered worthy
to suffer shame for
His name. 42 And
every day, in the
temple and from

NIV

and from house to house, they never stopped teaching and proclaiming the good news that Jesus is the Messiah.

The Choosing of the Seven

6 In those days when the number of disciples was increasing, the Hellenistic Jews[a] among them complained against the Hebraic Jews because their widows were being overlooked in the daily distribution of food. 2 So the Twelve gathered all the disciples together and said, "It would not be right for us to neglect the ministry of the word of God in order to wait on tables. 3 Brothers and sisters, choose seven men from among you who are known to be full of the Spirit and wisdom. We will turn this responsibility over to them 4 and will give our attention to prayer and the ministry of the word."

5 This proposal pleased the whole group. They chose Stephen, a man full of faith and of the Holy Spirit; also Philip, Procorus, Nicanor, Timon, Parmenas, and Nicolas from Antioch, a convert to Judaism. 6 They presented these men to the apostles, who prayed and laid their hands

[a] 1 That is, Jews who had adopted the Greek language and culture

---

καὶ κατ᾽ οἶκον ↱ ↱ οὐκ ἐπαύοντο διδάσκοντες καὶ εὐαγγελιζόμενοι τὸν
and at home, they did not stop teaching and preaching Jesus the
2779 2848 3875 4264 4264 4024 4264 1438 2779 2294 2652 3836
cj p.a n.asm pl v.imi.3p pt.pa.npm cj pt.pm.npm d.asm

χριστὸν Ἰησοῦν.
Christ. *Jesus*
5986 2652
n.asm n.asm

6:1 ἐν δὲ ταῖς ἡμέραις ταύταις →
Now in *Now* *{the}* these days *these* when the number of the disciples
1254 1877 1254 3836 4047 2465 4047 3836 3836 3412
p.d cj d.dpf n.dpf r.dpf

πληθυνόντων τῶν μαθητῶν ἐγένετο γογγυσμὸς τῶν Ἑλληνιστῶν πρὸς τοὺς
was increasing, *of the* *disciples* there was a complaint by the Hellenists against the
4437 3836 3412 1181 1198 3836 1821 4639 3836
pt.pa.gpm d.gpm n.gpm v.ami.3s n.nsm d.gpm n.gpm p.a d.apm

Ἑβραίους, ὅτι παρεθεωροῦντο ἐν τῇ διακονίᾳ τῇ
Hebrews because their widows were being neglected in the daily distribution of food. *{the}*
1578 4022 899 5939 4145 1877 3836 2766 1355 3836
n.apm cj v.ipi.3p p.d d.dsf n.dsf d.dsf

καθημερινῇ αἱ χῆραι αὐτῶν. 2 προσκαλεσάμενοι δὲ οἱ δώδεκα
daily *{the}* *widows* *their* So the twelve called together *So* *the* *twelve*
2766 3836 5939 899 1254 3836 1557 4673 1254 3836 1557
a.dsf d.npf n.npf r.gpm.3 pt.am.npm cj d.npm a.npm

τὸ πλῆθος τῶν μαθητῶν εἶπαν, οὐκ ἀρεστόν ἐστιν ἡμᾶς
the entire group of disciples and said, "It is not right *It is* for us
3836 4436 3836 3412 3306 1639 1639 4024 744 1639 7005
d.asn n.asn d.gpm n.gpm v.aai.3p pl a.nsn v.pai.3s r.ap.1

καταλείψαντας τὸν λόγον τοῦ θεοῦ διακονεῖν τραπέζαις. 3
to neglect the word of God ⌊in order to wait on⌋ tables. Therefore, brothers,
2901 3836 3364 3836 2536 1354 5544 1254 81
pt.aa.apm d.asm n.asm d.gsm n.gsm f.pa n.dpf

ἐπισκέψασθε δέ, ἀδελφοί, ἄνδρας ἐξ ὑμῶν
select *Therefore* *brothers* from among you seven men *from among* *you*
2170 1254 81 1666 1666 7007 2231 467 1666 7007
v.amm.2p cj n.vpm n.apm p.g r.gp.2

μαρτυρουμένους ἑπτά, πλήρεις → πνεύματος καὶ σοφίας, οὓς καταστήσομεν
of good standing, *seven* full of the Spirit and of wisdom, whom we will appoint
3455 2231 4441 4460 2779 5053 4005 2770
pt.pp.apm a.apm a.apm n.gsn cj n.gsf r.apm v.fai.1p

ἐπὶ τῆς χρείας ταύτης, 4 ἡμεῖς δὲ τῇ
to carry out *{the}* this responsibility. *this* But we *But* will devote ourselves to
2093 3836 4047 5970 4047 1254 7005 1254 4674 4674 4674 3836
p.g d.gsf n.gsf r.gsf r.np.1 cj d.dsf

προσευχῇ καὶ τῇ διακονίᾳ τοῦ λόγου προσκαρτερήσομεν. 5 καὶ
prayer and ⌊to the⌋ ministry of the word." *will devote ourselves* And the proposal
4666 2779 3836 1355 3836 3364 4674 2779 3836 3364
n.dsf cj d.dsf n.dsf d.gsm n.gsm v.fai.1p cj

ἤρεσεν ὁ λόγος ἐνώπιον παντὸς τοῦ πλήθους καὶ ἐξελέξαντο Στέφανον,
pleased *the* *proposal* *{before}* the entire *the* group, so they chose Stephen, a
743 3836 3364 1967 3836 4246 3836 4436 2779 1721 5108
v.aai.3s d.nsm n.nsm p.g a.gsn d.gsn n.gsn cj v.ami.3p n.asm

ἄνδρα πλήρης πίστεως καὶ → πνεύματος ἁγίου, καὶ Φίλιππον καὶ Πρόχορον
man full of faith and of the Holy Spirit; *Holy* also Philip and Prochorus
467 4441 4411 2779 41 4460 41 2779 5805 2779 4743
n.asm a.asm n.gsf cj n.gsn a.gsn cj n.asm cj n.asm

καὶ Νικάνορα καὶ Τίμωνα καὶ Παρμενᾶν καὶ Νικόλαον προσήλυτον Ἀντιοχέα,
and Nicanor and Timon and Parmenas and Nicolaus, a proselyte of Antioch.
2779 3770 2779 5511 2779 4226 2779 3775 4670 523
cj n.asm cj n.asm cj n.asm cj n.asm n.asm n.asm

6 οὓς ἔστησαν ἐνώπιον τῶν ἀποστόλων, καὶ προσευξάμενοι ἐπέθηκαν
These they set before the apostles, *{and}* who prayed and laid their hands
4005 2705 1967 3836 693 2779 4667 2202 3836 5931
r.apm v.aai.3p p.g d.gpm n.gpm cj pt.am.npm v.aai.3p

NASB

house to house, they kept right on teaching and preaching Jesus *as* the Christ.

Choosing of the Seven

6:1 Now at this time while the disciples were increasing *in number,* a complaint arose on the part of the [a]Hellenistic *Jews* against the *native* Hebrews, because their widows were being overlooked in the daily serving *of food.* 2 So the twelve summoned the congregation of the disciples and said, "It is not desirable for us to neglect the word of God in order to serve tables. 3 Therefore, brethren, select from among you seven men of good reputation, full of the Spirit and of wisdom, whom we may put in charge of this task. 4 But we will devote ourselves to prayer and to the ministry of the word."

5 The statement found approval with the whole congregation; and they chose Stephen, a man full of faith and of the Holy Spirit, and Philip, Prochorus, Nicanor, Timon, Parmenas and Nicolas, a [b]proselyte from Antioch. 6 And these they brought before the apostles; and after praying, they laid their hands on them.

[a] Jews who adopted the Gr language and much of Gr culture through acculturation
[b] I.e. a Gentile convert to Judaism

NIV

on them.
[7]So the word of God spread. The number of disciples in Jerusalem increased rapidly, and a large number of priests became obedient to the faith.

Stephen Seized

[8]Now Stephen, a man full of God's grace and power, performed great wonders and signs among the people. [9]Opposition arose, however, from members of the Synagogue of the Freedmen (as it was called)—Jews of Cyrene and Alexandria as well as the provinces of Cilicia and Asia—who began to argue with Stephen. [10]But they could not stand up against the wisdom the Spirit gave him as he spoke.
[11]Then they secretly persuaded some men to say, "We have heard Stephen speak blasphemous words against Moses and against God."
[12]So they stirred up the people and the elders and the teachers of the law. They seized Stephen and brought him before the Sanhedrin. [13]They produced false witnesses, who testified, "This fellow never stops speaking against this holy place and against the law. [14]For we have heard him say that this Jesus of Nazareth will destroy this place and change the customs Moses handed down to us."

← αὐτοῖς τὰς χεῖρας. [7] καὶ ὁ λόγος τοῦ θεοῦ ηὔξανεν καὶ
on them. *their hands* And the word of God ⌊continued to spread,⌋ and the number
899 3836 5931 2779 3836 3364 3836 2536 889 2779 3836 750
r.dpm.3 d.apf n.apf cj d.nsm n.nsm d.gsm n.gsm v.iai.3s cj

ἐπληθύνετο ὁ ἀριθμὸς τῶν μαθητῶν ἐν Ἰερουσαλὴμ σφόδρα,
of disciples increased *the number of disciples* greatly in Jerusalem, *greatly*
3836 3412 4437 3836 750 3836 3412 5379 1877 2647 5379
v.ipi.3s d.nsm n.nsm d.gpm n.gpm p.d n.dsf adv

πολύς τε ὄχλος τῶν ἱερέων ὑπήκουον τῇ πίστει. [8] Στέφανος δὲ
and a large *and* group of priests became obedient ⌊to the⌋ faith. And Stephen, *And*
5445 4498 5445 4063 3836 2636 5634 3836 4411 1254 5108 1254
a.nsm cj n.nsm d.gpm n.gpm v.iai.3p d.dsf n.dsf n.nsm cj

πλήρης χάριτος καὶ δυνάμεως ἐποίει τέρατα καὶ σημεῖα μεγάλα ἐν τῷ
full of grace and power, was doing great wonders and signs *great* among the
4441 5921 2779 1539 4472 3489 5469 2779 4956 3489 1877 3836
a.nsm n.gsf cj n.gsf v.iai.3s n.apn cj n.apn a.apn p.d d.dsm

λαῷ. [9] ἀνέστησαν δέ τινες τῶν ἐκ τῆς συναγωγῆς τῆς
people. But there rose up *But* some of those of the synagogue of the Freedmen
3295 1254 482 1254 5516 3836 1666 3836 5252 3836 3339
n.dsm v.aai.3p cj r.npm d.gpm p.g d.gsf n.gsf d.gsf

λεγομένης Λιβερτίνων καὶ Κυρηναίων καὶ Ἀλεξανδρέων καὶ τῶν ἀπὸ
(as it was called), *Freedmen* both Cyrenians and Alexandrians, ⌊as well as⌋ those from
3306 3339 2779 3254 2779 233 2779 3836 608
pt.pp.gsf n.gpm cj n.gpm cj n.gpm cj d.gpm p.g

Κιλικίας καὶ Ἀσίας συζητοῦντες τῷ Στεφάνῳ, [10] καὶ οὐκ ἴσχυον
Cilicia and Asia, disputing with *{the}* Stephen. Yet they could not *they could*
3070 2779 823 5184 3836 5108 2779 2710 2710 4024 2710
n.gsf cj n.gsf pt.pa.npm d.dsm n.dsm cj pl v.iai.3p

ἀντιστῆναι τῇ σοφίᾳ καὶ τῷ πνεύματι ᾧ ἐλάλει. [11] τότε
withstand the wisdom and the Spirit ⌊with which⌋ he was speaking. Then
468 3836 5053 2779 3836 4460 4005 3281 5538
f.aa d.dsf n.dsf cj d.dsn n.dsn r.dsn v.iai.3s adv

ὑπέβαλον ἄνδρας λέγοντας ὅτι ἀκηκόαμεν αὐτοῦ λαλοῦντος
⌊they secretly talked⌋ some men into saying, ~ "We have heard him speak
5680 467 3306 4022 201 899 3281
v.aai.3p n.apm pt.pa.apm cj v.rai.1p r.gsm.3 pt.pa.gsm

ῥήματα βλάσφημα εἰς Μωϋσῆν καὶ τὸν θεόν. [12] συνεκίνησάν τε
blasphemous words *blasphemous* against Moses and *{the}* God." And they incited *And*
1061 4839 1061 1650 3707 2779 3836 2536 5445 5167 5445
n.apn a.apn p.a n.asm cj d.asm n.asm v.aai.3p cj

τὸν λαὸν καὶ τοὺς πρεσβυτέρους καὶ τοὺς γραμματεῖς καὶ ↱ ἐπιστάντες
the people and the elders and the scribes, and they ⌊suddenly moved in⌋ and
3836 3295 2779 3836 4565 2779 3836 1208 2779 5275 2392
d.asm n.asm cj d.apm a.apm cj d.apm n.apm cj pt.aa.npm

συνήρπασαν αὐτὸν καὶ ἤγαγον εἰς τὸ συνέδριον, [13] ἔστησάν τε
seized him and brought him before the council, and they set up *and* false
5275 899 2779 72 1650 3836 5284 5445 2705 5445 6014
v.aai.3p r.asm.3 cj v.aai.3p p.a d.asn n.asn v.aai.3p cj

μάρτυρας ψευδεῖς λέγοντας, ὁ ἄνθρωπος οὗτος ↱ οὐ παύεται λαλῶν
witnesses *false* who said, *{the}* "This man *This* does not stop saying
3459 6014 3306 3836 4047 476 4047 4264 4024 4264 3281
n.apm a.apm pt.pa.apm d.nsm n.nsm r.nsm pl v.pmi.3s pt.pa.nsm

ῥήματα κατὰ τοῦ τόπου τοῦ ἁγίου τούτου[a] καὶ τοῦ νόμου, [14]
words against *{the}* this holy place *{the} holy this* and the law, for
4839 2848 3836 4047 41 5536 3836 41 4047 2779 3836 3795 1142
n.apn p.g d.gsm n.gsm d.gsm a.gsm r.gsm cj d.gsm n.gsm

ἀκηκόαμεν γὰρ αὐτοῦ λέγοντος ὅτι Ἰησοῦς ὁ Ναζωραῖος οὗτος καταλύσει
we have heard *for* him say that this Jesus the Nazarene *this* will destroy
201 1142 899 3306 4022 4047 2652 3836 3717 4047 2907
v.rai.1p cj r.gsm.3 pt.pa.gsm cj n.nsm d.nsm n.nsm r.nsm v.fai.3s

τὸν τόπον τοῦτον καὶ ἀλλάξει τὰ ἔθη ἃ παρέδωκεν ἡμῖν
{the} this place *this* and will change the customs that Moses handed down to us."
3836 4047 5536 4047 2779 248 3836 1621 4005 3707 4140 7005
d.asm n.asm r.asm cj v.fai.3s d.apn n.apn r.apn v.aai.3s r.dp.1

[a] [τούτου] UBS.

NASB

[7]The word of God kept on spreading; and the number of the disciples continued to increase greatly in Jerusalem, and a great many of the priests were becoming obedient to the faith.
[8]And Stephen, full of grace and power, was performing great wonders and signs among the people. [9]But some men from what was called the Synagogue of the Freedmen, *including* both Cyrenians and Alexandrians, and some from Cilicia and Asia, rose up and argued with Stephen. [10]But they were unable to cope with the wisdom and the Spirit with which he was speaking. [11]Then they secretly induced men to say, "We have heard him speak blasphemous words against Moses and *against* God."
[12]And they stirred up the people, the elders and the scribes, and they came up to him and dragged him away and brought him before the Council.
[13]They put forward false witnesses who said, "This man incessantly speaks against this holy place and the Law; [14]for we have heard him say that this Nazarene, Jesus, will destroy this place and alter the customs which Moses handed down to us."

NIV

15 All who were sit-
ting in the Sanhe-
drin looked intent-
ly at Stephen, and
they saw that his
face was like the
face of an angel.

Stephen's Speech to the Sanhedrin

7 Then the high
priest asked
Stephen, "Are
these charges
true?"
2 To this he re-
plied: "Brothers
and fathers, listen
to me! The God of
glory appeared to
our father Abra-
ham while he was
still in Mesopo-
tamia, before he
lived in Harran.
3 'Leave your
country and your
people,' God said,
'and go to the land
I will show you.'[a]
4 "So he left the
land of the Chal-
deans and settled
in Harran. After
the death of his fa-
ther, God sent him
to this land where
you are now living.
5 He gave him no
inheritance here,
not even enough
ground to set his
foot on. But God
promised him that
he and his descen-
dants after him
would possess the
land, even though
at that time Abra-
ham had no child.
6 God spoke to him
in this way: 'For
four hundred years
your descendants
will be strangers
in a country not
their own, and
they will

[a] 3 Gen. 12:1

Μωϋσῆς. 15 καὶ ἀτενίσαντες εἰς αὐτὸν
Moses And everyone who was sitting in the council, looking intently at him,
3707 2779 4246 3836 2757 2757 1877 3836 5284 867 1650 899
n.nsm cj pt.aa.npm p.a r.asm.3

πάντες οἱ καθεζόμενοι ἐν τῷ συνεδρίῳ εἶδον τὸ πρόσωπον αὐτοῦ ὡσεὶ
everyone who was sitting in the council saw *{the}* his face *his* like the
4246 3836 2757 1877 3836 5284 1625 3836 899 4725 899 6059
a.npm d.npm pt.pm.npm p.d d.dsn n.dsn v.aai.3p d.asn n.asn r.gsm.3 pl

πρόσωπον → ἀγγέλου.
face of an angel.
4725 34
n.asn n.gsm

7:1 εἶπεν δὲ ὁ ἀρχιερεύς, εἰ ταῦτα οὕτως ἔχει;
And the high priest said, *And the high priest {if}* "Are these things true?" *Are*
1254 3836 797 797 3306 1254 3836 797 1623 2400 4047 4048 2400
v.aai.3s cj d.nsm n.nsm cj r.npn adv v.pai.3s

2 ὁ δὲ ἔφη, ⌞ἄνδρες ἀδελφοί⌟ καὶ πατέρες, ἀκούσατε. ὁ θεὸς τῆς
And Stephen *And* said: "My brothers and fathers, hear me. The God of
1254 3836 1254 5774 467 81 2779 4252 201 3836 2536 3836
d.nsm cj v.iai.3s n.vpm n.vpm cj n.vpm v.aam.2p d.nsm n.nsm d.gsf

δόξης ὤφθη τῷ πατρὶ ἡμῶν Ἀβραὰμ ὄντι ἐν τῇ Μεσοποταμίᾳ
glory appeared to our father *our* Abraham ⌞when he was⌟ in *{the}* Mesopotamia,
1518 3972 3836 7005 4252 7005 11 1639 1877 3836 3544
n.gsf v.api.3s d.dsm n.dsm r.gp.1 n.dsm pt.pa.dsm p.d d.dsf n.dsf

⌞πρὶν ἢ⌟ κατοικῆσαι αὐτὸν ἐν Χαρρὰν 3 καὶ εἶπεν πρὸς αὐτόν, ἔξελθε ἐκ
before he lived *he* in Haran, and said to him, 'Go out from
4570 2445 899 2997 899 1877 5924 2779 3306 4639 899 2002 1666
cj pl f.aa r.asm.3 p.d n.dsf cj v.aai.3s p.a r.asm.3 v.aam.2s p.g

τῆς γῆς σου καὶ ἐκ[a] τῆς συγγενείας σου, καὶ δεῦρο εἰς τὴν γῆν ἣν ἂν
{the} your land *your* and from *{the}* your relatives *your* and come to the land that ~
3836 5148 1178 5148 2779 1666 3836 5148 5149 5148 2779 1306 1650 3836 1178 4005 323
d.gsf n.gsf r.gs.2 cj p.g d.gsf n.gsf r.gs.2 cj j p.a d.asf n.asf r.asf pl

σοι δείξω. 4 τότε ἐξελθὼν ἐκ γῆς → Χαλδαίων
I will show you.' *I will show* Then he went out from the land of the Chaldeans and
1259 1259 1259 5148 1259 5538 2002 1666 1178 5900
r.ds.2 v.aas.1s adv pt.aa.nsm p.g n.gsf n.gpm

κατῴκησεν ἐν Χαρράν. κἀκεῖθεν μετὰ τὸ ἀποθανεῖν τὸν πατέρα αὐτοῦ
lived in Haran. And after *{the}* his father died, *{the} father his*
2997 1877 5924 2796 3552 3836 899 4252 633 3836 4252 899
v.aai.3s p.d n.dsf crasis p.a d.asn f.aa d.asm n.asm r.gsm.3

→ μετῴκισεν αὐτὸν εἰς τὴν γῆν ταύτην εἰς ἣν ὑμεῖς ↱ νῦν
God had him move *him* to *{the}* this land *this* in which you are now
899 3579 899 1650 3836 4047 1178 4047 1650 4005 7007 2997 3814
v.aai.3s r.asm.3 p.a d.asf n.asf r.asf p.a r.asf r.np.2 adv

κατοικεῖτε, 5 καὶ οὐκ ἔδωκεν αὐτῷ κληρονομίαν ἐν αὐτῇ οὐδὲ
living. Yet he gave him no *he gave him* inheritance in it, not even a foot
2997 2779 1443 1443 899 4024 1443 899 3100 1877 899 4028 4546
v.pai.2p cj pl v.aai.3s r.dsm.3 n.asf p.d r.dsf.3 cj

βῆμα ποδὸς καὶ ἐπηγγείλατο δοῦναι αὐτῷ εἰς κατάσχεσιν αὐτὴν καὶ τῷ
of ground, *foot* but promised to give it to him as a possession, *it* and to
1037 4546 2779 2040 1443 899 899 1650 2959 899 2779 3836
n.asn n.gsm cj v.ami.3s f.aa r.dsm.3 p.a n.asf r.asf.3 cj d.dsn

σπέρματι αὐτοῦ μετ᾽ αὐτόν, οὐκ ὄντος
his descendants *his* after him, though as yet Abraham had no *though as yet had*
899 5065 899 3552 899 1639 1639 1639 899 1639 4024 1639
n.dsn r.gsm.3 p.a r.asm.3 pl pt.pa.gsn

αὐτῷ τέκνου. 6 ἐλάλησεν δὲ οὕτως ὁ θεὸς ὅτι
Abraham child. And God spoke *And* thus, *{the} God* that Abraham's descendants
899 5451 1254 2536 3281 1254 4048 3836 2536 4022 899 5065
r.dsm.3 n.gsn v.aai.3s cj adv d.nsm n.nsm cj

ἔσται τὸ σπέρμα αὐτοῦ πάροικον ἐν γῇ ἀλλοτρίᾳ καὶ
⌞would be⌟ *{the} descendants Abraham's* sojourners in a foreign land, *foreign* and that the
1639 3836 5065 899 4230 1877 259 1178 259 2779
v.fmi.3s d.nsn n.nsn r.gsm.3 a.nsn p.d n.dsf a.dsf cj

[a] [ἐκ] UBS, omitted by TNIV.

NASB

15 And fixing their
gaze on him, all
who were sitting in
the Council saw his
face like the face of
an angel.

Stephen's Defense

7:1 The high priest
said, "Are these
things so?"
2 And he said,
"Hear me, breth-
ren and fathers!
The God of glory
appeared to our
father Abraham
when he was in
Mesopotamia,
before he lived in
Haran, 3 and said
to him, 'LEAVE
YOUR COUNTRY AND
YOUR RELATIVES,
AND COME INTO THE
LAND THAT I WILL
SHOW YOU.' 4 Then
he left the land of
the Chaldeans and
settled in Haran.
From there, after
his father died,
God had him move
to this country in
which you are now
living. 5 But He
gave him no inheri-
tance in it, not even
a foot of ground,
and *yet,* even when
he had no child, He
promised that HE
WOULD GIVE IT TO
HIM AS A POSSESSION,
AND TO HIS DESCEN-
DANTS AFTER HIM.
6 But God spoke
to this effect, that
his DESCENDANTS
WOULD BE ALIENS
IN A FOREIGN LAND,
AND THAT THEY

NIV

be enslaved and
mistreated. [7]But I
will punish the na-
tion they serve as
slaves,' God said,
'and afterward
they will come
out of that country
and worship me in
this place.'[a] [8]Then
he gave Abraham
the covenant of
circumcision. And
Abraham became
the father of Isaac
and circumcised
him eight days af-
ter his birth. Later
Isaac became the
father of Jacob,
and Jacob became
the father of the
twelve patriarchs.
[9]"Because the
patriarchs were
jealous of Joseph,
they sold him as a
slave into Egypt.
But God was with
him [10]and rescued
him from all his
troubles. He gave
Joseph wisdom
and enabled him to
gain the goodwill
of Pharaoh king of
Egypt. So Pharaoh
made him ruler
over Egypt and all
his palace.
[11]"Then a famine
struck all Egypt
and Canaan,
bringing great suf-
fering, and our an-
cestors could not
find food. [12]When
Jacob heard that
there was grain
in Egypt, he sent
our forefathers on
their first visit.
[13]On their second
visit, Joseph told
his brothers who
he was, and Phar-
aoh learned about
Joseph's family.
[14]After this, Joseph

δουλώσουσιν αὐτὸ καὶ κακώσουσιν ἔτη τετρακόσια· [7]καὶ
people would enslave *{them}* and mistreat them four hundred years. *four hundred* But,
1530 899 2779 2808 5484 5484 2291 5484 2779
v.fai.3p r.asn.3 cj v.fai.3p n.apn a.apn cj

τὸ ἔθνος ⌊ᾧ ἐὰν⌋ δουλεύσουσιν κρινῶ ἐγώ, ὁ θεὸς
'Whatever *{the}* nation *Whatever* they serve as slaves, I will punish,' *I* said *{the}* God,
4005 3836 1620 4005 1569 1526 1609 3212 1609 3306 3836 2536
d.asn n.asn r.dsn pl v.fai.3p v.fai.1s r.ns.1 d.nsm n.nsm

εἶπεν, καὶ μετὰ ταῦτα ἐξελεύσονται καὶ λατρεύσουσίν μοι ἐν τῷ τόπῳ
said 'and after this ⌊they will come out⌋ and they will worship me in *{the}* this place.'
3306 2779 3552 4047 2002 2779 3302 1609 1877 3836 4047 5536
v.aai.3s cj p.a r.apn v.fmi.3p cj v.fai.3p r.ds.1 p.d d.dsm n.dsm

τούτῳ. [8]καὶ ἔδωκεν αὐτῷ διαθήκην περιτομῆς· καὶ οὕτως
this And he gave him a covenant of circumcision; and so Abraham
4047 2779 1443 899 1347 4364 2779 4048
r.dsm cj v.aai.3s r.dsm.3 n.asf n.gsf cj adv

ἐγέννησεν τὸν Ἰσαὰκ καὶ περιέτεμεν αὐτὸν τῇ ἡμέρᾳ τῇ ὀγδόῃ,
⌊became the father of⌋ *{the}* Isaac and circumcised him ⌊on the⌋ eighth day; *{the}* *eighth*
1164 3836 2693 2779 4362 899 3836 3838 2465 3836 3838
v.aai.3s d.asm n.asm cj v.aai.3s r.asm.3 d.dsf n.dsf d.dsf a.dsf

καὶ Ἰσαὰκ τὸν Ἰακώβ, καὶ Ἰακὼβ τοὺς δώδεκα πατριάρχας.
and Isaac became the father of *{the}* Jacob, and Jacob of the twelve patriarchs.
2779 2693 3836 2609 2779 2609 3836 1557 4256
cj n.nsm d.asm n.asm cj n.nsm d.apm a.apm n.apm

[9]καὶ οἱ πατριάρχαι ζηλώσαντες τὸν Ἰωσὴφ ἀπέδοντο εἰς Αἴγυπτον. καὶ
"And the patriarchs, jealous of Joseph, sold him into Egypt; but God
2779 3836 4256 2420 3836 2737 625 1650 131 2779 2536
cj d.npm n.npm pt.aa.npm d.asm n.asm v.ami.3p p.a n.asf cj

ἦν ὁ θεὸς μετ' αὐτοῦ [10]καὶ ἐξείλατο αὐτὸν ἐκ πασῶν τῶν θλίψεων
was *{the}* *God* with him, and rescued him ⌊out of⌋ all *{the}* his afflictions
1639 3836 2536 3552 899 2779 1975 899 1666 4246 3836 899 2568
v.iai.3s d.nsm n.nsm p.g r.gsm.3 cj v.ami.3s r.asm.3 p.g a.gpf d.gpf n.gpf

αὐτοῦ καὶ ἔδωκεν αὐτῷ χάριν καὶ σοφίαν ἐναντίον Φαραὼ βασιλέως Αἰγύπτου καὶ
his and gave him favor and wisdom before Pharaoh, king of Egypt, who
899 2779 1443 899 5921 2779 5053 1883 5755 995 131 2779
r.gsm.3 cj v.aai.3s r.dsm.3 n.asf cj n.asf p.g n.gsm n.gsm n.gsf cj

κατέστησεν αὐτὸν ἡγούμενον ἐπ' Αἴγυπτον καὶ ἐφ'[a] ὅλον τὸν οἶκον
appointed him ruler over Egypt and over all *{the}* his royal household.
2770 899 2451 2093 131 2779 2093 3910 3836 899 3875
v.aai.3s r.asm.3 pt.pm.asm p.a n.asf cj p.a a.asm d.asm n.asm

αὐτοῦ. [11]ἦλθεν δὲ λιμὸς ἐφ' ὅλην τὴν Αἴγυπτον καὶ Χανάαν καὶ
his Now there came *Now* a famine upon all *{the}* Egypt and Canaan, *{and}*
899 1254 2262 1254 3350 2093 3910 3836 131 2779 5913 2779
r.gsm.3 v.aai.3s cj n.nsm p.a a.asf d.asf n.asf cj n.asf cj

θλῖψις μεγάλη, καὶ οὐχ ηὕρισκον χορτάσματα οἱ
bringing great affliction, *great* and our fathers could find no *could find* food. *{the}*
3489 2568 3489 2779 7005 4252 2351 2351 4024 2351 5964 3836
n.nsf a.nsf cj pl v.iai.3p n.apn d.npm

πατέρες ἡμῶν. [12]ἀκούσας δὲ Ἰακὼβ ὄντα σιτία εἰς Αἴγυπτον
fathers *our* But Jacob, hearing *But* *Jacob* that ⌊there was⌋ grain in Egypt,
4252 7005 1254 2609 201 1254 2609 1639 4989 1650 131
n.npm r.gp.1 pt.aa.nsm cj n.nsm pt.pa.apn n.apn p.a n.asf

ἐξαπέστειλεν τοὺς πατέρας ἡμῶν ↰ πρῶτον. [13]καὶ ἐν τῷ
sent *{the}* our fathers *our* out on their first visit. *{and}* On their
1990 3836 7005 4252 7005 1990 4754 2779 1877 3836
v.aai.3s d.apm n.apm r.gp.1 adv cj p.d d.dsn

δευτέρῳ ἀνεγνωρίσθη Ἰωσὴφ τοῖς ἀδελφοῖς αὐτοῦ καὶ
second visit Joseph made himself known *Joseph* to his brothers, *his* and the lineage
1311 2737 341 2737 3836 899 81 899 2779 3836 1169
a.dsn v.api.3s n.nsm d.dpm n.dpm r.gsm.3 cj

φανερὸν ἐγένετο τῷ Φαραὼ τὸ γένος τοῦ[b] Ἰωσήφ. [14]
of Joseph became clear *became* to Pharaoh. *the* *lineage* *of* *Joseph* Then Joseph
3836 2737 1181 5745 1181 3836 5755 3836 1169 3836 2737 1254 2737
a.nsn v.ami.3s d.dsm n.dsm d.nsn n.nsn d.gsm n.gsm

NASB

WOULD BE ENSLAVED
AND MISTREATED
FOR FOUR HUNDRED
YEARS. [7]'AND
WHATEVER NATION
TO WHICH THEY
WILL BE IN BONDAGE
I MYSELF WILL
JUDGE,' said God,
'AND AFTER THAT
THEY WILL COME OUT
AND [a]SERVE ME IN
THIS PLACE.' [8]And
He gave him the
covenant of cir-
cumcision; and so
Abraham became
the father of Isaac,
and circumcised
him on the eighth
day; and Isaac
became the father
of Jacob, and
Jacob *of* the twelve
patriarchs.
[9]"The patriarchs
became jealous of
Joseph and sold
him into Egypt. *Yet*
God was with him,
[10]and rescued him
from all his afflic-
tions, and granted
him favor and
wisdom in the sight
of Pharaoh, king
of Egypt, and he
made him governor
over Egypt and all
his household.
[11]"Now a famine
came over all
Egypt and Canaan,
and great afflic-
tion *with it,* and
our fathers could
find no food. [12]But
when Jacob heard
that there was grain
in Egypt, he sent
our fathers *there*
the first time. [13]On
the second *visit* Jo-
seph made himself
known to his broth-
ers, and Joseph's
family was dis-
closed to Pharaoh.
[14]Then Joseph

[a] 7 Gen. 15:13,14

[a] [ἐφ'] UBS, omitted by TNIV.
[b] [τοῦ] UBS, omitted by TNIV.

[a] Or *worship*

NIV

sent for his fa-
ther Jacob and
his whole family,
seventy-five in all.
15Then Jacob went
down to Egypt,
where he and our
ancestors died.
16Their bodies
were brought back
to Shechem and
placed in the tomb
that Abraham had
bought from the
sons of Hamor at
Shechem for a cer-
tain sum of money.
17“As the time
drew near for
God to fulfill his
promise to Abra-
ham, the number
of our people in
Egypt had greatly
increased. 18Then
‘a new king, to
whom Joseph
meant nothing,
came to power in
Egypt.’[a] 19He dealt
treacherously with
our people and
oppressed our an-
cestors by forcing
them to throw out
their newborn ba-
bies so that they
would die.
20“At that time
Moses was born,
and he was no or-
dinary child.[b] For
three months he
was cared for by
his family. 21When
he was placed out-
side, Pharaoh’s
daughter took him
and brought him
up as her own son.
22Moses was ed-
ucated in all the
wisdom

ἀποστείλας δὲ Ἰωσὴφ μετεκαλέσατο Ἰακὼβ τὸν πατέρα αὐτοῦ καὶ πᾶσαν
sent *Then Joseph* and summoned Jacob *{the}* his father *his* and all
690 1254 2737 3559 2609 3836 899 4252 899 2779 4246
pt.aa.nsm cj n.nsm v.ami.3s n.asm d.asm n.asm r.gsm.3 cj a.asf

τὴν συγγένειαν ἐν ψυχαῖς ⌊ἑβδομήκοντα πέντε.⌋ 15 καὶ κατέβη
his relatives, *{in}* seventy-five persons. *seventy-five* And Jacob went down
3836 5149 1877 1573 6034 1573 4297 2779 2609 2849
d.asf n.asf p.d n.dpf a.dpf a.dpf cj v.aai.3s

Ἰακὼβ εἰς Αἴγυπτον καὶ → ἐτελεύτησεν αὐτὸς καὶ οἱ
Jacob into Egypt, and he himself died *himself* there, ⌊along with⌋ *{the}* our
2609 1650 131 2779 899 5462 899 2779 3836 7005
n.nsm p.a n.asf cj v.aai.3s r.nsm cj d.npm

πατέρες ἡμῶν, 16 καὶ μετετέθησαν εἰς Συχὲμ καὶ ἐτέθησαν ἐν τῷ μνήματι
fathers, *our* and ⌊they were brought back⌋ to Shechem and laid in the tomb
4252 7005 2779 3572 1650 5374 2779 5502 1877 3836 3645
n.npm r.gp.1 cj v.api.3p p.a n.asf cj v.api.3p p.d d.dsn n.dsn

ᾧ ὠνήσατο Ἀβραὰμ τιμῆς ἀργυρίου παρὰ τῶν υἱῶν Ἑμμὼρ ἐν
that Abraham had bought for *Abraham* a sum of silver from the sons of Hamor in
4005 11 6050 11 5507 736 4123 3836 5626 1846 1877
r.dsn v.ami.3s n.nsm n.gsf n.gsn p.g d.gpm n.gpm n.gsm p.d

Συχέμ. 17 καθὼς δὲ ἤγγιζεν ὁ χρόνος τῆς
Shechem. “But as *But* the time of the promise drew near, *the time of the*
5374 1254 2777 1254 3836 5989 3836 3836 2039 1581 3836 5989 3836
n.dsf cj cj v.iai.3s d.nsm n.nsm d.gsf

ἐπαγγελίας ἧς ὡμολόγησεν ὁ θεὸς τῷ Ἀβραάμ, ηὔξησεν ὁ
promise which God had granted *{the} God* to Abraham, our people increased *our*
2039 4005 2536 3933 3836 2536 3836 11 3836 3295 889 3836
n.gsf r.gsf v.aai.3s d.nsm n.nsm d.dsm n.dsm v.aai.3s d.nsm

λαὸς καὶ ἐπληθύνθη ἐν Αἰγύπτῳ 18 ⌊ἄχρι οὗ⌋ ἀνέστη βασιλεὺς ἕτερος
people and multiplied in Egypt, until there arose another king *another*
3295 2779 4437 1877 131 948 4005 482 2283 995 2283
n.nsm cj v.api.3s p.d n.dsf p.g r.gsm v.aai.3s n.nsm r.nsm

[a]ἐπ' Αἴγυπτον ὃς ↱ οὐκ ᾔδει τὸν Ἰωσήφ. 19 οὗτος κατασοφισάμενος τὸ
over Egypt who did not know *{the}* Joseph. He took advantage of *{the}* our
2093 131 4005 3857 4024 3857 3836 2737 4047 2947 3836 7005
p.a n.asf r.nsm pl v.lai.3s d.asm n.asm r.nsm pt.am.nsm d.asn

γένος ἡμῶν ἐκάκωσεν τοὺς πατέρας ἡμῶν[b] τοῦ ποιεῖν τὰ
nation *our* and mistreated *{the}* our fathers, *our* *{the}* making them expose *{the}* their
1169 7005 2808 3836 7005 4252 7005 3836 4472 1704 3836 899
n.asn r.gp.1 v.aai.3s d.apm n.apm r.gp.1 d.gsn f.pa d.apn

βρέφη ἔκθετα αὐτῶν εἰς τὸ ↱ ↱ μὴ ζῳογονεῖσθαι. 20 ἐν ᾧ καιρῷ
infants, *expose* *their* ⌊so that⌋ ~ they would not be kept alive. At which time
1100 1704 899 1650 3836 2441 2441 3590 2441 1877 4005 2789
n.apn a.apn r.gpm.3 p.a d.asn pl f.pp p.d r.dsm n.dsm

ἐγεννήθη Μωϋσῆς καὶ ἦν ἀστεῖος τῷ θεῷ· ὃς ἀνετράφη
Moses was born, *Moses* and ⌊he was⌋ beautiful before God. He ⌊was brought up⌋ for three
3707 1164 3707 2779 1639 842 3836 2536 4005 427 5552
v.api.3s n.nsm cj v.iai.3s a.nsm d.dsm n.dsm r.nsm v.api.3s

μῆνας τρεῖς ἐν τῷ οἴκῳ τοῦ πατρός, 21 → ἐκτεθέντος δὲ
months *three* in *{the}* his father's house; *his* *father's* and when he was abandoned, *and*
3604 5552 1877 3836 3836 4252 3875 3836 4252 1254 899 1758 1254
n.apm a.apm p.d d.dsm n.dsm d.gsm n.gsm pt.ap.gsm cj

αὐτοῦ ἀνείλατο αὐτὸν ἡ θυγάτηρ Φαραὼ καὶ ἀνεθρέψατο
he the daughter of Pharaoh rescued him *the* *daughter* *of Pharaoh* and brought
899 3836 2588 5755 5755 359 899 3836 2588 5755 2779 427
r.gsm.3 v.ami.3s r.asm.3 d.nsf n.nsf n.gsm cj v.ami.3s

αὐτὸν ↞ ἑαυτῇ εἰς υἱόν. 22 καὶ ἐπαιδεύθη Μωϋσῆς ἐν[c] πάσῃ σοφίᾳ
him up for herself as a son. So Moses was trained *Moses* in all the wisdom
899 427 1571 1650 5626 2779 3707 4084 3707 1877 4246 5053
r.asm.3 r.dsf.3 p.a n.asm cj v.api.3s n.nsm p.d a.dsf n.dsf

NASB

sent *word* and
invited Jacob his
father and all his
relatives to come
to him, seventy-
five persons *in all.*
15And Jacob went
down to Egypt
and *there* he and
our fathers died.
16*From there* they
were removed to
Shechem and laid
in the tomb which
Abraham had pur-
chased for a sum
of money from the
sons of Hamor in
Shechem.
17“But as the time
of the promise was
approaching which
God had assured
to Abraham, the
people increased
and multiplied in
Egypt, 18until THERE
AROSE ANOTHER
KING OVER EGYPT
WHO KNEW NOTHING
ABOUT JOSEPH. 19It
was he who took
shrewd advantage
of our race and
mistreated our
fathers so that they
would expose their
infants and they
would not survive.
20It was at this
time that Moses
was born; and he
was lovely in the
sight of God, and
he was nurtured
three months in
his father’s home.
21And after he had
been set outside,
Pharaoh’s daughter
took him away and
nurtured him as her
own son. 22Moses
was educated in all
the learning of the

[a] 18 Exodus 1:8
[b] 20 Or *was fair in the sight of God*

[a] [ἐπ' Αἴγυπτον] UBS.
[b] [ἡμῶν] UBS, omitted by TNIV.
[c] [ἐν] UBS, omitted by TNIV.

NIV

of the Egyptians
and was power-
ful in speech and
action.
23 “When Moses
was forty years
old, he decided
to visit his own
people, the Isra-
elites. 24 He saw
one of them being
mistreated by an
Egyptian, so he
went to his de-
fense and avenged
him by killing the
Egyptian. 25 Moses
thought that his
own people would
realize that God
was using him to
rescue them, but
they did not. 26 The
next day Moses
came upon two Is-
raelites who were
fighting. He tried
to reconcile them
by saying, ‘Men,
you are brothers;
why do you want
to hurt each oth-
er?’
27 “But the man
who was mis-
treating the other
pushed Moses
aside and said,
‘Who made you
ruler and judge
over us? 28 Are you
thinking of killing
me as you killed
the Egyptian yes-
terday?’[a] 29 When
Moses heard this,
he fled to Midian,
where he settled
as a foreigner and
had two sons.
30 “After forty
years had passed,
an angel appeared
to Moses in the
flames of a burn-
ing bush in the
desert near Mount
Sinai. 31 When he
saw this, he was
amazed at the

→ Αἰγυπτίων, ἦν δὲ δυνατὸς ἐν λόγοις καὶ ἔργοις αὐτοῦ. 23 ὡς
of the Egyptians and was {and} powerful in his words and deeds. {his} “When
130 1254 1639 1254 1543 1877 899 3364 2779 2240 899 6055
n.gpm v.iai.3s cj a.nsm p.d n.dpm cj n.dpn r.gsm.3 cj

δὲ ἐπληροῦτο αὐτῷ τεσσερακονταετὴς χρόνος, ⌞ἀνέβη ἐπὶ⌟ τὴν καρδίαν
{and} he was {he} about forty years old, it entered {the} his mind
1254 899 4444 899 5478 5989 326 2093 3836 899 2840
cj v.ipi.3s r.dsm.3 a.nsm n.nsm v.aai.3s p.a d.asf n.asf

αὐτοῦ ἐπισκέψασθαι τοὺς ἀδελφοὺς αὐτοῦ τοὺς υἱοὺς Ἰσραήλ. 24 καὶ ἰδών
{his} to visit {the} his brothers, {his} the sons of Israel. And seeing
899 2170 3836 899 81 899 3836 5626 2702 2779 1625
r.gsm.3 f.am d.apm n.apm r.gsm.3 d.apm n.apm n.gsm cj pt.aa.nsm

τινα ἀδικούμενον ἠμύνατο καὶ ἐποίησεν ἐκδίκησιν τῷ
one of them being treated unjustly, he defended him and brought justice ⌞to the⌟
5516 92 310 2779 4472 1689 3836
r.asm pt.pp.asm v.ami.3s cj v.aai.3s n.asf d.dsm

καταπονουμένῳ πατάξας τὸν Αἰγύπτιον. 25 ἐνόμιζεν δὲ
one being mistreated ⌞by striking down⌟ the Egyptian. He thought {and} that his brothers
2930 4250 3836 130 3787 1254 899 81
pt.pp.dsm pt.aa.nsm d.asm n.asm v.iai.3s cj

συνιέναι τοὺς ἀδελφοὺς αὐτοῦ[a] ὅτι ὁ θεὸς διὰ χειρὸς αὐτοῦ δίδωσιν
would understand {the} brothers {his} that {the} God, by his hand, {his} was granting
5317 3836 81 899 4022 3836 2536 1328 899 5931 899 1443
f.pa d.apm n.apm r.gsm.3 cj d.nsm n.nsm p.g n.gsf r.gsm.3 v.pai.3s

σωτηρίαν αὐτοῖς, οἱ δὲ ↱ οὐ συνῆκαν. 26 τῇ τε ἐπιούσῃ ἡμέρᾳ
them deliverance; {them} but they {but} did not understand. ⌞On the⌟ ~ following day
899 5401 899 1254 3836 1254 5317 4024 5317 3836 5445 2079 2465
n.asf r.dpm.3 d.npm cj pl v.aai.3p d.dsf cj pt.pa.dsf n.dsf

ὤφθη αὐτοῖς μαχομένοις καὶ συνήλλασσεν αὐτοὺς εἰς εἰρήνην
he appeared to them ⌞as they were quarreling⌟ and tried to reconcile them to be at peace,
3972 899 3481 2779 5261 899 1650 1645
v.api.3s r.dpm.3 pt.pm.dpm cj v.iai.3s r.apm.3 p.a n.asf

εἰπών, ἄνδρες, ἀδελφοί ἐστε· ἱνατί ἀδικεῖτε ἀλλήλους; 27 ὁ δὲ
saying, ‘Men, you are brothers. {you are} Why are you hurting one another?’ But the {But}
3306 467 1639 1639 81 1639 2672 92 253 1254 3836 1254
pt.aa.nsm n.vpm n.npm v.pai.2p cj v.pai.2p r.apm d.nsm cj

ἀδικῶν τὸν πλησίον ἀπώσατο αὐτὸν ↰ εἰπών, τίς σε
⌞one who was trying to injure⌟ his neighbor pushed Moses aside, saying, ‘Who made you
92 3836 4446 723 899 723 3306 5515 2770 5148
pt.pa.nsm d.asm adv v.ami.3s r.asm.3 pt.aa.nsm r.nsm r.as.2

κατέστησεν ἄρχοντα καὶ δικαστὴν ἐφ’ ἡμῶν; 28 μὴ ἀνελεῖν με
{made} a ruler and a judge over us? {not} Do you want to kill me
2770 807 2779 1471 2093 7005 3590 2527 5148 2527 359 1609
v.aai.3s n.asm cj n.asm p.g r.gp.1 pl f.aa r.as.1

σὺ θέλεις ⌞ὃν τρόπον⌟ ἀνεῖλες ἐχθὲς τὸν Αἰγύπτιον; 29
{you} {Do want} as yesterday you killed {yesterday} the Egyptian?’ At this remark,
5148 2527 4005 5573 2396 359 2396 3836 130 1877 4047 3364
r.ns.2 v.pai.2s r.asm n.asm v.aai.2s adv d.asm n.asm

ἔφυγεν δὲ Μωϋσῆς ἐν τῷ λόγῳ τούτῳ καὶ ἐγένετο πάροικος ἐν γῇ
Moses fled {and} {Moses} {At} {the} {remark} {this} and became an exile in the land
3707 5771 1254 3707 1877 3836 3364 4047 2779 1181 4230 1877 1178
v.aai.3s cj n.nsm p.d d.dsm n.dsm r.dsm cj v.ami.3s n.nsm p.d n.dsf

Μαδιάμ, οὗ ἐγέννησεν υἱοὺς δύο. 30 καὶ → πληρωθέντων ἐτῶν
of Midian, where he had two sons. {two} “Now when forty years had passed, {years}
3409 4023 1164 1545 5626 1545 2779 5477 2291 4444 2291
n.gsm adv v.aai.3s n.apm a.apm cj pt.ap.gpn n.gpn

τεσσεράκοντα ὤφθη αὐτῷ ἐν τῇ ἐρήμῳ τοῦ ὄρους Σινᾶ ἄγγελος ἐν
{forty} there appeared to him in the desert near Mount Sinai an angel in the
5477 3972 899 1877 3836 2245 3836 4001 4982 34 1877
a.gpn v.api.3s r.dsm.3 p.d d.dsf n.dsf d.gsn n.gsn n.gsn n.nsm p.d

φλογὶ → πυρὸς βάτου. 31 ↱ ὁ δὲ Μωϋσῆς ἰδὼν ἐθαύμαζεν τὸ
flame of a burning bush. When {the} {and} Moses saw it, ⌞he wondered at⌟ the
5825 4786 1004 1625 3836 1254 3707 1625 2513 3836
n.dsf n.gsn n.gsm d.nsm cj n.nsm pt.aa.nsm v.iai.3s d.asn

NASB

Egyptians, and
he was a man of
power in words
and deeds. 23 But
when he was ap-
proaching the age
of forty, it entered
his mind to visit
his brethren, the
sons of Israel.
24 And when he saw
one *of them* being
treated unjustly, he
defended him and
took vengeance for
the oppressed by
striking down the
Egyptian. 25 And he
supposed that his
brethren under-
stood that God was
granting them de-
liverance through
him, but they did
not understand.
26 On the following
day he appeared
to them as they
were fighting
together, and he
tried to reconcile
them in peace,
saying, ‘Men, you
are brethren, why
do you injure one
another?’ 27 But the
one who was injur-
ing his neighbor
pushed him away,
saying, ‘WHO MADE
YOU A RULER AND
JUDGE OVER US?
28 YOU DO NOT MEAN
TO KILL ME AS YOU
KILLED THE EGYP-
TIAN YESTERDAY,
DO YOU?’ 29 At this
remark, MOSES
FLED AND BECAME
AN ALIEN IN THE
LAND OF MIDIAN,
where he became
the father of two
sons.
30 “After forty
years had passed,
AN ANGEL APPEARED
TO HIM IN THE WIL-
DERNESS OF MOUNT
Sinai, IN THE FLAME
OF A BURNING THORN
BUSH. 31 When
Moses saw it, he
marveled at the

[a] 28 Exodus 2:14

[a] [αὐτοῦ] UBS, omitted by TNIV.

NIV

sight. As he went
over to get a closer
look, he heard the
Lord say: 32 'I am
the God of your
fathers, the God
of Abraham, Isaac
and Jacob.'[a] Moses
trembled with fear
and did not dare to
look.
33 "Then the Lord
said to him, 'Take
off your sandals,
for the place where
you are standing
is holy ground.
34 I have indeed
seen the oppres-
sion of my people
in Egypt. I have
heard their groan-
ing and have come
down to set them
free. Now come, I
will send you back
to Egypt.'[b]
35 "This is the
same Moses they
had rejected with
the words, 'Who
made you ruler
and judge?' He
was sent to be their
ruler and deliverer
by God himself,
through the angel
who appeared to
him in the bush.
36 He led them out
of Egypt and per-
formed wonders
and signs in Egypt,
at the Red Sea and
for forty years in
the wilderness.
37 "This is the
Moses who told
the Israelites, 'God
will raise up for
you a prophet like
me from your own
people.'[c] 38 He was
in the assembly
in the wilderness,
with the angel who
spoke to him on
Mount Sinai, and

ὅραμα, → προσερχομένου δὲ αὐτοῦ κατανοῆσαι ἐγένετο φωνὴ →
sight; and as he came closer *and* *he* to look at it, there came the voice of the
3969 1254 899 4665 1254 899 2917 1181 5889
n.asn pt.pm.gsm cj r.gsm.3 f.aa v.ami.3s n.nsf

κυρίου· 32 ἐγὼ ὁ θεὸς τῶν πατέρων σου, ὁ θεὸς Ἀβραὰμ καὶ Ἰσαὰκ
Lord: 'I am the God of your forefathers, *your* the God of Abraham and of Isaac
3261 1609 3836 2536 3836 5148 4252 5148 3836 2536 11 2779 2693
n.gsm r.ns.1 d.nsm n.nsm d.gpm n.gpm r.gs.2 d.nsm n.nsm n.gsm cj n.gsm

καὶ Ἰακώβ. ἔντρομος δὲ γενόμενος Μωϋσῆς ↱ οὐκ ἐτόλμα
and of Jacob.' And Moses began to tremble *And* *began* *Moses* and did not dare
2779 2609 1254 3707 1181 1958 1254 1181 3707 5528 4024 5528
cj n.gsm a.nsm cj pt.am.nsm n.nsm pl v.iai.3s

κατανοῆσαι. 33 εἶπεν δὲ αὐτῷ ὁ κύριος, λῦσον τὸ ὑπόδημα τῶν
to look. And the Lord said *And* to him, *the* *Lord* 'Take off the sandals from
2917 1254 3836 3261 3306 1254 899 3836 3261 3395 3836 5687 3836
f.aa v.aai.3s cj r.dsm.3 d.nsm n.nsm v.aam.2s d.asn n.asn d.gpm

ποδῶν σου, ὁ γὰρ τόπος ἐφ᾽ ᾧ ἕστηκας γῆ ἁγία ἐστίν.
your feet, *your* for the *for* place on which you stand is holy ground. *holy* *is*
5148 4546 5148 1142 3836 1142 5536 2093 4005 2705 1639 41 1178 41 1639
n.gpm r.gs.2 d.nsm cj n.nsm p.d r.dsm v.rai.2s n.nsf a.nsf v.pai.3s

34 ἰδὼν εἶδον τὴν κάκωσιν τοῦ λαοῦ μου τοῦ ἐν Αἰγύπτῳ καὶ
Surely ⌊I have seen⌋ the oppression of my people *my* *{the}* in Egypt, and I have
1625 1625 3836 2810 3836 1609 3295 1609 3836 1877 131 2779 201 201
pt.aa.nsm v.aai.1s d.asf n.asf d.gsm n.gsm r.gs.1 d.gsm p.d n.dsf cj

τοῦ στεναγμοῦ αὐτῶν ἤκουσα, καὶ κατέβην ἐξελέσθαι αὐτούς·
heard *{the}* their groaning, *their* *I have heard* and ⌊I have come down⌋ to deliver them.
201 3836 899 5099 899 201 2779 2849 1975 899
d.gsm n.gsm r.gpm.3 v.aai.1s cj v.aai.1s f.am r.apm.3

καὶ νῦν δεῦρο ἀποστείλω σε ↰ εἰς Αἴγυπτον. 35 τοῦτον τὸν Μωϋσῆν ὃν
{and} Now come, I will send you back to Egypt.' This *{the}* Moses, whom
2779 3814 1306 690 5148 690 1650 131 4047 3836 3707 4005
cj adv j v.aas.1s r.as.2 p.a n.asf r.asm d.asm n.asm r.asm

ἠρνήσαντο εἰπόντες, τίς σε κατέστησεν ἄρχοντα καὶ δικαστήν; τοῦτον
they rejected, saying, 'Who made you *made* a ruler and a judge?' — this man
766 3306 5515 2770 5148 2770 807 2779 1471 4047
v.ami.3p pt.aa.npm r.nsm r.as.2 v.aai.3s n.asm cj n.asm r.asm

ὁ θεὸς καὶ[a] ἄρχοντα καὶ λυτρωτὴν ἀπέσταλκεν σὺν χειρὶ → ἀγγέλου
{the} God sent both as ruler and redeemer *sent* by the hand of the angel
3836 2536 690 2779 807 2779 3392 690 5250 5931 34
d.nsm n.nsm cj n.asm cj n.asm v.rai.3s p.d n.dsf n.gsm

τοῦ ὀφθέντος αὐτῷ ἐν τῇ βάτῳ. 36 οὗτος ἐξήγαγεν αὐτοὺς ↰ ποιήσας τέρατα
who appeared to him in the bush. He led them out, performing wonders
3836 3972 899 1877 3836 1004 4047 1974 899 1974 4472 5469
d.gsm pt.ap.gsm r.dsm.3 p.d d.dsf n.dsf r.nsm v.aai.3s r.apm.3 pt.aa.nsm n.apn

καὶ σημεῖα ἐν γῇ Αἰγύπτῳ καὶ ἐν ἐρυθρᾷ θαλάσσῃ καὶ ἐν τῇ ἐρήμῳ
and signs in the land of Egypt and at the Red Sea and in the wilderness
2779 4956 1877 1178 131 2779 1877 2261 2498 2779 1877 3836 2245
cj n.apn p.d n.dsf n.dsf cj p.d a.dsf n.dsf cj p.d d.dsf n.dsf

→ ἔτη τεσσεράκοντα. 37 οὗτός ἐστιν ὁ Μωϋσῆς ὁ εἴπας τοῖς υἱοῖς
for forty years. *forty* This is the Moses who said to the sons
5477 2291 5477 4047 1639 3836 3707 3836 3306 3836 5626
n.apn a.apn r.nsm v.pai.3s d.nsm n.nsm d.nsm pt.aa.nsm d.dpm n.dpm

Ἰσραήλ, προφήτην ὑμῖν ἀναστήσει ὁ θεὸς ἐκ τῶν
of Israel, 'God will raise up a prophet for you *will raise up* *{the}* *God* ⌊from among⌋ *{the}* your
2702 2536 482 482 482 4737 7007 482 3836 2536 1666 3836 7007
n.gsm n.asm r.dp.2 v.fai.3s d.nsm n.nsm p.g d.gpm

ἀδελφῶν ὑμῶν ὡς ἐμέ. 38 οὗτός ἐστιν ὁ γενόμενος ἐν τῇ ἐκκλησίᾳ
brothers, *your* as he raised up me.' He is the one who was in the congregation
81 7007 6055 1609 4047 1639 3836 1181 1877 3836 1711
n.gpm r.gp.2 pl r.as.1 r.nsm v.pai.3s d.nsm pt.am.nsm p.d d.dsf n.dsf

ἐν τῇ ἐρήμῳ μετὰ τοῦ ἀγγέλου τοῦ λαλοῦντος αὐτῷ ἐν τῷ ὄρει Σινᾶ καὶ
in the wilderness with the angel who spoke to him on *{the}* Mount Sinai, and
1877 3836 2245 3552 3836 34 3836 3281 899 1877 3836 4001 4982 2779
p.d d.dsf n.dsf p.g d.gsm n.gsm d.gsm pt.pa.gsm r.dsm.3 p.d d.dsn n.dsn n.dsn cj

NASB

sight; and as he
approached to look
more closely, there
came the voice of
the Lord: 32 'I AM
THE GOD OF YOUR
FATHERS, THE GOD
OF ABRAHAM AND
ISAAC AND JACOB.'
Moses shook with
fear and would not
venture to look.
33 BUT THE LORD
SAID TO HIM, 'TAKE
OFF THE SANDALS
FROM YOUR FEET,
FOR THE PLACE ON
WHICH YOU ARE
STANDING IS HOLY
GROUND. 34 I HAVE
CERTAINLY SEEN THE
OPPRESSION OF MY
PEOPLE IN EGYPT
AND HAVE HEARD
THEIR GROANS, AND
I HAVE COME DOWN
TO RESCUE THEM;
COME NOW, AND I
WILL SEND YOU TO
EGYPT.'
35 "This Moses
whom they dis-
owned, saying,
'WHO MADE YOU
A RULER AND A
JUDGE?' is the one
whom God sent *to*
be both a ruler and
a deliverer with the
help of the angel
who appeared to
him in the thorn
bush. 36 This man
led them out, per-
forming wonders
and signs in the
land of Egypt and
in the Red Sea and
in the wilderness
for forty years.
37 This is the Moses
who said to the
sons of Israel,
'GOD WILL RAISE UP
FOR YOU A PROPHET
LIKE ME FROM YOUR
BRETHREN.' 38 This
is the one who was
in the congregation
in the wilderness
together with the
angel who was
speaking to him on
Mount Sinai, and

[a] 32 Exodus 3:6
[b] 34 Exodus 3:5,7,8,10
[c] 37 Deut. 18:15

[a] [καὶ] UBS.

NIV

with our ancestors;
and he received
living words to
pass on to us.
39"But our an-
cestors refused to
obey him. Instead,
they rejected him
and in their hearts
turned back to
Egypt. 40They told
Aaron, 'Make us
gods who will go
before us. As for
this fellow Moses
who led us out
of Egypt—we
don't know what
has happened to
him!'[a] 41That was
the time they made
an idol in the form
of a calf. They
brought sacrifices
to it and reveled
in what their own
hands had made.
42But God turned
away from them
and gave them
over to the worship
of the sun, moon
and stars. This
agrees with what is
written in the book
of the prophets:

"'Did you bring
me sacrifices
and offerings
forty years
in the
wilderness,
people of
Israel?
43You have taken
up the
tabernacle of
Molek
and the star of
your god
Rephan,
the idols you
made to
worship.
Therefore I will
send you
into exile'[b]
beyond
Babylon.

44"Our ancestors
had the tabernacle
of the covenant law
with them in the
wilderness. It had
been made as God
directed Moses, ac-
cording to the pat-
tern he had seen.
45After

[a] 40 Exodus 32:1
[b] 43 Amos 5:25-27 (see Septuagint)

τῶν πατέρων ἡμῶν, ὃς ἐδέξατο λόγια ζῶντα δοῦναι ἡμῖν,[a]
with {the} our fathers, our and he received living oracles living to give to us.
3836 7005 4252 7005 4005 1312 2409 3359 2409 1443 7005
d.gpm n.gpm r.gp.1 r.nsm v.ami.3s n.apn pt.pa.apn f.aa r.dp.1

39 ᾧ οὐκ ἠθέλησαν ὑπήκοοι γενέσθαι οἱ πατέρες ἡμῶν,
⌞To him⌟ our fathers were not willing to be obedient, to be {the} fathers our
4005 7005 4252 2527 4024 2527 1181 1181 5675 1181 3836 4252 7005
r.dsm pl v.aai.3p a.npm f.am d.npm n.npm r.gp.1

ἀλλὰ ἀπώσαντο καὶ ἐστράφησαν ἐν ταῖς καρδίαις αὐτῶν εἰς
but thrust him aside, and turned in {the} their hearts their to
247 723 2779 5138 1877 3836 899 2840 899 1650
cj v.ami.3p cj v.api.3p p.d d.dpf n.dpf r.gpm.3 p.a

Αἴγυπτον 40 εἰπόντες τῷ Ἀαρών, ποίησον ἡμῖν θεοὺς οἳ προπορεύσονται ἡμῶν·
Egypt, saying to Aaron, 'Make for us gods who will go before us,
131 3306 3836 2 4472 7005 2536 4005 4638 7005
n.asf pt.aa.npm d.dsm n.dsm v.aam.2s r.dp.1 n.apm r.npm v.fmi.3p r.gp.1

ὁ γὰρ Μωϋσῆς οὗτος, ὃς ἐξήγαγεν ἡμᾶς ἐκ γῆς Αἰγύπτου, οὐκ
{the} for this Moses this who brought us from the land of Egypt, we do not
3836 1142 4047 3707 4047 4005 1974 7005 1666 1178 131 3857 3857 4024
d.nsm cj n.nsm r.nsm r.nsm v.aai.3s r.ap.1 p.g n.gsf n.gsf pl

οἴδαμεν τί ἐγένετο αὐτῷ. 41 καὶ ἐμοσχοποίησαν ἐν ταῖς ἡμέραις ἐκείναις
know what has happened to him.' And they made a calf in {the} those days those
3857 5515 1181 899 2779 3674 1877 3836 1697 2465 1697
v.rai.1p r.nsn v.ami.3s r.dsm.3 cj v.aai.3p p.d d.dpf n.dpf r.dpf

καὶ ἀνήγαγον θυσίαν τῷ εἰδώλῳ καὶ εὐφραίνοντο ἐν τοῖς ἔργοις τῶν
and offered a sacrifice ⌞to the⌟ idol and began rejoicing in the works of their
2779 343 2602 3836 1631 2779 2370 1877 3836 2240 3836 899
cj v.aai.3p n.asf d.dsn n.dsn cj v.ipi.3p p.d d.dpn n.dpn d.gpf

χειρῶν αὐτῶν. 42 ἔστρεψεν δὲ ὁ θεὸς καὶ παρέδωκεν αὐτοὺς
hands. their But God turned away But {the} God and gave them over
5931 899 1254 2536 5138 1254 3836 2536 2779 4140 899 4140
n.gpf r.gpm.3 v.aai.3s cj d.nsm n.nsm cj v.aai.3s r.apm.3

λατρεύειν τῇ στρατιᾷ τοῦ οὐρανοῦ καθὼς γέγραπται ἐν βίβλῳ τῶν προφητῶν,
to worship the host of heaven, as it is written in the book of the prophets:
3302 3836 5131 3836 4041 2777 1211 1877 1047 3836 4737
f.pa d.dsf n.dsf d.gsm n.gsm cj v.rpi.3s p.d n.dsf d.gpm n.gpm

μὴ σφάγια καὶ θυσίας προσηνέγκατέ μοι ἔτη
No 'Did you bring to me slain beasts and sacrifices Did you bring to me forty years
3590 4712 4712 4712 1609 1609 5376 2779 2602 4712 1609 5477 2291
pl n.apn cj n.apf v.aai.2p r.ds.1 n.apn

τεσσεράκοντα ἐν τῇ ἐρήμῳ, οἶκος Ἰσραήλ; 43 καὶ ἀνελάβετε τὴν
forty in the wilderness, O house of Israel? No; {and} You took along the
5477 1877 3836 2245 3875 2702 3590 2779 377 3836
a.apn p.d d.dsf n.dsf n.vsm n.gsm cj v.aai.2p d.asf

σκηνὴν τοῦ Μόλοχ καὶ τὸ ἄστρον τοῦ θεοῦ ὑμῶν[b] Ῥαιφάν, τοὺς τύπους οὓς
shrine of Moloch and the star of your god your Rephan, the images that
5008 3836 3661 2779 3836 849 3836 7007 2536 7007 4818 3836 5596 4005
n.asf d.gsm n.gsm cj d.asn n.asn d.gsm n.gsm r.gp.2 n.gsm d.apm n.apm r.apm

ἐποιήσατε προσκυνεῖν αὐτοῖς, καὶ μετοικιῶ ὑμᾶς ἐπέκεινα
you made, to worship them, so I will make you move you beyond
4472 4686 899 2779 7007 3579 7007 2084
v.aai.2p f.pa r.dpm.3 cj v.fai.1s r.ap.2 p.g

Βαβυλῶνος. 44 ἡ σκηνὴ τοῦ μαρτυρίου ἦν τοῖς πατράσιν ἡμῶν ἐν τῇ
Babylon.' "The tabernacle of witness was with our fathers our in the
956 3836 5008 3836 3457 1639 3836 7005 4252 7005 1877 3836
n.gsf d.nsf n.nsf d.gsn n.gsn v.iai.3s d.dpm n.dpm r.gp.1 p.d d.dsf

ἐρήμῳ καθὼς διετάξατο ὁ λαλῶν τῷ
wilderness just as the one who spoke to Moses ordered him the one who spoke to
2245 2777 3836 3281 3281 3281 3836 3707 1411 3836 3281 3836
n.dsf cj v.ami.3s d.nsm pt.pa.nsm d.dsm

Μωϋσῇ ποιῆσαι αὐτὴν κατὰ τὸν τύπον ὃν ἑωράκει· 45
Moses to make it ⌞according to⌟ the pattern that he had seen. And when our fathers
3707 4472 899 2848 3836 5596 4005 3972 1342 7005 4252
n.dsm f.aa r.asf.3 p.a d.asm n.asm r.asm v.lai.3s

[a] ἡμῖν UBS, TNIV. ὑμῖν NET.
[b] [ὑμῶν] UBS.

NASB

who was with our
fathers; and he
received living or-
acles to pass on to
you. 39Our fathers
were unwilling to
be obedient to him,
but repudiated him
and in their hearts
turned back to
Egypt, 40SAYING TO
AARON, 'MAKE FOR
US GODS WHO WILL
GO BEFORE US; FOR
THIS MOSES WHO
LED US OUT OF THE
LAND OF EGYPT—WE
DO NOT KNOW WHAT
HAPPENED TO HIM.'
41At that time they
made a calf and
brought a sacrifice
to the idol, and
were rejoicing in
the works of their
hands. 42But God
turned away and
delivered them up
to serve the host
of heaven; as it is
written in the book
of the prophets,
'IT WAS NOT TO ME
THAT YOU OFFERED
VICTIMS AND SACRI-
FICES FORTY YEARS
IN THE WILDERNESS,
WAS IT, O HOUSE
OF ISRAEL? 43YOU
ALSO TOOK ALONG
THE TABERNACLE
OF MOLOCH AND
THE STAR OF THE
GOD ROMPHA, THE
IMAGES WHICH YOU
MADE TO WOR-
SHIP. I ALSO WILL
REMOVE YOU BEYOND
BABYLON.'
44"Our fathers had
the tabernacle of
testimony in the
wilderness, just
as He who spoke
to Moses directed
him to make it ac-
cording to the pat-
tern which he had
seen. 45And having
received it in their
turn, our fathers

NIV

receiving the tab-
ernacle, our ances-
tors under Joshua
brought it with them
when they took
the land from the
nations God drove
out before them. It
remained in the land
until the time of Da-
vid, [46]who enjoyed
God's favor and
asked that he might
provide a dwelling
place for the God of
Jacob.[a] [47]But it was
Solomon who built
a house for him.
[48]"However, the
Most High does not
live in houses made
by human hands.
As the prophet says:

[49]" 'Heaven is my
throne,
and the earth is
my footstool.
What kind of
house will
you build for
me?
says the
Lord.
Or where will
my resting
place be?
[50]Has not my
hand made
all these
things?'[b]

[51]"You stiffnecked
people! Your hearts
and ears are still
uncircumcised. You
are just like your
ancestors: You al-
ways resist the Holy
Spirit! [52]Was there
ever a prophet your
ancestors did not per-
secute? They even
killed those who pre-
dicted the coming of
the Righteous One.
And now you have
betrayed and mur-
dered him— [53]you
who have received
the law that was giv-
en through angels but
have not obeyed it."

The Stoning of Stephen

[54]When the mem-
bers of the Sanhedrin
heard this, they were
furious

[a] 46 Some early manuscripts *the house of Jacob*
[b] 50 Isaiah 66:1,2

ἣν καὶ εἰσήγαγον ← διαδεξάμενοι οἱ πατέρες ἡμῶν μετὰ
received it in return, *{also}* they brought it in *when received in return* *{the}* *fathers* *our* with
1342 4005 1342 1342 2779 1652 1342 3836 4252 7005 3552
r.asf adv v.aai.3p pt.am.npm d.npm n.npm r.gp.1 p.g

Ἰησοῦ ἐν τῇ κατασχέσει τῶν ἐθνῶν, ὧν ἐξῶσεν ὁ θεὸς ἀπὸ
Joshua in *{the}* taking possession of the nations, whom God drove out *{the}* *God* before the
2652 1877 3836 2959 3836 1620 4005 2536 2034 3836 2536 608
n.gsm p.d d.dsf n.dsf d.gpn n.gpn r.gpn v.aai.3s d.nsm n.nsm p.g

προσώπου τῶν πατέρων ἡμῶν ἕως τῶν ἡμερῶν Δαυίδ, 46 ὃς εὗρεν χάριν
face of our fathers, *our* until the days of David, who found favor
4725 3836 7005 4252 7005 2401 3836 2465 1253 4005 2351 5921
n.gsn d.gpm n.gpm r.gp.1 p.g d.gpf n.gpf n.gsm r.nsm v.aai.3s n.asf

ἐνώπιον τοῦ θεοῦ καὶ ᾐτήσατο εὑρεῖν σκήνωμα τῷ οἴκῳ[a] Ἰακώβ. 47
in the sight of God and asked to find a dwelling place ⌊for the⌋ God of Jacob. But it
1967 3836 2536 2779 160 2351 5013 3836 3875 2609 1254
p.g d.gsm n.gsm cj v.ami.3s f.aa n.asn d.dsm n.dsm n.gsm

Σολομὼν δὲ οἰκοδόμησεν αὐτῷ οἶκον. 48 ἀλλ᾽ οὐχ
was Solomon *But* who built a house for him. *house* Yet the Most High does not
5048 1254 3868 3875 899 3875 247 3836 5736 5736 2997 4024
n.nsm cj v.aai.3s r.dsm.3 n.asm cj pl

ὁ ὕψιστος ἐν χειροποιήτοις κατοικεῖ, καθὼς ὁ προφήτης λέγει,
the *Most High* dwell in ⌊houses made by hands;⌋ *does dwell* as the prophet says,
3836 5736 2997 1877 5935 2997 2777 3836 4737 3306
d.nsm a.nsm.s p.d a.dpm v.pai.3s cj d.nsm n.nsm v.pai.3s

49 ὁ οὐρανός μοι θρόνος, ἡ δὲ γῆ ὑποπόδιον τῶν ποδῶν μου·
{the} 'Heaven is my throne, *{the}* and earth is the footstool for my feet. *my*
3836 4041 1609 2585 3836 1254 1178 5711 3836 1609 4546 1609
d.nsm n.nsm r.ds.1 n.nsm d.nsf cj n.nsf n.nsn d.gpm n.gpm r.gs.1

ποῖον οἶκον οἰκοδομήσετέ μοι, λέγει κύριος, ἢ τίς τόπος τῆς
⌊What sort of⌋ house will you build for me, says the Lord, or what is the place of my
4481 3875 3868 1609 3306 3261 2445 5515 5536 3836 1609
r.asm n.asm v.fai.2p r.ds.1 v.pai.3s n.nsm cj r.nsm n.nsm d.gsf

καταπαύσεώς μου; 50 ↱ οὐχὶ ἡ χείρ μου ἐποίησεν ταῦτα πάντα;
rest? *my* Did not *{the}* my hand *my* make all these things?' *all*
2923 1609 4472 4049 3836 1609 5931 1609 4472 4246 4047 4246
n.gsf r.gs.1 pl d.nsf n.nsf r.gs.1 v.aai.3s r.apn a.apn

51 Σκληροτράχηλοι καὶ ἀπερίτμητοι καρδίαις καὶ τοῖς ὠσίν, ὑμεῖς ἀεὶ
"You stiff-necked people, *{and}* uncircumcised in heart and *{the}* ears! You are always
5019 2779 598 2840 2779 3836 4044 7007 528 107
a.vpm cj a.vpm n.dpf cj d.dpn n.dpn r.np.2 adv

τῷ πνεύματι τῷ ἁγίῳ ἀντιπίπτετε ὡς οἱ πατέρες ὑμῶν
resisting the Holy Spirit. *{the}* *Holy* *are resisting* As *{the}* your fathers *your* were, so
528 3836 41 4460 3836 41 528 6055 3836 7007 4252 7007
d.dsn n.dsn d.dsn a.dsn v.pai.2p cj d.npm n.npm r.gp.2

καὶ ὑμεῖς. 52 τίνα τῶν προφητῶν ↱ οὐκ ἐδίωξαν οἱ πατέρες
also are you. Which of the prophets did not your fathers persecute? *{the}* *fathers*
2779 7007 5515 3836 4737 1503 4024 7007 4252 1503 3836 4252
adv r.np.2 r.asm d.gpm n.gpm pl v.aai.3p d.npm n.npm

ὑμῶν; καὶ ἀπέκτειναν τοὺς προκαταγγείλαντας περὶ τῆς ἐλεύσεως τοῦ
your *{and}* They killed those who announced beforehand concerning the coming of the
7007 2779 650 3836 4615 4309 3836 1803 3836
r.gp.2 cj v.aai.3p d.apm pt.aa.apm p.g d.gsf n.gsf d.gsm

δικαίου, οὗ νῦν ὑμεῖς προδόται καὶ φονεῖς ἐγένεσθε,
⌊Righteous One,⌋ ⌊of whom⌋ you have now *you* become betrayers and murderers! *have become*
1465 4005 7007 1181 3814 7007 1181 4595 2779 5838 1181
a.gsm r.gsm adv r.np.2 n.npm cj n.npm v.ami.2p

53 οἵτινες ἐλάβετε τὸν νόμον εἰς διαταγὰς ἀγγέλων καὶ ↱ οὐκ
You, who received the law by decrees given by angels and did not
4015 3284 3836 3795 1650 1408 34 2779 5875 4024
r.npm v.aai.2p d.asm n.asm p.a n.apf n.gpm cj pl

ἐφυλάξατε. 54 ἀκούοντες δὲ ταῦτα ⌊διεπρίοντο ταῖς καρδίαις
keep it." Now when they heard *Now* these things, they became furious
5875 1254 201 1254 4047 1391 3836 2840
v.aai.2p pt.pa.npm cj r.apn v.ipi.3p d.dpf n.dpf

[a] οἴκῳ UBS, NET. θεῷ TNIV.

NASB

brought it in with
Joshua upon
dispossessing the
nations whom God
drove out before
our fathers, until
the time of David.
[46]*David* found favor
in God's sight, and
asked that he might
find a dwelling
place for the [a]God
of Jacob. [47]But it
was Solomon who
built a house for
Him. [48]However,
the Most High does
not dwell in *houses*
made by *human*
hands; as the
prophet says:

[49]' HEAVEN IS MY
THRONE,
AND EARTH
IS THE FOOT-
STOOL OF MY
FEET;
WHAT KIND OF
HOUSE WILL
YOU BUILD FOR
ME?' says the
Lord,
' OR WHAT PLACE
IS THERE FOR
MY REPOSE?
[50]' WAS IT NOT
MY HAND
WHICH MADE
ALL THESE
THINGS?'
[51]"You men who
are stiff-necked
and uncircumcised
in heart and ears
are always resist-
ing the Holy Spirit;
you are doing just
as your fathers did.
[52]Which one of the
prophets did your
fathers not perse-
cute? They killed
those who had pre-
viously announced
the coming of the
Righteous One,
whose betrayers
and murderers you
have now become;
[53]you who received
the law as ordained
by angels, and *yet*
did not keep it."

Stephen Put to Death

[54]Now when they

[a] The earliest mss read *house* instead of *God;* the Septuagint reads *God*

NIV

and gnashed their
teeth at him. 55 But
Stephen, full of
the Holy Spirit,
looked up to heav-
en and saw the
glory of God, and
Jesus standing at
the right hand of
God. 56 "Look," he
said, "I see heaven
open and the Son
of Man standing at
the right hand of
God."
57 At this they
covered their ears
and, yelling at the
top of their voic-
es, they all rushed
at him, 58 dragged
him out of the city
and began to stone
him. Meanwhile,
the witnesses laid
their coats at the
feet of a young
man named Saul.
59 While they
were stoning him,
Stephen prayed,
"Lord Jesus, re-
ceive my spirit."
60 Then he fell
on his knees and
cried out, "Lord,
do not hold this
sin against them."
When he had said
this, he fell asleep.
8 And Saul ap-
proved of their
killing him.

The Church Persecuted and Scattered

On that day a
great persecution
broke out against
the church in Je-
rusalem, and all
except the apostles
were scattered
throughout Ju-
dea and Samaria.
2 Godly men buried

αὐτῶν⌋ καὶ ἔβρυχον τοὺς ὀδόντας ἐπ᾽ αὐτόν. 55 ὑπάρχων δὲ πλήρης →
and ground their teeth at him. But Stephen, being *But* full of
899 2779 1107 3836 3848 2093 899 1254 5639 1254 4441
r.gpm.3 cj v.iai.3p d.apm n.apm p.a r.asm.3 pt.pa.nsm cj a.nsm

πνεύματος ἁγίου ἀτενίσας εἰς τὸν οὐρανὸν εἶδεν δόξαν θεοῦ καὶ
the Holy Spirit, *Holy* looked right into *{the}* heaven and saw the glory of God, and
41 4460 41 867 1650 3836 4041 1625 1518 2536 2779
n.gsn a.gsn pt.aa.nsm p.a d.asm n.asm v.aai.3s n.asf n.gsm cj

Ἰησοῦν ἑστῶτα ἐκ δεξιῶν τοῦ θεοῦ 56 καὶ εἶπεν, ἰδοὺ θεωρῶ τοὺς
Jesus standing at the right hand of God. And he said, "Behold, I see the
2652 2705 1666 1288 3836 2536 2779 3306 2627 2555 3836
n.asm pt.ra.asm p.g a.gpf d.gsm n.gsm cj v.aai.3s j v.pai.1s d.apm

οὐρανοὺς διηνοιγμένους καὶ τὸν υἱὸν τοῦ ἀνθρώπου ἐκ δεξιῶν
heavens opened, and the Son of Man standing at the right hand
4041 1380 2779 3836 5626 3836 476 2705 1666 1288
n.apm pt.rp.apm cj d.asm n.asm d.gsm n.gsm p.g a.gpf

ἑστῶτα τοῦ θεοῦ. 57 ↱ κράξαντες δὲ → φωνῇ μεγάλῃ συνέσχον
standing of God." But they cried out *But* with a loud voice *loud* and covered
2705 3836 2536 1254 5309 3189 1254 3489 5889 3489 5309
pt.ra.asm d.gsm n.gsm pt.aa.npm cj n.dsf a.dsf v.aai.3p

τὰ ὦτα αὐτῶν καὶ ὥρμησαν ὁμοθυμαδὸν ἐπ᾽ αὐτὸν 58 καὶ ἐκβαλόντες
{the} their ears *their* and rushed together at him. *{and}* ⌊When they had driven⌋
3836 899 4044 899 2779 3994 3924 2093 899 2779 1675
d.apn n.apn r.gpm.3 cj v.aai.3p adv p.a r.asm.3 cj pt.aa.npm

ἔξω τῆς πόλεως ἐλιθοβόλουν. καὶ οἱ μάρτυρες ἀπέθεντο τὰ
him ⌊out of⌋ the city, they began to stone him; and the witnesses laid *{the}* their
2032 3836 4484 3344 2779 3836 3459 700 3836 899
p.g d.gsf n.gsf v.iai.3p cj d.npm n.npm v.ami.3p d.apn

ἱμάτια αὐτῶν παρὰ τοὺς πόδας → νεανίου καλουμένου Σαύλου, 59 καὶ
cloaks *their* at the feet of a young man named Saul. *{and}*
2668 899 4123 3836 4546 3733 2813 4930 2779
n.apn r.gpm.3 p.a d.apm n.apm n.gsm pt.pp.gsm n.gsm cj

ἐλιθοβόλουν τὸν Στέφανον ἐπικαλούμενον καὶ λέγοντα, κύριε Ἰησοῦ,
They kept stoning *{the}* Stephen ⌊as he was calling on⌋ God and saying, "Lord Jesus,
3344 3836 5108 2126 2779 3306 3261 2652
v.iai.3p d.asm n.asm pt.pm.asm cj pt.pa.asm n.vsm n.vsm

δέξαι τὸ πνεῦμά μου. 60 θεὶς δὲ τὰ γόνατα ἔκραξεν →
receive *{the}* my spirit!" *my* And falling *And* to his knees he cried out in a loud
1312 3836 1609 4460 1609 1254 5502 1254 3836 1205 3189 3489
v.amm.2s d.asn n.asn r.gs.1 pt.aa.nsm cj d.apn n.apn v.aai.3s

φωνῇ μεγάλῃ, κύριε, ↱ μὴ στήσῃς αὐτοῖς ταύτην τὴν ἁμαρτίαν. καὶ
voice, *loud* "Lord, do not hold this sin ⌊against them."⌋ *this* *{the}* *sin* And
5889 3489 3261 2705 3590 2705 4047 281 899 4047 3836 281 2779
n.dsf a.dsf n.vsm pl v.aas.2s r.dpm.3 r.asf d.asf n.asf cj

τοῦτο εἰπὼν ἐκοιμήθη.
when he had said this, *when he had said* he fell asleep.
3306 3306 3306 3306 4047 3306 3121
r.asn pt.aa.nsm v.api.3s

8:1 Σαῦλος δὲ ἦν συνευδοκῶν τῇ ἀναιρέσει αὐτοῦ. ἐγένετο δὲ
Now Saul *Now* was in agreement with his execution. *his* There arose *{and}*
1254 4930 1254 1639 5306 3836 899 358 899 1181 1254
n.nsm cj v.iai.3s pt.pa.nsm d.dsf n.dsf r.gsm.3 v.ami.3s cj

ἐν ἐκείνῃ τῇ ἡμέρᾳ διωγμὸς μέγας ἐπὶ τὴν ἐκκλησίαν τὴν ἐν
on that *{the}* day a great persecution *great* against the church *{the}* in
1877 1697 3836 2465 3489 1501 3489 2093 3836 1711 3836 1877
p.d r.dsf d.dsf n.dsf n.nsm a.nsm p.a d.asf n.asf d.asf p.d

Ἱεροσολύμοις, ↱ ↱ πάντες δὲ διεσπάρησαν κατὰ τὰς χώρας τῆς
Jerusalem, and they were all *and* scattered throughout the regions of
2642 1254 1401 1401 4246 1254 1401 2848 3836 6001 3836
n.dpn a.npm cj v.api.3p p.a d.apf n.apf d.gsf

Ἰουδαίας καὶ Σαμαρείας πλὴν τῶν ἀποστόλων. 2 συνεκόμισαν δὲ τὸν
Judea and Samaria, except the apostles. Devout men buried *{and}* *{the}*
2677 2779 4899 4440 3836 693 2327 467 5172 1254 3836
n.gsf cj n.gsf p.g d.gpm n.gpm v.aai.3p cj d.asm

NASB

heard this, they
were cut to the
quick, and they
began gnashing
their teeth at him.
55 But being full of
the Holy Spirit, he
gazed intently into
heaven and saw the
glory of God, and
Jesus standing at
the right hand of
God; 56 and he said,
"Behold, I see the
heavens opened up
and the Son of Man
standing at the
right hand of God."
57 But they cried out
with a loud voice,
and covered their
ears and rushed at
him with one im-
pulse. 58 When they
had driven him out
of the city, they
began stoning *him;*
and the witnesses
laid aside their
robes at the feet
of a young man
named Saul. 59 They
went on stoning
Stephen as he
called on *the Lord*
and said, "Lord
Jesus, receive my
spirit!" 60 Then fall-
ing on his knees,
he cried out with a
loud voice, "Lord,
do not hold this
sin against them!"
Having said this,
he fell asleep.

Saul Persecutes the Church

8:1 Saul was in
hearty agreement
with putting him to
death.
And on that day
a great persecution
began against the
church in Jeru-
salem, and they
were all scattered
throughout the re-
gions of Judea and
Samaria, except the
apostles. 2 *Some* de-
vout men buried

NIV

Stephen and mourned deeply for him. 3 But Saul began to destroy the church. Going from house to house, he dragged off both men and women and put them in prison.

Philip in Samaria

4 Those who had been scattered preached the word wherever they went. 5 Philip went down to a city in Samaria and proclaimed the Messiah there. 6 When the crowds heard Philip and saw the signs he performed, they all paid close attention to what he said. 7 For with shrieks, impure spirits came out of many, and many who were paralyzed or lame were healed. 8 So there was great joy in that city.

Simon the Sorcerer

9 Now for some time a man named Simon had practiced sorcery in the city and amazed all the people of Samaria. He boasted that he was someone great, 10 and all the people, both high and low, gave him their attention and exclaimed, "This man is rightly called the Great Power of God." 11 They followed him because he had amazed them for a long time

Στέφανον ἄνδρες εὐλαβεῖς καὶ ἐποίησαν κοπετὸν μέγαν ἐπ' αὐτῷ. 3
Stephen *men* *Devout* and made great lamentation *great* over him. But
5108 467 2327 2779 4472 3489 3157 3489 2093 899 1254
n.asm n.npm a.npm cj v.aai.3p n.asm a.asm p.d r.dsm.3

Σαῦλος δὲ ἐλυμαίνετο τὴν ἐκκλησίαν κατὰ τοὺς οἴκους
Saul *But* ⌊was making havoc of⌋ the church; entering every *{the}* house,
4930 1254 3381 3836 1711 1660 2848 3836 3875
n.nsm cj v.imi.3s d.asf n.asf p.a d.apm n.apm

εἰσπορευόμενος, → σύρων τε ἄνδρας καὶ γυναῖκας παρεδίδου εἰς
entering he ⌊dragged off⌋ both men and women and put them in
1660 4140 5359 5445 467 2779 1222 4140 1650
pt.pm.nsm pt.pa.nsm cj n.apm cj n.apf v.iai.3s p.a

φυλακήν. 4 οἱ μὲν οὖν διασπαρέντες διῆλθον εὐαγγελιζόμενοι
prison. Now those ~ *Now* who were scattered ⌊went from place to place⌋ preaching
5871 4036 3836 3525 4036 1401 1451 2294
n.asf d.npm pl cj pt.ap.npm v.aai.3p pt.pm.npm

τὸν λόγον. 5 Φίλιππος δὲ κατελθὼν εἰς τὴν[a] πόλιν τῆς Σαμαρείας
the word. Philip *{and}* went down to the main city of Samaria and
3836 3364 5805 1254 2982 1650 3836 4484 3836 4899
d.asm n.asm n.nsm cj pt.aa.nsm p.a d.asf n.asf d.gsf n.gsf

ἐκήρυσσεν αὐτοῖς τὸν Χριστόν. 6 προσεῖχον
began proclaiming to them the Christ. And with one accord the crowds ⌊paid attention to⌋
3062 899 3836 5986 1254 3924 3924 3924 3836 4063 4668
v.iai.3s r.dpm.3 d.asm n.asm v.iai.3p

δὲ οἱ ὄχλοι τοῖς λεγομένοις ὑπὸ τοῦ Φιλίππου ὁμοθυμαδὸν ἐν τῷ
And *the* *crowds* what was being said by *{the}* Philip *with one accord* as *{the}* they
1254 3836 4063 3836 3306 5679 3836 5805 3924 1877 3836 899
cj d.npm n.npm d.dpn pt.pp.dpn p.g d.gsm n.gsm adv p.d d.dsn

ἀκούειν αὐτοὺς καὶ βλέπειν τὰ σημεῖα ἃ ἐποίει. 7 πολλοὶ γὰρ
heard *they* him and saw the signs that ⌊he was performing.⌋ For many *For*
201 899 2779 1063 3836 4956 4005 4472 1142 4498 1142
f.pa r.apm.3 cj f.pa d.apn n.apn r.apn v.iai.3s a.npm cj

τῶν ἐχόντων πνεύματα ἀκάθαρτα βοῶντα → φωνῇ μεγάλῃ ἐξήρχοντο,
of those who had unclean spirits, *unclean* crying with a loud voice, *loud* came out;
3836 2400 176 4460 176 1066 3489 5889 3489 2002
d.gpm pt.pa.gpm n.apn a.apn pt.pa.apn n.dsf a.dsf v.imi.3p

πολλοὶ δὲ παραλελυμένοι καὶ χωλοὶ ἐθεραπεύθησαν· 8 ἐγένετο δὲ πολλὴ
and many *and* paralyzed and lame were healed. So there was *So* great
1254 4498 1254 4168 2779 6000 2543 1254 1181 1254 4498
a.npm cj pt.rp.npm cj a.npm v.api.3p v.ami.3s cj a.nsf

χαρὰ ἐν τῇ πόλει ἐκείνῃ. 9 ἀνὴρ δέ τις ὀνόματι Σίμων
joy in *{the}* that city. *that* Now there was a man *Now* *a* named Simon,
5915 1877 3836 1697 4484 1697 1254 4732 4732 5516 467 1254 5516 3950 4981
n.nsf p.d d.dsf n.dsf r.dsf n.nsm cj r.nsm n.dsn n.nsm

προϋπῆρχεν ἐν τῇ πόλει μαγεύων καὶ
there was who had been practicing magic in the city *who had been practicing magic* and
4732 3405 3405 3405 3405 3405 1877 3836 4484 3405 2779
v.iai.3s p.d d.dsf n.dsf pt.pa.nsm cj

ἐξιστάνων τὸ ἔθνος τῆς Σαμαρείας, λέγων → εἶναί τινα ἑαυτὸν μέγαν,
amazing the people of Samaria, saying that he himself was someone *himself* great.
2014 3836 1620 3836 4899 3306 1571 1639 5516 1571 3489
pt.pa.nsm d.asn n.asn d.gsf n.gsf pt.pa.nsm f.pa r.asm r.asm.3 a.asm

10 ᾧ προσεῖχον πάντες ἀπὸ μικροῦ ἕως μεγάλου
They all paid attention ⌊to him,⌋ *They paid attention* *all* from the least to the greatest,
4668 4246 4668 4668 4005 4668 4246 608 3625 2401 3489
r.dsm v.iai.3p a.npm p.g a.gsm p.g a.gsm

λέγοντες, οὗτός ἐστιν ἡ δύναμις τοῦ θεοῦ ἡ καλουμένη μεγάλη. 11
saying, "This man is the power of God, which is called Great." And
3306 4047 1639 3836 1539 3836 2536 3836 2813 3489 1254
pt.pa.npm r.nsm v.pai.3s d.nsf n.nsf d.gsm n.gsm d.nsf pt.pp.nsf a.nsf

προσεῖχον δὲ αὐτῷ διὰ τὸ → ἱκανῷ χρόνῳ ταῖς
they paid attention *And* to him because *{the}* for a long time he had amazed them by his
4668 1254 899 1328 3836 2653 5989 2014 2014 2014 899 3836
v.iai.3p cj r.dsm.3 p.a d.asn a.dsm n.dsm d.dpf

NASB

Stephen, and made loud lamentation over him. 3 But Saul *began* ravaging the church, entering house after house, and dragging off men and women, he would put them in prison.

Philip in Samaria

4 Therefore, those who had been scattered went about preaching the word. 5 Philip went down to the city of Samaria and *began* proclaiming Christ to them. 6 The crowds with one accord were giving attention to what was said by Philip, as they heard and saw the signs which he was performing. 7 For *in the case of* many who had unclean spirits, they were coming out *of them* shouting with a loud voice; and many who had been paralyzed and lame were healed. 8 So there was much rejoicing in that city.

9 Now there was a man named Simon, who formerly was practicing magic in the city and astonishing the people of Samaria, claiming to be someone great; 10 and they all, from smallest to greatest, were giving attention to him, saying, "This man is what is called the Great Power of God." 11 And they were giving him attention because he had for a long time astonished them

[a] [τὴν] UBS, omitted by TNIV.

NIV

with his sorcery.
12 But when they
believed Philip as
he proclaimed the
good news of the
kingdom of God
and the name of
Jesus Christ, they
were baptized,
both men and
women. 13 Simon
himself believed
and was baptized.
And he followed
Philip everywhere,
astonished by the
great signs and
miracles he saw.
14 When the apos-
tles in Jerusalem
heard that Samaria
had accepted the
word of God, they
sent Peter and
John to Samaria.
15 When they ar-
rived, they prayed
for the new be-
lievers there that
they might receive
the Holy Spirit,
16 because the Holy
Spirit had not yet
come on any of
them; they had
simply been bap-
tized in the name
of the Lord Jesus.
17 Then Peter and
John placed their
hands on them,
and they received
the Holy Spirit.
18 When Simon
saw that the Spirit
was given at the
laying on of the
apostles' hands,
he offered them
money 19 and said,
"Give me also this
ability so that ev-
eryone on whom I
lay my hands may
receive the Holy
Spirit."
20 Peter answered:
"May your money
perish with you,

μαγείαις ἐξεστακέναι αὐτούς. 12 ὅτε δὲ ἐπίστευσαν τῷ Φιλίππῳ
magic. *he had amazed* *them* But when *But* they believed *{the}* Philip
3404 2014 899 1254 4021 1254 4409 3836 5805
n.dpf f.ra r.apm.3 cj cj v.aai.3p d.dsm n.dsm

εὐαγγελιζομένῳ περὶ τῆς βασιλείας τοῦ θεοῦ καὶ τοῦ ὀνόματος Ἰησοῦ Χριστοῦ,
as he preached about the kingdom of God and the name of Jesus Christ,
2294 4309 3836 993 3836 2536 2779 3836 3950 2652 5986
pt.pm.dsm p.g d.gsf n.gsf d.gsm n.gsm cj d.gsn n.gsn n.gsm n.gsm

ἐβαπτίζοντο ἄνδρες τε καὶ γυναῖκες. 13 ὁ δὲ Σίμων καὶ αὐτὸς
they were baptized, both men *both* and women. *{the}* *{and}* Even Simon *Even* himself
966 5445 467 5445 2779 1222 3836 1254 2779 4981 2779 899
v.ipi.3p n.npm cj cj n.npf d.nsm cj n.nsm adv r.nsm

ἐπίστευσεν καὶ βαπτισθεὶς ⌊ἦν προσκαρτερῶν⌋ τῷ Φιλίππῳ,
believed, and after being baptized he stayed constantly with *{the}* Philip.
4409 2779 966 1639 4674 3836 5805
v.aai.3s cj pt.ap.nsm v.iai.3s pt.pa.nsm d.dsm n.dsm

θεωρῶν τε σημεῖα καὶ δυνάμεις μεγάλας γινομένας ἐξίστατο.
And seeing *And* signs and great miracles *great* happening, he was amazed.
5445 2555 5445 4956 2779 3489 1539 3489 1181 2014
pt.pa.nsm cj n.apn cj n.apf a.apf pt.pm.apf v.imi.3s

14 ἀκούσαντες δὲ οἱ ἐν Ἱεροσολύμοις ἀπόστολοι ὅτι
when heard Now when the apostles in Jerusalem *apostles* heard that Samaria
201 1254 201 3836 693 1877 2642 693 201 4022 4899
pt.aa.npm cj d.npm p.d n.dpn n.npm cj

δέδεκται ἡ Σαμάρεια τὸν λόγον τοῦ θεοῦ, ἀπέστειλαν πρὸς αὐτοὺς Πέτρον καὶ
had received *{the}* *Samaria* the word of God, they sent to them Peter and
1312 3836 4899 3836 3364 3836 2536 690 4639 899 4377 2779
v.rmi.3s d.nsf n.nsf d.asm n.asm d.gsm n.gsm v.aai.3p p.a r.apm.3 n.asm cj

Ἰωάννην, 15 οἵτινες καταβάντες προσηύξαντο περὶ αὐτῶν ὅπως λάβωσιν
John, who went down and prayed for them that ⌊they might receive⌋
2722 4015 2849 4667 4309 899 3968 3284
n.asm r.npm pt.aa.npm v.ami.3p p.g r.gpm.3 cj v.aas.3p

πνεῦμα ἅγιον. 16 οὐδέπω γὰρ ἦν ἐπ' οὐδενὶ αὐτῶν
the Holy Spirit, *Holy* for he had not yet *for* *he had* fallen on any one of them,
41 4460 41 1142 1639 1639 4031 1142 1639 2158 2093 4029 899
n.asn a.asn adv cj v.iai.3s p.d a.dsm r.gpm.3

ἐπιπεπτωκός, μόνον δὲ βεβαπτισμένοι ὑπῆρχον εἰς τὸ ὄνομα τοῦ
fallen but they had simply *but* been baptized *they had* in the name of the
2158 1254 5639 5639 3667 1254 966 5639 1650 3836 3950 3836
pt.ra.nsn adv cj pt.rp.npm v.iai.3p p.a d.asn n.asn d.gsm

κυρίου Ἰησοῦ. 17 τότε ἐπετίθεσαν τὰς χεῖρας ἐπ' αὐτοὺς καὶ
Lord Jesus. Then Peter and John laid *{the}* hands on them and
3261 2652 5538 2202 3836 5931 2093 899 2779
n.gsm n.gsm adv v.iai.3p d.apf n.apf p.a r.apm.3 cj

ἐλάμβανον πνεῦμα ἅγιον. 18 → ἰδὼν δὲ ὁ Σίμων ὅτι
they received the Holy Spirit. *Holy* But when Simon saw *But* *{the}* *Simon* that it was
3284 41 4460 41 1254 4981 1625 1254 3836 4981 4022
v.iai.3p n.asn a.asn pt.aa.nsm cj d.nsm n.nsm cj

διὰ τῆς ἐπιθέσεως τῶν χειρῶν τῶν ἀποστόλων δίδοται τὸ
through the laying on of the hands of the apostles that the Spirit was given, *the*
1328 3836 2120 3836 5931 3836 693 3836 4460 1443 3836
p.g d.gsf n.gsf d.gpf n.gpf d.gpm n.gpm v.ppi.3s d.nsn

πνεῦμα, προσήνεγκεν αὐτοῖς χρήματα 19 λέγων, δότε κἀμοὶ τὴν ἐξουσίαν
Spirit he offered them money, saying, "Give me also *{the}* this power,
4460 4712 899 5975 3306 1443 2743 3836 4047 2026
n.nsn v.aai.3s r.dpm.3 n.apn pt.pa.nsm v.aam.2p crasis d.asf n.asf

ταύτην ἵνα ⌊ᾧ ἐὰν⌋ ἐπιθῶ τὰς χεῖρας λαμβάνῃ πνεῦμα ἅγιον.
this that anyone on whom I lay *{the}* hands may receive the Holy Spirit." *Holy*
4047 2671 4005 1569 2202 3836 5931 3284 41 4460 41
r.asf cj r.dsm pl v.aas.1s d.apf n.apf v.pas.3s n.asn a.asn

20 Πέτρος δὲ εἶπεν πρὸς αὐτόν, τὸ ἀργύριόν σου σὺν σοὶ εἴη
But Peter *But* said to him, "May *{the}* your silver *your* go with you *May go*
1254 4377 1254 3306 4639 899 1639 3836 5148 736 5148 1639 5250 5148 1639
n.nsm cj v.aai.3s p.a r.asm.3 d.nsn n.nsn r.gs.2 p.d r.ds.2 v.pao.3s

NASB

with his magic
arts. 12 But when
they believed
Philip preaching
the good news
about the kingdom
of God and the
name of Jesus
Christ, they were
being baptized,
men and women
alike. 13 Even
Simon himself
believed; and after
being baptized, he
continued on with
Philip, and as he
observed signs and
great miracles tak-
ing place, he was
constantly amazed.
14 Now when
the apostles in
Jerusalem heard
that Samaria had
received the word
of God, they sent
them Peter and
John, 15 who came
down and prayed
for them that they
might receive the
Holy Spirit. 16 For
He had not yet
fallen upon any
of them; they had
simply been bap-
tized in the name
of the Lord Jesus.
17 Then they *began*
laying their hands
on them, and they
were receiving the
Holy Spirit. 18 Now
when Simon saw
that the Spirit was
bestowed through
the laying on of the
apostles' hands, he
offered them mon-
ey, 19 saying, "Give
this authority to
me as well, so that
everyone on whom
I lay my hands may
receive the Holy
Spirit." 20 But Peter
said to him, "May
your silver perish
with you, because

NIV

because you
thought you could
buy the gift of
God with money!
21 You have no part
or share in this
ministry, because
your heart is not
right before God.
22 Repent of this
wickedness and
pray to the Lord
in the hope that he
may forgive you
for having such
a thought in your
heart. 23 For I see
that you are full of
bitterness and cap-
tive to sin."
24 Then Simon
answered, "Pray
to the Lord for me
so that nothing you
have said may hap-
pen to me."
25 After they had
further proclaimed
the word of the
Lord and testified
about Jesus, Peter
and John returned
to Jerusalem,
preaching the gos-
pel in many Sa-
maritan villages.

Philip and the Ethiopian

26 Now an angel
of the Lord said to
Philip, "Go south
to the road—the
desert road—that
goes down from
Jerusalem to
Gaza." 27 So he
started out, and on
his way he met an
Ethiopian[a] eunuch,
an important offi-
cial in charge of all
the treasury of the
Kandake (which
means "queen of
the Ethiopians").
This man had gone
to Jerusalem to
worship,

[a] 27 That is, from the southern Nile region

εἰς ἀπώλειαν ὅτι τὴν δωρεὰν τοῦ θεοῦ ἐνόμισας διὰ
to destruction, because you thought you could obtain the gift of God *you thought* with
1650 724 4022 3787 3787 3227 3227 3227 3836 1561 3836 2536 3787 1328
p.a n.asf cj d.asf n.asf d.gsm n.gsm v.aai.2s p.g

χρημάτων κτᾶσθαι· 21 οὐκ ἔστιν σοι μερὶς οὐδὲ κλῆρος ἐν τῷ
money! *you could obtain* There is not *There is* ⌞for you⌟ a part or share in *{the}*
5975 3227 1639 1639 4024 1639 5148 3535 4028 3102 1877 3836
n.gpn f.pm pl v.pai.3s r.ds.2 n.nsf cj n.nsm p.d d.dsm

λόγῳ τούτῳ, ἡ γὰρ καρδία σου οὐκ ἔστιν εὐθεῖα ἔναντι τοῦ θεοῦ.
this matter, *this* *{the}* for your heart *your* is not *is* upright before *{the}* God.
4047 3364 4047 3836 1142 5148 2840 5148 1639 4024 1639 2318 1882 3836 2536
n.dsm r.dsm d.nsf cj n.nsf r.gs.2 pl v.pai.3s a.nsf p.g d.gsm n.gsm

22 μετανόησον οὖν ἀπὸ τῆς κακίας σου ταύτης καὶ δεήθητι τοῦ
Repent, therefore, of *{the}* this wickedness of yours, *this* and pray to the
3566 4036 608 3836 4047 2798 5148 4047 2779 1289 3836
v.aam.2s cj p.g d.gsf n.gsf r.gs.2 r.gsf cj v.apm.2s d.gsm

κυρίου, εἰ ἄρα ἀφεθήσεταί σοι ἡ ἐπίνοια τῆς
Lord that, if possible, the intent of your heart may be forgiven you. *the* *intent* *of*
3261 1623 726 3836 2154 3836 5148 2840 918 5148 3836 2154 3836
n.gsm cj cj v.fpi.3s r.ds.2 d.nsf n.nsf d.gsf

καρδίας σου. 23 εἰς γὰρ χολὴν πικρίας καὶ
heart *your* For I see that you are in *For* the gall of bitterness and in the
2840 5148 1142 3972 3972 5148 1639 1650 1142 5958 4394 2779 1650
n.gsf r.gs.2 p.a cj n.asf n.gsf cj

σύνδεσμον ἀδικίας ὁρῶ σε ὄντα. 24 ἀποκριθεὶς δὲ ὁ Σίμων
bond of unrighteousness." *I see* *you* *are* And answering, *And* *{the}* Simon
5278 94 3972 5148 1639 1254 646 1254 3836 4981
n.asm n.gsf v.pai.1s r.as.2 pt.pa.asm pt.ap.nsm cj d.nsm n.nsm

εἶπεν, δεήθητε ὑμεῖς ὑπὲρ ἐμοῦ πρὸς τὸν κύριον ὅπως μηδὲν
said, "You pray *You* for me to the Lord so that nothing of what you have
3306 7007 1289 7007 5642 1609 4639 3836 3261 3968 3594 4005 4005 3306 3306
v.aai.3s v.apm.2p r.np.2 p.g r.gs.1 p.a d.asm n.asm cj a.nsn

ἐπέλθῃ ἐπ' ἐμὲ ὧν εἰρήκατε. 25 οἱ μὲν οὖν διαμαρτυράμενοι καὶ
said may come upon me." *of what* *you have said* *{the}* ~ Now after solemnly testifying and
3306 2088 2093 1609 4005 3306 3836 3525 4036 1371 2779
v.aas.3s p.a r.as.1 r.gpn v.rai.2p d.npm pl cj pt.am.npm cj

λαλήσαντες τὸν λόγον τοῦ κυρίου ὑπέστρεφον εἰς Ἱεροσόλυμα,
speaking the word of the Lord, they returned to Jerusalem, preaching the gospel
3281 3836 3364 3836 3261 5715 1650 2642 2294 2294 2294
pt.aa.npm d.asm n.asm d.gsm n.gsm v.iai.3p p.a n.apn

πολλάς τε κώμας τῶν Σαμαριτῶν εὐηγγελίζοντο. 26 ἄγγελος δὲ
to many ~ villages of the Samaritans. *preaching the gospel to* Now an angel *Now* of
2294 4498 5445 3267 3836 4901 2294 1254 34 1254
a.apf cj n.apf d.gpm n.gpm v.imi.3p n.nsm cj

κυρίου ἐλάλησεν πρὸς Φίλιππον λέγων, ἀνάστηθι καὶ πορεύου κατὰ
the Lord spoke to Philip, saying, "Rise and go toward the
3261 3281 4639 5805 3306 482 2779 4513 2848
n.gsm v.aai.3s p.a n.asm pt.pa.nsm v.aam.2s cj v.pmm.2s p.a

μεσημβρίαν ἐπὶ τὴν ὁδὸν τὴν καταβαίνουσαν ἀπὸ Ἰερουσαλὴμ εἰς Γάζαν, αὕτη
south on the road that goes down from Jerusalem to Gaza." This
3540 2093 3836 3847 3836 2849 608 2647 1650 1124 4047
n.asf p.a d.asf n.asf d.asf pt.pa.asf p.g n.gsf p.a n.asf r.nsf

ἐστὶν ἔρημος. 27 καὶ ἀναστὰς ἐπορεύθη. καὶ ἰδοὺ ⌞ἀνὴρ
is a desert place. And he rose and went. And ⌞there was⌟ an Ethiopian,
1639 2245 2779 4513 482 4513 2779 2627 467
v.pai.3s a.nsf cj pt.aa.nsm v.api.3s cj j n.nsm

Αἰθίοψ⌟ εὐνοῦχος δυνάστης Κανδάκης βασιλίσσης Αἰθιόπων, ὃς ἦν
a eunuch, a court official of Candace, queen of the Ethiopians, who was
134 2336 1541 2833 999 134 4005 1639
n.nsm n.nsm n.nsm n.gsf n.gsf n.gpm r.nsm v.iai.3s

ἐπὶ πάσης τῆς γάζης αὐτῆς, ὃς ἐληλύθει προσκυνήσων
⌞in charge of⌟ all *{the}* her treasure, *her* who had come to Jerusalem to worship
2093 4246 3836 899 1125 899 4005 2262 1650 2647 4686
p.g a.gsf d.gsf n.gsf r.gsf.3 r.nsm v.lai.3s pt.fa.nsm

NASB

you thought you
could obtain the
gift of God with
money! 21 You have
no part or portion
in this matter, for
your heart is not
right before God.
22 Therefore repent
of this wickedness
of yours, and pray
the Lord that, if
possible, the inten-
tion of your heart
may be forgiven
you. 23 For I see
that you are in the
gall of bitterness
and in the bondage
of iniquity." 24 But
Simon answered
and said, "Pray to
the Lord for me
yourselves, so that
nothing of what
you have said may
come upon me."

An Ethiopian Receives Christ

25 So, when they
had solemnly testi-
fied and spoken the
word of the Lord,
they started back
to Jerusalem, and
were preaching
the gospel to many
villages of the Sa-
maritans.
26 But an angel of
the Lord spoke to
Philip saying, "Get
up and go south
to the road that
descends from Je-
rusalem to Gaza."
(This is a desert
road.) 27 So he
got up and went;
and there was an
Ethiopian eunuch,
a court official of
Candace, queen
of the Ethiopians,
who was in charge
of all her treasure;
and he had come to
Jerusalem to

NIV

[28]and on his way
home was sitting
in his chariot read-
ing the Book of
Isaiah the prophet.
[29]The Spirit told
Philip, "Go to that
chariot and stay
near it."
[30]Then Philip ran
up to the chariot
and heard the man
reading Isaiah the
prophet. "Do you
understand what
you are reading?"
Philip asked.
[31]"How can I,"
he said, "unless
someone explains
it to me?" So he
invited Philip to
come up and sit
with him.
[32]This is the pas-
sage of Scripture
the eunuch was
reading:

"He was led like
a sheep
to the
slaughter,
and as a lamb
before its
shearer is
silent,
so he did not
open his
mouth.
[33]In his
humiliation
he was
deprived of
justice.
Who can
speak of
his descendants?
For his life
was taken
from the
earth."[a]

[34]The eunuch
asked Philip, "Tell
me, please, who is
the prophet talking
about, himself or
someone else?"
[35]Then Philip be-
gan with that very
passage of Scrip-
ture and told him
the good news
about Jesus.
[36]As they traveled
along the

εἰς Ἰερουσαλήμ, 28 ἦν τε ὑποστρέφων καὶ καθήμενος ἐπὶ τοῦ ἅρματος
to Jerusalem and was and returning, {and} seated in {the} his carriage,
1650 2647 5445 1639 5445 5715 2779 2764 2093 3836 899 761
p.a n.asf v.iai.3s cj pt.pa.nsm cj pt.pm.nsm p.g d.gsn n.gsn

αὐτοῦ καὶ ἀνεγίνωσκεν τὸν προφήτην Ἠσαΐαν. 29 εἶπεν δὲ τὸ
his and he was reading the prophet Isaiah. And the Spirit said And the
899 2779 336 3836 4737 2480 1254 3836 4460 3306 1254 3836
r.gsm.3 cj v.iai.3s d.asm n.asm n.asm v.aai.3s cj d.nsn

πνεῦμα τῷ Φιλίππῳ, πρόσελθε καὶ κολλήθητι τῷ ἅρματι τούτῳ. 30
Spirit to Philip, "Go over and join {the} this carriage." this So Philip
4460 3836 5805 4665 2779 3140 3836 4047 761 4047 1254 5805
n.nsn d.dsm n.dsm v.aam.2s cj v.apm.2s d.dsn n.dsn r.dsn

προσδραμὼν δὲ ὁ Φίλιππος ἤκουσεν αὐτοῦ ἀναγινώσκοντος Ἠσαΐαν τὸν
ran to So {the} Philip him and heard him reading Isaiah the
4708 1254 3836 5805 201 899 336 2480 3836
pt.aa.nsm cj d.nsm n.nsm v.aai.3s r.gsm.3 pt.pa.gsm n.asm d.asm

προφήτην καὶ εἶπεν, ἆρά γε γινώσκεις ἃ ἀναγινώσκεις; 31 ὁ δὲ
prophet and he said, {then} ~ "Do you understand what you are reading?" And he And
4737 2779 3306 727 1145 1182 4005 336 1254 3836 1254
n.asm cj v.aai.3s pl pl v.pai.2s r.apn v.pai.2s d.nsm cj

εἶπεν, πῶς γὰρ ⌊ἂν δυναίμην⌋ ⌊ἐὰν μή⌋ τις ὁδηγήσει με; παρεκάλεσέν
said, "How {for} could I unless someone guide me?" And he invited
3306 4802 1142 323 1538 1569 3590 5516 3842 1609 5445 4151
v.aai.3s cj cj pl v.ppo.1s cj pl r.nsm v.fai.3s r.as.1 v.aai.3s

τε τὸν Φίλιππον ἀναβάντα καθίσαι σὺν αὐτῷ. 32 ἡ δὲ περιοχὴ τῆς
And {the} Philip to come up and sit with him. Now the Now passage of
5445 3836 5805 326 2767 5250 899 1254 3836 1254 4343 3836
cj d.asm n.asm pt.aa.asm f.aa p.d r.dsm.3 d.nsf cj n.nsf d.gsf

γραφῆς ἣν ἀνεγίνωσκεν ἦν αὕτη· ὡς πρόβατον ἐπὶ σφαγὴν
scripture the man was reading was this: "As a sheep to the slaughter
1210 4005 336 1639 4047 6055 4585 2093 5375
n.gsf r.asf v.iai.3s v.iai.3s r.nsf pl n.nsn p.a n.asf

ἤχθη καὶ ὡς ἀμνὸς ἐναντίον τοῦ κείραντος αὐτὸν ἄφωνος, οὕτως
⌊he was led,⌋ and as a lamb dumb before {the} its shearer, its dumb so
72 2779 6055 303 936 1883 3836 899 3025 899 936 4048
v.api.3s cj cj n.nsm p.g d.gsm pt.aa.gsm r.asm.3 a.nsm adv

οὐκ ἀνοίγει τὸ στόμα αὐτοῦ. 33 ἐν τῇ ταπεινώσει[a] ἡ κρίσις
he opens not he opens {the} his mouth. his In {the} humiliation {the} justice was
487 487 4024 487 3836 899 5125 899 1877 3836 5428 3836 3213 149
pl v.pai.3s d.asn n.asn r.gsm.3 p.d d.dsf n.dsf d.nsf n.nsf

αὐτοῦ ἤρθη· τὴν γενεὰν αὐτοῦ τίς διηγήσεται; ὅτι
taken from him. was taken {the} His family history His who will declare? For his life
149 899 149 3836 899 1155 899 5515 1455 4022 899 2437
r.gsm.3 v.api.3s d.asf n.asf r.gsm.3 r.nsm v.fmi.3s cj

αἴρεται ἀπὸ τῆς γῆς ἡ ζωὴ αὐτοῦ. 34 ἀποκριθεὶς δὲ ὁ εὐνοῦχος
is taken away from the earth." {the} life his And in answer And the eunuch said
149 608 3836 1178 3836 2437 899 1254 646 1254 3836 2336 3306
v.ppi.3s p.g d.gsf n.gsf d.nsf n.nsf r.gsm.3 pt.ap.nsm cj d.nsm n.nsm

τῷ Φιλίππῳ εἶπεν, δέομαί σου, περὶ τίνος ↱ ὁ προφήτης λέγει τοῦτο; περὶ
to Philip, said "I ask you, about whom does the prophet say this, about
3836 5805 3306 1289 5148 4309 5515 3306 3836 4737 3306 4047 4309
d.dsm n.dsm v.aai.3s v.pmi.1s r.gs.2 p.g r.gsm d.nsm n.nsm v.pai.3s r.asn p.g

ἑαυτοῦ ἢ περὶ ἑτέρου τινός; 35 ἀνοίξας δὲ ὁ Φίλιππος τὸ
himself or about someone else?" someone Then Philip opened Then {the} Philip {the}
1571 2445 4309 5516 2283 5516 1254 5805 487 1254 3836 5805 3836
r.gsm.3 cj p.g r.gsm r.gsm pt.aa.nsm cj d.nsm n.nsm d.asn

στόμα αὐτοῦ καὶ ἀρξάμενος ἀπὸ τῆς γραφῆς ταύτης
his mouth, his and beginning from {the} this Scripture this
899 5125 899 2779 806 608 3836 4047 1210 4047
n.asn r.gsm.3 cj pt.am.nsm p.g d.gsf n.gsf r.gsf

εὐηγγελίσατο αὐτῷ τὸν Ἰησοῦν. 36 ὡς δὲ ἐπορεύοντο κατὰ τὴν
⌊he announced the good news⌋ to him, {the} Jesus. And as And they traveled along the
2294 899 3836 2652 1254 6055 1254 4513 2848 3836
v.ami.3s r.dsm.3 d.asm n.asm cj cj v.imi.3p p.a d.asf

NASB

worship, [28]and
he was returning
and sitting in his
chariot, and was
reading the prophet
Isaiah. [29]Then
the Spirit said to
Philip, "Go up and
join this chariot."
[30]Philip ran up and
heard him reading
Isaiah the prophet,
and said, "Do you
understand what
you are reading?"
[31]And he said,
"Well, how could
I, unless someone
guides me?" And
he invited Philip
to come up and sit
with him. [32]Now
the passage of
Scripture which he
was reading was
this:
"HE WAS LED AS
A SHEEP TO
SLAUGHTER;
AND AS A LAMB
BEFORE ITS
SHEARER IS
SILENT,
SO HE DOES
NOT OPEN HIS
MOUTH.
[33]"IN HUMILIATION
HIS JUDGMENT
WAS TAKEN
AWAY;
WHO WILL
RELATE HIS
GENERATION?
FOR HIS LIFE
IS REMOVED
FROM THE
EARTH."
[34]The eunuch an-
swered Philip and
said, "Please *tell
me,* of whom does
the prophet say
this? Of himself or
of someone else?"
[35]Then Philip
opened his mouth,
and beginning from
this Scripture he
preached Jesus to
him. [36]As they went
along the road they

[a] 33 Isaiah 53:7,8
(see Septuagint)

[a] αὐτοῦ included by UBS after ταπεινώσει.

NIV

road, they came
to some water and
the eunuch said,
"Look, here is
water. What can
stand in the way
of my being bap-
tized?" [37][a] 38 And
he gave orders to
stop the chariot.
Then both Philip
and the eunuch
went down into
the water and Phil-
ip baptized him.
39 When they came
up out of the wa-
ter, the Spirit of
the Lord suddenly
took Philip away,
and the eunuch
did not see him
again, but went on
his way rejoicing.
40 Philip, however,
appeared at Azo-
tus and traveled
about, preaching
the gospel in all
the towns until he
reached Caesarea.

Saul's Conversion

9 Meanwhile,
Saul was still
breathing out
murderous threats
against the Lord's
disciples. He went
to the high priest
2 and asked him
for letters to the
synagogues in Da-
mascus, so that if
he found any there
who belonged to
the Way, whether
men or women,
he might take
them as prison-
ers to Jerusalem.
3 As he neared
Damascus on his
journey, suddenly
a light from heav-
en flashed around
him. 4 He fell to the
ground and heard
a voice say to him,
"Saul,

ὁδόν, ἦλθον ἐπί τι ὕδωρ, καί φησιν ὁ εὐνοῦχος, ἰδοὺ ὕδωρ, τί
road they came to some water; and the eunuch said, *the eunuch* "Look! Water! What
3847 2262 2093 5516 5623 2779 3836 2336 5774 3836 2336 2627 5623 5515
n.asf v.aai.3p p.a r.asn n.asn cj v.pai.3s d.nsm n.nsm j n.nsn r.nsn

κωλύει με ↰ βαπτισθῆναι;[a] 38 καὶ ἐκέλευσεν στῆναι τὸ ἅρμα καὶ
prevents me from being baptized?" And he ordered the carriage to stop, *the carriage* and
3266 1609 3266 966 2779 3027 3836 761 2705 3836 761 2779
v.pai.3s r.as.1 f.ap cj v.aai.3s f.aa d.asn n.asn cj

→ κατέβησαν ἀμφότεροι εἰς τὸ ὕδωρ, ὅ τε Φίλιππος καὶ ὁ εὐνοῦχος,
they both went down *both* into the water, *{the}* both Philip and the eunuch;
317 2849 317 1650 3836 5623 3836 5445 5805 2779 3836 2336
v.aai.3p a.npm p.a d.asn n.asn d.nsm cj n.nsm cj d.nsm n.nsm

καὶ ἐβάπτισεν αὐτόν. 39 ὅτε δὲ ἀνέβησαν ἐκ τοῦ ὕδατος, πνεῦμα →
and he baptized him. And when *And* they came up ⌊out of⌋ the water, the Spirit of the
2779 966 899 1254 4021 1254 326 1666 3836 5623 4460
cj v.aai.3s r.asm.3 cj cj v.aai.3p p.g d.gsn n.gsn n.nsn

κυρίου ἥρπασεν τὸν Φίλιππον ↰ καὶ οὐκ εἶδεν αὐτὸν οὐκέτι
Lord ⌊suddenly took⌋ *{the}* Philip away, and *{not}* the eunuch saw him no more,
3261 773 3836 5805 773 2779 4024 3836 2336 1625 899 4033
n.gsm v.aai.3s d.asm n.asm cj pl v.aai.3s r.asm.3 adv

ὁ εὐνοῦχος, ἐπορεύετο γὰρ τὴν ὁδὸν αὐτοῦ χαίρων. 40 Φίλιππος δὲ
the eunuch but went on *but* *{the}* his way *his* rejoicing. But Philip *But*
3836 2336 1142 4513 1142 3836 899 3847 899 5897 1254 5805 1254
d.nsm n.nsm v.imi.3s cj d.asf n.asf r.gsm.3 pt.pa.nsm n.nsm cj

εὑρέθη εἰς Ἄζωτον· καὶ διερχόμενος εὐηγγελίζετο
was found at Azotus; and ⌊as he traveled through⌋ the area ⌊he announced the good news to⌋
2351 1650 111 2779 1451 2294
v.api.3s p.a n.asf cj pt.pm.nsm v.imi.3s

τὰς πόλεις πάσας ἕως τοῦ ἐλθεῖν αὐτὸν εἰς Καισάρειαν.
all the towns, *all* until *{the}* he came *he* to Caesarea.
4246 3836 4484 4246 2401 3836 899 2262 899 1650 2791
d.apf n.apf a.apf p.g d.gsn f.aa r.asm.3 p.a n.asf

9:1 ὁ δὲ Σαῦλος ἔτι ἐμπνέων ἀπειλῆς καὶ φόνου εἰς τοὺς μαθητὰς τοῦ
{the} But Saul, still breathing threat and murder against the disciples of the
3836 1254 4930 2285 1863 581 2779 5840 1650 3836 3412 3836
d.nsm cj n.nsm adv pt.pa.nsm n.gsf cj n.gsm p.a d.apm n.apm d.gsm

κυρίου, προσελθὼν τῷ ἀρχιερεῖ 2 ᾐτήσατο παρ᾽ αὐτοῦ ἐπιστολὰς εἰς Δαμασκὸν
Lord, went to the high priest and requested from him letters to Damascus
3261 4665 3836 797 160 4123 899 2186 1650 1242
n.gsm pt.aa.nsm d.dsm n.dsm v.ami.3s p.g r.gsm.3 n.apf p.a n.asf

πρὸς τὰς συναγωγάς, ὅπως ἐάν τινας εὕρῃ τῆς ὁδοῦ
addressed to the synagogues, that if he found any *he found* who were of the Way,
4639 3836 5252 3968 1569 2351 2351 5516 2351 1639 1639 3836 3847
p.a d.apf n.apf cj cj r.apm v.aas.3s d.gsf n.gsf

ὄντας, ἄνδρας τε καὶ γυναῖκας, δεδεμένους ἀγάγῃ εἰς
who were men ~ or women, he should bring them bound *he should bring* to
1639 467 5445 2779 1222 72 72 72 1313 72 1650
pt.pa.apm n.apm cj cj n.apf pt.rp.apm v.aas.3s p.a

Ἰερουσαλήμ. 3 ἐν δὲ τῷ πορεύεσθαι ἐγένετο αὐτὸν ἐγγίζειν τῇ
Jerusalem. As *{and}* ~ he traveled along, *{it happened that}* *he* approaching *{the}*
2647 1877 1254 3836 899 4513 1181 899 1581 3836
n.asf p.d cj d.dsn f.pm v.ami.3s r.asm.3 f.pa d.dsf

Δαμασκῷ, ἐξαίφνης τε αὐτὸν περιήστραψεν φῶς ἐκ τοῦ
Damascus, suddenly ~ *him* a light from heaven shone all around him; *light from {the}*
1242 1978 5445 899 5890 1666 4041 4313 899 5890 1666 3836
n.dsf adv cj r.asm.3 v.aai.3s n.nsn p.g d.gsm

οὐρανοῦ 4 καὶ πεσὼν ἐπὶ τὴν γῆν ἤκουσεν φωνὴν λέγουσαν αὐτῷ, Σαοὺλ
heaven and falling to the ground, he heard a voice saying to him, "Saul,
4041 2779 4406 2093 3836 1178 201 5889 3306 899 4910
n.gsm cj pt.aa.nsm p.a d.asf n.asf v.aai.3s n.asf pt.pa.asf r.dsm.3 n.vsm

NASB

came to some wa-
ter; and the eunuch
*said, "Look! Wa-
ter! What prevents
me from being
baptized?" 37 [[a]And
Philip said, "If
you believe with
all your heart, you
may." And he an-
swered and said, "I
believe that Jesus
Christ is the Son of
God."] 38 And he or-
dered the chariot to
stop; and they both
went down into
the water, Philip as
well as the eunuch,
and he baptized
him. 39 When they
came up out of the
water, the Spirit of
the Lord snatched
Philip away; and
the eunuch no lon-
ger saw him, but
went on his way re-
joicing. 40 But Philip
found himself at
Azotus, and as he
passed through he
kept preaching the
gospel to all the
cities until he came
to Caesarea.

The Conversion of Saul

9:1 Now Saul, still
breathing threats
and murder against
the disciples of
the Lord, went to
the high priest,
2 and asked for let-
ters from him to
the synagogues at
Damascus, so that
if he found any
belonging to the
Way, both men and
women, he might
bring them bound
to Jerusalem. 3 As
he was traveling,
it happened that
he was approach-
ing Damascus,
and suddenly a
light from heaven
flashed around
him; 4 and he fell
to the ground and
heard a voice say-
ing to him, "Saul,

[a] 37 Some manuscripts include here *Philip said, "If you believe with all your heart, you may." The eunuch answered, "I believe that Jesus Christ is the Son of God."*

a 37 εἶπε δὲ ὁ Φίλιππος, Εἰ πιστεύεις ἐξ ὅλης τῆς καρδίας, ἔξεστιν. ἀποκριθεὶς δὲ εἶπε, Πιστεύω τὸν υἱὸν τοῦ Θεοῦ εἶναι τὸν Ἰησοῦν Χριστόν. included by TR after βαπτισθῆναι.

[a] Early mss do not contain this v

NIV

Saul, why do you
persecute me?”
[5]“Who are you,
Lord?” Saul asked.
“I am Jesus,
whom you are
persecuting,” he
replied. [6]“Now get
up and go into the
city, and you will
be told what you
must do.”
[7]The men trav-
eling with Saul
stood there
speechless; they
heard the sound
but did not see
anyone. [8]Saul
got up from the
ground, but when
he opened his eyes
he could see noth-
ing. So they led
him by the hand
into Damascus.
[9]For three days he
was blind, and did
not eat or drink
anything.
[10]In Damascus
there was a disci-
ple named Anani-
as. The Lord called
to him in a vision,
“Ananias!”
“Yes, Lord,” he
answered.
[11]The Lord told
him, “Go to the
house of Judas
on Straight Street
and ask for a
man from Tarsus
named Saul, for he
is praying. [12]In a
vision he has seen
a man named An-
anias come and
place his hands on
him to restore his
sight.”

Σαούλ, τί με διώκεις; [5] εἶπεν δέ, τίς εἶ,
Saul, why are you persecuting me?” *are you persecuting* And he said, *And* “Who ⌊are you,⌋
4910 5515 1503 1503 1503 1609 1503 1254 3306 1254 5515 1639
n.vsm r.asn r.as.1 v.pai.2s v.aai.3s cj r.nsm v.pai.2s

κύριε; ὁ δέ, ἐγώ εἰμι Ἰησοῦς ὃν σὺ διώκεις· [6]ἀλλὰ ἀνάστηθι
Lord?” And he *And* said, “I am Jesus, whom you are persecuting. But rise
3261 1254 3836 1254 1609 1639 2652 4005 5148 1503 247 482
n.vsm d.nsm cj r.ns.1 v.pai.1s n.nsm r.asm r.ns.2 v.pai.2s cj v.aam.2s

καὶ εἴσελθε εἰς τὴν πόλιν καὶ λαληθήσεταί σοι ⌊ὅ τί⌋ σε δεῖ ποιεῖν. [7]οἱ
and go into the city, and it will be told you what you must do.” The
2779 1656 1650 3836 4484 2779 3281 5148 4005 5515 5148 1256 4472 3836
cj v.aam.2s p.a d.asf n.asf cj v.fpi.3s r.ds.2 r.asn r.asn r.as.2 v.pai.3s f.pa d.npm

δὲ ἄνδρες οἱ συνοδεύοντες αὐτῷ εἱστήκεισαν ἐνεοί, ἀκούοντες μὲν τῆς
{and} men who were traveling with him stood speechless, hearing ~ the
1254 467 3836 5321 899 2705 1917 201 3525 3836
cj n.npm d.npm pt.pa.npm r.dsm.3 v.lai.3p a.npm pt.pa.npm pl d.gsf

φωνῆς μηδένα δὲ θεωροῦντες. [8] ἠγέρθη δὲ Σαῦλος ἀπὸ τῆς
voice but seeing no one. *but* *seeing* So Saul got up *So* *Saul* from the
5889 1254 2555 3594 1254 2555 1254 4930 1586 1254 4930 608 3836
n.gsf a.asm cj pt.pa.npm v.api.3s cj n.nsm p.g d.gsf

γῆς, → ἀνεῳγμένων δὲ τῶν ὀφθαλμῶν αὐτοῦ
ground, but although his eyes were open, *but* *{the}* *eyes* *his* he could see
1178 1254 899 4057 487 1254 3836 4057 899 1063 1063 1063
n.gsf pt.rp.gpm cj d.gpm n.gpm r.gsm.3

οὐδὲν ἔβλεπεν· χειραγωγοῦντες ← ← ← δὲ αὐτὸν εἰσήγαγον
nothing. *he could see* So they led him by the hand *So* and brought him *brought*
4029 1063 1254 5932 1254 1652 899 1652
a.asn v.iai.3s pt.pa.npm cj r.asm.3 v.aai.3p

εἰς Δαμασκόν. [9]καὶ ἦν ἡμέρας τρεῖς μὴ βλέπων καὶ οὐκ ἔφαγεν οὐδὲ
into Damascus. And ⌊he was⌋ three days *three* without sight and neither ate nor
1650 1242 2779 1639 5552 2465 5552 3590 1063 2779 4024 2266 4028
p.a n.asf cj v.iai.3s n.apf a.apf pl pt.pa.nsm cj pl v.aai.3s cj

ἔπιεν. ↰ [10] ἦν δέ τις μαθητὴς ἐν Δαμασκῷ ὀνόματι Ἁνανίας,
drank anything. Now ⌊there was⌋ *Now* a disciple at Damascus named Ananias;
4403 4028 1254 1639 1254 5516 3412 1877 1242 3950 393
v.aai.3s v.iai.3s cj r.nsm n.nsm p.d n.dsf n.dsn n.nsm

καὶ εἶπεν πρὸς αὐτὸν ἐν ὁράματι ὁ κύριος, Ἁνανία. ὁ δὲ
and the Lord said to him in a vision, *the* *Lord* “Ananias.” And he *And*
2779 3836 3261 3306 4639 899 1877 3969 3836 3261 393 1254 3836 1254
cj v.aai.3s p.a r.asm.3 p.d n.dsn d.nsm n.nsm n.vsm d.nsm cj

εἶπεν, ἰδοὺ ἐγώ, κύριε. [11] ὁ δὲ κύριος πρὸς αὐτόν, ἀναστὰς
replied, “Here I am, Lord.” Then the *Then* Lord told him, “Get up and
3306 2627 1609 3261 1254 3836 1254 3261 4639 899 482
v.aai.3s j r.ns.1 n.vsm d.nsm cj n.nsm p.a r.asm.3 pt.aa.nsm

πορεύθητι ἐπὶ τὴν ῥύμην τὴν καλουμένην Εὐθεῖαν καὶ ζήτησον ἐν οἰκίᾳ Ἰούδα
go to the street *{the}* called ‘Straight,’ and inquire at the house of Judas
4513 2093 3836 4860 3836 2813 2318 2779 2426 1877 3864 2683
v.apm.2s p.a d.asf n.asf d.asf pt.pp.asf a.asf cj v.aam.2s p.d n.dsf n.gsm

→ Σαῦλον ὀνόματι Ταρσέα, ἰδοὺ γὰρ προσεύχεται
for a man from Tarsus named Saul, *named* *from Tarsus* for ⌊even now⌋ *for* he is praying,
5432 5432 3950 4930 3950 5432 1142 2627 1142 4667
n.asm n.dsn n.asm j cj v.pmi.3s

[12] καὶ εἶδεν ἄνδρα [a]ἐν ὁράματι[b] Ἁνανίαν ὀνόματι
and in a vision ⌊he has seen⌋ a man *in* *vision* named Ananias *named*
2779 1877 3969 1625 467 1877 3969 3950 393 3950
cj v.aai.3s n.asm p.d n.dsn n.asm n.dsn

εἰσελθόντα καὶ ἐπιθέντα ← αὐτῷ τὰς[c] χεῖρας ὅπως ἀναβλέψῃ.
come in and lay his hands on him *his* *hands* so that ⌊he might regain his sight.”⌋
1656 2779 2202 3836 5931 899 3836 5931 3968 329
pt.aa.asm cj pt.aa.asm r.dsm.3 d.apf n.apf cj v.aas.3s

[a] [ἐν ὁράματι] UBS, , NET.
[b] ὁράματι omitted in NET.
[c] [τὰς] UBS.

NASB

Saul, why are you
persecuting Me?”
[5]And he said,
“Who are You,
Lord?” And He
said, “I am Jesus
whom you are
persecuting, [6]but
get up and enter
the city, and it will
be told you what
you must do.” [7]The
men who traveled
with him stood
speechless, hearing
the voice but see-
ing no one. [8]Saul
got up from the
ground, and though
his eyes were open,
he could see noth-
ing; and leading
him by the hand,
they brought him
into Damascus.
[9]And he was three
days without sight,
and neither ate nor
drank.
[10]Now there
was a disciple at
Damascus named
Ananias; and the
Lord said to him
in a vision, “Anan-
ias.” And he said,
“Here I am, Lord.”
[11]And the Lord *said*
to him, “Get up
and go to the street
called Straight,
and inquire at the
house of Judas for
a man from Tarsus
named Saul, for he
is praying, [12]and he
has seen [a]in a vi-
sion a man named
Ananias come in
and lay his hands
on him, so that he
might regain his
sight.” [13]But

[a] A few early mss do not contain *in a vision*

NIV

13“Lord,” Anani-
as answered, “I
have heard many
reports about this
man and all the
harm he has done
to your holy peo-
ple in Jerusalem.
14And he has come
here with author-
ity from the chief
priests to arrest all
who call on your
name.”
15But the Lord
said to Ananias,
“Go! This man is
my chosen instru-
ment to proclaim
my name to the
Gentiles and their
kings and to the
people of Israel. 16I
will show him how
much he must suf-
fer for my name.”
17Then Ananias
went to the house
and entered it.
Placing his hands
on Saul, he said,
“Brother Saul,
the Lord—Jesus,
who appeared to
you on the road as
you were coming
here—has sent
me so that you
may see again and
be filled with the
Holy Spirit.” 18Im-
mediately, some-
thing like scales
fell from Saul’s
eyes, and he could
see again. He got
up and was bap-
tized, 19and after
taking some food,
he regained his
strength.

Saul in Damascus and Jerusalem

Saul spent sev-
eral days with the
disciples in Da-
mascus. 20At once
he began to preach
in the synagogues
that Jesus

13 ἀπεκρίθη δὲ Ἁνανίας, κύριε, ἤκουσα ἀπὸ πολλῶν περὶ τοῦ
But Ananias answered, *But Ananias* “Lord, I have heard from many about *{the}* this
1254 393 646 1254 393 3261 201 608 4498 4309 3836 4047
v.api.3s cj n.nsm n.vsm v.aai.1s p.g a.gpm p.g d.gsm

ἀνδρὸς τούτου ὅσα κακὰ τοῖς ἁγίοις σου ἐποίησεν ἐν
man, *this* ⌊how much⌋ harm he did to your saints *your he did* at
467 4047 4012 2805 4472 4472 3836 5148 41 5148 4472 1877
n.gsm r.gsm r.apn a.apn d.dpm a.dpm r.gs.2 v.aai.3s p.d

Ἰερουσαλήμ· 14 καὶ ὧδε ἔχει ἐξουσίαν παρὰ τῶν ἀρχιερέων δῆσαι πάντας τοὺς
Jerusalem. And here he has authority from the chief priests to imprison all who
2647 2779 6045 2400 2026 4123 3836 797 1313 4246 3836
n.dsf cj adv v.pai.3s n.asf p.g d.gpm n.gpm f.aa a.apm d.apm

ἐπικαλουμένους τὸ ὄνομά σου. 15 εἶπεν δὲ πρὸς αὐτὸν ὁ
call on *{the}* your name.” *your* But the Lord said *But* to him, *the*
2126 3836 5148 3950 5148 1254 3836 3261 3306 1254 4639 899 3836
pt.pm.apm d.asn n.asn r.gs.2 v.aai.3s cj p.a r.asm.3 d.nsm

κύριος, πορεύου, ὅτι σκεῦος ἐκλογῆς ἐστίν μοι
Lord “Go, for this man is for me a chosen instrument *chosen is for me*
3261 4513 4022 4047 4047 1639 1609 1609 1724 5007 1724 1639 1609
n.nsm v.pmm.2s cj n.nsn n.gsf v.pai.3s r.ds.1

οὗτος τοῦ βαστάσαι τὸ ὄνομά μου ἐνώπιον ἐθνῶν τε καὶ βασιλέων
this man to carry *{the}* my name *my* before both Gentiles *both* and kings and
4047 3836 1002 3836 1609 3950 1609 1967 5445 1620 5445 2779 995 5445
r.nsm d.gsn f.aa d.asn n.asn r.gs.1 p.g n.gpn cj cj n.gpm

υἱῶν τε Ἰσραήλ· 16 ἐγὼ γὰρ ὑποδείξω αὐτῷ ὅσα δεῖ αὐτὸν
the sons *and* of Israel, for I *for* will show him ⌊how much⌋ he must *he* suffer
5626 5445 2702 1142 1609 1142 5683 899 4012 899 1256 899 4248
n.gpm cj n.gsm r.ns.1 cj v.fai.1s r.dsm.3 r.apn v.pai.3s r.asm.3

ὑπὲρ τοῦ ὀνόματός μου παθεῖν. 17 ἀπῆλθεν δὲ Ἁνανίας καὶ
⌊for the sake⌋ of my name.” *my suffer* So Ananias went *So Ananias* and
5642 3836 1609 3950 1609 4248 1254 393 599 1254 393 2779
p.g d.gsn n.gsn r.gs.1 f.aa v.aai.3s cj n.nsm cj

⌊εἰσῆλθεν εἰς⌋ τὴν οἰκίαν καὶ ↱ ἐπιθεὶς ἐπ᾿ αὐτὸν τὰς χεῖρας
entered the house; *{and}* he placed his hands on Saul *his hands* and
1656 1650 3836 3864 2779 3306 2202 3836 5931 2093 899 3836 5931
v.aai.3s p.a d.asf n.asf cj pt.aa.nsm p.a r.asm.3 d.apf n.apf

εἶπεν, Σαοὺλ ἀδελφέ, ὁ κύριος ἀπέσταλκέν με, Ἰησοῦς ὁ ὀφθείς σοι
said, “Brother Saul, *Brother* the Lord *has sent me* Jesus, who appeared to you
3306 81 4910 81 3836 3261 690 1609 2652 3836 3972 5148
v.aai.3s n.vsm n.vsm d.nsm n.nsm v.rai.3s r.as.1 n.nsm d.nsm pt.ap.nsm r.ds.2

ἐν τῇ ὁδῷ ᾗ ἤρχου, ὅπως ἀναβλέψῃς καὶ
on the road ⌊by which⌋ you came, has sent me so that ⌊you may recover your sight⌋ and
1877 3836 3847 4005 2262 690 690 1609 3968 329 2779
p.d d.dsf n.dsf r.dsf v.imi.2s cj v.aas.2s cj

πλησθῇς πνεύματος ἁγίου. 18 καὶ εὐθέως ἀπέπεσαν
be filled with the Holy Spirit.” *Holy* And immediately something like flakes fell
4398 41 4460 41 2779 2311 6055 3318 674
v.aps.2s n.gsn a.gsn cj adv v.aai.3p

αὐτοῦ ἀπὸ τῶν ὀφθαλμῶν ὡς λεπίδες, ἀνέβλεψέν τε καὶ ↱
from his *from {the}* eyes, *like flakes* and ⌊he regained his sight.⌋ *and* Then he
608 899 608 3836 4057 6055 3318 5445 329 5445 2779 966
r.gsm.3 p.g d.gpm n.gpm pl n.npf v.aai.3s cj cj

ἀναστὰς ἐβαπτίσθη 19 καὶ λαβὼν τροφὴν ἐνίσχυσεν. ἐγένετο δὲ μετὰ
got up and was baptized; and taking food, he was strengthened. And he was *And* with
482 966 2779 3284 5575 1932 1254 1181 1254 3552
pt.aa.nsm v.api.3s cj pt.aa.nsm n.asf v.aai.3s v.ami.3s cj p.g

τῶν ἐν Δαμασκῷ μαθητῶν → ἡμέρας τινὰς 20 καὶ εὐθέως
the disciples in Damascus *disciples* for several days. *several* And right away he
3836 3412 1877 1242 3412 5516 2465 5516 2779 2311 3062
d.gpm p.d n.dsf n.gpm n.apf r.apf cj adv

ἐν ταῖς συναγωγαῖς ἐκήρυσσεν τὸν Ἰησοῦν ὅτι οὗτός
began proclaiming Jesus in the synagogues, *he began proclaiming {the} Jesus* that this man
3062 3062 2652 1877 3836 5252 3062 3836 2652 4022 4047
p.d d.dpf n.dpf v.iai.3s d.asm n.asm cj r.nsm

NASB

Ananias answered,
“Lord, I have heard
from many about
this man, how
much harm he did
to Your saints at
Jerusalem; 14and
here he has author-
ity from the chief
priests to bind all
who call on Your
name.” 15But the
Lord said to him,
“Go, for he is a
chosen [a]instrument
of Mine, to bear
My name before
the Gentiles and
kings and the sons
of Israel; 16for I
will show him how
much he must suf-
fer for My name’s
sake.” 17So Ananias
departed and
entered the house,
and after laying his
hands on him said,
“Brother Saul, the
Lord Jesus, who
appeared to you
on the road by
which you were
coming, has sent
me so that you may
regain your sight
and be filled with
the Holy Spirit.”
18And immediately
there fell from his
eyes something
like scales, and he
regained his sight,
and he got up and
was baptized; 19and
he took food and
was strengthened.

Saul Begins to Preach Christ

Now for several
days he was with
the disciples who
were at Damascus,
20and immediately
he *began* to pro-
claim Jesus in the
synagogues, say-
ing, “He

[a] Or *vessel*

NIV

is the Son of God.
[21] All those who
heard him were
astonished and
asked, "Isn't he the
man who raised
havoc in Jerusa-
lem among those
who call on this
name? And hasn't
he come here to
take them as pris-
oners to the chief
priests?" [22] Yet
Saul grew more
and more power-
ful and baffled the
Jews living in Da-
mascus by proving
that Jesus is the
Messiah.
[23] After many
days had gone by,
there was a con-
spiracy among the
Jews to kill him,
[24] but Saul learned
of their plan. Day
and night they kept
close watch on the
city gates in order
to kill him. [25] But
his followers took
him by night and
lowered him in
a basket through
an opening in the
wall.
[26] When he came
to Jerusalem, he
tried to join the
disciples, but they
were all afraid of
him, not believing
that he really was
a disciple. [27] But
Barnabas took him
and brought him
to the apostles.
He told them how
Saul on his jour-
ney had seen the
Lord and that the
Lord had spoken

ἐστιν ὁ υἱὸς τοῦ θεοῦ. 21 ἐξίσταντο δὲ πάντες οἱ
is the Son of God. And all who heard him were astonished *And all who*
1639 3836 5626 3836 2536 1254 4246 3836 201 2014 1254 4246 3836
v.pai.3s d.nsm n.nsm d.gsm n.gsm v.imi.3p cj a.npm d.npm

ἀκούοντες καὶ ἔλεγον, οὐχ οὗτός ἐστιν ὁ → →
heard and said, "Is not this *Is* the man who in Jerusalem
201 2779 3306 1639 4024 4047 1639 3836 1650 2647
pt.pa.npm cj v.iai.3p pl r.nsm v.pai.3s d.nsm

πορθήσας εἰς Ἰερουσαλὴμ τοὺς ἐπικαλουμένους τὸ ὄνομα τοῦτο, καὶ
⌊was trying to destroy⌋ *in Jerusalem* those who called on *{the}* this name? *this* And
4514 1650 2647 3836 2126 3836 4047 3950 4047 2779
pt.aa.nsm p.a n.asf d.apm pt.pm.apm d.asn n.asn r.asn cj

ὧδε εἰς τοῦτο ἐληλύθει ἵνα δεδεμένους αὐτοὺς
has he not come here for the very purpose *has he come* of bringing them bound *them*
2262 2262 2262 6045 1650 4047 2262 2671 72 899 1313 899
adv p.a r.asn v.lai.3s cj pt.rp.apm r.apm.3

ἀγάγῃ ἐπὶ τοὺς ἀρχιερεῖς; 22 Σαῦλος δὲ ↱ μᾶλλον ἐνεδυναμοῦτο
bringing before the chief priests?" But Saul *But* became ⌊more and more⌋ capable,
72 2093 3836 797 1254 4930 1254 1904 3437 1904
v.aas.3s p.a d.apm n.apm n.nsm cj adv.c v.ipi.3s

καὶ συνέχυννεν τοὺς[a] Ἰουδαίους τοὺς κατοικοῦντας ἐν Δαμασκῷ συμβιβάζων
and threw into confusion the Jews who lived in Damascus by proving
2779 5177 3836 2681 3836 2997 1877 1242 5204
cj v.iai.3s d.apm a.apm d.apm pt.pa.apm p.d n.dsf pt.pa.nsm

ὅτι οὗτός ἐστιν ὁ χριστός. 23 Ὡς δὲ ἐπληροῦντο ἡμέραι
that this man Jesus is the Christ. Now after *Now* some days had passed, *days*
4022 4047 1639 3836 5986 1254 6055 1254 2653 2465 4444 2465
cj r.nsm v.pai.3s d.nsm n.nsm cj cj v.ipi.3p n.npf

ἱκαναί, συνεβουλεύσαντο οἱ Ἰουδαῖοι ἀνελεῖν αὐτόν, 24
some the Jews plotted together *the Jews* to kill him, but their plot
2653 3836 2681 5205 3836 2681 359 899 1254 899 2101
a.npf v.ami.3p d.npm a.npm f.aa r.asm.3

ἐγνώσθη δὲ τῷ Σαύλῳ ἡ ἐπιβουλὴ αὐτῶν. παρετηροῦντο δὲ
⌊was made known⌋ *but* to Saul. *{the} plot their* ⌊They kept close watch on⌋ *{and}*
1182 1254 3836 4930 3836 2101 899 4190 1254
v.api.3s cj d.dsm n.dsm d.nsf n.nsf r.gpm.3 v.imi.3p cj

καὶ τὰς πύλας ἡμέρας τε καὶ νυκτὸς ὅπως αὐτὸν ἀνέλωσιν,
{also} the gates day ~ and night so that they might kill him; *they might kill*
2779 3836 4783 2465 5445 2779 3816 3968 359 359 359 899 359
adv d.apf n.apf n.gsf cj cj n.gsf cj r.asm.3 v.aas.3p

25 λαβόντες δὲ οἱ μαθηταὶ αὐτοῦ νυκτὸς
but his disciples took *but {the} disciples his* him by night and let him down
1254 899 3412 3284 1254 3836 3412 899 3816 2768 899 2768
pt.aa.npm cj d.npm n.npm r.gsm.3 n.gsf

διὰ τοῦ τείχους καθῆκαν αὐτὸν χαλάσαντες ἐν σπυρίδι.
through an opening in the wall, *let down him* lowering him in a basket.
1328 3836 5446 2768 899 5899 1877 5083
p.g d.gsn n.gsn v.aai.3p r.asm.3 pt.aa.npm p.d n.dsf

26 παραγενόμενος δὲ εἰς Ἰερουσαλὴμ ἐπείραζεν κολλᾶσθαι τοῖς μαθηταῖς, καὶ
When he came *{and}* to Jerusalem, he attempted to join the disciples; but
4134 1254 1650 2647 4279 3140 3836 3412 2779
pt.am.nsm cj p.a n.asf v.iai.3s f.pp d.dpm n.dpm cj

↱ ↱ πάντες ἐφοβοῦντο αὐτὸν μὴ πιστεύοντες ὅτι ἐστὶν μαθητής. 27
they were all afraid of him, not believing that he was a disciple. But
5828 5828 4246 5828 899 3590 4409 4022 1639 3412 1254
a.npm v.ipi.3p r.asm.3 pl pt.pa.npm cj v.pai.3s n.nsm

Βαρναβᾶς δὲ ἐπιλαβόμενος αὐτὸν ἤγαγεν πρὸς τοὺς ἀποστόλους καὶ
Barnabas *But* took him and brought him to the apostles and
982 1254 2138 899 72 4639 3836 693 2779
n.nsm cj pt.am.nsm r.asm.3 v.aai.3s p.a d.apm n.apm cj

διηγήσατο αὐτοῖς πῶς ἐν τῇ ὁδῷ εἶδεν τὸν κύριον καὶ ὅτι ἐλάλησεν
he related to them how on the road ⌊he had seen⌋ the Lord, and that the Lord had spoken
1455 899 4802 1877 3836 3847 1625 3836 3261 2779 4022 3281
v.ami.3s r.dpm.3 cj p.d d.dsf n.dsf v.aai.3s d.asm n.asm cj cj v.aai.3s

[a] [τοὺς] UBS.

NASB

is the Son of God."
[21] All those hearing
him continued to
be amazed, and
were saying, "Is
this not he who
in Jerusalem
destroyed those
who called on this
name, and *who* had
come here for the
purpose of bringing
them bound before
the chief priests?"
[22] But Saul kept in-
creasing in strength
and confounding
the Jews who lived
at Damascus by
proving that this
Jesus is the Christ.
[23] When many
days had elapsed,
the Jews plotted
together to do
away with him,
[24] but their plot
became known to
Saul. They were
also watching the
gates day and night
so that they might
put him to death;
[25] but his disciples
took him by night
and let him down
through *an opening
in* the wall, lower-
ing him in a large
basket.
[26] When he came
to Jerusalem, he
was trying to as-
sociate with the
disciples; but they
were all afraid of
him, not believ-
ing that he was
a disciple. [27] But
Barnabas took hold
of him and brought
him to the apostles
and described to
them how he had
seen the Lord on
the road, and that
He had talked to

NIV

to him, and how in
Damascus he had
preached fearless-
ly in the name of
Jesus. 28 So Saul
stayed with them
and moved about
freely in Jeru-
salem, speaking
boldly in the name
of the Lord. 29 He
talked and debated
with the Hellenis-
tic Jews,[a] but they
tried to kill him.
30 When the be-
lievers learned of
this, they took him
down to Caesarea
and sent him off to
Tarsus.
31 Then the church
throughout Judea,
Galilee and Sa-
maria enjoyed a
time of peace and
was strengthened.
Living in the fear
of the Lord and
encouraged by
the Holy Spirit, it
increased in num-
bers.

Aeneas and Dorcas

32 As Peter trav-
eled about the
country, he went
to visit the Lord's
people who lived
in Lydda. 33 There
he found a man
named Aeneas,
who was paralyzed
and had been bed-
ridden for eight
years. 34 "Aeneas,"
Peter said to him,
"Jesus Christ heals
you. Get up and
roll up your mat."
Immediately Ae-
neas got up. 35 All
those who lived in
Lydda and Shar-
on saw him and
turned to the Lord.
36 In Joppa there
was a disciple
named Tabitha

[a] 29 That is, Jews who had adopted the Greek language and culture

αὐτῷ καὶ πῶς ἐν Δαμασκῷ ἐπαρρησιάσατο ἐν τῷ ὀνόματι τοῦ Ἰησοῦ.
to him, and how in Damascus ⌊he had spoken out boldly⌋ in the name of Jesus.
899 2779 4802 1877 1242 4245 1877 3836 3950 3836 2652
r.dsm.3 cj cj p.d n.dsf v.ami.3s p.d d.dsn n.dsn d.gsm n.gsm

28 καὶ ἦν μετ᾽ αὐτῶν εἰσπορευόμενος καὶ ἐκπορευόμενος εἰς Ἰερουσαλήμ,
And ⌊he was⌋ with them, going in and out at Jerusalem,
2779 1639 3552 899 1660 2779 1744 1650 2647
cj v.iai.3s p.g r.gpm.3 pt.pm.nsm cj pt.pm.nsm p.a n.asf

παρρησιαζόμενος ἐν τῷ ὀνόματι τοῦ κυρίου, 29 ἐλάλει τε καὶ συνεζήτει
speaking out boldly in the name of the Lord. ⌊He was talking⌋ ~ and disputing
4245 1877 3836 3950 3836 3261 3281 5445 2779 5184
pt.pm.nsm p.d d.dsn n.dsn d.gsm n.gsm v.iai.3s cj cj v.iai.3s

πρὸς τοὺς Ἑλληνιστάς, οἱ δὲ ἐπεχείρουν ἀνελεῖν αὐτόν.
with the ⌊Greek-speaking Jews,⌋ but they *but* ⌊were looking for a way⌋ to kill him.
4639 3836 1821 1254 3836 1254 2217 359 899
p.a d.apm n.apm d.npm cj v.iai.3p f.aa r.asm.3

30 → ἐπιγνόντες δὲ οἱ ἀδελφοὶ κατήγαγον αὐτὸν ↰ εἰς
And when the brothers learned about *And the brothers* this, they took him down to
1254 3836 81 2105 1254 3836 81 2864 899 2864 1650
pt.aa.npm cj d.npm n.npm v.aai.3p r.asm.3 p.a

Καισάρειαν καὶ ἐξαπέστειλαν αὐτὸν ↰ εἰς Ταρσόν. 31 ἡ μὲν οὖν ἐκκλησία
Caesarea and sent him off to Tarsus. So the ~ *So* church
2791 2779 1990 899 1990 1650 5433 4036 3836 3525 4036 1711
n.asf cj v.aai.3p r.asm.3 p.a n.asf d.nsf pl cj n.nsf

καθ᾽ ὅλης τῆς Ἰουδαίας καὶ Γαλιλαίας καὶ Σαμαρείας εἶχεν εἰρήνην
throughout all *{the}* Judea and Galilee and Samaria had peace;
2848 3910 3836 2677 2779 1133 2779 4899 2400 1645
p.g a.gsf d.gsf n.gsf cj n.gsf cj n.gsf v.iai.3s n.asf

οἰκοδομουμένη καὶ πορευομένη τῷ φόβῳ τοῦ κυρίου καὶ τῇ παρακλήσει τοῦ
being built up, and walking ⌊in the⌋ fear of the Lord and ⌊in the⌋ comfort of the
3868 2779 4513 3836 5832 3836 3261 2779 3836 4155 3836
pt.pp.nsf cj pt.pp.nsf d.dsm n.dsm d.gsm n.gsm cj d.dsf n.dsf d.gsn

ἁγίου πνεύματος ἐπληθύνετο. 32 ἐγένετο δὲ Πέτρον διερχόμενον
Holy Spirit, ⌊it increased in number.⌋ *{it happened that}* Now as Peter was traveling
41 4460 4437 1181 1254 4377 1451
a.gsn n.gsn v.ipi.3s v.ami.3s cj n.asm pt.pm.asm

διὰ πάντων → κατελθεῖν καὶ πρὸς τοὺς ἁγίους τοὺς κατοικοῦντας
through the entire region, he also came down *also* to the saints who were living in
1328 4246 2779 2982 2779 4639 3836 41 3836 2997
p.g a.gpn f.aa adv p.a d.apm a.apm d.apm pt.pa.apm

Λύδδα. 33 εὗρεν δὲ ἐκεῖ ἄνθρωπόν τινα ὀνόματι Αἰνέαν ἐξ
Lydda. And he found *And* there a man *a* named Aeneas, bedridden for eight
3375 1254 2351 1254 1695 5516 476 5516 3950 138 2879 1666 3893
n.asf v.aai.3s cj adv n.asm r.asm n.dsn n.asm p.g

ἐτῶν ὀκτὼ ⌊κατακείμενον ἐπὶ κραβάττου,⌋ ὃς ἦν παραλελυμένος. 34 καὶ
years, *eight bedridden* who was paralyzed. *{and}* Peter
2291 3893 2879 2093 3187 4005 1639 4168 2779 4377
n.gpn a.gpn pt.pm.asm p.g n.gsm r.nsm v.iai.3s pt.rp.nsm cj

εἶπεν αὐτῷ ὁ Πέτρος, Αἰνέα, ἰᾶταί σε Ἰησοῦς Χριστός· ἀνάστηθι
said to him, *{the} Peter* "Aeneas, Jesus Christ heals you. *Jesus Christ* Get up
3306 899 3836 4377 138 2652 5986 2615 5148 2652 5986 482
v.aai.3s r.dsm.3 d.nsm n.nsm n.vsm v.pmi.3s r.as.2 n.nsm n.nsm v.aam.2s

καὶ στρῶσον σεαυτῷ. ↰ καὶ εὐθέως ἀνέστη. 35 καὶ εἶδαν αὐτὸν πάντες οἱ
and make your own bed!" And immediately he got up. And *saw him* all who
2779 5143 4932 5143 2779 2311 482 2779 1625 899 4246 3836
cj v.aam.2s r.dsm.2 cj adv v.aai.3s cj v.aai.3p r.asm.3 a.npm d.npm

κατοικοῦντες Λύδδα καὶ τὸν Σαρῶνα, οἵτινες ἐπέστρεψαν ἐπὶ τὸν
lived in Lydda and *{the}* Sharon saw him, and they turned to the
2997 3375 2779 3836 4926 1625 899 4015 2188 2093 3836
pt.pa.npm n.asf cj d.asm n.asm r.npm v.aai.3p p.a d.asm

κύριον. 36 ἐν Ἰόππῃ δέ τις ἦν μαθήτρια ὀνόματι Ταβιθά, ἣ
Lord. Now in Joppa *Now* there was a *there was* disciple named Tabitha, which
3261 1254 1877 2673 1254 1639 1639 5516 1639 3413 3950 5412 4005
n.asm p.d n.dsf cj r.nsf v.iai.3s n.nsf n.dsn n.nsf r.nsf

NASB

him, and how at
Damascus he had
spoken out boldly
in the name of
Jesus. 28 And he was
with them, moving
about freely in
Jerusalem, speak-
ing out boldly in
the name of the
Lord. 29 And he was
talking and arguing
with the Hellenistic
Jews; but they
were attempting to
put him to death.
30 But when the
brethren learned
of it, they brought
him down to Cae-
sarea and sent him
away to Tarsus.
31 So the church
throughout all
Judea and Galilee
and Samaria en-
joyed peace, being
built up; and going
on in the fear of
the Lord and in
the comfort of the
Holy Spirit, it con-
tinued to increase.

Peter's Ministry

32 Now as Peter
was traveling
through all *those*
regions, he came
down also to the
saints who lived
at Lydda. 33 There
he found a man
named Aeneas,
who had been bed-
ridden eight years,
for he was para-
lyzed. 34 Peter said
to him, "Aeneas,
Jesus Christ heals
you; get up and
make your bed."
Immediately he got
up. 35 And all who
lived at Lydda and
Sharon saw him,
and they turned to
the Lord.
36 Now in Joppa
there was a disciple
named Tabitha

NIV

(in Greek her
name is Dorcas);
she was always
doing good and
helping the poor.
37 About that time
she became sick
and died, and her
body was washed
and placed in an
upstairs room.
38 Lydda was near
Joppa; so when
the disciples heard
that Peter was in
Lydda, they sent
two men to him
and urged him,
"Please come at
once!"
39 Peter went with
them, and when
he arrived he was
taken upstairs
to the room. All
the widows stood
around him, cry-
ing and showing
him the robes and
other clothing that
Dorcas had made
while she was still
with them.
40 Peter sent them
all out of the room;
then he got down
on his knees and
prayed. Turning
toward the dead
woman, he said,
"Tabitha, get up."
She opened her
eyes, and see-
ing Peter she sat
up. 41 He took her
by the hand and
helped her to her
feet. Then he
called for the be-
lievers, especially
the widows, and
presented her to
them alive. 42 This
became known all
over Joppa, and
many people be-
lieved in the Lord.

διερμηνευομένη λέγεται Δορκάς· αὕτη ἦν πλήρης → ἔργων ἀγαθῶν καὶ
when translated means Dorcas. She was full of good works *good* and
1450 3306 1520 4047 1639 4441 19 2240 19 2779
pt.pp.nsf v.ppi.3s n.nsf r.nsf v.iai.3s a.nsf n.gpn a.gpn cj

ἐλεημοσυνῶν ὧν ἐποίει. 37 ἐγένετο δὲ ἐν ταῖς
acts of charity, which ⌊she was always doing.⌋ In those days she became *{and}* *In* *{the}*
1797 4005 4472 1877 1697 2465 899 1181 1254 1877 3836
n.gpf r.gpf v.iai.3s v.ami.3s cj p.d d.dpf

ἡμέραις ἐκείναις ἀσθενήσασαν αὐτὴν ἀποθανεῖν· λούσαντες δὲ
days *those* ill *she* and died; and ⌊when they had washed⌋ her, *and*
2465 1697 820 899 633 1254 3374 1254
n.dpf r.dpf pt.aa.asf r.asf.3 f.aa pt.aa.npm cj

ἔθηκαν αὐτὴν[a] ἐν ὑπερῴῳ. 38 ἐγγὺς δὲ οὔσης Λύδδας τῇ
they laid her in an upper room. Since Lydda is near *{and}* *Since is* *Lydda* *{the}*
5502 899 1877 5673 1639 3375 1639 1584 1254 1639 3375 3836
v.aai.3p r.asf.3 p.d n.dsn adv cj pt.pa.gsf n.gsf d.dsf

Ἰόππῃ οἱ μαθηταὶ ἀκούσαντες ὅτι Πέτρος ἐστὶν ⌊ἐν αὐτῇ⌋ ἀπέστειλαν δύο
Joppa, the disciples, hearing that Peter was there, sent two
2673 3836 3412 201 4022 4377 1639 1877 899 690 1545
n.dsf d.npm n.npm pt.aa.npm cj n.nsm v.pai.3s p.d r.dsf.3 v.aai.3p a.apm

ἄνδρας πρὸς αὐτὸν παρακαλοῦντες, ↱ μὴ ὀκνήσῃς διελθεῖν ἕως ἡμῶν. 39
men to him urging him, "Do not delay in coming to us." So
467 4639 899 4151 3890 3590 3890 1451 2401 7005 1254
n.apm p.a r.asm.3 pt.pa.npm pl v.aas.2s f.aa p.g r.gp.1

ἀναστὰς δὲ Πέτρος συνῆλθεν αὐτοῖς· ὃν παραγενόμενον ἀνήγαγον
Peter got up *So* *Peter* and went with them; and when he arrived, they took him
4377 482 1254 4377 5302 899 4005 4134 343
pt.aa.nsm cj n.nsm v.aai.3s r.dpm.3 r.asm pt.am.asm v.aai.3p

εἰς τὸ ὑπερῷον καὶ παρέστησαν αὐτῷ πᾶσαι αἱ χῆραι
to the upper room. *{and}* All the widows stood beside him, *All* *the* *widows*
1650 3836 5673 2779 4246 3836 5939 4225 899 4246 3836 5939
p.a d.asn n.asn cj v.aai.3p r.dsm.3 a.npf d.npf n.npf

κλαίουσαι καὶ ἐπιδεικνύμεναι χιτῶνας καὶ ἱμάτια ὅσα ἐποίει
weeping and showing the tunics and other clothing *other* Dorcas ⌊used to make⌋
3081 2779 2109 5945 2779 4012 2668 4012 1520 4472
pt.pa.npf cj pt.pm.npf n.apm cj n.apn r.apn v.iai.3s

μετ᾽ αὐτῶν οὖσα ἡ Δορκάς. 40 ἐκβαλὼν δὲ
while she was still with them. *while she was* *{the}* *Dorcas* But Peter put *But* them
1639 1639 1639 3552 899 1639 3836 1520 1254 4377 1675 1254
p.g r.gpf.3 pt.pa.nsf d.nsf n.nsf pt.aa.nsm cj

ἔξω πάντας ὁ Πέτρος καὶ θεὶς τὰ γόνατα προσηύξατο καὶ
all outside, *all* *{the}* *Peter* and falling to his knees he prayed; then
4246 2032 4246 3836 4377 2779 5502 3836 1205 4667 2779
adv a.apm d.nsm n.nsm cj pt.aa.nsm d.apn n.apn v.ami.3s cj

ἐπιστρέψας πρὸς τὸ σῶμα εἶπεν, Ταβιθά, ἀνάστηθι. ἡ δὲ ἤνοιξεν τοὺς
turning toward the dead body, he said, "Tabitha, get up!" And she *And* opened *{the}*
2188 4639 3836 5393 3306 5412 482 1254 3836 1254 487 3836
pt.aa.nsm p.a d.asn n.asn v.aai.3s n.vsf v.aam.2s d.nsf cj v.aai.3s d.apm

ὀφθαλμοὺς αὐτῆς, καὶ ἰδοῦσα τὸν Πέτρον ἀνεκάθισεν. 41 δοὺς δὲ αὐτῇ
her eyes, *her* and seeing *{the}* Peter, she sat up. And he gave *And* her
899 4057 899 2779 1625 3836 4377 361 1254 1443 1254 899
n.apm r.gsf.3 cj pt.aa.nsf d.asm n.asm v.aai.3s pt.aa.nsm cj r.dsf.3

χεῖρα ἀνέστησεν αὐτήν· ↰ φωνήσας δὲ τοὺς ἁγίους καὶ τὰς χήρας
his hand and raised her up; then he called *then* the saints and *{the}* widows and
5931 482 899 482 1254 5888 1254 3836 41 2779 3836 5939
n.asf v.aai.3s r.asf.3 pt.aa.nsm cj d.apm a.apm cj d.apf n.apf

παρέστησεν αὐτὴν ζῶσαν. 42 γνωστὸν δὲ ἐγένετο καθ᾽ ὅλης τῆς
presented her alive. And it became known *And* *it became* throughout all *{the}*
4225 899 2409 1254 1181 1181 1196 1254 1181 2848 3910 3836
v.aai.3s r.asf.3 pt.pa.asf a.nsn cj v.ami.3s p.g a.gsf d.gsf

Ἰόππης καὶ ἐπίστευσαν πολλοὶ ἐπὶ τὸν κύριον. 43 ἐγένετο
Joppa, and many believed *many* on the Lord. *{it happened that}* And he
2673 2779 4498 4409 4498 2093 3836 3261 1181 1254 3531
n.gsf cj v.aai.3p a.npm p.a d.asm n.asm v.ami.3s

NASB

(which trans-
lated *in Greek* is
called Dorcas);
this woman was
abounding with
deeds of kindness
and charity which
she continually did.
37 And it happened
at that time that she
fell sick and died;
and when they
had washed her
body, they laid it
in an upper room.
38 Since Lydda was
near Joppa, the
disciples, having
heard that Peter
was there, sent
two men to him,
imploring him,
"Do not delay in
coming to us." 39 So
Peter arose and
went with them.
When he arrived,
they brought him
into the upper
room; and all the
widows stood
beside him, weep-
ing and showing
all the [a]tunics and
garments that Dor-
cas used to make
while she was with
them. 40 But Peter
sent them all out
and knelt down
and prayed, and
turning to the body,
he said, "Tabitha,
arise." And she
opened her eyes,
and when she saw
Peter, she sat up.
41 And he gave
her his hand and
raised her up; and
calling the saints
and widows, he
presented her alive.
42 It became known
all over Joppa, and
many believed in
the Lord. 43 And

[a] [αὐτὴν] UBS.

[a] Or *inner garments*

NIV

[43]Peter stayed in Joppa for some time with a tanner named Simon.

Cornelius Calls for Peter

10 At Caesarea there was a man named Cornelius, a centurion in what was known as the Italian Regiment. [2]He and all his family were devout and God-fearing; he gave generously to those in need and prayed to God regularly. [3]One day at about three in the afternoon he had a vision. He distinctly saw an angel of God, who came to him and said, "Cornelius!"

[4]Cornelius stared at him in fear. "What is it, Lord?" he asked.

The angel answered, "Your prayers and gifts to the poor have come up as a memorial offering before God. [5]Now send men to Joppa to bring back a man named Simon who is called Peter. [6]He is staying with Simon the tanner, whose house is by the sea."

[7]When the angel who spoke to him had gone, Cornelius called two of his servants and a devout soldier who was one of his attendants. [8]He told them everything that had happened and sent them to Joppa.

	δὲ		ἡμέρας	ἱκανὰς	μεῖναι	ἐν	Ἰόππῃ	παρά	τινι	Σίμωνι	
stayed	*And*	a number	of days	*number*	*he stayed*	in	Joppa	with	a certain	Simon,	a
3531	1254	2653	2465	2653	3531	1877	2673	4123	5516	4981	
	cj		n.apf	a.apf	f.aa	p.d	n.dsf	p.d	r.dsm	n.dsm	

βυρσεῖ.
tanner.
1114
n.dsm

10:1	ἀνὴρ	δέ	τις	ἐν	Καισαρείᾳ	ὀνόματι	Κορνήλιος,	
There was a	man	*{and}*	*a*	in	Caesarea	named	Cornelius,	a
5516	467	1254	5516	1877	2791	3950	3173	
	n.nsm	cj	r.nsm	p.d	n.dsf	n.dsn	n.nsm	

ἑκατοντάρχης	ἐκ		σπείρης	τῆς	καλουμένης		Ἰταλικῆς,	[2]	εὐσεβὴς	καὶ
centurion	from	the	cohort	that	was called	the	Italian,	a	devout man	and
1672	1666		5061	3836	2813		2713		2356	2779
n.nsm	p.g		n.gsf	d.gsf	pt.pp.gsf		a.gsf		a.nsm	cj

φοβούμενος	τὸν	θεὸν	σὺν	παντὶ	τῷ		οἴκῳ	αὐτοῦ,	ποιῶν	ἐλεημοσύνας
one who feared	*{the}*	God	with	all	*{the}*	his	household,	*his*	gave	alms
5828	3836	2536	5250	4246	3836	899	3875	899	4472	1797
pt.pp.nsm	d.asm	n.asm	p.d	a.dsm	d.dsm		n.dsm	r.gsm.3	pt.pa.nsm	n.apf

πολλὰς	τῷ	λαῷ	καὶ	δεόμενος	τοῦ	θεοῦ	⌞διὰ	παντός,⌟	[3]εἶδεν	ἐν	
generously	⌞to the⌟	people,	and	prayed	to	God	continually.		He saw	in	a
4498	3836	3295	2779	1289	3836	2536	1328	4246	1625	1877	
a.apf	d.dsm	n.dsm	cj	pt.pp.nsm	d.gsm	n.gsm	p.g	a.gsn	v.aai.3s	p.d	

ὁράματι	φανερῶς	⌞ὡσεὶ	περὶ⌟		ὥραν	ἐνάτην	τῆς	ἡμέρας		ἄγγελον	τοῦ	θεοῦ
vision	clearly,	about		the ninth	hour	*ninth*	of the	day,	an	angel	of	God
3969	5747	6059	4309	1888	6052	1888	3836	2465		34	3836	2536
n.dsn	adv	pl	p.a		n.asf	a.asf	d.gsf	n.gsf		n.asm	d.gsm	n.gsm

εἰσελθόντα	πρὸς	αὐτὸν	καὶ	εἰπόντα	αὐτῷ,	Κορνήλιε.	[4]ὁ	δὲ	ἀτενίσας	αὐτῷ	καὶ
coming	to	him	and	saying	to him,	"Cornelius."	*he*	*{and}*	Staring at	him	and
1656	4639	899	2779	3306	899	3173	3836	1254	867	899	2779
pt.aa.asm	p.a	r.asm.3	cj	pt.aa.asm	r.dsm.3	n.vsm	d.nsm	cj	pt.aa.nsm	r.dsm.3	cj

	ἔμφοβος	γενόμενος		εἶπεν,	τί	ἐστιν,	κύριε;		εἶπεν	δὲ	αὐτῷ,	αἱ
becoming	afraid,	*becoming*	he	said,	"What	is it,	Lord?"	And	he said	*And*	to him,	*{the}*
1181	1873	1181	3836	3306	5515	1639	3261	1254	3306	1254	899	3836
	a.nsm	pt.am.nsm		v.aai.3s	r.nsn	v.pai.3s	n.vsm		v.aai.3s	cj	r.dsm.3	d.npf

	προσευχαί	σου	καὶ	αἱ		ἐλεημοσύναι	σου	ἀνέβησαν	εἰς	μνημόσυνον
"Your	prayers	*Your*	and	*{the}*	your	acts of charity	*your*	have gone up	as	a memorial
5148	4666	5148	2779	3836	5148	1797	5148	326	1650	3649
	n.npf	r.gs.2	cj	d.npf		n.npf	r.gs.2	v.aai.3p	p.a	n.asn

ἔμπροσθεν	τοῦ	θεοῦ.	[5]καὶ	νῦν	πέμψον	ἄνδρας	εἰς	Ἰόππην	καὶ	μετάπεμψαι		
before	*{the}*	God.	And	now	send	men	to	Joppa	and	send for	a	man
1869	3836	2536	2779	3814	4287	467	1650	2673	2779	3569	5516	5516
p.g	d.gsm	n.gsm	cj	adv	v.aam.2s	n.apm	p.a	n.asf	cj	v.amm.2s		

	Σίμωνά	τινα	ὅς	ἐπικαλεῖται	Πέτρος·	[6]οὗτος	ξενίζεται	παρά	τινι
named	Simon	*a man*	who	is called	Peter.	He	is lodging	with	a man named
	4981	5516	4005	2126	4377	4047	3826	4123	5516
	n.asm	r.asm	r.nsm	v.ppi.3s	n.nsm	r.nsm	v.ppi.3s	p.d	r.dsm

Σίμωνι		βυρσεῖ,	ᾧ		ἐστιν	οἰκία	παρὰ	θάλασσαν.[a]	[7]ὡς	δὲ
Simon,	a	tanner,	whose	house	is	*house*	by	the sea."	When	*{and}*
4981		1114	4005	3864	1639	3864	4123	2498	6055	1254
n.dsm		n.dsm	r.dsm		v.pai.3s	n.nsf	p.a	n.asf	cj	cj

ἀπῆλθεν	ὁ	ἄγγελος	ὁ	λαλῶν	αὐτῷ,				φωνήσας	δύο	τῶν	οἰκετῶν
had gone away	the	angel	who	spoke	to him	had	gone	away,	he called	two	of his	servants
599	3836	34	3836	3281	899	599	599	599	5888	1545	3836	3860
v.aai.3s	d.nsm	n.nsm	d.nsm	pt.pa.nsm	r.dsm.3				pt.aa.nsm	a.apm	d.gpm	n.gpm

καὶ		στρατιώτην	εὐσεβῆ	τῶν	προσκαρτερούντων	αὐτῷ	[8]καὶ
and	a devout	soldier	*devout*	⌞from among⌟	those who waited on	him,	and
2779	2356	5132	2356	3836	4674	899	2779
cj		n.asm	a.asm	d.gpm	pt.pa.gpm	r.dsm.3	cj

ἐξηγησάμενος	ἅπαντα	αὐτοῖς	ἀπέστειλεν	αὐτοὺς	εἰς	τὴν	Ἰόππην.	[9]τῇ	δὲ
when he had related	everything	to them,	he sent	them	to	*{the}*	Joppa.	The	*{and}*
2007	570	899	690	899	1650	3836	2673	3836	1254
pt.am.nsm	a.apn	r.dpm.3	v.aai.3s	r.apm.3	p.a	d.asf	n.asf	d.dsf	cj

[a] οὗτος λαλήσει σοι τί σε δεῖ ποιεῖν included by TR after θάλασσαν.

NASB

Peter stayed many days in Joppa with a tanner *named* Simon.

Cornelius's Vision

[10:1]Now *there was* a man at Caesarea named Cornelius, a centurion of what was called the Italian [a]cohort, [2]a devout man and one who feared God with all his household, and gave many [b]alms to the *Jewish* people and prayed to God continually. [3]About the [c]ninth hour of the day he clearly saw in a vision an angel of God who had *just* come in and said to him, "Cornelius!" [4]And fixing his gaze on him and being much alarmed, he said, "What is it, Lord?" And he said to him, "Your prayers and [d]alms have ascended as a memorial before God. [5]Now dispatch *some* men to Joppa and send for a man *named* Simon, who is also called Peter; [6]he is staying with a tanner *named* Simon, whose house is by the sea." [7]When the angel who was speaking to him had left, he summoned two of his servants and a devout soldier of those who were his personal attendants, [8]and after he had explained everything to them, he sent them to Joppa.

[a] Or *battalion*
[b] Or *gifts of charity*
[c] I.e. 3 p.m.
[d] Or *deeds of charity*

NIV

Peter's Vision

9 About noon the
following day as
they were on their
journey and ap-
proaching the city,
Peter went up on
the roof to pray.
10 He became hun-
gry and wanted
something to eat,
and while the meal
was being pre-
pared, he fell into
a trance. 11 He saw
heaven opened and
something like a
large sheet being
let down to earth
by its four corners.
12 It contained all
kinds of four-foot-
ed animals, as
well as reptiles
and birds. 13 Then
a voice told him,
"Get up, Peter. Kill
and eat."
14 "Surely not,
Lord!" Peter re-
plied. "I have
never eaten any-
thing impure or
unclean."
15 The voice spoke
to him a second
time, "Do not call
anything impure
that God has made
clean."
16 This happened
three times, and
immediately the
sheet was taken
back to heaven.
17 While Peter was
wondering about
the meaning of the
vision, the men
sent by Cornelius
found out where
Simon's house was
and stopped at the
gate. 18 They called
out, asking if Si-
mon who

ἐπαύριον, → ὁδοιπορούντων ἐκείνων καὶ τῇ πόλει ἐγγιζόντων,
following day, as they were on their journey *they* and approaching the city, *approaching*
2069 1697 3844 1697 2779 1581 3836 4484 1581
adv pt.pa.gpm r.gpm cj d.dsf n.dsf pt.pa.gpm

ἀνέβη Πέτρος ἐπὶ τὸ δῶμα προσεύξασθαι περὶ ὥραν ἕκτην. 10
Peter went up *Peter* on the housetop to pray about the sixth hour. *sixth* And
4377 326 4377 2093 3836 1560 4667 4309 1761 6052 1761 1254
v.aai.3s n.nsm p.a d.asn n.asn f.am p.a n.asf a.asf

ἐγένετο δὲ πρόσπεινος καὶ ἤθελεν γεύσασθαι. → παρασκευαζόντων δὲ
he became *And* hungry and wanted to eat, but while they were preparing *but*
1181 1254 4698 2779 2527 1174 1254 899 4186 1254
v.ami.3s cj a.nsm cj v.iai.3s f.am pt.pa.gpm cj

αὐτῶν ἐγένετο ἐπ' αὐτὸν ἔκστασις 11 καὶ θεωρεῖ τὸν οὐρανὸν ἀνεῳγμένον
they it, he fell into *he* a trance, and he saw the heavens opened
899 899 1181 2093 899 1749 2779 2555 3836 4041 487
r.gpm.3 v.ami.3s p.a r.asm.3 n.nsf cj v.pai.3s d.asm n.asm pt.rp.asm

καὶ καταβαῖνον σκεῦός τι ὡς ὀθόνην μεγάλην
and a certain object descending, *object* *certain* like a great sheet, *great* being let down
2779 5516 5007 2849 5007 5516 6055 3489 3855 3489 2768 2768 2768
cj pt.pa.asn n.asn r.asn pl n.asf a.asf

→ τέσσαρσιν ἀρχαῖς καθιέμενον ἐπὶ τῆς γῆς, 12 ἐν ᾧ ὑπῆρχεν πάντα τὰ
by its four corners *being let down* upon the earth. In it were ⌞all kinds of⌟ *{the}*
5475 794 2768 2093 3836 1178 1877 4005 5639 4246 3836
a.dpf n.dpf pt.pp.asn p.g d.gsf n.gsf p.d r.dsn v.iai.3s a.npn d.npn

τετράποδα καὶ ἑρπετὰ τῆς γῆς καὶ πετεινὰ τοῦ οὐρανοῦ. 13 καὶ
four-footed animals, and reptiles of the earth, and birds of the air. Then a voice
5488 2779 2260 3836 1178 2779 4374 3836 4041 2779 5889
n.npn cj n.npn d.gsf n.gsf cj n.npn d.gsm n.gsm cj

ἐγένετο φωνὴ πρὸς αὐτόν, ἀναστάς, Πέτρε, θῦσον καὶ φάγε. 14 ὁ δὲ Πέτρος
came *voice* to him, "Get up, Peter; slaughter and eat!" *{the}* But Peter
1181 5889 4639 899 482 4377 2604 2779 2266 3836 1254 4377
v.ami.3s n.nsf p.a r.asm.3 pt.aa.nsm n.vsm v.aam.2s cj v.aam.2s d.nsm cj n.nsm

εἶπεν, μηδαμῶς, κύριε, ὅτι ↱ ↱ οὐδέποτε ἔφαγον πᾶν κοινὸν καὶ
said, "By no means, Lord; for I have never eaten anything common or
3306 3592 3261 4022 2266 2266 4030 2266 4246 3123 2779
v.aai.3s adv n.vsm cj adv v.aai.1s a.asn a.asn cj

ἀκάθαρτον. 15 καὶ φωνὴ πάλιν ⌞ἐκ δευτέρου⌟ πρὸς αὐτόν, ἃ ὁ
unclean." And a voice came again, a second time, to him, "What *{the}*
176 2779 5889 4099 1666 1311 4639 899 4005 3836
a.asn cj n.nsf adv p.g a.gsn p.a r.asm.3 r.apn d.nsm

θεὸς ἐκαθάρισεν, σὺ ↱ μὴ κοίνου. 16 τοῦτο δὲ ἐγένετο ⌞ἐπὶ
God has made clean, you must not ⌞consider common."⌟ This *{and}* happened three times,
2536 2751 5148 3124 3590 3124 4047 1254 1181 2093
n.nsm v.aai.3s r.ns.2 pl v.pam.2s r.nsn cj v.ami.3s p.a

τρὶς⌟ καὶ εὐθὺς ἀνελήμφθη τὸ σκεῦος εἰς τὸν οὐρανόν. 17 ὡς
and immediately the object was taken up *the* *object* to *{the}* heaven. Now while
5565 2779 2318 3836 5007 377 3836 5007 1650 3836 4041 1254 6055
adv cj adv v.api.3s d.nsn n.nsn p.a d.asm n.asm cj

δὲ ἐν ἑαυτῷ διηπόρει ὁ Πέτρος τί
Now Peter was perplexed within himself *was perplexed* *{the}* *Peter* as to what the vision that
1254 4377 1389 1389 1877 1571 1389 3836 4377 5515 3836 3969 4005
cj p.d r.dsm.3 v.iai.3s d.nsm n.nsm r.nsn

ἂν εἴη τὸ ὅραμα ὃ εἶδεν, ἰδοὺ οἱ ἄνδρες οἱ
he had seen might mean, *the* *vision* *that* *he had seen* behold, the men *{the}*
1625 1625 1625 323 1639 3836 3969 4005 1625 2627 3836 467 3836
pl v.pao.3s d.nsn n.nsn r.asn v.aai.3s j d.npm n.npm d.npm

ἀπεσταλμένοι ὑπὸ τοῦ Κορνηλίου διερωτήσαντες τὴν οἰκίαν τοῦ Σίμωνος
sent by *{the}* Cornelius, ⌞having made inquiry for⌟ the house of Simon,
690 5679 3836 3173 1452 3836 3864 3836 4981
pt.rp.npm p.g d.gsm n.gsm pt.aa.npm d.asf n.asf d.gsm n.gsm

ἐπέστησαν ἐπὶ τὸν πυλῶνα, 18 καὶ φωνήσαντες ἐπυνθάνοντο εἰ Σίμων ὁ
stood at the gate and called out to ask whether Simon who
2392 2093 3836 4784 2779 5888 4785 1623 4981 3836
v.aai.3p p.a d.asm n.asm cj pt.aa.npm v.imi.3p cj n.nsm d.nsm

NASB

9 On the next
day, as they were
on their way and
approaching the
city, Peter went up
on the housetop
about the [a]sixth
hour to pray. 10 But
he became hungry
and was desiring
to eat; but while
they were making
preparations, he
fell into a trance;
11 and he *saw the
sky opened up, and
an [b]object like a
great sheet com-
ing down, lowered
by four corners to
the ground, 12 and
there were in it
all *kinds of* four-
footed animals and
[c]crawling creatures
of the earth and
birds of the air. 13 A
voice came to him,
"Get up, Peter,
kill and eat!" 14 But
Peter said, "By
no means, Lord,
for I have never
eaten anything un-
holy and unclean."
15 Again a voice
came to him a sec-
ond time, "What
God has cleansed,
no *longer* consider
unholy." 16 This
happened three
times, and imme-
diately the object
was taken up into
the sky.
17 Now while Peter
was greatly per-
plexed in mind as
to what the vision
which he had seen
might be, behold,
the men who
had been sent by
Cornelius, having
asked directions
for Simon's house,
appeared at the
gate; 18 and calling
out, they were ask-
ing whether Simon,
who was also

a I.e. noon
b Or *vessel*
c Or *reptiles*

NIV

was known as Pe-
ter was staying
there.
[19] While Peter
was still thinking
about the vision,
the Spirit said
to him, "Simon,
three[a] men are
looking for you.
[20] So get up and go
downstairs. Do not
hesitate to go with
them, for I have
sent them."
[21] Peter went
down and said to
the men, "I'm the
one you're looking
for. Why have you
come?"
[22] The men re-
plied, "We have
come from Cornel-
ius the centurion.
He is a righteous
and God-fearing
man, who is re-
spected by all the
Jewish people. A
holy angel told
him to ask you to
come to his house
so that he could
hear what you have
to say." [23] Then Pe-
ter invited the men
into the house to
be his guests.

Peter at Cornelius's House

The next day Pe-
ter started out with
them, and some of
the believers from
Joppa went along.
[24] The following
day he arrived in
Caesarea. Cornel-
ius was expecting
them and had
called together his
relatives and close
friends. [25] As Peter
entered the house,
Cornelius met him
and fell at his feet
in reverence. [26] But
Peter made him
get up.

[a] 19 One early manuscript *two*; other manuscripts do not have the number.

ἐπικαλούμενος Πέτρος ἐνθάδε ξενίζεται. [19] τοῦ δὲ ↱ Πέτρου
was called Peter was staying there. *was staying* *{the}* *{and}* As Peter
2126 4377 3826 3826 1924 3826 3836 1254 1445 4377
pt.pp.nsm n.nsm adv v.ppi.3s d.gsm cj n.gsm

διενθυμουμένου περὶ τοῦ ὁράματος εἶπεν αὐτῷ[a] τὸ πνεῦμα, ἰδοὺ
was thinking about the vision, the Spirit said to him, *the* *Spirit* "Behold, three
1445 4309 3836 3969 3836 4460 3306 899 3836 4460 2627 5552
pt.pm.gsm p.g d.gsn n.gsn v.aai.3s r.dsm.3 d.nsn n.nsn j

ἄνδρες τρεῖς ζητοῦντές σε, [20] ἀλλὰ ἀναστὰς κατάβηθι καὶ ⌊πορεύου σὺν⌋
men *three* ⌊are looking for⌋ you. But get up, go down, and accompany
467 5552 2426 5148 247 482 2849 2779 4513 5250
n.npm a.npm pt.pa.npm r.as.2 cj pt.aa.nsm v.aam.2s cj v.pmm.2s p.d

αὐτοῖς μηδὲν διακρινόμενος ὅτι ἐγὼ ἀπέσταλκα αὐτούς. [21] καταβὰς
them without hesitation, because I have sent them." And Peter went down
899 3594 1359 4022 1609 690 899 1254 4377 2849
r.dpm.3 a.asn pt.pm.nsm cj r.ns.1 v.rai.1s r.apm.3 pt.aa.nsm

δὲ Πέτρος πρὸς τοὺς ἄνδρας[b] εἶπεν, ἰδοὺ ἐγώ εἰμι ὃν ζητεῖτε·
And *Peter* to the men and said, "Behold, I am the one ⌊you are looking for.⌋
1254 4377 4639 3836 467 3306 2627 1609 1639 4005 2426
cj n.nsm p.a d.apm n.apm v.aai.3s j r.ns.1 v.pai.1s r.asm v.pai.2p

τίς ἡ αἰτία δι' ἣν πάρεστε; [22] οἱ δὲ εἶπαν, Κορνήλιος
What is the reason for which you have come?" And they *And* said, "Cornelius, a
5515 3836 162 1328 4005 4205 1254 3836 1254 3306 3173
r.nsf d.nsf n.nsf p.a r.asf v.pai.2p d.npm cj v.aai.3p n.nsm

ἑκατοντάρχης, ἀνὴρ δίκαιος καὶ φοβούμενος τὸν θεόν, μαρτυρούμενός
centurion, an upright man *upright* and one who fears *{the}* God, ⌊who is well spoken of⌋
1672 1465 467 1465 2779 5828 3836 2536 3455
n.nsm n.nsm a.nsm cj pt.pp.nsm d.asm n.asm pt.pp.nsm

τε ὑπὸ ὅλου τοῦ ἔθνους τῶν Ἰουδαίων, ἐχρηματίσθη ὑπὸ ἀγγέλου ἁγίου
~ by the whole *the* nation of the Jews, was directed by a holy angel *holy*
5445 5679 3836 3910 3836 1620 3836 2681 5976 5679 41 34 41
cj p.g a.gsn d.gsn n.gsn d.gpm a.gpm v.api.3s p.g n.gsm a.gsm

μεταπέμψασθαί σε ↰ ↰ εἰς τὸν οἶκον αὐτοῦ καὶ ἀκοῦσαι ῥήματα παρὰ
to send for you to come to *{the}* his house *his* and to hear words from
3569 5148 3569 3569 1650 3836 899 3875 899 2779 201 4839 4123
f.am r.as.2 p.a d.asm n.asm r.gsm.3 cj f.aa n.apn p.g

σοῦ. [23] εἰσκαλεσάμενος ← οὖν αὐτοὺς ἐξένισεν. τῇ δὲ
you." So he invited them in *So* *them* and ⌊gave them lodging.⌋ ⌊On the⌋ *{and}*
5148 4036 1657 899 4036 899 3826 3836 1254
r.gs.2 pt.am.nsm cj r.apm.3 v.aai.3s d.dsf cj

ἐπαύριον ↱ ἀναστὰς ἐξῆλθεν σὺν αὐτοῖς καί τινες τῶν ἀδελφῶν τῶν ἀπὸ
next day he got up and set out with them, and some of the brothers *{the}* from
2069 2002 482 2002 5250 899 2779 5516 3836 81 3836 608
adv pt.aa.nsm v.aai.3s p.d r.dpm.3 cj r.npm d.gpm n.gpm d.gpm p.g

Ἰόππης συνῆλθον αὐτῷ. [24] τῇ δὲ ἐπαύριον ⌊εἰσῆλθεν εἰς⌋ τὴν
Joppa went with him. And ⌊on the⌋ *And* following day they entered *{the}*
2673 5302 899 1254 3836 1254 2069 1656 1650 3836
n.gsf v.aai.3p r.dsm.3 d.dsf cj adv v.aai.3s p.a d.asf

Καισάρειαν. ὁ δὲ Κορνήλιος ἦν προσδοκῶν αὐτοὺς συγκαλεσάμενος τοὺς
Caesarea. *{the}* *{and}* Cornelius was expecting them and had called together *{the}*
2791 3836 1254 3173 1639 4659 899 5157 3836
n.asf d.nsm cj n.nsm v.iai.3s pt.pa.nsm r.apm.3 pt.am.nsm d.apm

συγγενεῖς αὐτοῦ καὶ τοὺς ἀναγκαίους φίλους. [25] ὡς δὲ ἐγένετο τοῦ
his relatives *his* and *{the}* close friends. When *{and}* *{it happened that}* ~
899 5150 899 2779 3836 338 5813 6055 1254 1181 3836
n.apm r.gsm.3 cj d.apm a.apm n.apm cj cj v.ami.3s d.gsn

εἰσελθεῖν τὸν Πέτρον, συναντήσας αὐτῷ ὁ Κορνήλιος πεσὼν
Peter entered, *{the}* *Peter* Cornelius met him *{the}* *Cornelius* and fell
4377 1656 3836 4377 3173 5267 899 3836 3173 4406
f.aa d.asm n.asm pt.aa.nsm r.dsm.3 d.nsm n.nsm pt.aa.nsm

ἐπὶ τοὺς πόδας προσεκύνησεν. [26] ὁ δὲ Πέτρος → ἤγειρεν αὐτὸν
at his feet and worshiped him. *{the}* But Peter made him get up, *him*
2093 3836 4546 4686 3836 1254 4377 899 1586 899
p.a d.apm n.apm v.aai.3s d.nsm cj n.nsm v.aai.3s r.asm.3

[a] [αὐτῷ] UBS.
[b] τοὺς ἀπεσταλμένους ἀπὸ τοῦ Κορνηλίου πρὸς αὐτόν included by TR after ἄνδρας.

NASB

called Peter, was
staying there.
[19] While Peter
was reflecting on
the vision, the
Spirit said to him,
"Behold, three men
are looking for
you. [20] But get up,
go downstairs and
accompany them
without misgiv-
ings, for I have
sent them Myself."
[21] Peter went down
to the men and
said, "Behold, I
am the one you are
looking for; what
is the reason for
which you have
come?" [22] They
said, "Cornelius,
a centurion, a
righteous and
God-fearing man
well spoken of by
the entire nation
of the Jews, was
divinely directed
by a holy angel
to send for you *to*
come to his house
and hear a message
from you." [23] So he
invited them in and
gave them lodging.

Peter at Caesarea

And on the next
day he got up and
went away with
them, and some of
the brethren from
Joppa accompa-
nied him. [24] On the
following day he
entered Caesarea.
Now Cornelius was
waiting for them
and had called to-
gether his relatives
and close friends.
[25] When Peter en-
tered, Cornelius
met him, and fell
at his feet and wor-
shiped *him.* [26] But
Peter raised him
up, saying,

NIV

"Stand up," he
said, "I am only a
man myself."
27 While talking
with him, Peter
went inside and
found a large
gathering of peo-
ple. 28 He said to
them: "You are
well aware that it
is against our law
for a Jew to asso-
ciate with or visit
a Gentile. But God
has shown me that
I should not call
anyone impure or
unclean. 29 So when
I was sent for, I
came without rais-
ing any objection.
May I ask why you
sent for me?"
30 Cornelius an-
swered: "Three
days ago I was in
my house pray-
ing at this hour, at
three in the after-
noon. Suddenly
a man in shining
clothes stood be-
fore me 31 and said,
'Cornelius, God
has heard your
prayer and remem-
bered your gifts to
the poor. 32 Send to
Joppa for Simon
who is called Pe-
ter. He is a guest in
the home of Simon
the tanner, who
lives by the sea.'
33 So I sent for you
immediately, and
it was good of you
to come. Now we
are all here in the
presence of God
to listen to every-
thing the Lord has
commanded you to
tell us."

λέγων, ἀνάστηθι· καὶ ἐγὼ αὐτὸς ἄνθρωπός εἰμι. 27 καὶ
saying, "Stand up; I myself am also *I* *myself* just a man." *am* And
3306 482 1609 899 1639 2779 1609 899 476 1639 2779
pt.pa.nsm v.aam.2s adv r.ns.1 r.nsm n.nsm v.pai.1s cj

συνομιλῶν αὐτῷ εἰσῆλθεν καὶ εὑρίσκει συνεληλυθότας πολλούς,
⌊as he talked with⌋ him, he went inside and found many people gathered. *many people*
5326 899 1656 2779 2351 4498 4498 5302 4498
pt.pa.nsm r.dsm.3 v.aai.3s cj v.pai.3s pt.ra.apm a.apm

28 ἔφη τε πρός αὐτούς, ↱ ὑμεῖς ἐπίστασθε ὡς ἀθέμιτόν ἐστιν
And he said *And* to them, "You yourselves know how unlawful it is for a
5445 5774 5445 4639 899 2179 7007 2179 6055 116 1639
v.iai.3s cj p.a r.apm.3 r.np.2 v.ppi.2p cj a.nsn v.pai.3s

ἀνδρὶ Ἰουδαίῳ κολλᾶσθαι ἢ προσέρχεσθαι ἀλλοφύλῳ· κἀμοὶ
man who is a Jew to associate with or to visit anyone of another race, but
467 2681 3140 2445 4665 260 2743
n.dsm a.dsm f.pp cj f.pm a.dsm crasis

← ὁ θεὸς ἔδειξεν μηδένα κοινὸν ἢ
God showed me *{the}* *God* *showed* that I should call no person common or
2536 1259 3836 2536 1259 3306 3306 3306 3594 476 3123 2445
d.nsm n.nsm v.aai.3s a.asm a.asm cj

ἀκάθαρτον λέγειν ἄνθρωπον· 29 διὸ καὶ
unclean. *I should call* *person* Therefore, *{also}* when I was summoned, I came
176 3306 476 1475 2779 3569 3569 3569 3569 2262 2262
a.asm f.pa n.asm cj adv

ἀναντιρρήτως ἦλθον μεταπεμφθείς. πυνθάνομαι οὖν τίνι λόγῳ
⌊without raising any objection.⌋ *I came* *when I was summoned* So I ask *So* for what reason
395 2262 3569 4036 4785 4036 5515 3364
adv v.aai.1s pt.ap.nsm v.pmi.1s cj r.dsm n.dsm

μετεπέμψασθέ με; 30 καὶ ὁ Κορνήλιος ἔφη, ἀπὸ τετάρτης ἡμέρας μέχρι ταύτης
did you send for me?" And *{the}* Cornelius said, *ago* "Four days ago at this
3569 1609 2779 3836 3173 5774 608 5480 2465 608 3588 4047
v.ami.2p r.as.1 cj d.nsm n.nsm v.iai.3s p.g a.gsf n.gsf p.g r.gsf

τῆς ὥρας ἤμην τὴν ἐνάτην προσευχόμενος ἐν τῷ οἴκῳ μου, καὶ
{the} hour, I was praying at the ninth hour *praying* in *{the}* my house, *my* and
3836 6052 1639 4667 3836 1888 4667 1877 3836 1609 3875 1609 2779
d.gsf n.gsf v.imi.1s d.asf a.asf pt.pm.nsm p.d d.dsm n.dsm r.gs.1 cj

ἰδοὺ ἀνὴρ ἔστη ἐνώπιόν μου ἐν ἐσθῆτι λαμπρᾷ 31 καὶ φησίν, Κορνήλιε,
behold, a man stood before me in bright clothing *bright* and he said, 'Cornelius,
2627 467 2705 1967 1609 1877 3287 2264 3287 2779 5774 3173
j n.nsm v.aai.3s p.g r.gs.1 p.d n.dsf a.dsf cj v.pai.3s n.vsm

εἰσηκούσθη σου ἡ προσευχὴ καὶ αἱ ἐλεημοσύναι σου
your prayer has been heard *your* *{the}* *prayer* and *{the}* your acts of charity *your*
5148 4666 1653 5148 3836 4666 2779 3836 5148 1797 5148
v.api.3s r.gs.2 d.nsf n.nsf cj d.npf n.npf r.gs.2

ἐμνήσθησαν ἐνώπιον τοῦ θεοῦ. 32 πέμψον οὖν εἰς Ἰόππην καὶ
have been remembered before *{the}* God. Send therefore to Joppa and
3630 1967 3836 2536 4287 4036 1650 2673 2779
v.api.3p p.g d.gsm n.gsm v.aam.2s cj p.a n.asf cj

μετακάλεσαι Σίμωνα ὃς ἐπικαλεῖται Πέτρος, οὗτος ξενίζεται ἐν οἰκίᾳ Σίμωνος
invite Simon who is called Peter. He is staying in the house of Simon, a
3559 4981 4005 2126 4377 4047 3826 1877 3864 4981
v.amm.2s n.asm r.nsm v.ppi.3s n.nsm r.nsm v.ppi.3s p.d n.dsf n.gsm

βυρσέως παρὰ θάλασσαν.[a] 33 ἐξαυτῆς οὖν ἔπεμψα πρὸς σέ, σύ τε
tanner, by the sea.' So immediately *So* I sent for you, and you *and*
1114 4123 2498 4036 1994 4036 4287 4639 5148 5445 5148 5445
n.gsm p.a n.asf adv cj v.aai.1s p.a r.as.2 r.ns.2 cj

καλῶς ἐποίησας παραγενόμενος. νῦν οὖν πάντες ἡμεῖς
did well *did* by coming. Now therefore we are all *we* here
4472 2822 4472 4134 3814 4036 7005 4205 4246 7005 4205
adv v.aai.2s pt.am.nsm adv cj a.npm r.np.1

ἐνώπιον τοῦ θεοῦ πάρεσμεν ἀκοῦσαι πάντα τὰ προστεταγμένα σοι ὑπὸ τοῦ
in the presence of God *are here* to hear all that has been commanded you by the
1967 3836 2536 4205 201 4246 3836 4705 5148 5679 3836
p.g d.gsm n.gsm v.pai.1p f.aa a.apn d.apn pt.rp.apn r.ds.2 p.g d.gsm

NASB

"Stand up; I too am
just a man." 27 As he
talked with him, he
entered and *found
many people as-
sembled. 28 And he
said to them, "You
yourselves know
how unlawful it is
for a man who is
a Jew to associate
with a foreigner or
to visit him; and
yet God has shown
me that I should
not call any man
unholy or unclean.
29 That is why I
came without
even raising any
objection when I
was sent for. So I
ask for what reason
you have sent for
me."
30 Cornelius said,
"Four days ago to
this hour, I was
praying in my
house during the
[a] ninth hour; and
behold, a man
stood before me in
shining garments,
31 and he *said,
'Cornelius, your
prayer has been
heard and your
alms have been
remembered before
God. 32 Therefore
send to Joppa and
invite Simon, who
is also called Peter,
to come to you; he
is staying at the
house of Simon *the*
tanner by the sea.'
33 So I sent for you
immediately, and
you have been kind
enough to come.
Now then, we are
all here present be-
fore God to hear all
that you have been
commanded by the
Lord."

[a] ὃς παραγενόμενος λαλήσει σοι included by TR after θάλασσαν.

[a] I.e. 3 to 4 p.m.

NIV

34 Then Peter be-
gan to speak: "I
now realize how
true it is that God
does not show
favoritism 35 but
accepts from ev-
ery nation the one
who fears him and
does what is right.
36 You know the
message God sent
to the people of
Israel, announc-
ing the good news
of peace through
Jesus Christ, who
is Lord of all.
37 You know what
has happened
throughout the
province of Ju-
dea, beginning in
Galilee after the
baptism that John
preached— 38 how
God anointed
Jesus of Naza-
reth with the Holy
Spirit and power,
and how he went
around doing good
and healing all
who were under
the power of the
devil, because God
was with him.
39 "We are wit-
nesses of every-
thing he did in
the country of the
Jews and in Jeru-
salem. They killed
him by hanging
him on a cross,
40 but God raised
him from the dead
on the third day
and caused him to
be seen. 41 He was
not seen by all the
people, but by wit-
nesses whom God
had already cho-
sen—by us who
ate and drank with
him after he rose
from the dead.

κυρίου. 34 ἀνοίξας δὲ Πέτρος τὸ στόμα εἶπεν, ⸤ἐπ' ἀληθείας⸥
Lord." So Peter opened *So* *Peter* his mouth and said: "Truly
3261 1254 4377 487 1254 4377 3836 5125 3306 2093 237
n.gsm pt.aa.nsm cj n.nsm d.asn n.asn v.aai.3s p.g n.gsf

καταλαμβάνομαι ὅτι οὐκ ἔστιν προσωπολήμπτης ὁ θεός, 35 ἀλλ' ἐν
I understand that God is not *is* one who shows partiality; *{the}* *God* but in
2898 4022 2536 1639 4024 1639 4720 3836 2536 247 1877
v.pmi.1s cj pl v.pai.3s n.nsm d.nsm n.nsm cj p.d

παντὶ ἔθνει ὁ φοβούμενος αὐτὸν καὶ ἐργαζόμενος δικαιοσύνην δεκτὸς
every nation *{the}* anyone who fears him and does what is right is acceptable
4246 1620 3836 5828 899 2779 2237 1466 1639 1283
a.dsn n.dsn d.nsm pt.pp.nsm r.asm.3 cj pt.pm.nsm n.asf a.nsm

αὐτῷ ἐστιν. 36 τὸν λόγον ὃν[a] ἀπέστειλεν τοῖς υἱοῖς Ἰσραὴλ εὐαγγελιζόμενος
to him *is* As for the word that he sent to the sons of Israel, preaching good news
899 1639 3836 3364 4005 690 3836 5626 2702 2294
r.dsm.3 v.pai.3s d.asm n.asm r.asm v.aai.3s d.dpm n.dpm n.gsm pt.pm.nsm

εἰρήνην διὰ Ἰησοῦ Χριστοῦ, οὗτός ἐστιν πάντων κύριος, 37 ↱ ὑμεῖς
of peace through Jesus Christ (he is Lord of all), *Lord* you yourselves
1645 1328 2652 5986 4047 1639 3261 4246 3261 3857 7007
n.asf p.g n.gsm n.gsm r.nsm v.pai.3s a.gpm n.nsm r.np.2

οἴδατε τὸ γενόμενον ῥῆμα καθ' ὅλης τῆς Ἰουδαίας, ἀρξάμενος ἀπὸ
know the account that spread *account* throughout all *{the}* Judea, beginning from
3857 4839 3836 1181 4839 2848 3910 3836 2677 806 608
v.rai.2p d.asn pt.am.asn n.asn p.g a.gsf d.gsf n.gsf pt.am.nsm p.g

τῆς Γαλιλαίας μετὰ τὸ βάπτισμα ὃ ἐκήρυξεν Ἰωάννης, 38 Ἰησοῦν τὸν ἀπὸ
{the} Galilee after the baptism that John proclaimed, *John* Jesus *{the}* of
3836 1133 3552 3836 967 4005 2722 3062 2722 2652 3836 608
d.gsf n.gsf p.a d.asn n.asn r.asn v.aai.3s n.nsm n.asm d.asm p.g

Ναζαρέθ, ὡς ἔχρισεν αὐτὸν ὁ θεὸς → πνεύματι ἁγίῳ καὶ →
Nazareth, how God anointed him *{the}* *God* with the Holy Spirit *Holy* and with
3714 6055 2536 5987 899 3836 2536 41 4460 41 2779
n.gsf cj v.aai.3s r.asm.3 d.nsm n.nsm n.dsn a.dsn cj

δυνάμει, ὃς διῆλθεν εὐεργετῶν καὶ ἰώμενος πάντας τοὺς καταδυναστευομένους
power; who went about doing good and healing all who were oppressed
1539 4005 1451 2308 2779 2615 4246 3836 2872
n.dsf r.nsm v.aai.3s pt.pa.nsm cj pt.pm.nsm a.apm d.apm pt.pp.apm

ὑπὸ τοῦ διαβόλου, ὅτι ὁ θεὸς ἦν μετ' αὐτοῦ. 39 καὶ ἡμεῖς μάρτυρες
by the devil, because *{the}* God was with him. And we are witnesses
5679 3836 1333 4022 3836 2536 1639 3552 899 2779 7005 3459
p.g d.gsm n.gsm cj d.nsm n.nsm v.iai.3s p.g r.gsm.3 cj r.np.1 n.npm

πάντων ὧν ἐποίησεν ἔν τε τῇ χώρᾳ τῶν Ἰουδαίων καὶ ἐν[b] Ἰερουσαλήμ.
of all that he did both in *both* the country of the Jews and in Jerusalem,
4246 4005 4472 5445 1877 5445 3836 6001 3836 2681 2779 1877 2647
a.gpn r.gpn v.aai.3s p.d cj d.dsf n.dsf d.gpm a.gpm cj p.d n.dsf

ὃν καὶ ἀνεῖλαν κρεμάσαντες ἐπὶ ξύλου. 40 τοῦτον ὁ θεὸς ἤγειρεν
whom also ⸤they put to death⸥ by hanging him on a tree. This man *{the}* God raised up
4005 2779 359 3203 2093 3833 4047 3836 2536 1586
r.asm adv v.aai.3p pt.aa.npm p.g n.gsm r.asm d.nsm n.nsm v.aai.3s

ἐν[c] τῇ τρίτῃ ἡμέρᾳ καὶ ἔδωκεν αὐτὸν ἐμφανῆ γενέσθαι, 41 οὐ παντὶ τῷ
on the third day and allowed him to be seen, *to be* not to all the
1877 3836 5569 2465 2779 1443 899 1181 1181 1871 1181 4024 4246 3836
p.d d.dsf a.dsf n.dsf cj v.aai.3s r.asm.3 a.asm f.am pl a.dsm d.dsm

λαῷ, ἀλλὰ μάρτυσιν τοῖς προκεχειροτονημένοις ὑπὸ τοῦ θεοῦ, ἡμῖν, οἵτινες
people but to witnesses who had been previously chosen by *{the}* God, to us, who
3295 247 3459 3836 4742 5679 3836 2536 7005 4015
n.dsm cj n.dpm d.dpm pt.rp.dpm p.g d.gsm n.gsm r.dp.1 r.npm

συνεφάγομεν καὶ συνεπίομεν αὐτῷ μετὰ τὸ ἀναστῆναι αὐτὸν ἐκ νεκρῶν·
ate and drank with him after he *{the}* rose *he* from the dead.
5303 2779 5228 899 3552 899 3836 482 899 1666 3738
v.aai.1p cj v.aai.1p r.dsm.3 p.a d.asn f.aa r.asm.3 p.g a.gpm

NASB

Gentiles Hear Good News

34 Opening his
mouth, Peter said:
"**I** most certainly
understand *now*
that God is not one
to show partiality,
35 but in every na-
tion the man who
fears Him and does
what is right is
welcome to Him.
36 The word which
He sent to the sons
of Israel, preach-
ing peace through
Jesus Christ (He is
Lord of all)— 37 you
yourselves know
the thing which
took place through-
out all Judea, start-
ing from Galilee,
after the baptism
which John pro-
claimed. 38 *You
know of* Jesus of
Nazareth, how God
anointed Him with
the Holy Spirit
and with power,
and *how* He went
about doing good
and healing all who
were oppressed by
the devil, for God
was with Him.
39 We are witnesses
of all the things He
did both in the land
of the Jews and in
Jerusalem. They
also put Him to
death by hanging
Him on a cross.
40 God raised Him
up on the third day
and granted that
He become vis-
ible, 41 not to all the
people, but to wit-
nesses who were
chosen beforehand
by God, *that is,*
to us who ate and
drank with Him
after He arose from
the dead.

[a] [ὃν] UBS.
[b] [ἐν] UBS, omitted by TNIV.
[c] [ἐν] UBS.

NIV

[42]He command-
ed us to preach
to the people and
to testify that he
is the one whom
God appointed as
judge of the liv-
ing and the dead.
[43]All the prophets
testify about him
that everyone who
believes in him re-
ceives forgiveness
of sins through his
name."
[44]While Peter
was still speaking
these words, the
Holy Spirit came
on all who heard
the message. [45]The
circumcised be-
lievers who had
come with Peter
were astonished
that the gift of the
Holy Spirit had
been poured out
even on Gentiles.
[46]For they heard
them speaking
in tongues[a] and
praising God.
Then Peter said,
[47]"Surely no one
can stand in the
way of their be-
ing baptized with
water. They have
received the Holy
Spirit just as we
have." [48]So he or-
dered that they
be baptized in
the name of Jesus
Christ. Then they
asked Peter to stay
with them for a
few days.

Peter Explains His Actions

11 The apostles
and the be-
lievers throughout
Judea heard that
the Gentiles also
had received the
word of God.

[a] 46 Or *other languages*

42 καὶ παρήγγειλεν ἡμῖν κηρύξαι τῷ λαῷ καὶ διαμαρτύρασθαι ὅτι οὗτός ἐστιν
And he commanded us to preach ⌞to the⌟ people and to testify that this is
2779 4133 7005 3062 3836 3295 2779 1371 4022 4047 1639
cj v.aai.3s r.dp.1 f.aa d.dsm n.dsm cj f.am cj r.nsm v.pai.3s

ὁ ὡρισμένος ὑπὸ τοῦ θεοῦ κριτὴς → ζώντων καὶ νεκρῶν. 43 τούτῳ
he who is appointed by *{the}* God to be judge of the living and the dead. To him
3836 3988 5679 3836 2536 3216 2409 2779 3738 4047
d.nsm pt.rp.nsm p.g d.gsm n.gsm n.nsm pt.pa.gpm cj a.gpm r.dsm

πάντες οἱ προφῆται μαρτυροῦσιν ἄφεσιν
all the prophets bear witness, that everyone who believes in him receives forgiveness
4246 3836 4737 3455 4246 3836 4409 1650 899 3284 912
a.npm d.npm n.npm v.pai.3p n.asf

ἁμαρτιῶν λαβεῖν διὰ τοῦ ὀνόματος αὐτοῦ πάντα τὸν πιστεύοντα εἰς αὐτόν.
of sins *receives* through *{the}* his name." *his* *everyone* *who* *believes* *in* *him*
281 3284 1328 3836 899 3950 899 4246 3836 4409 1650 899
n.gpf f.aa p.g d.gsn n.gsn r.gsm.3 a.asm d.asm pt.pa.asm p.a r.asm.3

44 ↱ ↱ ἔτι λαλοῦντος τοῦ Πέτρου τὰ ῥήματα ταῦτα
While Peter was still speaking *{the}* *Peter* *{the}* these words, *these* the Holy Spirit
3281 4377 3281 2285 3281 3836 4377 3836 4047 4839 4047 3836 41 4460
adv pt.pa.gsm d.gsm n.gsm d.apn n.apn r.apn

ἐπέπεσεν τὸ πνεῦμα τὸ ἅγιον ἐπὶ πάντας τοὺς ἀκούοντας τὸν λόγον.
came *the* *Spirit* *{the}* *Holy* on all those ⌞who were listening to⌟ the message.
2158 3836 4460 3836 41 2093 4246 3836 201 3836 3364
v.aai.3s d.nsn n.nsn d.nsn a.nsn p.a a.apm d.apm pt.pa.apm d.asm n.asm

45 καὶ ἐξέστησαν οἱ ἐκ περιτομῆς πιστοὶ ὅσοι συνῆλθαν τῷ
And *were amazed* the believers, ⌞from among⌟ the circumcised, *believers* who came with *{the}*
2779 2014 3836 4412 1666 4364 4412 4012 5302 3836
cj v.aai.3p d.npm p.g n.gsf a.npm r.npm v.aai.3p d.dsm

Πέτρῳ, ὅτι καὶ ἐπὶ τὰ ἔθνη ↱ ἡ δωρεὰ τοῦ ἁγίου πνεύματος
Peter, were amazed that even on the Gentiles was the gift of the Holy Spirit
4377 2014 2014 4022 2779 2093 3836 1620 1773 3836 1561 3836 41 4460
n.dsm cj adv p.a d.apn n.apn d.nsf n.nsf d.gsn a.gsn n.gsn

ἐκκέχυται· 46 ἤκουον γὰρ αὐτῶν λαλούντων γλώσσαις καὶ
poured out. For ⌞they were hearing⌟ *For* them speaking with tongues and
1773 1142 201 1142 899 3281 1185 2779
v.rpi.3s v.iai.3p cj r.gpm.3 pt.pa.gpm n.dpf cj

μεγαλυνόντων τὸν θεόν. τότε ἀπεκρίθη Πέτρος, 47 μήτι
magnifying *{the}* God. Then Peter declared, *Peter* ⌞"Surely no⌟ one is able to
3486 3836 2536 5538 4377 646 4377 3614 5516 1538 1538 3266
pt.pa.gpm d.asm n.asm adv v.api.3s n.nsm pl

τὸ ὕδωρ δύναται κωλῦσαί τις τοῦ μὴ βαπτισθῆναι
withhold the water *is able* *to withhold* *one* so that these people cannot be baptized
3266 3836 5623 1538 3266 5516 3836 4047 4047 3590 966
d.asn n.asn v.ppi.3s f.aa r.nsm d.gsn pl f.ap

τούτους, οἵτινες τὸ πνεῦμα τὸ ἅγιον ἔλαβον ὡς καὶ ἡμεῖς;
these people who received the Holy Spirit *{the}* *Holy* *received* just as *just* we did,
4047 4015 3284 3836 41 4460 3836 41 3284 2779 6055 2779 7005
r.apm r.npm d.asn n.asn d.asn a.asn v.aai.3p cj adv r.np.1

↰ ↰ 48 προσέταξεν δὲ αὐτοὺς ἐν τῷ ὀνόματι Ἰησοῦ
can he? And he ordered *And* them to be baptized in the name of Jesus
3614 3614 1254 4705 1254 899 966 966 966 1877 3836 3950 2652
v.aai.3s cj r.apm.3 p.d d.dsn n.dsn n.gsm

Χριστοῦ βαπτισθῆναι. τότε ἠρώτησαν αὐτὸν ἐπιμεῖναι → ἡμέρας τινάς.
Christ. *to be baptized* Then they asked him to remain for some days. *some*
5986 966 5538 2263 899 2152 5516 2465 5516
n.gsm f.ap adv v.aai.3p r.asm.3 f.aa n.apf r.apf

11:1 ἤκουσαν δὲ οἱ ἀπόστολοι καὶ οἱ ἀδελφοὶ οἱ ὄντες κατὰ τὴν
heard Now the apostles and the brothers who were throughout *{the}*
201 1254 3836 693 2779 3836 81 3836 1639 2848 3836
v.aai.3p cj d.npm n.npm cj d.npm n.npm d.npm pt.pa.npm p.a d.asf

Ἰουδαίαν ὅτι καὶ τὰ ἔθνη ἐδέξαντο τὸν λόγον τοῦ θεοῦ.
Judea heard that the Gentiles too *the* *Gentiles* had accepted the word of God.
2677 201 4022 3836 1620 2779 3836 1620 1312 3836 3364 3836 2536
n.asf cj adv d.npn n.npn v.ami.3p d.asm n.asm d.gsm n.gsm

NASB

[42]And He ordered
us to preach to
the people, and
solemnly to testify
that this is the One
who has been
appointed by God
as Judge of the liv-
ing and the dead.
[43]Of Him all the
prophets bear wit-
ness that through
His name everyone
who believes in
Him receives for-
giveness of sins."
[44]While Peter was
still speaking these
words, the Holy
Spirit fell upon all
those who were
listening to the
message. [45]All the
circumcised be-
lievers who came
with Peter were
amazed, because
the gift of the Holy
Spirit had been
poured out on the
Gentiles also. [46]For
they were hearing
them speaking
with tongues and
exalting God. Then
Peter answered,
[47]"Surely no one
can refuse the wa-
ter for these to be
baptized who have
received the Holy
Spirit just as we
did, can he?" [48]And
he ordered them
to be baptized in
the name of Jesus
Christ. Then they
asked him to stay
on for a few days.

Peter Reports at Jerusalem

[11:1]Now the
apostles and the
brethren who were
throughout Judea
heard that the
Gentiles also had
received the word
of God.

NIV

2 So when Pe-
ter went up to
Jerusalem, the cir-
cumcised believers
criticized him 3 and
said, "You went
into the house of
uncircumcised
men and ate with
them."
4 Starting from
the beginning, Pe-
ter told them the
whole story: 5 "I
was in the city of
Joppa praying, and
in a trance I saw a
vision. I saw some-
thing like a large
sheet being let
down from heaven
by its four corners,
and it came down
to where I was. 6 I
looked into it and
saw four-footed
animals of the
earth, wild beasts,
reptiles and birds.
7 Then I heard a
voice telling me,
'Get up, Peter. Kill
and eat.'
8 "I replied,
'Surely not, Lord!
Nothing impure
or unclean has
ever entered my
mouth.'
9 "The voice
spoke from heaven
a second time, 'Do
not call anything
impure that God
has made clean.'
10 This happened
three times, and
then it was all
pulled up to heav-
en again.
11 "Right then
three men who
had been sent to
me from Caes-
area stopped at
the house where I
was staying. 12 The
Spirit told

2 ὅτε δὲ ἀνέβη Πέτρος εἰς Ἰερουσαλήμ,
So when *So* Peter went up *Peter* to Jerusalem, they who were of the circumcision
1254 4021 1254 4377 326 4377 1650 2647 3836 1666 4364
cj cj v.aai.3s n.nsm p.a n.asf

διεκρίνοντο πρὸς αὐτὸν οἱ ἐκ περιτομῆς 3 λέγοντες ὅτι εἰσῆλθες πρὸς
took issue with him, *they of circumcision* saying, ~ "You went to a house of
1359 4639 899 3836 1666 4364 3306 4022 1656 4639 2400
v.imi.3p p.a r.asm.3 d.npm p.g n.gsf pt.pa.npm cj v.aai.2s p.a

ἄνδρας ἀκροβυστίαν ἔχοντας καὶ συνέφαγες αὐτοῖς. 4
uncircumcised men *uncircumcised of* and ate with them." But Peter
213 467 213 2400 2779 5303 899 1254 4377
n.apm n.asf pt.pa.apm cj v.aai.2s r.dpm.3

ἀρξάμενος δὲ Πέτρος ἐξετίθετο αὐτοῖς → καθεξῆς λέγων, 5 ἐγὼ ἤμην ἐν
began *But Peter* and explained to them in an orderly fashion, saying, "I was in
806 1254 4377 1758 899 2759 3306 1609 1639 1877
pt.am.nsm cj n.nsm v.imi.3s r.dpm.3 adv pt.pa.nsm r.ns.1 v.imi.1s p.d

πόλει Ἰόππῃ προσευχόμενος καὶ εἶδον ἐν ἐκστάσει ὅραμα,
the city of Joppa, praying, and in a trance I saw *in trance* a vision, an
4484 2673 4667 2779 1877 1749 1625 1877 1749 3969 5516
n.dsf n.dsf pt.pm.nsm cj v.aai.1s p.d n.dsf n.asn

καταβαῖνον σκεῦός τι ὡς ὀθόνην μεγάλην →
object descending, *object an* like a great sheet *great* being let down by its
5007 2849 5007 5516 6055 3489 3855 3489 2768 2768 2768
pt.pa.asn n.asn r.asn pl n.asf a.asf

τέσσαρσιν ἀρχαῖς καθιεμένην ἐκ τοῦ οὐρανοῦ, καὶ ἦλθεν ἄχρι ἐμοῦ. 6
four corners *being let down* from *{the}* heaven, and it came ⌊close to⌋ me. I
5475 794 2768 1666 3836 4041 2779 2262 948 1609 2917
a.dpf n.dpf pt.pp.asf p.g d.gsm n.gsm cj v.aai.3s p.g r.gs.1

εἰς ἣν ἀτενίσας κατενόουν καὶ εἶδον τὰ τετράποδα τῆς γῆς καὶ
looked into it closely *I looked* and I saw *{the}* four-footed animals of the earth, *{and}*
2917 1650 4005 867 2917 2779 1625 3836 5488 3836 1178 2779
p.a r.asf pt.aa.nsm v.iai.1s cj v.aai.1s d.apn n.apn d.gsf n.gsf cj

τὰ θηρία καὶ τὰ ἑρπετὰ καὶ τὰ πετεινὰ τοῦ οὐρανοῦ. 7 → ἤκουσα
{the} wild animals, *{and} {the}* reptiles, and *{the}* birds of the air. I also heard
3836 2563 2779 3836 2260 2779 3836 4374 3836 4041 2779 201
d.apn n.apn cj d.apn n.apn cj d.apn n.apn d.gsm n.gsm v.aai.1s

δὲ καὶ φωνῆς λεγούσης μοι, ἀναστάς, Πέτρε, θῦσον καὶ φάγε. 8 εἶπον δέ,
{and} also a voice saying to me, 'Get up, Peter; slaughter and eat!' But I said, *But*
1254 2779 5889 3306 1609 482 4377 2604 2779 2266 1254 3306 1254
cj adv n.gsf pt.pa.gsf r.ds.1 pt.aa.nsm n.vsm v.aam.2s cj v.aam.2s v.aai.1s cj

μηδαμῶς, κύριε, ὅτι κοινὸν ἢ ἀκάθαρτον οὐδέποτε → ← εἰσῆλθεν εἰς
'By no means, Lord; for nothing common or unclean *nothing* has ever entered into
3592 3261 4022 4030 3123 2445 176 4030 1656 1650
adv n.vsm cj a.nsn cj a.nsn adv v.aai.3s p.a

τὸ στόμα μου. 9 ἀπεκρίθη δὲ φωνὴ ⌊ἐκ δευτέρου⌋ ἐκ
{the} my mouth.' *my* But the voice replied *But voice* a second time from
3836 1609 5125 1609 1254 5889 646 1254 5889 1666 1311 1666
d.asn n.asn r.gs.1 v.api.3s cj n.nsf p.g a.gsn p.g

τοῦ οὐρανοῦ, ἃ ὁ θεὸς ἐκαθάρισεν, σὺ ↱ μὴ κοίνου. 10 τοῦτο
{the} heaven, 'What *{the}* God has made clean, you must not ⌊consider common.'⌋ This
3836 4041 4005 3836 2536 2751 5148 3124 3590 3124 4047
d.gsm n.gsm r.apn d.nsm n.nsm v.aai.3s r.ns.2 pl v.pam.2s r.nsn

δὲ ἐγένετο ⌊ἐπὶ τρίς,⌋ καὶ ἀνεσπάσθη πάλιν ἅπαντα εἰς τὸν
{and} happened three times, and again everything was drawn up *again everything* into *{the}*
1254 1181 2093 5565 2779 4099 570 413 4099 570 1650 3836
cj v.ami.3s p.a adv cj v.api.3s adv a.npn p.a d.asm

οὐρανόν. 11 καὶ ἰδοὺ ἐξαυτῆς τρεῖς ἄνδρες ἐπέστησαν ἐπὶ τὴν οἰκίαν ἐν
heaven. And behold, ⌊at that very moment⌋ three men arrived at the house, in
4041 2779 2627 1994 5552 467 2392 2093 3836 3864 1877
n.asm cj j adv a.npm n.npm v.aai.3p p.a d.asf n.asf p.d

ᾗ ἦμεν,[a] ἀπεσταλμένοι ἀπὸ Καισαρείας πρός με. 12 εἶπεν δὲ τὸ
which we were, sent from Caesarea to me. And the Spirit told *And the*
4005 1639 690 608 2791 4639 1609 1254 3836 4460 3306 1254 3836
r.dsf v.iai.1p pt.rp.npm p.g n.gsf p.a r.as.1 v.aai.3s cj d.nsn

[a] ἦμεν UBS, NET. ἤμην TNIV.

NASB

2 And when Peter
came up to Jeru-
salem, those who
were circumcised
took issue with
him, 3 saying, "You
went to uncircum-
cised men and ate
with them." 4 But
Peter began *speak-
ing* and *proceeded*
to explain to them
in orderly se-
quence, saying, 5 "I
was in the city of
Joppa praying; and
in a trance I saw a
vision, an object
coming down
like a great sheet
lowered by four
corners from the
sky; and it came
right down to me,
6 and when I had
fixed my gaze on it
and was observing
it I saw the four-
footed animals of
the earth and the
wild beasts and the
[a]crawling creatures
and the birds of the
air. 7 I also heard
a voice saying to
me, 'Get up, Peter;
kill and eat.' 8 But
I said, 'By no
means, Lord, for
nothing unholy or
unclean has ever
entered my mouth.'
9 But a voice from
heaven answered a
second time, 'What
God has cleansed,
no longer consider
unholy.' 10 This hap-
pened three times,
and everything
was drawn back
up into the sky.
11 And behold, at
that moment three
men appeared at
the house in which
we were *staying*,
having been sent to
me from Caesarea.
12 The Spirit told

[a] Or *reptiles*

NIV

me to have no hes-
itation about going
with them. These
six brothers also
went with me, and
we entered the
man's house. 13He
told us how he had
seen an angel ap-
pear in his house
and say, 'Send to
Joppa for Simon
who is called Pe-
ter. 14He will bring
you a message
through which
you and all your
household will be
saved.'
15"As I began to
speak, the Holy
Spirit came on
them as he had
come on us at the
beginning. 16Then
I remembered
what the Lord had
said: 'John bap-
tized with[a] water,
but you will be
baptized with[b] the
Holy Spirit.' 17So
if God gave them
the same gift he
gave us who be-
lieved in the Lord
Jesus Christ, who
was I to think that
I could stand in
God's way?"
18When they
heard this, they
had no further
objections and
praised God, say-
ing, "So then, even
to Gentiles God
has granted repen-
tance that leads to
life."

The Church in Antioch

19Now those who
had been scattered
by the persecu-
tion that broke out
when Stephen was
killed traveled as
far as Phoenicia,
Cyprus and Anti-
och, spreading the
word only among
Jews. 20Some of
them, however,
men from Cyprus

πνεῦμά μοι συνελθεῖν αὐτοῖς μηδὲν διακρίναντα. ἦλθον δὲ σὺν ἐμοὶ
Spirit me to go with them without hesitating. And with me went *And with me*
4460 1609 5302 899 3594 1359 1254 5250 1609 2262 1254 5250 1609
n.nsn r.ds.1 f.aa r.dpm.3 a.asn pt.aa.asm v.aai.3p cj p.d r.ds.1

καὶ οἱ ἐξ ἀδελφοὶ οὗτοι καὶ εἰσήλθομεν εἰς τὸν οἶκον τοῦ ἀνδρός.
also *{the}* these six brothers, *these* and we went into the house of the man.
2779 3836 4047 1971 81 4047 2779 1656 1650 3836 3875 3836 467
adv d.npm a.npm n.npm r.npm cj v.aai.1p p.a d.asm n.asm d.gsm n.gsm

13 ἀπήγγειλεν δὲ ἡμῖν πῶς εἶδεν τὸν[a] ἄγγελον ἐν τῷ οἴκῳ
And he told *And* us how ⌊he had seen⌋ the angel standing in *{the}* his house
1254 550 1254 7005 4802 1625 3836 34 2705 1877 3836 899 3875
v.aai.3s cj r.dp.1 cj v.aai.3s d.asm n.asm p.d d.dsm n.dsm

αὐτοῦ σταθέντα καὶ εἰπόντα, ἀπόστειλον εἰς Ἰόππην καὶ μετάπεμψαι Σίμωνα τὸν
his *standing* and saying, 'Send to Joppa and summon Simon, who
899 2705 2779 3306 690 1650 2673 2779 3569 4981 3836
r.gsm.3 pt.ap.asm cj pt.aa.asm v.aam.2s p.a n.asf cj v.amm.2s n.asm d.asm

ἐπικαλούμενον Πέτρον, 14 ὃς λαλήσει ῥήματα πρὸς σὲ ἐν οἷς
is called Peter, who will speak words to you by which you and your entire
2126 4377 4005 3281 4839 4639 5148 1877 4005 5148 2779 5148 4246
pt.pp.asm n.asm r.nsm v.fai.3s n.apn p.a r.as.2 p.d r.dpn

σωθήσῃ σὺ καὶ πᾶς ὁ οἶκός σου. 15 ἐν δὲ τῷ
household will be saved.' *you and entire {the} household your* And as *And* I ~
3875 5392 5148 2779 4246 3836 3875 5148 1254 1877 1254 1609 3836
v.fpi.2s r.ns.2 cj a.nsm d.nsm n.nsm r.gs.2 p.d cj d.dsn

ἄρξασθαί με λαλεῖν ἐπέπεσεν τὸ πνεῦμα τὸ ἅγιον ἐπ' αὐτοὺς
began *I* to speak, the Holy Spirit fell *the Spirit {the} Holy* upon them just
806 1609 3281 3836 41 4460 2158 3836 4460 3836 41 2093 899 2779
f.am r.as.1 f.pa v.aai.3s d.nsn n.nsn d.nsn a.nsn p.a r.apm.3

ὥσπερ καὶ ἐφ' ἡμᾶς ἐν ἀρχῇ. 16 ἐμνήσθην δὲ τοῦ ῥήματος
as *just* he did upon us at the beginning. And I remembered *And* the word
6061 2779 2093 7005 1877 794 1254 3630 1254 3836 4839
pl adv p.a r.ap.1 p.d n.dsf v.api.1s cj d.gsn n.gsn

τοῦ κυρίου ὡς ἔλεγεν, Ἰωάννης μὲν ἐβάπτισεν ὕδατι, ὑμεῖς δὲ
of the Lord, how he said, 'John indeed baptized with water, but you *but*
3836 3261 6055 3306 2722 3525 966 5623 1254 7007 1254
d.gsm n.gsm cj v.iai.3s n.nsm pl v.aai.3s n.dsn r.np.2 cj

βαπτισθήσεσθε ἐν πνεύματι ἁγίῳ. 17 εἰ οὖν τὴν ἴσην δωρεὰν
will be baptized with the Holy Spirit.' *Holy* If then God gave the same gift
966 1877 41 4460 41 1623 4036 2536 1443 3836 2698 1561
v.fpi.2p p.d n.dsn a.dsn cj cj d.asf a.asf n.asf

ἔδωκεν αὐτοῖς ὁ θεὸς ὡς καὶ ἡμῖν πιστεύσασιν ἐπὶ τὸν κύριον
gave to them *{the} God* as *{also}* he gave to us when we believed in the Lord
1443 899 3836 2536 6055 2779 7005 4409 2093 3836 3261
v.aai.3s r.dpm.3 d.nsm n.nsm cj adv r.dp.1 pt.aa.dpm p.a d.asm n.asm

Ἰησοῦν Χριστόν, ἐγὼ τίς ἤμην δυνατὸς κωλῦσαι ← τὸν
Jesus Christ, who was I *who was* to be able to stand in God's way?" *{the}*
2652 5986 5515 1639 1609 5515 1639 1543 3266 2536 3836
n.asm n.asm r.ns.1 r.nsm v.imi.1s a.nsm f.aa d.asm

θεόν; 18 Ἀκούσαντες δὲ ταῦτα ἡσύχασαν καὶ ἐδόξασαν τὸν θεὸν
God's When they heard *{and}* these things, they fell silent, and they glorified *{the}* God,
2536 201 1254 4047 2483 2779 1519 3836 2536
n.asm pt.aa.npm cj r.apn v.aai.3p cj v.aai.3p d.asm n.asm

λέγοντες, ἄρα καὶ τοῖς ἔθνεσιν ὁ θεὸς τὴν μετάνοιαν εἰς
saying, ⌊"So then⌋ even to the Gentiles *{the}* God has granted *{the}* repentance that leads to
3306 726 2779 3836 1620 3836 2536 1443 1443 3836 3567 1650
pt.pa.npm cj adv d.dpn n.dpn d.nsm n.nsm d.asf n.asf p.a

ζωὴν ἔδωκεν. 19 οἱ μὲν οὖν διασπαρέντες ἀπὸ τῆς θλίψεως τῆς
life." *has granted* Now those ~ *Now* who were scattered ⌊because of⌋ the persecution, which
2437 1443 4036 3836 3525 4036 1401 608 3836 2568 3836
n.asf v.aai.3s d.npm pl cj pt.ap.npm p.g d.gsf n.gsf d.gsf

γενομένης ἐπὶ Στεφάνῳ διῆλθον ἕως Φοινίκης καὶ Κύπρου καὶ
came to pass over Stephen, ⌊made their way⌋ ⌊as far as⌋ Phoenicia and Cyprus and
1181 2093 5108 1451 2401 5834 2779 3251 2779
pt.am.gsf p.d n.dsm v.aai.3p p.g n.gsf cj n.gsf cj

NASB

me to go with them
without misgiv-
ings. These six
brethren also went
with me and we
entered the man's
house. 13And he
reported to us how
he had seen the
angel standing in
his house, and say-
ing, 'Send to Joppa
and have Simon,
who is also called
Peter, brought here;
14and he will speak
words to you by
which you will be
saved, you and all
your household.'
15And as I began
to speak, the Holy
Spirit fell upon
them just as *He*
did upon us at the
beginning. 16And
I remembered the
word of the Lord,
how He used to
say, 'John baptized
with water, but you
will be baptized
with the Holy
Spirit.' 17Therefore
if God gave to
them the same gift
as *He gave* to us
also after believing
in the Lord Jesus
Christ, who was I
that I could stand
in God's way?"
18When they heard
this, they quieted
down and glori-
fied God, saying,
"Well then, God
has granted to the
Gentiles also the
repentance *that*
leads to life."

The Church at Antioch

19So then those
who were scat-
tered because of
the persecution
that occurred in
connection with
Stephen made their
way to Phoenicia
and Cyprus and

[a] 16 Or *in*
[b] 16 Or *in*

[a] [τὸν] UBS.

NIV

and Cyrene, went
to Antioch and
began to speak to
Greeks also, tell-
ing them the good
news about the
Lord Jesus. 21 The
Lord's hand was
with them, and a
great number of
people believed
and turned to the
Lord.
22 News of this
reached the church
in Jerusalem, and
they sent Barna-
bas to Antioch.
23 When he arrived
and saw what the
grace of God had
done, he was glad
and encouraged
them all to re-
main true to the
Lord with all their
hearts. 24 He was a
good man, full of
the Holy Spirit and
faith, and a great
number of people
were brought to
the Lord.
25 Then Barnabas
went to Tarsus
to look for Saul,
26 and when he
found him, he
brought him to
Antioch. So for a
whole year Barna-
bas and Saul met
with the church
and taught great
numbers of people.
The disciples were
called Christians
first at Antioch.

Ἀντιοχείας μηδενὶ λαλοῦντες τὸν λόγον ⌊εἰ μὴ⌋ μόνον
Antioch, speaking the word to no one *speaking* *the* *word* except Jews only.
522 3281 3836 3364 3594 3281 3836 3364 1623 3590 2681 3667
n.gsf a.dsm pt.pa.npm d.asm n.asm cj pl adv

Ἰουδαίοις. 20 ἦσαν δέ τινες ἐξ αὐτῶν ἄνδρες Κύπριοι καὶ Κυρηναῖοι,
Jews But there were *But* some of them, men of Cyprus and Cyrene,
2681 1254 1639 1254 5516 1666 899 467 3250 2779 3254
a.dpm v.iai.3p cj r.npm p.g r.gpm.3 n.npm n.npm cj n.npm

οἵτινες ἐλθόντες εἰς Ἀντιόχειαν ἐλάλουν καὶ πρὸς τοὺς Ἑλληνιστὰς
who on coming to Antioch began to speak also to the Hellenists,
4015 2262 1650 522 3281 2779 4639 3836 1821
r.npm pt.aa.npm p.a n.asf v.iai.3p adv p.a d.apm n.apm

εὐαγγελιζόμενοι τὸν κύριον Ἰησοῦν. 21 καὶ ἦν χεὶρ κυρίου
preaching the Lord Jesus. And the hand of the Lord was *hand* *of Lord*
2294 3836 3261 2652 2779 5931 3261 3261 1639 5931 3261
pt.pm.npm d.asm n.asm n.asm cj v.iai.3s n.nsf n.gsm

μετ' αὐτῶν, πολύς τε ἀριθμὸς ὁ πιστεύσας ἐπέστρεψεν ἐπὶ τὸν
with them, and a great *and* number became *{the}* believers and turned to the
3552 899 5445 4498 5445 750 3836 4409 2188 2093 3836
p.g r.gpm.3 a.nsm cj n.nsm d.nsm pt.aa.nsm v.aai.3s p.a d.asm

κύριον. 22 ἠκούσθη δὲ ὁ λόγος εἰς τὰ ὦτα τῆς
Lord. The report of all this was heard *{and}* *The* *report* in the ears of the
3261 3836 3364 4309 899 201 1254 3836 3364 1650 3836 4044 3836
n.asm v.api.3s cj d.nsm n.nsm p.a d.apn n.apn d.gsf

ἐκκλησίας τῆς οὔσης ἐν Ἰερουσαλὴμ περὶ αὐτῶν καὶ ἐξαπέστειλαν Βαρναβᾶν[a]
church *{the}* *{being}* in Jerusalem, *of* *this* and they sent Barnabas
1711 3836 1639 1877 2647 4309 899 2779 1990 982
n.gsf d.gsf pt.pa.gsf p.d n.dsf p.g r.gpm.3 cj v.aai.3p n.asm

ἕως Ἀντιοχείας. 23 ↱ ὃς παραγενόμενος καὶ ἰδὼν τὴν χάριν τὴν[b] τοῦ
⌊as far as⌋ Antioch. When he came and saw the grace *{the}* of
2401 522 1625 4005 4134 2779 1625 3836 5921 3836 3836
p.g n.gsf r.nsm pt.am.nsm cj pt.aa.nsm d.asf n.asf d.asf d.gsm

θεοῦ, ἐχάρη καὶ παρεκάλει πάντας
God, ⌊he was glad,⌋ and ⌊he began to exhort⌋ them all to remain faithful to the Lord
2536 5897 2779 4151 4246 4693 4693 4693 3836 3836 3261
n.gsm v.api.3s cj v.iai.3s a.apm

τῇ προθέσει τῆς καρδίας προσμένειν τῷ κυρίῳ, 24 ὅτι ἦν ἀνὴρ
⌊in the⌋ purpose of their hearts, *to remain faithful* *to the* *Lord* for ⌊he was⌋ a good man,
3836 4606 3836 2840 4693 3836 3261 4022 1639 19 467
d.dsf n.dsf d.gsf n.gsf f.pa d.dsm n.dsm cj v.iai.3s n.nsm

ἀγαθὸς καὶ πλήρης → πνεύματος ἁγίου καὶ πίστεως. καὶ
good *{and}* full of the Holy Spirit *Holy* and of faith. And a considerable number
19 2779 4441 41 4460 41 2779 4411 2779 2653 2653
a.nsm cj a.nsm n.gsn a.gsn cj n.gsf cj

προσετέθη ὄχλος ἱκανὸς τῷ κυρίῳ. 25 ἐξῆλθεν δὲ
of people were brought *people* *considerable number* ⌊to the⌋ Lord. So Barnabas went *So*
4063 4707 4063 2653 3836 3261 1254 2002 1254
v.api.3s n.nsm a.nsm d.dsm n.dsm v.aai.3s cj

εἰς Ταρσὸν ἀναζητῆσαι Σαῦλον, 26 καὶ εὑρὼν ἤγαγεν εἰς
to Tarsus to look for Saul, and ⌊when he had found⌋ him, he brought him to
1650 5433 349 4930 2779 2351 72 1650
p.a n.asf f.aa n.asm cj pt.aa.nsm v.aai.3s p.a

Ἀντιόχειαν. ἐγένετο δὲ αὐτοῖς καὶ → ἐνιαυτὸν ὅλον
Antioch. *{it happened that}* *{and}* *they* *{also}* For a whole year *whole* they
522 1181 1254 899 2779 3910 1929 3910 899
n.asf v.ami.3s cj r.dpm.3 adv n.asm a.asm

συναχθῆναι ἐν τῇ ἐκκλησίᾳ καὶ διδάξαι ὄχλον
met with the church and taught a considerable number of people.
5251 1877 3836 1711 2779 1438 2653 2653 4063
f.ap p.d d.dsf n.dsf cj f.aa n.asm

ἱκανόν, χρηματίσαι τε πρώτως ἐν Ἀντιοχείᾳ
considerable number *were called* And in Antioch the disciples were first *in* *Antioch*
2653 5976 5445 1877 522 3836 3412 5976 4759 1877 522
a.asm f.aa cj adv p.d n.dsf

NASB

Antioch, speaking
the word to no one
except to Jews
alone. 20 But there
were some of them,
men of Cyprus and
Cyrene, who came
to Antioch and
began speaking to
the [a]Greeks also,
preaching the Lord
Jesus. 21 And the
hand of the Lord
was with them,
and a large number
who believed
turned to the Lord.
22 The news about
them reached the
ears of the church
at Jerusalem,
and they sent
Barnabas off to
Antioch. 23 Then
when he arrived
and witnessed the
grace of God, he
rejoiced and *began*
to encourage them
all with resolute
heart to remain
true to the Lord;
24 for he was a good
man, and full of
the Holy Spirit and
of faith. And con-
siderable numbers
were brought to
the Lord. 25 And he
left for Tarsus to
look for Saul; 26 and
when he had found
him, he brought
him to Antioch.
And for an entire
year they met with
the church and
taught considerable
numbers; and the
disciples were first
called Christians in
Antioch.

[a] διελθεῖν included by UBS after Βαρναβᾶν.
[b] [τὴν] UBS.

[a] Lit *Hellenists;* people who lived by Greek customs and culture

NIV

[27]During this time some prophets came down from Jerusalem to Antioch. [28]One of them, named Agabus, stood up and through the Spirit predicted that a severe famine would spread over the entire Roman world. (This happened during the reign of Claudius.) [29]The disciples, as each one was able, decided to provide help for the brothers and sisters living in Judea. [30]This they did, sending their gift to the elders by Barnabas and Saul.

Peter's Miraculous Escape From Prison

12 It was about this time that King Herod arrested some who belonged to the church, intending to persecute them. [2]He had James, the brother of John, put to death with the sword. [3]When he saw that this met with approval among the Jews, he proceeded to seize Peter also. This happened during the Festival of Unleavened Bread. [4]After arresting him, he put him in prison, handing him over to be guarded by four squads of four soldiers each. Herod intended to bring him out for public trial after the Passover.
[5]So Peter was kept in

τοὺς μαθητὰς Χριστιανούς. 27 ἐν ταύταις δὲ ταῖς ἡμέραις
the disciples called Christians. During these *{and} {the}* days prophets
3836 3412 5976 5985 1877 4047 1254 3836 2465 4737
d.apm n.apm n.apm p.d r.dpf cj d.dpf n.dpf

κατῆλθον ἀπὸ Ἱεροσολύμων προφῆται εἰς Ἀντιόχειαν. 28 ἀναστὰς
came down from Jerusalem *prophets* to Antioch. And one of them stood up,
2982 608 2642 4737 1650 522 1254 1651 1666 899 482
v.aai.3p p.g n.gpn n.npm p.a n.asf pt.aa.nsm

δὲ εἷς ἐξ αὐτῶν ὀνόματι Ἅγαβος ἐσήμανεν διὰ τοῦ πνεύματος
And one of them named Agabus, and indicated by the Spirit that there would
1254 1651 1666 899 3950 13 4955 1328 3836 4460 3516 3516
cj a.nsm p.g r.gpm.3 n.dsn n.nsm v.aai.3s p.g d.gsn n.gsn

λιμὸν μεγάλην μέλλειν ἔσεσθαι ἐφ᾽ ὅλην τὴν οἰκουμένην, ἥτις ἐγένετο
be a great famine *great there would be* over all the world (which took place
1639 3489 3350 3489 3516 1639 2093 3910 3836 3876 4015 1181
n.asf a.asf f.pa f.fm p.a a.asf d.asf n.asf r.nsf v.ami.3s

ἐπὶ Κλαυδίου. 29 τῶν δὲ μαθητῶν, καθὼς εὐπορεῖτό
in the days of Claudius). So each of the *So* disciples, ⌊according to⌋ his financial ability,
2093 3087 1254 1667 3836 1254 3412 2777 5516 2344
p.g n.gsm d.gpm cj n.gpm cj v.imi.3s

τις, ὥρισαν ἕκαστος ⌊αὐτῶν εἰς διακονίαν⌋ πέμψαι τοῖς
his resolved *each* to send relief *to send* to the brothers
5516 3988 1667 4287 4287 899 1650 1355 4287 3836 81
r.nsm v.aai.3p r.nsm r.gpm.3 p.a n.asf f.aa d.dpm

κατοικοῦσιν ἐν τῇ Ἰουδαίᾳ ἀδελφοῖς· 30 ὃ καὶ ἐποίησαν
living in *{the}* Judea, *brothers* and they did so, *and they did*
2997 1877 3836 2677 81 2779 4472 4472 4005 2779 4472
pt.pa.dpm p.d d.dsf n.dsf n.dpm r.asn adv v.aai.3p

ἀποστείλαντες πρὸς τοὺς πρεσβυτέρους διὰ χειρὸς → Βαρναβᾶ καὶ Σαύλου.
sending it to the elders by the hand of Barnabas and Saul.
690 4639 3836 4565 1328 5931 982 2779 4930
pt.aa.npm p.a d.apm a.apm p.g n.gsf n.gsm cj n.gsm

12:1 κατ᾽ ἐκεῖνον δὲ τὸν καιρὸν ἐπέβαλεν Ἡρῴδης ὁ
About that *{and} {the}* time Herod the king set *Herod the*
2848 1697 1254 3836 2789 2476 3836 995 2095 2476 3836
p.a r.asm cj d.asm n.asm v.aai.3s n.nsm d.nsm

βασιλεὺς τὰς χεῖρας κακῶσαί τινας τῶν ἀπὸ τῆς ἐκκλησίας. 2 → →
king his hand to mistreat some *{the}* ⌊belonging to⌋ the church. He had James
995 3836 5931 2808 5516 3836 608 3836 1711 2610
n.nsm d.apf n.apf f.aa r.apm d.gpm p.g d.gsf n.gsf

ἀνεῖλεν δὲ Ἰάκωβον τὸν ἀδελφὸν Ἰωάννου → μαχαίρῃ.
the brother of John put to death *{and} James the brother of John* with the sword,
3836 81 2722 2722 359 1254 2610 3836 81 2722 3479
v.aai.3s cj n.asm d.asm n.asm n.gsm n.dsf

3 ἰδὼν δὲ ὅτι ⌊ἀρεστόν ἐστιν⌋ τοῖς Ἰουδαίοις, προσέθετο συλλαβεῖν
and ⌊when he saw⌋ *and* that it pleased the Jews, he proceeded to arrest
1254 1625 1254 4022 744 1639 3836 2681 4707 5197
pt.aa.nsm cj cj a.nsn v.pai.3s d.dpm a.dpm v.ami.3s f.aa

καὶ Πέτρον, ἦσαν δὲ αἱ[a] ἡμέραι τῶν ἀζύμων 4
Peter also. *Peter* This was *{and}* during the days of ⌊Unleavened Bread.⌋ When he
4377 2779 4377 1639 1254 3836 2465 3836 109 4389 4389
adv n.asm v.iai.3p cj d.npf n.npf d.gpn n.gpn

ὃν καὶ πιάσας ἔθετο εἰς φυλακὴν παραδοὺς ←
had seized him, *{also} When he had seized* he put him in prison, handing him over
4389 4389 4005 2779 4389 5502 1650 5871 4140
r.asm adv pt.aa.nsm v.ami.3s p.a n.asf pt.aa.nsm

τέσσαρσιν τετραδίοις στρατιωτῶν φυλάσσειν αὐτόν, βουλόμενος μετὰ τὸ
to four squads of four soldiers each to guard him, intending after the
5475 5482 5132 5875 899 1089 3552 3836
a.dpn n.dpn n.gpm f.pa r.asm.3 pt.pm.nsm p.a d.asn

πάσχα ἀναγαγεῖν αὐτὸν ↰ τῷ λαῷ. 5 ὁ μὲν οὖν Πέτρος ἐτηρεῖτο ἐν τῇ
Passover to bring him out ⌊to the⌋ people. *{the}* ~ So Peter was kept in *{the}*
4247 343 899 343 3836 3295 3836 3525 4036 4377 5498 1877 3836
n.asn f.aa r.asm.3 d.dsm n.dsm d.nsm pl cj n.nsm v.ipi.3s p.d d.dsf

[a] [αἱ] UBS, omitted by TNIV.

NASB

[27]Now at this time some prophets came down from Jerusalem to Antioch. [28]One of them named Agabus stood up and *began* to indicate by the Spirit that there would certainly be a great famine all over the world. And this took place in the *reign* of Claudius. [29]And in the proportion that any of the disciples had means, each of them determined to send *a contribution* for the relief of the brethren living in Judea. [30]And this they did, sending it in charge of Barnabas and Saul to the elders.

Peter's Arrest and Deliverance

[12:1]Now about that time Herod the king laid hands on some who belonged to the church in order to mistreat them. [2]And he had James the brother of John put to death with a sword. [3]When he saw that it pleased the Jews, he proceeded to arrest Peter also. Now it was during the days of Unleavened Bread. [4]When he had seized him, he put him in prison, delivering him to four squads of soldiers to guard him, intending after the Passover to bring him out before the people. [5]So Peter was kept

NIV

prison, but the
church was ear-
nestly praying to
God for him.
6The night be-
fore Herod was to
bring him to trial,
Peter was sleep-
ing between two
soldiers, bound
with two chains,
and sentries stood
guard at the en-
trance. 7Suddenly
an angel of the
Lord appeared and
a light shone in
the cell. He struck
Peter on the side
and woke him up.
"Quick, get up!"
he said, and the
chains fell off Pe-
ter's wrists.
8Then the angel
said to him, "Put
on your clothes
and sandals."
And Peter did so.
"Wrap your cloak
around you and
follow me," the an-
gel told him. 9Peter
followed him out
of the prison, but
he had no idea
that what the an-
gel was doing was
really happening;
he thought he was
seeing a vision.
10They passed the
first and second
guards and came
to the iron gate
leading to the city.
It opened for them
by itself, and they
went through it.
When they had
walked the length
of one street, sud-
denly the angel left
him.
11Then Peter
came to himself

φυλακῇ· προσευχὴ δὲ ἦν ἐκτενῶς γινομένη ὑπὸ τῆς
prison, but prayer *but* was made earnestly *made* to God for him by the
5871 1254 4666 1254 1639 1181 1757 1181 4639 2536 4309 899 5679 3836
n.dsf n.nsf cj v.iai.3s adv pt.pm.nsf p.g d.gsf

ἐκκλησίας πρὸς τὸν θεὸν περὶ αὐτοῦ. 6 ὅτε δὲ ἤμελλεν προαγαγεῖν
church. *to* *{the}* *God* *for* *him* Now when *Now* Herod was about to bring
1711 4639 3836 2536 4309 899 1254 4021 1254 2476 3516 4575
n.gsf p.a d.asm n.asm p.g r.gsm.3 cj cj v.iai.3s f.aa

αὐτὸν ↰ ὁ Ἡρῴδης, τῇ νυκτὶ ἐκείνῃ ἦν ὁ Πέτρος
him out, *{the}* *Herod* on that very night, *that very* Peter was *{the}* *Peter*
899 4575 3836 2476 3836 1697 1697 3816 1697 4377 1639 3836 4377
r.asm.3 d.nsm n.nsm d.dsf n.dsf r.dsf v.iai.3s d.nsm n.nsm

κοιμώμενος μεταξὺ δύο στρατιωτῶν δεδεμένος → ἁλύσεσιν δυσὶν φύλακές
asleep between two soldiers, bound with two chains; *two* and guards
3121 3568 1545 5132 1313 1545 268 1545 5445 5874
pt.pp.nsm p.g a.gpm n.gpm pt.rp.nsm n.dpf a.dpf n.npm

τε πρὸ τῆς θύρας ἐτήρουν τὴν φυλακήν. 7 καὶ ἰδοὺ ἄγγελος → κυρίου
and before the door were guarding the prison. And behold, an angel of the Lord
5445 4574 3836 2598 5498 3836 5871 2779 2627 34 3261
cj p.g d.gsf n.gsf v.iai.3p d.asf n.asf cj j n.nsm n.gsm

ἐπέστη καὶ φῶς ἔλαμψεν ἐν τῷ οἰκήματι· ↱ πατάξας δὲ τὴν
⌞suddenly appeared,⌟ and a light shone in the cell. He struck *{and}* the
2392 2779 5890 3290 1877 3836 3862 1586 4250 1254 3836
v.aai.3s cj n.nsn v.aai.3s p.d d.dsn n.dsn pt.aa.nsm cj d.asf

πλευρὰν τοῦ Πέτρου ἤγειρεν αὐτὸν λέγων, ἀνάστα ⌞ἐν τάχει.⌟ καὶ
side of Peter and woke him, saying, "Get up quickly." And his chains
4433 3836 4377 1586 899 3306 482 1877 5443 2779 899 268
n.asf d.gsm n.gsm v.aai.3s r.asm.3 pt.pa.nsm v.aam.2s p.d n.dsn cj

ἐξέπεσαν αὐτοῦ αἱ ἁλύσεις ἐκ τῶν χειρῶν. 8 εἶπεν δὲ ὁ ἄγγελος
fell *his* *{the}* *chains* off his hands. And the angel said *And* *the* *angel*
1738 899 3836 268 1666 3836 5931 1254 3836 34 3306 1254 3836 34
v.aai.3p r.gsm.3 d.npf n.npf p.g d.gpf n.gpf v.aai.3s cj d.nsm n.nsm

πρὸς αὐτόν, ζῶσαι καὶ ὑπόδησαι τὰ σανδάλιά σου. ἐποίησεν δὲ
to him, ⌞"Dress yourself⌟ and put on *{the}* your sandals." *your* And he did *And*
4639 899 2439 2779 5686 3836 5148 4908 5148 1254 4472 1254
p.a r.asm.3 v.amm.2s cj v.amm.2s d.apn n.apn r.gs.2 v.aai.3s cj

οὕτως. καὶ λέγει αὐτῷ, περιβαλοῦ τὸ ἱμάτιόν σου ↰ ↰ καὶ ἀκολούθει
so. And he said to him, "Wrap *{the}* your cloak *your* around yourself and follow
4048 2779 3306 899 4314 3836 5148 2668 5148 4314 4314 2779 199
adv cj v.pai.3s r.dsm.3 v.amm.2s d.asn n.asn r.gs.2 cj v.pam.2s

μοι. 9 καὶ ↱ ἐξελθὼν ἠκολούθει καὶ ↱ ↱ οὐκ ᾔδει ὅτι ἀληθές ἐστιν
me." And he went out and followed him, and he did not know that *real* *was*
1609 2779 199 2002 199 2779 3857 3857 4024 3857 4022 239 1639
r.ds.1 cj pt.aa.nsm v.iai.3s cj pl v.lai.3s cj a.nsn v.pai.3s

τὸ γινόμενον διὰ τοῦ ἀγγέλου· ἐδόκει δὲ ὅραμα
what was being done by the angel was real, but thought *but* he was seeing a vision.
3836 1181 1328 3836 34 1639 239 1254 1506 1254 1063 1063 1063 3969
d.nsn pt.pm.nsn p.g d.gsm n.gsm v.iai.3s cj n.asn

βλέπειν. 10 διελθόντες δὲ πρώτην φυλακὴν καὶ δευτέραν ἦλθαν
he was seeing ⌞When they had passed⌟ *{and}* the first guard and the second, they came
1063 1451 1254 4755 5871 2779 1311 2262
f.pa pt.aa.npm cj a.asf n.asf cj a.asf v.aai.3p

ἐπὶ τὴν πύλην τὴν σιδηρᾶν τὴν φέρουσαν εἰς τὴν πόλιν, ἥτις αὐτομάτη
to the iron gate *{the}* *iron* that leads into the city, which of its own accord
2093 3836 4971 4783 3836 4971 3836 5770 1650 3836 4484 4015 897
p.a d.asf n.asf d.asf a.asf d.asf pt.pa.asf p.a d.asf n.asf r.nsf a.nsf

ἠνοίγη αὐτοῖς καὶ ↱ ἐξελθόντες προῆλθον ῥύμην μίαν, καὶ εὐθέως
opened for them, and they went out and went down one street, *one* and immediately the
487 899 2779 4601 2002 4601 1651 4860 1651 2779 2311 3836
v.api.3s r.dpm.3 cj pt.aa.npm v.aai.3p n.asf a.asf cj adv

ἀπέστη ὁ ἄγγελος ἀπ' αὐτοῦ. 11 καὶ ὁ Πέτρος ἐν ἑαυτῷ
angel left *the* *angel* *{from}* him. *{and}* *{the}* When Peter came to himself,
34 923 3836 34 608 899 2779 3836 1181 4377 1181 1877 1571
v.aai.3s d.nsm n.nsm p.g r.gsm.3 cj d.nsm n.nsm p.d r.dsm.3

NASB

in the prison, but
prayer for him
was being made
fervently by the
church to God.
6On the very night
when Herod was
about to bring him
forward, Peter was
sleeping between
two soldiers, bound
with two chains,
and guards in front
of the door were
watching over
the prison. 7And
behold, an angel
of the Lord sud-
denly appeared
and a light shone
in the cell; and he
struck Peter's side
and woke him up,
saying, "Get up
quickly." And his
chains fell off his
hands. 8And the
angel said to him,
"Gird yourself and
put on your san-
dals." And he did
so. And he *said to
him, "Wrap your
cloak around you
and follow me."
9And he went out
and continued to
follow, and he did
not know that what
was being done
by the angel was
real, but thought
he was seeing a vi-
sion. 10When they
had passed the first
and second guard,
they came to the
iron gate that leads
into the city, which
opened for them
by itself; and they
went out and went
along one street,
and immediately
the angel departed
from him. 11When
Peter came to him-
self, he said,

NIV

and said, "Now
I know without
a doubt that the
Lord has sent his
angel and rescued
me from Herod's
clutches and from
everything the
Jewish people
were hoping would
happen."
12 When this had
dawned on him,
he went to the
house of Mary the
mother of John,
also called Mark,
where many peo-
ple had gathered
and were praying.
13 Peter knocked
at the outer en-
trance, and a ser-
vant named Rhoda
came to answer the
door. 14 When she
recognized Peter's
voice, she was
so overjoyed she
ran back without
opening it and ex-
claimed, "Peter is
at the door!"
15 "You're out of
your mind," they
told her. When
she kept insisting
that it was so, they
said, "It must be
his angel."
16 But Peter kept
on knocking, and
when they opened
the door and saw
him, they were as-
tonished. 17 Peter
motioned with his
hand for them to
be quiet and de-
scribed how the
Lord had brought
him out of prison.
"Tell James and
the other brothers
and sisters about
this," he said, and
then he left for an-
other place.
18 In the morning,

γενόμενος εἶπεν, νῦν οἶδα ἀληθῶς ὅτι ἐξαπέστειλεν ὁ[a] κύριος τὸν
When came he said, "Now I know for certain that the Lord has sent *the* *Lord* *{the}*
1181 3306 3814 3857 242 4022 3836 3261 1990 3836 3261 3836
pt.am.nsm v.aai.3s adv v.rai.1s adv cj v.aai.3s d.nsm n.nsm d.asm

ἄγγελον αὐτοῦ καὶ ἐξείλατό με ἐκ χειρὸς Ἡρῴδου καὶ ↰ πάσης τῆς
his angel *his* and rescued me from the hand of Herod and from all that the
899 34 899 2779 1975 1609 1666 5931 2476 2779 1666 4246 3836 3836
n.asm r.gsm.3 cj v.ami.3s r.as.1 p.g n.gsf n.gsm cj a.gsf d.gsf

προσδοκίας τοῦ λαοῦ τῶν Ἰουδαίων. 12 συνιδών τε
Jewish people were expecting." *the* *people* *{the}* *Jewish* ⌊When he realized⌋ ~ this,
2681 3295 4660 3836 3295 3836 2681 5328 5445
n.gsf d.gsm n.gsm d.gpm a.gpm pt.aa.nsm cj

ἦλθεν ἐπὶ τὴν οἰκίαν τῆς Μαρίας τῆς μητρὸς Ἰωάννου τοῦ ἐπικαλουμένου
he went to the house of Mary, the mother of John whose other name was
2262 2093 3836 3864 3836 3451 3836 3613 2722 3836 2126
v.aai.3s p.a d.asf n.asf d.gsf n.gsf d.gsf n.gsf n.gsm d.gsm pt.pp.gsm

Μάρκου, οὗ ἦσαν ἱκανοὶ συνηθροισμένοι καὶ προσευχόμενοι. 13 →
Mark, where there were many gathered together and praying. And when he
3453 4023 1639 2653 5255 2779 4667 1254 899
n.gsm adv v.iai.3p a.npm pt.rp.npm cj pt.pm.npm

κρούσαντος δὲ αὐτοῦ τὴν θύραν τοῦ πυλῶνος
knocked *And* *he* at the door of the gateway, a servant girl named Rhoda
3218 1254 899 3836 2598 3836 4784 4087 4087 3950 4851
pt.aa.gsm cj r.gsm.3 d.asf n.asf d.gsm n.gsm

προσῆλθεν παιδίσκη ὑπακοῦσαι ὀνόματι Ῥόδη, 14 καὶ ἐπιγνοῦσα τὴν
came *servant girl* to answer. *named* *Rhoda* *{and}* When she recognized *{the}* Peter's
4665 4087 5634 3950 4851 2779 2105 3836 4377
v.aai.3s n.nsf f.aa n.dsn n.nsf cj pt.aa.nsf d.asf

φωνὴν τοῦ Πέτρου ἀπὸ τῆς χαρᾶς ↱ ↱ οὐκ ἤνοιξεν τὸν πυλῶνα,
voice, *{the}* *Peter's* ⌊because of⌋ her joy she did not open the gate, but
5889 3836 4377 608 3836 5915 487 487 4024 487 3836 4784 1254
n.asf d.gsm n.gsm p.g d.gsf n.gsf pl v.aai.3s d.asm n.asm

εἰσδραμοῦσα δὲ ἀπήγγειλεν ἑστάναι τὸν Πέτρον πρὸ τοῦ πυλῶνος.
ran back inside *but* and reported that Peter was standing *{the}* *Peter* at the gate.
1661 1254 550 4377 2705 3836 4377 4574 3836 4784
pt.aa.nsf cj v.aai.3s f.ra d.asm n.asm p.g d.gsm n.gsm

15 οἱ δὲ πρὸς αὐτὴν εἶπαν, μαίνῃ. ἡ δὲ διϊσχυρίζετο
They *{and}* said to her, *said* ⌊"You are out of your mind."⌋ But she *But* insisted
3836 1254 3306 4639 899 3306 3419 1254 3836 1254 1462
d.npm cj p.a r.asf.3 v.aai.3p v.pmi.2s d.nsf cj v.imi.3s

οὕτως ἔχειν. οἱ δὲ ἔλεγον, ὁ ἄγγελός ἐστιν αὐτοῦ.
that it was so. *it was* They *{and}* kept saying, "It is his *{the}* angel!" *It is* *his*
2400 2400 4048 2400 3836 1254 3306 1639 1639 899 3836 34 1639 899
adv f.pa d.npm cj v.iai.3p d.nsm n.nsm v.pai.3s r.gsm.3

16 ὁ δὲ Πέτρος ἐπέμενεν κρούων· ἀνοίξαντες δὲ εἶδαν αὐτὸν καὶ
{the} But Peter continued knocking; and when they opened, *and* they saw him and
3836 1254 4377 2152 3218 1254 487 1254 1625 899 2779
d.nsm cj n.nsm v.iai.3s pt.pa.nsm pt.aa.npm cj v.aai.3p r.asm.3 cj

ἐξέστησαν. 17 κατασείσας δὲ αὐτοῖς τῇ χειρὶ σιγᾶν
were astonished. But Peter motioned *But* to them ⌊with his⌋ hand to be silent, and
2014 1254 2939 1254 899 3836 5931 4967
v.aai.3p pt.aa.nsm cj r.dpm.3 d.dsf n.dsf f.pa

διηγήσατο[b] πῶς ὁ κύριος αὐτὸν ἐξήγαγεν ἐκ τῆς φυλακῆς
he related how the Lord had brought him *had brought* ⌊out of⌋ the prison. And
1455 4802 3836 3261 1974 1974 899 1974 1666 3836 5871 5445
v.ami.3s cj d.nsm n.nsm r.asm.3 v.aai.3s p.g d.gsf n.gsf

εἶπέν τε, ἀπαγγείλατε Ἰακώβῳ καὶ τοῖς ἀδελφοῖς ταῦτα. καὶ ↱
he said, *And* "Tell these things to James and to the brothers." *these things* Then he
3306 5445 550 4047 4047 2610 2779 3836 81 4047 2779 4513
v.aai.3s cj v.aam.2p n.dsm cj d.dpm n.dpm r.apn cj

ἐξελθὼν ἐπορεύθη εἰς ἕτερον τόπον. 18 → γενομένης δὲ ἡμέρας
departed and went to another place. Now when day came, *Now* *day*
2002 4513 1650 2283 5536 1254 2465 1181 1254 2465
pt.aa.nsm v.api.3s p.a r.asm n.asm pt.am.gsf cj n.gsf

NASB

"Now I know for
sure that the Lord
has sent forth His
angel and rescued
me from the hand
of Herod and from
all that the Jew-
ish people were
expecting." 12 And
when he real-
ized *this,* he went
to the house of
Mary, the mother
of John who was
also called Mark,
where many were
gathered together
and were praying.
13 When he knocked
at the door of the
gate, a servant-girl
named Rhoda came
to answer. 14 When
she recognized
Peter's voice,
because of her joy
she did not open
the gate, but ran in
and announced that
Peter was standing
in front of the gate.
15 They said to her,
"You are out of
your mind!" But
she kept insisting
that it was so. They
kept saying, "It is
his angel." 16 But
Peter continued
knocking; and
when they had
opened *the door,*
they saw him and
were amazed.
17 But motioning
to them with his
hand to be silent,
he described to
them how the Lord
had led him out of
the prison. And he
said, "Report these
things to James and
the brethren." Then
he left and went to
another place.
18 Now when day

[a] [ὁ] UBS.
[b] αὐτοῖς included by UBS after διηγήσατο.

NIV

there was no small
commotion among
the soldiers as to
what had become
of Peter. [19]After
Herod had a thor-
ough search made
for him and did
not find him, he
cross-examined
the guards and or-
dered that they be
executed.

Herod's Death

Then Herod
went from Judea
to Caesarea and
stayed there. [20]He
had been quar-
reling with the
people of Tyre and
Sidon; they now
joined together
and sought an au-
dience with him.
After securing the
support of Blastus,
a trusted person-
al servant of the
king, they asked
for peace, because
they depended on
the king's coun-
try for their food
supply.
[21]On the appoint-
ed day Herod,
wearing his royal
robes, sat on his
throne and de-
livered a public
address to the peo-
ple. [22]They shout-
ed, "This is the
voice of a god, not
of a man." [23]Im-
mediately, because
Herod did not give
praise to God, an
angel of the Lord
struck him down,
and he was eat-
en by worms and
died.
[24]But the word of
God continued to
spread and flourish.

Barnabas and Saul Sent Off

[25]When Barnabas
and Saul had fin-
ished their mission,
they returned from[a]
Jerusalem, taking
with them John,
also called Mark.

[a] 25 Some manu-
scripts *to*

ἦν τάραχος οὐκ ὀλίγος ἐν τοῖς στρατιώταις τί ἄρα
⌊there was⌋ no little commotion *no* *little* among the soldiers as to what *{then}* had
1639 4024 3900 5431 4024 3900 1877 3836 5132 5515 726 1181
v.iai.3s n.nsm pl a.nsm p.d d.dpm n.dpm r.nsn cj

ὁ Πέτρος ἐγένετο. 19 ↱ Ἡρῴδης δὲ ἐπιζητήσας αὐτὸν καὶ ↱
become of *{the}* Peter. *had become* And after Herod *And* searched for him and could
1181 3836 4377 1181 1254 2118 2476 1254 2118 899 2779 2351
d.nsm n.nsm v.ami.3s n.nsm cj pt.aa.nsm r.asm.3 cj

μὴ εὑρών, ↱ ἀνακρίνας τοὺς φύλακας ἐκέλευσεν ἀπαχθῆναι, καὶ
not find him, he examined the guards and ordered them to be executed. Then
3590 2351 3027 373 3836 5874 3027 552 2779
pl pt.aa.nsm pt.aa.nsm d.apm n.apm v.aai.3s f.ap cj

↱ κατελθὼν ἀπὸ τῆς Ἰουδαίας εἰς Καισάρειαν διέτριβεν. 20
he went down from *{the}* Judea to Caesarea and stayed there. Now Herod
1417 2982 608 3836 2677 1650 2791 1417 1254
pt.aa.nsm p.g d.gsf n.gsf p.a n.asf v.iai.3s

ἦν δὲ θυμομαχῶν → Τυρίοις καὶ Σιδωνίοις· ὁμοθυμαδὸν δὲ
was *Now* very angry with the Tyrinians and the Sidonians, and with one accord *and*
1639 1254 2595 5601 2779 4973 1254 3924 1254
v.iai.3s cj pt.pa.nsm n.dpm cj a.dpm adv cj

παρῆσαν πρὸς αὐτὸν καὶ πείσαντες Βλάστον, τὸν ἐπὶ τοῦ
they came to him and ⌊when they had persuaded⌋ Blastus, who was ⌊in charge of⌋ the
4205 4639 899 2779 4275 1058 3836 2093 3836
v.iai.3p p.a r.asm.3 cj pt.aa.npm n.asm d.asm p.g d.gsm

κοιτῶνος τοῦ βασιλέως, ᾐτοῦντο εἰρήνην διὰ τὸ τρέφεσθαι
bed-chamber of the king, ⌊they asked for⌋ peace because *{the}* their country's food-supply
3131 3836 995 160 1645 1328 3836 899 6001 5555
n.gsm d.gsm n.gsm v.imi.3p n.asf p.a d.asn f.pp

αὐτῶν τὴν χώραν ἀπὸ τῆς βασιλικῆς. 21 → τακτῇ δὲ
their *{the}* *country's* was provided by the king's country. On an appointed *{and}*
899 3836 6001 608 3836 997 5414 1254
r.gpm.3 d.asf n.asf p.g d.gsf a.gsf a.dsf cj

ἡμέρᾳ ὁ Ἡρῴδης ἐνδυσάμενος ἐσθῆτα βασιλικὴν καὶ[a] καθίσας ἐπὶ τοῦ
day *{the}* Herod put on his royal robes, *royal* *{and}* sat down on the
2465 3836 2476 1907 997 2264 997 2779 2767 2093 3836
n.dsf d.nsm n.nsm pt.am.nsm n.asf a.asf cj pt.aa.nsm p.g d.gsn

βήματος ἐδημηγόρει πρὸς αὐτούς, 22 ὁ δὲ δῆμος ἐπεφώνει,
⌊judgment seat,⌋ and ⌊delivered an oration⌋ to them. But the *But* crowd began to shout,
1037 1319 4639 899 1254 3836 1254 1322 2215
n.gsn v.iai.3s p.a r.apm.3 d.nsm cj n.nsm v.iai.3s

→ θεοῦ φωνὴ καὶ οὐκ → ἀνθρώπου. 23 παραχρῆμα δὲ
"It is the voice of a god, *voice* and not of a man!" And immediately *And* an angel
5889 2536 5889 2779 4024 476 1254 4202 1254 34
n.gsm n.nsf cj pl n.gsm adv cj

→ ἐπάταξεν αὐτὸν ἄγγελος κυρίου ⌊ἀνθ' ὧν⌋ ↱ ↱ οὐκ
of the Lord struck Herod down *Herod* *angel* *of Lord* because he did not
3261 3261 899 4250 899 34 3261 505 4005 1443 1443 4024
v.aai.3s r.asm.3 n.nsm n.gsm p.g r.gpn pl

ἔδωκεν τὴν δόξαν τῷ θεῷ, καὶ γενόμενος σκωληκόβρωτος ἐξέψυξεν. 24 ὁ
give the glory to God, and he was eaten by worms and died. But the
1443 3836 1518 3836 2536 2779 1181 5037 1775 1254 3836
v.aai.3s d.asf n.asf d.dsm n.dsm cj pt.am.nsm a.nsm v.aai.3s d.nsm

δὲ λόγος τοῦ θεοῦ ηὔξανεν καὶ ἐπληθύνετο. 25 Βαρναβᾶς δὲ καὶ
But word of God ⌊continued to advance⌋ and gain adherents. And Barnabas *And* and
1254 3364 3836 2536 889 2779 4437 1254 982 1254 2779
cj n.nsm d.gsm n.gsm v.iai.3s cj v.ipi.3s n.nsm cj cj

Σαῦλος ὑπέστρεψαν εἰς[b] Ἰερουσαλὴμ πληρώσαντες τὴν διακονίαν,
Saul returned from Jerusalem having completed their mission,
4930 5715 1650 2647 4444 3836 1355
n.nsm v.aai.3p p.a n.asf pt.aa.npm d.asf n.asf

συμπαραλαβόντες Ἰωάννην τὸν ἐπικληθέντα Μᾶρκον.
taking with them John, whose other name was Mark.
5221 2722 3836 2126 3453
pt.aa.npm n.asm d.asm pt.ap.asm n.asm

[a] [καὶ] UBS, omitted by TNIV.
[b] εἰς UBS, NET. ἐξ TNIV.

NASB

came, there was no
small disturbance
among the soldiers
as to what could
have become of Pe-
ter. [19]When Herod
had searched for
him and had not
found him, he ex-
amined the guards
and ordered that
they be led away
to execution. Then
he went down from
Judea to Caesarea
and was spending
time there.

Death of Herod

[20]Now he was
very angry with the
people of Tyre and
Sidon; and with
one accord they
came to him, and
having won over
Blastus the king's
chamberlain, they
were asking for
peace, because
their country was
fed by the king's
country. [21]On an
appointed day
Herod, having put
on his royal ap-
parel, took his seat
on the rostrum and
began delivering
an address to them.
[22]The people kept
crying out, "The
voice of a god and
not of a man!"
[23]And immediately
an angel of the
Lord struck him
because he did not
give God the glory,
and he was eaten
by worms and died.
[24]But the word of
the Lord continued
to grow and to be
multiplied.
[25]And Barnabas
and Saul returned
from Jerusalem
when they had ful-
filled their mission,
taking along with
them John, who
was also called
Mark.

NIV

13 [1]Now in
the church
at Antioch there
were prophets and
teachers: Barna-
bas, Simeon called
Niger, Lucius of
Cyrene, Manaen
(who had been
brought up with
Herod the tetrarch)
and Saul. [2]While
they were worship-
ing the Lord and
fasting, the Holy
Spirit said, "Set
apart for me Bar-
nabas and Saul for
the work to which
I have called
them." [3]So after
they had fasted
and prayed, they
placed their hands
on them and sent
them off.

On Cyprus

[4]The two of them,
sent on their way
by the Holy Spirit,
went down to Se-
leucia and sailed
from there to Cy-
prus. [5]When they
arrived at Salamis,
they proclaimed
the word of God in
the Jewish syna-
gogues. John was
with them as their
helper.
[6]They traveled
through the whole
island until they
came to Paphos.
There they met a
Jewish sorcerer
and false prophet
named Bar-Jesus,
[7]who was an atten-
dant of the procon-
sul, Sergius Pau-
lus. The proconsul,
an intelligent man,
sent for Barnabas
and Saul because
he wanted to hear
the word of God.
[8]But Elymas the
sorcerer (for that
is what his name
means)

13:1 ἦσαν δὲ ἐν Ἀντιοχείᾳ κατὰ τὴν οὖσαν ἐκκλησίαν προφῆται καὶ
Now there were {Now} in Antioch in the local church prophets and
1254 1639 1254 1877 522 2848 3836 1639 1711 4737 2779
v.iai.3p cj p.d n.dsf p.a d.asf pt.pa.asf n.asf n.npm cj

διδάσκαλοι ὅ τε Βαρναβᾶς καὶ Συμεὼν ὁ καλούμενος Νίγερ καὶ Λούκιος
teachers, {the} both Barnabas and Simeon who was called Niger, {and} Lucius
1437 3836 5445 982 2779 5208 3836 2813 3769 2779 3372
n.npm d.nsm cj n.nsm cj n.nsm d.nsm pt.pp.nsm n.nsm cj n.nsm

ὁ Κυρηναῖος, Μαναήν τε Ἡρῴδου τοῦ τετραάρχου
the Cyrenian, and Manaen, {and} the foster-brother of Herod the tetrarch,
3836 3254 5445 3441 5445 5343 2476 3836 5490
d.nsm n.nsm n.nsm cj n.gsm d.gsm n.gsm

σύντροφος καὶ Σαῦλος. 2 → λειτουργούντων δὲ αὐτῶν τῷ
foster-brother and Saul. While they ⌞were performing their service⌟ {and} they ⌞to the⌟
5343 2779 4930 899 3310 1254 899 3836
n.nsm cj n.nsm pt.pa.gpm cj r.gpm.3 d.dsm

κυρίῳ καὶ νηστευόντων εἶπεν τὸ πνεῦμα τὸ ἅγιον, ἀφορίσατε δή
Lord and fasting, the Holy Spirit said, {the} {Spirit} {the} Holy "Set apart {then}
3261 2779 3764 3836 41 4460 3306 3836 4460 3836 41 928 1314
n.dsm cj pt.pa.gpm v.aai.3s d.nsn n.nsn d.nsn a.nsn v.aam.2p pl

μοι τὸν Βαρναβᾶν καὶ Σαῦλον εἰς τὸ ἔργον ↱ ὃ προσκέκλημαι αὐτούς.
⌞for me⌟ {the} Barnabas and Saul for the work to which I have called them."
1609 3836 982 2779 4930 1650 3836 2240 4673 4005 4673 899
r.ds.1 d.asm n.asm cj n.asm p.a d.asn n.asn r.asn v.rmi.1s r.apm.3

3 τότε νηστεύσαντες καὶ προσευξάμενοι καὶ ↱ ἐπιθέντες τὰς χεῖρας αὐτοῖς
Then after fasting and praying {and} they laid their hands on them and
5538 3764 2779 4667 2779 668 2202 3836 5931 899
adv pt.aa.npm cj pt.am.npm cj pt.aa.npm d.apf n.apf r.dpm.3

ἀπέλυσαν. ← 4 αὐτοὶ μὲν οὖν ἐκπεμφθέντες ὑπὸ τοῦ ἁγίου πνεύματος
sent them off. So they, ~ {So} being sent out by the Holy Spirit,
668 4036 899 3525 4036 1734 5679 3836 41 4460
v.aai.3p r.npm pl cj pt.ap.npm p.g d.gsn a.gsn n.gsn

κατῆλθον εἰς Σελεύκειαν, ἐκεῖθέν τε ἀπέπλευσαν εἰς Κύπρον 5 καὶ
went down to Seleucia, and from there {and} they sailed to Cyprus. And
2982 1650 4942 5445 1696 5445 676 1650 3251 2779
v.aai.3p p.a n.asf adv cj v.aai.3p p.a n.asf cj

γενόμενοι ἐν Σαλαμῖνι κατήγγελλον τὸν λόγον τοῦ θεοῦ ἐν ταῖς
when they arrived in Salamis, they began to proclaim the word of God in the
1181 1877 4887 2859 3836 3364 3836 2536 1877 3836
pt.am.npm p.d n.dsf v.iai.3p d.asm n.asm d.gsm n.gsm p.d d.dpf

συναγωγαῖς τῶν Ἰουδαίων. → εἶχον δὲ καὶ Ἰωάννην → ὑπηρέτην.
synagogues of the Jews, and they also had {and} {also} John as their assistant.
5252 3836 2681 1254 2779 2400 1254 2779 2722 5677
n.dpf d.gpm a.gpm v.iai.3p cj adv n.asm n.asm

6 διελθόντες δὲ ὅλην τὴν νῆσον ἄχρι Πάφου εὗρον
⌞When they had gone through⌟ {and} the whole {the} island ⌞as far as⌟ Paphos, they met a certain
1451 1254 3836 3910 3836 3762 948 4265 2351 5516
pt.aa.npm cj a.asf d.asf n.asf p.g n.gsf v.aai.3p

ἄνδρα τινὰ μάγον ψευδοπροφήτην Ἰουδαῖον ⌞ᾧ ὄνομα⌟ Βαριησοῦ
man, {certain} a magician, a Jewish false prophet {Jewish} named Bar-Jesus,
467 5516 3407 2681 6021 2681 4005 3950 979
n.asm r.asm n.asm n.asm a.asm r.dsm n.nsn n.nsm

7 ὃς ἦν σὺν τῷ ἀνθυπάτῳ Σεργίῳ Παύλῳ, ἀνδρὶ συνετῷ. οὗτος
who was with the proconsul Sergius Paulus, an intelligent man. {intelligent} This man
4005 1639 5250 3836 478 4950 4263 5305 467 5305 4047
r.nsm v.iai.3s p.d d.dsm n.dsm n.dsm n.dsm n.dsm a.dsm r.nsm

προσκαλεσάμενος Βαρναβᾶν καὶ Σαῦλον ἐπεζήτησεν ἀκοῦσαι τὸν λόγον τοῦ
summoned Barnabas and Saul and wanted to hear the word of
4673 982 2779 4930 2118 201 3836 3364 3836
pt.am.nsm n.asm cj n.asm v.aai.3s f.aa d.asm n.asm d.gsm

θεοῦ. 8 ἀνθίστατο δὲ αὐτοῖς Ἐλύμας ὁ μάγος, οὕτως γὰρ
God. {opposed} But {them} Elymas the magician (for ⌞that is the way⌟ {for} his name
2536 468 1254 899 1829 3836 3407 1142 4048 1142 899 3950
n.gsm v.imi.3s cj r.dpm.3 n.nsm d.nsm n.nsm adv cj

NASB

First Missionary Journey

[13:1]Now there were
at Antioch, in the
church that was
there, prophets and
teachers: Barnabas,
and Simeon who
was called Niger,
and Lucius of
Cyrene, and Ma-
naen who had been
brought up with
Herod the tetrarch,
and Saul. [2]While
they were minis-
tering to the Lord
and fasting, the
Holy Spirit said,
"Set apart for Me
Barnabas and Saul
for the work to
which I have called
them." [3]Then,
when they had
fasted and prayed
and laid their hands
on them, they sent
them away.
[4]So, being sent
out by the Holy
Spirit, they went
down to Seleucia
and from there
they sailed to
Cyprus. [5]When
they reached Sa-
lamis, they *began*
to proclaim the
word of God in the
synagogues of the
Jews; and they also
had John as their
helper. [6]When they
had gone through
the whole island as
far as Paphos, they
found a magician, a
Jewish false proph-
et whose name
was Bar-Jesus,
[7]who was with the
proconsul, Sergius
Paulus, a man of
intelligence. This
man summoned
Barnabas and Saul
and sought to hear
the word of God.
[8]But Elymas the
magician (for so
his name is

NIV

opposed them and
tried to turn the
proconsul from
the faith. [9]Then
Saul, who was
also called Paul,
filled with the
Holy Spirit, looked
straight at Elymas
and said, [10]"You
are a child of the
devil and an ene-
my of everything
that is right! You
are full of all kinds
of deceit and trick-
ery. Will you never
stop perverting the
right ways of the
Lord? [11]Now the
hand of the Lord is
against you. You
are going to be
blind for a time,
not even able to
see the light of the
sun."
Immediately mist
and darkness came
over him, and he
groped about,
seeking someone
to lead him by the
hand. [12]When the
proconsul saw
what had hap-
pened, he believed,
for he was amazed
at the teaching
about the Lord.

In Pisidian Antioch

[13]From Paphos,
Paul and his com-
panions sailed to
Perga in Pamphyl-
ia, where John left
them to return to
Jerusalem. [14]From
Perga they went
on to Pisidian An-
tioch. On the Sab-
bath they entered
the synagogue and
sat down. [15]After
the reading from
the Law and the
Prophets, the lead-
ers of the syna-
gogue sent word to

μεθερμηνεύεται τὸ ὄνομα αὐτοῦ, ζητῶν διαστρέψαι τὸν ἀνθύπατον
is translated) *{the}* *name* *his* opposed them, trying to turn the proconsul
3493 3836 3950 899 468 899 2426 1406 3836 478
v.ppi.3s d.nsn n.nsn r.gsm.3 pt.pa.nsm f.aa d.asm n.asm

ἀπὸ τῆς πίστεως. 9 Σαῦλος δέ, ὁ καὶ Παῦλος, πλησθεὶς →
⌊away from⌋ the faith. But Saul, *But* who is also Paul, filled with the Holy
608 3836 4411 1254 4930 1254 3836 2779 4263 4398 41
p.g d.gsf n.gsf n.nsm cj d.nsm adv n.nsm pt.ap.nsm

πνεύματος ἁγίου ἀτενίσας εἰς αὐτὸν 10 εἶπεν, ὦ πλήρης παντὸς
Spirit, *Holy* looked intently at him and said, "O man full of all kinds
4460 41 867 1650 899 3306 6043 4441 4246
n.gsn a.gsn pt.aa.nsm p.a r.asm.3 v.aai.3s j a.vsm a.gsm

δόλου καὶ πάσης ῥᾳδιουργίας, υἱὲ → διαβόλου, ἐχθρὲ πάσης δικαιοσύνης, ↱
of deceit and all fraud, son of the devil, enemy of all righteousness, will
1515 2779 4246 4816 5626 1333 2398 4246 1466 4264
n.gsm cj a.gsf n.gsf n.vsm n.gsm a.vsm a.gsf n.gsf

↱ οὐ παύσῃ διαστρέφων τὰς ὁδοὺς τοῦ[a] κυρίου τὰς εὐθείας; 11 καὶ νῦν
you not stop making crooked the straight paths of the Lord? *{the}* *straight* And now,
4264 4024 4264 1406 3836 2318 3847 3836 3261 3836 2318 2779 3814
pl v.fmi.2s pt.pa.nsm d.apf n.apf d.gsm n.gsm d.apf a.apf cj adv

ἰδοὺ χεὶρ → κυρίου ἐπὶ σὲ καὶ ἔσῃ τυφλὸς μὴ βλέπων τὸν ἥλιον
behold, the hand of the Lord is upon you, and ⌊you will be⌋ blind, not seeing the sun
2627 5931 3261 2093 5148 2779 1639 5603 3590 1063 3836 2463
j n.nsf n.gsm p.a r.as.2 cj v.fmi.2s a.nsm pl pt.pa.nsm d.asm n.asm

ἄχρι καιροῦ. παραχρῆμά τε ἔπεσεν ἐπ᾽ αὐτὸν ἀχλὺς καὶ σκότος καὶ
for a time." And immediately *And* fell upon him mist and darkness, and
948 2789 5445 4202 5445 4406 2093 899 944 2779 5030 2779
p.g n.gsm adv cj v.aai.3s p.a r.asm.3 n.nsf cj n.nsn cj

περιάγων ἐζήτει χειραγωγούς. 12 τότε
⌊as he went about⌋ he sought ⌊someone to lead him by the hand.⌋ Then the proconsul believed,
4310 2426 5933 5538 3836 478 4409
pt.pa.nsm v.iai.3s n.apm adv

ἰδὼν ὁ ἀνθύπατος τὸ γεγονὸς ἐπίστευσεν ἐκπλησσόμενος ἐπὶ τῇ
⌊when he saw⌋ *the* *proconsul* what had occurred, *believed* for he was astonished at the
1625 3836 478 3836 1181 4409 1742 2093 3836
pt.aa.nsm d.nsm n.nsm d.asn pt.ra.asn v.aai.3s pt.pp.nsm p.d d.dsf

διδαχῇ τοῦ κυρίου. 13 ἀναχθέντες δὲ ἀπὸ τῆς Πάφου
teaching of the Lord. Then Paul and those with him put out to sea *Then* from *{the}* Paphos
1439 3836 3261 1254 4263 3836 4309 343 1254 608 3836 4265
n.dsf d.gsm n.gsm pt.ap.npm cj p.g d.gsf n.gsf

οἱ περὶ Παῦλον ἦλθον εἰς Πέργην τῆς Παμφυλίας, Ἰωάννης δὲ
those *with* *Paul* and came to Perga of Pamphylia. John, however,
3836 4309 4263 2262 1650 4308 3836 4103 2722 1254
d.npm p.a n.asm v.aai.3p p.a n.asf d.gsf n.gsf n.nsm cj

ἀποχωρήσας ἀπ᾽ αὐτῶν ὑπέστρεψεν εἰς Ἱεροσόλυμα. 14 αὐτοὶ δὲ
left *{from}* them and returned to Jerusalem; but they *but*
713 608 899 5715 1650 2642 1254 899 1254
pt.aa.nsm p.g r.gpm.3 v.aai.3s p.a n.apn r.npm cj

διελθόντες ἀπὸ τῆς Πέργης παρεγένοντο εἰς Ἀντιόχειαν τὴν Πισιδίαν,
went on from *{the}* Perga and arrived at Pisidian Antioch. *{the}*
1451 608 3836 4308 4134 1650 4407 522 3836 4407
pt.aa.npm p.g d.gsf n.gsf v.ami.3p p.a n.asf d.asf n.asf

καὶ ↱ ἐλθόντες[b] εἰς τὴν συναγωγὴν τῇ ἡμέρᾳ τῶν
{and} On the sabbath day they went into the synagogue *On the* *day* *{the}*
2779 3836 3836 4879 2465 2767 2262 1650 3836 5252 3836 2465 3836
cj pt.aa.npm p.a d.asf n.asf d.dsf n.dsf d.gpn

σαββάτων ἐκάθισαν. 15 μετὰ δὲ τὴν ἀνάγνωσιν τοῦ νόμου καὶ τῶν
sabbath and sat down. After *{and}* the reading ⌊from the⌋ Law and the
4879 2767 3552 1254 3836 342 3836 3795 2779 3836
n.gpn v.aai.3p p.a cj d.asf n.asf d.gsm n.gsm cj d.gpm

προφητῶν ἀπέστειλαν οἱ ἀρχισυνάγωγοι πρὸς
Prophets, the rulers of the synagogue sent *the* *rulers of the synagogue* a message to
4737 3836 801 801 801 801 690 3836 801 4639
n.gpm v.aai.3p d.npm n.npm p.a

NASB

translated) was
opposing them,
seeking to turn the
proconsul away
from the faith. [9]But
Saul, who was also
known as Paul,
filled with the Holy
Spirit, fixed his
gaze on him, [10]and
said, "You who are
full of all deceit
and fraud, you
son of the devil,
you enemy of all
righteousness, will
you not cease to
make crooked the
straight ways of
the Lord? [11]Now,
behold, the hand
of the Lord is
upon you, and you
will be blind and
not see the sun
for a time." And
immediately a mist
and a darkness fell
upon him, and he
went about seeking
those who would
lead him by the
hand. [12]Then the
proconsul believed
when he saw what
had happened,
being amazed at
the teaching of the
Lord.
[13]Now Paul and
his companions
put out to sea
from Paphos and
came to Perga in
Pamphylia; but
John left them and
returned to Jerusa-
lem. [14]But going on
from Perga, they
arrived at Pisidian
Antioch, and on
the Sabbath day
they went into the
synagogue and sat
down. [15]After the
reading of the Law
and the Prophets
the synagogue offi-
cials sent to them,

[a] [τοῦ] UBS.
[b] ἐλθόντες TNIV, NET. [εἰσ]ελθόντες UBS.

NIV

them, saying,
"Brothers, if you
have a word of
exhortation for
the people, please
speak."
16 Standing up,
Paul motioned
with his hand and
said: "Fellow Is-
raelites and you
Gentiles who
worship God, lis-
ten to me! 17 The
God of the people
of Israel chose
our ancestors; he
made the people
prosper during
their stay in Egypt;
with mighty pow-
er he led them out
of that country;
18 for about forty
years he endured
their conduct[a] in
the wilderness;
19 and he overthrew
seven nations in
Canaan, giving
their land to his
people as their
inheritance. 20 All
this took about 450
years.
"After this, God
gave them judges
until the time of
Samuel the proph-
et. 21 Then the
people asked for a
king, and he gave
them Saul son of
Kish, of the tribe
of Benjamin, who
ruled forty years.
22 After removing
Saul, he made Da-
vid their king. God
testified concern-
ing him: 'I have
found David son of
Jesse, a man after
my own heart; he
will do everything
I want him to do.'
23 "From this
man's descendants
God

[a] 18 Some manuscripts *he cared for them*

αὐτοὺς λέγοντες, ⌞ἄνδρες ἀδελφοί,⌟ εἴ τίς ἐστιν ἐν ὑμῖν
them, saying, "My brothers, if there is any *there is* among you with a
899 3306 467 81 1623 1639 1639 5516 1639 1877 7007
r.apm.3 pt.pa.npm n.vpm n.vpm cj r.nsm v.pai.3s p.d r.dp.2

λόγος παρακλήσεως πρὸς τὸν λαόν, λέγετε. 16 ἀναστὰς δὲ Παῦλος
word of encouragement for the people, say it." So Paul stood up, *So* *Paul*
3364 4155 4639 3836 3295 3306 1254 4263 482 1254 4263
n.nsm n.gsf p.a d.asm n.asm v.pam.2p pt.aa.nsm cj n.nsm

καὶ κατασείσας τῇ χειρὶ εἶπεν, ἄνδρες Ἰσραηλῖται καὶ οἱ φοβούμενοι τὸν
and gesturing ⌞with his⌟ hand, said, "Men of Israel and ⌞you who⌟ fear *{the}*
2779 2939 3836 5931 3306 467 2703 2779 3836 5828 3836
cj pt.aa.nsm d.dsf n.dsf v.aai.3s n.vpm n.vpm cj d.vpm pt.pp.vpm d.asm

θεόν, ἀκούσατε. 17 ὁ θεὸς τοῦ λαοῦ τούτου Ἰσραὴλ ἐξελέξατο τοὺς
God, listen: The God of this people *this* Israel chose *{the}* our
2536 201 3836 2536 3836 4047 3295 4047 2702 1721 3836 7005
n.asm v.aam.2p d.nsm n.nsm d.gsm n.gsm r.gsm n.gsm v.ami.3s d.apm

πατέρας ἡμῶν καὶ ➦ τὸν λαὸν ὕψωσεν ἐν τῇ παροικίᾳ ἐν γῇ Αἰγύπτου
fathers *our* and made the people great during their stay in the land of Egypt;
4252 7005 2779 5738 3836 3295 5738 1877 3836 4229 1877 1178 131
n.apm r.gp.1 cj d.asm n.asm v.aai.3s p.d d.dsf n.dsf p.d n.dsf n.gsf

καὶ μετὰ βραχίονος ὑψηλοῦ ἐξήγαγεν αὐτοὺς ἐξ αὐτῆς, 18 καὶ ὡς
then with uplifted arm *uplifted* he led them ⌞out of⌟ it. And for about
2779 3552 5734 1098 5734 1974 899 1666 899 2779 5989 6055
cj p.g n.gsm a.gsm v.aai.3s r.apm.3 p.g r.gsf.3 cj pl

τεσσερακονταετῆ χρόνον ἐτροποφόρησεν αὐτοὺς ἐν τῇ ἐρήμῳ 19 καὶ
forty years *for* he put up with their ways in the wilderness. *{and}*
5478 5989 5574 899 1877 3836 2245 2779
a.asm n.asm v.aai.3s r.apm.3 p.d d.dsf n.dsf cj

καθελὼν ἔθνη ἑπτὰ ἐν γῇ Χανάαν κατεκληρονόμησεν
⌞After he had destroyed⌟ seven nations *seven* in the land of Canaan, he gave them
2747 2231 1620 2231 1877 1178 5913 2883
pt.aa.nsm n.apn a.apn p.d n.dsf n.gsf v.aai.3s

τὴν γῆν αὐτῶν ↰ ↰ ↰ 20 ὡς ἔτεσιν
{the} their land *their* as an inheritance. All this took about four hundred fifty years.
3836 899 1178 899 2883 2883 2883 6055 5484 5484 4299 2291
d.asf n.asf r.gpn.3 pl n.dpn

τετρακοσίοις καὶ πεντήκοντα. καὶ μετὰ ταῦτα ἔδωκεν κριτὰς ἕως Σαμουὴλ
four hundred *{and}* *fifty* *{and}* After this he gave them judges until Samuel
5484 2779 4299 2779 3552 4047 1443 3216 2401 4905
a.dpn cj a.dpn cj p.a r.apn v.aai.3s n.apm p.g n.gsm

τοῦ[a] προφήτου. 21 κἀκεῖθεν ᾐτήσαντο βασιλέα καὶ ἔδωκεν αὐτοῖς ὁ θεὸς
the prophet. Then ⌞they asked for⌟ a king, and God gave them *{the}* *God*
3836 4737 2796 160 995 2779 2536 1443 899 3836 2536
d.gsm n.gsm crasis v.ami.3p n.asm cj v.aai.3s r.dpm.3 d.nsm n.nsm

τὸν Σαοὺλ υἱὸν Κίς, ἄνδρα ἐκ φυλῆς Βενιαμίν, ἔτη
{the} Saul, son of Kish, a man from the tribe of Benjamin, who ruled forty years.
3836 4910 5626 3078 467 1666 5876 1021 5477 2291
d.asm n.asm n.asm n.gsm n.asm p.g n.gsf n.gsm n.apn

τεσσεράκοντα, 22 καὶ μεταστήσας αὐτὸν ἤγειρεν τὸν Δαυὶδ αὐτοῖς
forty *{and}* After removing him, ⌞he raised up⌟ *{the}* David to be their
5477 2779 3496 899 1586 3836 1253 1650 1650 899
a.apn cj pt.aa.nsm r.asm.3 v.aai.3s d.asm n.asm r.dpm.3

εἰς βασιλέα ᾧ καὶ εἶπεν μαρτυρήσας, εὗρον Δαυὶδ τὸν
to be king, ⌞of whom⌟ *{also}* he said by way of testimony: ⌞'I have found⌟ in David the son
1650 995 4005 2779 3306 3455 2351 1253 3836
p.a n.asm r.dsm adv v.aai.3s pt.aa.nsm v.aai.1s n.asm d.asm

τοῦ Ἰεσσαί, ἄνδρα κατὰ τὴν καρδίαν μου, ὃς ποιήσει πάντα τὰ
of Jesse a man after *{the}* my heart, *my* who will do everything *{the}* I
3836 2649 467 2848 3836 1609 2840 1609 4005 4472 4246 3836 1609
d.gsm n.gsm n.asm p.a d.asf n.asf r.gs.1 r.nsm v.fai.3s a.apn d.apn

θελήματά μου. 23 τούτου ὁ θεὸς ἀπὸ τοῦ
want *I* him to.' It was from the offspring of this man that *{the}* God *from* *the*
2525 1609 608 3836 5065 4047 3836 2536 608 3836
n.apn r.gs.1 r.gsm d.nsm n.nsm p.g d.gsn

[a] [τοῦ] UBS, omitted by TNIV.

NASB

saying, "Brethren,
if you have any
word of exhorta-
tion for the people,
say it." 16 Paul stood
up, and motioning
with his hand said,
"Men of Israel,
and you who fear
God, listen: 17 The
God of this people
Israel chose our fa-
thers and made the
people great during
their stay in the
land of Egypt, and
with an uplifted
arm He led them
out from it. 18 For
a period of about
forty years He put
up with them in the
wilderness. 19 When
He had destroyed
seven nations in
the land of Canaan,
He distributed
their land as an
inheritance—*all of
which took* about
four hundred and
fifty years. 20 After
these things He
gave *them* judges
until Samuel the
prophet. 21 Then
they asked for a
king, and God
gave them Saul
the son of Kish, a
man of the tribe of
Benjamin, for forty
years. 22 After He
had removed him,
He raised up David
to be their king,
concerning whom
He also testified
and said, 'I HAVE
FOUND DAVID the
son of Jesse, A MAN
AFTER MY HEART,
who will do all My
will.' 23 From the
descendants of this
man, according to
promise, God has

NIV

has brought to
Israel the Savior
Jesus, as he prom-
ised. 24 Before the
coming of Jesus,
John preached re-
pentance and bap-
tism to all the peo-
ple of Israel. 25 As
John was complet-
ing his work, he
said: 'Who do you
suppose I am? I am
not the one you are
looking for. But
there is one com-
ing after me whose
sandals I am not
worthy to untie.'
26 "Fellow chil-
dren of Abraham
and you God-fear-
ing Gentiles, it
is to us that this
message of sal-
vation has been
sent. 27 The people
of Jerusalem and
their rulers did not
recognize Jesus,
yet in condemning
him they fulfilled
the words of the
prophets that are
read every Sab-
bath. 28 Though
they found no
proper ground for
a death sentence,
they asked Pilate
to have him exe-
cuted. 29 When they
had carried out all
that was written
about him, they
took him down
from the cross and
laid him in a tomb.
30 But God raised
him from the dead,
31 and for many
days he was seen
by those who had
traveled with him
from Galilee to

σπέρματος κατ᾽ ἐπαγγελίαν ἤγαγεν τῷ Ἰσραὴλ σωτῆρα Ἰησοῦν, 24
offspring ⌊according to⌋ promise brought to Israel a savior, Jesus. Before
5065 2848 2039 72 3836 2702 5400 2652 4574
n.gsn p.a n.asf v.aai.3s d.dsm n.dsm n.asm n.asm

προκηρύξαντος Ἰωάννου ⌊πρὸ προσώπου⌋ τῆς εἰσόδου αὐτοῦ
John Before {the} coming his
his coming John had proclaimed a
899 1658 2722 4619 2722 4574 4725 3836 1658 899
pt.aa.gsm n.gsm p.g n.gsn d.gsf n.gsf r.gsm.3

βάπτισμα μετανοίας παντὶ τῷ λαῷ Ἰσραήλ. 25 ὡς δὲ ἐπλήρου
And
baptism of repentance to all the people of Israel. And as John was completing
967 3567 4246 3836 3295 2702 1254 6055 1254 2722 4444
n.asn n.gsf a.dsm d.dsm n.dsm n.gsm cj cj v.iai.3s

Ἰωάννης τὸν δρόμον, ἔλεγεν, τί ἐμὲ ὑπονοεῖτε εἶναι;
John do you suppose
his ministry, he said repeatedly, 'What do you suppose me to be?
2722 3836 1536 3306 5515 5706 5706 5706 1609 5706 1639
n.nsm d.asm n.asm v.iai.3s r.asn r.as.1 v.pai.2p f.pa

οὐκ εἰμὶ ἐγώ· ἀλλ᾽ ἰδοὺ ἔρχεται μετ᾽ ἐμὲ οὗ οὐκ
am I
I am not he. But behold, one is coming after me ⌊of whom⌋ I am not
1609 1639 4024 1639 1609 247 2627 2262 3552 1609 4005 1639 1639 4024
pl v.pai.1s r.ns.1 cj j v.pmi.3s p.a r.as.1 r.gsm pl

εἰμὶ ἄξιος τὸ ὑπόδημα τῶν ποδῶν λῦσαι. 26 ⌊ἄνδρες ἀδελφοί,⌋ υἱοὶ
I am to untie
worthy to untie the sandals for his feet.' "My brothers, sons
1639 545 3395 3395 3836 5687 3836 4546 3395 467 81 5626
v.pai.1s a.nsm d.asn n.asn d.gpm n.gpm f.aa n.vpm n.vpm n.vpm

→ γένους Ἀβραὰμ καὶ οἱ ἐν ὑμῖν φοβούμενοι τὸν θεόν, ἡμῖν ὁ
{the}
of the family of Abraham, and those among you who fear God, it is to us that the
1169 11 2779 3836 1877 7007 5828 3836 2536 7005 3836
n.gsn n.gsm cj d.vpm p.d r.dp.2 pt.pp.vpm d.asm n.asm r.dp.1 d.nsm

λόγος τῆς σωτηρίας ταύτης ἐξαπεστάλη. 27 οἱ γὰρ κατοικοῦντες ἐν
this For
message of this salvation has been sent. For those who live in
3364 3836 4047 5401 4047 1990 1142 3836 1142 2997 1877
n.nsm d.gsf n.gsf r.gsf v.api.3s d.npm cj pt.pa.npm p.d

Ἰερουσαλὴμ καὶ οἱ ἄρχοντες αὐτῶν τοῦτον ἀγνοήσαντες καὶ
{the} their him
Jerusalem and their rulers, ⌊because they did not recognize⌋ him nor
2647 2779 3836 899 807 899 4047 51 4047 2779
n.dsf cj d.npm n.npm r.gpm.3 r.asm pt.aa.npm cj

τὰς φωνὰς τῶν προφητῶν τὰς κατὰ πᾶν σάββατον
{on}
understand the utterances of the prophets, which are read every Sabbath,
3836 5889 3836 4737 3836 336 336 2848 4246 4879
d.apf n.apf d.gpm n.gpm d.apf p.a a.asn n.asn

ἀναγινωσκομένας κρίναντες ἐπλήρωσαν, 28 καὶ
are read fulfilled
fulfilled them by condemning him. And though they found
336 4444 3212 4444 2779 2351 2351 2351
pt.pp.apf pt.aa.npm v.aai.3p cj

μηδεμίαν αἰτίαν θανάτου εὑρόντες ᾐτήσαντο Πιλᾶτον → →
though they found
no crime ⌊deserving death,⌋ they asked Pilate to have him
3594 162 2505 2351 160 4397 899
a.asf n.asf n.gsm pt.aa.npm v.ami.3p n.asm

ἀναιρεθῆναι αὐτόν. 29 ὡς δὲ ἐτέλεσαν πάντα τὰ περὶ
him And
executed. And when ⌊they had carried out⌋ everything that was written about
359 899 1254 6055 1254 5464 4246 3836 1211 1211 4309
f.ap r.asm.3 cj cj v.aai.3p a.apn d.apn p.g

αὐτοῦ γεγραμμένα, ↱ καθελόντες ← ἀπὸ τοῦ ξύλου ἔθηκαν εἰς
was written
him, they took him down from the tree and laid him in a
899 1211 5502 2747 608 3836 3833 5502 1650
r.gsm.3 pt.rp.apn pt.aa.npm p.g d.gsn n.gsn v.aai.3p p.a

μνημεῖον. 30 ὁ δὲ θεὸς ἤγειρεν αὐτὸν ἐκ νεκρῶν, 31 ὃς ὤφθη ἐπὶ
{the}
tomb. But God raised him from the dead, and he was seen for
3646 3836 1254 2536 1586 899 1666 3738 4005 3972 2093
n.asn d.nsm cj n.nsm v.aai.3s r.asm.3 p.g a.gpm r.nsm v.api.3s p.a

ἡμέρας πλείους τοῖς συναναβᾶσιν αὐτῷ ἀπὸ τῆς Γαλιλαίας εἰς
many {the}
many days by those ⌊who had gone up with⌋ him from Galilee to
4498 2465 4498 3836 5262 899 608 3836 1133 1650
n.apf a.apf.c d.dpm pt.aa.dpm r.dsm.3 p.g d.gsf n.gsf p.a

NASB

brought to Israel
a Savior, Jesus,
24 after John had
proclaimed before
His coming a bap-
tism of repentance
to all the people of
Israel. 25 And while
John was complet-
ing his course, he
kept saying, 'What
do you suppose
that I am? I am not
He. But behold,
one is coming after
me the sandals of
whose feet I am not
worthy to untie.'
26 "Brethren, sons
of Abraham's
family, and those
among you who
fear God, to us the
message of this
salvation has been
sent. 27 For those
who live in Jeru-
salem, and their
rulers, recognizing
neither Him nor
the utterances of
the prophets which
are read every Sab-
bath, fulfilled *these*
by condemning
Him. 28 And though
they found no
ground for *putting*
Him to death, they
asked Pilate that
He be executed.
29 When they had
carried out all that
was written con-
cerning Him, they
took Him down
from the cross and
laid Him in a tomb.
30 But God raised
Him from the dead;
31 and for many
days He appeared
to those who came
up with Him from
Galilee to

NIV

Jerusalem. They
are now his wit-
nesses to our
people.
32 “We tell you the
good news: What
God promised our
ancestors 33 he has
fulfilled for us,
their children, by
raising up Jesus.
As it is written in
the second Psalm:

“ ‘You are my
son;
today I have
become
your
father.’[a]

34 God raised him
from the dead so
that he will never
be subject to de-
cay. As God has
said,

“ ‘I will give you
the holy
and sure
blessings
promised to
David.’[b]

35 So it is also stat-
ed elsewhere:

“ ‘You will not
let your
holy one
see decay.’[c]

36 “Now when
David had served
God’s purpose in
his own genera-
tion, he fell asleep;
he was buried with
his ancestors and
his body decayed.
37 But the one
whom God raised
from the dead did
not see decay.
38 “Therefore, my
friends, I want
you to know that
through Jesus the
forgiveness of sins
is proclaimed to
you. 39 Through
him everyone who
believes is set free
from every sin, a
justification you
were not able to
obtain under the
law of Moses.

Ἰερουσαλήμ, οἵτινες νῦν[a] εἰσιν μάρτυρες αὐτοῦ πρὸς τὸν λαόν. 32 καὶ
Jerusalem, who are now *are* his witnesses *his* to the people. And
2647 4015 1639 3814 1639 899 3459 899 4639 3836 3295 2779
n.asf r.npm adv v.pai.3p n.npm r.gsm.3 p.a d.asm n.asm cj

ἡμεῖς ↱ ↱ ὑμᾶς εὐαγγελιζόμεθα τὴν πρὸς τοὺς
we are telling you the good news regarding the promise that was made to the
7005 2294 2294 7007 2294 3836 2039 1181 1181 4639 3836
r.np.1 r.ap.2 v.pmi.1p d.asf p.a d.apm

πατέρας ἐπαγγελίαν γενομένην, 33 ὅτι ταύτην ὁ θεὸς
fathers, *promise* *was made* that God has fulfilled this *{the}* *God*
4252 2039 1181 4022 2536 1740 1740 4047 3836 2536
n.apm n.asf pt.am.asf cj r.asf d.nsm n.nsm

ἐκπεπλήρωκεν τοῖς τέκνοις αὐτῶν[b] ἡμῖν ἀναστήσας Ἰησοῦν ὡς καὶ
has fulfilled for us, *{the}* their children, *their* *for us* by raising Jesus; as also
1740 7005 7005 3836 899 5451 899 7005 482 2652 6055 2779
v.rai.3s d.dpn n.dpn r.gpm.3 r.dp.1 pt.aa.nsm n.asm cj adv

ἐν τῷ ψαλμῷ γέγραπται τῷ δευτέρῳ, υἱός μου εἶ σύ,
in the second Psalm it is written, *{the}* *second* ‘You are my Son; *my* *are* *You*
1877 3836 1311 6011 1211 3836 1311 5148 1639 1609 5626 1609 1639 5148
p.d d.dsm n.dsm v.rpi.3s d.dsm a.dsm n.nsm r.gs.1 v.pai.2s r.ns.2

ἐγὼ σήμερον γεγέννηκά σε. 34 ὅτι δὲ ἀνέστησεν αὐτὸν
today I *today* have begotten you.’ But regarding the fact that *But* he has raised Jesus
4958 1609 4958 1164 5148 1254 4022 1254 482 899
r.ns.1 adv v.rai.1s r.as.2 cj cj v.aai.3s r.asm.3

ἐκ νεκρῶν μηκέτι μέλλοντα ὑποστρέφειν εἰς διαφθοράν, οὕτως εἴρηκεν ὅτι
from the dead, no more about to return to corruption, thus he said: ~
1666 3738 3600 3516 5715 1650 1426 4048 3306 4022
p.g a.gpm adv pt.pa.asm f.pa p.a n.asf adv v.rai.3s cj

δώσω ὑμῖν τὰ ὅσια Δαυὶδ τὰ πιστά. 35 διότι καὶ
⌊‘I will give⌋ to you the sacred and sure promises made to David.’ *{the}* *sure* So also
1443 7007 3836 4008 4412 1253 3836 4412 1484 2779
v.fai.1s r.dp.2 d.apn a.apn n.gsm d.apn a.apn cj adv

ἐν ἑτέρῳ λέγει, ↱ ↱ οὐ δώσεις τὸν ὅσιόν σου ἰδεῖν διαφθοράν.
in another psalm he says, ‘You will not let *{the}* your Holy One *your* see corruption.’
1877 2283 3306 1443 1443 4024 1443 3836 5148 4008 5148 1625 1426
p.d r.dsm v.pai.3s pl v.fai.2s d.asm a.asm r.gs.2 f.aa n.asf

36 Δαυὶδ μὲν γὰρ ἰδίᾳ γενεᾷ
For David, ~ *For* after he had served the purpose of God ⌊in his own⌋ generation,
1142 1253 3525 1142 5676 5676 5676 5676 3836 1087 3836 2536 2625 1155
n.nsm pl cj a.dsf n.dsf

ὑπηρετήσας τῇ τοῦ θεοῦ βουλῇ ἐκοιμήθη καὶ προσετέθη πρὸς τοὺς πατέρας
after he had served *the* *of* *God* *purpose* fell asleep and was laid with *{the}* his fathers
5676 3836 3836 2536 1087 3121 2779 4707 4639 3836 899 4252
pt.aa.nsm d.dsf d.gsm n.gsm n.dsf v.api.3s cj v.api.3s p.a d.apm n.apm

αὐτοῦ καὶ εἶδεν διαφθοράν, 37 ↱ ὃν δὲ ὁ θεὸς ἤγειρεν, ↱ οὐκ εἶδεν
his and saw corruption, but he whom *but* *{the}* God raised up did not see
899 2779 1625 1426 1254 1625 4005 1254 3836 2536 1586 1625 4024 1625
r.gsm.3 cj v.aai.3s n.asf r.asm cj d.nsm n.nsm v.aai.3s pl v.aai.3s

διαφθοράν. 38 γνωστὸν οὖν ἔστω ὑμῖν, ⌊ἄνδρες
corruption. Therefore let it be known *Therefore* *let it be* to you, my brothers,
1426 4036 1639 1639 1639 1196 4036 1639 7007 467
n.asf a.nsn cj v.pam.3s r.dp.2 n.vpm

ἀδελφοί,⌋ ὅτι διὰ τούτου ὑμῖν ἄφεσις ἁμαρτιῶν καταγγέλλεται, καὶ[c]
that through this one *to you* forgiveness of sins is being proclaimed to you; and
81 4022 1328 4047 7007 912 281 2859 7007 7007 2779
n.vpm cj p.g r.gsm r.dp.2 n.nsf n.gpf v.ppi.3s adv

ἀπὸ πάντων ὧν οὐκ ἠδυνήθητε ἐν νόμῳ Μωϋσέως
from all ⌊from which⌋ you could not *you could* be set free by the law of Moses,
608 4246 4005 1538 1538 4024 1538 1467 1467 1467 1877 3795 3707
p.g a.gpn r.gpn pl v.api.2p p.d n.dsm n.gsm

NASB

Jerusalem, the very
ones who are now
His witnesses to
the people. 32 And
we preach to you
the good news of
the promise made
to the fathers, 33 that
God has fulfilled
this *promise* to our
children in that He
raised up Jesus, as
it is also writ-
ten in the second
Psalm, ‘YOU ARE
MY SON; TODAY
I HAVE BEGOTTEN
YOU.’ 34 *As for the*
fact that He raised
Him up from the
dead, no longer to
return to decay, He
has spoken in this
way: ‘I WILL GIVE
YOU THE HOLY *and*
SURE *blessings* OF
DAVID.’ 35 Therefore
He also says in an-
other *Psalm,* ‘YOU
WILL NOT ALLOW
YOUR HOLY ONE TO
UNDERGO DECAY.’
36 For David, after
he had served the
purpose of God in
his own generation,
fell asleep, and
was laid among
his fathers and
underwent decay;
37 but He whom
God raised did not
undergo decay.
38 Therefore let
it be known to
you, brethren,
that through Him
forgiveness of sins
is proclaimed to
you, 39 and through
Him everyone who
believes is freed
from all things,
from which you
could not be freed
through the Law of
Moses. 40 Therefore

---

[a] 33 Psalm 2:7
[b] 34 Isaiah 55:3
[c] 35 Psalm 16:10 (see Septuagint)

[a] [νῦν] UBS.
[b] [αὐτῶν] UBS, omitted by TNIV.
[c] [καὶ] UBS.

NIV

40 Take care that
what the prophets
have said does not
happen to you:
41 "'Look, you
scoffers,
wonder and
perish,
for I am going
to do
something
in your
days
that you
would
never
believe,
even if
someone
told you.'[a]"
42 As Paul and
Barnabas were
leaving the syn-
agogue, the peo-
ple invited them
to speak further
about these things
on the next Sab-
bath. 43 When the
congregation was
dismissed, many
of the Jews and
devout converts to
Judaism followed
Paul and Barna-
bas, who talked
with them and
urged them to con-
tinue in the grace
of God.
44 On the next
Sabbath almost the
whole city gath-
ered to hear the
word of the Lord.
45 When the Jews
saw the crowds,
they were filled
with jealousy.
They began to
contradict what
Paul was saying
and heaped abuse
on him.
46 Then Paul
and Barnabas
answered them
boldly: "We had to
speak the word of
God to you first.

δικαιωθῆναι, 39 ἐν τούτῳ πᾶς ὁ πιστεύων δικαιοῦται. 40 βλέπετε οὖν μὴ
be set free by this man everyone who believes is set free. Take care then *not*
1467 1877 4047 4246 3836 4409 1467 1063 4036 3590
f.ap p.d r.dsm a.nsm d.nsm pt.pa.nsm v.ppi.3s v.pam.2p cj cj

ἐπέλθῃ τὸ εἰρημένον ἐν τοῖς προφήταις, 41 ἴδετε,
does happen that what was spoken in the prophets does not happen to you. 'Look,
2088 3836 3306 1877 3836 4737 2088 3590 2088 1625
v.aas.3s d.nsn pt.rp.nsn p.d d.dpm n.dpm v.aam.2p

οἱ καταφρονηταί, καὶ θαυμάσατε καὶ ἀφανίσθητε, ὅτι ἔργον
you scoffers; *{and}* be amazed and perish! For I am doing a work
3836 2970 2779 2513 2779 906 4022 1609 2237 2237 2240
d.vpm n.vpm cj v.aam.2p cj v.apm.2p cj n.asn

ἐργάζομαι ἐγὼ ἐν ταῖς ἡμέραις ὑμῶν, ἔργον ὃ ↱ ↱ ⌊οὐ μὴ⌋ πιστεύσητε
am doing *I* in *{the}* your days, *your* a work that you will not believe,
2237 1609 1877 3836 7007 2465 7007 2240 4005 4409 4409 4024 3590 4409
v.pmi.1s r.ns.1 p.d d.dpf n.dpf r.gp.2 n.asn r.asn pl pl v.aas.2p

ἐάν τις ἐκδιηγῆται ὑμῖν. ↰ ↰ 42 → ἐξιόντων δὲ αὐτῶν
⌊even though⌋ someone should tell you in detail.'" As they went out, *{and}* *they* the
1569 5516 1687 7007 1687 1687 899 1997 1254 899
cj r.nsm v.pms.3s r.dp.2 pt.pa.gpm cj r.gpm.3

παρεκάλουν εἰς τὸ μεταξὺ σάββατον
people begged that these things be discussed with them on the next Sabbath.
4151 4047 4839 3281 3281 899 899 1650 3836 3568 4879
v.iai.3p p.a d.asn adv n.asn

λαληθῆναι αὐτοῖς τὰ ῥήματα ταῦτα. 43 →
be discussed *with them* *{the}* *things* *these* And after the meeting of the synagogue
3281 899 3836 4839 4047 1254 3836 3836 5252
f.ap r.dpm.3 d.apn n.apn r.apn

λυθείσης δὲ τῆς συναγωγῆς ἠκολούθησαν πολλοὶ τῶν Ἰουδαίων καὶ τῶν
broke up, *And* *of the* *synagogue* *followed* many *{the}* Jews and *{the}*
3395 1254 3836 5252 199 4498 3836 2681 2779 3836
pt.ap.gsf cj d.gsf n.gsf v.aai.3p a.npm d.gpm a.gpm cj d.gpm

σεβομένων προσηλύτων τῷ Παύλῳ καὶ τῷ Βαρναβᾷ, οἵτινες
devout converts followed *{the}* Paul and *{the}* Barnabas, who,
4936 4670 199 3836 4263 2779 3836 982 4015
pt.pm.gpm n.gpm d.dsm n.dsm cj d.dsm n.dsm r.npm

προσλαλοῦντες αὐτοῖς ἔπειθον αὐτοὺς προσμένειν τῇ χάριτι τοῦ θεοῦ.
as they spoke with them, were persuading them to continue in the grace of God.
4688 899 4275 899 4693 3836 5921 3836 2536
pt.pa.npm r.dpm.3 v.iai.3p r.apm.3 f.pa d.dsf n.dsf d.gsm n.gsm

44 τῷ δὲ ἐρχομένῳ σαββάτῳ σχεδὸν πᾶσα ἡ πόλις συνήχθη
⌊On the⌋ *{and}* following Sabbath almost the whole *the* city ⌊assembled together⌋
3836 1254 2262 4879 5385 3836 4246 3836 4484 5251
d.dsn cj pt.pm.dsn n.dsn adv a.nsf d.nsf n.nsf v.api.3s

ἀκοῦσαι τὸν λόγον τοῦ κυρίου. 45 → ἰδόντες δὲ οἱ Ἰουδαῖοι
to hear the word of the Lord. But when the Jews saw *But* *the* *Jews*
201 3836 3364 3836 3261 1254 3836 2681 1625 1254 3836 2681
f.aa d.asm n.asm d.gsm n.gsm pt.aa.npm cj d.npm a.npm

τοὺς ὄχλους ἐπλήσθησαν ζήλου καὶ ἀντέλεγον τοῖς
the crowds, ⌊they were filled with⌋ jealousy; and blaspheming, ⌊they began to contradict⌋ what was
3836 4063 4398 2419 2779 1059 515 3836 3281
d.apm n.apm v.api.3p n.gsm cj v.iai.3p d.dpn

ὑπὸ Παύλου λαλουμένοις βλασφημοῦντες. 46
being said by Paul. *was being said* *blaspheming* Both Paul and Barnabas
3281 3281 5679 4263 3281 1059 5445 4263 2779 982
p.g n.gsm pt.pp.dpn pt.pa.npm

παρρησιασάμενοί τε ὁ Παῦλος καὶ ὁ Βαρναβᾶς εἶπαν,
spoke boldly *Both* *{the}* *Paul* *and* *{the}* *Barnabas* and said, "It was necessary
4245 5445 3836 4263 2779 3836 982 3306 1639 1639 338
pt.am.npm cj d.nsm n.nsm cj d.nsm n.nsm v.aai.3p

ὑμῖν ἦν ἀναγκαῖον πρῶτον λαληθῆναι τὸν
that the word of God be spoken first to you. *It was* *necessary* *first* *be spoken* *the*
3836 3364 3836 2536 3281 3281 4754 7007 1639 338 4754 3281 3836
r.dp.2 v.iai.3s a.nsn adv f.ap d.asm

NASB

take heed, so that
the thing spoken
of in the Prophets
may not come
upon *you:*
41 'BEHOLD, YOU
SCOFFERS, AND
MARVEL, AND
PERISH;
FOR I AM AC-
COMPLISHING A
WORK IN YOUR
DAYS,
A WORK WHICH
YOU WILL NEV-
ER BELIEVE,
THOUGH SOME-
ONE SHOULD
DESCRIBE IT TO
YOU.'"
42 As Paul and
Barnabas were go-
ing out, the people
kept begging that
these things might
be spoken to them
the next Sabbath.
43 Now when *the*
meeting of the
synagogue had
broken up, many
of the Jews and of
the God-fearing
proselytes followed
Paul and Barnabas,
who, speaking to
them, were urging
them to continue in
the grace of God.

Paul Turns to the Gentiles

44 The next Sab-
bath nearly the
whole city as-
sembled to hear
the word of the
Lord. 45 But when
the Jews saw the
crowds, they were
filled with jealousy
and *began* contra-
dicting the things
spoken by Paul,
and were blas-
pheming. 46 Paul
and Barnabas
spoke out boldly
and said, "It was
necessary that the
word of God be
spoken to you first;

[a] 41 Hab. 1:5

NIV

Since you reject
it and do not con-
sider yourselves
worthy of eternal
life, we now turn
to the Gentiles.
47 For this is what
the Lord has com-
manded us:

"'I have made
you[a] a light
for the
Gentiles,
that you[b]
may bring
salvation
to the ends
of the
earth.'[c]"

48 When the Gen-
tiles heard this,
they were glad and
honored the word
of the Lord; and all
who were appoint-
ed for eternal life
believed.
49 The word of
the Lord spread
through the whole
region. 50 But the
Jewish leaders
incited the God-
fearing women of
high standing and
the leading men
of the city. They
stirred up persecu-
tion against Paul
and Barnabas,
and expelled them
from their region.
51 So they shook
the dust off their
feet as a warning
to them and went
to Iconium. 52 And
the disciples were
filled with joy
and with the Holy
Spirit.

In Iconium

14 At Iconium
Paul and
Barnabas went
as usual into the
Jewish synagogue.
There they spoke
so effectively that
a great number of
Jews and Greeks
believed.

[a] 47 The Greek is singular.
[b] 47 The Greek is singular.
[c] 47 Isaiah 49:6

λόγον τοῦ θεοῦ· ἐπειδὴ ἀπωθεῖσθε αὐτὸν καὶ οὐκ ἀξίους
word of God Since you reject it and do not consider yourselves worthy
3364 3836 2536 2076 723 899 2779 3212 4024 3212 1571 545
n.asm d.gsm n.gsm cj v.pmi.2p r.asm.3 cj pl a.apm

κρίνετε ἑαυτοὺς τῆς αἰωνίου ζωῆς, ἰδοὺ στρεφόμεθα εἰς τὰ ἔθνη.
do consider yourselves of eternal life, *{behold}* we are now turning to the Gentiles.
3212 1571 3836 173 2437 2627 5138 1650 3836 1620
v.pai.2p r.apm.2 d.gsf a.gsf n.gsf j v.ppi.1p p.a d.apn n.apn

47 οὕτως γὰρ ἐντέταλται ἡμῖν ὁ κύριος, τέθεικά σε εἰς
For thus *For* the Lord has commanded us: *the Lord* 'I have appointed you to be a
1142 4048 1142 3836 3261 1948 7005 3836 3261 5502 5148 1650
adv cj v.rmi.3s r.dp.1 d.nsm n.nsm v.rai.1s r.as.2 p.a

φῶς → ἐθνῶν τοῦ εἶναί σε εἰς σωτηρίαν ἕως ἐσχάτου τῆς γῆς.
light for the Gentiles, to bring *{you} {to}* salvation to the ends of the earth.'"
5890 1620 3836 1639 5148 1650 5401 2401 2274 3836 1178
n.asn n.gpn d.gsn f.pa r.as.2 p.a n.asf p.g a.gsn d.gsf n.gsf

48 → ἀκούοντα δὲ τὰ ἔθνη ἔχαιρον καὶ ἐδόξαζον
When the Gentiles heard *{and} the Gentiles* this, ⌊they began rejoicing⌋ and glorifying
3836 1620 201 1254 3836 1620 5897 2779 1519
pt.pa.npn cj d.npn n.npn v.iai.3p cj v.iai.3p

τὸν λόγον τοῦ κυρίου καὶ ἐπίστευσαν ὅσοι ἦσαν τεταγμένοι εἰς ζωὴν
the word of the Lord, and *believed* ⌊as many as⌋ were appointed to eternal life
3836 3364 3836 3261 2779 4409 4012 1639 5435 1650 173 2437
d.asm n.asm d.gsm n.gsm cj v.aai.3p r.npm v.iai.3p pt.rp.npm p.a n.asf

αἰώνιον· 49 διεφέρετο δὲ ὁ λόγος τοῦ
eternal believed. So the word of the Lord ⌊was being spread⌋ *So the word of the*
173 4409 1254 3836 3364 3836 3836 3261 1422 1254 3836 3364 3836
a.asf v.ipi.3s cj d.nsm n.nsm d.gsm

κυρίου δι' ὅλης τῆς χώρας. 50 οἱ δὲ Ἰουδαῖοι παρώτρυναν τὰς
Lord throughout the whole *the* region. But the *But* Jews incited the
3261 1328 3836 3910 3836 6001 1254 3836 1254 2681 4241 3836
n.gsm p.g a.gsf d.gsf n.gsf d.npm cj a.npm v.aai.3p d.apf

σεβομένας γυναῖκας τὰς εὐσχήμονας καὶ τοὺς πρώτους τῆς πόλεως καὶ
devout women of honorable rank and the leading men of the city, and
4936 1222 3836 2363 2779 3836 4755 3836 4484 2779
pt.pm.apf n.apf d.apf a.apf cj d.apm a.apm d.gsf n.gsf cj

ἐπήγειραν διωγμὸν ἐπὶ τὸν Παῦλον καὶ Βαρναβᾶν καὶ ἐξέβαλον αὐτοὺς ↰
⌊they stirred up⌋ persecution against *{the}* Paul and Barnabas, and drove them out
2074 1501 2093 3836 4263 2779 982 2779 1675 899 1675
v.aai.3p n.asm p.a d.asm n.asm cj n.asm cj v.aai.3p r.apm.3

ἀπὸ τῶν ὁρίων αὐτῶν. 51 οἱ δὲ ἐκτιναξάμενοι τὸν κονιορτὸν τῶν
of *{the}* their district. *their* So they *So* shook off the dust ⌊from their⌋
608 3836 899 3990 899 1254 3836 1254 1759 3836 3155 3836
p.g d.gpn n.gpn r.gpm.3 d.npm cj pt.am.npm d.asm n.asm d.gpm

ποδῶν ἐπ' αὐτοὺς ἦλθον εἰς Ἰκόνιον, 52 οἵ τε μαθηταὶ ἐπληροῦντο
feet against them and went on to Iconium. And the *And* disciples were filled with
4546 2093 899 2262 1650 2658 5445 3836 5445 3412 4444
n.gpm p.a r.apm.3 v.aai.3p p.a n.asn d.npm cj n.npm v.ipi.3p

χαρᾶς καὶ ↰ πνεύματος ἁγίου.
joy and with the Holy Spirit. *Holy*
5915 2779 4444 41 4460 41
n.gsf cj n.gsn a.gsn

14:1 ἐγένετο δὲ ἐν Ἰκονίῳ ↰ κατὰ τὸ αὐτὸ
⌊It came to pass⌋ *{and}* in Iconium that Paul and Barnabas went as *{the}* usual
1181 1254 1877 2658 1181 899 899 899 1656 2848 3836 899
v.ami.3s cj p.d n.dsn p.a d.asn r.asn

εἰσελθεῖν αὐτοὺς εἰς τὴν συναγωγὴν τῶν Ἰουδαίων καὶ λαλῆσαι
went Paul and Barnabas into the synagogue of the Jews and spoke
1656 899 1650 3836 5252 3836 2681 2779 3281
f.aa r.apm.3 p.a d.asf n.asf d.gpm a.gpm cj f.aa

οὕτως ὥστε πιστεῦσαι Ἰουδαίων τε καὶ
⌊in such a way⌋ that a large group of both Jews and Greeks believed. *Jews both and*
4048 6063 4498 4436 5445 2681 2779 1818 4409 2681 5445 2779
adv cj f.aa a.gpm cj cj

NASB

since you repudiate
it and judge your-
selves unworthy of
eternal life, behold,
we are turning to
the Gentiles. 47 For
so the Lord has
commanded us,
'I HAVE PLACED
YOU AS A
LIGHT FOR THE
GENTILES,
THAT YOU MAY
BRING SALVA-
TION TO THE
END OF THE
EARTH.'"
48 When the Gen-
tiles heard this,
they *began* rejoic-
ing and glorifying
the word of the
Lord; and as many
as had been ap-
pointed to eternal
life believed. 49 And
the word of the
Lord was being
spread through the
whole region. 50 But
the Jews incited
the devout women
of prominence and
the leading men
of the city, and
instigated a perse-
cution against Paul
and Barnabas, and
drove them out of
their district. 51 But
they shook off the
dust of their feet
in protest against
them and went to
Iconium. 52 And the
disciples were con-
tinually filled with
joy and with the
Holy Spirit.

Acceptance and Opposition

14:1 In Iconium they
entered the syna-
gogue of the Jews
together, and spoke
in such a manner
that a large number
of people believed,
both of Jews and of

NIV

[2]But the Jews who
refused to believe
stirred up the oth-
er Gentiles and
poisoned their
minds against
the brothers. [3]So
Paul and Barnabas
spent consider-
able time there,
speaking boldly
for the Lord, who
confirmed the
message of his
grace by enabling
them to perform
signs and wonders.
[4]The people of the
city were divided;
some sided with
the Jews, others
with the apostles.
[5]There was a plot
afoot among both
Gentiles and Jews,
together with their
leaders, to mistreat
them and stone
them. [6]But they
found out about
it and fled to the
Lycaonian cities of
Lystra and Derbe
and to the sur-
rounding country,
[7]where they con-
tinued to preach
the gospel.

In Lystra and Derbe

[8]In Lystra there
sat a man who
was lame. He had
been that way
from birth and had
never walked. [9]He
listened to Paul as
he was speaking.
Paul looked direct-
ly at him, saw that
he had faith to be
healed [10]and called
out, "Stand up on
your feet!" At that,
the man jumped up
and began to walk.
[11]When the crowd
saw what Paul

Ἑλλήνων πολὺ πλῆθος. [2] οἱ δὲ ἀπειθήσαντες Ἰουδαῖοι ἐπήγειραν καὶ
Greeks large group But the *But* Jews who did not believe *Jews* stirred up and
1818 4498 4436 1254 3836 1254 2681 578 2681 2074 2779
n.gpm a.asn n.asn d.npm cj pt.aa.npm a.npm v.aai.3p cj

ἐκάκωσαν τὰς ψυχὰς τῶν ἐθνῶν κατὰ τῶν ἀδελφῶν. [3] →
embittered the minds of the Gentiles against their brothers. So they stayed there for a
2808 3836 6034 3836 1620 2848 3836 81 4036 1417 1417 1417
v.aai.3p d.apf n.apf d.gpn n.gpn p.g d.gpm n.gpm

ἱκανὸν μὲν οὖν χρόνον διέτριψαν παρρησιαζόμενοι ἐπὶ τῷ κυρίῳ τῷ
considerable ~ *So* time, *they stayed there* speaking out boldly about the Lord, who
2653 3525 4036 5989 1417 4245 2093 3836 3261 3836
a.asm pl cj n.asm v.aai.3p pt.pm.npm p.d d.dsm n.dsm d.dsm

μαρτυροῦντι ἐπὶ[a] τῷ λόγῳ τῆς χάριτος αὐτοῦ, διδόντι σημεῖα καὶ τέρατα
witnessed to the message of his grace, *his* granting signs and wonders
3455 2093 3836 3364 3836 899 5921 899 1443 4956 2779 5469
pt.pa.dsm p.d d.dsm n.dsm d.gsf n.gsf r.gsm.3 pt.pa.dsm n.apn cj n.apn

γίνεσθαι διὰ τῶν χειρῶν αὐτῶν. [4] ἐσχίσθη δὲ
to be done through *{the}* their hands. *their* But the people of the city were divided; *But*
1181 1328 3836 899 5931 899 1254 3836 4436 3836 3836 4484 5387 1254
f.pm p.g d.gpf n.gpf r.gpm.3 v.api.3s cj

τὸ πλῆθος τῆς πόλεως, καὶ οἱ μὲν ἦσαν σὺν τοῖς Ἰουδαίοις, οἱ δὲ
the people of the city while some ~ sided with the Jews, others *{and}* sided
3836 4436 3836 4484 2779 3836 3525 1639 5250 3836 2681 3836 1254
d.nsn n.nsn d.gsf n.gsf cj d.npm pl v.iai.3p p.d d.dpm a.dpm d.npm pl

σὺν τοῖς ἀποστόλοις. [5]ὡς δὲ ἐγένετο ὁρμὴ τῶν ἐθνῶν τε καὶ
with the apostles. When *{and}* there was an attempt by both Gentiles *both* and
5250 3836 693 6055 1254 1181 3995 3836 5445 1620 5445 2779
p.d d.dpm n.dpm cj cj v.ami.3s n.nsf d.gpn n.gpn cj cj

Ἰουδαίων σὺν τοῖς ἄρχουσιν αὐτῶν ὑβρίσαι καὶ λιθοβολῆσαι
Jews ⌊along with⌋ *{the}* their rulers, *their* to mistreat them and to stone
2681 5250 3836 899 807 899 5614 2779 3344
a.gpm p.d d.dpm n.dpm r.gpm.3 f.aa cj f.aa

αὐτούς, [6]→ συνιδόντες κατέφυγον εἰς τὰς πόλεις τῆς Λυκαονίας
them, they ⌊became aware of⌋ it and fled to the cities of Lycaonia,
899 2966 5328 2966 1650 3836 4484 3836 3377
r.apm.3 pt.aa.npm v.aai.3p p.a d.apf n.apf d.gsf n.gsf

Λύστραν καὶ Δέρβην καὶ τὴν περίχωρον, [7]κἀκεῖ
Lystra and Derbe, and to the ⌊surrounding region,⌋ and there they were
3388 2779 1292 2779 3836 4369 2795 1639 1639
n.asf cj n.asf cj d.asf a.asf crasis

εὐαγγελιζόμενοι ἦσαν. [8]καί τις ἀνήρ
⌊preaching the good news.⌋ *they were* Now there was a man sitting in Lystra, whose feet
2294 1639 2779 5516 467 2764 1877 3388 3836 4546
pt.pm.npm v.iai.3p cj r.nsm n.nsm

ἀδύνατος ἐν Λύστροις τοῖς ποσὶν ἐκάθητο, χωλὸς ἐκ κοιλίας → μητρὸς
were useless, *in Lystra whose feet sitting* lame from the womb of his mother,
105 1877 3388 3836 4546 2764 6000 1666 3120 899 3613
a.nsm p.d n.dpn d.dpm n.dpm v.imi.3s a.nsm p.g n.gsf n.gsf

αὐτοῦ ὃς → οὐδέποτε περιεπάτησεν. [9]οὗτος ἤκουσεν τοῦ Παύλου λαλοῦντος·
his who had never walked. This man listened to *{the}* Paul speaking.
899 4005 4344 4030 4344 4047 201 3836 4263 3281
r.gsm.3 r.nsm adv v.aai.3s r.nsm v.aai.3s d.gsm n.gsm pt.pa.gsm

ὃς ἀτενίσας αὐτῷ καὶ ἰδὼν ὅτι ἔχει πίστιν τοῦ
Looking intently at him, Paul *Looking intently at him {and}* saw that he had faith ~
867 867 867 899 4005 867 899 2779 1625 4022 2400 4411 3836
r.nsm pt.aa.nsm r.dsm.3 cj pt.aa.nsm cj v.pai.3s n.asf d.gsn

σωθῆναι, [10] εἶπεν → μεγάλῃ φωνῇ, ἀνάστηθι ἐπὶ τοὺς πόδας σου
to be healed, and said in a loud voice, "Stand upright on *{the}* your feet." *your*
5392 3306 3489 5889 482 3981 2093 3836 5148 4546 5148
f.ap v.aai.3s a.dsf n.dsf v.aam.2s p.a d.apm n.apm r.gs.2

ὀρθός. καὶ ἥλατο καὶ περιεπάτει. [11] οἵ τε ὄχλοι ἰδόντες ὃ
upright And ⌊he jumped up⌋ and began to walk. And the *And* crowds, seeing what Paul
3981 2779 256 2779 4344 5445 3836 5445 4063 1625 4005 4263
a.nsm cj v.ami.3s cj v.iai.3s d.npm cj n.npm pt.aa.npm r.asn

NASB

Greeks. [2]But
the Jews who
disbelieved stirred
up the minds of
the Gentiles and
embittered them
against the breth-
ren. [3]Therefore
they spent a long
time *there* speak-
ing boldly *with*
reliance upon the
Lord, who was
testifying to the
word of His grace,
granting that signs
and wonders be
done by their
hands. [4]But the
people of the city
were divided; and
some sided with
the Jews, and some
with the apostles.
[5]And when an at-
tempt was made by
both the Gentiles
and the Jews with
their rulers, to mis-
treat and to stone
them, [6]they became
aware of it and
fled to the cities of
Lycaonia, Lystra
and Derbe, and
the surrounding
region; [7]and there
they continued to
preach the gospel.
[8]At Lystra a man
was sitting who
had no strength
in his feet, lame
from his mother's
womb, who had
never walked.
[9]This man was
listening to Paul
as he spoke, who,
when he had fixed
his gaze on him
and had seen that
he had faith to be
made well, [10]said
with a loud voice,
"Stand upright on
your feet." And
he leaped up and
began to walk.
[11]When the crowds
saw what Paul had

[a] [ἐπὶ] UBS.

NIV

had done, they
shouted in the Lyc-
aonian language,
"The gods have
come down to us
in human form!"
12 Barnabas they
called Zeus, and
Paul they called
Hermes because
he was the chief
speaker. 13 The
priest of Zeus,
whose temple was
just outside the
city, brought bulls
and wreaths to the
city gates because
he and the crowd
wanted to offer
sacrifices to them.
14 But when the
apostles Barnabas
and Paul heard
of this, they tore
their clothes and
rushed out into the
crowd, shouting:
15 "Friends, why
are you doing this?
We too are only
human, like you.
We are bringing
you good news,
telling you to turn
from these worth-
less things to the
living God, who
made the heavens
and the earth and
the sea and every-
thing in them. 16 In
the past, he let all
nations go their
own way. 17 Yet he
has not left himself
without testimo-
ny: He has shown
kindness by giv-
ing you rain from
heaven and crops
in their seasons; he
provides you with
plenty of food and
fills your hearts
with joy."

ἐποίησεν Παῦλος ἐπῆραν τὴν φωνὴν αὐτῶν → Λυκαονιστὶ λέγοντες,
had done, *Paul* lifted up *{the}* their voices, *their* saying in the dialect of Lycaonia, *saying*
4472 4263 2048 3836 899 5889 899 3306 3378 3306
v.aai.3s n.nsm v.aai.3p d.asf n.asf r.gpm.3 adv pt.pa.npm

οἱ θεοὶ ὁμοιωθέντες ἀνθρώποις κατέβησαν πρὸς ἡμᾶς,
"The gods have come down to us in the likeness of men!" *have come down* *to* *us*
3836 2536 2849 2849 2849 4639 7005 3929 476 2849 4639 7005
d.npm n.npm pt.ap.npm n.dpm v.aai.3p p.a r.ap.1

12 ἐκάλουν τε τὸν Βαρναβᾶν Δία, τὸν δὲ Παῦλον Ἑρμῆν, ἐπειδὴ αὐτὸς
Barnabas they called ~ *{the}* *Barnabas* Zeus, *{the}* and Paul, Hermes, because he
982 2813 5445 3836 982 2416 3836 1254 4263 2258 2076 899
v.iai.3p cj d.asm n.asm n.asm d.asm cj n.asm n.asm cj r.nsm

ἦν ὁ ἡγούμενος τοῦ λόγου. 13 ὅ τε ἱερεὺς τοῦ Διὸς τοῦ ὄντος
was the chief *{the}* speaker. The ~ priest of Zeus, whose temple was
1639 3836 2451 3836 3364 3836 5445 2636 3836 2416 3836 1639
v.iai.3s d.nsm pt.pm.nsm d.gsm n.gsm d.nsm cj n.nsm d.gsm n.gsm d.gsm pt.pa.gsm

πρὸ τῆς πόλεως ταύρους καὶ στέμματα ἐπὶ τοὺς πυλῶνας ἐνέγκας
⌞at the entrance to⌟ the city, brought oxen and garlands to the gates, *brought*
4574 3836 4484 5770 5436 2779 5098 2093 3836 4784 5770
p.g d.gsf n.gsf n.apm cj n.apn p.a d.apm n.apm pt.aa.nsm

σὺν τοῖς ὄχλοις ἤθελεν θύειν. 14 →
intending to offer sacrifice ⌞along with⌟ the crowds. *intending* *to offer sacrifice* But when the
2527 2604 2604 2604 5250 3836 4063 2527 2604 1254 3836
p.d d.dpm n.dpm v.iai.3s f.pa

ἀκούσαντες δὲ οἱ ἀπόστολοι Βαρναβᾶς καὶ Παῦλος
apostles Barnabas and Paul heard of it, *But* *the* *apostles* *Barnabas* *and* *Paul*
693 982 2779 4263 201 1254 3836 693 982 2779 4263
pt.aa.npm cj d.npm n.npm n.nsm cj n.nsm

↱ διαρρήξαντες τὰ ἱμάτια αὐτῶν ἐξεπήδησαν εἰς τὸν ὄχλον κράζοντες
they tore *{the}* their clothes, *their* rushed out into the crowd, and shouted,
899 1396 3836 899 2668 899 1737 1650 3836 4063 3189
pt.aa.npm d.apn n.apn r.gpm.3 v.aai.3p p.a d.asm n.asm pt.pa.npm

15 καὶ λέγοντες, ἄνδρες, τί ταῦτα ποιεῖτε; καὶ ἡμεῖς
{and} saying, "Men, why are you doing these things? *are you doing* For we too *we*
2779 3306 467 5515 4472 4472 4472 4047 4472 7005 2779 7005
cj pt.pa.npm n.vpm r.asn r.apn v.pai.2p adv r.np.1

ὁμοιοπαθεῖς ἐσμεν ὑμῖν ἄνθρωποι εὐαγγελιζόμενοι ὑμᾶς ↰
are men ⌞subject to the same frailties⌟ *are* as you, *men* bringing you good
1639 476 3926 1639 7007 476 2294 7007 2294
a.npm v.pai.1p r.dp.2 n.npm pt.pm.npm r.ap.2

↰ ἀπὸ τούτων τῶν ματαίων ἐπιστρέφειν ἐπὶ θεὸν ζῶντα,
news to turn away from these *{the}* vain things *to turn away* to the living God, *living*
2294 2188 2188 2188 608 4047 3836 3469 2188 2093 2409 2536 2409
p.g r.gpn d.gpn a.gpn f.pa p.a n.asm pt.pa.asm

ὃς ἐποίησεν τὸν οὐρανὸν καὶ τὴν γῆν καὶ τὴν θάλασσαν καὶ πάντα τὰ ἐν
who made the heaven and the earth and the sea and everything *{the}* in
4005 4472 3836 4041 2779 3836 1178 2779 3836 2498 2779 4246 3836 1877
r.nsm v.aai.3s d.asm n.asm cj d.asf n.asf cj d.asf n.asf cj a.apn d.apn p.d

αὐτοῖς· 16 ὃς ἐν ταῖς παρῳχημέναις γενεαῖς εἴασεν πάντα τὰ ἔθνη πορεύεσθαι
them, who in *{the}* past generations allowed all the nations to walk
899 4005 1877 3836 4233 1155 1572 4246 3836 1620 4513
r.dpm.3 r.nsm p.d d.dpf pt.rp.dpf n.dpf v.aai.3s a.apn d.apn n.apn f.pm

ταῖς ὁδοῖς αὐτῶν· 17 καίτοι οὐκ ἀμάρτυρον αὐτὸν
in their own ways; *their own* yet he did not leave himself without witness, *himself*
3836 899 899 3847 899 2792 918 918 4024 918 899 282 899
d.dpf n.dpf r.gpn.3 cj pl a.asm r.asm.3

ἀφῆκεν ἀγαθουργῶν, οὐρανόθεν ὑμῖν ὑετοὺς διδοὺς καὶ
he did leave for he did good, giving you rains from heaven *you* *rains* *giving* and fruitful
918 14 1443 7007 5624 4040 7007 5624 1443 2779 2845
v.aai.3s pt.pa.nsm adv r.dp.2 n.apm pt.pa.nsm cj

καιροὺς καρποφόρους, ἐμπιπλῶν → τροφῆς καὶ εὐφροσύνης τὰς καρδίας
seasons, *fruitful* filling your hearts with food and gladness." *{the}* *hearts*
2789 2845 1858 7007 2840 5575 2779 2372 3836 2840
n.apm a.apm pt.pa.nsm n.gsf cj n.gsf d.apf n.apf

NASB

done, they raised
their voice, saying
in the Lycaonian
language, "The
gods have become
like men and have
come down to us."
12 And they *began*
calling Barnabas,
Zeus, and Paul,
Hermes, because
he was the chief
speaker. 13 The
priest of Zeus,
whose *temple* was
just outside the
city, brought oxen
and garlands to the
gates, and wanted
to offer sacrifice
with the crowds.
14 But when the
apostles Barnabas
and Paul heard of
it, they tore their
robes and rushed
out into the crowd,
crying out 15 and
saying, "Men,
why are you doing
these things? We
are also men of
the same nature as
you, and preach the
gospel to you that
you should turn
from these [a]vain
things to a living
God, WHO MADE
THE HEAVEN AND
THE EARTH AND THE
SEA AND ALL THAT
IS IN THEM. 16 In the
generations gone
by He permitted
all the nations to
go their own ways;
17 and yet He did
not leave Himself
without witness, in
that He did good
and gave you rains
from heaven and
fruitful seasons,
satisfying your
hearts with food
and gladness."

[a] I.e. idols

NIV

[18]Even with these
words, they had
difficulty keeping
the crowd from
sacrificing to
them.
[19]Then some Jews
came from Anti-
och and Iconium
and won the crowd
over. They stoned
Paul and dragged
him outside the
city, thinking he
was dead. [20]But
after the disci-
ples had gathered
around him, he got
up and went back
into the city. The
next day he and
Barnabas left for
Derbe.

The Return to Antioch in Syria

[21]They preached
the gospel in that
city and won a
large number of
disciples. Then
they returned to
Lystra, Iconi-
um and Antioch,
[22]strengthening the
disciples and en-
couraging them to
remain true to the
faith. "We must
go through many
hardships to enter
the kingdom of
God," they said.
[23]Paul and Bar-
nabas appointed
elders[a] for them in
each church and,
with prayer and
fasting, commit-
ted them to the
Lord, in whom
they had put their
trust. [24]After going
through Pisidia,
they came into
Pamphylia, [25]and
when they had
preached the word
in Perga, they went
down to Attalia.
[26]From Attalia
they sailed back
to Antioch, where
they had been
committed to the
grace of God for

[a] 23 Or *Barnabas ordained elders*; or *Barnabas had elders elected*

ὑμῶν. [18] καὶ ταῦτα λέγοντες ↱ μόλις κατέπαυσαν τοὺς ὄχλους τοῦ μὴ
your Even saying these things, *saying* they barely restrained the crowds *{the}* from
7007 2779 3306 4047 3306 2924 3660 2924 3836 4063 3836 3590
r.gp.2 cj r.apn pt.pa.npm adv v.aai.3p d.apm n.apm d.gsn pl

θύειν αὐτοῖς. [19] ἐπῆλθαν δὲ ἀπὸ Ἀντιοχείας καὶ Ἰκονίου
⌞offering sacrifice⌟ to them. But there came *But* Jews from Antioch and Iconium,
2604 899 1254 2088 1254 2681 608 522 2779 2658
f.pa r.dpm.3 v.aai.3p cj p.g n.gsf cj n.gsn

Ἰουδαῖοι καὶ πείσαντες τοὺς ὄχλους καὶ ↱ λιθάσαντες τὸν Παῦλον
Jews and having persuaded the crowd *{and}* they stoned *{the}* Paul and
2681 2779 4275 3836 4063 2779 5359 3342 3836 4263
a.npm cj pt.aa.npm d.apm n.apm cj pt.aa.npm d.asm n.asm

ἔσυρον ἔξω τῆς πόλεως νομίζοντες αὐτὸν τεθνηκέναι. [20] →
dragged him outside the city, thinking him to be dead. But when the disciples
5359 2032 3836 4484 3787 899 2569 1254 3836 3412
v.iai.3p p.g d.gsf n.gsf pt.pa.npm r.asm.3 f.ra

κυκλωσάντων δὲ τῶν μαθητῶν αὐτὸν ↱ ἀναστὰς εἰσῆλθεν εἰς τὴν πόλιν.
gathered around *But* *the* *disciples* him, he got up and went into the city;
3240 1254 3836 3412 899 1656 482 1656 1650 3836 4484
pt.aa.gpm cj d.gpm n.gpm r.asm.3 pt.aa.nsm v.aai.3s p.a d.asf n.asf

καὶ τῇ ἐπαύριον ἐξῆλθεν σὺν τῷ Βαρναβᾷ εἰς Δέρβην.
and ⌞on the⌟ following day he set off with *{the}* Barnabas for Derbe.
2779 3836 2069 2002 5250 3836 982 1650 1292
cj d.dsf adv v.aai.3s p.d d.dsm n.dsm p.a n.asf

[21] εὐαγγελισάμενοί τε τὴν πόλιν ἐκείνην καὶ →
⌞After they had preached the good news⌟ ~ *{the}* in that city *that* and made many
2294 5445 3836 1697 4484 1697 2779 2653
pt.am.npm cj d.asf n.asf r.asf cj

μαθητεύσαντες ἱκανοὺς ὑπέστρεψαν εἰς τὴν Λύστραν καὶ εἰς Ἰκόνιον καὶ εἰς
disciples, *many* they returned to *{the}* Lystra, then ⌞on to⌟ Iconium and to
3411 2653 5715 1650 3836 3388 2779 1650 2658 2779 1650
pt.aa.npm a.apm v.aai.3p p.a d.asf n.asf cj p.a n.asn cj p.a

Ἀντιόχειαν [22] ἐπιστηρίζοντες τὰς ψυχὰς τῶν μαθητῶν, παρακαλοῦντες
Antioch, strengthening the souls of the disciples, encouraging them
522 2185 3836 6034 3836 3412 4151
n.asf pt.pa.npm d.apf n.apf d.gpm n.gpm pt.pa.npm

ἐμμένειν τῇ πίστει καὶ ὅτι διὰ πολλῶν θλίψεων δεῖ
to continue ⌞in the⌟ faith, and saying, ~ "It is through many tribulations that we must
1844 3836 4411 2779 4022 1328 4498 2568 7005 1256
f.pa d.dsf n.dsf cj cj p.g a.gpf n.gpf v.pai.3s

ἡμᾶς ⌞εἰσελθεῖν εἰς⌟ τὴν βασιλείαν τοῦ θεοῦ. [23] χειροτονήσαντες δὲ
we enter the kingdom of God." And when they had appointed *And* elders
7005 1656 1650 3836 993 3836 2536 1254 5936 1254 4565
r.ap.1 f.aa p.a d.asf n.asf d.gsm n.gsm pt.aa.npm cj

αὐτοῖς κατ' ἐκκλησίαν πρεσβυτέρους, προσευξάμενοι μετὰ νηστειῶν παρέθεντο
for them in every church, *elders* praying with fasting, they committed
899 2848 1711 4565 4667 3552 3763 4192
r.dpm.3 p.a n.asf a.apm pt.am.npm p.g n.gpf v.ami.3p

αὐτοὺς τῷ κυρίῳ εἰς ὃν πεπιστεύκεισαν. [24] καὶ διελθόντες τὴν Πισιδίαν
them ⌞to the⌟ Lord in whom they had believed. And going through *{the}* Pisidia,
899 3836 3261 1650 4005 4409 2779 1451 3836 4407
r.apm.3 d.dsm n.dsm p.a r.asm v.lai.3p cj pt.aa.npm d.asf n.asf

ἦλθον εἰς τὴν Παμφυλίαν [25] καὶ λαλήσαντες ἐν Πέργῃ τὸν
they came to *{the}* Pamphylia. And ⌞when they had spoken⌟ the word in Perga, *the*
2262 1650 3836 4103 2779 3281 3836 3364 1877 4308 3836
v.aai.3p p.a d.asf n.asf cj pt.aa.npm p.d n.dsf d.asm

λόγον κατέβησαν εἰς Ἀττάλειαν [26] κἀκεῖθεν ἀπέπλευσαν εἰς Ἀντιόχειαν,
word they went down to Attalia, and from there they sailed to Antioch,
3364 2849 1650 877 2796 676 1650 522
n.asm v.aai.3p p.a n.asf crasis v.aai.3p p.a n.asf

ὅθεν ἦσαν παραδεδομένοι τῇ χάριτι τοῦ θεοῦ εἰς τὸ ἔργον ὃ
where ⌞they had been⌟ commended ⌞to the⌟ grace of God for the work that
3854 1639 4140 3836 5921 3836 2536 1650 3836 2240 4005
cj v.iai.3p pt.rp.npm d.dsf n.dsf d.gsm n.gsm p.a d.asn n.asn r.asn

NASB

[18]*Even* saying
these things, with
difficulty they re-
strained the crowds
from offering
sacrifice to them.
[19]But Jews came
from Antioch
and Iconium, and
having won over
the crowds, they
stoned Paul and
dragged him out
of the city, sup-
posing him to be
dead. [20]But while
the disciples stood
around him, he got
up and entered the
city. The next day
he went away with
Barnabas to Derbe.
[21]After they had
preached the gos-
pel to that city and
had made many
disciples, they
returned to Lystra
and to Iconium
and to Antioch,
[22]strengthening the
souls of the dis-
ciples, encouraging
them to continue
in the faith, and
saying, "Through
many tribulations
we must enter the
kingdom of God."
[23]When they had
appointed elders
for them in every
church, having
prayed with fast-
ing, they com-
mended them to
the Lord in whom
they had believed.
[24]They passed
through Pisidia
and came into
Pamphylia. [25]When
they had spoken
the word in Perga,
they went down
to Attalia. [26]From
there they sailed
to Antioch, from
which they had
been commended
to the grace of God
for the work that

NIV

the work they had
now completed.
27 On arriving
there, they gath-
ered the church
together and re-
ported all that God
had done through
them and how he
had opened a door
of faith to the Gen-
tiles. 28 And they
stayed there a long
time with the dis-
ciples.

The Council at Jerusalem

15 Certain
people
came down from
Judea to Antioch
and were teach-
ing the believers:
"Unless you are
circumcised, ac-
cording to the
custom taught by
Moses, you cannot
be saved." 2 This
brought Paul and
Barnabas into
sharp dispute
and debate with
them. So Paul and
Barnabas were
appointed, along
with some other
believers, to go
up to Jerusalem
to see the apostles
and elders about
this question. 3 The
church sent them
on their way, and
as they traveled
through Phoenicia
and Samaria, they
told how the Gen-
tiles had been con-
verted. This news
made all the be-
lievers very glad.
4 When they came
to Jerusalem, they
were welcomed
by the church and
the apostles and
elders, to whom
they reported
everything God
had done through
them.
5 Then some of
the believers who
belonged to the
party of the Phari-
sees stood up

ἐπλήρωσαν. 27 παραγενόμενοι δὲ καὶ συναγαγόντες τὴν ἐκκλησίαν ↰
they had fulfilled. And when they arrived, *And* and had gathered the church together,
4444 1254 4134 1254 2779 5251 3836 1711 5251
v.aai.3p pt.am.npm cj cj pt.aa.npm d.asf n.asf

ἀνήγγελλον ὅσα ἐποίησεν ὁ θεὸς μετ᾽ αὐτῶν καὶ ὅτι ἤνοιξεν
they reported all that God had done *{the} God* with them and how he had opened a door of
334 4012 2536 4472 3836 2536 3552 899 2779 4022 487 2598 4411
v.iai.3p r.apn v.aai.3s d.nsm n.nsm p.g r.gpm.3 cj cj v.aai.3s

τοῖς ἔθνεσιν θύραν πίστεως. 28 διέτριβον δὲ χρόνον οὐκ ὀλίγον
faith to the Gentiles. *door of faith* And they spent *And* no little time *no little*
4411 3836 1620 2598 4411 1254 1417 1254 4024 3900 5989 4024 3900
d.dpn n.dpn n.asf n.gsf v.iai.3p cj n.asm pl a.asm

σὺν τοῖς μαθηταῖς.
there with the disciples.
5250 3836 3412
p.d d.dpm n.dpm

15:1 καί τινες κατελθόντες ἀπὸ τῆς Ἰουδαίας ἐδίδασκον τοὺς
Now ⌞some men⌟ came down from *{the}* Judea and began to teach the
2779 5516 2982 608 3836 2677 1438 3836
cj r.npm pt.aa.npm p.g d.gsf n.gsf v.iai.3p d.apm

ἀδελφοὺς ὅτι, ⌞ἐὰν μὴ⌟ περιτμηθῆτε τῷ ἔθει τῷ Μωϋσέως,
brothers, ~ "Unless you are circumcised ⌞according to the⌟ custom of Moses,
81 4022 1569 3590 4362 3836 1621 3836 3707
n.apm cj cj pl v.aps.2p d.dsn n.dsn d.dsn n.gsm

⌞οὐ δύνασθε⌟ σωθῆναι. 2 → γενομένης δὲ
you cannot be saved." And when Paul and Barnabas had *And* no small
4024 1538 5392 1254 4263 2779 982 1181 1254 4024 3900
pl v.ppi.2p f.ap pt.am.gsf cj

στάσεως καὶ ζητήσεως οὐκ ὀλίγης τῷ Παύλῳ καὶ τῷ Βαρναβᾷ πρὸς αὐτούς,
argument and debate *no small {the} Paul and {the} Barnabas* with them, the
5087 2779 2428 4024 3900 3836 4263 2779 3836 982 4639 899
n.gsf cj n.gsf pl a.gsf d.dsm n.dsm cj d.dsm n.dsm p.a r.apm.3

ἔταξαν ἀναβαίνειν Παῦλον καὶ Βαρναβᾶν καί τινας ἄλλους ἐξ αὐτῶν
brethren appointed *to go up* Paul and Barnabas and some others among them
5435 326 4263 2779 982 2779 5516 257 1666 899
v.aai.3p f.pa n.asm cj n.asm cj r.apm r.apm p.g r.gpm.3

πρὸς τοὺς ἀποστόλους καὶ πρεσβυτέρους εἰς Ἰερουσαλὴμ
to go up to Jerusalem to the apostles and elders *to Jerusalem*
326 326 326 1650 2647 4639 3836 693 2779 4565 1650 2647
p.a d.apm n.apm cj a.apm p.a n.asf

περὶ τοῦ ζητήματος τούτου. 3 οἱ μὲν οὖν προπεμφθέντες ὑπὸ τῆς
regarding *{the}* this issue. *this they* ~ So ⌞being sent on their way⌟ by the
4309 3836 4047 2427 4047 3836 3525 4036 4636 5679 3836
p.g d.gsn n.gsn r.gsn d.npm pl cj pt.ap.npm p.g d.gsf

ἐκκλησίας διήρχοντο τήν τε Φοινίκην καὶ Σαμάρειαν ἐκδιηγούμενοι τὴν
church, they went through *{the}* both Phoenicia and Samaria, narrating in detail the
1711 3836 1451 3836 5445 5834 2779 4899 1687 3836
n.gsf v.imi.3p d.asf cj n.asf cj n.asf pt.pm.npm d.asf

ἐπιστροφὴν τῶν ἐθνῶν καὶ ἐποίουν χαρὰν μεγάλην πᾶσιν τοῖς ἀδελφοῖς.
conversion of the Gentiles, and brought great joy *great* to all the brothers.
2189 3836 1620 2779 4472 3489 5915 3489 4246 3836 81
n.asf d.gpn n.gpn cj v.iai.3p n.asf a.asf a.dpm d.dpm n.dpm

4 παραγενόμενοι δὲ εἰς Ἰερουσαλὴμ παρεδέχθησαν ἀπὸ τῆς ἐκκλησίας καὶ
And when they arrived *And* in Jerusalem, they were welcomed by the church and
1254 4134 1254 1650 2647 4138 608 3836 1711 2779
pt.am.npm cj p.a n.asf v.api.3p p.g d.gsf n.gsf cj

τῶν ἀποστόλων καὶ τῶν πρεσβυτέρων, ἀνήγγειλάν τε ὅσα ὁ θεὸς
the apostles and the elders, and they reported *and* all that *{the}* God
3836 693 2779 3836 4565 5445 334 5445 4012 3836 2536
d.gpm n.gpm cj d.gpm a.gpm v.aai.3p cj r.apn d.nsm n.nsm

ἐποίησεν μετ᾽ αὐτῶν. 5 ἐξανέστησαν δέ τινες τῶν ἀπὸ τῆς αἱρέσεως τῶν
had done with them. But some arose *But some {the}* from the party of the
4472 3552 899 1254 5516 1985 1254 5516 3836 608 3836 146 3836
v.aai.3s p.g r.gpm.3 v.aai.3p cj r.npm d.gpm p.g d.gsf n.gsf d.gpm

NASB

they had accom-
plished. 27 When
they had arrived
and gathered the
church together,
they *began* to
report all things
that God had done
with them and how
He had opened
a door of faith
to the Gentiles.
28 And they spent a
long time with the
disciples.

The Council at Jerusalem

15:1 Some men
came down from
Judea and *began*
teaching the breth-
ren, "Unless you
are circumcised ac-
cording to the cus-
tom of Moses, you
cannot be saved."
2 And when Paul
and Barnabas had
great dissension
and debate with
them, *the brethren*
determined that
Paul and Barnabas
and some others of
them should go up
to Jerusalem to the
apostles and elders
concerning this
issue. 3 Therefore,
being sent on their
way by the church,
they were passing
through both Phoe-
nicia and Samaria,
describing in detail
the conversion of
the Gentiles, and
were bringing great
joy to all the breth-
ren. 4 When they ar-
rived at Jerusalem,
they were received
by the church and
the apostles and
the elders, and they
reported all that
God had done with
them. 5 But some of
the sect of the

NIV

and said, "The
Gentiles must be
circumcised and
required to keep
the law of Moses."
6 The apostles and
elders met to con-
sider this question.
7 After much dis-
cussion, Peter got
up and addressed
them: "Brothers,
you know that
some time ago
God made a choice
among you that
the Gentiles might
hear from my lips
the message of the
gospel and believe.
8 God, who knows
the heart, showed
that he accepted
them by giving
the Holy Spirit to
them, just as he
did to us. 9 He did
not discriminate
between us and
them, for he puri-
fied their hearts by
faith. 10 Now then,
why do you try to
test God by put-
ting on the necks
of Gentiles a yoke
that neither we nor
our ancestors have
been able to bear?
11 No! We believe
it is through the
grace of our Lord
Jesus that we are
saved, just as they
are."
12 The whole as-
sembly became
silent as they lis-
tened to Barnabas
and Paul telling
about the signs and
wonders God had
done among the
Gentiles through
them.

Φαρισαίων πεπιστευκότες λέγοντες ὅτι δεῖ περιτέμνειν αὐτοὺς
Pharisees, believers, and said, ~ ⌞"It is necessary⌟ to circumcise them and
5757 4409 3306 4022 1256 4362 899 5445
n.gpm pt.ra.npm pt.pa.npm cj v.pai.3s f.pa r.apm.3

παραγγέλλειν τε τηρεῖν τὸν νόμον Μωϋσέως. 6
order *and* them to keep the law of Moses." The apostles and the elders
4133 5445 5498 3836 3795 3707 3836 693 2779 3836 4565
f.pa cj f.pa d.asm n.asm n.gsm

συνήχθησάν τε οἱ ἀπόστολοι καὶ οἱ πρεσβύτεροι ἰδεῖν περὶ τοῦ λόγου
were gathered ~ *The apostles and the elders* to see about *{the}* this matter.
5251 5445 3836 693 2779 3836 4565 1625 4309 3836 4047 3364
v.api.3p cj d.npm n.npm cj d.npm a.npm f.aa p.g d.gsm n.gsm

τούτου. 7 πολλῆς δὲ ζητήσεως γενομένης ἀναστὰς
this After there had been much *{and}* debate, *After there had been* Peter stood up
4047 1181 1181 1181 1181 4498 1254 2428 1181 4377 482
r.gsn a.gsf cj n.gsf pt.am.gsf pt.aa.nsm

Πέτρος εἶπεν πρὸς αὐτούς, ⌞ἄνδρες ἀδελφοί,⌟ ὑμεῖς ἐπίστασθε ὅτι ἀφ᾽ ἡμερῶν
Peter and said to them, "My brothers, you know that in days
4377 3306 4639 899 467 81 7007 2179 4022 608 2465
n.nsm v.aai.3s p.a r.apm.3 n.vpm n.vpm r.np.2 v.ppi.2p cj p.g n.gpf

ἀρχαίων ἐν ὑμῖν ἐξελέξατο ὁ θεὸς διὰ τοῦ
of old God made a choice among you, *made a choice {the} God* that through *{the}* my
792 2536 1721 1721 1721 1877 7007 1721 3836 2536 1328 3836 1609
a.gpf p.d r.dp.2 v.ami.3s d.nsm n.nsm p.g d.gsn

στόματός μου ἀκοῦσαι τὰ ἔθνη τὸν λόγον τοῦ εὐαγγελίου καὶ
mouth *my* the Gentiles should hear *the Gentiles* the message of the gospel and
5125 1609 3836 1620 201 3836 1620 3836 3364 3836 2295 2779
n.gsn r.gs.1 f.aa d.apn n.apn d.asm n.asm d.gsn n.gsn cj

πιστεῦσαι. 8 καὶ ὁ καρδιογνώστης θεὸς ἐμαρτύρησεν αὐτοῖς δοὺς
believe. And *{the}* God, who knows the heart, *God* confirmed this, *to them* by giving
4409 2779 3836 2536 2841 2536 3455 899 1443
f.aa cj d.nsm n.nsm n.nsm v.aai.3s r.dpn.3 pt.aa.nsm

τὸ πνεῦμα τὸ ἅγιον καθὼς καὶ ἡμῖν 9 καὶ ↱ ↱ οὐθὲν
the Holy Spirit *{the} Holy* to them just as *{also}* he did to us, and he made no
3836 41 4460 3836 41 899 899 2777 2779 7005 2779 1359 1359 4032
d.asn n.asn d.asn a.asn pl adv r.dp.1 cj a.asn

διέκρινεν μεταξὺ ἡμῶν τε καὶ αὐτῶν τῇ πίστει καθαρίσας τὰς
distinction between us ~ and them, cleansing their hearts by faith. *cleansing {the}*
1359 3568 7005 5445 2779 899 2751 899 2840 3836 4411 2751 3836
v.aai.3s p.g r.gp.1 cj cj r.gpn.3 d.dsf n.dsf pt.aa.nsm d.apf

καρδίας αὐτῶν. 10 νῦν οὖν τί πειράζετε τὸν θεὸν ἐπιθεῖναι ζυγὸν ἐπὶ
hearts their So now *So* why are you testing *{the}* God by putting a yoke on
2840 899 4036 3814 4036 5515 4279 3836 2536 2202 2433 2093
n.apf r.gpn.3 adv cj r.asn v.pai.2p d.asm n.asm f.aa n.asm p.a

τὸν τράχηλον τῶν μαθητῶν ὃν οὔτε οἱ πατέρες ἡμῶν οὔτε ἡμεῖς
the neck of the disciples, which neither *{the}* our ancestors *our* nor we
3836 5549 3836 3412 4005 4046 3836 7005 4252 7005 4046 7005
d.asm n.asm d.gpm n.gpm r.asm cj d.npm n.npm r.gp.1 cj r.np.1

ἰσχύσαμεν βαστάσαι; 11 ἀλλὰ διὰ τῆς χάριτος τοῦ κυρίου Ἰησοῦ πιστεύομεν
have been able to bear? But through the grace of the Lord Jesus we believe
2710 1002 247 1328 3836 5921 3836 3261 2652 4409
v.aai.1p f.aa cj p.g d.gsf n.gsf d.gsm n.gsm n.gsm v.pai.1p

σωθῆναι καθ᾽ ὃν τρόπον κἀκεῖνοι. 12
that ⌞we will be saved,⌟ in the same way as those also." And the entire assembly
5392 2848 4005 5573 2797 1254 3836 4246 4436
f.ap p.a r.asm n.asm adv

ἐσίγησεν δὲ πᾶν τὸ πλῆθος καὶ ἤκουον Βαρναβᾶ καὶ Παύλου ἐξηγουμένων ὅσα
fell silent, *And entire the assembly* and ⌞listened to⌟ Barnabas and Paul recounting all
4967 1254 4246 3836 4436 2779 201 982 2779 4263 2007 4012
v.aai.3s cj a.nsn d.nsn n.nsn cj v.iai.3p n.gsm cj n.gsm pt.pm.gpm r.apn

ἐποίησεν ὁ θεὸς σημεῖα καὶ τέρατα ἐν
the signs and wonders that God had done *{the} God signs and wonders* through them among
4956 2779 5469 2536 4472 3836 2536 4956 2779 5469 1328 899 1877
v.aai.3s d.nsm n.nsm n.apn cj n.apn p.d

NASB

Pharisees who had
believed stood up,
saying, "It is neces-
sary to circumcise
them and to direct
them to observe the
Law of Moses."
6 The apostles and
the elders came to-
gether to look into
this matter. 7 After
there had been
much debate, Peter
stood up and said
to them, "Brethren,
you know that in
the early days God
made a choice
among you, that by
my mouth the Gen-
tiles would hear the
word of the gospel
and believe. 8 And
God, who knows
the heart, testified
to them giving
them the Holy
Spirit, just as He
also did to us; 9 and
He made no dis-
tinction between us
and them, cleans-
ing their hearts
by faith. 10 Now
therefore why do
you put God to
the test by placing
upon the neck of
the disciples a yoke
which neither our
fathers nor we have
been able to bear?
11 But we believe
that we are saved
through the grace
of the Lord Jesus,
in the same way as
they also are."
12 All the people
kept silent, and
they were listening
to Barnabas and
Paul as they were
relating what signs
and wonders God
had done through
them among the
Gentiles.

NIV

[13]When they finished, James spoke up. "Brothers," he said, "listen to me. [14]Simon[a] has described to us how God first intervened to choose a people for his name from the Gentiles. [15]The words of the prophets are in agreement with this, as it is written:

[16]" 'After this I will return
and rebuild David's fallen tent.
Its ruins I will rebuild,
and I will restore it,
[17]that the rest of mankind may seek the Lord,
even all the Gentiles who bear my name,
says the Lord, who does these things'[b]—
[18] things known from long ago.[c]

[19]"It is my judgment, therefore, that we should not make it difficult for the Gentiles who are turning to God. [20]Instead we should write to them, telling them to abstain from food polluted by idols, from sexual immorality, from the meat of strangled animals and from blood. [21]For the law of Moses has been preached in every city from the earliest times and is read in the synagogues on every Sabbath."

[a] 14 Greek *Simeon*, a variant of *Simon*; that is, Peter
[b] 17 Amos 9:11,12 (see Septuagint)
[c] 17,18 Some manuscripts *things'— / [18]the Lord's work is known to him from long ago*

τοῖς ἔθνεσιν δι᾽ αὐτῶν. [13] μετὰ δὲ τὸ σιγῆσαι αὐτοὺς
the Gentiles. *through them* When *{and}* ~ they finished speaking, *they* James
3836 1620 1328 899 3552 1254 3836 899 4967 899 2610
d.dpn n.dpn p.g r.gpm.3 p.a cj d.asn f.aa r.apm.3

ἀπεκρίθη Ἰάκωβος λέγων, ˌἄνδρες ἀδελφοί,˩ ἀκούσατέ μου. [14] Συμεὼν
replied, *James* saying, "My brothers, listen to me. Simeon
646 2610 3306 467 81 201 1609 5208
v.api.3s n.nsm pt.pa.nsm n.vpm n.vpm v.aam.2p r.gs.1 n.nsm

ἐξηγήσατο καθὼς πρῶτον ὁ θεὸς ἐπεσκέψατο λαβεῖν ἐξ
has recounted how God first *{the} God* ˌconcerned himself about˩ taking ˌfrom among˩ the
2007 2777 2536 4754 3836 2536 2170 3284 1666
v.ami.3s cj adv d.nsm n.nsm v.ami.3s f.aa p.g

ἐθνῶν λαὸν τῷ ὀνόματι αὐτοῦ. [15] καὶ τούτῳ συμφωνοῦσιν οἱ λόγοι τῶν
Gentiles a people for his name. *his* And with this agree the words of the
1620 3295 3836 899 3950 899 2779 4047 5244 3836 3364 3836
n.gpn n.asm d.dsn n.dsn r.gsm.3 cj r.dsn v.pai.3p d.npm n.npm d.gpm

προφητῶν καθὼς γέγραπται, [16] μετὰ ταῦτα ἀναστρέψω καὶ ἀνοικοδομήσω τὴν
prophets, as it is written, 'After this I will return, and I will rebuild the
4737 2777 1211 3552 4047 418 2779 488 3836
n.gpm cj v.rpi.3s p.a r.apn v.fai.1s cj v.fai.1s d.asf

σκηνὴν Δαυὶδ τὴν πεπτωκυῖαν καὶ τὰ κατεσκαμμένα αὐτῆς
tent of David, which has fallen, and I will rebuild the ruins of it,
5008 1253 3836 4406 2779 488 488 488 3836 2940 899
n.asf n.gsm d.asf pt.ra.asf cj d.apn pt.rp.apn r.gsf.3

ἀνοικοδομήσω καὶ ἀνορθώσω αὐτήν, [17] ὅπως ἂν ἐκζητήσωσιν
I will rebuild and I will restore it, so that the rest of men may seek
488 2779 494 899 3968 3836 2905 3836 476 323 1699
v.fai.1s cj v.fai.1s r.asf.3 cj pl v.aas.3p

οἱ κατάλοιποι τῶν ἀνθρώπων τὸν κύριον καὶ πάντα τὰ ἔθνη ἐφ᾽ οὓς
the rest of men the Lord, namely, all the Gentiles on whom my
3836 2905 3836 476 3836 3261 2779 4246 3836 1620 2093 4005 1609
d.npm a.npm d.gpm n.gpm d.asm n.asm cj a.npn d.npn n.npn p.a r.apm

ἐπικέκληται τὸ ὄνομά μου ἐπ᾽ αὐτούς, λέγει κύριος ποιῶν ταῦτα
name has been called, *{the} name my {on} {them}* says the Lord, who makes these things
3950 2126 3836 3950 1609 2093 899 3306 3261 4472 4047
v.rpi.3s d.nsn n.nsn r.gs.1 p.a r.apm.3 v.pai.3s n.nsm pt.pa.nsm r.apn

[18] γνωστὰ ἀπ᾽ αἰῶνος.[a] [19] διὸ ἐγὼ κρίνω ↱ ↱ μὴ παρενοχλεῖν τοῖς
known from long ago.' Therefore I conclude that we should not trouble those
1196 608 172 1475 1609 3212 4214 4214 3590 4214 3836
a.apn p.g n.gsm cj r.ns.1 v.pai.1s pl f.pa d.dpm

ἀπὸ τῶν ἐθνῶν ἐπιστρέφουσιν ἐπὶ τὸν θεόν, [20] ἀλλὰ ἐπιστεῖλαι αὐτοῖς τοῦ
from the Gentiles who are turning to *{the}* God, but should write to them ~
608 3836 1620 2188 2093 3836 2536 247 2182 899 3836
p.g d.gpn n.gpn pt.pa.dpm p.a d.asm n.asm cj f.aa r.dpm.3 d.gsn

ἀπέχεσθαι τῶν ἀλισγημάτων τῶν εἰδώλων καὶ τῆς πορνείας καὶ τοῦ
to abstain from the pollutions of idols, and from sexual immorality, and from
600 3836 246 3836 1631 2779 3836 4518 2779 3836
f.pm d.gpn n.gpn d.gpn n.gpn cj d.gsf n.gsf cj d.gsn

πνικτοῦ καὶ τοῦ αἵματος. [21] Μωϋσῆς γὰρ
ˌwhat has been strangled,˩ and from blood. For from ancient generations Moses *For*
4465 2779 3836 135 1142 1666 792 1155 3707 1142
a.gsn cj d.gsn n.gsn n.nsm cj

ἐκ γενεῶν ἀρχαίων κατὰ πόλιν τοὺς κηρύσσοντας αὐτὸν ἔχει
from generations ancient has had in every city those who proclaim him, *has had* because
1666 1155 792 2400 2400 2848 4484 3836 3062 899 2400 336
p.g n.gpf n.gpf p.a n.asf d.apm pt.pa.apm r.asm.3 v.pai.3s

ἐν ταῖς συναγωγαῖς ˌκατὰ πᾶν˩ σάββατον ἀναγινωσκόμενος.
he is read aloud in the synagogues every Sabbath." *because he is read aloud*
336 336 336 336 1877 3836 5252 2848 4246 4879 336
p.d d.dpf n.dpf p.a a.asn n.asn pt.pp.nsm

[a] 34 ἐστι τῷ Θεῷ πάντα τὰ ἔργα αὐτοῦ included by TR after αἰῶνος.

NASB

James's Judgment

[13]After they had stopped speaking, James answered, saying, "Brethren, listen to me. [14]Simeon has related how God first concerned Himself about taking from among the Gentiles a people for His name. [15]With this the words of the Prophets agree, just as it is written,

[16]' AFTER THESE THINGS I will return,
AND I WILL REBUILD THE TABERNACLE OF DAVID WHICH HAS FALLEN,
AND I WILL REBUILD ITS RUINS,
AND I WILL RESTORE IT,
[17] SO THAT THE REST OF MANKIND MAY SEEK THE LORD,
AND ALL THE GENTILES WHO ARE CALLED BY MY NAME,'
[18] SAYS THE LORD, WHO MAKES THESE THINGS KNOWN FROM LONG AGO.

[19]Therefore it is my judgment that we do not trouble those who are turning to God from among the Gentiles, [20]but that we write to them that they abstain from things contaminated by idols and from fornication and from what is strangled and from blood. [21]For Moses from ancient generations has in every city those who preach him, since he is read in the synagogues every Sabbath."

NIV

The Council's Letter to Gentile Believers

22 Then the apos-
tles and elders,
with the whole
church, decided
to choose some of
their own men and
send them to Anti-
och with Paul and
Barnabas. They
chose Judas (called
Barsabbas) and Si-
las, men who were
leaders among the
believers. 23 With
them they sent the
following letter:

The apostles
and elders, your
brothers,

To the Gentile
believers in An-
tioch, Syria and
Cilicia:

Greetings.

24 We have
heard that some
went out from us
without our au-
thorization and
disturbed you,
troubling your
minds by what
they said. 25 So
we all agreed to
choose some men
and send them to
you with our dear
friends Barna-
bas and Paul—
26 men who have
risked their lives
for the name of
our Lord Jesus
Christ. 27 There-
fore we are send-
ing Judas and Si-
las to confirm by
word of mouth

22 τότε ἔδοξε τοῖς ἀποστόλοις καὶ τοῖς πρεσβυτέροις σὺν ὅλῃ
Then ⌞it seemed good⌟ to the apostles and the elders, ⌞together with⌟ the whole
5538 1506 3836 693 2779 3836 4565 5250 3836 3910
adv v.aai.3s d.dpm n.dpm cj d.dpm a.dpm p.d a.dsf

τῇ ἐκκλησίᾳ ἐκλεξαμένους ἄνδρας ἐξ αὐτῶν πέμψαι εἰς
the church, to send men chosen *men* ⌞from among⌟ them *to send* to
3836 1711 4287 4287 467 1721 467 1666 899 4287 1650
d.dsf n.dsf pt.am.apm n.apm p.g r.gpm.3 f.aa p.a

Ἀντιόχειαν σὺν τῷ Παύλῳ καὶ Βαρναβᾷ, Ἰούδαν τὸν καλούμενον Βαρσαββᾶν
Antioch with *{the}* Paul and Barnabas — Judas *{the}* called Barsabbas,
522 5250 3836 4263 2779 982 2683 3836 2813 984
n.asf p.d d.dsm n.dsm cj n.dsm n.asm d.asm pt.pp.asm n.asm

καὶ Σιλᾶν, ἄνδρας ἡγουμένους ἐν τοῖς ἀδελφοῖς, 23 γράψαντες διὰ
and Silas, leading men *leading* among the brothers — writing by their
2779 4976 2451 467 2451 1877 3836 81 1211 1328 899
cj n.asm n.apm pt.pm.apm p.d d.dpm n.dpm pt.aa.npm p.g

χειρὸς αὐτῶν· οἱ ἀπόστολοι καὶ οἱ πρεσβύτεροι ἀδελφοὶ τοῖς
hand, *their* "From the apostles and *{the}* elders, your brothers, to the Gentile
5931 899 3836 693 2779 3836 4565 81 3836 1620
n.gsf r.gpm.3 d.npm n.npm cj d.npm a.npm n.npm d.dpm

κατὰ τὴν Ἀντιόχειαν καὶ Συρίαν καὶ Κιλικίαν ἀδελφοῖς τοῖς ἐξ ἐθνῶν
brothers in *{the}* Antioch and Syria and Cilicia, *brothers* *{the}* *{from}* *Gentile*
81 2848 3836 522 2779 5353 2779 3070 81 3836 1666 1620
p.a d.asf n.asf cj n.asf cj n.asf n.dpm d.dpm p.g n.gpn

χαίρειν. 24 ἐπειδὴ ἠκούσαμεν ὅτι τινὲς ἐξ ἡμῶν ἐξελθόντες[a] ἐτάραξαν
Greetings! Since we have heard that some ⌞from among⌟ us have gone out and troubled
5897 2076 201 4022 5516 1666 7005 2002 5429
f.pa cj v.aai.1p cj r.npm p.g r.gp.1 pt.aa.npm v.aai.3p

ὑμᾶς → λόγοις ἀνασκευάζοντες τὰς ψυχὰς ὑμῶν[b] ↱ ↱ ↱ οἷς
you with their words, unsettling *{the}* your minds *your* — we had given them
7007 3364 412 3836 7007 6034 7007 1403 1403 1403 4005
r.ap.2 n.dpm pt.pa.npm d.apf n.apf r.gp.2 r.dpm

οὐ διεστειλάμεθα, 25 ἔδοξεν ἡμῖν γενομένοις ὁμοθυμαδὸν
⌞no such⌟ instructions — ⌞it seemed good⌟ to us, having reached agreement,
4024 1403 1506 7005 1181 3924
pl v.ami.1p v.aai.3s r.dp.1 pt.am.dpm adv

ἐκλεξαμένοις ἄνδρας πέμψαι πρὸς ὑμᾶς σὺν τοῖς ἀγαπητοῖς ἡμῶν Βαρναβᾷ καὶ
to select men to send to you with *{the}* our beloved *our* Barnabas and
1721 467 4287 4639 7007 5250 3836 7005 28 7005 982 2779
pt.am.dpm n.apm f.aa p.a r.ap.2 p.d d.dpm a.dpm r.gp.1 n.dsm cj

Παύλῳ, 26 ἀνθρώποις παραδεδωκόσι τὰς ψυχὰς αὐτῶν ὑπὲρ τοῦ ὀνόματος τοῦ
Paul, men who have risked *{the}* their lives *their* for the name of
4263 476 4140 3836 899 6034 899 5642 3836 3950 3836
n.dsm n.dpm pt.ra.dpm d.apf n.apf r.gpm.3 p.g d.gsn n.gsn d.gsm

κυρίου ἡμῶν Ἰησοῦ Χριστοῦ. 27 ἀπεστάλκαμεν οὖν Ἰούδαν καὶ
our Lord *our* Jesus Christ. Therefore we have sent *Therefore* Judas and
7005 3261 7005 2652 5986 4036 690 4036 2683 2779
n.gsm r.gp.1 n.gsm n.gsm v.rai.1p cj n.asm cj

Σιλᾶν καὶ αὐτοὺς ⌞διὰ λόγου⌟ ἀπαγγέλλοντας τὰ
Silas, and they will tell you the same things verbally. *will tell* *the*
4976 2779 899 550 550 3836 899 899 1328 3364 550 3836
n.asm adv r.apm.3 p.g n.gsm pt.pa.apm d.apn

[a] [ἐξελθόντες] UBS.
[b] λέγοντες περιτέμνεσθαι καὶ τηρεῖν τὸν νόμον included by TR after ὑμῶν.

NASB

22 Then it seemed
good to the apos-
tles and the elders,
with the whole
church, to choose
men from among
them to send to An-
tioch with Paul and
Barnabas—Judas
called Barsabbas,
and Silas, leading
men among the
brethren, 23 and they
sent this letter by
them,
"The apostles
and the breth-
ren who are
elders, to the
brethren in
Antioch and
Syria and
Cilicia who
are from the
Gentiles,
greetings.
24 "Since we
have heard
that some of
our number
to whom we
gave no in-
struction have
disturbed you
with *their*
words, unset-
tling your
souls,
25 it seemed
good to
us, having
become of
one mind, to
select men to
send to you
with our be-
loved Barna-
bas and Paul,
26 men who
have risked
their lives
for the name
of our Lord
Jesus Christ.
27 "Therefore
we have sent
Judas and
Silas, who
themselves
will also
report the
same things
by word *of
mouth.*

NIV

what we are writ-
ing. [28]It seemed
good to the Holy
Spirit and to us not
to burden you with
anything beyond
the following re-
quirements: [29]You
are to abstain from
food sacrificed to
idols, from blood,
from the meat of
strangled animals
and from sexual
immorality. You
will do well to
avoid these things.
Farewell.

[30]So the men
were sent off and
went down to
Antioch, where
they gathered the
church together
and delivered the
letter. [31]The people
read it and were
glad for its encour-
aging message.
[32]Judas and Silas,
who themselves
were prophets, said
much to encourage
and strengthen the
believers. [33]After
spending some
time there, they
were sent off by
the believers with
the blessing of
peace to return to
those who had sent
them. [34][a] [35]But
Paul and Barna-
bas remained in
Antioch, where
they and many
others taught and
preached the word
of the Lord.

Disagreement Between Paul and Barnabas

[36]Some time later
Paul said to Bar-
nabas, "Let us go
back and

[a] 34 Some manuscripts include here *But Silas decided to remain there.*

αὐτά. 28 ἔδοξεν γὰρ τῷ πνεύματι τῷ ἁγίῳ καὶ ἡμῖν
same things For ⌊it seemed good⌋ *For* ⌊to the⌋ Holy Spirit *{the}* *Holy* and to us to
899 1142 1506 1142 3836 41 4460 3836 41 2779 7005 2202
r.apn v.aai.3s cj d.dsn n.dsn d.dsn a.dsn cj r.dp.1

μηδὲν πλέον ἐπιτίθεσθαι ὑμῖν βάρος πλὴν τούτων τῶν
impose on you no further *to impose* *on you* burden than these *{the}*
2202 7007 7007 3594 4498 2202 7007 983 4440 4047 3836
a.asn a.asn.c f.pm r.dp.2 n.asn p.g r.gpn d.gpn

ἐπάναγκες, 29 ἀπέχεσθαι εἰδωλοθύτων καὶ αἵματος καὶ
essential requirements: that ⌊you abstain from⌋ ⌊meat sacrificed to idols,⌋ and from blood, and
2055 600 1628 2779 135 2779
adv f.pm n.gpn cj n.gsn cj

πνικτῶν καὶ πορνείας, ἐξ
from things strangled, and from sexual immorality. If you keep yourselves from doing
4465 2779 4518 1413 1413 1413 1571 1666
a.gpn cj n.gsf p.g

ὧν διατηροῦντες ἑαυτοὺς εὖ πράξετε. ἔρρωσθε. 30 οἱ
⌊these things,⌋ *If you keep* *yourselves* you will do well. *you will do* Farewell." So they
4005 1413 1571 4556 4556 4556 2292 4556 4874 4036 3836
r.gpn pt.pa.npm r.apm.2 adv v.fai.2p v.rpm.2p d.npm

μὲν οὖν ἀπολυθέντες κατῆλθον εἰς Ἀντιόχειαν, καὶ συναγαγόντες τὸ
~ *So* were sent off and went down to Antioch, and gathering the
3525 4036 668 2982 1650 522 2779 5251 3836
pl cj pt.ap.npm v.aai.3p p.a n.asf cj pt.aa.npm d.asn

πλῆθος ↰ ἐπέδωκαν τὴν ἐπιστολήν. 31 ἀναγνόντες ← δὲ
entire group together, they delivered the letter. And when they read it aloud, *And* the
4436 5251 2113 3836 2186 1254 336 1254
n.asn v.aai.3p d.asf n.asf pt.aa.npm cj

ἐχάρησαν ἐπὶ τῇ παρακλήσει. 32 Ἰούδας τε καὶ Σιλᾶς καὶ
people rejoiced at its encouragement. Both Judas *Both* and Silas, also being
5897 2093 3836 4155 5445 2683 5445 2779 4976 2779 1639
v.api.3p p.d d.dsf n.dsf n.nsm cj cj n.nsm adv

αὐτοὶ προφῆται ὄντες διὰ
prophets themselves, *prophets* *being* encouraged and strengthened the brothers with a long
4737 899 4737 1639 4151 2779 2185 3836 81 1328 4498
r.npm n.npm pt.pa.npm p.g

λόγου πολλοῦ παρεκάλεσαν τοὺς ἀδελφοὺς καὶ ἐπεστήριξαν, 33
speech. *long* *encouraged* *the* *brothers* *and* *strengthened* And
3364 4498 4151 3836 81 2779 2185 1254
n.gsm n.gsm v.aai.3p d.apm n.apm cj v.aai.3p

ποιήσαντες δὲ χρόνον ἀπελύθησαν μετ' εἰρήνης
⌊when they had spent⌋ *And* some time there, they were despatched with a greeting of peace
4472 1254 5989 668 3552 1645
pt.aa.npm cj n.asm v.api.3p p.g n.gsf

ἀπὸ τῶν ἀδελφῶν πρὸς τοὺς ἀποστείλαντας αὐτούς.[a] 35 Παῦλος δὲ καὶ
from the brothers to those who had sent them. But Paul *But* and
608 3836 81 4639 3836 690 899 1254 4263 1254 2779
p.g d.gpm n.gpm p.a d.apm pt.aa.apm r.apm.3 n.nsm cj cj

Βαρναβᾶς διέτριβον ἐν Ἀντιοχείᾳ διδάσκοντες καὶ εὐαγγελιζόμενοι
Barnabas continued on in Antioch, teaching and preaching the word of
982 1417 1877 522 1438 2779 2294 3836 3364 3836
n.nsm v.iai.3p p.d n.dsf pt.pa.npm cj pt.pm.npm

μετὰ καὶ ἑτέρων πολλῶν τὸν λόγον τοῦ κυρίου. 36 μετὰ
the Lord, with many others also. *others* *many* *the* *word* *of the* *Lord* And after
3836 3261 3552 4498 2283 2779 2283 4498 3836 3364 3836 3261 1254 3552
p.g adv r.gpm a.gpm d.asm n.asm d.gsm n.gsm p.a

δέ τινας ἡμέρας εἶπεν πρὸς Βαρναβᾶν Παῦλος, ἐπιστρέψαντες δὴ
And some days Paul said to Barnabas, *Paul* "Let us return indeed and
1254 5516 2465 4263 3306 4639 982 4263 2188 1314
cj r.apf n.apf v.aai.3s p.a n.asm n.nsm pt.aa.npm pl

[a] ἔδοξε δὲ τῷ Σίλᾳ ἐπιμεῖναι αὐτοῦ. included by TR after αὐτούς.

NASB

[28]"For it seemed
good to the
Holy Spirit
and to us to
lay upon you
no greater
burden than
these essen-
tials:
[29]that you
abstain from
things sacri-
ficed to idols
and from
blood and
from things
strangled and
from fornica-
tion; if you
keep your-
selves free
from such
things, you
will do well.
Farewell."
[30]So when they
were sent away,
they went down
to Antioch; and
having gathered
the congregation
together, they
delivered the let-
ter. [31]When they
had read it, they
rejoiced because
of its encourage-
ment. [32]Judas and
Silas, also being
prophets them-
selves, encouraged
and strengthened
the brethren with a
lengthy message.
[33]After they had
spent time *there,*
they were sent
away from the
brethren in peace
to those who had
sent them out.
[34][[a]But it seemed
good to Silas to
remain there.]
[35]But Paul and
Barnabas stayed in
Antioch, teaching
and preaching with
many others also,
the word of the
Lord.

Second Missionary Journey

[36]After some days
Paul said to Barna-
bas, "Let us return

[a] Early mss do not contain this v

NIV

visit the believers
in all the towns
where we preached
the word of the
Lord and see how
they are doing."
37 Barnabas wanted
to take John, also
called Mark, with
them, 38 but Paul
did not think it
wise to take him,
because he had
deserted them in
Pamphylia and
had not contin-
ued with them in
the work. 39 They
had such a sharp
disagreement that
they parted com-
pany. Barnabas
took Mark and
sailed for Cyprus,
40 but Paul chose
Silas and left,
commended by
the believers to the
grace of the Lord.
41 He went through
Syria and Cilicia,
strengthening the
churches.

Timothy Joins Paul and Silas

16 Paul came
to Derbe
and then to Lystra,
where a disciple
named Timothy
lived, whose moth-
er was Jewish
and a believer but
whose father was
a Greek. 2 The be-
lievers at Lystra
and Iconium spoke
well of him. 3 Paul
wanted to take him
along on the jour-
ney, so he circum-
cised him because
of the Jews who
lived in that area,
for they

ἐπισκεψώμεθα τοὺς ἀδελφοὺς κατὰ πόλιν πᾶσαν ἐν αἷς κατηγγείλαμεν τὸν
visit the brothers in every city *every* in which we announced the
2170 3836 81 2848 4246 4484 4246 1877 4005 2859 3836
v.ams.1p d.apm n.apm p.a n.asf a.asf p.d r.dpf v.aai.1p d.asm

λόγον τοῦ κυρίου πῶς ἔχουσιν. 37 Βαρναβᾶς δὲ ἐβούλετο συμπαραλαβεῖν
word of the Lord to see how they are." Now Barnabas *Now* wanted to take with
3364 3836 3261 4802 2400 1254 982 1254 1089 5221
n.asm d.gsm n.gsm cj v.pai.3p n.nsm cj v.imi.3s f.aa

καὶ τὸν Ἰωάννην τὸν καλούμενον Μᾶρκον· 38 Παῦλος δὲ →
{also} them *{the}* John who is called Mark. But Paul *But* did not
2779 3836 2722 3836 2813 3453 1254 4263 1254 3590
adv d.asm n.asm d.asm pt.pp.asm n.asm n.nsm cj

ἠξίου, τὸν ἀποστάντα ἀπ' αὐτῶν ἀπὸ Παμφυλίας
⌊think it wise⌋ to take with them this one who had withdrawn from them in Pamphylia
546 5221 5221 5221 4047 4047 3836 923 608 899 608 4103
v.iai.3s d.asm pt.aa.asm p.g r.gpm.3 p.g n.gsf

καὶ ↱ μὴ συνελθόντα αὐτοῖς εἰς τὸ ἔργον μὴ συμπαραλαμβάνειν τοῦτον.
and had not gone with them to the work. *not* *to take with* *this one*
2779 5302 3590 5302 899 1650 3836 2240 3590 5221 4047
cj pl pt.aa.asm r.dpm.3 p.a d.asn n.asn pl f.pa r.asm

39 ἐγένετο δὲ παροξυσμὸς ὥστε ἀποχωρισθῆναι αὐτοὺς ἀπ' ἀλλήλων,
There arose *{and}* a sharp disagreement, so that they parted *they* from one another.
1181 1254 4237 6063 899 714 899 608 253
v.ami.3s cj n.nsm cj f.ap r.apm.3 p.g r.gpm

τόν τε Βαρναβᾶν παραλαβόντα τὸν Μᾶρκον ἐκπλεῦσαι εἰς Κύπρον, 40
{the} ~ Barnabas took *{the}* Mark and sailed off to Cyprus, but
3836 5445 982 4161 3836 3453 1739 1650 3251 1254
d.asm cj n.asm pt.aa.asm d.asm n.asm f.aa p.a n.asf

Παῦλος δὲ ἐπιλεξάμενος Σιλᾶν ἐξῆλθεν παραδοθεὶς τῇ χάριτι τοῦ
Paul *but* chose Silas and departed, having been commended ⌊to the⌋ grace of the
4263 1254 2141 4976 2002 4140 3836 5921 3836
n.nsm cj pt.am.nsm n.asm v.aai.3s pt.ap.nsm d.dsf n.dsf d.gsm

κυρίου ὑπὸ τῶν ἀδελφῶν. 41 διήρχετο δὲ τὴν Συρίαν καὶ τὴν[a]
Lord by the brothers. And ⌊he traveled through⌋ *And* *{the}* Syria and *{the}*
3261 5679 3836 81 1254 1451 1254 3836 5353 2779 3836
n.gsm p.g d.gpm n.gpm v.imi.3s cj d.asf n.asf cj d.asf

Κιλικίαν ἐπιστηρίζων τὰς ἐκκλησίας.
Cilicia, strengthening the churches.
3070 2185 3836 1711
n.asf pt.pa.nsm d.apf n.apf

16:1 κατήντησεν δὲ καὶ[b] εἰς Δέρβην καὶ εἰς Λύστραν. καὶ ἰδοὺ
Paul went *{and}* also to Derbe and to Lystra; and *{behold}* there
2918 1254 2779 1650 1292 2779 1650 3388 2779 2627 1639
v.aai.3s cj adv p.a n.asf cj p.a n.asf cj j

μαθητής τις ἦν ἐκεῖ ὀνόματι Τιμόθεος, υἱὸς →
was a certain disciple *certain there was* there named Timothy, the son of a converted Jewish
1639 5516 3412 5516 1639 1695 3950 5510 5626 4412 2681
n.nsm r.nsm v.iai.3s adv n.dsn n.nsm n.nsm

γυναικὸς Ἰουδαίας πιστῆς, πατρὸς δὲ Ἕλληνος, 2 ὃς ἐμαρτυρεῖτο
woman, *Jewish* *converted* whose father *{and}* was a Greek. He was well attested
1222 2681 4412 4252 1254 1818 4005 3455
n.gsf a.gsf a.gsf n.gsm cj n.gsm r.nsm v.ipi.3s

ὑπὸ τῶν ἐν Λύστροις καὶ Ἰκονίῳ ἀδελφῶν. 3 τοῦτον ἠθέλησεν
by the brothers at Lystra and Iconium. *brothers* Paul wanted Timothy *wanted*
5679 3836 81 1877 3388 2779 2658 81 4263 2527 4047 2527
p.g d.gpm p.d n.dpn cj n.dsn n.gpm r.asm v.aai.3s

ὁ Παῦλος σὺν αὐτῷ ἐξελθεῖν, καὶ ↱ λαβὼν περιέτεμεν
{the} *Paul* to accompany *{with}* him, *to accompany* so he took him and circumcised
3836 4263 2002 2002 5250 899 2002 2779 4362 3284 4362
d.nsm n.nsm p.d r.dsm.3 f.aa cj pt.aa.nsm v.aai.3s

αὐτὸν διὰ τοὺς Ἰουδαίους τοὺς ὄντας ἐν τοῖς τόποις ἐκείνοις, →
him ⌊because of⌋ the Jews who were in *{the}* those places; *those* for they
899 1328 3836 2681 3836 1639 1877 3836 1697 5536 1697 1142
r.asm.3 p.a d.apm a.apm d.apm pt.pa.apm p.d d.dpm n.dpm r.dpm

[a] [τὴν] UBS.
[b] [καὶ] UBS.

NASB

and visit the breth-
ren in every city
in which we pro-
claimed the word
of the Lord, *and*
see how they are."
37 Barnabas wanted
to take John, called
Mark, along with
them also. 38 But
Paul kept insisting
that they should
not take him along
who had deserted
them in Pamphylia
and had not gone
with them to the
work. 39 And there
occurred such a
sharp disagreement
that they separated
from one another,
and Barnabas took
Mark with him
and sailed away to
Cyprus. 40 But Paul
chose Silas and
left, being commit-
ted by the brethren
to the grace of the
Lord. 41 And he was
traveling through
Syria and Cilicia,
strengthening the
churches.

The Macedonian Vision

16:1 Paul came
also to Derbe and
to Lystra. And a
disciple was there,
named Timothy,
the son of a Jewish
woman who was
a believer, but his
father was a Greek,
2 and he was well
spoken of by the
brethren who were
in Lystra and Ico-
nium. 3 Paul wanted
this man to go with
him; and he took
him and circum-
cised him because
of the Jews who
were in those parts,

NIV

all knew that
his father was a
Greek. 4 As they
traveled from
town to town, they
delivered the de-
cisions reached by
the apostles and
elders in Jerusa-
lem for the people
to obey. 5 So the
churches were
strengthened in the
faith and grew dai-
ly in numbers.

Paul's Vision of the Man of Macedonia

6 Paul and his
companions trav-
eled throughout
the region of
Phrygia and Ga-
latia, having been
kept by the Holy
Spirit from preach-
ing the word in the
province of Asia.
7 When they came
to the border of
Mysia, they tried
to enter Bithynia,
but the Spirit of
Jesus would not
allow them to. 8 So
they passed by
Mysia and went
down to Troas.
9 During the night
Paul had a vision
of a man of Mac-
edonia standing
and begging him,
"Come over to
Macedonia and
help us." 10 After
Paul had seen the
vision, we got
ready at once to
leave for Mace-
donia, conclud-
ing that God had
called us to preach
the gospel to them.

Lydia's Conversion in Philippi

11 From Troas we
put out to sea and
sailed straight for
Samothrace, and
the next day we
went on to Neap-
olis. 12 From there
we traveled to
Philippi, a Roman
colony and the
leading city of that

ᾔδεισαν γὰρ ἅπαντες ὅτι Ἕλλην ὁ πατὴρ αὐτοῦ ὑπῆρχεν.
all knew *for* *all* that his father was a Greek. *{the}* *father* *his* *was*
570 3857 1142 570 4022 899 4252 5639 1818 3836 4252 899 5639
v.lai.3p cj a.npm cj n.nsm d.nsm n.nsm r.gsm.3 v.iai.3s

4 ὡς δὲ διεπορεύοντο τὰς πόλεις, παρεδίδοσαν αὐτοῖς φυλάσσειν τὰ δόγματα
As *{and}* they went through the cities, they delivered to them for observance the decrees
6055 1254 1388 3836 4484 4140 899 5875 3836 1504
cj cj v.imi.3p d.apf n.apf v.iai.3p r.dpm.3 f.pa d.apn n.apn

τὰ κεκριμένα ὑπὸ τῶν ἀποστόλων καὶ πρεσβυτέρων τῶν ἐν
that ⌊had been decided on⌋ by the apostles and elders who were in
3836 3212 5679 3836 693 2779 4565 3836 1877
d.apn pt.rp.apn p.g d.gpm n.gpm cj a.gpm d.gpm p.d

Ἱεροσολύμοις. 5 αἱ μὲν οὖν ἐκκλησίαι ἐστερεοῦντο τῇ πίστει καὶ
Jerusalem. So the ~ *So* churches were strengthened ⌊in the⌋ faith, and
2642 4036 3836 3525 4036 1711 5105 3836 4411 2779
n.dpn d.npf pl cj n.npf v.ipi.3p d.dsf n.dsf cj

ἐπερίσσευον τῷ ἀριθμῷ ⌊καθ' ἡμέραν.⌋ 6 διῆλθον δὲ τὴν Φρυγίαν
they increased in number daily. And ⌊they went through⌋ *And* the Phrygian
4355 3836 750 2848 2465 1254 1451 1254 3836 5867
v.iai.3p d.dsm n.dsm p.a n.asf v.aai.3p cj d.asf n.asf

καὶ Γαλατικὴν χώραν κωλυθέντες ὑπὸ τοῦ ἁγίου πνεύματος ↰ λαλῆσαι
and Galatian region, having been prevented by the Holy Spirit from speaking
2779 1131 6001 3266 5679 3836 41 4460 3266 3281
cj a.asf n.asf pt.ap.npm p.g d.gsn a.gsn n.gsn f.aa

τὸν λόγον ἐν τῇ Ἀσίᾳ· 7 ἐλθόντες δὲ κατὰ τὴν Μυσίαν ἐπείραζον
the message in *{the}* Asia. And ⌊when they came⌋ *And* to *{the}* Mysia, they tried
3836 3364 1877 3836 823 1254 2262 1254 2848 3836 3695 4279
d.asm n.asm p.d d.dsf n.dsf pt.aa.npm cj p.a d.asf n.asf v.iai.3p

εἰς τὴν Βιθυνίαν πορευθῆναι, καὶ ↱ οὐκ εἴασεν
to go into *{the}* Bithynia, *to go* but the Spirit of Jesus did not allow
4513 4513 1650 3836 1049 4513 2779 3836 4460 2652 2652 1572 4024 1572
p.a d.asf n.asf f.ap cj pl v.aai.3s

αὐτοὺς τὸ πνεῦμα Ἰησοῦ· 8 παρελθόντες δὲ τὴν Μυσίαν κατέβησαν
them, *the* *Spirit* *of Jesus* so they passed through *so* *{the}* Mysia and went down
899 3836 4460 2652 1254 4216 1254 3836 3695 2849
r.apm.3 d.nsn n.nsn n.gsm pt.aa.npm cj d.asf n.asf v.aai.3p

εἰς Τρῳάδα. 9 καὶ ὅραμα διὰ τῆς[a] νυκτὸς τῷ Παύλῳ ὤφθη, ἀνὴρ
to Troas. And a vision in the night appeared to Paul: *appeared* a man
1650 5590 2779 3969 1328 3836 3816 3972 3836 4263 3972 5516 467
p.a n.asf cj n.nsn p.g d.gsf n.gsf d.dsm n.dsm v.api.3s n.nsm

Μακεδών τις ἦν ἑστὼς καὶ παρακαλῶν αὐτὸν καὶ λέγων, διαβὰς
of Macedonia *a* was standing there, *{and}* urging him and saying, ⌊"Come over⌋
3424 5516 1639 2705 2779 4151 899 2779 3306 1329
n.nsm r.nsm v.iai.3s pt.ra.nsm cj pt.pa.nsm r.asm.3 cj pt.pa.nsm pt.aa.nsm

εἰς Μακεδονίαν βοήθησον ἡμῖν. 10 ὡς δὲ τὸ ὅραμα εἶδεν,
to Macedonia and help us!" And when *And* Paul had seen the vision, *had seen*
1650 3423 1070 7005 1254 6055 1254 1625 1625 3836 3969 1625
p.a n.asf v.aam.2s r.dp.1 cj cj d.asn n.asn v.aai.3s

εὐθέως ἐζητήσαμεν ἐξελθεῖν εἰς Μακεδονίαν συμβιβάζοντες ὅτι
immediately we tried to go into Macedonia, concluding that God
2311 2426 2002 1650 3423 5204 4022 2536
adv v.aai.1p f.aa p.a n.asf pt.pa.npm cj

προσκέκληται ἡμᾶς ὁ θεὸς εὐαγγελίσασθαι αὐτούς. 11 ἀναχθέντες δὲ ἀπὸ
had called us *{the}* *God* ⌊to preach the gospel to⌋ them. So, setting sail *So* from
4673 7005 3836 2536 2294 899 1254 343 1254 608
v.rmi.3s r.ap.1 d.nsm n.nsm f.am r.apm.3 pt.ap.npm cj p.g

Τρῳάδος εὐθυδρομήσαμεν εἰς Σαμοθρᾴκην, τῇ δὲ ἐπιούσῃ εἰς
Troas, ⌊we sailed on a direct course⌋ to Samothrace, and ⌊on the⌋ *and* ⌊following day⌋ to
5590 2312 1650 4903 1254 3836 1254 2079 1650
n.gsf v.aai.1p p.a n.asf d.dsf cj a.dsf p.a

⌊Νέαν πόλιν,⌋ 12 κἀκεῖθεν εἰς Φιλίππους, ἥτις ἐστὶν πρώτη[b] →
Neapolis, and from there to Philippi, which is a leading city of that
3742 4484 2796 1650 5804 4015 1639 4755 4484
a.asf n.asf crasis p.a n.apm r.nsf v.pai.3s a.nsf

[a] [τῆς] UBS, omitted by TNIV.
[b] πρώτη TNIV, NET. πρώτη[ς] UBS.

NASB

for they all knew
that his father was
a Greek. 4 Now
while they were
passing through
the cities, they
were delivering the
decrees which had
been decided upon
by the apostles and
elders who were in
Jerusalem, for them
to observe. 5 So
the churches were
being strengthened
in the faith, and
were increasing in
number daily.
6 They passed
through the Phry-
gian and Galatian
region, having
been forbidden by
the Holy Spirit to
speak the word
in Asia; 7 and af-
ter they came to
Mysia, they were
trying to go into
Bithynia, and the
Spirit of Jesus did
not permit them;
8 and passing by
Mysia, they came
down to Troas. 9 A
vision appeared to
Paul in the night: a
man of Macedonia
was standing and
appealing to him,
and saying, "Come
over to Macedo-
nia and help us."
10 When he had seen
the vision, immedi-
ately we sought to
go into Macedonia,
concluding that
God had called us
to preach the gos-
pel to them.
11 So putting
out to sea from
Troas, we ran a
straight course to
Samothrace, and
on the day follow-
ing to Neapolis;
12 and from there to
Philippi, which is a
leading city of the

NIV

district[a] of Mac-
edonia. And we
stayed there sever-
al days.
13 On the Sabbath
we went outside
the city gate to the
river, where we
expected to find
a place of prayer.
We sat down and
began to speak to
the women who
had gathered there.
14 One of those lis-
tening was a wom-
an from the city
of Thyatira named
Lydia, a dealer in
purple cloth. She
was a worship-
er of God. The
Lord opened her
heart to respond
to Paul's mes-
sage. 15 When she
and the members
of her household
were baptized, she
invited us to her
home. "If you con-
sider me a believer
in the Lord," she
said, "come and
stay at my house."
And she persuad-
ed us.

Paul and Silas in Prison

16 Once when we
were going to the
place of prayer,
we were met by a
female slave who
had a spirit by
which she predict-
ed the future. She
earned a great deal
of money for her
owners by fortune-
telling. 17 She fol-
lowed Paul and the
rest of us, shout-
ing, "These men
are servants of the
Most High God,
who are telling
you the way to be
saved." 18 She kept
this up for many
days. Finally Paul

μερίδος τῆς Μακεδονίας πόλις, κολωνία. ἦμεν δὲ ἐν ταύτῃ τῇ
district of Macedonia, *city* a Roman colony. We *{and}* remained in that *{the}*
3535 3836 3423 4484 3149 1639 1254 1417 1877 4047 3836
n.gsf d.gsf n.gsf n.nsf n.nsf v.iai.1p cj p.d r.dsf d.dsf

πόλει διατρίβοντες → ἡμέρας τινάς. 13 τῇ τε ἡμέρᾳ τῶν
city *remained* for several days. *several* And ⌊on the⌋ *And* Sabbath day *{the}*
4484 1417 5516 2465 5516 5445 3836 5445 4879 2465 3836
n.dsf pt.pa.npm n.apf r.apf d.dsf cj n.dsf d.gpn

σαββάτων ἐξήλθομεν ἔξω τῆς πύλης παρὰ ποταμὸν οὗ ἐνομίζομεν
Sabbath we went outside the gate to the riverside, where we thought there would
4879 2002 2032 3836 4783 4123 4532 4023 3787 1639 1639
n.gpn v.aai.1p p.g d.gsf n.gsf p.a n.asm adv v.iai.1p

προσευχὴν εἶναι, καὶ ↱ καθίσαντες ἐλαλοῦμεν ταῖς
be a place of prayer, *there would be* and we sat down and spoke to the women
1639 4666 1639 2779 3281 2767 3281 3836 1222
n.asf f.pa cj pt.aa.npm v.iai.1p d.dpf

συνελθούσαις γυναιξίν. 14 καί τις γυνὴ ὀνόματι Λυδία,
who had gathered there. *women* And a certain woman, named Lydia, a
5302 1222 2779 5516 1222 3950 3376
pt.aa.dpf n.dpf cj r.nsf n.nsf n.dsn n.nsf

πορφυρόπωλις → πόλεως Θυατείρων σεβομένη τὸν θεόν, ἤκουεν, ἧς
seller of purple cloths from the city of Thyatira, a ⌊worshipper of⌋ *{the}* God, listened; *her*
4527 4484 2587 4936 3836 2536 201 4005
n.nsf n.gsf n.gpn pt.pm.nsf d.asm n.asm v.iai.3s r.gsf

ὁ κύριος διήνοιξεν τὴν καρδίαν προσέχειν τοῖς λαλουμένοις ὑπὸ τοῦ
and the Lord opened *{the}* her heart to respond to what was said by *{the}*
3836 3261 1380 3836 4005 2840 4668 3836 3281 5679 3836
d.nsm n.nsm v.aai.3s d.asf n.asf f.pa d.dpn pt.pp.dpn p.g d.gsm

Παύλου. 15 ὡς δὲ ἐβαπτίσθη καὶ ὁ οἶκος αὐτῆς,
Paul. And when *And* she was baptized, and *{the}* her household *her* as well,
4263 1254 6055 1254 966 2779 3836 899 3875 899
n.gsm cj cj v.api.3s cj d.nsm n.nsm r.gsf.3

παρεκάλεσεν λέγουσα, εἰ κεκρίκατέ με πιστὴν τῷ κυρίῳ εἶναι,
she urged us, saying, "If you have judged me to be faithful ⌊to the⌋ Lord, *to be*
4151 3306 1623 3212 1609 1639 1639 4412 3836 3261 1639
v.aai.3s pt.pa.nsf cj v.rai.2p r.as.1 a.asf d.dsm n.dsm f.pa

εἰσελθόντες εἰς τὸν οἶκόν μου μένετε· καὶ παρεβιάσατο ἡμᾶς.
come to *{the}* my house *my* and stay." And she prevailed upon us.
1656 1650 3836 1609 3875 1609 3531 2779 4128 7005
pt.aa.npm p.a d.asm n.asm r.gs.1 v.pam.2p cj v.ami.3s r.ap.1

16 ἐγένετο δὲ → πορευομένων ἡμῶν εἰς τὴν προσευχὴν
{it happened that} Now as we were going *we* to the place of prayer, a
1181 1254 7005 4513 7005 1650 3836 4666 5516
v.ami.3s cj pt.pm.gpm r.gp.1 p.a d.asf n.asf

παιδίσκην τινὰ ἔχουσαν πνεῦμα πύθωνα ὑπαντῆσαι ἡμῖν, ἥτις
slave girl *a* who had a spirit of divination, met us. She brought great
4087 5516 2400 4460 4780 5636 7005 4015 4218 4498
n.asf r.asf pt.pa.asf n.asn n.asm f.aa r.dp.1 r.nsf

ἐργασίαν πολλὴν παρεῖχεν τοῖς κυρίοις αὐτῆς μαντευομένη. 17 αὕτη
profit *great* *brought* to her masters *her* by fortune-telling. She
2238 4498 4218 3836 899 3261 899 3446 4047
n.asf a.asf v.iai.3s d.dpm n.dpm r.gsf.3 pt.pm.nsf r.nsf

κατακολουθοῦσα τῷ Παύλῳ καὶ ἡμῖν ἔκραζεν λέγουσα, οὗτοι οἱ ἄνθρωποι
followed after *{the}* Paul and us, crying out, saying, "These *{the}* men are
2887 3836 4263 2779 7005 3189 3306 4047 3836 476 1639
pt.pa.nsf d.dsm n.dsm cj r.dp.1 v.iai.3s pt.pa.nsf r.npm d.npm n.npm

δοῦλοι τοῦ θεοῦ τοῦ ὑψίστου εἰσίν, οἵτινες καταγγέλλουσιν ὑμῖν
servants of the Most High God, *{the}* *Most High* *are* who proclaim to you the
1529 3836 5736 5736 2536 3836 5736 1639 4015 2859 7007
n.npm d.gsm n.gsm d.gsm a.gsm.s v.pai.3p r.npm v.pai.3p r.dp.2

ὁδὸν σωτηρίας. 18 τοῦτο δὲ ἐποίει ἐπὶ πολλὰς ἡμέρας.
way of salvation." And this *And* ⌊she kept doing⌋ for many days. But Paul
3847 5401 1254 4047 1254 4472 2093 4498 2465 1254 4263
n.asf n.gsf r.asn cj v.iai.3s p.a a.apf n.apf

NASB

district of Mace-
donia, a *Roman*
colony; and we
were staying in this
city for some days.
13 And on the Sab-
bath day we went
outside the gate to
a riverside, where
we were supposing
that there would be
a place of prayer;
and we sat down
and began speaking
to the women who
had assembled.

First Convert in Europe

14 A woman named
Lydia, from the
city of Thyatira,
a seller of purple
fabrics, a wor-
shiper of God, was
listening; and the
Lord opened her
heart to respond to
the things spoken
by Paul. 15 And
when she and her
household had
been baptized,
she urged us, say-
ing, "If you have
judged me to be
faithful to the Lord,
come into my
house and stay."
And she prevailed
upon us.
16 It happened that
as we were going
to the place of
prayer, a slave-girl
having a spirit of
divination met us,
who was bringing
her masters much
profit by fortune-
telling. 17 Following
after Paul and us,
she kept crying
out, saying, "These
men are bond-
servants of the
Most High God,
who are proclaim-
ing to you the way
of salvation." 18 She
continued doing
this for many days.
But Paul was

[a] 12 The text and meaning of the Greek for *the leading city of that district* are uncertain.

NIV

became so annoyed that he turned around and said to the spirit, "In the name of Jesus Christ I command you to come out of her!" At that moment the spirit left her.
19 When her owners realized that their hope of making money was gone, they seized Paul and Silas and dragged them into the marketplace to face the authorities.
20 They brought them before the magistrates and said, "These men are Jews, and are throwing our city into an uproar
21 by advocating customs unlawful for us Romans to accept or practice."
22 The crowd joined in the attack against Paul and Silas, and the magistrates ordered them to be stripped and beaten with rods.
23 After they had been severely flogged, they were thrown into prison, and the jailer was commanded to guard them carefully.
24 When he received these orders, he put them in the inner cell and fastened their feet in the stocks.
25 About midnight Paul and Silas were praying and singing hymns to God, and the other prisoners were listening to them.

διαπονηθεὶς δὲ Παῦλος καὶ ἐπιστρέψας τῷ πνεύματι εἶπεν, παραγγέλλω σοι
became annoyed, *But* *Paul* and turning ⌊to the⌋ spirit, said, "I charge you
1387 1254 4263 2779 2188 3836 4460 3306 4133 5148
pt.ap.nsm cj n.nsm cj pt.aa.nsm d.dsn n.dsn v.aai.3s v.pai.1s r.ds.2

ἐν ὀνόματι Ἰησοῦ Χριστοῦ ἐξελθεῖν ἀπ᾽ αὐτῆς· καὶ ἐξῆλθεν αὐτῇ τῇ
in the name of Jesus Christ to come out of her." And it came out that very *that*
1877 3950 2652 5986 2002 608 899 2779 2002 3836 899 3836
p.d n.dsn n.gsm n.gsm f.aa p.g r.gsf.3 cj v.aai.3s r.dsf d.dsf

ὥρᾳ. 19 → ἰδόντες δὲ οἱ κύριοι αὐτῆς ὅτι
hour. When her owners saw *{and}* *{the}* *owners* *her* that their hope of profit
6052 899 3261 1625 1254 3836 3261 899 4022 899 1828 3836 2238
n.dsf pt.aa.npm cj d.npm n.npm r.gsf.3 cj

ἐξῆλθεν ἡ ἐλπὶς τῆς ἐργασίας αὐτῶν, ↱ ἐπιλαβόμενοι τὸν Παῦλον καὶ τὸν
was gone, *{the}* *hope* *of* *profit* *their* they seized *{the}* Paul and *{the}*
2002 3836 1828 3836 2238 899 1816 2138 3836 4263 2779 3836
v.aai.3s d.nsf n.nsf d.gsf n.gsf r.gpm.3 pt.am.npm d.asm n.asm cj d.asm

Σιλᾶν εἵλκυσαν εἰς τὴν ἀγορὰν ἐπὶ τοὺς ἄρχοντας 20 καὶ
Silas and dragged them into the marketplace before the rulers. And
4976 1816 1650 3836 59 2093 3836 807 2779
n.asm v.aai.3p p.a d.asf n.asf p.a d.apm n.apm cj

προσαγαγόντες αὐτοὺς τοῖς στρατηγοῖς εἶπαν, οὗτοι οἱ ἄνθρωποι
when they had brought them to the magistrates, they said, "These *{the}* men are Jews,
4642 899 3836 5130 3306 4047 3836 476 5639 2681
pt.aa.npm r.apm.3 d.dpm n.dpm v.aai.3p r.npm d.npm n.npm

ἐκταράσσουσιν ἡμῶν τὴν πόλιν, Ἰουδαῖοι ὑπάρχοντες, 21 καὶ καταγγέλλουσιν
and they are disturbing our *{the}* city *Jews* *are* *{and}* by advocating
1752 7005 3836 4484 2681 5639 2779 2859
v.pai.3p r.gp.1 d.asf n.asf a.npm pt.pa.npm cj v.pai.3p

ἔθη ἃ ↱ οὐκ ἔξεστιν ἡμῖν παραδέχεσθαι οὐδὲ ποιεῖν Ῥωμαίοις
customs that are not lawful for us to accept or practice, since we are Romans.
1621 4005 1997 4024 1997 7005 4138 4028 4472 1639 1639 1639 4871
n.apn r.npn pl v.pai.3s r.dp.1 f.pm cj f.pa n.dpm

οὖσιν. 22 καὶ συνεπέστη ὁ ὄχλος κατ᾽ αὐτῶν καὶ οἱ
since we are *{and}* The crowd joined in attacking *The* *crowd* *{against}* them, and the
1639 2779 3836 4063 5308 3836 4063 2848 899 2779 3836
pt.pa.dpm cj v.aai.3s d.nsm n.nsm p.g r.gpm.3 cj d.npm

στρατηγοὶ περιρήξαντες ← αὐτῶν τὰ ἱμάτια ἐκέλευον ῥαβδίζειν,
magistrates tore the clothes off them *the* *clothes* and gave orders to beat them
5130 4351 3836 2668 899 3836 2668 3027 4810
n.npm pt.aa.npm r.gpm.3 d.apn n.apn v.iai.3p f.pa

← ← 23 πολλάς τε ἐπιθέντες αὐτοῖς πληγὰς
with rods. And when they had laid many *And* *when they had laid* stripes on them, *stripes*
5445 2202 2202 2202 2202 4498 5445 2202 4435 899 4435
a.apf cj pt.aa.npm r.dpm.3 n.apf

ἔβαλον εἰς φυλακὴν παραγγείλαντες τῷ δεσμοφύλακι ἀσφαλῶς
they threw them into prison, charging the jailer to keep them securely,
965 1650 5871 4133 3836 1302 5498 5498 899 857
v.aai.3p p.a n.asf pt.aa.npm d.dsm n.dsm adv

τηρεῖν αὐτούς. 24 ὃς παραγγελίαν τοιαύτην λαβὼν ἔβαλεν
to keep *them* who, having received such a charge, *such* *having received* put
5498 899 4005 3284 3284 5525 4132 5525 3284 965
f.pa r.apm.3 r.nsm n.asf r.asf pt.aa.nsm v.aai.3s

αὐτοὺς εἰς τὴν ἐσωτέραν φυλακὴν καὶ τοὺς πόδας ἠσφαλίσατο αὐτῶν
them into the inner prison and fastened *{the}* their feet *fastened* *their*
899 1650 3836 2278 5871 2779 856 3836 899 4546 856 899
r.apm.3 p.a d.asf a.asf n.asf cj d.apm n.apm v.ami.3s r.gpm.3

εἰς τὸ ξύλον. 25 κατὰ δὲ τὸ μεσονύκτιον Παῦλος καὶ Σιλᾶς προσευχόμενοι
in the stocks. About *{and}* *{the}* midnight Paul and Silas were praying and
1650 3836 3833 2848 1254 3836 3543 4263 2779 4976 4667
p.a d.asn n.asn p.a cj d.asn n.asn n.nsm cj n.nsm pt.pm.npm

ὕμνουν τὸν θεόν, ἐπηκροῶντο δὲ αὐτῶν οἱ δέσμιοι.
⌊singing hymns to⌋ *{the}* God, and the prisoners ⌊were listening to⌋ *and* them. *the* *prisoners*
5630 3836 2536 1254 3836 1300 2053 1254 899 3836 1300
v.iai.3p d.asm n.asm v.imi.3p cj r.gpm.3 d.npm n.npm

NASB

greatly annoyed, and turned and said to the spirit, "I command you in the name of Jesus Christ to come out of her!" And it came out at that very moment.
19 But when her masters saw that their hope of profit was gone, they seized Paul and Silas and dragged them into the market place before the authorities,
20 and when they had brought them to the chief magistrates, they said, "These men are throwing our city into confusion, being Jews,
21 and are proclaiming customs which it is not lawful for us to accept or to observe, being Romans."

Paul and Silas Imprisoned

22 The crowd rose up together against them, and the chief magistrates tore their robes off them and proceeded to order *them* to be beaten with rods.
23 When they had struck them with many blows, they threw them into prison, commanding the jailer to guard them securely;
24 and he, having received such a command, threw them into the inner prison and fastened their feet in the stocks.
25 But about midnight Paul and Silas were praying and singing hymns of praise to God, and the prisoners were listening to

NIV

[26]Suddenly there
was such a violent
earthquake that
the foundations
of the prison were
shaken. At once all
the prison doors
flew open, and
everyone's chains
came loose. [27]The
jailer woke up, and
when he saw the
prison doors open,
he drew his sword
and was about to
kill himself be-
cause he thought
the prisoners had
escaped. [28]But
Paul shouted,
"Don't harm your-
self! We are all
here!"
[29]The jailer called
for lights, rushed
in and fell trem-
bling before Paul
and Silas. [30]He
then brought them
out and asked,
"Sirs, what must I
do to be saved?"
[31]They replied,
"Believe in the
Lord Jesus,
and you will be
saved—you and
your household."
[32]Then they spoke
the word of the
Lord to him and
to all the others in
his house. [33]At that
hour of the night
the jailer took
them and washed
their wounds; then
immediately he
and all his house-
hold were bap-
tized. [34]The jailer
brought

26 ἄφνω δὲ σεισμὸς ἐγένετο μέγας ὥστε σαλευθῆναι τὰ
Suddenly {and} there was a violent earthquake, there was violent so that were shaken the
924 1254 1181 1181 3489 4939 1181 3489 6063 4888 3836
adv cj n.nsm v.ami.3s a.nsm cj f.ap d.apn

θεμέλια τοῦ δεσμωτηρίου· ἠνεῴχθησαν δὲ παραχρῆμα αἱ θύραι
foundations of the prison were shaken; were opened and immediately all the doors
2528 3836 1303 4888 4888 487 1254 4202 4246 3836 2598
n.apn d.gsn n.gsn v.api.3p cj adv d.npf n.npf

πᾶσαι καὶ πάντων τὰ δεσμὰ ἀνέθη. 27 ⸂ἔξυπνος
all were opened and everyone's {the} chains were unfastened. When the jailer woke up
4246 487 487 2779 4246 3836 1301 479 1625 3836 1302 2031
a.npf cj a.gpm d.npn n.npn v.api.3s a.nsm

δὲ γενόμενος⸃ ὁ δεσμοφύλαξ καὶ ἰδὼν ἀνεῳγμένας τὰς θύρας τῆς φυλακῆς,
the jailer and saw standing open the doors of the prison
1254 1181 3836 1302 2779 1625 487 3836 2598 3836 5871
cj pt.am.nsm d.nsm n.nsm cj pt.aa.nsm pt.rp.apf d.apf n.apf d.gsf n.gsf

σπασάμενος τὴν[a] μάχαιραν ἤμελλεν ἑαυτὸν ἀναιρεῖν
standing open, he drew his sword and was about to kill himself, to kill
487 487 3516 5060 3836 3479 3516 359 359 1571 359
pt.am.nsm d.asf n.asf v.iai.3s r.asm.3 f.pa

νομίζων ἐκπεφευγέναι τοὺς δεσμίους. 28 ἐφώνησεν δὲ
for he thought the prisoners had escaped. the prisoners But Paul called out But in a
3787 3836 1300 1767 3836 1300 1254 4263 5888 1254
pt.pa.nsm f.ra d.apm n.apm v.aai.3s cj

μεγάλῃ φωνῇ ὁ[b] Παῦλος λέγων, μηδὲν πράξῃς σεαυτῷ κακόν,
loud voice, {the} Paul saying, "Do not Do harm yourself, harm for we are
3489 5889 3836 4263 3306 4556 3594 4556 2805 4932 2805 1142 1639 1639
a.dsf n.dsf d.nsm n.nsm pt.pa.nsm a.asn v.aas.2s r.dsm.2 a.asn

ἅπαντες γάρ ἐσμεν ἐνθάδε. 29 αἰτήσας δὲ φῶτα εἰσεπήδησεν καὶ
all for we are here." Then, calling for Then lights, the jailer rushed in and
570 1142 1639 1924 1254 160 1254 5890 1659 2779
a.npm cj v.pai.1p adv pt.aa.nsm cj n.apn v.aai.3s cj

⸂ἔντρομος γενόμενος⸃ προσέπεσεν τῷ Παύλῳ καὶ τῷ[c] Σιλᾷ 30 καὶ
trembling with fear he fell down before {the} Paul and {the} Silas. Then he
1958 1181 4700 3836 4263 2779 3836 4976 2779 5774
a.nsm pt.am.nsm v.aai.3s d.dsm n.dsm cj d.dsm n.dsm cj

προαγαγὼν αὐτοὺς ἔξω ἔφη, κύριοι, τί με δεῖ ποιεῖν ἵνα σωθῶ;
brought them outside and asked, "Sirs, what must I must do to be saved?"
4575 899 2032 5774 3261 5515 1256 1609 1256 4472 2671 5392
pt.aa.nsm r.apm.3 adv v.iai.3s n.vpm r.asn r.as.1 v.pai.3s f.pa cj v.aps.1s

31 οἱ δὲ εἶπαν, πίστευσον ἐπὶ τὸν κύριον Ἰησοῦν καὶ σωθήσῃ σὺ
And they And said, "Believe in the Lord Jesus, and ⸂you will be saved,⸃ you
1254 3836 1254 3306 4409 2093 3836 3261 2652 2779 5392 5148
d.npm cj v.aai.3p v.aam.2s p.a d.asm n.asm n.asm cj v.fpi.2s r.ns.2

καὶ ὁ οἶκός σου. 32 καὶ ἐλάλησαν αὐτῷ τὸν λόγον τοῦ κυρίου
and {the} your household." your And they spoke to him the word of the Lord to him,
2779 3836 5148 3875 5148 2779 3281 899 3836 3364 3836 3261 899 899
cj d.nsm n.nsm r.gs.2 cj v.aai.3p r.dsm.3 d.asm n.asm d.gsm n.gsm

σὺν πᾶσιν τοῖς ἐν τῇ οἰκίᾳ αὐτοῦ. 33 καὶ παραλαβὼν αὐτοὺς ἐν
⸂along with⸃ all who were in {the} his house. his And taking them in
5250 4246 3836 1877 3836 899 3864 899 2779 4161 899 1877
p.d a.dpm d.dpm p.d d.dsf n.dsf r.gsm.3 cj pt.aa.nsm r.apm.3 p.d

ἐκείνῃ τῇ ὥρᾳ τῆς νυκτὸς ἔλουσεν ἀπὸ τῶν πληγῶν, καὶ ἐβαπτίσθη
that {the} hour of the night, he washed {from} their wounds; then he was baptized at once,
1697 3836 6052 3836 3816 3374 608 3836 4435 2779 966 4202 4202
r.dsf d.dsf n.dsf d.gsf n.gsf v.aai.3s p.g d.gpf n.gpf cj v.api.3s

αὐτὸς καὶ οἱ αὐτοῦ πάντες παραχρῆμα, 34 ἀναγαγών τε
he and {the} all his all family. at once And ⸂when he had brought⸃ And
899 2779 3836 4246 899 4246 4202 5445 343 5445
r.nsm cj d.npm r.gsm.3 a.npm adv pt.aa.nsm cj

NASB

them; [26]and sud-
denly there came a
great earthquake,
so that the founda-
tions of the prison
house were shaken;
and immediately
all the doors were
opened and every-
one's chains were
unfastened. [27]When
the jailer awoke
and saw the prison
doors opened, he
drew his sword and
was about to kill
himself, supposing
that the prisoners
had escaped. [28]But
Paul cried out with
a loud voice, say-
ing, "Do not harm
yourself, for we
are all here!" [29]And
he called for lights
and rushed in, and
trembling with
fear he fell down
before Paul and
Silas, [30]and after he
brought them out,
he said, "Sirs, what
must I do to be
saved?"

The Jailer Converted

[31]They said, "Be-
lieve in the Lord
Jesus, and you
will be saved, you
and your house-
hold." [32]And they
spoke the word of
the Lord to him
together with all
who were in his
house. [33]And he
took them that *very*
hour of the night
and washed their
wounds, and im-
mediately he was
baptized, he and
all his *household*.
[34]And he brought

[a] [τὴν] UBS.
[b] [ὁ] UBS, omitted by TNIV.
[c] [τῷ] UBS, omitted by TNIV.

NIV

them into his
house and set a
meal before them;
he was filled with
joy because he had
come to believe in
God—he and his
whole household.
35 When it was
daylight, the
magistrates sent
their officers to
the jailer with the
order: "Release
those men." 36 The
jailer told Paul,
"The magistrates
have ordered that
you and Silas be
released. Now you
can leave. Go in
peace."
37 But Paul said to
the officers: "They
beat us publicly
without a trial,
even though we
are Roman citi-
zens, and threw us
into prison. And
now do they want
to get rid of us qui-
etly? No! Let them
come themselves
and escort us out."
38 The officers re-
ported this to the
magistrates, and
when they heard
that Paul and Silas
were Roman cit-
izens, they were
alarmed. 39 They
came to appease
them and escort-
ed them from the
prison, requesting
them to leave the
city. 40 After Paul
and Silas came out
of the prison, they
went to Lydia's
house, where they
met with the broth-
ers and sisters and
encouraged them.
Then they left.

αὐτοὺς ↰ εἰς τὸν οἶκον παρέθηκεν τράπεζαν ↰ καὶ ἠγαλλιάσατο
them up into his house, he set food before them; and he rejoiced, having
899 343 1650 3836 3875 4192 5544 4192 2779 22 4409
r.apm.3 p.a d.asm n.asm v.aai.3s n.asf cj v.ami.3s

πανοικεὶ πεπιστευκὼς τῷ θεῷ.
placed his faith in God ⌊along with his entire household.⌋ *having placed his faith in God*
4409 4409 4409 3836 2536 4109 4409 3836 2536
adv pt.ra.nsm d.dsm n.dsm

35 ἡμέρας δὲ γενομένης ἀπέστειλαν οἱ στρατηγοὶ
But when it was day, *But when it was* the magistrates sent *the magistrates*
1254 1181 1181 1181 2465 1254 1181 3836 5130 690 3836 5130
n.gsf cj pt.am.gsf v.aai.3p d.npm n.npm

τοὺς ῥαβδούχους λέγοντες, ἀπόλυσον τοὺς ἀνθρώπους ἐκείνους. 36
their constables, saying, "Release *{the}* those men." *those* And the jailer
3836 4812 3306 668 3836 1697 476 1697 1254 3836 1302
d.apm n.apm pt.pa.npm v.aam.2s d.apm n.apm r.apm

ἀπήγγειλεν δὲ ὁ δεσμοφύλαξ τοὺς λόγους τούτους[a] πρὸς τὸν Παῦλον
reported *And the jailer {the}* these words *these* to *{the}* Paul, saying,
550 1254 3836 1302 3836 4047 3364 4047 4639 3836 4263
v.aai.3s cj d.nsm n.nsm d.apm n.apm r.apm p.a d.asm n.asm

ὅτι ἀπέσταλκαν οἱ στρατηγοὶ ἵνα ἀπολυθῆτε· νῦν
~ "The magistrates have sent orders *The magistrates* to release you. So depart now
4022 3836 5130 690 3836 5130 2671 668 4036 2002 3814
cj v.rai.3p d.npm n.npm cj v.aps.2p adv

οὖν ἐξελθόντες πορεύεσθε ἐν εἰρήνῃ. 37 ὁ δὲ Παῦλος ἔφη πρὸς αὐτούς,
So depart and go in peace." *{the}* But Paul said to them,
4036 2002 4513 1877 1645 3836 1254 4263 5774 4639 899
cj pt.aa.npm v.pmm.2p p.d n.dsf d.nsm cj n.nsm v.iai.3s p.a r.apm.3

δείραντες ἡμᾶς δημοσίᾳ ἀκατακρίτους, ἀνθρώπους Ῥωμαίους
⌊"They have beaten⌋ us publicly, uncondemned, men who are Roman citizens,
1296 7005 1323 185 476 5639 5639 4871
pt.aa.npm r.ap.1 a.dsf a.apm n.apm n.apm

ὑπάρχοντας, ἔβαλον εἰς φυλακήν, καὶ νῦν λάθρᾳ
who are and have thrown us into prison; and now would they send us away in secret?
5639 965 1650 5871 2779 3814 1675 1675 1675 7005 1675 3277
pt.pa.apm v.aai.3p p.a n.asf cj adv adv

ἡμᾶς ἐκβάλλουσιν; οὐ γάρ, ἀλλὰ → ἐλθόντες αὐτοὶ ἡμᾶς
us would they send away No *{for}* indeed! They themselves must come *themselves* and *us*
7005 1675 4024 1142 247 899 2262 899 7005
r.ap.1 v.pai.3p pl cj cj pt.aa.npm r.npm r.ap.1

ἐξαγαγέτωσαν. ← 38 ἀπήγγειλαν δὲ τοῖς στρατηγοῖς
escort us out." The constables reported *{and}* these words to the magistrates.
1974 7005 3836 4812 550 1254 4047 4839 3836 5130
v.aam.3p v.aai.3p cj d.dpm n.dpm

οἱ ῥαβδοῦχοι τὰ ῥήματα ταῦτα. ἐφοβήθησαν δὲ ἀκούσαντες ὅτι
The constables {the} words these And they were afraid *And* when they heard that they were
3836 4812 3836 4839 4047 1254 5828 1254 201 4022 1639 1639
d.npm n.npm d.apn n.apn r.apn v.api.3p cj pt.aa.npm cj

Ῥωμαῖοί εἰσιν, 39 καὶ ↱ ἐλθόντες παρεκάλεσαν αὐτοὺς ↰ ↰ ↰
Roman citizens. *they were* So they came and spoke to them in a friendly
4871 1639 2779 4151 2262 4151 899 4151 4151 4151
n.npm v.pai.3p cj pt.aa.npm v.aai.3p r.apm.3

↰ καὶ ἐξαγαγόντες ← ἠρώτων ⌊ἀπελθεῖν ἀπὸ⌋ τῆς πόλεως. 40
manner; and having taken them out, they asked them to leave the city. So
4151 2779 1974 2263 599 608 3836 4484 1254
cj pt.aa.npm v.iai.3p f.aa p.g d.gsf n.gsf

ἐξελθόντες δὲ ἀπὸ τῆς φυλακῆς εἰσῆλθον πρὸς τὴν Λυδίαν καὶ
⌊when they had left⌋ *So {from}* the prison, they went to *{the}* Lydia's house; and
2002 1254 608 3836 5871 1656 4639 3836 3376 2779
pt.aa.npm cj p.g d.gsf n.gsf v.aai.3p p.a d.asf n.asf cj

ἰδόντες παρεκάλεσαν τοὺς ἀδελφοὺς καὶ ἐξῆλθαν.
⌊when they saw⌋ the brothers, they encouraged *the brothers* them and departed.
1625 3836 81 4151 3836 81 2779 2002
pt.aa.npm v.aai.3p d.apm n.apm cj v.aai.3p

[a] [τούτους] UBS.

NASB

them into his house
and set food before
them, and rejoiced
greatly, having
believed in God
with his whole
household.
35 Now when day
came, the chief
magistrates sent
their policemen,
saying, "Release
those men." 36 And
the jailer reported
these words to
Paul, *saying,* "The
chief magistrates
have sent to release
you. Therefore
come out now
and go in peace."
37 But Paul said to
them, "They have
beaten us in public
without trial, men
who are Romans,
and have thrown
us into prison; and
now are they send-
ing us away se-
cretly? No indeed!
But let them come
themselves and
bring us out." 38 The
policemen reported
these words to the
chief magistrates.
They were afraid
when they heard
that they were
Romans, 39 and
they came and
appealed to them,
and when they had
brought them out,
they kept begging
them to leave the
city. 40 They went
out of the prison
and entered *the
house of* Lydia, and
when they saw the
brethren, they en-
couraged them and
departed.

NIV

In Thessalonica

17 When Paul
and his
companions had
passed through
Amphipolis and
Apollonia, they
came to Thes-
salonica, where
there was a Jewish
synagogue. 2 As
was his custom,
Paul went into the
synagogue, and
on three Sabbath
days he reasoned
with them from
the Scriptures,
3 explaining and
proving that the
Messiah had to
suffer and rise
from the dead.
"This Jesus I am
proclaiming to you
is the Messiah,"
he said. 4 Some of
the Jews were per-
suaded and joined
Paul and Silas, as
did a large num-
ber of God-fearing
Greeks and quite
a few prominent
women.
5 But other Jews
were jealous; so
they rounded up
some bad charac-
ters from the mar-
ketplace, formed
a mob and started
a riot in the city.
They rushed to
Jason's house in
search of Paul and
Silas in order to
bring them out to
the crowd.[a] 6 But
when they did not
find them, they
dragged Jason and
some other believ-
ers before the city
officials, shouting:
"These men who
have caused trou-
ble all over the
world have now
come here, 7 and
Jason has wel-
comed them

[a] 5 Or *the assembly of the people*

17:1 διοδεύσαντες δὲ τὴν Ἀμφίπολιν καὶ τὴν Ἀπολλωνίαν
˻Having passed through˼ *{and}* *{the}* Amphipolis and *{the}* Apollonia, Paul and Silas
1476 1254 3836 315 2779 3836 662
pt.aa.npm cj d.asf n.asf cj d.asf n.asf

ἦλθον εἰς Θεσσαλονίκην ὅπου ἦν συναγωγὴ τῶν Ἰουδαίων. 2
came to Thessalonica, where ˻there was˼ a synagogue of the Jews. And
2262 1650 2553 3963 1639 5252 3836 2681 1254
v.aai.3p p.a n.asf cj v.iai.3s n.nsf d.gpm a.gpm

κατὰ δὲ τὸ εἰωθὸς τῷ Παύλῳ εἰσῆλθεν πρὸς αὐτοὺς καὶ ἐπὶ
˻according to˼ *And* *{the}* Paul's custom, *{the}* *Paul's* he went to them and for three
2848 1254 3836 4263 1665 3836 4263 1656 4639 899 2779 2093 5552
p.a cj d.asn pt.ra.asn d.dsm n.dsm v.aai.3s p.a r.apm.3 cj p.a

σάββατα τρία διελέξατο αὐτοῖς ἀπὸ τῶν γραφῶν, 3 διανοίγων καὶ
Sabbath days *three* ˻he reasoned with˼ them from the Scriptures, explaining and
4879 5552 1363 899 608 3836 1210 1380 2779
n.apn a.apn v.ami.3s r.dpm.3 p.g d.gpf n.gpf pt.pa.nsm cj

παρατιθέμενος ὅτι τὸν χριστὸν ἔδει παθεῖν καὶ
demonstrating that it was necessary for the Messiah *it was necessary for* to suffer and
4192 4022 1256 1256 1256 1256 3836 5986 1256 4248 2779
pt.pm.nsm cj d.asm n.asm v.iai.3s f.aa cj

ἀναστῆναι ἐκ νεκρῶν καὶ ὅτι οὗτός ἐστιν ὁ χριστὸς ὁ[a] Ἰησοῦς ὃν
to rise from the dead, and that, "This one is the Messiah, this Jesus whom
482 1666 3738 2779 4022 4047 1639 3836 5986 3836 2652 4005
f.aa p.g a.gpm cj cj r.nsm v.pai.3s d.nsm n.nsm d.nsm n.nsm r.asm

ἐγὼ καταγγέλλω ὑμῖν. 4 καί τινες ἐξ αὐτῶν ἐπείσθησαν καὶ προσεκληρώθησαν
I am proclaiming to you." And some of them were persuaded and cast their lot with
1609 2859 7007 2779 5516 1666 899 4275 2779 4677
r.ns.1 v.pai.1s r.dp.2 cj r.npm p.g r.gpm.3 v.api.3p cj v.api.3p

τῷ Παύλῳ καὶ τῷ Σιλᾷ, τῶν τε σεβομένων Ἑλλήνων πλῆθος πολύ,
{the} Paul and *{the}* Silas, *{the}* both a great number of devout Greeks *number* *great*
3836 4263 2779 3836 4976 3836 5445 4498 4436 4936 1818 4436 4498
d.dsm n.dsm cj d.dsm n.dsm d.gpm cj pt.pm.gpm n.gpm n.nsn a.nsn

γυναικῶν τε τῶν πρώτων οὐκ ὀλίγαι. 5
women and not a few of the leading *not* *few* women. But the Jews,
1222 5445 4024 3900 3836 4755 4024 3900 1222 1254 3836 2681
n.gpf cj d.gpf a.gpf pl a.npf

ζηλώσαντες δὲ οἱ Ἰουδαῖοι καὶ προσλαβόμενοι τῶν
moved by envy, *But* *the* *Jews* *{and}* recruited certain wicked men of the
2420 1254 3836 2681 2779 4689 5516 4505 467 3836
pt.aa.npm cj d.npm a.npm cj pt.am.npm d.gpm

ἀγοραίων ἄνδρας τινὰς πονηροὺς καὶ ὀχλοποιήσαντες → → → →
marketplace *men* *certain* *wicked* and, forming a mob, they set the city in an
61 467 5516 4505 2779 4062 3836 4484
n.gpm n.apm r.apm a.apm cj pt.aa.npm

ἐθορύβουν τὴν πόλιν καὶ ↱ ἐπιστάντες τῇ οἰκίᾳ Ἰάσονος ἐζήτουν
uproar. *the* *city* *{and}* They attacked the house of Jason, trying to bring
2572 3836 4484 2779 2426 2392 3836 3864 2619 2426 4575 4575
v.iai.3p d.asf n.asf cj pt.aa.npm d.dsf n.dsf n.gsm v.iai.3p

αὐτοὺς προαγαγεῖν εἰς τὸν δῆμον· 6 ↱ ↱ ↱ μὴ εὑρόντες δὲ
them *to bring out* out to the people. But when they could not find *But*
899 4575 4575 1650 3836 1322 1254 2351 2351 2351 3590 2351 1254
r.apm.3 f.aa p.a d.asm n.asm pl pt.aa.npm cj

αὐτοὺς ἔσυρον Ἰάσονα καί τινας ἀδελφοὺς ἐπὶ τοὺς πολιτάρχας βοῶντες
them, they dragged Jason and some fellow believers before the city authorities, shouting,
899 5359 2619 2779 5516 81 2093 3836 4485 1066
r.apm.3 v.iai.3p n.asm cj r.apm n.apm p.a d.apm n.apm pt.pa.npm

ὅτι οἱ ↱ ↱ τὴν οἰκουμένην ἀναστατώσαντες οὗτοι
~ "These men who have turned the world upside down *These men* have come
4022 4047 4047 3836 415 415 3836 3876 415 4047 4205 4205
cj d.npm d.asf n.asf pt.aa.npm r.npm

καὶ ἐνθάδε πάρεισιν, 7 οὓς ὑποδέδεκται Ἰάσων·
here too, *here* *have come* and Jason has received them *has received as guests* *Jason* as
1924 2779 1924 4205 2619 5685 5685 4005 5685 2619 5685
adv adv v.pai.3p r.apm v.rmi.3s n.nsm

[a] [ὁ] UBS.

NASB

Paul at Thessalonica

17:1 Now when
they had traveled
through Amphipo-
lis and Apollonia,
they came to
Thessalonica,
where there was
a synagogue of
the Jews. 2 And ac-
cording to Paul's
custom, he went to
them, and for three
Sabbaths reasoned
with them from
the Scriptures, 3 ex-
plaining and giving
evidence that the
Christ had to suf-
fer and rise again
from the dead,
and *saying,* "This
Jesus whom I am
proclaiming to you
is the Christ." 4 And
some of them were
persuaded and
joined Paul and
Silas, along with
a large number of
the God-fearing
Greeks and a num-
ber of the leading
women. 5 But the
Jews, becoming
jealous and taking
along some wicked
men from the mar-
ket place, formed
a mob and set the
city in an uproar;
and attacking the
house of Jason,
they were seek-
ing to bring them
out to the people.
6 When they did not
find them, they *be-
gan* dragging Jason
and some brethren
before the city au-
thorities, shouting,
"These men who
have upset [a] the
world have come
here also; 7 and Ja-
son has welcomed
them, and they all

[a] Lit *the inhabited earth*

NIV

into his house.
They are all defy-
ing Caesar's de-
crees, saying that
there is another
king, one called
Jesus." 8 When
they heard this,
the crowd and
the city officials
were thrown into
turmoil. 9 Then
they made Jason
and the others
post bond and let
them go.

In Berea

10 As soon as it
was night, the be-
lievers sent Paul
and Silas away
to Berea. On ar-
riving there, they
went to the Jewish
synagogue. 11 Now
the Berean Jews
were of more no-
ble character than
those in Thessalo-
nica, for they re-
ceived the message
with great eager-
ness and examined
the Scriptures
every day to see
if what Paul said
was true. 12 As a re-
sult, many of them
believed, as did
also a number of
prominent Greek
women and many
Greek men.
13 But when the
Jews in Thessalo-
nica learned that
Paul was preach-
ing the word of
God at Berea,
some of them went
there too, agitat-
ing the crowds and
stirring them up.
14 The believers
immediately sent
Paul to the coast,
but Silas

καὶ οὗτοι πάντες ἀπέναντι τῶν δογμάτων Καίσαρος
guests; and all these men *all* are acting contrary to the decrees of Caesar,
5685 2779 4246 4047 4246 4556 4556 595 3836 1504 2790
cj r.npm a.npm p.g d.gpn n.gpn n.gsm

πράσσουσιν βασιλέα ἕτερον λέγοντες εἶναι Ἰησοῦν. 8
are acting saying that there is another king, *another saying there is* Jesus." And
4556 3306 1639 1639 2283 995 2283 3306 1639 2652 1254
v.pai.3p n.asm r.asm pt.pa.npm f.pa n.asm

ἐτάραξαν δὲ τὸν ὄχλον καὶ τοὺς πολιτάρχας ἀκούοντας ταῦτα, 9 καὶ
⌞they stirred up⌟ *And* the people and the city authorities who heard these things. And
5429 1254 3836 4063 2779 3836 4485 201 4047 2779
v.aai.3p cj d.asm n.asm cj d.apm n.apm pt.pa.apm r.apn cj

λαβόντες τὸ ἱκανὸν παρὰ τοῦ Ἰάσονος καὶ τῶν λοιπῶν ἀπέλυσαν
⌞when they had taken⌟ *{the}* bail from *{the}* Jason and the others, they let
3284 3836 2653 4123 3836 2619 2779 3836 3370 668
pt.aa.npm d.asn a.asn p.g d.gsm n.gsm cj d.gpm a.gpm v.aai.3p

αὐτούς. ↶ 10 οἱ δὲ ἀδελφοὶ εὐθέως διὰ νυκτὸς
them go. And the *And* brothers immediately sent Paul and Silas off by night
899 668 1254 3836 1254 81 2311 1734 4263 2779 4976 1734 1328 3816
r.apm.3 d.npm cj n.npm adv p.g n.gsf

ἐξέπεμψαν τόν τε Παῦλον καὶ τὸν Σιλᾶν εἰς Βέροιαν, ↱ οἵτινες
sent off {the} ~ Paul and {the} Silas to Berea. When they
1734 3836 5445 4263 2779 3836 4976 1650 1023 4134 4015
v.aai.3p d.asm cj n.asm cj d.asm n.asm p.a n.asf r.npm

παραγενόμενοι εἰς τὴν συναγωγὴν τῶν Ἰουδαίων ἀπῄεσαν. 11 οὗτοι
got there, they went to the synagogue of the Jews. *they went* These Jews
4134 583 583 1650 3836 5252 3836 2681 583 4047
pt.am.npm p.a d.asf n.asf d.gpm a.gpm v.iai.3p r.npm

δὲ ἦσαν εὐγενέστεροι τῶν ἐν Θεσσαλονίκῃ, οἵτινες ἐδέξαντο τὸν
{and} were more open-minded ⌞than those⌟ in Thessalonica, for they received the
1254 1639 2302 3836 1877 2553 4015 1312 3836
cj v.iai.3p a.npm.c d.gpm p.d n.dsf r.npm v.ami.3p d.asm

λόγον μετὰ πάσης προθυμίας καθ᾽ ἡμέραν ἀνακρίνοντες τὰς
message with all eagerness, examining the scriptures every day *examining the*
3364 3552 4246 4608 373 3836 1210 2848 2465 373 3836
n.asm p.g a.gsf n.gsf p.a n.asf pt.pa.npm d.apf

γραφὰς εἰ ἔχοι ταῦτα οὕτως. 12 πολλοὶ μὲν οὖν ἐξ αὐτῶν
scriptures to see if *were* these things were so. So many ~ *So* of them
1210 1623 2400 4047 2400 4048 4036 4498 3525 4036 1666 899
n.apf cj v.pao.3s r.npn adv a.npm pl cj p.g r.gpm.3

ἐπίστευσαν καὶ τῶν Ἑλληνίδων γυναικῶν τῶν εὐσχημόνων καὶ
believed, with not a few *{the}* prominent Greek women *{the} prominent* and
4409 2779 4024 3900 3836 2363 1820 1222 3836 2363 2779
v.aai.3p cj d.gpf a.gpf n.gpf d.gpf a.gpf cj

ἀνδρῶν οὐκ ὀλίγοι. 13 ὡς δὲ ἔγνωσαν οἱ ἀπὸ τῆς Θεσσαλονίκης
men. *not few* But when *But learned* the Jews from *{the}* Thessalonica
467 4024 3900 1254 6055 1254 1182 3836 2681 608 3836 2553
n.gpm pl a.npm cj cj v.aai.3p d.npm p.g d.gsf n.gsf

Ἰουδαῖοι ὅτι καὶ ἐν τῇ Βεροίᾳ κατηγγέλη ὑπὸ τοῦ
Jews learned that also in *{the}* Berea the word of God was proclaimed by *{the}*
2681 1182 4022 2779 1877 3836 1023 3836 3364 3836 2536 2859 5679 3836
a.npm cj adv p.d d.dsf n.dsf v.api.3s p.g d.gsm

Παύλου ὁ λόγος τοῦ θεοῦ, ἦλθον κἀκεῖ σαλεύοντες καὶ ταράσσοντες τοὺς
Paul, *the word of God* they came there too, inciting and stirring up the
4263 3836 3364 3836 2536 2262 2795 4888 2779 5429 3836
n.gsm d.nsm n.nsm d.gsm n.gsm v.aai.3p crasis pt.pa.npm cj pt.pa.npm d.apm

ὄχλους. 14 εὐθέως δὲ τότε τὸν Παῦλον ἐξαπέστειλαν ←
crowds. Then immediately *{and} Then {the} Paul* the brothers sent Paul away,
4063 5538 2311 1254 5538 3836 4263 3836 81 1990 4263
n.apm adv cj adv d.asm n.asm v.aai.3p

οἱ ἀδελφοὶ πορεύεσθαι ἕως ἐπὶ τὴν θάλασσαν, ὑπέμεινάν τε ὅ τε Σιλᾶς
the brothers to go ⌞as far as⌟ to the sea, *remained* but *{the}* both Silas
3836 81 4513 2401 2093 3836 2498 5702 5445 3836 5445 4976
d.npm n.npm f.pm p.g p.a d.asf n.asf v.aai.3p cj d.nsm cj n.nsm

NASB

act contrary to the
decrees of Caesar,
saying that there is
another king, Je-
sus." 8They stirred
up the crowd and
the city authorities
who heard these
things. 9And when
they had received a
pledge from Jason
and the others, they
released them.

Paul at Berea

10The brethren im-
mediately sent Paul
and Silas away by
night to Berea, and
when they arrived,
they went into the
synagogue of the
Jews. 11Now these
were more noble-
minded than those
in Thessalonica, for
they received the
word with great ea-
gerness, examining
the Scriptures daily
to see whether
these things were
so. 12Therefore
many of them be-
lieved, along with
a number of promi-
nent Greek women
and men. 13But
when the Jews of
Thessalonica found
out that the word
of God had been
proclaimed by Paul
in Berea also, they
came there as well,
agitating and stir-
ring up the crowds.
14Then immediately
the brethren sent
Paul out to go as
far as the sea; and
Silas

NIV

and Timothy
stayed at Be-
rea. 15 Those who
escorted Paul
brought him to
Athens and then
left with instruc-
tions for Silas and
Timothy to join
him as soon as
possible.

In Athens

16 While Paul was
waiting for them
in Athens, he was
greatly distressed
to see that the city
was full of idols.
17 So he reasoned
in the synagogue
with both Jews
and God-fearing
Greeks, as well
as in the market-
place day by day
with those who
happened to be
there. 18 A group
of Epicurean and
Stoic philosophers
began to debate
with him. Some of
them asked, "What
is this babbler
trying to say?"
Others remarked,
"He seems to be
advocating for-
eign gods." They
said this because
Paul was preach-
ing the good news
about Jesus and
the resurrection.
19 Then they took
him and brought
him to a meeting
of the Areopagus,
where they said
to him, "May we
know what this
new teaching is
that you are pre-
senting? 20 You
are bringing some
strange ideas to
our ears, and we
would like to know
what they mean."
21 (All the Atheni-
ans and the for-
eigners

καὶ ὁ Τιμόθεος ἐκεῖ. 15 οἱ δὲ καθιστάνοντες τὸν Παῦλον ἤγαγον
and {the} Timothy remained there. Those {and} who conducted {the} Paul brought
2779 3836 5510 5702 1695 3836 1254 2770 3836 4263 72
cj d.nsm n.nsm adv d.npm cj pt.pa.npm d.asm n.asm v.aai.3p

ἕως Ἀθηνῶν, καὶ λαβόντες ἐντολὴν πρὸς τὸν Σιλᾶν καὶ τὸν Τιμόθεον
him ⌊as far as⌋ Athens, and receiving an order for {the} Silas and {the} Timothy
2401 121 2779 3284 1953 4639 3836 4976 2779 3836 5510
p.g n.gpf cj pt.aa.npm n.asf p.a d.asm n.asm cj d.asm n.asm

ἵνα ὡς τάχιστα ἔλθωσιν πρὸς αὐτὸν ἐξῄεσαν. 16 ἐν δὲ ταῖς
to come to him as soon as possible, come to him they left. at Now {the}
2671 2262 4639 899 6055 5441 2262 4639 899 1997 1877 1254 3836
cj pl adv.s v.aas.3p p.a r.asm.3 v.iai.3p p.d cj d.dpf

Ἀθήναις → ἐκδεχομένου αὐτοὺς τοῦ Παύλου παρωξύνετο
Athens while Paul was waiting for them {the} Paul at Athens, his spirit was stirred up
121 4263 1683 899 3836 4263 1877 121 899 4460 4236
n.dpf pt.pm.gsm r.apm.3 d.gsm n.gsm v.ipi.3s

τὸ πνεῦμα αὐτοῦ ἐν αὐτῷ θεωροῦντος κατείδωλον οὖσαν τὴν πόλιν.
{the} spirit his within him on seeing the city full of idols. {being} the city
3836 4460 899 1877 899 2555 3836 4484 2977 1639 3836 4484
d.nsn n.nsn r.gsm.3 p.d r.dsm.3 pt.pa.gsm a.asf pt.pa.asf d.asf n.asf

17 διελέγετο μὲν οὖν ἐν τῇ συναγωγῇ τοῖς Ἰουδαίοις καὶ τοῖς σεβομένοις
So he reasoned ~ So in the synagogue ⌊with the⌋ Jews and the worshippers,
4036 1363 3525 4036 1877 3836 5252 3836 2681 2779 3836 4936
v.imi.3s pl cj p.d d.dsf n.dsf d.dpm a.dpm cj d.dpm pt.pm.dpm

καὶ ἐν τῇ ἀγορᾷ ⌊κατὰ πᾶσαν⌋ ἡμέραν πρὸς τοὺς παρατυγχάνοντας.
and in the marketplace every day with those who happened to be there.
2779 1877 3836 59 2848 4246 2465 4639 3836 4193
cj p.d d.dsf n.dsf p.a a.asf n.asf p.a d.apm pt.pa.apm

18 τινὲς δὲ καὶ τῶν Ἐπικουρείων καὶ Στοϊκῶν φιλοσόφων συνέβαλλον
Also some {and} Also of the Epicurean and Stoic philosophers ⌊were conversing with⌋
2779 5516 1254 2779 3836 2134 2779 5121 5815 5202
r.npm cj adv d.gpm n.gpm cj a.gpm n.gpm v.iai.3p

αὐτῷ, καί τινες ἔλεγον, τί ἂν → θέλοι ὁ σπερμολόγος οὗτος
him, and some were asking, "What ~ does this babbler want {the} babbler this
899 2779 5516 3306 5515 323 4047 5066 2527 3836 5066 4047
r.dsm.3 cj r.npm v.iai.3p r.asn pl v.pao.3s d.nsm n.nsm r.nsm

λέγειν; οἱ δέ, ξένων δαιμονίων δοκεῖ
to say?" Others said, {and} "He seems to be a proclaimer of strange gods," He seems
3306 3836 1254 1506 1506 1639 1639 2858 3828 1228 1506
f.pa d.npm pl a.gpn n.gpn v.pai.3s

καταγγελεὺς εἶναι, ὅτι τὸν Ἰησοῦν καὶ τὴν
proclaimer to be for he was announcing the good news about {the} Jesus and the
2858 1639 4022 2294 2294 2294 2294 2294 2294 3836 2652 2779 3836
n.nsm f.pa cj d.asm n.asm cj d.asf

ἀνάστασιν εὐηγγελίζετο. 19 ἐπιλαβόμενοί τε αὐτοῦ
resurrection. he was announcing the good news And they took hold of And him and brought him
414 2294 5445 2138 5445 899 72
n.asf v.imi.3s pt.am.npm cj r.gsm.3

ἐπὶ τὸν ⌊Ἄρειον πάγον⌋ ἤγαγον λέγοντες, δυνάμεθα γνῶναι τίς ἡ καινὴ
to the Areopagus, brought saying, "May we know what is {the} this new
2093 3836 740 4076 72 3306 1538 1182 5515 3836 4047 2785
p.a d.asm a.asm n.asm v.aai.3p pt.pa.npm v.ppi.1p f.aa r.nsf d.nsf a.nsf

αὕτη ἡ ὑπὸ σοῦ λαλουμένη διδαχή; 20
this {the} teaching being presented by you? being presented teaching For you bring some
4047 3836 1439 3281 3281 5679 5148 3281 1439 1142 1662 1662 5516
r.nsf d.nsf p.g r.gs.2 pt.pp.nsf n.nsf

ξενίζοντα γάρ τινα εἰσφέρεις εἰς τὰς ἀκοὰς ἡμῶν· βουλόμεθα οὖν γνῶναι
strange things For some you bring to {the} our ears, our so we want so to know
3826 1142 5516 1662 1650 3836 7005 198 7005 4036 1089 4036 1182
pt.pa.apn cj r.apn v.pai.2s p.a d.apf n.apf r.gp.1 v.pmi.1p cj f.aa

τίνα θέλει ταῦτα εἶναι. 21 Ἀθηναῖοι δὲ πάντες καὶ οἱ
what {it wills} these things mean." (Now all the Athenians Now all and the foreigners
5515 2527 4047 1639 1254 4246 122 1254 4246 2779 3836 3828
r.apn v.pai.3s r.apn f.pa n.npm cj a.npm cj d.npm

NASB

and Timothy
remained there.
15 Now those who
escorted Paul
brought him as
far as Athens; and
receiving a com-
mand for Silas and
Timothy to come to
him as soon as pos-
sible, they left.

Paul at Athens

16 Now while Paul
was waiting for
them at Athens, his
spirit was being
provoked within
him as he was
observing the city
full of idols. 17 So
he was reasoning
in the synagogue
with the Jews and
the God-fearing
Gentiles, and in the
market place every
day with those who
happened to be
present. 18 And also
some of the Epi-
curean and Stoic
philosophers were
conversing with
him. Some were
saying, "What
would this idle
babbler wish to
say?" Others, "He
seems to be a pro-
claimer of strange
deities,"—because
he was preach-
ing Jesus and the
resurrection. 19 And
they took him and
brought him to the
Areopagus, saying,
"May we know
what this new
teaching is which
you are proclaim-
ing? 20 For you are
bringing some
strange things to
our ears; so we
want to know what
these things mean."
21 (Now all the
Athenians and the
strangers visiting
there used to

NIV

who lived there
spent their time
doing nothing but
talking about and
listening to the lat-
est ideas.)
22Paul then stood
up in the meeting
of the Areopagus
and said: "People
of Athens! I see
that in every way
you are very re-
ligious. 23For as I
walked around and
looked carefully
at your objects of
worship, I even
found an altar with
this inscription: TO
AN UNKNOWN GOD.
So you are igno-
rant of the very
thing you wor-
ship—and this is
what I am going to
proclaim to you.
24"The God who
made the world
and everything in
it is the Lord of
heaven and earth
and does not live
in temples built
by human hands.
25And he is not
served by human
hands, as if he
needed anything.
Rather, he himself
gives everyone
life and breath and
everything else.
26From one man
he made all the
nations, that they
should inhabit the
whole earth; and
he marked out
their appointed
times in history
and the boundaries
of their lands.
27God did this so
that they would
seek him and per-
haps reach out for
him and find him,
though he is not
far from any one
of us. 28'For in him
we live and move
and have our be-
ing.'[a] As some

[a] 28 From the Cretan philosopher Epimenides

ἐπιδημοῦντες ξένοι εἰς οὐδὲν ἕτερον ηὐκαίρουν
living there *foreigners* used to spend their time in nothing else *used to spend their time*
2111 3828 2320 2320 2320 2320 2320 1650 4029 2283 2320
pt.pa.npm n.npm p.a a.asn r.asn v.iai.3p

ἢ λέγειν τι ἢ ἀκούειν τι καινότερον. 22 σταθεὶς δὲ ὁ[a]
than to tell *{something}* or to hear something new.) So Paul, standing *So* *{the}*
2445 3306 5516 2445 201 5516 2785 1254 4263 2705 1254 3836
pl f.pa r.asn cj f.pa r.asn a.asn.c pt.ap.nsm cj d.nsm

Παῦλος ἐν μέσῳ τοῦ ⌞Ἀρείου πάγου⌟ ἔφη, ἄνδρες Ἀθηναῖοι,
Paul in the midst of the Areopagus, said: "Men of Athens, I perceive that
4263 1877 3545 3836 740 4076 5774 467 122 2555 2555 6055
n.nsm p.d n.dsn d.gsm a.gsm n.gsm v.iai.3s n.vpm n.vpm

κατὰ πάντα ὡς δεισιδαιμονεστέρους ὑμᾶς θεωρῶ. 23 διερχόμενος
in every way *that* you are a very devout people. *you* *I perceive* For as I went around
2848 4246 6055 7007 1273 7007 2555 1142 1451
p.a a.apn pl a.apm.c r.ap.2 v.pai.1s pt.pm.nsm

γὰρ καὶ ἀναθεωρῶν τὰ σεβάσματα ὑμῶν εὗρον καὶ βωμὸν ἐν ᾧ
For and observed *{the}* your objects of worship, *your* I found also an altar on which
1142 2779 355 3836 7007 4934 7007 2351 2779 1117 1877 4005
cj cj pt.pa.nsm d.apn n.apn r.gp.2 v.aai.1s adv n.asm p.d r.dsm

ἐπεγέγραπτο, → ἀγνώστῳ θεῷ. ὃ οὖν ἀγνοοῦντες εὐσεβεῖτε,
was inscribed, 'To an unknown god.' So what *So* you worship without knowing, *you worship*
2108 58 2536 4036 4005 4036 2355 2355 51 2355
v.lpi.3s a.dsm n.dsm r.asn cj pt.pa.npm v.pai.2p

τοῦτο ἐγὼ καταγγέλλω ὑμῖν. 24 ὁ θεὸς ὁ ποιήσας τὸν κόσμον καὶ πάντα
this I proclaim to you. The God who made the world and everything
4047 1609 2859 7007 3836 2536 3836 4472 3836 3180 2779 4246
r.asn r.ns.1 v.pai.1s r.dp.2 d.nsm n.nsm d.nsm pt.aa.nsm d.asm n.asm cj a.apn

τὰ ἐν αὐτῷ, οὗτος οὐρανοῦ καὶ γῆς ὑπάρχων κύριος οὐκ
{the} in it, *{this one}* being Lord of heaven and earth, *being* *Lord* does not live
3836 1877 899 4047 5639 3261 4041 2779 1178 5639 3261 2997 4024 2997
d.apn p.d r.dsm.3 r.nsm n.gsm cj n.gsf pt.pa.nsm n.nsm pl

ἐν χειροποιήτοις ναοῖς κατοικεῖ 25 οὐδὲ ὑπὸ
in shrines ⌞made by human hands,⌟ *shrines* *does live* nor is he served by human
1877 3724 5935 3724 2997 4028 2543 2543 2543 5679 474
p.d a.dpm n.dpm v.pai.3s cj p.g

χειρῶν ἀνθρωπίνων θεραπεύεται προσδεόμενός τινος, ↱ ↱ αὐτὸς διδοὺς
hands, *human* *is he served* as though he needed anything, since he himself gives
5931 474 2543 4656 5516 1443 1443 899 1443
n.gpf a.gpf v.ppi.3s pt.pm.nsm r.gsn r.nsm pt.pa.nsm

πᾶσι ζωὴν καὶ πνοὴν καὶ τὰ πάντα· 26 ἐποίησέν τε ἐξ ἑνὸς πᾶν ἔθνος
to all life and breath and *{the}* everything. And he made *And* from one man every race
4246 2437 2779 4466 2779 3836 4246 5445 4472 5445 1666 1651 4246 1620
a.dpm n.asf cj n.asf cj d.apn a.apn v.aai.3s cj p.g a.gsm a.asn n.asn

ἀνθρώπων κατοικεῖν ἐπὶ παντὸς προσώπου τῆς γῆς, ὁρίσας
of men to live on all the face of the earth, ⌞having determined⌟
476 2997 2093 4246 4725 3836 1178 3988
n.gpm f.pa p.g a.gsn n.gsn d.gsf n.gsf pt.aa.nsm

προστεταγμένους καιροὺς καὶ τὰς ὁροθεσίας τῆς κατοικίας ← ←
allotted epochs and the fixed boundaries of the places where they would live,
4705 2789 2779 3836 3999 3836 3000 899
pt.rp.apm n.apm cj d.apf n.apf d.gsf n.gsf

αὐτῶν 27 ζητεῖν τὸν θεόν, εἰ ⌞ἄρα γε⌟ ψηλαφήσειαν αὐτὸν
they ⌞that they should seek⌟ *{the}* God, if perhaps that ⌞they might grope for⌟ him
899 2426 3836 2536 1623 726 1145 6027 899
r.gpm.3 f.pa d.asm n.asm cj cj pl v.aao.3p r.asm.3

καὶ εὕροιεν, καί γε οὐ μακρὰν ἀπὸ ἑνὸς ἑκάστου ἡμῶν
and find him, though indeed he is not far from each one *each* of us.
2779 2351 2779 1145 5639 5639 4024 3426 608 1667 1651 1667 7005
cj v.aao.3p cj pl pl adv p.g a.gsm r.gsm r.gp.1

ὑπάρχοντα. 28 ἐν αὐτῷ γὰρ ζῶμεν καὶ κινούμεθα καὶ ἐσμέν, ὡς καί τινες
he is 'For in him *For* we live and move about and exist,' as even some
5639 1142 1877 899 1142 2409 2779 3075 2779 1639 6055 2779 5516
pt.pa.asm p.d r.dsm.3 cj v.pai.1p cj v.ppi.1p cj v.pai.1p cj adv r.npm

[a] [ὁ] UBS, omitted by TNIV.

NASB

spend their time in
nothing other than
telling or hearing
something new.)

Sermon on Mars Hill

22So Paul stood
in the midst of
the Areopagus
and said, "Men of
Athens, I observe
that you are very
religious in all
respects. 23For
while I was pass-
ing through and
examining the
objects of your
worship, I also
found an altar with
this inscription,
'TO AN UNKNOWN
GOD.' Therefore
what you worship
in ignorance, this
I proclaim to you.
24The God who
made the world
and all things in it,
since He is Lord of
heaven and earth,
does not dwell
in temples made
with hands; 25nor
is He served by
human hands, as
though He needed
anything, since
He Himself gives
to all *people* life
and breath and all
things; 26and He
made from one
man every nation
of mankind to live
on all the face of
the earth, having
determined *their*
appointed times
and the boundaries
of their habitation,
27that they would
seek God, if per-
haps they might
grope for Him and
find Him, though
He is not far from
each one of us;
28for in Him we live
and move and ex-
ist, as even some

NIV

of your own poets
have said, 'We are
his offspring.'[a]
29 "Therefore
since we are
God's offspring,
we should not
think that the di-
vine being is like
gold or silver or
stone—an image
made by human
design and skill.
30 In the past God
overlooked such
ignorance, but now
he commands all
people everywhere
to repent. 31 For he
has set a day when
he will judge the
world with justice
by the man he has
appointed. He has
given proof of this
to everyone by
raising him from
the dead."
32 When they
heard about the
resurrection of
the dead, some
of them sneered,
but others said,
"We want to hear
you again on this
subject." 33 At that,
Paul left the Coun-
cil. 34 Some of the
people became fol-
lowers of Paul and
believed. Among
them was Diony-
sius, a member of
the Areopagus,
also a woman
named Damaris,
and a number of
others.

In Corinth

18 After this,
Paul left
Athens and went to
Corinth. 2 There he
met a Jew named
Aquila, a native of
Pontus, who had
recently

τῶν ⌞καθ' ὑμᾶς⌟ ποιητῶν εἰρήκασιν, τοῦ γὰρ καὶ γένος
of your own poets have said, 'For we too are his *For* *too* offspring.'
3836 2848 7007 4475 3306 1142 1639 2779 1639 3836 1142 2779 1169
d.gpm p.a r.ap.2 n.gpm v.rai.3p d.gsm cj adv n.nsn

ἐσμέν. 29 γένος οὖν ὑπάρχοντες τοῦ θεοῦ οὐκ
we are So since we are the offspring *So* *since we are* of God, we ought not
1639 4036 5639 5639 5639 1169 4036 5639 3836 2536 4053 4053 4024
v.pai.1p n.nsn cj pt.pa.npm d.gsm n.gsm pl

ὀφείλομεν νομίζειν χρυσῷ ἢ ἀργύρῳ ἢ
we ought to think that the divine being is like an image carved in gold or silver or
4053 3787 3836 2521 2521 1639 3927 5916 5916 5996 2445 738 2445
v.pai.1p f.pa n.dsm cj n.dsm cj

λίθῳ, χαράγματι → τέχνης καὶ ἐνθυμήσεως ἀνθρώπου, τὸ θεῖον εἶναι
stone *image carved* by human skill and imagination. *human* *the* *divine being* *is*
3345 5916 476 5492 2779 1927 476 3836 2521 1639
n.dsm n.dsn n.gsf cj n.gsf n.gsm d.asn a.asn f.pa

ὅμοιον. 30 τοὺς μὲν οὖν χρόνους τῆς ἀγνοίας ὑπεριδὼν
like So then, God overlooked the ~ *So then* times of ignorance, *overlooked*
3927 4036 4036 2536 5666 3836 3525 4036 5989 3836 53 5666
a.asn d.apm pl cj n.apm d.gsf n.gsf pt.aa.nsm

ὁ θεός, τὰ νῦν παραγγέλλει τοῖς ἀνθρώποις πάντας
{the} *God* *{the}* but now he orders *{the}* men to repent, all of them in
3836 2536 3836 3814 4133 3836 476 3566 3566 4246
d.nsm n.nsm d.apn adv v.pai.3s d.dpm n.dpm a.apm

πανταχοῦ μετανοεῖν, 31 καθότι ἔστησεν ἡμέραν ἐν ᾗ μέλλει κρίνειν τὴν
all places, *to repent* because he has appointed a day on which he will judge the
4116 3566 2776 2705 2465 1877 4005 3516 3212 3836
adv f.pa cj v.aai.3s n.asf p.d r.dsf v.pai.3s f.pa d.asf

οἰκουμένην ἐν δικαιοσύνῃ, ἐν ἀνδρὶ ᾧ ὥρισεν, πίστιν
world in righteousness by the man whom he has appointed, having provided proof
3876 1877 1466 1877 467 4005 3988 4218 4218 4411
n.asf p.d n.dsf p.d n.dsm r.dsm v.aai.3s n.asf

παρασχὼν πᾶσιν ἀναστήσας αὐτὸν ἐκ νεκρῶν. 32 ἀκούσαντες δὲ
having provided to all by raising him from the dead." Now ⌞when they heard of⌟ *Now*
4218 4246 482 899 1666 3738 1254 201 1254
pt.aa.nsm a.dpm pt.aa.nsm r.asm.3 p.g a.gpm pt.aa.npm cj

ἀνάστασιν → νεκρῶν οἱ μὲν ἐχλεύαζον, οἱ δὲ εἶπαν, ἀκουσόμεθά
the resurrection of the dead, some ~ mocked, but others *but* said, "We will hear
414 3738 3836 3525 5949 1254 3836 1254 3306 201
n.asf a.gpm d.npm pl v.iai.3p d.npm pl v.aai.3p v.fmi.1p

σου περὶ τούτου καὶ πάλιν. 33 οὕτως ὁ Παῦλος ἐξῆλθεν ἐκ μέσου
you again about this." *{also}* *again* So *{the}* Paul departed from their midst.
5148 4099 4309 4047 2779 4099 4048 3836 4263 2002 1666 899 3545
r.gs.2 p.g r.gsn adv adv adv d.nsm n.nsm v.aai.3s p.g n.gsn

αὐτῶν. 34 τινὲς δὲ ἄνδρες κολληθέντες αὐτῷ ἐπίστευσαν, ἐν οἷς καὶ
their But some *But* men joined him and believed; among whom also
899 1254 5516 1254 467 3140 899 4409 1877 4005 2779
r.gpm.3 r.npm cj n.npm pt.ap.npm r.dsm.3 v.aai.3p p.d r.dpm cj

Διονύσιος ὁ Ἀρεοπαγίτης καὶ γυνὴ ὀνόματι Δάμαρις καὶ ἕτεροι σὺν
were Dionysius the Areopagite and a woman named Damaris and others with
1477 3836 741 2779 1222 3950 1240 2779 2283 5250
n.nsm d.nsm n.nsm cj n.nsf n.dsn n.nsf cj r.npm p.d

αὐτοῖς.
them.
899
r.dpm.3

18:1 μετὰ ταῦτα χωρισθεὶς ἐκ τῶν Ἀθηνῶν ἦλθεν εἰς Κόρινθον. 2 καὶ
After this Paul departed from *{the}* Athens and went to Corinth. And
3552 4047 6004 1666 3836 121 2262 1650 3172 2779
p.a r.apn pt.ap.nsm p.g d.gpf n.gpf v.aai.3s p.a n.asf cj

εὑρών τινα Ἰουδαῖον ὀνόματι Ἀκύλαν, Ποντικὸν τῷ γένει προσφάτως
finding a certain Jew named Aquila, a native of Pontus, *{the}* *native* recently
2351 5516 2681 3950 217 1169 4507 3836 1169 4711
pt.aa.nsm r.asm a.asm n.dsn n.asm a.asm d.dsn n.dsn adv

NASB

of your own poets
have said, 'For
we also are His
children.' 29 Being
then the children
of God, we ought
not to think that the
Divine Nature is
like gold or silver
or stone, an image
formed by the art
and thought of
man. 30 Therefore
having overlooked
the times of
ignorance, God is
now declaring to
men that all *people*
everywhere should
repent, 31 because
He has fixed a day
in which He will
judge the world
in righteousness
through a Man
whom He has
appointed, having
furnished proof to
all men by raising
Him from the
dead."
32 Now when
they heard of the
resurrection of the
dead, some *began*
to sneer, but oth-
ers said, "We shall
hear you again
concerning this."
33 So Paul went out
of their midst. 34 But
some men joined
him and believed,
among whom also
were Dionysius
the Areopagite and
a woman named
Damaris and others
with them.

Paul at Corinth

18:1 After these
things he left Ath-
ens and went to
Corinth. 2 And he
found a Jew named
Aquila, a native
of Pontus, having
recently come

[a] 28 From the Cili-
cian Stoic philoso-
pher Aratus

NIV

come from Ita-
ly with his wife
Priscilla, because
Claudius had or-
dered all Jews to
leave Rome. Paul
went to see them,
3and because he
was a tentmaker
as they were, he
stayed and worked
with them. 4Every
Sabbath he rea-
soned in the syn-
agogue, trying to
persuade Jews and
Greeks.
5When Silas and
Timothy came
from Macedonia,
Paul devoted him-
self exclusively to
preaching, testi-
fying to the Jews
that Jesus was
the Messiah. 6But
when they opposed
Paul and became
abusive, he shook
out his clothes in
protest and said to
them, "Your blood
be on your own
heads! I am inno-
cent of it. From
now on I will go to
the Gentiles."
7Then Paul left
the synagogue and
went next door to
the house of Titius
Justus, a worshiper
of God. 8Crispus,
the synagogue
leader, and his
entire household
believed in the
Lord; and many
of the Corinthians
who heard Paul
believed and were
baptized.
9One night the
Lord spoke

ἐληλυθότα ἀπὸ τῆς Ἰταλίας καὶ Πρίσκιλλαν γυναῖκα αὐτοῦ, διὰ τὸ
come from *{the}* Italy with his wife Priscilla *wife* *his* because *{the}*
2262 608 3836 2712 2779 899 1222 4572 1222 899 1328 3836
pt.ra.asm p.g d.gsf n.gsf cj n.asf n.asf r.gsm.3 p.a d.asn

διατεταχέναι Κλαύδιον χωρίζεσθαι πάντας τοὺς Ἰουδαίους ἀπὸ
Claudius had commanded *Claudius* all the Jews to depart *all* *the* *Jews* from
3087 1411 3087 4246 3836 2681 6004 4246 3836 2681 608
f.ra n.asm f.pp a.apm d.apm a.apm p.g

τῆς Ῥώμης, προσῆλθεν αὐτοῖς 3καὶ διὰ τὸ ὁμότεχνον εἶναι
{the} Rome, he approached them, and because ~ he was of the same trade *he was*
3836 4873 4665 899 2779 1328 3836 1639 1639 3937 1639
d.gsf n.gsf v.aai.3s r.dpm.3 cj p.a d.asn a.asm f.pa

ἔμενεν παρ᾽ αὐτοῖς, καὶ ἠργάζετο· ἦσαν γὰρ σκηνοποιοὶ τῇ τέχνῃ. 4
he stayed with them and worked, for they were *for* tentmakers by trade. And
3531 4123 899 2779 2237 1142 1639 1142 5010 3836 5492 1254
v.iai.3s p.d r.dpm.3 cj v.imi.3s v.iai.3p cj n.npm d.dsf n.dsf

διελέγετο δὲ ἐν τῇ συναγωγῇ ⌊κατὰ πᾶν⌋ σάββατον ἔπειθέν τε
he reasoned *And* in the synagogue every Sabbath and tried to persuade *and*
1363 1254 1877 3836 5252 2848 4246 4879 5445 4275 5445
v.imi.3s cj p.d d.dsf n.dsf p.a a.asn n.asn v.iai.3s cj

Ἰουδαίους καὶ Ἕλληνας. 5ὡς δὲ κατῆλθον ἀπὸ τῆς
Jews and Greeks. When *{and}* Silas and Timothy came down from *{the}*
2681 2779 1818 6055 1254 4976 2779 5510 2982 608 3836
a.apm cj n.apm cj cj v.aai.3p p.g d.gsf

Μακεδονίας ὅ τε Σιλᾶς καὶ ὁ Τιμόθεος, συνείχετο
Macedonia, *{the}* *{both}* *Silas* *and* *{the}* *Timothy* Paul ⌊was wholly absorbed⌋ with preaching
3423 3836 5445 4976 2779 3836 5510 4263 5309
n.gsf d.nsm cj n.nsm cj d.nsm n.nsm v.ipi.3s

τῷ λόγῳ ὁ Παῦλος διαμαρτυρόμενος τοῖς Ἰουδαίοις εἶναι τὸν χριστὸν
the word, *{the}* *Paul* testifying to the Jews that Jesus was the Messiah.
3836 3364 3836 4263 1371 3836 2681 2652 1639 3836 5986
d.dsm n.dsm d.nsm n.nsm pt.pm.nsm d.dpm a.dpm f.pa d.asm n.asm

Ἰησοῦν. 6 → ἀντιτασσομένων δὲ αὐτῶν καὶ βλασφημούντων ↱
Jesus But when they opposed *But* *they* and reviled him, he
2652 1254 899 530 1254 899 2779 1059 3306
n.asm pt.pm.gpm cj r.gpm.3 cj pt.pa.gpm

ἐκτιναξάμενος τὰ ἱμάτια εἶπεν πρὸς αὐτούς, τὸ αἷμα ὑμῶν ἐπὶ τὴν
shook out his garments and said to them, *{the}* "Your blood *Your* be on *{the}*
1759 3836 2668 3306 4639 899 3836 7007 135 7007 2093 3836
pt.am.nsm d.apn n.apn v.aai.3s p.a r.apm.3 d.nsn n.nsn r.gp.2 p.a d.asf

κεφαλὴν ὑμῶν· καθαρὸς ἐγὼ ἀπὸ τοῦ νῦν εἰς τὰ
your own head! *your own* I am guiltless. *I* From *{the}* now on I will go to the
7007 7007 3051 7007 1609 2754 1609 608 3836 3814 4513 4513 4513 1650 3836
n.asf r.gp.2 a.nsm r.ns.1 p.g d.gsm adv p.a d.apn

ἔθνη πορεύσομαι. 7καὶ ↱ μεταβὰς ἐκεῖθεν εἰσῆλθεν εἰς οἰκίαν τινὸς
Gentiles." *I will go* And he left there and went to the house of one
1620 4513 2779 1656 3553 1696 1656 1650 3864 5516
n.apn v.fmi.1s cj pt.aa.nsm adv v.aai.3s p.a n.asf r.gsm

ὀνόματι Τιτίου Ἰούστου σεβομένου τὸν θεόν, οὗ ἡ οἰκία ἦν συνομοροῦσα
named Titius Justus, a worshiper of *{the}* God, whose *{the}* house was next door
3950 5517 2688 4936 3836 2536 4005 3836 3864 1639 5327
n.dsn n.gsm n.gsm pt.pm.gsm d.asm n.asm r.gsm d.nsf n.nsf v.iai.3s pt.pa.nsf

τῇ συναγωγῇ. 8Κρίσπος δὲ ὁ ἀρχισυνάγωγος ἐπίστευσεν τῷ κυρίῳ
⌊to the⌋ synagogue. Crispus, *{and}* the ruler of the synagogue, believed ⌊in the⌋ Lord,
3836 5252 3214 1254 3836 801 4409 3836 3261
d.dsf n.dsf n.nsm cj d.nsm n.nsm v.aai.3s d.dsm n.dsm

σὺν ὅλῳ τῷ οἴκῳ αὐτοῦ, καὶ πολλοὶ τῶν Κορινθίων
⌊together with⌋ his entire *{the}* household; *his* and many of the Corinthians
5250 899 3910 3836 3875 899 2779 4498 3836 3171
p.d a.dsm d.dsm n.dsm r.gsm.3 cj a.npm d.gpm a.gpm

ἀκούοντες ἐπίστευον καὶ ἐβαπτίζοντο. 9 εἶπεν δὲ ὁ κύριος
⌊upon hearing about⌋ it, believed and were baptized. And the Lord said *And* *the* *Lord*
201 4409 2779 966 1254 3836 3261 3306 1254 3836 3261
pt.pa.npm v.iai.3p cj v.ipi.3p v.aai.3s cj d.nsm n.nsm

NASB

from Italy with
his wife Priscilla,
because Claudius
had commanded all
the Jews to leave
Rome. He came to
them, 3and because
he was of the same
trade, he stayed
with them and they
were working, for
by trade they were
tent-makers. 4And
he was reasoning
in the synagogue
every Sabbath and
trying to persuade
Jews and Greeks.
5But when Silas
and Timothy came
down from Mace-
donia, Paul *began*
devoting himself
completely to the
word, solemnly
testifying to the
Jews that Jesus was
the Christ. 6But
when they resisted
and blasphemed,
he shook out his
garments and said
to them, "Your
blood *be* on your
own heads! I am
clean. From now
on I will go to the
Gentiles." 7Then he
left there and went
to the house of a
man named Titius
Justus, a worshiper
of God, whose
house was next
to the synagogue.
8Crispus, the leader
of the synagogue,
believed in the
Lord with all
his household,
and many of the
Corinthians when
they heard were
believing and being
baptized. 9And the
Lord said to Paul

NIV

to Paul in a vision:
"Do not be afraid;
keep on speaking,
do not be silent.
10 For I am with
you, and no one is
going to attack and
harm you, because
I have many peo-
ple in this city."
11 So Paul stayed in
Corinth for a year
and a half, teach-
ing them the word
of God.
12 While Gallio
was proconsul of
Achaia, the Jews
of Corinth made
a united attack on
Paul and brought
him to the place
of judgment.
13 "This man," they
charged, "is per-
suading the people
to worship God in
ways contrary to
the law."
14 Just as Paul
was about to
speak, Gallio said
to them, "If you
Jews were mak-
ing a complaint
about some misde-
meanor or serious
crime, it would be
reasonable for me
to listen to you.
15 But since it in-
volves questions
about words and
names and your
own law — settle
the matter your-
selves. I will not
be a judge of such
things." 16 So he
drove them off.
17 Then the crowd
there turned on
Sosthenes the syn-
agogue leader and
beat him in front
of the

ἐν νυκτὶ δι' ὁράματος τῷ Παύλῳ, ↱ μὴ φοβοῦ, ἀλλὰ
to Paul during the night in a vision, *to* *Paul* "Do not be afraid, but
3836 4263 1877 3816 1328 3969 3836 4263 5828 3590 5828 247
p.d n.dsf p.g n.gsn d.dsm n.dsm pl v.ppm.2s cj

λάλει καὶ ↱ μὴ σιωπήσῃς, 10 διότι ἐγώ εἰμι μετὰ σοῦ καὶ οὐδεὶς
⌞go on speaking⌟ and do not be silent, because I am with you and no one
3281 2779 4995 3590 4995 1484 1609 1639 3552 5148 2779 4029
v.pam.2s cj pl v.aas.2s cj r.ns.1 v.pai.1s p.g r.gs.2 cj a.nsm

ἐπιθήσεταί ← σοι τοῦ → κακῶσαί σε, διότι λαός ἐστί
will lay a hand on you to do you harm, *you* for I have many people *have*
2202 5148 3836 5148 2808 5148 1484 1609 1639 4498 3295 1639
v.fmi.3s r.ds.2 d.gsn f.aa r.as.2 cj n.nsm v.pai.3s

μοι πολὺς ἐν τῇ πόλει ταύτῃ. 11 ἐκάθισεν δὲ ἐνιαυτὸν καὶ
I *many* in *{the}* this city." *this* So he stayed *So* there a year and six
1609 4498 1877 3836 4047 4484 4047 1254 2767 1254 1929 2779 1971
r.ds.1 a.nsm p.d d.dsf n.dsf r.dsf v.aai.3s cj n.asm cj

μῆνας ἓξ διδάσκων ἐν αὐτοῖς τὸν λόγον τοῦ θεοῦ. 12 Γαλλίωνος
months, *six* teaching among them the word of God. But when Gallio
3604 1971 1438 1877 899 3836 3364 3836 2536 1254 1639 1136
n.apm a.apm pt.pa.nsm p.d r.dpm.3 d.asm n.asm d.gsm n.gsm n.gsm

δὲ ἀνθυπάτου ὄντος τῆς Ἀχαΐας κατεπέστησαν ὁμοθυμαδὸν ↰
But was proconsul *when was* of Achaia, the Jews rose up with one accord against
1254 1639 478 1639 3836 938 3836 2681 2987 3924 2987
cj n.gsm pt.pa.gsm d.gsf n.gsf v.aai.3p adv

οἱ Ἰουδαῖοι τῷ Παύλῳ καὶ ἤγαγον αὐτὸν ἐπὶ τὸ βῆμα 13 λέγοντες ὅτι
the *Jews* *{the}* Paul and brought him before the tribunal, saying, ~
3836 2681 3836 4263 2779 72 899 2093 3836 1037 3306 4022
d.npm a.npm d.dsm n.dsm cj v.aai.3p r.asm.3 p.a d.asn n.asn pt.pa.npm cj

παρὰ τὸν νόμον ἀναπείθει οὗτος τοὺς ἀνθρώπους σέβεσθαι τὸν
contrary to the *law* "This man is persuading *This man* *{the}* men to worship *{the}*
4123 3836 3795 4047 4047 400 4047 3836 476 4936 3836
p.a d.asm n.asm v.pai.3s r.nsm d.apm n.apm f.pm d.asm

θεόν. 14 → μέλλοντος δὲ τοῦ Παύλου
God in a way contrary to the law." But when Paul was about *But* *{the}* *Paul*
2536 4123 4123 3836 3795 1254 4263 3516 1254 3836 4263
n.asm pt.pa.gsm cj d.gsm n.gsm

ἀνοίγειν τὸ στόμα εἶπεν ὁ Γαλλίων πρὸς τοὺς Ἰουδαίους, εἰ μὲν ἦν
to open his mouth, Gallio said *{the}* *Gallio* to the Jews, "If ~ it were a
487 3836 5125 1136 3306 3836 1136 4639 3836 2681 1623 3525 1639
f.pa d.asn n.asn v.aai.3s d.nsm n.nsm p.a d.apm a.apm cj pl v.iai.3s

ἀδίκημά τι ἢ ῥᾳδιούργημα πονηρόν, ὦ Ἰουδαῖοι,
matter of wrongdoing *matter* or a serious piece of villainy, *serious piece* O Jews, it
5516 93 5516 2445 4505 4505 4815 4505 6043 2681
n.nsn r.nsn cj n.nsn a.nsn j a.vpm

⌞κατὰ λόγον⌟ ἂν ἀνεσχόμην ὑμῶν, 15 εἰ δὲ ζητήματά
would be reasonable *would* for me to put up with you. But if *But* the questions
323 2848 3364 323 462 7007 1254 1623 1254 2427
p.a n.asm pl v.ami.1s r.gp.2 cj cj n.npn

ἐστιν περὶ λόγου καὶ ὀνομάτων καὶ νόμου ⌞τοῦ καθ'⌟ ὑμᾶς, ὄψεσθε
are about a word and names and your own law, *own* *your* see to it
1639 4309 3364 2779 3950 2779 7007 3836 3795 3836 2848 7007 3972
v.pai.3s p.g n.gsm cj n.gpn cj n.gsm d.gsm p.a r.ap.2 v.fmi.2p

αὐτοί· κριτὴς ἐγὼ τούτων οὐ βούλομαι
yourselves. I do not wish to be a judge *I* ⌞of these matters."⌟ *not* *I do wish*
899 1609 1089 4024 1089 1639 1639 3216 1609 4047 4024 1089
r.npm n.nsm r.ns.1 r.gpn pl v.pmi.1s

εἶναι. 16 καὶ ἀπήλασεν αὐτοὺς ἀπὸ τοῦ βήματος. 17 ↱ ἐπιλαβόμενοι δὲ
to be And he drove them from the tribunal. And they all took hold of *And*
1639 2779 590 899 608 3836 1037 1254 5597 4246 2138 1254
f.pa cj v.aai.3s r.apm.3 p.g d.gsn n.gsn pt.am.npm cj

πάντες Σωσθένην τὸν ἀρχισυνάγωγον ἔτυπτον ἔμπροσθεν τοῦ
all Sosthenes, the ruler of the synagogue, and ⌞began to beat⌟ him in front of the
4246 5398 3836 801 5597 1869 3836
a.npm n.asm d.asm n.asm v.iai.3p p.g d.gsn

NASB

in the night by a
vision, "Do not be
afraid *any longer,*
but go on speaking
and do not be si-
lent; 10 for I am with
you, and no man
will attack you in
order to harm you,
for I have many
people in this city."
11 And he settled
there a year and six
months, teaching
the word of God
among them.
12 But while Gallio
was proconsul of
Achaia, the Jews
with one accord
rose up against
Paul and brought
him before the
judgment seat,
13 saying, "This
man persuades
men to worship
God contrary to the
law." 14 But when
Paul was about to
open his mouth,
Gallio said to the
Jews, "If it were a
matter of wrong or
of vicious crime,
O Jews, it would
be reasonable for
me to put up with
you; 15 but if there
are questions about
words and names
and your own
law, look after it
yourselves; I am
unwilling to be
a judge of these
matters." 16 And he
drove them away
from the judgment
seat. 17 And they all
took hold of Sos-
thenes, the leader
of the synagogue,
and *began* beating
him in front of the

NIV

proconsul; and
Gallio showed no
concern whatever.

Priscilla, Aquila and
Apollos

[18]Paul stayed
on in Corinth for
some time. Then
he left the broth-
ers and sisters and
sailed for Syria,
accompanied by
Priscilla and Aq-
uila. Before he
sailed, he had his
hair cut off at Cen-
chreae because of
a vow he had tak-
en. [19]They arrived
at Ephesus, where
Paul left Priscilla
and Aquila. He
himself went into
the synagogue and
reasoned with the
Jews. [20]When they
asked him to spend
more time with
them, he declined.
[21]But as he left, he
promised, "I will
come back if it is
God's will." Then
he set sail from
Ephesus. [22]When
he landed at Caes-
area, he went up
to Jerusalem and
greeted the church
and then went
down to Antioch.
[23]After spend-
ing some time in
Antioch, Paul set
out from there
and traveled from
place to place
throughout the re-
gion of Galatia and
Phrygia, strength-
ening all the dis-
ciples.
[24]Meanwhile a
Jew named Apol-
los, a native of Al-
exandria, came to
Ephesus. He was a
learned man, with
a thorough knowl-
edge of the Scrip-
tures. [25]He had
been instructed in
the way of the

βήματος· καὶ οὐδὲν τούτων τῷ Γαλλίωνι ἔμελεν.
tribunal. But none ˻of these things˼ were of concern to Gallio. *were of concern*
1037 2779 4029 4047 3508 3508 3508 3836 1136 3508
n.gsn cj a.nsn r.gpn d.dsm n.dsm v.iai.3s

[18] ὁ δὲ Παῦλος ἔτι προσμείνας → ἡμέρας ἱκανὰς
{the} {and} Paul, *{still}* ˻after remaining there˼ for a number of days, *number of* said
3836 1254 4263 2285 4693 2653 2653 2465 2653 698
d.nsm cj n.nsm adv pt.aa.nsm n.apf a.apf

τοῖς ἀδελφοῖς ἀποταξάμενος ἐξέπλει εἰς τὴν Συρίαν, καὶ σὺν αὐτῷ
farewell to the brothers *said farewell* and sailed away to *{the}* Syria, and with him
698 3836 81 698 1739 1650 3836 5353 2779 5250 899
d.dpm n.dpm pt.am.nsm v.iai.3s p.a d.asf n.asf cj p.d r.dsm.3

Πρίσκιλλα καὶ Ἀκύλας, → → κειράμενος ἐν Κεγχρεαῖς
were Priscilla and Aquila. At Cenchreae he had his head shaved, *At* *Cenchreae*
4572 2779 217 1877 3020 3836 3051 3025 1877 3020
n.nsf cj n.nsm pt.am.nsm p.d n.dpf

τὴν κεφαλήν, εἶχεν γὰρ εὐχήν. [19] κατήντησαν δὲ εἰς Ἔφεσον, →
his head for ˻he had taken˼ *for* a vow. And they went *And* to Ephesus, and
3836 3051 1142 2400 1142 2376 1254 2918 1254 1650 2387
d.asf n.asf v.iai.3s cj n.asf v.aai.3p cj p.a n.asf

κἀκεῖνους κατέλιπεν αὐτοῦ, ↱ αὐτὸς δὲ εἰσελθὼν εἰς τὴν
he left them *he left* there but he himself *but* went into the
2901 2901 2797 2901 7000 1254 1656 899 1254 1656 1650 3836
cj v.aai.3s adv r.nsm cj pt.aa.nsm p.a d.asf

συναγωγὴν διελέξατο τοῖς Ἰουδαίοις. [20] → ἐρωτώντων δὲ αὐτῶν
synagogue and reasoned with the Jews. When they asked *{and}* *they* him
5252 1363 3836 2681 899 2263 1254 899
n.asf v.ami.3s d.dpm a.dpm pt.pa.gpm cj r.gpm.3

ἐπὶ πλείονα χρόνον μεῖναι ↱ ↱ οὐκ ἐπένευσεν, [21] ἀλλὰ
to stay *{for}* a longer time, *to stay* he would not consent but
3531 3531 2093 4498 5989 3531 2153 2153 4024 2153 247
p.a a.asm.c n.asm f.aa pl v.aai.3s cj

ἀποταξάμενος καὶ εἰπών,[a] πάλιν ἀνακάμψω πρὸς ὑμᾶς τοῦ θεοῦ
bade farewell, *{and}* saying, *again* ˻"I will come back˼ to you again, *{the}* God
698 2779 3306 4099 366 4639 7007 4099 3836 2536
pt.am.nsm cj pt.aa.nsm adv v.fai.1s p.a r.ap.2 d.gsm n.gsm

θέλοντος, ἀνήχθη ἀπὸ τῆς Ἐφέσου, [22] καὶ κατελθὼν εἰς Καισάρειαν,
willing." Then he set sail from *{the}* Ephesus, and ˻when he touched land˼ at Caesarea,
2527 343 608 3836 2387 2779 2982 1650 2791
pt.pa.gsm v.api.3s p.g d.gsf n.gsf cj pt.aa.nsm p.a n.asf

↱ ἀναβὰς καὶ ἀσπασάμενος τὴν ἐκκλησίαν κατέβη εἰς Ἀντιόχειαν.
he went up and greeted the church and then went down to Antioch.
2849 326 2779 832 3836 1711 2849 1650 522
pt.aa.nsm cj pt.am.nsm d.asf n.asf v.aai.3s p.a n.asf

[23] καὶ ποιήσας χρόνον τινὰ ἐξῆλθεν διερχόμενος
{and} After spending some time *some* there, he departed and made his way
2779 4472 5516 5989 5516 2002 1451
cj pt.aa.nsm n.asm r.asm v.aai.3s pt.pm.nsm

καθεξῆς ↰ τὴν Γαλατικὴν χώραν καὶ Φρυγίαν, ἐπιστηρίζων πάντας
˻from place to place˼ through the Galatian country and Phrygia, strengthening all
2759 1451 3836 1131 6001 2779 5867 2185 4246
adv d.asf a.asf n.asf cj n.asf pt.pa.nsm a.apm

τοὺς μαθητάς. [24] Ἰουδαῖος δέ τις Ἀπολλῶς ὀνόματι,
the disciples. Now a Jew *Now a* named Apollos, *named* an
3836 3412 1254 5516 2681 1254 5516 3950 663 3950
d.apm n.apm a.nsm cj r.nsm n.nsm n.dsn

Ἀλεξανδρεὺς τῷ γένει, ἀνὴρ λόγιος, κατήντησεν εἰς Ἔφεσον,
Alexandrian by race, *man eloquent* arrived in Ephesus. He was an eloquent man,
233 3836 1169 467 3360 2918 1650 2387 3360 467
n.nsm d.dsn n.dsn n.nsm a.nsm v.aai.3s p.a n.asf

˻δυνατὸς ὢν˼ ἐν ταῖς γραφαῖς. [25] οὗτος ἦν κατηχημένος τὴν ὁδὸν τοῦ
well-versed in the Scriptures. He ˻had been˼ instructed in the way of the
1543 1639 1877 3836 1210 4047 1639 2994 3836 3847 3836
a.nsm pt.pa.nsm p.d d.dpf n.dpf r.nsm v.iai.3s pt.rp.nsm d.asf n.asf d.gsm

[a] δεῖ με πάντως τὴν ἑορτὴν τὴν ἐρχομένην ποιῆσαι εἰς Ἱεροσόλυμα included by TR after εἰπών.

NASB

judgment seat. But
Gallio was not con-
cerned about any
of these things.
[18]Paul, having
remained many
days longer, took
leave of the breth-
ren and put out to
sea for Syria, and
with him were
Priscilla and Aq-
uila. In Cenchrea
he had his hair cut,
for he was keep-
ing a vow. [19]They
came to Ephesus,
and he left them
there. Now he
himself entered
the synagogue and
reasoned with the
Jews. [20]When they
asked him to stay
for a longer time,
he did not consent,
[21]but taking leave
of them and say-
ing, "I will return
to you again if God
wills," he set sail
from Ephesus.
[22]When he had
landed at Caesarea,
he went up and
greeted the church,
and went down to
Antioch.

Third Missionary Journey

[23]And having spent
some time *there,* he
left and passed suc-
cessively through
the Galatian re-
gion and Phrygia,
strengthening all
the disciples.
[24]Now a Jew
named Apollos,
an Alexandrian by
birth, an eloquent
man, came to
Ephesus; and he
was mighty in the
Scriptures. [25]This
man had been in-
structed in the way
of the

NIV

Lord, and he spoke
with great fervor[a]
and taught about
Jesus accurately,
though he knew
only the baptism of
John. 26He began
to speak boldly
in the synagogue.
When Priscilla and
Aquila heard him,
they invited him to
their home and ex-
plained to him the
way of God more
adequately.
27When Apol-
los wanted to go
to Achaia, the
brothers and sis-
ters encouraged
him and wrote to
the disciples there
to welcome him.
When he arrived,
he was a great
help to those who
by grace had be-
lieved. 28For he
vigorously refuted
his Jewish oppo-
nents in public de-
bate, proving from
the Scriptures that
Jesus was the Mes-
siah.

Paul in Ephesus

19 While
Apollos
was at Corinth,
Paul took the road
through the inte-
rior and arrived at
Ephesus. There he
found some dis-
ciples 2and asked
them, "Did you
receive the Holy
Spirit when[b] you
believed?"
They answered,
"No, we have not
even heard that
there is a Holy
Spirit."
3So Paul asked,
"Then what bap-
tism did you re-
ceive?"
"John's baptism,"
they replied.

[a] 25 Or *with fervor in the Spirit*
[b] 2 Or *after*

κυρίου καὶ ζέων τῷ πνεύματι ἐλάλει καὶ ἐδίδασκεν ἀκριβῶς τὰ περὶ
Lord; and ⌞being fervent⌟ in spirit, he spoke and taught accurately the facts about
3261 2779 2417 3836 4460 3281 2779 1438 209 3836 4309
n.gsm cj pt.pa.nsm d.dsn n.dsn v.iai.3s cj v.iai.3s adv d.apn p.g

τοῦ Ἰησοῦ, ἐπιστάμενος μόνον τὸ βάπτισμα Ἰωάννου· 26 οὗτός τε ἤρξατο
{the} Jesus, though he knew only the baptism of John. He ~ began
3836 2652 2179 3667 3836 967 2722 4047 5445 806
d.gsm n.gsm pt.pp.nsm adv d.asn n.asn n.gsm r.nsm cj v.ami.3s

παρρησιάζεσθαι ἐν τῇ συναγωγῇ. ἀκούσαντες δὲ αὐτοῦ Πρίσκιλλα καὶ
to speak boldly in the synagogue, but when they heard *but* him, Priscilla and
4245 1877 3836 5252 1254 201 1254 899 4572 2779
f.pm p.d d.dsf n.dsf pt.aa.npm cj r.gsm.3 n.nsf cj

Ἀκύλας προσελάβοντο αὐτὸν καὶ ἀκριβέστερον αὐτῷ ἐξέθεντο τὴν ὁδὸν
Aquila took him and explained more accurately to him *explained* the way
217 4689 899 2779 1758 209 899 1758 3836 3847
n.nsm v.ami.3p r.asm.3 cj adv.c r.dsm.3 v.ami.3p d.asf n.asf

[a]τοῦ θεοῦ. 27 → βουλομένου δὲ αὐτοῦ διελθεῖν εἰς τὴν Ἀχαΐαν,
of God. And when he wanted *And* *he* ⌞to continue on⌟ into *{the}* Achaia,
3836 2536 1254 899 1089 1254 899 1451 1650 3836 938
d.gsm n.gsm pt.pm.gsm cj r.gsm.3 f.aa p.a d.asf n.asf

προτρεψάμενοι οἱ ἀδελφοὶ ἔγραψαν τοῖς μαθηταῖς ἀποδέξασθαι
the brothers encouraged *the* *brothers* him and wrote to the disciples to welcome
3836 81 4730 3836 81 1211 3836 3412 622
pt.am.npm d.npm n.npm v.aai.3p d.dpm n.dpm f.am

αὐτόν, ↱ ὃς παραγενόμενος → συνεβάλετο πολὺ τοῖς
him. When he arrived there, he greatly helped *greatly* those
899 4134 4005 4134 4498 5202 4498 3836
r.asm.3 r.nsm pt.am.nsm v.ami.3s adv d.dpm

πεπιστευκόσιν διὰ τῆς χάριτος· 28 εὐτόνως γὰρ τοῖς
⌞who had come to believe⌟ through *{the}* grace, for he powerfully *for* refuted the
4409 1328 3836 5921 1142 1352 2364 1142 1352 3836
pt.ra.dpm p.g d.gsf n.gsf adv cj d.dpm

Ἰουδαίοις διακατηλέγχετο δημοσίᾳ ἐπιδεικνὺς διὰ τῶν γραφῶν εἶναι τὸν
Jews *he refuted* in public, demonstrating by the Scriptures that Jesus was the
2681 1352 1323 2109 1328 3836 1210 2652 1639 3836
a.dpm v.imi.3s a.dsf pt.pa.nsm p.g d.gpf n.gpf f.pa d.asm

χριστὸν Ἰησοῦν.
Messiah. *Jesus*
5986 2652
n.asm n.asm

19:1 ἐγένετο δὲ ἐν τῷ τὸν Ἀπολλῶ εἶναι ἐν Κορίνθῳ Παῦλον
And ⌞it happened that⌟ *And* while ~ *{the}* Apollos was at Corinth, Paul
1254 1181 1254 1877 3836 3836 663 1639 1877 3172 4263
v.ami.3s cj p.d d.dsn d.asm n.asm f.pa p.d n.dsf n.asm

διελθόντα τὰ ἀνωτερικὰ μέρη ἐλθεῖν[b] εἰς Ἔφεσον καὶ εὑρεῖν τινας
went through the inland regions and came to Ephesus. *{and}* There he found some
1451 3836 541 3538 2262 1650 2387 2779 2351 5516
pt.aa.asm d.apn a.apn n.apn f.aa p.a n.asf cj f.aa r.apm

μαθητὰς 2 εἶπέν τε πρὸς αὐτούς, εἰ πνεῦμα ἅγιον
disciples and said *and* to them, *{if}* "Did you receive the Holy Spirit *Holy*
3412 5445 3306 5445 4639 899 1623 3284 3284 3284 41 4460 41
n.apm v.aai.3s cj p.a r.apm.3 cj n.asn a.asn

ἐλάβετε πιστεύσαντες; οἱ δὲ πρὸς αὐτόν, ἀλλ᾽ οὐδ᾽
Did you receive when you believed?" They *{and}* said to him, "Why, we have not even heard
3284 4409 3836 1254 4639 899 247 201 201 4028 201
v.aai.2p pt.aa.npm d.npm cj p.a r.asm.3 cj adv

εἰ πνεῦμα ἅγιον ἔστιν ἠκούσαμεν. 3 εἶπέν τε, εἰς τί
if there is a Holy Spirit." *Holy* *there is* *we have heard* So Paul asked, *So* "Into what
1623 1639 1639 41 4460 41 1639 201 5445 3306 5445 1650 5515
cj n.nsn a.nsn v.pai.3s v.aai.1p v.aai.3s cj p.a r.asn

οὖν ἐβαπτίσθητε; οἱ δὲ εἶπαν, εἰς τὸ Ἰωάννου βάπτισμα.
then were you baptized?" And they *And* replied, "Into the baptism of John." *baptism*
4036 966 1254 3836 1254 3306 1650 3836 967 2722 967
cj v.api.2p d.npm cj v.aai.3p p.a d.asn n.gsm n.asn

[a] [τοῦ θεοῦ] UBS.
[b] ἐλθεῖν TNIV, NET. [κατ]ελθεῖν UBS.

NASB

Lord; and being
fervent in spirit, he
was speaking and
teaching accurately
the things concern-
ing Jesus, being
acquainted only
with the baptism
of John; 26and he
began to speak
out boldly in the
synagogue. But
when Priscilla and
Aquila heard him,
they took him aside
and explained to
him the way of
God more accu-
rately. 27And when
he wanted to go
across to Achaia,
the brethren en-
couraged him and
wrote to the dis-
ciples to welcome
him; and when
he had arrived,
he greatly helped
those who had
believed through
grace, 28for he
powerfully refuted
the Jews in public,
demonstrating
by the Scriptures
that Jesus was the
Christ.

Paul at Ephesus

19:1It happened that
while Apollos was
at Corinth, Paul
passed through the
upper country and
came to Ephesus,
and found some
disciples. 2He said
to them, "Did you
receive the Holy
Spirit when you
believed?" And
they *said* to him,
"No, we have not
even heard whether
there is a Holy
Spirit." 3And he
said, "Into what
then were you bap-
tized?" And they
said, "Into John's
baptism."

NIV

[4]Paul said, "John's
baptism was a
baptism of repen-
tance. He told the
people to believe
in the one com-
ing after him, that
is, in Jesus." [5]On
hearing this, they
were baptized in
the name of the
Lord Jesus. [6]When
Paul placed his
hands on them, the
Holy Spirit came
on them, and they
spoke in tongues[a]
and prophesied.
[7]There were about
twelve men in all.
[8]Paul entered the
synagogue and
spoke boldly there
for three months,
arguing persua-
sively about the
kingdom of God.
[9]But some of them
became obstinate;
they refused to be-
lieve and publicly
maligned the Way.
So Paul left them.
He took the disci-
ples with him and
had discussions
daily in the lecture
hall of Tyrannus.
[10]This went on for
two years, so that
all the Jews and
Greeks who lived
in the province
of Asia heard the
word of the Lord.
[11]God did extra-
ordinary miracles
through Paul, [12]so
that even handker-
chiefs and aprons
that had touched
him were taken to
the sick, and

4 εἶπεν δὲ Παῦλος, Ἰωάννης ἐβάπτισεν → βάπτισμα μετανοίας τῷ
Paul said, {and} Paul "John baptized with a baptism of repentance, telling the
4263 3306 1254 4263 2722 966 967 3567 3306 3836
v.aai.3s cj n.nsm n.nsm v.aai.3s n.asn n.gsf d.dsm

λαῷ λέγων εἰς τὸν ἐρχόμενον μετ' αὐτὸν ἵνα πιστεύσωσιν, τοῦτ' ἔστιν
people telling to believe in the one coming after him, to believe that is,
3295 3306 2671 4409 1650 3836 2262 3552 899 2671 4409 4047 1639
n.dsm pt.pa.nsm p.a d.asm pt.pm.asm p.a r.asm.3 cj v.aas.3p r.nsn v.pai.3s

εἰς τὸν Ἰησοῦν. 5 ἀκούσαντες δὲ ἐβαπτίσθησαν εἰς τὸ ὄνομα τοῦ κυρίου
in {the} Jesus." Upon hearing this, {and} they were baptized in the name of the Lord
1650 3836 2652 201 1254 966 1650 3836 3950 3836 3261
p.a d.asm n.asm pt.aa.npm cj v.api.3p p.a d.asn n.asn d.gsm n.gsm

Ἰησοῦ. 6 καὶ → ἐπιθέντος ← αὐτοῖς τοῦ Παύλου τὰς[a] χεῖρας
Jesus. And when Paul laid his hands on them, {the} Paul his hands the
2652 2779 4263 2202 3836 5931 899 3836 4263 3836 5931 3836
n.gsm cj pt.aa.gsm r.dpm.3 d.gsm n.gsm d.apf n.apf

ἦλθε τὸ πνεῦμα τὸ ἅγιον ἐπ' αὐτούς, ἐλάλουν τε → γλώσσαις
Holy Spirit came the Spirit {the} Holy on them, and they spoke and in tongues
41 4460 2262 3836 4460 3836 41 2093 899 5445 3281 5445 1185
v.aai.3s d.nsn n.nsn d.nsn a.nsn p.a r.apm.3 v.iai.3p cj n.dpf

καὶ ἐπροφήτευον. 7 ἦσαν δὲ οἱ πάντες ἄνδρες ὡσεὶ δώδεκα. 8
and prophesied. And the men were And the in all men about twelve. And
2779 4736 1254 3836 467 1639 1254 3836 4246 467 6059 1557 1254
cj v.iai.3p v.iai.3p cj d.npm a.npm n.npm pl a.npm

↱ εἰσελθὼν δὲ εἰς τὴν συναγωγὴν ἐπαρρησιάζετο ἐπὶ μῆνας τρεῖς
he went And into the synagogue and spoke boldly for three months, three
4245 1656 1254 1650 3836 5252 4245 2093 5552 3604 5552
pt.aa.nsm cj p.a d.asf n.asf v.imi.3s p.a n.apm a.apm

διαλεγόμενος καὶ πείθων τὰ[b] περὶ τῆς βασιλείας τοῦ
reasoning and persuading them concerning the concerning things of the kingdom of
1363 2779 4275 4309 3836 4309 3836 993 3836
pt.pm.nsm cj pt.pa.nsm d.apn p.g d.gsf n.gsf d.gsm

θεοῦ. 9 ὡς δέ τινες ἐσκληρύνοντο καὶ ἠπείθουν κακολογοῦντες τὴν
God. But when But some became stubborn and refused to believe, speaking evil of the
2536 1254 6055 1254 5516 5020 2779 578 2800 3836
n.gsm cj cj r.npm v.ipi.3p cj v.iai.3p pt.pa.npm d.asf

ὁδὸν ἐνώπιον τοῦ πλήθους, ↱ ἀποστὰς ἀπ' αὐτῶν ἀφώρισεν τοὺς μαθητὰς
Way before the congregation, he withdrew from them, taking the disciples with
3847 1967 3836 4436 928 923 608 899 928 3836 3412
n.asf p.g d.gsn n.gsn pt.aa.nsm p.g r.gpm.3 v.aai.3s d.apm n.apm

↱ ⌊καθ' ἡμέραν⌋ διαλεγόμενος ἐν τῇ σχολῇ Τυράννου.
him, and continued daily to discourse in the ⌊lecture hall⌋ of Tyrannus.
1363 2848 2465 1363 1877 3836 5391 5598
p.a n.asf pt.pm.nsm p.d d.dsf n.dsf n.gsm

10 τοῦτο δὲ ἐγένετο ἐπὶ ἔτη δύο, ὥστε πάντας τοὺς κατοικοῦντας τὴν
This {and} went on for two years, two so that all the residents of {the}
4047 1254 1181 2093 1545 2291 1545 6063 4246 3836 2997 3836
r.nsn cj v.ami.3s p.a n.apn a.apn cj a.apm d.apm pt.pa.apm d.asf

Ἀσίαν ἀκοῦσαι τὸν λόγον τοῦ κυρίου, Ἰουδαίους τε καὶ Ἕλληνας. 11
Asia heard the word of the Lord, both Jews both and Greeks. They
823 201 3836 3364 3836 3261 5445 2681 5445 2779 1818
n.asf f.aa d.asm n.asm d.gsm n.gsm a.apm cj cj n.apm

δυνάμεις τε οὐ τὰς τυχούσας ὁ θεὸς ἐποίει διὰ τῶν
were no ordinary miracles ~ no {the} ordinary that {the} God was doing by the
4024 5593 1539 5445 4024 3836 5593 3836 2536 4472 1328 3836
n.apf cj pl d.apf pt.aa.apf d.nsm n.nsm v.iai.3s p.g d.gpf

χειρῶν Παύλου, 12 ὥστε καὶ ἐπὶ τοὺς ἀσθενοῦντας
hands of Paul, so that {also} for the sick handkerchiefs and aprons
5931 4263 6063 2779 2093 3836 820 5051 2445 4980
n.gpf n.gsm cj adv p.a d.apm pt.pa.apm

ἀποφέρεσθαι ἀπὸ τοῦ χρωτὸς αὐτοῦ σουδάρια ἢ σιμικίνθια καὶ
were carried off from {the} his body his handkerchiefs and aprons for the sick, and
708 608 3836 899 5999 899 5051 2445 4980 2093 3836 820 2779
f.pp p.g d.gsm n.gsm r.gsm.3 n.apn cj n.apn cj

NASB

[4]Paul said, "John
baptized with the
baptism of repen-
tance, telling the
people to believe
in Him who was
coming after him,
that is, in Jesus."
[5]When they heard
this, they were
baptized in the
name of the Lord
Jesus. [6]And when
Paul had laid his
hands upon them,
the Holy Spirit
came on them, and
they *began* speak-
ing with tongues
and prophesying.
[7]There were in all
about twelve men.
[8]And he entered
the synagogue and
continued speaking
out boldly for three
months, reasoning
and persuading
them about the
kingdom of God.
[9]But when some
were becoming
hardened and dis-
obedient, speaking
evil of the Way
before the people,
he withdrew from
them and took
away the disciples,
reasoning daily
in the school of
Tyrannus. [10]This
took place for two
years, so that all
who lived in Asia
heard the word of
the Lord, both Jews
and Greeks.

Miracles at Ephesus

[11]God was per-
forming extraordi-
nary miracles by
the hands of Paul,
[12]so that handker-
chiefs or aprons
were even carried
from his body to
the sick, and the

[a] 6 Or *other languages*

[a] [τὰς] UBS, omitted by TNIV.
[b] [τὰ] UBS, omitted by TNIV.

NIV

their illnesses
were cured and
the evil spirits left
them.
13 Some Jews who
went around driv-
ing out evil spirits
tried to invoke
the name of the
Lord Jesus over
those who were
demon-possessed.
They would say,
"In the name of the
Jesus whom Paul
preaches, I com-
mand you to come
out." 14 Seven sons
of Sceva, a Jewish
chief priest, were
doing this. 15 One
day the evil spirit
answered them,
"Jesus I know,
and Paul I know
about, but who are
you?" 16 Then the
man who had the
evil spirit jumped
on them and over-
powered them
all. He gave them
such a beating that
they ran out of the
house naked and
bleeding.
17 When this be-
came known to the
Jews and Greeks
living in Ephe-
sus, they were all
seized with fear,
and the name of
the Lord Jesus was
held in high honor.
18 Many of those
who believed now
came and openly
confessed what
they had done. 19 A
number who had
practiced sorcery

ἀπαλλάσσεσθαι ἀπ᾽ αὐτῶν τὰς νόσους, τά τε πνεύματα τὰ πονηρὰ
diseases were driven away by them {the} diseases {the} and evil spirits {the} evil
3798 557 608 899 3836 3798 3836 5445 4505 4460 3836 4505
f.pp p.g r.gpm.3 d.apf n.apf d.apn cj n.apn d.apn a.apn

ἐκπορεύεσθαι. 13 ἐπεχείρησαν δέ τινες καὶ τῶν περιερχομένων Ἰουδαίων
came out. tried But some also of the itinerant Jews,
1744 2217 1254 5516 2779 3836 4320 2681
f.pm v.aai.3p cj r.npm adv d.gpm pt.pm.gpm a.gpm

ἐξορκιστῶν ὀνομάζειν ἐπὶ τοὺς ἔχοντας τὰ
exorcists, tried to invoke the name of the Lord Jesus over those having {the} evil
2020 2217 3951 3836 3950 3836 3836 3261 2652 2093 3836 2400 3836 4505
n.gpm f.pa p.a d.apm pt.pa.apm d.apn

πνεύματα τὰ πονηρὰ τὸ ὄνομα τοῦ κυρίου Ἰησοῦ λέγοντες, ὁρκίζω ὑμᾶς ↰ τὸν
spirits, {the} evil the name of the Lord Jesus saying, "I adjure you by that
4460 3836 4505 3836 3950 3836 3261 2652 3306 3991 7007 3991 3836
n.apn d.apn a.apn d.asn n.asn d.gsm n.gsm n.gsm pt.pa.npm v.pai.1s r.ap.2 d.asm

Ἰησοῦν ὃν Παῦλος κηρύσσει. 14 ἦσαν δέ → τινος
Jesus whom Paul proclaims." ⌊There were⌋ {and} seven sons of a man named
2652 4005 4263 3062 1639 1254 2231 5626 5516
n.asm r.asm n.nsm v.pai.3s v.iai.3p cj r.gsm

Σκευᾶ Ἰουδαίου ἀρχιερέως ἑπτὰ υἱοὶ τοῦτο ποιοῦντες. 15
Sceva, a Jewish high priest, seven sons who were doing this. who were doing But the
5005 2681 797 2231 5626 4472 4472 4472 4047 4472 1254 3836
n.gsm a.gsm n.gsm a.npm n.npm r.asn pt.pa.npm

ἀποκριθὲν δὲ τὸ πνεῦμα τὸ πονηρὸν εἶπεν αὐτοῖς, τὸν μὲν[a] Ἰησοῦν
evil spirit answering But the spirit {the} evil said to them, {the} ~ "Jesus
4505 4460 646 1254 3836 4460 3836 4505 3306 899 3836 3525 2652
pt.ap.nsn cj d.nsn n.nsn d.nsn a.nsn v.aai.3s r.dpm.3 d.asm pl n.asm

γινώσκω καὶ τὸν Παῦλον ἐπίσταμαι, ὑμεῖς δὲ τίνες ἐστέ; 16 καὶ ἐφαλόμενος
I know, and {the} Paul I recognize, you but who are you?" And leaped
1182 2779 3836 4263 2179 7007 1254 5515 1639 7007 2779 2383
v.pai.1s cj d.asm n.asm v.ppi.1s r.np.2 cj r.npm v.pai.2p cj pt.am.nsm

ὁ ἄνθρωπος ἐπ᾽ αὐτοὺς ἐν ᾧ ἦν τὸ πνεῦμα τὸ πονηρόν,
the man on them in whom was the evil spirit {the} evil leaped on
3836 476 2093 899 1877 4005 1639 3836 4505 4460 3836 4505 2383 2093
d.nsm n.nsm p.a r.apm.3 p.d r.dsm v.iai.3s d.nsn n.nsn d.nsn a.nsn

κατακυριεύσας ἀμφοτέρων ἴσχυσεν κατ᾽ αὐτῶν ὥστε
them, took control all and overpowered all seven of them, so that they fled,
899 2894 317 2710 317 2848 899 6063 1767 1767
pt.aa.nsm a.gpm v.aai.3s p.g r.gpm.3 cj

γυμνοὺς καὶ τετραυματισμένους ἐκφυγεῖν ἐκ τοῦ οἴκου ἐκείνου. 17
naked and wounded, they fled ⌊out of⌋ {the} that house. that And
1218 2779 5547 1767 1666 3836 1697 3875 1697 1254
a.apm cj pt.rp.apm f.aa p.g d.gsm n.gsm r.gsm

τοῦτο δὲ ἐγένετο γνωστὸν πᾶσιν Ἰουδαίοις τε καὶ Ἕλλησιν τοῖς κατοικοῦσιν
this And became known to all the Jews ~ and Greeks who lived in
4047 1254 1181 1196 4246 2681 5445 2779 1818 3836 2997
r.nsn cj v.ami.3s a.nsn a.dpm a.dpm cj cj n.dpm d.dpm pt.pa.dpm

τὴν Ἔφεσον καὶ ἐπέπεσεν φόβος ἐπὶ πάντας αὐτοὺς καὶ ἐμεγαλύνετο τὸ
{the} Ephesus. And fear fell fear upon them all, them and was exalted the
3836 2387 2779 5832 2158 5832 2093 899 4246 899 2779 3486 3836
d.asf n.asf cj v.aai.3s n.nsm p.a a.apm r.apm.3 cj v.ipi.3s d.nsn

ὄνομα τοῦ κυρίου Ἰησοῦ. 18 πολλοί τε τῶν
name of the Lord Jesus was exalted. Also many Also of those
3950 3836 3261 2652 3486 3486 5445 4498 5445 3836
n.nsn d.gsm n.gsm n.gsm a.npm cj d.gpm

πεπιστευκότων ἤρχοντο ἐξομολογούμενοι καὶ ἀναγγέλλοντες τὰς
⌊who had become believers⌋ kept coming, confessing and divulging {the} their
4409 2262 2018 2779 334 3836 899
pt.ra.gpm v.imi.3p pt.pm.npm cj pt.pa.npm d.apf

πράξεις αὐτῶν. 19 ἱκανοὶ δὲ τῶν τὰ περίεργα
practices. their And a number And of those who had practiced {the} magic arts
4552 899 1254 2653 1254 3836 4556 4556 4556 3836 4319
n.apf r.gpm.3 a.npm cj d.gpm d.apn n.apn

NASB

diseases left them
and the evil spirits
went out. 13 But
also some of the
Jewish exorcists,
who went from
place to place,
attempted to name
over those who
had the evil spirits
the name of the
Lord Jesus, saying,
"I adjure you by
Jesus whom Paul
preaches." 14 Seven
sons of one Sceva,
a Jewish chief
priest, were doing
this. 15 And the evil
spirit answered
and said to them,
"I recognize Jesus,
and I know about
Paul, but who are
you?" 16 And the
man, in whom
was the evil spirit,
leaped on them
and subdued all of
them and overpow-
ered them, so that
they fled out of that
house naked and
wounded. 17 This
became known
to all, both Jews
and Greeks, who
lived in Ephesus;
and fear fell upon
them all and the
name of the Lord
Jesus was being
magnified. 18 Many
also of those who
had believed kept
coming, confessing
and disclosing their
practices. 19 And
many of those who
practiced magic

[a] [μὲν] UBS.

NIV

brought their
scrolls together
and burned them
publicly. When
they calculated
the value of the
scrolls, the total
came to fifty thou-
sand drachmas.[a]
20 In this way the
word of the Lord
spread widely and
grew in power.
21 After all this
had happened,
Paul decided[b] to
go to Jerusalem,
passing through
Macedonia and
Achaia. "After I
have been there,"
he said, "I must
visit Rome also."
22 He sent two of
his helpers, Timo-
thy and Erastus, to
Macedonia, while
he stayed in the
province of Asia a
little longer.

The Riot in Ephesus

23 About that
time there arose a
great disturbance
about the Way.
24 A silversmith
named Demetrius,
who made silver
shrines of Arte-
mis, brought in
a lot of business
for the craftsmen
there. 25 He called
them together,
along with the
workers in related
trades, and said:
"You know, my
friends, that we
receive a good
income from this
business. 26 And
you see and hear
how this fellow
Paul has convinced
and led astray
large numbers

πραξάντων συνενέγκαντες τὰς βίβλους κατέκαιον ← ἐνώπιον πάντων,
who had practiced collected their books and burned them up in the sight of all.
4556 5237 3836 1047 2876 1967 4246
pt.aa.gpm pt.aa.npm d.apf n.apf v.iai.3p p.g a.gpm

καὶ συνεψήφισαν τὰς τιμὰς αὐτῶν καὶ εὗρον ἀργυρίου ⌊μυριάδας πέντε.⌋
And they calculated the value of them and found *pieces of silver* it to be fifty thousand
2779 5248 3836 5507 899 2779 2351 736 3689 4297
cj v.aai.3p d.apf n.apf r.gpf.3 cj v.aai.3p n.gsn n.apf a.apf

20 οὕτως κατὰ κράτος τοῦ κυρίου ὁ λόγος
pieces of silver. So *in* *power* the word of the Lord *the* *word*
736 736 736 4048 2848 3197 3836 3364 3836 3261 3836 3364
adv p.a n.asn d.gsm n.gsm d.nsm n.nsm

ηὔξανεν καὶ ἴσχυεν. 21 ὡς δὲ ἐπληρώθη
⌊continued to spread⌋ and grow in power. Now after *Now* all these things had taken place,
889 2779 2710 2848 3197 1254 6055 1254 4047 4047 4444
v.iai.3s cj v.iai.3s cj cj v.api.3s

ταῦτα, ἔθετο ὁ Παῦλος ἐν τῷ πνεύματι ↱ διελθὼν τὴν
these things Paul resolved *{the}* *Paul* in *{the}* spirit to pass through *{the}*
4047 4263 5502 3836 4263 1877 3836 4460 4513 1451 3836
r.npn v.ami.3s d.nsm n.nsm p.d d.dsn n.dsn pt.aa.nsm d.asf

Μακεδονίαν καὶ Ἀχαΐαν πορεύεσθαι εἰς Ἱεροσόλυμα εἰπὼν ὅτι μετὰ τὸ
Macedonia and Achaia and go on to Jerusalem, saying, ~ "After *{the}* I
3423 2779 938 4513 1650 2642 3306 4022 3552 3836 1609
n.asf cj n.asf f.pm p.a n.apn pt.aa.nsm cj p.a d.asn

γενέσθαι με ἐκεῖ δεῖ με καὶ Ῥώμην ἰδεῖν. 22 ἀποστείλας δὲ εἰς
have been *I* there, I must *I* also see Rome." *see* So after sending *So* to
1181 1609 1695 1609 1256 1609 2779 1625 4873 1625 1254 690 1254 1650
f.am r.as.1 adv v.pai.3s r.as.1 adv n.asf f.aa pt.aa.nsm cj p.a

τὴν Μακεδονίαν δύο τῶν διακονούντων αὐτῷ, Τιμόθεον καὶ Ἔραστον, ↱
{the} Macedonia two of those who were helping him, Timothy and Erastus, he
3836 3423 1545 3836 1354 899 5510 2779 2235 2091
d.asf n.asf a.apm d.gpm pt.pa.gpm r.dsm.3 n.asm cj n.asm

αὐτὸς ἐπέσχεν → χρόνον εἰς τὴν Ἀσίαν. 23 ἐγένετο δὲ
himself stayed for a time in *{the}* Asia. About that time ⌊there broke out⌋ *{and}*
899 2091 5989 1650 3836 823 2848 1697 2789 1181 1254
r.nsm v.aai.3s n.asm p.a d.asf n.asf v.ami.3s cj

κατὰ τὸν καιρὸν ἐκεῖνον τάραχος οὐκ ὀλίγος περὶ τῆς ὁδοῦ. 24
About *{the}* *time* *that* no little disturbance *no* *little* concerning the Way. For a
2848 3836 2789 1697 4024 3900 5431 4024 3900 4309 3836 3847 1142
p.a d.asm n.asm r.asm n.nsm pl a.nsm p.g d.gsf n.gsf

Δημήτριος γάρ τις ὀνόματι, ἀργυροκόπος, ποιῶν ναοὺς ἀργυροῦς
man named Demetrius, *For* *man* *named* a silversmith, who made silver shrines *silver*
5516 3950 1320 1142 5516 3950 737 4472 739 3724 739
n.nsm cj r.nsm n.dsn n.nsm pt.pa.nsm n.apm a.apm

Ἀρτέμιδος παρείχετο τοῖς τεχνίταις οὐκ ὀλίγην ἐργασίαν, 25 ↱
of Artemis, brought no little business to the craftsmen. *no* *little* *business* He
783 4218 4024 3900 2238 3836 5493 4024 3900 2238 3306
n.gsf v.imi.3s d.dpm n.dpm pl a.asf n.asf

↱ οὓς συναθροίσας καὶ τοὺς περὶ τὰ τοιαῦτα ἐργάτας εἶπεν,
called them together with *{the}* workmen in *{the}* similar trades, *workmen* and said,
5255 4005 5255 2779 3836 2239 4309 3836 5525 2239 3306
r.apm pt.aa.nsm adv d.apm p.a d.apn r.apn n.apm v.aai.3s

ἄνδρες, ἐπίστασθε ὅτι ἐκ ταύτης τῆς ἐργασίας ἡ εὐπορία ἡμῖν ἐστιν
"Men, you know that from this *{the}* trade *{the}* prosperity comes to us. *comes*
467 2179 4022 1666 4047 3836 2238 3836 2345 1639 7005 1639
n.vpm v.ppi.2p cj p.g r.gsf d.gsf n.gsf d.nsf n.nsf r.dp.1 v.pai.3s

26 καὶ θεωρεῖτε καὶ ἀκούετε ὅτι οὐ μόνον Ἐφέσου ἀλλὰ σχεδὸν πάσης τῆς
And you see and hear that not only in Ephesus but in almost all of
2779 2555 2779 201 4022 4024 3667 2387 247 5385 4246 3836
cj v.pai.2p cj v.pai.2p cj pl adv n.gsf cj adv a.gsf d.gsf

Ἀσίας ὁ Παῦλος οὗτος πείσας μετέστησεν ἱκανὸν
Asia *{the}* this Paul *this* has persuaded and turned away a considerable
823 3836 4047 4263 4047 4275 3496 2653
n.gsf d.nsm n.nsm r.nsm pt.aa.nsm v.aai.3s a.asm

NASB

brought their books
together and *began*
burning them in the
sight of everyone;
and they counted
up the price of
them and found
it fifty thousand
pieces of silver.
20 So the word of
the Lord was grow-
ing mightily and
prevailing.
21 Now after
these things were
finished, Paul pur-
posed in the Spirit
to go to Jerusalem
after he had passed
through Macedonia
and Achaia, saying,
"After I have been
there, I must also
see Rome." 22 And
having sent into
Macedonia two of
those who minis-
tered to him, Timo-
thy and Erastus, he
himself stayed in
Asia for a while.
23 About that time
there occurred no
small disturbance
concerning the
Way. 24 For a man
named Demetrius,
a silversmith,
who made silver
shrines of Artemis,
was bringing no
little business to
the craftsmen;
25 these he gathered
together with the
workmen of similar
trades, and said,
"Men, you know
that our prosperity
depends upon this
business. 26 You see
and hear that not
only in Ephesus,
but in almost all
of Asia, this Paul
has persuaded and
turned away a con-
siderable number

[a] *19* A drachma was a silver coin worth about a day's wages.
[b] *21* Or *decided in the Spirit*

NIV

of people here in
Ephesus and in
practically the
whole province of
Asia. He says that
gods made by hu-
man hands are no
gods at all. 27 There
is danger not only
that our trade
will lose its good
name, but also that
the temple of the
great goddess Ar-
temis will be dis-
credited; and the
goddess herself,
who is worshiped
throughout the
province of Asia
and the world, will
be robbed of her
divine majesty."
28 When they
heard this, they
were furious and
began shouting:
"Great is Artemis
of the Ephesians!"
29 Soon the whole
city was in an
uproar. The peo-
ple seized Gaius
and Aristarchus,
Paul's traveling
companions from
Macedonia, and
all of them rushed
into the theater
together. 30 Paul
wanted to appear
before the crowd,
but the disciples
would not let him.
31 Even some of
the officials of the
province, friends
of Paul, sent him a
message begging
him not to venture
into the theater.
32 The assembly
was in confusion:
Some were shout-
ing one thing,
some another.
Most of the peo-
ple did not even
know why they
were there. 33 The
Jews in the crowd
pushed Alexander

ὄχλον λέγων ὅτι οὐκ εἰσὶν θεοὶ οἱ διὰ
⌊number of people,⌋ saying that gods made by hand are not *are* gods at all. *gods* *by*
4063 3306 4022 3836 1181 1328 5931 1639 4024 1639 2536 3836 1328
n.asm pt.pa.nsm cj pl v.pai.3p n.npm d.npm p.g

χειρῶν γινόμενοι. 27 οὐ μόνον δὲ τοῦτο κινδυνεύει
hand *made* There is danger not only *{and}* that this *There is danger* trade
5931 1181 3073 3073 3073 4024 3667 1254 4047 3073 3538
n.gpf pt.pm.npm pl adv cj r.asn v.pai.3s

ἡμῖν τὸ μέρος εἰς ἀπελεγμὸν ἐλθεῖν ἀλλὰ καὶ τὸ τῆς
of ours *{the}* *trade* will fall into disrepute, *will fall* but also that the temple of the
7005 3836 3538 2262 2262 1650 591 2262 247 2779 3836 2639 3836
r.dp.1 d.asn n.asn p.a n.asm f.aa cj adv d.asn d.gsf

μεγάλης θεᾶς Ἀρτέμιδος ἱερὸν εἰς οὐθὲν λογισθῆναι,
great goddess Artemis *temple* is in danger of being regarded as worthless *being regarded*
3489 2516 783 2639 3357 3357 1650 4032 3357
a.gsf n.gsf n.gsf n.asn p.a a.asn f.ap

μέλλειν τε καὶ καθαιρεῖσθαι τῆς μεγαλειότητος αὐτῆς
and her magnificence ⌊in danger of⌋ *and* *{also}* being destroyed, *{the}* *magnificence* *her*
5445 899 3484 3516 5445 2779 2747 3836 3484 899
f.pa cj adv f.pp d.gsf n.gsf r.gsf.3

ἣν ὅλη ἡ Ἀσία καὶ ἡ οἰκουμένη σέβεται. 28 ἀκούσαντες δὲ καὶ
⌊she whom⌋ all *{the}* Asia and the world worship." When they heard *{and}* *{and}* this,
4005 3910 3836 823 2779 3836 3876 4936 201 1254 2779
r.asf a.nsf d.nsf n.nsf cj d.nsf n.nsf v.pmi.3s pt.aa.npm cj cj

γενόμενοι πλήρεις θυμοῦ ἔκραζον λέγοντες, μεγάλη ἡ Ἄρτεμις →
they were filled with anger and ⌊began to cry out,⌋ saying, "Great is *{the}* Artemis of the
1181 4441 2596 3189 3306 3489 3836 783
pt.am.npm a.npm n.gsm v.iai.3p pt.pa.npm a.nsf d.nsf n.nsf

Ἐφεσίων. 29 καὶ ἐπλήσθη ἡ πόλις τῆς συγχύσεως, ὥρμησάν τε
Ephesians!" So the city ⌊was filled with⌋ *the* *city* the confusion, and they rushed *and*
2386 2779 3836 4484 4398 3836 4484 3836 5180 5445 3994 5445
a.gpm cj v.api.3s d.nsf n.nsf d.gsf n.gsf v.aai.3p cj

→ ὁμοθυμαδὸν εἰς τὸ θέατρον συναρπάσαντες Γάϊον καὶ Ἀρίσταρχον
with a single purpose into the theater, dragging with them Gaius and Aristarchus,
3924 1650 3836 2519 5275 1127 2779 752
adv p.a d.asn n.asn pt.aa.npm n.asm cj n.asm

Μακεδόνας, συνεκδήμους Παύλου. 30 ↱ Παύλου δὲ βουλομένου
Macedonians, traveling-companions of Paul. But when Paul *But* wanted
3424 5292 4263 1254 1089 4263 1254 1089
n.apm n.apm n.gsm n.gsm cj pt.pm.gsm

εἰσελθεῖν εἰς τὸν δῆμον ↱ οὐκ εἴων αὐτὸν οἱ μαθηταί· 31
to go in among the people, the disciples would not let him. *the* *disciples* And
1656 1650 3836 1322 3836 3412 1572 4024 1572 899 3836 3412 1254
f.aa p.a d.asm n.asm pl v.iai.3p r.asm.3 d.npm n.npm

τινὲς δὲ καὶ τῶν Ἀσιαρχῶν, ὄντες αὐτῷ φίλοι, πέμψαντες πρὸς
also some *And* *also* of the Asiarchs, being friendly to him, *friendly* sent to
2779 5516 1254 2779 3836 825 1639 5813 899 5813 4287 4639
r.npm cj adv d.gpm n.gpm pt.pa.npm r.dsm.3 n.npm pt.aa.npm p.a

αὐτὸν παρεκάλουν μὴ δοῦναι ἑαυτὸν εἰς τὸ θέατρον. 32 ἄλλοι
him and urged him not to commit himself to the theater. So then some
899 4151 3590 1443 1571 1650 3836 2519 4036 4036 257
r.asm.3 v.iai.3p pl f.aa r.asm.3 p.a d.asn n.asn r.npm

μὲν οὖν ἄλλο τι ἔκραζον· ἦν γὰρ
~ *So then* were shouting one thing, *were shouting* some another, for the assembly was *for*
3525 4036 3189 3189 257 5516 3189 1142 3836 1711 1639 1142
pl cj r.asn r.asn v.iai.3p v.iai.3s cj

ἡ ἐκκλησία συγκεχυμένη καὶ οἱ πλείους ↱ οὐκ ᾔδεισαν ⌊τίνος ἕνεκα⌋
the *assembly* in confusion, and *{the}* most of them did not know why
3836 1711 5177 2779 3836 4498 3857 4024 3857 5515 1914
d.nsf n.nsf pt.rp.nsf cj d.npm a.npm.c pl v.lai.3p r.gsn p.g

συνεληλύθεισαν. 33 ἐκ δὲ τοῦ ὄχλου συνεβίβασαν Ἀλέξανδρον,
they had assembled. And ⌊some of⌋ *And* the crowd prompted Alexander, the Jews
5302 1254 1666 1254 3836 4063 5204 235 3836 2681
v.lai.3p p.g cj d.gsm n.gsm v.aai.3p n.asm

NASB

of people, saying
that gods made
with hands are
no gods *at all.*
27 Not only is there
danger that this
trade of ours fall
into disrepute,
but also that the
temple of the great
goddess Artemis be
regarded as worth-
less and that she
whom all of Asia
and the world wor-
ship will even be
dethroned from her
magnificence."
28 When they heard
this and were filled
with rage, they
began crying out,
saying, "Great is
Artemis of the
Ephesians!" 29 The
city was filled with
the confusion, and
they rushed with
one accord into the
theater, dragging
along Gaius and
Aristarchus, Paul's
traveling compan-
ions from Mace-
donia. 30 And when
Paul wanted to go
into the assem-
bly, the disciples
would not let him.
31 Also some of
the [a]Asiarchs who
were friends of his
sent to him and re-
peatedly urged him
not to venture into
the theater. 32 So
then, some were
shouting one thing
and some another,
for the assembly
was in confusion
and the majority
did not know for
what reason they
had come together.
33 Some of the
crowd concluded
it was Alexander,
since the Jews had

[a] I.e. political or religious officials of the province of Asia

NIV

to the front, and
they shouted in-
structions to him.
He motioned for
silence in order
to make a defense
before the people.
34But when they
realized he was a
Jew, they all shout-
ed in unison for
about two hours:
"Great is Artemis
of the Ephesians!"
35The city clerk
quieted the crowd
and said: "Fel-
low Ephesians,
doesn't all the
world know that
the city of Ephe-
sus is the guardian
of the temple of
the great Artemis
and of her image,
which fell from
heaven? 36There-
fore, since these
facts are undeni-
able, you ought
to calm down and
not do anything
rash. 37You have
brought these
men here, though
they have neither
robbed temples nor
blasphemed our
goddess. 38If, then,
Demetrius and his
fellow craftsmen
have a grievance
against anybody,
the courts are open
and there are pro-
consuls. They can
press charges. 39If
there is anything
further you want
to bring up, it
must be settled in
a legal assembly.
40As it is, we are
in danger of be-
ing charged with
rioting because
of what happened
today. In that case
we would not be
able to account for
this commotion,
since there is no
reason

προβαλόντων αὐτὸν ↰ τῶν Ἰουδαίων· ὁ δὲ Ἀλέξανδρος κατασείσας τὴν
pushing him forward. *the* *Jews* *{the}* And Alexander motioned with his
4582 899 4582 3836 2681 3836 1254 235 2939 3836
pt.aa.gpm r.asm.3 d.gpm a.gpm d.nsm cj n.nsm pt.aa.nsm d.asf

χεῖρα ἤθελεν ἀπολογεῖσθαι τῷ δήμῳ. 34 ἐπιγνόντες δὲ ὅτι
hand and wanted to make a defense ⌊to the⌋ crowd. But when they recognized *But* that he
5931 2527 664 3836 1322 1254 2105 1254 4022 1639
n.asf v.iai.3s f.pm d.dsm n.dsm pt.aa.npm cj cj

Ἰουδαῖός ἐστιν, φωνὴ ἐγένετο μία ἐκ πάντων ὡς
was a Jew, *he was* a single cry went up *single* from them all as they cried out for
1639 2681 1639 1651 5889 1181 1651 1666 4246 6055 3189 3189 3189
a.nsm v.pai.3s n.nsf v.ami.3s a.nsf p.g a.gpm pl

ἐπὶ ὥρας δύο κραζόντων, μεγάλη ἡ Ἄρτεμις → Ἐφεσίων. 35 →
about two hours, *two* *they cried out* "Great is *{the}* Artemis of the Ephesians!" And when
2093 1545 6052 1545 3189 3489 3836 783 2386 1254
p.a n.apf a.apf pt.pa.gpm a.nsf d.nsf n.nsf a.gpm

καταστείλας δὲ ὁ γραμματεὺς τὸν ὄχλον φησίν, ἄνδρες Ἐφέσιοι,
the city clerk had quieted *And* *the* *city clerk* the crowd, he said, "Men of Ephesus,
3836 1208 1208 2948 1254 3836 1208 3836 4063 5774 467 2386
pt.aa.nsm cj d.nsm n.nsm d.asm n.asm v.pai.3s n.vpm a.vpm

τίς γάρ ἐστιν ἀνθρώπων ὃς ↱ οὐ γινώσκει τὴν → Ἐφεσίων
what *{for}* man is there *man* who does not know that the city of the Ephesians
5515 1142 476 1639 476 4005 1182 4024 1182 3836 4484 2386
r.nsm cj v.pai.3s n.gpm r.nsm pl v.pai.3s d.asf a.gpm

πόλιν νεωκόρον οὖσαν τῆς μεγάλης Ἀρτέμιδος καὶ τοῦ
city is the temple keeper *is* of the great Artemis and of her image
4484 1639 3753 1639 3836 3489 783 2779 3836
n.asf n.asm pt.pa.asf d.gsf a.gsm n.gsf cj d.gsn

διοπετοῦς; 36 ↱ ἀναντιρρήτων οὖν ὄντων τούτων
⌊that fell from heaven?⌋ So, since these things are indisputable, *So* *are* *these things*
1479 4036 1639 4047 4047 1639 394 4036 1639 4047
a.gsn a.gpn cj pt.pa.gpn r.gpn

⌊δέον ἐστὶν⌋ ὑμᾶς κατεσταλμένους ὑπάρχειν καὶ μηδὲν προπετὲς
you must *you* be quiet *be* and do nothing rash.
7007 1256 1639 7007 5639 2948 5639 2779 4556 3594 4637
pt.pa.nsn v.pai.3s r.ap.2 pt.rp.apm f.pa cj a.asn a.asn

πράσσειν. 37 ἠγάγετε γὰρ τοὺς ἄνδρας τούτους οὔτε
do For ⌊you have brought⌋ *For* *{the}* these men, *these* who are neither
4556 1142 72 1142 3836 4047 467 4047 4046
f.pa v.aai.2p cj d.apm n.apm r.apm cj

ἱεροσύλους οὔτε βλασφημοῦντας τὴν θεὸν ἡμῶν. 38 εἰ μὲν οὖν Δημήτριος
temple robbers nor blasphemers against *{the}* our goddess. *our* If ~ then Demetrius
2645 4046 1059 3836 7005 2536 7005 1623 3525 4036 1320
n.apm cj pt.pa.apm d.asf n.asf r.gp.1 cj pl cj n.nsm

καὶ οἱ σὺν αὐτῷ τεχνῖται ἔχουσι πρός τινα λόγον,
and the craftsmen with him *craftsmen* have a complaint against anyone, *complaint* the
2779 3836 5493 5250 899 5493 2400 3364 4639 5516 3364
cj d.npm p.d r.dsm.3 n.npm v.pai.3p p.a r.asm n.asm

ἀγοραῖοι ἄγονται καὶ ἀνθύπατοί εἰσιν, ἐγκαλείτωσαν
courts are open, and there are proconsuls. *there are* ⌊Let them bring charges against⌋
61 72 2779 1639 1639 478 1639 1592
n.npf v.ppi.3p cj n.npm v.pai.3p v.pam.3p

ἀλλήλοις. 39 εἰ δέ τι περαιτέρω ἐπιζητεῖτε,
one another there. But if *But* you want anything in addition, *you want* it shall be
253 1254 1623 1254 2118 2118 5516 4304 2118 2147 2147 2147
r.dpm cj cj r.asn adv.c v.pai.2p

ἐν τῇ ἐννόμῳ ἐκκλησίᾳ ἐπιλυθήσεται. 40 καὶ γὰρ κινδυνεύομεν
settled in the legal assembly. *it shall be settled* For indeed *For* ⌊we are in danger of⌋
2147 1877 3836 1937 1711 2147 1142 2779 1142 3073
p.d d.dsf a.dsf n.dsf v.fpi.3s adv cj v.pai.1p

ἐγκαλεῖσθαι στάσεως περὶ τῆς σήμερον, μηδενὸς αἰτίου
being charged *riot* ⌊in connection with⌋ this day's riot, there being no cause
1592 5087 4309 3836 4958 5087 5639 5639 3594 165
f.pp n.gsf p.g d.gsf adv a.gsn n.gsn

NASB

put him forward;
and having
motioned with his
hand, Alexander
was intending to
make a defense to
the assembly. 34But
when they recog-
nized that he was a
Jew, a *single* outcry
arose from them all
as they shouted for
about two hours,
"Great is Artemis
of the Ephesians!"
35After quieting the
crowd, the town
clerk *said, "Men
of Ephesus, what
man is there after
all who does not
know that the city
of the Ephesians
is guardian of the
temple of the great
Artemis and of
the *image* which
fell down from
heaven? 36So, since
these are undeni-
able facts, you
ought to keep calm
and to do nothing
rash. 37For you
have brought these
men *here* who are
neither robbers
of temples nor
blasphemers of our
goddess. 38So then,
if Demetrius and
the craftsmen who
are with him have
a complaint against
any man, the courts
are in session
and proconsuls
are *available;*
let them bring
charges against one
another. 39But if
you want anything
beyond this, it shall
be settled in the
lawful assembly.
40For indeed we are
in danger of being
accused of a riot in
connection with to-
day's events, since
there is no *real*
cause *for it,* and

NIV

for it." 41 After he
had said this, he
dismissed the as-
sembly.

Through Macedonia and Greece

20 When the
uproar had
ended, Paul sent
for the disciples
and, after encour-
aging them, said
goodbye and set
out for Macedo-
nia. 2 He traveled
through that area,
speaking many
words of encour-
agement to the
people, and finally
arrived in Greece,
3 where he stayed
three months. Be-
cause some Jews
had plotted against
him just as he was
about to sail for
Syria, he decided
to go back through
Macedonia. 4 He
was accompanied
by Sopater son of
Pyrrhus from Be-
rea, Aristarchus
and Secundus
from Thessalo-
nica, Gaius from
Derbe, Timothy
also, and Tychicus
and Trophimus
from the province
of Asia. 5 These
men went on ahead
and waited for us
at Troas. 6 But we
sailed from Philip-
pi after the Festi-
val of Unleavened
Bread, and five
days later joined
the others at Troas,
where we stayed
seven days.

Eutychus Raised From the Dead at Troas

7 On the first day
of the week we
came together to
break bread. Paul
spoke to the peo-
ple and,

ὑπάρχοντος περὶ οὗ ↱ ↱ οὐ[a] δυνησόμεθα ἀποδοῦναι λόγον περὶ τῆς
there being for it; and we will not be able to give an explanation for *{the}*
5639 4309 4005 1538 1538 4024 1538 625 3364 4309 3836
pt.pa.gsn p.g r.gsn pl v.fmi.1p f.aa n.asm p.g d.gsf

συστροφῆς ταύτης. καὶ ταῦτα εἰπὼν ἀπέλυσεν τὴν ἐκκλησίαν.
this commotion." *this* And having said this, *having said* he dismissed the assembly.
4047 5371 4047 2779 3306 3306 4047 3306 668 3836 1711
n.gsf r.gsf cj r.apn pt.aa.nsm v.aai.3s d.asf n.asf

20:1 μετὰ δὲ τὸ παύσασθαι τὸν θόρυβον μεταπεμψάμενος ὁ
After *{and}* ~ the uproar ceased, *the* *uproar* Paul sent for *{the}*
3552 1254 3836 3836 2573 4264 3836 2573 4263 3569 3836
p.a cj d.asn f.am d.asm n.asm pt.am.nsm d.nsm

Παῦλος τοὺς μαθητὰς καὶ παρακαλέσας, ἀσπασάμενος ⌊ἐξῆλθεν
Paul the disciples, and after encouraging them and saying farewell, he left
4263 3836 3412 2779 4151 832 2002
n.nsm d.apm n.apm cj pt.aa.nsm pt.am.nsm v.aai.3s

πορεύεσθαι⌋ εἰς Μακεδονίαν. 2 διελθὼν δὲ τὰ μέρη ἐκεῖνα
for Macedonia. ⌊When he had gone through⌋ *{and}* *{the}* those parts *those*
4513 1650 3423 1451 1254 3836 1697 3538 1697
f.pm p.a n.asf pt.aa.nsm cj d.apn n.apn r.apn

καὶ παρακαλέσας αὐτοὺς → λόγῳ πολλῷ ἦλθεν εἰς τὴν Ἑλλάδα 3 ποιήσας
and encouraged them with many words, *many* he came to *{the}* Greece. He spent
2779 4151 899 4498 3364 4498 2262 1650 3836 1817 4472
cj pt.aa.nsm r.apm.3 n.dsm a.dsm v.aai.3s p.a d.asf n.asf pt.aa.nsm

τε μῆνας τρεῖς· → γενομένης ἐπιβουλῆς αὐτῷ ὑπὸ τῶν
~ three months *three* there, and when a plot was hatched *plot* ⌊against him⌋ by the
5445 5552 3604 5552 2101 1181 2101 899 5679 3836
cj n.apm a.apm pt.am.gsf n.gsf r.dsm.3 p.g d.gpm

Ἰουδαίων μέλλοντι ἀνάγεσθαι εἰς τὴν Συρίαν, ⌊ἐγένετο γνώμης⌋ τοῦ
Jews ⌊as he was about⌋ to set sail for *{the}* Syria, he decided to
2681 3516 343 1650 3836 5353 1181 1191 3836
a.gpm pt.pa.dsm f.pm p.a d.asf n.asf v.ami.3s n.gsf d.gsn

ὑποστρέφειν διὰ Μακεδονίας. 4 συνείπετο δὲ αὐτῷ Σώπατρος
return through Macedonia. *went with* *{and}* *him* Sopater of Berea, the son
5715 1328 3423 5299 1254 899 5396
f.pa p.g n.gsf v.imi.3s cj r.dsm.3 n.nsm

Πύρρου Βεροιαῖος, Θεσσαλονικέων δὲ Ἀρίσταρχος καὶ Σεκοῦνδος,
of Pyrrhus from Berea, went with him, *from Thessalonians* as did Aristarchus and Secundus
4795 1024 5299 5299 899 2552 1254 752 2779 4941
n.gsm a.nsm n.gpm cj n.nsm cj n.nsm

καὶ Γάϊος Δερβαῖος καὶ Τιμόθεος, Ἀσιανοὶ δὲ
from Thessalonians, *{and}* Gaius a resident of Derbe, *{and}* Timothy, and the Asians, *and*
2552 2552 2779 1127 1291 2779 5510 1254 824 1254
cj n.nsm a.nsm cj n.nsm n.npm cj

Τύχικος καὶ Τρόφιμος. 5 οὗτοι δὲ προελθόντες ἔμενον ἡμᾶς ἐν
Tychicus and Trophimus. ⌊These men⌋ *{and}* had gone on ahead and ⌊were waiting for⌋ us in
5608 2779 5576 4047 1254 4601 3531 7005 1877
n.nsm cj n.nsm r.npm cj pt.aa.npm v.iai.3p r.ap.1 p.d

Τρῳάδι, 6 ἡμεῖς δὲ ἐξεπλεύσαμεν μετὰ τὰς ἡμέρας τῶν ἀζύμων ἀπὸ
Troas. We *{and}* sailed away after the days of ⌊Unleavened Bread⌋ from
5590 7005 1254 1739 3552 3836 2465 3836 109 608
n.dsf r.np.1 cj v.aai.1p p.a d.apf n.apf d.gpn n.gpn p.g

Φιλίππων καὶ ⌊ἤλθομεν πρὸς⌋ αὐτοὺς εἰς τὴν Τρῳάδα ἄχρι ἡμερῶν
Philippi and joined the others in *{the}* Troas five days later, *days*
5804 2779 2262 4639 899 1650 3836 5590 4297 2465 948 2465
n.gpm cj v.aai.1p p.a r.apm.3 p.a d.asf n.asf p.g n.gpf

πέντε, ὅπου διετρίψαμεν → ἡμέρας ἑπτά. 7 ἐν δὲ τῇ μιᾷ τῶν σαββάτων
five where we stayed for seven days. *seven* On *{and}* the first day of the week,
4297 3963 1417 2231 2465 2231 1877 1254 3836 1651 3836 4879
a.gpf cj v.aai.1p n.apf a.apf p.d cj d.dsf a.dsf d.gpn n.gpn

→ συνηγμένων ἡμῶν κλάσαι ἄρτον, ὁ Παῦλος διελέγετο αὐτοῖς
when we had gathered *we* to break bread, *{the}* Paul addressed them, and
7005 5251 7005 3089 788 3836 4263 1363 899
pt.rp.gpm r.gp.1 f.aa n.asm d.nsm n.nsm v.imi.3s r.dpm.3

NASB

in this connection
we will be unable
to account for this
disorderly gather-
ing." 41 After saying
this he dismissed
the assembly.

Paul in Macedonia and Greece

20:1 After the up-
roar had ceased,
Paul sent for the
disciples, and when
he had exhorted
them and taken his
leave of them, he
left to go to Mace-
donia. 2 When he
had gone through
those districts and
had given them
much exhortation,
he came to Greece.
3 And *there* he spent
three months, and
when a plot was
formed against him
by the Jews as he
was about to set
sail for Syria, he
decided to return
through Macedo-
nia. 4 And he was
accompanied by
Sopater of Berea,
the son of Pyrrhus,
and by Aristarchus
and Secundus of
the Thessalonians,
and Gaius of Der-
be, and Timothy,
and Tychicus and
Trophimus of Asia.
5 But these had
gone on ahead and
were waiting for us
at Troas. 6 We sailed
from Philippi after
the days of Unleav-
ened Bread, and
came to them at
Troas within five
days; and there we
stayed seven days.
7 On the first day
of the week, when
we were gathered
together to break
bread, Paul *began*
talking to them,

[a] [οὐ] UBS.

NIV

because he intend-
ed to leave the
next day, kept on
talking until mid-
night. 8 There were
many lamps in
the upstairs room
where we were
meeting. 9 Seated
in a window was a
young man named
Eutychus, who
was sinking into
a deep sleep as
Paul talked on and
on. When he was
sound asleep, he
fell to the ground
from the third sto-
ry and was picked
up dead. 10 Paul
went down, threw
himself on the
young man and put
his arms around
him. "Don't be
alarmed," he said.
"He's alive!"
11 Then he went
upstairs again and
broke bread and
ate. After talking
until daylight, he
left. 12 The people
took the young
man home alive
and were greatly
comforted.

Paul's Farewell to the Ephesian Elders

13 We went on
ahead to the ship
and sailed for
Assos, where we
were going to take
Paul aboard. He
had made this ar-
rangement because
he was going there
on foot. 14 When
he met us at As-
sos, we took him
aboard and went
on to Mitylene.
15 The next day we
set sail from there
and arrived off
Chios. The day af-
ter that we crossed
over to

μέλλων ἐξιέναι τῇ ἐπαύριον, παρέτεινέν τε τὸν λόγον μέχρι μεσονυκτίου.
⌊since he intended⌋ to leave the next day, he continued his message until midnight.
3516 1997 3836 2069 4189 5445 3836 3364 3588 3543
pt.pa.nsm f.pa d.dsf adv v.iai.3s cj d.asm n.asm p.g n.gsn

8 ἦσαν δὲ λαμπάδες ἱκαναὶ ἐν τῷ ὑπερῴῳ οὗ ἦμεν
⌊There were⌋ *{and}* a number of lamps *number of* in the upper room where we had
1639 1254 2653 2653 3286 2653 1877 3836 5673 4023 1639
v.iai.3p cj n.npf a.npf p.d d.dsn n.dsn adv v.iai.1p

συνηγμένοι. 9 καθεζόμενος δέ τις νεανίας ὀνόματι Εὔτυχος ἐπὶ τῆς
gathered. *sitting* And a young man, named Eutychus, sitting on the
5251 2757 1254 5516 3733 3950 2366 2757 2093 3836
pt.rp.npm pt.pm.nsm cj r.nsm n.nsm n.dsn n.nsm p.g d.gsf

θυρίδος, καταφερόμενος ὕπνῳ βαθεῖ ↱ διαλεγομένου τοῦ Παύλου
window ledge, was sinking into a deep sleep *deep* as Paul continued to speak *{the}* *Paul*
2600 2965 960 5678 960 4263 1363 3836 4263
n.gsf pt.pp.nsm n.dsm a.dsm pt.pm.gsm d.gsm n.gsm

⌊ἐπὶ πλεῖον,⌋ κατενεχθεὶς ἀπὸ τοῦ ὕπνου ἔπεσεν ἀπὸ τοῦ τριστέγου κάτω καὶ
on and on. Overcome by *{the}* sleep, he fell from the third floor *{down}* and
2093 4498 2965 608 3836 5678 4406 608 3836 5566 3004 2779
p.a adv.c pt.ap.nsm p.g d.gsm n.gsm v.aai.3s p.g d.gsn n.gsn adv cj

ἤρθη νεκρός. 10 καταβὰς δὲ ὁ Παῦλος ἐπέπεσεν
⌊was picked up⌋ for dead. But Paul went down *But* *{the}* *Paul* and ⌊threw himself on⌋
149 3738 1254 4263 2849 1254 3836 4263 2158
v.api.3s a.nsm pt.aa.nsm cj d.nsm n.nsm v.aai.3s

αὐτῷ καὶ συμπεριλαβὼν εἶπεν, ↱ μὴ θορυβεῖσθε, ἡ γὰρ ψυχὴ
him, and ⌊putting his arms around⌋ him, said, "Do not be alarmed, *{the}* for his life
899 2779 5227 3306 2572 3590 2572 3836 1142 899 6034
r.dsm.3 cj pt.aa.nsm v.aai.3s pl v.ppm.2p d.nsf cj n.nsf

αὐτοῦ ἐν αὐτῷ ἐστιν. 11 ἀναβὰς δὲ καὶ κλάσας
his is in him." *is* Then Paul ⌊went back upstairs,⌋ *Then* and ⌊after he had broken⌋
899 1639 1877 899 1639 1254 326 1254 2779 3089
r.gsm.3 p.d r.dsm.3 v.pai.3s pt.aa.nsm cj cj pt.aa.nsm

τὸν ἄρτον καὶ γευσάμενος ⌊ἐφ᾽ ἱκανόν⌋ τε
{the} bread and eaten, he spoke with them a considerable time, ~
3836 788 2779 1174 3917 3917 3917 2093 2653 5445
d.asm n.asm cj pt.am.nsm p.a a.asm cj

ὁμιλήσας ἄχρι αὐγῆς, οὕτως ἐξῆλθεν. 12 ἤγαγον δὲ τὸν παῖδα
he spoke with until dawn, and so he departed. And they took *And* the boy home
3917 948 879 4048 2002 1254 72 1254 3836 4090
pt.aa.nsm p.g n.gsf adv v.aai.3s v.aai.3p cj d.asm n.asm

ζῶντα καὶ παρεκλήθησαν οὐ μετρίως. 13 ἡμεῖς δὲ προελθόντες ἐπὶ τὸ πλοῖον
alive and were encouraged not a little. We, then, went on to the ship
2409 2779 4151 4024 3585 7005 1254 4601 2093 3836 4450
pt.pa.asm cj v.api.3p pl adv r.np.1 cj pt.aa.npm p.a d.asn n.asn

ἀνήχθημεν ἐπὶ τὴν Ἆσσον ἐκεῖθεν μέλλοντες ἀναλαμβάνειν τὸν Παῦλον· ↰
and set sail for *{the}* Assos, where we planned to take *{the}* Paul on
343 2093 3836 840 1696 3516 377 3836 4263 377
v.api.1p p.a d.asf n.asf adv pt.pa.npm f.pa d.asm n.asm

↰ ↱ οὕτως γὰρ διατεταγμένος ἦν μέλλων αὐτὸς πεζεύειν.
board; for he had made this *for* arrangement, *he had* intending himself ⌊to travel by land.⌋
377 1142 1639 1639 1411 4048 1142 1411 1639 3516 899 4269
adv cj pt.rp.nsm v.iai.3s pt.pa.nsm r.nsm f.pa

14 ὡς δὲ συνέβαλλεν ἡμῖν εἰς τὴν Ἆσσον, ↱ ἀναλαβόντες αὐτὸν ↰ ↰
When *{and}* he met us at *{the}* Assos, we took him on board and
6055 1254 5202 7005 1650 3836 840 2262 377 899 377 377
cj cj v.iai.3s r.dp.1 p.a d.asf n.asf pt.aa.npm r.asm.3

ἤλθομεν εἰς Μιτυλήνην, 15 κἀκεῖθεν ↱ ἀποπλεύσαντες τῇ
⌊continued on⌋ to Mitylene. ⌊And from there⌋ we sailed away ⌊on the⌋
2262 1650 3639 2796 2918 676 3836
v.aai.1p p.a n.asf crasis pt.aa.npm d.dsf

ἐπιούσῃ κατηντήσαμεν ἄντικρυς Χίου, τῇ δὲ ἑτέρᾳ παρεβάλομεν
⌊following day⌋ and arrived ⌊off the shore of⌋ Chios, the *{and}* next day we touched
2079 2918 513 5944 3836 1254 2283 4125
pt.pa.dsf v.aai.1p p.g n.gsf d.dsf cj r.dsf v.aai.1p

NASB

intending to leave
the next day, and
he prolonged his
message until
midnight. 8 There
were many lamps
in the upper room
where we were
gathered together.
9 And there was a
young man named
Eutychus sitting
on the window sill,
sinking into a deep
sleep; and as Paul
kept on talking, he
was overcome by
sleep and fell down
from the third floor
and was picked up
dead. 10 But Paul
went down and
fell upon him, and
after embracing
him, he said, "Do
not be troubled,
for his life is in
him." 11 When he
had gone *back* up
and had broken the
bread and eaten, he
talked with them
a long while until
daybreak, and then
left. 12 They took
away the boy alive,
and were greatly
comforted.

Troas to Miletus

13 But we, going
ahead to the ship,
set sail for Assos,
intending from
there to take Paul
on board; for so he
had arranged it, in-
tending himself to
go by land. 14 And
when he met us at
Assos, we took him
on board and came
to Mitylene. 15 Sail-
ing from there, we
arrived the follow-
ing day opposite
Chios; and the next
day we crossed

NIV

Samos, and on
the following day
arrived at Mile-
tus. 16 Paul had
decided to sail past
Ephesus to avoid
spending time in
the province of
Asia, for he was
in a hurry to reach
Jerusalem, if pos-
sible, by the day of
Pentecost.
17 From Miletus,
Paul sent to Eph-
esus for the elders
of the church.
18 When they ar-
rived, he said to
them: “You know
how I lived the
whole time I was
with you, from the
first day I came
into the province
of Asia. 19 I served
the Lord with
great humility and
with tears and in
the midst of se-
vere testing by the
plots of my Jewish
opponents. 20 You
know that I have
not hesitated to
preach anything
that would be help-
ful to you but have
taught you publicly
and from house to
house. 21 I have de-
clared to both Jews
and Greeks that
they must turn to
God in repentance
and have faith in
our Lord Jesus.
22 “And now,
compelled by the
Spirit, I am going
to Jerusalem, not
knowing what
will happen to me
there.

εἰς Σάμον,[a] τῇ δὲ ἐχομένῃ ἤλθομεν εἰς Μίλητον. 16
at Samos, and the *and* day after that we went to Miletus. For Paul
1650 4904 1254 3836 1254 2400 2262 1650 3626 1142 4263
p.a n.asf d.dsf cj pt.pm.dsf v.aai.1p p.a n.asf

κεκρίκει γὰρ ὁ Παῦλος παραπλεῦσαι τὴν Ἔφεσον, ὅπως ↱ μὴ γένηται
had decided *For* *{the}* *Paul* to sail past *{the}* Ephesus, so that he might not have
3212 1142 3836 4263 4179 3836 2387 3968 899 1181 3590 1181
v.lai.3s cj d.nsm n.nsm f.aa d.asf n.asf cj pl v.ams.3s

αὐτῷ χρονοτριβῆσαι ἐν τῇ Ἀσίᾳ· ἔσπευδεν γὰρ εἰ δυνατὸν
he to spend time in *{the}* Asia, for he was hastening, *for* if it were possible
899 5990 1877 3836 823 1142 5067 1142 1623 1639 1639 1543
r.dsm.3 f.aa p.d d.dsf n.dsf v.iai.3s cj cj n.nsn

εἴη αὐτῷ τὴν ἡμέραν τῆς πεντηκοστῆς γενέσθαι εἰς
it were for him, to be in Jerusalem for the day of Pentecost. *to be* *in*
1639 899 1181 1181 1650 2642 3836 2465 3836 4300 1181 1650
v.pao.3s r.dsm.3 d.asf n.asf d.gsf n.gsf f.am p.a

Ἱεροσόλυμα. 17 ἀπὸ δὲ τῆς Μιλήτου ↱ πέμψας εἰς Ἔφεσον μετεκαλέσατο τοὺς
Jerusalem From *{and}* *{the}* Miletus he sent to Ephesus, asking the
2642 608 1254 3836 3626 3559 4287 1650 2387 3559 3836
n.apn p.g cj d.gsf n.gsf pt.aa.nsm p.a n.asf v.ami.3s d.apm

πρεσβυτέρους τῆς ἐκκλησίας. ↰ ↰ 18 ὡς δὲ παρεγένοντο πρὸς
elders of the church to come to him. And when *And* they came to
4565 3836 1711 3559 3559 1254 6055 1254 4134 4639
a.apm d.gsf n.gsf cj cj v.ami.3p p.a

αὐτὸν εἶπεν αὐτοῖς, ὑμεῖς ἐπίστασθε,
him, he said to them: “You yourselves know how I lived among you the whole time
899 3306 899 7007 2179 4802 1181 1181 3552 7007 3836 4246 5989
r.asm.3 v.aai.3s r.dpm.3 r.np.2 v.ppi.2p

ἀπὸ πρώτης ἡμέρας ἀφ᾽ ἧς ἐπέβην εἰς τὴν Ἀσίαν, πῶς μεθ᾽ ὑμῶν τὸν πάντα
from the first day on which I set foot in *{the}* Asia, *how* *among* *you* *the* *whole*
608 4755 2465 608 4005 2094 1650 3836 823 4802 3552 7007 3836 4246
p.g a.gsf n.gsf p.g r.gsf v.aai.1s p.a d.asf n.asf cj p.g r.gp.2 d.asm a.asm

χρόνον ἐγενόμην, 19 δουλεύων τῷ κυρίῳ μετὰ πάσης ταπεινοφροσύνης καὶ ↰
time *I lived* serving the Lord with all humility and with
5989 1181 1526 3836 3261 3552 4246 5425 2779 3552
n.asm v.ami.1s pt.pa.nsm d.dsm n.dsm p.g a.gsf n.gsf cj

δακρύων καὶ πειρασμῶν τῶν συμβάντων μοι ἐν ταῖς ἐπιβουλαῖς τῶν
tears, *{and}* enduring the trials that fell on me by the plots of the
1232 2779 4280 3836 5201 1609 1877 3836 2101 3836
n.gpn cj n.gpm d.gpm pt.aa.gpm r.ds.1 p.d d.dpf n.dpf d.gpm

Ἰουδαίων, 20 ὡς οὐδὲν → → ὑπεστειλάμην τῶν συμφερόντων τοῦ μὴ
Jews; how *anything* I did not hold back *that* *would be helpful* *{the}* *not* from
2681 6055 4029 3590 5713 3836 5237 3836 3590
a.gpm cj a.asn v.ami.1s d.gpn pt.pa.gpn d.gsn pl

ἀναγγεῖλαι ὑμῖν καὶ διδάξαι ὑμᾶς δημοσίᾳ καὶ
proclaiming to you anything that would be helpful, and from teaching you publicly *{and}*
334 7007 4029 3836 5237 5237 5237 2779 1438 7007 1323 2779
f.aa r.dp.2 cj f.aa r.ap.2 a.dsf cj

⌊κατ᾽ οἴκους,⌋ 21 διαμαρτυρόμενος Ἰουδαίοις τε καὶ Ἕλλησιν
from house to house, testifying both to Jews *both* and to Greeks about
2848 3875 1371 5445 2681 5445 2779 1818
p.a n.apm pt.pm.nsm a.dpm cj cj n.dpm

τὴν εἰς θεὸν μετάνοιαν καὶ πίστιν εἰς τὸν κύριον ἡμῶν
{the} repentance toward God *repentance* and about faith in *{the}* our Lord *our*
3836 3567 1650 2536 3567 2779 4411 1650 3836 7005 3261 7005
d.asf p.a n.asm n.asf cj n.asf p.a d.asm n.asm r.gp.1

Ἰησοῦν. 22 καὶ νῦν ἰδοὺ δεδεμένος ἐγὼ τῷ πνεύματι πορεύομαι εἰς
Jesus. And now, *{behold}* ⌊compelled by⌋ the Spirit, I *the* *Spirit* am going to
2652 2779 3814 2627 1313 3836 4460 1609 3836 4460 4513 1650
n.asm cj adv j pt.rp.nsm r.ns.1 d.dsn n.dsn v.pmi.1s p.a

Ἰερουσαλὴμ τὰ ⌊ἐν αὐτῇ⌋ συναντήσοντά μοι μὴ
Jerusalem, not knowing what will happen to me there, *will happen* *to me* *not*
2647 3590 3857 3836 5267 5267 1609 1609 1877 899 5267 1609 3590
n.asf d.apn p.d r.dsf.3 pt.fa.apn r.ds.1 pl

[a] καὶ μείναντες ἐν Τρωγυλλίῳ included by TR after Σάμον.

NASB

over to Samos; and
the day following
we came to Mil-
etus. 16 For Paul had
decided to sail past
Ephesus so that he
would not have to
spend time in Asia;
for he was hurrying
to be in Jerusalem,
if possible, on the
day of Pentecost.

Farewell to Ephesus

17 From Miletus
he sent to Ephesus
and called to him
the elders of the
church. 18 And when
they had come to
him, he said to
them,
“You yourselves
know, from the first
day that I set foot
in Asia, how I was
with you the whole
time, 19 serving
the Lord with all
humility and with
tears and with trials
which came upon
me through the
plots of the Jews;
20 how I did not
shrink from declar-
ing to you anything
that was profitable,
and teaching you
publicly and from
house to house,
21 solemnly testify-
ing to both Jews
and Greeks of
repentance toward
God and faith in
our Lord Jesus
Christ. 22 And now,
behold, bound by
the Spirit, I am on
my way to Jerusa-
lem, not knowing
what will happen
to me there,

NIV

23 I only know that
in every city the
Holy Spirit warns
me that prison and
hardships are fac-
ing me. 24 However,
I consider my life
worth nothing to
me; my only aim is
to finish the race
and complete the
task the Lord Jesus
has given me — the
task of testifying
to the good news
of God's grace.
25 "Now I know
that none of you
among whom I
have gone about
preaching the
kingdom will ever
see me again.
26 Therefore, I de-
clare to you today
that I am innocent
of the blood of
any of you. 27 For I
have not hesitated
to proclaim to you
the whole will of
God. 28 Keep watch
over yourselves
and all the flock
of which the Holy
Spirit has made
you overseers. Be
shepherds of the
church of God,[a]
which he bought
with his own
blood.[b] 29 I know
that after I leave,
savage wolves will
come in among
you and will not
spare the flock.
30 Even from your
own number men
will arise and dis-
tort the truth in
order to draw away
disciples after
them.

εἰδώς, 23 πλὴν ὅτι τὸ πνεῦμα τὸ ἅγιον κατὰ πόλιν διαμαρτύρεταί μοι
knowing except that the Holy Spirit {the} Holy in every city testifies to me,
3857 4440 4022 3836 41 4460 3836 41 2848 4484 1371 1609
pt.ra.nsm cj cj d.nsn n.nsn d.nsn a.nsn p.a n.asf v.pmi.3s r.ds.1

λέγον ὅτι δεσμὰ καὶ θλίψεις με μένουσιν.
saying that in every city imprisonment and persecutions are waiting for me. are waiting for
3306 4022 2848 2848 4484 1301 2779 2568 3531 3531 3531 1609 3531
pt.pa.nsn cj n.npn cj n.npf r.as.1 v.pai.3p

24 ἀλλ᾽ οὐδενὸς λόγου ποιοῦμαι τὴν ψυχὴν τιμίαν
But I make my life of no account I make my life as of any value
247 4472 4472 3836 6034 4029 3364 4472 3836 6034 5508
cj a.gsm n.gsm v.pmi.1s d.asf n.asf a.asf

ἐμαυτῷ ὡς τελειώσαι τὸν δρόμον μου καὶ τὴν διακονίαν ἣν ἔλαβον παρὰ
to me, that I may finish {the} my task my and the ministry that I received from
1831 6055 5457 3836 1609 1536 1609 2779 3836 1355 4005 3284 4123
r.dsm.1 cj f.aa d.asm n.asm r.gs.1 cj d.asf n.asf r.asf v.aai.1s p.g

τοῦ κυρίου Ἰησοῦ, διαμαρτύρασθαι τὸ εὐαγγέλιον τῆς χάριτος τοῦ θεοῦ.
the Lord Jesus, to testify to the good news of the grace of God.
3836 3261 2652 1371 3836 2295 3836 5921 3836 2536
d.gsm n.gsm n.gsm f.am d.asn n.asn d.gsf n.gsf d.gsm n.gsm

25 καὶ νῦν ἰδοὺ ἐγὼ οἶδα ὅτι οὐκέτι ὄψεσθε τὸ πρόσωπόν μου ↰
"And now {behold} I know that none of ⌊you will see⌋ {the} my face my again,
2779 3814 2627 1609 3857 4022 4033 3972 3836 1609 4725 1609 4033
cj adv j r.ns.1 v.rai.1s cj adv v.fmi.2p d.asn n.asn r.gs.1

ὑμεῖς πάντες ἐν οἷς διῆλθον κηρύσσων τὴν βασιλείαν. 26 διότι μαρτύρομαι
you {all} among whom I went about proclaiming the kingdom. Therefore I testify
7007 4246 1877 4005 1451 3062 3836 993 1484 3458
r.np.2 a.npm p.d r.dpm v.aai.1s pt.pa.nsm d.asf n.asf cj v.pmi.1s

ὑμῖν ἐν τῇ ⌊σήμερον ἡμέρᾳ⌋ ὅτι καθαρός εἰμι ἀπὸ τοῦ αἵματος →
to you this {the} day that I am innocent I am of the blood of you
7007 1877 3836 4958 2465 4022 1639 1639 2754 1639 608 3836 135
r.dp.2 p.d d.dsf adv n.dsf cj a.nsm v.pai.1s p.g d.gsn n.gsn

πάντων· 27 ↱ ↱ οὐ γὰρ ὑπεστειλάμην τοῦ μὴ ἀναγγεῖλαι
all, for I did not for shrink ~ from announcing to you the
4246 1142 5713 5713 4024 1142 5713 3836 3590 334 7007 7007 3836
a.gpm pl cj v.ami.1s d.gsn pl f.aa

πᾶσαν τὴν βουλὴν τοῦ θεοῦ ὑμῖν. 28 προσέχετε ἑαυτοῖς καὶ παντὶ τῷ ποιμνίῳ,
whole the purpose of God. to you Watch out for yourselves and for all the flock
4246 3836 1087 3836 2536 7007 4668 1571 2779 4246 3836 4480
a.asf d.asf n.asf d.gsm n.gsm r.dp.2 v.pam.2p r.dpm.2 cj a.dsn d.dsn n.dsn

ἐν ᾧ ὑμᾶς τὸ πνεῦμα τὸ ἅγιον ἔθετο ἐπισκόπους ποιμαίνειν τὴν
in which you the Holy Spirit {the} Holy has placed you overseers, to shepherd the
1877 4005 7007 3836 41 4460 3836 41 5502 7007 2176 4477 3836
p.d r.dsn r.ap.2 d.nsn n.nsn d.nsn a.nsn v.ami.3s n.apm f.pa d.asf

ἐκκλησίαν τοῦ θεοῦ, ἣν περιεποιήσατο διὰ τοῦ αἵματος τοῦ ἰδίου. 29 ἐγὼ
church of God, which he purchased with the blood of his own Son. I
1711 3836 2536 4005 4347 1328 3836 135 3836 2625 1609
n.asf d.gsm n.gsm r.asf v.ami.3s p.g d.gsn n.gsn d.gsn a.gsn r.ns.1

οἶδα ὅτι εἰσελεύσονται μετὰ τὴν ἄφιξίν μου λύκοι βαρεῖς εἰς
know that there will come to you after {the} my departure my savage wolves, savage to
3857 4022 1656 1650 7007 3552 3836 1609 922 1609 987 3380 987 1650
v.rai.1s cj v.fmi.3p p.a d.asf n.asf r.gs.1 n.npm a.npm p.a

ὑμᾶς μὴ φειδόμενοι τοῦ ποιμνίου, 30 καὶ ἐξ ὑμῶν αὐτῶν →
you not sparing the flock. Even ⌊from among⌋ your own group will men
7007 3590 5767 3836 4480 2779 1666 7007 899 467
r.ap.2 pl pt.pm.npm d.gsn n.gsn cj p.g r.gp.2 r.gpm

ἀναστήσονται ἄνδρες λαλοῦντες διεστραμμένα τοῦ ἀποσπᾶν τοὺς μαθητὰς
arise, men speaking distortions of the truth, to draw the disciples
482 467 3281 1406 3836 685 3836 3412
v.fmi.3p n.npm pt.pa.npm pt.rp.apn d.gsn f.pa d.apm n.apm

↰ ὀπίσω αὐτῶν. 31 διὸ γρηγορεῖτε μνημονεύοντες ὅτι τριετίαν νύκτα καὶ
away after them. Therefore be alert, remembering that for three years, night or
685 3958 899 1475 1213 3648 4022 5562 3816 2779
p.g r.gpm.3 cj v.pam.2p pt.pa.npm cj n.asf n.asf cj

NASB

23 except that
the Holy Spirit
solemnly testifies
to me in every city,
saying that bonds
and afflictions
await me. 24 But I
do not consider my
life of any account
as dear to myself,
so that I may finish
my course and the
ministry which
I received from
the Lord Jesus, to
testify solemnly of
the gospel of the
grace of God.
25 "And now, be-
hold, I know that
all of you, among
whom I went about
preaching the
kingdom, will no
longer see my face.
26 Therefore, I tes-
tify to you this day
that I am innocent
of the blood of all
men. 27 For I did
not shrink from de-
claring to you the
whole purpose of
God. 28 Be on guard
for yourselves and
for all the flock,
among which the
Holy Spirit has
made you over-
seers, to shepherd
the church of
God which He
purchased with
His own blood. 29 I
know that after my
departure savage
wolves will come
in among you, not
sparing the flock;
30 and from among
your own selves
men will arise,
speaking perverse
things, to draw
away the disciples
after them. 31 There-
fore be on the alert,
remembering that
night and day for a
period of three

[a] 28 Many manuscripts *of the Lord*
[b] 28 Or *with the blood of his own Son.*

NIV

31 So be on your
guard! Remember
that for three years
I never stopped
warning each of
you night and day
with tears.
32 "Now I commit
you to God and
to the word of his
grace, which can
build you up and
give you an in-
heritance among
all those who are
sanctified. 33 I
have not coveted
anyone's silver or
gold or clothing.
34 You yourselves
know that these
hands of mine
have supplied my
own needs and
the needs of my
companions. 35 In
everything I did,
I showed you that
by this kind of
hard work we must
help the weak,
remembering the
words the Lord
Jesus himself said:
'It is more blessed
to give than to re-
ceive.' "
36 When Paul had
finished speaking,
he knelt down with
all of them and
prayed. 37 They all
wept as they em-
braced him and
kissed him. 38 What
grieved them most
was his statement
that they would
never see his face
again. Then they
accompanied him
to the ship.

ἡμέραν ↱ ↱ οὐκ ἐπαυσάμην μετὰ δακρύων νουθετῶν ἕνα
day, I did not cease warning each one of you with tears. *warning* *one*
2465 4264 4264 4024 4264 3805 1667 1651 3552 1232 3805 1651
n.asf pl v.ami.1s p.g n.gpn pt.pa.nsm a.asm

ἕκαστον. 32 καὶ τὰ νῦν παρατίθεμαι ὑμᾶς τῷ θεῷ καὶ τῷ λόγῳ τῆς
each And *{the}* now I commend you to God and ⌊to the⌋ word of his
1667 2779 3836 3814 4192 7007 3836 2536 2779 3836 3364 3836 899
r.asm cj d.apn adv v.pmi.1s r.ap.2 d.dsm n.dsm cj d.dsm n.dsm d.gsf

χάριτος αὐτοῦ, τῷ δυναμένῳ οἰκοδομῆσαι ← καὶ δοῦναι τὴν κληρονομίαν
grace, *his* which is able to build you up and to give you an inheritance
5921 899 3836 1538 3868 2779 1443 3836 3100
n.gsf r.gsm.3 d.dsm pt.pp.dsm f.aa cj f.aa d.asf n.asf

ἐν τοῖς ἡγιασμένοις πᾶσιν. 33 ἀργυρίου ἢ
among all those who are sanctified. *all* I have not coveted anyone's silver or
1877 4246 3836 39 4246 2121 2121 4029 2121 4029 736 2445
p.d d.dpm pt.rp.dpm a.dpm n.gsn cj

χρυσίου ἢ ἱματισμοῦ οὐδενὸς ἐπεθύμησα· 34 ↱ αὐτοὶ γινώσκετε ὅτι
gold or clothing. *not anyone's* *I have coveted* You yourselves know that these
5992 2445 2669 4029 2121 1182 899 1182 4022 4047
n.gsn cj n.gsm n.gsm v.aai.1s r.npm v.pai.2p cj

ταῖς χρείαις μου καὶ τοῖς οὖσιν
hands of mine provided for *{the}* my own needs *my own* ⌊as well as⌋ the needs of those *{being}*
5931 5676 5676 3836 1609 1609 5970 1609 2779 3836 1639
d.dpf n.dpf r.gs.1 cj d.dpm pt.pa.dpm

μετ᾽ ἐμοῦ ὑπηρέτησαν αἱ χεῖρες αὗται. 35 πάντα ὑπέδειξα ὑμῖν ὅτι
with me. *provided for* *{the}* *hands* *these* In all this I have shown you that by
3552 1609 5676 3836 5931 4047 4246 5683 7007 4022 3159
p.g r.gs.1 v.aai.3p d.npf n.npf r.npf a.apn v.aai.1s r.dp.2 cj

οὕτως κοπιῶντας δεῖ ἀντιλαμβάνεσθαι τῶν ἀσθενούντων,
working ⌊in this way⌋ *by working* ⌊you must⌋ help the weak,
3159 4048 3159 1256 514 3836 820
adv pt.pa.apm v.pai.3s f.pm d.gpm pt.pa.gpm

μνημονεύειν τε τῶν λόγων τοῦ κυρίου Ἰησοῦ ὅτι ↱ αὐτὸς εἶπεν, μακάριόν
remembering ~ the words of the Lord Jesus, how he himself said, *blessed*
3648 5445 3836 3364 3836 3261 2652 4022 3306 899 3306 3421
f.pa cj d.gpm n.gpm d.gsm n.gsm n.gsm cj r.nsm v.aai.3s a.nsn

ἐστιν μᾶλλον διδόναι ἢ λαμβάνειν. 36 καὶ ταῦτα
'It is more blessed to give than to receive.'" And when he had said these things,
1639 3437 3421 1443 2445 3284 2779 3306 3306 3306 3306 4047
v.pai.3s adv.c f.pa pl f.pa cj r.apn

εἰπὼν ↱ ⌊θεὶς τὰ γόνατα αὐτοῦ⌋ σὺν πᾶσιν αὐτοῖς
when he had said he knelt down with them all *them* and
3306 4667 5502 3836 1205 899 5250 899 4246 899
pt.aa.nsm pt.aa.nsm d.apn n.apn r.gsm.3 p.d a.dpm r.dpm.3

προσηύξατο. 37 ἱκανὸς δὲ κλαυθμὸς ἐγένετο πάντων καὶ ↱
prayed. And there was much *And* weeping *there was* on the part of all, and they
4667 1254 1181 1181 2653 1254 3088 1181 4246 2779 2968
v.ami.3s a.nsm cj n.nsm v.ami.3s a.gpm cj

ἐπιπεσόντες ἐπὶ τὸν τράχηλον τοῦ Παύλου κατεφίλουν αὐτόν, ↰
fell on the neck of Paul and kissed him lovingly,
2158 2093 3836 5549 3836 4263 2968 899 2968
pt.aa.npm p.a d.asm n.asm d.gsm n.gsm v.iai.3p r.asm.3

38 ὀδυνώμενοι μάλιστα ἐπὶ τῷ λόγῳ ᾧ εἰρήκει, ὅτι οὐκέτι
being saddened most of all ⌊because of⌋ the word *{which}* he had spoken, that no longer
3849 3436 2093 3836 3364 4005 3306 4022 4033
pt.pp.npm adv.s p.d d.dsm n.dsm r.dsm v.lai.3s cj adv

μέλλουσιν τὸ πρόσωπον αὐτοῦ θεωρεῖν. προέπεμπον δὲ αὐτὸν
were they going to see *{the}* his face. *his* *to see* And they escorted *And* him
3516 2555 2555 3836 899 4725 899 2555 1254 4636 1254 899
v.pai.3p d.asn n.asn r.gsm.3 f.pa v.iai.3p cj r.asm.3

εἰς τὸ πλοῖον.
to the ship.
1650 3836 4450
p.a d.asn n.asn

NASB

years I did not
cease to admon-
ish each one with
tears. 32 And now
I commend you
to God and to the
word of His grace,
which is able to
build *you* up and
to give *you* the
inheritance among
all those who are
sanctified. 33 I have
coveted no one's
silver or gold or
clothes. 34 You
yourselves know
that these hands
ministered to my
own needs and to
the men who were
with me. 35 In every-
thing I showed you
that by working
hard in this manner
you must help the
weak and remem-
ber the words of
the Lord Jesus, that
He Himself said,
'It is more blessed
to give than to
receive.' "
36 When he had
said these things,
he knelt down and
prayed with them
all. 37 And they *be-*
gan to weep aloud
and embraced Paul,
and repeatedly
kissed him, 38 griev-
ing especially over
the word which he
had spoken, that
they would not
see his face again.
And they were ac-
companying him to
the ship.

NIV

On to Jerusalem

21 After we had torn ourselves away from them, we put out to sea and sailed straight to Kos. The next day we went to Rhodes and from there to Patara. 2 We found a ship crossing over to Phoenicia, went on board and set sail. 3 After sighting Cyprus and passing to the south of it, we sailed on to Syria. We landed at Tyre, where our ship was to unload its cargo. 4 We sought out the disciples there and stayed with them seven days. Through the Spirit they urged Paul not to go on to Jerusalem. 5 When it was time to leave, we left and continued on our way. All of them, including wives and children, accompanied us out of the city, and there on the beach we knelt to pray. 6 After saying goodbye to each other, we went aboard the ship, and they returned home.

7 We continued our voyage from Tyre and landed at Ptolemais, where we greeted the brothers and sisters and stayed with them for a day. 8 Leaving the next day, we reached Caesarea

21:1 ὡς δὲ ἐγένετο ἀναχθῆναι ἡμᾶς
And when *And* *{it happened that}* we had parted from them, we put out to sea *we*
1254 6055 1254 1181 685 685 685 608 899 7005 343 7005
cj cj v.ami.3s f.ap r.ap.1

ἀποσπασθέντας ἀπ᾽ αὐτῶν, ⌞εὐθυδρομήσαντες ἤλθομεν⌟ εἰς τὴν Κῶ,
we had parted *from* *them* and sailed on a straight course to *{the}* Cos, then
685 608 899 2312 2262 1650 3836 3271 1254
pt.ap.apm p.g r.gpm.3 pt.aa.npm v.aai.1p p.a d.asf n.asf

τῇ δὲ ἑξῆς εἰς τὴν Ῥόδον κἀκεῖθεν εἰς Πάταρα, 2 καὶ εὑρόντες
⌞on the⌟ *then* ⌞next day⌟ to *{the}* Rhodes, and from there to Patara. And finding a
3836 1254 2009 1650 3836 4852 2796 1650 4249 2779 2351
d.dsf cj adv p.a d.asf n.asf crasis p.a n.apn cj pt.aa.npm

πλοῖον διαπερῶν εἰς Φοινίκην ↱ ἐπιβάντες ἀνήχθημεν. 3 ἀναφάναντες δὲ
ship bound for Phoenicia, we went aboard and set sail. ⌞We came in sight of⌟ *{and}*
4450 1385 1650 5834 343 2094 343 428 1254
n.asn pt.pa.asn p.a n.asf pt.aa.npm v.api.1p pt.aa.npm cj

τὴν Κύπρον καὶ καταλιπόντες αὐτὴν ↰ εὐώνυμον ἐπλέομεν εἰς Συρίαν
{the} Cyprus, and leaving it behind ⌞on our port side,⌟ ⌞we sailed on⌟ to Syria
3836 3251 2779 2901 899 2901 2381 4434 1650 5353
d.asf n.asf cj pt.aa.npm r.asf.3 a.asf v.iai.1p p.a n.asf

καὶ κατήλθομεν εἰς Τύρον· ἐκεῖσε γὰρ τὸ πλοῖον ἦν ἀποφορτιζόμενον τὸν
and landed at Tyre, for there *for* the ship was to unload its
2779 2982 1650 5602 1142 1698 1142 3836 4450 1639 711 3836
cj v.aai.1p p.a n.asf adv cj d.nsn n.nsn v.iai.3s pt.pm.nsn d.asm

γόμον. 4 ἀνευρόντες δὲ τοὺς μαθητὰς ἐπεμείναμεν αὐτοῦ ἡμέρας ἑπτά,
cargo. After locating *{and}* the disciples, we stayed there seven days; *seven* and
1203 461 1254 3836 3412 2152 7000 2231 2465 2231
n.asm pt.aa.npm cj d.apm n.apm v.aai.1p adv n.apf a.apf

οἵτινες τῷ Παύλῳ ἔλεγον διὰ τοῦ πνεύματος μὴ ἐπιβαίνειν εἰς
they kept telling *{the}* Paul *kept telling* through the Spirit not to set foot in
4015 3306 3306 3836 4263 3306 1328 3836 4460 3590 2094 1650
r.npm d.dsm n.dsm v.iai.3p p.g d.gsn n.gsn pl f.pa p.a

Ἱεροσόλυμα. 5 ὅτε δὲ ἐγένετο ἡμᾶς ἐξαρτίσαι τὰς ἡμέρας, ↱
Jerusalem. When *{and}* *{it happened that}* our days there were ended, *{the}* *days* we
2642 4021 1254 1181 7005 2465 1992 3836 2465 4513
n.apn cj cj v.ami.3s r.ap.1 f.aa d.apf n.apf

ἐξελθόντες ἐπορευόμεθα προπεμπόντων ἡμᾶς πάντων σὺν γυναιξὶ καὶ
departed and went on our journey, and *accompanied* *us* they all, with wives and
2002 4513 4636 7005 4246 5250 1222 2779
pt.aa.npm v.imi.1p pt.pa.gpm r.ap.1 a.gpm p.d n.dpf cj

τέκνοις ἕως ἔξω τῆς πόλεως, καὶ ⌞θέντες τὰ
children, accompanied us until we were outside the city. Then kneeling down
5451 4636 7005 2401 2032 3836 4484 2779 5502 3836
n.dpn p.g p.g d.gsf n.gsf cj pt.aa.npm d.apn

γόνατα⌟ ἐπὶ τὸν αἰγιαλὸν προσευξάμενοι 6 ἀπησπασάμεθα ἀλλήλους καὶ
on the beach, we prayed and said farewell to one another. Then
1205 2093 3836 129 4667 571 253 2779
n.apn p.a d.asm n.asm pt.am.npm v.ami.1p r.apm cj

ἀνέβημεν εἰς τὸ πλοῖον, ἐκεῖνοι δὲ ὑπέστρεψαν εἰς τὰ ἴδια.
we went ⌞on board⌟ the ship, and they *and* returned to *{the}* their own homes.
326 1650 3836 4450 1254 1697 1254 5715 1650 3836 2625
v.aai.1p p.a d.asn n.asn r.npm cj v.aai.3p p.a d.apn a.apn

7 ἡμεῖς δὲ τὸν πλοῦν διανύσαντες ἀπὸ Τύρου κατηντήσαμεν
we And having completed the voyage *having completed* from Tyre, we came
7005 1254 1382 1382 3836 4452 1382 608 5602 7005 2918
r.np.1 cj d.asm n.asm pt.aa.npm p.g n.gsf v.aai.1p

εἰς Πτολεμαΐδα καὶ ↱ ἀσπασάμενοι τοὺς ἀδελφοὺς ἐμείναμεν ἡμέραν μίαν
to Ptolemais, and we greeted the brothers and stayed one day *one*
1650 4767 2779 3531 832 3836 81 3531 1651 2465 1651
p.a n.asf cj pt.am.npm d.apm n.apm v.aai.1p n.asf a.asf

παρ᾽ αὐτοῖς. 8 τῇ δὲ ἐπαύριον ↱ ἐξελθόντες ἤλθομεν εἰς Καισάρειαν
with them. ⌞On the⌟ *{and}* next day we departed and went to Caesarea.
4123 899 3836 1254 2069 2262 2002 2262 1650 2791
p.d r.dpm.3 d.dsf cj adv pt.aa.npm v.aai.1p p.a n.asf

NASB

Paul Sails from Miletus

21:1 When we had parted from them and had set sail, we ran a straight course to Cos and the next day to Rhodes and from there to Patara; 2 and having found a ship crossing over to Phoenicia, we went aboard and set sail. 3 When we came in sight of Cyprus, leaving it on the left, we kept sailing to Syria and landed at Tyre; for there the ship was to unload its cargo. 4 After looking up the disciples, we stayed there seven days; and they kept telling Paul through the Spirit not to set foot in Jerusalem. 5 When our days there were ended, we left and started on our journey, while they all, with wives and children, escorted us until *we were* out of the city. After kneeling down on the beach and praying, we said farewell to one another. 6 Then we went on board the ship, and they returned home again.

7 When we had finished the voyage from Tyre, we arrived at Ptolemais, and after greeting the brethren, we stayed with them for a day. 8 On the next day we left and came to Caesarea, and entering

NIV

and stayed at the
house of Philip the
evangelist, one of
the Seven. 9 He had
four unmarried
daughters who
prophesied.
10 After we had
been there a num-
ber of days, a
prophet named
Agabus came
down from Judea.
11 Coming over to
us, he took Paul's
belt, tied his own
hands and feet
with it and said,
"The Holy Spirit
says, 'In this way
the Jewish leaders
in Jerusalem will
bind the owner of
this belt and will
hand him over to
the Gentiles.'"
12 When we heard
this, we and the
people there plead-
ed with Paul not
to go up to Jerusa-
lem. 13 Then Paul
answered, "Why
are you weeping
and breaking my
heart? I am ready
not only to be
bound, but also to
die in Jerusalem
for the name of
the Lord Jesus."
14 When he would
not be dissuaded,
we gave up and
said, "The Lord's
will be done."
15 After this, we
started on our
way up

καὶ ↱ εἰσελθόντες εἰς τὸν οἶκον Φιλίππου τοῦ εὐαγγελιστοῦ, ὄντος
{and} There we went into the house of Philip the evangelist, who was one
2779 3531 1656 1650 3836 3875 5805 3836 2296 1639
cj pt.aa.npm p.a d.asm n.asm n.gsm d.gsm n.gsm pt.pa.gsm

ἐκ τῶν ἑπτά, ἐμείναμεν παρ' αὐτῷ. 9 τούτῳ δὲ ἦσαν θυγατέρες
of the seven, and stayed with him. (He {and} had four unmarried daughters
1666 3836 2231 3531 4123 899 4047 1254 1639 5475 4221 2588
p.g d.gpm a.gpm v.aai.1p p.d r.dsm.3 r.dsm cj v.iai.3p n.npf

τέσσαρες παρθένοι προφητεύουσαι. 10 ἐπιμενόντων δὲ → ἡμέρας
four unmarried who prophesied.) ⌊While we were staying⌋ {and} for many days,
5475 4221 4736 2152 1254 4498 2465
a.npf n.npf pt.pa.npf pt.pa.gpm cj n.apf

πλείους κατῆλθέν τις ἀπὸ τῆς Ἰουδαίας προφήτης ὀνόματι
many a prophet named Agabus came down a from {the} Judea. prophet named
4498 5516 4737 3950 13 2982 5516 608 3836 2677 4737 3950
a.apf.c v.aai.3s r.nsm p.g d.gsf n.gsf n.nsm n.dsn

Ἄγαβος, 11 καὶ ἐλθὼν πρὸς ἡμᾶς καὶ ἄρας τὴν ζώνην τοῦ Παύλου, ↱
Agabus {and} He came to us and, taking {the} Paul's belt, {the} Paul's he
13 2779 2262 4639 7005 2779 149 3836 4263 2438 3836 4263 3306
n.nsm cj pt.aa.nsm p.a r.ap.1 cj pt.aa.nsm d.asf n.asf d.gsm n.gsm

δήσας ἑαυτοῦ τοὺς πόδας καὶ τὰς χεῖρας εἶπεν,
tied his own {the} hands and feet and {the} hands with it and said, "The Holy Spirit
1313 1571 3836 5931 2779 4546 2779 3836 5931 3306 3836 41 4460
pt.aa.nsm r.gsm.3 d.apm n.apm cj d.apf n.apf v.aai.3s

τάδε λέγει τὸ πνεῦμα τὸ ἅγιον,
says this: says The Spirit {the} Holy 'This is how the Jews will tie up in
3306 3840 3306 3836 4460 3836 41 4048 4048 4048 3836 2681 1313 1313 1313 1877
r.apn v.pai.3s d.nsn n.nsn d.nsn a.nsn

τὸν ἄνδρα οὗ ἐστιν ἡ ζώνη αὕτη, οὕτως δήσουσιν ἐν
Jerusalem the man whose belt this is, {the} belt this This is how will tie up in
2647 3836 467 4005 2438 4047 1639 3836 2438 4047 4048 1313 1877
d.asm n.asm r.gsm v.pai.3s d.nsf n.nsf r.nsf adv v.fai.3p p.d

Ἰερουσαλὴμ οἱ Ἰουδαῖοι καὶ παραδώσουσιν εἰς χεῖρας → ἐθνῶν.
Jerusalem the Jews and will deliver him into the hands of the Gentiles.'"
2647 3836 2681 2779 4140 1650 5931 1620
n.dsf d.npm a.npm cj v.fai.3p p.a n.apf n.gpn

12 ὡς δὲ ἠκούσαμεν ταῦτα, παρεκαλοῦμεν ἡμεῖς τε καὶ οἱ ἐντόπιοι
When {and} we heard this, urged both we both and the local people
6055 1254 201 4047 4151 5445 7005 5445 2779 3836 1954
cj cj v.aai.1p r.apn v.iai.1p r.np.1 cj cj d.npm a.npm

τοῦ μὴ ἀναβαίνειν αὐτὸν εἰς Ἰερουσαλήμ. 13 τότε ἀπεκρίθη ὁ
urged him ~ not to go up him to Jerusalem. Then Paul answered, {the}
4151 899 3836 3590 326 899 1650 2647 5538 4263 646 3836
d.gsn pl f.pa r.asm.3 p.a n.asf adv v.api.3s d.nsm

Παῦλος, τί ποιεῖτε κλαίοντες καὶ συνθρύπτοντές μου τὴν καρδίαν;
Paul "What ⌊are you doing,⌋ weeping and breaking my {the} heart? For
4263 5515 4472 3081 2779 5316 1609 3836 2840 1142
n.nsm r.asn v.pai.2p pt.pa.npm cj pt.pa.npm r.gs.1 d.asf n.asf

ἐγὼ γὰρ οὐ μόνον δεθῆναι ἀλλὰ καὶ ἀποθανεῖν εἰς Ἰερουσαλὴμ
I For am ready not only ⌊to be tied up⌋ but also to die in Jerusalem
1609 1142 2400 2290 4024 3667 1313 247 2779 633 1650 2647
r.ns.1 cj pl adv f.ap cj adv f.aa p.a n.asf

ἑτοίμως ἔχω ὑπὲρ τοῦ ὀνόματος τοῦ κυρίου Ἰησοῦ. 14 ↱ ↱ μὴ
ready am for the name of the Lord Jesus." And since he would not
2290 2400 5642 3836 3950 3836 3261 2652 1254 4275 899 4275 3590
adv v.pai.1s p.g d.gsn n.gsn d.gsm n.gsm n.gsm pl

πειθομένου δὲ αὐτοῦ ἡσυχάσαμεν εἰπόντες, ↱ τοῦ κυρίου τὸ θέλημα
be persuaded, And he we fell silent, saying, "Let the will of the Lord the will
4275 1254 899 2483 3306 1181 3836 2525 3836 3261 3836 2525
pt.pp.gsm cj r.gsm.3 v.aai.1p pt.aa.npm d.gsm n.gsm d.nsn n.nsn

γινέσθω. 15 μετὰ δὲ τὰς ἡμέρας ταύτας ↱ ἐπισκευασάμενοι ἀναβαίνομεν
be done." After {and} {the} these days these we got ready and started up
1181 3552 1254 3836 4047 2465 4047 326 2171 326
v.pmm.3s p.a cj d.apf n.apf r.apf pt.am.npm v.iai.1p

NASB

the house of Philip
the evangelist, who
was one of the
seven, we stayed
with him. 9 Now
this man had four
virgin daughters
who were prophet-
esses. 10 As we
were staying there
for some days, a
prophet named
Agabus came down
from Judea. 11 And
coming to us, he
took Paul's belt
and bound his own
feet and hands,
and said, "This
is what the Holy
Spirit says: 'In
this way the Jews
at Jerusalem will
bind the man who
owns this belt and
deliver him into
the hands of the
Gentiles.'" 12 When
we had heard this,
we as well as the
local residents
began begging
him not to go up to
Jerusalem. 13 Then
Paul answered,
"What are you
doing, weeping and
breaking my heart?
For I am ready not
only to be bound,
but even to die at
Jerusalem for the
name of the Lord
Jesus." 14 And since
he would not be
persuaded, we fell
silent, remarking,
"The will of the
Lord be done!"

Paul at Jerusalem

15 After these days
we got ready and
started on our way

NIV

to Jerusalem.
16 Some of the dis-
ciples from Caes-
area accompanied
us and brought
us to the home of
Mnason, where we
were to stay. He
was a man from
Cyprus and one of
the early disciples.

Paul's Arrival at Jerusalem

17 When we ar-
rived at Jerusalem,
the brothers and
sisters received
us warmly. 18 The
next day Paul and
the rest of us went
to see James, and
all the elders were
present. 19 Paul
greeted them and
reported in de-
tail what God had
done among the
Gentiles through
his ministry.
20 When they
heard this, they
praised God. Then
they said to Paul:
"You see, brother,
how many thou-
sands of Jews have
believed, and all
of them are zeal-
ous for the law.
21 They have been
informed that you
teach all the Jews
who live among
the Gentiles to
turn away from
Moses, telling
them not to cir-
cumcise their
children or live
according to our
customs. 22 What
shall we do? They
will certainly
hear that you have
come, 23 so do what
we tell you. There
are four men with
us who have made
a vow. 24 Take

εἰς Ἱεροσόλυμα· 16 συνῆλθον δὲ καὶ τῶν μαθητῶν ἀπὸ Καισαρείας
to Jerusalem. *came* And *{also}* ⌊some of the⌋ disciples from Caesarea came
1650 2642 5302 1254 2779 3836 3412 608 2791 5302
p.a n.apn v.aai.3p cj adv d.gpm n.gpm p.g n.gsf

σὺν ἡμῖν, ἄγοντες παρ᾽ ᾧ ξενισθῶμεν
with us, bringing Mnason of Cyprus, an early disciple, with whom we should lodge.
5250 7005 72 3643 3250 3250 5516 792 3412 4123 4005 3826
p.d r.dp.1 pt.pa.npm p.d r.dsm v.aps.1p

Μνάσωνί τινι Κυπρίῳ, ἀρχαίῳ μαθητῇ. 17 → γενομένων δὲ ἡμῶν εἰς
Mnason an of Cyprus early disciple When we arrived *{and} we* in
3643 5516 3250 792 3412 7005 1181 1254 7005 1650
n.dsm r.dsm n.dsm a.dsm n.dsm pt.am.gpm cj r.gp.1 p.a

Ἱεροσόλυμα ἀσμένως ἀπεδέξαντο ἡμᾶς οἱ ἀδελφοί. 18 τῇ δὲ
Jerusalem, *gladly* the brothers welcomed us gladly. *the brothers* ⌊On the⌋ *{and}*
2642 830 3836 81 622 7005 830 3836 81 3836 1254
n.apn adv v.ami.3p r.ap.1 d.npm n.npm d.dsf cj

ἐπιούσῃ εἰσῄει ὁ Παῦλος σὺν ἡμῖν πρὸς Ἰάκωβον, πάντες τε
⌊following day⌋ Paul went *{the} Paul* with us to James, and all *and* the
2079 4263 1655 3836 4263 5250 7005 4639 2610 5445 4246 5445 3836
pt.pa.dsf v.iai.3s d.nsm n.nsm p.d r.dp.1 p.a n.asm a.npm cj

παρεγένοντο οἱ πρεσβύτεροι. 19 καὶ ἀσπασάμενος αὐτοὺς ἐξηγεῖτο
elders were present. *the elders {and}* After he greeted them, ⌊he began to relate⌋
4565 4134 3836 4565 2779 832 899 2007
v.ami.3p d.npm a.npm cj pt.am.nsm r.apm.3 v.imi.3s

καθ᾽ ἓν ἕκαστον, ὧν ἐποίησεν ὁ θεὸς ἐν τοῖς ἔθνεσιν διὰ τῆς
one by one *one* what God had done *{the} God* among the Gentiles through *{the}* his
1667 2848 1651 1667 4005 2536 4472 3836 2536 1877 3836 1620 1328 3836 899
p.a a.asn r.asn r.gpn v.aai.3s d.nsm n.nsm p.d d.dpn n.dpn p.g d.gsf

διακονίας αὐτοῦ. 20 ↱ οἱ δὲ ἀκούσαντες ἐδόξαζον τὸν θεὸν
ministry. *his* And when they *And* heard it, ⌊they began to praise⌋ *{the}* God.
1355 899 1254 201 3836 1254 201 1519 3836 2536
n.gsf r.gsm.3 d.npm cj pt.aa.npm v.iai.3p d.asm n.asm

εἶπόν τε αὐτῷ, θεωρεῖς, ἀδελφέ, πόσαι μυριάδες εἰσὶν
And they said *And* to him, "You see, brother, how many thousands of believers ⌊there are⌋
5445 3306 5445 899 2555 81 4531 3689 3836 4409 1639
v.aai.3p cj r.dsm.3 v.pai.2s n.vsm r.npf n.npf v.pai.3p

ἐν τοῖς Ἰουδαίοις τῶν πεπιστευκότων καὶ πάντες ζηλωταὶ τοῦ νόμου
among the Jews, *of believers* and they are all zealous for the law.
1877 3836 2681 3836 4409 2779 5639 5639 4246 2421 3836 3795
p.d d.dpm a.dpm d.gpm pt.ra.gpm cj a.npm n.npm d.gsm n.gsm

ὑπάρχουσιν· 21 κατηχήθησαν δὲ περὶ σοῦ ὅτι ἀποστασίαν διδάσκεις ἀπὸ
they are But they were told *But* about you that *to forsake* you are teaching *{from}*
5639 1254 2994 1254 4309 5148 4022 686 1438 608
v.pai.3p v.api.3p cj p.g r.gs.2 cj n.asf v.pai.2s p.g

Μωϋσέως τοὺς κατὰ τὰ ἔθνη πάντας Ἰουδαίους
Moses all the Jews who are among the Gentiles *all Jews* to forsake
3707 4246 3836 2681 2848 3836 1620 4246 2681 686 686
n.gsm d.apm p.a d.apn n.apn a.apm a.apm

λέγων μὴ περιτέμνειν αὐτοὺς τὰ τέκνα μηδὲ
Moses, telling them not to circumcise *them* their children and not to walk according to
3707 3306 899 3590 4362 899 3836 5451 3593 4344 4344 4344 4344
pt.pa.nsm pl f.pa r.apm.3 d.apn n.apn cj

τοῖς ἔθεσιν περιπατεῖν. 22 τί οὖν ἐστιν; ↱ ↱ πάντως ἀκούσονται
our customs. *to walk according to* What then is to be done? They will certainly hear
3836 1621 4344 5515 4036 1639 201 201 4122 201
d.dpn n.dpn f.pa r.nsn cj v.pai.3s adv v.fmi.3p

ὅτι ἐλήλυθας. 23 τοῦτο οὖν ποίησον ὅ σοι λέγομεν, εἰσὶν
that you have come. *{this}* Therefore, do what we tell you. *we tell* ⌊There are⌋
4022 2262 4047 4036 4472 4005 3306 3306 5148 3306 1639
cj v.rai.2s r.asn cj v.aam.2s r.asn r.ds.2 v.pai.1p v.pai.3p

ἡμῖν ἄνδρες τέσσαρες εὐχὴν ἔχοντες ἐφ᾽ ἑαυτῶν. 24
⌊with us⌋ four men *four vow* ⌊who have taken⌋ upon themselves a vow. Take
7005 5475 467 5475 2376 2400 2093 1571 2376 4161
r.dp.1 n.npm a.npm n.asf pt.pa.npm p.g r.gpm.3

NASB

up to Jerusalem.
16 *Some* of the
disciples from
Caesarea also came
with us, taking us
to Mnason of Cy-
prus, a disciple of
long standing with
whom we were to
lodge.
17 After we arrived
in Jerusalem, the
brethren received
us gladly. 18 And the
following day Paul
went in with us to
James, and all the
elders were pres-
ent. 19 After he had
greeted them, he
began to relate one
by one the things
which God had
done among the
Gentiles through
his ministry. 20 And
when they heard it
they *began* glorify-
ing God; and they
said to him, "You
see, brother, how
many thousands
there are among the
Jews of those who
have believed, and
they are all zealous
for the Law; 21 and
they have been told
about you, that you
are teaching all
the Jews who are
among the Gentiles
to forsake Moses,
telling them not to
circumcise their
children nor to
walk according
to the customs.
22 What, then, is *to
be done?* They will
certainly hear that
you have come.
23 Therefore do this
that we tell you.
We have four men
who are under a
vow; 24 take them

NIV

these men, join
in their purifica-
tion rites and pay
their expenses, so
that they can have
their heads shaved.
Then everyone
will know there is
no truth in these
reports about you,
but that you your-
self are living in
obedience to the
law. 25 As for the
Gentile believers,
we have written to
them our decision
that they should
abstain from food
sacrificed to idols,
from blood, from
the meat of stran-
gled animals and
from sexual immo-
rality."
26 The next day
Paul took the men
and purified him-
self along with
them. Then he
went to the temple
to give notice of
the date when the
days of purifica-
tion would end and
the offering would
be made for each
of them.

Paul Arrested

27 When the seven
days were nearly
over, some Jews
from the prov-
ince of Asia saw
Paul at the temple.
They stirred up
the whole crowd
and seized him,
28 shouting, "Fel-
low Israelites, help
us! This is the man
who teaches ev-
eryone everywhere
against our people
and our law and
this place. And
besides, he has
brought Greeks
into the temple and
defiled this holy
place."

τούτους παραλαβὼν ἁγνίσθητι σὺν αὐτοῖς καὶ → δαπάνησον ἐπ᾽
these men *Take* and purify yourself ⌞along with⌟ them and pay their expenses *{to}*
4047 4161 49 5250 899 2779 899 1251 2093
r.apm pt.aa.nsm v.apm.2s p.d r.dpm.3 cj v.aam.2s p.d

αὐτοῖς ἵνα ξυρήσονται τὴν κεφαλήν, καὶ γνώσονται πάντες ὅτι
their that they may shave their heads, and everyone will know *everyone* that there is
899 2671 3834 3836 3051 2779 4246 1182 4246 4022 1639 1639
r.dpm.3 cj v.fmi.3p d.asf n.asf cj v.fmi.3p a.npm cj

ὧν κατήχηνται περὶ σοῦ οὐδέν ἐστιν ἀλλὰ → στοιχεῖς
nothing in what ⌞they have been told⌟ about you, *nothing there is* but that you yourself walk
4029 4005 2994 4309 5148 4029 1639 247 899 5123
r.gpn v.rpi.3p p.g r.gs.2 a.nsn v.pai.3s cj v.pai.2s

καὶ αὐτὸς φυλάσσων τὸν νόμον. 25 περὶ δὲ τῶν πεπιστευκότων
{also} *yourself* keeping the law. But as for *But* the Gentiles who have believed,
2779 899 5875 3836 3795 1254 4309 1254 3836 1620 4409
adv r.nsm pt.pa.nsm d.asm n.asm p.g cj d.gpn pt.ra.gpn

ἐθνῶν ἡμεῖς ἐπεστείλαμεν ← κρίναντες φυλάσσεσθαι αὐτοὺς
Gentiles we sent a letter with our judgment that they should abstain from *they*
1620 7005 2182 3212 899 5875 899
n.gpn r.np.1 v.aai.1p pt.aa.npm f.pm r.apm.3

τό τε εἰδωλόθυτον καὶ αἷμα καὶ πνικτὸν καὶ
what ~ ⌞has been sacrificed to idols,⌟ and from blood, and from ⌞what has been strangled,⌟ and
3836 5445 1628 2779 135 2779 4465 2779
d.asn cj n.asn cj n.asn cj a.asn cj

πορνείαν. 26 τότε ὁ Παῦλος παραλαβὼν τοὺς ἄνδρας τῇ
from sexual immorality." Then *{the}* Paul took the men and ⌞on the⌟
4518 5538 3836 4263 4161 3836 467 3836
n.asf adv d.nsm n.nsm pt.aa.nsm d.apm n.apm d.dsf

ἐχομένῃ ἡμέρᾳ σὺν αὐτοῖς ἁγνισθείς, εἰσῄει εἰς τὸ ἱερὸν
next day he purified himself with them *purified himself* and went into the temple,
2400 2465 49 49 5250 899 49 1655 1650 3836 2639
pt.pm.dsf n.dsf p.d r.dpm.3 pt.ap.nsm v.iai.3s p.a d.asn n.asn

διαγγέλλων τὴν ἐκπλήρωσιν τῶν ἡμερῶν τοῦ ἁγνισμοῦ ἕως οὗ ←
⌞giving notice of⌟ the completion of the days of the purification, at which time the
1334 3836 1741 3836 2465 3836 50 2401 4005 2401 3836
pt.pa.nsm d.asf n.asf d.gpf n.gpf d.gsm n.gsm p.g r.gsm

προσηνέχθη ὑπὲρ ἑνὸς ἑκάστου αὐτῶν ἡ προσφορά. 27 ὡς
sacrifice would be offered ⌞on behalf of⌟ each one *each* of them. *the* *sacrifice* When
4714 4712 5642 1667 1651 1667 899 3836 4714 6055
v.api.3s p.g a.gsm r.gsm r.gpm.3 d.nsf n.nsf cj

δὲ ἔμελλον αἱ ἑπτὰ ἡμέραι συντελεῖσθαι, οἱ ἀπὸ τῆς
{and} the seven days were about *the seven days* to be completed, the Jews from *{the}*
1254 3836 2231 2465 3516 3836 2231 2465 5334 3836 2681 608 3836
cj v.iai.3p d.npf a.npf n.npf f.pp d.npm p.g d.gsf

Ἀσίας Ἰουδαῖοι θεασάμενοι αὐτὸν ἐν τῷ ἱερῷ συνέχεον πάντα τὸν ὄχλον
Asia, *Jews* upon seeing him in the temple, stirred up the whole *the* crowd
823 2681 2517 899 1877 3836 2639 5177 3836 4246 3836 4063
n.gsf a.npm pt.am.npm r.asm.3 p.d d.dsn n.dsn v.iai.3p a.asm d.asm n.asm

καὶ ἐπέβαλον ἐπ᾽ αὐτὸν τὰς χεῖρας 28 κράζοντες, ἄνδρες Ἰσραηλῖται, βοηθεῖτε·
and laid hands on him, *{the}* *hands* crying out, "Men of Israel, help!
2779 2095 5931 2093 899 3836 5931 3189 467 2703 1070
cj v.aai.3p p.a r.asm.3 d.apf n.apf pt.pa.npm n.vpm n.vpm v.pam.2p

οὗτός ἐστιν ὁ ἄνθρωπος ὁ κατὰ τοῦ λαοῦ καὶ
This is the man who is teaching everyone everywhere against our people, *{and}*
4047 1639 3836 476 3836 1438 1438 4246 4114 2848 3836 3295 2779
r.nsm v.pai.3s d.nsm n.nsm d.nsm p.g d.gsm n.gsm cj

τοῦ νόμου καὶ τοῦ τόπου τούτου πάντας πανταχῇ διδάσκων, ἔτι τε
our law, and *{the}* this place. *this* *everyone* *everywhere* *is teaching* And besides, *And*
3836 3795 2779 3836 4047 5536 4047 4246 4114 1438 5445 2285 5445
d.gsm n.gsm cj d.gsm n.gsm r.gsm a.apm adv pt.pa.nsm adv cj

καὶ Ἕλληνας εἰσήγαγεν εἰς τὸ ἱερὸν καὶ → →
he even brought Greeks *he brought* into the temple and has made this holy place
1652 2779 1652 1818 1652 1650 3836 2639 2779 4047 41 5536
adv n.apm v.aai.3s p.a d.asn n.asn cj

NASB

and purify yourself
along with them,
and pay their
expenses so that
they may shave
their heads; and
all will know that
there is nothing to
the things which
they have been told
about you, but that
you yourself also
walk orderly, keep-
ing the Law. 25 But
concerning the
Gentiles who have
believed, we wrote,
having decided
that they should
abstain from meat
sacrificed to idols
and from blood
and from what
is strangled and
from fornication."
26 Then Paul took
the men, and the
next day, purifying
himself along with
them, went into the
temple giving no-
tice of the comple-
tion of the days of
purification, until
the sacrifice was
offered for each
one of them.

Paul Seized in the Temple

27 When the seven
days were almost
over, the Jews from
Asia, upon seeing
him in the temple,
began to stir up
all the crowd and
laid hands on him,
28 crying out, "Men
of Israel, come to
our aid! This is the
man who preaches
to all men every-
where against our
people and the Law
and this place; and
besides he has even
brought Greeks
into the temple and
has defiled this
holy place."

NIV

29 (They had previously seen Trophimus the Ephesian in the city with Paul and assumed that Paul had brought him into the temple.)

30 The whole city was aroused, and the people came running from all directions. Seizing Paul, they dragged him from the temple, and immediately the gates were shut.

31 While they were trying to kill him, news reached the commander of the Roman troops that the whole city of Jerusalem was in an uproar. 32 He at once took some officers and soldiers and ran down to the crowd. When the rioters saw the commander and his soldiers, they stopped beating Paul.

33 The commander came up and arrested him and ordered him to be bound with two chains. Then he asked who he was and what he had done. 34 Some in the crowd shouted one thing and some another, and since the commander could not get at the truth because of the uproar, he ordered that Paul be taken into the barracks. 35 When Paul reached the steps, the violence of the mob was so great he had to be carried

κεκοίνωκεν τὸν ἅγιον τόπον τοῦτον. 29 ἦσαν γὰρ προεωρακότες Τρόφιμον τὸν
unclean." *{the}* *holy* *place* *this* For they had *For* previously seen Trophimus the
3124 3836 41 5536 4047 1142 1639 1142 4632 5576 3836
v.rai.3s d.asm a.asm n.asm r.asm v.iai.3p cj pt.ra.npm n.asm d.asm

Ἐφέσιον ἐν τῇ πόλει σὺν αὐτῷ, ὃν ἐνόμιζον ὅτι εἰς τὸ
Ephesian in the city with him, and *him* they assumed that Paul had taken him into the
2386 1877 3836 4484 5250 899 4005 3787 4022 4263 1652 1652 4005 1650 3836
n.asm p.d d.dsf n.dsf p.d r.dsm.3 r.asm v.iai.3p cj p.a d.asn

ἱερὸν εἰσήγαγεν ὁ Παῦλος. 30 ἐκινήθη τε ἡ πόλις ὅλη
temple. *had taken* *{the}* *Paul* Then all the city ⌞was stirred up,⌟ *Then* *the* *city* *all*
2639 1652 3836 4263 5445 3910 3836 4484 3075 5445 3836 4484 3910
n.asn v.aai.3s d.nsm n.nsm v.api.3s cj d.nsf n.nsf a.nsf

καὶ ↱ ἐγένετο συνδρομὴ τοῦ λαοῦ, καὶ ↱ ἐπιλαβόμενοι τοῦ
and a mob of people quickly formed. *mob* *of* *people* *{and}* They seized *{the}*
2779 5282 3836 3295 5282 1181 5282 3836 3295 2779 1816 2138 3836
cj v.ami.3s n.nsf d.gsm n.gsm cj pt.am.npm d.gsm

Παύλου εἷλκον αὐτὸν ἔξω τοῦ ἱεροῦ καὶ εὐθέως ἐκλείσθησαν
Paul and dragged him outside the temple, and immediately the gates were shut.
4263 1816 899 2032 3836 2639 2779 2311 3836 2598 3091
n.gsm v.iai.3p r.asm.3 p.g d.gsn n.gsn cj adv v.api.3p

αἱ θύραι. 31 ζητούντων τε αὐτὸν ἀποκτεῖναι
the *gates* And ⌞while they were trying⌟ *And* to kill him, *to kill* a report
3836 2598 5445 2426 5445 650 650 899 650 5762
d.npf n.npf pt.pa.gpm cj r.asm.3 f.aa

ἀνέβη φάσις τῷ χιλιάρχῳ τῆς σπείρης ὅτι ὅλη
⌞was sent up⌟ *report* ⌞to the⌟ ⌞commanding officer⌟ of the detachment that all Jerusalem
326 5762 3836 5941 3836 5061 4022 3910 2647
v.aai.3s n.nsf d.dsm n.dsm d.gsf n.gsf cj a.nsf

συγχύννεται Ἰερουσαλήμ. 32 ὃς ἐξαυτῆς παραλαβὼν στρατιώτας καὶ
was in an uproar. *Jerusalem* At once he *At once* took along some soldiers and
5177 2647 1994 1994 4005 1994 4161 5132 2779
v.ppi.3s n.nsf r.nsm adv pt.aa.nsm n.apm cj

ἑκατοντάρχας κατέδραμεν ἐπ' αὐτούς, ↱ οἱ δὲ ἰδόντες τὸν
centurions and ran down to them; and when they *and* saw the
1672 2963 2093 899 1254 1625 3836 1254 1625 3836
n.apm v.aai.3s p.a r.apm.3 d.npm cj pt.aa.npm d.asm

χιλίαρχον καὶ τοὺς στρατιώτας ἐπαύσαντο τύπτοντες τὸν Παῦλον. 33 τότε
⌞commanding officer⌟ and the soldiers, they stopped beating *{the}* Paul. Then
5941 2779 3836 5132 4264 5597 3836 4263 5538
n.asm cj d.apm n.apm v.ami.3p pt.pa.npm d.asm n.asm adv

ἐγγίσας ὁ χιλίαρχος ἐπελάβετο αὐτοῦ καὶ ἐκέλευσεν
came up the ⌞commanding officer⌟ came up and arrested him and ordered him
1581 3836 5941 1581 1581 2138 899 2779 3027
pt.aa.nsm d.nsm n.nsm v.ami.3s r.gsm.3 cj v.aai.3s

δεθῆναι → ἁλύσεσι δυσί, καὶ ἐπυνθάνετο τίς εἴη καὶ τί ἐστιν
⌞to be tied up⌟ with two chains. *two* Then he asked who ⌞he might be⌟ and what he had
1313 1545 268 1545 2779 4785 5515 1639 2779 5515 1639
f.ap n.dpf a.dpf cj v.imi.3s r.nsm v.pao.3s cj r.asn v.pai.3s

πεποιηκώς. 34 ἄλλοι δὲ ἄλλο τι ἐπεφώνουν ἐν τῷ
done. Some *{and}* in the crowd were shouting one thing, *were shouting* *in* *the*
4472 257 1254 1877 3836 4063 2215 2215 257 5516 2215 1877 3836
pt.ra.nsm r.npm cj r.asn r.asn v.iai.3p p.d d.dsm

ὄχλῳ. ↱ ↱ ⌞μὴ δυναμένου⌟ δὲ αὐτοῦ γνῶναι τὸ
crowd some another, and since he was unable *and* *he* to find out the
4063 1254 1538 899 1538 3590 1538 1254 899 1182 3836
n.dsm pl pt.pp.gsm cj r.gsm.3 f.aa d.asn

ἀσφαλὲς διὰ τὸν θόρυβον ἐκέλευσεν ἄγεσθαι αὐτὸν εἰς τὴν
truth ⌞because of⌟ the uproar, he ordered him to be brought *him* into the
855 1328 3836 2573 3027 899 72 899 1650 3836
a.asn p.a d.asm n.asm v.aai.3s f.pp r.asm.3 p.a d.asf

παρεμβολήν. 35 ὅτε δὲ ἐγένετο ἐπὶ τοὺς ἀναβαθμούς, συνέβη βαστάζεσθαι
barracks. When *{and}* he got to the stairs, Paul had to be carried
4213 4021 1254 1181 2093 3836 325 899 5201 1002
n.asf cj cj v.ami.3s p.a d.apm n.apm v.aai.3s f.pp

NASB

29 For they had previously seen Trophimus the Ephesian in the city with him, and they supposed that Paul had brought him into the temple. 30 Then all the city was provoked, and the people rushed together, and taking hold of Paul they dragged him out of the temple, and immediately the doors were shut. 31 While they were seeking to kill him, a report came up to the [a]commander of the *Roman* cohort that all Jerusalem was in confusion. 32 At once he took along *some* soldiers and centurions and ran down to them; and when they saw the commander and the soldiers, they stopped beating Paul. 33 Then the commander came up and took hold of him, and ordered him to be bound with two chains; and he *began* asking who he was and what he had done. 34 But among the crowd some were shouting one thing *and* some another, and when he could not find out the facts because of the uproar, he ordered him to be brought into the barracks. 35 When he got to the stairs, he was carried

[a] I.e. chiliarch, in command of one thousand troops

NIV

by the soldiers.
36 The crowd that
followed kept
shouting, "Get rid
of him!"

Paul Speaks to the Crowd

37 As the soldiers
were about to take
Paul into the bar-
racks, he asked the
commander, "May
I say something to
you?"
"Do you speak
Greek?" he re-
plied. 38 "Aren't
you the Egyptian
who started a re-
volt and led four
thousand terrorists
out into the wil-
derness some time
ago?"
39 Paul answered,
"I am a Jew, from
Tarsus in Cilicia,
a citizen of no or-
dinary city. Please
let me speak to the
people."
40 After receiving
the commander's
permission, Paul
stood on the steps
and motioned to
the crowd. When
they were all si-
lent, he said to
them in Aramaic[a]:
22 1 "Brothers
and fathers,
listen now to my
defense."
2 When they heard
him speak to them
in Aramaic, they
became very quiet.
Then Paul said:
3 "I am a Jew, born
in Tarsus

[a] 40 Or possibly *Hebrew*; also in 22:2

αὐτὸν ὑπὸ τῶν στρατιωτῶν διὰ τὴν βίαν τοῦ ὄχλου, 36 ἠκολούθει γὰρ
Paul by the soldiers ⌞because of⌟ the violence of the mob, *kept following* for
899 5679 3836 5132 1328 3836 1040 3836 4063 199 1142
r.asm.3 p.g d.gpm n.gpm p.a d.asf n.asf d.gsm n.gsm v.iai.3s cj

τὸ πλῆθος τοῦ λαοῦ κράζοντες, αἶρε αὐτόν.
the crowd of people kept following and shouting, ⌞"Away with⌟ him!"
3836 4436 3836 3295 199 199 3189 149 899
d.nsn n.nsn d.gsm n.gsm pt.pa.npm v.pam.2s r.asm.3

37 μέλλων τε εἰσάγεσθαι εἰς τὴν παρεμβολὴν ὁ Παῦλος λέγει τῷ
⌞As he was about⌟ ~ to be brought into the barracks, *{the}* Paul said ⌞to the⌟
3516 5445 1652 1650 3836 4213 3836 4263 3306 3836
pt.pa.nsm cj f.pp p.a d.asf n.asf d.nsm n.nsm v.pai.3s d.dsm

χιλιάρχῳ, εἰ ἔξεστίν μοι εἰπεῖν τι πρὸς σέ; ὁ δὲ ἔφη,
⌞commanding officer,⌟ *{if}* "Is it allowed ⌞for me⌟ to say something to you?" He *{and}* replied,
5941 1623 1997 1609 3306 5516 4639 5148 3836 1254 5774
n.dsm cj v.pai.3s r.ds.1 f.aa r.asn p.a r.as.2 d.nsm cj v.iai.3s

Ἑλληνιστὶ γινώσκεις; 38 οὐκ ἄρα σὺ εἶ ὁ
"Do you know Greek? *Do you know* Then you are not *Then you are* the
1182 1182 1182 1822 1182 726 5148 1639 4024 726 5148 1639 3836
adv v.pai.2s pl cj r.ns.2 v.pai.2s d.nsm

Αἰγύπτιος ὁ πρὸ τούτων τῶν ἡμερῶν ἀναστατώσας καὶ ἐξαγαγὼν εἰς τὴν
Egyptian who ⌞prior to⌟ these *{the}* days stirred up a revolt and led into the
130 3836 4574 4047 3836 2465 415 2779 1974 1650 3836
n.nsm d.nsm p.g r.gpf d.gpf n.gpf pt.aa.nsm cj pt.aa.nsm p.a d.asf

ἔρημον τοὺς τετρακισχιλίους ἄνδρας τῶν σικαρίων; 39 εἶπεν δὲ ὁ
desert the four thousand men of the Assassins?" But Paul replied, *But* *{the}*
2245 3836 5483 467 3836 4974 1254 4263 3306 1254 3836
n.asf d.apm a.apm n.apm d.gpm n.gpm v.aai.3s cj d.nsm

Παῦλος, ἐγὼ ἄνθρωπος μέν εἰμι Ἰουδαῖος, Ταρσεὺς τῆς Κιλικίας, οὐκ
Paul "I *{person}* ~ am a Jew, from Tarsus in Cilicia, a citizen of no
4263 1609 476 3525 1639 2681 5432 3836 3070 4489 4024
n.nsm r.ns.1 n.nsm pl v.pai.1s a.nsm n.nsm d.gsf n.gsf pl

ἀσήμου πόλεως πολίτης· δέομαι δέ σου, ἐπίτρεψόν μοι λαλῆσαι πρὸς τὸν λαόν.
obscure city. *citizen* I beg *{and}* you, allow me to speak to the people."
817 4484 4489 1289 1254 5148 2205 1609 3281 4639 3836 3295
a.gsf n.gsf n.nsm v.ppi.1s cj r.gs.2 v.aam.2s r.ds.1 f.aa p.a d.asm n.asm

40 → ἐπιτρέψαντος ← δὲ αὐτοῦ ὁ Παῦλος ἑστὼς ἐπὶ τῶν
And when he had given him permission, *And he* *{the}* Paul stood on the
1254 899 2205 1254 899 3836 4263 2705 2093 3836
pt.aa.gsm cj r.gsm.3 d.nsm n.nsm pt.ra.nsm p.g d.gpm

ἀναβαθμῶν κατέσεισεν τῇ χειρὶ τῷ λαῷ. πολλῆς δὲ
steps and motioned with his hand ⌞to the⌟ people. And when there was a great *And*
325 2939 3836 5931 3836 3295 1254 1181 1181 1181 4498 1254
n.gpm v.aai.3s d.dsf n.dsf d.dsm n.dsm a.gsf cj

σιγῆς γενομένης προσεφώνησεν τῇ Ἑβραΐδι διαλέκτῳ λέγων,
hush, *when there was* he addressed them ⌞in the⌟ Hebrew language, saying:
4968 1181 4715 3836 1579 1365 3306
n.gsf pt.am.gsf v.aai.3s d.dsf a.dsf n.dsf pt.pa.nsm

22:1 ⌞ἄνδρες ἀδελφοὶ⌟ καὶ πατέρες, ἀκούσατέ ← μου τῆς
"My brothers and fathers, listen now to me *{the}* as I make my
467 81 2779 4252 201 3815 1609 3836
n.vpm n.vpm cj n.vpm v.aam.2p r.gs.1 d.gsf

πρὸς ὑμᾶς νυνὶ ἀπολογίας. 2 ἀκούσαντες δὲ ὅτι
defense to you." *now* *defense* And when they heard *And* that he was addressing them
665 4639 7007 3815 665 1254 201 1254 4022 4715 4715 4715 899
p.a r.ap.2 adv n.gsf pt.aa.npm cj cj

τῇ Ἑβραΐδι διαλέκτῳ προσεφώνει αὐτοῖς, μᾶλλον παρέσχον
⌞in the⌟ Hebrew language, *he was addressing* *them* they became even more *they became*
3836 1579 1365 4715 899 4218 4218 3437 4218
d.dsf a.dsf n.dsf v.iai.3s r.dpm.3 adv.c v.aai.3p

ἡσυχίαν. καὶ φησίν, 3 ἐγώ εἰμι ἀνὴρ Ἰουδαῖος, γεγεννημένος ἐν Ταρσῷ
quiet. And he said: "I am a Jewish man, *Jewish* born in Tarsus
2484 2779 5774 1609 1639 2681 467 2681 1164 1877 5433
n.asf cj v.pai.3s r.ns.1 v.pai.1s n.nsm a.nsm pt.rp.nsm p.d n.dsf

NASB

by the soldiers
because of the vio-
lence of the mob;
36 for the multitude
of the people kept
following them,
shouting, "Away
with him!"
37 As Paul was
about to be brought
into the barracks,
he said to the com-
mander, "May I say
something to you?"
And he *said, "Do
you know Greek?
38 Then you are not
the Egyptian who
some time ago
stirred up a revolt
and led the four
thousand men of
the Assassins out
into the wilder-
ness?" 39 But Paul
said, "I am a Jew
of Tarsus in Cilicia,
a citizen of no in-
significant city; and
I beg you, allow
me to speak to the
people." 40 When
he had given him
permission, Paul,
standing on the
stairs, motioned to
the people with his
hand; and when
there was a great
hush, he spoke
to them in the
Hebrew dialect,
saying,

Paul's Defense before the Jews

22:1 "Brethren and
fathers, hear my
defense which I
now *offer* to you."
2 And when they
heard that he was
addressing them in
the Hebrew dialect,
they became even
more quiet; and he
*said,
3 "I am a Jew, born
in Tarsus of Cilicia,

NIV

of Cilicia, but
brought up in this
city. I studied un-
der Gamaliel and
was thoroughly
trained in the law
of our ancestors.
I was just as zeal-
ous for God as any
of you are today.
[4]I persecuted the
followers of this
Way to their death,
arresting both men
and women and
throwing them
into prison, [5]as the
high priest and all
the Council can
themselves testify.
I even obtained
letters from them
to their associates
in Damascus, and
went there to bring
these people as
prisoners to Jeru-
salem to be pun-
ished.
[6]"About noon as
I came near Da-
mascus, suddenly
a bright light from
heaven flashed
around me. [7]I fell
to the ground and
heard a voice say
to me, 'Saul! Saul!
Why do you perse-
cute me?'
[8]" 'Who are you,
Lord?' I asked.
" 'I am Jesus of
Nazareth, whom
you are persecut-
ing,' he replied.
[9]My companions
saw the light, but
they did not un-
derstand the voice
of him who was
speaking to me.
[10]" 'What

τῆς Κιλικίας, ἀνατεθραμμένος δὲ ἐν τῇ πόλει ταύτῃ, παρὰ τοὺς πόδας
of Cilicia, but brought up *but* in *{the}* this city *this* at the feet
3836 3070 1254 427 1254 1877 3836 4047 4484 4047 4123 3836 4546
d.gsf n.gsf pt.rp.nsm cj p.d d.dsf n.dsf r.dsf p.a d.apm n.apm

Γαμαλιὴλ πεπαιδευμένος κατὰ ἀκρίβειαν τοῦ πατρῴου νόμου,
of Gamaliel, educated ⌞according to⌟ the strictness of the ancestral law, being
1137 4084 2848 205 3836 4262 3795 5639
n.gsm pt.rp.nsm p.a n.asf d.gsm a.gsm n.gsm

ζηλωτὴς ὑπάρχων τοῦ θεοῦ καθὼς πάντες ὑμεῖς ἐστε σήμερον· [4]ὃς
zealous *being* for God just as you all *you* are today. *{who}* I
2421 5639 3836 2536 2777 7007 4246 7007 1639 4958 4005 1503
n.nsm pt.pa.nsm d.gsm n.gsm cj a.npm r.np.2 v.pai.2p adv r.nsm

ταύτην τὴν ὁδὸν ἐδίωξα ἄχρι θανάτου δεσμεύων
persecuted the followers of this *{the}* Way *I persecuted* ⌞even to⌟ their death, putting in chains
1503 4047 3836 3847 1503 948 2505 1297
r.asf d.asf n.asf v.aai.1s p.g n.gsm pt.pa.nsm

καὶ παραδιδοὺς εἰς φυλακὰς ἄνδρας τε καὶ γυναῖκας,
both men and women and delivering them to prison, *men* *both* *and* *women*
5445 467 2779 1222 2779 4140 1650 5871 467 5445 2779 1222
cj pt.pa.nsm p.a n.apf n.apm cj cj n.apf

[5]ὡς καὶ ὁ ἀρχιερεὺς μαρτυρεῖ μοι καὶ πᾶν τὸ πρεσβυτέριον,
as also the high priest *can bear witness* *me* and the whole *{the}* council of elders can bear
6055 2779 3836 797 3455 1609 2779 4246 3836 4564 3455 3455
cj adv d.nsm n.nsm v.pai.3s r.ds.1 cj a.nsn d.nsn n.nsn

παρ' ὧν καὶ ἐπιστολὰς δεξάμενος πρὸς τοὺς ἀδελφοὺς
me witness. From them *{also}* I received letters *received* to the brothers, and I
1609 3455 4123 4005 2779 1312 2186 1312 4639 3836 81 4513
p.g r.gpm adv n.apf pt.am.nsm p.a d.apm n.apm

εἰς Δαμασκὸν ἐπορευόμην, ἄξων καὶ τοὺς ἐκεῖσε ὄντας
went toward Damascus *I went* to take those also *those* who were there *who were* and
4513 1650 1242 4513 72 3836 2779 3836 1639 1639 1698 1639
p.a n.asf v.imi.1s pt.fa.nsm adv d.apm adv pt.pa.apm

δεδεμένους ← ← εἰς Ἰερουσαλὴμ ἵνα τιμωρηθῶσιν. [6]ἐγένετο δέ ↱
bring them in bonds to Jerusalem to be punished. *{it happened that}* *{and}* As
1313 1650 2647 2671 5512 1181 1254 4513
pt.rp.apm p.a n.asf cj v.aps.3p v.ami.3s cj

μοι πορευομένῳ καὶ ἐγγίζοντι τῇ Δαμασκῷ περὶ μεσημβρίαν ἐξαίφνης ἐκ τοῦ
I journeyed and came near to Damascus, about noon suddenly ⌞out of⌟ *{the}*
1609 4513 2779 1581 3836 1242 4309 3540 1978 1666 3836
r.ds.1 pt.pm.dsm cj pt.pa.dsm d.dsf n.dsf p.a n.asf adv p.g d.gsm

οὐρανοῦ περιαστράψαι φῶς ἱκανὸν περὶ ἐμέ, [7]ἔπεσά τε εἰς τὸ
heaven flashed a brilliant light *brilliant* all around me. I fell ~ to the
4041 4313 2653 5890 2653 4309 1609 4406 5445 1650 3836
n.gsm f.aa n.asn a.asn p.a r.as.1 v.aai.1s cj p.a d.asn

ἔδαφος καὶ ἤκουσα φωνῆς λεγούσης μοι, Σαοὺλ Σαούλ, τί
ground and heard a voice saying to me, 'Saul, Saul, why are you persecuting
1611 2779 201 5889 3306 1609 4910 4910 5515 1503 1503 1503
n.asn cj v.aai.1s n.gsf pt.pa.gsf r.ds.1 n.vsm n.vsm r.asn

με διώκεις; [8] ἐγὼ δὲ ἀπεκρίθην, τίς εἶ, κύριε; εἶπέν τε
me?' *are you persecuting* And I *And* answered, 'Who ⌞are you,⌟ Lord?' And he said *And*
1609 1503 1254 1609 1254 646 5515 1639 3261 5445 3306 5445
r.as.1 v.pai.2s r.ns.1 cj v.api.1s r.nsm v.pai.2s n.vsm v.aai.3s cj

πρός με, ἐγώ εἰμι Ἰησοῦς ὁ Ναζωραῖος, ὃν σὺ διώκεις. [9] οἱ δὲ
to me, 'I am Jesus of Nazareth, whom you are persecuting.' Now those *Now*
4639 1609 1609 1639 2652 3836 3717 4005 5148 1503 1254 3836 1254
p.a r.as.1 r.ns.1 v.pai.1s n.nsm d.nsm n.nsm r.asm r.ns.2 v.pai.2s d.npm cj

σὺν ἐμοὶ ὄντες τὸ μὲν φῶς ἐθεάσαντο[a] τὴν δὲ
who were with me *who were* saw the ~ light *saw* but did not understand the *but*
1639 1639 5250 1609 1639 2517 3836 3525 5890 2517 1254 201 4024 201 3836 1254
p.d r.ds.1 pt.pa.npm d.asn pl n.asn v.ami.3p d.asf cj

φωνὴν οὐκ ἤκουσαν τοῦ λαλοῦντός μοι. [10] εἶπον δέ, τί
voice *not* *did understand* of the ⌞one who was speaking to⌟ me. And I said, *And* 'What
5889 4024 201 3836 3281 1609 1254 3306 1254 5515
n.asf pl v.aai.3p d.gsm pt.pa.gsm r.ds.1 v.aai.1s cj r.asn

NASB

but brought up in
this city, educated
under Gamaliel,
strictly accord-
ing to the law of
our fathers, being
zealous for God
just as you all are
today. [4]I persecuted
this Way to the
death, binding and
putting both men
and women into
prisons, [5]as also the
high priest and all
the Council of the
elders can testify.
From them I also
received letters
to the brethren,
and started off
for Damascus in
order to bring even
those who were
there to Jerusalem
as prisoners to be
punished.
[6]"But it happened
that as I was on my
way, approaching
Damascus about
noontime, a very
bright light sud-
denly flashed from
heaven all around
me, [7]and I fell to
the ground and
heard a voice say-
ing to me, 'Saul,
Saul, why are you
persecuting Me?'
[8]And I answered,
'Who are You,
Lord?' And He
said to me, 'I am
Jesus the Nazarene,
whom you are
persecuting.' [9]And
those who were
with me saw the
light, to be sure,
but did not under-
stand the voice of
the One who was
speaking to me.
[10]And I said,

[a] καὶ ἔμφοβοι ἐγένοντο included by TR after ἐθεάσαντο.

NIV

shall I do, Lord?' I asked.

"'Get up,' the Lord said, 'and go into Damascus. There you will be told all that you have been assigned to do.' [11]My companions led me by the hand into Damascus, because the brilliance of the light had blinded me.

[12]"A man named Ananias came to see me. He was a devout observer of the law and highly respected by all the Jews living there. [13]He stood beside me and said, 'Brother Saul, receive your sight!' And at that very moment I was able to see him.

[14]"Then he said: 'The God of our ancestors has chosen you to know his will and to see the Righteous One and to hear words from his mouth. [15]You will be his witness to all people of what you have seen and heard. [16]And now what are you waiting for? Get up, be baptized and wash your sins away, calling on his name.'

[17]"When I returned to Jerusalem and was praying at the temple, I fell into a trance [18]and saw the Lord speaking to me. 'Quick!' he said. 'Leave Jerusalem immediately,

ποιήσω, κύριε; ὁ δὲ κύριος εἶπεν πρός με, ἀναστὰς πορεύου εἰς
shall I do, Lord?' And the *And* Lord said to me, 'Get up and go on into
4472 3261 1254 3836 1254 3261 3306 4639 1609 482 4513 1650
v.aas.1s n.vsm d.nsm cj n.nsm v.aai.3s p.a r.as.1 pt.aa.nsm v.pmm.2s p.a

Δαμασκὸν κἀκεῖ σοι λαληθήσεταί περὶ πάντων ὧν τέτακταί σοι
Damascus, and there *you* it will be told you about all that has been assigned to you
1242 2795 5148 3281 5148 4309 4246 4005 5435 5148
n.asf crasis r.ds.2 v.fpi.3s p.g a.gpn r.gpn v.rpi.3s r.ds.2

ποιῆσαι. 11 ὡς δὲ ↱ ↱ οὐκ ἐνέβλεπον ἀπὸ τῆς δόξης τοῦ φωτὸς
to do.' Since {and} I could not see ⌊due to⌋ the brilliance of that light,
4472 6055 1254 1838 1838 4024 1838 608 3836 1518 3836 1697 5890
f.aa cj cj pl v.iai.1s p.g d.gsf n.gsf d.gsn n.gsn

ἐκείνου, χειραγωγούμενος ὑπὸ τῶν συνόντων μοι ἦλθον εἰς Δαμασκόν. 12
that being led by the hand by those who were with me, I went to Damascus. "Then
1697 5932 5679 3836 5289 1609 2262 1650 1242 1254
r.gsn pt.pp.nsm p.g d.gpm pt.pa.gpm r.ds.1 v.aai.1s p.a n.asf

Ἁνανίας δέ τις, ἀνὴρ εὐλαβὴς κατὰ τὸν νόμον,
a certain Ananias, *Then* *certain* a devout man *devout* ⌊according to⌋ the law,
5516 393 1254 5516 2327 467 2327 2848 3836 3795
n.nsm cj r.nsm n.nsm a.nsm p.a d.asm n.asm

μαρτυρούμενος ὑπὸ πάντων τῶν κατοικούντων Ἰουδαίων, 13 ἐλθὼν πρός
well spoken of by all the Jews who lived there, *Jews* came to
3455 5679 4246 3836 2681 2997 2681 2262 4639
pt.pp.nsm p.g a.gpm d.gpm pt.pa.gpm a.gpm pt.aa.nsm p.a

με καὶ ἐπιστὰς εἶπέν μοι, Σαοὺλ ἀδελφέ, ἀνάβλεψον. κἀγὼ
me, and standing there said to me, 'Brother Saul, *Brother* recover your sight.' And at
1609 2779 2392 3306 1609 81 4910 81 329 2743 3836
r.as.1 cj pt.aa.nsm v.aai.3s r.ds.1 n.vsm n.vsm v.aam.2s crasis

← αὐτῇ τῇ ὥρᾳ ⌊ἀνέβλεψα εἰς⌋ αὐτόν. 14
that very hour I *very* *at that* *hour* recovered my sight and saw him. And
3836 899 6052 899 3836 6052 329 1650 899 1254
r.dsf d.dsf n.dsf v.aai.1s p.a r.asm.3

ὁ δὲ εἶπεν, ὁ θεὸς τῶν πατέρων ἡμῶν προεχειρίσατό σε γνῶναι τὸ
he *And* said, 'The God of our fathers *our* has chosen you to know {the} his
3836 1254 3306 3836 2536 3836 7005 4252 7005 4741 5148 1182 3836 899
d.nsm cj v.aai.3s d.nsm n.nsm d.gpm n.gpm r.gp.1 v.ami.3s r.as.2 f.aa d.asn

θέλημα αὐτοῦ καὶ ἰδεῖν τὸν δίκαιον καὶ ἀκοῦσαι φωνὴν ἐκ τοῦ
will, *his* {and} to see the ⌊Righteous One⌋ and to hear a voice from {the} his
2525 899 2779 1625 3836 1465 2779 201 5889 1666 3836 899
n.asn r.gsm.3 cj f.aa d.asm a.asm cj f.aa n.asf p.g d.gsn

στόματος αὐτοῦ, 15 ὅτι ἔσῃ μάρτυς αὐτῷ πρὸς ⌊πάντας ἀνθρώπους⌋ ὧν
mouth. *his* For ⌊you will be⌋ a witness for him to everyone of what
5125 899 4022 1639 3459 899 4639 4246 476 4005
n.gsn r.gsm.3 cj v.fmi.2s n.nsm r.dsm.3 p.a a.apm n.apm r.gpn

ἑώρακας καὶ ἤκουσας. 16 καὶ νῦν τί μέλλεις; ἀναστὰς βάπτισαι καὶ
you have seen and heard. And now why are you waiting? Rise and be baptized and
3972 2779 201 2779 3814 5515 3516 482 966 2779
v.rai.2s cj v.aai.2s cj adv r.asn v.pai.2s pt.aa.nsm v.amm.2s cj

ἀπόλουσαι τὰς ἁμαρτίας σου ἐπικαλεσάμενος τὸ ὄνομα αὐτοῦ.
wash away {the} your sins, *your* calling on {the} his name.' *his*
666 3836 5148 281 5148 2126 3836 899 3950 899
v.amm.2s d.apf n.apf r.gs.2 pt.am.nsm d.asn n.asn r.gsm.3

17 ἐγένετο δέ ↱ μοι ὑποστρέψαντι εἰς Ἰερουσαλὴμ καὶ
{it happened that} {and} When I had returned to Jerusalem and I
1181 1254 5715 1609 5715 1650 2647 2779 1609
v.ami.3s cj r.ds.1 pt.aa.dsm p.a n.asf cj

προσευχομένου μου ἐν τῷ ἱερῷ γενέσθαι με ἐν ἐκστάσει 18 καὶ ἰδεῖν
was praying *I* in the temple, I fell *I* into a trance and I saw
4667 1609 1877 3836 2639 1609 1181 1609 1877 1749 2779 1625
pt.pm.gsm r.gs.1 p.d d.dsn n.dsn f.am r.as.1 p.d n.dsf cj f.aa

αὐτὸν λέγοντά μοι, σπεῦσον καὶ ἔξελθε ⌊ἐν τάχει⌋ ἐξ
him saying to me, 'Make haste and get out of Jerusalem quickly, *of*
899 3306 1609 5067 2779 2002 1666 2647 1877 5443 1666
r.asm.3 pt.pa.asm r.ds.1 v.aam.2s cj v.aam.2s p.d n.dsn p.g

NASB

'What shall I do, Lord?' And the Lord said to me, 'Get up and go on into Damascus, and there you will be told of all that has been appointed for you to do.' [11]But since I could not see because of the brightness of that light, I was led by the hand by those who were with me and came into Damascus.

[12]"A certain Ananias, a man who was devout by the standard of the Law, *and* well spoken of by all the Jews who lived there, [13]came to me, and standing near said to me, 'Brother Saul, receive your sight!' And at that very time I looked up at him. [14]And he said, 'The God of our fathers has appointed you to know His will and to see the Righteous One and to hear an utterance from His mouth. [15]For you will be a witness for Him to all men of what you have seen and heard. [16]Now why do you delay? Get up and be baptized, and wash away your sins, calling on His name.'

[17]"It happened when I returned to Jerusalem and was praying in the temple, that I fell into a trance, [18]and I saw Him saying to me, 'Make haste, and get out of Jerusalem quickly,

NIV

because the people
here will not ac-
cept your testimo-
ny about me.'
[19] " 'Lord,' I
replied, 'these
people know that
I went from one
synagogue to an-
other to imprison
and beat those who
believe in you.
[20] And when the
blood of your mar-
tyr[a] Stephen was
shed, I stood there
giving my approv-
al and guarding
the clothes of those
who were killing
him.'
[21] "Then the Lord
said to me, 'Go; I
will send you far
away to the Gen-
tiles.' "

Paul the Roman Citizen

[22] The crowd lis-
tened to Paul until
he said this. Then
they raised their
voices and shout-
ed, "Rid the earth
of him! He's not fit
to live!"
[23] As they were
shouting and
throwing off their
cloaks and fling-
ing dust into the
air, [24] the com-
mander ordered
that Paul be taken
into the barracks.
He directed that
he be flogged and
interrogated in or-
der to find out why
the people were
shouting at him
like this. [25] As they
stretched him out
to flog him, Paul
said to the centuri-
on standing there,
"Is it legal for you
to flog a

[a] 20 Or *witness*

Ἰερουσαλήμ, διότι ↱ ↱ οὐ παραδέξονταί σου μαρτυρίαν περὶ ἐμοῦ. [19] κἀγὼ
Jerusalem because they will not accept your testimony about me.' And I
2647 1484 4138 4138 4024 4138 5148 3456 4309 1609 2743
n.gsf cj pl v.fmi.3p r.gs.2 n.asf p.g r.gs.1 crasis

εἶπον, κύριε, αὐτοὶ ἐπίστανται ὅτι ἐγὼ ἤμην
said, 'Lord, they themselves know that I used to go from one synagogue to
3306 3261 899 2179 4022 1609 1639 2848 2848 2848 2848
v.aai.1s n.vsm r.npm v.ppi.3p cj r.ns.1 v.imi.1s

φυλακίζων καὶ δέρων ⌊κατὰ τὰς συναγωγὰς⌋ τοὺς
another imprisoning and flogging *from one synagogue to another* those
2848 5872 2779 1296 2848 3836 5252 3836
pt.pa.nsm cj pt.pa.nsm p.a d.apf n.apf d.apm

πιστεύοντας ἐπὶ σέ, [20] καὶ ὅτε ἐξεχύννετο τὸ αἷμα Στεφάνου τοῦ μάρτυρός
who believed in you. And when *was being shed* the blood of Stephen, *{the}* your witness,
4409 2093 5148 2779 4021 1773 3836 135 5108 3836 5148 3459
pt.pa.apm p.a r.as.2 cj cj v.ipi.3s d.nsn n.nsn n.gsm d.gsm n.gsm

σου, καὶ ↱ αὐτὸς ἤμην ἐφεστὼς καὶ συνευδοκῶν[a] καὶ
your was being shed, *{and}* I myself was ⌊standing by⌋ *{and}* approving and
5148 1773 1773 1773 2779 1639 899 1639 2392 2779 5306 2779
r.gs.2 cj r.nsm v.imi.1s pt.ra.nsm cj pt.pa.nsm cj

φυλάσσων τὰ ἱμάτια τῶν ἀναιρούντων αὐτόν. [21] καὶ εἶπεν πρός με, πορεύου,
guarding the cloaks of those who were killing him.' And he said to me, 'Go,
5875 3836 2668 3836 359 899 2779 3306 4639 1609 4513
pt.pa.nsm d.apn n.apn d.gpm pt.pa.gpm r.asm.3 cj v.aai.3s p.a r.as.1 v.pmm.2s

ὅτι ἐγὼ εἰς ἔθνη μακρὰν ἐξαποστελῶ σε.
for I will send you far away to the Gentiles.'" *far away* *will send* *you*
4022 1609 1990 1990 5148 3426 3426 1650 1620 3426 1990 5148
cj r.ns.1 p.a n.apn adv v.fai.1s r.as.2

[22] ἤκουον δὲ αὐτοῦ ἄχρι τούτου τοῦ λόγου καὶ ἐπῆραν τὴν
⌊They listened to⌋ *{and}* him until this *{the}* word, but then they raised *{the}* their
201 1254 899 948 4047 3836 3364 2779 2048 3836 899
v.iai.3p cj r.gsm.3 p.g r.gsm d.gsm n.gsm cj v.aai.3p d.asf

φωνὴν αὐτῶν λέγοντες, αἶρε ἀπὸ τῆς γῆς τὸν τοιοῦτον,
voices *their* saying, ⌊"Away with⌋ such a fellow from the earth, *{the}* *such a fellow* for
5889 899 3306 149 5525 5525 5525 608 3836 1178 3836 5525 1142
n.asf r.gpm.3 pt.pa.npm v.pam.2s p.g d.gsf n.gsf d.asm r.asm

↱ ↱ οὐ γὰρ καθῆκεν αὐτὸν ζῆν. [23] → κραυγαζόντων τε αὐτῶν καὶ
it is not *for* right for him to live!" While they were crying out ~ *they* and
2763 2763 4024 1142 2763 899 2409 899 3198 5445 899 2779
pl cj v.iai.3s r.asm.3 f.pa pt.pa.gpm cj r.gpm.3 cj

ῥιπτούντων τὰ ἱμάτια καὶ κονιορτὸν βαλλόντων εἰς τὸν ἀέρα, [24]
throwing off their cloaks and flinging dust *flinging* in the air, the
4848 3836 2668 2779 965 3155 965 1650 3836 113 3836
pt.pa.gpm d.apn n.apn cj n.asm pt.pa.gpm p.a d.asm n.asm

ἐκέλευσεν ὁ χιλίαρχος εἰσάγεσθαι αὐτὸν εἰς τὴν
commanding officer ordered *the* *commanding officer* Paul ⌊to be brought back⌋ *Paul* into the
5941 5941 3027 3836 5941 899 1652 899 1650 3836
v.aai.3s d.nsm n.nsm f.pp r.asm.3 p.a d.asf

παρεμβολήν, εἴπας μάστιξιν ἀνετάζεσθαι αὐτὸν ἵνα
barracks, saying that *whips* he ⌊should be examined with⌋ whips *he* so that
4213 3306 3465 899 458 3465 899 2671
n.asf pt.aa.nsm n.dpf f.pp r.asm.3 cj

ἐπιγνῷ δι' ἣν αἰτίαν οὕτως ἐπεφώνουν αὐτῷ.
⌊he might know⌋ the reason why *the* *reason* *that way* ⌊they were shouting at⌋ him that way.
2105 4005 162 1328 4005 162 4048 2215 899 4048 4048
v.aas.3s p.a r.asf n.asf adv v.iai.3p r.dsm.3

[25] ὡς δὲ προέτειναν αὐτὸν ↰ τοῖς ἱμᾶσιν, εἶπεν πρὸς τὸν
But when *But* they had stretched him out for the lash, Paul said to the centurion
1254 6055 1254 4727 899 4727 3836 2666 4263 3306 4639 3836 1672
cj cj v.aai.3p r.asm.3 d.dpm n.dpm v.aai.3s p.a d.asm

ἑστῶτα ἑκατόνταρχον ὁ Παῦλος, εἰ
⌊standing by,⌋ *centurion* *{the}* *Paul* *{if}* "Is it lawful for you to flog a
2705 1672 3836 4263 1623 1997 1997 1997 7007 7007 3464 3464
pt.ra.asm n.asm d.nsm n.nsm cj

[a] τῇ ἀναιρέσει αὐτοῦ included by TR after συνευδοκῶν.

NASB

because they will
not accept your tes-
timony about Me.'
[19] And I said, 'Lord,
they themselves
understand that
in one synagogue
after another I
used to imprison
and beat those
who believed in
You. [20] And when
the blood of Your
witness Stephen
was being shed, I
also was standing
by approving, and
watching out for
the coats of those
who were slaying
him.' [21] And He
said to me, 'Go!
For I will send you
far away to the
Gentiles.' "
[22] They listened
to him up to this
statement, and
then they raised
their voices and
said, "Away with
such a fellow from
the earth, for he
should not be al-
lowed to live!"
[23] And as they were
crying out and
throwing off their
cloaks and tossing
dust into the air,
[24] the [a]commander
ordered him to be
brought into the
barracks, stating
that he should
be examined by
scourging so that
he might find out
the reason why
they were shouting
against him that
way. [25] But when
they stretched him
out with thongs,
Paul said to the
centurion who was
standing by, "Is it
lawful for you to
scourge a man who

[a] I.e. chiliarch, in command of one thousand troops

NIV

Roman citi-
zen who hasn't
even been found
guilty?"
26 When the cen-
turion heard this,
he went to the
commander and
reported it. "What
are you going to
do?" he asked.
"This man is a Ro-
man citizen."
27 The commander
went to Paul and
asked, "Tell me,
are you a Roman
citizen?"
"Yes, I am," he
answered.
28 Then the com-
mander said, "I
had to pay a lot of
money for my citi-
zenship."
"But I was born
a citizen," Paul re-
plied.
29 Those who were
about to interro-
gate him withdrew
immediately. The
commander him-
self was alarmed
when he realized
that he had put
Paul, a Roman citi-
zen, in chains.

Paul Before the Sanhedrin

30 The commander
wanted to find out
exactly why Paul
was being accused
by the Jews. So
the next day he
released him and
ordered the chief
priests and all the
members of the
Sanhedrin to as-
semble. Then he
brought Paul and
had him stand be-
fore them.
23 Paul looked
straight at
the Sanhedrin and
said,

ἄνθρωπον Ῥωμαῖον καὶ ἀκατάκριτον ἔξεστιν ὑμῖν μαστίζειν; 26 →
man who is a Roman citizen and uncondemned?" *Is it lawful for you to flog* When
476 4871 2779 185 1997 7007 3464
n.asm n.asm cj a.asm v.pai.3s r.dp.2 f.pa

ἀκούσας δὲ ὁ ἑκατοντάρχης ↱ προσελθὼν τῷ
the centurion heard *{and} the centurion* this, he went and reported ⌞to the⌟
3836 1672 201 1254 3836 1672 550 4665 550 3836
pt.aa.nsm cj d.nsm n.nsm pt.aa.nsm d.dsm

χιλιάρχῳ ἀπήγγειλεν λέγων, τί μέλλεις ποιεῖν; ὁ γὰρ
⌞commanding officer,⌟ *reported* saying, "What are you about to do? *{the}* For this
5941 550 3306 5515 3516 4472 3836 1142 4047
n.dsm v.aai.3s pt.pa.nsm r.asn v.pai.2s f.pa d.nsm cj

ἄνθρωπος οὗτος Ῥωμαῖός ἐστιν. 27 προσελθὼν δὲ
man *this* is a Roman citizen." *is* The commanding officer came to *{and}*
476 4047 1639 4871 1639 3836 5941 5941 4665 1254
n.nsm r.nsm n.nsm v.pai.3s pt.aa.nsm cj

ὁ χιλίαρχος εἶπεν αὐτῷ, λέγε μοι, σὺ Ῥωμαῖος εἶ;
The commanding officer him and said, *him* "Tell me, are you a Roman citizen?" *are*
3836 5941 899 3306 899 3306 1609 1639 5148 4871 1639
d.nsm n.nsm v.aai.3s r.dsm.3 v.pam.2s r.ds.1 r.ns.2 n.nsm v.pai.2s

ὁ δὲ ἔφη, ναί. 28 ἀπεκρίθη δὲ ὁ χιλίαρχος,
He *{and}* replied, "Yes." The commanding officer answered, *{and} The commanding officer*
3836 1254 5774 3721 3836 5941 5941 646 1254 3836 5941
d.nsm cj v.iai.3s pl v.api.3s cj d.nsm n.nsm

ἐγὼ → πολλοῦ κεφαλαίου τὴν πολιτείαν ταύτην
"I obtained this citizenship with a large sum of money." *{the} citizenship this*
1609 3227 4047 4486 4498 3049 3836 4486 4047
r.ns.1 a.gsn n.gsn d.asf n.asf r.asf

ἐκτησάμην. ὁ δὲ Παῦλος ἔφη, ἐγὼ δὲ ↱ καὶ γεγέννημαι.
obtained *{the} {and}* Paul answered, "But I *But* was even born one."
3227 3836 1254 4263 5774 1254 1609 1254 1164 2779 1164
v.ami.1s d.nsm cj n.nsm v.iai.3s r.ns.1 cj adv v.rpi.1s

29 εὐθέως οὖν ἀπέστησαν ἀπ' αὐτοῦ οἱ μέλλοντες αὐτὸν
Immediately *{then} drew back from him* those who were about to examine him
2311 4036 923 608 899 3836 3516 458 458 899
adv cj v.aai.3p p.g r.gsm.3 d.npm pt.pa.npm r.asm.3

ἀνετάζειν, καὶ ὁ χιλίαρχος δὲ ἐφοβήθη ἐπιγνοὺς ὅτι
to examine drew back from him; and the ⌞commanding officer⌟ *{and}* was afraid, realizing that
458 923 923 608 899 2779 3836 5941 1254 5828 2105 4022
f.pa cj d.nsm n.nsm cj v.api.3s pt.aa.nsm cj

Ῥωμαῖός ἐστιν καὶ ὅτι αὐτὸν ἦν δεδεκώς. 30
Paul was a Roman citizen *was* and that he had bound him. *he had bound* But
1639 4871 1639 2779 4022 1639 1639 1313 899 1639 1313 1254
n.nsm v.pai.3s cj cj r.asm.3 v.iai.3s pt.ra.nsm

τῇ δὲ ἐπαύριον βουλόμενος γνῶναι τὸ ἀσφαλές, τὸ τί
⌞on the⌟ *But* next day, wanting to know *{the}* for sure *{the}* what
3836 1254 2069 1089 1182 3836 855 3836 5515
d.dsf cj adv pt.pm.nsm f.aa d.asn a.asn d.asn r.asn

κατηγορεῖται ὑπὸ τῶν Ἰουδαίων, ἔλυσεν αὐτὸν καὶ
⌞was the accusation being made against⌟ him by the Jews, he released him and
2989 5679 3836 2681 3395 899 2779
v.ppi.3s p.g d.gpm a.gpm v.aai.3s r.asm.3 cj

ἐκέλευσεν συνελθεῖν τοὺς ἀρχιερεῖς καὶ πᾶν τὸ συνέδριον, καὶ ↱
ordered *to meet* the chief priests and all the council to meet, and he
3027 5302 3836 797 2779 4246 3836 5284 5302 5302 2779 2705
v.aai.3s f.aa d.apm n.apm cj a.asn d.asn n.asn cj

καταγαγὼν τὸν Παῦλον ↰ ἔστησεν εἰς αὐτούς.
brought *{the}* Paul down and set him before them.
2864 3836 4263 2864 2705 1650 899
pt.aa.nsm d.asm n.asm v.aai.3s p.a r.apm.3

23:1 ἀτενίσας δὲ ὁ Παῦλος τῷ συνεδρίῳ εἶπεν,
⌞Looking intently at⌟ *{and}* the council, *{the}* Paul *the council* said,
867 1254 3836 5284 3836 4263 3836 5284 3306
pt.aa.nsm cj d.nsm n.nsm d.dsn n.dsn v.aai.3s

NASB

is a Roman and
uncondemned?"
26 When the centu-
rion heard *this,* he
went to the com-
mander and told
him, saying, "What
are you about to
do? For this man
is a Roman." 27 The
commander came
and said to him,
"Tell me, are you
a Roman?" And he
said, "Yes." 28 The
commander an-
swered, "I acquired
this citizenship
with a large sum
of money." And
Paul said, "But
I was actually
born *a citizen.*"
29 Therefore those
who were about
to examine him
immediately let
go of him; and the
commander also
was afraid when he
found out that he
was a Roman, and
because he had put
him in chains.
30 But on the next
day, wishing to
know for certain
why he had been
accused by the
Jews, he released
him and ordered
the chief priests
and all the Council
to assemble, and
brought Paul down
and set him before
them.

Paul before the Council

23:1 Paul, look-
ing intently at the
Council, said,

NIV

"My brothers, I
have fulfilled my
duty to God in all
good conscience
to this day." 2 At
this the high priest
Ananias ordered
those standing
near Paul to strike
him on the mouth.
3 Then Paul said
to him, "God will
strike you, you
whitewashed wall!
You sit there to
judge me accord-
ing to the law,
yet you yourself
violate the law by
commanding that I
be struck!"
4 Those who were
standing near Paul
said, "How dare
you insult God's
high priest!"
5 Paul replied,
"Brothers, I did
not realize that
he was the high
priest; for it is
written: 'Do not
speak evil about
the ruler of your
people.'[a]"
6 Then Paul,
knowing that
some of them were
Sadducees and
the others Phar-
isees, called out
in the Sanhedrin,
"My brothers, I
am a Pharisee,
descended from
Pharisees. I stand
on trial because
of the hope of the
resurrection of the
dead." 7 When he
said this, a dispute
broke out between
the Pharisees and
the Sadducees,
and the assembly
was divided. 8 (The
Sadducees say that
there is no resur-
rection, and that
there are neither
angels nor spirits,
but the Pharisees
believe

˻ἄνδρες ἀδελφοί,˼ ἐγὼ πάσῃ συνειδήσει ἀγαθῇ πεπολίτευμαι τῷ
"My brothers, I have lived in all good conscience *good* *have lived* before
467 81 1609 4488 4488 4246 19 5287 19 4488 3836
n.vpm n.vpm r.ns.1 a.dsf n.dsf a.dsf v.rmi.1s d.dsm

θεῷ ἄχρι ταύτης τῆς ἡμέρας. 2 ὁ δὲ ἀρχιερεὺς Ἁνανίας ἐπέταξεν τοῖς
God up to this *{the}* day." At that the *{and}* high priest Ananias ordered those
2536 948 4047 3836 2465 3836 1254 797 393 2199 3836
n.dsm p.g r.gsf d.gsf n.gsf d.nsm cj n.nsm n.nsm v.aai.3s d.dpm

παρεστῶσιν αὐτῷ τύπτειν αὐτοῦ ↰ τὸ στόμα. 3 τότε ὁ Παῦλος πρὸς αὐτὸν
standing near him to strike him on the mouth. Then *{the}* Paul said to him,
4225 899 5597 899 5597 3836 5125 5538 3836 4263 3306 4639 899
pt.ra.dpm r.dsm.3 f.pa r.gsm.3 d.asn n.asn adv d.nsm n.nsm p.a r.asm.3

εἶπεν, τύπτειν σε μέλλει ὁ θεός, → τοῖχε κεκονιαμένε·
said "God is about to strike you, *is about* *{the}* *God* you whitewashed wall! *whitewashed*
3306 2536 3516 3516 5597 5148 3516 3836 2536 3154 5526 3154
v.aai.3s f.pa r.as.2 v.pai.3s d.nsm n.nsm n.vsm pt.rp.vsm

καὶ ↱ σὺ κάθῃ κρίνων με κατὰ τὸν νόμον καὶ παρανομῶν
indeed Do you indeed sit judging me ˻according to˼ the law yet ˻contrary to the law˼
2779 2764 5148 2779 2764 3212 1609 2848 3836 3795 2779 4174
cj r.ns.2 v.pmi.2s pt.pa.nsm r.as.1 p.a d.asm n.asm cj pt.pa.nsm

κελεύεις με τύπτεσθαι; 4 οἱ δὲ παρεστῶτες εἶπαν, τὸν
order me to be struck?" Those *{and}* standing near him said, "Dare you insult God's *{the}*
3027 1609 5597 3836 1254 4225 3306 3366 3366 2536 3836
v.pai.2s r.as.1 f.pp d.npm cj pt.ra.npm v.aai.3p d.asm

ἀρχιερέα τοῦ θεοῦ λοιδορεῖς; 5 ἔφη τε ὁ Παῦλος, ↱ ↱ οὐκ ᾔδειν,
high priest?" *{the}* *God's* *you insult* And Paul said, *And* *{the}* *Paul* "I did not realize,
797 3836 2536 3366 5445 4263 5774 5445 3836 4263 3857 3857 4024 3857
n.asm d.gsm n.gsm v.pai.2s v.iai.3s cj d.nsm n.nsm pl v.lai.1s

ἀδελφοί, ὅτι ἐστὶν ἀρχιερεύς, γέγραπται γὰρ ὅτι
brothers, that he was high priest; for it is written, *for* ~ 'You shall not speak evil about the
81 4022 1639 797 1142 1211 1142 4022 3306 3306 4024 3306 2809 3306
n.vpm cj v.pai.3s n.nsm v.rpi.3s cj cj

ἄρχοντα τοῦ λαοῦ σου οὐκ ἐρεῖς κακῶς. 6 → γνοὺς
ruler of your people.'" *your* *not* *You shall speak about* *evil* Now when Paul perceived
807 3836 5148 3295 5148 4024 3306 2809 1254 4263 1182
n.asm d.gsm n.gsm r.gs.2 pl v.fai.2s adv pt.aa.nsm

δὲ ὁ Παῦλος ὅτι τὸ ἓν μέρος ἐστὶν Σαδδουκαίων τὸ δὲ ἕτερον
Now *{the}* *Paul* that *{the}* one part were Sadducees and the *and* other
1254 3836 4263 4022 3836 1651 3538 1639 4881 1254 3836 1254 2283
cj d.nsm n.nsm cj d.nsn a.nsn n.nsn v.pai.3s n.gpm d.nsn cj r.nsn

Φαρισαίων ἔκραζεν ἐν τῷ συνεδρίῳ, ˻ἄνδρες ἀδελφοί,˼ ἐγὼ
Pharisees, ˻he cried out˼ in the council, "My brothers, I am a
5757 3189 1877 3836 5284 467 81 1609 1639
n.gpm v.iai.3s p.d d.dsn n.dsn n.vpm n.vpm r.ns.1

Φαρισαῖός εἰμι, υἱὸς Φαρισαίων, περὶ ἐλπίδος καὶ → ἀναστάσεως →
Pharisee, *am* a son of Pharisees. It is regarding my hope *{and}* of a resurrection for
5757 1639 5626 5757 4309 1828 2779 414
n.nsm v.pai.1s n.nsm n.gpm p.g n.gsf cj n.gsf

νεκρῶν ἐγὼ[a] κρίνομαι. 7 τοῦτο δὲ αὐτοῦ εἰπόντος
the dead that I am on trial." When he said this, *{and}* *he* *When said* an argument
3738 1609 3212 3306 899 3306 4047 1254 899 3306 5087
a.gpm r.ns.1 v.ppi.1s r.asn cj r.gsm.3 pt.aa.gsm

ἐγένετο στάσις τῶν Φαρισαίων καὶ Σαδδουκαίων καὶ
broke out *argument* between the Pharisees and the Sadducees, and the assembly
1181 5087 3836 5757 2779 4881 2779 3836 4436
v.ami.3s n.nsf d.gpm n.gpm cj n.gpm cj

ἐσχίσθη τὸ πλῆθος. 8 σαδδουκαῖοι μὲν γὰρ λέγουσιν μὴ
was divided. *the* *assembly* (For the Sadducees ~ *For* say that there is no
5387 3836 4436 1142 4881 3525 1142 3306 1639 1639 3590
v.api.3s d.nsn n.nsn n.npm pl cj v.pai.3p pl

εἶναι ἀνάστασιν μήτε ἄγγελον μήτε πνεῦμα, Φαρισαῖοι δὲ ὁμολογοῦσιν τὰ
there is resurrection, nor angel nor spirit, but the Pharisees *but* confess *{the}*
1639 414 3612 34 3612 4460 1254 5757 1254 3933 3836
f.pa n.asf cj n.asm cj n.asn n.npm pl v.pai.3p d.apn

NASB

"Brethren, I have
lived my life with a
perfectly good con-
science before God
up to this day."
2 The high priest
Ananias command-
ed those standing
beside him to strike
him on the mouth.
3 Then Paul said to
him, "God is going
to strike you, you
whitewashed wall!
Do you sit to try
me according to
the Law, and in
violation of the
Law order me to be
struck?" 4 But the
bystanders said,
"Do you revile
God's high priest?"
5 And Paul said,
"I was not aware,
brethren, that he
was high priest; for
it is written, 'YOU
SHALL NOT SPEAK
EVIL OF A RULER OF
YOUR PEOPLE.'"
6 But perceiving
that one group
were Sadducees
and the other Phar-
isees, Paul *began*
crying out in the
Council, "Brethren,
I am a Pharisee, a
son of Pharisees; I
am on trial for the
hope and resurrec-
tion of the dead!"
7 As he said this,
there occurred a
dissension between
the Pharisees and
Sadducees, and
the assembly was
divided. 8 For the
Sadducees say
that there is no
resurrection, nor an
angel, nor a spirit,
but the Pharisees
acknowledge them

[a] 5 Exodus 22:28

[a] [ἐγὼ] UBS, omitted by TNIV.

NIV

all these things.)
[9]There was a
great uproar, and
some of the teach-
ers of the law who
were Pharisees
stood up and ar-
gued vigorously.
"We find nothing
wrong with this
man," they said.
"What if a spirit or
an angel has spo-
ken to him?" [10]The
dispute became
so violent that the
commander was
afraid Paul would
be torn to pieces
by them. He or-
dered the troops to
go down and take
him away from
them by force and
bring him into the
barracks.
[11]The following
night the Lord
stood near Paul
and said, "Take
courage! As you
have testified
about me in Je-
rusalem, so you
must also testify in
Rome."

The Plot to Kill Paul

[12]The next morn-
ing some Jews
formed a conspir-
acy and bound
themselves with
an oath not to eat
or drink until they
had killed Paul.
[13]More than forty
men were involved
in this plot. [14]They
went to the chief
priests and the
elders and said,
"We have taken a
solemn oath not to
eat anything un-
til we have killed
Paul. [15]Now then,
you and

ἀμφότερα. 9 ἐγένετο δὲ κραυγὴ μεγάλη, καὶ ἀναστάντες τινὲς τῶν
both.) Then there arose *Then* a great uproar, *great* and *stood up* certain of the
317 1254 1181 1254 3489 3199 3489 2779 482 5516 3836
a.apn v.ami.3s cj n.nsf a.nsf cj pt.aa.npm r.npm d.gpm

γραμματέων τοῦ μέρους τῶν Φαρισαίων διεμάχοντο λέγοντες,
scribes of the party of the Pharisees stood up and protested vigorously, saying,
1208 3836 3538 3836 5757 482 482 1372 3306
n.gpm d.gsn n.gsn d.gpm n.gpm v.imi.3p pt.pa.npm

οὐδὲν κακὸν εὑρίσκομεν ἐν τῷ ἀνθρώπῳ τούτῳ· εἰ δὲ
"We find nothing evil *We find* in *{the}* this man. *this* What if *{and}* a
2351 2351 4029 2805 2351 1877 3836 4047 476 4047 1623 1254
a.asn a.asn v.pai.1p p.d d.dsm n.dsm r.dsm cj cj

πνεῦμα ἐλάλησεν αὐτῷ ἢ ἄγγελος;[a] 10
spirit or an angel has spoken to him?" *or* *angel* And when the argument became
4460 2445 34 3281 899 2445 34 1254 1181 5087 1181
n.nsn v.aai.3s r.dsm.3 cj n.nsm

Πολλῆς δὲ γινομένης στάσεως φοβηθεὶς ὁ χιλίαρχος
violent, *And* *when became* *argument* the commanding officer, afraid *the* *commanding officer*
4498 1254 1181 5087 3836 5941 5941 5828 3836 5941
a.gsf cj pt.pm.gsf n.gsf pt.ap.nsm d.nsm n.nsm

μὴ διασπασθῇ ὁ Παῦλος ὑπ᾽ αὐτῶν ἐκέλευσεν τὸ στράτευμα
{not} that Paul ⌞would be torn apart⌟ *{the}* *Paul* by them, commanded the soldiers
3590 4263 1400 3836 4263 5679 899 3027 3836 5128
cj v.aps.3s d.nsm n.nsm p.g r.gpm.3 v.aai.3s d.asn n.asn

καταβὰν ἁρπάσαι αὐτὸν ↰ ἐκ μέσου αὐτῶν ↰ ↰ ἄγειν τε εἰς
to go down and take him away from among them by force and bring *and* him into
2849 773 899 773 1666 3545 899 773 773 5445 72 5445 1650
pt.aa.asn f.aa r.asm.3 p.g n.gsn r.gpm.3 f.pa cj p.a

τὴν παρεμβολήν. 11 τῇ δὲ ἐπιούσῃ νυκτὶ ἐπιστὰς αὐτῷ ὁ κύριος
the barracks. The *{and}* following night the Lord stood by him *the* *Lord* and
3836 4213 3836 1254 2079 3816 3836 3261 2392 899 3836 3261
d.asf n.asf d.dsf cj pt.pa.dsf n.dsf pt.aa.nsm r.dsm.3 d.nsm n.nsm

εἶπεν, θάρσει· ὡς γὰρ διεμαρτύρω τὰ περὶ ἐμοῦ εἰς
said, "Take courage, for as *for* ⌞you have testified to⌟ the facts about me in
3306 2510 1142 6055 1142 1371 3836 4309 1609 1650
v.aai.3s v.pam.2s cj cj v.ami.2s d.apn p.g r.gs.1 p.a

Ἰερουσαλήμ, οὕτω σε δεῖ καὶ εἰς Ῥώμην μαρτυρῆσαι. 12 γενομένης
Jerusalem, so must you *must* also testify in Rome." *testify* When it was
2647 4048 1256 5148 1256 2779 3455 1650 4873 3455 1181
n.asf adv r.as.2 v.pai.3s adv p.a n.asf f.aa pt.am.gsf

δὲ ἡμέρας ποιήσαντες συστροφὴν οἱ Ἰουδαῖοι ἀνεθεμάτισαν
{and} day, the Jews made a plot *the* *Jews* and bound
1254 2465 3836 2681 4472 5371 3836 2681 354
cj n.gsf pt.aa.npm n.asf d.npm a.npm v.aai.3p

ἑαυτοὺς ↰ ↰ ↰ λέγοντες μήτε φαγεῖν μήτε πιεῖν ⌞ἕως οὗ⌟
themselves by an oath saying that they would neither eat nor drink until
1571 354 354 354 3306 3612 2266 3612 4403 2401 4005
r.apm.3 pt.pa.npm cj f.aa cj f.aa p.g r.gsm

ἀποκτείνωσιν τὸν Παῦλον. 13 ἦσαν δὲ πλείους τεσσεράκοντα οἱ
they had killed *{the}* Paul. ⌞There were⌟ *{and}* more than forty who made
650 3836 4263 1639 1254 4498 5477 3836 4472
v.aas.3p d.asm n.asm v.iai.3p cj a.npm.c a.npm d.npm

ταύτην τὴν συνωμοσίαν ποιησάμενοι, 14 οἵτινες προσελθόντες τοῖς ἀρχιερεῦσιν καὶ
this *{the}* conspiracy. *made* These went to the chief priests and
4047 3836 5350 4472 4015 4665 3836 797 2779
r.asf d.asf n.asf pt.am.npm r.npm pt.aa.npm d.dpm n.dpm cj

τοῖς πρεσβυτέροις εἶπαν, ἀναθέματι ἀνεθεματίσαμεν ἑαυτοὺς
{the} elders and said, *by oath* "We have bound ourselves by an oath to taste
3836 4565 3306 353 354 1571 353 353 1174 1174
d.dpm a.dpm v.aai.3p n.dsn v.aai.1p r.apm.1

μηδενὸς γεύσασθαι ⌞ἕως οὗ⌟ ἀποκτείνωμεν τὸν Παῦλον. 15 νῦν οὖν ὑμεῖς
no food *to taste* until we have killed *{the}* Paul. So now *So* you and
3594 1174 2401 4005 650 3836 4263 4036 3814 4036 7007 5250
a.gsn f.am p.g r.gsm v.aas.1p d.asm n.asm adv cj r.np.2

[a] μὴ θεομαχῶμεν included by TR after ἄγγελος.

NASB

all. [9]And there
occurred a great
uproar; and some
of the scribes of
the Pharisaic party
stood up and *began*
to argue heatedly,
saying, "We find
nothing wrong
with this man;
suppose a spirit
or an angel has
spoken to him?"
[10]And as a great
dissension was
developing, the
[a]commander was
afraid Paul would
be torn to pieces by
them and ordered
the troops to go
down and take
him away from
them by force, and
bring him into the
barracks.
[11]But on the night
immediately fol-
lowing, the Lord
stood at his side
and said, "Take
courage; for as you
have solemnly wit-
nessed to My cause
at Jerusalem, so
you must witness
at Rome also."

A Conspiracy to Kill Paul

[12]When it was day,
the Jews formed
a conspiracy and
bound themselves
under an oath,
saying that they
would neither eat
nor drink until they
had killed Paul.
[13]There were more
than forty who
formed this plot.
[14]They came to the
chief priests and
the elders and said,
"We have bound
ourselves under
a solemn oath to
taste nothing until
we have killed
Paul. [15]Now there-
fore, you and

[a] I.e. chiliarch, in command of one thousand troops

NIV

the Sanhedrin
petition the com-
mander to bring
him before you
on the pretext of
wanting more ac-
curate information
about his case. We
are ready to kill
him before he gets
here."
16But when the
son of Paul's sister
heard of this plot,
he went into the
barracks and told
Paul.
17Then Paul
called one of the
centurions and
said, "Take this
young man to the
commander; he
has something to
tell him." 18So he
took him to the
commander.
The centurion
said, "Paul, the
prisoner, sent for
me and asked me
to bring this young
man to you be-
cause he has some-
thing to tell you."
19The command-
er took the young
man by the hand,
drew him aside
and asked, "What
is it you want to
tell me?"
20He said: "Some
Jews have agreed
to ask you to bring
Paul before the
Sanhedrin tomor-
row on the pretext
of wanting more
accurate informa-
tion about him.

ἐμφανίσατε τῷ χιλιάρχῳ σὺν τῷ συνεδρίῳ ὅπως καταγάγῃ
the council give notice ⌊to the⌋ ⌊commanding officer⌋ *and the council* to bring
3836 5284 1872 3836 5941 5250 3836 5284 3968 2864
v.aam.2p d.dsm n.dsm p.d d.dsn n.dsn cj v.aas.3s

αὐτὸν ↰ εἰς ὑμᾶς ὡς μέλλοντας διαγινώσκειν ἀκριβέστερον
him down to you, as ⌊though you were going⌋ to examine his case more accurately;
899 2864 1650 7007 6055 3516 1336 899 3836 209
r.asm.3 p.a r.ap.2 pl pt.pa.apm f.pa adv.c

τὰ περὶ αὐτοῦ· ἡμεῖς δὲ πρὸ τοῦ ἐγγίσαι
case his and we *and* will be ready to kill him before *{the}* he gets there."
3836 4309 899 1254 7005 1254 1639 1639 2289 359 359 899 4574 3836 899 1581
d.apn p.g r.gsm.3 r.np.1 cj p.g d.gsn f.aa

αὐτὸν ἕτοιμοί ἐσμεν τοῦ ἀνελεῖν αὐτόν. 16 ἀκούσας δὲ ὁ υἱὸς τῆς
he ready will be {the} to kill him when heard about But when the son of
899 2289 1639 3836 359 899 201 1254 201 3836 5626 3836
r.asm.3 a.npm v.pai.1p d.gsn f.aa r.asm.3 pt.aa.nsm cj d.nsm n.nsm d.gsf

ἀδελφῆς Παύλου τὴν ἐνέδραν, ↱ παραγενόμενος καὶ ⌊εἰσελθὼν
Paul's sister *Paul's* heard about the ambush, he went and entered
4263 80 4263 201 201 3836 1909 550 4134 2779 1656
n.gsf n.gsm d.asf n.asf pt.am.nsm cj pt.aa.nsm

εἰς⌋ τὴν παρεμβολὴν ἀπήγγειλεν τῷ Παύλῳ. 17 προσκαλεσάμενος
the barracks and reported it to Paul. Then Paul called
1650 3836 4213 550 3836 4263 1254 4263 4673
p.a d.asf n.asf v.aai.3s d.dsm n.dsm pt.am.nsm

δὲ ὁ Παῦλος ἕνα τῶν ἑκατονταρχῶν ἔφη, τὸν νεανίαν τοῦτον
Then {the} Paul one of the centurions and said, "Take *{the}* this young man *this*
1254 3836 4263 1651 3836 1672 5774 552 3836 4047 3733 4047
cj d.nsm n.nsm a.asm d.gpm n.gpm v.iai.3s d.asm n.asm r.asm

ἀπάγαγε πρὸς τὸν χιλίαρχον, ἔχει γάρ ἀπαγγεῖλαί τι
Take to the ⌊commanding officer,⌋ for he has *for* something to report *something*
552 4639 3836 5941 1142 2400 1142 5516 550 5516
v.aam.2s p.a d.asm n.asm v.pai.3s cj f.aa r.asn

αὐτῷ. 18 ὁ μὲν οὖν παραλαβὼν αὐτὸν ἤγαγεν πρὸς τὸν
to him." So he ~ *So* took him and brought him to the
899 4036 3836 3525 4036 4161 899 72 4639 3836
r.dsm.3 d.nsm pl cj pt.aa.nsm r.asm.3 v.aai.3s p.a d.asm

χιλίαρχον καὶ φησίν, ὁ δέσμιος Παῦλος προσκαλεσάμενός με
⌊commanding officer⌋ and said, "The prisoner Paul called me and
5941 2779 5774 3836 1300 4263 4673 1609
n.asm cj v.pai.3s d.nsm n.nsm n.nsm pt.am.nsm r.as.1

ἠρώτησεν τοῦτον τὸν νεανίσκον ἀγαγεῖν πρὸς σὲ ἔχοντά τι
asked me to bring this *{the}* young man *to bring* to you, as he has something
2263 72 72 4047 3836 3734 72 4639 5148 2400 5516
v.aai.3s r.asm d.asm n.asm f.aa p.a r.as.2 pt.pa.asm r.asn

λαλῆσαί σοι. 19 ἐπιλαβόμενος ← δὲ τῆς χειρὸς αὐτοῦ
to say to you." The commanding officer took him by *{and}* the hand, *him*
3281 5148 3836 5941 5941 2138 899 1254 3836 5931 899
f.aa r.ds.2 pt.am.nsm cj d.gsf n.gsf r.gsm.3

ὁ χιλίαρχος καὶ ἀναχωρήσας ⌊κατ' ἰδίαν⌋ ἐπυνθάνετο, τί ἐστιν
The commanding officer {and} drew him aside and asked, "What is it
3836 5941 2779 432 2848 2625 4785 5515 1639
d.nsm n.nsm cj pt.aa.nsm p.a a.asf v.imi.3s r.nsn v.pai.3s

ὃ ἔχεις ἀπαγγεῖλαί μοι; 20 εἶπεν δὲ ὅτι οἱ Ἰουδαῖοι συνέθεντο τοῦ
that you have to report to me?" And he said, *And* ~ "The Jews have agreed to
4005 2400 550 1609 1254 3306 1254 4022 3836 2681 5338 3836
r.asn v.pai.2s f.aa r.ds.1 v.aai.3s cj cj d.npm a.npm v.ami.3p d.gsn

ἐρωτῆσαί σε ὅπως αὔριον τὸν Παῦλον καταγάγῃς εἰς τὸ
ask you to bring Paul down tomorrow *{the} Paul bring down* to the
2263 5148 3968 2864 4263 2864 892 3836 4263 2864 1650 3836
f.aa r.as.2 cj adv d.asm n.asm v.aas.2s p.a d.asn

συνέδριον ὡς → μέλλον τι ἀκριβέστερον
council, as though the case against him was going *case* to be examined more closely.
5284 6055 5516 4309 899 3516 5516 4785 4785 4785 209
n.asn pl pt.pa.asn r.asn adv.c

NASB

the Council notify
the commander to
bring him down
to you, as though
you were going to
determine his case
by a more thorough
investigation; and
we for our part are
ready to slay him
before he comes
near *the place.*"
16But the son of
Paul's sister heard
of their ambush,
and he came and
entered the bar-
racks and told Paul.
17Paul called one
of the centurions
to him and said,
"Lead this young
man to the com-
mander, for he has
something to report
to him." 18So he
took him and led
him to the com-
mander and *said,
"Paul the prisoner
called me to him
and asked me to
lead this young
man to you since
he has something
to tell you." 19The
commander took
him by the hand
and stepping aside,
began to inquire
of him privately,
"What is it that you
have to report to
me?" 20And he said,
"The Jews have
agreed to ask you
to bring Paul down
tomorrow to the
Council, as though
they were going to
inquire somewhat
more thoroughly
about him.

NIV

[21]Don't give in
to them, because
more than forty of
them are waiting
in ambush for him.
They have taken
an oath not to eat
or drink until they
have killed him.
They are ready
now, waiting for
your consent to
their request."
[22]The command-
er dismissed the
young man with
this warning:
"Don't tell anyone
that you have re-
ported this to me."

Paul Transferred to Caesarea

[23]Then he called
two of his centu-
rions and ordered
them, "Get ready a
detachment of two
hundred soldiers,
seventy horsemen
and two hundred
spearmen[a] to go to
Caesarea at nine
tonight. [24]Provide
horses for Paul so
that he may be tak-
en safely to Gover-
nor Felix."
[25]He wrote a let-
ter as follows:

[26]Claudius Lys-
ias,

To His Excel-
lency, Governor
Felix:

Greetings.

[27]This man was
seized by the
Jews and they
were about to kill
him, but I came
with my troops
and rescued him,
for I had learned
that he is a

[a] 23 The meaning of the Greek for this word is uncertain.

πυνθάνεσθαι περὶ αὐτοῦ. 21 σὺ οὖν ↱ μὴ πεισθῇς αὐτοῖς,
to be examined *against* *him* But you *But* should not be persuaded by them, for more
4785 4309 899 4036 5148 4036 4275 3590 4275 899 1142 4498
f.pm p.g r.gsm.3 r.ns.2 cj pl v.aps.2s r.dpm.3

ἐνεδρεύουσιν γὰρ αὐτὸν ἐξ αὐτῶν ἄνδρες πλείους
than forty of their men ⌞are lying in wait for⌟ *for* him *of* *their* *men* *more than*
4498 5477 1666 899 467 1910 1142 899 1666 899 467 4498
v.pai.3p cj r.asm.3 p.g r.gpm.3 n.npm a.npm.c

τεσσεράκοντα, οἵτινες ἀνεθεμάτισαν ἑαυτοὺς ↰ ↰ μήτε φαγεῖν μήτε πιεῖν
forty and *{who}* have bound themselves by an oath neither to eat nor drink
5477 4015 354 1571 354 354 3612 2266 3612 4403
a.npm r.npm v.aai.3p r.apm.3 cj f.aa cj f.aa

⌞ἕως οὗ⌟ ἀνέλωσιν αὐτόν, καὶ νῦν εἰσιν ἕτοιμοι προσδεχόμενοι τὴν ἀπὸ σοῦ
until they kill him. And now they are ready, awaiting *{the}* *{from}* your
2401 4005 359 899 2779 3814 1639 2289 4657 3836 608 5148
p.g r.gsm v.aas.3p r.asm.3 cj adv v.pai.3p a.npm pt.pm.npm d.asf p.g r.gs.2

ἐπαγγελίαν. 22 ὁ μὲν οὖν χιλίαρχος ἀπέλυσε τὸν νεανίσκον
consent." So the ~ *So* ⌞commanding officer⌟ dismissed the young man,
2039 4036 3836 3525 4036 5941 668 3836 3734
n.asf d.nsm pl cj n.nsm v.aai.3s d.asm n.asm

παραγγείλας μηδενὶ ἐκλαλῆσαι ὅτι ταῦτα
charging him to tell no one *to tell* that you have reported these things
4133 1718 1718 3594 1718 4022 1872 1872 1872 4047
pt.aa.nsm a.dsm f.aa cj r.apn

ἐνεφάνισας πρός με. 23 καί προσκαλεσάμενος δύο τινὰς[a] τῶν ἑκατονταρχῶν
you have reported to me." Then he called two *{certain}* of the centurions
1872 4639 1609 2779 4673 1545 5516 3836 1672
v.aai.2s p.a r.as.1 cj pt.am.nsm a.apm r.apm d.gpm n.gpm

εἶπεν, ἑτοιμάσατε στρατιώτας
and said, "Get ready by the third hour of the night two hundred soldiers,
3306 2286 608 5569 6052 3836 3836 3816 1357 1357 5132
v.aai.3s v.aam.2p n.apm

διακοσίους, ὅπως πορευθῶσιν ἕως
two hundred seventy horsemen, and two hundred spearmen to go ⌞as far as⌟
1357 1573 2689 1357 1357 1287 3968 4513 2401
a.apm cj v.aps.3p p.g

Καισαρείας, καὶ ἱππεῖς ἑβδομήκοντα καὶ δεξιολάβους διακοσίους ἀπὸ τρίτης ὥρας
Caesarea." *{and}* *horsemen* *seventy* *{and}* *spearmen* *two hundred* *by* *third* *hour*
2791 2779 2689 1573 2779 1287 1357 608 5569 6052
n.gsf cj n.apm a.apm cj n.apm a.apm p.g a.gsf n.gsf

τῆς νυκτός, 24 κτήνη τε παραστῆσαι ἵνα
of the *night* And he told them to provide mounts *And* *to provide* so that
3836 3816 5445 4225 4225 3229 5445 4225 2671
d.gsf n.gsf n.apn cj f.aa cj

ἐπιβιβάσαντες τὸν Παῦλον ↰ διασώσωσι ← πρὸς Φήλικα τὸν
having put *{the}* Paul on them they might bring him safely to Felix the
2097 3836 4263 2097 1407 4639 5772 3836
pt.aa.npm d.asm n.asm v.aas.3p p.a n.asm d.asm

ἡγεμόνα, 25 γράψας ἐπιστολὴν ἔχουσαν τὸν τύπον τοῦτον· 26 Κλαύδιος
governor. And he wrote a letter having *{the}* this form: *this* "Claudius
2450 1211 2186 2400 3836 4047 5596 4047 3087
n.asm pt.aa.nsm n.asf pt.pa.asf d.asm n.asm r.asm n.nsm

Λυσίας τῷ κρατίστῳ ἡγεμόνι Φήλικι χαίρειν. 27 τὸν ἄνδρα τοῦτον
Lysias, ⌞to the⌟ most excellent governor, Felix, greetings. *{the}* This man *This*
3385 3836 3196 2450 5772 5897 3836 4047 467 4047
n.nsm d.dsm a.dsm.s n.dsm n.dsm f.pa d.asm n.asm r.asm

συλλημφθέντα ὑπὸ τῶν Ἰουδαίων καὶ μέλλοντα ἀναιρεῖσθαι ὑπ' αὐτῶν →
was seized by the Jews and was about to be killed by them, when I
5197 5679 3836 2681 2779 3516 359 5679 899
pt.ap.asm p.g d.gpm a.gpm cj pt.pa.asm f.pp p.g r.gpm.3

ἐπιστὰς σὺν τῷ στρατεύματι ἐξειλάμην μαθὼν ὅτι
came upon him and, with the soldiers, rescued him, ⌞having learned⌟ that he was a
2392 5250 3836 5128 1975 3443 4022 1639 1639
pt.aa.nsm p.d d.dsn n.dsn v.ami.1s pt.aa.nsm cj

[a] [τινὰς] UBS.

NASB

[21]So do not listen
to them, for more
than forty of them
are lying in wait
for him who have
bound themselves
under a curse not
to eat or drink until
they slay him; and
now they are ready
and waiting for the
promise from you."
[22]So the command-
er let the young
man go, instructing
him, "Tell no one
that you have noti-
fied me of these
things."

Paul Moved to Caesarea

[23]And he called to
him two of the cen-
turions and said,
"Get two hundred
soldiers ready by
[a]the third hour of
the night to pro-
ceed to Caesarea,
with seventy horse-
men and two hun-
dred spearmen."
[24]*They were* also
to provide mounts
to put Paul on and
bring him safely to
Felix the governor.
[25]And he wrote a
letter having this
form:

[26]"Claudius
Lysias, to the
most excel-
lent governor
Felix, greet-
ings.

[27]"When this
man was ar-
rested by the
Jews and was
about to be
slain by them,
I came up to
them with
the troops
and rescued
him, having
learned that
he was a

[a] I.e. 9 p.m.

NIV

Roman citizen. 28I
wanted to know
why they were
accusing him, so
I brought him to
their Sanhedrin.
29I found that the
accusation had to
do with questions
about their law,
but there was no
charge against
him that deserved
death or impris-
onment. 30When I
was informed of a
plot to be carried
out against the
man, I sent him
to you at once. I
also ordered his
accusers to present
to you their case
against him.

31So the soldiers,
carrying out their
orders, took Paul
with them dur-
ing the night and
brought him as
far as Antipatris.
32The next day
they let the cav-
alry go on with
him, while they
returned to the
barracks. 33When
the cavalry arrived
in Caesarea, they
delivered the let-
ter to the governor
and handed Paul
over to him. 34The
governor read the
letter and asked
what province he
was from. Learn-
ing that he was
from Cilicia, 35he
said, "I will hear
your case when
your accusers get
here." Then he or-
dered that Paul be
kept under guard
in Herod's palace.

Ῥωμαῖός ἐστιν. 28 βουλόμενός τε ἐπιγνῶναι τὴν αἰτίαν δι᾽ ἣν
Roman citizen. *he was* And wanting *And* to know the charge for which
4871 1639 5445 1089 5445 2105 3836 162 1328 4005
n.nsm v.pai.3s pt.pm.nsm cj f.aa d.asf n.asf p.a r.asf

ἐνεκάλουν αὐτῷ, κατήγαγον ← εἰς τὸ συνέδριον αὐτῶν 29
they were accusing him, I brought him down to *{the}* their council. *their* I
1592 899 2864 1650 3836 899 5284 899 2351
v.iai.3p r.dsm.3 v.aai.1s p.a d.asn n.asn r.gpm.3

ὃν εὗρον ἐγκαλούμενον περὶ ζητημάτων τοῦ νόμου αὐτῶν,
found him *I found* accused ⌊in regard to⌋ questions of their law, *their* but with
2351 4005 2351 1592 4309 2427 3836 899 3795 899 1254 2400
r.asm v.aai.1s pt.pp.asm p.g n.gpn d.gsm n.gsm r.gpm.3

μηδὲν δὲ ἄξιον θανάτου ἢ δεσμῶν ἔχοντα ἔγκλημα. 30
no charge *but* deserving death or imprisonment. *with* *charge* And
3594 1598 1254 545 2505 2445 1301 2400 1598 1254
a.asn cj a.asn n.gsm cj n.gpm pt.pa.asm n.asn

μηνυθείσης δέ μοι ἐπιβουλῆς εἰς τὸν ἄνδρα
when it was disclosed *And* to me that there would be a plot against the man,
3606 1254 1609 1639 1639 1639 2101 1650 3836 467
pt.ap.gsf cj r.ds.1 n.gsf p.a d.asm n.asm

ἔσεσθαι ἐξαυτῆς ἔπεμψα πρὸς σέ παραγγείλας καὶ τοῖς
there would be *at once* I sent him to you at once, ordering his accusers also *his*
1639 1994 4287 4639 5148 1994 1994 4133 3836 2991 2779 3836
f.fm adv v.aai.1s p.a r.as.2 pt.aa.nsm adv d.dpm

κατηγόροις λέγειν τὰ[a] πρὸς αὐτὸν ἐπὶ σοῦ. 31 οἱ μὲν οὖν στρατιῶται
accusers to speak *{the}* against him to you." So the ~ *So* soldiers,
2991 3306 3836 4639 899 2093 5148 4036 3836 3525 4036 5132
n.dpm f.pa d.apn p.a r.asm.3 p.g r.gs.2 d.npm pl cj n.npm

κατὰ τὸ διατεταγμένον αὐτοῖς ἀναλαβόντες τὸν Παῦλον ἤγαγον διὰ
⌊according to⌋ the directions given to them, took *{the}* Paul and brought him by
2848 3836 1411 899 377 3836 4263 72 1328
p.a d.asn pt.rp.asn r.dpm.3 pt.aa.npm d.asm n.asm v.aai.3p p.g

νυκτὸς εἰς τὴν Ἀντιπατρίδα, 32 τῇ δὲ ἐπαύριον ἐάσαντες τοὺς ἱππεῖς
night to *{the}* Antipatris. The *{and}* next day they let the horsemen
3816 1650 3836 526 3836 1254 2069 1572 3836 2689
n.gsf p.a d.asf n.asf d.dsf cj adv pt.aa.npm d.apm n.apm

ἀπέρχεσθαι σὺν αὐτῷ ὑπέστρεψαν εἰς τὴν παρεμβολήν· 33 ↱ οἵτινες
go on with him, and they returned to the barracks. When the horsemen
599 5250 899 5715 1650 3836 4213 1656 4015
f.pm p.d r.dsm.3 v.aai.3p p.a d.asf n.asf r.npm

εἰσελθόντες εἰς τὴν Καισάρειαν καὶ ↱ ἀναδόντες τὴν ἐπιστολὴν τῷ ἡγεμόνι
arrived in *{the}* Caesarea, *{and}* they delivered the letter ⌊to the⌋ governor
1656 1650 3836 2791 2779 4225 347 3836 2186 3836 2450
pt.aa.npm p.a d.asf n.asf cj pt.aa.npm d.asf n.asf d.dsm n.dsm

παρέστησαν καὶ τὸν Παῦλον αὐτῷ. 34 ἀναγνοὺς δὲ καὶ
and turned over *and* *{the}* Paul to him. ⌊When he had read⌋ the letter, *{and}* *{and}*
2779 4225 2779 3836 4263 899 336 1254 2779
v.aai.3p cj d.asm n.asm r.dsm.3 pt.aa.nsm cj cj

ἐπερωτήσας ἐκ ποίας ἐπαρχείας ἐστίν, καὶ πυθόμενος ὅτι ἀπὸ Κιλικίας,
he asked from what province he was. *{and}* Learning that he was from Cilicia,
2089 1666 4481 2065 1639 2779 4785 4022 608 3070
pt.aa.nsm p.g r.gsf n.gsf v.pai.3s cj pt.am.nsm cj p.g n.gsf

35 → → → διακούσομαί σου, ἔφη, ὅταν καὶ οἱ κατήγοροί
he said, "I will give you a hearing *you* *he said* when *{also}* *{the}* your accusers
5774 5774 5148 1358 5148 5774 4020 2779 3836 5148 2991
v.fmi.1s r.gs.2 v.iai.3s cj adv d.npm n.npm

σου παραγένωνται· κελεύσας ἐν τῷ πραιτωρίῳ
your arrive." Then he commanded that Paul be guarded in *{the}* Herod's headquarters.
5148 4134 3027 899 5875 5875 1877 3836 2476 4550
r.gs.2 v.ams.3p pt.aa.nsm p.d d.dsn n.dsn

τοῦ Ἡρῴδου φυλάσσεσθαι αὐτόν.
{the} *Herod's* *be guarded* *Paul*
3836 2476 5875 899
d.gsm n.gsm f.pp r.asm.3

[a] [τὰ] UBS.

NASB

Roman.
28 "And wanting
to ascertain
the charge for
which they
were accus-
ing him, I
brought him
down to their
Council;
29 and I found
him to be
accused over
questions
about their
Law, but
under no ac-
cusation de-
serving death
or imprison-
ment.
30 "When I was
informed that
there would
be a plot
against the
man, I sent
him to you at
once, also in-
structing his
accusers to
bring charges
against him
before you."
31So the soldiers,
in accordance with
their orders, took
Paul and brought
him by night to An-
tipatris. 32But the
next day, leaving
the horsemen to go
on with him, they
returned to the bar-
racks. 33When these
had come to Cae-
sarea and delivered
the letter to the
governor, they also
presented Paul to
him. 34When he had
read it, he asked
from what province
he was, and when
he learned that he
was from Cilicia,
35he said, "I will
give you a hearing
after your accusers
arrive also," giving
orders for him to
be kept in Herod's
[a]Praetorium.

[a] I.e. governor's official residence

NIV

Paul's Trial Before Felix

24 Five days
later the
high priest Ana-
nias went down
to Caesarea with
some of the el-
ders and a lawyer
named Tertullus,
and they brought
their charges
against Paul be-
fore the governor.
2 When Paul was
called in, Tertul-
lus presented his
case before Felix:
"We have enjoyed
a long period of
peace under you,
and your foresight
has brought about
reforms in this na-
tion. 3 Everywhere
and in every way,
most excellent
Felix, we acknowl-
edge this with pro-
found gratitude.
4 But in order not to
weary you further,
I would request
that you be kind
enough to hear us
briefly.
5 "We have found
this man to be
a troublemaker,
stirring up riots
among the Jews all
over the world. He
is a ringleader of
the Nazarene sect
6 and even tried to
desecrate the tem-
ple; so we seized
him. [7][a] 8 By exam-
ining him yourself
you will be able
to learn the truth
about all these
charges we are
bringing against
him."

[a] 6-8 Some manuscripts include here *him, and we would have judged him in accordance with our law. 7 But the commander Lysias came and took him from us with much violence, 8 ordering his accusers to come before you.*

24:1 μετὰ δὲ πέντε ἡμέρας κατέβη ὁ ἀρχιερεὺς Ἁνανίας μετὰ
And after *And* five days *went down* the high priest Ananias went down with
1254 3552 1254 4297 2465 2849 3836 797 393 2849 2849 3552
p.a cj a.apf n.apf v.aai.3s d.nsm n.nsm n.nsm p.g

πρεσβυτέρων τινῶν καὶ ῥήτορος Τερτύλλου τινός, οἵτινες
some elders *some* and a ⌊prosecuting attorney,⌋ one Tertullus; *one* and they
5516 4565 5516 2779 4842 5516 5472 5516 4015
a.gpm r.gpm cj n.gsm n.gsm r.gsm r.npm

ἐνεφάνισαν τῷ ἡγεμόνι ↰ ↰ κατὰ τοῦ Παύλου. 2 → κληθέντος
laid before the governor their case against *{the}* Paul. And when he was summoned,
1872 3836 2450 1872 1872 2848 3836 4263 1254 899 2813
v.aai.3p d.dsm n.dsm p.g d.gsm n.gsm pt.ap.gsm

δὲ αὐτοῦ ἤρξατο κατηγορεῖν ὁ Τέρτυλλος λέγων,
And *he* Tertullus began to accuse him, *{the}* *Tertullus* saying: "Since we have
1254 899 5472 806 2989 3836 5472 3306 5593 5593 5593
cj r.gsm.3 v.ami.3s f.pa d.nsm n.nsm pt.pa.nsm

πολλῆς εἰρήνης τυγχάνοντες διὰ σοῦ καὶ ↱ διορθωμάτων
enjoyed a long period of peace *Since we have enjoyed* through your rule, and since reforms
5593 4498 1645 5593 1328 5148 2779 1181 1480
a.gsf n.gsf pt.pa.npm p.g r.gs.2 cj n.gpn

γινομένων τῷ ἔθνει τούτῳ διὰ τῆς σῆς προνοίας, 3 πάντῃ τε καὶ
are being made in the nation *the* by *{the}* your foresight, ⌊in every way⌋ ~ and
1181 3836 4047 1620 4047 1328 3836 5050 4630 4118 5445 2779
pt.pm.gpn d.dsn n.dsn r.dsn p.g d.gsf r.gsf.2 n.gsf adv cj cj

πανταχοῦ ἀποδεχόμεθα, κράτιστε Φῆλιξ, μετὰ πάσης εὐχαριστίας. 4 ἵνα
everywhere we accept them, most excellent Felix, with all gratitude. But, that
4116 622 3196 5772 3552 4246 2374 1254 2671
adv v.pmi.1p a.vsm.s n.vsm p.g a.gsf n.gsf cj

δὲ μὴ ἐπὶ πλεῖόν σε ἐγκόπτω, παρακαλῶ ἀκοῦσαί σε
But I may not detain you any longer, *you* *I may detain* I beg you to hear *you*
1254 1601 1601 3590 1601 5148 2093 4498 5148 1601 4151 5148 201 5148
cj pl p.a adv.c r.as.2 v.pas.1s v.pai.1s f.aa r.as.2

ἡμῶν συντόμως τῇ σῇ ἐπιεικείᾳ. 5 εὑρόντες γὰρ τὸν ἄνδρα τοῦτον
us briefly in your kindness. For we found *For* *{the}* this man *this* to be a
7005 5339 3836 5050 2116 1142 2351 1142 3836 4047 467 4047
r.gp.1 adv d.dsf r.dsf.2 n.dsf pt.aa.npm cj d.asm n.asm r.asm

λοιμὸν καὶ κινοῦντα στάσεις πᾶσιν τοῖς Ἰουδαίοις τοῖς κατὰ τὴν
troublemaker, *{and}* ⌊one who stirs up⌋ riots ⌊among all⌋ the Jews *{the}* throughout the
3369 2779 3075 5087 4246 3836 2681 3836 2848 3836
n.asm cj pt.pa.asm n.apf a.dpm d.dpm a.dpm d.dpm p.a d.asf

οἰκουμένην πρωτοστάτην τε τῆς τῶν Ναζωραίων αἱρέσεως, 6 ὃς καὶ
world, and a ringleader *and* of the sect of the Nazarenes. *sect* He even
3876 5445 4756 5445 3836 146 3836 3717 146 4005 2779
n.asf n.asm cj d.gsf d.gpm n.gpm n.gsf r.nsm adv

τὸ ἱερὸν ἐπείρασεν βεβηλῶσαι ὃν καὶ ἐκρατήσαμεν,[a] 8 παρ᾽
tried to desecrate the temple, *tried* *to desecrate* *him* so we laid hold of him. *from*
4279 1014 1014 3836 2639 4279 1014 4005 2779 3195 4005 4123
d.asn n.asn v.aai.3s f.aa r.asm adv v.aai.1p p.g

οὗ δυνήσῃ αὐτὸς ἀνακρίνας
him *you will be able* When you examine him yourself, *When you examine* you will be able to
4005 1538 373 373 373 899 373 1538 1538 1538 1538 2105
r.gsm v.fpi.2s r.nsm pt.aa.nsm

περὶ πάντων τούτων ἐπιγνῶναι ὧν ἡμεῖς κατηγοροῦμεν αὐτοῦ.
learn from him about all these things *to learn* of which we are accusing him."
2105 4123 4005 4309 4246 4047 2105 4005 7005 2989 899
p.g a.gpn r.gpn f.aa r.gpn r.np.1 v.pai.1p r.gsm.3

[a] καὶ κατὰ τὸν ἡμέτερον νόμον ἠθελήσαμεν κρίνειν. [7] παρελθὼν δὲ Λυσίας ὁ χιλίαρχος μετὰ πολλῆς βίας ἐκ τῶν χειρῶν ἡμῶν ἀπήγαγε, [8] κελεύσας τοὺς κατηγόρους αὐτοῦ ἔρχεσθαι ἐπὶ σέ· included by TR after ἐκρατήσαμεν.

NASB

Paul before Felix

24:1 After five days
the high priest
Ananias came
down with some
elders, with an
attorney *named*
Tertullus, and they
brought charges
to the governor
against Paul. 2 After
Paul had been
summoned, Tertul-
lus began to accuse
him, saying *to the*
governor,
"Since we have
through you at-
tained much peace,
and since by your
providence reforms
are being carried
out for this nation,
3 we acknowledge
this in every way
and everywhere,
most excellent Fe-
lix, with all thank-
fulness. 4 But, that I
may not weary you
any further, I beg
you to grant us, by
your kindness, a
brief hearing. 5 For
we have found this
man a real pest
and a fellow who
stirs up dissension
among all the Jews
throughout [a] the
world, and a ring-
leader of the sect
of the Nazarenes.
6 And he even tried
to desecrate the
temple; and then
we arrested him.
[[b] We wanted to
judge him accord-
ing to our own
Law. 7 But Lysias
the commander
came along, and
with much violence
took him out of our
hands, 8 ordering his
accusers to come
before you.] By ex-
amining him your-
self concerning
all these matters
you will be able to
ascertain the things
of which we accuse

[a] Lit *the inhabited earth*
[b] The early mss do not contain the remainder of v 6, v 7, nor the first part of v 8

NIV

[9]The other Jews
joined in the accu-
sation, asserting
that these things
were true.
[10]When the gov-
ernor motioned for
him to speak, Paul
replied: "I know
that for a number
of years you have
been a judge over
this nation; so I
gladly make my
defense. [11]You
can easily verify
that no more than
twelve days ago I
went up to Jeru-
salem to worship.
[12]My accusers did
not find me argu-
ing with anyone
at the temple, or
stirring up a crowd
in the synagogues
or anywhere else
in the city. [13]And
they cannot prove
to you the charges
they are now mak-
ing against me.
[14]However, I admit
that I worship the
God of our ances-
tors as a follower
of the Way, which
they call a sect.
I believe every-
thing that is in
accordance with
the Law and that
is written in the
Prophets, [15]and
I have the same
hope in God as
these men them-
selves have, that
there will be a res-
urrection of both
the righteous and
the wicked. [16]So
I strive always
to keep my con-
science clear

[9]συνεπέθεντο δὲ καὶ οἱ Ἰουδαῖοι φάσκοντες ταῦτα
joined the attack And the Jews also *the* *Jews* joined the attack, saying that it
5298 1254 3836 2681 2779 3836 2681 5298 5298 5298 5763 4047
v.ami.3p cj adv d.npm a.npm pt.pa.npm r.apn

οὕτως ἔχειν. [10] ἀπεκρίθη τε ὁ Παῦλος → νεύσαντος
was so. *was* And Paul responded, *And* *{the}* *Paul* when the governor motioned
2400 4048 2400 5445 4263 646 5445 3836 4263 3836 2450 3748
adv f.pa v.api.3s cj d.nsm n.nsm pt.aa.gsm

αὐτῷ τοῦ ἡγεμόνος λέγειν, ἐκ πολλῶν ἐτῶν ὄντα σε
to him *he* *governor* to speak: "Knowing that for many years you ˪have been˩ *you* a
899 3836 2450 3306 2179 2179 1666 4498 2291 5148 1639 5148
r.dsm.3 d.gsm n.gsm f.pa p.g a.gpn n.gpn pt.pa.asm r.as.2

κριτὴν τῷ ἔθνει τούτῳ ἐπιστάμενος εὐθύμως τὰ περὶ ἐμαυτοῦ → → →
judge over this nation, *this* *Knowing that* gladly *things* *concerning* *my own* do I make
3216 3836 4047 1620 4047 2179 2315 3836 4309 1831
n.asm d.dsn n.dsn r.dsn pt.pp.nsm adv d.apn p.g r.gsm.1

ἀπολογοῦμαι, [11] → δυναμένου σου ἐπιγνῶναι
my own defense concerning these things. As you are able *you* to verify for
1831 1831 664 4309 3836 5148 1538 5148 2105
v.pmi.1s pt.pp.gsm r.gs.2 f.aa

ὅτι οὐ πλείους εἰσίν μοι ἡμέραι δώδεκα ˪ἀφ᾽ ἧς˩
yourself, *{that}* it is not more than *it is* *{to me}* twelve days *twelve* since
4022 1639 1639 4024 4498 1639 1609 1557 2465 1557 608 4005
cj pl a.npf.c v.pai.3p r.ds.1 n.npf a.npf p.g r.gsf

ἀνέβην προσκυνήσων εἰς Ἰερουσαλήμ. [12] καὶ οὔτε ἐν τῷ ἱερῷ → →
I went up to worship in Jerusalem, and *not either* *in* *the* *temple* they did not
326 4686 1650 2647 2779 4046 1877 3836 2639 4046
v.aai.1s pt.fa.nsm p.a n.asf cj cj p.d d.dsn n.dsn

εὗρόν με πρός τινα διαλεγόμενον ἢ ˪ἐπίστασιν ποιοῦντα˩ ὄχλου
find me arguing with anyone *arguing* or stirring up a crowd, either
2351 1609 1363 4639 5516 1363 2445 2180 4472 4063 4046
v.aai.3p r.as.1 p.a r.asm pt.pm.asm cj n.asf pt.pa.asm n.gsm

οὔτε ἐν ταῖς συναγωγαῖς οὔτε κατὰ τὴν πόλιν, [13] οὐδὲ
in the temple or in the synagogues or in the city. Neither can they
1877 3836 2639 4046 1877 3836 5252 4046 2848 3836 4484 4028 1538 1538
cj p.d d.dpf n.dpf cj p.a d.asf n.asf cj

παραστῆσαι δύνανταί σοι περὶ ὧν ↱ ↱ νυνὶ κατηγοροῦσίν
provide proof *can they* to you regarding the things of which they are now accusing
4225 1538 5148 4309 4005 2989 2989 3815 2989
f.aa v.ppi.3p r.ds.2 p.g r.gpn adv v.pai.3p

μου. [14] ὁμολογῶ δὲ τοῦτό σοι ὅτι κατὰ τὴν ὁδὸν ἣν λέγουσιν
me. But this I confess *But* *this* to you, that ˪according to˩ the Way, which they call a
1609 1254 4047 3933 1254 4047 5148 4022 2848 3836 3847 4005 3306
r.gs.1 v.pai.1s cj r.asn r.ds.2 cj p.a d.asf n.asf r.asf v.pai.3p

αἵρεσιν, οὕτως λατρεύω τῷ → πατρῴῳ θεῷ πιστεύων πᾶσι τοῖς
sect, thus I worship the God of our fathers, *God* believing all things that are
146 4048 3302 3836 2536 4262 2536 4409 4246 3836
n.asf adv v.pai.1s d.dsm a.dsm n.dsm pt.pa.nsm a.dpn d.dpn

κατὰ τὸν νόμον καὶ τοῖς ἐν τοῖς προφήταις γεγραμμένοις, [15]
˪according to˩ the Law and *{the}* written in the Prophets, *written* having a
2848 3836 3795 2779 3836 1211 1877 3836 4737 1211 2400
p.a d.asm n.asm cj d.dpn p.d d.dpm n.dpm pt.rp.dpn

ἐλπίδα ἔχων εἰς τὸν θεὸν ἣν καὶ αὐτοὶ οὗτοι προσδέχονται,
hope *having* in *{the}* God, which *{also}* these men themselves *these men* accept,
1828 2400 1650 3836 2536 4005 2779 4047 4047 899 4047 4657
n.asf pt.pa.nsm p.a d.asm n.asm r.asf adv r.npm r.npm v.pmi.3p

ἀνάστασιν μέλλειν ἔσεσθαι → δικαίων τε καὶ →
that there is to be a resurrection *there is* *to be* both of the just *both* and of the
3516 3516 1639 1639 414 3516 1639 5445 1465 5445 2779
n.asf f.pa f.fm a.gpm cj cj

ἀδίκων. [16] ἐν τούτῳ καὶ αὐτὸς ἀσκῶ ἀπρόσκοπον
unjust. In view of this *{also}* I ˪do my best˩ to have a clear
96 1877 4047 2779 899 828 2400 2400 718
a.gpm p.d r.dsn adv r.nsm v.pai.1s a.asf

NASB

him." [9]The Jews
also joined in the
attack, asserting
that these things
were so.
[10]When the gover-
nor had nodded for
him to speak, Paul
responded:
"**K**nowing that
for many years you
have been a judge
to this nation, I
cheerfully make
my defense, [11]since
you can take note
of the fact that no
more than twelve
days ago I went
up to Jerusalem to
worship. [12]Neither
in the temple, nor
in the synagogues,
nor in the city
itself did they find
me carrying on a
discussion with
anyone or caus-
ing a riot. [13]Nor
can they prove to
you *the charges* of
which they now
accuse me. [14]But
this I admit to you,
that according to
the Way which
they call a sect I do
serve the God of
our fathers, believ-
ing everything that
is in accordance
with the Law and
that is written
in the Prophets;
[15]having a hope in
God, which these
men cherish them-
selves, that there
shall certainly be
a resurrection of
both the righteous
and the wicked.
[16]In view of this, I
also do my best to
maintain always a
blameless

NIV

before God and
man.
[17]“After an ab-
sence of several
years, I came to
Jerusalem to bring
my people gifts
for the poor and to
present offerings.
[18]I was ceremo-
nially clean when
they found me in
the temple courts
doing this. There
was no crowd
with me, nor was
I involved in any
disturbance. [19]But
there are some
Jews from the
province of Asia,
who ought to be
here before you
and bring charges
if they have any-
thing against me.
[20]Or these who are
here should state
what crime they
found in me when
I stood before the
Sanhedrin— [21]un-
less it was this one
thing I shouted
as I stood in their
presence: ‘It is
concerning the
resurrection of the
dead that I am on
trial before you to-
day.’ ”
[22]Then Felix, who
was well acquaint-
ed with the Way,
adjourned the pro-
ceedings. “When
Lysias the com-
mander comes,”
he said, “I will
decide your case.”
[23]He ordered the
centurion to keep
Paul under guard
but to give him
some freedom and
permit his friends
to take care of his
needs.
[24]Several days
later Felix came
with his wife Dru-
silla, who was
Jewish.

συνείδησιν ἔχειν πρὸς τὸν θεὸν καὶ τοὺς ἀνθρώπους ⌞διὰ παντός.⌟ [17]
conscience *to have* toward *{the}* God and *{the}* men at all times. “Now,
5287 2400 4639 3836 2536 2779 3836 476 1328 4246 1254
n.asf f.pa p.a d.asm n.asm cj d.apm n.apm p.g a.gsn

δι' ἐτῶν δὲ πλειόνων ἐλεημοσύνας ποιήσων
after several years, *Now* *several* I came to my people bringing gifts for the poor *bringing*
1328 4498 2291 1254 4498 4134 4134 1650 1609 1620 4472 1797 4472
p.g n.gpn cj a.gpn.c n.apf pt.fa.nsm

εἰς τὸ ἔθνος μου παρεγενόμην καὶ προσφοράς, [18] ἐν αἷς
to *{the}* *people* *my* *I came* and presenting offerings, *when* which I was doing
1650 3836 1620 1609 4134 2779 4714 1877 4005
p.a d.asn n.asn r.gs.1 v.ami.1s cj n.apf p.d r.dpf

εὗρόν με ἡγνισμένον ἐν τῷ ἱερῷ ⌞οὐ μετὰ⌟ ὄχλου ⌞οὐδὲ
when they found me, ritually purified in the temple, without a crowd and without
1877 2351 1609 49 1877 3836 2639 4024 3552 4063 4028
v.aai.3p r.as.1 pt.rp.asm p.d d.dsn n.dsn pl p.g n.gsm cj

μετὰ⌟ θορύβου, [19] τινὲς δὲ ἀπὸ τῆς Ἀσίας Ἰουδαῖοι, οὓς
a commotion. But there are some *But* Jews from *{the}* Asia *Jews* who
3552 2573 1254 5516 1254 2681 608 3836 823 2681 4005
p.g n.gsm r.npm cj p.g d.gsf n.gsf a.npm r.apm

ἔδει ἐπὶ σοῦ παρεῖναι καὶ κατηγορεῖν εἴ τι ἔχοιεν
⌞ought to⌟ be here before you *be here* and bring charges, if they have anything *they have*
1256 4205 4205 2093 5148 4205 2779 2989 1623 2400 2400 5516 2400
v.iai.3s p.g r.gs.2 f.pa cj f.pa cj r.asn v.pao.3p

πρὸς ἐμέ. [20] ἢ ↱ αὐτοὶ οὗτοι εἰπάτωσαν τί εὗρον
against me. Or let these men themselves *these men* tell what wrongdoing they found
4639 1609 2445 3306 4047 4047 899 4047 3306 5515 93 2351
p.a r.as.1 cj r.npm r.npm v.aam.3p r.asn v.aai.3p

ἀδίκημα → στάντος μου ἐπὶ τοῦ συνεδρίου, [21] ἢ περὶ
wrongdoing when I stood *I* before the council, ⌞other than⌟ *{concerning}* this
93 1609 2705 1609 2093 3836 5284 2445 4309 4047
n.asn pt.aa.gsm r.gs.1 p.g d.gsn n.gsn pl p.g

μιᾶς ταύτης φωνῆς ἧς ἐκέκραξα ἐν αὐτοῖς ἑστὼς ὅτι
one *this* utterance that I cried out while standing among them: *while standing* ~ ‘It is
1651 4047 5889 4005 3189 2705 2705 1877 899 2705 4022
a.gsf r.gsf n.gsf r.gsf v.aai.1s p.d r.dpm.3 pt.ra.nsm cj

περὶ ἀναστάσεως → νεκρῶν ἐγὼ κρίνομαι σήμερον ἐφ' ὑμῶν.
regarding a resurrection for the dead that I am on trial before you this day.’” *before* *you*
4309 414 3738 1609 3212 2093 7007 4958 2093 7007
p.g n.gsf a.gpm r.ns.1 v.ppi.1s adv p.g r.gp.2

[22] ἀνεβάλετο δὲ αὐτοὺς ὁ Φῆλιξ, ἀκριβέστερον εἰδὼς τὰ περὶ
put off But *them* *{the}* Felix, knowing more exactly *knowing* the facts concerning
327 1254 899 3836 5772 3857 209 3857 3836 4309
v.ami.3s cj r.apm.3 d.nsm n.nsm adv.c pt.ra.nsm d.apn p.g

τῆς ὁδοῦ εἴπας, ὅταν Λυσίας ὁ χιλίαρχος καταβῇ,
the Way, put them off, saying, “When Lysias the ⌞commanding officer⌟ comes down,
3836 3847 327 899 327 3306 4020 3385 3836 5941 2849
d.gsf n.gsf pt.aa.nsm cj n.nsm d.nsm n.nsm v.aas.3s

διαγνώσομαι τὰ ⌞καθ' ὑμᾶς·⌟ [23] διαταξάμενος τῷ ἑκατοντάρχῃ τηρεῖσθαι
I will decide *{the}* your case.” Then he commanded the centurion to keep
1336 3836 2848 7007 1411 3836 1672 5498
v.fmi.1s d.apn p.a r.ap.2 pt.am.nsm d.dsm n.dsm f.pp

αὐτὸν → → ἔχειν τε ἄνεσιν καὶ μηδένα κωλύειν ↰ τῶν
him in custody, but to let him have *but* some freedom and not to prevent any of his
899 5445 2400 5445 457 2779 3594 3266 3594 3836 899
r.asm.3 f.pa cj n.asf cj a.asm f.pa d.gpm

ἰδίων αὐτοῦ ↰ ὑπηρετεῖν αὐτῷ. ↰ [24] μετὰ δὲ ἡμέρας τινὰς
friends *his* from ⌞taking care of⌟ his needs. After *{and}* some days *some* Felix
2625 899 3266 5676 899 5676 3552 1254 5516 2465 5516 5772
a.gpm r.gsm.3 f.pa r.dsm.3 p.a cj n.apf r.apf

παραγενόμενος ὁ Φῆλιξ σὺν Δρουσίλλῃ τῇ ἰδίᾳ γυναικὶ οὔσῃ Ἰουδαίᾳ
arrived *{the}* *Felix* with his wife Drusilla, *{the}* *his* *wife* who was Jewish.
4134 3836 5772 5250 2625 1222 1537 3836 2625 1222 1639 2681
pt.am.nsm d.nsm n.nsm p.d n.dsf d.dsf a.dsf n.dsf pt.pa.dsf a.dsf

NASB

conscience *both*
before God and
before men. [17]Now
after several years
I came to bring
[a]alms to my nation
and to present
offerings; [18]in
which they found
me *occupied* in
the temple, having
been purified,
without *any* crowd
or uproar. But *there*
were some Jews
from Asia— [19]who
ought to have been
present before
you and to make
accusation, if they
should have any-
thing against me.
[20]Or else let these
men themselves
tell what misdeed
they found when
I stood before the
Council, [21]other
than for this one
statement which I
shouted out while
standing among
them, ‘For the
resurrection of the
dead I am on trial
before you today.’”
[22]But Felix, hav-
ing a more exact
knowledge about
the Way, put them
off, saying, “When
Lysias the [b]com-
mander comes
down, I will decide
your case.” [23]Then
he gave orders to
the centurion for
him to be kept in
custody and *yet*
have *some* free-
dom, and not to
prevent any of his
friends from minis-
tering to him.
[24]But some days
later Felix arrived
with Drusilla, his
wife who was a
Jewess, and sent

[a] *Or gifts to charity*
[b] I.e. chiliarch, in command of one thousand troops

NIV

He sent for Paul and listened to him as he spoke about faith in Christ Jesus. [25]As Paul talked about righteousness, self-control and the judgment to come, Felix was afraid and said, "That's enough for now! You may leave. When I find it convenient, I will send for you." [26]At the same time he was hoping that Paul would offer him a bribe, so he sent for him frequently and talked with him.
[27]When two years had passed, Felix was succeeded by Porcius Festus, but because Felix wanted to grant a favor to the Jews, he left Paul in prison.

Paul's Trial Before Festus

25 Three days after arriving in the province, Festus went up from Caesarea to Jerusalem, [2]where the chief priests and the Jewish leaders appeared before him and presented the charges against Paul. [3]They requested Festus, as a favor to them, to have Paul transferred to Jerusalem, for they were preparing an ambush to kill him along the way. [4]Festus answered, "Paul is being held at Caesarea, and I myself

μετεπέμψατο τὸν Παῦλον καὶ ἤκουσεν αὐτοῦ περὶ τῆς εἰς Χριστὸν
He sent for *{the}* Paul and heard him speak about *{the}* faith in Christ
3569 3836 4263 2779 201 899 4309 3836 4411 1650 5986
v.ami.3s d.asm n.asm cj v.aai.3s r.gsm.3 p.g d.gsf p.a n.asm

Ἰησοῦν πίστεως. [25] → διαλεγομένου δὲ αὐτοῦ περὶ δικαιοσύνης καὶ
Jesus. *faith* And as he reasoned with *And he* him about righteousness and
2652 4411 1254 899 1363 1254 899 4309 1466 2779
n.asm n.gsf pt.pm.gsm cj r.gsm.3 p.g n.gsf cj

ἐγκρατείας καὶ τοῦ κρίματος τοῦ μέλλοντος, ἔμφοβος γενόμενος ὁ
self-control and the judgment *{the}* to come, Felix became frightened *became* *{the}*
1602 2779 3836 3210 3836 3516 5772 1181 1873 1181 3836
n.gsf cj d.gsn n.gsn d.gsn pt.pa.gsn a.nsm pt.am.nsm d.nsm

Φῆλιξ ἀπεκρίθη, τὸ νῦν ⌞ἔχον πορεύου,⌟ καιρὸν δὲ
Felix and said, "For the present go away, but when I find time *but*
5772 646 3836 3814 2400 4513 1254 3561 3561 3561 2789 1254
n.nsm v.api.3s d.asn adv pt.pa.asn v.pmm.2s n.asm cj

μεταλαβὼν μετακαλέσομαί σε, [26] ἅμα καὶ ἐλπίζων ὅτι χρήματα
when I find I will send for you." ⌞At the same time⌟ *{and}* he hoped that money
3561 3559 5148 275 2779 1827 4022 5975
pt.aa.nsm v.fmi.1s r.as.2 adv cj pt.pa.nsm cj n.npn

δοθήσεται αὐτῷ ὑπὸ τοῦ Παύλου· διὸ καὶ πυκνότερον αὐτὸν
would be given to him by *{the}* Paul. So *{also}* he sent for him frequently *him*
1443 899 5679 3836 4263 1475 2779 3569 3569 3569 899 4781 899
v.fpi.3s r.dsm.3 p.g d.gsm n.gsm cj adv adv.c r.asm.3

μεταπεμπόμενος ὡμίλει αὐτῷ. [27] ↱ διετίας δὲ πληρωθείσης
he sent for and ⌞conversed with⌟ him. When two years *{and}* had passed, Felix
3569 3917 899 4444 1454 1254 4444 5772
pt.pm.nsm v.iai.3s r.dsm.3 n.gsf cj pt.ap.gsf

⌞ἔλαβεν διάδοχον⌟ ὁ Φῆλιξ Πόρκιον Φῆστον, θέλων τε
was replaced *{the}* *Felix* by Porcius Festus, and wanting *and* to curry
3284 1345 3836 5772 4517 5776 5445 2527 5445 2960 2960
v.aai.3s n.asm d.nsm n.nsm n.asm n.asm pt.pa.nsm cj

χάριτα καταθέσθαι τοῖς Ἰουδαίοις ὁ Φῆλιξ κατέλιπε τὸν Παῦλον δεδεμένον.
favor *to curry with* with the Jews, *{the}* Felix left *{the}* Paul in prison.
5921 2960 2960 3836 2681 3836 5772 2901 3836 4263 1313
n.asf f.am d.dpm a.dpm d.nsm n.nsm v.aai.3s d.asm n.asm pt.rp.asm

[25:1] Φῆστος οὖν ἐπιβὰς τῇ ἐπαρχείᾳ μετὰ τρεῖς ἡμέρας
Festus *{then}* Three days after arriving ⌞in the⌟ province, *after* *Three* *days* Festus
5776 4036 5552 2465 3552 2094 3836 2065 3552 5552 2465 5776
n.nsm cj pt.aa.nsm d.dsf n.dsf p.a a.apf n.apf

ἀνέβη εἰς Ἱεροσόλυμα ἀπὸ Καισαρείας, [2]ἐνεφάνισάν τε αὐτῷ οἱ
went up to Jerusalem from Caesarea. *brought formal charges* So *{to him}* the
326 1650 2642 608 2791 1872 5445 899 3836
v.aai.3s p.a n.apn p.g n.gsf v.aai.3p cj r.dsm.3 d.npm

ἀρχιερεῖς καὶ οἱ πρῶτοι τῶν Ἰουδαίων κατὰ τοῦ
chief priests and the Jewish leaders *{the}* *Jewish* brought formal charges against *{the}*
797 2779 3836 2681 4755 3836 2681 1872 1872 1872 2848 3836
n.npm cj d.npm a.npm d.gpm a.gpm p.g d.gsm

Παύλου καὶ παρεκάλουν αὐτὸν [3] αἰτούμενοι χάριν κατ᾽ αὐτοῦ
Paul, *{and}* begging him and asking him to do them a favor against Paul;
4263 2779 4151 899 160 5921 2848 899
n.gsm cj v.iai.3p r.asm.3 pt.pm.npm n.asf p.g r.gsm.3

ὅπως μεταπέμψηται αὐτὸν εἰς Ἰερουσαλήμ,
{so that} they urged Festus to transfer him to Jerusalem, for they were forming a
3968 3569 899 1650 2647 4472 4472 4472 4472
cj v.ams.3s r.asm.3 p.a n.asf

ἐνέδραν ποιοῦντες ἀνελεῖν αὐτὸν κατὰ τὴν ὁδόν. [4]ὁ μὲν οὖν Φῆστος
plot *for they were forming* to kill him along the way. *{the}* ~ So then Festus
1909 4472 359 899 2848 3836 3847 3836 3525 4036 5776
n.asf pt.pa.npm f.aa r.asm.3 p.a d.asf n.asf d.nsm pl cj n.nsm

ἀπεκρίθη τηρεῖσθαι τὸν Παῦλον εἰς Καισάρειαν, ἑαυτὸν δὲ
replied that Paul was being kept *{the}* *Paul* at Caesarea but that he himself *but*
646 4263 5498 3836 4263 1650 2791 1254 1571 1254
v.api.3s f.pp d.asm n.asm p.a n.asf r.asm.3 cj

NASB

for Paul and heard him *speak* about faith in Christ Jesus. [25]But as he was discussing righteousness, self-control and the judgment to come, Felix became frightened and said, "Go away for the present, and when I find time I will summon you." [26]At the same time too, he was hoping that money would be given him by Paul; therefore he also used to send for him quite often and converse with him. [27]But after two years had passed, Felix was succeeded by Porcius Festus, and wishing to do the Jews a favor, Felix left Paul imprisoned.

Paul before Festus

[25:1]Festus then, having arrived in the province, three days later went up to Jerusalem from Caesarea. [2]And the chief priests and the leading men of the Jews brought charges against Paul, and they were urging him, [3]requesting a concession against Paul, that he might have him brought to Jerusalem (*at the same time,* setting an ambush to kill him on the way). [4]Festus then answered that Paul was being kept in custody at Caesarea and that he

NIV

am going there
soon. 5 Let some of
your leaders come
with me, and if the
man has done any-
thing wrong, they
can press charges
against him there."
6 After spending
eight or ten days
with them, Fes-
tus went down to
Caesarea. The next
day he convened
the court and or-
dered that Paul
be brought before
him. 7 When Paul
came in, the Jews
who had come
down from Jerusa-
lem stood around
him. They brought
many serious
charges against
him, but they
could not prove
them.
8 Then Paul made
his defense: "I
have done noth-
ing wrong against
the Jewish law or
against the temple
or against Caesar."
9 Festus, wishing
to do the Jews a
favor, said to Paul,
"Are you willing
to go up to Jerusa-
lem and stand trial
before me there on
these charges?"
10 Paul answered:
"I am now stand-
ing before Caesar's
court, where I
ought to be tried. I
have not done any
wrong to the Jews,
as you yourself
know very well.
11 If, however, I am
guilty of doing
anything

μέλλειν ⌊ἐν τάχει⌋ ἐκπορεύεσθαι· 5 οἱ οὖν ↱ ἐν
intended to go there shortly. *to go there* *{the}* "So," he said, "let *{among}*
3516 1744 1744 1744 1877 5443 1744 3836 4036 5774 5774 5160 1877
f.pa p.d n.dsn f.pm d.npm cj p.d

ὑμῖν, φησίν, δυνατοὶ συγκαταβάντες εἴ τι ἐστιν ἐν τῷ ἀνδρὶ
your leaders *he said* *leaders* go down there with me, and if *anything* there is in this man
7007 1543 5774 1543 5160 1623 5516 1639 1877 3836 467
r.dp.2 v.pai.3s a.npm pt.aa.npm cj r.nsn v.pai.3s p.d d.dsm n.dsm

ἄτοπον κατηγορείτωσαν αὐτοῦ. 6 διατρίψας δὲ ἐν αὐτοῖς
anything improper, ⌊let them bring charges against⌋ him." After he stayed *{and}* among them
5516 876 2989 899 1417 1254 1877 899
a.nsn v.pam.3p r.gsm.3 pt.aa.nsm cj p.d r.dpm.3

ἡμέρας οὐ πλείους ὀκτὼ ἢ δέκα, καταβὰς εἰς Καισάρειαν, τῇ
days not more than eight or ten days, he went down to Caesarea, and the
2465 4024 4498 3893 2445 1274 2465 2849 1650 2791 3836
n.apf pl a.apf.c a.gpf cj a.gpf pt.aa.nsm p.a n.asf d.dsf

ἐπαύριον ↱ καθίσας ἐπὶ τοῦ βήματος ἐκέλευσεν τὸν Παῦλον ἀχθῆναι.
next day he took his seat on the judge's bench and ordered *{the}* Paul to be brought.
2069 3027 2767 2093 3836 1037 3027 3836 4263 72
adv pt.aa.nsm p.g d.gsn n.gsn v.aai.3s d.asm n.asm f.ap

7 → παραγενομένου δὲ αὐτοῦ περιέστησαν αὐτὸν οἱ
When he arrived, *{and}* *he* *stood around* *him* the Jews who had come
899 4134 1254 899 4325 899 3836 2681 2849 2849 2849
pt.am.gsm cj r.gsm.3 v.aai.3p r.asm.3 d.npm

ἀπὸ Ἱεροσολύμων καταβεβηκότες Ἰουδαῖοι πολλὰ καὶ
down from Jerusalem *who had come down* *Jews* stood around him, bringing many and
2849 608 2642 2849 2681 4325 4325 899 2965 4498 2779
p.g n.gpn pt.ra.npm a.npm a.apn cj

βαρέα αἰτιώματα καταφέροντες ἃ ↱ ↱ οὐκ ἴσχυον ἀποδεῖξαι,
serious charges *bringing against* against him, which they were not able to prove.
987 166 2965 2965 4005 2710 2710 4024 2710 617
a.apn n.apn pt.pa.npm r.apn pl v.iai.3p f.aa

8 τοῦ Παύλου ἀπολογουμένου ὅτι οὔτε εἰς τὸν νόμον τῶν Ἰουδαίων οὔτε
{the} Paul argued in his defense, ~ "Neither against the law of the Jews, nor
3836 4263 664 4022 4046 1650 3836 3795 3836 2681 4046
d.gsm n.gsm pt.pm.gsm cj cj p.a d.asm n.asm d.gpm a.gpm cj

εἰς τὸ ἱερὸν οὔτε εἰς Καίσαρά ↱ ↱ ↱ τι ἥμαρτον. 9 ὁ
against the temple, nor against Caesar have I committed any offense." But *{the}*
1650 3836 2639 4046 1650 2790 279 279 279 5516 279 1254 3836
p.a d.asn n.asn cj p.a n.asm r.asn v.aai.1s d.nsm

Φῆστος δὲ θέλων τοῖς Ἰουδαίοις χάριν καταθέσθαι ἀποκριθεὶς
Festus, *But* wanting to curry favor with the Jews, *favor* *to curry with* responded
5776 1254 2527 2960 2960 5921 2960 3836 2681 5921 2960 646
n.nsm cj pt.pa.nsm d.dpm a.dpm n.asf f.am pt.ap.nsm

τῷ Παύλῳ εἶπεν, θέλεις εἰς Ἱεροσόλυμα ἀναβὰς ἐκεῖ
to Paul, saying, ⌊"Do you want⌋ to go up to Jerusalem *to go up* and there be tried
3836 4263 3306 2527 326 326 326 1650 2642 326 1695 3212 3212
d.dsm n.dsm v.aai.3s v.pai.2s p.a n.apn pt.aa.nsm adv

περὶ τούτων κριθῆναι ἐπ' ἐμοῦ; 10 εἶπεν δὲ ὁ Παῦλος,
on these charges *be tried* before me?" Paul answered, *{and}* *{the}* *Paul* "I am now
4309 4047 3212 2093 1609 4263 3306 1254 3836 4263 1639 1639
p.g r.gpn f.ap p.g r.gs.1 v.aai.3s cj d.nsm n.nsm

ἐπὶ τοῦ βήματος Καίσαρος ἑστώς εἰμι, οὗ με δεῖ
standing before *{the}* Caesar's ⌊judgment seat,⌋ *Caesar's* *standing* *I am* where I ought
2705 2093 3836 2790 1037 2790 2705 1639 4023 1609 1256
p.g d.gsn n.gsn n.gsm pt.ra.nsm v.pai.1s adv r.as.1 v.pai.3s

κρίνεσθαι. Ἰουδαίους ↱ ↱ ↱ οὐδὲν ἠδίκησα ὡς καὶ σὺ
to be tried. Against the Jews I have done nothing wrong, as *{also}* you yourself
3212 2681 92 92 92 4029 92 6055 2779 2105 5148
f.pp a.apm a.asn v.aai.1s cj adv r.ns.2

κάλλιον ἐπιγινώσκεις. 11 εἰ μὲν οὖν ἀδικῶ καὶ
know very well. *you know* If ~ then ⌊I am a wrongdoer⌋ and have done anything
2105 2822 2105 1623 3525 4036 92 2779 4556 4556 5516
adv.c v.pai.2s cj pl cj v.pai.1s cj

NASB

himself was about
to leave shortly.
5 "Therefore," he
*said, "let the influ-
ential men among
you go there with
me, and if there is
anything wrong
about the man, let
them prosecute
him."
6 After he had
spent not more
than eight or ten
days among them,
he went down to
Caesarea, and on
the next day he
took his seat on
the tribunal and
ordered Paul to
be brought. 7 After
Paul arrived, the
Jews who had
come down from
Jerusalem stood
around him, bring-
ing many and seri-
ous charges against
him which they
could not prove,
8 while Paul said in
his own defense,
"I have committed
no offense either
against the Law
of the Jews or
against the temple
or against Caesar."
9 But Festus, wish-
ing to do the Jews
a favor, answered
Paul and said, "Are
you willing to go
up to Jerusalem
and stand trial
before me on these
charges?" 10 But
Paul said, "I am
standing before
Caesar's tribunal,
where I ought to be
tried. I have done
no wrong to *the*
Jews, as you also
very well know.
11 If, then, I am a
wrongdoer and
have committed
anything worthy

NIV

deserving death,
I do not refuse
to die. But if the
charges brought
against me by
these Jews are not
true, no one has
the right to hand
me over to them. I
appeal to Caesar!"
12 After Festus
had conferred with
his council, he de-
clared: "You have
appealed to Cae-
sar. To Caesar you
will go!"

Festus Consults King Agrippa

13 A few days later
King Agrippa and
Bernice arrived at
Caesarea to pay
their respects to
Festus. 14 Since
they were spend-
ing many days
there, Festus dis-
cussed Paul's case
with the king. He
said: "There is a
man here whom
Felix left as a pris-
oner. 15 When I
went to Jerusalem,
the chief priests
and the elders of
the Jews brought
charges against
him and asked that
he be condemned.
16 "I told them
that it is not the
Roman custom to
hand over anyone
before they have
faced their accus-
ers and have had
an opportunity to
defend themselves
against the charg-
es. 17 When they
came here with
me, I did not delay
the case,

ἄξιον θανάτου πέπραχά τι, οὐ παραιτοῦμαι τὸ ἀποθανεῖν· εἰ δὲ
worthy of death, *have done* *anything* I am not trying to escape ~ death; but if *but*
545 2505 4556 5516 4024 4148 3836 633 1254 1623 1254
a.asn n.gsm v.rai.1s r.asn pl v.pmi.1s d.asn f.aa cj cj

οὐδέν ἐστιν ⌊ὧν οὗτοι⌋ κατηγοροῦσίν μου, οὐδείς με δύναται
there is nothing *there is* to their charges against me, no one *me* has a right to turn
1639 1639 4029 1639 4005 4047 2989 1609 4029 1609 1538 5919 5919
a.nsn v.pai.3s r.gpn r.npm v.pai.3p r.gs.1 a.nsm r.as.1 v.ppi.3s

αὐτοῖς χαρίσασθαι· Καίσαρα ἐπικαλοῦμαι. 12 τότε ὁ
me over to them. *to turn over* I appeal to Caesar." *I appeal to* Then *{the}*
1609 5919 899 5919 2126 2126 2126 2790 2126 5538 3836
r.dpm.3 f.am n.asm v.pmi.1s adv d.nsm

Φῆστος συλλαλήσας μετὰ τοῦ συμβουλίου ἀπεκρίθη, Καίσαρα ἐπικέκλησαι,
Festus, after conferring with the council, replied, "To Caesar you have appealed;
5776 5196 3552 3836 5206 646 2126 2790 2126
n.nsm pt.aa.nsm p.g d.gsn n.gsn v.api.3s n.asm v.rmi.2s

ἐπὶ Καίσαρα πορεύσῃ. 13 ἡμερῶν δὲ διαγενομένων τινῶν Ἀγρίππας
to Caesar you will go." Now after some days *Now* had passed, *some* Agrippa
2093 2790 4513 1254 1335 5516 2465 1254 1335 5516 68
p.a n.asm v.fmi.2s n.gpf cj pt.am.gpf r.gpf n.nsm

ὁ βασιλεὺς καὶ Βερνίκη κατήντησαν εἰς Καισάρειαν ἀσπασάμενοι τὸν
the king and Bernice came down to Caesarea and ⌊paid their respects to⌋ *{the}*
3836 995 2779 1022 2918 1650 2791 832 3836
d.nsm n.nsm cj n.nsf v.aai.3p p.a n.asf pt.am.npm d.asm

Φῆστον. 14 ὡς δὲ πλείους ἡμέρας διέτριβον ἐκεῖ, ὁ
Festus. Since *{and}* they were staying there several days, *they were staying* *there* *{the}*
5776 6055 1254 1417 1417 1417 1695 4498 2465 1417 1695 3836
n.asm cj cj a.apf.c n.apf v.iai.3p adv d.nsm

Φῆστος τῷ βασιλεῖ ἀνέθετο τὰ κατὰ τὸν Παῦλον λέγων,
Festus laid Paul's case before the king, *laid before* *{the}* *case* *{the}* *Paul's* saying,
5776 423 4263 2848 423 3836 995 423 3836 2848 3836 4263 3306
n.nsm d.dsm n.dsm v.ami.3s d.apn p.a d.asm n.asm pt.pa.nsm

ἀνήρ τίς ἐστιν καταλελειμμένος ὑπὸ Φήλικος δέσμιος, 15 περὶ οὗ
"There is a man *a* *There is* left by Felix, a prisoner. *about him*
1639 1639 5516 467 5516 1639 2901 5679 5772 1300 4309 4005
n.nsm r.nsm v.pai.3s pt.rp.nsm p.g n.gsm n.nsm p.g r.gsm

γενομένου μου εἰς Ἱεροσόλυμα ἐνεφάνισαν οἱ ἀρχιερεῖς καὶ οἱ
When I came *I* to Jerusalem, *informed* the chief priests and the
1609 1181 1609 1650 2642 1872 3836 797 2779 3836
pt.am.gsm r.gs.1 p.a n.apn v.aai.3p d.npm n.npm cj d.npm

πρεσβύτεροι τῶν Ἰουδαίων αἰτούμενοι κατ᾽
elders of the Jews informed me about him, asking for a guilty verdict against
4565 3836 2681 1872 4309 4005 160 2869 2869 2848
a.npm d.gpm a.gpm pt.pm.npm p.g

αὐτοῦ καταδίκην. 16 πρὸς οὓς ἀπεκρίθην ὅτι οὐκ ἔστιν
him. *guilty verdict* I answered *{to}* them *I answered* that it was not *it was* the
899 2869 646 646 4639 4005 646 4022 1639 1639 4024 1639
r.gsm.3 n.asf p.a r.apm v.api.1s cj pl v.pai.3s

ἔθος Ῥωμαίοις χαρίζεσθαί τινα ἄνθρωπον ⌊πρὶν ἢ⌋ ὁ
custom of the Romans to turn anyone *{person}* over before the
1621 4871 5919 5516 476 5919 4570 2445 3836
n.nsn n.dpm f.pm r.asm n.asm cj pl d.nsm

κατηγορούμενος ⌊κατὰ πρόσωπον⌋ ἔχοι τοὺς κατηγόρους
accused has met the accusers face to face *has* *the* *accusers*
2989 2400 3836 2991 2848 4725 2400 3836 2991
pt.pp.nsm p.a n.asn v.pao.3s d.apm n.apm

τόπον τε ἀπολογίας λάβοι περὶ τοῦ ἐγκλήματος.
and had an opportunity *and* to make his defense *to make* against the charge.
5445 5536 5445 3284 3284 665 3284 4309 3836 1598
n.asm cj n.gsf v.aao.3s p.g d.gsn n.gsn

17 συνελθόντων οὖν αὐτῶν[a] ἐνθάδε ἀναβολὴν μηδεμίαν
So when they met *So* *they* here, I made no delay, *no*
4036 899 5302 4036 899 1924 3027 4472 3594 332 3594
pt.aa.gpm cj r.gpm.3 adv n.asf a.asf

NASB

of death, I do not
refuse to die; but
if none of those
things is *true* of
which these men
accuse me, no one
can hand me over
to them. I appeal
to Caesar." 12 Then
when Festus had
conferred with
his council, he
answered, "You
have appealed to
Caesar, to Caesar
you shall go."
13 Now when
several days had
elapsed, King
Agrippa and Ber-
nice arrived at Cae-
sarea and paid their
respects to Festus.
14 While they were
spending many
days there, Festus
laid Paul's case
before the king,
saying, "There is a
man who was left
as a prisoner by
Felix; 15 and when I
was at Jerusalem,
the chief priests
and the elders of
the Jews brought
charges against
him, asking for a
sentence of con-
demnation against
him. 16 I answered
them that it is not
the custom of the
Romans to hand
over any man be-
fore the accused
meets his accusers
face to face and has
an opportunity to
make his defense
against the charges.
17 So after they had
assembled here, I
did not delay, but

[a] [αὐτῶν] UBS.

NIV

but convened the
court the next day
and ordered the
man to be brought
in. 18 When his ac-
cusers got up to
speak, they did not
charge him with
any of the crimes
I had expected.
19 Instead, they had
some points of
dispute with him
about their own
religion and about
a dead man named
Jesus who Paul
claimed was alive.
20 I was at a loss
how to investigate
such matters; so I
asked if he would
be willing to go
to Jerusalem and
stand trial there
on these charges.
21 But when Paul
made his appeal
to be held over for
the Emperor's de-
cision, I ordered
him held until I
could send him to
Caesar."
22 Then Agrippa
said to Festus, "I
would like to hear
this man myself."
He replied, "To-
morrow you will
hear him."

Paul Before Agrippa

23 The next day
Agrippa and Ber-
nice came with
great pomp and
entered the audi-
ence room with
the high-ranking
military officers
and the prominent
men of the city. At
the command of
Festus, Paul was
brought in. 24 Fes-
tus said:

ποιησάμενος τῇ ἑξῆς καθίσας ἐπὶ τοῦ βήματος ἐκέλευσα
made but ⌊on the⌋ next day took my seat on the judge's bench and ordered the man
4472 3836 2009 2767 2093 3836 1037 3027 3836 467
pt.am.nsm d.dsf adv pt.aa.nsm p.g d.gsn n.gsn v.aai.1s

ἀχθῆναι τὸν ἄνδρα· 18 περὶ οὗ → σταθέντες οἱ κατήγοροι
to be brought. *the* *man* *against him* When the accusers stood up, *the* *accusers* they
72 3836 467 4309 4005 3836 2991 2705 3836 2991 5770
f.ap d.asm n.asm p.g r.gsm pt.ap.npm d.npm n.npm

οὐδεμίαν αἰτίαν ἔφερον ὧν ἐγὼ ὑπενόουν πονηρῶν,
brought no charge *they brought* against him of such evils as I was expecting, *evils*
5770 4029 162 5770 4309 4005 4005 4505 1609 5706 4505
a.asf n.asf v.iai.3p r.gpn r.ns.1 v.iai.1s a.gpn

19 ζητήματα δέ τινα περὶ τῆς ἰδίας δεισιδαιμονίας εἶχον
but had certain questions *but* *certain* about *{the}* their own religion *had* to put
1254 2400 5516 2427 1254 5516 4309 3836 2625 1272 2400
n.apn cj r.apn p.g d.gsf a.gsf n.gsf v.iai.3p

πρὸς αὐτὸν καὶ περί τινος Ἰησοῦ τεθνηκότος ὃν ἔφασκεν ὁ Παῦλος
to him and about a certain Jesus, who was dead, whom Paul claimed *{the}* *Paul*
4639 899 2779 4309 5516 2652 2569 4005 4263 5763 3836 4263
p.a r.asm.3 cj p.g r.gsm n.gsm pt.ra.gsm r.asm v.iai.3s d.nsm n.nsm

ζῆν. 20 → ἀπορούμενος δὲ ἐγὼ τὴν περὶ
⌊to be alive.⌋ Since I was uncertain *{and}* *I* *{the}* about how to investigate
2409 1609 679 1254 1609 3836 4309 2428 2428 2428
f.pa pt.pm.nsm cj r.ns.1 d.asf p.g

τούτων ζήτησιν ἔλεγον εἰ βούλοιτο πορεύεσθαι εἰς Ἱεροσόλυμα
such questions, *how to investigate* I asked if he wanted to go to Jerusalem to
4047 2428 3306 1623 1089 4513 1650 2642 3212
r.gpn n.asf v.iai.1s cj v.pmo.3s f.pm p.a n.apn

κἀκεῖ κρίνεσθαι περὶ τούτων. 21 τοῦ δὲ → Παύλου ἐπικαλεσαμένου
be tried there *to be tried* on these charges. *{the}* But when Paul had appealed
3212 3212 2795 3212 4309 4047 3836 1254 2126 4263 2126
crasis f.pp p.g r.gpn d.gsm cj n.gsm pt.am.gsm

τηρηθῆναι αὐτὸν εἰς τὴν τοῦ Σεβαστοῦ διάγνωσιν, ἐκέλευσα
⌊to be kept in custody⌋ *{him}* for the decision of the emperor, *decision* I ordered him
5498 899 1650 3836 1338 3836 4935 1338 3027 899
f.ap r.asm.3 p.a d.asf d.gsm a.gsm n.asf v.aai.1s

τηρεῖσθαι αὐτὸν ⌊ἕως οὗ⌋ ἀναπέμψω αὐτὸν πρὸς Καίσαρα. 22 Ἀγρίππας δὲ
to be held *him* until I could send him to Caesar." Then Agrippa *Then*
5498 899 2401 4005 402 899 4639 2790 1254 68 1254
f.pp r.asm.3 p.g r.gsm v.aas.1s r.asm.3 p.a n.asm n.nsm cj

πρὸς τὸν Φῆστον, → ἐβουλόμην καὶ αὐτὸς τοῦ ἀνθρώπου
said to *{the}* Festus, "I too would like *too* to hear the man myself." *the* *man*
4639 3836 5776 2779 1089 2779 201 201 3836 476 899 3836 476
p.a d.asm n.asm v.imi.1s adv r.nsm d.gsm n.gsm

ἀκοῦσαι. αὔριον, φησίν, ἀκούσῃ αὐτοῦ. 23 τῇ οὖν ἐπαύριον →
to hear "Tomorrow," said he, ⌊"you will hear⌋ him." So ⌊on the⌋ *So* next day when
201 892 5774 201 899 4036 3836 4036 2069
f.aa adv v.pai.3s v.fmi.2s r.gsm.3 d.dsf cj adv

ἐλθόντος τοῦ Ἀγρίππα καὶ τῆς Βερνίκης μετὰ πολλῆς φαντασίας
Agrippa and Bernice came *{the}* *Agrippa* *and* *{the}* *Bernice* with great pomp
68 2779 1022 2262 3836 68 2779 3836 1022 3552 4498 5752
pt.aa.gsm d.gsm n.gsm cj d.gsf n.gsf p.g a.gsf n.gsf

καὶ ⌊εἰσελθόντων εἰς⌋ τὸ ἀκροατήριον σύν τε χιλιάρχοις καὶ
and entered the audience hall ⌊along with⌋ *{both}* the ⌊commanding officers⌋ and
2779 1656 1650 3836 211 5250 5445 5941 2779
cj pt.aa.gpm p.a d.asn n.asn p.d cj n.dpm cj

ἀνδράσιν τοῖς κατ' ἐξοχὴν τῆς πόλεως καὶ →
the prominent men *the* *{according to}* *prominent* of the city, and when Festus
3836 2029 467 3836 2848 2029 3836 4484 2779 5776
n.dpm d.dpm p.a n.asf d.gsf n.gsf cj

κελεύσαντος τοῦ Φήστου ἤχθη ὁ Παῦλος. 24 καί φησιν
had given the order, *{the}* *Festus* Paul ⌊was brought in.⌋ *{the}* *Paul* And Festus said,
3027 3836 5776 4263 72 3836 4263 2779 5776 5774
pt.aa.gsm d.gsm n.gsm v.api.3s d.nsm n.nsm cj v.pai.3s

NASB

on the next day
took my seat on
the tribunal and
ordered the man to
be brought before
me. 18 When the
accusers stood
up, they *began*
bringing charges
against him not
of such crimes as
I was expecting,
19 but they *simply*
had some points of
disagreement with
him about their
own religion and
about a dead man,
Jesus, whom Paul
asserted to be alive.
20 Being at a loss
how to investigate
such matters, I
asked whether he
was willing to go
to Jerusalem and
there stand trial
on these matters.
21 But when Paul
appealed to be
held in custody
for [a]the Emperor's
decision, I ordered
him to be kept in
custody until I send
him to Caesar."
22 Then Agrippa
said to Festus, "I
also would like to
hear the man my-
self." "Tomorrow,"
he *said, "you shall
hear him."

Paul before Agrippa

23 So, on the next
day when Agrippa
came together with
Bernice amid great
pomp, and entered
the auditorium
[b]accompanied by
the commanders
and the prominent
men of the city, at
the command of
Festus, Paul was
brought in. 24 Festus

[a] Lit *the Augustus's* (in this case Nero)
[b] Lit *and with*

NIV

"King Agrippa,
and all who are
present with us,
you see this man!
The whole Jew-
ish community
has petitioned me
about him in Jeru-
salem and here in
Caesarea, shouting
that he ought not
to live any longer.
25 I found he had
done nothing de-
serving of death,
but because he
made his appeal to
the Emperor I de-
cided to send him
to Rome. 26 But I
have nothing def-
inite to write to
His Majesty about
him. Therefore I
have brought him
before all of you,
and especially
before you, King
Agrippa, so that
as a result of this
investigation I may
have something to
write. 27 For I think
it is unreasonable
to send a prisoner
on to Rome with-
out specifying the
charges against
him."

26 Then
Agrippa
said to Paul, "You
have permission
to speak for your-
self."
So Paul motioned
with his hand and
began his defense:
2 "King Agrippa,
I consider myself
fortunate to stand
before you today
as I make my de-
fense against all
the accusations
of the Jews, 3 and
especially so be-
cause you are well
acquainted with
all the Jewish cus-
toms and contro-
versies.

ὁ Φῆστος, Ἀγρίππα βασιλεῦ καὶ πάντες οἱ συμπαρόντες ἡμῖν ἄνδρες,
{the} *Festus* "King Agrippa, *King* and all *{the}* men present with us, *men*
3836 5776 995 68 995 2779 4246 3836 467 5223 7005 467
d.nsm n.nsm n.vsm n.vsm cj a.vpm d.vpm pt.pa.vpm r.dp.1 n.vpm

θεωρεῖτε τοῦτον περὶ οὗ ἅπαν τὸ πλῆθος τῶν Ἰουδαίων ἐνέτυχόν μοι
you see this man about whom the whole *the* Jewish people *{the}* *Jewish* petitioned me,
2555 4047 4309 4005 3836 570 3836 2681 4436 3836 2681 1961 1609
v.pai.2p r.asm p.g r.gsm a.nsn d.nsn n.nsn d.gpm a.gpm v.aai.3p r.ds.1

ἔν τε Ἱεροσολύμοις καὶ ἐνθάδε βοῶντες μὴ δεῖν αὐτὸν ζῆν
both in *both* Jerusalem and here, crying out that he ought not *ought* *he* to live
5445 1877 5445 2642 2779 1924 1066 899 1256 3590 1256 899 2409
p.d cj n.dpn cj adv pt.pa.npm pl f.pa r.asm.3 f.pa

μηκέτι. 25 ἐγὼ δὲ κατελαβόμην μηδὲν ἄξιον αὐτὸν θανάτου
any longer. But I *But* found that he had done nothing worthy *he* of death;
3600 1254 1609 1254 2898 899 4556 4556 3594 545 899 2505
adv r.ns.1 cj v.ami.1s a.asn a.asn r.asm.3 n.gsm

πεπραχέναι, ↱ αὐτοῦ δὲ τούτου ἐπικαλεσαμένου τὸν Σεβαστὸν ἔκρινα
had done and since he *and* himself appealed to the emperor, I decided
4556 1254 2126 899 1254 4047 2126 3836 4935 3212
f.ra r.gsm.3 cj r.gsm pt.am.gsm d.asm a.asm v.aai.1s

πέμπειν. 26 περὶ οὗ ἀσφαλές τι γράψαι
to send him. But I do not have anything definite about him *definite* *anything* to write
4287 2400 2400 4024 2400 5516 855 4309 4005 855 5516 1211
f.pa p.g r.gsm a.asn r.asn f.aa

τῷ κυρίῳ οὐκ ἔχω, διὸ προήγαγον αὐτὸν ἐφ᾽ ὑμῶν καὶ μάλιστα
⌞to my⌟ lord. *not* *I do have* Therefore I have brought him before you all, and especially
3836 3261 4024 2400 1475 4575 899 2093 7007 2779 3436
d.dsm n.dsm pl v.pai.1s cj v.aai.1s r.asm.3 p.g r.gp.2 cj adv.s

ἐπὶ σοῦ, βασιλεῦ Ἀγρίππα, ὅπως ↱ τῆς ἀνακρίσεως γενομένης
before you, King Agrippa, so that, when the examination has been conducted,
2093 5148 995 68 3968 1181 3836 374 1181
p.g r.gs.2 n.vsm n.vsm cj d.gsf n.gsf pt.am.gsf

σχῶ τί γράψω, 27 ἄλογον γάρ μοι δοκεῖ πέμποντα
⌞I may have⌟ something to write. For it seems unreasonable *For* to me, *it seems* in sending
2400 5515 1211 1142 1506 1506 263 1142 1609 1506 4287
v.aas.1s r.asn v.aas.1s a.nsn cj r.ds.1 v.pai.3s pt.pa.asm

δέσμιον μὴ καὶ τὰς κατ᾽ αὐτοῦ αἰτίας σημᾶναι.
a prisoner, not to also report the charges against him." *charges* *to report*
1300 3590 4955 2779 4955 3836 162 2848 899 162 4955
n.asm pl adv d.apf p.g r.gsm.3 n.apf f.aa

26:1 Ἀγρίππας δὲ πρὸς τὸν Παῦλον ἔφη, ἐπιτρέπεταί σοι
So Agrippa *So* said to *{the}* Paul, *said* "You have permission *You* to
1254 68 1254 5774 4639 3836 4263 5774 5148 2205 5148 3306
n.nsm cj p.a d.asm n.asm v.iai.3s v.ppi.3s r.ds.2

περὶ σεαυτοῦ λέγειν. τότε ὁ Παῦλος ἐκτείνας τὴν χεῖρα
speak for yourself." *to speak* Then *{the}* Paul ⌞stretched out⌟ his hand and
3306 4309 4932 3306 5538 3836 4263 1753 3836 5931
p.g r.gsm.2 f.pa adv d.nsm n.nsm pt.aa.nsm d.asf n.asf

ἀπελογεῖτο· 2 περὶ πάντων ὧν ἐγκαλοῦμαι ὑπὸ
⌞began to make his defense:⌟ "Regarding all the things of which I am being accused by the
664 4309 4246 4005 1592 5679
v.imi.3s p.g a.gpn r.gpn v.ppi.1s p.g

Ἰουδαίων, βασιλεῦ Ἀγρίππα, ἥγημαι ἐμαυτὸν μακάριον ἐπὶ σοῦ
Jews, King Agrippa, I consider myself fortunate that it is before you that
2681 995 68 2451 1831 3421 2093 5148
a.gpm n.vsm n.vsm v.rmi.1s r.asm.1 a.asm p.g r.gs.2

μέλλων σήμερον ἀπολογεῖσθαι 3 μάλιστα
I am about to make my defense today, *to make my defense* especially because you are
3516 664 664 664 664 4958 664 3436 1639 5148 1639
pt.pa.nsm adv f.pm adv.s

γνώστην ὄντα σε πάντων τῶν κατὰ Ἰουδαίους
well acquainted *because are you* with all the customs and controversies of the Jews.
1195 1639 5148 4246 3836 1621 2779 2427 2848 2681
n.asm pt.pa.asm r.as.2 a.gpn d.gpn p.a a.apm

NASB

*said, "King
Agrippa, and all
you gentlemen here
present with us,
you see this man
about whom all the
people of the Jews
appealed to me,
both at Jerusalem
and here, loudly
declaring that he
ought not to live
any longer. 25 But I
found that he had
committed nothing
worthy of death;
and since he him-
self appealed to the
Emperor, I decided
to send him. 26 Yet
I have nothing
definite about him
to write to my lord.
Therefore I have
brought him before
you *all* and espe-
cially before you,
King Agrippa, so
that after the inves-
tigation has taken
place, I may have
something to write.
27 For it seems
absurd to me in
sending a prisoner,
not to indicate also
the charges against
him."

Paul's Defense before Agrippa

26:1 Agrippa said
to Paul, "You are
permitted to speak
for yourself." Then
Paul stretched out
his hand and *pro-
ceeded* to make his
defense:
2 "In regard to all
the things of which
I am accused by
the Jews, I consider
myself fortunate,
King Agrippa, that
I am about to make
my defense before
you today; 3 espe-
cially because you
are an expert in all
customs and ques-
tions among *the*
Jews; therefore

NIV

Therefore, I beg
you to listen to me
patiently.
4"The Jewish
people all know
the way I have
lived ever since I
was a child, from
the beginning
of my life in my
own country, and
also in Jerusalem.
5They have known
me for a long time
and can testify, if
they are willing,
that I conformed
to the strictest sect
of our religion,
living as a Phari-
see. 6And now it
is because of my
hope in what God
has promised our
ancestors that I
am on trial today.
7This is the prom-
ise our twelve
tribes are hoping
to see fulfilled
as they earnestly
serve God day and
night. King Agrip-
pa, it is because
of this hope that
these Jews are ac-
cusing me. 8Why
should any of you
consider it incredi-
ble that God raises
the dead?
9"I too was con-
vinced that I ought
to do all that was
possible to oppose
the name of Jesus
of Nazareth. 10And
that is just what I
did in Jerusalem.
On the authority
of the chief priests
I put many of the
Lord's people in
prison,

ἐθῶν τε καὶ ζητημάτων, διὸ δέομαι μακροθύμως
customs {both} and controversies Therefore I beg you to listen to me patiently.
1621 5445 2779 2427 1475 1289 201 201 201 1609 3430
n.gpn cj cj n.gpn cj v.pmi.1s adv

ἀκοῦσαί μου. 4 τὴν μὲν οὖν βίωσίν μου τὴν[a] ἐκ
to listen to me All the Jews know *{the} ~ {then}* my ⌊manner of life⌋ *my {the}* from my
201 1609 4246 3836 2681 3857 3836 3525 4036 1609 1052 1609 3836 1666
f.aa r.gs.1 d.asf pl cj n.asf r.gs.1 d.asf p.g

νεότητος τὴν ἀπ᾽ ἀρχῆς γενομένην ἐν τῷ ἔθνει μου ἔν τε
youth, which from the beginning was spent among *{the}* my own people *my own* in ~
3744 3836 608 794 1181 1877 3836 1609 1609 1620 1609 1877 5445
n.gsf d.asf p.g n.gsf pt.am.asf p.d d.dsn n.dsn r.gs.1 p.d cj

Ἱεροσολύμοις ἴσασι πάντες οἱ[b] Ἰουδαῖοι 5προγινώσκοντές με → ἄνωθεν,
Jerusalem, *know All the Jews* for they have known me from the first,
2642 3857 4246 3836 2681 4589 1609 540
n.dpn v.rai.3p a.npm d.npm a.npm pt.pa.npm r.as.1 adv

ἐὰν θέλωσι μαρτυρεῖν, ὅτι κατὰ τὴν
if ⌊they are willing⌋ to go on record, that I lived as a Pharisee ⌊according to⌋ the
1569 2527 3455 4022 2409 2409 5757 2848 3836
cj v.pas.3p f.pa cj p.a d.asf

ἀκριβεστάτην αἵρεσιν τῆς ἡμετέρας θρησκείας ἔζησα Φαρισαῖος. 6καὶ νῦν
strictest party of our religious system. *I lived Pharisee* And now I
207 146 3836 2466 2579 2409 5757 2779 3814 2705
a.asf.s n.asf d.gsf r.gsf.1 n.gsf v.aai.1s n.nsm cj adv

ἐπ᾽ ἐλπίδι τῆς εἰς τοὺς
stand here on trial ⌊because of⌋ my hope in the promise made by God to *{the}* our
2705 3212 3212 2093 1828 3836 2039 1181 5679 2536 1650 3836 7005
p.d n.dsf d.gsf p.a d.apm

πατέρας ἡμῶν ἐπαγγελίας γενομένης ὑπὸ τοῦ θεοῦ ἕστηκα κρινόμενος, 7εἰς ἣν
fathers, *our promise made by {the} God I stand on trial* to which
4252 7005 2039 1181 5679 3836 2536 2705 3212 1650 4005
n.apm r.gp.1 n.gsf pt.am.gsf p.g d.gsm n.gsm v.rai.1s pt.pp.nsm p.a r.asf

τὸ δωδεκάφυλον ἡμῶν ⌊ἐν ἐκτενείᾳ⌋ νύκτα
{the} our twelve tribes *our* hope to attain, worshipping strenuously night
3836 7005 1559 7005 1827 2918 2918 3302 1877 1755 3816
d.nsn n.nsn r.gp.1 p.d n.dsf n.asf

καὶ ἡμέραν λατρεῦον ἐλπίζει καταντῆσαι, περὶ ἧς ἐλπίδος
and day. *worshipping hope to attain* It is for this hope, your Excellency, that
2779 2465 3302 1827 2918 4309 4005 1828 995
cj n.asf pt.pa.nsn v.pai.3s f.aa p.g r.gsf n.gsf

ἐγκαλοῦμαι ὑπὸ Ἰουδαίων, βασιλεῦ.[c] 8τί ἄπιστον κρίνεται
I am being accused by Jews! *Excellency* Why is it thought incredible *is it thought*
1592 5679 2681 995 5515 3212 3212 3212 603 3212
v.ppi.1s p.g a.gpm n.vsm r.asn a.nsn v.ppi.3s

παρ᾽ ὑμῖν εἰ ὁ θεὸς νεκροὺς ἐγείρει; 9Ἐγὼ μὲν οὖν ἔδοξα ἐμαυτῷ
among you that *{the}* God raises the dead? *raises* I ~ *{then}* thought to myself
4123 7007 1623 3836 2536 1586 3738 1586 1609 3525 4036 1506 1831
p.d r.dp.2 cj d.nsm n.nsm a.apm v.pai.3s r.ns.1 pl cj v.aai.1s r.dsm.1

πρὸς τὸ ὄνομα Ἰησοῦ τοῦ Ναζωραίου δεῖν
that I ought to do many deeds hostile to the name of Jesus of Nazareth. *I ought*
1256 1256 4556 4556 4498 1885 1885 4639 3836 3950 2652 3836 3717 1256
p.a d.asn n.asn n.gsm d.gsm n.gsm f.pa

πολλὰ ἐναντία πρᾶξαι, 10 ὃ καὶ ἐποίησα ἐν Ἱεροσολύμοις, καὶ
many hostile deeds to do And I did so *{also} I did* in Jerusalem; *{and}*
4498 1885 4556 4472 4472 4005 2779 4472 1877 2642 2779
a.apn a.apn f.aa r.asn adv v.aai.1s p.d n.dpn cj

πολλούς τε τῶν ἁγίων ἐγὼ ἐν φυλακαῖς
not only did I lock up in prison many *not only* of the saints, *I in prison*
5445 5445 2881 1609 2881 2881 1877 5871 4498 5445 3836 41 1609 1877 5871
a.apm cj d.gpm a.gpm r.ns.1 p.d n.dpf

NASB

I beg you to listen
to me patiently.
4"So then, all
Jews know my
manner of life
from my youth up,
which from the be-
ginning was spent
among my *own*
nation and at Jeru-
salem; 5since they
have known about
me for a long time,
if they are willing
to testify, that I
lived *as* a Pharisee
according to the
strictest sect of our
religion. 6And now
I am standing trial
for the hope of the
promise made by
God to our fathers;
7*the promise* to
which our twelve
tribes hope to
attain, as they ear-
nestly serve *God*
night and day. And
for this hope, O
King, I am being
accused by Jews.
8Why is it consid-
ered incredible
among you *people*
if God does raise
the dead?
9"So then, I
thought to myself
that I had to do
many things hostile
to the name of
Jesus of Nazareth.
10And this is just
what I did in Je-
rusalem; not only
did I lock up many
of the saints in
prisons,

[a] [τὴν] UBS, omitted by TNIV.
[b] [οἱ] UBS.
[c] Ἀγρίππα, ὑπὸ τῶν Ἰουδαίων included by TR after βασιλεῦ.

NIV

and when they
were put to death,
I cast my vote
against them.
11 Many a time I
went from one
synagogue to an-
other to have them
punished, and I
tried to force them
to blaspheme. I
was so obsessed
with persecuting
them that I even
hunted them down
in foreign cities.
12 "On one of
these journeys
I was going to
Damascus with
the authority and
commission of
the chief priests.
13 About noon,
King Agrippa, as
I was on the road,
I saw a light from
heaven, bright-
er than the sun,
blazing around
me and my com-
panions. 14 We all
fell to the ground,
and I heard a voice
saying to me in
Aramaic,[a] 'Saul,
Saul, why do you
persecute me? It
is hard for you to
kick against the
goads.'
15 "Then I asked,
'Who are you,
Lord?'
" 'I am Jesus,
whom you are per-
secuting,' the Lord
replied. 16 'Now get
up and stand on
your feet. I have
appeared to you
to appoint you as
a servant and as
a witness of what
you have seen and
will see of me.

κατέκλεισα τὴν παρὰ τῶν ἀρχιερέων ἐξουσίαν λαβὼν
did lock up {the} after receiving authority from the chief priests, authority after receiving but
2881 3836 3284 3284 2026 4123 3836 797 2026 3284 5445
v.aai.1s d.asf p.g d.gpm n.gpm n.asf pt.aa.nsm

→ ἀναιρουμένων τε αὐτῶν κατήνεγκα ψῆφον. ← 11 καὶ
also when they were put to death but also they I cast my vote against them. And
5445 899 359 5445 899 2965 6029 2965 2779
pt.pp.gpm cj r.gpm.3 v.aai.1s n.asf cj

↱ κατὰ πάσας τὰς συναγωγὰς πολλάκις τιμωρῶν αὐτοὺς
I punished them often in all the synagogues often punished them and
337 5512 899 4490 2848 4246 3836 5252 4490 5512 899
p.a a.apf d.apf n.apf adv pt.pa.nsm r.apm.3

ἠνάγκαζον βλασφημεῖν ↱ ↱ περισσῶς τε ἐμμαινόμενος αὐτοῖς
tried to make them blaspheme; and since I was so vehemently and angry at them,
337 1059 5445 1841 1841 4360 5445 1841 899
v.iai.1s f.pa adv cj pt.pm.nsm r.dpm.3

ἐδίωκον ἕως καὶ εἰς τὰς ἔξω πόλεις. 12 ἐν οἷς
I pursued them even {also} to {the} foreign cities. "On one of these journeys I
1503 2401 2779 1650 3836 2032 4484 1877 4005
v.iai.1s cj adv p.a d.apf adv n.apf p.d r.dpn

πορευόμενος εἰς τὴν Δαμασκὸν μετ᾽ ἐξουσίας καὶ ἐπιτροπῆς τῆς τῶν ἀρχιερέων
was going to {the} Damascus with authority and commission from the chief priests,
4513 1650 3836 1242 3552 2026 2779 2207 3836 3836 797
pt.pm.nsm p.a d.asf n.asf p.g n.gsf cj n.gsf d.gsf d.gpm n.gpm

13 ⌊ἡμέρας μέσης⌋ κατὰ τὴν ὁδὸν εἶδον, βασιλεῦ, οὐρανόθεν
and at midday I saw on the way, I saw O king, a light from heaven,
2465 3545 1625 1625 2848 3836 3847 1625 995 5890 4040
n.gsf a.gsf p.a d.asf n.asf v.aai.1s n.vsm adv

⌊ὑπὲρ τὴν λαμπρότητα⌋ τοῦ ἡλίου περιλάμψαν με φῶς καὶ τοὺς
brighter than the sun, that shone around me light and those who
5642 3836 3288 3836 2463 4334 1609 5890 2779 3836 4513
p.a d.asf n.asf d.gsm n.gsm pt.aa.asn r.as.1 n.asn cj d.apm

σὺν ἐμοὶ πορευομένους. 14 ↱ ↱ πάντων τε καταπεσόντων
journeyed with me. who journeyed And when we had all And fallen
4513 5250 1609 4513 5445 2928 7005 2928 4246 5445 2928
p.d r.ds.1 pt.pm.apm a.gpm cj pt.aa.gpm

ἡμῶν εἰς τὴν γῆν ἤκουσα φωνὴν λέγουσαν πρός με τῇ Ἑβραΐδι διαλέκτῳ,
we to the ground, I heard a voice saying to me ⌊in the⌋ Hebrew language,
7005 1650 3836 1178 201 5889 3306 4639 1609 3836 1579 1365
r.gp.1 p.a d.asf n.asf v.aai.1s n.asf pt.pa.asf p.a r.as.1 d.dsf a.dsf n.dsf

Σαοὺλ Σαούλ, τί με διώκεις; σκληρόν σοι
'Saul, Saul, why are you persecuting me? are you persecuting It is hard ⌊for you⌋ to
4910 4910 5515 1503 1503 1503 1609 1503 5017 5148 3280
n.vsm n.vsm r.asn r.as.1 v.pai.2s a.nsn r.ds.2

πρὸς κέντρα λακτίζειν. 15 ἐγὼ δὲ εἶπα, τίς εἶ, κύριε; ὁ
kick against the goads.' to kick And I And said, 'Who ⌊are you,⌋ Lord?' And the
3280 4639 3034 3280 1254 1609 1254 3306 5515 1639 3261 1254 3836
p.a n.apn f.pa r.ns.1 cj v.aai.1s r.nsm v.pai.2s n.vsm d.nsm

δὲ κύριος εἶπεν, ἐγώ εἰμι Ἰησοῦς ὃν σὺ διώκεις. 16 ἀλλὰ ἀνάστηθι καὶ
And Lord said, 'I am Jesus whom you are persecuting. But get up and
1254 3261 3306 1609 1639 2652 4005 5148 1503 247 482 2779
cj n.nsm v.aai.3s r.ns.1 v.pai.1s n.nsm r.asm r.ns.2 v.pai.2s cj v.aam.2s cj

στῆθι ἐπὶ τοὺς πόδας σου· εἰς τοῦτο γὰρ
stand on {the} your feet; your for I have appeared to you for this purpose, for
2705 2093 3836 5148 4546 5148 1142 3972 3972 3972 5148 5148 1650 4047 1142
v.aam.2s p.a d.apm n.apm r.gs.2 p.a r.asn cj

ὤφθην σοι, προχειρίσασθαί σε ὑπηρέτην καὶ μάρτυρα
I have appeared to you to appoint you a servant and witness both to the things
3972 5148 4741 5148 5677 2779 3459 5445
v.api.1s r.ds.2 f.am r.as.2 n.asm cj n.asm

ὧν τε εἶδές με[a] ὧν τε ὀφθήσομαί σοι,
in which both ⌊you have seen⌋ me and to those in which and I will appear to you.
4005 5445 1625 1609 5445 4005 5445 3972 5148
r.gpn cj v.aai.2s r.as.1 r.gpn cj v.fpi.1s r.ds.2

NASB

having received
authority from the
chief priests, but
also when they
were being put to
death I cast my
vote against them.
11 And as I punished
them often in all
the synagogues, I
tried to force them
to blaspheme; and
being furiously
enraged at them, I
kept pursuing them
even to foreign
cities.
12 "While so en-
gaged as I was
journeying to
Damascus with
the authority and
commission of the
chief priests, 13 at
midday, O King, I
saw on the way a
light from heaven,
brighter than the
sun, shining all
around me and
those who were
journeying with
me. 14 And when
we had all fallen
to the ground, I
heard a voice say-
ing to me in the
Hebrew dialect,
'Saul, Saul, why
are you persecuting
Me? It is hard for
you to kick against
the goads.' 15 And
I said, 'Who are
You, Lord?' And
the Lord said, 'I am
Jesus whom you
are persecuting.
16 But get up and
stand on your feet;
for this purpose I
have appeared to
you, to appoint you
a minister and a
witness not only to
the things which
you have seen, but
also to the things in
which I will appear
to you;

a 14 Or *Hebrew*

a [με] UBS, omitted by NET.

NIV

17 I will rescue you
from your own
people and from
the Gentiles. I
am sending you
to them 18 to open
their eyes and turn
them from dark-
ness to light, and
from the power of
Satan to God, so
that they may re-
ceive forgiveness
of sins and a place
among those who
are sanctified by
faith in me.'
19 "So then, King
Agrippa, I was not
disobedient to the
vision from heav-
en. 20 First to those
in Damascus, then
to those in Jeru-
salem and in all
Judea, and then
to the Gentiles,
I preached that
they should repent
and turn to God
and demonstrate
their repentance
by their deeds.
21 That is why some
Jews seized me in
the temple courts
and tried to kill
me. 22 But God
has helped me to
this very day; so
I stand here and
testify to small
and great alike. I
am saying noth-
ing beyond what
the prophets and
Moses said would
happen— 23 that
the Messiah would
suffer and, as the
first to rise from
the dead, would
bring the message
of light to his own
people and to the
Gentiles."
24 At this point
Festus interrupted
Paul's defense.

17 ἐξαιρούμενός σε ἐκ τοῦ λαοῦ καὶ ἐκ τῶν ἐθνῶν εἰς οὓς ἐγὼ ἀποστέλλω
I will rescue you from your people and from the Gentiles, to whom I am sending
1975 5148 1666 3836 3295 2779 1666 3836 1620 1650 4005 1609 690
pt.pm.nsm r.as.2 p.g d.gsm n.gsm cj p.g d.gpn n.gpn p.a r.apm r.ns.1 v.pai.1s

σε 18 ἀνοῖξαι ὀφθαλμοὺς αὐτῶν, τοῦ ἐπιστρέψαι ἀπὸ σκότους εἰς φῶς καὶ
you to open their eyes, *their* that they may turn from darkness to light, and
5148 487 899 4057 899 3836 2188 608 5030 1650 5890 2779
r.as.2 f.aa n.apm r.gpm.3 d.gsn f.aa p.g n.gsn p.a n.asn cj

τῆς ἐξουσίας τοῦ σατανᾶ ἐπὶ τὸν θεόν, τοῦ λαβεῖν αὐτοὺς ἄφεσιν
⌊from the⌋ power of Satan to *{the}* God, that they may receive *they* forgiveness
3836 2026 3836 4928 2093 3836 2536 3836 899 3284 899 912
d.gsf n.gsf d.gsm n.gsm p.a d.asm n.asm d.gsn f.aa r.apm.3 n.asf

ἁμαρτιῶν καὶ κλῆρον ἐν τοῖς ἡγιασμένοις πίστει τῇ εἰς ἐμέ. 19 ὅθεν,
of sins and a place among those who are sanctified by faith *{the}* in me.' So then,
281 2779 3102 1877 3836 39 4411 3836 1650 1609 3854
n.gpf cj n.asm p.d d.dpm pt.rp.dpm n.dsf d.dsf p.a r.as.1 cj

βασιλεῦ Ἀγρίππα, οὐκ ἐγενόμην ἀπειθὴς τῇ οὐρανίῳ ὀπτασίᾳ 20 ἀλλὰ
King Agrippa, I was not *I was* disobedient ⌊to the⌋ heavenly vision, but
995 68 1181 1181 4024 1181 579 3836 4039 3965 247
n.vsm n.vsm pl v.ami.1s a.nsm d.dsf a.dsf n.dsf cj

τοῖς ἐν Δαμασκῷ πρῶτόν τε καὶ → Ἱεροσολύμοις,
I declared to those in Damascus first, then also to those in Jerusalem and through
550 550 3836 1877 1242 4754 5445 2779 2642 5445
d.dpm p.d n.dsf adv cj cj n.dpn

πᾶσάν τε τὴν χώραν τῆς Ἰουδαίας καὶ τοῖς ἔθνεσιν ἀπήγγελλον
all *and* the region of Judea, and to the Gentiles, *I declared* that
4246 5445 3836 6001 3836 2677 2779 3836 1620 550
a.asf cj d.asf n.asf d.gsf n.gsf cj d.dpn n.dpn v.iai.1s

μετανοεῖν καὶ ἐπιστρέφειν ἐπὶ τὸν θεόν, ἄξια τῆς μετανοίας
⌊they should repent⌋ and turn to *{the}* God, performing works worthy of repentance.
3566 2779 2188 2093 3836 2536 4556 2240 545 3836 3567
f.pa cj f.pa p.a d.asm n.asm a.apn d.gsf n.gsf

ἔργα πράσσοντας. 21 ἕνεκα τούτων ↰ με Ἰουδαῖοι συλλαβόμενοι
works performing It was for that reason *me* that the Jews seized
2240 4556 1914 4047 1914 1609 2681 5197
n.apn pt.pa.apm p.g r.gpn r.as.1 a.npm pt.am.npm

[a]ἐν τῷ ἱερῷ ἐπειρῶντο διαχειρίσασθαι. 22 ἐπικουρίας οὖν
me in the temple and tried to kill me. Obtaining help, therefore,
1609 1877 3836 2639 4281 1429 5593 2135 4036
p.d d.dsn n.dsn v.imi.3p f.am n.gsf cj

τυχὼν τῆς ἀπὸ τοῦ θεοῦ ἄχρι τῆς ἡμέρας ταύτης ἕστηκα μαρτυρόμενος
Obtaining {the} from *{the}* God, until *{the}* this day *this* I have stood testifying both
5593 3836 608 3836 2536 948 3836 4047 2465 4047 2705 3455 5445
pt.aa.nsm d.gsf p.g d.gsm n.gsm p.g d.gsf n.gsf r.gsf v.rai.1s pt.pm.nsm

μικρῷ τε καὶ μεγάλῳ οὐδὲν ἐκτὸς λέγων ὧν τε οἱ προφῆται
to small *both* and great, saying nothing beyond *saying* what the prophets and Moses
3625 5445 2779 3489 3306 4029 1760 3306 4005 5445 3836 4737 2779 3707
a.dsm cj cj a.dsm a.asn p.g pt.pa.nsm r.gpn cj d.npm n.npm

ἐλάλησαν μελλόντων γίνεσθαι καὶ Μωϋσῆς, 23 εἰ παθητὸς ὁ
said would come to pass: *and Moses* that the Christ was to suffer *the*
3281 3516 1181 2779 3707 1623 3836 5986 4078 3836
v.aai.3p pt.pa.gpn f.pm cj n.nsm cj a.nsm d.nsm

χριστός, εἰ πρῶτος ἐξ ἀναστάσεως → νεκρῶν φῶς
Christ and, as the first to rise from the dead, he would proclaim light
5986 1623 4755 1666 414 3738 3516 3516 2859 5890
n.nsm cj a.nsm p.g n.gsf a.gpm n.asn

μέλλει καταγγέλλειν τῷ τε λαῷ καὶ τοῖς ἔθνεσιν. 24 ↱
he would proclaim both ⌊to our⌋ *both* people and to the Gentiles." As Paul was saying
3516 2859 5445 3836 5445 3295 2779 3836 1620 664 899 664 664
v.pai.3s f.pa d.dsm cj n.dsm cj d.dpn n.dpn

ταῦτα δὲ αὐτοῦ ἀπολογουμένου ὁ Φῆστος → μεγάλῃ
these things *{and} Paul was saying in his defense* in his defense, *{the}* Festus said in a loud
4047 1254 899 664 664 664 664 3836 5776 5774 3489
r.apn cj r.gsm.3 pt.pm.gsm d.nsm n.nsm a.dsf

[a] ὄντα included by UBS before ἐν.

NASB

17 rescuing you from
the *Jewish* people
and from the
Gentiles, to whom
I am sending you,
18 to open their eyes
so that they may
turn from darkness
to light and from
the dominion of
Satan to God, that
they may receive
forgiveness of sins
and an inheritance
among those who
have been sancti-
fied by faith in
Me.'
19 "So, King Agrip-
pa, I did not prove
disobedient to the
heavenly vision,
20 but *kept* declaring
both to those of
Damascus first, and
also at Jerusalem
and *then* through-
out all the region
of Judea, and *even*
to the Gentiles,
that they should
repent and turn to
God, performing
deeds appropriate
to repentance. 21 For
this reason *some*
Jews seized me
in the temple and
tried to put me to
death. 22 So, having
obtained help from
God, I stand to this
day testifying both
to small and great,
stating nothing but
what the Prophets
and Moses said
was going to take
place; 23 that the
Christ was to suf-
fer, *and* that by
reason of *His* res-
urrection from the
dead He would be
the first to proclaim
light both to the
Jewish people and
to the Gentiles."
24 While *Paul* was
saying this in his
defense, Festus
*said in a loud

NIV

"You are out of
your mind, Paul!"
he shouted. "Your
great learning is
driving you in-
sane."
25"I am not in-
sane, most excel-
lent Festus," Paul
replied. "What I
am saying is true
and reasonable.
26The king is fa-
miliar with these
things, and I can
speak freely to
him. I am con-
vinced that none
of this has escaped
his notice, be-
cause it was not
done in a corner.
27King Agrippa,
do you believe the
prophets? I know
you do."
28Then Agrippa
said to Paul, "Do
you think that in
such a short time
you can persuade
me to be a Chris-
tian?"
29Paul replied,
"Short time or
long—I pray to
God that not only
you but all who
are listening to me
today may become
what I am, except
for these chains."
30The king rose,
and with him the
governor and Ber-
nice and those
sitting with them.
31After they left
the room, they
began saying to
one another, "This
man is not doing
anything that de-
serves death or
imprisonment."

τῇ φωνῇ φησιν, μαίνῃ, Παῦλε· τὰ πολλά σε γράμματα
{the} voice, *said* ˪"You are out of your mind,˩ Paul! {the} Much *you* learning is driving
3836 5889 5774 3419 4263 3836 4498 5148 1207 4365 4365
d.dsf n.dsf v.pai.3s v.pmi.2s n.vsm d.npn a.npn r.as.2 n.npn

˪εἰς μανίαν˩ περιτρέπει. 25 ὁ δὲ Παῦλος, ↱ ↱ οὐ μαίνομαι,
you insane!" *is driving* {the} But Paul said, "I am not out of my mind,
5148 1650 3444 4365 3836 1254 4263 5774 3419 3419 4024 3419
p.a n.asf v.pai.3s d.nsm cj n.nsm pl v.pmi.1s

φησίν, κράτιστε Φῆστε, ἀλλὰ ἀληθείας καὶ σωφροσύνης ῥήματα
said most excellent Festus, but true and rational are the words that
5774 3196 5776 247 237 2779 5408 4839
v.pai.3s a.vsm.s n.vsm cj n.gsf cj n.gsf n.apn

ἀποφθέγγομαι. 26 ἐπίσταται γὰρ περὶ τούτων ὁ βασιλεὺς πρὸς
I declare. For the king knows *For* about these matters, *the* *king* and to
710 1142 3836 995 2179 1142 4309 4047 3836 995 4639
v.pmi.1s v.ppi.3s cj p.g r.gpn d.nsm n.nsm p.a

ὃν καὶ παρρησιαζόμενος λαλῶ, λανθάνειν γὰρ αὐτόν
him {also} I am speaking boldly, *I am speaking* *has escaped notice* for *his* I
4005 2779 3281 3281 3281 4245 3281 3291 1142 899 4275
r.asm adv pt.pm.nsm v.pai.1s f.pa cj r.asm.3

τι[a] τούτων οὐ πείθομαι οὐθέν,
am persuaded that ~ none ˪of these things,˩ {not} *I am persuaded* *none* has escaped his notice,
4275 4275 5516 4032 4047 4024 4275 4032 3291 3291 899 3291
r.asn r.gpn pl v.ppi.1s a.asn

οὐ γάρ ἐστιν ἐν γωνίᾳ πεπραγμένον τοῦτο. 27 πιστεύεις,
for this was not *for* *was* done in a corner. *done* *this* Do you believe,
1142 4047 1639 4024 1142 1639 4556 1877 1224 4556 4047 4409
pl cj v.pai.3s p.d n.dsf pt.rp.nsn r.nsn v.pai.2s

βασιλεῦ Ἀγρίππα, τοῖς προφήταις; οἶδα ὅτι πιστεύεις. 28 ὁ δὲ Ἀγρίππας
King Agrippa, in the prophets? I know that you believe." {the} Then Agrippa said
995 68 3836 4737 3857 4022 4409 3836 1254 68
n.vsm n.vsm d.dpm n.dpm v.rai.1s cj v.pai.2s d.nsm cj n.nsm

πρὸς τὸν Παῦλον, ἐν ὀλίγῳ με πείθεις Χριστιανὸν
to {the} Paul, "In too short a time *me* you believe you are making a Christian of
4639 3836 4263 1877 3900 1609 4275 4472 5985
p.a d.asm n.asm p.d a.dsn r.as.1 v.pai.2s n.asm

ποιῆσαι. 29 ὁ δὲ Παῦλος, ˪εὐξαίμην ἂν˩ τῷ θεῷ καὶ
me." *making* {the} {and} Paul replied, "I would to God that whether the
1609 4472 3836 1254 4263 2377 323 3836 2536 2779
f.aa d.nsm cj n.nsm v.amo.1s pl d.dsm n.dsm cj

˪ἐν ὀλίγῳ˩ καὶ ˪ἐν μεγάλῳ˩ οὐ μόνον σὲ ἀλλὰ καὶ πάντας τοὺς
time be short or long, not only you but also all those
1877 3900 2779 1877 3489 4024 3667 5148 247 2779 4246 3836
p.d a.dsn cj p.d a.dsn pl adv r.as.2 cj adv a.apm d.apm

ἀκούοντάς μου σήμερον → γενέσθαι ˪τοιούτους ὁποῖος˩ καὶ ἐγώ
˪who are listening to˩ me today would also become as *also* I
201 1609 4958 2779 1181 5525 3961 2779 1609
pt.pa.apm r.gs.1 adv f.am r.apm r.nsm adv r.ns.1

εἰμι παρεκτὸς τῶν δεσμῶν τούτων. 30 ἀνέστη τε ὁ βασιλεὺς
am, except for {the} these chains." *these* Then the king stood up, *Then* *the* *king*
1639 4211 3836 4047 1301 4047 5445 3836 995 482 5445 3836 995
v.pai.1s p.g d.gpm n.gpm r.gpm v.aai.3s cj d.nsm n.nsm

καὶ ὁ ἡγεμὼν ἥ τε Βερνίκη καὶ οἱ συγκαθήμενοι αὐτοῖς, 31 καὶ
and the governor {the} and Bernice and those sitting with them; and
2779 3836 2450 3836 5445 1022 2779 3836 5153 899 2779
cj d.nsm n.nsm d.nsf cj n.nsf cj d.npm pt.pm.npm r.dpm.3 cj

ἀναχωρήσαντες ἐλάλουν πρὸς ἀλλήλους λέγοντες ὅτι
˪after they had left the room,˩ they spoke to one another, saying, ~ "This man is doing
432 3281 4639 253 3306 4022 4047 476 4556 4556
pt.aa.npm v.iai.3p p.a r.apm pt.pa.npm cj

οὐδὲν θανάτου ἢ δεσμῶν ἄξιόν τι[b] πράσσει ὁ ἄνθρωπος οὗτος.
nothing worthy of death or imprisonment." *worthy* ~ *is doing* {the} *man* *This*
4029 545 2505 2445 1301 545 5516 4556 3836 476 4047
a.asn n.gsm cj n.gpm a.asn r.asn v.pai.3s d.nsm n.nsm r.nsm

[a] [τι] UBS, omitted by TNIV.
[b] [τι] UBS.

NASB

voice, "Paul, you
are out of your
mind! *Your* great
learning is driving
you mad." 25But
Paul *said, "I am
not out of my
mind, most excel-
lent Festus, but I
utter words of so-
ber truth. 26For the
king knows about
these matters, and
I speak to him also
with confidence,
since I am per-
suaded that none of
these things escape
his notice; for this
has not been done
in a corner. 27King
Agrippa, do you
believe the Proph-
ets? I know that
you do." 28Agrippa
replied to Paul,
"In a short time
you will persuade
me to become a
Christian." 29And
Paul *said,* "I would
wish to God, that
whether in a short
or long time, not
only you, but also
all who hear me
this day, might
become such as
I am, except for
these chains."
30The king stood
up and the gover-
nor and Bernice,
and those who
were sitting with
them, 31and when
they had gone
aside, they *began*
talking to one an-
other, saying, "This
man is not doing
anything worthy of
death or imprison-
ment."

NIV

32 Agrippa said to
Festus, "This man
could have been
set free if he had
not appealed to
Caesar."

Paul Sails for Rome

27 When it
was decided
that we would sail
for Italy, Paul and
some other pris-
oners were handed
over to a centuri-
on named Julius,
who belonged to
the Imperial Regi-
ment. 2 We boarded
a ship from Adra-
myttium about to
sail for ports along
the coast of the
province of Asia,
and we put out to
sea. Aristarchus, a
Macedonian from
Thessalonica, was
with us.
3 The next day
we landed at Si-
don; and Julius, in
kindness to Paul,
allowed him to go
to his friends so
they might pro-
vide for his needs.
4 From there we put
out to sea again
and passed to the
lee of Cyprus be-
cause the winds
were against us.
5 When we had
sailed across the
open sea off the
coast of Cilicia
and Pamphylia, we
landed at Myra in
Lycia. 6 There the
centurion found
an Alexandrian
ship sailing for It-
aly and put us on
board. 7 We made
slow headway for
many days

32 Ἀγρίππας δὲ τῷ Φήστῳ ἔφη, ἀπολελύσθαι ἐδύνατο
And Agrippa *And* said to Festus, *said* "This man could have been set free *could have*
1254 68 1254 5774 3836 5776 5774 4047 476 1538 1538 668 1538
n.nsm cj d.dsm n.dsm v.iai.3s f.rp v.ipi.3s

ὁ ἄνθρωπος οὗτος εἰ ↱ ↱ μὴ ἐπεκέκλητο Καίσαρα.
{the} *man* *This* if he had not appealed to Caesar."
3836 476 4047 1623 2126 2126 3590 2126 2790
d.nsm n.nsm r.nsm cj pl v.lmi.3s n.asm

27:1 ὡς δὲ ἐκρίθη τοῦ ἀποπλεῖν ἡμᾶς εἰς τὴν Ἰταλίαν,
And when *And* it was decided that we would sail *we* for *{the}* Italy,
1254 6055 1254 3212 3836 7005 676 7005 1650 3836 2712
cj cj v.api.3s d.gsn f.pa r.ap.1 p.a d.asf n.asf

παρεδίδουν τόν τε Παῦλον καί τινας ἑτέρους δεσμώτας → ἑκατοντάρχῃ ὀνόματι
they delivered *{the}* *{both}* Paul and some other prisoners to a centurion, named
4140 3836 5445 4263 2779 5516 2283 1304 1672 3950
v.iai.3p d.asm cj n.asm cj r.apm r.apm n.apm n.dsm n.dsn

Ἰουλίῳ → σπείρης Σεβαστῆς. 2 ἐπιβάντες δὲ πλοίῳ
Julius, of the Augustan Cohort. *Augustan* And ⌞embarking on⌟ *And* a ship
2685 4935 5061 4935 1254 2094 1254 4450
n.dsm n.gsf a.gsf pt.aa.npm cj n.dsn

Ἀδραμυττηνῷ μέλλοντι πλεῖν εἰς τοὺς κατὰ τὴν Ἀσίαν
from Adramyttium, ⌞which was about⌟ to sail to *{the}* ports ⌞along the coast of⌟ *{the}* Asia,
101 3516 4434 1650 3836 5536 2848 3836 823
a.dsn pt.pa.dsn f.pa p.a d.apm p.a d.asf n.asf

τόπους ἀνήχθημεν ὄντος σὺν ἡμῖν
ports we put to sea. Aristarchus, a Macedonian from Thessalonica was with us.
5536 343 752 3424 2552 2552 1639 5250 7005
n.apm v.api.1p pt.pa.gsm p.d r.dp.1

Ἀριστάρχου Μακεδόνος Θεσσαλονικέως. 3 τῇ τε ἑτέρᾳ κατήχθημεν εἰς
Aristarchus *Macedonian* *from Thessalonica* The ~ next day we put in at
752 3424 2552 3836 5445 2283 2864 1650
n.gsm n.gsm n.gsm d.dsf cj r.dsf v.api.1p p.a

Σιδῶνα, φιλανθρώπως τε ὁ Ἰούλιος τῷ Παύλῳ χρησάμενος
Sidon; and Julius treated Paul kindly *and* *{the}* *Julius* *{the}* *Paul* *treated*
4972 5445 2685 5968 4263 5793 5445 3836 2685 3836 4263 5968
n.asf adv cj d.nsm n.nsm d.dsm n.dsm pt.am.nsm

ἐπέτρεψεν πρὸς τοὺς φίλους πορευθέντι ἐπιμελείας τυχεῖν.
and allowed him to go to his friends *to go* and be cared for. *be*
2205 4513 4513 4639 3836 5813 4513 5593 2149 5593
v.aai.3s p.a d.apm n.apm pt.ap.dsm n.gsf f.aa

4 → κἀκεῖθεν ἀναχθέντες ὑπεπλεύσαμεν τὴν Κύπρον
And putting out to sea from there, *putting out to sea* ⌞we sailed under the lee of⌟ *{the}* Cyprus,
343 343 343 343 2796 343 5709 3836 3251
crasis pt.ap.npm v.aai.1p d.asf n.asf

διὰ τὸ τοὺς ἀνέμους εἶναι ἐναντίους, 5 τό τε
because *{the}* the winds were against us. And when we had sailed across the ~
1328 3836 3836 449 1639 1885 1386 1386 1386 1386 1386 3836 5445
p.a d.asn d.apm n.apm f.pa a.apm d.asn cj

πέλαγος τὸ κατὰ τὴν Κιλικίαν καὶ Παμφυλίαν διαπλεύσαντες
open sea *{the}* ⌞along the coast of⌟ *{the}* Cilicia and Pamphylia, *when we had sailed across*
4283 3836 2848 3836 3070 2779 4103 1386
n.asn d.asn p.a d.asf n.asf cj n.asf pt.aa.npm

κατήλθομεν εἰς Μύρα τῆς Λυκίας. 6 κἀκεῖ εὑρὼν ὁ ἑκατοντάρχης
we came to Myra in Lycia. There the centurion found *the* *centurion* a
2982 1650 3688 3836 3379 2795 3836 1672 2351 3836 1672
v.aai.1p p.a n.apn d.gsf n.gsf crasis pt.aa.nsm d.nsm n.nsm

πλοῖον Ἀλεξανδρῖνον πλέον εἰς τὴν Ἰταλίαν → ἐνεβίβασεν ἡμᾶς εἰς
ship from Alexandria sailing for *{the}* Italy and put us on board *us* *{onto}*
4450 234 4434 1650 3836 2712 7005 1837 7005 1650
n.asn a.asn pt.pa.asn p.a d.asf n.asf v.aai.3s r.ap.1 p.a

αὐτό. 7 ἐν ἱκαναῖς δὲ ἡμέραις βραδυπλοοῦντες καὶ
it. We sailed slowly for a number of *{and}* days *sailed slowly* and arrived
899 1095 1095 1877 2653 1254 2465 1095 2779 1181
r.asn.3 p.d a.dpf cj n.dpf pt.pa.npm cj

NASB

32 And Agrippa said
to Festus, "This
man might have
been set free if he
had not appealed to
Caesar."

Paul Is Sent to Rome

27:1 When it was
decided that we
would sail for
Italy, they pro-
ceeded to deliver
Paul and some
other prisoners to
a centurion of the
Augustan [a]cohort
named Julius. 2 And
embarking in an
Adramyttian ship,
which was about to
sail to the regions
along the coast of
Asia, we put out to
sea accompanied
by Aristarchus,
a Macedonian of
Thessalonica. 3 The
next day we put in
at Sidon; and Julius
treated Paul with
consideration and
allowed him to go
to his friends and
receive care. 4 From
there we put out
to sea and sailed
under the shelter
of Cyprus because
the winds were
contrary. 5 When we
had sailed through
the sea along the
coast of Cilicia
and Pamphylia, we
landed at Myra in
Lycia. 6 There the
centurion found
an Alexandrian
ship sailing for
Italy, and he put us
aboard it. 7 When
we had sailed
slowly for a good
many days, and

[a] Or *battalion*

NIV

and had difficulty
arriving off Cni-
dus. When the
wind did not al-
low us to hold our
course, we sailed
to the lee of Crete,
opposite Salmone.
8 We moved along
the coast with dif-
ficulty and came
to a place called
Fair Havens, near
the town of Lasea.
9 Much time had
been lost, and sail-
ing had already
become dangerous
because by now it
was after the Day
of Atonement.[a] So
Paul warned them,
10 "Men, I can see
that our voyage is
going to be disas-
trous and bring
great loss to ship
and cargo, and
to our own lives
also." 11 But the
centurion, instead
of listening to
what Paul said, fol-
lowed the advice
of the pilot and of
the owner of the
ship. 12 Since the
harbor was unsuit-
able to winter in,
the majority decid-
ed that we should
sail on, hoping
to reach Phoenix
and winter there.
This was a harbor
in Crete, facing
both southwest and
northwest.

The Storm

13 When a gentle
south wind began
to blow, they saw
their opportunity;

[a] 9 That is, Yom Kippur

μόλις	γενόμενοι	κατὰ	τὴν	Κνίδον,	↱			↱	μὴ	προσεῶντος	ἡμᾶς
with difficulty	*arrived*	off	*{the}*	Cnidus,	and as	the	wind	did	not	allow	us
3660	1181	2848	3836	3118	4661	3836	449	4661	3590	4661	7005
adv	pt.am.npm	p.a	d.asf	n.asf					pl	pt.pa.gsm	r.ap.1

↰	↰	↰	τοῦ	ἀνέμου	ὑπεπλεύσαμεν	τὴν	Κρήτην	κατὰ	Σαλμώνην,
to	go	farther,	*the*	*wind*	⌊we sailed under the lee of⌋	*{the}*	Crete	off	Salmone.
4661	4661	4661	3836	449	5709	3836	3207	2848	4892
			d.gsm	n.gsm	v.aai.1p	d.asf	n.asf	p.a	n.asf

8

			μόλις	τε	παραλεγόμενοι	αὐτὴν	ἤλθομεν	εἰς		τόπον	τινὰ
Sailing	past	it	with difficulty,	~	*Sailing past*	*it*	we came	to	a	place	*a*
4162	4162	899	3660	5445	4162	899	2262	1650	5516	5536	5516
			adv	cj	pt.pm.npm	r.asf.3	v.aai.1p	p.a		n.asm	r.asm

καλούμενον	Καλοὺς	λιμένας		ᾧ	ἐγγὺς			πόλις	ἦν	Λασαία.	9
called	Fair	Havens,	near	⌊to which⌋	*near*	was	the	city	*was*	Lasea.	Since
2813	2819	3348	1584	4005	1584	1639		4484	1639	3297	1254
pt.pp.asm	a.apm	n.apm		r.dsm	adv			n.nsf	v.iai.3s	n.nsf	

ἱκανοῦ	δὲ	χρόνου	διαγενομένου	καὶ			ὄντος	ἤδη	ἐπισφαλοῦς	τοῦ
considerable	*Since*	time	had passed	and	the	voyage	was	now	dangerous	*the*
2653	1254	5989	1335	2779	3836	4452	1639	2453	2195	3836
a.gsm	cj	n.gsm	pt.am.gsm	cj			pt.pa.gsm	adv	a.gsm	d.gsm

πλοὸς	διὰ	τὸ	καὶ	τὴν	νηστείαν	↱	ἤδη	παρεληλυθέναι		παρῄνει	ὁ
voyage	because	*{the}*	*{also}*	the	fast	had	already	gone by,	Paul	advised	*{the}*
4452	1328	3836	2779	3836	3763	4216	2453	4216	4263	4147	3836
n.gsm	p.a	d.asn	adv	d.asf	n.asf		adv	f.ra		v.iai.3s	d.nsm

Παῦλος		10 λέγων	αὐτοῖς,	ἄνδρες,	θεωρῶ	ὅτι						
Paul	them,	saying,	*{to them}*	"Gentlemen,	I perceive	that	the	voyage	that	is	about	to
4263		3306	899	467	2555	4022	3836	4452		3516	3516	1639
n.nsm		pt.pa.nsm	r.dpm.3	n.vpm	v.pai.1s	cj						

		μετὰ	ὕβρεως	καὶ	πολλῆς	ζημίας	οὐ	μόνον	τοῦ	φορτίου	καὶ	τοῦ
take	place	will involve	injury	and	much	loss,	not	only	of the	cargo	and	the
1639	1639	3552	5615	2779	4498	2422	4024	3667	3836	5845	2779	3836
		p.g	n.gsf	cj	a.gsf	n.gsf	pl	adv	d.gsn	n.gsn	cj	d.gsn

πλοίου	ἀλλὰ	καὶ	τῶν		ψυχῶν	ἡμῶν	μέλλειν	ἔσεσθαι	τὸν	πλοῦν.	11	ὁ
ship,	but	also	of	our	lives."	*our*	*is about*	*to take place*	*the*	*voyage*	But	the
4450	247	2779	3836	7005	6034	7005	3516	1639	3836	4452	1254	3836
n.gsn	cj	adv	d.gpf		n.gpf	r.gp.1	f.pa	f.fm	d.asm	n.asm		d.nsm

δὲ	ἑκατοντάρχης					τῷ	κυβερνήτῃ	καὶ	τῷ	ναυκλήρῳ	μᾶλλον
But	centurion	was	more	convinced	by	the	captain	and	the	ship's owner	*more*
1254	1672	4275	3437	4275	4275	3836	3237	2779	3836	3729	3437
cj	n.nsm					d.dsm	n.dsm	cj	d.dsm	n.dsm	adv.c

ἐπείθετο	ἢ		τοῖς	ὑπὸ	Παύλου	λεγομένοις.	12 ἀνευθέτου	δὲ	↱	τοῦ
was convinced by	than	by	what	*by*	Paul	was saying.	*unsuitable*	And	since	the
4275	2445	5679	3836	5679	4263	3306	460	1254	5639	3836
v.ipi.3s	pl		d.dpn	p.g	n.gsm	pt.pp.dpn	a.gsm	cj		d.gsm

λιμένος	ὑπάρχοντος		πρὸς	παραχειμασίαν	οἱ	πλείονες	ἔθεντο		βουλὴν
harbor	was	unsuitable	to	winter in,	the	majority	made	a	decision
3348	5639	460	4639	4200	3836	4498	5502		1087
n.gsm	pt.pa.gsm		p.a	n.asf	d.npm	a.npm.c	v.ami.3p		n.asf

ἀναχθῆναι	ἐκεῖθεν,	εἴ	πως	δύναιντο	καταντήσαντες	εἰς	Φοίνικα
⌊to put out to sea⌋	from there,	if	somehow	⌊they might be able⌋	to reach	*{to}*	Phoenix,
343	1696	1623	4803	1538	2918	1650	5837
f.ap	adv	cj	pl	v.ppo.3p	pt.aa.npm	p.a	n.asm

παραχειμάσαι	λιμένα	τῆς	Κρήτης	βλέποντα		⌊κατὰ	λίβα⌋	καὶ	⌊κατὰ
spend the winter	a harbor	of	Crete,	facing	both	southwest		and	northwest,
4199	3348	3836	3207	1063		2848	3355	2779	2848
f.aa	n.asm	d.gsf	n.gsf	pt.pa.asm		p.a	n.asm	cj	p.a

χῶρον.⌋				13	→			ὑποπνεύσαντος	δὲ
	and spend	the	winter there.	Now	when	the south	wind	blew gently,	*Now*
6008	4199	4199	4199	1254		3803	3803	5710	1254
n.asm								pt.aa.gsm	cj

νότου	δόξαντες					τῆς	προθέσεως	κεκρατηκέναι,	
south wind	thinking	that	they	had	obtained	their	purpose,	*they had obtained*	they
3803	1506		3195	3195	3195	3836	4606	3195	
n.gsm	pt.aa.npm					d.gsf	n.gsf	f.ra	

NASB

with difficulty had
arrived off Cnidus,
since the wind did
not permit us *to go*
farther, we sailed
under the shelter of
Crete, off Salmone;
8 and with difficulty
sailing past it we
came to a place
called Fair Havens,
near which was the
city of Lasea.
9 When consider-
able time had
passed and the
voyage was now
dangerous, since
even the [a]fast was
already over, Paul
began to admonish
them, 10 and said to
them, "Men, I per-
ceive that the voy-
age will certainly
be with damage
and great loss, not
only of the cargo
and the ship, but
also of our lives."
11 But the centu-
rion was more per-
suaded by the pilot
and the captain of
the ship than by
what was being
said by Paul. 12 Be-
cause the harbor
was not suitable
for wintering, the
majority reached
a decision to put
out to sea from
there, if somehow
they could reach
Phoenix, a harbor
of Crete, facing
southwest and
northwest, and
spend the winter
there.
13 When a moder-
ate south wind
came up, suppos-
ing that they had
attained their pur-
pose, they

[a] I.e. Day of Atonement in September or October, which was a dangerous time of year for navigation

NIV

so they weighed
anchor and sailed
along the shore
of Crete. [14]Be-
fore very long,
a wind of hurri-
cane force, called
the Northeaster,
swept down from
the island. [15]The
ship was caught
by the storm and
could not head
into the wind; so
we gave way to
it and were driv-
en along. [16]As we
passed to the lee
of a small island
called Cauda, we
were hardly able
to make the life-
boat secure, [17]so
the men hoisted it
aboard. Then they
passed ropes un-
der the ship itself
to hold it together.
Because they were
afraid they would
run aground on the
sandbars of Syr-
tis, they lowered
the sea anchor[a]
and let the ship be
driven along. [18]We
took such a violent
battering from the
storm that the next
day they began to
throw the cargo
overboard. [19]On
the third day, they
threw the ship's
tackle overboard
with their own
hands. [20]When nei-
ther sun nor stars
appeared for many
days and the storm
continued raging,
we finally gave up
all hope of being
saved.
[21]After they had
gone a long time
without food, Paul

[a] 17 Or *the sails*

ἄραντες ἆσσον παρελέγοντο τὴν Κρήτην. [14]
⌊weighed anchor⌋ *close to the shore* and sailed along *{the}* Crete, close to the shore. But
149 839 4162 3836 3207 839 839 839 839 1254
pt.aa.npm adv.c v.imi.3p d.asf n.asf

⌊μετ' οὐ πολὺ⌋ δὲ ἔβαλεν κατ' αὐτῆς ἄνεμος
soon *But* a violent wind, called the northeaster, rushed ⌊down from⌋ Crete. *wind*
3552 4024 4498 1254 5607 449 2813 2350 965 2848 899 449
p.a pl adv cj v.aai.3s p.g r.gsf.3 n.nsm

τυφωνικὸς ὁ καλούμενος εὐρακύλων· [15] → συναρπασθέντος δὲ
violent *{the}* *called* *northeaster* And when the ship was caught by it *And*
5607 3836 2813 2350 1254 3836 4450 5275 1254
a.nsm d.nsm pt.pp.nsm n.nsm pt.ap.gsn cj

τοῦ πλοίου καὶ μὴ δυναμένου ἀντοφθαλμεῖν τῷ ἀνέμῳ ↱ ἐπιδόντες
the ship and could not *could* head into the wind, we gave way and
3836 4450 2779 1538 3590 1538 535 3836 449 5770 2113
d.gsn n.gsn cj pl pt.pp.gsn f.pa d.dsm n.dsm pt.aa.npm

ἐφερόμεθα. [16] νησίον δέ τι ὑποδραμόντες
⌊allowed ourselves to be driven along.⌋ *small island* *{and}* *a* ⌊Running under the lee of⌋ a small
5770 3761 1254 5516 5720 5516 3761
v.ipi.1p n.asn cj r.asn pt.aa.npm

καλούμενον Καῦδα ἰσχύσαμεν μόλις περικρατεῖς
island called Cauda, we were able with difficulty to get the dinghy under control.
3761 2813 3007 2710 3660 1181 1181 3836 5002 4331
pt.pp.asn n.asf v.aai.1p adv a.npm

γενέσθαι τῆς σκάφης, [17] ἣν ἄραντες βοηθείαις
to get *the* *dinghy* After hoisting it *After hoisting up* up, they passed cables
1181 3836 5002 149 149 4005 149 149 5968 5968 1069
f.am d.gsf n.gsf r.asf pt.aa.npm n.dpf

ἐχρῶντο → ὑποζωννύντες ← τὸ πλοῖον, φοβούμενοί τε μὴ
they passed under the ship to hold it together. *the* *ship* Then, fearing *Then* that
5968 3836 4450 5690 3836 4450 5445 5828 5445 3590
v.imi.3p pt.pa.npm d.asn n.asn pt.pp.npm cj cj

εἰς τὴν Σύρτιν ἐκπέσωσιν, χαλάσαντες τὸ σκεῦος,
they would run aground on the Syrtis, *they would run aground* they lowered the sea anchor,
1738 1738 1738 1738 1650 3836 5358 1738 5899 3836 5007
p.a d.asf n.asf v.aas.3p pt.aa.npm d.asn n.asn

οὕτως → → ἐφέροντο. [18] σφοδρῶς δὲ → χειμαζομένων
and thus they let the ship be driven along. *so violently* *{and}* Since we were being pounded
4048 5770 5380 1254 7005 5928
adv v.ipi.3p adv cj pt.pp.gpm

← ← ← ἡμῶν τῇ ἑξῆς ἐκβολὴν
so violently by the storm, *we* the next day they began to ⌊throw cargo overboard;⌋
5380 5380 7005 3836 2009 4472 4472 4472 1678
r.gp.1 d.dsf adv n.asf

ἐποιοῦντο [19] καὶ τῇ τρίτῃ αὐτόχειρες ↱ ↱ τὴν σκευὴν τοῦ
they began to and ⌊on the⌋ third day *their own hands* they threw the ship's tackle *{the}*
4472 2779 3836 5569 901 4849 4849 3836 4450 5006 3836
v.imi.3p cj d.dsf a.dsf n.npm d.asf n.asf d.gsn

πλοίου ἔρριψαν. [20] ↱ μήτε δὲ ἡλίου μήτε ἄστρων
ship's overboard with their own hands. When neither *{and}* sun nor stars
4450 4849 901 901 901 2210 3612 1254 2463 3612 849
n.gsn v.aai.3p cj cj n.gsm cj n.gpn

ἐπιφαινόντων ἐπὶ πλείονας ἡμέρας, χειμῶνός τε οὐκ ὀλίγου
appeared for many days, and no small storm *and* *no* *small*
2210 2093 4498 2465 5445 4024 3900 5930 5445 4024 3900
pt.pa.gpn p.a a.apf.c n.apf n.gsm cj pl a.gsm

ἐπικειμένου, λοιπὸν περιῃρεῖτο ἐλπὶς πᾶσα τοῦ σῴζεσθαι ἡμᾶς.
continued to rage, *at last* *was abandoned* all hope *all* of our being saved *our* was at
2130 3370 4311 4246 1828 4246 3836 7005 5392 7005 4311 3370
pt.pm.gsm adv v.ipi.3s n.nsf a.nsf d.gsn f.pp r.ap.1

[21] πολλῆς τε ἀσιτίας ὑπαρχούσης τότε
last abandoned. Since they had long ~ been without food, *Since had been* *{then}* Paul
3370 4311 5639 5639 4498 5445 5639 826 5639 5538 4263
a.gsf cj n.gsf pt.pa.gsf adv

NASB

weighed anchor
and *began* sailing
along Crete, close
inshore.

Shipwreck

[14]But before very
long there rushed
down from the land
a violent wind,
called [a]Euraquilo;
[15]and when the ship
was caught *in it*
and could not face
the wind, we gave
way *to it* and let
ourselves be driven
along. [16]Running
under the shelter
of a small island
called Clauda,
we were scarcely
able to get the
ship's boat under
control. [17]After
they had hoisted it
up, they used sup-
porting cables in
undergirding the
ship; and fearing
that they might
run aground on *the
shallows* of Syrtis,
they let down the
sea anchor and in
this way let them-
selves be driven
along. [18]The next
day as we were
being violently
storm-tossed, they
began to jettison
the cargo; [19]and on
the third day they
threw the ship's
tackle overboard
with their own
hands. [20]Since nei-
ther sun nor stars
appeared for many
days, and no small
storm was assailing
us, from then on all
hope of our being
saved was gradu-
ally abandoned.
[21]When they had
gone a long time
without food, then

[a] I.e. a northeaster

NIV

stood up before
them and said:
“Men, you should
have taken my
advice not to sail
from Crete; then
you would have
spared yourselves
this damage and
loss. 22 But now I
urge you to keep
up your courage,
because not one
of you will be
lost; only the ship
will be destroyed.
23 Last night an
angel of the God
to whom I belong
and whom I serve
stood beside me
24 and said, ‘Do not
be afraid, Paul.
You must stand
trial before Cae-
sar; and God has
graciously given
you the lives of all
who sail with you.’
25 So keep up your
courage, men, for
I have faith in God
that it will happen
just as he told me.
26 Nevertheless, we
must run aground
on some island.”

The Shipwreck

27 On the four-
teenth night we
were still being
driven across the
Adriatic[a] Sea,
when about mid-
night the sailors
sensed they were
approaching land.
28 They took sound-
ings and found
that the water was
a hundred and
twenty feet[b] deep.
A short time later
they took sound-
ings again and
found it was ninety
feet[c] deep. 29 Fear-
ing that we would
be dashed against
the rocks,

[a] 27 In ancient times the name referred to an area extending well south of Italy.
[b] 28 Or about 37 meters
[c] 28 Or about 27 meters

σταθεὶς ὁ Παῦλος ἐν μέσῳ αὐτῶν εἶπεν, ἔδει μέν, ὦ
stood up *{the}* *Paul* in their midst *their* and said, “Men, ⌊you should have⌋ ~ *{O}*
2705 3836 4263 1877 899 3545 899 3306 467 1256 3525 6043
pt.ap.nsm d.nsm n.nsm p.d n.dsn r.gpm.3 v.aai.3s v.iai.3s pl j

ἄνδρες, πειθαρχήσαντάς μοι ↰ μὴ ἀνάγεσθαι ἀπὸ τῆς Κρήτης κερδῆσαί
Men followed my advice and not set sail from *{the}* Crete and incurred
467 4272 1609 4272 3590 343 608 3836 3207 5445 3045
n.vpm pt.aa.apm r.ds.1 pl f.pp p.g d.gsf n.gsf f.aa

τε τὴν ὕβριν ταύτην καὶ τὴν ζημίαν. 22 καὶ τὰ νῦν παραινῶ ὑμᾶς
and *{the}* this injury *this* and *{the}* loss. And *{the}* now I advise you
5445 3836 4047 5615 4047 2779 3836 2422 2779 3836 3814 4147 7007
cj d.asf n.asf r.asf cj d.asf n.asf cj d.apn adv v.pai.1s r.ap.2

εὐθυμεῖν, ἀποβολὴ γὰρ ψυχῆς οὐδεμία ἔσται ἐξ
⌊to be of good courage;⌋ *loss* for *of life* *no* ⌊there will be⌋ no loss of life among
2313 613 1142 6034 4029 1639 4029 613 6034 6034 1666
f.pa n.nsf cj n.gsf a.nsf v.fmi.3s p.g

ὑμῶν πλὴν τοῦ πλοίου. 23 παρέστη γάρ μοι ταύτῃ τῇ νυκτὶ
you, but only of the ship. For ⌊there stood by⌋ *For* me this *{the}* night an angel
7007 4440 3836 4450 1142 4225 1142 1609 4047 3836 3816 34
r.gp.2 p.g d.gsn n.gsn v.aai.3s cj r.ds.1 r.dsf d.dsf n.dsf

τοῦ θεοῦ, οὗ εἰμι ἐγώ[a] ᾧ καὶ λατρεύω, ἄγγελος 24 λέγων, ↱ μὴ
of the God whose I am *I* and whom *and* I serve, *angel* saying, ‘Do not
3836 2536 4005 1609 1639 1609 2779 4005 2779 3302 34 3306 5828 3590
d.gsm n.gsm r.gsm v.pai.1s r.ns.1 r.dsm cj v.pai.1s n.nsm pt.pa.nsm pl

φοβοῦ, Παῦλε, Καίσαρί σε δεῖ παραστῆναι, καὶ ἰδοὺ κεχάρισταί
be afraid, Paul; *Caesar* you must stand before Caesar; and behold, God has granted
5828 4263 2790 5148 1256 4225 2790 2779 2627 2536 5919
v.ppm.2s n.vsm n.dsm r.as.2 v.pai.3s f.aa cj j v.rmi.3s

σοι ↰ ↰ ↰ ὁ θεὸς πάντας τοὺς πλέοντας μετὰ σοῦ. 25 διὸ εὐθυμεῖτε,
you as a gift *{the}* *God* all those who sail with you.’ So be of good courage,
5148 5919 5919 5919 3836 2536 4246 3836 4434 3552 5148 1475 2313
r.ds.2 d.nsm n.nsm a.apm d.apm pt.pa.apm p.g r.gs.2 cj v.pam.2p

ἄνδρες, πιστεύω γὰρ τῷ θεῷ ὅτι οὕτως ἔσται καθ᾽ ὃν
men, for I have faith *for* in God that it will be so, *it will be* just as it
467 1142 4409 1142 3836 2536 4022 1639 1639 1639 4048 1639 5573 2848 4005
n.vpm v.pai.1s cj d.dsm n.dsm cj adv v.fmi.3s p.a r.asm

τρόπον λελάληταί μοι. 26 εἰς νῆσον δέ τινα δεῖ ἡμᾶς ἐκπεσεῖν.
just has been told me. *on* *island* But *some* we must *we* run aground on some
5573 3281 1609 1650 3762 1254 5516 7005 1256 7005 1738 1650 5516
n.asm v.rpi.3s r.ds.1 p.a n.asf cj r.asf v.pai.3s r.ap.1 f.aa

ὡς δὲ τεσσαρεσκαιδεκάτη νὺξ ἐγένετο →
island.” 27 And when *And* it was the fourteenth night, *it was* as we
3762 1254 6055 1254 1181 1181 5476 3816 1181 7005
cj cj a.nsf n.nsf v.ami.3s

διαφερομένων ἡμῶν ἐν τῷ Ἀδρίᾳ, κατὰ ⌊μέσον τῆς νυκτὸς⌋
⌊were being driven about⌋ *we* in the Adriatic Sea, about midnight the sailors
1422 7005 1877 3836 102 2848 3545 3836 3816 3836 3731
pt.pp.gpm r.gp.1 p.d d.dsm n.dsm p.a n.asn d.gsf n.gsf

ὑπενόουν οἱ ναῦται προσάγειν τινὰ αὐτοῖς χώραν. 28 καὶ ↱
suspected *the* *sailors* that they were nearing *{some}* *they* land. So they
5706 3836 3731 899 4642 5516 899 6001 2779 2351
v.iai.3p d.npm n.npm f.pa r.asf r.dpm.3 n.asf cj

βολίσαντες εὗρον ὀργυιὰς εἴκοσι, βραχὺ δὲ
took soundings and found twenty fathoms; *twenty* and after a short distance *and*
1075 2351 1633 3976 1633 1254 1460 1099 1460 1254
pt.aa.npm v.aai.3p n.apf a.apf adv cj

διαστήσαντες ↱ καὶ πάλιν βολίσαντες εὗρον ὀργυιὰς
after distance they took soundings again and *again* *took soundings* found fifteen fathoms.
1460 2351 1075 1075 4099 2779 4099 1075 2351 1278 3976
pt.aa.npm cj adv pt.aa.npm v.aai.3p n.apf

δεκαπέντε· 29 φοβούμενοί τε μή που κατὰ τραχεῖς
fifteen Fearing ~ that *{somewhere}* we might run aground on the rocky
1278 5828 5445 3590 4543 1738 1738 1738 1738 2848 5550
a.apf pt.pp.npm cj cj pl p.a a.apm

[a] [ἐγώ] UBS.

NASB

Paul stood up in
their midst and
said, “Men, you
ought to have fol-
lowed my advice
and not to have
set sail from Crete
and incurred this
damage and loss.
22 *Yet* now I urge
you to keep up
your courage, for
there will be no
loss of life among
you, but *only* of the
ship. 23 For this very
night an angel of
the God to whom I
belong and whom I
serve stood before
me, 24 saying, ‘Do
not be afraid, Paul;
you must stand
before Caesar;
and behold, God
has granted you
all those who are
sailing with you.’
25 Therefore, keep
up your courage,
men, for I believe
God that it will
turn out exactly as
I have been told.
26 But we must
run aground on a
certain island.”
27 But when the
fourteenth night
came, as we were
being driven about
in the Adriatic Sea,
about midnight the
sailors *began* to
surmise that they
were approaching
some land. 28 They
took soundings
and found *it to be*
twenty fathoms;
and a little far-
ther on they took
another sounding
and found *it to be*
fifteen fathoms.
29 Fearing that we
might run aground
somewhere on the
rocks, they

NIV

they dropped four
anchors from the
stern and prayed
for daylight. [30]In
an attempt to es-
cape from the
ship, the sailors let
the lifeboat down
into the sea, pre-
tending they were
going to lower
some anchors from
the bow. [31]Then
Paul said to the
centurion and the
soldiers, "Unless
these men stay
with the ship, you
cannot be saved."
[32]So the soldiers
cut the ropes that
held the lifeboat
and let it drift
away.
[33]Just before
dawn Paul urged
them all to eat.
"For the last four-
teen days," he
said, "you have
been in constant
suspense and
have gone without
food—you haven't
eaten anything.
[34]Now I urge you
to take some food.
You need it to
survive. Not one
of you will lose a
single hair from
his head." [35]After
he said this, he
took some bread
and gave thanks
to God in front of
them all. Then he
broke it and began
to eat. [36]They were
all encouraged
and ate some food
themselves.

τόπους ἐκπέσωμεν, ↱ ἐκ πρύμνης ῥίψαντες ἀγκύρας
coast, *we might run aground* they dropped four anchors from the stern *dropped* *anchors*
5536 1738 2377 4849 5475 46 1666 4744 4849 46
n.apm v.aas.1p p.g n.gsf pt.aa.npm n.apf

τέσσαρας ηὔχοντο ἡμέραν γενέσθαι. 30 ↱ τῶν δὲ ναυτῶν ζητούντων
four and prayed for day to come. But when the *But* sailors tried
5475 2377 2465 1181 1254 2426 3836 1254 3731 2426
a.apf v.imi.3p n.asf f.am d.gpm cj n.gpm pt.pa.gpm

φυγεῖν ἐκ τοῦ πλοίου καὶ χαλασάντων τὴν σκάφην εἰς τὴν θάλασσαν προφάσει
to escape from the ship and had lowered the dinghy into the sea pretending
5771 1666 3836 4450 2779 5899 3836 5002 1650 3836 2498 4733
f.aa p.g d.gsn n.gsn cj pt.aa.gpm d.asf n.asf p.a d.asf n.asf n.dsf

ὡς ἐκ πρῴρης ἀγκύρας μελλόντων ἐκτείνειν,
{that} they intended to let down anchors from the bow, *anchors* *they intended* *to let down*
6055 3516 3516 1753 1753 1753 46 1666 4749 46 3516 1753
pl p.g n.gsf n.apf pt.pa.gpm f.pa

31 εἶπεν ὁ Παῦλος τῷ ἑκατοντάρχῃ καὶ τοῖς στρατιώταις, ἐὰν
Paul said *{the}* *Paul* ⸤to the⸥ centurion and the soldiers, "If these men
4263 3306 3836 4263 3836 1672 2779 3836 5132 1569 4047 4047
v.aai.3s d.nsm n.nsm d.dsm n.dsm cj d.dpm n.dpm cj

↱ μὴ οὗτοι μείνωσιν ἐν τῷ πλοίῳ, ὑμεῖς σωθῆναι ⸤οὐ δύνασθε.⸥
do not *these men* remain in the ship, you cannot be saved." *cannot*
3531 3590 4047 3531 1877 3836 4450 7007 4024 5392 4024 1538
pl r.npm v.aas.3p p.d d.dsn n.dsn r.np.2 f.ap pl v.ppi.2p

32 τότε ἀπέκοψαν οἱ στρατιῶται τὰ σχοινία τῆς σκάφης καὶ
Then the soldiers cut *the* *soldiers* the ropes ⸤from the⸥ dinghy and
5538 3836 5132 644 3836 5132 3836 5389 3836 5002 2779
adv v.aai.3p d.npm n.npm d.apn n.apn d.gsf n.gsf cj

εἴασαν αὐτὴν ἐκπεσεῖν. 33 ἄχρι δὲ οὗ ἡμέρα ἤμελλεν γίνεσθαι, παρεκάλει
let it drift away. As *{and}* *{which}* day was about to dawn, Paul urged
1572 899 1738 948 1254 4005 2465 3516 1181 4263 4151
v.aai.3p r.asf.3 f.aa p.g cj r.gsm n.nsf v.iai.3s f.pm v.iai.3s

ὁ Παῦλος ἅπαντας μεταλαβεῖν τροφῆς λέγων,
{the} *Paul* them all to take some food, saying, "Today is the
3836 4263 570 3561 5575 3306 4958
d.nsm n.nsm a.apm f.aa n.gsf pt.pa.nsm

τεσσαρεσκαιδεκάτην σήμερον ἡμέραν προσδοκῶντες
fourteenth *Today* day that you have continued in suspense and been
5476 4958 2465 1412 1412 1412 4659
a.asf adv n.asf pt.pa.npm

ἄσιτοι διατελεῖτε μηθὲν προσλαβόμενοι. 34 διὸ παρακαλῶ
⸤without food,⸥ *you have continued* having taken nothing. *having taken* Therefore I urge
827 1412 4689 4689 3594 4689 1475 4151
a.npm v.pai.2p a.asn pt.am.npm cj v.pai.1s

ὑμᾶς μεταλαβεῖν τροφῆς· τοῦτο γὰρ πρὸς τῆς ὑμετέρας σωτηρίας
you to take some food; for this *for* is for *{the}* your survival,
7007 3561 5575 1142 4047 1142 5639 4639 3836 5629 5401
r.ap.2 f.aa n.gsf r.nsn cj p.g d.gsf r.gsf.2 n.gsf

ὑπάρχει, οὐδενὸς γὰρ ὑμῶν θρὶξ ἀπὸ τῆς κεφαλῆς ἀπολεῖται.
is for not *for* *of you* a hair will perish from the head *will perish* of any
5639 1142 4029 1142 7007 2582 660 660 608 3836 3051 660
v.pai.3s a.gsm cj r.gp.2 n.nsf p.g d.gsf n.gsf v.fmi.3s

35 εἴπας δὲ ταῦτα καὶ λαβὼν ἄρτον εὐχαρίστησεν
of you." And ⸤when he had said⸥ *And* these things, *and* he took bread, and giving thanks
7007 7007 1254 3306 1254 4047 2779 3284 788 2779 2373
pt.aa.nsm cj r.apn cj pt.aa.nsm n.asm v.aai.3s

τῷ θεῷ ἐνώπιον πάντων καὶ ↱ κλάσας ἤρξατο ἐσθίειν. 36
to God before them all, *{and}* he broke it and began to eat. So everyone
3836 2536 1967 4246 2779 806 3089 806 2266 1254 4246
d.dsm n.dsm p.g a.gpm cj pt.aa.nsm v.ami.3s f.pa

εὔθυμοι δὲ γενόμενοι πάντες καὶ ↱ αὐτοὶ προσελάβοντο τροφῆς.
was encouraged *So* *was* *everyone* and they themselves took food.
1181 2314 1254 1181 4246 2779 4689 899 4689 5575
a.npm cj pt.am.npm a.npm adv r.npm v.ami.3p n.gsf

NASB

cast four anchors
from the stern
and wished for
daybreak. [30]But as
the sailors were
trying to escape
from the ship and
had let down the
ship's boat into the
sea, on the pretense
of intending to lay
out anchors from
the bow, [31]Paul said
to the centurion
and to the soldiers,
"Unless these men
remain in the ship,
you yourselves
cannot be saved."
[32]Then the soldiers
cut away the ropes
of the *ship's* boat
and let it fall away.
[33]Until the day
was about to dawn,
Paul was encour-
aging them all to
take some food,
saying, "Today
is the fourteenth
day that you have
been constantly
watching and go-
ing without eating,
having taken noth-
ing. [34]Therefore I
encourage you to
take some food,
for this is for your
preservation, for
not a hair from
the head of any of
you will perish."
[35]Having said this,
he took bread and
gave thanks to God
in the presence of
all, and he broke it
and began to eat.
[36]All of them were
encouraged and
they themselves
also took food.

NIV

37 Altogether there
were 276 of us on
board. 38 When
they had eaten
as much as they
wanted, they light-
ened the ship by
throwing the grain
into the sea.
39 When day-
light came, they
did not recognize
the land, but they
saw a bay with
a sandy beach,
where they decid-
ed to run the ship
aground if they
could. 40 Cutting
loose the anchors,
they left them in
the sea and at the
same time untied
the ropes that
held the rudders.
Then they hoisted
the foresail to the
wind and made for
the beach. 41 But
the ship struck a
sandbar and ran
aground. The bow
stuck fast and
would not move,
and the stern was
broken to pieces
by the pounding of
the surf.
42 The soldiers
planned to kill
the prisoners to
prevent any of
them from swim-
ming away and
escaping. 43 But the
centurion want-
ed to spare Paul's
life and kept them
from carrying out
their plan. He or-
dered those who
could swim to
jump overboard
first and get to
land. 44 The rest
were to get there
on planks or on
other pieces of the
ship.

37 ἤμεθα δὲ αἱ πᾶσαι ψυχαὶ ἐν τῷ πλοίῳ διακόσιαι
We were *{and}* in *{the}* all two hundred seventy-six persons on the ship. *two hundred*
1639 1254 3836 4246 1357 1357 1573 6034 1877 3836 4450 1357
v.imi.1p cj d.npf a.npf n.npf p.d d.dsn n.dsn a.npf

⌊ἑβδομήκοντα ἕξ.⌋ 38 → → → κορεσθέντες δὲ τροφῆς ἐκούφιζον τὸ
seventy-six And when they had eaten enough, *And eaten* they lightened the
1573 1971 1254 5575 3170 1254 5575 3185 3836
a.npf a.npf pt.ap.npm cj n.gsf v.iai.3p d.asn

πλοῖον ἐκβαλλόμενοι τὸν σῖτον ↰ εἰς τὴν θάλασσαν. 39 ὅτε δὲ
ship, throwing the wheat out into the sea. Now when *Now* it was
4450 1675 3836 4992 1675 1650 3836 2498 1254 4021 1254 1181 1181
n.asn pt.pm.npm d.asm n.asm p.a d.asf n.asf cj cj

ἡμέρα ἐγένετο, τὴν γῆν οὐκ ἐπεγίνωσκον,
day, *it was* they did not recognize the land, *not they did recognize* but they noticed a
2465 1181 2105 2105 4024 2105 3836 1178 4024 2105 1254 2917 2917 5516
n.nsf v.ami.3s d.asf n.asf pl v.iai.3p

κόλπον δέ τινα κατενόουν ἔχοντα αἰγιαλὸν εἰς ὃν ἐβουλεύοντο εἰ δύναιντο
bay *but a they noticed* that had a beach, on which they planned, if possible,
3146 1254 5516 2917 2400 129 1650 4005 1086 1623 1538
n.asm cj r.asm v.iai.3p pt.pa.asm n.asm p.a r.asm v.imi.3p cj v.ppo.3p

ἐξῶσαι τὸ πλοῖον. ↰ 40 καὶ ↱ τὰς ἀγκύρας περιελόντες εἴων
to run the ship ashore. So they cut loose the anchors, *cut loose* left them
2034 3836 4450 2034 2779 1572 4311 4311 3836 46 4311 1572
f.aa d.asn n.asn cj d.apf n.apf pt.aa.npm v.iai.3p

εἰς τὴν θάλασσαν, ἅμα ἀνέντες τὰς ζευκτηρίας τῶν πηδαλίων
in the sea, and ⌊at the same time⌋ untied the ropes that held the rudders.
1650 3836 2498 275 479 3836 2415 3836 4382
p.a d.asf n.asf adv pt.aa.npm d.apf n.apf d.gpn n.gpn

καὶ ἐπάραντες τὸν ἀρτέμωνα τῇ πνεούσῃ κατεῖχον εἰς τὸν αἰγιαλόν. 41
Then hoisting the foresail ⌊to the⌋ wind, they made for the beach. But
2779 2048 3836 784 3836 4463 2988 1650 3836 129 1254
cj pt.aa.npm d.asm n.asm d.dsf pt.pa.dsf v.iai.3p p.a d.asm n.asm

περιπεσόντες δὲ εἰς τόπον διθάλασσον ἐπέκειλαν τὴν ναῦν ↰ καὶ ἡ μὲν
caught *But* in some crosscurrents, they ran the ship aground; *{and}* the ~
4346 1254 1650 5536 1458 2131 3836 3730 2131 2779 3836 3525
pt.aa.npm cj p.a n.asm a.asm v.aai.3p d.asf n.asf cj d.nsf pl

πρῷρα ἐρείσασα ἔμεινεν ἀσάλευτος, ἡ δὲ πρύμνα ἐλύετο ὑπὸ
bow stuck and remained immovable, but the *but* stern ⌊began to break up⌋ by
4749 2242 3531 810 1254 3836 1254 4744 3395 5679
n.nsf pt.aa.nsf v.aai.3s a.nsf d.nsf cj n.nsf v.ipi.3s p.g

τῆς βίας [a]τῶν κυμάτων. 42 τῶν δὲ στρατιωτῶν βουλὴ ἐγένετο ἵνα
the force of the waves. It was the plan of the *{and}* soldiers *plan It was* to
3836 1040 3836 3246 1181 1181 1087 3836 1254 5132 1087 1181 2671
d.gsf n.gsf d.gpn n.gpn d.gpm cj n.gpm n.nsf v.ami.3s cj

τοὺς δεσμώτας ἀποκτείνωσιν, ⌊μή τις⌋ ἐκκολυμβήσας διαφύγῃ.
kill the prisoners, *kill* so none could escape by swimming away. *could escape*
650 3836 1304 650 3590 5516 1423 1423 1713 1423
d.apm n.apm v.aas.3p cj r.nsm pt.aa.nsm v.aas.3s

43 ὁ δὲ ἑκατοντάρχης βουλόμενος διασῶσαι τὸν Παῦλον ἐκώλυσεν
But the *But* centurion, wanting to spare *{the}* Paul's life, prevented
1254 3836 1254 1672 1089 1407 3836 4263 3266
d.nsm cj n.nsm pt.pm.nsm f.aa d.asm n.asm v.aai.3s

αὐτοὺς ↰ τοῦ βουλήματος, ἐκέλευσέν τε τοὺς δυναμένους κολυμβᾶν
them from *{the}* ⌊carrying out their plan;⌋ and he ordered *and* those who could swim
899 3266 3836 1088 5445 3027 5445 3836 1538 3147
r.apm.3 d.gsn n.gsn v.aai.3s cj d.apm pt.pp.apm f.pa

ἀπορίψαντας πρώτους ἐπὶ τὴν γῆν ἐξιέναι 44 καὶ τοὺς
⌊to throw themselves overboard⌋ first and make for the land, *make* and the
681 4755 1997 2093 3836 1178 1997 2779 3836
pt.aa.apm a.apm p.a d.asf n.asf f.pa cj d.apm

λοιποὺς ⌊οὓς μὲν⌋ ἐπὶ σανίσιν, οὓς δὲ ἐπὶ τινων τῶν ἀπὸ τοῦ πλοίου. καὶ
rest, some on planks and others *and* on pieces *{the}* of the ship. And
3370 4005 3525 2093 4909 1254 4005 1254 2093 5516 3836 608 3836 4450 2779
a.apm r.apm pl p.d n.dpf r.apm pl p.g r.gpn d.gpn p.g d.gsn n.gsn cj

[a] [τῶν κυμάτων] UBS.

NASB

37 All of us in the
ship were two hun-
dred and seventy-
six persons. 38 When
they had eaten
enough, they *began*
to lighten the ship
by throwing out the
wheat into the sea.
39 When day
came, they could
not recognize the
land; but they did
observe a bay with
a beach, and they
resolved to drive
the ship onto it if
they could. 40 And
casting off the
anchors, they left
them in the sea
while at the same
time they were
loosening the ropes
of the rudders; and
hoisting the fore-
sail to the wind,
they were heading
for the beach. 41 But
striking a reef
where two seas
met, they ran the
vessel aground;
and the prow stuck
fast and remained
immovable, but the
stern *began* to be
broken up by the
force *of the waves.*
42 The soldiers' plan
was to kill the pris-
oners, so that none
of them would
swim away and
escape; 43 but the
centurion, wanting
to bring Paul safely
through, kept
them from their
intention, and com-
manded that those
who could swim
should jump over-
board first and get
to land, 44 and the
rest *should follow,*
some on planks,
and others on vari-
ous things from the
ship. And so it

NIV

In this way every-
one reached land
safely.

Paul Ashore on Malta

28 Once safely
on shore,
we found out that
the island was
called Malta. 2The
islanders showed
us unusual kind-
ness. They built a
fire and welcomed
us all because it
was raining and
cold. 3Paul gath-
ered a pile of
brushwood and,
as he put it on the
fire, a viper, driv-
en out by the heat,
fastened itself on
his hand. 4When
the islanders saw
the snake hanging
from his hand,
they said to each
other, "This man
must be a mur-
derer; for though
he escaped from
the sea, the god-
dess Justice has
not allowed him
to live." 5But Paul
shook the snake
off into the fire
and suffered no
ill effects. 6The
people expected
him to swell up or
suddenly fall dead;
but after waiting a
long time and see-
ing nothing unusu-
al happen to him,
they changed their
minds and said he
was a god.

οὕτως ἐγένετο πάντας διασωθῆναι ἐπὶ τὴν γῆν.
so it came about that all escaped safely to the land.
4048 1181 4246 1407 2093 3836 1178
adv v.ami.3s a.apm f.ap p.a d.asf n.asf

28:1 καὶ διασωθέντες τότε ἐπέγνωμεν ὅτι Μελίτη
And ⌊when we had escaped safely,⌋ then we learned that the island was called Malta.
2779 1407 5538 2105 4022 3836 3762 2813 2813 3514
cj pt.ap.npm adv v.aai.1p cj n.nsf

ἡ νῆσος καλεῖται. 2οἵ τε βάρβαροι παρεῖχον οὐ τὴν τυχοῦσαν
the island was called The ~ native people showed us no *{the}* ordinary
3836 3762 2813 3836 5445 975 4218 7005 4024 3836 5593
d.nsf n.nsf v.ppi.3s d.npm cj n.npm v.iai.3p pl d.asf pt.aa.asf

φιλανθρωπίαν ἡμῖν, ↱ ἅψαντες γὰρ πυρὰν προσελάβοντο πάντας
kindness, *us* for they kindled *for* a fire and welcomed us all,
5792 7005 1142 4689 721 1142 4787 4689 7005 4246
n.asf r.dp.1 pt.aa.npm cj n.asf v.ami.3p a.apm

ἡμᾶς διὰ τὸν ὑετὸν τὸν ἐφεστῶτα καὶ διὰ τὸ
us because it had begun to *{the}* rain *{the} it had begun to* and ⌊because of⌋ the
7005 1328 2392 2392 2392 2392 3836 5624 3836 2392 2779 1328 3836
r.ap.1 p.a d.asm n.asm d.asm pt.ra.asm cj p.a d.asn

ψῦχος. 3→ συστρέψαντος δὲ τοῦ Παύλου φρυγάνων τι
cold. When Paul had gathered *{and} {the} Paul* a bundle of sticks *a*
6036 4263 5370 1254 3836 4263 5516 4436 5866 5516
n.asn pt.aa.gsm cj d.gsm n.gsm n.gpn r.asn

πλῆθος καὶ ἐπιθέντος ἐπὶ τὴν πυράν, ἔχιδνα ἀπὸ τῆς θέρμης
bundle and put them on the fire, a viper came out from the heat
4436 2779 2202 2093 3836 4787 2399 2002 2002 608 3836 2549
n.asn cj pt.aa.gsm p.a d.asf n.asf n.nsf p.g d.gsf n.gsf

ἐξελθοῦσα καθῆψεν τῆς χειρὸς αὐτοῦ. 4ὡς δὲ εἶδον
came out and fastened onto *{the}* his hand. *his* When *{and}* the native people saw
2002 2750 3836 899 5931 899 6055 1254 3836 975 975 1625
pt.aa.nsf v.aai.3s d.gsf n.gsf r.gsm.3 cj cj v.aai.3p

οἱ βάρβαροι κρεμάμενον τὸ θηρίον ἐκ τῆς χειρὸς αὐτοῦ,
the native people the creature hanging *the creature* from *{the}* his hand, *his* they
3836 975 3836 2563 3203 3836 2563 1666 3836 899 5931 899 3306
d.npm n.npm pt.pm.asn d.asn n.asn p.g d.gsf n.gsf r.gsm.3

πρὸς ἀλλήλους ἔλεγον, πάντως φονεύς ἐστιν ὁ ἄνθρωπος
said to each other, *they said* "Certainly this man is a murderer, *is {the} man*
3306 4639 253 3306 4122 4047 476 1639 5838 1639 3836 476
p.a r.apm v.iai.3p adv n.nsm v.pai.3s d.nsm n.nsm

οὗτος ↱ ὃν διασωθέντα ἐκ τῆς θαλάσσης ἡ δίκη
this and though he has escaped from the sea, *{the}* justice has not allowed him
4047 1407 4005 1407 1666 3836 2498 3836 1472 1572 4024 1572
r.nsm r.asm pt.ap.asm p.g d.gsf n.gsf d.nsf n.nsf

ζῆν οὐκ εἴασεν. 5 ὁ μὲν οὖν ἀποτινάξας τὸ θηρίον ↰ εἰς τὸ πῦρ
to live." *not has allowed* But Paul ~ *But* shook the creature off into the fire and
2409 4024 1572 4036 3836 3525 4036 701 3836 2563 701 1650 3836 4786
f.pa pl v.aai.3s d.nsm pl cj pt.aa.nsm d.asn n.asn p.a d.asn n.asn

ἔπαθεν οὐδὲν κακόν, 6οἱ δὲ προσεδόκων αὐτὸν μέλλειν πίμπρασθαι ἢ
suffered no harm. They *{and}* were expecting that he was going to swell up or
4248 4029 2805 3836 1254 4659 899 3516 4399 2445
v.aai.3s a.asn a.asn d.npm cj v.iai.3p r.asm.3 f.pa f.pp cj

καταπίπτειν ἄφνω νεκρόν. ⌊ἐπὶ πολὺ⌋ δὲ αὐτῶν
suddenly fall down *suddenly* dead; but when they waited a long time *but they*
924 2928 924 3738 1254 4659 899 4659 2093 4498 1254 899
f.pa adv a.asm p.a adv cj r.gpm.3

προσδοκώντων καὶ θεωρούντων μηδὲν ἄτοπον εἰς αὐτὸν γινόμενον
when waited and saw no misfortune happen to him, *happen*
4659 2779 2555 3594 876 1181 1650 899 1181
pt.pa.gpm cj pt.pa.gpm a.asn a.asn p.a r.asm.3 pt.pm.asn

μεταβαλόμενοι ἔλεγον αὐτὸν εἶναι θεόν. 7 ἐν δὲ τοῖς
⌊they changed their minds⌋ and said that he was a god. Now in *Now* the region
3554 3306 899 1639 2536 1254 1877 1254 3836
pt.am.npm v.iai.3p r.asm.3 f.pa n.asm p.d cj d.dpn

NASB

happened that they
all were brought
safely to land.

Safe at Malta

28:1When they
had been brought
safely through,
then we found out
that the island was
called Malta. 2The
natives showed us
extraordinary kind-
ness; for because
of the rain that had
set in and because
of the cold, they
kindled a fire and
received us all.
3But when Paul had
gathered a bundle
of sticks and laid
them on the fire,
a viper came out
because of the heat
and fastened itself
on his hand. 4When
the natives saw
the creature hang-
ing from his hand,
they *began* saying
to one another,
"Undoubtedly this
man is a murderer,
and though he has
been saved from
the sea, justice has
not allowed him to
live." 5However he
shook the creature
off into the fire and
suffered no harm.
6But they were
expecting that he
was about to swell
up or suddenly fall
down dead. But af-
ter they had waited
a long time and
had seen nothing
unusual happen to
him, they changed
their minds and
began to say that
he was a god.
7Now in the

NIV

[7]There was an es-
tate nearby that be-
longed to Publius,
the chief official
of the island. He
welcomed us to his
home and showed
us generous hos-
pitality for three
days. [8]His father
was sick in bed,
suffering from fe-
ver and dysentery.
Paul went in to
see him and, after
prayer, placed his
hands on him and
healed him. [9]When
this had happened,
the rest of the sick
on the island came
and were cured.
[10]They honored
us in many ways;
and when we were
ready to sail, they
furnished us with
the supplies we
needed.

Paul's Arrival at Rome

[11]After three
months we put out
to sea in a ship
that had wintered
in the island—it
was an Alexandri-
an ship with the
figurehead of the
twin gods Castor
and Pollux. [12]We
put in at Syra-
cuse and stayed
there three days.
[13]From there we
set sail and arrived
at Rhegium. The
next day the south
wind came up, and
on the following
day we reached
Puteoli. [14]There
we found some
brothers and sis-
ters who invited
us to spend a week
with them. And so
we came to Rome.
[15]The brothers and
sisters there had
heard that we were
coming,

περὶ τὸν τόπον ἐκεῖνον ὑπῆρχεν χωρία τῷ πρώτῳ τῆς νήσου
around {the} that place *that* were fields belonging ⌞to the⌟ ⌞leading man⌟ of the island,
4309 3836 1697 5536 1697 5639 6005 3836 4755 3836 3762
p.a d.asm n.asm r.asm v.iai.3s n.npn d.dsm a.dsm d.gsf n.gsf

ὀνόματι Ποπλίῳ, ὃς ἀναδεξάμενος ἡμᾶς τρεῖς ἡμέρας φιλοφρόνως
by name Publius, who welcomed us and for three days entertained us hospitably.
3950 4511 4005 346 7005 5552 2465 3826 5819
n.dsn n.dsm r.nsm pt.am.nsm r.ap.1 a.apf n.apf adv

ἐξένισεν. [8]ἐγένετο δὲ τὸν πατέρα τοῦ Ποπλίου
entertained ⌞It happened that⌟ {and} the father of Publius lay sick with bouts of
3826 1181 1254 3836 4252 3836 4511 2879 5309 5309
v.aai.3s v.ami.3s cj d.asm n.asm d.gsm n.gsm

πυρετοῖς καὶ δυσεντερίῳ συνεχόμενον κατακεῖσθαι, πρὸς ὃν ὁ
fever and with dysentery. *with bouts* *lay* Paul visited {with} him, {the}
4790 2779 1548 5309 2879 4263 1656 4639 4005 3836
n.dpm cj n.dsn pt.pp.asm f.pm p.a r.asm d.nsm

Παῦλος εἰσελθὼν καὶ προσευξάμενος ↱ ἐπιθεὶς τὰς χεῖρας ↰ αὐτῷ ἰάσατο
Paul *visited* and when he had prayed, he laid his hands on him and healed
4263 1656 2779 4667 2615 2202 3836 5931 2202 899 2615
n.nsm pt.aa.nsm cj pt.am.nsm pt.aa.nsm d.apf n.apf r.dsm.3 v.ami.3s

αὐτόν. [9] ↱ τούτου δὲ γενομένου καὶ οἱ λοιποὶ οἱ ἐν τῇ νήσῳ
him. And when this *And* happened, *also* the rest of the people on the island
899 1254 1181 4047 1254 1181 2779 3836 3370 3836 1877 3836 3762
r.asm.3 r.gsn cj pt.am.gsn adv d.npm a.npm d.npm p.d d.dsf n.dsf

ἔχοντες ἀσθενείας προσήρχοντο καὶ ἐθεραπεύοντο, [10]οἳ καὶ
who had diseases also came and were cured. They also honored us with
2400 819 2779 4665 2779 2543 4005 2779 5506 7005
pt.pa.npm n.apf v.imi.3p cj v.ipi.3p r.npm adv

πολλαῖς τιμαῖς ἐτίμησαν ἡμᾶς καὶ ἀναγομένοις ἐπέθεντο τὰ
many honors, *honored* *us* and ⌞when we were getting ready to sail,⌟ they put {the}
4498 5507 5506 7005 2779 343 2202 3836
a.dpf n.dpf v.aai.3p r.ap.1 cj pt.pp.dpm v.ami.3p d.apn

πρὸς τὰς χρείας. [11]μετὰ δὲ τρεῖς μῆνας ἀνήχθημεν ἐν πλοίῳ
on board whatever we needed. After {and} three months ⌞we put out to sea⌟ in a ship
4639 3836 5970 3552 1254 5552 3604 343 1877 4450
p.a d.apf n.apf p.a cj a.apm n.apm v.api.1p p.d n.dsn

παρακεχειμακότι ἐν τῇ νήσῳ, Ἀλεξανδρίνῳ,
that had wintered at the island, a ship of Alexandria, with the "Heavenly Twins" as a
4199 1877 3836 3762 234 1483 1483
pt.ra.dsn p.d d.dsf n.dsf a.dsn

παρασήμῳ Διοσκούροις. [12]καὶ καταχθέντες εἰς Συρακούσας ἐπεμείναμεν
figurehead. *Heavenly Twins* And when we put in at Syracuse, we stayed there three
4185 1483 2779 2864 1650 5352 2152 5552
a.dsn n.dpm cj pt.ap.npm p.a n.apf v.aai.1p

ἡμέρας τρεῖς, [13]ὅθεν ↱ περιελόντες κατηντήσαμεν εἰς Ῥήγιον. καὶ μετὰ
days. *three* ⌞From there⌟ we circled round and came to Rhegium; and after
2465 5552 3854 2918 4311 2918 1650 4836 2779 3552
n.apf a.apf cj pt.aa.npm v.aai.1p p.a n.asn cj p.a

μίαν ἡμέραν ἐπιγενομένου νότου δευτεραῖοι ἤλθομεν εἰς
one day a south wind came up, *south wind* and ⌞on the following day⌟ we arrived in
1651 2465 3803 3803 2104 3803 1308 2262 1650
a.asf n.asf pt.am.gsm n.gsm a.npm v.aai.1p p.a

Ποτιόλους, [14]οὗ εὑρόντες ἀδελφοὺς παρεκλήθημεν παρ' αὐτοῖς
Puteoli, where we found brethren, and were invited to stay with them
4541 4023 2351 81 4151 2152 2152 4123 899
n.apm adv pt.aa.npm n.apm v.api.1p p.d r.dpm.3

ἐπιμεῖναι ἡμέρας ἑπτά· καὶ οὕτως εἰς τὴν Ῥώμην ἤλθαμεν. [15] →
to stay seven days. *seven* And so we went toward {the} Rome. *we went* And
2152 2231 2465 2231 2779 4048 2262 2262 1650 3836 4873 2262
f.aa n.apf a.apf cj adv p.a d.asf n.asf v.aai.1p

κἀκεῖθεν οἱ ἀδελφοὶ ἀκούσαντες τὰ περὶ ἡμῶν ἦλθαν εἰς
the brothers there, *the* *brothers* when they heard {the} about us, came *to*
3836 81 2796 3836 81 201 3836 4309 7005 2262 1650
crasis d.npm n.npm pt.aa.npm d.apn p.g r.gp.1 v.aai.3p p.a

NASB

neighborhood of
that place were
lands belonging
to the leading
man of the island,
named Publius,
who welcomed us
and entertained
us courteously
three days. [8]And it
happened that the
father of Publius
was lying *in bed*
afflicted with
recurrent fever
and dysentery; and
Paul went in *to*
see him and after
he had prayed, he
laid his hands on
him and healed
him. [9]After this
had happened, the
rest of the people
on the island who
had diseases were
coming to him
and getting cured.
[10]They also hon-
ored us with many
marks of respect;
and when we were
setting sail, they
supplied *us* with all
we needed.

Paul Arrives at Rome

[11]At the end of
three months we
set sail on an Alex-
andrian ship which
had wintered at
the island, and
which had the Twin
Brothers for its fig-
urehead. [12]After we
put in at Syracuse,
we stayed there for
three days. [13]From
there we sailed
around and arrived
at Rhegium, and
a day later a south
wind sprang up,
and on the second
day we came to
Puteoli. [14]There
we found *some*
brethren, and were
invited to stay with
them for seven
days; and thus we
came to Rome.
[15]And the brethren,
when they heard
about us, came

NIV

and they traveled
as far as the Forum
of Appius and the
Three Taverns to
meet us. At the
sight of these peo-
ple Paul thanked
God and was en-
couraged. [16]When
we got to Rome,
Paul was allowed
to live by himself,
with a soldier to
guard him.

Paul Preaches at Rome Under Guard

[17]Three days later
he called together
the local Jewish
leaders. When
they had assem-
bled, Paul said to
them: "My broth-
ers, although I
have done nothing
against our people
or against the cus-
toms of our ances-
tors, I was arrested
in Jerusalem and
handed over to the
Romans. [18]They
examined me and
wanted to release
me, because I was
not guilty of any
crime deserving
death. [19]The Jews
objected, so I was
compelled to make
an appeal to Cae-
sar. I certainly did
not intend to bring
any charge against
my own people.
[20]For this reason I
have asked to see
you and talk with
you. It is because
of the hope of Isra-
el that I am bound
with this chain."
[21]They replied,
"We have not re-
ceived any letters
from Judea

ἀπάντησιν ἡμῖν ἄχρι Ἀππίου φόρου καὶ Τριῶν ταβερνῶν,
meet us ⌊as far as⌋ the Forum of Appius *Forum* and Three Taverns to meet us.
561 7005 948 5842 716 5842 2779 5552 5411 1650 561 7005
n.asf r.dp.1 p.g n.gsm n.gsn cj a.gpf n.gpf

οὓς ἰδὼν ὁ Παῦλος εὐχαριστήσας τῷ θεῷ ἔλαβε θάρσος.
On seeing them, *On seeing* *{the}* Paul gave thanks to God and took courage.
1625 1625 4005 1625 3836 4263 2373 3836 2536 3284 2511
r.apm pt.aa.nsm d.nsm n.nsm pt.aa.nsm d.dsm n.dsm v.aai.3s n.asn

16 ὅτε δὲ ⌊εἰσήλθομεν εἰς⌋ Ῥώμην, ἐπετράπη τῷ Παύλῳ μένειν καθ᾽
And when *And* we entered Rome, Paul was allowed *{the}* *Paul* to stay by
1254 4021 1254 1656 1650 4873 4263 2205 3836 4263 3531 2848
cj cj v.aai.1p p.a n.asf v.api.3s d.dsm n.dsm f.pa p.a

ἑαυτὸν σὺν τῷ φυλάσσοντι αὐτὸν στρατιώτῃ. 17 ἐγένετο δὲ
himself, with a soldier *{the}* guarding him. *soldier* And ⌊it happened that⌋ *And*
1571 5250 5132 3836 5875 899 5132 1254 1181 1254
r.asm.3 p.d d.dsm pt.pa.dsm r.asm.3 n.dsm v.ami.3s cj

μετὰ ἡμέρας τρεῖς συγκαλέσασθαι αὐτὸν τοὺς ὄντας τῶν Ἰουδαίων
after three days *three* Paul called together *Paul* the *{being}* leaders of the Jews.
3552 5552 2465 5552 899 5157 899 3836 1639 4755 3836 2681
p.a n.apf a.apf f.am r.asm.3 d.apm pt.pa.apm d.gpm a.gpm

πρώτους· → συνελθόντων δὲ αὐτῶν ἔλεγεν πρὸς αὐτούς, ἐγώ, ⌊ἄνδρες
leaders And when they gathered, *And* *they* he said to them: *I* "My brothers,
4755 1254 899 5302 1254 899 3306 4639 899 1609 467
a.apm pt.aa.gpm cj r.gpm.3 v.iai.3s p.a r.apm.3 r.ns.1 n.vpm

ἀδελφοί,⌋ οὐδὲν ἐναντίον ποιήσας τῷ λαῷ ἢ τοῖς
though I have done nothing against *though have done* our people or the
81 4472 1609 4472 4472 4029 1883 4472 3836 3295 2445 3836
n.vpm a.asn p.g pt.aa.nsm d.dsm n.dsm cj d.dpn

ἔθεσι τοῖς πατρῴοις δέσμιος ἐξ Ἱεροσολύμων παρεδόθην
customs of our fathers, yet I was delivered as a prisoner from Jerusalem *I was delivered*
1621 3836 4262 4140 4140 4140 1300 1666 2642 4140
n.dpn d.dpn a.dpn n.nsm p.g n.gpn v.api.1s

εἰς τὰς χεῖρας τῶν Ῥωμαίων, 18 οἵτινες ἀνακρίναντές με ἐβούλοντο ἀπολῦσαι
into the hands of the Romans. They examined me and wanted to release
1650 3836 5931 3836 4871 4015 373 1609 1089 668
p.a d.apf n.apf d.gpm n.gpm r.npm pt.aa.npm r.as.1 v.imi.3p f.aa

διὰ τὸ μηδεμίαν αἰτίαν → θανάτου ὑπάρχειν ἐν ἐμοί.
me, because *{the}* there was no basis for a death sentence *there was* against me.
1328 3836 5639 5639 3594 162 2505 5639 1877 1609
p.a d.asn a.asf n.asf n.gsm f.pa p.d r.ds.1

19 → ἀντιλεγόντων δὲ τῶν Ἰουδαίων ἠναγκάσθην ἐπικαλέσασθαι
But when the Jews objected, *But* *the* *Jews* I was compelled to appeal to
1254 3836 2681 515 1254 3836 2681 337 2126
pt.pa.gpm cj d.gpm a.gpm v.api.1s f.am

Καίσαρα οὐχ ὡς τοῦ ἔθνους
Caesar, but not as though I had some charge to bring against *{the}* my own people.
2790 4024 6055 2400 2400 2400 5516 2989 2989 2989 2989 3836 1609 1609 1620
n.asm pl pl d.gsn n.gsn

μου ἔχων τι κατηγορεῖν. 20 διὰ ταύτην οὖν τὴν
my own *though I had* *some* *charge to bring against* For this reason, therefore, *{the}* I have
1609 2400 5516 2989 1328 4047 4036 3836 4151 4151
r.gs.1 pt.pa.nsm r.asn f.pa p.a r.asf cj d.asf

αἰτίαν παρεκάλεσα ὑμᾶς ἰδεῖν καὶ προσλαλῆσαι, ἕνεκεν
asked *I have* to see you *to see* and speak with you, since it is ⌊because of⌋
162 4151 1625 1625 7007 1625 2779 4688 1142 1914
n.asf v.aai.1s r.ap.2 f.aa cj f.aa p.g

γὰρ τῆς ἐλπίδος τοῦ Ἰσραὴλ τὴν ἅλυσιν ταύτην περίκειμαι.
since the hope of Israel that I wear *{the}* this chain." *this* *I wear*
1142 3836 1828 3836 2702 4329 4329 3836 4047 268 4047 4329
cj d.gsf n.gsf d.gsm n.gsm d.asf n.asf r.asf v.pmi.1s

21 οἱ δὲ πρὸς αὐτὸν εἶπαν, ἡμεῖς οὔτε γράμματα
And they *And* said to him, *said* "We have received no letters from Judea
1254 3836 1254 3306 4639 899 3306 7005 1312 1312 4046 1207 608 2677
d.npm cj p.a r.asm.3 v.aai.3p r.np.1 cj n.apn

NASB

from there as far
as the Market of
Appius and Three
Inns to meet us;
and when Paul saw
them, he thanked
God and took
courage.
[16]When we en-
tered Rome, Paul
was allowed to stay
by himself, with
the soldier who
was guarding him.
[17]After three days
Paul called togeth-
er those who were
the leading men of
the Jews, and when
they came together,
he *began* saying to
them, "Brethren,
though I had done
nothing against our
people or the cus-
toms of our fathers,
yet I was delivered
as a prisoner from
Jerusalem into the
hands of the Ro-
mans. [18]And when
they had examined
me, they were
willing to release
me because there
was no ground
for putting me to
death. [19]But when
the Jews objected,
I was forced to ap-
peal to Caesar, not
that I had any accu-
sation against my
nation. [20]For this
reason, therefore,
I requested to see
you and to speak
with you, for I am
wearing this chain
for the sake of the
hope of Israel."
[21]They said to him,
"We have neither
received letters
from Judea

NIV

concerning you,
and none of our
people who have
come from there
has reported or
said anything bad
about you. 22 But
we want to hear
what your views
are, for we know
that people every-
where are talking
against this sect."
23 They arranged
to meet Paul on a
certain day, and
came in even larg-
er numbers to the
place where he
was staying. He
witnessed to them
from morning
till evening, ex-
plaining about the
kingdom of God,
and from the Law
of Moses and from
the Prophets he
tried to persuade
them about Jesus.
24 Some were con-
vinced by what
he said, but others
would not believe.
25 They disagreed
among themselves
and began to leave
after Paul had
made this final
statement: "The
Holy Spirit spoke
the truth to your
ancestors when he
said through Isaiah
the prophet:
26 "'Go to this
people and
say,
"You will be
ever hearing
but never
under-
standing;
you will be
ever seeing
but never
perceiving."
27 For this people's
heart has
become
calloused;
they hardly hear
with their
ears,
and they have
closed their
eyes.

περὶ σοῦ ἐδεξάμεθα ἀπὸ τῆς Ἰουδαίας οὔτε παραγενόμενός ↱ τις τῶν ἀδελφῶν
about you, *have received* from *{the}* Judea nor *come from there* have any of the brothers
4309 5148 1312 608 3836 2677 4046 4134 550 5516 3836 81
p.g r.gs.2 v.ami.1p p.g d.gsf n.gsf cj pt.am.nsm r.nsm d.gpm n.gpm

ἀπήγγειλεν ἢ ἐλάλησέν τι περὶ σοῦ πονηρόν. 22
come from there and reported or spoken any bad about you. *bad* But
4134 4134 4134 550 2445 3281 5516 4505 4309 5148 4505 1254
v.aai.3s cj v.aai.3s r.asn p.g r.gs.2 a.asn

ἀξιοῦμεν δὲ παρὰ σοῦ ἀκοῦσαι ἃ φρονεῖς, περὶ μὲν γὰρ τῆς
we desire *But* to hear from you *to hear* what you think, for ˪with regard to˩ ~ *for* *{the}*
546 1254 201 201 4123 5148 201 4005 5858 1142 4309 3525 1142 3836
v.pai.1p cj p.g r.gs.2 f.aa r.apn v.pai.2s p.g pl cj d.gsf

αἱρέσεως ταύτης γνωστὸν ἡμῖν ἐστιν ὅτι πανταχοῦ ἀντιλέγεται.
this sect *this* it is known to us *it is* that everywhere it is spoken against."
4047 146 4047 1639 1639 1196 7005 1639 4022 4116 515
n.gsf r.gsf a.nsn r.dp.1 v.pai.3s cj adv v.ppi.3s

23 ταξάμενοι δὲ αὐτῷ ἡμέραν ἦλθον πρὸς αὐτὸν
˪When they had arranged˩ *{and}* a day to meet with him, *day* many came to him
5435 1254 2465 899 2465 4498 2262 4639 899
pt.am.npm cj r.dsm.3 n.asf v.aai.3p p.a r.asm.3

εἰς τὴν ξενίαν πλείονες οἷς ἐξετίθετο διαμαρτυρόμενος τὴν
at his lodging, *many* and he expounded to them, *he expounded* testifying to the
1650 3836 3825 4498 1758 1758 4005 1758 1371 3836
p.a d.asf n.asf a.npm.c r.dpm v.imi.3s pt.pm.nsm d.asf

βασιλείαν τοῦ θεοῦ, πείθων τε αὐτοὺς περὶ τοῦ Ἰησοῦ ἀπό
kingdom of God and trying to convince *and* them about *{the}* Jesus both from
993 3836 2536 5445 4275 5445 899 4309 3836 2652 5445 608
n.asf d.gsm n.gsm pt.pa.nsm cj r.apm.3 p.g d.gsm n.gsm p.g

τε τοῦ νόμου Μωϋσέως καὶ ↰ τῶν προφητῶν, ἀπὸ πρωῒ ἕως ἑσπέρας. 24 καὶ
both the Law of Moses and from the Prophets, from morning till evening. And
5445 3836 3795 3707 2779 608 3836 4737 608 4745 2401 2270 2779
cj d.gsm n.gsm n.gsm cj d.gpm n.gpm p.g adv p.g n.gsf cj

˪οἱ μὲν˩ ἐπείθοντο τοῖς λεγομένοις, οἱ δὲ ἠπίστουν· 25 →
some were convinced by what he said, but others *but* refused to believe. And not
3836 3525 4275 3836 3306 1254 3836 1254 601 1254
d.npm pl v.ipi.3p d.dpn pt.pp.dpn d.npm pl v.iai.3p

ἀσύμφωνοι δὲ ὄντες πρὸς ἀλλήλους ἀπελύοντο → εἰπόντος τοῦ
being in harmony *And* *being* among themselves, they departed after Paul made *{the}*
1639 851 1254 1639 4639 253 668 4263 3306 3836
a.npm cj pt.pa.npm p.a r.apm v.imi.3p pt.aa.gsm d.gsm

Παύλου ῥῆμα ἕν, ὅτι καλῶς τὸ πνεῦμα τὸ ἅγιον
Paul one further statement. *one* ~ *right* "The Holy Spirit *{the}* *Holy* was right in
4263 1651 4839 1651 4022 2822 3836 41 4460 3836 41 2822
n.gsm n.asn a.asn cj adv d.nsn n.nsn d.nsn a.nsn

ἐλάλησεν διὰ Ἠσαΐου τοῦ προφήτου πρὸς τοὺς πατέρας ὑμῶν
saying to your fathers through Isaiah the prophet: *to* *{the}* *fathers* *your*
3281 4639 7007 4252 1328 2480 3836 4737 4639 3836 4252 7007
v.aai.3s p.g n.gsm d.gsm n.gsm p.a d.apm n.apm r.gp.2

26 λέγων, πορεύθητι πρὸς τὸν λαὸν τοῦτον καὶ εἰπόν, ˪ἀκοῇ
{saying} 'Go to *{the}* this people, *this* and say, "You will indeed hear
3306 4513 4639 3836 4047 3295 4047 2779 3306 198
pt.pa.nsm v.apm.2s p.a d.asm n.asm r.asm cj v.aam.2s n.dsf

ἀκούσετε˩ καὶ ˪οὐ μὴ˩ συνῆτε καὶ ˪βλέποντες βλέψετε˩ καὶ ˪οὐ μὴ˩
but never understand, and you will indeed see but never
201 2779 4024 3590 5317 2779 1063 1063 2779 4024 3590
v.fai.2p cj pl pl v.aas.2p cj pt.pa.npm v.fai.2p cj pl pl

ἴδητε· 27 ἐπαχύνθη γὰρ ἡ καρδία τοῦ λαοῦ τούτου καὶ
perceive; *has become dull* for the heart of this people *this* has become dull, and
1625 4266 1142 3836 2840 3836 4047 3295 4047 4266 4266 4266 2779
v.aas.2p v.api.3s cj d.nsf n.nsf d.gsm n.gsm r.gsm cj

τοῖς ὠσὶν βαρέως ἤκουσαν καὶ τοὺς ὀφθαλμοὺς
they hear with difficultly ˪with their˩ ears, *with difficultly* *they hear* and *{the}* their eyes
201 201 977 977 3836 4044 977 201 2779 3836 899 4057
d.dpn n.dpn adv v.aai.3p cj d.apm n.apm

NASB

concerning you,
nor have any of
the brethren come
here and reported
or spoken anything
bad about you.
22 But we desire
to hear from you
what your views
are; for concern-
ing this sect, it is
known to us that it
is spoken against
everywhere."
23 When they had
set a day for Paul,
they came to him
at his lodging in
large numbers; and
he was explain-
ing to them by
solemnly testifying
about the kingdom
of God and trying
to persuade them
concerning Jesus,
from both the Law
of Moses and from
the Prophets, from
morning until eve-
ning. 24 Some were
being persuaded by
the things spoken,
but others would
not believe. 25 And
when they did not
agree with one
another, they *began*
leaving after Paul
had spoken one
parting word, "The
Holy Spirit rightly
spoke through
Isaiah the prophet
to your fathers,
26 saying,
'GO TO THIS
PEOPLE AND
SAY,
"YOU WILL KEEP
ON HEARING,
BUT WILL NOT
UNDERSTAND;
AND YOU WILL
KEEP ON SEE-
ING, BUT WILL
NOT PERCEIVE;
27 FOR THE HEART
OF THIS PEOPLE
HAS BECOME
DULL,
AND WITH THEIR
EARS THEY
SCARCELY
HEAR,
AND THEY HAVE
CLOSED THEIR
EYES;

NIV

Otherwise they
might see
with their
eyes,
hear with
their ears,
understand
with their
hearts and turn,
and I would
heal them.’[a]

28“Therefore I
want you to know
that God’s salva-
tion has been sent
to the Gentiles,
and they will lis-
ten!” [29][b]
30For two whole
years Paul stayed
there in his own
rented house and
welcomed all who
came to see him.
31He proclaimed
the kingdom of
God and taught
about the Lord
Jesus Christ—
with all boldness
and without hin-
drance!

αὐτῶν ἐκάμμυσαν· μήποτε ἴδωσιν τοῖς ὀφθαλμοῖς καὶ τοῖς
their they have closed, lest ⌊they should see⌋ ⌊with their⌋ eyes and hear ⌊with their⌋
899 2826 3607 1625 3836 4057 2779 201 3836
r.gpm.3 v.aai.3p cj v.aas.3p d.dpm n.dpm cj d.dpn

ὠσὶν ἀκούσωσιν καὶ τῇ καρδίᾳ συνῶσιν καὶ ἐπιστρέψωσιν, καὶ
ears *hear* and understand ⌊with their⌋ heart *understand* and turn, and
4044 201 2779 5317 3836 2840 5317 2779 2188 2779
n.dpn v.aas.3p cj d.dsf n.dsf v.aas.3p cj v.aas.3p cj

ἰάσομαι αὐτούς. 28 γνωστὸν οὖν ἔστω ὑμῖν ὅτι
I should heal them.”’” So let it be known *So* *let it be* to you that this salvation
2615 899 4036 1639 1639 1639 1196 4036 1639 7007 4022 4047 5402
v.fmi.1s r.apm.3 a.nsn cj v.pam.3s r.dp.2 cj

τοῖς ἔθνεσιν ἀπεστάλη τοῦτο τὸ σωτήριον τοῦ θεοῦ·
of God has been sent to the Gentiles; *has been sent* *this* *{the}* *salvation* *of* *God* even
3836 2536 690 690 690 3836 1620 690 4047 3836 5402 3836 2536 2779
d.dpn n.dpn v.api.3s r.nsn d.nsn n.nsn d.gsm n.gsm

αὐτοὶ καὶ ἀκούσονται.[a] 30 ἐνέμεινεν δὲ διετίαν ← ὅλην ἐν ἰδίῳ
they *even* will listen.” Paul lived there *{and}* two whole years *whole* in his own
899 2779 201 1844 1254 1454 3910 3910 1877 2625
r.npm cj v.fmi.3p v.aai.3s cj n.asf a.asf p.d a.dsn

μισθώματι καὶ ἀπεδέχετο πάντας τοὺς εἰσπορευομένους πρὸς αὐτόν, 31 κηρύσσων
rented house and welcomed all who came to him, proclaiming
3637 2779 622 4246 3836 1660 4639 899 3062
n.dsn cj v.imi.3s a.apm d.apm pt.pm.apm p.a r.asm.3 pt.pa.nsm

τὴν βασιλείαν τοῦ θεοῦ καὶ διδάσκων τὰ περὶ τοῦ κυρίου Ἰησοῦ Χριστοῦ μετὰ
the kingdom of God and teaching *{the}* about the Lord Jesus Christ with
3836 993 3836 2536 2779 1438 3836 4309 3836 3261 2652 5986 3552
d.asf n.asf d.gsm n.gsm cj pt.pa.nsm d.apn p.g d.gsm n.gsm n.gsm n.gsm p.g

πάσης παρρησίας ἀκωλύτως.
all boldness, without hindrance.
4246 4244 219
a.gsf n.gsf adv

NASB

OTHERWISE
THEY MIGHT
SEE WITH THEIR
EYES,
AND HEAR WITH
THEIR EARS,
AND UNDER-
STAND WITH
THEIR HEART
AND RETURN,
AND I WOULD
HEAL THEM.”’
28Therefore let it be
known to you that
this salvation of
God has been sent
to the Gentiles;
they will also lis-
ten.” 29[[a]When he
had spoken these
words, the Jews
departed, having
a great dispute
among them-
selves.]
30And he stayed
two full years in
his own rented
quarters and was
welcoming all
who came to him,
31preaching the
kingdom of God
and teaching con-
cerning the Lord
Jesus Christ with
all openness, un-
hindered.

[a] 27 Isaiah 6:9,10 (see Septuagint)
[b] 29 Some manuscripts include here *After he said this, the Jews left, arguing vigorously among themselves.*

[a] 29 καὶ ταῦτα αὐτοῦ εἰπόντος, ἀπῆλθον οἱ Ἰουδαῖοι, πολλὴν ἔχοντες ἐν ἑαυτοῖς συζήτησιν. included by TR after ἀκούσονται.

[a] Early mss do not contain this v

Romans

NIV

1 Paul, a servant of Christ Jesus, called to be an apostle and set apart for the gospel of God— 2 the gospel he promised beforehand through his prophets in the Holy Scriptures 3 regarding his Son, who as to his earthly life[a] was a descendant of David, 4 and who through the Spirit of holiness was appointed the Son of God in power[b] by his resurrection from the dead: Jesus Christ our Lord. 5 Through him we received grace and apostleship to call all the Gentiles to the obedience that comes from[c] faith for his name's sake. 6 And you also are among those Gentiles who are called to belong to Jesus Christ.

7 To all in Rome who are loved by God and called to be his holy people:

Grace and peace to you from God our Father and from the Lord Jesus Christ.

Paul's Longing to Visit Rome

8 First, I thank my God through Jesus Christ for all of you, because your faith is being reported all over the world. 9 God, whom I serve in

[a] 3 Or *who according to the flesh*
[b] 4 Or *was declared with power to be the Son of God*
[c] 5 Or *that is*

1:1 Παῦλος δοῦλος Χριστοῦ Ἰησοῦ, κλητὸς ἀπόστολος ἀφωρισμένος εἰς
Paul, a servant of Christ Jesus, called to be an apostle, set apart for
4263 1529 5986 2652 3105 693 928 1650
n.nsm n.nsm n.gsm n.gsm a.nsm n.nsm pt.rp.nsm p.a

εὐαγγέλιον θεοῦ, 2 ὃ προεπηγγείλατο διὰ τῶν προφητῶν αὐτοῦ
the gospel of God, which he promised beforehand through *{the}* his prophets *his*
2295 2536 4005 4600 1328 3836 899 4737 899
n.asn n.gsm r.asn v.ami.3s p.g d.gpm n.gpm r.gsm.3

ἐν γραφαῖς ἁγίαις 3 περὶ τοῦ υἱοῦ αὐτοῦ τοῦ
in the holy scriptures, *holy* the gospel concerning *{the}* his Son, *his* who
1877 41 1210 41 4309 3836 899 5626 899 3836
p.d n.dpf a.dpf p.g d.gsm n.gsm r.gsm.3 d.gsm

γενομένου ἐκ σπέρματος Δαυὶδ κατὰ σάρκα, 4 τοῦ ὁρισθέντος
was descended from *{seed}* David ⌊according to⌋ the flesh, and *{the}* was designated
1181 1666 5065 1253 2848 4922 3836 3988
pt.am.gsm p.g n.gsn n.gsm p.a n.asf d.gsm pt.ap.gsm

υἱοῦ θεοῦ ἐν δυνάμει κατὰ πνεῦμα ἁγιωσύνης ἐξ ἀναστάσεως →
Son of God with power ⌊according to⌋ the spirit of holiness by the resurrection from
5626 2536 1877 1539 2848 4460 43 1666 414
n.gsm n.gsm p.d n.dsf p.a n.asn n.gsf p.g n.gsf

νεκρῶν, Ἰησοῦ Χριστοῦ τοῦ κυρίου ἡμῶν, 5 δι᾽ οὗ ἐλάβομεν χάριν
the dead, Jesus Christ *{the}* our Lord. *our* Through him we have received grace
3738 2652 5986 3836 7005 3261 7005 1328 4005 3284 5921
a.gpm n.gsm n.gsm d.gsm n.gsm r.gp.1 p.g r.gsm v.aai.1p n.asf

καὶ ἀποστολὴν εἰς ὑπακοὴν πίστεως ἐν πᾶσιν τοῖς ἔθνεσιν
and apostleship ⌊to bring about⌋ the obedience of faith among all the nations
2779 692 1650 5633 4411 1877 4246 3836 1620
cj n.asf p.a n.asf n.gsf p.d a.dpn d.dpn n.dpn

ὑπὲρ τοῦ ὀνόματος αὐτοῦ, 6 ἐν οἷς ἐστε καὶ ὑμεῖς κλητοὶ
⌊on behalf of⌋ *{the}* his name, *his* among whom are you also, *you* called to
5642 3836 899 3950 899 1877 4005 1639 7007 2779 7007 3105
p.g d.gsn n.gsn r.gsm.3 p.d r.dpn v.pai.2p adv r.np.2 a.npm

Ἰησοῦ Χριστοῦ, 7 πᾶσιν τοῖς οὖσιν ἐν Ῥώμῃ ἀγαπητοῖς θεοῦ, κλητοῖς
belong to Jesus Christ. To all who are in Rome, loved by God and called
2652 5986 4246 3836 1639 1877 4873 28 2536 3105
n.gsm n.gsm a.dpm d.dpm pt.pa.dpm p.d n.dsf a.dpm n.gsm a.dpm

ἁγίοις, χάρις ὑμῖν καὶ εἰρήνη ἀπὸ θεοῦ πατρὸς ἡμῶν καὶ κυρίου Ἰησοῦ
to be saints: Grace to you and peace from God our Father *our* and the Lord Jesus
41 5921 7007 2779 1645 608 2536 7005 4252 7005 2779 3261 2652
a.dpm n.nsf r.dp.2 cj n.nsf p.g n.gsm n.gsm r.gp.1 cj n.gsm n.gsm

Χριστοῦ. 8 πρῶτον μὲν εὐχαριστῶ τῷ θεῷ μου διὰ Ἰησοῦ Χριστοῦ περὶ
Christ. First of all, ~ I thank *{the}* my God *my* through Jesus Christ for
5986 4754 3525 2373 3836 1609 2536 1609 1328 2652 5986 4309
n.gsm adv pl v.pai.1s d.dsm n.dsm r.gs.1 p.g n.gsm n.gsm p.g

πάντων ὑμῶν ὅτι ἡ πίστις ὑμῶν καταγγέλλεται ἐν ὅλῳ τῷ
all of you, because *{the}* your faith *your* is being proclaimed throughout the whole *the*
4246 7007 4022 3836 7007 4411 7007 2859 1877 3836 3910 3836
a.gpm r.gp.2 cj d.nsf n.nsf r.gp.2 v.ppi.3s p.d a.dsm d.dsm

κόσμῳ. 9 μάρτυς γάρ μού ἐστιν ὁ θεός, ᾧ λατρεύω ἐν τῷ
world. For God is my witness, *For my is {the} God* whom I serve with *{the}*
3180 1142 2536 1639 1609 3459 1142 1609 1639 3836 2536 4005 3302 1877 3836
n.dsm n.nsm cj r.gs.1 v.pai.3s d.nsm n.nsm r.dsm v.pai.1s p.d d.dsn

NASB

The Gospel Exalted

1:1 Paul, a bond-servant of Christ Jesus, called *as* an apostle, set apart for the gospel of God, 2 which He promised beforehand through His prophets in the holy Scriptures, 3 concerning His Son, who was born of a descendant of David according to the flesh, 4 who was declared the Son of God with power [a]by the resurrection from the dead, according to the Spirit of holiness, Jesus Christ our Lord, 5 through whom we have received grace and apostleship to bring about *the* obedience of faith among all the Gentiles for His name's sake, 6 among whom you also are the called of Jesus Christ;

7 to all who are beloved of God in Rome, called *as* saints: Grace to you and peace from God our Father and the Lord Jesus Christ.

8 First, I thank my God through Jesus Christ for you all, because your faith is being proclaimed throughout the whole world. 9 For God, whom I serve

[a] Or *as a result of*

NIV

my spirit in preach-
ing the gospel of
his Son, is my wit-
ness how constantly
I remember you
10in my prayers at
all times; and I pray
that now at last by
God's will the way
may be opened for
me to come to you.
11I long to see you
so that I may im-
part to you some
spiritual gift to
make you strong—
12that is, that you
and I may be mutu-
ally encouraged by
each other's faith.
13I do not want
you to be unaware,
brothers and sis-
ters,[a] that I planned
many times to
come to you (but
have been prevent-
ed from doing so
until now) in order
that I might have a
harvest among you,
just as I have had
among the other
Gentiles.
14I am obligated
both to Greeks and
non-Greeks, both
to the wise and the
foolish. 15That is
why I am so eager
to preach the gos-
pel also to you who
are in Rome.
16For I am not
ashamed of the
gospel, because it
is the power of God
that brings salva-
tion to everyone
who believes: first
to the Jew, then to
the Gentile. 17For in
the gospel the righ-
teousness of God is
revealed—a righ-
teousness that is
by faith from first
to last,[b] just as it is
written: "The

[a] 13 The Greek word for *brothers and sisters* (*adelphoi*) refers here to believers, both men and women, as part of God's family; also in 7:1, 4; 8:12, 29; 10:1; 11:25; 12:1; 15:14, 30; 16:14, 17.
[b] 17 Or *is from faith to faith*

πνεύματί μου ἐν τῷ εὐαγγελίῳ τοῦ υἱοῦ αὐτοῦ, ὡς ἀδιαλείπτως
my spirit *my* in the gospel of his Son, *his* how unceasingly I make
1609 4460 1609 1877 3836 2295 3836 899 5626 899 6055 90 4472 4472
n.dsn r.gs.1 p.d d.dsn n.dsn d.gsm n.gsm r.gsm.3 cj adv

μνείαν ὑμῶν ποιοῦμαι 10 πάντοτε ἐπὶ τῶν προσευχῶν μου δεόμενος εἴ πως
mention of you *I make* always in *{the}* my prayers, *my* asking if perhaps
3644 7007 4472 4121 2093 3836 1609 4666 1609 1289 1623 4803
n.asf r.gp.2 v.pmi.1s adv p.g d.gpf n.gpf r.gs.1 pt.pm.nsm cj pl

ἤδη ποτὲ εὐοδωθήσομαι ἐν τῷ θελήματι τοῦ θεοῦ ⌞ἐλθεῖν πρὸς⌟ ὑμᾶς. 11
now at last I may be able, by the will of God, to visit you. For
2453 4537 2338 1877 3836 2525 3836 2536 2262 4639 7007 1142
adv adv v.fpi.1s p.d d.dsn n.dsn d.gsm n.gsm f.aa p.a r.ap.2

ἐπιποθῶ γὰρ ἰδεῖν ὑμᾶς, ἵνα τι μεταδῶ χάρισμα ὑμῖν
I long *For* to see you so that *some* ⌞I may share with⌟ you some spiritual gift *you*
2160 1142 1625 7007 2671 5516 3556 7007 5516 4461 5922 7007
v.pai.1s cj f.aa r.ap.2 cj r.asn v.aas.1s n.asn r.dp.2

πνευματικὸν εἰς τὸ στηριχθῆναι ὑμᾶς, 12 τοῦτο δέ ἐστιν
spiritual to *{the}* strengthen you — that *{and}* is, that
4461 1650 3836 5114 7007 4047 1254 1639
a.asn p.a d.asn f.ap r.ap.2 r.nsn cj v.pai.3s

⌞συμπαρακληθῆναι ἐν ὑμῖν⌟ διὰ τῆς ἐν ἀλλήλοις πίστεως ὑμῶν τε
we may be mutually encouraged by *{the}* *{in}* each other's faith, I by yours ~
5220 1877 7007 1328 3836 1877 253 4411 7007 5445
f.ap p.d r.dp.2 p.g d.gsf p.d r.dpm n.gsf r.gp.2 cj

καὶ ἐμοῦ. 13 ➝ ➝ οὐ θέλω δὲ ὑμᾶς ἀγνοεῖν, ἀδελφοί, ὅτι ➝
and you by mine. I do not want *{and}* you to be unaware, brethren, that I
2779 1609 2527 2527 4024 2527 1254 7007 51 81 4022 4729
cj r.gs.1 pl v.pai.1s cj r.ap.2 f.pa n.vpm cj

πολλάκις προεθέμην ἐλθεῖν πρὸς ὑμᾶς, καὶ ἐκωλύθην ἄχρι τοῦ δεῦρο, ἵνα
often intended to come to you (but have been prevented until *{the}* now) so that
4490 4729 2262 4639 7007 2779 3266 948 3836 1306 2671
adv v.ami.1s f.aa p.a r.ap.2 cj v.api.1s p.g d.gsm adv cj

τινὰ καρπὸν σχῶ καὶ ἐν ὑμῖν καθὼς καὶ ἐν τοῖς
I might have some fruit *I might have* *{also}* among you, just as *{also}* among the
2400 2400 2400 5516 2843 2400 2779 1877 7007 2777 2779 1877 3836
r.asm n.asm v.aas.1s adv p.d r.dp.2 pl adv p.d d.dpn

λοιποῖς ἔθνεσιν. 14 ➝ Ἕλλησίν τε καὶ ➝
rest of the Gentiles. I am a debtor both to the Greeks *both* and to the
3370 1620 1639 1639 4050 5445 1818 5445 2779
a.dpn n.dpn n.dpm cj cj

βαρβάροις, ➝ σοφοῖς τε καὶ ➝ ἀνοήτοις ὀφειλέτης εἰμί, 15 οὕτως τὸ
barbarians, to the wise *{both}* ⌞as well as⌟ to the foolish. *debtor* *I am* So *part*
975 5055 5445 2779 485 4050 1639 4048 3836
n.dpm a.dpm cj cj a.dpm n.nsm v.pai.1s adv d.nsn

κατ᾽ ἐμὲ πρόθυμον καὶ ὑμῖν τοῖς ἐν
for my part I am eager to preach the gospel to you also *to you* who are in
2848 1609 3836 4609 2294 2294 2294 2294 7007 7007 2779 7007 3836 1877
p.a r.as.1 a.nsn adv r.dp.2 d.dpm p.d

Ῥώμῃ εὐαγγελίσασθαι. 16 ➝ ➝ οὐ γὰρ ἐπαισχύνομαι τὸ εὐαγγέλιον,[a]
Rome. *to preach the gospel* For I am not *For* ashamed of the gospel; it
4873 2294 1142 2049 2049 4024 1142 2049 3836 2295 1639
n.dsf f.am pl cj v.pmi.1s d.asn n.asn

δύναμις γὰρ θεοῦ ἐστιν εἰς σωτηρίαν παντὶ τῷ πιστεύοντι, ➝
is the power *{for}* of God *it is* for salvation to everyone who believes, to the
1639 1539 1142 2536 1639 1650 5401 4246 3836 4409
n.nsf cj n.gsm v.pai.3s p.a n.asf a.dsm d.dsm pt.pa.dsm

Ἰουδαίῳ τε πρῶτον καὶ ➝ Ἕλληνι. 17 δικαιοσύνη γὰρ θεοῦ
Jew ~ first ⌞and also⌟ to the Greek. For in it the righteousness *For* of God
2681 5445 4754 2779 1818 1142 1877 899 1466 1142 2536
a.dsm cj adv cj n.dsm n.nsf cj n.gsm

ἐν αὐτῷ ἀποκαλύπτεται ἐκ πίστεως εἰς πίστιν, καθὼς γέγραπται, ὁ δὲ
in *it* is revealed from faith to faith; as it is written, "The *{and}*
1877 899 636 1666 4411 1650 4411 2777 1211 3836 1254
p.d r.dsn.3 v.ppi.3s p.g n.gsf p.a n.asf cj v.rpi.3s d.nsm cj

[a] τοῦ Χριστοῦ included by TR after εὐαγγέλιον.

NASB

in my spirit in the
preaching of the
gospel of His Son,
is my witness *as to*
how unceasingly I
make mention of
you, 10always in
my prayers making
request, if perhaps
now at last by the
will of God I may
succeed in coming
to you. 11For I long
to see you so that
I may impart some
spiritual gift to
you, that you may
be established;
12that is, that I may
be encouraged
together with you
while among you,
each of us by the
other's faith, both
yours and mine. 13I
do not want you
to be unaware,
brethren, that often
I have planned to
come to you (and
have been pre-
vented so far) so
that I may obtain
some fruit among
you also, even as
among the rest of
the Gentiles. 14I am
[a]under obligation
both to Greeks and
to barbarians, both
to the wise and to
the foolish. 15So,
for my part, I am
eager to preach the
gospel to you also
who are in Rome.
16For I am not
ashamed of the
gospel, for it is the
power of God for
salvation to every-
one who believes,
to the Jew first and
also to the Greek.
17For in it *the* righ-
teousness of God
is revealed from
faith to faith; as it
is written,

[a] Lit *debtor*

NIV

righteous will live
by faith."[a]

God's Wrath Against Sinful Humanity

[18]The wrath of
God is being re-
vealed from heav-
en against all the
godlessness and
wickedness of
people, who sup-
press the truth by
their wickedness,
[19]since what may
be known about
God is plain to
them, because God
has made it plain
to them. [20]For
since the creation
of the world God's
invisible quali-
ties—his eternal
power and divine
nature—have
been clearly seen,
being understood
from what has
been made, so that
people are without
excuse.
[21]For although
they knew God,
they neither glo-
rified him as God
nor gave thanks
to him, but their
thinking became
futile and their
foolish hearts
were darkened.
[22]Although they
claimed to be wise,
they became fools
[23]and exchanged
the glory of the
immortal God for
images made to
look like a mortal
human being and
birds and animals
and reptiles.
[24]Therefore God
gave them over in
the sinful desires
of their hearts to
sexual impurity
for the degrading
of their bodies
with one another.
[25]They exchanged
the truth about
God for a lie, and
worshiped and
served created
things rather than
the Creator—who

[a] 17 Hab. 2:4

δίκαιος ἐκ πίστεως ζήσεται. 18 ἀποκαλύπτεται γὰρ ὀργὴ θεοῦ
righteous by faith will live." For the wrath of God is being revealed *For* *wrath* *of God*
1465 1666 4411 2409 1142 3973 2536 2536 636 1142 3973 2536
a.nsm p.g n.gsf v.fmi.3s v.ppi.3s cj n.nsf n.gsm

ἀπ᾽ οὐρανοῦ ἐπὶ πᾶσαν ἀσέβειαν καὶ ἀδικίαν ἀνθρώπων τῶν
from heaven against all ungodliness and the unrighteousness of those who suppress
608 4041 2093 4246 813 2779 94 476 3836 2988
p.g n.gsm p.a a.asf n.asf cj n.asf n.gpm d.gpm

τὴν ἀλήθειαν ἐν ἀδικίᾳ κατεχόντων, 19 διότι τὸ γνωστὸν
the truth by their unrighteousness, *suppress* because what ⌞can be known about⌟
3836 237 1877 94 2988 1484 3836 1196
d.asf n.asf p.d n.dsf pt.pa.gpm cj d.nsn a.nsn

τοῦ θεοῦ φανερόν ἐστιν ἐν αὐτοῖς, ὁ θεὸς γὰρ αὐτοῖς
{the} God is plain *is* to them, for *{the}* God *for* has revealed it to them.
3836 2536 1639 5745 1639 1877 899 1142 3836 2536 1142 5746 5746 899
d.gsm n.gsm a.nsn v.pai.3s p.d r.dpm.3 d.nsm n.nsm cj r.dpm.3

ἐφανέρωσεν. 20 τὰ γὰρ ἀόρατα αὐτοῦ
has revealed Ever since the creation of the world, *{the}* *{for}* his ⌞invisible attributes,⌟ *his*
5746 608 608 3232 3180 3836 1142 899 548 899
v.aai.3s d.npn cj a.npn r.gsm.3

ἀπὸ κτίσεως κόσμου τοῖς ποιήμασιν νοούμενα καθορᾶται, ἥ
Ever since *creation* *world* *through what* *has been made* *being understood* *have been clearly seen* *{the}*
608 3232 3180 3836 4473 3783 2775 3836
p.g n.gsf n.gsm d.dpn n.dpn pt.pp.npn v.ppi.3s d.nsf

τε ἀΐδιος αὐτοῦ δύναμις καὶ θειότης,
⌞that is,⌟ his eternal *his* power and divine nature, have been clearly seen, being understood
5445 899 132 899 1539 2779 2522 2775 2775 2775 2775 3783 3783
cj a.nsf r.gsm.3 n.nsf cj n.nsf

εἰς τὸ εἶναι αὐτοὺς ἀναπολογήτους, 21 διότι
through what has been made. So ~ they are *they* without excuse. ⌞Even though⌟
3836 3836 4473 4473 4473 1650 3836 899 1639 899 406 1484
p.a d.asn f.pa r.apm.3 a.apm cj

γνόντες τὸν θεὸν οὐχ ὡς θεὸν ἐδόξασαν ἢ ηὐχαρίστησαν,
they knew *{the}* God, they did not honor him as God *they did honor* or give
1182 3836 2536 1519 1519 4024 1519 6055 2536 1519 2445 2373
pt.aa.npm d.asm n.asm pl pl n.asm v.aai.3p cj v.aai.3p

← ἀλλ᾽ ἐματαιώθησαν ἐν τοῖς διαλογισμοῖς αὐτῶν καὶ ἐσκοτίσθη
him thanks, but they became futile in *{the}* their speculations *their* and *were darkened*
247 3471 1877 3836 899 1369 899 2779 5029
cj v.api.3p p.d d.dpm n.dpm r.gpm.3 cj v.api.3s

ἡ ἀσύνετος αὐτῶν καρδία. 22 φάσκοντες εἶναι σοφοὶ
{the} their foolish *their* hearts were darkened. Professing to be wise,
3836 899 852 899 2840 5029 5029 5763 1639 5055
d.nsf a.nsf r.gpm.3 n.nsf pt.pa.npm f.pa a.npm

ἐμωράνθησαν 23 καὶ ἤλλαξαν τὴν δόξαν τοῦ ἀφθάρτου θεοῦ ἐν
they became fools, and exchanged the glory of the incorruptible God for images
3701 2779 248 3836 1518 3836 915 2536 1877 1635
v.api.3p cj v.aai.3p d.asf n.asf d.gsm a.gsm n.gsm p.d

ὁμοιώματι εἰκόνος φθαρτοῦ ἀνθρώπου καὶ πετεινῶν καὶ τετραπόδων καὶ
resembling *images* corruptible man and birds and four-footed animals and
3930 1635 5778 476 2779 4374 2779 5488 2779
n.dsn n.gsf a.gsm n.gsm cj n.gpn cj n.gpn cj

ἑρπετῶν. 24 διὸ παρέδωκεν αὐτοὺς ↰ ὁ θεὸς ἐν ταῖς ἐπιθυμίαις
crawling creatures. Therefore God gave them over *{the}* *God* in the lusts
2260 1475 2536 4140 899 4140 3836 2536 1877 3836 2123
n.gpn cj v.aai.3s r.apm.3 d.nsm n.nsm p.d d.dpf n.dpf

τῶν καρδιῶν αὐτῶν εἰς ἀκαθαρσίαν τοῦ ἀτιμάζεσθαι τὰ σώματα αὐτῶν
of their hearts *their* to impurity, so that they dishonored *{the}* their bodies *their*
3836 899 2840 899 1650 174 3836 869 3836 899 5393 899
d.gpf n.gpf r.gpm.3 p.a n.asf d.gsn f.pp d.apn n.apn r.gpm.3

ἐν αὐτοῖς, 25 οἵτινες μετήλλαξαν τὴν ἀλήθειαν τοῦ θεοῦ ἐν τῷ ψεύδει καὶ
among themselves. They exchanged the truth of God for a lie and
1877 899 4015 3563 3836 237 3836 2536 1877 3836 6022 2779
p.d r.dpm.3 r.npm v.aai.3p d.asf n.asf d.gsm n.gsm p.d d.dsn n.dsn cj

---

NASB

"BUT THE RIGHTEOUS
man SHALL LIVE BY
FAITH."

Unbelief and Its Consequences

[18]For the wrath
of God is revealed
from heaven
against all ungodli-
ness and unrigh-
teousness of men
who suppress the
truth in unrigh-
teousness, [19]be-
cause that which is
known about God
is evident within
them; for God
made it evident to
them. [20]For since
the creation of the
world His invis-
ible attributes, His
eternal power and
divine nature, have
been clearly seen,
being understood
through what has
been made, so that
they are without
excuse. [21]For even
though they knew
God, they did not
[a]honor Him as God
or give thanks, but
they became futile
in their specula-
tions, and their
foolish heart was
darkened. [22]Pro-
fessing to be wise,
they became fools,
[23]and exchanged
the glory of the
incorruptible God
for an image in the
form of corruptible
man and of birds
and four-footed
animals and [b]crawl-
ing creatures.
[24]Therefore God
gave them over in
the lusts of their
hearts to impu-
rity, so that their
bodies would be
dishonored among
them. [25]For they
exchanged the truth
of God for a lie,

[a] Lit *glorify*
[b] Or *reptiles*

NIV

is forever praised. Amen.
26 Because of this, God gave them over to shameful lusts. Even their women exchanged natural sexual relations for unnatural ones. 27 In the same way the men also abandoned natural relations with women and were inflamed with lust for one another. Men committed shameful acts with other men, and received in themselves the due penalty for their error.
28 Furthermore, just as they did not think it worthwhile to retain the knowledge of God, so God gave them over to a depraved mind, so that they do what ought not to be done. 29 They have become filled with every kind of wickedness, evil, greed and depravity. They are full of envy, murder, strife, deceit and malice. They are gossips, 30 slanderers, God-haters, insolent, arrogant and boastful; they invent ways of doing evil; they disobey their parents; 31 they have no understanding, no fidelity, no love, no mercy. 32 Although they know God's righteous decree that those who do such things deserve death, they not only

ἐσεβάσθησαν καὶ ἐλάτρευσαν τῇ κτίσει παρὰ τὸν κτίσαντα, ὅς ἐστιν
worshiped and served the creature ⌊rather than⌋ the Creator, who is
4933 2779 3302 3836 3232 4123 3836 3231 4005 1639
v.api.3p cj v.aai.3p d.dsf n.dsf p.a d.asm pt.aa.asm r.nsm v.pai.3s

εὐλογητὸς εἰς τοὺς αἰῶνας, ἀμήν. 26 διὰ τοῦτο παρέδωκεν αὐτοὺς ↰ ὁ
blessed for all time. Amen. For this reason God gave them over *{the}*
2329 1650 3836 172 297 1328 4047 2536 4140 899 4140 3836
a.nsm p.a d.apm n.apm pl p.a r.asn v.aai.3s r.apm.3 d.nsm

θεὸς εἰς πάθη ἀτιμίας, αἵ τε γὰρ θήλειαι αὐτῶν μετήλλαξαν τὴν
God to degrading passions. *degrading* *{the}* *~* *{for}* Their women *Their* exchanged the
2536 1650 871 4079 871 3836 5445 1142 899 2559 899 3563 3836
n.nsm p.a n.apn n.gsf d.npf cj cj a.npf r.gpm.3 v.aai.3p d.asf

φυσικὴν χρῆσιν εἰς τὴν ⌊παρὰ φύσιν,⌋ 27 ὁμοίως τε
natural sexual function for ⌊one that⌋ is unnatural, and likewise *and* the men
5879 5979 1650 3836 4123 5882 5445 3931 5445 3836 781
a.asf n.asf p.a d.asf p.a n.asf adv cj

καὶ οἱ ἄρσενες ἀφέντες τὴν φυσικὴν χρῆσιν τῆς θηλείας ἐξεκαύθησαν
also *the* *men* abandoned the natural sexual relation with women and burned
2779 3836 781 918 3836 5879 5979 3836 2559 1706
adv d.npm a.npm pt.aa.npm d.asf a.asf n.asf d.gsf a.gsf v.api.3p

ἐν τῇ ὀρέξει αὐτῶν εἰς ἀλλήλους, ἄρσενες ἐν ἄρσεσιν τὴν
in *{the}* their passion *their* for one another — men with men committing *{the}*
1877 3836 899 3979 899 1650 253 781 1877 781 2981 3836
p.d d.dsf n.dsf r.gpm.3 p.a r.apm a.npm p.d a.dpm d.asf

ἀσχημοσύνην κατεργαζόμενοι καὶ τὴν ἀντιμισθίαν ἣν
shameless acts *committing* and receiving in themselves the due penalty *{that}*
859 2981 2779 655 1877 1571 3836 1256 521 4005
n.asf pt.pm.npm cj d.asf n.asf r.asf

ἔδει τῆς πλάνης αὐτῶν ἐν ἑαυτοῖς ἀπολαμβάνοντες. 28 καὶ καθὼς ↱ ↱
due for their error. *their* *in* *themselves* *receiving* And as they did
1256 3836 899 4415 899 1877 1571 655 2779 2777 1507 1507
v.iai.3s d.gsf n.gsf r.gpm.3 p.d r.dpm.3 pt.pa.npm cj cj

οὐκ ἐδοκίμασαν τὸν θεὸν ⌊ἔχειν ἐν ἐπιγνώσει,⌋
not see fit to acknowledge *{the}* God, *to acknowledge* God
4024 1507 2400 2400 3836 2536 2400 1877 2106 2536
pl v.aai.3p d.asm n.asm f.pa p.d n.dsf

παρέδωκεν αὐτοὺς ↰ ὁ θεὸς εἰς ἀδόκιμον νοῦν, ποιεῖν τὰ ↱ μὴ
gave them over *{the}* *God* to a debased mind, to do things that ought not
4140 899 4140 3836 2536 1650 99 3808 4472 3836 2763 3590
v.aai.3s r.apm.3 d.nsm n.nsm p.a a.asm n.asm f.pa d.apn pl

καθήκοντα, 29 πεπληρωμένους πάσῃ ἀδικίᾳ πονηρίᾳ πλεονεξίᾳ
to be done. They are filled with ⌊every kind of⌋ unrighteousness, wickedness, covetousness,
2763 4444 4246 94 4504 4432
pt.pa.apn pt.rp.apm a.dsf n.dsf n.dsf n.dsf

κακίᾳ, μεστοὺς φθόνου φόνου ἔριδος δόλου κακοηθείας, ψιθυριστὰς
malice. They are full of envy, murder, strife, deceit, meanness. They are gossips,
2798 3550 5784 5840 2251 1515 2799 6031
n.dsf a.apm n.gsm n.gsm n.gsf n.gsm n.gsf n.apm

30 καταλάλους θεοστυγεῖς ὑβριστὰς ὑπερηφάνους ἀλαζόνας, ἐφευρετὰς κακῶν,
slanderers, haters of God, insolent, arrogant, boastful, inventors of evil,
2897 2539 5616 5662 225 2388 2805
n.apm a.apm n.apm a.apm n.apm n.apm a.gpn

γονεῦσιν ἀπειθεῖς, 31 ἀσυνέτους ἀσυνθέτους ἀστόργους ἀνελεήμονας·
disobedient to parents, *disobedient* foolish, covenant-breakers, unloving, ruthless.
579 1204 579 852 853 845 446
n.dpm a.apm a.apm a.apm a.apm a.apm

32 οἵτινες τὸ δικαίωμα τοῦ θεοῦ ἐπιγνόντες ὅτι οἱ
Though they understand the righteous requirement of God, *Though understand* that those
2105 4015 2105 3836 1468 3836 2536 2105 4022 3836
r.npm d.asn n.asn d.gsm n.gsm pt.aa.npm cj d.npm

τὰ τοιαῦτα πράσσοντες ἄξιοι θανάτου εἰσίν, οὐ μόνον
who practice *{the}* such things *who practice* are worthy of death, *are* they not only
4556 4556 3836 5525 4556 1639 545 2505 1639 4472 4024 3667
d.apn r.apn pt.pa.npm a.npm n.gsm v.pai.3p pl adv

NASB

and worshiped and served the creature rather than the Creator, who is blessed forever. Amen.
26 For this reason God gave them over to degrading passions; for their women exchanged the natural function for that which is unnatural, 27 and in the same way also the men abandoned the natural function of the woman and burned in their desire toward one another, men with men committing indecent acts and receiving in their own persons the due penalty of their error.
28 And just as they did not see fit to acknowledge God any longer, God gave them over to a depraved mind, to do those things which are not proper, 29 being filled with all unrighteousness, wickedness, greed, evil; full of envy, murder, strife, deceit, malice; *they are* gossips, 30 slanderers, haters of God, insolent, arrogant, boastful, inventors of evil, disobedient to parents, 31 without understanding, untrustworthy, unloving, unmerciful; 32 and although they know the ordinance of God, that those who practice such things are worthy of death, they not

NIV

continue to do
these very things
but also approve of
those who practice
them.

God's Righteous Judgment

2 You, therefore,
have no ex-
cuse, you who pass
judgment on some-
one else, for at
whatever point you
judge another, you
are condemning
yourself, because
you who pass
judgment do the
same things. [2]Now
we know that
God's judgment
against those who
do such things is
based on truth. [3]So
when you, a mere
human being, pass
judgment on them
and yet do the
same things, do
you think you will
escape God's judg-
ment? [4]Or do you
show contempt for
the riches of his
kindness, forbear-
ance and patience,
not realizing that
God's kindness is
intended to lead
you to repentance?
[5]But because of
your stubbornness
and your unrepen-
tant heart, you are
storing up wrath
against yourself
for the day of
God's wrath, when
his righteous judg-
ment will be re-
vealed. [6]God "will
repay each person
according to what
they have done."[a]
[7]To those who by
persistence in do-
ing good

αὐτὰ ποιοῦσιν ἀλλὰ καὶ συνευδοκοῦσιν τοῖς
continue to do them *they continue to do* but also ⌊to heartily approve of⌋ others
4472 4472 4472 899 4472 247 2779 5306 3836
r.apn.3 v.pai.3p cj adv v.pai.3p d.dpm

πράσσουσιν.
who practice them.
4556
pt.pa.dpm

2:1 διὸ ἀναπολόγητος εἶ, ⌊ὦ ἄνθρωπε πᾶς⌋ ↱ ὁ
Therefore you are without excuse, *you are* whoever you are, when you
1475 1639 1639 406 1639 6043 476 4246 3212 3836
cj a.nsm v.pai.2s j n.vsm a.vsm d.vsm

κρίνων· ἐν ᾧ γὰρ κρίνεις τὸν ἕτερον, σεαυτὸν
judge someone else, for in ⌊that which⌋ *for* you judge *{the}* another, you condemn yourself,
3212 1142 1877 4005 1142 3212 3836 2283 2891 2891 4932
pt.pa.vsm p.d r.dsn cj v.pai.2s d.asm r.asm r.asm.2

κατακρίνεις, τὰ γὰρ αὐτὰ πράσσεις ὁ κρίνων.
you condemn *the* for *same things* *are practicing* you who judge are practicing the same things.
2891 3836 1142 899 4556 3836 3212 4556 4556 3836 899 899
v.pai.2s d.apn cj r.apn v.pai.2s d.nsm pt.pa.nsm

2 οἴδαμεν δὲ ὅτι τὸ κρίμα τοῦ θεοῦ ἐστιν κατὰ ἀλήθειαν
And we know *And* that the judgment of God is ⌊according to⌋ truth
1254 3857 1254 4022 3836 3210 3836 2536 1639 2848 237
v.rai.1p cj cj d.nsn n.nsn d.gsm n.gsm v.pai.3s p.a n.asf

ἐπὶ τοὺς τὰ τοιαῦτα πράσσοντας. 3 λογίζῃ δὲ
⌊with respect to⌋ those who practice *{the}* such things. *who practice* ⌊Do you suppose,⌋ *{and}*
2093 3836 4556 4556 3836 5525 4556 3357 1254
p.a d.apm d.apn r.apn pt.pa.apm v.pmi.2s cj

τοῦτο, ⌊ὦ ἄνθρωπε⌋ ↱ ὁ κρίνων τοὺς τὰ τοιαῦτα
this, whoever you are, when you judge those who practice *{the}* such things
4047 6043 476 3212 3836 3212 3836 4556 4556 3836 5525
r.asn j n.vsm d.vsm pt.pa.vsm d.apm d.apn r.apn

πράσσοντας καὶ ποιῶν αὐτά, ὅτι σὺ ἐκφεύξῃ τὸ κρίμα τοῦ θεοῦ;
who practice yet do them yourself, that you will escape the judgment of God?
4556 2779 4472 899 4022 5148 1767 3836 3210 3836 2536
pt.pa.apm cj pt.pa.vsm r.apn cj r.ns.2 v.fmi.2s d.asn n.asn d.gsm n.gsm

4 ἢ τοῦ πλούτου τῆς χρηστότητος αὐτοῦ καὶ τῆς
Or do you hold in contempt the riches of his kindness *his* and *{the}*
2445 2969 2969 2969 2969 2969 3836 4458 3836 899 5983 899 2779 3836
cj d.gsm n.gsm d.gsf n.gsf r.gsm.3 cj d.gsf

ἀνοχῆς καὶ τῆς μακροθυμίας καταφρονεῖς, ἀγνοῶν ὅτι τὸ
forbearance and *{the}* patience, *do you hold in contempt* not knowing that *{the}* God's
496 2779 3836 3429 2969 51 4022 3836 2536
n.gsf cj d.gsf n.gsf v.pai.2s pt.pa.nsm cj d.nsn

χρηστὸν τοῦ θεοῦ εἰς μετάνοιάν σε ἄγει; 5
kindness *{the}* *God's* is meant to lead you to repentance? *you* *is meant to lead* But
5982 3836 2536 72 72 72 72 5148 1650 3567 5148 72 1254
a.nsn d.gsm n.gsm p.a n.asf r.as.2 v.pai.3s

κατὰ δὲ τὴν σκληρότητά σου καὶ ἀμετανόητον καρδίαν
⌊because of⌋ *But* *{the}* your stubbornness *your* and your unrepentant heart,
2848 1254 3836 5148 5018 5148 2779 295 2840
p.a cj d.asf n.asf r.gs.2 cj a.asf n.asf

θησαυρίζεις σεαυτῷ ὀργὴν ἐν ἡμέρᾳ ὀργῆς καὶ
⌊you are storing up⌋ wrath for yourself *wrath* on the day of wrath, when God's righteous
2564 3973 4932 3973 1877 2465 3973 2779 2536 1464
v.pai.2s r.dsm.2 n.asf p.d n.dsf n.gsf cj

ἀποκαλύψεως δικαιοκρισίας τοῦ θεοῦ 6 ὃς ἀποδώσει ἑκάστῳ
judgment will be revealed, *righteous judgment* *{the}* *God's* who will give to each person
1464 637 1464 3836 2536 4005 625 1667
n.gsf n.gsf d.gsm n.gsm r.nsm v.fai.3s r.dsm

κατὰ τὰ ἔργα αὐτοῦ· 7 τοῖς μὲν καθ᾽ ὑπομονὴν ἔργου
⌊according to⌋ what he has done: *he* to those ~ who by patiently doing good works
2848 3836 899 2240 899 3836 3525 2426 2848 5705 19 2240
p.a d.apn n.apn r.gsm.3 d.dpm pl p.a n.asf n.gsn

NASB

only do the same,
but also give hearty
approval to those
who practice them.

The Impartiality of God

[2:1]Therefore you
have no excuse, ev-
eryone of you who
passes judgment,
for in that which
you judge another,
you condemn your-
self; for you who
judge practice the
same things. [2]And
we know that the
judgment of God
rightly falls upon
those who practice
such things. [3]But
do you suppose
this, O man, when
you pass judg-
ment on those
who practice such
things and do the
same *yourself,* that
you will escape
the judgment of
God? [4]Or do you
think lightly of
the riches of His
kindness and toler-
ance and patience,
not knowing that
the kindness of
God leads you to
repentance? [5]But
because of your
stubbornness and
unrepentant heart
you are storing up
wrath for yourself
in the day of wrath
and revelation
of the righteous
judgment of God,
[6]who WILL RENDER
TO EACH PERSON
ACCORDING TO HIS
DEEDS: [7]to those
who by persever-
ance in doing good

[a] 6 Psalm 62:12; Prov. 24:12

NIV

seek glory, honor
and immortality,
he will give eter-
nal life. [8]But for
those who are self-
seeking and who
reject the truth and
follow evil, there
will be wrath and
anger. [9]There will
be trouble and
distress for every
human being who
does evil: first
for the Jew, then
for the Gentile;
[10]but glory, honor
and peace for ev-
eryone who does
good: first for the
Jew, then for the
Gentile. [11]For God
does not show fa-
voritism.
[12]All who sin
apart from the law
will also perish
apart from the law,
and all who sin un-
der the law will be
judged by the law.
[13]For it is not those
who hear the law
who are righteous
in God's sight,
but it is those who
obey the law who
will be declared
righteous. [14](In-
deed, when Gen-
tiles, who do not
have the law, do by
nature things re-
quired by the law,
they are a law for
themselves, even
though they do
not have the law.
[15]They show that
the requirements
of the law are writ-
ten on their hearts,
their consciences
also bearing wit-
ness, and their
thoughts

ἀγαθοῦ δόξαν καὶ τιμὴν καὶ ἀφθαρσίαν ζητοῦσιν ζωὴν
good seek for glory and honor and immortality, *who seek for* he will give eternal life;
19 2426 2426 1518 2779 5507 2779 914 2426 173 2437
a.gsn n.asf cj n.asf cj n.asf pt.pa.dpm n.asf

αἰώνιον, 8 τοῖς δὲ ⌞ἐξ ἐριθείας⌟ καὶ ἀπειθοῦσι τῇ ἀληθείᾳ
eternal but to those *but* who are self-seeking and do not obey the truth
173 1254 3836 1254 1666 2249 2779 578 3836 237
a.asf d.dpm pl p.g n.gsf cj pt.pa.dpm d.dsf n.dsf

πειθομένοις δὲ τῇ ἀδικίᾳ ὀργὴ καὶ θυμός. 9
but obey *but* *{the}* unrighteousness, there will be wrath and fury. There will be
1254 4275 1254 3836 94 3973 2779 2596
pt.pm.dpm cj d.dsf n.dsf n.nsf cj n.nsm

θλῖψις καὶ στενοχωρία ἐπὶ πᾶσαν ψυχὴν ἀνθρώπου τοῦ κατεργαζομένου
tribulation and distress for every human being *human* who does
2568 2779 5103 2093 4246 476 6034 476 3836 2981
n.nsf cj n.nsf p.a a.asf n.asf n.gsm d.gsm pt.pm.gsm

τὸ κακόν, → Ἰουδαίου τε πρῶτον καὶ → Ἕλληνος, 10 δόξα δὲ
{the} evil, for the Jew ~ first and also for the Greek, but glory *but*
3836 2805 2681 5445 4754 2779 1818 1254 1518 1254
d.asn a.asn a.gsm cj adv cj n.gsm n.nsf cj

καὶ τιμὴ καὶ εἰρήνη παντὶ τῷ ἐργαζομένῳ τὸ ἀγαθόν, → Ἰουδαίῳ τε
and honor and peace for everyone who does *{the}* good, for the Jew ~
2779 5507 2779 1645 4246 3836 2237 3836 19 2681 5445
cj n.nsf cj n.nsf a.dsm d.dsm pt.pm.dsm d.asn a.asn a.dsm cj

πρῶτον καὶ → Ἕλληνι· 11 οὐ γάρ ἐστιν προσωπολημψία παρὰ
first and also for the Greek. For there is no *For* *There is* favoritism with
4754 2779 1818 1142 1639 1639 4024 1142 1639 4721 4123
adv cj n.dsm pl cj v.pai.3s n.nsf p.d

τῷ θεῷ. 12 ὅσοι γὰρ ἀνόμως ἥμαρτον,
{the} God: for all who *for* have sinned ⌞apart from the law⌟ *have sinned* will also perish
3836 2536 1142 4012 1142 279 279 492 279 660 2779 660
d.dsm n.dsm r.npm cj adv v.aai.3p

ἀνόμως καὶ ἀπολοῦνται, καὶ ὅσοι ἐν νόμῳ ἥμαρτον,
⌞apart from the law,⌟ *also* *will perish* and all who have sinned under the law *have sinned* will
492 2779 660 2779 4012 279 279 1877 3795 279 3212
adv adv v.fmi.3p cj r.npm p.d n.dsm v.aai.3p

διὰ νόμου κριθήσονται· 13 οὐ γὰρ οἱ ἀκροαταὶ → νόμου
be judged by the law; *will be judged* for it is not *for* the hearers of the law
3212 3212 1328 3795 3212 1142 4024 1142 3836 212 3795
p.g n.gsm v.fpi.3p pl cj d.npm n.npm n.gsm

δίκαιοι παρὰ τῷ[a] θεῷ, ἀλλ᾽ οἱ ποιηταὶ → νόμου
who are righteous before *{the}* God, but the doers of the law who
1465 4123 3836 2536 247 3836 4475 3795
a.npm p.d d.dsm n.dsm cj d.npm n.npm n.gsm

δικαιωθήσονται. 14 ὅταν γὰρ ἔθνη τὰ μὴ νόμον
will be declared righteous. For whenever *For* the Gentiles, who do not have the law,
1467 1142 4020 1142 1620 3836 2400 3590 2400 3795
v.fpi.3p cj cj n.npn d.npn pl n.asm

ἔχοντα φύσει τὰ τοῦ νόμου ποιῶσιν, οὗτοι νόμον ↱ ↱
do have do by nature ⌞the things⌟ ⌞required by the⌟ law, *do* these, *law* although they
2400 4472 5882 3836 3836 3795 4472 4047 3795 2400 2400
pt.pa.npn n.dsf d.apn d.gsm n.gsm v.pas.3p r.npm n.asm

↱ μὴ ἔχοντες ἑαυτοῖς εἰσιν νόμος· 15 οἵτινες ἐνδείκνυνται
do not have the law, are a law to themselves. *are* *law* They show
2400 3590 2400 3795 1639 3795 1571 1639 3795 4015 1892
pl pt.pa.npm r.dpm.3 v.pai.3p n.nsm r.npm v.pmi.3p

τὸ ἔργον τοῦ νόμου γραπτὸν ἐν ταῖς καρδίαις αὐτῶν,
that the work of the law is written on *{the}* their hearts, *their* their conscience
3836 2240 3836 3795 1209 1877 3836 899 2840 899 899 5287
d.asn n.asn d.gsm n.gsm a.asn p.d d.dpf n.dpf r.gpm.3

συμμαρτυρούσης αὐτῶν τῆς συνειδήσεως καὶ μεταξὺ ἀλλήλων τῶν λογισμῶν
bearing witness *their* *{the}* *conscience* and their conflicting *their* *{the}* thoughts
5210 899 3836 5287 2779 253 3568 253 3836 3361
pt.pa.gsf r.gpm.3 d.gsf n.gsf cj p.g r.gpm d.gpm n.gpm

NASB

seek for glory and
honor and immor-
tality, eternal life;
[8]but to those who
are selfishly ambi-
tious and do not
obey the truth, but
obey unrighteous-
ness, wrath and
indignation. [9]*There*
will be tribulation
and distress for
every soul of man
who does evil, of
the Jew first and
also of the Greek,
[10]but glory and
honor and peace to
everyone who does
good, to the Jew
first and also to the
Greek. [11]For there
is no partiality with
God.
[12]For all who have
sinned without
the Law will also
perish without the
Law, and all who
have sinned under
the Law will be
judged by the Law;
[13]for *it is* not the
hearers of the Law
who are just before
God, but the doers
of the Law will
be justified. [14]For
when Gentiles who
do not have the
Law do instinc-
tively the things of
the Law, these, not
having the Law,
are a law to them-
selves, [15]in that
they show the work
of the Law writ-
ten in their hearts,
their conscience
bearing witness
and their thoughts
alternately

[a] [τῷ] UBS.

NIV

sometimes accus-
ing them and at
other times even
defending them.)
16 This will take
place on the day
when God judges
people's secrets
through Jesus
Christ, as my gos-
pel declares.

The Jews and the Law

17 Now you, if
you call yourself a
Jew; if you rely on
the law and boast
in God; 18 if you
know his will and
approve of what is
superior because
you are instructed
by the law; 19 if you
are convinced that
you are a guide for
the blind, a light
for those who are
in the dark, 20 an
instructor of the
foolish, a teacher
of little children,
because you have
in the law the
embodiment of
knowledge and
truth— 21 you,
then, who teach
others, do you not
teach yourself?
You who preach
against stealing,
do you steal?
22 You who say that
people should not
commit adultery,
do you commit
adultery? You who
abhor idols, do
you rob temples?
23 You who boast
in the law, do you
dishonor God by
breaking the law?
24 As it is written:
"God's name is
blasphemed among
the Gentiles be-
cause of you."[a]
25 Circumcision
has value if you
observe the law,
but if you break
the law, you have
become as though
you had not been
circumcised.

[a] 24 Isaiah 52:5 (see Septuagint); Ezek. 36:20,22

κατηγορούντων ἢ καὶ ἀπολογουμένων, 16 ἐν ἡμέρᾳ ὅτε κρίνει ὁ θεὸς
accusing or else defending them, on the day when God judges {the} God
2989 2445 2779 664 1877 2465 4021 2536 3212 3836 2536
pt.pa.gpm cj adv pt.pm.gpm p.d n.dsf cj v.pai.3s d.nsm n.nsm

τὰ κρυπτὰ τῶν ἀνθρώπων κατὰ τὸ εὐαγγέλιόν μου διὰ Χριστοῦ
the secrets of everyone ⌊according to⌋ {the} my gospel my through Christ
3836 3220 3836 476 2848 3836 1609 2295 1609 1328 5986
d.apn a.apn d.gpm n.gpm p.a d.asn n.asn r.gs.1 p.g n.gsm

Ἰησοῦ.[a] 17 εἰ δὲ σὺ Ἰουδαῖος ἐπονομάζῃ καὶ ἐπαναπαύῃ
Jesus. But if But you call yourself a Jew, call yourself and rely on the
2652 1254 1623 1254 5148 2226 2226 2681 2226 2779 2058
n.gsm cj cj r.ns.2 a.nsm v.ppi.2s cj v.pmi.2s

νόμῳ καὶ καυχᾶσαι ἐν θεῷ 18 καὶ γινώσκεις τὸ θέλημα καὶ δοκιμάζεις τὰ
law, and boast in God, and know his will, and approve the
3795 2779 3016 1877 2536 2779 1182 3836 2525 2779 1507 3836
n.dsm cj v.pmi.2s p.d n.dsm cj v.pai.2s d.asn n.asn cj v.pai.2s d.apn

διαφέροντα κατηχούμενος ἐκ τοῦ νόμου, 19 πέποιθάς τε
things that excel ⌊because you are instructed⌋ by the law, and are convinced and that you
1422 2994 1666 3836 3795 5445 4275 5445
pt.pa.apn pt.pp.nsm p.g d.gsm n.gsm v.rai.2s cj

σεαυτὸν ὁδηγὸν εἶναι → τυφλῶν, φῶς τῶν ἐν σκότει, 20
yourself are a guide are of the blind, a light for those who are in darkness, a
4932 1639 3843 1639 5603 5890 3836 1877 5030
r.asm.2 n.asm f.pa a.gpm n.asn d.gpm p.d n.dsn

παιδευτὴν → ἀφρόνων, διδάσκαλον νηπίων, ἔχοντα τὴν
corrector of the foolish, a teacher of little children, having in the law the
4083 933 1437 3758 2400 1877 3836 3795 3836
n.asm a.gpm n.asm a.gpm pt.pa.asm d.asf

μόρφωσιν τῆς γνώσεως καὶ τῆς ἀληθείας ἐν τῷ νόμῳ· 21 ὁ οὖν διδάσκων
embodiment of knowledge and of truth in the law — you, then, who teach
3673 3836 1194 2779 3836 237 1877 3836 3795 3836 4036 1438
n.asf d.gsf n.gsf cj d.gsf n.gsf p.d d.dsm n.dsm d.vsm cj pt.pa.vsm

ἕτερον σεαυτὸν ↱ ↱ οὐ διδάσκεις; ὁ κηρύσσων μὴ κλέπτειν
others, yourself will you not teach yourself? You who preach against stealing,
2283 4932 1438 1438 4024 1438 4932 3836 3062 3590 3096
r.asm r.asm.2 pl v.pai.2s d.vsm pt.pa.vsm pl f.pa

κλέπτεις; 22 ὁ λέγων μὴ μοιχεύειν μοιχεύεις; ὁ
do you steal? You who tell others not ⌊to commit adultery,⌋ ⌊do you commit adultery?⌋ You
3096 3836 3306 3590 3658 3658 3836
v.pai.2s d.vsm pt.pa.vsm pl f.pa v.pai.2s d.vsm

βδελυσσόμενος τὰ εἴδωλα ἱεροσυλεῖς; 23 ὃς ἐν νόμῳ καυχᾶσαι,
who abhor {the} idols, do you rob temples? You who boast in the law, boast
1009 3836 1631 2644 4005 3016 1877 3795 3016
pt.pm.vsm d.apn n.apn v.pai.2s r.nsm p.d n.dsm v.pmi.2s

διὰ τῆς παραβάσεως τοῦ νόμου τὸν θεὸν ἀτιμάζεις· 24
by your breaking of the law you dishonor {the} God! you dishonor For as it is
1328 3836 4126 3836 3795 869 869 3836 2536 869 1142 2777 1211 1211
p.g d.gsf n.gsf d.gsm n.gsm d.asm n.asm v.pai.2s

τὸ γὰρ ὄνομα τοῦ θεοῦ δι' ὑμᾶς
written, "On account of you the For name of God On account of you
1211 1328 1328 1328 7007 3836 1142 3950 3836 2536 1328 7007
d.nsn cj n.nsn d.gsm n.gsm p.a r.ap.2

βλασφημεῖται ἐν τοῖς ἔθνεσιν, καθὼς γέγραπται. 25
is being blasphemed among the Gentiles." as it is written For to be sure,
1059 1877 3836 1620 2777 1211 1142 3525 3525 3525
v.ppi.3s p.d d.dpn n.dpn cj v.rpi.3s

περιτομὴ μὲν γὰρ ὠφελεῖ ἐὰν νόμον πράσσῃς· ἐὰν δὲ
circumcision to be sure For is of value if you practice the law, you practice but if but you
4364 3525 1142 6067 1569 4556 4556 3795 4556 1254 1569 1254 1639
n.nsf pl cj v.pai.3s cj n.asm v.pas.2s cj cj

παραβάτης → νόμου ἦς, ἡ περιτομή σου ἀκροβυστία
are a transgressor of the law, you are {the} your circumcision your has become uncircumcision.
1639 4127 3795 1639 3836 5148 4364 5148 1181 1181 213
n.nsm n.gsm v.pas.2s d.nsf n.nsf r.gs.2 n.nsf

[a] Ἰησοῦ omitted in TNIV.

NASB

accusing or else
defending them,
16 on the day when,
according to my
gospel, God will
judge the secrets of
men through Christ
Jesus.

The Jew Is Condemned by the Law

17 But if you bear
the name "Jew"
and rely upon the
Law and boast in
God, 18 and know
His will and ap-
prove the things
that are essential,
being instructed
out of the Law,
19 and are confident
that you yourself
are a guide to
the blind, a light
to those who are
in darkness, 20 a
corrector of the
foolish, a teacher
of the immature,
having in the Law
the embodiment
of knowledge
and of the truth,
21 you, therefore,
who teach another,
do you not teach
yourself? You who
preach that one
shall not steal, do
you steal? 22 You
who say that one
should not commit
adultery, do you
commit adultery?
You who abhor
idols, do you rob
temples? 23 You
who boast in the
Law, through your
breaking the Law,
do you dishonor
God? 24 For "THE
NAME OF GOD IS
BLASPHEMED AMONG
THE GENTILES BE-
CAUSE OF YOU," just
as it is written.
25 For indeed
circumcision is of
value if you prac-
tice the Law; but
if you are a trans-
gressor of the Law,
your circumcision
has become uncir-
cumcision. 26 So if

NIV

[26]So then, if those
who are not cir-
cumcised keep
the law's require-
ments, will they
not be regarded
as though they
were circumcised?
[27]The one who is
not circumcised
physically and yet
obeys the law will
condemn you who,
even though you
have the[a] written
code and circum-
cision, are a law-
breaker.
[28]A person is not
a Jew who is one
only outwardly,
nor is circumcision
merely outward
and physical. [29]No,
a person is a Jew
who is one inward-
ly; and circumci-
sion is circumci-
sion of the heart,
by the Spirit, not
by the written
code. Such a per-
son's praise is not
from other people,
but from God.

God's Faithfulness

3 What advan-
tage, then, is
there in being a
Jew, or what value
is there in circum-
cision? [2]Much in
every way! First
of all, the Jews
have been entrust-
ed with the very
words of God.
[3]What if some
were unfaithful?
Will their unfaith-
fulness nullify
God's faithful-
ness? [4]Not at all!
Let God be true,
and every human
being a liar. As it
is written:

"So that you may
be proved
right when

γέγονεν. 26 ἐὰν οὖν ἡ ἀκροβυστία τὰ δικαιώματα
has become Therefore if *Therefore* the ⌊uncircumcised man⌋ keeps the righteous requirements
1181 4036 1569 4036 3836 213 5875 3836 1468
v.rai.3s cj cj d.nsf n.nsf d.apn n.apn

τοῦ νόμου φυλάσσῃ, οὐχ ἡ ἀκροβυστία αὐτοῦ εἰς
of the law, *keeps* will not *{the}* his uncircumcision *his* be counted as
3836 3795 5875 3357 4024 3836 899 213 899 3357 3357 1650
d.gsm n.gsm v.pas.3s pl d.nsf n.nsf r.gsm.3 p.a

περιτομὴν λογισθήσεται; 27 καὶ κρινεῖ ἡ ἐκ φύσεως
circumcision? *will be counted* And *will judge* will not the one who by nature is
4364 3357 2779 3212 3212 3836 5464 5464 1666 5882
n.asf v.fpi.3s cj v.fai.3s d.nsf p.g n.gsf

ἀκροβυστία τὸν νόμον τελοῦσα σὲ τὸν διὰ γράμματος καὶ
uncircumcised yet fulfills the law *one who fulfills* judge you who have the written code and
213 5464 3836 3795 5464 3212 5148 3836 1328 1207 2779
n.nsf d.asm n.asm pt.pa.nsf r.as.2 d.asm p.g n.gsn cj

περιτομῆς παραβάτην → νόμου. 28 οὐ γὰρ ὁ
circumcision yet are a transgressor of the law? For that person is not *For* a Jew who
4364 4127 3795 1142 4024 1142 3836 2681
n.gsf n.asm n.gsm pl cj d.nsm

⌊ἐν τῷ φανερῷ⌋ Ἰουδαῖός ἐστιν οὐδὲ ἡ
is one outwardly, *Jew* *is* nor is *{the}* circumcision that which is
1639 1877 3836 5745 2681 1639 4028 3836 4364
p.d d.dsn a.dsn a.nsm v.pai.3s cj d.nsf

⌊ἐν τῷ φανερῷ⌋ ἐν σαρκὶ περιτομή, 29 ἀλλ' ὁ
outward in the flesh. *circumcision* But a person is a Jew who is one
1877 3836 5745 1877 4922 4364 247 2681 3836
p.d d.dsn a.dsn p.d n.dsf n.nsf cj d.nsm

⌊ἐν τῷ κρυπτῷ⌋ Ἰουδαῖος, καὶ περιτομὴ → καρδίας ἐν
inwardly, *Jew* and circumcision is a matter of the heart, by the
1877 3836 3220 2681 2779 4364 2840 1877
p.d d.dsn a.dsn a.nsm cj n.nsf n.gsf p.d

πνεύματι οὐ → γράμματι, οὗ ὁ ἔπαινος οὐκ ἐξ
Spirit and not by the written code. ⌊That person's⌋ *{the}* praise comes not from
4460 4024 1207 4005 3836 2047 4024 1666
n.dsn pl n.dsn r.gsm d.nsm n.nsm pl p.g

ἀνθρώπων ἀλλ' ἐκ τοῦ θεοῦ.
man but from *{the}* God.
476 247 1666 3836 2536
n.gpm cj p.g d.gsm n.gsm

3:1 τί οὖν τὸ περισσὸν τοῦ Ἰουδαίου ἢ τίς ἡ ὠφέλεια
What advantage then *{the}* *advantage* has the Jew? Or what is the value
5515 4356 4036 3836 4356 3836 2681 2445 5515 3836 6066
r.nsn cj d.nsn a.nsn d.gsm a.gsm cj r.nsf d.nsf n.nsf

τῆς περιτομῆς; 2 πολὺ κατὰ πάντα τρόπον. πρῶτον μὲν γάρ[a] ὅτι
of circumcision? Much in every way. For first of all, ~ *For* *{that}*
3836 4364 4498 2848 4246 5573 1142 4754 3525 1142 4022
d.gsf n.gsf a.nsn p.a a.asm n.asm adv pl cj cj

ἐπιστεύθησαν τὰ λόγια τοῦ θεοῦ. 3 τί γάρ; εἰ ἠπίστησάν
⌊they were entrusted with⌋ the oracles of God. But what *But* if some were unfaithful,
4409 3836 3359 3836 2536 1142 5515 1142 1623 5516 601
v.api.3p d.apn n.apn d.gsm n.gsm r.nsn cj cj v.aai.3p

τινες, μὴ ἡ ἀπιστία αὐτῶν τὴν πίστιν τοῦ θεοῦ καταργήσει;
some *{not}* will *{the}* their lack of faith *their* nullify the faithfulness of God? *will nullify*
5516 3590 2934 3836 899 602 899 2934 3836 4411 3836 2536 2934
r.npm pl d.nsf n.nsf r.gpm.3 d.asf n.asf d.gsm n.gsm v.fai.3s

4 ⌊μὴ γένοιτο⌋ → γινέσθω δὲ ὁ θεὸς ἀληθής, πᾶς δὲ
By no means! Let God be *{and}* *{the}* *God* true and every *and*
3590 1181 2536 1181 1254 3836 2536 239 1254 4246 1254
pl v.amo.3s v.pmm.3s cj d.nsm n.nsm a.nsm a.nsm cj

ἄνθρωπος ψεύστης, καθὼς γέγραπται, ὅπως ↱ ἂν δικαιωθῇς ἐν τοῖς
man a liar. As it is written, "so that you may be justified in *{the}* your
476 6026 2777 1211 3968 1467 323 1467 1877 3836 5148
n.nsm n.nsm cj v.rpi.3s cj pl v.aps.2s p.d d.dpm

NASB

the uncircumcised
man keeps the
requirements of
the Law, will not
his uncircumci-
sion be regarded
as circumcision?
[27]And he who
is physically
uncircumcised, if
he keeps the Law,
will he not judge
you who though
having the letter
of the Law and
circumcision are
a transgressor of
the Law? [28]For he
is not a Jew who is
one outwardly, nor
is circumcision that
which is outward
in the flesh. [29]But
he is a Jew who is
one inwardly; and
circumcision is
that which is of the
heart, by the Spirit,
not by the letter;
and his praise is
not from men, but
from God.

All the World Guilty

[3:1]Then what
advantage has the
Jew? Or what is
the benefit of cir-
cumcision? [2]Great
in every respect.
First of all, that
they were entrusted
with the oracles of
God. [3]What then?
If some did not
believe, their unbe-
lief will not nullify
the faithfulness of
God, will it? [4]May
it never be! Rather,
let God be found
true, though every
man *be found* a
liar, as it is written,
" THAT YOU MAY
BE JUSTIFIED IN

---

[a] 27 Or *who, by means of a*

[a] [γὰρ] UBS, omitted by NET.

NIV

you speak
and prevail
when you
judge."[a]
5 But if our un-
righteousness
brings out God's
righteousness
more clearly, what
shall we say?
That God is un-
just in bringing
his wrath on us?
(I am using a hu-
man argument.)
6 Certainly not! If
that were so, how
could God judge
the world? 7 Some-
one might argue,
"If my falsehood
enhances God's
truthfulness and
so increases his
glory, why am I
still condemned as
a sinner?" 8 Why
not say—as some
slanderously claim
that we say—"Let
us do evil that
good may result"?
Their condemna-
tion is just!

No One Is Righteous

9 What shall we
conclude then?
Do we have any
advantage? Not at
all! For we have
already made the
charge that Jews
and Gentiles alike
are all under the
power of sin. 10 As
it is written:

"There is no one
righteous,
not even one;
11 there is no one
who understands;
there is no one
who seeks
God.
12 All have turned
away,
they have
together
become
worthless;
there is no one
who does
good,
not even

λόγοις σου καὶ νικήσεις ἐν τῷ κρίνεσθαί σε. 5 εἰ δὲ ἡ
words *your* and prevail when *{the}* you are judged." *you* But if *But* *{the}* our
3364 5148 2779 3771 1877 3836 5148 3212 5148 1254 1623 1254 3836 7005
n.dpm r.gs.2 cj v.fai.2s p.d d.dsn f.pp r.as.2 cj cj d.nsf

ἀδικία ἡμῶν θεοῦ δικαιοσύνην συνίστησιν, τί
unrighteousness *our* demonstrates the righteousness of God, *righteousness* *demonstrates* what
94 7005 5319 1466 2536 1466 5319 5515
n.nsf r.gp.1 n.gsm n.asf v.pai.3s r.asn

ἐροῦμεν; μὴ ἄδικος ὁ θεὸς ὁ ἐπιφέρων τὴν ὀργήν; ↱ ↱
shall we say? *{not}* That God is unjust *{the}* *God* *{the}* to inflict *{the}* wrath on us? (I use
3306 3590 2536 96 3836 2536 3836 2214 3836 3973 3306 3306
v.fai.1p pl a.nsm d.nsm n.nsm d.nsm pt.pa.nsm d.asf n.asf

⌊κατὰ ἄνθρωπον⌋ λέγω. 6 ⌊μὴ γένοιτο·⌋ ἐπεὶ πῶς →
a human argument!) By no means! For otherwise how could God
2848 476 3306 3590 1181 2075 4802 2536
p.a n.asm v.pai.1s pl v.amo.3s cj cj

κρινεῖ ὁ θεὸς τὸν κόσμον; 7 εἰ δὲ ἡ ἀλήθεια τοῦ
judge *{the}* *God* the world? But if *But* by my lie *{the}* God's truthfulness *{the}*
3212 3836 2536 3836 3180 1254 1623 1254 1877 1847 6025 3836 2536 237 3836
v.fai.3s d.nsm n.nsm d.asm n.asm cj cj d.nsf n.nsf d.gsm

θεοῦ ἐν τῷ ἐμῷ ψεύσματι ἐπερίσσευσεν εἰς τὴν δόξαν αὐτοῦ, τί
God's *by* *{the}* *my* *lie* abounds to *{the}* his glory, *his* why am I
2536 1877 3836 1847 6025 4355 1650 3836 899 1518 899 5515 3212 2743
n.gsm p.d d.dsn r.dsn.1 n.dsn v.aai.3s p.a d.asf n.asf r.gsm.3 r.asn

ἔτι κἀγὼ ὡς ἁμαρτωλὸς κρίνομαι; 8 καὶ μὴ καθὼς
still *I* being condemned as a sinner? *am being condemned* And why not say (as
2285 2743 3212 3212 6055 283 3212 2779 3590 2777
adv crasis pl a.nsm v.ppi.1s cj pl cj

βλασφημούμεθα καὶ καθώς φασίν τινες ἡμᾶς λέγειν ὅτι ποιήσωμεν τὰ
some slanderously *{and}* *{as}* claim *some* that we are saying), ~ "Let us do *{the}*
5516 1059 2779 2777 5774 5516 7005 3306 4022 4472 3836
v.ppi.1p cj cj v.pai.3p r.npm r.ap.1 f.pa cj v.aas.1p d.apn

κακά, ἵνα ἔλθῃ τὰ ἀγαθά; ὧν τὸ κρίμα ἔνδικόν
evil so that good ⌊may come⌋ *{the}* *good* of it"? Their *{the}* condemnation is well deserved!
2805 2671 19 2262 3836 19 4005 3836 3210 1639 1899
a.apn cj v.aas.3s d.npn a.npn r.gpm d.nsn n.nsn a.nsn

ἐστιν. 9 τί οὖν; προεχόμεθα; οὐ πάντως· προῃτιασάμεθα γὰρ
is What then? ⌊Are we better off?⌋ Not at all, for we have already charged *for* that both
1639 5515 4036 4604 4024 4122 1142 4577 1142 5445
v.pai.3s r.nsn cj v.pmi.1p pl adv v.ami.1p cj

Ἰουδαίους τε καὶ Ἕλληνας πάντας ὑφ᾽ ἁμαρτίαν εἶναι, 10 καθὼς
Jews *both* and Greeks are all under the power of sin, *are* as
2681 5445 2779 1818 1639 4246 5679 281 1639 2777
a.apm cj cj n.apm a.apm p.a n.asf f.pa cj

γέγραπται ὅτι οὐκ ἔστιν δίκαιος οὐδὲ εἷς, 11 οὐκ ἔστιν ὁ συνίων, οὐκ
it is written, ~ "No one is righteous, not even one; no one is *{the}* understanding; no
1211 4022 4024 1639 1465 4028 1651 4024 1639 3836 5317 4024
v.rpi.3s cj pl v.pai.3s a.nsm adv a.nsm pl v.pai.3s d.nsm pt.pa.nsm pl

ἔστιν ὁ ἐκζητῶν τὸν θεόν. 12 ↱ ↱ πάντες ἐξέκλιναν ἅμα
one is *{the}* seeking for *{the}* God. They have all turned away; together
1639 3836 1699 3836 2536 1712 1712 4246 1712 275
v.pai.3s d.nsm pt.pa.nsm d.asm n.asm a.npm v.aai.3p adv

ἠχρεώθησαν· οὐκ ἔστιν ὁ ποιῶν χρηστότητα, [a]οὐκ ἔστιν ἕως
⌊they have become worthless.⌋ No one is *{the}* doing good, there is not *there is* even
946 4024 1639 3836 4472 5983 1639 1639 4024 1639 2401
v.api.3p pl v.pai.3s d.nsm pt.pa.nsm n.asf pl v.pai.3s p.g

NASB

YOUR WORDS,
AND PREVAIL
WHEN YOU ARE
JUDGED."
5 But if our un-
righteousness
demonstrates the
righteousness of
God, what shall we
say? The God who
inflicts wrath is
not unrighteous, is
He? (I am speaking
in human terms.)
6 May it never be!
For otherwise, how
will God judge
the world? 7 But
if through my lie
the truth of God
abounded to His
glory, why am I
also still being
judged as a sinner?
8 And why not *say*
(as we are slander-
ously reported and
as some claim that
we say), "Let us do
evil that good may
come"? Their con-
demnation is just.
9 What then? Are
we better than
they? Not at all; for
we have already
charged that both
Jews and Greeks
are all under sin;
10 as it is written,
"THERE IS NONE
RIGHTEOUS,
NOT EVEN ONE;
11 THERE IS NONE
WHO UNDER-
STANDS,
THERE IS NONE
WHO SEEKS
FOR GOD;
12 ALL HAVE
TURNED ASIDE,
TOGETHER
THEY HAVE BE-
COME USELESS;
THERE IS NONE
WHO DOES
GOOD,
THERE IS NOT
EVEN ONE."

[a] 4 Psalm 51:4

[a] [οὐκ ἔστιν] UBS.

NIV

one."[a]
13 "Their throats
are open
graves;
their tongues
practice deceit."[b]
"The poison of
vipers is on
their lips."[c]
14 "Their mouths
are full of
cursing and
bitterness."[d]
15 "Their feet are
swift to
shed blood;
16 ruin and
misery mark
their ways,
17 and the way of
peace they do
not know."[e]
18 "There is no
fear of God
before their
eyes."[f]
19 Now we know
that whatever the
law says, it says to
those who are un-
der the law, so that
every mouth may
be silenced and the
whole world held
accountable to God.
20 Therefore no one
will be declared
righteous in God's
sight by the works
of the law; rather,
through the law we
become conscious
of our sin.

Righteousness Through Faith

21 But now apart
from the law the
righteousness of
God has been made
known, to which the
Law and the Proph-
ets testify. 22 This
righteousness is giv-
en through faith in[g]
Jesus Christ to all
who believe. There
is no difference be-
tween Jew and Gen-
tile, 23 for all have
sinned and fall short
of the glory of God,
24 and all are justi-
fied freely by his

[a] 12 Psalms 14:1-3; 53:1-3; Eccles. 7:20
[b] 13 Psalm 5:9
[c] 13 Psalm 140:3
[d] 14 Psalm 10:7 (see Septuagint)
[e] 17 Isaiah 59:7,8
[f] 18 Psalm 36:1
[g] 22 Or *through the faithfulness of*

ἑνός. 13 τάφος ἀνεῳγμένος ὁ λάρυγξ αὐτῶν, ταῖς γλώσσαις
one. Their throat is an open grave; *open* *{the}* *throat* *Their* with their tongues
1651 899 3296 487 5439 487 3836 3296 899 3836 899 1185
a.gsm n.nsm pt.rp.nsm d.nsm n.nsm r.gpm.3 d.dpf n.dpf

αὐτῶν ἐδολιοῦσαν, ἰὸς ἀσπίδων ὑπὸ τὰ χείλη αὐτῶν· 14 ὧν τὸ
their they deceive; the poison of asps is under *{the}* their lips; *their* their *{the}*
899 1514 2675 835 5679 3836 899 5927 899 4005 3836
r.gpm.3 v.iai.3p n.nsm n.gpf p.a d.apn n.apn r.gpm.3 r.gpm d.nsn

στόμα ἀρᾶς καὶ πικρίας γέμει, 15 ὀξεῖς οἱ πόδες αὐτῶν
mouth is full of cursing and bitterness; *is full of* *swift* *{the}* their feet *their* are swift
5125 1154 1154 1154 725 2779 4394 1154 3955 3836 899 4546 899 3955
n.nsn n.gsf cj n.gsf v.pai.3s a.npm d.npm n.npm r.gpm.3

ἐκχέαι αἷμα, 16 σύντριμμα καὶ ταλαιπωρία ἐν ταῖς ὁδοῖς αὐτῶν, 17 καὶ
to shed blood; destruction and misery are in *{the}* their paths; *their* and the
1772 135 5342 2779 5416 1877 3836 899 3847 899 2779
f.aa n.asn n.nsn cj n.nsf p.d d.dpf n.dpf r.gpm.3 cj

ὁδὸν εἰρήνης ↱ ↱ οὐκ ἔγνωσαν. 18 οὐκ ἔστιν φόβος θεοῦ ἀπέναντι
way of peace they have not known. There is no *There is* fear of God before
3847 1645 1182 1182 4024 1182 1639 1639 4024 1639 5832 2536 595
n.asf n.gsf pl v.aai.3p pl v.pai.3s n.nsm n.gsm p.g

τῶν ὀφθαλμῶν αὐτῶν 19 οἴδαμεν δὲ ὅτι ὅσα ὁ νόμος λέγει
{the} their eyes." *their* Now we know *Now* that whatever the law says, it
3836 899 4057 899 1254 3857 1254 4022 4012 3836 3795 3306 3281
d.gpm n.gpm r.gpm.3 v.rai.1p cj cj r.apn d.nsm n.nsm v.pai.3s

τοῖς ἐν τῷ νόμῳ λαλεῖ, ἵνα πᾶν στόμα φραγῇ καὶ
speaks to those who are under the law, *it says* so that every mouth ⌊may be silenced⌋ and the
3281 3836 1877 3836 3795 3281 2671 4246 5125 5852 2779 3836
d.dpm p.d d.dsm n.dsm v.pai.3s cj a.nsn n.nsn v.aps.3s cj

ὑπόδικος γένηται πᾶς ὁ κόσμος τῷ θεῷ· 20 διότι ἐξ
whole world may be held accountable *may be* *whole* *the* *world* to God. So by the
4246 3180 1181 1181 5688 1181 4246 3836 3180 3836 2536 1484 1666
a.nsm v.ams.3s a.nsm d.nsm n.nsm d.dsm n.dsm cj p.g

ἔργων → νόμου οὐ δικαιωθήσεται πᾶσα σὰρξ ἐνώπιον αὐτοῦ,
works of the law no flesh at all will be justified *at all* *flesh* before him, because
2240 3795 4024 4922 4246 4246 1467 4246 4922 1967 899 1142
n.gpn n.gsm pl v.fpi.3s a.nsf n.nsf p.g r.gsm.3

διὰ γὰρ νόμου ἐπίγνωσις ἁμαρτίας. 21 νυνὶ δὲ χωρὶς
through *because* the law comes the knowledge of sin. But now, *But* apart from the
1328 1142 3795 2106 281 1254 3815 1254 6006
p.g cj n.gsm n.nsf n.gsf adv cj p.g

νόμου δικαιοσύνη θεοῦ
law (although attested by the law and the prophets) the righteousness of God
3795 3455 3455 5679 3836 3795 2779 3836 4737 1466 2536
n.gsm n.nsf n.gsm

πεφανέρωται μαρτυρουμένη ὑπὸ τοῦ νόμου καὶ τῶν προφητῶν, 22
has been disclosed. *although attested* *by* *the* *law* *and* *the* *prophets* It is the
5746 3455 5679 3836 3795 2779 3836 4737
v.rpi.3s pt.pp.nsf p.g d.gsm n.gsm cj d.gpm n.gpm

δικαιοσύνη δὲ θεοῦ διὰ πίστεως → Ἰησοῦ Χριστοῦ εἰς πάντας τοὺς
righteousness *{and}* of God available through faith in Jesus Christ for all who
1466 1254 2536 1328 4411 2652 5986 1650 4246 3836
n.nsf cj n.gsm p.g n.gsf n.gsm n.gsm p.a a.apm d.apm

πιστεύοντας. οὐ γάρ ἐστιν διαστολή, 23 πάντες γὰρ ἥμαρτον
believe. (For there is no *For* *there is* distinction, since all *since* have sinned
4409 1142 1639 1639 4024 1142 1639 1405 1142 4246 1142 279
pt.pa.apm pl cj v.pai.3s n.nsf a.npm cj v.aai.3p

καὶ ὑστεροῦνται τῆς δόξης τοῦ θεοῦ 24 δικαιούμενοι δωρεὰν τῇ αὐτοῦ
and ⌊continue to fall short⌋ of the glory of God.) They are justified freely by his
2779 5728 3836 1518 3836 2536 1467 1562 3836 899
cj v.pmi.3p d.gsf n.gsf d.gsm n.gsm pt.pp.npm adv d.dsf r.gsm.3

NASB

13 "THEIR THROAT
IS AN OPEN
GRAVE,
WITH THEIR
TONGUES THEY
KEEP DECEIV-
ING,"
"THE POISON OF
ASPS IS UNDER
THEIR LIPS";
14 "WHOSE MOUTH
IS FULL OF
CURSING AND
BITTERNESS";
15 "THEIR FEET ARE
SWIFT TO SHED
BLOOD,
16 DESTRUCTION
AND MISERY
ARE IN THEIR
PATHS,
17 AND THE PATH
OF PEACE THEY
HAVE NOT
KNOWN."
18 "THERE IS NO
FEAR OF GOD
BEFORE THEIR
EYES."
19 Now we know
that whatever the
Law says, it speaks
to those who are
under the Law, so
that every mouth
may be closed and
all the world may
become account-
able to God; 20 be-
cause by the works
of the Law no flesh
will be justified
in His sight; for
through the Law
comes the knowl-
edge of sin.

Justification by Faith

21 But now apart
from the Law *the*
righteousness
of God has been
manifested, be-
ing witnessed by
the Law and the
Prophets, 22 even *the*
righteousness of
God through faith
in Jesus Christ
for all those who
believe; for there is
no distinction; 23 for
all have sinned and
fall short of the
glory of God, 24 be-
ing justified as a

NIV

grace through the
redemption that
came by Christ
Jesus. 25 God pre-
sented Christ as a
sacrifice of atone-
ment,[a] through the
shedding of his
blood—to be re-
ceived by faith. He
did this to demon-
strate his righteous-
ness, because in his
forbearance he had
left the sins com-
mitted beforehand
unpunished— 26 he
did it to demonstrate
his righteousness
at the present time,
so as to be just and
the one who justi-
fies those who have
faith in Jesus.
27 Where, then,
is boasting? It is
excluded. Because
of what law? The
law that requires
works? No, because
of the law that re-
quires faith. 28 For
we maintain that a
person is justified
by faith apart from
the works of the
law. 29 Or is God the
God of Jews only?
Is he not the God of
Gentiles too? Yes,
of Gentiles too,
30 since there is only
one God, who will
justify the circum-
cised by faith and
the uncircumcised
through that same
faith. 31 Do we, then,
nullify the law by
this faith? Not at
all! Rather, we up-
hold the law.

Abraham Justified by Faith

4 What then
shall we say
that Abraham, our
forefather accord-
ing to the flesh,
discovered in this
matter? 2 If, in fact,
Abraham was jus-
tified by

[a] 25 The Greek for *sacrifice of atonement* refers to the atonement cover on the ark of the covenant (see Lev. 16:15,16).

χάριτι διὰ τῆς ἀπολυτρώσεως τῆς ἐν Χριστῷ Ἰησοῦ. 25 ὃν προέθετο
grace through the redemption that is in Christ Jesus, whom God set forth
5921 1328 3836 667 3836 1877 5986 2652 4005 2536 4729
n.dsf p.g d.gsf n.gsf d.gsf p.d n.dsm n.dsm r.asm v.ami.3s

ὁ θεὸς ἱλαστήριον διὰ τῆς[a] πίστεως ἐν τῷ
{the} *God* as an atoning sacrifice by his blood, obtainable through *{the}* faith. *by* *{the}*
3836 2536 2663 1877 899 135 1328 3836 4411 1877 3836
d.nsm n.nsm n.asn p.g d.gsf n.gsf p.d d.dsn

αὐτοῦ αἵματι εἰς ἔνδειξιν τῆς δικαιοσύνης αὐτοῦ διὰ
his *blood* This was to demonstrate *{the}* his righteousness, *his* because God in his
899 135 1650 1893 3836 899 1466 899 1328
r.gsm.3 n.dsn p.a n.asf d.gsf n.gsf r.gsm.3 p.a

τὴν πάρεσιν τῶν προγεγονότων ἁμαρτημάτων 26 ἐν τῇ ἀνοχῇ
forbearance *{the}* ⌊had passed over⌋ *{the}* previous sins. *{the}*
3836 4217 3836 4588 280 1877 3836 496
d.asf n.asf d.gpn pt.ra.gpn n.gpn p.d d.dsf n.dsf

τοῦ θεοῦ, πρὸς τὴν ἔνδειξιν τῆς δικαιοσύνης αὐτοῦ ἐν τῷ νῦν
{the} It was also to *{the}* demonstrate *{the}* his righteousness *his* at the present
3836 2536 4639 3836 1893 3836 899 1466 899 1877 3836 3814
d.gsm n.gsm p.a d.asf n.asf d.gsf n.gsf r.gsm.3 p.d d.dsm adv

καιρῷ, εἰς τὸ εἶναι αὐτὸν δίκαιον καὶ δικαιοῦντα τὸν ἐκ
time, that *{the}* he ⌊might be⌋ *he* just and the justifier of ⌊the one⌋ who has
2789 1650 3836 899 1639 899 1465 2779 1467 3836 1666
n.dsm p.a d.asn f.pa r.asm.3 n.asm cj pt.pa.asm d.asm p.g

πίστεως Ἰησοῦ. 27 ποῦ οὖν ἡ καύχησις; ἐξεκλείσθη. διὰ ποίου νόμου;
faith in Jesus. Where then is *{the}* boasting? It has been excluded. By what kind of law?
4411 2652 4543 4036 3836 3018 1710 1328 4481 3795
n.gsf n.gsm cj cj d.nsf n.nsf v.api.3s p.g r.gsm n.gsm

τῶν ἔργων; οὐχί, ἀλλὰ διὰ νόμου πίστεως. 28 λογιζόμεθα γὰρ
By a law of works? No, but by the law of faith. For we hold *For* that a
3836 2240 4049 247 1328 3795 4411 1142 3357 1142
d.gpn n.gpn pl cj p.g n.gsm n.gsf v.pmi.1p cj

δικαιοῦσθαι πίστει ἄνθρωπον χωρὶς ἔργων → νόμου. 29 ἢ
person is justified by faith *person* apart from the works of the law. Or is God the
476 1467 4411 476 6006 2240 3795 2445 3836
f.pp n.dsf n.asm p.g n.gpn n.gsm cj

Ἰουδαίων ὁ θεὸς μόνον; οὐχὶ καὶ ἐθνῶν; ναὶ
God of Jews *the* *God* only? Is he not the God of Gentiles as well? *of Gentiles* Yes, of
2536 2681 3836 2536 3667 4049 1620 1620 2779 1620 3721 1620
a.gpm d.nsm n.nsm adv pl adv n.gpn pl

καὶ ἐθνῶν, 30 εἴπερ εἷς ὁ θεὸς ὃς δικαιώσει περιτομὴν
Gentiles as well. *of Gentiles* Since God is one, *{the}* *God* he will justify the circumcised
1620 2779 1620 1642 2536 1651 3836 2536 4005 1467 4364
adv n.gpn cj a.nsm d.nsm n.nsm r.nsm v.fai.3s n.asf

ἐκ πίστεως καὶ ἀκροβυστίαν διὰ τῆς πίστεως. 31
⌊on the basis of⌋ their faith and the uncircumcised by the same faith. Do we
1666 4411 2779 213 1328 3836 4411 2934 2934
p.g n.gsf cj n.asf p.g d.gsf n.gsf

νόμον οὖν καταργοῦμεν διὰ τῆς πίστεως; μὴ
therefore nullify the law *therefore* *Do we nullify* through *{the}* faith? By no means!
4036 2934 3795 4036 2934 1328 3836 4411 3590
n.asm cj v.pai.1p p.g d.gsf n.gsf pl

γένοιτο·⌋ ἀλλὰ νόμον ἱστάνομεν.
⌊On the contrary,⌋ we uphold the law. *we uphold*
1181 247 2705 2705 3795 2705
v.amo.3s cj n.asm v.pai.1p

4:1 τί οὖν ἐροῦμεν εὑρηκέναι Ἀβραὰμ τὸν προπάτορα ἡμῶν
What then ⌊shall we say⌋ *has discovered* that Abraham, *{the}* our forefather *our*
5515 4036 3306 2351 11 3836 7005 4635 7005
r.asn cj v.fai.1p f.ra n.asm d.asm n.asm r.gp.1

κατὰ σάρκα; 2 εἰ γὰρ Ἀβραὰμ ἐξ
⌊according to⌋ the flesh, has discovered about this? For if *For* Abraham was justified by
2848 4922 2351 2351 1142 1623 1142 11 1467 1467 1666
p.a n.asf cj cj n.nsm p.g

[a] [τῆς] UBS, omitted by TNIV.

NASB

gift by His
grace through
the redemption
which is in Christ
Jesus; 25 whom God
displayed publicly
as a propitiation in
His blood through
faith. *This was* to
demonstrate His
righteousness,
because in the
forbearance of God
He passed over
the sins previously
committed; 26 for
the demonstra-
tion, *I say,* of His
righteousness at
the present time, so
that He would be
just and the justi-
fier of the one who
has faith in Jesus.
27 Where then
is boasting? It is
excluded. By what
kind of law? Of
works? No, but by
a law of faith. 28 For
we maintain that
a man is justified
by faith apart from
works of the Law.
29 Or is God *the God*
of Jews only? Is
He not *the God* of
Gentiles also? Yes,
of Gentiles also,
30 since indeed God
who will justify
the circumcised by
faith and the uncir-
cumcised through
faith is one.
31 Do we then
nullify the Law
through faith? May
it never be! On the
contrary, we estab-
lish the Law.

Justification by Faith Evidenced in Old Testament

4:1 What then shall
we say that Abra-
ham, our forefather
according to the
flesh, has found?
2 For if Abraham
was justified by

NIV

works, he had
something to boast
about—but not
before God. ³What
does Scripture say?
"Abraham believed
God, and it was
credited to him as
righteousness."[a]
⁴Now to the one
who works, wages
are not credit-
ed as a gift but
as an obligation.
⁵However, to the
one who does not
work but trusts
God who justifies
the ungodly, their
faith is credited
as righteousness.
⁶David says the
same thing when
he speaks of the
blessedness of the
one to whom God
credits righteous-
ness apart from
works:

⁷"Blessed are those whose transgressions are forgiven, whose sins are covered.
⁸Blessed is the one whose sin the Lord will never count against them."[b]

⁹Is this blessed-
ness only for the
circumcised, or
also for the un-
circumcised? We
have been saying
that Abraham's
faith was credited
to him as righ-
teousness. ¹⁰Under
what circumstanc-
es was it credited?
Was it after he was
circumcised, or
before? It was not
after, but before!
¹¹And he received
circumcision as a
sign, a seal of the
righteousness that
he had by faith
while he was still
uncircumcised. So
then, he is the fa-
ther of all who

[a] 3 Gen. 15:6; also in verse 22
[b] 8 Psalm 32:1,2

ἔργων ἐδικαιώθη, ἔχει καύχημα, ἀλλ᾽ οὐ πρὸς θεόν. ³ τί γὰρ ↱
works, *was justified* he has ⌊something to boast about⌋ (but not before God). For what *For* does
2240 1467 2400 3017 247 4024 4639 2536 1142 5515 1142 3306
n.gpn v.api.3s v.pai.3s n.asn cj pl p.a n.asm r.asn cj

ἡ γραφὴ λέγει; ἐπίστευσεν δὲ Ἀβραὰμ τῷ θεῷ καὶ ἐλογίσθη
the scripture say? "And Abraham believed *And Abraham {the}* God, and it was credited
3836 1210 3306 1254 11 4409 1254 11 3836 2536 2779 3357
d.nsf n.nsf v.pai.3s v.aai.3s cj n.nsm d.dsm n.dsm cj v.api.3s

αὐτῷ εἰς δικαιοσύνην. ⁴ τῷ δὲ ἐργαζομένῳ ὁ μισθὸς ↱ οὐ λογίζεται
to him as righteousness." Now ⌊to the⌋ *Now* one who works, his wages are not credited
899 1650 1466 1254 3836 1254 2237 3836 3635 3357 4024 3357
r.dsm.3 p.a n.asf d.dsm cj pt.pm.dsm d.nsm n.nsm pl v.ppi.3s

κατὰ χάριν ἀλλὰ κατὰ ὀφείλημα, ⁵ τῷ δὲ ↱ ↱ ↱ μὴ ἐργαζομένῳ
as a gift, but as an obligation. But ⌊to the⌋ *But* one who does not work,
2848 5921 247 2848 4052 1254 3836 1254 2237 2237 2237 3590 2237
p.a n.asf cj p.a n.asn d.dsm cj pl pt.pm.dsm

πιστεύοντι δὲ ἐπὶ τὸν δικαιοῦντα τὸν ἀσεβῆ λογίζεται ἡ
but entrusts himself *but* to the one who justifies the ungodly, his faith is credited *{the}*
1254 4409 1254 2093 3836 1467 3836 815 899 4411 3357 3836
pt.pa.dsm cj p.a d.asm pt.pa.asm d.asm a.asm v.ppi.3s d.nsf

πίστις αὐτοῦ εἰς δικαιοσύνην· ⁶καθάπερ καὶ Δαυὶδ λέγει τὸν μακαρισμὸν
faith his as righteousness. So also David ⌊speaks of⌋ the blessedness
4411 899 1650 1466 2749 2779 1253 3306 3836 3422
n.nsf r.gsm.3 p.a n.asf cj adv n.nsm v.pai.3s d.asm n.asm

τοῦ ἀνθρώπου ᾧ ὁ θεὸς λογίζεται δικαιοσύνην χωρὶς ἔργων·
of the one ⌊to whom⌋ *{the}* God credits righteousness apart from works:
3836 476 4005 3836 2536 3357 1466 6006 2240
d.gsm n.gsm r.dsm d.nsm n.nsm v.pmi.3s n.asf p.g n.gpn

⁷μακάριοι ὧν ἀφέθησαν αἱ ἀνομίαι καὶ ὧν
"Blessed are those whose lawless deeds are forgiven, *{the} lawless deeds* and whose sins
3421 4005 490 490 918 3836 490 2779 4005 281
a.npm r.gpm v.api.3p d.npf n.npf cj r.gpm

ἐπεκαλύφθησαν αἱ ἁμαρτίαι· ⁸μακάριος ἀνὴρ οὗ ↱ ⌊οὐ μὴ⌋
are covered. *{the} sins* Blessed is the man whose sin the Lord will not
2128 3836 281 3421 467 4005 281 3261 3357 4024 3590
v.api.3p d.npf n.npf a.nsm n.nsm r.gsm pl pl

λογίσηται κύριος ἁμαρτίαν. ⁹ὁ μακαρισμὸς οὖν οὗτος ἐπὶ
take into account." *Lord sin {the} blessedness* Therefore, is this blessedness for
3357 3261 281 3836 3422 4036 4047 3422 2093
v.ams.3s n.nsm n.asf d.nsm n.nsm cj r.nsm p.a

τὴν περιτομὴν ἢ καὶ ἐπὶ τὴν ἀκροβυστίαν; λέγομεν γάρ, ἐλογίσθη
the circumcised alone, or is it also for the uncircumcised? For we say, *For was credited*
3836 4364 2445 2779 2093 3836 213 1142 3306 1142 3357
d.asf n.asf cj adv p.a d.asf n.asf v.pai.1p cj v.api.3s

τῷ Ἀβραὰμ ἡ πίστις εἰς δικαιοσύνην. ¹⁰πῶς οὖν ἐλογίσθη;
"It was to Abraham that faith was credited as righteousness." How then was it credited
3836 11 3836 4411 3357 3357 1650 1466 4802 4036 3357
d.dsm n.dsm d.nsf n.nsf p.a n.asf cj cj v.api.3s

ἐν περιτομῇ ὄντι ἢ ⌊ἐν ἀκροβυστίᾳ;⌋ οὐκ ἐν
to him? Was it after he was circumcised *he was* or before? It was not after
1877 1639 1639 4364 1639 2445 1877 213 4024 1877
p.d n.dsf pt.pa.dsm cj p.d n.dsf pl p.d

περιτομῇ ἀλλ᾽ ⌊ἐν ἀκροβυστίᾳ·⌋ ¹¹καὶ σημεῖον ἔλαβεν
his circumcision but before. *{and}* He received the sign *He received*
4364 247 1877 213 2779 3284 3284 4956 3284
n.dsf cj p.d n.dsf cj n.asn v.aai.3s

περιτομῆς σφραγῖδα τῆς δικαιοσύνης τῆς πίστεως τῆς
of circumcision as a seal of the righteousness that he had by faith *{the}* while he was
4364 5382 3836 1466 3836 4411 3836
n.gsf n.asf d.gsf n.gsf d.gsf n.gsf d.gsf

ἐν τῇ ἀκροβυστίᾳ, εἰς τὸ εἶναι αὐτὸν πατέρα πάντων τῶν
still *{the}* uncircumcised, ⌊so that⌋ ~ he ⌊would be⌋ *he* the father of all who
1877 3836 213 1650 3836 899 1639 899 4252 4246 3836
p.d d.dsf n.dsf p.a d.asn f.pa r.asm.3 n.asm a.gpm d.gpm

NASB

works, he has
something to
boast about, but
not before God.
³For what does
the Scripture
say? "ABRAHAM
BELIEVED GOD, AND
IT WAS CREDITED TO
HIM AS RIGHTEOUS-
NESS." ⁴Now to the
one who works,
his wage is not
credited as a favor,
but as what is due.
⁵But to the one who
does not work,
but believes in
Him who justifies
the ungodly, his
faith is credited
as righteousness,
⁶just as David also
speaks of the bless-
ing on the man to
whom God credits
righteousness apart
from works:

⁷"BLESSED ARE THOSE WHOSE LAWLESS DEEDS HAVE BEEN FORGIVEN,
AND WHOSE SINS HAVE BEEN COVERED.
⁸"BLESSED IS THE MAN WHOSE SIN THE LORD WILL NOT TAKE INTO ACCOUNT."

⁹Is this bless-
ing then on the
circumcised, or on
the uncircumcised
also? For we say,
"FAITH WAS CRED-
ITED TO ABRAHAM
AS RIGHTEOUSNESS."
¹⁰How then was it
credited? While he
was circumcised,
or uncircumcised?
Not while circum-
cised, but while
uncircumcised;
¹¹and he received
the sign of circum-
cision, a seal of the
righteousness of
the faith which he
had while uncir-
cumcised, so that
he might be the
father of all who

NIV

believe but have
not been circum-
cised, in order
that righteousness
might be credited
to them. 12 And he
is then also the fa-
ther of the circum-
cised who not only
are circumcised but
who also follow
in the footsteps of
the faith that our
father Abraham
had before he was
circumcised.
13 It was not
through the law
that Abraham and
his offspring re-
ceived the promise
that he would be
heir of the world,
but through the
righteousness that
comes by faith.
14 For if those who
depend on the law
are heirs, faith
means nothing
and the prom-
ise is worthless,
15 because the law
brings wrath. And
where there is no
law there is no
transgression.
16 Therefore, the
promise comes by
faith, so that it may
be by grace and
may be guaranteed
to all Abraham's
offspring—not
only to those who
are of the law but
also to those who
have the faith of
Abraham. He is
the father of us all.
17 As it is written:
"I have made you a
father of many na-
tions."[a] He is our
father in the sight
of God, in whom
he believed—the
God who gives
life to

πιστευόντων ⌞δι᾽ ἀκροβυστίας,⌟ εἰς τὸ → → →
believe but have never been circumcised, that ~ they too might have
4409 1328 213 1650 3836 2779
pt.pa.gpm p.g n.gsf p.a d.asn

λογισθῆναι καὶ[a] αὐτοῖς τὴν[b] δικαιοσύνην, 12 καὶ πατέρα →
righteousness credited *too* to them. *{the}* *righteousness* He is also the father of the
1466 3357 2779 899 3836 1466 2779 4252
f.ap adv r.dpm.3 d.asf n.asf cj n.asm

περιτομῆς τοῖς οὐκ ἐκ περιτομῆς μόνον ἀλλὰ καὶ τοῖς στοιχοῦσιν τοῖς
circumcised who are not merely *{of}* circumcised *merely* but also *{the}* walk in the
4364 3836 4024 3667 1666 4364 3667 247 2779 3836 5123 3836
n.gsf d.dpm pl p.g n.gsf adv cj adv d.dpm pt.pa.dpm d.dpn

ἴχνεσιν τῆς ἐν ἀκροβυστίᾳ πίστεως τοῦ πατρὸς ἡμῶν Ἀβραάμ.
footsteps of the *still* *uncircumcised* faith that *{the}* our father *our* Abraham had while
2717 3836 1877 213 4411 3836 7005 4252 7005 11
n.dpn d.gsf p.d n.dsf n.gsf d.gsm n.gsm r.gp.1 n.gsm

13 οὐ γὰρ διὰ νόμου ἡ ἐπαγγελία
he was still uncircumcised. *not* For *through* *law* the promise that he would be heir
1877 213 4024 1142 1328 3795 3836 2039 899 1639 1639 3101
pl cj p.g n.gsm d.nsf n.nsf

τῷ Ἀβραὰμ ἢ τῷ σπέρματι αὐτοῦ,
of the world did not come to Abraham or to his descendants *his* through the law,
3180 3180 4024 3836 11 2445 3836 899 5065 899 1328 3795
d.dsm n.dsm cj d.dsn n.dsn r.gsm.3

τὸ κληρονόμον αὐτὸν εἶναι κόσμου, ἀλλὰ διὰ δικαιοσύνης πίστεως. 14
{the} *heir* *he* *would be* *of world* but through the righteousness of faith. For
3836 3101 899 1639 3180 247 1328 1466 4411 1142
d.nsn n.nsn r.asm.3 f.pa n.gsm cj p.g n.gsf n.gsf

εἰ γὰρ οἱ ἐκ νόμου κληρονόμοι, κεκένωται ἡ
if *For* the heirs are those who follow the law, *heirs* then faith is meaningless *{the}*
1623 1142 3836 3101 1666 3795 3101 4411 3033 3836
cj cj d.npm p.g n.gsm n.npm v.rpi.3s d.nsf

πίστις καὶ κατήργηται ἡ ἐπαγγελία· 15 ὁ γὰρ νόμος
faith and the promise is void. *the* *promise* For the *For* Law brings about
4411 2779 3836 2039 2934 3836 2039 1142 3836 1142 3795 2981 2981
n.nsf cj v.rpi.3s d.nsf n.nsf d.nsm cj n.nsm

ὀργὴν κατεργάζεται· οὗ δὲ οὐκ ἔστιν νόμος οὐδὲ
wrath, *brings about* but where *but* there is no *there is* law, there can be no
3973 2981 1254 4023 1254 1639 1639 4024 1639 3795 4028
n.asf v.pmi.3s adv cj pl v.pai.3s n.nsm adv

παράβασις. 16 διὰ τοῦτο ἐκ πίστεως, ἵνα κατὰ
violation. For this reason the promise ⌞is based on⌟ faith, that it may ⌞depend on⌟
4126 1328 4047 3836 2039 1666 4411 2671 2848
n.nsf p.a r.asn p.g n.gsf cj p.a

χάριν, εἰς τὸ εἶναι βεβαίαν τὴν ἐπαγγελίαν παντὶ τῷ σπέρματι,
grace and ⌞so that⌟ ~ ⌞it may be made⌟ certain *the* *promise* to all his descendants,
5921 1650 3836 1639 1010 3836 2039 4246 3836 5065
n.asf p.a d.asn f.pa a.asf d.asf n.asf a.dsn d.dsn n.dsn

οὐ τῷ ἐκ τοῦ νόμου μόνον ἀλλὰ καὶ τῷ ἐκ
not only ⌞to those⌟ who are under the law, *only* but also ⌞to those⌟ who share the
4024 3667 3836 1666 3836 3795 3667 247 2779 3836 1666
pl d.dsn p.g d.gsm n.gsm adv cj adv d.dsn p.g

πίστεως Ἀβραάμ, ὅς ἐστιν πατὴρ → πάντων ἡμῶν, 17 καθὼς γέγραπται ὅτι
faith of Abraham, who is the father of us all. *us* As it is written, ~
4411 11 4005 1639 4252 7005 4246 7005 2777 1211 4022
n.gsf n.gsm r.nsm v.pai.3s n.nsm a.gpm r.gp.1 cj v.rpi.3s cj

πατέρα πολλῶν ἐθνῶν τέθεικά σε,
"I have made you the father of many nations." *I have made* *you* He is our father,
5502 5502 5502 5148 4252 4498 1620 5502 5148
n.asm a.gpn n.gpn v.rai.1s r.as.2

κατέναντι οὗ ἐπίστευσεν θεοῦ τοῦ ζῳοποιοῦντος
⌞in the presence of⌟ *whom* *he believed in* God in whom he believed, the God who gives life to
2978 4005 4409 2536 4409 4005 4409 4409 3836 2443
p.g r.gsm v.aai.3s n.gsm d.gsm pt.pa.gsm

NASB

believe without
being circumcised,
that righteousness
might be credited
to them, 12 and the
father of circumci-
sion to those who
not only are of the
circumcision, but
who also follow
in the steps of the
faith of our father
Abraham which
he had while
uncircumcised.
13 For the promise
to Abraham or to
his descendants
that he would be
heir of the world
was not through
the Law, but
through the righ-
teousness of faith.
14 For if those who
are of the Law
are heirs, faith is
made void and the
promise is nulli-
fied; 15 for the Law
brings about wrath,
but where there is
no law, there also
is no violation.
16 For this reason
it is by faith, in
order that *it may*
be in accordance
with grace, so that
the promise will be
guaranteed to all
the descendants,
not only to those
who are of the
Law, but also to
those who are of
the faith of Abra-
ham, who is the fa-
ther of us all, 17 (as
it is written, "A
FATHER OF MANY NA-
TIONS HAVE I MADE
YOU") in the pres-
ence of Him whom
he believed, *even*
God, who gives life

[a] 17 Gen. 17:5

[a] [καὶ] UBS.
[b] [τὴν] UBS.

NIV

the dead and calls
into being things
that were not.
[18]Against all
hope, Abraham
in hope believed
and so became the
father of many na-
tions, just as it had
been said to him,
"So shall your
offspring be."[a]
[19]Without weak-
ening in his faith,
he faced the fact
that his body was
as good as dead—
since he was about
a hundred years
old—and that
Sarah's womb was
also dead. [20]Yet
he did not waver
through unbe-
lief regarding the
promise of God,
but was strength-
ened in his faith
and gave glory to
God, [21]being ful-
ly persuaded that
God had power
to do what he had
promised. [22]This
is why "it was
credited to him as
righteousness."
[23]The words "it
was credited to
him" were written
not for him alone,
[24]but also for us,
to whom God will
credit righteous-
ness—for us who
believe in him
who raised Jesus
our Lord from the
dead. [25]He was
delivered over to
death for our sins
and was raised to
life for our justifi-
cation.

Peace and Hope

5 Therefore,
since we have
been justified
through faith, we[b]
have peace with

τοὺς νεκροὺς καὶ καλοῦντος τὰ ↱ μὴ ὄντα ὡς ὄντα.
the dead and calls into being ⌊the things⌋ that do not exist. *into being*
3836 3738 2779 2813 6055 1639 3836 1639 3590 1639 6055 1639
d.apm a.apm cj pt.pa.gsm d.apn pl pt.pa.apn pl pt.pa.apn

18 ὃς παρ' ἐλπίδα ἐπ' ἐλπίδι ἐπίστευσεν εἰς τὸ γενέσθαι
Abraham *{from}* Hoping against hope, Abraham believed that ~ he would become
4005 4123 1828 2093 1828 4005 4409 1650 3836 899 1181
r.nsm p.a n.asf p.d n.dsf v.aai.3s p.a d.asn f.am

αὐτὸν πατέρα πολλῶν ἐθνῶν κατὰ τὸ εἰρημένον, οὕτως →
he the father of many nations ⌊according to⌋ what had been spoken, "So will your
899 4252 4498 1620 2848 3836 3306 4048 5148
r.asm.3 n.asm a.gpn n.gpn p.a d.asn pt.rp.asn adv

ἔσται τὸ σπέρμα σου, 19 καὶ μὴ ἀσθενήσας τῇ πίστει κατενόησεν
descendants be." *{the}* *descendants* *your* *{and}* Not being weak in faith, he considered
5065 1639 3836 5065 5148 2779 3590 820 3836 4411 2917
v.fmi.3s d.nsn n.nsn r.gs.2 cj pl pt.aa.nsm d.dsf n.dsf v.aai.3s

τὸ ἑαυτοῦ σῶμα → [a]νενεκρωμένον, ἑκατονταετής που
{the} his own body as dead (since he was about a hundred years old), *about*
3836 1571 5393 3739 5639 5639 5639 4543 1670 4543
d.asn r.gsm.3 n.asn pt.rp.asn a.nsm pl

ὑπάρχων, καὶ τὴν νέκρωσιν τῆς μήτρας Σάρρας· 20
since he was and the barrenness of Sarah's womb. *Sarah's* He did not waver in
5639 2779 3836 3740 3836 4925 3616 4925 1359 1359 4024 1359 3836
pt.pa.nsm cj d.asf n.asf d.gsf n.gsf n.gsf

εἰς δὲ τὴν ἐπαγγελίαν τοῦ θεοῦ οὐ διεκρίθη τῇ ἀπιστίᾳ ἀλλ'
unbelief regarding *{and}* the promise of God *not* *He did waver* *in* *unbelief* but
602 1650 1254 3836 2039 3836 2536 4024 1359 3836 602 247
p.a cj d.asf n.asf d.gsm n.gsm pl v.api.3s d.dsf n.dsf cj

ἐνεδυναμώθη τῇ πίστει, δοὺς δόξαν τῷ θεῷ 21 καὶ πληροφορηθεὶς ὅτι ὃ
was strengthened in faith, giving glory to God, *{and}* fully convinced that what
1904 3836 4411 1443 1518 3836 2536 2779 4442 4022 4005
v.api.3s d.dsf n.dsf pt.aa.nsm n.asf d.dsm n.dsm cj pt.ap.nsm cj r.asn

ἐπήγγελται δυνατός ἐστιν καὶ ποιῆσαι. 22 διὸ καὶ [b]
God had promised, he was also able *he was* *also* to do. ⌊That is why⌋ *{also}* his faith
2040 1639 1639 2779 1543 1639 2779 4472 1475 2779
v.rmi.3s a.nsm v.pai.3s adv f.aa cj adv

ἐλογίσθη αὐτῷ εἰς δικαιοσύνην. 23 ↱
was credited to him as righteousness. But the statement, "it was credited to him," was
3357 899 1650 1466 1254 3357 3357 3357 899 899 1211
v.api.3s r.dsm.3 p.a n.asf

οὐκ ἐγράφη δὲ δι' αὐτὸν μόνον ὅτι ἐλογίσθη αὐτῷ 24 ἀλλὰ καὶ
not written *But* for his sake alone, ~ *it was credited* *to him* but for our sake as well,
4024 1211 1254 1328 899 3667 4022 3357 899 247 1328 7005 1328 2779
pl v.api.3s cj p.a r.asm.3 adv cj v.api.3s r.dsm.3 cj adv

δι' ἡμᾶς, οἷς μέλλει λογίζεσθαι, τοῖς πιστεύουσιν ἐπὶ τὸν ἐγείραντα
for sake *our* to whom it will be credited, those who believe in the one who raised
1328 7005 4005 3516 3357 3836 4409 2093 3836 1586
p.a r.ap.1 r.dpm v.pai.3s f.pp d.dpm pt.pa.dpm p.a d.asm pt.aa.asm

Ἰησοῦν τὸν κύριον ἡμῶν ἐκ νεκρῶν, 25 ὃς παρεδόθη διὰ
Jesus *{the}* our Lord *our* from the dead, who ⌊was delivered over⌋ to death for
2652 3836 7005 3261 7005 1666 3738 4005 4140 1328
n.asm d.asm n.asm r.gp.1 p.g a.gpm r.nsm v.api.3s p.a

τὰ παραπτώματα ἡμῶν καὶ ἠγέρθη διὰ τὴν δικαίωσιν ἡμῶν.
{the} our transgressions *our* and raised for *{the}* our justification. *our*
3836 7005 4183 7005 2779 1586 1328 3836 7005 1470 7005
d.apn n.apn r.gp.1 cj v.api.3s p.a d.asf n.asf r.gp.1

5:1 δικαιωθέντες οὖν ἐκ πίστεως εἰρήνην ἔχομεν πρὸς
Therefore, since we are justified *Therefore* by faith, we have peace *we have* with
4036 1467 4036 1666 4411 2400 2400 1645 2400 4639
pt.ap.npm cj p.g n.gsf n.asf v.pai.1p p.a

NASB

to the dead and
calls into being
that which does
not exist. [18]In hope
against hope he
believed, so that
he might become
a father of many
nations accord-
ing to that which
had been spoken,
"SO SHALL YOUR
DESCENDANTS BE."
[19]Without becom-
ing weak in faith
he contemplated
his own body, now
as good as dead
since he was about
a hundred years
old, and the dead-
ness of Sarah's
womb; [20]yet, with
respect to the
promise of God,
he did not waver in
unbelief but grew
strong in faith, giv-
ing glory to God,
[21]and being fully
assured that what
God had promised,
He was able
also to perform.
[22]Therefore IT WAS
ALSO CREDITED TO
HIM AS RIGHTEOUS-
NESS. [23]Now not for
his sake only was it
written that it was
credited to him,
[24]but for our sake
also, to whom it
will be credited, as
those who believe
in Him who raised
Jesus our Lord
from the dead, [25]*He*
who was delivered
over because of our
transgressions, and
was raised because
of our justification.

Results of Justification

[5:1]Therefore, hav-
ing been justified
by faith, we have
peace with God

[a] 18 Gen. 15:5
[b] 1 Many manu-
scripts *let us*

[a] ἤδη included by UBS before νενεκρωμένον.
[b] [καὶ] UBS.

NIV

God through our
Lord Jesus Christ,
2through whom we
have gained access
by faith into this
grace in which we
now stand. And
we[a] boast in the
hope of the glory
of God. 3Not only
so, but we[b] also
glory in our suf-
ferings, because
we know that
suffering produc-
es perseverance;
4perseverance,
character; and
character, hope.
5And hope does not
put us to shame,
because God's love
has been poured
out into our hearts
through the Holy
Spirit, who has
been given to us.
6You see, at just
the right time,
when we were still
powerless, Christ
died for the un-
godly. 7Very rarely
will anyone die for
a righteous person,
though for a good
person someone
might possibly
dare to die. 8But
God demonstrates
his own love for us
in this: While we
were still sinners,
Christ died for us.
9Since we have
now been justi-
fied by his blood,
how much more
shall we be saved
from God's wrath
through him! 10For
if, while we were
God's enemies, we
were reconciled to
him through the
death of his Son,
how much more,

[a] 2 Or *let us*
[b] 3 Or *let us*

τὸν θεὸν διὰ τοῦ κυρίου ἡμῶν Ἰησοῦ Χριστοῦ 2δι' οὗ καὶ
{the} God through *{the}* our Lord *our* Jesus Christ, through whom we have also
3836 2536 1328 3836 7005 3261 7005 2652 5986 1328 4005 2400 2400 2779
d.asm n.asm p.g d.gsm n.gsm r.gp.1 n.gsm n.gsm p.g r.gsm adv

τὴν προσαγωγὴν ἐσχήκαμεν [a]τῇ πίστει εἰς τὴν χάριν ταύτην ἐν
obtained *{the}* access *we have obtained* by faith into *{the}* this grace *this* in
2400 3836 4643 2400 3836 4411 1650 3836 4047 5921 4047 1877
d.asf n.asf v.rai.1p d.dsf n.dsf p.a d.asf n.asf r.asf p.d

ᾗ ἑστήκαμεν καὶ καυχώμεθα ἐπ' ἐλπίδι τῆς δόξης τοῦ θεοῦ. 3 οὐ
which we stand, and we rejoice in hope of sharing the glory of God. And not
4005 2705 2779 3016 2093 1828 3836 1518 3836 2536 1254 4024
r.dsf v.rai.1p cj v.pmi.1p p.d n.dsf d.gsf n.gsf d.gsm n.gsm pl

μόνον δέ, ἀλλὰ ➝ καὶ καυχώμεθα ἐν ταῖς θλίψεσιν, εἰδότες ὅτι ἡ θλῖψις
only *And* that, but we also rejoice in our sufferings, knowing that *{the}* suffering
3667 1254 247 3016 2779 3016 1877 3836 2568 3857 4022 3836 2568
adv cj cj adv v.pmi.1p p.d d.dpf n.dpf pt.ra.npm cj d.nsf n.nsf

ὑπομονὴν κατεργάζεται, 4ἡ δὲ ὑπομονὴ δοκιμήν, ἡ δὲ
produces endurance, *produces* *{the}* and endurance produces character, *{the}* and
2981 5705 2981 3836 1254 5705 1509 3836 1254
n.asf v.pmi.3s d.nsf cj n.nsf n.asf d.nsf cj

δοκιμὴ ἐλπίδα. 5ἡ δὲ ἐλπὶς ➝ οὐ καταισχύνει, ὅτι ἡ ἀγάπη
character produces hope, *{the}* and hope does not disappoint us, because the love
1509 1828 3836 1254 1828 2875 4024 2875 4022 3836 27
n.nsf n.asf d.nsf cj n.nsf pl v.pai.3s cj d.nsf n.nsf

τοῦ θεοῦ ἐκκέχυται ἐν ταῖς καρδίαις ἡμῶν διὰ πνεύματος
of God ⌊has been poured out⌋ into *{the}* our hearts *our* through the Holy Spirit
3836 2536 1773 1877 3836 7005 2840 7005 1328 41 4460
d.gsm n.gsm v.rpi.3s p.d d.dpf n.dpf r.gp.1 p.g n.gsn

ἁγίου τοῦ δοθέντος ἡμῖν. 6ἔτι γὰρ Χριστὸς ὄντων ἡμῶν ἀσθενῶν
Holy who was given to us. *while* For *Christ* while we were *we* still helpless,
41 3836 1443 7005 2285 1142 5986 2285 7005 1639 7005 2285 822
a.gsn d.gsn pt.ap.gsn r.dp.1 adv cj n.nsm pt.pa.gpm r.gp.1 a.gpm

ἔτι κατὰ καιρὸν ὑπὲρ ἀσεβῶν ἀπέθανεν. 7 μόλις γὰρ
still at the right time Christ died for the ungodly. *died* For rarely *For* will one
2285 2848 2789 5986 633 5642 815 633 1142 3660 1142 633 5516
adv p.a n.asm p.g a.gpm v.aai.3s adv cj

ὑπὲρ δικαίου τις ἀποθανεῖται· ὑπὲρ γὰρ τοῦ
die for an upright person *one* *will die* — though perhaps for *though* *{the}* a genuinely
633 5642 1465 5516 633 1142 5440 5642 1142 3836
p.g a.gsm r.nsm v.fmi.3s p.g cj d.gsm

ἀγαθοῦ τάχα τις καὶ τολμᾷ ἀποθανεῖν· 8 συνίστησιν δὲ
good person *perhaps* one *{also}* ⌊might actually dare⌋ to die. But God demonstrates *But*
19 5440 5516 2779 5528 633 1254 2536 5319 1254
a.gsm adv r.nsm adv v.pai.3s f.aa v.pai.3s cj

τὴν ἑαυτοῦ ἀγάπην εἰς ἡμᾶς ὁ θεός, ὅτι ἔτι ἁμαρτωλῶν
{the} his love for us *{the}* *God* in that while we were still sinners
3836 1571 27 1650 7005 3836 2536 4022 1639 7005 1639 2285 283
d.asf r.gsm.3 n.asf p.a r.ap.1 d.nsm n.nsm cj adv a.gpm

ὄντων ἡμῶν Χριστὸς ὑπὲρ ἡμῶν ἀπέθανεν. 9πολλῷ οὖν μᾶλλον ➝ ➝
while were *we* Christ died for us. *died* *much* Since *more* we have now
1639 7005 5986 633 5642 7005 633 4498 4036 3437 3814
pt.pa.gpm r.gp.1 n.nsm p.g r.gp.1 v.aai.3s a.dsn cj adv.c

δικαιωθέντες νῦν ἐν τῷ αἵματι αὐτοῦ σωθησόμεθα
been justified *now* by *{the}* his blood, *his* much more will we be saved from the wrath of
1467 3814 1877 3836 899 135 899 4498 3437 5392 608 3836 3973
pt.ap.npm adv p.d d.dsn n.dsn r.gsm.3 v.fpi.1p

δι' αὐτοῦ ἀπὸ τῆς ὀργῆς. 10 εἰ γὰρ ἐχθροὶ ὄντες
God through him. *from* *the* *wrath* For if *For* while we were enemies *while we were*
1328 899 608 3836 3973 1142 1623 1142 1639 1639 1639 2398 1639
p.g r.gsm.3 p.g d.gsf n.gsf cj cj a.npm pt.pa.npm

κατηλλάγημεν τῷ θεῷ διὰ τοῦ θανάτου τοῦ υἱοῦ αὐτοῦ, πολλῷ μᾶλλον
we were reconciled to God through the death of his Son, *his* much more,
2904 3836 2536 1328 3836 2505 3836 899 5626 899 4498 3437
v.api.1p d.dsm n.dsm p.g d.gsm n.gsm d.gsm n.gsm r.gsm.3 a.dsn adv.c

[a] [τῇ πίστει] UBS.

NASB

through our Lord
Jesus Christ,
2through whom
also we have
obtained our
introduction by
faith into this grace
in which we stand;
and we exult in
hope of the glory
of God. 3And not
only this, but we
also exult in our
tribulations, know-
ing that tribula-
tion brings about
perseverance;
4and perseverance,
proven charac-
ter; and proven
character, hope;
5and hope does not
disappoint, because
the love of God has
been poured out
within our hearts
through the Holy
Spirit who was
given to us.
6For while we
were still helpless,
at the right time
Christ died for the
ungodly. 7For one
will hardly die for
a righteous man;
though perhaps
for the good man
someone would
dare even to die.
8But God demon-
strates His own
love toward us, in
that while we were
yet sinners, Christ
died for us. 9Much
more then, having
now been justified
by His blood, we
shall be saved from
the wrath *of God*
through Him. 10For
if while we were
enemies we were
reconciled to God
through the death
of His Son, much
more, having

NIV

having been rec-
onciled, shall we
be saved through
his life! [11]Not
only is this so, but
we also boast in
God through our
Lord Jesus Christ,
through whom we
have now received
reconciliation.

Death Through Adam, Life Through Christ

[12]Therefore, just
as sin entered the
world through one
man, and death
through sin, and
in this way death
came to all peo-
ple, because all
sinned—
[13]To be sure, sin
was in the world
before the law
was given, but
sin is not charged
against anyone's
account where
there is no law.
[14]Nevertheless,
death reigned from
the time of Adam
to the time of
Moses, even over
those who did not
sin by breaking a
command, as did
Adam, who is a
pattern of the one
to come.
[15]But the gift is
not like the tres-
pass. For if the
many died by the
trespass of the one
man, how much
more did God's
grace and the gift
that came by the
grace of the one
man, Jesus Christ,
overflow to the
many! [16]Nor can
the gift of God be
compared with the
result of one man's
sin: The judgment

καταλλαγέντες σωθησόμεθα ἐν τῇ ζωῇ αὐτοῦ· 11 οὐ μόνον δέ,
now that we are reconciled, will we be saved by {the} his life. *his* And not only *And*
2904 5392 1877 3836 899 2437 899 1254 4024 3667 1254
pt.ap.npm v.fpi.1p p.d d.dsf n.dsf r.gsm.3 pl adv cj

ἀλλὰ ↱ καὶ καυχώμενοι ἐν τῷ θεῷ διὰ τοῦ κυρίου ἡμῶν Ἰησοῦ
that, but we also rejoice in {the} God through {the} our Lord *our* Jesus
247 3016 2779 3016 1877 3836 2536 1328 3836 7005 3261 7005 2652
cj adv pt.pm.npm p.d d.dsm n.dsm p.g d.gsm n.gsm r.gp.1 n.gsm

Χριστοῦ δι᾿ οὗ νῦν τὴν καταλλαγὴν ἐλάβομεν.
Christ, through whom we now have received {the} reconciliation. *we have received*
5986 1328 4005 3284 3814 3284 3284 3836 2903 3284
n.gsm p.g r.gsm adv d.asf n.asf v.aai.1p

12 ⌞διὰ τοῦτο⌟ ὥσπερ δι᾿ ἑνὸς ἀνθρώπου ἡ ἁμαρτία
Therefore, just as sin came into the world through one man, {the} *sin*
1328 4047 6061 281 1656 1650 3836 3180 1328 1651 476 3836 281
p.a r.asn cj p.g a.gsm n.gsm d.nsf n.nsf

εἰς τὸν κόσμον εἰσῆλθεν καὶ διὰ τῆς ἁμαρτίας ὁ θάνατος, καὶ οὕτως
into the world came and death through {the} sin, {the} *death* and so
1650 3836 3180 1656 2779 2505 1328 3836 281 3836 2505 2779 4048
p.a d.asm n.asm v.aai.3s cj p.g d.gsf n.gsf d.nsm n.nsm cj adv

εἰς πάντας ἀνθρώπους ὁ θάνατος διῆλθεν, ⌞ἐφ᾿ ᾧ⌟ πάντες
death spread to all men, {the} *death spread* because all
2505 1451 1650 4246 476 3836 2505 1451 2093 4005 4246
p.a a.apm n.apm d.nsm n.nsm v.aai.3s p.d r.dsn a.npm

ἥμαρτον· 13 ἄχρι γὰρ νόμου ἁμαρτία ἦν ἐν κόσμῳ,
have sinned, *before* For *law* sin was in the world before the law was given,
279 948 1142 3795 281 1639 1877 3180 948 3795
v.aai.3p p.g cj n.gsm n.nsf v.iai.3s p.d n.dsm

ἁμαρτία δὲ ↱ οὐκ ἐλλογεῖται μὴ ὄντος νόμου,
but sin *but* is not charged when there is no *when there is* law.
1254 281 1254 1824 4024 1824 1639 1639 1639 3590 1639 3795
n.nsf cj pl v.ppi.3s pl pt.pa.gsm n.gsm

14 ἀλλὰ ἐβασίλευσεν ὁ θάνατος ἀπὸ Ἀδὰμ μέχρι Μωϋσέως καὶ ἐπὶ
Nevertheless death reigned {the} *death* from Adam until Moses, even over
247 2505 996 3836 2505 608 77 3588 3707 2779 2093
cj v.aai.3s d.nsm n.nsm p.g n.gsm p.g n.gsm adv p.a

τοὺς μὴ ἁμαρτήσαντας ⌞ἐπὶ τῷ ὁμοιώματι⌟ τῆς παραβάσεως
those whose sinning was not *whose sinning* like the transgression
3836 279 279 3590 279 2093 3836 3930 3836 4126
d.apm pl pt.aa.apm p.d d.dsn n.dsn d.gsf n.gsf

Ἀδὰμ ὅς ἐστιν τύπος τοῦ μέλλοντος. 15 ἀλλ᾿ οὐχ ὡς τὸ
of Adam, who was a type of the coming one. But the free gift is not like the
77 4005 1639 5596 3836 3516 247 3836 5922 5922 4024 6055 3836
n.gsm r.nsm v.pai.3s n.nsm d.gsm pt.pa.gsm cj pl cj d.nsn

παράπτωμα, οὕτως καὶ τὸ χάρισμα· εἰ γὰρ τῷ
transgression. *{thus} {also} the free gift* For if *For* the many died ⌞through the⌟
4183 4048 2779 3836 5922 1142 1623 1142 3836 4498 633 3836
n.nsn adv adv d.nsn n.nsn cj cj d.dsn

τοῦ ἑνὸς παραπτώματι οἱ πολλοὶ ἀπέθανον, πολλῷ μᾶλλον ἡ
transgression of the one, *transgression the many died* much more did the
4183 3836 1651 4183 3836 4498 633 4498 3437 4355 3836
d.gsm a.gsm n.dsn d.npm a.npm v.aai.3p a.dsn adv.c d.nsf

χάρις τοῦ θεοῦ καὶ ἡ δωρεὰ ἐν χάριτι τῇ τοῦ ἑνὸς ἀνθρώπου
grace of God and the gift that came by the grace {the} of the one man
5921 3836 2536 2779 3836 1561 1877 5921 3836 3836 1651 476
n.nsf d.gsm n.gsm cj d.nsf n.nsf p.d n.dsf d.dsf d.gsm a.gsm n.gsm

Ἰησοῦ Χριστοῦ εἰς τοὺς πολλοὺς ἐπερίσσευσεν. 16 καὶ οὐχ ὡς
Jesus Christ overflow to the many. *did overflow* And the gift is not like
2652 5986 4355 1650 3836 4498 4355 2779 3836 1564 4024 6055
n.gsm n.gsm p.a d.apm a.apm v.aai.3s cj pl cj

δι᾿ ἑνὸς ἁμαρτήσαντος τὸ δώρημα· τὸ μὲν γὰρ κρίμα
the ⌞result of⌟ that one man's sin; *the gift* for the ~ *for* judgment
1328 1651 279 3836 1564 1142 3836 3525 1142 3210
p.g a.gsm pt.aa.gsm d.nsn n.nsn d.nsn pl cj n.nsn

NASB

been reconciled,
we shall be saved
by His life. [11]And
not only this, but
we also exult in
God through our
Lord Jesus Christ,
through whom we
have now received
the reconciliation.
[12]Therefore, just
as through one man
sin entered into the
world, and death
through sin, and so
death spread to all
men, because all
sinned— [13]for until
the Law sin was
in the world, but
sin is not imputed
when there is no
law. [14]Neverthe-
less death reigned
from Adam until
Moses, even over
those who had not
sinned in the like-
ness of the offense
of Adam, who is a
[a]type of Him who
was to come.
[15]But the free
gift is not like the
transgression. For
if by the transgres-
sion of the one the
many died, much
more did the grace
of God and the gift
by the grace of the
one Man, Jesus
Christ, abound to
the many. [16]The
gift is not like
that which came
through the one
who sinned; for on
the one hand the
judgment *arose*

[a] Or *foreshadowing*

NIV

followed one sin
and brought con-
demnation, but
the gift followed
many trespasses
and brought justi-
fication. 17For if,
by the trespass of
the one man, death
reigned through
that one man, how
much more will
those who receive
God's abundant
provision of grace
and of the gift of
righteousness reign
in life through the
one man, Jesus
Christ!
18Consequently,
just as one tres-
pass resulted in
condemnation for
all people, so also
one righteous act
resulted in justifi-
cation and life for
all people. 19For
just as through the
disobedience of
the one man the
many were made
sinners, so also
through the obe-
dience of the one
man the many will
be made righteous.
20The law was
brought in so
that the trespass
might increase.
But where sin
increased, grace
increased all the
more, 21so that,
just as sin reigned
in death, so also
grace might reign
through righteous-
ness to bring eter-
nal life through
Jesus Christ our
Lord.

ἐξ ἑνὸς εἰς κατάκριμα, τὸ δὲ χάρισμα ἐκ
following the one transgression ˻led to˼ condemnation, but the *but* free gift following the
1666 1651 1650 2890 1254 3836 1254 5922 1666
p.g a.gsn p.a n.asn d.nsn cj n.nsn p.g

πολλῶν παραπτωμάτων εἰς δικαίωμα. 17 εἰ γὰρ τῷ τοῦ
many transgressions ˻led to˼ justification. For if *For* ˻by the˼ transgression of the
4498 4183 1650 1468 1142 1623 1142 3836 4183 3836
a.gpn n.gpn p.a n.asn cj cj d.dsn d.gsm

ἑνὸς παραπτώματι ὁ θάνατος ἐβασίλευσεν διὰ τοῦ ἑνός, πολλῷ μᾶλλον
one man *transgression* *{the}* death reigned through that one, much more will
1651 4183 3836 2505 996 1328 3836 1651 4498 3437 996
a.gsm n.dsn d.nsm n.nsm v.aai.3s p.g d.gsm a.gsm a.dsn adv.c

οἱ τὴν περισσείαν τῆς χάριτος καὶ τῆς δωρεᾶς τῆς δικαιοσύνης
those who receive the abundance of grace and the gift of righteousness
3836 3284 3284 3836 4353 3836 5921 2779 3836 1561 3836 1466
d.npm d.asf n.asf d.gsf n.gsf cj d.gsf n.gsf d.gsf n.gsf

λαμβάνοντες ἐν ζωῇ βασιλεύσουσιν διὰ τοῦ ἑνὸς Ἰησοῦ Χριστοῦ.
who receive reign in life *will reign* through the one, Jesus Christ.
3284 996 1877 2437 996 1328 3836 1651 2652 5986
pt.pa.npm p.d n.dsf v.fai.3p p.g d.gsm a.gsm n.gsm n.gsm

18 ˻ἄρα οὖν˼ ὡς δι᾽ ἑνὸς παραπτώματος εἰς
Therefore, ˻just as˼ *{through}* one man's transgression brought condemnation for
726 4036 6055 1328 1651 4183 1650 2890 1650
cj cj cj p.g a.gsn n.gsn p.a

πάντας ἀνθρώπους εἰς κατάκριμα, οὕτως καὶ δι᾽ ἑνὸς δικαιώματος
all men, *brought condemnation* so also *{through}* one man's righteous act
4246 476 1650 2890 4048 2779 1328 1651 1468
a.apm n.apm p.a n.asn adv adv p.g a.gsn n.gsn

εἰς πάντας ἀνθρώπους εἰς δικαίωσιν ζωῆς· 19 ὥσπερ
brought justification and life for all men. *brought justification* *life* For just as
1650 1470 2437 1650 4246 476 1650 1470 2437 1142 6061
p.a a.apm n.apm p.a n.asf n.gsf cj

γὰρ διὰ τῆς παρακοῆς τοῦ ἑνὸς ἀνθρώπου
For through one man's *{the}* disobedience *{the}* *one* *man's* the many were made
1142 1328 1651 476 3836 4157 3836 1651 476 3836 4498 2770 2770
cj p.g d.gsf n.gsf d.gsm a.gsm n.gsm

ἁμαρτωλοὶ κατεστάθησαν οἱ πολλοί, οὕτως καὶ διὰ τῆς ὑπακοῆς τοῦ
sinners, *were made* *the* *many* so also through the one man's obedience *{the}*
283 2770 3836 4498 4048 2779 1328 3836 1651 5633 3836
a.npm v.api.3p d.npm a.npm adv adv p.g d.gsf n.gsf d.gsm

ἑνὸς δίκαιοι κατασταθήσονται οἱ πολλοί. 20 νόμος
one the many will be made righteous. *will be made* *the* *many* Now the law
1651 3836 4498 2770 2770 2770 1465 2770 3836 4498 1254 3795
a.gsm a.npm v.fpi.3p d.npm a.npm n.nsm

δὲ παρεισῆλθεν, ἵνα πλεονάσῃ τὸ παράπτωμα, οὗ δὲ
Now came in so that the transgression might increase; *the* *transgression* but where *but*
1254 4209 2671 3836 4183 4429 3836 4183 1254 4023 1254
cj v.aai.3s cj v.aas.3s d.nsn n.nsn adv cj

ἐπλεόνασεν ἡ ἁμαρτία, ὑπερεπερίσσευσεν ἡ χάρις, 21 ἵνα ὥσπερ
sin increased, *{the}* *sin* grace increased all the more, *{the}* *grace* so that just as sin
281 4429 3836 281 5921 5668 3836 5921 2671 6061 281
v.aai.3s d.nsf n.nsf v.aai.3s d.nsf n.nsf cj cj

ἐβασίλευσεν ἡ ἁμαρτία ἐν τῷ θανάτῳ, οὕτως καὶ ἡ χάρις βασιλεύσῃ διὰ
reigned *{the}* *sin* in *{the}* death, so also *{the}* grace might reign through
996 3836 281 1877 3836 2505 4048 2779 3836 5921 996 1328
v.aai.3s d.nsf n.nsf p.d d.dsm n.dsm adv adv d.nsf n.nsf v.aas.3s p.g

δικαιοσύνης εἰς ζωὴν αἰώνιον διὰ Ἰησοῦ Χριστοῦ τοῦ κυρίου
righteousness ˻leading to˼ eternal life *eternal* through Jesus Christ *{the}* our Lord.
1466 1650 173 2437 173 1328 2652 5986 3836 7005 3261
n.gsf p.a n.asf a.asf p.g n.gsm n.gsm d.gsm n.gsm

ἡμῶν.
our
7005
r.gp.1

NASB

from one *trans-*
gression resulting
in condemnation,
but on the other
hand the free gift
arose from many
transgressions re-
sulting in justifica-
tion. 17For if by the
transgression of the
one, death reigned
through the one,
much more those
who receive the
abundance of grace
and of the gift
of righteousness
will reign in life
through the One,
Jesus Christ.
18So then as
through one trans-
gression there
resulted condem-
nation to all men,
even so through
one act of righ-
teousness there re-
sulted justification
of life to all men.
19For as through the
one man's disobe-
dience the many
were made sinners,
even so through the
obedience of the
One the many will
be made righteous.
20The Law came in
so that the trans-
gression would
increase; but where
sin increased,
grace abounded
all the more, 21so
that, as sin reigned
in death, even so
grace would reign
through righteous-
ness to eternal
life through Jesus
Christ our Lord.

NIV

Dead to Sin, Alive in Christ

6 What shall we say, then? Shall we go on sinning so that grace may increase? [2]By no means! We are those who have died to sin; how can we live in it any longer? [3]Or don't you know that all of us who were baptized into Christ Jesus were baptized into his death? [4]We were therefore buried with him through baptism into death in order that, just as Christ was raised from the dead through the glory of the Father, we too may live a new life.

[5]For if we have been united with him in a death like his, we will certainly also be united with him in a resurrection like his. [6]For we know that our old self was crucified with him so that the body ruled by sin might be done away with,[a] that we should no longer be slaves to sin— [7]because anyone who has died has been set free from sin.

[8]Now if we died with Christ, we believe that we will also live with him. [9]For we know that since Christ was raised from the dead, he cannot die again; death no longer has mastery over him. [10]The death he died, he died to sin once for all; but the life

[a] 6 Or *be rendered powerless*

6:1 τί οὖν ἐροῦμεν; ἐπιμένωμεν τῇ ἁμαρτίᾳ, ἵνα ἡ χάρις
What then shall we say? — "Let us continue in sin so that {the} grace
5515 4036 3306 2152 3836 281 2671 3836 5921
r.asn cj v.fai.1p v.pas.1p d.dsf n.dsf cj d.nsf n.nsf

πλεονάσῃ; [2]⌞μὴ γένοιτο.⌟ ↱ ↱ οἵτινες ἀπεθάνομεν τῇ ἁμαρτίᾳ,
may increase"? By no means! How can we who died to sin
4429 3590 1181 4802 2409 633 4015 633 3836 281
v.aas.3s pl v.amo.3s r.npm v.aai.1p d.dsf n.dsf

πῶς ἔτι ζήσομεν ἐν αὐτῇ; [3]ἢ ἀγνοεῖτε ὅτι, ↱ ὅσοι ἐβαπτίσθημεν εἰς
How ⌞go on⌟ living in it? Or ⌞do you not know⌟ that we who were baptized into
4802 2285 2409 1877 899 2445 51 4022 966 4012 966 1650
pl adv v.fai.1p p.d r.dsf.3 cj v.pai.2p cj r.npm v.api.1p p.a

Χριστὸν Ἰησοῦν, εἰς τὸν θάνατον αὐτοῦ ἐβαπτίσθημεν; [4]
Christ Jesus were baptized into {the} his death? *his* *were baptized* Therefore
5986 2652 966 966 1650 3836 899 2505 899 966 4036
n.asm n.asm p.a d.asm n.asm r.gsm.3 v.api.1p

συνετάφημεν οὖν αὐτῷ διὰ τοῦ βαπτίσματος εἰς τὸν θάνατον, ἵνα ὥσπερ
⌞we were buried with⌟ *Therefore* him by {the} baptism into {the} death, so that just as
5313 4036 899 1328 3836 967 1650 3836 2505 2671 6061
v.api.1p cj r.dsm.3 p.g d.gsn n.gsn p.a d.asm n.asm cj cj

ἠγέρθη Χριστὸς ἐκ νεκρῶν διὰ τῆς δόξης τοῦ πατρός, οὕτως καὶ ἡμεῖς
Christ was raised *Christ* from the dead by the glory of the Father, so also we
5986 1586 5986 1666 3738 1328 3836 1518 3836 4252 4048 2779 7005
v.api.3s n.nsm p.g a.gpm p.g d.gsf n.gsf d.gsm n.gsm adv adv r.np.1

ἐν καινότητι ζωῆς περιπατήσωμεν. [5] εἰ γὰρ
might walk in newness of life. *might walk* For if *For* we have become
4344 4344 1877 2786 2437 4344 1142 1623 1142 1181 1181 1181
p.d n.dsf n.gsf v.aas.1p cj cj

σύμφυτοι γεγόναμεν τῷ ὁμοιώματι τοῦ θανάτου αὐτοῦ, ἀλλὰ
united with him *we have become* ⌞in the⌟ likeness of his death, *his* we will certainly
5242 1181 3836 3930 3836 899 2505 899 1639 1639 247
a.npm v.rai.1p d.dsn n.dsn d.gsm n.gsm r.gsm.3 cj

καὶ τῆς ἀναστάσεως ἐσόμεθα· [6] τοῦτο
also be united with him in the likeness of his resurrection. *we will be* We know this,
2779 1639 3836 414 1639 1182 1182 4047
adv d.gsf n.gsf v.fmi.1p r.asn

γινώσκοντες ὅτι ὁ παλαιὸς ἡμῶν ἄνθρωπος συνεσταυρώθη, ἵνα
We know that {the} our old *our* self was crucified with him, so that the
1182 4022 3836 7005 4094 7005 476 5365 2671 3836
pt.pa.npm cj d.nsm a.nsm r.gp.1 n.nsm v.api.3s cj

καταργηθῇ τὸ σῶμα τῆς ἁμαρτίας, τοῦ ↱
body of sin ⌞would be rendered powerless,⌟ *the* *body* *of* *sin* so that we would
5393 3836 281 2934 3836 5393 3836 281 3836 7005 1526
v.aps.3s d.nsn n.nsn d.gsf n.gsf d.gsn

μηκέτι δουλεύειν ἡμᾶς τῇ ἁμαρτίᾳ· [7] ὁ γὰρ ἀποθανὼν δεδικαίωται
no longer be enslaved *we* by sin; for the *for* ⌞one who has died⌟ has been set free
3600 1526 7005 3836 281 1142 3836 1142 633 1467
adv f.pa r.ap.1 d.dsf n.dsf d.nsm cj pt.aa.nsm v.rpi.3s

ἀπὸ τῆς ἁμαρτίας. [8] εἰ δὲ ἀπεθάνομεν σὺν Χριστῷ, πιστεύομεν ὅτι ↱ ↱
from {the} sin. Now if *Now* we have died with Christ, we believe that we will
608 3836 281 1254 1623 1254 633 5250 5986 4409 4022 5182 5182
p.g d.gsf n.gsf cj cj v.aai.1p p.d n.dsm v.pai.1p cj

καὶ συζήσομεν αὐτῷ, [9]εἰδότες ὅτι Χριστὸς ἐγερθεὶς ἐκ νεκρῶν
also live with him. We know that Christ, ⌞having been raised⌟ from the dead, will
2779 5182 899 3857 4022 5986 1586 1666 3738 633
adv v.fai.1p r.dsm.3 pt.ra.npm cj n.nsm pt.ap.nsm p.g a.gpm

→ οὐκέτι ἀποθνήσκει, θάνατος αὐτοῦ οὐκέτι κυριεύει.
never die again; *will die* death no longer has mastery over him. *no longer* *has mastery*
633 4033 633 2505 4033 4033 3259 3259 899 4033 3259
adv v.pai.3s n.nsm r.gsm.3 adv v.pai.3s

10 ὃ γὰρ ἀπέθανεν, τῇ ἁμαρτίᾳ ἀπέθανεν ἐφάπαξ, ὃ
For the death *For* he died, he died to sin *he died* ⌞once for all;⌟ but the life
1142 4005 1142 633 633 633 3836 281 633 2384 1254 4005
r.asn cj v.aai.3s d.dsf n.dsf v.aai.3s adv r.asn

NASB

Believers Are Dead to Sin, Alive to God

6:1What shall we say then? Are we to continue in sin so that grace may increase? [2]May it never be! How shall we who died to sin still live in it? [3]Or do you not know that all of us who have been baptized into Christ Jesus have been baptized into His death? [4]Therefore we have been buried with Him through baptism into death, so that as Christ was raised from the dead through the glory of the Father, so we too might walk in newness of life. [5]For if we have become united with *Him* in the likeness of His death, certainly we shall also be *in the likeness* of His resurrection, [6]knowing this, that our old self was crucified with *Him,* in order that our body of sin might be done away with, so that we would no longer be slaves to sin; [7]for he who has died is freed from sin.

[8]Now if we have died with Christ, we believe that we shall also live with Him, [9]knowing that Christ, having been raised from the dead, is never to die again; death no longer is master over Him. [10]For the death that He died, He died to sin once for all; but the life

NIV

he lives, he lives
to God.
[11]In the same
way, count your-
selves dead to sin
but alive to God
in Christ Jesus.
[12]Therefore do
not let sin reign in
your mortal body
so that you obey its
evil desires. [13]Do
not offer any part
of yourself to sin
as an instrument
of wickedness, but
rather offer your-
selves to God as
those who have
been brought from
death to life; and
offer every part
of yourself to him
as an instrument
of righteousness.
[14]For sin shall no
longer be your
master, because
you are not under
the law, but under
grace.

Slaves to Righteousness

[15]What then?
Shall we sin be-
cause we are not
under the law
but under grace?
By no means!
[16]Don't you know
that when you of-
fer yourselves to
someone as obedi-
ent slaves, you are
slaves of the one
you obey—wheth-
er you are slaves
to sin, which leads
to death, or to
obedience, which
leads to righteous-
ness? [17]But thanks
be to God that,
though you used
to be slaves to sin,
you have come to
obey from your
heart the pattern of
teaching that has
now claimed your
allegiance. [18]You
have been set free
from sin and have
become slaves to
righteousness.
[19]I am using an
example

δὲ ζῇ, ζῇ τῷ θεῷ. [11] οὕτως καὶ ὑμεῖς λογίζεσθε ἑαυτοὺς εἶναι[a]
but ⌊he lives,⌋ ⌊he lives⌋ to God. So you too *you* consider yourselves to be
1254 2409 2409 3836 2536 4048 7007 2779 7007 3357 1571 1639
cj v.pai.3s v.pai.3s d.dsm n.dsm adv adv r.np.2 v.pmm.2p r.apm.2 f.pa

νεκροὺς μὲν τῇ ἁμαρτίᾳ ζῶντας δὲ τῷ θεῷ ἐν Χριστῷ Ἰησοῦ. [12]
dead ~ to sin but alive *but* to God in Christ Jesus. Therefore
3738 3525 3836 281 1254 2409 1254 3836 2536 1877 5986 2652 4036
a.apm pl d.dsf n.dsf pt.pa.apm cj d.dsm n.dsm p.d n.dsm n.dsm

μὴ οὖν βασιλευέτω ἡ ἁμαρτία ἐν τῷ θνητῷ ὑμῶν σώματι
do not *Therefore* let sin reign *{the}* *sin* in *{the}* your mortal *your* body
996 3590 4036 281 996 3836 281 1877 3836 7007 2570 7007 5393
pl cj v.pam.3s d.nsf n.nsf p.d d.dsn a.dsn r.gp.2 n.dsn

εἰς τὸ ὑπακούειν ταῖς ἐπιθυμίαις αὐτοῦ, [13] μηδὲ παριστάνετε τὰ
⌊so that⌋ ~ you obey *{the}* its desires. *its* Do not continue to present *{the}*
1650 3836 5634 3836 899 2123 899 4225 3593 4225 3836
p.a d.asn f.pa d.dpf n.dpf r.gsn.3 cj v.pam.2p d.apn

μέλη ὑμῶν ὅπλα ἀδικίας τῇ ἁμαρτίᾳ, ἀλλὰ
your members *your* to sin as instruments for unrighteousness, *to* *sin* but
7007 3517 7007 3836 281 3960 94 3836 281 247
n.apn r.gp.2 n.apn n.gsf d.dsf n.dsf cj

παραστήσατε ἑαυτοὺς τῷ θεῷ ὡσεὶ ἐκ νεκρῶν ζῶντας καὶ τὰ
present yourselves to God as alive from the dead, *alive* and *{the}* your
4225 1571 3836 2536 6059 2409 1666 3738 2409 2779 3836 7007
v.aam.2p r.apm.2 d.dsm n.dsm pl p.g a.gpm pt.pa.apm cj d.apn

μέλη ὑμῶν ὅπλα δικαιοσύνης τῷ θεῷ. [14] ἁμαρτία γὰρ
members *your* to God as instruments for righteousness. *to* *God* For sin *For* will
3517 7007 3836 2536 3960 1466 3836 2536 1142 281 1142 3259
n.apn r.gp.2 n.apn n.gsf d.dsm n.dsm n.nsf cj

ὑμῶν οὐ κυριεύσει, οὐ γάρ ἐστε ὑπὸ νόμον
not have mastery over you, *not* *will have mastery* since you are not *since* *you are* under law
4024 3259 3259 7007 4024 3259 1142 1639 1639 4024 1142 1639 5679 3795
r.gp.2 pl v.fai.3s pl cj v.pai.2p p.a n.asm

ἀλλὰ ὑπὸ χάριν. [15] τί οὖν; ἁμαρτήσωμεν, ὅτι οὐκ ἐσμὲν ὑπὸ νόμον
but under grace. What then? Should we sin because we are not *we are* under law
247 5679 5921 5515 4036 279 4022 1639 1639 4024 1639 5679 3795
cj p.a n.asf r.nsn cj v.aas.1p cj pl v.pai.1p p.a n.asm

ἀλλὰ ὑπὸ χάριν; ⌊μὴ γένοιτο.⌋ [16] οὐκ οἴδατε ὅτι
but under grace? By no means! Do you not know that if you present
247 5679 5921 3590 1181 3857 3857 4024 3857 4022 4225 4225
cj p.a n.asf pl v.amo.3s pl v.rai.2p cj

ᾧ παριστάνετε ἑαυτοὺς δούλους εἰς ὑπακοήν,
yourselves ⌊to someone⌋ *you present* *yourselves* as obedient slaves, *as* *obedient* you
1571 4005 4225 1571 1650 5633 1529 1650 5633 1639
r.dsm v.pai.2p r.apm.2 n.apm p.a n.asf

δοῦλοί ἐστε ᾧ ὑπακούετε, ἤτοι ἁμαρτίας εἰς θάνατον
are slaves *you are* of the ⌊one whom⌋ you obey, either of sin, which ⌊leads to⌋ death,
1639 1529 1639 4005 5634 2486 281 1650 2505
n.npm v.pai.2p r.dsm v.pai.2p cj n.gsf p.a n.asm

ἢ ὑπακοῆς εἰς δικαιοσύνην; [17] χάρις δὲ τῷ θεῷ ὅτι
or of obedience, which ⌊leads to⌋ righteousness? But thanks *But* be to God that
2445 5633 1650 1466 1254 5921 1254 3836 2536 4022
cj n.gsf p.a n.asf n.nsf cj d.dsm n.dsm cj

ἦτε δοῦλοι τῆς ἁμαρτίας ὑπηκούσατε δὲ ἐκ καρδίας εἰς
⌊though you were⌋ slaves of sin, you became obedient *{and}* from the heart to that
1639 1529 3836 281 5634 1254 1666 2840 1650
v.iai.2p n.npm d.gsf n.gsf v.aai.2p cj p.g n.gsf p.a

ὃν παρεδόθητε τύπον διδαχῆς, [18] ἐλευθερωθέντες
pattern of teaching to which you were committed, *pattern* *of teaching* and having been set free
5596 1439 1439 4005 4140 5596 1439 1254 1802
r.asm v.api.2p n.asm n.gsf pt.ap.npm

δὲ ἀπὸ τῆς ἁμαρτίας ἐδουλώθητε τῇ δικαιοσύνῃ. [19]
and from *{the}* sin, you became slaves of righteousness. (I am speaking in
1254 608 3836 281 1530 3836 1466 3306 3306 3306
cj p.g d.gsf n.gsf v.api.2p d.dsf n.dsf

[a] [εἶναι] UBS, omitted by NET.

NASB

that He lives,
He lives to God.
[11]Even so consider
yourselves to be
dead to sin, but
alive to God in
Christ Jesus.
[12]Therefore do
not let sin reign in
your mortal body
so that you obey
its lusts, [13]and do
not go on present-
ing the members
of your body to
sin *as* instruments
of unrighteous-
ness; but present
yourselves to God
as those alive from
the dead, and your
members *as* instru-
ments of righteous-
ness to God. [14]For
sin shall not be
master over you,
for you are not un-
der law but under
grace.
[15]What then? Shall
we sin because we
are not under law
but under grace?
May it never be!
[16]Do you not know
that when you
present yourselves
to someone *as*
slaves for obedi-
ence, you are
slaves of the one
whom you obey,
either of sin result-
ing in death, or of
obedience resulting
in righteousness?
[17]But thanks be to
God that though
you were slaves of
sin, you became
obedient from the
heart to that form
of teaching to
which you were
committed, [18]and
having been freed
from sin, you
became slaves of
righteousness. [19]I
am speaking in

NIV

from everyday life
because of your
human limitations.
Just as you used to
offer yourselves as
slaves to impurity
and to ever-in-
creasing wick-
edness, so now
offer yourselves
as slaves to righ-
teousness leading
to holiness. 20 When
you were slaves to
sin, you were free
from the control
of righteousness.
21 What benefit
did you reap at
that time from the
things you are now
ashamed of? Those
things result in
death! 22 But now
that you have been
set free from sin
and have become
slaves of God, the
benefit you reap
leads to holiness,
and the result is
eternal life. 23 For
the wages of sin is
death, but the gift
of God is eternal
life in[a] Christ Jesus
our Lord.

Released From the Law, Bound to Christ

7 Do you not
know, brothers
and sisters—for
I am speaking to
those who know
the law—that the
law has authori-
ty over someone
only as long as that
person lives? 2 For
example, by law a
married woman is
bound to her hus-
band as long as he
is alive, but if her
husband dies, she
is released from
the law that binds
her to him. 3 So
then, if she has
sexual relations
with

[a] 23 Or *through*

ἀνθρώπινον λέγω διὰ τὴν ἀσθένειαν τῆς σαρκὸς ὑμῶν.
human terms *I am speaking* ⌞because of⌟ *{the}* your natural limitations.) *{the}* *natural* *your* For
474 3306 1328 3836 7007 4922 819 3836 4922 7007 1142
a.asn v.pai.1s p.a d.asf n.asf d.gsf n.gsf r.gp.2

ὥσπερ γὰρ παρεστήσατε τὰ μέλη ὑμῶν δοῦλα τῇ ἀκαθαρσίᾳ καὶ τῇ
just as *For* you presented *{the}* your members *your* as slaves to impurity and to
6061 1142 4225 3836 7007 3517 7007 1529 3836 174 2779 3836
cj cj v.aai.2p d.apn n.apn r.gp.2 a.apn d.dsf n.dsf cj d.dsf

ἀνομίᾳ εἰς τὴν ἀνομίαν, οὕτως νῦν παραστήσατε τὰ μέλη
lawlessness ⌞leading to⌟ *{the}* more lawlessness, so now present *{the}* your members
490 1650 3836 490 4048 3814 4225 3836 7007 3517
n.dsf p.a d.asf n.asf adv adv v.aam.2p d.apn n.apn

ὑμῶν δοῦλα τῇ δικαιοσύνῃ εἰς ἁγιασμόν. 20 ὅτε γὰρ
your as slaves to righteousness, ⌞leading to⌟ sanctification. For when *For* you were
7007 1529 3836 1466 1650 40 1142 4021 1142 1639 1639
r.gp.2 a.apn d.dsf n.dsf p.a n.asm cj cj

δοῦλοι ἦτε τῆς ἁμαρτίας, ἐλεύθεροι ἦτε τῇ δικαιοσύνῃ.
slaves *you were* of sin, you were free *you were* ⌞with regard to⌟ righteousness.
1529 1639 3836 281 1639 1639 1801 1639 3836 1466
n.npm v.iai.2p d.gsf n.gsf a.npm v.iai.2p d.dsf n.dsf

21 τίνα οὖν καρπὸν εἴχετε τότε; ἐφ᾽ οἷς ➝
Therefore what *Therefore* fruit ⌞were you getting⌟ ⌞at that time⌟ from the things of which you
4036 5515 4036 2843 2400 5538 2093 4005 2049
r.asm cj n.asm v.iai.2p adv p.d r.dpn

➝ νῦν ἐπαισχύνεσθε, τὸ γὰρ τέλος ἐκείνων θάνατος. 22 νυνὶ δὲ
are now ashamed? For the *For* end of those things is death. But now, *But*
2049 3814 2049 1142 3836 1142 5465 1697 2505 1254 3815 1254
adv v.ppi.2p d.nsn cj n.nsn r.gpn n.nsm adv cj

ἐλευθερωθέντες ἀπὸ τῆς ἁμαρτίας δουλωθέντες δὲ τῷ θεῷ ἔχετε
freed from *{the}* sin and enslaved *and* to God, the fruit you get
1802 608 3836 281 1254 1530 1254 3836 2536 3836 2843 7007 2400
pt.ap.npm p.g d.gsf n.gsf pt.ap.npm cj d.dsm n.dsm v.pai.2p

τὸν καρπὸν ὑμῶν εἰς ἁγιασμόν, τὸ δὲ τέλος ζωὴν αἰώνιον.
the *fruit* *you* ⌞leads to⌟ sanctification, and its *and* outcome, eternal life. *eternal*
3836 2843 7007 1650 40 1254 3836 1254 5465 173 2437 173
d.asm n.asm r.gp.2 p.a n.asm d.asn cj n.asn n.asf a.asf

23 τὰ γὰρ ὀψώνια τῆς ἁμαρτίας θάνατος, τὸ δὲ χάρισμα τοῦ θεοῦ
For the *For* wages of sin is death, but the *but* free gift of God is
1142 3836 1142 4072 3836 281 2505 1254 3836 1254 5922 3836 2536
d.npn cj n.npn d.gsf n.gsf n.nsm d.nsn cj n.nsn d.gsm n.gsm

ζωὴ αἰώνιος ἐν Χριστῷ Ἰησοῦ τῷ κυρίῳ ἡμῶν.
eternal life *eternal* in Christ Jesus *{the}* our Lord. *our*
173 2437 173 1877 5986 2652 3836 7005 3261 7005
n.nsf a.nsf p.d n.dsm n.dsm d.dsm n.dsm r.gp.1

7:1 ἢ ἀγνοεῖτε, ἀδελφοί, γινώσκουσιν γὰρ
Or ⌞do you not know,⌟ brethren (for I am speaking to those who know *for* the
2445 51 81 1142 3281 3281 3281 1182 1142
cj v.pai.2p n.vpm pt.pa.dpm cj

νόμον λαλῶ, ὅτι ὁ νόμος κυριεύει τοῦ ἀνθρώπου ἐφ᾽ ὅσον χρόνον ↰
law), *I am speaking* that the law ⌞is binding on⌟ a person only so long as
3795 3281 4022 3836 3795 3259 3836 476 2093 4012 5989 4012
n.asm v.pai.1s cj d.nsm n.nsm v.pai.3s d.gsm n.gsm p.a r.asm n.asm

ζῇ; 2 ἡ γὰρ ὕπανδρος γυνὴ τῷ
⌞he lives?⌟ Thus a *Thus* married woman is bound by law ⌞to her⌟ husband
2409 1142 3836 1142 5635 1222 1313 1313 3795 3795 3836 467
v.pai.3s d.nsf cj a.nsf n.nsf d.dsm

ζῶντι ἀνδρὶ δέδεται νόμῳ· ἐὰν δὲ ἀποθάνῃ ὁ ἀνήρ,
⌞while he is living;⌟ *husband* *is bound* *by law* but if *but* her husband dies, *her* *husband*
2409 467 1313 3795 1254 1569 1254 3836 467 633 3836 467
pt.pa.dsm n.dsm v.rpi.3s n.dsm cj cj v.aas.3s d.nsm n.nsm

κατήργηται ἀπὸ τοῦ νόμου τοῦ ἀνδρός. 3 ⌞ἄρα οὖν⌟
she is released from the law of marriage. Accordingly, if she is joined to
2934 608 3836 3795 3836 467 726 4036 1569 1181 1181 1181 467
v.rpi.3s p.g d.gsm n.gsm d.gsm n.gsm cj cj

NASB

human terms
because of the
weakness of your
flesh. For just as
you presented your
members as slaves
to impurity and
to lawlessness,
resulting in *further*
lawlessness, so
now present your
members as slaves
to righteous-
ness, resulting in
sanctification.
20 For when you
were slaves of sin,
you were free in
regard to righteous-
ness. 21 Therefore
what benefit were
you then deriving
from the things of
which you are now
ashamed? For the
outcome of those
things is death.
22 But now having
been freed from
sin and enslaved
to God, you derive
your benefit, result-
ing in sanctifica-
tion, and the out-
come, eternal life.
23 For the wages of
sin is death, but
the free gift of God
is eternal life in
Christ Jesus our
Lord.

Believers United to Christ

7:1 Or do you not
know, brethren (for
I am speaking to
those who know
the law), that the
law has jurisdiction
over a person as
long as he lives?
2 For the married
woman is bound
by law to her hus-
band while he is
living; but if her
husband dies, she
is released from the
law concerning the
husband. 3 So then,
if while her hus-
band is living she
is joined to

NIV

another man while her husband is still alive, she is called an adulteress. But if her husband dies, she is released from that law and is not an adulteress if she marries another man.
4 So, my brothers and sisters, you also died to the law through the body of Christ, that you might belong to another, to him who was raised from the dead, in order that we might bear fruit for God. 5 For when we were in the realm of the flesh,[a] the sinful passions aroused by the law were at work in us, so that we bore fruit for death. 6 But now, by dying to what once bound us, we have been released from the law so that we serve in the new way of the Spirit, and not in the old way of the written code.

The Law and Sin

7 What shall we say, then? Is the law sinful? Certainly not! Nevertheless, I would not have known what sin was had it not been for the law. For I would not have known what coveting really was if the law had not said, "You shall not covet."[b] 8 But sin, seizing the opportunity afforded by the

[a] 5 In contexts like this, the Greek word for *flesh* (*sarx*) refers to the sinful state of human beings, often presented as a power in opposition to the Spirit.
[b] 7 Exodus 20:17; Deut. 5:21

→ ζῶντος τοῦ ἀνδρὸς μοιχαλὶς
another man while her husband is alive, *her* *husband* she will be called an adulteress;
2283 467 3836 467 2409 3836 467 5976 5976 5976 5976 3655
pt.pa.gsm d.gsm n.gsm n.nsf

χρηματίσει ἐὰν γένηται ἀνδρὶ ἑτέρῳ· ἐὰν δὲ ἀποθάνῃ ὁ
she will be called *if* *she is joined* *to man* *another* but if *but* her husband dies, *her*
5976 1569 1181 467 2283 1254 1569 1254 3836 467 633 3836
v.fai.3s cj v.ams.3s n.dsm r.dsm cj cj v.aas.3s d.nsm

ἀνήρ, ἐλευθέρα ἐστὶν ἀπὸ τοῦ νόμου, τοῦ μὴ εἶναι αὐτὴν
husband she is free *she is* from that law, so that she is not *is* *she* an
467 1639 1639 1801 1639 608 3836 3795 3836 899 1639 3590 1639 899
n.nsm a.nsf v.pai.3s p.g d.gsm n.gsm d.gsn pl f.pa r.asf.3

μοιχαλίδα γενομένην ἀνδρὶ ἑτέρῳ. 4 ὥστε, ἀδελφοί μου, καὶ ὑμεῖς
adulteress if she marries another man. *another* So then, my brothers, *my* you also *you*
3655 1181 2283 467 2283 6063 1609 81 1609 7007 2779 7007
n.asf pt.am.asf n.dsm r.dsm cj n.vpm r.gs.1 adv r.np.2

ἐθανατώθητε τῷ νόμῳ διὰ τοῦ σώματος τοῦ Χριστοῦ, εἰς τὸ γενέσθαι
have died ⌊to the⌋ law through the body of Christ that ~ you might belong
2506 3836 3795 1328 3836 5393 3836 5986 1650 3836 7007 1181
v.api.2p d.dsm n.dsm p.g d.gsn n.gsn d.gsm n.gsm p.a d.asn f.am

ὑμᾶς ἑτέρῳ, τῷ ἐκ νεκρῶν ἐγερθέντι, ἵνα
you to another, ⌊to the⌋ one who was raised from the dead, *one who was raised* so that
7007 2283 3836 1586 1586 1586 1586 1666 3738 1586 2671
r.ap.2 r.dsm d.dsm p.g a.gpm pt.ap.dsm cj

καρποφορήσωμεν τῷ θεῷ. 5 ὅτε γὰρ ἦμεν ἐν τῇ σαρκί, τὰ
we might bear fruit for God. For while *For* ⌊we were living⌋ in the flesh, our sinful
2844 3836 2536 1142 4021 1142 1639 1877 3836 4922 3836 281
v.aas.1p d.dsm n.dsm cj cj v.iai.1p p.d d.dsf n.dsf d.npn

παθήματα τῶν ἁμαρτιῶν τὰ διὰ τοῦ νόμου ἐνηργεῖτο ἐν τοῖς
passions, *{the}* *sinful* *{the}* aroused by the law, *aroused* were at work in *{the}*
4077 3836 281 3836 1919 1328 3836 3795 1919 1877 3836
n.npn d.gpf n.gpf d.npn p.g d.gsm n.gsm v.imi.3s p.d d.dpn

μέλεσιν ἡμῶν, εἰς τὸ καρποφορῆσαι τῷ θανάτῳ· 6 νυνὶ δὲ
our bodies *our* to ~ bear fruit for death. But now *But*
7005 3517 7005 1650 3836 2844 3836 2505 1254 3815 1254
n.dpn r.gp.1 p.a d.asn f.aa d.dsm n.dsm adv cj

κατηργήθημεν ἀπὸ τοῦ νόμου ἀποθανόντες ἐν ᾧ κατειχόμεθα, ὥστε
we have been released from the law, having died to ⌊that which⌋ held us captive, so that
2934 608 3836 3795 633 1877 4005 2988 6063
v.api.1p p.g d.gsm n.gsm pt.aa.npm p.d r.dsm v.ipi.1p cj

δουλεύειν ἡμᾶς ἐν καινότητι → πνεύματος καὶ οὐ παλαιότητι
we serve *we* in newness of the Spirit and not under the old
7005 1526 7005 1877 2786 4460 2779 4024 4095
f.pa r.ap.1 p.d n.dsf n.gsn cj pl n.dsf

γράμματος. 7 τί οὖν ἐροῦμεν; ὁ νόμος ἁμαρτία; ⌊μὴ γένοιτο·⌋
written code. What then shall we say? Is the law sin? By no means!
1207 5515 4036 3306 3836 3795 281 3590 1181
n.gsn r.asn cj v.fai.1p d.nsm n.nsm n.nsf pl v.amo.3s

ἀλλὰ τὴν ἁμαρτίαν οὐκ ἔγνων ⌊εἰ
⌊On the contrary,⌋ I would not have known *{the}* sin *not* *I would have known* except
247 1182 1182 4024 1182 1182 3836 281 4024 1182 1623
cj d.asf n.asf pl v.aai.1s cj

μὴ⌋ διὰ νόμου, τήν τε γὰρ
through the law; *{the}* ~ ⌊that is,⌋ I would not have known what it means
3590 1328 3795 3836 5445 1142 3857 3857 4024 3857 3857
pl p.g n.gsm d.asf cj cj

ἐπιθυμίαν οὐκ ᾔδειν ↱ ⌊εἰ μὴ⌋ ὁ νόμος ἔλεγεν, ↱ ↱ οὐκ
to covet *not* *I would have known* had not the law said, "You shall not
2123 4024 3857 3306 1623 3590 3836 3795 3306 2121 2121 4024
n.asf pl v.lai.1s cj pl d.nsm n.nsm v.iai.3s pl

ἐπιθυμήσεις. 8 ἀφορμὴν δὲ λαβοῦσα ἡ ἁμαρτία διὰ τῆς
covet." *opportunity* But sin, seizing the opportunity *{the}* *sin* through the
2121 929 1254 281 3284 929 3836 281 1328 3836
v.fai.2s n.asf cj pt.aa.nsf d.nsf n.nsf p.g d.gsf

NASB

another man, she shall be called an adulteress; but if her husband dies, she is free from the law, so that she is not an adulteress though she is joined to another man.
4 Therefore, my brethren, you also were made to die to the Law through the body of Christ, so that you might be joined to another, to Him who was raised from the dead, in order that we might bear fruit for God. 5 For while we were in the flesh, the sinful passions, which were *aroused* by the Law, were at work in the members of our body to bear fruit for death. 6 But now we have been released from the Law, having died to that by which we were bound, so that we serve in newness of the [a]Spirit and not in oldness of the letter.
7 What shall we say then? Is the Law sin? May it never be! On the contrary, I would not have come to know sin except through the Law; for I would not have known about coveting if the Law had not said, "YOU SHALL NOT COVET." 8 But sin, taking opportunity through

[a] Or *spirit*

NIV

commandment,
produced in me ev-
ery kind of covet-
ing. For apart from
the law, sin was
dead. 9Once I was
alive apart from
the law; but when
the commandment
came, sin sprang to
life and I died. 10I
found that the very
commandment that
was intended to
bring life actual-
ly brought death.
11For sin, seizing
the opportunity
afforded by the
commandment,
deceived me, and
through the com-
mandment put me
to death. 12So then,
the law is holy, and
the commandment
is holy, righteous
and good.
13Did that which
is good, then, be-
come death to me?
By no means! Nev-
ertheless, in order
that sin might be
recognized as
sin, it used what
is good to bring
about my death, so
that through the
commandment sin
might become ut-
terly sinful.
14We know that
the law is spiritual;
but I am unspiritu-
al, sold as a slave
to sin. 15I do not
understand what
I do. For what I
want to do I do not
do, but what I hate
I do. 16And if I do
what I do not want
to do, I agree that
the law is

ἐντολῆς κατειργάσατο ἐν ἐμοὶ πᾶσαν ἐπιθυμίαν· χωρὶς γὰρ
commandment, produced in me ⌞all kinds of⌟ covetousness. (For apart from *For* the
1953 2981 1877 1609 4246 2123 1142 6006 1142
n.gsf v.ami.3s p.d r.ds.1 a.asf n.asf p.g cj

νόμου ἁμαρτία νεκρά. 9 ἐγὼ δὲ → ἔζων χωρὶς νόμου ποτέ, →
law, sin is dead.) I *{and}* was once alive apart from the law, *once* but when
3795 281 3738 1609 1254 4537 2409 6006 3795 4537 1254
n.gsm n.nsf a.nsf r.ns.1 cj v.iai.1s p.g n.gsm adv

ἐλθούσης δὲ τῆς ἐντολῆς ἡ ἁμαρτία ἀνέζησεν,[a] 10 ἐγὼ
the commandment came, *but the commandment {the}* sin came to life and I
3836 1953 2262 1254 3836 1953 3836 281 348 1254 1609
pt.aa.gsf cj d.gsf n.gsf d.nsf n.nsf v.aai.3s r.ns.1

δὲ ἀπέθανον καὶ εὑρέθη μοι ἡ ἐντολὴ ἡ εἰς ζωήν, αὕτη
and died. *{and}* I found *to me!* that the very commandment that promised life *very*
1254 633 2779 2351 1609 3836 4047 1953 3836 1650 2437 4047
cj v.aai.1s cj v.api.3s r.ds.1 d.nsf n.nsf d.nsf p.a n.asf r.nsf

εἰς θάνατον· 11 ἡ γὰρ ἁμαρτία ἀφορμὴν λαβοῦσα διὰ τῆς
brought death to me! *{the}* For sin, seizing the opportunity *seizing* through the
1650 2505 1609 1609 3836 1142 281 3284 929 3284 1328 3836
p.a n.asm d.nsf cj n.nsf n.asf pt.aa.nsf p.g d.gsf

ἐντολῆς ἐξηπάτησέν με καὶ δι᾽ αὐτῆς ἀπέκτεινεν. 12 ὥστε ὁ μὲν
commandment, deceived me and through it killed me. So then, the ~
1953 1987 1609 2779 1328 899 650 6063 3836 3525
n.gsf v.aai.3s r.as.1 cj p.g r.gsf.3 v.aai.3s cj d.nsm pl

νόμος ἅγιος καὶ ἡ ἐντολὴ ἁγία καὶ δικαία καὶ ἀγαθή. 13 τὸ οὖν
law is holy, and the commandment is holy and righteous and good. Did that *then*
3795 41 2779 3836 1953 41 2779 1465 2779 19 1181 3836 4036
n.nsm a.nsm cj d.nsf n.nsf a.nsf cj a.nsf cj a.nsf d.nsn cj

ἀγαθὸν ἐμοὶ ἐγένετο θάνατος; ⌞μὴ γένοιτο·⌟ ἀλλὰ
which is good, then, become death to me? *Did become death* By no means! But
19 4036 1181 2505 1609 1181 2505 3590 1181 247
a.nsn r.ds.1 v.ami.3s n.nsm pl v.amo.3s cj

ἡ ἁμαρτία, ἵνα φανῇ ἁμαρτία, διὰ
{the} sin, ⌞in order that⌟ ⌞it might be shown⌟ to be sin, produced death in me through
3836 281 2671 5743 281 2981 2505 1609 1609 1328
d.nsf n.nsf cj v.aps.3s n.nsf p.g

τοῦ ἀγαθοῦ μοι κατεργαζομένη θάνατον, ἵνα
that which is good *in me produced death* so that sin, through the commandment,
3836 19 1609 2981 2505 2671 281 1328 3836 1953
d.gsn a.gsn r.ds.1 pt.pm.nsf n.asm cj

γένηται καθ᾽ ὑπερβολὴν ἁμαρτωλὸς ἡ ἁμαρτία διὰ τῆς ἐντολῆς.
might be sinful beyond measure *sinful {the} sin through the commandment*
1181 283 2848 5651 283 3836 281 1328 3836 1953
v.ams.3s p.a n.asf a.nsf d.nsf n.nsf p.g d.gsf n.gsf

14 οἴδαμεν γὰρ ὅτι ὁ νόμος πνευματικός ἐστιν, ἐγὼ δὲ σάρκινός
For we know *For* that the law is spiritual; *is* but I *but* am unspiritual,
1142 3857 1142 4022 3836 3795 1639 4461 1639 1254 1609 1254 1639 4921
v.rai.1p cj cj d.nsm n.nsm a.nsm v.pai.3s r.ns.1 cj a.nsm

εἰμι πεπραμένος ὑπὸ τὴν ἁμαρτίαν. 15 ↱ ὃ
am sold as a slave to *{the}* sin. For I do not understand my own
1639 4405 5679 3836 281 1142 1182 1182 4024 1182 2981 4005
v.pai.1s pt.rp.nsm p.a d.asf n.asf r.asn

γὰρ κατεργάζομαι οὐ γινώσκω· οὐ γὰρ ὃ θέλω τοῦτο
For actions; *not I do understand* for I am not *for* doing what I want *{this}*
1142 2981 4024 1182 1142 4556 4556 4024 1142 4556 4005 2527 4047
cj v.pmi.1s pl v.pai.1s pl cj r.asn v.pai.1s r.asn

πράσσω, ἀλλ᾽ ὃ μισῶ τοῦτο ποιῶ. 16 εἰ δὲ
I am doing to do, but I am doing what I hate. *{this} I am doing* But if *But* I am
4556 247 4472 4472 4472 4005 3631 4047 4472 1254 1623 1254 4472 4472
v.pai.1s cj r.asn v.pai.1s r.asn v.pai.1s cj cj

ὃ ↱ ↱ οὐ θέλω τοῦτο ποιῶ, σύμφημι τῷ νόμῳ ὅτι
doing what I do not want *{this} I am doing* to do, I agree with the law, that it is
4472 4005 2527 2527 4024 2527 4047 4472 5238 3836 3795 4022
r.asn pl v.pai.1s r.asn v.pai.1s v.pai.1s d.dsm n.dsm cj

[a] ἐγὼ δὲ ἀπέθανον included by TR after ἀνέζησεν.

NASB

the commandment,
produced in me
coveting of every
kind; for apart
from the Law sin *is*
dead. 9I was once
alive apart from
the Law; but when
the commandment
came, sin became
alive and I died;
10and this com-
mandment, which
was to result in life,
proved to result in
death for me; 11for
sin, taking an op-
portunity through
the commandment,
deceived me and
through it killed
me. 12So then, the
Law is holy, and
the commandment
is holy and righ-
teous and good.
13Therefore did
that which is good
become *a cause of*
death for me? May
it never be! Rather
it was sin, in order
that it might be
shown to be sin
by effecting my
death through that
which is good, so
that through the
commandment sin
would become ut-
terly sinful.

The Conflict of Two Natures

14For we know
that the Law is
spiritual, but I am
of flesh, sold into
bondage to sin.
15For what I am
doing, I do not un-
derstand; for I am
not practicing what
I *would* like to *do,*
but I am doing the
very thing I hate.
16But if I do the
very thing I do not
want *to do,* I agree
with the Law, *con-
fessing* that the

NIV

good. [17]As it is, it
is no longer I my-
self who do it, but
it is sin living in
me. [18]For I know
that good itself
does not dwell in
me, that is, in my
sinful nature.[a] For
I have the desire to
do what is good,
but I cannot carry
it out. [19]For I do
not do the good I
want to do, but the
evil I do not want
to do—this I keep
on doing. [20]Now if
I do what I do not
want to do, it is no
longer I who do it,
but it is sin living
in me that does it.
[21]So I find this
law at work: Al-
though I want to
do good, evil is
right there with
me. [22]For in my
inner being I de-
light in God's law;
[23]but I see another
law at work in
me, waging war
against the law of
my mind and mak-
ing me a prisoner
of the law of sin at
work within me.
[24]What a wretched
man I am! Who
will rescue me
from this body that
is subject to death?
[25]Thanks be to
God, who delivers
me through Jesus
Christ our Lord!
So then, I myself
in my mind am a
slave to God's law,
but in my sinful
nature[b] a

καλός. 17 νυνὶ δὲ οὐκέτι ↱ ἐγὼ κατεργάζομαι αὐτὸ ἀλλὰ ἡ
good. So now *So* it is no longer I myself doing it, but *{the}* sin
2819 1254 3815 1254 4033 2981 1609 2981 899 247 3836 281
a.nsm adv cj adv r.ns.1 v.pmi.1s r.asn.3 cj d.nsf

οἰκοῦσα ἐν ἐμοὶ ἁμαρτία. 18 οἶδα γὰρ ὅτι οὐκ οἰκεῖ ἐν ἐμοί, τοῦτ'
living in me. *sin* For I know *For* that nothing good dwells in me, that
3861 1877 1609 281 1142 3857 1142 4022 4024 19 3861 1877 1609 4047
pt.pa.nsf p.d r.ds.1 n.nsf v.rai.1s cj cj pl v.pai.3s p.d r.ds.1 r.nsn

ἔστιν ἐν τῇ σαρκί μου, ἀγαθόν· τὸ γὰρ θέλειν παράκειταί μοι,
is, in *{the}* my flesh; *my* *good* for I have the *for* desire *have* *I*
1639 1877 3836 1609 4922 1609 19 1142 1609 4154 3836 1142 2527 4154 1609
v.pai.3s p.d d.dsf n.dsf r.gs.1 a.nsn d.nsn cj f.pa v.pmi.3s r.ds.1

τὸ δὲ → → κατεργάζεσθαι τὸ καλὸν οὔ· 19
to do what is right, *{the}* but I am unable to do it. *what* *right* *unable* For I
3836 2819 3836 1254 4024 2981 3836 2819 4024 1142 4472
d.nsn cj f.pm d.asn a.asn pl

οὐ γὰρ ὃ θέλω ποιῶ ἀγαθόν, ἀλλὰ ὃ ↱ ↱ οὐ
do not *For* do the good *{that}* I want, *I do* *good* but the evil *{that}* I do not
4472 4024 1142 19 4005 2527 4472 19 247 2805 4005 2527 2527 4024
pl cj r.asn v.pai.1s v.pai.1s a.asn cj r.asn pl

θέλω κακὸν τοῦτο πράσσω. 20 εἰ δὲ ὃ ↱ ↱ οὐ θέλω ἐγὼ[a]
want *evil* is what I do. Now if *Now* I do what I do not want, *I*
2527 2805 4047 4556 1254 1623 1254 1609 4472 4005 2527 2527 4024 2527 1609
v.pai.1s a.asn r.asn v.pai.1s cj cj r.asn pl v.pai.1s r.ns.1

τοῦτο ποιῶ, οὐκέτι ἐγὼ κατεργάζομαι αὐτὸ ἀλλὰ ἡ οἰκοῦσα ἐν
{this} *do* it is no longer I who do it, but *{the}* sin that lives in
4047 4472 4033 1609 2981 899 247 3836 281 3861 1877
r.asn v.pai.1s adv r.ns.1 v.pmi.1s r.asn.3 cj d.nsf pt.pa.nsf p.d

ἐμοὶ ἁμαρτία. 21 εὑρίσκω ἄρα τὸν νόμον, τῷ → θέλοντι ἐμοὶ
me. *sin* So I find *So* it to be a law that when I want *I*
1609 281 726 2351 726 3836 3795 3836 1609 2527 1609
r.ds.1 n.nsf v.pai.1s cj d.asm n.asm d.dsm pt.pa.dsm r.ds.1

ποιεῖν τὸ καλόν, ὅτι ἐμοὶ τὸ κακὸν παράκειται· 22
to do *{the}* good, *{that}* evil is present in me. *{the}* *evil* *is present* For
4472 3836 2819 4022 2805 4154 4154 1609 3836 2805 4154 1142
f.pa d.asn a.asn cj r.ds.1 d.nsn a.nsn v.pmi.3s

συνήδομαι γὰρ τῷ νόμῳ τοῦ θεοῦ κατὰ τὸν ἔσω ἄνθρωπον, 23 βλέπω
⌞I joyfully agree with⌟ *For* the law of God in the inner man, but I see
5310 1142 3836 3795 3836 2536 2848 3836 2276 476 1254 1063
v.pmi.1s cj d.dsm n.dsm d.gsm n.gsm p.a d.asm adv n.asm v.pai.1s

δὲ ἕτερον νόμον ἐν τοῖς μέλεσίν μου ἀντιστρατευόμενον τῷ νόμῳ τοῦ
but a different law in *{the}* my members; *my* it wages war against the law of my
1254 2283 3795 1877 3836 1609 3517 1609 529 3836 3795 3836 1609
cj r.asm n.asm p.d d.dpn n.dpn r.gs.1 pt.pm.asm d.dsm n.dsm d.gsm

νοός μου καὶ → αἰχμαλωτίζοντά με ἐν τῷ νόμῳ τῆς ἁμαρτίας τῷ
mind *my* and makes me captive *me* to the law of sin *{the}*
3808 1609 2779 1609 170 1609 1877 3836 3795 3836 281 3836
n.gsm r.gs.1 cj pt.pa.asm r.as.1 p.d d.dsm n.dsm d.gsf n.gsf d.dsm

ὄντι ἐν τοῖς μέλεσίν μου. 24 ταλαίπωρος ἐγὼ ἄνθρωπος· τίς
dwelling in *{the}* my members. *my* Wretched man that I *man* am! Who
1639 1877 3836 1609 3517 1609 5417 476 1609 476 5515
pt.pa.dsm p.d d.dpn n.dpn r.gs.1 a.nsm r.ns.1 n.nsm r.nsm

με ῥύσεται ἐκ τοῦ σώματος τοῦ θανάτου τούτου; 25 χάρις δὲ[b]
will deliver me *will deliver* from *{the}* this body of death? *this* Thanks *{and}*
4861 4861 1609 4861 1666 3836 4047 5393 3836 2505 4047 5921 1254
r.as.1 v.fmi.3s p.g d.gsn n.gsn d.gsm n.gsm r.gsm n.nsf cj

τῷ θεῷ διὰ Ἰησοῦ Χριστοῦ τοῦ κυρίου ἡμῶν. ἄρα οὖν αὐτὸς ἐγὼ
be to God through Jesus Christ *{the}* our Lord! *our* So then, I myself *I*
3836 2536 1328 2652 5986 3836 7005 3261 7005 726 4036 1609 899 1609
d.dsm n.dsm p.g n.gsm n.gsm d.gsm n.gsm r.gp.1 cj cj r.nsm r.ns.1

τῷ μὲν νοῒ δουλεύω νόμῳ θεοῦ τῇ δὲ σαρκὶ
serve the law of God ⌞with my⌟ ~ mind, *serve* *law* *of God* but ⌞with my⌟ *but* flesh I
1526 3795 2536 2536 3836 3525 3808 1526 3795 2536 1254 3836 1254 4922
d.dsm pl n.dsm v.pai.1s n.dsm n.gsm d.dsf cj n.dsf

NASB

Law is good. [17]So
now, no longer am
I the one doing
it, but sin which
dwells in me. [18]For
I know that nothing
good dwells in me,
that is, in my flesh;
for the willing is
present in me, but
the doing of the
good *is* not. [19]For
the good that I
want, I do not do,
but I practice the
very evil that I do
not want. [20]But if I
am doing the very
thing I do not want,
I am no longer the
one doing it, but
sin which dwells
in me.
[21]I find then the
principle that evil
is present in me,
the one who wants
to do good. [22]For
I joyfully concur
with the law of
God in the inner
man, [23]but I see a
different law in
the members of
my body, waging
war against the
law of my mind
and making me
a prisoner of the
law of sin which
is in my members.
[24]Wretched man
that I am! Who will
set me free from
the body of this
death? [25]Thanks
be to God through
Jesus Christ our
Lord! So then, on
the one hand I my-
self with my mind
am serving the law
of God, but on the
other, with

[a] 18 Or *my flesh*
[b] 25 Or *in the flesh*

[a] [ἐγὼ] UBS.
[b] δέ omitted by NET.

NIV

slave to the law
of sin.

Life Through the Spirit

8 Therefore,
there is now
no condemnation
for those who are
in Christ Jesus,
[2]because through
Christ Jesus the
law of the Spirit
who gives life has
set you[a] free from
the law of sin and
death. [3]For what
the law was power-
less to do because
it was weakened
by the flesh,[b] God
did by sending his
own Son in the
likeness of sinful
flesh to be a sin of-
fering.[c] And so he
condemned sin in
the flesh, [4]in order
that the righteous
requirement of the
law might be fully
met in us, who do
not live according
to the flesh but
according to the
Spirit.
[5]Those who live
according to the
flesh have their
minds set on what
the flesh desires;
but those who live
in accordance with
the Spirit have
their minds set on
what the Spirit de-
sires. [6]The mind
governed by the
flesh is death, but
the mind governed
by the Spirit is life
and peace. [7]The
mind governed by
the flesh is hostile
to God; it does not
submit to God's
law, nor can it do
so. [8]Those

[a] 2 The Greek is singular; some manuscripts *me*
[b] 3 In contexts like this, the Greek word for *flesh* (*sarx*) refers to the sinful state of human beings, often presented as a power in opposition to the Spirit; also in verses 4-13.
[c] 3 Or *flesh, for sin*

νόμῳ ἁμαρτίας.
serve the law of sin.
3795 281
n.dsm n.gsf

8:1 οὐδὲν ἄρα νῦν κατάκριμα τοῖς ἐν Χριστῷ
There is therefore now no *therefore* *now* condemnation for those who are in Christ
726 3814 4029 726 3814 2890 3836 1877 5986
a.nsn cj adv n.nsn d.dpm p.d n.dsm

Ἰησοῦ.[a] 2 ὁ γὰρ νόμος τοῦ πνεύματος τῆς ζωῆς ἐν Χριστῷ Ἰησοῦ → →
Jesus. For the *For* law of the Spirit of life in Christ Jesus has set
2652 1142 3836 1142 3795 3836 4460 3836 2437 1877 5986 2652
n.dsm d.nsm cj n.nsm d.gsn n.gsn d.gsf n.gsf p.d n.dsm n.dsm

ἠλευθέρωσέν σε ἀπὸ τοῦ νόμου τῆς ἁμαρτίας καὶ τοῦ θανάτου. 3 τὸ
you free *you* from the law of sin and of death. For what
5148 1802 5148 608 3836 3795 3836 281 2779 3836 2505 1142 3836
v.aai.3s r.as.2 p.g d.gsm n.gsm d.gsf n.gsf cj d.gsm n.gsm d.asn

γὰρ ἀδύνατον τοῦ νόμου ἐν ᾧ ἠσθένει διὰ τῆς σαρκός, ὁ
For the law could not do, *the* *law* *{in}* *{that}* ⌊weak as it was⌋ through the flesh, *{the}*
1142 3836 3795 105 3836 3795 1877 4005 820 1328 3836 4922 3836
cj a.asn d.gsm n.gsm p.d r.dsn v.iai.3s p.g d.gsf n.gsf d.nsm

θεὸς τὸν ἑαυτοῦ υἱὸν πέμψας ἐν ὁμοιώματι → σαρκὸς
God, by sending *{the}* his own Son *by sending* in the likeness of sinful flesh
2536 4287 4287 3836 1571 5626 4287 1877 3930 281 4922
n.nsm d.asm r.gsm.3 n.asm pt.aa.nsm p.d n.dsn n.gsf

ἁμαρτίας καὶ περὶ ἁμαρτίας κατέκρινεν τὴν ἁμαρτίαν ἐν τῇ σαρκί, 4 ἵνα τὸ
sinful and as a sin offering, condemned *{the}* sin in the flesh, so that the
281 2779 4309 281 2891 3836 281 1877 3836 4922 2671 3836
n.gsf cj p.g n.gsf v.aai.3s d.asf n.asf p.d d.dsf n.dsf cj d.nsn

δικαίωμα τοῦ νόμου πληρωθῇ ἐν ἡμῖν τοῖς μὴ κατὰ
righteous requirement of the law might be fulfilled in us, who do not walk ⌊according to⌋
1468 3836 3795 4444 1877 7005 3836 4344 3590 4344 2848
n.nsn d.gsm n.gsm v.aps.3s p.d r.dp.1 d.dpm pl p.a

σάρκα περιπατοῦσιν ἀλλὰ κατὰ πνεῦμα. 5 οἱ γὰρ
the flesh *do walk* but ⌊according to⌋ the Spirit. For those *For* who live
4922 4344 247 2848 4460 1142 3836 1142 1639 1639
n.asf pt.pa.dpm cj p.a n.asn d.npm cj

κατὰ σάρκα ὄντες τὰ τῆς σαρκὸς
⌊according to⌋ the flesh *who live* have set their minds on ⌊the things⌋ of the flesh,
2848 4922 1639 5858 5858 5858 5858 3836 3836 4922
p.a n.asf pt.pa.npm d.apn d.gsf n.gsf

φρονοῦσιν, οἱ δὲ κατὰ πνεῦμα
have set their minds but those *but* who live ⌊according to⌋ the Spirit have set their minds on
5858 1254 3836 1254 2848 4460
v.pai.3p d.npm cj p.a n.asn

τὰ τοῦ πνεύματος. 6 τὸ γὰρ φρόνημα τῆς σαρκὸς θάνατος,
⌊the things⌋ of the Spirit. To set the *{for}* mind ⌊on the⌋ flesh leads to death,
3836 3836 4460 3836 1142 5859 3836 4922 2505
d.apn d.gsn n.gsn d.nsn cj n.nsn d.gsf n.gsf n.nsm

τὸ δὲ φρόνημα τοῦ πνεύματος ζωὴ καὶ εἰρήνη· 7 διότι τὸ
but to set the *{and}* mind on the Spirit brings life and peace, because the
3836 1254 5859 3836 4460 2437 2779 1645 1484 3836
d.nsn cj n.nsn d.gsn n.gsn n.nsf cj n.nsf cj d.nsn

φρόνημα τῆς σαρκὸς ἔχθρα εἰς θεόν, τῷ γὰρ νόμῳ
mind set on the flesh is hostile to God; it does not submit ⌊to the⌋ *{for}* law
5859 3836 4922 2397 1650 2536 5718 5718 4024 5718 3836 1142 3795
n.nsn d.gsf n.gsf n.nsf p.a n.asm d.dsm cj n.dsm

τοῦ θεοῦ οὐχ ὑποτάσσεται, οὐδὲ γὰρ δύναται· 8 οἱ δὲ
of God; *not* *it does submit* in fact, it is not even *in fact* able to do so. Those *{and}*
3836 2536 4024 5718 1142 1142 4028 1142 1538 3836 1254
d.gsm n.gsm pl v.ppi.3s cj cj v.ppi.3s d.npm cj

[a] μὴ κατὰ σάρκα περιπατοῦσιν, ἀλλὰ κατὰ πνεῦμα included by TR after Ἰησοῦ.

NASB

my flesh the law
of sin.

Deliverance from Bondage

8:1Therefore there
is now no condem-
nation for those
who are in Christ
Jesus. [2]For the law
of the Spirit of life
in Christ Jesus has
set you free from
the law of sin and
of death. [3]For what
the Law could not
do, weak as it was
through the flesh,
God *did:* sending
His own Son in the
likeness of sinful
flesh and *as an of-*
fering for sin, He
condemned sin in
the flesh, [4]so that
the requirement
of the Law might
be fulfilled in us,
who do not walk
according to the
flesh but according
to the Spirit. [5]For
those who are ac-
cording to the flesh
set their minds on
the things of the
flesh, but those
who are according
to the Spirit, the
things of the Spirit.
[6]For the mind set
on the flesh is
death, but the mind
set on the Spirit
is life and peace,
[7]because the mind
set on the flesh
is hostile toward
God; for it does not
subject itself to the
law of God, for it is
not even able *to do*
so, [8]and those who

NIV

who are in the realm of
the flesh cannot please
God.
9You, however, are
not in the realm of the
flesh but are in the
realm of the Spirit, if
indeed the Spirit of
God lives in you. And
if anyone does not have
the Spirit of Christ,
they do not belong to
Christ. 10But if Christ
is in you, then even
though your body is
subject to death be-
cause of sin, the Spirit
gives life[a] because of
righteousness. 11And if
the Spirit of him who
raised Jesus from the
dead is living in you,
he who raised Christ
from the dead will also
give life to your mortal
bodies because of[b] his
Spirit who lives in you.
12Therefore, brothers
and sisters, we have an
obligation—but it is
not to the flesh, to live
according to it. 13For if
you live according to
the flesh, you will die;
but if by the Spirit you
put to death the mis-
deeds of the body, you
will live.
14For those who are
led by the Spirit of
God are the children
of God. 15The Spirit
you received does not
make you slaves, so
that you live in fear
again; rather, the Spirit
you received brought
about your adoption
to sonship.[c] And by
him we cry, *"Abba,*[d]
Father." 16The Spirit
himself testifies with
our spirit that we are
God's children. 17Now
if we are children,

[a] *10* Or *you, your body is dead because of sin, yet your spirit is alive*
[b] *11* Some manuscripts *bodies through*
[c] *15* The Greek word for *adoption to sonship* is a term referring to the full legal standing of an adopted male heir in Roman culture; also in verse 23.
[d] *15* Aramaic for *father*

ἐν σαρκὶ ὄντες θεῷ ἀρέσαι οὐ δύνανται.
controlled by the flesh *controlled* are not able to please God. *to please not are able*
1639 1877 4922 1639 1538 4024 1538 743 743 2536 743 4024 1538
p.d n.dsf pt.pa.npm n.dsm f.aa pl v.ppi.3p

9 ὑμεῖς δὲ οὐκ ἐστὲ ἐν σαρκὶ ἀλλὰ ἐν πνεύματι, εἴπερ
You, however, are not *are* controlled by the flesh but by the Spirit, if indeed
7007 1254 1639 4024 1639 1877 4922 247 1877 4460 1642
r.np.2 cj pl v.pai.2p p.d n.dsf cj p.d n.dsn cj

πνεῦμα θεοῦ οἰκεῖ ἐν ὑμῖν. εἰ δέ τις πνεῦμα Χριστοῦ
the Spirit of God lives in you. *{if} {and}* Whoever does not have the Spirit of Christ
4460 2536 3861 1877 7007 1623 1254 5516 2400 4024 2400 4460 5986
n.nsn n.gsm v.pai.3s p.d r.dp.2 cj cj r.nsm n.asn n.gsm

οὐκ ἔχει, οὗτος → οὐκ ἔστιν αὐτοῦ. 10 εἰ δὲ Χριστὸς ἐν ὑμῖν,
not does have {this one} does not ⌊belong to⌋ him. But if *But* Christ is in you,
4024 2400 4047 1639 4024 1639 899 1254 1623 1254 5986 1877 7007
pl v.pai.3s r.nsm pl v.pai.3s r.gsm.3 cj cj n.nsm p.d r.dp.2

τὸ μὲν σῶμα νεκρὸν διὰ ἁμαρτίαν τὸ δὲ πνεῦμα ζωὴ
although the *although* body is dead ⌊because of⌋ sin, the *{and}* Spirit is life
3525 3836 3525 5393 3738 1328 281 3836 1254 4460 2437
d.nsn pl n.nsn a.nsn p.a n.asf d.nsn cj n.nsn n.nsf

διὰ δικαιοσύνην. 11 εἰ δὲ τὸ πνεῦμα τοῦ ἐγείραντος τὸν Ἰησοῦν
⌊because of⌋ righteousness. But if *But* the Spirit of him who raised *{the}* Jesus
1328 1466 1254 1623 1254 3836 4460 3836 1586 3836 2652
p.a n.asf cj cj d.nsn n.nsn d.gsm pt.aa.gsm d.asm n.asm

ἐκ νεκρῶν οἰκεῖ ἐν ὑμῖν, ὁ ἐγείρας Χριστὸν ἐκ νεκρῶν →
from the dead lives in you, the ⌊one who raised⌋ Christ Jesus from the dead will
1666 3738 3861 1877 7007 3836 1586 5986 1666 3738
p.g a.gpm v.pai.3s p.d r.dp.2 d.nsm pt.aa.nsm n.asm p.g a.gpm

ζῳοποιήσει καὶ τὰ θνητὰ σώματα ὑμῶν διὰ τοῦ ἐνοικοῦντος
also give life to *also {the}* your mortal bodies *your* through his Spirit who lives
2779 2443 2779 3836 7007 2570 5393 7007 1328 899 4460 3836 1940
v.fai.3s adv d.apn a.apn n.apn r.gp.2 p.g d.gsn pt.pa.gsn

αὐτοῦ πνεύματος ἐν ὑμῖν. 12 ἄρα οὖν, ἀδελφοί, ὀφειλέται ἐσμὲν οὐ τῇ
his Spirit in you. So then, brethren, we are debtors, *we are* not ⌊to the⌋
899 4460 1877 7007 726 4036 81 1639 1639 4050 1639 4024 3836
r.gsm.3 n.gsn p.d r.dp.2 cj cj n.vpm n.npm v.pai.1p pl d.dsf

σαρκὶ τοῦ κατὰ σάρκα ζῆν, 13 εἰ γὰρ κατὰ
flesh, ~ to live ⌊according to⌋ the flesh, *to live* for if *for* you live ⌊according to⌋
4922 3836 2409 2409 2848 4922 2409 1142 1623 1142 2409 2409 2848
n.dsf d.gsn p.a n.asf f.pa cj cj p.a

σάρκα ζῆτε, μέλλετε ἀποθνῄσκειν· εἰ δὲ → πνεύματι
the flesh, *you live* ⌊you will certainly⌋ die; but if *but* by the Spirit you put
4922 2409 3516 633 1254 1623 1254 4460 2506 2506
n.asf v.pai.2p v.pai.2p f.pa cj cj n.dsn

τὰς πράξεις τοῦ σώματος θανατοῦτε, ζήσεσθε. 14 ὅσοι γὰρ
to death the deeds of the body, *you put to death* you will live. For it is those *For* who
2506 2506 3836 4552 3836 5393 2506 2409 1142 4012 1142 72
d.apf n.apf d.gsn n.gsn v.pai.2p v.fmi.2p r.npm cj

→ πνεύματι θεοῦ ἄγονται, οὗτοι υἱοὶ θεοῦ εἰσιν. 15 → →
are led by the Spirit of God *who are led* who are the sons of God. *are* For you did
72 72 4460 2536 72 4047 1639 5626 2536 1639 1142 3284 3284
n.dsn n.gsm v.ppi.3p r.npm n.npm n.gsm v.pai.3p

οὐ γὰρ ἐλάβετε πνεῦμα δουλείας πάλιν εἰς φόβον ἀλλὰ ἐλάβετε
not *For* receive the spirit of slavery leading back to fear, but you received the
4024 1142 3284 4460 1525 4099 1650 5832 247 3284
pl cj v.aai.2p n.asn n.gsf adv p.a n.asm cj v.aai.2p

πνεῦμα υἱοθεσίας ἐν ᾧ κράζομεν, αββα ὁ πατήρ. 16 αὐτὸ τὸ
Spirit of adoption. By him we cry out, "Abba! *{the}* Father!" The Spirit himself *The*
4460 5625 1877 4005 3189 5 3836 4252 3836 4460 899 3836
n.asn n.gsf p.d r.dsn v.pai.1p n.vsm d.vsm n.vsm r.nsn d.nsn

πνεῦμα συμμαρτυρεῖ τῷ πνεύματι ἡμῶν ὅτι ἐσμὲν τέκνα θεοῦ. 17 εἰ
Spirit bears witness with *{the}* our spirit *our* that we are children of God, and if
4460 5210 3836 7005 4460 7005 4022 1639 5451 2536 1254 1623
n.nsn v.pai.3s d.dsn n.dsn r.gp.1 cj v.pai.1p n.npn n.gsm cj

NASB

are in the flesh can-
not please God.
9However, you
are not in the flesh
but in the Spirit, if
indeed the Spirit of
God dwells in you.
But if anyone does
not have the Spirit
of Christ, he does
not belong to Him.
10If Christ is in you,
though the body
is dead because of
sin, yet the spirit
is alive because
of righteousness.
11But if the Spirit of
Him who raised Je-
sus from the dead
dwells in you, He
who raised Christ
Jesus from the
dead will also give
life to your mortal
bodies [a]through
His Spirit who
dwells in you.
12So then, breth-
ren, we are under
obligation, not to
the flesh, to live
according to the
flesh— 13for if you
are living accord-
ing to the flesh,
you must die; but
if by the Spirit you
are putting to death
the deeds of the
body, you will live.
14For all who are
being led by the
Spirit of God, these
are sons of God.
15For you have not
received a spirit
of slavery leading
to fear again, but
you have received
a spirit of adoption
as sons by which
we cry out, "Abba!
Father!" 16The Spir-
it Himself testifies
with our spirit that
we are children of
God, 17and if

[a] One early ms reads *because of*

NIV

then we are
heirs—heirs of
God and co-heirs
with Christ, if in-
deed we share in
his sufferings in
order that we may
also share in his
glory.

Present Suffering and Future Glory

[18]I consider that
our present suffer-
ings are not worth
comparing with
the glory that will
be revealed in us.
[19]For the creation
waits in eager ex-
pectation for the
children of God to
be revealed. [20]For
the creation was
subjected to frus-
tration, not by its
own choice, but by
the will of the one
who subjected it,
in hope [21]that[a] the
creation itself will
be liberated from
its bondage to de-
cay and brought
into the freedom
and glory of the
children of God.
[22]We know that
the whole creation
has been groaning
as in the pains of
childbirth right up
to the present time.
[23]Not only so, but
we ourselves, who
have the firstfruits
of the Spirit, groan
inwardly as we
wait eagerly for
our adoption to
sonship, the re-
demption of our
bodies. [24]For in
this hope we were
saved. But hope
that is seen is no
hope at all. Who
hopes for what
they already have?
[25]But if we hope
for what we do not
yet have, we wait
for it patiently.

δὲ τέκνα, καὶ κληρονόμοι· κληρονόμοι μὲν θεοῦ, συγκληρονόμοι δὲ Χριστοῦ,
and children, then heirs, heirs ~ of God and fellow heirs with *and* Christ,
1254 5451 2779 3101 3101 3525 2536 1254 5169 1254 5986
cj n.npn adv n.npm n.npm pl n.gsm n.npm cj n.gsm

εἴπερ συμπάσχομεν ἵνα ↱ ↱ καὶ συνδοξασθῶμεν.
18 λογίζομαι
provided we suffer with him so that we may also be glorified with him. For I consider
1642 5224 2671 5280 5280 2779 5280 1142 3357
cj v.pai.1p cj adv v.aps.1p v.pmi.1s

γὰρ ὅτι οὐκ ἄξια τὰ παθήματα τοῦ
For that the sufferings of this present time are not ⌊worth comparing⌋ *the sufferings of this*
1142 4022 3836 4077 3836 3836 3814 2789 4024 545 3836 4077 3836
cj cj pl a.npn d.npn n.npn d.gsm

νῦν καιροῦ πρὸς τὴν μέλλουσαν δόξαν ἀποκαλυφθῆναι εἰς ἡμᾶς.
19 ἡ γὰρ
present time with the glory that will *glory* be revealed to us. *{the}* For
3814 2789 4639 3836 1518 3516 1518 636 1650 7005 3836 1142
adv n.gsm p.a d.asf pt.pa.asf n.asf f.ap p.a r.ap.1 d.nsf cj

ἀποκαραδοκία τῆς κτίσεως τὴν ἀποκάλυψιν τῶν υἱῶν τοῦ θεοῦ
the creation eagerly waits for *the creation* the revealing of the sons of God.
3836 3232 638 587 3836 3232 3836 637 3836 5626 3836 2536
n.nsf d.gsf n.gsf d.asf n.asf d.gpm n.gpm d.gsm n.gsm

ἀπεκδέχεται.
20 τῇ γὰρ ματαιότητι ἡ κτίσις
waits For the creation was subjected to *For* futility, *the creation*
587 1142 3836 3232 5718 5718 3836 1142 3470 3836 3232
v.pmi.3s d.dsf cj n.dsf d.nsf n.nsf

ὑπετάγη, οὐχ ἑκοῦσα ἀλλὰ διὰ τὸν ὑποτάξαντα, ἐφ᾽ ἐλπίδι
was subjected not ⌊of its own choosing,⌋ but ⌊because of⌋ him who subjected it, in hope
5718 4024 1776 247 1328 3836 5718 2093 1828
v.api.3s pl a.nsf cj p.a d.asm pt.aa.asm p.d n.dsf

21 ὅτι καὶ αὐτὴ ἡ κτίσις ἐλευθερωθήσεται ἀπὸ τῆς δουλείας τῆς
that *{also}* the creation itself *the creation* will be set free from its bondage to
4022 2779 3836 3232 899 3836 3232 1802 608 3836 1525 3836
cj adv r.nsf d.nsf n.nsf v.fpi.3s p.g d.gsf n.gsf d.gsf

φθορᾶς εἰς τὴν ἐλευθερίαν τῆς δόξης τῶν τέκνων τοῦ θεοῦ.
22 οἴδαμεν
decay into the glorious freedom *{the} glorious* of the children of God. For we know
5785 1650 3836 1518 1800 3836 1518 3836 5451 3836 2536 1142 3857
n.gsf p.a d.asf n.asf d.gsf n.gsf d.gpn n.gpn d.gsm n.gsm v.rai.1p

γὰρ ὅτι πᾶσα ἡ κτίσις συστενάζει καὶ συνωδίνει ἄχρι τοῦ νῦν·
For that the entire *the* creation has been groaning and suffering together up to the present
1142 4022 3836 4246 3836 3232 5367 2779 5349 948 3836 3814
cj cj a.nsf d.nsf n.nsf v.pai.3s cj v.pai.3s p.g d.gsm adv

23 οὐ μόνον δέ, ἀλλὰ καὶ αὐτοὶ τὴν ἀπαρχὴν τοῦ
hour. And not only this, *And* but *{also}* we ourselves, who have the first fruits of the
1254 4024 3667 1254 247 2779 5100 899 2400 2400 3836 569 3836
pl adv cj cj adv r.npm d.asf n.asf d.gsn

πνεύματος ἔχοντες, ἡμεῖς καὶ αὐτοὶ ⌊ἐν ἑαυτοῖς⌋ στενάζομεν
Spirit, *who have* groan inwardly as we *{also} {ourselves} inwardly we groan*
4460 2400 5100 1877 7005 2779 899 1877 1571 5100
n.gsn pt.pa.npm r.np.1 adv r.npm p.d r.dpm.1 v.pai.1p

υἱοθεσίαν ἀπεκδεχόμενοι, τὴν ἀπολύτρωσιν τοῦ σώματος ἡμῶν.
eagerly await our adoption, *eagerly await* the redemption of our bodies. *our*
587 587 5625 587 3836 667 3836 7005 5393 7005
n.asf pt.pm.npm d.asf n.asf d.gsn n.gsn r.gp.1

24 τῇ γὰρ ἐλπίδι ἐσώθημεν· ἐλπὶς δὲ βλεπομένη οὐκ ἔστιν ἐλπίς·
For ⌊in this⌋ *For* hope we were saved. Now hope *Now* that is seen is not *is* hope,
1142 3836 1142 1828 5392 1254 1828 1254 1063 1639 4024 1639 1828
d.dsf cj n.dsf v.api.1p n.nsf cj pt.pp.nsf pl v.pai.3s n.nsf

ὃ γὰρ βλέπει τίς ἐλπίζει;
25 εἰ δὲ ὃ ↱
for who hopes for what *for* he sees? *who hopes for* But if *But* we hope for what we
1142 5515 1827 1827 4005 1142 1063 5515 1827 1254 1623 1254 1827 1827 1827 4005 1063
r.asn cj v.pai.3s r.nsm v.pai.3s cj cj r.asn

↱ οὐ βλέπομεν ἐλπίζομεν, δι᾽ ὑπομονῆς ἀπεκδεχόμεθα.
do not see, *we hope for* we wait for it with patience. *we wait for*
1063 4024 1063 1827 587 587 587 1328 5705 587
pl v.pai.1p v.pai.1p p.g n.gsf v.pmi.1p

NASB

children, heirs also,
heirs of God and
fellow heirs with
Christ, if indeed we
suffer with *Him* so
that we may also
be glorified with
Him.
[18]For I consider
that the sufferings
of this present time
are not worthy to
be compared with
the glory that is to
be revealed to us.
[19]For the anxious
longing of the cre-
ation waits eagerly
for the revealing
of the sons of God.
[20]For the creation
was subjected to
futility, not willing-
ly, but because of
Him who subjected
it, [a]in hope [21]that
the creation itself
also will be set free
from its slavery
to corruption into
the freedom of
the glory of the
children of God.
[22]For we know that
the whole creation
groans and suffers
the pains of child-
birth together until
now. [23]And not
only this, but also
we ourselves, hav-
ing the first fruits
of the Spirit, even
we ourselves groan
within ourselves,
waiting eagerly for
our adoption as
sons, the redemp-
tion of our body.
[24]For in hope we
have been saved,
but hope that is
seen is not hope;
for who hopes for
what he *already*
sees? [25]But if we
hope for what we
do not see, with
perseverance we
wait eagerly for it.

[a] 20,21 Or *subjected it in hope.* [21]*For*

[a] Or *in hope; because the creation*

NIV

[26]In the same way,
the Spirit helps us
in our weakness.
We do not know
what we ought to
pray for, but the
Spirit himself in-
tercedes for us
through wordless
groans. [27]And he
who searches our
hearts knows the
mind of the Spirit,
because the Spir-
it intercedes for
God's people in ac-
cordance with the
will of God.
[28]And we know
that in all things
God works for
the good of those
who love him,
who[a] have been
called according
to his purpose.
[29]For those God
foreknew he also
predestined to be
conformed to the
image of his Son,
that he might be the
firstborn among
many brothers and
sisters. [30]And those
he predestined, he
also called; those
he called, he also
justified; those he
justified, he also
glorified.

More Than Conquerors

[31]What, then,
shall we say in
response to these
things? If God is
for us, who can be
against us? [32]He
who did not spare
his own Son, but
gave him up for us
all—how will he
not also, along with
him, graciously
give us all things?
[33]Who will bring
any charge against
those whom God
has chosen? It is
God who

[a] 28 Or *that all things work together for good to those who love God, who*; or *that in all things God works together with those who love him to bring about what is good—with those who*

26 ὡσαύτως δὲ καὶ τὸ πνεῦμα συναντιλαμβάνεται τῇ ἀσθενείᾳ
⌊In the same way,⌋ *{and}* *{also}* the Spirit helps us in our weakness;
6058 1254 2779 3836 4460 5269 3836 7005 819
adv cj adv d.nsn n.nsn v.pmi.3s d.dsf n.dsf

ἡμῶν· τὸ γὰρ τί προσευξώμεθα καθὸ ↰ δεῖ οὐκ οἴδαμεν,
our *{the}* for we do not know how to pray as we ought, *not* *we do know*
7005 3836 1142 3857 3857 4024 3857 5515 4667 2771 4667 1256 4024 3857
r.gp.1 d.asn cj r.asn v.ams.1p cj v.pai.3s pl v.rai.1p

ἀλλὰ αὐτὸ τὸ πνεῦμα ὑπερεντυγχάνει στεναγμοῖς
but the Spirit himself *the* *Spirit* intercedes for us with groanings
247 3836 4460 899 3836 4460 5659 5099
cj r.nsn d.nsn n.nsn v.pai.3s n.dpm

ἀλαλήτοις· 27 ὁ δὲ ἐραυνῶν τὰς καρδίας οἶδεν τί τὸ φρόνημα
⌊too deep for words.⌋ *{the}* And God, who searches our hearts, knows *{what}* the desire
227 3836 1254 2236 3836 2840 3857 5515 3836 5859
a.dpm d.nsm cj pt.pa.nsm d.apf n.apf v.rai.3s r.nsn d.nsn n.nsn

τοῦ πνεύματος, ὅτι κατὰ θεὸν
of the Spirit, because the Spirit intercedes for the saints ⌊according to⌋ the will of God.
3836 4460 4022 1961 5642 41 2848 2536
d.gsn n.gsn cj p.a n.asm

ἐντυγχάνει ὑπὲρ ἁγίων. 28 οἴδαμεν δὲ ὅτι
intercedes *for* *saints* And we know *And* that all things work together for good
1961 5642 41 1254 3857 1254 4022 4246 4246 5300 5300 1650 19
v.pai.3s p.g a.gpm v.rai.1p cj cj

τοῖς ἀγαπῶσιν τὸν θεὸν πάντα συνεργεῖ εἰς ἀγαθόν, τοῖς
for those who love *{the}* God, *all things* *work together* *for* *good* for those who are called
3836 26 3836 2536 4246 5300 1650 19 3836 1639 1639 3105
d.dpm pt.pa.dpm d.asm n.asm a.apn v.pai.3s p.a a.asn d.dpm

κατὰ πρόθεσιν κλητοῖς οὖσιν. 29 ὅτι οὓς προέγνω, ↱ καὶ προώρισεν
⌊according to⌋ his purpose, *called* *who are* because those he foreknew he also predestined
2848 4606 3105 1639 4022 4005 4589 4633 2779 4633
p.a n.asf a.dpm pt.pa.dpm cj r.apm v.aai.3s adv v.aai.3s

συμμόρφους τῆς εἰκόνος τοῦ υἱοῦ αὐτοῦ, εἰς τὸ εἶναι αὐτὸν
to become conformed to the image of his Son, *his* that ~ he ⌊might be⌋ *he* the
5215 3836 1635 3836 899 5626 899 1650 3836 899 1639 899
a.apm d.gsf n.gsf d.gsm n.gsm r.gsm.3 p.a d.asn f.pa r.asm.3

πρωτότοκον ἐν πολλοῖς ἀδελφοῖς· 30 οὓς δὲ προώρισεν, τούτους ↱ καὶ
firstborn among many brethren. And those *And* he predestined, these he also
4758 1877 4498 81 1254 4005 1254 4633 4047 2813 2779
a.asm p.d a.dpm n.dpm r.apm cj v.aai.3s r.apm adv

ἐκάλεσεν· καὶ οὓς ἐκάλεσεν, τούτους ↱ καὶ ἐδικαίωσεν· οὓς δὲ ἐδικαίωσεν,
called; and those he called, these he also justified; and those *and* he justified,
2813 2779 4005 2813 4047 1467 2779 1467 1254 4005 1254 1467
v.aai.3s cj r.apm v.aai.3s r.apm adv v.aai.3s r.apm cj v.aai.3s

τούτους ↱ καὶ ἐδόξασεν. 31 τί οὖν ἐροῦμεν πρὸς ταῦτα; εἰ
these he also glorified. What then ⌊shall we say⌋ in response to these things? If
4047 1519 2779 1519 5515 4036 3306 4639 4047 1623
r.apm adv v.aai.3s r.asn cj v.fai.1p p.a r.apn cj

ὁ θεὸς ὑπὲρ ἡμῶν, τίς καθ᾽ ἡμῶν; 32 ὅς γε τοῦ
{the} God is for us, who can be against us? He who ~ did not spare *{the}*
3836 2536 5642 7005 5515 2848 7005 5767 4005 1145 5767 4024 5767 3836
d.nsm n.nsm p.g r.gp.1 r.nsm p.g r.gp.1 r.nsm pl d.gsm

ἰδίου υἱοῦ οὐκ ἐφείσατο ἀλλὰ ὑπὲρ ἡμῶν πάντων παρέδωκεν
his own Son, *not* *He did spare* but delivered him up for us all, *delivered up*
2625 5626 4024 5767 247 4140 899 4140 5642 7005 4246 4140
a.gsm n.gsm pl v.ami.3s cj p.g r.gp.1 a.gpm v.aai.3s

αὐτόν, πῶς οὐχὶ καὶ σὺν αὐτῷ τὰ πάντα ἡμῖν
him how will he not also, ⌊along with⌋ him, graciously give us *{the}* all things? *us*
899 4802 5919 5919 4049 2779 5250 899 5919 5919 7005 3836 4246 7005
r.asm.3 pl pl adv p.d r.dsm.3 d.apn a.apn r.dp.1

χαρίσεται; 33 τίς ἐγκαλέσει κατὰ ἐκλεκτῶν θεοῦ; θεὸς ὁ
will he graciously give Who ⌊will bring a charge⌋ against God's elect? *God's* It is God who
5919 5515 1592 2848 2536 1723 2536 2536 3836
v.fmi.3s r.nsm v.fai.3s p.g a.gpm n.gsm n.nsm d.nsm

NASB

Our Victory in Christ

[26]In the same
way the Spirit also
helps our weak-
ness; for we do not
know how to pray
as we should, but
the Spirit Himself
intercedes for *us*
with groanings too
deep for words;
[27]and He who
searches the hearts
knows what the
mind of the Spirit
is, because He
intercedes for the
saints according to
the will of God.
[28]And we know
that [a]God causes
all things to work
together for good
to those who love
God, to those who
are called accord-
ing to *His* purpose.
[29]For those whom
He foreknew, He
also predestined *to*
become conformed
to the image of
His Son, so that
He would be the
firstborn among
many brethren;
[30]and these whom
He predestined,
He also called;
and these whom
He called, He also
justified; and these
whom He justified,
He also glorified.
[31]What then shall
we say to these
things? If God
is for us, who *is*
against us? [32]He
who did not spare
His own Son, but
delivered Him over
for us all, how will
He not also with
Him freely give us
all things? [33]Who
will bring a charge
against God's
elect? God is the

[a] One early ms reads *all things work together for good*

NIV

justifies. [34]Who
then is the one who
condemns? No
one. Christ Jesus
who died—more
than that, who was
raised to life—is
at the right hand
of God and is also
interceding for us.
[35]Who shall sep-
arate us from the
love of Christ?
Shall trouble or
hardship or perse-
cution or famine or
nakedness or dan-
ger or sword? [36]As
it is written:

> "For your sake we face death all day long;
> we are considered as sheep to be slaughtered."[a]

[37]No, in all these
things we are more
than conquerors
through him who
loved us. [38]For I
am convinced that
neither death nor
life, neither angels
nor demons,[b] nei-
ther the present
nor the future,
nor any powers,
[39]neither height
nor depth, nor
anything else in
all creation, will
be able to separate
us from the love
of God that is in
Christ Jesus our
Lord.

Paul's Anguish Over Israel

9 I speak the
truth in
Christ—I am not
lying, my con-
science confirms
it through the Holy
Spirit— [2]I have
great sorrow and
unceasing anguish
in my heart. [3]For
I could wish that
I myself were
cursed and cut off
from Christ for the
sake of my people,
those of my own

[a] 36 Psalm 44:22
[b] 38 Or *nor heavenly rulers*

δικαιῶν· 34 τίς ὁ κατακρινῶν; Χριστὸς Ἰησοῦς[a] ὁ ἀποθανών,
justifies. Who is it that condemns? Christ Jesus is the one who died — and
1467 5515 3836 2891 5986 2652 3836 633 1254
pt.pa.nsm r.nsm d.nsm pt.pa.nsm n.nsm n.nsm d.nsm pt.aa.nsm

μᾶλλον δὲ ἐγερθείς, ὅς καί ἐστιν ἐν δεξιᾷ τοῦ θεοῦ, ὃς καὶ
more than that, *and* he was raised — who *{also}* is at the right hand of God, who also
3437 1254 1586 4005 2779 1639 1877 1288 3836 2536 4005 2779
adv.c cj pt.ap.nsm r.nsm adv v.pai.3s p.d a.dsf d.gsm n.gsm r.nsm adv

ἐντυγχάνει ὑπὲρ ἡμῶν. 35 τίς ἡμᾶς χωρίσει ἀπὸ τῆς ἀγάπης τοῦ
is interceding for us. Who can separate us *can separate* from the love of
1961 5642 7005 5515 6004 6004 7005 6004 608 3836 27 3836
v.pai.3s p.g r.gp.1 r.nsm r.ap.1 v.fai.3s p.g d.gsf n.gsf d.gsm

Χριστοῦ; θλῖψις ἢ στενοχωρία ἢ διωγμὸς ἢ λιμὸς ἢ γυμνότης ἢ
Christ? Can tribulation, or distress, or persecution, or famine, or nakedness, or
5986 2568 2445 5103 2445 1501 2445 3350 2445 1219 2445
n.gsm n.nsf cj n.nsf cj n.nsm cj n.nsm cj n.nsf cj

κίνδυνος ἢ μάχαιρα; 36 καθὼς γέγραπται ὅτι → ἕνεκεν σοῦ θανατούμεθα
danger, or sword? As it is written, ~ "For your sake *your* we face death
3074 2445 3479 2777 1211 4022 5148 1914 5148 2506
n.nsm cj n.nsf cj v.rpi.3s cj p.g r.gs.2 v.ppi.1p

ὅλην τὴν ἡμέραν, ↞ ἐλογίσθημεν ὡς πρόβατα σφαγῆς. 37 ἀλλ᾽ ἐν
all *{the}* day long; we are regarded as sheep to be slaughtered." No, in all
3910 3836 2465 3910 3357 6055 4585 5375 247 1877 4246
a.asf d.asf n.asf v.api.1p cj n.npn n.gsf cj p.d

τούτοις πᾶσιν ὑπερνικῶμεν διὰ τοῦ ἀγαπήσαντος ἡμᾶς.
these things *all* ⌊we are winning a most glorious victory⌋ through him who loved us.
4047 4246 5664 1328 3836 26 7005
r.dpn a.dpn v.pai.1p p.g d.gsm pt.aa.gsm r.ap.1

38 πέπεισμαι γὰρ ὅτι οὔτε θάνατος οὔτε ζωὴ οὔτε ἄγγελοι οὔτε ἀρχαὶ οὔτε
For I am convinced *For* that neither death, nor life, nor angels, nor rulers, nor
1142 4275 1142 4022 4046 2505 4046 2437 4046 34 4046 794 4046
v.rpi.1s cj cj cj n.nsm cj n.nsf cj n.npm cj n.npf cj

ἐνεστῶτα οὔτε μέλλοντα οὔτε δυνάμεις 39 οὔτε ὕψωμα οὔτε βάθος οὔτε τις
things present, nor things to come, nor powers, nor height, nor depth, nor any
1931 4046 3516 4046 1539 4046 5739 4046 958 4046 5516
pt.ra.npn cj pt.pa.npn cj n.npf cj n.nsn cj n.nsn cj r.nsf

κτίσις ἑτέρα δυνήσεται ἡμᾶς χωρίσαι ἀπὸ τῆς ἀγάπης τοῦ
other ⌊created thing⌋ *other* will be able to separate us *to separate* from the love of
2283 3232 2283 1538 6004 6004 7005 6004 608 3836 27 3836
n.nsf r.nsf v.fpi.3s r.ap.1 f.aa p.g d.gsf n.gsf d.gsm

θεοῦ τῆς ἐν Χριστῷ Ἰησοῦ τῷ κυρίῳ ἡμῶν.
God *{the}* in Christ Jesus *{the}* our Lord. *our*
2536 3836 1877 5986 2652 3836 7005 3261 7005
n.gsm d.gsf p.d n.dsm n.dsm d.dsm n.dsm r.gp.1

9:1 ἀλήθειαν λέγω ἐν Χριστῷ, ↱ ↱ οὐ ψεύδομαι,
I am telling the truth *I am telling* in Christ — I am not lying;
3306 3306 3306 237 3306 1877 5986 6017 6017 4024 6017
n.asf v.pai.1s p.d n.dsm pl v.pmi.1s

συμμαρτυρούσης μοι τῆς συνειδήσεώς μου ἐν πνεύματι
my conscience bears witness with me *{the} conscience* *my* in the Holy Spirit
1609 5287 5210 1609 3836 5287 1609 1877 41 4460
pt.pa.gsf r.ds.1 d.gsf n.gsf r.gs.1 p.d n.dsn

ἁγίῳ, 2 ὅτι λύπη μοί ἐστιν μεγάλη καὶ ἀδιάλειπτος ὀδύνη τῇ
Holy — that I have great sorrow *I* *have* *great* and unceasing anguish in my
41 4022 1609 1639 3489 3383 1609 1639 3489 2779 89 3850 3836 1609
a.dsn cj n.nsf r.ds.1 v.pai.3s a.nsf cj a.nsf n.nsf d.dsf

καρδίᾳ μου. 3 ηὐχόμην γὰρ ἀνάθεμα εἶναι αὐτὸς ἐγὼ
heart. *my* For I could wish *For* that I myself were accursed, *were* *myself* *I* cut off
2840 1609 1142 2377 1142 1609 899 1639 353 1639 899 1609
n.dsf r.gs.1 v.imi.1s cj n.nsn f.pa r.nsm r.ns.1

ἀπὸ τοῦ Χριστοῦ ὑπὲρ τῶν ἀδελφῶν μου τῶν συγγενῶν μου
from *{the}* Christ, ⌊for the sake⌋ of my brethren, *my* *{the}* my kinsmen *my*
608 3836 5986 5642 3836 1609 81 1609 3836 1609 5150 1609
p.g d.gsm n.gsm p.g d.gpm n.gpm r.gs.1 d.gpm n.gpm r.gs.1

[a] [Ἰησοῦς] UBS, omitted by NET.

NASB

one who justifies;
[34]who is the one
who condemns?
Christ Jesus is He
who died, yes,
rather who was
[a]raised, who is at
the right hand of
God, who also
intercedes for us.
[35]Who will separate
us from the love of
[b]Christ? Will tribu-
lation, or distress,
or persecution, or
famine, or naked-
ness, or peril, or
sword? [36]Just as it
is written,

> "For Your sake we are being put to death all day long;
> We were considered as sheep to be slaughtered."

[37]But in all these
things we over-
whelmingly con-
quer through Him
who loved us. [38]For
I am convinced
that neither death,
nor life, nor angels,
nor principalities,
nor things present,
nor things to come,
nor powers, [39]nor
height, nor depth,
nor any other cre-
ated thing, will be
able to separate us
from the love of
God, which is in
Christ Jesus our
Lord.

Solicitude for Israel

[9:1]I am telling the
truth in Christ, I
am not lying, my
conscience testi-
fies with me in the
Holy Spirit, [2]that I
have great sorrow
and unceasing grief
in my heart. [3]For
I could wish that
I myself were ac-
cursed, *separated*
from Christ for the
sake of my breth-
ren, my kinsmen

[a] One early ms reads *raised from the dead*
[b] Two early mss read *God*

NIV

race, [4]the people
of Israel. Theirs
is the adoption to
sonship; theirs the
divine glory, the
covenants, the re-
ceiving of the law,
the temple worship
and the promises.
[5]Theirs are the pa-
triarchs, and from
them is traced the
human ancestry of
the Messiah, who
is God over all,
forever praised![a]
Amen.

God's Sovereign Choice

[6]It is not as
though God's word
had failed. For not
all who are de-
scended from Isra-
el are Israel. [7]Nor
because they are
his descendants
are they all Abra-
ham's children. On
the contrary, "It is
through Isaac that
your offspring will
be reckoned."[b] [8]In
other words, it is
not the children by
physical descent
who are God's
children, but it is
the children of the
promise who are
regarded as Abra-
ham's offspring.
[9]For this was how
the promise was
stated: "At the ap-
pointed time I will
return, and Sarah
will have a son."[c]
[10]Not only that, but
Rebekah's children
were conceived at
the same time by
our father Isaac.
[11]Yet, before the
twins were born or
had done anything
good or bad—in
order that God's
purpose in election
might stand: [12]not
by works but by him
who calls—she was
told, "The

[a] 5 Or *Messiah, who is over all. God be forever praised!* Or *Messiah. God who is over all be forever praised!*
[b] 7 Gen. 21:12
[c] 9 Gen. 18:10,14

κατὰ σάρκα, [4]οἵτινές εἰσιν Ἰσραηλῖται, ὧν ἡ υἱοθεσία καὶ
⌞according to⌟ the flesh, who are Israelites. ⌞To them⌟ belong the adoption, *{and}*
2848 4922 4015 1639 2703 4005 3836 5625 2779
p.a n.asf r.npm v.pai.3p n.npm r.gpm d.nsf n.nsf cj

ἡ δόξα καὶ αἱ διαθῆκαι καὶ ἡ νομοθεσία καὶ ἡ λατρεία καὶ
the glory, *{and}* the covenants, *{and}* the ⌞giving of the law,⌟ *{and}* the temple worship, and
3836 1518 2779 3836 1347 2779 3836 3792 2779 3836 3301 2779
d.nsf n.nsf cj d.npf n.npf cj d.nsf n.nsf cj d.nsf n.nsf cj

αἱ ἐπαγγελίαι, [5]ὧν οἱ πατέρες καὶ ἐξ ὧν
the promises. ⌞To them⌟ belong the patriarchs, and from them by human descent came
3836 2039 4005 3836 4252 2779 1666 4005 2848 4922 4922
d.npf n.npf r.gpm d.npm n.npm cj p.g r.gpm

ὁ Χριστὸς τὸ κατὰ σάρκα, ὁ ὢν ἐπὶ πάντων θεὸς εὐλογητὸς εἰς
the Christ, *{the}* *by* *human descent* who is God over all, *God* blessed for
3836 5986 3836 2848 4922 3836 1639 2536 2093 4246 2536 2329 1650
d.nsm n.nsm d.asn p.a n.asf d.nsm pt.pa.nsm p.g a.gpn n.nsm a.nsm p.a

τοὺς αἰῶνας, ἀμήν. [6] οὐχ οἷον δὲ ὅτι ἐκπέπτωκεν ὁ
all time. Amen. But it is not as *But* though the word of God had failed. *the*
3836 172 297 1254 4024 3888 1254 4022 3836 3364 3836 2536 1738 3836
d.apm n.apm pl pl r.nsn cj cj v.rai.3s d.nsm

λόγος τοῦ θεοῦ. οὐ γὰρ πάντες οἱ ἐξ Ἰσραὴλ οὗτοι
word *of* *God* For not *For* all who are descended from Israel are actually *{these}*
3364 3836 2536 1142 4024 1142 4246 3836 1666 2702 4047
n.nsm d.gsm n.gsm pl cj a.npm d.npm p.g n.gsm r.npm

Ἰσραήλ, [7]οὐδ' ὅτι εἰσὶν σπέρμα Ἀβραάμ
Israel; neither are they all children of Abraham because they are his descendants; *of Abraham*
2702 4028 4246 5451 11 11 4022 1639 5065 11
n.nsm cj cj v.pai.3p n.nsn n.gsm

πάντες τέκνα, ἀλλ', ἐν Ἰσαάκ κληθήσεταί σοι
all *children* ⌞on the contrary,⌟ "It is through Isaac that your descendants will be named." *your*
4246 5451 247 1877 2693 5148 5065 2813 5148
a.npm n.npn cj p.d n.dsm v.fpi.3s r.ds.2

σπέρμα. [8]τοῦτ' ἔστιν, οὐ τὰ τέκνα τῆς σαρκὸς ταῦτα τέκνα τοῦ θεοῦ
descendants This means it is not the children of the flesh who are children of God,
5065 4047 1639 4024 3836 5451 3836 4922 4047 5451 3836 2536
n.nsn r.nsn v.pai.3s pl d.npn n.npn d.gsf n.gsf r.npn n.npn d.gsm n.gsm

ἀλλὰ τὰ τέκνα τῆς ἐπαγγελίας λογίζεται εἰς σπέρμα. [9]
but the children of the promise are counted as descendants. For this is what the
247 3836 5451 3836 2039 3357 1650 5065 1142 4047 3836
cj d.npn n.npn d.gsf n.gsf v.ppi.3s p.a n.asn

ἐπαγγελίας γὰρ ὁ λόγος οὗτος· κατὰ τὸν καιρὸν τοῦτον ἐλεύσομαι
promise *For* *what* said: *this* "About *{the}* this time *this* next year I will return
2039 1142 3836 3364 4047 2848 3836 4047 2789 4047 2262
n.gsf cj d.nsm n.nsm r.nsm p.a d.asm n.asm r.asm v.fmi.1s

καὶ ἔσται τῇ Σάρρᾳ υἱός. [10]οὐ μόνον δέ, ἀλλὰ καὶ Ῥεβέκκα
and Sarah will have *{the}* *Sarah* a son." Not only that, *{and}* but *{also}* when Rebecca
2779 4925 1639 3836 4925 5626 4024 3667 1254 247 2779 2400 4831
cj v.fmi.3s d.dsf n.dsf n.nsm pl adv cj cj adv n.nsf

ἐξ ἑνὸς κοίτην ἔχουσα, Ἰσαὰκ τοῦ πατρὸς
had conceived twins by one man, *conceived* *when had* our forefather Isaac *{the}* *forefather*
2400 3130 1666 1651 3130 2400 7005 4252 2693 3836 4252
p.g a.gsm n.asf pt.pa.nsf n.gsm d.gsm n.gsm

ἡμῶν, [11] μήπω γὰρ γεννηθέντων μηδὲ πραξάντων τι ἀγαθὸν ἢ
our — for even before *for* they were born or had done anything either good or
7005 1142 3609 1142 1164 3593 4556 5516 19 2445
r.gp.1 adv cj pt.ap.gpm cj pt.aa.gpm r.asn a.asn cj

φαῦλον, ἵνα ἡ κατ' ἐκλογὴν πρόθεσις τοῦ θεοῦ μένη,
bad so that *{the}* God's purpose ⌞according to⌟ election *purpose* *{the}* *God's* ⌞might stand,⌟
5765 2671 3836 2536 4606 2848 1724 4606 3836 2536 3531
a.asn cj d.nsf p.a n.asf n.nsf d.gsm n.gsm v.pas.3s

[12]οὐκ ἐξ ἔργων ἀλλ' ἐκ τοῦ καλοῦντος, ἐρρέθη αὐτῇ ὅτι ὁ
not ⌞because of⌟ works, but ⌞because of⌟ his call — it was said to her, ~ "The
4024 1666 2240 247 1666 3836 2813 3306 899 4022 3836
pl p.g n.gpn cj p.g d.gsm pt.pa.gsm v.api.3s r.dsf.3 cj d.nsm

NASB

according to the
flesh, [4]who are
Israelites, to whom
belongs the adop-
tion as sons, and
the glory and the
covenants and the
giving of the Law
and the *temple*
service and the
promises, [5]whose
are the fathers, and
from whom is the
Christ according
to the flesh, who
is over all, God
blessed forever.
Amen.
[6]But *it is* not as
though the word
of God has failed.
For they are not all
Israel who are *de-*
scended from Isra-
el; [7]nor are they all
children because
they are Abraham's
descendants, but:
"THROUGH ISAAC
YOUR DESCENDANTS
WILL BE NAMED."
[8]That is, it is not
the children of
the flesh who are
children of God,
but the children
of the promise
are regarded as
descendants. [9]For
this is the word of
promise: "AT THIS
TIME I WILL COME,
AND SARAH SHALL
HAVE A SON." [10]And
not only this, but
there was Rebekah
also, when she had
conceived *twins*
by one man, our
father Isaac; [11]for
though *the twins*
were not yet born
and had not done
anything good or
bad, so that God's
purpose accord-
ing to *His* choice
would stand, not
because of works
but because of Him
who calls, [12]it was
said to her, "THE

NIV

older will serve the
younger."[a] 13 Just as
it is written: "Jacob
I loved, but Esau I
hated."[b]
14 What then shall
we say? Is God
unjust? Not at all!
15 For he says to
Moses,

"I will have mercy
on whom I
have mercy,
and I will
have compa-
ssion on
whom I
have compa-
ssion."[c]

16 It does not,
therefore, depend
on human desire
or effort, but on
God's mercy. 17 For
Scripture says to
Pharaoh: "I raised
you up for this
very purpose, that
I might display
my power in you
and that my name
might be pro-
claimed in all the
earth."[d] 18 There-
fore God has mer-
cy on whom he
wants to have mer-
cy, and he hardens
whom he wants to
harden.
19 One of you will
say to me: "Then
why does God still
blame us? For who
is able to resist his
will?" 20 But who
are you, a human
being, to talk back
to God? "Shall
what is formed
say to the one who
formed it, 'Why
did you make
me like this?' "[e]
21 Does not the pot-
ter have the right
to make out of the
same lump of clay
some pottery for
special purposes
and some for com-
mon use?
22 What if God,

μείζων δουλεύσει τῷ ἐλάσσονι, 13 καθὼς γέγραπται, τὸν Ἰακὼβ ἠγάπησα, τὸν δὲ
older will serve the younger." As it is written, {the} "Jacob I loved, {the} but
3489 1526 3836 1781 2777 1211 3836 2609 26 3836 1254
a.nsm.c v.fai.3s d.dsm a.dsm.c cj v.rpi.3s d.asm n.asm v.aai.1s d.asm cj

Ἠσαῦ ἐμίσησα. 14 τί οὖν ἐροῦμεν; μὴ ἀδικία → παρὰ τῷ θεῷ;
Esau I hated." What then shall we say? Is there not injustice on God's part? {the} God's
2481 3631 5515 4036 3306 3590 94 2536 4123 3836 2536
n.asm v.aai.1s r.asn cj v.fai.1p pl n.nsf p.d d.dsm n.dsm

μὴ γένοιτο.⌟ 15 τῷ Μωϋσεῖ γὰρ λέγει, ἐλεήσω
By no means! For he says to Moses, For he says ⌞"I will have mercy on⌟
3590 1181 1142 3306 3306 3836 3707 1142 3306 1796
pl v.amo.3s d.dsm n.dsm cj v.pai.3s v.fai.1s

ὃν ἂν ἐλεῶ καὶ οἰκτιρήσω ὃν ἂν οἰκτίρω. 16 ἄρα
whom ~ ⌞I have mercy,⌟ and ⌞I will have compassion on⌟ whom ~ I have compassion." So
4005 323 1796 2779 3882 4005 323 3882 726
r.asm pl v.pas.1s cj v.fai.1s r.asm pl v.pas.1s cj

οὖν οὐ τοῦ θέλοντος οὐδὲ τοῦ τρέχοντος ἀλλὰ τοῦ ἐλεῶντος
then, it does not depend on human desire or {the} exertion, but on God's mercy.
4036 4024 3836 2527 4028 3836 5556 247 3836 2536 1790
cj pl d.gsm pt.pa.gsm cj d.gsm pt.pa.gsm cj d.gsm pt.pa.gsm

θεοῦ. 17 λέγει γὰρ ἡ γραφὴ τῷ Φαραὼ ὅτι εἰς ➚ αὐτὸ τοῦτο
God's For the scripture says For the scripture to Pharaoh, ~ "For this very purpose
2536 1142 3836 1210 3306 1142 3836 1210 3836 5755 4022 1650 4047 899 4047
n.gsm v.pai.3s cj d.nsf n.nsf d.dsm n.dsm cj p.a r.asn r.asn

ἐξήγειρά σε ↰ ὅπως ἐνδείξωμαι ἐν σοὶ τὴν δύναμίν μου καὶ ὅπως
I have raised you up, that I might display my power in you, {the} power my and that
1995 5148 1995 3968 1892 1609 1539 1877 5148 3836 1539 1609 2779 3968
v.aai.1s r.as.2 cj v.ams.1s p.d r.ds.2 d.asf n.asf r.gs.1 cj cj

διαγγελῇ τὸ ὄνομά μου ἐν πάσῃ τῇ γῇ. 18 ἄρα οὖν
my name might be proclaimed {the} name my in all the earth." So then, God has
1609 3950 1334 3836 3950 1609 1877 4246 3836 1178 726 4036 1796
v.aps.3s d.asn n.asn r.gs.1 p.d a.dsf d.dsf n.dsf cj cj

ὃν θέλει ἐλεεῖ, ὃν δὲ θέλει σκληρύνει.
mercy on whomever he wills, has mercy on and he hardens whomever and he wills. he hardens
1796 1796 4005 2527 1796 1254 5020 5020 4005 1254 2527 5020
r.asm v.pai.3s v.pai.3s r.asm cj v.pai.3s v.pai.3s

19 ἐρεῖς μοι οὖν, τί οὖν[a] ➚ ➚ ἔτι μέμφεται; τῷ
So ⌞you will say⌟ to me, So "Why then does he still find fault? For who can resist {the}
4036 3306 1609 4036 5515 4036 3522 3522 2285 3522 1142 5515 468 468 3836
v.fai.2s r.ds.1 cj r.asn cj adv v.pmi.3s d.dsn

γὰρ βουλήματι αὐτοῦ τίς ἀνθέστηκεν; 20 ὦ ἄνθρωπε,
For his will?" his who can resist But who are you, a mere mortal,
1142 899 1088 899 5515 468 3529 5515 1639 5148 6043 476
cj n.dsn r.gsm.3 r.nsm v.rai.3s j n.vsm

μενοῦνγε σὺ τίς εἶ ὁ ἀνταποκρινόμενος τῷ θεῷ;
But you who are {the} to criticize {the} God? Certainly the thing that is
3529 5148 5515 1639 3836 503 3836 2536 3836 4420
pl r.ns.2 r.nsm v.pai.2s d.nsm pt.pm.nsm d.dsm n.dsm

➚ μὴ ἐρεῖ τὸ πλάσμα τῷ πλάσαντι, τί με
molded may not say the thing molded ⌞to the⌟ one who molded it, "Why have you made me
4420 3306 3590 3306 3836 4420 3836 4421 5515 4472 4472 4472 1609
pl v.fai.3s d.nsn n.nsn d.dsm pt.aa.dsm r.asn r.as.1

ἐποίησας οὕτως; 21 ἢ οὐκ ἔχει ἐξουσίαν ὁ κεραμεὺς τοῦ
have you made like this?" {or} Has the potter no Has right the potter of
4472 4048 2445 2400 3836 3038 4024 2400 2026 3836 3038 3836
v.aai.2s adv cj pl v.pai.3s n.asf d.nsm n.nsm d.gsm

πηλοῦ ἐκ τοῦ αὐτοῦ φυράματος ποιῆσαι ⌞ὃ μὲν⌟ εἰς
clay to make from the same lump of clay to make some pottery for a
4384 4472 4472 1666 3836 899 5878 3836 4384 4472 4005 3525 5007 1650
n.gsm p.g d.gsn r.gsn n.gsn f.aa r.asn pl p.a

τιμὴν σκεῦος ὃ δὲ εἰς ἀτιμίαν; 22 εἰ δὲ θέλων
special occasion pottery and other and for common use? What if What God, willing
5507 5007 1254 4005 1254 1650 871 1254 1623 1254 2536 2527
n.asf n.asn r.asn pl p.a n.asf cj cj pt.pa.nsm

NASB

OLDER WILL SERVE
THE YOUNGER."
13 Just as it is
written, "JACOB I
LOVED, BUT ESAU I
HATED."
14 What shall we
say then? There is
no injustice with
God, is there? May
it never be! 15 For
He says to Moses,
"I WILL HAVE MERCY
ON WHOM I HAVE
MERCY, AND I WILL
HAVE COMPASSION
ON WHOM I HAVE
COMPASSION." 16 So
then it *does* not
depend on the man
who wills or the
man who runs,
but on God who
has mercy. 17 For
the Scripture says
to Pharaoh, "FOR
THIS VERY PURPOSE
I RAISED YOU UP,
TO DEMONSTRATE
MY POWER IN YOU,
AND THAT MY NAME
MIGHT BE PRO-
CLAIMED THROUGH-
OUT THE WHOLE
EARTH." 18 So then
He has mercy on
whom He desires,
and He hardens
whom He desires.
19 You will say to
me then, "Why
does He still find
fault? For who
resists His will?"
20 On the contrary,
who are you, O
man, who answers
back to God? The
thing molded will
not say to the
molder, "Why did
you make me like
this," will it? 21 Or
does not the potter
have a right over
the clay, to make
from the same
lump one vessel for
honorable use and
another for com-
mon use? 22 What if
God, although

a 12 Gen. 25:23
b 13 Mal. 1:2,3
c 15 Exodus 33:19
d 17 Exodus 9:16
e 20 Isaiah 29:16; 45:9

a [οὖν] UBS.

NIV

although choosing
to show his wrath
and make his pow-
er known, bore
with great patience
the objects of his
wrath—prepared
for destruction?
23 What if he did
this to make the
riches of his glory
known to the ob-
jects of his mercy,
whom he prepared
in advance for
glory— 24 even
us, whom he also
called, not only
from the Jews but
also from the Gen-
tiles? 25 As he says
in Hosea:

"I will call them
'my people'
who are not
my people;
and I will call
her 'my
loved one'
who is not
my loved
one,"[a]

26 and,

"In the very place
where it was
said to them,
'You are not my
people,'
there they will
be called
'children of
the living
God.'"[b]

27 Isaiah cries out con-
cerning Israel:

"Though the
number of
the Israelites
be like the
sand by the
sea,
only the
remnant will
be saved.
28 For the Lord will
carry out
his sentence on
earth with
speed and
finality."[c]

29 It is just as Isaiah
said previously:

"Unless the Lord
Almighty

ὁ θεὸς ἐνδείξασθαι τὴν ὀργὴν καὶ γνωρίσαι τὸ δυνατὸν αὐτοῦ ἤνεγκεν
{the} God to display his wrath and make known {the} his power, his has endured
3836 2536 1892 3836 3973 2779 1192 3836 899 1543 899 5770
d.nsm n.nsm f.am d.asf n.asf cj f.aa d.asn a.asn r.gsm.3 v.aai.3s

ἐν πολλῇ μακροθυμίᾳ σκεύη ὀργῆς κατηρτισμένα εἰς ἀπώλειαν, 23 καὶ
with great patience the objects of wrath prepared for destruction? And what if
1877 4498 3429 5007 3973 2936 1650 724 2779
p.d a.dsf n.dsf n.apn n.gsf pt.rp.apn p.a n.asf cj

ἵνα γνωρίσῃ τὸν πλοῦτον τῆς δόξης αὐτοῦ ἐπὶ σκεύη
he did so ⌊in order to⌋ make known the riches of his glory his to the objects
2671 1192 3836 4458 3836 899 1518 899 2093 5007
cj v.aas.3s d.asm n.asm d.gsf n.gsf r.gsm.3 p.a n.apn

ἐλέους ἃ προητοίμασεν εἰς δόξαν; 24 Οὓς καὶ ἐκάλεσεν
of mercy, which he prepared beforehand for glory — even us, whom even he has called,
1799 4005 4602 1650 1518 2779 7005 4005 2779 2813
n.gsn r.apn v.aai.3s p.a n.asf r.apm adv v.aai.3s

ἡμᾶς οὐ μόνον ἐξ Ἰουδαίων ἀλλὰ καὶ ἐξ ἐθνῶν, 25 ὡς καὶ ἐν
us not only from the Jews, but also from the Gentiles. As he also says in
7005 4024 3667 1666 2681 247 2779 1666 1620 6055 3306 2779 3306 1877
r.ap.1 pl adv p.g a.gpm cj adv p.g n.gpn cj adv p.d

τῷ Ὡσηὲ λέγει, καλέσω τὸν οὐ λαόν μου
{the} Hosea, he says "Those who were not my people, I will call Those not people my 'my
3836 6060 3306 3836 4024 1609 3295 2813 3836 4024 3295 1609 1609
d.dsm n.dsm v.pai.3s v.fai.1s d.asm pl n.asm r.gs.1

λαόν μου καὶ τὴν ↱ ↱ οὐκ ἠγαπημένην ἠγαπημένην· 26 καὶ
people,' my and her who was not beloved, I will call 'beloved.'" "And
3295 1609 2779 3836 26 26 4024 26 26 2779
n.asm r.gs.1 cj d.asf pl pt.rp.asf pt.rp.asf cj

ἔσται ἐν τῷ τόπῳ οὗ ἐρρέθη αὐτοῖς, οὐ λαός
⌊it will happen that⌋ in ⌊the very⌋ place where God said to them, 'You are not my people,'
1639 1877 3836 5536 4023 3306 899 7007 4024 1609 3295
v.fmi.3s p.d d.dsm n.dsm adv v.api.3s r.dpm.3 pl n.nsm

μου ὑμεῖς, ἐκεῖ κληθήσονται υἱοὶ → θεοῦ ζῶντος. 27 Ἠσαΐας δὲ κράζει
my You there they will be called 'sons of the living God.'" living Isaiah {and} cries out
1609 7007 1695 2813 5626 2409 2536 2409 2480 1254 3189
r.gs.1 r.np.2 adv v.fpi.3p n.npm n.gsm pt.pa.gsm n.nsm cj v.pai.3s

ὑπὲρ τοῦ Ἰσραήλ, ἐὰν ᾖ ὁ ἀριθμὸς τῶν υἱῶν Ἰσραὴλ ὡς ἡ
concerning {the} Israel, ⌊"Even if⌋ were the number of the sons of Israel were as the
5642 3836 2702 1569 1639 3836 750 3836 5626 2702 1639 6055 3836
p.g d.gsm n.gsm cj v.pas.3s d.nsm n.nsm d.gpm n.gpm n.gsm pl d.nsf

ἄμμος τῆς θαλάσσης, τὸ ὑπόλειμμα σωθήσεται. 28
sand of the sea, only a remnant will be saved; for the Lord will carry out his
302 3836 2498 3836 5698 5392 1142 3261 4472 4472 4472
n.nsf d.gsf n.gsf d.nsn n.nsn v.fpi.3s

λόγον γὰρ συντελῶν καὶ συντέμνων[a] ποιήσει κύριος ἐπὶ τῆς γῆς.
sentence for on the earth, thoroughly and without delay." will carry out Lord on the earth
3364 1142 2093 3836 1178 5334 2779 5335 4472 3261 2093 3836 1178
n.asm cj pt.pa.nsm cj pt.pa.nsm v.fai.3s n.nsm p.g d.gsf n.gsf

29 καὶ καθὼς προείρηκεν Ἠσαΐας, εἰ ↱ μὴ κύριος σαβαὼθ
And as Isaiah predicted, Isaiah "If the Lord of hosts had not Lord of hosts
2779 2777 2480 4597 2480 1623 3261 4877 4877 1593 3590 3261 4877
cj cj v.rai.3s n.nsm cj pl n.nsm n.gpm

NASB

willing to demon-
strate His wrath
and to make His
power known,
endured with much
patience vessels of
wrath prepared for
destruction? 23 And
He did so to make
known the riches
of His glory upon
vessels of mercy,
which He prepared
beforehand for glo-
ry, 24 *even* us, whom
He also called, not
from among Jews
only, but also from
among Gentiles.
25 As He says also
in Hosea,

"I WILL CALL
THOSE WHO
WERE NOT MY
PEOPLE, 'MY
PEOPLE,'
AND HER WHO
WAS NOT
BELOVED, 'BE-
LOVED.'"
26 "AND IT SHALL
BE THAT IN THE
PLACE WHERE
IT WAS SAID TO
THEM, 'YOU
ARE NOT MY
PEOPLE,'
THERE THEY
SHALL BE
CALLED SONS
OF THE LIVING
GOD."
27 Isaiah cries
out concerning
Israel, "THOUGH
THE NUMBER OF THE
SONS OF ISRAEL BE
LIKE THE SAND OF
THE SEA, IT IS THE
REMNANT THAT WILL
BE SAVED; 28 FOR THE
LORD WILL EXECUTE
HIS WORD ON THE
EARTH, THOROUGHLY
AND QUICKLY."
29 And just as Isaiah
foretold,
"UNLESS THE
LORD OF SA-
BAOTH HAD

[a] 25 Hosea 2:23
[b] 26 Hosea 1:10
[c] 28 Isaiah 10:22,23 (see Septuagint)

[a] ἐν δικαιοσύνῃ· ὅτι λόγον συντετμημένον included by TR after συντέμνων.

NIV

had
left us
descendants,
we would have
become like
Sodom,
we would have
been like
Gomorrah."[a]

Israel's Unbelief

[30]What then shall
we say? That the
Gentiles, who did
not pursue righ-
teousness, have
obtained it, a righ-
teousness that is
by faith; [31]but the
people of Israel,
who pursued the
law as the way
of righteousness,
have not attained
their goal. [32]Why
not? Because they
pursued it not by
faith but as if it
were by works.
They stumbled
over the stumbling
stone. [33]As it is
written:

"See, I lay in
Zion a stone
that causes
people to
stumble
and a rock that
makes them
fall,
and the one
who believes
in him will
never be put
to shame."[b]

10 Brothers
and sisters,
my heart's desire
and prayer to God
for the Israelites
is that they may
be saved. [2]For I
can testify about
them that they are
zealous for God,
but their zeal is not
based on knowl-
edge. [3]Since they
did not know the
righteousness of
God and sought
to establish their
own, they did not
submit to God's
righteousness.
[4]Christ is the cul-
mination of the
law

ἐγκατέλιπεν ἡμῖν σπέρμα, ὡς Σόδομα ἂν ἐγενήθημεν καὶ
left to us descendants, we would have become like Sodom, *would we have become* and
1593 7005 5065 1181 323 1181 1181 6055 5047 323 1181 2779
v.aai.3s r.dp.1 n.asn pl n.npn pl v.api.1p cj

ὡς Γόμορρα ἂν ὡμοιώθημεν. [30] τί οὖν ἐροῦμεν; ὅτι
would have resembled *{like}* Gomorrah." *would have resembled* What then shall we say? — that
323 3929 3929 6055 1202 323 3929 5515 4036 3306 4022
pl n.nsf pl v.api.1p r.asn cj v.fai.1p cj

ἔθνη τὰ ➝ μὴ διώκοντα δικαιοσύνην κατέλαβεν δικαιοσύνην,
the Gentiles who did not pursue righteousness have obtained it, the
1620 3836 1503 3590 1503 1466 2898 1466
n.npn d.npn pl pt.pa.npn n.asf v.aai.3s n.asf

δικαιοσύνην δὲ τὴν ἐκ πίστεως, [31] Ἰσραὴλ δὲ διώκων νόμον
righteousness *{and}* that is by faith; but Israel, *but* ⌊even though it pursued⌋ a law
1466 1254 3836 1666 4411 1254 2702 1254 1503 3795
n.asf cj d.asf p.g n.gsf n.nsm cj pt.pa.nsm n.asm

δικαιοσύνης εἰς νόμον[a] ➝ οὐκ ἔφθασεν. [32] ⌊διὰ τί;⌋
that would produce righteousness, *{to} it* did not attain it? Why not?
1466 1650 3795 5777 4024 5777 3795 1328 5515
n.gsf p.a n.asm pl v.aai.3s p.a r.asn

ὅτι οὐκ ἐκ πίστεως ἀλλ᾽ ὡς ἐξ ἔργων·
Because they did not pursue it by faith, but ⌊as though⌋ it were by works.
4022 4024 1666 4411 247 6055 1666 2240
cj pl p.g n.gsf cj pl p.g n.gpn

προσέκοψαν τῷ λίθῳ τοῦ προσκόμματος, [33] καθὼς γέγραπται,
⌊They stumbled over⌋ the stumbling stone, *{the} stumbling* as it is written,
4684 3836 4682 3345 3836 4682 2777 1211
v.aai.3p d.dsm n.dsm d.gsn n.gsn cj v.rpi.3s

ἰδοὺ τίθημι ἐν Σιὼν λίθον προσκόμματος καὶ πέτραν
"Behold, I am laying in Zion a stone that makes them stumble and a rock that
2627 5502 1877 4994 3345 4682 2779 4376
j v.pai.1s p.d n.dsf n.asm n.gsn cj n.asf

σκανδάλου, ← καὶ ὁ πιστεύων ἐπ᾽ αὐτῷ ➝ οὐ καταισχυνθήσεται.
trips them up; but the one who believes in him will not be put to shame."
4998 2779 3836 4409 2093 899 2875 4024 2875
n.gsn cj d.nsm pt.pa.nsm p.d r.dsm.3 pl v.fpi.3s

[10:1] ἀδελφοί, ἡ μὲν εὐδοκία τῆς ἐμῆς καρδίας καὶ ἡ δέησις πρὸς
Brethren, *{the}* ~ my heart's desire *{the} my heart's* and *{the}* prayer to
81 3836 3525 1847 2840 2306 3836 1847 2840 2779 3836 1255 4639
n.vpm d.nsf pl n.nsf d.gsf r.gsf.1 n.gsf cj d.nsf n.nsf p.a

τὸν θεὸν ὑπὲρ αὐτῶν εἰς σωτηρίαν. [2] ➝ ➝ μαρτυρῶ γὰρ
{the} God for the Israelites is that they may be saved. For I bear them witness *For*
3836 2536 5642 899 1650 5401 1142 899 3455 1142
d.asm n.asm p.g r.gpm.3 p.a n.asf v.pai.1s cj

αὐτοῖς ὅτι ζῆλον θεοῦ ἔχουσιν ἀλλ᾽ οὐ κατ᾽ ἐπίγνωσιν· [3]
them that they have a zeal for God, *they have* but not ⌊according to⌋ knowledge. For
899 4022 2400 2400 2419 2536 2400 247 4024 2848 2106 1142
r.dpm.3 cj n.asm n.gsm v.pai.3p cj pl p.a n.asf

ἀγνοοῦντες γὰρ τὴν τοῦ θεοῦ δικαιοσύνην καὶ
ignoring *For* the righteousness that comes from God, *righteousness* and seeking to
51 1142 3836 1466 3836 2536 1466 2779 2426 2705
pt.pa.npm cj d.asf d.gsm n.gsm n.asf cj

τὴν ἰδίαν δικαιοσύνην[b] ζητοῦντες στῆσαι, τῇ
establish *{the}* their own, *{righteousness}* *seeking* *to establish* they did not submit to God's
2705 3836 2625 1466 2426 2705 5718 5718 4024 5718 3836 2536
d.asf a.asf n.asf pt.pa.npm f.aa d.dsf

δικαιοσύνῃ τοῦ θεοῦ οὐχ ὑπετάγησαν. [4] τέλος γὰρ → νόμου
righteousness. *{the} God's not they did submit* For Christ is the end *For* of the law,
1466 3836 2536 4024 5718 1142 5986 5465 1142 3795
n.dsf d.gsm n.gsm pl v.api.3p n.nsn cj n.gsm

NASB

LEFT TO US A
POSTERITY,
WE WOULD
HAVE BECOME
LIKE SODOM,
AND WOULD
HAVE RESEM-
BLED GOMOR-
RAH."
[30]What shall we
say then? That
Gentiles, who did
not pursue righ-
teousness, attained
righteousness,
even the righteous-
ness which is by
faith; [31]but Israel,
pursuing a law
of righteousness,
did not arrive at
that law. [32]Why?
Because *they did*
not *pursue it* by
faith, but as though
it were by works.
They stumbled
over the stumbling
stone, [33]just as it is
written,

"BEHOLD, I
LAY IN ZION
A STONE OF
STUMBLING
AND A ROCK OF
OFFENSE,
AND HE WHO
BELIEVES IN
HIM WILL
NOT BE DISAP-
POINTED."

The Word of Faith Brings Salvation

[10:1]Brethren, my
heart's desire and
my prayer to God
for them is for *their*
salvation. [2]For I
testify about them
that they have a
zeal for God, but
not in accordance
with knowledge.
[3]For not know-
ing about God's
righteousness and
seeking to establish
their own, they did
not subject them-
selves to the righ-
teousness of God.
[4]For Christ is the
end of the law

---

[a] 29 Isaiah 1:9
[b] 33 Isaiah 8:14; 28:16

[a] δικαιοσύνης included by TR after νόμον.
[b] [δικαιοσύνῃ] UBS, omitted by TNIV.

NIV

so that there may
be righteousness
for everyone who
believes.
[5]Moses writes
this about the righ-
teousness that is
by the law: "The
person who does
these things will
live by them."[a]
[6]But the righteous-
ness that is by
faith says: "Do not
say in your heart,
'Who will ascend
into heaven?'"[b]
(that is, to bring
Christ down) [7]"or
'Who will descend
into the deep?'"[c]
(that is, to bring
Christ up from
the dead). [8]But
what does it say?
"The word is near
you; it is in your
mouth and in your
heart,"[d] that is, the
message concern-
ing faith that we
proclaim: [9]If you
declare with your
mouth, "Jesus is
Lord," and believe
in your heart that
God raised him
from the dead,
you will be saved.
[10]For it is with
your heart that you
believe and are
justified, and it is
with your mouth
that you profess
your faith and are
saved. [11]As Scrip-
ture says, "Anyone
who believes in
him will never be
put to shame."[e]
[12]For there is no
difference between
Jew and Gentile—
the same Lord is
Lord of all and
richly blesses all
who call on him,
[13]for, "Everyone
who calls on

[a] 5 Lev. 18:5
[b] 6 Deut. 30:12
[c] 7 Deut. 30:13
[d] 8 Deut. 30:14
[e] 11 Isaiah 28:16 (see Septuagint)

Χριστὸς εἰς δικαιοσύνην παντὶ τῷ πιστεύοντι. [5] Μωϋσῆς γὰρ
Christ so now there is righteousness for everyone who believes. For Moses *For*
5986 1650 1466 4246 3836 4409 1142 3707 1142
n.nsm p.a n.asf a.dsm d.dsm pt.pa.dsm n.nsm cj

γράφει τὴν δικαιοσύνην τὴν ἐκ τοῦ[a] νόμου ὅτι ὁ
writes regarding the righteousness that is ⌊based on⌋ the law, "The person
1211 3836 1466 3836 1666 3836 3795 4022 3836 476
v.pai.3s d.asf n.asf d.asf p.g d.gsm n.gsm cj d.nsm

ποιήσας αὐτὰ ἄνθρωπος ζήσεται ἐν αὐτοῖς. [6] ἡ δὲ
⌊committed to⌋ ⌊these things⌋ *person* must live by them." But the *But* righteousness
4472 899 476 2409 1877 899 1254 3836 1254 1466
pt.aa.nsm r.apn.3 n.nsm v.fmi.3s p.d r.dpn.3 d.nsf cj

ἐκ πίστεως δικαιοσύνη οὕτως λέγει, ➝ μὴ εἴπῃς ἐν τῇ καρδίᾳ σου,
⌊based on⌋ faith *righteousness* *{this}* says, "Do not say in *{the}* your heart, *your*
1666 4411 1466 4048 3306 3306 3590 3306 1877 3836 5148 2840 5148
p.g n.gsf n.nsf adv v.pai.3s pl v.aas.2s p.d d.dsf n.dsf r.gs.2

τίς ἀναβήσεται εἰς τὸν οὐρανόν; τοῦτ᾽ ἔστιν ➝ ➝ Χριστὸν καταγαγεῖν· [7] ἤ,
'Who will ascend into *{the}* heaven?' (that is, to bring Christ down), or,
5515 326 1650 3836 4041 4047 1639 2864 2864 5986 2864 2445
r.nsm v.fmi.3s p.a d.asm n.asm r.nsn v.pai.3s n.asm f.aa cj

τίς καταβήσεται εἰς τὴν ἄβυσσον; τοῦτ᾽ ἔστιν Χριστὸν ἐκ νεκρῶν
'Who will descend into the abyss?' (that is, to bring Christ up from the dead)."
5515 2849 1650 3836 12 4047 1639 343 343 5986 343 1666 3738
r.nsm v.fmi.3s p.a d.asf n.asf r.nsn v.pai.3s n.asm p.g a.gpm

ἀναγαγεῖν. [8] ἀλλὰ τί λέγει; ἐγγύς σου τὸ ῥῆμά ἐστιν ἐν τῷ
to bring up But what ⌊does it say?⌋ "The word is near you, *The* *word* *is* in *{the}*
343 247 5515 3306 3836 4839 1639 1584 5148 3836 4839 1639 1877 3836
f.aa cj r.asn v.pai.3s adv r.gs.2 d.nsn n.nsn v.pai.3s p.d d.dsn

στόματί σου καὶ ἐν τῇ καρδίᾳ σου, τοῦτ᾽ ἔστιν τὸ ῥῆμα τῆς πίστεως
your mouth *your* and in *{the}* your heart," *your* that is, the word of faith
5148 5125 5148 2779 1877 3836 5148 2840 5148 4047 1639 3836 4839 3836 4411
n.dsn r.gs.2 cj p.d d.dsf n.dsf r.gs.2 r.nsn v.pai.3s d.nsn n.nsn d.gsf n.gsf

ὃ κηρύσσομεν. [9] ὅτι ἐὰν ὁμολογήσῃς ἐν τῷ στόματί σου κύριον
that we proclaim: that if you confess with *{the}* your mouth, *your* "Jesus is Lord,"
4005 3062 4022 1569 3933 1877 3836 5148 5125 5148 2652 3261
r.asn v.pai.1p cj cj v.aas.2s p.d d.dsn n.dsn r.gs.2 n.asm

Ἰησοῦν καὶ πιστεύσῃς ἐν τῇ καρδίᾳ σου ὅτι ὁ θεὸς αὐτὸν ἤγειρεν
Jesus and believe in *{the}* your heart *your* that *{the}* God raised him *raised*
2652 2779 4409 1877 3836 5148 2840 5148 4022 3836 2536 1586 899 1586
n.asm cj v.aas.2s p.d d.dsf n.dsf r.gs.2 cj d.nsm n.nsm r.asm.3 v.aai.3s

ἐκ νεκρῶν, σωθήσῃ· [10] ➝ καρδίᾳ γὰρ πιστεύεται
from the dead, ⌊you will be saved.⌋ For with the heart *For* a person believes and
1666 3738 5392 1142 2840 1142 4409
p.g a.gpm v.fpi.2s n.dsf cj v.ppi.3s

εἰς δικαιοσύνην, ➝ στόματι δὲ ὁμολογεῖται εἰς σωτηρίαν. [11]
is made righteous, and with the mouth *and* he confesses and is saved. For
1650 1466 1254 5125 1254 3933 1650 5401 1142
p.a n.asf n.dsn cj v.ppi.3s p.a n.asf

λέγει γὰρ ἡ γραφή, ⌊πᾶς ὁ⌋ πιστεύων ἐπ᾽ αὐτῷ ➝ οὐ
the Scripture says, *For* *the* *scripture* "Whoever believes in him will not
3836 1210 3306 1142 3836 1210 4246 3836 4409 2093 899 2875 4024
v.pai.3s cj d.nsf n.nsf a.nsm d.nsm pt.pa.nsm p.d r.dsm.3 pl

καταισχυνθήσεται. [12] οὐ γάρ ἐστιν διαστολὴ Ἰουδαίου
be put to shame." For there is no *For* *there is* distinction between the Jew
2875 1142 1639 1639 4024 1142 1639 1405 5445 2681
v.fpi.3s pl cj v.pai.3s n.nsf a.gsm

τε καὶ Ἕλληνος, ὁ γὰρ αὐτὸς κύριος πάντων, πλουτῶν
between and the Greek; for the *for* same Lord is Lord of all, giving generously
5445 2779 1818 1142 3836 1142 899 3261 4246 4456
cj cj n.gsm d.nsm cj r.nsm n.nsm a.gpm pt.pa.nsm

εἰς πάντας τοὺς ἐπικαλουμένους αὐτόν· [13] πᾶς γὰρ ὃς ἂν ἐπικαλέσηται
to all who call on him; for "everyone *for* who ~ calls on
1650 4246 3836 2126 899 1142 4246 1142 4005 323 2126
p.a a.apm d.apm pt.pm.apm r.asm.3 a.nsm cj r.nsm pl v.ams.3s

[a] [τοῦ] UBS.

NASB

for righteousness
to everyone who
believes.
[5]For Moses writes
that the man who
practices the righ-
teousness which
is based on law
shall live by that
righteousness. [6]But
the righteousness
based on faith
speaks as follows:
"DO NOT SAY IN
YOUR HEART, 'WHO
WILL ASCEND INTO
HEAVEN?' (that is,
to bring Christ
down), [7]or 'WHO
WILL DESCEND INTO
THE ABYSS?' (that
is, to bring Christ
up from the dead)."
[8]But what does it
say? "THE WORD IS
NEAR YOU, IN YOUR
MOUTH AND IN YOUR
HEART"—that is,
the word of faith
which we are
preaching, [9]that if
you confess with
your mouth Jesus
as Lord, and be-
lieve in your heart
that God raised
Him from the dead,
you will be saved;
[10]for with the heart
a person believes,
resulting in righ-
teousness, and
with the mouth he
confesses, resulting
in salvation. [11]For
the Scripture says,
"WHOEVER BELIEVES
IN HIM WILL NOT BE
DISAPPOINTED." [12]For
there is no distinc-
tion between Jew
and Greek; for the
same *Lord* is Lord
of all, abounding in
riches for all who
call on Him; [13]for
"WHOEVER WILL
CALL ON THE NAME

NIV

the name of the
Lord will be
saved."[a]
14How, then, can
they call on the
one they have not
believed in? And
how can they be-
lieve in the one of
whom they have
not heard? And
how can they hear
without someone
preaching to them?
15And how can
anyone preach un-
less they are sent?
As it is written:
"How beautiful are
the feet of those
who bring good
news!"[b]
16But not all the
Israelites accepted
the good news. For
Isaiah says, "Lord,
who has believed
our message?"[c]
17Consequent-
ly, faith comes
from hearing the
message, and the
message is heard
through the word
about Christ. 18But
I ask: Did they not
hear? Of course
they did:

"Their voice has
gone out into
all the earth,
their words to
the ends of
the world."[d]

19Again I ask: Did
Israel not under-
stand? First, Mo-
ses says,

"I will make you
envious by
those who
are not a
nation;
I will make you
angry by a
nation
that has no
understand-
ing."[e]

20And Isaiah boldly
says,

"I was found by
those who
did not seek
me;

[a] 13 Joel 2:32
[b] 15 Isaiah 52:7
[c] 16 Isaiah 53:1
[d] 18 Psalm 19:4
[e] 19 Deut. 32:21

τὸ ὄνομα → κυρίου σωθήσεται. 14 πῶς οὖν ἐπικαλέσωνται εἰς ὃν
the name of the Lord will be saved." But how *But* are they to call on one in whom
3836 3950 3261 5392 4036 4802 4036 2126 1650 4005
d.asn n.asn n.gsm v.fpi.3s cj cj v.ams.3p p.a r.asm

↱ ↱ οὐκ ἐπίστευσαν; πῶς δὲ πιστεύσωσιν οὗ ↱ ↱ οὐκ
they have not believed? And how *And* ⌞are they to believe in⌟ one ⌞of whom⌟ they have never
4409 4409 4024 4409 1254 4802 1254 4409 4005 201 201 4024
pl v.aai.3p cj cj v.aas.3p r.gsm pl

ἤκουσαν; πῶς δὲ ἀκούσωσιν χωρὶς κηρύσσοντος; 15 πῶς
heard? And how *And* are they to hear unless someone proclaims the message? And how
201 1254 4802 1254 201 6006 3062 1254 4802
v.aai.3p cj cj v.aas.3p p.g pt.pa.gsm cj

δὲ κηρύξωσιν ⌞ἐὰν μὴ⌟ ἀποσταλῶσιν; καθὼς γέγραπται, ὡς
And ⌞are they to proclaim the message⌟ unless they are sent? As it is written, "How
1254 3062 1569 3590 690 2777 1211 6055
cj v.aas.3p cj pl v.aps.3p cj v.rpi.3s pl

ὡραῖοι οἱ πόδες τῶν εὐαγγελιζομένων τὰ[a] ἀγαθά. 16 ἀλλ᾽ οὐ πάντες
timely are the feet of those who preach *{the}* good news!" However, not all
6053 3836 4546 3836 2294 3836 19 247 4024 4246
a.npm d.npm n.npm d.gpm pt.pm.gpm d.apn a.apn cj pl a.npm

ὑπήκουσαν τῷ εὐαγγελίῳ. Ἠσαΐας γὰρ λέγει, κύριε, τίς ἐπίστευσεν τῇ
of them have obeyed the good news, for Isaiah *for* says, "Lord, who has believed *{the}*
5634 3836 2295 1142 2480 1142 3306 3261 5515 4409 3836
v.aai.3p d.dsn n.dsn n.nsm cj v.pai.3s n.vsm r.nsm v.aai.3s d.dsf

ἀκοῇ ἡμῶν; 17 ἄρα ἡ πίστις ἐξ ἀκοῆς, ἡ δὲ
our message?" *our* So *{the}* faith ⌞comes from⌟ hearing the message, and what *and* is
7005 198 7005 726 3836 4411 1666 198 1254 3836 1254
n.dsf r.gp.1 cj d.nsf n.nsf p.g n.gsf d.nsf cj

ἀκοὴ διὰ ῥήματος Χριστοῦ. 18 ἀλλὰ λέγω, μὴ ↱ ↱ οὐκ
heard ⌞comes through⌟ the word of Christ. But I ask, *they have* have they not
198 1328 4839 5986 247 3306 3590 201 201 4024
n.nsf p.g n.gsn n.gsm cj v.pai.1s pl pl

ἤκουσαν; μενοῦνγε, εἰς πᾶσαν τὴν γῆν
heard? Indeed they have, for, "Their voice has gone out to all the earth,
201 3529 3590 3590 899 5782 2002 2002 2002 1650 4246 3836 1178
v.aai.3p pl p.a a.asf d.asf n.asf

ἐξῆλθεν ὁ φθόγγος αὐτῶν καὶ εἰς τὰ πέρατα τῆς οἰκουμένης τὰ
has gone out *{the}* *voice* *Their* and their words to the ends of the world." *{the}*
2002 3836 5782 899 2779 899 4839 1650 3836 4306 3836 3876 3836
v.aai.3s d.nsm n.nsm r.gpm.3 cj p.a d.apn n.apn d.gsf n.gsf d.npn

ῥήματα αὐτῶν. 19 ἀλλὰ λέγω, μὴ ↱ Ἰσραὴλ οὐκ ἔγνω; πρῶτος Μωϋσῆς
words *their* But I ask, *{not}* did Israel not understand? First of all, Moses
4839 899 247 3306 3590 1182 2702 4024 1182 4755 3707
n.npn r.gpm.3 cj v.pai.1s pl n.nsm pl v.aai.3s a.nsm n.nsm

λέγει, ἐγὼ → → παραζηλώσω ὑμᾶς ἐπ᾽ οὐκ ἔθνει, ἐπ᾽ ἔθνει
says, "I will make you jealous *you* by those who are not a nation; by a nation
3306 1609 7007 4143 7007 2093 4024 1620 2093 1620
v.pai.3s r.ns.1 v.fai.1s r.ap.2 p.d pl n.dsn p.d n.dsn

ἀσυνέτῳ → → → παροργιῶ ὑμᾶς. 20 Ἠσαΐας δὲ ἀποτολμᾷ
void of understanding I will make you angry." *you* Then Isaiah *Then* very boldly
852 7007 4239 7007 1254 2480 1254 703
a.dsn v.fai.1s r.ap.2 n.nsm cj v.pai.3s

καὶ λέγει, εὑρέθην ἐν[b] τοῖς ἐμὲ μὴ ζητοῦσιν,
{and} says, "I was found by those who were not looking for me; *not* *who were looking for*
2779 3306 2351 1877 3836 2426 2426 3590 2426 2426 1609 3590 2426
cj v.pai.3s v.api.1s p.d d.dpm r.as.1 pl pt.pa.dpm

[a] [τὰ] UBS, omitted by TNIV.
[b] [ἐν] UBS, omitted by TNIV.

NASB

OF THE LORD WILL
BE SAVED."
14How then will
they call on Him
in whom they have
not believed? How
will they believe
in Him whom they
have not heard?
And how will they
hear without a
preacher? 15How
will they preach
unless they are
sent? Just as it
is written, "HOW
BEAUTIFUL ARE THE
FEET OF THOSE WHO
BRING GOOD NEWS OF
GOOD THINGS!"
16However, they
did not all heed
the good news; for
Isaiah says, "LORD,
WHO HAS BELIEVED
OUR REPORT?" 17So
faith *comes* from
hearing, and hear-
ing by the word of
Christ.
18But I say, surely
they have never
heard, have they?
Indeed they have;

"THEIR VOICE
HAS GONE OUT
INTO ALL THE
EARTH,
AND THEIR
WORDS TO THE
ENDS OF THE
WORLD."

19But I say, surely
Israel did not
know, did they?
First Moses says,

"I WILL MAKE
YOU JEALOUS
BY THAT WHICH
IS NOT A NA-
TION,
BY A NATION
WITHOUT UN-
DERSTANDING
WILL I ANGER
YOU." 20And
Isaiah is very
bold and
says,

20"I WAS FOUND
BY THOSE WHO
DID NOT SEEK
ME,

NIV

I revealed
myself to
those who
did not ask
for me."[a]
[21] But concerning Is-
rael he says,
"All day long I
have held out
my hands
to a disobedient
and obstinate
people."[b]

The Remnant of Israel

11 I ask then:
Did God
reject his people?
By no means! I am
an Israelite myself,
a descendant of
Abraham, from the
tribe of Benjamin.
[2] God did not reject
his people, whom
he foreknew. Don't
you know what
Scripture says in
the passage about
Elijah—how he
appealed to God
against Israel:
[3] "Lord, they have
killed your proph-
ets and torn down
your altars; I am
the only one left,
and they are trying
to kill me"[c]? [4] And
what was God's
answer to him? "I
have reserved for
myself seven thou-
sand who have not
bowed the knee to
Baal."[d] [5] So too, at
the present time
there is a remnant
chosen by grace.
[6] And if by grace,
then it cannot be
based on works;
if it were, grace
would no longer be
grace.
[7] What then?
What the people
of Israel sought so
earnestly they did
not obtain.

[a] 20 Isaiah 65:1
[b] 21 Isaiah 65:2
[c] 3 1 Kings 19:10,14
[d] 4 1 Kings 19:18

ἐμφανὴς ἐγενόμην τοῖς ἐμὲ μὴ
I became well known *I became* to those who were not asking for me." *not*
1181 1181 1871 1181 3836 2089 2089 3590 2089 2089 1609 3590
a.nsm v.ami.1s d.dpm r.as.1 pl

ἐπερωτῶσιν. 21 πρὸς δὲ τὸν Ἰσραὴλ λέγει, ὅλην τὴν ἡμέραν
who were asking for But concerning *But* *{the}* Israel he says, "All *{the}* day long
2089 1254 4639 1254 3836 2702 3306 3910 3836 2465
pt.pa.dpm p.a cj d.asm n.asm v.pai.3s a.asf d.asf n.asf

ἐξεπέτασα τὰς χεῖράς μου πρὸς λαὸν
⌞I have held out⌟ *{the}* my hands *my* to a disobedient and argumentative people."
1736 3836 1609 5931 1609 4639 578 2779 515 3295
v.aai.1s d.apf n.apf r.gs.1 p.a n.asm

ἀπειθοῦντα καὶ ἀντιλέγοντα.
disobedient *and* *argumentative*
578 2779 515
pt.pa.asm cj pt.pa.asm

11:1 λέγω οὖν, μὴ → ἀπώσατο ὁ θεὸς τὸν λαὸν αὐτοῦ;
So I ask, *So* *{not}* has God repudiated *{the}* *God* *{the}* his people? *his*
4036 3306 4036 3590 2536 723 3836 2536 3836 899 3295 899
v.pai.1s cj pl v.ami.3s d.nsm n.nsm d.asm n.asm r.gsm.3

⌞μὴ γένοιτο·⌟ καὶ γὰρ ἐγὼ Ἰσραηλίτης εἰμί, ⌞ἐκ
By no means! *{and}* For I myself am an Israelite, *am* a descendant
3590 1181 2779 1142 1609 1639 2703 1639 1666
pl v.amo.3s cj cj r.ns.1 n.nsm v.pai.1s p.g

σπέρματος⌟ Ἀβραάμ, → φυλῆς Βενιαμίν. 2 ↱ οὐκ ἀπώσατο ὁ θεὸς
of Abraham, from the tribe of Benjamin. God has not repudiated *{the}* *God*
5065 11 5876 1021 2536 723 4024 723 3836 2536
n.gsn n.gsm n.gsf n.asf pl v.ami.3s d.nsm n.nsm

τὸν λαὸν αὐτοῦ ὃν προέγνω. ἢ ↱ ↱ οὐκ οἴδατε
{the} his people *his* whom he foreknew. Or do you not know what the Scripture says
3836 899 3295 899 4005 4589 2445 3857 3857 4024 3857 5515 3836 1210 3306
d.asm n.asm r.gsm.3 r.asm v.aai.3s cj pl v.rai.2p

ἐν Ἠλίᾳ τί λέγει ἡ γραφή, ὡς ἐντυγχάνει τῷ θεῷ κατὰ τοῦ
in the passage about Elijah, *what* *says* *the* *scripture* how he pleads with God against *{the}*
1877 2460 5515 3306 3836 1210 6055 1961 3836 2536 2848 3836
p.d n.dsm r.asn v.pai.3s d.nsf n.nsf cj v.pai.3s d.dsm n.dsm p.g d.gsm

Ἰσραήλ; 3 κύριε, τοὺς προφήτας σου ἀπέκτειναν,
Israel? "Lord, they have killed *{the}* your prophets, *your* *they have killed* they have torn
2702 3261 650 650 650 3836 5148 4737 5148 650 2940 2940 2940
n.gsm n.vsm d.apm n.apm r.gs.2 v.aai.3p

τὰ θυσιαστήριά σου κατέσκαψαν, κἀγὼ ὑπελείφθην μόνος καὶ
down *{the}* your altars, *your* *they have torn down* and I alone am left, *alone* and
2940 3836 5148 2603 5148 2940 2743 3668 5699 3668 2779
d.apn n.apn r.gs.2 v.aai.3p crasis v.api.1s a.nsm cj

ζητοῦσιν τὴν ψυχήν μου. 4 ἀλλὰ τί → λέγει αὐτῷ ὁ
they are seeking *{the}* my life." *my* But what was the divine reply saying to him?
2426 3836 1609 6034 1609 247 5515 3836 5977 5977 3306 899 3836
v.pai.3p d.asf n.asf r.gs.1 cj r.asn v.pai.3s r.dsm.3 d.nsm

χρηματισμός; κατέλιπον ἐμαυτῷ ἑπτακισχιλίους ἄνδρας, οἵτινες ↱ οὐκ ἔκαμψαν
God's "I have kept for myself seven thousand men who have not bowed
5977 2901 1831 2233 467 4015 2828 4024 2828
n.nsm v.aai.1s r.dsm.1 a.apm n.apm r.npm pl v.aai.3p

γόνυ τῇ Βάαλ. 5 οὕτως οὖν καὶ ἐν τῷ νῦν καιρῷ λεῖμμα κατ᾽
the knee to Baal." So *{then}* too at the present time there is a remnant, *by*
1205 3836 955 4048 4036 2779 1877 3836 3814 2789 1181 1181 3307 2848
n.asn d.dsf n.dsm adv cj adv p.d d.dsm adv n.dsm n.nsn p.a

ἐκλογὴν χάριτος γέγονεν· 6 εἰ δὲ χάριτι, οὐκέτι ἐξ
chosen by grace. *there is* And if *And* it is by grace, it is no longer ⌞on the basis of⌟
1724 2848 5921 1181 1254 1623 1254 5921 4033 1666
n.asf n.gsf v.rai.3s cj cj n.dsf adv p.g

ἔργων, ἐπεὶ ἡ χάρις ↱ οὐκέτι γίνεται χάρις.[a] 7 τί οὖν;
works, otherwise *{the}* grace would no longer be grace. What then? Israel failed to
2240 2075 3836 5921 1181 4033 1181 5921 5515 4036 2702 4024 2209
n.gpn cj d.nsf n.nsf adv v.pmi.3s n.nsf r.nsn cj

[a] εἰ δὲ ἐξ ἔργων, οὐκέτι ἐστὶ χάρις· ἐπεὶ τὸ ἔργον οὐκέτι ἐστὶν ἔργον included by TR after χάρις.

NASB

I BECAME MANI-
FEST TO THOSE
WHO DID NOT
ASK FOR ME."
[21] But as for Israel
He says, "ALL THE
DAY LONG I HAVE
STRETCHED OUT MY
HANDS TO A DISOBE-
DIENT AND OBSTI-
NATE PEOPLE."

Israel Is Not Cast Away

[11:1] I say then, God
has not rejected
His people, has
He? May it never
be! For I too am an
Israelite, a descen-
dant of Abraham,
of the tribe of
Benjamin. [2] God
has not rejected
His people whom
He foreknew. Or
do you not know
what the Scripture
says in *the passage*
about Elijah, how
he pleads with
God against Israel?
[3] "Lord, THEY HAVE
KILLED YOUR PROPH-
ETS, THEY HAVE TORN
DOWN YOUR ALTARS,
AND I ALONE AM
LEFT, AND THEY ARE
SEEKING MY LIFE."
[4] But what is the
divine response to
him? "I HAVE KEPT
for Myself SEVEN
THOUSAND MEN WHO
HAVE NOT BOWED
THE KNEE TO BAAL."
[5] In the same way
then, there has
also come to be at
the present time a
remnant according
to *God's* gracious
choice. [6] But if it is
by grace, it is no
longer on the basis
of works, other-
wise grace is no
longer grace.
[7] What then? What

NIV

The elect among
them did, but the
others were hard-
ened, [8]as it is
written:

> "God gave them
> a spirit of
> stupor,
> eyes that could
> not see
> and ears that
> could not
> hear,
> to this very day."[a]

[9]And David says:

> "May their table
> become a
> snare and a
> trap,
> a stumbling
> block and a
> retribution
> for them.
> [10]May their eyes be
> darkened so
> they cannot
> see,
> and their backs
> be bent
> forever."[b]

Ingrafted Branches

[11]Again I ask: Did
they stumble so as
to fall beyond re-
covery? Not at all!
Rather, because
of their transgres-
sion, salvation has
come to the Gen-
tiles to make Israel
envious. [12]But if
their transgres-
sion means riches
for the world, and
their loss means
riches for the Gen-
tiles, how much
greater riches will
their full inclusion
bring!
[13]I am talking to
you Gentiles. Inas-
much as I am the
apostle to the Gen-
tiles, I take pride
in my ministry
[14]in the hope that
I may somehow
arouse my own
people to envy and
save some of them.
[15]For if their rejec-
tion brought rec-
onciliation to the
world, what will
their acceptance

[a] 8 Deut. 29:4; Isaiah 29:10
[b] 10 Psalm 69:22,23

ὃ ἐπιζητεῖ Ἰσραήλ, τοῦτο οὐκ ἐπέτυχεν, ἡ δὲ ἐκλογὴ ἐπέτυχεν,
obtain what it was seeking, *Israel* *{this}* *failed* *to obtain* but the *but* elect obtained it.
2209 4005 2118 2702 4047 4024 2209 1254 3836 1254 1724 2209
r.asn v.pai.3s n.nsm r.asn pl v.aai.3s d.nsf cj n.nsf v.aai.3s

οἱ δὲ λοιποὶ ἐπωρώθησαν, [8]καθὼς γέγραπται, ἔδωκεν αὐτοῖς ὁ θεὸς
The *{and}* rest were hardened, as it is written, "God gave them *{the}* *God* a
3836 1254 3370 4800 2777 1211 2536 1443 899 3836 2536
d.npm cj a.npm v.api.3p cj v.rpi.3s v.aai.3s r.dpm.3 d.nsm n.nsm

πνεῦμα κατανύξεως, ὀφθαλμοὺς τοῦ ↱ μὴ βλέπειν καὶ ὦτα τοῦ ↱ μὴ
spirit of stupor, eyes that would not see and ears that would not
4460 2919 4057 3836 1063 3590 1063 2779 4044 3836 201 3590
n.asn n.gsf n.apm d.gsn pl f.pa cj n.apn d.gsn pl

ἀκούειν, ἕως τῆς σήμερον ἡμέρας. [9]καὶ Δαυὶδ λέγει, → γενηθήτω ἡ
hear, to this very day." And David says, "May their table become *{the}*
201 2401 3836 4958 2465 2779 1253 3306 899 5544 1181 3836
f.pa p.g d.gsf adv n.gsf cj n.nsm v.pai.3s v.apm.3s d.nsf

τράπεζα αὐτῶν εἰς παγίδα καὶ εἰς θήραν καὶ εἰς σκάνδαλον καὶ εἰς
table *their* *{for}* a snare and *{for}* a trap, *{and}* *{for}* a stumbling block and *{for}* a
5544 899 1650 4075 2779 1650 2560 2779 1650 4998 2779 1650
n.nsf r.gpm.3 p.a n.asf cj p.a n.asf cj p.a n.asn cj p.a

ἀνταπόδομα αὐτοῖς, [10] → σκοτισθήτωσαν οἱ ὀφθαλμοὶ αὐτῶν τοῦ ↱
retribution for them. May their eyes be darkened *{the}* *eyes* *their* so they
501 899 899 4057 5029 3836 4057 899 3836 1063
n.asn r.dpm.3 v.apm.3p d.npm n.npm r.gpm.3 d.gsn

μὴ βλέπειν καὶ ↱ τὸν νῶτον αὐτῶν ˻διὰ παντὸς˼ σύγκαμψον. [11]
cannot see, and keep *{the}* their backs *their* constantly bent." So
3590 1063 2779 5159 3836 899 3822 899 1328 4246 5159 4036
pl f.pa cj d.asm n.asm r.gpm.3 p.g a.gsm v.aam.2s

λέγω οὖν, μὴ ἔπταισαν ἵνα πέσωσιν; ˻μὴ γένοιτο·˼ ἀλλὰ τῷ
I ask, *So* *{not}* did they stumble so as to fall? By no means! But ˻because of˼
3306 4036 3590 4760 2671 4406 3590 1181 247 3836
v.pai.1s cj pl v.aai.3p cj v.aas.3p pl v.amo.3s cj d.dsn

αὐτῶν παραπτώματι ἡ σωτηρία τοῖς ἔθνεσιν εἰς τὸ → →
their transgression *{the}* salvation has come to the Gentiles ˻so as˼ ~ to make Israel
899 4183 3836 5401 3836 1620 1650 3836 899
r.gpm.3 n.dsn d.nsf n.nsf d.dpn n.dpn p.a d.asn

παραζηλῶσαι αὐτούς. [12] εἰ δὲ τὸ παράπτωμα αὐτῶν πλοῦτος →
jealous. *Israel* Now if *Now* *{the}* their transgression *their* means riches for
4143 899 1254 1623 1254 3836 899 4183 899 4458
f.aa r.apm.3 cj cj d.nsn n.nsn r.gpm.3 n.nsm

κόσμου καὶ τὸ ἥττημα αὐτῶν πλοῦτος → ἐθνῶν, πόσῳ μᾶλλον
the world and *{the}* their failure *their* means riches for the Gentiles, how much more
3180 2779 3836 899 2488 899 4458 1620 4531 3437
n.gsm cj d.nsn n.nsn r.gpm.3 n.nsm n.gpn r.dsn adv.c

τὸ πλήρωμα αὐτῶν. [13] ὑμῖν δὲ λέγω τοῖς
will *{the}* their full inclusion *their* mean! I am speaking to you *{and}* *I am speaking* *{the}*
3836 899 4445 899 3306 3306 3306 7007 1254 3306 3836
d.nsn n.nsn r.gpm.3 r.dp.2 cj v.pai.1s d.dpn

ἔθνεσιν, ˻ἐφ᾽ ὅσον˼ μὲν οὖν εἰμι ἐγὼ ἐθνῶν ἀπόστολος,
Gentiles. Inasmuch ~ then as I am *I* an apostle to the Gentiles, *apostle*
1620 2093 4012 3525 4036 1609 1639 1609 693 1620 693
n.dpn p.a r.asn pl cj v.pai.1s r.ns.1 n.gpn n.nsm

τὴν διακονίαν μου δοξάζω, [14] εἴ πως παραζηλώσω
I take pride in *{the}* my ministry, *my* *I take pride in* if somehow I could provoke
1519 1519 1519 1519 3836 1609 1355 1609 1519 1623 4803 4143
d.asf n.asf r.gs.1 v.pai.1s cj pl v.fai.1s

μου τὴν σάρκα ↰ ↰ καὶ σώσω τινὰς ἐξ αὐτῶν. [15] εἰ γὰρ ἡ
my own *{the}* countrymen to jealousy and save some of them. For if *For* *{the}*
1609 3836 4922 4143 4143 2779 5392 5516 1666 899 1142 1623 1142 3836
r.gs.1 d.asf n.asf cj v.fai.1s r.apm p.g r.gpm.3 cj cj d.nsf

ἀποβολὴ αὐτῶν καταλλαγὴ → κόσμου, τίς ἡ πρόσλημψις
their rejection *their* leads to the reconciliation of the world, what will their acceptance
899 613 899 2903 3180 5515 3836 4691
n.nsf r.gpm.3 n.nsf n.gsm r.nsf d.nsf n.nsf

NASB

Israel is seeking, it
has not obtained,
but those who were
chosen obtained it,
and the rest were
hardened; [8]just as it
is written,

> "GOD GAVE THEM
> A SPIRIT OF
> STUPOR,
> EYES TO SEE
> NOT AND EARS
> TO HEAR NOT,
> DOWN TO THIS
> VERY DAY."

[9]And David says,

> "LET THEIR
> TABLE BECOME
> A SNARE AND A
> TRAP,
> AND A STUM-
> BLING BLOCK
> AND A RET-
> RIBUTION TO
> THEM.
> [10]"LET THEIR EYES
> BE DARKENED
> TO SEE NOT,
> AND BEND
> THEIR BACKS
> FOREVER."

[11]I say then, they
did not stumble
so as to fall, did
they? May it never
be! But by their
transgression sal-
vation *has come*
to the Gentiles, to
make them jeal-
ous. [12]Now if their
transgression is
riches for the world
and their failure is
riches for the Gen-
tiles, how much
more will their ful-
fillment be! [13]But I
am speaking to you
who are Gentiles.
Inasmuch then as
I am an apostle of
Gentiles, I magnify
my ministry, [14]if
somehow I might
move to jealousy
my fellow country-
men and save some
of them. [15]For if
their rejection is
the reconciliation
of the world, what
will *their* accep-
tance be but

NIV

be but life from
the dead? [16]If the
part of the dough
offered as first-
fruits is holy, then
the whole batch
is holy; if the root
is holy, so are the
branches.
[17]If some of the
branches have
been broken off,
and you, though a
wild olive shoot,
have been grafted
in among the oth-
ers and now share
in the nourishing
sap from the olive
root, [18]do not con-
sider yourself to be
superior to those
other branches. If
you do, consider
this: You do not
support the root,
but the root sup-
ports you. [19]You
will say then,
"Branches were
broken off so that
I could be grafted
in." [20]Granted. But
they were broken
off because of
unbelief, and you
stand by faith. Do
not be arrogant,
but tremble. [21]For
if God did not
spare the natural
branches, he will
not spare you ei-
ther.
[22]Consider there-
fore the kindness
and sternness of
God: sternness to
those who fell, but
kindness to you,
provided that you
continue in his
kindness. Other-
wise, you also will
be cut off. [23]And
if they do not per-
sist in unbelief,
they will be graft-
ed in, for God is
able to graft them
in again. [24]After
all, if

ˌεἰ μὴˌ ζωὴ ἐκ νεκρῶν; [16] εἰ δὲ ἡ ἀπαρχὴ ἁγία,
mean but life from the dead? If *{and}* the dough offered as first fruits is holy, so
1623 3590 2437 1666 3738 1623 1254 3836 569 41
cj pl n.nsf p.g a.gpm cj cj d.nsf n.nsf a.nsf

καὶ τὸ φύραμα· καὶ εἰ ἡ ῥίζα ἁγία, καὶ οἱ κλάδοι. [17] εἰ
also is the whole lump; and if the root is holy, so also are the branches. But if
2779 3836 5878 2779 1623 3836 4844 41 2779 3836 3080 1254 1623
adv d.nsn n.nsn cj cj d.nsf n.nsf a.nsf adv d.npm n.npm cj

δέ τινες τῶν κλάδων ἐξεκλάσθησαν, σὺ δὲ ἀγριέλαιος ὢν
But some of the branches were broken off, and you, *and* although a wild olive shoot, *although*
1254 5516 3836 3080 1709 1254 5148 1254 1639 66 1639
cj r.npm d.gpm n.gpm v.api.3p r.ns.2 cj n.nsf pt.pa.nsm

ἐνεκεντρίσθης ἐν αὐτοῖς καὶ συγκοινωνὸς τῆς ῥίζης τῆς
were grafted in among the others and you now share in the nourishing root *{the}*
1596 1877 899 2779 1181 1181 5171 3836 4404 4844 3836
v.api.2s p.d r.dpm.3 cj n.nsm d.gsf n.gsf d.gsf

πιότητος τῆς ἐλαίας ἐγένου, [18] ↱ μὴ κατακαυχῶ τῶν κλάδων·
nourishing of the olive tree, *you now* do not ˌbecome arrogant towardˌ the branches. But
4404 3836 1777 1181 2878 3590 2878 3836 3080 1254
n.gsf d.gsf n.gsf v.ami.2s pl v.pmm.2s d.gpm n.gpm

εἰ δὲ κατακαυχᾶσαι οὐ σὺ τὴν ῥίζαν βαστάζεις ἀλλὰ
if *But* you do, consider this: it is not you who support the root, *who support* but
1623 1254 2878 4024 5148 1002 1002 3836 4844 1002 247
cj cj v.pmi.2s pl r.ns.2 d.asf n.asf v.pai.2s cj

ἡ ῥίζα σέ. [19] ἐρεῖς οὖν, ἐξεκλάσθησαν κλάδοι
the root that supports you. Then ˌyou will say,ˌ *Then* "The branches were broken off *branches*
3836 4844 5148 4036 3306 4036 3080 1709 3080
d.nsf n.nsf r.as.2 v.fai.2s cj v.api.3p n.npm

ἵνα ἐγὼ ἐγκεντρισθῶ. [20] καλῶς· τῇ ἀπιστίᾳ
so I ˌcould be grafted in."ˌ That is true. They were broken off ˌbecause ofˌ unbelief,
2671 1609 1596 2822 1709 1709 1709 1709 3836 602
cj r.ns.1 v.aps.1s adv d.dsf n.dsf

ἐξεκλάσθησαν, σὺ δὲ τῇ πίστει ἕστηκας. μὴ ὑψηλὰ φρόνει
They were broken off and you *and* stand by faith. *stand* Do not be proud, *Do be*
1709 1254 5148 1254 2705 3836 4411 2705 5858 3590 5858 5734 5858
v.api.3p r.ns.2 cj d.dsf n.dsf v.rai.2s pl a.apn v.pam.2s

ἀλλὰ φοβοῦ· [21] εἰ γὰρ ὁ θεὸς τῶν ˌκατὰ φύσινˌ κλάδων
but ˌstand in awe.ˌ For if *For {the}* God did not spare the natural branches,
247 5828 1142 1623 1142 3836 2536 5767 4024 5767 3836 2848 5882 3080
cj v.ppm.2s cj cj d.nsm n.nsm d.gpm p.a n.asf n.gpm

οὐκ ἐφείσατο, [a]ˌμή πωςˌ[b] οὐδὲ σοῦ ↰ φείσεται. [22] ἴδε
not did spare perhaps he will not spare you either. *he will spare* Consider
4024 5767 3590 4803 5767 5767 4028 5767 5148 4028 5767 2623
pl v.ami.3s cj pl adv r.gs.2 v.fmi.3s v.aam.2s

οὖν χρηστότητα καὶ ἀποτομίαν θεοῦ· ἐπὶ μὲν τοὺς
therefore the kindness and the severity of God — severity to ~ those
4036 5983 2779 704 2536 704 2093 3525 3836
cj n.asf cj n.asf n.gsm p.a pl d.apm

πεσόντας ἀποτομία, ἐπὶ δὲ σὲ χρηστότης θεοῦ, ἐὰν
ˌwho have fallen,ˌ *severity* but God's kindness to *but* you, *kindness* *God's* provided
4406 704 1254 2536 5983 2093 1254 5148 5983 2536 1569
pt.aa.apm n.nsf p.a cj r.as.2 n.nsf n.gsm cj

ἐπιμένῃς τῇ χρηστότητι, ἐπεὶ καὶ σὺ ἐκκοπήσῃ. [23] κἀκεῖνοι
ˌyou continue inˌ his kindness. Otherwise you too *you* will be cut off. And even they,
2152 3836 5983 2075 5148 2779 5148 1716 1254 2797
v.pas.2s d.dsf n.dsf cj adv r.ns.2 v.fpi.2s adv

δέ, ἐὰν ↱ ↱ μὴ ἐπιμένωσιν τῇ ἀπιστίᾳ, ἐγκεντρισθήσονται,
And if they do not continue in their unbelief, will be grafted in, for God is
1254 1569 2152 2152 3590 2152 3836 602 1596 1142 2536 1639
cj cj pl v.pas.3p d.dsf n.dsf v.fpi.3p

δυνατὸς γάρ ἐστιν ὁ θεὸς πάλιν ἐγκεντρίσαι αὐτούς. [24] εἰ
able *for is {the} God* to graft them in again. *to graft in* *them* For if
1543 1142 1639 3836 2536 1596 1596 899 1596 4099 1596 899 1142 1623
a.nsm cj v.pai.3s d.nsm n.nsm adv f.aa r.apm.3 cj

[a] [μή πως] UBS, omitted by TNIV.
[b] πως omitted in TNIV.

NASB

life from the dead?
[16]If the first piece *of*
dough is holy, the
lump is also; and if
the root is holy, the
branches are too.
[17]But if some of
the branches were
broken off, and
you, being a wild
olive, were grafted
in among them and
became partaker
with them of the
rich root of the
olive tree, [18]do not
be arrogant toward
the branches; but
if you are arrogant,
remember that it is
not you who sup-
ports the root, but
the root *supports*
you. [19]You will say
then, "Branches
were broken off
so that I might be
grafted in." [20]Quite
right, they were
broken off for
their unbelief, but
you stand by your
faith. Do not be
conceited, but fear;
[21]for if God did not
spare the natural
branches, He will
not spare you, ei-
ther. [22]Behold then
the kindness and
severity of God; to
those who fell, se-
verity, but to you,
God's kindness, if
you continue in His
kindness; other-
wise you also will
be cut off. [23]And
they also, if they
do not continue in
their unbelief, will
be grafted in, for
God is able to graft
them in again. [24]For

NIV

you were cut out of
an olive tree that is
wild by nature, and
contrary to nature
were grafted into
a cultivated olive
tree, how much
more readily will
these, the natural
branches, be graft-
ed into their own
olive tree!

All Israel Will Be Saved

25 I do not want
you to be ignorant
of this mystery,
brothers and sis-
ters, so that you
may not be con-
ceited: Israel has
experienced a
hardening in part
until the full num-
ber of the Gentiles
has come in, 26 and
in this way[a] all Is-
rael will be saved.
As it is written:

> "The deliverer will come from Zion;
> he will turn godlessness away from Jacob.
> 27 And this is[b] my covenant with them
> when I take away their sins."[c]

28 As far as the
gospel is con-
cerned, they are
enemies for your
sake; but as far as
election is con-
cerned, they are
loved on account
of the patriarchs,
29 for God's gifts
and his call are
irrevocable. 30 Just
as you who were
at one time dis-
obedient to God
have now received
mercy as a result
of their disobedi-
ence, 31 so they too
have now become
disobedient in or-
der that

[a] 26 Or *and so*
[b] 27 Or *will be*
[c] 27 Isaiah 59:20,21; 27:9 (see Septuagint); Jer. 31:33,34

γὰρ σὺ ἐκ τῆς κατὰ φύσιν ἐξεκόπης ἀγριελαίου καὶ
For you were cut from what is by nature *were cut* a wild olive tree, and grafted
1142 5148 1716 1716 1666 3836 2848 5882 1716 66 2779 1596
cj r.ns.2 p.g d.gsf p.a n.asf v.api.2s n.gsf cj

παρὰ φύσιν ἐνεκεντρίσθης εἰς καλλιέλαιον, πόσῳ μᾶλλον ↱ οὗτοι
⌊contrary to⌋ nature *grafted* into a ⌊cultivated olive tree,⌋ how much more will these,
4123 5882 1596 1650 2814 4531 3437 1596 4047
p.a n.asf v.api.2s p.a n.asf r.dsn adv.c r.npm

οἱ ⌊κατὰ φύσιν⌋ ἐγκεντρισθήσονται τῇ ἰδίᾳ ἐλαίᾳ. 25 ↱
the natural branches, be grafted back into *{the}* ⌊their own⌋ olive tree? For I
3836 2848 5882 1596 3836 2625 1777 1142 2527
d.npm p.a n.asf v.fpi.3p d.dsf a.dsf n.dsf

↱ οὐ γὰρ θέλω ὑμᾶς ἀγνοεῖν, ἀδελφοί, τὸ μυστήριον τοῦτο, —
do not *For* want you to be uninformed, my brothers, of *{the}* this mystery *this*
2527 4024 1142 2527 7007 51 81 3836 4047 3696 4047
pl cj v.pai.1s r.ap.2 f.pa n.vpm d.asn n.asn r.asn

ἵνα ↱ ↱ μὴ ἦτε παρ᾽[a] ἑαυτοῖς φρόνιμοι, ὅτι
so that you may not be wise in ⌊your own conceits⌋ *wise* — that a partial
2671 1639 1639 3590 1639 5861 4123 1571 5861 4022 608
cj pl v.pas.2p p.d r.dpm.2 a.npm cj

πώρωσις ⌊ἀπὸ μέρους⌋ τῷ Ἰσραὴλ γέγονεν ⌊ἄχρι οὗ⌋ τὸ πλήρωμα
hardening *partial* has happened to Israel *has happened* until the full number
4801 608 3538 1181 1181 3836 2702 1181 948 4005 3836 4445
n.nsf p.g n.gsn d.dsm n.dsm v.rai.3s p.g r.gsm d.nsn n.nsn

τῶν ἐθνῶν εἰσέλθῃ 26 καὶ οὕτως πᾶς Ἰσραὴλ σωθήσεται, καθὼς
of the Gentiles ⌊has come in.⌋ And ⌊in this way⌋ all Israel will be saved: as
3836 1620 1656 2779 4048 4246 2702 5392 2777
d.gpn n.gpn v.aas.3s cj adv a.nsm n.nsm v.fpi.3s cj

γέγραπται, ἥξει ἐκ Σιὼν ὁ ῥυόμενος, ἀποστρέψει ἀσεβείας
it is written, "Out of Zion ⌊will come⌋ *Out of Zion* the Deliverer; he will remove ungodliness
1211 1666 1666 4994 2457 1666 4994 3836 4861 695 813
v.rpi.3s v.fai.3s p.g n.gsf d.nsm pt.pm.nsm v.fai.3s n.apf

ἀπὸ Ἰακώβ. 27 καὶ αὕτη αὐτοῖς ἡ παρ᾽ ἐμοῦ διαθήκη, ὅταν
from Jacob." "And this will be my covenant with them, *{the}* *{from}* *my* *covenant* when
608 2609 2779 4047 1609 1347 899 3836 4123 1609 1347 4020
p.g n.gsm cj r.nsf r.dpm.3 d.nsf p.g r.gs.1 n.nsf cj

ἀφέλωμαι τὰς ἁμαρτίας αὐτῶν. 28 κατὰ μὲν τὸ εὐαγγέλιον ἐχθροὶ
I take away *{the}* their sins." *their* ⌊In regard to⌋ ~ the gospel they are enemies
904 3836 899 281 899 2848 3525 3836 2295 2398
v.ams.1s d.apf n.apf r.gpm.3 p.a pl d.asn n.asn a.npm

δι᾽ ὑμᾶς, ↰ κατὰ δὲ τὴν ἐκλογὴν ἀγαπητοὶ διὰ τοὺς
for your sake, but ⌊in regard to⌋ *but* *{the}* election they are dearly loved ⌊for the sake of⌋ their
1328 7007 1328 1254 2848 1254 3836 1724 28 1328 3836
p.a r.ap.2 p.a cj d.asf n.asf a.npm p.a d.apm

πατέρας· 29 ἀμεταμέλητα γὰρ τὰ χαρίσματα καὶ ἡ κλῆσις τοῦ θεοῦ.
forefathers. *irrevocable* For the gifts and the calling of God are
4252 294 1142 3836 5922 2779 3836 3104 3836 2536
n.apm a.npn cj d.npn n.npn cj d.nsf n.nsf d.gsm n.gsm

30 ὥσπερ γὰρ ὑμεῖς ↱ ποτε ἠπειθήσατε τῷ θεῷ, νῦν δὲ
irrevocable. For just as *For* you were ⌊at one time⌋ disobedient to God but now *but*
294 1142 6061 1142 7007 578 4537 578 3836 2536 1254 3814 1254
cj cj r.np.2 adv v.aai.2p d.dsm n.dsm adv cj

ἠλεήθητε τῇ τούτων ἀπειθείᾳ, 31 οὕτως καὶ οὗτοι
⌊have received mercy⌋ ⌊because of⌋ their disobedience, so *{also}* they
1796 3836 4047 577 4048 2779 4047
v.api.2p d.dsf r.gpm n.dsf adv adv r.npm

νῦν ἠπείθησαν τῷ ὑμετέρῳ ἐλέει,
⌊at the present time⌋ have been disobedient in order that ⌊by the⌋ mercy shown to you *mercy*
3814 578 2671 2671 2671 3836 1799 5629 1799
adv v.aai.3p d.dsn r.dsn.2 n.dsn

[a] παρ᾽ UBS, NET. ἐν TNIV.

NASB

if you were cut
off from what
is by nature a
wild olive tree,
and were grafted
contrary to nature
into a cultivated
olive tree, how
much more will
these who are the
natural *branches* be
grafted into their
own olive tree?
25 For I do not
want you, brethren,
to be uninformed
of this mystery—so
that you will not be
wise in your own
estimation—that a
partial hardening
has happened to
Israel until the full-
ness of the Gentiles
has come in; 26 and
so all Israel will be
saved; just as it is
written,

> "THE DELIVERER WILL COME FROM ZION,
> HE WILL REMOVE UNGODLINESS FROM JACOB."
> 27 "THIS IS MY COVENANT WITH THEM,
> WHEN I TAKE AWAY THEIR SINS."

28 From the stand-
point of the gospel
they are enemies
for your sake, but
from the standpoint
of *God's* choice
they are beloved
for the sake of
the fathers; 29 for
the gifts and the
calling of God are
irrevocable. 30 For
just as you once
were disobedient
to God, but now
have been shown
mercy because of
their disobedience,
31 so these also now
have been disobe-
dient, that because
of the mercy
shown to you they

NIV

they too may now[a]
receive mercy as a
result of God's mer-
cy to you. 32 For God
has bound everyone
over to disobedience
so that he may have
mercy on them all.

Doxology

33 Oh, the depth of the
riches of the
wisdom and[b]
knowledge of
God!
How
unsearchable
his
judgments,
and his paths
beyond
tracing out!
34 "Who has known
the mind of
the Lord?
Or who has
been his
counselor?"[c]
35 "Who has ever
given to God,
that God should
repay them?"[d]
36 For from him and
through him
and for him
are all things.
To him be the
glory forever!
Amen.

A Living Sacrifice

12 Therefore,
I urge you,
brothers and sisters,
in view of God's
mercy, to offer your
bodies as a living
sacrifice, holy and
pleasing to God—
this is your true and
proper worship.
2 Do not conform
to the pattern of
this world, but be
transformed by the
renewing of your
mind. Then you will
be able to test and
approve what God's
will is—his good,
pleasing and perfect
will.

Humble Service in the Body of Christ

3 For by the grace
given me I say

[a] 31 Some manuscripts do not have *now*.
[b] 33 Or *riches and the wisdom and the*
[c] 34 Isaiah 40:13
[d] 35 Job 41:11

ἵνα καὶ αὐτοὶ ➝ νῦν[a] ἐλεηθῶσιν. 32 συνέκλεισεν γὰρ ὁ θεὸς
in order that they also *they* may now receive mercy. For God has consigned *For {the} God*
2671 899 2779 899 1796 3814 1796 1142 2536 5168 1142 3836 2536
cj adv r.npm adv v.aps.3p v.aai.3s cj d.nsm n.nsm

τοὺς πάντας εἰς ἀπείθειαν, ἵνα τοὺς πάντας
{the} all to disobedience so that he may show mercy to *{the}* all.
3836 4246 1650 577 2671 1796 1796 1796 1796 1796 3836 4246
d.apm a.apm p.a n.asf cj d.apm a.apm

ἐλεήσῃ. 33 ὦ βάθος ➝ πλούτου καὶ σοφίας καὶ γνώσεως θεοῦ·
he may show mercy to O the depth of the riches and wisdom and knowledge of God!
1796 6043 958 4458 2779 5053 2779 1194 2536
v.aas.3s j n.nsn n.gsm cj n.gsf cj n.gsf n.gsm

ὡς ἀνεξεραύνητα τὰ κρίματα αὐτοῦ καὶ ἀνεξιχνίαστοι αἱ ὁδοὶ
How unsearchable are *{the}* his judgments *his* and how inscrutable *{the}* his ways!
6055 451 3836 899 3210 899 2779 453 3836 899 3847
pl a.npn d.npn n.npn r.gsm.3 cj n.npf d.npf n.npf

αὐτοῦ. 34 τίς γὰρ ἔγνω νοῦν ➝ κυρίου; ἢ τίς
his For who *For* has known the mind of the Lord, or who has been his
899 1142 5515 1142 1182 3808 3261 2445 5515 1181 1181 899
r.gsm.3 r.nsm cj v.aai.3s n.asm n.gsm cj r.nsm

σύμβουλος αὐτοῦ ἐγένετο; 35 ἢ τίς προέδωκεν αὐτῷ, καὶ ἀνταποδοθήσεται
counselor? *his* *has been* Or who has given to God that God must pay
5207 899 1181 2445 5515 4594 899 2779 500
n.nsm r.gsm.3 v.ami.3s cj r.nsm v.aai.3s r.dsm.3 cj v.fpi.3s

αὐτῷ; ↩ 36 ὅτι ἐξ αὐτοῦ καὶ δι᾿ αὐτοῦ καὶ εἰς αὐτὸν τὰ πάντα·
him back? For from him and through him and to him are *{the}* all things.
899 500 4022 1666 899 2779 1328 899 2779 1650 899 3836 4246
r.dsm.3 cj p.g r.gsm.3 cj p.g r.gsm.3 cj p.a r.asm.3 d.npn a.npn

αὐτῷ ἡ δόξα εἰς τοὺς αἰῶνας, ἀμήν.
To him be *{the}* glory for all time! Amen.
899 3836 1518 1650 3836 172 297
r.dsm.3 d.nsf n.nsf p.a d.apm n.apm pl

12:1 παρακαλῶ οὖν ὑμᾶς, ἀδελφοί, διὰ τῶν οἰκτιρμῶν τοῦ θεοῦ
I appeal to you therefore, *you* brethren, by the mercies of God,
4151 7007 4036 7007 81 1328 3836 3880 3836 2536
v.pai.1s cj r.ap.2 n.vpm p.g d.gpm n.gpm d.gsm n.gsm

παραστῆσαι τὰ σώματα ὑμῶν θυσίαν ζῶσαν ἁγίαν εὐάρεστον τῷ
to present *{the}* your bodies *your* as a living sacrifice, *living* holy and acceptable to
4225 3836 7007 5393 7007 2409 2602 2409 41 2298 3836
f.aa d.apn n.apn r.gp.2 n.asf pt.pa.asf a.asf a.asf d.dsm

θεῷ, τὴν λογικὴν λατρείαν ὑμῶν· 2 καὶ ➝ μὴ συσχηματίζεσθε τῷ
God — this is a reasonable act of worship for you. And do not be conformed to this
2536 3836 3358 3301 7007 2779 5372 3590 5372 3836 4047
n.dsm d.asf a.asf n.asf r.gp.2 cj pl v.ppm.2p d.dsm

αἰῶνι τούτῳ, ἀλλὰ μεταμορφοῦσθε τῇ ἀνακαινώσει τοῦ νοὸς εἰς τὸ
world, *this* but be transformed ⌞by the⌟ renewing of your mind, ⌞so that⌟ ~ you
172 4047 247 3565 3836 364 3836 3808 1650 3836 7007
n.dsm r.dsm cj v.ppm.2p d.dsf n.dsf d.gsm n.gsm p.a d.asn

δοκιμάζειν ὑμᾶς τί τὸ θέλημα τοῦ θεοῦ, τὸ ἀγαθὸν καὶ
may discern *you* the will of God, what *the will of God* is *{the}* good and
1507 7007 3836 2525 3836 2536 5515 3836 2525 3836 2536 3836 19 2779
f.pa r.ap.2 r.nsn d.nsn n.nsn d.gsm n.gsm d.nsn a.nsn cj

εὐάρεστον καὶ τέλειον. 3 λέγω γὰρ διὰ τῆς χάριτος τῆς δοθείσης μοι
acceptable and perfect. *I say* For by the grace *{the}* given to me I say
2298 2779 5455 3306 1142 1328 3836 5921 3836 1443 1609 3306 3306
a.nsn cj a.nsn v.pai.1s cj p.g d.gsf n.gsf d.gsf pt.ap.gsf r.ds.1

[a] [νῦν] UBS, omitted by TR.

NASB

also may now be
shown mercy. 32 For
God has shut up all
in disobedience so
that He may show
mercy to all.
33 Oh, the depth
of the riches both
of the wisdom and
knowledge of God!
How unsearchable
are His judgments
and unfathomable
His ways! 34 For
WHO HAS KNOWN THE
MIND OF THE LORD,
OR WHO BECAME
HIS COUNSELOR?
35 Or WHO HAS FIRST
GIVEN TO HIM THAT
IT MIGHT BE PAID
BACK TO HIM AGAIN?
36 For from Him
and through Him
and to Him are all
things. To Him *be*
the glory forever.
Amen.

Dedicated Service

12:1 Therefore I
urge you, brethren,
by the mercies of
God, to present
your bodies a liv-
ing and holy sacri-
fice, acceptable to
God, *which is* your
spiritual service of
worship. 2 And do
not be conformed
to this world, but
be transformed by
the renewing of
your mind, so that
you may prove
what the will of
God is, that which
is good and accept-
able and perfect.
3 For through the
grace given to me I
say to everyone

NIV

to every one of
you: Do not think
of yourself more
highly than you
ought, but rather
think of your-
self with sober
judgment, in ac-
cordance with
the faith God has
distributed to each
of you. 4 For just
as each of us has
one body with
many members,
and these members
do not all have
the same function,
5 so in Christ we,
though many, form
one body, and each
member belongs to
all the others. 6 We
have different gifts,
according to the
grace given to each
of us. If your gift is
prophesying, then
prophesy in accor-
dance with your[a]
faith; 7 if it is serv-
ing, then serve; if
it is teaching, then
teach; 8 if it is to en-
courage, then give
encouragement; if
it is giving, then
give generously; if
it is to lead,[b] do it
diligently; if it is to
show mercy, do it
cheerfully.

Love in Action

9 Love must be
sincere. Hate what
is evil; cling to
what is good. 10 Be
devoted to one
another in love.
Honor one another
above yourselves.
11 Never be lacking
in zeal, but keep
your spiritual fer-
vor, serving the
Lord. 12 Be joy-
ful in

[a] 6 Or *the*
[b] 8 Or *to provide for others*

παντὶ τῷ ὄντι ἐν ὑμῖν ↱ ↱ μὴ ὑπερφρονεῖν παρ'
⌊to every one⌋ who is among you that he should not ⌊think of himself more highly⌋ than
4246 3836 1639 1877 7007 5672 5672 3590 5672 4123
a.dsm d.dsm pt.pa.dsm p.d r.dp.2 pl f.pa p.a

ὃ δεῖ φρονεῖν ἀλλὰ φρονεῖν εἰς τὸ σωφρονεῖν, ἑκάστῳ
he ought to think; but to think with *{the}* sober judgment, as God has assigned to each
4005 1256 5858 247 5858 1650 3836 5404 6055 2536 3532 3532 1667
r.asn v.pai.3s f.pa cj f.pa p.a d.asn f.pa r.dsm

ὡς ὁ θεὸς ἐμέρισεν μέτρον πίστεως. 4 καθάπερ γὰρ ἐν ἑνὶ σώματι
as *{the}* *God* *has assigned* a measure of faith. For as *For* in our one body
6055 3836 2536 3532 3586 4411 1142 2749 1142 1877 1651 5393
cj d.nsm n.nsm v.aai.3s n.asn n.gsf cj cj p.d a.dsn n.dsn

πολλὰ μέλη ἔχομεν, τὰ δὲ μέλη πάντα οὐ τὴν
we have many members, *we have* and the *and* members do not all *not* have the
2400 2400 4498 3517 2400 1254 3836 1254 3517 2400 4024 4246 4024 2400 3836
a.apn n.apn v.pai.1p d.npn cj n.npn a.npn pl d.asf

αὐτὴν ἔχει πρᾶξιν, 5 οὕτως οἱ πολλοὶ ἕν σῶμά ἐσμεν ἐν Χριστῷ,
same *do have* function, so we who are many are one body *we are* in Christ,
899 2400 4552 4048 1639 3836 4498 1639 1651 5393 1639 1877 5986
r.asf v.pai.3s n.asf adv d.npm a.npm a.nsn n.nsn v.pai.1p p.d n.dsm

τὸ δὲ ⌊καθ' εἷς⌋ ἀλλήλων μέλη. 6 ἔχοντες δὲ
{the} and individually members who belong to one another, *members* having *{and}*
3836 1254 2848 1651 3517 253 3517 2400 1254
d.asn cj p.a a.nsm r.gpm n.npn pt.pa.npm cj

χαρίσματα κατὰ τὴν χάριν τὴν δοθεῖσαν ἡμῖν διάφορα, εἴτε
gifts that differ ⌊according to⌋ the grace *{the}* given to us. *differ* If your gift is
5922 1427 2848 3836 5921 3836 1443 7005 1427 1664
n.apn p.a d.asf n.asf d.asf pt.ap.asf r.dp.1 a.apn cj

προφητείαν κατὰ τὴν ἀναλογίαν τῆς πίστεως, 7 εἴτε
prophecy, then prophesy in *{the}* proportion to your faith; if your gift is
4735 2848 3836 381 3836 4411 1664
n.asf p.a d.asf n.asf d.gsf n.gsf cj

διακονίαν ἐν τῇ διακονίᾳ, εἴτε ὁ διδάσκων ἐν τῇ διδασκαλίᾳ,
service, use it to *{the}* serve; if you are a *{the}* teacher, then *{the}* teach;
1355 1877 3836 1355 1664 3836 1438 1877 3836 1436
n.asf p.d d.dsf n.dsf cj d.nsm pt.pa.nsm p.d d.dsf n.dsf

8 εἴτε ὁ παρακαλῶν ἐν τῇ παρακλήσει,
if you have the gift of encouragement, then use it to *{the}* encourage; if you are able
1664 3836 4151 1877 3836 4155
cj d.nsm pt.pa.nsm p.d d.dsf n.dsf

ὁ μεταδιδοὺς ⌊ἐν ἁπλότητι,⌋ ὁ προϊστάμενος ἐν
{the} to give, give generously; if your gift is *{the}* leadership, lead with
3836 3556 1877 605 3836 4613 1877
d.nsm pt.pa.nsm p.d n.dsf d.nsm pt.pm.nsm p.d

σπουδῇ, ὁ ἐλεῶν ἐν ἱλαρότητι. 9 ἡ ἀγάπη
zeal; if it is *{the}* ⌊showing mercy,⌋ then do it with cheerfulness. Let *{the}* love be
5082 3836 1790 1877 2660 3836 27
n.dsf d.nsm pt.pa.nsm p.d n.dsf d.nsf n.nsf

ἀνυπόκριτος. ἀποστυγοῦντες τὸ πονηρόν, κολλώμενοι τῷ ἀγαθῷ, 10
genuine. Abhor what is evil; hold fast to what is good. Love one
537 696 3836 4505 3140 3836 19 5816 253
a.nsf pt.pa.npm d.asn a.asn pt.pp.npm d.dsn a.dsn

τῇ φιλαδελφίᾳ εἰς ἀλλήλους φιλόστοργοι,
another with brotherly affection; *{to}* *one another* *Love* outdo one another in showing
253 3836 5789 1650 253 5816 4605 253 253 4605 4605
d.dsf n.dsf p.a r.apm a.npm

τῇ τιμῇ ἀλλήλους προηγούμενοι, 11 τῇ σπουδῇ μὴ ὀκνηροί,
{the} honor; *one another* *outdo in showing* do not lag in zeal; *not* *do lag* be
3836 5507 253 4605 3891 3590 3891 3836 5082 3590 3891 2417
d.dsf n.dsf r.apm pt.pm.npm d.dsf n.dsf pl a.npm

τῷ πνεύματι ζέοντες, τῷ κυρίῳ δουλεύοντες, 12 τῇ
enthusiastic in spirit; *be enthusiastic* serve the Lord; *serve* rejoice in
2417 3836 4460 2417 1526 3836 3261 1526 5897 3836
d.dsn n.dsn pt.pa.npm d.dsm n.dsm pt.pa.npm d.dsf

NASB

among you not to
think more highly
of himself than
he ought to think;
but to think so
as to have sound
judgment, as God
has allotted to
each a measure
of faith. 4 For just
as we have many
members in one
body and all the
members do not
have the same
function, 5 so we,
who are many, are
one body in Christ,
and individually
members one of
another. 6 Since we
have gifts that dif-
fer according to the
grace given to us,
*each of us is to ex-
ercise them accord-
ingly:* if prophecy,
according to the
proportion of his
faith; 7 if service,
in his serving; or
he who teaches, in
his teaching; 8 or
he who exhorts,
in his exhortation;
he who gives,
with [a]liberality; he
who leads, with
diligence; he who
shows mercy, with
cheerfulness.
9 *Let* love *be*
without hypocrisy.
Abhor what is evil;
cling to what is
good. 10 *Be* devoted
to one another in
brotherly love; give
preference to one
another in honor;
11 not lagging be-
hind in diligence,
fervent in spirit,
serving the Lord;
12 rejoicing in

[a] Or *simplicity*

NIV

hope, patient in
affliction, faithful
in prayer. 13 Share
with the Lord's
people who are in
need. Practice hos-
pitality.
14 Bless those who
persecute you;
bless and do not
curse. 15 Rejoice
with those who re-
joice; mourn with
those who mourn.
16 Live in harmony
with one another.
Do not be proud,
but be willing to
associate with
people of low po-
sition.[a] Do not be
conceited.
17 Do not repay
anyone evil for
evil. Be careful to
do what is right
in the eyes of ev-
eryone. 18 If it is
possible, as far as
it depends on you,
live at peace with
everyone. 19 Do
not take revenge,
my dear friends,
but leave room for
God's wrath, for
it is written: "It is
mine to avenge; I
will repay,"[b] says
the Lord. 20 On the
contrary:

"If your enemy is hungry, feed him;
if he is thirsty, give him something to drink.
In doing this, you will heap burning coals on his head."[c]

21 Do not be over-
come by evil, but
overcome evil with
good.

Submission to Governing Authorities

13 Let every-
one be sub-
ject to the govern-
ing authorities,

[a] 16 Or *willing to do menial work*
[b] 19 Deut. 32:35
[c] 20 Prov. 25:21,22

ἐλπίδι χαίροντες, τῇ θλίψει ὑπομένοντες, τῇ προσευχῇ
hope, *rejoice* be patient in suffering, *be patient* devote yourself to prayer;
1828 5897 5702 5702 3836 2568 5702 4674 4674 3836 4666
n.dsf pt.pa.npm d.dsf n.dsf pt.pa.npm d.dsf n.dsf

προσκαρτεροῦντες, 13 ταῖς χρείαις τῶν ἁγίων κοινωνοῦντες,
devote yourself contribute to the needs of the saints, *contribute to* seek to
4674 3125 3125 3836 5970 3836 41 3125 1503 1503
pt.pa.npm d.dpf n.dpf d.gpm a.gpm pt.pa.npm

τὴν φιλοξενίαν διώκοντες. 14 εὐλογεῖτε τοὺς διώκοντας ὑμᾶς,[a] εὐλογεῖτε καὶ
show *{the}* hospitality. *seek to show* Bless those who persecute you; bless and
1503 3836 5810 1503 2328 3836 1503 7007 2328 2779
d.asf n.asf pt.pa.npm v.pam.2p d.apm pt.pa.apm r.ap.2 v.pam.2p cj

➞ μὴ καταρᾶσθε. 15 χαίρειν μετὰ χαιρόντων, κλαίειν μετὰ κλαιόντων.
do not curse them. Rejoice with those who rejoice; weep with those who weep.
2933 3590 2933 5897 3552 5897 3081 3552 3081
pl v.pmm.2p f.pa p.g pt.pa.gpm f.pa p.g pt.pa.gpm

16 τὸ αὐτὸ εἰς ἀλλήλους φρονοῦντες, μὴ τὰ ὑψηλὰ φρονοῦντες
Live *{the}* in harmony with one another; *Live* do not be *{the}* haughty *do be*
5858 3836 899 1650 253 5858 5858 3590 5858 3836 5734 5858
d.asn r.asn p.a r.apm pt.pa.npm pl d.apn a.apn pt.pa.npm

ἀλλὰ τοῖς ταπεινοῖς συναπαγόμενοι. ➞ μὴ γίνεσθε φρόνιμοι παρ'
but associate with the lowly. *associate with* Do not be wise in
247 5270 5270 3836 5424 5270 1181 3590 1181 5861 4123
cj d.dpm a.dpm pt.pp.npm pl v.pmm.2p a.npm p.d

ἑαυτοῖς. 17 μηδενὶ κακὸν ἀντὶ κακοῦ ἀποδιδόντες, προνοούμενοι
your own estimation. Repay no one evil for evil; *Repay* give careful thought to
1571 625 3594 2805 505 2805 625 4629
r.dpm.2 a.dsm a.asn p.g a.gsn pt.pa.npm pt.pm.npm

καλὰ ἐνώπιον πάντων ἀνθρώπων· 18 εἰ δυνατὸν τὸ ἐξ
what is good in the sight of all people. If possible, so far as it ⌞depends on⌟
2819 1967 4246 476 1623 1543 3836 1666
a.apn p.g a.gpm n.gpm cj a.nsn d.asn p.g

ὑμῶν, μετὰ πάντων ἀνθρώπων εἰρηνεύοντες· 19 μὴ ἑαυτοὺς
you, be at peace with all people. *be at peace* Never avenge yourselves,
7007 1644 1644 1644 3552 4246 476 1644 3590 1688 1571
r.gp.2 p.g a.gpm n.gpm pt.pa.npm pl r.apm.2

ἐκδικοῦντες, ἀγαπητοί, ἀλλὰ δότε τόπον τῇ ὀργῇ, γέγραπται γάρ,
avenge dear friends, but leave room ⌞for the⌟ wrath of God, for it is written, *for*
1688 28 247 1443 5536 3836 3973 1142 1211 1142
pt.pa.npm a.vpm cj v.aam.2p n.asm d.dsf n.dsf v.rpi.3s cj

ἐμοὶ ἐκδίκησις, ἐγὼ ἀνταποδώσω, λέγει κύριος. 20 ἀλλὰ
"Vengeance is mine, *Vengeance* I will repay, says the Lord." ⌞To the contrary,⌟
1689 1609 1689 1609 500 3306 3261 247
r.ds.1 n.nsf r.ns.1 v.fai.1s v.pai.3s n.nsm cj

ἐὰν πεινᾷ ὁ ἐχθρός σου, ψώμιζε αὐτόν· ἐὰν διψᾷ, ➞
"if your enemy is hungry, *{the}* *enemy* *your* feed him; if he is thirsty, give him
1569 5148 2398 4277 3836 2398 5148 6039 899 1569 1498 899
cj v.pas.3s d.nsm a.nsm r.gs.2 v.pam.2s r.asm.3 cj v.pas.3s

πότιζε αὐτόν· τοῦτο γὰρ ποιῶν
⌞something to drink;⌟ *him* for by doing this *for* *by doing* you will heap burning
4540 899 1142 4472 4472 4047 1142 4472 5397 5397 5397 4786
v.pam.2s r.asm.3 r.asn cj pt.pa.nsm

ἄνθρακας πυρὸς σωρεύσεις ἐπὶ τὴν κεφαλὴν αὐτοῦ. 21 ➞ μὴ νικῶ ὑπὸ
coals *burning* *you will heap* on *{the}* his head." *his* Do not be overcome by
472 4786 5397 2093 3836 899 3051 899 3771 3590 3771 5679
n.apm n.gsn v.fai.2s p.a d.asf n.asf r.gsm.3 pl v.ppm.2s p.g

τοῦ κακοῦ ἀλλὰ νίκα ἐν τῷ ἀγαθῷ τὸ κακόν.
{the} evil, but overcome evil with *{the}* good. *{the}* *evil*
3836 2805 247 3771 2805 1877 3836 19 3836 2805
d.gsn a.gsn cj v.pam.2s p.d d.dsn a.dsn d.asn a.asn

13:1 πᾶσα ψυχὴ ἐξουσίαις ὑπερεχούσαις
Every person must be subject to the governing authorities *governing*
4246 6034 5718 5718 5718 5718 5660 2026 5660
a.nsf n.nsf n.dpf pt.pa.dpf

[a] [ὑμᾶς] UBS, omitted by TNIV.

NASB

hope, persever-
ing in tribulation,
devoted to prayer,
13 contributing to
the needs of the
saints, practicing
hospitality.
14 Bless those who
persecute [a]you;
bless and do not
curse. 15 Rejoice
with those who
rejoice, and weep
with those who
weep. 16 Be of the
same mind toward
one another; do
not be haughty in
mind, but associate
with the lowly. Do
not be wise in your
own estimation.
17 Never pay back
evil for evil to any-
one. Respect what
is right in the sight
of all men. 18 If
possible, so far as
it depends on you,
be at peace with
all men. 19 Never
take your own re-
venge, beloved, but
leave room for the
wrath *of God*, for
it is written, "VEN-
GEANCE IS MINE, I
WILL REPAY," says
the Lord. 20 "BUT IF
YOUR ENEMY IS HUN-
GRY, FEED HIM, AND
IF HE IS THIRSTY,
GIVE HIM A DRINK;
FOR IN SO DOING YOU
WILL HEAP BURNING
COALS ON HIS HEAD."
21 Do not be over-
come by evil, but
overcome evil with
good.

Be Subject to Government

13:1 Every person is
to be in subjection
to the governing
authorities. For

[a] Two early mss do not contain *you*

NIV

for there is no
authority except
that which God
has established.
The authorities
that exist have
been established
by God. 2 Conse-
quently, whoever
rebels against the
authority is rebel-
ling against what
God has instituted,
and those who
do so will bring
judgment on them-
selves. 3 For rulers
hold no terror for
those who do right,
but for those who
do wrong. Do you
want to be free
from fear of the
one in authority?
Then do what is
right and you will
be commended.
4 For the one in
authority is God's
servant for your
good. But if you do
wrong, be afraid,
for rulers do not
bear the sword for
no reason. They
are God's servants,
agents of wrath to
bring punishment
on the wrongdoer.
5 Therefore, it is
necessary to submit
to the authorities,
not only because
of possible pun-
ishment but also
as a matter of con-
science.
6 This is also why
you pay taxes, for
the authorities are
God's servants,
who give their full
time to governing.
7 Give to every-
one what you owe
them: If you owe
taxes, pay taxes;
if revenue, then
revenue; if respect,
then respect;

ὑποτασσέσθω. οὐ γὰρ ἔστιν ἐξουσία ⌞εἰ μὴ⌟ ὑπὸ θεοῦ,
must be subject to because there is no *because* *there is* authority except by God's
5718 1142 1639 1639 4024 1142 1639 2026 1623 3590 5679 2536
v.ppm.3s pl cj v.pai.3s n.nsf cj pl p.g n.gsm

αἱ δὲ οὖσαι ὑπὸ θεοῦ τεταγμέναι
appointment, and those *and* ⌞that presently exist⌟ have been instituted by God. *instituted*
1254 3836 1254 1639 1639 1639 5435 5679 2536 5435
d.npf cj pt.pa.npf p.g n.gsm pt.rp.npf

εἰσίν. 2 ὥστε ὁ ἀντιτασσόμενος τῇ ἐξουσίᾳ τῇ τοῦ θεοῦ
have been Therefore whoever resists *{the}* authority resists what *{the}* God
1639 6063 3836 530 3836 2026 468 3836 3836 2536
v.pai.3p cj d.nsm pt.pm.nsm d.dsf n.dsf d.dsf d.gsm n.gsm

διαταγῇ ἀνθέστηκεν, οἱ δὲ ἀνθεστηκότες ἑαυτοῖς
has decreed, *resists* and those *and* who resist will bring judgment on themselves.
1408 468 1254 3836 1254 468 3284 3284 3210 3284 1571
n.dsf v.rai.3s d.npm cj pt.ra.npm r.dpm.3

κρίμα λήμψονται. 3 οἱ γὰρ ἄρχοντες οὐκ εἰσὶν φόβος τῷ
judgment *will bring on* *{the}* For rulers are not *are* a source of fear ⌞for those⌟ who
3210 3284 3836 1142 807 1639 4024 1639 5832 3836
n.asn v.fmi.3p d.npm cj n.npm pl v.pai.3p n.nsm d.dsn

ἀγαθῷ ἔργῳ ἀλλὰ τῷ κακῷ. θέλεις δὲ ↱ μὴ φοβεῖσθαι τὴν
do good, *do* but ⌞for those⌟ who do wrong. ⌞Would you⌟ *{and}* have no fear of the
2240 19 2240 247 3836 2805 2527 1254 5828 3590 5828 3836
a.dsn n.dsn cj d.dsn a.dsn v.pai.2s cj pl f.pp d.asf

ἐξουσίαν· τὸ ἀγαθὸν ποίει, καὶ ἕξεις ἔπαινον ἐξ αὐτῆς,
one in authority? Then do what is right *do* and ⌞you will receive⌟ approval from him,
2026 4472 3836 19 4472 2779 2400 2047 1666 899
n.asf d.asn a.asn v.pam.2s cj v.fai.2s n.asm p.g r.gsf.3

4 θεοῦ γὰρ διάκονός ἐστιν σοὶ εἰς τὸ ἀγαθόν. ἐὰν
for he is a servant of God *for* *servant* *he is* for your *for* *{the}* good. But if
1142 1639 1639 1356 2536 1142 1356 1639 1650 5148 1650 3836 19 1254 1569
n.gsm cj n.nsm v.pai.3s r.ds.2 p.a d.asn a.asn cj

δὲ τὸ κακὸν ποιῇς, φοβοῦ, οὐ γὰρ εἰκῇ
But you do what is wrong, *you do* be afraid; for he does not *for* bear the sword in vain.
1254 4472 4472 3836 2805 4472 5828 1142 5841 5841 4024 1142 5841 3836 3479 1632
cj d.asn a.asn v.pas.2s v.ppm.2s pl cj adv

τὴν μάχαιραν φορεῖ· θεοῦ γὰρ διάκονός ἐστιν ἔκδικος
the *sword* *he does bear* For he is a servant of God, *For* *servant* *He is* an avenger
3836 3479 5841 1142 1639 1639 1356 2536 1142 1356 1639 1690
d.asf n.asf v.pai.3s n.gsm cj n.nsm v.pai.3s n.nsm

εἰς ὀργὴν τῷ τὸ κακὸν πράσσοντι. 5 διὸ ἀνάγκη
⌞to carry out⌟ wrath ⌞on the⌟ one who does *{the}* wrong. *one who does* Therefore one must
1650 3973 3836 4556 4556 4556 3836 2805 4556 1475 340
p.a n.asf d.dsm d.asn a.asn pt.pa.dsm cj n.nsf

ὑποτάσσεσθαι, οὐ μόνον διὰ τὴν ὀργὴν ἀλλὰ καὶ διὰ τὴν συνείδησιν.
be subject, not only ⌞because of⌟ *{the}* wrath, but also ⌞because of⌟ *{the}* conscience.
5718 4024 3667 1328 3836 3973 247 2779 1328 3836 5287
f.pp pl adv p.a d.asf n.asf cj adv p.a d.asf n.asf

6 διὰ τοῦτο γὰρ καὶ φόρους τελεῖτε,
For this is also why *this* *For* *also* you pay taxes, *you pay* for authorities are
1142 4047 2779 1328 4047 1142 2779 5464 5464 5843 5464 1142 1639
p.a r.asn cj adv n.apm v.pai.2p

λειτουργοὶ γὰρ θεοῦ εἰσιν εἰς αὐτὸ τοῦτο προσκαρτεροῦντες.
servants *for* of God, *are* devoted to this very thing. *this* *devoted*
3313 1142 2536 1639 4674 1650 4047 899 4047 4674
n.npm cj n.gsm v.pai.3p p.a r.asn r.asn pt.pa.npm

7 ἀπόδοτε πᾶσιν τὰς ὀφειλάς, τῷ τὸν φόρον τὸν φόρον,
Pay everyone what is owed to them: taxes ⌞to whom⌟ *{the}* taxes are due; *{the}* *taxes*
625 4246 3836 4051 5843 3836 3836 5843 3836 5843
v.aam.2p a.dpm d.apf n.apf d.dsm d.asm n.asm d.asm n.asm

τῷ τὸ τέλος τὸ τέλος, τῷ τὸν φόβον τὸν
revenue ⌞to whom⌟ *{the}* revenue is due; *{the}* *revenue* respect ⌞to whom⌟ *{the}* respect is due; *{the}*
5465 3836 3836 5465 3836 5465 5832 3836 3836 5832 3836
d.dsm d.asn n.asn d.asn n.asn d.dsm d.asm n.asm d.asm

NASB

there is no author-
ity except from
God, and those
which exist are
established by
God. 2 Therefore
whoever resists au-
thority has opposed
the ordinance of
God; and they who
have opposed will
receive condemna-
tion upon them-
selves. 3 For rulers
are not a cause
of fear for good
behavior, but for
evil. Do you want
to have no fear of
authority? Do what
is good and you
will have praise
from the same;
4 for it is a minister
of God to you for
good. But if you
do what is evil, be
afraid; for it does
not bear the sword
for nothing; for it is
a minister of God,
an avenger who
brings wrath on the
one who practices
evil. 5 Therefore it
is necessary to be
in subjection, not
only because of
wrath, but also for
conscience' sake.
6 For because of
this you also pay
taxes, for *rulers*
are servants of
God, devoting
themselves to this
very thing. 7 Render
to all what is due
them: tax to whom
tax *is due;* custom
to whom custom;
fear to whom fear;

NIV

if honor, then honor.

Love Fulfills the Law

8 Let no debt remain outstanding, except the continuing debt to love one another, for whoever loves others has fulfilled the law. 9 The commandments, "You shall not commit adultery," "You shall not murder," "You shall not steal," "You shall not covet,"[a] and whatever other command there may be, are summed up in this one command: "Love your neighbor as yourself."[b] 10 Love does no harm to a neighbor. Therefore love is the fulfillment of the law.

The Day Is Near

11 And do this, understanding the present time: The hour has already come for you to wake up from your slumber, because our salvation is nearer now than when we first believed. 12 The night is nearly over; the day is almost here. So let us put aside the deeds of darkness and put on the armor of light. 13 Let us behave decently, as in the daytime, not in carousing and drunkenness, not in sexual immorality and debauchery, not in dissension and jealousy. 14 Rather, clothe yourselves with the Lord Jesus Christ, and do not think about how to gratify the desires of the flesh.[c]

[a] 9 Exodus 20:13-15,17; Deut. 5:17-19,21
[b] 9 Lev. 19:18
[c] *14* In contexts like this, the Greek word for *flesh* (*sarx*) refers to the sinful state of human beings, often presented as a power in opposition to the Spirit.

Interlinear

φόβον, τῷ τὴν τιμὴν τὴν τιμήν. 8 μηδενὶ μηδὲν ὀφείλετε ⌊εἰ
respect honor ⌊to whom⌋ *{the}* honor is due. *{the}* *honor* Owe no one anything, *Owe* except
5832 5507 3836 3836 5507 3836 5507 4053 3594 3594 4053 1623
n.asm d.dsm d.asf n.asf d.asf n.asf a.dsm a.asn v.pam.2p cj

μὴ⌋ τὸ ἀλλήλους ἀγαπᾶν, ὁ γὰρ ἀγαπῶν τὸν ἕτερον
{the} to love one another; *to love* for the *for* ⌊one who loves⌋ his neighbor has
3590 3836 26 26 253 26 1142 3836 1142 26 3836 2283 4444
pl d.asn r.apm f.pa d.nsm cj pt.pa.nsm d.asm r.asm

νόμον πεπλήρωκεν. 9 τὸ γὰρ ↱ ↱ οὐ
fulfilled the law. *has fulfilled* For the commandments, *For* "You shall not
4444 3795 4444 1142 3836 1142 3658 3658 4024
n.asm v.rai.3s d.nsn cj pl

μοιχεύσεις, ↱ ↱ οὐ φονεύσεις, ↱ ↱ οὐ κλέψεις, ↱ ↱ οὐκ
commit adultery, You shall not murder, You shall not steal, You shall not
3658 5839 5839 4024 5839 3096 3096 4024 3096 2121 2121 4024
v.fai.2s pl v.fai.2s pl v.fai.2s pl

ἐπιθυμήσεις, καὶ εἴ τις ἑτέρα ἐντολή, ἐν
covet," (and *there may be* any other commandment there may be) are summed up in
2121 2779 1623 5516 2283 1953 1623 1623 1623 368 368 368 1877
v.fai.2s cj cj r.nsf r.nsf n.nsf p.d

τῷ λόγῳ τούτῳ ἀνακεφαλαιοῦται [a]ἐν τῷ· ἀγαπήσεις τὸν πλησίον σου
{the} this saying, *this* *are summed up* *{in}* *{the}* "You shall love *{the}* your neighbor *your*
3836 4047 3364 4047 368 1877 3836 26 3836 5148 4446 5148
d.dsm n.dsm r.dsm v.ppi.3s p.d d.dsm v.fai.2s d.asm adv r.gs.2

ὡς σεαυτόν. 10 ἡ ἀγάπη τῷ πλησίον κακὸν οὐκ ἐργάζεται·
as yourself." *{the}* Love does no wrong to its neighbor. *wrong* *no* *does to*
6055 4932 3836 27 2237 4024 2805 2237 3836 4446 2805 4024 2237
cj r.asm.2 d.nsf n.nsf d.dsm adv a.asn pl v.pmi.3s

πλήρωμα οὖν → νόμου ἡ ἀγάπη. 11 καὶ τοῦτο
Therefore love is the fulfillment *Therefore* of the law. *{the}* *love* And live this way
4036 27 4445 4036 3795 3836 27 2779 4047
n.nsn cj n.gsm d.nsf n.nsf cj r.asn

εἰδότες τὸν καιρόν, ὅτι ὥρα ἤδη ὑμᾶς ἐξ ὕπνου
⌊because you are aware of⌋ the time, that the hour ⌊has come⌋ for us to wake from sleep,
3857 3836 2789 4022 6052 2453 7007 1586 1586 1666 5678
pt.ra.npm d.asm n.asm cj n.nsf adv r.ap.2 p.g n.gsm

ἐγερθῆναι, νῦν γὰρ ἐγγύτερον ἡμῶν ἡ σωτηρία ἢ ὅτε
to wake for our salvation is nearer now *for* *nearer* *our* *{the}* *salvation* than when
1586 1142 7005 5401 1584 3814 1142 1584 7005 3836 5401 2445 4021
f.ap adv cj adv.c r.gp.1 d.nsf n.nsf pl cj

→ ἐπιστεύσαμεν. 12 ἡ νὺξ προέκοψεν, ἡ δὲ ἡμέρα ἤγγικεν.
we first believed. The night is nearly over and the *and* day is at hand. So
4409 3836 3816 4621 1254 3836 1254 2465 1581 4036
v.aai.1p d.nsf n.nsf v.aai.3s d.nsf cj n.nsf v.rai.3s

ἀποθώμεθα οὖν τὰ ἔργα τοῦ σκότους, ἐνδυσώμεθα δὲ[b] τὰ ὅπλα τοῦ
we must lay aside *So* the works of darkness and put on *and* the armor of
700 4036 3836 2240 3836 5030 1254 1907 1254 3836 3960 3836
v.ams.1p cj d.apn n.apn d.gsn n.gsn v.ams.1p cj d.apn n.apn d.gsn

φωτός. 13 ὡς ἐν ἡμέρᾳ εὐσχημόνως περιπατήσωμεν,
light. Let us live becomingly, as in the daytime, *becomingly* *Let us live*
5890 4344 4344 4344 2361 6055 1877 2465 2361 4344
n.gsn pl p.d n.dsf adv v.aas.1p

μὴ κώμοις καὶ μέθαις, μὴ κοίταις καὶ ἀσελγείαις, μὴ ἔριδι
not in carousing and drunkenness, not ⌊in sexual promiscuity⌋ and sensuality, not in strife
3590 3269 2779 3494 3590 3130 2779 816 3590 2251
pl n.dpm cj n.dpf pl n.dpf cj n.dpf pl n.dsf

καὶ ζήλῳ, 14 ἀλλὰ ἐνδύσασθε τὸν κύριον Ἰησοῦν Χριστὸν καὶ
and jealousy. Rather, put on the Lord Jesus Christ, and make no provision
2779 2419 247 1907 3836 3261 2652 5986 2779 4472 3590 4630
cj n.dsm cj v.amm.2p d.asm n.asm n.asm n.asm cj

τῆς σαρκὸς πρόνοιαν μὴ ποιεῖσθε εἰς ἐπιθυμίας.
for the sinful nature *provision for* *no* *make* to gratify its desires.
4630 3836 4922 4630 3590 4472 1650 2123
d.gsf n.gsf n.asf pl v.pmm.2p p.a n.apf

[a] [ἐν τῷ] UBS.
[b] [δὲ] UBS.

NASB

honor to whom honor.

8 Owe nothing to anyone except to love one another; for he who loves his neighbor has fulfilled *the* law. 9 For this, "YOU SHALL NOT COMMIT ADULTERY, YOU SHALL NOT MURDER, YOU SHALL NOT STEAL, YOU SHALL NOT COVET," and if there is any other commandment, it is summed up in this saying, "YOU SHALL LOVE YOUR NEIGHBOR AS YOURSELF." 10 Love does no wrong to a neighbor; therefore love is the fulfillment of *the* law.

11 *Do* this, knowing the time, that it is already the hour for you to awaken from sleep; for now [a]salvation is nearer to us than when we believed. 12 The night is almost gone, and the day is near. Therefore let us lay aside the deeds of darkness and put on the armor of light. 13 Let us behave properly as in the day, not in carousing and drunkenness, not in sexual promiscuity and sensuality, not in strife and jealousy. 14 But put on the Lord Jesus Christ, and make no provision for the flesh in regard to *its* lusts.

[a] Or *our salvation is nearer than when*

NIV

The Weak and the Strong

14 Accept the
one whose
faith is weak, with-
out quarreling over
disputable matters.
2 One person's faith
allows them to
eat anything, but
another, whose
faith is weak, eats
only vegetables.
3 The one who eats
everything must
not treat with con-
tempt the one who
does not, and the
one who does not
eat everything
must not judge the
one who does, for
God has accepted
them. 4 Who are
you to judge some-
one else's servant?
To their own mas-
ter, servants stand
or fall. And they
will stand, for the
Lord is able to
make them stand.
5 One person
considers one day
more sacred than
another; another
considers every
day alike. Each
of them should be
fully convinced in
their own mind.
6 Whoever regards
one day as spe-
cial does so to the
Lord. Whoever
eats meat does so
to the Lord, for
they give thanks
to God; and who-
ever abstains does
so to the Lord and
gives thanks to
God. 7 For none of
us lives for our-
selves alone, and
none of us dies for
ourselves alone. 8 If
we live, we live for
the Lord; and if we
die, we die for the
Lord.

14:1 τὸν δὲ ἀσθενοῦντα τῇ πίστει προσλαμβάνεσθε, ↱ μὴ
Accept the *{and}* one who is weak in faith, *Accept* but do not
4689 3836 1254 820 3836 4411 4689 1360 3590
d.asm cj pt.pa.asm d.dsf n.dsf v.pmm.2p pl

⌞εἰς διακρίσεις⌟ διαλογισμῶν. 2 ὃς μὲν πιστεύει φαγεῖν πάντα,
argue about his personal opinions. ⌞One person⌟ ~ believes he can eat anything,
1650 1360 1369 4005 3525 4409 2266 4246
p.a n.apf n.gpm r.nsm pl v.pai.3s f.aa a.apn

ὁ δὲ ἀσθενῶν λάχανα ἐσθίει. 3 ὁ ἐσθίων
while the *while* weak brother eats only vegetables. *eats* The ⌞one who eats⌟ everything
1254 3836 1254 820 2266 3303 2266 3836 2266
d.nsm pl pt.pa.nsm n.apn v.pai.3s d.nsm pt.pa.nsm

τὸν ↱ ↱ ↱ μὴ ἐσθίοντα μὴ ἐξουθενείτω,
must not hold in contempt the one who does not eat, *not* *must hold in contempt* and
2024 3590 2024 2024 2024 3836 2266 2266 2266 3590 2266 3590 2024 1254
d.asm pl pt.pa.asm pl v.pam.3s

ὁ δὲ ↱ ↱ μὴ ἐσθίων τὸν ἐσθίοντα μὴ κρινέτω,
the *and* one who ⌞abstains from⌟ eating must not judge the one who eats, *not* *must judge*
3836 1254 2266 2266 3590 2266 3212 3590 3212 3836 2266 3590 3212
d.nsm cj pl pt.pa.nsm d.asm pt.pa.asm pl v.pam.3s

ὁ θεὸς γὰρ αὐτὸν προσελάβετο. 4 σὺ τίς εἶ ὁ
for *{the}* God *for* has accepted him. *has accepted* Who are you *Who* *are* *{the}*
1142 3836 2536 1142 4689 4689 899 4689 5515 1639 5148 5515 1639 3836
d.nsm n.nsm cj r.asm.3 v.ami.3s r.ns.2 r.nsm v.pai.2s d.nsm

κρίνων ἀλλότριον οἰκέτην; τῷ ἰδίῳ κυρίῳ στήκει ἢ
⌞to pass judgment on⌟ someone else's servant? It is before his own master that ⌞he will stand⌟ or
3212 259 3860 3836 2625 3261 5112 2445
pt.pa.nsm a.asm n.asm d.dsm a.dsm n.dsm v.pai.3s cj

πίπτει· σταθήσεται δέ, δυνατεῖ γὰρ ὁ κύριος → → στῆσαι
fall. And he will stand, *And* for the Lord is able *for* *the* *Lord* to make him stand.
4406 1254 2705 1254 1142 3836 3261 1542 1142 3836 3261 899 2705
v.pai.3s v.fpi.3s cj v.pai.3s cj d.nsm n.nsm f.aa

αὐτόν. 5 ὃς μὲν γὰρ[a] κρίνει ἡμέραν παρ' ἡμέραν,
him For ⌞one person⌟ ~ *For* regards one day more sacred than another, while
899 1142 4005 3525 1142 3212 2465 4123 2465 1254
r.asm.3 r.nsm pl cj v.pai.3s n.asf p.a n.asf

ὃς δὲ κρίνει πᾶσαν ἡμέραν· ἕκαστος
⌞another person⌟ *while* regards all days the same. Each person must be fully convinced
4005 1254 3212 4246 2465 1667 4442 4442 4442 4442
r.nsm pl v.pai.3s a.asf n.asf r.nsm

ἐν τῷ ἰδίῳ νοΐ πληροφορείσθω. 6 ὁ φρονῶν τὴν ἡμέραν
in *{the}* his own mind. *must be fully convinced* The ⌞one who observes⌟ the day observes it
1877 3836 2625 3808 4442 3836 5858 3836 2465 5858
p.d d.dsm a.dsm n.dsm v.ppm.3s d.nsm pt.pa.nsm d.asf n.asf

→ κυρίῳ φρονεῖ· καὶ ὁ ἐσθίων → κυρίῳ ἐσθίει,
for the Lord. *observes* And the ⌞one who eats,⌟ eats for the Lord, *eats* because
3261 5858 2779 3836 2266 2266 3261 2266 1142
n.dsm v.pai.3s cj d.nsm pt.pa.nsm n.dsm v.pai.3s

εὐχαριστεῖ γὰρ τῷ θεῷ· καὶ ὁ ↱ ↱ μὴ ἐσθίων →
he gives thanks *because* to God; and the one who ⌞abstains from⌟ eating, does not eat for
2373 1142 3836 2536 2779 3836 2266 2266 3590 2266 2266 4024 2266
v.pai.3s cj d.dsm n.dsm cj d.nsm pl pt.pa.nsm

κυρίῳ οὐκ ἐσθίει καὶ εὐχαριστεῖ τῷ θεῷ. 7 οὐδεὶς γὰρ ἡμῶν ἑαυτῷ
the Lord *not* *does eat* and gives thanks to God. For none *For* of us lives for himself,
3261 4024 2266 2779 2373 3836 2536 1142 4029 1142 7005 2409 1571
n.dsm pl v.pai.3s cj v.pai.3s d.dsm n.dsm a.nsm cj r.gp.1 r.dsm.3

ζῇ καὶ οὐδεὶς ἑαυτῷ ἀποθνῄσκει· 8 ἐάν τε γὰρ ζῶμεν,
lives and none dies for himself. *dies* For if ~ *For* we live, we live
2409 2779 4029 633 1571 633 1142 1569 5445 1142 2409 2409 2409
v.pai.3s cj a.nsm r.dsm.3 v.pai.3s cj cj cj v.pas.1p

τῷ κυρίῳ ζῶμεν, ἐάν τε ἀποθνῄσκωμεν, τῷ κυρίῳ
⌞for the⌟ Lord, *we live* and if *and* we die, we die ⌞for the⌟ Lord.
3836 3261 2409 5445 1569 5445 633 633 633 3836 3261
d.dsm n.dsm v.pai.1p cj cj v.pas.1p d.dsm n.dsm

NASB

Principles of Conscience

14:1 Now accept the
one who is weak
in faith, *but* not
for *the purpose of*
passing judgment
on his opinions.
2 One person has
faith that he may
eat all things, but
he who is weak
eats vegetables
only. 3 The one who
eats is not to regard
with contempt the
one who does not
eat, and the one
who does not eat
is not to judge the
one who eats, for
God has accepted
him. 4 Who are you
to judge the servant
of another? To his
own master he
stands or falls; and
he will stand, for
the Lord is able to
make him stand.
5 One person
regards one day
above another,
another regards
every day *alike.*
Each person must
be fully convinced
in his own mind.
6 He who observes
the day, observes
it for the Lord, and
he who eats, does
so for the Lord,
for he gives thanks
to God; and he
who eats not, for
the Lord he does
not eat, and gives
thanks to God. 7 For
not one of us lives
for himself, and
not one dies for
himself; 8 for if we
live, we live for the
Lord, or if we die,
we die for the

[a] [γὰρ] UBS.

NIV

So, whether we live or die, we belong to the Lord. 9 For this very reason, Christ died and returned to life so that he might be the Lord of both the dead and the living.

10 You, then, why do you judge your brother or sister[a]? Or why do you treat them with contempt? For we will all stand before God's judgment seat. 11 It is written:

"'As surely as I live,' says the Lord,
'every knee will bow before me;
every tongue will acknowledge God.'"[b]

12 So then, each of us will give an account of ourselves to God.

13 Therefore let us stop passing judgment on one another. Instead, make up your mind not to put any stumbling block or obstacle in the way of a brother or sister. 14 I am convinced, being fully persuaded in the Lord Jesus, that nothing is unclean in itself. But if anyone regards something as unclean, then for that person it is unclean. 15 If your brother or sister is distressed because of what you eat, you are no longer acting in love. Do not by your eating destroy

ἀποθνῄσκομεν. ἐάν τε οὖν ζῶμεν ἐάν τε ἀποθνῄσκωμεν,
we die So then, whether *So* *then* we live or whether *or* we die, we
633 5445 4036 1569 5445 4036 2409 5445 1569 5445 633 1639
v.pai.1p cj cj cj v.pas.1p cj cj v.pas.1p

τοῦ κυρίου ἐσμέν. 9 ⌞εἰς τοῦτο⌟ γὰρ Χριστὸς ἀπέθανεν
belong to the Lord. *we belong to* For the reason why *For* Christ died
1639 1639 3836 3261 1639 1142 1650 4047 1142 5986 633
d.gsm n.gsm v.pai.1p p.a r.asn cj n.nsm v.aai.3s

καὶ ἔζησεν, ἵνα καὶ → νεκρῶν καὶ → ζώντων
and rose to life again was that he might be Lord both of the dead and of the living.
2779 2409 2671 3259 3259 3259 3259 2779 3738 2779 2409
cj v.aai.3s cj cj a.gpm cj pt.pa.gpm

κυριεύσῃ. 10 ↱ σὺ δὲ τί κρίνεις τὸν ἀδελφόν σου; ἢ
he might be Lord Why do you *{and}* *Why* ⌞pass judgment on⌟ *{the}* your brother? *your* Or
3259 5515 3212 5148 1254 5515 3212 3836 5148 81 5148 2445
v.aas.3s r.ns.2 cj r.asn v.pai.2s d.asm n.asm r.gs.2 cj

καὶ ↱ σὺ τί ἐξουθενεῖς τὸν ἀδελφόν σου; ↰ ↰ ↱ ↱
again, why do you *why* hold *{the}* your brother *your* in contempt? For we will
2779 5515 2024 5148 5515 2024 3836 5148 81 5148 2024 2024 1142 4225 4225
adv r.ns.2 r.asn v.pai.2s d.asm n.asm r.gs.2

πάντες γὰρ παραστησόμεθα τῷ βήματι τοῦ θεοῦ, 11 γέγραπται γάρ, →
all *For* stand before the ⌞judgment seat⌟ of God. For it is written, *For* "As
4246 1142 4225 3836 1037 3836 2536 1142 1211 1142
a.npm cj v.fmi.1p d.dsn n.dsn d.gsm n.gsm v.rpi.3s cj

ζῶ ἐγώ, λέγει κύριος, ὅτι ἐμοὶ κάμψει πᾶν γόνυ καὶ
I live, *I* says the Lord, ~ every knee will bow to me, *will bow* *every* *knee* and
1609 2409 1609 3306 3261 4022 4246 1205 2828 2828 1609 2828 4246 1205 2779
v.pai.1s r.ns.1 v.pai.3s n.nsm cj r.ds.1 v.fai.3s a.nsn n.nsn cj

πᾶσα γλῶσσα ἐξομολογήσεται τῷ θεῷ. 12 ἄρα οὖν[a] ἕκαστος ἡμῶν
every tongue will give praise to God." So then each of us will give an
4246 1185 2018 3836 2536 726 4036 1667 7005 1443 1443
a.nsf n.nsf v.fmi.3s d.dsm n.dsm cj cj r.nsm r.gp.1

περὶ ἑαυτοῦ λόγον δώσει [b]τῷ θεῷ.[c] 13 μηκέτι οὖν
account of himself *account* *will give* to God. Therefore let us stop *Therefore*
3364 4309 1571 3364 1443 3836 2536 4036 3212 3212 3600 4036
p.g r.gsm.3 n.asm v.fai.3s d.dsm n.dsm adv cj

ἀλλήλους κρίνωμεν· ἀλλὰ τοῦτο κρίνατε
passing judgment on one another, *let us passing judgment on* but resolve this *resolve*
3212 3212 3212 253 3212 247 3212 4047 3212
r.apm v.pas.1p cj r.asn v.aam.2p

μᾶλλον, τὸ μὴ τιθέναι πρόσκομμα τῷ ἀδελφῷ ↰ ἢ σκάνδαλον.
instead, ~ never to put an obstacle or a trap in a brother's way. *or* *trap*
3437 3836 3590 5502 4682 2445 4998 3836 81 3836 2445 4998
adv.c d.asn pl f.pa n.asn d.dsm n.dsm cj n.asn

14 οἶδα καὶ πέπεισμαι ἐν κυρίῳ Ἰησοῦ ὅτι οὐδὲν κοινὸν δι' ἑαυτοῦ,
I know and am convinced in the Lord Jesus that nothing is unclean in itself;
3857 2779 4275 1877 3261 2652 4022 4029 3123 1328 1571
v.rai.1s cj v.rpi.1s p.d n.dsm n.dsm cj a.nsn a.nsn p.g r.gsn.3

⌞εἰ μὴ⌟ τῷ λογιζομένῳ τι κοινὸν εἶναι, ἐκείνῳ κοινόν.
however, ⌞to the⌟ one who considers something to be unclean, *to be* to him it is unclean.
1623 3590 3836 3357 5516 1639 1639 3123 1639 1697 3123
cj pl d.dsm pt.pm.dsm r.asn a.asn f.pa r.dsm a.nsn

15 εἰ γὰρ διὰ βρῶμα ὁ ἀδελφός σου λυπεῖται,
For if *For* your brother is being hurt by ⌞what you eat,⌟ *{the}* *brother* *your* *is being hurt*
1142 1623 1142 5148 81 3382 3382 3382 1328 1109 3836 81 5148 3382
cj cj p.a n.asn d.nsm n.nsm r.gs.2 v.ppi.3s

οὐκέτι κατὰ ἀγάπην περιπατεῖς· μὴ τῷ →
you are no longer walking in love. *you are walking* Do not destroy by what you
4344 4344 4033 4344 2848 27 4344 660 3590 660 3836 5148
adv p.a n.asf v.pai.2s pl d.dsn

NASB

Lord; therefore whether we live or die, we are the Lord's. 9 For to this end Christ died and lived again, that He might be Lord both of the dead and of the living.

10 But you, why do you judge your brother? Or you again, why do you regard your brother with contempt? For we will all stand before the judgment seat of God. 11 For it is written,

"As I live, says the Lord, every knee shall bow to Me,
And every tongue shall give praise to God."

12 So then each one of us will give an account of himself to God.

13 Therefore let us not judge one another anymore, but rather determine this—not to put an obstacle or a stumbling block in a brother's way. 14 I know and am convinced in the Lord Jesus that nothing is unclean in itself; but to him who thinks anything to be unclean, to him it is unclean. 15 For if because of food your brother is hurt, you are no longer walking according to love. Do not destroy with

[a] *10* The Greek word for *brother or sister* (*adelphos*) refers here to a believer, whether man or woman, as part of God's family; also in verses 13, 15 and 21.
[b] *11* Isaiah 45:23

[a] [οὖν] UBS.
[b] [τῷ θεῷ] UBS, , NET.
[c] θεῷ omitted in NET.

NIV

someone for
whom Christ died.
16Therefore do not
let what you know
is good be spoken
of as evil. 17For the
kingdom of God
is not a matter of
eating and drink-
ing, but of righ-
teousness, peace
and joy in the Holy
Spirit, 18because
anyone who serves
Christ in this way
is pleasing to God
and receives hu-
man approval.
19Let us therefore
make every effort
to do what leads to
peace and to mutu-
al edification. 20Do
not destroy the
work of God for
the sake of food.
All food is clean,
but it is wrong for
a person to eat
anything that caus-
es someone else
to stumble. 21It is
better not to eat
meat or drink wine
or to do anything
else that will cause
your brother or sis-
ter to fall.
22So whatever
you believe about
these things keep
between yourself
and God. Blessed
is the one who
does not con-
demn himself by
what he approves.
23But whoever
has doubts is con-
demned if they
eat, because their
eating is not from
faith; and every-
thing that does not
come from faith
is sin.[a]

15 We who
are strong
ought to bear with
the

[a] 23 Some manuscripts place 16:25-27 here; others after 15:33.

βρώματί σου ἐκεῖνον ἀπόλλυε ὑπὲρ οὗ Χριστὸς ἀπέθανεν. 16 ↱ μὴ →
eat *you* that brother *Do destroy* for whom Christ died. Therefore do not let
1109 5148 1697 660 5642 4005 5986 633 4036 1059 3590
n.dsn r.gs.2 r.asm v.pam.2s p.g r.gsm n.nsm v.aai.3s pl

βλασφημείσθω οὖν ὑμῶν τὸ ἀγαθόν. 17
what you regard as good be spoken of as evil. *Therefore* *you* *what good* For the kingdom
3836 7007 19 1059 4036 7007 3836 19 1142 3836 993
v.ppm.3s cj r.gp.2 d.nsn a.nsn

οὐ γάρ ἐστιν ἡ βασιλεία τοῦ θεοῦ βρῶσις καὶ πόσις
of God is not *For* *is* *the* *kingdom* *of* *God* a matter of eating and drinking,
3836 2536 1639 4024 1142 1639 3836 993 3836 2536 1111 2779 4530
pl cj v.pai.3s d.nsf n.nsf d.gsm n.gsm n.nsf cj n.nsf

ἀλλὰ δικαιοσύνη καὶ εἰρήνη καὶ χαρὰ ἐν πνεύματι ἁγίῳ· 18 ὁ
but of righteousness and peace and joy in the Holy Spirit. *Holy* For whoever
247 1466 2779 1645 2779 5915 1877 41 4460 41 1142 3836
cj n.nsf cj n.nsf cj n.nsf p.d n.dsn a.dsn d.nsm

γὰρ ἐν τούτῳ δουλεύων τῷ Χριστῷ εὐάρεστος τῷ θεῷ καὶ δόκιμος
For serves Christ in this way *serves* *{the}* *Christ* is pleasing to God and approved
1142 1526 5986 1877 4047 1526 3836 5986 2298 3836 2536 2779 1511
cj p.d r.dsn pt.pa.nsm d.dsm n.dsm a.nsm d.dsm n.dsm cj a.nsm

τοῖς ἀνθρώποις. 19 ἄρα οὖν τὰ τῆς εἰρήνης διώκωμεν καὶ τὰ
by men. So then let us pursue what makes for peace *let us pursue* and *{the}*
3836 476 726 4036 1503 1503 1503 3836 3836 1645 1503 2779 3836
d.dpm n.dpm cj cj d.apn d.gsf n.gsf v.pas.1p cj d.apn

τῆς οἰκοδομῆς τῆς ⸤εἰς ἀλλήλους.⸥ 20 ↱ μὴ ἕνεκεν βρώματος
for mutual upbuilding. *{the}* *mutual* Do not, ⸤for the sake of⸥ food,
3836 1650 3869 3836 1650 253 2907 3590 1914 1109
d.gsf n.gsf d.gsf p.a r.apm pl p.g n.gsn

κατάλυε τὸ ἔργον τοῦ θεοῦ. πάντα μὲν καθαρά, ἀλλὰ κακὸν
destroy the work of God. All food is indeed clean, but it is wrong to cause
2907 3836 2240 3836 2536 4246 3525 2754 247 2805 1328
v.pam.2s d.asn n.asn d.gsm n.gsm a.npn pl a.npn cj a.asn

τῷ ἀνθρώπῳ τῷ διὰ προσκόμματος ἐσθίοντι. 21 καλὸν τὸ
{the} another to stumble ⸤by what⸥ *cause* *to stumble* you eat. It is good *{the}*
3836 476 4682 4682 3836 1328 4682 2266 2819 3836
d.dsm n.dsm d.dsm p.g n.gsn pt.pa.dsm a.nsn d.nsn

μὴ φαγεῖν κρέα μηδὲ πιεῖν οἶνον μηδὲ ⸤ἐν ᾧ⸥ ↱ ὁ ἀδελφός
not to eat meat or to drink wine or to do anything that makes *{the}* your brother
3590 2266 3200 3593 4403 3885 3593 1877 4005 4684 3836 5148 81
pl f.aa n.apn cj f.aa n.asm cj p.d r.dsn d.nsm n.nsm

σου προσκόπτει.[a] 22 σὺ πίστιν ἣν[b] ἔχεις κατὰ σεαυτὸν
your stumble. The faith that you *faith* *that* have, keep as your own conviction
5148 4684 4411 4005 5148 4411 4005 2400 2400 2848 4932
r.gs.2 v.pai.3s r.ns.2 n.asf r.asf v.pai.2s p.a r.asm.2

ἔχε ἐνώπιον τοῦ θεοῦ. μακάριος ὁ ↱ ↱ ↱ μὴ κρίνων ἑαυτὸν
keep before *{the}* God. Blessed is the one who has no ⸤reason to condemn⸥ himself
2400 1967 3836 2536 3421 3836 3212 3212 3212 3590 3212 1571
v.pam.2s p.g d.gsm n.gsm a.nsm d.nsm pl pt.pa.nsm r.asm.3

ἐν ᾧ δοκιμάζει· 23 ὁ δὲ διακρινόμενος ἐὰν φάγῃ
for what he approves. But the *But* one who doubts is condemned if he eats,
1877 4005 1507 1254 3836 1254 1359 2891 2891 1569 2266
p.d r.dsn v.pai.3s d.nsm cj pt.pm.nsm cj v.aas.3s

κατακέκριται, ὅτι οὐκ ἐκ πίστεως· πᾶν δὲ ὃ οὐκ ἐκ
is condemned because his eating is not from faith; and whatever *and* ~ is not from
2891 4022 4024 1666 4411 1254 4246 1254 4005 4024 1666
v.rpi.3s cj pl p.g n.gsf a.nsn cj r.nsn pl p.g

πίστεως ἁμαρτία ἐστίν.
faith is sin. *is*
4411 1639 281 1639
n.gsf n.nsf v.pai.3s

15:1 ὀφείλομεν δὲ ἡμεῖς οἱ δυνατοὶ τὰ
We who are strong have an obligation *{and}* *We* *who* *strong* to bear with the
7005 3836 1543 4053 1254 7005 3836 1543 1002 1002 1002 3836
v.pai.1p cj r.np.1 d.npm a.npm d.apn

[a] ἢ σκανδαλίζεται ἢ ἀσθενεῖ included by TR after προσκόπτει.
[b] [ἣν] UBS, omitted by NET.

NASB

your food him for
whom Christ died.
16Therefore do not
let what is for you
a good thing be
spoken of as evil;
17for the kingdom
of God is not eat-
ing and drinking,
but righteousness
and peace and joy
in the Holy Spirit.
18For he who in this
way serves Christ
is acceptable to
God and approved
by men. 19So then
[a]we pursue the
things which make
for peace and the
building up of
one another. 20Do
not tear down the
work of God for
the sake of food.
All things indeed
are clean, but they
are evil for the man
who eats and gives
offense. 21It is good
not to eat meat
or to drink wine,
or *to do anything*
by which your
brother stumbles.
22The faith which
you have, have as
your own convic-
tion before God.
Happy is he who
does not condemn
himself in what he
approves. 23But he
who doubts is con-
demned if he eats,
because *his eating*
is not from faith;
and whatever is not
from faith is sin.

Self-denial on Behalf of Others

15:1Now we who
are strong ought to

[a] Later mss read *let us pursue*

NIV

failings of the
weak and not to
please ourselves.
2 Each of us should
please our neigh-
bors for their good,
to build them up.
3 For even Christ
did not please
himself but, as it
is written: "The in-
sults of those who
insult you have
fallen on me."[a]
4 For everything
that was written in
the past was writ-
ten to teach us, so
that through the en-
durance taught in
the Scriptures and
the encouragement
they provide we
might have hope.
5 May the God
who gives endur-
ance and encour-
agement give you
the same attitude
of mind toward
each other that
Christ Jesus had,
6 so that with one
mind and one
voice you may glo-
rify the God and
Father of our Lord
Jesus Christ.
7 Accept one an-
other, then, just as
Christ accepted
you, in order to
bring praise to
God. 8 For I tell
you that Christ has
become a servant
of the Jews[b] on be-
half of God's truth,
so that the promis-
es made to the pa-
triarchs might be
confirmed 9 and,
moreover, that the
Gentiles might
glorify God for
his mercy. As it is
written:

> "Therefore I will
> praise you
> among the
> Gentiles;
> I will sing the
> praises of
> your name."[c]

ἀσθενήματα τῶν ἀδυνάτων βαστάζειν καὶ μὴ ἑαυτοῖς ἀρέσκειν. 2
failings of the weak, *to bear with* and not to please ourselves. *to please* Let
821 3836 105 1002 2779 3590 743 743 1571 743 743
n.apn d.gpm a.gpm f.pa cj pl r.dpm.1 f.pa

ἕκαστος ἡμῶν τῷ πλησίον ἀρεσκέτω εἰς τὸ ἀγαθὸν πρὸς οἰκοδομήν· ←
each of us please his neighbor *Let please* for his good, to build him up.
1667 7005 743 3836 4446 743 1650 3836 19 4639 3869
r.nsm r.gp.1 d.dsm adv v.pam.3s p.a d.asn a.asn p.a n.asf

3 καὶ γὰρ ὁ Χριστὸς οὐχ ἑαυτῷ ἤρεσεν, ἀλλὰ καθὼς γέγραπται, οἱ
{also} For *{the}* Christ did not please himself; *did please* but as it is written, "The
2779 1142 3836 5986 743 4024 743 1571 743 247 2777 1211 3836
adv cj d.nsm n.nsm pl r.dsm.3 v.aai.3s cj cj v.rpi.3s d.npm

ὀνειδισμοὶ τῶν ὀνειδιζόντων σε ἐπέπεσαν ἐπ' ἐμέ. 4 ὅσα γὰρ
insults of those who insult you have fallen on me." For whatever *For*
3944 3836 3943 5148 2158 2093 1609 1142 4012 1142
n.npm d.gpm pt.pa.gpm r.as.2 v.aai.3p p.a r.as.1 r.npn cj

προεγράφη, εἰς τὴν ἡμετέραν διδασκαλίαν ἐγράφη, ἵνα
⌊was written at an earlier time⌋ was written for *{the}* our instruction, *was written* that
4592 1211 1211 1650 3836 2466 1436 1211 2671
v.api.3s p.a d.asf r.asf.1 n.asf v.api.3s cj

διὰ τῆς ὑπομονῆς καὶ διὰ τῆς παρακλήσεως τῶν γραφῶν τὴν
through *{the}* endurance and through the encouragement of the scriptures we might have *{the}*
1328 3836 5705 2779 1328 3836 4155 3836 1210 2400 2400 2400 3836
p.g d.gsf n.gsf cj p.g d.gsf n.gsf d.gpf n.gpf d.asf

ἐλπίδα ἔχωμεν. 5 ὁ δὲ θεὸς τῆς ὑπομονῆς καὶ τῆς παρακλήσεως δῴη
hope. *we might have* May the *{and}* God of endurance and *{the}* encouragement enable
1828 2400 1443 3836 1254 2536 3836 5705 2779 3836 4155 1443
n.asf v.pas.1p d.nsm cj n.nsm d.gsf n.gsf cj d.gsf n.gsf v.aao.3s

ὑμῖν ⌊τὸ αὐτὸ φρονεῖν⌋ ἐν ἀλλήλοις κατὰ Χριστὸν Ἰησοῦν,
you to live in harmony with one another, ⌊according to⌋ Christ Jesus,
7007 3836 899 5858 1877 253 2848 5986 2652
r.dp.2 d.asn r.asn f.pa p.d r.dpm p.a n.asm n.asm

6 ἵνα ὁμοθυμαδὸν ἐν ἑνὶ στόματι δοξάζητε τὸν θεὸν καὶ πατέρα τοῦ
so that together you may with one voice glorify the God and Father of our
2671 3924 1519 1519 1877 1651 5125 1519 3836 2536 2779 4252 3836 7005
cj adv p.d a.dsn n.dsn v.pas.2p d.asm n.asm cj n.asm d.gsm

κυρίου ἡμῶν Ἰησοῦ Χριστοῦ. 7 διὸ προσλαμβάνεσθε ἀλλήλους, καθὼς
Lord *our* Jesus Christ. Therefore accept one another even as Christ has
3261 7005 2652 5986 1475 4689 253 2777 5986 4689
n.gsm r.gp.1 n.gsm n.gsm cj v.pmm.2p r.apm cj

καὶ ὁ Χριστὸς προσελάβετο ὑμᾶς εἰς δόξαν τοῦ θεοῦ. 8 λέγω γὰρ
also *{the}* *Christ* accepted you, for the glory of God. For I tell *For* you that
2779 3836 5986 4689 7007 1650 1518 3836 2536 1142 3306 1142
adv d.nsm n.nsm v.ami.3s r.ap.2 p.a n.asf d.gsm n.gsm v.pai.1s cj

Χριστὸν διάκονον γεγενῆσθαι → περιτομῆς ὑπὲρ ἀληθείας
Christ has become a servant *has become* of the circumcised ⌊on behalf of⌋ the truth
5986 1181 1181 1356 1181 4364 5642 237
n.asm n.asm f.rp n.gsf p.g n.gsf

θεοῦ, εἰς τὸ βεβαιῶσαι τὰς ἐπαγγελίας τῶν πατέρων, 9 τὰ
of God, ⌊in order to⌋ ~ confirm the promises made to the patriarchs, and that the
2536 1650 3836 1011 3836 2039 3836 4252 1254 3836
n.gsm p.a d.asn f.aa d.apf n.apf d.gpm n.gpm d.apn

δὲ ἔθνη ὑπὲρ ἐλέους δοξάσαι τὸν θεόν, καθὼς γέγραπται,
and Gentiles might glorify God for his mercy. *might glorify* *{the}* *God* As it is written,
1254 1620 1519 1519 2536 5642 1799 1519 3836 2536 2777 1211
cj n.apn p.g n.gsn f.aa d.asm n.asm cj v.rpi.3s

διὰ τοῦτο ἐξομολογήσομαί σοι ἐν ἔθνεσιν καὶ τῷ ὀνόματί
"For this reason I will acknowledge you among the Gentiles and sing praises to your name."
1328 4047 2018 5148 1877 1620 2779 6010 6010 3836 5148 3950
p.a r.asn v.fmi.1s r.ds.2 p.d n.dpn cj d.dsn n.dsn

NASB

bear the weak-
nesses of those
without strength
and not *just* please
ourselves. 2 Each
of us is to please
his neighbor for
his good, to his
edification. 3 For
even Christ did not
please Himself;
but as it is written,
"THE REPROACHES
OF THOSE WHO
REPROACHED YOU
FELL ON ME." 4 For
whatever was
written in earlier
times was written
for our instruction,
so that through
perseverance and
the encouragement
of the Scriptures
we might have
hope. 5 Now may
the God who gives
perseverance and
encouragement
grant you to be
of the same mind
with one another
according to Christ
Jesus, 6 so that with
one accord you
may with one voice
glorify the God and
Father of our Lord
Jesus Christ.
7 Therefore, accept
one another, just as
Christ also accept-
ed us to the glory
of God. 8 For I say
that Christ has be-
come a servant to
the circumcision on
behalf of the truth
of God to confirm
the promises *given*
to the fathers, 9 and
for the Gentiles
to glorify God for
His mercy; as it is
written,

> "THEREFORE
> I WILL GIVE
> PRAISE TO YOU
> AMONG THE
> GENTILES,
> AND I WILL
> SING TO YOUR
> NAME."

[a] 3 Psalm 69:9
[b] 8 Greek *circumcision*
[c] 9 2 Samuel 22:50; Psalm 18:49

NIV

10 Again, it says,
"Rejoice, you
Gentiles,
with his
people."[a]
11 And again,
"Praise the Lord,
all you
Gentiles;
let all the
peoples extol
him."[b]
12 And again, Isaiah
says,
"The Root of Jesse
will spring
up,
one who will
arise to rule
over the
nations;
in him the
Gentiles will
hope."[c]
13 May the God
of hope fill you
with all joy and
peace as you trust
in him, so that you
may overflow with
hope by the power
of the Holy Spirit.

Paul the Minister to the Gentiles

14 I myself am con-
vinced, my broth-
ers and sisters, that
you yourselves
are full of good-
ness, filled with
knowledge and
competent to in-
struct one another.
15 Yet I have written
you quite boldly on
some points to re-
mind you of them
again, because of
the grace God gave
me 16 to be a minis-
ter of Christ Jesus
to the Gentiles. He
gave me the priest-
ly duty of pro-
claiming the gospel
of God, so that the
Gentiles might be-
come an offering
acceptable to God,
sanctified by the
Holy Spirit.
17 Therefore I glo-
ry in Christ Jesus
in my service to
God. 18 I will

σου ψαλῶ. 10 καὶ πάλιν λέγει, εὐφράνθητε, ἔθνη, μετὰ τοῦ λαοῦ αὐτοῦ.
your *sing praises* And again it says, "Rejoice, O Gentiles, with *{the}* his people." *his*
5148 6010 2779 4099 3306 2370 1620 3552 3836 899 3295 899
r.gs.2 v.fai.1s cj adv v.pai.3s v.apm.2p n.vpn p.g d.gsm n.gsm r.gsm.3

11 καὶ πάλιν, αἰνεῖτε, πάντα τὰ ἔθνη, τὸν κύριον καὶ →
And again, "Praise the Lord all you Gentiles, *the* *Lord* and let all the nations
2779 4099 140 3836 3261 4246 3836 1620 3836 3261 2779 4246 3836 3295
cj adv v.pam.2p a.vpn d.vpn n.vpn d.asm n.asm cj

ἐπαινεσάτωσαν αὐτὸν πάντες οἱ λαοί. 12 καὶ πάλιν Ἠσαΐας λέγει,
extol him." *all* *the* *nations* And again Isaiah says, "The root of
2046 899 4246 3836 3295 2779 4099 2480 3306 3836 4844 3836
v.aam.3p r.asm.3 a.npm d.npm n.npm cj adv n.nsm v.pai.3s

ἔσται ἡ ῥίζα τοῦ Ἰεσσαὶ καὶ ὁ ἀνιστάμενος ἄρχειν ἐθνῶν, ἐπ'
Jesse will come, *The* *root* *of* *Jesse* even he who rises ⌞to rule over⌟ the Gentiles; in
2649 1639 3836 4844 3836 2649 2779 3836 482 806 1620 2093
v.fmi.3s d.nsf n.nsf d.gsm n.gsm cj d.nsm pt.pm.nsm f.pa n.gpn p.d

αὐτῷ ↱ ἔθνη ἐλπιοῦσιν. 13 ↱ ὁ δὲ θεὸς τῆς ἐλπίδος πληρώσαι
him will the Gentiles hope." Now may the *Now* God of hope fill
899 1827 1620 1827 1254 4444 3836 1254 2536 3836 1828 4444
r.dsm.3 n.npn v.fai.3p d.nsm cj n.nsm d.gsf n.gsf v.aao.3s

ὑμᾶς ↰ πάσης χαρᾶς καὶ εἰρήνης ἐν τῷ πιστεύειν, εἰς τὸ περισσεύειν
you with all joy and peace in *{the}* believing, ⌞so that⌟ ~ you may abound
7007 4444 4246 5915 2779 1645 1877 3836 4409 1650 3836 7007 4355
r.ap.2 a.gsf n.gsf cj n.gsf p.d d.dsn f.pa p.a d.asn f.pa

ὑμᾶς ἐν τῇ ἐλπίδι ἐν δυνάμει → πνεύματος ἁγίου. 14
you in *{the}* hope by the power of the Holy Spirit. *Holy* I myself
7007 1877 3836 1828 1877 1539 41 4460 41 1609 899
r.ap.2 p.d d.dsf n.dsf p.d n.dsf n.gsn a.gsn

πέπεισμαι δέ, ἀδελφοί μου, καὶ αὐτὸς ἐγὼ περὶ ὑμῶν ὅτι καὶ
am convinced about you, *{and}* my brethren, *my* *{also}* *myself* *I* *about* *you* that *{also}* you
4275 4309 7007 1254 1609 81 1609 2779 899 1609 4309 7007 4022 2779 1639
v.rpi.1s cj n.vpm r.gs.1 adv r.nsm r.ns.1 p.g r.gp.2 cj adv

αὐτοὶ μεστοί ἐστε ἀγαθωσύνης, πεπληρωμένοι πάσης τῆς[a] γνώσεως,
yourselves are full *you are* of goodness, filled with all *{the}* knowledge, and
899 1639 3550 1639 20 4444 4246 3836 1194
r.npm a.npm v.pai.2p n.gsf pt.rp.npm a.gsf d.gsf n.gsf

δυνάμενοι καὶ ἀλλήλους νουθετεῖν. 15 τολμηρότερον δὲ
able also to instruct one another. *to instruct* *rather boldly* Nevertheless on certain
1538 2779 3805 3805 253 3805 5529 1254 608 3538
pt.pp.npm cj r.apm f.pa adv.c cj

ἔγραψα ὑμῖν ἀπὸ μέρους ὡς ἐπαναμιμνῄσκων ὑμᾶς
subjects I have written to you *on* *certain subjects* rather boldly ⌞so as⌟ to refresh your
3538 1211 7007 608 3538 5529 5529 6055 2057 7007
v.aai.1s r.dp.2 p.g n.gsn pl pt.pa.nsm r.ap.2

↰ διὰ τὴν χάριν τὴν δοθεῖσάν μοι ὑπὸ τοῦ θεοῦ 16 εἰς τὸ εἶναί με
memory, ⌞because of⌟ the grace that was given me by *{the}* God to ~ be *{I}* a
2057 1328 3836 5921 3836 1443 1609 5679 3836 2536 1650 3836 1639 1609
p.a d.asf n.asf d.asf pt.ap.asf r.ds.1 p.g d.gsm n.gsm p.a d.asn f.pa r.as.1

λειτουργὸν Χριστοῦ Ἰησοῦ εἰς τὰ ἔθνη, ἱερουργοῦντα τὸ εὐαγγέλιον τοῦ θεοῦ,
minister of Christ Jesus to the Gentiles, serving the gospel of God
3313 5986 2652 1650 3836 1620 2646 3836 2295 3836 2536
n.asm n.gsm n.gsm p.a d.apn n.apn pt.pa.asm d.asn n.asn d.gsm n.gsm

↰ ↰ ↰ ἵνα γένηται ἡ προσφορὰ τῶν ἐθνῶν
as a priest, so that my offering of the Gentiles may become *my* *offering* *of the* *Gentiles*
2646 2646 2646 2671 3836 4714 3836 3836 1620 1181 3836 4714 3836 1620
cj v.ams.3s d.nsf n.nsf d.gpn n.gpn

εὐπρόσδεκτος, ἡγιασμένη ἐν πνεύματι ἁγίῳ. 17 ἔχω
acceptable, sanctified by the Holy Spirit. *Holy* In Christ Jesus, then, I have
2347 39 1877 41 4460 41 1877 5986 2652 4036 2400
a.nsf pt.rp.nsf p.d n.dsn a.dsn v.pai.1s

οὖν τὴν[b] καύχησιν ἐν Χριστῷ Ἰησοῦ τὰ πρὸς τὸν θεόν· 18 ↱ ↱
then *{the}* reason to boast *In* *Christ* *Jesus* of my work for *{the}* God. For I will
4036 3836 3018 1877 5986 2652 3836 4639 3836 2536 1142 5528 5528
cj d.asf n.asf p.d n.dsm n.dsm d.apn p.a d.asm n.asm

NASB

10 Again he says,
"REJOICE, O
GENTILES,
WITH HIS
PEOPLE."
11 And again,
"PRAISE THE
LORD ALL YOU
GENTILES,
AND LET ALL
THE PEOPLES
PRAISE HIM."
12 Again Isaiah says,
"THERE SHALL
COME THE
ROOT OF JESSE,
AND HE WHO
ARISES TO
RULE OVER THE
GENTILES,
IN HIM SHALL
THE GENTILES
HOPE."
13 Now may the God
of hope fill you
with all joy and
peace in believing,
so that you will
abound in hope by
the power of the
Holy Spirit.
14 And concerning
you, my brethren,
I myself also am
convinced that you
yourselves are full
of goodness, filled
with all knowledge
and able also to
admonish one an-
other. 15 But I have
written very boldly
to you on some
points so as to
remind you again,
because of the
grace that was giv-
en me from God,
16 to be a minister of
Christ Jesus to the
Gentiles, minister-
ing as a priest the
gospel of God, so
that *my* offering of
the Gentiles may
become accept-
able, sanctified by
the Holy Spirit.
17 Therefore in
Christ Jesus I have
found reason for
boasting in things
pertaining to God.
18 For I will not

[a] *10* Deut. 32:43
[b] *11* Psalm 117:1
[c] *12* Isaiah 11:10 (see Septuagint)

[a] [τῆς] UBS.
[b] [τὴν] UBS, omitted by NET.

NIV

not venture to
speak of anything
except what Christ
has accomplished
through me in lead-
ing the Gentiles to
obey God by what
I have said and
done— 19by the
power of signs and
wonders, through
the power of the
Spirit of God. So
from Jerusalem
all the way around
to Illyricum, I
have fully pro-
claimed the gospel
of Christ. 20It has
always been my
ambition to preach
the gospel where
Christ was not
known, so that I
would not be build-
ing on someone
else's foundation.
21Rather, as it is
written:

> "Those who were
> not told
> about him
> will see,
> and those who
> have not
> heard
> will under-
> stand."[a]

22This is why I
have often been
hindered from
coming to you.

Paul's Plan to Visit Rome

23But now that
there is no more
place for me to
work in these re-
gions, and since I
have been longing
for many years to
visit you, 24I plan
to do so when I go
to Spain. I hope
to see you while
passing through
and to have you
assist me on my
journey there, af-
ter I have enjoyed
your company for a
while. 25Now, how-
ever, I am on my
way to Jerusalem
in the service of
the Lord's people
there. 26For Mace-
donia and Achaia

[a] 21 Isaiah 52:15 (see Septuagint)

οὐ γὰρ τολμήσω τι λαλεῖν ὧν οὐ κατειργάσατο
not *For* venture to speak of anything *to speak of* except what *except* Christ has accomplished
4024 1142 5528 3281 3281 3281 5516 3281 4024 4005 4024 5986 2981
pl cj v.fai.1s r.asn f.pa r.gpn pl v.ami.3s

Χριστὸς δι᾽ ἐμοῦ εἰς ὑπακοὴν ἐθνῶν, λόγῳ καὶ ἔργῳ,
Christ through me in bringing the Gentiles to obedience, *Gentiles* by word and deed,
5986 1328 1609 1620 1650 5633 1620 3364 2779 2240
n.nsm p.g r.gs.1 p.a n.asf n.gpn n.dsm cj n.dsn

19 ἐν δυνάμει σημείων καὶ τεράτων, ἐν δυνάμει → πνεύματος θεοῦ·[a] ὥστε
by the power of signs and wonders, by the power of the Spirit of God, so that
1877 1539 4956 2779 5469 1877 1539 4460 2536 6063
p.d n.dsf n.gpn cj n.gpn p.d n.dsf n.gsn n.gsm cj

με ἀπὸ Ἰερουσαλὴμ καὶ κύκλῳ μέχρι τοῦ Ἰλλυρικοῦ πεπληρωκέναι
I from Jerusalem *{and}* ⌊all the way around⌋ to *{the}* Illyricum I have fulfilled
1609 608 2647 2779 3241 3588 3836 2665 1609 4444
r.as.1 p.g n.gsf cj adv p.g d.gsn n.gsn f.ra

τὸ εὐαγγέλιον τοῦ Χριστοῦ, 20 οὕτως δὲ
my ministry of proclaiming the gospel of Christ. And thus *And*
3836 2295 3836 5986 1254 4048 1254
d.asn n.asn d.gsm n.gsm adv cj

φιλοτιμούμενον εὐαγγελίζεσθαι οὐχ ὅπου ὠνομάσθη Χριστός, ⌊ἵνα
⌊I have always made it my aim⌋ to preach the gospel, not where Christ was known, *Christ* lest
5818 2294 4024 3963 5986 3951 5986 2671
pt.pm.asm f.pm pl cj v.api.3s n.nsm cj

μὴ⌋ ἐπ᾽ ἀλλότριον θεμέλιον οἰκοδομῶ, 21 ἀλλὰ καθὼς γέγραπται,
I should build on someone else's foundation; *I should build* rather, as it is written,
3590 3868 3868 3868 2093 259 2529 3868 247 2777 1211
pl p.a a.asm n.asm v.pas.1s cj cj v.rpi.3s

οἷς ↱ ↱ οὐκ ἀνηγγέλη περὶ αὐτοῦ ὄψονται, καὶ οἳ ↱ ↱ οὐκ ἀκηκόασιν
"Those who were not told of him will see, and those who have not heard
4005 334 334 4024 334 4309 899 3972 2779 4005 201 201 4024 201
r.dpm pl v.api.3s p.g r.gsm.3 v.fmi.3p cj r.npm pl v.rai.3p

συνήσουσιν. 22 διὸ καὶ ἐνεκοπτόμην τὰ
of him will understand." ⌊This is why⌋ *{also}* on so many occasions I was kept from *{the}*
5317 1475 2779 4498 4498 4498 4498 1601 3836
v.fai.3p cj adv v.ipi.1s d.apn

πολλὰ τοῦ ἐλθεῖν πρὸς ὑμᾶς· 23 νυνὶ δὲ μηκέτι
on so many occasions ~ coming to you; but now *but* I no longer have a
4498 3836 2262 4639 7007 1254 3815 1254 2400 3600 2400
a.apn d.gsn f.aa p.a r.ap.2 adv cj adv

τόπον ἔχων ἐν τοῖς κλίμασι τούτοις,
⌊reason for remaining⌋ *I have* in *{the}* these regions, *these* and for many years I have
5536 2400 1877 3836 4047 3107 4047 1254 608 4498 2291 2400 2400
n.asm pt.pa.nsm p.d d.dpn n.dpn r.dpn

ἐπιποθίαν δὲ ἔχων τοῦ ἐλθεῖν πρὸς ὑμᾶς ἀπὸ πολλῶν ἐτῶν, 24 ⌊ὡς ἂν⌋
desired *and* *I have* ~ to come to visit you. *for* *many* *years* When
2163 1254 2400 3836 2262 4639 7007 608 4498 2291 6055 323
n.asf cj pt.pa.nsm d.gsn f.aa p.a r.ap.2 p.g a.gpn n.gpn cj pl

πορεύωμαι εἰς τὴν Σπανίαν· ἐλπίζω γὰρ διαπορευόμενος θεάσασθαι
I do go to *{the}* Spain, I hope *{for}* to see you as I pass through *to see*
4513 1650 3836 5056 1827 1142 2517 2517 7007 1388 2517
v.pms.1s p.a d.asf n.asf v.pai.1s cj pt.pm.nsm f.am

ὑμᾶς καὶ ὑφ᾽ ὑμῶν προπεμφθῆναι ἐκεῖ ἐὰν
you and be helped on my way there by you, *be helped on my way* *there* *{if}* after I
7007 2779 4636 4636 4636 4636 4636 1695 5679 7007 4636 1695 1569 4754 1858
r.ap.2 cj p.g r.gp.2 f.ap adv cj

ὑμῶν πρῶτον ἀπὸ μέρους ἐμπλησθῶ. 25 νυνὶ δὲ
have enjoyed your company *after* for a while. *I have enjoyed* But for now, *But*
1858 1858 7007 4754 608 3538 1858 1254 3815 1254
r.gp.2 adv p.g n.gsn v.aps.1s adv cj

πορεύομαι εἰς Ἰερουσαλὴμ → διακονῶν τοῖς ἁγίοις. 26
I am going to Jerusalem in a service for the saints. For Macedonia and Achaia
4513 1650 2647 1354 3836 41 1142 3423 2779 938
v.pmi.1s p.a n.asf pt.pa.nsm d.dpm a.dpm

[a] [θεοῦ] UBS.

NASB

presume to speak
of anything except
what Christ has
accomplished
through me,
resulting in the
obedience of the
Gentiles by word
and deed, 19in the
power of signs
and wonders, in
the power of the
Spirit; so that from
Jerusalem and
round about as far
as Illyricum I have
fully preached the
gospel of Christ.
20And thus I aspired
to preach the
gospel, not where
Christ was *already*
named, so that I
would not build
on another man's
foundation; 21but as
it is written,

> "THEY WHO HAD
> NO NEWS OF
> HIM SHALL
> SEE,
> AND THEY WHO
> HAVE NOT
> HEARD SHALL
> UNDERSTAND."

22For this reason
I have often been
prevented from
coming to you;
23but now, with
no further place
for me in these
regions, and since I
have had for many
years a longing
to come to you
24whenever I go
to Spain—for I
hope to see you in
passing, and to be
helped on my way
there by you, when
I have first enjoyed
your company for a
while— 25but now,
I am going to Jeru-
salem serving the
saints. 26For Mace-
donia and Achaia

NIV

were pleased to make a contribution for the poor among the Lord's people in Jerusalem. 27 They were pleased to do it, and indeed they owe it to them. For if the Gentiles have shared in the Jews' spiritual blessings, they owe it to the Jews to share with them their material blessings. 28 So after I have completed this task and have made sure that they have received this contribution, I will go to Spain and visit you on the way. 29 I know that when I come to you, I will come in the full measure of the blessing of Christ.

30 I urge you, brothers and sisters, by our Lord Jesus Christ and by the love of the Spirit, to join me in my struggle by praying to God for me. 31 Pray that I may be kept safe from the unbelievers in Judea and that the contribution I take to Jerusalem may be favorably received by the Lord's people there, 32 so that I may come to you with joy, by God's will, and in your company be refreshed. 33 The God of peace be with

εὐδόκησαν γὰρ Μακεδονία καὶ Ἀχαΐα ˪κοινωνίαν τινὰ˩ ποιήσασθαι εἰς
were pleased *For* *Macedonia* *and* *Achaia* to make a contribution *to make* to
2305 1142 3423 2779 938 4472 4472 3126 5516 4472 1650
v.aai.3p cj n.nsf cj n.nsf n.asf r.asf f.am p.a

τοὺς πτωχοὺς τῶν ἁγίων τῶν ἐν Ἰερουσαλήμ. 27 εὐδόκησαν γὰρ
the poor ˪among the˩ saints *{the}* in Jerusalem. They were pleased *{for}* to do so,
3836 4777 3836 41 3836 1877 2647 2305 1142
d.apm a.apm d.gpm a.gpm d.gpm p.d n.dsf v.aai.3p cj

καὶ ὀφειλέται εἰσὶν αὐτῶν· εἰ γὰρ
in fact, they are obligated *they are* to them; for if *for* the Gentiles have come to share
2779 1639 1639 4050 1639 899 1142 1623 1142 3836 1620 3125 3125 3125 3125
cj n.npm v.pai.3p r.gpm.3 cj cj

τοῖς πνευματικοῖς αὐτῶν ἐκοινώνησαν τὰ ἔθνη, ὀφείλουσιν καὶ
in *{the}* their spiritual blessings, *their* *have come to share in* *the* *Gentiles* they ought also to
3125 3836 899 4461 899 3125 3836 1620 4053 2779 3310
d.dpn a.dpn r.gpm.3 v.aai.3p d.npn n.npn v.pai.3p adv

ἐν τοῖς σαρκικοῖς λειτουργῆσαι αὐτοῖς. 28
be of service to them in *{the}* material things. *to be of service* *to them* Therefore, when
3310 3310 3310 899 899 1877 3836 4920 3310 899 4036 2200
p.d d.dpn a.dpn f.aa r.dpm.3

τοῦτο οὖν ἐπιτελέσας καὶ σφραγισάμενος αὐτοῖς τὸν
I have completed this task *Therefore* *when I have completed* and have delivered to them *{the}*
2200 2200 2200 4047 4036 2200 2779 5381 899 3836
r.asn cj pt.aa.nsm cj pt.am.nsm r.dpm.3 d.asm

καρπὸν τοῦτον, ἀπελεύσομαι δι᾽ ὑμῶν εἰς Σπανίαν· 29
what was raised, *what* I will leave for Spain ˪by way of˩ you. *for* *Spain* And
4047 2843 4047 599 1650 5056 1328 7007 1650 5056 1254
n.asm r.asm v.fmi.1s p.g r.gp.2 p.a n.asf

οἶδα δὲ ὅτι ἐρχόμενος πρὸς ὑμᾶς ἐν πληρώματι → εὐλογίας
I know *And* that when I come to you, I will come in the fulness of the blessing
3857 1254 4022 2262 4639 7007 2262 2262 2262 1877 4445 2330
v.rai.1s cj cj pt.pm.nsm p.a r.ap.2 p.d n.dsn n.gsf

Χριστοῦ ἐλεύσομαι. 30 παρακαλῶ δὲ ὑμᾶς, ἀδελφοί, διὰ τοῦ κυρίου ἡμῶν
of Christ. *I will come* Now I urge *Now* you, brethren, by *{the}* our Lord *our*
5986 2262 1254 4151 1254 7007 81 1328 3836 7005 3261 7005
n.gsm v.fmi.1s v.pai.1s cj r.ap.2 n.vpm p.g d.gsm n.gsm r.gp.1

Ἰησοῦ Χριστοῦ καὶ διὰ τῆς ἀγάπης τοῦ πνεύματος συναγωνίσασθαί μοι ἐν ταῖς
Jesus Christ and by the love of the Spirit, to join me in *{the}*
2652 5986 2779 1328 3836 27 3836 4460 5253 1609 1877 3836
n.gsm n.gsm cj p.g d.gsf n.gsf d.gsn n.gsn f.am r.ds.1 p.d d.dpf

προσευχαῖς ὑπὲρ ἐμοῦ ↰ πρὸς τὸν θεόν, 31 ἵνα ῥυσθῶ ἀπὸ
fervent prayer to God on my behalf, *to* *{the}* *God* that ˪I may be delivered˩ from
4666 4639 2536 5642 1609 5642 4639 3836 2536 2671 4861 608
n.dpf p.g r.gs.1 p.a d.asm n.asm cj v.aps.1s p.g

τῶν ἀπειθούντων ἐν τῇ Ἰουδαίᾳ καὶ ἡ διακονία μου
those in Judea who refuse to believe, *in* *{the}* *Judea* and that *{the}* my service *my*
3836 1877 2677 578 1877 3836 2677 2779 3836 1609 1355 1609
d.gpm pt.pa.gpm p.d d.dsf n.dsf cj d.nsf n.nsf r.gs.1

ἡ εἰς Ἰερουσαλὴμ εὐπρόσδεκτος τοῖς ἁγίοις γένηται, 32 ἵνα
{the} to Jerusalem may prove truly acceptable to the saints, *may prove* so that by God's
3836 1650 2647 1181 1181 2347 3836 41 1181 2671 1328 2536
d.nsf p.a n.asf a.nsf d.dpm a.dpm v.ams.3s cj

ἐν χαρᾷ ἐλθὼν πρὸς ὑμᾶς διὰ θελήματος θεοῦ
will I may come to you with joy *I may come* *to* *you* *by* *will* *God's* and
2525 2262 2262 2262 4639 7007 1877 5915 2262 4639 7007 1328 2525 2536
p.d n.dsf pt.aa.nsm p.a r.ap.2 p.g n.gsn n.gsm

συναναπαύσωμαι ὑμῖν. ↰ 33 ὁ δὲ θεὸς τῆς εἰρήνης μετὰ
be refreshed in your company. Now may the *Now* God of peace be with
5265 7007 5265 1254 3836 1254 2536 3836 1645 3552
v.ams.1s r.dp.2 d.nsm cj n.nsm d.gsf n.gsf p.g

πάντων ὑμῶν, ἀμήν.
all of you. Amen.
4246 7007 297
a.gpm r.gp.2 pl

NASB

have been pleased to make a contribution for the poor among the saints in Jerusalem. 27 Yes, they were pleased *to do so,* and they are indebted to them. For if the Gentiles have shared in their spiritual things, they are indebted to minister to them also in material things. 28 Therefore, when I have finished this, and have put my seal on this fruit of theirs, I will go on by way of you to Spain. 29 I know that when I come to you, I will come in the fullness of the blessing of Christ.

30 Now I urge you, brethren, by our Lord Jesus Christ and by the love of the Spirit, to strive together with me in your prayers to God for me, 31 that I may be rescued from those who are disobedient in Judea, and *that* my service for Jerusalem may prove acceptable to the saints; 32 so that I may come to you in joy by the will of God and find *refreshing* rest in your company. 33 Now the God of peace be with you all. Amen.

NIV

you all. Amen.

Personal Greetings

16 I commend to you our sister
Phoebe, a deacon[a,b]
of the church in Cen-
chreae. 2I ask you
to receive her in the
Lord in a way worthy
of his people and to
give her any help she
may need from you,
for she has been the
benefactor of many
people, including me.
3Greet Priscilla[c]
and Aquila, my
co-workers in
Christ Jesus.
4They risked
their lives for
me. Not only
I but all the
churches of
the Gentiles
are grateful to
them.
5Greet also the
church that
meets at their
house.
Greet my dear
friend Epene-
tus, who was
the first convert
to Christ in the
province of
Asia.
6Greet Mary, who
worked very
hard for you.
7Greet Andronicus
and Junia, my
fellow Jews
who have been
in prison with
me. They are
outstanding
among[d] the
apostles, and
they were in
Christ before I
was.
8Greet Ampliatus,
my dear friend
in the Lord.
9Greet Urbanus,
our co-worker
in Christ, and
my dear friend
Stachys.
10Greet Apelles,

16:1 συνίστημι δὲ ὑμῖν Φοίβην τὴν ἀδελφὴν ἡμῶν, οὖσαν καὶ[a]
I commend *{and}* to you our sister Phoebe, *{the}* *sister* *our* who is *{also}* a
5319 1254 7007 7005 80 5833 3836 80 7005 1639 2779
v.pai.1s cj r.dp.2 n.asf d.asf n.asf r.gp.1 pt.pa.asf cj

διάκονον τῆς ἐκκλησίας τῆς ἐν Κεγχρεαῖς, 2ἵνα αὐτὴν
servant of the church *{the}* in Cenchrea, so that you may receive her
1356 3836 1711 3836 1877 3020 2671 4657 4657 4657 899
n.asf d.gsf n.gsf d.gsf p.d n.dpf cj r.asf.3

προσδέξησθε ἐν κυρίῳ ἀξίως τῶν ἁγίων καὶ παραστῆτε αὐτῇ ⌊ἐν
you may receive in the Lord ⌊in a manner worthy⌋ of the saints, and give her any
4657 1877 3261 547 3836 41 2779 4225 899 1877
v.ams.2p p.d n.dsm adv d.gpm a.gpm cj v.aas.2p r.dsf.3 p.d

ᾧ ἄν⌋ ὑμῶν χρῄζῃ πράγματι· καὶ γὰρ αὐτὴ
help she may need from you; *she may need* *help* *{also}* for she has been of
4005 323 4547 5974 5974 5974 7007 5974 4547 2779 1142 899 1181 1181
r.dsn pl r.gp.2 v.pas.3s n.dsn adv cj r.nsf

προστάτις πολλῶν ἐγενήθη καὶ ἐμοῦ αὐτοῦ. 3ἀσπάσασθε Πρίσκαν καὶ
great assistance to many, *has been* including myself. *{herself}* Greet Prisca and
4706 4498 1181 2779 1609 899 832 4571 2779
n.nsf a.gpm v.api.3s cj r.gs.1 r.gsm v.amm.2p n.asf cj

Ἀκύλαν τοὺς συνεργούς μου ἐν Χριστῷ Ἰησοῦ, 4οἵτινες
Aquila, *{the}* my fellow workers *my* in Christ Jesus, who risked their own necks
217 3836 1609 5301 1609 1877 5986 2652 4015 5719 1571 1571 5549
n.asm d.apm n.apm r.gs.1 p.d n.dsm n.dsm r.npm

ὑπὲρ τῆς ψυχῆς μου τὸν ἑαυτῶν τράχηλον ὑπέθηκαν, οἷς οὐκ ἐγὼ μόνος
for *{the}* my life. *my* *{the}* *their own* *necks* *risked* *to them* Not only I *only*
5642 3836 1609 6034 1609 3836 1571 5549 5719 4005 4024 3668 1609 3668
p.g d.gsf n.gsf r.gs.1 d.asm r.gpm.3 n.asm v.aai.3p r.dpm pl r.ns.1 a.nsm

εὐχαριστῶ ἀλλὰ καὶ πᾶσαι αἱ ἐκκλησίαι
but also all the churches of the Gentiles are grateful *but* *also* *all* *the* *churches*
247 2779 4246 3836 1711 3836 3836 1620 2373 247 2779 4246 3836 1711
v.pai.1s cj adv a.npf d.npf n.npf

τῶν ἐθνῶν, 5καὶ τὴν κατ᾿ οἶκον αὐτῶν ἐκκλησίαν.
of the *Gentiles* to them. Also greet the church in their house. *their* *church*
3836 1620 4005 4005 2779 3836 1711 2848 899 3875 899 1711
d.gpn n.gpn cj d.asf p.a n.asm r.gpm.3 n.asf

ἀσπάσασθε Ἐπαίνετον τὸν ἀγαπητόν μου, ὅς ἐστιν ἀπαρχὴ
Greet my dear friend Epaenetus, *{the}* *dear friend* *my* who was the first convert
832 1609 28 28 2045 3836 28 1609 4005 1639 569
v.amm.2p n.asm d.asm a.asm r.gs.1 r.nsm v.pai.3s n.nsf

τῆς Ἀσίας εἰς Χριστόν. 6ἀσπάσασθε Μαρίαν, ἥτις πολλὰ
to Christ in Asia. *to* *Christ* Greet Mary, who has worked ⌊so very hard⌋
1650 5986 3836 823 1650 5986 832 3451 4015 3159 3159 4498
d.gsf n.gsf p.a n.asm v.amm.2p n.asf r.nsf a.apn

ἐκοπίασεν εἰς ὑμᾶς. 7ἀσπάσασθε Ἀνδρόνικον καὶ Ἰουνιᾶν τοὺς συγγενεῖς μου
has worked for you. Greet Andronicus and Junia, *{the}* my compatriots *my*
3159 1650 7007 832 438 2779 2687 3836 1609 5150 1609
v.aai.3s p.a r.ap.2 v.amm.2p n.asm cj n.asm d.apm n.apm r.gs.1

καὶ συναιχμαλώτους μου, οἵτινές εἰσιν ἐπίσημοι ἐν τοῖς ἀποστόλοις, οἳ
and my fellow prisoners; *my* they were well known to the apostles, and they
2779 1609 5257 1609 4015 1639 2168 1877 3836 693 4005
cj n.apm r.gs.1 r.npm v.pai.3p a.npm p.d d.dpm n.dpm r.npm

καὶ πρὸ ἐμοῦ γέγοναν ἐν Χριστῷ. 8ἀσπάσασθε Ἀμπλιᾶτον τὸν
also were in Christ before me. *were* *in* *Christ* Greet Ampliatus, *{the}*
2779 1181 1877 5986 4574 1609 1181 1877 5986 832 309 3836
adv p.g r.gs.1 v.rai.3p p.d n.dsm v.amm.2p n.asm d.asm

ἀγαπητόν μου ἐν κυρίῳ. 9ἀσπάσασθε Οὐρβανὸν τὸν συνεργὸν ἡμῶν
my dear friend *my* in the Lord. Greet Urbanus, *{the}* our fellow worker *our*
1609 28 1609 1877 3261 832 4042 3836 7005 5301 7005
a.asm r.gs.1 p.d n.dsm v.amm.2p n.asm d.asm n.asm r.gp.1

ἐν Χριστῷ καὶ Στάχυν τὸν ἀγαπητόν μου. 10ἀσπάσασθε Ἀπελλῆν
in Christ, and my dear friend Stachys. *{the}* *dear friend* *my* Greet Apelles,
1877 5986 2779 1609 28 28 5093 3836 28 1609 832 593
p.d n.dsm cj n.asm d.asm a.asm r.gs.1 v.amm.2p n.asm

NASB

Greetings and Love Expressed

16:1I commend
to you our sister
Phoebe, who is
a servant of the
church which is
at Cenchrea; 2that
you receive her in
the Lord in a man-
ner worthy of the
saints, and that you
help her in whatev-
er matter she may
have need of you;
for she herself has
also been a helper
of many, and of
myself as well.
3Greet Prisca
and Aquila, my
fellow workers in
Christ Jesus, 4who
for my life risked
their own necks, to
whom not only do
I give thanks, but
also all the church-
es of the Gentiles;
5also *greet* the
church that is in
their house. Greet
Epaenetus, my
beloved, who is
the first convert to
Christ from Asia.
6Greet Mary, who
has worked hard
for you. 7Greet
Andronicus and
Junias, my kins-
men and my fellow
prisoners, who are
outstanding among
the apostles, who
also were in Christ
before me. 8Greet
Ampliatus, my
beloved in the
Lord. 9Greet Ur-
banus, our fellow
worker in Christ,
and Stachys my
beloved. 10Greet
Apelles, the

[a] 1 Or *servant*
[b] 1 The word *deacon* refers here to a Christian designated to serve with the overseers/elders of the church in a variety of ways; similarly in Phil. 1:1 and 1 Tim. 3:8,12.
[c] 3 Greek *Prisca*, a variant of *Priscilla*
[d] 7 Or *are esteemed by*

[a] [καὶ] UBS, omitted by TNIV.

NIV

whose fidelity
to Christ has
stood the test.
Greet those who
belong to the
household of
Aristobulus.
11 Greet Herodion,
my fellow Jew.
Greet those in the
household of
Narcissus who
are in the Lord.
12 Greet Tryphena
and Tryphosa,
those women
who work hard
in the Lord.
Greet my dear
friend Persis,
another woman
who has worked
very hard in the
Lord.
13 Greet Rufus, cho-
sen in the Lord,
and his mother,
who has been a
mother to me,
too.
14 Greet Asyncritus,
Phlegon, Her-
mes, Patrobas,
Hermas and the
other brothers
and sisters with
them.
15 Greet Philologus,
Julia, Nereus
and his sister,
and Olympas
and all the
Lord's people
who are with
them.
16 Greet one another
with a holy kiss.
All the churches
of Christ send
greetings.
17 I urge you,
brothers and sis-
ters, to watch out
for those who
cause divisions
and put obstacles
in your way that
are contrary to
the teaching you
have learned. Keep
away from them.
18 For such people
are not serving our
Lord Christ, but
their own appe-
tites. By smooth
talk and flattery
they deceive the
minds of naive
people. 19 Everyone

τὸν δόκιμον ⌞ἐν Χριστῷ.⌟ ἀσπάσασθε τοὺς ἐκ τῶν
{the} a ⌞tried and true⌟ Christian. Greet those who ⌞belong to⌟ the household
3836 1511 1877 5986 832 3836 1666 3836
d.asm a.asm p.d n.dsm v.amm.2p d.apm p.g d.gpm

Ἀριστοβούλου. 11 ἀσπάσασθε Ἡρῳδίωνα τὸν συγγενῆ μου. ἀσπάσασθε τοὺς
of Aristobulus. Greet Herodion, {the} my compatriot. my Greet those
755 832 2479 3836 1609 5150 1609 832 3836
n.gsm v.amm.2p n.asm d.asm n.asm r.gs.1 v.amm.2p d.apm

ἐκ τῶν Ναρκίσσου τοὺς ὄντας ἐν κυρίῳ.
in the Lord who ⌞belong to⌟ the household of Narcissus. {the} {who are} in Lord
1877 3261 1666 3836 3727 3836 1639 1877 3261
p.g d.gpm n.gsm d.apm pt.pa.apm p.d n.dsm

12 ἀσπάσασθε Τρύφαιναν καὶ Τρυφῶσαν τὰς κοπιώσας ἐν κυρίῳ. ἀσπάσασθε
Greet Tryphaena and Tryphosa, {the} diligent workers in the Lord. Greet
832 5586 2779 5589 3836 3159 1877 3261 832
v.amm.2p n.asf cj n.asf d.apf pt.pa.apf p.d n.dsm v.amm.2p

Περσίδα τὴν ἀγαπητήν, ἥτις πολλὰ ἐκοπίασεν ἐν
my dear friend Persis, my dear friend who has worked ⌞so very hard⌟ has worked in the
3836 28 28 4372 3836 28 4015 3159 3159 4498 3159 1877
n.asf d.asf a.asf r.nsf a.apn v.aai.3s p.d

κυρίῳ. 13 ἀσπάσασθε Ῥοῦφον τὸν ἐκλεκτὸν ⌞ἐν κυρίῳ⌟ καὶ τὴν μητέρα
Lord. Greet Rufus, an outstanding Christian, also {the} his mother
3261 832 4859 3836 1723 1877 3261 2779 3836 899 3613
n.dsm v.amm.2p n.asm d.asm a.asm p.d n.dsm cj d.asf n.asf

αὐτοῦ καὶ ἐμοῦ. 14 ἀσπάσασθε Ἀσύγκριτον, Φλέγοντα, Ἑρμῆν, Πατροβᾶν, Ἑρμᾶν
his and mine. Greet Asyncritus, Phlegon, Hermes, Patrobas, Hermas,
899 2779 1609 832 850 5823 2258 4259 2254
r.gsm.3 cj r.gs.1 v.amm.2p n.asm n.asm n.asm n.asm n.asm

καὶ τοὺς σὺν αὐτοῖς ἀδελφούς. 15 ἀσπάσασθε Φιλόλογον καὶ Ἰουλίαν, Νηρέα
and the brethren with them. brethren Greet Philologus and Julia, Nereus
2779 3836 81 5250 899 81 832 5807 2779 2684 3759
cj d.apm p.d r.dpm.3 n.apm v.amm.2p n.asm cj n.asf n.asm

καὶ τὴν ἀδελφὴν αὐτοῦ, καὶ Ὀλυμπᾶν καὶ τοὺς σὺν αὐτοῖς
and {the} his sister, his and Olympas, and all the saints who are with them.
2779 3836 899 80 899 2779 3912 2779 4246 3836 41 5250 899
cj d.asf n.asf r.gsm.3 cj n.asm cj d.apm p.d r.dpm.3

πάντας ἁγίους. 16 ἀσπάσασθε ἀλλήλους ἐν φιλήματι ἁγίῳ.
all saints Greet one another with a holy kiss. holy All the churches
4246 41 832 253 1877 41 5799 41 4246 3836 1711
a.apm a.apm v.amm.2p r.apm p.d n.dsn a.dsn

ἀσπάζονται ὑμᾶς αἱ ἐκκλησίαι πᾶσαι τοῦ Χριστοῦ. 17 παρακαλῶ
of Christ greet you. the churches All of Christ Now I urge
3836 5986 832 7007 3836 1711 4246 3836 5986 1254 4151
v.pmi.3p r.ap.2 d.npf n.npf a.npf d.gsm n.gsm v.pai.1s

δὲ ὑμᾶς, ἀδελφοί, σκοπεῖν τοὺς τὰς διχοστασίας καὶ τὰ
Now you, brethren, ⌞to watch out for⌟ people who cause {the} divisions and {the}
1254 7007 81 5023 3836 3836 1496 2779 3836
cj r.ap.2 n.vpm f.pa d.apm d.apf n.apf cj d.apn

σκάνδαλα παρὰ τὴν διδαχὴν ἣν ὑμεῖς ⌞ἐμάθετε ποιοῦντας,⌟
upset people's faith ⌞contrary to⌟ the teaching that you have received.
4998 4123 3836 1439 4005 7007 3443 4472
n.apn p.a d.asf n.asf r.asf r.np.2 v.aai.2p pt.pa.apm

καὶ ⌞ἐκκλίνετε ἀπ᾽⌟ αὐτῶν· 18 οἱ γὰρ τοιοῦτοι τῷ κυρίῳ
{and} Avoid them. {the} For such people do not serve {the} our Lord
2779 1712 608 899 3836 1142 5525 1526 4024 1526 3836 7005 3261
cj v.pam.2p p.g r.gpm.3 d.npm cj r.npm d.dsm n.dsm

ἡμῶν Χριστῷ οὐ δουλεύουσιν ἀλλὰ τῇ ἑαυτῶν κοιλίᾳ, καὶ διὰ τῆς
our Christ not do serve but {the} their own appetites. {and} By their
7005 5986 4024 1526 247 3836 1571 3120 2779 1328 3836
r.gp.1 n.dsm pl v.pai.3p cj d.dsf r.gpm.3 n.dsf cj p.g d.gsf

χρηστολογίας καὶ εὐλογίας ἐξαπατῶσιν τὰς καρδίας τῶν ἀκάκων. 19 ἡ γὰρ ὑμῶν
smooth talk and flattery they deceive the hearts of the guileless. {the} {for} Your
5981 2779 2330 1987 3836 2840 3836 179 3836 1142 7007
n.gsf cj n.gsf v.pai.3p d.apf n.apf d.gpm a.gpm d.nsf cj r.gp.2

NASB

approved in
Christ. Greet
those who are of
the *household* of
Aristobulus. 11Greet
Herodion, my kins-
man. Greet those
of the *household* of
Narcissus, who are
in the Lord. 12Greet
Tryphaena and
Tryphosa, workers
in the Lord. Greet
Persis the beloved,
who has worked
hard in the Lord.
13Greet Rufus,
a choice man in
the Lord, also his
mother and mine.
14Greet Asyncritus,
Phlegon, Hermes,
Patrobas, Hermas
and the brethren
with them. 15Greet
Philologus and
Julia, Nereus and
his sister, and
Olympas, and all
the saints who are
with them. 16Greet
one another with a
holy kiss. All the
churches of Christ
greet you.
17Now I urge you,
brethren, keep your
eye on those who
cause dissensions
and hindrances
contrary to the
teaching which you
learned, and turn
away from them.
18For such men are
slaves, not of our
Lord Christ but of
their own appe-
tites; and by their
smooth and flatter-
ing speech they de-
ceive the hearts of
the unsuspecting.
19For the report

NIV

has heard about
your obedience, so
I rejoice because
of you; but I want
you to be wise
about what is good,
and innocent about
what is evil.
[20]The God of
peace will soon
crush Satan under
your feet.
The grace of our
Lord Jesus be with
you.
[21]Timothy, my
co-worker, sends
his greetings to
you, as do Lucius,
Jason and Sosip-
ater, my fellow
Jews.
[22]I, Tertius, who
wrote down this
letter, greet you in
the Lord.
[23]Gaius, whose
hospitality I and
the whole church
here enjoy, sends
you his greetings.
Erastus, who is
the city's director
of public works,
and our brother
Quartus send you
their greetings. [24][a]
[25]Now to him
who is able to
establish you in
accordance with
my gospel, the
message I pro-
claim about Jesus
Christ, in keeping
with the revelation
of the mystery hid-
den for long ages
past, [26]but now
revealed and made
known through the
prophetic writings
by the command
of the eternal God,
so that all the Gen-
tiles might come
to the obedience
that comes from[b]
faith—

ὑπακοὴ εἰς πάντας ἀφίκετο·
obedience is known to all *is known* and thus I am rejoicing over you. *thus*
5633 919 919 1650 4246 919 4036 5897 5897 5897 2093 7007 4036
n.nsf p.a a.apm v.ami.3s p.d r.dp.2 cj
ἐφ᾽ ὑμῖν οὖν

χαίρω, θέλω δὲ ὑμᾶς σοφοὺς εἶναι εἰς τὸ ἀγαθόν,
I am rejoicing But I want *But* you to be wise *to be* as to what is good, and
5897 1254 2527 1254 7007 1639 1639 5055 1639 1650 3836 19 1254
v.pai.1s v.pai.1s cj r.ap.2 a.apm f.pa p.a d.asn a.asn

ἀκεραίους δὲ εἰς τὸ κακόν. [20] ὁ δὲ θεὸς τῆς εἰρήνης → συντρίψει
innocent *and* as to what is evil. The *{and}* God of peace will soon crush
193 1254 1650 3836 2805 3836 1254 2536 3836 1645 1877 5341
a.apm cj p.a d.asn a.asn d.nsm cj n.nsm d.gsf n.gsf v.fai.3s

τὸν σατανᾶν ὑπὸ τοὺς πόδας ὑμῶν ⌞ἐν τάχει.⌟ ἡ χάρις τοῦ κυρίου
{the} Satan under *{the}* your feet. *your* *soon* May the grace of our Lord
3836 4928 5679 3836 7007 4546 7007 1877 5443 3836 5921 3836 7005 3261
d.asm n.asm p.a d.apm n.apm r.gp.2 p.d n.dsn d.nsf n.nsf d.gsm n.gsm

ἡμῶν Ἰησοῦ μεθ᾽ ὑμῶν. [21] ἀσπάζεται ὑμᾶς Τιμόθεος ὁ
our Jesus be with you. Timothy my fellow worker greets you, *Timothy* *{the}*
7005 2652 3552 7007 5510 1609 5301 5301 832 7007 5510 3836
r.gp.1 n.gsm p.g r.gp.2 v.pmi.3s r.ap.2 n.nsm d.nsm

συνεργός μου καὶ Λούκιος καὶ Ἰάσων καὶ Σωσίπατρος οἱ συγγενεῖς μου.
fellow worker *my* as do Lucius and Jason and Sosipater, *{the}* my compatriots. *my*
5301 1609 2779 3372 2779 2619 2779 5399 3836 1609 5150 1609
n.nsm r.gs.1 cj n.nsm cj n.nsm cj n.nsm d.npm n.npm r.gs.1

[22] ἀσπάζομαι ὑμᾶς ἐγὼ Τέρτιος ὁ γράψας τὴν ἐπιστολὴν
greet *you* I, Tertius, the ⌞one who is writing down⌟ this letter, greet you
832 7007 1609 5470 3836 1211 3836 2186 832 7007
v.pmi.1s r.ap.2 r.ns.1 n.nsm d.nsm pt.aa.nsm d.asf n.asf

ἐν κυρίῳ. [23] ἀσπάζεται ὑμᾶς Γάϊος ὁ ξένος μου καὶ ὅλης τῆς
in the Lord. *greets* *you* Gaius, a host to me ⌞as well as⌟ to the whole *to the*
1877 3261 832 7007 1127 3836 3828 1609 2779 3836 3836 3910 3836
p.d n.dsm v.pmi.3s r.ap.2 n.nsm d.nsm n.nsm r.gs.1 cj a.gsf d.gsf

ἐκκλησίας. ἀσπάζεται ὑμᾶς Ἔραστος ὁ
church, greets you. Erastus, the city treasurer greets you, *Erastus* *the*
1711 832 7007 2235 3836 4484 3874 832 7007 2235 3836
n.gsf v.pmi.3s r.ap.2 n.nsm d.nsm

οἰκονόμος τῆς πόλεως καὶ Κούαρτος ὁ ἀδελφός.[a] [25] [b]τῷ δὲ
treasurer *{the}* *city* as does our brother Quartus. *our* *brother* Now to *Now*
3874 3836 4484 2779 3836 81 3181 3836 81 1254 3836 1254
n.nsm d.gsf n.gsf cj n.nsm d.nsm n.nsm d.dsm cj

δυναμένῳ ὑμᾶς στηρίξαι κατὰ τὸ εὐαγγέλιόν μου καὶ
⌞him who is able⌟ to establish you *to establish* ⌞according to⌟ *{the}* my gospel *my* and
1538 5114 5114 7007 5114 2848 3836 1609 2295 1609 2779
pt.pp.dsm r.ap.2 f.aa p.a d.asn n.asn r.gs.1 cj

τὸ κήρυγμα Ἰησοῦ Χριστοῦ, κατὰ ἀποκάλυψιν → μυστηρίου
the preaching of Jesus Christ, ⌞according to⌟ the revelation of the mystery that has
3836 3060 2652 5986 2848 637 3696 4967 4967
d.asn n.asn n.gsm n.gsm p.a n.asf n.gsn

χρόνοις αἰωνίοις ↰ σεσιγημένου, [26] φανερωθέντος
been kept secret for long ages past, *which has been kept secret* but now is manifested,
4967 4967 4967 5989 173 5989 4967 1254 3814 5746
n.dpm a.dpm pt.rp.gsn pt.ap.gsn

δὲ νῦν διά τε γραφῶν → προφητικῶν κατ᾽ ἐπιταγὴν τοῦ
but *now* and by *and* the Scriptures of the prophets, ⌞according to⌟ the commandment of the
1254 3814 5445 1328 5445 1210 4738 2848 2198 3836
cj adv p.g cj n.gpf a.gpf p.a n.asf d.gsm

αἰωνίου θεοῦ εἰς ὑπακοὴν πίστεως εἰς
eternal God, has been made known to all the nations, ⌞leading to⌟ obedience of faith; *to*
173 2536 1192 1192 1192 1192 1650 4246 3836 1620 1650 5633 4411 1650
a.gsm n.gsm p.a n.asf n.gsf p.a

NASB

of your obedience
has reached to
all; therefore I am
rejoicing over you,
but I want you to
be wise in what is
good and innocent
in what is evil.
[20]The God of peace
will soon crush
Satan under your
feet.
The grace of our
Lord Jesus be with
you.
[21]Timothy my fel-
low worker greets
you, and *so do*
Lucius and Jason
and Sosipater, my
kinsmen.
[22]I, Tertius, who
write this letter,
greet you in the
Lord.
[23]Gaius, host
to me and to the
whole church,
greets you. Erastus,
the city treasurer
greets you, and
Quartus, the broth-
er. [24][[a]The grace
of our Lord Jesus
Christ be with you
all. Amen.]
[25]Now to Him
who is able to es-
tablish you accord-
ing to my gospel
and the preaching
of Jesus Christ,
according to the
revelation of the
mystery which has
been kept secret
for long ages past,
[26]but now is mani-
fested, and by the
Scriptures of the
prophets, according
to the command-
ment of the eternal
God, has been
made known to all
the nations, *leading*
to obedience of

[a] 24 Some manuscripts include here *May the grace of our Lord Jesus Christ be with all of you. Amen.*
[b] 26 Or *that is*

[a] 24 ἡ χάρις τοῦ Κυρίου ἡμῶν Ἰησοῦ Χριστοῦ μετὰ πάντων ὑμῶν. ἀμήν. included by TR after ἀδελφός.
[b] UBS brackets vv25-27.

[a] Early mss do not contain this v

NIV

27 to the only wise God be glory forever through Jesus Christ! Amen.

πάντα	τὰ	ἔθνη	γνωρισθέντος,	27 →	μόνῳ	σοφῷ	θεῷ,	διὰ	Ἰησοῦ	Χριστοῦ,
all	*the*	*nations*	*has been made known*	to the	only	wise	God,	through	Jesus	Christ,
4246	3836	1620	1192		3668	5055	2536	1328	2652	5986
a.apn	d.apn	n.apn	pt.ap.gsn		a.dsm	a.dsm	n.dsm	p.g	n.gsm	n.gsm

ᾧ		ἡ	δόξα	εἰς	τοὺς	αἰῶνας,	ἀμήν.[a]
{to him}	be	the	glory	for	all	time.	Amen.
4005		3836	1518	1650	3836	172	297
r.dsm		d.nsf	n.nsf	p.a	d.apm	n.apm	pl

NASB

faith; 27 to the only wise God, through Jesus Christ, be the glory forever. Amen.

[a] πρὸς Ῥωμαίους ἐγράφη ἀπὸ Κορίνθου διὰ Φοίβης τῆς διακόνου τῆς ἐν Κεγχρεαῖς ἐκκλησίας included by TR after ἀμήν.

1 Corinthians

NIV

1 Paul, called to
be an apostle
of Christ Jesus by
the will of God,
and our brother
Sosthenes,

2 To the church of
God in Corinth,
to those sanctified
in Christ Jesus
and called to be
his holy people,
together with all
those everywhere
who call on the
name of our Lord
Jesus Christ—
their Lord and
ours:

3 Grace and peace
to you from God
our Father and the
Lord Jesus Christ.

Thanksgiving

4 I always thank
my God for you
because of his
grace given you in
Christ Jesus. 5 For
in him you have
been enriched
in every way—
with all kinds
of speech and
with all knowl-
edge— 6 God thus
confirming our
testimony about
Christ among you.
7 Therefore you do
not lack any spiri-
tual gift as you ea-
gerly wait for our
Lord Jesus Christ
to be revealed. 8 He
will also keep you
firm to the end,
so that you will be
blameless on the
day of our Lord
Jesus Christ. 9 God
is faithful, who has
called you into fel-
lowship with his

1:1 Παῦλος κλητὸς ἀπόστολος Χριστοῦ Ἰησοῦ διὰ θελήματος θεοῦ
Paul, called to be an apostle of Christ Jesus by the will of God,
4263 3105 693 5986 2652 1328 2525 2536
n.nsm a.nsm n.nsm n.gsm n.gsm p.g n.gsn n.gsm

καὶ Σωσθένης ὁ ἀδελφὸς 2 τῇ ἐκκλησίᾳ τοῦ θεοῦ τῇ οὔσῃ ἐν Κορίνθῳ,
and Sosthenes our brother, ⌊to the⌋ church of God that is in Corinth,
2779 5398 3836 81 3836 1711 3836 2536 3836 1639 1877 3172
cj n.nsm d.nsm n.nsm d.dsf n.dsf d.gsm n.gsm d.dsf pt.pa.dsf p.d n.dsf

ἡγιασμένοις ἐν Χριστῷ Ἰησοῦ, κλητοῖς ἁγίοις, σὺν πᾶσιν τοῖς
to those sanctified in Christ Jesus and called to be saints ⌊together with⌋ all those
39 1877 5986 2652 3105 41 5250 4246 3836
pt.rp.dpm p.d n.dsm n.dsm a.dpm a.dpm p.d a.dpm d.dpm

ἐπικαλουμένοις τὸ ὄνομα τοῦ κυρίου ἡμῶν Ἰησοῦ Χριστοῦ ἐν
in every place who call on the name of our Lord *our* Jesus Christ, *in*
1877 4246 5536 2126 3836 3950 3836 7005 3261 7005 2652 5986 1877
pt.pm.dpm d.asn n.asn d.gsm n.gsm r.gp.1 n.gsm n.gsm p.d

παντὶ τόπῳ, αὐτῶν καὶ ἡμῶν· 3 χάρις ὑμῖν καὶ εἰρήνη ἀπὸ θεοῦ πατρὸς
every place both their Lord and ours: Grace to you and peace from God our Father
4246 5536 899 2779 7005 5921 7007 2779 1645 608 2536 7005 4252
a.dsm n.dsm r.gpm.3 cj r.gp.1 n.nsf r.dp.2 cj n.nsf p.g n.gsm n.gsm

ἡμῶν καὶ κυρίου Ἰησοῦ Χριστοῦ. 4 → → εὐχαριστῶ τῷ θεῷ μου
our and the Lord Jesus Christ. I am always giving thanks to my God *my*
7005 2779 3261 2652 5986 4121 2373 3836 1609 2536 1609
r.gp.1 cj n.gsm n.gsm n.gsm v.pai.1s d.dsm n.dsm r.gs.1

πάντοτε περὶ ὑμῶν ἐπὶ τῇ χάριτι τοῦ θεοῦ τῇ δοθείσῃ ὑμῖν ἐν Χριστῷ
always for you ⌊because of⌋ the grace of God that was given to you in Christ
4121 4309 7007 2093 3836 5921 3836 2536 3836 1443 7007 1877 5986
adv p.g r.gp.2 p.d d.dsf n.dsf d.gsm n.gsm d.dsf pt.ap.dsf r.dp.2 p.d n.dsm

Ἰησοῦ, 5 ὅτι ἐν παντὶ ἐπλουτίσθητε ἐν αὐτῷ, ἐν παντὶ λόγῳ καὶ πάσῃ
Jesus, that in ⌊every way⌋ you were enriched in him in all speech and all
2652 4022 1877 4246 4457 1877 899 1877 4246 3364 2779 4246
n.dsm cj p.d a.dsn v.api.2p p.d r.dsm.3 p.d a.dsm n.dsm cj a.dsf

γνώσει, 6 καθὼς τὸ μαρτύριον τοῦ Χριστοῦ ἐβεβαιώθη ἐν ὑμῖν,
knowledge — just as the testimony about Christ was confirmed among you —
1194 2777 3836 3457 3836 5986 1011 1877 7007
n.dsf cj d.nsn n.nsn d.gsm n.gsm v.api.3s p.d r.dp.2

7 ὥστε ὑμᾶς ↱ μὴ ὑστερεῖσθαι ἐν μηδενὶ χαρίσματι ἀπεκδεχομένους τὴν
so that you do not lack in any spiritual gift as you wait for the
6063 7007 5728 3590 5728 1877 3594 5922 587 3836
cj r.ap.2 pl f.pp p.d a.dsn n.dsn pt.pm.apm d.asf

ἀποκάλυψιν τοῦ κυρίου ἡμῶν Ἰησοῦ Χριστοῦ, 8 ὃς καὶ βεβαιώσει ὑμᾶς
revealing of our Lord *our* Jesus Christ. He *{also}* will keep you
637 3836 7005 3261 7005 2652 5986 4005 2779 1011 7007
n.asf d.gsm n.gsm r.gp.1 n.gsm n.gsm r.nsm adv v.fai.3s r.ap.2

↰ ἕως τέλους ἀνεγκλήτους ἐν τῇ ἡμέρᾳ τοῦ κυρίου ἡμῶν Ἰησοῦ
steadfast to the end, guiltless in the day of our Lord *our* Jesus
1011 2401 5465 441 1877 3836 2465 3836 7005 3261 7005 2652
p.g n.gsn a.apm p.d d.dsf n.dsf d.gsm n.gsm r.gp.1 n.gsm

Χριστοῦ.[a] 9 πιστὸς ὁ θεός, δι' οὗ ἐκλήθητε εἰς κοινωνίαν τοῦ
Christ. God is faithful, *{the} God* by whom you were called into fellowship with his
5986 2536 4412 3836 2536 1328 4005 2813 1650 3126 3836 899
n.gsm a.nsm d.nsm n.nsm p.g r.gsm v.api.2p p.a n.asf d.gsm

NASB

Appeal to Unity

1:1 Paul, called *as*
an apostle of Jesus
Christ by the will
of God, and Sos-
thenes our brother,
2 To the church of
God which is at
Corinth, to those
who have been
sanctified in Christ
Jesus, saints by
calling, with all
who in every place
call on the name
of our Lord Jesus
Christ, their *Lord*
and ours:
3 Grace to you and
peace from God
our Father and the
Lord Jesus Christ.
4 I thank [a]my God
always concerning
you for the grace
of God which was
given you in Christ
Jesus, 5 that in ev-
erything you were
enriched in Him, in
all speech and all
knowledge, 6 even
as the testimony
concerning Christ
was confirmed in
you, 7 so that you
are not lacking in
any gift, awaiting
eagerly the revela-
tion of our Lord
Jesus Christ, 8 who
will also confirm
you to the end,
blameless in the
day of our Lord
Jesus Christ. 9 God
is faithful, through
whom you were
called into fellow-
ship with His Son,

[a] [Χριστοῦ] UBS.

[a] Two early mss do not contain *my*

NIV

Son, Jesus Christ
our Lord.

A Church Divided Over Leaders

10 I appeal to you,
brothers and sis-
ters,[a] in the name
of our Lord Jesus
Christ, that all of
you agree with one
another in what
you say and that
there be no divi-
sions among you,
but that you be
perfectly united in
mind and thought.
11 My brothers and
sisters, some from
Chloe's household
have informed me
that there are quar-
rels among you.
12 What I mean is
this: One of you
says, "I follow
Paul"; another, "I
follow Apollos";
another, "I follow
Cephas[b]"; still
another, "I follow
Christ."
13 Is Christ di-
vided? Was Paul
crucified for you?
Were you bap-
tized in the name
of Paul? 14 I thank
God that I did not
baptize any of you
except Crispus and
Gaius, 15 so no one
can say that you
were baptized in
my name. 16 (Yes,
I also baptized
the household of
Stephanas; be-
yond that, I don't
remember if I bap-
tized anyone else.)
17 For Christ did not
send me to bap-
tize, but to preach
the gospel — not
with wisdom and
eloquence, lest

[a] 10 The Greek word for *brothers and sisters* (*adelphoi*) refers here to believers, both men and women, as part of God's family; also in verses 11 and 26; and in 2:1; 3:1; 4:6; 6:8; 7:24, 29; 10:1; 11:33; 12:1; 14:6, 20, 26, 39; 15:1, 6, 50, 58; 16:15, 20.

[b] 12 That is, Peter

υἱοῦ αὐτοῦ Ἰησοῦ Χριστοῦ τοῦ κυρίου ἡμῶν. 10 παρακαλῶ δὲ ὑμᾶς, ἀδελφοί,
Son, *his* Jesus Christ *{the}* our Lord. *our* I appeal to *{and}* you, brothers,
5626 899 2652 5986 3836 7005 3261 7005 4151 1254 7007 81
n.gsm r.gsm.3 n.gsm n.gsm d.gsm n.gsm r.gp.1 v.pai.1s cj r.ap.2 n.vpm

διὰ τοῦ ὀνόματος τοῦ κυρίου ἡμῶν Ἰησοῦ Χριστοῦ, ἵνα →
by the name of our Lord *our* Jesus Christ, that you all
1328 3836 3950 3836 7005 3261 7005 2652 5986 2671 4246
p.g d.gsn n.gsn d.gsm n.gsm r.gp.1 n.gsm n.gsm cj

⌊τὸ αὐτὸ λέγητε⌋ πάντες καὶ μὴ ᾖ ἐν ὑμῖν
come to agreement *all* and that there be no *there be* divisions among you,
3836 899 3306 4246 2779 1639 1639 3590 1639 5388 1877 7007
d.asn r.asn v.pas.2p a.npm cj pl v.pas.3s p.d r.dp.2

σχίσματα, ἦτε δὲ κατηρτισμένοι ἐν τῷ αὐτῷ νοῒ καὶ ἐν
divisions but that ⌊you be⌋ *but* united in the same ⌊frame of mind⌋ and *{in}*
5388 1254 1639 1254 2936 1877 3836 899 3808 2779 1877
n.npn v.pas.2p cj pt.rp.npm p.d d.dsm r.dsm n.dsm cj p.d

τῇ αὐτῇ γνώμῃ. 11 ἐδηλώθη γάρ μοι περὶ ὑμῶν, ἀδελφοί μου, ὑπὸ
the same judgment. For ⌊it has been reported⌋ *For* to me *{about}* *{you}* *brothers* *my* by
3836 899 1191 1142 1317 1142 1609 4309 7007 81 1609 5679
d.dsf r.dsf n.dsf v.api.3s cj r.ds.1 p.g r.gp.2 n.vpm r.gs.1 p.g

τῶν Χλόης ὅτι ἔριδες ἐν ὑμῖν εἰσιν.
members of Chloe's household that there are quarrels among you, *there are* my brothers.
3836 5951 4022 1639 1639 2251 1877 7007 1639 1609 81
d.gpm n.gsf cj n.npf p.d r.dp.2 v.pai.3p

12 λέγω δὲ τοῦτο ὅτι ἕκαστος ὑμῶν λέγει, ἐγὼ μέν εἰμι Παύλου,
What I mean *{and}* is this: ~ each of you is saying, "I ~ am with Paul," or,
3306 1254 4047 4022 1667 7007 3306 1609 3525 1639 4263 1254
v.pai.1s cj r.asn cj r.nsm r.gp.2 v.pai.3s r.ns.1 pl v.pai.1s n.gsm

ἐγὼ δὲ Ἀπολλῶ, ἐγὼ δὲ Κηφᾶ, ἐγὼ δὲ Χριστοῦ.
"I *or* am with Apollos," or, "I *or* am with Cephas," or, "I *or* am with Christ."
1609 1254 663 1254 1609 1254 3064 1254 1609 1254 5986
r.ns.1 cj n.gsm r.ns.1 cj n.gsm r.ns.1 cj n.gsm

13 → μεμέρισται ὁ Χριστός; μὴ ↱ Παῦλος ἐσταυρώθη ὑπὲρ ὑμῶν, ἢ
Has Christ been divided? *{the}* *Christ* *{not}* Was Paul crucified for you? Or
5986 3532 3836 5986 3590 5090 4263 5090 5642 7007 2445
v.rpi.3s d.nsm n.nsm pl n.nsm v.api.3s p.g r.gp.2 cj

εἰς τὸ ὄνομα Παύλου ἐβαπτίσθητε; 14 εὐχαριστῶ [a] τῷ θεῷ ὅτι
were you baptized in the name of Paul? *were you baptized* I thank *{the}* God that
966 966 966 1650 3836 3950 4263 966 2373 3836 2536 4022
p.a d.asn n.asn n.gsm v.api.2p v.pai.1s d.dsm n.dsm cj

→ οὐδένα ὑμῶν ἐβάπτισα ⌊εἰ μή⌋ Κρίσπον καὶ Γάϊον, 15 ἵνα μή
I did not baptize any of you *I did baptize* except Crispus and Gaius, so that no
966 966 966 4029 7007 966 1623 3590 3214 2779 1127 2671 3590
a.asm r.gp.2 v.aai.1s cj pl n.asm cj n.asm cj pl

τις εἴπῃ ὅτι εἰς τὸ ἐμὸν ὄνομα ἐβαπτίσθητε. 16 →
one can say that you were baptized in *{the}* my name. *you were baptized* (I also
5516 3306 4022 966 966 966 1650 3836 1847 3950 966 2779
r.nsm v.aas.3s cj p.a d.asn r.asn.1 n.asn v.api.2p

ἐβάπτισα δὲ καὶ τὸν Στεφανᾶ οἶκον, λοιπὸν ↱ ↱ οὐκ οἶδα
baptized *{and}* *also* the household of Stephanas; *household* ⌊beyond that⌋ I do not know
966 1254 2779 3836 3875 5107 3875 3370 3857 3857 4024 3857
v.aai.1s cj adv d.asm n.gsm n.asm adv pl v.rai.1s

εἴ τινα ἄλλον ἐβάπτισα. 17 ↱ οὐ γὰρ ἀπέστειλέν με
if I baptized anyone else.) *I baptized* For Christ did not *For* send me
1623 966 966 5516 257 966 1142 5986 690 4024 1142 690 1609
cj r.asm r.asm v.aai.1s pl cj v.aai.3s r.as.1

Χριστὸς βαπτίζειν ἀλλὰ εὐαγγελίζεσθαι, οὐκ ἐν σοφίᾳ λόγου, ⌊ἵνα
Christ to baptize but to preach the gospel, and not with eloquent wisdom, *eloquent* lest
5986 966 247 2294 4024 1877 3364 5053 3364 2671
n.nsm f.pa cj f.pm pl p.d n.dsf n.gsm cj

μὴ⌋ κενωθῇ ὁ σταυρὸς τοῦ Χριστοῦ. 18 ὁ
the cross of Christ ⌊be rendered ineffective.⌋ *the* *cross* *of* *Christ* For the
3590 3836 5089 3836 5986 3033 3836 5089 3836 5986 1142 3836
pl v.aps.3s d.nsm n.nsm d.gsm n.gsm d.nsm

[a] [τῷ θεῷ] UBS.

NASB

Jesus Christ our
Lord.
10 Now I exhort
you, brethren, by
the name of our
Lord Jesus Christ,
that you all agree
and that there be
no divisions among
you, but that you
be made complete
in the same mind
and in the same
judgment. 11 For
I have been in-
formed concerning
you, my brethren,
by Chloe's *people,*
that there are quar-
rels among you.
12 Now I mean this,
that each one of
you is saying, "I
am of Paul," and
"I of Apollos," and
"I of Cephas," and
"I of Christ." 13 Has
Christ been divid-
ed? Paul was not
crucified for you,
was he? Or were
you baptized in the
name of Paul? 14[a] I
thank God that I
baptized none of
you except Crispus
and Gaius, 15 so that
no one would say
you were baptized
in my name. 16 Now
I did baptize also
the household of
Stephanas; beyond
that, I do not know
whether I baptized
any other. 17 For
Christ did not send
me to baptize,
but to preach the
gospel, not in clev-
erness of speech,
so that the cross of
Christ would not
be made void.

[a] Two early mss read *I give thanks that*

NIV

the cross of Christ
be emptied of its
power.

Christ Crucified Is God's Power and Wisdom

18 For the message
of the cross is fool-
ishness to those
who are perishing,
but to us who are
being saved it is
the power of God.
19 For it is written:

"I will destroy
the wisdom
of the wise;
the
intelligence
of the
intelligent
I will
frustrate."[a]

20 Where is the
wise person?
Where is the
teacher of the law?
Where is the phi-
losopher of this
age? Has not God
made foolish the
wisdom of the
world? 21 For since
in the wisdom of
God the world
through its wis-
dom did not know
him, God was
pleased through
the foolishness of
what was preached
to save those who
believe. 22 Jews
demand signs
and Greeks look
for wisdom, 23 but
we preach Christ
crucified: a stum-
bling block to Jews
and foolishness to
Gentiles, 24 but to
those whom God
has called, both
Jews and Greeks,
Christ the power
of God and the
wisdom of God.
25 For the foolish-
ness of God is
wiser than human
wisdom, and the
weakness of God
is stronger than
human strength.
26 Brothers and
sisters, think of
what you were
when you were

[a] 19 Isaiah 29:14

λόγος γὰρ ὁ τοῦ σταυροῦ τοῖς μὲν ἀπολλυμένοις μωρία
message *For* *{the}* of the cross is foolishness to those ~ who are perishing, *foolishness*
3364 1142 3836 3836 5089 1639 3702 3836 3525 660 3702
n.nsm cj d.nsm d.gsm n.gsm d.dpm pl pt.pm.dpm n.nsf

ἐστίν, τοῖς δὲ σῳζομένοις ἡμῖν δύναμις θεοῦ ἐστιν.
is but to us *but* ⌊who are being saved⌋ *us* it is the power of God. *it is*
1639 1254 3836 7005 1254 5392 7005 1639 1639 1539 2536 1639
v.pai.3s d.dpm cj pt.pp.dpm r.dp.1 n.nsf n.gsm v.pai.3s

19 γέγραπται γάρ, ἀπολῶ τὴν σοφίαν τῶν σοφῶν καὶ τὴν σύνεσιν τῶν
For it is written, *For* "I will destroy the wisdom of the wise, and the shrewdness of the
1142 1211 1142 660 3836 5053 3836 5055 2779 3836 5304 3836
v.rpi.3s cj v.fai.1s d.asf n.asf d.gpm a.gpm cj d.asf n.asf d.gpm

συνετῶν ἀθετήσω. 20 ποῦ σοφός; ποῦ γραμματεύς; ποῦ
intelligent I will thwart." Where is the wise person? Where is the scholar? Where is the
5305 119 4543 5055 4543 1208 4543
a.gpm v.fai.1s cj a.nsm cj n.nsm cj

συζητητὴς τοῦ αἰῶνος τούτου; ↱ οὐχὶ ἐμώρανεν ὁ θεὸς τὴν σοφίαν
brilliant debater of this age? *this* Has not God made foolish *{the}* *God* the wisdom
5186 3836 4047 172 4047 3701 4049 2536 3701 3836 2536 3836 5053
n.nsm d.gsm n.gsm r.gsm pl v.aai.3s d.nsm n.nsm d.asf n.asf

τοῦ κόσμου; 21 ἐπειδὴ γὰρ ἐν τῇ σοφίᾳ τοῦ θεοῦ ↱ οὐκ
of the world? For since *For* in the wisdom of God the world did not
3836 3180 1142 2076 1142 1877 3836 5053 3836 2536 3836 3180 1182 4024
d.gsm n.gsm cj cj p.d d.dsf n.dsf d.gsm n.gsm pl

ἔγνω ὁ κόσμος διὰ τῆς σοφίας τὸν θεόν, εὐδόκησεν ὁ θεὸς
⌊come to know⌋ *the* *world* God through *{the}* wisdom, *{the}* *God* God was pleased *{the}* *God*
1182 3836 3180 2536 1328 3836 5053 3836 2536 2536 2305 3836 2536
v.aai.3s d.nsm n.nsm p.g d.gsf n.gsf d.asm n.asm v.aai.3s d.nsm n.nsm

διὰ τῆς μωρίας τοῦ κηρύγματος σῶσαι τοὺς πιστεύοντας· 22 ἐπειδὴ καὶ
through the foolishness of what we preach to save those who believe. For *{and}*
1328 3836 3702 3836 3060 5392 3836 4409 2076 2779
p.g d.gsf n.gsf d.gsn n.gsn f.aa d.apm pt.pa.apm cj cj

Ἰουδαῖοι σημεῖα αἰτοῦσιν καὶ Ἕλληνες σοφίαν ζητοῦσιν,
Jews demand signs *demand* and Greeks are looking for wisdom, *are looking for*
2681 160 4956 160 2779 1818 2426 2426 2426 5053 2426
a.npm n.apn v.pai.3p cj n.npm n.asf v.pai.3p

23 ἡμεῖς δὲ κηρύσσομεν Χριστὸν ἐσταυρωμένον, Ἰουδαίοις μὲν
but we *but* preach Christ crucified, a stumbling block to Jews ~
1254 7005 1254 3062 5986 5090 4998 4998 2681 3525
r.np.1 cj v.pai.1p n.asm pt.rp.asm a.dpm pl

σκάνδαλον, ἔθνεσιν δὲ μωρίαν, 24 αὐτοῖς δὲ τοῖς κλητοῖς,
stumbling block and foolishness to Gentiles. *and* *foolishness* Yet to those *Yet* who are called,
4998 1254 3702 1620 1254 3702 1254 899 1254 3836 3105
n.asn n.dpn cj n.asf r.dpm.3 cj d.dpm a.dpm

Ἰουδαίοις τε καὶ Ἕλλησιν, Χριστὸν θεοῦ δύναμιν καὶ
both Jews *both* and Greeks, Christ is the power of God *power* and the wisdom
5445 2681 5445 2779 1818 5986 1539 2536 1539 2779 5053
a.dpm cj cj n.dpm n.asm n.gsm n.asf cj

θεοῦ σοφίαν· 25 ὅτι τὸ μωρὸν τοῦ θεοῦ σοφώτερον → τῶν
of God. *wisdom* For the foolishness of God is wiser than the wisdom of
2536 5053 4022 3836 3704 3836 2536 1639 5055 3836
n.gsm n.asf cj d.nsn a.nsn d.gsm n.gsm a.nsn.c d.gpm

ἀνθρώπων ἐστὶν καὶ τὸ ἀσθενὲς τοῦ θεοῦ ἰσχυρότερον → τῶν
men, *is* and the weakness of God is stronger than the strength of
476 1639 2779 3836 822 3836 2536 2708 3836
n.gpm v.pai.3s cj d.nsn a.nsn d.gsm n.gsm a.nsn.c d.gpm

ἀνθρώπων. 26 βλέπετε γὰρ τὴν κλῆσιν ὑμῶν, ἀδελφοί, ὅτι
men. Consider *{for}* *{the}* your calling, *your* brothers: ~ according to worldly
476 1063 1142 3836 7007 3104 7007 81 4022 2848 2848 4922
n.gpm v.pai.2p cj d.asf n.asf r.gp.2 n.vpm cj

οὐ πολλοὶ σοφοὶ κατὰ σάρκα, οὐ πολλοὶ
standards, not many of you were wise, *according to* *worldly standards* not many were
4922 4024 4498 5055 2848 4922 4024 4498
pl a.npm a.npm p.a n.asf pl a.npm

NASB

The Wisdom of God

18 For the word of
the cross is foolish-
ness to those who
are perishing, but
to us who are being
saved it is the pow-
er of God. 19 For it
is written,

"I WILL DESTROY
THE WISDOM
OF THE WISE,
AND THE CLEV-
ERNESS OF THE
CLEVER I WILL
SET ASIDE."

20 Where is the wise
man? Where is
the scribe? Where
is the debater of
this age? Has not
God made foolish
the wisdom of the
world? 21 For since
in the wisdom of
God the world
through its wisdom
did not *come to*
know God, God
was well-pleased
through the fool-
ishness of the mes-
sage preached to
save those who be-
lieve. 22 For indeed
Jews ask for signs
and Greeks search
for wisdom; 23 but
we preach [a]Christ
crucified, to Jews
a stumbling block
and to Gentiles
foolishness, 24 but to
those who are the
called, both Jews
and Greeks, Christ
the power of God
and the wisdom of
God. 25 Because the
foolishness of God
is wiser than men,
and the weakness
of God is stronger
than men.
26 For consider
your calling, breth-
ren, that there were
not many wise
according to the
flesh, not many

[a] I.e. Messiah

NIV

called. Not many
of you were wise
by human stan-
dards; not many
were influential;
not many were
of noble birth.
[27]But God chose
the foolish things
of the world to
shame the wise;
God chose the
weak things of the
world to shame
the strong. [28]God
chose the low-
ly things of this
world and the
despised things—
and the things
that are not—to
nullify the things
that are, [29]so that
no one may boast
before him. [30]It
is because of him
that you are in
Christ Jesus, who
has become for
us wisdom from
God—that is, our
righteousness, ho-
liness and redemp-
tion. [31]Therefore,
as it is written:
"Let the one who
boasts boast in the
Lord."[a]

2 And so it
was with me,
brothers and sis-
ters. When I came
to you, I did not
come with elo-
quence or human
wisdom as I pro-
claimed to you the
testimony about
God.[b] [2]For I re-
solved to know
nothing while I
was with you ex-
cept Jesus Christ
and him crucified.
[3]I came to you in
weakness with
great fear and
trembling. [4]My
message and my

[a] 31 Jer. 9:24
[b] 1 Some manu-
scripts *proclaimed to*
you God's mystery

δυνατοί, οὐ πολλοὶ εὐγενεῖς· [27] ἀλλὰ τὰ μωρὰ τοῦ
influential, not many were of noble birth. But God chose the ⌊foolish things⌋ of the
1543 4024 4498 2302 247 2536 1721 3836 3704 3836
a.npm pl a.npm a.npm cj d.apn a.apn d.gsm

κόσμου ἐξελέξατο ὁ θεός, ἵνα καταισχύνῃ τοὺς σοφούς, καὶ τὰ
world *chose* *{the}* *God* to shame the wise; *{and}* God chose the
3180 1721 3836 2536 2671 2875 3836 5055 2779 2536 1721 3836
n.gsm v.ami.3s d.nsm n.nsm cj v.pas.3s d.apm a.apm cj d.apn

ἀσθενῆ τοῦ κόσμου ἐξελέξατο ὁ θεός, ἵνα καταισχύνῃ τὰ ἰσχυρά, [28] καὶ
weak things of the world *chose* *{the}* *God* to shame the strong; *{and}*
822 3836 3180 1721 3836 2536 2671 2875 3836 2708 2779
a.apn d.gsm n.gsm v.ami.3s d.nsm n.nsm cj v.pas.3s d.apn a.apn cj

τὰ → ἀγενῆ τοῦ κόσμου καὶ τὰ
God chose the things that the world considers insignificant *the* *world* and *{the}*
2536 1721 3836 3836 3180 38 3836 3180 2779 3836
d.apn a.apn d.gsm n.gsm cj d.apn

ἐξουθενημένα ἐξελέξατο ὁ θεός, τὰ μὴ ὄντα, ἵνα
contemptible, *chose* *{the}* *God* what is regarded as nothing, *is regarded* to render
2024 1721 3836 2536 3836 1639 1639 3590 1639 2671 2934
pt.rp.apn v.ami.3s d.nsm n.nsm d.apn pl pt.pa.apn cj

τὰ ὄντα καταργήσῃ, [29] ὅπως μὴ καυχήσηται ⌊πᾶσα σὰρξ⌋
useless the ⌊things that are,⌋ *render useless* so that no one can boast *one*
2934 3836 1639 2934 3968 3590 4246 3016 4246 4922
d.apn pt.pa.apn v.aas.3s cj pl v.ams.3s a.nsf n.nsf

ἐνώπιον τοῦ θεοῦ. [30] ἐξ αὐτοῦ δὲ ὑμεῖς ἐστε ἐν Χριστῷ
in the presence of God. But you are of him *But* *you* *are* in Christ
1967 3836 2536 1254 7007 1639 1666 899 1254 7007 1639 1877 5986
p.g d.gsm n.gsm p.g r.gsm.3 cj r.np.2 v.pai.2p p.d n.dsm

Ἰησοῦ, ὃς ἐγενήθη σοφία ἡμῖν ἀπὸ θεοῦ, δικαιοσύνη τε καὶ
Jesus, who became for us wisdom *for us* from God, and righteousness *and* and
2652 4005 1181 7005 7005 5053 7005 608 2536 5445 1466 5445 2779
n.dsm r.nsm v.api.3s n.nsf r.dp.1 p.g n.gsm n.nsf cj cj

ἁγιασμὸς καὶ ἀπολύτρωσις, [31] ἵνα καθὼς γέγραπται, ὁ καυχώμενος
sanctification and redemption, so that, as it is written, "Let the one who boasts, boast
40 2779 667 2671 2777 1211 3016 3836 3016 3016
n.nsm cj n.nsf cj cj v.rpi.3s d.nsm pt.pm.nsm

ἐν κυρίῳ καυχάσθω.
in the Lord." *Let boast*
1877 3261 3016
p.d n.dsm v.pmm.3s

2:1 ↱ κἀγὼ ἐλθὼν πρὸς ὑμᾶς, ἀδελφοί, → → ἦλθον οὐ καθ' ὑπεροχὴν
When I came to you, brothers, I did not come *not* with excellence
2262 2743 2262 4639 7007 81 4024 2262 4024 2848 5667
crasis pt.aa.nsm p.a r.ap.2 n.vpm v.aai.1s pl p.a n.asf

λόγου ἢ σοφίας καταγγέλλων ὑμῖν ↰ τὸ μαρτύριον[a] τοῦ θεοῦ. [2] οὐ γὰρ
of speech or of wisdom as I told you about the secret purpose of God. *{not}* For
3364 2445 5053 2859 7007 2859 3836 3457 3836 2536 4024 1142
n.gsm cj n.gsf pt.pa.nsm r.dp.2 d.asn n.asn d.gsm n.gsm pl cj

ἔκρινά τι εἰδέναι ἐν ὑμῖν ⌊εἰ μὴ⌋ Ἰησοῦν Χριστὸν καὶ
I had decided to know nothing *to know* among you except Jesus Christ and
3212 3857 3857 5516 3857 1877 7007 1623 3590 2652 5986 2779
v.aai.1s r.asn f.ra p.d r.dp.2 cj pl n.asm n.asm cj

τοῦτον ἐσταυρωμένον. [3] κἀγὼ ἐν ἀσθενείᾳ καὶ ἐν φόβῳ καὶ ἐν
him crucified. So I came to you in weakness and *{in}* fear, and with
4047 5090 2743 1181 4639 7007 1877 819 2779 1877 5832 2779 1877
r.asm pt.rp.asm crasis p.d n.dsf cj p.d n.dsm cj p.d

τρόμῳ πολλῷ ἐγενόμην πρὸς ὑμᾶς, [4] καὶ ὁ λόγος μου καὶ τὸ
much trembling. *much* *came* *to* *you* *{and}* *{the}* My word *My* and *{the}* my
4498 5571 4498 1181 4639 7007 2779 3836 1609 3364 1609 2779 3836 1609
n.dsm a.dsm v.ami.1s p.a r.ap.2 cj d.nsm n.nsm r.gs.1 cj d.nsn

[a] μαρτύριον TNIV, NET. μυστήριον UBS.

NASB

mighty, not many
noble; [27]but God
has chosen the
foolish things of
the world to shame
the wise, and God
has chosen the
weak things of the
world to shame
the things which
are strong, [28]and
the base things
of the world and
the despised God
has chosen, the
things that are not,
so that He may
nullify the things
that are, [29]so that
no man may boast
before God. [30]But
by His doing you
are in Christ Jesus,
who became to us
wisdom from God,
and righteousness
and sanctification,
and redemption,
[31]so that, just as it
is written, "LET HIM
WHO BOASTS, BOAST
IN THE LORD."

Paul's Reliance upon the Spirit

[2:1]And when
I came to you,
brethren, I did not
come with superi-
ority of speech or
of wisdom, pro-
claiming to you the
[a]testimony of God.
[2]For I determined
to know nothing
among you except
Jesus Christ, and
Him crucified. [3]I
was with you in
weakness and in
fear and in much
trembling, [4]and my
message and my

[a] One early ms reads *mystery*

NIV

preaching were not
with wise and per-
suasive words, but
with a demonstra-
tion of the Spirit's
power, [5]so that
your faith might
not rest on human
wisdom, but on
God's power.

God's Wisdom Revealed by the Spirit

[6]We do, however,
speak a message of
wisdom among the
mature, but not the
wisdom of this age
or of the rulers of
this age, who are
coming to nothing.
[7]No, we declare
God's wisdom, a
mystery that has
been hidden and
that God destined
for our glory be-
fore time began.
[8]None of the rulers
of this age under-
stood it, for if they
had, they would
not have crucified
the Lord of glory.
[9]However, as it is
written:

"What no eye
has seen,
what no ear
has heard,
and what
no human
mind
has conceived"[a]—
the things
God has
prepared
for those
who love
him—

[10]these are the
things God has re-
vealed to us by his
Spirit.
The Spirit search-
es all things, even
the deep things of
God. [11]For who
knows a person's
thoughts except
their own

κήρυγμά μου οὐκ ἐν πειθοῖς[a] σοφίας λόγοις[b] ἀλλ᾽ ἐν
message *my* were not delivered with persuasive words of wisdom, *words* but with a
3060 1609 4024 1877 4273 3364 5053 3364 247 1877
n.nsn r.gs.1 pl p.d a.dpm n.gsf n.dpm cj p.d

ἀποδείξει → πνεύματος καὶ δυνάμεως, [5]ἵνα ἡ πίστις ὑμῶν ↱ μὴ
demonstration of the Spirit and of power, so that *{the}* your faith *your* would not
618 4460 2779 1539 2671 3836 7007 4411 7007 1639 3590
n.dsf n.gsn cj n.gsf cj d.nsf n.nsf r.gp.2 pl

ᾖ ἐν σοφίᾳ ἀνθρώπων ἀλλ᾽ ἐν δυνάμει θεοῦ. [6]
⌊be based⌋ on the wisdom of men but on the power of God. However, we do
1639 1877 5053 476 247 1877 1539 2536 1254 3281 3281
v.pas.3s p.d n.dsf n.gpm cj p.d n.dsf n.gsm

σοφίαν δὲ λαλοῦμεν ἐν τοῖς τελείοις, σοφίαν
speak wisdom *However* *we do speak* among those who are mature, although it is not the wisdom
3281 5053 1254 3281 1877 3836 5455 1254 4024 5053
n.asf cj v.pai.1p p.d d.dpm a.dpm n.asf

δὲ οὐ τοῦ αἰῶνος τούτου οὐδὲ τῶν ἀρχόντων τοῦ αἰῶνος τούτου
although not of this age *this* or of the rulers of this age, *this*
1254 4024 3836 4047 172 4047 4028 3836 807 3836 4047 172 4047
cj pl d.gsm n.gsm r.gsm cj d.gpm n.gpm d.gsm n.gsm r.gsm

τῶν καταργουμένων· [7]ἀλλὰ λαλοῦμεν θεοῦ σοφίαν
who are doomed to perish. Rather, we speak the wisdom of God; *wisdom* a wisdom that was
3836 2934 247 3281 5053 2536 5053 3836 648
d.gpm pt.pp.gpm cj v.pai.1p n.gsm n.asf

ἐν μυστηρίῳ τὴν ἀποκεκρυμμένην, ἣν προώρισεν ὁ θεὸς πρὸ
hidden in mystery *that was hidden* and that God had determined *{the} God* before
648 1877 3696 3836 648 4005 2536 4633 3836 2536 4574
p.d n.dsn d.asf pt.rp.asf r.asf v.aai.3s d.nsm n.nsm p.g

τῶν αἰώνων εἰς δόξαν ἡμῶν. [8]ἣν οὐδεὶς τῶν ἀρχόντων τοῦ αἰῶνος
the ages for our glory. *our* *it* None of the rulers of this age
3836 172 1650 7005 1518 7005 4005 4029 3836 807 3836 4047 172
d.gpm n.gpm p.a n.asf r.gp.1 r.asf a.nsm d.gpm n.gpm d.gsm n.gsm

τούτου ἔγνωκεν· εἰ γὰρ ἔγνωσαν, οὐκ ἂν τὸν
this understood it, for if *for* they had, they would not *would* have crucified the
4047 1182 4005 1142 1623 1142 1182 5090 323 4024 323 5090 5090 3836
r.gsm v.rai.3s cj cj v.aai.3p pl pl d.asm

κύριον τῆς δόξης ἐσταύρωσαν. [9]ἀλλὰ καθὼς γέγραπται, ἃ ὀφθαλμὸς οὐκ
Lord of glory. *they have crucified* But, as it is written, *{that}* "No eye *No*
3261 3836 1518 5090 247 2777 1211 4005 4024 4057 4024
n.asm d.gsf n.gsf v.aai.3p cj cj v.rpi.3s r.apn n.nsm pl

εἶδεν καὶ οὖς οὐκ ἤκουσεν καὶ ἐπὶ ↱ καρδίαν ἀνθρώπου οὐκ
has seen, *{and}* no ear *no* has heard, *{and}* nor *{to}* has the mind of man *nor*
1625 2779 4024 4044 4024 201 2779 4024 2093 326 2840 476 4024
v.aai.3s cj n.nsn pl v.aai.3s cj p.a n.asf n.gsm pl

ἀνέβη, ἃ ἡτοίμασεν ὁ θεὸς τοῖς ἀγαπῶσιν αὐτόν. [10]
imagined, the ⌊things that⌋ God has prepared *{the} God* for those who love him." But God
326 4005 2536 2286 3836 2536 3836 26 899 1254 2536
v.aai.3s r.apn v.aai.3s d.nsm n.nsm d.dpm pt.pa.dpm r.asm.3

ἡμῖν δὲ[c] ἀπεκάλυψεν ὁ θεὸς διὰ τοῦ πνεύματος· τὸ γὰρ
has revealed them to us *But* *has revealed* *{the} God* through his Spirit; for the *for*
636 636 7005 1254 636 3836 2536 1328 3836 4460 1142 3836 1142
r.dp.1 cj v.aai.3s d.nsm n.nsm p.g d.gsn n.gsn d.nsn cj

πνεῦμα πάντα ἐραυνᾷ, καὶ τὰ βάθη τοῦ θεοῦ. [11] τίς γὰρ
Spirit searches everything, *searches* even the ⌊deep things⌋ of God. For who *For*
4460 2236 4246 2236 2779 3836 958 3836 2536 1142 5515 1142
n.nsn a.apn v.pai.3s cj d.apn n.apn d.gsm n.gsm r.nsm cj

οἶδεν ἀνθρώπων τὰ τοῦ ἀνθρώπου ⌊εἰ μὴ⌋ τὸ
among men can know *among men* the thoughts of a man except the man's own
476 476 3857 476 3836 3836 476 1623 3590 3836 476 476
v.rai.3s n.gpm d.apn d.gsm n.gsm cj pl d.nsn

NASB

preaching were
not in persuasive
words of wisdom,
but in demonstra-
tion of the Spirit
and of power, [5]so
that your faith
would not rest on
the wisdom of
men, but on the
power of God.
[6]Yet we do speak
wisdom among
those who are
mature; a wisdom,
however, not of
this age nor of the
rulers of this age,
who are passing
away; [7]but we
speak God's wis-
dom in a mystery,
the hidden *wisdom*
which God pre-
destined before the
ages to our glory;
[8]*the wisdom* which
none of the rul-
ers of this age has
understood; for if
they had under-
stood it they would
not have crucified
the Lord of glory;
[9]but just as it is
written,

"Things which
eye has not
seen and
ear has not
heard,
And *which*
have not
entered the
heart of man,
All that God
has prepared
for those
who love
Him."

[10a]For to us God
revealed *them*
through the
Spirit; for the Spirit
searches all things,
even the depths
of God. [11]For who
among men knows
the *thoughts* of a
man except the

[a] πειθοῖς TNIV, NET. πειθοῖ[ς] UBS.
[b] [λόγοις] UBS.
[c] δὲ UBS, NET. γὰρ TNIV.

[a] 9 Isaiah 64:4

[a] One early ms reads *But*

NIV

spirit within them?
In the same way
no one knows the
thoughts of God
except the Spirit
of God. 12 What
we have received
is not the spirit of
the world, but the
Spirit who is from
God, so that we
may understand
what God has free-
ly given us. 13 This
is what we speak,
not in words taught
us by human wis-
dom but in words
taught by the
Spirit, explaining
spiritual realities
with Spirit-taught
words.[a] 14 The per-
son without the
Spirit does not
accept the things
that come from
the Spirit of God
but considers them
foolishness, and
cannot understand
them because they
are discerned only
through the Spirit.
15 The person with
the Spirit makes
judgments about
all things, but such
a person is not
subject to merely
human judgments,
16 for,

"Who has known the mind of the Lord
so as to instruct him?"[b]

But we have the mind of Christ.

The Church and Its Leaders

3 Brothers and
sisters, I could
not address you
as people who
live by the Spirit
but as people who
are still world-
ly—mere infants
in Christ. 2 I gave
you milk, not solid
food, for you were
not yet ready for it.
Indeed, you

[a] 13 Or *Spirit, interpreting spiritual truths to those who are spiritual*
[b] 16 Isaiah 40:13

πνεῦμα τοῦ ἀνθρώπου τὸ ἐν αὐτῷ; οὕτως καὶ
spirit *{the}* *man's own* that is in him? ⌞In the same way,⌟ *{also}* no one can understand
4460 3836 476 3836 1877 899 4048 2779 4029 4029 1182 1182
n.nsn d.gsm n.gsm d.nsn p.d r.dsm.3 adv adv

τὰ τοῦ θεοῦ οὐδεὶς ἔγνωκεν ⌞εἰ μὴ⌟ τὸ πνεῦμα τοῦ θεοῦ. 12 ἡμεῖς
the thoughts of God *no one* *can understand* except the Spirit of God. *we*
3836 3836 2536 4029 1182 1623 3590 3836 4460 3836 2536 7005
d.apn d.gsm n.gsm a.nsm v.rai.3s cj pl d.nsn n.nsn d.gsm n.gsm r.np.1

δὲ οὐ τὸ πνεῦμα τοῦ κόσμου ἐλάβομεν ἀλλὰ τὸ πνεῦμα τὸ
{and} It was not the spirit of the world that we received, but the Spirit *{the}* sent
1254 4024 3836 4460 3836 3180 7005 3284 247 3836 4460 3836
cj pl d.asn n.asn d.gsm n.gsm v.aai.1p cj d.asn n.asn d.asn

ἐκ τοῦ θεοῦ, ἵνα εἰδῶμεν τὰ ὑπὸ τοῦ θεοῦ
from *{the}* God, that ⌞we might understand⌟ the gifts freely given to us by *{the}* God.
1666 3836 2536 2671 3857 3836 5919 5919 5919 7005 7005 5679 3836 2536
p.g d.gsm n.gsm cj v.ras.1p d.apn p.g d.gsm n.gsm

χαρισθέντα ἡμῖν· 13 ἃ καὶ λαλοῦμεν οὐκ
gifts freely given *to us* And we speak about ⌞these things⌟ *And* *we speak about* in words not
5919 7005 2779 3281 3281 3281 4005 2779 3281 1877 3364 4024
pt.ap.apn r.dp.1 r.apn adv v.pai.1p pl

ἐν διδακτοῖς ἀνθρωπίνης σοφίας λόγοις ἀλλ᾽ ἐν διδακτοῖς → πνεύματος,
in taught by human wisdom *words* but *{in}* taught by the Spirit,
1877 1435 474 5053 3364 247 1877 1435 4460
p.d a.dpm a.gsf n.gsf n.dpm cj p.d a.dpm n.gsn

πνευματικοῖς πνευματικὰ συγκρίνοντες. 14 ψυχικὸς δὲ
expressing spiritual truths in spiritual words. *spiritual truths* *expressing* The natural *{and}*
5173 4461 4461 4461 4461 5173 6035 1254
a.dpn a.apn pt.pa.npm a.nsm cj

ἄνθρωπος ↱ οὐ δέχεται τὰ τοῦ πνεύματος τοῦ θεοῦ,
man does not receive the things of the Spirit of God, for they are
476 1312 4024 1312 3836 3836 4460 3836 2536 1142 1639 1639
n.nsm pl v.pmi.3s d.apn d.gsn n.gsn d.gsm n.gsm

μωρία γὰρ αὐτῷ ἐστιν καὶ ⌞οὐ δύναται⌟ γνῶναι, ὅτι ↱ ↱
foolishness *for* to him; *they are* *{and}* he cannot understand them because they are
3702 1142 899 1639 2779 4024 1538 1182 4022 373 373
n.nsf cj r.dsm.3 v.pai.3s cj pl v.ppi.3s f.aa cj

πνευματικῶς ἀνακρίνεται. 15 ὁ δὲ πνευματικὸς ἀνακρίνει τὰ[a] πάντα,
spiritually discerned. But the *But* spiritual person discerns *{the}* all things, and
4462 373 1254 3836 1254 4461 373 3836 4246 1254
adv v.ppi.3s d.nsm cj a.nsm v.pai.3s d.apn a.apn

↱ ↱ αὐτὸς δὲ ↱ ὑπ᾽ οὐδενὸς ἀνακρίνεται. 16 τίς γὰρ ἔγνω
is not himself *and* subject to anyone's scrutiny. For, "Who *For* has known the
373 4029 899 1254 373 5679 4029 373 1142 5515 1142 1182
r.nsm cj p.g a.gsm v.ppi.3s r.nsm cj v.aai.3s

νοῦν → κυρίου, ὃς συμβιβάσει αὐτόν; ἡμεῖς δὲ νοῦν Χριστοῦ
mind of the Lord, *{who}* so as to advise him?" But we *But* have the mind of Christ.
3808 3261 4005 5204 899 1254 7005 1254 2400 3808 5986
n.asm n.gsm r.nsm v.fai.3s r.asm.3 r.np.1 cj n.asm n.gsm

ἔχομεν.
have
2400
v.pai.1p

3:1 κἀγώ, ἀδελφοί, ↰ οὐκ ἠδυνήθην λαλῆσαι ὑμῖν ὡς πνευματικοῖς
And so, brothers, I could not *could* speak to you as spiritual people,
2743 81 2743 1538 4024 1538 3281 7007 6055 4461
crasis n.vpm pl v.api.1s f.aa r.dp.2 pl a.dpm

ἀλλ᾽ ὡς σαρκίνοις, ὡς νηπίοις ἐν Χριστῷ. 2 γάλα ὑμᾶς
but rather as ⌞people of the flesh,⌟ as infants in Christ. I gave you milk, *you*
247 6055 4921 6055 3758 1877 5986 4540 4540 7007 1128 7007
cj pl a.dpm pl a.dpm p.d n.dsm n.asn r.ap.2

ἐπότισα, οὐ βρῶμα, ↱ ↱ οὔπω γὰρ ἐδύνασθε. ἀλλ᾽ → ↱ ↱
I gave not solid food, for you were not *for* ready for it. And even now you are
4540 4024 1109 1142 1538 1538 4037 1142 1538 247 3814 1538 1538
v.aai.1s pl n.asn adv cj v.ipi.2p cj

[a] τὰ UBS, NET. μὲν TNIV.

NASB

spirit of the man
which is in him?
Even so the
thoughts of God no
one knows except
the Spirit of God.
12 Now we have
received, not the
spirit of the world,
but the Spirit who
is from God, so
that we may know
the things freely
given to us by God,
13 which things we
also speak, not in
words taught by
human wisdom,
but in those taught
by the Spirit, com-
bining spiritual
thoughts with spiri-
tual *words.*
14 But a natural
man does not ac-
cept the things
of the Spirit of
God, for they are
foolishness to him;
and he cannot
understand them,
because they are
spiritually ap-
praised. 15 But he
who is spiritual ap-
praises all things,
yet he himself is
appraised by no
one. 16 For WHO HAS
KNOWN THE MIND OF
THE LORD, THAT HE
WILL INSTRUCT HIM?
But we have the
mind of Christ.

Foundations for Living

3:1 And I, brethren,
could not speak
to you as to spiri-
tual men, but as to
men of flesh, as to
infants in Christ.
2 I gave you milk
to drink, not solid
food; for you were
not yet able *to*
receive it. Indeed,
even now you are

NIV

are still not ready.
3You are still
worldly. For since
there is jealousy
and quarreling
among you, are
you not worldly?
Are you not acting
like mere humans?
4For when one
says, "I follow
Paul," and another,
"I follow Apollos,"
are you not mere
human beings?
5What, after all,
is Apollos? And
what is Paul? Only
servants, through
whom you came
to believe—as the
Lord has assigned
to each his task. 6I
planted the seed,
Apollos watered it,
but God has been
making it grow.
7So neither the one
who plants nor the
one who waters is
anything, but only
God, who makes
things grow. 8The
one who plants and
the one who wa-
ters have one pur-
pose, and they will
each be rewarded
according to their
own labor. 9For we
are co-workers in
God's service; you
are God's field,
God's building.
10By the grace
God has given me,
I laid a foundation
as a wise build-
er, and someone
else is building on
it. But each one
should build with
care. 11For no one
can lay any foun-
dation other than
the one already
laid, which is Jesus
Christ. 12If

οὐδὲ ἔτι νῦν δύνασθε, 3 ἔτι γὰρ σαρκικοί ἐστε. ὅπου γὰρ
not yet *now* ready, for you are still *for* of the flesh. *you are* For while *For* there is
4028 2285 3814 1538 1142 1639 1639 2285 1142 4920 1639 1142 3963 1142
adv adv adv v.ppi.2p adv cj a.npm v.pai.2p cj cj

ἐν ὑμῖν ζῆλος καὶ ἔρις, οὐχὶ σαρκικοί ἐστε καὶ
jealousy and strife among you, *jealousy and strife* are you not of the flesh *are you* and
2419 2779 2251 1877 7007 2419 2779 2251 1639 1639 4049 4920 1639 2779
p.d r.dp.2 n.nsm cj n.nsf pl a.npm v.pai.2p cj

κατὰ ἄνθρωπον περιπατεῖτε; 4 ὅταν γὰρ λέγῃ τις, ἐγὼ μέν εἰμι
behaving like mere men? *behaving* For when *For* one says, *one* "I ~ follow
4344 2848 476 4344 1142 4020 1142 5516 3306 5516 1609 3525 1639
p.a n.asm v.pai.2p cj cj v.pas.3s r.nsm r.ns.1 pl v.pai.1s

Παύλου, ἕτερος δέ, ἐγὼ Ἀπολλῶ, οὐκ ἄνθρωποί ἐστε;
Paul," and another, *and* "I follow Apollos," are you not like everyone else? *are you*
4263 1254 2283 1254 1609 663 1639 1639 4024 476 1639
n.gsm r.nsm pl r.ns.1 n.gsm pl n.npm v.pai.2p

5 Τί οὖν ἐστιν Ἀπολλῶς; τί δέ ἐστιν Παῦλος; διάκονοι δι' ὧν
What then is Apollos? What *{and}* is Paul? Servants through whom
5515 4036 1639 663 5515 1254 1639 4263 1356 1328 4005
r.nsn cj v.pai.3s n.nsm r.nsn cj v.pai.3s n.nsm n.npm p.g r.gpm

ἐπιστεύσατε, καὶ ἑκάστῳ ὡς ὁ κύριος ἔδωκεν.
you came to believe, even as the Lord assigned to each of us. *as the Lord assigned*
4409 2779 6055 3836 3261 1443 1667 6055 3836 3261 1443
v.aai.2p cj r.dsm cj d.nsm n.nsm v.aai.3s

6 ἐγὼ ἐφύτευσα, Ἀπολλῶς ἐπότισεν, ἀλλὰ ὁ θεὸς ηὔξανεν· 7 ὥστε
I planted, Apollos watered, but *{the}* God ⌊has been causing the growth.⌋ So
1609 5885 663 4540 247 3836 2536 889 6063
r.ns.1 v.aai.1s n.nsm v.aai.3s cj d.nsm n.nsm v.iai.3s cj

οὔτε ὁ φυτεύων ἐστίν τι οὔτε ὁ ποτίζων
neither the one who plants nor the one who waters is anything, *nor the one who waters*
4046 3836 5885 4046 3836 4540 4540 4540 1639 5516 4046 3836 4540
cj d.nsm pt.pa.nsm v.pai.3s r.nsn cj d.nsm pt.pa.nsm

ἀλλ' ὁ αὐξάνων θεός. 8 ὁ φυτεύων δὲ καὶ ὁ
but God is the ⌊one who gives the growth.⌋ *God* The one who plants *{and}* and the
247 2536 3836 889 2536 3836 5885 1254 2779 3836
cj d.nsm pt.pa.nsm n.nsm d.nsm pt.pa.nsm cj cj d.nsm

ποτίζων ἕν εἰσιν, ἕκαστος δὲ τὸν ἴδιον
⌊one who waters⌋ have a ⌊common purpose,⌋ *have* and each *and* will receive *{the}* his
4540 1639 1651 1639 1254 1667 1254 3284 3284 3836 2625
pt.pa.nsm a.nsn v.pai.3p r.nsm cj d.asm a.asm

μισθὸν λήμψεται κατὰ τὸν ἴδιον κόπον· 9
wages *will receive* ⌊on the basis of⌋ *{the}* his work. For we are coworkers
3635 3284 2848 3836 2625 3160 1142 1639 1639 5301
n.asm v.fmi.3s p.a d.asm a.asm n.asm

θεοῦ γάρ ἐσμεν συνεργοί, θεοῦ γεώργιον, θεοῦ οἰκοδομή ἐστε.
⌊belonging to God.⌋ *For we are coworkers* You are God's field, God's building. *You are*
2536 1142 1639 5301 1639 1639 2536 1176 2536 3869 1639
n.gsm cj v.pai.1p n.npm n.gsm n.nsn n.gsm n.nsf v.pai.2p

10 κατὰ τὴν χάριν τοῦ θεοῦ τὴν δοθεῖσάν μοι ὡς σοφὸς ἀρχιτέκτων
⌊According to⌋ the grace of God *{the}* given to me, like a skilled master builder I
2848 3836 5921 3836 2536 3836 1443 1609 6055 5055 802 5502
p.a d.asf n.asf d.gsm n.gsm d.asf pt.ap.asf r.ds.1 pl a.nsm n.nsm

θεμέλιον ἔθηκα, ἄλλος δὲ ἐποικοδομεῖ. ↱ ἕκαστος δὲ
laid a foundation, *I laid* but ⌊someone else⌋ *but* is building on it. Let each one *{and}*
5502 2529 5502 1254 257 1254 2224 1063 1667 1254
n.asm v.aai.1s r.nsm cj v.pai.3s r.nsm cj

βλεπέτω πῶς ἐποικοδομεῖ. 11 θεμέλιον γὰρ ἄλλον
take care how he builds on it. For no one is able to lay a foundation *For* other
1063 4802 2224 1142 4029 4029 1538 1538 5502 5502 2529 1142 257
v.pam.3s cj v.pai.3s n.asm cj r.asm

οὐδεὶς δύναται θεῖναι παρὰ τὸν κείμενον, ὅς ἐστιν Ἰησοῦς Χριστός. 12 εἰ
no one is able to lay than that which is laid, which is Jesus Christ. If
4029 1538 5502 4123 3836 3023 4005 1639 2652 5986 1623
a.nsm v.ppi.3s f.aa p.a d.asm pt.pm.asm r.nsm v.pai.3s n.nsm n.nsm cj

NASB

not yet able, 3for
you are still fleshly.
For since there is
jealousy and strife
among you, are
you not fleshly,
and are you not
walking like mere
men? 4For when
one says, "I am of
Paul," and another,
"I am of Apollos,"
are you not *mere*
men?
5What then is
Apollos? And what
is Paul? Servants
through whom you
believed, even as
the Lord gave *op-*
portunity to each
one. 6I planted,
Apollos watered,
but God was caus-
ing the growth. 7So
then neither the
one who plants nor
the one who waters
is anything, but
God who causes
the growth. 8Now
he who plants and
he who waters are
one; but each will
receive his own
reward according
to his own labor.
9For we are God's
fellow workers;
you are God's field,
God's building.
10According to
the grace of God
which was given
to me, like a wise
master builder I
laid a foundation,
and another is
building on it. But
each man must
be careful how he
builds on it. 11For
no man can lay a
foundation other
than the one which
is laid, which is Je-
sus Christ. 12Now

NIV

anyone builds on
this foundation
using gold, sil-
ver, costly stones,
wood, hay or
straw, 13 their work
will be shown
for what it is, be-
cause the Day will
bring it to light. It
will be revealed
with fire, and the
fire will test the
quality of each
person's work.
14 If what has been
built survives, the
builder will re-
ceive a reward. 15 If
it is burned up, the
builder will suffer
loss but yet will
be saved—even
though only as one
escaping through
the flames.
16 Don't you know
that you your-
selves are God's
temple and that
God's Spirit dwells
in your midst? 17 If
anyone destroys
God's temple, God
will destroy that
person; for God's
temple is sacred,
and you together
are that temple.
18 Do not deceive
yourselves. If any
of you think you
are wise by the
standards of this
age, you should
become "fools" so
that you may be-
come wise. 19 For
the wisdom of
this world is fool-
ishness in God's
sight. As it is writ-
ten: "He catches
the wise in their
craftiness"[a]; 20 and
again, "The Lord
knows that the
thoughts of the

δέ τις ἐποικοδομεῖ ἐπὶ τὸν θεμέλιον χρυσόν, ἄργυρον, ⸂λίθους τιμίους,⸃
{and} anyone is building on the foundation with gold, silver, gems,
1254 5516 2224 2093 3836 2529 5996 738 3345 5508
cj r.nsm v.pai.3s p.a d.asm n.asm n.asm n.asm n.apm a.apm

ξύλα, χόρτον, καλάμην, 13 ἑκάστου τὸ ἔργον φανερὸν
wood, hay, straw — the work of each person *the* *work* will become evident,
3833 5965 2811 3836 2240 1667 3836 2240 1181 1181 5745
n.apn n.asm n.asf r.gsm d.nsn n.nsn a.nsn

γενήσεται, ἡ γὰρ ἡμέρα δηλώσει, ὅτι ἐν πυρὶ
will become for the *for* Day will disclose it, because it will be revealed by fire.
1181 1142 3836 1142 2465 1317 4022 636 636 636 636 1877 4786
v.fmi.3s d.nsf cj n.nsf v.fai.3s cj p.d n.dsn

ἀποκαλύπτεται, καὶ ἑκάστου τὸ ἔργον ὁποῖόν
it will be revealed And the fire will test what sort of work each *{the}* *work* *what sort of*
636 2779 3836 4786 1507 1507 3961 3961 3961 2240 1667 3836 2240 3961
v.ppi.3s cj r.gsm d.asn n.asn r.nsn

ἐστιν τὸ πῦρ αὐτὸ[a] δοκιμάσει. 14 εἴ τινος τὸ ἔργον
has done. *the* *fire* *{it}* *will test* If the work that someone *the* *work* has built
1639 3836 4786 899 1507 1623 3836 2240 4005 5516 3836 2240 2224 2224
v.pai.3s d.nsn n.nsn r.nsn v.fai.3s cj r.gsm d.nsn n.nsn

μενεῖ ὃ ἐποικοδόμησεν, μισθὸν λήμψεται· 15 εἴ
on it remains, *which* *has built on* he will receive a reward. *he will receive* If
2224 3531 4005 2224 3284 3284 3284 3635 3284 1623
v.fai.3s r.asn v.aai.3s n.asm v.fmi.3s cj

τινος τὸ ἔργον κατακαήσεται, ζημιωθήσεται, ↱ αὐτὸς δὲ
someone's *{the}* work is burned up, he will suffer loss; however, he himself *however*
5516 3836 2240 2876 2423 1254 5392 899 1254
r.gsm d.nsn n.nsn v.fpi.3s v.fpi.3s r.nsm cj

σωθήσεται, οὕτως δὲ ὡς διὰ πυρός. 16 ↱ ↱ οὐκ οἴδατε ὅτι
will be saved, but only *but* as through fire. Do you not know that you are
5392 1254 4048 1254 6055 1328 4786 3857 3857 4024 3857 4022 1639 1639
v.fpi.3s adv cj pl p.g n.gsn pl v.rai.2p cj

ναὸς θεοῦ ἐστε καὶ ↰ τὸ πνεῦμα τοῦ θεοῦ οἰκεῖ ἐν ὑμῖν; 17 εἴ
God's temple *God's* *you are* and that *{the}* God's Spirit *{the}* *God's* lives in you? If
2536 3724 2536 1639 2779 4022 3836 2536 4460 3836 2536 3861 1877 7007 1623
n.nsm n.gsm v.pai.2p cj d.nsn n.nsn d.gsm n.gsm v.pai.3s p.d r.dp.2 cj

τις τὸν ναὸν τοῦ θεοῦ φθείρει, φθερεῖ τοῦτον ὁ θεός·
anyone destroys *{the}* God's temple, *{the}* *God's* *destroys* God will destroy him. *{the}* *God*
5516 5780 3836 2536 3724 3836 2536 5780 2536 5780 4047 3836 2536
r.nsm d.asm n.asm d.gsm n.gsm v.pai.3s v.fai.3s r.asm d.nsm n.nsm

ὁ γὰρ ναὸς τοῦ θεοῦ ἅγιός ἐστιν, οἵτινές ἐστε ὑμεῖς.
{the} For God's temple *{the}* *God's* is holy, *is* and that is what you are. *you*
3836 1142 2536 3724 3836 2536 1639 41 1639 4015 7007 1639 7007
d.nsm cj n.nsm d.gsm n.gsm a.nsm v.pai.3s r.npm v.pai.2p r.np.2

18 μηδεὶς ἑαυτὸν ἐξαπατάτω· εἴ τις δοκεῖ σοφὸς
Let no one deceive himself. *Let deceive* If someone among you thinks he is wise
1987 3594 1987 1571 1987 1623 5516 1877 7007 1506 1639 1639 5055
a.nsm r.asm.3 v.pam.3s cj r.nsm v.pai.3s a.nsm

εἶναι ἐν ὑμῖν ἐν τῷ αἰῶνι τούτῳ, μωρὸς γενέσθω, ἵνα
he is *among* *you* in *{the}* this age, *this* let him become foolish *let him become* so that
1639 1877 7007 1877 3836 4047 172 4047 1181 1181 1181 3704 1181 2671
f.pa p.d r.dp.2 p.d d.dsm n.dsm r.dsm a.nsm v.amm.3s cj

γένηται σοφός. 19 ἡ γὰρ σοφία τοῦ κόσμου τούτου μωρία παρὰ
he may become wise. For the *For* wisdom of this world *this* is folly with
1181 5055 1142 3836 1142 5053 3836 4047 3180 4047 1639 3702 4123
v.ams.3s a.nsm d.nsf cj n.nsf d.gsm n.gsm r.gsm n.nsf p.d

τῷ θεῷ ἐστιν. γέγραπται γάρ, ὁ δρασσόμενος τοὺς σοφοὺς ἐν τῇ
{the} God. *is* For it is written, *For* "He traps the wise with *{the}* their own
3836 2536 1639 1142 1211 1142 3836 1533 3836 5055 1877 3836 899 899
d.dsm n.dsm v.pai.3s v.rpi.3s cj d.nsm pt.pm.nsm d.apm a.apm p.d d.dsf

πανουργίᾳ αὐτῶν· 20 καὶ πάλιν, κύριος γινώσκει τοὺς διαλογισμοὺς τῶν
craftiness." *their own* And again, "The Lord knows the reasonings of the
4111 899 2779 4099 3261 1182 3836 1369 3836
n.dsf r.gpm.3 cj adv n.nsm v.pai.3s d.apm n.apm d.gpm

NASB

if any man builds
on the foundation
with gold, silver,
precious stones,
wood, hay, straw,
13 each man's
work will become
evident; for the
day will show it
because it is *to be*
revealed with fire,
and the fire itself
will test the qual-
ity of each man's
work. 14 If any
man's work which
he has built on it
remains, he will
receive a reward.
15 If any man's work
is burned up, he
will suffer loss;
but he himself will
be saved, yet so as
through fire.
16 Do you not
know that you are
a temple of God
and *that* the Spirit
of God dwells in
you? 17 If any man
destroys the temple
of God, God will
destroy him, for
the temple of God
is holy, and that is
what you are.
18 Let no man
deceive himself.
If any man among
you thinks that he
is wise in this age,
he must become
foolish, so that he
may become wise.
19 For the wisdom
of this world is
foolishness before
God. For it is writ-
ten, "*He is* THE
ONE WHO CATCHES
THE WISE IN THEIR
CRAFTINESS"; 20 and
again, "THE LORD
KNOWS THE REASON-
INGS of

a 19 Job 5:13

a [αὐτὸ] UBS.

NIV

wise are futile."[a]
21 So then, no more
boasting about hu-
man leaders! All
things are yours,
22 whether Paul or
Apollos or Ce-
phas[b] or the world
or life or death or
the present or the
future—all are
yours, 23 and you
are of Christ, and
Christ is of God.

The Nature of True Apostleship

4 This, then, is
how you ought
to regard us: as
servants of Christ
and as those en-
trusted with the
mysteries God has
revealed. 2 Now
it is required that
those who have
been given a trust
must prove faith-
ful. 3 I care very
little if I am judged
by you or by any
human court; in-
deed, I do not even
judge myself. 4 My
conscience is clear,
but that does not
make me innocent.
It is the Lord who
judges me. 5 There-
fore judge nothing
before the appoint-
ed time; wait until
the Lord comes.
He will bring to
light what is hid-
den in darkness
and will expose
the motives of the
heart. At that time
each will receive
their praise from
God.
6 Now, broth-
ers and sisters, I
have applied these
things to myself
and Apollos for
your benefit,

[a] 20 Psalm 94:11
[b] 22 That is, Peter

σοφῶν ὅτι εἰσὶν μάταιοι. 21 ὥστε → μηδεὶς καυχάσθω ἐν ἀνθρώποις·
wise, that they are futile." So then, let no one boast ⌊with respect to⌋ men.
5055 4022 1639 3469 6063 3016 3594 3016 1877 476
a.gpm cj v.pai.3p a.npm cj a.nsm v.pmm.3s p.d n.dpm

πάντα γὰρ ὑμῶν ἐστιν, 22 εἴτε Παῦλος εἴτε Ἀπολλῶς εἴτε Κηφᾶς, εἴτε
For all things *For* are yours, *are* whether Paul or Apollos or Cephas or the
1142 4246 1142 1639 7007 1639 1664 4263 1664 663 1664 3064 1664
a.npn cj r.gp.2 v.pai.3s cj n.nsm cj n.nsm cj n.nsm cj

κόσμος εἴτε ζωὴ εἴτε θάνατος, εἴτε ἐνεστῶτα εἴτε μέλλοντα· πάντα ὑμῶν,
world or life or death or the present or the future — all are yours,
3180 1664 2437 1664 2505 1664 1931 1664 3516 4246 7007
n.nsm cj n.nsf cj n.nsm cj pt.ra.npn cj pt.pa.npn a.npn r.gp.2

23 ὑμεῖς δὲ Χριστοῦ, Χριστὸς δὲ θεοῦ.
and you *and* are Christ's, and Christ *and* is God's.
1254 7007 1254 5986 1254 5986 1254 2536
r.np.2 cj n.gsm n.nsm cj n.gsm

4:1 οὕτως ἡμᾶς λογιζέσθω ἄνθρωπος ὡς ὑπηρέτας Χριστοῦ
⌊This is how⌋ one should regard us, *should regard one* as servants of Christ
4048 476 3357 3357 7005 3357 476 6055 5677 5986
adv r.ap.1 v.pmm.3s n.nsm pl n.apm n.gsm

καὶ οἰκονόμους → μυστηρίων θεοῦ. 2 ὧδε λοιπὸν ζητεῖται ἐν
and stewards of God's mysteries. *God's* ⌊In this connection⌋ then, it is required of
2779 3874 2536 3696 2536 6045 3370 2426 1877
cj n.apm n.gpn n.gsm adv adv v.ppi.3s p.d

τοῖς οἰκονόμοις, ἵνα πιστός τις εὑρεθῇ. 3 ἐμοὶ δὲ εἰς
{the} stewards that they be found trustworthy. *they be found* But for me *But {for}* it
3836 3874 2671 5516 2351 2351 4412 5516 2351 1254 1609 1254 1650 1639
d.dpm n.dpm cj a.nsm r.nsm v.aps.3s r.ds.1 cj p.a

ἐλάχιστόν ἐστιν, ἵνα ὑφ' ὑμῶν
is a ⌊matter of the least consequence⌋ *it is* that I should be judged by you
1639 1788 1639 2671 373 373 373 373 5679 7007
a.asn.s v.pai.3s cj p.g r.gp.2

ἀνακριθῶ ἢ ὑπὸ ἀνθρωπίνης ἡμέρας· ἀλλ' οὐδὲ ἐμαυτὸν
I should be judged or by any human court. In fact, I do not even judge myself.
373 2445 5679 474 2465 247 373 373 4028 373 1831
v.aps.1s cj p.g a.gsf n.gsf cj adv r.asm.1

ἀνακρίνω. 4 → οὐδὲν γὰρ ἐμαυτῷ σύνοιδα, ἀλλ' οὐκ
I do judge For I am not aware of anything *For* against myself, *I am aware of* yet not
373 1142 5323 5323 5323 5323 4029 1142 1831 5323 247 4024
v.pai.1s a.asn cj r.dsm.1 v.rai.1s cj pl

ἐν τούτῳ δεδικαίωμαι, ὁ δὲ ἀνακρίνων με κύριός ἐστιν.
⌊because of⌋ this am I acquitted. It is the *{and}* Lord who judges me. *Lord It is*
1877 4047 1467 1639 1639 3836 1254 3261 373 1609 3261 1639
p.d r.dsn v.rpi.1s d.nsm cj pt.pa.nsm r.as.1 n.nsm v.pai.3s

5 ὥστε μὴ πρὸ καιροῦ τι κρίνετε
So then, stop passing judgment on anything before the time, *anything passing judgment on*
6063 3590 3212 3212 3212 5516 4574 2789 5516 3212
cj pl p.g n.gsm r.asn v.pam.2p

⌊ἕως ἄν⌋ ἔλθῃ ὁ κύριος, ὃς καὶ φωτίσει τὰ κρυπτὰ τοῦ
before the Lord comes. *the Lord* He *{and}* ⌊will bring to light⌋ the hidden things of
2401 323 3836 3261 2262 3836 3261 4005 2779 5894 3836 3220 3836
cj pl v.aas.3s d.nsm n.nsm r.nsm cj v.fai.3s d.apn a.apn d.gsn

σκότους καὶ φανερώσει τὰς βουλὰς τῶν καρδιῶν· καὶ τότε ὁ ἔπαινος
darkness and will disclose the motives of the heart. *{and}* ⌊At that time⌋ *{the}* praise
5030 2779 5746 3836 1087 3836 2840 2779 5538 3836 2047
n.gsn cj v.fai.3s d.apf n.apf d.gpf n.gpf cj adv d.nsm n.nsm

γενήσεται ἑκάστῳ ἀπὸ τοῦ θεοῦ. 6 ταῦτα δέ,
will come to each from *{the}* God. I have applied all this *{and}* to myself and Apollos
1181 1667 608 3836 2536 3571 3571 3571 4047 1254 1650 1831 2779 663
v.fmi.3s r.dsm p.g d.gsm n.gsm r.apn cj

ἀδελφοί, μετεσχημάτισα εἰς ἐμαυτὸν καὶ Ἀπολλῶν δι' ὑμᾶς,
for your benefit, brothers, *I have applied to myself and Apollos for benefit your*
1328 7007 1328 81 3571 1650 1831 2779 663 1328 7007
n.vpm v.aai.1s p.a r.asm.1 cj n.asm p.a r.ap.2

NASB

the wise, THAT THEY
ARE USELESS." 21 So
then let no one
boast in men. For
all things belong to
you, 22 whether Paul
or Apollos or Ce-
phas or the world
or life or death or
things present or
things to come;
all things belong
to you, 23 and you
belong to Christ;
and Christ belongs
to God.

Servants of Christ

4:1 Let a man
regard us in this
manner, as ser-
vants of Christ
and stewards of
the mysteries of
God. 2 In this case,
moreover, it is re-
quired of stewards
that one be found
trustworthy. 3 But
to me it is a very
small thing that I
may be examined
by you, or by *any*
human court; in
fact, I do not even
examine myself.
4 For I am conscious
of nothing against
myself, yet I am
not by this acquit-
ted; but the one
who examines me
is the Lord. 5 There-
fore do not go on
passing judgment
before [a]the time,
but wait until the
Lord comes who
will both bring to
light the things hid-
den in the darkness
and disclose the
motives of *men's*
hearts; and then
each man's praise
will come to him
from God.
6 Now these
things, brethren, I
have figuratively
applied to myself
and Apollos for
your sakes, so that

[a] I.e. the appointed time of judgment

NIV

so that you may
learn from us the
meaning of the
saying, "Do not
go beyond what
is written." Then
you will not be
puffed up in being
a follower of one
of us over against
the other. 7 For who
makes you differ-
ent from anyone
else? What do you
have that you did
not receive? And if
you did receive it,
why do you boast
as though you did
not?
8 Already you
have all you want!
Already you have
become rich! You
have begun to
reign—and that
without us! How
I wish that you
really had begun
to reign so that we
also might reign
with you! 9 For it
seems to me that
God has put us
apostles on display
at the end of the
procession, like
those condemned
to die in the arena.
We have been
made a spectacle
to the whole uni-
verse, to angels as
well as to human
beings. 10 We are
fools for Christ,
but you are so wise
in Christ! We are
weak, but you are
strong! You are
honored, we are
dishonored! 11 To
this very hour we
go hungry and
thirsty, we are in
rags, we are bru-
tally treated, we
are homeless. 12 We
work hard with our
own hands. When
we are cursed, we
bless; when we are
persecuted, we en-
dure it; 13 when we
are slandered, we
answer kindly. We
have become the
scum of the earth,
the garbage of the
world—right up to
this moment.

ἵνα ἐν ἡμῖν μάθητε τὸ μὴ ὑπὲρ ἃ γέγραπται, ἵνα μὴ
that you may learn by us *you may learn* {the} not to go beyond what is written, that none
2671 3443 3443 3443 1877 7005 3443 3836 3590 5642 4005 1211 2671 3590
cj p.d r.dp.1 v.aas.2p d.asn pl p.a r.apn v.rpi.3s cj pl

εἷς ὑπὲρ τοῦ ἑνὸς φυσιοῦσθε κατὰ τοῦ
of you may be puffed up ⌊in favor of⌋ {the} one *you may be puffed up* against {the}
1651 5881 5881 5881 5881 5881 5642 3836 1651 5881 2848 3836
a.nsm p.g d.gsm a.gsm v.ppi.2p p.g d.gsm

ἑτέρου. 7 τίς γάρ σε διακρίνει; τί δὲ
another. For who *For* sees anything superior in you? *sees anything superior in* What {and}
2283 1142 5515 1142 1359 1359 1359 1359 5148 1359 5515 1254
r.gsm r.nsm cj r.as.2 v.pai.3s r.asn cj

ἔχεις ὃ οὐκ ἔλαβες; εἰ δὲ καὶ ἔλαβες, τί καυχᾶσαι
⌊do you have⌋ that you did not receive? And if *And* {also} you received it, why do you boast
2400 4005 3284 3284 4024 3284 1254 1623 1254 2779 3284 5515 3016
v.pai.2s r.asn pl v.aai.2s cj cj adv v.aai.2s r.asn v.pmi.2s

ὡς μὴ λαβών; 8 ἤδη κεκορεσμένοι ἐστέ, ἤδη
⌊as if⌋ you did not receive it? Already you have all you want! *you have* Already
6055 3284 3284 3590 3284 2453 1639 1639 3170 1639 2453
pl pl pt.aa.nsm adv pt.rp.npm v.pai.2p adv

ἐπλουτήσατε, χωρὶς ἡμῶν ἐβασιλεύσατε· καὶ ὄφελόν γε ἐβασιλεύσατε,
you are rich! Without us ⌊you have begun to reign!⌋ And would that ~ you did reign,
4456 6006 7005 996 2779 4054 1145 996
v.aai.2p p.g r.gp.1 v.aai.2p cj pt.aa.nsn pl v.aai.2p

ἵνα καὶ ἡμεῖς ὑμῖν συμβασιλεύσωμεν. 9 δοκῶ γάρ,
so that {also} we could reign with you! *could reign with* For ⌊it seems to me⌋ *For* that
2671 2779 7005 5203 5203 5203 7007 5203 1142 1506 1142
cj adv r.np.1 r.dp.2 v.aas.1p v.pai.1s cj

ὁ θεὸς ἡμᾶς τοὺς ἀποστόλους ἐσχάτους ἀπέδειξεν ὡς
{the} God has displayed us, the apostles, last, *has displayed* as
3836 2536 617 617 7005 3836 693 2274 617 6055
d.nsm n.nsm r.ap.1 d.apm n.apm a.apm v.aai.3s pl

ἐπιθανατίους, ὅτι θέατρον ἐγενήθημεν τῷ κόσμῳ καὶ
⌊men sentenced to death,⌋ because we have become a spectacle *we have become* ⌊to the⌋ world, both
2119 4022 1181 1181 1181 2519 1181 3836 3180 2779
a.apm cj n.nsn v.api.1p d.dsm n.dsm cj

ἀγγέλοις καὶ ἀνθρώποις. 10 ἡμεῖς μωροὶ διὰ Χριστόν, ὑμεῖς δὲ
to angels and to men. We are fools for Christ, but you *but* are
34 2779 476 7005 3704 1328 5986 1254 7007 1254
n.dpm cj n.dpm r.np.1 a.npm p.a n.asm r.np.2 cj

φρόνιμοι ἐν Χριστῷ· ἡμεῖς ἀσθενεῖς, ὑμεῖς δὲ ἰσχυροί· ὑμεῖς
men of wisdom in Christ! We are weak, but you *but* are strong! You are
5861 1877 5986 7005 822 1254 7007 1254 2708 7007
a.npm p.d n.dsm r.np.1 a.npm r.np.2 cj a.npm r.np.2

ἔνδοξοι, ἡμεῖς δὲ ἄτιμοι. 11 ἄχρι τῆς ἄρτι ὥρας καὶ πεινῶμεν
distinguished, but we *but* are dishonored! To this present hour {and} we are hungry
1902 1254 7005 1254 872 948 3836 785 6052 2779 4277
a.npm r.np.1 cj a.npm p.g d.gsf adv n.gsf cj v.pai.1p

καὶ διψῶμεν καὶ γυμνιτεύομεν καὶ κολαφιζόμεθα καὶ ἀστατοῦμεν 12 καὶ
and thirsty, {and} poorly clothed, {and} knocked about, and homeless. {and}
2779 1498 2779 1217 2779 3139 2779 841 2779
cj v.pai.1p cj v.pai.1p cj v.ppi.1p cj v.pai.1p cj

κοπιῶμεν ἐργαζόμενοι ταῖς ἰδίαις χερσίν· λοιδορούμενοι εὐλογοῦμεν, διωκόμενοι
We labor, working with our own hands. When reviled, we bless; when persecuted,
3159 2237 3836 2625 5931 3366 2328 1503
v.pai.1p pt.pm.npm d.dpf a.dpf n.dpf pt.pp.npm v.pai.1p pt.pp.npm

ἀνεχόμεθα, 13 δυσφημούμενοι παρακαλοῦμεν· ὡς
we endure; when slandered, we respond kindly. We have become, ⌊as it were,⌋ the
462 1555 4151 1181 1181 1181 6055
v.pmi.1p pt.pp.npm v.pai.1p pl

περικαθάρματα τοῦ κόσμου ἐγενήθημεν, πάντων περίψημα ἕως ἄρτι.
scum of the world, *We have become* the refuse of all things, *refuse* even now.
4326 3836 3180 1181 4370 4246 4370 2401 785
n.npn d.gsm n.gsm v.api.1p a.gpn n.nsn p.g adv

NASB

in us you may learn
not to exceed what
is written, so that
no one of you will
become arrogant
in behalf of one
against the other.
7 For who regards
you as superior?
What do you have
that you did not
receive? And if
you did receive it,
why do you boast
as if you had not
received it?
8 You are already
filled, you have al-
ready become rich,
you have become
kings without
us; and indeed, *I*
wish that you had
become kings so
that we also might
reign with you.
9 For, I think, God
has exhibited us
apostles last of all,
as men condemned
to death; because
we have become
a spectacle to the
world, both to
angels and to men.
10 We are fools for
Christ's sake, but
you are prudent
in Christ; we are
weak, but you are
strong; you are
distinguished, but
we are without
honor. 11 To this
present hour we
are both hungry
and thirsty, and are
poorly clothed, and
are roughly treated,
and are home-
less; 12 and we toil,
working with our
own hands; when
we are reviled, we
bless; when we
are persecuted, we
endure; 13 when we
are slandered, we
try to conciliate;
we have become
as the scum of the
world, the dregs
of all things, *even*
until now.

NIV

Paul's Appeal and Warning

14 I am writing
this not to shame
you but to warn
you as my dear
children. 15 Even if
you had ten thou-
sand guardians in
Christ, you do not
have many fathers,
for in Christ Jesus
I became your fa-
ther through the
gospel. 16 Therefore
I urge you to imi-
tate me. 17 For this
reason I have sent
to you Timothy,
my son whom I
love, who is faith-
ful in the Lord. He
will remind you
of my way of life
in Christ Jesus,
which agrees with
what I teach ev-
erywhere in every
church.
18 Some of you
have become arro-
gant, as if I were
not coming to you.
19 But I will come
to you very soon,
if the Lord is will-
ing, and then I will
find out not only
how these arrogant
people are talking,
but what power
they have. 20 For
the kingdom of
God is not a mat-
ter of talk but of
power. 21 What do
you prefer? Shall I
come to you with
a rod of discipline,
or shall I come in
love and with a
gentle spirit?

Dealing With a Case of Incest

5 It is actually
reported that
there is sexual im-
morality among
you, and of a kind
that even pagans
do not tolerate: A
man

14 οὐκ ἐντρέπων ὑμᾶς γράφω ταῦτα ἀλλʼ
I am not writing these things to shame you, *I am writing* *these things* but to admonish
1211 1211 4024 1211 4047 4047 1956 7007 1211 4047 247 3805 3805
pl pt.pa.nsm r.ap.2 v.pai.1s r.apn cj

ὡς τέκνα μου ἀγαπητὰ νουθετῶν[a] 15 ἐὰν γὰρ
you as my dear children. *my* *dear* *to admonish* For though *For* you have
6055 1609 28 5451 1609 28 3805 1142 1569 1142 2400 2400
pl n.apn r.gs.1 a.apn pt.pa.nsm cj cj

μυρίους παιδαγωγοὺς ἔχητε ἐν Χριστῷ ἀλλʼ οὐ πολλοὺς πατέρας·
innumerable guardians *you have* in Christ, *{but}* you do not have many fathers,
3692 4080 2400 1877 5986 247 4024 4498 4252
a.apm n.apm v.pas.2p p.d n.dsm cj pl a.apm n.apm

ἐν γὰρ Χριστῷ Ἰησοῦ διὰ τοῦ εὐαγγελίου ἐγὼ
because I became your father in *because* Christ Jesus through the gospel. *I*
1142 1609 1164 7007 1164 1877 1142 5986 2652 1328 3836 2295 1609
p.d cj n.dsm n.dsm p.g d.gsn n.gsn r.ns.1

ὑμᾶς ἐγέννησα. 16 παρακαλῶ οὖν ὑμᾶς, μιμηταί μου γίνεσθε.
your *became father* I urge you, therefore, *you* be imitators of me. *be*
7007 1164 4151 7007 4036 7007 1181 3629 1609 1181
r.ap.2 v.aai.1s v.pai.1s cj r.ap.2 n.npm r.gs.1 v.pmm.2p

17 ⌞διὰ τοῦτο⌟ ἔπεμψα ὑμῖν Τιμόθεον, ὅς ἐστίν μου τέκνον
That is why I sent to you Timothy, who is my beloved and faithful child
1328 4047 4287 7007 5510 4005 1639 1609 28 2779 4412 5451
p.a r.asn v.aai.1s r.dp.2 n.asm r.nsm v.pai.3s r.gs.1 n.nsn

ἀγαπητὸν καὶ πιστὸν ἐν κυρίῳ, ὃς ὑμᾶς ἀναμνήσει τὰς ὁδούς
beloved *and* *faithful* in the Lord. He will remind you *will remind* of my ways
28 2779 4412 1877 3261 4005 389 389 7007 389 3836 1609 3847
a.nsn cj a.nsn p.d n.dsm r.nsm r.ap.2 v.fai.3s d.apf n.apf

μου τὰς ἐν Χριστῷ Ἰησοῦ,[b] καθὼς πανταχοῦ ἐν πάσῃ ἐκκλησίᾳ
my *{the}* in Christ Jesus, as I teach them everywhere in every church.
1609 3836 1877 5986 2652 2777 1438 1438 4116 1877 4246 1711
r.gs.1 d.apf p.d n.dsm n.dsm cj adv p.d a.dsf n.dsf

διδάσκω. 18 ὡς ↱ ↱ μὴ ἐρχομένου δέ μου
I teach Some have become arrogant, as though I were not coming *{and}* *I*
1438 5516 5881 5881 5881 6055 2262 1609 2262 3590 2262 1254 1609
v.pai.1s pl pl pt.pm.gsm cj r.gs.1

πρὸς ὑμᾶς ἐφυσιώθησάν τινες· 19 ἐλεύσομαι δὲ ταχέως πρὸς ὑμᾶς
to you. *have become arrogant* *Some* But I will come *But* to you soon, *to* *you*
4639 7007 5881 5516 1254 2262 1254 4639 7007 5441 4639 7007
p.a r.ap.2 v.api.3p r.npm v.fmi.1s cj adv p.a r.ap.2

ἐὰν ὁ κύριος θελήσῃ, καὶ γνώσομαι οὐ τὸν λόγον τῶν πεφυσιωμένων ἀλλὰ
if the Lord wills, and I will find out not the speech of these arrogant people but
1569 3836 3261 2527 2779 1182 4024 3836 3364 3836 5881 247
cj d.nsm n.nsm v.aas.3s cj v.fmi.1s pl d.asm n.asm d.gpm pt.rp.gpm cj

τὴν δύναμιν· 20 οὐ γὰρ ἐν λόγῳ ἡ βασιλεία
their power. For the kingdom of God is not *For* a matter of talk *the* *kingdom*
3836 1539 1142 3836 993 3836 2536 4024 1142 1877 3364 3836 993
d.asf n.asf pl cj p.d n.dsm d.nsf n.nsf

τοῦ θεοῦ ἀλλʼ ἐν δυνάμει. 21 τί θέλετε; ἐν
of *God* but of power. What ⌞would you prefer?⌟ Shall I come to you with a
3836 2536 247 1877 1539 5515 2527 2262 2262 2262 4639 7007 1877
d.gsm n.gsm cj p.d n.dsf r.asn v.pai.2p p.d

ῥάβδῳ ἔλθω πρὸς ὑμᾶς ἢ ἐν ἀγάπῃ → πνεύματί τε πραΰτητος;
rod of correction *Shall I come* *to* *you* or with love in a spirit ~ of gentleness?
4811 2262 4639 7007 2445 1877 27 4460 5445 4559
n.dsf v.aas.1s p.a r.ap.2 cj p.d n.dsf n.dsn cj n.gsf

5:1 ↱ ↱ Ὅλως ἀκούεται ἐν ὑμῖν πορνεία,
It is actually reported that there is sexual immorality among you, *sexual immorality*
201 201 3914 201 4518 4518 1877 7007 4518
adv v.ppi.3s p.d r.dp.2 n.nsf

καὶ τοιαύτη πορνεία ἥτις οὐδὲ ← ἐν τοῖς ἔθνεσιν, ὥστε
{and} a kind of immorality that is not tolerated even among *{the}* Gentiles, for a man
2779 5525 4518 4015 4028 1877 3836 1620 6063 5516
cj r.nsf n.nsf r.nsf adv p.d d.dpn n.dpn cj

[a] νουθετῶν TNIV, NET. νουθετῶ[ν] UBS.
[b] [Ἰησοῦ] UBS, omitted by NET.

NASB

14 I do not write
these things to
shame you, but
to admonish you
as my beloved
children. 15 For if
you were to have
countless tutors
in Christ, yet *you*
would not *have*
many fathers, for
in Christ Jesus I
became your father
through the gospel.
16 Therefore I exhort
you, be imitators
of me. 17 For this
reason I have sent
to you Timothy,
who is my beloved
and faithful child
in the Lord, and he
will remind you of
my ways which are
in Christ, just as I
teach everywhere
in every church.
18 Now some have
become arrogant,
as though I were
not coming to you.
19 But I will come
to you soon, if the
Lord wills, and I
shall find out, not
the words of those
who are arrogant
but their power.
20 For the kingdom
of God does not
consist in words
but in power.
21 What do you de-
sire? Shall I come
to you with a rod,
or with love and
a spirit of gentle-
ness?

Immorality Rebuked

5:1 It is actually
reported that there
is immorality
among you, and
immorality of such
a kind as does not
exist even among
the Gentiles, that
someone has his

NIV

is sleeping with his
father's wife. [2]And
you are proud!
Shouldn't you
rather have gone
into mourning
and have put out
of your fellowship
the man who has
been doing this?
[3]For my part, even
though I am not
physically present,
I am with you in
spirit. As one who
is present with you
in this way, I have
already passed
judgment in the
name of our Lord
Jesus on the one
who has been do-
ing this. [4]So when
you are assembled
and I am with you
in spirit, and the
power of our Lord
Jesus is present,
[5]hand this man
over to Satan for
the destruction of
the flesh,[a,b] so that
his spirit may be
saved on the day of
the Lord.
[6]Your boasting
is not good. Don't
you know that a
little yeast leavens
the whole batch of
dough? [7]Get rid
of the old yeast,
so that you may
be a new unleav-
ened batch—as
you really are. For
Christ, our Pass-
over lamb, has
been sacrificed.
[8]Therefore let us
keep the Festival,
not with the old
bread leavened
with malice and
wickedness, but
with the unleav-
ened bread of sin-
cerity and truth.
[9]I wrote to you in
my letter not to as-
sociate with

[a] 5 In contexts like this, the Greek word for *flesh* (*sarx*) refers to the sinful state of human beings, often presented as a power in opposition to the Spirit.
[b] 5 Or *of his body*

γυναῖκά τινα τοῦ πατρὸς ἔχειν. [2]καὶ
is living in sin with his father's wife. *man his father's is living in sin with* And
2400 2400 2400 2400 2400 3836 4252 1222 5516 3836 4252 2400 2779
n.asf r.asm d.gsm n.gsm f.pa cj

ὑμεῖς πεφυσιωμένοι ἐστὲ καὶ ↱ ↱ οὐχὶ μᾶλλον ἐπενθήσατε, ἵνα
you are arrogant! *are {and}* Ought you not rather to have mourned, so that the
7007 1639 5881 1639 2779 4291 4291 4049 3437 4291 2671 3836
r.np.2 pt.rp.npm v.pai.2p cj pl adv.c v.aai.2p cj

ἀρθῇ ἐκ μέσου ὑμῶν ὁ τὸ ἔργον τοῦτο
man who did this deed ⌊would be removed⌋ from your midst? *your the {the} deed this*
4556 4556 4556 4047 2240 149 1666 7007 3545 7007 3836 3836 2240 4047
v.aps.3s p.g n.gsn r.gp.2 d.nsm d.asn n.asn r.asn

πράξας; [3] ↱ ἐγὼ μὲν γάρ, ἀπὼν τῷ σώματι παρὼν δὲ τῷ πνεύματι,
who did For though I ~ *For* am absent in body, I am present *{and}* in spirit;
4556 1142 583 1609 3525 1142 583 3836 5393 4205 1254 3836 4460
pt.aa.nsm r.ns.1 pl cj pt.pa.nsm d.dsn n.dsn pt.pa.nsm cj d.dsn n.dsn

↱ ↱ ἤδη κέκρικα ὡς παρὼν
and I have already ⌊passed judgment on⌋ the one who did this, ⌊just as⌋ ⌊though I were present.⌋
3212 3212 2453 3212 3836 2981 2981 2981 4047 6055 4205
adv v.rai.1s pl pt.pa.nsm

τὸν οὕτως τοῦτο κατεργασάμενον· [4] ἐν τῷ ὀνόματι τοῦ
the {so} this one who did When you are assembled in the name of
3836 4048 4047 2981 5251 7007 5251 5251 1877 3836 3950 3836
d.asm adv r.asn pt.am.asm p.d d.dsn n.dsn d.gsm

κυρίου ἡμῶν[a] Ἰησοῦ συναχθέντων ὑμῶν καὶ τοῦ ἐμοῦ
our Lord *our* Jesus *When are assembled you* and *{the}* I am with you in
7005 3261 7005 2652 5251 7007 2779 3836 1847
n.gsm r.gp.1 n.gsm pt.ap.gpm r.gp.2 cj d.gsn r.gs.1

πνεύματος σὺν τῇ δυνάμει τοῦ κυρίου ἡμῶν Ἰησοῦ, [5]παραδοῦναι ←
spirit, with the power of our Lord *our* Jesus, hand this man over
4460 5250 3836 1539 3836 7005 3261 7005 2652 4140 5525 5525
n.gsn p.d d.dsf n.dsf d.gsm n.gsm r.gp.1 n.gsm f.aa

τὸν τοιοῦτον τῷ σατανᾷ εἰς ὄλεθρον τῆς σαρκός, ἵνα τὸ πνεῦμα
{the} this man to Satan for the destruction of the flesh, so that the spirit
3836 5525 3836 4928 1650 3897 3836 4922 2671 3836 4460
d.asm r.asm d.dsm n.dsm p.a n.asm d.gsf n.gsf cj d.nsn n.nsn

σωθῇ ἐν τῇ ἡμέρᾳ τοῦ κυρίου. [6] οὐ καλὸν τὸ καύχημα
⌊may be saved⌋ on the Day of the Lord. Your boasting is not good. *{the} boasting*
5392 1877 3836 2465 3836 3261 7007 3017 4024 2819 3836 3017
v.aps.3s p.d d.dsf n.dsf d.gsm n.gsm pl a.nsn d.nsn n.nsn

ὑμῶν. ↱ ↱ οὐκ οἴδατε ὅτι μικρὰ ζύμη ὅλον τὸ φύραμα
Your Do you not know that a little leaven leavens the whole *{the}* ⌊batch of dough?⌋
7007 3857 3857 4024 3857 4022 3625 2434 2435 3910 3836 5878
r.gp.2 pl v.rai.2p cj a.nsf n.nsf a.asn d.asn n.asn

ζυμοῖ; [7]ἐκκαθάρατε τὴν παλαιὰν ζύμην, ἵνα ἦτε νέον φύραμα, καθώς
leavens Get rid of the old leaven so that ⌊you may be⌋ a new batch of dough, just as
2435 1705 3836 4094 2434 2671 1639 3742 5878 2777
v.pai.3s v.aam.2p d.asf a.asf n.asf cj v.pas.2p a.nsn n.nsn cj

→ ἐστε ἄζυμοι· καὶ γὰρ τὸ πάσχα ἡμῶν
you really are unleavened. *{also}* For Christ, *{the}* our ⌊Passover lamb,⌋ *our*
1639 109 2779 1142 5986 3836 7005 4247 7005
v.pai.2p a.npm adv cj d.nsn n.nsn r.gp.1

ἐτύθη Χριστός. [8]ὥστε ἑορτάζωμεν μὴ ἐν ζύμῃ
⌊has been sacrificed.⌋ *Christ* So ⌊let us celebrate the festival,⌋ not with the old leaven,
2604 5986 6063 2037 3590 1877 4094 2434
v.api.3s n.nsm cj v.pas.1p pl p.d n.dsf

παλαιᾷ μηδὲ ἐν ζύμῃ κακίας καὶ πονηρίας ἀλλ' ἐν ἀζύμοις →
old not with the leaven of malice and wickedness, but with the ⌊unleavened bread⌋ of
4094 3593 1877 2434 2798 2779 4504 247 1877 109
a.dsf cj p.d n.dsf n.gsf cj n.gsf cj p.d a.dpn

εἰλικρινείας καὶ ἀληθείας. [9]ἔγραψα ὑμῖν ἐν τῇ ἐπιστολῇ μὴ συναναμίγνυσθαι
sincerity and truth. I wrote to you in my letter not to associate with
1636 2779 237 1211 7007 1877 3836 2186 3590 5264
n.gsf cj n.gsf v.aai.1s r.dp.2 p.d d.dsf n.dsf pl f.pm

[a] [ἡμῶν] UBS.

NASB

father's wife. [2]You
have become arro-
gant and have not
mourned instead,
so that the one who
had done this deed
would be removed
from your midst.
[3]For I, on my part,
though absent in
body but present in
spirit, have already
judged him who
has so committed
this, as though I
were present. [4]In
the name of our
Lord Jesus, when
you are assembled,
and I with you in
spirit, with the
power of our Lord
Jesus, [5]*I have*
decided to deliver
such a one to Satan
for the destruction
of his flesh, so that
his spirit may be
saved in the day of
the Lord [a]Jesus.
[6]Your boasting is
not good. Do you
not know that a
little leaven leav-
ens the whole lump
of dough? [7]Clean
out the old leaven
so that you may be
a new lump, just
as you are *in fact*
unleavened. For
Christ our Passover
also has been sac-
rificed. [8]Therefore
let us celebrate
the feast, not with
old leaven, nor
with the leaven of
malice and wicked-
ness, but with the
unleavened bread
of sincerity and
truth.
[9]I wrote you in
my letter not to as-
sociate with

[a] Two early mss do not contain *Jesus*

NIV

sexually immoral people— [10]not at all meaning the people of this world who are immoral, or the greedy and swindlers, or idolaters. In that case you would have to leave this world. [11]But now I am writing to you that you must not associate with anyone who claims to be a brother or sister[a] but is sexually immoral or greedy, an idolater or slanderer, a drunkard or swindler. Do not even eat with such people.

[12]What business is it of mine to judge those outside the church? Are you not to judge those inside? [13]God will judge those outside. "Expel the wicked person from among you."[b]

Lawsuits Among Believers

6 If any of you has a dispute with another, do you dare to take it before the ungodly for judgment instead of before the Lord's people? [2]Or do you not know that the Lord's people will judge the world? And if you are to judge the world, are you not competent to judge trivial cases? [3]Do you not know that we will judge angels? How much more the things of this life! [4]Therefore, if you have disputes about such matters, do you ask for a ruling from those whose way of life is scorned in the church?

[a] *11* The Greek word for *brother or sister* (*adelphos*) refers here to a believer, whether man or woman, as part of God's family; also in 8:11, 13.

[b] *13* Deut. 13:5; 17:7; 19:19; 21:21; 22:21,24; 24:7

πόρνοις, [10]οὐ πάντως τοῖς πόρνοις τοῦ
⌊sexually immoral people⌋ — not at all meaning the ⌊sexually immoral⌋ of this
4521 4024 4122 3836 4521 3836 4047
n.dpm pl adv d.dpm n.dpm d.gsm

κόσμου τούτου ἢ τοῖς πλεονέκταις καὶ ἅρπαξιν ἢ εἰδωλολάτραις, ἐπεὶ
world, *this* or the greedy and swindlers, or idolaters, since then
3180 4047 2445 3836 4431 2779 774 2445 1629 2075 726
n.gsm r.gsm cj d.dpm n.dpm cj a.dpm cj n.dpm cj

ὠφείλετε ἄρα ἐκ τοῦ κόσμου ἐξελθεῖν. [11] νῦν δὲ ἔγραψα
⌊you would have⌋ *then* to go ⌊out of⌋ the world. *to go* But now *But* I am writing
4053 726 2002 2002 1666 3836 3180 2002 1254 3814 1254 1211
v.iai.2p cj p.g d.gsm n.gsm f.aa adv cj v.aai.1s

ὑμῖν μὴ συναναμίγνυσθαι ⌊ἐάν τις⌋ ἀδελφὸς
to you not to associate with anyone who bears the name of brother
7007 3590 5264 1569 5516 3951 3951 3951 3951 3951 81
r.dp.2 pl f.pm cj r.nsm n.nsm

ὀνομαζόμενος ᾖ πόρνος ἢ πλεονέκτης ἢ εἰδωλολάτρης ἢ
who bears the name of ⌊if he is⌋ a ⌊sexually immoral⌋ or greedy person, *{or}* an idolater, *{or}*
3951 1639 4521 2445 4431 2445 1629 2445
pt.pp.nsm v.pas.3s n.nsm cj n.nsm cj n.nsm cj

λοίδορος ἢ μέθυσος ἢ ἅρπαξ, τῷ τοιούτῳ μηδὲ
slanderer, *{or}* drunkard, or swindler — not even to eat with *{the}* such a one. *not even*
3368 2445 3500 2445 774 3593 3593 5303 5303 5303 3836 5525 3593
n.nsm cj n.nsm cj a.nsm d.dsm r.dsm adv

συνεσθίειν. [12] τί γάρ μοι τοὺς ἔξω κρίνειν;
to eat with For what business *For* is it of mine to judge *{the}* outsiders? *to judge* Is it
5303 1142 5515 1142 1609 3212 3212 3836 2032 3212
f.pa r.nsn cj r.ds.1 d.apm adv f.pa

οὐχὶ τοὺς ἔσω ὑμεῖς κρίνετε; [13] τοὺς δὲ ἔξω
not those inside the church that you are to judge? But God will judge those *But* outside.
4049 3836 2276 7007 3212 1254 2536 3212 3212 3836 1254 2032
pl d.apm adv r.np.2 v.pai.2p d.apm cj adv

ὁ θεὸς κρινεῖ. ἐξάρατε τὸν πονηρὸν ἐξ ὑμῶν αὐτῶν.[a]
{the} *God* *will judge* "Remove the evil person ⌊from among⌋ you." *{yourselves}*
3836 2536 3212 1976 3836 4505 1666 7007 899
d.nsm n.nsm v.fai.3s v.aam.2p d.asm a.asm p.g r.gp.2 r.gpm

[6:1] τολμᾷ τις ὑμῶν πρᾶγμα ἔχων πρὸς τὸν ἕτερον
how dare he When any of you has a legal dispute *When has* against *{the}* another, how dare
5528 2400 5516 7007 2400 4547 2400 4639 3836 2283 5528 5528
v.pai.3s r.nsm r.gp.2 n.asn pt.pa.nsm p.a d.asm r.asm

κρίνεσθαι ἐπὶ τῶν ἀδίκων καὶ οὐχὶ ἐπὶ τῶν ἁγίων; [2]ἢ ↱ ↱
he go to law before *{the}* ⌊heathen judges⌋ and not before the saints? Or do you
5528 3212 2093 3836 96 2779 4049 2093 3836 41 2445 3857 3857
f.pm p.g d.gpm a.gpm cj pl p.g d.gpm a.gpm cj

οὐκ οἴδατε ὅτι οἱ ἅγιοι τὸν κόσμον κρινοῦσιν; καὶ εἰ
not know that the saints will judge the world? *will judge* And if the world is
4024 3857 4022 3836 41 3212 3212 3836 3180 3212 2779 1623 3836 3180 3212
pl v.rai.2p cj d.npm a.npm d.asm n.asm v.fai.3p cj cj

ἐν ὑμῖν κρίνεται ὁ κόσμος, ἀνάξιοί ἐστε
to be judged by you, *is to be judged* *the* *world* are you incompetent *are you*
3212 3212 3212 1877 7007 3212 3836 3180 1639 1639 396 1639
p.d r.dp.2 v.ppi.3s d.nsm n.nsm a.npm v.pai.2p

κριτηρίων ἐλαχίστων; [3]↱ ↱ οὐκ οἴδατε ὅτι ἀγγέλους κρινοῦμεν,
to try minor cases? Do you not know that we will judge angels, *we will judge*
3215 1788 3857 3857 4024 3857 4022 3212 3212 3212 34 3212
n.gpn a.gpn.s pl v.rai.2p cj n.apm v.fai.1p

μήτι γε βιωτικά; [4] βιωτικὰ μὲν οὖν κριτήρια
not to mention ~ ⌊everyday affairs?⌋ So if you have ordinary cases, ~ *So* *cases*
3614 1145 1053 4036 1569 2400 2400 1053 3215 3525 4036 3215
pl pl a.apn a.apn pl cj n.apn

ἐὰν ἔχητε, τοὺς ἐξουθενημένους ἐν τῇ ἐκκλησίᾳ,
if *you have* do you appoint as judges those who have no standing in the church?
1569 2400 2767 2767 2767 4047 3836 2024 1877 3836 1711
cj v.pas.2p d.apm pt.rp.apm p.d d.dsf n.dsf

[a] τολμᾷ τις ὑμῶν, πρᾶγμα ἔχων πρὸς τὸν ἕτερον, κρίνεσθαι ἐπὶ τῶν ἀδικῶν, καὶ οὐχὶ ἐπὶ τῶν ἁγίων included by TR after αὐτῶν.

NASB

immoral people; [10]I *did* not at all *mean* with the immoral people of this world, or with the covetous and swindlers, or with idolaters, for then you would have to go out of the world. [11]But actually, I wrote to you not to associate with any so-called brother if he is an immoral person, or covetous, or an idolater, or a reviler, or a drunkard, or a swindler—not even to eat with such a one. [12]For what have I to do with judging outsiders? Do you not judge those who are within *the church?* [13]But those who are outside, God judges. REMOVE THE WICKED MAN FROM AMONG YOURSELVES.

Lawsuits Discouraged

[6:1]Does any one of you, when he has a case against his neighbor, dare to go to law before the unrighteous and not before the saints? [2]Or do you not know that the saints will judge the world? If the world is judged by you, are you not competent *to constitute* the smallest law courts? [3]Do you not know that we will judge angels? How much more matters of this life? [4]So if you have law courts dealing with matters of this life, do you appoint them as judges who are of no account in the church?

NIV

5 I say this to shame you. Is it possible that there is nobody among you wise enough to judge a dispute between believers? 6 But instead, one brother takes another to court—and this in front of unbelievers! 7 The very fact that you have lawsuits among you means you have been completely defeated already. Why not rather be wronged? Why not rather be cheated? 8 Instead, you yourselves cheat and do wrong, and you do this to your brothers and sisters. 9 Or do you not know that wrongdoers will not inherit the kingdom of God? Do not be deceived: Neither the sexually immoral nor idolaters nor adulterers nor men who have sex with men[a] 10 nor thieves nor the greedy nor drunkards nor slanderers nor swindlers will inherit the kingdom of God. 11 And that is what some of you were. But you were washed, you were sanctified, you were justified in the name of the Lord Jesus Christ and by the Spirit of our God.

Sexual Immorality

12 "I have the right to do anything," you say—but not everything is beneficial. "I have the right to do anything"—but I will not be mastered by anything. 13 You say, "Food for the stomach and the stomach

[a] 9 The words *men who have sex with men* translate two Greek words that refer to the passive and active participants in homosexual acts.

τούτους καθίζετε; 5 πρὸς ἐντροπὴν ὑμῖν λέγω. οὕτως οὐκ ἔνι
those *do you appoint* I say this to your shame! *your* *I say* *{thus}* *{not}* Is there
4047 2767 3306 3306 4639 7007 1959 7007 3306 4048 4024 1928
r.apm v.pai.2p p.a n.asf r.dp.2 v.pai.1s adv pl v.pai.3s

ἐν ὑμῖν οὐδεὶς σοφός, ὃς δυνήσεται διακρῖναι ⌊ἀνὰ μέσον⌋ τοῦ
no one among you *no one* wise *{who}* enough to settle a dispute between *{the}*
4029 4029 1877 7007 4029 5055 4005 1538 1359 324 3545 3836
p.d r.dp.2 a.nsm a.nsm r.nsm v.fpi.3s f.aa p.a n.asn d.gsm

ἀδελφοῦ αὐτοῦ; 6 ἀλλὰ ἀδελφὸς μετὰ ἀδελφοῦ κρίνεται καὶ τοῦτο
his brothers, *his* but brother goes to court against brother, *goes to court* and that
899 81 899 247 81 3212 3212 3212 3552 81 3212 2779 4047
n.gsm r.gsm.3 cj n.nsm p.g n.gsm v.pmi.3s cj r.asn

ἐπὶ ἀπίστων; 7 Ἤδη μὲν οὖν[a] ὅλως ἥττημα ὑμῖν ἐστιν ὅτι
before unbelievers? Already ~ *{then}* it is altogether a defeat for you, *it is* that you
2093 603 2453 3525 4036 1639 1639 3914 2488 7007 1639 4022 2400
p.g a.gpm adv pl cj adv n.nsn r.dp.2 v.pai.3s cj

κρίματα ἔχετε μεθ᾽ ἑαυτῶν. ⌊διὰ τί⌋ οὐχὶ μᾶλλον ἀδικεῖσθε; ⌊διὰ τί⌋ οὐχὶ
have lawsuits *you have* with one another. Why not rather be wronged? Why not
2400 3210 2400 3552 1571 1328 5515 4049 3437 92 1328 5515 4049
n.apn v.pai.2p p.g r.gpm.2 p.a r.asn pl adv.c v.pmi.2p p.a r.asn pl

μᾶλλον ἀποστερεῖσθε; 8 ἀλλὰ ↱ ὑμεῖς ἀδικεῖτε καὶ ἀποστερεῖτε, καὶ τοῦτο
rather be defrauded? But you yourselves wrong and defraud, and this to
3437 691 247 92 7007 92 2779 691 2779 4047
adv.c v.pmi.2p cj r.np.2 v.pai.2p cj v.pai.2p cj r.asn

ἀδελφούς. 9 ἢ ↱ ↱ οὐκ οἴδατε ὅτι ἄδικοι
your own brothers! *{or}* Do you not know that the unrighteous will not inherit the
81 2445 3857 3857 4024 3857 4022 96 3099 4024 3099
n.apm cj pl v.rai.2p cj a.npm

θεοῦ βασιλείαν οὐ κληρονομήσουσιν; ↱ μὴ πλανᾶσθε· οὔτε
kingdom of God? *kingdom* *not* *will inherit* Do not be deceived: neither the
993 2536 993 4024 3099 4414 3590 4414 4046
n.gsm n.asf pl v.fai.3p pl v.ppm.2p cj

πόρνοι οὔτε εἰδωλολάτραι οὔτε μοιχοὶ οὔτε μαλακοὶ οὔτε
⌊sexually immoral,⌋ nor idolaters, nor adulterers, nor male prostitutes, nor
4521 4046 1629 4046 3659 4046 3434 4046
n.npm cj n.npm cj n.npm cj a.npm cj

ἀρσενοκοῖται 10 οὔτε κλέπται οὔτε πλεονέκται, οὐ μέθυσοι, οὐ λοίδοροι, οὐχ
homosexuals, nor thieves, nor the greedy, nor drunkards, nor slanderers, nor
780 4046 3095 4046 4431 4024 3500 4024 3368 4024
n.npm cj n.npm cj n.npm pl n.npm pl n.npm pl

ἅρπαγες βασιλείαν θεοῦ κληρονομήσουσιν. 11 καὶ
swindlers will inherit the kingdom of God. *will inherit* And some of you were
774 3099 3099 993 2536 3099 2779 5516 1639 1639
a.npm n.asf n.gsm v.fai.3p cj

ταῦτά τινες ἦτε· ἀλλὰ ἀπελούσασθε, ἀλλὰ ἡγιάσθητε,
guilty of these abominations! *some* *you were* But you were washed, *{but}* you were sanctified,
4047 5516 1639 247 666 247 39
r.npn r.npm v.iai.2p cj v.ami.2p cj v.api.2p

ἀλλὰ ἐδικαιώθητε ἐν τῷ ὀνόματι τοῦ κυρίου Ἰησοῦ Χριστοῦ καὶ ἐν τῷ
{but} you were justified in the name of the Lord Jesus Christ and by the
247 1467 1877 3836 3950 3836 3261 2652 5986 2779 1877 3836
cj v.api.2p p.d d.dsn n.dsn d.gsm n.gsm n.gsm n.gsm cj p.d d.dsn

πνεύματι τοῦ θεοῦ ἡμῶν. 12 πάντα μοι ἔξεστιν ἀλλ᾽ οὐ
Spirit of our God. *our* "All things are lawful ⌊for me,"⌋ *are lawful* — but not
4460 3836 7005 2536 7005 4246 1997 1997 1609 1997 247 4024
n.dsn d.gsm n.gsm r.gp.1 a.npn r.ds.1 v.pai.3s cj pl

πάντα συμφέρει· πάντα μοι ἔξεστιν ἀλλ᾽ ↱ οὐκ ἐγὼ
all things are helpful. "All things are lawful ⌊for me"⌋ *are lawful* — but I will not *I*
4246 5237 4246 1997 1997 1609 1997 247 1609 2027 4024 1609
a.npn v.pai.3s a.npn r.ds.1 v.pai.3s cj pl r.ns.1

ἐξουσιασθήσομαι ὑπό τινος. 13 τὰ βρώματα τῇ κοιλίᾳ καὶ ἡ κοιλία
be overpowered by anything. *{the}* "Food is ⌊for the⌋ stomach and the stomach is
2027 5679 5516 3836 1109 3836 3120 2779 3836 3120
v.fpi.1s p.g r.gsn d.npn n.npn d.dsf n.dsf cj d.nsf n.nsf

[a] [οὖν] UBS.

NASB

5 I say *this* to your shame. *Is it* so, *that* there is not among you one wise man who will be able to decide between his brethren, 6 but brother goes to law with brother, and that before unbelievers?

7 Actually, then, it is already a defeat for you, that you have lawsuits with one another. Why not rather be wronged? Why not rather be defrauded? 8 On the contrary, you yourselves wrong and defraud. *You do* this even to *your* brethren.

9 Or do you not know that the unrighteous will not inherit the kingdom of God? Do not be deceived; neither fornicators, nor idolaters, nor adulterers, nor [a]effeminate, nor homosexuals, 10 nor thieves, nor *the* covetous, nor drunkards, nor revilers, nor swindlers, will inherit the kingdom of God. 11 Such were some of you; but you were washed, but you were sanctified, but you were justified in the name of the Lord Jesus Christ and in the Spirit of our God.

The Body Is the Lord's

12 All things are lawful for me, but not all things are profitable. All things are lawful for me, but I will not be mastered by anything. 13 Food is for the stomach and the stomach is

[a] I.e. effeminate by perversion

NIV

for food, and God will destroy them both." The body, however, is not meant for sexual immorality but for the Lord, and the Lord for the body. [14]By his power God raised the Lord from the dead, and he will raise us also. [15]Do you not know that your bodies are members of Christ himself? Shall I then take the members of Christ and unite them with a prostitute? Never! [16]Do you not know that he who unites himself with a prostitute is one with her in body? For it is said, "The two will become one flesh."[a] [17]But whoever is united with the Lord is one with him in spirit.[b]

[18]Flee from sexual immorality. All other sins a person commits are outside the body, but whoever sins sexually, sins against their own body. [19]Do you not know that your bodies are temples of the Holy Spirit, who is in you, whom you have received from God? You are not your own; [20]you were bought at a price. Therefore honor God with your bodies.

Concerning Married Life

7 Now for the matters you wrote about: "It is good for a man not

---

τοῖς βρώμασιν, ὁ δὲ θεὸς καὶ ταύτην καὶ ταῦτα καταργήσει.
for food" — *{the}* and God will destroy both the one and the other. *will destroy*
3836 1109 3836 1254 2536 2934 2934 2779 4047 2779 4047 2934
d.dpn n.dpn d.nsm cj n.nsm cj r.asf cj r.apn v.fai.3s

τὸ δὲ σῶμα οὐ τῇ πορνείᾳ ἀλλὰ τῷ κυρίῳ, καὶ ὁ κύριος
But the *But* body is not for sexual immorality, but ⌊for the⌋ Lord, and the Lord
1254 3836 1254 5393 4024 3836 4518 247 3836 3261 2779 3836 3261
d.nsn cj n.nsn pl d.dsf n.dsf cj d.dsm n.dsm cj d.nsm n.nsm

τῷ σώματι· [14] ὁ δὲ θεὸς καὶ τὸν κύριον ἤγειρεν καὶ ↱ ↱
⌊for the⌋ body; *{the}* and God both has raised the Lord *has raised* and will raise
3836 5393 3836 1254 2536 2779 1586 1586 3836 3261 1586 2779 1995 1995
d.dsn n.dsn d.nsm cj n.nsm cj d.asm n.asm v.aai.3s cj

ἡμᾶς ἐξεγερεῖ διὰ τῆς δυνάμεως αὐτοῦ. [15] ↱ ↱ οὐκ οἴδατε ὅτι τὰ
us up by *{the}* his power. *his* Do you not know that *{the}* your
7005 1995 1328 3836 899 1539 899 3857 3857 4024 3857 4022 3836 7007
r.ap.1 v.fai.3s p.g d.gsf n.gsf r.gsm.3 pl v.rai.2p cj d.npn

σώματα ὑμῶν μέλη Χριστοῦ ἐστιν; ↱ ↱ ἄρας οὖν τὰ μέλη τοῦ
bodies *your* are members of Christ? *are* Shall I then take *then* the members of
5393 7007 1639 3517 5986 1639 4472 4472 4036 149 4036 3836 3517 3836
n.npn r.gp.2 n.npn n.gsm v.pai.3s pt.aa.nsm cj d.apn n.apn d.gsm

Χριστοῦ ποιήσω → πόρνης μέλη; ⌊μὴ γένοιτο.⌋ [16] ἢ[a] ↱
Christ and make them members of a prostitute? *members* Never! Or do
5986 4472 3517 4520 3517 3590 1181 2445 3857
n.gsm v.aas.1s n.gsf n.apn pl v.amo.3s cj

↱ οὐκ οἴδατε ὅτι ὁ κολλώμενος τῇ πόρνῃ ἓν σῶμά ἐστιν;
you not know that he ⌊who joins himself to⌋ a prostitute is one body *is* with her?
3857 4024 3857 4022 3836 3140 3836 4520 1639 1651 5393 1639
pl v.rai.2p cj d.nsm pt.pp.nsm d.dsf n.dsf a.nsn n.nsn v.pai.3s

ἔσονται γάρ, φησίν, οἱ δύο εἰς σάρκα μίαν. [17]
For it says, "The two will become *For* *it says* *The* *two* *{into}* one flesh." *one* But
1142 5774 5774 3836 1545 1639 1142 5774 3836 1545 1650 1651 4922 1651 1254
v.fmi.3p cj v.pai.3s d.npm a.npm p.a n.asf a.asf

ὁ δὲ κολλώμενος τῷ κυρίῳ ἓν πνεῦμά ἐστιν.
the *But* ⌊one who joins himself to⌋ the Lord is one spirit *is* with him.
3836 1254 3140 3836 3261 1639 1651 4460 1639
d.nsm cj pt.pp.nsm d.dsm n.dsm a.nsn n.nsn v.pai.3s

[18] φεύγετε τὴν πορνείαν. πᾶν ἁμάρτημα ⌊ὃ ἐὰν⌋ ποιήσῃ
Flee *{the}* sexual immorality! Every other sin *other* a person commits
5771 3836 4518 4246 4005 280 4005 1569 476 4472
v.pam.2p d.asf n.asf a.nsn n.nsn r.asn pl v.aas.3s

ἄνθρωπος ἐκτὸς τοῦ σώματός ἐστιν· ὁ δὲ πορνεύων
person is outside the body, *is* but the *but* ⌊sexually immoral person⌋ sins
476 1639 1760 3836 5393 1639 1254 3836 1254 4519 279
n.nsm p.g d.gsn n.gsn v.pai.3s d.nsm cj pt.pa.nsm

εἰς τὸ ἴδιον σῶμα ἁμαρτάνει. [19] ἢ ↱ ↱ οὐκ οἴδατε ὅτι τὸ σῶμα
against *{the}* his own body. *sins* Or do you not know that *{the}* your body
1650 3836 2625 5393 279 2445 3857 3857 4024 3857 4022 3836 7007 5393
p.a d.asn a.asn n.asn v.pai.3s cj pl v.rai.2p cj d.nsn n.nsn

ὑμῶν ναὸς τοῦ ἐν ὑμῖν ἁγίου πνεύματός ἐστιν οὗ
your is a temple of the Holy Spirit who is in you, *Holy* *Spirit* *is* whom
7007 1639 3724 3836 41 4460 1877 7007 41 4460 1639 4005
r.gp.2 n.nsm d.gsn p.d r.dp.2 a.gsn n.gsn v.pai.3s r.gsn

ἔχετε ἀπὸ θεοῦ, καὶ οὐκ ἐστὲ ἑαυτῶν; [20] ἠγοράσθητε γὰρ
⌊you have received⌋ from God, and you are not *you are* your own? For you were bought *For*
2400 608 2536 2779 1639 1639 4024 1639 1571 1142 60 1142
v.pai.2p p.g n.gsm cj pl v.pai.2p r.gpm.2 v.api.2p cj

→ τιμῆς· δοξάσατε δὴ τὸν θεὸν ἐν τῷ σώματι ὑμῶν.[b]
with a price; therefore glorify *therefore* *{the}* God with *{the}* your body. *your*
5507 1314 1519 1314 3836 2536 1877 3836 7007 5393 7007
n.gsf v.aam.2p pl d.asm n.asm p.d d.dsn n.dsn r.gp.2

7:1 περὶ δὲ ὧν ἐγράψατε, καλὸν → ἀνθρώπῳ
Now concerning *Now* the matters you wrote about. Yes, "It is good for a man not
1254 4309 1254 4005 1211 2819 476 3590
p.g cj r.gpn v.aai.2p a.nsn n.dsm

NASB

for food, but God will do away with both of them. Yet the body is not for immorality, but for the Lord, and the Lord is for the body. [14]Now God has not only raised the Lord, but will also raise us up through His power. [15]Do you not know that your bodies are members of Christ? Shall I then take away the members of Christ and make them members of a prostitute? May it never be! [16]Or do you not know that the one who joins himself to a prostitute is one body *with her?* For He says, "THE TWO SHALL BECOME ONE FLESH." [17]But the one who joins himself to the Lord is one spirit *with Him.* [18]Flee immorality. Every *other* sin that a man commits is outside the body, but the immoral man sins against his own body. [19]Or do you not know that your body is a temple of the Holy Spirit who is in you, whom you have from God, and that you are not your own? [20]For you have been bought with a price: therefore glorify God in your body.

Teaching on Marriage

[7:1]Now concerning the things about which you wrote, it is good for a man

---

[a] 16 Gen. 2:24
[b] 17 Or *in the Spirit*

[a] [ἢ] UBS.
[b] καὶ ἐν τῷ πνεύματι ὑμῶν, ἅτινά ἐστι τοῦ Θεοῦ included by TR after ὑμῶν.

NIV

to have sexual
relations with a
woman.” 2But
since sexual im-
morality is occur-
ring, each man
should have sexual
relations with his
own wife, and
each woman with
her own husband.
3The husband
should fulfill
his marital duty
to his wife, and
likewise the wife
to her husband.
4The wife does
not have author-
ity over her own
body but yields it
to her husband.
In the same way,
the husband does
not have authority
over his own body
but yields it to his
wife. 5Do not de-
prive each other
except perhaps by
mutual consent
and for a time, so
that you may de-
vote yourselves to
prayer. Then come
together again so
that Satan will not
tempt you because
of your lack of
self-control. 6I say
this as a conces-
sion, not as a com-
mand. 7I wish that
all of you were as
I am. But each of
you has your own
gift from God; one
has this gift, an-
other has that.
8Now to the un-
married[a] and the
widows I say: It is
good for them to
stay unmarried, as
I do. 9But if they
cannot control
themselves, they
should marry, for
it is better to mar-
ry than to burn
with passion.

[a] 8 Or *widowers*

→ γυναικὸς μὴ ἅπτεσθαι· 2 διὰ δὲ τὰς
to have sexual contact with a woman.” *not* *to have sexual contact* But ⌊because of⌋ *But* cases
721 721 721 721 1222 3590 721 1254 1328 1254 3836
n.gsf pl f.pm p.a cj d.apf

πορνείας ἕκαστος τὴν ἑαυτοῦ γυναῖκα ἐχέτω καὶ ἑκάστη
of sexual immorality, each man should have *{the}* his own wife *should have* and each woman
4518 1667 2400 2400 3836 1571 1222 2400 2779 1667
n.apf r.nsm d.asf r.gsm.3 n.asf v.pam.3s cj r.nsf

τὸν ἴδιον ἄνδρα ἐχέτω. 3 τῇ
{the} her own husband. *{should have}* The husband should fulfill his marital responsibility ⌊to his⌋
3836 2625 467 2400 3836 467 625 625 3836 4051 4051 3836
d.asm a.asm n.asm v.pam.3s d.dsf

γυναικὶ ὁ ἀνὴρ τὴν ὀφειλὴν ἀποδιδότω, ὁμοίως δὲ καὶ ἡ γυνὴ
wife, *The* *husband* *his* *marital responsibility* *should fulfill* and likewise *and* *{also}* the wife
1222 3836 467 3836 4051 625 1254 3931 1254 2779 3836 1222
n.dsf d.nsm n.nsm d.asf n.asf v.pam.3s adv cj adv d.nsf n.nsf

τῷ ἀνδρί. 4 ἡ γυνὴ τοῦ ἰδίου σώματος οὐκ
⌊to her⌋ husband. For the wife does not have authority over her own body, *not*
3836 467 3836 1222 2027 4024 2027 2027 3836 2625 5393 4024
d.dsm n.dsm d.nsf n.nsf d.gsn a.gsn n.gsn pl

ἐξουσιάζει ἀλλὰ ὁ ἀνήρ, ὁμοίως δὲ καὶ ὁ ἀνὴρ
does have authority but the husband does. ⌊In the same way,⌋ *{and}* *{also}* the husband does not
2027 247 3836 467 3931 1254 2779 3836 467 2027 4024
v.pai.3s cj d.nsm n.nsm adv cj adv d.nsm n.nsm

τοῦ ἰδίου σώματος οὐκ ἐξουσιάζει ἀλλὰ ἡ γυνή. 5 ↱ μὴ
have authority over his own body, *not* *does have authority* but the wife does. Do not
2027 2027 3836 2625 5393 4024 2027 247 3836 1222 691 3590
d.gsn a.gsn n.gsn pl v.pai.3s cj d.nsf n.nsf pl

ἀποστερεῖτε ἀλλήλους, εἰ ⌊μήτι ἂν⌋ ἐκ συμφώνου πρὸς καιρόν, ἵνα
deprive one another, except perhaps by agreement for a set time, so that
691 253 1623 3614 323 1666 5247 4639 2789 2671
v.pam.2p r.apm cj pl pl p.g n.gsn p.a n.asm cj

σχολάσητε τῇ προσευχῇ καὶ[a] πάλιν ⌊ἐπὶ τὸ αὐτὸ⌋
⌊you may devote yourselves⌋ to prayer; then come together again, *together*
5390 3836 4666 2779 1639 2093 4099 2093 3836 899
v.aas.2p d.dsf n.dsf cj adv p.a d.asn r.asn

ἦτε, ἵνα ↱ μὴ πειράζῃ ὑμᾶς ὁ σατανᾶς διὰ τὴν
come so that Satan may not tempt you *{the}* *Satan* ⌊because of⌋ *{the}* your
1639 2671 4928 4279 3590 4279 7007 3836 4928 1328 3836 7007
v.pas.2p cj pl v.pas.3s r.ap.2 d.nsm n.nsm p.a d.asf

ἀκρασίαν ὑμῶν. 6 τοῦτο δὲ λέγω κατὰ συγγνώμην οὐ κατ᾽ ἐπιταγήν.
lack of self-control. *your* This *{and}* I say ⌊by way of⌋ concession, not of command.
202 7007 4047 1254 3306 2848 5152 4024 2848 2198
n.asf r.gp.2 r.asn cj v.pai.1s p.a n.asf pl p.a n.asf

7 θέλω δὲ πάντας ἀνθρώπους εἶναι ὡς καὶ ἐμαυτόν· ἀλλὰ ἕκαστος
I wish *{and}* that all men were as *{also}* I myself am. But each has
2527 1254 4246 476 1639 6055 2779 1831 247 1667 2400
v.pai.1s cj a.apm n.apm f.pa pl adv r.asm.1 cj r.nsm

ἴδιον ἔχει χάρισμα ἐκ θεοῦ, ὁ μὲν οὕτως, ὁ δὲ οὕτως. 8 λέγω
his own *has* gift from God, one ~ of one kind and one *and* of another. *I say*
2625 2400 5922 1666 2536 3836 3525 4048 1254 3836 1254 4048 3306
a.asn v.pai.3s n.asn p.g n.gsm d.nsm pl adv d.nsm pl adv v.pai.1s

δὲ τοῖς ἀγάμοις καὶ ταῖς χήραις, καλὸν αὐτοῖς ἐὰν μείνωσιν
Now to the unmarried and to the widows I say that it is good for them if they remain
1254 3836 23 2779 3836 5939 3306 3306 2819 899 1569 3531
cj d.dpm a.dpm cj d.dpf n.dpf a.nsn r.dpm.3 cj v.aas.3p

ὡς κἀγώ· 9 εἰ δὲ ↱ ↱ οὐκ ἐγκρατεύονται, γαμησάτωσαν,
single, as I am. But if *But* they are not practicing self-control, they should marry;
6055 2743 1254 1623 1254 1603 1603 4024 1603 1138
cj crasis cj cj pl v.pmi.3p v.aam.3p

κρεῖττον γάρ ἐστιν γαμῆσαι ἢ πυροῦσθαι. 10 τοῖς
for it is better *for* *it is* to marry than to burn with sexual passion. To the
1142 1639 1639 3202 1142 1639 1138 2445 4792 3836
a.nsn.c cj v.pai.3s f.aa pl f.pp d.dpm

[a] τῇ προσευχῇ included by TR after καί.

NASB

not to touch a
woman. 2But
because of im-
moralities, each
man is to have his
own wife, and each
woman is to have
her own husband.
3The husband must
fulfill his duty to
his wife, and like-
wise also the wife
to her husband.
4The wife does not
have authority over
her own body, but
the husband *does;*
and likewise also
the husband does
not have authority
over his own body,
but the wife *does.*
5Stop depriving
one another, except
by agreement for
a time, so that you
may devote your-
selves to prayer,
and come together
again so that Satan
will not tempt you
because of your
lack of self-control.
6But this I say by
way of concession,
not of command.
7[a]Yet I wish that
all men were even
as I myself am.
However, each
man has his own
gift from God, one
in this manner, and
another in that.
8But I say to the
unmarried and to
widows that it is
good for them if
they remain even
as I. 9But if they
do not have self-
control, let them
marry; for it is bet-
ter to marry than to
burn *with passion.*

[a] One early ms reads *For*

NIV

10 To the married
I give this com-
mand (not I, but
the Lord): A wife
must not separate
from her husband.
11 But if she does,
she must remain
unmarried or else
be reconciled to
her husband. And
a husband must not
divorce his wife.
12 To the rest I
say this (I, not
the Lord): If any
brother has a wife
who is not a be-
liever and she is
willing to live with
him, he must not
divorce her. 13 And
if a woman has a
husband who is not
a believer and he is
willing to live with
her, she must not
divorce him. 14 For
the unbelieving
husband has been
sanctified through
his wife, and the
unbelieving wife
has been sancti-
fied through her
believing husband.
Otherwise your
children would be
unclean, but as it
is, they are holy.
15 But if the unbe-
liever leaves, let it
be so. The broth-
er or the sister is
not bound in such
circumstances;
God has called us
to live in peace.
16 How do you
know, wife, wheth-
er you will save
your husband? Or,
how do you know,
husband, whether
you will save your
wife?

Concerning Change of Status

17 Nevertheless,

δὲ γεγαμηκόσιν παραγγέλλω, οὐκ ἐγὼ ἀλλὰ ὁ κύριος, γυναῖκα
{and} married I give this command (not I, but the Lord): a wife should not
1254 1138 4133 4024 1609 247 3836 3261 1222 6004 3590
cj pt.ra.dpm v.pai.1s pl r.ns.1 cj d.nsm n.nsm n.asf

ἀπὸ ἀνδρὸς μὴ χωρισθῆναι, 11 ἐὰν δὲ καὶ χωρισθῇ,
separate from her husband *not* *should separate* (however if *however* *{also}* she does,
6004 608 467 3590 6004 1254 1569 1254 2779 6004
p.g n.gsm pl f.ap cj cj adv v.aps.3s

μενέτω ἄγαμος ἢ τῷ ἀνδρὶ καταλλαγήτω καὶ ἄνδρα
let her remain unmarried or else be reconciled ⌊to her⌋ husband), *be reconciled* and a husband
3531 23 2445 2904 2904 3836 467 2904 2779 467
v.pam.3s a.nsf cj d.dsm n.dsm v.apm.3s cj n.asm

γυναῖκα μὴ ἀφιέναι. 12 τοῖς δὲ λοιποῖς λέγω ἐγὼ οὐχ
should not divorce his wife. *not* *should divorce* To the *{and}* rest I say (I, not
918 3590 918 1222 3590 918 3836 1254 3370 3306 1609 4024
n.asf pl f.pa d.dpm cj a.dpm v.pai.1s r.ns.1 pl

ὁ κύριος, εἴ τις ἀδελφὸς γυναῖκα ἔχει ἄπιστον καὶ αὕτη
the Lord): If some brother has a wife *has* who is not a believer, and she
3836 3261 1623 5516 81 2400 1222 2400 603 2779 4047
d.nsm n.nsm cj r.nsm n.nsm n.asf v.pai.3s a.asf cj r.nsf

συνευδοκεῖ οἰκεῖν μετ᾽ αὐτοῦ, ↱ ↱ μὴ ἀφιέτω αὐτήν· 13 καὶ γυνὴ
is willing to live with him, he should not divorce her. And if some woman
5306 3861 3552 899 918 918 3590 918 899 2779 1623 5516 1222
v.pai.3s f.pa p.g r.gsm.3 pl v.pam.3s r.asf.3 cj n.nsf

εἴ τις ἔχει ἄνδρα ἄπιστον καὶ οὗτος συνευδοκεῖ οἰκεῖν μετ᾽ αὐτῆς,
if *some* has a husband who is not a believer, and he is willing to live with her,
1623 5516 2400 467 603 2779 4047 5306 3861 3552 899
cj r.nsf v.pai.3s n.asm a.asm cj r.nsm v.pai.3s f.pa p.g r.gsf.3

↱ ↱ μὴ ἀφιέτω τὸν ἄνδρα. 14 ἡγίασται γὰρ ὁ
she should not divorce *{the}* him. For the unbelieving husband is consecrated *For* *the*
918 918 3590 918 3836 467 1142 3836 603 467 39 1142 3836
pl v.pam.3s d.asm n.asm v.rpi.3s cj d.nsm

ἀνὴρ ὁ ἄπιστος ἐν τῇ γυναικὶ καὶ
husband *{the}* *unbelieving* through union with his wife, and the unbelieving wife
467 3836 603 1877 3836 1222 2779 3836 603 1222
n.nsm d.nsm a.nsm p.d d.dsf n.dsf cj

ἡγίασται ἡ γυνὴ ἡ ἄπιστος ἐν τῷ ἀδελφῷ· ⌊ἐπεὶ ἄρα⌋ τὰ
is consecrated *the* *wife* *{the}* *unbelieving* through union with her husband. Otherwise *{the}*
39 3836 1222 3836 603 1877 3836 81 2075 726 3836
v.rpi.3s d.nsf n.nsf d.nsf a.nsf p.d d.dsm n.dsm cj cj d.npn

τέκνα ὑμῶν ἀκάθαρτά ἐστιν, νῦν δὲ ἅγιά ἐστιν.
your children *your* would be defiled, *would be* but ⌊as it is,⌋ *but* they are holy. *they are*
7007 5451 7007 1639 1639 176 1639 1254 3814 1254 1639 1639 41 1639
n.npn r.gp.2 a.npn v.pai.3s adv cj a.npn v.pai.3s

15 εἰ δὲ ὁ ἄπιστος χωρίζεται, χωριζέσθω·
But if *But* the unbelieving partner separates, let it be so. In such cases the brother
1254 1623 1254 3836 603 6004 6004 1877 5525 5525 3836 81
cj cj d.nsm a.nsm v.ppi.3s v.ppm.3s

↱ οὐ δεδούλωται ὁ ἀδελφὸς ἢ ἡ ἀδελφὴ ἐν τοῖς τοιούτοις·
or the sister is not bound. *the* *brother* *or* *the* *sister* *In* *{the}* *such cases* It
2445 3836 80 1530 4024 1530 3836 81 2445 3836 80 1877 3836 5525
pl v.rpi.3s d.nsm n.nsm cj d.nsf n.nsf p.d d.dpn r.dpn

ἐν δὲ εἰρήνῃ κέκληκεν ὑμᾶς[a] ὁ θεός. 16 τί γὰρ οἶδας,
is to *{and}* peace that God has called us. *{the}* *God* For how *For* ⌊do you know,⌋
1877 1254 1645 2536 2813 7007 3836 2536 1142 5515 1142 3857
p.d cj n.dsf v.rai.3s r.ap.2 d.nsm n.nsm r.asn cj v.rai.2s

γύναι, εἰ τὸν ἄνδρα σώσεις; ἢ τί οἶδας, ἄνερ,
wife, whether you will save your husband? *you will save* Or how ⌊do you know,⌋ husband,
1222 1623 5392 5392 5392 3836 467 5392 2445 5515 3857 467
n.vsf cj d.asm n.asm v.fai.2s cj r.asn v.rai.2s n.vsm

εἰ τὴν γυναῖκα σώσεις; 17 ⌊Εἰ μὴ⌋
whether you will save your wife? *you will save* Only, as the Lord has assigned
1623 5392 5392 5392 3836 1222 5392 1623 3590 6055 3836 3261 3532 3532
cj d.asf n.asf v.fai.2s cj pl

NASB

10 But to the mar-
ried I give instruc-
tions, not I, but the
Lord, that the wife
should not leave
her husband 11 (but
if she does leave,
she must remain
unmarried, or else
be reconciled to
her husband), and
that the husband
should not divorce
his wife.
12 But to the rest I
say, not the Lord,
that if any brother
has a wife who is
an unbeliever, and
she consents to
live with him, he
must not divorce
her. 13 And a woman
who has an unbe-
lieving husband,
and he consents
to live with her,
she must not send
her husband away.
14 For the unbeliev-
ing husband is
sanctified through
his wife, and the
unbelieving wife is
sanctified through
her believing hus-
band; for otherwise
your children are
unclean, but now
they are holy. 15 Yet
if the unbelieving
one leaves, let him
leave; the brother
or the sister is not
under bondage in
such *cases,* but
God has called
[a]us to peace. 16 For
how do you know,
O wife, whether
you will save your
husband? Or how
do you know, O
husband, whether
you will save your
wife?
17 Only, as the
Lord has assigned

[a] ὑμᾶς UBS, NET. ἡμᾶς TNIV.

[a] One early ms reads *you*

NIV

each person should live as a believer in whatever situation the Lord has assigned to them, just as God has called them. This is the rule I lay down in all the churches. [18]Was a man already circumcised when he was called? He should not become uncircumcised. Was a man uncircumcised when he was called? He should not be circumcised. [19]Circumcision is nothing and uncircumcision is nothing. Keeping God's commands is what counts. [20]Each person should remain in the situation they were in when God called them.

[21]Were you a slave when you were called? Don't let it trouble you—although if you can gain your freedom, do so. [22]For the one who was a slave when called to faith in the Lord is the Lord's freed person; similarly, the one who was free when called is Christ's slave. [23]You were bought at a price; do not become slaves of human beings. [24]Brothers and sisters, each person, as responsible to God, should remain in the situation they were in when God called them.

Concerning the Unmarried

[25]Now about virgins: I have no command from the Lord, but I give

ἑκάστῳ ὡς ἐμέρισεν ὁ κύριος, ἕκαστον ὡς κέκληκεν
to each person, *as* *has assigned* *the* *Lord* as God has called each one, *as* *has called*
1667 6055 3532 3836 3261 6055 2536 2813 2813 1667 6055 2813
r.dsm cj v.aai.3s d.nsm n.nsm r.asm cj v.rai.3s

ὁ θεός, οὕτως περιπατείτω. καὶ οὕτως ἐν ταῖς
{the} *God* so ⌊let that person conduct his life.⌋ And thus I prescribe in all the
3836 2536 4048 4344 2779 4048 1411 1411 1877 4246 3836
d.nsm n.nsm adv v.pam.3s cj adv p.d d.dpf

ἐκκλησίαις πάσαις διατάσσομαι. [18] → περιτετμημένος τις
churches. *all* *I prescribe* If a man was already circumcised *man*
1711 4246 1411 5516 4362 5516
n.dpf a.dpf v.pmi.1s pt.rp.nsm r.nsm

ἐκλήθη, ↱ ↱ μὴ ἐπισπάσθω· ⌊ἐν
⌊when he was called,⌋ he should not conceal his circumcision. If a man was not circumcised
2813 2177 2177 3590 2177 5516 1877
v.api.3s pl v.pmm.3s p.d

ἀκροβυστίᾳ⌋ κέκληταί τις, ↱ ↱ μὴ περιτεμνέσθω. [19] ἡ
⌊when he was called,⌋ *man* he should not submit to circumcision. *{the}*
213 2813 5516 4362 4362 3590 4362 3836
n.dsf v.rpi.3s r.nsm pl v.ppm.3s d.nsf

περιτομὴ οὐδέν ἐστιν καὶ ἡ ἀκροβυστία οὐδέν ἐστιν, ἀλλὰ
Circumcision is nothing *is* and *{the}* uncircumcision is nothing. *is* Rather, it is
4364 1639 4029 1639 2779 3836 213 1639 4029 1639 247
n.nsf a.nsn v.pai.3s cj d.nsf n.nsf a.nsn v.pai.3s cj

τήρησις ἐντολῶν θεοῦ. [20] ἕκαστος
keeping God's commandments *God's* that counts. Let each person continue in that
5499 2536 1953 2536 3531 1667 3531 1877 4047
n.nsf n.gpf n.gsm r.nsm

ἐν τῇ κλήσει ᾗ ἐκλήθη, ἐν ταύτῃ μενέτω. [21] ↱
condition *{in}* *{the}* *{calling}* ⌊in which⌋ he was called. *in* *that condition* *Let continue* If you
4047 1877 3836 3104 4005 2813 1877 4047 3531 2813
p.d d.dsf n.dsf r.dsf v.api.3s p.d r.dsf v.pam.3s

↱ δοῦλος ἐκλήθης, ↱ μή σοι μελέτω· ἀλλ᾽ εἰ καὶ
were a slave when called, do not *{to you}* ⌊be concerned about⌋ it. However, if *{also}*
2813 1529 2813 3508 3590 5148 3508 247 1623 2779
n.nsm v.api.2s pl r.ds.2 v.pam.3s cj cj adv

δύνασαι ἐλεύθερος γενέσθαι, ↱ μᾶλλον χρῆσαι. [22]
you are able to gain your freedom, *to gain* make the most of the opportunity. For
1538 1181 1181 1801 1181 5968 3437 5968 1142
v.ppi.2s a.nsm f.am adv.c v.amm.2s

ὁ γὰρ ἐν κυρίῳ κληθεὶς → δοῦλος
the *For* one who was called by the Lord *one who was called* as a slave is a
3836 1142 2813 2813 2813 2813 1877 3261 2813 1529 1639
d.nsm cj p.d n.dsm pt.ap.nsm n.nsm

ἀπελεύθερος → κυρίου ἐστίν, ὁμοίως ὁ → ἐλεύθερος
freedman of the Lord. *is* Likewise, the one who was called as a free person
592 3261 1639 3931 3836 2813 2813 2813 2813 1801
n.nsm n.gsm v.pai.3s adv d.nsm a.nsm

κληθεὶς δοῦλός ἐστιν Χριστοῦ. [23] → τιμῆς
one who was called is a slave *is* of Christ. You were bought with a price;
2813 1639 1529 1639 5986 60 60 60 5507
pt.ap.nsm n.nsm v.pai.3s n.gsm n.gsf

ἠγοράσθητε· ↱ μὴ γίνεσθε δοῦλοι ἀνθρώπων. [24] ἕκαστος ἐν ᾧ
You were bought do not become slaves of men. Each one in the condition in which
60 1181 3590 1181 1529 476 1667 1877 4005
v.api.2p pl v.pmm.2p n.npm n.gpm r.nsm p.d r.dsn

ἐκλήθη, ἀδελφοί, ἐν τούτῳ μενέτω παρὰ θεῷ. [25] περὶ δὲ
he was called, brothers, in that condition ⌊let him remain⌋ with God. Now concerning *Now*
2813 81 1877 4047 3531 4123 2536 1254 4309 1254
v.api.3s n.vpm p.d r.dsn v.pam.3s p.d n.dsm p.g cj

τῶν παρθένων ἐπιταγὴν → κυρίου οὐκ ἔχω,
{the} virgins: I have no command from the Lord, *no* *I have* but I give my
3836 4221 2400 2400 4024 2198 3261 4024 2400 1254 1443 1443
d.gpf n.gpf n.asf n.gsm pl v.pai.1s

NASB

to each one, as God has called each, in this manner let him walk. And so I direct in all the churches. [18]Was any man called *when he was already* circumcised? He is not to become uncircumcised. Has anyone been called in uncircumcision? He is not to be circumcised. [19]Circumcision is nothing, and uncircumcision is nothing, but *what matters is* the keeping of the commandments of God. [20]Each man must remain in that condition in which he was called.

[21]Were you called while a slave? Do not worry about it; but if you are able also to become free, rather do that. [22]For he who was called in the Lord while a slave, is the Lord's freedman; likewise he who was called while free, is Christ's slave. [23]You were bought with a price; do not become slaves of men. [24]Brethren, each one is to remain with God in that *condition* in which he was called.

[25]Now concerning virgins I have no command of the Lord, but I give an

NIV

a judgment as one
who by the Lord's
mercy is trustwor-
thy. 26 Because of
the present crisis,
I think that it is
good for a man to
remain as he is.
27 Are you pledged
to a woman? Do
not seek to be re-
leased. Are you
free from such a
commitment? Do
not look for a wife.
28 But if you do
marry, you have
not sinned; and if a
virgin marries, she
has not sinned. But
those who marry
will face many
troubles in this
life, and I want to
spare you this.
29 What I mean,
brothers and sis-
ters, is that the
time is short. From
now on those who
have wives should
live as if they do
not; 30 those who
mourn, as if they
did not; those
who are happy, as
if they were not;
those who buy
something, as if it
were not theirs to
keep; 31 those who
use the things of
the world, as if not
engrossed in them.
For this world in
its present form is
passing away.
32 I would like you
to be free from
concern. An un-
married man is
concerned about
the Lord's af-
fairs—how he can
please the Lord.
33 But a married
man is concerned
about the affairs
of this

γνώμην δὲ δίδωμι ὡς ἠλεημένος ὑπὸ κυρίου πιστὸς
opinion *but* *I give* as ⌊one who has been shown mercy⌋ by the Lord and is trustworthy.
1191 1254 1443 6055 1796 5679 3261 1639 4412
n.asf cj v.pai.1s pl pt.rp.nsm p.g n.gsm a.nsm

εἶναι. 26 νομίζω οὖν τοῦτο καλὸν ὑπάρχειν διὰ τὴν ἐνεστῶσαν
is I think, then, that this is good *is* ⌊because of⌋ the present
1639 3787 4036 4047 5639 2819 5639 1328 3836 1931
f.pa v.pai.1s cj r.asn a.asn f.pa p.a d.asf pt.ra.asf

ἀνάγκην, ὅτι καλὸν → ἀνθρώπῳ τὸ οὕτως εἶναι. 27 δέδεσαι →
distress — that it is good for a man *{the}* to remain as he is. ⌊If you are married⌋ to a
340 4022 2819 476 3836 4048 1639 1313
n.asf cj a.asn n.dsm d.nsn adv f.pa v.rpi.2s

γυναικί, μὴ ζήτει λύσιν· λέλυσαι ἀπὸ γυναικός, → μὴ ζήτει
wife, do not seek ⌊to be set free;⌋ ⌊if you are free⌋ from a wife, do not seek a
1222 3590 2426 3386 3395 608 1222 2426 3590 2426
n.dsf pl v.pam.2s n.asf v.rpi.2s p.g n.gsf pl v.pam.2s

γυναῖκα. 28 ἐὰν δὲ καὶ γαμήσῃς, → → οὐχ ἥμαρτες, καὶ ἐὰν
wife. But if *But* *{also}* you do marry, you have not sinned, and if a virgin
1222 1254 1569 1254 2779 1138 279 279 4024 279 2779 1569 4221
n.asf cj cj adv v.aas.2s pl v.aai.2s cj cj

γήμῃ ἡ παρθένος, → → οὐχ ἥμαρτεν·
marries, *{the}* *virgin* she has not sinned. However those who do marry will have worldly
1138 3836 4221 279 279 4024 279 1254 5525 2400 2400 4922
v.aas.3s d.nsf n.nsf pl v.aai.3s

θλῖψιν δὲ τῇ σαρκὶ ἕξουσιν οἱ τοιοῦτοι, ἐγὼ δὲ
trouble, *However* *{the}* *worldly* *will have* *{the}* *those* and I *and* am trying to spare
2568 1254 3836 4922 2400 3836 5525 1254 1609 1254 5767 5767 5767 5767
n.asf cj d.dsf n.dsf v.fai.3p d.npm r.npm r.ns.1 cj

ὑμῶν φείδομαι. 29 τοῦτο δέ φημι, ἀδελφοί, ὁ καιρὸς
you. *am trying to spare* And I say this, *And* *I say* my brothers: the time has
7007 5767 1254 5774 5774 4047 1254 5774 81 3836 2789 1639
r.gp.2 v.pmi.1s r.asn cj v.pai.1s n.vpm d.nsm n.nsm

συνεσταλμένος ἐστίν· ⌊τὸ λοιπόν,⌋ ἵνα καὶ οἱ
grown short. *has* From now on those who have wives should *{and}* *those*
5366 1639 3836 3370 3836 2400 2400 1222 2671 2779 3836
pt.rp.nsm v.pai.3s d.asn adv cj cj d.npm

ἔχοντες γυναῖκας ὡς μὴ ἔχοντες ὦσιν 30 καὶ οἱ
who have *wives* be as though they had none, *though they had* *be* and those
2400 1222 1639 6055 2400 2400 2400 3590 2400 1639 2779 3836
pt.pa.npm n.apf pl pl pt.pa.npm v.pas.3p cj d.npm

κλαίοντες ὡς → → → μὴ κλαίοντες καὶ οἱ χαίροντες ὡς → → →
who mourn as though they were not mourning, and those who rejoice as though they were
3081 6055 3081 3081 3081 3590 3081 2779 3836 5897 6055 5897 5897 5897
pt.pa.npm pl pl pt.pa.npm cj d.npm pt.pa.npm pl

μὴ χαίροντες καὶ οἱ ἀγοράζοντες ὡς → → → μὴ κατέχοντες, 31 καὶ οἱ
not rejoicing, and those who buy as though they had no possessions, and those
3590 5897 2779 3836 60 6055 2988 2988 2988 3590 2988 2779 3836
pl pt.pa.npm cj d.npm pt.pa.npm pl pl pt.pa.npm cj d.npm

χρώμενοι τὸν κόσμον ὡς → → → μὴ καταχρώμενοι· παράγει γὰρ τὸ
who use the world as though they were not absorbed in it. *is passing away* For the
5968 3836 3180 6055 2974 2974 2974 3590 2974 4135 1142 3836
pt.pm.npm d.asm n.asm pl pl pt.pm.npm v.pai.3s cj d.nsn

σχῆμα τοῦ κόσμου τούτου. 32 θέλω δὲ ὑμᾶς
form of this world *this* is passing away. I want *{and}* you to be
5386 3836 4047 3180 4047 4135 4135 4135 2527 1254 7007 1639 1639
n.nsn d.gsm n.gsm r.gsm v.pai.1s cj r.ap.2

ἀμερίμνους εἶναι. ὁ ἄγαμος μεριμνᾷ τὰ τοῦ κυρίου, πῶς
free from concern. *to be* An ⌊unmarried man⌋ ⌊is concerned about⌋ ⌊the things⌋ of the Lord, how
291 1639 3836 23 3534 3836 3836 3261 4802
a.apm f.pa d.nsm a.nsm v.pai.3s d.apn d.gsm n.gsm cj

ἀρέσῃ τῷ κυρίῳ· 33 ὁ δὲ γαμήσας μεριμνᾷ τὰ τοῦ
to please the Lord. But a *But* married man ⌊is concerned about⌋ ⌊the things⌋ of the
743 3836 3261 1254 3836 1254 1138 3534 3836 3836
v.aas.3s d.dsm n.dsm d.nsm cj pt.aa.nsm v.pai.3s d.apn d.gsm

NASB

opinion as one
who by the mercy
of the Lord is
trustworthy. 26 I
think then that this
is good in view of
the present distress,
that it is good for
a man to remain
as he is. 27 Are you
bound to a wife?
Do not seek to be
released. Are you
released from a
wife? Do not seek
a wife. 28 But if you
marry, you have
not sinned; and if
a virgin marries,
she has not sinned.
Yet such will have
trouble in this life,
and I am trying to
spare you. 29 But
this I say, brethren,
the time has been
shortened, so
that from now on
those who have
wives should be
as though they
had none; 30 and
those who weep,
as though they
did not weep; and
those who rejoice,
as though they did
not rejoice; and
those who buy, as
though they did not
possess; 31 and those
who use the world,
as though they did
not make full use
of it; for the form
of this world is
passing away.
32 But I want you
to be free from
concern. One who
is unmarried is
concerned about
the things of the
Lord, how he may
please the Lord;
33 but one who is
married is con-
cerned about the
things of the world,

NIV

world—how he
can please his
wife— [34]and his
interests are divid-
ed. An unmarried
woman or virgin
is concerned about
the Lord's affairs:
Her aim is to be
devoted to the
Lord in both body
and spirit. But a
married woman is
concerned about
the affairs of this
world—how she
can please her hus-
band. [35]I am say-
ing this for your
own good, not to
restrict you, but
that you may live
in a right way in
undivided devo-
tion to the Lord.
[36]If anyone is
worried that he
might not be act-
ing honorably to-
ward the virgin he
is engaged to, and
if his passions are
too strong[a] and he
feels he ought to
marry, he should
do as he wants.
He is not sinning.
They should get
married. [37]But the
man who has set-
tled the matter in
his own mind, who
is under no com-
pulsion but has
control over his
own will, and who
has made up his
mind not to marry
the virgin—this
man also does the
right thing. [38]So
then, he who mar-
ries the virgin

κόσμου, πῶς ἀρέσῃ τῇ γυναικί, 34 καὶ μεμέρισται. καὶ ἡ γυνὴ ἡ
world, how to please his wife, and he is divided. *{and}* An unmarried woman *{the}*
3180 4802 743 3836 1222 2779 3532 2779 3836 23 1222 3836
n.gsm cj v.aas.3s d.dsf n.dsf cj v.rpi.3s cj d.nsf n.nsf d.nsf

ἄγαμος καὶ ἡ παρθένος[a] μεριμνᾷ τὰ τοῦ κυρίου, ἵνα ᾖ
unmarried or a virgin ⌊is concerned about⌋ ⌊the things⌋ of the Lord, that ⌊she may be⌋
23 2779 3836 4221 3534 3836 3836 3261 2671 1639
a.nsf cj d.nsf n.nsf v.pai.3s d.apn d.gsm n.gsm cj v.pas.3s

ἁγία καὶ τῷ σώματι καὶ τῷ πνεύματι· ἡ δὲ γαμήσασα μεριμνᾷ
holy both in body and *{the}* spirit. But a *But* married woman ⌊is concerned about⌋
41 2779 3836 5393 2779 3836 4460 1254 3836 1254 1138 3534
a.nsf cj d.dsn n.dsn cj d.dsn n.dsn d.nsf cj pt.aa.nsf v.pai.3s

τὰ τοῦ κόσμου, πῶς ἀρέσῃ τῷ ἀνδρί. 35 τοῦτο δὲ πρὸς
⌊the things⌋ of the world, how to please her husband. I am saying this *{and}* for
3836 3836 3180 4802 743 3836 467 3306 3306 3306 4047 1254 4639
d.apn d.gsm n.gsm cj v.aas.3s d.dsm n.dsm r.asn cj p.a

τὸ ⌊ὑμῶν αὐτῶν⌋ σύμφορον λέγω, οὐχ ἵνα βρόχον ὑμῖν ἐπιβάλω ἀλλὰ
{the} your benefit, *I am saying* not to put a restraint on you, *put on* but
3836 7007 899 5239 3306 4024 2671 2095 1105 2095 7007 2095 247
d.asn r.gp.2 r.gpm n.asn v.pai.1s pl cj n.asm r.dp.2 v.aas.1s cj

πρὸς τὸ εὔσχημον καὶ εὐπάρεδρον τῷ κυρίῳ ἀπερισπάστως. 36 εἰ
to promote *{the}* propriety and undivided devotion ⌊to the⌋ Lord. *undivided* If
4639 3836 2363 2779 597 2339 3836 3261 597 1623
p.a d.asn a.asn cj n.asn d.dsm n.dsm adv cj

δέ τις ⌊ἀσχημονεῖν ἐπὶ⌋ τὴν παρθένον αὐτοῦ ↰ ↰ ↰
{and} someone believes he is not treating *{the}* his virgin *his* in an appropriate
1254 5516 3787 858 2093 3836 899 4221 899 858 858 858
cj r.nsm f.pa p.a d.asf n.asf r.gsm.3

↰ νομίζει, ἐὰν ↱ ↱ ᾖ ὑπέρακμος καὶ οὕτως ὀφείλει γίνεσθαι,
manner, *believes* if his passions are strong, and so it has to be, he
858 3787 1569 5644 5644 1639 5644 2779 4048 4053 1181 4472
v.pai.3s cj v.pas.3s a.nsf cj adv v.pai.3s f.pm

ὃ θέλει ποιείτω, ↱ ↱ οὐχ ἁμαρτάνει, γαμείτωσαν. 37
should do what he desires, *he should do* it is no sin — let them marry. However,
4472 4472 4005 2527 4472 279 279 4024 279 1138 1254
r.asn v.pai.3s v.pam.3s pl v.pai.3s v.pam.3p

ὃς δὲ ἕστηκεν ἐν τῇ καρδίᾳ αὐτοῦ ἑδραῖος μὴ
the man who *However* stands firm in *{the}* his resolve *his* *firm* is under no
4005 1254 2705 1612 1877 3836 899 2840 899 1612 2400 2400 3590
r.nsm cj v.rai.3s p.d d.dsf n.dsf r.gsm.3 a.nsm pl

ἔχων ἀνάγκην, ἐξουσίαν δὲ ἔχει περὶ τοῦ ἰδίου θελήματος καὶ
is under compulsion but has control *but* *has* over *{the}* his desire, and has
2400 340 1254 2400 2026 1254 2400 4309 3836 2625 2525 2779 3212
pt.pa.nsm n.asf n.asf cj v.pai.3s p.g d.gsn a.gsn n.gsn cj

τοῦτο κέκρικεν ἐν τῇ ἰδίᾳ καρδίᾳ, τηρεῖν τὴν ἑαυτοῦ παρθένον,
determined this *has determined* in *{the}* his heart to keep her as his virgin,
3212 4047 3212 1877 3836 2625 2840 5498 3836 1571 4221
r.asn v.rai.3s p.d d.dsf a.dsf n.dsf f.pa d.asf r.gsm.3 n.asf

καλῶς ποιήσει. 38 ὥστε καὶ ὁ γαμίζων[b] τὴν ἑαυτοῦ παρθένον
he will do well. *he will do* So then *{and}* the one who marries *{the}* his virgin
4472 4472 4472 2822 4472 6063 2779 3836 1139 3836 1571 4221
adv v.fai.3s cj cj d.nsm pt.pa.nsm d.asf r.gsm.3 n.asf

NASB

how he may please
his wife, [34]and *his
interests* are di-
vided. The woman
who is unmarried,
and the virgin, is
concerned about
the things of the
Lord, that she may
be holy both in
body and spirit; but
one who is married
is concerned about
the things of the
world, how she
may please her
husband. [35]This I
say for your own
benefit; not to put a
restraint upon you,
but to promote
what is appropriate
and *to secure* un-
distracted devotion
to the Lord.
[36]But if any man
thinks that he is
acting unbecom-
ingly toward his
virgin *daughter,*
if she is past her
youth, and if it
must be so, let him
do what he wishes,
he does not sin; let
her marry. [37]But he
who stands firm in
his heart, being un-
der no constraint,
but has authority
over his own will,
and has decided
this in his own
heart, to keep his
own virgin *daugh-
ter,* he will do well.
[38]So then both he
who gives his own
virgin *daughter* in
marriage does

[a] 36 Or *if she is getting beyond the usual age for marriage*

[a] ἡ ἄγαμος included by TR after παρθένος.
[b] γαμίζων UBS, TNIV, NET. ἐκγαμίζων TR.

NIV

does right, but he
who does not mar-
ry her does better.[a]
[39]A woman is
bound to her hus-
band as long as he
lives. But if her
husband dies, she
is free to marry
anyone she wishes,
but he must belong
to the Lord. [40]In
my judgment, she
is happier if she
stays as she is—
and I think that I
too have the Spirit
of God.

Concerning Food Sacrificed to Idols

8 Now about
food sac-
rificed to idols:
We know that
"We all possess
knowledge." But
knowledge puffs
up while love
builds up. [2]Those
who think they
know something
do not yet know
as they ought to
know. [3]But who-
ever loves God is
known by God.[b]
[4]So then, about

[a] 36-38 Or *[36]If anyone thinks he is not treating his daughter properly, and if she is getting along in years* (or *if her passions are too strong*), *and he feels she ought to marry, he should do as he wants. He is not sinning. He should let her get married. [37]But the man who has settled the matter in his own mind, who is under no compulsion but has control over his own will, and who has made up his mind to keep the virgin unmarried—this man also does the right thing. [38]So then, he who gives his virgin in marriage does right, but he who does not give her in marriage does better.*

[b] 2,3 An early manuscript and another ancient witness *think they have knowledge do not yet know as they ought to know. [3]But whoever loves truly knows.*

καλῶς ποιεῖ καὶ ὁ ↱ ↱ ↱ μὴ γαμίζων[a] κρεῖσσον ποιήσει.
does well, *does* and the one who does not marry will do even better. *will do*
4472 2822 4472 2779 3836 1139 1139 1139 3590 1139 4472 4472 3202 4472
adv v.pai.3s cj d.nsm pl pt.pa.nsm adv.c v.fai.3s

39 γυνὴ δέδεται ἐφ᾽ ὅσον χρόνον ζῇ ὁ ἀνὴρ αὐτῆς· ἐὰν
A wife is bound for such a time as her husband ⌊is alive.⌋ *{the}* *husband* *her* But if
1222 1313 2093 4012 5989 899 467 2409 3836 467 899 1254 1569
n.nsf v.rpi.3s p.a r.asm n.asm v.pai.3s d.nsm n.nsm r.gsf.3 cj

δὲ κοιμηθῇ ὁ ἀνήρ, ἐλευθέρα ἐστὶν ᾧ
But her husband should die, *her* *husband* she is free *she is* to marry whom
1254 3836 467 3121 3836 467 1639 1639 1801 1639 1138 1138 4005
cj v.aps.3s d.nsm n.nsm a.nsf v.pai.3s r.dsm

θέλει γαμηθῆναι, μόνον ἐν κυρίῳ. 40
she wishes, *to marry* only in the Lord. But in my opinion she will be
2527 1138 3667 1877 3261 1254 2848 1847 1191 1639 1639 1639
v.pai.3s f.ap adv p.d n.dsm

μακαριωτέρα δέ ἐστιν ἐὰν οὕτως μείνῃ, κατὰ τὴν ἐμὴν γνώμην·
happier *But* *she will be* if she remains as she is. *she remains* *in* *{the}* *my* *opinion*
3421 1254 1639 1569 3531 3531 4048 3531 2848 3836 1847 1191
a.nsf.c cj v.pai.3s cj adv v.aas.3s p.a d.asf r.asf.1 n.asf

δοκῶ δὲ κἀγὼ πνεῦμα θεοῦ ἔχειν.
And I believe *And* that I too have the Spirit of God. *have*
1254 1506 1254 2743 2400 4460 2536 2400
v.pai.1s cj crasis n.asn n.gsm f.pa

8:1 περὶ δὲ τῶν εἰδωλοθύτων, οἴδαμεν ὅτι πάντες
Now concerning *Now* *{the}* ⌊food sacrificed to idols:⌋ we know that "we all have
1254 4309 1254 3836 1628 3857 4022 2400 4246 2400
p.g cj d.gpn n.gpn v.rai.1p cj a.npm

γνῶσιν ἔχομεν. ἡ γνῶσις φυσιοῖ, ἡ δὲ ἀγάπη οἰκοδομεῖ· 2 εἴ τις
knowledge." *we have* *{the}* Knowledge puffs up, *{the}* but love builds up. If someone
1194 2400 3836 1194 5881 3836 1254 27 3868 1623 5516
n.asf v.pai.1p d.nsf n.nsf v.pai.3s d.nsf cj n.nsf v.pai.3s cj r.nsm

δοκεῖ ἐγνωκέναι τι, ↱ ↱ οὔπω ἔγνω καθὼς δεῖ γνῶναι· 3 εἰ
presumes to know something, he does not yet know as ⌊he ought⌋ to know. But if
1506 1182 5516 1182 1182 4037 1182 2777 1256 1182 1254 1623
v.pai.3s f.ra r.asn adv v.aai.3s cj v.pai.3s f.aa cj

δέ τις ἀγαπᾷ τὸν θεόν, οὗτος ἔγνωσται ὑπ᾽ αὐτοῦ. 4 περὶ
But someone loves *{the}* God, he is known by God. Therefore, as to the eating
1254 5516 26 3836 2536 4047 1182 5679 899 4036 4309
cj r.nsm v.pai.3s d.asm n.asm r.nsm v.rpi.3s p.g r.gsm.3 p.g

τῆς βρώσεως οὖν τῶν εἰδωλοθύτων, οἴδαμεν ὅτι οὐδὲν εἴδωλον
of food *Therefore* *{the}* sacrificed to idols, we know that "an idol has no *idol*
3836 1111 4036 3836 1628 3857 4022 1631 4029 1631
d.gsf n.gsf cj d.gpn n.gpn v.rai.1p cj a.nsn n.nsn

⌊ἐν κόσμῳ⌋ καὶ ὅτι οὐδεὶς θεὸς ⌊εἰ μὴ⌋ εἷς. 5 καὶ γὰρ εἴπερ
genuine reality" and that "there is no God but one." For even *For* if
1877 3180 2779 4022 4029 2536 1623 3590 1651 1142 2779 1142 1642
p.d n.dsm cj cj a.nsm n.nsm cj pl a.nsm adv cj cj

[a] γαμίζων UBS, TNIV, NET. ἐκγαμίζων TR.

NASB

well, and he who
does not give her
in marriage will do
better.
[39]A wife is bound
as long as her
husband lives; but
if her husband is
dead, she is free
to be married to
whom she wishes,
only in the Lord.
[40]But in my opinion
she is happier if
she remains as she
is; and I think that I
also have the Spirit
of God.

Take Care with Your Liberty

[8:1]Now concerning
things sacrificed to
idols, we know that
we all have knowl-
edge. Knowledge
makes arrogant,
but love edifies. [2]If
anyone supposes
that he knows any-
thing, he has not
yet known as he
ought to know; [3]but
if anyone loves
God, he is known
by Him.
[4]Therefore con-
cerning the eating
of things sacrificed
to idols, we know
that [a]there is no
such thing as an
idol in the world,
and that there is no
God but one. [5]For
even if there

[a] Lit *nothing is an idol in the world;* i.e. an idol has no real existence

NIV

eating food sac-
rificed to idols:
We know that "An
idol is nothing at
all in the world"
and that "There is
no God but one."
5For even if there
are so-called gods,
whether in heav-
en or on earth (as
indeed there are
many "gods" and
many "lords"), 6yet
for us there is but
one God, the Fa-
ther, from whom
all things came and
for whom we live;
and there is but one
Lord, Jesus Christ,
through whom all
things came and
through whom we
live.
7But not every-
one possesses this
knowledge. Some
people are still
so accustomed to
idols that when
they eat sacrificial
food they think
of it as having
been sacrificed to
a god, and since
their conscience is
weak, it is defiled.
8But food does
not bring us near
to God; we are no
worse if we do not
eat, and no better
if we do.
9Be careful, how-
ever, that the exer-
cise of your rights
does not become
a stumbling block
to the weak. 10For
if someone with a
weak conscience
sees you, with all
your knowledge,
eating in an idol's
temple, won't that
person be embold-
ened to eat what is
sacrificed to idols?
11So this weak
brother or sister,
for whom Christ
died, is destroyed
by your knowl-
edge. 12When you
sin against

εἰσὶν λεγόμενοι θεοὶ εἴτε ἐν οὐρανῷ εἴτε ἐπὶ γῆς, ὥσπερ εἰσὶν
⌞there are⌟ so-called gods, whether in heaven or on earth (as indeed ⌞there are⌟ many
1639 3306 2536 1664 1877 4041 1664 2093 1178 6061 1639 4498
v.pai.3p pt.pp.npm n.npm cj p.d n.dsm cj p.g n.gsf cj v.pai.3p

θεοὶ πολλοὶ καὶ κύριοι πολλοί, 6ἀλλ᾽ ἡμῖν εἷς θεὸς ὁ πατὴρ
"gods" *many* and many "lords"), *many* yet for us there is but one God, the Father,
2536 4498 2779 4498 3261 4498 247 7005 1651 2536 3836 4252
n.npm a.npm cj n.npm a.npm cj r.dp.1 a.nsm n.nsm d.nsm n.nsm

ἐξ οὗ τὰ πάντα καὶ ἡμεῖς εἰς αὐτόν, καὶ εἷς κύριος
from whom are *{the}* all things and for whom we exist, *for* *whom* and one Lord,
1666 4005 3836 4246 2779 1650 899 7005 1650 899 2779 1651 3261
p.g r.gsm d.npn a.npn cj r.np.1 p.a r.asm.3 cj a.nsm n.nsm

Ἰησοῦς Χριστὸς δι᾽ οὗ τὰ πάντα καὶ ἡμεῖς δι᾽
Jesus Christ, through whom are *{the}* all things and through whom we exist. *through*
2652 5986 1328 4005 3836 4246 2779 1328 899 7005 1328
n.nsm n.nsm p.g r.gsm d.npn a.npn cj r.np.1 p.g

αὐτοῦ. 7ἀλλ᾽ οὐκ ἐν πᾶσιν ἡ γνῶσις· τινὲς δὲ
whom However, not everyone has *everyone* this knowledge. But some, *But* because in
899 247 4024 4246 1877 4246 3836 1194 1254 5516 1254 2401
r.gsm.3 cj pl p.d a.dpm d.nsf n.nsf r.npm cj

τῇ συνηθείᾳ ἕως ἄρτι τοῦ εἰδώλου
former times they were *{the}* involved with *in former times* *{the}* idols, eat this food
2401 2401 3836 5311 2401 785 3836 1631 2266
d.dsf n.dsf p.g adv d.gsn n.gsn

ὡς εἰδωλόθυτον ἐσθίουσιν, καὶ ἡ συνείδησις αὐτῶν
⌞as though⌟ it were an idol sacrifice, *eat* and thus *{the}* their conscience, *their* being
6055 1628 2266 2779 3836 899 5287 899 1639
pl n.asn v.pai.3p cj d.nsf n.nsf r.gpm.3

ἀσθενὴς οὖσα μολύνεται. 8βρῶμα δὲ ↱ ↱ ἡμᾶς οὐ παραστήσει τῷ θεῷ·
weak, *being* is defiled. Food *{and}* does not bring us *not* close to God.
822 1639 3662 1109 1254 4225 4024 4225 7005 4024 4225 3836 2536
a.nsf pt.pa.nsf v.ppi.3s n.nsn cj r.ap.1 pl v.fai.3s d.dsm n.dsm

οὔτε ἐὰν ↱ ↱ μὴ φάγωμεν ὑστερούμεθα, οὔτε ἐὰν φάγωμεν
We are no worse if we do not eat, *We are worse* and no better if we do.
5728 5728 4046 5728 1569 2266 2266 3590 2266 5728 4046 4355 1569 2266
cj cj pl v.aas.1p v.ppi.1p cj cj v.aas.1p

περισσεύομεν. 9 βλέπετε δὲ μή πως ἡ ἐξουσία
better But take care *But* that this right of yours does not *that* *{the}* *right*
4355 1254 1063 1254 4803 4047 2026 7007 7007 1181 3590 4803 3836 2026
v.pai.1p v.pam.2p cj cj pl d.nsf n.nsf

ὑμῶν αὕτη πρόσκομμα γένηται τοῖς ἀσθενέσιν. 10 ἐὰν γάρ τις
of yours *this* become a stumbling block *does become* to the weak. For if *For* someone
7007 4047 1181 4682 1181 3836 822 1142 1569 1142 5516
r.gp.2 r.nsf n.nsn v.ams.3s d.dpm a.dpm cj cj r.nsm

ἴδῃ σὲ τὸν ἔχοντα γνῶσιν ἐν εἰδωλείῳ κατακείμενον, ↱ οὐχὶ
⌞should see⌟ you who have knowledge, dining in an idol's temple, *dining* will not
1625 5148 3836 2400 1194 2879 1877 1627 2879 3868 4049
v.aas.3s r.as.2 d.asm pt.pa.asm n.asf p.d n.dsn pt.pm.asm pl

ἡ συνείδησις → αὐτοῦ ἀσθενοῦς ὄντος οἰκοδομηθήσεται εἰς τὸ
the conscience of the one who is weak be emboldened to ~ eat
3836 5287 899 822 1639 3868 1650 3836 2266
d.nsf n.nsf r.gsm.3 a.gsm pt.pa.gsm v.fpi.3s p.a d.asn

τὰ εἰδωλόθυτα ἐσθίειν; 11
food sacrificed to idols? *eat* And so the one who is weak, the brother for whom
3836 1628 2266 1142 1142 3836 820 820 820 820 3836 81 1328 4005
d.apn n.apn f.pa

ἀπόλλυται γὰρ ὁ ἀσθενῶν ἐν τῇ σῇ γνώσει, ὁ
Christ died, will be destroyed *And so* *the* *one who is weak* by *{the}* your knowledge. *the*
5986 633 660 1142 3836 820 1877 3836 5050 1194 3836
v.pmi.3s cj d.nsm pt.pa.nsm p.d d.dsf r.dsf.2 n.dsf d.nsm

ἀδελφὸς δι᾽ ὃν Χριστὸς ἀπέθανεν. 12οὕτως δὲ ἁμαρτάνοντες εἰς τοὺς
brother *for* *whom* *Christ* *died* So *{and}* when you sin against your
81 1328 4005 5986 633 4048 1254 279 1650 3836
n.nsm p.a r.asm n.nsm v.aai.3s adv cj pt.pa.npm p.a d.apm

NASB

are so-called gods
whether in heaven
or on earth, as
indeed there are
many gods and
many lords, 6yet for
us there is *but* one
God, the Father,
from whom are all
things and we *exist*
for Him; and one
Lord, Jesus Christ,
by whom are all
things, and we *exist*
through Him.
7However not
all men have this
knowledge; but
some, being ac-
customed to the
idol until now,
eat *food* as if it
were sacrificed to
an idol; and their
conscience being
weak is defiled.
8But food will not
commend us to
God; we are nei-
ther the worse if
we do not eat, nor
the better if we do
eat. 9But take care
that this liberty
of yours does not
somehow become
a stumbling block
to the weak. 10For if
someone sees you,
who have knowl-
edge, dining in an
idol's temple, will
not his conscience,
if he is weak, be
strengthened to eat
things sacrificed to
idols? 11For through
your knowledge
he who is weak is
ruined, the brother
for whose sake
Christ died. 12And
so, by sinning

NIV

them in this way
and wound their
weak conscience,
you sin against
Christ. [13]Therefore, if what I eat
causes my brother
or sister to fall into
sin, I will never eat
meat again, so that
I will not cause
them to fall.

Paul's Rights as an Apostle

9 Am I not free?
Am I not an
apostle? Have I
not seen Jesus our
Lord? Are you not
the result of my
work in the Lord?
[2]Even though I
may not be an
apostle to others,
surely I am to you!
For you are the
seal of my apostle-
ship in the Lord.
[3]This is my de-
fense to those who
sit in judgment
on me. [4]Don't we
have the right to
food and drink?
[5]Don't we have the
right to take a be-
lieving wife along
with us, as do the
other apostles and
the Lord's broth-
ers and Cephas[a]?
[6]Or is it only I and
Barnabas who lack
the right to not
work for a living?
[7]Who serves as a
soldier at his own
expense? Who
plants a vineyard
and does not eat
its grapes? Who
tends a flock and
does not drink the
milk?

[a] 5 That is, Peter

ἀδελφοὺς καὶ τύπτοντες αὐτῶν τὴν συνείδησιν ἀσθενοῦσαν εἰς
brothers and wound their {the} conscience, being weak, you are sinning against
81 2779 5597 899 3836 5287 820 279 279 279 1650
n.apm cj pt.pa.npm r.gpm.3 d.asf n.asf pt.pa.asf p.a

Χριστὸν ἁμαρτάνετε. [13] διόπερ εἰ βρῶμα → σκανδαλίζει τὸν
Christ. *you are sinning* Therefore, if food causes my brother to stumble, {the}
5986 279 1478 1623 1109 1609 81 4997 3836
n.asm v.pai.2p cj cj n.nsn v.pai.3s d.asm

ἀδελφόν μου, ↱ ↱ ⌞οὐ μὴ⌟ φάγω κρέα εἰς τὸν αἰῶνα, ⌞ἵνα μὴ⌟ ↱ ↱ τὸν
brother *my* I will never eat meat, {for} {all} {time} lest I cause {the}
81 1609 2266 2266 4024 3590 2266 3200 1650 3836 172 2671 3590 4997 4997 3836
n.asm r.gs.1 pl pl v.aas.1s n.apn p.a d.asm n.asm cj pl d.asm

ἀδελφόν μου σκανδαλίσω.
my brother *my* to stumble.
1609 81 1609 4997
n.asm r.gs.1 v.aas.1s

9:1 οὐκ εἰμὶ ἐλεύθερος; οὐκ εἰμὶ ἀπόστολος; οὐχὶ
Am I not *Am I* free? Am I not *Am I* an apostle? Have I not
1639 1639 4024 1639 1801 1639 1639 4024 1639 693 3972 3972 4049
pl v.pai.1s a.nsm pl v.pai.1s n.nsm pl

Ἰησοῦν τὸν κύριον ἡμῶν ἑόρακα; οὐ τὸ ἔργον
seen Jesus {the} our Lord? *our* *Have I seen* Are you not the result of {the} my labor
3972 2652 3836 7005 3261 7005 3972 1639 7007 4024 3836 1609 2240
n.asm d.asm n.asm r.gp.1 v.rai.1s pl d.nsn n.nsn

μου ὑμεῖς ἐστε ἐν κυρίῳ; [2] εἰ ἄλλοις οὐκ εἰμὶ ἀπόστολος, ἀλλά
my *you* *Are* in the Lord? If to others I am not *I am* an apostle, at least
1609 7007 1639 1877 3261 1623 257 1639 1639 4024 1639 693 247
r.gs.1 r.np.2 v.pai.2p p.d n.dsm cj r.dpm pl v.pai.1s n.nsm cj

γε ὑμῖν εἰμι· ἡ γάρ σφραγίς μου τῆς ἀποστολῆς ὑμεῖς
~ I am to you, *I am* for you are the *for* proof of my *of* apostleship *you*
1145 1639 1639 7007 1639 1142 7007 1639 3836 1142 5382 3836 1609 3836 692 7007
pl r.dp.2 v.pai.1s d.nsf cj n.nsf r.gs.1 d.gsf n.gsf r.np.2

ἐστε ἐν κυρίῳ. [3] ἡ ἐμὴ ἀπολογία τοῖς ἐμὲ
are in the Lord. {the} This is my defense to those who sit in judgment on me.
1639 1877 3261 3836 4047 1639 1847 665 3836 373 373 373 373 373 1609
v.pai.2p p.d n.dsm d.nsf r.nsf.1 n.nsf d.dpm r.as.1

ἀνακρίνουσίν ἐστιν αὕτη. [4] μὴ ↱ ↱ οὐκ ἔχομεν ἐξουσίαν φαγεῖν καὶ
who sit in judgment on *is* *This* ~ Do we not have the right to eat and
373 1639 4047 3590 2400 2400 4024 2400 2026 2266 2779
pt.pa.dpm v.pai.3s r.nsf pl pl v.pai.1p n.asf f.aa cj

πεῖν; [5] μὴ ↱ ↱ οὐκ ἔχομεν ἐξουσίαν ἀδελφὴν γυναῖκα
drink? {not} Do we not have the right to the company of a believing wife,
4403 3590 2400 2400 4024 2400 2026 4310 4310 4310 4310 80 1222
f.aa pl pl v.pai.1p n.asf n.asf n.asf

περιάγειν ὡς καὶ οἱ λοιποὶ ἀπόστολοι καὶ οἱ ἀδελφοὶ τοῦ κυρίου
to the company of as also the other apostles, {and} the Lord's brothers, {the} *Lord's*
4310 6055 2779 3836 3370 693 2779 3836 3261 81 3836 3261
f.pa pl adv d.npm a.npm n.npm cj d.npm n.npm d.gsm n.gsm

καὶ Κηφᾶς; [6] ἢ μόνος ἐγὼ καὶ Βαρναβᾶς οὐκ ἔχομεν ἐξουσίαν ↱
and Cephas do? Or is it only I and Barnabas who have no *have* right to
2779 3064 2445 3668 1609 2779 982 2400 4024 2400 2026 2237
cj n.nsm cj a.nsm r.ns.1 cj n.nsm pl v.pai.1p n.asf

μὴ ἐργάζεσθαι; [7] Τίς στρατεύεται ἰδίοις ὀψωνίοις ποτέ; τίς
⌞refrain from⌟ working? Who ever serves in the army at his own expense? *ever* Who
3590 2237 5515 4537 5129 2625 4072 4537 5515
pl f.pm r.nsm v.pmi.3s a.dpn n.dpn adv r.nsm

φυτεύει ἀμπελῶνα καὶ τὸν καρπὸν αὐτοῦ οὐκ ἐσθίει; ἢ τίς
plants a vineyard and does not eat {the} its fruit? *its* *not* *does eat* Or who
5885 308 2779 2266 4024 2266 3836 899 2843 899 4024 2266 2445 5515
v.pai.3s n.asm cj d.asm n.asm r.gsm.3 pl v.pai.3s cj r.nsm

ποιμαίνει ποίμνην καὶ ἐκ τοῦ γάλακτος τῆς ποίμνης οὐκ
tends a flock and does not drink of {the} its milk? {the} *its* *not*
4477 4479 2779 2266 4024 2266 1666 3836 4479 1128 3836 4479 4024
v.pai.3s n.asf cj p.g d.gsn n.gsn d.gsf n.gsf pl

NASB

against the brethren
and wounding their
conscience when
it is weak, you
sin against Christ.
[13]Therefore, if food
causes my brother
to stumble, I will
never eat meat
again, so that I
will not cause my
brother to stumble.

Paul's Use of Liberty

[9:1]Am I not free?
Am I not an
apostle? Have I
not seen Jesus our
Lord? Are you not
my work in the
Lord? [2]If to others
I am not an apostle,
at least I am to
you; for you are the
seal of my apostle-
ship in the Lord.
[3]My defense to
those who examine
me is this: [4]Do we
not have a right
to eat and drink?
[5]Do we not have a
right to take along
a believing wife,
even as the rest of
the apostles and
the brothers of the
Lord and Cephas?
[6]Or do only Barna-
bas and I not have
a right to refrain
from working?
[7]Who at any time
serves as a soldier
at his own ex-
pense? Who plants
a vineyard and
does not eat the
fruit of it? Or who
tends a flock and
does not use the
milk of the flock?

NIV

8Do I say this
merely on human
authority? Doesn't
the Law say the
same thing? 9For
it is written in the
Law of Moses:
"Do not muzzle
an ox while it is
treading out the
grain."[a] Is it about
oxen that God is
concerned? 10Sure-
ly he says this for
us, doesn't he?
Yes, this was writ-
ten for us, because
whoever plows and
threshes should be
able to do so in the
hope of sharing in
the harvest. 11If we
have sown spiri-
tual seed among
you, is it too much
if we reap a ma-
terial harvest from
you? 12If others
have this right of
support from you,
shouldn't we have
it all the more?
But we did not
use this right. On
the contrary, we
put up with any-
thing rather than
hinder the gospel
of Christ.
13Don't you know
that those who
serve in the tem-
ple get their food
from the temple,
and that those who
serve at the altar
share in what is of-
fered on the altar?
14In the same way,
the Lord has com-
manded that those
who preach

ἐσθίει; 8Μὴ κατὰ ἄνθρωπον ↰ ↰ ↰
does drink *{not}* Am I saying these things from a merely human point of view?
2266 3590 3281 3281 3281 4047 4047 2848 476 2848 2848 2848
v.pai.3s pl p.a n.asm

ταῦτα λαλῶ ἢ καὶ ὁ νόμος ταῦτα οὐ λέγει; 9 ἐν
these things *Am I saying* Or *{also}* does not the Law say the same? *not* *does say* For in
4047 3281 2445 2779 3306 4024 3836 3795 3306 4047 4024 3306 1142 1877
r.apn v.pai.1s cj adv d.nsm n.nsm r.apn pl v.pai.3s p.d

γὰρ τῷ Μωϋσέως νόμῳ γέγραπται, ↱ ↱ οὐ κημώσεις βοῦν
For the Law of Moses *Law* it is written, "You shall not muzzle an ox
1142 3836 3795 3707 3795 1211 3055 3055 4024 3055 1091
cj d.dsm n.gsm n.dsm v.rpi.3s pl v.fai.2s n.asm

ἀλοῶντα. μὴ τῶν βοῶν μέλει τῷ θεῷ ↰
⌊while it is treading out⌋ the grain." It is not for oxen that God is concerned, *{the}* *God* is
262 3590 3836 1091 2536 3508 3836 2536 3590
pt.pa.asm pl d.gpm n.gpm v.pai.3s d.dsm n.dsm

↰ 10 ἢ δι' ἡμᾶς ↰ πάντως λέγει;
it? Or does he not speak entirely for our sake. *entirely* *does he speak* To be sure,
3590 2445 3306 3306 3306 4122 1328 7005 1328 4122 3306 1142 1142 1142
cj p.a r.ap.1 adv v.pai.3s

δι' ἡμᾶς ↰ γὰρ ἐγράφη ὅτι ὀφείλει
it was written for our sake, *To be sure* *it was written* because the one plowing should plow
1211 1211 1211 1328 7005 1328 1142 1211 4022 3836 769 769 4053 769
p.a r.ap.1 cj v.api.3s cj v.pai.3s

ἐπ' ἐλπίδι ὁ ἀροτριῶν ἀροτριᾶν καὶ ὁ ἀλοῶν ἐπ' ἐλπίδι τοῦ
in hope *the* *one plowing* *plow* and the one threshing thresh in hope of
2093 1828 3836 769 769 2779 3836 262 2093 1828 3836
p.d n.dsf d.nsm pt.pa.nsm f.pa cj d.nsm pt.pa.nsm p.d n.dsf d.gsn

μετέχειν. 11εἰ ἡμεῖς ὑμῖν τὰ πνευματικὰ
sharing in the crop. If we sowed spiritual things ⌊among you,⌋ *{the}* *spiritual things*
3576 1623 7005 5062 4461 4461 7007 3836 4461
f.pa cj r.np.1 r.dp.2 d.apn a.apn

ἐσπείραμεν, μέγα εἰ ἡμεῖς ὑμῶν τὰ σαρκικὰ
sowed is it too much if we reap material things from you? *{the}* *material things*
5062 3489 1623 7005 2545 4920 4920 7007 3836 4920
v.aai.1p a.nsn cj r.np.1 r.gp.2 d.apn a.apn

θερίσομεν; 12Εἰ ἄλλοι τῆς ὑμῶν ἐξουσίας μετέχουσιν,
reap If others have a share in this right over you, *right* *have a share in* do
2545 1623 257 3576 3576 3576 3576 2026 3836 7007 2026 3576
v.fai.1p cj r.npm d.gsf r.gp.2 n.gsf v.pai.3p

οὐ μᾶλλον ἡμεῖς; ἀλλ' ↱ ↱ οὐκ ἐχρησάμεθα τῇ ἐξουσίᾳ
not we even more? *we* Nevertheless, we have not made use of *{the}* this right,
4024 7005 3437 7005 247 5968 5968 4024 5968 3836 4047 2026
pl adv.c r.np.1 cj pl v.ami.1p d.dsf n.dsf

ταύτῃ, ἀλλὰ πάντα στέγομεν, ⌊ἵνα μὴ⌋ τινα ἐγκοπὴν δῶμεν
this but endure all things *endure* lest we place some ⌊obstacle in the way⌋ *we place*
4047 247 5095 4246 5095 2671 3590 1443 1443 5516 1600 1443
r.dsf cj a.apn v.pai.1p cj pl r.asf n.asf v.aas.1p

τῷ εὐαγγελίῳ τοῦ Χριστοῦ. 13↱ ↱ οὐκ οἴδατε ὅτι οἱ τὰ
⌊of the⌋ gospel of Christ. Do you not know that those who perform *{the}*
3836 2295 3836 5986 3857 3857 4024 3857 4022 3836 2237 2237 3836
d.dsn n.dsn d.gsm n.gsm pl v.rai.2p cj d.npm d.apn

ἱερὰ ἐργαζόμενοι τὰ[a] ἐκ τοῦ ἱεροῦ ἐσθίουσιν, οἱ
⌊sacred rites⌋ *who perform* *{the}* in the temple eat food from the temple, *eat food* and those
2641 2237 3836 2266 2266 1666 3836 2639 2266 3836
n.apn pt.pm.npm d.apn p.g d.gsn n.gsn v.pai.3p d.npm

τῷ θυσιαστηρίῳ παρεδρεύοντες τῷ θυσιαστηρίῳ
who serve ⌊at the⌋ altar *who serve* share in the sacrificial offerings?
4204 4204 3836 2603 4204 5211 5211 3836 2603
d.dsn n.dsn pt.pa.npm d.dsn n.dsn

συμμερίζονται; 14οὕτως καὶ ὁ κύριος διέταξεν τοῖς
share in ⌊In the same way,⌋ *{and}* the Lord gave instructions to those who proclaim
5211 4048 2779 3836 3261 1411 3836 2859 2859
v.pmi.3p adv cj d.nsm n.nsm v.aai.3s d.dpm

NASB

8I am not speak-
ing these things
according to hu-
man judgment, am
I? Or does not the
Law also say these
things? 9For it is
written in the Law
of Moses, "YOU
SHALL NOT MUZZLE
THE OX WHILE HE IS
THRESHING." God
is not concerned
about oxen, is He?
10Or is He speaking
altogether for our
sake? Yes, for our
sake it was writ-
ten, because the
plowman ought
to plow in hope,
and the thresher *to*
thresh in hope of
sharing *the crops.*
11If we sowed
spiritual things in
you, is it too much
if we reap material
things from you?
12If others share the
right over you, do
we not more? Nev-
ertheless, we did
not use this right,
but we endure all
things so that we
will cause no hin-
drance to the gos-
pel of Christ. 13Do
you not know that
those who perform
sacred services
eat the *food* of the
temple, *and* those
who attend regular-
ly to the altar have
their share from the
altar? 14So also the
Lord directed those
who proclaim the

[a] 9 Deut. 25:4

[a] [τὰ] UBS.

NIV

the gospel should
receive their living
from the gospel.
15 But I have not
used any of these
rights. And I am
not writing this in
the hope that you
will do such things
for me, for I would
rather die than
allow anyone to
deprive me of this
boast. 16 For when
I preach the gos-
pel, I cannot boast,
since I am com-
pelled to preach.
Woe to me if I do
not preach the gos-
pel! 17 If I preach
voluntarily, I have
a reward; if not
voluntarily, I am
simply discharging
the trust commit-
ted to me. 18 What
then is my reward?
Just this: that in
preaching the gos-
pel I may offer it
free of charge, and
so not make full
use of my rights as
a preacher of the
gospel.

Paul's Use of His Freedom

19 Though I am
free and belong
to no one, I have
made myself a
slave to everyone,
to win as many
as possible. 20 To
the Jews I became
like a Jew, to win
the Jews. To those
under the law I
became like one
under the law
(though I myself
am not under the
law), so as to win
those under

τὸ εὐαγγέλιον καταγγέλλουσιν ἐκ τοῦ εὐαγγελίου ζῆν.
the gospel *who proclaim* that they should get their living from the gospel. *living*
3836 2295 2859 2409 1666 3836 2295 2409
d.asn n.asn pt.pa.dpm p.g d.gsn n.gsn f.pa

15 ἐγὼ δὲ ↱ οὐ κέχρημαι οὐδενὶ τούτων. οὐκ ἔγραψα δὲ
But I *But* have not used any of these rights. And I am not writing *And*
1254 1609 1254 5968 4024 5968 4029 4047 1254 4024 1211 1254
r.ns.1 cj pl v.rmi.1s a.dsn r.gpn pl v.aai.1s cj

ταῦτα, ἵνα οὕτως γένηται ἐν ἐμοί· καλὸν γάρ μοι
this so that *{thus}* something will be done for me; for it would be better *for* ⌊for me⌋
4047 2671 4048 1181 1877 1609 1142 2819 1142 1609
r.apn cj adv v.ams.3s p.d r.ds.1 a.nsn cj r.ds.1

μᾶλλον ἀποθανεῖν ἢ τὸ καύχημά μου
rather to die *{than}* — no one shall take away *{the}* my ⌊ground for boasting!⌋ *my*
3437 633 2445 4029 4029 3033 3033 3033 3836 1609 3017 1609
adv.c f.aa pl d.asn n.asn r.gs.1

οὐδεὶς κενώσει. 16 ἐὰν γὰρ εὐαγγελίζωμαι, ↱ οὐκ ἔστιν μοι
no one *shall take away* If *{for}* I preach the gospel, I do not have *I* a
4029 3033 1569 1142 2294 1609 1639 4024 1639 1609
a.nsm v.fai.3s cj cj v.pms.1s pl v.pai.3s r.ds.1

καύχημα· ↱ ἀνάγκη γάρ μοι ἐπίκειται· οὐαὶ γάρ μοί ἐστιν
⌊ground for boasting,⌋ for I am compelled *for* *I* to do so. Woe *{for}* is me *is*
3017 1142 1609 2130 340 1142 1609 2130 4026 1142 1639 1609 1639
n.nsn n.nsf cj r.ds.1 v.pmi.3s j cj r.ds.1 v.pai.3s

ἐὰν ↱ ↱ μὴ εὐαγγελίσωμαι. 17 εἰ γὰρ ἑκὼν τοῦτο πράσσω,
if I do not preach the gospel! For if *For* I do this willingly, *this* *I do*
1569 2294 2294 3590 2294 1142 1623 1142 4556 4556 4047 1776 4047 4556
cj pl v.ams.1s cj cj a.nsm r.asn v.pai.1s

μισθὸν ἔχω· εἰ δὲ ἄκων,
I have a reward. *I have* But if *But* unwillingly, I have been entrusted with a
2400 2400 3635 2400 1254 1623 1254 220 4409 4409 4409 4409 4409
n.asm v.pai.1s cj cj a.nsm

οἰκονομίαν πεπίστευμαι· 18 τίς οὖν μού ἐστιν ὁ μισθός; ἵνα
charge. *I have been entrusted with* What then is my *is* *{the}* reward? That
3873 4409 5515 4036 1639 1609 1639 3836 3635 2671
n.asf v.rpi.1s r.nsm cj r.gs.1 v.pai.3s d.nsm n.nsm cj

εὐαγγελιζόμενος ἀδάπανον θήσω τὸ εὐαγγέλιον
when I preach I may present the gospel free of charge, *I may present* *the* *gospel* and
2294 5502 5502 5502 3836 2295 78 5502 3836 2295
pt.pm.nsm a.asn v.fai.1s d.asn n.asn

εἰς τὸ μὴ καταχρήσασθαι τῇ ἐξουσίᾳ μου ἐν τῷ εὐαγγελίῳ. 19
so ~ not make full use of *{the}* my right *my* in the gospel. For though
1650 3836 3590 2974 3836 1609 2026 1609 1877 3836 2295 1142 1639
p.a d.asn pl f.am d.dsf n.dsf r.gs.1 p.d d.dsn n.dsn

ἐλεύθερος γὰρ ὢν ἐκ πάντων πᾶσιν
I am free *For* *though I am* from all, I have made myself a servant to all,
1639 1639 1801 1142 1639 1666 4246 1530 1530 1530 1831 1530 1530 4246
a.nsm cj pt.pa.nsm p.g a.gpm a.dpm

ἐμαυτὸν ἐδούλωσα, ἵνα τοὺς πλείονας κερδήσω·
myself *I have made a servant* so that I might win *{the}* ⌊as many as possible.⌋ *I might win*
1831 1530 2671 3045 3045 3045 3836 4498 3045
r.asm.1 v.aai.1s cj d.apm a.apm.c v.aas.1s

20 καὶ ἐγενόμην τοῖς Ἰουδαίοις ὡς Ἰουδαῖος, ἵνα
{and} To the Jews I became *To the* *Jews* as a Jew that I might win
2779 3836 3836 2681 1181 3836 2681 6055 2681 2671 3045 3045 3045
cj v.ami.1s d.dpm a.dpm pl a.nsm cj

Ἰουδαίους κερδήσω· τοῖς ὑπὸ νόμον ὡς ὑπὸ νόμον,
Jews. *I might win* To those under the law I became as one under the law (though
2681 3045 3836 5679 3795 6055 5679 3795 1639
a.apm v.aas.1s d.dpm p.a n.asm pl p.a n.asm

μὴ ὢν αὐτὸς ὑπὸ νόμον, ἵνα τοὺς ὑπὸ
I myself am not *though I am* *myself* under the law) that I might win those under the
1639 899 1639 3590 1639 899 5679 3795 2671 3045 3045 3045 3836 5679
pl pt.pa.nsm r.nsm p.a n.asm cj d.apm p.a

NASB

gospel to get their
living from the
gospel.
15 But I have used
none of these
things. And I am
not writing these
things so that it
will be done so
in my case; for it
would be better
for me to die than
have any man
make my boast an
empty one. 16 For if
I preach the gospel,
I have nothing to
boast of, for I am
under compulsion;
for woe is me if I
do not preach the
gospel. 17 For if I do
this voluntarily, I
have a reward; but
if against my will,
I have a steward-
ship entrusted to
me. 18 What then is
my reward? That,
when I preach the
gospel, I may offer
the gospel without
charge, so as not
to make full use
of my right in the
gospel.
19 For though I
am free from all
men, I have made
myself a slave to
all, so that I may
win more. 20 To the
Jews I became as a
Jew, so that I might
win Jews; to those
who are under the
Law, as under the
Law though not
being myself under
the Law, so that I
might win those
who are under the

NIV

the law. 21 To those
not having the law
I became like one
not having the law
(though I am not
free from God's
law but am under
Christ's law), so
as to win those not
having the law.
22 To the weak I be-
came weak, to win
the weak. I have
become all things
to all people so
that by all possi-
ble means I might
save some. 23 I do
all this for the sake
of the gospel, that
I may share in its
blessings.

The Need for Self-Discipline

24 Do you not
know that in a race
all the runners
run, but only one
gets the prize? Run
in such a way as
to get the prize.
25 Everyone who
competes in the
games goes into
strict training.
They do it to get
a crown that will
not last, but we do
it to get a crown
that will last for-
ever. 26 Therefore
I do not run like
someone running
aimlessly; I do not
fight like a boxer
beating the air.
27 No, I strike a
blow to my body
and make it my
slave so that after
I have preached
to others, I myself
will not be dis-
qualified for the
prize.

Warnings From Israel's History

10 For I do not
want you to
be ignorant of the
fact, brothers and
sisters, that our
ancestors were all
under the cloud
and that they all
passed through
the sea.

νόμον κερδήσω· 21 τοῖς ἀνόμοις ὡς ἄνομος,
law. *I might win* To those ⌊outside the law⌋ I became as ⌊one outside the law⌋ (though I
3795 3045 3836 491 6055 491 1639 1639
n.asm v.aas.1s d.dpm a.dpm pl a.nsm

μὴ ὢν ἄνομος θεοῦ ἀλλ᾽ ἔννομος Χριστοῦ, ἵνα κερδάνω
am not *though I am* ⌊free from the law⌋ of God but ⌊subject to the law⌋ of Christ) that I might win
1639 3590 1639 491 2536 247 1937 5986 2671 3045
pl pt.pa.nsm a.nsm n.gsm cj a.nsm n.gsm cj v.aas.1s

τοὺς ἀνόμους· 22 ἐγενόμην τοῖς ἀσθενέσιν ἀσθενής, ἵνα
those ⌊outside the law.⌋ To the weak I became *To the weak* weak that I might
3836 491 3836 3836 822 1181 3836 822 822 2671 3045 3045
d.apm a.apm v.ami.1s d.dpm a.dpm a.nsm cj

τοὺς ἀσθενεῖς κερδήσω· τοῖς πᾶσιν γέγονα
win the weak. *I might win* I have become all things to all people, *I have become*
3045 3836 822 3045 1181 1181 1181 4246 4246 3836 4246 1181
d.apm a.apm v.aas.1s d.dpm a.dpm v.rai.1s

πάντα, ἵνα πάντως τινὰς σώσω. 23 πάντα δὲ ποιῶ
all things that by all means I might save some. *I might save* I do all things *{and}* *I do*
4246 2671 4122 5392 5392 5392 5516 5392 4472 4472 4246 1254 4472
a.npn cj adv r.apm v.aas.1s a.apn cj v.pai.1s

διὰ τὸ εὐαγγέλιον, ἵνα → → → συγκοινωνὸς αὐτοῦ
⌊for the sake of⌋ the gospel, that I may share with them in its benefits. *its*
1328 3836 2295 2671 1181 1181 899 5171 899
p.a d.asn n.asn cj n.nsm r.gsn.3

γένωμαι. 24 ↱ ↱ οὐκ οἴδατε ὅτι οἱ ἐν σταδίῳ τρέχοντες πάντες
I may Do you not know that all who run in the stadium *run* *all*
1181 3857 3857 4024 3857 4022 4246 3836 5556 1877 5084 5556 4246
v.ams.1s pl v.rai.2p cj d.npm p.d n.dsn pt.pa.npm a.npm

μὲν τρέχουσιν, εἷς δὲ λαμβάνει τὸ βραβεῖον; οὕτως τρέχετε ἵνα
~ compete but only one *but* receives the prize? So run that
3525 5556 1254 1651 1254 3284 3836 1092 4048 5556 2671
pl v.pai.3p a.nsm cj v.pai.3s d.asn n.asn adv v.pam.2p cj

καταλάβητε. 25 πᾶς δὲ ὁ ἀγωνιζόμενος πάντα
you may win. Everyone *{and}* who competes exercises self-control in all things.
2898 4246 1254 3836 76 1603 1603 1603 4246
v.aas.2p a.nsm cj d.nsm pt.pm.nsm a.apn

ἐγκρατεύεται, ἐκεῖνοι μὲν οὖν ἵνα φθαρτὸν στέφανον λάβωσιν,
exercises self-control in They ~ *{then}* do it to receive a perishable wreath, *receive*
1603 1697 3525 4036 2671 3284 5778 5109 3284
v.pmi.3s r.npm pl cj cj a.asm n.asm v.aas.3p

ἡμεῖς δὲ ἄφθαρτον. 26 ἐγὼ τοίνυν οὕτως → τρέχω ὡς
but we *but* for an imperishable one. So I *So* *{in this way}* do not run *{like}*
1254 7005 1254 915 5523 1609 5523 4048 4024 5556 6055
r.np.1 cj a.asm r.ns.1 cj adv v.pai.1s pl

οὐκ ἀδήλως, οὕτως → → πυκτεύω ὡς οὐκ ἀέρα δέρων·
not aimlessly; *{in this way}* I do not box like *not* one flailing the air. *one flailing*
4024 85 4048 4024 4782 6055 4024 1296 1296 113 1296
pl adv adv v.pai.1s pl pl n.asm pt.pa.nsm

27 ἀλλὰ ὑπωπιάζω μου τὸ σῶμα καὶ δουλαγωγῶ, μή πως
But I discipline my *{the}* body and bring it into subjection, *not* so that having preached
247 5724 1609 3836 5393 2779 1524 3590 4803 3062 3062
cj v.pai.1s r.gs.1 d.asn n.asn cj v.pai.1s cj pl

ἄλλοις κηρύξας αὐτὸς ἀδόκιμος γένωμαι.
to others *having preached* I myself should not be disqualified. *I should be*
257 3062 1181 899 1181 3590 1181 99 1181
r.dpm pt.aa.nsm r.nsm a.nsm v.ams.1s

10:1 ↱ ↱ οὐ θέλω γὰρ ὑμᾶς ἀγνοεῖν, ἀδελφοί, ὅτι οἱ πατέρες
For I do not want *For* you to be unaware, brothers, that *{the}* our fathers
1142 2527 2527 4024 2527 1142 7007 51 81 4022 3836 7005 4252
pl v.pai.1s cj r.ap.2 f.pa n.vpm cj d.npm n.npm

ἡμῶν πάντες ὑπὸ τὴν νεφέλην ἦσαν καὶ πάντες διὰ τῆς θαλάσσης
our were all under the cloud *were* and all passed through the sea,
7005 1639 4246 5679 3836 3749 1639 2779 4246 1451 1328 3836 2498
r.gp.1 a.npm p.a d.asf n.asf v.iai.3p cj a.npm p.g d.gsf n.gsf

---

NASB

Law; 21 to those
who are without
law, as without
law, though not be-
ing without the law
of God but under
the law of Christ,
so that I might
win those who are
without law. 22 To
the weak I became
weak, that I might
win the weak; I
have become all
things to all men,
so that I may by all
means save some.
23 I do all things for
the sake of the gos-
pel, so that I may
become a fellow
partaker of it.
24 Do you not
know that those
who run in a race
all run, but *only*
one receives the
prize? Run in such
a way that you may
win. 25 Everyone
who competes in
the games exer-
cises self-control
in all things. They
then *do it* to re-
ceive a perishable
wreath, but we
an imperishable.
26 Therefore I run in
such a way, as not
without aim; I box
in such a way, as
not beating the air;
27 but I discipline
my body and make
it my slave, so
that, after I have
preached to others,
I myself will not be
disqualified.

Avoid Israel's Mistakes

10:1 For I do not
want you to be
unaware, brethren,
that our fathers
were all under
the cloud and all
passed through the

NIV

[2]They were all
baptized into Mo-
ses in the cloud
and in the sea.
[3]They all ate the
same spiritual
food [4]and drank
the same spiri-
tual drink; for
they drank from
the spiritual rock
that accompanied
them, and that
rock was Christ.
[5]Nevertheless,
God was not
pleased with most
of them; their bod-
ies were scattered
in the wilderness.
[6]Now these
things occurred as
examples to keep
us from setting
our hearts on evil
things as they did.
[7]Do not be idol-
aters, as some of
them were; as it
is written: "The
people sat down to
eat and drink and
got up to indulge
in revelry."[a] [8]We
should not commit
sexual immorality,
as some of them
did—and in one
day twenty-three
thousand of them
died. [9]We should
not test Christ,[b]
as some of them
did—and were
killed by snakes.
[10]And do not
grumble, as some
of them did—and
were killed by the
destroying angel.
[11]These things
happened to them
as examples and
were written down
as warnings for
us, on whom the
culmination of the
ages has come.

[a] 7 Exodus 32:6
[b] 9 Some manu-
scripts *test the Lord*

διῆλθον [2]καὶ πάντες εἰς τὸν Μωϋσῆν ἐβαπτίσθησαν[a] ἐν τῇ νεφέλῃ
passed and all were baptized into *{the}* Moses *were baptized* in the cloud
1451 2779 4246 966 966 1650 3836 3707 966 1877 3836 3749
v.aai.3p cj a.npm p.a d.asm n.asm v.api.3p p.d d.dsf n.dsf

καὶ ἐν τῇ θαλάσσῃ [3]καὶ πάντες τὸ αὐτὸ πνευματικὸν βρῶμα ἔφαγον [4]καὶ
and in the sea, and all ate the same spiritual food, *ate* and
2779 1877 3836 2498 2779 4246 2266 3836 899 4461 1109 2266 2779
cj p.d d.dsf n.dsf cj a.npm d.asn r.asn a.asn n.asn v.aai.3p cj

πάντες τὸ αὐτὸ πνευματικὸν ἔπιον πόμα· ἔπινον γὰρ ἐκ
all drank the same spiritual *drank* drink; for ⌊they used to drink⌋ *for* from the
4246 4403 3836 899 4461 4403 4503 1142 4403 1142 1666
a.npm d.asn r.asn a.asn v.aai.3p n.asn v.iai.3p cj p.g

πνευματικῆς ἀκολουθούσης πέτρας, ἡ πέτρα δὲ ἦν ὁ Χριστός.
spiritual rock that followed *rock* them, and that rock *and* was *{the}* Christ.
4461 4376 199 4376 1254 3836 4376 1254 1639 3836 5986
a.gsf pt.pa.gsf n.gsf d.nsf n.nsf cj v.iai.3s d.nsm n.nsm

[5]ἀλλ' ↱ οὐκ ἐν τοῖς πλείοσιν αὐτῶν εὐδόκησεν ὁ θεός,
But with most of them God was not *with* *{the}* *most* *of them* pleased, *{the}* *God*
247 1877 4498 899 899 2536 2305 4024 1877 3836 4498 899 2305 3836 2536
cj pl p.d d.dpm a.dpm.c r.gpm.3 v.aai.3s d.nsm n.nsm

κατεστρώθησαν γὰρ ἐν τῇ ἐρήμῳ. [6] ταῦτα δὲ
for their corpses were scattered *for* over the desert. Now these things *Now* took place as
1142 2954 1142 1877 3836 2245 1254 4047 1254 1181 1181
v.api.3p cj p.d d.dsf n.dsf r.npn cj

τύποι ἡμῶν ἐγενήθησαν, εἰς τὸ μὴ εἶναι ἡμᾶς ἐπιθυμητὰς κακῶν,
examples for us, *took place* ⌊so that⌋ ~ we would not *would* *we* crave evil things,
5596 7005 1181 1650 3836 7005 1639 3590 1639 7005 2122 2805
n.npm r.gp.1 v.api.3p p.a d.asn pl f.pa r.ap.1 n.apm a.gpn

↱ καθὼς κἀκεῖνοι ἐπεθύμησαν. [7]→ μηδὲ εἰδωλολάτραι γίνεσθε καθώς
even as they did. So do not become idolaters, *do become* as
2797 2777 2797 2121 1181 3593 1181 1629 1181 2777
cj adv v.aai.3p cj n.npm v.pmm.2p cj

τινες αὐτῶν, ὥσπερ γέγραπται, ἐκάθισεν ὁ λαὸς φαγεῖν καὶ πεῖν
some of them were. As it is written, "The people sat down *The* *people* to eat and drink
5516 899 6061 1211 3836 3295 2767 3836 3295 2266 2779 4403
r.npm r.gpm.3 cj v.rpi.3s v.aai.3s d.nsm n.nsm f.aa cj f.aa

καὶ ἀνέστησαν παίζειν. [8]↱ ↱ μηδὲ πορνεύωμεν, καθώς τινες αὐτῶν
and rose up to play." We must not ⌊indulge in sexual immorality,⌋ as some of them
2779 482 4089 4519 4519 3593 4519 2777 5516 899
cj v.aai.3p f.pa cj v.pas.1p cj r.npm r.gpm.3

ἐπόρνευσαν καὶ ἔπεσαν → μιᾷ ἡμέρᾳ ⌊εἴκοσι τρεῖς⌋ χιλιάδες.
did, and twenty-three thousand fell in a single day. *twenty-three* *thousand*
4519 2779 1633 5942 4406 1651 2465 1633 5552 5942
v.aai.3p cj v.aai.3p a.dsf n.dsf a.npf a.npf n.npf

[9]→ ↱ ↱ μηδὲ → ἐκπειράζωμεν τὸν Χριστόν, καθώς τινες αὐτῶν
And let us not put Christ to the test, *{the}* *Christ* as some of them
1733 1733 3593 5986 1733 3836 5986 2777 5516 899
cj v.pas.1p d.asm n.asm cj r.npm r.gpm.3

ἐπείρασαν καὶ ὑπὸ τῶν ὄφεων ἀπώλλυντο. [10]→ ↱ μηδὲ γογγύζετε,
did, and were destroyed by *{the}* serpents. *were destroyed* And do not grumble,
4279 2779 660 660 5679 3836 4058 660 1197 3593 1197
v.aai.3p cj p.g d.gpm n.gpm v.imi.3p cj v.pam.2p

καθάπερ τινὲς αὐτῶν ἐγόγγυσαν καὶ ἀπώλοντο ὑπὸ τοῦ ὀλοθρευτοῦ. [11]
as some of them did, and were killed by the destroyer. Now
2749 5516 899 1197 2779 660 5679 3836 3904 1254
cj r.npm r.gpm.3 v.aai.3p cj v.ami.3p p.g d.gsm n.gsm

ταῦτα δὲ τυπικῶς συνέβαινεν ἐκείνοις, ἐγράφη
these events *Now* happened to them as examples, *happened* *to them* but ⌊were written down⌋
4047 1254 5201 1697 1697 5595 5201 1697 1254 1211
r.npn cj adv v.iai.3s r.dpm v.api.3s

δὲ πρὸς νουθεσίαν ἡμῶν, εἰς οὓς τὰ τέλη τῶν αἰώνων κατήντηκεν.
but as warnings for *warnings* us, on whom the end of the ages has come.
1254 3804 4639 3804 7005 1650 4005 3836 5465 3836 172 2918
cj p.a n.asf r.gp.1 p.a r.apm d.npn n.npn d.gpm n.gpm v.rai.3s

[a] ἐβαπτίσθησαν UBS, TNIV. ἐβαπτίζοντο NET.

NASB

sea; [2]and all were
baptized into
Moses in the cloud
and in the sea; [3]and
all ate the same
spiritual food; [4]and
all drank the same
spiritual drink, for
they were drinking
from a spiri-
tual rock which
followed them;
and the rock was
Christ. [5]Neverthe-
less, with most of
them God was not
well-pleased; for
they were laid low
in the wilderness.
[6]Now these
things happened as
examples for us,
so that we would
not crave evil
things as they also
craved. [7]Do not be
idolaters, as some
of them were; as
it is written, "THE
PEOPLE SAT DOWN
TO EAT AND DRINK,
AND STOOD UP TO
PLAY." [8]Nor let us
act immorally, as
some of them did,
and twenty-three
thousand fell in
one day. [9]Nor let
us try the Lord, as
some of them did,
and were destroyed
by the serpents.
[10]Nor grumble, as
some of them did,
and were destroyed
by the destroyer.
[11]Now these things
happened to them
as an example, and
they were written
for our instruction,
upon whom the
ends of the ages
have come.

NIV

12 So, if you think you
are standing firm, be
careful that you don't
fall! 13 No temptation[a]
has overtaken you
except what is com-
mon to mankind.
And God is faithful;
he will not let you
be tempted[b] beyond
what you can bear.
But when you are
tempted,[c] he will
also provide a way
out so that you can
endure it.

Idol Feasts and the Lord's Supper

14 Therefore, my
dear friends, flee
from idolatry. 15 I
speak to sensible
people; judge for
yourselves what I
say. 16 Is not the cup
of thanksgiving
for which we give
thanks a participa-
tion in the blood of
Christ? And is not
the bread that we
break a participa-
tion in the body of
Christ? 17 Because
there is one loaf, we,
who are many, are
one body, for we all
share the one loaf.
18 Consider the peo-
ple of Israel: Do not
those who eat the
sacrifices participate
in the altar? 19 Do I
mean then that food
sacrificed to an idol
is anything, or that
an idol is anything?
20 No, but the sacri-
fices of pagans are
offered to demons,
not to God, and I do
not want you to be
participants with de-
mons. 21 You cannot
drink the cup of the
Lord and the

[a] *13* The Greek for *temptation* and *tempted* can also mean *testing* and *tested.*
[b] *13* The Greek for *temptation* and *tempted* can also mean *testing* and *tested.*
[c] *13* The Greek for *temptation* and *tempted* can also mean *testing* and *tested.*

12 ὥστε ↱ ὁ δοκῶν ἑστάναι βλεπέτω μὴ πέσῃ. 13 πειρασμὸς
So let the ⌊one who thinks⌋ he stands watch out lest he fall. No trial has
6063 1063 3836 1506 2705 1063 3590 4406 4024 4280 3284
cj d.nsm pt.pa.nsm f.ra v.pam.3s cj v.aas.3s n.nsm

ὑμᾶς οὐκ εἴληφεν ⌊εἰ μὴ⌋ ἀνθρώπινος· πιστὸς δὲ
overtaken you *No* *has overtaken* that is not distinctively human; and God is faithful; *and*
3284 7007 4024 3284 1623 3590 474 1254 2536 4412 1254
r.ap.2 pl v.rai.3s cj pl a.nsm a.nsm cj

ὁ θεός, ὃς ↱ οὐκ ἐάσει ὑμᾶς πειρασθῆναι ὑπὲρ ὃ δύνασθε ἀλλὰ
{the} *God* he will not let you be tested beyond what you can bear, but with the
3836 2536 4005 1572 4024 1572 7007 4279 5642 4005 1538 247 5250 3836
d.nsm n.nsm r.nsm pl v.fai.3s r.ap.2 f.ap p.a r.asn v.ppi.2p cj

→ ποιήσει σὺν τῷ πειρασμῷ καὶ τὴν ἔκβασιν τοῦ δύνασθαι
trial will also provide *with* *the* *trial* *also* the way through, so that ⌊you will be able⌋
4280 2779 4472 5250 3836 4280 2779 3836 1676 3836 1538
v.fai.3s p.d d.dsm n.dsm adv d.asf n.asf d.gsn f.pp

ὑπενεγκεῖν. 14 διόπερ, ἀγαπητοί μου, φεύγετε ἀπὸ τῆς εἰδωλολατρίας.
to endure it. Therefore, my dear friends, *my* flee from the worship of idols.
5722 1478 1609 28 1609 5771 608 3836 1630
f.aa cj a.vpm r.gs.1 v.pam.2p p.g d.gsf n.gsf

15 ὡς φρονίμοις λέγω, κρίνατε ὑμεῖς ὅ φημι.
I speak as ⌊to sensible people;⌋ *I speak* judge for yourselves what ⌊I am about to say.⌋
3306 3306 6055 5861 3306 3212 7007 4005 5774
pl a.dpm v.pai.1s v.aam.2p r.np.2 r.asn v.pai.1s

16 τὸ ποτήριον τῆς εὐλογίας ὃ εὐλογοῦμεν, οὐχὶ κοινωνία ἐστὶν τοῦ
The cup of blessing that we bless, is it not a sharing in the
3836 4539 3836 2330 4005 2328 1639 1639 4049 3126 1639 3836
d.nsn n.nsn d.gsf n.gsf r.asn v.pai.1p pl n.nsf v.pai.3s d.gsn

αἵματος τοῦ Χριστοῦ; τὸν ἄρτον ὃν κλῶμεν, οὐχὶ κοινωνία τοῦ
blood of Christ? The bread that we break, is it not a sharing in the
135 3836 5986 3836 788 4005 3089 1639 1639 4049 3126 3836
n.gsn d.gsm n.gsm d.asm n.asm r.asm v.pai.1p pl n.nsf d.gsn

σώματος τοῦ Χριστοῦ ἐστιν; 17 ὅτι εἷς ἄρτος, ἓν
body of Christ? *is it* Because there is one loaf, we who are many are one
5393 3836 5986 1639 4022 1651 788 1639 3836 4498 1639 1651
n.gsn d.gsm n.gsm v.pai.3s cj a.nsm n.nsm a.nsn

σῶμα οἱ πολλοί ἐσμεν, οἱ γὰρ πάντες ἐκ τοῦ ἑνὸς ἄρτου μετέχομεν.
body, *who* *many* *we are* *{the}* for we all partake of the one loaf. *we partake*
5393 3836 4498 1639 3836 1142 3576 4246 3576 1666 3836 1651 788 3576
n.nsn d.npm a.npm v.pai.1p d.npm cj a.npm p.g d.gsm a.gsm n.gsm v.pai.1p

18 βλέπετε τὸν Ἰσραὴλ κατὰ σάρκα· οὐχ οἱ ἐσθίοντες τὰς θυσίας
Consider *{the}* Israel ⌊according to⌋ the flesh: are not those who eat the sacrifices
1063 3836 2702 2848 4922 1639 4024 3836 2266 3836 2602
v.pam.2p d.asm n.asm p.a n.asf pl d.npm pt.pa.npm d.apf n.apf

κοινωνοὶ τοῦ θυσιαστηρίου εἰσίν; 19 Τί οὖν φημι; ὅτι
sharers in the altar? *are* So what *So* am I implying? That
3128 3836 2603 1639 4036 5515 4036 5774 4022
n.npm d.gsn n.gsn v.pai.3p r.asn cj v.pai.1s cj

εἰδωλόθυτόν τί ἐστιν ἢ ὅτι εἴδωλόν τί ἐστιν; 20 ἀλλ'
⌊food offered to idols⌋ is anything, *is* or that an idol is anything? *is* No,
1628 1639 5516 1639 2445 4022 1631 1639 5516 1639 247
n.nsn r.nsn v.pai.3s cj cj n.nsn r.nsn v.pai.3s cj

ὅτι ἃ θύουσιν, δαιμονίοις καὶ οὐ
what I am implying is that the ⌊things that⌋ people sacrifice, they sacrifice to demons and not
4022 4005 2604 2604 2604 1228 2779 4024
cj r.apn v.pai.3p n.dpn cj pl

θεῷ θύουσιν·[a] ↱ ↱ οὐ θέλω δὲ ὑμᾶς κοινωνοὺς τῶν δαιμονίων
to God; *they sacrifice* and I do not want *and* you to be sharers with demons.
2536 2604 1254 2527 2527 4024 2527 1254 7007 1181 1181 3128 3836 1228
n.dsm v.pai.3p pl v.pai.1s cj r.ap.2 n.apm d.gpn n.gpn

γίνεσθαι. 21 ⌊οὐ δύνασθε⌋ ποτήριον → κυρίου πίνειν καὶ
to be You cannot drink the cup of the Lord *drink* and the
1181 4024 1538 4403 4539 3261 4403 2779
f.pm pl v.ppi.2p n.asn n.gsm f.pa cj

[a] [θύουσιν] UBS.

NASB

12 Therefore let
him who thinks he
stands take heed
that he does not
fall. 13 No tempta-
tion has overtaken
you but such as is
common to man;
and God is faithful,
who will not allow
you to be tempted
beyond what you
are able, but with
the temptation will
provide the way of
escape also, so that
you will be able to
endure it.
14 Therefore, my
beloved, flee from
idolatry. 15 I speak
as to wise men;
you judge what I
say. 16 Is not the cup
of blessing which
we bless a shar-
ing in the blood of
Christ? Is not the
bread which we
break a sharing in
the body of Christ?
17 Since there is
one bread, we who
are many are one
body; for we all
partake of the one
bread. 18 Look at
the nation Israel;
are not those who
eat the sacrifices
sharers in the altar?
19 What do I mean
then? That a thing
sacrificed to idols
is anything, or that
an idol is anything?
20 *No,* but *I say* that
the things which
the Gentiles sacri-
fice, they sacrifice
to demons and not
to God; and I do
not want you to
become sharers in
demons. 21 You can-
not drink the cup of
the Lord and the

NIV

cup of demons
too; you cannot
have a part in both
the Lord's table
and the table of
demons. [22]Are we
trying to arouse the
Lord's jealousy?
Are we stronger
than he?

The Believer's Freedom

[23]"I have the right
to do anything,"
you say—but not
everything is ben-
eficial. "I have the
right to do any-
thing"—but not
everything is con-
structive. [24]No one
should seek their
own good, but the
good of others.
[25]Eat anything
sold in the meat
market without
raising questions
of conscience,
[26]for, "The earth is
the Lord's, and ev-
erything in it."[a]
[27]If an unbeliev-
er invites you to
a meal and you
want to go, eat
whatever is put
before you without
raising questions
of conscience.
[28]But if someone
says to you, "This
has been offered
in sacrifice," then
do not eat it, both
for the sake of the
one who told you
and for the sake
of conscience. [29]I
am referring to
the other person's
conscience, not
yours. For why is
my freedom being
judged by anoth-
er's conscience?
[30]If I take part
in the meal with
thankfulness, why
am I denounced
because of some-
thing I thank God
for?
[31]So whether
you eat

ποτήριον δαιμονίων, ⌞οὐ δύνασθε⌟ → τραπέζης → κυρίου μετέχειν
cup of demons; you cannot partake of the table of the Lord *partake of*
4539 1228 4024 1538 3576 5544 3261 3576
n.asn n.gpn pl v.ppi.2p n.gsf n.gsm f.pa

καὶ τραπέζης δαιμονίων. 22 ἢ παραζηλοῦμεν τὸν κύριον; ↰ ↰
and the table of demons. Or are we trying to provoke the Lord to jealousy?
2779 5544 1228 2445 4143 3836 3261 4143 4143
cj n.gsf n.gpn cj v.pai.1p d.asm n.asm

μὴ ἰσχυρότεροι αὐτοῦ ἐσμεν; 23 Πάντα ἔξεστιν ἀλλ᾽ οὐ πάντα
{not} Are we stronger than he? *Are we* "All things are permissible," but not all things
3590 1639 1639 2708 899 1639 4246 1997 247 4024 4246
pl a.npm.c r.gsm.3 v.pai.1p a.npn v.pai.3s cj pl a.npn

συμφέρει· πάντα ἔξεστιν ἀλλ᾽ οὐ πάντα οἰκοδομεῖ. 24 μηδεὶς τὸ
are helpful. "All things are permissible," but not all things build up. Let no one seek *{the}*
5237 4246 1997 247 4024 4246 3868 2426 3594 2426 3836
v.pai.3s a.npn v.pai.3s cj pl a.npn v.pai.3s a.nsm d.asn

ἑαυτοῦ ζητείτω ἀλλὰ τὸ τοῦ ἑτέρου. 25 πᾶν τὸ ἐν
his own advantage *Let seek* but that of the other. Eat whatever *{the}* is sold in the
1571 2426 247 3836 3836 2283 2266 4246 3836 4797 4797 1877
r.gsm.3 v.pam.3s cj d.asn d.gsm r.gsm a.asn d.asn p.d

μακέλλῳ πωλούμενον ἐσθίετε ↱ μηδὲν ἀνακρίνοντες διὰ τὴν συνείδησιν·
marketplace, *is sold* *Eat* asking no question ⌞based on⌟ *{the}* conscience,
3425 4797 2266 373 3594 373 1328 3836 5287
n.dsn pt.pp.asn v.pam.2p a.asn pt.pa.npm p.a d.asf n.asf

26 τοῦ κυρίου γὰρ ἡ γῆ καὶ τὸ πλήρωμα
for the earth and its fullness ⌞belong to the⌟ Lord. *for the earth and {the} fullness*
1142 3836 1178 2779 899 4445 3836 3261 1142 3836 1178 2779 3836 4445
d.gsm n.gsm cj d.nsf n.nsf cj d.nsn n.nsn

αὐτῆς. 27 εἴ τις καλεῖ ὑμᾶς τῶν ἀπίστων καὶ
its If one of the unbelievers invites you *of the unbelievers* to a meal and
899 1623 5516 3836 3836 603 2813 7007 3836 603 2779
r.gsf.3 cj r.nsm v.pai.3s r.ap.2 d.gpm a.gpm cj

θέλετε πορεύεσθαι, πᾶν τὸ παρατιθέμενον ὑμῖν ἐσθίετε ↱ μηδὲν
you decide to go, eat whatever *{the}* is set before you, *eat* asking no
2527 4513 2266 4246 3836 4192 7007 2266 373 3594
v.pai.2p f.pm a.asn d.asn pt.pp.asn r.dp.2 v.pam.2p a.asn

ἀνακρίνοντες διὰ τὴν συνείδησιν. 28 ἐὰν δέ τις
question ⌞based on⌟ *{the}* conscience. However, if *However* someone should say
373 1328 3836 5287 1254 1569 1254 5516 3306 3306
pt.pa.npm p.a d.asf n.asf cj cj r.nsm

ὑμῖν εἴπῃ, τοῦτο ἱερόθυτόν ἐστιν, ↱ μὴ ἐσθίετε
to you, *should say* "This has been offered in sacrifice," *has been* then do not eat it,
7007 3306 4047 1639 1639 2638 1639 2266 3590 2266
r.dp.2 v.aas.3s r.nsn a.nsn v.pai.3s pl v.pam.2p

δι᾽ ἐκεῖνον τὸν μηνύσαντα καὶ ↰ ↰ ↰ ↰ τὴν συνείδησιν·[a]
⌞for the sake of⌟ the one who told you, and for the sake of *{the}* conscience
1328 1697 3836 3606 2779 1328 1328 1328 1328 3836 5287
p.a r.asm d.asm pt.aa.asm cj d.asf n.asf

29 συνείδησιν δὲ λέγω οὐχὶ τὴν ἑαυτοῦ
— I mean the conscience *{and}* *I mean* of the other person, not *{the}* your own.
3306 3306 3836 5287 1254 3306 3836 3836 2283 2283 4049 3836 1571
n.asf cj v.pai.1s pl d.asf r.gsm.3

ἀλλὰ τὴν τοῦ ἑτέρου. ἱνατί γὰρ ↱ ἡ ἐλευθερία μου κρίνεται ὑπὸ
{rather} *the of the other person* Why then should *{the}* my liberty *my* be determined by
247 3836 3836 2283 2672 1142 3212 3836 1609 1800 1609 3212 5679
cj d.asf d.gsm r.gsm cj cj d.nsf n.nsf r.gs.1 v.ppi.3s p.g

ἄλλης συνειδήσεως; 30 εἰ ἐγὼ χάριτι μετέχω, τί
the conscience of another? *conscience* If I partake with thankfulness, *partake* why
5287 257 5287 1623 1609 3576 5921 3576 5515
r.gsf n.gsf cj r.ns.1 n.dsf v.pai.1s r.asn

βλασφημοῦμαι ὑπὲρ οὗ ἐγὼ εὐχαριστῶ; 31 Εἴτε οὖν ἐσθίετε
am I blamed because of that for which I give thanks? So, whether *So* you eat
1059 5642 4005 1609 2373 4036 1664 4036 2266
v.ppi.1s p.g r.gsn r.ns.1 v.pai.1s cj cj v.pai.2p

NASB

cup of demons;
you cannot partake
of the table of the
Lord and the table
of demons. [22]Or
do we provoke the
Lord to jealousy?
We are not stronger
than He, are we?
[23]All things are
lawful, but not all
things are profit-
able. All things are
lawful, but not all
things edify. [24]Let
no one seek his
own *good,* but that
of his neighbor.
[25]Eat anything that
is sold in the meat
market without
asking questions
for conscience'
sake; [26]FOR THE
EARTH IS THE
LORD'S, AND ALL IT
CONTAINS. [27]If one
of the unbelievers
invites you and
you want to go,
eat anything that
is set before you
without asking
questions for con-
science' sake. [28]But
if anyone says to
you, "This is meat
sacrificed to idols,"
do not eat *it,* for
the sake of the
one who informed
you, and for con-
science' sake; [29]I
mean not your own
conscience, but the
other *man's;* for
why is my freedom
judged by an-
other's conscience?
[30]If I partake with
thankfulness, why
am I slandered
concerning that
for which I give
thanks?
[31]Whether, then,
you eat or drink or

[a] 26 Psalm 24:1

[a] τοῦ γὰρ Κυρίου ἡ γῆ καὶ τὸ πλήρωμα αὐτῆς included by TR after συνείδησιν.

NIV

or drink or what-
ever you do, do it
all for the glory
of God. 32 Do not
cause anyone to
stumble, whether
Jews, Greeks or the
church of God—
33 even as I try to
please everyone in
every way. For I
am not seeking my
own good but the
good of many, so
that they may be
saved.
11 1 Follow my
example, as
I follow the exam-
ple of Christ.

On Covering the Head in Worship

2 I praise you for
remembering me
in everything and
for holding to the
traditions just as I
passed them on to
you. 3 But I want
you to realize that
the head of every
man is Christ, and
the head of the
woman is man,[a]
and the head of
Christ is God. 4 Ev-
ery man who prays
or prophesies with
his head covered
dishonors his
head. 5 But every
woman who prays
or prophesies with
her head uncov-
ered dishonors her
head—it is the
same as having
her head shaved.
6 For if a woman
does not cover her
head, she might as
well have her hair
cut off; but if it is
a disgrace for a
woman to have her
hair cut off or her
head shaved, then
she should cover
her head.
7 A man

[a] 3 Or *of the wife is her husband*

εἴτε πίνετε εἴτε τι ποιεῖτε, πάντα εἰς δόξαν θεοῦ ποιεῖτε. 32 →
or drink, or whatever you do, do everything for the glory of God. *do* Do not
1664 4403 1664 5516 4472 4472 4246 1650 1518 2536 4472 1181
cj v.pai.2p cj r.asn v.pai.2p a.apn p.a n.asf n.gsm v.pam.2p

ἀπρόσκοποι καὶ Ἰουδαίοις γίνεσθε καὶ Ἕλλησιν καὶ τῇ ἐκκλησίᾳ τοῦ
be a stumbling block to either Jews *Do be* or Greeks, or ⌊to the⌋ church of
1181 718 2779 2681 1181 2779 1818 2779 3836 1711 3836
a.npm cj a.dpm v.pmm.2p cj n.dpm cj d.dsf n.dsf d.gsm

θεοῦ, 33 → καθὼς κἀγὼ πάντα πᾶσιν ἀρέσκω μὴ ζητῶν
God; even as I try to please everyone in everything *try to please* I do, not seeking
2536 2743 2777 2743 743 743 743 4246 4246 743 3590 2426
n.gsm cj crasis a.apn a.dpm v.pai.1s pl pt.pa.nsm

τὸ ἐμαυτοῦ σύμφορον ἀλλὰ τὸ τῶν πολλῶν, ἵνα σωθῶσιν.
{the} my own advantage, but that of the many, so that ⌊they may be saved.⌋
3836 1831 5239 247 3836 3836 4498 2671 5392
d.asn r.gsm.1 n.asn cj d.asn d.gpm a.gpm cj v.aps.3p

11:1 μιμηταί μου γίνεσθε καθὼς κἀγὼ Χριστοῦ. 2 ἐπαινῶ δὲ ὑμᾶς
Be imitators of me, *Be* as I also am of Christ. I commend *{and}* you
1181 3629 1609 1181 2777 2743 5986 2046 1254 7007
n.npm r.gs.1 v.pmm.2p cj crasis n.gsm v.pai.1s cj r.ap.2

ὅτι πάντα μου μέμνησθε καί,
because you remember me in everything *me* *you remember* and hold firmly to the traditions
4022 3630 3630 1609 4246 1609 3630 2779 2988 2988 2988 3836 4142
cj a.apn r.gs.1 v.rpi.2p cj

καθὼς παρέδωκα ὑμῖν, τὰς παραδόσεις κατέχετε. 3 θέλω δὲ ὑμᾶς
just as ⌊I passed them on⌋ to you. *the* *traditions* *hold firmly to* But I want *But* you
2777 4140 7007 3836 4142 2988 1254 2527 1254 7007
cj v.aai.1s r.dp.2 d.apf n.apf v.pai.2p v.pai.1s cj r.ap.2

εἰδέναι ὅτι παντὸς ἀνδρὸς ἡ κεφαλὴ ὁ Χριστός ἐστιν,
to understand that the head of every man *the* *head* is *{the}* Christ, *is* and the
3857 4022 3836 3051 4246 467 3836 3051 1639 3836 5986 1639 1254
f.ra cj a.gsm n.gsm d.nsf n.nsf d.nsm n.nsm v.pai.3s

κεφαλὴ δὲ → γυναικὸς ὁ ἀνήρ, κεφαλὴ δὲ τοῦ Χριστοῦ ὁ
head *and* of a wife is her husband, and the head *and* of Christ is *{the}*
3051 1254 1222 3836 467 1254 3051 1254 3836 5986 3836
n.nsf cj n.gsf d.nsm n.nsm n.nsf cj d.gsm n.gsm d.nsm

θεός. 4 πᾶς ἀνὴρ προσευχόμενος ἢ προφητεύων κατὰ κεφαλῆς ἔχων
God. Any man who prays or prophesies with his head covered *head* *with*
2536 4246 467 4667 2445 4736 2400 3051 2848 3051 2400
n.nsm a.nsm n.nsm pt.pm.nsm cj pt.pa.nsm p.g n.gsf pt.pa.nsm

καταισχύνει τὴν κεφαλὴν αὐτοῦ. 5 πᾶσα δὲ γυνὴ προσευχομένη ἢ
disgraces *{the}* his head, *his* but any *but* wife who prays or
2875 3836 899 3051 899 1254 4246 1254 1222 4667 2445
v.pai.3s d.asf n.asf r.gsm.3 a.nsf cj n.nsf pt.pm.nsf cj

προφητεύουσα → ἀκατακαλύπτῳ τῇ κεφαλῇ καταισχύνει τὴν
prophesies with her head uncovered *her* *head* disgraces *{the}* her
4736 3836 3051 184 3836 3051 2875 3836 899
pt.pa.nsf a.dsf d.dsf n.dsf v.pai.3s d.asf

κεφαλὴν αὐτῆς· ἓν γάρ ἐστιν καὶ τὸ αὐτὸ τῇ
head, *her* for it is one *for* *it is* and the same as a woman
3051 899 1142 1639 1639 1651 1142 1639 2779 3836 899 3836
n.asf r.gsf.3 a.nsn cj v.pai.3s cj d.nsn r.nsn d.dsf

ἐξυρημένῃ. 6 εἰ γὰρ → οὐ κατακαλύπτεται γυνή,
⌊who has her head shaved.⌋ For if *For* a woman will not cover her head, *woman*
3834 1142 1623 1142 1222 2877 4024 2877 1222
pt.rp.dsf cj cj pl v.pmi.3s n.nsf

καὶ κειράσθω· εἰ δὲ αἰσχρὸν → γυναικὶ τὸ
{also} ⌊she should cut her hair short.⌋ But if *But* it is disgraceful for a woman *{the}*
2779 3025 1254 1623 1254 156 1222 3836
adv v.amm.3s cj cj a.nsn n.dsf d.nsn

κείρασθαι ἢ ξυρᾶσθαι, κατακαλυπτέσθω. 7 ἀνὴρ μὲν
⌊to have her hair cut short⌋ or ⌊have her head shaved,⌋ she should cover her head. For a man ~
3025 2445 3834 2877 1142 467 3525
f.am cj f.pm v.pmm.3s n.nsm pl

NASB

whatever you do,
do all to the glory
of God. 32 Give no
offense either to
Jews or to Greeks
or to the church of
God; 33 just as I also
please all men in
all things, not seek-
ing my own profit
but the *profit* of the
many, so that they
may be saved.

Christian Order

11:1 Be imitators of
me, just as I also
am of Christ.
2 Now I praise
you because you
remember me in
everything and
hold firmly to the
traditions, just as I
delivered them to
you. 3 But I want
you to understand
that Christ is the
head of every man,
and the man is the
head of a woman,
and God is the
head of Christ. 4 Ev-
ery man who has
something on his
head while pray-
ing or prophesying
disgraces his head.
5 But every woman
who has her head
uncovered while
praying or prophe-
sying disgraces her
head, for she is one
and the same as the
woman whose head
is shaved. 6 For if
a woman does not
cover her head, let
her also have her
hair cut off; but if
it is disgraceful for
a woman to have
her hair cut off or
her head shaved,
let her cover her
head. 7 For a man

NIV

ought not to cover
his head,[a] since he
is the image and
glory of God; but
woman is the glory
of man. 8For man
did not come from
woman, but woman
from man; 9neither
was man created for
woman, but wom-
an for man. 10It is
for this reason that
a woman ought to
have authority over
her own[b] head, be-
cause of the angels.
11Nevertheless, in
the Lord woman
is not independent
of man, nor is man
independent of
woman. 12For as
woman came from
man, so also man is
born of woman. But
everything comes
from God.
13Judge for your-
selves: Is it proper
for a woman to pray
to God with her
head uncovered?
14Does not the very
nature of things
teach you that if a
man has long hair,
it is a disgrace to
him, 15but that if
a woman has long
hair, it is her glo-
ry? For long hair
is given to her as a
covering. 16If any-
one wants to be
contentious about
this, we have no
other practice—nor
do the churches of
God.

γὰρ οὐκ ὀφείλει → κατακαλύπτεσθαι τὴν κεφαλὴν
For should not *should* have his head covered, *his* *head* since he is the
1142 4053 4024 4053 3836 3051 2877 3836 3051 5639 5639 5639
cj pl v.pai.3s f.pm d.asf n.asf

εἰκὼν καὶ δόξα θεοῦ ὑπάρχων· ἡ γυνὴ δὲ δόξα ἀνδρός ἐστιν.
image and glory of God, *since he is* but *{the}* woman *but* is the glory of man. *is*
1635 2779 1518 2536 5639 1254 3836 1222 1254 1639 1518 467 1639
n.nsf cj n.nsf n.gsm pt.pa.nsm d.nsf n.nsf cj n.nsf n.gsm v.pai.3s

8 ↱ οὐ γάρ ἐστιν ἀνὴρ ἐκ γυναικός ἀλλὰ γυνὴ ἐξ ἀνδρός· 9 καὶ γὰρ
For man did not *For* come *man* from woman, but woman from man. *{also}* *{for}*
1142 467 1639 4024 1142 1639 467 1666 1222 247 1222 1666 467 2779 1142
pl cj v.pai.3s n.nsm p.g n.gsf cj n.nsf p.g n.gsm adv cj

οὐκ → ἐκτίσθη ἀνὴρ διὰ τὴν γυναῖκα ἀλλὰ γυνὴ διὰ τὸν ἄνδρα. 10 διὰ
Neither was man created *man* for *{the}* woman, but woman for *{the}* man. For
4024 467 3231 467 1328 3836 1222 247 1222 1328 3836 467 1328
pl v.api.3s n.nsm p.a d.asf n.asf cj n.nsf p.a d.asm n.asm p.a

τοῦτο ὀφείλει ἡ γυνὴ ἐξουσίαν ἔχειν ἐπὶ τῆς
this reason a woman ought *{the}* *woman* to have a sign of authority *to have* on her
4047 1222 4053 3836 1222 2400 2400 2026 2400 2093 3836
r.asn v.pai.3s d.nsf n.nsf n.asf f.pa p.g d.gsf

κεφαλῆς διὰ τοὺς ἀγγέλους. 11 πλὴν οὔτε γυνὴ
head, ⌞because of⌟ the angels. Nevertheless, in the Lord woman is not *woman*
3051 1328 3836 34 4440 1877 3261 1222 4046 1222
n.gsf p.a d.apm n.apm cj cj n.nsf

χωρὶς ἀνδρὸς οὔτε ἀνὴρ χωρὶς γυναικὸς ἐν κυρίῳ· 12 ὥσπερ γὰρ ἡ
independent of man nor is man independent of woman; *in* *Lord* for just as *for* the
6006 467 4046 467 6006 1222 1877 3261 1142 6061 1142 3836
p.g n.gsm cj n.nsm p.g n.gsf p.d n.dsm cj cj d.nsf

γυνὴ ἐκ τοῦ ἀνδρός, οὕτως καὶ ὁ ἀνὴρ διὰ τῆς γυναικός·
woman came from *{the}* man, so also the man now comes through *{the}* woman.
1222 1666 3836 467 4048 2779 3836 467 1328 3836 1222
n.nsf p.g d.gsm n.gsm adv adv d.nsm n.nsm p.g d.gsf n.gsf

τὰ δὲ πάντα ἐκ τοῦ θεοῦ. 13 ἐν ⌞ὑμῖν αὐτοῖς⌟ κρίνατε·
{the} And all things come from *{the}* God. Judge for yourselves: *Judge* is
3836 1254 4246 1666 3836 2536 3212 1877 7007 899 3212 1639
d.npn cj a.npn p.g d.gsm n.gsm p.d r.dp.2 r.dpm v.aam.2p

πρέπον ἐστὶν → γυναῖκα ἀκατακάλυπτον τῷ θεῷ
it proper *is it* for a wife to pray to God with her head uncovered? *to* *God*
1639 4560 1639 1222 4667 4667 3836 2536 184 3836 2536
pt.pa.nsn v.pai.3s n.asf a.asf d.dsm n.dsm

προσεύχεσθαι; 14 ↱ οὐδὲ ἡ φύσις αὐτὴ διδάσκει ὑμᾶς ὅτι ἀνὴρ μὲν ἐὰν
to pray Does not *{the}* nature itself teach you that if a man ~ *if*
4667 1438 4028 3836 5882 899 1438 7007 4022 1569 467 3525 1569
f.pm pl d.nsf n.nsf r.nsf v.pai.3s r.ap.2 cj n.nsm pl cj

κομᾷ ἀτιμία αὐτῷ ἐστιν, 15 γυνὴ δὲ ἐὰν κομᾷ
⌞has long hair,⌟ it is a disgrace for him, *it is* but if a woman *but* *if* ⌞has long hair,⌟
3150 1639 1639 871 899 1639 1254 1569 1222 1254 1569 3150
v.pas.3s n.nsf r.dsm.3 v.pai.3s n.nsf cj cj v.pas.3s

δόξα αὐτῇ ἐστιν; ὅτι ἡ κόμη ἀντὶ περιβολαίου
it is her glory? *her* *it is* For her long hair is given to her for a covering.
1639 1639 899 1518 899 1639 4022 3836 3151 1443 1443 899 899 505 4316
n.nsf r.dsf.3 v.pai.3s cj d.nsf n.nsf p.g n.gsn

δέδοται αὐτῇ.[a] 16 εἰ δέ τις δοκεῖ φιλόνεικος εἶναι, ἡμεῖς
is given *to her* If *{and}* anyone is inclined to be quarrelsome, *to be* we have no
1443 899 1623 1254 5516 1506 1639 1639 5809 1639 7005 2400 4024
v.rpi.3s r.dsf.3 cj cj r.nsm v.pai.3s a.nsm f.pa r.np.1

τοιαύτην συνήθειαν οὐκ ἔχομεν οὐδὲ αἱ ἐκκλησίαι τοῦ θεοῦ. 17
such practice, *no* *have* nor do the churches of God. But in giving
5525 5311 4024 2400 4028 3836 1711 3836 2536 1254 4133 4133
r.asf n.asf pl v.pai.1p cj d.npf n.npf d.gsm n.gsm

NASB

ought not to have
his head covered,
since he is the
image and glory
of God; but the
woman is the glory
of man. 8For man
does not originate
from woman, but
woman from man;
9for indeed man
was not created
for the woman's
sake, but woman
for the man's sake.
10Therefore the
woman ought to
have *a symbol of*
authority on her
head, because of
the angels. 11How-
ever, in the Lord,
neither is woman
independent of
man, nor is man
independent of
woman. 12For as the
woman originates
from the man, so
also the man *has*
his birth through
the woman; and
all things originate
from God. 13Judge
for yourselves:
is it proper for a
woman to pray to
God *with her head*
uncovered? 14Does
not even nature
itself teach you that
if a man has long
hair, it is a dishon-
or to him, 15but if
a woman has long
hair, it is a glory to
her? For her hair
is given to her for
a covering. 16But
if one is inclined
to be contentious,
we have no other
practice, nor have
the churches of
God.
17But in giving

[a] 4-7 Or *4Every man who prays or prophesies with long hair dishonors his head. 5But every woman who prays or prophesies with no covering of hair dishonors her head—she is just like one of the "shorn women." 6If a woman has no covering, let her be for now with short hair; but since it is a disgrace for a woman to have her hair shorn or shaved, she should grow it again. 7A man ought not to have long hair*

[b] 10 Or *have a sign of authority on her*

[a] [αὐτῇ] UBS.

NIV

Correcting an Abuse of the Lord's Supper

[17]In the following
directives I have
no praise for you,
for your meetings
do more harm than
good. [18]In the first
place, I hear that
when you come to-
gether as a church,
there are divisions
among you, and to
some extent I be-
lieve it. [19]No doubt
there have to be
differences among
you to show which
of you have God's
approval. [20]So
then, when you
come together, it
is not the Lord's
Supper you eat,
[21]for when you are
eating, some of
you go ahead with
your own private
suppers. As a re-
sult, one person
remains hungry
and another gets
drunk. [22]Don't you
have homes to eat
and drink in? Or
do you despise the
church of God by
humiliating those
who have nothing?
What shall I say to
you? Shall I praise
you? Certainly not
in this matter!
[23]For I received
from the Lord
what I also passed
on to you: The
Lord Jesus, on the
night he was be-
trayed, took bread,
[24]and when he had
given thanks, he
broke it and said,
"This

τοῦτο δὲ παραγγέλλων ↱ ↱ οὐκ ἐπαινῶ ὅτι
the following instructions *But* *in giving instructions* I do not commend you, because when you
4047 4133 1254 4133 2046 2046 4024 2046 4022 5302 5302
r.asn cj pt.pa.nsm pl v.pai.1s cj

οὐκ εἰς τὸ κρεῖσσον ἀλλὰ εἰς τὸ ἧσσον συνέρχεσθε.
come together it is not for the better but for the worse. *when you come together*
5302 5302 4024 1650 3836 3202 247 1650 3836 2482 5302
pl p.a d.asn a.asn.c cj p.a d.asn a.asn.c v.pmi.2p

18 πρῶτον μὲν γὰρ → συνερχομένων ὑμῶν ἐν
For ⌊in the first place,⌋ ~ *For* I hear that when you gather *you* as a
1142 4754 3525 1142 201 201 7007 5302 7007 1877
adv pl cj pt.pm.gpm r.gp.2 p.d

ἐκκλησίᾳ ἀκούω σχίσματα ἐν ὑμῖν ὑπάρχειν καὶ μέρος τι
church *I hear* there are divisions among you, *there are* and in part I believe it,
1711 201 5639 5639 5388 1877 7007 5639 2779 3538 4409 4409 5516
n.dsf v.pai.1s n.apn p.d r.dp.2 f.pa cj n.asn r.asn

πιστεύω. 19 δεῖ γὰρ καὶ αἱρέσεις ἐν ὑμῖν εἶναι, ἵνα καὶ [a]
I believe for ⌊there must⌋ be *for* *{also}* factions among you *be* so that *{also}* it
4409 1142 1256 1639 1142 2779 146 1877 7007 1639 2671 2779 1181
v.pai.1s v.pai.3s cj adv n.apf p.d r.dp.2 f.pa cj adv

οἱ δόκιμοι φανεροὶ γένωνται ἐν ὑμῖν.
may become clear who among you are genuine. *clear* *it may become* *among* *you*
1181 1181 5745 3836 1877 7007 1511 5745 1181 1877 7007
d.npm a.npm a.npm v.ams.3p p.d r.dp.2

20 → συνερχομένων οὖν ὑμῶν ἐπὶ τὸ αὐτὸ οὐκ ἔστιν
Therefore when you gather *Therefore* *you* in the assembly, it is not *it is*
4036 7007 5302 4036 7007 2093 3836 899 1639 1639 4024 1639
pt.pm.gpm cj r.gp.2 p.a d.asn r.asn pl v.pai.3s

κυριακὸν δεῖπνον φαγεῖν· 21
to eat a supper ⌊in honor of the Lord.⌋ *supper* *to eat* For when it comes time to eat,
2266 2266 1270 3258 1270 2266 1142 1877 2266 2266
a.asn n.asn f.aa

ἕκαστος γὰρ τὸ ἴδιον δεῖπνον προλαμβάνει ἐν τῷ φαγεῖν, καὶ ὃς
each one *For* goes ahead with *{the}* his own supper; *goes ahead with* *when* ~ *to eat* and one
1667 1142 4624 4624 4624 3836 2625 1270 4624 1877 3836 2266 2779 4005
r.nsm cj d.asn a.asn n.asn v.pai.3s p.d d.dsn f.aa cj r.nsm

μὲν πεινᾷ ὃς δὲ μεθύει. 22 μὴ γὰρ
~ ⌊remains hungry⌋ while another *while* ⌊becomes drunk.⌋ *{not}* *{for}* Can it be that you do
3525 4277 1254 4005 1254 3501 3590 1142 2400 2400
pl v.pai.3s r.nsm pl v.pai.3s pl cj

οἰκίας οὐκ ἔχετε εἰς τὸ ἐσθίειν καὶ πίνειν; ἢ
not have houses *not* *you do have* in which to eat and drink? Or are you trying to
4024 2400 3864 4024 2400 1650 3836 2266 2779 4403 2445 2969 2969 2969 2969
n.apf pl v.pai.2p p.a d.asn f.pa cj f.pa cj

τῆς ἐκκλησίας τοῦ θεοῦ καταφρονεῖτε, καὶ
show contempt for the church of God *are you trying to show contempt for* by
2969 2969 2969 3836 1711 3836 2536 2969 2779
d.gsf n.gsf d.gsm n.gsm v.pai.2p cj

καταισχύνετε τοὺς μὴ ἔχοντας; τί εἴπω ὑμῖν; ἐπαινέσω
humiliating those who have nothing? *who have* What ⌊should I say⌋ to you? Should I commend
2875 3836 2400 2400 3590 2400 5515 3306 7007 2046
v.pai.2p d.apm pl pt.pa.apm r.asn v.aas.1s r.dp.2 v.aas.1s

ὑμᾶς; ἐν τούτῳ ↱ ↱ οὐκ ἐπαινῶ. 23 ἐγὼ γὰρ παρέλαβον ἀπὸ τοῦ
you? For this I will not commend you. For I *For* received from the
7007 1877 4047 2046 2046 4024 2046 1142 1609 1142 4161 608 3836
r.ap.2 p.d r.dsn pl v.pai.1s r.ns.1 cj v.aai.1s p.g d.gsm

κυρίου, ὃ ↱ καὶ παρέδωκα ὑμῖν, ὅτι ὁ κύριος Ἰησοῦς ἐν τῇ νυκτὶ
Lord ⌊that which⌋ I also passed on to you: that the Lord Jesus on the night
3261 4005 4140 2779 4140 7007 4022 3836 3261 2652 1877 3836 3816
n.gsm r.asn adv v.aai.1s r.dp.2 cj d.nsm n.nsm n.nsm p.d d.dsf n.dsf

ᾗ παρεδίδετο ἔλαβεν ἄρτον 24 καὶ εὐχαριστήσας ἔκλασεν καὶ εἶπεν, τοῦτό
when he was betrayed took bread, and after giving thanks, he broke it, and said, "This
4005 4140 3284 788 2779 2373 3089 2779 3306 4047
r.dsf v.ipi.3s v.aai.3s n.asm cj pt.aa.nsm v.aai.3s cj v.aai.3s r.nsn

---

NASB

[s]this instruction, I
do not praise you,
because you come
together not for the
better but for the
worse. [18]For, in the
first place, when
you come together
as a church, I hear
that divisions exist
among you; and
in part I believe it.
[19]For there must
also be factions
among you, so
that those who
are approved may
become evident
among you.
[20]Therefore when
you meet together,
it is not to eat the
Lord's Supper, [21]for
in your eating each
one takes his own
supper first; and
one is hungry and
another is drunk.
[22]What! Do you
not have houses in
which to eat and
drink? Or do you
despise the church
of God and shame
those who have
nothing? What
shall I say to you?
Shall I praise you?
In this I will not
praise you.

The Lord's Supper

[23]For I received
from the Lord that
which I also deliv-
ered to you, that
the Lord Jesus in
the night in which
He was betrayed
took bread; [24]and
when He had given
thanks, He broke it
and said, "This

---

[a] [καὶ] UBS.

NIV

is my body, which
is for you; do this
in remembrance of
me.” 25 In the same
way, after supper
he took the cup,
saying, “This cup
is the new cov-
enant in my blood;
do this, whenever
you drink it, in
remembrance of
me.” 26 For when-
ever you eat this
bread and drink
this cup, you pro-
claim the Lord’s
death until he
comes.
27 So then, who-
ever eats the bread
or drinks the cup
of the Lord in an
unworthy manner
will be guilty of
sinning against
the body and
blood of the Lord.
28 Everyone ought
to examine them-
selves before they
eat of the bread
and drink from the
cup. 29 For those
who eat and drink
without discerning
the body of Christ
eat and drink
judgment on them-
selves. 30 That is
why many among
you are weak and
sick, and a number
of you have fall-
en asleep. 31 But
if we were more
discerning with re-
gard to ourselves,
we would not
come under such
judgment. 32 Nev-
ertheless, when we
are judged in this
way by the Lord,
we are being dis-
ciplined so that we
will not be finally
condemned with
the

μού ἐστιν τὸ σῶμα τὸ ὑπὲρ ὑμῶν· τοῦτο ποιεῖτε εἰς τὴν
is my *is* *{the}* body which is for you. Do this *Do* in *{the}* remembrance
1639 1609 1639 3836 5393 3836 5642 7007 4472 4047 4472 1650 3836 390
r.gs.1 v.pai.3s d.nsn n.nsn d.nsn p.g r.gp.2 r.asn v.pam.2p p.a d.asf

ἐμὴν ἀνάμνησιν. 25 ὡσαύτως καὶ τὸ ποτήριον μετὰ τὸ
of me.” *remembrance of* ⌞In the same way,⌟ he took the cup also, *the* *cup* after *{the}*
390 1847 390 6058 3836 4539 2779 3836 4539 3552 3836
r.asf.1 n.asf adv adv d.asn n.asn p.a d.asn

δειπνῆσαι λέγων, τοῦτο τὸ ποτήριον ἡ καινὴ διαθήκη ἐστὶν ἐν τῷ ἐμῷ
supper, saying, “This *{the}* cup is the new covenant *is* in *{the}* my
1268 3306 4047 3836 4539 1639 3836 2785 1347 1639 1877 3836 1847
f.aa pt.pa.nsm r.nsn d.nsn n.nsn d.nsf a.nsf n.nsf v.pai.3s p.d d.dsn r.dsn.1

αἵματι· τοῦτο ποιεῖτε, ⌞ὁσάκις ἐὰν⌟ πίνητε, εἰς τὴν ἐμὴν
blood. Do this, *Do* as often as you drink it, in *{the}* remembrance of me.”
135 4472 4047 4472 4006 1569 4403 1650 3836 390 390 1847
n.dsn r.asn v.pam.2p adv pl v.pas.2p p.a d.asf r.asf.1

ἀνάμνησιν. 26 ὁσάκις γὰρ ἐὰν ἐσθίητε τὸν ἄρτον τοῦτον καὶ τὸ
remembrance of For ⌞as often as⌟ *For* ~ you eat *{the}* this bread *this* and drink this
390 1142 4006 1142 1569 2266 3836 4047 788 4047 2779 4403 3836
n.asf adv cj pl v.pas.2p d.asm n.asm r.asm cj d.asn

ποτήριον πίνητε, τὸν θάνατον τοῦ κυρίου καταγγέλλετε ⌞ἄχρι
cup, *drink* you proclaim the Lord’s death *{the}* *Lord’s* *you proclaim* until
4539 4403 2859 2859 3836 3261 2505 3836 3261 2859 948
n.asn v.pas.2p d.asm n.asm d.gsm n.gsm v.pai.2p p.g

οὗ⌟ ἔλθῃ. 27 ὥστε ⌞ὃς ἂν⌟ ἐσθίῃ τὸν ἄρτον ἢ πίνῃ τὸ
he comes. Whoever, therefore, *Whoever* eats this bread or drinks this
4005 2262 4005 6063 4005 323 2266 3836 788 2445 4403 3836
r.gsm v.aas.3s cj r.nsm pl v.pas.3s d.asm n.asm cj v.pas.3s d.asn

ποτήριον τοῦ κυρίου ἀναξίως, ἔνοχος ἔσται τοῦ σώματος καὶ
cup of the Lord ⌞in an unworthy manner⌟ will be guilty *will be* of the body and
4539 3836 3261 397 1639 1639 1944 1639 3836 5393 2779
n.asn d.gsm n.gsm adv a.nsm v.fmi.3s d.gsn n.gsn cj

τοῦ αἵματος τοῦ κυρίου. 28 δοκιμαζέτω δὲ ἄνθρωπος ἑαυτὸν καὶ
{the} blood of the Lord. A person should examine *{and}* *person* himself, then, and
3836 135 3836 3261 476 1507 1254 476 1571 2779
d.gsn n.gsn d.gsm n.gsm v.pam.3s cj n.nsm r.asm.3 cj

οὕτως ἐκ τοῦ ἄρτου ἐσθιέτω καὶ ἐκ τοῦ ποτηρίου πινέτω· 29 ὁ
so eat of the bread *eat* and drink of the cup. *drink* For the
4048 2266 1666 3836 788 2266 2779 4403 1666 3836 4539 4403 1142 3836
adv p.g d.gsm n.gsm v.pam.3s cj p.g d.gsn n.gsn v.pam.3s d.nsm

γὰρ ἐσθίων καὶ πίνων κρίμα
For ⌞one who eats⌟ and drinks without discerning the body eats and drinks judgment
1142 2266 2779 4403 3590 1359 3836 5393 2266 2779 4403 3210
cj pt.pa.nsm cj pt.pa.nsm n.asn

ἑαυτῷ ἐσθίει καὶ πίνει μὴ διακρίνων τὸ σῶμα. 30 ⌞διὰ τοῦτο⌟ ἐν
on himself. *eats* *and* *drinks* *without* *discerning* *the* *body* That is why many of
1571 2266 2779 4403 3590 1359 3836 5393 1328 4047 4498 1877
r.dsm.3 v.pai.3s cj v.pai.3s pl pt.pa.nsm d.asn n.asn p.a r.asn p.d

ὑμῖν πολλοὶ ἀσθενεῖς καὶ ἄρρωστοι καὶ κοιμῶνται ἱκανοί. 31
you *many* are weak and sick, and quite a few are dead. *quite a few* But
7007 4498 822 2779 779 2779 2653 2653 2653 3121 2653 1254
r.dp.2 a.npm a.npm cj a.npm cj v.ppi.3p a.npm

εἰ δὲ ἑαυτοὺς διεκρίνομεν, ↱ οὐκ ἂν
if *But* we had been examining ourselves, *we had been examining* we would not *would*
1623 1254 1359 1359 1359 1359 1571 1359 3212 323 4024 323
cj cj r.apm.2 v.iai.1p pl pl

ἐκρινόμεθα· 32 κρινόμενοι δὲ ὑπὸ τοῦ[a] κυρίου
come under judgment. But ⌞when we are judged⌟ *But* by the Lord,
3212 1254 3212 1254 5679 3836 3261
v.ipi.1p pt.pp.npm cj p.g d.gsm n.gsm

παιδευόμεθα, ἵνα μὴ σὺν τῷ
⌞we are being corrected by discipline,⌟ so that we will not be condemned ⌞along with⌟ the
4084 2671 2891 2891 3590 2891 2891 5250 3836
v.ppi.1p cj pl p.d d.dsm

[a] [τοῦ] UBS.

NASB

is My body, which
is for you; do this
in remembrance of
Me.” 25 In the same
way *He took* the
cup also after sup-
per, saying, “This
cup is the new
covenant in My
blood; do this, as
often as you drink
it, in remembrance
of Me.” 26 For as of-
ten as you eat this
bread and drink the
cup, you proclaim
the Lord’s death
until He comes.
27 Therefore who-
ever eats the bread
or drinks the cup
of the Lord in an
unworthy manner,
shall be guilty of
the body and the
blood of the Lord.
28 But a man must
examine himself,
and in so doing
he is to eat of the
bread and drink
of the cup. 29 For
he who eats and
drinks, eats and
drinks judgment
to himself if he
does not judge the
body rightly. 30 For
this reason many
among you are
weak and sick, and
a number sleep.
31 But if we judged
ourselves rightly,
we would not be
judged. 32 But when
we are judged, we
are disciplined by
the Lord so that we
will not be con-
demned along with
the world.

NIV

world.
33 So then, my
brothers and sis-
ters, when you
gather to eat, you
should all eat to-
gether. 34 Anyone
who is hungry
should eat some-
thing at home,
so that when you
meet together it
may not result in
judgment.
And when I come
I will give further
directions.

Concerning Spiritual Gifts

12 Now about
the gifts of
the Spirit, broth-
ers and sisters, I
do not want you
to be uninformed.
2 You know that
when you were
pagans, somehow
or other you were
influenced and
led astray to mute
idols. 3 Therefore I
want you to know
that no one who
is speaking by
the Spirit of God
says, "Jesus be
cursed," and no
one can say, "Jesus
is Lord," except by
the Holy Spirit.
4 There are dif-
ferent kinds of
gifts, but the same
Spirit distributes
them. 5 There are
different kinds of
service, but the
same Lord. 6 There
are different kinds
of working, but in
all of them and in
everyone it is the
same God at work.
7 Now to each
one the manifes-
tation of the Spirit
is given for the
common good. 8 To
one there is given
through the Spirit
a message of wis-
dom, to another a
message of knowl-
edge

κόσμῳ κατακριθῶμεν. 33 ὥστε, ἀδελφοί μου, συνερχόμενοι εἰς τὸ
world. *we will be condemned* So then, my brothers, *my* ⌊when you come together⌋ to ~
3180 2891 6063 1609 81 1609 5302 1650 3836
n.dsm v.aps.1p cj n.vpm r.gs.1 pt.pm.npm p.a d.asn

φαγεῖν ἀλλήλους ἐκδέχεσθε. 34 εἴ τις πεινᾷ, ἐν οἴκῳ
eat, wait for one another. *wait for* If anyone is hungry, he should eat at home,
2266 1683 1683 253 1683 1623 5516 4277 2266 2266 2266 1877 3875
f.aa r.apm v.pmm.2p cj r.nsm v.pai.3s p.d n.dsm

ἐσθιέτω, ἵνα μὴ εἰς κρίμα συνέρχησθε.
he should eat so that when you come together it does not lead to judgment. *when you come together*
2266 2671 5302 5302 5302 5302 3590 1650 3210 5302
v.pam.3s cj pl p.a n.asn v.pms.2p

τὰ δὲ λοιπὰ ὡς ἂν ἔλθω διατάξομαι.
I will give directions about *{the} {and}* other matters when ~ I come. *I will give directions*
1411 1411 1411 1411 3836 1254 3370 6055 323 2262 1411
d.apn cj a.apn cj pl v.aas.1s v.fmi.1s

12:1 περὶ δὲ τῶν πνευματικῶν, ἀδελφοί, ↱ ↱ οὐ θέλω ὑμᾶς
Now concerning *Now {the}* spiritual gifts, brothers, I do not want you
1254 4309 1254 3836 4461 81 2527 2527 4024 2527 7007
p.g cj d.gpn a.gpn n.vpm pl v.pai.1s r.ap.2

ἀγνοεῖν. 2 οἴδατε ὅτι ὅτε ἔθνη ἦτε
to be uninformed. You know that when you were pagans *you were* you were somehow seduced
51 3857 4022 4021 1639 1639 1620 1639 72 72 6055 72
f.pa v.rai.2p cj cj n.npn v.iai.2p

πρὸς τὰ εἴδωλα τὰ ἄφωνα ὡς ἂν ἤγεσθε
and led astray to *{the}* idols that ⌊could not speak.⌋ *somehow* ~ *you were seduced*
552 552 4639 3836 1631 3836 936 6055 323 72
p.a d.apn n.apn d.apn a.apn cj pl v.ipi.2p

ἀπαγόμενοι. 3 διὸ → → γνωρίζω ὑμῖν ὅτι οὐδεὶς ἐν
led astray Therefore I want you to understand *you* that no one speaking by the
552 1475 7007 1192 7007 4022 4029 3281 1877
pt.pp.npm cj v.pai.1s r.dp.2 cj a.nsm p.d

πνεύματι θεοῦ λαλῶν λέγει, ἀνάθεμα Ἰησοῦς, καὶ οὐδεὶς δύναται εἰπεῖν,
Spirit of God *speaking* says, "Jesus is accursed!" *Jesus* and no one can say,
4460 2536 3281 3306 2652 353 2652 2779 4029 1538 3306
n.dsn n.gsm pt.pa.nsm v.pai.3s n.nsn n.nsm cj a.nsm v.ppi.3s f.aa

κύριος Ἰησοῦς, ⌊εἰ μὴ⌋ ἐν πνεύματι ἁγίῳ. 4
"Jesus is Lord," *Jesus* except by the Holy Spirit. *Holy* Now there are
2652 3261 2652 1623 3590 1877 41 4460 41 1254 1639 1639
n.nsm n.nsm cj pl p.d n.dsn a.dsn

διαιρέσεις δὲ χαρισμάτων εἰσίν, τὸ δὲ αὐτὸ πνεῦμα· 5 καὶ
different kinds *Now* of gifts, *there are* but the *but* same Spirit; and there are
1348 1254 5922 1639 1254 3836 1254 899 4460 2779 1639 1639
n.npf cj n.gpn v.pai.3p d.nsn cj r.nsn n.nsn cj

διαιρέσεις διακονιῶν εἰσιν, καὶ ὁ αὐτὸς κύριος· 6 καὶ διαιρέσεις
different kinds of ministries, *there are* but the same Lord; and there are different
1348 1355 1639 2779 3836 899 3261 2779 1639 1639 1348
n.npf n.gpf v.pai.3p cj d.nsm r.nsm n.nsm cj n.npf

ἐνεργημάτων εἰσίν, ὁ δὲ αὐτὸς θεὸς ὁ ἐνεργῶν τὰ πάντα
accomplishments, *there are* but it is the *but* same God who produces *{the}* all of them
1920 1639 1254 3836 1254 899 2536 3836 1919 3836 4246
n.gpn v.pai.3p d.nsm cj r.nsm n.nsm d.nsm pt.pa.nsm d.apn a.apn

ἐν πᾶσιν. 7 ἑκάστῳ δὲ δίδοται ἡ
in everyone. But the manifestation of the Spirit is given to each one *But* *is given* *the*
1877 4246 1254 3836 5748 3836 3836 4460 1443 1443 1667 1254 1443 3836
p.d a.dpm r.dsm cj v.ppi.3s d.nsf

φανέρωσις τοῦ πνεύματος πρὸς τὸ συμφέρον. 8 ᾧ μὲν γὰρ διὰ
manifestation *of the* *Spirit* for the good of all. For ⌊to one⌋ ~ *For* is given through
5748 3836 4460 4639 3836 5237 1142 4005 3525 1142 1443 1443 1328
n.nsf d.gsn n.gsn p.g d.asn pt.pa.asn r.dsm pl cj p.g

τοῦ πνεύματος δίδοται λόγος σοφίας, ἄλλῳ δὲ λόγος γνώσεως
the Spirit *is given* a message of wisdom, to another *{and}* a message of knowledge
3836 4460 1443 3364 5053 257 1254 3364 1194
d.gsn n.gsn v.ppi.3s n.nsm n.gsf r.dsm pl n.nsm n.gsf

NASB

33 So then, my
brethren, when you
come together to
eat, wait for one
another. 34 If anyone
is hungry, let him
eat at home, so
that you will not
come together for
judgment. The
remaining matters
I will arrange when
I come.

The Use of Spiritual Gifts

12:1 Now concern-
ing spiritual *gifts,*
brethren, I do not
want you to be un-
aware. 2 You know
that when you were
pagans, *you were*
led astray to the
mute idols, how-
ever you were led.
3 Therefore I make
known to you that
no one speaking
by the Spirit of
God says, "Jesus is
accursed"; and no
one can say, "Jesus
is Lord," except by
the Holy Spirit.
4 Now there are
varieties of gifts,
but the same Spirit.
5 And there are vari-
eties of ministries,
and the same Lord.
6 There are variet-
ies of effects, but
the same God who
works all things in
all *persons.* 7 But to
each one is given
the manifestation
of the Spirit for the
common good. 8 For
to one is given the
word of wisdom
through the Spirit,
and to another the
word of knowledge

NIV

by means of the
same Spirit, 9to
another faith by
the same Spirit,
to another gifts
of healing by that
one Spirit, 10to
another miracu-
lous powers, to
another prophecy,
to another distin-
guishing between
spirits, to another
speaking in dif-
ferent kinds of
tongues,[a] and to
still another the
interpretation of
tongues.[b] 11All
these are the work
of one and the
same Spirit, and he
distributes them to
each one, just as he
determines.

Unity and Diversity in the Body

12Just as a body,
though one, has
many parts, but
all its many parts
form one body, so
it is with Christ.
13For we were all
baptized by[c] one
Spirit so as to
form one body—
whether Jews or
Gentiles, slave
or free—and we
were all given the
one Spirit to drink.
14Even so the body
is not made up of
one part but of
many.
15Now if the foot
should say, "Be-
cause I am not a
hand, I do not be-
long to the body,"
it would not for
that reason stop
being part of the
body. 16And if the
ear should say,
"Because I am
not an eye, I do
not belong to the
body," it would
not for that reason
stop being part of
the body. 17If the
whole body were

[a] 10 Or *languages*; also in verse 28
[b] 10 Or *languages*; also in verse 28
[c] 13 Or *with*; or *in*

κατὰ τὸ αὐτὸ πνεῦμα, 9 ἑτέρῳ πίστις ἐν τῷ αὐτῷ πνεύματι, ἄλλῳ
⌊according to⌋ the same Spirit, to another faith by the same Spirit, to another
2848 3836 899 4460 2283 4411 1877 3836 899 4460 257
p.a d.asn r.asn n.asn r.dsm n.nsf p.d d.dsn r.dsn n.dsn r.dsm

δὲ χαρίσματα ἰαμάτων ἐν τῷ ἑνὶ πνεύματι, 10 ἄλλῳ δὲ ἐνεργήματα
{and} gifts of healing by the one Spirit, to another *{and}* performance
1254 5922 2611 1877 3836 1651 4460 257 1254 1920
pl n.npn n.gpn p.d d.dsn a.dsn n.dsn r.dsm pl n.npn

δυνάμεων, ἄλλῳ δὲ[a] προφητεία, ἄλλῳ δὲ[b] διακρίσεις πνευμάτων, ἑτέρῳ
of miracles, to another *{and}* prophecy, to another *{and}* discerning of spirits, to another
1539 257 1254 4735 257 1254 1360 4460 2283
n.gpf r.dsm pl n.nsf r.dsm pl n.npf n.gpn r.dsm

γένη γλωσσῶν, ἄλλῳ δὲ ἑρμηνεία γλωσσῶν· 11 πάντα δὲ ταῦτα
⌊various kinds⌋ of tongues, and to another *and* interpretation of tongues. *all* But *these things*
1169 1185 1254 257 1254 2255 1185 4246 1254 4047
n.npn n.gpf r.dsm pl n.nsf n.gpf a.apn cj r.apn

ἐνεργεῖ τὸ ἓν καὶ τὸ αὐτὸ πνεῦμα διαιροῦν ⌊ἰδίᾳ ἑκάστῳ⌋ καθὼς
who produces it is the one and *{the}* same Spirit, distributing to each as
1919 3836 1651 2779 3836 899 4460 1349 2625 1667 2777
v.pai.3s d.nsn a.nsn cj d.nsn r.nsn n.nsn pt.pa.nsn a.dsf r.dsm cj

βούλεται. 12 καθάπερ γὰρ τὸ σῶμα
he determines, who produces all these things. For just as *For* the ⌊physical body⌋ is
1089 1919 1919 4246 4047 4047 1142 2749 1142 3836 5393 1639
v.pmi.3s cj cj d.nsn n.nsn

ἕν ἐστιν καὶ μέλη πολλὰ ἔχει, πάντα δὲ τὰ μέλη τοῦ
one *is* yet has many members, *many* *has* and all *and* the members of the
1651 1639 2779 2400 4498 3517 4498 2400 1254 4246 1254 3836 3517 3836
a.nsn v.pai.3s cj n.apn a.apn v.pai.3s a.npn cj d.npn n.npn d.gsn

σώματος πολλὰ ὄντα ἕν ἐστιν σῶμα, οὕτως καὶ ὁ Χριστός·
body, though many, *though* are one *are* body, so also is the body of Christ.
5393 1639 4498 1639 1639 1651 1639 5393 4048 2779 3836 5986
n.gsn a.npn pt.pa.npn a.nsn v.pai.3s n.nsn adv adv d.nsm n.nsm

13 καὶ γὰρ ἐν ἑνὶ πνεύματι ἡμεῖς πάντες εἰς ἓν σῶμα ἐβαπτίσθημεν,
{also} For in one Spirit we were all baptized into one body, *were baptized*
2779 1142 1877 1651 4460 7005 966 4246 966 1650 1651 5393 966
adv cj p.d a.dsn n.dsn r.np.1 a.npm p.a a.asn n.asn v.api.1p

εἴτε Ἰουδαῖοι εἴτε Ἕλληνες εἴτε δοῦλοι εἴτε ἐλεύθεροι, καὶ πάντες
whether Jews or Greeks, *{whether}* slaves or free, and we were all
1664 2681 1664 1818 1664 1529 1664 1801 2779 4540 4540 4246
cj a.npm cj n.npm cj n.npm cj a.npm cj a.npm

ἓν πνεῦμα ἐποτίσθημεν. 14 καὶ γὰρ τὸ σῶμα οὐκ ἔστιν
imbued with one Spirit. *we were imbued with* For indeed *For* the body is not *is* a
4540 4540 1651 4460 4540 1142 2779 1142 3836 5393 1639 4024 1639
a.asn n.asn v.api.1p adv cj d.nsn n.nsn pl v.pai.3s

ἓν μέλος ἀλλὰ πολλά. 15 ἐὰν εἴπῃ ὁ πούς, ὅτι οὐκ
single member, but many. If the foot ⌊should say,⌋ *the* *foot* "Since I am not
1651 3517 247 4498 1569 3836 4546 3306 3836 4546 4022 1639 1639 4024
a.nsn n.nsn cj a.npn cj v.aas.3s d.nsm n.nsm cj pl

εἰμὶ χείρ, οὐκ εἰμὶ ἐκ τοῦ σώματος, ↱ ↱ οὐ παρὰ τοῦτο
I am a hand, I am not *I am* ⌊part of⌋ the body," it would not for that reason
1639 5931 1639 1639 4024 1639 1666 3836 5393 1639 1639 4024 4123 4047
v.pai.1s n.nsf pl v.pai.1s p.g d.gsn n.gsn pl p.a r.asn

οὐκ ἔστιν ἐκ τοῦ σώματος; 16 καὶ ἐὰν εἴπῃ τὸ οὖς, ὅτι
cease to be ⌊part of⌋ the body. And if the ear ⌊should say,⌋ *the* *ear* "Since I
4024 1639 1666 3836 5393 2779 1569 3836 4044 3306 3836 4044 4022 1639
pl v.pai.3s p.g d.gsn n.gsn cj cj v.aas.3s d.nsn n.nsn cj

οὐκ εἰμὶ ὀφθαλμός, οὐκ εἰμὶ ἐκ τοῦ σώματος, ↱ ↱ οὐ
am not *I am* an eye, I am not *I am* ⌊part of⌋ the body," it would not
1639 4024 1639 4057 1639 1639 4024 1639 1666 3836 5393 1639 1639 4024
pl v.pai.1s n.nsm pl v.pai.1s p.g d.gsn n.gsn pl

παρὰ τοῦτο οὐκ ἔστιν ἐκ τοῦ σώματος; 17 εἰ ὅλον τὸ σῶμα
for that reason cease to be ⌊part of⌋ the body. If the whole *the* body were an
4123 4047 4024 1639 1666 3836 5393 1623 3836 3910 3836 5393
p.a r.asn pl v.pai.3s p.g d.gsn n.gsn cj a.nsn d.nsn n.nsn

[a] [δὲ] UBS.
[b] [δὲ] UBS.

NASB

according to the
same Spirit; 9to
another faith by the
same Spirit, and
to another gifts of
healing by the one
Spirit, 10and to an-
other the effecting
of miracles, and to
another prophecy,
and to another the
distinguishing of
spirits, to another
various kinds of
tongues, and to an-
other the interpre-
tation of tongues.
11But one and the
same Spirit works
all these things,
distributing to each
one individually
just as He wills.
12For even as
the body is one
and *yet* has many
members, and all
the members of the
body, though they
are many, are one
body, so also is
Christ. 13For by one
Spirit we were all
baptized into one
body, whether Jews
or Greeks, whether
slaves or free, and
we were all made
to drink of one
Spirit.
14For the body is
not one member,
but many. 15If the
foot says, "Because
I am not a hand, I
am not *a part* of
the body," it is not
for this reason any
the less *a part* of
the body. 16And if
the ear says, "Be-
cause I am not an
eye, I am not *a part*
of the body," it is
not for this reason
any the less *a part*
of the body. 17If the
whole body were

NIV

an eye, where
would the sense
of hearing be? If
the whole body
were an ear, where
would the sense
of smell be? 18 But
in fact God has
placed the parts
in the body, every
one of them, just
as he wanted them
to be. 19 If they
were all one part,
where would the
body be? 20 As it
is, there are many
parts, but one
body.
21 The eye cannot
say to the hand, "I
don't need you!"
And the head can-
not say to the feet,
"I don't need you!"
22 On the contrary,
those parts of the
body that seem
to be weaker are
indispensable,
23 and the parts that
we think are less
honorable we treat
with special honor.
And the parts that
are unpresentable
are treated with
special modesty,
24 while our pre-
sentable parts
need no special
treatment. But
God has put the
body together, giv-
ing greater honor
to the parts that
lacked it, 25 so that
there should be
no division in the
body, but that its
parts should have
equal concern for
each other. 26 If one
part suffers,

ὀφθαλμός, ποῦ ἡ ἀκοή; εἰ ὅλον ἀκοή, ποῦ
eye, where would the ⌊sense of hearing⌋ be? If the whole body were an ear, where
4057 4543 3836 198 1623 3910 198 4543
n.nsm cj d.nsf n.nsf cj a.nsn n.nsf cj

ἡ ὄσφρησις; 18 νυνὶ δὲ ὁ θεὸς ἔθετο τὰ μέλη,
would the sense of smell be? But ⌊as it is,⌋ *But* *{the}* God arranged the members in the
3836 4018 1254 3815 1254 3836 2536 5502 3836 3517 1877 3836
d.nsf n.nsf adv cj d.nsm n.nsm v.ami.3s d.apn n.apn

ἓν ἕκαστον αὐτῶν ἐν τῷ σώματι καθὼς ἠθέλησεν. 19 εἰ δὲ
body, every one *every* of them, *in* *the* *body* just as he chose. If *{and}*
5393 1667 1651 1667 899 1877 3836 5393 2777 2527 1623 1254
a.asn r.asn r.gpn.3 p.d d.dsn n.dsn cj v.aai.3s cj cj

ἦν τὰ πάντα ἓν μέλος, ποῦ τὸ σῶμα; 20 νῦν δὲ
⌊they were⌋ *{the}* all a single member, where would the body be? But ⌊as it is,⌋ *But* there
1639 3836 4246 1651 3517 4543 3836 5393 1254 3814 1254
v.iai.3s d.npn a.npn a.nsn n.nsn cj d.nsn n.nsn adv cj

πολλὰ μὲν μέλη, ἓν δὲ σῶμα. 21 ⌊οὐ δύναται⌋ δὲ ὁ
are many ~ members, but one *but* body. The eye cannot *{and}* *The*
4498 3525 3517 1254 1651 1254 5393 3836 4057 4024 1538 1254 3836
a.npn pl n.npn a.nsn cj n.nsn pl v.ppi.3s cj d.nsm

ὀφθαλμὸς εἰπεῖν τῇ χειρί, χρείαν σου οὐκ ἔχω, ἢ πάλιν ἡ
eye say ⌊to the⌋ hand, "I have no need of you"; *no* *I have* nor again the
4057 3306 3836 5931 2400 2400 4024 5970 5148 4024 2400 2445 4099 3836
n.nsm f.aa d.dsf n.dsf n.asf r.gs.2 pl v.pai.1s cj adv d.nsf

κεφαλὴ τοῖς ποσίν· χρείαν ὑμῶν οὐκ ἔχω· 22 ἀλλὰ πολλῷ
head to the feet, "I have no need of you." *no* *I have* Quite the contrary, *Quite*
3051 3836 4546 2400 2400 4024 5970 7007 4024 2400 4498 247 4498
n.nsf d.dpm n.dpm n.asf r.gp.2 pl v.pai.1s cj a.dsn

μᾶλλον τὰ δοκοῦντα μέλη τοῦ σώματος
{rather} those members of the body that seem *members* *of the* *body* to be
3437 3836 3517 3836 3836 5393 1506 3517 3836 5393 5639 5639
adv.c d.npn pt.pa.npn n.npn d.gsn n.gsn

ἀσθενέστερα ὑπάρχειν ἀναγκαῖά ἐστιν, 23 καὶ ἃ
weaker *to be* are indispensable, *are* and those members of the body that
822 5639 1639 338 1639 2779 4047 4047 3836 3836 5393 4005
a.npn.c f.pa a.npn v.pai.3s cj r.apn

δοκοῦμεν ἀτιμότερα εἶναι τοῦ σώματος τούτοις τιμὴν
we consider less honorable *{to be}* *of the* *body* *those members* we clothe with greater honor,
1506 872 1639 3836 5393 4047 4363 4363 4363 4358 5507
v.pai.1p a.apn.c f.pa d.gsn n.gsn r.dpn n.asf

περισσοτέραν περιτίθεμεν, καὶ τὰ ἀσχήμονα ἡμῶν
greater *we clothe with* and *{the}* our ⌊unpresentable members⌋ *our* are treated with
4358 4363 2779 3836 7005 860 7005 2400 2400 2400
a.asf.c v.pai.1p cj d.npn a.npn r.gp.1

εὐσχημοσύνην περισσοτέραν ἔχει, 24 τὰ δὲ εὐσχήμονα
greater modesty, *greater* *are treated with* *{the}* whereas our presentable members
4358 2362 4358 2400 3836 1254 7005 2363
n.asf a.asf.c v.pai.3s d.npn cj a.npn

ἡμῶν οὐ χρείαν ἔχει. ἀλλὰ ὁ θεὸς συνεκέρασεν τὸ σῶμα
our have no such need. *have* Instead, *{the}* God has so arranged the body, giving greater
7005 2400 4024 5970 2400 247 3836 2536 5166 3836 5393 1443 4358
r.gp.1 pl n.asf v.pai.3s cj d.nsm n.nsm v.aai.3s d.asn n.asn

τῷ ὑστερουμένῳ περισσοτέραν δοὺς τιμήν, 25 ἵνα
honor ⌊to the⌋ member that lacked it, *greater* *giving* *honor* so that there would be
5507 3836 5728 4358 1443 5507 2671 1639 1639 1639
d.dsn pt.pp.dsn a.asf.c pt.aa.nsm n.asf cj

μὴ ᾖ σχίσμα ἐν τῷ σώματι ἀλλὰ τὸ αὐτὸ
no *there would be* division in the body, but that the members would have the same
3590 1639 5388 1877 3836 5393 247 3836 3517 3534 3534 3836 899
pl v.pas.3s n.nsn p.d d.dsn n.dsn cj d.asn r.asn

ὑπὲρ ἀλλήλων μεριμνῶσιν τὰ μέλη. 26 καὶ εἴτε πάσχει ἓν
care for one another. *would have care* *the* *members* And if one member suffers, *one*
3534 5642 253 3534 3836 3517 2779 1664 1651 3517 4248 1651
p.g r.gpn v.pas.3p d.npn n.npn cj cj v.pai.3s a.nsn

NASB

an eye, where
would the hearing
be? If the whole
were hearing,
where would the
sense of smell be?
18 But now God has
placed the mem-
bers, each one of
them, in the body,
just as He desired.
19 If they were all
one member, where
would the body be?
20 But now there are
many members,
but one body. 21 And
the eye cannot say
to the hand, "I have
no need of you";
or again the head
to the feet, "I have
no need of you."
22 On the contrary, it
is much truer that
the members of the
body which seem
to be weaker are
necessary; 23 and
those *members* of
the body which
we deem less
honorable, on these
we bestow more
abundant honor,
and our less pre-
sentable members
become much
more presentable,
24 whereas our more
presentable mem-
bers have no need
of it. But God has
so composed the
body, giving more
abundant honor
to that *member*
which lacked, 25 so
that there may be
no division in the
body, but *that* the
members may have
the same care for
one another. 26 And
if one member

NIV

every part suffers with it; if one part is honored, every part rejoices with it.

[27]Now you are the body of Christ, and each one of you is a part of it. [28]And God has placed in the church first of all apostles, second prophets, third teachers, then miracles, then gifts of healing, of helping, of guidance, and of different kinds of tongues. [29]Are all apostles? Are all prophets? Are all teachers? Do all work miracles? [30]Do all have gifts of healing? Do all speak in tongues[a]? Do all interpret? [31]Now eagerly desire the greater gifts.

Love Is Indispensable

And yet I will show you the most excellent way.

13 If I speak in the tongues[b] of men or of angels, but do not have love, I am only a resounding gong or a clanging cymbal. [2]If I have the gift of prophecy and can fathom all mysteries and all knowledge, and if I have a faith

μέλος, συμπάσχει πάντα τὰ μέλη· εἴτε δοξάζεται ἓν[a]
member every member suffers with it; *every* *{the}* *member* if one member is honored, *one*
3517 4246 3517 5224 4246 3836 3517 1664 1651 3517 1519 1651
n.nsn v.pai.3s a.npn d.npn n.npn cj v.ppi.3s a.nsn

μέλος, συγχαίρει πάντα τὰ μέλη. 27 ὑμεῖς δέ ἐστε
member every member rejoices with it. *every* *{the}* *member* Now you *Now* are Christ's
3517 4246 3517 5176 4246 3836 3517 1254 7007 1254 1639 5986
n.nsn v.pai.3s a.npn d.npn n.npn r.np.2 cj v.pai.2p

σῶμα Χριστοῦ καὶ μέλη ἐκ μέρους. 28 καὶ οὓς μὲν
body *Christ's* and each of you is a member of it. And *{whom}* ~ God
5393 5986 2779 3517 1666 3538 2779 4005 3525 2536
n.nsn n.gsm cj n.npn p.g n.gsn cj r.apm pl

ἔθετο ὁ θεὸς ἐν τῇ ἐκκλησίᾳ πρῶτον ἀποστόλους, δεύτερον προφήτας,
has appointed *{the}* *God* in the church first apostles, second prophets,
5502 3836 2536 1877 3836 1711 4754 693 1311 4737
v.ami.3s d.nsm n.nsm p.d d.dsf n.dsf adv n.apm adv n.apm

τρίτον διδασκάλους, ἔπειτα δυνάμεις, ἔπειτα χαρίσματα ἰαμάτων,
third teachers, then miracles, then gifts of healing,
5568 1437 2083 1539 2083 5922 2611
adv n.apm adv n.apf adv n.apn n.gpn

ἀντιλήμψεις, κυβερνήσεις, γένη γλωσσῶν. 29 μὴ
⌞those able to help others,⌟ ⌞those who can provide guidance,⌟ and ⌞various kinds⌟ of tongues. Not
516 3236 1169 1185 3590
n.apf n.apf n.apn n.gpf pl

πάντες ἀπόστολοι; ↰ ↰ μὴ πάντες προφῆται; ↰ ↰ μὴ πάντες
all are apostles, are they? Not all are prophets, are they? Not all are
4246 693 3590 3590 3590 4246 4737 3590 3590 3590 4246
a.npm n.npm pl a.npm n.npm pl a.npm

διδάσκαλοι; ↰ ↰ μὴ πάντες δυνάμεις; ↰ ↰ 30 μὴ πάντες
teachers, are they? Not all work miracles, do they? Not all have
1437 3590 3590 3590 4246 1539 3590 3590 3590 4246 2400
n.npm pl a.npm n.npf pl a.npm

χαρίσματα ἔχουσιν ἰαμάτων; ↰ ↰ μὴ πάντες γλώσσαις λαλοῦσιν; ↰ ↰
gifts *have* of healing, do they? Not all speak in tongues, *speak* do they?
5922 2400 2611 3590 3590 3590 4246 3281 1185 3281 3590 3590
n.apn v.pai.3p n.gpn pl a.npm n.dpf v.pai.3p

μὴ πάντες διερμηνεύουσιν; ↰ ↰ 31 ζηλοῦτε δὲ ↰ τὰ χαρίσματα
Not all are able to interpret, are they? ⌞Set your hearts⌟ then on the higher gifts.
3590 4246 1450 3590 3590 2420 1254 2420 3836 3489 5922
pl a.npm v.pai.3p v.pam.2p cj d.apn n.apn

τὰ μείζονα. καὶ ἔτι καθ᾽ ὑπερβολὴν ὁδὸν ὑμῖν
{the} *higher* And now I will show you a way that is beyond comparison. *way* *you*
3836 3489 2779 2285 1259 1259 1259 7007 3847 2848 5651 3847 7007
d.apn a.apn.c cj adv p.a n.asf n.asf r.dp.2

δείκνυμι.
I will show
1259
v.pai.1s

13:1 ἐὰν ταῖς γλώσσαις τῶν ἀνθρώπων λαλῶ καὶ τῶν ἀγγέλων,
If I speak in the tongues of men *I speak* and of angels, but
1569 3281 3281 3836 1185 3836 476 3281 2779 3836 34 1254
cj d.dpf n.dpf d.gpm n.gpm v.pas.1s cj d.gpm n.gpm

ἀγάπην δὲ μὴ ἔχω, γέγονα χαλκὸς ἠχῶν ἢ
do not have love, *but* *not* *do have* I am a resounding gong *resounding* or a
2400 3590 2400 27 1254 3590 2400 1181 2490 5910 2490 2445
n.asf cj pl v.pas.1s v.rai.1s n.nsm pt.pa.nsm cj

κύμβαλον ἀλαλάζον. 2 καὶ ἐὰν ἔχω προφητείαν καὶ εἰδῶ τὰ
clanging cymbal. *clanging* And if I have the gift of prophecy, and understand *{the}*
226 3247 226 2779 1569 2400 4735 2779 3857 3836
n.nsn pt.pa.nsn cj cj v.pas.1s n.asf cj v.ras.1s d.apn

μυστήρια πάντα καὶ πᾶσαν τὴν γνῶσιν καὶ ἐὰν ἔχω πᾶσαν τὴν πίστιν
all mysteries *all* and all *{the}* knowledge, and if I have all *{the}* faith
4246 3696 4246 2779 4246 3836 1194 2779 1569 2400 4246 3836 4411
n.apn a.apn cj a.asf d.asf n.asf cj cj v.pas.1s a.asf d.asf n.asf

NASB

suffers, all the members suffer with it; if *one* member is honored, all the members rejoice with it.

[27]Now you are Christ's body, and individually members of it. [28]And God has appointed in the church, first apostles, second prophets, third teachers, then miracles, then gifts of healings, helps, administrations, *various* kinds of tongues. [29]All are not apostles, are they? All are not prophets, are they? All are not teachers, are they? All are not *workers of* miracles, are they? [30]All do not have gifts of healings, do they? All do not speak with tongues, do they? All do not interpret, do they? [31]But earnestly desire the greater gifts.

And I show you a still more excellent way.

The Excellence of Love

[13:1]If I speak with the tongues of men and of angels, but do not have love, I have become a noisy gong or a clanging cymbal. [2]If I have *the gift of* prophecy, and know all mysteries and all knowledge; and if I have all

[a] 30 Or *other languages*
[b] 1 Or *languages*

[a] [ἓν] UBS, omitted by NET.

NIV

that can move
mountains, but do
not have love, I am
nothing. [3]If I give
all I possess to the
poor and give over
my body to hard-
ship that I may
boast,[a] but do not
have love, I gain
nothing.
[4]Love is patient,
love is kind. It
does not envy, it
does not boast, it
is not proud. [5]It
does not dishon-
or others, it is not
self-seeking, it is
not easily angered,
it keeps no record
of wrongs. [6]Love
does not delight in
evil but rejoices
with the truth. [7]It
always protects,
always trusts,
always hopes, al-
ways perseveres.
[8]Love never fails.
But where there
are prophecies,
they will cease;
where there are
tongues, they will
be stilled; where
there is knowl-
edge, it will pass
away. [9]For we
know in part and
we prophesy in
part, [10]but when
completeness
comes, what is in
part disappears.
[11]When I was a
child, I talked like
a child, I thought
like a child, I rea-
soned like a child.
When I became
a man, I put the
ways of childhood
behind me. [12]For
now we see only a
reflection as in

ὥστε ὄρη μεθιστάναι, ἀγάπην δὲ μὴ ἔχω,
so that I can remove mountains, *I can remove* but do not have love, *but* *not* *do have*
6063 3496 3496 3496 4001 3496 1254 2400 3590 2400 27 1254 3590 2400
cj n.apn f.pa n.asf cj pl v.pas.1s

οὐθέν εἰμι. [3]κἂν ψωμίσω πάντα τὰ ὑπάρχοντά μου καὶ ἐὰν
I am nothing. *I am* If I give away everything *{the}* I own, *I* and if
1639 1639 4032 1639 2829 6039 4246 3836 1609 5639 1609 2779 1569
a.nsn v.pai.1s crasis v.aas.1s a.apn d.apn pt.pa.apn r.gs.1 cj cj

παραδῶ τὸ σῶμά μου ἵνα καυχήσωμαι, ἀγάπην δὲ μὴ
I surrender *{the}* my body *my* to be burned, but do not have love, *but* *not*
4140 3836 1609 5393 1609 2671 3016 1254 2400 3590 2400 27 1254 3590
v.aas.1s d.asn n.asn r.gs.1 cj v.ams.1s n.asf cj pl

ἔχω, οὐδὲν ὠφελοῦμαι. [4]ἡ ἀγάπη μακροθυμεῖ, χρηστεύεται
do have it benefits me nothing. *it benefits me* *{the}* Love is patient, love is kind,
2400 6067 6067 6067 4029 6067 3836 27 3428 27 5980
v.pas.1s a.asn v.ppi.1s d.nsf n.nsf v.pai.3s v.pmi.3s

ἡ ἀγάπη, ↱ ↱ οὐ ζηλοῖ, [a]ἡ ἀγάπη[b] ↱ οὐ περπερεύεται, ↱ ↱ οὐ
{the} *love* it does not envy. *{the}* Love does not brag, it is not
3836 27 2420 2420 4024 2420 3836 27 4371 4024 4371 5881 5881 4024
d.nsf n.nsf pl v.pai.3s d.nsf n.nsf pl v.pmi.3s pl

φυσιοῦται, [5]↱ ↱ οὐκ ἀσχημονεῖ, ↱ ↱ οὐ ⌊ζητεῖ τὰ ἑαυτῆς,⌋ ↱ ↱
arrogant, it is not rude, it is not self-seeking, it is
5881 858 858 4024 858 2426 2426 4024 2426 3836 1571 4236 4236
v.ppi.3s pl v.pai.3s pl v.pai.3s d.apn r.gsf.3

οὐ παροξύνεται, ↱ ↱ οὐ λογίζεται τὸ κακόν, [6]↱ ↱ οὐ χαίρει ἐπὶ τῇ
not easily angered, it keeps no account of wrongs, it takes no pleasure in *{the}*
4024 4236 3357 3357 4024 3357 3836 2805 5897 5897 4024 5897 2093 3836
pl v.ppi.3s pl v.pmi.3s d.asn a.asn pl v.pai.3s p.d d.dsf

ἀδικίᾳ, συγχαίρει δὲ τῇ ἀληθείᾳ· [7] πάντα στέγει,
wrongdoing, but rejoices in *but* the truth. Love bears all things, *bears* believes
94 1254 5176 1254 3836 237 5095 4246 5095 4409
n.dsf v.pai.3s cj d.dsf n.dsf a.apn v.pai.3s

πάντα πιστεύει, πάντα ἐλπίζει, πάντα ὑπομένει. [8]ἡ ἀγάπη
all things, *believes* hopes all things, *hopes* endures all things. *endures* *{the}* Love
4246 4409 1827 4246 1827 5702 4246 5702 3836 27
a.apn v.pai.3s a.apn v.pai.3s a.apn v.pai.3s d.nsf n.nsf

οὐδέποτε πίπτει· εἴτε δὲ προφητεῖαι, καταργηθήσονται· εἴτε
never ⌊comes to an end.⌋ But if *But* there are prophecies, they will be set aside; if there
4030 4406 1254 1664 1254 4735 2934 1664
adv v.pai.3s cj cj n.npf v.fpi.3p cj

γλῶσσαι, παύσονται· εἴτε γνῶσις, καταργηθήσεται. [9] ἐκ
are tongues, they will cease; if there is knowledge, it will be set aside. For we know in
1185 4264 1664 1194 2934 1142 1182 1182 1666
n.npf v.fmi.3p cj n.nsf v.fpi.3s p.g

μέρους γὰρ γινώσκομεν καὶ ἐκ μέρους προφητεύομεν· [10] ὅταν δὲ
part *For* *we know* and we prophesy in part, *we prophesy* but when *but*
3538 1142 1182 2779 4736 4736 1666 3538 4736 1254 4020 1254
n.gsn cj v.pai.1p cj p.g n.gsn v.pai.1p cj cj

ἔλθῃ τὸ τέλειον, τὸ ⌊ἐκ μέρους⌋ καταργηθήσεται. [11]ὅτε ἤμην
what is complete comes, *what complete* the partial will be set aside. When I was a
3836 5455 2262 3836 5455 3836 1666 3538 2934 4021 1639
v.aas.3s d.nsn a.nsn d.nsn p.g n.gsn v.fpi.3s cj v.imi.1s

νήπιος, ἐλάλουν ὡς νήπιος, ἐφρόνουν ὡς νήπιος, ἐλογιζόμην ὡς νήπιος· ὅτε
child, I talked like a child, I thought like a child, I reasoned like a child. When
3758 3281 6055 3758 5858 6055 3758 3357 6055 3758 4021
a.nsm v.iai.1s pl a.nsm v.iai.1s pl a.nsm v.imi.1s pl a.nsm cj

γέγονα ἀνήρ, κατήργηκα τὰ τοῦ νηπίου. [12] βλέπομεν
I became a man, I set aside childish ways. *{the}* *childish* For the present we are looking
1181 467 2934 3758 3836 3836 3758 1142 785 1063
v.rai.1s n.nsm v.rai.1s d.apn d.gsm a.gsm v.pai.1p

NASB

faith, so as to
remove mountains,
but do not have
love, I am nothing.
[3]And if I give all
my possessions to
feed *the poor,* and
if I surrender my
body [a]to be burned,
but do not have
love, it profits me
nothing.
[4]Love is patient,
love is kind *and* is
not jealous; love
does not brag *and*
is not arrogant,
[5]does not act unbe-
comingly; it does
not seek its own,
is not provoked,
does not take into
account a wrong
suffered, [6]does
not rejoice in
unrighteousness,
but rejoices with
the truth; [7]bears all
things, believes all
things, hopes all
things, endures all
things.
[8]Love never fails;
but if *there are*
gifts of prophecy,
they will be done
away; if *there are*
tongues, they will
cease; if *there is*
knowledge, it will
be done away. [9]For
we know in part
and we prophesy
in part; [10]but when
the perfect comes,
the partial will be
done away. [11]When
I was a child, I
used to speak like
a child, think like
a child, reason like
a child; when I be-
came a man, I did
away with childish
things. [12]For now
we see in a mirror

[a] 3 Some manu-
scripts *body to the*
flames

[a] [ἡ ἀγάπη] UBS, omitted by TNIV.
[b] ἀγάπη omitted in TNIV.

[a] Early mss read
that I may boast

NIV

a mirror; then we
shall see face to
face. Now I know
in part; then I
shall know fully,
even as I am fully
known.
13 And now these
three remain: faith,
hope and love.
But the greatest of
these is love.

Intelligibility in Worship

14 Follow the
way of love
and eagerly desire
gifts of the Spirit,
especially proph-
ecy. 2 For anyone
who speaks in a
tongue[a] does not
speak to people but
to God. Indeed, no
one understands
them; they utter
mysteries by the
Spirit. 3 But the one
who prophesies
speaks to people for
their strengthening,
encouraging and
comfort. 4 Any-
one who speaks in
a tongue edifies
themselves, but the
one who prophesies
edifies the church.
5 I would like every
one of you to speak
in tongues,[b] but I
would rather have
you prophesy. The
one who prophesies
is greater than the
one who speaks in
tongues,[c] unless
someone interprets,
so that the church
may be edified.
6 Now, brothers
and sisters, if I
come to you and
speak in tongues,
what good will I
be to you, unless I
bring you some rev-
elation or knowl-
edge

[a] 2 Or *in another language*; also in verses 4, 13, 14, 19, 26 and 27
[b] 5 Or *in other languages*; also in verses 6, 18, 22, 23 and 39
[c] 5 Or *in other languages*; also in verses 6, 18, 22, 23 and 39

γὰρ ἄρτι δι᾿ ἐσόπτρου ⌞ἐν αἰνίγματι,⌟ τότε δὲ πρόσωπον πρὸς
For *present* through a mirror obscurely, but then *but* face to
1142 785 1328 2269 1877 141 1254 5538 1254 4725 4639
cj adv p.g n.gsn p.d n.dsn adv cj n.asn p.a

πρόσωπον· ἄρτι γινώσκω ἐκ μέρους, τότε δὲ ἐπιγνώσομαι καθὼς καὶ
face. Now I know in part; then *{and}* I will know fully, just as *{also}*
4725 785 1182 1666 3538 5538 1254 2105 2777 2779
n.asn adv v.pai.1s p.g n.gsn adv cj v.fmi.1s cj adv

ἐπεγνώσθην. 13 νυνὶ δὲ μένει πίστις, ἐλπίς, ἀγάπη, τὰ τρία
⌞I have been fully known.⌟ And now *And* remain faith, hope, and love; *{the}* these three.
2105 1254 3815 1254 3531 4411 1828 27 3836 4047 5552
v.api.1s adv cj v.pai.3s n.nsf n.nsf n.nsf d.npn a.npn

ταῦτα· μείζων δὲ τούτων ἡ ἀγάπη.
these And the greatest *And* of these is *{the}* love.
4047 1254 3489 1254 4047 3836 27
r.npn a.nsf.c cj r.gpn d.nsf n.nsf

14:1 διώκετε τὴν ἀγάπην, ζηλοῦτε δὲ τὰ πνευματικά, μᾶλλον
Pursue *{the}* love, and ⌞earnestly desire⌟ *and* the spiritual gifts, but especially
1503 3836 27 1254 2420 1254 3836 4461 1254 3437
v.pam.2p d.asf n.asf v.pam.2p cj d.apn a.apn adv.c

δὲ ἵνα προφητεύητε. 2 ὁ γὰρ λαλῶν → γλώσσῃ οὐκ ἀνθρώποις
but that you may prophesy. For the *For* one speaking in a tongue speaks not to men
1254 2671 4736 1142 3836 1142 3281 1185 3281 4024 476
cj cj v.pas.2p d.nsm cj pt.pa.nsm n.dsf pl n.dpm

λαλεῖ ἀλλὰ θεῷ· οὐδεὶς γὰρ ἀκούει, →
speaks but to God; indeed, no one *indeed* understands him, yet he is speaking mysteries by
3281 247 2536 1142 4029 1142 201 1254 3281 3281 3281 3696
v.pai.3s cj n.dsm a.nsm cj v.pai.3s

πνεύματι δὲ λαλεῖ μυστήρια· 3 ὁ δὲ
the Spirit. *yet* *he is speaking* *mysteries* On the other hand, the *On the other hand*
4460 1254 3281 3696 1254 1254 1254 1254 3836 1254
n.dsn cj v.pai.3s n.apn d.nsm cj

προφητεύων ἀνθρώποις λαλεῖ → οἰκοδομὴν καὶ παράκλησιν καὶ
one who prophesies speaks to people *speaks* for their edification, *{and}* encouragement, and
4736 3281 476 3281 3869 2779 4155 2779
pt.pa.nsm n.dpm v.pai.3s n.asf cj n.asf cj

παραμυθίαν. 4 ὁ λαλῶν → γλώσσῃ ἑαυτὸν οἰκοδομεῖ· ὁ δὲ
consolation. The ⌞one who speaks⌟ in a tongue edifies himself, *edifies* but the *but*
4171 3836 3281 1185 3868 1571 3868 1254 3836 1254
n.asf d.nsm pt.pa.nsm n.dsf r.asm.3 v.pai.3s d.nsm cj

προφητεύων ἐκκλησίαν οἰκοδομεῖ. 5 θέλω δὲ πάντας ὑμᾶς
one who prophesies edifies the church. *edifies* Now ⌞I would like⌟ *Now* all of you
4736 3868 1711 3868 1254 2527 1254 4246 7007
pt.pa.nsm n.asf v.pai.3s v.pai.1s cj a.apm r.ap.2

λαλεῖν γλώσσαις, μᾶλλον δὲ ἵνα προφητεύητε· μείζων
to speak in tongues, but even more *but* to prophesy. The one who prophesies is greater
3281 1185 1254 3437 1254 2671 4736 3836 4736 4736 4736 3489
f.pa n.dpf adv.c cj cj v.pas.2p a.nsm.c

δὲ ὁ προφητεύων ἢ ὁ λαλῶν γλώσσαις ⌞ἐκτὸς εἰ μή⌟
{and} *The* *one who prophesies* than the ⌞one who speaks⌟ in tongues, unless
1254 3836 4736 2445 3836 3281 1185 1760 1623 3590
cj d.nsm pt.pa.nsm pl d.nsm pt.pa.nsm n.dpf adv cj pl

διερμηνεύῃ, ἵνα ἡ ἐκκλησία οἰκοδομὴν λάβῃ. 6 νῦν δέ,
he interprets so that the church may receive edification. *may receive* But ⌞as it is,⌟ *But*
1450 2671 3836 1711 3284 3284 3869 3284 1254 3814 1254
v.pas.3s cj d.nsf n.nsf n.asf v.aas.3s adv cj

ἀδελφοί, ἐὰν ἔλθω πρὸς ὑμᾶς γλώσσαις λαλῶν, τί ὑμᾶς
brothers, if I come to you speaking in tongues, *speaking* how will I benefit you
81 1569 2262 4639 7007 3281 1185 3281 5515 6067 6067 6067 7007
n.vpm cj v.aas.1s p.a r.ap.2 n.dpf pt.pa.nsm r.asn r.ap.2

ὠφελήσω ⌞ἐὰν μή⌟ ὑμῖν λαλήσω ἢ ἐν ἀποκαλύψει ἢ ἐν γνώσει
will I benefit unless I impart to you *I impart* some *{in}* revelation or *{in}* knowledge
6067 1569 3590 3281 3281 7007 3281 2445 1877 637 2445 1877 1194
v.fai.1s cj pl r.dp.2 v.aas.1s cj p.d n.dsf cj p.d n.dsf

NASB

dimly, but then
face to face; now
I know in part, but
then I will know
fully just as I also
have been fully
known. 13 But now
faith, hope, love,
abide these three;
but the greatest of
these is love.

Prophecy a Superior Gift

14:1 Pursue love,
yet desire earnestly
spiritual *gifts,* but
especially that you
may prophesy. 2 For
one who speaks in
a tongue does not
speak to men but
to God; for no one
understands, but in
his spirit he speaks
mysteries. 3 But one
who prophesies
speaks to men for
edification and
exhortation and
consolation. 4 One
who speaks in a
tongue edifies him-
self; but one who
prophesies edifies
the church. 5 Now
I wish that you all
spoke in tongues,
but *even* more that
you would proph-
esy; and greater is
one who proph-
esies than one who
speaks in tongues,
unless he inter-
prets, so that the
church may receive
edifying.
6 But now, breth-
ren, if I come to
you speaking in
tongues, what
will I profit you
unless I speak to
you either by way
of revelation or of
knowledge

NIV

or prophecy or
word of instruc-
tion? 7Even in the
case of lifeless
things that make
sounds, such as the
pipe or harp, how
will anyone know
what tune is being
played unless there
is a distinction in
the notes? 8Again,
if the trumpet does
not sound a clear
call, who will get
ready for battle?
9So it is with you.
Unless you speak
intelligible words
with your tongue,
how will anyone
know what you are
saying? You will
just be speaking
into the air. 10Un-
doubtedly there
are all sorts of
languages in the
world, yet none
of them is without
meaning. 11If then
I do not grasp the
meaning of what
someone is saying,
I am a foreigner to
the speaker, and
the speaker is a
foreigner to me.
12So it is with you.
Since you are ea-
ger for gifts of the
Spirit, try to excel
in those that build
up the church.
13For this rea-
son the one who
speaks in a tongue
should pray that
they may inter-
pret what they say.
14For if I pray in a
tongue, my spirit
prays, but my mind
is unfruitful. 15So
what shall I do? I
will pray with my
spirit, but I will
also pray with my
understanding; I
will sing with my
spirit, but I will
also sing with my
understanding.
16Otherwise when
you are praising
God in the Spirit,
how can someone
else, who is now
put in the position

ἢ ἐν προφητείᾳ ἢ ἐν[a] διδαχῇ; 7 ὅμως τὰ ἄψυχα
or {in} prophecy or {in} teaching? It is the same with {the} ⌞lifeless things⌟ that produce
2445 1877 4735 2445 1877 1439 3940 3836 953 1443 1443
cj p.d n.dsf cj p.d n.dsf adv d.npn a.npn

φωνὴν διδόντα, εἴτε αὐλὸς εἴτε κιθάρα, ἐὰν διαστολὴν
sound, that produce whether flute or harp; if they do not make a difference
5889 1443 1664 888 1664 3067 1569 1443 1443 3590 1443 1405
n.asf pt.pa.npn cj n.nsm cj n.nsf cj n.asf

τοῖς φθόγγοις μὴ δῷ, πῶς →
between notes, not they do make how will what is being played on the flute or the harp
3836 5782 3590 1443 4802 3836 884 884 884 884 884 884 2445 3836 3068
d.dpm n.dpm pl v.aas.3s cj

γνωσθήσεται τὸ αὐλούμενον ἢ τὸ κιθαριζόμενον; 8 καὶ γὰρ ἐὰν
be understood? what is being played on the flute or the harp Again, {for} if the
1182 3836 884 2445 3836 3068 2779 1142 1569
v.fpi.3s d.nsn pt.pp.nsn cj d.nsn pt.pp.nsn adv cj cj

ἄδηλον σάλπιγξ φωνὴν δῷ, τίς παρασκευάσεται εἰς πόλεμον;
bugle gives an uncertain bugle call, gives who will get ready for battle?
4894 1443 83 4894 5889 1443 5515 4186 1650 4483
a.asf n.nsf n.asf v.aas.3s r.nsm v.fmi.3s p.a n.asm

9 οὕτως καὶ ὑμεῖς διὰ τῆς γλώσσης ἐὰν
So {also} it is with you; if you do not speak a clear message with your tongue, if
4048 2779 7007 1569 1443 1443 3590 1443 2358 3364 1328 3836 1185 1569
adv adv r.np.2 p.g d.gsf n.gsf cj

μὴ εὔσημον λόγον δῶτε, πῶς γνωσθήσεται τὸ λαλούμενον; ἔσεσθε γὰρ
not clear message you do speak how will anyone know what is being said? ⌞You will be⌟ {for}
3590 2358 3364 1443 4802 1182 3836 3281 1639 1142
pl a.asm n.asm v.aas.2p cj v.fpi.3s d.nsn pt.pp.nsn v.fmi.2p cj

εἰς ἀέρα λαλοῦντες. 10 ⌞τοσαῦτα εἰ τύχοι⌟ γένη
speaking into the air. speaking There are who-knows-how-many kinds
3281 1650 113 3281 1639 1639 5537 1623 5593 1169
p.a n.asm pt.pa.npm r.npn cj v.aao.3s n.npn

φωνῶν εἰσιν ἐν κόσμῳ καὶ οὐδὲν ἄφωνον· 11 ἐὰν οὖν ↱ ↱
of languages There are in the world, and none is without meaning. But if But I do
5889 1639 1877 3180 2779 4029 936 4036 1569 4036 3857 3857
n.gpf v.pai.3p p.d n.dsm cj a.nsn a.nsn cj cj

μὴ εἰδῶ τὴν δύναμιν τῆς φωνῆς, ἔσομαι τῷ λαλοῦντι βάρβαρος καὶ
not grasp the meaning of the language, I will be a foreigner ⌞to the⌟ speaker foreigner and
3590 3857 3836 1539 3836 5889 1639 975 3836 3281 975 2779
pl v.ras.1s d.asf n.asf d.gsf n.gsf v.fmi.1s d.dsm pt.pa.dsm n.nsm cj

ὁ λαλῶν ἐν ἐμοὶ βάρβαρος. 12 οὕτως καὶ ὑμεῖς, ἐπεὶ
the speaker a foreigner to me. foreigner So {also} it is with you. Since you are
3836 3281 975 1877 1609 975 4048 2779 7007 2075 1639 1639
d.nsm pt.pa.nsm p.d r.ds.1 n.nsm adv adv r.np.2 cj

ζηλωταί ἐστε → → → πνευμάτων, πρὸς τὴν οἰκοδομὴν
eager you are for manifestations of the Spirit, seek to excel for the edification
2421 1639 4460 2426 2671 4355 4639 3836 3869
n.npm v.pai.2p n.gpn p.a d.asf n.asf

τῆς ἐκκλησίας ζητεῖτε ἵνα περισσεύητε. 13 διὸ ὁ λαλῶν →
of the church. seek to excel ⌞For this reason,⌟ the ⌞one who speaks⌟ in a
3836 1711 2426 2671 4355 1475 3836 3281
d.gsf n.gsf v.pam.2p cj v.pas.2p cj d.nsm pt.pa.nsm

γλώσσῃ προσευχέσθω ἵνα διερμηνεύῃ. 14 ἐὰν γὰρ[b] προσεύχωμαι →
tongue should pray that ⌞he will be able to interpret.⌟ For if For I pray in a
1185 4667 2671 1450 1142 1569 1142 4667
n.dsf v.pmm.3s cj v.pas.3s cj cj v.pms.1s

γλώσσῃ, τὸ πνεῦμά μου προσεύχεται, ὁ δὲ νοῦς μου ἄκαρπός
tongue, {the} my spirit my prays {the} but my mind my is unproductive.
1185 3836 1609 4460 1609 4667 3836 1254 1609 3808 1609 1639 182
n.dsf d.nsn n.nsn r.gs.1 v.pmi.3s d.nsm cj n.nsm r.gs.1 a.nsm

ἐστιν. 15 τί οὖν ἐστιν; προσεύξομαι τῷ πνεύματι, → →
is What then ⌞shall I do?⌟ I will pray ⌞with my⌟ spirit, but I will also
1639 5515 4036 1639 4667 3836 4460 1254 2779
v.pai.3s r.nsn cj v.pai.3s v.fmi.1s d.dsn n.dsn

[a] [ἐν] UBS.
[b] [γὰρ] UBS, omitted by NET.

NASB

or of prophecy or
of teaching? 7Yet
even lifeless things,
either flute or
harp, in producing
a sound, if they
do not produce a
distinction in the
tones, how will it
be known what is
played on the flute
or on the harp?
8For if the bugle
produces an indis-
tinct sound, who
will prepare him-
self for battle? 9So
also you, unless
you utter by the
tongue speech that
is clear, how will
it be known what
is spoken? For you
will be speaking
into the air. 10There
are, perhaps, a
great many kinds
of languages in
the world, and no
kind is without
meaning. 11If then
I do not know the
meaning of the
language, I will
be to the one who
speaks a barbarian,
and the one who
speaks will be a
barbarian to me.
12So also you, since
you are zealous of
spiritual *gifts,* seek
to abound for the
edification of the
church.
13Therefore let
one who speaks in
a tongue pray that
he may interpret.
14For if I pray
in a tongue, my
spirit prays, but my
mind is unfruitful.
15What is *the out-*
come then? I will
pray with the spirit
and I will

NIV

of an inquirer,[a]
say "Amen" to
your thanksgiving,
since they do not
know what you are
saying? 17 You are
giving thanks well
enough, but no one
else is edified.
18 I thank God that
I speak in tongues
more than all of
you. 19 But in the
church I would
rather speak five
intelligible words
to instruct others
than ten thousand
words in a tongue.
20 Brothers and
sisters, stop think-
ing like children.
In regard to evil be
infants, but in your
thinking be adults.
21 In the Law it is
written:

> "With other
> tongues
> and through
> the lips of
> foreigners
> I will speak to
> this people,
> but even then
> they will
> not listen to
> me,
> says the
> Lord."[b]

22 Tongues, then,
are a sign, not
for believers but
for unbelievers;
prophecy, how-
ever, is not for
unbelievers but for
believers. 23 So if
the whole church
comes togeth-
er and everyone
speaks in tongues,
and inquirers or

[a] 16 The Greek word for *inquirer* is a technical term for someone not fully initiated into a religion; also in verses 23 and 24.
[b] 21 Isaiah 28:11,12

προσεύξομαι δὲ καὶ τῷ νοΐ· ψαλῶ τῷ πνεύματι, →
pray *but* *also* ⌊with my⌋ understanding. ⌊I will sing praises⌋ ⌊with my⌋ spirit, but I
4667 1254 2779 3836 3808 6010 3836 4460 1254
v.fmi.1s cj adv d.dsm n.dsm v.fai.1s d.dsn n.dsn

→ ψαλῶ δὲ καὶ τῷ νοΐ. 16 ἐπεὶ ἐὰν εὐλογῇς
will also sing praises *but* *also* ⌊with my⌋ understanding. Otherwise, if you are praising God
2779 6010 1254 2779 3836 3808 2075 1569 2328
v.fai.1s cj adv d.dsm n.dsm cj cj v.pas.2s

ἐν[a] πνεύματι, ↱ ὁ ἀναπληρῶν τὸν τόπον τοῦ ἰδιώτου πῶς ἐρεῖ
by the Spirit, how can anyone in the position of an outsider *how* say,
1877 4460 4802 3306 3836 405 3836 5536 3836 2626 4802 3306
p.d n.dsn d.nsm pt.pa.nsm d.asm n.asm d.gsm n.gsm cj v.fai.3s

τὸ ἀμὴν ἐπὶ τῇ σῇ εὐχαριστίᾳ; ἐπειδὴ τί λέγεις
{the} "Amen," to *{the}* your thanksgiving since he does not know what ⌊you are saying?⌋
3836 297 2093 3836 5050 2374 2076 3857 3857 4024 3857 5515 3306
d.asn pl p.d d.dsf r.dsf.2 n.dsf cj r.asn v.pai.2s

οὐκ οἶδεν· 17 σὺ μὲν γὰρ καλῶς εὐχαριστεῖς ἀλλ᾽
not *he does know* For you ~ *For* are giving thanks well enough, *are giving thanks* but
4024 3857 1142 5148 3525 1142 2373 2373 2373 2822 2373 247
pl v.rai.3s r.ns.2 pl cj adv v.pai.2s cj

ὁ ἕτερος ↱ οὐκ οἰκοδομεῖται. 18 εὐχαριστῶ τῷ θεῷ,
the other person is not being edified. I thank *{the}* God I speak in tongues
3836 2283 3868 4024 3868 2373 3836 2536 3281 3281 1185 1185
d.nsm r.nsm pl v.ppi.3s v.pai.1s d.dsm n.dsm

πάντων ὑμῶν μᾶλλον γλώσσαις λαλῶ· 19 ἀλλὰ ἐν ἐκκλησίᾳ θέλω
more than all of you; *more* *in tongues* *I speak* however, in church I would rather
3437 4246 7007 3437 1185 3281 247 1877 1711 2527
a.gpm r.gp.2 adv.c n.dpf v.pai.1s cj p.d n.dsf v.pai.1s

πέντε λόγους τῷ νοΐ μου λαλῆσαι, ἵνα καὶ
speak five words with my understanding, *my* *speak* ⌊so as to⌋ instruct others also,
3281 4297 3364 3836 1609 3808 1609 3281 2671 2994 257 2779
a.apm n.apm d.dsm n.dsm r.gs.1 f.aa cj adv

ἄλλους κατηχήσω, ἢ μυρίους λόγους ἐν γλώσσῃ. 20 ἀδελφοί, μὴ
others *instruct* than ten thousand words in a tongue. Brothers, do not be
257 2994 2445 3692 3364 1877 1185 81 1181 3590 1181
r.apm v.aas.1s pl a.apm n.apm p.d n.dsf n.vpm pl

παιδία γίνεσθε ταῖς φρεσὶν ἀλλὰ τῇ κακίᾳ νηπιάζετε, ταῖς δὲ φρεσὶν
children *do be* in your thinking. Rather, in evil be infants, but in your *but* thinking be
4086 1181 3836 5856 247 3836 2798 3757 1254 3836 1254 5856 1181
n.npn v.pmm.2p d.dpf n.dpf cj d.dsf n.dsf v.pam.2p d.dpf cj n.dpf

τέλειοι γίνεσθε. 21 ἐν τῷ νόμῳ γέγραπται ὅτι ἐν ἑτερογλώσσοις καὶ
adults. *be* In the Law it is written, ~ "By ⌊people with strange tongues⌋ and
5455 1181 1877 3836 3795 1211 4022 1877 2280 2779
a.npm v.pmm.2p p.d d.dsm n.dsm v.rpi.3s cj p.d a.dpm cj

ἐν χείλεσιν ἑτέρων λαλήσω τῷ λαῷ τούτῳ καὶ οὐδ᾽ οὕτως
by the lips of foreigners will I speak to this people, *this* yet not even ⌊in this way⌋
1877 5927 2283 3281 3836 4047 3295 4047 2779 4028 4048
p.d n.dpn r.gpm v.fai.1s d.dsm n.dsm r.dsm cj adv adv

εἰσακούσονταί μου, λέγει κύριος. 22 ὥστε αἱ γλῶσσαι εἰς σημεῖόν
will they listen to me, says the Lord." So then *{the}* tongues are for a sign,
1653 1609 3306 3261 6063 3836 1185 1639 1650 4956
v.fmi.3p r.gs.1 v.pai.3s n.nsm cj d.npf n.npf p.a n.asn

εἰσιν οὐ τοῖς πιστεύουσιν ἀλλὰ τοῖς ἀπίστοις, ἡ δὲ προφητεία οὐ τοῖς
are not for believers but for unbelievers, *{the}* while prophecy is not for
1639 4024 3836 4409 247 3836 603 3836 1254 4735 4024 3836
v.pai.3p pl d.dpm pt.pa.dpm cj d.dpm a.dpm d.nsf cj n.nsf pl d.dpm

ἀπίστοις ἀλλὰ τοῖς πιστεύουσιν. 23 ἐὰν οὖν συνέλθῃ ἡ
unbelievers but for believers. So if *So* the whole church assembles *the*
603 247 3836 4409 4036 1569 4036 3836 3910 1711 5302 3836
a.dpm cj d.dpm pt.pa.dpm cj cj v.aas.3s d.nsf

ἐκκλησία ὅλη ἐπὶ τὸ αὐτὸ καὶ πάντες λαλῶσιν γλώσσαις,
church *whole* in the ⌊same place⌋ and everyone is speaking in tongues, and outsiders or
1711 3910 2093 3836 899 2779 4246 3281 1185 1254 2626 2445
n.nsf a.nsf p.a d.asn r.asn cj a.npm v.pas.3p n.dpf

[a] [ἐν] UBS.

NASB

pray with the mind
also; I will sing
with the spirit and
I will sing with the
mind also. 16 Other-
wise if you bless
in the spirit *only,*
how will the one
who fills the place
of the ungifted say
the "Amen" at your
giving of thanks,
since he does not
know what you are
saying? 17 For you
are giving thanks
well enough, but
the other person
is not edified. 18 I
thank God, I speak
in tongues more
than you all; 19 how-
ever, in the church
I desire to speak
five words with my
mind so that I may
instruct others also,
rather than ten
thousand words in
a tongue.

Instruction for the Church

20 Brethren, do
not be children in
your thinking; yet
in evil be infants,
but in your think-
ing be mature. 21 In
the Law it is writ-
ten, "BY MEN OF
STRANGE TONGUES
AND BY THE LIPS
OF STRANGERS I
WILL SPEAK TO THIS
PEOPLE, AND EVEN
SO THEY WILL NOT
LISTEN TO ME,"
says the Lord. 22 So
then tongues are
for a sign, not to
those who believe
but to unbelievers;
but prophecy *is*
for a sign, not to
unbelievers but to
those who believe.
23 Therefore if the
whole church as-
sembles together
and all speak in
tongues, and un-
gifted men or

NIV

unbelievers come
in, will they not
say that you are
out of your mind?
24But if an un-
believer or an
inquirer comes in
while everyone is
prophesying, they
are convicted of
sin and are brought
under judgment by
all, 25as the secrets
of their hearts are
laid bare. So they
will fall down and
worship God, ex-
claiming, "God is
really among you!"

Good Order in Worship

26What then shall
we say, brothers
and sisters? When
you come together,
each of you has a
hymn, or a word of
instruction, a reve-
lation, a tongue or
an interpretation.
Everything must
be done so that
the church may
be built up. 27If
anyone speaks in
a tongue, two—
or at the most
three—should
speak, one at a
time, and someone
must interpret. 28If
there is no inter-
preter, the speaker
should keep quiet
in the church and
speak to himself
and to God.
29Two or three
prophets should
speak, and the oth-
ers should weigh
carefully what is
said. 30And if a
revelation comes
to someone who
is sitting down,
the first speaker
should stop. 31For
you can all prophe-
sy in turn so that

εἰσέλθωσιν δὲ ἰδιῶται ἢ ἄπιστοι, ↱ ↱ οὐκ ἐροῦσιν ὅτι
unbelievers come in, *and* *outsiders* *or* *unbelievers* will they not say that
603 1656 1254 2626 2445 603 3306 3306 4024 3306 4022
v.aas.3p cj n.npm cj a.npm pl v.fai.3p cj

μαίνεσθε; 24 ἐὰν δὲ πάντες προφητεύωσιν,
⌊you are out of your minds?⌋ But if *But* all are prophesying, and an unbeliever or
3419 1254 1569 1254 4246 4736 1254 5516 603 2445
v.pmi.2p cj cj a.npm v.pas.3p

εἰσέλθῃ δέ τις ἄπιστος ἢ ἰδιώτης, ἐλέγχεται ὑπὸ πάντων,
outsider comes in, *and* *an* *unbeliever* *or* *outsider* he is convicted by all,
2626 1656 1254 5516 603 2445 2626 1794 5679 4246
v.aas.3s cj r.nsm a.nsm cj n.nsm v.ppi.3s p.g a.gpm

ἀνακρίνεται ὑπὸ πάντων, 25 τὰ κρυπτὰ τῆς καρδίας αὐτοῦ
⌊he is called to account⌋ by all, and the secrets of his heart *his* are
373 5679 4246 3836 3220 3836 899 2840 899 1181
v.ppi.3s p.g a.gpm d.npn a.npn d.gsf n.gsf r.gsm.3

φανερὰ γίνεται, καὶ οὕτως πεσὼν ἐπὶ πρόσωπον προσκυνήσει τῷ θεῷ
laid bare. *are* *{and}* Thus ⌊he will fall⌋ on his face and worship *{the}* God,
5745 1181 2779 4048 4406 2093 4725 4686 3836 2536
a.npn v.pmi.3s cj adv pt.aa.nsm p.a n.asn v.fai.3s d.dsm n.dsm

ἀπαγγέλλων ὅτι ὄντως ὁ θεὸς ἐν ὑμῖν ἐστιν. 26 τί οὖν
declaring, ~ "God is really *{the}* *God* among you." *is* What then
550 4022 2536 1639 3953 3836 2536 1877 7007 1639 5515 4036
pt.pa.nsm cj adv d.nsm n.nsm p.d r.dp.2 v.pai.3s r.nsn cj

ἐστιν, ἀδελφοί; ὅταν συνέρχησθε, ἕκαστος ψαλμὸν ἔχει,
is the outcome, brothers? When you come together, each one has a hymn, *has* a
1639 81 4020 5302 1667 2400 6011 2400
v.pai.3s n.vpm cj v.pms.2p r.nsm n.asm v.pai.3s

διδαχὴν ἔχει, ἀποκάλυψιν ἔχει, γλῶσσαν ἔχει, ἑρμηνείαν ἔχει·
word of instruction, *{has}* a revelation, *{has}* a tongue, *{has}* an interpretation. *{has}* Let
1439 2400 637 2400 1185 2400 2255 2400 1181
n.asf v.pai.3s n.asf v.pai.3s n.asf v.pai.3s n.asf v.pai.3s

πάντα πρὸς οἰκοδομὴν γινέσθω. 27 εἴτε → γλώσσῃ τις λαλεῖ,
all things be done for edification. *Let be done* If any speak in a tongue, *any* *speak* it
4246 1181 1181 4639 3869 1181 1664 5516 3281 1185 5516 3281
a.npn p.a n.asf v.pmm.3s cj n.dsf r.nsm v.pai.3s

κατὰ δύο ἢ τὸ πλεῖστον τρεῖς καὶ ἀνὰ μέρος, καὶ εἷς
should be only two, or at the most three, and each in turn; and someone
2848 1545 2445 3836 4498 5552 2779 324 3538 2779 1651
p.a a.apm cj d.asn a.asn.s a.apm cj p.a n.asn cj a.nsm

διερμηνευέτω· 28 ἐὰν δὲ μὴ ᾖ διερμηνευτής,
must interpret. But if *But* there is no *there is* one who can interpret, the
1450 1254 1569 1254 1639 1639 3590 1639 1449
v.pam.3s cj cj pl v.pas.3s n.nsm

σιγάτω ἐν ἐκκλησίᾳ, ἑαυτῷ δὲ λαλείτω καὶ τῷ θεῷ.
⌊speaker should remain silent⌋ in church and speak to himself *and* *speak* and to God.
4967 1877 1711 1254 3281 1571 1254 3281 2779 3836 2536
v.pam.3s p.d n.dsf r.dsm.3 cj v.pam.3s cj d.dsm n.dsm

29 προφῆται δὲ δύο ἢ τρεῖς λαλείτωσαν καὶ οἱ ἄλλοι
prophets *{and}* Two or three should speak as prophets and *{the}* others
4737 1254 1545 2445 5552 3281 4737 2779 3836 257
n.npm cj a.npm cj a.npm v.pam.3p cj d.npm r.npm

διακρινέτωσαν· 30 ἐὰν δὲ ἄλλῳ
should weigh carefully what is said. But if *But* a revelation comes ⌊to another person⌋
1359 1254 1569 1254 636 636 257
v.pam.3p cj cj r.dsm

ἀποκαλυφθῇ καθημένῳ, ὁ πρῶτος σιγάτω. 31
revelation comes ⌊who is sitting down,⌋ the first ⌊speaker should stop.⌋ For in this way all
636 2764 3836 4755 4967 1142 4246
v.aps.3s pt.pm.dsm d.nsm a.nsm v.pam.3s

δύνασθε γὰρ ⌊καθ' ἕνα⌋ πάντες προφητεύειν, ἵνα
will be able *For* to prophesy one by one, *all* *to prophesy* ⌊with the result that⌋
1538 1142 4736 4736 2848 1651 4246 4736 2671
v.ppi.2p cj p.a a.asm a.npm f.pa cj

NASB

unbelievers
enter, will they
not say that you
are mad? 24But
if all prophesy,
and an unbeliever
or an ungifted
man enters, he is
convicted by all, he
is called to account
by all; 25the secrets
of his heart are
disclosed; and so
he will fall on his
face and worship
God, declaring that
God is certainly
among you.
26What is *the*
outcome then,
brethren? When
you assemble, each
one has a psalm,
has a teaching, has
a revelation, has
a tongue, has an
interpretation. Let
all things be done
for edification. 27If
anyone speaks in
a tongue, *it should*
be by two or at the
most three, and
each in turn, and
one must interpret;
28but if there is no
interpreter, he must
keep silent in the
church; and let him
speak to himself
and to God. 29Let
two or three proph-
ets speak, and let
the others pass
judgment. 30But if a
revelation is made
to another who is
seated, the first one
must keep silent.
31For you can all
prophesy one by
one, so that all

NIV

everyone may be instructed and encouraged. [32]The spirits of prophets are subject to the control of prophets. [33]For God is not a God of disorder but of peace—as in all the congregations of the Lord's people.

[34]Women[a] should remain silent in the churches. They are not allowed to speak, but must be in submission, as the law says. [35]If they want to inquire about something, they should ask their own husbands at home; for it is disgraceful for a woman to speak in the church.[b]

[36]Or did the word of God originate with you? Or are you the only people it has reached? [37]If anyone thinks they are a prophet or otherwise gifted by the Spirit, let them acknowledge that what I am writing to you is the Lord's command. [38]But if anyone ignores this, they will themselves be ignored.[c]

[39]Therefore, my brothers and sisters, be eager to prophesy, and do not forbid speaking in tongues. [40]But everything should be done in a fitting and orderly way.

[a] 33,34 Or *peace. As in all the congregations of the Lord's people, [34]women*
[b] 34,35 In a few manuscripts these verses come after verse 40.
[c] 38 Some manuscripts *But anyone who is ignorant of this will be ignorant*

πάντες μανθάνωσιν καὶ πάντες παρακαλῶνται. [32] καὶ πνεύματα προφητῶν
all may learn and all be encouraged, Indeed, the spirits of prophets are
4246 3443 2779 4246 4151 2779 4460 4737 5718
a.npm v.pas.3p cj a.npm v.pps.3p cj n.npn n.gpm

προφήταις ὑποτάσσεται, [33] οὐ γάρ ἐστιν ἀκαταστασίας
subject to prophets, *are subject* for God is not *for* *is* a God of confusion
5718 4737 5718 1142 2536 1639 4024 1142 1639 189
n.dpm v.ppi.3s pl cj v.pai.3s n.gsf

ὁ θεὸς ἀλλὰ εἰρήνης. ὡς ἐν πάσαις ταῖς ἐκκλησίαις τῶν ἁγίων [34] αἱ γυναῖκες
{the} *God* but of peace. As in all the churches of the saints, the women
3836 2536 247 1645 6055 1877 4246 3836 1711 3836 41 3836 1222
d.nsm n.nsm cj n.gsf pl p.d a.dpf d.dpf n.dpf d.gpm a.gpm d.npf n.npf

ἐν ταῖς ἐκκλησίαις σιγάτωσαν· ➝ οὐ γὰρ ἐπιτρέπεται
are to be silent in the churches, *are to be silent* for they are not *for* permitted
4967 4967 4967 4967 1877 3836 1711 4967 1142 899 2205 4024 1142 2205
p.d d.dpf n.dpf v.pam.3p pl cj v.ppi.3s

αὐταῖς λαλεῖν, ἀλλὰ ὑποτασσέσθωσαν, καθὼς καὶ ὁ νόμος λέγει. [35] εἰ
they to speak. Rather, they are to be submissive, as in fact the law says. And if
899 3281 247 5718 2777 2779 3836 3795 3306 1254 1623
r.dpf.3 f.pa cj v.ppm.3p cj adv d.nsm n.nsm v.pai.3s cj

δέ τι μαθεῖν θέλουσιν,
And they want to find out about something, *to find out about* *they want* they should ask their
1254 2527 2527 3443 3443 3443 3443 5516 3443 2527 2089 2089 2089 2625
cj r.asn f.aa v.pai.3p

ἐν οἴκῳ τοὺς ἰδίους ἄνδρας ἐπερωτάτωσαν· αἰσχρὸν γάρ
own husbands at home; *{the}* *their own* *husbands* *they should ask* for it is improper *for*
2625 467 1877 3875 3836 2625 467 2089 1142 1639 1639 156 1142
p.d n.dsm d.apm a.apm n.apm v.pam.3p a.nsn cj

ἐστιν ➝ γυναικὶ λαλεῖν ἐν ἐκκλησίᾳ. [36] ἢ ἀφ'
it is for a woman to speak in church. Or did the word of God originate with
1639 1222 3281 1877 1711 2445 2002 3836 3364 3836 2536 2002 608
v.pai.3s n.dsf f.pa p.d n.dsf cj p.g

ὑμῶν ὁ λόγος τοῦ θεοῦ ἐξῆλθεν, ἢ εἰς ὑμᾶς μόνους κατήντησεν;
you? *the* *word* *of* *God* *did originate* Or did it come to you alone? *did it come*
7007 3836 3364 3836 2536 2002 2445 2918 2918 2918 1650 7007 3668 2918
r.gp.2 d.nsm n.nsm d.gsm n.gsm v.aai.3s cj p.a r.ap.2 a.apm v.aai.3s

[37] Εἴ τις δοκεῖ προφήτης εἶναι ἢ πνευματικός,
If anyone considers himself to be a prophet *to be* or spiritual,
1623 5516 1506 1639 1639 4737 1639 2445 4461
cj r.nsm v.pai.3s n.nsm f.pa cj a.nsm

ἐπιγινωσκέτω ἃ γράφω ὑμῖν ὅτι ➝ κυρίου ἐστὶν
let him acknowledge that what I am writing to you *that* is a command of the Lord. *is*
2105 4022 4005 1211 7007 4022 1639 1953 3261 1639
v.pam.3s r.apn v.pai.1s r.dp.2 cj n.gsm v.pai.3s

ἐντολή· [38] εἰ δέ τις ἀγνοεῖ, ἀγνοεῖται.[a] [39] ὥστε,
command If *{and}* anyone fails to acknowledge this, ⌊he will not be acknowledged.⌋ So,
1953 1623 1254 5516 51 51 6063
n.nsf cj cj r.nsm v.pai.3s v.pmi.3s cj

ἀδελφοί μου,[b] ζηλοῦτε τὸ προφητεύειν καὶ τὸ λαλεῖν μὴ
my brothers, *my* be eager ~ to prophesy, and do not forbid ~ speaking *not*
1609 81 1609 2420 3836 4736 2779 3266 3590 3266 3836 3281 3590
n.vpm r.gs.1 v.pam.2p d.asn f.pa cj d.asn f.pa pl

κωλύετε γλώσσαις· [40] πάντα δὲ ➝ εὐσχημόνως καὶ
do forbid in tongues. But everything *But* should be done in a proper and
3266 1185 1254 4246 1254 1181 1181 1181 2361 2779
v.pam.2p n.dpf a.npn cj adv cj

⌊κατὰ τάξιν⌋ γινέσθω.
orderly way. *should be done*
2848 5423 1181
p.a n.asf v.pmm.3s

15:1 γνωρίζω δὲ ὑμῖν, ἀδελφοί, τὸ εὐαγγέλιον ὃ εὐηγγελισάμην
Now I make known *Now* to you, brothers, the gospel that I preached
1254 1192 1254 7007 81 3836 2295 4005 2294
v.pai.1s cj r.dp.2 n.vpm d.asn n.asn r.asn v.ami.1s

[a] ἀγνοεῖτω included by TR after ἀγνοεῖται.
[b] [μου] UBS.

NASB

may learn and all may be exhorted; [32]and the spirits of prophets are subject to prophets; [33]for God is not *a God* of confusion but of peace, as in all the churches of the saints.

[34]The women are to keep silent in the churches; for they are not permitted to speak, but are to subject themselves, just as the Law also says. [35]If they desire to learn anything, let them ask their own husbands at home; for it is improper for a woman to speak in church. [36]Was it from you that the word of God *first* went forth? Or has it come to you only?

[37]If anyone thinks he is a prophet or spiritual, let him recognize that the things which I write to you are the Lord's commandment. [38]But if anyone does not recognize *this,* he [a]is not recognized.

[39]Therefore, my brethren, desire earnestly to prophesy, and do not forbid to speak in tongues. [40]But all things must be done properly and in an orderly manner.

The Fact of Christ's Resurrection

[15:1]Now I make known to you, brethren, the gospel which I preached to you,

[a] Two early mss read *is not to be recognized*

NIV

The Resurrection of Christ

15 Now, broth-
ers and
sisters, I want to
remind you of the
gospel I preached
to you, which you
received and on
which you have
taken your stand.
2By this gospel
you are saved, if
you hold firm-
ly to the word I
preached to you.
Otherwise, you
have believed in
vain.
3For what I re-
ceived I passed
on to you as of
first importance[a]:
that Christ died
for our sins ac-
cording to the
Scriptures, 4that
he was buried,
that he was raised
on the third day
according to the
Scriptures, 5and
that he appeared
to Cephas,[b] and
then to the Twelve.
6After that, he
appeared to more
than five hundred
of the brothers
and sisters at the
same time, most of
whom are still liv-
ing, though some
have fallen asleep.
7Then he appeared
to James, then to
all the apostles,
8and last of all he
appeared to me
also, as to one ab-
normally born.
9For I am the
least of the apos-
tles and do not
even deserve to be
called an apostle,
because I perse-
cuted the church of
God. 10But by the
grace of God I am
what I am, and his
grace to me was
not without ef-
fect. No, I worked
harder than all of
them—yet not I,
but the grace of

[a] 3 Or *you at the first*
[b] 5 That is, Peter

ὑμῖν, ὃ καὶ παρελάβετε, ἐν ᾧ καὶ ἑστήκατε, 2δι' οὗ καὶ
to you, which also you received, in which also you stand, through which also
7007 4005 2779 4161 1877 4005 2779 2705 1328 4005 2779
r.dp.2 r.asn adv v.aai.2p p.d r.dsn adv v.rai.2p p.g r.gsn adv

σῴζεσθε, τίνι λόγῳ εὐηγγελισάμην ὑμῖν εἰ
⌊you are being saved,⌋ if you hold firmly to the message I preached to you *if*
5392 1623 2988 2988 2988 5515 3364 2294 7007 1623
v.ppi.2p r.dsm n.dsm v.ami.1s r.dp.2 cj

κατέχετε, ⌊ἐκτὸς εἰ μὴ⌋ εἰκῇ ἐπιστεύσατε. 3
you hold firmly — unless you have believed in vain. *you have believed* For
2988 1760 1623 3590 4409 4409 4409 1632 4409 1142
v.pai.2p adv cj pl adv v.aai.2p

παρέδωκα γὰρ ὑμῖν ἐν πρώτοις, ὃ ↱ καὶ παρέλαβον, ὅτι Χριστὸς
I passed on *For* to you ⌊as of⌋ first importance what I also received: that Christ
4140 1142 7007 1877 4755 4005 4161 2779 4161 4022 5986
v.aai.1s cj r.dp.2 p.d a.dpn r.asn adv v.aai.1s cj n.nsm

ἀπέθανεν ὑπὲρ τῶν ἁμαρτιῶν ἡμῶν κατὰ τὰς γραφὰς 4καὶ ὅτι
died for *{the}* our sins *our* ⌊according to⌋ the Scriptures, and that
633 5642 3836 7005 281 7005 2848 3836 1210 2779 4022
v.aai.3s p.g d.gpf n.gpf r.gp.1 p.a d.apf n.apf cj cj

ἐτάφη καὶ ὅτι ἐγήγερται τῇ ἡμέρᾳ τῇ τρίτῃ κατὰ τὰς
⌊he was buried,⌋ and that ⌊he has been raised⌋ ⌊on the⌋ third day *{the}* *third* ⌊according to⌋ the
2507 2779 4022 1586 3836 5569 2465 3836 5569 2848 3836
v.api.3s cj cj v.rpi.3s d.dsf n.dsf d.dsf a.dsf p.a d.apf

γραφὰς 5καὶ ὅτι ὤφθη Κηφᾷ εἶτα τοῖς δώδεκα· 6ἔπειτα ὤφθη ↱
Scriptures, and that he appeared to Cephas, then to the twelve. Then he appeared to
1210 2779 4022 3972 3064 1663 3836 1557 2083 3972 81
n.apf cj cj v.api.3s n.dsm adv d.dpm a.dpm adv v.api.3s

ἐπάνω πεντακοσίοις ἀδελφοῖς ἐφάπαξ, ἐξ ὧν οἱ πλείονες →
more than five hundred brothers ⌊at the same time,⌋ most of whom *{the}* *most* are still
2062 4296 81 2384 4498 1666 4005 3836 4498 2401
adv a.dpm n.dpm adv p.g r.gpm d.npm a.npm.c

μένουσιν ⌊ἕως ἄρτι,⌋ τινὲς δὲ ἐκοιμήθησαν· 7ἔπειτα ὤφθη Ἰακώβῳ
living, *still* although some *although* have fallen asleep. Then he appeared to James,
3531 2401 785 1254 5516 1254 3121 2083 3972 2610
v.pai.3p p.g adv r.npm cj v.api.3p adv v.api.3s n.dsm

εἶτα → τοῖς ἀποστόλοις πᾶσιν· 8ἔσχατον δὲ πάντων ὡσπερεὶ τῷ
then to all the apostles. *all* Last *{and}* of all, as ⌊to one⌋
1663 4246 3836 693 4246 2274 1254 4246 6062 3836
adv d.dpm n.dpm a.dpm adv cj a.gpm pl d.dsn

ἐκτρώματι ὤφθη κἀμοί. 9 ἐγὼ γάρ εἰμι ὁ ἐλάχιστος τῶν
⌊abnormally born,⌋ he appeared ⌊even to me.⌋ For I *For* am the least of the
1765 3972 2743 1142 1609 1142 1639 3836 1788 3836
n.dsn v.api.3s crasis r.ns.1 cj v.pai.1s d.nsm a.nsm.s d.gpm

ἀποστόλων ὃς οὐκ εἰμὶ ἱκανὸς καλεῖσθαι ἀπόστολος, διότι ἐδίωξα
apostles, and I am not *am* worthy to be called an apostle, because I persecuted
693 4005 1639 4024 1639 2653 2813 693 1484 1503
n.gpm r.nsm pl v.pai.1s a.nsm f.pp n.nsm cj v.aai.1s

τὴν ἐκκλησίαν τοῦ θεοῦ· 10 → χάριτι δὲ θεοῦ εἰμι ὅ εἰμι, καὶ ἡ
the church of God. But by the grace *But* of God I am what I am, and *{the}* his
3836 1711 3836 2536 1254 5921 1254 2536 1639 4005 1639 2779 3836 899
d.asf n.asf d.gsm n.gsm n.dsf cj n.gsm v.pai.1s r.nsn v.pai.1s cj d.nsf

χάρις αὐτοῦ ἡ εἰς ἐμὲ οὐ κενὴ ἐγενήθη, ἀλλὰ περισσότερον
grace *his* *{the}* toward me was not in vain. *was* No, I worked harder
5921 899 3836 1650 1609 1181 4024 3031 1181 247 3159 3159 4358
n.nsf r.gsm.3 d.nsf p.a r.as.1 pl a.nsf v.api.3s cj adv.c

→ αὐτῶν πάντων ἐκοπίασα, οὐκ ἐγὼ δὲ ἀλλὰ ἡ χάρις τοῦ θεοῦ
than any of them *any* *I worked* — yet not I, *yet* but the grace of God
4246 899 4246 3159 1254 4024 1609 1254 247 3836 5921 3836 2536
r.gpm.3 a.gpm v.aai.1s pl r.ns.1 cj cj d.nsf n.nsf d.gsm n.gsm

ἡ[a] σὺν ἐμοί. 11εἴτε οὖν ἐγὼ εἴτε ἐκεῖνοι, οὕτως κηρύσσομεν καὶ οὕτως
that is with me. Whether then it was I or they, so we preach and so
3836 5250 1609 1664 4036 1609 1664 1697 4048 3062 2779 4048
d.nsf p.d r.ds.1 cj cj r.ns.1 cj r.npm adv v.pai.1p cj adv

[a] [ἡ] UBS, omitted by TNIV.

NASB

which also you
received, in which
also you stand, 2by
which also you
are saved, if you
hold fast the word
which I preached
to you, unless you
believed in vain.
3For I delivered
to you as of first
importance what I
also received, that
Christ died for our
sins according to
the Scriptures, 4and
that He was buried,
and that He was
raised on the third
day according to
the Scriptures, 5and
that He appeared
to Cephas, then to
the twelve. 6After
that He appeared
to more than five
hundred brethren
at one time, most
of whom remain
until now, but some
have fallen asleep;
7then He appeared
to James, then to
all the apostles;
8and last of all, as
to one untimely
born, He appeared
to me also. 9For I
am the least of the
apostles, and not
fit to be called an
apostle, because
I persecuted the
church of God.
10But by the grace
of God I am what I
am, and His grace
toward me did not
prove vain; but I
labored even more
than all of them,
yet not I, but the
grace of God with
me. 11Whether then
it was I or they, so
we preach and so

NIV

God that was with
me. [11]Whether,
then, it is I or they,
this is what we
preach, and this is
what you believed.

The Resurrection of the Dead

[12]But if it is
preached that
Christ has been
raised from the
dead, how can
some of you say
that there is no
resurrection of the
dead? [13]If there is
no resurrection of
the dead, then not
even Christ has
been raised. [14]And
if Christ has not
been raised, our
preaching is use-
less and so is your
faith. [15]More than
that, we are then
found to be false
witnesses about
God, for we have
testified about
God that he raised
Christ from the
dead. But he did
not raise him if in
fact the dead are
not raised. [16]For
if the dead are not
raised, then Christ
has not been raised
either. [17]And if
Christ has not
been raised, your
faith is futile; you
are still in your
sins. [18]Then those
also who have
fallen asleep in
Christ are lost. [19]If
only for this life
we have hope in
Christ, we are of
all people most to
be pitied.
[20]But Christ has
indeed been raised
from the dead,
the firstfruits of
those who have
fallen asleep. [21]For
since death came
through a man,

ἐπιστεύσατε. 12 εἰ δὲ Χριστὸς κηρύσσεται ὅτι ἐκ νεκρῶν
you came to believe. Now if *Now* Christ is proclaimed as raised from the dead,
4409 1254 1623 1254 5986 3062 4022 1586 1666 3738
v.aai.2p cj cj n.nsm v.ppi.3s cj p.g a.gpm

ἐγήγερται, πῶς → λέγουσιν ἐν ὑμῖν τινες ὅτι ἀνάστασις
raised how can some of you say *of* *you* *some* that there is no resurrection
1586 4802 5516 1877 7007 3306 1877 7007 5516 4022 1639 1639 4024 414
v.rpi.3s cj v.pai.3p p.d r.dp.2 r.npm cj n.nsf

→ νεκρῶν οὐκ ἔστιν; 13 εἰ δὲ ἀνάστασις → νεκρῶν οὐκ
of the dead? *no* *there is* But if *But* there is no resurrection of the dead, *no*
3738 4024 1639 1254 1623 1254 1639 1639 4024 414 3738 4024
a.gpm pl v.pai.3s cj cj n.nsf a.gpm pl

ἔστιν, οὐδὲ Χριστὸς ἐγήγερται· 14 εἰ δὲ Χριστὸς ↱ οὐκ ἐγήγερται,
there is not even Christ has been raised. And if *And* Christ has not been raised, then
1639 4028 5986 1586 1254 1623 1254 5986 1586 4024 1586 726
v.pai.3s adv n.nsm v.rpi.3s cj cj n.nsm pl v.rpi.3s

κενὸν ἄρα καὶ[a] τὸ κήρυγμα ἡμῶν,
our proclamation is groundless, *then* *{also}* *{the}* *proclamation* *our* and your faith is to
7005 3060 3031 726 2779 3836 3060 7005 2779 7007 4411
a.nsn cj adv d.nsn n.nsn r.gp.1

κενὴ καὶ ἡ πίστις ὑμῶν· 15 → → εὑρισκόμεθα δὲ καὶ
no purpose. *and* *{the}* *faith* *your* Beyond that, we are even found *Beyond that* *even*
3031 2779 3836 4411 7007 1254 1254 2779 2351 1254 2779
a.nsf cj d.nsf n.nsf r.gp.2 v.ppi.1p cj adv

ψευδομάρτυρες τοῦ θεοῦ, ὅτι ἐμαρτυρήσαμεν κατὰ τοῦ θεοῦ ὅτι ἤγειρεν
to be false witnesses about God, because we have borne witness about *{the}* God that he raised
6020 3836 2536 4022 3455 2848 3836 2536 4022 1586
n.npm d.gsm n.gsm cj v.aai.1p p.g d.gsm n.gsm cj v.aai.3s

τὸν Χριστόν, ὃν ↱ ↱ οὐκ ἤγειρεν εἴπερ ἄρα νεκροὶ ↱ οὐκ
{the} Christ, whom he did not raise ⌞if it is true that⌟ *{then}* the dead are not
3836 5986 4005 1586 1586 4024 1586 1642 726 3738 1586 4024
d.asm n.asm r.asm pl v.aai.3s cj cj a.npm pl

ἐγείρονται. 16 εἰ γὰρ νεκροὶ ↱ οὐκ ἐγείρονται, οὐδὲ Χριστὸς
raised. For if *For* the dead are not raised, not even Christ
1586 1142 1623 1142 3738 1586 4024 1586 4028 5986
v.ppi.3p cj cj a.npm pl v.ppi.3p adv n.nsm

ἐγήγερται· 17 εἰ δὲ Χριστὸς ↱ οὐκ ἐγήγερται, ματαία ἡ
has been raised. And if *And* Christ has not been raised, your faith is useless; *{the}*
1586 1254 1623 1254 5986 1586 4024 1586 7007 4411 3469 3836
v.rpi.3s cj cj n.nsm pl v.rpi.3s a.nsf d.nsf

πίστις ὑμῶν, ἔτι ἐστὲ ἐν ταῖς ἁμαρτίαις ὑμῶν, 18 ἄρα καὶ οἱ
faith *your* you are still *you are* in *{the}* your sins. *your* Then those also *those*
4411 7007 1639 1639 2285 1639 1877 3836 7007 281 7007 726 3836 2779 3836
n.nsf r.gp.2 adv v.pai.2p p.d d.dpf n.dpf r.gp.2 cj adv d.npm

κοιμηθέντες ἐν Χριστῷ ἀπώλοντο. 19 εἰ ἐν τῇ
⌞who have fallen asleep⌟ in Christ have perished. If our hope in Christ is for *{the}*
3121 1877 5986 660 1623 1639 1827 1877 5986 1639 1877 3836
pt.ap.npm p.d n.dsm v.ami.3p cj p.d d.dsf

ζωῇ ταύτῃ ἐν Χριστῷ ἠλπικότες ἐσμὲν μόνον,
this life *this* *in* *Christ* *hope* *our is* only, we are of all men
4047 2437 4047 1877 5986 1827 1639 3667 1639 1639 4246 4246 476
n.dsf r.dsf p.d n.dsm pt.ra.npm v.pai.1p adv

ἐλεεινότεροι πάντων ἀνθρώπων ἐσμέν. 20 νυνὶ δὲ Χριστὸς ἐγήγερται ἐκ
most to be pitied. *of all* *men* *we are* But in fact *But* Christ has been raised from
1795 4246 476 1639 1254 3815 1254 5986 1586 1666
a.npm.c a.gpm n.gpm v.pai.1p adv cj n.nsm v.rpi.3s p.g

νεκρῶν ἀπαρχὴ τῶν κεκοιμημένων. 21 ἐπειδὴ γὰρ δι'
the dead, the firstfruits of those who have fallen asleep. For since *For* death came through
3738 569 3836 3121 1142 2076 1142 2505 1328
a.gpm n.nsf d.gpm pt.rp.gpm cj cj p.g

ἀνθρώπου θάνατος, καὶ δι' ἀνθρώπου ἀνάστασις
a man, *death* the resurrection of the dead also comes through a man. *resurrection*
476 2505 414 3738 2779 1328 476 414
n.gsm n.nsm adv p.g n.gsm n.nsf

NASB

you believed.
[12]Now if Christ
is preached, that
He has been raised
from the dead, how
do some among
you say that there
is no resurrection
of the dead? [13]But
if there is no resur-
rection of the dead,
not even Christ has
been raised; [14]and if
Christ has not been
raised, then our
preaching is vain,
your faith also is
vain. [15]Moreover
we are even found
to be false wit-
nesses of God, be-
cause we testified
against God that
He raised [a]Christ,
whom He did not
raise, if in fact the
dead are not raised.
[16]For if the dead
are not raised, not
even Christ has
been raised; [17]and if
Christ has not been
raised, your faith is
worthless; you are
still in your sins.
[18]Then those also
who have fallen
asleep in Christ
have perished. [19]If
we have hoped in
Christ in this life
only, we are of all
men most to be
pitied.

The Order of Resurrection

[20]But now Christ
has been raised
from the dead, the
first fruits of those
who are asleep.
[21]For since by a
man *came* death,
by a man also *came*
the resurrection of
the dead.

[a] [καὶ] UBS, omitted by TNIV.

[a] I.e. the Messiah

NIV

the resurrection
of the dead comes
also through a
man. [22]For as in
Adam all die, so
in Christ all will
be made alive.
[23]But each in turn:
Christ, the first-
fruits; then, when
he comes, those
who belong to him.
[24]Then the end
will come, when
he hands over the
kingdom to God
the Father after
he has destroyed
all dominion, au-
thority and power.
[25]For he must reign
until he has put all
his enemies under
his feet. [26]The last
enemy to be de-
stroyed is death.
[27]For he "has put
everything under
his feet."[a] Now
when it says that
"everything" has
been put under
him, it is clear that
this does not in-
clude God himself,
who put every-
thing under Christ.
[28]When he has
done this, then the
Son himself will
be made subject
to him who put
everything under
him, so that God
may be all in all.
[29]Now if there is
no resurrection,
what will those do
who are baptized
for the dead? If the
dead are not raised
at all, why are peo-
ple baptized for
them? [30]And as for
us, why do we en-
danger ourselves

νεκρῶν. [22] ὥσπερ γὰρ ἐν τῷ Ἀδὰμ πάντες ἀποθνῄσκουσιν, οὕτως καὶ ἐν
dead For just as *For* in *{the}* Adam all die, so also in
3738 1142 6061 1142 1877 3836 77 4246 633 4048 2779 1877
a.gpm cj cj p.d d.dsm n.dsm a.npm v.pai.3p adv adv p.d

τῷ Χριστῷ πάντες ζῳοποιηθήσονται. [23] ἕκαστος δὲ ἐν τῷ ἰδίῳ τάγματι·
{the} Christ all will be made alive. But each *But* in *{the}* his own order:
3836 5986 4246 2443 1254 1667 1254 1877 3836 2625 5413
d.dsm n.dsm a.npm v.fpi.3p r.nsm cj p.d d.dsn a.dsn n.dsn

ἀπαρχὴ Χριστός, ἔπειτα οἱ τοῦ Χριστοῦ ἐν τῇ παρουσίᾳ
Christ, the firstfruits; *Christ* then, those ⌞who belong to⌟ Christ, when *{the}* he comes.
5986 569 5986 2083 3836 3836 5986 1877 3836 899 4242
n.nsf n.nsm adv d.npm d.gsm n.gsm p.d d.dsf n.dsf

αὐτοῦ, [24] εἶτα τὸ τέλος, ὅταν παραδιδῷ τὴν βασιλείαν τῷ θεῷ καὶ
he ⌞Then comes⌟ the end, when he hands over the kingdom to God *{and}* the
899 1663 3836 5465 4020 4140 3836 993 3836 2536 2779
r.gsm.3 adv d.nsn n.nsn cj v.pas.3s d.asf n.asf d.dsm n.dsm cj

πατρί, ὅταν καταργήσῃ πᾶσαν ἀρχὴν καὶ πᾶσαν ἐξουσίαν καὶ δύναμιν. [25]
Father, when he has destroyed every dominion, *{and}* every authority and power. For
4252 4020 2934 4246 794 2779 4246 2026 2779 1539 1142
n.dsm cj v.aas.3s a.asf n.asf cj a.asf n.asf cj n.asf

δεῖ γὰρ αὐτὸν βασιλεύειν ⌞ἄχρι οὗ⌟ θῇ πάντας τοὺς ἐχθροὺς ὑπὸ τοὺς
he must *For* *he* reign until ⌞he has put⌟ all his enemies under *{the}*
899 1256 1142 899 996 948 4005 5502 4246 3836 2398 5679 3836
v.pai.3s cj r.asm.3 f.pa p.g r.gsm v.aas.3s a.apm d.apm a.apm p.a d.apm

πόδας αὐτοῦ. [26] ἔσχατος ἐχθρὸς καταργεῖται ὁ θάνατος· [27] ↱ ↱
his feet. *his* The last enemy to be destroyed is *{the}* death. For "he has
899 4546 899 2274 2398 2934 3836 2505 1142 5718 5718
n.apm r.gsm.3 a.nsm a.nsm v.ppi.3s d.nsm n.nsm

↱ πάντα γὰρ ὑπέταξεν ὑπὸ τοὺς πόδας αὐτοῦ. ὅταν δὲ εἴπῃ ὅτι
put everything *For* in subjection under *{the}* his feet." *his* Now when *Now* it says that
5718 4246 1142 5718 5679 3836 899 4546 899 1254 4020 1254 3306 4022
a.apn cj v.aai.3s p.a d.apm n.apm r.gsm.3 cj cj v.aas.3s cj

πάντα ὑποτέτακται, δῆλον ὅτι ἐκτὸς τοῦ → → →
"everything ⌞has been put in subjection,"⌟ it is clear that this does not include the one who put
4246 5718 1316 4022 1760 3836
a.npn v.rpi.3s a.nsn cj p.g d.gsm

ὑποτάξαντος αὐτῷ τὰ πάντα. [28] ὅταν δὲ ὑποταγῇ αὐτῷ
everything in subjection to him. *{the}* *everything* And when *And* everything is subjected to him,
4246 5718 899 3836 4246 1254 4020 1254 4246 5718 899
pt.aa.gsm r.dsm.3 d.apn a.apn cj cj v.aps.3s r.dsm.3

τὰ πάντα, τότε ↱ καὶ[a] αὐτὸς ὁ υἱὸς ὑποταγήσεται τῷ
{the} *everything* then the Son himself will also *himself* *the* *Son* be subjected ⌞to the⌟
3836 4246 5538 3836 5626 899 5718 2779 899 3836 5626 5718 3836
d.npn a.npn adv adv r.nsm d.nsm n.nsm v.fpi.3s d.dsm

ὑποτάξαντι αὐτῷ τὰ πάντα, ἵνα ᾖ ὁ θεὸς τὰ[b] πάντα
one who subjected everything to him, *{the}* *everything* so that God ⌞may be⌟ *{the}* *God* *{the}* all
5718 4246 899 3836 4246 2671 2536 1639 3836 2536 3836 4246
pt.aa.dsm r.dsm.3 d.apn a.apn cj v.pas.3s d.nsm n.nsm d.npn a.npn

ἐν πᾶσιν. [29] ἐπεὶ τί ποιήσουσιν οἱ βαπτιζόμενοι ὑπὲρ τῶν
in all. Otherwise, what will they accomplish, those who are being baptized for the
1877 4246 2075 5515 4472 3836 966 5642 3836
p.d a.dpn cj r.asn v.fai.3p d.npm pt.pp.npm p.g d.gpm

νεκρῶν; εἰ ↱ ὅλως νεκροὶ οὐκ ἐγείρονται, τί καὶ
dead? If the dead are not actually *dead* *not* raised, why then
3738 1623 3738 1586 4024 3914 3738 4024 1586 5515 2779
a.gpm cj adv a.npm pl v.ppi.3p r.asn adv

βαπτίζονται ὑπὲρ αὐτῶν; [30] Τί καὶ ↱ ἡμεῖς κινδυνεύομεν
⌞are they being baptized⌟ for them? And why *And* are we ⌞putting ourselves in danger⌟
966 5642 899 2779 5515 2779 3073 7005 3073
v.ppi.3p p.g r.gpm.3 r.asn cj r.np.1 v.pai.1p

NASB

[22]For as in Adam
all die, so also in
Christ all will be
made alive. [23]But
each in his own
order: Christ the
first fruits, after
that those who
are Christ's at His
coming, [24]then
comes the end,
when He hands
over the kingdom
to the God and
Father, when He
has abolished all
rule and all author-
ity and power. [25]For
He must reign until
He has put all His
enemies under
His feet. [26]The last
enemy that will
be abolished is
death. [27]For HE HAS
PUT ALL THINGS IN
SUBJECTION UNDER
HIS FEET. But when
He says, "All
things are put in
subjection," it is
evident that He
is excepted who
put all things in
subjection to Him.
[28]When all things
are subjected to
Him, then the Son
Himself also will
be subjected to the
One who subjected
all things to Him,
so that God may be
all in all.
[29]Otherwise, what
will those do who
are baptized for the
dead? If the dead
are not raised at all,
why then are they
baptized for them?
[30]Why are we also
in danger

[a] [καὶ] UBS, omitted by TNIV.
[b] [τὰ] UBS, omitted by TNIV.

[a] 27 Psalm 8:6

NIV

every hour? [31]I
face death ev-
ery day—yes,
just as surely as I
boast about you in
Christ Jesus our
Lord. [32]If I fought
wild beasts in
Ephesus with no
more than human
hopes, what have I
gained? If the dead
are not raised,

"Let us eat and
drink,
for tomorrow
we die."[a]

[33]Do not be mis-
led: "Bad com-
pany corrupts
good character."[b]
[34]Come back to
your senses as you
ought, and stop
sinning; for there
are some who are
ignorant of God—
I say this to your
shame.

The Resurrection Body

[35]But someone
will ask, "How are
the dead raised?
With what kind
of body will they
come?" [36]How
foolish! What you
sow does not come
to life unless it
dies. [37]When you
sow, you do not
plant the body that
will be, but just a
seed, perhaps of
wheat or of some-
thing else. [38]But
God gives it a body
as he has deter-
mined, and to each
kind of seed he
gives its own body.
[39]Not all flesh is
the same: People
have one kind of
flesh, animals
have another, birds
another and fish
another. [40]There
are also heavenly
bodies and there
are earthly bodies;
but the splendor of
the heavenly bod-
ies is one kind, and
the splendor

[a] 32 Isaiah 22:13
[b] 33 From the Greek poet Menander

πᾶσαν ὥραν; [31] καθ' ἡμέραν ἀποθνῄσκω, νὴ τὴν ὑμετέραν
every hour? Every day ⌊I am in danger of dying!⌋ ⌊I swear by⌋ my boasting in you,
4246 6052 2848 2465 633 3755 3836 3018 5629
a.asf n.asf p.a n.asf v.pai.1s pl d.asf a.asf

καύχησιν,[a] ἣν ἔχω ἐν Χριστῷ Ἰησοῦ τῷ κυρίῳ ἡμῶν. [32] εἰ κατὰ
boasting which I have in Christ Jesus *{the}* our Lord. *our* If as a
3018 4005 2400 1877 5986 2652 3836 7005 3261 7005 1623 2848
n.asf r.asf v.pai.1s p.d n.dsm n.dsm d.dsm n.dsm r.gp.1 cj p.a

ἄνθρωπον ἐθηριομάχησα ἐν Ἐφέσῳ, τί μοι τὸ ὄφελος; εἰ νεκροὶ
mere man ⌊I fought with wild beasts⌋ at Ephesus, what have I *{the}* gained? If the dead
476 2562 1877 2387 5515 1609 3836 4055 1623 3738
n.asm v.aai.1s p.d n.dsf r.nsn r.ds.1 d.nsn n.nsn cj a.npm

↱ οὐκ ἐγείρονται, φάγωμεν καὶ πίωμεν, αὔριον γὰρ ἀποθνῄσκομεν. [33] ↱ μὴ
are not raised, let us eat and drink, for tomorrow *for* we die. Do not
1586 4024 1586 2266 2779 4403 1142 892 1142 633 4414 3590
pl v.ppi.3p v.aas.1p cj v.aas.1p adv cj v.pai.1p pl

πλανᾶσθε· φθείρουσιν ἤθη χρηστὰ ὁμιλίαι κακαί. [34] ἐκνήψατε
be deceived: "Bad company corrupts good morals." *good* *company* *Bad* Sober up
4414 2805 3918 5780 5982 2456 5982 3918 2805 1729
v.ppm.2p v.pai.3p n.apn a.apn n.npf a.npf v.aam.2p

→ δικαίως καὶ μὴ ἁμαρτάνετε, ἀγνωσίαν γὰρ θεοῦ τινες
as you ought, and stop sinning; for some have no knowledge *for* of God. *some*
1469 2779 3590 279 1142 5516 2400 57 1142 2536 5516
adv cj pl v.pam.2p n.asf cj n.gsm r.npm

ἔχουσιν, πρὸς ἐντροπὴν ὑμῖν λαλῶ. [35] ἀλλὰ ἐρεῖ τις,
have I say this to your shame. *your* *I say* But someone ⌊will ask,⌋ *someone*
2400 3281 3281 4639 7007 1959 7007 3281 247 5516 3306 5516
v.pai.3p p.a n.asf r.dp.2 v.pai.1s cj v.fai.3s r.nsm

πῶς → ἐγείρονται οἱ νεκροί; ποίῳ δὲ σώματι
"How are the dead raised? *the* *dead* And ⌊with what kind of⌋ *And* body
4802 3836 3738 1586 3836 3738 1254 4481 1254 5393
cj v.ppi.3p d.npm a.npm r.dsn cj n.dsn

ἔρχονται; [36] ἄφρων, σὺ ὃ σπείρεις, ↱ οὐ ζῳοποιεῖται ⌊ἐὰν μὴ⌋
will they come?" You fool! *You* What you sow does not come to life unless
2262 5148 933 5148 4005 5062 2443 4024 2443 1569 3590
v.pmi.3p n.vsm r.ns.2 r.asn v.pai.2s pl v.ppi.3s cj pl

ἀποθάνῃ· [37] καὶ ὃ σπείρεις, οὐ τὸ σῶμα τὸ γενησόμενον σπείρεις ἀλλὰ
it dies. And what you sow is not the body that is to be, *{you sow}* but a
633 2779 4005 5062 4024 3836 5393 3836 1181 5062 247
v.aas.3s cj r.asn v.pai.2s pl d.asn n.asn d.asn pt.fm.asn v.pai.2s cj

γυμνὸν κόκκον ⌊εἰ τύχοι⌋ σίτου ἤ τινος τῶν λοιπῶν· [38] ὁ δὲ θεὸς
bare seed, perhaps of wheat or something *{the}* else. *{the}* But God
1218 3133 1623 5593 4992 2445 5516 3836 3370 3836 1254 2536
a.asm n.asm cj v.aao.3s n.gsm cj r.gsn d.gpn a.gpn d.nsm cj n.nsm

δίδωσιν αὐτῷ σῶμα καθὼς ἠθέλησεν, καὶ ἑκάστῳ τῶν σπερμάτων ἴδιον
gives it a body as he has determined, and to each kind of seed its own
1443 899 5393 2777 2527 2779 1667 3836 5065 2625
v.pai.3s r.dsm.3 n.asn cj v.aai.3s cj r.dsn d.gpn n.gpn a.asn

σῶμα. [39] οὐ πᾶσα σὰρξ ἡ αὐτὴ σὰρξ ἀλλὰ ἄλλη μὲν ἀνθρώπων,
body. Not all flesh is the same; *{flesh}* *{but}* people have one kind, ~ *people*
5393 4024 4246 4922 3836 899 4922 247 476 257 3525 476
n.asn pl a.nsf n.nsf d.nsf r.nsf n.nsf cj r.nsf pl n.gpm

ἄλλη δὲ σὰρξ κτηνῶν, ἄλλη δὲ σὰρξ πτηνῶν, ἄλλη δὲ
animals another, *{and}* *{flesh}* *animals* birds another, *{and}* *{flesh}* *birds* fish another. *{and}*
3229 257 1254 4922 3229 4764 257 1254 4922 4764 2716 257 1254
r.nsf pl n.nsf n.gpn r.nsf pl n.nsf n.gpn r.nsf pl

ἰχθύων. [40] καὶ σώματα ἐπουράνια, καὶ σώματα ἐπίγεια· ἀλλὰ
fish And there are heavenly bodies *heavenly* and earthly bodies; *earthly* but
2716 2779 2230 5393 2230 2779 2103 5393 2103 247
n.gpm cj n.npn a.npn cj n.npn a.npn cj

ἑτέρα μὲν ἡ τῶν ἐπουρανίων δόξα,
the glory of heavenly bodies is of one kind ~ *the* *of* *heavenly* *glory* and the glory
3836 1518 3836 2230 2283 3525 3836 3836 2230 1518 1254 3836
r.nsf pl d.nsf d.gpn a.gpn n.nsf

[a] ἀδελφοί included by UBS after καύχησιν.

NASB

every hour? [31]I
affirm, brethren,
by the boasting in
you which I have
in Christ Jesus our
Lord, I die daily.
[32]If from human
motives I fought
with wild beasts at
Ephesus, what does
it profit me? If the
dead are not raised,
LET US EAT AND
DRINK, FOR TOMOR-
ROW WE DIE. [33]Do
not be deceived:
"Bad company
corrupts good
morals." [34]Become
sober-minded as
you ought, and stop
sinning; for some
have no knowledge
of God. I speak *this*
to your shame.
[35]But someone
will say, "How are
the dead raised?
And with what
kind of body do
they come?" [36]You
fool! That which
you sow does not
come to life unless
it dies; [37]and that
which you sow,
you do not sow
the body which is
to be, but a bare
grain, perhaps of
wheat or of some-
thing else. [38]But
God gives it a body
just as He wished,
and to each of the
seeds a body of its
own. [39]All flesh is
not the same flesh,
but there is one
flesh of men, and
another flesh of
beasts, and another
flesh of birds, and
another of fish.
[40]There are also
heavenly bodies
and earthly bodies,
but the glory of the
heavenly is one,
and the *glory* of the

NIV

of the earthly
bodies is another.
41 The sun has one
kind of splendor,
the moon anoth-
er and the stars
another; and star
differs from star in
splendor.
42 So will it be
with the resurrec-
tion of the dead.
The body that is
sown is perish-
able, it is raised
imperishable; 43 it
is sown in dishon-
or, it is raised in
glory; it is sown
in weakness, it
is raised in pow-
er; 44 it is sown a
natural body, it is
raised a spiritual
body.
If there is a nat-
ural body, there
is also a spiritual
body. 45 So it is
written: "The first
man Adam became
a living being"[a];
the last Adam, a
life-giving spirit.
46 The spiritual did
not come first, but
the natural, and af-
ter that the spiritu-
al. 47 The first man
was of the dust
of the earth; the
second man is of
heaven. 48 As was
the earthly man, so
are those who are
of the earth; and
as is the heavenly
man, so also are
those who are of
heaven. 49 And just
as we have borne
the image of the
earthly man, so
shall we[b] bear the
image of the heav-
enly man.
50 I declare to you,
brothers and sis-
ters, that flesh and
blood cannot in-
herit the kingdom
of God, nor

ἑτέρα δὲ ἡ τῶν ἐπιγείων. 41 ἄλλη δόξα
of earthly bodies is of another. *and the of earthly* The sun has ⌊one kind of⌋ glory,
3836 2103 2283 1254 3836 3836 2103 2463 257 1518
r.nsf pl d.nsf d.gpn a.gpn r.nsf n.nsf

ἡλίου, καὶ ἄλλη δόξα σελήνης, καὶ ἄλλη δόξα
sun {and} the moon ⌊another kind of⌋ glory, *moon {and}* the stars ⌊another kind of⌋ glory;
2463 2779 4943 257 1518 4943 2779 843 257 1518
n.gsm cj r.nsf n.nsf n.gsf cj r.nsf n.nsf

ἀστέρων· ἀστὴρ γὰρ ἀστέρος διαφέρει ἐν δόξῃ. 42 οὕτως καὶ ἡ
stars and star *and* differs from star *differs from* in glory. So also is the
843 1142 843 1142 1422 1422 843 1422 1877 1518 4048 2779 3836
n.gpm n.nsm cj n.gsm v.pai.3s p.d n.dsf adv adv d.nsf

ἀνάστασις τῶν νεκρῶν. σπείρεται ἐν φθορᾷ, ἐγείρεται ἐν
resurrection of the dead. The body is sown in a ⌊perishable state,⌋ it is raised *{in}*
414 3836 3738 5062 1877 5785 1586 1877
n.nsf d.gpm a.gpm v.ppi.3s p.d n.dsf v.ppi.3s p.d

ἀφθαρσίᾳ· 43 σπείρεται ἐν ἀτιμίᾳ, ἐγείρεται ἐν δόξῃ· σπείρεται ἐν ἀσθενείᾳ,
imperishable. It is sown in humiliation, it is raised in glory; it is sown in weakness,
914 5062 1877 871 1586 1877 1518 5062 1877 819
n.dsf v.ppi.3s p.d n.dsf v.ppi.3s p.d n.dsf v.ppi.3s p.d n.dsf

ἐγείρεται ἐν δυνάμει· 44 σπείρεται σῶμα ψυχικόν, ἐγείρεται σῶμα
it is raised in power; it is sown a natural body, *natural* it is raised a spiritual body.
1586 1877 1539 5062 6035 5393 6035 1586 4461 5393
v.ppi.3s p.d n.dsf v.ppi.3s n.nsn a.nsn v.ppi.3s n.nsn

πνευματικόν. εἰ ἔστιν σῶμα ψυχικόν, ἔστιν καὶ πνευματικόν.
spiritual If there is a natural body, *natural* there is also a spiritual body.
4461 1623 1639 6035 5393 6035 1639 2779 4461
a.nsn cj v.pai.3s n.nsn a.nsn v.pai.3s adv a.nsn

45 οὕτως καὶ γέγραπται, ἐγένετο ὁ πρῶτος ἄνθρωπος Ἀδὰμ
So also it is written, "The first man, Adam, became *The first man Adam*
4048 2779 1211 3836 4755 476 77 1181 3836 4755 476 77
adv adv v.rpi.3s v.ami.3s d.nsm a.nsm n.nsm n.nsm

εἰς ψυχὴν ζῶσαν, ὁ ἔσχατος Ἀδὰμ εἰς πνεῦμα
{into} a living soul." *living* The last Adam became *{into}* a life-giving spirit.
1650 2409 6034 2409 3836 2274 77 1650 2443 4460
p.a n.asf pt.pa.asf d.nsm a.nsm n.nsm p.a n.asn

ζωοποιοῦν. 46 ἀλλ᾽ οὐ πρῶτον τὸ πνευματικὸν ἀλλὰ τὸ
life-giving However, the spiritual did not come first, *the spiritual* but the
2443 247 3836 4461 4024 4754 3836 4461 247 3836
pt.pa.asn cj pl adv d.nsn a.nsn cj d.nsn

ψυχικόν, ἔπειτα τὸ πνευματικόν. 47 ὁ πρῶτος ἄνθρωπος ἐκ γῆς
natural, then the spiritual. The first man was of the earth,
6035 2083 3836 4461 3836 4755 476 1666 1178
a.nsn adv d.nsn a.nsn d.nsm a.nsm n.nsm p.g n.gsf

χοϊκός, ὁ δεύτερος ἄνθρωπος ἐξ οὐρανοῦ. 48 οἷος ὁ χοϊκός,
⌊made of dust;⌋ the second man is of heaven. As was the man of dust,
5954 3836 1311 476 1666 4041 3888 3836 5954
a.nsm d.nsm a.nsm n.nsm p.g n.gsm r.nsm d.nsm a.nsm

τοιοῦτοι καὶ οἱ χοϊκοί, καὶ οἷος ὁ ἐπουράνιος, τοιοῦτοι καὶ οἱ
so also are those ⌊who are of dust;⌋ and as is the man of heaven, so also are those
5525 2779 3836 5954 2779 3888 3836 2230 5525 2779 3836
r.npm adv d.npm a.npm cj r.nsm d.nsm a.nsm r.npm adv d.npm

ἐπουράνιοι· 49 καὶ καθὼς ἐφορέσαμεν τὴν εἰκόνα τοῦ χοϊκοῦ, → →
who are of heaven. And even as we have borne the image of the man of dust, let us also
2230 2779 2777 5841 3836 1635 3836 5954 2779
a.npm cj cj v.aai.1p d.asf n.asf d.gsm a.gsm

φορέσομεν[a] καὶ τὴν εἰκόνα τοῦ ἐπουρανίου. 50 τοῦτο δέ φημι, ἀδελφοί, ὅτι
bear *also* the likeness of the man of heaven Now this *Now* I declare, brothers, that
5841 2779 3836 1635 3836 2230 1254 4047 1254 5774 81 4022
v.fai.1p adv d.asf n.asf d.gsm a.gsm r.asn cj v.pai.1s n.vpm cj

σὰρξ καὶ αἷμα βασιλείαν θεοῦ κληρονομῆσαι ⌊οὐ δύναται⌋ οὐδὲ
flesh and blood cannot inherit the kingdom of God, *inherit cannot* nor
4922 2779 135 4024 3099 993 2536 3099 4024 1538 4028
n.nsf cj n.nsn n.asf n.gsm f.aa pl v.ppi.3s cj

NASB

earthly is another.
41 There is one glory
of the sun, and an-
other glory of the
moon, and another
glory of the stars;
for star differs from
star in glory.
42 So also is the
resurrection of the
dead. It is sown a
perishable *body,* it
is raised an imper-
ishable *body;* 43 it is
sown in dishonor,
it is raised in glory;
it is sown in weak-
ness, it is raised in
power; 44 it is sown
a natural body, it
is raised a spiritual
body. If there is a
natural body, there
is also a spiritual
body. 45 So also it
is written, "The
first MAN, Adam,
BECAME A LIVING
SOUL." The last
Adam *became* a
life-giving spirit.
46 However, the
spiritual is not first,
but the natural;
then the spiritual.
47 The first man is
from the earth,
earthy; the sec-
ond man is from
heaven. 48 As is
the earthy, so also
are those who are
earthy; and as is
the heavenly, so
also are those who
are heavenly. 49 Just
as we have borne
the image of the
earthy, [a]we will
also bear the image
of the heavenly.

The Mystery of Resurrection

50 Now I say this,
brethren, that flesh
and blood cannot
inherit the kingdom
of God; nor does

a 45 Gen. 2:7
b 49 Some early manuscripts *so let us*

a φορέσομεν UBS, TNIV. φορέσωμεν NET.

a Two early mss read *let us also*

NIV

does the perish-
able inherit the
imperishable.
51 Listen, I tell you
a mystery: We
will not all sleep,
but we will all be
changed— 52 in a
flash, in the twin-
kling of an eye, at
the last trumpet.
For the trumpet
will sound, the
dead will be raised
imperishable,
and we will be
changed. 53 For the
perishable must
clothe itself with
the imperishable,
and the mortal
with immortality.
54 When the per-
ishable has been
clothed with the
imperishable, and
the mortal with
immortality, then
the saying that is
written will come
true: "Death has
been swallowed up
in victory."[a]

55 "Where,
O death,
is your
victory?
Where,
O death,
is your
sting?"[b]

56 The sting of
death is sin, and
the power of sin
is the law. 57 But
thanks be to God!
He gives us the
victory through
our Lord Jesus
Christ.
58 Therefore, my
dear brothers and
sisters, stand firm.
Let nothing move
you. Always give
yourselves fully
to the work of the
Lord, because you
know that your la-
bor in the Lord is
not in vain.

[a] 54 Isaiah 25:8
[b] 55 Hosea 13:14

ἡ φθορὰ τὴν ἀφθαρσίαν κληρονομεῖ. 51 ἰδοὺ
does the perishable inherit the imperishable. *does inherit* Listen, I tell you a
3099 3836 5785 3099 3836 914 3099 2627 3306 3306 7007
d.nsf n.nsf d.asf n.asf v.pai.3s j

μυστήριον ὑμῖν λέγω, ↱ ↱ πάντες οὐ κοιμηθησόμεθα, ↱ ↱ πάντες δὲ
mystery: *you* *I tell* we will not all *not* die, but we will all *but*
3696 7007 3306 3121 3121 4024 4246 4024 3121 1254 248 248 4246 1254
n.asn r.dp.2 v.pai.1s a.npm pl v.fpi.1p a.npm cj

ἀλλαγησόμεθα, 52 ἐν ἀτόμῳ, ἐν ῥιπῇ → ὀφθαλμοῦ, ἐν τῇ ἐσχάτῃ
be changed — in an instant, in the twinkling of an eye, at the last
248 1877 875 1877 4846 4057 1877 3836 2274
v.fpi.1p p.d a.dsn p.d n.dsf n.gsm p.d d.dsf a.dsf

σάλπιγγι· σαλπίσει γὰρ καὶ οἱ νεκροὶ ἐγερθήσονται ἄφθαρτοι καὶ
trumpet. For the ⌊trumpet will sound,⌋ *For* and the dead will be raised imperishable, and
4894 1142 4895 1142 2779 3836 3738 1586 915 2779
n.dsf v.fai.3s cj cj d.npm a.npm v.fpi.3p a.npm cj

ἡμεῖς ἀλλαγησόμεθα. 53 δεῖ γὰρ τὸ φθαρτὸν τοῦτο
we will be changed. For this perishable body must *For* *{the}* *perishable* *this*
7005 248 1142 4047 5778 1256 1142 3836 5778 4047
r.np.1 v.fpi.1p v.pai.3s cj d.asn a.asn r.asn

ἐνδύσασθαι ἀφθαρσίαν καὶ τὸ θνητὸν τοῦτο ↰ ἐνδύσασθαι
put on imperishability, and *{the}* this mortal body *this* must put on
1907 914 2779 3836 4047 2570 4047 1256 1907
f.am n.asf cj d.asn a.asn r.asn f.am

ἀθανασίαν. 54 ὅταν δὲ τὸ φθαρτὸν τοῦτο ἐνδύσηται ἀφθαρσίαν
immortality. So when *So* *{the}* this perishable body *this* puts on imperishability,
114 1254 4020 1254 3836 4047 5778 4047 1907 914
n.asf cj cj d.nsn a.nsn r.nsn v.ams.3s n.asf

καὶ τὸ θνητὸν τοῦτο ἐνδύσηται ἀθανασίαν, τότε
and *{the}* this mortal body *this* puts on immortality, then the saying that is written
2779 3836 4047 2570 4047 1907 114 5538 3836 3364 3836 1211 1211
cj d.nsn a.nsn r.nsn v.ams.3s n.asf adv

γενήσεται ὁ λόγος ὁ γεγραμμένος, κατεπόθη ὁ θάνατος
will be fulfilled: *the* *saying* *that* *is written* "Death ⌊has been swallowed up⌋ *{the}* *Death*
1181 3836 3364 3836 1211 2505 2927 3836 2505
v.fmi.3s d.nsm n.nsm d.nsm pt.rp.nsm v.api.3s d.nsm n.nsm

εἰς νῖκος. 55 ποῦ σου, θάνατε, τὸ νῖκος; ποῦ σου,
in victory." "Where, O death, is your *O death* *{the}* victory? Where, O death, is your
1650 3777 4543 2505 2505 5148 2505 3836 3777 4543 2505 2505 5148
p.a n.asn cj r.gs.2 n.vsm d.nsn n.nsn cj r.gs.2

θάνατε, τὸ κέντρον; 56 τὸ δὲ κέντρον τοῦ θανάτου ἡ ἁμαρτία, ἡ δὲ
O death *{the}* sting?" The *{and}* sting of death is *{the}* sin, and the *and*
2505 3836 3034 3836 1254 3034 3836 2505 3836 281 1254 3836 1254
n.vsm d.nsn n.nsn d.nsn cj n.nsn d.gsm n.gsm d.nsf n.nsf d.nsf cj

δύναμις τῆς ἁμαρτίας ὁ νόμος· 57 τῷ δὲ θεῷ χάρις τῷ διδόντι
power of sin is the law. But thanks be to *But* God, *thanks* who gives
1539 3836 281 3836 3795 1254 5921 3836 1254 2536 5921 3836 1443
n.nsf d.gsf n.gsf d.nsm n.nsm d.dsm cj n.dsm n.nsf d.dsm pt.pa.dsm

ἡμῖν τὸ νῖκος διὰ τοῦ κυρίου ἡμῶν Ἰησοῦ Χριστοῦ. 58 ὥστε,
us the victory through *{the}* our Lord *our* Jesus Christ! So then, my dear
7005 3836 3777 1328 3836 7005 3261 7005 2652 5986 6063 1609 28
r.dp.1 d.asn n.asn p.g d.gsm n.gsm r.gp.1 n.gsm n.gsm cj

ἀδελφοί μου ἀγαπητοί, ἑδραῖοι γίνεσθε, ἀμετακίνητοι, περισσεύοντες ἐν
brothers, *my* *dear* be steadfast, *be* immovable, always abounding in
81 1609 28 1181 1612 1181 293 4121 4355 1877
n.vpm r.gs.1 a.vpm a.npm v.pmm.2p a.npm pt.pa.npm p.d

τῷ ἔργῳ τοῦ κυρίου πάντοτε, εἰδότες ὅτι ὁ κόπος ὑμῶν οὐκ
the work of the Lord, *always* ⌊since you know⌋ that *{the}* your labor *your* is not
3836 2240 3836 3261 4121 3857 4022 3836 7007 3160 7007 1639 4024
d.dsn n.dsn d.gsm n.gsm adv pt.ra.npm cj d.nsm n.nsm r.gp.2 pl

ἐστιν κενὸς ἐν κυρίῳ.
is in vain in the Lord.
1639 3031 1877 3261
v.pai.3s a.nsm p.d n.dsm

NASB

the perishable
inherit the imper-
ishable. 51 Behold, I
tell you a mystery;
we will not all
sleep, but we will
all be changed,
52 in a moment, in
the twinkling of
an eye, at the last
trumpet; for the
trumpet will sound,
and the dead will
be raised imperish-
able, and we will
be changed. 53 For
this perishable
must put on the
imperishable, and
this mortal must
put on immortal-
ity. 54 But when
this perishable
will have put on
the imperishable,
and this mortal
will have put on
immortality, then
will come about
the saying that is
written, "DEATH IS
SWALLOWED UP in
victory. 55 O DEATH,
WHERE IS YOUR
VICTORY? O DEATH,
WHERE IS YOUR
STING?" 56 The sting
of death is sin, and
the power of sin
is the law; 57 but
thanks be to God,
who gives us the
victory through our
Lord Jesus Christ.
58 Therefore, my
beloved brethren,
be steadfast, im-
movable, always
abounding in the
work of the Lord,
knowing that your
toil is not *in* vain in
the Lord.

NIV

The Collection for the Lord's People

16 Now about
the collec-
tion for the Lord's
people: Do what I
told the Galatian
churches to do.
2On the first day of
every week, each
one of you should
set aside a sum of
money in keeping
with your income,
saving it up, so
that when I come
no collections will
have to be made.
3Then, when I ar-
rive, I will give
letters of intro-
duction to the men
you approve and
send them with
your gift to Jeru-
salem. 4If it seems
advisable for me to
go also, they will
accompany me.

Personal Requests

5After I go
through Macedo-
nia, I will come
to you—for I will
be going through
Macedonia. 6Per-
haps I will stay
with you for a
while, or even
spend the winter,
so that you can
help me on my
journey, wherever
I go. 7For I do not
want to see you
now and make
only a passing
visit; I hope to
spend some time
with you, if the
Lord permits. 8But
I will stay on at
Ephesus until Pen-
tecost, 9because
a great door for
effective work has
opened to me,

16:1 περὶ δὲ τῆς λογείας τῆς εἰς τοὺς ἁγίους ὥσπερ διέταξα ταῖς
Now concerning *Now* the collection *{the}* for the saints: as I directed the
1254 4309 1254 3836 3356 3836 1650 3836 41 6061 1411 3836
p.g cj d.gsf n.gsf d.gsf p.a d.apm a.apm cj v.aai.1s d.dpf

ἐκκλησίαις τῆς Γαλατίας, οὕτως καὶ ὑμεῖς ποιήσατε. 2 κατὰ μίαν →
churches of Galatia, so you also *you* are to do. On the first day of the
1711 3836 1130 4048 7007 2779 7007 4472 2848 1651
n.dpf d.gsf n.gsf adv adv r.np.2 v.aam.2p p.a a.asf

σαββάτου ἕκαστος ὑμῶν ⌊παρ᾽ ἑαυτῷ⌋ τιθέτω
week, each of you should put something aside *should put* as he may
4879 1667 7007 5502 5502 4005 4123 1571 5502 1569 2338 2338
n.gsn r.nsm r.gp.2 p.d r.dsm.3 v.pam.3s

θησαυρίζων ⌊ὅ τι⌋ ἐὰν εὐοδῶται, ἵνα
prosper and save it, *something* *as* *he may prosper* so that when I come, collections
2338 2564 4005 5516 1569 2338 2671 4020 2262 2262 3356
pt.pa.nsm r.asn r.asn pl v.pps.3s cj

→ μὴ ὅταν ἔλθω τότε λογεῖαι γίνωνται. 3 ὅταν δὲ παραγένωμαι,
will not *when* *I come* *{then}* *collections* have to be made. And when *And* I arrive, I
1181 3590 4020 2262 5538 3356 1181 1254 4020 1254 4134 4287
pl cj v.aas.1s adv n.npf v.pms.3p cj cj v.ams.1s

⌊οὓς ἐὰν⌋ δοκιμάσητε, δι᾽ ἐπιστολῶν
will dispatch with letters of introduction whomever you approve *with* *letters*
4287 4287 1328 2186 4005 1569 1507 1328 2186
r.apm pl v.aas.2p p.g n.gpf

τούτους πέμψω ἀπενεγκεῖν τὴν χάριν ὑμῶν εἰς Ἰερουσαλήμ· 4 ἐὰν δὲ
{these} *I will dispatch* to carry *{the}* your gift *your* to Jerusalem. And if *And*
4047 4287 708 3836 7007 5921 7007 1650 2647 1254 1569 1254
r.apm v.fai.1s f.aa d.asf n.asf r.gp.2 p.a n.asf cj cj

ἄξιον ᾖ τοῦ → κἀμὲ πορεύεσθαι, σὺν ἐμοὶ
it seems advisable *it seems* that I should go also, *should go* they will go with me.
1639 1639 545 1639 3836 4513 4513 2743 4513 4513 4513 4513 5250 1609
a.nsn v.pas.3s d.gsn crasis f.pm p.d r.ds.1

πορεύσονται. 5 ἐλεύσομαι δὲ πρὸς ὑμᾶς ὅταν Μακεδονίαν
they will go But I will come *But* to you after I have gone through Macedonia
4513 1254 2262 1254 4639 7007 4020 1451 1451 1451 1451 3423
v.fmi.3p v.fmi.1s cj p.a r.ap.2 cj n.asf

διέλθω· Μακεδονίαν γὰρ διέρχομαι,
I have gone through — for I intend to go through Macedonia *for* *I intend to go through*
1451 1142 1451 1451 1451 1451 1451 3423 1142 1451
v.aas.1s n.asf cj v.pmi.1s

6 πρὸς ὑμᾶς δὲ τυχὸν παραμενῶ
— and it may be that I will stay awhile with you, *and* *it may be that* *I will stay*
1254 5593 5593 5593 5593 4169 4169 4169 4639 7007 1254 5593 4169
p.a r.ap.2 cj pt.aa.asn v.fai.1s

ἢ καὶ παραχειμάσω, ἵνα ὑμεῖς → → με προπέμψητε ⌊οὗ ἐὰν⌋
or even spend the winter, so that you can help me continue my journey, wherever
2445 2779 4199 2671 7007 4636 4636 1609 4636 4023 1569
cj adv v.fai.1s cj r.np.2 r.as.1 v.aas.2p adv pl

πορεύωμαι. 7 → → οὐ θέλω γὰρ ὑμᾶς ἄρτι ἐν παρόδῳ ἰδεῖν,
I go. For I do not want *For* to see you now just in passing, *to see*
4513 1142 2527 2527 4024 2527 1142 1625 1625 7007 785 1877 4227 1625
v.pms.1s pl v.pai.1s cj r.ap.2 adv p.d n.dsf f.aa

ἐλπίζω γὰρ χρόνον τινὰ ἐπιμεῖναι πρὸς ὑμᾶς ἐὰν ὁ κύριος
for I hope *for* to spend some time *some* *to spend* with you, if the Lord
1142 1827 1142 2152 2152 5516 5989 5516 2152 4639 7007 1569 3836 3261
v.pai.1s cj n.asm r.asm f.aa p.a r.ap.2 cj d.nsm n.nsm

ἐπιτρέψῃ. 8 ἐπιμενῶ δὲ ἐν Ἐφέσῳ ἕως τῆς πεντηκοστῆς· 9 θύρα γάρ
permits. But I will stay *But* in Ephesus until *{the}* Pentecost, for a door *for* that
2205 1254 2152 1254 1877 2387 2401 3836 4300 1142 2598 1142
v.aas.3s v.fai.1s cj p.d n.dsf p.g d.gsf n.gsf n.nsf cj

μοι ἀνέῳγεν μεγάλη καὶ ἐνεργής, καὶ
offers wide and effective ministry stands open ⌊for me,⌋ *stands open* *wide* *and* *effective* *{and}*
3489 2779 1921 487 487 1609 487 3489 2779 1921 2779
r.ds.1 v.rai.3s a.nsf cj a.nsf cj

NASB

Instructions and Greetings

16:1Now concern-
ing the collection
for the saints,
as I directed the
churches of Gala-
tia, so do you also.
2On the first day of
every week each
one of you is to put
aside and save, as
he may prosper, so
that no collections
be made when I
come. 3When I
arrive, whomever
you may approve,
I will send them
with letters to carry
your gift to Jeru-
salem; 4and if it is
fitting for me to go
also, they will go
with me.
5But I will come
to you after I go
through Macedo-
nia, for I am going
through Macedo-
nia; 6and perhaps I
will stay with you,
or even spend the
winter, so that you
may send me on
my way wherever
I may go. 7For I
do not wish to see
you now *just* in
passing; for I hope
to remain with you
for some time, if
the Lord permits.
8But I will remain
in Ephesus until
Pentecost; 9for a
wide door for ef-
fective *service* has
opened to me, and

NIV

and there are many
who oppose me.
10When Timothy
comes, see to it
that he has nothing
to fear while he is
with you, for he
is carrying on the
work of the Lord,
just as I am. 11No
one, then, should
treat him with
contempt. Send
him on his way in
peace so that he
may return to me.
I am expecting
him along with the
brothers.
12Now about our
brother Apollos: I
strongly urged him
to go to you with
the brothers. He
was quite unwill-
ing to go now, but
he will go when
he has the oppor-
tunity.
13Be on your
guard; stand firm
in the faith; be
courageous; be
strong. 14Do every-
thing in love.
15You know that
the household of
Stephanas were
the first converts
in Achaia, and
they have devot-
ed themselves to
the service of the
Lord's people. I
urge you, brothers
and sisters, 16to
submit to such
people and to ev-
eryone who joins
in the work and
labors at it. 17I was
glad when Steph-
anas, Fortunatus
and Achaicus
arrived, because
they have supplied
what was lacking
from you. 18For
they refreshed my
spirit and

→ → → ἀντικείμενοι πολλοί. 10 ἐὰν δὲ ἔλθῃ Τιμόθεος,
although there are many adversaries. *many* Now if *Now* Timothy comes, *Timothy*
4498 512 4498 1254 1569 1254 5510 2262 5510
pt.pm.npm a.npm cj cj v.aas.3s n.nsm

βλέπετε, ἵνα ἀφόβως γένηται πρὸς ὑμᾶς·
see that he has ⌞nothing to fear⌟ *he has* while he is with you, for he is doing
1063 2671 1181 1181 925 1181 4639 7007 1142 2237 2237 2237
v.pam.2p cj adv v.ams.3s p.a r.ap.2

τὸ γὰρ ἔργον κυρίου ἐργάζεται ↱ ὡς κἀγώ· 11 μή τις οὖν ↱
the *for* Lord's work, *Lord's* *he is doing* just as I am. So no one *So* should
3836 1142 3261 2240 3261 2237 2743 6055 2743 4036 3590 5516 4036 2024
d.asn cj n.asn n.gsm v.pmi.3s cj crasis pl r.nsm cj

↱ αὐτὸν ἐξουθενήσῃ. προπέμψατε δὲ αὐτὸν ↰ ↰ ↰ ἐν εἰρήνῃ, ἵνα
treat him with contempt. Help *{and}* him continue his journey in peace, that
2024 899 2024 4636 1254 899 4636 4636 4636 1877 1645 2671
r.asm.3 v.aas.3s v.aam.2p cj r.asm.3 p.d n.dsf cj

ἔλθῃ πρός με· ἐκδέχομαι γὰρ αὐτὸν μετὰ τῶν ἀδελφῶν. 12
⌞he may come⌟ to me; for I am expecting *for* him with the brothers. Now
2262 4639 1609 1142 1683 1142 899 3552 3836 81 1254
v.aas.3s p.a r.as.1 v.pmi.1s cj r.asm.3 p.g d.gpm n.gpm

περὶ δὲ Ἀπολλῶ τοῦ ἀδελφοῦ, ↱ πολλὰ παρεκάλεσα αὐτόν, ἵνα ἔλθῃ πρὸς
concerning *Now* Apollos our brother: I strongly urged him to go to
4309 1254 663 3836 81 4151 4498 4151 899 2671 2262 4639
p.g cj n.gsm d.gsm n.gsm a.apn v.aai.1s r.asm.3 cj v.aas.3s p.a

ὑμᾶς μετὰ τῶν ἀδελφῶν· καὶ πάντως οὐκ ἦν θέλημα ἵνα
you with the other brothers, but it was not at all *not* *it was* his intention to go
7007 3552 3836 81 2779 1639 1639 4024 4122 4024 1639 2525 2671 2262
r.ap.2 p.g d.gpm n.gpm cj adv pl v.iai.3s n.nsn cj

νῦν ἔλθῃ· ἐλεύσεται δὲ ὅταν εὐκαιρήσῃ. 13 γρηγορεῖτε, στήκετε
now. *go* He will go *{and}* when he has an opportunity. Stay on guard, ⌞continue to stand firm⌟
3814 2262 2262 1254 4020 2320 1213 5112
adv v.aas.3s v.fmi.3s cj cj v.aas.3s v.pam.2p v.pam.2p

ἐν τῇ πίστει, ἀνδρίζεσθε, κραταιοῦσθε. 14 πάντα ὑμῶν
in the faith, be men of courage, grow in strength. Everything you do should be done
1877 3836 4411 437 3194 4246 7007 1181 1181 1181
p.d d.dsf n.dsf v.pmm.2p v.ppm.2p a.npn r.gp.2

ἐν ἀγάπῃ γινέσθω. 15 παρακαλῶ δὲ ὑμᾶς, ἀδελφοί· οἴδατε τὴν οἰκίαν
in love. *should be done* *I urge* *So* *you* *brothers* You know that the household
1877 27 1181 4151 1254 7007 81 3857 4022 3836 3864
p.d n.dsf v.pmm.3s v.pai.1s cj r.ap.2 n.vpm v.rai.2p d.asf n.asf

Στεφανᾶ, ὅτι ἐστὶν ἀπαρχὴ τῆς Ἀχαΐας καὶ
of Stephanus *that* were the first converts in the province of Achaia, and that they devoted
5107 4022 1639 569 3836 938 2779 5435 5435
n.gsm cj v.pai.3s n.nsf d.gsf n.gsf cj

εἰς διακονίαν τοῖς ἁγίοις ἔταξαν ἑαυτούς·
themselves to the service of the saints. *they devoted* *themselves* So I urge you, brothers,
1571 1650 1355 3836 41 5435 1571 1254 4151 4151 7007 81
p.a n.asf d.dpm a.dpm v.aai.3p r.apm.3

16 ἵνα καὶ ὑμεῖς ὑποτάσσησθε τοῖς τοιούτοις καὶ παντὶ τῷ
that you also *you* submit to such as these, and to everyone who
2671 7007 2779 7007 5718 3836 5525 2779 4246 3836
cj adv r.np.2 v.pps.2p d.dpm r.dpm cj a.dsm d.dsm

συνεργοῦντι καὶ κοπιῶντι. 17 χαίρω δὲ ἐπὶ τῇ παρουσίᾳ Στεφανᾶ
assists in the work and labors in it. But I rejoice *But* at the coming of Stephanas,
5300 2779 3159 1254 5897 1254 2093 3836 4242 5107
pt.pa.dsm cj pt.pa.dsm v.pai.1s cj p.d d.dsf n.dsf n.gsm

καὶ Φορτουνάτου καὶ Ἀχαϊκοῦ, ὅτι τὸ ὑμέτερον
{and} Fortunatus, and Achaicus because they have supplied what was lacking from you,
2779 5847 2779 939 4022 4047 405 405 3836 5729 5729 5629
cj n.gsm cj n.gsm cj d.asn r.asn.2

ὑστέρημα οὗτοι ἀνεπλήρωσαν· 18 ἀνέπαυσαν γὰρ τὸ ἐμὸν πνεῦμα καὶ τὸ
was lacking *they* *have supplied* for they have refreshed *for* *{the}* my spirit and *{the}*
5729 4047 405 1142 399 1142 3836 1847 4460 2779 3836
n.asn r.npm v.aai.3p v.aai.3p cj d.asn r.asn.1 n.asn cj d.asn

NASB

there are many
adversaries.
10Now if Timothy
comes, see that he
is with you without
cause to be afraid,
for he is doing the
Lord's work, as I
also am. 11So let no
one despise him.
But send him on
his way in peace,
so that he may
come to me; for I
expect him with
the brethren.
12But concern-
ing Apollos our
brother, I encour-
aged him greatly to
come to you with
the brethren; and
it was not at all
his desire to come
now, but he will
come when he has
opportunity.
13Be on the alert,
stand firm in the
faith, act like men,
be strong. 14Let all
that you do be done
in love.
15Now I urge you,
brethren (you know
the household of
Stephanas, that
they were the first
fruits of Achaia,
and that they have
devoted themselves
for ministry to the
saints), 16that you
also be in subjec-
tion to such men
and to everyone
who helps in the
work and labors.
17I rejoice over the
coming of Stepha-
nas and Fortunatus
and Achaicus,
because they have
supplied what was
lacking on your
part. 18For they
have refreshed my
spirit and yours.

NIV

yours also. Such
men deserve rec-
ognition.

Final Greetings

[19]The churches
in the province
of Asia send you
greetings. Aqui-
la and Priscilla[a]
greet you warmly
in the Lord, and
so does the church
that meets at their
house. [20]All the
brothers and sis-
ters here send you
greetings. Greet
one another with a
holy kiss.
[21]I, Paul, write
this greeting in my
own hand.
[22]If anyone does
not love the Lord,
let that person be
cursed! Come,
Lord[b]!
[23]The grace of the
Lord Jesus be with
you.
[24]My love to all
of you in Christ
Jesus. Amen.[c]

[a] 19 Greek *Prisca*, a variant of *Priscilla*
[b] 22 The Greek for *Come, Lord* reproduces an Aramaic expression (*Marana tha*) used by early Christians.
[c] 24 Some manuscripts do not have *Amen.*

ὑμῶν. ἐπιγινώσκετε οὖν τοὺς τοιούτους. 19
yours. Therefore recognize the worth *Therefore* of such men. The churches of Asia
7007 4036 2105 4036 3836 5525 3836 1711 3836 823
r.gp.2 v.pam.2p cj d.apm r.apm

ἀσπάζονται ὑμᾶς αἱ ἐκκλησίαι τῆς Ἀσίας.
⌊send their greetings to⌋ you. *The churches of Asia* Aquila and Prisca, along with the
832 7007 3836 1711 3836 823 217 2779 4571 5250 5250 3836
v.pmi.3p r.ap.2 d.npf n.npf d.gsf n.gsf

→ ἀσπάζεται ὑμᾶς ἐν κυρίῳ πολλὰ
church that meets in their house, send their special greetings *{you}* in the Lord. *special*
1711 2848 899 3875 4498 832 7007 1877 3261 4498
v.pmi.3s r.ap.2 p.d n.dsm a.apn

Ἀκύλας καὶ Πρίσκα σὺν τῇ κατʼ οἶκον αὐτῶν ἐκκλησίᾳ. 20
Aquila and Prisca along with the in house their church All the brothers
217 2779 4571 5250 3836 2848 3875 899 1711 4246 3836 81
n.nsm cj n.nsf p.d d.dsf p.a n.asm r.gpm.3 n.dsf

→ ἀσπάζονται ὑμᾶς οἱ ἀδελφοὶ πάντες. ἀσπάσασθε ἀλλήλους ἐν
send you greetings. *you the brothers All* Greet one another with a holy
7007 832 7007 3836 81 4246 832 253 1877 41
v.pmi.3p r.ap.2 d.npm n.npm a.npm v.amm.2p r.apm p.d

φιλήματι ἁγίῳ. 21 ὁ ἀσπασμὸς τῇ ἐμῇ χειρὶ Παύλου. 22 εἴ τις ↱ οὐ
kiss. *holy* This greeting is in ⌊my own⌋ hand, Paul. If anyone does not
5799 41 3836 833 3836 1847 5931 4263 1623 5516 5797 4024
n.dsn a.dsn d.nsm n.nsm d.dsf r.dsf.1 n.dsf n.gsm cj r.nsm pl

φιλεῖ τὸν κύριον, ἤτω ἀνάθεμα. ⌊μαράνα θα.⌋ 23 ἡ χάρις τοῦ
love the Lord, ⌊let him be⌋ accursed. Our Lord has come! May the grace of the
5797 3836 3261 1639 353 3448 3448 3836 5921 3836
v.pai.3s d.asm n.asm v.pam.3s n.nsn j j d.nsf n.nsf d.gsm

κυρίου Ἰησοῦ μεθʼ ὑμῶν. 24 ἡ ἀγάπη μου μετὰ πάντων ὑμῶν ἐν
Lord Jesus be with you. *{the}* My love *My* be with you all *you* in
3261 2652 3552 7007 3836 1609 27 1609 3552 7007 4246 7007 1877
n.gsm n.gsm p.g r.gp.2 d.nsf n.nsf r.gs.1 p.g a.gpm r.gp.2 p.d

Χριστῷ Ἰησοῦ.[a]
Christ Jesus.
5986 2652
n.dsm n.dsm

[a] ἀμὴν included by TNIV.

NASB

Therefore ac-
knowledge such
men.
[19]The churches
of Asia greet you.
Aquila and Prisca
greet you heartily
in the Lord, with
the church that is
in their house. [20]All
the brethren greet
you. Greet one
another with a holy
kiss.
[21]The greeting is
in my own hand—
Paul. [22]If anyone
does not love the
Lord, he is to be
accursed. Marana-
tha. [23]The grace
of the Lord Jesus
be with you. [24]My
love be with you
all in Christ Jesus.
Amen.

2 Corinthians

NIV

1 Paul, an apos-
tle of Christ
Jesus by the will of
God, and Timothy
our brother,

To the church of
God in Corinth,
together with all
his holy people
throughout Acha-
ia:

[2]Grace and peace
to you from God
our Father and the
Lord Jesus Christ.

Praise to the God of All Comfort

[3]Praise be to the
God and Father
of our Lord Jesus
Christ, the Father
of compassion
and the God of
all comfort, [4]who
comforts us in
all our troubles,
so that we can
comfort those in
any trouble with
the comfort we
ourselves receive
from God. [5]For
just as we share
abundantly in
the sufferings of
Christ, so also our
comfort abounds
through Christ. [6]If
we are distressed,
it is for your com-
fort and salvation;
if we are comfort-
ed, it is for your
comfort, which
produces in you
patient endurance
of the same suf-
ferings we suffer.
[7]And our hope
for you is firm,
because we know
that just as you
share in

1:1 Παῦλος ἀπόστολος Χριστοῦ Ἰησοῦ διὰ θελήματος θεοῦ καὶ Τιμόθεος
Paul, an apostle of Christ Jesus by the will of God, and Timothy
4263 693 5986 2652 1328 2525 2536 2779 5510
n.nsm n.nsm n.gsm n.gsm p.g n.gsn n.gsm cj n.nsm

ὁ ἀδελφὸς τῇ ἐκκλησίᾳ τοῦ θεοῦ τῇ οὔσῃ ἐν Κορίνθῳ σὺν τοῖς ἁγίοις
our brother, ⌞to the⌟ church of God that is at Corinth, with all the saints
3836 81 3836 1711 3836 2536 3836 1639 1877 3172 5250 4246 3836 41
d.nsm n.nsm d.dsf n.dsf d.gsm n.gsm d.dsf pt.pa.dsf p.d n.dsf p.d d.dpm a.dpm

πᾶσιν τοῖς οὖσιν ἐν ὅλῃ τῇ Ἀχαΐᾳ, [2]χάρις ὑμῖν καὶ εἰρήνη ἀπὸ θεοῦ
all who are in all *{the}* Achaia: Grace to you and peace from God our
4246 3836 1639 1877 3910 3836 938 5921 7007 2779 1645 608 2536 7005
a.dpm d.dpm pt.pa.dpm p.d a.dsf d.dsf n.dsf n.nsf r.dp.2 cj n.nsf p.g n.gsm

πατρὸς ἡμῶν καὶ κυρίου Ἰησοῦ Χριστοῦ. [3]εὐλογητὸς ὁ θεὸς καὶ πατὴρ τοῦ
Father *our* and the Lord Jesus Christ. Blessed be the God and Father of
4252 7005 2779 3261 2652 5986 2329 3836 2536 2779 4252 3836
n.gsm r.gp.1 cj n.gsm n.gsm n.gsm a.nsm d.nsm n.nsm cj n.nsm d.gsm

κυρίου ἡμῶν Ἰησοῦ Χριστοῦ, ὁ πατὴρ τῶν οἰκτιρμῶν καὶ θεὸς πάσης
our Lord *our* Jesus Christ, the Father of mercies and God of all
7005 3261 7005 2652 5986 3836 4252 3836 3880 2779 2536 4246
n.gsm r.gp.1 n.gsm n.gsm d.nsm n.nsm d.gpm n.gpm cj n.nsm a.gsf

παρακλήσεως, [4]ὁ παρακαλῶν ἡμᾶς ἐπὶ πάσῃ τῇ θλίψει ἡμῶν εἰς τὸ
encouragement, who encourages us in all *{the}* our troubles, *our* ⌞so that⌟ ~
4155 3836 4151 7005 2093 4246 3836 7005 2568 7005 1650 3836
n.gsf d.nsm pt.pa.nsm r.ap.1 p.d a.dsf d.dsf n.dsf r.gp.1 p.a d.asn

δύνασθαι ἡμᾶς παρακαλεῖν τοὺς ἐν πάσῃ θλίψει διὰ τῆς παρακλήσεως
we may be able *we* to encourage those experiencing any trouble with the encouragement
7005 1538 7005 4151 3836 1877 4246 2568 1328 3836 4155
f.pp r.ap.1 f.pa d.apm p.d a.dsf n.dsf p.g d.gsf n.gsf

ἧς → παρακαλούμεθα αὐτοὶ ὑπὸ τοῦ θεοῦ. [5]ὅτι καθὼς
⌞with which⌟ we ourselves are encouraged *ourselves* by *{the}* God. For just as the
4005 899 4151 899 5679 3836 2536 4022 2777 3836
r.gsf v.ppi.1p r.npm p.g d.gsm n.gsm cj cj

περισσεύει τὰ παθήματα τοῦ Χριστοῦ εἰς ἡμᾶς, οὕτως ↱
sufferings of Christ overflow *the sufferings of Christ* to us, so also does
4077 3836 5986 4355 3836 4077 3836 5986 1650 7005 4048 2779 4355
v.pai.3s d.npn n.npn d.gsm n.gsm p.a r.ap.1 adv

διὰ τοῦ Χριστοῦ περισσεύει καὶ ἡ παράκλησις
the encouragement we receive through *{the}* Christ overflow. *also the encouragement*
3836 4155 7005 7005 1328 3836 5986 4355 2779 3836 4155
p.g d.gsm n.gsm v.pai.3s adv d.nsf n.nsf

ἡμῶν. [6]εἴτε δὲ θλιβόμεθα, ὑπὲρ τῆς ὑμῶν παρακλήσεως καὶ σωτηρίας·
we receive If *{and}* we are distressed, it is for *{the}* your encouragement and salvation;
7005 1664 1254 2567 5642 3836 7007 4155 2779 5401
r.gp.1 cj cj v.ppi.1p p.g d.gsf r.gp.2 n.gsf cj n.gsf

εἴτε παρακαλούμεθα, ὑπὲρ τῆς ὑμῶν παρακλήσεως τῆς ἐνεργουμένης ἐν
if we are encouraged, it is for *{the}* your encouragement that you experience in your
1664 4151 5642 3836 7007 4155 3836 1919 1877
cj v.ppi.1p p.g d.gsf r.gp.2 n.gsf d.gsf pt.pm.gsf p.d

ὑπομονῇ τῶν αὐτῶν παθημάτων ὧν καὶ ἡμεῖς πάσχομεν. [7]καὶ ἡ
patient endurance of the same sufferings that we also *we* suffer. And *{the}* our
5705 3836 899 4077 4005 7005 2779 7005 4248 2779 3836 7005
n.dsf d.gpn r.gpn n.gpn r.gpn adv r.np.1 v.pai.1p cj d.nsf

ἐλπὶς ἡμῶν βεβαία ὑπὲρ ὑμῶν εἰδότες ὅτι ὡς ⌞κοινωνοί ἐστε⌟
hope *our* for you is firm, *for you* ⌞because we know⌟ that as you share in
1828 7005 5642 7007 1010 5642 7007 3857 4022 6055 3128 1639
n.nsf r.gp.1 a.nsf p.g r.gp.2 pt.ra.npm cj cj n.npm v.pai.2p

NASB

Introduction

1:1Paul, an apostle
of Christ Jesus by
the will of God,
and Timothy *our*
brother,

To the church of
God which is at
Corinth with all
the saints who are
throughout Achaia:
[2]Grace to you and
peace from God
our Father and the
Lord Jesus Christ.
[3]Blessed *be* the
God and Father
of our Lord Jesus
Christ, the Father
of mercies and
God of all comfort,
[4]who comforts us
in all our affliction
so that we will be
able to comfort
those who are in
any affliction with
the comfort with
which we ourselves
are comforted by
God. [5]For just as
the sufferings of
Christ are ours
in abundance, so
also our comfort is
abundant through
Christ. [6]But if we
are afflicted, it is
for your comfort
and salvation; or
if we are com-
forted, it is for your
comfort, which
is effective in the
patient enduring of
the same sufferings
which we also suf-
fer; [7]and our hope
for you is firmly
grounded, know-
ing that as you are
shares of our

NIV

our sufferings, so also you share in our comfort.
[8]We do not want you to be uninformed, brothers and sisters,[a] about the troubles we experienced in the province of Asia. We were under great pressure, far beyond our ability to endure, so that we despaired of life itself. [9]Indeed, we felt we had received the sentence of death. But this happened that we might not rely on ourselves but on God, who raises the dead. [10]He has delivered us from such a deadly peril, and he will deliver us again. On him we have set our hope that he will continue to deliver us, [11]as you help us by your prayers. Then many will give thanks on our behalf for the gracious favor granted us in answer to the prayers of many.

Paul's Change of Plans

[12]Now this is our boast: Our conscience testifies that we have conducted ourselves in the world, and especially in our relations with you, with integrity[b] and godly sincerity. We have done so, relying not on worldly wisdom but on God's grace. [13]For we do not write you anything you cannot read or understand. And I

[a] 8 The Greek word for *brothers and sisters* (*adelphoi*) refers here to believers, both men and women, as part of God's family; also in 8:1; 13:11.
[b] 12 Many manuscripts *holiness*

Interlinear

τῶν παθημάτων, οὕτως καὶ τῆς παρακλήσεως. 8 ↱ ↱ οὐ γὰρ
our sufferings, so also you will share in our encouragement. For we do not *For*
3836 4077 4048 2779 3836 4155 1142 2527 2527 4024 1142
d.gpn n.gpn adv adv d.gsf n.gsf pl cj

θέλομεν ὑμᾶς ἀγνοεῖν, ἀδελφοί, ὑπὲρ τῆς θλίψεως ἡμῶν τῆς γενομένης ἐν τῇ
want you to be unaware, brothers, about the affliction we *{the}* suffered in *{the}*
2527 7007 51 81 5642 3836 2568 7005 3836 1181 1877 3836
v.pai.1p r.ap.2 f.pa n.vpm p.g d.gsf n.gsf r.gp.1 d.gsf pt.am.gsf p.d d.dsf

Ἀσίᾳ, ὅτι ⌊καθ' ὑπερβολὴν⌋ ὑπὲρ δύναμιν
Asia, that we were burdened excessively beyond our power to cope,
823 4022 976 976 976 2848 5651 5642 1539
n.dsf cj p.a n.asf p.a n.asf

ἐβαρήθημεν ὥστε ἐξαπορηθῆναι ἡμᾶς καὶ τοῦ ζῆν· 9 ἀλλὰ αὐτοὶ
we were burdened so that we despaired *we* even of living. Indeed, we had the
976 6063 7005 1989 7005 2779 3836 2409 247 899 2400 3836
v.api.1p cj f.ap r.ap.1 adv d.gsn f.pa cj r.npm

ἐν ἑαυτοῖς τὸ ἀπόκριμα τοῦ θανάτου ἐσχήκαμεν, ἵνα
sentence of death within ourselves, *the sentence of death had* that we
645 3836 2505 1877 1571 3836 645 3836 2505 2400 2671 1639
p.d r.dpm.1 d.asn n.asn d.gsm n.gsm v.rai.1p cj

μὴ πεποιθότες ὦμεν ἐφ' ἑαυτοῖς ἀλλ' ἐπὶ τῷ θεῷ τῷ ἐγείροντι
should ⌊no longer⌋ trust *we should* in ourselves, but in the God who raises
1639 3590 4275 1639 2093 1571 247 2093 3836 2536 3836 1586
pl pt.ra.npm v.pas.1p p.d r.dpm.1 cj p.d d.dsm n.dsm d.dsm pt.pa.dsm

τοὺς νεκρούς· 10 ὃς ἐκ τηλικούτου θανάτου ἐρρύσατο ἡμᾶς καὶ
the dead. He delivered us from so great a risk of death *delivered us* and
3836 3738 4005 4861 7005 1666 5496 2505 4861 7005 2779
d.apm a.apm r.nsm p.g r.gsm n.gsm v.ami.3s r.ap.1 cj

ῥύσεται, εἰς ὃν ἠλπίκαμεν ὅτι[a] καὶ ἔτι
will deliver us. On him ⌊we have set our hope⌋ that he will deliver us yet again, *yet*
4861 1650 4005 1827 4022 4861 4861 4861 2285 2779 2285
v.fmi.3s p.a r.asm v.rai.1p cj adv adv

ῥύσεται, 11 → συνυπουργούντων καὶ ὑμῶν ὑπὲρ ἡμῶν τῇ δεήσει, ἵνα
he will deliver as you also join in helping *also you {for}* us by prayer, so that
4861 7007 2779 5348 2779 7007 5642 7005 3836 1255 2671
v.fmi.3s pt.pa.gpm adv r.gp.2 p.g r.gp.1 d.dsf n.dsf cj

ἐκ πολλῶν προσώπων τὸ
thanks may be given by many people on our behalf for the gracious gift granted
2373 2373 2373 2373 1666 4498 4725 5642 7005 5642 3836 5922 5922
p.g a.gpn n.gpn d.nsn

εἰς ἡμᾶς χάρισμα διὰ πολλῶν εὐχαριστηθῇ ὑπὲρ ἡμῶν. 12 ἡ γὰρ
to us *gracious gift* through the help of many. *thanks may be given on behalf our {the}* For
1650 7005 5922 1328 4498 2373 5642 7005 3836 1142
p.a r.ap.1 n.nsn p.g a.gpm v.aps.3s p.g r.gp.1 d.nsf cj

καύχησις ἡμῶν αὕτη ἐστίν, τὸ μαρτύριον τῆς συνειδήσεως ἡμῶν, ὅτι
our confidence *our* is this, *is* the testimony of our conscience, *our* that
7005 3018 7005 1639 4047 1639 3836 3457 3836 7005 5287 7005 4022
n.nsf r.gp.1 r.nsf v.pai.3s d.nsn n.nsn d.gsf n.gsf r.gp.1 cj

ἐν ἁπλότητι καὶ εἰλικρινείᾳ τοῦ θεοῦ, καὶ[b] οὐκ ἐν σοφίᾳ σαρκικῇ
with simplicity and sincerity like that of God, and not with earthly wisdom *earthly*
1877 605 2779 1636 3836 2536 2779 4024 1877 4920 5053 4920
p.d n.dsf cj n.dsf d.gsm n.gsm cj pl p.d n.dsf a.dsf

ἀλλ' ἐν χάριτι θεοῦ, ἀνεστράφημεν ἐν τῷ κόσμῳ, περισσοτέρως δὲ
but by the grace of God, we conducted ourselves in the world, and all the more *and*
247 1877 5921 2536 418 1877 3836 3180 1254 4359 1254
cj p.d n.dsf n.gsm v.api.1p p.d d.dsm n.dsm adv.c cj

πρὸς ὑμᾶς. 13 οὐ γὰρ ἄλλα γράφομεν ὑμῖν ἀλλ' ἢ
toward you. Now we are not *Now* writing you anything *we are writing you* other than
4639 7007 1142 1211 1211 4024 1142 1211 7007 257 1211 7007 247 2445
p.a r.ap.2 pl cj r.apn v.pai.1p r.dp.2 cj pl

ἃ ἀναγινώσκετε ἢ καὶ ἐπιγινώσκετε· ἐλπίζω δὲ ὅτι ⌊ἕως
what you can read and also understand. But I hope *But* that you will understand fully,
4005 336 2445 2779 2105 1254 1827 1254 4022 2105 2105 2105 2401
r.apn v.pai.2p cj adv v.pai.2p v.pai.1s cj cj p.g

[a] [ὅτι] UBS.
[b] [καὶ] UBS, omitted by TNIV.

NASB

sufferings, so also you are *sharers* of our comfort.
[8]For we do not want you to be unaware, brethren, of our affliction which came *to us* in Asia, that we were burdened excessively, beyond our strength, so that we despaired even of life; [9]indeed, we had the sentence of death within ourselves so that we would not trust in ourselves, but in God who raises the dead; [10]who delivered us from so great a *peril of* death, and will deliver *us*, He on whom we have set our hope. And He will yet deliver us, [11]you also joining in helping us through your prayers, so that thanks may be given by many persons on our behalf for the favor bestowed on us through *the prayers of* many.

Paul's Integrity

[12]For our proud confidence is this: the testimony of our conscience, that in holiness and godly sincerity, not in fleshly wisdom but in the grace of God, we have conducted ourselves in the world, and especially toward you. [13]For we write nothing else to you than what you read and understand, and I hope you will understand until

NIV

hope that, [14]as you have understood us in part, you will come to understand fully that you can boast of us just as we will boast of you in the day of the Lord Jesus.

[15]Because I was confident of this, I wanted to visit you first so that you might benefit twice. [16]I wanted to visit you on my way to Macedonia and to come back to you from Macedonia, and then to have you send me on my way to Judea. [17]Was I fickle when I intended to do this? Or do I make my plans in a worldly manner so that in the same breath I say both "Yes, yes" and "No, no"?

[18]But as surely as God is faithful, our message to you is not "Yes" and "No." [19]For the Son of God, Jesus Christ, who was preached among you by us—by me and Silas[a] and Timothy—was not "Yes" and "No," but in him it has always been "Yes." [20]For no matter how many promises God has made, they are "Yes" in Christ. And so through him the "Amen"

τέλους˩ ἐπιγνώσεσθε, 14 καθὼς καὶ ἐπέγνωτε ἡμᾶς ˪ἀπὸ μέρους,˩ ὅτι
you will understand just as also you have understood us partially, that
5465 2105 2777 2779 2105 7005 608 3538 4022
n.gsn v.fmi.2p cj adv v.aai.2p r.ap.1 p.g n.gsn cj

καύχημα ὑμῶν ἐσμεν καθάπερ καὶ ὑμεῖς ἡμῶν ἐν τῇ ἡμέρᾳ
we are your source of pride, *your* *we are* as you also *you* are ours, in the day
1639 1639 7007 3017 7007 1639 2749 7007 2779 7007 7005 1877 3836 2465
n.nsn r.gp.2 v.pai.1p cj adv r.np.2 r.gp.1 p.d d.dsf n.dsf

τοῦ κυρίου[a] Ἰησοῦ. 15 καὶ ταύτῃ τῇ πεποιθήσει ἐβουλόμην
of the Lord Jesus. And ˪because of this˩ *{the}* confidence, I was intending to come
3836 3261 2652 2779 4047 3836 4301 1089 2262 2262
d.gsm n.gsm n.gsm cj r.dsf d.dsf n.dsf v.imi.1s

πρότερον πρὸς ὑμᾶς ἐλθεῖν, ἵνα δευτέραν χάριν
to you first, *to* *you* *to come* so that you might have a second benefit
4639 7007 4728 4639 7007 2262 2671 2400 2400 2400 1311 5921
adv.c p.a r.ap.2 f.aa cj a.asf n.asf

σχῆτε, 16 καὶ δι' ὑμῶν διελθεῖν εἰς Μακεδονίαν καὶ
you might have — *{and}* through your help, to go on to Macedonia, and from Macedonia
2400 2779 1328 7007 1451 1650 3423 2779 608 3423
v.aas.2p cj p.g r.gp.2 f.aa p.a n.asf cj

πάλιν ἀπὸ Μακεδονίας ἐλθεῖν πρὸς ὑμᾶς καὶ ↱ ↱ ↱ ὑφ' ὑμῶν
to come back *from Macedonia* *to come* to you and to be helped by you
2262 2262 4099 608 3423 2262 4639 7007 2779 4636 4636 4636 5679 7007
adv p.g n.gsf f.aa p.a r.ap.2 cj p.g r.gp.2

προπεμφθῆναι εἰς τὴν Ἰουδαίαν. 17 τοῦτο οὖν
on my way to *{the}* Judea. Therefore when I was planning this, *Therefore*
4636 1650 3836 2677 4036 1089 1089 1089 1089 4047 4036
f.ap p.a d.asf n.asf r.asn cj

βουλόμενος μήτι ἄρα τῇ ἐλαφρίᾳ ἐχρησάμην; ↰ ↰ ἢ ἃ
when I was planning I was not *{then}* *{the}* capricious, *I was* was I? Or ˪the things˩
1089 5968 5968 3614 726 3836 1786 5968 3614 3614 2445 4005
pt.pm.nsm pl cj d.dsf n.dsf v.ami.1s cj r.apn

βουλεύομαι κατὰ σάρκα βουλεύομαι, ἵνα ᾖ
I plan, do I plan ˪according to˩ the flesh, *do I plan* so that with me ˪it would be˩
1086 1086 1086 1086 2848 4922 1086 2671 4123 1609 1639
v.pmi.1s p.a n.asf v.pmi.1s cj v.pas.3s

παρ' ἐμοὶ τὸ ναὶ ναὶ καὶ τὸ οὒ οὔ; 18
with *me* *{the}* "Yes, yes" and *{the}* "No, no" at the same time? But as surely as God is
4123 1609 3836 3721 3721 2779 3836 4024 4024 1254 2536
p.d r.ds.1 d.nsn pl pl cj d.nsn pl pl

πιστὸς δὲ ὁ θεὸς ὅτι ὁ λόγος ἡμῶν ὁ πρὸς ὑμᾶς ↱ οὐκ ἔστιν
trustworthy, *But* *{the}* *God* *{that}* *{the}* our word *our* *{the}* to you has not been
4412 1254 3836 2536 4022 3836 7005 3364 7005 3836 4639 7007 1639 4024 1639
a.nsm cj d.nsm n.nsm cj d.nsm n.nsm r.gp.1 d.nsm p.a r.ap.2 pl v.pai.3s

ναὶ καὶ οὔ. 19 ὁ τοῦ θεοῦ γὰρ υἱὸς Ἰησοῦς Χριστὸς ὁ
"Yes" and "No." For the Son of God, *For* *Son* Jesus Christ, the one who was
3721 2779 4024 1142 3836 5626 3836 2536 1142 5626 2652 5986 3836 3062 3062 3062
pl cj pl d.nsm d.gsm n.gsm cj n.nsm n.nsm n.nsm d.nsm

ἐν ὑμῖν δι' ἡμῶν κηρυχθείς, δι' ἐμοῦ καὶ Σιλουανοῦ καὶ
proclaimed among you by us *one who was proclaimed* — by me, *{and}* Silvanus, and
3062 1877 7007 1328 7005 3062 1328 1609 2779 4977 2779
p.d r.dp.2 p.g r.gp.1 pt.ap.nsm p.g r.gs.1 cj n.gsm cj

Τιμοθέου, οὐκ ἐγένετο ναὶ καὶ οὒ ἀλλὰ ναὶ
Timothy — was not *was* "Yes" and "No," but in him it has always been "Yes."
5510 1181 4024 1181 3721 2779 4024 247 1877 899 1181 1181 1181 1181 3721
n.gsm pl v.ami.3s pl cj pl cj pl

ἐν αὐτῷ γέγονεν. 20 ὅσαι γὰρ ἐπαγγελίαι θεοῦ, ἐν
in *him* *it has always been* For all *For* the promises of God find their "Yes" in
1877 899 1181 1142 4012 1142 2039 2536 3836 3721 1877
p.d r.dsm.3 v.rai.3s r.npf cj n.npf n.gsm p.d

αὐτῷ τὸ ναί· διὸ καὶ δι' αὐτοῦ τὸ ἀμὴν τῷ θεῷ
him; *their* *Yes* and ˪that is why˩ *{also}* it is through him that we say our "Amen" to God
899 3836 3721 1475 2779 1328 899 7005 3836 297 3836 2536
r.dsm.3 d.nsn pl cj adv p.g r.gsm.3 d.nsn pl d.dsm n.dsm

NASB

the end; [14]just as you also partially did understand us, that we are your reason to be proud as you also are ours, in the day of our Lord Jesus.

[15]In this confidence I intended at first to come to you, so that you might twice receive a blessing; [16]that is, to pass your way into Macedonia, and again from Macedonia to come to you, and by you to be helped on my journey to Judea. [17]Therefore, I was not vacillating when I intended to do this, was I? Or what I purpose, do I purpose according to the flesh, so that with me there will be yes, yes and no, no *at the same time?* [18]But as God is faithful, our word to you is not yes and no. [19]For the Son of God, Christ Jesus, who was preached among you by us—by me and Silvanus and Timothy—was not yes and no, but is yes in Him. [20]For as many as are the promises of God, in Him they are yes; therefore also through Him is our Amen to the glory

[a] 19 Greek *Silvanus*, a variant of *Silas*

[a] ἡμῶν included by UBS after κυρίου.

NIV

is spoken by us to
the glory of God.
[21]Now it is God
who makes both
us and you stand
firm in Christ. He
anointed us, [22]set
his seal of owner-
ship on us, and put
his Spirit in our
hearts as a deposit,
guaranteeing what
is to come.
[23]I call God as
my witness—and
I stake my life on
it—that it was
in order to spare
you that I did not
return to Corinth.
[24]Not that we lord
it over your faith,
but we work with
you for your joy,
because it is by
faith you stand
firm.
2 [1]So I made up
my mind that
I would not make
another painful
visit to you. [2]For if
I grieve you, who
is left to make me
glad but you whom
I have grieved? [3]I
wrote as I did, so
that when I came I
would not be dis-
tressed by those
who should have
made me rejoice. I
had confidence in
all of you, that you
would all share my
joy. [4]For I wrote
you out of great
distress and an-
guish of heart and
with many tears,
not to grieve you
but to let you know
the depth of my
love for you.

πρὸς δόξαν δι᾽ ἡμῶν. 21 ὁ δὲ βεβαιῶν ἡμᾶς
for his glory. {through} we Now God is the Now ⌊one who strengthens⌋ us,
4639 1518 1328 7005 1254 2536 3836 1254 1011 7005
p.a n.asf p.g r.gp.1 d.nsm cj pt.pa.nsm r.ap.1

σὺν ὑμῖν εἰς Χριστὸν καὶ χρίσας ἡμᾶς θεός, 22 ὁ ↱ καὶ
⌊together with⌋ you, in Christ, and has anointed us, God and who has also
5250 7007 1650 5986 2779 5987 7005 2536 3836 5381 2779
p.d r.dp.2 p.a n.asm cj pt.aa.nsm r.ap.1 n.nsm d.nsm adv

σφραγισάμενος ἡμᾶς καὶ δοὺς τὸν ἀρραβῶνα τοῦ
sealed us and given us his Spirit in our hearts as a pledge. his
5381 7005 2779 1443 3836 4460 1877 7005 2840 3836 775 3836
pt.am.nsm r.ap.1 cj pt.aa.nsm d.asm n.asm d.gsn

πνεύματος ἐν ταῖς καρδίαις ἡμῶν. 23 ἐγὼ δὲ μάρτυρα τὸν θεὸν
Spirit in {the} hearts our I {and} call God as a witness {the} God
4460 1877 3836 2840 7005 1609 1254 2126 2536 3459 3836 2536
n.gsn p.d d.dpf n.dpf r.gp.1 r.ns.1 cj n.asm d.asm n.asm

ἐπικαλοῦμαι ἐπὶ τὴν ἐμὴν ψυχήν, ὅτι φειδόμενος ὑμῶν →
call against {the} my soul, that it was to spare you that I did not come
2126 2093 3836 1847 6034 4022 5767 7007 2262 2262 2262
v.pmi.1s p.a d.asf r.asf.1 n.asf cj pt.pm.nsm r.gp.2

οὐκέτι ἦλθον εἰς Κόρινθον. 24 οὐχ ὅτι κυριεύομεν ὑμῶν τῆς πίστεως ἀλλὰ
again I did come to Corinth. Not that we are ruling over your {the} faith, but
4033 2262 1650 3172 4024 4022 3259 7007 3836 4411 247
adv v.aai.1s p.a n.asf pl cj v.pai.1p r.gp.2 d.gsf n.gsf cj

συνεργοί ἐσμεν τῆς χαρᾶς ὑμῶν· τῇ γὰρ πίστει
we are workers with you we are for your joy; your for by for faith
1639 1639 5301 1639 3836 7007 5915 7007 1142 3836 1142 4411
n.npm v.pai.1p d.gsf n.gsf r.gp.2 d.dsf cj n.dsf

ἑστήκατε.
⌊you have stood firm.⌋
2705
v.rai.2p

2:1 ἔκρινα γὰρ ἐμαυτῷ τοῦτο τὸ μὴ πάλιν ἐν
So I decided So this within myself, this ~ not to come to you again with
1142 3212 1142 4047 1831 4047 3836 3590 2262 2262 4639 7007 4099 1877
v.aai.1s cj r.dsm.1 r.asn d.asn pl adv p.d

λύπῃ πρὸς ὑμᾶς ἐλθεῖν. 2 εἰ γὰρ ἐγὼ → λυπῶ ὑμᾶς, καὶ τίς ὁ →
sorrow. to you to come For if For I cause you sorrow, you then who is there to
3383 4639 7007 2262 1142 1623 1142 1609 7007 3382 7007 2779 5515 3836
n.dsf p.a r.ap.2 f.aa cj cj r.ns.1 v.pai.1s r.ap.2 cj r.nsm d.nsm

→ εὐφραίνων με ⌊εἰ μὴ⌋ ὁ λυπούμενος ἐξ ἐμοῦ; 3 καὶ ἔγραψα
make me glad me except the one made sorrowful by me? And I wrote
1609 2370 1609 1623 3590 3836 3382 1666 1609 2779 1211
pt.pa.nsm r.as.1 cj pl d.nsm pt.pp.nsm p.g r.gs.1 cj v.aai.1s

τοῦτο αὐτό, ἵνα μὴ ἐλθὼν λύπην σχῶ
this very thing so that when I came, I would not when I came have sorrow I would have
4047 899 2671 2262 2262 2262 2400 2400 3590 2262 2400 3383 2400
r.asn r.asn cj pl pt.aa.nsm n.asf v.aas.1s

ἀφ᾽ ὧν ἔδει ↱ ↱ με χαίρειν, πεποιθὼς ἐπὶ πάντας ὑμᾶς ὅτι
from those ⌊who ought⌋ to make me rejoice, having confidence in you all you that
608 4005 1256 5897 5897 1609 5897 4275 2093 7007 4246 7007 4022
p.g r.gpm v.iai.3s r.as.1 f.pa pt.ra.nsm p.a a.apm r.ap.2 cj

ἡ ἐμὴ χαρὰ πάντων ὑμῶν ἐστιν. 4 ἐκ γὰρ
{the} my joy would be the joy of you all. of you would be For ⌊out of⌋ For
3836 1847 5915 1639 1639 7007 7007 4246 7007 1639 1142 1666 1142
d.nsf r.nsf.1 n.nsf a.gpm r.gp.2 v.pai.3s p.g cj

πολλῆς θλίψεως καὶ συνοχῆς καρδίας ἔγραψα ὑμῖν διὰ πολλῶν δακρύων, οὐχ ἵνα
much distress and anguish of heart I wrote to you, with many tears, not to
4498 2568 2779 5330 2840 1211 7007 1328 4498 1232 4024 2671
a.gsf n.gsf cj n.gsf n.gsf v.aai.1s r.dp.2 p.g a.gpn n.gpn pl cj

λυπηθῆτε ἀλλὰ τὴν ἀγάπην ἵνα γνῶτε ἣν ἔχω
cause you sorrow but to let you know the love to let you know that I have
3382 247 2671 1182 1182 1182 3836 27 2671 1182 4005 2400
v.aps.2p cj d.asf n.asf cj v.aas.2p r.asf v.pai.1s

NASB

of God through
us. [21]Now He who
establishes us with
you in Christ and
anointed us is God,
[22]who also sealed
us and gave *us* the
Spirit in our hearts
as a pledge.
[23]But I call God as
witness to my soul,
that to spare you I
did not come again
to Corinth. [24]Not
that we lord it over
your faith, but are
workers with you
for your joy; for in
your faith you are
standing firm.

Reaffirm Your Love

2:1 But I deter-
mined this for my
own sake, that I
would not come
to you in sorrow
again. [2]For if I
cause you sorrow,
who then makes
me glad but the one
whom I made sor-
rowful? [3]This is the
very thing I wrote
you, so that when I
came, I would not
have sorrow from
those who ought to
make me rejoice;
having confidence
in you all that my
joy would be *the*
joy of you all. [4]For
out of much afflic-
tion and anguish
of heart I wrote
to you with many
tears; not so that
you would be made
sorrowful, but that
you might know
the love which I

NIV

Forgiveness for the Offender

[5]If anyone has
caused grief, he
has not so much
grieved me as he
has grieved all of
you to some ex-
tent—not to put
it too severely.
[6]The punishment
inflicted on him
by the majority is
sufficient. [7]Now
instead, you ought
to forgive and
comfort him, so
that he will not be
overwhelmed by
excessive sorrow.
[8]I urge you, there-
fore, to reaffirm
your love for him.
[9]Another reason I
wrote you was to
see if you would
stand the test and
be obedient in ev-
erything. [10]Anyone
you forgive, I also
forgive. And what
I have forgiven—
if there was any-
thing to forgive—
I have forgiven in
the sight of Christ
for your sake, [11]in
order that Satan
might not outwit
us. For we are not
unaware of his
schemes.

Ministers of the New Covenant

[12]Now when I
went to Troas to
preach the gos-
pel of Christ and
found that the
Lord had opened
a door for me, [13]I
still had no peace
of mind, because
I did not find my
brother Titus there.
So I said goodbye
to them and went
on to

περισσοτέρως εἰς ὑμᾶς. 5 εἰ δέ τις λελύπηκεν,
especially for you. But if *But* anyone has caused sorrow, he has caused sorrow
4359 1650 7007 1254 1623 1254 5516 3382 3382 3382 3382 3382
adv.c p.a r.ap.2 cj cj r.nsm v.rai.3s

οὐκ ἐμὲ λελύπηκεν, ἀλλὰ ἀπὸ μέρους, ἵνα μὴ ἐπιβαρῶ,
not for me, *he has caused sorrow* but in some measure — not to *not* ⌊overstate the case⌋ —
4024 1609 3382 247 608 3538 3590 2671 3590 2096
pl r.as.1 v.rai.3s cj p.g n.gsn cj pl v.pas.1s

πάντας ὑμᾶς. 6 ἱκανὸν τῷ τοιούτῳ ἡ ἐπιτιμία αὕτη ἡ
for all of you. *enough* This punishment on such a person *{the}* *punishment* *This* *{the}*
4246 7007 2653 4047 2204 3836 5525 3836 2204 4047 3836
a.apm r.ap.2 a.nsn d.dsm r.dsm d.nsf n.nsf r.nsf d.nsf

ὑπὸ τῶν πλειόνων, 7 ὥστε τοὐναντίον ↱ μᾶλλον ὑμᾶς
by the majority is enough for him, so that *him* you should rather *you*
5679 3836 4498 2653 6063 5539 7007 5919 3437 7007
p.g d.gpm a.gpm.c cj crasis.asn adv.c r.ap.2

χαρίσασθαι καὶ παρακαλέσαι, ⌊μή πως⌋ τῇ περισσοτέρᾳ
forgive and console him, lest he be swallowed up by excessive
5919 2779 4151 5539 3590 4803 5525 2927 2927 2927 3836 4358
f.am cj f.aa cj pl d.dsf a.dsf.c

λύπῃ καταποθῇ ὁ τοιοῦτος. 8 διὸ παρακαλῶ ὑμᾶς → →
sorrow. *be swallowed up* *{the}* *he* So I urge you to show that your love for him
3383 2927 3836 5525 1475 4151 7007 27 1650 899
n.dsf v.aps.3s d.nsm r.nsm cj v.pai.1s r.ap.2

κυρῶσαι εἰς αὐτὸν ἀγάπην· 9 εἰς τοῦτο γὰρ καὶ ἔγραψα, ἵνα γνῶ
is real. *for* *him* *love* For this reason *{for}* also I wrote you: to discover whether
3263 1650 899 27 1650 4047 1142 2779 1211 2671 1182
f.aa p.a r.asm.3 n.asf p.a r.asn cj adv v.aai.1s cj v.aas.1s

τὴν δοκιμὴν ὑμῶν, εἰ εἰς πάντα ὑπήκοοί ἐστε.
you could *{the}* ⌊stand the test⌋ *you* — if in everything you are obedient. *you are*
7007 3836 1509 7007 1623 1650 4246 1639 1639 5675 1639
d.asf n.asf r.gp.2 cj p.a a.apn a.npm v.pai.2p

10 ᾧ δέ τι χαρίζεσθε, κἀγώ·
Now the one ⌊to whom⌋ *Now* you forgive anything, *you forgive* I also do the same; for
1254 4005 1254 5919 5919 5516 5919 2743 1142
r.dsm cj r.asn v.pmi.2p crasis

καὶ γὰρ ἐγὼ ὃ κεχάρισμαι, εἴ τι κεχάρισμαι,
indeed, *for* what I *what* have forgiven — if I have forgiven anything *I have forgiven* — I
2779 1142 4005 1609 4005 5919 1623 5919 5919 5919 5516 5919
adv cj r.ns.1 r.asn v.rmi.1s cj r.asn v.rmi.1s

δι' ὑμᾶς ↰ ἐν προσώπῳ Χριστοῦ, 11 ⌊ἵνα μὴ⌋ πλεονεκτηθῶμεν
did so for your benefit in the presence of Christ, lest ⌊we be taken advantage of⌋
1328 7007 1328 1877 4725 5986 2671 3590 4430
p.a r.ap.2 p.d n.dsn n.gsm cj pl v.aps.1p

ὑπὸ τοῦ σατανᾶ· οὐ γὰρ αὐτοῦ τὰ νοήματα ἀγνοοῦμεν.
by *{the}* Satan; for we are not *for* unaware of his *{the}* intentions. *we are unaware of*
5679 3836 4928 1142 51 51 4024 1142 51 51 899 3836 3784 51
p.g d.gsm n.gsm pl cj r.gsm.3 d.apn n.apn v.pai.1p

12 ἐλθὼν δὲ εἰς τὴν Τρῳάδα εἰς τὸ εὐαγγέλιον τοῦ Χριστοῦ καὶ
⌊When I came⌋ *{and}* to *{the}* Troas to proclaim the gospel of Christ, even
2262 1254 1650 3836 5590 1650 3836 2295 3836 5986 2779
pt.aa.nsm cj p.a d.asf n.asf p.a d.asn n.asn d.gsm n.gsm cj

θύρας μοι ἀνεῳγμένης ἐν κυρίῳ, 13
though a door had been opened ⌊for me⌋ *though had been opened* by the Lord, I had
487 2598 487 487 487 1609 487 1877 3261 2400 2400
n.gsf r.ds.1 pt.rp.gsf p.d n.dsm

οὐκ ἔσχηκα ἄνεσιν τῷ πνεύματί μου τῷ ↱ ↱ μὴ εὑρεῖν με
no *I had* relief for my spirit, *my* *{the}* because I could not find *I* my
4024 2400 457 3836 1609 4460 1609 3836 2351 1609 2351 3590 2351 1609 1609
pl v.rai.1s n.asf d.dsn n.dsn r.gs.1 d.dsn pl f.aa r.as.1

Τίτον τὸν ἀδελφόν μου, ἀλλὰ ἀποταξάμενος αὐτοῖς ἐξῆλθον εἰς
brother Titus *{the}* *brother* *my* there. So I said good-bye to them and went on to
81 5519 3836 81 1609 247 698 899 2002 1650
n.asm d.asm n.asm r.gs.1 cj pt.am.nsm r.dpm.3 v.aai.1s p.a

NASB

have especially for
you.
[5]But if any has
caused sorrow, he
has caused sorrow
not to me, but in
some degree—in
order not to say
too much—to all
of you. [6]Sufficient
for such a one is
this punishment
which *was inflicted*
by the majority, [7]so
that on the contrary
you should rather
forgive and com-
fort *him,* otherwise
such a one might
be overwhelmed by
excessive sorrow.
[8]Wherefore I urge
you to reaffirm
your love for him.
[9]For to this end
also I wrote, so that
I might put you to
the test, whether
you are obedient
in all things. [10]But
one whom you
forgive anything,
I *forgive* also; for
indeed what I have
forgiven, if I have
forgiven anything,
I did it for your
sakes in the pres-
ence of Christ, [11]so
that no advantage
would be taken of
us by Satan, for we
are not ignorant of
his schemes.
[12]Now when I
came to Troas for
the gospel of Christ
and when a door
was opened for me
in the Lord, [13]I had
no rest for my spir-
it, not finding Titus
my brother; but
taking my leave of
them, I went on to
Macedonia.

NIV

Macedonia.
[14]But thanks
be to God, who
always leads us
as captives in
Christ's triumphal
procession and
uses us to spread
the aroma of the
knowledge of
him everywhere.
[15]For we are to
God the pleasing
aroma of Christ
among those who
are being saved
and those who are
perishing. [16]To
the one we are an
aroma that brings
death; to the oth-
er, an aroma that
brings life. And
who is equal to
such a task? [17]Un-
like so many, we
do not peddle the
word of God for
profit. On the con-
trary, in Christ we
speak before God
with sincerity, as
those sent from
God.
3 Are we begin-
ning to com-
mend ourselves
again? Or do we
need, like some
people, letters of
recommendation
to you or from
you? [2]You your-
selves are our let-
ter, written on our
hearts, known and
read by everyone.
[3]You show that
you are a letter
from Christ, the
result of our min-
istry, written not
with ink but with
the Spirit of the
living God, not on

Μακεδονίαν. 14 τῷ δὲ θεῷ χάρις τῷ ↱ πάντοτε θριαμβεύοντι
Macedonia. But thanks be to *But* God, *thanks* who is always leading
3423 1254 5921 3836 1254 2536 5921 3836 2581 4121 2581
n.asf d.dsm cj n.dsm n.nsf d.dsm adv pt.pa.dsm

ἡμᾶς ↰ ↰ ἐν τῷ Χριστῷ καὶ τὴν ὀσμὴν τῆς
us in triumph in *{the}* Christ, and through us is making known the fragrance of the
7005 2581 2581 1877 3836 5986 2779 1328 7005 5746 5746 5746 3836 4011 3836
r.ap.1 p.d d.dsm n.dsm cj d.asf n.asf d.gsf

γνώσεως αὐτοῦ φανεροῦντι δι᾽ ἡμῶν ἐν παντὶ τόπῳ· 15 ὅτι
knowledge of him *is making known* *through* *us* in every place. For we are an aroma
1194 899 5746 1328 7005 1877 4246 5536 4022 1639 1639 2380
n.gsf r.gsm.3 pt.pa.dsm p.g r.gp.1 p.d a.dsm n.dsm cj

Χριστοῦ εὐωδία ἐσμὲν τῷ θεῷ ἐν τοῖς σῳζομένοις καὶ ἐν τοῖς
of Christ *aroma* *we are* to God among those ⌊who are being saved.⌋ *{and}* Among those
5986 2380 1639 3836 2536 1877 3836 5392 2779 1877 3836
n.gsm n.nsf v.pai.1p d.dsm n.dsm p.d d.dpm pt.pp.dpm cj p.d d.dpm

ἀπολλυμένοις, 16 οἷς μὲν ὀσμὴ ⌊ἐκ θανάτου⌋ εἰς θάνατον,
who are perishing *{to them}* ~ we are a deadly fume *deadly* that kills, but
660 4005 3525 1666 4011 1666 2505 1650 2505 1254
pt.pm.dpm r.dpm pl n.nsf p.g n.gsm p.a n.asm

οἷς δὲ ὀσμὴ ⌊ἐκ ζωῆς⌋ εἰς ζωήν. καὶ
⌊to the former⌋ *but* we are a life-giving fragrance *life-giving* ⌊that brings⌋ life. And who is
4005 1254 1666 4011 1666 2437 1650 2437 2779 5515
r.dpm pl n.nsf p.g n.gsf p.a n.asf cj

πρὸς ταῦτα τίς ἱκανός; 17 οὐ γάρ ἐσμεν ὡς οἱ
adequate for ministry like this? *who* *adequate* For we are not *For* *we are* like *{the}*
2653 4639 4047 5515 2653 1142 1639 1639 4024 1142 1639 6055 3836
p.a r.apn r.nsm a.nsm pl cj v.pai.1p pl d.npm

πολλοὶ καπηλεύοντες τὸν λόγον τοῦ θεοῦ, ἀλλ᾽
so many, peddling the word of God. ⌊To the contrary,⌋ in Christ we speak in
4498 2836 3836 3364 3836 2536 247 1877 5986 3281 3281 2978
a.npm pt.pa.npm d.asm n.asm d.gsm n.gsm cj

ὡς ἐξ εἰλικρινείας, ἀλλ᾽ ὡς ἐκ θεοῦ κατέναντι
the sight of God as men of sincerity, *{but}* as men sent from God. *in the sight*
2978 2978 2536 2536 6055 1666 1636 247 6055 1666 2536 2978
pl p.g n.gsf cj pl p.g n.gsm p.g

θεοῦ ἐν Χριστῷ λαλοῦμεν.
of God *in* *Christ* *we speak*
2536 1877 5986 3281
n.gsm p.d n.dsm v.pai.1p

3:1 ἀρχόμεθα πάλιν ἑαυτοὺς συνιστάνειν; ἢ ↱
Are we beginning to recommend ourselves again? *ourselves* *to recommend* *{or}* We
806 5319 5319 1571 4099 1571 5319 2445 5974
v.pmi.1p adv r.apm.1 f.pa cj

↱ μὴ χρῄζομεν ὥς τινες συστατικῶν ἐπιστολῶν πρὸς ὑμᾶς ἢ ἐξ
do not need, as some do, letters of recommendation *letters* to you or from
5974 3590 5974 6055 5516 2186 5364 2186 4639 7007 2445 1666
pl v.pai.1p cj r.npm a.gpf n.gpf p.a r.ap.2 cj p.g

ὑμῶν; ↰ ↰ 2 ἡ ἐπιστολὴ ἡμῶν ὑμεῖς ἐστε,
you, do we? You yourselves are *{the}* our letter, *our* *yourselves* *You are*
7007 3590 3590 1639 7007 1639 3836 7005 2186 7005 7007 1639
r.gp.2 d.nsf n.nsf r.gp.1 r.np.2 v.pai.2p

ἐγγεγραμμένη ἐν ταῖς καρδίαις ἡμῶν, γινωσκομένη καὶ ἀναγινωσκομένη ὑπὸ
written on *{the}* our hearts, *our* known and read by
1582 1877 3836 7005 2840 7005 1182 2779 336 5679
pt.rp.nsf p.d d.dpf n.dpf r.gp.1 pt.pp.nsf cj pt.pp.nsf p.g

πάντων ἀνθρώπων, 3 φανερούμενοι ὅτι ἐστὲ ἐπιστολὴ Χριστοῦ διακονηθεῖσα ὑφ᾽
all people; making known that you are a letter of Christ, delivered by
4246 476 5746 4022 1639 2186 5986 1354 5679
a.gpm n.gpm pt.pp.npm cj v.pai.2p n.nsf n.gsm pt.ap.nsf p.g

ἡμῶν, ἐγγεγραμμένη οὐ μέλανι ἀλλὰ → πνεύματι → θεοῦ ζῶντος, οὐκ ἐν
us, written not in ink but by the Spirit of the living God, *living* not on
7005 1582 4024 3506 247 4460 2409 2536 2409 4024 1877
r.gp.1 pt.rp.nsf pl a.dsn cj n.dsn n.gsm pt.pa.gsm pl p.d

NASB

[14]But thanks be to
God, who always
leads us in triumph
in Christ, and
manifests through
us the sweet aroma
of the knowledge
of Him in every
place. [15]For we
are a fragrance
of Christ to God
among those who
are being saved
and among those
who are perishing;
[16]to the one an aro-
ma from death to
death, to the other
an aroma from life
to life. And who is
adequate for these
things? [17]For we
are not like many,
[a]peddling the word
of God, but as
from sincerity, but
as from God, we
speak in Christ in
the sight of God.

Ministers of a New Covenant

[3:1]Are we begin-
ning to commend
ourselves again?
Or do we need, as
some, letters of
commendation to
you or from you?
[2]You are our let-
ter, written in our
hearts, known and
read by all men;
[3]being manifested
that you are a letter
of Christ, cared for
by us, written not
with ink but with
the Spirit of the liv-
ing God, not on

[a] Or *corrupting*

NIV

tablets of stone but
on tablets of hu-
man hearts.
4 Such confidence
we have through
Christ before God.
5 Not that we are
competent in our-
selves to claim
anything for our-
selves, but our
competence comes
from God. 6 He has
made us compe-
tent as ministers of
a new covenant—
not of the letter
but of the Spirit;
for the letter kills,
but the Spirit gives
life.

The Greater Glory of the New Covenant

7 Now if the min-
istry that brought
death, which was
engraved in letters
on stone, came
with glory, so that
the Israelites could
not look steadily
at the face of Mo-
ses because of its
glory, transitory
though it was,
8 will not the min-
istry of the Spirit
be even more glo-
rious? 9 If the min-
istry that brought
condemnation
was glorious, how
much more glori-
ous is the ministry
that brings righ-
teousness! 10 For
what was glorious
has no glory now
in comparison
with the surpass-
ing glory. 11 And
if what was tran-
sitory came with
glory, how much
greater is the glory
of that which lasts!
12 Therefore, since
we have

πλαξὶν λιθίναις ἀλλʼ ἐν πλαξὶν → καρδίαις σαρκίναις. 4 πεποίθησιν
tablets of stone but on tablets of human hearts. *human* Such is the confidence
4419 3343 247 1877 4419 4921 2840 4921 5525 4301
n.dpf a.dpf cj p.d n.dpf n.dpf a.dpf n.asf

δὲ τοιαύτην ἔχομεν διὰ τοῦ Χριστοῦ πρὸς τὸν θεόν. 5 οὐχ ὅτι
{and} *Such* we have through *{the}* Christ toward *{the}* God. Not that we are
1254 5525 2400 1328 3836 5986 4639 3836 2536 4024 4022 1639 1639
cj r.asf v.pai.1p p.g d.gsm n.gsm p.a d.asm n.asm pl cj

ἀφʼ ἑαυτῶν ἱκανοί ἐσμεν λογίσασθαί τι ὡς ἐξ ἑαυτῶν, ἀλλʼ
adequate in ourselves *adequate* *we are* to consider anything as coming from us, but
2653 608 1571 2653 1639 3357 5516 6055 1666 1571 247
p.g r.gpm.1 a.npm v.pai.1p f.am r.asn pl p.g r.gpm.1 cj

ἡ ἱκανότης ἡμῶν ἐκ τοῦ θεοῦ, 6 ὃς καὶ → ἱκάνωσεν ἡμᾶς
{the} our adequacy *our* comes from *{the}* God, who indeed made us adequate *us* as
3836 7005 2654 7005 1666 3836 2536 4005 2779 7005 2655 7005
d.nsf n.nsf r.gp.1 p.g d.gsm n.gsm r.nsm adv v.aai.3s r.ap.1

διακόνους → καινῆς διαθήκης, οὐ → γράμματος ἀλλὰ → πνεύματος·
servants of a new covenant, based not on the letter but on the Spirit;
1356 2785 1347 4024 1207 247 4460
n.apm a.gsf n.gsf pl n.gsn cj n.gsn

τὸ γὰρ γράμμα ἀποκτέννει, τὸ δὲ πνεῦμα ζῳοποιεῖ. 7 εἰ δὲ ἡ
for the *for* letter kills, but the *but* Spirit imparts life. Now if *Now* the
1142 3836 1142 1207 650 1254 3836 1254 4460 2443 1254 1623 1254 3836
d.nsn cj n.nsn v.pai.3s d.nsn cj n.nsn v.pai.3s cj cj d.nsf

διακονία τοῦ θανάτου ἐν γράμμασιν ἐντετυπωμένη λίθοις ἐγενήθη ἐν
ministry of death, engraved in letters *engraved* on stones, came with
1355 3836 2505 1963 1877 1207 1963 3345 1181 1877
n.nsf d.gsm n.gsm p.d n.dpn pt.rp.nsf n.dpm v.api.3s p.d

δόξῃ, ὥστε ⌊μὴ δύνασθαι⌋ ἀτενίσαι τοὺς ⌊υἱοὺς Ἰσραὴλ⌋
such glory that the Israelites were unable to gaze steadily *the* *Israelites*
1518 6063 3836 5626 3590 1538 867 3836 5626 2702
n.dsf cj pl f.pp f.aa d.apm n.apm n.gsm

εἰς τὸ πρόσωπον Μωϋσέως διὰ τὴν δόξαν τοῦ προσώπου αὐτοῦ ↱ ↱
into the face of Moses ⌊due to⌋ the glory of his face, *his* fading as
1650 3836 4725 3707 1328 3836 1518 3836 899 4725 899 2934 2934
p.a d.asn n.asn n.gsm p.a d.asf n.asf d.gsn n.gsn r.gsm.3

τὴν καταργουμένην, 8 πῶς οὐχὶ μᾶλλον ἡ διακονία τοῦ
it was, how *{not}* much more glorious will be the ministry of the
3836 2934 4802 4049 3437 1877 1639 1639 3836 1355 3836
d.asf pt.pp.asf pl pl adv.c d.nsf n.nsf d.gsn

πνεύματος ἔσται ⌊ἐν δόξῃ;⌋ 9 εἰ γὰρ τῇ διακονίᾳ τῆς
Spirit? *will be* *glorious* For if *For* there was glory ⌊in the⌋ ministry of
4460 1639 1877 1518 1142 1623 1142 1518 3836 1355 3836
n.gsn v.fmi.3s p.d n.dsf cj cj d.dsf n.dsf d.gsf

κατακρίσεως δόξα, πολλῷ μᾶλλον → περισσεύει ἡ
condemnation, *glory* how much more will the ministry of righteousness exceed *the*
2892 1518 4498 3437 3836 1355 3836 1466 4355 3836
n.gsf n.nsf a.dsn adv.c v.pai.3s d.nsf

διακονία τῆς δικαιοσύνης δόξῃ. 10 καὶ γὰρ
ministry *of* *righteousness* it in glory! For indeed, *For* what had been glorious, in this
1355 3836 1466 1518 1142 2779 1142 3836 1519 1519 1519 1877 4047
n.nsf d.gsf n.gsf n.dsf adv cj

↱ οὐ δεδόξασται τὸ δεδοξασμένον ἐν τούτῳ τῷ μέρει εἵνεκεν τῆς
case has no glory *what had been glorious* *in* *this* *{the}* *case* ⌊because of⌋ the glory
3538 1519 4024 1519 3836 1519 1877 4047 3836 3538 1641 3836 1518
pl v.rpi.3s d.nsn pt.rp.nsn p.d r.dsn d.dsn n.dsn p.g d.gsf

ὑπερβαλλούσης δόξης. 11 εἰ γὰρ τὸ καταργούμενον διὰ δόξης,
that surpasses it. *glory* For if *For* what was fading away ⌊came with⌋ glory,
5650 1518 1142 1623 1142 3836 2934 1328 1518
pt.pa.gsf n.gsf cj cj d.nsn pt.pp.nsn p.g n.gsf

πολλῷ μᾶλλον τὸ μένον ἐν δόξῃ. 12 ἔχοντες
how much more will that ⌊which is permanent⌋ be filled with glory. Therefore ⌊since we have⌋
4498 3437 3836 3531 1877 1518 4036 2400
a.dsn adv.c d.nsn pt.pa.nsn p.d n.dsf pt.pa.npm

NASB

tablets of stone
but on tablets of
human hearts.
4 Such confidence
we have through
Christ toward God.
5 Not that we are
adequate in our-
selves to consider
anything as *coming*
from ourselves,
but our adequacy
is from God, 6 who
also made us ad-
equate *as* servants
of a new covenant,
not of the letter but
of the Spirit; for
the letter kills, but
the Spirit gives life.
7 But if the min-
istry of death, in
letters engraved on
stones, came with
glory, so that the
sons of Israel could
not look intently at
the face of Moses
because of the glo-
ry of his face, fad-
ing *as* it was, 8 how
will the ministry
of the Spirit fail
to be even more
with glory? 9 For
if the ministry of
condemnation has
glory, much more
does the ministry
of righteousness
abound in glory.
10 For indeed what
had glory, in this
case has no glory
because of the glo-
ry that surpasses *it.*
11 For if that which
fades away *was*
with glory, much
more that which re-
mains *is* in glory.
12 Therefore hav-
ing such a hope,

NIV

such a hope, we
are very bold. [13]We
are not like Moses,
who would put a
veil over his face
to prevent the Isra-
elites from seeing
the end of what
was passing away.
[14]But their minds
were made dull,
for to this day the
same veil remains
when the old cov-
enant is read. It
has not been re-
moved, because
only in Christ
is it taken away.
[15]Even to this day
when Moses is
read, a veil covers
their hearts. [16]But
whenever anyone
turns to the Lord,
the veil is taken
away. [17]Now the
Lord is the Spir-
it, and where the
Spirit of the Lord
is, there is free-
dom. [18]And we all,
who with unveiled
faces contemplate[a]
the Lord's glory,
are being trans-
formed into his
image with ever-
increasing glory,
which comes from
the Lord, who is
the Spirit.

Present Weakness and Resurrection Life

4 Therefore,
since through
God's mercy we
have this minis-
try, we do not lose
heart. [2]Rather, we
have renounced se-
cret and shameful

οὖν τοιαύτην ἐλπίδα πολλῇ παρρησίᾳ χρώμεθα 13 καὶ οὐ
Therefore such a hope, we behave with great boldness, *we behave* and not
4036 5525 1828 5968 5968 4498 4244 5968 2779 4024
cj r.asf n.asf a.dsf n.dsf v.pmi.1p cj pl

καθάπερ Μωϋσῆς ἐτίθει κάλυμμα ἐπὶ τὸ πρόσωπον αὐτοῦ πρὸς τὸ
like Moses ⌊who used to put⌋ a veil over *{the}* his face *his* so that ~
2749 3707 5502 2820 2093 3836 899 4725 899 4639 3836
cj n.nsm v.iai.3s n.asn p.a d.asn n.asn r.gsm.3 p.a d.asn

μὴ ἀτενίσαι τοὺς υἱοὺς Ἰσραὴλ εἰς τὸ τέλος τοῦ
the sons of Israel would not gaze *the sons of Israel* at the end of
3836 5626 2702 2702 3590 867 3836 5626 2702 1650 3836 5465 3836
pl f.aa d.apm n.apm n.gsm p.a d.asn n.asn d.gsn

καταργουμένου. 14 ἀλλὰ ἐπωρώθη τὰ νοήματα αὐτῶν. ἄχρι γὰρ
what was fading away. But their minds were closed. *{the} minds their* For until *For*
2934 247 899 3784 4800 3836 3784 899 1142 948 1142
pt.pp.gsn cj v.api.3s d.npn n.npn r.gpm.3 p.g cj

τῆς σήμερον ἡμέρας τὸ αὐτὸ κάλυμμα ἐπὶ τῇ ἀναγνώσει τῆς παλαιᾶς
the present day the same veil remains at the reading of the old
3836 4958 2465 3836 899 2820 3531 2093 3836 342 3836 4094
d.gsf adv n.gsf d.nsn r.nsn n.nsn p.d d.dsf n.dsf d.gsf a.gsf

διαθήκης μένει, ↱ ↱ μὴ ἀνακαλυπτόμενον ὅτι ἐν Χριστῷ
covenant. *remains* Since the veil is not removed, it is clear that only in Christ
1347 3531 365 365 3590 365 4022 1877 5986
n.gsf v.pai.3s pl pt.pp.nsn cj p.d n.dsm

καταργεῖται· 15 ἀλλ᾽ ἕως σήμερον ⌊ἡνίκα ἂν⌋ ἀναγινώσκηται Μωϋσῆς,
is it taken away. But until today, whenever Moses is being read, *Moses* a
2934 247 2401 4958 2471 323 3707 336 3707
v.ppi.3s cj p.g adv cj pl v.pps.3s n.nsm

κάλυμμα ἐπὶ τὴν καρδίαν αὐτῶν κεῖται· 16 ἡνίκα δὲ ἐὰν ἐπιστρέψῃ
veil lies over *{the}* their heart; *their lies* yet whenever *yet* ~ one turns
2820 3023 2093 3836 899 2840 899 3023 1254 2471 1254 1569 2188
n.nsn p.a d.asf n.asf r.gpm.3 v.pmi.3s cj cj pl v.aas.3s

πρὸς κύριον, περιαιρεῖται τὸ κάλυμμα. 17 ὁ δὲ κύριος τὸ
to the Lord, the veil is removed. *the veil* Now the *Now* Lord is the
4639 3261 3836 2820 4311 3836 2820 1254 3836 1254 3261 1639 3836
p.a n.asm v.ppi.3s d.nsn n.nsn d.nsm cj n.nsm d.nsn

πνεῦμά ἐστιν· οὗ δὲ τὸ πνεῦμα → κυρίου, ἐλευθερία. 18
Spirit, *is* and where *and* the Spirit of the Lord is, there is freedom. And
4460 1639 1254 4023 1254 3836 4460 3261 1800 1254
n.nsn v.pai.3s adv cj d.nsn n.nsn n.gsm n.nsf

ἡμεῖς δὲ πάντες ἀνακεκαλυμμένῳ προσώπῳ τὴν δόξαν →
we *And* all, with unveiled faces, beholding as in a mirror the glory of
7005 1254 4246 365 4725 3002 3002 3002 3002 3002 3836 1518
r.np.1 cj a.npm pt.rp.dsn n.dsn d.asf n.asf

κυρίου κατοπτριζόμενοι τὴν αὐτὴν εἰκόνα
the Lord, *beholding as in a mirror* are being transformed into the same image
3261 3002 3565 3565 3565 3565 3836 899 1635
n.gsm pt.pm.npm d.asf r.asf n.asf

μεταμορφούμεθα ἀπὸ δόξης εἰς δόξαν καθάπερ ἀπὸ κυρίου
are being transformed into from one degree of glory to another, just as from the Lord, who
3565 608 1518 1650 1518 2749 608 3261
v.ppi.1p p.g n.gsf p.a n.asf pl p.g n.gsm

πνεύματος.
is the Spirit.
4460
n.gsn

4:1 ⌊διὰ τοῦτο,⌋ ἔχοντες τὴν διακονίαν ταύτην καθὼς
Therefore ⌊since we have⌋ *{the}* this ministry, *this* just as
1328 4047 2400 3836 4047 1355 4047 2777
p.a r.asn pt.pa.npm d.asf n.asf r.asf cj

ἠλεήθημεν, ↱ ↱ οὐκ ἐγκακοῦμεν 2 ἀλλὰ ἀπειπάμεθα τὰ
⌊we have received mercy,⌋ we are not discouraged. But we have renounced *{the}* shameful
1796 1591 1591 4024 1591 247 584 3836 158
v.api.1p pl v.pai.1p cj v.ami.1p d.apn

NASB

we use great
boldness in *our*
speech, [13]and *are*
not like Moses,
who used to put a
veil over his face
so that the sons of
Israel would not
look intently at the
end of what was
fading away. [14]But
their minds were
hardened; for until
this very day at the
reading of the old
covenant the same
veil remains un-
lifted, because it is
removed in Christ.
[15]But to this day
whenever Moses
is read, a veil lies
over their heart;
[16]but whenever a
person turns to the
Lord, the veil is
taken away. [17]Now
the Lord is the
Spirit, and where
the Spirit of the
Lord is, *there* is
liberty. [18]But we all,
with unveiled face,
beholding as in a
mirror the glory of
the Lord, are being
transformed into
the same image
from glory to glory,
just as from the
Lord, the Spirit.

Paul's Apostolic Ministry

[4:1]Therefore, since
we have this minis-
try, as we received
mercy, we do not
lose heart, [2]but we
have renounced the
things hidden

[a] 18 Or *reflect*

NIV

ways; we do not
use deception, nor
do we distort the
word of God. On
the contrary, by
setting forth the
truth plainly we
commend our-
selves to every-
one's conscience
in the sight of God.
3 And even if our
gospel is veiled, it
is veiled to those
who are perishing.
4 The god of this
age has blinded
the minds of un-
believers, so that
they cannot see the
light of the gospel
that displays the
glory of Christ,
who is the im-
age of God. 5 For
what we preach
is not ourselves,
but Jesus Christ
as Lord, and our-
selves as your
servants for Jesus'
sake. 6 For God,
who said, "Let
light shine out of
darkness,"[a] made
his light shine in
our hearts to give
us the light of
the knowledge of
God's glory dis-
played in the face
of Christ.
7 But we have this
treasure in jars
of clay to show
that this all-sur-
passing power is
from God and not
from us. 8 We are
hard pressed on
every side, but
not crushed; per-
plexed, but not
in despair; 9 per-
secuted, but not
abandoned; struck
down, but not de-
stroyed. 10 We al-
ways carry around

κρυπτὰ τῆς αἰσχύνης, ↱ ↱ μὴ ⌞περιπατοῦντες ἐν⌟ πανουργίᾳ μηδὲ
hidden deeds. *{the}* *shameful* We do not practice cunning, nor
3220 3836 158 4344 4344 3590 4344 1877 4111 3593
a.apn d.gsf n.gsf pl pt.pa.npm p.d n.dsf cj

δολοῦντες τὸν λόγον τοῦ θεοῦ ἀλλὰ τῇ φανερώσει τῆς ἀληθείας
⌞do we tamper with⌟ the word of God, but ⌞by the⌟ open declaration of truth
1516 3836 3364 3836 2536 247 3836 5748 3836 237
pt.pa.npm d.asm n.asm d.gsm n.gsm cj d.dsf n.dsf d.gsf n.gsf

συνιστάνοντες ἑαυτοὺς πρὸς πᾶσαν συνείδησιν ἀνθρώπων ἐνώπιον τοῦ
we commend ourselves to every person's conscience *person's* ⌞in the sight of⌟ *{the}*
5319 1571 4639 4246 476 5287 476 1967 3836
pt.pa.npm r.apm.3 p.a a.asf n.asf n.gpm p.g d.gsm

θεοῦ. 3 εἰ δὲ καὶ ἔστιν κεκαλυμμένον τὸ εὐαγγέλιον ἡμῶν,
God. But even if *But* *even* our gospel is veiled, *{the}* *gospel* *our*
2536 1254 2779 1623 1254 2779 7005 2295 1639 2821 3836 2295 7005
n.gsm cj cj adv v.pai.3s pt.rp.nsn d.nsn n.nsn r.gp.1

ἐν τοῖς ἀπολλυμένοις ἐστὶν κεκαλυμμένον, 4 ἐν οἷς
it is veiled only to those who are perishing, *it is* *veiled* in ⌞whose case⌟
1639 1639 2821 1877 3836 660 1639 2821 1877 4005
p.d d.dpm pt.pm.dpm v.pai.3s pt.rp.nsn p.d r.dpm

ὁ θεὸς τοῦ αἰῶνος τούτου ἐτύφλωσεν τὰ νοήματα τῶν ἀπίστων εἰς
the god of this world *this* has blinded the minds of the unbelievers, ⌞so that⌟
3836 2536 3836 4047 172 4047 5604 3836 3784 3836 603 1650
d.nsm n.nsm d.gsm n.gsm r.gsm v.aai.3s d.apn n.apn d.gpm a.gpm p.a

τὸ ↱ μὴ αὐγάσαι τὸν φωτισμὸν τοῦ εὐαγγελίου τῆς δόξης τοῦ Χριστοῦ,
~ they cannot see the light of the gospel of the glory of Christ,
3836 878 3590 878 3836 5895 3836 2295 3836 1518 3836 5986
d.asn pl f.aa d.asm n.asm d.gsn n.gsn d.gsf n.gsf d.gsm n.gsm

ὅς ἐστιν εἰκὼν τοῦ θεοῦ. 5 οὐ γὰρ ἑαυτοὺς κηρύσσομεν
who is the image of God. For we do not *For* proclaim ourselves, *we do proclaim*
4005 1639 1635 3836 2536 1142 3062 3062 4024 1142 3062 1571 3062
r.nsm v.pai.3s n.nsf d.gsm n.gsm pl cj r.apm.1 v.pai.1p

ἀλλὰ Ἰησοῦν Χριστὸν κύριον, ἑαυτοὺς δὲ δούλους ὑμῶν διὰ Ἰησοῦν.
but Jesus Christ as Lord, and ourselves *and* as your slaves *your* for Jesus'
247 2652 5986 3261 1254 1571 1254 7007 1529 7007 1328 2652
cj n.asm n.asm n.asm r.apm.1 cj n.apm r.gp.2 p.a n.asm

↤ 6 ὅτι ὁ θεὸς ὁ εἰπών, ἐκ σκότους φῶς λάμψει, ὃς ⌞ἔλαμψεν
sake. For it is the God who said, ⌞"Out of⌟ darkness light will shine," who has flooded
1328 4022 3836 2536 3836 3306 1666 5030 5890 3290 4005 3290
cj d.nsm n.nsm d.nsm pt.aa.nsm p.g n.gsn n.nsn v.fai.3s r.nsm v.aai.3s

ἐν⌟ ταῖς καρδίαις ἡμῶν πρὸς φωτισμὸν τῆς γνώσεως τῆς δόξης τοῦ
{the} our hearts *our* with the light of the glorious knowledge *{the}* *glorious* of
1877 3836 7005 2840 7005 4639 5895 3836 1518 1194 3836 1518 3836
p.d d.dpf n.dpf r.gp.1 p.a n.asm d.gsf n.gsf d.gsf n.gsf d.gsm

θεοῦ ἐν προσώπῳ[a] Χριστοῦ. 7 ἔχομεν δὲ τὸν θησαυρὸν τοῦτον ἐν
God in the face of Christ. But we have *But* *{the}* this treasure *this* in
2536 1877 4725 5986 1254 2400 1254 3836 4047 2565 4047 1877
n.gsm p.d n.dsn n.gsm v.pai.1p cj d.asm n.asm r.asm p.d

ὀστρακίνοις σκεύεσιν, ἵνα ἡ ὑπερβολὴ τῆς δυνάμεως ᾖ τοῦ θεοῦ καὶ
clay pots, so that the surpassing *{the}* power belongs to God and does
4017 5007 2671 3836 5651 3836 1539 1639 3836 2536 2779
a.dpn n.dpn cj d.nsf n.nsf d.gsf n.gsf v.pas.3s d.gsm n.gsm cj

μὴ ἐξ ἡμῶν· 8 ἐν παντὶ θλιβόμενοι ἀλλ᾽ οὐ
not come from us. We are under pressure from ⌞every side,⌟ *We are under pressure* but not
3590 1666 7005 2567 2567 2567 2567 1877 4246 2567 247 4024
pl p.g r.gp.1 p.d a.dsn pt.pp.npm cj pl

στενοχωρούμενοι, ἀπορούμενοι ἀλλ᾽ οὐκ ἐξαπορούμενοι, 9 διωκόμενοι ἀλλ᾽ οὐκ
crushed; bewildered, but not driven to despair; persecuted, but not
5102 679 247 4024 1989 1503 247 4024
pt.pp.npm pt.pm.npm cj pl pt.pm.npm pt.pp.npm cj pl

ἐγκαταλειπόμενοι, καταβαλλόμενοι ἀλλ᾽ οὐκ ἀπολλύμενοι, 10 πάντοτε
abandoned; knocked down, but not knocked out; always carrying about
1593 2850 247 4024 660 4121 4367 4367
pt.pp.npm pt.pp.npm cj pl pt.pm.npm adv

NASB

because of shame,
not walking in
craftiness or adul-
terating the word
of God, but by the
manifestation of
truth commending
ourselves to every
man's conscience
in the sight of God.
3 And even if our
gospel is veiled, it
is veiled to those
who are perishing,
4 in whose case
the god of this
world has blinded
the minds of the
unbelieving so
that they might
not see the light of
the gospel of the
glory of Christ,
who is the image
of God. 5 For we
do not preach our-
selves but Christ
Jesus as Lord, and
ourselves as your
bond-servants for
Jesus' sake. 6 For
God, who said,
"Light shall shine
out of darkness,"
is the One who has
shone in our hearts
to give the Light of
the knowledge of
the glory of God in
the face of Christ.
7 But we have this
treasure in earthen
vessels, so that the
surpassing great-
ness of the power
will be of God and
not from ourselves;
8 *we are* afflicted in
every way, but not
crushed; perplexed,
but not despairing;
9 persecuted, but not
forsaken; struck
down, but not de-
stroyed; 10 always
carrying about in

[a] 6 Gen. 1:3

[a] Ἰησοῦ included by UBS after προσώπῳ.

NIV

in our body the
death of Jesus,
so that the life of
Jesus may also be
revealed in our
body. 11 For we
who are alive are
always being given
over to death for
Jesus' sake, so that
his life may also
be revealed in our
mortal body. 12 So
then, death is at
work in us, but life
is at work in you.
13 It is written: "I
believed; therefore
I have spoken."[a]
Since we have that
same spirit of[b]
faith, we also be-
lieve and therefore
speak, 14 because
we know that the
one who raised the
Lord Jesus from
the dead will also
raise us with Jesus
and present us
with you to him-
self. 15 All this is
for your benefit, so
that the grace that
is reaching more
and more people
may cause thanks-
giving to overflow
to the glory of
God.
16 Therefore we
do not lose heart.
Though outward-
ly we are wasting
away, yet inwardly
we are being re-
newed day by day.
17 For our light and
momentary trou-
bles are achieving
for us an eternal
glory that far out-
weighs them all.
18 So we fix our
eyes

τὴν νέκρωσιν τοῦ Ἰησοῦ ἐν τῷ σώματι περιφέροντες, ἵνα
in the body the dying of Jesus, *in the body carrying about* so that the life
1877 3836 5393 3836 3740 3836 2652 1877 3836 5393 4367 2671 3836 2437
d.asf n.asf d.gsm n.gsm p.d d.dsn n.dsn pt.pa.npm cj

καὶ ἡ ζωὴ τοῦ Ἰησοῦ ἐν τῷ σώματι ἡμῶν
of Jesus may also *the life of Jesus* be displayed in *{the}* our bodies. *our*
3836 2652 5746 2779 3836 2437 3836 2652 5746 5746 1877 3836 7005 5393 7005
adv d.nsf n.nsf d.gsm n.gsm p.d d.dsn n.dsn r.gp.1

φανερωθῇ. 11 ἀεὶ γὰρ ἡμεῖς οἱ ζῶντες
may be displayed For we who live are constantly *For we who live* being handed over
5746 1142 7005 3836 2409 4140 107 1142 7005 3836 2409 4140 4140 4140
v.aps.3s adv cj r.np.1 d.npm pt.pa.npm

εἰς θάνατον παραδιδόμεθα διὰ Ἰησοῦν, ἵνα καὶ ἡ
to death *are being handed over* ⌊for the sake of⌋ Jesus, so that the life of Jesus also *the*
1650 2505 4140 1328 2652 2671 3836 2437 3836 2652 2779 3836
p.a n.asm v.ppi.1p p.a n.asm cj adv d.nsf

ζωὴ τοῦ Ἰησοῦ φανερωθῇ ἐν τῇ θνητῇ σαρκὶ ἡμῶν. 12 ὥστε ὁ
life of Jesus may be manifested in *{the}* our mortal flesh. *our* Thus *{the}*
2437 3836 2652 5746 1877 3836 7005 2570 4922 7005 6063 3836
n.nsf d.gsm n.gsm v.aps.3s p.d d.dsf a.dsf n.dsf r.gp.1 cj d.nsm

θάνατος ἐν ἡμῖν ἐνεργεῖται, ἡ δὲ ζωὴ ἐν ὑμῖν. 13
death is at work in us, *is at work* *{the}* but life in you. But
2505 1919 1919 1919 1877 7005 1919 3836 1254 2437 1877 7007 1254
n.nsm p.d r.dp.1 v.pmi.3s d.nsf cj n.nsf p.d r.dp.2

ἔχοντες δὲ τὸ αὐτὸ πνεῦμα τῆς πίστεως κατὰ τὸ γεγραμμένον, ἐπίστευσα,
⌊since we have⌋ *But* the same spirit of faith as that which stands written, "I believed;
2400 1254 3836 899 4460 3836 4411 2848 3836 1211 4409
pt.pa.npm cj d.asn r.asn n.asn d.gsf n.gsf p.a d.asn pt.rp.asn v.aai.1s

διὸ ἐλάλησα, καὶ ἡμεῖς πιστεύομεν, διὸ καὶ λαλοῦμεν, 14 εἰδότες ὅτι
therefore I spoke," we too *we* believe, and thus *and* we speak, knowing that
1475 3281 7005 2779 7005 4409 2779 1475 2779 3281 3857 4022
cj v.aai.1s adv r.np.1 v.pai.1p cj adv v.pai.1p pt.ra.npm cj

ὁ ἐγείρας τὸν κύριον[a] Ἰησοῦν καὶ ἡμᾶς σὺν Ἰησοῦ ἐγερεῖ
the ⌊one who raised⌋ the Lord Jesus will raise us also *us* with Jesus *will raise*
3836 1586 3836 3261 2652 1586 1586 7005 2779 7005 5250 2652 1586
d.nsm pt.aa.nsm d.asm n.asm n.asm cj r.ap.1 p.d n.dsm v.fai.3s

καὶ παραστήσει σὺν ὑμῖν. ↰ 15 τὰ γὰρ πάντα ← δι'
and bring us, ⌊together with⌋ you, before him. *{the}* For all these things are for
2779 4225 5250 7007 4225 3836 1142 4246 1328
cj v.fai.3s p.d r.dp.2 d.npn cj a.npn p.a

ὑμᾶς, ↰ ἵνα ↱ ἡ χάρις πλεονάσασα διὰ τῶν πλειόνων
your sake, so that as *{the}* grace extends to *{the}* ⌊more and more people,⌋ it may
7007 1328 2671 4429 3836 5921 4429 1328 3836 4498 4355 4355
r.ap.2 cj d.nsf n.nsf pt.aa.nsf p.g d.gpm a.gpm.c

τὴν εὐχαριστίαν περισσεύσῃ εἰς τὴν δόξαν τοῦ θεοῦ. 16 διὸ ↱ ↱ οὐκ
increase *{the}* thanksgiving *it may increase* to the glory of God. So we are not
4355 3836 2374 4355 1650 3836 1518 3836 2536 1475 1591 1591 4024
d.asf n.asf v.aas.3s p.a d.asf n.asf d.gsm n.gsm cj pl

ἐγκακοῦμεν, ἀλλ' εἰ καὶ ὁ ἔξω ἡμῶν ἄνθρωπος διαφθείρεται, ἀλλ'
discouraged, but even if *even {the}* our outward *our* man is wasting away, *{but}*
1591 247 2779 1623 2779 3836 7005 2032 7005 476 1425 247
v.pai.1p cj cj adv d.nsm adv r.gp.1 n.nsm v.ppi.3s cj

ὁ ἔσω ἡμῶν ἀνακαινοῦται ἡμέρᾳ καὶ ἡμέρᾳ. 17 τὸ γὰρ παραυτίκα
{the} our inward *our* man is being renewed day by day. *{the}* For our momentary
3836 7005 2276 7005 363 2465 2779 2465 3836 1142 7005 4194
d.nsm adv r.gp.1 v.ppi.3s n.dsf cj n.dsf d.nsn cj adv

ἐλαφρὸν τῆς θλίψεως ἡμῶν καθ'
lightness of affliction *our* is producing for us an eternal weight of glory far
1787 3836 2568 7005 2981 2981 7005 7005 173 983 1518 1518 2848
a.nsn d.gsf n.gsf r.gp.1 p.a

ὑπερβολὴν εἰς ὑπερβολὴν αἰώνιον βάρος δόξης κατεργάζεται ἡμῖν, 18
beyond all comparison, *eternal weight of glory is producing for us* as we look
5651 1650 5651 173 983 1518 2981 7005 5023 7005 5023
n.asf p.a n.asf a.asn n.asn n.gsf v.pmi.3s r.dp.1

NASB

the body the dying
of Jesus, so that the
life of Jesus also
may be manifested
in our body. 11 For
we who live are
constantly being
delivered over to
death for Jesus'
sake, so that the
life of Jesus also
may be manifested
in our mortal flesh.
12 So death works in
us, but life in you.
13 But having the
same spirit of faith,
according to what
is written, "I BE-
LIEVED, THEREFORE I
SPOKE," we also be-
lieve, therefore we
also speak, 14 know-
ing that He who
raised the Lord
Jesus will raise us
also with Jesus and
will present us with
you. 15 For all things
are for your sakes,
so that the grace
which is spread-
ing to more and
more people may
cause the giving of
thanks to abound to
the glory of God.
16 Therefore we do
not lose heart, but
though our outer
man is decaying,
yet our inner man
is being renewed
day by day. 17 For
momentary, light
affliction is pro-
ducing for us an
eternal weight of
glory far beyond
all comparison,
18 while we look

[a] 13 Psalm 116:10 (see Septuagint)
[b] 13 Or *Spirit-given*

[a] κύριον omitted in NET.

NIV

not on what is
seen, but on what
is unseen, since
what is seen is
temporary, but
what is unseen is
eternal.

Awaiting the New Body

5 For we know
that if the
earthly tent we live
in is destroyed,
we have a build-
ing from God, an
eternal house in
heaven, not built
by human hands.
[2]Meanwhile we
groan, longing to
be clothed instead
with our heavenly
dwelling, [3]be-
cause when we
are clothed, we
will not be found
naked. [4]For while
we are in this tent,
we groan and are
burdened, because
we do not wish to
be unclothed but to
be clothed instead
with our heavenly
dwelling, so that
what is mortal
may be swallowed
up by life. [5]Now
the one who has
fashioned us for
this very purpose
is God, who has
given us the Spirit
as a deposit, guar-
anteeing what is to
come.
[6]Therefore we are
always confident
and know that as
long as we are at
home in the body
we are away from
the Lord. [7]For
we live by faith,
not by sight. [8]We
are confident, I
say, and would
prefer to be away
from the body
and at home with
the Lord. [9]So we
make it our goal to
please him, wheth-
er we are at home
in the body or
away from it.

μὴ σκοπούντων ἡμῶν τὰ βλεπόμενα ἀλλὰ τὰ ⌊μὴ βλεπόμενα·⌋ τὰ
not *as look on* *we* on what can be seen, but on the unseen; for what
3590 5023 7005 5023 3836 1063 247 3836 3590 1063 1142 3836
pl pt.pa.gpm r.gp.1 d.apn pt.pp.apn cj d.apn pl pt.pp.apn d.npn

γὰρ βλεπόμενα πρόσκαιρα, τὰ δὲ μὴ βλεπόμενα αἰώνια.
for can be seen is temporary, but what *but* cannot be seen is eternal.
1142 1063 4672 1254 3836 1254 3590 1063 173
cj pt.pp.npn a.npn d.npn cj pl pt.pp.npn a.npn

5:1 οἴδαμεν γὰρ ὅτι ἐὰν ἡ ἐπίγειος ἡμῶν οἰκία τοῦ σκήνους
For we know *For* that if *{the}* our earthly *our* house, the ⌊tent we live in,⌋
1142 3857 1142 4022 1569 3836 7005 2103 7005 3864 3836 5011
v.rai.1p cj cj cj d.nsf a.nsf r.gp.1 n.nsf d.gsn n.gsn

καταλυθῇ, οἰκοδομὴν ἐκ θεοῦ ἔχομεν, οἰκίαν ἀχειροποίητον
is taken down, we have a building from God, *we have* a house not made with hands,
2907 2400 2400 3869 1666 2536 2400 3864 942
v.aps.3s n.asf p.g n.gsm v.pai.1p n.asf a.asf

αἰώνιον ἐν τοῖς οὐρανοῖς. 2 καὶ γὰρ ἐν τούτῳ στενάζομεν
eternal, in the heavens. For indeed *For* in this tent we groan, longing to
173 1877 3836 4041 1142 2779 1142 1877 4047 5100 2160 2086
a.asf p.d d.dpm n.dpm adv cj p.d r.dsn v.pai.1p

τὸ οἰκητήριον ἡμῶν τὸ ⌊ἐξ οὐρανοῦ⌋ ἐπενδύσασθαι
put on *{the}* our heavenly dwelling place, *our* *{the}* *heavenly* *to put on*
2086 2086 3836 7005 1666 3863 7005 3836 1666 4041 2086
d.asn n.asn r.gp.1 d.asn p.g n.gsm f.am

ἐπιποθοῦντες, 3 ⌊εἴ γε καὶ⌋ ἐνδυσάμενοι[a] οὐ
longing so that ⌊after we have taken off⌋ our earthly house we will not be
2160 1623 1145 2779 1907 2351 2351 4024 2351
pt.pa.npm cj pl adv pt.am.npm pl

γυμνοὶ εὑρεθησόμεθα. 4 καὶ γὰρ ➝ οἱ ὄντες ἐν τῷ σκήνει στενάζομεν
found naked. *we will be found* *{also}* For while we remain in this tent, we groan
2351 1218 2351 2779 1142 1639 3836 1639 1877 3836 5011 5100
a.npm v.fpi.1p adv cj d.npm pt.pa.npm p.d d.dsn n.dsn v.pai.1p

βαρούμενοι, ⌊ἐφ' ᾧ⌋ οὐ θέλομεν ἐκδύσασθαι ἀλλ' ἐπενδύσασθαι, ἵνα
and are burdened, not because *not* we want to be unclothed, but clothed, so that
976 4024 2093 4005 4024 2527 1694 247 2086 2671
pt.pp.npm p.d r.dsn pl v.pai.1p f.am cj f.am cj

καταποθῇ τὸ θνητὸν ὑπὸ τῆς ζωῆς. 5 ὁ δὲ
what is mortal ⌊may be swallowed up⌋ *what is mortal* by *{the}* life. The *{and}*
3836 2570 2570 2927 3836 2570 5679 3836 2437 3836 1254
v.aps.3s d.nsn a.nsn p.g d.gsf n.gsf d.nsm cj

κατεργασάμενος ἡμᾶς εἰς ➝ αὐτὸ τοῦτο θεός, ὁ δοὺς ἡμῖν τὸν
one who prepared us for this very thing is God, who gave us the Spirit as a
2981 7005 1650 4047 899 4047 2536 3836 1443 7005 3836 4460 3836
pt.am.nsm r.ap.1 p.a r.asn r.asn n.nsm d.nsm pt.aa.nsm r.dp.1 d.asm

ἀρραβῶνα τοῦ πνεύματος. 6 ➝ ➝ θαρροῦντες οὖν πάντοτε καὶ
pledge. *the* *Spirit* Therefore we are always confident, *Therefore* *always* *{and}*
775 3836 4460 4036 4121 2509 4036 4121 2779
n.asm d.gsn n.gsn pt.pa.npm cj adv cj

εἰδότες ὅτι ἐνδημοῦντες ἐν τῷ σώματι ἐκδημοῦμεν ἀπὸ τοῦ κυρίου· 7
knowing that ⌊while we are at home⌋ in the body we are away from the Lord, for
3857 4022 1897 1877 3836 5393 1685 608 3836 3261 1142
pt.ra.npm cj pt.pa.npm p.d d.dsn n.dsn v.pai.1p p.g d.gsm n.gsm

διὰ πίστεως γὰρ περιπατοῦμεν, οὐ διὰ εἴδους· 8 θαρροῦμεν δὲ
we live by faith, *for* *we live* not by sight. Thus we are confident *Thus*
4344 4344 1328 4411 1142 4344 4024 1328 1626 1254 2509 1254
p.g n.gsf cj v.pai.1p pl p.g n.gsn v.pai.1p cj

καὶ εὐδοκοῦμεν μᾶλλον ἐκδημῆσαι ἐκ τοῦ σώματος καὶ ἐνδημῆσαι πρὸς τὸν
and would rather be away from the body and at home with the
2779 2305 3437 1685 1666 3836 5393 2779 1897 4639 3836
cj v.pai.1p adv.c f.aa p.g d.gsn n.gsn cj f.aa p.a d.asm

κύριον. 9 διὸ καὶ φιλοτιμούμεθα, εἴτε ἐνδημοῦντες εἴτε ἐκδημοῦντες,
Lord. So then we make it our goal, whether at home or away, to be
3261 1475 2779 5818 1664 1897 1664 1685 1639 1639
n.asm cj adv v.pmi.1p cj pt.pa.npm cj pt.pa.npm

NASB

not at the things
which are seen, but
at the things which
are not seen; for
the things which
are seen are tempo-
ral, but the things
which are not seen
are eternal.

The Temporal and Eternal

5:1 For we know
that if the earthly
tent which is our
house is torn down,
we have a build-
ing from God, a
house not made
with hands, eternal
in the heavens.
[2]For indeed in this
house we groan,
longing to be
clothed with our
dwelling from
heaven, [3]inasmuch
as we, having put
it on, will not be
found naked. [4]For
indeed while we
are in this tent,
we groan, being
burdened, because
we do not want to
be unclothed but
to be clothed, so
that what is mortal
will be swallowed
up by life. [5]Now
He who prepared
us for this very
purpose is God,
who gave to us the
Spirit as a pledge.
[6]Therefore, be-
ing always of
good courage, and
knowing that while
we are at home in
the body we are
absent from the
Lord— [7]for we
walk by faith, not
by sight— [8]we are
of good courage,
I say, and prefer
rather to be absent
from the body and
to be at home with
the Lord. [9]There-
fore we also have
as our ambition,
whether at home or
absent, to be

[a] ἐνδυσάμενοι TNIV, NET. ἐκδυσάμενοι UBS.

NIV

10For we must all
appear before the
judgment seat of
Christ, so that
each of us may re-
ceive what is due
us for the things
done while in the
body, whether
good or bad.

The Ministry of Reconciliation

11Since, then, we
know what it is to
fear the Lord, we
try to persuade
others. What we
are is plain to
God, and I hope
it is also plain to
your conscience.
12We are not try-
ing to commend
ourselves to you
again, but are giv-
ing you an oppor-
tunity to take pride
in us, so that you
can answer those
who take pride in
what is seen rath-
er than in what is
in the heart. 13If
we are "out of our
mind," as some
say, it is for God;
if we are in our
right mind, it is for
you. 14For Christ's
love compels us,
because we are
convinced that one
died for all, and
therefore all died.
15And he died for
all, that those who
live should no lon-
ger live for them-
selves but for him
who died for them
and was raised
again.
16So from now
on we regard no
one from a world-
ly point of view.
Though we once
regarded Christ in
this way, we

εὐάρεστοι αὐτῷ εἶναι. 10 τοὺς γὰρ πάντας ἡμᾶς φανερωθῆναι δεῖ
pleasing to him. *to be* *{the}* For we must all *we* appear *must*
2298 899 1639 3836 1142 7005 1256 4246 7005 5746 1256
a.npm r.dsm.3 f.pa d.apm cj a.apm r.ap.1 f.ap v.pai.3s

ἔμπροσθεν τοῦ βήματος τοῦ Χριστοῦ, ἵνα κομίσηται ἕκαστος τὰ
before the ⌊judgment seat⌋ of Christ, so that each one may be repaid *each one* *{the}*
1869 3836 1037 3836 5986 2671 1667 1667 3152 1667 3836
p.g d.gsn n.gsn d.gsm n.gsm cj v.ams.3s r.nsm d.apn

διὰ τοῦ σώματος πρὸς ἃ ἔπραξεν, εἴτε
according to what he has done ⌊while in⌋ the body, *according to* *what* *he has done* whether
4639 4639 4005 4556 4556 4556 1328 3836 5393 4639 4005 4556 1664
p.g d.gsn n.gsn p.a r.apn v.aai.3s cj

ἀγαθὸν εἴτε φαῦλον. 11 εἰδότες οὖν τὸν φόβον τοῦ κυρίου
good or bad. Therefore ⌊since we know⌋ *Therefore* the fear of the Lord, we
19 1664 5765 4036 3857 4036 3836 5832 3836 3261 4275
a.asn cj a.asn pt.ra.npm cj d.asm n.asm d.gsm n.gsm

ἀνθρώπους πείθομεν, θεῷ δὲ
attempt to persuade others; *we attempt to persuade* we stand open to God, *{and}*
4275 4275 4275 476 4275 5746 5746 5746 2536 1254
n.apm v.pai.1p n.dsm cj

πεφανερώμεθα· ἐλπίζω δὲ καὶ ἐν ταῖς συνειδήσεσιν ὑμῶν πεφανερῶσθαι.
we stand open and, I trust, *and* also to *{the}* your conscience. *your* *{to stand open}*
5746 1254 1827 1254 2779 1877 3836 7007 5287 7007 5746
v.rpi.1p v.pai.1s cj adv p.d d.dpf n.dpf r.gp.2 f.rp

12 οὐ πάλιν ἑαυτοὺς συνιστάνομεν ὑμῖν ἀλλὰ
For we are not again recommending ourselves *we are recommending* to you but giving you
5319 5319 4024 4099 5319 1571 5319 7007 247 1443 7007
pl adv r.apm.1 v.pai.1p r.dp.2 cj

ἀφορμὴν διδόντες ὑμῖν καυχήματος ὑπὲρ ἡμῶν, ἵνα ἔχητε
an occasion *giving* *you* to boast on our behalf, so that ⌊you may be able⌋
929 1443 7007 3017 5642 7005 5642 2671 2400
n.asf pt.pa.npm r.dp.2 n.gsn p.g r.gp.1 cj v.pas.2p

πρὸς τοὺς ἐν προσώπῳ καυχωμένους καὶ μὴ ἐν
to answer those who boast ⌊of what⌋ is seen *who boast* and not of what is in the
4639 3836 3016 3016 1877 4725 3016 2779 3590 1877
p.a d.apm p.d n.dsn pt.pm.apm cj pl p.d

καρδίᾳ. 13 εἴτε γὰρ ἐξέστημεν, θεῷ· εἴτε σωφρονοῦμεν,
heart. For if *For* ⌊we are out of our minds,⌋ it is for God; if ⌊we are of sound mind,⌋ it is
2840 1142 1664 1142 2014 2536 1664 5404
n.dsf cj cj v.aai.1p n.dsm cj v.pai.1p

ὑμῖν. 14 ἡ γὰρ ἀγάπη τοῦ Χριστοῦ συνέχει ἡμᾶς, κρίναντας
for you. For the *For* love of Christ controls us, ⌊since we have concluded⌋
7007 1142 3836 1142 27 3836 5986 5309 7005 3212
r.dp.2 d.nsf cj n.nsf d.gsm n.gsm v.pai.3s r.ap.1 pt.aa.apm

τοῦτο, ὅτι εἷς ὑπὲρ πάντων ἀπέθανεν, ἄρα οἱ πάντες ἀπέθανον·
this: that one has died for all; *has died* therefore *{the}* all have died.
4047 4022 1651 633 633 5642 4246 633 726 3836 4246 633
r.asn cj a.nsm p.g a.gpm v.aai.3s cj d.npm a.npm v.aai.3p

15 καὶ ὑπὲρ πάντων ἀπέθανεν, ἵνα οἱ ζῶντες μηκέτι
And he died for all *he died* so that those ⌊who are living⌋ might no longer live
2779 633 633 5642 4246 633 2671 3836 2409 2409 3600 2409
cj p.g a.gpm v.aai.3s cj d.npm pt.pa.npm adv

ἑαυτοῖς ζῶσιν ἀλλὰ τῷ ὑπὲρ αὐτῶν ἀποθανόντι καὶ ἐγερθέντι.
for themselves *might live* but ⌊for the⌋ one who died for them *one who died* and was raised.
1571 2409 247 3836 633 633 633 5642 899 633 2779 1586
r.dpm.3 v.pas.3p cj d.dsm p.g r.gpm.3 pt.aa.dsm cj pt.ap.dsm

16 ὥστε ἡμεῖς ἀπὸ τοῦ νῦν οὐδένα οἴδαμεν κατὰ σάρκα·
So from now on we *from* *{the}* *now* regard no one *regard* ⌊according to⌋ the flesh.
6063 608 3814 7005 608 3836 3814 3857 4029 3857 2848 4922
cj r.np.1 p.g d.gsn adv a.asm v.rai.1p p.a n.asf

εἰ καὶ ἐγνώκαμεν κατὰ σάρκα Χριστόν, ἀλλὰ νῦν
Even though *Even* we once regarded Christ ⌊according to⌋ the flesh, *Christ* yet now we
2779 1623 2779 1182 5986 2848 4922 5986 247 3814 1182
cj adv v.rai.1p p.a n.asf n.asm cj adv

NASB

pleasing to Him.
10For we must all
appear before the
judgment seat of
Christ, so that
each one may be
recompensed for
his deeds in the
body, according to
what he has done,
whether good or
bad.
11Therefore,
knowing the fear of
the Lord, we per-
suade men, but we
are made manifest
to God; and I hope
that we are made
manifest also in
your consciences.
12We are not again
commending
ourselves to you
but *are* giving you
an occasion to be
proud of us, so that
you will have *an*
answer for those
who take pride in
appearance and
not in heart. 13For
if we are beside
ourselves, it is for
God; if we are of
sound mind, it
is for you. 14For
the love of Christ
controls us, having
concluded this, that
one died for all,
therefore all died;
15and He died for
all, so that they
who live might
no longer live for
themselves, but for
Him who died and
rose again on their
behalf.
16Therefore from
now on we recog-
nize no one accord-
ing to the flesh;
even though we
have known Christ
according to the
flesh, yet now

NIV

do so no longer.
17Therefore, if any-
one is in Christ,
the new creation
has come:[a] The
old has gone, the
new is here! 18All
this is from God,
who reconciled us
to himself through
Christ and gave
us the ministry
of reconciliation:
19that God was
reconciling the
world to himself in
Christ, not count-
ing people's sins
against them. And
he has committed
to us the message
of reconciliation.
20We are therefore
Christ's ambas-
sadors, as though
God were making
his appeal through
us. We implore
you on Christ's be-
half: Be reconciled
to God. 21God
made him who
had no sin to be
sin[b] for us, so that
in him we might
become the righ-
teousness of God.

6 As God's co-
workers we
urge you not to re-
ceive God's grace
in vain. 2For he
says,

"In the time of
my favor I
heard you,
and in the day
of salvation
I helped
you."[c]

I tell you, now is
the time of God's
favor, now is the
day of salvation.

Paul's Hardships

3We put no stum-
bling block in
anyone's path, so
that our

[a] 17 Or *Christ, that person is a new creation.*
[b] 21 Or *be a sin offering*
[c] 2 Isaiah 49:8

οὐκέτι γινώσκομεν. 17 ὥστε εἴ τις ἐν Χριστῷ,
regard him in that way no longer. *we regard* Therefore if anyone is in Christ, there is
1182 4033 1182 6063 1623 5516 1877 5986
adv v.pai.1p cj cj r.nsm p.d n.dsm

καινὴ κτίσις· τὰ ἀρχαῖα παρῆλθεν, ἰδοὺ γέγονεν καινά·
a new creation; what is old has passed away; behold, what is new has come! *what is new*
2785 3232 3836 792 4216 2627 2785 2785 2785 1181 2785
a.nsf n.nsf d.npn a.npn v.aai.3s j v.rai.3s a.npn

18 τὰ δὲ πάντα ἐκ τοῦ θεοῦ τοῦ καταλλάξαντος ἡμᾶς ἑαυτῷ διὰ Χριστοῦ
{the} And all this is from *{the}* God, who has reconciled us to himself through Christ
3836 1254 4246 1666 3836 2536 3836 2904 7005 1571 1328 5986
d.npn cj a.npn p.g d.gsm n.gsm d.gsm pt.aa.gsm r.ap.1 r.dsm.3 p.g n.gsm

καὶ δόντος ἡμῖν τὴν διακονίαν τῆς καταλλαγῆς, 19 ὡς ὅτι θεὸς ἦν ἐν
and given us the ministry of reconciliation; ⌞that is,⌟ God was in
2779 1443 7005 3836 1355 3836 2903 6055 4022 2536 1639 1877
cj pt.aa.gsm r.dp.1 d.asf n.asf d.gsf n.gsf pl cj n.nsm v.iai.3s p.d

Χριστῷ κόσμον καταλλάσσων ἑαυτῷ, μὴ λογιζόμενος
Christ reconciling the world *reconciling* to himself, not counting their trespasses
5986 2904 3180 2904 1571 3590 3357 899 4183
n.dsm n.asm pt.pa.nsm r.dsm.3 pl pt.pm.nsm

αὐτοῖς τὰ παραπτώματα αὐτῶν καὶ θέμενος ἐν ἡμῖν τὸν λόγον
⌞against them.⌟ *{the}* *trespasses* *their* And he has entrusted us with *us* the message
899 3836 4183 899 2779 5502 7005 1877 7005 3836 3364
r.dpm.3 d.apn n.apn r.gpm.3 cj pt.am.nsm p.d r.dp.1 d.asm n.asm

τῆς καταλλαγῆς. 20 ὑπὲρ Χριστοῦ οὖν
of reconciliation. Therefore we are ambassadors for Christ, *Therefore*
3836 2903 4036 4563 4563 4563 5642 5986 4036
d.gsf n.gsf p.g n.gsm cj

πρεσβεύομεν ὡς τοῦ θεοῦ παρακαλοῦντος δι' ἡμῶν· δεόμεθα
we are ambassadors ⌞as though⌟ *{the}* God were making his appeal through us. We implore you
4563 6055 3836 2536 4151 1328 7005 1289
v.pai.1p pl d.gsm n.gsm pt.pa.gsm p.g r.gp.1 v.pmi.1p

ὑπὲρ Χριστοῦ, καταλλάγητε τῷ θεῷ. 21 τὸν μὴ γνόντα
⌞on behalf of⌟ Christ, "Be reconciled to God." He made him who knew no *who knew*
5642 5986 2904 3836 2536 4472 4472 3836 1182 1182 3590 1182
p.g n.gsm v.apm.2p d.dsm n.dsm d.asm pl pt.aa.asm

ἁμαρτίαν ὑπὲρ ἡμῶν ἁμαρτίαν ἐποίησεν, ἵνα ἡμεῖς
sin to be a sin-offering for us, *sin-offering* *He made* so that in him we
281 281 5642 7005 281 4472 2671 1877 899 7005
n.asf p.g r.gp.1 n.asf v.aai.3s cj r.np.1

γενώμεθα δικαιοσύνη θεοῦ ἐν αὐτῷ.
might become the righteousness of God. *in* *him*
1181 1466 2536 1877 899
v.ams.1p n.nsf n.gsm p.d r.dsm.3

6:1 συνεργοῦντες δὲ καὶ παρακαλοῦμεν μὴ
Thus as coworkers with him, *Thus* *{also}* we urge you not to receive the
1254 5300 1254 2779 4151 7007 3590 1312 1312 3836
pt.pa.npm cj adv v.pai.1p pl

εἰς κενὸν τὴν χάριν τοῦ θεοῦ δέξασθαι ὑμᾶς· 2 λέγει γάρ, →
grace of God in vain. *the* *grace* *of* *God* *to receive* *you* For he says, *For* "In the
5921 3836 2536 1650 3031 3836 5921 3836 2536 1312 7007 1142 3306 1142
p.a a.asn d.asf n.asf d.gsm n.gsm f.am r.ap.2 v.pai.3s cj

καιρῷ → δεκτῷ ἐπήκουσά σου καὶ ἐν ἡμέρᾳ σωτηρίας ἐβοήθησά σοι. ἰδοὺ
time of my favor I heard you, *{and}* in the day of salvation I helped you." Behold,
2789 1283 2052 5148 2779 1877 2465 5401 1070 5148 2627
n.dsm a.dsm v.aai.1s r.gs.2 cj p.d n.dsf n.gsf v.aai.1s r.ds.2 j

νῦν καιρὸς εὐπρόσδεκτος, ἰδοὺ νῦν ἡμέρα σωτηρίας. 3
now is the acceptable time; *acceptable* behold, now is the day of salvation! We do
3814 2347 2789 2347 2627 3814 2465 5401 1443 1443
adv n.nsm a.nsm j adv n.nsf n.gsf

μηδεμίαν ← ἐν μηδενὶ διδόντες προσκοπήν, ἵνα
not put a stumbling block in ⌞anyone's way,⌟ *We do put* *stumbling block* so that our
3594 1443 4683 4683 1877 3594 1443 4683 2671 3836
a.asf p.d a.dsn pt.pa.npm n.asf cj

NASB

we know *Him in
this way* no longer.
17Therefore if any-
one is in Christ, *he
is* a new creature;
the old things
passed away;
behold, new things
have come. 18Now
all *these* things are
from God, who
reconciled us to
Himself through
Christ and gave
us the ministry
of reconciliation,
19namely, that
God was in Christ
reconciling the
world to Himself,
not counting their
trespasses against
them, and He
has committed
to us the word of
reconciliation.
20Therefore, we
are ambassadors
for Christ, as
though God were
making an appeal
through us; we beg
you on behalf of
Christ, be recon-
ciled to God. 21He
made Him who
knew no sin *to be*
sin on our behalf,
so that we might
become the righ-
teousness of God
in Him.

Their Ministry Commended

6:1And working
together *with Him,*
we also urge you
not to receive the
grace of God in
vain— 2for He
says,

"At the accept-
able time I
listened to
you,
And on the
day of salva-
tion I helped
you."

Behold, now is
"the acceptable
time," behold, now
is "the day of sal-
vation"— 3giving
no cause for of-
fense in anything,

NIV

ministry will
not be discred-
ited. [4]Rather, as
servants of God
we commend
ourselves in ev-
ery way: in great
endurance; in
troubles, hardships
and distresses;
[5]in beatings, im-
prisonments and
riots; in hard work,
sleepless nights
and hunger; [6]in
purity, under-
standing, patience
and kindness; in
the Holy Spir-
it and in sincere
love; [7]in truthful
speech and in the
power of God;
with weapons of
righteousness in
the right hand
and in the left;
[8]through glory
and dishonor, bad
report and good
report; genuine,
yet regarded as im-
postors; [9]known,
yet regarded as
unknown; dying,
and yet we live on;
beaten, and yet
not killed; [10]sor-
rowful, yet always
rejoicing; poor, yet
making many rich;
having nothing,
and yet possessing
everything.
[11]We have spo-
ken freely to you,
Corinthians, and
opened wide our
hearts to you. [12]We
are not withhold-
ing our affection
from you, but you
are withholding
yours from us.
[13]As a fair ex-
change — I speak
as to my chil-
dren — open wide
your hearts also.

↱ μὴ μωμηθῇ ἡ διακονία, [4]ἀλλ᾽
ministry may not be faulted. *our ministry* Rather, as servants of God, we commend
1355 3699 3590 3699 3836 1355 247 6055 1356 2536 2536 5319 5319
pl v.aps.3s d.nsf n.nsf cj

ἐν παντὶ συνιστάντες ἑαυτοὺς ὡς θεοῦ διάκονοι, ἐν ὑπομονῇ
ourselves in ⌊every way:⌋ *we commend ourselves as of God servants* in great endurance,
1571 1877 4246 5319 1571 6055 2536 1356 1877 4498 5705
p.d a.dsn pt.pa.npm r.apm.1 pl n.gsm n.npm p.d n.dsf

πολλῇ, ἐν θλίψεσιν, ἐν ἀνάγκαις, ἐν στενοχωρίαις, [5]ἐν πληγαῖς, ἐν
great in times of affliction, *{in}* hardship, and *{in}* distress; in beatings, in
4498 1877 2568 1877 340 1877 5103 1877 4435 1877
a.dsf p.d n.dpf p.d n.dpf p.d n.dpf p.d n.dpf p.d

φυλακαῖς, ἐν ἀκαταστασίαις, ἐν κόποις, ἐν ἀγρυπνίαις, ἐν
imprisonments, in riots, in labors, in times of sleeplessness and *{in}*
5871 1877 189 1877 3160 1877 71 1877
n.dpf p.d n.dpf p.d n.dpm p.d n.dpf p.d

νηστείαις, [6]ἐν ἁγνότητι, ἐν γνώσει, ἐν μακροθυμίᾳ, ἐν χρηστότητι, ἐν
hunger; by purity, by knowledge, by patience, by kindness, by the
3763 1877 55 1877 1194 1877 3429 1877 5983 1877
n.dpf p.d n.dsf p.d n.dsf p.d n.dsf p.d n.dsf p.d

πνεύματι ἁγίῳ, ἐν ἀγάπῃ ἀνυποκρίτῳ, [7]ἐν λόγῳ ἀληθείας, ἐν
Holy Spirit, *Holy* by sincere love; *sincere* by the word of truth, by the
41 4460 41 1877 537 27 537 1877 3364 237 1877
n.dsn a.dsn p.d n.dsf a.dsf p.d n.dsm n.gsf p.d

δυνάμει θεοῦ· διὰ τῶν ὅπλων τῆς δικαιοσύνης τῶν δεξιῶν καὶ →
power of God; with the weapons of righteousness both for the right hand and for the
1539 2536 1328 3836 3960 3836 1466 3836 1288 2779
n.dsf n.gsm p.g d.gpn n.gpn d.gsf n.gsf d.gpf a.gpf cj

ἀριστερῶν, [8]διὰ δόξης καὶ ἀτιμίας, διὰ δυσφημίας καὶ εὐφημίας· ὡς πλάνοι
left; through glory and dishonor, through slander and praise; as deceivers,
754 1328 1518 2779 871 1328 1556 2779 2367 6055 4418
a.gpf p.g n.gsf cj n.gsf p.g n.gsf cj n.gsf pl a.npm

καὶ ἀληθεῖς, [9]ὡς ἀγνοούμενοι καὶ ἐπιγινωσκόμενοι, ὡς ἀποθνῄσκοντες
⌊and yet⌋ true men; as unknown, ⌊and yet⌋ well-known; as dying,
2779 239 6055 51 2779 2105 6055 633
cj a.npm pl pt.pp.npm cj pt.pp.npm pl pt.pa.npm

καὶ ἰδοὺ ζῶμεν, ὡς παιδευόμενοι καὶ μὴ θανατούμενοι,
⌊and yet⌋ — look! — ⌊we continue to live;⌋ as scourged, ⌊and yet⌋ not killed;
2779 2627 2409 6055 4084 2779 3590 2506
cj j v.pai.1p pl pt.pp.npm cj pl pt.pp.npm

[10]ὡς λυπούμενοι ἀεὶ δὲ χαίροντες, ὡς πτωχοὶ ↱ πολλοὺς δὲ
as sorrowing, yet always *yet* rejoicing; as poor, yet making many *yet*
6055 3382 1254 107 1254 5897 6055 4777 1254 4457 4498 1254
pl pt.pp.npm adv cj pt.pa.npm pl a.npm a.apm cj

πλουτίζοντες, ὡς μηδὲν ἔχοντες καὶ πάντα κατέχοντες. [11]
rich; as having nothing, *having* ⌊and yet⌋ possessing everything. *possessing* We
4457 6055 2400 3594 2400 2779 2988 4246 2988 487
pt.pa.npm pl a.asn pt.pa.npm cj a.apn pt.pa.npm

τὸ στόμα ἡμῶν ἀνέῳγεν πρὸς ὑμᾶς, Κορίνθιοι, ἡ
have opened *{the}* our mouth *our* freely *We have opened* to you, Corinthians; *{the}* our
487 487 3836 7005 5125 7005 487 4639 7007 3171 3836 7005
d.nsn n.nsn r.gp.1 v.rai.3s p.a r.ap.2 n.vpm d.nsf

καρδία ἡμῶν πεπλάτυνται· [12] οὐ στενοχωρεῖσθε ← ←
heart *our* ⌊has been opened wide.⌋ We are not withholding our affection from you,
2840 7005 4425 4024 5102 7005 5073
n.nsf r.gp.1 v.rpi.3s pl v.ppi.2p

ἐν ἡμῖν, στενοχωρεῖσθε ← δὲ ἐν τοῖς σπλάγχνοις ὑμῶν· [13]τὴν
{in} *our* but you are withholding yours from us. *but {in} {the} affection yours {the}*
1877 7005 1254 5102 7007 1254 1877 3836 5073 7007 3836
p.d r.dp.1 v.ppi.2p cj p.d d.dpn n.dpn r.gp.2 d.asf

δὲ αὐτὴν ἀντιμισθίαν, ὡς τέκνοις λέγω, πλατύνθητε
Now as a fair exchange — I speak as to children *I speak* — open wide your hearts
1254 899 521 3306 3306 6055 5451 3306 4425 7007
cj r.asf n.asf pl n.dpn v.pai.1s v.apm.2p

NASB

so that the ministry
will not be discred-
ited, [4]but in every-
thing commend-
ing ourselves as
servants of God, in
much endurance, in
afflictions, in hard-
ships, in distresses,
[5]in beatings, in
imprisonments, in
tumults, in labors,
in sleeplessness, in
hunger, [6]in purity,
in knowledge, in
patience, in kind-
ness, in the Holy
Spirit, in genuine
love, [7]in the word
of truth, in the
power of God;
by the weapons
of righteousness
for the right hand
and the left, [8]by
glory and dishonor,
by evil report
and good report;
regarded as deceiv-
ers and yet true; [9]as
unknown yet well-
known, as dying
yet behold, we live;
as punished yet
not put to death,
[10]as sorrowful yet
always rejoic-
ing, as poor yet
making many rich,
as having nothing
yet possessing all
things.
[11]Our mouth has
spoken freely to
you, O Corinthi-
ans, our heart is
opened wide. [12]You
are not restrained
by us, but you are
restrained in your
own affections.
[13]Now in a like ex-
change—I speak as
to children—open
wide *to us* also.

NIV

Warning Against Idolatry

14 Do not be yoked together with unbelievers. For what do righteousness and wickedness have in common? Or what fellowship can light have with darkness? 15 What harmony is there between Christ and Belial[a]? Or what does a believer have in common with an unbeliever? 16 What agreement is there between the temple of God and idols? For we are the temple of the living God. As God has said:

"I will live with them
and walk among them,
and I will be their God,
and they will be my people."[b]

17 Therefore,

"Come out from them
and be separate,
says the Lord.
Touch no unclean thing,
and I will receive you."[c]

18 And,

"I will be a Father to you,
and you will be my sons and daughters,
says the Lord Almighty."[d]

7 Therefore, since we have these promises, dear friends, let us purify ourselves from everything that contaminates body and spirit, perfecting holiness out of reverence for God.

Paul's Joy Over the Church's Repentance

2 Make room for us in your hearts. We have wronged no one, we have corrupted no

[a] 15 Greek *Beliar*, a variant of *Belial*
[b] 16 Lev. 26:12; Jer. 32:38; Ezek. 37:27
[c] 17 Isaiah 52:11; Ezek. 20:34,41
[d] 18 2 Samuel 7:14; 7:8

καὶ ὑμεῖς. 14 μὴ γίνεσθε ἑτεροζυγοῦντες ἀπίστοις· τίς γὰρ
to us also. *your* Do not be unevenly yoked with unbelievers; for what *for* is there
2779 7007 1181 3590 1181 2282 603 1142 5515 1142
cj r.np.2 pl v.pmm.2p pt.pa.npm a.dpm r.nsf cj

μετοχὴ δικαιοσύνῃ καὶ ἀνομίᾳ, ἢ τίς κοινωνία φωτὶ πρὸς
in common between righteousness and lawlessness? Or what fellowship has light with
3580 1466 2779 490 2445 5515 3126 5890 4639
n.nsf n.dsf cj n.dsf cj r.nsf n.nsf n.dsn p.a

σκότος; 15 τίς δὲ συμφώνησις Χριστοῦ πρὸς Βελιάρ, ἢ τίς
darkness? What *{and}* harmony is there between Christ *between* and Belial? Or what
5030 5515 1254 5245 4639 5986 4639 1016 2445 5515
n.asn r.nsf cj n.nsf n.gsm p.a n.asm cj r.nsf

μερὶς πιστῷ μετὰ ἀπίστου; 16 τίς δὲ συγκατάθεσις
does a believer have in common *believer* with an unbeliever? What *{and}* agreement can
4412 3535 4412 3552 603 5515 1254 5161
n.nsf a.dsm p.g a.gsm r.nsf cj n.nsf

ναῷ θεοῦ μετὰ εἰδώλων; ἡμεῖς γὰρ ναὸς θεοῦ ἐσμεν
the temple of God have with idols? For we *For* are the temple of the living God; *are*
3724 2536 3552 1631 1142 7005 1142 1639 3724 2409 2536 1639
n.dsm n.gsm p.g n.gpn r.np.1 cj n.nsm n.gsm v.pai.1p

ζῶντος, καθὼς εἶπεν ὁ θεὸς ὅτι ἐνοικήσω ἐν αὐτοῖς καὶ ἐμπεριπατήσω
living just as God said: *{the}* *God* ~ "I will dwell in their midst and walk among
2409 2777 2536 3306 3836 2536 4022 1940 1877 899 1877 2779 1853
pt.pa.gsm cj v.aai.3s d.nsm n.nsm cj v.fai.1s p.d r.dpm.3 cj v.fai.1s

καὶ ἔσομαι αὐτῶν θεὸς καὶ αὐτοὶ ἔσονταί μου λαός. 17 διὸ ἐξέλθατε
them; *{and}* I will be their God and they will be my people." Therefore, "come out
2779 1639 899 2536 2779 899 1639 1609 3295 1475 2002
cj v.fmi.1s r.gpm.3 n.nsm cj r.npm v.fmi.3p r.gs.1 n.nsm cj v.aam.2p

ἐκ μέσου αὐτῶν καὶ ἀφορίσθητε, λέγει κύριος, καὶ ἀκαθάρτου
from their midst *their* and be separate," says the Lord, and "touch no unclean thing;
1666 899 3545 899 2779 928 3306 3261 2779 721 3590 176
p.g n.gsn r.gpm.3 cj v.apm.2p v.pai.3s n.nsm cj a.gsn

μὴ ἅπτεσθε· κἀγὼ εἰσδέξομαι ὑμᾶς 18 καὶ ἔσομαι ὑμῖν εἰς πατέρα καὶ
no *touch* then I will receive you, and I will be a father to you, *{for}* *father* and
3590 721 2743 1654 7007 2779 1639 4252 7007 1650 4252 2779
pl v.pmm.2p crasis v.fmi.1s r.ap.2 cj v.fmi.1s r.dp.2 p.a n.asm cj

ὑμεῖς ἔσεσθέ μοι εἰς υἱοὺς καὶ θυγατέρας, λέγει κύριος
you will be sons and daughters to me," *{for}* *sons* *and* *daughters* says the Lord
7007 1639 5626 2779 2588 1609 1650 5626 2779 2588 3306 3261
r.np.2 v.fmi.2p r.ds.1 p.a n.apm cj n.apf v.pai.3s n.nsm

παντοκράτωρ.
Almighty.
4120
n.nsm

7:1 ταύτας οὖν ἔχοντες τὰς ἐπαγγελίας, ἀγαπητοί,
Since then we have these *then* *Since we have* *{the}* promises, dear friends,
2400 4036 2400 2400 4047 4036 2400 3836 2039 28
r.apf cj pt.pa.npm d.apf n.apf a.vpm

καθαρίσωμεν ἑαυτοὺς ἀπὸ παντὸς μολυσμοῦ σαρκὸς καὶ πνεύματος, ἐπιτελοῦντες
let us cleanse ourselves from every defilement of flesh and spirit, perfecting
2751 1571 608 4246 3663 4922 2779 4460 2200
v.aas.1p r.apm.1 p.g a.gsm n.gsm n.gsf cj n.gsn pt.pa.npm

ἁγιωσύνην ἐν φόβῳ θεοῦ. 2 χωρήσατε ἡμᾶς·
holiness in the fear of God. ⌊Make room for⌋ us in your hearts; we have wronged
43 1877 5832 2536 6003 7005 92 92 92
n.asf p.d n.dsm n.gsm v.aam.2p r.ap.1

οὐδένα ἠδικήσαμεν, οὐδένα ἐφθείραμεν,
no one, *we have wronged* we have corrupted no one, *we have corrupted* we have taken advantage
4029 92 5780 5780 5780 4029 5780 4430 4430 4430 4430
a.asm v.aai.1p a.asm v.aai.1p

NASB

14 Do not be bound together with unbelievers; for what partnership have righteousness and lawlessness, or what fellowship has light with darkness? 15 Or what harmony has Christ with Belial, or what has a believer in common with an unbeliever? 16 Or what agreement has the temple of God with idols? For we are the temple of the living God; just as God said,

"I WILL DWELL IN THEM AND WALK AMONG THEM;
AND I WILL BE THEIR GOD, AND THEY SHALL BE MY PEOPLE.

17 "Therefore, COME OUT FROM THEIR MIDST AND BE SEPARATE,"
says the Lord.
"AND DO NOT TOUCH WHAT IS UNCLEAN;
And I will welcome you.
18 "And I will be a father to you,
And you shall be sons and daughters to Me,"
Says the Lord Almighty.

Paul Reveals His Heart

7:1 Therefore, having these promises, beloved, let us cleanse ourselves from all defilement of flesh and spirit, perfecting holiness in the fear of God.

2 Make room for us *in your hearts;* we wronged no one, we corrupted no one, we took advantage of no

NIV

one, we have exploited
no one. 3 I do not
say this to con-
demn you; I have
said before that
you have such a
place in our hearts
that we would live
or die with you. 4 I
have spoken to you
with great frank-
ness; I take great
pride in you. I am
greatly encour-
aged; in all our
troubles my joy
knows no bounds.
5 For when we
came into Mace-
donia, we had no
rest, but we were
harassed at every
turn—conflicts on
the outside, fears
within. 6 But God,
who comforts the
downcast, com-
forted us by the
coming of Titus,
7 and not only by
his coming but
also by the com-
fort you had given
him. He told us
about your long-
ing for me, your
deep sorrow, your
ardent concern for
me, so that my joy
was greater than
ever.
8 Even if I caused
you sorrow by my
letter, I do not re-
gret it. Though I
did regret it—I
see that my letter
hurt you, but only
for a little while—
9 yet now I am
happy, not because
you were made
sorry, but because
your sorrow led
you to repentance.
For you became
sorrowful as God
intended and so

οὐδένα ἐπλεονεκτήσαμεν. 3 πρὸς κατάκρισιν οὐ
of no one. *we have taken advantage of* I do not say this to condemn you, *not*
4430 4029 4430 3306 3306 4024 3306 4639 2892 4024
a.asm v.aai.1p p.a n.asf pl

λέγω, προείρηκα γὰρ ὅτι ἐν ταῖς καρδίαις ἡμῶν ἐστε εἰς
I do say for I have said previously *for* that you are in *{the}* our hearts; *our* *you are* thus
3306 1142 4597 1142 4022 1639 1639 1877 3836 7005 2840 7005 1639 1650
v.pai.1s v.rai.1s cj cj p.d d.dpf n.dpf r.gp.1 v.pai.2p p.a

τὸ → συναποθανεῖν καὶ συζῆν. 4 πολλή μοι παρρησία πρὸς ὑμᾶς,
~ we live and die together. *and* *live* I have great *I* confidence in you;
3836 5182 2779 5271 2779 5182 1609 4498 1609 4244 4639 7007
d.asn f.aa cj f.pa a.nsf r.ds.1 n.nsf p.a r.ap.2

πολλή μοι καύχησις ὑπὲρ ὑμῶν· πεπλήρωμαι τῇ παρακλήσει,
I take great *I* pride in you. I am filled with encouragement;
1609 4498 1609 3018 5642 7007 4444 3836 4155
a.nsf r.ds.1 n.nsf p.g r.gp.2 v.rpi.1s d.dsf n.dsf

ὑπερπερισσεύομαι τῇ χαρᾷ ἐπὶ πάσῃ τῇ θλίψει ἡμῶν. 5 καὶ γὰρ →
I am overflowing with joy in all *{the}* our distress. *our* For even *For* when we
5668 3836 5915 2093 4246 3836 7005 2568 7005 1142 2779 1142 7005
v.pmi.1s d.dsf n.dsf p.d a.dsf d.dsf n.dsf r.gp.1 adv cj

ἐλθόντων ἡμῶν εἰς Μακεδονίαν οὐδεμίαν ἔσχηκεν ἄνεσιν ἡ σάρξ
came *we* to Macedonia, our bodies had no *had* rest, *{the}* *bodies*
2262 7005 1650 3423 7005 4922 2400 4029 2400 457 3836 4922
pt.aa.gpm r.gp.1 p.a n.asf a.asf v.rai.3s n.asf d.nsf n.nsf

ἡμῶν ἀλλ' ἐν παντὶ θλιβόμενοι· ἔξωθεν μάχαι, ἔσωθεν
our but on all sides we were distressed — ⌊from the outside⌋ came conflicts, from within there
7005 247 1877 4246 2567 2033 3480 2277
r.gp.1 cj p.d a.dsn pt.pp.npm adv n.npf adv

φόβοι. 6 ἀλλ' ὁ παρακαλῶν τοὺς ταπεινοὺς παρεκάλεσεν ἡμᾶς ὁ θεός
were fears. But God, who encourages the downcast, encouraged us *{the}* *God*
5832 247 2536 3836 4151 3836 5424 4151 7005 3836 2536
n.npm cj d.nsm pt.pa.nsm d.apm a.apm v.aai.3s r.ap.1 d.nsm n.nsm

ἐν τῇ παρουσίᾳ Τίτου, 7 οὐ μόνον δὲ ἐν τῇ παρουσίᾳ αὐτοῦ ἀλλὰ
with the arrival of Titus. And not only *And* by *{the}* his arrival *his* but
1877 3836 4242 5519 1254 4024 3667 1254 1877 3836 899 4242 899 247
p.d d.dsf n.dsf n.gsm pl adv cj p.d d.dsf n.dsf r.gsm.3 cj

καὶ ἐν τῇ παρακλήσει ᾗ παρεκλήθη ἐφ' ὑμῖν, ἀναγγέλλων ἡμῖν τὴν
also by the encouragement ⌊with which⌋ he was encouraged by you, as he reported to us *{the}*
2779 1877 3836 4155 4005 4151 2093 7007 334 7005 3836
adv p.d d.dsf n.dsf r.dsf v.api.3s p.d r.dp.2 pt.pa.nsm r.dp.1 d.asf

ὑμῶν ἐπιπόθησιν, τὸν ὑμῶν ὀδυρμόν, τὸν ὑμῶν ζῆλον ὑπὲρ ἐμοῦ ὥστε
your strong affection, *{the}* your deep sorrow, *{the}* your ⌊ardent concern⌋ for me, so that
7007 2161 3836 7007 3851 3836 7007 2419 5642 1609 6063
r.gp.2 n.asf d.asm r.gp.2 n.asm d.asm r.gp.2 n.asm p.g r.gs.1 cj

με μᾶλλον χαρῆναι. 8 ὅτι εἰ καὶ → → ἐλύπησα ὑμᾶς ἐν
I rejoiced ⌊more than ever.⌋ *rejoiced* For even if *even* I made you sad *you* by
1609 5897 3437 5897 4022 2779 1623 2779 7007 3382 7007 1877
r.as.1 adv.c f.ap cj cj adv v.aai.1s r.ap.2 p.d

τῇ ἐπιστολῇ, ↱ ↱ οὐ μεταμέλομαι· εἰ καὶ μετεμελόμην, βλέπω
my letter, I do not regret it. Even if *Even* I did regret it — for I see
3836 2186 3564 3564 4024 3564 2779 1623 2779 3564 1142 1063
d.dsf n.dsf pl v.ppi.1s cj adv v.ipi.1s v.pai.1s

γὰρ[a] ὅτι ἡ ἐπιστολὴ ἐκείνη εἰ καὶ πρὸς ὥραν
for that *{the}* that letter *that* did make you sad, though only for a ⌊short time⌋
1142 4022 3836 1697 2186 1697 3382 3382 7007 3382 1623 2779 4639 6052
cj cj d.nsf n.nsf r.nsf cj adv p.a n.asf

ἐλύπησεν ὑμᾶς, 9 νῦν χαίρω, οὐχ ὅτι ἐλυπήθητε ἀλλ' ὅτι
did make sad *you* — now I rejoice, not because ⌊you were made sad,⌋ but because
3382 7007 3814 5897 4024 4022 3382 247 4022
v.aai.3s r.ap.2 adv v.pai.1s pl cj v.api.2p cj cj

ἐλυπήθητε εἰς μετάνοιαν· ἐλυπήθητε γὰρ κατὰ θεόν, ↰ ἵνα ἐν
your sadness ⌊led to⌋ repentance; for ⌊you were made sad⌋ *for* as God intended, so that in
3382 1650 3567 1142 3382 1142 2848 2536 2848 2671 1877
v.api.2p p.a n.asf v.api.2p cj p.a n.asm cj p.d

NASB

one. 3 I do not speak
to condemn you,
for I have said
before that you are
in our hearts to die
together and to live
together. 4 Great is
my confidence in
you; great is my
boasting on your
behalf. I am filled
with comfort; I
am overflowing
with joy in all our
affliction.
5 For even when
we came into
Macedonia our
flesh had no rest,
but we were afflict-
ed on every side:
conflicts without,
fears within. 6 But
God, who comforts
the depressed,
comforted us by
the coming of Ti-
tus; 7 and not only
by his coming, but
also by the comfort
with which he was
comforted in you,
as he reported to us
your longing, your
mourning, your
zeal for me; so that
I rejoiced even
more. 8 For though
I caused you sor-
row by my letter,
I do not regret it;
though I did regret
it—*for* I see that
that letter caused
you sorrow, though
only for a while—
9 I now rejoice,
not that you were
made sorrowful,
but that you were
made sorrowful to
the point of repen-
tance; for you were
made sorrowful ac-
cording to *the will
of* God, so that you

[a] [γὰρ] UBS, omitted by TNIV.

NIV

were not harmed
in any way by us.
10 Godly sorrow
brings repentance
that leads to salva-
tion and leaves no
regret, but world-
ly sorrow brings
death. 11 See what
this godly sorrow
has produced in
you: what ear-
nestness, what
eagerness to clear
yourselves, what
indignation, what
alarm, what long-
ing, what concern,
what readiness to
see justice done.
At every point you
have proved your-
selves to be inno-
cent in this matter.
12 So even though
I wrote to you, it
was neither on ac-
count of the one
who did the wrong
nor on account of
the injured party,
but rather that be-
fore God you could
see for yourselves
how devoted to us
you are. 13 By all
this we are encour-
aged.
In addition to our
own encourage-
ment, we were es-
pecially delighted
to see how happy
Titus was, because
his spirit has been
refreshed by all of
you. 14 I had boast-
ed to him about
you, and you have
not embarrassed
me. But just as ev-
erything we said
to you was true, so
our boasting about
you to Titus has
proved to be true
as well. 15 And his
affection for you

μηδενὶ ζημιωθῆτε ἐξ ἡμῶν. 10 ἡ γὰρ κατὰ θεὸν λύπη
nothing ⌊you suffered loss⌋ by us. *{the}* For sadness ⌊as intended by⌋ God *sadness* produces
3594 2423 1666 7005 3836 1142 3383 2848 2536 3383 2237
a.dsn v.aps.2p p.g r.gp.1 d.nsf cj p.a n.asm n.nsf

μετάνοιαν εἰς σωτηρίαν ἀμεταμέλητον ἐργάζεται· ἡ δὲ τοῦ κόσμου
a repentance that ⌊leads to⌋ salvation, leaving no regret; *produces* *{the}* but *{the}* worldly
3567 1650 5401 294 2237 3836 1254 3836 3180
n.asf p.a n.asf a.asf v.pmi.3s d.nsf cj d.gsm n.gsm

λύπη θάνατον κατεργάζεται. 11 ἰδοὺ γὰρ αὐτὸ
sadness produces death. *produces* For see *For* what eagerness this very thing
3383 2981 2505 2981 1142 2627 1142 4531 5082 4047 899
n.nsf n.asm v.pmi.3s j cj r.nsn

τοῦτο τὸ κατὰ θεὸν ↰ λυπηθῆναι πόσην κατειργάσατο ὑμῖν
this — this sadness as God intended *sadness* *what* — has produced in you;
4047 3836 3382 2848 2536 2848 3382 4531 2981 7007
r.nsn d.nsn p.a n.asm f.ap r.asf v.ami.3s r.dp.2

σπουδήν, ἀλλὰ ἀπολογίαν, ἀλλὰ ἀγανάκτησιν, ἀλλὰ φόβον, ἀλλὰ
eagerness what defense of yourselves, what indignation, what alarm, what
5082 247 665 247 25 247 5832 247
n.asf cj n.asf cj n.asf cj n.asm cj

ἐπιπόθησιν, ἀλλὰ ζῆλον, ἀλλὰ ἐκδίκησιν. ἐν παντὶ συνεστήσατε ἑαυτοὺς
longing, what deep concern, what punishment! In everything you have proved yourselves
2161 247 2419 247 1689 1877 4246 5319 1571
n.asf cj n.asm cj n.asf p.d a.dsn v.aai.2p r.apm.2

ἁγνοὺς εἶναι τῷ πράγματι. 12 ἄρα εἰ καὶ ἔγραψα ὑμῖν,
to be innocent *to be* ⌊in this⌋ matter. So then, even though *even* I wrote to you, it was
1639 1639 54 1639 3836 4547 726 2779 1623 2779 1211 7007
a.apm f.pa d.dsn n.dsn cj cj adv v.aai.1s r.dp.2

οὐχ ἕνεκεν τοῦ ἀδικήσαντος οὐδὲ ἕνεκεν τοῦ ἀδικηθέντος ἀλλ᾽ ἕνεκεν
not ⌊on account of⌋ the offender, nor ⌊on account of⌋ the one offended, but that
4024 1914 3836 92 4028 1914 3836 92 247 1914
pl p.g d.gsm pt.aa.gsm cj p.g d.gsm pt.ap.gsm cj p.g

τοῦ φανερωθῆναι τὴν σπουδὴν ὑμῶν τὴν ὑπὲρ ἡμῶν
your earnestness toward us ~ might be revealed *{the}* *earnestness* *your* *{the}* *toward* *us*
7007 5082 5642 7005 3836 5746 3836 5082 7007 3836 5642 7005
d.gsn f.ap d.asf n.asf r.gp.2 d.asf p.g r.gp.1

πρὸς ὑμᾶς ἐνώπιον τοῦ θεοῦ. 13 διὰ τοῦτο παρακεκλήμεθα. ἐπὶ
to you in the sight of God. ⌊Because of⌋ this we are encouraged. And in addition
4639 7007 1967 3836 2536 1328 4047 4151 1254 2093
p.a r.ap.2 p.g d.gsm n.gsm p.a r.asn v.rpi.1p p.d

δὲ τῇ παρακλήσει ἡμῶν περισσοτέρως μᾶλλον ἐχάρημεν
And to our own encouragement, *our own* we rejoiced more than ever *more* *we rejoiced*
1254 3836 7005 7005 4155 7005 5897 5897 3437 4359 3437 5897
cj d.dsf n.dsf r.gp.1 adv.c adv.c v.api.1p

ἐπὶ τῇ χαρᾷ Τίτου, ὅτι ἀναπέπαυται τὸ πνεῦμα αὐτοῦ ἀπὸ πάντων
at the joy of Titus, because his spirit has been refreshed *{the}* *spirit* *his* by all
2093 3836 5915 5519 4022 899 4460 399 3836 4460 899 608 4246
p.d d.dsf n.dsf n.gsm cj v.rpi.3s d.nsn n.nsn r.gsm.3 p.g a.gpm

ὑμῶν· 14 ὅτι εἴ τι αὐτῷ ὑπὲρ ὑμῶν
of you. For if I have boasted to him about anything *to him* regarding you,
7007 4022 1623 3016 3016 3016 899 899 3016 5516 899 5642 7007
r.gp.2 cj cj r.asn r.dsm.3 p.g r.gp.2

κεκαύχημαι, ↱ ↱ οὐ κατῃσχύνθην, ἀλλ᾽ ὡς πάντα
I have boasted about I have not been embarrassed, but ⌊just as⌋ everything we said to you
3016 2875 2875 4024 2875 247 6055 4246 3281 3281 7007 7007
v.rmi.1s pl v.api.1s cj cj a.apn

⌊ἐν ἀληθείᾳ⌋ ἐλαλήσαμεν ὑμῖν, οὕτως καὶ ἡ καύχησις ἡμῶν ἡ ἐπὶ
was true, *we said* *to you* so also *{the}* our boast *our* *{the}* to
1877 237 3281 7007 4048 2779 3836 7005 3018 7005 3836 2093
p.d n.dsf v.aai.1p r.dp.2 adv adv d.nsf n.nsf r.gp.1 d.nsf p.g

Τίτου ἀλήθεια ἐγενήθη. 15 καὶ τὰ σπλάγχνα αὐτοῦ
Titus about you has proved true. *has proved* And *{the}* his affection *his* for you
5519 1181 1181 237 1181 2779 3836 899 5073 899 1650 7007
n.gsm n.nsf v.api.3s cj d.npn n.npn r.gsm.3

NASB

might not suffer
loss in anything
through us.
10 For the sorrow
that is accord-
ing to *the will of*
God produces a
repentance without
regret, *leading*
to salvation, but
the sorrow of the
world produces
death. 11 For behold
what earnestness
this very thing, this
godly sorrow, has
produced in you:
what vindication of
yourselves, what
indignation, what
fear, what longing,
what zeal, what
avenging of wrong!
In everything you
demonstrated
yourselves to
be innocent in
the matter. 12 So
although I wrote
to you, *it was* not
for the sake of the
offender nor for
the sake of the one
offended, but that
your earnestness on
our behalf might
be made known
to you in the sight
of God. 13 For this
reason we have
been comforted.
And besides our
comfort, we re-
joiced even much
more for the joy of
Titus, because his
spirit has been re-
freshed by you all.
14 For if in anything
I have boasted to
him about you,
I was not put to
shame; but as we
spoke all things
to you in truth, so
also our boasting
before Titus proved
to be *the* truth.
15 His affection

NIV

is all the greater
when he remem-
bers that you were
all obedient, re-
ceiving him with
fear and trembling.
[16]I am glad I can
have complete
confidence in you.

The Collection for the Lord's People

8 And now,
brothers and
sisters, we want
you to know about
the grace that God
has given the Mac-
edonian churches.
[2]In the midst of a
very severe trial,
their overflow-
ing joy and their
extreme poverty
welled up in rich
generosity. [3]For
I testify that they
gave as much as
they were able,
and even beyond
their ability. En-
tirely on their own,
[4]they urgently
pleaded with us
for the privilege of
sharing in this ser-
vice to the Lord's
people. [5]And they
exceeded our ex-
pectations: They
gave themselves
first of all to the
Lord, and then by
the will of God
also to us. [6]So we
urged Titus, just
as he had earlier
made a beginning,
to bring also to
completion this act
of grace on your
part. [7]But since
you excel in every-
thing—in faith, in
speech, in knowl-
edge, in complete
earnestness and in
the love we have
kindled in you[a]—

[a] 7 Some manuscripts *and in your love for us*

περισσοτέρως εἰς ὑμᾶς ἐστιν ἀναμιμνησκομένου τὴν πάντων
is even greater *for you is* when he recalls the obedience of you all,
1639 4359 1650 7007 1639 389 3836 5633 7007 7007 4246
adv.c p.a r.ap.2 v.pai.3s pt.pp.gsm d.asf a.gpm

ὑμῶν ὑπακοήν, ὡς μετὰ φόβου καὶ τρόμου ἐδέξασθε αὐτόν. [16] χαίρω ὅτι
of you obedience how with fear and trembling you welcomed him. I rejoice because
7007 5633 6055 3552 5832 2779 5571 1312 899 5897 4022
r.gp.2 n.asf cj p.g n.gsm cj n.gsm v.ami.2p r.asm.3 v.pai.1s cj

ἐν παντὶ θαρρῶ ἐν ὑμῖν.
in everything ˻I have complete confidence˼ in you.
1877 4246 2509 1877 7007
p.d a.dsn v.pai.1s p.d r.dp.2

8:1 → → γνωρίζομεν δὲ ὑμῖν, ἀδελφοί, ↰ τὴν χάριν τοῦ θεοῦ τὴν
We want you to know, *{and} you* brothers, about the grace of God *{the}*
7007 1192 1254 7007 81 1192 3836 5921 3836 2536 3836
v.pai.1p cj r.dp.2 n.vpm d.asf n.asf d.gsm n.gsm d.asf

δεδομένην ἐν ταῖς ἐκκλησίαις τῆς Μακεδονίας, [2] ὅτι ἐν πολλῇ δοκιμῇ
shown among the churches of Macedonia, how that in a severe test
1443 1877 3836 1711 3836 3423 4022 1877 4498 1509
pt.rp.asf p.d d.dpf n.dpf d.gsf n.gsf cj p.d a.dsf n.dsf

θλίψεως ἡ περισσεία τῆς χαρᾶς αὐτῶν καὶ ἡ ˻κατὰ βάθους˼
of affliction, the fullness of their joy *their* and *{the}* their extreme
2568 3836 4353 3836 899 5915 899 2779 3836 899 2848 958
n.gsf d.nsf n.nsf d.gsf n.gsf r.gpm.3 cj d.nsf p.g n.gsn

πτωχεία αὐτῶν ἐπερίσσευσεν εἰς τὸ πλοῦτος τῆς ἁπλότητος αὐτῶν· [3]ὅτι
poverty *their* have overflowed in the richness of their generosity. *their* For — as
4775 899 4355 1650 3836 4458 3836 899 605 899 4022
n.nsf r.gpm.3 v.aai.3s p.a d.asn n.asn d.gsf n.gsf r.gpm.3 cj

κατὰ δύναμιν, μαρτυρῶ, καὶ παρὰ
I can testify — they gave ˻according to˼ their means, *I can testify* and even beyond their
3455 3455 3455 2848 1539 3455 2779 4123
p.a n.asf v.pai.1s cj p.a

δύναμιν, αὐθαίρετοι [4] μετὰ πολλῆς παρακλήσεως δεόμενοι ἡμῶν
means; acting spontaneously, begging us with great insistence *begging us*
1539 882 1289 7005 3552 4498 4155 1289 7005
n.asf a.npm p.g a.gsf n.gsf pt.pp.npm r.gp.1

τὴν χάριν καὶ τὴν κοινωνίαν τῆς διακονίας τῆς εἰς τοὺς ἁγίους, [5]καὶ
˻for the˼ ˻privilege of˼ *{and} {the}* joining in this ministry *{the}* to the saints. And
3836 5921 2779 3836 3126 3836 1355 3836 1650 3836 41 2779
d.asf n.asf cj d.asf n.asf d.gsf n.gsf d.gsf p.a d.apm a.apm cj

οὐ καθὼς ἠλπίσαμεν ἀλλὰ ἑαυτοὺς ἔδωκαν
they did this, not simply as we had hoped, but first they gave themselves *they gave*
4024 2777 1827 247 4754 1443 1443 1571 1443
pl cj v.aai.1p cj r.apm.3 v.aai.3p

πρῶτον τῷ κυρίῳ καὶ ἡμῖν διὰ θελήματος θεοῦ [6]εἰς τὸ
first ˻to the˼ Lord and then to us, by the will of God. So ~ we
4754 3836 3261 2779 7005 1328 2525 2536 1650 3836 7005
adv d.dsm n.dsm cj r.dp.1 p.g n.gsn n.gsm p.a d.asn

παρακαλέσαι ἡμᾶς Τίτον, ἵνα καθὼς προενήρξατο οὕτως καὶ
urged *we* Titus that just as ˻he had previously begun the work,˼ so now
4151 7005 5519 2671 2777 4599 4048 2779
f.aa r.ap.1 n.asm cj cj v.ami.3s adv cj

ἐπιτελέσῃ εἰς ὑμᾶς καὶ τὴν χάριν ταύτην.
he should complete this act of kindness among you. *{also} {the} act of kindness this*
2200 4047 5921 5921 5921 1650 7007 2779 3836 5921 4047
v.aas.3s p.a r.ap.2 adv d.asf n.asf r.asf

[7]ἀλλ᾽ ὥσπερ ἐν παντὶ περισσεύετε, πίστει καὶ λόγῳ καὶ
But as you excel in everything *you excel* — in faith, *{and}* in speech, *{and}*
247 6061 4355 4355 1877 4246 4355 4411 2779 3364 2779
cj cj p.d a.dsn v.pai.2p n.dsf cj n.dsm cj

γνώσει καὶ πάσῃ σπουδῇ καὶ τῇ ἐξ ἡμῶν ἐν ὑμῖν[a]
in knowledge, *{and}* in all eagerness, and ˻in the˼ love we ˻have aroused˼ *we* in you
1194 2779 4246 5082 2779 3836 27 7005 1666 7005 1877 7007
n.dsf cj a.dsf n.dsf cj d.dsf p.g r.gp.1 p.d r.dp.2

[a] ἐξ ὑμῶν ἐν ἡμῖν included by TR after ὑμῖν.

NASB

abounds all the
more toward you,
as he remembers
the obedience of
you all, how you
received him with
fear and trembling.
[16]I rejoice that in
everything I have
confidence in you.

Great Generosity

[8:1]Now, brethren,
we *wish to* make
known to you the
grace of God which
has been given in
the churches of
Macedonia, [2]that
in a great ordeal
of affliction their
abundance of joy
and their deep
poverty overflowed
in the wealth of
their liberality.
[3]For I testify that
according to their
ability, and beyond
their ability, *they*
gave of their own
accord, [4]begging
us with much urg-
ing for the favor
of participation
in the support of
the saints, [5]and
this, not as we had
expected, but they
first gave them-
selves to the Lord
and to us by the
will of God. [6]So we
urged Titus that as
he had previously
made a beginning,
so he would also
complete in you
this gracious work
as well.
[7]But just as you
abound in ev-
erything, in faith
and utterance and
knowledge and in
all earnestness and
in the [a]love we in-
spired in you, *see*

[a] Lit *love from us in you;* one early ms reads *your love for us*

NIV

see that you also
excel in this grace
of giving.
8 I am not com-
manding you, but
I want to test the
sincerity of your
love by comparing
it with the ear-
nestness of others.
9 For you know the
grace of our Lord
Jesus Christ, that
though he was
rich, yet for your
sake he became
poor, so that you
through his pover-
ty might become
rich.
10 And here is my
judgment about
what is best for
you in this matter.
Last year you were
the first not only
to give but also to
have the desire to
do so. 11 Now finish
the work, so that
your eager willing-
ness to do it may
be matched by
your completion
of it, according to
your means. 12 For
if the willingness
is there, the gift is
acceptable accord-
ing to what one
has, not according
to what one does
not have.
13 Our desire is
not that others
might be relieved
while you are hard
pressed, but that
there might be
equality. 14 At the
present time your
plenty will supply
what they need, so
that in turn their
plenty will supply
what you need.
The goal is equali-
ty, 15 as

ἀγάπη, ἵνα καὶ ἐν ταύτῃ τῇ χάριτι περισσεύητε.
love — make sure that *{also}* you excel in this *{the}* act of kindness. *you excel*
27 2671 2779 4355 4355 1877 4047 3836 5921 4355
n.dsf cj adv p.d r.dsf d.dsf n.dsf v.pas.2p

8 οὐ κατ᾽ ἐπιταγὴν λέγω ἀλλὰ
I am not saying this as an order, *I am saying* but as a way of testing the
3306 3306 4024 3306 2848 2198 3306 247 1507 1507 1507 1507 1507 3836
pl p.a n.asf v.pai.1s cj

διὰ τῆς ἑτέρων σπουδῆς καὶ τὸ τῆς
genuineness of your love by comparison ⌞with the⌟ eagerness of others. *eagerness* *{and}* *the* *of*
1188 3836 5629 27 1328 3836 5082 2283 5082 2779 3836 3836
p.g d.gsf r.gpm n.gsf cj d.asn d.gsf

ὑμετέρας ἀγάπης γνήσιον δοκιμάζων· 9 γινώσκετε γὰρ τὴν χάριν τοῦ
your *love* *genuineness* *as a way of testing* For you know *For* the grace of our
5629 27 1188 1507 1142 1182 1142 3836 5921 3836 7005
r.gsf.2 n.gsf a.asn pt.pa.nsm v.pai.2p cj d.asf n.asf d.gsm

κυρίου ἡμῶν Ἰησοῦ Χριστοῦ, ὅτι δι᾽ ὑμᾶς ↰ ἐπτώχευσεν
Lord *our* Jesus Christ, that though he was rich, yet for your sakes he became poor,
3261 7005 2652 5986 4022 1639 1639 1639 4454 1328 7007 1328 4776
n.gsm r.gp.1 n.gsm n.gsm cj p.a r.ap.2 v.aai.3s

πλούσιος ὤν, ἵνα ὑμεῖς τῇ ἐκείνου πτωχείᾳ πλουτήσητε. 10 καὶ
rich *though he was* so that you by his poverty ⌞might become rich.⌟ And in
4454 1639 2671 7007 3836 1697 4775 4456 2779 1877
a.nsm pt.pa.nsm cj r.np.2 d.dsf r.gsm n.dsf v.aas.2p cj

γνώμην ἐν τούτῳ δίδωμι· τοῦτο γὰρ
this matter I am giving my opinion; *in* *this matter* *I am giving* for this *for* is beneficial
4047 4047 1443 1443 1443 1191 1877 4047 1443 1142 4047 1142 5237 5237
n.asf p.d r.dsn v.pai.1s r.nsn cj

ὑμῖν συμφέρει, οἵτινες οὐ μόνον τὸ ποιῆσαι ἀλλὰ καὶ τὸ
for you, *is beneficial* who last year not only began ~ to do this work but also ~
7007 5237 4015 4373 4373 4024 3667 4599 3836 4472 247 2779 3836
r.dp.2 v.pai.3s r.npm pl adv d.asn f.aa cj cj d.asn

θέλειν προενήρξασθε ἀπὸ πέρυσι· 11 νυνὶ δὲ καὶ τὸ ποιῆσαι
to desire to do it. *began* *{from}* *last year* So now *So* *{also}* ~ finish doing
2527 4599 608 4373 1254 3815 1254 2779 3836 2200 4472
f.pa v.ami.2p p.g adv adv cj adv d.asn f.aa

ἐπιτελέσατε, ὅπως καθάπερ ἡ προθυμία τοῦ θέλειν, οὕτως καὶ τὸ
finish it, so that *{just as}* your readiness ~ in desiring it ⌞may be matched⌟ *{also}* ~
2200 3968 2749 3836 4608 3836 2527 4048 2779 3836
v.aam.2p cj cj d.nsf n.nsf d.gsn f.pa adv adv d.nsn

ἐπιτελέσαι ἐκ τοῦ ἔχειν. 12 εἰ γὰρ ἡ προθυμία πρόκειται,
by your completing it, as ~ ⌞your means allow.⌟ For if *For* the readiness is present,
2200 1666 3836 2400 1142 1623 1142 3836 4608 4618
f.aa p.g d.gsn f.pa cj cj d.nsf n.nsf v.pmi.3s

καθὸ ἐὰν ἔχῃ εὐπρόσδεκτος, οὐ καθὸ
the gift is acceptable ⌞according to⌟ whatever a person has, *acceptable* not ⌞according to⌟
2347 2771 1569 2400 2347 4024 2771
cj pl v.pas.3s a.nsm pl cj

↱ ↱ οὐκ ἔχει. 13 οὐ γὰρ ἵνα ἄλλοις ἄνεσις,
what he does not have. For this is not *For* for the ease of others *ease* and a burden
2400 2400 4024 2400 1142 4024 1142 2671 457 257 457 2568
pl v.pai.3s pl cj cj r.dpm n.nsf

ὑμῖν θλῖψις, ἀλλ᾽ ἐξ ἰσότητος· 14 ἐν τῷ νῦν καιρῷ τὸ ὑμῶν
for you, *burden* but a ⌞matter of⌟ equality; at the present time *{the}* your
7007 2568 247 1666 2699 1877 3836 3814 2789 3836 7007
r.dp.2 n.nsf cj p.g n.gsf p.d d.dsm adv n.dsm d.nsn r.gp.2

περίσσευμα εἰς τὸ ἐκείνων ὑστέρημα, ἵνα καὶ τὸ ἐκείνων περίσσευμα
abundance ⌞should supply⌟ what they need, so that then *{the}* their abundance
4354 1650 3836 1697 5729 2671 2779 3836 1697 4354
n.nsn p.a d.asn r.gpm n.asn cj adv d.nsn r.gpm n.nsn

γένηται εἰς τὸ ὑμῶν ὑστέρημα, ὅπως γένηται ἰσότης, 15 καθὼς
may supply *{the}* your need; ⌞in this way⌟ ⌞there will be⌟ equality. As
1181 1650 3836 7007 5729 3968 1181 2699 2777
v.ams.3s p.a d.asn r.gp.2 n.asn cj v.ams.3s n.nsf cj

NASB

that you abound
in this gracious
work also. 8 I am
not speaking *this*
as a command, but
as proving through
the earnestness of
others the sincerity
of your love also.
9 For you know the
grace of our Lord
Jesus Christ, that
though He was
rich, yet for your
sake He became
poor, so that you
through His pov-
erty might become
rich. 10 I give *my*
opinion in this
matter, for this is
to your advantage,
who were the first
to begin a year ago
not only to do *this,*
but also to desire
to do it. 11 But now
finish doing it also,
so that just as *there*
was the readiness
to desire it, so *there*
may be also the
completion of it by
your ability. 12 For
if the readiness is
present, it is ac-
ceptable according
to what *a person*
has, not according
to what he does
not have. 13 For *this*
is not for the ease
of others *and* for
your affliction,
but by way of
equality— 14 at this
present time your
abundance *being*
a supply for their
need, so that their
abundance also
may become *a sup-*
ply for your need,
that there may be
equality; 15 as it is

NIV

it is written: "The
one who gathered
much did not have
too much, and the
one who gathered
little did not have
too little."[a]

Titus Sent to Receive the Collection

16 Thanks be to
God, who put into
the heart of Titus
the same concern I
have for you. 17 For
Titus not only wel-
comed our appeal,
but he is coming
to you with much
enthusiasm and
on his own initia-
tive. 18 And we are
sending along with
him the brother
who is praised by
all the churches for
his service to the
gospel. 19 What is
more, he was cho-
sen by the church-
es to accompany
us as we carry the
offering, which
we administer in
order to honor the
Lord himself and
to show our eager-
ness to help. 20 We
want to avoid any
criticism of the
way we administer
this liberal gift.
21 For we are taking
pains to do what
is right, not only
in the eyes of the
Lord but also in
the eyes of man.
22 In addition, we
are sending with
them our broth-
er who has often
proved to us in
many ways that
he is zealous, and
now even more
so because of his
great

[a] *15* Exodus 16:18

γέγραπται, ὁ τὸ πολὺ ↱ οὐκ ἐπλεόνασεν, καὶ ὁ
it is written, "The one who gathered *{the}* much did not have a surplus, and the one who
1211 3836 3836 4498 4429 4024 4429 2779 3836
v.rpi.3s d.nsm d.asn a.asn pl v.aai.3s cj d.nsm

τὸ ὀλίγον ↱ οὐκ ἠλαττόνησεν. 16 χάρις δὲ τῷ θεῷ τῷ δόντι
gathered *{the}* little did not have too little." But thanks *But* be to God who put
3836 3900 1782 4024 1782 1254 5921 1254 3836 2536 3836 1443
d.asn a.asn pl v.aai.3s n.nsf cj d.dsm n.dsm d.dsm pt.aa.dsm

τὴν αὐτὴν σπουδὴν ὑπὲρ ὑμῶν ↰ ἐν τῇ καρδίᾳ Τίτου, 17 ὅτι
the same eagerness on your behalf in the heart of Titus, because he not only
3836 899 5082 5642 7007 5642 1877 3836 2840 5519 4022 1312 3525 3525
d.asf r.asf n.asf p.g r.gp.2 p.d d.dsf n.dsf n.gsm cj

τὴν μὲν παράκλησιν ἐδέξατο, σπουδαιότερος δὲ ὑπάρχων
accepted our *not only* request, *he accepted* but being very eager *but* and acting
1312 3836 3525 4155 1312 1254 5080 1254 5639
d.asf pl n.asf v.ami.3s a.nsm.c cj pt.pa.nsm

αὐθαίρετος ἐξῆλθεν πρὸς ὑμᾶς. 18 συνεπέμψαμεν δὲ μετ' αὐτοῦ
on his own initiative, ⌞he is on his way⌟ to you. And we sent along *And* with him
882 2002 4639 7007 1254 5225 1254 3552 899
a.nsm v.aai.3s p.a r.ap.2 v.aai.1p cj p.g r.gsm.3

τὸν ἀδελφὸν οὗ ὁ ἔπαινος ἐν τῷ
the brother who is *{the}* highly respected throughout all the churches for his work in the
3836 81 4005 3836 2047 1328 4246 3836 1711 1877 3836
d.asm n.asm r.gsm d.nsm n.nsm p.d d.dsn

εὐαγγελίῳ διὰ πασῶν τῶν ἐκκλησιῶν, 19 οὐ μόνον δέ, ἀλλὰ καὶ
gospel. *throughout all the churches* And not only this, *And* but *{also}*
2295 1328 4246 3836 1711 1254 4024 3667 1254 247 2779
n.dsn p.g a.gpf d.gpf n.gpf pl adv cj cj adv

χειροτονηθεὶς ὑπὸ τῶν ἐκκλησιῶν συνέκδημος ἡμῶν
he has been appointed by the churches to be our traveling companion *our* as we carry
5936 5679 3836 1711 7005 5292 7005 7005 1354
pt.ap.nsm p.g d.gpf n.gpf n.nsm r.gp.1

σὺν τῇ χάριτι ταύτῃ τῇ διακονουμένῃ ὑφ' ἡμῶν πρὸς τὴν
out *{with}* *{the}* this act of kindness *this* *{the}* *carry out* *{by}* *we* for the glory
1354 5250 3836 4047 5921 4047 3836 1354 5679 7005 4639 3836 1518
p.d d.dsf n.dsf r.dsf d.dsf pt.pp.dsf p.g r.gp.1 p.a d.asf

αὐτοῦ[a] τοῦ κυρίου δόξαν καὶ προθυμίαν ἡμῶν, 20 → →
of the Lord himself, *of the Lord* *glory* and to show our readiness. *our* We are
3836 3836 3261 899 3836 3261 1518 2779 7005 4608 7005
r.gsm d.gsm n.gsm n.asf cj n.asf r.gp.1

→ στελλόμενοι τοῦτο, μή τις ἡμᾶς μωμήσηται
taking this precaution *this* so that no one should blame us *should blame* for the way
4047 5097 4047 3590 5516 3699 3699 7005 3699
pt.pm.npm r.asn cj r.nsm r.ap.1 v.ams.3s

ἐν τῇ ἁδρότητι ταύτῃ τῇ διακονουμένῃ ὑφ' ἡμῶν·
we are administering *{in}* *{the}* this generous gift, *this* *{the}* *are administering* *{by}* *we*
7005 1354 1354 1877 3836 4047 103 4047 3836 1354 5679 7005
p.d d.dsf n.dsf r.dsf d.dsf pt.pp.dsf p.g r.gp.1

21 προνοοῦμεν γὰρ καλὰ οὐ μόνον ἐνώπιον κυρίου ἀλλὰ καὶ
for ⌞we are concerned to do⌟ *for* ⌞what is right,⌟ not only before the Lord but also
1142 4629 1142 2819 4024 3667 1967 3261 247 2779
v.pai.1p cj a.apn pl adv p.g n.gsm cj adv

ἐνώπιον ἀνθρώπων. 22 συνεπέμψαμεν δὲ αὐτοῖς τὸν ἀδελφὸν ἡμῶν
before men. And ⌞we are sending along with⌟ *And* them *{the}* our brother *our*
1967 476 1254 5225 1254 899 3836 7005 81 7005
p.g n.gpm v.aai.1p cj r.dpm.3 d.asm n.asm r.gp.1

ὃν → → ἐδοκιμάσαμεν ἐν πολλοῖς πολλάκις
whom we have often tested in many matters *often* and found to be
4005 4490 1507 1877 4498 4490 1639 1639
r.asm v.aai.1p p.d a.dpn adv

σπουδαῖον ὄντα, νυνὶ δὲ πολὺ σπουδαιότερον → →
eager, *to be* and now *and* he is all the more eager because of his great
5080 1639 1254 3815 1254 4498 5080 4498
a.asm pt.pa.asm adv cj adv a.asm.c

[a] [αὐτοῦ] UBS.

NASB

written, "HE WHO
gathered MUCH DID
NOT HAVE TOO MUCH,
AND HE WHO *gath-
ered* LITTLE HAD NO
LACK."
16 But thanks be to
God who puts the
same earnestness
on your behalf in
the heart of Titus.
17 For he not only
accepted our ap-
peal, but being
himself very ear-
nest, he has gone
to you of his own
accord. 18 We have
sent along with
him the brother
whose fame in *the
things of* the gospel
has spread through
all the churches;
19 and not only *this,*
but he has also
been appointed
by the churches to
travel with us in
this gracious work,
which is being
administered by
us for the glory of
the Lord Himself,
and *to show* our
readiness, 20 taking
precaution so that
no one will dis-
credit us in our ad-
ministration of this
generous gift; 21 for
we have regard for
what is honorable,
not only in the
sight of the Lord,
but also in the sight
of men. 22 We have
sent with them our
brother, whom we
have often tested
and found diligent
in many things,
but now even more
diligent because of

NIV

confidence in you.
23 As for Titus, he
is my partner and
co-worker among
you; as for our
brothers, they are
representatives of
the churches and
an honor to Christ.
24 Therefore show
these men the
proof of your love
and the reason for
our pride in you,
so that the church-
es can see it.
9 There is no
need for me to
write to you about
this service to the
Lord's people.
2 For I know your
eagerness to help,
and I have been
boasting about it to
the Macedonians,
telling them that
since last year you
in Achaia were
ready to give; and
your enthusiasm
has stirred most
of them to action.
3 But I am sending
the brothers in or-
der that our boast-
ing about you in
this matter should
not prove hollow,
but that you may
be ready, as I said
you would be. 4 For
if any Macedoni-
ans come with me
and find you un-
prepared, we—not
to say anything
about you—would
be ashamed of
having been so
confident. 5 So I
thought it neces-
sary to urge the
brothers to visit
you in advance

πεποιθήσει πολλῇ τῇ εἰς ὑμᾶς. 23 εἴτε ὑπὲρ Τίτου, κοινωνὸς ἐμὸς καὶ
confidence *great* *{the}* in you. As for Titus, he is my companion *my* and
4301 4498 3836 1650 7007 1664 5642 5519 1847 3128 1847 2779
n.dsf a.dsf d.dsf p.a r.ap.2 cj p.g n.gsm n.nsm r.nsm.1 cj

εἰς ὑμᾶς συνεργός· εἴτε ἀδελφοὶ ἡμῶν, ἀπόστολοι →
fellow worker among you. *fellow worker* As for our brothers, *our* they are delegates of
5301 5301 1650 7007 5301 1664 7005 81 7005 693
p.a r.ap.2 n.nsm cj n.npm r.gp.1 n.npm

ἐκκλησιῶν, δόξα Χριστοῦ. 24 τὴν
the churches, an honor to Christ. Therefore show them openly before the churches the
1711 1518 5986 4036 1892 899 1892 4725 3836 1711 3836
n.gpf n.nsf n.gsm d.asf

οὖν ἔνδειξιν τῆς ἀγάπης ὑμῶν καὶ ἡμῶν καυχήσεως ὑπὲρ ὑμῶν
Therefore proof of your love *your* and the reason for our pride in you.
4036 1893 3836 7007 27 7007 2779 7005 3018 5642 7007
cj n.asf d.gsf n.gsf r.gp.2 cj r.gp.1 n.gsf p.g r.gp.2

εἰς αὐτοὺς ἐνδεικνύμενοι εἰς πρόσωπον τῶν ἐκκλησιῶν.
{to} *them* *show openly* *{to}* *before* *the* *churches*
1650 899 1892 1650 4725 3836 1711
p.a r.apm.3 pt.pm.npm p.a n.asn d.gpf n.gpf

9:1 περὶ μὲν γὰρ τῆς διακονίας τῆς εἰς τοὺς ἁγίους
Now concerning ~ *Now* the service *{the}* to the saints, there is
1142 4309 3525 1142 3836 1355 3836 1650 3836 41 1639 1639
p.g pl cj d.gsf n.gsf d.gsf p.a d.apm a.apm

περισσόν μοί ἐστιν τὸ γράφειν ὑμῖν, 2 οἶδα γὰρ τὴν προθυμίαν ὑμῶν
no necessity ⌊for me⌋ *there is* ~ to write to you, for I know *for* *{the}* your readiness *your*
4356 1609 1639 3836 1211 7007 1142 3857 1142 3836 7007 4608 7007
a.nsn r.ds.1 v.pai.3s d.nsn f.pa r.dp.2 v.rai.1s cj d.asf n.asf r.gp.2

↱ ἣν ὑπὲρ ὑμῶν καυχῶμαι → Μακεδόσιν, ὅτι Ἀχαΐα
to help, about which *{for}* *{you}* I keep boasting to the Macedonians, saying that Achaia
3016 4005 5642 7007 3016 3424 4022 938
r.asf p.g r.gp.2 v.pmi.1s n.dpm cj n.nsf

παρεσκεύασται ἀπὸ πέρυσι, καὶ τὸ ὑμῶν ζῆλος ἠρέθισεν τοὺς πλείονας.
has been ready since last year, and *{the}* your zeal ⌊has stirred up⌋ *{the}* most of them.
4186 608 4373 2779 3836 7007 2419 2241 3836 4498
v.rmi.3s p.g adv cj d.nsn r.gp.2 n.nsn v.aai.3s d.apm a.apm.c

3 ἔπεμψα δὲ τοὺς ἀδελφούς, ἵνα ↱ μὴ
But I am sending *But* these brothers so that what we say in praise of you may not
1254 4287 1254 3836 81 2671 3836 7005 3017 3017 3017 5642 7007 3033 3590
v.aai.1s cj d.apm n.apm cj pl

τὸ καύχημα ἡμῶν τὸ ὑπὲρ ὑμῶν κενωθῇ ἐν τῷ μέρει τούτῳ, ἵνα
what *say in praise* *we* *{the}* *of* *you* ⌊be an empty boast⌋ in *{the}* this instance, *this* that
3836 3017 7005 3836 5642 7007 3033 1877 3836 4047 3538 4047 2671
d.nsn n.nsn r.gp.1 d.nsn p.g r.gp.2 v.aps.3s p.d d.dsn n.dsn r.dsn cj

καθὼς ἔλεγον παρεσκευασμένοι ἦτε, 4 μή
you may be ready just as I said *ready* *you may be* you would be. Lest
1639 1639 1639 4186 2777 3306 4186 1639 3590
cj v.iai.3p pt.rm.npm v.pas.2p cj

πως ἐὰν ἔλθωσιν σὺν ἐμοὶ Μακεδόνες καὶ ↱ εὕρωσιν ὑμᾶς
perhaps if some Macedonians should come with me *Macedonians* and not find you
4803 1569 3424 2262 5250 1609 3424 2779 564 2351 7007
pl cj v.aas.3p p.d r.ds.1 n.npm cj v.aas.3p r.ap.2

ἀπαρασκευάστους καταισχυνθῶμεν ἡμεῖς, ἵνα μὴ
ready, we — to say nothing of you — would be humiliated *we* *to* *nothing*
564 7005 2671 3306 3590 7007 2875 7005 2671 3590
a.apm v.aps.1p r.np.1 cj pl

λέγω ὑμεῖς, ἐν τῇ ὑποστάσει ταύτῃ. 5 ἀναγκαῖον
say *you* by *{the}* this confidence. *this* Therefore I considered it necessary
3306 7007 1877 3836 4047 5712 4047 4036 2451 2451 338
v.pas.1s r.np.2 p.d d.dsf n.dsf r.dsf a.nsn

οὖν ἡγησάμην παρακαλέσαι τοὺς ἀδελφούς, ἵνα προέλθωσιν εἰς ὑμᾶς ↰ ↰
Therefore *I considered* to urge the brothers to go to you in advance
4036 2451 4151 3836 81 2671 4601 1650 7007 4601 4601
cj v.ami.1s f.aa d.apm n.apm cj v.aas.3p p.a r.ap.2

NASB

his great confi-
dence in you. 23 As
for Titus, *he is* my
partner and fellow
worker among
you; as for our
brethren, *they are*
messengers of the
churches, a glory to
Christ. 24 Therefore
openly before the
churches, show
them the proof
of your love and
of our reason for
boasting about you.

God Gives Most

9:1 For it is super-
fluous for me to
write to you about
this ministry to the
saints; 2 for I know
your readiness, of
which I boast about
you to the Macedo-
nians, *namely,* that
Achaia has been
prepared since
last year, and your
zeal has stirred
up most of them.
3 But I have sent the
brethren, in order
that our boasting
about you may not
be made empty in
this case, so that, as
I was saying, you
may be prepared;
4 otherwise if any
Macedonians come
with me and find
you unprepared,
we—not to speak
of you—will be put
to shame by this
confidence. 5 So I
thought it neces-
sary to urge the
brethren that they
would go on ahead

NIV

and finish the ar-
rangements for
the generous gift
you had promised.
Then it will be
ready as a gener-
ous gift, not as one
grudgingly given.

Generosity Encouraged

6 Remember this:
Whoever sows
sparingly will also
reap sparingly,
and whoever sows
generously will
also reap gener-
ously. 7 Each of you
should give what
you have decided
in your heart to
give, not reluctant-
ly or under com-
pulsion, for God
loves a cheerful
giver. 8 And God is
able to bless you
abundantly, so that
in all things at all
times, having all
that you need, you
will abound in
every good work.
9 As it is written:

> "They have freely scattered
> their gifts to the poor;
> their righteousness endures
> forever."[a]

10 Now he who sup-
plies seed to the
sower and bread
for food will also
supply and in-
crease your store
of seed and will
enlarge the harvest
of your righteous-
ness. 11 You will be
enriched in every
way so that you
can be generous
on every occa-
sion, and through
us your generos-
ity will result in
thanksgiving to
God.
12 This service
that you perform is
not only supplying
the needs of the
Lord's people but
is also

καὶ προκαταρτίσωσιν τὴν προεπηγγελμένην
and to arrange beforehand the generous contribution you had previously promised,
2779 4616 3836 2330 2330 7007 4600
cj v.aas.3p d.asf pt.rp.asf

εὐλογίαν ὑμῶν, ταύτην ἑτοίμην εἶναι οὕτως ὡς
generous contribution *you* so that it would be ready *so that would be* *{thus}* as a
2330 7007 1639 1639 4047 1639 1639 2289 1639 4048 6055
n.asf r.gp.2 r.asf a.asf f.pa adv pl

εὐλογίαν καὶ μὴ ὡς πλεονεξίαν. 6 τοῦτο δέ, ὁ
generous gift and not as ⌊something you had to do.⌋ Remember this: *{and}* the
2330 2779 3590 6055 4432 4047 1254 3836
n.asf cj pl pl n.asf r.asn cj d.nsm

σπείρων φειδομένως φειδομένως καὶ θερίσει, καὶ ὁ σπείρων
one who sows sparingly will also reap sparingly, *also* *will reap* and the one who sows
5062 5768 2545 2779 2545 5768 2779 2545 2779 3836 5062
pt.pa.nsm adv adv adv v.fai.3s cj d.nsm pt.pa.nsm

⌊ἐπ᾿ εὐλογίαις⌋ ⌊ἐπ᾿ εὐλογίαις⌋ καὶ θερίσει. 7 ἕκαστος
generously will also reap generously. *also* *will reap* Each one must
2093 2330 2545 2779 2545 2093 2330 2779 2545 1667
p.d n.dpf p.d n.dpf adv v.fai.3s r.nsm

καθὼς προῄρηται τῇ καρδίᾳ, μὴ ⌊ἐκ λύπης⌋ ἢ ἐξ ἀνάγκης·
give as he has decided ⌊in his⌋ heart, not reluctantly nor under constraint, for it
2777 4576 3836 2840 3590 1666 3383 2445 1666 340 1142
cj v.rmi.3s d.dsf n.dsf pl p.g n.gsf cj p.g n.gsf

ἱλαρὸν γὰρ δότην ἀγαπᾷ ὁ θεός. 8 δυνατεῖ δὲ ὁ θεὸς
is the cheerful *for* giver whom God loves. *{the}* *God* And God is able *And* *{the}* *God*
2659 1142 1522 2536 26 3836 2536 1254 2536 1542 1254 3836 2536
a.asm cj n.asm v.pai.3s d.nsm n.nsm v.pai.3s cj d.nsm n.nsm

↱ ↱ πᾶσαν χάριν περισσεῦσαι εἰς ὑμᾶς, ἵνα ἐν παντὶ πάντοτε
to make all grace overflow to you, so that, in all things and at all times, having
4355 4355 4246 5921 4355 1650 7007 2671 1877 4246 4121 2400
a.asf n.asf f.aa p.a r.ap.2 cj p.d a.dsn adv

πᾶσαν αὐτάρκειαν ἔχοντες περισσεύητε εἰς πᾶν ἔργον ἀγαθόν,
all you need, *having* you may overflow in ⌊every kind⌋ of good work. *good*
4246 894 2400 4355 1650 4246 19 2240 19
a.asf n.asf pt.pa.npm v.pas.2p p.a a.asn n.asn a.asn

9 καθὼς γέγραπται, ἐσκόρπισεν, ἔδωκεν τοῖς πένησιν, ἡ
As it is written, ⌊"He has distributed generously,⌋ he has given to the poor; *{the}* his
2777 1211 5025 1443 3836 4288 3836 899
cj v.rpi.3s v.aai.3s v.aai.3s d.dpm n.dpm d.nsf

δικαιοσύνη αὐτοῦ μένει εἰς τὸν αἰῶνα. 10 ὁ δὲ ἐπιχορηγῶν σπόρον τῷ
righteousness *his* endures for all time." The *{and}* one who supplies seed ⌊to the⌋
1466 899 3531 1650 3836 172 3836 1254 2220 5078 3836
n.nsf r.gsm.3 v.pai.3s p.a d.asm n.asm d.nsm cj pt.pa.nsm n.asm d.dsm

σπείροντι καὶ ἄρτον εἰς βρῶσιν χορηγήσει καὶ πληθυνεῖ τὸν σπόρον ὑμῶν καὶ
sower and bread for food will supply and multiply *{the}* your seed *your* and
5062 2779 788 1650 1111 5961 2779 4437 3836 7007 5078 7007 2779
pt.pa.dsm cj n.asm p.a n.asf v.fai.3s adv v.fai.3s d.asm n.asm r.gp.2 cj

αὐξήσει τὰ γενήματα τῆς δικαιοσύνης ὑμῶν. 11 ἐν παντὶ
enlarge the harvest of your righteousness. *your* In ⌊every way⌋
889 3836 1163 3836 7007 1466 7007 1877 4246
v.fai.3s d.apn n.apn d.gsf n.gsf r.gp.2 p.d a.dsn

πλουτιζόμενοι εἰς πᾶσαν ἁπλότητα, ἥτις κατεργάζεται δι᾿ ἡμῶν
⌊you will be made rich⌋ for all your generosity, which is producing through us
4457 1650 4246 605 4015 2981 1328 7005
pt.pp.npm p.a a.asf n.asf r.nsf v.pmi.3s p.g r.gp.1

εὐχαριστίαν τῷ θεῷ· 12 ὅτι ἡ διακονία τῆς λειτουργίας ταύτης οὐ
thanksgiving to God, because the service of this ministry *this* is not
2374 3836 2536 4022 3836 1355 3836 4047 3311 4047 1639 4024
n.asf d.dsm n.dsm cj d.nsf n.nsf d.gsf n.gsf r.gsf pl

μόνον ἐστὶν προσαναπληροῦσα τὰ ὑστερήματα τῶν ἁγίων, ἀλλὰ ↱ καὶ
only *is* providing for the needs of the saints, but is also
3667 1639 4650 3836 5729 3836 41 247 4355 2779
adv v.pai.3s pt.pa.nsf d.apn n.apn d.gpm a.gpm cj adv

NASB

to you and arrange
beforehand your
previously prom-
ised bountiful gift,
so that the same
would be ready
as a bountiful gift
and not affected by
covetousness.
6 Now this *I say,*
he who sows spar-
ingly will also reap
sparingly, and he
who sows bounti-
fully will also reap
bountifully. 7 Each
one *must do* just
as he has purposed
in his heart, not
grudgingly or
under compulsion,
for God loves a
cheerful giver.
8 And God is able
to make all grace
abound to you, so
that always having
all sufficiency in
everything, you
may have an abun-
dance for every
good deed; 9 as it is
written,

> "HE SCATTERED
> ABROAD, HE
> GAVE TO THE
> POOR,
> HIS RIGHTEOUS-
> NESS ENDURES
> FOREVER."

10 Now He who sup-
plies seed to the
sower and bread
for food will sup-
ply and multiply
your seed for sow-
ing and increase
the harvest of
your righteous-
ness; 11 you will
be enriched in
everything for all
liberality, which
through us is pro-
ducing thanksgiv-
ing to God. 12 For
the ministry of this
service is not only
fully supplying the
needs of the saints,
but is also

[a] 9 Psalm 112:9

NIV

overflowing in
many expressions
of thanks to God.
13 Because of the
service by which
you have proved
yourselves, others
will praise God
for the obedience
that accompanies
your confession
of the gospel of
Christ, and for
your generosity in
sharing with them
and with everyone
else. 14 And in their
prayers for you
their hearts will go
out to you, because
of the surpassing
grace God has giv-
en you. 15 Thanks
be to God for his
indescribable gift!

Paul's Defense of His Ministry

10 By the
humility
and gentleness of
Christ, I appeal to
you—I, Paul, who
am "timid" when
face to face with
you, but "bold"
toward you when
away! 2 I beg you
that when I come
I may not have to
be as bold as I ex-
pect to be toward
some people who
think that we live
by the standards
of this world. 3 For
though we live in
the world, we do
not wage war as
the world does.
4 The weapons we
fight with are not
the weapons of
the world. On the
contrary, they have
divine power to
demolish strong-
holds. 5 We demol-
ish arguments and
every pretension
that sets itself up
against the knowl-
edge of God, and
we take captive
every thought to
make it

περισσεύουσα διὰ πολλῶν εὐχαριστιῶν τῷ θεῷ. 13 διὰ τῆς δοκιμῆς τῆς
overflowing through many thanksgivings to God. By their approval of this
4355 1328 4498 2374 3836 2536 1328 3836 1509 3836 4047
pt.pa.nsf p.g a.gpf n.gpf d.dsm n.dsm p.g d.gsf n.gsf d.gsf

διακονίας ταύτης δοξάζοντες τὸν θεὸν ἐπὶ τῇ ὑποταγῇ τῆς ὁμολογίας
service, *this* they glorify *{the}* God for your obedience ⌊stemming from⌋ your confession
1355 4047 1519 3836 2536 2093 3836 5717 3836 7007 3934
n.gsf r.gsf pt.pa.npm d.asm n.asm p.d d.dsf n.dsf d.gsf n.gsf

ὑμῶν εἰς τὸ εὐαγγέλιον τοῦ Χριστοῦ καὶ → ἁπλότητι τῆς κοινωνίας εἰς
your in the gospel of Christ, and for the generosity of your partnership with
7007 1650 3836 2295 3836 5986 2779 605 3836 3126 1650
r.gp.2 p.a d.asn n.asn d.gsm n.gsm cj n.dsf d.gsf n.gsf p.a

αὐτοὺς καὶ εἰς πάντας, 14 καὶ ↱ αὐτῶν δεήσει ὑπὲρ ὑμῶν ↰ ἐπιποθούντων
them and with everyone. And in their prayers on your behalf they yearn for
899 2779 1650 4246 2779 1255 899 1255 5642 7007 5642 2160
r.apm.3 cj p.a a.apm cj r.gpm.3 n.dsf p.g r.gp.2 pt.pa.gpm

ὑμᾶς διὰ τὴν ὑπερβάλλουσαν χάριν τοῦ θεοῦ ἐφ' ὑμῖν. 15 χάρις
you ⌊because of⌋ the surpassing grace of God ⌊bestowed on⌋ you. Thanks be
7007 1328 3836 5650 5921 3836 2536 2093 7007 5921
r.ap.2 p.a d.asf pt.pa.asf n.asf d.gsm n.gsm p.d r.dp.2 n.nsf

τῷ θεῷ ἐπὶ τῇ ἀνεκδιηγήτῳ αὐτοῦ δωρεᾷ.
to God for *{the}* his inexpressible *his* gift!
3836 2536 2093 3836 899 442 899 1561
d.dsm n.dsm p.d d.dsf a.dsf r.gsm.3 n.dsf

10:1 αὐτὸς δὲ ἐγὼ Παῦλος παρακαλῶ ὑμᾶς διὰ τῆς πραΰτητος
Now I, Paul myself, *Now I* *Paul* appeal to you by the meekness
1254 1609 4263 899 1254 1609 4263 4151 7007 1328 3836 4559
r.nsm cj r.ns.1 n.nsm v.pai.1s r.ap.2 p.g d.gsf n.gsf

καὶ ἐπιεικείας τοῦ Χριστοῦ, ὃς κατὰ πρόσωπον μὲν ταπεινὸς ἐν ὑμῖν,
and gentleness of Christ — I who when present ~ am "timid" among you,
2779 2116 3836 5986 4005 2848 4725 3525 5424 1877 7007
cj n.gsf d.gsm n.gsm r.nsm p.a n.asn pl a.nsm p.d r.dp.2

ἀπὼν δὲ θαρρῶ εἰς ὑμᾶς· 2 δέομαι δὲ τὸ
but ⌊when away⌋ *but* am "bold" toward you. I ask *{and}* ~ that when I am present
1254 583 1254 2509 1650 7007 1289 1254 3836 4205 4205 4205 4205
pt.pa.nsm cj v.pai.1s p.a r.ap.2 v.ppi.1s cj d.asn

↱ ↱ μὴ παρὼν θαρρῆσαι τῇ → πεποιθήσει ᾗ λογίζομαι
I may not *when I am present* have to be "bold," with such a confidence as I expect
2509 2509 3590 4205 2509 3836 4301 4005 3357
pl pt.pa.nsm f.aa d.dsf n.dsf r.dsf v.pmi.1s

τολμῆσαι ἐπί τινας τοὺς λογιζομένους ἡμᾶς ὡς κατὰ
⌊I will dare to use⌋ against those who think that we are walking *{as}* ⌊according to⌋
5528 2093 5516 3836 3357 7005 4344 4344 6055 2848
f.aa p.a r.apm d.apm pt.pm.apm r.ap.1 pl p.a

σάρκα περιπατοῦντας. 3 ἐν σαρκὶ γὰρ περιπατοῦντες
the flesh. *are walking* For though we walk in the flesh, *For* *though we walk* we
4922 4344 1142 4344 4344 4344 1877 4922 1142 4344 5129
n.asf pt.pa.apm p.d n.dsf cj pt.pa.npm

οὐ κατὰ σάρκα στρατευόμεθα, 4 τὰ γὰρ ὅπλα τῆς
are not waging war ⌊according to⌋ the flesh, *we are waging war* for the *for* weapons of
5129 4024 5129 5129 2848 4922 5129 1142 3836 1142 3960 3836
pl p.a n.asf v.pmi.1p d.npn cj n.npn d.gsf

στρατείας ἡμῶν οὐ → σαρκικὰ ἀλλὰ δυνατὰ τῷ θεῷ πρὸς
our warfare *our* are not of the flesh, but are empowered by God for
7005 5127 7005 4024 4920 247 1543 3836 2536 4639
n.gsf r.gp.1 pl a.npn cj a.npn d.dsm n.dsm p.a

καθαίρεσιν ὀχυρωμάτων, λογισμοὺς καθαιροῦντες 5 καὶ πᾶν ὕψωμα
tearing down strongholds. We tear down arguments *We tear down* and every lofty idea
2746 4065 2747 2747 2747 3361 2747 2779 4246 5739
n.asf n.gpn n.apm pt.pa.npm cj a.asn n.asn

ἐπαιρόμενον κατὰ τῆς γνώσεως τοῦ θεοῦ, καὶ αἰχμαλωτίζοντες πᾶν νόημα εἰς
that is raised against the knowledge of God, and we take captive every thought to make it
2048 2848 3836 1194 3836 2536 2779 170 4246 3784 1650
pt.pp.asn p.g d.gsf n.gsf d.gsm n.gsm cj pt.pa.npm a.asn n.asn p.a

NASB

overflowing
through many
thanksgivings to
God. 13 Because of
the proof given by
this ministry, they
will glorify God
for *your* obedience
to your confession
of the gospel of
Christ and for the
liberality of your
contribution to
them and to all,
14 while they also,
by prayer on your
behalf, yearn for
you because of the
surpassing grace
of God in you.
15 Thanks be to God
for His indescrib-
able gift!

Paul Describes Himself

10:1 Now I, Paul,
myself urge you
by the meekness
and gentleness of
Christ—I who am
meek when face
to face with you,
but bold toward
you when absent!
2 I ask that when I
am present I *need*
not be bold with
the confidence with
which I propose
to be courageous
against some, who
regard us as if we
walked according
to the flesh. 3 For
though we walk
in the flesh, we do
not war according
to the flesh, 4 for
the weapons of our
warfare are not of
the flesh, but di-
vinely powerful for
the destruction of
fortresses. 5 *We are*
destroying specula-
tions and every
lofty thing raised
up against the
knowledge of God,
and *we are* taking
every thought cap-
tive to the

NIV

obedient to Christ.
[6]And we will be
ready to punish
every act of dis-
obedience, once
your obedience is
complete.
[7]You are judging
by appearances.[a]
If anyone is con-
fident that they
belong to Christ,
they should con-
sider again that we
belong to Christ
just as much as
they do. [8]So even
if I boast some-
what freely about
the authority the
Lord gave us for
building you up
rather than tearing
you down, I will
not be ashamed of
it. [9]I do not want
to seem to be try-
ing to frighten you
with my letters.
[10]For some say,
"His letters are
weighty and force-
ful, but in person
he is unimpressive
and his speaking
amounts to noth-
ing." [11]Such people
should realize that
what we are in
our letters when
we are absent, we
will be in our ac-
tions when we are
present.
[12]We do not dare
to classify or com-
pare ourselves
with some who
commend them-
selves. When they
measure them-
selves by them-
selves and com-
pare themselves
with themselves,
they are not

[a] 7 Or *Look at the obvious facts*

τὴν ὑπακοὴν τοῦ Χριστοῦ, [6]καὶ ⌞ἐν ἑτοίμῳ⌟ ἔχοντες ἐκδικῆσαι πᾶσαν
{the} obey *{the}* Christ. And we are ready *we are* to avenge every
3836 5633 3836 5986 2779 2400 2400 1877 2289 2400 1688 4246
d.asf n.asf d.gsm n.gsm cj p.d a.dsn pt.pa.npm f.aa a.asf

παρακοήν, ὅταν πληρωθῇ ὑμῶν ἡ ὑπακοή. [7]
act of disobedience, whenever your obedience becomes complete. *your* *{the}* *obedience* You are
4157 4020 7007 5633 4444 7007 3836 5633 1063 1063
n.asf cj v.aps.3s r.gp.2 d.nsf n.nsf

τὰ κατὰ πρόσωπον βλέπετε. εἴ τις πέποιθεν ἑαυτῷ
looking *{the}* at outward appearances. *You are looking* If anyone has persuaded himself that
1063 3836 2848 4725 1063 1623 5516 4275 1571
d.apn p.a n.asn v.pai.2p cj r.nsm v.rai.3s r.dsm.3

Χριστοῦ εἶναι, τοῦτο ⌞λογιζέσθω πάλιν⌟ ⌞ἐφ' ἑαυτοῦ,⌟ ὅτι καθὼς
he belongs to Christ, *he belongs* *{this}* he should remind himself that just as
1639 1639 5986 1639 4047 3357 4099 2093 1571 4022 2777
n.gsm f.pa r.asn v.pmm.3s adv p.g r.gsm.3 cj cj

αὐτὸς Χριστοῦ, οὕτως καὶ ἡμεῖς. [8] ἐάν τε[a] γὰρ
he belongs to Christ, so also do we. For even if *even* *For* I boast about it,
899 5986 4048 2779 7005 1142 5445 1569 5445 1142 3016 3016 3016 5516
r.nsm n.gsm adv adv r.np.1 cj cj cj

περισσότερόν τι καυχήσωμαι περὶ τῆς ἐξουσίας ἡμῶν ἧς
and more than that, *it* *I boast about* about the authority which the Lord gave us *which*
4358 5516 3016 4309 3836 2026 4005 3836 3261 1443 7005 4005
adv.c r.asn v.ams.1s p.g d.gsf n.gsf r.gp.1 r.gsf

ἔδωκεν ὁ κύριος εἰς οἰκοδομὴν ← καὶ οὐκ εἰς καθαίρεσιν ὑμῶν, ↰ ↱ ↱
gave *the* *Lord* for building you up and not for tearing you down, I will
1443 3836 3261 1650 3869 2779 4024 1650 2746 7007 2746 159 159
v.aai.3s d.nsm n.nsm p.a n.asf cj pl p.a n.asf r.gp.2

οὐκ αἰσχυνθήσομαι. [9]↱ ↱ ἵνα μὴ δόξω ὡς ἂν
not be ashamed. I do not ⌞want to⌟ *not* seem ⌞as though⌟ ~
4024 159 1506 1506 3590 2671 3590 1506 6055 323
pl v.fpi.1s cj pl v.aas.1s pl pl

ἐκφοβεῖν ὑμᾶς διὰ τῶν ἐπιστολῶν· [10]ὅτι αἱ ἐπιστολαὶ
⌞I am trying to frighten⌟ you with my letters. For some are saying, "His letters
1768 7007 1328 3836 2186 4022 5774 5774 3836 2186
f.pa r.ap.2 p.g d.gpf n.gpf cj d.npf n.npf

μέν, φησίν, βαρεῖαι καὶ ἰσχυραί, ἡ δὲ παρουσία τοῦ σώματος
~ *are saying* are weighty and forceful, but his *but* physical presence *{the}* *physical* is
3525 5774 987 2779 2708 1254 3836 1254 5393 4242 3836 5393
pl v.pai.3s a.npf cj a.npf d.nsf cj n.nsf d.gsn n.gsn

ἀσθενὴς καὶ ὁ λόγος ἐξουθενημένος. [11] τοῦτο
weak, and his rhetoric amounts to nothing." Let such a person consider this,
822 2779 3836 3364 2024 3357 5525 5525 5525 3357 4047
a.nsf cj d.nsm n.nsm pt.rp.nsm r.asn

λογιζέσθω ὁ τοιοῦτος, ὅτι οἷοί ἐσμεν τῷ λόγῳ δι' ἐπιστολῶν ἀπόντες,
Let consider *{the}* *such a person* that what we are in word through letters when absent,
3357 3836 5525 4022 3888 1639 3836 3364 1328 2186 583
v.pmm.3s d.nsm r.nsm cj r.npm v.pai.1p d.dsm n.dsm p.g n.gpf pt.pa.npm

τοιοῦτοι καὶ παρόντες τῷ ἔργῳ. [12] ↱ ↱ οὐ γὰρ
such we also are in act when present. *in* *act* For we would not *For*
5525 2779 3836 2240 4205 3836 2240 1142 5528 5528 4024 1142
r.npm adv pt.pa.npm d.dsn n.dsn pl cj

τολμῶμεν ἐγκρῖναι ἢ συγκρῖναι ἑαυτούς τισιν τῶν
dare to classify or compare ourselves with some of those who are recommending
5528 1605 2445 5173 1571 5516 3836 5319 5319 5319
v.pai.1p f.aa cj f.aa r.apm.1 r.dpm d.gpm

ἑαυτοὺς συνιστανόντων, ἀλλὰ αὐτοὶ ἐν ἑαυτοῖς
themselves. *who are recommending* Rather, when they measure themselves by themselves
1571 5319 247 3582 899 3582 1571 1877 1571
r.apm.3 pt.pa.gpm cj r.npm p.d r.dpm.3

ἑαυτοὺς μετροῦντες καὶ συγκρίνοντες ἑαυτοὺς ἑαυτοῖς ↱ ↱ οὐ
themselves *when measure* and compare themselves by themselves, they are without
1571 3582 2779 5173 1571 1571 5317 5317 4024
r.apm.3 pt.pa.npm cj pt.pa.npm r.apm.3 r.dpm.3 pl

[a] [τε] UBS.

NASB

obedience of
Christ, [6]and we are
ready to punish
all disobedience,
whenever your
obedience is
complete.
[7]You are looking
at things as they
are outwardly. If
anyone is confi-
dent in himself
that he is Christ's,
let him consider
this again within
himself, that just
as he is Christ's,
so also are we.
[8]For even if I boast
somewhat further
about our author-
ity, which the Lord
gave for building
you up and not for
destroying you, I
will not be put to
shame, [9]for I do
not wish to seem
as if I would terrify
you by my letters.
[10]For they say, "His
letters are weighty
and strong, but his
personal presence
is unimpressive
and his speech con-
temptible." [11]Let
such a person con-
sider this, that what
we are in word by
letters when ab-
sent, such persons
we are also in deed
when present.
[12]For we are not
bold to class or
compare ourselves
with some of those
who commend
themselves; but
when they measure
themselves by
themselves and
compare them-
selves with them-
selves, they are

NIV

wise. 13We, how-
ever, will not
boast beyond
proper limits, but
will confine our
boasting to the
sphere of service
God himself has
assigned to us, a
sphere that also
includes you. 14We
are not going too
far in our boast-
ing, as would be
the case if we had
not come to you,
for we did get as
far as you with the
gospel of Christ.
15Neither do we
go beyond our
limits by boasting
of work done by
others. Our hope
is that, as your
faith continues to
grow, our sphere
of activity among
you will greatly
expand, 16so that
we can preach the
gospel in the re-
gions beyond you.
For we do not want
to boast about
work already done
in someone else's
territory. 17But,
"Let the one who
boasts boast in the
Lord."[a] 18For it is
not the one who
commends himself
who is approved,
but the one whom
the Lord com-
mends.

Paul and the False Apostles

11 I hope you
will put up
with me in a little
foolishness. Yes,
please put up with
me! 2I am jealous
for you with a god-
ly jealousy.

συνιᾶσιν. 13 ἡμεῖς δὲ οὐκ εἰς τὰ ἄμετρα καυχησόμεθα
understanding. We, however, will not boast beyond {the} proper limits, *will boast*
5317 7005 1254 3016 4024 3016 1650 3836 296 3016
v.pai.3p r.np.1 cj pl p.a d.apn a.apn v.fmi.1p

ἀλλὰ κατὰ τὸ μέτρον τοῦ κανόνος οὗ ἐμέρισεν ἡμῖν ὁ θεὸς →
but only within the measure of the ⌊sphere of action⌋ which God has assigned to us {the} *God* as a
247 2848 3836 3586 3836 2834 4005 2536 3532 7005 3836 2536
cj p.a d.asn n.asn d.gsm n.gsm r.gsm v.aai.3s r.dp.1 d.nsm n.nsm

μέτρου, ἐφικέσθαι ἄχρι καὶ ὑμῶν. 14 οὐ γὰρ ὡς ↱ ↱ μὴ
measure, extending even ⌊as far as⌋ *even* you. For it is not *For* ⌊as though⌋ we had not
3586 2391 2779 948 2779 7007 1142 4024 1142 6055 2391 2391 3590
n.gsn f.am p.g adv r.gp.2 pl cj pl pl

ἐφικνούμενοι εἰς ὑμᾶς ὑπερεκτείνομεν ἑαυτούς, ἄχρι γὰρ
come to you, over-reaching ourselves, for we did come even ⌊as far as⌋ *for*
2391 1650 7007 5657 1571 1142 5777 5777 5777 2779 948 1142
pt.pm.npm p.a r.ap.2 v.pai.1p r.apm.1 p.g cj

καὶ ὑμῶν ἐφθάσαμεν ἐν τῷ εὐαγγελίῳ τοῦ Χριστοῦ, 15 οὐκ εἰς τὰ
even you *we did come* with the gospel of Christ. We will not ⌊go beyond⌋ {the}
2779 7007 5777 1877 3836 2295 3836 5986 4024 1650 3836
adv r.gp.2 v.aai.1p p.d d.dsn n.dsn d.gsm n.gsm pl p.a d.apn

ἄμετρα καυχώμενοι ἐν ἀλλοτρίοις κόποις, ἐλπίδα δὲ
proper limits by boasting in the labors of others, *labors* but we have hope *but*
296 3016 1877 3160 259 3160 1254 2400 2400 1828 1254
a.apn pt.pm.npm p.d a.dpm n.dpm n.asf cj

ἔχοντες → αὐξανομένης τῆς πίστεως ὑμῶν ἐν
we have that as your faith continues to grow, {the} *faith* *your* our area of activity among
2400 7007 4411 889 3836 4411 7007 7005 2834 2834 2834 1877
pt.pa.npm pt.pp.gsf d.gsf n.gsf r.gp.2 p.d

ὑμῖν → → μεγαλυνθῆναι κατὰ τὸν κανόνα ἡμῶν ⌊εἰς
you will be greatly enlarged, *{according to}* *{the}* *area of activity* *our* *greatly*
7007 1650 3486 2848 3836 2834 7005 1650
r.dp.2 f.ap p.a d.asm n.asm r.gp.1 p.a

περισσείαν⌋ 16 εἰς τὰ ὑπερέκεινα ὑμῶν
⌊so that⌋ we may preach the gospel in places beyond you,
4353 1650 2294 2294 2294 2294 2294 3836 5654 7007
n.asf p.a d.apn p.g r.gp.2

εὐαγγελίσασθαι, οὐκ ἐν ἀλλοτρίῳ κανόνι
we may preach the gospel not boasting about the work already done in another person's territory.
2294 4024 3016 3016 1650 1877 259 2834
f.am pl p.d a.dsm n.dsm

⌊εἰς τὰ ἕτοιμα⌋ καυχήσασθαι. 17 ὁ δὲ καυχώμενος
already *boasting about* But rather, "Let the *But rather* one who boasts, boast
1650 3836 2289 3016 1254 1254 3016 3836 1254 3016 3016
p.a d.apn a.apn f.am d.nsm cj pt.pm.nsm

ἐν κυρίῳ καυχάσθω· 18 οὐ γὰρ ὁ ἑαυτὸν
in the Lord." *Let boast* For it is not *For* the one who recommends himself
1877 3261 3016 1142 4024 1142 3836 5319 5319 5319 1571
p.d n.dsm v.pmm.3s pl cj d.nsm r.asm.3

συνιστάνων, ἐκεῖνός ἐστιν δόκιμος, ἀλλὰ ὃν ὁ κύριος συνίστησιν.
one who recommends who is approved, but the ⌊one whom⌋ the Lord recommends.
5319 1697 1639 1511 247 4005 3836 3261 5319
pt.pa.nsm r.nsm v.pai.3s a.nsm cj r.asm d.nsm n.nsm v.pai.3s

11:1 ὄφελον ἀνείχεσθέ μου μικρόν τι ἀφροσύνης· ἀλλὰ καὶ
O that ⌊you would put up with⌋ me in a little *a* foolishness! *{but}* *{also}*
4054 462 1609 5516 3625 5516 932 247 2779
pt.aa.nsn v.imi.2p r.gs.1 a.asn r.asn n.gsf cj adv

ἀνέχεσθέ μου. 2 ζηλῶ ↱ γὰρ ὑμᾶς θεοῦ
⌊Do put up with⌋ me! For I am jealous for *For* you with a jealousy God inspires,
462 1609 1142 2420 7007 1142 7007 2419 2419 2536
v.pmi.2p r.gs.1 v.pai.1s cj r.ap.2 n.gsm

NASB

without under-
standing. 13But
we will not boast
beyond *our* mea-
sure, but within
the measure of the
sphere which God
apportioned to us
as a measure, to
reach even as far as
you. 14For we are
not overextending
ourselves, as if we
did not reach to
you, for we were
the first to come
even as far as
you in the gospel
of Christ; 15not
boasting beyond
our measure, *that*
is, in other men's
labors, but with the
hope that as your
faith grows, we
will be, within our
sphere, enlarged
even more by you,
16so as to preach
the gospel even to
the regions beyond
you, *and* not to
boast in what has
been accomplished
in the sphere of an-
other. 17But HE WHO
BOASTS IS TO BOAST
IN THE LORD. 18For
it is not he who
commends himself
that is approved,
but he whom the
Lord commends.

Paul Defends His Apostleship

11:1I wish that you
would bear with
me in a little fool-
ishness; but indeed
you are bearing
with me. 2For I am
jealous for you
with a godly

[a] 17 Jer. 9:24

NIV

I promised you
to one husband,
to Christ, so that
I might present
you as a pure vir-
gin to him. 3But
I am afraid that
just as Eve was
deceived by the
serpent's cunning,
your minds may
somehow be led
astray from your
sincere and pure
devotion to Christ.
4For if someone
comes to you and
preaches a Jesus
other than the
Jesus we preached,
or if you receive
a different spirit
from the Spirit
you received, or
a different gospel
from the one you
accepted, you put
up with it easily
enough.
5I do not think
I am in the least
inferior to those
"super-apostles."[a]
6I may indeed be
untrained as a
speaker, but I do
have knowledge.
We have made this
perfectly clear to
you in every way.
7Was it a sin for
me to lower myself
in order to elevate
you by preach-
ing the gospel of
God to you free of
charge? 8I robbed
other churches by
receiving support
from them so as to
serve you. 9And
when I was with
you and needed
something, I was
not

ζήλω, ἡρμοσάμην γὰρ ὑμᾶς ἑνὶ ἀνδρὶ
with jealousy for I have promised for you in marriage to a single husband, to Christ, that
2419 1142 764 1142 7007 764 764 1651 467 3836 5986 4225
n.dsm v.ami.1s cj r.ap.2 a.dsm n.dsm

παρθένον ἁγνὴν παραστῆσαι τῷ
I might present you to him as an undefiled virgin. undefiled that I might present to
4225 4225 4225 54 4221 54 4225 3836
n.asf a.asf f.aa d.dsm

Χριστῷ· 3 φοβοῦμαι δὲ ⌊μή πως,⌋ ὡς ὁ ὄφις ἐξηπάτησεν Εὕαν
Christ But I am afraid, But however, that ⌊just as⌋ the serpent deceived Eve
5986 1254 5828 1254 3590 4803 6055 3836 4058 1987 2293
n.dsm v.ppi.1s cj cj pl cj d.nsm n.nsm v.aai.3s n.asf

ἐν τῇ πανουργίᾳ αὐτοῦ, φθαρῇ τὰ νοήματα ὑμῶν ἀπὸ
by {the} his craftiness, his so your minds ⌊may be led astray⌋ {the} minds your from
1877 3836 899 4111 899 7007 3784 5780 3836 3784 7007 608
p.d d.dsf n.dsf r.gsm.3 v.aps.3s d.npn n.npn r.gp.2 p.g

τῆς ἁπλότητος [a]καὶ τῆς ἁγνότητος τῆς εἰς τὸν Χριστόν. 4 εἰ μὲν γὰρ ὁ
the simplicity and {the} purity that is in {the} Christ. For if For one
3836 605 2779 3836 55 3836 1650 3836 5986 1142 1623 3525 1142 3836
d.gsf n.gsf cj d.gsf n.gsf d.gsf p.a d.asm n.asm cj pl cj d.nsm

ἐρχόμενος ἄλλον Ἰησοῦν κηρύσσει ὃν οὐκ ἐκηρύξαμεν, ἢ
comes and proclaims a different Jesus proclaims whom we did not proclaim, or
2262 3062 257 2652 3062 4005 3062 3062 4024 3062 2445
pt.pm.nsm r.asm n.asm v.pai.3s r.asm pl v.aai.1p cj

πνεῦμα ἕτερον λαμβάνετε ὃ οὐκ ἐλάβετε, ἢ
if you welcome a different spirit different you welcome which you did not welcome, or a
3284 3284 2283 4460 2283 3284 4005 3284 3284 4024 3284 2445
n.asn r.asn v.pai.2p r.asn pl v.aai.2p cj

εὐαγγέλιον ἕτερον ὃ οὐκ ἐδέξασθε, καλῶς
different gospel different which you did not welcome, you put up with it easily.
2283 2295 2283 4005 1312 1312 4024 1312 462 462 462 462 2822
n.asn r.asn r.asn pl v.ami.2p adv

ἀνέχεσθε. 5 λογίζομαι γὰρ μηδὲν ὑστερηκέναι τῶν
you put up with For I consider myself For to be in no way inferior to those
462 1142 3357 1142 5728 5728 3594 5728 3836
v.pmi.2p v.pmi.1s cj a.asn f.ra d.gpm

⌊ὑπερλίαν ἀποστόλων.⌋ 6 εἰ δὲ καὶ ἰδιώτης τῷ λόγῳ,
"super-apostles." But even if But even I am an amateur in speaking, I am
5663 693 1254 2779 1623 1254 2779 2626 3836 3364
adv n.gpm cj cj adv n.nsm d.dsm n.dsm

⌊ἀλλ᾽ οὐ⌋ τῇ γνώσει, ἀλλ᾽ ἐν παντὶ φανερώσαντες
certainly not in knowledge. Rather, in ⌊every way⌋ ⌊we have made this plain⌋ to you as
247 4024 3836 1194 247 1877 4246 5746 1650 7007
cj pl d.dsf n.dsf cj p.d a.dsn pt.aa.npm

ἐν πᾶσιν εἰς ὑμᾶς. 7 ἢ ἁμαρτίαν ἐποίησα
to all. to you Or did I commit a sin did I commit in humbling
1877 4246 1650 7007 2445 4472 4472 4472 281 4472 5427 5427
p.d a.dpn p.a r.ap.2 cj n.asf v.aai.1s

ἐμαυτὸν ταπεινῶν ἵνα ὑμεῖς ὑψωθῆτε, ὅτι
myself in humbling so that you could be exalted, because I proclaimed the gospel of God
1831 5427 2671 7007 5738 4022 2294 2294 3836 2295 3836 2536
r.asm.1 pt.pa.nsm cj r.np.2 v.aps.2p cj

δωρεὰν τὸ τοῦ θεοῦ εὐαγγέλιον εὐηγγελισάμην ὑμῖν; 8
to you ⌊without a charge?⌋ the of God gospel I proclaimed to you I robbed
7007 7007 1562 3836 3836 2536 2295 2294 7007 5195 5195
adv d.asn d.gsm n.gsm n.asn v.ami.1s r.dp.2

ἄλλας ἐκκλησίας ἐσύλησα λαβὼν ὀψώνιον πρὸς τὴν ὑμῶν
other churches, I robbed taking support from them ⌊to carry out⌋ my service to you.
257 1711 5195 3284 4072 4639 3836 1355 7007
r.apf n.apf v.aai.1s pt.aa.nsm n.asn p.a d.asf r.gp.2

διακονίαν, 9 καὶ παρὼν πρὸς ὑμᾶς καὶ ὑστερηθεὶς οὐ
service And ⌊when I was present⌋ with you and in need, I did not
1355 2779 4205 4639 7007 2779 5728 2915 2915 4024
n.asf cj pt.pa.nsm p.a r.ap.2 cj pt.ap.nsm pl

NASB

jealousy; for I be-
trothed you to one
husband, so that to
Christ I might pres-
ent you *as* a pure
virgin. 3But I am
afraid that, as the
serpent deceived
Eve by his crafti-
ness, your minds
will be led astray
from the simplicity
and purity *of devo-
tion* to Christ. 4For
if one comes and
preaches another
Jesus whom we
have not preached,
or you receive a
different spirit
which you have
not received, or a
different gospel
which you have not
accepted, you bear
this beautifully.
5For I consider
myself not in the
least inferior to
the most eminent
apostles. 6But even
if I am unskilled
in speech, yet I am
not *so* in knowl-
edge; in fact, in
every way we have
made *this* evident
to you in all things.
7Or did I commit
a sin in humbling
myself so that you
might be exalted,
because I preached
the gospel of God
to you without
charge? 8I robbed
other churches by
taking wages *from
them* to serve you;
9and when I was
present with you
and was in need, I

[a] 5 Or *to the most eminent apostles*

[a] [καὶ τῆς ἁγνότητος] UBS.

NIV

a burden to any-
one, for the broth-
ers who came from
Macedonia sup-
plied what I need-
ed. I have kept
myself from being
a burden to you in
any way, and will
continue to do so.
10 As surely as the
truth of Christ is in
me, nobody in the
regions of Acha-
ia will stop this
boasting of mine.
11 Why? Because
I do not love you?
God knows I do!
12 And I will keep
on doing what I
am doing in order
to cut the ground
from under those
who want an op-
portunity to be
considered equal
with us in the
things they boast
about. 13 For such
people are false
apostles, deceitful
workers, masquer-
ading as apostles
of Christ. 14 And no
wonder, for Satan
himself masquer-
ades as an angel
of light. 15 It is not
surprising, then, if
his servants also
masquerade as ser-
vants of righteous-
ness. Their end
will be what their
actions deserve.

Paul Boasts About His Sufferings

16 I repeat: Let no
one take me for a
fool. But if you do,
then tolerate me
just as you would a
fool, so that I may
do a little boasting.

κατενάρκησα οὐθενός· τὸ γὰρ
burden anyone, for when the brothers came from Macedonia they supplied {the} for
2915 4032 1142 2262 3836 81 2262 608 3423 4650 4650 3836 1142
v.aai.1s a.gsm d.asn cj

ὑστέρημά μου προσανεπλήρωσαν οἱ ἀδελφοὶ ἐλθόντες ἀπὸ Μακεδονίας, καὶ
my need. my they supplied the brothers when came from Macedonia {and}
1609 5729 1609 4650 3836 81 2262 608 3423 2779
n.asn r.gs.1 v.aai.3p d.npm n.npm pt.aa.npm p.g n.gsf cj

ἐν παντὶ ἀβαρῆ ἐμαυτὸν ὑμῖν
I kept myself from being a burden to you in any way, being a burden myself to you
5498 5498 1831 5498 4 4 4 7007 7007 1877 4246 4 1831 7007
p.d a.dsn a.asm r.asm.1 r.dp.2

ἐτήρησα καὶ τηρήσω. 10 → ἔστιν ἀλήθεια Χριστοῦ ἐν
I kept from and ⌊will continue to do so.⌋ As the truth of Christ is truth of Christ in
5498 2779 5498 237 5986 5986 1639 237 5986 1877
v.aai.1s cj v.fai.1s v.pai.3s n.nsf n.gsm p.d

ἐμοὶ ὅτι ἡ καύχησις αὕτη ↱ οὐ φραγήσεται εἰς ἐμὲ ἐν τοῖς
me, ~ {the} this boasting this of mine will not be put to silence of mine in the
1609 4022 3836 4047 3018 4047 1650 1609 5852 4024 5852 1650 1609 1877 3836
r.ds.1 cj d.nsf n.nsf r.nsf pl v.fpi.3s p.a r.as.1 p.d d.dpn

κλίμασιν τῆς Ἀχαΐας. 11 διὰ τί; ὅτι ↱ ↱ οὐκ ἀγαπῶ ὑμᾶς; ὁ θεὸς
districts of Achaia. Why is that? Is it because I do not love you? {the} God
3107 3836 938 1328 5515 4022 26 26 4024 26 7007 3836 2536
n.dpn d.gsf n.gsf p.a r.asn cj pl v.pai.1s r.ap.2 d.nsm n.nsm

οἶδεν. 12 ὃ δὲ ποιῶ, καὶ ποιήσω, ἵνα ἐκκόψω τὴν
knows I do. And what And I am doing {also} ⌊I will continue to do,⌋ so as to remove any
3857 1254 4005 1254 4472 2779 4472 2671 1716 3836
v.rai.3s r.asn cj v.pai.1s adv v.fai.1s cj v.aas.1s d.asf

ἀφορμὴν τῶν θελόντων ἀφορμήν, ἵνα ἐν ᾧ
opportunity from those desiring an opportunity to be regarded, in the things in which
929 3836 2527 929 2671 2351 2351 1877 4005
n.asf d.gpm pt.pa.gpm n.asf cj p.d r.dsn

καυχῶνται εὑρεθῶσιν καθὼς καὶ ἡμεῖς. 13 οἱ γὰρ τοιοῦτοι
they boast, be regarded to be just as {also} we are. {the} For such men are
3016 2351 2777 2779 7005 3836 1142 5525
v.pmi.3p v.aps.3p cj adv r.np.1 d.npm cj r.npm

ψευδαπόστολοι, ἐργάται δόλιοι, μετασχηματιζόμενοι εἰς ἀποστόλους
false apostles, deceitful workers, deceitful disguising themselves as apostles
6013 1513 2239 1513 3571 1650 693
n.npm n.npm a.npm pt.pm.npm p.a n.apm

Χριστοῦ. 14 καὶ οὐ θαῦμα· αὐτὸς γὰρ ὁ σατανᾶς μετασχηματίζεται εἰς
of Christ. And no wonder! For Satan himself For {the} Satan disguises himself as
5986 2779 4024 2512 1142 4928 899 1142 3836 4928 3571 1650
n.gsm cj pl n.nsn r.nsm cj d.nsm n.nsm v.pmi.3s p.a

ἄγγελον φωτός. 15 οὐ μέγα οὖν εἰ καὶ οἱ διάκονοι
an angel of light. So it is no great surprise So if his servants, too, {the} servants
34 5890 4036 4024 3489 4036 1623 899 1356 2779 3836 1356
n.asm n.gsn pl a.nsn cj cj adv d.npm n.npm

αὐτοῦ μετασχηματίζονται ὡς διάκονοι δικαιοσύνης· ὧν τὸ τέλος ἔσται
his disguise themselves as servants of righteousness. Their {the} end will be
899 3571 6055 1356 1466 4005 3836 5465 1639
r.gsm.3 v.pmi.3p pl n.npm n.gsf r.gpm d.nsn n.nsn v.fmi.3s

κατὰ τὰ ἔργα αὐτῶν. 16 πάλιν λέγω, μή τίς με δόξῃ
⌊according to⌋ {the} their works. their Again I say, let no one think me let think
2848 3836 899 2240 899 4099 3306 1506 3590 5516 1506 1609 1506
p.a d.apn n.apn r.gpm.3 adv v.pai.1s pl r.nsm r.as.1 v.aas.3s

ἄφρονα εἶναι· εἰ δὲ μή γε, κἂν ὡς ἄφρονα
foolish. {to be} But even if But ~ even you do, ⌊then at least⌋ accept me as a fool,
933 1639 1254 1145 1623 1254 3590 1145 2829 1312 1609 6055 933
a.asm f.pa cj cj pl pl crasis pl a.asm

δέξασθέ με, ἵνα κἀγὼ μικρόν τι καυχήσωμαι. 17 ὃ λαλῶ,
accept me so that I too may boast a little. a may boast What I am saying,
1312 1609 2671 2743 3016 3016 5516 3625 5516 3016 4005 3281
v.amm.2p r.as.1 cj crasis a.asn r.asn v.ams.1s r.asn v.pai.1s

NASB

was not a burden to
anyone; for when
the brethren came
from Macedonia
they fully supplied
my need, and in
everything I kept
myself from being
a burden to you,
and will continue
to do so. 10 As the
truth of Christ is in
me, this boasting
of mine will not
be stopped in the
regions of Achaia.
11 Why? Because I
do not love you?
God knows *I do!*
12 But what I
am doing I will
continue to do, so
that I may cut off
opportunity from
those who desire
an opportunity to
be regarded just
as we are in the
matter about which
they are boasting.
13 For such men
are false apostles,
deceitful workers,
disguising them-
selves as apostles
of Christ. 14 No
wonder, for even
Satan disguises
himself as an angel
of light. 15 Therefore
it is not surprising
if his servants also
disguise them-
selves as servants
of righteousness,
whose end will be
according to their
deeds.
16 Again I say,
let no one think
me foolish; but if
you do, receive
me even as fool-
ish, so that I also
may boast a little.
17 What I am saying,

NIV

[17]In this self-confi-
dent boasting I am
not talking as the
Lord would, but
as a fool. [18]Since
many are boast-
ing in the way the
world does, I too
will boast. [19]You
gladly put up with
fools since you
are so wise! [20]In
fact, you even put
up with anyone
who enslaves you
or exploits you or
takes advantage
of you or puts on
airs or slaps you in
the face. [21]To my
shame I admit that
we were too weak
for that!
Whatever any-
one else dares to
boast about—I
am speaking as a
fool—I also dare
to boast about.
[22]Are they He-
brews? So am I.
Are they Israel-
ites? So am I. Are
they Abraham's
descendants? So
am I. [23]Are they
servants of Christ?
(I am out of my
mind to talk like
this.) I am more.
I have worked
much harder, been
in prison more
frequently, been
flogged more se-
verely, and been
exposed to death
again and again.
[24]Five times I re-
ceived from the
Jews the forty
lashes minus one.
[25]Three times I
was beaten with
rods, once I was
pelted with stones,
three times I was
shipwrecked, I
spent a night and
a day in the open
sea, [26]I have been
constantly

οὐ κατὰ κύριον λαλῶ ἀλλ᾽ ὡς ἐν ἀφροσύνῃ, ἐν
I am not saying ⌊according to⌋ the Lord, *I am saying* but as in foolishness, in
3281 3281 4024 3281 2848 3261 3281 247 6055 1877 932 1877
pl p.a n.asm v.pai.1s cj pl p.d n.dsf p.d

ταύτῃ τῇ ὑποστάσει τῆς καυχήσεως. 18 ἐπεὶ πολλοὶ καυχῶνται
this *{the}* confidence of boasting. Since there are many who are boasting
4047 3836 5712 3836 3018 2075 4498 3016
r.dsf d.dsf n.dsf d.gsf n.gsf cj a.npm v.pmi.3p

κατὰ σάρκα, κἀγὼ καυχήσομαι. 19 ἡδέως γὰρ ἀνέχεσθε τῶν
⌊according to⌋ the flesh, I too will boast. For gladly *For* ⌊you put up with⌋ *{the}*
2848 4922 2743 3016 1142 2452 1142 462 3836
p.a n.asf crasis v.fmi.1s adv cj v.pmi.2p d.gpm

ἀφρόνων φρόνιμοι ὄντες· 20 ἀνέχεσθε γὰρ εἴ τις
fools, since you are so wise! *since you are* For ⌊you put up with⌋ *For* it if anyone
933 1639 1639 1639 5861 1639 1142 462 1142 1623 5516
a.gpm a.npm pt.pa.npm v.pmi.2p cj cj r.nsm

ὑμᾶς καταδουλοῖ, εἴ τις κατεσθίει, εἴ τις λαμβάνει,
enslaves you, *enslaves* if anyone exploits you, if anyone ⌊takes advantage of⌋ you,
2871 7007 2871 1623 5516 2983 1623 5516 3284
r.ap.2 v.pai.3s cj r.nsm v.pai.3s cj r.nsm v.pai.3s

εἴ τις ἐπαίρεται, εἴ τις εἰς πρόσωπον ὑμᾶς δέρει. 21
if anyone puts on airs, if anyone strikes you in the face. *you* *strikes* I say
1623 5516 2048 1623 5516 1296 7007 1650 4725 7007 1296 3306 3306
cj r.nsm v.pmi.3s cj r.nsm p.a n.asn r.ap.2 v.pai.3s

κατὰ ἀτιμίαν λέγω, ὡς ὅτι ἡμεῖς ἠσθενήκαμεν. ἐν ᾧ δ᾽
this to my shame, *I say* *{as}* that in this we have been weak. But ⌊as to⌋ whatever *But*
2848 871 3306 6055 4022 7005 820 1254 1877 4005 1254
p.a n.asf v.pai.1s pl cj r.np.1 v.rai.1p p.d r.dsn cj

ἄν τις τολμᾷ, ἐν ἀφροσύνῃ λέγω,
~ ⌊anyone else⌋ dares to boast about — I am talking like a fool *I am talking* — I
323 5516 5528 3306 3306 3306 1877 932 3306 2743
pl r.nsm v.pas.3s p.d n.dsf v.pai.1s

τολμῶ κἀγώ. 22 Ἑβραῖοί εἰσιν; → κἀγώ. Ἰσραηλῖταί
also ⌊dare to boast.⌋ *I also* Are they Hebrews? *Are they* So am I. Are they Israelites?
2743 5528 2743 1639 1639 1578 1639 2743 1639 1639 2703
v.pai.1s crasis n.npm v.pai.3p crasis n.npm

εἰσιν; → κἀγώ. σπέρμα Ἀβραάμ εἰσιν; → κἀγώ. 23
Are they So am I. Are they descendants of Abraham? *Are they* So am I. Are they
1639 2743 1639 1639 5065 11 1639 2743 1639 1639
v.pai.3p crasis n.nsn n.gsm v.pai.3p crasis

διάκονοι Χριστοῦ εἰσιν; → παραφρονῶν λαλῶ,
servants of Christ? *Are they* — I am talking like a madman! *I am talking* — I am
1356 5986 1639 3281 3281 3281 4196 3281 1609
n.npm n.gsm v.pai.3p pt.pa.nsm v.pai.1s

ὑπὲρ ἐγώ· ἐν κόποις περισσοτέρως, ἐν φυλακαῖς περισσοτέρως,
⌊even more so:⌋ *I* in far more labors, *far more* in prison more often,
5642 1609 1877 4359 4359 3160 4359 1877 5871 4359
adv r.ns.1 p.d n.dpm adv.c p.d n.dpf adv.c

ἐν πληγαῖς ὑπερβαλλόντως, ἐν θανάτοις πολλάκις. 24
in beatings more severe, facing death again and again. Five times I received
1877 4435 5649 1877 2505 4490 4294 4294 3284 3284
p.d n.dpf adv p.d n.dpm adv

ὑπὸ Ἰουδαίων πεντάκις τεσσεράκοντα παρὰ μίαν ἔλαβον, 25 τρὶς
from the Jews *Five times* the forty lashes less one. *I received* ⌊Three times⌋
5679 2681 4294 5477 4123 1651 3284 5565
p.g a.gpm adv a.apf p.a a.asf v.aai.1s adv

ἐρραβδίσθην, ἅπαξ ἐλιθάσθην, τρὶς ἐναυάγησα,
⌊I was beaten with a rod.⌋ Once I was stoned. ⌊Three times⌋ I was shipwrecked. I have been adrift
4810 562 3342 5565 3728 4472 4472 4472 4472
v.api.1s adv v.api.1s adv v.aai.1s

νυχθήμερον ἐν τῷ βυθῷ πεποίηκα· 26 →
on the open sea ⌊for twenty-four hours.⌋ *on* *the* *open sea* *I have been adrift* On my frequent
1877 3836 1113 1113 3819 1877 3836 1113 4472 4490
n.asn p.d d.dsm n.dsm v.rai.1s

NASB

I am not say-
ing as the Lord
would, but as in
foolishness, in
this confidence of
boasting. [18]Since
many boast accord-
ing to the flesh,
I will boast also.
[19]For you, being
so wise, tolerate
the foolish gladly.
[20]For you tolerate it
if anyone enslaves
you, anyone de-
vours you, anyone
takes advantage of
you, anyone exalts
himself, anyone
hits you in the face.
[21]To *my* shame I
must say that we
have been weak *by*
comparison.
But in whatever
respect anyone *else*
is bold—I speak
in foolishness—I
am just as bold
myself. [22]Are they
Hebrews? So am I.
Are they Israelites?
So am I. Are they
descendants of
Abraham? So am I.
[23]Are they servants
of Christ?—I speak
as if insane—I
more so; in far
more labors, in
far more impris-
onments, beaten
times without num-
ber, often in danger
of death. [24]Five
times I received
from the Jews
thirty-nine *lashes.*
[25]Three times I was
beaten with rods,
once I was stoned,
three times I was
shipwrecked, a
night and a day I
have spent in the
deep. [26]*I have been*

NIV

on the move. I
have been in dan-
ger from rivers,
in danger from
bandits, in danger
from my fellow
Jews, in danger
from Gentiles;
in danger in the
city, in danger in
the country, in
danger at sea; and
in danger from
false believers. [27]I
have labored and
toiled and have
often gone with-
out sleep; I have
known hunger and
thirst and have of-
ten gone without
food; I have been
cold and naked.
[28]Besides every-
thing else, I face
daily the pressure
of my concern for
all the churches.
[29]Who is weak,
and I do not feel
weak? Who is led
into sin, and I do
not inwardly burn?
[30]If I must boast,
I will boast of the
things that show
my weakness.
[31]The God and
Father of the Lord
Jesus, who is to
be praised forev-
er, knows that I
am not lying. [32]In
Damascus the gov-
ernor under King
Aretas had the city
of the Damascenes
guarded in order
to arrest me. [33]But
I was lowered in
a basket from a
window in the
wall and slipped
through his hands.

Paul's Vision and His Thorn

12 I must go
on boasting.
Although there
is nothing to be
gained, I will go
on to visions and
revelations from
the Lord.

ὁδοιπορίαις πολλάκις, κινδύνοις ποταμῶν, κινδύνοις λῃστῶν,
journeys *frequent* I have been exposed to dangers from rivers, dangers from bandits,
3845 4490 3074 4532 3074 3334
n.dpf adv n.dpm n.gpm n.dpm n.gpm

κινδύνοις ἐκ γένους, κινδύνοις ἐξ ἐθνῶν, κινδύνοις ἐν πόλει,
dangers from ⌊my own people,⌋ dangers from Gentiles, dangers in the city,
3074 1666 1169 3074 1666 1620 3074 1877 4484
n.dpm p.g n.gsn n.dpm p.g n.gpn n.dpm p.d n.dsf

κινδύνοις ἐν ἐρημίᾳ, κινδύνοις ἐν θαλάσσῃ, κινδύνοις ἐν
dangers in the countryside, dangers at sea, dangers at the hands of
3074 1877 2244 3074 1877 2498 3074 1877
n.dpm p.d n.dsf n.dpm p.d n.dsf n.dpm p.d

ψευδαδέλφοις, [27] κόπῳ καὶ μόχθῳ, ἐν ἀγρυπνίαις πολλάκις, ἐν λιμῷ καὶ
false brothers; in toil and hard work, often in need of sleep, *often* in hunger and
6012 3160 2779 3677 4490 1877 71 4490 1877 3350 2779
n.dpm n.dsm cj n.dsm p.d n.dpf adv p.d n.dsm cj

δίψει, ⌊ἐν νηστείαις⌋ πολλάκις, ἐν ψύχει καὶ γυμνότητι·
thirst, many times without food, *many times* in cold and nakedness.
1499 4490 4490 1877 3763 4490 1877 6036 2779 1219
n.dsn p.d n.dpf adv p.d n.dsn cj n.dsf

[28] χωρὶς τῶν παρεκτὸς ἡ ἐπίστασίς μοι ἡ ⌊καθ' ἡμέραν,⌋
⌊Apart from⌋ *{the}* other things, there is the daily pressure ⌊on me⌋ *{the}* *daily* of
6006 3836 4211 3836 2848 2180 1609 3836 2848 2465
p.g d.gpn adv d.nsf n.nsf r.ds.1 d.nsf p.a n.asf

ἡ μέριμνα πασῶν τῶν ἐκκλησιῶν. [29] τίς ἀσθενεῖ καὶ ↱ ↱ οὐκ ἀσθενῶ;
my anxious concern for all the churches. Who is weak, and I am not weak?
3836 3533 4246 3836 1711 5515 820 2779 820 820 4024 820
d.nsf n.nsf a.gpf d.gpf n.gpf r.nsm v.pai.3s cj pl v.pai.1s

τίς σκανδαλίζεται καὶ ↱ οὐκ ἐγὼ πυροῦμαι; [30] Εἰ
Who is made to stumble, and I do not *I* burn with indignation? If there must
5515 4997 2779 1609 4792 4024 1609 4792 1623 1256 1256
r.nsm v.ppi.3s cj pl r.ns.1 v.ppi.1s cj

καυχᾶσθαι δεῖ, τὰ τῆς ἀσθενείας μου
be boasting, *there must* I will boast of ⌊the things⌋ that display my weakness. *my*
3016 1256 3016 3016 3016 3016 3836 3836 1609 819 1609
f.pm v.pai.3s d.apn d.gsf n.gsf r.gs.1

καυχήσομαι. [31] ὁ θεὸς καὶ πατὴρ τοῦ κυρίου Ἰησοῦ
I will boast of The God and Father of our Lord Jesus, he who is blessed for all
3016 3836 2536 2779 4252 3836 3261 2652 3836 1639 1639 2329 1650 3836
v.fmi.1s d.nsm n.nsm cj n.nsm d.gsm n.gsm n.gsm

οἶδεν, ὁ ὢν εὐλογητὸς εἰς τοὺς αἰῶνας, ὅτι ↱ ↱ οὐ ψεύδομαι.
time, knows *he* *who is* *blessed* *for* *all* *time* that I am not lying.
172 3857 3836 1639 2329 1650 3836 172 4022 6017 6017 4024 6017
v.rai.3s d.nsm pt.pa.nsm a.nsm p.a d.apm n.apm cj pl v.pmi.1s

[32] ἐν Δαμασκῷ ὁ ἐθνάρχης Ἁρέτα τοῦ βασιλέως ἐφρούρει τὴν πόλιν
At Damascus the ethnarch under king Aretas *under* *king* was guarding the city
1877 1242 3836 1617 3836 995 745 3836 995 5864 3836 4484
p.d n.dsf d.nsm n.nsm n.gsm d.gsm n.gsm v.iai.3s d.asf n.asf

Δαμασκηνῶν πιάσαι με, [33] καὶ διὰ
of Damascus ⌊in order to arrest⌋ me, but I was lowered in a basket through an
1241 4389 1609 2779 5899 5899 5899 1877 4914 1328
a.gpm f.aa r.as.1 cj p.g

θυρίδος ἐν σαργάνῃ ἐχαλάσθην διὰ τοῦ τείχους καὶ ἐξέφυγον τὰς χεῖρας αὐτοῦ.
opening *in* *basket* *I was lowered* in the wall and escaped *{the}* his hands. *his*
2600 1877 4914 5899 1328 3836 5446 2779 1767 3836 899 5931 899
n.gsf p.d n.dsf v.api.1s p.g d.gsn n.gsn cj v.aai.1s d.apf n.apf r.gsm.3

12:1 καυχᾶσθαι δεῖ, ↱ ↱ οὐ
It is necessary for me to continue boasting. *It is necessary* Though it is not
1256 1256 1256 3016 1256 3525 5237 5237 4024
f.pm v.pai.3s pl

συμφέρον μέν, ἐλεύσομαι δὲ εἰς ὀπτασίας καὶ ἀποκαλύψεις → κυρίου.
profitable, *Though* I will go on *{and}* to visions and revelations from the Lord.
5237 3525 2262 1254 1650 3965 2779 637 3261
pt.pa.nsn pl v.fmi.1s cj p.a n.apf cj n.apf n.gsm

NASB

on frequent jour-
neys, in dangers
from rivers,
dangers from rob-
bers, dangers from
my countrymen,
dangers from the
Gentiles, dangers
in the city, dangers
in the wilderness,
dangers on the sea,
dangers among
false brethren;
[27]*I have been* in
labor and hardship,
through many
sleepless nights, in
hunger and thirst,
often without
food, in cold and
exposure. [28]Apart
from *such* external
things, there is the
daily pressure on
me *of* concern for
all the churches.
[29]Who is weak
without my being
weak? Who is led
into sin without my
intense concern?
[30]If I have to
boast, I will boast
of what pertains
to my weakness.
[31]The God and
Father of the Lord
Jesus, He who is
blessed forever,
knows that I am
not lying. [32]In
Damascus the eth-
narch under Aretas
the king was
guarding the city
of the Damascenes
in order to seize
me, [33]and I was let
down in a basket
through a window
in the wall, and *so*
escaped his hands.

Paul's Vision

[12:1]Boasting is
necessary, though
it is not profitable;
but I will go on to
visions and revela-
tions of the Lord.

NIV

2 I know a man in
Christ who four-
teen years ago
was caught up to
the third heaven.
Whether it was
in the body or out
of the body I do
not know—God
knows. 3 And I
know that this
man—whether in
the body or apart
from the body I do
not know, but God
knows— 4 was
caught up to para-
dise and heard in-
expressible things,
things that no one
is permitted to tell.
5 I will boast about
a man like that,
but I will not boast
about myself,
except about my
weaknesses. 6 Even
if I should choose
to boast, I would
not be a fool, be-
cause I would be
speaking the truth.
But I refrain, so
no one will think
more of me than
is warranted by
what I do or say,
7 or because of
these surpassingly
great revelations.
Therefore, in order
to keep me from
becoming conceit-
ed, I was given a
thorn in my flesh,
a messenger of
Satan, to torment
me. 8 Three times
I pleaded with
the Lord to take
it away from me.
9 But he said to me,
"My grace is suffi-
cient for you,

2 οἶδα ἄνθρωπον ἐν Χριστῷ πρὸ ἐτῶν δεκατεσσάρων, εἴτε
I know a man in Christ who fourteen years ago *years fourteen* — whether
3857 476 1877 5986 1280 2291 4574 2291 1280 1664
v.rai.1s n.asm p.d n.dsm p.g n.gpn a.gpn cj

ἐν σώματι ↱ ↱ οὐκ οἶδα, εἴτε ἐκτὸς τοῦ σώματος ↱ ↱ οὐκ οἶδα, ὁ
in the body I do not know or apart from the body I do not know, only
1877 5393 3857 3857 4024 3857 1664 1760 3836 5393 3857 3857 4024 3857 3836
p.d n.dsn pl v.rai.1s cj p.g d.gsn n.gsn pl v.rai.1s d.nsm

θεὸς οἶδεν, ἁρπαγέντα τὸν τοιοῦτον ἕως τρίτου οὐρανοῦ. 3 καὶ
God knows — such a man was caught up *{the} such a man* to the third heaven. And
2536 3857 5525 5525 5525 773 3836 5525 2401 5569 4041 2779
n.nsm v.rai.3s pt.ap.asm d.asm r.asm p.g a.gsm n.gsm cj

οἶδα τὸν τοιοῦτον ἄνθρωπον, εἴτε ἐν σώματι εἴτε χωρὶς τοῦ
I know that *{the}* this man — whether in the body or apart from the
3857 3836 5525 476 1664 1877 5393 1664 6006 3836
v.rai.1s d.asm r.asm n.asm cj p.d n.dsn cj p.g d.gsn

σώματος ↱ ↱ οὐκ οἶδα, ὁ θεὸς οἶδεν, 4 ὅτι ἡρπάγη εἰς τὸν
body I do not know, only God knows — that ⌊he was caught up⌋ into *{the}*
5393 3857 3857 4024 3857 3836 2536 3857 4022 773 1650 3836
n.gsn pl v.rai.1s d.nsm n.nsm v.rai.3s cj v.api.3s p.a d.asm

παράδεισον καὶ ἤκουσεν ἄρρητα ῥήματα ἃ οὐκ ἐξὸν → ἀνθρώπῳ
paradise and heard unspeakable words which are not permitted for a man
4137 2779 201 777 4839 4005 4024 1997 476
n.asm cj v.aai.3s a.apn n.apn r.apn pl pt.pa.nsn n.dsm

λαλῆσαι. 5 ὑπὲρ τοῦ τοιούτου καυχήσομαι, → ὑπὲρ δὲ
to utter. ⌊On behalf of⌋ *{the}* this man I will boast, but on my own behalf *but*
3281 5642 3836 5525 3016 1254 1831 1831 5642 1254
f.aa p.g d.gsm r.gsm v.fmi.1s p.g cj

ἐμαυτοῦ ↱ ↱ οὐ καυχήσομαι ⌊εἰ μὴ⌋ ἐν ταῖς ἀσθενείαις. 6 ἐὰν γὰρ
my own I will not boast, except in my weakness. For ⌊even if⌋ *For*
1831 3016 3016 4024 3016 1623 3590 1877 3836 819 1142 1569 1142
r.gsm.1 pl v.fmi.1s cj pl p.d d.dpf n.dpf cj cj

θελήσω καυχήσασθαι, ↱ ↱ οὐκ ἔσομαι ἄφρων,
⌊I should choose⌋ to boast, I would not be foolish, because I would be telling
2527 3016 1639 1639 4024 1639 933 1142 3306 3306 3306 3306
v.aas.1s f.am pl v.fmi.1s a.nsm

ἀλήθειαν γὰρ ἐρῶ, φείδομαι δέ, μή τις
the truth. *because I would be telling* But I refrain from this, *But* so that no one will give
237 1142 3306 1254 5767 1254 3590 5516 3357 3357
n.asf cj v.fai.1s v.pmi.1s cj cj r.nsm

εἰς ἐμὲ λογίσηται ὑπὲρ ὃ βλέπει με ἢ ἀκούει τι[a] ἐξ ἐμοῦ
credit to me *will give credit* beyond what he sees in me or he hears *{what}* from me,
3357 1650 1609 3357 5642 4005 1063 1609 2445 201 5516 1666 1609
p.a r.as.1 v.ams.3s p.a r.asn v.pai.3s r.as.1 cj v.pai.3s r.asn p.g r.gs.1

7 καὶ τῇ ὑπερβολῇ τῶν ἀποκαλύψεων. διὸ ἵνα
especially ⌊because of the⌋ ⌊extraordinary character⌋ of my revelations. Therefore ⌊in order that⌋
2779 3836 5651 3836 637 1475 2671
cj d.dsf n.dsf d.gpf n.gpf cj cj

↱ ↱ μὴ ὑπεραίρωμαι, ἐδόθη μοι σκόλοψ τῇ σαρκί, ἄγγελος
I should not become conceited, ⌊there was given⌋ to me a thorn ⌊in the⌋ flesh, a messenger
5643 5643 3590 5643 1443 1609 5022 3836 4922 34
pl v.pps.1s v.api.3s r.ds.1 n.nsm d.dsf n.dsf n.nsm

σατανᾶ, ἵνα με κολαφίζῃ, ἵνα ↱ ↱ μὴ ὑπεραίρωμαι. 8
of Satan to torment me, *torment* that I should not become conceited. Three times
4928 2671 3139 1609 3139 2671 5643 5643 3590 5643 5565 5565
n.gsm cj r.as.1 v.pas.3s cj pl v.pps.1s

ὑπὲρ τούτου τρὶς τὸν κύριον παρεκάλεσα ἵνα
I pleaded with the Lord about this, *Three times the Lord I pleaded with* that
4151 4151 4151 3836 3261 5642 4047 5565 3836 3261 4151 2671
p.g r.gsn adv d.asm n.asm v.aai.1s cj

⌊ἀποστῇ ἀπ'⌋ ἐμοῦ. 9 καὶ εἴρηκέν μοι, ἀρκεῖ σοι ἡ χάρις
it would leave me. But he said to me, "My grace is sufficient ⌊for you,⌋ *{the} grace*
923 608 1609 2779 3306 1609 1609 5921 758 5148 3836 5921
v.aas.3s p.g r.gs.1 cj v.rai.3s r.ds.1 v.pai.3s r.ds.2 d.nsf n.nsf

[a] [τι] UBS, omitted by TNIV.

NASB

2 I know a man
in Christ who
fourteen years
ago—whether
in the body I do
not know, or out
of the body I do
not know, God
knows—such a
man was caught
up to the third
heaven. 3 And I
know how such a
man—whether in
the body or apart
from the body I
do not know, God
knows— 4 was
caught up into
Paradise and heard
inexpressible
words, which a
man is not permit-
ted to speak. 5 On
behalf of such a
man I will boast;
but on my own
behalf I will not
boast, except in
regard to *my* weak-
nesses. 6 For if I do
wish to boast I will
not be foolish, for
I will be speak-
ing the truth; but I
refrain *from this,*
so that no one will
credit me with
more than he sees
in me or hears
from me.

A Thorn in the Flesh

7 Because of the
surpassing great-
ness of the rev-
elations, for this
reason, to keep
me from exalting
myself, there was
given me a thorn
in the flesh, a mes-
senger of Satan to
torment me—to
keep me from
exalting myself!
8 Concerning this I
implored the Lord
three times that it
might leave me.
9 And He has said to
me, "My grace is
sufficient for you,

NIV

for my power is
made perfect in
weakness." There-
fore I will boast
all the more gladly
about my weak-
nesses, so that
Christ's power
may rest on me.
10 That is why, for
Christ's sake, I
delight in weak-
nesses, in insults,
in hardships, in
persecutions, in
difficulties. For
when I am weak,
then I am strong.

Paul's Concern for the Corinthians

11 I have made
a fool of myself,
but you drove me
to it. I ought to
have been com-
mended by you,
for I am not in the
least inferior to
the "super-apos-
tles,"[a] even though
I am nothing. 12 I
persevered in dem-
onstrating among
you the marks
of a true apostle,
including signs,
wonders and mir-
acles. 13 How were
you inferior to the
other churches,
except that I was
never a burden to
you? Forgive me
this wrong!
14 Now I am ready
to visit you for
the third time,
and I will not be a
burden to you, be-
cause what I want
is not your pos-
sessions but you.
After all, children
should not have to
save up for their
parents, but par-
ents for their chil-
dren. 15 So I will
very gladly spend

μου, ἡ γὰρ δύναμις ἐν ἀσθενείᾳ τελεῖται. ↱ ↱
My for my *for* power is fulfilled in weakness." *is fulfilled* Therefore I will most
1609 1142 3836 1142 1539 5464 5464 1877 819 5464 4036 3016 3016 3437
r.gs.1 d.nsf cj n.nsf p.d n.dsf v.ppi.3s

ἥδιστα οὖν μᾶλλον καυχήσομαι ἐν ταῖς ἀσθενείαις μου, ἵνα
gladly *Therefore* *most* boast in *{the}* my weaknesses, *my* ⌊in order that⌋ the
2452 4036 3437 3016 1877 3836 1609 819 1609 2671 3836
adv.s cj adv.c v.fmi.1s p.d d.dpf n.dpf r.gs.1 cj

ἐπισκηνώσῃ ἐπ᾽ ἐμὲ ἡ δύναμις τοῦ Χριστοῦ. 10 διὸ
power of Christ may dwell in me. *the* *power* *of* *Christ* ⌊For this reason⌋
1539 3836 5986 2172 2093 1609 3836 1539 3836 5986 1475
v.aas.3s p.a r.as.1 d.nsf n.nsf d.gsm n.gsm cj

εὐδοκῶ ἐν ἀσθενείαις, ἐν ὕβρεσιν, ἐν ἀνάγκαις, ἐν διωγμοῖς καὶ
I am content with weaknesses, with insults, with hardships, with persecutions and
2305 1877 819 1877 5615 1877 340 1877 1501 2779
v.pai.1s p.d n.dpf p.d n.dpf p.d n.dpf p.d n.dpm cj

στενοχωρίαις, ὑπὲρ Χριστοῦ· ὅταν γὰρ ἀσθενῶ, τότε δυνατός
difficulties ⌊for the sake of⌋ Christ; for whenever *for* I am weak, then I am strong.
5103 5642 5986 1142 4020 1142 820 5538 1639 1639 1543
n.dpf p.g n.gsm cj cj v.pas.1s adv a.nsm

εἰμι. 11 γέγονα ἄφρων, ὑμεῖς με ἠναγκάσατε. ἐγὼ γὰρ
I am ⌊I am acting like⌋ a fool, but you drove me *drove* to it. I *{for}*
1639 1181 933 7007 337 1609 337 1609 1142
v.pai.1s v.rai.1s a.nsm r.np.2 r.as.1 v.aai.2p r.ns.1 cj

ὤφειλον ὑφ᾽ ὑμῶν συνίστασθαι· οὐδὲν γὰρ ὑστέρησα
ought to be commended by you, *to be commended* for in no way *for* ⌊am I inferior to⌋
4053 5319 5319 5319 5679 7007 5319 1142 4029 1142 5728
v.iai.1s p.g r.gp.2 f.pp a.asn cj v.aai.1s

τῶν ⌊ὑπερλίαν ἀποστόλων⌋ εἰ καὶ οὐδέν εἰμι. 12 τὰ μὲν
the "super-apostles" — even though *even* I am nothing. *I am* The ~
3836 5663 693 2779 1623 2779 1639 1639 4029 1639 3836 3525
d.gpm adv n.gpm cj adv a.nsn v.pai.1s d.npn pl

σημεῖα τοῦ ἀποστόλου κατειργάσθη ἐν ὑμῖν ἐν πάσῃ ὑπομονῇ,
marks of an apostle were done among you with all persistence, along with
4956 3836 693 2981 1877 7007 1877 4246 5705 5445 5445
n.npn d.gsm n.gsm v.api.3s p.d r.dp.2 p.d a.dsf n.dsf

σημείοις τε καὶ τέρασιν καὶ δυνάμεσιν. 13 τί γάρ ἐστιν ὃ
signs *along with* and wonders and powerful deeds. For ⌊in what way⌋ *For* were *{that}*
4956 5445 2779 5469 2779 1539 1142 5515 1142 1639 4005
n.dpn cj cj n.dpn cj n.dpf r.asn cj v.pai.3s r.asn

ἡσσώθητε ὑπὲρ τὰς λοιπὰς → ἐκκλησίας, ⌊εἰ μὴ⌋ ὅτι αὐτὸς ἐγὼ ↱
you less favored than the rest of the churches, except that I myself *I* was
2273 5642 3836 3370 1711 1623 3590 4022 1609 899 1609 2915
v.api.2p p.a d.apf a.apf n.apf cj pl cj r.nsm r.ns.1

οὐ κατενάρκησα ὑμῶν; χαρίσασθέ μοι τὴν ἀδικίαν ταύτην. 14 ἰδοὺ
not a burden to you? Forgive me *{the}* this injustice! *this* Look, for the
4024 2915 7007 5919 1609 3836 4047 94 4047 2627 4047 4047
pl v.aai.1s r.gp.2 v.amm.2p r.ds.1 d.asf n.asf r.asf j

τρίτον τοῦτο ἑτοίμως ἔχω ἐλθεῖν πρὸς ὑμᾶς, καὶ ↱ ↱ οὐ
third time *for the* I am ready *I am* to come to you, and I will not
5568 4047 2400 2400 2290 2400 2262 4639 7007 2779 2915 2915 4024
adv r.asn adv v.pai.1s f.aa p.a r.ap.2 cj pl

καταναρκήσω· ↱ ↱ οὐ γὰρ ζητῶ τὰ ὑμῶν ἀλλὰ ὑμᾶς.
be a burden, because I am not *because* seeking what you have, but you. For children
2915 1142 2426 2426 4024 1142 2426 3836 7007 247 7007 1142 5451
v.fai.1s pl cj v.pai.1s d.npn r.gp.2 cj r.ap.2

οὐ γὰρ ὀφείλει τὰ τέκνα τοῖς γονεῦσιν θησαυρίζειν ἀλλὰ οἱ
ought not *For* *ought* *{the}* *children* save up for their parents, *save up* but the
4053 4024 1142 4053 3836 5451 2564 2564 3836 1204 2564 247 3836
pl cj v.pai.3s d.npn n.npn d.dpm n.dpm f.pa cj d.npm

γονεῖς τοῖς τέκνοις. 15 ἐγὼ δὲ ↱ ἥδιστα δαπανήσω καὶ ἐκδαπανηθήσομαι
parents for the children. I *{and}* will most gladly spend and be spent
1204 3836 5451 1609 1254 1251 2452 1251 2779 1682
n.npm d.dpn n.dpn r.ns.1 cj adv.s v.fai.1s cj v.fpi.1s

NASB

for power is
perfected in weak-
ness." Most gladly,
therefore, I will
rather boast about
my weaknesses, so
that the power of
Christ may dwell
in me. 10 Therefore
I am well content
with weaknesses,
with insults, with
distresses, with
persecutions, with
difficulties, for
Christ's sake; for
when I am weak,
then I am strong.
11 I have become
foolish; you your-
selves compelled
me. Actually I
should have been
commended by
you, for in no
respect was I in-
ferior to the most
eminent apostles,
even though I am a
nobody. 12 The signs
of a true apostle
were performed
among you with all
perseverance, by
signs and wonders
and miracles. 13 For
in what respect
were you treated as
inferior to the rest
of the churches,
except that I my-
self did not become
a burden to you?
Forgive me this
wrong!
14 Here for this
third time I am
ready to come to
you, and I will not
be a burden to you;
for I do not seek
what is yours, but
you; for children
are not responsible
to save up for *their*
parents, but parents
for *their* children.
15 I will most gladly
spend and be ex-
pended for your

[a] 11 Or *the most eminent apostles*

NIV

for you everything
I have and expend
myself as well. If
I love you more,
will you love me
less? 16Be that as
it may, I have not
been a burden to
you. Yet, crafty
fellow that I am,
I caught you by
trickery! 17Did
I exploit you
through any of the
men I sent to you?
18I urged Titus to
go to you and I
sent our brother
with him. Titus did
not exploit you,
did he? Did we not
walk in the same
footsteps by the
same Spirit?
19Have you been
thinking all along
that we have been
defending our-
selves to you? We
have been speak-
ing in the sight of
God as those in
Christ; and every-
thing we do, dear
friends, is for your
strengthening.
20For I am afraid
that when I come
I may not find you
as I want you to
be, and you may
not find me as you
want me to be. I
fear that there may
be discord, jeal-
ousy, fits of rage,
selfish ambition,
slander, gossip,
arrogance and dis-
order. 21I am afraid
that when I come
again my God will
humble me before
you, and I will be
grieved over many
who have sinned
earlier and have
not repented

ὑπὲρ τῶν ψυχῶν ὑμῶν. εἰ περισσοτέρως ὑμᾶς ἀγαπῶ,[a]
⌊on behalf of⌋ *{the}* your souls. *your* If I love you more, *you* *I love* am I
5642 3836 7007 6034 7007 1623 26 26 7007 4359 7007 26 26 26
p.g d.gpf n.gpf r.gp.2 cj adv.c r.ap.2 v.pai.1s

ἧσσον ἀγαπῶμαι; 16 Ἔστω δέ, ἐγὼ οὐ κατεβάρησα
to be loved less? *am I to be loved* But ⌊be that as it may,⌋ *But* I did not burden
26 26 26 2482 26 1254 1639 1254 1609 2851 4024 2851
adv.c v.ppi.1s v.pam.3s cj r.ns.1 pl v.aai.1s

ὑμᾶς· ἀλλὰ ὑπάρχων πανοῦργος δόλῳ ὑμᾶς ἔλαβον. 17
you; yet being crafty, I took you in by deceit! *you* *I took in* I did
7007 247 5639 4112 3284 3284 7007 3284 1515 7007 3284 4430 4430
r.ap.2 cj pt.pa.nsm a.nsm n.dsm r.ap.2 v.aai.1s

μή τινα ὧν ἀπέσταλκα πρὸς ὑμᾶς, δι᾽
not take advantage of you through anyone *{whom}* I sent to you, did I? *through*
3590 4430 4430 4430 7007 1328 5516 4005 690 4639 7007 3590 3590 1328
pl r.asm r.gpm v.rai.1s p.a r.ap.2 p.g

αὐτοῦ ἐπλεονέκτησα ὑμᾶς; 18 παρεκάλεσα Τίτον καὶ συναπέστειλα
{him} *I did take advantage of* *you* I urged Titus to visit you and I sent
899 4430 7007 4151 5519 4151 4151 2779 5273
r.gsm.3 v.aai.1s r.ap.2 v.aai.1s n.asm cj v.aai.1s

τὸν ἀδελφόν· μήτι ἐπλεονέκτησεν ὑμᾶς Τίτος; οὐ
the brother with him. Titus did not take advantage of you, *Titus* did he? Did we not
3836 81 5273 5519 4430 3614 4430 7007 5519 4344 4344 4024
d.asm n.asm pl v.aai.3s r.ap.2 n.nsm pl

τῷ αὐτῷ πνεύματι περιεπατήσαμεν; οὐ τοῖς
conduct ourselves ⌊in the⌋ same spirit? *Did we conduct ourselves* Did we not behave in the
4344 4344 3836 899 4460 4344 2717 2717 4024 2717 3836
d.dsn r.dsn n.dsn v.aai.1p pl d.dpn

αὐτοῖς ἴχνεσιν; 19 Πάλαι δοκεῖτε ὅτι
same way? *Did we behave* Have you been thinking all along *Have you been thinking* that we are
899 2717 1506 1506 1506 1506 4093 1506 4022 664 664
r.dpn n.dpn adv v.pai.2p cj

ὑμῖν ἀπολογούμεθα. κατέναντι θεοῦ
defending ourselves to you? *we are defending ourselves* We are speaking before God as those
664 664 7007 664 3281 3281 3281 2978 2536
r.dp.2 v.pmi.1p p.g n.gsm

ἐν Χριστῷ λαλοῦμεν· τὰ δὲ πάντα, ἀγαπητοί, ὑπὲρ τῆς ὑμῶν
in Christ; *We are speaking* *{the}* and all that we do, dear friends, is for *{the}* your
1877 5986 3281 3836 1254 4246 28 5642 3836 7007
p.d n.dsm v.pai.1p d.npn cj a.npn a.vpm p.g d.gsf r.gp.2

οἰκοδομῆς. 20 φοβοῦμαι γὰρ ⌊μή πως⌋ ἐλθὼν οὐχ
upbuilding. For I am afraid *For* that perhaps ⌊when I come⌋ I may find you not
3869 1142 5828 1142 3590 4803 2262 2351 2351 2351 7007 4024
n.gsf v.ppi.1s cj cj pl pt.aa.nsm pl

οἵους θέλω εὕρω ὑμᾶς κἀγὼ εὑρεθῶ ὑμῖν οἷον οὐ
as ⌊I would wish,⌋ *I may find* *you* and that I may be found by you not as *not*
3888 2527 2351 7007 2743 2351 7007 4024 3888 4024
r.apm v.pai.1s v.aas.1s r.ap.2 crasis v.aps.1s r.dp.2 r.asm pl

θέλετε· ⌊μή πως⌋ ἔρις, ζῆλος, θυμοί, ἐριθεῖαι,
⌊you would wish;⌋ perhaps there will be strife, jealousy, ⌊flaring anger,⌋ selfish ambition,
2527 3590 4803 2251 2419 2596 2249
v.pai.2p cj pl n.nsf n.nsm n.npm n.npf

καταλαλιαί, ψιθυρισμοί, φυσιώσεις, ἀκαταστασίαι· 21 μὴ
backbiting, gossiping, conceit, disorder. *{not}* I am afraid that when I
2896 6030 5883 189 3590 2262 1609
n.npf n.npm n.npf n.npf cj

πάλιν ἐλθόντος μου ταπεινώσῃ με ὁ θεός μου πρὸς ὑμᾶς καὶ
come, my God may again *when come* *I* humble me *{the}* *God* *my* before you, and
2262 1609 2536 5427 4099 2262 1609 5427 1609 3836 2536 1609 4639 7007 2779
adv pt.aa.gsm r.gs.1 v.aas.3s r.as.1 d.nsm n.nsm r.gs.1 p.a r.ap.2 cj

πενθήσω πολλοὺς τῶν προημαρτηκότων καὶ μὴ μετανοησάντων ἐπὶ τῇ
that I will mourn for many who have sinned earlier and have not repented of the
4291 4498 3836 4579 2779 3566 3590 3566 2093 3836
v.aas.1s a.apm d.gpm pt.ra.gpm cj pl pt.aa.gpm p.d d.dsf

[a] ἀγαπῶ TNIV, NET. ἀγαπῶ[ν] UBS.

NASB

souls. If I love you
more, am I to be
loved less? 16But
be that as it may, I
did not burden you
myself; neverthe-
less, crafty fellow
that I am, I took
you in by deceit.
17*Certainly* I have
not taken advan-
tage of you through
any of those whom
I have sent to you,
have I? 18I urged
Titus *to go,* and
I sent the brother
with him. Titus
did not take any
advantage of you,
did he? Did we not
conduct ourselves
in the same spirit
and walk in the
same steps?
19All this time you
have been thinking
that we are defend-
ing ourselves to
you. *Actually,* it
is in the sight of
God that we have
been speaking in
Christ; and all for
your upbuilding,
beloved. 20For I am
afraid that perhaps
when I come I may
find you to be not
what I wish and
may be found by
you to be not what
you wish; that
perhaps *there will
be* strife, jealousy,
angry tempers,
disputes, slanders,
gossip, arrogance,
disturbances; 21I am
afraid that when
I come again my
God may humili-
ate me before you,
and I may mourn
over many of those
who have sinned
in the past and not
repented of the

NIV

of the impurity,
sexual sin and
debauchery in
which they have
indulged.

Final Warnings

13 This will
be my third
visit to you. "Ev-
ery matter must
be established
by the testimony
of two or three
witnesses."[a] ²I
already gave you
a warning when I
was with you the
second time. I now
repeat it while ab-
sent: On my return
I will not spare
those who sinned
earlier or any of
the others, ³since
you are demanding
proof that Christ is
speaking through
me. He is not weak
in dealing with
you, but is pow-
erful among you.
⁴For to be sure,
he was crucified
in weakness, yet
he lives by God's
power. Likewise,
we are weak in
him, yet by God's
power we will live
with him in our
dealing with you.
⁵Examine your-
selves to see
whether you are
in the faith; test
yourselves. Do you
not realize that
Christ Jesus is in
you — unless, of
course, you fail the
test? ⁶And I trust
that you will dis-
cover that we have
not failed the test.
⁷Now we pray to
God that you will
not do anything
wrong — not so
that people will
see that we have
stood the test but
so that you will do
what is right even
though

[a] 1 Deut. 19:15

ἀκαθαρσίᾳ καὶ πορνείᾳ καὶ ἀσελγείᾳ ᾗ ἔπραξαν.
impurity, *{and}* sexual immorality, and debauchery ⌊in which⌋ they indulged.
174 2779 4518 2779 816 4005 4556
n.dsf cj n.dsf cj n.dsf r.dsf v.aai.3p

13:1 ↱ τρίτον τοῦτο ἔρχομαι πρὸς ὑμᾶς· ἐπὶ στόματος δύο
This will be my third *This* visit to you. On the evidence of two or
4047 2262 5568 4047 2262 4639 7007 2093 5125 1545 2779
adv r.asn v.pmi.1s p.a r.ap.2 p.g n.gsn a.gpm

μαρτύρων καὶ τριῶν σταθήσεται πᾶν ῥῆμα. ²προείρηκα
three witnesses *or* *three* every accusation is to be confirmed. *every* *accusation* I said before
5552 3459 2779 5552 4246 4839 2705 4246 4839 4597
n.gpm cj a.gpm v.fpi.3s a.nsn n.nsn v.rai.1s

καὶ προλέγω, ὡς
when I was with you the second time, and now, though absent, ⌊I say ahead of time⌋ *when*
6055 4205 4205 4205 3836 1311 1311 2779 3814 583 583 4625 6055
cj v.pai.1s pl

παρὼν τὸ δεύτερον καὶ ἀπὼν νῦν, τοῖς προημαρτηκόσιν καὶ
I was with *the* *second time* *{and}* *though absent* *now* to those who have sinned previously and to
4205 3836 1311 2779 583 3814 3836 4579 2779 4246
pt.pa.nsm d.asn adv cj pt.pa.nsm adv d.dpm pt.ra.dpm cj

τοῖς λοιποῖς πᾶσιν, ὅτι ἐὰν ἔλθω εἰς τὸ πάλιν ↱ ↱ οὐ φείσομαι,
all the rest, *to all* that if I come *{to}* *{the}* again I will not spare anyone,
4246 3836 3370 4246 4022 1569 2262 1650 3836 4099 5767 5767 4024 5767
d.dpm a.dpm a.dpm cj cj v.aas.1s p.a d.asn adv pl v.fmi.1s

³ἐπεὶ δοκιμὴν ζητεῖτε τοῦ ἐν ἐμοὶ λαλοῦντος Χριστοῦ,
since you seek proof *you seek* that Christ is speaking through me. *is speaking* *Christ*
2075 2426 2426 1509 2426 3836 5986 3281 3281 1877 1609 3281 5986
cj n.asf v.pai.2p d.gsm p.d r.ds.1 pt.pa.gsm n.gsm

ὃς εἰς ὑμᾶς οὐκ ἀσθενεῖ ἀλλὰ δυνατεῖ ἐν ὑμῖν. ⁴ καὶ γὰρ
He is not weak toward you *not* *is weak* but is powerful among you. For indeed *For*
4005 820 4024 820 1650 7007 4024 820 247 1542 1877 7007 1142 2779 1142
r.nsm p.a r.ap.2 pl v.pai.3s cj v.pai.3s p.d r.dp.2 adv cj

ἐσταυρώθη ἐξ ἀσθενείας, ἀλλὰ ζῇ ἐκ δυνάμεως θεοῦ. καὶ γὰρ
he was crucified in weakness, but ⌊he lives⌋ by the power of God. For indeed *For*
5090 1666 819 247 2409 1666 1539 2536 1142 2779 1142
v.api.3s p.g n.gsf cj v.pai.3s p.g n.gsf n.gsm adv cj

ἡμεῖς ἀσθενοῦμεν ἐν αὐτῷ, ἀλλὰ ζήσομεν σὺν αὐτῷ ἐκ δυνάμεως θεοῦ εἰς
we are weak in him, but we will live with him by the power of God toward
7005 820 1877 899 247 2409 5250 899 1666 1539 2536 1650
r.np.1 v.pai.1p p.d r.dsm.3 cj v.fai.1p p.d r.dsm.3 p.g n.gsf n.gsm p.a

ὑμᾶς. ⁵ ἑαυτοὺς πειράζετε εἰ ἐστὲ ἐν τῇ πίστει, ἑαυτοὺς
you. Examine yourselves *Examine* to see if you are in the faith. Test yourselves.
7007 4279 1571 4279 1623 1639 1877 3836 4411 1507 1571
r.ap.2 r.apm.2 v.pam.2p cj v.pai.2p p.d d.dsf n.dsf r.apm.2

δοκιμάζετε· ἢ ↱ ↱ οὐκ ἐπιγινώσκετε ἑαυτοὺς ὅτι Ἰησοῦς[a] Χριστὸς ἐν
Test Or do you not realize about yourselves, that Jesus Christ is in
1507 2445 2105 2105 4024 2105 1571 4022 2652 5986 1877
v.pam.2p cj pl v.pai.2p r.apm.2 cj n.nsm n.nsm p.d

ὑμῖν; εἰ μήτι ⌊ἀδόκιμοί ἐστε.⌋ ⁶ ἐλπίζω δὲ ὅτι γνώσεσθε
you? — unless, of course, you fail the test! And I hope *And* that ⌊you will find out⌋
7007 1623 3614 99 1639 1254 1827 1254 4022 1182
r.dp.2 cj pl a.npm v.pai.2p v.pai.1s cj cj v.fmi.2p

ὅτι ἡμεῖς ↱ οὐκ ⌊ἐσμὲν ἀδόκιμοι.⌋ ⁷ εὐχόμεθα δὲ πρὸς τὸν θεὸν
that we do not fail the test! Now we pray *Now* to *{the}* God that you
4022 7005 1639 4024 1639 99 1254 2377 1254 4639 3836 2536 7007
cj r.np.1 pl v.pai.1p a.npm v.pmi.1p cj p.a d.asm n.asm

↱ μὴ ποιῆσαι ὑμᾶς κακὸν μηδέν, οὐχ ἵνα ἡμεῖς
may not do *you* anything wrong, *anything* not that we would appear as
4472 3590 4472 7007 3594 2805 3594 4024 2671 7005 5743 5743
pl f.aa r.ap.2 a.asn a.asn pl cj r.np.1

δόκιμοι φανῶμεν, ἀλλ᾽ ἵνα ὑμεῖς τὸ καλὸν ποιῆτε,
⌊having passed the test,⌋ *would appear* but that you may do what is right *may do* even though
1511 5743 247 2671 7007 4472 4472 3836 2819 4472 1254 1254
a.npm v.aps.1p cj cj r.np.2 d.asn a.asn v.pas.2p

[a] Ἰησοῦς omitted in TNIV.

NASB

impurity, immoral-
ity and sensuality
which they have
practiced.

Examine Yourselves

13:1 This is the third
time I am coming
to you. EVERY FACT
IS TO BE CONFIRMED
BY THE TESTIMONY
OF TWO OR THREE
WITNESSES. ²I have
previously said
when present the
second time, and
though now absent
I say in advance
to those who have
sinned in the past
and to all the rest
as well, that if I
come again I will
not spare *anyone,*
³since you are
seeking for proof
of the Christ who
speaks in me, and
who is not weak
toward you, but
mighty in you. ⁴For
indeed He was
crucified because
of weakness, yet
He lives because of
the power of God.
For we also are
weak [a]in Him, yet
we will live with
Him because of the
power of God *di-*
rected toward you.
⁵Test yourselves
to see if you are in
the faith; examine
yourselves! Or do
you not recognize
this about your-
selves, that Jesus
Christ is in you —
unless indeed you
fail the test? ⁶But I
trust that you will
realize that we our-
selves do not fail
the test. ⁷Now we
pray to God that
you do no wrong;
not that we our-
selves may appear
approved, but that
you may do what is
right, even though

[a] One early ms reads *with Him*

NIV

we may seem to
have failed. 8For
we cannot do any-
thing against the
truth, but only for
the truth. 9We are
glad whenever we
are weak but you
are strong; and
our prayer is that
you may be fully
restored. 10This is
why I write these
things when I am
absent, that when
I come I may not
have to be harsh in
my use of authori-
ty—the authority
the Lord gave me
for building you
up, not for tearing
you down.

Final Greetings

11Finally, brothers
and sisters, rejoice!
Strive for full res-
toration, encour-
age one another,
be of one mind,
live in peace. And
the God of love
and peace will be
with you.
12Greet one an-
other with a holy
kiss. 13All God's
people here send
their greetings.
14May the grace
of the Lord Jesus
Christ, and the
love of God, and
the fellowship of
the Holy Spirit be
with you all.

ἡμεῖς δὲ ὡς ἀδόκιμοι ὦμεν. 8 ↱ ↱ οὐ γὰρ δυνάμεθά
we *even though* may appear as having failed. *may appear* For we are not *For* able
7005 1254 1639 1639 6055 99 1639 1142 1538 1538 4024 1142 1538
r.np.1 cj pl a.npm v.pas.1p pl cj v.ppi.1p

τι κατὰ τῆς ἀληθείας ἀλλὰ ὑπὲρ τῆς ἀληθείας. 9 χαίρομεν γὰρ
to do anything against the truth, but only for the truth. For we rejoice *For*
5516 2848 3836 237 247 5642 3836 237 1142 5897 1142
r.asn p.g d.gsf n.gsf cj p.g d.gsf n.gsf v.pai.1p cj

ὅταν ἡμεῖς ἀσθενῶμεν, ὑμεῖς δὲ δυνατοὶ ἦτε· τοῦτο καὶ
whenever we are weak, but you *but* are strong. *are* And this *And* is what
4020 7005 820 1254 7007 1254 1639 1543 1639 2779 4047 2779
cj r.np.1 v.pas.1p r.np.2 cj a.npm v.pas.2p r.asn adv

εὐχόμεθα, τὴν ὑμῶν κατάρτισιν. 10 ⌊διὰ τοῦτο⌋ ταῦτα
we pray for, *{the}* your Christian maturity. Therefore I write these things
2377 3836 7007 2937 1328 4047 1211 1211 4047
v.pmi.1p d.asf r.gp.2 n.asf p.a r.asn r.apn

ἀπὼν γράφω, ἵνα παρὼν μὴ
⌊while I am absent,⌋ *I write* so that ⌊when I am present⌋ I may not have to treat you
583 1211 2671 4205 5968 5968 3590 5968 5968 5968
pt.pa.nsm v.pai.1s cj pt.pa.nsm pl

ἀποτόμως χρήσωμαι κατὰ τὴν ἐξουσίαν ἣν ὁ κύριος ἔδωκέν μοι εἰς
harshly *I may have to treat* ⌊according to⌋ the authority which the Lord gave me for
705 5968 2848 3836 2026 4005 3836 3261 1443 1609 1650
adv v.ams.1s p.a d.asf n.asf r.asf d.nsm n.nsm v.aai.3s r.ds.1 p.a

οἰκοδομὴν καὶ οὐκ εἰς καθαίρεσιν. 11 λοιπόν, ἀδελφοί, χαίρετε, καταρτίζεσθε,
building up and not *{for}* tearing down. Finally, brothers, rejoice, strive for maturity,
3869 2779 4024 1650 2746 3370 81 5897 2936
n.asf cj pl p.a n.asf adv n.vpm v.pam.2p v.ppm.2p

παρακαλεῖσθε, τὸ ⌊αὐτὸ φρονεῖτε,⌋ εἰρηνεύετε, καὶ ὁ θεὸς τῆς ἀγάπης
take courage, *{the}* be like-minded, live in peace; and the God of love
4151 3836 899 5858 1644 2779 3836 2536 3836 27
v.ppm.2p d.asn r.asn v.pam.2p v.pam.2p cj d.nsm n.nsm d.gsf n.gsf

καὶ εἰρήνης ἔσται μεθ᾽ ὑμῶν. 12 ἀσπάσασθε ἀλλήλους ἐν ἁγίῳ φιλήματι.
and peace will be with you. Greet one another with a holy kiss. All the
2779 1645 1639 3552 7007 832 253 1877 41 5799 4246 3836
cj n.gsf v.fmi.3s p.g r.gp.2 v.amm.2p r.apm p.d a.dsn n.dsn

→ ἀσπάζονται ὑμᾶς οἱ ἅγιοι πάντες. 13 ἡ χάρις τοῦ κυρίου Ἰησοῦ
saints send you their greetings. *you the saints All* The grace of the Lord Jesus
41 7007 832 7007 3836 41 4246 3836 5921 3836 3261 2652
v.pmi.3p r.ap.2 d.npm a.npm a.npm d.nsf n.nsf d.gsm n.gsm n.gsm

Χριστοῦ καὶ ἡ ἀγάπη τοῦ θεοῦ καὶ ἡ κοινωνία τοῦ ἁγίου πνεύματος μετὰ
Christ and the love of God and the fellowship of the Holy Spirit be with
5986 2779 3836 27 3836 2536 2779 3836 3126 3836 41 4460 3552
n.gsm cj d.nsf n.nsf d.gsm n.gsm cj d.nsf n.nsf d.gsn a.gsn n.gsn p.g

πάντων ὑμῶν.[a]
you all. *you*
7007 4246 7007
a.gpm r.gp.2

NASB

we may appear
unapproved. 8For
we can do nothing
against the truth,
but *only* for the
truth. 9For we
rejoice when we
ourselves are weak
but you are strong;
this we also pray
for, that you be
made complete.
10For this reason I
am writing these
things while ab-
sent, so that when
present I *need* not
use severity, in ac-
cordance with the
authority which the
Lord gave me for
building up and not
for tearing down.
11Finally, breth-
ren, rejoice, be
made complete,
be comforted, be
like-minded, live
in peace; and the
God of love and
peace will be with
you. 12Greet one
another with a holy
kiss. 13All the saints
greet you.
14The grace of
the Lord Jesus
Christ, and the
love of God, and
the fellowship of
the Holy Spirit, be
with you all.

[a] ἀμήν. πρὸς Κορινθίους Δευτέρα ἐγράφη ἀπὸ Φιλίππων τῆς Μακεδονίας διὰ Τίτου καὶ Λουκᾶ included by TR after ὑμῶν.

Galatians

NIV

1 Paul, an apos-
tle—sent not
from men nor by a
man, but by Jesus
Christ and God the
Father, who raised
him from the
dead— [2]and all
the brothers and
sisters[a] with me,

To the churches
in Galatia:

[3]Grace and peace
to you from God
our Father and the
Lord Jesus Christ,
[4]who gave him-
self for our sins to
rescue us from the
present evil age,
according to the
will of our God and
Father, [5]to whom
be glory for ever
and ever. Amen.

No Other Gospel

[6]I am astonished
that you are so
quickly deserting
the one who called
you to live in the
grace of Christ and
are turning to a
different gospel—
[7]which is really no
gospel at all. Evi-
dently some peo-
ple are throwing
you into confusion
and are trying to
pervert the gos-
pel of Christ. [8]But
even if we or an
angel from heav-
en should preach
a gospel other
than the one we
preached to you,
let them be under
God's curse! [9]As

[a] 2 The Greek word for *brothers and sisters* (*adelphoi*) refers here to believers, both men and women, as part of God's family; also in verse 11; and in 3:15; 4:12, 28, 31; 5:11, 13; 6:1, 18.

1:1 Παῦλος ἀπόστολος οὐκ ἀπ᾽ ἀνθρώπων οὐδὲ δι᾽ ἀνθρώπου ἀλλὰ
From Paul, an apostle — not from men, nor through man, but
4263 693 4024 608 476 4028 1328 476 247
n.nsm n.nsm pl p.g n.gpm cj p.g n.gsm cj

διὰ Ἰησοῦ Χριστοῦ καὶ θεοῦ πατρὸς τοῦ ἐγείραντος αὐτὸν ἐκ νεκρῶν,
through Jesus Christ and God the Father who raised him from the dead —
1328 2652 5986 2779 2536 4252 3836 1586 899 1666 3738
p.g n.gsm n.gsm cj n.gsm n.gsm d.gsm pt.aa.gsm r.asm.3 p.g a.gpm

[2]καὶ οἱ σὺν ἐμοὶ πάντες ἀδελφοὶ ταῖς ἐκκλησίαις τῆς
and all the brothers who are with me, *all* *brothers* to the churches of
2779 4246 3836 81 5250 1609 4246 81 3836 1711 3836
cj d.npm p.d r.ds.1 a.npm n.npm d.dpf n.dpf d.gsf

Γαλατίας, [3]χάρις ὑμῖν καὶ εἰρήνη ἀπὸ θεοῦ πατρὸς ἡμῶν[a] καὶ κυρίου
Galatia: Grace to you and peace from God our Father *our* and the Lord
1130 5921 7007 2779 1645 608 2536 7005 4252 7005 2779 3261
n.gsf n.nsf r.dp.2 cj n.nsf p.g n.gsm n.gsm r.gp.1 cj n.gsm

Ἰησοῦ Χριστοῦ [4]τοῦ δόντος ἑαυτὸν ὑπὲρ τῶν ἁμαρτιῶν ἡμῶν, ὅπως
Jesus Christ, who gave himself for *{the}* our sins *our* ⌞in order to⌟
2652 5986 3836 1443 1571 5642 3836 7005 281 7005 3968
n.gsm n.gsm d.gsm pt.aa.gsm r.asm.3 p.g d.gpf n.gpf r.gp.1 cj

ἐξέληται ἡμᾶς ἐκ τοῦ αἰῶνος τοῦ ἐνεστῶτος πονηροῦ κατὰ τὸ
rescue us from this present evil age, *{the}* *present* *evil* ⌞according to⌟ the
1975 7005 1666 3836 1931 4505 172 3836 1931 4505 2848 3836
v.ams.3s r.ap.1 p.g d.gsm n.gsm d.gsm pt.ra.gsm a.gsm p.a d.asn

θέλημα τοῦ θεοῦ καὶ πατρὸς ἡμῶν, [5]ᾧ ἡ δόξα εἰς τοὺς ⌞αἰῶνας
will of our God and Father, *our* ⌞to whom⌟ be *{the}* glory for all time!
2525 3836 7005 2536 2779 4252 7005 4005 3836 1518 1650 3836 172
n.asn d.gsm n.gsm cj n.gsm r.gp.1 r.dsm d.nsf n.nsf p.a d.apm n.apm

τῶν αἰώνων,⌟ ἀμήν. [6]Θαυμάζω ὅτι ↱ ↱ οὕτως ταχέως ⌞μετατίθεσθε ἀπὸ⌟
Amen. I am astonished that you are so quickly deserting
3836 172 297 2513 4022 3572 3572 4048 5441 3572 608
d.gpm n.gpm pl v.pai.1s cj adv adv v.ppi.2p p.g

τοῦ καλέσαντος ὑμᾶς ἐν χάριτι Χριστοῦ[b] εἰς ἕτερον
the one who called you by the grace of Christ and are turning to a different
3836 2813 7007 1877 5921 5986 1650 2283
d.gsm pt.aa.gsm r.ap.2 p.d n.dsf n.gsm p.a r.asn

εὐαγγέλιον, [7]ὃ οὐκ ἔστιν ἄλλο, ⌞εἰ μὴ⌟ τινές εἰσιν οἱ
gospel — not that *not* there is another gospel, but there are some *there are* who
2295 4024 4005 4024 1639 257 1623 3590 1639 1639 5516 1639 3836
n.asn r.nsn pl v.pai.3s r.nsn cj pl r.npm v.pai.3p d.npm

ταράσσοντες ὑμᾶς καὶ θέλοντες μεταστρέψαι τὸ εὐαγγέλιον τοῦ Χριστοῦ.
are trying to confuse you and want to pervert the gospel of Christ.
5429 7007 2779 2527 3570 3836 2295 3836 5986
pt.pa.npm r.ap.2 cj pt.pa.npm f.aa d.asn n.asn d.gsm n.gsm

[8]ἀλλὰ καὶ ἐὰν ἡμεῖς ἢ ἄγγελος ἐξ οὐρανοῦ εὐαγγελίζηται[c] ←
But even if we, or an angel from heaven, should preach a gospel
247 2779 1569 7005 2445 34 1666 4041 2294
cj adv cj r.np.1 cj n.nsm p.g n.gsm v.pms.3s

παρ᾽ ὃ εὐηγγελισάμεθα ὑμῖν, ἀνάθεμα ἔστω. [9]ὡς
⌞at odds with⌟ the one we already preached to you, let him be accursed. *let him be* As
4123 4005 2294 7007 1639 1639 1639 353 1639 6055
p.a r.asn v.ami.1p r.dp.2 n.nsn v.pam.3s cj

[a] ἡμῶν omitted in NET.
[b] [Χριστοῦ] UBS.
[c] εὐαγγελίζηται UBS, NET. εὐαγγελίσηται TNIV.

NASB

Introduction

[1:1]Paul, an apostle
(not *sent* from men
nor through the
agency of man,
but through Jesus
Christ and God the
Father, who raised
Him from the
dead), [2]and all the
brethren who are
with me,
To the churches
of Galatia:
[3]Grace to you and
peace from God
our Father and the
Lord Jesus Christ,
[4]who gave Himself
for our sins so that
He might rescue us
from this present
evil age, according
to the will of our
God and Father,
[5]to whom *be* the
glory forevermore.
Amen.

Perversion of the Gospel

[6]I am amazed that
you are so quickly
deserting Him who
called you by the
grace of Christ, for
a different gospel;
[7]which is *really* not
another; only there
are some who are
disturbing you and
want to distort the
gospel of Christ.
[8]But even if we,
or an angel from
heaven, should
preach to you a
gospel contrary
to what we have
preached to you, he
is to be accursed!

NIV

we have already
said, so now I say
again: If anybody
is preaching to you
a gospel other than
what you accepted,
let them be under
God's curse!
10 Am I now try-
ing to win the
approval of human
beings, or of God?
Or am I trying to
please people? If
I were still trying
to please people, I
would not be a ser-
vant of Christ.

Paul Called by God

11 I want you to
know, brothers and
sisters, that the
gospel I preached
is not of human
origin. 12 I did not
receive it from any
man, nor was I
taught it; rather, I
received it by rev-
elation from Jesus
Christ.
13 For you have
heard of my pre-
vious way of life
in Judaism, how
intensely I perse-
cuted the church
of God and tried
to destroy it. 14 I
was advancing in
Judaism beyond
many of my own
age among my
people and was
extremely zealous
for the traditions
of my fathers.
15 But when God,
who set me apart
from my mother's
womb and called
me by his

προειρήκαμεν καὶ ἄρτι πάλιν λέγω, εἴ τις ὑμᾶς
we have said before, and now I say again: *I say* If anyone is preaching to you
4597 2779 785 3306 3306 4099 3306 1623 5516 2294 2294 7007
v.rai.1p cj adv adv v.pai.1s cj r.nsm r.ap.2

εὐαγγελίζεται παρ' ὃ παρελάβετε,
is preaching gospel a gospel ˪at odds with˩ the one ˪you have already received,˩ let him be
2294 2294 4123 4005 4161 1639 1639 1639
v.pmi.3s p.a r.asn v.aai.2p

ἀνάθεμα ἔστω. 10 ἄρτι γὰρ ἀνθρώπους
accursed. *let him be* For am I now *For* seeking the approval of men,
353 1639 1142 4275 4275 785 1142 4275 4275 4275 4275 476
n.nsn v.pam.3s adv cj n.apm

πείθω ἢ τὸν θεόν; ἢ ζητῶ ἀνθρώποις ἀρέσκειν;
am I seeking the approval of or of *{the}* God? Or ˪am I trying˩ to please men? *to please*
4275 2445 3836 2536 2445 2426 743 743 476 743
v.pai.1s cj d.asm n.asm cj v.pai.1s n.dpm f.pa

εἰ ἔτι ἀνθρώποις ἤρεσκον,
If I were still trying to please men, *I were trying to please* I would not be a
1623 743 743 2285 743 743 743 476 743 1639 323 4024 1639
cj adv n.dpm v.iai.1s

Χριστοῦ δοῦλος οὐκ ἂν ἤμην. 11 → → γνωρίζω γάρ[a] ὑμῖν, ἀδελφοί,
servant of Christ. *servant not would I be* I want you to know, *{for} you* brothers,
1529 5986 1529 4024 323 1639 7007 1192 1142 7007 81
n.gsm n.nsm pl pl v.imi.1s v.pai.1s cj r.dp.2 n.vpm

τὸ εὐαγγέλιον τὸ εὐαγγελισθὲν ὑπ' ἐμοῦ ὅτι οὐκ ἔστιν κατὰ ἄνθρωπον·
that the gospel *{the}* preached by me *that* is not *is* of human
4022 3836 2295 3836 2294 5679 1609 4022 1639 4024 1639 2848 476
d.asn n.asn d.asn pt.ap.asn p.g r.gs.1 cj pl v.pai.3s p.a n.asm

↰ 12 οὐδὲ γὰρ ἐγὼ παρὰ ἀνθρώπου παρέλαβον αὐτό οὔτε
origin. For I did not *For I* receive it from man, *did receive* *it* nor
2848 1142 1609 4161 4028 1142 1609 4161 899 4123 476 4161 899 4046
cj cj r.ns.1 p.g n.gsm v.aai.1s r.asn.3 cj

ἐδιδάχθην ἀλλὰ δι' ἀποκαλύψεως Ἰησοῦ Χριστοῦ. 13
was I taught it; instead I received it by a revelation from Jesus Christ. For
1438 247 1328 637 2652 5986 1142
v.api.1s cj p.g n.gsf n.gsm n.gsm

ἠκούσατε γὰρ τὴν ἐμὴν ἀναστροφήν ποτε ἐν τῷ Ἰουδαϊσμῷ, ὅτι
˪you have heard of˩ *For {the}* my former way of life *former* in *{the}* Judaism, how
201 1142 3836 1847 4537 419 4537 1877 3836 2682 4022
v.aai.2p cj d.asf r.asf.1 n.asf adv p.d d.dsm n.dsm cj

˪καθ' ὑπερβολὴν˩ ἐδίωκον τὴν ἐκκλησίαν τοῦ θεοῦ καὶ
intensely ˪I used to persecute˩ the church of God and
2848 5651 1503 3836 1711 3836 2536 2779
p.a n.asf v.iai.1s d.asf n.asf d.gsm n.gsm cj

ἐπόρθουν αὐτήν, 14 καὶ προέκοπτον ἐν τῷ Ἰουδαϊσμῷ ὑπὲρ πολλοὺς →
˪was trying to destroy˩ it. And I was advancing in *{the}* Judaism beyond many of
4514 899 2779 4621 1877 3836 2682 5642 4498
v.iai.1s r.asf.3 cj v.iai.1s p.d d.dsm n.dsm p.a a.apm

συνηλικιώτας ἐν τῷ γένει μου, περισσοτέρως ζηλωτὴς ὑπάρχων
my own age in the ˪entire nation,˩ *my* being extremely zealous for *being*
1609 5312 1877 3836 1169 1609 5639 4359 2421 5639
n.apm p.d d.dsn n.dsn r.gs.1 adv.c n.nsm pt.pa.nsm

τῶν πατρικῶν μου παραδόσεων. 15 ὅτε δὲ εὐδόκησεν [b]ὁ θεός[c] ὁ → →
the traditions of my ancestors. But when *But was pleased {the}* God, who had set
3836 4257 1609 4142 1254 4021 1254 2305 3836 2536 3836
d.gpf a.gpf r.gs.1 n.gpf cj cj v.aai.3s d.nsm n.nsm d.nsm

ἀφορίσας με ἐκ κοιλίας μητρός μου καὶ καλέσας διὰ τῆς
me apart *me* from my mother's womb *mother's my* and called me by *{the}* his
1609 928 1609 1666 1609 3613 3120 3613 1609 2779 2813 1328 3836 899
pt.aa.nsm r.as.1 p.g n.gsf n.gsf r.gs.1 cj pt.aa.nsm p.g d.gsf

[a] γάρ UBS, TNIV. δέ NET.
[b] [ὁ θεὸς] UBS, not included in NET.
[c] θεός omitted in NET.

NASB

9 As we have said
before, so I say
again now, if any
man is preaching
to you a gospel
contrary to what
you received, he is
to be accursed!
10 For am I now
seeking the favor
of men, or of God?
Or am I striving
to please men? If
I were still trying
to please men, I
would not be a
bond-servant of
Christ.

Paul Defends His Ministry

11 For I would
have you know,
brethren, that the
gospel which was
preached by me is
not according to
man. 12 For I neither
received it from
man, nor was I
taught it, but *I re-*
ceived it through a
revelation of Jesus
Christ.
13 For you have
heard of my former
manner of life in
Judaism, how I
used to persecute
the church of God
beyond measure
and tried to destroy
it; 14 and I was ad-
vancing in Judaism
beyond many of
my contemporaries
among my coun-
trymen, being more
extremely zealous
for my ancestral
traditions. 15 But
when God, who
had set me apart
even from my
mother's womb
and called me

NIV

grace, was pleased
[16]to reveal his
Son in me so that
I might preach
him among the
Gentiles, my im-
mediate response
was not to consult
any human being.
[17]I did not go up to
Jerusalem to see
those who were
apostles before I
was, but I went
into Arabia. Later
I returned to Da-
mascus.
[18]Then after three
years, I went up
to Jerusalem to
get acquainted
with Cephas[a] and
stayed with him
fifteen days. [19]I
saw none of the
other apostles—
only James, the
Lord's brother. [20]I
assure you before
God that what I
am writing you is
no lie.
[21]Then I went to
Syria and Cilicia.
[22]I was personally
unknown to the
churches of Judea
that are in Christ.
[23]They only heard
the report: "The
man who formerly
persecuted us is
now preaching the
faith he once tried
to destroy." [24]And
they praised God
because of me.

Paul Accepted by the Apostles

2 Then after
fourteen years,
I went up again
to Jerusalem, this
time with Barna-
bas. I took Titus
along also. [2]I went
in response to a

[a] 18 That is, Peter

χάριτος αὐτοῦ [16] ἀποκαλύψαι τὸν υἱὸν αὐτοῦ ἐν ἐμοί, ἵνα
grace, *his* was pleased to reveal *{the}* his Son *his* in me so that
5921 899 2305 2305 636 3836 899 5626 899 1877 1609 2671
n.gsf r.gsm.3 f.aa d.asm n.asm r.gsm.3 p.d r.ds.1 cj

εὐαγγελίζωμαι αὐτὸν ἐν τοῖς ἔθνεσιν, εὐθέως ↱ ↱ οὐ προσανεθέμην
I might preach him among the Gentiles, *{immediately}* I did not consult with
2294 899 1877 3836 1620 2311 4651 4651 4024 4651
v.pms.1s r.asm.3 p.d d.dpn n.dpn adv pl v.ami.1s

σαρκὶ καὶ αἵματι [17] οὐδὲ ἀνῆλθον εἰς Ἱεροσόλυμα πρὸς τοὺς πρὸ
flesh and blood, nor did I go up to Jerusalem to those who were apostles before
4922 2779 135 4028 456 1650 2642 4639 3836 693 4574
n.dsf cj n.dsn cj v.aai.1s p.a n.apn p.a d.apm p.g

ἐμοῦ ἀποστόλους, ἀλλὰ ἀπῆλθον εἰς Ἀραβίαν καὶ πάλιν ὑπέστρεψα εἰς
me; *apostles* but I went away into Arabia and returned again *returned* to
1609 693 247 599 1650 728 2779 5715 4099 5715 1650
r.gs.1 n.apm cj v.aai.1s p.a n.asf cj adv v.aai.1s p.a

Δαμασκόν. [18] ἔπειτα μετὰ ἔτη τρία ἀνῆλθον εἰς Ἱεροσόλυμα
Damascus. Then after three years *three* I went up to Jerusalem
1242 2083 3552 5552 2291 5552 456 1650 2642
n.asf adv p.a n.apn a.apn v.aai.1s p.a n.apn

ἱστορῆσαι Κηφᾶν καὶ ἐπέμεινα πρὸς αὐτὸν ἡμέρας δεκαπέντε, [19]
⌞to get acquainted with⌟ Cephas and stayed with him fifteen days. *fifteen* But
2707 3064 2779 2152 4639 899 1278 2465 1278 1254
f.aa n.asm cj v.aai.1s p.a r.asm.3 n.apf a.apf

→ ἕτερον δὲ τῶν ἀποστόλων οὐκ εἶδον ⌞εἰ μὴ⌟
I did not see any of the other *But* *of the* apostles *not* *I did see* — except
1625 1625 4024 1625 3836 3836 2283 1254 3836 693 4024 1625 1623 3590
r.asm cj d.gpm n.gpm pl v.aai.1s cj pl

Ἰάκωβον τὸν ἀδελφὸν τοῦ κυρίου. [20] ἃ δὲ γράφω ὑμῖν, ἰδοὺ
James, the Lord's brother. *{the}* *Lord's* In what *{and}* I am writing to you, I swear
2610 3836 3261 81 3836 3261 4005 1254 1211 7007 2627
n.asm d.asm n.asm d.gsm n.gsm r.apn cj v.pai.1s r.dp.2 j

ἐνώπιον τοῦ θεοῦ ὅτι ↱ ↱ οὐ ψεύδομαι. [21] ἔπειτα ἦλθον εἰς τὰ κλίματα
before *{the}* God, *{that}* I am not lying! After that I went to the regions
1967 3836 2536 4022 6017 6017 4024 6017 2083 2262 1650 3836 3107
p.g d.gsm n.gsm cj pl v.pmi.1s adv v.aai.1s p.a d.apn n.apn

τῆς Συρίας καὶ τῆς Κιλικίας· [22] ἤμην δὲ ἀγνοούμενος τῷ
of Syria and *{the}* Cilicia. But I was *But* still personally unknown *{the}*
3836 5353 2779 3836 3070 1254 1639 1254 4725 51 3836
d.gsf n.gsf cj d.gsf n.gsf v.imi.1s cj pt.pp.nsm d.dsn

προσώπῳ ταῖς ἐκκλησίαις τῆς Ἰουδαίας ταῖς ἐν Χριστῷ. [23] μόνον δὲ
personally to the churches of Judea that are in Christ. They only *{and}* kept
4725 3836 1711 3836 2677 3836 1877 5986 1639 3667 1254 1639
n.dsn d.dpf n.dpf d.gsf n.gsf d.dpf p.d n.dsm adv cj

ἀκούοντες ἦσαν ὅτι ὁ → → διώκων ἡμᾶς ποτε ↱ νῦν
hearing, *They kept* ~ "The one who formerly persecuted us *formerly* is now
201 1639 4022 3836 4537 1503 7005 4537 2294 3814
pt.pa.npm v.iai.3p cj d.nsm pt.pa.nsm r.ap.1 adv adv

εὐαγγελίζεται τὴν πίστιν ἥν ↱ ποτε ἐπόρθει, [24] καὶ ἐδόξαζον ἐν
preaching the faith that he once tried to destroy." So they praised God ⌞because of⌟
2294 3836 4411 4005 4514 4537 4514 2779 1519 2536 1877
v.pmi.3s d.asf n.asf r.asf adv v.iai.3s cj v.iai.3p p.d

ἐμοὶ τὸν θεόν.
me. *{the}* *God*
1609 3836 2536
r.ds.1 d.asm n.asm

[2:1] ἔπειτα διὰ δεκατεσσάρων ἐτῶν πάλιν ἀνέβην εἰς Ἱεροσόλυμα
Then after fourteen years I went up again *I went up* to Jerusalem
2083 1328 1280 2291 326 326 326 4099 326 1650 2642
adv p.g a.gpn n.gpn adv v.aai.1s p.a n.apn

μετὰ Βαρναβᾶ συμπαραλαβὼν ← καὶ Τίτον· [2] ἀνέβην δὲ κατὰ
with Barnabas, taking Titus along as well. *Titus* I went up *{and}* ⌞in response to⌟ a
3552 982 5221 5519 2779 5519 326 1254 2848
p.g n.gsm pt.aa.nsm adv n.asm v.aai.1s cj p.a

NASB

through His grace,
was pleased [16]to
reveal His Son in
me so that I might
preach Him among
the Gentiles, I did
not immediately
consult with flesh
and blood, [17]nor did
I go up to Jerusa-
lem to those who
were apostles be-
fore me; but I went
away to Arabia,
and returned once
more to Damascus.
[18]Then three years
later I went up to
Jerusalem to be-
come acquainted
with Cephas,
and stayed with
him fifteen days.
[19]But I did not see
any other of the
apostles except
James, the Lord's
brother. [20](Now in
what I am writing
to you, I assure you
before God that
I am not lying.)
[21]Then I went into
the regions of Syria
and Cilicia. [22]I
was *still* unknown
by sight to the
churches of Judea
which were in
Christ; [23]but only,
they kept hearing,
"He who once per-
secuted us is now
preaching the faith
which he once tried
to destroy." [24]And
they were glorify-
ing God because
of me.

The Council at Jerusalem

[2:1]Then after an
interval of fourteen
years I went up
again to Jerusalem
with Barnabas,
taking Titus along
also. [2]It was be-
cause of

NIV

revelation and,
meeting privately
with those es-
teemed as leaders,
I presented to them
the gospel that I
preach among the
Gentiles. I wanted
to be sure I was not
running and had
not been running
my race in vain.
3 Yet not even Titus,
who was with me,
was compelled to
be circumcised,
even though he
was a Greek. 4 This
matter arose be-
cause some false
believers had infil-
trated our ranks to
spy on the freedom
we have in Christ
Jesus and to make
us slaves. 5 We did
not give in to them
for a moment, so
that the truth of the
gospel might be
preserved for you.
6 As for those who
were held in high
esteem—whatever
they were makes
no difference to
me; God does not
show favoritism—
they added nothing
to my message.
7 On the contrary,
they recognized
that I had been
entrusted with the
task of preaching
the gospel to the
uncircumcised,[a]
just as Peter had
been to the cir-
cumcised.[b] 8 For
God, who was at
work in Peter as
an apostle to the
circumcised, was
also at work in

[a] 7 That is, Gentiles

[b] 7 That is, Jews; also in verses 8 and 9

ἀποκάλυψιν· καὶ ἀνεθέμην αὐτοῖς
revelation and laid out before them — though privately before the acknowledged leaders
637 2779 423 899 1254 2848 3836 1506
n.asf cj v.ami.1s r.dpm.3

τὸ εὐαγγέλιον ὃ κηρύσσω ἐν τοῖς ἔθνεσιν, ⌊κατ᾽ ἰδίαν⌋ δὲ τοῖς
— the gospel that I proclaim among the Gentiles, *privately* *though* *the*
3836 2295 4005 3062 1877 3836 1620 2848 2625 1254 3836
d.asn n.asn r.asn v.pai.1s p.d d.dpn n.dpn p.a a.asf cj d.dpm

δοκοῦσιν, μή πως εἰς κενὸν τρέχω ἢ
acknowledged lest somehow I was running, or had run, in vain. *I was running* *or*
1506 3590 4803 5556 5556 5556 2445 5556 5556 1650 3031 5556 2445
pt.pa.dpm cj pl p.a a.asn v.pas.1s cj

ἔδραμον. 3 ἀλλ᾽ οὐδὲ Τίτος ὁ σὺν ἐμοί,
had run Yet not even Titus, who was with me, was compelled to be circumcised,
5556 247 4028 5519 3836 5250 1609 337 337 4362 4362 4362
v.aai.1s cj adv n.nsm d.nsm p.d r.ds.1

Ἕλλην ὤν, ἠναγκάσθη περιτμηθῆναι· 4
though he was a Greek. *though he was* *was compelled* *to be circumcised* This matter came up
1639 1639 1639 1818 1639 337 4362
n.nsm pt.pa.nsm v.api.3s f.ap

διὰ δὲ τοὺς παρεισάκτους ψευδαδέλφους, οἵτινες
⌊because of⌋ *{and}* some false brothers ⌊secretly brought in⌋ *false brothers* — they
1328 1254 3836 6012 6012 4207 6012 4015
p.a cj d.apm a.apm n.apm r.npm

παρεισῆλθον κατασκοπῆσαι τὴν ἐλευθερίαν ἡμῶν ἣν ἔχομεν ἐν Χριστῷ
had slipped in to spy out *{the}* our freedom *our* that we have in Christ
4209 2945 3836 7005 1800 7005 4005 2400 1877 5986
v.aai.3p f.aa d.asf n.asf r.gp.1 r.asf v.pai.1p p.d n.dsm

Ἰησοῦ, ἵνα ἡμᾶς καταδουλώσουσιν, 5 οἷς
Jesus so that they might make slaves of us *they might make slaves of* — but to them we
2652 2671 2871 2871 2871 2871 2871 7005 2871 4005 1634
n.dsm cj r.ap.1 v.fai.3p r.dpm

οὐδὲ ← πρὸς ὥραν εἴξαμεν τῇ ὑποταγῇ, ἵνα ἡ
did not yield in submission even for a moment, *we did yield* *in* *submission* so that the
1634 4028 1634 3836 5717 4639 6052 1634 3836 5717 2671 3836
adv p.a n.asf v.aai.1p d.dsf n.dsf cj d.nsf

ἀλήθεια τοῦ εὐαγγελίου διαμείνῃ πρὸς ὑμᾶς. 6 ἀπὸ δὲ τῶν
truth of the gospel would be preserved for you. But from *But* those
237 3836 2295 1373 4639 7007 1254 608 1254 3836
n.nsf d.gsn n.gsn v.aas.3s p.a r.ap.2 p.g cj d.gpm

δοκούντων εἶναι ← τι, ὁποῖοί ποτε ἦσαν οὐδέν
who were supposed to be acknowledged leaders (what *{then}* they were makes no difference
1506 1639 1506 5516 3961 4537 1639 1422 4029 1422
pt.pa.gpm f.pa r.asn r.npm pl v.iai.3p a.asn

μοι διαφέρει· πρόσωπον ὁ [a] θεὸς ἀνθρώπου οὐ λαμβάνει —
to me; *makes difference* God shows no partiality) *{the}* *God* *{of man}* *no* *shows*
1609 1422 2536 3284 4024 4725 3836 2536 476 4024 3284
r.ds.1 v.pai.3s n.asn d.nsm n.nsm n.gsm pl v.pai.3s

ἐμοὶ γὰρ οἱ δοκοῦντες οὐδὲν προσανέθεντο 7 ἀλλὰ
those leaders contributed nothing to me. *{for}* *those* *leaders* *nothing* *contributed* But
3836 1506 4651 4029 1609 1142 3836 1506 4029 4651 247
r.ds.1 cj d.npm pt.pa.npm a.asn v.ami.3p cj

τοὐναντίον ἰδόντες ὅτι πεπίστευμαι τὸ εὐαγγέλιον τῆς
on the contrary, ⌊when they saw⌋ that ⌊I had been entrusted with⌋ the gospel ⌊for the⌋
5539 1625 4022 4409 3836 2295 3836
crasis.asn pt.aa.npm cj v.rpi.1s d.asn n.asn d.gsf

ἀκροβυστίας καθὼς Πέτρος τῆς περιτομῆς, 8
uncircumcised just as Peter had been entrusted with the gospel ⌊for the⌋ circumcised (for
213 2777 4377 3836 4364 1142
n.gsf cj n.nsm d.gsf n.gsf

ὁ γὰρ ἐνεργήσας Πέτρῳ εἰς ἀποστολὴν τῆς περιτομῆς ἐνήργησεν
the *for* one who empowered Peter for his apostleship to the circumcised also empowered
3836 1142 1919 4377 1650 692 3836 4364 2779 1919
d.nsm cj pt.aa.nsm n.dsm p.a n.asf d.gsf n.gsf v.aai.3s

[a] [ὁ] UBS.

NASB

a revelation that
I went up; and I
submitted to them
the gospel which
I preach among
the Gentiles, but *I*
did so in private to
those who were of
reputation, for fear
that I might be run-
ning, or had run, in
vain. 3 But not even
Titus, who was
with me, though he
was a Greek, was
compelled to be
circumcised. 4 But
it was because of
the false brethren
secretly brought in,
who had sneaked
in to spy out our
liberty which we
have in Christ
Jesus, in order
to bring us into
bondage. 5 But we
did not yield in
subjection to them
for even an hour,
so that the truth of
the gospel would
remain with you.
6 But from those
who were of high
reputation (what
they were makes
no difference to
me; God shows no
partiality)—well,
those who were of
reputation contrib-
uted nothing to me.
7 But on the con-
trary, seeing that I
had been entrusted
with the gospel
to the uncircum-
cised, just as Peter
had been to the
circumcised 8 (for
He who effectually
worked for Peter in
his apostleship to
the circumcised ef-
fectually worked

NIV

me as an apostle
to the Gentiles.
9 James, Cephas[a]
and John, those
esteemed as pil-
lars, gave me and
Barnabas the right
hand of fellowship
when they recog-
nized the grace
given to me. They
agreed that we
should go to the
Gentiles, and they
to the circumcised.
10 All they asked
was that we should
continue to remem-
ber the poor, the
very thing I had
been eager to do all
along.

Paul Opposes Cephas

11 When Cephas
came to Antioch, I
opposed him to his
face, because he
stood condemned.
12 For before cer-
tain men came
from James, he
used to eat with
the Gentiles. But
when they arrived,
he began to draw
back and separate
himself from the
Gentiles because
he was afraid of
those who be-
longed to the cir-
cumcision group.
13 The other Jews
joined him in his
hypocrisy, so that
by their hypocrisy
even Barnabas was
led astray.
14 When I saw that
they were not act-
ing in line with the
truth of the gospel,
I said to Cephas in
front of them all,
"You are a Jew,
yet you live like
a Gentile and not
like a Jew. How is
it, then, that you

καὶ ἐμοὶ εἰς τὰ ἔθνη, 9 καὶ →
also me for mine to the Gentiles) and when James and Cephas and John, who were
2779 1609 1650 3836 1620 2779 2610 2779 3064 2779 2722 3836 1639
adv r.ds.1 p.a d.apn n.apn cj

γνόντες τὴν χάριν τὴν δοθεῖσάν μοι, Ἰάκωβος καὶ Κηφᾶς
acknowledged pillars, recognized the grace that had been given to me, *James and Cephas*
1506 5146 1182 3836 5921 3836 1443 1609 2610 2779 3064
pt.aa.npm d.asf n.asf d.asf pt.ap.asf r.ds.1 n.nsm cj n.nsm

καὶ Ἰωάννης, οἱ δοκοῦντες στῦλοι εἶναι,
and John who acknowledged pillars were they gave to Barnabas and me the
2779 2722 3836 1506 5146 1639 1443 1443 982 982 2779 1609
cj n.nsm d.npm pt.pa.npm n.npm f.pa

δεξιὰς ἔδωκαν ἐμοὶ καὶ Βαρναβᾷ κοινωνίας, ἵνα ἡμεῖς εἰς τὰ
right hand *they gave me and to Barnabas* of fellowship, agreeing that we should go to the
1288 1443 1609 2779 982 3126 2671 7005 1650 3836
a.apf v.aai.3p r.ds.1 cj n.dsm n.gsf cj r.np.1 p.a d.apn

ἔθνη, αὐτοὶ δὲ εἰς τὴν περιτομήν· 10 μόνον
Gentiles and they *and* to the circumcised. They asked only that we should continue
1620 1254 899 1254 1650 3836 4364 3667 2671 3648 3648 3648
n.apn r.npm cj p.a d.asf n.asf adv

τῶν πτωχῶν ἵνα μνημονεύωμεν, ὃ ↱ καὶ
to remember the poor, *that we should continue to remember* the very thing I too
3648 3648 3836 4777 2671 3648 4005 899 4047 5079 2779
d.gpm a.gpm cj v.pas.1p r.asn adv

ἐσπούδασα αὐτὸ τοῦτο ποιῆσαι. 11 ὅτε δὲ ἦλθεν Κηφᾶς εἰς
was eager *very thing* to do. But when *But* Cephas came *Cephas* to
5079 899 4047 4472 1254 4021 1254 3064 2262 3064 1650
v.aai.1s r.asn r.asn f.aa cj cj v.aai.3s n.nsm p.a

Ἀντιόχειαν, κατὰ πρόσωπον αὐτῷ ἀντέστην, ὅτι
Antioch, I opposed him to his face, *his I opposed* because he stood
522 468 468 2848 899 4725 899 468 4022 1639 1639
n.asf p.a n.asn r.dsm.3 v.aai.1s cj

κατεγνωσμένος ἦν. 12 πρὸ τοῦ γὰρ ἐλθεῖν τινας ἀπὸ Ἰακώβου
condemned. *he stood* For until ~ *For* certain men came *certain men* from James,
2861 1639 1142 4574 3836 1142 5516 5516 2262 5516 608 2610
pt.rp.nsm v.iai.3s p.g d.gsn cj f.aa r.apm p.g n.gsm

μετὰ τῶν ἐθνῶν συνήσθιεν· ὅτε δὲ ἦλθον,
he used to eat with the Gentiles; *he used to eat* but when *but* they arrived,
5303 5303 5303 5303 3552 3836 1620 5303 1254 4021 1254 2262
p.g d.gpn n.gpn v.iai.3s cj cj v.aai.3p

ὑπέστελλεν καὶ ἀφώριζεν ἑαυτὸν φοβούμενος τοὺς ἐκ
⌊he began to draw back⌋ and separate himself because he feared those of the
5713 2779 928 1571 5828 3836 1666
v.iai.3s cj v.iai.3s r.asm.3 pt.pp.nsm d.apm p.g

περιτομῆς. 13 καὶ συνυπεκρίθησαν αὐτῷ ↰ ↰ ↰
⌊circumcision party.⌋ And the rest of the Jews joined him in playing the
4364 2779 3836 3370 2681 5347 899 5347 5347 5347
n.gsf cj v.api.3p r.dsm.3

↰ καὶ[a] οἱ λοιποὶ Ἰουδαῖοι, ὥστε καὶ Βαρναβᾶς συναπήχθη αὐτῶν τῇ
hypocrite, *{and} the rest Jews* so that even Barnabas was led astray by their *by*
5347 2779 3836 3370 2681 6063 2779 982 5270 3836 899 3836
cj d.npm a.npm a.npm cj adv n.nsm v.api.3s r.gpm.3 d.dsf

ὑποκρίσει. 14 ἀλλ᾿ ὅτε εἶδον ὅτι ↱ ↱ οὐκ ὀρθοποδοῦσιν πρὸς τὴν
hypocrisy. But when I saw that they were not ⌊behaving in a manner consistent⌋ with the
5694 247 4021 1625 4022 3980 3980 4024 3980 4639 3836
n.dsf cj cj v.aai.1s cj pl v.pai.3p p.a d.asf

ἀλήθειαν τοῦ εὐαγγελίου, εἶπον τῷ Κηφᾷ ἔμπροσθεν πάντων, εἰ σὺ
truth of the gospel, I said to Cephas before them all, "If you, born a
237 3836 2295 3306 3836 3064 1869 4246 1623 5148 5639
n.asf d.gsn n.gsn v.aai.1s d.dsm n.dsm p.g a.gpm cj r.ns.2

Ἰουδαῖος ὑπάρχων ἐθνικῶς καὶ οὐχὶ Ἰουδαϊκῶς ζῇς, πῶς
Jew, *born* live like a Gentile and not like a Jew, *live* ⌊by what right⌋ are you
2681 5639 2409 1619 2779 4049 2680 2409 4802 337 337
a.nsm pt.pa.nsm adv cj pl adv v.pai.2s cj

NASB

for me also to the
Gentiles), 9 and
recognizing the
grace that had
been given to me,
James and Cephas
and John, who
were reputed to
be pillars, gave to
me and Barnabas
the right hand of
fellowship, so that
we *might go* to the
Gentiles and they
to the circumcised.
10 *They* only *asked*
us to remember
the poor—the very
thing I also was
eager to do.

Peter (Cephas) Opposed by Paul

11 But when Ce-
phas came to Anti-
och, I opposed him
to his face, because
he stood con-
demned. 12 For prior
to the coming of
certain men from
James, he used to
eat with the Gen-
tiles; but when they
came, he *began*
to withdraw and
hold himself aloof,
fearing the party
of the circumci-
sion. 13 The rest of
the Jews joined
him in hypocrisy,
with the result that
even Barnabas was
carried away by
their hypocrisy.
14 But when I saw
that they were not
straightforward
about the truth of
the gospel, I said to
Cephas in the pres-
ence of all, "If you,
being a Jew, live
like the Gentiles
and not like the
Jews, how *is it that*

[a] 9 That is, Peter; also in verses 11 and 14

[a] [καὶ] UBS, omitted by TNIV.

NIV

force Gentiles to
follow Jewish cus-
toms?
15"We who are
Jews by birth and
not sinful Gentiles
16know that a per-
son is not justified
by the works of the
law, but by faith
in Jesus Christ. So
we, too, have put
our faith in Christ
Jesus that we may
be justified by
faith in[a] Christ and
not by the works
of the law, because
by the works of the
law no one will be
justified.
17"But if, in seek-
ing to be justified
in Christ, we Jews
find ourselves also
among the sin-
ners, doesn't that
mean that Christ
promotes sin? Ab-
solutely not! 18If
I rebuild what I
destroyed, then I
really would be a
lawbreaker.
19"For through
the law I died to
the law so that I
might live for God.
20I have been cru-
cified with Christ
and I no longer
live, but Christ
lives in me. The
life I now live in
the body, I live by
faith in the Son of
God, who loved
me and gave him-
self for me. 21I do
not set aside the
grace of God, for
if righteousness
could be gained
through the law,

τὰ ἔθνη ἀναγκάζεις ἰουδαΐζειν; 15 Ἡμεῖς
trying to make the Gentiles *are you trying to make* live like Jews?" We ourselves are Jews
337 337 337 3836 1620 337 2678 7005 2681
d.apn n.apn v.pai.2s f.pa r.np.1

φύσει Ἰουδαῖοι καὶ οὐκ ἐξ ἐθνῶν ἁμαρτωλοί· 16 εἰδότες δὲ[a] ὅτι οὐ
by birth *Jews* and not *{from}* Gentile sinners; yet we know *yet* that no one
5882 2681 2779 4024 1666 1620 283 1254 3857 1254 4022 4024 476
n.dsf a.npm cj pl p.g n.gpn a.npm pt.ra.npm cj cj pl

δικαιοῦται ἄνθρωπος ἐξ ἔργων → νόμου ⌊ἐὰν μὴ⌋ διὰ πίστεως Ἰησοῦ
is justified *one* by the works of the law but through faith in Jesus
1467 476 1666 2240 3795 1569 3590 1328 4411 2652
v.ppi.3s n.nsm p.g n.gpn n.gsm cj pl p.g n.gsf n.gsm

Χριστοῦ, καὶ ἡμεῖς εἰς Χριστὸν Ἰησοῦν ἐπιστεύσαμεν, ἵνα
Christ. And we have come to believe in Christ Jesus, *have come to believe* so that
5986 2779 7005 4409 4409 4409 4409 1650 5986 2652 4409 2671
n.gsm cj r.np.1 p.a n.asm n.asm v.aai.1p cj

δικαιωθῶμεν ἐκ πίστεως Χριστοῦ καὶ οὐκ ἐξ ἔργων → νόμου, ὅτι
we might be justified by faith in Christ, and not ⌊by doing⌋ the works of the law, since
1467 1666 4411 5986 2779 4024 1666 2240 3795 4022
v.aps.1p p.g n.gsf n.gsm cj pl p.g n.gpn n.gsm cj

ἐξ ἔργων → νόμου οὐ δικαιωθήσεται πᾶσα σάρξ.
no one will be justified by the works of the law. *no* *will be justified* *{one}* *{flesh}*
4024 4246 1467 1467 1467 1666 2240 3795 4024 1467 4246 4922
p.g n.gpn n.gsm pl v.fpi.3s a.nsf n.nsf

17 εἰ δὲ ζητοῦντες δικαιωθῆναι ἐν Χριστῷ → → εὑρέθημεν
But if, *But* while seeking to be justified in Christ, we ourselves have also been found
1254 1623 1254 2426 1467 1877 5986 899 2779 2351
cj cj pt.pa.npm f.ap p.d n.dsm v.api.1p

καὶ αὐτοὶ ἁμαρτωλοί, ἆρα Χριστὸς ἁμαρτίας διάκονος;
also *ourselves* to be sinners, is Christ then *Christ* a servant of sin? *servant*
2779 899 283 5986 727 5986 1356 281 1356
adv r.npm a.npm pl n.nsm n.gsf n.nsm

⌊μὴ γένοιτο.⌋ 18 εἰ γὰρ ἃ κατέλυσα
Of course not! But if *But* I build up again those things I once tore down,
3590 1181 1142 1623 1142 3868 3868 3868 4099 4047 4005 2907
pl v.amo.3s cj cj r.apn v.aai.1s

ταῦτα πάλιν οἰκοδομῶ, παραβάτην ἐμαυτὸν
those *again* *I build up* then I demonstrate that I am a lawbreaker. *I*
4047 4099 3868 5319 5319 1831 4127 1831
r.apn adv v.pai.1s n.asm r.asm.1

συνιστάνω. 19 ἐγὼ γὰρ διὰ νόμου → νόμῳ ἀπέθανον,
I demonstrate For through the law I *For* *through* *law* died to the law *died*
5319 1142 1328 3795 1609 1142 1328 3795 633 3795 633
v.pai.1s r.ns.1 cj p.g n.gsm n.dsm v.aai.1s

ἵνα θεῷ ζήσω. Χριστῷ συνεσταύρωμαι·
so that I might live for God. *I might live* I have been crucified with Christ; *I have been crucified*
2671 2409 2409 2409 2536 2409 5365 5365 5365 5365 5986 5365
cj n.dsm v.aas.1s n.dsm v.rpi.1s

20 ζῶ δὲ οὐκέτι ἐγώ, ζῇ δὲ ἐν ἐμοὶ Χριστός·
and I no longer live, *and* *no longer I* but Christ lives *but* in me. *Christ*
1254 1609 4033 4033 2409 1254 4033 1609 1254 5986 2409 1254 1877 1609 5986
v.pai.1s cj adv r.ns.1 v.pai.3s cj p.d r.ds.1 n.nsm

ὃ δὲ → νῦν ζῶ ἐν σαρκί, ἐν πίστει ζῶ τῇ τοῦ υἱοῦ
And the life *And* I now live in the flesh, I live by faith *I live* in the Son
1254 4005 1254 2409 3814 2409 1877 4922 2409 2409 1877 4411 2409 3836 3836 5626
r.asn cj adv v.pai.1s p.d n.dsf p.d n.dsf v.pai.1s d.dsf d.gsm n.gsm

τοῦ θεοῦ τοῦ ἀγαπήσαντός με καὶ παραδόντος ἑαυτὸν ὑπὲρ ἐμοῦ. 21 ↱ ↱ οὐκ
of God, who loved me and gave himself for me. I do not
3836 2536 3836 26 1609 2779 4140 1571 5642 1609 119 119 4024
d.gsm n.gsm d.gsm pt.aa.gsm r.as.1 cj pt.aa.gsm r.asm.3 p.g r.gs.1 pl

ἀθετῶ τὴν χάριν τοῦ θεοῦ· εἰ γὰρ διὰ νόμου
nullify the grace of God; for if *for* righteousness could be gained through the law,
119 3836 5921 3836 2536 1142 1623 1142 1466 1328 3795
v.pai.1s d.asf n.asf d.gsm n.gsm cj cj p.g n.gsm

NASB

you compel the
Gentiles to live like
Jews?
15"We *are* Jews by
nature and not sin-
ners from among
the Gentiles; 16nev-
ertheless knowing
that a man is not
justified by the
works of the Law
but through faith in
Christ Jesus, even
we have believed
in Christ Jesus,
so that we may be
justified by faith in
Christ and not by
the works of the
Law; since by the
works of the Law
no flesh will be
justified. 17But if,
while seeking to be
justified in Christ,
we ourselves have
also been found
sinners, is Christ
then a minister of
sin? May it never
be! 18For if I re-
build what I have
once destroyed, I
prove myself to be
a transgressor. 19For
through the Law
I died to the Law,
so that I might live
to God. 20I have
been crucified with
Christ; and it is no
longer I who live,
but Christ lives in
me; and the *life*
which I now live
in the flesh I live
by faith in the Son
of God, who loved
me and gave Him-
self up for me. 21I
do not nullify the
grace of God, for
if righteousness
comes through the

[a] 16 Or *but through the faithfulness of . . . justified on the basis of the faithfulness of*

[a] [δὲ] UBS.

NIV

Christ died for noth-
ing!"[a]

Faith or Works of the Law

3 You foolish Ga-
latians! Who
has bewitched you?
Before your very
eyes Jesus Christ was
clearly portrayed as
crucified. 2I would
like to learn just one
thing from you: Did
you receive the Spirit
by the works of the
law, or by believing
what you heard?
3Are you so foolish?
After beginning by
means of the Spirit,
are you now trying
to finish by means
of the flesh?[b] 4Have
you experienced[c] so
much in vain—if it
really was in vain?
5So again I ask, does
God give you his
Spirit and work mir-
acles among you by
the works of the law,
or by your believing
what you heard? 6So
also Abraham "be-
lieved God, and it
was credited to him
as righteousness."[d]
7Understand, then,
that those who have
faith are children of
Abraham. 8Scripture
foresaw that God
would justify the
Gentiles by faith,
and announced the
gospel in advance to
Abraham: "All na-
tions will be blessed
through you."[e] 9So
those who rely on
faith are blessed
along with Abraham,
the man of faith.
10For all who rely on
the works of the law
are under a curse, as it
is written: "Cursed is

[a] 21 Some interpreters end the quotation after verse 14.
[b] 3 In contexts like this, the Greek word for *flesh* (*sarx*) refers to the sinful state of human beings, often presented as a power in opposition to the Spirit.
[c] 4 Or *suffered*
[d] 6 Gen. 15:6
[e] 8 Gen. 12:3; 18:18; 22:18

δικαιοσύνη, ἄρα Χριστὸς δωρεὰν ἀπέθανεν.
righteousness then Christ died for nothing! *died*
1466 726 5986 633 1562 633
n.nsf cj n.nsm adv v.aai.3s

3:1 ὦ ἀνόητοι Γαλάται, τίς ὑμᾶς ἐβάσκανεν,[a] οἷς κατ᾽
O foolish Galatians! Who has bewitched you, *has bewitched* before whose *before*
6043 485 1129 5515 1001 1001 7007 1001 2848 4005 2848
j a.vpm n.vpm r.nsm r.ap.2 v.aai.3s r.dpm p.a

ὀφθαλμοὺς Ἰησοῦς Χριστὸς προεγράφη ἐσταυρωμένος; 2 τοῦτο μόνον
eyes Jesus Christ ˻was publicly exhibited˼ as crucified? Only this *Only*
4057 2652 5986 4592 5090 3667 4047 3667
n.apm n.nsm n.nsm v.api.3s pt.rp.nsm r.asn adv

θέλω μαθεῖν ἀφ᾽ ὑμῶν· ἐξ ἔργων → νόμου τὸ πνεῦμα
I want to learn from you: Did you receive the Spirit by works of the law *the Spirit*
2527 3443 608 7007 3284 3284 3284 3836 4460 1666 2240 3795 3836 4460
v.pai.1s f.aa p.g r.gp.2 p.g n.gpn n.gsm d.asn n.asn

ἐλάβετε ἢ ἐξ ἀκοῆς πίστεως; 3 οὕτως ἀνόητοί ἐστε, ἐναρξάμενοι →
Did you receive or by hearing with faith? Are you so foolish? *Are you* Having begun by
3284 2445 1666 198 4411 1639 1639 4048 485 1639 1887
v.aai.2p cj p.g n.gsf n.gsf adv a.npm v.pai.2p pt.am.npm

πνεύματι νῦν → σαρκὶ ἐπιτελεῖσθε; 4
the Spirit, would you now attain your goal by the flesh? *would you attain your goal* Have you
4460 2200 2200 3814 2200 2200 2200 4922 2200 4248 4248
n.dsn adv n.dsf v.ppi.2p

τοσαῦτα ἐπάθετε εἰκῇ; εἴ γε καὶ εἰκῇ.
suffered so many things *Have you suffered* ˻for no purpose?˼ — if ~ it really was ˻for no purpose.˼
4248 5537 4248 1632 1623 1145 2779 1632
r.apn v.aai.2p adv cj pl adv adv

5 ὁ οὖν ἐπιχορηγῶν ὑμῖν τὸ πνεῦμα καὶ ἐνεργῶν δυνάμεις ἐν ὑμῖν,
So does the *So* one who gives you the Spirit and works miracles among you
4036 3836 4036 2220 7007 3836 4460 2779 1919 1539 1877 7007
d.nsm cj pt.pa.nsm r.dp.2 d.asn n.asn cj pt.pa.nsm n.apf p.d r.dp.2

ἐξ ἔργων → νόμου ἢ ἐξ ἀκοῆς πίστεως; 6 Καθὼς Ἀβραὰμ ἐπίστευσεν
do it by works of the law, or by hearing with faith? Consider Abraham: "He believed
1666 2240 3795 2445 1666 198 4411 2777 11 4409
p.g n.gpn n.gsm cj p.g n.gsf n.gsf cj n.nsm v.aai.3s

τῷ θεῷ, καὶ ἐλογίσθη αὐτῷ εἰς δικαιοσύνην· 7 γινώσκετε ἄρα ὅτι οἱ
{the} God, and it was reckoned to him as righteousness." Know then that it is those
3836 2536 2779 3357 899 1650 1466 1182 726 4022 3836
d.dsm n.dsm cj v.api.3s r.dsm.3 p.a n.asf v.pam.2p cj cj d.npm

ἐκ πίστεως, οὗτοι υἱοί εἰσιν Ἀβραάμ. 8 προϊδοῦσα δὲ
of faith who are the sons *are* of Abraham. And the Scripture, foreseeing *And*
1666 4411 4047 1639 5626 1639 11 1254 3836 1210 4632 1254
p.g n.gsf r.npm n.npm v.pai.3p n.gsm pt.aa.nsf cj

ἡ γραφὴ ὅτι ἐκ πίστεως δικαιοῖ τὰ ἔθνη ὁ
the Scripture that God would justify the Gentiles by faith, *would justify* *the Gentiles {the}*
3836 1210 4022 2536 1467 1467 3836 1620 1666 4411 1467 3836 1620 3836
d.nsf n.nsf cj p.g n.gsf v.pai.3s d.apn n.apn d.nsm

θεός, προευηγγελίσατο τῷ Ἀβραὰμ ὅτι →
God ˻preached the gospel beforehand˼ to Abraham, saying, "In you will all nations
2536 4603 3836 11 4022 1877 5148 4246 1620
n.nsm v.ami.3s d.dsm n.dsm cj

ἐνευλογηθήσονται ἐν σοὶ πάντα τὰ ἔθνη· 9 ὥστε οἱ ἐκ πίστεως εὐλογοῦνται
be blessed." *In you all {the} nations* So then, those who believe are blessed
1922 1877 5148 4246 3836 1620 6063 3836 1666 4411 2328
v.fpi.3p p.d r.ds.2 a.npn d.npn n.npn cj d.npm p.g n.gsf v.ppi.3p

σὺν τῷ πιστῷ Ἀβραάμ. 10 ὅσοι γὰρ ἐξ ἔργων →
˻along with˼ Abraham, the believer. *Abraham* For all *For* who rely on works of the
5250 11 3836 4412 11 1142 4012 1142 1639 1639 1666 2240
p.d d.dsm a.dsm n.dsm r.npm cj p.g n.gpn

νόμου εἰσίν, ὑπὸ κατάραν εἰσίν· γέγραπται γὰρ ὅτι ἐπικατάρατος
law *who rely* are under a curse; *are* for it is written, *for* ~ "Cursed is
3795 1639 1639 5679 2932 1639 1142 1211 1142 4022 2129
n.gsm v.pai.3p p.a n.asf v.pai.3p v.rpi.3s cj cj a.nsm

[a] τῇ ἀληθείᾳ μὴ πείθεσθαι included by TR after ἐβάσκανεν.

NASB

Law, then Christ
died needlessly."

Faith Brings Righteousness

3:1You foolish
Galatians, who has
bewitched you,
before whose eyes
Jesus Christ was
publicly portrayed
as crucified? 2This
is the only thing
I want to find out
from you: did you
receive the Spirit
by the works of
the Law, or by
hearing with faith?
3Are you so fool-
ish? Having begun
by the Spirit, are
you now being
perfected by the
flesh? 4Did you suf-
fer so many things
in vain—if indeed
it was in vain?
5So then, does He
who provides you
with the Spirit and
works miracles
among you, do it
by the works of the
Law, or by hearing
with faith?
6Even so Abraham
BELIEVED GOD, AND
IT WAS RECKONED TO
HIM AS RIGHTEOUS-
NESS. 7Therefore,
be sure that it is
those who are of
faith who are sons
of Abraham. 8The
Scripture, forësee-
ing that God would
justify the Gentiles
by faith, preached
the gospel before-
hand to Abraham,
saying, "ALL THE
NATIONS WILL BE
BLESSED IN YOU."
9So then those who
are of faith are
blessed with Abra-
ham, the believer.
10For as many as
are of the works of
the Law are under
a curse; for it is
written, "CURSED

NIV

everyone who does
not continue to do
everything written
in the Book of the
Law."[a] 11 Clearly
no one who re-
lies on the law is
justified before
God, because "the
righteous will live
by faith."[b] 12 The
law is not based on
faith; on the con-
trary, it says, "The
person who does
these things will
live by them."[c]
13 Christ redeemed
us from the curse
of the law by be-
coming a curse for
us, for it is written:
"Cursed is every-
one who is hung
on a pole."[d] 14 He
redeemed us in or-
der that the bless-
ing given to Abra-
ham might come
to the Gentiles
through Christ
Jesus, so that by
faith we might re-
ceive the promise
of the Spirit.

The Law and the Promise

15 Brothers and
sisters, let me take
an example from
everyday life. Just
as no one can set
aside or add to a
human covenant
that has been duly
established, so
it is in this case.
16 The promises
were spoken to
Abraham and to
his seed. Scripture
does not say "and
to seeds," mean-
ing many people,
but "and to your
seed,"[e] meaning
one person, who
is Christ. 17 What I
mean is this: The
law,

πᾶς ὅς ↱ οὐκ ἐμμένει πᾶσιν τοῖς γεγραμμένοις ἐν τῷ βιβλίῳ τοῦ νόμου
everyone who does not continue in all things written in the book of the law,
4246 4005 1844 4024 1844 4246 3836 1211 1877 3836 1046 3836 3795
a.nsm r.nsm pl v.pai.3s a.dpn d.dpn pt.rp.dpn p.d d.dsn n.dsn d.gsm n.gsm

τοῦ ποιῆσαι αὐτά. 11 ὅτι δὲ ἐν
~ to do them." Now it is clear that *Now* no one is justified before God by
3836 4472 899 1254 1316 1316 1316 4022 1254 4029 4029 1467 1467 4123 2536 1877
d.gsn f.aa r.apn.3 cj cj p.d

νόμῳ οὐδεὶς δικαιοῦται παρὰ τῷ θεῷ δῆλον, ὅτι ὁ
the law, *no one* *is justified* *before* *{the}* *God* *it is clear* because "it is by faith that the
3795 4029 1467 4123 3836 2536 1316 4022 1666 4411 3836
n.dsm a.nsm v.ppi.3s p.d d.dsm n.dsm a.nsn cj d.nsm

δίκαιος ἐκ πίστεως ζήσεται· 12 ὁ δὲ νόμος οὐκ ἔστιν
⌊righteous person⌋ *by* *faith* will live." However, the *However* law is not *is*
1465 1666 4411 2409 1254 3836 1254 3795 1639 4024 1639
a.nsm p.g n.gsf v.fmi.3s d.nsm cj n.nsm pl v.pai.3s

ἐκ πίστεως, ἀλλ᾽ ὁ ποιήσας αὐτὰ ζήσεται ἐν αὐτοῖς.
of faith; ⌊on the contrary,⌋ it teaches that "the one who does them will live by them."
1666 4411 247 3836 4472 899 2409 1877 899
p.g n.gsf cj d.nsm pt.aa.nsm r.apn.3 v.fmi.3s p.d r.dpn.3

13 Χριστὸς ἡμᾶς ἐξηγόρασεν ἐκ τῆς κατάρας τοῦ νόμου γενόμενος
Christ redeemed us *redeemed* from the curse of the law by becoming a curse
5986 1973 7005 1973 1666 3836 2932 3836 3795 1181 2932
n.nsm r.ap.1 v.aai.3s p.g d.gsf n.gsf d.gsm n.gsm pt.am.nsm

ὑπὲρ ἡμῶν κατάρα, ὅτι γέγραπται, ἐπικατάρατος πᾶς ὁ κρεμάμενος ἐπὶ
for us *curse* — for it is written, "Cursed is everyone who is hung on a
5642 7005 2932 4022 1211 2129 4246 3836 3203 2093
p.g r.gp.1 n.nsf cj v.rpi.3s a.nsm a.nsm d.nsm pt.pm.nsm p.g

ξύλου, 14 ἵνα εἰς τὰ
tree" — ⌊in order that⌋ in Christ Jesus the blessing of Abraham might come to the
3833 2671 1877 5986 2652 3836 2330 3836 11 1181 1181 1650 3836
n.gsn cj p.a d.apn

ἔθνη ἡ εὐλογία τοῦ Ἀβραὰμ γένηται ἐν Χριστῷ Ἰησοῦ, ἵνα
Gentiles, *the* *blessing* *of* *Abraham* *might come* *in* *Christ* *Jesus* so that we might
1620 3836 2330 3836 11 1181 1877 5986 2652 2671 3284 3284
n.apn d.nsf n.nsf d.gsm n.gsm v.ams.3s p.d n.dsm n.dsm cj

τὴν ἐπαγγελίαν τοῦ πνεύματος λάβωμεν διὰ τῆς πίστεως. 15
receive the promise of the Spirit *we might receive* through *{the}* faith. To
3284 3836 2039 3836 4460 3284 1328 3836 4411 3306
d.asf n.asf d.gsn n.gsn v.aas.1p p.g d.gsf n.gsf

ἀδελφοί, κατὰ ἄνθρωπον λέγω, ὅμως
speak in human terms, brothers: *in* *human terms* *To speak* ⌊even though⌋ a covenant is one
3306 2848 476 476 81 2848 476 3306 3940 1347
n.vpm p.a n.asm v.pai.1s adv

ἀνθρώπου κεκυρωμένην διαθήκην οὐδεὶς → → ἀθετεῖ ἢ
made by man, yet ⌊when it has been ratified,⌋ *covenant* no one can set it aside or
476 3263 1347 4029 119 2445
n.gsm pt.rp.asf n.asf a.nsm v.pai.3s cj

ἐπιδιατάσσεται. 16 τῷ δὲ Ἀβραὰμ ἐρρέθησαν αἱ
add anything to it. Now the promises were made to *Now* Abraham *were made* *the*
2112 1254 3836 2039 3306 3306 3836 1254 11 3306 3836
v.pmi.3s d.dsm cj n.dsm v.api.3p d.npf

ἐπαγγελίαι καὶ τῷ σπέρματι αὐτοῦ. ↱ οὐ λέγει, καὶ τοῖς σπέρμασιν,
promises and to his descendant. *his* Scripture does not say, "and to descendants,"
2039 2779 3836 899 5065 899 3306 4024 3306 2779 3836 5065
n.npf cj d.dsn n.dsn r.gsm.3 pl v.pai.3s cj d.dpn n.dpn

ὡς ἐπὶ πολλῶν ἀλλ᾽ ὡς ἐφ᾽ ἑνός· καὶ τῷ σπέρματί
referring to many, but "and to your descendant," referring to one, *and* *to* *descendant*
6055 2093 4498 247 2779 3836 5148 5065 6055 2093 1651 2779 3836 5065
pl p.g a.gpn cj pl p.g a.gsn cj d.dsn n.dsn

σου, ὅς ἐστιν Χριστός. 17 τοῦτο δὲ λέγω,
your who is Christ. What I am saying is this: *{and}* *I am saying* the law, which
5148 4005 1639 5986 3306 3306 3306 4047 1254 3306 3836 3795 1181
r.gs.2 r.nsm v.pai.3s n.nsm r.asn cj v.pai.1s

NASB

IS EVERYONE WHO
DOES NOT ABIDE BY
ALL THINGS WRITTEN
IN THE BOOK OF THE
LAW, TO PERFORM
THEM." 11 Now that
no one is justified
by the Law before
God is evident; for,
"THE RIGHTEOUS
MAN SHALL LIVE BY
FAITH." 12 How-
ever, the Law is
not of faith; on
the contrary, "HE
WHO PRACTICES
THEM SHALL LIVE
BY THEM." 13 Christ
redeemed us
from the curse of
the Law, having
become a curse for
us—for it is writ-
ten, "CURSED IS EV-
ERYONE WHO HANGS
ON A TREE"— 14 in
order that in Christ
Jesus the bless-
ing of Abraham
might come to the
Gentiles, so that
we would receive
the promise of
the Spirit through
faith.

Intent of the Law

15 Brethren, I speak
in terms of human
relations: even
though it is *only* a
man's covenant,
yet when it has
been ratified, no
one sets it aside or
adds conditions to
it. 16 Now the prom-
ises were spoken
to Abraham and to
his seed. He does
not say, "And to
seeds," as *referring*
to many, but *rather*
to one, "And to
your seed," that is,
Christ. 17 What I am
saying is this: the
Law, which came

[a] *10* Deut. 27:26
[b] *11* Hab. 2:4
[c] *12* Lev. 18:5
[d] *13* Deut. 21:23
[e] *16* Gen. 12:7; 13:15; 24:7

NIV

introduced 430
years later, does
not set aside the
covenant previ-
ously established
by God and thus
do away with the
promise. 18 For if
the inheritance de-
pends on the law,
then it no longer
depends on the
promise; but God
in his grace gave
it to Abraham
through a promise.
19 Why, then, was
the law given at
all? It was added
because of trans-
gressions until the
Seed to whom the
promise referred
had come. The law
was given through
angels and entrust-
ed to a mediator.
20 A mediator, how-
ever, implies more
than one party; but
God is one.
21 Is the law,
therefore, opposed
to the promises of
God? Absolutely
not! For if a law
had been given
that could impart
life, then righ-
teousness would
certainly have
come by the law.
22 But Scripture
has locked up ev-
erything under
the control of sin,
so that what was
promised, being
given through faith
in Jesus Christ,
might be given to
those who believe.

Children of God

23 Before the com-
ing of this faith,[a]
we were held in
custody under the
law, locked up
until the faith that
was to come would
be revealed. 24 So
the law was our
guardian until

[a] 22,23 Or *through the faithfulness of Jesus . . .* [23]*Before faith came*

διαθήκην προκεκυρωμένην ὑπὸ
came four hundred and thirty years later, does not annul a covenant previously established by
1181 5484 5484 2779 5558 2291 3552 4024 218 1347 4623 5679
n.asf pt.rp.asf p.g

τοῦ θεοῦ ὁ μετὰ τετρακόσια καὶ τριάκοντα ἔτη γεγονὼς νόμος οὐκ ἀκυροῖ εἰς
{the} God, *the* *later* *four hundred* *and* *thirty* *years* *which came* *law* *not* *annul* ⌊so as⌋
3836 2536 3836 3552 5484 2779 5558 2291 1181 3795 4024 218 1650
d.gsm n.gsm d.nsm p.a a.apn cj a.apn n.apn pt.ra.nsm n.nsm pl v.pai.3s p.a

τὸ καταργῆσαι τὴν ἐπαγγελίαν. ↰ 18 εἰ γὰρ ἐκ νόμου
~ to make the promise void. For if *For* the inheritance is ⌊based on⌋ law,
3836 2934 3836 2039 2934 1142 1623 1142 3836 3100 1666 3795
d.asn f.aa d.asf n.asf cj cj p.g n.gsm

ἡ κληρονομία, οὐκέτι ἐξ ἐπαγγελίας· τῷ δὲ Ἀβραὰμ
the *inheritance* it is no longer ⌊based on⌋ a promise; but God gave it to *but* Abraham
3836 3100 4033 1666 2039 1254 2536 5919 3836 1254 11
d.nsf n.nsf adv p.g n.gsf d.dsm cj n.dsm

δι᾽ ἐπαγγελίας κεχάρισται ὁ θεός. 19 τί οὖν ὁ νόμος;
through a promise. *gave* *{the}* *God* Why then was the law given? It was
1328 2039 5919 3836 2536 5515 4036 3836 3795 4707 4707
p.g n.gsf v.rmi.3s d.nsm n.nsm r.asn cj d.nsm n.nsm

τῶν παραβάσεων χάριν προσετέθη, ⌊ἄχρις οὗ⌋
added because of *{the}* transgressions, *because of* *It was added* until the descendant
4707 5920 5920 3836 4126 5920 4707 948 4005 3836 5065
d.gpf n.gpf p.g v.api.3s p.g r.gsm

ἔλθῃ τὸ σπέρμα ᾧ ἐπήγγελται, διαταγεὶς δι᾽
⌊should come⌋ *the* *descendant* ⌊to whom⌋ ⌊the promise had been made.⌋ It was established through
2262 3836 5065 4005 2040 1411 1328
v.aas.3s d.nsn n.nsn r.dsm v.rpi.3s pt.ap.nsm p.g

ἀγγέλων ἐν ⌊χειρὶ μεσίτου.⌋ 20 ὁ δὲ μεσίτης ἑνὸς
angels by a mediator. Now a *Now* mediator is not for one party only,
34 1877 5931 3542 1254 3836 1254 3542 1639 4024 1651
n.gpm p.d n.dsf n.gsm d.nsm cj n.nsm a.gsm

οὐκ ἔστιν, ὁ δὲ θεὸς εἷς ἐστιν. 21 ὁ οὖν νόμος κατὰ τῶν
not *is* *{the}* but God is one. *is* Is the law, therefore, *law* ⌊opposed to⌋ the
4024 1639 3836 1254 2536 1639 1651 1639 3836 3795 4036 3795 2848 3836
pl v.pai.3s d.nsm cj n.nsm a.nsm v.pai.3s d.nsm cj n.nsm p.g d.gpf

ἐπαγγελιῶν [a]τοῦ θεοῦ; ⌊μὴ γένοιτο·⌋ εἰ γὰρ ἐδόθη νόμος
promises of God? Certainly not! For if *For* a law ⌊had been given⌋ *law*
2039 3836 2536 3590 1181 1142 1623 1142 3795 1443 3795
n.gpf d.gsm n.gsm pl v.amo.3s cj cj v.api.3s n.nsm

ὁ δυνάμενος ζῳοποιῆσαι, ὄντως ἐκ νόμου ἂν
that could impart life, then righteousness would indeed be by the law. *would*
3836 1538 2443 1466 323 3953 1639 1666 3795 323
d.nsm pt.pp.nsm f.aa adv p.g n.gsm pl

ἦν ἡ δικαιοσύνη. 22 ἀλλὰ συνέκλεισεν ἡ γραφὴ τὰ πάντα
be *{the}* *righteousness* But the Scripture confined *the* *Scripture* *{the}* everything
1639 3836 1466 247 3836 1210 5168 3836 1210 3836 4246
v.iai.3s d.nsf n.nsf cj v.aai.3s d.nsf n.nsf d.apn a.apn

ὑπὸ ἁμαρτίαν, ἵνα ἡ ἐπαγγελία ἐκ πίστεως Ἰησοῦ Χριστοῦ δοθῇ
under sin, so that what was promised through faith in Jesus Christ ⌊might be given⌋
5679 281 2671 3836 2039 1666 4411 2652 5986 1443
p.a n.asf cj d.nsf n.nsf p.g n.gsf n.gsm n.gsm v.aps.3s

τοῖς πιστεύουσιν. 23 πρὸ τοῦ δὲ ἐλθεῖν τὴν πίστιν
to those who believe. Now before ~ *Now* faith came, *{the}* *faith* we were held in
3836 4409 1254 4574 3836 1254 4411 2262 3836 4411 5864 5864 5864 5864
d.dpm pt.pa.dpm p.g d.gsn cj f.aa d.asf n.asf

ὑπὸ νόμον ἐφρουρούμεθα συγκλειόμενοι εἰς τὴν μέλλουσαν πίστιν
custody under the law, *we were held in custody* imprisoned until the coming faith
5864 5679 3795 5864 5168 1650 3836 3516 4411
p.a n.asm v.ipi.1p pt.pp.npm p.a d.asf pt.pa.asf n.asf

ἀποκαλυφθῆναι, 24 ὥστε ὁ νόμος παιδαγωγὸς ἡμῶν γέγονεν εἰς
would be revealed. Thus the law was our disciplinarian *our* *was* until the time of
636 6063 3836 3795 1181 7005 4080 7005 1181 1650
f.ap cj d.nsm n.nsm n.nsm r.gp.1 v.rai.3s p.a

[a] [τοῦ θεοῦ] UBS.

NASB

four hundred
and thirty years
later, does not
invalidate a cov-
enant previously
ratified by God,
so as to nullify the
promise. 18 For if
the inheritance is
based on law, it is
no longer based on
a promise; but God
has granted it to
Abraham by means
of a promise.
19 Why the Law
then? It was added
because of trans-
gressions, having
been ordained
through angels by
the agency of a
mediator, until the
seed would come
to whom the prom-
ise had been made.
20 Now a mediator
is not for one *party
only;* whereas God
is *only* one. 21 Is the
Law then contrary
to the promises of
God? May it never
be! For if a law had
been given which
was able to impart
life, then righteous-
ness would indeed
have been based
on law. 22 But the
Scripture has shut
up everyone under
sin, so that the
promise by faith in
Jesus Christ might
be given to those
who believe.
23 But before faith
came, we were
kept in custody
under the law, be-
ing shut up to the
faith which was
later to be revealed.
24 Therefore the
Law has become
our tutor *to lead us*

NIV

Christ came that
we might be jus-
tified by faith.
25 Now that this
faith has come, we
are no longer un-
der a guardian.
26 So in Christ
Jesus you are all
children of God
through faith, 27 for
all of you who
were baptized
into Christ have
clothed your-
selves with Christ.
28 There is neither
Jew nor Gentile,
neither slave nor
free, nor is there
male and female,
for you are all one
in Christ Jesus.
29 If you belong to
Christ, then you
are Abraham's
seed, and heirs
according to the
promise.
4 What I am
saying is that
as long as an heir
is underage, he is
no different from
a slave, although
he owns the whole
estate. 2 The heir is
subject to guard-
ians and trustees
until the time set
by his father. 3 So
also, when we
were underage, we
were in slavery un-
der the elemental
spiritual forces[a]
of the world. 4 But
when the set time
had fully come,
God sent his Son,
born of a woman,

Χριστόν, ἵνα ἐκ πίστεως δικαιωθῶμεν·
Christ, so that we might be declared righteous by faith. *we might be declared righteous*
5986 2671 1467 1467 1467 1467 1467 1666 4411 1467
n.asm cj p.g n.gsf v.aps.1p

25 → → ἐλθούσης δὲ τῆς πίστεως οὐκέτι ὑπὸ παιδαγωγόν
But now that faith has come, *But {the} faith* we are no longer under a guardian.
1254 4411 2262 1254 3836 4411 1639 1639 4033 5679 4080
pt.aa.gsf cj d.gsf n.gsf adv p.a n.asm

ἐσμεν. 26 πάντες γὰρ υἱοὶ θεοῦ ἐστε διὰ τῆς πίστεως ἐν Χριστῷ
we are For you are all *For* sons of God *you are* through *{the}* faith in Christ
1639 1142 1639 1639 4246 1142 5626 2536 1639 1328 3836 4411 1877 5986
v.pai.1p a.npm cj n.npm n.gsm v.pai.2p p.g d.gsf n.gsf p.d n.dsm

Ἰησοῦ· 27 ὅσοι ← γὰρ εἰς Χριστὸν ἐβαπτίσθητε,
Jesus. For as many of you as *For* were baptized into Christ *you were baptized* have
2652 1142 4012 966 1142 966 966 1650 5986 966 1907
n.dsm r.npm cj p.a n.asm v.api.2p

Χριστὸν ἐνεδύσασθε. 28 οὐκ ἔνι
clothed yourselves with Christ. *have clothed yourselves with* Now there is neither *there is*
1907 1907 1907 5986 1907 1928 1928 4024 1928
n.asm v.ami.2p pl v.pai.3s

Ἰουδαῖος οὐδὲ Ἕλλην, οὐκ ἔνι δοῦλος οὐδὲ ἐλεύθερος, οὐκ ἔνι ἄρσεν
Jew nor Greek, neither *{there is}* slave nor free, neither *{there is}* male
2681 4028 1818 4024 1928 1529 4028 1801 4024 1928 781
a.nsm cj n.nsm pl v.pai.3s n.nsm cj a.nsm pl v.pai.3s a.nsn

καὶ θῆλυ· πάντες γὰρ ὑμεῖς εἷς ἐστε ἐν Χριστῷ Ἰησοῦ. 29 εἰ
nor female; for you are all *for you* one *are* in Christ Jesus. And if
2779 2559 1142 7007 1639 4246 1142 7007 1651 1639 1877 5986 2652 1254 1623
cj a.nsn a.npm cj r.np.2 a.nsm v.pai.2p p.d n.dsm n.dsm cj

δὲ ὑμεῖς Χριστοῦ, ἄρα τοῦ Ἀβραὰμ σπέρμα ἐστέ,
And you belong to Christ, then you are descendants of Abraham, *descendants you are* heirs
1254 7007 5986 726 1639 1639 5065 3836 11 5065 1639 3101
cj r.np.2 n.gsm cj d.gsm n.gsm n.nsn v.pai.2p

κατ' ἐπαγγελίαν κληρονόμοι.
⌊according to⌋ the promise. *heirs*
2848 2039 3101
p.a n.asf n.npm

4:1 λέγω δέ, ⌊ἐφ' ὅσον χρόνον⌋ ὁ κληρονόμος
What I am saying *{and}* is that as long as the heir is a
3306 1254 2093 4012 5989 3836 3101 1639
v.pai.1s cj p.a r.asm n.asm d.nsm n.nsm

νήπιός ἐστιν, οὐδὲν διαφέρει → δούλου κύριος
minor, *is* he differs not at all *he differs* from a slave, even though in fact he owns
3758 1639 1422 1422 4029 1422 1529 1639 1639 1639 1639 3261
a.nsm v.pai.3s a.asn v.pai.3s n.gsm n.nsm

πάντων ὤν, 2 ἀλλὰ ὑπὸ ἐπιτρόπους
the entire estate. *even though in fact* However, he remains under the care of guardians
4246 1639 247 1639 1639 5679 2207
a.gpn pt.pa.nsm cj p.a n.apm

ἐστὶν καὶ οἰκονόμους ἄχρι τῆς προθεσμίας τοῦ πατρός. 3 οὕτως καὶ
he remains and managers until the time determined by his father. And so it is *And* with
1639 2779 3874 948 3836 4607 3836 4252 2779 4048 2779
v.pai.3s cj n.apm p.g d.gsf n.gsf d.gsm n.gsm adv adv

ἡμεῖς, ὅτε ἦμεν νήπιοι, ὑπὸ τὰ στοιχεῖα τοῦ κόσμου
us. While we were minors, we were enslaved to the ⌊elementary principles⌋ of the world.
7005 4021 1639 3758 1639 1639 1530 5679 3836 5122 3836 3180
r.np.1 cj v.iai.1p a.npm p.a d.apn n.apn d.gsm n.gsm

ἤμεθα δεδουλωμένοι· 4 ὅτε δὲ ἦλθεν τὸ πλήρωμα τοῦ
we were enslaved But when *But* the fullness of time had come, *the fullness of*
1639 1530 1254 4021 1254 3836 4445 3836 5989 2262 3836 4445 3836
v.imi.1p pt.rp.npm cj cj v.aai.3s d.nsn n.nsn d.gsm

χρόνου, ἐξαπέστειλεν ὁ θεὸς τὸν υἱὸν αὐτοῦ, γενόμενον ἐκ γυναικός,
time God sent forth *{the} God {the}* his Son, *his* born of a woman,
5989 2536 1990 3836 2536 3836 899 5626 899 1181 1666 1222
n.gsm v.aai.3s d.nsm n.nsm d.asm n.asm r.gsm.3 pt.am.asm p.g n.gsf

NASB

to Christ, so that
we may be justified
by faith. 25 But now
that faith has come,
we are no longer
under a tutor. 26 For
you are all sons of
God through faith
in Christ Jesus.
27 For all of you
who were baptized
into Christ have
clothed yourselves
with Christ. 28 There
is neither Jew nor
Greek, there is
neither slave nor
free man, there is
neither male nor
female; for you are
all one in Christ
Jesus. 29 And if you
belong to Christ,
then you are Abra-
ham's descendants,
heirs according to
promise.

Sonship in Christ

4:1 Now I say, as
long as the heir is a
child, he does not
differ at all from
a slave although
he is owner of
everything, 2 but he
is under guardians
and managers until
the date set by the
father. 3 So also
we, while we were
children, were held
in bondage under
the elemental
things of the world.
4 But when the full-
ness of the time
came, God sent
forth His Son, born
of a woman, born

[a] 3 Or *under the basic principles*

NIV

born under the
law, [5]to redeem
those under the
law, that we might
receive adoption
to sonship.[a] [6]Be-
cause you are his
sons, God sent the
Spirit of his Son
into our hearts, the
Spirit who calls
out, *"Abba,*[b] Fa-
ther." [7]So you are
no longer a slave,
but God's child;
and since you are
his child, God has
made you also an
heir.

Paul's Concern for the Galatians

[8]Formerly, when
you did not know
God, you were
slaves to those
who by nature
are not gods. [9]But
now that you know
God—or rath-
er are known by
God—how is it
that you are turn-
ing back to those
weak and miser-
able forces[c]? Do
you wish to be en-
slaved by them all
over again? [10]You
are observing
special days and
months and sea-
sons and years! [11]I
fear for you, that
somehow I have
wasted my efforts
on you.
[12]I plead with
you, brothers and
sisters, become
like me, for I be-
came like you. You
did me no wrong.
[13]As you know, it
was because of an
illness that I first
preached the gos-
pel to you, [14]and
even though my
illness was a trial
to you, you

[a] 5 The Greek word for *adoption to sonship* is a legal term referring to the full legal standing of an adopted male heir in Roman culture.
[b] 6 Aramaic for *Father*
[c] 9 Or *principles*

γενόμενον ὑπὸ νόμον, 5 ἵνα τοὺς ὑπὸ νόμον ἐξαγοράσῃ, ἵνα
born under law, to redeem those who were under law, *redeem* so that we
1181 5679 3795 2671 1973 3836 5679 3795 1973 2671 655
pt.am.asm p.a n.asm cj d.apm p.a n.asm v.aas.3s cj

τὴν υἱοθεσίαν ἀπολάβωμεν. 6 ὅτι δέ ἐστε υἱοί,
might receive *{the}* ⌊adoption as sons.⌋ *we might receive* And because *And* you are sons, God
655 655 3836 5625 655 1254 4022 1254 1639 5626 2536
d.asf n.asf v.aas.1p cj cj v.pai.2p n.npm

ἐξαπέστειλεν ὁ θεὸς τὸ πνεῦμα τοῦ υἱοῦ αὐτοῦ εἰς τὰς καρδίας ἡμῶν
sent *{the} God* the Spirit of his Son *his* into *{the}* our hearts, *our*
1990 3836 2536 3836 4460 3836 899 5626 899 1650 3836 7005 2840 7005
v.aai.3s d.nsm n.nsm d.asn n.asn d.gsm n.gsm r.gsm.3 p.a d.apf n.apf r.gp.1

κρᾶζον, αββα ὁ πατήρ. 7 ὥστε οὐκέτι εἶ δοῦλος ἀλλὰ υἱός·
⌊who cries out⌋ "Abba! *{the}* Father!" So you are no longer *you are* a slave, but a son;
3189 5 3836 4252 6063 1639 1639 4033 1639 1529 247 5626
pt.pa.asn n.vsm d.vsm n.vsm cj adv v.pai.2s n.nsm cj n.nsm

εἰ δὲ υἱός, καὶ κληρονόμος διὰ θεοῦ. 8 ⌊ἀλλὰ τότε⌋
and since *and* you are a son, then you are an heir through God. Formerly,
1254 1623 1254 5626 2779 3101 1328 2536 247 5538
cj cj n.nsm adv n.nsm p.g n.gsm cj adv

μὲν οὐκ εἰδότες θεὸν ἐδουλεύσατε τοῖς φύσει μὴ
~ when you did not know God, you were enslaved to those who by nature are not
3525 3857 3857 3857 4024 3857 2536 1526 3836 1639 5882 1639 3590
pl pl pt.ra.npm n.asm v.aai.2p d.dpm n.dsf pl

οὖσιν θεοῖς· 9 νῦν δὲ γνόντες θεόν, μᾶλλον δὲ
who are gods. But now *But* that ⌊you have come to know⌋ God — or rather, *or*
1639 2536 1254 3814 1254 1182 2536 1254 3437 1254
pt.pa.dpm n.dpm adv cj pt.aa.npm n.asm adv.c cj

γνωσθέντες ὑπὸ θεοῦ, πῶς ἐπιστρέφετε πάλιν ἐπὶ τὰ ἀσθενῆ καὶ πτωχὰ
are known by God — how can you turn back again to the feeble and inferior
1182 5679 2536 4802 2188 4099 2093 3836 822 2779 4777
pt.ap.npm p.g n.gsm pl v.pai.2p adv p.a d.apn a.apn cj a.apn

στοιχεῖα οἷς πάλιν
⌊elementary principles of the world?⌋ How can you want to be their slaves all over again?
5122 2527 2527 2527 2527 1526 1526 4005 1526 540 540 4099
n.apn r.dpn adv

ἄνωθεν δουλεύειν θέλετε; 10 ἡμέρας
all over *to be slaves* *How can you want* You scrupulously observe special days
540 1526 2527 4190 4190 4190 2465
adv f.pa v.pai.2p n.apf

παρατηρεῖσθε καὶ μῆνας καὶ καιροὺς καὶ ἐνιαυτούς, 11 φοβοῦμαι ὑμᾶς μή
You scrupulously observe and months and seasons and years! I am afraid *{you}* *{not}*
4190 2779 3604 2779 2789 2779 1929 5828 7007 3590
v.pmi.2p cj n.apm cj n.apm cj n.apm v.ppi.1s r.ap.2 cj

πως εἰκῇ κεκοπίακα εἰς ὑμᾶς. 12 γίνεσθε ὡς
that I may have labored over you ⌊to no avail.⌋ *I may have labored* *over* *you* Become as
4803 3159 3159 3159 3159 1650 7007 1632 3159 1650 7007 1181 6055
pl adv v.rai.1s p.a r.ap.2 v.pmm.2p cj

ἐγώ, ὅτι κἀγὼ ὡς ὑμεῖς, ἀδελφοί, δέομαι
I am, because I have become as you are; I plead with you, brothers. *I plead*
1609 4022 2743 6055 7007 1289 1289 7007 7007 81 1289
r.ns.1 cj crasis cj r.np.2 n.vpm v.ppi.1s

ὑμῶν. οὐδέν με ἠδικήσατε· 13 οἴδατε δὲ ὅτι
with you You have done me no wrong. *me* *You have done wrong* You know *{and}* that it
7007 92 92 92 1609 4029 92 1609 92 3857 1254 4022
r.gp.2 a.asn r.as.1 v.aai.2p v.rai.2p cj cj

δι' ἀσθένειαν τῆς σαρκὸς εὐηγγελισάμην ὑμῖν τὸ πρότερον,
was ⌊due to⌋ a physical infirmity *{the}* *physical* that I preached the gospel to you at first;
1328 4922 819 3836 4922 2294 7007 3836 4728
p.a n.asf d.gsf n.gsf v.ami.1s r.dp.2 d.asn adv.c

14 καὶ τὸν πειρασμὸν ὑμῶν ἐν τῇ σαρκί μου οὐκ
and though my condition was a trial to you, *{in}* *{the}* *condition* *my* you did not
2779 1609 4922 3836 4280 7007 1877 3836 4922 1609 2024 2024 4024
cj d.asm n.asm r.gp.2 p.d d.dsf n.dsf r.gs.1 pl

NASB

under the Law,
[5]so that He might
redeem those
who were under
the Law, that we
might receive the
adoption as sons.
[6]Because you are
sons, God has sent
forth the Spirit of
His Son into our
hearts, crying,
"Abba! Father!"
[7]Therefore you are
no longer a slave,
but a son; and if a
son, then an heir
through God.
[8]However at that
time, when you
did not know God,
you were slaves
to those which
by nature are no
gods. [9]But now
that you have come
to know God, or
rather to be known
by God, how is it
that you turn back
again to the weak
and worthless el-
emental things, to
which you desire
to be enslaved all
over again? [10]You
observe days and
months and sea-
sons and years. [11]I
fear for you, that
perhaps I have
labored over you
in vain.
[12]I beg of you,
brethren, become
as I *am,* for I also
have become as
you *are.* You have
done me no wrong;
[13]but you know
that it was because
of a bodily illness
that I preached the
gospel to you the
first time; [14]and that
which was a trial to
you in my bodily
condition you did

NIV

did not treat me
with contempt or
scorn. Instead, you
welcomed me as if
I were an angel of
God, as if I were
Christ Jesus him-
self. [15]Where, then,
is your blessing
of me now? I can
testify that, if you
could have done
so, you would have
torn out your eyes
and given them to
me. [16]Have I now
become your ene-
my by telling you
the truth?
[17]Those peo-
ple are zealous
to win you over,
but for no good.
What they want
is to alienate you
from us, so that
you may have zeal
for them. [18]It is
fine to be zealous,
provided the pur-
pose is good, and
to be so always,
not just when I am
with you. [19]My
dear children, for
whom I am again
in the pains of
childbirth until
Christ is formed in
you, [20]how I wish I
could be with you
now and change
my tone, because
I am perplexed
about you!

Hagar and Sarah

[21]Tell me, you
who want to be
under the law, are
you not aware of
what the law says?
[22]For it is written
that Abraham had
two sons, one by
the slave woman
and the other by
the free woman.
[23]His son by the
slave woman was
born according to
the flesh, but his
son by the free
woman was born
as the result of a
divine promise.
[24]These things

ἐξουθενήσατε οὐδὲ ἐξεπτύσατε, ἀλλὰ ὡς ἄγγελον θεοῦ
despise or reject me, but you welcomed me as an angel of God,
2024 4028 1746 247 1312 1312 1609 6055 34 2536
v.aai.2p cj v.aai.2p cj cj n.asm n.gsm

ἐδέξασθέ με, ὡς Χριστὸν Ἰησοῦν. 15 ποῦ οὖν ὁ
you welcomed me as though I were Christ Jesus. What then became of the
1312 1609 6055 5986 2652 4543 4036 3836
v.ami.2p r.as.1 cj n.asm n.asm cj cj d.nsm

μακαρισμὸς ὑμῶν; μαρτυρῶ γὰρ ὑμῖν ὅτι εἰ δυνατὸν
blessing you enjoyed? For I testify about *For* you that, if possible, you would have
3422 7007 1142 3455 1142 7007 4022 1623 1543 2021 2021 2021
n.nsm r.gp.2 v.pai.1s cj r.dp.2 cj cj a.nsn

τοὺς ὀφθαλμοὺς ὑμῶν ἐξορύξαντες ἐδώκατέ μοι.
torn out *{the}* your eyes *your you would have torn out* and given them to me!
2021 2021 3836 7007 4057 7007 2021 1443 1609
d.apm n.apm r.gp.2 pt.aa.npm v.aai.2p r.ds.1

16 ὥστε ἐχθρὸς ὑμῶν γέγονα → → ἀληθεύων ὑμῖν;
So then, have I become your enemy *your have I become* by telling you the truth? *you*
6063 1181 1181 1181 7007 2398 7007 1181 7007 238 7007
cj a.nsm r.gp.2 v.rai.1s pt.pa.nsm r.dp.2

17 ζηλοῦσιν ὑμᾶς οὐ καλῶς, ἀλλὰ ἐκκλεῖσαι ὑμᾶς
⌊They zealously seek⌋ your favor, but for no good purpose. Rather, they want to separate you
2420 7007 4024 2822 247 2527 2527 1710 7007
v.pai.3p r.ap.2 pl adv cj f.aa r.ap.2

θέλουσιν, ↰ ἵνα αὐτοὺς ζηλοῦτε· 18
they want from us so that you will seek them. *you will seek* Now to be zealous for a
2527 1710 2671 2420 2420 2420 899 2420 1254 2420 2420 2420 1877
v.pai.3p cj r.apm.3 v.pai.2p

καλὸν δὲ ζηλοῦσθαι ἐν καλῷ πάντοτε καὶ μὴ μόνον
good purpose is always good, *Now to be zealous for good purpose always {and}* not just
2819 2819 4121 2819 1254 2420 1877 2819 4121 2779 3590 3667
a.nsn cj f.pp p.d a.dsn adv cj pl adv

ἐν τῷ παρεῖναί με πρὸς ὑμᾶς. 19 τέκνα μου, οὓς ↱ ↱
when ~ I am present *I* with you. My little children, *My* ⌊for whom⌋ I am
1877 3836 1609 4205 1609 4639 7007 1609 5451 1609 4005 6048 6048
p.d d.dsn f.pa r.as.1 p.a r.ap.2 n.vpn r.gs.1 r.apm

πάλιν ὠδίνω μέχρις οὗ μορφωθῇ Χριστὸς ἐν ὑμῖν· 20 ἤθελον
again ⌊in the pain of childbirth⌋ until *{when}* Christ is formed *Christ* in you, I wish
4099 6048 3588 4005 5986 3672 5986 1877 7007 2527
adv v.pai.1s p.g r.gsm v.aps.3s n.nsm p.d r.dp.2 v.iai.1s

δὲ παρεῖναι πρὸς ὑμᾶς ἄρτι καὶ ἀλλάξαι τὴν φωνήν μου, ὅτι ἀπορούμαι
{and} I could be with you now and change *{the}* my tone, *my* for I am perplexed
1254 4205 4639 7007 785 2779 248 3836 1609 5889 1609 4022 679
cj f.pa p.a r.ap.2 adv cj f.aa d.asf n.asf r.gs.1 cj v.pmi.1s

ἐν ὑμῖν. 21 λέγετέ μοι, οἱ ὑπὸ νόμον θέλοντες εἶναι,
about you. Tell me, ⌊you who⌋ want to be under the law, *want to be* will you
1877 7007 3306 1609 3836 2527 1639 1639 5679 3795 2527 1639 201 201
p.d r.dp.2 v.pam.2p r.ds.1 d.vpm p.a n.asm pt.pa.vpm f.pa

τὸν νόμον οὐκ ἀκούετε; 22 γέγραπται γὰρ ὅτι Ἀβραὰμ
not listen to the law? *not will you listen to* For it is written *For* that Abraham had
4024 201 201 3836 3795 4024 201 1142 1211 1142 4022 11 2400
d.asm n.asm pl v.pai.2p v.rpi.3s cj cj n.nsm

δύο υἱοὺς ἔσχεν, ἕνα ἐκ τῆς παιδίσκης καὶ ἕνα ἐκ τῆς ἐλευθέρας. 23 ἀλλ᾽ ὁ
two sons, *had* one by the slave woman and one by the free woman. *{but}* The
1545 5626 2400 1651 1666 3836 4087 2779 1651 1666 3836 1801 247 3836
a.apm n.apm v.aai.3s a.asm p.g d.gsf n.gsf cj a.asm p.g d.gsf a.gsf cj d.nsm

μὲν ἐκ τῆς παιδίσκης κατὰ σάρκα γεγέννηται, ὁ δὲ
~ son by the slave woman was born ⌊according to⌋ the flesh, *was born* but the *but*
3525 1666 3836 4087 1164 1164 2848 4922 1164 1254 3836 1254
pl p.g d.gsf n.gsf p.a n.asf v.rpi.3s d.nsm cj

ἐκ τῆς ἐλευθέρας δι᾽ ἐπαγγελίας. 24 ἅτινά ἐστιν
son by the free woman was born ⌊as the result of⌋ promise. This may be
1666 3836 1801 1328 2039 4015 1639
p.g d.gsf a.gsf p.g n.gsf r.npn v.pai.3s

NASB

not despise or
loathe, but you
received me as
an angel of God,
as Christ Jesus
Himself. [15]Where
then is that sense
of blessing you
had? For I bear you
witness that, if pos-
sible, you would
have plucked out
your eyes and
given them to me.
[16]So have I become
your enemy by tell-
ing you the truth?
[17]They eagerly seek
you, not commend-
ably, but they wish
to shut you out so
that you will seek
them. [18]But it is
good always to be
eagerly sought in
a commendable
manner, and not
only when I am
present with you.
[19]My children,
with whom I am
again in labor until
Christ is formed in
you— [20]but I could
wish to be present
with you now and
to change my tone,
for I am perplexed
about you.

Bond and Free

[21]Tell me, you
who want to be un-
der law, do you not
listen to the law?
[22]For it is written
that Abraham had
two sons, one by
the bondwoman
and one by the free
woman. [23]But the
son by the bond-
woman was born
according to the
flesh, and the son
by the free woman
through the prom-
ise. [24]This is

NIV

are being taken
figuratively: The
women represent
two covenants.
One covenant is
from Mount Sinai
and bears chil-
dren who are to be
slaves: This is Ha-
gar. 25Now Hagar
stands for Mount
Sinai in Arabia and
corresponds to the
present city of Je-
rusalem, because
she is in slavery
with her children.
26But the Jerusa-
lem that is above is
free, and she is our
mother. 27For it is
written:

"Be glad, barren
woman,
you who
never bore
a child;
shout for joy and
cry aloud,
you who were
never in
labor;
because more
are the
children of
the desolate
woman
than of her
who has a
husband."[a]

28Now you, broth-
ers and sisters, like
Isaac, are children
of promise. 29At
that time the son
born according to
the flesh perse-
cuted the son born
by the power of
the Spirit. It is the
same now. 30But
what does Scrip-
ture say? "Get rid
of the slave woman
and her son, for
the slave woman's
son will never
share in the inheri-
tance with the free
woman's son."[b]
31Therefore, broth-
ers and sisters, we
are not children
of the slave wom-
an, but of the free
woman.

[a] 27 Isaiah 54:1
[b] 30 Gen. 21:10

ἀλληγορούμενα· αὗται γὰρ εἰσιν δύο διαθῆκαι, μία μὲν ἀπὸ ὄρους
interpreted allegorically, for these women *for* represent two covenants. One ~ is from Mount
251 1142 4047 1142 1639 1545 1347 1651 3525 608 4001
pt.pp.npn r.npf cj v.pai.3p a.npf n.npf a.nsf pl p.g n.gsn

Σινᾶ εἰς δουλείαν γεννῶσα, ἥτις ἐστὶν Ἁγάρ. 25 τὸ δὲ Ἁγὰρ
Sinai, bearing children to be slaves; *bearing children* she is Hagar. *{the}* Now Hagar
4982 1164 1164 1650 1525 1164 4015 1639 29 3836 1254 29
n.gsn p.a n.asf pt.pa.nsf r.nsf v.pai.3s n.nsf d.nsn pl n.nsf

Σινᾶ ὄρος ἐστὶν ἐν τῇ Ἀραβίᾳ· συστοιχεῖ δὲ τῇ
represents Mount Sinai *Mount represents* in *{the}* Arabia and ⌊corresponds to⌋ *and* the
1639 4001 4982 4001 1639 1877 3836 728 1254 5368 1254 3836
n.nsn n.nsn v.pai.3s p.d d.dsf n.dsf v.pai.3s cj d.dsf

νῦν Ἰερουσαλήμ, δουλεύει γὰρ μετὰ τῶν τέκνων αὐτῆς. 26 ἡ
present Jerusalem, for she is in slavery *for* with *{the}* her children. *her* But the
3814 2647 1142 1526 1142 3552 3836 899 5451 899 1254 3836
adv n.dsf v.pai.3s cj p.g d.gpn n.gpn r.gsf.3 d.nsf

δὲ ἄνω Ἰερουσαλὴμ ἐλευθέρα ἐστίν, ἥτις ἐστὶν μήτηρ
But Jerusalem above *Jerusalem* is the free woman, *is* and she is our mother.
1254 2647 539 2647 1639 1801 1639 4015 1639 7005 3613
pl adv n.nsf a.nsf v.pai.3s r.nsf v.pai.3s n.nsf

ἡμῶν· 27 γέγραπται γάρ, εὐφράνθητι, στεῖρα ἡ ↱ οὐ τίκτουσα,
our For it is written, *For* "Rejoice, ⌊O barren woman,⌋ ⌊you who⌋ bear no children;
7005 1142 1211 1142 2370 5096 3836 5503 4024 5503
r.gp.1 v.rpi.3s cj v.apm.2s n.vsf d.vsf pl pt.pa.vsf

ῥῆξον καὶ βόησον, ἡ ↱ οὐκ ὠδίνουσα· ὅτι πολλὰ τὰ
⌊break forth⌋ and cry aloud, ⌊you who⌋ are not ⌊in the pain of childbirth!⌋ For *in number* the
4838 2779 1066 3836 6048 4024 6048 4022 4498 3836
v.aam.2s cj v.aam.2s d.vsf pl pt.pa.vsf cj a.npn d.npn

τέκνα τῆς ἐρήμου μᾶλλον ἢ τῆς ἐχούσης τὸν
children of the desolate will be more in number than those ⌊of the woman who has⌋ a
5451 3836 2245 3437 4498 4498 2445 3836 2400 3836
n.npn d.gsf a.gsf adv.c pl d.gsf pt.pa.gsf d.asm

ἄνδρα. 28 ὑμεῖς δέ, ἀδελφοί, κατὰ Ἰσαὰκ ἐπαγγελίας τέκνα
husband. But you, *But* my brothers, like Isaac, are children of promise. *children*
467 1254 7007 1254 81 2848 2693 1639 5451 2039 5451
n.asm r.np.2 cj n.vpm p.a n.asm n.gsf n.npn

ἐστέ. 29 ἀλλ᾽ ὥσπερ τότε ὁ κατὰ σάρκα
are But just as ⌊at that time⌋ the one who was born ⌊according to⌋ the flesh
1639 247 6061 5538 3836 1164 1164 1164 1164 2848 4922
v.pai.2p cj cj adv d.nsm p.a n.asf

γεννηθεὶς ἐδίωκεν τὸν κατὰ πνεῦμα, οὕτως καὶ
one who was born persecuted the one who was born ⌊according to⌋ the Spirit, so also it is
1164 1503 3836 2848 4460 4048 2779
pt.ap.nsm v.iai.3s d.asm p.a n.asn adv adv

νῦν. 30 ἀλλὰ τί → λέγει ἡ γραφή; ἔκβαλε τὴν παιδίσκην καὶ
now. But what does the Scripture say? *the Scripture* "Drive away the slave woman and
3814 247 5515 3836 1210 3306 3836 1210 1675 3836 4087 2779
adv cj r.asn v.pai.3s d.nsf n.nsf v.aam.2s d.asf n.asf cj

τὸν υἱὸν αὐτῆς· ↱ οὐ γὰρ μὴ
{the} her son, *her* for the son of the slave woman must not *for* *{not}*
3836 899 5626 899 1142 3836 5626 3836 3836 4087 4087 3099 4024 1142 3590
d.asm n.asm r.gsf.3 pl cj pl

κληρονομήσει ὁ υἱὸς τῆς παιδίσκης μετὰ τοῦ υἱοῦ τῆς ἐλευθέρας.
share the inheritance *the son of the slave woman* with the son of the free woman."
3099 3836 5626 3836 4087 3552 3836 5626 3836 1801
v.fai.3s d.nsm n.nsm d.gsf n.gsf p.g d.gsm n.gsm d.gsf a.gsf

31 διό, ἀδελφοί, οὐκ ἐσμὲν → παιδίσκης τέκνα ἀλλὰ τῆς
So then, brothers, we are not *we are* children of a slave woman *children* but of the
1475 81 1639 1639 4024 1639 5451 4087 5451 247 3836
cj n.vpm pl v.pai.1p n.gsf n.npn cj d.gsf

ἐλευθέρας.
free woman.
1801
a.gsf

NASB

allegorically
speaking, for
these *women* are
two covenants:
one *proceed-
ing* from Mount
Sinai bearing
children who are
to be slaves; she is
Hagar. 25Now this
Hagar is Mount
Sinai in Arabia and
corresponds to the
present Jerusalem,
for she is in slavery
with her children.
26But the Jerusalem
above is free; she
is our mother. 27For
it is written,

"REJOICE, BAR-
REN WOMAN
WHO DOES NOT
BEAR;
BREAK FORTH
AND SHOUT,
YOU WHO ARE
NOT IN LABOR;
FOR MORE NU-
MEROUS ARE
THE CHILDREN
OF THE DESO-
LATE
THAN OF THE
ONE WHO HAS
A HUSBAND."

28And you brethren,
like Isaac, are chil-
dren of promise.
29But as at that time
he who was born
according to the
flesh persecuted
him *who was born*
according to the
Spirit, so it is now
also. 30But what
does the Scripture
say?

"CAST OUT THE
BONDWOMAN
AND HER SON,
FOR THE SON
OF THE BOND-
WOMAN SHALL
NOT BE AN
HEIR WITH THE
SON OF THE
FREE WOMAN."

31So then, brethren,
we are not children
of a bondwoman,
but of the free
woman.

NIV

Freedom in Christ

5 It is for free-
dom that
Christ has set us
free. Stand firm,
then, and do not let
yourselves be bur-
dened again by a
yoke of slavery.
2 Mark my words!
I, Paul, tell you
that if you let
yourselves be cir-
cumcised, Christ
will be of no val-
ue to you at all.
3 Again I declare
to every man who
lets himself be
circumcised that
he is obligated to
obey the whole
law. 4 You who are
trying to be jus-
tified by the law
have been alien-
ated from Christ;
you have fallen
away from grace.
5 For through the
Spirit we eagerly
await by faith the
righteousness for
which we hope.
6 For in Christ
Jesus neither cir-
cumcision nor
uncircumcision
has any value.
The only thing
that counts is faith
expressing itself
through love.
7 You were run-
ning a good race.
Who cut in on you
to keep you from
obeying the truth?
8 That kind of per-
suasion does not
come from the one
who calls you. 9 "A
little yeast works
through the whole
batch of dough."
10 I am confident in
the Lord that you
will take no oth-
er view. The one
who is throwing
you into confu-
sion, whoever that
may be, will have
to pay the penal-
ty. 11 Brothers and
sisters, if I am still
preaching circum-
cision, why

5:1 τῇ ἐλευθερίᾳ ↱ ↱ ἡμᾶς Χριστὸς ἠλευθέρωσεν· στήκετε οὖν
For freedom Christ has set us *Christ* free. Stand firm, therefore,
3836 1800 5986 1802 1802 7005 5986 1802 5112 4036
d.dsf n.dsf r.ap.1 n.nsm v.aai.3s v.pam.2p cj

καὶ μὴ πάλιν → ζυγῷ δουλείας ἐνέχεσθε. 2 ἴδε ἐγὼ Παῦλος
and do not be subject again to a yoke of slavery. *do be subject* Listen! I, Paul,
2779 1923 3590 1923 1923 4099 2433 1525 1923 2623 1609 4263
cj pl adv n.dsm n.gsf v.ppm.2p pl r.ns.1 n.nsm

λέγω ὑμῖν ὅτι ἐὰν περιτέμνησθε, Χριστὸς ὑμᾶς
tell you that if you agree to circumcision, Christ will be of no benefit to you.
3306 7007 4022 1569 4362 5986 6067 6067 6067 4029 6067 6067 7007
v.pai.1s r.dp.2 cj cj v.pps.2p n.nsm r.ap.2

οὐδὲν ὠφελήσει. 3 μαρτύρομαι δὲ πάλιν παντὶ ἀνθρώπῳ
no *will be of benefit to* And furthermore I declare *And furthermore* to every man
4029 6067 1254 4099 3458 1254 4099 4246 476
a.asn v.fai.3s v.pmi.1s cj adv a.dsm n.dsm

περιτεμνομένῳ ὅτι ὀφειλέτης ἐστὶν ὅλον τὸν νόμον
who agrees to circumcision that he is obligated *he is* to obey the entire *the* law.
4362 4022 1639 1639 4050 1639 4472 4472 3836 3910 3836 3795
pt.pp.dsm cj n.nsm v.pai.3s a.asm d.asm n.asm

ποιῆσαι. 4 κατηργήθητε ἀπὸ Χριστοῦ, οἵτινες
to obey ⌞You have cut yourself off⌟ from Christ, you who are trying to be justified
4472 2934 608 5986 1467 4015 1467 1467 1467 1467 1467
f.aa v.api.2p p.g n.gsm r.npm

ἐν νόμῳ δικαιοῦσθε, τῆς χάριτος ἐξεπέσατε.
by the law; *you trying to be justified* you have fallen away from grace. *you have fallen away*
1877 3795 1467 1738 1738 1738 1738 3836 5921 1738
p.d n.dsm v.ppi.2p d.gsf n.gsf v.aai.2p

5 ἡμεῖς γὰρ → πνεύματι ἐκ πίστεως
For we *For* by the Spirit, through faith, eagerly await the righteousness for which we
1142 7005 1142 4460 1666 4411 587 587 1466
r.np.1 cj n.dsn p.g n.gsf

ἐλπίδα δικαιοσύνης ἀπεκδεχόμεθα. 6 ἐν γὰρ Χριστῷ Ἰησοῦ οὔτε περιτομή
hope. *righteousness* *eagerly await* For in *For* Christ Jesus neither circumcision
1828 1466 587 1142 1877 1142 5986 2652 4046 4364
n.asf n.gsf v.pmi.1p p.d cj n.dsm n.dsm cj n.nsf

τι ἰσχύει οὔτε ἀκροβυστία ἀλλὰ πίστις
nor uncircumcision counts for anything, *counts for* *nor* *uncircumcision* but only faith expressing
4046 213 2710 2710 5516 2710 4046 213 247 4411 1919
r.asn v.pai.3s cj n.nsf cj n.nsf

δι' ἀγάπης ἐνεργουμένη. 7 ἐτρέχετε καλῶς· τίς ὑμᾶς ἐνέκοψεν
itself through love. *expressing itself* ⌞You were running⌟ well; who hindered you *hindered*
1919 1328 27 1919 5556 2822 5515 1601 7007 1601
p.g n.gsf pt.pm.nsf v.iai.2p adv r.nsm r.ap.2 v.aai.3s

τῇ[a] ἀληθείᾳ μὴ πείθεσθαι; 8 ἡ πεισμονὴ οὐκ ἐκ τοῦ
from obeying the truth? *from* *obeying* Such persuasion does not come from the
3590 4275 3836 237 3590 4275 3836 4282 4024 1666 3836
d.dsf n.dsf pl f.pp d.nsf n.nsf pl p.g d.gsm

καλοῦντος ὑμᾶς. 9 μικρὰ ζύμη ὅλον τὸ φύραμα ζυμοῖ. 10 ἐγὼ
one who calls you. A little leaven leavens the whole *the* lump of dough! *leavens* I
2813 7007 3625 2434 2435 3836 3910 3836 5878 2435 1609
pt.pa.gsm r.ap.2 a.nsf n.nsf a.asn d.asn n.asn v.pai.3s r.ns.1

πέποιθα εἰς ὑμᾶς ἐν κυρίῳ ὅτι οὐδὲν ἄλλο φρονήσετε·
am confident about you in the Lord that you will not think otherwise. *you will think* But
4275 1650 7007 1877 3261 4022 5858 5858 4029 5858 257 5858 1254
v.rai.1s p.a r.ap.2 p.d n.dsm cj a.asn r.asn v.fai.2p

ὁ δὲ ταράσσων ὑμᾶς βαστάσει τὸ κρίμα, ⌞ὅστις ἐὰν⌟ ᾖ.
the *But* ⌞one who is trying to confuse⌟ you will pay the penalty, whoever ⌞he may be.⌟
3836 1254 5429 7007 1002 3836 3210 4015 1569 1639
d.nsm cj pt.pa.nsm r.ap.2 v.fai.3s d.asn n.asn r.nsm pl v.pas.3s

11 ἐγὼ δέ, ἀδελφοί, εἰ περιτομὴν ἔτι κηρύσσω, τί
But I, *But* brothers, if I am still preaching circumcision, *still* *I am preaching* why
1254 1609 1254 81 1623 3062 3062 2285 3062 4364 2285 3062 5515
r.ns.1 cj n.vpm cj n.asf adv v.pai.1s r.asn

[a] [τῇ] UBS.

NASB

Walk by the Spirit

5:1 It was for free-
dom that Christ set
us free; therefore
keep standing firm
and do not be sub-
ject again to a yoke
of slavery.
2 Behold I, Paul,
say to you that
if you receive
circumcision,
Christ will be of
no benefit to you.
3 And I testify again
to every man who
receives circumci-
sion, that he is
under obligation
to keep the whole
Law. 4 You have
been severed from
Christ, you who are
seeking to be justi-
fied by law; you
have fallen from
grace. 5 For we
through the Spirit,
by faith, are wait-
ing for the hope of
righteousness. 6 For
in Christ Jesus nei-
ther circumcision
nor uncircumcision
means anything,
but faith working
through love.
7 You were run-
ning well; who
hindered you from
obeying the truth?
8 This persuasion
did not *come* from
Him who calls you.
9 A little leaven
leavens the whole
lump *of dough.* 10 I
have confidence
in you in the Lord
that you will adopt
no other view;
but the one who
is disturbing you
will bear his judg-
ment, whoever he
is. 11 But I, brethren,
if I still preach cir-
cumcision, why am

NIV

am I still being
persecuted? In that
case the offense of
the cross has been
abolished. 12As for
those agitators, I
wish they would go
the whole way and
emasculate them-
selves!

Life by the Spirit

13You, my broth-
ers and sisters,
were called to be
free. But do not use
your freedom to
indulge the flesh[a];
rather, serve one
another humbly in
love. 14For the en-
tire law is fulfilled
in keeping this one
command: "Love
your neighbor as
yourself."[b] 15If you
bite and devour
each other, watch
out or you will be
destroyed by each
other.
16So I say, walk
by the Spirit, and
you will not grat-
ify the desires of
the flesh. 17For
the flesh desires
what is contrary
to the Spirit, and
the Spirit what is
contrary to the
flesh. They are in
conflict with each
other, so that you
are not to do what-
ever[c] you want.
18But if you are
led by the Spirit,
you are not under
the law.
19The acts of the
flesh are obvious:
sexual immorality,
impurity and de-
bauchery; 20idolatry
and witchcraft; ha-
tred, discord, jeal-
ousy, fits of rage,

[a] 13 In contexts like this, the Greek word for *flesh* (*sarx*) refers to the sinful state of human beings, often presented as a power in opposition to the Spirit; also in verses 16, 17, 19 and 24; and in 6:8.
[b] 14 Lev. 19:18
[c] 17 Or *you do not do what*

↱ ↱ ἔτι διώκομαι; ἄρα κατήργηται τὸ
am I still being persecuted? ⌞In that case⌟ the offense of the cross has been removed. *the*
1503 1503 2285 1503 726 3836 4998 3836 3836 5089 2934 3836
adv v.ppi.1s cj v.rpi.3s d.nsn

σκάνδαλον τοῦ σταυροῦ. 12 ὄφελον καὶ
offense *of the* *cross* I wish *{and}* those who are disturbing you
4998 3836 5089 4054 2779 3836 415 415 415 7007
n.nsn d.gsm n.gsm pt.aa.nsn cj

ἀποκόψονται οἱ ἀναστατοῦντες ὑμᾶς. 13 ὑμεῖς γὰρ
⌞would mutilate themselves!⌟ *those* *who are disturbing* *you* For you, *For* brothers, were called
644 3836 415 7007 1142 7007 1142 81 2813 2813
v.fmi.3p d.npm pt.pa.npm r.ap.2 r.np.2 cj

ἐπ' ἐλευθερίᾳ ἐκλήθητε, ἀδελφοί· μόνον μὴ τὴν ἐλευθερίαν εἰς ἀφορμὴν
to freedom. *were called* *brothers* Only do not use your freedom as an opportunity
2093 1800 2813 81 3667 3590 3836 1800 1650 929
p.d n.dsf v.api.2p n.vpm adv pl d.asf n.asf p.a n.asf

τῇ σαρκί, ἀλλὰ διὰ τῆς ἀγάπης δουλεύετε ἀλλήλοις. 14 ὁ γὰρ πᾶς
⌞for the⌟ flesh, but through *{the}* love serve one another. For the *For* entire
3836 4922 247 1328 3836 27 1526 253 1142 3836 1142 4246
d.dsf n.dsf cj p.g d.gsf n.gsf v.pam.2p r.dpm d.nsm cj a.nsm

νόμος ἐν ἑνὶ λόγῳ πεπλήρωται, ἐν τῷ· ἀγαπήσεις τὸν
law is summed up in a single command: *is summed up* *{in}* *{this}* "You shall love *{the}*
3795 4444 4444 4444 1877 1651 3364 4444 1877 3836 26 3836
n.nsm p.d a.dsm n.dsm v.rpi.3s p.d d.dsn v.fai.2s d.asm

πλησίον σου ὡς σεαυτόν. 15 εἰ δὲ
your neighbor *your* as yourself." But if *But* you keep on biting and devouring
5148 4446 5148 6055 4932 1254 1623 1254 1231 1231 1231 1231 2779 2983
adv r.gs.2 cj r.asm.2 cj cj

ἀλλήλους δάκνετε καὶ κατεσθίετε, βλέπετε μὴ ὑπ'
one another, *you keep on biting* *and* *devouring* watch out that you are not consumed by
253 1231 2779 2983 1063 384 384 3590 384 5679
r.apm v.pai.2p cj v.pai.2p v.pam.2p cj p.g

ἀλλήλων ἀναλωθῆτε. 16 λέγω δέ, → πνεύματι περιπατεῖτε καὶ
one another. *you are consumed* So I say, *So* live by the Spirit *live* and you
253 384 1254 3306 1254 4344 4460 4344 2779 5464
r.gpm v.aps.2p v.pai.1s cj n.dsn v.pam.2p cj

ἐπιθυμίαν → σαρκὸς ⌞οὐ μὴ⌟ τελέσητε. 17 ἡ γὰρ
will not gratify the desires of the flesh. *not* *you will gratify* For the *For* desires
5464 4024 5464 2123 4922 4024 3590 5464 1142 3836 1142 2121
n.asf n.gsf pl pl v.aas.2p d.nsf cj

σὰρξ ἐπιθυμεῖ κατὰ τοῦ πνεύματος, τὸ δὲ πνεῦμα
of the flesh *desires* are against the Spirit, and the desires of the *and* Spirit are
4922 2121 2848 3836 4460 1254 3836 1254 4460
n.nsf v.pai.3s p.g d.gsn n.gsn d.nsn cj n.nsn

κατὰ τῆς σαρκός, ταῦτα γὰρ ἀλλήλοις ἀντίκειται, ἵνα → μὴ
against the flesh; for these *for* are opposed to one other, *are opposed* to keep you from
2848 3836 4922 1142 4047 1142 512 512 253 512 2671 4472 3590
p.g d.gsf n.gsf r.npn cj r.dpn v.pmi.3s cj pl

⌞ἃ ἐὰν⌟ θέλητε ταῦτα ποιῆτε. 18 εἰ δὲ
doing the things *{whatever}* you want *things* *you doing* to do. But if *But* you are led
4472 4047 4005 1569 2527 4047 4472 1254 1623 1254 72 72 72
r.apn pl v.pas.2p r.apn v.pas.2p cj cj

→ πνεύματι ἄγεσθε, οὐκ ἐστὲ ὑπὸ νόμον. 19
by the Spirit, *you are led* you are not *you are* under the law. Now the works of the
4460 72 1639 1639 4024 1639 5679 3795 1254 3836 2240 3836 3836
n.dsn v.ppi.2p pl v.pai.2p p.a n.asm

φανερὰ δέ ἐστιν τὰ ἔργα τῆς σαρκός, ἅτινά ἐστιν πορνεία,
flesh are obvious: *Now* *are* *the* *works* *of the* *flesh* *{which}* *{are}* sexual immorality,
4922 1639 5745 1254 1639 3836 2240 3836 4922 4015 1639 4518
a.npn cj v.pai.3s d.npn n.npn d.gsf n.gsf r.npn v.pai.3s n.nsf

ἀκαθαρσία, ἀσέλγεια, 20 εἰδωλολατρία, φαρμακεία, ἔχθραι, ἔρις, ζῆλος, θυμοί,
impurity, debauchery, idolatry, sorcery, quarrels, strife, jealousy, fits of rage,
174 816 1630 5758 2397 2251 2419 2596
n.nsf n.nsf n.nsf n.nsf n.npf n.nsf n.nsm n.npm

NASB

I still persecuted?
Then the stumbling
block of the cross
has been abolished.
12I wish that those
who are trou-
bling you would
even mutilate
themselves.
13For you were
called to freedom,
brethren; only
do not *turn* your
freedom into an
opportunity for the
flesh, but through
love serve one
another. 14For the
whole Law is ful-
filled in one word,
in the *statement,*
"YOU SHALL LOVE
YOUR NEIGHBOR AS
YOURSELF." 15But
if you bite and de-
vour one another,
take care that you
are not consumed
by one another.
16But I say, walk
by the Spirit, and
you will not carry
out the desire of
the flesh. 17For
the flesh sets its
desire against the
Spirit, and the
Spirit against the
flesh; for these
are in opposition
to one another, so
that you may not
do the things that
you please. 18But
if you are led by
the Spirit, you are
not under the Law.
19Now the deeds
of the flesh are
evident, which are:
immorality, im-
purity, sensuality,
20idolatry, sorcery,
enmities, strife,
jealousy, outbursts

NIV

selfish ambition,
dissensions, fac-
tions [21]and envy;
drunkenness, or-
gies, and the like. I
warn you, as I did
before, that those
who live like this
will not inherit the
kingdom of God.
[22]But the fruit of
the Spirit is love,
joy, peace, forbear-
ance, kindness,
goodness, faithful-
ness, [23]gentleness
and self-control.
Against such
things there is no
law. [24]Those who
belong to Christ
Jesus have cruci-
fied the flesh with
its passions and
desires. [25]Since we
live by the Spirit,
let us keep in step
with the Spirit.
[26]Let us not be-
come conceited,
provoking and en-
vying each other.

Doing Good to All

6 Brothers and
sisters, if
someone is caught
in a sin, you who
live by the Spirit
should restore that
person gently. But
watch yourselves,
or you also may
be tempted. [2]Car-
ry each other's
burdens, and in
this way you will
fulfill the law of
Christ. [3]If anyone
thinks they are
something when
they are not, they
deceive them-
selves. [4]Each one
should test their
own actions.

ἐριθεῖαι, διχοστασίαι, αἱρέσεις, 21 φθόνοι, μέθαι, κῶμοι καὶ τὰ ὅμοια
selfish rivalries, dissensions, divisions, envyings, drunkenness, orgies, and things like
2249 1496 146 5784 3494 3269 2779 3836 3927
n.npf n.npf n.npf n.npm n.npf n.npm cj d.npn a.npn

τούτοις, ἃ προλέγω ὑμῖν, καθὼς προεῖπον ← ὅτι οἱ τὰ
these. {that} I warn you, as I warned you before: {that} those who practice {the}
4047 4005 4625 7007 2777 4597 4022 3836 4556 4556 3836
r.dpn r.apn v.pai.1s r.dp.2 cj v.aai.1s cj d.npm d.apn

τοιαῦτα πράσσοντες βασιλείαν θεοῦ οὐ κληρονομήσουσιν.
such things who practice will not inherit the kingdom of God! not will inherit
5525 4556 3099 4024 3099 993 2536 4024 3099
r.apn pt.pa.npm n.asf n.gsm pl v.fai.3p

22 ὁ δὲ καρπὸς τοῦ πνεύματός ἐστιν ἀγάπη χαρὰ εἰρήνη,
By contrast, the By contrast fruit of the Spirit is love, joy, peace,
1254 1254 3836 1254 2843 3836 4460 1639 27 5915 1645
d.nsm cj n.nsm d.gsn n.gsn v.pai.3s n.nsf n.nsf n.nsf

μακροθυμία χρηστότης ἀγαθωσύνη, πίστις 23 πραΰτης ἐγκράτεια· κατὰ τῶν
patience, kindness, generosity, faithfulness, gentleness, self-control; against {the}
3429 5983 20 4411 4559 1602 2848 3836
n.nsf n.nsf n.nsf n.nsf n.nsf n.nsf p.g d.gpn

τοιούτων οὐκ ἔστιν νόμος. 24 οἱ δὲ τοῦ Χριστοῦ Ἰησοῦ[a]
such things there is no there is law. And those And who belong to Christ Jesus have
5525 1639 1639 4024 1639 3795 1254 3836 1254 5090 3836 5986 2652 5090
r.gpn pl v.pai.3s n.nsm d.npm cj d.gsm n.gsm n.gsm

τὴν σάρκα ἐσταύρωσαν σὺν τοῖς παθήμασιν καὶ ταῖς ἐπιθυμίαις. 25 εἰ
crucified the flesh who have crucified with its passions and {the} desires. Since
5090 3836 4922 5090 5250 3836 4077 2779 3836 2123 1623
d.asf n.asf v.aai.3p p.d d.dpn n.dpn cj d.dpf n.dpf cj

ζῶμεν → πνεύματι, → πνεύματι καὶ στοιχῶμεν.
we live by the Spirit, let us also be guided by the Spirit. also let us be guided
2409 4460 5123 5123 2779 5123 5123 4460 2779 5123
v.pai.1p n.dsn n.dsn cj v.pas.1p

26 ↱ ↱ μὴ γινώμεθα κενόδοξοι, ἀλλήλους προκαλούμενοι,
Let us not become conceited, provoking one another, provoking being jealous
1181 1181 3590 1181 3030 4614 253 4614 5783 5783
pl v.pms.1p a.npm r.apm pt.pm.npm

ἀλλήλοις φθονοῦντες.
of one another. being jealous of
5783 253 5783
r.dpm pt.pa.npm

6:1 ἀδελφοί, ἐὰν καὶ προλημφθῇ ἄνθρωπος ἔν τινι παραπτώματι,
My brothers, if {also} someone is detected someone in some wrongdoing,
81 1569 2779 476 4624 476 1877 5516 4183
n.vpm cj adv v.aps.3s n.nsm p.d r.dsn n.dsn

ὑμεῖς οἱ πνευματικοὶ καταρτίζετε τὸν τοιοῦτον ἐν πνεύματι πραΰτητος,
you who are spiritual should restore that one in a spirit of gentleness,
7007 3836 4461 2936 3836 5525 1877 4460 4559
r.np.2 d.npm a.npm v.pam.2p d.asm r.asm p.d n.dsn n.gsf

σκοπῶν σεαυτὸν μὴ καὶ σὺ πειρασθῇς. 2 ἀλλήλων τὰ βάρη
taking care lest you yourself lest {also} you be tempted. Bear one another's {the} burdens,
5023 3590 5148 4932 3590 2779 5148 4279 1002 253 3836 983
pt.pa.nsm r.asm.2 cj adv r.ns.2 v.aps.2s r.gpm d.apn n.apn

βαστάζετε καὶ οὕτως ἀναπληρώσετε τὸν νόμον τοῦ Χριστοῦ. 3 εἰ γὰρ
Bear and ⸤in this way⸥ you will fulfill the law of Christ. For if For
1002 2779 4048 405 3836 3795 3836 5986 1142 1623 1142
v.pam.2p cj adv v.fai.2p d.asm n.asm d.gsm n.gsm cj cj

δοκεῖ τις εἶναί τι μηδὲν ὤν, φρεναπατᾷ ἑαυτόν.
anyone thinks anyone he is something, when he is nothing, when he is he deceives himself.
5516 1506 5516 1639 5516 1639 1639 1639 3594 1639 5854 1571
v.pai.3s r.nsm f.pa r.nsn a.nsn pt.pa.nsm v.pai.3s r.asm.3

4 τὸ δὲ ἔργον ἑαυτοῦ δοκιμαζέτω ἕκαστος, καὶ
But let each one examine {the} But his own work, his own let examine each one and
1254 1507 1667 1667 1507 3836 1254 1571 1571 2240 1571 1507 1667 2779
d.asn cj n.asn r.gsm.3 v.pam.3s r.nsm cj

[a] [Ἰησοῦ] UBS, omitted by NET.

NASB

of anger, disputes,
dissensions, fac-
tions, [21]envying,
drunkenness, ca-
rousing, and things
like these, of which
I forewarn you,
just as I have fore-
warned you, that
those who practice
such things will not
inherit the kingdom
of God. [22]But the
fruit of the Spirit
is love, joy, peace,
patience, kindness,
goodness, faithful-
ness, [23]gentleness,
self-control;
against such things
there is no law.
[24]Now those who
belong to Christ
Jesus have cruci-
fied the flesh with
its passions and
desires.
[25]If we live by
the Spirit, let us
also walk by the
Spirit. [26]Let us not
become boastful,
challenging one
another, envying
one another.

Bear One Another's Burdens

[6:1]Brethren, even if
anyone is caught in
any trespass, you
who are spiritual,
restore such a one
in a spirit of gentle-
ness; *each one*
looking to yourself,
so that you too will
not be tempted.
[2]Bear one another's
burdens, and
thereby fulfill the
law of Christ. [3]For
if anyone thinks he
is something when
he is nothing, he
deceives himself.
[4]But each one must
examine his own
work, and then he

NIV

Then they can take
pride in themselves
alone, without
comparing them-
selves to someone
else, 5 for each
one should carry
their own load.
6 Nevertheless, the
one who receives
instruction in the
word should share
all good things
with their instruc-
tor.
7 Do not be de-
ceived: God can-
not be mocked. A
man reaps what he
sows. 8 Whoever
sows to please
their flesh, from
the flesh will reap
destruction; who-
ever sows to please
the Spirit, from
the Spirit will reap
eternal life. 9 Let us
not become weary
in doing good, for
at the proper time
we will reap a har-
vest if we do not
give up. 10 There-
fore, as we have
opportunity, let us
do good to all peo-
ple, especially to
those who belong
to the family of be-
lievers.

Not Circumcision but the New Creation

11 See what large
letters I use as I
write to you with
my own hand!
12 Those who want
to impress people
by means of the
flesh are trying to
compel you to be
circumcised. The
only reason they
do this is to avoid
being persecuted
for the cross of
Christ. 13 Not even
those who are cir-
cumcised keep the
law,

τότε εἰς ἑαυτὸν μόνον τὸ καύχημα ἕξει
then he will have reason for boasting in himself alone, *{the}* *reason for boasting* *he will have*
5538 2400 2400 2400 3017 3017 3017 1650 1571 3668 3836 3017 2400
adv p.a r.asm.3 adv d.asn n.asn v.fai.3s

καὶ οὐκ εἰς τὸν ἕτερον· 5 ἕκαστος γὰρ τὸ ἴδιον
and not ⌊in comparison with⌋ *{the}* ⌊someone else.⌋ For each one *For* will bear *{the}* his own
2779 4024 1650 3836 2283 1142 1667 1142 1002 1002 3836 2625
cj pl p.a d.asm r.asm r.nsm cj d.asn a.asn

φορτίον βαστάσει. 6 κοινωνείτω δὲ ὁ
load. *will bear* Now the one who is taught the word must share *Now* *the*
5845 1002 1254 3836 2994 2994 2994 2994 3836 3364 3125 1254 3836
n.asn v.fai.3s v.pam.3s cj d.nsm

κατηχούμενος τὸν λόγον τῷ κατηχοῦντι ἐν πᾶσιν ἀγαθοῖς.
one who is taught *the* *word* all good things ⌊with the⌋ one who teaches. *{in}* *all* *good things*
2994 3836 3364 4246 19 19 3836 2994 1877 4246 19
pt.pp.nsm d.asm n.asm d.dsm pt.pa.dsm p.d a.dpn a.dpn

7 → μὴ πλανᾶσθε, θεὸς → οὐ μυκτηρίζεται. ὃ γὰρ ἐὰν σπείρῃ
Do not be deceived: God is not mocked. For whatever *For* ~ a person sows,
4414 3590 4414 2536 3682 4024 3682 1142 4005 1142 1569 476 5062
pl v.ppm.2p n.nsm pl v.ppi.3s r.asn cj pl v.pas.3s

ἄνθρωπος, τοῦτο → → καὶ θερίσει· 8 ὅτι ὁ σπείρων εἰς τὴν
person that will he also reap. For the one who sows to *{the}* his own
476 4047 2545 2545 2779 2545 4022 3836 5062 1650 3836 1571 1571
n.nsm r.asn adv v.fai.3s cj d.nsm pt.pa.nsm p.a d.asf

σάρκα ἑαυτοῦ ἐκ τῆς σαρκὸς θερίσει φθοράν, ὁ δὲ σπείρων εἰς τὸ
flesh, *his own* from the flesh will reap corruption; but the *but* one who sows to the
4922 1571 1666 3836 4922 2545 5785 1254 3836 1254 5062 1650 3836
n.asf r.gsm.3 p.g d.gsf n.gsf v.fai.3s n.asf d.nsm cj pt.pa.nsm p.a d.asn

πνεῦμα ἐκ τοῦ πνεύματος θερίσει ζωὴν αἰώνιον. 9
Spirit, from the Spirit will reap eternal life. *eternal* So let us not grow tired
4460 1666 3836 4460 2545 173 2437 173 1254 1591 1591 3590 1591 1591
n.asn p.g d.gsn n.gsn v.fai.3s n.asf a.asf

τὸ δὲ καλὸν ποιοῦντες μὴ ἐγκακῶμεν, → καιρῷ γὰρ ἰδίῳ
of doing what *So* is right, *doing* *not* *let us grow tired of* for in due time *for* *due*
1591 4472 3836 1254 2819 4472 3590 1591 1142 2625 2789 1142 2625
d.asn cj a.asn pt.pa.npm pl v.pas.1p n.dsm cj a.dsm

θερίσομεν → → → μὴ ἐκλυόμενοι. 10 ἄρα οὖν ὡς καιρὸν ἔχομεν,
we will reap, if we do not give up. So then, as we have opportunity, *we have*
2545 1725 1725 1725 3590 1725 726 4036 6055 2400 2400 2789 2400
v.fai.1p pl pt.pp.npm cj cj cj n.asm v.pai.1p

ἐργαζώμεθα τὸ ἀγαθὸν πρὸς πάντας, μάλιστα δὲ πρὸς τοὺς οἰκείους
let us do *{the}* good to everyone, and especially *and* to those of the family
2237 3836 19 4639 4246 1254 3436 1254 4639 3836 3858
v.pms.1p d.asn a.asn p.a a.apm adv.s cj p.a d.apm n.apm

τῆς πίστεως. 11 ἴδετε πηλίκοις ὑμῖν γράμμασιν ἔγραψα
of faith. See ⌊with what large⌋ letters I am writing to you *letters* *I am writing*
3836 4411 1625 4383 1207 1211 1211 1211 7007 1207 1211
d.gsf n.gsf v.aam.2p r.dpn r.dp.2 n.dpn v.aai.1s

τῇ ἐμῇ χειρί. 12 ὅσοι θέλουσιν εὐπροσωπῆσαι ἐν σαρκί, οὗτοι
with ⌊my own⌋ hand! Those who want to make a good showing in the flesh, they
3836 1847 5931 4012 2527 2349 1877 4922 4047
d.dsf r.dsf.1 n.dsf r.npm v.pai.3p f.aa p.d n.dsf r.npm

ἀναγκάζουσιν ὑμᾶς περιτέμνεσθαι, μόνον ἵνα
⌊are the ones trying to force⌋ you to be circumcised — only so that they may not be
337 7007 4362 3667 2671 1503 1503 3590 1503
v.pai.3p r.ap.2 f.pp adv cj

τῷ σταυρῷ τοῦ Χριστοῦ μὴ διώκωνται.[a] 13 οὐδὲ γὰρ οἱ
persecuted ⌊for the⌋ cross of Christ. *not* *they may be persecuted* For even *For* those
1503 3836 5089 3836 5986 3590 1503 1142 4028 1142 3836
d.dsm n.dsm d.gsm n.gsm pl v.pps.3p adv cj d.npm

περιτεμνόμενοι ↰ αὐτοὶ νόμον φυλάσσουσιν ἀλλὰ θέλουσιν ὑμᾶς
who are circumcised do not themselves keep the law, *do keep* but they want you
4362 5875 4028 899 5875 3795 5875 247 2527 7007
pt.pp.npm r.npm n.asm v.pai.3p cj v.pai.3p r.ap.2

[a] διώκωνται UBS, TNIV. διώκονται NET.

NASB

will have *reason*
for boasting in
regard to himself
alone, and not in
regard to another.
5 For each one will
bear his own load.
6 The one who is
taught the word is
to share all good
things with the
one who teaches
him. 7 Do not be
deceived, God is
not mocked; for
whatever a man
sows, this he will
also reap. 8 For the
one who sows to
his own flesh will
from the flesh reap
corruption, but the
one who sows to
the Spirit will from
the Spirit reap eter-
nal life. 9 Let us not
lose heart in doing
good, for in due
time we will reap
if we do not grow
weary. 10 So then,
while we have op-
portunity, let us do
good to all people,
and especially to
those who are of
the household of
the faith.
11 See with what
large letters I am
writing to you with
my own hand.
12 Those who desire
to make a good
showing in the
flesh try to compel
you to be circum-
cised, simply so
that they will not
be persecuted for
the cross of Christ.
13 For those who
[a]are circumcised do
not even keep the
Law themselves,
but they desire

[a] Two early mss read *have been*

NIV

yet they want you
to be circumcised
that they may
boast about your
circumcision in
the flesh. 14 May I
never boast except
in the cross of our
Lord Jesus Christ,
through which[a]
the world has been
crucified to me,
and I to the world.
15 Neither circumci-
sion nor uncircum-
cision means any-
thing; what counts
is the new creation.
16 Peace and mercy
to all who follow
this rule—to[b] the
Israel of God.
17 From now on,
let no one cause
me trouble, for I
bear on my body
the marks of Jesus.
18 The grace of
our Lord Jesus
Christ be with
your spirit, broth-
ers and sisters.
Amen.

περιτέμνεσθαι, ἵνα ἐν τῇ ὑμετέρᾳ σαρκὶ καυχήσωνται. 14
to be circumcised so that they may boast in *{the}* your flesh. *they may boast* But may
4362 2671 3016 3016 3016 1877 3836 5629 4922 3016 1254 1181
f.pp cj p.d d.dsf r.dsf.2 n.dsf v.ams.3p

ἐμοὶ δὲ μὴ γένοιτο καυχᾶσθαι ⌊εἰ μὴ⌋ ἐν τῷ σταυρῷ τοῦ κυρίου ἡμῶν
I *But* never *may* boast, except in the cross of our Lord *our*
1609 1254 3590 1181 3016 1623 3590 1877 3836 5089 3836 7005 3261 7005
r.ds.1 cj pl v.amo.3s f.pm cj pl p.d d.dsm n.dsm d.gsm n.gsm r.gp.1

Ἰησοῦ Χριστοῦ, δι᾽ οὗ ἐμοὶ κόσμος ἐσταύρωται
Jesus Christ, through which the world has been crucified to me, *world* *has been crucified*
2652 5986 1328 4005 3180 5090 5090 5090 1609 3180 5090
n.gsm n.gsm p.g r.gsm r.ds.1 n.nsm v.rpi.3s

κἀγὼ → κόσμῳ. 15 οὔτε γάρ περιτομή τί ἐστιν
and I to the world. For neither *For* circumcision nor uncircumcision is anything, *is*
2743 3180 1142 4046 1142 4364 4046 213 1639 5516 1639
crasis n.dsm cj cj n.nsf r.nsn v.pai.3s

οὔτε ἀκροβυστία ἀλλὰ καινὴ κτίσις. 16 καὶ ὅσοι τῷ κανόνι
nor *uncircumcision* but a new creation. As for all who will follow *{the}* this rule
4046 213 247 2785 3232 2779 4012 5123 5123 5123 3836 4047 2834
cj n.nsf cj a.nsf n.nsf cj r.npm d.dsm n.dsm

τούτῳ στοιχήσουσιν, εἰρήνη ἐπ᾽ αὐτοὺς καὶ ἔλεος καὶ ἐπὶ τὸν
this *who will follow* — may peace and mercy be upon them, *and* *mercy* even upon the
4047 5123 1645 2779 1799 2093 899 2779 1799 2779 2093 3836
r.dsm v.fai.3p n.nsf p.a r.apm.3 cj n.nsn cj p.a d.asm

Ἰσραὴλ τοῦ θεοῦ. 17 ⌊τοῦ λοιποῦ⌋ κόπους μοι μηδεὶς
Israel of God. From now on let no one cause me trouble, *me* *no one*
2702 3836 2536 3836 3370 4218 3594 3594 4218 1609 3160 1609 3594
n.asm d.gsm n.gsm d.gsn adv n.apm r.ds.1 a.nsm

παρεχέτω· ἐγὼ γὰρ τὰ στίγματα τοῦ Ἰησοῦ ἐν τῷ σώματί μου
let cause for I *for* bear the marks of Jesus on *{the}* my body. *my*
4218 1142 1609 1142 1002 3836 5116 3836 2652 1877 3836 1609 5393 1609
v.pam.3s r.ns.1 cj d.apn n.apn d.gsm n.gsm p.d d.dsn n.dsn r.gs.1

βαστάζω. 18 ἡ χάρις τοῦ κυρίου ἡμῶν Ἰησοῦ Χριστοῦ μετὰ τοῦ
bear May the grace of our Lord *our* Jesus Christ be with *{the}* your
1002 3836 5921 3836 7005 3261 7005 2652 5986 3552 3836 7007
v.pai.1s d.nsf n.nsf d.gsm n.gsm r.gp.1 n.gsm n.gsm p.g d.gsn

πνεύματος ὑμῶν, ἀδελφοί. ἀμήν.[a]
spirit, *your* my brothers. Amen.
4460 7007 81 297
n.gsn r.gp.2 n.vpm pl

NASB

to have you
circumcised so that
they may boast in
your flesh. 14 But
may it never be
that I would boast,
except in the cross
of our Lord Jesus
Christ, through
which the world
has been crucified
to me, and I to the
world. 15 For neither
is circumcision
anything, nor un-
circumcision, but a
new creation. 16 And
those who will
walk by this rule,
peace and mercy
be upon them, and
upon the Israel of
God.
17 From now on
let no one cause
trouble for me, for
I bear on my body
the brand-marks of
Jesus.
18 The grace of our
Lord Jesus Christ
be with your spirit,
brethren. Amen.

[a] 14 Or *whom*
[b] 16 Or *rule and to*

[a] πρὸς Γαλάτας ἐγράφη ἀπὸ Ῥώμης included by TR after ἀμήν.

Ephesians

NIV

1 Paul, an apostle
of Christ Jesus
by the will of God,
To God's holy people
in Ephesus,[a] the faith-
ful in Christ Jesus:
2Grace and peace
to you from God
our Father and the
Lord Jesus Christ.

Praise for Spiritual Blessings in Christ

3Praise be to the
God and Father of our
Lord Jesus Christ,
who has blessed us in
the heavenly realms
with every spiritual
blessing in Christ.
4For he chose us in
him before the crea-
tion of the world to be
holy and blameless
in his sight. In love
5he[b] predestined us
for adoption to son-
ship[c] through Jesus
Christ, in accordance
with his pleasure and
will— 6to the praise
of his glorious grace,
which he has freely
given us in the One
he loves. 7In him we
have redemption
through his blood, the
forgiveness of sins, in
accordance with the
riches of God's grace
8that he lavished on
us. With all wisdom
and understanding,
9he[d] made known
to us the mystery of
his will

[a] 1 Some early manuscripts do not have *in Ephesus.*
[b] 4,5 Or *sight in love. 5He*
[c] 5 The Greek word for *adoption to sonship* is a legal term referring to the full legal standing of an adopted male heir in Roman culture.
[d] 8,9 Or *us with all wisdom and understanding. 9And he*

1:1 Παῦλος ἀπόστολος Χριστοῦ Ἰησοῦ διὰ θελήματος θεοῦ τοῖς ἁγίοις
Paul, an apostle of Christ Jesus by the will of God, to the saints
4263 693 5986 2652 1328 2525 2536 3836 41
n.nsm n.nsm n.gsm n.gsm p.g n.gsn n.gsm d.dpm a.dpm

τοῖς οὖσιν [a]ἐν Ἐφέσῳ καὶ πιστοῖς ἐν Χριστῷ Ἰησοῦ, 2 χάρις ὑμῖν καὶ
who are in Ephesus, {and} the faithful in Christ Jesus: Grace to you and
3836 1639 1877 2387 2779 4412 1877 5986 2652 5921 7007 2779
d.dpm pt.pa.dpm p.d n.dsf cj a.dpm p.d n.dsm n.dsm n.nsf r.dp.2 cj

εἰρήνη ἀπὸ θεοῦ πατρὸς ἡμῶν καὶ → κυρίου Ἰησοῦ Χριστοῦ. 3 εὐλογητὸς
peace from God our Father *our* and from the Lord Jesus Christ. Blessed be
1645 608 2536 7005 4252 7005 2779 3261 2652 5986 2329
n.nsf p.g n.gsm n.gsm r.gp.1 cj n.gsm n.gsm n.gsm a.nsm

ὁ θεὸς καὶ πατὴρ τοῦ κυρίου ἡμῶν Ἰησοῦ Χριστοῦ, ὁ εὐλογήσας ἡμᾶς ἐν
the God and Father of our Lord *our* Jesus Christ, who has blessed us with
3836 2536 2779 4252 3836 7005 3261 7005 2652 5986 3836 2328 7005 1877
d.nsm n.nsm cj n.nsm d.gsm n.gsm r.gp.1 n.gsm n.gsm d.nsm pt.aa.nsm r.ap.1 p.d

πάσῃ εὐλογίᾳ πνευματικῇ ἐν τοῖς ἐπουρανίοις ἐν Χριστῷ, 4 καθὼς ἐξελέξατο ἡμᾶς
every spiritual blessing in the heavenly places in Christ, even as he chose us
4246 2330 4461 1877 3836 2230 1877 5986 2777 1721 7005
a.dsf n.dsf a.dsf p.d d.dpn a.dpn p.d n.dsm cj v.ami.3s r.ap.1

ἐν αὐτῷ πρὸ καταβολῆς → κόσμου εἶναι ἡμᾶς ἁγίους καὶ ἀμώμους
in him before the creation of the world to be *{we}* holy and blameless
1877 899 4574 2856 3180 1639 7005 41 2779 320
p.d r.dsm.3 p.g n.gsf n.gsm f.pa r.ap.1 a.apm cj a.apm

κατενώπιον αὐτοῦ ἐν ἀγάπῃ, 5 προορίσας ἡμᾶς εἰς υἱοθεσίαν ←
before him. In love he predestined us for adoption as his own sons
2979 899 1877 27 4633 7005 1650 5625 1650 899 899
p.g r.gsm.3 p.d n.dsf pt.aa.nsm r.ap.1 p.a n.asf

διὰ Ἰησοῦ Χριστοῦ εἰς αὐτόν, κατὰ τὴν εὐδοκίαν τοῦ θελήματος
through Jesus Christ, *as* *his own* ⌊according to⌋ the good pleasure of his will,
1328 2652 5986 1650 899 2848 3836 2306 3836 899 2525
p.g n.gsm n.gsm p.a r.asm.3 p.a d.asf n.asf d.gsn n.gsn

αὐτοῦ, 6 εἰς ἔπαινον → δόξης τῆς χάριτος αὐτοῦ ἧς
his to the praise of his glorious *{the}* grace *his* ⌊with which⌋
899 1650 2047 899 1518 3836 5921 899 4005
r.gsm.3 p.a n.asm n.gsf d.gsf n.gsf r.gsm.3 r.gsf

ἐχαρίτωσεν ἡμᾶς ἐν τῷ ἠγαπημένῳ. 7 ἐν ᾧ ἔχομεν τὴν
⌊he has highly favored⌋ us in the Beloved. In him ⌊we have received⌋ *{the}*
5923 7005 1877 3836 26 1877 4005 2400 3836
v.aai.3s r.ap.1 p.d d.dsm pt.rp.dsm p.d r.dsm v.pai.1p d.asf

ἀπολύτρωσιν διὰ τοῦ αἵματος αὐτοῦ, τὴν ἄφεσιν τῶν παραπτωμάτων,
redemption through *{the}* his blood, *his* the forgiveness of our trespasses,
667 1328 3836 899 135 899 3836 912 3836 4183
n.asf p.g d.gsn n.gsn r.gsm.3 d.asf n.asf d.gpn n.gpn

κατὰ τὸ πλοῦτος τῆς χάριτος αὐτοῦ 8 ἧς ἐπερίσσευσεν εἰς ἡμᾶς, ἐν
⌊according to⌋ the rich benefits of his grace, *his* which he lavished on us in
2848 3836 4458 3836 899 5921 899 4005 4355 1650 7005 1877
p.a d.asn n.asn d.gsf n.gsf r.gsm.3 r.gsf v.aai.3s p.a r.ap.1 p.d

πάσῃ σοφίᾳ καὶ φρονήσει, 9 γνωρίσας ἡμῖν τὸ μυστήριον τοῦ θελήματος
all wisdom and insight. ⌊He has made known⌋ to us the mystery of his will,
4246 5053 2779 5860 1192 7005 3836 3696 3836 899 2525
a.dsf n.dsf cj n.dsf pt.aa.nsm r.dp.1 d.asn n.asn d.gsn n.gsn

[a] [ἐν Ἐφέσῳ] UBS.

NASB

The Blessings of Redemption

1:1Paul, an apostle
of Christ Jesus by
the will of God,
To the saints who
are [a]at Ephesus and
who are faithful
in Christ Jesus:
2Grace to you and
peace from God
our Father and the
Lord Jesus Christ.
3Blessed *be* the
God and Father
of our Lord Jesus
Christ, who has
blessed us with ev-
ery spiritual bless-
ing in the heavenly
places in Christ,
4just as He chose
us in Him before
the foundation of
the world, that we
would be holy and
blameless before
[b]Him. In love 5He
predestined us to
adoption as sons
through Jesus
Christ to Himself,
according to the
kind intention of
His will, 6to the
praise of the glory
of His grace, which
He freely bestowed
on us in the Be-
loved. 7In Him we
have redemption
through His blood,
the forgiveness
of our trespasses,
according to the
riches of His grace
8which He lavished
on us. In all wis-
dom and insight
9He made known to
us the mystery of

[a] Three early mss do not contain *at Ephesus*
[b] Or *Him, in love*

NIV

according to his
good pleasure,
which he purposed
in Christ, [10]to be
put into effect
when the times
reach their fulfill-
ment—to bring
unity to all things
in heaven and on
earth under Christ.
[11]In him we were
also chosen,[a]
having been pre-
destined accord-
ing to the plan of
him who works
out everything in
conformity with
the purpose of his
will, [12]in order
that we, who were
the first to put our
hope in Christ,
might be for the
praise of his glo-
ry. [13]And you also
were included in
Christ when you
heard the mes-
sage of truth, the
gospel of your
salvation. When
you believed, you
were marked in
him with a seal,
the promised Holy
Spirit, [14]who is a
deposit guarantee-
ing our inheritance
until the redemp-
tion of those who
are God's pos-
session—to the
praise of his glory.

Thanksgiving and Prayer

[15]For this reason,
ever since I heard
about your faith in
the Lord Jesus and
your love for all
God's people, [16]I
have not stopped
giving thanks for
you, remembering
you in my prayers.
[17]I keep asking
that the God of our
Lord Jesus Christ,
the glorious Fa-
ther, may give
you the

[a] 11 Or *were made heirs*

αὐτοῦ, κατὰ τὴν εὐδοκίαν αὐτοῦ ἣν προέθετο ἐν αὐτῷ 10 εἰς
his ⌊according to⌋ {the} his good pleasure, his which he purposed in Christ, as a
899 2848 3836 899 2306 899 4005 4729 1877 899 1650
r.gsm.3 p.a d.asf n.asf r.gsm.3 r.asf v.ami.3s p.d r.dsm.3 p.a

οἰκονομίαν τοῦ πληρώματος τῶν καιρῶν, ἀνακεφαλαιώσασθαι τὰ πάντα
plan ⌊for the⌋ fullness of time, to bring {the} everything
3873 3836 4445 3836 2789 368 3836 4246
n.asf d.gsn n.gsn d.gpm n.gpm f.am d.apn a.apn

↤ ἐν τῷ Χριστῷ, τὰ ἐπὶ τοῖς οὐρανοῖς καὶ τὰ ἐπὶ τῆς γῆς ἐν αὐτῷ.
together in {the} Christ, things in {the} heaven and things on {the} earth. {in} {him}
368 1877 3836 5986 3836 2093 3836 4041 2779 3836 2093 3836 1178 1877 899
p.d d.dsm n.dsm d.apn p.d d.dpm n.dpm cj d.apn p.g d.gsf n.gsf p.d r.dsm.3

11 ἐν ᾧ καὶ ἐκληρώθημεν προορισθέντες κατὰ
In Christ {also} ⌊we have obtained an inheritance,⌋ having been predestined ⌊according to⌋ the
1877 4005 2779 3103 4633 2848
p.d r.dsm adv v.api.1p pt.ap.npm p.a

πρόθεσιν τοῦ τὰ πάντα ἐνεργοῦντος κατὰ τὴν βουλὴν
purpose of him who accomplishes {the} all things who accomplishes ⌊according to⌋ the counsel
4606 3836 1919 1919 3836 4246 1919 2848 3836 1087
n.asf d.gsm d.apn a.apn pt.pa.gsm p.a d.asf n.asf

τοῦ θελήματος αὐτοῦ 12 εἰς τὸ
of his will, his ⌊so that⌋ we, who have already set our hope in Christ, ~
3836 899 2525 899 1650 7005 3836 4598 4598 4598 4598 4598 1877 5986 3836
d.gsn n.gsn r.gsm.3 p.a d.asn

εἶναι ἡμᾶς εἰς ἔπαινον → δόξης αὐτοῦ τοὺς προηλπικότας ἐν τῷ
⌊might be⌋ we for the praise of his glory. his who have already set our hope in {the}
1639 7005 1650 2047 899 1518 899 3836 4598 1877 3836
f.pa r.ap.1 p.a n.asm n.gsf r.gsm.3 d.apm pt.ra.apm p.d d.dsm

Χριστῷ. 13 ἐν ᾧ καὶ ὑμεῖς ἀκούσαντες τὸν λόγον τῆς ἀληθείας, τὸ
Christ You also are in him, also You having heard the word of truth, the
5986 7007 2779 1877 4005 2779 7007 201 3836 3364 3836 237 3836
n.dsm p.d r.dsm adv r.np.2 pt.aa.npm d.asm n.asm d.gsf n.gsf d.asn

εὐαγγέλιον τῆς σωτηρίας ὑμῶν, ἐν ᾧ καὶ πιστεύσαντες
good news of your salvation; your in him also, when you believed,
2295 3836 7007 5401 7007 1877 4005 2779 4409
n.asn d.gsf n.gsf r.gp.2 p.d r.dsm adv pt.aa.npm

ἐσφραγίσθητε τῷ πνεύματι τῆς ἐπαγγελίας τῷ ἁγίῳ,
⌊you were marked with the seal⌋ of the promised Holy Spirit, {the} promised {the} Holy
5381 3836 2039 41 4460 3836 2039 3836 41
v.api.2p d.dsn n.dsn d.gsf n.gsf d.dsn a.dsn

14 ὅ ἐστιν ἀρραβὼν τῆς κληρονομίας ἡμῶν, εἰς
which is the guarantee of our inheritance our vouching for God's
4005 1639 775 3836 7005 3100 7005 1650
r.nsn v.pai.3s n.nsm d.gsf n.gsf r.gp.1 p.a

ἀπολύτρωσιν τῆς περιποιήσεως, εἰς ἔπαινον τῆς δόξης αὐτοῦ. 15 διὰ
redemption of his possession, to the praise of his glory. his For
667 3836 4348 1650 2047 3836 899 1518 899 1328
n.asf d.gsf n.gsf p.a n.asm d.gsf n.gsf r.gsm.3 p.a

τοῦτο κἀγὼ ἀκούσας τὴν καθ' ὑμᾶς πίστιν ἐν τῷ κυρίῳ Ἰησοῦ καὶ τὴν
this reason, {I also} having heard {the} about your faith in the Lord Jesus and the
4047 2743 201 3836 2848 7007 4411 1877 3836 3261 2652 2779 3836
r.asn crasis pt.aa.nsm d.asf p.a r.ap.2 n.asf p.d d.dsm n.dsm n.dsm cj d.asf

ἀγάπην τὴν εἰς πάντας τοὺς ἁγίους 16 ↱ ↱ οὐ παύομαι εὐχαριστῶν
love {the} you extend to all the saints, I do not cease giving thanks
27 3836 1650 4246 3836 41 4264 4264 4024 4264 2373
n.asf d.asf p.a a.apm d.apm a.apm pl v.pmi.1s pt.pa.nsm

ὑπὲρ ὑμῶν μνείαν ποιούμενος ἐπὶ τῶν προσευχῶν μου, 17 ἵνα ὁ
for you, making mention making of you in {the} my prayers, my that the
5642 7007 4472 3644 4472 2093 3836 1609 4666 1609 2671 3836
p.g r.gp.2 n.asf pt.pm.nsm p.g d.gpf n.gpf r.gs.1 cj d.nsm

θεὸς τοῦ κυρίου ἡμῶν Ἰησοῦ Χριστοῦ, ὁ πατὴρ τῆς δόξης, δώῃ ὑμῖν
God of our Lord our Jesus Christ, the Father of glory, ⌊may give⌋ you a
2536 3836 7005 3261 7005 2652 5986 3836 4252 3836 1518 1443 7007
n.nsm d.gsm n.gsm r.gp.1 n.gsm n.gsm d.nsm n.nsm d.gsf n.gsf v.aas.3s r.dp.2

NASB

His will, accord-
ing to His kind
intention which He
purposed in Him
[10]with a view to an
administration suit-
able to the fullness
of the times, *that
is,* the summing
up of all things in
Christ, things in
the heavens and
things on the earth.
In Him [11]also we
have obtained an
inheritance, having
been predestined
according to His
purpose who works
all things after the
counsel of His will,
[12]to the end that we
who were the first
to hope in [a]Christ
would be to the
praise of His glory.
[13]In Him, you also,
after listening to
the message of
truth, the gospel of
your salvation—
having also
believed, you were
sealed in Him with
the Holy Spirit of
promise, [14]who is
given as a pledge
of our inheritance,
with a view to
the redemption of
God's own posses-
sion, to the praise
of His glory.
[15]For this reason I
too, having heard
of the faith in the
Lord Jesus which
exists among you
and [b]your love for
all the saints, [16]do
not cease giving
thanks for you,
while making men-
tion *of you* in my
prayers; [17]that the
God of our Lord
Jesus Christ, the
Father of glory,
may give to you a

[a] I.e. the Messiah
[b] Three early mss do not contain *your love*

NIV

Spirit[a] of wisdom
and revelation, so
that you may know
him better. [18] I pray
that the eyes of
your heart may be
enlightened in or-
der that you may
know the hope to
which he has called
you, the riches of
his glorious inher-
itance in his holy
people, [19] and his
incomparably great
power for us who
believe. That pow-
er is the same as
the mighty strength
[20] he exerted when
he raised Christ
from the dead and
seated him at his
right hand in the
heavenly realms,
[21] far above all rule
and authority, pow-
er and dominion,
and every name
that is invoked, not
only in the pres-
ent age but also in
the one to come.
[22] And God placed
all things under his
feet and appoint-
ed him to be head
over everything
for the church,
[23] which is his body,
the fullness of him
who fills every-
thing in every way.

Made Alive in Christ

2 As for you,
you were dead
in your transgres-
sions and sins, [2] in
which you used
to live when you
followed the ways
of this world and
of the ruler of the
kingdom of the air,
the spirit who is

πνεῦμα σοφίας καὶ ἀποκαλύψεως ἐν ἐπιγνώσει αὐτοῦ, 18 →
spirit of wisdom and revelation by ⌊coming to know more⌋ of him. I pray that, with
4460 5053 2779 637 1877 2106 899 1650
n.asn n.gsf cj n.gsf p.d n.dsf r.gsm.3

πεφωτισμένους τοὺς ὀφθαλμοὺς τῆς καρδίας ὑμῶν[a] εἰς τὸ
the eyes of your heart enlightened, *the eyes of heart your that* ~
3836 4057 3836 7007 2840 5894 3836 4057 3836 2840 7007 1650 3836
pt.rp.apm d.apm n.apm d.gsf n.gsf r.gp.2 p.a d.asn

εἰδέναι ὑμᾶς τίς ἐστιν ἡ ἐλπὶς τῆς κλήσεως αὐτοῦ, τίς
you may comprehend *you {what} {is}* the hope to which he has called *he* you, what
7007 3857 7007 5515 1639 3836 1828 3836 899 3104 899 5515
f.ra r.ap.2 r.nsf v.pai.3s d.nsf n.nsf d.gsf n.gsf r.gsm.3 r.nsm

ὁ πλοῦτος τῆς δόξης τῆς κληρονομίας αὐτοῦ ἐν τοῖς ἁγίοις, 19 καὶ
are the rich benefits of his glorious *{the}* inheritance *his* among the saints, and
3836 4458 3836 899 1518 3836 3100 899 1877 3836 41 2779
d.nsm n.nsm d.gsf n.gsf d.gsf n.gsf r.gsm.3 p.d d.dpm a.dpm cj

τί τὸ ὑπερβάλλον μέγεθος τῆς δυνάμεως αὐτοῦ εἰς ἡμᾶς τοὺς
what is the incomparable greatness of his power *his* ⌊available for⌋ us who
5515 3836 5650 3490 3836 899 1539 899 1650 7005 3836
r.nsn d.nsn pt.pa.nsn n.nsn d.gsf n.gsf r.gsm.3 p.a r.ap.1 d.apm

πιστεύοντας κατὰ τὴν ἐνέργειαν τοῦ κράτους τῆς ἰσχύος αὐτοῦ. 20 ἣν
believe, ⌊according to⌋ the exercise of his mighty *{the}* strength, *his* which
4409 2848 3836 1918 3836 899 3197 3836 2709 899 4005
pt.pa.apm p.a d.asf n.asf d.gsn n.gsn d.gsf n.gsf r.gsm.3 r.asf

ἐνήργησεν ἐν τῷ Χριστῷ ἐγείρας αὐτὸν ἐκ νεκρῶν καὶ καθίσας
he accomplished in *{the}* Christ ⌊when he raised⌋ him from the dead and seated him
1919 1877 3836 5986 1586 899 1666 3738 2779 2767
v.aai.3s p.d d.dsm n.dsm pt.aa.nsm r.asm.3 p.g a.gpm cj pt.aa.nsm

ἐν δεξιᾷ αὐτοῦ ἐν τοῖς ἐπουρανίοις 21 ὑπεράνω πάσης ἀρχῆς καὶ
at his right hand *his* in the heavenly realms, infinitely superior to every ruler, *{and}*
1877 899 1288 899 1877 3836 2230 5645 4246 794 2779
p.d a.dsf r.gsm.3 p.d d.dpn a.dpn p.g a.gsf n.gsf cj

ἐξουσίας καὶ δυνάμεως καὶ κυριότητος καὶ παντὸς ὀνόματος ὀνομαζομένου,
authority, *{and}* power, or dominion — *{and}* every name that can be named, —
2026 2779 1539 2779 3262 2779 4246 3950 3951
n.gsf cj n.gsf cj n.gsf cj a.gsn n.gsn pt.pp.gsn

οὐ μόνον ἐν τῷ αἰῶνι τούτῳ ἀλλὰ καὶ ἐν τῷ μέλλοντι· 22 καὶ
not only in *{the}* this age *this* but also in the age to come. And he
4024 3667 1877 3836 4047 172 4047 247 2779 1877 3836 3516 2779 5718
pl adv p.d d.dsm n.dsm r.dsm cj adv p.d d.dsm pt.pa.dsm cj

πάντα ὑπέταξεν ὑπὸ τοὺς πόδας αὐτοῦ καὶ αὐτὸν ἔδωκεν
placed all things *he placed* under *{the}* Christ's feet *Christ's* and gave him *gave* as
5718 4246 5718 5679 3836 899 4546 899 2779 1443 899 1443
a.apn v.aai.3s p.a d.apm n.apm r.gsm.3 cj r.asm.3 v.aai.3s

κεφαλὴν ὑπὲρ πάντα τῇ ἐκκλησίᾳ, 23 ἥτις ἐστὶν τὸ σῶμα αὐτοῦ, τὸ
head over all things ⌊to the⌋ church, which is *{the}* his body, *his* the
3051 5642 4246 3836 1711 4015 1639 3836 899 5393 899 3836
n.asf p.a a.apn d.dsf n.dsf r.nsf v.pai.3s d.nsn n.nsn r.gsm.3 d.nsn

πλήρωμα τοῦ τὰ πάντα ἐν πᾶσιν πληρουμένου.
fullness of the one who fills *{the}* all things in every way. *one who fills*
4445 3836 4444 4444 4444 3836 4246 1877 4246 4444
n.nsn d.gsm d.apn a.apn p.d a.dpn pt.pm.gsm

2:1 καὶ ὑμᾶς ὄντας νεκροὺς τοῖς παραπτώμασιν καὶ ταῖς ἁμαρτίαις
And you were dead ⌊by reason of⌋ your trespasses and *{the}* sins,
2779 7007 1639 3738 3836 7007 4183 2779 3836 281
cj r.ap.2 pt.pa.apm a.apm d.dpn n.dpn cj d.dpf n.dpf

ὑμῶν, 2 ἐν αἷς ↱ ποτε περιεπατήσατε κατὰ τὸν αἰῶνα τοῦ κόσμου
your in which you once lived ⌊according to⌋ the course of this world,
7007 1877 4005 4344 4537 4344 2848 3836 172 3836 4047 3180
r.gp.2 p.d r.dpf adv v.aai.2p p.a d.asm n.asm d.gsm n.gsm

τούτου, κατὰ τὸν ἄρχοντα τῆς ἐξουσίας τοῦ ἀέρος, τοῦ πνεύματος τοῦ
this ⌊according to⌋ the ruler of the realm of the air, of the spirit that is
4047 2848 3836 807 3836 2026 3836 113 3836 4460 3836
r.gsm p.a d.asm n.asm d.gsf n.gsf d.gsm n.gsm d.gsn n.gsn d.gsn

NASB

spirit of wisdom
and of revelation
in the knowledge
of Him. [18] *I pray*
that the eyes of
your heart may be
enlightened, so
that you will know
what is the hope of
His calling, what
are the riches of
the glory of His
inheritance in the
saints, [19] and what
is the surpassing
greatness of His
power toward us
who believe. *These*
are in accordance
with the working
of the strength of
His might [20] which
He brought about
in Christ, when
He raised Him
from the dead and
seated Him at His
right hand in the
heavenly *places,*
[21] far above all
rule and author-
ity and power and
dominion, and
every name that is
named, not only in
this age but also in
the one to come.
[22] And He put all
things in subjection
under His feet, and
gave Him as head
over all things to
the church, [23] which
is His body, the
fullness of Him
who fills all in all.

Made Alive in Christ

2:1 And you were
dead in your tres-
passes and sins,
[2] in which you
formerly walked
according to the
course of this
world, according
to the prince of the
power of the air, of
the spirit that is

[a] 17 Or *a spirit*

[a] [ὑμῶν] UBS, omitted by NET.

NIV

now at work in
those who are
disobedient. 3All
of us also lived
among them at one
time, gratifying
the cravings of our
flesh[a] and follow-
ing its desires and
thoughts. Like the
rest, we were by
nature deserving of
wrath. 4But because
of his great love
for us, God, who
is rich in mercy,
5made us alive with
Christ even when
we were dead in
transgressions—it
is by grace you
have been saved.
6And God raised
us up with Christ
and seated us with
him in the heaven-
ly realms in Christ
Jesus, 7in order
that in the coming
ages he might show
the incomparable
riches of his grace,
expressed in his
kindness to us in
Christ Jesus. 8For
it is by grace you
have been saved,
through faith—and
this is not from
yourselves, it is the
gift of God— 9not
by works, so that no
one can boast. 10For
we are God's hand-
iwork, created in
Christ Jesus to do
good works, which
God prepared in ad-
vance for us to do.

Jew and Gentile Reconciled Through Christ

11Therefore, re-
member that for-
merly you who are
Gentiles by birth
and called "uncir-
cumcised" by those
who call them-
selves "the circum-
cision" (which is
done in

[a] 3 In contexts like this, the Greek word for *flesh* (*sarx*) refers to the sinful state of human beings, often presented as a power in opposition to the Spirit.

νῦν ⌊ἐνεργοῦντος ἐν⌋ τοῖς υἱοῖς τῆς ἀπειθείας· 3ἐν οἷς καὶ ἡμεῖς πάντες
now energizing the sons of disobedience. Among them we also *we* all
3814 1919 1877 3836 5626 3836 577 1877 4005 7005 2779 7005 4246
adv pt.pa.gsn p.d d.dpm n.dpm d.gsf n.gsf p.d r.dpm adv r.np.1 a.npm

ἀνεστράφημέν ποτε ἐν ταῖς ἐπιθυμίαις τῆς σαρκὸς ἡμῶν ποιοῦντες τὰ
once lived *once* in the passions of our flesh, *our* gratifying the
4537 418 4537 1877 3836 2123 3836 7005 4922 7005 4472 3836
v.api.1p adv p.d d.dpf n.dpf d.gsf n.gsf r.gp.1 pt.pa.npm d.apn

θελήματα τῆς σαρκὸς καὶ τῶν διανοιῶν, καὶ ἤμεθα τέκνα
desires and impulses of the flesh, *and {the} impulses* and were by nature children
2525 2779 1379 3836 4922 2779 3836 1379 2779 1639 5882 5882 5451
n.apn d.gsf n.gsf cj d.gpf n.gpf cj v.imi.1p n.npn

φύσει ὀργῆς ὡς καὶ οἱ λοιποί· 4ὁ δὲ θεὸς πλούσιος
by nature of wrath, just like *just {the}* ⌊everyone else.⌋ *{the}* But God, being rich
5882 3973 2779 6055 2779 3836 3370 3836 1254 2536 1639 4454
n.dsf n.gsf cj adv d.npm a.npm d.nsm cj n.nsm a.nsm

ὢν ἐν ἐλέει, διὰ τὴν πολλὴν ἀγάπην αὐτοῦ ἣν ἠγάπησεν
being in mercy, ⌊because of⌋ *{the}* his great love *his* ⌊with which⌋ he loved
1639 1877 1799 1328 3836 899 4498 27 899 4005 26
pt.pa.nsm p.d n.dsn p.a d.asf a.asf n.asf r.gsm.3 r.asf v.aai.3s

ἡμᾶς, 5καὶ → ὄντας ἡμᾶς νεκροὺς τοῖς παραπτώμασιν →
us, even though we were *we* dead in our trespasses, made us
7005 2779 7005 1639 7005 3738 3836 4183
r.ap.1 adv pt.pa.apm r.ap.1 a.apm d.dpn n.dpn

συνεζωοποίησεν τῷ Χριστῷ, χάριτί ἐστε σεσῳσμένοι 6καὶ
alive together with *{the}* Christ — by grace ⌊you have been⌋ saved — and
5188 3836 5986 5921 1639 5392 2779
v.aai.3s d.dsm n.dsm n.dsf v.pai.2p pt.rp.npm cj

συνήγειρεν ← ← καὶ συνεκάθισεν ← ἐν τοῖς ἐπουρανίοις ἐν
raised us up with him and seated us with him in the heavenly places in
5283 2779 5154 1877 3836 2230 1877
v.aai.3s cj v.aai.3s p.d d.dpn a.dpn p.d

Χριστῷ Ἰησοῦ, 7ἵνα ἐνδείξηται ἐν τοῖς αἰῶσιν τοῖς ἐπερχομένοις τὸ ὑπερβάλλον
Christ Jesus, to demonstrate in the ages *{the}* to come the incomparable
5986 2652 2671 1892 1877 3836 172 3836 2088 3836 5650
n.dsm n.dsm cj v.ams.3s p.d d.dpm n.dpm d.dpm pt.pm.dpm d.asn pt.pa.asn

πλοῦτος τῆς χάριτος αὐτοῦ ἐν χρηστότητι ἐφ' ἡμᾶς ἐν Χριστῷ Ἰησοῦ. 8
riches of his grace *his* in kindness to us in Christ Jesus. For
4458 3836 899 5921 899 1877 5983 2093 7005 1877 5986 2652 1142
n.asn d.gsf n.gsf r.gsm.3 p.d n.dsf p.a r.ap.1 p.d n.dsm n.dsm

τῇ γὰρ χάριτί ἐστε σεσῳσμένοι διὰ πίστεως· καὶ τοῦτο οὐκ ἐξ
by *For* grace ⌊you have been⌋ saved through faith, and this is not of
3836 1142 5921 1639 5392 1328 4411 2779 4047 4024 1666
d.dsf cj n.dsf v.pai.2p pt.rp.npm p.g n.gsf cj r.nsn pl p.g

ὑμῶν, θεοῦ τὸ δῶρον· 9 οὐκ ἐξ ἔργων, ἵνα μή τις
yourselves, it is the gift of God; *the gift* it is not of works, so that no one
7007 3836 1565 2536 3836 1565 4024 1666 2240 2671 3590 5516
r.gp.2 n.gsm d.nsn n.nsn pl p.g n.gpn cj pl r.nsm

καυχήσηται. 10 αὐτοῦ γάρ ἐσμεν ποίημα, κτισθέντες ἐν Χριστῷ Ἰησοῦ
may boast. For we are his *For we are* work, created in Christ Jesus
3016 1142 1639 1639 899 1142 1639 4473 3231 1877 5986 2652
v.ams.3s r.gsm.3 cj v.pai.1p n.nsn pt.ap.npm p.d n.dsm n.dsm

ἐπὶ ἔργοις ἀγαθοῖς οἷς προητοίμασεν ὁ θεὸς, ἵνα ἐν
for good works, *good* which God prepared in advance *{the} God* that we should do *{in}*
2093 19 2240 19 4005 2536 4602 3836 2536 2671 4344 4344 4344 1877
p.d n.dpn a.dpn r.dpn v.aai.3s d.nsm n.nsm cj p.d

αὐτοῖς περιπατήσωμεν. 11διὸ μνημονεύετε ὅτι ποτὲ ὑμεῖς τὰ ἔθνη ἐν
them. *we should do* So remember that ⌊at one time⌋ you *{the}* Gentiles in the
899 4344 1475 3648 4022 4537 7007 3836 1620 1877
r.dpn.3 v.aas.1p cj v.pam.2p cj adv r.np.2 d.npn n.npn p.d

σαρκί, οἱ λεγόμενοι ἀκροβυστία ὑπὸ τῆς λεγομένης περιτομῆς ↱ ἐν
flesh, *{the}* called the uncircumcision by those called the circumcision — made in
4922 3836 3306 213 5679 3836 3306 4364 5935 1877
n.dsf d.npm pt.pp.npm n.nsf p.g d.gsf pt.pp.gsf n.gsf p.d

NASB

now working in the
sons of disobedi-
ence. 3Among them
we too all formerly
lived in the lusts of
our flesh, indulging
the desires of the
flesh and of the
mind, and were
by nature children
of wrath, even
as the rest. 4But
God, being rich in
mercy, because of
His great love with
which He loved
us, 5even when we
were dead in our
transgressions,
made us alive to-
gether [a]with Christ
(by grace you have
been saved), 6and
raised us up with
Him, and seated
us with Him in the
heavenly *places* in
Christ Jesus, 7so
that in the ages to
come He might
show the surpass-
ing riches of His
grace in kindness
toward us in Christ
Jesus. 8For by
grace you have
been saved through
faith; and that not
of yourselves, *it
is* the gift of God;
9not as a result of
works, so that no
one may boast.
10For we are His
workmanship, cre-
ated in Christ Jesus
for good works,
which God pre-
pared beforehand
so that we would
walk in them.
11Therefore
remember that
formerly you, the
Gentiles in the
flesh, who are
called "Uncir-
cumcision" by the
so-called "Circum-
cision," *which is*
performed in the

[a] Two early mss read *in Christ*

NIV

the body by human
hands)— [12]re-
member that at that
time you were sep-
arate from Christ,
excluded from
citizenship in Isra-
el and foreigners
to the covenants
of the promise,
without hope and
without God in the
world. [13]But now
in Christ Jesus you
who once were far
away have been
brought near by the
blood of Christ.
[14]For he himself
is our peace, who
has made the two
groups one and has
destroyed the bar-
rier, the dividing
wall of hostility,
[15]by setting aside
in his flesh the law
with its commands
and regulations.
His purpose was to
create in himself
one new humanity
out of the two, thus
making peace,
[16]and in one body
to reconcile both
of them to God
through the cross,
by which he put to
death their hostil-
ity. [17]He came and
preached peace to
you who were far
away and peace
to those who were
near. [18]For through
him we both have
access to the Fa-
ther by one Spirit.
[19]Consequently,
you are no longer
foreigners and
strangers, but fel-
low citizens with
God's people and
also members of
his household,
[20]built on the foun-
dation of the

σαρκὶ χειροποιήτου, 12 ὅτι ἦτε τῷ καιρῷ ἐκείνῳ
the flesh by hands — remember that at that time ⌊you were⌋ *at* *time* *that*
4922 5935 4022 3836 1697 2789 1639 3836 2789 1697
n.dsf a.gsf cj v.iai.2p d.dsm n.dsm r.dsm

χωρὶς Χριστοῦ, ἀπηλλοτριωμένοι τῆς πολιτείας τοῦ Ἰσραὴλ καὶ ξένοι τῶν
apart from Christ, excluded from the commonwealth of Israel and strangers to the
6006 5986 558 3836 4486 3836 2702 2779 3828 3836
p.g n.gsm pt.rp.npm d.gsf n.gsf d.gsm n.gsm cj n.npm d.gpf

διαθηκῶν τῆς ἐπαγγελίας, ἐλπίδα μὴ ἔχοντες καὶ ἄθεοι ἐν τῷ
covenants of promise, having no hope *no* *having* and ⌊without God⌋ in the
1347 3836 2039 2400 3590 1828 3590 2400 2779 117 1877 3836
n.gpf d.gsf n.gsf n.asf pl pt.pa.npm cj a.npm p.d d.dsm

κόσμῳ. 13 νυνὶ δὲ ἐν Χριστῷ Ἰησοῦ ὑμεῖς οἵ ποτε ὄντες μακρὰν
world. But now *But* in Christ Jesus you who were ⌊at that time⌋ *were* far away
3180 1254 3815 1254 1877 5986 2652 7007 4005 1639 4537 1639 3426
n.dsm adv cj p.d n.dsm n.dsm r.np.2 d.npm adv pt.pa.npm adv

ἐγενήθητε ἐγγὺς ἐν τῷ αἵματι τοῦ Χριστοῦ. 14 αὐτὸς γάρ ἐστιν ἡ
have come near through the blood of Christ. For he *For* is *{the}* our
1181 1584 1877 3836 135 3836 5986 1142 899 1142 1639 3836 7005
v.api.2p adv p.d d.dsn n.dsn d.gsm n.gsm r.nsm cj v.pai.3s d.nsf

εἰρήνη ἡμῶν, ὁ ποιήσας τὰ ἀμφότερα ἓν καὶ τὸ μεσότοιχον
peace, *our* who has made us *{the}* both one and has broken down the dividing
1645 7005 3836 4472 3836 317 1651 2779 3395 3395 3395 3836 3546
n.nsf r.gp.1 d.nsm pt.aa.nsm d.apn a.apn a.asn cj d.asn n.asn

τοῦ φραγμοῦ λύσας, τὴν ἔχθραν ἐν τῇ σαρκὶ
{the} wall, *has broken down* having abolished in his flesh the hostility, *in* *{the}* *flesh*
3836 5850 3395 1877 899 4922 3836 2397 1877 3836 4922
d.gsm n.gsm pt.aa.nsm d.asf n.asf p.d d.dsf n.dsf

αὐτοῦ, 15 τὸν νόμον τῶν ἐντολῶν ἐν δόγμασιν καταργήσας, ἵνα
his the law of commandments and regulations, ⌊so as to⌋ create in
899 3836 3795 3836 1953 1877 1504 2934 2671 3231 1877
r.gsm.3 d.asm n.asm d.gpf n.gpf p.d n.dpn pt.aa.nsm cj

τοὺς δύο κτίσῃ ἐν αὐτῷ εἰς ἕνα καινὸν ἄνθρωπον
himself one new man from the two, *create* *in* *himself* *{into}* *one* *new* *man*
899 1651 2785 476 3836 1545 3231 1877 899 1650 1651 2785 476
d.apm a.apm v.aas.3s p.d r.dsm.3 p.a a.asm a.asm n.asm

ποιῶν εἰρήνην 16 καὶ ἀποκαταλλάξῃ τοὺς ἀμφοτέρους ἐν ἑνὶ σώματι
thus making peace, and to reconcile *{the}* both to God in one body
4472 1645 2779 639 3836 317 3836 2536 1877 1651 5393
pt.pa.nsm n.asf cj v.aas.3s d.apm a.apm p.d a.dsn n.dsn

τῷ θεῷ διὰ τοῦ σταυροῦ, → → ἀποκτείνας τὴν ἔχθραν ἐν
to *God* through the cross, having put the hostility to death *the* *hostility* in
3836 2536 1328 3836 5089 3836 2397 650 3836 2397 1877
d.dsm n.dsm p.g d.gsm n.gsm pt.aa.nsm d.asf n.asf p.d

αὐτῷ. 17 καὶ → ἐλθὼν εὐηγγελίσατο εἰρήνην ὑμῖν τοῖς μακρὰν
himself. And he came and ⌊preached the good news⌋ of peace to you who were far off
899 2779 2294 2262 2294 1645 7007 3836 3426
r.dsm.3 cj pt.aa.nsm v.ami.3s n.asf r.dp.2 d.dpm adv

καὶ εἰρήνην τοῖς ἐγγύς· 18 ὅτι δι᾽ αὐτοῦ → ἔχομεν τὴν
and of peace ⌊to those who⌋ were near; for through him we both have *{the}*
2779 1645 3836 1584 4022 1328 899 317 2400 3836
cj n.asf d.dpm adv cj p.g r.gsm.3 v.pai.1p d.asf

προσαγωγὴν οἱ ἀμφότεροι ἐν ἑνὶ πνεύματι πρὸς τὸν πατέρα. 19 ἄρα οὖν
access *{the}* *both* by the one Spirit to the Father. So then you
4643 3836 317 1877 1651 4460 4639 3836 4252 726 4036 1639
n.asf d.npm a.npm p.d a.dsn n.dsn p.a d.asm n.asm cj cj

οὐκέτι ἐστὲ ξένοι καὶ πάροικοι ἀλλὰ ἐστὲ συμπολῖται τῶν ἁγίων
are no longer *you are* strangers and aliens, but you are ⌊fellow citizens with⌋ the saints
1639 4033 1639 3828 2779 4230 247 1639 5232 3836 41
adv v.pai.2p n.npm cj n.npm cj v.pai.2p n.npm d.gpm a.gpm

καὶ οἰκεῖοι τοῦ θεοῦ, 20 ἐποικοδομηθέντες ἐπὶ τῷ θεμελίῳ τῶν
and ⌊members of the household⌋ of God, built on the foundation of the
2779 3858 3836 2536 2224 2093 3836 2529 3836
cj n.npm d.gsm n.gsm pt.ap.npm p.d d.dsm n.dsm d.gpm

NASB

flesh by human
hands— [12]*remem-
ber* that you were
at that time sepa-
rate from Christ,
excluded from the
commonwealth of
Israel, and strang-
ers to the cov-
enants of promise,
having no hope and
without God in the
world. [13]But now
in Christ Jesus you
who formerly were
far off have been
brought near by
the blood of Christ.
[14]For He Himself
is our peace,
who made both
groups into one
and broke down
the barrier of the
dividing wall, [15]by
abolishing in His
flesh the enmity,
which is the Law
of commandments
contained in ordi-
nances, so that in
Himself He might
make the two into
one new man, *thus*
establishing peace,
[16]and might recon-
cile them both in
one body to God
through the cross,
by it having put to
death the enmity.
[17]AND HE CAME AND
PREACHED PEACE TO
YOU WHO WERE FAR
AWAY, AND PEACE
TO THOSE WHO WERE
NEAR; [18]for through
Him we both have
our access in one
Spirit to the Father.
[19]So then you are
no longer strangers
and aliens, but you
are fellow citizens
with the saints,
and are of God's
household, [20]having
been built on the
foundation of the

NIV

apostles and proph-
ets, with Christ
Jesus himself as
the chief corner-
stone. 21 In him the
whole building is
joined together and
rises to become a
holy temple in the
Lord. 22 And in him
you too are being
built together to
become a dwelling
in which God lives
by his Spirit.

God's Marvelous Plan for the Gentiles

3 For this rea-
son I, Paul, the
prisoner of Christ
Jesus for the sake
of you Gentiles—
2 Surely you have
heard about the
administration
of God's grace
that was given to
me for you, 3 that
is, the mystery
made known to
me by revelation,
as I have already
written briefly.
4 In reading this,
then, you will be
able to understand
my insight into
the mystery of
Christ, 5 which was
not made known
to people in oth-
er generations as
it has now been
revealed by the
Spirit to God's
holy apostles and
prophets. 6 This
mystery is that
through the gospel
the Gentiles are
heirs together with
Israel, members
together of one
body, and sharers
together in the
promise in Christ
Jesus.
7 I became a ser-
vant of this gos-
pel by the gift of
God's grace given
me through the

ἀποστόλων καὶ προφητῶν, ὄντος ἀκρογωνιαίου αὐτοῦ
apostles and prophets, the cornerstone being *cornerstone* Christ Jesus himself,
693 2779 4737 214 1639 214 5986 2652 899
n.gpm cj n.gpm pt.pa.gsm a.gsm r.gsm

Χριστοῦ Ἰησοῦ, 21 ἐν ᾧ πᾶσα οἰκοδομὴ συναρμολογουμένη αὔξει εἰς
Christ *Jesus* in whom the whole structure, being joined together, grows into a holy
5986 2652 1877 4005 4246 3869 5274 891 1650 41
n.gsm n.gsm p.d r.dsm a.nsf n.nsf pt.pp.nsf v.pai.3s p.a

ναὸν ἅγιον ἐν κυρίῳ, 22 ἐν ᾧ καὶ ὑμεῖς συνοικοδομεῖσθε εἰς
temple *holy* in the Lord, in whom you also *you* are being built together into a
3724 41 1877 3261 1877 4005 7007 2779 7007 5325 1650
n.asm a.asm p.d n.dsm p.d r.dsm adv r.np.2 v.ppi.2p p.a

κατοικητήριον τοῦ θεοῦ ἐν πνεύματι.
dwelling place for God by the Spirit.
2999 3836 2536 1877 4460
n.asn d.gsm n.gsm p.d n.dsn

3:1 ↱ τούτου χάριν ἐγὼ Παῦλος ὁ δέσμιος τοῦ Χριστοῦ Ἰησοῦ[a]
For this reason I, Paul, a prisoner of Christ Jesus
5920 4047 5920 1609 4263 3836 1300 3836 5986 2652
r.gsn p.g r.ns.1 n.nsm d.nsm n.nsm d.gsm n.gsm n.gsm

ὑπὲρ ὑμῶν τῶν ἐθνῶν 2 ⌞εἴ γε⌟ ἠκούσατε τὴν
⌞for the sake of⌟ you *{the}* Gentiles — assuming that ⌞you have heard about⌟ the
5642 7007 3836 1620 1623 1145 201 3836
p.g r.gp.2 d.gpn n.gpn cj pl v.aai.2p d.asf

οἰκονομίαν τῆς χάριτος τοῦ θεοῦ τῆς δοθείσης μοι εἰς ὑμᾶς, 3 ὅτι[b] κατὰ
stewardship of the grace of God that was given to me for you, that by
3873 3836 5921 3836 2536 3836 1443 1609 1650 7007 4022 2848
n.asf d.gsf n.gsf d.gsm n.gsm d.gsf pt.ap.gsf r.ds.1 p.a r.ap.2 cj p.a

ἀποκάλυψιν ἐγνωρίσθη μοι τὸ μυστήριον, καθὼς
revelation the mystery was made known to me, *the* *mystery* as
637 3836 3696 1192 1609 3836 3696 2777
n.asf v.api.3s r.ds.1 d.nsn n.nsn cj

προέγραψα ⌞ἐν ὀλίγῳ,⌟ 4 πρὸς ὃ δύνασθε
⌞I have already written⌟ briefly. Accordingly, when you read this ⌞you will be able⌟
4592 1877 3900 4639 336 336 336 4005 1538
v.aai.1s p.d a.dsn p.a r.asn v.ppi.2p

ἀναγινώσκοντες νοῆσαι τὴν σύνεσίν μου ἐν τῷ μυστηρίῳ τοῦ Χριστοῦ,
when you read to understand *{the}* my insight *my* into the mystery of Christ,
336 3783 3836 1609 5304 1609 1877 3836 3696 3836 5986
pt.pa.npm f.aa d.asf n.asf r.gs.1 p.d d.dsn n.dsn d.gsm n.gsm

5 ὃ ἑτέραις γενεαῖς οὐκ ἐγνωρίσθη
which was not made known to the sons of men in other generations *not* *was made known*
4005 1192 4024 1192 1192 3836 3836 5626 3836 476 2283 1155 4024 1192
r.nsn r.dpf n.dpf pl v.api.3s

τοῖς υἱοῖς τῶν ἀνθρώπων ὡς ↱ ↱ νῦν ἀπεκαλύφθη τοῖς ἁγίοις ἀποστόλοις
to the *sons* *of* *men* as it has now been revealed to his holy apostles
3836 5626 3836 476 6055 636 636 3814 636 3836 899 41 693
d.dpm n.dpm d.gpm n.gpm cj adv v.api.3s d.dpm a.dpm n.dpm

αὐτοῦ καὶ προφήταις ἐν πνεύματι, 6 εἶναι τὰ ἔθνη
his and prophets by the Spirit, namely, that the Gentiles are *the* *Gentiles*
899 2779 4737 1877 4460 3836 1620 1639 3836 1620
r.gsm.3 cj n.dpm p.d n.dsn f.pa d.apn n.apn

συγκληρονόμα καὶ σύσσωμα καὶ συμμέτοχα τῆς ἐπαγγελίας
joint heirs, *{and}* ⌞fellow members of the body⌟ and ⌞sharers together in⌟ the promise
5169 2779 5362 2779 5212 3836 2039
a.apn cj a.apn cj a.apn d.gsf n.gsf

ἐν Χριστῷ Ἰησοῦ διὰ τοῦ εὐαγγελίου, 7 οὗ ἐγενήθην διάκονος
in Christ Jesus through the gospel. ⌞Of this⌟ gospel I became a servant
1877 5986 2652 1328 3836 2295 4005 1181 1356
p.d n.dsm n.dsm p.g d.gsn n.gsn r.gsn v.api.1s n.nsm

κατὰ τὴν δωρεὰν τῆς χάριτος τοῦ θεοῦ τῆς δοθείσης μοι κατὰ τὴν
⌞according to⌟ the gift of God's grace, *{the}* *God's* which was given to me by the
2848 3836 1561 3836 2536 5921 3836 2536 3836 1443 1609 2848 3836
p.a d.asf n.asf d.gsf n.gsf d.gsm n.gsm d.gsf pt.ap.gsf r.ds.1 p.a d.asf

NASB

apostles and proph-
ets, Christ Jesus
Himself being the
corner *stone,* 21 in
whom the whole
building, being
fitted together, is
growing into a
holy temple in the
Lord, 22 in whom
you also are being
built together into a
dwelling of God in
the Spirit.

Paul's Stewardship

3:1 For this reason
I, Paul, the prisoner
of Christ Jesus
for the sake of
you Gentiles— 2 if
indeed you have
heard of the stew-
ardship of God's
grace which was
given to me for
you; 3 that by rev-
elation there was
made known to
me the mystery,
as I wrote before
in brief. 4 By refer-
ring to this, when
you read you can
understand my
insight into the
mystery of Christ,
5 which in other
generations was
not made known to
the sons of men, as
it has now been re-
vealed to His holy
apostles and proph-
ets in the Spirit; 6 *to
be specific,* that the
Gentiles are fellow
heirs and fellow
members of the
body, and fellow
partakers of the
promise in Christ
Jesus through the
gospel, 7 of which
I was made a min-
ister, according to
the gift of God's
grace which was
given to me ac-
cording to the

a [Ἰησοῦ] UBS.
b [ὅτι] UBS.

NIV

working of his power. [8]Although I am less than the least of all the Lord's people, this grace was given me: to preach to the Gentiles the boundless riches of Christ, [9]and to make plain to everyone the administration of this mystery, which for ages past was kept hidden in God, who created all things. [10]His intent was that now, through the church, the manifold wisdom of God should be made known to the rulers and authorities in the heavenly realms, [11]according to his eternal purpose that he accomplished in Christ Jesus our Lord. [12]In him and through faith in him we may approach God with freedom and confidence. [13]I ask you, therefore, not to be discouraged because of my sufferings for you, which are your glory.

A Prayer for the Ephesians

[14]For this reason I kneel before the Father, [15]from whom every family[a] in heaven and on earth derives its name. [16]I pray that out of his glorious riches he may strengthen you with power through his

ἐνέργειαν τῆς δυνάμεως αὐτοῦ. [8]ἐμοὶ τῷ ἐλαχιστοτέρῳ πάντων ἁγίων
exercise of his power. *his* To me, the very least of all the saints, this
1918 3836 899 1539 899 1609 3836 1788 4246 41 4047
n.asf d.gsf n.gsf r.gsm.3 r.ds.1 d.dsm a.dsm.c a.gpm a.gpm

ἐδόθη ἡ χάρις αὕτη, τοῖς ἔθνεσιν εὐαγγελίσασθαι τὸ
grace was given: *{the}* *grace* *this* to preach to the Gentiles *to preach* the
5921 1443 3836 5921 4047 2294 2294 3836 1620 2294 3836
v.api.3s d.nsf n.nsf r.nsf d.dpn n.dpn f.am d.asn

ἀνεξιχνίαστον πλοῦτος τοῦ Χριστοῦ [9]καὶ → → φωτίσαι πάντας[a] τίς ἡ
unsearchable riches of Christ, and to make it plain to all what is the
453 4458 3836 5986 2779 5894 4246 5515 3836
a.asn n.asn d.gsm n.gsm cj f.aa a.apm r.nsf d.nsf

οἰκονομία τοῦ μυστηρίου τοῦ ἀποκεκρυμμένου ἀπὸ τῶν αἰώνων ἐν τῷ θεῷ
administration of the mystery, which was kept hidden for *{the}* ages in *{the}* God
3873 3836 3696 3836 648 608 3836 172 1877 3836 2536
n.nsf d.gsn n.gsn d.gsn pt.rp.gsn p.g d.gpm n.gpm p.d d.dsm n.dsm

τῷ τὰ πάντα κτίσαντι,[b] [10]ἵνα
who created *{the}* all things, *created* ⌊in order that⌋ now, through the church, the manifold
3836 3231 3836 4246 3231 2671 3814 1328 3836 1711 3836 4497
d.dsm d.apn a.apn pt.aa.dsm cj

γνωρισθῇ νῦν ταῖς ἀρχαῖς καὶ ταῖς ἐξουσίαις ἐν τοῖς
wisdom of God ⌊should be made known⌋ *now* to the rulers and *{the}* authorities in the
5053 3836 2536 1192 3814 3836 794 2779 3836 2026 1877 3836
v.aps.3s adv d.dpf n.dpf cj d.dpf n.dpf p.d d.dpn

ἐπουρανίοις διὰ τῆς ἐκκλησίας ἡ πολυποίκιλος σοφία τοῦ θεοῦ,
heavenly realms, *through* *the* *church* *the* *manifold* *wisdom* *of* *God*
2230 1328 3836 1711 3836 4497 5053 3836 2536
a.dpn p.g d.gsf n.gsf d.nsf a.nsf n.nsf d.gsm n.gsm

[11]κατὰ πρόθεσιν τῶν αἰώνων ἣν ἐποίησεν ἐν τῷ Χριστῷ
⌊according to⌋ the eternal purpose *{the}* *eternal* that he accomplished in *{the}* Christ
2848 172 4606 3836 172 4005 4472 1877 3836 5986
p.a n.asf d.gpm n.gpm r.asf v.aai.3s p.d d.dsm n.dsm

Ἰησοῦ τῷ κυρίῳ ἡμῶν, [12]ἐν ᾧ ἔχομεν τὴν παρρησίαν καὶ
Jesus *{the}* our Lord, *our* in whom we have *{the}* boldness and confident
2652 3836 7005 3261 7005 1877 4005 2400 3836 4244 2779 4301
n.dsm d.dsm n.dsm r.gp.1 p.d r.dsm v.pai.1p d.asf n.asf cj

προσαγωγὴν ἐν πεποιθήσει διὰ τῆς πίστεως αὐτοῦ. [13] διὸ
access *{in}* *confident* through *{the}* faith in him. I ask you, therefore,
4643 1877 4301 1328 3836 4411 899 160 160 1475
n.asf p.d n.dsf p.g d.gsf n.gsf r.gsm.3 cj

αἰτοῦμαι μὴ ἐγκακεῖν ἐν ταῖς θλίψεσίν μου ὑπὲρ ὑμῶν, ↰
I ask not to be discouraged ⌊because of⌋ *{the}* my sufferings *my* on your behalf,
160 3590 1591 1877 3836 1609 2568 1609 5642 7007 5642
v.pmi.1s pl f.pa p.d d.dpf n.dpf r.gs.1 p.g r.gp.2

ἥτις ἐστὶν δόξα ὑμῶν. [14] ↱ τούτου χάριν κάμπτω τὰ γόνατά μου πρὸς
which are your glory. *your* For this reason I bow *{the}* my knees *my* before
4015 1639 7007 1518 7007 5920 4047 5920 2828 3836 1609 1205 1609 4639
r.nsf v.pai.3s n.nsf r.gp.2 r.gsn p.g v.pai.1s d.apn n.apn r.gs.1 p.a

τὸν πατέρα,[c] [15]ἐξ οὗ πᾶσα πατριὰ ἐν οὐρανοῖς καὶ ἐπὶ γῆς ὀνομάζεται,
the Father, from whom every family in heaven and on earth derives its name,
3836 4252 1666 4005 4246 4255 1877 4041 2779 2093 1178 3951
d.asm n.asm p.g r.gsm a.nsf n.nsf p.d n.dpm cj p.g n.gsf v.ppi.3s

[16]ἵνα δῷ ὑμῖν κατὰ τὸ
⌊in order that⌋ according to the riches of his glory ⌊he may grant⌋ you *according to* *the*
2671 2848 2848 3836 4458 3836 899 1518 1443 7007 2848 3836
cj v.aas.3s r.dp.2 p.a d.asn

πλοῦτος τῆς δόξης αὐτοῦ δυνάμει κραταιωθῆναι διὰ τοῦ
riches *of* *glory* *his* to be strengthened with power *to be strengthened* through *{the}* his
4458 3836 1518 899 3194 3194 3194 1539 3194 1328 3836 899
n.asn d.gsf n.gsf r.gsm.3 n.dsf f.ap p.g d.gsn

NASB

working of His power. [8]To me, the very least of all saints, this grace was given, to preach to the Gentiles the unfathomable riches of Christ, [9]and to bring to light what is the administration of the mystery which for ages has been hidden in God who created all things; [10]so that the manifold wisdom of God might now be made known through the church to the rulers and the authorities in the heavenly *places.* [11]*This was* in accordance with the eternal purpose which He carried out in Christ Jesus our Lord, [12]in whom we have boldness and confident access through faith in Him. [13]Therefore I ask you not to lose heart at my tribulations on your behalf, for they are your glory.

[14]For this reason I bow my knees before the Father, [15]from whom every family in heaven and on earth derives its name, [16]that He would grant you, according to the riches of His glory, to be strengthened with power through His

[a] 15 The Greek for *family* (*patria*) is derived from the Greek for *father* (*pater*).

[a] [πάντας] UBS.
[b] διὰ Ἰησοῦ Χριστοῦ included by TR after κτίσαντι.
[c] τοῦ Κυρίου ἡμῶν Ἰησοῦ Χριστοῦ included by TR after πατέρα.

NIV

Spirit in your in-
ner being, 17 so that
Christ may dwell
in your hearts
through faith. And
I pray that you,
being rooted and
established in love,
18 may have pow-
er, together with
all the Lord's holy
people, to grasp
how wide and
long and high and
deep is the love
of Christ, 19 and to
know this love that
surpasses knowl-
edge—that you
may be filled to the
measure of all the
fullness of God.
20 Now to him
who is able to do
immeasurably
more than all we
ask or imagine,
according to his
power that is at
work within us,
21 to him be glory
in the church and
in Christ Jesus
throughout all gen-
erations, for ever
and ever! Amen.

Unity and Maturity in the Body of Christ

4 As a prisoner
for the Lord,
then, I urge you to
live a life worthy
of the calling you
have received. 2 Be
completely humble
and gentle; be pa-
tient, bearing with
one another in
love. 3 Make every
effort to keep the
unity of the Spirit
through the bond
of peace. 4 There is
one body and one
Spirit, just as you
were called to one
hope when you
were called; 5 one
Lord,

πνεύματος αὐτοῦ εἰς τὸν ἔσω ἄνθρωπον, 17 κατοικῆσαι τὸν Χριστὸν

Spirit *his* in your inner being, that Christ may dwell *{the}* *Christ* in

4460 899 1650 3836 2276 476 5986 2997 3836 5986 1877

n.gsn r.gsm.3 p.a d.asm adv n.asm f.aa d.asm n.asm

διὰ τῆς πίστεως ἐν ταῖς καρδίαις ὑμῶν, ἐν ἀγάπῃ

your hearts through *{the}* faith, *in* *{the}* *hearts* *your* rooted and grounded in love,

7007 2840 1328 3836 4411 1877 3836 2840 7007 4845 2779 2530 1877 27

p.g d.gsf n.gsf p.d d.dpf n.dpf r.gp.2 p.d n.dsf

ἐρριζωμένοι καὶ τεθεμελιωμένοι, 18 ἵνα ἐξισχύσητε καταλαβέσθαι

rooted *and* *grounded* ⌞in order that⌟ you may be empowered to grasp

4845 2779 2530 2671 2015 2898

pt.rp.npm cj pt.rp.npm cj v.aas.2p f.am

σὺν πᾶσιν τοῖς ἁγίοις τί τὸ πλάτος καὶ μῆκος καὶ ὕψος καὶ βάθος, 19

with all the saints what is the breadth and length and height and depth, and

5250 4246 3836 41 5515 3836 4424 2779 3601 2779 5737 2779 958 5445

p.d a.dpm d.dpm a.dpm r.nsn d.nsn n.nsn cj n.nsn cj n.nsn cj n.nsn

γνῶναί τε τὴν ὑπερβάλλουσαν τῆς γνώσεως ἀγάπην τοῦ Χριστοῦ,

to know *and* the love of Christ which surpasses *{the}* knowledge, *love* *of* *Christ*

1182 5445 3836 27 3836 5986 5650 3836 1194 27 3836 5986

f.aa cj d.asf pt.pa.asf d.gsf n.gsf n.asf d.gsm n.gsm

ἵνα πληρωθῆτε εἰς πᾶν τὸ πλήρωμα τοῦ θεοῦ. 20 τῷ δὲ

that ⌞you may be filled up⌟ to all the fullness of God. Now ⌞to the⌟ *Now*

2671 4444 1650 4246 3836 4445 3836 2536 1254 3836 1254

cj v.aps.2p p.a a.asn d.asn n.asn d.gsm n.gsm d.dsm cj

δυναμένῳ ὑπὲρ πάντα ποιῆσαι ὑπερεκπερισσοῦ ὧν

⌞one who is able⌟ to do far more abundantly beyond all *to do* *far more abundantly* that

1538 4472 4472 5655 5655 5655 5642 4246 4472 5655 4005

pt.pp.dsm p.a a.apn f.aa adv r.gpn

αἰτούμεθα ἢ νοοῦμεν κατὰ τὴν δύναμιν τὴν ἐνεργουμένην ἐν ἡμῖν,

we ask or imagine, ⌞according to⌟ the power that is working within us,

160 2445 3783 2848 3836 1539 3836 1919 1877 7005

v.pmi.1p cj v.pai.1p p.a d.asf n.asf d.asf pt.pm.asf p.d r.dp.1

21 αὐτῷ ἡ δόξα ἐν τῇ ἐκκλησίᾳ καὶ ἐν Χριστῷ Ἰησοῦ εἰς πάσας τὰς

to him be *{the}* glory in the church and in Christ Jesus throughout all *{the}*

899 3836 1518 1877 3836 1711 2779 1877 5986 2652 1650 4246 3836

r.dsm.3 d.nsf n.nsf p.d d.dsf n.dsf cj p.d n.dsm n.dsm p.a a.apf d.apf

γενεᾶς τοῦ αἰῶνος τῶν αἰώνων, ἀμήν.

generations, *{the}* forever and *{the}* ever! Amen.

1155 3836 172 3836 172 297

n.apf d.gsm n.gsm d.gpm n.gpm pl

4:1 παρακαλῶ οὖν ὑμᾶς ἐγὼ ὁ

I therefore, the prisoner in the Lord, exhort *therefore* you *I* *the*

1609 4036 3836 1300 1877 3261 4151 4036 7007 1609 3836

v.pai.1s cj r.ap.2 r.ns.1 d.nsm

δέσμιος ἐν κυρίῳ ἀξίως περιπατῆσαι τῆς κλήσεως ἧς

prisoner *in* *Lord* to lead a life worthy *to lead a life* of the calling ⌞with which⌟

1300 1877 3261 4344 4344 4344 4344 547 4344 3836 3104 4005

n.nsm p.d n.dsm adv f.aa d.gsf n.gsf r.gsf

ἐκλήθητε, 2 μετὰ πάσης ταπεινοφροσύνης καὶ πραΰτητος, μετὰ μακροθυμίας,

you were called, with all humility and gentleness, with patience,

2813 3552 4246 5425 2779 4559 3552 3429

v.api.2p p.g a.gsf n.gsf cj n.gsf p.g n.gsf

ἀνεχόμενοι ἀλλήλων ἐν ἀγάπῃ, 3 σπουδάζοντες τηρεῖν τὴν ἑνότητα τοῦ

bearing with one another in love, making every effort to preserve the unity of the

462 253 1877 27 5079 5498 3836 1942 3836

pt.pm.npm r.gpm p.d n.dsf pt.pa.npm f.pa d.asf n.asf d.gsn

πνεύματος ἐν τῷ συνδέσμῳ τῆς εἰρήνης· 4 Ἓν σῶμα καὶ ἓν πνεῦμα,

Spirit by the bond of peace. There is one body and one Spirit,

4460 1877 3836 5278 3836 1645 1651 5393 2779 1651 4460

n.gsn p.d d.dsm n.dsm d.gsf n.gsf a.nsn n.nsn cj a.nsn n.nsn

καθὼς καὶ ἐκλήθητε ἐν μιᾷ ἐλπίδι τῆς κλήσεως ὑμῶν· 5 εἷς κύριος,

just as you also were called to the one hope of your calling; *your* one Lord,

2777 2779 2813 1877 1651 1828 3836 7007 3104 7007 1651 3261

cj adv v.api.2p p.d a.dsf n.dsf d.gsf n.gsf r.gp.2 a.nsm n.nsm

NASB

Spirit in the inner
man, 17 so that
Christ may dwell in
your hearts through
faith; *and* that you,
being rooted and
grounded in love,
18 may be able to
comprehend with
all the saints what
is the breadth and
length and height
and depth, 19 and to
know the love of
Christ which sur-
passes knowledge,
that you may be
filled up to all the
fullness of God.
20 Now to Him
who is able to do
far more abundant-
ly beyond all that
we ask or think,
according to the
power that works
within us, 21 to Him
be the glory in
the church and in
Christ Jesus to all
generations forever
and ever. Amen.

Unity of the Spirit

4:1 Therefore I,
the prisoner of
the Lord, implore
you to walk in a
manner worthy of
the calling with
which you have
been called, 2 with
all humility and
gentleness, with
patience, showing
tolerance for one
another in love,
3 being diligent to
preserve the unity
of the Spirit in the
bond of peace.
4 *There is* one body
and one Spirit, just
as also you were
called in one hope
of your calling;
5 one Lord,

NIV

one faith, one bap-
tism; [6]one God
and Father of all,
who is over all and
through all and
in all.
[7]But to each one
of us grace has
been given as
Christ apportioned
it. [8]This is why it[a]
says:

"When he
ascended
on high,
he took many
captives
and gave
gifts to his
people."[b]

[9](What does "he
ascended" mean
except that he also
descended to the
lower, earthly re-
gions[c]? [10]He who
descended is the
very one who as-
cended higher than
all the heavens,
in order to fill the
whole universe.)
[11]So Christ himself
gave the apostles,
the prophets, the
evangelists, the
pastors and teach-
ers, [12]to equip his
people for works
of service, so that
the body of Christ
may be built up
[13]until we all reach
unity in the faith
and in the knowl-
edge of the Son of
God and become
mature, attaining
to the whole mea-
sure of the fullness
of Christ.
[14]Then we will no
longer be infants,
tossed back and
forth by the waves,
and blown here
and there by every
wind of teaching
and by the cunning
and craftiness of
people in their de-
ceitful scheming.

[a] 8 Or *God*
[b] 8 Psalm 68:18
[c] 9 Or *the depths of the earth*

μία πίστις, ἓν βάπτισμα, [6]εἷς θεὸς καὶ πατὴρ πάντων, ὁ ἐπὶ πάντων καὶ
one faith, one baptism; one God and Father of all, who is above all and
1651 4411 1651 967 1651 2536 2779 4252 4246 3836 2093 4246 2779
a.nsf n.nsf a.nsn n.nsn a.nsm n.nsm cj n.nsm a.gpm d.nsm p.g a.gpm cj

διὰ πάντων καὶ ἐν πᾶσιν. [7] → ἑνὶ δὲ ἑκάστῳ ἡμῶν ἐδόθη ἡ
through all and in all. But to each one *But* *each* of us grace was given *{the}*
1328 4246 2779 1877 4246 1254 1667 1651 1254 1667 7005 5921 1443 3836
p.g a.gpm cj p.d a.dpm a.dsm cj r.dsm r.gp.1 v.api.3s d.nsf

χάρις κατὰ τὸ μέτρον τῆς δωρεᾶς τοῦ Χριστοῦ. [8]διὸ λέγει,
grace ⌊according to⌋ the measure of the gift of Christ. Therefore it says,
5921 2848 3836 3586 3836 1561 3836 5986 1475 3306
n.nsf p.a d.asn n.asn d.gsf n.gsf d.gsm n.gsm cj v.pai.3s

ἀναβὰς εἰς ὕψος ᾐχμαλώτευσεν αἰχμαλωσίαν, ↰ ἔδωκεν δόματα
⌊"When he ascended⌋ on high he led a host of prisoners captive; he gave gifts
326 1650 5737 169 168 169 1443 1517
pt.aa.nsm p.a n.asn v.aai.3s n.asf v.aai.3s n.apn

τοῖς ἀνθρώποις. [9] τὸ δὲ ἀνέβη τί ἐστιν, ⌊εἰ μὴ⌋
to men." Now the *Now* expression "he ascended," what ⌊does it imply⌋ except
3836 476 1254 3836 1254 326 5515 1639 1623 3590
d.dpm n.dpm d.nsn cj v.aai.3s r.nsn v.pai.3s cj pl

ὅτι ↱ καὶ κατέβη εἰς τὰ κατώτερα μέρη[a] τῆς γῆς; [10]ὁ καταβὰς
that he also descended to the lower regions, to the earth? He who descended is
4022 2849 2779 2849 1650 3836 3005 3538 3836 1178 3836 2849 1639
cj adv v.aai.3s p.a d.apn a.apn.c n.apn d.gsf n.gsf d.nsm pt.aa.nsm

αὐτός ἐστιν ↱ ↱ καὶ ὁ ἀναβὰς ὑπεράνω πάντων τῶν οὐρανῶν, ἵνα
himself *is* the one who also *the* ascended far above all the heavens, so that
899 1639 3836 326 326 2779 3836 326 5645 4246 3836 4041 2671
r.nsm v.pai.3s adv d.nsm pt.aa.nsm p.g a.gpm d.gpm n.gpm cj

πληρώσῃ τὰ πάντα. [11]καὶ αὐτὸς ἔδωκεν τοὺς μὲν ἀποστόλους, τοὺς δὲ
he might fill *{the}* all things. And it was he who gave the ~ apostles, the *{and}*
4444 3836 4246 2779 899 1443 3836 3525 693 3836 1254
v.aas.3s d.apn a.apn cj r.nsm v.aai.3s d.apm pl n.apm d.apm pl

προφήτας, τοὺς δὲ εὐαγγελιστάς, τοὺς δὲ ποιμένας καὶ διδασκάλους, [12]πρὸς
prophets, the *{and}* evangelists, the *{and}* pastors and teachers, to
4737 3836 1254 2296 3836 1254 4478 2779 1437 4639
n.apm d.apm pl n.apm d.apm pl n.apm cj n.apm p.a

τὸν καταρτισμὸν τῶν ἁγίων εἰς ἔργον διακονίας, εἰς οἰκοδομὴν τοῦ σώματος
{the} equip the saints for the work of ministry, to build up the body
3836 2938 3836 41 1650 2240 1355 1650 3869 3836 5393
d.asm n.asm d.gpm a.gpm p.a n.asn n.gsf p.a n.asf d.gsn n.gsn

τοῦ Χριστοῦ, [13]μέχρι → καταντήσωμεν οἱ πάντες εἰς τὴν ἑνότητα τῆς
of Christ, until we all attain *{the}* *all* to the unity of the
3836 5986 3588 4246 2918 3836 4246 1650 3836 1942 3836
d.gsm n.gsm cj v.aas.1p d.npm a.npm p.a d.asf n.asf d.gsf

πίστεως καὶ τῆς ἐπιγνώσεως τοῦ υἱοῦ τοῦ θεοῦ, εἰς ἄνδρα τέλειον, εἰς
faith and of the knowledge of the Son of God, to mature adulthood, *mature* to
4411 2779 3836 2106 3836 5626 3836 2536 1650 5455 467 5455 1650
n.gsf cj d.gsf n.gsf d.gsm n.gsm d.gsm n.gsm p.a n.asm a.asm p.a

μέτρον → ἡλικίας τοῦ πληρώματος τοῦ Χριστοῦ, [14]ἵνα ↱ ↱ μηκέτι
the measure of the stature of the fullness of Christ, so that we may no longer
3586 2461 3836 4445 3836 5986 2671 1639 1639 3600
n.asn n.gsf d.gsn n.gsn d.gsm n.gsm cj adv

ὦμεν νήπιοι, κλυδωνιζόμενοι καὶ περιφερόμενοι παντὶ ἀνέμῳ τῆς διδασκαλίας ἐν
be children, tossed to and fro and blown about by every wind of doctrine, by
1639 3758 3115 2779 4367 4246 449 3836 1436 1877
v.pas.1p n.npm pt.pp.npm cj pt.pp.npm a.dsm n.dsm d.gsf n.gsf p.d

τῇ κυβείᾳ τῶν ἀνθρώπων, ἐν πανουργίᾳ πρὸς τὴν μεθοδείαν τῆς
{the} human cunning, *{the}* *human* by craftiness in *{the}* deceitful scheming; *{the}*
3836 476 3235 3836 476 1877 4111 4639 3836 4415 3497 3836
d.dsf n.dsf d.gpm n.gpm p.d n.dsf p.a d.asf n.asf d.gsf

[a] [μέρη] UBS.

NASB

one faith, one
baptism, [6]one God
and Father of all
who is over all and
through all and
in all.
[7]But to each one
of us grace was
given according
to the measure
of Christ's gift.
[8]Therefore it says,

"When He
ascended on
high,
He led captive
a host of
captives,
And He gave
gifts to men."

[9](Now this *ex-
pression,* "He
ascended," what
does it mean ex-
cept that He also
had descended into
the lower parts of
the earth? [10]He who
descended is Him-
self also He who
ascended far above
all the heavens, so
that He might fill
all things.) [11]And
He gave some
as apostles, and
some *as* proph-
ets, and some *as*
evangelists, and
some *as* pastors
and teachers, [12]for
the equipping of
the saints for the
work of service, to
the building up of
the body of Christ;
[13]until we all at-
tain to the unity of
the faith, and of
the knowledge of
the Son of God,
to a mature man,
to the measure of
the stature which
belongs to the full-
ness of Christ. [14]As
a result, we are no
longer to be chil-
dren, tossed here
and there by waves
and carried about
by every wind of
doctrine, by the
trickery of men, by
craftiness in deceit-
ful scheming;

NIV

15 Instead, speaking
the truth in love,
we will grow to
become in every
respect the mature
body of him who
is the head, that is,
Christ. 16 From him
the whole body,
joined and held
together by every
supporting liga-
ment, grows and
builds itself up in
love, as each part
does its work.

Instructions for Christian Living

17 So I tell you
this, and insist
on it in the Lord,
that you must no
longer live as the
Gentiles do, in the
futility of their
thinking. 18 They
are darkened in
their understand-
ing and separated
from the life of
God because of the
ignorance that is
in them due to the
hardening of their
hearts. 19 Having
lost all sensitivity,
they have given
themselves over to
sensuality so as to
indulge in every
kind of impurity,
and they are full of
greed.
20 That, however,
is not the way of
life you learned
21 when you heard
about Christ and
were taught in him
in accordance with
the truth that is in
Jesus. 22 You were
taught, with regard
to your former
way of life, to put
off your old self,
which is being
corrupted

πλάνης, 15 ἀληθεύοντες δὲ ἐν ἀγάπῃ αὐξήσωμεν εἰς αὐτὸν τὰ
deceitful but, speaking the truth *but* in love, may grow up in every way into him *{the}*
4415 1254 238 1254 1877 27 889 4246 4246 1650 899 3836
n.gsf pt.pa.npm cj p.d n.dsf v.aas.1p p.a r.asm.3 d.apn

πάντα, ὅς ἐστιν ἡ κεφαλή, Χριστός, 16 ἐξ οὗ πᾶν τὸ σῶμα
every way who is the head, Christ, from whom the whole *the* body,
4246 4005 1639 3836 3051 5986 1666 4005 3836 4246 3836 5393
a.apn r.nsm v.pai.3s d.nsf n.nsf n.nsm p.g r.gsm a.nsn d.nsn n.nsn

συναρμολογούμενον καὶ συμβιβαζόμενον διὰ πάσης ἁφῆς τῆς
joined and brought together by every supporting ligament, *{the}*
5274 2779 5204 1328 4246 2221 913 3836
pt.pp.nsn cj pt.pp.nsn p.g a.gsf n.gsf d.gsf

ἐπιχορηγίας κατ' ἐνέργειαν ἐν μέτρῳ ἑνὸς ἑκάστου μέρους
supporting ⌊according to⌋ the working of *{measure}* each individual *each* part,
2221 2848 1918 1877 3586 1667 1651 1667 3538
n.gsf p.a n.asf p.d n.dsn a.gsn r.gsn n.gsn

τὴν αὔξησιν τοῦ σώματος ποιεῖται εἰς οἰκοδομὴν ἑαυτοῦ ↰
makes the body *{the}* grow *the* *body* *makes* ⌊so that⌋ it builds itself up
4472 3836 5393 3836 890 3836 5393 4472 1650 3869 1571 3869
d.asf n.asf d.gsn n.gsn v.pmi.3s p.a n.asf r.gsn.3

ἐν ἀγάπῃ. 17 τοῦτο οὖν λέγω καὶ μαρτύρομαι ἐν κυρίῳ, ↱
in love. Now this *Now* I say and testify in the Lord, that you are
1877 27 4036 4047 4036 3306 2779 3458 1877 3261 7007 4344
p.d n.dsf r.asn cj v.pai.1s cj v.pmi.1s p.d n.dsm

μηκέτι ὑμᾶς περιπατεῖν, καθὼς καὶ τὰ ἔθνη περιπατεῖ ἐν ματαιότητι τοῦ
no longer *you* to live as *{also}* the Gentiles live, in the futility of
3600 7007 4344 2777 2779 3836 1620 4344 1877 3470 3836
adv r.ap.2 f.pa cj adv d.npn n.npn v.pai.3s p.d n.dsf d.gsm

νοὸς αὐτῶν, 18 ἐσκοτωμένοι τῇ διανοίᾳ ὄντες, ἀπηλλοτριωμένοι
their minds, *their* being darkened ⌊in their⌋ understanding, *being* separated from
899 3808 899 1639 5031 3836 1379 1639 558
n.gsm r.gpm.3 pt.rp.npm d.dsf n.dsf pt.pa.npm pt.rp.npm

τῆς ζωῆς τοῦ θεοῦ διὰ τὴν ἄγνοιαν τὴν οὖσαν ἐν αὐτοῖς, διὰ τὴν
the life of God ⌊because of⌋ the ignorance that is in them ⌊due to⌋ the
3836 2437 3836 2536 1328 3836 53 3836 1639 1877 899 1328 3836
d.gsf n.gsf d.gsm n.gsm p.a d.asf n.asf d.asf pt.pa.asf p.d r.dpm.3 p.a d.asf

πώρωσιν τῆς καρδίας αὐτῶν, 19 οἵτινες
hardening of their hearts. *their* Having lost all feeling of shame, they
4801 3836 899 2840 899 556 556 556 556 556 556 4015
n.asf d.gsf n.gsf r.gpm.3 r.npm

ἀπηλγηκότες ↱ ↱ ἑαυτοὺς παρέδωκαν τῇ ἀσελγείᾳ εἰς
Having lost all feeling of shame have given themselves over to debauchery for the
556 4140 4140 1571 4140 3836 816 1650
pt.ra.npm r.apm.3 v.aai.3p d.dsf n.dsf p.a

ἐργασίαν → ἀκαθαρσίας πάσης ἐν πλεονεξίᾳ. 20
practice of every kind of impurity *every kind* with covetousness. But that is not
2238 4246 4246 174 4246 1877 4432 1254 4048 4048 4024
n.asf n.gsf a.gsf p.d n.dsf

ὑμεῖς δὲ οὐχ οὕτως ἐμάθετε τὸν Χριστόν, 21 ⌊εἴ γε⌋
the way you *But* *not* *that is the way* learned *{the}* Christ! — assuming that you
4048 4048 7007 1254 4024 4048 3443 3836 5986 1623 1145 201
r.np.2 cj pl adv v.aai.2p d.asm n.asm cj pl

αὐτὸν ἠκούσατε καὶ ἐν αὐτῷ ἐδιδάχθητε, καθώς
have heard of him *you have heard of* and were taught in him, *were taught* as the truth
201 201 201 899 201 2779 1438 1438 1877 899 1438 2777 237
r.asm.3 v.aai.2p cj p.d r.dsm.3 v.api.2p cj

ἐστιν ἀλήθεια ἐν τῷ Ἰησοῦ, 22 ἀποθέσθαι ὑμᾶς κατὰ τὴν προτέραν
is *truth* in *{the}* Jesus. *to put away* *you* Regarding your former
1639 237 1877 3836 2652 700 7007 2848 3836 4728
v.pai.3s n.nsf p.d d.dsm n.dsm f.am r.ap.2 p.a d.asf a.asf.c

ἀναστροφὴν τὸν παλαιὸν ἄνθρωπον τὸν φθειρόμενον
way of life, you were taught to put away your old self, which is being corrupted
419 7007 700 700 700 3836 4094 476 3836 5780
n.asf d.asm a.asm n.asm d.asm pt.pp.asm

NASB

15 but speaking the
truth in love, we
are to grow up in
all *aspects* into
Him who is the
head, *even* Christ,
16 from whom the
whole body, being
fitted and held
together by what
every joint sup-
plies, according to
the proper working
of each individual
part, causes the
growth of the body
for the building up
of itself in love.

The Christian's Walk

17 So this I say,
and affirm together
with the Lord, that
you walk no longer
just as the Gentiles
also walk, in the
futility of their
mind, 18 being dark-
ened in their under-
standing, excluded
from the life of
God because of the
ignorance that is
in them, because
of the hardness of
their heart; 19 and
they, having be-
come callous, have
given themselves
over to sensuality
for the practice of
every kind of im-
purity with greedi-
ness. 20 But you did
not learn Christ in
this way, 21 if indeed
you have heard
Him and have been
taught in Him, just
as truth is in Jesus,
22 that, in reference
to your former
manner of life, you
lay aside the old
self, which is being
corrupted in

NIV

by its deceitful de-
sires; [23]to be made
new in the attitude
of your minds;
[24]and to put on the
new self, created to
be like God in true
righteousness and
holiness.
[25]Therefore each
of you must put
off falsehood and
speak truthfully
to your neigh-
bor, for we are all
members of one
body. [26]"In your
anger do not sin"[a]:
Do not let the sun
go down while
you are still an-
gry, [27]and do not
give the devil a
foothold. [28]Any-
one who has been
stealing must steal
no longer, but must
work, doing some-
thing useful with
their own hands,
that they may have
something to share
with those in need.
[29]Do not let any
unwholesome talk
come out of your
mouths, but only
what is helpful for
building others up
according to their
needs, that it may
benefit those who
listen. [30]And do
not grieve the Holy
Spirit of God, with
whom you were
sealed for the day
of redemption.
[31]Get rid of all bit-
terness, rage and
anger, brawling
and slander, along
with every form of
malice. [32]Be kind
and compassionate
to one another, for-
giving

κατὰ τὰς ἐπιθυμίας τῆς ἀπάτης, 23 ἀνανεοῦσθαι δὲ τῷ πνεύματι
and deluded by its desires, {the} deluded and to be renewed and ⌊in the⌋ spirit
573 2848 3836 2123 3836 573 1254 391 1254 3836 4460
p.a d.apf n.apf d.gsf n.gsf f.pp cj d.dsn n.dsn

τοῦ νοὸς ὑμῶν 24 καὶ ἐνδύσασθαι τὸν καινὸν ἄνθρωπον τὸν κατὰ
of your minds. your And to put on the new self, {the} created in
3836 7007 3808 7007 2779 1907 3836 2785 476 3836 3231 2848
d.gsm n.gsm r.gp.2 cj f.am d.asm a.asm n.asm d.asm p.a

θεὸν ↰ κτισθέντα ἐν δικαιοσύνῃ καὶ ὁσιότητι τῆς ἀληθείας.
God's likeness, created in the righteousness and holiness ⌊that come from the⌋ truth.
2536 2848 3231 1877 1466 2779 4009 3836 237
n.asm pt.ap.asm p.d n.dsf cj n.dsf d.gsf n.gsf

25 διὸ ἀποθέμενοι τὸ ψεῦδος → λαλεῖτε ἀλήθειαν ἕκαστος μετὰ
Therefore put off {the} falsehood and let each one speak the truth each one with
1475 700 3836 6022 1667 1667 3281 237 1667 3552
cj pt.am.npm d.asn n.asn v.pam.2p n.asf r.nsm p.g

τοῦ πλησίον αὐτοῦ, ὅτι ἐσμὲν ἀλλήλων μέλη. 26 ὀργίζεσθε καὶ
{the} his neighbor, his for we are members of one another. members If you get angry, {and}
3836 899 4446 899 4022 1639 3517 253 3517 3974 2779
d.gsm adv r.gsm.3 cj v.pai.1p r.gpm n.npn v.ppm.2p cj

↱ μὴ ἁμαρτάνετε· ↱ ↱ ὁ ἥλιος μὴ ἐπιδυέτω ἐπὶ τῷ[a] παροργισμῷ
do not sin; do not allow the sun not to go down on {the} your anger
279 3590 279 2115 3590 2115 3836 2463 3590 2115 2093 3836 7007 4240
pl v.pam.2p d.nsm n.nsm pl v.pam.3s p.d d.dsm n.dsm

ὑμῶν, 27 μηδὲ → ← δίδοτε τόπον τῷ διαβόλῳ. 28 ↱ ὁ κλέπτων μηκέτι
your and do not give an opportunity ⌊to the⌋ devil. Let the thief no longer
7007 3593 1443 5536 3836 1333 3096 3836 3096 3600
r.gp.2 cj v.pam.2p n.asm d.dsm n.dsm d.nsm pt.pa.nsm adv

κλεπτέτω, μᾶλλον δὲ κοπιάτω ἐργαζόμενος ταῖς ἰδίαις[b] χερσὶν τὸ
steal, but rather but ⌊let him work hard,⌋ doing good with his own hands, {the}
3096 1254 3437 1254 3159 2237 19 3836 2625 5931 3836
v.pam.3s adv.c cj v.pam.3s pt.pm.nsm d.dpf a.dpf n.dpf d.asn

ἀγαθόν, ἵνα ἔχῃ μεταδιδόναι τῷ χρείαν ἔχοντι. 29
good so that ⌊he may have⌋ ⌊something to share with⌋ the one in need. one in Let
19 2671 2400 3556 3836 2400 2400 5970 2400 1744
a.asn cj v.pas.3s f.pa d.dsm n.asf pt.pa.dsm

⌊πᾶς λόγος⌋ σαπρὸς ἐκ τοῦ στόματος ὑμῶν μὴ ἐκπορευέσθω,
no evil talk evil come ⌊out of⌋ {the} your mouth, your no Let come
3590 4911 4246 3364 4911 1744 1666 3836 7007 5125 7007 3590 1744
a.nsm n.nsm a.nsm p.g d.gsn n.gsn r.gp.2 pl v.pmm.3s

ἀλλὰ εἴ τις ἀγαθὸς πρὸς οἰκοδομὴν τῆς χρείας, ἵνα ⌊δῷ χάριν⌋
but only what is useful for building up, as the need arises, that it may benefit
247 1623 5516 19 4639 3869 3836 5970 2671 1443 5921
cj cj r.nsm a.nsm p.a n.asf d.gsf n.gsf cj v.aas.3s n.asf

τοῖς ἀκούουσιν. 30 καὶ ↱ μὴ λυπεῖτε τὸ πνεῦμα τὸ ἅγιον τοῦ θεοῦ, ἐν
those who hear. And do not grieve the Holy Spirit {the} holy of God, in
3836 201 2779 3382 3590 3382 3836 41 4460 3836 41 3836 2536 1877
d.dpm pt.pa.dpm cj pl v.pam.2p d.asn n.asn d.asn a.asn d.gsm n.gsm p.d

ᾧ ἐσφραγίσθητε εἰς ἡμέραν ἀπολυτρώσεως. 31 ↱ πᾶσα πικρία καὶ θυμὸς
whom you were sealed for the day of redemption. Let all bitterness and wrath
4005 5381 1650 2465 667 149 4246 4394 2779 2596
r.dsn v.api.2p p.a n.asf n.gsf a.nsf n.nsf cj n.nsm

καὶ ὀργὴ καὶ κραυγὴ καὶ βλασφημία ἀρθήτω ἀφ' ὑμῶν σὺν πάσῃ κακίᾳ.
and anger and clamor and slander be removed from you, ⌊along with⌋ all malice.
2779 3973 2779 3199 2779 1060 149 608 7007 5250 4246 2798
cj n.nsf cj n.nsf cj n.nsf v.apm.3s p.g r.gp.2 p.d a.dsf n.dsf

32 γίνεσθε δὲ[c] εἰς ἀλλήλους χρηστοί, εὔσπλαγχνοι, χαριζόμενοι
Instead, be Instead kind to one another, kind tenderhearted, forgiving
1254 1181 1254 5982 1650 253 5982 2359 5919
v.pmm.2p cj p.a r.apm a.npm a.npm pt.pm.npm

NASB

accordance with
the lusts of deceit,
[23]and that you be
renewed in the
spirit of your mind,
[24]and put on the
new self, which in
the likeness of God
has been created
in righteousness
and holiness of the
truth.
[25]Therefore, lay-
ing aside false-
hood, SPEAK TRUTH
EACH ONE *of you*
WITH HIS NEIGHBOR,
for we are mem-
bers of one another.
[26]BE ANGRY, AND *yet*
DO NOT SIN; do not
let the sun go down
on your anger,
[27]and do not give
the devil an op-
portunity. [28]He who
steals must steal no
longer; but rather
he must labor, per-
forming with his
own hands what
is good, so that he
will have *some-
thing* to share with
one who has need.
[29]Let no unwhole-
some word proceed
from your mouth,
but only such *a
word* as is good for
edification accord-
ing to the need *of
the moment,* so that
it will give grace
to those who hear.
[30]Do not grieve
the Holy Spirit of
God, by whom you
were sealed for the
day of redemption.
[31]Let all bitterness
and wrath and
anger and clamor
and slander be put
away from you,
along with all
malice. [32]Be kind
to one another,
tender-hearted, for-
giving each

[a] 26 Psalm 4:4 (see Septuagint)

[a] [τῷ] UBS.
[b] [ἰδίαις] UBS.
[c] [δὲ] UBS, omitted by NET.

NIV

each other, just as
in Christ God for-
gave you.
5 [1]Follow God's
example,
therefore, as dear-
ly loved children
[2]and walk in the
way of love, just
as Christ loved us
and gave himself
up for us as a fra-
grant offering and
sacrifice to God.
[3]But among you
there must not be
even a hint of sex-
ual immorality, or
of any kind of im-
purity, or of greed,
because these are
improper for God's
holy people. [4]Nor
should there be
obscenity, foolish
talk or coarse jok-
ing, which are out
of place, but rather
thanksgiving. [5]For
of this you can be
sure: No immoral,
impure or greedy
person—such a
person is an idol-
ater—has any
inheritance in the
kingdom of Christ
and of God.[a] [6]Let
no one deceive you
with empty words,
for because of such
things God's wrath
comes on those
who are disobe-
dient. [7]Therefore
do not be partners
with them.
[8]For you were
once darkness, but
now you are light
in the Lord. Live
as children of light
[9](for the fruit of
the light consists
in all goodness,
righteousness and
truth) [10]and find
out what pleases
the Lord. [11]Have
nothing to do

[a] 5 Or *kingdom of the Messiah and God*

ἑαυτοῖς, καθὼς καὶ ὁ θεὸς ἐν Χριστῷ ἐχαρίσατο ὑμῖν.
one another, just as *{also}* *{the}* God in Christ forgave you.
1571 2777 2779 3836 2536 1877 5986 5919 7007
r.dpm.2 cj adv d.nsm n.nsm p.d n.dsm v.ami.3s r.dp.2

5:1 γίνεσθε οὖν μιμηταὶ τοῦ θεοῦ ὡς τέκνα ἀγαπητά
Therefore be *Therefore* imitators of God as his dear children, *dear*
4036 1181 4036 3629 3836 2536 6055 28 5451 28
v.pmm.2p cj n.npm d.gsm n.gsm pl n.npn a.npn

2 καὶ περιπατεῖτε ἐν ἀγάπῃ, καθὼς καὶ ὁ Χριστὸς ἠγάπησεν ἡμᾶς καὶ
and live in love, just as *{also}* *{the}* Christ loved us and
2779 4344 1877 27 2777 2779 3836 5986 26 7005 2779
cj v.pam.2p p.d n.dsf cj adv d.nsm n.nsm v.aai.3s r.ap.1 cj

παρέδωκεν ἑαυτὸν ὑπὲρ ἡμῶν προσφορὰν καὶ θυσίαν τῷ θεῷ εἰς
gave himself for us as a fragrant offering and sacrifice to God. *as*
4140 1571 5642 7005 1650 4011 4714 2779 2602 3836 2536 1650
v.aai.3s r.asm.3 p.g r.gp.1 n.asf cj n.asf d.dsm n.dsm p.a

⌞ὀσμὴν εὐωδίας.⌟ 3 πορνεία δὲ καὶ ἀκαθαρσία πᾶσα
fragrant But sexual immorality *But* and every kind of impurity *every kind of*
4011 2380 1254 4518 1254 2779 4246 4246 4246 174 4246
n.asf n.gsf n.nsf cj cj n.nsf a.nsf

ἢ πλεονεξία ➝ μηδὲ ὀνομαζέσθω ἐν ὑμῖν, καθὼς πρέπει → ἁγίοις,
or covetousness must not even be mentioned among you, as is proper among the saints;
2445 4432 3951 3593 3951 1877 7007 2777 4560 41
cj n.nsf adv v.ppm.3s p.d r.dp.2 cj v.pai.3s a.dpm

4 καὶ αἰσχρότης καὶ μωρολογία ἢ εὐτραπελία, ἃ ➝ οὐκ ἀνῆκεν, ἀλλὰ μᾶλλον
nor obscenity, *{and}* foolish talk, or coarse joking, which are not fitting, but rather
2779 157 2779 3703 2445 2365 4005 465 4024 465 247 3437
cj n.nsf cj n.nsf cj n.nsf r.npn pl v.iai.3s cj adv.c

εὐχαριστία. 5 τοῦτο γὰρ ⌞ἴστε γινώσκοντες,⌟ ὅτι
thanksgiving. For you may be sure of this, *For* *you may be sure of* that
2374 1142 3857 3857 3857 3857 3857 4047 1142 3857 1182 4022
n.nsf r.asn cj v.ram.2p pt.pa.npm cj

πᾶς πόρνος ἢ ἀκάθαρτος ἢ πλεονέκτης, ὅ ἐστιν
{every} no fornicator or impure or covetous person ⌞(such a one⌟ is an
4246 4024 4521 2445 176 2445 4431 4005 1639
a.nsm n.nsm cj a.nsm cj n.nsm r.nsn v.pai.3s

εἰδωλολάτρης, οὐκ ἔχει κληρονομίαν ἐν τῇ βασιλείᾳ τοῦ Χριστοῦ καὶ θεοῦ.
idolater) *no* has any inheritance in the kingdom of Christ and of God.
1629 4024 2400 3100 1877 3836 993 3836 5986 2779 2536
n.nsm pl v.pai.3s n.asf p.d d.dsf n.dsf d.gsm n.gsm cj n.gsm

6 μηδεὶς ὑμᾶς ἀπατάτω κενοῖς λόγοις· διὰ ταῦτα γὰρ
Let no one deceive you *Let deceive* with empty words, for ⌞because of⌟ these things *for* the
572 3594 572 7007 572 3031 3364 1142 1328 4047 1142 3836
a.nsm r.ap.2 v.pam.3s a.dpm n.dpm p.a r.apn cj

ἔρχεται ἡ ὀργὴ τοῦ θεοῦ ἐπὶ τοὺς υἱοὺς τῆς ἀπειθείας. 7
wrath of God comes *the* *wrath of* *God* upon the sons of disobedience. Therefore
3973 3836 2536 2262 3836 3973 3836 2536 2093 3836 5626 3836 577 4036
v.pmi.3s d.nsf n.nsf d.gsm n.gsm p.a d.apm n.apm d.gsf n.gsf

➝ μὴ οὖν γίνεσθε συμμέτοχοι αὐτῶν· 8 ἦτε γὰρ ποτε σκότος,
do not *Therefore* become partners with them; for once ⌞you were⌟ *for* *once* darkness, but
1181 3590 4036 1181 5212 899 1142 4537 1639 1142 4537 5030 1254
pl cj v.pmm.2p n.npm r.gpm.3 v.iai.2p cj adv n.nsn

νῦν δὲ φῶς ἐν κυρίῳ· ὡς τέκνα φωτὸς περιπατεῖτε 9 ὁ γὰρ
now *but* you are light in the Lord. Live as children of light *Live* (for the *for*
3814 1254 5890 1877 3261 4344 6055 5451 5890 4344 1142 3836 1142
adv cj n.nsn p.d n.dsm pl n.npn n.gsn v.pam.2p d.nsm cj

καρπὸς τοῦ φωτὸς ἐν πάσῃ ἀγαθωσύνῃ καὶ δικαιοσύνῃ καὶ ἀληθείᾳ
fruit of light consists in all goodness, *{and}* righteousness, and truth),
2843 3836 5890 1877 4246 20 2779 1466 2779 237
n.nsm d.gsn n.gsn p.d a.dsf n.dsf cj n.dsf cj n.dsf

10 δοκιμάζοντες τί ἐστιν εὐάρεστον τῷ κυρίῳ, 11 καὶ ➝ μὴ
⌞always trying to discern⌟ what is pleasing ⌞to the⌟ Lord. And do not
1507 5515 1639 2298 3836 3261 2779 5170 3590
pt.pa.npm r.nsn v.pai.3s a.nsn d.dsm n.dsm cj pl

NASB

other, just as God
in Christ also has
forgiven [a]you.

Be Imitators of God

[5:1]Therefore be
imitators of God,
as beloved chil-
dren; [2]and walk in
love, just as Christ
also loved [b]you and
gave Himself up
for us, an offering
and a sacrifice to
God as a fragrant
aroma.
[3]But immorality
or any impurity
or greed must not
even be named
among you, as
is proper among
saints; [4]and *there*
must be no filthi-
ness and silly talk,
or coarse jesting,
which are not fit-
ting, but rather giv-
ing of thanks. [5]For
this you know with
certainty, that no
immoral or impure
person or covet-
ous man, who is
an idolater, has an
inheritance in the
kingdom of Christ
and God.
[6]Let no one de-
ceive you with
empty words, for
because of these
things the wrath of
God comes upon
the sons of disobe-
dience. [7]Therefore
do not be partakers
with them; [8]for
you were formerly
darkness, but now
you are Light in
the Lord; walk as
children of Light
[9](for the fruit of the
Light *consists* in
all goodness and
righteousness and
truth), [10]trying to
learn what is pleas-
ing to the Lord.
[11]Do not participate

[a] Two early mss read *us*
[b] One early ms reads *us*

NIV

with the fruitless
deeds of darkness,
but rather ex-
pose them. [12]It is
shameful even to
mention what the
disobedient do in
secret. [13]But every-
thing exposed by
the light becomes
visible—and ev-
erything that is il-
luminated becomes
a light. [14]This is
why it is said:

"Wake up,
sleeper,
rise from the
dead,
and Christ
will shine
on you."

[15]Be very care-
ful, then, how you
live—not as un-
wise but as wise,
[16]making the most
of every oppor-
tunity, because
the days are evil.
[17]Therefore do not
be foolish, but un-
derstand what the
Lord's will is. [18]Do
not get drunk on
wine, which leads
to debauchery.
Instead, be filled
with the Spir-
it, [19]speaking to
one another with
psalms, hymns,
and songs from
the Spirit. Sing
and make music
from your heart to
the Lord, [20]always
giving thanks to
God the Father for
everything, in the
name of our Lord
Jesus Christ.

Instructions for Christian Households

[21]Submit to one
another out of rev-
erence for Christ.
[22]Wives, submit
yourselves

συγκοινωνεῖτε τοῖς ἔργοις τοῖς ἀκάρποις τοῦ σκότους, μᾶλλον δὲ καὶ
take part in the fruitless deeds {the} fruitless of darkness but instead but {also}
5170 3836 182 2240 3836 182 3836 5030 1254 3437 1254 2779
v.pam.2p d.dpn n.dpn d.dpn a.dpn d.gsn n.gsn adv.c cj adv

ἐλέγχετε. 12 τὰ γὰρ
expose them, for it is shameful even to speak of what for is done by them
1794 1142 1639 1639 156 2779 3306 3306 3836 1142 1181 1181 5679 899
v.pam.2p d.apn cj

κρυφῇ γινόμενα ὑπ' αὐτῶν αἰσχρόν ἐστιν καὶ λέγειν, 13 τὰ δὲ πάντα
in secret. is done by them shameful it is even to speak {the} But everything
3225 1181 5679 899 156 1639 2779 3306 3836 1254 4246
adv pt.pm.apn p.g r.gpm.3 a.nsn v.pai.3s adv f.pa d.npn cj a.npn

ἐλεγχόμενα ὑπὸ τοῦ φωτὸς φανεροῦται, 14 πᾶν γὰρ
that is exposed becomes illuminated by the light, becomes illuminated for everything for
1794 5746 5746 5679 3836 5890 5746 1142 4246 1142
pt.pp.npn p.g d.gsn n.gsn v.ppi.3s a.nsn cj

τὸ φανερούμενον φῶς ἐστιν. διὸ λέγει, ἔγειρε, ὁ καθεύδων, καὶ
that becomes illuminated is light. is Therefore it says, ⌊"Wake up,⌋ {the} sleeper, and
3836 5746 1639 5890 1639 1475 3306 1586 3836 2761 2779
d.nsn pt.pp.nsn n.nsn v.pai.3s cj v.pai.3s v.pam.2s d.vsm pt.pa.vsm cj

ἀνάστα ἐκ τῶν νεκρῶν, καὶ ἐπιφαύσει σοι ὁ Χριστός. 15 →
rise from the dead, and Christ will shine on you." {the} Christ So be very
482 1666 3836 3738 2779 5986 2213 5148 3836 5986 4036 209
v.aam.2s p.g d.gpm a.gpm cj v.fai.3s r.ds.2 d.nsm n.nsm

βλέπετε οὖν ἀκριβῶς πῶς περιπατεῖτε μὴ ὡς ἄσοφοι ἀλλ' ὡς σοφοί,
careful So very how you live, not as unwise people but as wise,
1063 4036 209 4802 4344 3590 6055 831 247 6055 5055
v.pam.2p cj adv cj v.pai.2p pl pl a.npm cj pl a.npm

16 ἐξαγοραζόμενοι τὸν καιρόν, ὅτι αἱ ἡμέραι πονηραί εἰσιν. 17 ⌊διὰ
making the most of the time, because the days are evil. are Therefore
1973 3836 2789 4022 3836 2465 1639 4505 1639 1328
pt.pm.npm d.asm n.asm cj d.npf n.npf a.npf v.pai.3p p.a

τοῦτο⌋ ↱ μὴ γίνεσθε ἄφρονες, ἀλλὰ συνίετε[a] τί τὸ θέλημα τοῦ κυρίου.
do not be foolish, but understand what the will of the Lord is.
4047 1181 3590 1181 933 247 5317 5515 3836 2525 3836 3261
r.asn pl v.pmm.2p a.npm cj v.pam.2p r.nsn d.nsn n.nsn d.gsm n.gsm

18 καὶ ↱ μὴ μεθύσκεσθε οἴνῳ, ἐν ᾧ ἐστιν ἀσωτία, ἀλλὰ πληροῦσθε
And do not get drunk with wine, in which is debauchery; instead, be filled
2779 3499 3590 3499 3885 1877 4005 1639 861 247 4444
cj pl v.ppm.2p n.dsm p.d r.dsm v.pai.3s n.nsf cj v.ppm.2p

ἐν πνεύματι, 19 λαλοῦντες ἑαυτοῖς ἐν[b] ψαλμοῖς καὶ ὕμνοις καὶ ᾠδαῖς
with the Spirit, speaking to one another in psalms and hymns and songs
1877 4460 3281 1571 1877 6011 2779 5631 2779 6046
p.d n.dsn pt.pa.npm r.dpm.2 p.d n.dpm cj n.dpm cj n.dpf

πνευματικαῖς, ᾄδοντες καὶ ψάλλοντες τῇ καρδίᾳ ὑμῶν τῷ κυρίῳ,
inspired by the Spirit; singing and making melody in your heart your ⌊to the⌋ Lord,
4461 106 2779 6010 3836 7007 2840 7007 3836 3261
a.dpf pt.pa.npm cj pt.pa.npm d.dsf n.dsf r.gp.2 d.dsm n.dsm

20 εὐχαριστοῦντες πάντοτε
giving thanks in the name of our Lord Jesus Christ to God the Father at all times and
2373 1877 3950 3836 7005 3261 2652 5986 3836 2536 4252 4121
pt.pa.npm adv

ὑπὲρ πάντων ἐν ὀνόματι τοῦ κυρίου ἡμῶν Ἰησοῦ Χριστοῦ τῷ θεῷ καὶ πατρί.
for everything. in name of Lord our Jesus Christ to God {and} Father
5642 4246 1877 3950 3836 3261 7005 2652 5986 3836 2536 2779 4252
p.g a.gpn p.d n.dsn d.gsm n.gsm r.gp.1 n.gsm n.gsm d.dsm n.dsm cj n.dsm

21 ὑποτασσόμενοι ἀλλήλοις ἐν φόβῳ Χριστοῦ, 22 αἱ γυναῖκες
Be subject to one another ⌊out of⌋ reverence for Christ. {the} Wives, be subject
5718 253 1877 5832 5986 3836 1222
pt.pp.npm r.dpm p.d n.dsm n.gsm d.vpf n.vpf

NASB

in the unfruitful
deeds of darkness,
but instead even
expose them; [12]for
it is disgraceful
even to speak of
the things which
are done by them
in secret. [13]But
all things become
visible when they
are exposed by the
light, for every-
thing that becomes
visible is light.
[14]For this reason it
says,

"Awake, sleep-
er,
And arise from
the dead,
And Christ
will shine on
you."

[15]Therefore be
careful how you
walk, not as un-
wise men but as
wise, [16]making the
most of your time,
because the days
are evil. [17]So then
do not be foolish,
but understand
what the will of
the Lord is. [18]And
do not get drunk
with wine, for that
is dissipation, but
be filled with the
Spirit, [19]speaking
to one another in
psalms and hymns
and spiritual songs,
singing and mak-
ing melody with
your heart to the
Lord; [20]always giv-
ing thanks for all
things in the name
of our Lord Jesus
Christ to God, even
the Father; [21]and
be subject to one
another in the fear
of Christ.

Marriage Like Christ and the Church

[22]Wives, *be sub-
ject* to your own

[a] συνίετε UBS, TNIV. συνίεντες NET.
[b] [ἐν] UBS.

NIV

to your own husbands as you do to the Lord. 23 For the husband is the head of the wife as Christ is the head of the church, his body, of which he is the Savior. 24 Now as the church submits to Christ, so also wives should submit to their husbands in everything.

25 Husbands, love your wives, just as Christ loved the church and gave himself up for her 26 to make her holy, cleansing[a] her by the washing with water through the word, 27 and to present her to himself as a radiant church, without stain or wrinkle or any other blemish, but holy and blameless. 28 In this same way, husbands ought to love their wives as their own bodies. He who loves his wife loves himself. 29 After all, no one ever hated their own body, but they feed and care for their body, just as Christ does the church— 30 for we are members of his body. 31 "For this reason a man will leave his father and mother and be united to his wife, and the two

[a] 26 Or *having cleansed*

τοῖς ἰδίοις ἀνδράσιν[a] ὡς τῷ κυρίῳ, 23 ὅτι ἀνήρ ἐστιν κεφαλὴ τῆς
to your husbands as ⌊to the⌋ Lord, for the husband is the head of the
3836 2625 467 6055 3836 3261 4022 467 1639 3051 3836
d.dpm a.dpm n.dpm pl d.dsm n.dsm cj n.nsm v.pai.3s n.nsf d.gsf

γυναικὸς ὡς καὶ ὁ Χριστὸς κεφαλὴ τῆς ἐκκλησίας, αὐτὸς
wife as Christ also *{the}* *Christ* is the head of the church, and is himself the
1222 6055 5986 2779 3836 5986 3051 3836 1711 899
n.gsf cj adv d.nsm n.nsm n.nsf d.gsf n.gsf r.nsm

σωτὴρ τοῦ σώματος· 24 ἀλλὰ ὡς ἡ ἐκκλησία ὑποτάσσεται τῷ Χριστῷ, οὕτως
savior of the body. But as the church is subject to Christ, so
5400 3836 5393 247 6055 3836 1711 5718 3836 5986 4048
n.nsm d.gsn n.gsn cj cj d.nsf n.nsf v.ppi.3s d.dsm n.dsm adv

καὶ αἱ γυναῖκες τοῖς ἀνδράσιν ἐν παντί. 25 οἱ ἄνδρες,
also should *{the}* wives be subject to their husbands in everything. *{the}* Husbands,
2779 3836 1222 3836 467 1877 4246 3836 467
adv d.npf n.npf d.dpm n.dpm p.d a.dsn d.vpm n.vpm

ἀγαπᾶτε τὰς γυναῖκας, καθὼς καὶ ὁ Χριστὸς ἠγάπησεν τὴν ἐκκλησίαν καὶ ↱
love your wives, just as *{also}* *{the}* Christ loved the church and gave
26 3836 1222 2777 2779 3836 5986 26 3836 1711 2779 4140
v.pam.2p d.apf n.apf cj adv d.nsm n.nsm v.aai.3s d.asf n.asf cj

ἑαυτὸν παρέδωκεν ὑπὲρ αὐτῆς, 26 ἵνα αὐτὴν ἁγιάσῃ καθαρίσας
himself up for her, that he might sanctify her, *he might sanctify* cleansing
1571 4140 5642 899 2671 39 39 39 899 39 2751
r.asm.3 v.aai.3s p.g r.gsf.3 cj r.asf.3 v.aas.3s pt.aa.nsm

τῷ λουτρῷ τοῦ ὕδατος ἐν ῥήματι, 27 ἵνα παραστήσῃ αὐτὸς
her ⌊by the⌋ washing of water through the word, so that he might present *he* the
3836 3373 3836 5623 1877 4839 2671 899 4225 899 3836
d.dsn n.dsn d.gsn n.gsn p.d n.dsn cj v.aas.3s r.nsm

ἑαυτῷ ἔνδοξον τὴν ἐκκλησίαν, μὴ ἔχουσαν σπίλον ἢ ῥυτίδα ἤ τι
church to himself in splendor, *the* *church* not having spot or wrinkle or any
1711 1571 1902 3836 1711 3590 2400 5070 2445 4869 2445 5516
r.dsm.3 a.asf d.asf n.asf pl pt.pa.asf n.asm cj n.asf cj r.asn

τῶν τοιούτων, ἀλλ᾽ ἵνα ᾖ ἁγία καὶ ἄμωμος. 28 οὕτως
{the} such thing, but that ⌊she might be⌋ holy and without blemish. ⌊In the same way⌋
3836 5525 247 2671 1639 41 2779 320 4048
d.gpn r.gpn cj cj v.pas.3s a.nsf cj a.nsf adv

ὀφείλουσιν καὶ[b] οἱ ἄνδρες ἀγαπᾶν τὰς ἑαυτῶν γυναῖκας ὡς τὰ
husbands also should *also* *{the}* *husbands* love *{the}* their wives as *{the}*
467 2779 4053 2779 3836 467 26 3836 1571 1222 6055 3836
v.pai.3p adv d.npm n.npm f.pa d.apf r.gpm.3 n.apf cj d.apn

ἑαυτῶν σώματα. ὁ ἀγαπῶν τὴν ἑαυτοῦ γυναῖκα ἑαυτὸν ἀγαπᾷ. 29
their own bodies. He who loves *{the}* his wife loves himself, *loves* for
1571 5393 3836 26 3836 1571 1222 26 1571 26 1142
r.gpm.3 n.apn d.nsm pt.pa.nsm d.asf r.gsm.3 n.asf r.asm.3 v.pai.3s

οὐδεὶς γάρ ποτε τὴν ἑαυτοῦ σάρκα ἐμίσησεν ἀλλὰ ἐκτρέφει καὶ θάλπει
no one *for* ever hates *{the}* his own body *hates* but nourishes and ⌊takes care of⌋
4029 1142 4537 3631 3836 1571 4922 3631 247 1763 2779 2499
a.nsm cj adv d.asf r.gsm.3 n.asf v.aai.3s cj v.pai.3s cj v.pai.3s

αὐτήν, καθὼς καὶ ὁ Χριστὸς τὴν ἐκκλησίαν, 30 ὅτι μέλη ἐσμὲν
it, just as *{also}* *{the}* Christ does the church, since we are members *we are*
899 2777 2779 3836 5986 3836 1711 4022 1639 1639 3517 1639
r.asf.3 cj adv d.nsm n.nsm d.asf n.asf cj n.npn v.pai.1p

τοῦ σώματος αὐτοῦ. 31 ἀντὶ τούτου καταλείψει ἄνθρωπος τὸν[c] πατέρα
of his body. *his* "For this reason a man shall leave *man* his father
3836 899 5393 899 505 4047 476 2901 476 3836 4252
d.gsn n.gsn r.gsm.3 p.g r.gsn v.fai.3s n.nsm d.asm n.asm

καὶ τὴν[d] μητέρα καὶ προσκολληθήσεται πρὸς τὴν γυναῖκα αὐτοῦ, καὶ
and his mother and be joined to *{the}* his wife, *his* and the two
2779 3836 3613 2779 4681 4639 3836 899 1222 899 2779 3836 1545
cj d.asf n.asf cj v.fpi.3s p.a d.asf n.asf r.gsm.3 cj

[a] ὑποτάσσεσθε included by TR after ἀνδράσιν.
[b] [καὶ] UBS.
[c] [τὸν] UBS.
[d] [τὴν] UBS.

NASB

husbands, as to the Lord. 23 For the husband is the head of the wife, as Christ also is the head of the church, He Himself *being* the Savior of the body. 24 But as the church is subject to Christ, so also the wives *ought to be* to their husbands in everything.

25 Husbands, love your wives, just as Christ also loved the church and gave Himself up for her, 26 so that He might sanctify her, having cleansed her by the washing of water with the word, 27 that He might present to Himself the church in all her glory, having no spot or wrinkle or any such thing; but that she would be holy and blameless. 28 So husbands ought also to love their own wives as their own bodies. He who loves his own wife loves himself; 29 for no one ever hated his own flesh, but nourishes and cherishes it, just as Christ also *does* the church, 30 because we are members of His body. 31 FOR THIS REASON A MAN SHALL LEAVE HIS FATHER AND MOTHER AND SHALL BE JOINED TO HIS WIFE, AND THE

NIV

will become one flesh."[a] 32This is a profound mystery—but I am talking about Christ and the church. 33However, each one of you also must love his wife as he loves himself, and the wife must respect her husband.

6 Children, obey your parents in the Lord, for this is right. 2"Honor your father and mother"—which is the first commandment with a promise— 3"so that it may go well with you and that you may enjoy long life on the earth."[b]

4Fathers,[c] do not exasperate your children; instead, bring them up in the training and instruction of the Lord.

5Slaves, obey your earthly masters with respect and fear, and with sincerity of heart, just as you would obey Christ. 6Obey them not only to win their favor when their eye is on you, but as slaves of Christ, doing the will of God from your heart. 7Serve wholeheartedly, as if you were serving the Lord, not people, 8because you know that the Lord will reward each one for whatever good they do,

ἔσονται οἱ δύο εἰς σάρκα μίαν. 32 τὸ μυστήριον τοῦτο μέγα
shall become *the* *two* *{into}* one flesh." *one* *{the}* This mystery *This* is profound,
1639 3836 1545 1650 1651 4922 1651 3836 4047 3696 4047 1639 3489
v.fmi.3p d.npm a.npm p.a n.asf a.asf d.nsn n.nsn r.nsn a.nsn

ἐστίν· ἐγὼ δὲ λέγω εἰς Χριστὸν καὶ εἰς τὴν ἐκκλησίαν. 33 πλὴν
is but I *but* am speaking about Christ and about the church. Nevertheless,
1639 1254 1609 1254 3306 1650 5986 2779 1650 3836 1711 4440
v.pai.3s r.ns.1 cj v.pai.1s p.a n.asm cj p.a d.asf n.asf cj

καὶ ὑμεῖς οἱ καθʼ ἕνα, ἕκαστος τὴν ἑαυτοῦ γυναῖκα
{also} each one of you *{the}* *of* *one* *each* is to love *{the}* his wife
2779 1667 1651 2848 7007 3836 2848 1651 1667 26 26 26 3836 1571 1222
adv r.np.2 d.npm p.a a.asm r.nsm d.asf r.gsm.3 n.asf

οὕτως ἀγαπάτω ὡς ἑαυτόν, ἡ δὲ γυνὴ ἵνα φοβῆται τὸν
{in this way} *is to love* as he loves himself, and the *and* wife *{that}* is to respect her
4048 26 6055 1571 1254 3836 1254 1222 2671 5828 3836
adv v.pam.3s cj r.asm.3 d.nsf cj n.nsf cj v.pps.3s d.asm

ἄνδρα.
husband.
467
n.asm

6:1 τὰ τέκνα, ὑπακούετε τοῖς γονεῦσιν ὑμῶν [a]ἐν κυρίῳ· τοῦτο γάρ
{the} Children, obey *{the}* your parents *your* in the Lord, for this *for*
3836 5451 5634 3836 7007 1204 7007 1877 3261 1142 4047 1142
d.vpn n.vpn v.pam.2p d.dpm n.dpm r.gp.2 p.d n.dsm r.nsn cj

ἐστιν δίκαιον. 2 τίμα τὸν πατέρα σου καὶ τὴν μητέρα, ἥτις ἐστὶν
is right. "Honor *{the}* your father *your* and *{the}* mother" — which is the first
1639 1465 5506 3836 5148 4252 5148 2779 3836 3613 4015 1639 4755
v.pai.3s a.nsn v.pam.2s d.asm n.asm r.gs.2 cj d.asf n.asf r.nsf v.pai.3s

ἐντολὴ πρώτη ἐν ἐπαγγελίᾳ, 3 ἵνα εὖ σοι γένηται καὶ
commandment *first* with a promise — "that it may go well ⌞with you⌟ *it may go* and
1953 4755 1877 2039 2671 1181 1181 1181 2292 5148 1181 2779
n.nsf a.nsf p.d n.dsf cj adv r.ds.2 v.ams.3s cj

ἔσῃ → μακροχρόνιος ἐπὶ τῆς γῆς. 4 καὶ οἱ πατέρες, ↱
that ⌞you may live⌟ in the land for a long time." *in* *the* *land* And *{the}* fathers, do
1639 2093 3836 1178 3432 2093 3836 1178 2779 3836 4252 4239
v.fmi.2s a.nsm p.g d.gsf n.gsf cj d.vpm n.vpm

μὴ παροργίζετε τὰ τέκνα ὑμῶν ↰ ↰ ἀλλὰ ἐκτρέφετε αὐτὰ ↰ ἐν
not provoke *{the}* your children *your* to anger, but raise them up in the
3590 4239 3836 7007 5451 7007 4239 4239 247 1763 899 1763 1877
pl v.pam.2p d.apn n.apn r.gp.2 cj v.pam.2p r.apn.3 p.d

παιδείᾳ καὶ νουθεσίᾳ → κυρίου. 5 οἱ δοῦλοι, ὑπακούετε τοῖς ⌞κατὰ σάρκα⌟
discipline and admonition of the Lord. *{the}* Slaves, obey your earthly
4082 2779 3804 3261 3836 1529 5634 3836 2848 4922
n.dsf cj n.dsf n.gsm d.vpm n.vpm v.pam.2p d.dpm p.a n.asf

κυρίοις μετὰ φόβου καὶ τρόμου ἐν ἁπλότητι τῆς καρδίας ὑμῶν ὡς
masters with fear and trembling, with sincerity of your heart, *your* ⌞as though⌟
3261 3552 5832 2779 5571 1877 605 3836 7007 2840 7007 6055
n.dpm p.g n.gsm cj n.gsm p.d n.dsf d.gsf n.gsf r.gp.2 cj

τῷ Χριστῷ, 6 μὴ κατʼ ὀφθαλμοδουλίαν ὡς ἀνθρωπάρεσκοι ἀλλʼ ὡς
obeying *{the}* Christ, not ⌞by way of⌟ eye-service, as people-pleasers, but as
3836 5986 3590 2848 4056 6055 473 247 6055
d.dsm n.dsm pl p.a n.asf pl a.npm cj pl

δοῦλοι Χριστοῦ ποιοῦντες τὸ θέλημα τοῦ θεοῦ ἐκ ψυχῆς, 7 μετʼ
slaves of Christ doing the will of God from the heart, serving with
1529 5986 4472 3836 2525 3836 2536 1666 6034 1526 3552
n.npm n.gsm pt.pa.npm d.asn n.asn d.gsm n.gsm p.g n.gsf p.g

εὐνοίας δουλεύοντες ὡς τῷ κυρίῳ καὶ οὐκ ἀνθρώποις, 8 εἰδότες ὅτι
enthusiasm *serving* ⌞as though⌟ serving the Lord and not men, knowing that
2334 1526 6055 3836 3261 2779 4024 476 3857 4022
n.gsf pt.pa.npm pl d.dsm n.dsm cj pl n.dpm pt.ra.npm cj

ἕκαστος ἐάν τι ποιήσῃ ἀγαθόν, τοῦτο
each person, if he does something *he does* good, will be repaid by the Lord for this,
1667 1569 4472 4472 5516 4472 19 3152 3152 3152 4123 3261 4047
r.nsm cj r.asn v.aas.3s a.asn r.asn

NASB

TWO SHALL BECOME ONE FLESH. 32This mystery is great; but I am speaking with reference to Christ and the church. 33Nevertheless, each individual among you also is to love his own wife even as himself, and the wife must *see to it* that she respects her husband.

Family Relationships

6:1Children, obey your parents in the Lord, for this is right. 2HONOR YOUR FATHER AND MOTHER (which is the first commandment with a promise), 3SO THAT IT MAY BE WELL WITH YOU, AND THAT YOU MAY LIVE LONG ON THE EARTH.

4Fathers, do not provoke your children to anger, but bring them up in the discipline and instruction of the Lord.

5Slaves, be obedient to those who are your masters according to the flesh, with fear and trembling, in the sincerity of your heart, as to Christ; 6not by way of eyeservice, as men-pleasers, but as slaves of Christ, doing the will of God from the heart. 7With good will render service, as to the Lord, and not to men, 8knowing that whatever good thing each one does, this he will receive back from the Lord,

a 31 Gen. 2:24
b 3 Deut. 5:16
c 4 Or *Parents*

a [ἐν κυρίῳ] UBS.

NIV

whether they are
slave or free.
9 And masters,
treat your slaves in
the same way. Do
not threaten them,
since you know
that he who is both
their Master and
yours is in heaven,
and there is no fa-
voritism with him.

The Armor of God

10 Finally, be
strong in the Lord
and in his mighty
power. 11 Put on the
full armor of God,
so that you can
take your stand
against the dev-
il's schemes. 12 For
our struggle is not
against flesh and
blood, but against
the rulers, against
the authorities,
against the powers
of this dark world
and against the
spiritual forces of
evil in the heaven-
ly realms. 13 There-
fore put on the full
armor of God, so
that when the day
of evil comes, you
may be able to
stand your ground,
and after you have
done everything,
to stand. 14 Stand
firm then, with the
belt of truth buck-
led around your
waist, with the
breastplate of righ-
teousness in place,
15 and with your
feet fitted with
the readiness that
comes from the
gospel of peace.
16 In addition to
all this, take up
the shield of faith,
with which you
can extinguish all
the flaming arrows
of the evil one.
17 Take the

κομίσεται παρὰ κυρίου εἴτε δοῦλος εἴτε ἐλεύθερος. 9 καὶ οἱ κύριοι,
will be repaid by Lord whether he is a slave or free. And *{the}* masters, do
3152 4123 3261 1664 1529 1664 1801 2779 3836 3261 4472
v.fmi.3s p.g n.gsm cj n.nsm cj a.nsm cj d.vpm n.vpm

τὰ αὐτὰ ποιεῖτε πρὸς αὐτούς, ἀνιέντες τὴν ἀπειλήν, εἰδότες ὅτι
the same *do* to them, ⌊giving up the use of⌋ *{the}* threats, knowing that the one
3836 899 4472 4639 899 479 3836 581 3857 4022 3836
d.apn r.apn v.pam.2p p.a r.apm.3 pt.pa.npm d.asf n.asf pt.ra.npm cj

καὶ αὐτῶν καὶ ὑμῶν ὁ κύριός ἐστιν ἐν οὐρανοῖς καὶ
who is both their master and yours *the master* is in heaven, and that there is
2779 899 3261 2779 7007 3836 3261 1639 1877 4041 2779 1639 1639
cj r.gpm.3 cj r.gp.2 d.nsm n.nsm v.pai.3s p.d n.dpm cj

προσωπολημψία οὐκ ἔστιν παρ᾽ αὐτῷ. 10 τοῦ λοιποῦ, ἐνδυναμοῦσθε ἐν
no favoritism *no there is* with him. *{the}* Finally, grow strong in the
4024 4721 4024 1639 4123 899 3836 3370 1904 1877
n.nsf pl v.pai.3s p.d r.dsm.3 d.gsn adv v.ppm.2p p.d

κυρίῳ καὶ ἐν τῷ κράτει τῆς ἰσχύος αὐτοῦ. 11 ἐνδύσασθε τὴν πανοπλίαν τοῦ
Lord and in the strength of his power. *his* Put on the full armor of
3261 2779 1877 3836 3197 3836 899 2709 899 1907 3836 4110 3836
n.dsm cj p.d d.dsn n.dsn d.gsf n.gsf r.gsm.3 v.amm.2p d.asf n.asf d.gsm

θεοῦ πρὸς τὸ δύνασθαι ὑμᾶς στῆναι πρὸς τὰς μεθοδείας τοῦ διαβόλου·
God, so that ~ you may be able *you* to stand against the schemes of the devil;
2536 4639 3836 7007 1538 7007 2705 4639 3836 3497 3836 1333
n.gsm p.a d.asn f.pp r.ap.2 f.aa p.a d.apf n.apf d.gsm n.gsm

12 ὅτι οὐκ ἔστιν ἡμῖν ἡ πάλη πρὸς αἷμα καὶ σάρκα
for our struggle is not *is our {the} struggle* against flesh and blood, *and flesh*
4022 7005 4097 1639 4024 1639 7005 3836 4097 4639 4922 2779 135 2779 4922
cj pl v.pai.3s r.dp.1 d.nsf n.nsf p.a n.asn cj n.asf

ἀλλὰ πρὸς τὰς ἀρχάς, πρὸς τὰς ἐξουσίας, πρὸς τοὺς κοσμοκράτορας τοῦ
but against the rulers, against the authorities, against the world rulers of this
247 4639 3836 794 4639 3836 2026 4639 3836 3179 3836 4047
cj p.a d.apf n.apf p.a d.apf n.apf p.a d.apm n.apm d.gsn

σκότους τούτου, πρὸς τὰ πνευματικὰ τῆς πονηρίας ἐν τοῖς ἐπουρανίοις.
darkness, *this* against the spiritual forces of evil in the heavenly realms.
5030 4047 4639 3836 4461 3836 4504 1877 3836 2230
n.gsn r.gsn p.a d.apn a.apn d.gsf n.gsf p.d d.dpm a.dpm

13 ⌊διὰ τοῦτο⌋ ἀναλάβετε τὴν πανοπλίαν τοῦ θεοῦ, ἵνα δυνηθῆτε
Therefore take up the full armor of God, so that ⌊you may be able⌋
1328 4047 377 3836 4110 3836 2536 2671 1538
p.a r.asn v.aam.2p d.asf n.asf d.gsm n.gsm cj v.aps.2p

ἀντιστῆναι ἐν τῇ ἡμέρᾳ τῇ πονηρᾷ καὶ ἅπαντα
⌊to stand your ground⌋ on the evil day, *{the} evil* and having done everything,
468 1877 3836 4505 2465 3836 4505 2779 2981 2981 570
f.aa p.d d.dsf n.dsf d.dsf a.dsf cj a.apn

κατεργασάμενοι στῆναι. 14 στῆτε οὖν περιζωσάμενοι τὴν ὀσφὺν ὑμῶν ἐν
having done to stand. Stand therefore, by girding *{the}* your waist *your* with
2981 2705 2705 4036 4322 3836 7007 4019 7007 1877
pt.am.npm f.aa v.aam.2p cj pt.am.npm d.asf n.asf r.gp.2 p.d

ἀληθείᾳ καὶ ἐνδυσάμενοι τὸν θώρακα τῆς δικαιοσύνης 15 καὶ ὑποδησάμενοι
truth, *{and}* by putting on the breastplate of righteousness, *{and}* by fitting
237 2779 1907 3836 2606 3836 1466 2779 5686
n.dsf cj pt.am.npm d.asm n.asm d.gsf n.gsf cj pt.am.npm

τοὺς πόδας ἐν ἑτοιμασίᾳ τοῦ εὐαγγελίου τῆς εἰρήνης, 16 ἐν πᾶσιν
your feet with the readiness of the gospel of peace; and besides all these,
3836 4546 1877 2288 3836 2295 3836 1645 1877 4246
d.apm n.apm p.d n.dsf d.gsn n.gsn d.gsf n.gsf p.d a.dpn

ἀναλαβόντες τὸν θυρεὸν τῆς πίστεως, ἐν ᾧ δυνήσεσθε πάντα
by taking up the shield of faith, with which you will be able to extinguish all
377 3836 2599 3836 4411 1877 4005 1538 4931 4931 4246
pt.aa.npm d.asm n.asm d.gsf n.gsf p.d r.dsm v.fmi.2p a.apn

τὰ βέλη τοῦ πονηροῦ τὰ[a] πεπυρωμένα σβέσαι· 17 καὶ τὴν
the flaming arrows of the evil one. *{the} flaming to extinguish* And take the
3836 4792 1018 3836 4505 3836 4792 4931 2779 1312 3836
d.apn n.apn d.gsm a.gsm d.apn pt.rp.apn f.aa cj d.asf

[a] [τὰ] UBS.

NASB

whether slave or
free.
9 And masters, do
the same things to
them, and give up
threatening, know-
ing that both their
Master and yours
is in heaven, and
there is no partial-
ity with Him.

The Armor of God

10 Finally, be
strong in the Lord
and in the strength
of His might. 11 Put
on the full armor
of God, so that
you will be able to
stand firm against
the schemes of
the devil. 12 For
our struggle is
not against flesh
and blood, but
against the rulers,
against the powers,
against the world
forces of this dark-
ness, against the
spiritual *forces* of
wickedness in the
heavenly *places.*
13 Therefore, take
up the full armor
of God, so that
you will be able
to resist in the evil
day, and having
done everything, to
stand firm. 14 Stand
firm therefore, HAV-
ING GIRDED YOUR
LOINS WITH TRUTH,
and HAVING PUT ON
THE BREASTPLATE
OF RIGHTEOUSNESS,
15 and having shod
YOUR FEET WITH THE
PREPARATION OF THE
GOSPEL OF PEACE;
16 in addition to all,
taking up the shield
of faith with which
you will be able to
extinguish all the
flaming arrows of
the evil *one.* 17 And

NIV

helmet of salvation and the sword of the Spirit, which is the word of God. [18]And pray in the Spirit on all occasions with all kinds of prayers and requests. With this in mind, be alert and always keep on praying for all the Lord's people. [19]Pray also for me, that whenever I speak, words may be given me so that I will fearlessly make known the mystery of the gospel, [20]for which I am an ambassador in chains. Pray that I may declare it fearlessly, as I should.

Final Greetings

[21]Tychicus, the dear brother and faithful servant in the Lord, will tell you everything, so that you also may know how I am and what I am doing. [22]I am sending him to you for this very purpose, that you may know how we are, and that he may encourage you.

[23]Peace to the brothers and sisters,[a] and love with faith from God the Father and the Lord Jesus Christ. [24]Grace to all who love our Lord Jesus Christ with an undying love.[b]

[a] 23 The Greek word for *brothers and sisters* (*adelphoi*) refers here to believers, both men and women, as part of God's family.

[b] 24 Or *Grace and immortality to all who love our Lord Jesus Christ.*

περικεφαλαίαν τοῦ σωτηρίου δέξασθε καὶ τὴν μάχαιραν τοῦ πνεύματος, ὅ ἐστιν
helmet of salvation, *take* and the sword of the Spirit, which is
4330 3836 5402 1312 2779 3836 3479 3836 4460 4005 1639
n.asf d.gsn n.gsn v.amm.2p cj d.asf n.asf d.gsn n.gsn r.nsn v.pai.3s

ῥῆμα θεοῦ. [18] διὰ πάσης προσευχῆς καὶ δεήσεως προσευχόμενοι ἐν
the word of God. ⌊By means of⌋ all prayer and petition, pray at
4839 2536 1328 4246 4666 2779 1255 4667 1877
n.nsn n.gsm p.g a.gsf n.gsf cj n.gsf pt.pm.npm p.d

παντὶ καιρῷ ἐν πνεύματι, καὶ εἰς αὐτὸ ↰ ἀγρυπνοῦντες ἐν πάσῃ
every time in the Spirit, and to this end keep alert with all
4246 2789 1877 4460 2779 1650 899 1650 70 1877 4246
a.dsm n.dsm p.d n.dsn cj p.a r.asn.3 pt.pa.npm p.d a.dsf

προσκαρτερήσει καὶ δεήσει περὶ πάντων τῶν ἁγίων [19] καὶ ὑπὲρ ἐμοῦ, ἵνα
perseverance and petition for all the saints, and for me, that when I
4675 2779 1255 4309 4246 3836 41 2779 5642 1609 2671 1877
n.dsf cj n.dsf p.g a.gpm d.gpm a.gpm cj p.g r.gs.1 cj

μοι δοθῇ λόγος ἐν ἀνοίξει τοῦ στόματός
open my mouth the word will be given to me *will be given* *word* *when* *open* *{the}* *mouth*
489 1609 5125 3364 1443 1443 1443 1609 1443 3364 1877 489 3836 5125
r.ds.1 v.aps.3s n.nsm p.d n.dsf d.gsn n.gsn

μου, ἐν παρρησίᾳ γνωρίσαι τὸ μυστήριον τοῦ εὐαγγελίου, [20] ὑπὲρ
my — that with boldness ⌊I will make known⌋ the mystery of the gospel, for
1609 1877 4244 1192 3836 3696 3836 2295 5642
r.gs.1 p.d n.dsf f.aa d.asn n.asn d.gsn n.gsn p.g

οὗ πρεσβεύω ἐν ἁλύσει, ἵνα ↱ ↱ ↱ ἐν αὐτῷ παρρησιάσωμαι
which I am an ambassador in chains. Pray that I may declare *{in}* it boldly,
4005 4563 1877 268 2671 4245 4245 4245 1877 899 4245
r.gsn v.pai.1s p.d n.dsf cj p.d r.dsn.3 v.ams.1s

ὡς δεῖ με λαλῆσαι. [21] ἵνα δὲ εἰδῆτε καὶ ὑμεῖς
as I ought *I* to speak. Now ⌊in order that⌋ *Now* you also may know *also* *you* my
6055 1609 1256 1609 3281 1254 2671 1254 7007 2779 3857 2779 7007 1609
cj v.pai.3s r.as.1 f.aa cj cj v.ras.2p adv r.np.2

⌊τὰ κατ'⌋ ἐμέ, τί πράσσω,
circumstances, *my* how I am doing, Tychicus, a dear brother and faithful servant in the
3836 2848 1609 5515 4556 5608 28 81 2779 4412 1356 1877
d.apn p.a r.as.1 r.asn v.pai.1s

πάντα γνωρίσει ὑμῖν Τύχικος ὁ ἀγαπητὸς ἀδελφὸς καὶ πιστὸς
Lord, will tell you everything. *will tell* *you* *Tychicus* *{the}* *dear* *brother* *and* *faithful*
3261 1192 1192 7007 4246 1192 7007 5608 3836 28 81 2779 4412
a.apn v.fai.3s r.dp.2 n.nsm d.nsm a.nsm n.nsm cj a.nsm

διάκονος ἐν κυρίῳ, [22] ὃν ἔπεμψα πρὸς ὑμᾶς εἰς αὐτὸ
servant *in* *Lord* I am sending him *I am sending* to you for this very
1356 1877 3261 4287 4287 4287 4005 4287 4639 7007 1650 4047 899
n.nsm p.d n.dsm r.asm v.aai.1s p.a r.ap.2 p.a r.asn

τοῦτο, ↰ ἵνα γνῶτε ⌊τὰ περὶ⌋ ἡμῶν ↰ καὶ παρακαλέσῃ τὰς
this purpose, that ⌊you may know⌋ how we are, and that he may encourage *{the}*
4047 1650 2671 1182 3836 4309 7005 3836 2779 4151 3836
r.asn cj v.aas.2p d.apn p.g r.gp.1 cj v.aas.3s d.apf

καρδίας ὑμῶν. [23] εἰρήνη τοῖς ἀδελφοῖς καὶ ἀγάπη μετὰ πίστεως ἀπὸ θεοῦ
your hearts. *your* Peace be to the brothers, and love with faith, from God the
7007 2840 7007 1645 3836 81 2779 27 3552 4411 608 2536
n.apf r.gp.2 n.nsf d.dpm n.dpm cj n.nsf p.g n.gsf p.g n.gsm

πατρὸς καὶ κυρίου Ἰησοῦ Χριστοῦ. [24] ἡ χάρις μετὰ πάντων τῶν ἀγαπώντων
Father and the Lord Jesus Christ. *{the}* Grace be with all who love
4252 2779 3261 2652 5986 3836 5921 3552 4246 3836 26
n.gsm cj n.gsm n.gsm n.gsm d.nsf n.nsf p.g a.gpm d.gpm pt.pa.gpm

τὸν κύριον ἡμῶν Ἰησοῦν Χριστὸν ἐν ἀφθαρσίᾳ.[a]
{the} our Lord *our* Jesus Christ, grace and immortality.
3836 7005 3261 7005 2652 5986 1877 914
d.asm n.asm r.gp.1 n.asm n.asm p.d n.dsf

[a] ἀμήν. πρὸς Ἐφεσίους ἐγράφη ἀπὸ Ῥώμης διὰ Τυχικοῦ included by TR after ἀφθαρσίᾳ.

NASB

take THE HELMET OF SALVATION, and the sword of the Spirit, which is the word of God.

[18]With all prayer and petition pray at all times in the Spirit, and with this in view, be on the alert with all perseverance and petition for all the saints, [19]and *pray* on my behalf, that utterance may be given to me in the opening of my mouth, to make known with boldness the mystery of the gospel, [20]for which I am an ambassador in chains; that [a]in *proclaiming* it I may speak boldly, as I ought to speak.

[21]But that you also may know about my circumstances, how I am doing, Tychicus, the beloved brother and faithful minister in the Lord, will make everything known to you. [22]I have sent him to you for this very purpose, so that you may know about us, and that he may comfort your hearts.

[23]Peace be to the brethren, and love with faith, from God the Father and the Lord Jesus Christ. [24]Grace be with all those who love our Lord Jesus Christ with incorruptible *love.*

[a] Two early mss read *I may speak it boldly*

Philippians

NIV

1 Paul and Tim-
othy, servants
of Christ Jesus,
To all God's holy
people in Christ
Jesus at Philippi,
together with the
overseers and dea-
cons[a]:
2 Grace and peace
to you from God
our Father and the
Lord Jesus Christ.

Thanksgiving and Prayer

3 I thank my God
every time I re-
member you. 4 In
all my prayers for
all of you, I al-
ways pray with joy
5 because of your
partnership in the
gospel from the
first day until now,
6 being confident
of this, that he who
began a good work
in you will carry it
on to completion
until the day of
Christ Jesus.
7 It is right for me
to feel this way
about all of you,
since I have you
in my heart and,
whether I am in
chains or defend-
ing and confirm-
ing the gospel, all
of you share in
God's grace with
me. 8 God can tes-
tify how I long for
all of you with the
affection of Christ
Jesus.
9 And this is my
prayer: that your
love may abound

[a] 1 The word *deacons* refers here to Christians designated to serve with the overseers/elders of the church in a variety of ways; similarly in Romans 16:1 and 1 Tim. 3:8,12.

1:1 Παῦλος καὶ Τιμόθεος δοῦλοι Χριστοῦ Ἰησοῦ πᾶσιν τοῖς ἁγίοις ἐν
From Paul and Timothy, servants of Christ Jesus, to all the saints in
4263 2779 5510 1529 5986 2652 4246 3836 41 1877
n.nsm cj n.nsm n.npm n.gsm n.gsm a.dpm d.dpm a.dpm p.d

Χριστῷ Ἰησοῦ τοῖς οὖσιν ἐν Φιλίπποις σὺν ἐπισκόποις καὶ διακόνοις.
Christ Jesus who are in Philippi, ⌊along with⌋ the overseers and deacons:
5986 2652 3836 1639 1877 5804 5250 2176 2779 1356
n.dsm n.dsm d.dpm pt.pa.dpm p.d n.dpm p.d n.dpm cj n.dpm

2 χάρις ὑμῖν καὶ εἰρήνη ἀπὸ θεοῦ πατρὸς ἡμῶν καὶ κυρίου Ἰησοῦ Χριστοῦ.
Grace to you and peace from God our Father *our* and the Lord Jesus Christ.
5921 7007 2779 1645 608 2536 7005 4252 7005 2779 3261 2652 5986
n.nsf r.dp.2 cj n.nsf p.g n.gsm n.gsm r.gp.1 cj n.gsm n.gsm n.gsm

3 εὐχαριστῶ τῷ θεῷ μου ⌊ἐπὶ πάσῃ⌋ τῇ μνείᾳ ὑμῶν 4 πάντοτε ἐν
I thank *{the}* my God *my* every time *{the}* I remember you. Always in
2373 3836 1609 2536 1609 2093 4246 3836 3644 7007 4121 1877
v.pai.1s d.dsm n.dsm r.gs.1 p.d a.dsf d.dsf n.dsf r.gp.2 adv p.d

πάσῃ δεήσει μου ὑπὲρ πάντων ὑμῶν, μετὰ χαρᾶς ⌊τὴν δέησιν
every prayer of mine for all of you I pray with joy, *I pray*
4246 1255 1609 5642 4246 7007 3836 3836 3552 5915 3836 1255
a.dsf n.dsf r.gs.1 p.g a.gpm r.gp.2 p.g n.gsf d.asf n.asf

ποιούμενος,⌋ 5 ἐπὶ τῇ κοινωνίᾳ ὑμῶν εἰς τὸ εὐαγγέλιον ἀπὸ τῆς
⌊because of⌋ *{the}* your partnership *your* in the gospel from the
4472 2093 3836 7007 3126 7007 1650 3836 2295 608 3836
pt.pm.nsm p.d d.dsf n.dsf r.gp.2 p.a d.asn n.asn p.g d.gsf

πρώτης ἡμέρας ἄχρι τοῦ νῦν, 6 πεποιθὼς ↱ αὐτὸ τοῦτο, ὅτι ὁ
first day until *{the}* now. For I am confident of this very thing, that he
4755 2465 948 3836 3814 4275 4047 899 4047 4022 3836
a.gsf n.gsf p.g d.gsm adv pt.ra.nsm r.asn r.asn cj d.nsm

ἐναρξάμενος ἐν ὑμῖν ἔργον ἀγαθὸν ἐπιτελέσει ἄχρι
who began a good work in you *work* *good* ⌊will bring it to completion⌋ at the
1887 19 2240 1877 7007 2240 19 2200 948
pt.am.nsm p.d r.dp.2 n.asn a.asn v.fai.3s p.g

ἡμέρας Χριστοῦ Ἰησοῦ· 7 καθώς ἐστιν δίκαιον ἐμοὶ τοῦτο φρονεῖν ὑπὲρ
day of Christ Jesus. *{just as}* It is right for me to feel this way *to feel* about
2465 5986 2652 2777 1639 1465 1609 5858 5858 4047 5858 5642
n.gsf n.gsm n.gsm cj v.pai.3s a.nsn r.ds.1 r.asn f.pa p.g

πάντων ὑμῶν διὰ τὸ ἔχειν με ἐν τῇ καρδίᾳ ὑμᾶς, ἔν τε
all of you, because ~ I have *I* you in my heart, *you* since both in *both*
4246 7007 1328 3836 1609 2400 1609 7007 1877 3836 2840 7007 5445 1877 5445
a.gpm r.gp.2 p.a d.asn f.pa r.as.1 p.d d.dsf n.dsf r.ap.2 p.d cj

τοῖς δεσμοῖς μου καὶ ἐν τῇ ἀπολογίᾳ καὶ βεβαιώσει τοῦ εὐαγγελίου
{the} my imprisonment *my* and in the defense and confirmation of the gospel,
3836 1609 1301 1609 2779 1877 3836 665 2779 1012 3836 2295
d.dpm n.dpm r.gs.1 cj p.d d.dsf n.dsf cj n.dsf d.gsn n.gsn

συγκοινωνούς μου ↰ τῆς χάριτος πάντας ὑμᾶς ὄντας. 8
you all share with me in the grace *all* *you* *{being}* of God. For God is
7007 4246 5171 1609 5171 3836 5921 4246 7007 1639 1142 2536
n.apm r.gs.1 d.gsf n.gsf a.apm r.ap.2 pt.pa.apm

μάρτυς γάρ μου ὁ θεὸς ὡς ἐπιποθῶ πάντας ὑμᾶς ἐν σπλάγχνοις
my witness *For* *my* *{the}* *God* that I long for all of you with the affection
1609 3459 1142 1609 3836 2536 6055 2160 4246 7007 1877 5073
n.nsm cj r.gs.1 d.nsm n.nsm cj v.pai.1s a.apm r.ap.2 p.d n.dpn

Χριστοῦ Ἰησοῦ. 9 καὶ τοῦτο προσεύχομαι, ἵνα ἡ ἀγάπη ὑμῶν ἔτι
of Christ Jesus. And this I pray, that *{the}* your love *your* may abound *{still}*
5986 2652 2779 4047 4667 2671 3836 7007 27 7007 4355 4355 2285
n.gsm n.gsm cj r.asn v.pmi.1s cj d.nsf n.nsf r.gp.2 adv

NASB

Thanksgiving

1:1 Paul and Timo-
thy, bond-servants
of Christ Jesus,
To all the saints
in Christ Jesus who
are in Philippi,
including the over-
seers and deacons:
2 Grace to you and
peace from God
our Father and the
Lord Jesus Christ.
3 I thank my God
in all my remem-
brance of you,
4 always offering
prayer with joy in
my every prayer
for you all, 5 in view
of your participa-
tion in the gospel
from the first day
until now. 6 *For I
am* confident of
this very thing, that
He who began a
good work in you
will perfect it until
the day of Christ
Jesus. 7 For it is
only right for me to
feel this way about
you all, because
I have you in my
heart, since both in
my imprisonment
and in the defense
and confirmation
of the gospel, you
all are partakers
of grace with me.
8 For God is my
witness, how I long
for you all with the
affection of Christ
Jesus. 9 And this I
pray, that your love
may abound still

NIV

more and more in
knowledge and
depth of insight,
[10]so that you may
be able to dis-
cern what is best
and may be pure
and blameless for
the day of Christ,
[11]filled with the
fruit of righteous-
ness that comes
through Jesus
Christ—to the
glory and praise of
God.

Paul's Chains Advance the Gospel

[12]Now I want you
to know, brothers
and sisters,[a] that
what has happened
to me has actually
served to advance
the gospel. [13]As a
result, it has become
clear throughout the
whole palace guard[b]
and to everyone else
that I am in chains
for Christ. [14]And be-
cause of my chains,
most of the brothers
and sisters have be-
come confident in
the Lord and dare
all the more to pro-
claim the gospel
without fear.
[15]It is true that
some preach Christ
out of envy and ri-
valry, but others out
of goodwill. [16]The
latter do so out of
love, knowing that
I am put here for
the defense of the
gospel. [17]The former
preach Christ out of
selfish ambition, not
sincerely, supposing
that they can stir up
trouble for me while
I am in chains. [18]But
what does it matter?
The important thing
is that in every way,

[a] 12 The Greek word for *brothers and sisters* (*adelphoi*) refers here to believers, both men and women, as part of God's family; also in verse 14; and in 3:1, 13, 17; 4:1, 8, 21.
[b] 13 Or *whole palace*

μᾶλλον καὶ μᾶλλον περισσεύῃ ἐν ἐπιγνώσει καὶ πάσῃ αἰσθήσει [10] εἰς τὸ
more and more, *may abound* with knowledge and all discernment, ⌞so that⌟ ~ you
3437 2779 3437 4355 1877 2106 2779 4246 151 1650 3836 7007
adv.c cj adv.c v.pas.3s p.d n.dsf cj a.dsf n.dsf p.a d.asn

δοκιμάζειν ὑμᾶς τὰ διαφέροντα, ἵνα ἦτε εἰλικρινεῖς καὶ ἀπρόσκοποι εἰς
may determine *you* what is essential, and so be pure and without blame on the
1507 7007 3836 1422 2671 1639 1637 2779 718 1650
f.pa r.ap.2 d.apn pt.pa.apn cj v.pas.2p a.npm cj a.npm p.a

ἡμέραν Χριστοῦ, [11] πεπληρωμένοι καρπὸν δικαιοσύνης τὸν διὰ Ἰησοῦ
day of Christ, filled with the fruit of righteousness that comes through Jesus
2465 5986 4444 2843 1466 3836 1328 2652
n.asf n.gsm pt.rp.npm n.asm n.gsf d.asm p.g n.gsm

Χριστοῦ εἰς δόξαν καὶ ἔπαινον θεοῦ. [12] γινώσκειν δὲ ὑμᾶς
Christ, to the glory and praise of God. Now I want you to know, *Now you*
5986 1650 1518 2779 2047 2536 1254 1089 1089 7007 1182 1254 7007
n.gsm p.a n.asf cj n.asm n.gsm f.pa cj r.ap.2

βούλομαι, ἀδελφοί, ὅτι τὰ κατ᾽ ἐμὲ
I want brothers, that what has happened to me has turned out to advance the gospel
1089 81 4022 3836 2848 1609 2262 2262 2262 1650 4620 3836 2295
v.pmi.1s n.vpm cj d.npn p.a r.as.1

μᾶλλον εἰς προκοπὴν τοῦ εὐαγγελίου ἐλήλυθεν, [13] ὥστε
even more, *to advance the gospel has turned out* so that it has become known
3437 1650 4620 3836 2295 2262 6063 1181 1181 1181 5745
adv.c p.a n.asf d.gsn n.gsn v.rai.3s cj

τοὺς δεσμούς μου
throughout the entire palace guard, and by everyone else, that *{the}* my imprisonment *my*
1877 3836 3910 4550 4550 2779 3836 4246 3370 3836 1609 1301 1609
d.apm n.apm r.gs.1

φανεροὺς ἐν Χριστῷ γενέσθαι ἐν ὅλῳ τῷ πραιτωρίῳ καὶ τοῖς λοιποῖς
known is for Christ, *it has become throughout entire the palace guard and by else*
5745 1877 5986 1181 1877 3910 3836 4550 2779 3836 3370
a.apm p.d n.dsm f.am p.d a.dsn d.dsn n.dsn cj d.dpm a.dpm

πᾶσιν, [14] καὶ τοὺς πλείονας τῶν ἀδελφῶν ἐν κυρίῳ
everyone and that *{the}* most of the brothers, having gained confidence in the Lord
4246 2779 3836 4498 3836 81 4275 4275 4275 1877 3261
a.dpm cj d.apm a.apm.c d.gpm n.gpm p.d n.dsm

πεποιθότας τοῖς δεσμοῖς μου περισσοτέρως τολμᾶν
having gained confidence by my imprisonment, *my* dare more than ever *dare* to speak
4275 3836 1609 1301 1609 5528 4359 5528 3281 3281
pt.ra.apm d.dpm n.dpm r.gs.1 adv f.pa

ἀφόβως τὸν λόγον λαλεῖν. [15] τινὲς μὲν καὶ
the word of God ⌞without fear.⌟ *the word to speak* To be sure, some *To be sure {also}*
3836 3364 925 3836 3364 3281 3525 3525 3525 5516 3525 2779
adv d.asm n.asm f.pa r.npm pl adv

διὰ φθόνον καὶ ἔριν, τινὲς δὲ καὶ δι᾽ εὐδοκίαν τὸν
are proclaiming Christ ⌞out of⌟ envy and strife, but others *but {also}* ⌞out of⌟ goodwill. *{the}*
3062 3062 5986 1328 5784 2779 2251 1254 5516 1254 2779 1328 2306 3836
p.a n.asm cj n.asf r.npm pl adv p.a n.asf d.asm

Χριστὸν κηρύσσουσιν· [16] οἱ μὲν ἐξ ἀγάπης, εἰδότες ὅτι εἰς
Christ are proclaiming The latter do it ⌞out of⌟ love, knowing that I am here for
5986 3062 3836 3525 1666 27 3857 4022 3023 3023 3023 1650
n.asm v.pai.3p d.npm pl p.g n.gsf pt.ra.npm cj p.a

ἀπολογίαν τοῦ εὐαγγελίου κεῖμαι, [17] οἱ δὲ ἐξ
the defense of the gospel. *I am here* The former proclaim Christ ⌞out of⌟ a
665 3836 2295 3023 3836 1254 2859 5986 1666
n.asf d.gsn n.gsn v.pmi.1s d.npm pl p.g

ἐριθείας τὸν Χριστὸν καταγγέλλουσιν, οὐχ ἁγνῶς, οἰόμενοι
sense of hostility, *{the} Christ proclaim* not sincerely, intending to increase my
2249 3836 5986 2859 4024 56 3887 1586 1586
n.gsf d.asm n.asm v.pai.3p pl adv pt.pm.npm

θλῖψιν ἐγείρειν τοῖς δεσμοῖς μου.[a] [18] τί γάρ; πλὴν ὅτι παντὶ τρόπῳ,
distress *to increase* while I am in prison. *I* What then? Only that in every way,
2568 1586 1609 3836 1301 1609 5515 1142 4440 4022 4246 5573
n.asf f.pa d.dpm n.dpm r.gs.1 r.nsn cj cj cj a.dsm n.dsm

[a] TR inverts the order of vv 16 and 17.

NASB

more and more in
real knowledge and
all discernment,
[10]so that you may
approve the things
that are excellent,
in order to be
sincere and blame-
less until the day
of Christ; [11]having
been filled with the
fruit of righteous-
ness which *comes*
through Jesus
Christ, to the glory
and praise of God.

The Gospel Is Preached

[12]Now I want you
to know, brethren,
that my circum-
stances have turned
out for the greater
progress of the
gospel, [13]so that my
imprisonment in
the cause of Christ
has become well
known throughout
the whole [a]prae-
torian guard and
to everyone else,
[14]and that most of
the brethren, trust-
ing in the Lord
because of my im-
prisonment, have
far more courage
to speak the word
of God without
fear. [15]Some, to be
sure, are preaching
Christ even from
envy and strife,
but some also from
good will; [16]the
latter *do it* out of
love, knowing that
I am appointed for
the defense of the
gospel; [17]the former
proclaim Christ
out of selfish ambi-
tion rather than
from pure motives,
thinking to cause
me distress in my
imprisonment.
[18]What then? Only
that in every way,

[a] Or *governor's palace*

NIV

whether from false
motives or true,
Christ is preached.
And because of
this I rejoice.
Yes, and I will
continue to re-
joice, 19 for I know
that through your
prayers and God's
provision of the
Spirit of Jesus
Christ what has
happened to me
will turn out for
my deliverance.[a]
20 I eagerly expect
and hope that I
will in no way be
ashamed, but will
have sufficient
courage so that
now as always
Christ will be ex-
alted in my body,
whether by life
or by death. 21 For
to me, to live is
Christ and to die
is gain. 22 If I am
to go on living in
the body, this will
mean fruitful labor
for me. Yet what
shall I choose? I
do not know! 23 I
am torn between
the two: I desire
to depart and be
with Christ, which
is better by far;
24 but it is more
necessary for you
that I remain in the
body. 25 Convinced
of this, I know that
I will remain, and
I will continue
with all of you for
your progress and
joy in the faith,
26 so that through
my being with you
again your boast-
ing in Christ Jesus
will abound on ac-
count of me.

εἴτε προφάσει εἴτε ἀληθείᾳ, Χριστὸς καταγγέλλεται, καὶ ἐν τούτῳ χαίρω. ἀλλὰ
whether in pretense or in truth, Christ is proclaimed; and in that I rejoice. Yes,
1664 4733 1664 237 5986 2859 2779 1877 4047 5897 247
cj n.dsf cj n.dsf n.nsm v.ppi.3s cj p.d r.dsn v.pai.1s cj

καὶ χαρήσομαι, 19 οἶδα γὰρ ὅτι τοῦτό μοι
and ⌞I will continue to rejoice.⌟ For I know *for* that this will turn out for my
2779 5897 1142 3857 1142 4022 4047 609 609 609 1650 1609
adv v.fpi.1s v.rai.1s cj cj r.nsn r.ds.1

ἀποβήσεται εἰς σωτηρίαν διὰ τῆς ὑμῶν δεήσεως καὶ ἐπιχορηγίας τοῦ
will turn out *for* deliverance through *{the}* your prayers and the help of the
609 1650 5401 1328 3836 7007 1255 2779 2221 3836
v.fmi.3s p.a n.asf p.g d.gsf r.gp.2 n.gsf cj n.gsf d.gsn

πνεύματος Ἰησοῦ Χριστοῦ 20 κατὰ τὴν ἀποκαραδοκίαν καὶ ἐλπίδα μου, ὅτι ➝
Spirit of Jesus Christ. It is *{the}* my earnest expectation and hope *my* that I
4460 2652 5986 2848 3836 1609 638 2779 1828 1609 4022 159
n.gsn n.gsm n.gsm p.a d.asf n.asf cj n.asf r.gs.1 cj

➝ ἐν οὐδενὶ αἰσχυνθήσομαι ἀλλ' ἐν πάσῃ παρρησίᾳ ὡς πάντοτε καὶ
will in no way be put to shame, but that with complete boldness, now as always, *{also}*
159 1877 4029 159 247 1877 4246 4244 3814 6055 4121 2779
p.d a.dsn v.fpi.1s cj p.d a.dsf n.dsf pl adv adv

νῦν μεγαλυνθήσεται Χριστὸς ἐν τῷ σώματί μου, εἴτε διὰ ζωῆς εἴτε
now Christ will be exalted *Christ* in *{the}* my body, *my* whether by life or
3814 5986 3486 5986 1877 3836 1609 5393 1609 1664 1328 2437 1664
adv v.fpi.3s n.nsm p.d d.dsn n.dsn r.gs.1 cj p.g n.gsf cj

διὰ θανάτου. 21 ἐμοὶ γὰρ τὸ ζῆν Χριστὸς καὶ τὸ ἀποθανεῖν κέρδος.
by death. For to me, *For* ~ to live is Christ and ~ to die is gain.
1328 2505 1142 1609 1142 3836 2409 5986 2779 3836 633 3046
p.g n.gsm r.ds.1 cj d.nsn f.pa n.nsm cj d.nsn f.aa n.nsn

22 εἰ δὲ τὸ ζῆν ἐν σαρκί, τοῦτό μοι
If *{and}* I am ~ ⌞to go on living⌟ in the flesh, that means fruitful labor ⌞for me;⌟
1623 1254 3836 2409 1877 4922 4047 2843 2240 1609
cj cj d.nsn f.pa p.d n.dsf r.nsn r.ds.1

καρπὸς ἔργου, καὶ τί αἱρήσομαι οὐ γνωρίζω.
fruitful *labor* yet I do not know which I would prefer. *not* *I do know*
2843 2240 2779 1192 1192 4024 1192 5515 145 4024 1192
n.nsm n.gsn cj r.asn v.fmi.1s pl v.pai.1s

23 συνέχομαι δὲ ἐκ τῶν δύο, τὴν ἐπιθυμίαν ἔχων εἰς τὸ
I am hard pressed *{and}* between the two, in that I have the desire *I have* to ~
5309 1254 1666 3836 1545 2400 2400 3836 2123 2400 1650 3836
v.ppi.1s cj p.g d.gpn a.gpn d.asf n.asf pt.pa.nsm p.a d.asn

ἀναλῦσαι καὶ σὺν Χριστῷ εἶναι, πολλῷ γὰρ[a] μᾶλλον
depart and be with Christ, *be* for that is much better by far, *for* *much*
386 2779 1639 5250 5986 1639 1142 3437 3202 4498 1142 3437
f.aa cj p.d n.dsm f.pa a.dsn cj adv.c

κρεῖσσον· 24 τὸ δὲ ἐπιμένειν ἐν[b] τῇ σαρκὶ
better ~ yet for your sake it is better that I remain in the flesh.
3202 3836 1254 1328 7007 1328 338 2152 1877 3836 4922
a.nsn.c d.nsn cj f.pa p.d d.dsf n.dsf

ἀναγκαιότερον δι' ὑμᾶς. 25 καὶ τοῦτο πεποιθὼς οἶδα ὅτι
better *for sake* *your* So, convinced of this, *convinced of* I know that
338 1328 7007 2779 4275 4275 4047 4275 3857 4022
a.nsn.c p.a r.ap.2 cj r.asn pt.ra.nsm v.rai.1s cj

μενῶ καὶ παραμενῶ πᾶσιν ὑμῖν εἰς τὴν ὑμῶν προκοπὴν καὶ χαρὰν
⌞I will remain,⌟ and ⌞I will continue with⌟ all of you for *{the}* your progress and joy
3531 2779 4169 4246 7007 1650 3836 7007 4620 2779 5915
v.fai.1s cj v.fai.1s a.dpm r.dp.2 p.a d.asf r.gp.2 n.asf cj n.asf

τῆς πίστεως, 26 ἵνα τὸ καύχημα ὑμῶν
in the faith, so that when I come again to you, *{the}* your boasting *your* in
3836 4411 2671 1328 1847 4242 4099 4639 7007 3836 7007 3017 7007 1877
d.gsf n.gsf cj d.nsn n.nsn r.gp.2

περισσεύῃ ἐν Χριστῷ Ἰησοῦ ἐν ἐμοὶ διὰ τῆς ἐμῆς παρουσίας
Christ Jesus might abound *in* *Christ* *Jesus* ⌞because of⌟ me. *when* *{the}* *I* *come*
5986 2652 4355 1877 5986 2652 1877 1609 1328 3836 1847 4242
v.pas.3s p.d n.dsm n.dsm p.d r.ds.1 p.g d.gsf r.gsf.1 n.gsf

NASB

whether in pretense
or in truth, Christ is
proclaimed; and in
this I rejoice.
Yes, and I will
rejoice, 19 for I
know that this will
turn out for my de-
liverance through
your prayers and
the provision of
the Spirit of Jesus
Christ, 20 accord-
ing to my earnest
expectation and
hope, that I will not
be put to shame in
anything, but *that*
with all boldness,
Christ will even
now, as always, be
exalted in my body,
whether by life or
by death.

To Live Is Christ

21 For to me, to live
is Christ and to
die is gain. 22 But if
I am to live *on* in
the flesh, this *will*
mean fruitful labor
for me; and I do
not know which to
choose. 23 But I am
hard-pressed from
both *directions,*
having the desire to
depart and be with
Christ, for *that* is
very much better;
24 yet to remain on
in the flesh is more
necessary for your
sake. 25 Convinced
of this, I know that
I will remain and
continue with you
all for your prog-
ress and joy in the
faith, 26 so that your
proud confidence
in me may abound
in Christ Jesus
through my coming
to you again.

[a] 19 Or *vindication*; or *salvation*

[a] [γὰρ] UBS.
[b] [ἐν] UBS, omitted by TNIV.

NIV

Life Worthy of the Gospel

[27]Whatever happens, conduct yourselves in a manner worthy of the gospel of Christ. Then, whether I come and see you or only hear about you in my absence, I will know that you stand firm in the one Spirit,[a] striving together as one for the faith of the gospel [28]without being frightened in any way by those who oppose you. This is a sign to them that they will be destroyed, but that you will be saved—and that by God. [29]For it has been granted to you on behalf of Christ not only to believe in him, but also to suffer for him, [30]since you are going through the same struggle you saw I had, and now hear that I still have.

Imitating Christ's Humility

2 Therefore if you have any encouragement from being united with Christ, if any comfort from his love, if any common sharing in the Spirit, if any tenderness and compassion, [2]then make my joy complete by being like-minded, having the same love, being one in spirit and of one mind. [3]Do nothing out of selfish ambition or vain conceit. Rather, in humility value others

[a] 27 Or *in one spirit*

πάλιν πρὸς ὑμᾶς. [27] μόνον ἀξίως τοῦ εὐαγγελίου τοῦ
again *to* *you* Only conduct yourselves ⌊in a manner worthy⌋ of the gospel of
4099 4639 7007 3667 4488 4488 547 3836 2295 3836
adv p.a r.ap.2 adv adv d.gsn n.gsn d.gsm

Χριστοῦ πολιτεύεσθε, ἵνα εἴτε ἐλθὼν καὶ ἰδὼν ὑμᾶς εἴτε ἀπὼν
Christ, *conduct yourselves* so that, whether I come and see you or ⌊remain away,⌋
5986 4488 2671 1664 2262 2779 1625 7007 1664 583
n.gsm v.pmm.2p cj cj pt.aa.nsm cj pt.aa.nsm r.ap.2 cj pt.pa.nsm

ἀκούω τὰ περὶ ὑμῶν, ὅτι στήκετε ἐν ἑνὶ πνεύματι,
I may hear *{the things}* *{concerning}* *{you}* that ⌊you are standing firm⌋ in one spirit, striving
201 3836 4309 7007 4022 5112 1877 1651 4460 5254
v.pas.1s d.apn p.g r.gp.2 cj v.pai.2p p.d a.dsn n.dsn

μιᾷ ψυχῇ συναθλοῦντες τῇ πίστει τοῦ εὐαγγελίου
side by side with one mind *striving side by side with* ⌊for the⌋ faith of the gospel,
5254 5254 5254 5254 1651 6034 5254 3836 4411 3836 2295
a.dsf n.dsf pt.pa.npm d.dsf n.dsf d.gsn n.gsn

[28] καὶ μὴ → πτυρόμενοι ἐν μηδενὶ ὑπὸ τῶν ἀντικειμένων, ἥτις ἐστὶν
and *{not}* are in no way frightened *in* *no way* by your opponents. This is
2779 3590 1877 3594 3594 4769 1877 3594 5679 3836 512 4015 1639
cj pl pt.pp.npm p.d a.dsn p.g d.gpm pt.pm.gpm r.nsf v.pai.3s

αὐτοῖς ἔνδειξις ἀπωλείας, ὑμῶν δὲ σωτηρίας,
a sign of destruction for them, *sign* *of destruction* but of salvation for you *but* *of salvation*
1893 724 724 899 1893 724 1254 5401 5401 7007 1254 5401
r.dpm.3 n.nsf n.gsf r.gp.2 cj n.gsf

καὶ τοῦτο ἀπὸ θεοῦ· [29] ὅτι ὑμῖν ἐχαρίσθη τὸ
— and that from God. For it has been granted to you *it has been granted* ~
2779 4047 608 2536 4022 5919 5919 5919 5919 7007 5919 3836
cj r.nsn p.g n.gsm cj r.dp.2 v.api.3s d.nsn

ὑπὲρ Χριστοῦ, οὐ μόνον τὸ εἰς αὐτὸν πιστεύειν ἀλλὰ καὶ τὸ
⌊on behalf of⌋ Christ, not only ~ to believe in him *to believe* but also ~
5642 5986 4024 3667 3836 4409 4409 1650 899 4409 247 2779 3836
p.g n.gsm pl adv d.nsn p.a r.asm.3 f.pa cj adv d.nsn

ὑπὲρ αὐτοῦ πάσχειν, [30] τὸν αὐτὸν ἀγῶνα
to suffer for him, *to suffer* since you are experiencing the same conflict
4248 4248 5642 899 4248 2400 2400 2400 2400 3836 899 74
p.g r.gsm.3 f.pa d.asm r.asm n.asm

ἔχοντες, οἷον εἴδετε ἐν ἐμοὶ καὶ νῦν ἀκούετε ἐν
since you are experiencing which you saw me in, *me* and now hear that I still face.
2400 3888 1625 1609 1877 1609 2779 3814 201 1609 1877
pt.pa.npm r.asm v.aai.2p p.d r.ds.1 cj adv v.pai.2p p.d

ἐμοί.
I
1609
r.ds.1

2:1 εἴ τις οὖν παράκλησις ἐν Χριστῷ, εἴ τι παραμύθιον
So if there is any *So* encouragement in Christ, if any comfort
4036 1623 5516 4036 4155 1877 5986 1623 5516 4172
cj r.nsf cj n.nsf p.d n.dsm cj r.nsn n.nsn

ἀγάπης, εἴ τις κοινωνία → πνεύματος, εἴ τις σπλάγχνα καὶ οἰκτιρμοί,
from love, if any fellowship in the Spirit, if any affection and compassion,
27 1623 5516 3126 4460 1623 5516 5073 2779 3880
n.gsf cj r.nsf n.nsf n.gsn cj r.nsm n.npn cj n.npm

[2] πληρώσατέ μου τὴν χαρὰν ↰ ἵνα τὸ ⌊αὐτὸ φρονῆτε,⌋ τὴν
make my *{the}* joy complete by *{the}* being like-minded, having the
4444 1609 3836 5915 4444 2671 3836 899 5858 2400 3836
v.aam.2p r.gs.1 d.asf n.asf cj d.asn r.asn v.pas.2p d.asf

αὐτὴν ἀγάπην ἔχοντες, σύμψυχοι, τὸ ἓν φρονοῦντες, [3] μηδὲν κατ᾽
same love, *having* united in spirit, ⌊with a⌋ single purpose. Do nothing out of
899 27 2400 5249 3836 1651 5858 3594 2848
r.asf n.asf pt.pa.npm a.npm d.asn a.asn pt.pa.npm a.asn p.a

ἐριθείαν μηδὲ κατὰ κενοδοξίαν ἀλλὰ τῇ ταπεινοφροσύνῃ ἀλλήλους
selfish ambition or *{out of}* vain conceit, but in humility consider others
2249 3593 2848 3029 247 3836 5425 2451 253
n.asf cj p.a n.asf cj d.dsf n.dsf r.apm

NASB

[27]Only conduct yourselves in a manner worthy of the gospel of Christ, so that whether I come and see you or remain absent, I will hear of you that you are standing firm in one spirit, with one mind striving together for the faith of the gospel; [28]in no way alarmed by *your* opponents—which is a sign of destruction for them, but of salvation for you, and that *too*, from God. [29]For to you it has been granted for Christ's sake, not only to believe in Him, but also to suffer for His sake, [30]experiencing the same conflict which you saw in me, and now hear *to be* in me.

Be Like Christ

[2:1]Therefore if there is any encouragement in Christ, if there is any consolation of love, if there is any fellowship of the Spirit, if any affection and compassion, [2]make my joy complete by being of the same mind, maintaining the same love, united in spirit, intent on one purpose. [3]Do nothing from selfishness or empty conceit, but with humility of mind regard one another

NIV

above yourselves, 4not looking to your own interests but each of you to the interests of the others.

5In your relationships with one another, have the same mindset as Christ Jesus:

6Who, being in very nature[a] God,
did not consider equality with God something to be used to his own advantage;
7rather, he made himself nothing
by taking the very nature[b] of a servant,
being made in human likeness.
8And being found in appearance as a man,
he humbled himself
by becoming obedient to death—
even death on a cross!
9Therefore God exalted him to the highest place
and gave him the name that is above every name,
10that at the name of Jesus every knee should bow,
in heaven and on earth and under the earth,
11and every tongue acknowledge that Jesus Christ is Lord,
to the glory of God the Father.

Do Everything Without Grumbling

12Therefore, my dear friends, as you have always obeyed—not only in my presence, but now much

[a] 6 Or *in the form of*
[b] 7 Or *the form*

ἡγούμενοι ὑπερέχοντας ἑαυτῶν, 4 μὴ[a]
consider more important than yourselves. Each person should look out not only for his own
2451 5660 1571 1667 1667 5023 5023 5023 3590 1571 1571
pt.pm.npm pt.pa.apm r.gpm.2 pl

τὰ ἑαυτῶν ἕκαστος σκοποῦντες ἀλλὰ καὶ[b] τὰ ἑτέρων ἕκαστοι.
interests, *his own* *Each person* *should look out* but also for ⌞the interests⌟ of others. *{each}*
3836 1571 1667 5023 247 2779 3836 2283 1667
d.apn r.gpm.2 r.nsm pt.pa.npm cj adv d.apn r.gpm r.npm

5 τοῦτο φρονεῖτε ἐν ὑμῖν ὃ καὶ ἐν
Your attitude toward one another should be the same *attitude* *{in}* *Your* as that *as* of
7007 5858 4047 5858 1877 7007 2779 4005 2779 1877
r.asn v.pam.2p p.d r.dp.2 r.nsn adv p.d

Χριστῷ Ἰησοῦ, 6ὃς ἐν μορφῇ θεοῦ ὑπάρχων οὐχ
Christ Jesus, who, although he was in the form of God, *although he was* did not
5986 2652 4005 5639 5639 5639 1877 3671 2536 5639 2451 4024
n.dsm n.dsm r.nsm p.d n.dsf n.gsm pt.pa.nsm pl

→ ἁρπαγμὸν ἡγήσατο τὸ εἶναι ἴσα θεῷ,
regard equality with God a thing to be grasped, *did regard* ~ *to be* *equality* *with God*
2451 2698 2536 2536 1639 1639 772 2451 3836 1639 2698 2536
n.asm v.ami.3s d.asn f.pa adv n.dsm

7ἀλλὰ ἑαυτὸν ἐκένωσεν μορφὴν → δούλου λαβών, ἐν
but emptied himself, *emptied* taking on the form of a servant, *taking on* being born in
247 3033 1571 3033 3284 3284 3671 1529 3284 1181 1181 1877
cj r.asm.3 v.aai.3s n.asf n.gsm pt.aa.nsm p.d

ὁμοιώματι ἀνθρώπων γενόμενος· καὶ σχήματι εὑρεθεὶς ὡς
the likeness of man. *being born* And being found in appearance *being found* as a
3930 476 1181 2779 2351 2351 5386 2351 6055
n.dsn n.gpm pt.am.nsm cj n.dsn pt.ap.nsm pl

ἄνθρωπος 8ἐταπείνωσεν ἑαυτὸν γενόμενος ὑπήκοος μέχρι θανάτου, θανάτου
man he humbled himself, becoming obedient ⌞to the point⌟ of death, even death
476 5427 1571 1181 5675 3588 2505 1254 2505
n.nsm v.aai.3s r.asm.3 pt.am.nsm a.nsm p.g n.gsm n.gsm

δὲ → σταυροῦ. 9διὸ καὶ ὁ θεὸς αὐτὸν ὑπερύψωσεν
even on a cross! Therefore *{also}* *{the}* God has highly exalted him *has highly exalted*
1254 5089 1475 2779 3836 2536 5671 5671 5671 899 5671
cj n.gsm cj adv d.nsm n.nsm r.asm.3 v.aai.3s

καὶ ἐχαρίσατο αὐτῷ τὸ ὄνομα τὸ ὑπὲρ πᾶν ὄνομα, 10ἵνα ἐν τῷ ὀνόματι
and bestowed on him the name that is above every name, so that at the name
2779 5919 899 3836 3950 3836 5642 4246 3950 2671 1877 3836 3950
cj v.ami.3s r.dsm.3 d.asn n.asn d.asn p.a a.asn n.asn cj p.d d.dsn n.dsn

Ἰησοῦ πᾶν γόνυ κάμψῃ ἐπουρανίων καὶ ἐπιγείων καὶ → καταχθονίων
of Jesus every knee should bow, in heaven, and on earth and under the earth,
2652 4246 1205 2828 2230 2779 2103 2779 2973
n.gsm a.nsn n.nsn v.aas.3s a.gpm cj a.gpm cj a.gpm

11καὶ πᾶσα γλῶσσα ἐξομολογήσηται ὅτι κύριος Ἰησοῦς Χριστὸς εἰς
and every tongue confess that Jesus Christ is Lord, *Jesus* *Christ* to the
2779 4246 1185 2018 4022 2652 5986 3261 2652 5986 1650
cj a.nsf n.nsf v.ams.3s cj n.nsm n.nsm n.nsm p.a

δόξαν θεοῦ πατρός. 12ὥστε, ἀγαπητοί μου, καθὼς ↱ ↱ πάντοτε
glory of God the Father. So then, my dear friends, *my* just as you have always
1518 2536 4252 6063 1609 28 1609 2777 5634 5634 4121
n.asf n.gsm n.gsm cj a.vpm r.gs.1 cj adv

ὑπηκούσατε, μὴ ὡς ἐν τῇ παρουσίᾳ μου μόνον ἀλλὰ νῦν
obeyed, not only *{as}* in *{the}* my presence *my* *only* but even more now
5634 3590 3667 6055 1877 3836 1609 4242 1609 3667 247 4498 3437 3814
v.aai.2p pl pl p.d d.dsf n.dsf r.gs.1 adv cj adv

[a] μή not included by TNIV.
[b] [καὶ] UBS.

NASB

as more important than yourselves; 4do not *merely* look out for your own personal interests, but also for the interests of others. 5Have this attitude in yourselves which was also in Christ Jesus, 6who, although He existed in the form of God, did not regard equality with God a thing to be grasped, 7but [a]emptied Himself, taking the form of a bond-servant, *and* being made in the likeness of men. 8Being found in appearance as a man, He humbled Himself by becoming obedient to the point of death, even death on a cross. 9For this reason also, God highly exalted Him, and bestowed on Him the name which is above every name, 10so that at the name of Jesus EVERY KNEE WILL BOW, of those who are in heaven and on earth and under the earth, 11and that every tongue will confess that Jesus Christ is Lord, to the glory of God the Father.

12So then, my beloved, just as you have always obeyed, not as in my presence only, but now much more in my

[a] I.e. laid aside His privileges

NIV

more in my ab-
sence—continue
to work out your
salvation with fear
and trembling,
13 for it is God who
works in you to
will and to act in
order to fulfill his
good purpose.
14 Do everything
without grumbling
or arguing, 15 so
that you may be-
come blameless
and pure, "children
of God without
fault in a warped
and crooked gener-
ation."[a] Then you
will shine among
them like stars in
the sky 16 as you
hold firmly to the
word of life. And
then I will be able
to boast on the day
of Christ that I did
not run or labor in
vain. 17 But even if
I am being poured
out like a drink of-
fering on the sac-
rifice and service
coming from your
faith, I am glad
and rejoice with
all of you. 18 So
you too should be
glad and rejoice
with me.

Timothy and Epaphroditus

19 I hope in the
Lord Jesus to send
Timothy to you
soon, that I also
may be cheered
when I receive
news about you.
20 I have no one
else like him, who
will show genuine
concern for your
welfare. 21 For ev-
eryone looks out
for their own in-
terests, not those
of Jesus Christ.
22 But you know
that Timothy has
proved himself,

πολλῷ μᾶλλον ἐν τῇ ἀπουσίᾳ μου, μετὰ
even *more* in *{the}* my absence, *my* continue to work out your salvation with
4498 3437 1877 3836 1609 707 1609 2981 2981 2981 2981 1571 5401 3552
a.dsn adv.c p.d d.dsf n.dsf r.gs.1 p.g

φόβου καὶ τρόμου τὴν ἑαυτῶν σωτηρίαν κατεργάζεσθε· 13 θεὸς γάρ
fear and trembling, *{the}* *your* *salvation* *continue to work out* for it is God *for*
5832 2779 5571 3836 1571 5401 2981 1142 1639 1639 2536 1142
n.gsm cj n.gsm d.asf r.gpm.2 n.asf v.pmm.2p n.nsm cj

ἐστιν ὁ ἐνεργῶν ἐν ὑμῖν καὶ τὸ θέλειν καὶ τὸ ἐνεργεῖν ὑπὲρ τῆς
it is who is at work in you, both ~ to will and ~ to work ⌞on behalf of⌟ his
1639 3836 1919 1877 7007 2779 3836 2527 2779 3836 1919 5642 3836
v.pai.3s d.nsm pt.pa.nsm p.d r.dp.2 cj d.asn f.pa cj d.asn f.pa p.g d.gsf

εὐδοκίας. 14 πάντα ποιεῖτε χωρὶς γογγυσμῶν καὶ διαλογισμῶν, 15 ἵνα
good pleasure. Do all things *Do* without grumbling or arguing, so that
2306 4472 4246 4472 6006 1198 2779 1369 2671
n.gsf a.apn v.pam.2p p.g n.gpm cj n.gpm cj

γένησθε ἄμεμπτοι καὶ ἀκέραιοι, τέκνα θεοῦ ἄμωμα μέσον →
⌞you may be⌟ blameless and innocent, children of God above reproach in the midst of a crooked
1181 289 2779 193 5451 2536 320 3545 5021
v.ams.2p a.npm cj a.npm n.npn n.gsm a.npn p.g

γενεᾶς σκολιᾶς καὶ διεστραμμένης, ἐν οἷς φαίνεσθε ὡς φωστῆρες
and perverse generation, *crooked* *and* *perverse* among whom you shine like stars
2779 1406 1155 5021 2779 1406 1877 4005 5743 6055 5891
n.gsf a.gsf cj pt.rp.gsf p.d r.dpm v.pmi.2p pl n.npm

ἐν κόσμῳ, 16 λόγον ζωῆς ἐπέχοντες, εἰς
in the universe, holding fast the word of life, *holding fast* ⌞so that⌟ I may have reason to
1877 3180 2091 2091 3364 2437 2091 1650 1609
p.d n.dsm n.asm n.gsf pt.pa.npm p.a

καύχημα ἐμοὶ εἰς ἡμέραν Χριστοῦ, ὅτι οὐκ εἰς κενὸν ἔδραμον οὐδὲ
boast *I* on the day of Christ that I did not run in vain *I did run* or
3017 1609 1650 2465 5986 4022 5556 5556 4024 5556 1650 3031 5556 4028
n.asn r.ds.1 p.a n.asf n.gsm cj pl p.a a.asn v.aai.1s cj

εἰς κενὸν ἐκοπίασα. 17 ἀλλὰ εἰ καὶ σπένδομαι
labor in vain. *labor* But even if *even* ⌞I am to be poured out as a drink offering⌟
3159 1650 3031 3159 247 2779 1623 2779 5064
p.a a.asn v.aai.1s cj cj adv v.ppi.1s

ἐπὶ τῇ θυσίᾳ καὶ λειτουργίᾳ τῆς πίστεως ὑμῶν, χαίρω καὶ συγχαίρω πᾶσιν
upon the sacrifice and service of your faith, *your* I am glad and rejoice with all
2093 3836 2602 2779 3311 3836 7007 4411 7007 5897 2779 5176 4246
p.d d.dsf n.dsf cj n.dsf d.gsf n.gsf r.gp.2 v.pai.1s cj v.pai.1s a.dpm

ὑμῖν· 18 ⌞τὸ δὲ αὐτὸ⌟ καὶ ὑμεῖς χαίρετε καὶ συγχαίρετέ μοι.
of you. Likewise you also *you* ⌞should be glad⌟ and rejoice with me.
7007 3836 1254 899 7007 2779 7007 5897 2779 5176 1609
r.dp.2 d.asn cj r.asn adv r.np.2 v.pam.2p cj v.pam.2p r.ds.1

19 ἐλπίζω δὲ ἐν κυρίῳ Ἰησοῦ Τιμόθεον ταχέως πέμψαι ὑμῖν,
I hope *{and}* in the Lord Jesus to send Timothy to you soon, *to send* *to you*
1827 1254 1877 3261 2652 4287 4287 5510 7007 7007 5441 4287 7007
v.pai.1s cj p.d n.dsm n.dsm n.asm adv f.aa r.dp.2

ἵνα κἀγὼ εὐψυχῶ γνοὺς τὰ περὶ ὑμῶν. 20 οὐδένα γὰρ
so that I too may be encouraged by news *{the}* about you. For I have no one else *For*
2671 2743 2379 1182 3836 4309 7007 1142 2400 2400 4029 1142
cj crasis v.pas.1s pt.aa.nsm d.apn p.g r.gp.2 a.asm cj

ἔχω ἰσόψυχον, ὅστις γνησίως τὰ περὶ ὑμῶν
I have of like mind who will be genuinely concerned for your welfare. *for* *your*
2400 2701 4015 3534 3534 1189 3534 4309 7007 3836 4309 7007
v.pai.1s a.asm r.nsm adv d.apn p.g r.gp.2

μεριμνήσει· 21 οἱ πάντες γὰρ τὰ ἑαυτῶν ζητοῦσιν,
will be concerned For they all *For* look out for their own interests, *their own* *look out for*
3534 1142 3836 4246 1142 2426 2426 2426 1571 1571 3836 1571 2426
v.fai.3s d.npm a.npm cj d.apn r.gpm.3 v.pai.3p

οὐ τὰ Ἰησοῦ Χριστοῦ. 22 τὴν δὲ δοκιμὴν αὐτοῦ
not for those of Jesus Christ. *{the}* But you know Timothy's proven character, *Timothy's*
4024 3836 2652 5986 3836 1254 1182 1182 899 1509 899
pl d.apn n.gsm n.gsm d.asf cj n.asf r.gsm.3

NASB

absence, work out
your salvation with
fear and trembling;
13 for it is God who
is at work in you,
both to will and to
work for *His* good
pleasure.
14 Do all things
without grumbling
or disputing; 15 so
that you will prove
yourselves to be
blameless and in-
nocent, children
of God above re-
proach in the midst
of a crooked and
perverse genera-
tion, among whom
you appear as
lights in the world,
16 holding fast the
word of life, so that
in the day of Christ
I will have reason
to glory because I
did not run in vain
nor toil in vain.
17 But even if I am
being poured out
as a drink offering
upon the sacrifice
and service of your
faith, I rejoice and
share my joy with
you all. 18 You too,
I urge you, rejoice
in the same way
and share your joy
with me.

Timothy and Epaphroditus

19 But I hope in
the Lord Jesus to
send Timothy to
you shortly, so
that I also may be
encouraged when
I learn of your
condition. 20 For I
have no one *else*
of kindred spirit
who will genuinely
be concerned for
your welfare. 21 For
they all seek after
their own interests,
not those of Christ
Jesus. 22 But you
know of his proven
worth, that he

[a] 15 Deut. 32:5

NIV

because as a son
with his father he
has served with me
in the work of the
gospel. [23]I hope,
therefore, to send
him as soon as I
see how things go
with me. [24]And I
am confident in
the Lord that I
myself will come
soon.
[25]But I think it
is necessary to
send back to you
Epaphroditus, my
brother, co-worker
and fellow soldier,
who is also your
messenger, whom
you sent to take
care of my needs.
[26]For he longs for
all of you and is
distressed because
you heard he was
ill. [27]Indeed he
was ill, and almost
died. But God had
mercy on him, and
not on him only
but also on me,
to spare me sor-
row upon sorrow.
[28]Therefore I am
all the more eager
to send him, so
that when you see
him again you may
be glad and I may
have less anxiety.
[29]So then, welcome
him in the Lord
with great joy, and
honor people like
him, [30]because he
almost died for the
work of Christ.
He risked his life
to make up for the
help you your-
selves could not

γινώσκετε, ὅτι ὡς → πατρὶ τέκνον σὺν ἐμοὶ ἐδούλευσεν
you know how as a child with his father *child* he served with me *he served*
1182 4022 6055 5451 4252 5451 1526 1526 5250 1609 1526
v.pai.2p cj cj n.dsm n.nsn p.d r.ds.1 v.aai.3s

εἰς τὸ εὐαγγέλιον. [23] τοῦτον μὲν οὖν ἐλπίζω πέμψαι
⌊in the furtherance of⌋ the gospel. *him* ~ Therefore I hope to send him just
1650 3836 2295 4047 3525 4036 1827 4287 4047 1994
p.a d.asn n.asn r.asm pl cj v.pai.1s f.aa

ὡς ἂν ἀφίδω τὰ περὶ ἐμὲ ἐξαυτῆς· [24] πέποιθα δὲ
as soon as ~ I see how things will turn out for me; *just as soon* and I trust *and*
1994 1994 6055 323 927 3836 4309 1609 1994 1254 4275 1254
cj pl v.aas.1s d.apn p.a r.as.1 adv v.rai.1s cj

ἐν κυρίῳ ὅτι καὶ αὐτὸς ταχέως ἐλεύσομαι. [25]
in the Lord that I myself also *myself* will be coming soon. *I will be coming* In
1877 3261 4022 2262 899 2779 899 2262 2262 2262 5441 2262 1254
p.d n.dsm cj adv r.nsm adv v.fmi.1s

ἀναγκαῖον δὲ ἡγησάμην
the meantime I think it necessary *In the meantime* *I think* to send to you
1254 1254 2451 2451 338 1254 2451 4287 4287 4639 7007
a.nsn cj v.ami.1s

Ἐπαφρόδιτον τὸν ἀδελφὸν καὶ συνεργὸν καὶ συστρατιώτην μου,
Epaphroditus, *{the}* my brother, *{and}* fellow worker, and fellow soldier, *my* as well as
2073 3836 1609 81 2779 5301 2779 5369 1609 1254 1254 1254
n.asm d.asm n.asm cj n.asm cj n.asm r.gs.1

ὑμῶν δὲ ἀπόστολον καὶ λειτουργὸν τῆς χρείας μου, πέμψαι πρὸς ὑμᾶς,
your *as well as* messenger and minister to my need, *my* *to send* *to* *you*
7007 1254 693 2779 3313 3836 1609 5970 1609 4287 4639 7007
r.gp.2 cj n.asm cj n.asm d.gsf n.gsf r.gs.1 f.aa p.a r.ap.2

[26] ἐπειδὴ ἐπιποθῶν ἦν πάντας ὑμᾶς καὶ ἀδημονῶν,
because he has been longing for *he has been* all of you and has been distressed
2076 1639 1639 1639 2160 1639 4246 7007 2779 86
cj pt.pa.nsm v.iai.3s a.apm r.ap.2 cj pt.pa.nsm

διότι ἠκούσατε ὅτι ἠσθένησεν. [27] ⌊καὶ γὰρ⌋ ἠσθένησεν παραπλήσιον θανάτῳ·
because you heard that he was ill. Indeed he was ill; he almost died.
1484 201 4022 820 2779 1142 820 4180 2505
cj v.aai.2p cj v.aai.3s adv cj v.aai.3s adv n.dsm

ἀλλὰ ὁ θεὸς ἠλέησεν αὐτόν, οὐκ αὐτὸν δὲ μόνον ἀλλὰ
But *{the}* God ⌊had mercy on⌋ him, and not only on him *and* *only* but on me
247 3836 2536 1796 899 1254 4024 3667 899 1254 3667 247 1609
cj d.nsm n.nsm v.aai.3s r.asm.3 pl r.asm.3 cj adv cj

καὶ ἐμέ, ἵνα μὴ λύπην ἐπὶ λύπην σχῶ. [28] ↱ ↱
as well, *me* so that I would not have sorrow upon sorrow. *I would have* Therefore I am
2779 1609 2671 2400 2400 3590 2400 3383 2093 3383 2400 4036 4287 4287
adv r.as.1 cj pl n.asf p.a n.asf v.aas.1s

σπουδαιοτέρως οὖν ἔπεμψα αὐτόν, ἵνα ἰδόντες αὐτὸν πάλιν χαρῆτε
all the more eager *Therefore* to send him, so that ⌊when you see⌋ him again ⌊you may rejoice⌋
5081 4036 4287 899 2671 1625 899 4099 5897
adv.c cj v.aai.1s r.asm.3 cj pt.aa.npm r.asm.3 adv v.aps.2p

κἀγὼ → → ἀλυπότερος ὦ. [29] προσδέχεσθε οὖν αὐτὸν ἐν
and I may no longer be anxious. *may be* Therefore welcome *Therefore* him in
2743 1639 1639 267 1639 4036 4657 4036 899 1877
crasis a.nsm.c v.pas.1s v.pmm.2p cj r.asm.3 p.d

κυρίῳ μετὰ πάσης χαρᾶς καὶ τοὺς τοιούτους ἐντίμους ἔχετε, [30] ὅτι
the Lord with great joy, and hold *{the}* such men in honor, *hold* because he
3261 3552 4246 5915 2779 2400 3836 5525 1952 2400 4022 1581
n.dsm p.g a.gsf n.gsf cj d.apm r.apm a.apm v.pam.2p cj

διὰ τὸ ἔργον Χριστοῦ μέχρι θανάτου ἤγγισεν
came close to death for the work of Christ, *to* *death* *he came close*
1581 1581 3588 2505 1328 3836 2240 5986 3588 2505 1581
p.a d.asn n.asn n.gsm p.g n.gsm v.aai.3s

παραβολευσάμενος τῇ ψυχῇ, ἵνα ἀναπληρώσῃ τὸ ὑμῶν ὑστέρημα τῆς
risking his life to make up for the help *{the}* you were not able *the*
4129 3836 6034 2671 405 3836 3311 3836 7007 5729 3836
pt.am.nsm d.dsf n.dsf cj v.aas.3s d.asn r.gp.2 n.asn d.gsf

NASB

served with me in
the furtherance of
the gospel like a
child *serving* his
father. [23]Therefore
I hope to send him
immediately, as
soon as I see how
things *go* with me;
[24]and I trust in the
Lord that I myself
also will be coming
shortly. [25]But I
thought it neces-
sary to send to you
Epaphroditus, my
brother and fellow
worker and fellow
soldier, who is also
your messenger
and minister to my
need; [26]because he
was longing [a]for
you all and was
distressed because
you had heard that
he was sick. [27]For
indeed he was
sick to the point of
death, but God had
mercy on him, and
not on him only
but also on me, so
that I would not
have sorrow upon
sorrow. [28]Therefore
I have sent him all
the more eagerly
so that when you
see him again you
may rejoice and I
may be less con-
cerned *about you.*
[29]Receive him then
in the Lord with all
joy, and hold men
like him in high
regard; [30]because
he came close to
death for the work
of Christ, risking
his life to complete
what was deficient
in your service
to me.

[a] One early ms reads *to see you all*

NIV

give me.

No Confidence in the Flesh

3 Further, my brothers and sisters, rejoice in the Lord! It is no trouble for me to write the same things to you again, and it is a safeguard for you. [2]Watch out for those dogs, those evildoers, those mutilators of the flesh. [3]For it is we who are the circumcision, we who serve God by his Spirit, who boast in Christ Jesus, and who put no confidence in the flesh— [4]though I myself have reasons for such confidence.

If someone else thinks they have reasons to put confidence in the flesh, I have more: [5]circumcised on the eighth day, of the people of Israel, of the tribe of Benjamin, a Hebrew of Hebrews; in regard to the law, a Pharisee; [6]as for zeal, persecuting the church; as for righteousness based on the law, faultless.

[7]But whatever were gains to me I now consider loss for the sake of Christ. [8]What is more, I consider everything a loss because of the surpassing worth of knowing Christ Jesus my Lord, for whose sake I have lost all things. I consider them garbage,

πρός με λειτουργίας.
to give me. *help*
4639 1609 3311
p.a r.as.1 n.gsf

3:1 τὸ λοιπόν, ἀδελφοί μου, χαίρετε ἐν κυρίῳ. τὰ αὐτὰ
{the} Finally, my brethren, *my* rejoice in the Lord. To write the ⌊same things⌋
3836 3370 1609 81 1609 5897 1877 3261 1211 1211 3836 899
d.asn adv n.vpm r.gs.1 v.pam.2p p.d n.dsm d.apn r.apn

γράφειν ὑμῖν ἐμοὶ μὲν οὐκ ὀκνηρόν, ὑμῖν
To write again to you is no trouble for me, ~ *no trouble* and it is a safeguard for you.
1211 7007 4024 3891 1609 3525 4024 3891 1254 855 7007
f.pa r.dp.2 r.ds.1 pl pl a.nsn r.dp.2

δὲ ἀσφαλές. [2]βλέπετε τοὺς κύνας, βλέπετε τοὺς κακοὺς ἐργάτας, βλέπετε τὴν
and safeguard Beware of the dogs, beware of the evil workers, beware of those
1254 855 1063 3836 3264 1063 3836 2805 2239 1063 3836
cj a.nsn v.pam.2p d.apm n.apm v.pam.2p d.apm a.apm n.apm v.pam.2p d.asf

κατατομήν. [3] ἡμεῖς γάρ ἐσμεν ἡ περιτομή, οἱ →
⌊who practice mutilation.⌋ For we *For* are the true circumcision, who worship by the
2961 1142 7005 1142 1639 3836 4364 3836 3302
n.asf r.np.1 cj v.pai.1p d.nsf n.nsf d.npm

πνεύματι θεοῦ λατρεύοντες καὶ καυχώμενοι ἐν Χριστῷ Ἰησοῦ καὶ οὐκ
Spirit of God *worship* and glory in Christ Jesus and have no
4460 2536 3302 2779 3016 1877 5986 2652 2779 4275 4024
n.dsn n.gsm pt.pa.npm cj pt.pm.npm p.d n.dsm n.dsm cj pl

ἐν σαρκὶ πεποιθότες, [4] καίπερ ἐγὼ ἔχων πεποίθησιν
confidence in the flesh *have confidence* — even though I have reason for confidence
4275 1877 4922 4275 2779 2788 1609 2400 4301
p.d n.dsf pt.ra.npm cj r.ns.1 pt.pa.nsm n.asf

καὶ ἐν σαρκί. εἴ τις δοκεῖ ἄλλος πεποιθέναι ἐν
even in the flesh. If anyone else thinks *else* ⌊he has reason for confidence⌋ in the
2779 1877 4922 1623 5516 257 1506 257 4275 1877
adv p.d n.dsf cj r.nsm v.pai.3s r.nsm f.ra p.d

σαρκί, ἐγὼ μᾶλλον· [5]περιτομῇ ὀκταήμερος, ἐκ γένους Ἰσραήλ,
flesh, I have more: circumcised on the eighth day, a member of the nation of Israel,
4922 1609 3437 4364 3892 1666 1169 2702
n.dsf r.ns.1 adv.c n.dsf a.nsm p.g n.gsn n.gsm

→ φυλῆς Βενιαμίν, Ἑβραῖος ἐξ Ἑβραίων, κατὰ νόμον
of the tribe of Benjamin, a Hebrew born of Hebrews. ⌊In regard to⌋ the law, I was a
5876 1021 1578 1666 1578 2848 3795
n.gsf n.gsm n.nsm p.g n.gpm p.a n.asm

Φαρισαῖος, [6]κατὰ ζῆλος διώκων τὴν ἐκκλησίαν, κατὰ δικαιοσύνην τὴν
Pharisee; as for zeal, a persecutor of the church; as for the righteousness *{the}* set
5757 2848 2419 1503 3836 1711 2848 1466 3836 1181
n.nsm p.a n.asn pt.pa.nsm d.asf n.asf p.a n.asf d.asf

ἐν νόμῳ γενόμενος ἄμεμπτος. [7]ἀλλὰ[a] ἅτινα ἦν μοι
forth in the law, *set forth* I was blameless. But ⌊whatever things⌋ were gain to me,
1181 1877 3795 1181 289 247 4015 1639 3046 1609
p.d n.dsm pt.am.nsm a.nsm cj r.npn v.iai.3s r.ds.1

κέρδη, ταῦτα ἥγημαι διὰ τὸν Χριστὸν ζημίαν.
gain these ⌊I have come to regard⌋ as loss ⌊because of⌋ *{the}* Christ. *loss*
3046 4047 2451 2422 1328 3836 5986 2422
n.npn r.apn v.rmi.1s p.a d.asm n.asm n.asf

[8]⌊ἀλλὰ μενοῦνγε καὶ⌋ ἡγοῦμαι πάντα ζημίαν εἶναι διὰ τὸ
More than that, I regard all things as loss *as* ⌊because of⌋ the
247 3529 2779 2451 4246 1639 2422 1639 1328 3836
cj pl adv v.pmi.1s a.apn n.asf f.pa p.a d.asn

ὑπερέχον τῆς γνώσεως Χριστοῦ Ἰησοῦ τοῦ κυρίου μου, δι᾽ ὃν
⌊surpassing worth⌋ of knowing Christ Jesus *{the}* my Lord, *my* for whom I have
5660 3836 1194 5986 2652 3836 1609 3261 1609 1328 4005 2423 2423
pt.pa.asn d.gsf n.gsf n.gsm n.gsm d.gsm n.gsm r.gs.1 p.a r.asm

τὰ πάντα ἐζημιώθην, καὶ ἡγοῦμαι → σκύβαλα,
suffered the loss of *{the}* all things *I have suffered the loss* and regard them as rubbish,
2423 2423 2423 3836 4246 2423 2779 2451 5032
d.apn a.apn v.api.1s cj v.pmi.1s n.apn

NASB

The Goal of Life

[3:1]Finally, my brethren, rejoice in the Lord. To write the same things *again* is no trouble to me, and it is a safeguard for you. [2]Beware of the dogs, beware of the evil workers, beware of the false circumcision; [3]for we are the *true* circumcision, who worship in the Spirit of God and glory in Christ Jesus and put no confidence in the flesh, [4]although I myself might have confidence even in the flesh. If anyone else has a mind to put confidence in the flesh, I far more: [5]circumcised the eighth day, of the nation of Israel, of the tribe of Benjamin, a Hebrew of Hebrews; as to the Law, a Pharisee; [6]as to zeal, a persecutor of the church; as to the righteousness which is in the Law, found blameless.

[7]But whatever things were gain to me, those things I have counted as loss for the sake of Christ. [8]More than that, I count all things to be loss in view of the surpassing value of knowing Christ Jesus my Lord, for whom I have suffered the loss of all things, and count them but rubbish

[a] [ἀλλὰ] UBS.

NIV

that I may gain
Christ [9]and be
found in him, not
having a righteous-
ness of my own
that comes from
the law, but that
which is through
faith in[a] Christ—
the righteousness
that comes from
God on the basis
of faith. [10]I want to
know Christ—yes,
to know the power
of his resurrection
and participation in
his sufferings, be-
coming like him in
his death, [11]and so,
somehow, attaining
to the resurrection
from the dead.
[12]Not that I have
already obtained
all this, or have
already arrived
at my goal, but I
press on to take
hold of that for
which Christ Jesus
took hold of me.
[13]Brothers and sis-
ters, I do not con-
sider myself yet to
have taken hold of
it. But one thing
I do: Forgetting
what is behind and
straining toward
what is ahead, [14]I
press on toward
the goal to win the
prize for which
God has called
me heavenward in
Christ Jesus.

Following Paul's Example

[15]All of us, then,
who are mature
should take such
a view of things.
And if on some
point you think
differently, that
too God will
make clear to you.
[16]Only let us live
up to what we have

ἵνα Χριστὸν κερδήσω [9]καὶ εὑρεθῶ ἐν αὐτῷ, μὴ ἔχων
⌊in order to⌋ gain Christ *gain* and be found in him, not having a righteousness of
2671 3045 5986 3045 2779 2351 1877 899 3590 2400 1466
cj n.asm v.aas.1s cj v.aps.1s p.d r.dsm.3 pl pt.pa.nsm

ἐμὴν δικαιοσύνην τὴν ἐκ νόμου ἀλλὰ τὴν διὰ πίστεως
my own *righteousness* that comes from the Law, but ⌊that which⌋ comes through faith
1847 1466 3836 1666 3795 247 3836 1328 4411
r.asf.1 n.asf d.asf p.g n.gsm cj d.asf p.g n.gsf

Χριστοῦ, τὴν ἐκ θεοῦ δικαιοσύνην ἐπὶ τῇ πίστει,
in Christ, the righteousness from God *righteousness* that is based on *{the}* faith —
5986 3836 1466 1666 2536 1466 2093 3836 4411
n.gsm d.asf p.g n.gsm n.asf p.d d.dsf n.dsf

[10] τοῦ γνῶναι αὐτὸν καὶ τὴν δύναμιν τῆς ἀναστάσεως αὐτοῦ καὶ τὴν[a]
that I may know him and the power of his resurrection *his* and the
3836 1182 899 2779 3836 1539 3836 899 414 899 2779 3836
d.gsn f.aa r.asm.3 cj d.asf n.asf d.gsf n.gsf r.gsm.3 cj d.asf

κοινωνίαν τῶν[b] παθημάτων αὐτοῦ, συμμορφιζόμενος τῷ θανάτῳ αὐτοῦ,
fellowship of his sufferings, *his* becoming like him in his death, *his*
3126 3836 899 4077 899 5214 3836 899 2505 899
n.asf d.gpn n.gpn r.gsm.3 pt.pp.nsm d.dsm n.dsm r.gsm.3

[11] εἴ πως καταντήσω εἰς τὴν ἐξανάστασιν τὴν ἐκ νεκρῶν. [12] οὐχ ὅτι ↱
if somehow I may attain *{to}* the resurrection *{the}* from the dead. Not that I
1623 4803 2918 1650 3836 1983 3836 1666 3738 4024 4022 3284
cj pl v.fai.1s p.a d.asf n.asf d.asf p.g a.gpm pl cj

↱ ἤδη ἔλαβον ἢ ↱ ἤδη τετελείωμαι, ← διώκω δὲ
have already obtained all this or have already reached my goal, but ⌊I press on⌋ *but*
3284 2453 3284 2445 5457 2453 5457 1254 1503 1254
adv v.aai.1s cj adv v.rpi.1s v.pai.1s cj

εἰ καὶ καταλάβω, ⌊ἐφ' ᾧ⌋ καὶ κατελήμφθην ὑπὸ
⌊in order to⌋ *{also}* make it my own because *{also}* Christ Jesus ⌊has made me his own.⌋ *{by}*
1623 2779 2898 2093 4005 2779 5986 2652 2898 5679
cj adv v.aas.1s p.d r.dsn adv v.api.1s p.g

Χριστοῦ Ἰησοῦ.[c] [13] ἀδελφοί, ἐγὼ ἐμαυτὸν οὐ[d]
Christ Jesus Brothers, I do not consider to have made it my own; *not*
5986 2652 81 1609 3357 4024 3357 2898 2898 2898 1831 4024
n.gsm n.gsm n.vpm r.ns.1 r.asm.1 pl

λογίζομαι κατειληφέναι· ἓν δέ, τὰ μὲν ὀπίσω
do consider *to have made* but this ⌊one thing⌋ *but* I do: forgetting what ~ lies behind
3357 2898 1254 1651 1254 2140 3836 3525 3958
v.pmi.1s f.ra a.asn cj d.apn pl adv

ἐπιλανθανόμενος τοῖς δὲ ἔμπροσθεν ἐπεκτεινόμενος, [14]
forgetting and reaching out to what *and* lies ahead, *reaching out to* I
2140 1254 2085 2085 2085 3836 1254 1869 2085 1503
pt.pm.nsm d.dpn cj adv pt.pm.nsm

κατὰ σκοπὸν διώκω εἰς τὸ βραβεῖον τῆς ἄνω κλήσεως τοῦ θεοῦ
press on toward the goal *I press on* for the prize of the upward call of God
1503 1503 2848 5024 1503 1650 3836 1092 3836 539 3104 3836 2536
p.a n.asm v.pai.1s p.a d.asn n.asn d.gsf adv n.gsf d.gsm n.gsm

ἐν Χριστῷ Ἰησοῦ. [15] ὅσοι ↱ οὖν τέλειοι, ↱ ↱ τοῦτο
in Christ Jesus. So those of us *So* ⌊who are mature⌋ should take this
1877 5986 2652 4036 4012 5858 4036 5455 5858 5858 4047
p.d n.dsm n.dsm r.npm cj a.npm r.asn

φρονῶμεν· καὶ εἴ τι ἑτέρως φρονεῖτε, καὶ τοῦτο ὁ θεὸς
point of view; and if in anything you think differently, *you think* that too *that* *{the}* God
5858 2779 1623 5516 5858 5858 2284 5858 4047 2779 4047 3836 2536
v.pas.1p cj cj r.asn adv v.pai.2p cj r.asn d.nsm n.nsm

ὑμῖν ἀποκαλύψει· [16] πλὴν ↱ ↱ εἰς ὃ → →
will make known to you. *will make known* ⌊In any case,⌋ let us live ⌊up to⌋ what we have
636 636 636 7007 636 4440 5777 5777 5123 1650 4005
r.dp.2 v.fai.3s cj p.a r.asn

NASB

so that I may gain
Christ, [9]and may
be found in Him,
not having a righ-
teousness of my
own derived from
the Law, but that
which is through
faith in Christ,
the righteousness
which *comes* from
God on the basis of
faith, [10]that I may
know Him and the
power of His resur-
rection and the
fellowship of His
sufferings, being
conformed to His
death; [11]in order
that I may attain
to the resurrection
from the dead.
[12]Not that I have
already obtained
it or have already
become perfect,
but I press on so
that I may lay hold
of that for which
also I was laid hold
of by Christ Jesus.
[13]Brethren, I do not
regard myself as
having laid hold of
it yet; but one thing
I do: forgetting
what *lies* behind
and reaching for-
ward to what *lies*
ahead, [14]I press on
toward the goal
for the prize of the
upward call of God
in Christ Jesus.
[15]Let us therefore,
as many as are
perfect, have this
attitude; and if in
anything you have
a different attitude,
God will reveal
that also to you;
[16]however, let us
keep living by that
same *standard* to

---

a [τὴν] UBS, omitted by TNIV.
b [τῶν] UBS, omitted by TNIV.
c [Ἰησοῦ] UBS.
d οὐ UBS, NET. οὔπω TNIV.

a 9 Or *through the faithfulness of*

NIV

already attained.
[17]Join together
in following my
example, brothers
and sisters, and
just as you have us
as a model, keep
your eyes on those
who live as we do.
[18]For, as I have of-
ten told you before
and now tell you
again even with
tears, many live
as enemies of the
cross of Christ.
[19]Their destiny
is destruction,
their god is their
stomach, and their
glory is in their
shame. Their mind
is set on earthly
things. [20]But our
citizenship is in
heaven. And we
eagerly await a
Savior from there,
the Lord Jesus
Christ, [21]who, by
the power that en-
ables him to bring
everything under
his control, will
transform our low-
ly bodies so that
they will be like
his glorious body.

Closing Appeal for Steadfastness and Unity

4 Therefore, my
brothers and
sisters, you whom
I love and long for,
my joy and crown,
stand firm in the
Lord in this way,
dear friends!
[2]I plead with Eu-
odia and I plead
with Syntyche to
be of the same
mind in the Lord.
[3]Yes, and I ask
you, my true com-
panion, help these
women since they
have contended
at my side in the
cause of the gos-
pel,

ἐφθάσαμεν, τῷ αὐτῷ στοιχεῖν.[a] 17 συμμιμηταί μου ↰ γίνεσθε,
already attained. {the} already live Join in following my example, Join
899 5777 3836 899 5123 1181 5213 1609 5213 1181
v.aai.1p d.dsn r.dsn f.pa n.npm r.gs.1 v.pmm.2p

ἀδελφοί, καὶ σκοπεῖτε τοὺς οὕτω περιπατοῦντας καθὼς
brothers, and ⌊pay close attention to⌋ those who are living this way, who are living as
81 2779 5023 3836 4344 4344 4344 4048 4344 2777
n.vpm cj v.pam.2p d.apm adv pt.pa.apm cj

ἔχετε → τύπον ἡμᾶς. 18 πολλοὶ γὰρ περιπατοῦσιν
you have us as an example. us For many For are living (I have often told
2400 7005 5596 7005 1142 4498 1142 4344 3306 3306 4490 3306
v.pai.2p n.asm r.ap.1 a.npm cj v.pai.3p

οὓς πολλάκις ἔλεγον ὑμῖν, νῦν δὲ καὶ κλαίων λέγω,
you about them often I have told about you but now but tell you even with tears) tell
7007 3306 4005 4490 3306 7007 1254 3814 1254 3306 2779 3081 3306
r.apm adv v.iai.1s r.dp.2 adv cj adv pt.pa.nsm v.pai.1s

τοὺς ἐχθροὺς τοῦ σταυροῦ τοῦ Χριστοῦ, 19 ὧν τὸ τέλος ἀπώλεια, ὧν ὁ
as enemies of the cross of Christ. Their {the} end is destruction, their {the}
3836 2398 3836 5089 3836 5986 4005 3836 5465 724 4005 3836
d.apm a.apm d.gsm n.gsm d.gsm n.gsm r.gpm d.nsn n.nsn n.nsf r.gpm d.nsm

θεὸς ἡ κοιλία καὶ ἡ δόξα ἐν τῇ αἰσχύνῃ αὐτῶν, οἱ
god is the belly, and they {the} glory in {the} their shame. their Their minds are
2536 3836 3120 2779 3836 1518 1877 3836 899 158 899 3836 5858 5858
n.nsm d.nsf n.nsf cj d.nsf n.nsf p.d d.dsf n.dsf r.gpm.3 d.npm

τὰ ἐπίγεια φρονοῦντες. 20 ἡμῶν γὰρ τὸ πολίτευμα ἐν
set on {the} earthly things. minds are set on But our But {the} citizenship is in
5858 5858 3836 2103 5858 1142 7005 1142 3836 4487 5639 1877
d.apn a.apn pt.pa.npm r.gp.1 cj d.nsn n.nsn p.d

οὐρανοῖς ὑπάρχει, ἐξ οὗ καὶ σωτῆρα ἀπεκδεχόμεθα
heaven, is and it is from there {also} that we eagerly await a Savior, we eagerly await
4041 5639 1666 4005 2779 587 587 587 5400 587
n.dpm v.pai.3s p.g r.gsm adv n.asm v.pmi.1p

κύριον Ἰησοῦν Χριστόν, 21 ὃς μετασχηματίσει τὸ σῶμα τῆς
the Lord Jesus Christ, who will transform {the} our lowly bodies {the}
3261 2652 5986 4005 3571 3836 7005 5428 5393 3836
n.asm n.asm n.asm r.nsm v.fai.3s d.asn n.asn d.gsf

ταπεινώσεως ἡμῶν σύμμορφον τῷ σώματι τῆς δόξης αὐτοῦ κατὰ
lowly our into the likeness of his glorious body, {the} glorious his by
5428 7005 5215 3836 899 1518 5393 3836 1518 899 2848
n.gsf r.gp.1 a.asn d.dsn n.dsn d.gsf n.gsf r.gsm.3 p.a

τὴν ἐνέργειαν τοῦ δύνασθαι αὐτὸν καὶ ὑποτάξαι αὐτῷ τὰ πάντα.
the power that also enables him also to subject all things to himself. {the} all things
3836 1918 3836 2779 1538 899 2779 5718 4246 4246 899 3836 4246
d.asf n.asf d.gsn f.pp r.asm.3 adv f.aa r.dsm.3 d.apn a.apn

4:1 ὥστε, ἀδελφοί μου ἀγαπητοὶ καὶ ἐπιπόθητοι, χαρὰ καὶ
Therefore, my brothers, my ⌊you whom I love⌋ and long for, my joy and
6063 1609 81 1609 28 2779 2162 1609 5915 2779
cj n.vpm r.gs.1 a.vpm cj a.vpm n.vsf cj

στέφανός μου, οὕτως στήκετε ἐν κυρίῳ, ἀγαπητοί.
crown, my stand firm in the Lord ⌊in this way,⌋ stand firm in Lord my dear friends!
5109 1609 5112 5112 1877 3261 4048 5112 1877 3261 28
n.vsm r.gs.1 adv v.pam.2p p.d n.dsm a.vpm

2 Εὐοδίαν παρακαλῶ καὶ Συντύχην παρακαλῶ ⌊τὸ αὐτὸ
I urge Euodia I urge and I urge Syntyche I urge to agree
4151 4151 2337 4151 2779 4151 4151 5345 4151 3836 899
n.asf v.pai.1s cj n.asf v.pai.1s d.asn r.asn

φρονεῖν⌋ ἐν κυρίῳ. 3 ναὶ ἐρωτῶ καὶ σέ, γνήσιε σύζυγε, συλλαμβάνου
in the Lord. Yes, I ask you also, you my true comrade, help
5858 1877 3261 3721 2263 5148 2779 5148 1188 5187 5197
f.pa p.d n.dsm pl v.pai.1s adv r.as.2 a.vsm n.vsm v.pmm.2s

αὐταῖς, αἵτινες ἐν τῷ εὐαγγελίῳ
these women who have labored side by side with me in the cause of the gospel,
899 4015 5254 5254 5254 5254 5254 5254 1609 1877 3836 2295
r.dpf.3 r.npf p.d d.dsn n.dsn

[a] κανόνι, τὸ αὐτὸ φρονεῖν included by TR after στοιχεῖν.

NASB

which we have
attained.
[17]Brethren, join in
following my ex-
ample, and observe
those who walk ac-
cording to the pat-
tern you have in us.
[18]For many walk, of
whom I often told
you, and now tell
you even weeping,
that they are en-
emies of the cross
of Christ, [19]whose
end is destruc-
tion, whose god is
their appetite, and
whose glory is in
their shame, who
set their minds
on earthly things.
[20]For our citizen-
ship is in heaven,
from which also
we eagerly wait for
a Savior, the Lord
Jesus Christ; [21]who
will transform
the body of our
humble state into
conformity with
the body of His
glory, by the exer-
tion of the power
that He has even to
subject all things to
Himself.

Think of Excellence

[4:1]Therefore, my
beloved brethren
whom I long *to
see,* my joy and
crown, in this way
stand firm in the
Lord, my beloved.
[2]I urge Euodia and
I urge Syntyche to
live in harmony in
the Lord. [3]Indeed,
true companion,
I ask you also to
help these women
who have shared
my struggle in *the
cause of* the gospel,

NIV

along with Clement
and the rest of my
co-workers, whose
names are in the
book of life.

Final Exhortations

4 Rejoice in the
Lord always. I
will say it again:
Rejoice! 5 Let your
gentleness be ev-
ident to all. The
Lord is near. 6 Do
not be anxious
about anything,
but in every sit-
uation, by prayer
and petition, with
thanksgiving, pre-
sent your requests
to God. 7 And the
peace of God,
which transcends
all understanding,
will guard your
hearts and your
minds in Christ
Jesus.
8 Finally, broth-
ers and sisters,
whatever is true,
whatever is noble,
whatever is right,
whatever is pure,
whatever is lovely,
whatever is admi-
rable—if anything
is excellent or
praiseworthy—
think about such
things. 9 Whatever
you have learned
or received or
heard from me, or
seen in me—put it
into practice. And
the God of peace
will be with you.

Thanks for Their Gifts

10 I rejoiced great-
ly in the Lord that
at last you renewed
your concern for
me. Indeed, you
were concerned,
but you had no op-
portunity to show
it. 11 I am not say-
ing this because I
am in need, for I
have learned to be
content

συνήθλησάν μοι μετὰ καὶ Κλήμεντος καὶ τῶν λοιπῶν →
have labored side by side with *me* along with *along* Clement and the rest of my
5254 1609 2779 3552 2779 3098 2779 3836 3370 1609
v.aai.3p r.ds.1 p.g adv n.gsm cj d.gpm a.gpm

συνεργῶν μου, ὧν τὰ ὀνόματα ἐν βίβλῳ ζωῆς. 4 χαίρετε ἐν κυρίῳ
fellow workers, *my* whose *{the}* names are in the book of life. Rejoice in the Lord
5301 1609 4005 3836 3950 1877 1047 2437 5897 1877 3261
n.gpm r.gs.1 r.gpm d.npn n.npn p.d n.dsf n.gsf v.pam.2p p.d n.dsm

πάντοτε· πάλιν ἐρῶ, χαίρετε. 5 ↱ τὸ ἐπιεικὲς ὑμῶν γνωσθήτω πᾶσιν
always; again I say, Rejoice! Let *{the}* your gentleness *your* be known to every
4121 4099 3306 5897 1182 3836 7007 2117 7007 1182 4246
adv adv v.fai.1s v.pam.2p d.nsn a.nsn r.gp.2 v.apm.3s a.dpm

ἀνθρώποις. ὁ κύριος ἐγγύς. 6 → μηδὲν μεριμνᾶτε,
person. The Lord is at hand. Do not be anxious about anything, *Do be anxious about*
476 3836 3261 1584 3534 3534 3534 3534 3594 3534
n.dpm d.nsm n.nsm adv a.asn v.pam.2p

ἀλλ᾽ ἐν παντὶ τῇ προσευχῇ καὶ τῇ δεήσει μετὰ εὐχαριστίας ↱ τὰ
but in everything by prayer and *{the}* supplication with thanksgiving let *{the}* your
247 1877 4246 3836 4666 2779 3836 1255 3552 2374 1192 3836 7007
cj p.d a.dsf d.dsf n.dsf cj d.dsf n.dsf p.g n.gsf d.npn

αἰτήματα ὑμῶν γνωριζέσθω πρὸς τὸν θεόν. 7 καὶ ἡ εἰρήνη τοῦ θεοῦ ἡ
requests *your* be made known to *{the}* God. And the peace of God, which
161 7007 1192 4639 3836 2536 2779 3836 1645 3836 2536 3836
n.npn r.gp.2 v.ppm.3s p.a d.asm n.asm cj d.nsf n.nsf d.gsm n.gsm d.nsf

ὑπερέχουσα πάντα νοῦν φρουρήσει τὰς καρδίας ὑμῶν καὶ τὰ
surpasses all understanding, will guard *{the}* your hearts *your* and *{the}* your
5660 4246 3808 5864 3836 7007 2840 7007 2779 3836 7007
pt.pa.nsf a.asm n.asm v.fai.3s d.apf n.apf r.gp.2 cj d.apn

νοήματα ὑμῶν ἐν Χριστῷ Ἰησοῦ. 8 τὸ λοιπόν, ἀδελφοί, ὅσα ἐστὶν ἀληθῆ,
minds *your* in Christ Jesus. *{the}* Finally, brothers, whatever is true,
3784 7007 1877 5986 2652 3836 3370 81 4012 1639 239
n.apn r.gp.2 p.d n.dsm n.dsm d.asn adv n.vpm r.npn v.pai.3s a.npm

ὅσα σεμνά, ὅσα δίκαια, ὅσα ἁγνά, ὅσα προσφιλῆ, ὅσα
whatever is honorable, whatever is just, whatever is pure, whatever is lovely, whatever is
4012 4948 4012 1465 4012 54 4012 4713 4012
r.npn a.npn r.npn a.npn r.npn a.npn r.npn a.npn r.npn

εὔφημα, εἴ τις ἀρετὴ καὶ εἴ τις ἔπαινος,
commendable, if there is any excellence, *{and}* if there is anything ⌞worthy of praise,⌟ let
2368 1623 5516 746 2779 1623 5516 2047 3357
a.npn cj r.nsf n.nsf cj cj r.nsm n.nsm

ταῦτα λογίζεσθε· 9 ἃ καὶ ἐμάθετε καὶ
your mind dwell on these things. *let your mind dwell on* What *{and}* ⌞you have learned⌟ and
3357 3357 3357 3357 4047 3357 4005 2779 3443 2779
r.apn v.pmm.2p r.apn cj v.aai.2p cj

παρελάβετε καὶ ἠκούσατε καὶ εἴδετε ἐν ἐμοί, ↱ ταῦτα πράσσετε· καὶ ὁ
received and heard and seen in me — put these things into practice, and the
4161 2779 201 2779 1625 1877 1609 4556 4047 4556 2779 3836
v.aai.2p cj v.aai.2p cj v.aai.2p p.d r.ds.1 r.apn v.pam.2p cj d.nsm

θεὸς τῆς εἰρήνης ἔσται μεθ᾽ ὑμῶν. 10 ἐχάρην δὲ ἐν κυρίῳ μεγάλως ὅτι ἤδη
God of peace will be with you. I rejoice *{and}* in the Lord greatly that now
2536 3836 1645 1639 3552 7007 5897 1254 1877 3261 3487 4022 2453
n.nsm d.gsf n.gsf v.fmi.3s p.g r.gp.2 v.api.1s cj p.d n.dsm adv cj adv

ποτὲ ἀνεθάλετε τὸ ὑπὲρ ἐμοῦ φρονεῖν, ⌞ἐφ᾽ ᾧ⌟
at last you have revived your concern for me. *concern* Indeed, you were concerned
4537 352 3836 5858 5642 1609 5858 2093 4005 5858 5858 5858
adv v.aai.2p d.asn p.g r.gs.1 f.pa p.d r.dsn

καὶ ἐφρονεῖτε, ἠκαιρεῖσθε δέ. 11 οὐχ ὅτι
before, *you were concerned* but you had no opportunity. *but* I am not saying this because I
2779 5858 1254 177 1254 3306 3306 4024 3306 4022
adv v.iai.2p v.imi.2p cj pl cj

καθ᾽ ὑστέρησιν λέγω, ἐγὼ γὰρ ἔμαθον ἐν
am in need, *I am saying* for I *for* have learned to be content in
2848 5730 3306 1142 1609 1142 3443 1639 1639 895 1877
p.a n.asf v.pai.1s r.ns.1 cj v.aai.1s p.d

NASB

together with
Clement also and
the rest of my
fellow workers,
whose names are in
the book of life.
4 Rejoice in the
Lord always; again
I will say, rejoice!
5 Let your gentle
spirit be known to
all men. The Lord
is near. 6 Be anxious
for nothing, but
in everything by
prayer and suppli-
cation with thanks-
giving let your
requests be made
known to God.
7 And the peace
of God, which
surpasses all com-
prehension, will
guard your hearts
and your minds in
Christ Jesus.
8 Finally, brethren,
whatever is true,
whatever is honor-
able, whatever is
right, whatever is
pure, whatever is
lovely, whatever
is of good repute,
if there is any
excellence and if
anything worthy
of praise, dwell
on these things.
9 The things you
have learned and
received and heard
and seen in me,
practice these
things, and the God
of peace will be
with you.

God's Provisions

10 But I rejoiced in
the Lord greatly,
that now at last you
have revived your
concern for me;
indeed, you were
concerned *before,*
but you lacked op-
portunity. 11 Not that
I speak from want,
for I have learned
to be content in

NIV

whatever the cir-
cumstances. 12 I
know what it is to
be in need, and I
know what it is to
have plenty. I have
learned the secret
of being content
in any and every
situation, whether
well fed or hungry,
whether living in
plenty or in want.
13 I can do all this
through him who
gives me strength.
14 Yet it was good
of you to share
in my troubles.
15 Moreover, as
you Philippians
know, in the early
days of your ac-
quaintance with
the gospel, when I
set out from Mac-
edonia, not one
church shared with
me in the matter
of giving and re-
ceiving, except
you only; 16 for
even when I was in
Thessalonica, you
sent me aid more
than once when I
was in need. 17 Not
that I desire your
gifts; what I de-
sire is that more
be credited to
your account. 18 I
have received full
payment and have
more than enough.
I am amply sup-
plied, now that
I have received
from Epaphrodi-
tus the gifts you
sent. They are a
fragrant offering,
an acceptable sac-
rifice, pleasing to
God. 19 And my
God will meet all
your needs accord-
ing to the riches of
his glory in Christ
Jesus.
20 To our God and
Father be glory
for ever and ever.
Amen.

Final Greetings

21 Greet all God's
people in Christ
Jesus.

οἷς εἰμι αὐτάρκης εἶναι. 12 οἶδα καὶ
⌞whatever circumstance⌟ ⌞I find myself.⌟ *content* *to be* I know *{and}* what it is
4005 1639 895 1639 3857 2779
r.dpn v.pai.1s n.nsm f.pa v.rai.1s cj

ταπεινοῦσθαι, οἶδα καὶ περισσεύειν· ἐν παντὶ καὶ ἐν
to be in want, and I know *and* what it is to have an abundance. In any and *{in}*
5427 2779 3857 2779 4355 1877 4246 2779 1877
f.pp v.rai.1s cj f.pa p.d a.dsn cj p.d

πᾶσιν μεμύημαι, καὶ χορτάζεσθαι καὶ πεινᾶν καὶ
every circumstance ⌞I have learned the secret,⌟ whether I am well-fed or hungry, *{and}*
4246 3679 2779 5963 2779 4277 2779
a.dpn v.rpi.1s cj f.pp cj f.pa cj

περισσεύειν καὶ ὑστερεῖσθαι· 13 πάντα ἰσχύω ἐν τῷ
have plenty or am in need. I can do all things *I can do* through the
4355 2779 5728 2710 2710 2710 4246 2710 1877 3836
f.pa cj f.pp a.apn v.pai.1s p.d d.dsm

ἐνδυναμοῦντί με. 14 πλὴν καλῶς ἐποιήσατε συγκοινωνήσαντές
one who strengthens me. However, you have acted nobly, *you have acted* sharing with
1904 1609 4440 4472 4472 4472 2822 4472 5170
pt.pa.dsm r.as.1 cj adv v.aai.2p pt.aa.npm

μου τῇ θλίψει. 15 οἴδατε δὲ καὶ ὑμεῖς, Φιλιππήσιοι, ὅτι ἐν
me ⌞in my⌟ distress. And you Philippians know *And* *{also}* *you* *Philippians* that in
1609 3836 2568 1254 7007 5803 3857 1254 2779 7007 5803 4022 1877
r.gs.1 d.dsf n.dsf v.rai.2p cj adv r.np.2 n.vpm cj p.d

ἀρχῇ τοῦ εὐαγγελίου, ὅτε ἐξῆλθον ἀπὸ Μακεδονίας, οὐδεμία
the beginning of my gospel ministry, when I left *{from}* Macedonia, no church joined
794 3836 2295 4021 2002 608 3423 4029 1711 3125
n.dsf d.gsn n.gsn cj v.aai.1s p.g n.gsf a.nsf

μοι ἐκκλησία ἐκοινώνησεν εἰς λόγον δόσεως καὶ λήμψεως ⌞εἰ μὴ⌟ ὑμεῖς μόνοι,
with me *church* *joined with* in *{matter}* giving and receiving but you only,
3125 1609 1711 3125 1650 3364 1521 2779 3331 1623 3590 7007 3668
r.ds.1 n.nsf v.aai.3s p.a n.asm n.gsf cj n.gsf cj pl r.np.2 a.npm

16 ὅτι καὶ ἐν Θεσσαλονίκῃ καὶ ⌞ἅπαξ καὶ δὶς⌟ εἰς τὴν
for even in Thessalonica *{and}* you sent something more than once for *{the}*
4022 2779 1877 2553 2779 4287 4287 562 2779 1489 1650 3836
cj adv p.d n.dsf cj adv cj adv p.a d.asf

χρείαν μοι ἐπέμψατε. 17 οὐχ ὅτι ἐπιζητῶ τὸ δόμα, ἀλλὰ ἐπιζητῶ τὸν καρπὸν
my need. *my* *you sent* Not that I seek the gift; rather, I seek the interest
1609 5970 1609 4287 4024 4022 2118 3836 1517 247 2118 3836 2843
n.asf r.ds.1 v.aai.2p pl cj v.pai.1s d.asn n.asn cj v.pai.1s d.asm n.asm

τὸν πλεονάζοντα εἰς λόγον ὑμῶν. 18 ἀπέχω δὲ πάντα καὶ
that accrues to your account. *your* I have received *{and}* all I need and
3836 4429 1650 7007 3364 7007 600 1254 4246 2779
d.asm pt.pa.asm p.a n.asm r.gp.2 v.pai.1s cj a.apn cj

περισσεύω· πεπλήρωμαι δεξάμενος παρὰ Ἐπαφροδίτου τὰ παρ᾿ ὑμῶν,
more. I am well supplied, having received from Epaphroditus the gift you sent, *you*
4355 4444 1312 4123 2073 3836 7007 4123 7007
v.pai.1s v.rpi.1s pt.am.nsm p.g n.gsm d.apn p.g r.gp.2

ὀσμὴν εὐωδίας, θυσίαν δεκτήν, εὐάρεστον τῷ θεῷ. 19 ὁ δὲ θεός
a fragrant offering, a sacrifice acceptable and pleasing to God. *{the}* And my God
4011 2380 2602 1283 2298 3836 2536 3836 1254 1609 2536
n.asf n.gsf n.asf a.asf a.asf d.dsm n.dsm d.nsm cj n.nsm

μου πληρώσει πᾶσαν χρείαν ὑμῶν κατὰ τὸ πλοῦτος αὐτοῦ ἐν
my will supply your every need *your* ⌞according to⌟ *{the}* his glorious riches *his* *{in}*
1609 4444 7007 4246 5970 7007 2848 3836 899 1518 4458 899 1877
r.gs.1 v.fai.3s a.asf n.asf r.gp.2 p.a d.asn n.asn r.gsm.3 p.d

δόξῃ ἐν Χριστῷ Ἰησοῦ. 20 τῷ δὲ θεῷ καὶ πατρὶ ἡμῶν ἡ δόξα εἰς
glorious in Christ Jesus. To *{and}* our God and Father *our* be *{the}* glory for
1518 1877 5986 2652 3836 1254 7005 2536 2779 4252 7005 3836 1518 1650
n.dsf p.d n.dsm n.dsm d.dsm cj n.dsm cj n.dsm r.gp.1 d.nsf n.nsf p.a

τοὺς ⌞αἰῶνας τῶν αἰώνων,⌟ ἀμήν. 21 ἀσπάσασθε πάντα ἅγιον ἐν Χριστῷ Ἰησοῦ.
all time. Amen. Greet every saint in Christ Jesus.
3836 172 3836 172 297 832 4246 41 1877 5986 2652
d.apm n.apm d.gpm n.gpm pl v.amm.2p a.asm a.asm p.d n.dsm n.dsm

---

NASB

whatever circum-
stances I am. 12 I
know how to get
along with humble
means, and I also
know how to live
in prosperity; in
any and every cir-
cumstance I have
learned the secret
of being filled and
going hungry, both
of having abun-
dance and suffering
need. 13 I can do all
things through Him
who strengthens
me. 14 Nevertheless,
you have done well
to share *with me* in
my affliction.
15 You yourselves
also know, Philip-
pians, that at the
first preaching of
the gospel, after I
left Macedonia, no
church shared with
me in the matter of
giving and receiv-
ing but you alone;
16 for even in Thes-
salonica you sent
a gift more than
once for my needs.
17 Not that I seek
the gift itself, but I
seek for the profit
which increases to
your account. 18 But
I have received
everything in full
and have an abun-
dance; I am amply
supplied, having
received from
Epaphroditus what
you have sent, a
fragrant aroma, an
acceptable sacri-
fice, well-pleasing
to God. 19 And my
God will supply all
your needs accord-
ing to His riches
in glory in Christ
Jesus. 20 Now to our
God and Father *be*
the glory forever
and ever. Amen.
21 Greet every saint
in Christ Jesus.

NIV

The brothers and
sisters who are
with me send
greetings. 22 All
God's people here
send you greetings,
especially those
who belong to Cae-
sar's household.
23 The grace of the
Lord Jesus Christ
be with your spirit.
Amen.[a]

[a] 23 Some manuscripts do not have *Amen*.

						ἀσπάζονται	ὑμᾶς	οἱ	σὺν	ἐμοὶ	ἀδελφοί.	22
The	brothers	who	are	with	me	⸤send their greetings to⸥	you.	*The*	*with*	*me*	*brothers*	All
3836	81			5250	1609	832	7007	3836	5250	1609	81	4246
						v.pmi.3p	r.ap.2	d.npm	p.d	r.ds.1	n.npm	

		ἀσπάζονται	ὑμᾶς	πάντες	οἱ	ἅγιοι,	μάλιστα	δὲ	οἱ	ἐκ	τῆς	Καίσαρος
the	saints	greet	you,	*All*	*the*	*saints*	especially	*{and}*	those	of	*{the}*	Caesar's
3836	41	832	7007	4246	3836	41	3436	1254	3836	1666	3836	2790
		v.pmi.3p	r.ap.2	a.npm	d.npm	a.npm	adv.s	cj	d.npm	p.g	d.gsf	n.gsm

οἰκίας.	23 ἡ	χάρις	τοῦ	κυρίου	Ἰησοῦ	Χριστοῦ		μετὰ	τοῦ		πνεύματος
household.	The	grace	of the	Lord	Jesus	Christ	be	with	*{the}*	your	spirit.
3864	3836	5921	3836	3261	2652	5986		3552	3836	7007	4460
n.gsf	d.nsf	n.nsf	d.gsm	n.gsm	n.gsm	n.gsm		p.g	d.gsn		n.gsn

ὑμῶν.[a]
your
7007
r.gp.2

[a] ἀμήν. πρὸς Φιλιππήσιους ἐγράφη ἀπὸ Ῥώμης δι᾽ Ἐπαφροδίτου included by TR after ὑμῶν.

NASB

The brethren
who are with me
greet you. 22 All
the saints greet
you, especially
those of Caesar's
household.
23 The grace of the
Lord Jesus Christ
be with your spirit.

Colossians

NIV

1 Paul, an apostle
of Christ Jesus by
the will of God, and
Timothy our brother,

[2]To God's holy peo-
ple in Colossae, the
faithful brothers and
sisters[a] in Christ:

Grace and peace
to you from God
our Father.[b]

Thanksgiving and Prayer

[3]We always thank
God, the Father of our
Lord Jesus Christ,
when we pray for you,
[4]because we have
heard of your faith in
Christ Jesus and of the
love you have for all
God's people—[5]the
faith and love that
spring from the hope
stored up for you in
heaven and about
which you have al-
ready heard in the true
message of the gospel
[6]that has come to
you. In the same way,
the gospel is bearing
fruit and growing
throughout the whole
world—just as it has
been doing among
you since the day you
heard it and truly un-
derstood God's grace.
[7]You learned it from
Epaphras, our dear
fellow servant,[c] who is
a faithful minister of
Christ on our[d] behalf,
[8]and who also told
us of your love in the
Spirit.

[a] 2 The Greek word for *brothers and sisters* (*adelphoi*) refers here to believers, both men and women, as part of God's family; also in 4:15.
[b] 2 Some manuscripts *Father and the Lord Jesus Christ*
[c] 7 Or *slave*
[d] 7 Some manuscripts *your*

1:1 Παῦλος ἀπόστολος Χριστοῦ Ἰησοῦ διὰ θελήματος θεοῦ καὶ Τιμόθεος
Paul, an apostle of Christ Jesus by the will of God, and Timothy
4263 693 5986 2652 1328 2525 2536 2779 5510
n.nsm n.nsm n.gsm n.gsm p.g n.gsn n.gsm cj n.nsm

ὁ ἀδελφὸς 2 τοῖς ἐν Κολοσσαῖς ἁγίοις καὶ πιστοῖς ἀδελφοῖς ἐν Χριστῷ,
our brother, to the *at* *Colossae* saints and faithful brothers in Christ at
3836 81 3836 1877 3145 41 2779 4412 81 1877 5986 1877
d.nsm n.nsm d.dpm p.d n.dpf a.dpm cj a.dpm n.dpm p.d n.dsm

χάρις ὑμῖν καὶ εἰρήνη ἀπὸ θεοῦ πατρὸς ἡμῶν.[a] 3 →
Colossae: Grace to you and peace from God our Father. *our* We always
3145 5921 7007 2779 1645 608 2536 7005 4252 7005 4121
n.nsf r.dp.2 cj n.nsf p.g n.gsm n.gsm r.gp.1

εὐχαριστοῦμεν τῷ θεῷ πατρὶ τοῦ κυρίου ἡμῶν Ἰησοῦ Χριστοῦ πάντοτε
thank *{the}* God, the Father of our Lord *our* Jesus Christ, *always*
2373 3836 2536 4252 3836 7005 3261 7005 2652 5986 4121
v.pai.1p d.dsm n.dsm n.dsm d.gsm n.gsm r.gp.1 n.gsm n.gsm adv

περὶ ὑμῶν προσευχόμενοι, 4 ἀκούσαντες τὴν πίστιν ὑμῶν
when we pray for you, *when we pray* ⌊for we have heard of⌋ *{the}* your faith *your*
4667 4667 4667 4309 7007 4667 201 3836 7007 4411 7007
p.g r.gp.2 pt.pm.npm pt.aa.npm d.asf n.asf r.gp.2

ἐν Χριστῷ Ἰησοῦ καὶ τὴν ἀγάπην ἣν ἔχετε εἰς πάντας τοὺς ἁγίους 5
in Christ Jesus and the love that you have for all the saints. Both
1877 5986 2652 2779 3836 27 4005 2400 1650 4246 3836 41
p.d n.dsm n.dsm cj d.asf n.asf r.asf v.pai.2p p.a a.apm d.apm a.apm

διὰ τὴν ἐλπίδα τὴν ἀποκειμένην ὑμῖν ἐν τοῖς οὐρανοῖς, ↱ ἣν
spring from the hope *{the}* laid up for you in *{the}* heaven. Of this
1328 3836 1828 3836 641 7007 1877 3836 4041 4578 4005
p.a d.asf n.asf d.asf pt.pm.asf r.dp.2 p.d d.dpm n.dpm r.asf

προηκούσατε ἐν τῷ λόγῳ τῆς ἀληθείας τοῦ εὐαγγελίου 6 τοῦ παρόντος
⌊you have heard before⌋ in the word of truth, the gospel, which has come
4578 1877 3836 3364 3836 237 3836 2295 3836 4205
v.aai.2p p.d d.dsm n.dsm d.gsf n.gsf d.gsn n.gsn d.gsn pt.pa.gsn

εἰς ὑμᾶς, καθὼς καὶ ἐν παντὶ τῷ κόσμῳ ἐστὶν καρποφορούμενον καὶ
to you. Just as *{and}* in the entire *the* world it is bearing fruit and
1650 7007 2777 2779 1877 3836 4246 3836 3180 1639 2844 2779
p.a r.ap.2 cj cj p.d a.dsm d.dsm n.dsm v.pai.3s pt.pm.nsn cj

αὐξανόμενον καθὼς καὶ ἐν ὑμῖν, ἀφ' ἧς ἡμέρας ἠκούσατε καὶ ἐπέγνωτε
growing, so also is it among you from the day you heard it and understood
889 2777 2779 1877 7007 608 4005 2465 201 2779 2105
pt.pp.nsn cj adv p.d r.dp.2 p.g r.gsf n.gsf v.aai.2p cj v.aai.2p

τὴν χάριν τοῦ θεοῦ ἐν ἀληθείᾳ· 7 καθὼς ἐμάθετε ἀπὸ Ἐπαφρᾶ τοῦ
the grace of God in truth; just as you learned it from Epaphras *{the}* our
3836 5921 3836 2536 1877 237 2777 3443 608 2071 3836 7005
d.asf n.asf d.gsm n.gsm p.d n.dsf cj v.aai.2p p.g n.gsm d.gsm

ἀγαπητοῦ συνδούλου ἡμῶν, ὅς ἐστιν πιστὸς ὑπὲρ ἡμῶν[b] ↰
beloved fellow servant, *our* who is a faithful minister of Christ on your behalf
28 5281 7005 4005 1639 4412 1356 3836 5986 5642 7005 5642
a.gsm n.gsm r.gp.1 r.nsm v.pai.3s a.nsm p.g r.gp.1

διάκονος τοῦ Χριστοῦ, 8 ὁ καὶ δηλώσας ἡμῖν τὴν ὑμῶν ἀγάπην ἐν πνεύματι.
minister *of* *Christ* *{the}* and has told us of your love in the Spirit.
1356 3836 5986 3836 2779 1317 7005 3836 7007 27 1877 4460
n.nsm d.gsm n.gsm d.nsm adv pt.aa.nsm r.dp.1 d.asf r.gp.2 n.asf p.d n.dsn

[a] καὶ Κυρίου Ἰησοῦ Χριστοῦ included by TR after ἡμῶν.
[b] ἡμῶν TNIV, NET. ὑμῶν UBS.

NASB

Thankfulness for Spiritual Attainments

1:1Paul, an apostle
of Jesus Christ by
the will of God,
and Timothy our
brother,
[2]To the saints and
faithful brethren
in Christ *who are*
at Colossae: Grace
to you and peace
from God our
Father.
[3]We give thanks
to God, the Father
of our Lord Jesus
Christ, praying
always for you,
[4]since we heard of
your faith in Christ
Jesus and the love
which you have
for all the saints;
[5]because of the
hope laid up for
you in heaven, of
which you previ-
ously heard in the
word of truth, the
gospel [6]which has
come to you, just
as in all the world
also it is constantly
bearing fruit and
increasing, even as
it has been doing
in you also since
the day you heard
of it and under-
stood the grace of
God in truth; [7]just
as you learned *it*
from Epaphras,
our beloved fel-
low bond-servant,
who is a faithful
servant of Christ
on our behalf, [8]and
he also informed us
of your love in the
Spirit.

NIV

9For this reason,
since the day we
heard about you, we
have not stopped
praying for you.
We continually ask
God to fill you with
the knowledge of
his will through
all the wisdom and
understanding that
the Spirit gives,[a]
10so that you may
live a life worthy of
the Lord and please
him in every way:
bearing fruit in
every good work,
growing in the
knowledge of God,
11being strength-
ened with all power
according to his
glorious might
so that you may
have great endur-
ance and patience,
12and giving joyful
thanks to the Fa-
ther, who has qual-
ified you[b] to share
in the inheritance
of his holy people
in the kingdom of
light. 13For he has
rescued us from the
dominion of dark-
ness and brought us
into the kingdom
of the Son he loves,
14in whom we have
redemption, the for-
giveness of sins.

The Supremacy of the Son of God

15The Son is the
image of the in-
visible God, the
firstborn over all
creation. 16For
in him all things
were created:
things in heaven
and on earth, vis-
ible and invisible,
whether thrones or
powers or rulers
or authorities; all
things have been
created through
him and for him.
17He is before all
things, and

[a] 9 Or *all spiritual wisdom and understanding*
[b] 12 Some manuscripts *us*

9 διὰ τοῦτο καὶ ἡμεῖς, ἀφ᾽ ἧς ἡμέρας ἠκούσαμεν, ↱ οὐ
For this reason, {also} we from the day we heard about you, we have not
1328 4047 2779 7005 608 4005 2465 201 7005 4264 4024
p.a r.asn adv r.np.1 p.g r.gsf n.gsf v.aai.1p pl

παυόμεθα ὑπὲρ ὑμῶν προσευχόμενοι καὶ αἰτούμενοι, ἵνα πληρωθῆτε
ceased praying for you *praying* and asking that ⌞you may be filled with⌟
4264 4667 5642 7007 4667 2779 160 2671 4444
v.pmi.1p p.g r.gp.2 pt.pm.npm cj pt.pm.npm cj v.aps.2p

τὴν ἐπίγνωσιν τοῦ θελήματος αὐτοῦ ἐν πάσῃ σοφίᾳ καὶ συνέσει
the knowledge of his will *his* in all spiritual wisdom and understanding,
3836 2106 3836 899 2525 899 1877 4246 4461 5053 2779 5304
d.asf n.asf d.gsn n.gsn r.gsm.3 p.d a.dsf n.dsf cj n.dsf

πνευματικῇ, 10 περιπατῆσαι ἀξίως τοῦ κυρίου ⌞εἰς πᾶσαν⌟ ἀρεσκείαν,
spiritual that you may walk worthy of the Lord, fully pleasing to him,
4461 4344 547 3836 3261 1650 4246 742
a.dsf f.aa adv d.gsm n.gsm p.a a.asf n.asf

ἐν παντὶ ἔργῳ ἀγαθῷ καρποφοροῦντες καὶ αὐξανόμενοι τῇ
bearing fruit in every good work, *good* *bearing fruit* and increasing ⌞in the⌟
2844 2844 1877 4246 19 2240 19 2844 2779 889 3836
p.d a.dsn n.dsn a.dsn pt.pa.npm cj pt.pp.npm d.dsf

ἐπιγνώσει τοῦ θεοῦ, 11 ἐν πάσῃ δυνάμει δυναμούμενοι κατὰ
knowledge of God, being strengthened with all power *being strengthened* ⌞according to⌟
2106 3836 2536 1540 1540 1877 4246 1539 1540 2848
n.dsf d.gsm n.gsm p.d a.dsf n.dsf pt.pp.npm p.a

τὸ κράτος τῆς δόξης αὐτοῦ εἰς πᾶσαν ὑπομονὴν καὶ
{the} his glorious might, {the} *glorious* *his* ⌞for the display of⌟ all endurance and
3836 899 1518 3197 3836 1518 899 1650 4246 5705 2779
d.asn n.asn d.gsf n.gsf r.gsm.3 p.a a.asf n.asf cj

μακροθυμίαν. ⌞μετὰ χαρᾶς⌟ 12 εὐχαριστοῦντες τῷ πατρὶ τῷ ἱκανώσαντι
patience; while joyfully giving thanks ⌞to the⌟ Father, who has qualified
3429 3552 5915 2373 3836 4252 3836 2655
n.asf p.g n.gsf pt.pa.npm d.dsm n.dsm d.dsm pt.aa.dsm

ὑμᾶς[a] εἰς τὴν μερίδα τοῦ κλήρου τῶν ἁγίων ἐν τῷ φωτί· 13 ὃς ἐρρύσατο
you to {the} share in the inheritance of the saints in the light. He has rescued
7007 1650 3836 3535 3836 3102 3836 41 1877 3836 5890 4005 4861
r.ap.2 p.a d.asf n.asf d.gsm n.gsm d.gpm a.gpm p.d d.dsn n.dsn r.nsm v.ami.3s

ἡμᾶς ἐκ τῆς ἐξουσίας τοῦ σκότους καὶ μετέστησεν εἰς τὴν βασιλείαν τοῦ
us from the tyranny of darkness and transferred us into the kingdom of his
7005 1666 3836 2026 3836 5030 2779 3496 1650 3836 993 3836 899
r.ap.1 p.g d.gsf n.gsf d.gsn n.gsn cj v.aai.3s p.a d.asf n.asf d.gsm

υἱοῦ τῆς ἀγάπης αὐτοῦ, 14 ἐν ᾧ ἔχομεν τὴν ἀπολύτρωσιν,[b] τὴν
beloved Son, {the} *beloved* *his* in whom we have {the} redemption, the
27 5626 3836 27 899 1877 4005 2400 3836 667 3836
n.gsm d.gsf n.gsf r.gsm.3 p.d r.dsm v.pai.1p d.asf n.asf d.asf

ἄφεσιν τῶν ἁμαρτιῶν· 15 ὅς ἐστιν εἰκὼν τοῦ θεοῦ τοῦ ἀοράτου,
forgiveness of sins. He is the image of the invisible God, {the} *invisible* the
912 3836 281 4005 1639 1635 3836 548 2536 3836 548
n.asf d.gpf n.gpf r.nsm v.pai.3s n.nsf d.gsm n.gsm d.gsm a.gsm

πρωτότοκος πάσης κτίσεως, 16 ὅτι ἐν αὐτῷ ἐκτίσθη τὰ πάντα ἐν
firstborn over all creation; for in him all things were created, *things* *all* in
4758 4246 3232 4022 1877 899 4246 3836 3231 3836 4246 1877
a.nsm a.gsf n.gsf cj p.d r.dsm.3 v.api.3s d.npn a.npn p.d

τοῖς οὐρανοῖς καὶ ἐπὶ τῆς γῆς, τὰ ὁρατὰ καὶ τὰ ἀόρατα, εἴτε θρόνοι εἴτε
{the} heaven and on {the} earth, things visible and {the} invisible, whether thrones or
3836 4041 2779 2093 3836 1178 3836 3971 2779 3836 548 1664 2585 1664
d.dpm n.dpm cj p.g d.gsf n.gsf d.npn a.npn cj d.npn a.npn cj n.npm cj

κυριότητες εἴτε ἀρχαὶ εἴτε ἐξουσίαι· τὰ πάντα
dominions, whether principalities or powers — all things *all* have been created
3262 1664 794 1664 2026 4246 3836 4246 3231 3231 3231
n.npf cj n.npf cj n.npf d.npn a.npn

δι᾽ αὐτοῦ καὶ εἰς αὐτὸν ἔκτισται· 17 καὶ αὐτός ἐστιν πρὸ πάντων καὶ
through him and for him. *have been created* And he is before all things, and
1328 899 2779 1650 899 3231 2779 899 1639 4574 4246 2779
p.g r.gsm.3 cj p.a r.asm.3 v.rpi.3s cj r.nsm v.pai.3s p.g a.gpn cj

[a] ἡμᾶς included by after ὑμᾶς.
[b] διὰ τοῦ αἵματος αὐτοῦ included by TR after ἀπολύτρωσιν.

NASB

9For this reason
also, since the day
we heard *of it,* we
have not ceased to
pray for you and to
ask that you may
be filled with the
knowledge of His
will in all spiritual
wisdom and under-
standing, 10so that
you will walk in a
manner worthy of
the Lord, to please
Him in all respects,
bearing fruit in
every good work
and increasing in
the knowledge of
God; 11strengthened
with all power,
according to His
glorious might, for
the attaining of all
steadfastness and
patience; joyously
12giving thanks to
the Father, who
has qualified us to
share in the inheri-
tance of the saints
in Light.

The Incomparable Christ

13For He rescued us
from the domain
of darkness, and
transferred us to
the kingdom of His
beloved Son, 14in
whom we have re-
demption, the for-
giveness of sins.
15He is the image
of the invisible
God, the firstborn
of all creation.
16For by Him all
things were cre-
ated, *both* in the
heavens and on
earth, visible and
invisible, whether
thrones or domin-
ions or rulers or
authorities—all
things have been
created through
Him and for Him.
17He is before all
things, and in Him

NIV

in him all things
hold together.
[18]And he is the
head of the body,
the church; he is
the beginning and
the firstborn from
among the dead, so
that in everything
he might have the
supremacy. [19]For
God was pleased
to have all his
fullness dwell in
him, [20]and through
him to reconcile to
himself all things,
whether things on
earth or things in
heaven, by making
peace through his
blood, shed on the
cross.
[21]Once you were
alienated from
God and were
enemies in your
minds because
of[a] your evil be-
havior. [22]But now
he has reconciled
you by Christ's
physical body
through death to
present you holy
in his sight, with-
out blemish and
free from accu-
sation— [23]if you
continue in your
faith, established
and firm, and do
not move from the
hope held out in
the gospel. This is
the gospel that you
heard and that has
been proclaimed to
every creature un-
der heaven, and of
which I, Paul, have
become a servant.

Paul's Labor for the Church

[24]Now I rejoice
in what I am suf-
fering for you,
and I fill up in my
flesh what is still
lacking in regard
to Christ's afflic-
tions, for the sake
of his

[a] 21 Or *minds, as shown by*

τὰ πάντα ἐν αὐτῷ συνέστηκεν, [18] καὶ αὐτός ἐστιν ἡ κεφαλὴ τοῦ
in him all things *all* *in* *him* hold together. And he is the head of the
1877 899 4246 3836 4246 1877 899 5319 2779 899 1639 3836 3051 3836
d.npn a.npn p.d r.dsm.3 v.rai.3s cj r.nsm v.pai.3s d.nsf n.nsf d.gsn

σώματος τῆς ἐκκλησίας· ὅς ἐστιν ἀρχή, πρωτότοκος ἐκ τῶν νεκρῶν,
body, the church. He is the beginning, the firstborn from the dead,
5393 3836 1711 4005 1639 794 4758 1666 3836 3738
n.gsn d.gsf n.gsf r.nsm v.pai.3s n.nsf a.nsm p.g d.gpm a.gpm

ἵνα γένηται ἐν πᾶσιν αὐτὸς πρωτεύων, [19] ὅτι ἐν αὐτῷ
⌊in order that⌋ he might be preeminent in everything. *he* *preeminent* For *in* *him*
2671 899 1181 4750 1877 4246 899 4750 4022 1877 899
cj v.ams.3s p.d a.dpn r.nsm pt.pa.nsm cj p.d r.dsm.3

εὐδόκησεν πᾶν τὸ πλήρωμα κατοικῆσαι [20] καὶ δι᾽ αὐτοῦ
God was pleased to have all his fullness dwell in him, and through him
2305 4246 3836 4445 2997 1877 899 2779 1328 899
v.aai.3s a.asn d.asn n.asn f.aa cj p.g r.gsm.3

ἀποκαταλλάξαι τὰ πάντα εἰς αὐτόν, εἰρηνοποιήσας διὰ τοῦ αἵματος τοῦ
to reconcile *{the}* all things to himself, *by making peace* *through* *{the}* *blood* *on the*
639 3836 4246 1650 899 1647 1328 3836 135 3836
f.aa d.apn a.apn p.a r.asm.3 pt.aa.nsm p.g d.gsn n.gsn d.gsm

σταυροῦ αὐτοῦ, [a]δι᾽ αὐτοῦ[b] εἴτε τὰ ἐπὶ τῆς γῆς εἴτε τὰ ἐν τοῖς
cross *his* *{through}* *{him}* whether *{the}* on *{the}* earth or *{the}* in *{the}*
5089 899 1328 899 1664 3836 2093 3836 1178 1664 3836 1877 3836
n.gsm r.gsm.3 p.g r.gsm.3 cj d.apn p.g d.gsf n.gsf cj d.apn p.d d.dpm

οὐρανοῖς. [21] καὶ ὑμᾶς
heaven, by making peace through his blood shed on the cross. And you who were
4041 1647 1647 1647 1328 899 135 3836 3836 5089 2779 7007 1639 1639
n.dpm cj r.ap.2

ποτε ὄντας ἀπηλλοτριωμένους καὶ ἐχθροὺς τῇ διανοίᾳ ⌊ἐν τοῖς ἔργοις⌋
⌊at one time⌋ *who were* alienated and hostile in mind, doing
4537 1639 558 2779 2398 3836 1379 1877 3836 2240
adv pt.pa.apm pt.rp.apm cj a.apm d.dsf n.dsf p.d d.dpn n.dpn

τοῖς πονηροῖς, [22] ↱ ↱ νυνὶ δὲ ἀποκατήλλαξεν ἐν τῷ σώματι
{the} evil deeds, he has now *{and}* reconciled in Christ's physical *{the}* body
3836 4505 639 639 3815 1254 639 1877 899 4922 3836 5393
d.dpn a.dpn adv cj v.aai.3s p.d d.dsn n.dsn

τῆς σαρκὸς αὐτοῦ διὰ τοῦ θανάτου παραστῆσαι ὑμᾶς ἁγίους καὶ
{the} *physical* *Christ's* through his death, in order to present you holy, *{and}*
3836 4922 899 1328 3836 2505 4225 7007 41 2779
d.gsf n.gsf r.gsm.3 p.g d.gsm n.gsm f.aa r.ap.2 a.apm cj

ἀμώμους καὶ ἀνεγκλήτους → κατενώπιον αὐτοῦ, [23] εἴ γε ἐπιμένετε
without blemish and beyond reproach in his sight *his* — if indeed you continue
320 2779 441 899 2979 899 1623 1145 2152
a.apm cj a.apm p.g r.gsm.3 cj pl v.pai.2p

τῇ πίστει τεθεμελιωμένοι καὶ ἑδραῖοι καὶ μὴ μετακινούμενοι ἀπὸ τῆς ἐλπίδος
⌊in the⌋ faith, stable and steadfast, *{and}* not shifting from the hope
3836 4411 2530 2779 1612 2779 3590 3560 608 3836 1828
d.dsf n.dsf pt.rp.npm cj a.npm cj pl pt.pp.npm p.g d.gsf n.gsf

τοῦ εὐαγγελίου οὗ ἠκούσατε, τοῦ κηρυχθέντος ἐν πάσῃ κτίσει τῇ ὑπὸ
of the gospel that you heard, which has been proclaimed to every creature *{the}* under
3836 2295 4005 201 3836 3062 1877 4246 3232 3836 5679
d.gsn n.gsn r.gsn v.aai.2p d.gsn pt.ap.gsn p.d a.dsf n.dsf d.dsf p.a

τὸν οὐρανόν, οὗ ἐγενόμην ἐγὼ Παῦλος διάκονος. [24] ↱ ↱ νῦν
{the} heaven, and ⌊of which⌋ *became* I, Paul, became a minister. I am now
3836 4041 4005 1181 1609 4263 1181 1356 5897 5897 3814
d.asm n.asm r.gsn v.ami.1s r.ns.1 n.nsm n.nsm adv

χαίρω ἐν τοῖς παθήμασιν ὑπὲρ ὑμῶν ↰ καὶ ἀνταναπληρῶ τὰ
rejoicing in my sufferings on your behalf, and in my flesh am completing what
5897 1877 3836 4077 5642 7007 5642 2779 1877 1609 4922 499 3836
v.pai.1s p.d d.dpn n.dpn p.g r.gp.2 cj v.pai.1s d.apn

ὑστερήματα τῶν θλίψεων τοῦ Χριστοῦ ἐν τῇ σαρκί μου ὑπὲρ τοῦ
is lacking in the afflictions of Christ *in* *{the}* *flesh* *my* ⌊for the sake of⌋ *{the}* his
5729 3836 2568 3836 5986 1877 3836 4922 1609 5642 3836 899
n.apn d.gpf n.gpf d.gsm n.gsm p.d d.dsf n.dsf r.gs.1 p.g d.gsn

[a] [δι᾽ αὐτοῦ] UBS, omitted by TNIV.
[b] αὐτοῦ omitted in TNIV.

NASB

all things hold to-
gether. [18]He is also
head of the body,
the church; and He
is the beginning,
the firstborn from
the dead, so that
He Himself will
come to have first
place in every-
thing. [19]For it was
the *Father's* good
pleasure for all the
fullness to dwell in
Him, [20]and through
Him to reconcile
all things to Him-
self, having made
peace through the
blood of His cross;
through Him, *I say,*
whether things on
earth or things in
heaven.
[21]And although
you were for-
merly alienated and
hostile in mind,
engaged in evil
deeds, [22]yet He has
now reconciled you
in His fleshly body
through death, in
order to present
you before Him
holy and blame-
less and beyond
reproach— [23]if
indeed you con-
tinue in the faith
firmly established
and steadfast, and
not moved away
from the hope of
the gospel that you
have heard, which
was proclaimed in
all creation under
heaven, and of
which I, Paul, was
made a minister.
[24]Now I rejoice in
my sufferings for
your sake, and in
my flesh I do my
share on behalf of
His body, which is
the church, in fill-
ing up what is lack-
ing in Christ's

NIV

body, which is the
church. 25 I have
become its servant
by the commission
God gave me to
present to you the
word of God in its
fullness— 26 the
mystery that has
been kept hidden
for ages and gener-
ations, but is now
disclosed to the
Lord's people. 27 To
them God has cho-
sen to make known
among the Gentiles
the glorious rich-
es of this mystery,
which is Christ in
you, the hope of
glory.
28 He is the one we
proclaim, admon-
ishing and teach-
ing everyone with
all wisdom, so that
we may present
everyone fully ma-
ture in Christ. 29 To
this end I stren-
uously contend
with all the energy
Christ so power-
fully works in me.
2 I want you
to know how
hard I am contend-
ing for you and for
those at Laodicea,
and for all who
have not met me
personally. 2 My
goal is that they
may be encour-
aged in heart and
united in love, so
that they may have
the full riches of
complete under-
standing, in order
that they may
know the mystery
of God, namely,
Christ, 3 in whom
are

σώματος αὐτοῦ, ὅ ἐστιν ἡ ἐκκλησία, 25 ἧς ἐγενόμην ἐγὼ διάκονος
body, *his* which is the church, ⌊of which⌋ I became *I* a minister
5393 899 4005 1639 3836 1711 4005 1609 1181 1609 1356
n.gsn r.gsm.3 r.nsn v.pai.3s d.nsf n.nsf r.gsf v.ami.1s r.ns.1 n.nsm

κατὰ τὴν οἰκονομίαν τοῦ θεοῦ τὴν δοθεῖσάν μοι εἰς ὑμᾶς ↰ πληρῶσαι
⌊according to⌋ the stewardship from God that was given to me for your benefit, to make
2848 3836 3873 3836 2536 3836 1443 1609 1650 7007 1650 4444
p.a d.asf n.asf d.gsm n.gsm d.asf pt.ap.asf r.ds.1 p.a r.ap.2 f.aa

τὸν λόγον τοῦ θεοῦ, ↰ ↰ 26 τὸ μυστήριον τὸ ἀποκεκρυμμένον ἀπὸ τῶν
the word of God fully known, the mystery that has been hidden for *{the}*
3836 3364 3836 2536 4444 4444 3836 3696 3836 648 608 3836
d.asm n.asm d.gsm n.gsm d.asn n.asn d.asn pt.rp.asn p.g d.gpm

αἰώνων καὶ ἀπὸ τῶν γενεῶν ↱ νῦν δὲ ἐφανερώθη τοῖς ἁγίοις αὐτοῦ,
ages and *{for}* *{the}* generations, but has now *but* been revealed to his saints. *his*
172 2779 608 3836 1155 1254 5746 3814 1254 5746 3836 899 41 899
n.gpm cj p.g d.gpf n.gpf adv cj v.api.3s d.dpm a.dpm r.gsm.3

27 οἷς ἠθέλησεν ὁ θεὸς γνωρίσαι τί τὸ
⌊To them⌋ God chose *{the}* *God* to make known how great among the Gentiles are the
4005 2536 2527 3836 2536 1192 5515 1877 3836 1620 3836
r.dpm v.aai.3s d.nsm n.nsm f.aa r.nsn d.nsn

πλοῦτος τῆς δόξης τοῦ μυστηρίου τούτου ἐν τοῖς ἔθνεσιν, ὅ ἐστιν
glorious riches *{the}* *glorious* of this mystery, *this* *among* *the* *Gentiles* which is
1518 4458 3836 1518 3836 4047 3696 4047 1877 3836 1620 4005 1639
n.nsn d.gsf n.gsf d.gsn n.gsn r.gsn p.d d.dpn n.dpn r.nsn v.pai.3s

Χριστὸς ἐν ὑμῖν, ἡ ἐλπὶς τῆς δόξης· 28 ὃν ἡμεῖς καταγγέλλομεν
Christ in you, the hope of glory. ⌊He is the one⌋ we proclaim,
5986 1877 7007 3836 1828 3836 1518 4005 7005 2859
n.nsm p.d r.dp.2 d.nsf n.nsf d.gsf n.gsf r.asm r.np.1 v.pai.1p

νουθετοῦντες ⌊πάντα ἄνθρωπον⌋ καὶ διδάσκοντες ⌊πάντα ἄνθρωπον⌋ ἐν πάσῃ
warning everyone and teaching everyone with all
3805 4246 476 2779 1438 4246 476 1877 4246
pt.pa.npm a.asm n.asm cj pt.pa.npm a.asm n.asm p.d a.dsf

σοφίᾳ, ἵνα παραστήσωμεν ⌊πάντα ἄνθρωπον⌋ τέλειον ἐν Χριστῷ· 29 εἰς ὃ
wisdom, so that we may present everyone mature in Christ. To ⌊this end⌋
5053 2671 4225 4246 476 5455 1877 5986 1650 4005
n.dsf cj v.aas.1p a.asm n.asm a.asm p.d n.dsm p.a r.asn

καὶ κοπιῶ ἀγωνιζόμενος κατὰ τὴν ἐνέργειαν αὐτοῦ τὴν ἐνεργουμένην
{also} I labor, striving ⌊according to⌋ *{the}* his power *his* that works
2779 3159 76 2848 3836 899 1918 899 3836 1919
adv v.pai.1s pt.pm.nsm p.a d.asf n.asf r.gsm.3 d.asf pt.pm.asf

ἐν ἐμοὶ ⌊ἐν δυνάμει.⌋
powerfully in me. *powerfully*
1877 1877 1609 1877 1539
p.d r.ds.1 p.d n.dsf

2:1 θέλω γὰρ ὑμᾶς εἰδέναι ἡλίκον ἀγῶνα ἔχω ὑπὲρ ὑμῶν καὶ τῶν
For I want *For* you to know how great a struggle I have for you and for those
1142 2527 1142 7007 3857 2462 74 2400 5642 7007 2779 3836
v.pai.1s cj r.ap.2 f.ra a.asm n.asm v.pai.1s p.g r.gp.2 cj d.gpm

ἐν Λαοδικείᾳ καὶ ὅσοι ↱ οὐχ ἑόρακαν τὸ πρόσωπόν μου ἐν σαρκί,
in Laodicea and for all who have not seen *{the}* my face *me* in the flesh.
1877 3293 2779 4012 3972 4024 3972 3836 1609 4725 1609 1877 4922
p.d n.dsf cj r.npm pl v.rai.3p d.asn n.asn r.gs.1 p.d n.dsf

2 ἵνα παρακληθῶσιν αἱ καρδίαι αὐτῶν συμβιβασθέντες ἐν
My goal is that their hearts may be encouraged *{the}* *hearts* *their* and knit together in
2671 899 2840 4151 3836 2840 899 5204 1877
cj v.aps.3p d.npf n.npf r.gpm.3 pt.ap.npm p.d

ἀγάπῃ καὶ εἰς πᾶν πλοῦτος τῆς πληροφορίας τῆς συνέσεως,
love, *{and}* ⌊so that⌋ they may have all the wealth of full assurance of understanding,
27 2779 1650 4246 4458 3836 4443 3836 5304
n.dsf cj p.a a.asn n.asn d.gsf n.gsf d.gsf n.gsf

εἰς ἐπίγνωσιν τοῦ μυστηρίου τοῦ θεοῦ, Χριστοῦ, 3 ἐν ᾧ εἰσιν
for knowledge of God's mystery, *{the}* *God's* which is Christ, in whom are
1650 2106 3836 2536 3696 3836 2536 5986 1877 4005 1639
p.a n.asf d.gsn n.gsn d.gsm n.gsm n.gsm p.d r.dsm v.pai.3p

NASB

afflictions. 25 Of
this church I was
made a minister
according to the
stewardship from
God bestowed
on me for your
benefit, so that I
might fully carry
out the *preach-*
ing of the word of
God, 26 *that is,* the
mystery which
has been hidden
from the *past* ages
and generations,
but has now been
manifested to His
saints, 27 to whom
God willed to
make known what
is the riches of
the glory of this
mystery among the
Gentiles, which
is Christ in you,
the hope of glory.
28 We proclaim
Him, admonish-
ing every man and
teaching every man
with all wisdom,
so that we may
present every man
complete in Christ.
29 For this purpose
also I labor, striv-
ing according to
His power, which
mightily works
within me.

You Are Built Up in Christ

2:1 For I want you
to know how great
a struggle I have
on your behalf and
for those who are
at Laodicea, and
for all those who
have not personally
seen my face, 2 that
their hearts may be
encouraged, having
been knit together
in love, and *at-*
taining to all the
wealth that comes
from the full assur-
ance of understand-
ing, *resulting* in a
true knowledge of
God's mystery, *that*
is, Christ *Himself,*
3 in whom are

NIV

hidden all the trea-
sures of wisdom and
knowledge. [4]I tell you
this so that no one
may deceive you by
fine-sounding argu-
ments. [5]For though I
am absent from you
in body, I am present
with you in spirit and
delight to see how dis-
ciplined you are and
how firm your faith in
Christ is.

Spiritual Fullness in Christ

[6]So then, just as you
received Christ Jesus
as Lord, continue to
live your lives in him,
[7]rooted and built up in
him, strengthened in
the faith as you were
taught, and over-
flowing with thank-
fulness.
[8]See to it that no
one takes you captive
through hollow and
deceptive philosophy,
which depends on
human tradition and
the elemental spiritual
forces[a] of this world
rather than on Christ.
[9]For in Christ all the
fullness of the Deity
lives in bodily form,
[10]and in Christ you
have been brought
to fullness. He is
the head over every
power and authority.
[11]In him you were
also circumcised with
a circumcision not
performed by human
hands. Your whole
self ruled by the flesh[b]
was put off when you
were circumcised by[c]
Christ, [12]having been
buried with him in
baptism, in which you
were also raised with
him through your
faith in the working

[a] *8* Or *the basic principles*; also in verse 20
[b] *11* In contexts like this, the Greek word for *flesh* (*sarx*) refers to the sinful state of human beings, often presented as a power in opposition to the Spirit; also in verse 13.
[c] *11* Or *put off in the circumcision of*

πάντες οἱ θησαυροὶ τῆς σοφίας καὶ γνώσεως ἀπόκρυφοι. [4]
hidden all the treasures of wisdom and knowledge. *hidden* I am telling
649 4246 3836 2565 3836 5053 2779 1194 649 3306 3306 3306
a.npm d.npm n.npm d.gsf n.gsf cj n.gsf a.npm

τοῦτο λέγω, ἵνα μηδεὶς ὑμᾶς παραλογίζηται ἐν πιθανολογίᾳ.
you this *I am telling* so that no one may deceive you *may deceive* with specious arguments.
4047 3306 2671 3594 4165 4165 7007 4165 1877 4391
r.asn v.pai.1s cj a.nsm r.ap.2 v.pms.3s p.d n.dsf

[5]εἰ γὰρ καὶ τῇ σαρκὶ ἄπειμι, ἀλλὰ τῷ
⌞Even though⌟ *{for}* *{also}* I am absent in body, *I am absent* *{but}* I am with you in
1623 1142 2779 583 583 583 3836 4922 583 247 1639 1639 5250 7007 3836
cj cj adv d.dsf n.dsf v.pai.1s cj d.dsn

πνεύματι σὺν ὑμῖν εἰμι, χαίρων καὶ βλέπων ὑμῶν τὴν τάξιν καὶ τὸ
spirit, *with* *you* *I am* and I rejoice *{and}* to see your *{the}* ⌞orderly conduct⌟ and the
4460 5250 7007 1639 5897 2779 1063 7007 3836 5423 2779 3836
n.dsn p.d r.dp.2 v.pai.1s pt.pa.nsm cj pt.pa.nsm r.gp.2 d.asf n.asf cj d.asn

στερέωμα τῆς εἰς Χριστὸν πίστεως ὑμῶν. [6] ὡς οὖν
stability of your faith in Christ. *faith* *your* So then, ⌞just as⌟ *So then*
5106 3836 7007 4411 1650 5986 4411 7007 4036 4036 6055 4036
n.asn d.gsf p.a n.asm n.gsf r.gp.2 cj cj

παρελάβετε τὸν Χριστὸν Ἰησοῦν τὸν κύριον, ἐν αὐτῷ περιπατεῖτε,
you received *{the}* Christ Jesus as Lord, continue to live in him, *continue to live*
4161 3836 5986 2652 3836 3261 4344 4344 4344 1877 899 4344
v.aai.2p d.asm n.asm n.asm d.asm n.asm p.d r.dsm.3 v.pam.2p

[7]ἐρριζωμένοι καὶ ἐποικοδομούμενοι ἐν αὐτῷ καὶ βεβαιούμενοι τῇ πίστει καθὼς
rooted and built up in him, *{and}* established ⌞in the⌟ faith just as
4845 2779 2224 1877 899 2779 1011 3836 4411 2777
pt.rp.npm cj pt.pp.npm p.d r.dsm.3 cj pt.pp.npm d.dsf n.dsf cj

ἐδιδάχθητε, περισσεύοντες ἐν εὐχαριστίᾳ. [8]βλέπετε μή τις ὑμᾶς
you were taught, and abounding in thanksgiving. See to it that no one takes you
1438 4355 1877 2374 1063 3590 5516 1639 7007
v.api.2p pt.pa.npm p.d n.dsf v.pam.2p cj r.nsm r.ap.2

ἔσται ὁ συλαγωγῶν διὰ τῆς φιλοσοφίας καὶ κενῆς ἀπάτης κατὰ τὴν
takes *{the}* captive ⌞by means of⌟ *{the}* philosophy and empty deceit, ⌞according to⌟ the
1639 3836 5194 1328 3836 5814 2779 3031 573 2848 3836
v.fmi.3s d.nsm pt.pa.nsm p.g d.gsf n.gsf cj a.gsf n.gsf p.a d.asf

παράδοσιν τῶν ἀνθρώπων, κατὰ τὰ στοιχεῖα τοῦ κόσμου καὶ οὐ
tradition of men, ⌞according to⌟ the ⌞elemental spirits⌟ of the world, and not
4142 3836 476 2848 3836 5122 3836 3180 2779 4024
n.asf d.gpm n.gpm p.a d.apn n.apn d.gsm n.gsm cj pl

κατὰ Χριστόν· [9]ὅτι ἐν αὐτῷ κατοικεῖ πᾶν τὸ πλήρωμα τῆς θεότητος
⌞according to⌟ Christ. For in him *dwells* the whole *the* fullness of deity
2848 5986 4022 1877 899 2997 3836 4246 3836 4445 3836 2540
p.a n.asm cj p.d r.dsm.3 v.pai.3s a.nsn d.nsn n.nsn d.gsf n.gsf

σωματικῶς, [10] καὶ ἐστὲ ἐν αὐτῷ πεπληρωμένοι, ὅς
dwells in bodily form, and you have come to fullness in him, *come to fullness* who
2997 5395 2779 1639 4444 4444 4444 1877 899 4444 4005
adv cj v.pai.2p p.d r.dsm.3 pt.rp.npm r.nsm

ἐστιν ἡ κεφαλὴ πάσης ἀρχῆς καὶ ἐξουσίας. [11]ἐν ᾧ ➝ καὶ περιετμήθητε
is the head of every principality and power. In him you also were circumcised
1639 3836 3051 4246 794 2779 2026 1877 4005 4362 2779 4362
v.pai.3s d.nsf n.nsf a.gsf n.gsf cj n.gsf p.d r.dsm cj v.api.2p

➝ περιτομῇ ἀχειροποιήτῳ ἐν τῇ ἀπεκδύσει τοῦ σώματος τῆς σαρκός,
with a circumcision not made with hands, by the putting off of the body of flesh,
4364 942 1877 3836 589 3836 5393 3836 4922
n.dsf a.dsf p.d d.dsf n.dsf d.gsn n.gsn d.gsf n.gsf

ἐν τῇ περιτομῇ τοῦ Χριστοῦ, [12] συνταφέντες αὐτῷ ἐν τῷ βαπτισμῷ,
by the circumcision of Christ. ⌞Having been buried with⌟ him in *{the}* baptism,
1877 3836 4364 3836 5986 5313 899 1877 3836 968
p.d d.dsf n.dsf d.gsm n.gsm pt.ap.npm r.dsm.3 p.d d.dsm n.dsm

ἐν ᾧ ➝ ➝ καὶ συνηγέρθητε διὰ τῆς πίστεως τῆς ἐνεργείας
{in} *{which}* you have also been raised with him through *{the}* faith in the powerful working
1877 4005 5283 5283 2779 5283 1328 3836 4411 3836 1918
p.d r.dsm adv v.api.2p p.g d.gsf n.gsf d.gsf n.gsf

NASB

hidden all the trea-
sures of wisdom
and knowledge.
[4]I say this so
that no one will
delude you with
persuasive argu-
ment. [5]For even
though I am absent
in body, neverthe-
less I am with you
in spirit, rejoicing
to see your good
discipline and the
stability of your
faith in Christ.
[6]Therefore as
you have received
Christ Jesus the
Lord, *so* walk in
Him, [7]having been
firmly rooted *and*
now being built
up in Him and
established [a]in your
faith, just as you
were instructed,
and overflowing
with gratitude.
[8]See to it that
no one takes you
captive through
philosophy and
empty deception,
according to the
tradition of men,
according to the
elementary prin-
ciples of the world,
rather than ac-
cording to Christ.
[9]For in Him all the
fullness of Deity
dwells in bodily
form, [10]and in Him
you have been
made complete,
and He is the head
over all rule and
authority; [11]and in
Him you were also
circumcised with a
circumcision made
without hands, in
the removal of the
body of the flesh
by the circumcision
of Christ; [12]having
been buried with
Him in baptism,
in which you were
also raised up with
Him through faith
in the working of

[a] Or *by*

NIV

of God, who raised
him from the dead.
13 When you were
dead in your sins
and in the uncir-
cumcision of your
flesh, God made
you[a] alive with
Christ. He forgave
us all our sins,
14 having canceled
the charge of our
legal indebted-
ness, which stood
against us and
condemned us;
he has taken it
away, nailing it to
the cross. 15 And
having disarmed
the powers and au-
thorities, he made
a public spectacle
of them, triumph-
ing over them by
the cross.[b]

Freedom From Human Rules

16 Therefore do
not let anyone
judge you by what
you eat or drink,
or with regard to a
religious festival,
a New Moon cel-
ebration or a Sab-
bath day. 17 These
are a shadow of
the things that
were to come; the
reality, however,
is found in Christ.
18 Do not let any-
one who delights
in false humility
and the worship
of angels disqual-
ify you. Such a
person also goes
into great detail
about what they
have seen; they are
puffed up with idle
notions by their
unspiritual mind.
19 They have lost
connection with
the head, from
whom the whole
body, supported
and held together
by its ligaments
and sinews, grows
as God causes it to
grow.

[a] 13 Some manuscripts *us*
[b] 15 Or *them in him*

τοῦ θεοῦ τοῦ ἐγείραντος αὐτὸν ἐκ νεκρῶν· 13 καὶ ὑμᾶς νεκροὺς
of God, who raised him from the dead. And although you were dead
3836 2536 3836 1586 899 1666 3738 2779 1639 7007 1639 3738
d.gsm n.gsm d.gsm pt.aa.gsm r.asm.3 p.g a.gpm cj r.ap.2 a.apm

ὄντας ἐν[a] τοῖς παραπτώμασιν καὶ τῇ ἀκροβυστίᾳ τῆς σαρκὸς ὑμῶν,
although were in your trespasses and the uncircumcision of your flesh, *your* God
1639 1877 3836 4183 2779 3836 213 3836 7007 4922 7007
pt.pa.apm p.d d.dpn n.dpn cj d.dsf n.dsf d.gsf n.gsf r.gp.2

→ συνεζωοποίησεν ὑμᾶς σὺν αὐτῷ, χαρισάμενος ἡμῖν πάντα τὰ
made you alive *you* with Christ. He forgave us all our
7007 5188 7007 5250 899 5919 7005 4246 3836
v.aai.3s r.ap.2 p.d r.dsm.3 pt.am.nsm r.dp.1 a.apn d.apn

παραπτώματα. 14 ἐξαλείψας τὸ καθ᾽ ἡμῶν χειρόγραφον τοῖς δόγμασιν
transgressions, having canceled the *against us* certificate of debt ⌊with its⌋ legal demands
4183 1981 3836 2848 7005 5934 3836 1504
n.apn pt.aa.nsm d.asn p.g r.gp.1 n.asn d.dpn n.dpn

ὃ ἦν ὑπεναντίον ἡμῖν, καὶ αὐτὸ ἦρκεν ⌊ἐκ τοῦ
against us, which was hostile to us. *{and}* He has taken it *He has taken* away
2848 7005 4005 1639 5641 7005 2779 149 149 149 899 149 1666 3836
r.nsn v.iai.3s a.nsn r.dp.1 cj r.asn.3 v.rai.3s p.g d.gsn

μέσου⌋ προσηλώσας αὐτὸ τῷ σταυρῷ· 15 ἀπεκδυσάμενος τὰς ἀρχὰς καὶ τὰς
by nailing it ⌊to the⌋ cross. He stripped the principalities and *{the}*
3545 4669 899 3836 5089 588 3836 794 2779 3836
n.gsn pt.aa.nsm r.asn.3 d.dsm n.dsm pt.am.nsm d.apf n.apf cj d.apf

ἐξουσίας ↰ ↰ ↰ ἐδειγμάτισεν ἐν παρρησίᾳ, θριαμβεύσας
powers of their authority and disgraced them in public ⌊by triumphing over⌋
2026 588 588 588 1258 1877 4244 2581
n.apf v.aai.3s p.d n.dsf pt.aa.nsm

αὐτοὺς ἐν αὐτῷ. 16 μὴ οὖν τις ὑμᾶς κρινέτω
them in Christ. Therefore do not *Therefore* let anyone judge you *do let judge*
899 1877 899 4036 3212 3590 4036 3212 5516 3212 7007 3212
r.apm.3 p.d r.dsm.3 pl cj r.nsm r.ap.2 v.pam.3s

ἐν βρώσει καὶ ἐν πόσει ἢ ἐν μέρει ἑορτῆς ἢ
⌊with respect to⌋ food and *{with respect to}* drink, or ⌊in regard to⌋ a religious festival, *{or}*
1877 1111 2779 1877 4530 2445 1877 3538 2038 2445
p.d n.dsf cj p.d n.dsf cj p.d n.dsn n.gsf cj

νεομηνίας ἢ σαββάτων· 17 ἅ ἐστιν σκιὰ τῶν μελλόντων, τὸ
a new moon, or a Sabbath day. These are but a shadow of what was to come, but the
3741 2445 4879 4005 1639 5014 3836 3516 1254 3836
n.gsf cj n.gpn r.npn v.pai.3s n.nsf d.gpn pt.pa.gpn d.nsn

δὲ σῶμα τοῦ Χριστοῦ. 18 μηδεὶς ὑμᾶς καταβραβευέτω
but reality is found in Christ. Let no one rob you *Let rob* of your prize,
1254 5393 3836 5986 2857 3594 2857 7007 2857
cj n.nsn d.gsm n.gsm a.nsm r.ap.2 v.pam.3s

θέλων ἐν ταπεινοφροσύνῃ καὶ θρησκείᾳ τῶν ἀγγέλων, ἃ
insisting on self-abasement and the worship of angels, taking his stand on
2527 1877 5425 2779 2579 3836 34 4005
pt.pa.nsm p.d n.dsf cj n.dsf d.gpm n.gpm r.apn

ἑόρακεν ἐμβατεύων, εἰκῇ φυσιούμενος ὑπὸ τοῦ νοὸς τῆς
visions, puffed up ⌊with empty⌋ notions by *{the}* his earthly ⌊way of thinking.⌋ *{the}*
3972 1836 1632 5881 5679 3836 899 4922 3808 3836
v.rai.3s pt.pa.nsm adv pt.pp.nsm p.g d.gsm n.gsm d.gsf

σαρκὸς αὐτοῦ, 19 καὶ οὐ κρατῶν τὴν κεφαλήν, ἐξ οὗ
earthly *his* *{and}* That person is not holding fast to the head, from whom the
4922 899 2779 4024 3195 3836 3051 1666 4005 3836
n.gsf r.gsm.3 cj pl pt.pa.nsm d.asf n.asf p.g r.gsm

πᾶν τὸ σῶμα διὰ τῶν ἁφῶν καὶ συνδέσμων
whole *the* body, nourished and held together by its joints and ligaments,
4246 3836 5393 2220 2779 5204 5204 1328 3836 913 2779 5278
a.nsn d.nsn n.nsn p.g d.gpf n.gpf cj n.gpm

ἐπιχορηγούμενον καὶ συμβιβαζόμενον αὔξει τὴν αὔξησιν τοῦ θεοῦ.
nourished *and* *held together* grows with a growth that is from God.
2220 2779 5204 891 3836 890 3836 2536
pt.pp.nsn cj pt.pp.nsn v.pai.3s d.asf n.asf d.gsm n.gsm

[a] [ἐν] UBS.

NASB

God, who raised
Him from the
dead. 13 When you
were dead in your
transgressions and
the uncircumcision
of your flesh, He
made you alive
together with Him,
having forgiven us
all our transgres-
sions, 14 having
canceled out the
certificate of debt
consisting of
decrees against us,
which was hostile
to us; and He has
taken it out of the
way, having nailed
it to the cross.
15 When He had
disarmed the rulers
and authorities,
He made a public
display of them,
having triumphed
over them through
Him.
16 Therefore no one
is to act as your
judge in regard to
food or drink or in
respect to a festival
or a new moon or
a Sabbath day—
17 things which are
a *mere* shadow of
what is to come;
but the substance
belongs to Christ.
18 Let no one keep
defrauding you
of your prize by
delighting in self-
abasement and
the worship of the
angels, taking his
stand on *visions* he
has seen, inflated
without cause by
his fleshly mind,
19 and not holding
fast to the head,
from whom the
entire body, be-
ing supplied and
held together by
the joints and liga-
ments, grows with
a growth which is
from God.

NIV

20 Since you died
with Christ to the
elemental spiri-
tual forces of this
world, why, as
though you still
belonged to the
world, do you sub-
mit to its rules:
21 "Do not han-
dle! Do not taste!
Do not touch!"?
22 These rules,
which have to do
with things that
are all destined
to perish with
use, are based on
merely human
commands and
teachings. 23 Such
regulations indeed
have an appear-
ance of wisdom,
with their self-im-
posed worship,
their false humility
and their harsh
treatment of the
body, but they lack
any value in re-
straining sensual
indulgence.

Living as Those Made Alive in Christ

3 Since, then,
you have been
raised with Christ,
set your hearts
on things above,
where Christ is,
seated at the right
hand of God. 2 Set
your minds on
things above, not
on earthly things.
3 For you died, and
your life is now
hidden with Christ
in God. 4 When
Christ, who is
your[a] life, appears,
then you also will
appear with him in
glory.
5 Put to death,
therefore, whatev-
er belongs to your
earthly nature:
sexual immorality,
impurity, lust, evil
desires and greed,
which is idolatry.
6 Because of these,
the wrath of

[a] 4 Some manuscripts *our*

20 εἰ ἀπεθάνετε σὺν Χριστῷ ἀπὸ τῶν στοιχείων τοῦ κόσμου, τί ὡς
Since you died with Christ to the elemental spirits of the world, why, ⌊as though⌋
1623 633 5250 5986 608 3836 5122 3836 3180 5515 6055
cj v.aai.2p p.d n.dsm p.g d.gpn n.gpn d.gsm n.gsm r.asn pl

ζῶντες ἐν κόσμῳ δογματίζεσθε; 21 ↱ μὴ ἅψῃ
⌊you were still living⌋ in the world, ⌊do you submit to regulations⌋ such as, "Do not handle!
2409 1877 3180 1505 721 3590 721
pt.pa.npm p.d n.dsm v.ppi.2p pl v.ams.2s

↱ μηδὲ γεύσῃ ↱ μηδὲ θίγῃς, 22 ἅ ἐστιν πάντα εἰς φθορὰν τῇ
Do not taste! Do not touch!"? These are all ⌊destined to⌋ perish with
1174 3593 1174 2566 3593 2566 4005 1639 4246 1650 5785 3836
cj v.ams.2s cj v.aas.2s r.npn v.pai.3s a.npn p.a n.asf d.dsf

ἀποχρήσει, κατὰ ← τὰ ἐντάλματα καὶ διδασκαλίας τῶν ἀνθρώπων,
use, based as they are on *{the}* human commands and teachings. *{the}* *human*
712 2848 3836 476 1945 2779 1436 3836 476
n.dsf p.a d.apn n.apn cj n.apf d.gpm n.gpm

23 ἅτινά ἐστιν λόγον μὲν ἔχοντα σοφίας ἐν
Such *{it is}* regulations indeed have the appearance of wisdom with their
4015 1639 3364 3525 2400 5053 1877
r.npn v.pai.3s n.asm pl pt.pa.npn n.gsf p.d

ἐθελοθρησκίᾳ καὶ ταπεινοφροσύνῃ καὶ[a] ἀφειδίᾳ → σώματος,
⌊self-imposed religious piety,⌋ *{and}* false humility, and harsh control over the body, but
1615 2779 5425 2779 910 5393
n.dsf cj n.dsf cj n.dsf n.gsn

οὐκ ⌊ἐν τιμῇ τινι⌋ πρὸς πλησμονὴν τῆς σαρκός.
they are of no value against the gratification of the flesh.
4024 1877 5507 5516 4639 4447 3836 4922
pl p.d n.dsf r.dsf p.a n.asf d.gsf n.gsf

3:1 εἰ οὖν συνηγέρθητε τῷ Χριστῷ, τὰ ἄνω
Therefore if *Therefore* ⌊you have been raised⌋ with Christ, seek ⌊the things⌋ above,
4036 1623 4036 5283 3836 5986 2426 3836 539
cj cj v.api.2p d.dsm n.dsm d.apn adv

ζητεῖτε, οὗ ὁ Χριστός ἐστιν ἐν δεξιᾷ τοῦ θεοῦ καθήμενος· 2
seek where *{the}* Christ is, seated at the right hand of God. *seated* Set
2426 4023 3836 5986 1639 2764 1877 1288 3836 2536 2764 5858
v.pam.2p adv d.nsm n.nsm v.pai.3s p.d a.dsf d.gsm n.gsm pt.pm.nsm

τὰ ἄνω φρονεῖτε, μὴ τὰ ἐπὶ τῆς γῆς. 3 ἀπεθάνετε
your minds on things above, *Set your minds on* not on things on *{the}* earth, for you died
5858 5858 5858 3836 539 5858 3590 3836 2093 3836 1178 1142 633
d.apn adv v.pam.2p pl d.apn p.g d.gsf n.gsf v.aai.2p

γὰρ καὶ ἡ ζωὴ ὑμῶν κέκρυπται σὺν τῷ Χριστῷ ἐν τῷ θεῷ· 4 ὅταν ὁ
for and *{the}* your life *your* is hidden with *{the}* Christ in *{the}* God. When *{the}*
1142 2779 3836 7007 2437 7007 3221 5250 3836 5986 1877 3836 2536 4020 3836
cj cj d.nsf n.nsf r.gp.2 v.rpi.3s p.d d.dsm n.dsm p.d d.dsm n.dsm cj d.nsm

Χριστὸς φανερωθῇ, ἡ ζωὴ ὑμῶν, τότε καὶ ὑμεῖς σὺν
Christ, who is your life, appears, *{the}* *life* *your* then you also *you* will appear with
5986 7007 2437 5746 3836 2437 7007 5538 7007 2779 7007 5746 5746 5250
n.nsm v.aps.3s d.nsf n.nsf r.gp.2 adv adv r.np.2 p.d

αὐτῷ φανερωθήσεσθε ἐν δόξῃ. 5 νεκρώσατε οὖν τὰ μέλη τὰ
him *will appear* in glory. Therefore put to death *Therefore* *{the}* whatever *{the}* is
899 5746 1877 1518 4036 3739 4036 3836 3517 3836
r.dsm.3 v.fpi.2p p.d n.dsf v.aam.2p cj d.apn n.apn d.apn

⌊ἐπὶ τῆς γῆς,⌋ πορνείαν ἀκαθαρσίαν πάθος ἐπιθυμίαν κακήν, καὶ
earthly in you: sexual immorality, impurity, lust, evil desire, *evil* and
2093 3836 1178 4518 174 4079 2805 2123 2805 2779
p.g d.gsf n.gsf n.asf n.asf n.asn n.asf a.asf cj

τὴν πλεονεξίαν, ἥτις ἐστὶν εἰδωλολατρία, 6 δι' ἃ ἔρχεται ἡ ὀργὴ τοῦ
{the} covetousness, which is idolatry. ⌊Because of⌋ these, *is coming* the wrath of
3836 4432 4015 1639 1630 1328 4005 2262 3836 3973 3836
d.asf n.asf r.nsf v.pai.3s n.nsf p.a r.apn v.pmi.3s d.nsf n.nsf d.gsm

[a] [καὶ] UBS, omitted by NET.

NASB

20 If you have
died with Christ
to the elementary
principles of the
world, why, as if
you were living in
the world, do you
submit yourself to
decrees, such as,
21 "Do not handle,
do not taste, do not
touch!" 22 (which
all *refer to* things
destined to perish
with use)—in ac-
cordance with the
commandments
and teachings of
men? 23 These are
matters which
have, to be sure,
the appearance of
wisdom in self-
made religion and
self-abasement and
severe treatment of
the body, *but are*
of no value against
fleshly indulgence.

Put On the New Self

3:1 Therefore if you
have been raised
up with Christ,
keep seeking the
things above,
where Christ is,
seated at the right
hand of God. 2 Set
your mind on the
things above, not
on the things that
are on earth. 3 For
you have died and
your life is hid-
den with Christ in
God. 4 When Christ,
who is our life,
is revealed, then
you also will be
revealed with Him
in glory.
5 Therefore con-
sider the members
of your earthly
body as dead to
immorality, impu-
rity, passion, evil
desire, and greed,
which amounts to
idolatry. 6 For it is
because of these
things that the
wrath of God

NIV

God is coming.[a]
7You used to walk
in these ways, in
the life you once
lived. 8But now
you must also rid
yourselves of all
such things as
these: anger, rage,
malice, slander,
and filthy lan-
guage from your
lips. 9Do not lie to
each other, since
you have taken off
your old self with
its practices 10and
have put on the
new self, which is
being renewed in
knowledge in the
image of its Crea-
tor. 11Here there is
no Gentile or Jew,
circumcised or un-
circumcised, bar-
barian, Scythian,
slave or free, but
Christ is all, and is
in all.
12Therefore, as
God's chosen peo-
ple, holy and dear-
ly loved, clothe
yourselves with
compassion, kind-
ness, humility,
gentleness and pa-
tience. 13Bear with
each other and for-
give one another
if any of you has a
grievance against
someone. Forgive
as the Lord for-
gave you. 14And
over all these vir-
tues put on love,
which binds them
all together in per-
fect unity.
15Let the peace
of Christ rule in
your hearts, since
as members of one
body you were
called to peace.
And be

[a] 6 Some early manuscripts *coming on those who are disobedient*

θεοῦ [a]ἐπὶ τοὺς υἱοὺς τῆς ἀπειθείας. 7 ἐν οἷς καὶ ὑμεῖς
God is coming upon the sons of disobedience. And in them you also *you* once
2536 2262 2262 2093 3836 5626 3836 577 1877 4005 7007 2779 7007 4537
n.gsm p.a d.apm n.apm d.gsf n.gsf p.d r.dpn cj r.np.2

περιεπατήσατέ ποτε, ὅτε ἐζῆτε ἐν τούτοις· 8 νυνὶ δὲ
walked, *once* when ⌊you were living⌋ among them. But now *But* you
4344 4537 4021 2409 1877 4047 1254 3815 1254 7007
v.aai.2p adv cj v.iai.2p p.d r.dpn adv cj

ἀπόθεσθε καὶ ὑμεῖς τὰ πάντα, ὀργήν, θυμόν, κακίαν,
must put away *{also}* *you* *those things* all those things: anger, rage, malice,
700 2779 7007 3836 4246 3836 3836 3973 2596 2798
v.amm.2p adv r.np.2 d.apn a.apn n.asf n.asm n.asf

βλασφημίαν, αἰσχρολογίαν ἐκ τοῦ στόματος ὑμῶν· 9 μὴ ψεύδεσθε εἰς
slander, and filthy talk from *{the}* your mouth. *your* Stop lying to
1060 155 1666 3836 7007 5125 7007 3590 6017 1650
n.asf n.asf p.g d.gsn n.gsn r.gp.2 pl v.pmm.2p p.a

ἀλλήλους, ἀπεκδυσάμενοι τὸν παλαιὸν ἄνθρωπον σὺν ταῖς πράξεσιν αὐτοῦ
one another, ⌊since you have put off⌋ the old man with *{the}* its practices, *its*
253 588 3836 4094 476 5250 3836 899 4552 899
r.apm pt.am.npm d.asm a.asm n.asm p.d d.dpf n.dpf r.gsm.3

10 καὶ ἐνδυσάμενοι τὸν νέον τὸν ἀνακαινούμενον εἰς ἐπίγνωσιν κατʼ
and have put on the ⌊new man,⌋ which is being renewed in knowledge after the
2779 1907 3836 3742 3836 363 1650 2106 2848
cj pt.am.npm d.asm a.asm d.asm pt.pp.asm p.a n.asf p.a

εἰκόνα τοῦ κτίσαντος αὐτόν, 11 ὅπου οὐκ ἔνι Ἕλλην καὶ
image of its creator. *its* Here there is no longer *there is* Greek and
1635 3836 899 3231 899 3963 1928 1928 4024 1928 1818 2779
n.asf d.gsm pt.aa.gsm r.asm.3 cj pl v.pai.3s n.nsm cj

Ἰουδαῖος, περιτομὴ καὶ ἀκροβυστία, βάρβαρος, Σκύθης, δοῦλος, ἐλεύθερος, ἀλλὰ
Jew, circumcised and uncircumcised, barbarian, Scythian, slave and free, but
2681 4364 2779 213 975 5033 1529 1801 247
a.nsm n.nsf cj n.nsf n.nsm n.nsm n.nsm a.nsm cj

τὰ [b] πάντα καὶ ἐν πᾶσιν Χριστός. 12 ἐνδύσασθε οὖν, ὡς
Christ is *{the}* all and in all. *Christ* *clothe yourselves with* Therefore, as the
5986 3836 4246 2779 1877 4246 5986 1907 4036 6055
d.npn a.npn cj p.d a.dpn n.nsm v.amm.2p cj pl

ἐκλεκτοὶ τοῦ θεοῦ ἅγιοι καὶ ἠγαπημένοι, σπλάγχνα οἰκτιρμοῦ
elect of God, holy and dearly loved, clothe yourselves with heartfelt compassion,
1723 3836 2536 41 2779 26 1907 1907 1907 5073 3880
a.npm d.gsm n.gsm a.npm cj pt.rp.npm n.apn n.gsm

χρηστότητα ταπεινοφροσύνην πραΰτητα μακροθυμίαν, 13 ἀνεχόμενοι ἀλλήλων
kindness, humility, gentleness, and patience. Bear with one another
5983 5425 4559 3429 462 253
n.asf n.asf n.asf n.asf pt.pm.npm r.gpm

καὶ χαριζόμενοι ἑαυτοῖς ἐάν τις πρός τινα ἔχῃ μομφήν·
and forgive each another, should anyone have a complaint against another. *have* *complaint*
2779 5919 1571 1569 5516 2400 3664 4639 5516 2400 3664
cj pt.pm.npm r.dpm.2 cj r.nsm p.a r.asm v.pas.3s n.asf

καθὼς καὶ ὁ κύριος ἐχαρίσατο ὑμῖν, οὕτως καὶ ὑμεῖς·
As *{also}* the Lord ⌊has graciously forgiven⌋ you, so also you must forgive.
2777 2779 3836 3261 5919 7007 4048 2779 7007
cj adv d.nsm n.nsm v.ami.3s r.dp.2 adv adv r.np.2

14 ἐπὶ πᾶσιν δὲ τούτοις τὴν ἀγάπην, ὅ ἐστιν σύνδεσμος
And cover all *And* these virtues with love, which is the bond
1254 2093 4246 1254 4047 3836 27 4005 1639 5278
p.d a.dpn cj r.dpn d.asf n.asf r.nsn v.pai.3s n.nsm

τῆς τελειότητος. 15 καὶ ↱ ἡ εἰρήνη τοῦ Χριστοῦ βραβευέτω ἐν
⌊that leads to⌋ perfection. And let the peace of Christ ⌊be the ruling principle⌋ in
3836 5456 2779 1093 3836 1645 3836 5986 1093 1877
d.gsf n.gsf cj d.nsf n.nsf d.gsm n.gsm v.pam.3s p.d

ταῖς καρδίαις ὑμῶν, εἰς ἣν καὶ ἐκλήθητε ἐν ἑνὶ σώματι· καὶ
{the} your heart, *your* to which indeed you were called in one body. And be
3836 7007 2840 7007 1650 4005 2779 2813 1877 1651 5393 2779 1181
d.dpf n.dpf r.gp.2 p.a r.asf adv v.api.2p p.d a.dsn n.dsn cj

[a] [ἐπὶ τοὺς υἱοὺς τῆς ἀπειθείας] UBS, omitted by TNIV.
[b] [τὰ] UBS.

NASB

will come [a]upon
the sons of dis-
obedience, 7and
in them you also
once walked, when
you were living
in them. 8But now
you also, put them
all aside: anger,
wrath, malice, slan-
der, *and* abusive
speech from your
mouth. 9Do not
lie to one another,
since you laid aside
the old self with
its *evil* practices,
10and have put on
the new self who
is being renewed
to a true knowl-
edge according to
the image of the
One who created
him— 11*a renewal*
in which there
is no *distinction
between* Greek and
Jew, circumcised
and uncircum-
cised, [b]barbarian,
Scythian, slave and
freeman, but Christ
is all, and in all.
12So, as those who
have been chosen
of God, holy and
beloved, put on a
heart of compas-
sion, kindness,
humility, gentle-
ness and patience;
13bearing with one
another, and for-
giving each other,
whoever has a
complaint against
anyone; just as the
Lord forgave you,
so also should you.
14Beyond all these
things *put on* love,
which is the perfect
bond of unity. 15Let
the peace of Christ
rule in your hearts,
to which indeed
you were called in
one body; and be

[a] Two early mss do not contain *upon the sons of disobedience*
[b] I.e. those who were not Greeks, either by birth or by culture

NIV

thankful. 16 Let the
message of Christ
dwell among you
richly as you teach
and admonish one
another with all
wisdom through
psalms, hymns,
and songs from
the Spirit, singing
to God with grati-
tude in your hearts.
17 And whatever
you do, whether in
word or deed, do it
all in the name of
the Lord Jesus, giv-
ing thanks to God
the Father through
him.

Instructions for Christian Households

18 Wives, submit
yourselves to your
husbands, as is fit-
ting in the Lord.
19 Husbands, love
your wives and do
not be harsh with
them.
20 Children, obey
your parents in ev-
erything, for this
pleases the Lord.
21 Fathers,[a] do not
embitter your chil-
dren, or they will
become discour-
aged.
22 Slaves, obey
your earthly mas-
ters in everything;
and do it, not only
when their eye
is on you and to
curry their favor,
but with sincer-
ity of heart and
reverence for the
Lord. 23 Whatev-
er you do, work
at it with all your
heart, as working
for the Lord, not
for human mas-
ters, 24 since you
know that you
will receive an
inheritance from
the Lord as a re-
ward. It is the Lord
Christ you are
serving. 25 Anyone
who does wrong
will be repaid for
their wrongs, and
there is no

[a] 21 Or *Parents*

εὐχάριστοι γίνεσθε. 16 ↱ ὁ λόγος τοῦ Χριστοῦ ἐνοικείτω ἐν ὑμῖν πλουσίως,
thankful. *be* Let the word of Christ dwell in you richly
2375 1181 1940 3836 3364 3836 5986 1940 1877 7007 4455
a.npm v.pmm.2p d.nsm n.nsm d.gsm n.gsm v.pam.3s p.d r.dp.2 adv

ἐν πάσῃ σοφίᾳ διδάσκοντες καὶ νουθετοῦντες ἑαυτούς,
with all wisdom as you teach and admonish one another with all wisdom
1877 4246 5053 1438 2779 3805 1571 1877 4246 5053
p.d a.dsf n.dsf pt.pa.npm cj pt.pa.npm r.apm.2

ψαλμοῖς ὕμνοις ᾠδαῖς πνευματικαῖς ἐν τῇ[a] χάριτι
⌞by means of psalms,⌟ hymns, and spiritual songs, *spiritual* singing with *{the}* gratitude
6011 5631 4461 6046 4461 106 1877 3836 5921
n.dpm n.dpm n.dpf a.dpf p.d d.dsf n.dsf

ᾄδοντες ἐν ταῖς καρδίαις ὑμῶν τῷ θεῷ· 17 καὶ ⌞πᾶν ὅ τι ἐὰν⌟ ποιῆτε
singing in *{the}* your heart *your* to God. And whatever you do
106 1877 3836 7007 2840 7007 3836 2536 2779 4246 4005 5516 1569 4472
pt.pa.npm p.d d.dpf n.dpf r.gp.2 d.dsm n.dsm cj a.asn r.asn r.asn pl v.pas.2p

ἐν λόγῳ ἢ ἐν ἔργῳ, πάντα ἐν ὀνόματι → κυρίου Ἰησοῦ,
in word or *{in}* deed, do everything in the name of the Lord Jesus,
1877 3364 2445 1877 2240 4246 1877 3950 3261 2652
p.d n.dsm cj p.d n.dsn a.apn p.d n.dsn n.gsm n.gsm

εὐχαριστοῦντες τῷ θεῷ πατρὶ δι᾽ αὐτοῦ. 18 αἱ γυναῖκες, ὑποτάσσεσθε
giving thanks to God the Father through him. *{the}* Wives, be subject
2373 3836 2536 4252 1328 899 3836 1222 5718
pt.pa.npm d.dsm n.dsm n.dsm p.g r.gsm.3 d.vpf n.vpf v.ppm.2p

τοῖς ἀνδράσιν ὡς ἀνῆκεν ἐν κυρίῳ. 19 οἱ ἄνδρες, ἀγαπᾶτε τὰς γυναῖκας
to your husbands, as is fitting in the Lord. *{the}* Husbands, love your wives
3836 467 6055 465 1877 3261 3836 467 26 3836 1222
d.dpm n.dpm cj v.iai.3s p.d n.dsm d.vpm n.vpm v.pam.2p d.apf n.apf

καὶ ↱ μὴ πικραίνεσθε πρὸς αὐτάς. 20 τὰ τέκνα, ὑπακούετε τοῖς γονεῦσιν
and do not become bitter toward them. *{the}* Children, obey your parents
2779 4393 3590 4393 4639 899 3836 5451 5634 3836 1204
cj pl v.ppm.2p p.a r.apf.3 d.vpn n.vpn v.pam.2p d.dpm n.dpm

κατὰ πάντα, τοῦτο γὰρ εὐάρεστόν ἐστιν ἐν κυρίῳ. 21 οἱ πατέρες,
in everything, for this *for* is pleasing *is* in the Lord. *{the}* Fathers,
2848 4246 1142 4047 1142 1639 2298 1639 1877 3261 3836 4252
p.a a.apn r.nsn cj a.nsn v.pai.3s p.d n.dsm d.vpm n.vpm

↱ μὴ ἐρεθίζετε τὰ τέκνα ὑμῶν, ⌞ἵνα μὴ⌟ ἀθυμῶσιν. 22 οἱ
do not provoke *{the}* your children, *your* lest ⌞they become discouraged.⌟ *{the}*
2241 3590 2241 3836 7007 5451 7007 2671 3590 126 3836
pl v.pam.2p d.apn n.apn r.gp.2 cj pl v.pas.3p d.vpm

δοῦλοι, ὑπακούετε κατὰ πάντα τοῖς ⌞κατὰ σάρκα⌟ κυρίοις,
Slaves, obey your earthly masters in every regard, *your earthly masters*
1529 5634 3836 2848 3261 2848 4246 3836 2848 4922 3261
n.vpm v.pam.2p p.a a.apn d.dpm p.a n.asf n.dpm

μὴ ἐν ὀφθαλμοδουλίᾳ ὡς ἀνθρωπάρεσκοι, ἀλλ᾽ ἐν ἁπλότητι καρδίας
not with ⌞a view to impressing others,⌟ as people-pleasers, but with sincerity of heart,
3590 1877 4056 6055 473 247 1877 605 2840
pl p.d n.dsf pl a.npm cj p.d n.dsf n.gsf

φοβούμενοι τὸν κύριον. 23 ⌞ὃ ἐὰν⌟ ποιῆτε, ⌞ἐκ ψυχῆς⌟ ἐργάζεσθε ὡς
fearing the Lord. Whatever you do, do it heartily, *do* as
5828 3836 3261 4005 1569 4472 2237 1666 6034 2237 6055
pt.pp.npm d.asm n.asm r.asn pl v.pas.2p p.g n.gsf v.pmm.2p pl

τῷ κυρίῳ καὶ οὐκ ἀνθρώποις, 24 εἰδότες ὅτι ἀπὸ κυρίου ἀπολήμψεσθε τὴν
⌞for the⌟ Lord, *{and}* not for men, ⌞for you know⌟ that *from Lord* you will receive an
3836 3261 2779 4024 476 3857 4022 608 3261 655 3836
d.dsm n.dsm cj pl n.dpm pt.ra.npm cj p.g n.gsm v.fmi.2p d.asf

ἀνταπόδοσιν τῆς κληρονομίας. τῷ κυρίῳ Χριστῷ δουλεύετε·
inheritance from the Lord as your reward. Serve the Lord Christ. *Serve*
502 608 3261 3836 3100 1526 3836 3261 5986 1526
n.asf d.gsf n.gsf d.dsm n.dsm n.dsm v.pam.2p

25 ὁ γὰρ ἀδικῶν κομίσεται ὃ ἠδίκησεν, καὶ οὐκ
But the *But* ⌞one who does wrong⌟ ⌞will be paid back⌟ for his wrong, and there is no
1142 3836 1142 92 3152 4005 92 2779 1639 1639 4024
d.nsm cj pt.pa.nsm v.fmi.3s r.asn v.aai.3s cj pl

[a] [τῇ] UBS.

NASB

thankful. 16 Let the
word of [a]Christ
richly dwell
within you, with all
wisdom teaching
and admonishing
one another with
psalms *and* hymns
and spiritual
songs, singing with
thankfulness in
your hearts to God.
17 Whatever you do
in word or deed, *do*
all in the name of
the Lord Jesus, giv-
ing thanks through
Him to God the
Father.

Family Relations

18 Wives, be
subject to your
husbands, as is
fitting in the Lord.
19 Husbands, love
your wives and
do not be embit-
tered against
them. 20 Children,
be obedient to
your parents in all
things, for this is
well-pleasing to
the Lord. 21 Fathers,
do not exasperate
your children, so
that they will not
lose heart.
22 Slaves, in all
things obey those
who are your
masters on earth,
not with external
service, as those
who *merely* please
men, but with
sincerity of heart,
fearing the Lord.
23 Whatever you
do, do your work
heartily, as for the
Lord rather than
for men, 24 knowing
that from the Lord
you will receive
the reward of the
inheritance. It is
the Lord Christ
whom you serve.
25 For he who does
wrong will receive
the consequences
of the wrong which
he has done, and

[a] One early ms reads *the Lord*

NIV

favoritism.

4 Masters, provide your slaves with what is right and fair, because you know that you also have a Master in heaven.

Further Instructions

2 Devote yourselves to prayer, being watchful and thankful. 3 And pray for us, too, that God may open a door for our message, so that we may proclaim the mystery of Christ, for which I am in chains. 4 Pray that I may proclaim it clearly, as I should. 5 Be wise in the way you act toward outsiders; make the most of every opportunity. 6 Let your conversation be always full of grace, seasoned with salt, so that you may know how to answer everyone.

Final Greetings

7 Tychicus will tell you all the news about me. He is a dear brother, a faithful minister and fellow servant[a] in the Lord. 8 I am sending him to you for the express purpose that you may know about our[b] circumstances and that he may encourage your hearts. 9 He is coming with Onesimus, our faithful and dear brother, who is one of you. They will tell you everything that is happening here.

[a] 7 Or *slave*; also in verse 12
[b] 8 Some manuscripts *that he may know about your*

ἔστιν προσωπολημψία.
there is favoritism.
1639 4721
v.pai.3s n.nsf

4:1 οἱ κύριοι, τὸ δίκαιον καὶ τὴν ἰσότητα τοῖς δούλοις
{the} Masters, treat your slaves *{the}* justly and *{the}* fairly, *your slaves*
3836 3261 4218 3836 1529 3836 1465 2779 3836 2699 3836 1529
d.vpm n.vpm d.asn a.asn cj d.asf n.asf d.dpm n.dpm

παρέχεσθε, εἰδότες ὅτι καὶ ὑμεῖς ἔχετε κύριον ἐν οὐρανῷ. 2 τῇ
treat knowing that you too *you* have a Master in heaven. Persevere in
4218 3857 4022 7007 2779 7007 2400 3261 1877 4041 4674 3836
v.pmm.2p pt.ra.npm cj adv r.np.2 v.pai.2p n.asm p.d n.dsm d.dsf

προσευχῇ προσκαρτερεῖτε, γρηγοροῦντες ἐν αὐτῇ ἐν εὐχαριστίᾳ, 3
prayer, *Persevere* being vigilant in it with thanksgiving. At the same time,
4666 4674 1213 1877 899 1877 2374 275 275 275 275
n.dsf v.pam.2p pt.pa.npm p.d r.dsf.3 p.d n.dsf

προσευχόμενοι ἅμα καὶ περὶ ἡμῶν, ἵνα ὁ θεὸς ἀνοίξῃ ἡμῖν θύραν
pray *At the same time* also for us, that *{the}* God will open a door for our *door*
4667 275 2779 4309 7005 2671 3836 2536 487 2598 7005 2598
pt.pm.npm adv adv p.g r.gp.1 cj d.nsm n.nsm v.aas.3s r.dp.1 n.asf

τοῦ λόγου λαλῆσαι τὸ μυστήριον τοῦ Χριστοῦ, δι᾽ ὃ καὶ
{the} message, ⌊so that we may declare⌋ the mystery of Christ, for which *{also}*
3836 3364 3281 3836 3696 3836 5986 1328 4005 2779
d.gsm n.gsm f.aa d.asn n.asn d.gsm n.gsm p.a r.asn adv

δέδεμαι, 4 ἵνα φανερώσω αὐτὸ ↰ ὡς δεῖ με λαλῆσαι. 5
I am in chains; that I may make it known as I should. *I* *{to speak}* Conduct
1313 2671 5746 899 5746 6055 1609 1256 1609 3281 4344
v.rpi.1s cj v.aas.1s r.asn.3 cj v.pai.3s r.as.1 f.aa

ἐν σοφίᾳ περιπατεῖτε πρὸς τοὺς ἔξω τὸν
yourselves with wisdom *Conduct yourselves* toward *{the}* outsiders, making the most of the
4344 1877 5053 4344 4639 3836 2032 1973 1973 1973 1973 3836
p.d n.dsf v.pam.2p p.a d.apm adv d.asm

καιρὸν ἐξαγοραζόμενοι. 6 ὁ λόγος ὑμῶν πάντοτε ⌊ἐν χάριτι,⌋
time. *making the most of* *{the}* Your speech *Your* should always be winsome,
2789 1973 3836 7007 3364 7007 4121 1877 5921
n.asm pt.pm.npm d.nsm n.nsm r.gp.2 adv p.d n.dsf

ἅλατι ἠρτυμένος, εἰδέναι πῶς δεῖ ὑμᾶς ⌊ἑνὶ
seasoned with salt, *seasoned* ⌊so that you will know⌋ how you must *you* answer each person.
789 229 789 3857 4802 7007 1256 7007 646 1651
n.dsn pt.rp.nsm f.ra cj v.pai.3s r.ap.2 a.dsm

ἑκάστῳ⌋ ἀποκρίνεσθαι. 7 τὰ κατ᾽ ἐμὲ πάντα γνωρίσει ὑμῖν Τύχικος ὁ
answer *the news about me all will tell you* Tychicus, a
1667 646 3836 2848 1609 4246 1192 7007 5608 3836
r.dsm f.pm d.apn p.a r.as.1 a.apn v.fai.3s r.dp.2 n.nsm d.nsm

ἀγαπητὸς ἀδελφὸς καὶ πιστὸς διάκονος καὶ σύνδουλος ἐν κυρίῳ,
beloved brother, *{and}* faithful minister and fellow servant in the Lord, will tell you
28 81 2779 4412 1356 2779 5281 1877 3261 1192 1192 7007
a.nsm n.nsm cj a.nsm n.nsm cj n.nsm p.d n.dsm

8 ὃν ἔπεμψα πρὸς ὑμᾶς εἰς
all the news about me. I am sending him *I am sending* to you for this
4246 3836 3836 2848 1609 4287 4287 4287 4005 4287 4639 7007 1650 4047
r.asm v.aai.1s p.a r.ap.2 p.a

αὐτὸ τοῦτο, ἵνα γνῶτε ⌊τὰ περὶ⌋ ἡμῶν[a] καὶ παρακαλέσῃ
⌊express purpose,⌋ *this* that ⌊you may know⌋ how we are and that he may encourage
899 4047 2671 1182 3836 4309 7005 2779 4151
r.asn r.asn cj v.aas.2p d.apn p.g r.gp.1 cj v.aas.3s

τὰς καρδίας ὑμῶν, 9 σὺν Ὀνησίμῳ τῷ πιστῷ καὶ ἀγαπητῷ ἀδελφῷ, ὅς
{the} your hearts. *your* With him is Onesimus, the faithful and beloved brother, who
3836 7007 2840 7007 5250 3946 3836 4412 2779 28 81 4005
d.apf n.apf r.gp.2 p.d n.dsm d.dsm a.dsm cj a.dsm n.dsm r.nsm

ἐστιν ἐξ ὑμῶν· πάντα ὑμῖν γνωρίσουσιν τὰ ὧδε.
is one of you; they will tell you about everything *you* *they will tell about* *{the}* here.
1639 1666 7007 1192 1192 1192 7007 1192 4246 7007 1192 3836 6045
v.pai.3s p.g r.gp.2 a.apn r.dp.2 v.fai.3p d.apn adv

[a] ὑμῶν included by after ἡμῶν.

NASB

that without partiality.

Fellow Workers

4:1 Masters, grant to your slaves justice and fairness, knowing that you too have a Master in heaven.

2 Devote yourselves to prayer, keeping alert in it with *an attitude of* thanksgiving; 3 praying at the same time for us as well, that God will open up to us a door for the word, so that we may speak forth the mystery of Christ, for which I have also been imprisoned; 4 that I may make it clear in the way I ought to speak.

5 Conduct yourselves with wisdom toward outsiders, making the most of the opportunity. 6 Let your speech always be with grace, *as though* seasoned with salt, so that you will know how you should respond to each person.

7 As to all my affairs, Tychicus, *our* beloved brother and faithful servant and fellow bond-servant in the Lord, will bring you information. 8 *For* I have sent him to you for this very purpose, that you may know about our circumstances and that he may encourage your hearts; 9 and with him Onesimus, *our* faithful and beloved brother, who is one of your *number*. They will inform you about the whole situation here.

NIV

10My fellow pris-
oner Aristarchus
sends you his
greetings, as does
Mark, the cousin
of Barnabas. (You
have received in-
structions about
him; if he comes
to you, welcome
him.) 11Jesus, who
is called Justus,
also sends greet-
ings. These are the
only Jews[a] among
my co-workers
for the kingdom
of God, and they
have proved a
comfort to me.
12Epaphras, who
is one of you and
a servant of Christ
Jesus, sends greet-
ings. He is always
wrestling in prayer
for you, that you
may stand firm
in all the will of
God, mature and
fully assured. 13I
vouch for him that
he is working hard
for you and for
those at Laodicea
and Hierapolis.
14Our dear friend
Luke, the doctor,
and Demas send
greetings. 15Give
my greetings to
the brothers and
sisters at Laodicea,
and to Nympha
and the church in
her house.
16After this let-
ter has been read
to you, see that it
is also read in the
church of the La-
odiceans and that
you in turn read
the letter from La-
odicea.
17Tell Archippus:

[a] *11 Greek only ones of the circumcision group*

10 ἀσπάζεται ὑμᾶς Ἀρίσταρχος ὁ συναιχμάλωτός μου
sends greetings *you* Aristarchus, *{the}* my fellow prisoner, *my* sends you greetings,
832 7007 752 3836 1609 5257 1609 832 7007 832
v.pmi.3s r.ap.2 n.nsm d.nsm n.nsm r.gs.1

καὶ Μᾶρκος ὁ ἀνεψιὸς Βαρναβᾶ περὶ οὗ ἐλάβετε ἐντολάς, ἐὰν ἔλθῃ
as does Mark, the cousin of Barnabas (about whom you received instructions; if he comes
2779 3453 3836 463 982 4309 4005 3284 1953 1569 2262
cj n.nsm d.nsm n.nsm n.gsm p.g r.gsm v.aai.2p n.apf cj v.aas.3s

πρὸς ὑμᾶς, δέξασθε αὐτόν 11 καὶ Ἰησοῦς ὁ λεγόμενος Ἰοῦστος, οἱ
to you, welcome him), and Jesus who is called Justus. These are the
4639 7007 1312 899 2779 2652 3836 3306 2688 4047 1639 3836
p.a r.ap.2 v.amm.2p r.asm.3 cj n.nsm d.nsm pt.pp.nsm n.nsm d.npm

ὄντες ⌞ἐκ περιτομῆς,⌟ οὗτοι μόνοι συνεργοὶ εἰς τὴν
are only Jewish *These* *only* Christians among my fellow workers for the
1639 3668 1666 4364 4047 3668 5301 1650 3836
pt.pa.npm p.g n.gsf r.npm a.npm n.npm p.a d.asf

βασιλείαν τοῦ θεοῦ, οἵτινες ἐγενήθησάν μοι παρηγορία.
kingdom of God, and they have been a comfort to me. *comfort*
993 3836 2536 4015 1181 4219 1609 4219
n.asf d.gsm n.gsm r.npm v.api.3p r.ds.1 n.nsf

12 ἀσπάζεται ὑμᾶς Ἐπαφρᾶς ὁ ἐξ ὑμῶν, δοῦλος Χριστοῦ Ἰησοῦ,[a]
sends greetings *you* Epaphras, who is one of you and a servant of Christ Jesus, sends
832 7007 2071 3836 1666 7007 1529 5986 2652 832
v.pmi.3s r.ap.2 n.nsm d.nsm p.g r.gp.2 n.nsm n.gsm n.gsm

πάντοτε ἀγωνιζόμενος ὑπὲρ ὑμῶν ↰ ἐν ταῖς προσευχαῖς, ἵνα
you greetings, always laboring on your behalf in his prayers, that
7007 832 4121 76 5642 7007 5642 1877 3836 4666 2671
adv pt.pm.nsm p.g r.gp.2 p.d d.dpf n.dpf cj

σταθῆτε τέλειοι καὶ πεπληροφορημένοι ἐν
⌞you may stand firm⌟ in everything that God wills, mature and fully assured. *in*
2705 1877 4246 2536 2525 5455 2779 4442 1877
v.aps.2p a.npm cj pt.rp.npm p.d

παντὶ θελήματι τοῦ θεοῦ. 13 → → μαρτυρῶ γὰρ αὐτῷ ὅτι ἔχει
everything *wills* *{the}* *God* For I bear him witness *For* *him* that he has worked
4246 2525 3836 2536 1142 899 3455 1142 899 4022 2400 4506
a.dsn n.dsn d.gsm n.gsm v.pai.1s cj r.dsm.3 cj v.pai.3s

πολὺν πόνον ὑπὲρ ὑμῶν καὶ τῶν ἐν Λαοδικείᾳ καὶ τῶν ἐν Ἱεραπόλει.
tirelessly *worked* for you and for those in Laodicea and *{the}* in Hierapolis.
4498 4506 5642 7007 2779 3836 1877 3293 2779 3836 1877 2631
a.asm n.asm p.g r.gp.2 cj d.gpm p.d n.dsf cj d.gpm p.d n.dsf

14 ἀσπάζεται ὑμᾶς Λουκᾶς ὁ ἰατρὸς ὁ ἀγαπητὸς
sends his greetings *you* Our dear friend Luke, the physician, *Our* *dear friend* sends you
832 7007 3836 28 28 3371 3836 2620 3836 28 832 7007
v.pmi.3s r.ap.2 n.nsm d.nsm n.nsm d.nsm a.nsm

καὶ Δημᾶς. 15 ἀσπάσασθε τοὺς ἐν Λαοδικείᾳ ἀδελφοὺς
his greetings, as does Demas. Give my greetings to the *at* *Laodicea* brothers who are
832 832 2779 1318 832 3836 1877 3293 81
cj n.nsm v.amm.2p d.apm p.d n.dsf n.apm

καὶ Νύμφαν καὶ τὴν κατ' οἶκον αὐτῆς ἐκκλησίαν.
at Laodicea ⌞as well as⌟ to Nympha and the *in* *house* *her* church that meets in
1877 3293 2779 3809 2779 3836 2848 3875 899 1711 2848
cj n.asf cj d.asf p.a n.asm r.gsf.3 n.asf

16 καὶ ὅταν ἀναγνωσθῇ παρ' ὑμῖν ἡ ἐπιστολή, ποιήσατε ἵνα
her house. And after this letter has been read among you, *this* *letter* see that
899 3875 2779 4020 3836 2186 336 4123 7007 3836 2186 4472 2671
cj cj v.aps.3s p.d r.dp.2 d.nsf n.nsf v.aam.2p cj

καὶ ἐν τῇ → Λαοδικέων ἐκκλησίᾳ ἀναγνωσθῇ, καὶ
it is read also in the church of the Laodiceans, *church* *it is read* and that you
336 336 336 2779 1877 3836 1711 3294 1711 336 2779 2671 7007
adv p.d d.dsf n.gpm n.dsf v.aps.3s cj

τὴν ἐκ Λαοδικείας ἵνα καὶ ὑμεῖς ἀναγνῶτε. 17 καὶ εἴπατε Ἀρχίππῳ,
read ⌞the one⌟ from Laodicea *that* as well. *you* *read* And tell Archippus,
336 3836 1666 3293 2671 2779 7007 336 2779 3306 800
d.asf p.g n.gsf cj adv r.np.2 v.aas.2p cj v.aam.2p n.dsm

[a] [Ἰησοῦ] UBS, omitted by NET.

NASB

10Aristarchus,
my fellow pris-
oner, sends you
his greetings; and
also Barnabas's
cousin Mark (about
whom you received
instructions; if he
comes to you, wel-
come him); 11and
also Jesus who is
called Justus; these
are the only fellow
workers for the
kingdom of God
who are from the
circumcision, and
they have proved
to be an encour-
agement to me.
12Epaphras, who is
one of your num-
ber, a bondslave of
Jesus Christ, sends
you his greetings,
always laboring
earnestly for you
in his prayers, that
you may stand
perfect and fully
assured in all the
will of God. 13For
I testify for him
that he has a deep
concern for you
and for those who
are in Laodicea and
Hierapolis. 14Luke,
the beloved physi-
cian, sends you his
greetings, and *also*
Demas. 15Greet the
brethren who are
in Laodicea and
also [a]Nympha and
the church that
is in her house.
16When this letter
is read among you,
have it also read in
the church of the
Laodiceans; and
you, for your part
read my letter *that*
is coming from
Laodicea. 17Say to
Archippus,

[a] Or *Nymphas* (masc)

NIV

"See to it that you complete the ministry you have received in the Lord."
[18]I, Paul, write this greeting in my own hand. Remember my chains. Grace be with you.

βλέπε την διακονίαν ἣν παρέλαβες ἐν κυρίῳ, ἵνα
⌊"See to it⌋ that you complete the ministry that you have received in the Lord." *that*
1063 2671 4444 4444 3836 1355 4005 4161 1877 3261 2671
v.pam.2s d.asf n.asf r.asf v.aai.2s p.d n.dsm cj

αὐτὴν πληροῖς. 18 ὁ ἀσπασμὸς τῇ ἐμῇ χειρὶ Παύλου.
{it} *you complete* I, Paul, write this greeting in ⌊my own⌋ hand. *Paul*
899 4444 4263 3836 833 3836 1847 5931 4263
r.asf.3 v.pas.2s d.nsm n.nsm d.dsf r.dsf.1 n.dsf n.gsm

μνημονεύετέ μου τῶν δεσμῶν. ἡ χάρις μεθ᾽ ὑμῶν.[a]
Remember my *{the}* chains. *{the}* Grace be with you.
3648 1609 3836 1301 3836 5921 3552 7007
v.pam.2p r.gs.1 d.gpm n.gpm d.nsf n.nsf p.g r.gp.2

NASB

"Take heed to the ministry which you have received in the Lord, that you may fulfill it."
[18]I, Paul, write this greeting with my own hand. Remember my imprisonment. Grace be with you.

[a] ἀμήν. πρὸς Κολοσσαεῖς ἐγράφη ἀπὸ Ῥώμης διὰ Τυχικοῦ καὶ Ὀνησίμου included by TR after ὑμῶν.

1 Thessalonians

NIV

1 Paul, Silas[a]
and Timothy,
To the church of the
Thessalonians in God
the Father and the
Lord Jesus Christ:
Grace and peace
to you.

Thanksgiving for the Thessalonians' Faith

2 We always thank
God for all of you
and continually
mention you in
our prayers. 3 We
remember before
our God and Father
your work produced
by faith, your labor
prompted by love,
and your endurance
inspired by hope
in our Lord Jesus
Christ.
4 For we know,
brothers and sisters[b]
loved by God, that
he has chosen you,
5 because our gos-
pel came to you not
simply with words
but also with power,
with the Holy Spirit
and deep convic-
tion. You know how
we lived among you
for your sake. 6 You
became imitators of
us and of the Lord,
for you welcomed
the message in the
midst of severe suf-
fering with the joy
given by the Holy
Spirit. 7 And so you
became a model to
all the believers in

[a] 1 Greek *Silvanus*, a variant of *Silas*
[b] 4 The Greek word for *brothers and sisters* (*adelphoi*) refers here to believers, both men and women, as part of God's family; also in 2:1, 9, 14, 17; 3:7; 4:1, 10, 13; 5:1, 4, 12, 14, 25, 27.

1:1 Παῦλος καὶ Σιλουανὸς καὶ Τιμόθεος τῇ ἐκκλησίᾳ → Θεσσαλονικέων
Paul, {and} Silvanus, and Timothy, ⌊to the⌋ church of the Thessalonians
4263 2779 4977 2779 5510 3836 1711 2552
n.nsm cj n.nsm cj n.nsm d.dsf n.dsf n.gpm

ἐν θεῷ πατρὶ καὶ κυρίῳ Ἰησοῦ Χριστῷ, χάρις ὑμῖν καὶ εἰρήνη.[a] 2 →
in God the Father and the Lord Jesus Christ: Grace to you and peace. We
1877 2536 4252 2779 3261 2652 5986 5921 7007 2779 1645
p.d n.dsm n.dsm cj n.dsm n.dsm n.dsm n.nsf r.dp.2 cj n.nsf

εὐχαριστοῦμεν τῷ θεῷ πάντοτε περὶ πάντων ὑμῶν μνείαν
continually give thanks to God *continually* for all of you, making mention
4121 2373 3836 2536 4121 4309 4246 7007 4472 3644
v.pai.1p d.dsm n.dsm adv p.g a.gpm r.gp.2 n.asf

ποιούμενοι ἐπὶ τῶν προσευχῶν ἡμῶν, ἀδιαλείπτως 3 μνημονεύοντες
making of you in {the} our prayers, *our* unceasingly remembering before
4472 2093 3836 7005 4666 7005 90 3648 1869
pt.pm.npm p.g d.gpf n.gpf r.gp.1 adv pt.pa.npm

ὑμῶν τοῦ ἔργου τῆς πίστεως καὶ τοῦ κόπου τῆς ἀγάπης καὶ
our God and Father your {the} work of faith, {and} your labor of love, and
7005 2536 2779 4252 7007 3836 2240 3836 4411 2779 3836 3160 3836 27 2779
r.gp.2 d.gsn n.gsn d.gsf n.gsf cj d.gsm n.gsm d.gsf n.gsf cj

τῆς ὑπομονῆς τῆς ἐλπίδος τοῦ κυρίου ἡμῶν Ἰησοῦ Χριστοῦ ἔμπροσθεν τοῦ
the steadfastness of your hope in our Lord *our* Jesus Christ. *before* {the}
3836 5705 3836 1828 3836 7005 3261 7005 2652 5986 1869 3836
d.gsf n.gsf d.gsf n.gsf d.gsm n.gsm r.gp.1 n.gsm n.gsm p.g d.gsm

θεοῦ καὶ πατρὸς ἡμῶν, 4 εἰδότες, ἀδελφοὶ ἠγαπημένοι ὑπὸ τοῦ[b] θεοῦ, τὴν
God and Father our We know, brothers loved by {the} God, that he has
2536 2779 4252 7005 3857 81 26 5679 3836 2536 3836
n.gsm cj n.gsm r.gp.1 pt.ra.npm n.vpm pt.rp.vpm p.g d.gsm n.gsm d.asf

ἐκλογὴν ὑμῶν, 5 ὅτι τὸ εὐαγγέλιον ἡμῶν ↱ οὐκ ἐγενήθη εἰς ὑμᾶς ἐν
chosen you, because {the} our gospel *our* did not come to you with
1724 7007 4022 3836 7005 2295 7005 1181 4024 1181 1650 7007 1877
n.asf r.gp.2 cj d.nsn n.nsn r.gp.1 pl v.api.3s p.a r.ap.2 p.d

λόγῳ μόνον ἀλλὰ καὶ ἐν δυνάμει καὶ ἐν πνεύματι ἁγίῳ καὶ ἐν[c]
words only, but also with power — {and} with the Holy Spirit *Holy* and {with} full
3364 3667 247 2779 1877 1539 2779 1877 41 4460 41 2779 1877 4498
n.dsm adv cj adv p.d n.dsf cj p.d n.dsn a.dsn cj p.d

πληροφορίᾳ πολλῇ, καθὼς οἴδατε οἷοι ἐγενήθημεν ἐν[d] ὑμῖν δι'
conviction *full* — as you know ⌊what kind of men⌋ we were among you for
4443 4498 2777 3857 3888 1181 1877 7007 1328
n.dsf a.dsf cj v.rai.2p r.npm v.api.1p p.d r.dp.2 p.a

ὑμᾶς. ↰ 6 καὶ ὑμεῖς μιμηταὶ ἡμῶν ἐγενήθητε καὶ τοῦ κυρίου,
your sakes. And you became imitators of us *became* and of the Lord,
7007 1328 2779 7007 1181 3629 7005 1181 2779 3836 3261
r.ap.2 cj r.np.2 n.npm r.gp.1 v.api.2p cj d.gsm n.gsm

δεξάμενοι τὸν λόγον ἐν θλίψει πολλῇ μετὰ χαρᾶς →
for you accepted the word ⌊in the midst of⌋ much affliction, *much* with the joy of the Holy
1312 3836 3364 1877 4498 2568 4498 3552 5915 41
pt.am.npm d.asm n.asm p.d n.dsf a.dsf p.g n.gsf

πνεύματος ἁγίου, 7 ὥστε γενέσθαι ὑμᾶς τύπον πᾶσιν τοῖς πιστεύουσιν ἐν
Spirit. *Holy* So you became *you* an example for all the believers in
4460 41 6063 7007 1181 7007 5596 4246 3836 4409 1877
n.gsn a.gsn cj f.am r.ap.2 n.asm a.dpm d.dpm pt.pa.dpm p.d

[a] ἀπὸ Θεοῦ πατρὸς ἡμῶν καὶ Κυρίου Ἰησοῦ Χριστοῦ included by TR after εἰρήνη.
[b] [τοῦ] UBS.
[c] [ἐν] UBS, omitted by TNIV.
[d] [ἐν] UBS.

NASB

Thanksgiving for These Believers

1:1 Paul and Sil-
vanus and Timothy,
To the church of
the Thessalonians
in God the Father
and the Lord Jesus
Christ: Grace to
you and peace.
2 We give thanks
to God always for
all of you, making
mention *of you*
in our prayers;
3 constantly bear-
ing in mind your
work of faith and
labor of love and
steadfastness of
hope in our Lord
Jesus Christ in the
presence of our
God and Father,
4 knowing, brethren
beloved by God,
His choice of you;
5 for our gospel did
not come to you in
word only, but also
in power and in
the Holy Spirit and
with full convic-
tion; just as you
know what kind
of men we proved
to be among you
for your sake. 6 You
also became imita-
tors of us and of
the Lord, having
received the word
in much tribulation
with the joy of the
Holy Spirit, 7 so
that you became an
example to all the
believers in

NIV

Macedonia and
Achaia. [8]The
Lord's message
rang out from you
not only in Mac-
edonia and Acha-
ia—your faith in
God has become
known every-
where. Therefore
we do not need to
say anything about
it, [9]for they them-
selves report what
kind of reception
you gave us. They
tell how you turned
to God from idols
to serve the living
and true God, [10]and
to wait for his
Son from heaven,
whom he raised
from the dead—
Jesus, who rescues
us from the coming
wrath.

Paul's Ministry in Thessalonica

2 You know,
brothers and
sisters, that our
visit to you was
not without results.
[2]We had previ-
ously suffered
and been treated
outrageously in
Philippi, as you
know, but with the
help of our God we
dared to tell you
his gospel in the
face of strong op-
position. [3]For the
appeal we make
does not spring
from error or im-
pure motives, nor
are we trying to
trick you. [4]On the
contrary, we speak
as those approved

τῇ Μακεδονίᾳ καὶ ἐν τῇ Ἀχαΐᾳ. 8 ἀφ'
{the} Macedonia and in {the} Achaia. The word of the Lord has echoed forth from
3836 3423 2779 1877 3836 938 3836 3364 3836 3836 3261 2010 2010 2010 608
d.dsf n.dsf cj p.d d.dsf n.dsf p.g

ὑμῶν γὰρ ἐξήχηται ὁ λόγος τοῦ κυρίου οὐ μόνον ἐν τῇ Μακεδονίᾳ καὶ
you {for} has echoed forth The word of the Lord not only in {the} Macedonia and
7007 1142 2010 3836 3364 3836 3261 4024 3667 1877 3836 3423 2779
r.gp.2 cj v.rpi.3s d.nsm n.nsm d.gsm n.gsm pl adv p.d d.dsf n.dsf cj

[a]ἐν τῇ[b] Ἀχαΐᾳ, ἀλλ' ἐν παντὶ τόπῳ ἡ πίστις ὑμῶν ἡ πρὸς τὸν θεὸν
{in} {the} Achaia, but in every place {the} your faith your {the} in {the} God
1877 3836 938 247 1877 4246 5536 3836 7007 4411 7007 3836 4639 3836 2536
p.d d.dsf n.dsf cj p.d a.dsm n.dsm d.nsf n.nsf r.gp.2 d.nsf p.a d.asm n.asm

ἐξελήλυθεν, ὥστε μὴ χρείαν ἔχειν ἡμᾶς λαλεῖν τι. 9
has become known, so we have no need have we to say anything. For they
2002 6063 7005 2400 3590 5970 2400 7005 3281 5516 1142 550
v.rai.3s cj pl n.asf f.pa r.ap.1 f.pa r.asn

αὐτοὶ γὰρ περὶ ἡμῶν ἀπαγγέλλουσιν ὁποίαν εἴσοδον ἔσχομεν πρὸς
themselves For report regarding us they report ⌞what kind of⌟ reception we had among
899 1142 550 4309 7005 550 3961 1658 2400 4639
r.npm cj p.g r.gp.1 v.pai.3p r.asf n.asf v.aai.1p p.a

ὑμᾶς, καὶ πῶς ἐπεστρέψατε πρὸς τὸν θεὸν ἀπὸ τῶν εἰδώλων δουλεύειν
you, and how you turned to {the} God from {the} idols to serve the living and
7007 2779 4802 2188 4639 3836 2536 608 3836 1631 1526 2409 2779
r.ap.2 cj cj v.aai.2p p.a d.asm n.asm p.g d.gpn n.gpn f.pa

θεῷ ζῶντι καὶ ἀληθινῷ 10 καὶ ἀναμένειν τὸν υἱὸν αὐτοῦ ἐκ τῶν
true God, living and true and to wait for {the} his Son his from {the}
240 2536 2409 2779 240 2779 388 3836 899 5626 899 1666 3836
n.dsm pt.pa.dsm cj a.dsm cj f.pa d.asm n.asm r.gsm.3 p.g d.gpm

οὐρανῶν, ὃν ἤγειρεν ἐκ τῶν[c] νεκρῶν, Ἰησοῦν τὸν ῥυόμενον ἡμᾶς ἐκ τῆς
heaven, whom he raised from the dead, Jesus, {the} our deliverer our from the
4041 4005 1586 1666 3836 3738 2652 3836 7005 4861 7005 1666 3836
n.gpm r.asm v.aai.3s p.g d.gpm a.gpm n.asm d.asm pt.pm.asm r.ap.1 p.g d.gsf

ὀργῆς τῆς ἐρχομένης.
coming wrath. {the} coming
2262 3973 3836 2262
n.gsf d.gsf pt.pm.gsf

2:1 ↱ αὐτοὶ γὰρ οἴδατε, ἀδελφοί, τὴν εἴσοδον ἡμῶν τὴν πρὸς
For you yourselves For know, brothers, that {the} our coming our {the} to
1142 3857 899 1142 3857 81 4022 3836 7005 1658 7005 3836 4639
r.npm cj v.rai.2p n.vpm d.asf n.asf r.gp.1 d.asf p.a

ὑμᾶς ὅτι οὐ κενὴ γέγονεν, 2 ἀλλὰ προπαθόντες καὶ
you that was not in vain. was but ⌞We had previously suffered⌟ and
7007 4022 1181 4024 3031 1181 247 4634 2779
r.ap.2 cj pl n.nsf v.rai.3s cj pt.aa.npm cj

ὑβρισθέντες, καθὼς οἴδατε, ἐν Φιλίπποις ἐπαρρησιασάμεθα
⌞been shamefully treated⌟ in Philippi, as you know, in Philippi but we had the courage
5614 1877 5804 2777 3857 1877 5804 247 4245
pt.ap.npm cj v.rai.2p p.d n.dpm v.ami.1p

ἐν τῷ θεῷ ἡμῶν λαλῆσαι πρὸς ὑμᾶς τὸ εὐαγγέλιον τοῦ θεοῦ ἐν
in {the} our God our to declare to you the gospel of God ⌞in spite of⌟
1877 3836 7005 2536 7005 3281 4639 7007 3836 2295 3836 2536 1877
p.d d.dsm n.dsm r.gp.1 f.aa p.a r.ap.2 d.asn n.asn d.gsm n.gsm p.d

πολλῷ ἀγῶνι. 3 ἡ γὰρ παράκλησις ἡμῶν οὐκ ἐκ πλάνης οὐδὲ
great opposition. {the} For our appeal our was not ⌞based on⌟ deceit, nor did it
4498 74 3836 1142 7005 4155 7005 4024 1666 4415 4028
a.dsm n.dsm d.nsf cj n.nsf r.gp.1 pl p.g n.gsf cj

ἐξ ἀκαθαρσίας οὐδὲ ἐν δόλῳ, 4 ἀλλὰ καθὼς δεδοκιμάσμεθα ὑπὸ
rise from impure motives or ⌞by way of⌟ trickery, but just as we have been approved by
1666 174 4028 1877 1515 247 2777 1507 5679
p.g n.gsf cj p.d n.dsm cj cj v.rpi.1p p.g

NASB

Macedonia and in
Achaia. [8]For the
word of the Lord
has sounded forth
from you, not only
in Macedonia and
Achaia, but also in
every place your
faith toward God
has gone forth,
so that we have
no need to say
anything. [9]For they
themselves report
about us what kind
of a reception we
had with you, and
how you turned to
God from idols to
serve a living and
true God, [10]and
to wait for His
Son from heaven,
whom He raised
from the dead,
that is Jesus, who
rescues us from the
wrath to come.

Paul's Ministry

[2:1]For you your-
selves know,
brethren, that our
coming to you was
not in vain, [2]but
after we had al-
ready suffered and
been mistreated
in Philippi, as you
know, we had the
boldness in our
God to speak to
you the gospel of
God amid much
opposition. [3]For
our exhortation
does not *come*
from error or im-
purity or by way of
deceit; [4]but just as
we have been ap-
proved by God

[a] [ἐν τῇ] UBS, omitted by TNIV.
[b] τῇ omitted in TNIV.
[c] [τῶν] UBS.

NIV

by God to be en-
trusted with the
gospel. We are not
trying to please
people but God,
who tests our
hearts. [5]You know
we never used flat-
tery, nor did we
put on a mask to
cover up greed—
God is our wit-
ness. [6]We were not
looking for praise
from people, not
from you or any-
one else, even
though as apostles
of Christ we could
have asserted our
authority. [7]In-
stead, we were like
young children[a]
among you.
Just as a nursing
mother cares for
her children, [8]so
we cared for you.
Because we loved
you so much, we
were delighted
to share with you
not only the gos-
pel of God but
our lives as well.
[9]Surely you re-
member, brothers
and sisters, our
toil and hardship;
we worked night
and day in order
not to be a burden
to anyone while
we preached the
gospel of God to
you. [10]You are
witnesses, and so
is God, of how
holy, righteous and
blameless we were
among you who
believed. [11]For you
know that we dealt
with each of you as
a father deals with
his own children,
[12]encouraging,
comforting and
urging you to

τοῦ θεοῦ πιστευθῆναι τὸ εὐαγγέλιον, οὕτως λαλοῦμεν, οὐχ ὡς
{the} God ⌞to be entrusted with⌟ the gospel, so we speak, not to please
3836 2536 4409 3836 2295 4048 3281 4024 6055 743
d.gsm n.gsm f.ap d.asn n.asn adv v.pai.1p pl pl

ἀνθρώποις ἀρέσκοντες ἀλλὰ θεῷ τῷ δοκιμάζοντι τὰς καρδίας ἡμῶν. [5]
man *please* but God who tests {the} our hearts. *our* For we
476 743 247 2536 3836 1507 3836 7005 2840 7005 1142 1181
n.dpm pt.pa.npm cj n.dsm d.dsm pt.pa.dsm d.apf n.apf r.gp.1

οὔτε γάρ ποτε ἐν λόγῳ κολακείας ἐγενήθημεν, καθὼς οἴδατε, οὔτε
never *For* {ever} came with flattering speech, *flattering* *we came* as you know, or
4046 1142 4537 1181 1877 3135 3364 3135 1181 2777 3857 4046
cj cj adv p.d n.dsm n.gsf v.api.1p cj v.rai.2p cj

ἐν προφάσει πλεονεξίας, θεὸς μάρτυς, [6]οὔτε ζητοῦντες ἐξ
with a pretext for greed — God is our witness. Neither did we seek praise from
1877 4733 4432 2536 3459 4046 2426 1518 1666
p.d n.dsf n.gsf n.nsm n.nsm cj pt.pa.npm p.g

ἀνθρώπων δόξαν οὔτε ἀφ᾽ ὑμῶν οὔτε ἀπ᾽ ἄλλων, [7]δυνάμενοι
men, *praise* whether from you or from others. ⌞Although we could⌟ have made
476 1518 4046 608 7007 4046 608 257 1538 1639 1639
n.gpm n.asf cj p.g r.gp.2 cj p.g r.gpm pt.pp.npm

⌞ἐν βάρει⌟ εἶναι ὡς Χριστοῦ ἀπόστολοι. ἀλλὰ ἐγενήθημεν νήπιοι
demands *have made* as apostles of Christ, *apostles* {but} we were gentle
1877 983 1639 6055 693 5986 693 247 1181 3758
p.d n.dsn f.pa pl n.gsm n.npm cj v.api.1p a.npm

⌞ἐν μέσῳ⌟ ὑμῶν, ⌞ὡς ἐὰν⌟ τροφὸς θάλπῃ τὰ ἑαυτῆς τέκνα, [8]οὕτως
among you, like a mother ⌞tenderly nursing⌟ {the} her own children. So deep
1877 3545 7007 6055 1569 5577 2499 3836 1571 5451 4048
p.d n.dsn r.gp.2 cj pl n.nsf v.pas.3s d.apn r.gsf.3 n.apn adv

ὁμειρόμενοι ὑμῶν εὐδοκοῦμεν μεταδοῦναι ὑμῖν οὐ μόνον τὸ
was our affection for you that we were pleased to share ⌞with you⌟ not only the
3916 7007 2305 3556 7007 4024 3667 3836
pt.pm.npm r.gp.2 v.iai.1p f.aa r.dp.2 pl adv d.asn

εὐαγγέλιον τοῦ θεοῦ ἀλλὰ καὶ τὰς ἑαυτῶν ψυχάς, διότι ἀγαπητοὶ
gospel of God but *as well* {the} our own selves as well, so dear had you
2295 3836 2536 247 2779 3836 1571 6034 2779 2779 1484 28 1181 1181
n.asn d.gsm n.gsm cj adv d.apf r.gpm.1 n.apf cj a.npm

ἡμῖν ἐγενήθητε. [9] μνημονεύετε γάρ, ἀδελφοί, τὸν κόπον ἡμῶν καὶ
become to us. *had you become* For you recall, *For* brothers, {the} our labor *our* and
1181 7005 1181 1142 3648 1142 81 3836 7005 3160 7005 2779
r.dp.1 v.api.2p v.pai.2p cj n.vpm d.asm n.asm r.gp.1 cj

τὸν μόχθον· νυκτὸς καὶ ἡμέρας ἐργαζόμενοι πρὸς τὸ μὴ
{the} toil. We worked night and day *We worked* so as ~ not
3836 3677 2237 2237 3816 2779 2465 2237 4639 3836 3590
d.asm n.asm n.gsf cj n.gsf pt.pm.npm p.a d.asn pl

ἐπιβαρῆσαί τινα ὑμῶν ἐκηρύξαμεν εἰς ὑμᾶς τὸ εὐαγγέλιον τοῦ θεοῦ.
⌞to become a burden to⌟ any of you, while proclaiming to you the gospel of God.
2096 5516 7007 3062 1650 7007 3836 2295 3836 2536
f.aa r.asm r.gp.2 v.aai.1p p.a r.ap.2 d.asn n.asn d.gsm n.gsm

[10] ὑμεῖς μάρτυρες καὶ ὁ θεός, ὡς ὁσίως καὶ δικαίως καὶ ἀμέμπτως
You are witnesses, and so is {the} God, how devout, {and} upright, and blameless was
7007 3459 2779 3836 2536 6055 4010 2779 1469 2779 290 1181
r.np.2 n.npm cj d.nsm n.nsm cj adv cj adv cj adv

ὑμῖν τοῖς πιστεύουσιν ἐγενήθημεν, [11] καθάπερ οἴδατε,
our conduct ⌞toward you⌟ {the} believers *was our conduct* — how, as you know,
1181 1181 7007 3836 4409 1181 2749 6055 3857
r.dp.2 d.dpm pt.pa.dpm v.api.1p cj v.rai.2p

ὡς ἕνα ἕκαστον ὑμῶν ὡς πατὴρ τέκνα ἑαυτοῦ
as we treated each one *each* of you as a father would treat his own children. *his own*
6055 1667 1651 1667 7007 6055 4252 1571 1571 5451 1571
cj a.asm r.asm r.gp.2 cj n.nsm n.apn r.gsm.3

[12] παρακαλοῦντες ὑμᾶς καὶ παραμυθούμενοι καὶ μαρτυρόμενοι εἰς τὸ
So we exhorted you, {and} encouraged you, and charged you to {the}
4151 7007 2779 4170 2779 3455 1650 3836
pt.pa.npm r.ap.2 cj pt.pm.npm cj pt.pm.npm p.a d.asn

NASB

to be entrusted
with the gospel, so
we speak, not as
pleasing men, but
God who examines
our hearts. [5]For we
never came with
flattering speech,
as you know, nor
with a pretext for
greed—God is
witness— [6]nor
did we seek glory
from men, either
from you or from
others, even though
as apostles of
Christ we might
have asserted our
authority. [7]But
we proved to be
[a]gentle among you,
as a nursing *mother*
tenderly cares for
her own children.
[8]Having so fond an
affection for you,
we were well-
pleased to impart
to you not only the
gospel of God but
also our own lives,
because you had
become very dear
to us.
[9]For you recall,
brethren, our labor
and hardship, *how*
working night and
day so as not to be
a burden to any of
you, we proclaimed
to you the gospel
of God. [10]You are
witnesses, and *so is*
God, how devoutly
and uprightly and
blamelessly we be-
haved toward you
believers; [11]just as
you know how we
were exhorting and
encouraging and
imploring each one
of you as a father
would his own
children, [12]so that

[a] 7 Some manu-
scripts *were gentle*

[a] Three early mss
read *babes*

NIV

live lives worthy
of God, who calls
you into his king-
dom and glory.
13 And we also
thank God con-
tinually because,
when you received
the word of God,
which you heard
from us, you ac-
cepted it not as a
human word, but
as it actually is,
the word of God,
which is indeed
at work in you
who believe. 14 For
you, brothers and
sisters, became
imitators of God's
churches in Ju-
dea, which are in
Christ Jesus: You
suffered from your
own people the
same things those
churches suffered
from the Jews
15 who killed the
Lord Jesus and the
prophets and also
drove us out. They
displease God and
are hostile to ev-
eryone 16 in their
effort to keep us
from speaking to
the Gentiles so that
they may be saved.
In this way they al-
ways heap up their
sins to the limit.
The wrath of God
has come upon
them at last.[a]

Paul's Longing to See the Thessalonians

17 But, brothers
and sisters, when
we were orphaned
by being sepa-
rated from you
for a short time
(in person, not
in thought), out
of our intense
longing

[a] 16 Or *them fully*

περιπατεῖν ὑμᾶς ἀξίως τοῦ θεοῦ τοῦ καλοῦντος ὑμᾶς εἰς τὴν
conduct yourselves ⌊in a manner worthy⌋ of God, who calls you into *{the}*
4344 7007 547 3836 2536 3836 2813 7007 1650 3836
f.pa r.ap.2 adv d.gsm n.gsm d.gsm pt.pa.gsm r.ap.2 p.a d.asf

ἑαυτοῦ βασιλείαν καὶ δόξαν. 13 καὶ διὰ τοῦτο καὶ ἡμεῖς
his own kingdom and glory. And for this reason we also *we* constantly
1571 993 2779 1518 2779 1328 4047 7005 2779 7005 90
r.gsm.3 n.asf cj n.asf cj p.a r.asn adv r.np.1

εὐχαριστοῦμεν τῷ θεῷ ἀδιαλείπτως, ὅτι παραλαβόντες λόγον
thank *{the}* God *constantly* that when you received the word of God which
2373 3836 2536 90 4022 4161 3364 3836 2536
v.pai.1p d.dsm n.dsm adv cj pt.aa.npm n.asm

ἀκοῆς παρ᾽ ἡμῶν τοῦ θεοῦ ἐδέξασθε οὐ → λόγον ἀνθρώπων ἀλλὰ
you heard from us, *of God* you accepted it not as a human word, *human* but
198 4123 7005 3836 2536 1312 4024 476 3364 476 247
n.gsf p.g r.gp.1 d.gsm n.gsm v.ami.2p pl n.asm n.gpm cj

καθώς → ἐστιν ἀληθῶς λόγον θεοῦ, ὃς καὶ ἐνεργεῖται ἐν ὑμῖν
as it truly is, *truly* the word of God, which even ⌊now is doing its work⌋ in you
2777 242 1639 242 3364 2536 4005 2779 1919 1877 7007
cj v.pai.3s adv n.asm n.gsm r.nsm cj v.pmi.3s p.d r.dp.2

τοῖς πιστεύουσιν. 14 ὑμεῖς γὰρ μιμηταὶ ἐγενήθητε, ἀδελφοί, τῶν
who believe. For you, *For* brothers, became imitators *became* *brothers* of the
3836 4409 1142 7007 1142 81 1181 3629 1181 81 3836
d.dpm pt.pa.dpm r.np.2 cj n.npm v.api.2p n.vpm d.gpf

ἐκκλησιῶν τοῦ θεοῦ τῶν οὐσῶν ἐν τῇ Ἰουδαίᾳ ἐν Χριστῷ Ἰησοῦ,
churches of God in Christ Jesus that are in *{the}* Judea; *in Christ Jesus*
1711 3836 2536 1877 5986 2652 3836 1639 1877 3836 2677 1877 5986 2652
n.gpf d.gsm n.gsm d.gpf pt.pa.gpf p.d d.dsf n.dsf p.d n.dsm n.dsm

ὅτι τὰ αὐτὰ ἐπάθετε καὶ ὑμεῖς ὑπὸ τῶν ἰδίων
because you too suffered the ⌊same things⌋ *suffered too you* from *{the}* your own
4022 7007 2779 4248 3836 899 4248 2779 7007 5679 3836 2625
cj d.apn r.apn v.aai.2p adv r.np.2 p.g d.gpm a.gpm

συμφυλετῶν καθὼς καὶ αὐτοὶ ὑπὸ τῶν Ἰουδαίων, 15 τῶν καὶ τὸν
countrymen, even as *{also}* they did from the Jews, who *{also}* killed the
5241 2777 2779 899 5679 3836 2681 3836 2779 650 3836
n.gpm cj adv r.npm p.g d.gpm a.gpm d.gpm adv d.asm

κύριον ἀποκτεινάντων Ἰησοῦν καὶ τοὺς προφήτας καὶ ↱ ↱ ἡμᾶς ἐκδιωξάντων
Lord *killed* Jesus and the prophets, and have driven us out,
3261 650 2652 2779 3836 4737 2779 1691 1691 7005 1691
n.asm pt.aa.gpm n.asm cj d.apm n.apm cj r.ap.1 pt.aa.gpm

καὶ θεῷ ⌊μὴ ἀρεσκόντων⌋ καὶ πᾶσιν
{and} who are displeasing to God *who are displeasing* and oppose all
2779 3590 3590 3590 2536 3590 743 2779 1885 4246
cj n.dsm pl pt.pa.gpm cj a.dpm

ἀνθρώποις ἐναντίων, 16 κωλυόντων ἡμᾶς ↰ τοῖς ἔθνεσιν λαλῆσαι ἵνα
mankind, *oppose* who prevent us from speaking to the Gentiles *speaking* that
476 1885 3266 7005 3266 3281 3836 1620 3281 2671
n.dpm a.gpm pt.pa.gpm r.ap.1 d.dpn n.dpn f.aa cj

σωθῶσιν, εἰς τὸ → ἀναπληρῶσαι αὐτῶν τὰς
⌊they might be saved.⌋ Their goal ~ has always ⌊been to complete the full number⌋ of their *{the}*
5392 1650 3836 4121 405 899 3836
v.aps.3p p.a d.asn f.aa r.gpm.3 d.apf

ἁμαρτίας πάντοτε. ἔφθασεν δὲ ἐπ᾽ αὐτοὺς ἡ ὀργὴ εἰς τέλος.
sins. *always* But God's wrath ⌊has caught up⌋ *But* with them *{the} wrath* at last!
281 4121 1254 3973 5777 1254 2093 899 3836 3973 1650 5465
n.apf adv v.aai.3s cj p.a r.apm.3 d.nsf n.nsf p.a n.asn

17 ἡμεῖς δέ, ἀδελφοί, ἀπορφανισθέντες ἀφ᾽ ὑμῶν πρὸς καιρὸν ὥρας,
As for us, *As for* brothers, when we were separated from you for a short time —
1254 1254 7005 1254 81 682 608 7007 4639 2789 6052
r.np.1 cj n.vpm pt.ap.npm p.g r.gp.2 p.a n.asm n.gsf

προσώπῳ οὐ καρδίᾳ, ↱ ↱ περισσοτέρως ἐσπουδάσαμεν
in person but not in heart — we were all the more eager, with intense longing,
4725 4024 2840 5079 5079 4359 5079 1877 4498 2123
n.dsn pl n.dsf adv.c v.aai.1p

NASB

you would walk in
a manner worthy of
the God who calls
you into His own
kingdom and glory.
13 For this reason
we also constantly
thank God that
when you received
the word of God
which you heard
from us, you ac-
cepted *it* not *as*
the word of men,
but *for* what it re-
ally is, the word
of God, which
also performs its
work in you who
believe. 14 For you,
brethren, became
imitators of the
churches of God
in Christ Jesus that
are in Judea, for
you also endured
the same suffer-
ings at the hands of
your own country-
men, even as they
did from the Jews,
15 who both killed
the Lord Jesus and
the prophets, and
drove us out. They
are not pleasing to
God, but hostile to
all men, 16 hindering
us from speaking
to the Gentiles so
that they may be
saved; with the
result that they
always fill up the
measure of their
sins. But wrath has
come upon them
[a] to the utmost.
17 But we, breth-
ren, having been
taken away from
you for a short
while—in person,
not in spirit—were
all the more eager
with great desire to

[a] Or *forever* or *alto-gether;* lit *to the end*

NIV

we made every
effort to see you.
18 For we wanted
to come to you —
certainly I, Paul,
did, again and
again — but Satan
blocked our way.
19 For what is our
hope, our joy, or
the crown in which
we will glory in
the presence of our
Lord Jesus when
he comes? Is it
not you? 20 Indeed,
you are our glory
and joy.
3 So when we
could stand
it no longer, we
thought it best
to be left by our-
selves in Athens.
2 We sent Timothy,
who is our broth-
er and co-worker
in God's service
in spreading the
gospel of Christ,
to strengthen and
encourage you in
your faith, 3 so that
no one would be
unsettled by these
trials. For you
know quite well
that we are des-
tined for them. 4 In
fact, when we were
with you, we kept
telling you that we
would be persecut-
ed. And it turned
out that way, as
you well know.
5 For this reason,
when I could stand
it no longer, I sent
to find out about
your faith. I was
afraid that in some
way the tempter
had tempted you
and that our labors
might have been
in vain.

τὸ πρόσωπον ὑμῶν ἰδεῖν ἐν πολλῇ ἐπιθυμίᾳ. 18 διότι ἠθελήσαμεν
to see you *{the}* in person. *you* *to see* *with* *intense* *longing* For we wanted
1625 1625 7007 3836 4725 7007 1625 1877 4498 2123 1484 2527
d.asn n.asn r.gp.2 f.aa p.d a.dsf n.dsf cj v.aai.1p

ἐλθεῖν πρὸς ὑμᾶς, ἐγὼ μὲν Παῦλος καὶ ἅπαξ καὶ δίς, καὶ ἐνέκοψεν
to come to you — I, ~ Paul, *{and}* time and again — but Satan hindered
2262 4639 7007 1609 3525 4263 2779 562 2779 1489 2779 4928 1601
f.aa p.a r.ap.2 r.ns.1 pl n.nsm cj adv cj adv cj v.aai.3s

ἡμᾶς ὁ σατανᾶς. 19 τίς γὰρ ἡμῶν ἐλπὶς ἢ χαρὰ ἢ στέφανος καυχήσεως
us. *{the}* *Satan* For what *For* is our hope, or joy, or crown of rejoicing
7005 3836 4928 1142 5515 1142 7005 1828 2445 5915 2445 5109 3018
r.ap.1 d.nsm n.nsm r.nsf cj r.gp.1 n.nsf cj n.nsf cj n.nsm n.gsf

ἢ οὐχὶ καὶ ὑμεῖς ἔμπροσθεν τοῦ κυρίου ἡμῶν Ἰησοῦ ἐν τῇ αὐτοῦ
{or} *not* *indeed* *you* before *{the}* our Lord *our* Jesus at *{the}* his
2445 4049 2779 7007 1869 3836 7005 3261 7005 2652 1877 3836 899
cj pl adv r.np.2 p.g d.gsm n.gsm r.gp.1 n.gsm p.d d.dsf r.gsm.3

παρουσίᾳ; 20 ὑμεῖς γάρ ἐστε ἡ δόξα ἡμῶν καὶ ἡ
coming? Is it not indeed you? Yes, you *Yes* are *{the}* our glory *our* and *{the}*
4242 4049 2779 7007 1142 7007 1142 1639 3836 7005 1518 7005 2779 3836
n.dsf r.np.2 cj v.pai.2p d.nsf n.nsf r.gp.1 cj d.nsf

χαρά.
joy!
5915
n.nsf

3:1 διὸ μηκέτι στέγοντες εὐδοκήσαμεν
So when we could bear it no longer, *when we could bear* we decided
1475 5095 5095 5095 5095 3600 5095 2305
cj adv pt.pa.npm v.aai.1p

καταλειφθῆναι ἐν Ἀθήναις μόνοι 2 καὶ ἐπέμψαμεν Τιμόθεον, τὸν ἀδελφὸν
to remain behind at Athens alone, and we sent Timothy, *{the}* our brother
2901 1877 121 3668 2779 4287 5510 3836 7005 81
f.ap p.d n.dpf a.npm cj v.aai.1p n.asm d.asm n.asm

ἡμῶν καὶ συνεργὸν τοῦ θεοῦ[a] ἐν τῷ εὐαγγελίῳ τοῦ Χριστοῦ, εἰς τὸ στηρίξαι
our and coworker for God in the gospel of Christ, to ~ establish
7005 2779 5301 3836 2536 1877 3836 2295 3836 5986 1650 3836 5114
r.gp.1 cj n.asm d.gsm n.gsm p.d d.dsn n.dsn d.gsm n.gsm p.a d.asn f.aa

ὑμᾶς καὶ παρακαλέσαι ὑπὲρ τῆς πίστεως ὑμῶν 3 τὸ μηδένα
you and encourage you in *{the}* your faith, *your* ⌊so that⌋ no one
7007 2779 4151 7007 5642 3836 7007 4411 7007 3836 3594
r.ap.2 cj f.aa p.g d.gsf n.gsf r.gp.2 d.asn a.asm

σαίνεσθαι ἐν ταῖς θλίψεσιν ταύταις. αὐτοὶ γὰρ οἴδατε ὅτι
would be moved by *{the}* these afflictions. *these* For you yourselves *For* know that we
4883 1877 3836 4047 2568 4047 1142 3857 899 1142 3857 4022 3023
f.pp p.d d.dpf n.dpf r.dpf r.npm cj v.rai.2p cj

εἰς τοῦτο κείμεθα· 4 καὶ γὰρ ὅτε πρὸς ὑμᾶς ἦμεν,
were destined for this. *we were destined* *{also}* In fact, when we were with you, *we were*
3023 3023 1650 4047 3023 2779 1142 4021 1639 1639 4639 7007 1639
p.a r.asn v.pmi.1p adv cj cj p.a r.ap.2 v.iai.1p

προελέγομεν ὑμῖν ὅτι μέλλομεν θλίβεσθαι, καθὼς καὶ
we told you in advance that we would suffer persecution; even as *{also}*
4625 7007 4625 4625 4022 3516 2567 2777 2779
v.iai.1p r.dp.2 cj v.pai.1p f.pp cj adv

ἐγένετο καὶ οἴδατε. 5 ⌊διὰ τοῦτο⌋ κἀγὼ μηκέτι στέγων
⌊it has turned out,⌋ as you know. So because I could bear it no longer, *could bear*
1181 2779 3857 2743 1328 4047 2743 5095 5095 3600 5095
v.ami.3s cj v.rai.2p p.a r.asn crasis adv pt.pa.nsm

ἔπεμψα εἰς τὸ γνῶναι τὴν πίστιν ὑμῶν, μή πως
I sent to ~ find out about your faith, *your* ⌊for fear that⌋ somehow the tempter
4287 1650 3836 1182 3836 7007 4411 7007 3590 4803 3836 4279
v.aai.1s p.a d.asn f.aa d.asf n.asf r.gp.2 cj pl

ἐπείρασεν ὑμᾶς ὁ πειράζων καὶ εἰς κενὸν γένηται ὁ κόπος
had tempted you *the* *tempter* and our labor had been in vain. *had been* *{the}* *labor*
4279 7007 3836 4279 2779 7005 3160 1181 1181 1650 3031 1181 3836 3160
v.aai.3s r.ap.2 d.nsm pt.pa.nsm cj p.a a.asn v.ams.3s d.nsm n.nsm

[a] διάκονον τοῦ Θεοῦ καὶ συνεργὸν ἡμῶν included by TR after θεοῦ.

NASB

see your face. 18 For
we wanted to come
to you — I, Paul,
more than once —
and *yet* Satan
hindered us. 19 For
who is our hope
or joy or crown
of exultation? Is
it not even you,
in the presence of
our Lord Jesus at
His coming? 20 For
you are our glory
and joy.

Encouragement of Timothy's Visit

3:1 Therefore when
we could endure
it no longer, we
thought it best to
be left behind at
Athens alone, 2 and
we sent Timothy,
our brother and
God's fellow
worker in the gos-
pel of Christ, to
strengthen and en-
courage you as to
your faith, 3 so that
no one would be
disturbed by these
afflictions; for you
yourselves know
that we have been
destined for this.
4 For indeed when
we were with you,
we *kept* telling you
in advance that we
were going to suf-
fer affliction; and
so it came to pass,
as you know. 5 For
this reason, when
I could endure *it*
no longer, I also
sent to find out
about your faith,
for fear that the
tempter might have
tempted you, and
our labor would be
in vain.

NIV

Timothy's Encouraging Report

6 But Timothy has
just now come to
us from you and
has brought good
news about your
faith and love. He
has told us that
you always have
pleasant memories
of us and that you
long to see us, just
as we also long to
see you. 7 There-
fore, brothers and
sisters, in all our
distress and per-
secution we were
encouraged about
you because of
your faith. 8 For
now we really
live, since you are
standing firm in
the Lord. 9 How
can we thank God
enough for you in
return for all the
joy we have in the
presence of our
God because of
you? 10 Night and
day we pray most
earnestly that we
may see you again
and supply what
is lacking in your
faith.
11 Now may our
God and Father
himself and our
Lord Jesus clear
the way for us
to come to you.
12 May the Lord
make your love
increase and over-
flow for each other
and for everyone
else, just as ours
does for you.
13 May he strength-
en your hearts so
that you will be
blameless and holy
in the presence
of our God and
Father when our
Lord Jesus comes
with all his holy
ones.

ἡμῶν. 6 ἄρτι δὲ ἐλθόντος Τιμοθέου πρὸς ἡμᾶς ἀφ᾽ ὑμῶν καὶ →
our But just now *But* Timothy has come *Timothy* to us from you, and has
7005 1254 785 1254 5510 2262 5510 4639 7005 608 7007 2779
r.gp.1 adv cj pt.aa.gsm n.gsm p.a r.ap.1 p.g r.gp.2 cj

→ εὐαγγελισαμένου ἡμῖν τὴν πίστιν καὶ τὴν ἀγάπην ὑμῶν καὶ ὅτι
brought us the good news *us* of your faith and *{the}* your love; *your* and that
7005 2294 7005 3836 4411 2779 3836 7007 27 7007 2779 4022
pt.am.gsm r.dp.1 d.asf n.asf cj d.asf n.asf r.gp.2 cj cj

→ ἔχετε μνείαν ἡμῶν ἀγαθὴν πάντοτε, ἐπιποθοῦντες
you always think of us with *think* *of us* affection *always* and long to see
4121 3644 7005 7005 2400 3644 7005 19 4121 2160 1625 1625
v.pai.2p n.asf r.gp.1 a.asf adv pt.pa.npm

ἡμᾶς ἰδεῖν καθάπερ καὶ ἡμεῖς ὑμᾶς, 7 ⌊διὰ τοῦτο⌋
us *to see* even as *{also}* we long to see you. So in all our distress
7005 1625 2749 2779 7005 7007 1328 4047 2093 4246 7005 340
r.ap.1 f.aa cj adv r.np.1 r.ap.2 p.a r.asn

παρεκλήθημεν, ἀδελφοί, ἐφ᾽ ὑμῖν ἐπὶ πάσῃ τῇ ἀνάγκῃ
and affliction, brothers, we have been reassured *brothers* about you *in* *all* *{the}* *distress*
2779 2568 81 4151 81 2093 7007 2093 4246 3836 340
v.api.1p n.vpm p.d r.dp.2 p.d a.dsf d.dsf n.dsf

καὶ θλίψει ἡμῶν διὰ τῆς ὑμῶν πίστεως, 8 ὅτι νῦν ζῶμεν ἐὰν ὑμεῖς στήκετε ἐν
and *affliction* *our* by *{the}* your faith. For now we live, if you stand firm in the
2779 2568 7005 1328 3836 7007 4411 4022 3814 2409 1569 7007 5112 1877
cj n.dsf r.gp.1 p.g d.gsf r.gp.2 n.gsf cj adv v.pai.1p cj r.np.2 v.pai.2p p.d

κυρίῳ. 9 τίνα γὰρ εὐχαριστίαν δυνάμεθα τῷ θεῷ ἀνταποδοῦναι περὶ ὑμῶν
Lord. For what *For* thanksgiving can we return to God *return* for you,
3261 1142 5515 1142 2374 1538 500 3836 2536 500 4309 7007
n.dsm r.asf cj n.asf v.ppi.1p d.dsm n.dsm f.aa p.g r.gp.2

ἐπὶ πάσῃ τῇ χαρᾷ ᾗ χαίρομεν δι᾽ ὑμᾶς ἔμπροσθεν
for all the joy ⌊with which⌋ we rejoice before our God ⌊because of⌋ you? *before*
2093 4246 3836 5915 4005 5897 1869 7005 2536 1328 7007 1869
p.d a.dsf d.dsf n.dsf r.dsf v.pai.1p p.a r.ap.2 p.g

τοῦ θεοῦ ἡμῶν, 10 νυκτὸς καὶ ἡμέρας ὑπερεκπερισσοῦ δεόμενοι εἰς τὸ
{the} *God* *our* Night and day we pray most earnestly *we pray* that ~
3836 2536 7005 3816 2779 2465 1289 1289 5655 1289 1650 3836
d.gsm n.gsm r.gp.1 n.gsf cj n.gsf adv pt.pp.npm p.a d.asn

ἰδεῖν ὑμῶν τὸ πρόσωπον καὶ καταρτίσαι τὰ ὑστερήματα τῆς πίστεως
⌊we may see⌋ your *{the}* face and supply what is lacking in your faith.
1625 7007 3836 4725 2779 2936 3836 5729 3836 7007 4411
f.aa r.gp.2 d.asn n.asn cj f.aa d.apn n.apn d.gsf n.gsf

ὑμῶν; 11 Αὐτὸς δὲ ↱ ὁ θεὸς καὶ πατὴρ ἡμῶν καὶ ὁ κύριος
your *himself* Now may *{the}* our God and Father *our* himself, and *{the}* our Lord
7007 899 1254 2985 3836 7005 2536 2779 4252 7005 899 2779 3836 7005 3261
r.gp.2 r.nsm cj d.nsm n.nsm cj n.nsm r.gp.1 cj d.nsm n.nsm

ἡμῶν Ἰησοῦς κατευθύναι τὴν ὁδὸν ἡμῶν πρὸς ὑμᾶς· 12 ὑμᾶς δὲ ↱ ὁ
our Jesus, direct *{the}* our way *our* to you. *you* And may the
7005 2652 2985 3836 7005 3847 7005 4639 7007 7007 1254 4429 3836
r.gp.1 n.nsm v.aao.3s d.asf n.asf r.gp.1 p.a r.ap.2 r.ap.2 cj d.nsm

κύριος → πλεονάσαι καὶ περισσεύσαι τῇ ἀγάπῃ εἰς ἀλλήλους καὶ εἰς
Lord cause you to increase and abound in love for one another and for
3261 7007 4429 2779 4355 3836 27 1650 253 2779 1650
n.nsm v.aao.3s cj v.aao.3s d.dsf n.dsf p.a r.apm cj p.a

πάντας καθάπερ καὶ ἡμεῖς εἰς ὑμᾶς, 13 εἰς τὸ στηρίξαι ὑμῶν τὰς καρδίας
all, even as *{also}* we do for you, ⌊so as to⌋ ~ establish your *{the}* hearts
4246 2749 2779 7005 1650 7007 1650 3836 5114 7007 3836 2840
a.apm cj adv r.np.1 p.a r.ap.2 p.a d.asn f.aa r.gp.2 d.apf n.apf

ἀμέμπτους ἐν ἁγιωσύνῃ ἔμπροσθεν τοῦ θεοῦ καὶ πατρὸς ἡμῶν ἐν τῇ
blameless in holiness before *{the}* our God and Father *our* at the
289 1877 43 1869 3836 7005 2536 2779 4252 7005 1877 3836
a.apf p.d n.dsf p.g d.gsm n.gsm cj n.gsm r.gp.1 p.d d.dsf

παρουσίᾳ τοῦ κυρίου ἡμῶν Ἰησοῦ μετὰ πάντων τῶν ἁγίων αὐτοῦ,[a]
coming of our Lord *our* Jesus with all *{the}* his saints. *his*
4242 3836 7005 3261 7005 2652 3552 4246 3836 899 41 899
n.dsf d.gsm n.gsm r.gp.1 n.gsm p.g a.gpm d.gpm a.gpm r.gsm.3

[a] ἀμήν included by UBS after αὐτοῦ.

NASB

6 But now that
Timothy has come
to us from you,
and has brought us
good news of your
faith and love, and
that you always
think kindly of us,
longing to see us
just as we also long
to see you, 7 for this
reason, brethren,
in all our distress
and affliction we
were comforted
about you through
your faith; 8 for
now we *really* live,
if you stand firm
in the Lord. 9 For
what thanks can
we render to God
for you in return
for all the joy with
which we rejoice
before our God on
your account, 10 as
we night and day
keep praying most
earnestly that we
may see your face,
and may complete
what is lacking in
your faith?
11 Now may our
God and Father
Himself and Jesus
our Lord direct our
way to you; 12 and
may the Lord cause
you to increase
and abound in love
for one another,
and for all people,
just as we also *do*
for you; 13 so that
He may establish
your hearts without
blame in holiness
before our God
and Father at the
coming of our Lord
Jesus with all His
saints.

NIV

Living to Please God

4 As for other matters, brothers and sisters, we instructed you how to live in order to please God, as in fact you are living. Now we ask you and urge you in the Lord Jesus to do this more and more. 2For you know what instructions we gave you by the authority of the Lord Jesus.

3It is God's will that you should be sanctified: that you should avoid sexual immorality; 4that each of you should learn to control your own body[a] in a way that is holy and honorable, 5not in passionate lust like the pagans, who do not know God; 6and that in this matter no one should wrong or take advantage of a brother or sister.[b] The Lord will punish all those who commit such sins, as we told you and warned you before. 7For God did not call us to be impure, but to live a holy life. 8Therefore, anyone who rejects this instruction does not reject a human being but God, the very God who gives you his Holy Spirit.

9Now about your love for one another we do not need to write to you, for you yourselves have been

[a] 4 Or *learn to live with your own wife*; or *learn to acquire a wife*

[b] 6 The Greek word for *brother or sister* (*adelphos*) refers here to a believer, whether man or woman, as part of God's family.

4:1 λοιπὸν οὖν, ἀδελφοί, ἐρωτῶμεν ὑμᾶς καὶ παρακαλοῦμεν ἐν κυρίῳ
Finally, then, brothers, we ask *you* and urge you in the Lord
3370 4036 81 2263 7007 2779 4151 7007 1877 3261
adv cj n.vpm v.pai.1p r.ap.2 cj v.pai.1p p.d n.dsm

Ἰησοῦ, ἵνα καθὼς παρελάβετε παρ᾽ ἡμῶν τὸ πῶς δεῖ ὑμᾶς περιπατεῖν καὶ
Jesus, that as you received from us ~ how you ought *you* to live so as
2652 2671 2777 4161 4123 7005 3836 4802 7007 1256 7007 4344 2779
n.dsm cj cj v.aai.2p p.g r.gp.1 d.asn cj v.pai.3s r.ap.2 f.pa cj

ἀρέσκειν θεῷ, καθὼς καὶ περιπατεῖτε, ἵνα περισσεύητε μᾶλλον. 2 οἴδατε
to please God (even as *{also}* you are doing), that you do so more and more. For you know
743 2536 2777 2779 4344 2671 4355 3437 1142 3857
f.pa n.dsm cj adv v.pai.2p cj v.pas.2p adv.c v.rai.2p

γὰρ τίνας παραγγελίας ἐδώκαμεν ὑμῖν διὰ τοῦ κυρίου Ἰησοῦ. 3 τοῦτο
For what commands we gave you ⌊by the authority⌋ of the Lord Jesus. For this
1142 5515 4132 1443 7007 1328 3836 3261 2652 1142 4047
cj r.apf n.apf v.aai.1p r.dp.2 p.g d.gsm n.gsm n.gsm r.nsn

γάρ ἐστιν θέλημα τοῦ θεοῦ, ὁ ἁγιασμὸς ὑμῶν, → ἀπέχεσθαι
For is the will of God — *{the}* your sanctification: *your* that you abstain
1142 1639 2525 3836 2536 3836 7007 40 7007 7007 600
cj v.pai.3s n.nsn d.gsm n.gsm d.nsm n.nsm r.gp.2 f.pm

ὑμᾶς ἀπὸ τῆς πορνείας, 4 → εἰδέναι ἕκαστον ὑμῶν
you from *{the}* sexual immorality, that each of you learn how *each* *of you* to maintain
7007 608 3836 4518 1667 7007 7007 3857 1667 7007 3227 3227
r.ap.2 p.g d.gsf n.gsf f.ra r.asm r.gp.2

τὸ ἑαυτοῦ σκεῦος κτᾶσθαι ἐν ἁγιασμῷ καὶ τιμῇ, 5 μὴ ἐν
control over *{the}* his own "vessel" *to maintain control over* in holiness and honor, not with
3227 3227 3836 1571 5007 3227 1877 40 2779 5507 3590 1877
d.asn r.gsm.3 n.asn f.pm p.d n.dsm cj n.dsf pl p.d

πάθει ἐπιθυμίας καθάπερ καὶ τὰ ἔθνη τὰ ↱ μὴ εἰδότα τὸν θεόν, 6 τὸ
the passion of lust, like *{also}* the Gentiles who do not know *{the}* God. ~
4079 2123 2749 2779 3836 1620 3836 3857 3590 3857 3836 2536 3836
n.dsn n.gsf pl adv d.npn n.npn d.npn pl pt.ra.npn d.asm n.asm d.asn

μὴ ὑπερβαίνειν καὶ πλεονεκτεῖν ἐν τῷ πράγματι τὸν ἀδελφὸν
⌊No one⌋ should sin against or ⌊take advantage of⌋ his brother in this matter, *{the}* *brother*
3590 5648 2779 4430 899 81 1877 3836 4547 3836 81
pl f.pa cj f.pa p.d d.dsn n.dsn d.asm n.asm

αὐτοῦ, διότι ἔκδικος κύριος περὶ πάντων τούτων, καθὼς καὶ
his because the Lord is the avenger *Lord* in all these things, as indeed
899 1484 3261 1690 3261 4309 4246 4047 2777 2779
r.gsm.3 cj n.nsm n.nsm p.g a.gpn r.gpn cj adv

προείπαμεν ὑμῖν ↰ καὶ διεμαρτυράμεθα. 7 ↱ οὐ γὰρ ἐκάλεσεν
we told you beforehand with solemn warning. For God has not *For* called
4597 7007 4597 2779 1371 1142 2536 2813 4024 1142 2813
v.aai.1p r.dp.2 cj v.ami.1p pl cj v.aai.3s

ἡμᾶς ὁ θεὸς ἐπὶ ἀκαθαρσίᾳ ἀλλ᾽ ἐν ἁγιασμῷ. 8 τοιγαροῦν ὁ ἀθετῶν
us *{the}* *God* for impurity, but in holiness. Consequently the ⌊one who rejects⌋
7005 3836 2536 2093 174 247 1877 40 5521 3836 119
r.ap.1 d.nsm n.nsm p.d n.dsf cj p.d n.dsm cj d.nsm pt.pa.nsm

οὐκ ἄνθρωπον ἀθετεῖ ἀλλὰ τὸν θεὸν τὸν καὶ[a] διδόντα τὸ
this is not rejecting man, *is rejecting* but *{the}* God, who also has given *{the}* his Holy
119 4024 119 476 119 247 3836 2536 3836 2779 1443 3836 899 41
pl n.asm v.pai.3s cj d.asm n.asm d.asm adv pt.pa.asm d.asn

πνεῦμα αὐτοῦ τὸ ἅγιον εἰς ὑμᾶς. 9 περὶ δὲ τῆς φιλαδελφίας
Spirit *his* *{the}* *Holy* to you. Now ⌊with regard to⌋ *Now* *{the}* brotherly love you
4460 899 3836 41 1650 7007 1254 4309 1254 3836 5789 2400
n.asn r.gsm.3 d.asn a.asn p.a r.ap.2 p.g cj d.gsf n.gsf

οὐ χρείαν ἔχετε[b] γράφειν ὑμῖν, αὐτοὶ γὰρ ὑμεῖς
have no need *you have* for us to write to you, for you yourselves *for* *you* have been
2400 4024 5970 2400 1211 7007 1142 7007 899 1142 7007 1639 1639
pl n.asf v.pai.2p f.pa r.dp.2 r.npm cj r.np.2

[a] [καὶ] UBS, omitted by TNIV.
[b] ἔχετε UBS, NET. ἔχομεν TNIV.

NASB

Sanctification and Love

4:1Finally then, brethren, we request and exhort you in the Lord Jesus, that as you received from us *instruction* as to how you ought to walk and please God (just as you actually do [a]walk), that you excel still more. 2For you know what commandments we gave you [b]by *the authority of* the Lord Jesus. 3For this is the will of God, your sanctification; *that is,* that you abstain from sexual immorality; 4that each of you know how to possess his own [c]vessel in sanctification and honor, 5not in lustful passion, like the Gentiles who do not know God; 6*and* that no man transgress and defraud his brother in the matter because the Lord is *the* avenger in all these things, just as we also told you before and solemnly warned *you.* 7For God has not called us for the purpose of impurity, but in sanctification. 8So, he who rejects *this* is not rejecting man but the God who gives His Holy Spirit to you.

9Now as to the love of the brethren, you have no need for *anyone* to write to you, for you yourselves are

[a] Or *conduct yourselves*
[b] Lit *through the Lord*
[c] I.e. body; or wife

NIV

taught by God
to love each oth-
er. 10And in fact,
you do love all
of God's family
throughout Mace-
donia. Yet we urge
you, brothers and
sisters, to do so
more and more,
11and to make it
your ambition to
lead a quiet life:
You should mind
your own business
and work with your
hands, just as we
told you, 12so that
your daily life may
win the respect of
outsiders and so
that you will not be
dependent on any-
body.

Believers Who Have Died

13Brothers and
sisters, we do not
want you to be
uninformed about
those who sleep in
death, so that you
do not grieve like
the rest of man-
kind, who have
no hope. 14For we
believe that Jesus
died and rose
again, and so we
believe that God
will bring with
Jesus those who
have fallen asleep
in him. 15Accord-
ing to the Lord's
word, we tell you
that we who are
still alive, who are
left until the com-
ing of the Lord,
will certainly not
precede those who
have fallen asleep.
16For the Lord
himself will come
down from heav-
en, with a loud
command, with
the voice of the
archangel and with
the trumpet call of
God, and the dead
in Christ will rise
first. 17After that,
we who are still
alive and are left

θεοδίδακτοί ἐστε εἰς τὸ ἀγαπᾶν ἀλλήλους, 10 ⌊καὶ γὰρ⌋ ποιεῖτε αὐτὸ
taught by God *have been* how ~ to love one another. Indeed you do show love
2531 1639 1650 3836 26 253 2779 1142 4472 899
a.npm v.pai.2p p.a d.asn f.pa r.apm adv cj v.pai.2p r.asn.3

εἰς πάντας τοὺς ἀδελφοὺς τοὺς[a] ⌊ἐν ὅλῃ⌋ τῇ Μακεδονίᾳ.
toward all the brothers *{the}* throughout *{the}* Macedonia, but
1650 4246 3836 81 3836 1877 3910 3836 3423 1254
p.a a.apm d.apm n.apm d.apm p.d a.dsf d.dsf n.dsf

παρακαλοῦμεν δὲ ὑμᾶς, ἀδελφοί, περισσεύειν μᾶλλον 11 καὶ φιλοτιμεῖσθαι
we urge *but* you, brothers, to do so more and more. *{and}* Make it your aim
4151 1254 7007 81 4355 3437 2779 5818
v.pai.1p cj r.ap.2 n.vpm f.pa adv.c cj f.pm

ἡσυχάζειν καὶ πράσσειν τὰ ἴδια καὶ ἐργάζεσθαι ταῖς ἰδίαις[b]
⌊to lead a quiet life,⌋ *{and}* to attend to *{the}* ⌊your own affairs,⌋ and to work with your own
2483 2779 4556 3836 2625 2779 2237 3836 7007 2625
f.pa cj f.pa d.apn a.apn cj f.pm d.dpf a.dpf

χερσὶν ὑμῶν, καθὼς ὑμῖν παρηγγείλαμεν, 12 ἵνα περιπατῆτε
hands, *your* as we commanded you. *we commanded* ⌊In this way⌋ you will live a
5931 7007 2777 4133 4133 7007 4133 2671 4344
n.dpf r.gp.2 cj r.dp.2 v.aai.1p cj v.pas.2p

εὐσχημόνως πρὸς τοὺς ἔξω καὶ μηδενὸς χρείαν ἔχητε.
proper life before *{the}* outsiders and be dependent on no one. *dependent on* *be*
2361 4639 3836 2032 2779 2400 5970 5970 3594 5970 2400
adv p.a d.apm adv cj a.gsn n.asf v.pas.2p

13 ➝ ➝ οὐ θέλομεν δὲ ὑμᾶς ἀγνοεῖν, ἀδελφοί, περὶ τῶν κοιμωμένων,
Now we do not want *Now* you to be uninformed, brothers, about those who are asleep,
1254 2527 2527 4024 2527 1254 7007 51 81 4309 3836 3121
pl v.pai.1p cj r.ap.2 f.pa n.vpm p.g d.gpm pt.pp.gpm

ἵνα ➝ ➝ μὴ λυπῆσθε καθὼς καὶ οἱ λοιποὶ οἱ μὴ ἔχοντες ἐλπίδα.
so that you will not grieve as *{also}* *{the}* others do who have no *have* hope.
2671 3382 3382 3590 3382 2777 2779 3836 3370 3836 2400 3590 2400 1828
cj pl v.pps.2p pl adv d.npm a.npm d.npm pl pt.pa.npm n.asf

14 εἰ γὰρ πιστεύομεν ὅτι Ἰησοῦς ἀπέθανεν καὶ ἀνέστη, οὕτως καὶ
For if *For* we believe that Jesus died and rose again, so also do we
1142 1623 1142 4409 4022 2652 633 2779 482 4048 2779
cj cj v.pai.1p cj n.nsm v.aai.3s cj v.aai.3s adv adv

ὁ θεὸς τοὺς κοιμηθέντας διὰ τοῦ Ἰησοῦ
believe that *{the}* God will bring with him those ⌊who have fallen asleep⌋ in *{the}* Jesus.
3836 2536 72 72 5250 899 3836 3121 1328 3836 2652
d.nsm n.nsm d.apm pt.ap.apm p.g d.gsm n.gsm

ἄξει σὺν αὐτῷ. 15 τοῦτο γὰρ ὑμῖν λέγομεν ἐν λόγῳ ➝
will bring *with* *him* For this *For* we say to you *we say* by the word of the
72 5250 899 1142 4047 1142 3306 3306 7007 3306 1877 3364
v.fai.3s p.d r.dsm.3 r.asn cj r.dp.2 v.pai.1p p.d n.dsm

κυρίου, ὅτι ἡμεῖς οἱ ζῶντες οἱ περιλειπόμενοι εἰς τὴν παρουσίαν τοῦ κυρίου
Lord, that we who are alive, who remain behind until the coming of the Lord,
3261 4022 7005 3836 2409 3836 4335 1650 3836 4242 3836 3261
n.gsm cj r.np.1 d.npm pt.pa.npm d.npm pt.pp.npm p.a d.asf n.asf d.gsm n.gsm

➝ ⌊οὐ μὴ⌋ φθάσωμεν τοὺς κοιμηθέντας· 16 ὅτι αὐτὸς
will by no means precede those ⌊who have fallen asleep,⌋ because the Lord himself
5777 4024 3590 5777 3836 3121 4022 3836 3261 899
pl pl v.aas.1p d.apm pt.ap.apm cj r.nsm

ὁ κύριος ἐν κελεύσματι, ἐν φωνῇ ➝ ἀρχαγγέλου
the *Lord* will descend from heaven with a cry of command, with the voice of an archangel,
3836 3261 2849 2849 608 4041 1877 3026 1877 5889 791
d.nsm n.nsm p.d n.dsn p.d n.dsf n.gsm

καὶ ἐν σάλπιγγι θεοῦ, καταβήσεται ἀπ' οὐρανοῦ καὶ οἱ νεκροὶ ἐν Χριστῷ
and with the trumpet of God, *will descend* *from* *heaven* and the dead in Christ
2779 1877 4894 2536 2849 608 4041 2779 3836 3738 1877 5986
cj p.d n.dsf n.gsm v.fmi.3s p.g n.gsm cj d.npm a.npm p.d n.dsm

ἀναστήσονται πρῶτον, 17 ἔπειτα ἡμεῖς οἱ ζῶντες οἱ περιλειπόμενοι ἅμα σὺν
will rise first. Then we who are alive, who remain behind, *together* *with*
482 4754 2083 7005 3836 2409 3836 4335 275 5250
v.fmi.3p adv adv r.np.1 d.npm pt.pa.npm d.npm pt.pp.npm adv p.d

[a] [τοὺς] UBS.
[b] [ἰδίαις] UBS, omitted by TNIV, NET.

NASB

taught by God to
love one another;
10for indeed you do
practice it toward
all the brethren
who are in all
Macedonia. But we
urge you, brethren,
to excel still more,
11and to make it
your ambition to
lead a quiet life
and attend to your
own business and
work with your
hands, just as we
commanded you,
12so that you will
behave properly
toward outsiders
and not be in any
need.

Those Who Died in Christ

13But we do not
want you to be un-
informed, brethren,
about those who
are asleep, so that
you will not grieve
as do the rest who
have no hope. 14For
if we believe that
Jesus died and
rose again, even
so God will bring
with Him those
who have fallen
asleep in Jesus.
15For this we say
to you by the word
of the Lord, that
we who are alive
and remain until
the coming of the
Lord, will not
precede those who
have fallen asleep.
16For the Lord
Himself will de-
scend from heaven
with a shout, with
the voice of *the*
archangel and with
the trumpet of
God, and the dead
in Christ will rise
first. 17Then we
who are alive and
remain will be

NIV

will be caught
up together with
them in the clouds
to meet the Lord
in the air. And so
we will be with
the Lord forever.
18 Therefore encour-
age one another
with these words.

The Day of the Lord

5 Now, brothers
and sisters,
about times and
dates we do not
need to write to
you, 2 for you know
very well that the
day of the Lord
will come like a
thief in the night.
3 While people are
saying, "Peace and
safety," destruc-
tion will come on
them suddenly, as
labor pains on a
pregnant woman,
and they will not
escape.
4 But you, broth-
ers and sisters, are
not in darkness
so that this day
should surprise
you like a thief.
5 You are all chil-
dren of the light
and children of
the day. We do not
belong to the night
or to the darkness.
6 So then, let us not
be like others, who
are asleep, but let
us be awake and
sober. 7 For those
who sleep, sleep
at night, and those
who get drunk,
get drunk at night.
8 But since we be-
long to the day, let
us be sober, put-
ting on faith and
love as a breast-
plate, and the hope

αὐτοῖς ἁρπαγησόμεθα ἐν νεφέλαις εἰς ἀπάντησιν τοῦ κυρίου
them will be caught up in the clouds together with them to meet the Lord
899 773 1877 3749 275 5250 899 1650 561 3836 3261
r.dpm.3 v.fpi.1p p.d n.dpf p.a n.asf d.gsm n.gsm

εἰς ἀέρα· καὶ οὕτως πάντοτε σὺν κυρίῳ ἐσόμεθα. 18 ὥστε
in the air. And so we will be forever with the Lord. *we will be* So
1650 113 2779 4048 1639 1639 1639 4121 5250 3261 1639 6063
p.a n.asm cj adv adv p.d n.dsm v.fmi.1p cj

παρακαλεῖτε ἀλλήλους ἐν τοῖς λόγοις τούτοις.
encourage one another with *{the}* these words. *these*
4151 253 1877 3836 4047 3364 4047
v.pam.2p r.apm p.d d.dpm n.dpm r.dpm

5:1 περὶ δὲ τῶν χρόνων καὶ τῶν καιρῶν, ἀδελφοί, οὐ
Now concerning *Now* the times and the seasons, brothers, you have no
1254 4309 1254 3836 5989 2779 3836 2789 81 2400 2400 4024
p.g cj d.gpm n.gpm cj d.gpm n.gpm n.vpm pl

χρείαν ἔχετε ὑμῖν γράφεσθαι, 2 αὐτοὶ γὰρ
need *you have* for anything to be written to you, *to be written* for you yourselves *for*
5970 2400 1211 1211 1211 7007 1211 1142 3857 899 1142
n.asf v.pai.2p r.dp.2 f.pp r.npm cj

ἀκριβῶς οἴδατε ὅτι ἡμέρα → κυρίου ὡς κλέπτης ἐν νυκτὶ
know full well *you know* that the day of the Lord will come like a thief by night.
3857 209 3857 4022 2465 3261 2262 2262 6055 3095 1877 3816
adv v.rai.2p cj n.nsf n.gsm pl n.nsm p.d n.dsf

οὕτως ἔρχεται. 3 ὅταν λέγωσιν, εἰρήνη καὶ ἀσφάλεια, τότε αἰφνίδιος
{in this way} *will come* When they are saying, "Peace and security," it is then that sudden
4048 2262 4020 3306 1645 2779 854 5538 167
adv v.pmi.3s cj v.pas.3p n.nsf cj n.nsf adv a.nsm

αὐτοῖς ἐφίσταται ὄλεθρος ὥσπερ ἡ ὠδὶν τῇ
destruction will come upon them, *will come* *destruction* like *{the}* ⌊labor pains⌋ upon a
3897 2392 2392 899 2392 3897 6061 3836 6047 3836
r.dpm.3 v.pmi.3s n.nsm cj d.nsf n.nsf d.dsf

⌊ἐν γαστρὶ ἐχούσῃ,⌋ καὶ ↱ ↱ ⌊οὐ μὴ⌋ ἐκφύγωσιν. 4 ὑμεῖς δέ,
woman with child, and they will not escape. But you, *But*
1877 1143 2400 2779 1767 1767 4024 3590 1767 1254 7007 1254
p.d n.dsf pt.pa.dsf cj pl pl v.aas.3p r.np.2 cj

ἀδελφοί, οὐκ ἐστὲ ἐν σκότει, ἵνα ἡ ἡμέρα ὑμᾶς ὡς
brothers, are not *are* in darkness, ⌊for that⌋ *{the}* day to take you by surprise like
81 1639 4024 1639 1877 5030 2671 3836 2465 2898 2898 7007 2898 2898 6055
n.vpm pl v.pai.2p p.d n.dsn cj d.nsf n.nsf r.ap.2 pl

κλέπτης καταλάβῃ· 5 πάντες γὰρ ὑμεῖς υἱοὶ φωτός ἐστε καὶ υἱοὶ
a thief; *to take by surprise* for you are all *for* *you* sons of light, *are* *{and}* sons
3095 2898 1142 7007 1639 4246 1142 7007 5626 5890 1639 2779 5626
n.nsm v.aas.3s a.npm cj r.np.2 n.npm n.gsn v.pai.2p cj n.npm

→ ἡμέρας. ↱ ↱ οὐκ ἐσμὲν νυκτὸς οὐδὲ σκότους· 6 ἄρα οὖν ↱ ↱ μὴ
of the day. We do not ⌊belong to⌋ night or darkness. So then let us not
2465 1639 1639 4024 1639 3816 4028 5030 726 4036 2761 2761 3590
n.gsf pl v.pai.1p n.gsf cj n.gsn cj cj pl

καθεύδωμεν ὡς οἱ λοιποί ἀλλὰ γρηγορῶμεν καὶ νήφωμεν. 7 οἱ γὰρ
fall asleep as *{the}* others do; rather let us stay awake and be sober. For those *For*
2761 6055 3836 3370 247 1213 2779 3768 1142 3836 1142
v.pas.1p cj d.npm a.npm cj v.pas.1p cj v.pas.1p d.npm cj

καθεύδοντες νυκτὸς καθεύδουσιν καὶ οἱ μεθυσκόμενοι νυκτὸς
who sleep, sleep at night, *sleep* and those who get drunk, are drunk at night;
2761 2761 3816 2761 2779 3836 3499 3501 3501 3816
pt.pa.npm n.gsf v.pai.3p cj d.npm pt.pp.npm n.gsf

μεθύουσιν· 8 ↱ ἡμεῖς δὲ ἡμέρας ὄντες νήφωμεν
are drunk but let us *but* who belong to the daylight *who belong to* stay sober,
3501 1254 3768 7005 1254 1639 1639 1639 2465 1639 3768
v.pai.3p r.np.1 cj n.gsf pt.pa.npm v.pas.1p

ἐνδυσάμενοι θώρακα πίστεως καὶ ἀγάπης καὶ → περικεφαλαίαν ἐλπίδα
putting on the breastplate of faith and love, and as a helmet the hope
1907 2606 4411 2779 27 2779 4330 1828
pt.am.npm n.asm n.gsf cj n.gsf cj n.asf n.asf

NASB

caught up together
with them in the
clouds to meet the
Lord in the air, and
so we shall always
be with the Lord.
18 Therefore comfort
one another with
these words.

The Day of the Lord

5:1 Now as to the
times and the
epochs, brethren,
you have no need
of anything to be
written to you. 2 For
you yourselves
know full well
that the day of the
Lord will come just
like a thief in the
night. 3 While they
are saying, "Peace
and safety!" then
destruction will
come upon them
suddenly like la-
bor pains upon a
woman with child,
and they will not
escape. 4 But you,
brethren, are not in
darkness, that the
day would overtake
you like a thief;
5 for you are all
sons of light and
sons of day. We are
not of night nor of
darkness; 6 so then
let us not sleep
as others do, but
let us be alert and
[a]sober. 7 For those
who sleep do their
sleeping at night,
and those who get
drunk get drunk at
night. 8 But since
we are of *the* day,
let us be [b]sober,
having put on the
breastplate of faith
and love, and as a
helmet, the hope of

[a] Or *self-controlled*
[b] Or *self-controlled*

NIV

of salvation as a
helmet. 9 For God
did not appoint us
to suffer wrath but
to receive salvation
through our Lord
Jesus Christ. 10 He
died for us so that,
whether we are
awake or asleep,
we may live to-
gether with him.
11 Therefore encour-
age one another
and build each oth-
er up, just as in fact
you are doing.

Final Instructions

12 Now we ask
you, brothers
and sisters, to ac-
knowledge those
who work hard
among you, who
care for you in
the Lord and who
admonish you.
13 Hold them in the
highest regard in
love because of
their work. Live
in peace with each
other. 14 And we
urge you, brothers
and sisters, warn
those who are idle
and disruptive,
encourage the dis-
heartened, help the
weak, be patient
with everyone.
15 Make sure that
nobody pays back
wrong for wrong,
but always strive
to do what is good
for each other and
for everyone else.
16 Rejoice always,
17 pray continually,
18 give thanks in all
circumstances; for
this is God's will
for you in Christ
Jesus.
19 Do not quench
the Spirit. 20 Do
not treat prophe-
cies with contempt
21 but test them all;
hold on to what is
good, 22 reject ev-
ery kind of evil.

σωτηρίας· 9 ὅτι ↱ οὐκ ἔθετο ἡμᾶς ὁ θεὸς εἰς ὀργὴν ἀλλὰ εἰς
of salvation. For God has not appointed us {the} God for wrath, but to
5401 4022 2536 5502 4024 5502 7005 3836 2536 1650 3973 247 1650
n.gsf cj pl v.ami.3s r.ap.1 d.nsm n.nsm p.a n.asf cj p.a

περιποίησιν σωτηρίας διὰ τοῦ κυρίου ἡμῶν Ἰησοῦ Χριστοῦ 10 τοῦ
obtain salvation through {the} our Lord our Jesus Christ, who
4348 5401 1328 3836 7005 3261 7005 2652 5986 3836
n.asf n.gsf p.g d.gsm n.gsm r.gp.1 n.gsm n.gsm d.gsm

ἀποθανόντος ὑπὲρ ἡμῶν, ἵνα εἴτε γρηγορῶμεν εἴτε καθεύδωμεν
died for us so that whether we are awake or asleep we will come to
633 5642 7005 2671 1664 1213 1664 2761 2409 2409 2409 2409
pt.aa.gsm p.g r.gp.1 cj cj v.pas.1p cj v.pas.1p

ἅμα σὺν αὐτῷ ζήσωμεν. 11 διὸ παρακαλεῖτε ἀλλήλους καὶ
life together with him. we will come to life Therefore encourage one another and
2409 275 5250 899 2409 1475 4151 253 2779
adv p.d r.dsm.3 v.aas.1p cj v.pam.2p r.apm cj

οἰκοδομεῖτε εἷς τὸν ἕνα, ↰ καθὼς καὶ ποιεῖτε. 12 ἐρωτῶμεν δὲ
build one {the} another up, as indeed you are doing. Now we ask Now
3868 1651 3836 1651 3868 2777 2779 4472 1254 2263 1254
v.pam.2p a.nsm d.asm a.asm cj adv v.pai.2p v.pai.1p cj

ὑμᾶς, ἀδελφοί, εἰδέναι τοὺς κοπιῶντας ἐν ὑμῖν καὶ προϊσταμένους ὑμῶν
you, brothers, to respect those who work tirelessly among you, {and} care for you
7007 81 3857 3836 3159 1877 7007 2779 4613 7007
r.ap.2 n.vpm f.ra d.apm pt.pa.apm p.d r.dp.2 cj pt.pm.apm r.gp.2

ἐν κυρίῳ καὶ νουθετοῦντας ὑμᾶς 13 καὶ ἡγεῖσθαι αὐτοὺς ὑπερεκπερισσοῦ ἐν
in the Lord, and instruct you, and to esteem them very highly in
1877 3261 2779 3805 7007 2779 2451 899 5655 1877
p.d n.dsm cj pt.pa.apm r.ap.2 cj f.pm r.apm.3 adv p.d

ἀγάπῃ διὰ τὸ ἔργον αὐτῶν. εἰρηνεύετε ἐν ἑαυτοῖς. 14
love ⌊because of⌋ {the} their work. their Be at peace among yourselves. Now
27 1328 3836 899 2240 899 1644 1877 1571 1254
n.dsf p.a d.asn n.asn r.gpm.3 v.pam.2p p.d r.dpm.2

παρακαλοῦμεν δὲ ὑμᾶς, ἀδελφοί, νουθετεῖτε τοὺς ἀτάκτους, παραμυθεῖσθε τοὺς
we appeal to Now you, brothers, admonish the disorderly, comfort the
4151 1254 7007 81 3805 3836 864 4170 3836
v.pai.1p cj r.ap.2 n.vpm v.pam.2p d.apm a.apm v.pmm.2p d.apm

ὀλιγοψύχους, ἀντέχεσθε τῶν ἀσθενῶν, μακροθυμεῖτε πρὸς πάντας. 15 ὁρᾶτε μή
discouraged, help the weak, be patient toward all. See that no
3901 504 3836 822 3428 4639 4246 3972 3590
a.apm v.pmm.2p d.gpm a.gpm v.pam.2p p.a a.apm v.pam.2p cj

τις κακὸν ἀντὶ κακοῦ τινι ἀποδῷ, ἀλλὰ πάντοτε τὸ
one pays back anyone evil for evil anyone pays back but always pursue what is
5516 625 625 5516 2805 505 2805 5516 625 247 4121 1503 3836
r.nsm a.asn p.g a.gsn r.dsm v.aas.3s cj adv d.asn

ἀγαθὸν διώκετε καὶ[a] εἰς ἀλλήλους καὶ εἰς πάντας. 16 πάντοτε χαίρετε,
good pursue both for one another and for all. Rejoice at all times, Rejoice
19 1503 2779 1650 253 2779 1650 4246 5897 4121 5897
a.asn v.pam.2p cj p.a r.apm cj p.a a.apm adv v.pam.2p

17 ἀδιαλείπτως προσεύχεσθε, 18 ἐν παντὶ εὐχαριστεῖτε· τοῦτο
pray without ceasing, pray give thanks in everything, give thanks for this
4667 90 4667 2373 2373 1877 4246 2373 1142 4047
adv v.pmm.2p p.d a.dsn v.pam.2p r.nsn

γὰρ θέλημα θεοῦ ἐν Χριστῷ Ἰησοῦ εἰς ὑμᾶς. 19 τὸ
for is God's will God's for you in Christ Jesus. for you Do not quench the
1142 2536 2525 2536 1650 7007 1877 5986 2652 1650 7007 4931 3590 4931 3836
cj n.nsn n.gsm p.d n.dsm n.dsm p.a r.ap.2 d.asn

πνεῦμα μὴ σβέννυτε, 20 προφητείας μὴ ἐξουθενεῖτε, 21
Spirit; not Do quench do not scoff at prophetic utterances, not do scoff at but
4460 3590 4931 2024 3590 2024 2024 4735 3590 2024 1254
n.asn pl v.pam.2p n.apf pl v.pam.2p

πάντα δὲ δοκιμάζετε, τὸ καλὸν κατέχετε, 22 ἀπὸ
test everything; but test hold fast what is good; hold fast abstain from evil
1507 4246 1254 1507 2988 2988 3836 2819 2988 600 608 4505
a.apn cj v.pam.2p d.asn a.asn v.pam.2p p.g

NASB

salvation. 9 For God
has not destined us
for wrath, but for
obtaining salva-
tion through our
Lord Jesus Christ,
10 who died for us,
so that whether
we are awake or
asleep, we will live
together with Him.
11 Therefore encour-
age one another
and build up one
another, just as you
also are doing.

Christian Conduct

12 But we request
of you, brethren,
that you appreci-
ate those who
diligently labor
among you, and
have charge over
you in the Lord
and give you
instruction, 13 and
that you esteem
them very highly
in love because of
their work. Live
in peace with one
another. 14 We urge
you, brethren,
admonish the
unruly, encourage
the fainthearted,
help the weak, be
patient with every-
one. 15 See that no
one repays another
with evil for evil,
but always seek
after that which
is good for one
another and for all
people. 16 Rejoice
always; 17 pray
without ceasing;
18 in everything give
thanks; for this is
God's will for you
in Christ Jesus.
19 Do not quench
the Spirit; 20 do not
despise prophetic
[a]utterances. 21 But
examine every-
thing *carefully;*
hold fast to that
which is good;
22 abstain from

[a] [καὶ] UBS, omitted by TNIV.

[a] Or *gifts*

NIV

23 May God him-
self, the God of
peace, sanctify
you through and
through. May
your whole spirit,
soul and body be
kept blameless at
the coming of our
Lord Jesus Christ.
24 The one who
calls you is faith-
ful, and he will
do it.

25 Brothers and
sisters, pray for us.
26 Greet all God's
people with a holy
kiss. 27 I charge
you before the
Lord to have this
letter read to all
the brothers and
sisters.
28 The grace of
our Lord Jesus
Christ be with you.

παντὸς εἴδους πονηροῦ ἀπέχεσθε. 23 αὐτὸς δὲ ↱ ὁ θεὸς τῆς εἰρήνης
of every kind. *evil* *abstain* *himself* Now may the God of peace himself
4246 1626 4505 600 899 1254 39 3836 2536 3836 1645 899
a.gsn n.gsn a.gsn v.pmm.2p r.nsm cj d.nsm n.nsm d.gsf n.gsf

ἁγιάσαι ὑμᾶς ὁλοτελεῖς, καὶ ὁλόκληρον ὑμῶν τὸ πνεῦμα καὶ ἡ ψυχὴ καὶ
sanctify you completely, and *completely whole* may your *{the}* spirit, *{and}* *{the}* soul, and
39 7007 3911 2779 3908 5498 7007 3836 4460 2779 3836 6034 2779
v.aao.3s r.ap.2 a.apm cj n.nsn r.gp.2 d.nsn n.nsn cj d.nsf n.nsf cj

τὸ σῶμα ἀμέμπτως ἐν τῇ παρουσίᾳ τοῦ
{the} body be preserved completely whole and blameless at the coming of our
3836 5393 5498 5498 3908 3908 290 1877 3836 4242 3836 7005
d.nsn n.nsn adv p.d d.dsf n.dsf d.gsm

κυρίου ἡμῶν Ἰησοῦ Χριστοῦ τηρηθείη. 24 πιστὸς ὁ καλῶν ὑμᾶς,
Lord *our* Jesus Christ. *may be preserved* *faithful* The ⌊one who calls⌋ you is
3261 7005 2652 5986 5498 4412 3836 2813 7007
n.gsm r.gp.1 n.gsm n.gsm v.apo.3s a.nsm d.nsm pt.pa.nsm r.ap.2

ὃς ↱ καὶ ποιήσει. 25 ἀδελφοί, προσεύχεσθε καὶ[a] περὶ ἡμῶν.
faithful, and he will surely do it. *brothers* Pray also for us, brothers.
4412 4005 4472 2779 4472 81 4667 2779 4309 7005 81
r.nsm adv v.fai.3s n.vpm v.pmm.2p adv p.g r.gp.1

26 ἀσπάσασθε τοὺς ἀδελφοὺς πάντας ἐν φιλήματι ἁγίῳ. 27 ἐνορκίζω ὑμᾶς
Greet all the brothers *all* with a holy kiss. *holy* I ask you
832 4246 3836 81 4246 1877 41 5799 41 1941 7007
v.amm.2p d.apm n.apm a.apm p.d n.dsn a.dsn v.pai.1s r.ap.2

↰ ↰ ↰ τὸν κύριον → → ἀναγνωσθῆναι τὴν ἐπιστολὴν
to swear by the name of the Lord to have this letter read *this* *letter*
1941 1941 1941 3836 3261 3836 2186 336 3836 2186
d.asm n.asm f.ap d.asf n.asf

πᾶσιν τοῖς ἀδελφοῖς. 28 ἡ χάρις τοῦ κυρίου ἡμῶν Ἰησοῦ Χριστοῦ μεθ'
to all the brothers. The grace of our Lord *our* Jesus Christ be with
4246 3836 81 3836 5921 3836 7005 3261 7005 2652 5986 3552
a.dpm d.dpm n.dpm d.nsf n.nsf d.gsm n.gsm r.gp.1 n.gsm n.gsm p.g

ὑμῶν.[b]
you.
7007
r.gp.2

[a] [καὶ] UBS, omitted by TNIV.
[b] ἀμήν. πρὸς Θεσσαλονικεῖς πρώτη ἐγράφη ἀπὸ Ἀθηνῶν included by TR after ὑμῶν.

NASB

every [a]form of evil.
23 Now may the
God of peace Him-
self sanctify you
entirely; and may
your spirit and soul
and body be pre-
served complete,
without blame at
the coming of our
Lord Jesus Christ.
24 Faithful is He
who calls you, and
He also will bring
it to pass.
25 Brethren, pray
for us[b].
26 Greet all the
brethren with a
holy kiss. 27 I adjure
you by the Lord to
have this letter read
to all the brethren.
28 The grace of our
Lord Jesus Christ
be with you.

[a] Or *appearance*
[b] Two early mss add *also*

2 Thessalonians

NIV

1 Paul, Silas[a]
and Timothy,

To the church of the Thessalonians in God our Father and the Lord Jesus Christ:

2 Grace and peace
to you from God the Father and the Lord Jesus Christ.

Thanksgiving and Prayer

3 We ought always
to thank God for you, brothers and sisters,[b] and rightly so, because your faith is growing more and more, and the love all of you have for one another is increasing.
4 Therefore,
among God's churches we boast about your perseverance and faith in all the persecutions and trials you are enduring.
5 All this is evi-
dence that God's judgment is right, and as a result you will be counted worthy of the kingdom of God, for which you are suffering.
6 God is
just: He will pay back trouble to those who trouble you
7 and give re-
lief to you who are troubled, and to us as well. This will happen when the Lord Jesus is revealed from heaven in blazing fire with his powerful angels.
8 He will
punish

[a] 1 Greek *Silvanus*, a variant of *Silas*
[b] 3 The Greek word for *brothers and sisters* (*adelphoi*) refers here to believers, both men and women, as part of God's family; also in 2:1, 13, 15; 3:1, 6, 13.

1:1 Παῦλος καὶ Σιλουανὸς καὶ Τιμόθεος τῇ ἐκκλησίᾳ → Θεσσαλονικέων
Paul, {and} Silvanus, and Timothy, ⌊to the⌋ church of the Thessalonians
4263 2779 4977 2779 5510 3836 1711 2552
n.nsm cj n.nsm cj n.nsm d.dsf n.dsf n.gpm

ἐν θεῷ πατρὶ ἡμῶν καὶ κυρίῳ Ἰησοῦ Χριστῷ, 2 χάρις ὑμῖν καὶ εἰρήνη ἀπὸ
in God our Father *our* and the Lord Jesus Christ: Grace to you and peace from
1877 2536 7005 4252 7005 2779 3261 2652 5986 5921 7007 2779 1645 608
p.d n.dsm n.dsm r.gp.1 cj n.dsm n.dsm n.dsm n.nsf r.dp.2 cj n.nsf p.g

θεοῦ πατρὸς ἡμῶν[a] καὶ κυρίου Ἰησοῦ Χριστοῦ. 3 εὐχαριστεῖν
God our Father *our* and the Lord Jesus Christ. We ought always to thank
2536 7005 4252 7005 2779 3261 2652 5986 4053 4053 4121 2373
n.gsm n.gsm r.gp.1 cj n.gsm n.gsm n.gsm f.pa

ὀφείλομεν τῷ θεῷ πάντοτε περὶ ὑμῶν, ἀδελφοί, καθὼς ἄξιόν ἐστιν, ὅτι
We ought {the} God *always* for you, brothers, as is fitting, *is* because your
4053 3836 2536 4121 4309 7007 81 2777 1639 545 1639 4022 7007
v.pai.1p d.dsm n.dsm adv p.g r.gp.2 n.vpm cj a.nsn v.pai.3s cj

ὑπεραυξάνει ἡ πίστις ὑμῶν καὶ πλεονάζει ἡ ἀγάπη ἑνὸς
faith is growing abundantly, {the} *faith* *your* and *is increasing* the love of each one
4411 5647 3836 4411 7007 2779 4429 3836 27 1667 1667 1651
v.pai.3s d.nsf n.nsf r.gp.2 cj v.pai.3s d.nsf n.nsf a.gsm

ἑκάστου πάντων ὑμῶν εἰς ἀλλήλους, 4 ὥστε αὐτοὺς ἡμᾶς
of each {*of all*} of you for one another is increasing, so that we ourselves *we* boast
1667 4246 7007 1650 253 4429 4429 6063 7005 899 7005 1595
r.gsm a.gpm r.gp.2 p.a r.apm cj r.apm r.ap.1

ἐν ὑμῖν ἐγκαυχᾶσθαι ἐν ταῖς ἐκκλησίαις τοῦ θεοῦ ὑπὲρ τῆς ὑπομονῆς ὑμῶν
about you *boast* in the churches of God for {the} your patience *your*
1877 7007 1595 1877 3836 1711 3836 2536 5642 3836 7007 5705 7007
p.d r.dp.2 f.pm p.d d.dpf n.dpf d.gsm n.gsm p.g d.gsf n.gsf r.gp.2

καὶ πίστεως ἐν πᾶσιν τοῖς διωγμοῖς ὑμῶν καὶ ταῖς θλίψεσιν αἷς ἀνέχεσθε,
and faith in all the persecutions {*your*} and {*the*} afflictions that you are enduring.
2779 4411 1877 4246 3836 1501 7007 2779 3836 2568 4005 462
cj n.gsf p.d a.dpm d.dpm n.dpm r.gp.2 cj d.dpf n.dpf r.dpf v.pmi.2p

5 ἔνδειγμα τῆς δικαίας κρίσεως τοῦ θεοῦ εἰς τὸ
This is evidence of the righteous judgment of God, and ⌊results in⌋ ~ your
1891 3836 1465 3213 3836 2536 1650 3836 7007
n.nsn d.gsf a.gsf n.gsf d.gsm n.gsm p.a d.asn

καταξιωθῆναι ὑμᾶς τῆς βασιλείας τοῦ θεοῦ, ὑπὲρ ἧς ↱ ↱ καὶ
⌊being considered worthy⌋ *your* of the kingdom of God, for which you are indeed
2921 7007 3836 993 3836 2536 5642 4005 4248 4248 2779
f.ap r.ap.2 d.gsf n.gsf d.gsm n.gsm p.g r.gsf adv

πάσχετε, 6 εἴπερ δίκαιον παρὰ θεῷ ἀνταποδοῦναι τοῖς
suffering. For it is a ⌊righteous thing⌋ for God to repay with affliction those
4248 1642 1465 4123 2536 500 2568 3836
v.pai.2p cj a.nsn p.d n.dsm f.aa d.dpm

θλίβουσιν ὑμᾶς θλῖψιν 7 καὶ ὑμῖν τοῖς θλιβομένοις ἄνεσιν μεθ'
who afflict you, *affliction* and to give relief to you who are afflicted, *relief* and to
2567 7007 2568 2779 457 7007 3836 2567 457 3552
pt.pa.dpm r.ap.2 n.asf cj r.dp.2 d.dpm pt.pp.dpm n.asf p.g

ἡμῶν, ↰ ↰ ἐν τῇ ἀποκαλύψει τοῦ κυρίου Ἰησοῦ ἀπ' οὐρανοῦ
us as well, when {*the*} the Lord Jesus is revealed *the* *Lord* *Jesus* from heaven
7005 3552 3552 1877 3836 3836 3261 2652 637 3836 3261 2652 608 4041
r.gp.1 p.d d.dsf n.dsf d.gsm n.gsm n.gsm p.g n.gsm

μετ' ἀγγέλων δυνάμεως αὐτοῦ 8 ἐν πυρὶ φλογός, διδόντος ἐκδίκησιν
with his mighty angels *mighty* *his* in flaming fire, *flaming* inflicting punishment
3552 899 1539 34 1539 899 1877 5825 4786 5825 1443 1689
p.g n.gpm n.gsf r.gsm.3 p.d n.dsn n.gsf pt.pa.gsm n.asf

[a] [ἡμῶν] UBS, omitted by NET.

NASB

Thanksgiving for Faith and Perseverance

1:1 Paul and Sil-
vanus and Timothy,
To the church of the Thessalonians in God our Father and the Lord Jesus Christ:
2 Grace to
you and peace from God the Father and the Lord Jesus Christ.
3 We ought always
to give thanks to God for you, brethren, as is *only* fitting, because your faith is greatly enlarged, and the love of each one of you toward one another grows *ever* greater;
4 therefore,
we ourselves speak proudly of you among the churches of God for your perseverance and faith in the midst of all your persecutions and afflictions which you endure.
5 *This is* a plain
indication of God's righteous judgment so that you will be considered worthy of the kingdom of God, for which indeed you are suffering.
6 For after
all it is *only* just for God to repay with affliction those who afflict you,
7 and *to give* relief
to you who are afflicted and to us as well when the Lord Jesus will be revealed from heaven with His mighty angels in flaming fire,
8 dealing out
retribution to

NIV

those who do not
know God and do
not obey the gospel
of our Lord Jesus.
9They will be pun-
ished with ever-
lasting destruction
and shut out from
the presence of the
Lord and from the
glory of his might
10on the day he
comes to be glo-
rified in his holy
people and to be
marveled at among
all those who have
believed. This
includes you, be-
cause you believed
our testimony to
you.
11With this in
mind, we constant-
ly pray for you,
that our God may
make you worthy
of his calling, and
that by his power
he may bring to
fruition your every
desire for good-
ness and your ev-
ery deed prompted
by faith. 12We
pray this so that
the name of our
Lord Jesus may be
glorified in you,
and you in him,
according to the
grace of our God
and the Lord Jesus
Christ.[a]

The Man of Lawlessness

2 Concerning
the coming
of our Lord Jesus
Christ and our
being gathered
to him, we ask
you, brothers and
sisters, 2not to
become easily un-
settled or alarmed
by the teaching
allegedly from
us—whether by
a prophecy or by
word of mouth or
by letter—assert-
ing that the day of
the Lord has al-
ready come. 3Don't
let anyone

[a] 12 *Or God and Lord, Jesus Christ*

τοῖς ↱ ↱ μὴ εἰδόσιν θεὸν καὶ τοῖς ↱ μὴ ὑπακούουσιν τῷ εὐαγγελίῳ τοῦ
on those who do not know God, and who do not obey the gospel of
3836 3857 3857 3590 3857 2536 2779 3836 5634 3590 5634 3836 2295 3836
d.dpm pl pt.ra.dpm n.asm cj d.dpm pl pt.pa.dpm d.dsn n.dsn d.gsm

κυρίου ἡμῶν Ἰησοῦ, 9οἵτινες δίκην τίσουσιν
our Lord *our* Jesus. They will experience the punishment *will experience* of eternal
7005 3261 7005 2652 4015 5514 5514 1472 5514 173
n.gsm r.gp.1 n.gsm r.npm n.asf v.fai.3p

ὄλεθρον αἰώνιον ἀπὸ προσώπου τοῦ κυρίου καὶ ἀπὸ τῆς δόξης τῆς
destruction, *eternal* ⌊away from⌋ the presence of the Lord and from the glory of his
3897 173 608 4725 3836 3261 2779 608 3836 1518 3836 899
n.asm a.asm p.g n.gsn d.gsm n.gsm cj p.g d.gsf n.gsf d.gsf

ἰσχύος αὐτοῦ, 10 ὅταν ἔλθῃ ἐνδοξασθῆναι ἐν τοῖς ἁγίοις αὐτοῦ
power *his* on that day when he comes to be glorified in *{the}* his saints, *his*
2709 899 1877 1697 2465 4020 2262 1901 1877 3836 899 41 899
n.gsf r.gsm.3 cj v.aas.3s f.ap p.d d.dpm a.dpm r.gsm.3

καὶ θαυμασθῆναι ἐν πᾶσιν τοῖς πιστεύσασιν, ὅτι
and to be marveled at by all who have believed, because our testimony to you
2779 2513 1877 4246 3836 4409 4022 7005 3457 2093 7007
cj f.ap p.d a.dpm d.dpm pt.aa.dpm cj

ἐπιστεύθη τὸ μαρτύριον ἡμῶν ἐφ' ὑμᾶς, ἐν τῇ ἡμέρᾳ ἐκείνῃ. 11 εἰς
was believed. *{the}* *testimony* *our* *to* *you* *on* *{the}* *day* *that* With this in view
4409 3836 3457 7005 2093 7007 1877 3836 2465 1697 2779 4005 1650
v.api.3s d.nsn n.nsn r.gp.1 p.a r.ap.2 p.d d.dsf n.dsf r.dsf p.a

ὃ καὶ προσευχόμεθα πάντοτε περὶ ὑμῶν, ἵνα ↱ ↱ ὑμᾶς
this *With* we pray for you constantly, *for* *you* that our God will count you
4005 2779 4667 4309 7007 4121 4309 7007 2671 7005 2536 546 546 7007
r.asn adv v.pmi.1p adv p.g r.gp.2 cj r.ap.2

ἀξιώσῃ τῆς κλήσεως ὁ θεὸς ἡμῶν καὶ πληρώσῃ πᾶσαν
worthy of his calling, *{the}* *God* *our* and by his power bring to fulfillment every
546 3836 3104 3836 2536 7005 2779 1877 1539 4444 4246
v.aas.3s d.gsf n.gsf d.nsm n.nsm r.gp.1 cj v.aas.3s a.asf

εὐδοκίαν ἀγαθωσύνης καὶ ἔργον πίστεως ἐν δυνάμει, 12 ὅπως ἐνδοξασθῇ τὸ
good resolve and work of faith, *by* *power* so that *may be glorified* the
2306 20 2779 2240 4411 1877 1539 3968 1901 3836
n.asf n.gsf cj n.asn n.gsf p.d n.dsf cj v.aps.3s d.nsn

ὄνομα τοῦ κυρίου ἡμῶν Ἰησοῦ ἐν ὑμῖν, καὶ ὑμεῖς ἐν αὐτῷ,
name of our Lord *our* Jesus may be glorified in you, and you in him,
3950 3836 7005 3261 7005 2652 1901 1901 1901 1877 7007 2779 7007 1877 899
n.nsn d.gsm n.gsm r.gp.1 n.gsm p.d r.dp.2 cj r.np.2 p.d r.dsm.3

κατὰ τὴν χάριν τοῦ θεοῦ ἡμῶν καὶ κυρίου Ἰησοῦ Χριστοῦ.
⌊according to⌋ the grace of our God *our* and the Lord Jesus Christ.
2848 3836 5921 3836 7005 2536 7005 2779 3261 2652 5986
p.a d.asf n.asf d.gsm n.gsm r.gp.1 cj n.gsm n.gsm n.gsm

2:1 ἐρωτῶμεν δὲ ὑμᾶς, ἀδελφοί, ὑπὲρ τῆς παρουσίας τοῦ κυρίου ἡμῶν
we ask Now *you* *brothers* concerning the coming of our Lord *our*
2263 1254 7007 81 5642 3836 4242 3836 7005 3261 7005
v.pai.1p cj r.ap.2 n.vpm p.g d.gsf n.gsf d.gsm n.gsm r.gp.1

Ἰησοῦ Χριστοῦ καὶ ἡμῶν ἐπισυναγωγῆς ἐπ' αὐτὸν 2εἰς τὸ
Jesus Christ and our assembling to him, we ask you, brothers, *{that}* ~
2652 5986 2779 7005 2191 2093 899 2263 2263 7007 81 1650 3836
n.gsm n.gsm cj r.gp.1 n.gsf p.a r.asm.3 p.a d.asn

μὴ ↱ ↱ ταχέως σαλευθῆναι ὑμᾶς ἀπὸ τοῦ νοὸς μηδὲ θροεῖσθαι, μήτε διὰ
not to be quickly shaken *{you}* out of your wits or disturbed, either by a
3590 4888 4888 5441 4888 7007 608 3836 3808 3593 2583 3612 1328
pl adv f.ap r.ap.2 p.g d.gsm n.gsm cj f.pp cj p.g

πνεύματος μήτε διὰ λόγου μήτε δι' ἐπιστολῆς ὡς δι' ἡμῶν,
prophecy or by a ⌊spoken word⌋ or by a letter ⌊purporting to come⌋ from us,
4460 3612 1328 3364 3612 1328 2186 6055 1328 7005
n.gsn cj p.g n.gsm cj p.g n.gsf pl p.g r.gp.1

ὡς ὅτι ἐνέστηκεν ἡ ἡμέρα τοῦ κυρίου· 3 μή
⌊to the effect⌋ that the day of the Lord is already here. *the* *day* *of the* *Lord* Let no
6055 4022 3836 2465 3836 3836 3261 1931 3836 2465 3836 3261 1987 3590
pl cj v.rai.3s d.nsf n.nsf d.gsm n.gsm pl

NASB

those who do not
know God and to
those who do not
obey the gospel
of our Lord Jesus.
9These will pay the
penalty of eternal
destruction, away
from the presence
of the Lord and
from the glory of
His power, 10when
He comes to be
glorified in His
saints on that day,
and to be marveled
at among all who
have believed—for
our testimony to
you was believed.
11To this end also
we pray for you
always, that our
God will count
you worthy of your
calling, and fulfill
every desire for
goodness and the
work of faith with
power, 12so that
the name of our
Lord Jesus will be
glorified in you,
and you in Him,
according to the
grace of our God
and *the* Lord Jesus
Christ.

Man of Lawlessness

2:1Now we request
you, brethren, with
regard to the com-
ing of our Lord
Jesus Christ and
our gathering to-
gether to Him, 2that
you not be quickly
shaken from your
composure or be
disturbed either by
a spirit or a mes-
sage or a letter as if
from us, to the ef-
fect that the day of
the Lord has come.
3Let no one in

NIV

deceive you in any
way, for that day
will not come until
the rebellion oc-
curs and the man
of lawlessness[a] is
revealed, the man
doomed to de-
struction. 4He will
oppose and will
exalt himself over
everything that is
called God or is
worshiped, so that
he sets himself up
in God's temple,
proclaiming him-
self to be God.
5Don't you re-
member that when
I was with you I
used to tell you
these things? 6And
now you know
what is holding
him back, so that
he may be revealed
at the proper time.
7For the secret
power of lawless-
ness is already at
work; but the one
who now holds it
back will contin-
ue to do so till he
is taken out of the
way. 8And then the
lawless one will
be revealed, whom
the Lord Jesus will
overthrow with
the breath of his
mouth and destroy
by the splendor of
his coming. 9The
coming of the law-
less one will be in
accordance with
how Satan works.
He will use all
sorts of displays
of power through
signs and wonders
that serve the lie,
10and all the ways
that wickedness
deceives those
who are perishing.
They perish be-
cause they refused
to love the truth

[a] 3 Some manu-
scripts *sin*

τις ὑμᾶς ἐξαπατήσῃ κατὰ μηδένα τρόπον. ὅτι → ⸤ἐὰν μὴ⸥
one deceive you *Let deceive* in any way; for that day will not come unless
5516 1987 7007 1987 2848 3594 5573 4022 2262 2262 1569 3590
r.nsm r.ap.2 v.aas.3s p.a a.asm n.asm cj cj pl

ἔλθῃ ἡ ἀποστασία πρῶτον καὶ ἀποκαλυφθῇ ὁ
will come the rebellion comes first and the man of lawlessness is revealed, *the*
2262 3836 686 4754 2779 3836 476 3836 490 636 3836
v.aas.3s d.nsf n.nsf adv cj v.aps.3s d.nsm

ἄνθρωπος τῆς ἀνομίας,[a] ὁ υἱὸς τῆς ἀπωλείας, 4ὁ ἀντικείμενος καὶ
man of lawlessness the son of destruction, who opposes and
476 3836 490 3836 5626 3836 724 3836 512 2779
n.nsm d.gsf n.gsf d.nsm n.nsm d.gsf n.gsf d.nsm pt.pm.nsm cj

ὑπεραιρόμενος ἐπὶ πάντα λεγόμενον θεὸν ἢ σέβασμα, ὥστε αὐτὸν
exalts himself above every so-called god or object of worship, so that he takes his
5643 2093 4246 3306 2536 2445 4934 6063 899 2767 2767
pt.pm.nsm p.a a.asm pt.pp.asm n.asm cj n.asn cj r.asm.3

εἰς τὸν ναὸν τοῦ θεοῦ καθίσαι ἀποδεικνύντα ↱ ἑαυτὸν ὅτι ἔστιν
seat in the temple of God, *takes his seat* proclaiming that he himself *that* is
2767 1650 3836 3724 3836 2536 2767 617 4022 1639 1571 4022 1639
p.a d.asm n.asm d.gsm n.gsm f.aa pt.pa.asm r.asm.3 cj v.pai.3s

θεός. 5↱ ↱ οὐ μνημονεύετε ὅτι ἔτι ὢν
God. Do you not remember that I told you this while I was still *while I was*
2536 3648 3648 4024 3648 4022 3306 3306 7007 4047 1639 1639 1639 2285 1639
n.nsm pl v.pai.2p cj adv pt.pa.nsm

πρὸς ὑμᾶς ταῦτα ἔλεγον ὑμῖν; 6καὶ νῦν τὸ → κατέχον οἴδατε
with you? *this I told you* And now you know what is holding him in check, *you know*
4639 7007 4047 3306 7007 2779 3814 3857 3857 3836 2988 3857
p.a r.ap.2 r.apn v.iai.1s r.dp.2 cj adv d.asn pt.pa.asn v.rai.2p

εἰς τὸ ἀποκαλυφθῆναι αὐτὸν ἐν τῷ ἑαυτοῦ καιρῷ. 7 τὸ γὰρ
⸤so that⸥ ~ he may be revealed *he* at *{the}* his proper time. For the *For*
1650 3836 899 636 899 1877 3836 1571 2789 1142 3836 1142
p.a d.asn f.ap r.asm.3 p.d d.dsm r.gsm.3 n.dsm d.nsn cj

μυστήριον ↱ ἤδη ἐνεργεῖται τῆς ἀνομίας· μόνον ὁ → → →
mystery of lawlessness is already at work; *of lawlessness* however, the one who is
3696 3836 490 1919 2453 1919 3836 490 3667 3836
n.nsn adv v.pmi.3s d.gsf n.gsf adv d.nsm

κατέχων ἄρτι ἕως ⸤ἐκ μέσου⸥ γένηται. 8καὶ
now restraining *now* will continue to do so until he is taken away. *he is taken* And
785 2988 785 2401 1181 1181 1181 1666 3545 1181 2779
pt.pa.nsm adv cj p.g n.gsn v.ams.3s cj

τότε ἀποκαλυφθήσεται ὁ ἄνομος, ὃν ὁ κύριος Ἰησοῦς[b]
then the lawless one will be revealed, *the lawless one* whom the Lord Jesus
5538 3836 491 491 636 3836 491 4005 3836 3261 2652
adv v.fpi.3s d.nsm a.nsm r.asm d.nsm n.nsm n.nsm

ἀνελεῖ τῷ πνεύματι τοῦ στόματος αὐτοῦ καὶ καταργήσει τῇ
will destroy ⸤with the⸥ breath of his mouth, *his* and bring to an end ⸤with the⸥
359 3836 4460 3836 899 5125 899 2779 2934 3836
v.fai.3s d.dsn n.dsn d.gsn n.gsn r.gsm.3 cj v.fai.3s d.dsf

ἐπιφανείᾳ τῆς παρουσίας αὐτοῦ, 9 οὗ ἐστιν ἡ
splendor of his coming. *his* The coming ⸤of the lawless one⸥ will be *The*
2211 3836 899 4242 899 3836 4242 4005 1639 3836
n.dsf d.gsf n.gsf r.gsm.3 r.gsm v.pai.3s d.nsf

παρουσία κατ' ἐνέργειαν τοῦ σατανᾶ ἐν πάσῃ δυνάμει καὶ
coming ⸤according to⸥ the activity of Satan, with ⸤all kinds of⸥ false miracles, *{and}*
4242 2848 1918 3836 4928 1877 4246 6022 1539 2779
n.nsf p.a n.asf d.gsm n.gsm p.d a.dsf n.dsf cj

σημείοις καὶ τέρασιν ψεύδους 10καὶ ἐν πάσῃ ἀπάτῃ ἀδικίας
signs, and wonders, *false* and with ⸤every kind of⸥ wicked deception *wicked*
4956 2779 5469 6022 2779 1877 4246 94 573 94
n.dpn cj n.dpn n.gsn cj p.d a.dsf n.dsf n.gsf

τοῖς ἀπολλυμένοις, ⸤ἀνθ' ὧν⸥ τὴν ἀγάπην τῆς ἀληθείας
for those who are perishing, because they did not accept the love of the truth
3836 660 505 4005 1312 1312 4024 1312 3836 27 3836 237
d.dpm pt.pm.dpm p.g r.gpn d.asf n.asf d.gsf n.gsf

[a] ἁμαρτίας included by TR after ἀνομίας.
[b] [Ἰησοῦς] UBS, omitted by NET.

NASB

any way deceive
you, for *it will not*
come unless the
[a]apostasy comes
first, and the man
of lawlessness is
revealed, the son of
destruction, 4who
opposes and exalts
himself above
every so-called
god or object of
worship, so that
he takes his seat in
the temple of God,
displaying himself
as being God. 5Do
you not remember
that while I was
still with you, I
was telling you
these things? 6And
you know what
restrains him now,
so that in his time
he will be revealed.
7For the mystery
of lawlessness is
already at work;
only he who now
restrains *will*
do so until he is
taken out of the
way. 8Then that
lawless one will
be revealed whom
the Lord will slay
with the breath
of His mouth and
bring to an end
by the appearance
of His coming;
9*that is,* the one
whose coming is
in accord with the
activity of Satan,
with all power and
signs and false
wonders, 10and with
all the deception
of wickedness for
those who perish,
because they did
not receive the love
of the truth so as to

[a] Or *falling away* from the faith

NIV

and so be saved.
11 For this reason
God sends them
a powerful delu-
sion so that they
will believe the lie
12 and so that all
will be condemned
who have not be-
lieved the truth but
have delighted in
wickedness.

Stand Firm

13 But we ought
always to thank
God for you,
brothers and sis-
ters loved by the
Lord, because God
chose you as first-
fruits[a] to be saved
through the sanc-
tifying work of the
Spirit and through
belief in the truth.
14 He called you to
this through our
gospel, that you
might share in the
glory of our Lord
Jesus Christ.
15 So then, broth-
ers and sisters,
stand firm and
hold fast to the
teachings[b] we
passed on to you,
whether by word
of mouth or by
letter.
16 May our Lord
Jesus Christ him-
self and God
our Father, who
loved us and by
his grace gave us
eternal encour-
agement and good
hope, 17 encourage
your hearts and
strengthen you in
every good deed
and word.

Request for Prayer

3 As for other
matters, broth-
ers and sisters,
pray for us that
the message of the
Lord

[a] 13 Some manuscripts *because from the beginning God chose you*
[b] 15 Or *traditions*

οὐκ ἐδέξαντο εἰς τὸ σωθῆναι αὐτούς. 11 καὶ διὰ τοῦτο πέμπει
not they did accept ⌞so as⌟ ~ to be saved. {they} {and} For this reason God will send
4024 1312 1650 3836 5392 899 2779 1328 4047 2536 4287
pl v.ami.3p p.a d.asn f.ap r.apm.3 cj p.a r.asn v.pai.3s

αὐτοῖς ὁ θεὸς ἐνέργειαν πλάνης εἰς τὸ πιστεῦσαι αὐτοὺς τῷ ψεύδει,
them {the} God an active delusion leading ~ them to believe them the lie,
899 3836 2536 1918 4415 1650 3836 899 4409 899 3836 6022
r.dpm.3 d.nsm n.nsm n.asf n.gsf p.a d.asn f.aa r.apm.3 d.dsn n.dsn

12 ἵνα → κριθῶσιν πάντες οἱ ↱ μὴ πιστεύσαντες τῇ ἀληθείᾳ ἀλλὰ
that they all may be condemned all who did not believe the truth but
2671 4246 3212 4246 3836 4409 3590 4409 3836 237 247
cj v.aps.3p a.npm d.npm pl pt.aa.npm d.dsf n.dsf cj

εὐδοκήσαντες τῇ ἀδικίᾳ. 13 ἡμεῖς δὲ ὀφείλομεν εὐχαριστεῖν τῷ
took pleasure in unrighteousness. But we But ought always to thank {the}
2305 3836 94 1254 7005 1254 4053 4121 2373 3836
pt.aa.npm d.dsf n.dsf r.np.1 cj v.pai.1p f.pa d.dsm

θεῷ πάντοτε περὶ ὑμῶν, ἀδελφοὶ ἠγαπημένοι ὑπὸ κυρίου, ὅτι εἵλατο ὑμᾶς
God always for you, brothers loved by the Lord, because God chose you
2536 4121 4309 7007 81 26 5679 3261 4022 2536 145 7007
n.dsm adv p.g r.gp.2 n.vpm pt.rp.vpm p.g n.gsm cj v.ami.3s r.ap.2

ὁ θεὸς ἀπαρχὴν[a] εἰς σωτηρίαν ἐν ἁγιασμῷ → πνεύματος καὶ πίστει →
{the} God as first fruits for salvation, by sanctification of the Spirit and belief in the
3836 2536 569 1650 5401 1877 40 4460 2779 4411
d.nsm n.nsm n.asf p.a n.asf p.d n.dsm n.gsn cj n.dsf

ἀληθείας, 14 εἰς ὃ καὶ[b] ἐκάλεσεν ὑμᾶς διὰ τοῦ
truth. to this And he called you to this salvation through {the} our
237 1650 4005 2779 2813 7007 1650 4005 1328 3836 7005
n.gsf p.a r.asn adv v.aai.3s r.ap.2 p.g d.gsn

εὐαγγελίου ἡμῶν εἰς περιποίησιν δόξης τοῦ κυρίου ἡμῶν
gospel, our ⌞that you might come⌟ to share the glory of our Lord our
2295 7005 1650 4348 1518 3836 7005 3261 7005
n.gsn r.gp.1 p.a n.asf n.gsf d.gsm n.gsm r.gp.1

Ἰησοῦ Χριστοῦ. 15 ἄρα οὖν, ἀδελφοί, στήκετε καὶ κρατεῖτε τὰς παραδόσεις ἃς
Jesus Christ. So then, brothers, stand firm and hold to the traditions that
2652 5986 726 4036 81 5112 2779 3195 3836 4142 4005
n.gsm n.gsm cj cj n.vpm v.pam.2p cj v.pam.2p d.apf n.apf r.apf

ἐδιδάχθητε εἴτε διὰ → λόγου εἴτε δι' → ἐπιστολῆς ἡμῶν. 16 αὐτὸς
you were taught, either by what we said or {by} what we wrote. we himself
1438 1664 1328 3364 1664 1328 7005 2186 7005 899
v.api.2p cj p.g n.gsm cj p.g n.gsf r.gp.1 r.nsm

δὲ ὁ κύριος ἡμῶν Ἰησοῦς Χριστὸς καὶ ὁ[c] θεὸς ὁ πατὴρ
Now may {the} our Lord our Jesus Christ himself and {the} God {the} our Father,
1254 3836 7005 3261 7005 2652 5986 899 2779 3836 2536 3836 7005 4252
cj d.nsm n.nsm r.gp.1 n.nsm n.nsm cj d.nsm n.nsm d.nsm n.nsm

ἡμῶν ὁ ἀγαπήσας ἡμᾶς καὶ δοὺς παράκλησιν αἰωνίαν καὶ ἐλπίδα
our who has loved us and given us eternal encouragement eternal and good hope
7005 3836 26 7005 2779 1443 173 4155 173 2779 19 1828
r.gp.1 d.nsm pt.aa.nsm r.ap.1 cj pt.aa.nsm n.asf a.asf cj n.asf

ἀγαθὴν ἐν χάριτι, 17 παρακαλέσαι ὑμῶν τὰς καρδίας καὶ στηρίξαι ἐν παντὶ
good by grace, encourage your {the} hearts and establish you in every
19 1877 5921 4151 7007 3836 2840 2779 5114 1877 4246
a.asf p.d n.dsf v.aao.3s r.gp.2 d.apf n.apf cj v.aao.3s p.d a.dsn

ἔργῳ καὶ λόγῳ ἀγαθῷ.
good work and word. good
19 2240 2779 3364 19
n.dsn cj n.dsm a.dsm

3:1 τὸ λοιπὸν προσεύχεσθε, ἀδελφοί, περὶ ἡμῶν, ἵνα ὁ λόγος τοῦ
{the} Finally, brothers, pray brothers for us, that the word of the
3836 3370 81 4667 81 4309 7005 2671 3836 3364 3836
d.asn adv v.pmm.2p n.vpm p.g r.gp.1 cj d.nsm n.nsm d.gsm

[a] ἀπαρχὴν UBS, TNIV. ἀπ' ἀρχῆς NET.
[b] [καὶ] UBS.
[c] [ὁ] UBS.

NASB

be saved. 11 For this
reason God will
send upon them a
deluding influence
so that they will
believe what is
false, 12 in order that
they all may be
judged who did not
believe the truth,
but took pleasure
in wickedness.
13 But we should
always give thanks
to God for you,
brethren beloved
by the Lord, be-
cause God has
chosen you [a]from
the beginning for
salvation through
sanctification by
the Spirit and faith
in the truth. 14 It was
for this He called
you through our
gospel, that you
may gain the glory
of our Lord Jesus
Christ. 15 So then,
brethren, stand firm
and hold to the
traditions which
you were taught,
whether by word *of
mouth* or by letter
from us.
16 Now may our
Lord Jesus Christ
Himself and God
our Father, who has
loved us and given
us eternal comfort
and good hope by
grace, 17 comfort
and strengthen
your hearts in ev-
ery good work and
word.

Exhortation

3:1 Finally, breth-
ren, pray for us that
the word of the

[a] One early ms reads *first fruits*

NIV

may spread rapidly
and be honored,
just as it was with
you. 2And pray that
we may be deliv-
ered from wicked
and evil people, for
not everyone has
faith. 3But the Lord
is faithful, and he
will strengthen you
and protect you
from the evil one.
4We have confi-
dence in the Lord
that you are doing
and will continue
to do the things we
command. 5May
the Lord direct
your hearts into
God's love and
Christ's persever-
ance.

Warning Against Idleness

6In the name of
the Lord Jesus
Christ, we com-
mand you, broth-
ers and sisters, to
keep away from
every believer who
is idle and disrup-
tive and does not
live according to
the teaching[a] you
received from us.
7For you your-
selves know how
you ought to fol-
low our example.
We were not idle
when we were with
you, 8nor did we
eat anyone's food
without paying for
it. On the contrary,
we worked night
and day, laboring
and toiling so that
we would not be a
burden to any of
you. 9We did this,
not because we do
not have the right
to such help, but in
order to offer our-
selves as a model
for you to imitate.
10For even when

[a] 6 Or *tradition*

κυρίου τρέχῃ καὶ δοξάζηται καθὼς καὶ πρὸς ὑμᾶς, 2 καὶ ἵνα
Lord ⌊may spread rapidly⌋ and be honored, as in fact it was among you. Pray also that
3261 5556 2779 1519 2777 2779 4639 7007 2779 2671
n.gsm v.pas.3s cj v.pps.3s cj adv p.a r.ap.2 cj cj

ῥυσθῶμεν ἀπὸ τῶν ἀτόπων καὶ πονηρῶν ἀνθρώπων· οὐ γὰρ πάντων
⌊we may be delivered⌋ from *{the}* unprincipled and wicked men; for not *for* all
4861 608 3836 876 2779 4505 476 1142 4024 1142 4246
v.aps.1p p.g d.gpm a.gpm cj a.gpm n.gpm pl cj a.gpm

ἡ πίστις. 3 πιστὸς δέ ἐστιν ὁ κύριος, ὃς
belong to the faith. But the Lord is faithful; *But is the Lord* he
3836 4411 1254 3836 3261 1639 4412 1254 1639 3836 3261 4005
d.nsf n.nsf a.nsm cj v.pai.3s d.nsm n.nsm r.nsm

στηρίξει ὑμᾶς καὶ φυλάξει ἀπὸ τοῦ πονηροῦ. 4 πεποίθαμεν δὲ ἐν
will establish you and guard you from the evil one. And we are confident *And* in the
5114 7007 2779 5875 608 3836 4505 1254 4275 1254 1877
v.fai.3s r.ap.2 cj v.fai.3s p.g d.gsm a.gsm v.rai.1p cj p.d

κυρίῳ ἐφ' ὑμᾶς, ὅτι ἃ παραγγέλλομεν καὶ[a] ποιεῖτε καὶ ποιήσετε.
Lord regarding you, that *things we require* *{and}* ⌊you are doing⌋ and ⌊will continue to do⌋
3261 2093 7007 4022 4005 4133 2779 4472 2779 4472
n.dsm p.a r.ap.2 cj r.apn v.pai.1p cj v.pai.2p cj v.fai.2p

5 ὁ δὲ κύριος κατευθύναι ὑμῶν τὰς καρδίας
the things we require of you. Now may the *Now* Lord direct your *{the}* hearts
4005 4133 4133 1254 2985 3836 1254 3261 2985 7007 3836 2840
d.nsm cj n.nsm v.aao.3s r.gp.2 d.apf n.apf

εἰς τὴν ἀγάπην τοῦ θεοῦ καὶ εἰς τὴν ὑπομονὴν τοῦ Χριστοῦ. 6
into the love of God and into the endurance of Christ. But
1650 3836 27 3836 2536 2779 1650 3836 5705 3836 5986 1254
p.a d.asf n.asf d.gsm n.gsm cj p.a d.asf n.asf d.gsm n.gsm

παραγγέλλομεν δὲ ὑμῖν, ἀδελφοί, ἐν ὀνόματι τοῦ κυρίου ἡμῶν[b] Ἰησοῦ
we charge *But* you, brothers, in the name of our Lord *our* Jesus
4133 1254 7007 81 1877 3950 3836 7005 3261 7005 2652
v.pai.1p cj r.dp.2 n.vpm p.d n.dsn d.gsm n.gsm r.gp.1 n.gsm

Χριστοῦ στέλλεσθαι ὑμᾶς ἀπὸ παντὸς ἀδελφοῦ
Christ, to stay away *{you}* from any brother who conducts himself
5986 5097 7007 608 4246 81 4344 4344 4344
n.gsm f.pm r.ap.2 p.g a.gsm n.gsm

ἀτάκτως περιπατοῦντος καὶ μὴ κατὰ τὴν παράδοσιν ἣν
⌊in a disorderly manner⌋ *who conducts himself* and not ⌊according to⌋ the tradition that
865 4344 2779 3590 2848 3836 4142 4005
adv pt.pa.gsm cj pl p.a d.asf n.asf r.asf

παρελάβοσαν παρ' ἡμῶν. 7 αὐτοὶ γὰρ οἴδατε πῶς δεῖ
they received from us. For you yourselves *For* know how our example should
4161 4123 7005 1142 3857 899 1142 3857 4802 7005 3628 1256
v.aai.3p p.g r.gp.1 r.npm cj v.rai.2p cj v.pai.3s

μιμεῖσθαι ἡμᾶς, ὅτι οὐκ ἠτακτήσαμεν ἐν ὑμῖν 8 οὐδὲ δωρεὰν
be followed, *our* because we did not ⌊lead disorderly lives⌋ among you, nor *without paying*
3628 7005 4022 863 863 4024 863 1877 7007 4028 1562
f.pm r.ap.1 cj pl v.aai.1p p.d r.dp.2 cj adv

ἄρτον ἐφάγομεν παρά τινος, ἀλλ'
food did we eat *{from}* anyone's food without paying for it. Instead we kept working night and
788 2266 4123 5515 788 1562 1562 247 2237 2237 2237 3816 2779
n.asm v.aai.1p p.g r.gsm cj

ἐν κόπῳ καὶ μόχθῳ νυκτὸς καὶ ἡμέρας ἐργαζόμενοι πρὸς τὸ μὴ
day with toil and hardship, *night and day we kept working* so ~ we would not
2465 1877 3160 2779 3677 3816 2779 2465 2237 4639 3836 2096 2096 3590
p.d n.dsm cj n.dsm n.gsf cj n.gsf pt.pm.npm p.a d.asn pl

ἐπιβαρῆσαί τινα ὑμῶν· 9 οὐχ ὅτι οὐκ ἔχομεν ἐξουσίαν, ἀλλ' ἵνα
be a burden to any of you, not because we do not have the right, but ⌊in order to⌋
2096 5516 7007 4024 4022 2400 2400 4024 2400 2026 247 2671
f.aa r.asm r.gp.2 pl cj pl v.pai.1p n.asf cj cj

ἑαυτοὺς τύπον δῶμεν ὑμῖν εἰς τὸ μιμεῖσθαι ἡμᾶς. 10 καὶ γὰρ ὅτε
make ourselves an example *make* for you to ~ imitate. *{us}* For even *For* when
1443 1571 5596 1443 7007 1650 3836 3628 7005 1142 2779 1142 4021
r.apm.3 n.asm v.aas.1p r.dp.2 p.a d.asn f.pm r.ap.1 adv cj cj

[a] [καὶ] UBS.
[b] [ἡμῶν] UBS, omitted by TNIV.

NASB

Lord will spread
rapidly and be
glorified, just as *it*
did also with you;
2and that we will be
rescued from per-
verse and evil men;
for not all have
faith. 3But the Lord
is faithful, and He
will strengthen and
protect you from
the evil *one.* 4We
have confidence in
the Lord concern-
ing you, that you
are doing and will
continue to do
what we command.
5May the Lord
direct your hearts
into the love of
God and into the
steadfastness of
Christ.
6Now we com-
mand you, breth-
ren, in the name
of our Lord Jesus
Christ, that you
keep away from
every brother who
leads an unruly life
and not according
to the tradition
which you received
from us. 7For you
yourselves know
how you ought
to follow our
example, because
we did not act in
an undisciplined
manner among
you, 8nor did we
eat anyone's bread
without paying for
it, but with labor
and hardship we
kept working night
and day so that we
would not be a bur-
den to any of you;
9not because we do
not have the right
to this, but in order
to offer ourselves
as a model for you,
so that you would
follow our exam-
ple. 10For even

NIV

we were with you,
we gave you this
rule: "The one who
is unwilling to
work shall not eat."
11 We hear that
some among you
are idle and dis-
ruptive. They are
not busy; they
are busybodies.
12 Such people we
command and
urge in the Lord
Jesus Christ to
settle down and
earn the food they
eat. 13 And as for
you, brothers and
sisters, never tire
of doing what is
good.
14 Take special
note of anyone
who does not obey
our instruction
in this letter. Do
not associate with
them, in order
that they may feel
ashamed. 15 Yet do
not regard them
as an enemy, but
warn them as you
would a fellow be-
liever.

Final Greetings

16 Now may the
Lord of peace him-
self give you peace
at all times and in
every way. The
Lord be with all
of you.
17 I, Paul, write
this greeting in my
own hand, which
is the distinguish-
ing mark in all my
letters. This is how
I write.
18 The grace of
our Lord Jesus
Christ be with
you all.

ἦμεν πρὸς ὑμᾶς, ↱ ↱ τοῦτο παρηγγέλλομεν ὑμῖν, ὅτι εἴ τις ↱ οὐ
we were with you, we gave you this charge: *you* ~ "If anyone is not
1639 4639 7007 4133 4133 7007 4047 4133 7007 4022 1623 5516 2527 4024
v.iai.1p p.a r.ap.2 r.asn v.iai.1p r.dp.2 cj cj r.nsm pl

θέλει ἐργάζεσθαι → ↱ ↱ μηδὲ ἐσθιέτω. 11 ἀκούομεν γάρ τινας
willing to work, then he should not eat." For we hear *For* that some among
2527 2237 2266 2266 3593 2266 1142 201 1142 5516 1877
v.pai.3s f.pm cj v.pam.3s v.pai.1p cj r.apm

περιπατοῦντας ἐν ὑμῖν ἀτάκτως ↱ μηδὲν ἐργαζομένους
you are conducting themselves *among you* ⌊in a disorderly manner,⌋ doing nothing themselves,
7007 4344 1877 7007 865 2237 3594 2237
pt.pa.apm p.d r.dp.2 adv a.asn pt.pm.apm

ἀλλὰ περιεργαζομένους· 12 τοῖς δὲ τοιούτοις παραγγέλλομεν καὶ
but ⌊meddling in the affairs of others.⌋ *{the}* *{and}* Such people we charge and
247 4318 3836 1254 5525 4133 2779
cj pt.pm.apm d.dpm cj r.dpm v.pai.1p cj

παρακαλοῦμεν ἐν κυρίῳ Ἰησοῦ Χριστῷ, ἵνα ⌊μετὰ ἡσυχίας⌋
exhort in the Lord Jesus Christ that they work quietly
4151 1877 3261 2652 5986 2671 2237 2237 3552 2484
v.pai.1p p.d n.dsm n.dsm n.dsm cj p.g n.gsf

ἐργαζόμενοι τὸν ἑαυτῶν ἄρτον ἐσθίωσιν. 13 ὑμεῖς δέ, ἀδελφοί, ↱ μὴ
they work and eat *{the}* their own food. *eat* But you, *But* brothers, must not
2237 2266 3836 1571 788 2266 1254 7007 1254 81 1591 3590
pt.pm.npm d.asm r.gpm.3 n.asm v.pas.3p r.np.2 cj n.vpm pl

ἐγκακήσητε καλοποιοῦντες. 14 εἰ δέ τις ↱ οὐχ ὑπακούει τῷ
become discouraged in doing what is right. Now if *Now* anyone does not obey what
1591 2818 1254 1623 1254 5516 5634 4024 5634 3836
v.aas.2p pt.pa.npm cj cj r.nsm pl v.pai.3s d.dsm

λόγῳ ἡμῶν διὰ τῆς ἐπιστολῆς, τοῦτον σημειοῦσθε ↱ μὴ
we say *we* in *{the}* this letter, *this* take note of that person and do not
7005 3364 7005 1328 3836 4047 2186 4047 4957 5264 3590
n.dsm r.gp.1 p.g d.gsf n.gsf r.asm v.pmm.2p pl

συναναμίγνυσθαι αὐτῷ, ἵνα ἐντραπῇ· 15 καὶ μὴ ὡς
associate with him, so that ⌊he will feel ashamed.⌋ *{and}* Do not regard him as an
5264 899 2671 1956 2779 2451 3590 2451 6055
f.pm r.dsm.3 cj v.aps.3s cj pl pl

ἐχθρὸν ἡγεῖσθε, ἀλλὰ νουθετεῖτε ὡς ἀδελφόν. 16 αὐτὸς δὲ ↱ ὁ κύριος
enemy, *Do regard* but admonish him as a brother. *himself* Now may the Lord
2398 2451 247 3805 6055 81 899 1254 1443 3836 3261
a.asm v.pmm.2p cj v.pam.2p pl n.asm r.nsm cj d.nsm n.nsm

τῆς εἰρήνης δῴη ὑμῖν τὴν εἰρήνην ⌊διὰ παντὸς⌋ ἐν παντὶ τρόπῳ. ὁ
of peace himself give you *{the}* peace always in every circumstance. The
3836 1645 899 1443 7007 3836 1645 1328 4246 1877 4246 5573 3836
d.gsf n.gsf v.aao.3s r.dp.2 d.asf n.asf p.g a.gsm p.d a.dsm n.dsm d.nsm

κύριος μετὰ πάντων ὑμῶν. 17 ὁ ἀσπασμὸς τῇ ἐμῇ χειρὶ Παύλου,
Lord be with you all. *you* The greeting is with ⌊my own⌋ hand — Paul's
3261 3552 7007 4246 7007 3836 833 3836 1847 5931 4263
n.nsm p.g a.gpm r.gp.2 d.nsm n.nsm d.dsf r.dsf.1 n.dsf n.gsm

ὅ ἐστιν σημεῖον ἐν πάσῃ ἐπιστολῇ· οὕτως γράφω. 18 ἡ χάρις
— which is a mark of genuineness in every letter; so I write. The grace
4005 1639 4956 1877 4246 2186 4048 1211 3836 5921
r.nsn v.pai.3s n.nsn p.d a.dsf n.dsf adv v.pai.1s d.nsf n.nsf

τοῦ κυρίου ἡμῶν Ἰησοῦ Χριστοῦ μετὰ πάντων ὑμῶν.[a]
of our Lord *our* Jesus Christ be with you all. *you*
3836 7005 3261 7005 2652 5986 3552 7007 4246 7007
d.gsm n.gsm r.gp.1 n.gsm n.gsm p.g a.gpm r.gp.2

NASB

when we were
with you, we used
to give you this
order: if anyone
is not willing to
work, then he is
not to eat, either.
11 For we hear that
some among you
are leading an
undisciplined life,
doing no work at
all, but acting like
busybodies. 12 Now
such persons we
command and
exhort in the Lord
Jesus Christ to
work in quiet fash-
ion and eat their
own bread. 13 But as
for you, brethren,
do not grow weary
of doing good.
14 If anyone does
not obey our in-
struction in this
letter, take special
note of that person
and do not associ-
ate with him, so
that he will be put
to shame. 15 *Yet* do
not regard him
as an enemy, but
admonish him as a
brother.
16 Now may the
Lord of peace
Himself continual-
ly grant you peace
in every circum-
stance. The Lord
be with you all!
17 I, Paul, write this
greeting with my
own hand, and this
is a distinguishing
mark in every let-
ter; this is the way
I write. 18 The grace
of our Lord Jesus
Christ be with you
all.

[a] ἀμήν. πρὸς Θεσσαλονικεῖς δευτέρα ἐγράφη ἀπὸ Ἀθηνῶν included by TR after ὑμῶν.

1 Timothy

NIV

1 Paul, an apos-
tle of Christ
Jesus by the com-
mand of God our
Savior and of
Christ Jesus our
hope,
2 To Timothy my
true son in the
faith:

Grace, mercy
and peace from
God the Father and
Christ Jesus our
Lord.

Timothy Charged to Oppose False Teachers

3 As I urged you
when I went into
Macedonia, stay
there in Ephesus
so that you may
command certain
people not to teach
false doctrines
any longer 4 or to
devote themselves
to myths and end-
less genealogies.
Such things pro-
mote controversial
speculations rather
than advancing
God's work—
which is by faith.
5 The goal of this
command is love,
which comes from
a pure heart and a
good conscience
and a sincere faith.
6 Some have de-
parted from these
and have turned to
meaningless talk.
7 They want to be
teachers of the law,
but they do not
know what they
are talking about
or what they so
confidently affirm.
8 We know that
the law is good if
one uses it proper-
ly. 9 We also know
that the law is

1:1 Παῦλος ἀπόστολος Χριστοῦ Ἰησοῦ κατ' ἐπιταγὴν θεοῦ
Paul, an apostle of Christ Jesus ⌞because of⌟ the command ⌞from God⌟ our
4263 693 5986 2652 2848 2198 2536 7005
n.nsm n.nsm n.gsm n.gsm p.a n.asf n.gsm

σωτῆρος ἡμῶν καὶ Χριστοῦ Ἰησοῦ τῆς ἐλπίδος ἡμῶν 2 Τιμοθέῳ γνησίῳ
Savior *our* and Christ Jesus our *{the}* hope, *our* to Timothy, my true
5400 7005 2779 5986 2652 7005 3836 1828 7005 5510 1188
n.gsm r.gp.1 cj n.gsm n.gsm d.gsf n.gsf r.gp.1 n.dsm a.dsn

τέκνῳ ⌞ἐν πίστει,⌟ χάρις ἔλεος εἰρήνη ἀπὸ θεοῦ πατρὸς καὶ Χριστοῦ
spiritual son: *spiritual* Grace, mercy, peace from God the Father and Christ
1877 5451 1877 4411 5921 1799 1645 608 2536 4252 2779 5986
n.dsn p.d n.dsf n.nsf n.nsn n.nsf p.g n.gsm n.gsm cj n.gsm

Ἰησοῦ τοῦ κυρίου ἡμῶν. 3 καθὼς παρεκάλεσά σε προσμεῖναι ἐν Ἐφέσῳ
Jesus our *{the}* Lord. *our* Just as I urged you to stay on in Ephesus
2652 7005 3836 3261 7005 2777 4151 5148 4693 1877 2387
n.gsm d.gsm n.gsm r.gp.1 cj v.aai.1s r.as.2 f.aa p.d n.dsf

πορευόμενος εἰς Μακεδονίαν, ἵνα παραγγείλῃς τισὶν μὴ
while I was traveling to Macedonia, so that you might command ⌞certain people⌟ not
4513 1650 3423 2671 4133 5516 3590
pt.pm.nsm p.a n.asf cj v.aas.2s r.dpm pl

ἑτεροδιδασκαλεῖν 4 μηδὲ προσέχειν → μύθοις καὶ
⌞to continue teaching any different doctrine⌟ or to devote themselves to endless myths and
2281 3593 4668 596 3680 2779
f.pa cj f.pa n.dpm cj

γενεαλογίαις ἀπεράντοις, αἵτινες ἐκζητήσεις παρέχουσιν μᾶλλον ἢ
genealogies, *endless* which produce speculations *produce* rather than the
1157 596 4015 4218 1700 4218 3437 2445
n.dpf a.dpf r.npf n.apf v.pai.3p adv.c pl

οἰκονομίαν θεοῦ τὴν ἐν πίστει. 5 τὸ δὲ τέλος τῆς παραγγελίας
stewardship ⌞from God⌟ which is by faith. But the *But* goal of this command
3873 2536 3836 1877 4411 1254 3836 1254 5465 3836 4132
n.asf n.gsm d.asf p.d n.dsf d.nsn cj n.nsn d.gsf n.gsf

ἐστὶν ἀγάπη ἐκ καθαρᾶς καρδίας καὶ συνειδήσεως ἀγαθῆς καὶ
is love from a clean heart and a clear conscience *clear* and a sincere
1639 27 1666 2754 2840 2779 19 5287 19 2779 537
v.pai.3s n.nsf p.g a.gsf n.gsf cj n.gsf a.gsf cj

πίστεως ἀνυποκρίτου, 6 ὧν τινες ἀστοχήσαντες
faith. *sincere* *of these things* Some, having fallen short of these things,
4411 537 4005 5516 846 4005 4005 4005
n.gsf a.gsf r.gpf r.npm pt.aa.npm

ἐξετράπησαν εἰς ματαιολογίαν 7 θέλοντες εἶναι νομοδιδάσκαλοι, ↱ ↱
⌞have wandered away⌟ into senseless babble, wishing to be teachers of the law even though
1762 1650 3467 2527 1639 3791 3783 3783
v.api.3p p.a n.asf pt.pa.npm f.pa n.npm

↱ ↱ μὴ νοοῦντες μήτε ἃ λέγουσιν μήτε περὶ τίνων
they do not understand either what they are saying or concerning what things
3783 3783 3590 3783 3612 4005 3306 3612 4309 5515
pl pt.pa.npm cj r.apn v.pai.3p cj p.g r.gpn

διαβεβαιοῦνται. 8 οἴδαμεν δὲ ὅτι καλὸς ὁ νόμος, ἐάν
⌞they are so dogmatically asserting.⌟ Now we know *Now* that *good* the law is good if
1331 1254 3857 1254 4022 2819 3836 3795 2819 1569
v.pmi.3p v.rai.1p cj cj a.nsm d.nsm n.nsm cj

τις αὐτῷ νομίμως χρῆται, 9 εἰδὼς τοῦτο, ὅτι δικαίῳ νόμος ↱
someone uses it lawfully, *uses* knowing this, that *for righteous person* law is
5516 5968 899 3789 5968 3857 4047 4022 1465 3795 3023
r.nsm r.dsm.3 adv v.pms.3s pt.ra.nsm r.asn cj a.dsm n.nsm

NASB

Misleadings in Doctrine and Living

1:1 Paul, an apostle
of Christ Jesus ac-
cording to the com-
mandment of God
our Savior, and of
Christ Jesus, *who*
is our hope,
2 To Timothy, *my*
true child in *the*
faith: Grace, mercy
and peace from
God the Father and
Christ Jesus our
Lord.
3 As I urged you
upon my departure
for Macedonia, re-
main on at Ephesus
so that you may in-
struct certain men
not to teach strange
doctrines, 4 nor to
pay attention to
myths and endless
genealogies, which
give rise to mere
speculation rather
than *furthering* the
administration of
God which is by
faith. 5 But the goal
of our instruction
is love from a pure
heart and a good
conscience and a
sincere faith. 6 For
some men, straying
from these things,
have turned aside
to fruitless discus-
sion, 7 wanting to
be teachers of the
Law, even though
they do not under-
stand either what
they are saying or
the matters about
which they make
confident asser-
tions.
8 But we know that
the Law is good,
if one uses it law-
fully, 9 realizing the
fact that law is

NIV

made not for the
righteous but for
lawbreakers and
rebels, the ungod-
ly and sinful, the
unholy and irre-
ligious, for those
who kill their
fathers or moth-
ers, for murderers,
10 for the sexually
immoral, for those
practicing homo-
sexuality, for slave
traders and liars
and perjurers—
and for whatever
else is contrary to
the sound doctrine
11 that conforms to
the gospel concern-
ing the glory of the
blessed God, which
he entrusted to me.

The Lord's Grace to Paul

12 I thank Christ
Jesus our Lord,
who has given
me strength, that
he considered me
trustworthy, ap-
pointing me to his
service. 13 Even
though I was once
a blasphemer and
a persecutor and
a violent man, I
was shown mercy
because I acted in
ignorance and un-
belief. 14 The grace
of our Lord was
poured out on me
abundantly, along
with the faith and
love that are in
Christ Jesus.
15 Here is a trust-
worthy saying
that deserves
full acceptance:
Christ Jesus came
into the world to
save sinners—of
whom I am the
worst. 16 But for
that very reason I
was shown mercy
so that in me, the
worst of sinners,
Christ Jesus might
display his im-
mense patience
as an example for
those

οὐ κεῖται, ἀνόμοις δὲ καὶ ἀνυποτάκτοις, ἀσεβέσι καὶ
not valid for a righteous person but for the lawless *but* and rebellious, irreligious and
4024 3023 1465 1465 1465 1254 491 1254 2779 538 815 2779
pl v.pmi.3s a.dpm cj cj a.dpm a.dpm cj

ἁμαρτωλοῖς, ἀνοσίοις καὶ βεβήλοις, πατρολῴαις καὶ μητρολῴαις,
sinners, unholy and profane, ⌞those who beat their fathers⌟ and mothers,
283 495 2779 1013 4260 2779 3618
a.dpm a.dpm cj a.dpm n.dpm cj n.dpm

ἀνδροφόνοις 10 πόρνοις ἀρσενοκοίταις ἀνδραποδισταῖς ψεύσταις
murderers, fornicators, ⌞men who practice homosexuality,⌟ kidnappers, liars,
439 4521 780 435 6026
n.dpm n.dpm n.dpm n.dpm n.dpm

ἐπιόρκοις, καὶ ⌞εἴ τι⌟ ἕτερον τῇ ὑγιαινούσῃ διδασκαλίᾳ
perjurers, and everything else that is contrary to healthy teaching,
2156 2779 1623 5516 2283 3836 512 512 512 5617 1436
n.dpm cj cj r.nsn r.nsn d.dsf pt.pa.dsf n.dsf

ἀντίκειται 11 κατὰ τὸ εὐαγγέλιον τῆς δόξης τοῦ μακαρίου θεοῦ,
is contrary to ⌞in conformity to⌟ the gospel of the glory of the blessed God
512 2848 3836 2295 3836 1518 3836 3421 2536
v.pmi.3s p.a d.asn n.asn d.gsf n.gsf d.gsm a.gsm n.gsm

ὃ ἐπιστεύθην ἐγώ. 12 χάριν ἔχω τῷ
⌞with which⌟ I was entrusted. *I* I continually thank *I continually* him who
4005 1609 4409 1609 2400 2400 5921 2400 3836
r.asn v.api.1s r.ns.1 n.asf v.pai.1s d.dsm

ἐνδυναμώσαντί με Χριστῷ Ἰησοῦ τῷ κυρίῳ ἡμῶν, ὅτι
strengthened me, Christ Jesus *{the}* our Lord, *our* since he considered that even
1904 1609 5986 2652 3836 7005 3261 7005 4022 2451 2451
pt.aa.dsm r.as.1 n.dsm n.dsm d.dsm n.dsm r.gp.1 cj

πιστόν με ἡγήσατο θέμενος εἰς διακονίαν
I would be faithful, *I* *he considered* ⌞as evidenced by his appointing⌟ me to service,
1609 4412 1609 2451 5502 1650 1355
a.asm r.as.1 v.ami.3s pt.am.nsm p.a n.asf

13 ↱ ↱ τὸ πρότερον ὄντα βλάσφημον καὶ διώκτην καὶ ὑβριστήν,
even though *{the}* formerly I was a blasphemer, *{and}* persecutor, and an insolent person.
1639 1639 3836 4728 1639 1061 2779 1502 2779 5616
d.asn adv.c pt.pa.asm a.asm cj n.asm cj n.asm

ἀλλὰ ἠλεήθην, ὅτι ἀγνοῶν ἐποίησα ἐν ἀπιστίᾳ·
But ⌞I was shown mercy⌟ since, being ignorant, I had acted in unbelief;
247 1796 4022 51 4472 1877 602
cj v.api.1s cj pt.pa.nsm v.aai.1s p.d n.dsf

14 ὑπερεπλεόνασεν δὲ ἡ χάρις τοῦ κυρίου ἡμῶν
completely overflowed and the grace of our Lord *our* completely overflowed for me
5670 1254 3836 5921 3836 7005 3261 7005 5670 5670
v.aai.3s cj d.nsf n.nsf d.gsm n.gsm r.gp.1

μετὰ πίστεως καὶ ἀγάπης τῆς ἐν Χριστῷ Ἰησοῦ. 15 πιστὸς ὁ λόγος καὶ
with faith and love that are in Christ Jesus. Trustworthy is the saying and
3552 4411 2779 27 3836 1877 5986 2652 4412 3836 3364 2779
p.g n.gsf cj n.gsf d.gsf p.d n.dsm n.dsm a.nsm d.nsm n.nsm cj

πάσης ἀποδοχῆς ἄξιος, ὅτι Χριστὸς Ἰησοῦς ἦλθεν εἰς τὸν κόσμον
worthy of complete acceptance: *worthy* ~ "Christ Jesus came into the world in
545 4246 628 545 4022 5986 2652 2262 1650 3836 3180 5392
a.gsf n.gsf a.nsm cj n.nsm n.nsm v.aai.3s p.a d.asm n.asm

ἁμαρτωλοὺς σῶσαι, ὧν πρῶτός εἰμι ἐγώ.
order to save sinners," *in order to save* of whom I am the foremost. *am* *I*
5392 5392 5392 283 5392 4005 1609 1639 4755 1639 1609
a.apm f.aa r.gpm a.nsm v.pai.1s r.ns.1

16 ἀλλὰ διὰ τοῦτο ἠλεήθην, ἵνα ἐν ἐμοὶ πρώτῳ
But for this reason ⌞I was shown mercy:⌟ so that in me as foremost Christ Jesus
247 1328 4047 1796 2671 1877 1609 4755 5986 2652
cj p.a r.asn v.api.1s cj p.d r.ds.1 a.dsm

ἐνδείξηται Χριστὸς Ἰησοῦς τὴν ἅπασαν μακροθυμίαν πρὸς ὑποτύπωσιν τῶν
might display *Christ* *Jesus* his complete patience as an illustration for those
1892 5986 2652 3836 570 3429 4639 5721 3836
v.ams.3s n.nsm n.nsm d.asf a.asf n.asf p.a n.asf d.gpm

NASB

not made for a
righteous person,
but for those who
are lawless and
rebellious, for the
ungodly and sin-
ners, for the unholy
and profane, for
those who kill their
fathers or mothers,
for murderers 10 and
immoral men and
homosexuals and
kidnappers and
liars and perjurers,
and whatever
else is contrary to
sound teaching,
11 according to the
glorious gospel of
the blessed God,
with which I have
been entrusted.
12 I thank Christ
Jesus our Lord,
who has strength-
ened me, because
He considered me
faithful, putting
me into service,
13 even though I
was formerly a
blasphemer and a
persecutor and a
violent aggressor.
Yet I was shown
mercy because I
acted ignorantly in
unbelief; 14 and the
grace of our Lord
was more than
abundant, with
the faith and love
which are *found* in
Christ Jesus. 15 It is
a trustworthy state-
ment, deserving
full acceptance,
that Christ Jesus
came into the
world to save sin-
ners, among whom
I am foremost *of
all.* 16 Yet for this
reason I found
mercy, so that in
me as the foremost,
Jesus Christ might
demonstrate His
perfect patience as
an example for

NIV

who would believe in him and receive eternal life. [17]Now to the King eternal, immortal, invisible, the only God, be honor and glory for ever and ever. Amen.

The Charge to Timothy Renewed

[18]Timothy, my son, I am giving you this command in keeping with the prophecies once made about you, so that by recalling them you may fight the battle well, [19]holding on to faith and a good conscience, which some have rejected and so have suffered shipwreck with regard to the faith. [20]Among them are Hymenaeus and Alexander, whom I have handed over to Satan to be taught not to blaspheme.

Instructions on Worship

2 I urge, then, first of all, that petitions, prayers, intercession and thanksgiving be made for all people— [2]for kings and all those in authority, that we may live peaceful and quiet lives in all godliness and holiness. [3]This is good, and pleases God our Savior, [4]who wants all people to be saved and to come to a knowledge of the truth. [5]For there is one God and one mediator between God

---

μελλόντων πιστεύειν ἐπ' αὐτῷ εἰς ζωὴν αἰώνιον. [17] τῷ δὲ βασιλεῖ
who were to believe in him for eternal life. *eternal* Now ⌞to the⌟ *Now* king
3516 4409 2093 899 1650 173 2437 173 1254 3836 1254 995
pt.pa.gpm f.pa p.d r.dsm.3 p.a n.asf a.asf d.dsm cj n.dsm

τῶν αἰώνων, ἀφθάρτῳ ἀοράτῳ μόνῳ θεῷ, τιμὴ καὶ δόξα εἰς τοὺς ⌞αἰῶνας
of ages, incorruptible, invisible, the only God, be honor and glory for all time.
3836 172 915 548 3668 2536 5507 2779 1518 1650 3836 172
d.gpm n.gpm a.dsm a.dsm a.dsm n.dsm n.nsf cj n.nsf p.a d.apm n.apm

τῶν αἰώνων, ἀμήν. [18] ταύτην τὴν παραγγελίαν παρατίθεμαί σοι, τέκνον Τιμόθεε,
{ages} Amen. This command I am entrusting to you, child Timothy,
3836 172 297 4047 3836 4132 4192 5148 5451 5510
d.gpm n.gpm pl r.asf d.asf n.asf v.pmi.1s r.ds.2 n.vsn n.vsm

κατὰ τὰς προαγούσας ἐπὶ σὲ προφητείας, ἵνα
in accordance with the prophecies previously made about you, *prophecies* so that by them
2848 3836 4735 4575 2093 5148 4735 2671 1877 899
p.a d.apf pt.pa.apf p.a r.as.2 n.apf cj

στρατεύῃ ἐν αὐταῖς τὴν καλὴν στρατείαν [19] ἔχων πίστιν καὶ ἀγαθὴν
you might fight *by* *them* the good fight, holding on to faith and a good
5129 1877 899 3836 2819 5127 2400 4411 2779 19
v.pms.2s p.d r.dpf.3 d.asf a.asf n.asf pt.pa.nsm n.asf cj a.asf

συνείδησιν, ἥν τινες ἀπωσάμενοι
conscience. *{which}* By rejecting their faith and good conscience, some *By rejecting* have
5287 4005 723 723 5516 723 3728
n.asf r.asf r.npm pt.am.npm

περὶ τὴν πίστιν ἐναυάγησαν, [20] ὧν ἐστιν Ὑμέναιος καὶ
shipwrecked *{in regard to}* the faith, *have shipwrecked* among whom are Hymenaeus and
3728 4309 3836 4411 3728 4005 1639 5628 2779
p.a d.asf n.asf v.aai.3p r.gpm v.pai.3s n.nsm cj

Ἀλέξανδρος, οὓς παρέδωκα τῷ σατανᾷ, ἵνα
Alexander, whom I have delivered over to Satan so that
235 4005 4140 3836 4928 2671
n.nsm r.apm v.aai.1s d.dsm n.dsm cj

παιδευθῶσιν μὴ βλασφημεῖν.
they might be taught through punishment not to blaspheme.
4084 3590 1059
v.aps.3p pl f.pa

2:1 παρακαλῶ οὖν πρῶτον πάντων ποιεῖσθαι δεήσεις προσευχάς
I urge *then* First of all, then, I urge you to make requests, prayers,
4151 4036 4754 4246 4036 4151 4151 4472 1255 4666
v.pai.1s cj adv a.gpn f.pp n.apf n.apf

ἐντεύξεις εὐχαριστίας ὑπὲρ πάντων ἀνθρώπων, [2] ὑπὲρ
petitions, and expressions of thanksgiving on behalf of all people — on behalf of
1950 2374 5642 4246 476 5642
n.apf n.apf p.g a.gpm n.gpm p.g

βασιλέων καὶ πάντων τῶν ἐν ὑπεροχῇ ὄντων, ἵνα
kings and all who are in positions of authority *are* — so that we might live
995 2779 4246 3836 1639 1877 5667 1639 2671 1341 1341 1341
n.gpm cj a.gpm d.gpm p.d n.dsf pt.pa.gpm cj

ἤρεμον καὶ ἡσύχιον βίον διάγωμεν ἐν πάσῃ εὐσεβείᾳ καὶ
out our lives in tranquility and calmness *lives* *we might live out* with complete reverence and
1341 1050 2475 2779 2485 1050 1341 1877 4246 2354 2779
a.asm cj a.asm n.asm v.pas.1p p.d a.dsf n.dsf cj

σεμνότητι. [3] τοῦτο καλὸν καὶ ἀπόδεκτον ἐνώπιον τοῦ σωτῆρος ἡμῶν
godly dignity. This is good and pleasing in the sight of God our Savior, *our*
4949 4047 2819 2779 621 1967 3836 2536 7005 5400 7005
n.dsf r.nsn a.nsn cj a.nsn p.g d.gsm n.gsm r.gp.1

θεοῦ, [4] ὃς πάντας ἀνθρώπους θέλει σωθῆναι καὶ εἰς ἐπίγνωσιν
God who wishes all people *wishes* to be saved and to come into a knowledge
2536 4005 2527 4246 476 2527 5392 2779 2262 2262 1650 2106
n.gsm r.nsm a.apm n.apm v.pai.3s f.ap cj p.a n.asf

→ ἀληθείας ἐλθεῖν. [5] εἷς γὰρ θεός, εἷς καὶ μεσίτης → θεοῦ
of the truth. *to come* For there is one *For* God, and one *and* mediator between God
237 2262 1142 1651 1142 2536 2779 1651 2779 3542 2536
n.gsf f.aa a.nsm cj n.nsm a.nsm cj n.nsm n.gsm

NASB

those who would believe in Him for eternal life. [17]Now to the King eternal, immortal, invisible, the only God, *be* honor and glory forever and ever. Amen.

[18]This command I entrust to you, Timothy, *my* son, in accordance with the prophecies previously made concerning you, that by them you fight the good fight, [19]keeping faith and a good conscience, which some have rejected and suffered shipwreck in regard to their faith. [20]Among these are Hymenaeus and Alexander, whom I have handed over to Satan, so that they will be taught not to blaspheme.

A Call to Prayer

[2:1]First of all, then, I urge that entreaties *and* prayers, petitions *and* thanksgivings, be made on behalf of all men, [2]for kings and all who are in authority, so that we may lead a tranquil and quiet life in all godliness and dignity. [3]This is good and acceptable in the sight of God our Savior, [4]who desires all men to be saved and to come to the knowledge of the truth. [5]For there is one God, *and* one mediator also between God and

NIV

and mankind, the
man Christ Jesus,
6who gave himself
as a ransom for
all people. This
has now been wit-
nessed to at the
proper time. 7And
for this purpose I
was appointed a
herald and an apos-
tle—I am telling
the truth, I am not
lying—and a true
and faithful teacher
of the Gentiles.
8Therefore I want
the men every-
where to pray, lift-
ing up holy hands
without anger or
disputing. 9I also
want the women
to dress modestly,
with decency and
propriety, adorn-
ing themselves,
not with elaborate
hairstyles or gold
or pearls or ex-
pensive clothes,
10but with good
deeds, appropriate
for women who
profess to worship
God.
11A woman[a]
should learn in
quietness and full
submission. 12I
do not permit a
woman to teach or
to assume author-
ity over a man;[b]
she must be quiet.
13For Adam was
formed first, then
Eve. 14And Adam
was not the one
deceived; it was
the woman who
was deceived and
became a sinner.
15But women[c] will
be saved through
childbearing—if
they continue in
faith, love and
holiness with pro-
priety.

[a] 11 Or *wife*; also in verse 12
[b] 12 Or *over her husband*
[c] 15 Greek *she*

καὶ ἀνθρώπων, ἄνθρωπος Χριστὸς Ἰησοῦς, 6 ὁ δοὺς ἑαυτὸν → ἀντίλυτρον
and people; a person, Christ Jesus, who gave himself as a ransom
2779 476 476 5986 2652 3836 1443 1571 519
cj n.gpm n.nsm n.nsm n.nsm d.nsm pt.aa.nsm r.asm.3 n.asn

ὑπὲρ πάντων, τὸ μαρτύριον → καιροῖς ἰδίοις. 7 εἰς ὃ
for all, the witness at the proper time. *proper* It is with reference to this
5642 4246 3836 3457 2625 2789 2625 1650 4005
p.g a.gpm d.nsn n.nsn n.dpm a.dpm p.a r.asn

ἐτέθην ἐγὼ κῆρυξ καὶ ἀπόστολος, ἀλήθειαν
witness that I was appointed *I* a herald and apostle — I am speaking the truth;
1609 5502 1609 3061 2779 693 3306 3306 3306 237
v.api.1s r.ns.1 n.nsm cj n.nsm n.asf

λέγω ↱ ↱ οὐ ψεύδομαι, διδάσκαλος → ἐθνῶν ἐν πίστει καὶ
I am speaking I am not lying — a teacher of the Gentiles in faith and
3306 6017 6017 4024 6017 1437 1620 1877 4411 2779
v.pai.1s pl v.pmi.1s n.nsm n.gpn p.d n.dsf cj

ἀληθείᾳ. 8 βούλομαι οὖν προσεύχεσθαι τοὺς ἄνδρας ἐν παντὶ τόπῳ
truth. I desire, then, that the men should pray *the men* in every place
237 1089 4036 3836 467 4667 3836 467 1877 4246 5536
n.dsf v.pmi.1s cj f.pm d.apm n.apm p.d a.dsm n.dsm

ἐπαίροντας ὁσίους χεῖρας χωρὶς ὀργῆς καὶ διαλογισμοῦ. 9 ὡσαύτως καὶ[a]
by lifting up holy hands, without anger and arguing. Likewise, I also desire that
2048 4008 5931 6006 3973 2779 1369 6058 2779
pt.pa.apm a.apf n.apf p.g n.gsf cj n.gsm adv adv

γυναῖκας ἐν καταστολῇ κοσμίῳ μετὰ αἰδοῦς
the women should adorn themselves in respectable attire, *respectable* with modesty
1222 3175 3175 1571 1877 3177 2950 3177 3552 133
n.apf p.d n.dsf a.dsf p.g n.gsf

καὶ σωφροσύνης κοσμεῖν ἑαυτάς, μὴ ἐν πλέγμασιν καὶ χρυσίῳ ἢ μαργαρίταις
and moderation, *should adorn themselves* not with braided hair and gold or pearls
2779 5408 3175 1571 3590 1877 4427 2779 5992 2445 3449
cj n.gsf f.pa r.apf.3 pl p.d n.dpn cj n.dsn cj n.dpm

ἢ ἱματισμῷ πολυτελεῖ, 10 ἀλλ᾽ ὃ πρέπει γυναιξὶν
or costly clothing, *costly* but with what is appropriate for women
2445 4500 2669 4500 247 4005 4560 1222
cj n.dsm a.dsm cj r.nsn v.pai.3s n.dpf

ἐπαγγελλομέναις θεοσέβειαν, δι᾽ ἔργων ἀγαθῶν. 11 γυνὴ
who are committed to godliness, namely, with good deeds. *good* A woman should learn
2040 2537 1328 19 2240 19 1222 3443 3443
pt.pm.dpf n.asf p.g n.gpn a.gpn n.nsf

ἐν ἡσυχίᾳ μανθανέτω ἐν πάσῃ ὑποταγῇ· 12 διδάσκειν δὲ
in quietness, *should learn* in all submissiveness; *to teach* but I do not permit
1877 2484 3443 1877 4246 5717 1438 1254 2205 2205 4024 2205
p.d n.dsf v.pam.3s p.d a.dsf n.dsf f.pa cj

γυναικὶ οὐκ ἐπιτρέπω οὐδὲ αὐθεντεῖν → ἀνδρός, ἀλλ᾽
a women *not I do permit* to teach or to exercise authority over a man; rather, she is
1222 4024 2205 1438 1438 4028 883 467 247
n.dsf pl v.pai.1s cj f.pa n.gsm cj

εἶναι ἐν ἡσυχίᾳ. 13 Ἀδὰμ γὰρ πρῶτος ἐπλάσθη, εἶτα Εὕα. 14 καὶ
to be in quietness. For Adam *For* was created first, *was created* then Eve. And
1639 1877 2484 1142 77 1142 4421 4421 4755 4421 1663 2293 2779
f.pa p.d n.dsf n.nsm cj a.nsm v.api.3s adv n.nsf cj

Ἀδὰμ οὐκ ἠπατήθη, ἡ δὲ γυνὴ ἐξαπατηθεῖσα ἐν
Adam was not deceived, but the *but* woman, having been deceived, has come into
77 4024 572 1254 3836 1254 1222 1987 1181 1181 1877
n.nsm pl v.api.3s d.nsf cj n.nsf pt.ap.nsf p.d

παραβάσει γέγονεν· 15 σωθήσεται δὲ διὰ τῆς τεκνογονίας, ἐὰν μείνωσιν
transgression; *has come* but she will be saved *but* through childbearing, if they remain
4126 1181 1254 5392 1254 1328 3836 5450 1569 3531
n.dsf v.rai.3s v.fpi.3s cj p.g d.gsf n.gsf cj v.aas.3p

ἐν πίστει καὶ ἀγάπῃ καὶ ἁγιασμῷ μετὰ σωφροσύνης.
in faith and love and holiness, with modesty.
1877 4411 2779 27 2779 40 3552 5408
p.d n.dsf cj n.dsf cj n.dsm p.g n.gsf

[a] [καὶ] UBS, omitted by NET.

NASB

men, *the* man
Christ Jesus, 6who
gave Himself as a
ransom for all, the
testimony *given*
at the proper time.
7For this I was ap-
pointed a preacher
and an apostle (I
am telling the truth,
I am not lying) as
a teacher of the
Gentiles in faith
and truth.
8Therefore I want
the men in every
place to pray, lift-
ing up holy hands,
without wrath and
dissension.

Women Instructed

9Likewise, *I want*
women to adorn
themselves with
proper clothing,
modestly and dis-
creetly, not with
braided hair and
gold or pearls or
costly garments,
10but rather by
means of good
works, as is proper
for women making
a claim to godli-
ness. 11A woman
must quietly re-
ceive instruction
with entire submis-
siveness. 12But I do
not allow a woman
to teach or exercise
authority over a
man, but to remain
quiet. 13For it was
Adam who was
first created, *and*
then Eve. 14And *it*
was not Adam *who*
was deceived, but
the woman being
deceived, fell into
transgression. 15But
women will be pre-
served through the
bearing of children
if they continue in
faith and love and
sanctity with self-
restraint.

NIV

Qualifications for Overseers and Deacons

3 Here is a trust-
worthy saying:
Whoever aspires to
be an overseer desires
a noble task. 2Now
the overseer is to be
above reproach, faith-
ful to his wife, tem-
perate, self-controlled,
respectable, hospita-
ble, able to teach, 3not
given to drunkenness,
not violent but gentle,
not quarrelsome, not
a lover of money. 4He
must manage his own
family well and see
that his children obey
him, and he must do
so in a manner wor-
thy of full[a] respect.
5(If anyone does not
know how to manage
his own family, how
can he take care of
God's church?) 6He
must not be a recent
convert, or he may
become conceited and
fall under the same
judgment as the devil.
7He must also have
a good reputation
with outsiders, so that
he will not fall into
disgrace and into the
devil's trap.
8In the same way, dea-
cons[b] are to be worthy
of respect, sincere, not
indulging in much
wine, and not pursuing
dishonest gain. 9They
must keep hold of
the deep truths of the
faith with a clear con-
science. 10They must
first be tested; and
then if there is nothing
against them, let them
serve as deacons.
11In the same way,
the women[c] are to be
worthy of respect, not

[a] 4 Or *him with proper*
[b] 8 The word *deacons* refers here to Christians designated to serve with the overseers/elders of the church in a variety of ways; similarly in verse 12; and in Romans 16:1 and Phil. 1:1.
[c] 11 Possibly deacons' wives or women who are deacons

3:1 πιστὸς ὁ λόγος· εἴ τις ἐπισκοπῆς ὀρέγεται,
Trustworthy is the saying. If anyone aspires to the office of overseer, *aspires to* he
4412 3836 3364 1623 5516 3977 3977 2175 3977 2121
a.nsm d.nsm n.nsm cj r.nsm n.gsf v.pmi.3s

καλοῦ ἔργου ἐπιθυμεῖ. 2 δεῖ οὖν τὸν
is desiring a good work. *he is desiring* Therefore, it is necessary *Therefore* for an
2121 2121 2819 2240 2121 4036 1256 4036 3836
a.gsn n.gsn v.pai.3s v.pai.3s cj d.asm

ἐπίσκοπον ἀνεπίλημπτον εἶναι, μιᾶς γυναικὸς ἄνδρα, νηφάλιον
overseer to be above reproach: *to be* a man of one woman, *man* clear-minded,
2176 1639 1639 455 1639 467 1651 1222 467 3767
n.asm a.asm f.pa a.gsf n.gsf n.asm a.asm

σώφρονα κόσμιον φιλόξενον διδακτικόν, 3μὴ πάροινον μὴ πλήκτην,[a]
self-controlled, dignified, hospitable, skilled in teaching, not a drunkard, not violent
5409 3177 5811 1434 3590 4232 3590 4438
a.asm a.asm a.asm a.asm pl n.asm pl n.asm

ἀλλὰ ἐπιεικῆ ἄμαχον ἀφιλάργυρον, 4 τοῦ ἰδίου οἴκου καλῶς
but gracious, not quarrelsome, not a lover of money, managing his own household well,
247 2117 285 921 4613 3836 2625 3875 2822
cj a.asm a.asm a.asm d.gsm a.gsm n.gsm adv

προϊστάμενον, τέκνα ἔχοντα ⌊ἐν ὑποταγῇ,⌋ μετὰ πάσης
managing having submissive children *having* *submissive* with all
4613 2400 1877 5451 2400 1877 5717 3552 4246
pt.pm.asm n.apn pt.pa.asm p.d n.dsf p.g a.gsf

σεμνότητος 5 εἰ δέ τις τοῦ ἰδίου οἴκου
dignity (for if *for* someone does not know how to manage *{the}* his own household,
4949 1254 1623 1254 5516 3857 4024 3857 3857 4613 4613 3836 2625 3875
n.gsf cj cj r.nsm d.gsm a.gsm n.gsm

προστῆναι οὐκ οἶδεν, πῶς ἐκκλησίας θεοῦ
to manage *not* *does know how* how will he care for the church of God?),
4613 4024 3857 4802 2150 2150 2150 2150 1711 2536
f.aa pl v.rai.3s cj n.gsf n.gsm

ἐπιμελήσεται; 6μὴ νεόφυτον, ⌊ἵνα μὴ⌋ τυφωθεὶς εἰς
will he care for not a recent convert, lest ⌊having become conceited,⌋ he fall into the
2150 3590 3745 2671 3590 5605 1860 1860 1650
v.fmi.3s pl a.asm cj pl pt.ap.nsm p.a

κρίμα ἐμπέσῃ τοῦ διαβόλου. 7 → → δεῖ δὲ καὶ
judgment *he fall* of the devil. And it is also necessary *And* *also* for an overseer to
3210 1860 3836 1333 1254 2779 1256 1254 2779 2400
n.asn v.aas.3s d.gsm n.gsm v.pai.3s cj adv

μαρτυρίαν καλὴν ἔχειν ἀπὸ τῶν ἔξωθεν, ⌊ἵνα μὴ⌋ εἰς
have a good reputation *good* *to have* with those outside, lest he fall into
2400 2819 3456 2819 2400 608 3836 2033 2671 3590 1860 1860 1650
n.asf a.asf f.pa p.g d.gpm adv cj pl p.a

ὀνειδισμὸν ἐμπέσῃ καὶ παγίδα τοῦ διαβόλου. 8διακόνους ὡσαύτως
reproach, *he fall* *{and}* which is the snare of the devil. Deacons, likewise, must
3944 1860 2779 4075 3836 1333 1356 6058
n.asm v.aas.3s cj n.asf d.gsm n.gsm n.apm adv

σεμνούς, μὴ διλόγους, μὴ οἴνῳ ⌊πολλῷ προσέχοντας,⌋ μὴ
be dignified, not gossips, not addicted to wine, *addicted* not
4948 3590 1474 3590 4498 3885 4498 4668 3590
a.apm pl a.apm pl n.dsm a.dsm pt.pa.apm pl

αἰσχροκερδεῖς, 9ἔχοντας τὸ μυστήριον τῆς πίστεως ἐν καθαρᾷ συνειδήσει.
greedy for gain, holding to the mystery of the faith with a clean conscience.
153 2400 3836 3696 3836 4411 1877 2754 5287
a.apm pt.pa.apm d.asn n.asn d.gsf n.gsf p.d a.dsf n.dsf

10 ↱ καὶ οὗτοι δὲ δοκιμαζέσθωσαν πρῶτον, εἶτα διακονείτωσαν
And they should also *they* *And* be tested first; then let them serve if they
1254 4047 1507 2779 4047 1254 1507 4754 1663 1354 1639 1639
adv r.npm cj v.ppm.3p adv adv v.pam.3p

ἀνέγκλητοι ὄντες. 11γυναῖκας ὡσαύτως σεμνάς, μὴ
are found above reproach. *if they are found* Wives likewise must be dignified, not
1639 1639 441 1639 1222 6058 4948 3590
a.npm pt.pa.npm n.apf adv a.apf pl

[a] μὴ αἰσχροκερδῆ included by TR after πλήκτην.

NASB

Overseers and Deacons

3:1It is a trustwor-
thy statement: if
any man aspires
to the office of
overseer, it is a fine
work he desires *to*
do. 2An overseer,
then, must be
above reproach,
the husband of one
wife, temperate,
prudent, respect-
able, hospitable,
able to teach, 3not
addicted to wine
or pugnacious, but
gentle, peaceable,
free from the love
of money. 4*He must*
be one who manag-
es his own house-
hold well, keeping
his children under
control with all
dignity 5(but if a
man does not know
how to manage his
own household,
how will he take
care of the church
of God?), 6*and* not
a new convert, so
that he will not
become conceited
and fall into the
condemnation in-
curred by the devil.
7And he must have
a good reputation
with those outside
the church, so that
he will not fall into
reproach and the
snare of the devil.
8Deacons likewise
must be men of
dignity, not double-
tongued, or addict-
ed to much wine
or fond of sordid
gain, 9*but* holding
to the mystery of
the faith with a
clear conscience.
10These men must
also first be tested;
then let them
serve as deacons
if they are beyond
reproach. 11Women
must likewise *be*
dignified, not

NIV

malicious talkers
but temperate and
trustworthy in ev-
erything.
12 A deacon must
be faithful to his
wife and must
manage his chil-
dren and his house-
hold well. 13 Those
who have served
well gain an excel-
lent standing and
great assurance in
their faith in Christ
Jesus.

Reasons for Paul's Instructions

14 Although I hope
to come to you
soon, I am writing
you these instruc-
tions so that, 15 if
I am delayed, you
will know how
people ought to
conduct them-
selves in God's
household, which
is the church of
the living God, the
pillar and founda-
tion of the truth.
16 Beyond all ques-
tion, the mystery
from which true
godliness springs
is great:

He appeared in the
flesh,
was vindicated
by the
Spirit,[a]
was seen by
angels,
was preached
among the
nations,
was believed on in
the world,
was taken up in
glory.

4 The Spirit
clearly says
that in later times
some will aban-
don the faith and
follow deceiving
spirits and things
taught by demons.
2 Such teachings
come through
hypocritical liars,
whose consciences
have been seared
as with a hot iron.
3 They forbid peo-
ple to marry

[a] 16 Or *vindicated in spirit*

διαβόλους, νηφαλίους, πιστὰς ἐν πᾶσιν. 12 διάκονοι ἔστωσαν μιᾶς
slanderers, clear-minded, faithful in all things. Deacons each should be men of one
1333 3767 4412 1877 4246 1356 1639 467 1651
a.apf a.apf a.apf p.d a.dpn n.npm v.pam.3p a.gsf

γυναικὸς ἄνδρες, τέκνων καλῶς προϊστάμενοι καὶ τῶν ἰδίων οἴκων.
woman, *men* managing children *well* *managing* and *{the}* their own households
1222 467 4613 5451 2822 4613 2779 3836 2625 3875
n.gsf n.npm n.gpn adv pt.pm.npm cj d.gpm a.gpm n.gpm

13 οἱ γὰρ καλῶς διακονήσαντες βαθμὸν
well. For those *For* who serve well *who serve* are acquiring a good standing
2822 1142 3836 1142 1354 1354 2822 1354 4347 4347 2819 957
d.npm cj adv pt.aa.npm n.asm

ἑαυτοῖς καλὸν περιποιοῦνται καὶ πολλὴν παρρησίαν ἐν πίστει τῇ ἐν
for themselves *good* *are acquiring* and great confidence in faith, which is in
1571 2819 4347 2779 4498 4244 1877 4411 3836 1877
r.dpm.3 a.asm v.pmi.3p cj a.asf n.asf p.d n.dsf d.dsf p.d

Χριστῷ Ἰησοῦ. 14 ταῦτά σοι γράφω ἐλπίζων
Christ Jesus. I am writing these things to you, *I am writing* ⌞even though I am hoping⌟
5986 2652 1211 1211 1211 4047 5148 1211 1827
n.dsm n.dsm r.apn r.ds.2 v.pai.1s pt.pa.nsm

ἐλθεῖν πρὸς σὲ ⌞ἐν τάχει·⌟ 15 ἐὰν δὲ βραδύνω, ἵνα εἰδῇς πῶς
to come to you quickly, but if *but* I wait, so that ⌞you may know⌟ how
2262 4639 5148 1877 5443 1254 1569 1254 1094 2671 3857 4802
f.aa p.a r.as.2 p.d n.dsn cj cj v.pas.1s cj v.ras.2s cj

δεῖ ἐν οἴκῳ θεοῦ ἀναστρέφεσθαι,
⌞it is necessary⌟ for people to conduct themselves in the house of God, *to conduct themselves*
1256 418 418 418 1877 3875 2536 418
v.pai.3s p.d n.dsm n.gsm f.pp

ἥτις ἐστὶν ἐκκλησία → θεοῦ ζῶντος, στῦλος καὶ ἑδραίωμα τῆς
which is the church of the living God, *living* a pillar and buttress of the
4015 1639 1711 2409 2536 2409 5146 2779 1613 3836
r.nsf v.pai.3s n.nsf n.gsm pt.pa.gsm n.nsm cj n.nsn d.gsf

ἀληθείας. 16 καὶ ὁμολογουμένως μέγα ἐστὶν τὸ τῆς εὐσεβείας μυστήριον·
truth. And undeniably great is the mystery of godliness, *mystery*
237 2779 3935 3489 1639 3836 3696 3836 2354 3696
n.gsf cj adv a.nsn v.pai.3s d.nsn d.gsf n.gsf n.nsn

ὃς[a] ἐφανερώθη ἐν σαρκί, ἐδικαιώθη ἐν πνεύματι, ὤφθη ἀγγέλοις, ἐκηρύχθη
who was revealed in flesh, was vindicated in spirit, appeared to angels; was preached
4005 5746 1877 4922 1467 1877 4460 3972 34 3062
r.nsm v.api.3s p.d n.dsf v.api.3s p.d n.dsn v.api.3s n.dpm v.api.3s

ἐν ἔθνεσιν, ἐπιστεύθη ἐν κόσμῳ, ἀνελήμφθη ἐν δόξῃ.
among the nations, was believed in the world, was taken up in glory.
1877 1620 4409 1877 3180 377 1877 1518
p.d n.dpn v.api.3s p.d n.dsm v.api.3s p.d n.dsf

4:1 τὸ δὲ πνεῦμα ῥητῶς λέγει ὅτι ἐν ὑστέροις καιροῖς
Now the *Now* Spirit clearly says that in the last times some of the
1254 3836 1254 4460 4843 3306 4022 1877 5731 2789 5516 3836 3836
d.nsn cj n.nsn adv v.pai.3s cj p.d a.dpm n.dpm

ἀποστήσονταί τινες τῆς πίστεως προσέχοντες πνεύμασιν πλάνοις
faith will apostasize *some* *of the* *faith* ⌞by being devoted to⌟ deceitful spirits *deceitful*
4411 923 5516 3836 4411 4668 4418 4460 4418
v.fmi.3p r.npm d.gsf n.gsf pt.pa.npm n.dpn a.dpn

καὶ διδασκαλίαις δαιμονίων, 2 ἐν ὑποκρίσει ψευδολόγων,
and teachings of demons, by the hypocrisy of liars whose own consciences
2779 1436 1228 1877 5694 6016 2625 2625 5287
cj n.dpf n.gpn p.d n.dsf n.gpm

κεκαυστηριασμένων τὴν ἰδίαν συνείδησιν, 3 κωλυόντων γαμεῖν,
have been seared, *{the}* *whose own* *consciences* forbidding to marry,
3013 3836 2625 5287 3266 1138
pt.rp.gpm d.asf a.asf n.asf pt.pa.gpm f.pa

[a] Θεὸς included by TR after ὃς.

NASB

malicious gossips,
but temperate,
faithful in all
things. 12 Deacons
must be husbands
of *only* one wife,
and good managers
of *their* children
and their own
households. 13 For
those who have
served well as
deacons obtain
for themselves a
high standing and
great confidence in
the faith that is in
Christ Jesus.
14 I am writing
these things to you,
hoping to come to
you before long;
15 but in case I am
delayed, *I write* so
that you will know
how one ought to
conduct himself in
the household of
God, which is the
church of the liv-
ing God, the pillar
and support of the
truth. 16 By common
confession, great
is the mystery of
godliness:

He who was
revealed in
the flesh,
Was vindicated
in the Spirit,
Seen by an-
gels,
Proclaimed
among the
nations,
Believed on in
the world,
Taken up in
glory.

Apostasy

4:1 But the Spirit
explicitly says that
in later times some
will fall away from
the faith, paying
attention to deceit-
ful spirits and doc-
trines of demons,
2 by means of the
hypocrisy of liars
seared in their own
conscience as with
a branding iron,
3 *men* who forbid
marriage *and*

NIV

and order them to
abstain from cer-
tain foods, which
God created to
be received with
thanksgiving by
those who believe
and who know the
truth. 4For every-
thing God created
is good, and noth-
ing is to be rejected
if it is received
with thanksgiv-
ing, 5because it is
consecrated by the
word of God and
prayer.
6If you point
these things out to
the brothers and
sisters,[a] you will
be a good minister
of Christ Jesus,
nourished on the
truths of the faith
and of the good
teaching that you
have followed.
7Have nothing to
do with godless
myths and old
wives' tales; rath-
er, train yourself
to be godly. 8For
physical training is
of some value, but
godliness has val-
ue for all things,
holding promise
for both the pres-
ent life and the life
to come. 9This is
a trustworthy say-
ing that deserves
full acceptance.
10That is why we
labor and strive,
because we have
put our hope in the
living God, who
is the Savior of all
people, and espe-
cially of those who
believe.
11Command and
teach these things.
12Don't let any-
one look down on
you because you
are young, but set
an example for
the believers in
speech, in

[a] 6 The Greek word for *brothers and sisters* (*adelphoi*) refers here to believers, both men and women, as part of God's family.

ἀπέχεσθαι βρωμάτων, ἃ ὁ θεὸς ἔκτισεν εἰς μετάλημψιν μετὰ
⌞demanding abstinence⌟ from foods that *{the}* God created to be received with
600 1109 4005 3836 2536 3231 1650 3562 3552
f.pm n.gpn r.apn d.nsm n.nsm v.aai.3s p.a n.asf p.g

εὐχαριστίας τοῖς πιστοῖς καὶ ἐπεγνωκόσι τὴν ἀλήθειαν. 4 ὅτι πᾶν
thanksgiving by those ⌞who are faithful⌟ and know the truth, since all of God's
2374 3836 4412 2779 2105 3836 237 4022 4246 2536
n.gsf d.dpm a.dpm cj pt.ra.dpm d.asf n.asf cj a.nsn

κτίσμα θεοῦ καλὸν καὶ οὐδὲν ἀπόβλητον μετὰ εὐχαριστίας
creation *God's* is good, and nothing is unclean if it is received with thanksgiving;
3233 2536 2819 2779 4029 612 3284 3284 3284 3284 3552 2374
n.nsn n.gsm a.nsn cj a.nsn a.nsn p.g n.gsf

λαμβανόμενον· 5 ἁγιάζεται γὰρ διὰ λόγου θεοῦ καὶ ἐντεύξεως. 6 ↱
if it is received for it is sanctified *for* through the word of God and prayer. By
3284 1142 39 1142 1328 3364 2536 2779 1950 5719
pt.pp.nsn v.ppi.3s cj p.g n.gsm n.gsm cj n.gsf

↱ ταῦτα ὑποτιθέμενος τοῖς ἀδελφοῖς καλὸς ἔσῃ διάκονος
placing these things before the brethren, you will be a good *you will be* servant
5719 4047 5719 3836 81 1639 1639 1639 2819 1639 1356
r.apn pt.pm.nsm d.dpm n.dpm a.nsm v.fmi.2s n.nsm

Χριστοῦ Ἰησοῦ, ἐντρεφόμενος τοῖς λόγοις τῆς πίστεως καὶ τῆς καλῆς
of Christ Jesus, being trained by the words of the faith and of the good
5986 2652 1957 3836 3364 3836 4411 2779 3836 2819
n.gsm n.gsm pt.pp.nsm d.dpm n.dpm d.gsf n.gsf cj d.gsf a.gsf

διδασκαλίας ᾗ παρηκολούθηκας· 7 τοὺς δὲ βεβήλους καὶ γραώδεις
teaching that you have followed. But reject the *But* profane and silly
1436 4005 4158 1254 4148 3836 1254 1013 2779 1212
n.gsf r.dsf v.rai.2s d.apm cj a.apm cj a.apm

μύθους παραιτοῦ. γύμναζε δὲ σεαυτὸν πρὸς εὐσέβειαν· 8 ἡ γὰρ σωματικὴ
myths; *reject* rather train *rather* yourself for godliness; *{the}* for bodily
3680 4148 1254 1214 1254 4932 4639 2354 3836 1142 5394
n.apm v.pmm.2s v.pam.2s cj r.asm.2 p.a n.asf d.nsf cj a.nsf

γυμνασία πρὸς ὀλίγον ἐστὶν ὠφέλιμος, ἡ δὲ εὐσέβεια
exercise is of value for a little while, *is* *of value* *{the}* but godliness is of
1215 1639 6068 6068 4639 3900 1639 6068 3836 1254 2354 1639 6068
n.nsf p.a a.asn v.pai.3s a.nsf d.nsf cj n.nsf

πρὸς πάντα ὠφέλιμός ἐστιν ἐπαγγελίαν ἔχουσα
value for all things *of value* *is* because it holds a promise *because it holds* for
6068 4639 4246 6068 1639 2400 2400 2400 2039 2400 3836
p.a a.apn a.nsf v.pai.3s n.asf pt.pa.nsf

ζωῆς τῆς νῦν καὶ τῆς μελλούσης. 9 πιστὸς ὁ λόγος καὶ
the present life *for the present* and ⌞for the⌟ coming life. Trustworthy is the saying and
3836 3814 2437 3836 3814 2779 3836 3516 4412 3836 3364 2779
n.gsf d.gsf adv cj d.gsf pt.pa.gsf a.nsm d.nsm n.nsm cj

πάσης ἀποδοχῆς ἄξιος· 10 εἰς τοῦτο γὰρ κοπιῶμεν καὶ
worthy of complete acceptance, *worthy* for ⌞with respect to⌟ this reason *for* we are toiling and
545 4246 628 545 1142 1650 4047 1142 3159 2779
a.gsf n.gsf a.nsm p.a r.asn cj v.pai.1p cj

ἀγωνιζόμεθα, ὅτι ἠλπίκαμεν ἐπὶ θεῷ ζῶντι, ὅς ἐστιν
struggling, since, ⌞"We have placed our hope⌟ in the living God, *living* who is the
76 4022 1827 2093 2409 2536 2409 4005 1639
v.pmi.1p cj v.rai.1p p.d n.dsm pt.pa.dsm r.nsm v.pai.3s

σωτὴρ πάντων ἀνθρώπων μάλιστα πιστῶν. 11 παράγγελλε
Savior of all people, particularly ⌞of those who believe."⌟ Command and teach
5400 4246 476 3436 4412 4133 2779 1438
n.nsm a.gpm n.gpm adv.s a.gpm v.pam.2s

ταῦτα καὶ δίδασκε. 12 μηδείς σου τῆς
these things. *and* *teach* Let no one treat you contemptuously because of your *{the}*
4047 2779 1438 2969 3594 2969 2969 5148 3836
r.apn cj v.pam.2s a.nsm r.gs.2 d.gsf

νεότητος καταφρονείτω, ἀλλὰ τύπος γίνου τῶν πιστῶν ἐν λόγῳ, ἐν
youth, *Let treat contemptuously* but be an example *be* for the faithful in speech, in
3744 2969 247 1181 5596 1181 3836 4412 1877 3364 1877
n.gsf v.pam.3s cj n.nsm v.pmm.2s d.gpm a.gpm p.d n.dsm p.d

NASB

advocate abstain-
ing from foods
which God has
created to be grate-
fully shared in by
those who believe
and know the truth.
4For everything
created by God is
good, and nothing
is to be rejected if
it is received with
gratitude; 5for it is
sanctified by means
of the word of God
and prayer.

A Good Minister's Discipline

6In pointing out
these things to the
brethren, you will
be a good servant
of Christ Jesus,
constantly nour-
ished on the words
of the faith and of
the sound doctrine
which you have
been following.
7But have nothing
to do with worldly
fables fit only for
old women. On
the other hand,
discipline yourself
for the purpose
of godliness; 8for
bodily discipline
is only of little
profit, but godli-
ness is profitable
for all things, since
it holds promise
for the present life
and *also* for the
life to come. 9It is a
trustworthy state-
ment deserving full
acceptance. 10For it
is for this we labor
and strive, because
we have fixed our
hope on the living
God, who is the
Savior of all men,
especially of be-
lievers.
11Prescribe and
teach these things.
12Let no one look
down on your
youthfulness, but
rather in speech,

NIV

conduct, in love, in
faith and in puri-
ty. 13 Until I come,
devote yourself to
the public reading
of Scripture, to
preaching and to
teaching. 14 Do not
neglect your gift,
which was given
you through proph-
ecy when the body
of elders laid their
hands on you.
15 Be diligent in
these matters; give
yourself wholly
to them, so that
everyone may see
your progress.
16 Watch your life
and doctrine close-
ly. Persevere in
them, because if
you do, you will
save both yourself
and your hearers.

Widows, Elders and Slaves

5 Do not rebuke
an older man
harshly, but exhort
him as if he were
your father. Treat
younger men as
brothers, 2 older
women as mothers,
and younger wom-
en as sisters, with
absolute purity.
3 Give proper rec-
ognition to those
widows who are
really in need.
4 But if a widow
has children or
grandchildren,
these should learn
first of all to put
their religion into
practice by caring
for their own fam-
ily and so repaying
their parents and
grandparents, for
this is pleasing to
God. 5 The wid-
ow who is really
in need and left
all alone puts her
hope in God and
continues night
and day to pray
and to ask God for
help. 6 But the

ἀναστροφῇ, ἐν ἀγάπῃ, ἐν πίστει, ἐν ἁγνείᾳ. 13 ἕως ἔρχομαι πρόσεχε τῇ
conduct, in love, in faith, in purity. Until I come, be devoted ˪to the˩
419 1877 27 1877 4411 1877 48 2401 2262 4668 3836
n.dsf p.d n.dsf p.d n.dsf p.d n.dsf cj v.pmi.1s v.pam.2s d.dsf

ἀναγνώσει, τῇ παρακλήσει, τῇ διδασκαλίᾳ. 14 ↱ μὴ ἀμέλει τοῦ
reading of Scripture, ˪to the˩ exhortation, ˪to the˩ teaching. Do not neglect the
342 3836 4155 3836 1436 288 3590 288 3836
n.dsf d.dsf n.dsf d.dsf n.dsf pl v.pam.2s d.gsn

ἐν σοὶ χαρίσματος, ὃ ἐδόθη σοι διὰ προφητείας μετὰ
gift that is in you, *gift* which was given to you through prophecy with the
5922 1877 5148 5922 4005 1443 5148 1328 4735 3552
p.d r.ds.2 n.gsn r.nsn v.api.3s r.ds.2 p.g n.gsf p.g

ἐπιθέσεως τῶν χειρῶν τοῦ πρεσβυτερίου. 15 ταῦτα
laying on of the hands of the body of elders. Continually practice these things,
2120 3836 5931 3836 4564 3509 3509 4047
n.gsf d.gpf n.gpf d.gsn n.gsn r.apn

μελέτα, ἐν τούτοις ἴσθι, ἵνα σου ἡ προκοπὴ
Continually practice immerse yourself in them, *immerse yourself* so that your *{the}* progress
3509 1639 1639 1877 4047 1639 2671 5148 3836 4620
v.pam.2s p.d r.dpn v.pam.2s cj r.gs.2 d.nsf n.nsf

φανερὰ ᾖ πᾶσιν. 16 ἔπεχε σεαυτῷ καὶ τῇ διδασκαλίᾳ, ἐπίμενε
might be visible *might be* to all. Watch yourself and the teaching; be persistent
1639 1639 5745 1639 4246 2091 4932 2779 3836 1436 2152
a.nsf v.pas.3s a.dpm v.pam.2s r.dsm.2 cj d.dsf n.dsf v.pam.2s

αὐτοῖς· ↱ τοῦτο γὰρ ποιῶν καὶ σεαυτὸν σώσεις καὶ τοὺς
in them; for by so *for* doing you will save both yourself *you will save* and those
899 1142 4472 4047 1142 4472 5392 5392 5392 2779 4932 5392 2779 3836
r.dpn.3 r.asn cj pt.pa.nsm cj r.asm.2 v.fai.2s cj d.apm

ἀκούοντάς σου.
hearing you.
201 5148
pt.pa.apm r.gs.2

5:1 πρεσβυτέρῳ ↱ μὴ ἐπιπλήξῃς ἀλλὰ παρακάλει ὡς πατέρα,
older man Do not rebuke but encourage an older man as a father,
4565 2159 3590 2159 247 4151 4565 4565 6055 4252
a.dsm pl v.aas.2s cj v.pam.2s pl n.asm

νεωτέρους ὡς ἀδελφούς, 2 πρεσβυτέρας ὡς μητέρας, νεωτέρας ὡς ἀδελφὰς ἐν
younger men as brothers, older women as mothers, younger women as sisters with
3742 6055 81 4565 6055 3613 3742 6055 80 1877
a.apm.c pl n.apm a.apf pl n.apf a.apf.c pl n.apf p.d

πάσῃ ἁγνείᾳ. 3 χήρας τίμα τὰς ὄντως χήρας. 4 εἰ δέ τις χήρα
all purity. Honor widows *Honor* who are truly widows. But if *But* a certain widow
4246 48 5506 5939 5506 3836 3953 5939 1254 1623 1254 5516 5939
a.dsf n.dsf n.apf v.pam.2s d.apf adv n.apf cj cj r.nsf n.nsf

τέκνα ἢ ἔκγονα ἔχει, μανθανέτωσαν πρῶτον τὸν
has children or grandchildren, *has* let them learn to show godliness first to *{the}*
2400 5451 2445 1681 2400 3443 2355 2355 2355 4754 2355 3836
n.apn cj n.apn v.pai.3s v.pam.3p adv d.asm

ἴδιον οἶκον εὐσεβεῖν καὶ ἀμοιβὰς ἀποδιδόναι τοῖς
their own household *to show godliness to* and to make some return *to make* to their
2625 3875 2355 2779 625 625 304 625 3836
a.asm n.asm f.pa cj n.apf f.pa d.dpm

προγόνοις· τοῦτο γάρ ἐστιν ἀπόδεκτον ἐνώπιον τοῦ θεοῦ. 5 ἡ δὲ ὄντως
parents; for this *for* is pleasing before *{the}* God. But the *But* true
4591 1142 4047 1142 1639 621 1967 3836 2536 1254 3836 1254 3953
n.dpm r.nsn cj v.pai.3s a.nsn p.g d.gsm n.gsm d.nsf cj adv

χήρα καὶ μεμονωμένη ἤλπικεν ἐπὶ θεὸν καὶ προσμένει ταῖς
widow, *{and}* ˪who has been left totally alone,˩ ˪has set her hope˩ on God and continues in
5939 2779 3670 1827 2093 2536 2779 4693 3836
n.nsf cj pt.rp.nsf v.rai.3s p.a n.asm cj v.pai.3s d.dpf

δεήσεσιν καὶ ταῖς προσευχαῖς νυκτὸς καὶ ἡμέρας, 6 ἡ δὲ
entreaties and *{the}* prayers night and day. But the *But*
1255 2779 3836 4666 3816 2779 2465 1254 3836 1254
n.dpf cj d.dpf n.dpf n.gsf cj n.gsf d.nsf cj

NASB

conduct, love,
faith *and* purity,
show yourself an
example of those
who believe.
13 Until I come, give
attention to the
public reading *of
Scripture,* to exhor-
tation and teaching.
14 Do not neglect the
spiritual gift within
you, which was
bestowed on you
through prophetic
utterance with the
laying on of hands
by the presbytery.
15 Take pains with
these things;
be *absorbed* in
them, so that your
progress will be
evident to all. 16 Pay
close attention
to yourself and
to your teaching;
persevere in these
things, for as you
do this you will
ensure salvation
both for yourself
and for those who
hear you.

Honor Widows

5:1 Do not sharply
rebuke an older
man, but *rather* ap-
peal to *him* as a fa-
ther, *to* the younger
men as brothers,
2 the older women
as mothers, *and* the
younger women as
sisters, in all purity.
3 Honor widows
who are widows
indeed; 4 but if any
widow has children
or grandchildren,
they must first
learn to practice
piety in regard to
their own family
and to make some
return to their
parents; for this is
acceptable in the
sight of God. 5 Now
she who is a widow
indeed and who
has been left alone,
has fixed her hope
on God and con-
tinues in entreaties
and prayers night
and day. 6 But she

NIV

widow who lives
for pleasure is
dead even while
she lives. 7 Give
the people these
instructions, so
that no one may
be open to blame.
8 Anyone who does
not provide for
their relatives, and
especially for their
own household,
has denied the faith
and is worse than
an unbeliever.
9 No widow may
be put on the list of
widows unless she
is over sixty, has
been faithful to
her husband, 10 and
is well known for
her good deeds,
such as bringing
up children, show-
ing hospitality,
washing the feet of
the Lord's people,
helping those in
trouble and de-
voting herself to
all kinds of good
deeds.
11 As for younger
widows, do not
put them on such
a list. For when
their sensual de-
sires overcome
their dedication
to Christ, they
want to marry.
12 Thus they bring
judgment on them-
selves, because
they have broken
their first pledge.
13 Besides, they
get into the habit
of being idle and
going about from
house to house.
And not only
do they become
idlers, but also
busybodies who
talk nonsense,
saying things they
ought not to. 14 So
I counsel younger
widows to marry,
to have children,
to manage their
homes and to give
the enemy no op-
portunity for slan-
der. 15 Some have

σπαταλῶσα ζῶσα τέθνηκεν. 7 καὶ
⌞one who has lived for pleasure,⌟ ⌞even though living,⌟ has died. Command these things as well,
5059 2409 2569 4133 4047 4047 2779
pt.pa.nsf pt.pa.nsf v.rai.3s cj

ταῦτα παράγγελλε, ἵνα ἀνεπίλημπτοι ὦσιν. 8 εἰ δέ
these things *Command* so that they may be above reproach. *they may be* But if *But*
4047 4133 2671 1639 1639 1639 455 1639 1254 1623 1254
r.apn v.pam.2s cj a.npm v.pas.3p cj cj

τις τῶν ἰδίων καὶ μάλιστα οἰκείων οὐ
anyone does not care for *{the}* his own, *{and}* especially ⌞his household members,⌟ *not*
5516 4629 4024 4629 4629 3836 2625 2779 3436 3858 4024
r.nsm d.gpm a.gpm cj adv.s n.gpm pl

προνοεῖ, τὴν πίστιν ἤρνηται καὶ ἔστιν → ἀπίστου
does care for he has disowned the faith *he has disowned* and is worse than an unbeliever.
4629 766 766 766 3836 4411 766 2779 1639 5937 603
v.pai.3s d.asf n.asf v.rmi.3s cj v.pai.3s a.gsm

χείρων. 9 ↱ χήρα καταλεγέσθω μὴ ἔλαττον ἐτῶν ἑξήκοντα
worse Let a widow be enrolled if she is not less than sixty ⌞years old,⌟ *sixty*
5937 2899 5939 2899 1181 1181 1181 3590 1781 2008 2291 2008
a.nsm.c n.nsf v.ppm.3s pl adv.c n.gpn a.gpn

γεγονυῖα, ἑνὸς ἀνδρὸς γυνή, 10 ἐν ἔργοις καλοῖς
if she is a woman of one man, *woman* being witnessed to by good deeds, *good*
1181 1222 1651 467 1222 3455 3455 3455 1877 2819 2240 2819
pt.ra.nsf a.gsm n.gsm n.nsf p.d n.dpn a.dpn

μαρτυρουμένη, εἰ ἐτεκνοτρόφησεν, εἰ ἐξενοδόχησεν, εἰ →
being witnessed to if she raised children, if she showed hospitality, if she washed the feet of
3455 1623 5452 1623 3827 1623 3782 3782 4546
pt.pp.nsf cj v.aai.3s cj v.aai.3s cj

ἁγίων πόδας ἔνιψεν, εἰ θλιβομένοις ἐπήρκεσεν, εἰ
the saints, *feet* *she washed* if she helped the afflicted, *she helped* if she earnestly
41 4546 3782 1623 2064 2064 2567 2064 1623 2051 2051
a.gpm n.apm v.aai.3s cj pt.pp.dpm v.aai.3s cj

παντὶ ἔργῳ ἀγαθῷ ἐπηκολούθησεν. 11 νεωτέρας δὲ
pursued every good work. *good* *she earnestly pursued* But refuse to enroll younger *But*
2051 4246 19 2240 19 2051 1254 4148 3742 1254
a.dsn n.dsn a.dsn v.aai.3s a.apf.c cj

χήρας παραιτοῦ· ὅταν γὰρ καταστρηνιάσωσιν τοῦ Χριστοῦ,
widows, *refuse* for when *for* ⌞their passions draw them away⌟ from Christ, they desire
5939 4148 1142 4020 1142 2952 3836 5986 2527 2527
n.apf v.pmm.2s cj cj v.aas.3p d.gsm n.gsm

γαμεῖν θέλουσιν 12 ἔχουσαι κρίμα ὅτι τὴν πρώτην πίστιν
to marry *they desire* and come under judgment since they abandoned their former faith.
1138 2527 2400 3210 4022 119 119 3836 4755 4411
f.pa v.pai.3p pt.pa.npf n.asn cj d.asf a.asf n.asf

ἠθέτησαν· 13 ἅμα δὲ καὶ ἀργαὶ μανθάνουσιν
they abandoned But ⌞at the same time⌟ *But* they also learn to be idlers, *they learn*
119 1254 275 1254 3443 2779 3443 734 3443
v.aai.3p adv cj adv a.npf v.pai.3p

περιερχόμεναι τὰς οἰκίας, οὐ μόνον δὲ ἀργαὶ ἀλλὰ καὶ φλύαροι καὶ
flitting about among *{the}* houses, but not only *but* idlers but also gossips and
4320 3836 3864 1254 4024 3667 1254 734 247 2779 5827 2779
pt.pm.npf d.apf n.apf pl adv cj a.npf cj adv a.npf cj

περίεργοι, λαλοῦσαι τὰ μὴ δέοντα. 14 βούλομαι οὖν
busybodies, speaking ⌞about things⌟ that they should not. *they should* So, I wish *So*
4319 3281 3836 1256 1256 3590 1256 4036 1089 4036
a.npf pt.pa.npf d.apn pl pt.pa.apn v.pmi.1s cj

νεωτέρας γαμεῖν, τεκνογονεῖν, οἰκοδεσποτεῖν,
younger widows to marry, to bear children, to manage their households, to give the Accuser
3742 1138 5449 3866 1443 1443 3836 512
a.apf.c f.pa f.pa f.pa

μηδεμίαν ἀφορμὴν διδόναι τῷ ἀντικειμένῳ λοιδορίας χάριν· 15 ↱
no occasion *to give* *the* *Accuser* for slander, *for* for some have
3594 929 1443 3836 512 5920 3367 5920 1142 5516 1762
a.asf n.asf f.pa d.dsm pt.pm.dsm n.gsf p.g

NASB

who gives herself
to wanton pleasure
is dead even
while she lives.
7 Prescribe these
things as well, so
that they may be
above reproach.
8 But if anyone does
not provide for his
own, and espe-
cially for those of
his household, he
has denied the faith
and is worse than
an unbeliever.
9 A widow is to
be put on the list
only if she is not
less than sixty
years old, *having*
been the wife of
one man, 10 having
a reputation for
good works; *and*
if she has brought
up children, if she
has shown hospi-
tality to strangers,
if she has washed
the saints' feet, if
she has assisted
those in distress,
and if she has
devoted herself to
every good work.
11 But refuse *to put*
younger widows
on the list, for
when they feel
sensual desires in
disregard of Christ,
they want to get
married, 12 *thus* in-
curring condemna-
tion, because they
have set aside their
previous pledge.
13 At the same time
they also learn *to*
be idle, as they go
around from house
to house; and not
merely idle, but
also gossips and
busybodies, talking
about things not
proper *to mention.*
14 Therefore, I want
younger *widows*
to get married,
bear children, keep
house, *and* give the
enemy no occasion
for reproach; 15 for
some have already

NIV

in fact already
turned away to fol-
low Satan.
16 If any woman
who is a believer
has widows in her
care, she should
continue to help
them and not let
the church be bur-
dened with them,
so that the church
can help those
widows who are
really in need.
17 The elders who
direct the affairs of
the church well are
worthy of double
honor, especially
those whose work
is preaching and
teaching. 18 For
Scripture says,
"Do not muzzle
an ox while it is
treading out the
grain,"[a] and "The
worker deserves
his wages."[b] 19 Do
not entertain an
accusation against
an elder unless it
is brought by two
or three witnesses.
20 But those elders
who are sinning
you are to reprove
before everyone,
so that the others
may take warning.
21 I charge you, in
the sight of God
and Christ Jesus
and the elect an-
gels, to keep these
instructions with-
out partiality, and
to do nothing out
of favoritism.
22 Do not be hasty
in the laying on of
hands, and do not
share in the sins of
others. Keep your-
self pure.
23 Stop drinking
only water, and
use a little wine
because of your
stomach and your
frequent illnesses.
24 The sins of
some

ἤδη γάρ τινες ἐξετράπησαν ὀπίσω τοῦ σατανᾶ. 16 εἴ τις πιστὴ ἔχει
already for some strayed after {the} Satan. If any ⌞believing woman⌟ has
2453 1142 5516 1762 3958 3836 4928 1623 5516 4412 2400
adv cj r.npf v.api.3p p.g d.gsm n.gsm cj r.nsf a.nsf v.pai.3s

χήρας, ἐπαρκείτω αὐταῖς καὶ → μὴ βαρείσθω ἡ ἐκκλησία, ἵνα
widows, ⌞let her care for⌟ them, and the church should not be burdened the church so that
5939 2064 899 2779 3836 1711 976 3590 976 3836 1711 2671
n.apf v.pam.3s r.dpf.3 cj pl v.ppm.3s d.nsf n.nsf cj

ταῖς ὄντως χήραις ἐπαρκέσῃ. 17 οἱ
it may care for the true widows. it may care for Let the elders who have been serving
2064 2064 2064 2064 3836 3953 5939 2064 546 3836 4565 4613 4613 4613 4613
d.dpf adv n.dpf v.aas.3s d.npm

καλῶς προεστῶτες πρεσβύτεροι διπλῆς τιμῆς
well who have been serving elders be considered worthy of double honor,
2822 4613 4565 546 546 546 546 1487 5507
adv pt.ra.npm a.npm a.gsf n.gsf

ἀξιούσθωσαν, μάλιστα οἱ κοπιῶντες ἐν λόγῳ καὶ
Let be considered worthy of namely, those ⌞who are laboring hard⌟ at preaching and
546 3436 3836 3159 1877 3364 2779
v.ppm.3p adv.s d.npm pt.pa.npm p.d n.dsm cj

διδασκαλίᾳ. 18 λέγει γὰρ ἡ γραφή, βοῦν
teaching. For Scripture says, For {the} Scripture "Do not muzzle an ox
1436 1142 1210 3306 1142 3836 1210 5821 4024 5821 1091
n.dsf v.pai.3s cj d.nsf n.nsf n.asm

ἀλοῶντα οὐ φιμώσεις, καί· ἄξιος ὁ ἐργάτης τοῦ μισθοῦ
⌞that is treading out⌟ the grain," not Do muzzle and, "Worthy is the worker of his wage."
262 4024 5821 2779 545 3836 2239 3836 899 3635
pt.pa.asm pl v.fai.2s cj a.nsm d.nsm n.nsm d.gsm n.gsm

αὐτοῦ. 19 κατὰ πρεσβυτέρου κατηγορίαν μὴ
his Do not accept an accusation against an elder, accusation not
899 4138 3590 4138 2990 2848 4565 2990 3590
r.gsm.3 p.g a.gsm n.asf pl

παραδέχου, ⌞ἐκτὸς εἰ μὴ⌟ ἐπὶ δύο ἢ τριῶν μαρτύρων. 20
Do accept except ⌞on the evidence of⌟ two or three witnesses. Confront
4138 1760 1623 3590 2093 1545 2445 5552 3459 1794
v.pmm.2s adv cj pl p.g a.gpm cj a.gpm n.gpm

τοὺς ἁμαρτάνοντας ἐνώπιον πάντων ἔλεγχε, ἵνα καὶ οἱ λοιποὶ
those who persist in sinning before everyone, Confront so that {also} the rest may stand in
3836 279 1967 4246 1794 2671 2779 3836 3370 2400 2400 2400
d.apm pt.pa.apm p.g a.gpm v.pam.2s cj adv d.npm a.npm

φόβον ἔχωσιν. 21 διαμαρτύρομαι ἐνώπιον τοῦ θεοῦ καὶ Χριστοῦ Ἰησοῦ καὶ
fear. may stand in I solemnly charge you before {the} God and Christ Jesus and
5832 2400 1371 1967 3836 2536 2779 5986 2652 2779
n.asm v.pas.3p v.pmi.1s p.g d.gsm n.gsm cj n.gsm n.gsm cj

τῶν ἐκλεκτῶν ἀγγέλων, ἵνα ταῦτα φυλάξῃς χωρὶς προκρίματος,
the elect angels, that you keep these things you keep without prejudging, doing
3836 1723 34 2671 5875 5875 4047 5875 6006 4622 4472
d.gpm a.gpm n.gpm cj r.apn v.aas.2s p.g n.gsn

μηδὲν ποιῶν κατὰ πρόσκλισιν. 22 χεῖρας ταχέως μηδενὶ
nothing doing with partiality. Do not lay hands on anyone quickly not on anyone
3594 4472 2848 4680 2202 3594 2202 5931 3594 3594 5441 3594
a.asn pt.pa.nsm p.a n.asf n.apf adv a.dsm

ἐπιτίθει μηδὲ κοινώνει ἁμαρτίαις ἀλλοτρίαις· σεαυτὸν ἁγνὸν τήρει.
Do lay or share in the sins of others; keep yourself pure. keep
2202 3593 3125 281 259 5498 4932 54 5498
v.pam.2s adv v.pam.2s n.dpf a.dpf r.asm.2 a.asm v.pam.2s

23 μηκέτι → ὑδροπότει, ἀλλὰ οἴνῳ ὀλίγῳ χρῶ διὰ
(No longer drink only water, but use a little wine, little use ⌞on account of⌟ your
3600 5621 247 5968 3900 3885 3900 5968 1328
adv v.pam.2s cj n.dsm a.dsm v.pmm.2s p.a

τὸν στόμαχον καὶ τὰς πυκνάς σου ἀσθενείας. 24 τινῶν ἀνθρώπων αἱ
{the} stomach and {the} your frequent your illnesses.) The sins of some people The
3836 5126 2779 3836 5148 4781 5148 819 3836 281 5516 476 3836
d.asm n.asm cj d.apf a.apf r.gs.2 n.apf r.gpm n.gpm d.npf

NASB

turned aside to
follow Satan.
16 If any woman
who is a believer
has *dependent*
widows, she must
assist them and the
church must not be
burdened, so that
it may assist those
who are widows
indeed.

Concerning Elders

17 The elders who
rule well are to be
considered worthy
of double honor,
especially those
who work hard
at preaching and
teaching. 18 For the
Scripture says,
"YOU SHALL NOT
MUZZLE THE OX
WHILE HE IS THRESH-
ING," and "The
laborer is worthy
of his wages." 19 Do
not receive an ac-
cusation against
an elder except on
the basis of two or
three witnesses.
20 Those who con-
tinue in sin, rebuke
in the presence of
all, so that the rest
also will be fear-
ful *of sinning.* 21 I
solemnly charge
you in the pres-
ence of God and
of Christ Jesus
and of *His* chosen
angels, to maintain
these *principles*
without bias, doing
nothing in a *spirit*
of partiality. 22 Do
not lay hands upon
anyone *too* hastily
and thereby share
responsibility for
the sins of others;
keep yourself free
from sin.
23 No longer drink
water *exclusively,*
but use a little wine
for the sake of your
stomach and your
frequent ailments.
24 The sins of some

[a] 18 Deut. 25:4
[b] 18 Luke 10:7

NIV

are obvious, reaching the place of judgment ahead of them; the sins of others trail behind them. 25 In the same way, good deeds are obvious, and even those that are not obvious cannot remain hidden forever.

6 All who are under the yoke of slavery should consider their masters worthy of full respect, so that God's name and our teaching may not be slandered. 2 Those who have believing masters should not show them disrespect just because they are fellow believers. Instead, they should serve them even better because their masters are dear to them as fellow believers and are devoted to the welfare[a] of their slaves.

False Teachers and the Love of Money

These are the things you are to teach and insist on. 3 If anyone teaches otherwise and does not agree to the sound instruction of our Lord Jesus Christ and to godly teaching, 4 they are conceited and understand nothing. They have an unhealthy interest in controversies and quarrels about words that result in envy, strife, malicious talk, evil suspicions 5 and constant friction between people of corrupt mind,

[a] 2 Or *and benefit from the service*

ἁμαρτίαι πρόδηλοί εἰσιν προάγουσαι εἰς κρίσιν, τισὶν δὲ ↱ καὶ
sins are conspicuous, *are* going before them into judgment, *some* but they also
281 1639 4593 1639 4575 1650 3213 5516 1254 2051 2779
n.npf a.npf v.pai.3p pt.pa.npf p.a n.asf r.dpm cj adv

ἐπακολουθοῦσιν· 25 ὡσαύτως καὶ τὰ ἔργα τὰ καλὰ
follow after some. So also the good works *{the} good* of some are
2051 5516 6058 2779 3836 2819 2240 3836 2819
v.pai.3p adv adv d.npn n.npn d.npn a.npn

πρόδηλα, καὶ τὰ ἄλλως ἔχοντα κρυβῆναι οὐ
conspicuous, and those that are not conspicuous *that are* are not able to be hidden. *not*
4593 2779 3836 2400 2400 261 2400 1538 4024 1538 3221 4024
a.npn cj d.npn adv pt.pa.npn f.ap pl

δύνανται.
are able
1538
v.ppi.3p

6:1 ὅσοι εἰσὶν ὑπὸ ζυγὸν δοῦλοι, τοὺς ἰδίους
˻As many as˼ are under the yoke as slaves should consider *{the}* their own
4012 1639 5679 2433 1529 2451 2451 3836 2625
r.npm v.pai.3p p.a n.asm n.npm d.apm a.apm

δεσπότας πάσης τιμῆς ἀξίους ἡγείσθωσαν, ἵνα μὴ τὸ ὄνομα τοῦ θεοῦ
masters as worthy of all honor *worthy* *should consider* so that *not* the name of God
1305 545 4246 5507 545 2451 2671 3590 3836 3950 3836 2536
n.apm a.gsf n.gsf a.apm v.pmm.3p cj pl d.nsn n.nsn d.gsm n.gsm

καὶ ἡ διδασκαλία → βλασφημῆται. 2 ↱ οἱ δὲ πιστοὺς
and the teaching might not be blasphemed. And let those *And* who have believing
2779 3836 1436 3590 1059 1254 2969 3836 1254 2400 2400 4412
cj d.nsf n.nsf v.pps.3s d.npm cj a.apm

ἔχοντες δεσπότας μὴ καταφρονείτωσαν, ὅτι ἀδελφοί εἰσιν, ἀλλὰ
who have masters not despise them because they are brothers; *they are* rather,
2400 1305 3590 2969 4022 1639 1639 81 1639 247
pt.pa.npm n.apm pl v.pam.3p cj n.npm v.pai.3p cj

μᾶλλον δουλευέτωσαν, ὅτι
let them serve all the more *let them serve* since those benefiting from their act of kindness
1526 1526 1526 3437 1526 4022 3836 514 514 3836 2307 2307 2307
adv.c v.pam.3p cj

πιστοί εἰσιν καὶ ἀγαπητοὶ οἱ τῆς εὐεργεσίας ἀντιλαμβανόμενοι. ταῦτα
are believers *are* and beloved. *those* *their* *act of kindness* *benefiting from* *these things*
1639 4412 1639 2779 28 3836 3836 2307 514 4047
a.npm v.pai.3p cj a.npm d.npm d.gsf n.gsf pt.pm.npm r.apn

δίδασκε καὶ παρακάλει. 3 εἴ τις ἑτεροδιδασκαλεῖ καὶ ↱ μὴ
Teach and urge these things. If someone teaches a different doctrine and does not
1438 2779 4151 4047 4047 1623 5516 2281 2779 4665 3590
v.pam.2s cj v.pam.2s cj r.nsm v.pai.3s cj pl

προσέρχεται ὑγιαίνουσιν λόγοις τοῖς τοῦ κυρίου ἡμῶν Ἰησοῦ Χριστοῦ καὶ
adhere to the healthy words *{the}* of our Lord *our* Jesus Christ and
4665 5617 3364 3836 3836 7005 3261 7005 2652 5986 2779
v.pmi.3s pt.pa.dpm n.dpm d.dpm d.gsm n.gsm r.gp.1 n.gsm n.gsm cj

τῇ κατ' εὐσέβειαν διδασκαλίᾳ, 4 τετύφωται,
the teaching that is ˻according to˼ godliness, *teaching* ˻he is puffed up with conceit,˼
3836 1436 2848 2354 1436 5605
d.dsf p.a n.asf n.dsf v.rpi.3s

μηδὲν ἐπιστάμενος, ἀλλὰ νοσῶν περὶ ζητήσεις καὶ
understanding nothing, *understanding* but ˻has a sickly craving˼ for speculations and
2179 3594 2179 247 3796 4309 2428 2779
a.asn pt.pp.nsm cj pt.pa.nsm p.a n.apf cj

λογομαχίας, ἐξ ὧν γίνεται φθόνος ἔρις βλασφημίαι, ὑπόνοιαι πονηραί,
fights about words ˻out of˼ which come envy, strife, slanders, evil suspicions, *evil*
3363 1666 4005 1181 5784 2251 1060 4505 5707 4505
n.apf p.g r.gpn v.pmi.3s n.nsm n.nsf n.npf n.npf a.npf

5 διαπαρατριβαὶ διεφθαρμένων ἀνθρώπων τὸν νοῦν καὶ
constant irritations among people who have been corrupted *among people* in their mind and
1384 476 476 1425 476 3836 3808 2779
n.npf pt.rp.gpm n.gpm d.asm n.asm cj

NASB

men are quite evident, going before them to judgment; for others, their *sins* follow after. 25 Likewise also, deeds that are good are quite evident, and those which are otherwise cannot be concealed.

Instructions to Those Who Minister

6:1 All who are under the yoke as slaves are to regard their own masters as worthy of all honor so that the name of God and *our* doctrine will not be spoken against. 2 Those who have believers as their masters must not be disrespectful to them because they are brethren, but must serve them all the more, because those who partake of the benefit are believers and beloved. Teach and preach these *principles.*

3 If anyone advocates a different doctrine and does not agree with sound words, those of our Lord Jesus Christ, and with the doctrine conforming to godliness, 4 he is conceited *and* understands nothing; but he has a morbid interest in controversial questions and disputes about words, out of which arise envy, strife, abusive language, evil suspicions, 5 and constant friction between men of depraved mind and

NIV

who have been
robbed of the truth
and who think
that godliness is a
means to financial
gain.
6But godliness
with contentment
is great gain. 7For
we brought noth-
ing into the world,
and we can take
nothing out of it.
8But if we have
food and cloth-
ing, we will be
content with that.
9Those who want
to get rich fall into
temptation and
a trap and into
many foolish and
harmful desires
that plunge people
into ruin and de-
struction. 10For the
love of money is a
root of all kinds of
evil. Some people,
eager for money,
have wandered
from the faith and
pierced themselves
with many griefs.

Final Charge to Timothy

11But you, man
of God, flee from
all this, and pur-
sue righteousness,
godliness, faith,
love, endurance
and gentleness.
12Fight the good
fight of the faith.
Take hold of the
eternal life to
which you were
called when you
made your good
confession in the
presence of many
witnesses. 13In
the sight of God,
who gives life to
everything, and of
Christ Jesus, who
while testifying
before Pontius
Pilate made the
good confession,
I charge you 14to
keep this com-
mand without spot
or blame

ἀπεστερημένων τῆς ἀληθείας, νομιζόντων πορισμὸν εἶναι τὴν
have been robbed of the truth, imagining that godliness is a means of profit. *is* *{the}*
691 3836 237 3787 2354 1639 4516 1639 3836
pt.rp.gpm d.gsf n.gsf pt.pa.gpm n.asm f.pa d.asf

εὐσέβειαν.[a] 6 ἔστιν δὲ πορισμὸς μέγας ἡ
godliness Now godliness with contentment is *Now* great profit. *great* *{the}*
2354 1254 2354 3552 894 1639 1254 3489 4516 3489 3836
n.asf v.pai.3s cj n.nsm a.nsm d.nsf

εὐσέβεια μετὰ αὐταρκείας· 7 οὐδὲν γὰρ εἰσηνέγκαμεν εἰς τὸν
godliness *with* *contentment* For we brought nothing *For* *we brought* into the
2354 3552 894 1142 1662 1662 4029 1142 1662 1650 3836
n.nsf p.g n.gsf a.asn cj v.aai.1p p.a d.asm

κόσμον, ὅτι οὐδὲ ἐξενεγκεῖν τι ↰ δυνάμεθα· 8 ἔχοντες δὲ
world, and neither are we able to take anything out; *are we able* but having *but*
3180 4022 4028 1538 1538 1538 1766 5516 1766 1538 1254 2400 1254
n.asm cj cj f.aa r.asn v.ppi.1p pt.pa.npm cj

διατροφὰς καὶ σκεπάσματα, τούτοις ἀρκεσθησόμεθα. 9 οἱ δὲ βουλόμενοι
food and clothing, with these we will be content. But those *But* wishing
1418 2779 5004 4047 758 1254 3836 1254 1089
n.apf cj n.apn r.dpn v.fpi.1p d.npm cj pt.pm.npm

πλουτεῖν ἐμπίπτουσιν εἰς πειρασμὸν καὶ παγίδα καὶ ἐπιθυμίας πολλὰς ἀνοήτους
to be rich fall into temptation and a snare and *passions* many foolish
4456 1860 1650 4280 2779 4075 2779 2123 4498 485
f.pa v.pai.3p p.a n.asm cj n.asf cj n.apf a.apf a.apf

καὶ βλαβεράς, αἵτινες βυθίζουσιν τοὺς ἀνθρώπους εἰς ὄλεθρον καὶ ἀπώλειαν.
and harmful passions that plunge the people into ruin and destruction.
2779 1054 2123 4015 1112 3836 476 1650 3897 2779 724
cj a.apf r.npf v.pai.3p d.apm n.apm p.a n.asm cj n.asf

10 ῥίζα γὰρ πάντων τῶν κακῶν ἐστιν ἡ φιλαργυρία, ἧς τινες
For a root *For* of all kinds of evils is the love of money, ⌊by which⌋ some,
1142 4844 1142 4246 3836 2805 1639 3836 5794 4005 5516
n.nsf cj a.gpn d.gpn a.gpn v.pai.3s d.nsf n.nsf r.gsf r.npm

ὀρεγόμενοι ἀπεπλανήθησαν ἀπὸ τῆς πίστεως καὶ ἑαυτοὺς περιέπειραν
by their craving, were led astray from the faith and have pierced themselves *have pierced*
3977 675 608 3836 4411 2779 4345 4345 1571 4345
pt.pm.npm v.api.3p p.g d.gsf n.gsf cj r.apm.3 v.aai.3p

→ ὀδύναις πολλαῖς. 11 σὺ δέ, ὦ ἄνθρωπε θεοῦ, ταῦτα φεῦγε·
with many pains. *many* But you, *But* *{O}* man of God, flee these things *flee*
4498 3850 4498 1254 5148 1254 6043 476 2536 5771 4047 5771
n.dpf a.dpf r.ns.2 cj j n.vsm n.gsm r.apn v.pam.2s

δίωκε δὲ δικαιοσύνην εὐσέβειαν πίστιν, ἀγάπην ὑπομονὴν πραϋπαθίαν.
and pursue *and* righteousness, godliness, faith, love, endurance, gentleness.
1254 1503 1254 1466 2354 4411 27 5705 4557
v.pam.2s cj n.asf n.asf n.asf n.asf n.asf n.asf

12 ἀγωνίζου τὸν καλὸν ἀγῶνα τῆς πίστεως, ἐπιλαβοῦ τῆς αἰωνίου ζωῆς, εἰς
Fight the good fight of the faith. ⌊Seize hold of⌋ the eternal life, to
76 3836 2819 74 3836 4411 2138 3836 173 2437 1650
v.pmm.2s d.asm a.asm n.asm d.gsf n.gsf v.amm.2s d.gsf a.gsf n.gsf p.a

ἣν ἐκλήθης καὶ ὡμολόγησας τὴν καλὴν ὁμολογίαν ἐνώπιον
which ⌊you were called⌋ and about which you confessed the good confession before
4005 2813 2779 3933 3836 2819 3934 1967
r.asf v.api.2s cj v.aai.2s d.asf a.asf n.asf p.g

πολλῶν μαρτύρων. 13 παραγγέλλω σοι[b] ἐνώπιον τοῦ θεοῦ τοῦ ζῳογονοῦντος
many witnesses. I urge you, in the presence of God who gives life to
4498 3459 4133 5148 1967 3836 2536 3836 2441
a.gpm n.gpm v.pai.1s r.ds.2 p.g d.gsm n.gsm d.gsm pt.pa.gsm

τὰ πάντα καὶ Χριστοῦ Ἰησοῦ τοῦ μαρτυρήσαντος ἐπὶ Ποντίου Πιλάτου
{the} all things and Christ Jesus who witnessed ⌊in the time of⌋ Pontius Pilate
3836 4246 2779 5986 2652 3836 3455 2093 4508 4397
d.apn a.apn cj n.gsm n.gsm d.gsm pt.aa.gsm p.g n.gsm n.gsm

τὴν καλὴν ὁμολογίαν, 14 τηρῆσαί σε τὴν ἐντολὴν ἄσπιλον ἀνεπίλημπτον
the good confession, to keep *{you}* the commandment unblemished and above reproach
3836 2819 3934 5498 5148 3836 1953 834 455
d.asf a.asf n.asf f.aa r.as.2 d.asf n.asf a.asf a.asf

NASB

deprived of the
truth, who suppose
that godliness is
a means of gain.
6But godliness
actually is a means
of great gain when
accompanied by
contentment. 7For
we have brought
nothing into the
world, so we can-
not take anything
out of it either. 8If
we have food and
covering, with
these we shall be
content. 9But those
who want to get
rich fall into temp-
tation and a snare
and many foolish
and harmful desires
which plunge men
into ruin and de-
struction. 10For the
love of money is a
root of all sorts of
evil, and some by
longing for it have
wandered away
from the faith and
pierced themselves
with many griefs.
11But flee from
these things, you
man of God, and
pursue righteous-
ness, godliness,
faith, love, per-
severance *and*
gentleness. 12Fight
the good fight of
faith; take hold of
the eternal life to
which you were
called, and you
made the good
confession in the
presence of many
witnesses. 13I
charge you in the
presence of God,
who gives life to
all things, and of
Christ Jesus, who
testified the good
confession before
Pontius Pilate,
14that you keep the
commandment
without stain or re-
proach until the

[a] ἀφίστασο ἀπὸ τῶν τοιούτων included by TR after εὐσέβειαν.
[b] [σοι] UBS, omitted by NET.

NIV

until the appearing
of our Lord Jesus
Christ, 15 which
God will bring
about in his own
time—God, the
blessed and only
Ruler, the King of
kings and Lord of
lords, 16 who alone
is immortal and
who lives in unap-
proachable light,
whom no one has
seen or can see.
To him be honor
and might forever.
Amen.

17 Command those
who are rich in this
present world not
to be arrogant nor
to put their hope
in wealth, which
is so uncertain,
but to put their
hope in God, who
richly provides us
with everything
for our enjoyment.
18 Command them
to do good, to be
rich in good deeds,
and to be gener-
ous and willing to
share. 19 In this way
they will lay up
treasure for them-
selves as a firm
foundation for the
coming age, so
that they may take
hold of the life that
is truly life.
20 Timothy, guard
what has been
entrusted to your
care. Turn away
from godless
chatter and the
opposing ideas
of what is falsely
called knowledge,
21 which some have
professed and in so
doing have depart-
ed from the faith.
Grace be with
you all.

μέχρι τῆς ἐπιφανείας τοῦ κυρίου ἡμῶν Ἰησοῦ Χριστοῦ, 15 ἣν
until the appearing of our Lord *our* Jesus Christ, which he will make
3588 3836 2211 3836 7005 3261 7005 2652 5986 4005 1259 1259 1259
p.g d.gsf n.gsf d.gsm n.gsm r.gp.1 n.gsm n.gsm r.asf

→ καιροῖς ἰδίοις δείξει ὁ μακάριος καὶ μόνος
known at the proper time. *proper* *he will make known* To the Blessed and only
1259 2625 2789 2625 1259 3836 3421 2779 3668
n.dpm a.dpm v.fai.3s d.nsm a.nsm cj a.nsm

δυνάστης, ὁ βασιλεὺς τῶν βασιλευόντων καὶ κύριος τῶν κυριευόντων, 16 ὁ
Sovereign, the King of kings and Lord of lords, the
1541 3836 995 3836 996 2779 3261 3836 3259 3836
n.nsm d.nsm n.nsm d.gpm pt.pa.gpm cj n.nsm d.gpm pt.pa.gpm d.nsm

μόνος ἔχων ἀθανασίαν, φῶς οἰκῶν
only one having immortality, the one dwelling in unapproachable light, *one dwelling in*
3668 2400 114 3861 3861 3861 717 5890 3861
a.nsm pt.pa.nsm n.asf n.asn pt.pa.nsm

ἀπρόσιτον, ὃν εἶδεν οὐδεὶς ἀνθρώπων οὐδὲ ἰδεῖν δύναται·
unapproachable whom no person has seen *no* *person* or is able to see, *is able*
717 4005 4029 476 1625 4029 476 4028 1538 1538 1625 1538
a.asn r.asm v.aai.3s a.nsm n.gpm cj f.aa v.ppi.3s

ᾧ τιμὴ καὶ κράτος αἰώνιον, ἀμήν. 17 τοῖς πλουσίοις ἐν τῷ νῦν
⌊to him⌋ be honor and might forever, Amen. Urge the rich in the present
4005 5507 2779 3197 173 297 4133 3836 4454 1877 3836 3814
r.dsm n.nsf cj n.nsn a.nsn pl d.dpm a.dpm p.d d.dsm adv

αἰῶνι παράγγελλε μὴ ὑψηλοφρονεῖν μηδὲ ἠλπικέναι ἐπὶ πλούτου
age *Urge* not to be haughty, or to set their hope on the uncertainty of riches
172 4133 3590 5735 3593 1827 2093 84 4458
n.dsm v.pam.2s pl f.pa cj f.ra p.g n.gsm

ἀδηλότητι ἀλλ᾽ ἐπὶ θεῷ τῷ παρέχοντι ἡμῖν πάντα πλουσίως εἰς ἀπόλαυσιν,
uncertainty but on God who grants to us all things richly for our enjoyment,
84 247 2093 2536 3836 4218 7005 4246 4455 1650 656
n.dsf cj p.d n.dsm d.dsm pt.pa.dsm r.dp.1 a.apn adv p.a n.asf

18 ἀγαθοεργεῖν, πλουτεῖν ἐν ἔργοις καλοῖς, εὐμεταδότους εἶναι,
to do good, to be rich in good deeds, *good* to be generous, *to be*
14 4456 1877 2819 2240 2819 1639 1639 2331 1639
f.pa f.pa p.d n.dpn a.dpn a.apm f.pa

κοινωνικούς, 19 ἀποθησαυρίζοντας ἑαυτοῖς θεμέλιον καλὸν εἰς τὸ
sharing, laying up for themselves a good foundation *good* for the
3127 631 1571 2819 2529 2819 1650 3836
a.apm pt.pa.apm r.dpm.3 n.asm a.asm p.a d.asn

μέλλον, ἵνα ἐπιλάβωνται τῆς ὄντως ζωῆς. 20 ὦ Τιμόθεε, τὴν
coming age, so that ⌊they might seize hold⌋ of what is truly life. O Timothy, guard the
3516 2671 2138 3836 3953 2437 6043 5510 5875 3836
pt.pa.asn cj v.ams.3p d.gsf adv n.gsf j n.vsm d.asf

παραθήκην φύλαξον ἐκτρεπόμενος τὰς βεβήλους κενοφωνίας καὶ
deposit entrusted to you, *guard* avoiding the unholy chatter and
4146 5875 1762 3836 1013 3032 2779
n.asf v.aam.2s pt.pm.nsm d.apf a.apf n.apf cj

ἀντιθέσεις τῆς ψευδωνύμου γνώσεως, 21 ἥν τινες
contradictions of what is falsely named "knowledge," for by professing it, some
509 3836 6024 1194 2040 2040 2040 4005 5516
n.apf d.gsf a.gsf n.gsf r.asf r.npm

ἐπαγγελλόμενοι περὶ τὴν πίστιν ἠστόχησαν. ἡ χάρις μεθ᾽ ὑμῶν.[a]
for by professing have swerved from the faith. *have swerved* {the} Grace be with you.
2040 846 846 4309 3836 4411 846 3836 5921 3552 7007
pt.pm.npm p.a d.asf n.asf v.aai.3p d.nsf n.nsf p.g r.gp.2

NASB

appearing of our
Lord Jesus Christ,
15 which He will
bring about at the
proper time—He
who is the blessed
and only Sover-
eign, the King of
kings and Lord of
lords, 16 who alone
possesses immor-
tality and dwells
in unapproachable
light, whom no
man has seen or
can see. To Him *be*
honor and eternal
dominion! Amen.
17 Instruct those
who are rich in this
present world not
to be conceited or
to fix their hope on
the uncertainty of
riches, but on God,
who richly supplies
us with all things
to enjoy. 18 *Instruct*
them to do good,
to be rich in good
works, to be gener-
ous and ready to
share, 19 storing up
for themselves the
treasure of a good
foundation for the
future, so that they
may take hold of
that which is life
indeed.
20 O Timothy,
guard what has
been entrusted
to you, avoid-
ing worldly *and*
empty chatter
and the opposing
arguments of what
is falsely called
"knowledge"—
21 which some have
professed and thus
gone astray from
the faith.
Grace be with
you.

[a] ἀμήν. πρὸς Τιμόθεον πρώτη ἐγράφη ἀπὸ Λαοδικείας ἥτις ἐστιν μητρόπολις Φρυγίας τῆς Πακατιανῆς included by TR after ὑμῶν.

2 Timothy

NIV

1 Paul, an apos-
tle of Christ
Jesus by the will
of God, in keeping
with the promise
of life that is in
Christ Jesus,
2 To Timothy, my
dear son:
Grace, mercy
and peace from
God the Father and
Christ Jesus our
Lord.

Thanksgiving

3 I thank God,
whom I serve, as
my ancestors did,
with a clear con-
science, as night
and day I con-
stantly remember
you in my prayers.
4 Recalling your
tears, I long to see
you, so that I may
be filled with joy.
5 I am reminded of
your sincere faith,
which first lived in
your grandmother
Lois and in your
mother Eunice
and, I am persuad-
ed, now lives in
you also.

Appeal for Loyalty to Paul and the Gospel

6 For this reason
I remind you to
fan into flame the
gift of God, which
is in you through
the laying on of
my hands. 7 For the
Spirit God gave
us does not make
us timid, but gives
us power, love and
self-discipline. 8 So
do not be ashamed
of the testimony
about our Lord or
of me his prisoner.
Rather, join with
me in suffering

1:1 Παῦλος ἀπόστολος Χριστοῦ Ἰησοῦ διὰ θελήματος θεοῦ κατ᾽
Paul, an apostle of Christ Jesus through the will of God ⌊according to⌋
4263 693 5986 2652 1328 2525 2536 2848
n.nsm n.nsm n.gsm n.gsm p.g n.gsn n.gsm p.a

ἐπαγγελίαν ζωῆς τῆς ἐν Χριστῷ Ἰησοῦ 2 Τιμοθέῳ ἀγαπητῷ τέκνῳ, χάρις
the promise of life that is in Christ Jesus, to Timothy, beloved son: Grace,
2039 2437 3836 1877 5986 2652 5510 28 5451 5921
n.asf n.gsf d.gsf p.d n.dsm n.dsm n.dsm a.dsn n.dsn n.nsf

ἔλεος εἰρήνη ἀπὸ θεοῦ πατρὸς καὶ Χριστοῦ Ἰησοῦ τοῦ κυρίου ἡμῶν.
mercy, peace from God the Father and Christ Jesus {the} our Lord. *our*
1799 1645 608 2536 4252 2779 5986 2652 3836 7005 3261 7005
n.nsn n.nsf p.g n.gsm n.gsm cj n.gsm n.gsm d.gsm n.gsm r.gp.1

3 ⌊χάριν ἔχω⌋ τῷ θεῷ, ᾧ λατρεύω ἀπὸ προγόνων ἐν καθαρᾷ
I continually thank {the} God, whom I serve, as did my ancestors, with a clean
5921 2400 3836 2536 4005 3302 608 4591 1877 2754
n.asf v.pai.1s d.dsm n.dsm r.dsm v.pai.1s p.g n.gpm p.d a.dsf

συνειδήσει, ὡς ἀδιάλειπτον → ἔχω τὴν περὶ σοῦ μνείαν ἐν ταῖς
conscience, as unceasingly I {have} remember {the} {about} you *remember* in {the} my
5287 6055 89 2400 3644 3836 4309 5148 3644 1877 3836 1609
n.dsf cj a.asf v.pai.1s d.asf p.g r.gs.2 n.asf p.d d.dpf

δεήσεσίν μου νυκτὸς καὶ ἡμέρας, 4 ἐπιποθῶν σε ἰδεῖν, μεμνημένος σου τῶν
prayers *my* night and day, yearning to see you, *to see* remembering your {the}
1255 1609 3816 2779 2465 2160 1625 1625 5148 1625 3630 5148 3836
n.dpf r.gs.1 n.gsf cj n.gsf pt.pa.nsm r.as.2 f.aa pt.rp.nsm r.gs.2 d.gpn

δακρύων, ἵνα χαρᾶς πληρωθῶ, 5 ↱ ὑπόμνησιν
tears, so that I may be filled with joy, *I may be filled with* because I remember
1232 2671 4444 4444 4444 4444 4444 5915 4444 3284 5704
n.gpn cj n.gsf v.aps.1s n.asf

λαβὼν τῆς ⌊ἐν σοὶ⌋ ἀνυποκρίτου πίστεως, ἥτις ἐνῴκησεν πρῶτον ἐν τῇ
{taking} {the} your sincere faith, which dwelt first in {the} your
3284 3836 1877 5148 537 4411 4015 1940 4754 1877 3836 5148
pt.aa.nsm d.gsf p.d r.ds.2 a.gsf n.gsf r.nsf v.aai.3s adv p.d d.dsf

μάμμῃ σου Λωΐδι καὶ τῇ μητρί σου Εὐνίκῃ, πέπεισμαι δὲ ὅτι
grandmother *your* Lois and {the} your mother *your* Eunice, and I am confident *and* that it is
3439 5148 3396 2779 3836 5148 3613 5148 2332 1254 4275 1254 4022
n.dsf r.gs.2 n.dsf cj d.dsf n.dsf r.gs.2 n.dsf v.rpi.1s cj cj

καὶ ἐν σοί. 6 δι᾽ ἣν αἰτίαν ἀναμιμνῄσκω σε ἀναζωπυρεῖν τὸ χάρισμα τοῦ
also in you. For which reason I remind you to fan into flame the gift of
2779 1877 5148 1328 4005 162 389 5148 351 3836 5922 3836
adv p.d r.ds.2 p.a r.asf n.asf v.pai.1s r.as.2 f.pa d.asn n.asn d.gsm

θεοῦ, ὅ ἐστιν ἐν σοὶ διὰ τῆς ἐπιθέσεως τῶν χειρῶν μου. 7 ↱
God, which is in you through the laying on of my hands, *my* for God did
2536 4005 1639 1877 5148 1328 3836 2120 3836 1609 5931 1609 1142 2536 1443
n.gsm r.nsn v.pai.3s p.d r.ds.2 p.g d.gsf n.gsf d.gpf n.gpf r.gs.1

οὐ γὰρ ἔδωκεν ἡμῖν ὁ θεὸς πνεῦμα δειλίας ἀλλὰ δυνάμεως καὶ ἀγάπης καὶ
not *for* give us {the} *God* a spirit of fear but of power and of love and
4024 1142 1443 7005 3836 2536 4460 1261 247 1539 2779 27 2779
pl cj v.aai.3s r.dp.1 d.nsm n.nsm n.asn n.gsf cj n.gsf cj n.gsf cj

σωφρονισμοῦ. 8 ↱ μὴ οὖν ἐπαισχυνθῇς τὸ μαρτύριον τοῦ
of self-control. Therefore do not *Therefore* be ashamed of the testimony concerning our
5406 4036 2049 3590 4036 2049 3836 3457 3836 7005
n.gsm pl cj v.aps.2s d.asn n.asn d.gsm

κυρίου ἡμῶν μηδὲ ἐμὲ τὸν δέσμιον αὐτοῦ, ἀλλὰ συγκακοπάθησον
Lord *our* nor of me {the} his prisoner, *his* but share in suffering
3261 7005 3593 1609 3836 899 1300 899 247 5155
n.gsm r.gp.1 cj r.as.1 d.asm n.asm r.gsm.3 cj v.aam.2s

NASB

Timothy Charged to Guard His Trust

1:1 Paul, an apostle
of Christ Jesus by
the will of God,
according to the
promise of life in
Christ Jesus,
2 To Timothy,
my beloved son:
Grace, mercy *and*
peace from God
the Father and
Christ Jesus our
Lord.
3 I thank God,
whom I serve
with a clear con-
science the way
my forefathers
did, as I constantly
remember you in
my prayers night
and day, 4 longing
to see you, even
as I recall your
tears, so that I may
be filled with joy.
5 For I am mindful
of the sincere faith
within you, which
first dwelt in your
grandmother Lois
and your mother
Eunice, and I am
sure that *it is* in
you as well. 6 For
this reason I re-
mind you to kindle
afresh the gift of
God which is in
you through the
laying on of my
hands. 7 For God
has not given us a
spirit of timidity,
but of power and
love and discipline.
8 Therefore do not
be ashamed of the
testimony of our
Lord or of me His
prisoner, but join
with *me* in suffer-
ing for the gospel

NIV

for the gospel, by
the power of God.
9 He has saved us
and called us to
a holy life—not
because of any-
thing we have done
but because of his
own purpose and
grace. This grace
was given us in
Christ Jesus before
the beginning of
time, 10 but it has
now been revealed
through the appear-
ing of our Savior,
Christ Jesus, who
has destroyed death
and has brought
life and immortal-
ity to light through
the gospel. 11 And
of this gospel I was
appointed a herald
and an apostle and
a teacher. 12 That
is why I am suf-
fering as I am. Yet
this is no cause for
shame, because I
know whom I have
believed, and am
convinced that he
is able to guard
what I have en-
trusted to him until
that day.
13 What you heard
from me, keep
as the pattern of
sound teaching,
with faith and love
in Christ Jesus.
14 Guard the good
deposit that was
entrusted to you—
guard it with the
help of the Holy
Spirit who lives
in us.

Examples of Disloyalty and Loyalty

15 You know that
everyone in the
province of Asia
has deserted me,
including Phygelus
and Hermogenes.
16 May the Lord
show mercy to
the household of
Onesiphorus,

τῷ εὐαγγελίῳ κατὰ δύναμιν θεοῦ, 9 τοῦ σώσαντος ἡμᾶς καὶ
⌊for the sake of the⌋ gospel by the power of God, who saved us and
3836 2295 2848 1539 2536 3836 5392 7005 2779
d.dsn n.dsn p.a n.asf n.gsm d.gsm pt.aa.gsm r.ap.1 cj

καλέσαντος → κλήσει ἁγίᾳ, οὐ κατὰ τὰ ἔργα ἡμῶν ἀλλὰ
called us to a holy calling, *holy* not ⌊because of⌋ *{the}* our works *our* but
2813 41 3104 41 4024 2848 3836 7005 2240 7005 247
pt.aa.gsm n.dsf a.dsf pl p.a d.apn n.apn r.gp.1 cj

κατὰ ἰδίαν πρόθεσιν καὶ χάριν, τὴν δοθεῖσαν ἡμῖν ἐν Χριστῷ Ἰησοῦ πρὸ
⌊because of⌋ his own purpose and grace, which was given to us in Christ Jesus before
2848 2625 4606 2779 5921 3836 1443 7005 1877 5986 2652 4574
p.a a.asf n.asf cj n.asf d.asf pt.ap.asf r.dp.1 p.d n.dsm n.dsm p.g

χρόνων αἰωνίων, 10 φανερωθεῖσαν δὲ νῦν διὰ τῆς ἐπιφανείας τοῦ
time eternal, but now has been made known *but* *now* through the appearing of
5989 173 1254 3814 5746 1254 3814 1328 3836 2211 3836
n.gpm a.gpm pt.ap.asf cj adv p.g d.gsf n.gsf d.gsm

σωτῆρος ἡμῶν Χριστοῦ Ἰησοῦ, καταργήσαντος μὲν
our Savior, *our* Christ Jesus, on the one hand, in order to abolish *on the one hand*
7005 5400 7005 5986 2652 3525 3525 3525 3525 2934 3525
n.gsm r.gp.1 n.gsm n.gsm pt.aa.gsm pl

τὸν θάνατον φωτίσαντος δὲ ζωὴν καὶ ἀφθαρσίαν
{the} death and, on the other, to bring to light *and on the other* life and incorruptibility
3836 2505 1254 1254 1254 1254 5894 1254 2437 2779 914
d.asm n.asm pt.aa.gsm cj n.asf cj n.asf

διὰ τοῦ εὐαγγελίου 11 εἰς ὃ ἐτέθην ἐγὼ κῆρυξ καὶ ἀπόστολος
through the gospel, for which I was appointed *I* a herald and an apostle
1328 3836 2295 1650 4005 1609 5502 1609 3061 2779 693
p.g d.gsn n.gsn p.a r.asn v.api.1s r.ns.1 n.nsm cj n.nsm

καὶ διδάσκαλος, 12 δι᾽ ἣν αἰτίαν καὶ ταῦτα πάσχω·
and a teacher, for which reason even I am suffering these things; *I am suffering*
2779 1437 1328 4005 162 2779 4248 4248 4248 4047 4248
cj n.nsm p.a r.asf n.asf adv r.apn v.pai.1s

ἀλλ᾽ ↱ ↱ οὐκ ἐπαισχύνομαι, οἶδα γὰρ ᾧ πεπίστευκα καὶ
but I am not ashamed, for I know *for* ⌊in whom⌋ I have trusted and
247 2049 2049 4024 2049 1142 3857 1142 4005 4409 2779
cj pl v.ppi.1s v.rai.1s cj r.dsm v.rai.1s cj

πέπεισμαι ὅτι δυνατός ἐστιν τὴν παραθήκην μου
I am fully convinced that he is able *he is* to guard *{the}* my deposit *my*
4275 4022 1639 1639 1543 1639 5875 5875 3836 1609 4146 1609
v.rpi.1s cj a.nsm v.pai.3s d.asf n.asf r.gs.1

φυλάξαι εἰς ἐκείνην τὴν ἡμέραν. 13 ὑποτύπωσιν ἔχε ὑγιαινόντων
to guard until that *{the}* day. Hold to the pattern *Hold to* of healthy
5875 1650 1697 3836 2465 2400 2400 5721 2400 5617
f.aa p.a r.asf d.asf n.asf n.asf v.pam.2s pt.pa.gpm

λόγων ὧν παρ᾽ ἐμοῦ ἤκουσας ἐν πίστει καὶ ἀγάπῃ τῇ
words that you have heard from me *you have heard* in the faith and the love that is
3364 4005 201 201 201 4123 1609 201 1877 4411 2779 27 3836
n.gpm r.gpm p.g r.gs.1 v.aai.2s p.d n.dsf cj n.dsf d.dsf

ἐν Χριστῷ Ἰησοῦ· 14 τὴν καλὴν παραθήκην φύλαξον διὰ πνεύματος
in Christ Jesus. Guard the good deposit *Guard* by the Holy Spirit
1877 5986 2652 5875 3836 2819 4146 5875 1328 41 4460
p.d n.dsm n.dsm d.asf a.asf n.asf v.aam.2s p.g n.gsn

ἁγίου τοῦ ⌊ἐνοικοῦντος ἐν⌋ ἡμῖν. 15 οἶδας τοῦτο, ὅτι
Holy that indwells us. You know this, that all those in Asia
41 3836 1940 1877 7005 3857 4047 4022 4246 3836 1877 823
a.gsn d.gsn pt.pa.gsn p.d r.dp.1 v.rai.2s r.asn cj

ἀπεστράφησάν με πάντες οἱ ἐν τῇ Ἀσίᾳ, ὧν ἐστιν Φύγελος καὶ
have deserted me, *all* *those* *in* *{the}* *Asia* ⌊among whom⌋ are Phygelus and
695 1609 4246 3836 1877 3836 823 4005 1639 5869 2779
v.api.3p r.as.1 a.npm d.npm p.d d.dsf n.dsf r.gpm v.pai.3s n.nsm cj

Ἑρμογένης. 16 → δῴη ἔλεος ὁ κύριος τῷ Ὀνησιφόρου
Hermogenes. May the Lord grant mercy *the* *Lord* ⌊to the⌋ household of Onesiphorus,
2259 3836 3261 1443 1799 3836 3261 3836 3875 3947
n.nsm v.aao.3s n.asn d.nsm n.nsm d.dsm n.gsm

NASB

according to the
power of God,
9 who has saved us
and called us with
a holy calling, not
according to our
works, but accord-
ing to His own
purpose and grace
which was granted
us in Christ Jesus
from all eternity,
10 but now has been
revealed by the
appearing of our
Savior Christ Je-
sus, who abolished
death and brought
life and immortal-
ity to light through
the gospel, 11 for
which I was ap-
pointed a preacher
and an apostle and
a teacher. 12 For this
reason I also suffer
these things, but I
am not ashamed;
for I know whom I
have believed and
I am convinced
that He is able to
guard what I have
entrusted to Him
until that day. 13 Re-
tain the standard
of sound words
which you have
heard from me, in
the faith and love
which are in Christ
Jesus. 14 Guard,
through the Holy
Spirit who dwells
in us, the treasure
which has been
entrusted to *you.*
15 You are aware
of the fact that all
who are in Asia
turned away from
me, among whom
are Phygelus and
Hermogenes. 16 The
Lord grant mercy
to the house of
Onesiphorus, for

NIV

because he often
refreshed me and
was not ashamed
of my chains. [17]On
the contrary, when
he was in Rome,
he searched hard
for me until he
found me. [18]May
the Lord grant that
he will find mer-
cy from the Lord
on that day! You
know very well in
how many ways he
helped me in Eph-
esus.

The Appeal Renewed

2 You then, my
son, be strong
in the grace that
is in Christ Jesus.
[2]And the things
you have heard me
say in the presence
of many witnesses
entrust to reliable
people who will
also be qualified to
teach others. [3]Join
with me in suffer-
ing, like a good
soldier of Christ
Jesus. [4]No one
serving as a sol-
dier gets entangled
in civilian affairs,
but rather tries to
please his com-
manding officer.
[5]Similarly, anyone
who competes as
an athlete does not
receive the victor's
crown except by
competing accord-
ing to the rules.
[6]The hardworking
farmer should be
the first to receive
a share of the
crops. [7]Reflect on
what I am saying,
for the Lord will
give you insight
into all this.
[8]Remember Jesus
Christ, raised from
the dead, descend-
ed from David.
This is my gospel,
[9]for

οἴκω, ὅτι πολλάκις με ἀνέψυξεν καὶ τὴν
household for often he refreshed me *he refreshed* and was not ashamed of *{the}* my
3875 4022 4490 434 434 1609 434 2779 2049 4024 2049 3836 1609
n.dsm cj adv r.as.1 v.aai.3s cj d.asf

ἅλυσίν μου οὐκ ἐπαισχύνθη, [17] ἀλλὰ γενόμενος ἐν Ῥώμῃ ➝ σπουδαίως ἐζήτησέν
chain, *my* *not* *was ashamed* but being in Rome, he earnestly searched for
268 1609 4024 2049 247 1181 1877 4873 2426 5081 2426
n.asf r.gs.1 pl v.api.3s cj pt.am.nsm p.d n.dsf adv v.aai.3s

με καὶ εὗρεν· [18] ➝ δῴη αὐτῷ ὁ κύριος εὑρεῖν ἔλεος παρὰ
me and found me. May the Lord grant him *the* *Lord* to find mercy from the
1609 2779 2351 3836 3261 1443 899 3836 3261 2351 1799 4123
r.as.1 cj v.aai.3s v.aao.3s r.dsm.3 d.nsm n.nsm f.aa n.asn p.g

κυρίου ἐν ἐκείνῃ τῇ ἡμέρᾳ. καὶ ὅσα ἐν Ἐφέσῳ διηκόνησεν,
Lord on that *{the}* day. And the services he performed in Ephesus *he performed*
3261 1877 1697 3836 2465 2779 4012 1354 1354 1877 2387 1354
n.gsm p.d r.dsf d.dsf n.dsf cj r.apn p.d n.dsf v.aai.3s

βέλτιον σὺ γινώσκεις.
you know very well. *you* *know*
5148 1182 1019 5148 1182
adv.c r.ns.2 v.pai.2s

[2:1] σὺ οὖν, τέκνον μου, ἐνδυναμοῦ ἐν τῇ χάριτι τῇ ἐν Χριστῷ
You, then, my child, *my* be strengthened by the grace that is in Christ
5148 4036 1609 5451 1609 1904 1877 3836 5921 3836 1877 5986
r.ns.2 cj n.vsn r.gs.1 v.ppm.2s p.d d.dsf n.dsf d.dsf p.d n.dsm

Ἰησοῦ, [2] καὶ ἃ ἤκουσας παρ᾿ ἐμοῦ διὰ πολλῶν μαρτύρων,
Jesus, and what you have heard from me ⌊in the presence of⌋ many witnesses, entrust
2652 2779 4005 201 4123 1609 1328 4498 3459 4192
n.dsm cj r.apn v.aai.2s p.g r.gs.1 p.g a.gpm n.gpm

ταῦτα παράθου πιστοῖς ἀνθρώποις, οἵτινες ἱκανοὶ ἔσονται καὶ
these things *entrust* to faithful men, who will also be able *will be* *also* to
4047 4192 4412 476 4015 1639 2779 1639 2653 1639 2779 1438
r.apn v.amm.2s a.dpm n.dpm r.npm a.npm v.fmi.3p adv

ἑτέρους διδάξαι. [3] συγκακοπάθησον ὡς καλὸς στρατιώτης Χριστοῦ Ἰησοῦ.
teach others. *to teach* Share in suffering as a good soldier of Christ Jesus.
1438 2283 1438 5155 6055 2819 5132 5986 2652
r.apm f.aa v.aam.2s pl a.nsm n.nsm n.gsm n.gsm

[4] οὐδεὶς στρατευόμενος ἐμπλέκεται ταῖς τοῦ βίου πραγματείαις,
No one serving in the military ⌊gets entangled in⌋ the affairs of ⌊daily life⌋ *affairs*
4029 5129 1861 3836 4548 3836 1050 4548
a.nsm pt.pm.nsm v.ppi.3s d.dpf d.gsm n.gsm n.dpf

ἵνα τῷ στρατολογήσαντι ἀρέσῃ. [5] ἐὰν δὲ καὶ
so that he pleases the one who enlisted him. *he pleases* Likewise, if *{and}* *Likewise* anyone
2671 743 743 3836 5133 743 2779 1569 1254 2779 5516
cj d.dsm pt.aa.dsm v.aas.3s cj cj adv

ἀθλῇ τις, ➝ ➝ οὐ στεφανοῦται ⌊ἐὰν μὴ⌋ νομίμως
⌊competes as an athlete,⌋ *anyone* he does not receive a wreath unless he competes lawfully.
123 5516 5110 5110 4024 5110 1569 3590 123 123 3789
v.pas.3s r.nsm pl v.ppi.3s cj pl adv

ἀθλήσῃ. [6] τὸν κοπιῶντα γεωργὸν δεῖ πρῶτον τῶν καρπῶν
he competes The hardworking farmer ⌊must be⌋ the first to receive the fruit.
123 3836 3159 1177 1256 4754 3561 3561 3836 2843
v.aas.3s d.asm pt.pa.asm n.asm v.pai.3s adv d.gpm n.gpm

μεταλαμβάνειν. [7] νόει ὃ λέγω, δώσει γάρ σοι ὁ κύριος
to receive ⌊Reflect on⌋ what I am saying, for the Lord will give *for* you *the* *Lord*
3561 3783 4005 3306 1142 3836 3261 1443 1142 5148 3836 3261
f.pa v.pam.2s r.asn v.pai.1s v.fai.3s cj r.ds.2 d.nsm n.nsm

σύνεσιν ἐν πᾶσιν. [8] μνημόνευε Ἰησοῦν Χριστὸν ἐγηγερμένον ἐκ νεκρῶν,
insight in all this. Remember Jesus Christ, risen from the dead,
5304 1877 4246 3648 2652 5986 1586 1666 3738
n.asf p.d a.dpn v.pam.2s n.asm n.asm pt.rp.asm p.g a.gpm

ἐκ σπέρματος Δαυίδ, κατὰ τὸ εὐαγγέλιόν μου, [9] ἐν
from the seed of David, ⌊in accordance with⌋ *{the}* my gospel, *my* ⌊because of⌋
1666 5065 1253 2848 3836 1609 2295 1609 1877
p.g n.gsn n.gsm p.a d.asn n.asn r.gs.1 p.d

NASB

he often refreshed
me and was not
ashamed of my
chains; [17]but when
he was in Rome, he
eagerly searched
for me and found
me— [18]the Lord
grant to him to find
mercy from the
Lord on that day—
and you know very
well what services
he rendered at
Ephesus.

Be Strong

[2:1]You therefore,
my son, be strong
in the grace that
is in Christ Jesus.
[2]The things which
you have heard
from me in the
presence of many
witnesses, entrust
these to faithful
men who will be
able to teach others
also. [3]Suffer hard-
ship with *me,* as
a good soldier of
Christ Jesus. [4]No
soldier in active
service entangles
himself in the af-
fairs of everyday
life, so that he may
please the one who
enlisted him as a
soldier. [5]Also if
anyone competes
as an athlete, he
does not win the
prize unless he
competes accord-
ing to the rules.
[6]The hard-working
farmer ought to be
the first to receive
his share of the
crops. [7]Consider
what I say, for the
Lord will give you
understanding in
everything.
[8]Remember Jesus
Christ, risen from
the dead, descen-
dant of David,
according to my
gospel, [9]for which

NIV

which I am suf-
fering even to
the point of be-
ing chained like
a criminal. But
God's word is not
chained. [10]There-
fore I endure ev-
erything for the
sake of the elect,
that they too may
obtain the salvation
that is in Christ
Jesus, with eternal
glory.
[11]Here is a trust-
worthy saying:

If we died with
him,
we will also live
with him;
[12]if we endure,
we will also
reign with
him.
If we disown him,
he will also
disown us;
[13]if we are faithless,
he remains
faithful,
for he cannot
disown
himself.

Dealing With False Teachers

[14]Keep reminding
God's people of
these things. Warn
them before God
against quarrel-
ing about words;
it is of no value,
and only ruins
those who listen.
[15]Do your best to
present yourself
to God as one ap-
proved, a worker
who does not need
to be ashamed
and who correctly
handles the word
of truth. [16]Avoid
godless chatter,
because those who
indulge in it will
become more and
more ungodly.
[17]Their teaching
will spread like
gangrene. Among
them are Hyme-
naeus and Phile-
tus, [18]who have
departed from the
truth.

ᾧ κακοπαθῶ μέχρι δεσμῶν ὡς κακοῦργος, ἀλλὰ ὁ
which ⌞I am suffering evil⌟ ⌞even to the point⌟ of imprisonment as a serious criminal, but the
4005 2802 3588 1301 6055 2806 247 3836
r.dsn v.pai.1s p.g n.gpm pl n.nsm cj d.nsm

λόγος τοῦ θεοῦ ↱ οὐ δέδεται· [10] διὰ τοῦτο πάντα
word of God is not bound. ⌞On account of⌟ this I am enduring all things
3364 3836 2536 1313 4024 1313 1328 4047 5702 5702 5702 4246
n.nsm d.gsm n.gsm pl v.rpi.3s p.a r.asn a.apn

ὑπομένω διὰ τοὺς ἐκλεκτούς, ἵνα καὶ αὐτοὶ
I am enduring ⌞for the sake of⌟ the elect, that they also *they* may experience the
5702 1328 3836 1723 2671 899 2779 899 5593 5593
v.pai.1s p.a d.apm a.apm cj adv r.npm

σωτηρίας τύχωσιν τῆς ἐν Χριστῷ Ἰησοῦ μετὰ δόξης αἰωνίου.
salvation *may experience* that is in Christ Jesus with eternal glory. *eternal*
5401 5593 3836 1877 5986 2652 3552 173 1518 173
n.gsf v.aas.3p d.gsf p.d n.dsm n.dsm p.g n.gsf a.gsf

[11] πιστὸς ὁ λόγος εἰ γὰρ συναπεθάνομεν, ↱ ↱ καὶ συζήσομεν·
Trustworthy is the saying, for: "If *for* we died together, we will also live together.
4412 3836 3364 1142 1623 1142 5271 5182 5182 2779 5182
a.nsm d.nsm n.nsm cj cj v.aai.1p adv v.fai.1p

[12] εἰ ὑπομένομεν, ↱ ↱ καὶ συμβασιλεύσομεν· εἰ ἀρνησόμεθα, κἀκεῖνος
If we endure, we will also reign together. If we will deny Christ, he
1623 5702 5203 5203 2779 5203 1623 766 2797
cj v.pai.1p adv v.fai.1p cj v.fmi.1p crasis

→ ἀρνήσεται ἡμᾶς· [13] εἰ ἀπιστοῦμεν, ἐκεῖνος πιστὸς μένει,
will also deny us. If we are faithless, he remains faithful, *remains* for he
766 7005 1623 601 1697 3531 4412 3531 1142 1538
v.fmi.3s r.ap.1 cj v.pai.1p r.nsm a.nsm v.pai.3s

ἀρνήσασθαι γὰρ ἑαυτὸν οὐ δύναται. [14] ταῦτα
is not able to deny *for* himself." *not* *he is able* Remind them of these things,
1538 4024 1538 766 1142 1571 4024 1538 5703 4047
f.am cj r.asm.3 pl v.ppi.3s r.apn

ὑπομίμνῃσκε διαμαρτυρόμενος ἐνώπιον τοῦ θεοῦ[a] μὴ
Remind solemnly charging them before *{the}* God not
5703 1371 1967 3836 2536 3590
v.pam.2s pt.pm.nsm p.g d.gsm n.gsm pl

λογομαχεῖν, ἐπ' οὐδὲν χρήσιμον, ἐπὶ
⌞to continue fighting about words,⌟ which ⌞results in⌟ nothing beneficial but only in the
3362 2093 4029 5978 2093
f.pa p.a a.asn a.asn p.d

καταστροφῇ τῶν ἀκουόντων. [15] σπούδασον σεαυτὸν
ruin of those listening. Be diligent to present yourself before God as
2953 3836 201 5079 4225 4225 4932 3836 2536
n.dsf d.gpm pt.pa.gpm v.aam.2s r.asm.2

δόκιμον παραστῆσαι τῷ θεῷ, ἐργάτην ἀνεπαίσχυντον,
⌞one tried and true,⌟ *to present* *before* *God* an unashamed worker, *unashamed*
1511 4225 3836 2536 454 2239 454
a.asm f.aa d.dsm n.dsm n.asm a.asm

ὀρθοτομοῦντα τὸν λόγον τῆς ἀληθείας. [16] τὰς δὲ βεβήλους κενοφωνίας
correctly handling the word of truth. But shun the *But* unholy chatter,
3982 3836 3364 3836 237 1254 4325 3836 1254 1013 3032
pt.pa.asm d.asm n.asm d.gsf n.gsf d.apf cj a.apf n.apf

περιΐστασο· ἐπὶ πλεῖον γὰρ προκόψουσιν ἀσεβείας [17] καὶ ὁ
shun for they will advance into greater *for* *they will advance* ungodliness and *{the}*
4325 1142 4621 4621 4621 2093 4498 1142 4621 813 2779 3836
v.pmm.2s p.a adv.c cj v.fai.3p n.gsf cj d.nsm

λόγος αὐτῶν ὡς γάγγραινα ⌞νομὴν ἕξει.⌟ ὧν ἐστιν
their talk *their* will spread like gangrene, *will spread* ⌞among whom⌟ are
899 3364 899 3786 3786 6055 1121 3786 2400 4005 1639
n.nsm r.gpm.3 pl n.nsf n.asf v.fai.3s r.gpm v.pai.3s

Ὑμέναιος καὶ Φίλητος, [18] οἵτινες περὶ τὴν ἀλήθειαν ἠστόχησαν,
Hymenaeus and Philetus, who have swerved from the truth, *have swerved*
5628 2779 5801 4015 846 846 4309 3836 237 846
n.nsm cj n.nsm r.npm p.a d.asf n.asf v.aai.3p

[a] θεοῦ UBS, TNIV. κυρίου NET.

NASB

I suffer hardship
even to imprison-
ment as a criminal;
but the word
of God is not
imprisoned. [10]For
this reason I endure
all things for the
sake of those who
are chosen, so
that they also may
obtain the salvation
which is in Christ
Jesus *and* with *it*
eternal glory. [11]It
is a trustworthy
statement:
For if we died
with Him, we
will also live
with Him;
[12]If we endure,
we will also
reign with
Him;
If we deny
Him, He also
will deny us;
[13]If we are
faithless, He
remains faith-
ful, for He
cannot deny
Himself.

An Unashamed Workman

[14]Remind *them* of
these things, and
solemnly charge
them in the pres-
ence of God not
to wrangle about
words, which is
useless *and leads*
to the ruin of
the hearers. [15]Be
diligent to pres-
ent yourself ap-
proved to God as
a workman who
does not need to
be ashamed, ac-
curately handling
the word of truth.
[16]But avoid worldly
and empty chatter,
for it will lead to
further ungodli-
ness, [17]and their
talk will spread
like [a]gangrene.
Among them are
Hymenaeus and
Philetus, [18]*men* who
have gone astray
from the truth

[a] Or *cancer*

NIV

They say that the
resurrection has al-
ready taken place,
and they destroy
the faith of some.
[19]Nevertheless,
God's solid foun-
dation stands firm,
sealed with this
inscription: "The
Lord knows those
who are his," and,
"Everyone who
confesses the name
of the Lord must
turn away from
wickedness."
[20]In a large house
there are articles
not only of gold
and silver, but also
of wood and clay;
some are for spe-
cial purposes and
some for common
use. [21]Those who
cleanse themselves
from the latter will
be instruments for
special purposes,
made holy, useful
to the Master and
prepared to do any
good work.
[22]Flee the evil
desires of youth
and pursue righ-
teousness, faith,
love and peace,
along with those
who call on the
Lord out of a pure
heart. [23]Don't
have anything to
do with foolish
and stupid argu-
ments, because
you know they
produce quarrels.
[24]And the Lord's
servant must not
be quarrelsome but
must be kind to
everyone, able to
teach, not resent-
ful. [25]Opponents
must be gently
instructed, in the
hope that God will
grant them repen-
tance leading them
to a knowledge of
the truth, [26]and

λέγοντες τὴν[a] ἀνάστασιν ↱ ἤδη γεγονέναι, καὶ ἀνατρέπουσιν τήν τινων
saying the resurrection has already occurred, and they are upsetting the faith of some.
3306 3836 414 1181 2453 1181 2779 426 3836 4411 5516
pt.pa.npm d.asf n.asf adv f.ra cj v.pai.3p d.asf r.gpm

πίστιν. 19 ὁ μέντοι στερεὸς θεμέλιος τοῦ θεοῦ ἕστηκεν, ἔχων
faith Nevertheless, the *Nevertheless* firm foundation of God stands firm, having
4411 3530 3836 3530 5104 2529 3836 2536 2705 2400
n.asf d.nsm cj a.nsm n.nsm d.gsm n.gsm v.rai.3s pt.pa.nsm

τὴν σφραγῖδα ταύτην· ἔγνω κύριος τοὺς ὄντας αὐτοῦ, καί, →
{the} this seal, *this* "The Lord knew *Lord* those who were his," and, "Let
3836 4047 5382 4047 3261 1182 3261 3836 1639 899 2779
d.asf n.asf r.asf v.aai.3s n.nsm d.apm pt.pa.apm r.gsm.3 cj

ἀποστήτω ἀπὸ ἀδικίας πᾶς ὁ
everyone naming the name of the Lord depart from unrighteousness." *everyone* *{the}*
4246 3951 3836 3950 3261 3261 923 608 94 4246 3836
v.aam.3s p.g n.gsf a.nsm d.nsm

ὀνομάζων τὸ ὄνομα κυρίου. 20 ἐν μεγάλῃ δὲ οἰκίᾳ οὐκ ἔστιν
naming *the* *name* *of Lord* And in a large *And* house there are not *there are*
3951 3836 3950 3261 1254 1877 3489 1254 3864 1639 1639 4024 1639
pt.pa.nsm d.asn n.asn n.gsm p.d a.dsf cj n.dsf pl v.pai.3s

μόνον σκεύη χρυσᾶ καὶ ἀργυρᾶ ἀλλὰ καὶ ξύλινα καὶ ὀστράκινα, καὶ ἃ
only vessels of gold and silver but also of wood and clay, ˻that is,˼ some
3667 5007 5997 2779 739 247 2779 3832 2779 4017 2779 4005
adv n.npn a.npn cj a.npn cj adv a.npn cj a.npn cj r.npn

μὲν εἰς τιμὴν ἃ δὲ εἰς ἀτιμίαν· 21 ἐὰν οὖν τις ἐκκαθάρῃ ἑαυτὸν
~ for honor and others *and* for dishonor. If, therefore, someone cleanses himself
3525 1650 5507 1254 4005 1254 1650 871 1569 4036 5516 1705 1571
pl p.a n.asf r.npn pl p.a n.asf cj cj r.nsm v.aas.3s r.asm.3

ἀπὸ τούτων, ἔσται σκεῦος εἰς τιμήν, ἡγιασμένον, εὔχρηστον
from these things, that person will be a vessel for honor, having been sanctified, useful
608 4047 1639 5007 1650 5507 39 2378
p.g r.gpn v.fmi.3s n.nsn p.a n.asf pt.rp.nsn a.nsn

τῷ δεσπότῃ, εἰς πᾶν ἔργον ἀγαθὸν ἡτοιμασμένον. 22 τὰς δὲ
˻to the˼ master, prepared for every good work. *prepared* *{the}* So flee
3836 1305 2286 1650 4246 2240 19 2286 3836 1254 5771
d.dsm n.dsm p.a a.asn n.asn a.asn pt.rp.nsn d.apf cj

νεωτερικὰς ἐπιθυμίας φεῦγε, δίωκε δὲ δικαιοσύνην πίστιν ἀγάπην εἰρήνην μετὰ
youthful passions *flee* and pursue *and* righteousness, faith, love, peace, with
3754 2123 5771 1254 1503 1254 1466 4411 27 1645 3552
a.apf n.apf v.pam.2s v.pam.2s cj n.asf n.asf n.asf n.asf p.g

τῶν ἐπικαλουμένων τὸν κύριον ἐκ καθαρᾶς καρδίας. 23 τὰς δὲ
those who call upon the Lord ˻out of˼ a clean heart. But avoid the *But*
3836 2126 3836 3261 1666 2754 2840 1254 4148 3836 1254
d.gpm pt.pm.gpm d.asm n.asm p.g a.gsf n.gsf d.apf cj

μωρὰς καὶ ἀπαιδεύτους ζητήσεις παραιτοῦ, εἰδὼς ὅτι γεννῶσιν μάχας· 24
foolish and uneducated speculations, *avoid* knowing that they breed quarrels. But
3704 2779 553 2428 4148 3857 4022 1164 3480 1254
a.apf cj a.apf n.apf v.pmm.2s pt.ra.nsm cj v.pai.3p n.apf

δοῦλον δὲ → κυρίου οὐ δεῖ μάχεσθαι ἀλλὰ
it is necessary that a servant *But* of the Lord not *it is necessary* be quarrelsome but
1256 1256 1256 1529 1254 3261 4024 1256 3481 247
n.asm cj n.gsm pl v.pai.3s f.pm cj

ἤπιον εἶναι πρὸς πάντας, διδακτικόν, ἀνεξίκακον, 25 ἐν
be gentle *be* to all, skilled in teaching, ˻patient even in the midst of evil,˼ in
1639 2473 1639 4639 4246 1434 452 1877
a.asm f.pa p.a a.apm a.asm a.asm p.d

πραΰτητι παιδεύοντα τοὺς ἀντιδιατιθεμένους, μήποτε δώῃ αὐτοῖς
meekness instructing those who oppose you, if perhaps God ˻might grant˼ them
4559 4084 3836 507 3607 2536 1443 899
n.dsf pt.pa.asm d.apm pt.pm.apm cj v.aas.3s r.dpm.3

ὁ θεὸς μετάνοιαν εἰς ἐπίγνωσιν → ἀληθείας 26 καὶ
{the} *God* repentance ˻leading to˼ a knowledge of the truth, and
3836 2536 3567 1650 2106 237 2779
d.nsm n.nsm n.asf p.a n.asf n.gsf cj

NASB

saying that the
resurrection has al-
ready taken place,
and they upset
the faith of some.
[19]Nevertheless, the
firm foundation of
God stands, having
this seal, "The
Lord knows those
who are His,"
and, "Everyone
who names the
name of the Lord
is to abstain from
wickedness."
[20]Now in a large
house there are
not only gold and
silver vessels,
but also vessels
of wood and of
earthenware, and
some to honor and
some to dishonor.
[21]Therefore, if
anyone cleanses
himself from these
things, he will be
a vessel for honor,
sanctified, use-
ful to the Master,
prepared for every
good work. [22]Now
flee from youthful
lusts and pursue
righteousness,
faith, love *and*
peace, with those
who call on the
Lord from a pure
heart. [23]But refuse
foolish and igno-
rant speculations,
knowing that they
produce quarrels.
[24]The Lord's bond-
servant must not be
quarrelsome, but
be kind to all, able
to teach, patient
when wronged,
[25]with gentleness
correcting those
who are in opposi-
tion, if perhaps
God may grant
them repentance
leading to the
knowledge of the
truth, [26]and they

[a] [τὴν] UBS.

NIV

that they will come
to their senses and
escape from the
trap of the dev-
il, who has taken
them captive to do
his will.
3 But mark this:
There will be
terrible times in
the last days. [2]Peo-
ple will be lovers
of themselves,
lovers of money,
boastful, proud,
abusive, disobe-
dient to their par-
ents, ungrateful,
unholy, [3]without
love, unforgiving,
slanderous, with-
out self-control,
brutal, not lov-
ers of the good,
[4]treacherous, rash,
conceited, lovers
of pleasure rath-
er than lovers of
God— [5]having a
form of godliness
but denying its
power. Have noth-
ing to do with such
people.
[6]They are the
kind who worm
their way into
homes and gain
control over gul-
lible women, who
are loaded down
with sins and
are swayed by
all kinds of evil
desires, [7]always
learning but never
able to come to a
knowledge of the
truth. [8]Just as Jan-
nes and Jambres
opposed Moses, so
also these teachers
oppose the truth.
They are men of
depraved minds,
who, as far as the
faith is concerned,
are rejected. [9]But
they will not get
very far because,
as in the case of
those men, their
folly will be clear
to everyone.

ἀνανήψωσιν ἐκ τῆς τοῦ διαβόλου παγίδος, *snare*
⌊they might return to soberness⌋ ⌊out of⌋ the snare of the devil
392 1666 3836 4075 3836 1333 4075
v.aas.3p p.g d.gsf d.gsm n.gsm n.gsf

ἐζωγρημένοι ὑπ᾽ αὐτοῦ εἰς τὸ ἐκείνου θέλημα.
⌊(having been captured alive⌋ by him) ⌊in order to do⌋ *{the}* his will.
2436 5679 899 1650 3836 1697 2525
pt.rp.npm p.g r.gsm.3 p.a d.asn r.gsm n.asn

3:1 τοῦτο δὲ γίνωσκε, ὅτι ἐν ἐσχάταις ἡμέραις
But take note of this, *But* *take note of* that in the last days
1254 1182 1182 1182 4047 1254 1182 4022 1877 2274 2465
r.asn cj v.pam.2s cj p.d a.dpf n.dpf

ἐνστήσονται καιροὶ χαλεποί· *difficult* 2 ἔσονται γὰρ οἱ ἄνθρωποι
there will be difficult times; for the people will be *for* *the* *people*
1931 5901 2789 5901 1142 3836 476 1639 1142 3836 476
v.fmi.3p n.npm a.npm v.fmi.3p cj d.npm n.npm

φίλαυτοι φιλάργυροι ἀλαζόνες ὑπερήφανοι βλάσφημοι, γονεῦσιν
lovers of self, lovers of money, braggarts, arrogant, abusive, disobedient to parents,
5796 5795 225 5662 1061 579 1204
a.npm a.npm n.npm a.npm a.npm n.dpm

ἀπειθεῖς, *disobedient* ἀχάριστοι ἀνόσιοι [3]ἄστοργοι ἄσπονδοι διάβολοι ἀκρατεῖς ἀνήμεροι
ungrateful, unholy, unloving, unforgiving, slanderous, uncontrolled, untamed,
579 940 495 845 836 1333 203 466
a.npm a.npm a.npm a.npm a.npm a.npm a.npm a.npm

ἀφιλάγαθοι [4]προδόται προπετεῖς τετυφωμένοι, φιλήδονοι μᾶλλον ἢ
⌊not loving the good,⌋ treacherous, reckless, conceited, loving pleasure rather than
920 4595 4637 5605 5798 3437 2445
a.npm n.npm a.npm pt.rp.npm a.npm adv.c pl

φιλόθεοι, [5]ἔχοντες μόρφωσιν εὐσεβείας τὴν *{the}* δὲ δύναμιν αὐτῆς *its*
loving God, having the appearance of godliness but denying its power;
5806 2400 3673 2354 3836 1254 766 899 1539 899
a.npm pt.pa.npm n.asf n.gsf d.asf cj n.asf r.gsf.3

ἠρνημένοι· *denying* καὶ τούτους ἀποτρέπου. *avoid* 6 ἐκ τούτων γάρ *For* εἰσιν οἱ *{the}*
⌊and so⌋ avoid these people. For ⌊some of⌋ these are
766 2779 706 4047 706 1142 1666 4047 1142 1639 3836
pt.rp.npm adv r.apm v.pmm.2s p.g r.gpn cj v.pai.3p d.npm

ἐνδύνοντες εἰς τὰς οἰκίας καὶ αἰχμαλωτίζοντες γυναικάρια σεσωρευμένα
creeping into the homes and capturing weak women ⌊who have been burdened⌋
1905 1650 3836 3864 2779 170 1220 5397
pt.pa.npm p.a d.apf n.apf cj pt.pa.npm n.apn pt.rp.apn

ἁμαρτίαις, ἀγόμενα → ἐπιθυμίαις ποικίλαις, *various* [7]πάντοτε μανθάνοντα καὶ
with sins, ⌊being led astray⌋ by various passions, always learning and
281 72 4476 2123 4476 4121 3443 2779
n.dpf pt.pp.apn n.dpf a.dpf adv pt.pa.apn cj

μηδέποτε εἰς ἐπίγνωσιν → ἀληθείας ἐλθεῖν *to come* δυνάμενα. *being able* 8
never being able to come to a knowledge of the truth. But
3595 1538 1538 2262 2262 1650 2106 237 2262 1538 1254
adv p.a n.asf n.gsf f.aa pt.pp.apn

⌊ὃν τρόπον⌋ δὲ *But* Ἰάννης καὶ Ἰαμβρῆς ἀντέστησαν Μωϋσεῖ, οὕτως καὶ οὗτοι
just as Jannes and Jambres opposed Moses, so also these men
4005 5573 1254 2614 2779 2612 468 3707 4048 2779 4047
r.asm n.asm cj n.nsm cj n.nsm v.aai.3p n.dsm adv adv r.npm

ἀνθίστανται τῇ ἀληθείᾳ, ἄνθρωποι κατεφθαρμένοι τὸν νοῦν, ἀδόκιμοι
are opposing the truth, men ⌊who have been corrupted in⌋ the mind, worthless
468 3836 237 476 2967 3836 3808 99
v.pmi.3p d.dsf n.dsf n.npm pt.rp.npm d.asm n.asm a.npm

περὶ τὴν πίστιν. [9]ἀλλ᾽ ↱ ↱ οὐ προκόψουσιν ἐπὶ πλεῖον· ἡ *{the}* γὰρ
concerning the faith. But they will not progress very far; for their
4309 3836 4411 247 4621 4621 4024 4621 2093 4498 3836 1142 899
p.a d.asf n.asf cj pl v.fai.3p p.a adv.c d.nsf cj

ἄνοια αὐτῶν *their* ἔκδηλος ἔσται *will be* πᾶσιν, ὡς καὶ ἡ ἐκείνων ἐγένετο. *was*
folly will be very clear to all, as also was the folly of those men.
486 899 1639 1639 1684 1639 4246 6055 2779 1181 3836 1697 1181
n.nsf r.gpm.3 a.nsf v.fmi.3s a.dpm cj adv d.nsf r.gpm v.ami.3s

NASB

may come to their
senses *and escape*
from the snare of
the devil, having
been held captive
by him to do his
will.

"Difficult Times Will Come"

[3:1]But realize this,
that in the last days
difficult times will
come. [2]For men
will be lovers of
self, lovers of mon-
ey, boastful, arro-
gant, revilers, dis-
obedient to parents,
ungrateful, unholy,
[3]unloving, irrecon-
cilable, malicious
gossips, without
self-control, brutal,
haters of good,
[4]treacherous, reck-
less, conceited,
lovers of pleasure
rather than lovers
of God, [5]holding
to a form of godli-
ness, although they
have denied its
power; Avoid such
men as these. [6]For
among them are
those who enter
into households
and captivate weak
women weighed
down with sins,
led on by various
impulses, [7]always
learning and never
able to come to
the knowledge of
the truth. [8]Just as
Jannes and Jambres
opposed Moses, so
these *men* also op-
pose the truth, men
of depraved mind,
rejected in regard
to the faith. [9]But
they will not make
further progress;
for their folly will
be obvious to all,
just as Jannes's
and Jambres's folly
was also.

NIV

A Final Charge to Timothy

[10]You, however,
know all about
my teaching, my
way of life, my
purpose, faith,
patience, love,
endurance, [11]per-
secutions, suf-
ferings — what
kinds of things
happened to me
in Antioch, Ico-
nium and Lystra,
the persecutions I
endured. Yet the
Lord rescued me
from all of them.
[12]In fact, every-
one who wants to
live a godly life in
Christ Jesus will
be persecuted,
[13]while evildoers
and impostors
will go from bad
to worse, deceiv-
ing and being
deceived. [14]But as
for you, continue
in what you have
learned and have
become convinced
of, because you
know those from
whom you learned
it, [15]and how from
infancy you have
known the Holy
Scriptures, which
are able to make
you wise for salva-
tion through faith
in Christ Jesus.
[16]All Scripture
is God-breathed
and is useful for
teaching, rebuk-
ing, correcting
and training in
righteousness, [17]so
that the servant of
God[a] may be thor-
oughly equipped
for every good
work.

4 In the presence
of God and of
Christ Jesus, who
will judge the liv-
ing and the dead,
and in view of his
appearing and his

[a] 17 Or *that you, a man of God,*

10 σὺ δὲ παρηκολούθησάς μου τῇ διδασκαλίᾳ, τῇ ἀγωγῇ, τῇ προθέσει,
But you *But* followed my *{the}* teaching, my way of life, my purpose,
1254 5148 1254 4158 1609 3836 1436 3836 73 3836 4606
r.ns.2 cj v.aai.2s r.gs.1 d.dsf n.dsf d.dsf n.dsf d.dsf n.dsf

τῇ πίστει, τῇ μακροθυμίᾳ, τῇ ἀγάπῃ, τῇ ὑπομονῇ, 11 τοῖς διωγμοῖς, τοῖς
my faith, my patience, my love, my steadfastness, my persecutions, my
3836 4411 3836 3429 3836 27 3836 5705 3836 1501 3836
d.dsf n.dsf d.dsf n.dsf d.dsf n.dsf d.dsf n.dsf d.dpm n.dpm d.dpm

παθήμασιν, οἷά μοι ἐγένετο ἐν Ἀντιοχείᾳ, ἐν Ἰκονίῳ, ἐν Λύστροις,
sufferings, which happened to me *happened* in Antioch, in Iconium, in Lystra,
4077 3888 1181 1609 1181 1877 522 1877 2658 1877 3388
n.dpn r.npn r.ds.1 v.ami.3s p.d n.dsf p.d n.dsn p.d n.dpn

οἵους διωγμοὺς ὑπήνεγκα καὶ ἐκ πάντων με ἐρρύσατο ὁ
which persecutions I endured, and ⌞out of⌟ all these the Lord rescued me. *rescued* *the*
3888 1501 5722 2779 1666 4246 3836 3261 4861 1609 4861 3836
r.apm n.apm v.aai.1s cj p.g a.gpn r.as.1 v.ami.3s d.nsm

κύριος. 12 καὶ πάντες δὲ οἱ θέλοντες εὐσεβῶς ζῆν ἐν Χριστῷ
Lord Indeed also all *Indeed* *{the}* wishing to live godly lives *to live* in Christ
3261 1254 2779 4246 1254 3836 2527 2409 2409 2357 2409 1877 5986
n.nsm adv a.npm cj d.npm pt.pa.npm adv f.pa p.d n.dsm

Ἰησοῦ διωχθήσονται. 13 πονηροὶ δὲ ἄνθρωποι καὶ γόητες προκόψουσιν
Jesus will be persecuted, while wicked *while* people and impostors will advance from
2652 1503 1254 4505 1254 476 2779 1200 4621
n.dsm v.fpi.3p a.npm cj n.npm cj n.npm v.fai.3p

ἐπὶ τὸ χεῖρον πλανῶντες καὶ πλανώμενοι. 14 σὺ δὲ μένε ἐν οἷς
bad to *{the}* worse, deceiving and being deceived. But you, *But* remain in what
2093 3836 5937 4414 2779 4414 1254 5148 1254 3531 1877 4005
p.a d.asn a.asn.c pt.pa.npm cj pt.pp.npm r.ns.2 cj v.pam.2s p.d r.dpn

ἔμαθες καὶ ἐπιστώθης, εἰδὼς παρὰ τίνων ἔμαθες, 15 καὶ ὅτι
⌞you have learned⌟ and ⌞have been convinced of,⌟ knowing from whom you learned and that
3443 2779 4413 3857 4123 5515 3443 2779 4022
v.aai.2s cj v.api.2s pt.ra.nsm p.g r.gpm v.aai.2s cj cj

ἀπὸ βρέφους τὰ[a] ἱερὰ γράμματα οἶδας, τὰ δυνάμενά ↱
from childhood you have known the sacred writings, *you have known* which are able to
608 1100 3857 3857 3857 3836 2641 1207 3857 3836 1538 5054
p.g n.gsn d.apn a.apn n.apn v.rai.2s d.apn pt.pp.apn

↱ σε σοφίσαι εἰς σωτηρίαν διὰ πίστεως τῆς ἐν Χριστῷ Ἰησοῦ. 16 πᾶσα
make you wise for salvation through faith that is in Christ Jesus. All
5054 5148 5054 1650 5401 1328 4411 3836 1877 5986 2652 4246
r.as.2 f.aa p.a n.asf p.g n.gsf d.gsf p.d n.dsm n.dsm a.nsf

γραφὴ θεόπνευστος καὶ ὠφέλιμος πρὸς διδασκαλίαν, πρὸς ἐλεγμόν, πρὸς
Scripture ⌞is breathed out by God⌟ and is profitable for teaching, for reproof, for
1210 2535 2779 6068 4639 1436 4639 1791 4639
n.nsf a.nsf cj a.nsf p.a n.asf p.a n.asm p.a

ἐπανόρθωσιν, πρὸς παιδείαν τὴν ἐν δικαιοσύνῃ, 17 ἵνα
correcting, for training *{the}* in righteousness, so that the man of God may be
2061 4639 4082 3836 1877 1466 2671 3836 476 3836 2536 1639 1639
n.asf p.a n.asf d.asf p.d n.dsf cj

ἄρτιος ᾖ ὁ τοῦ θεοῦ ἄνθρωπος, πρὸς πᾶν ἔργον ἀγαθὸν
proficient, *may be* *the* *of* *God* *man* fully equipped for every good work. *good*
787 1639 3836 3836 2536 476 1992 1992 4639 4246 19 2240 19
a.nsm v.pas.3s d.nsm d.gsm n.gsm n.nsm p.a a.asn n.asn a.asn

ἐξηρτισμένος.
fully equipped
1992
pt.rp.nsm

4:1 διαμαρτύρομαι ἐνώπιον τοῦ θεοῦ καὶ Χριστοῦ Ἰησοῦ τοῦ μέλλοντος
I solemnly charge you in the presence of God and Christ Jesus, who is about
1371 1967 3836 2536 2779 5986 2652 3836 3516
v.pmi.1s p.g d.gsm n.gsm cj n.gsm n.gsm d.gsm pt.pa.gsm

κρίνειν ζῶντας καὶ νεκρούς, καὶ τὴν ἐπιφάνειαν αὐτοῦ καὶ τὴν
to judge the living and the dead, and by his appearing *his* and by his
3212 2409 2779 3738 2779 3836 899 2211 899 2779 3836 899
f.pa pt.pa.apm cj a.apm cj d.asf n.asf r.gsm.3 cj d.asf

[a] [τὰ] UBS.

NASB

[10]Now you fol-
lowed my teaching,
conduct, purpose,
faith, patience,
love, perseverance,
[11]persecutions,
and sufferings,
such as happened
to me at Antioch,
at Iconium *and* at
Lystra; what perse-
cutions I endured,
and out of them all
the Lord rescued
me! [12]Indeed, all
who desire to live
godly in Christ
Jesus will be per-
secuted. [13]But evil
men and impostors
will proceed *from*
bad to worse, de-
ceiving and being
deceived. [14]You,
however, continue
in the things you
have learned and
become convinced
of, knowing from
whom you have
learned *them*, [15]and
that from child-
hood you have
known the sacred
writings which are
able to give you
the wisdom that
leads to salvation
through faith which
is in Christ Jesus.
[16]All Scripture is
inspired by God
and profitable
for teaching, for
reproof, for correc-
tion, for training
in righteousness;
[17]so that the man of
God may be ade-
quate, equipped for
every good work.

"Preach the Word"

[4:1]I solemnly
charge *you* in the
presence of God
and of Christ Jesus,
who is to judge the
living and the dead,
and by His appear-
ing and His

NIV

kingdom, I give
you this charge:
2 Preach the word;
be prepared in
season and out of
season; correct,
rebuke and en-
courage—with
great patience and
careful instruc-
tion. 3 For the time
will come when
people will not
put up with sound
doctrine. Instead,
to suit their own
desires, they will
gather around them
a great number
of teachers to say
what their itching
ears want to hear.
4 They will turn
their ears away
from the truth and
turn aside to myths.
5 But you, keep
your head in all
situations, endure
hardship, do the
work of an evan-
gelist, discharge all
the duties of your
ministry.
6 For I am already
being poured out
like a drink offer-
ing, and the time
for my departure
is near. 7 I have
fought the good
fight, I have fin-
ished the race,
I have kept the
faith. 8 Now there
is in store for me
the crown of righ-
teousness, which
the Lord, the
righteous Judge,
will award to me
on that day—and
not only to me,
but also to all who
have longed for his
appearing.

Personal Remarks

9 Do your best to
come to me quick-
ly, 10 for Demas,
because he loved
this world, has de-
serted me and has
gone to Thessalo-
nica. Crescens has
gone to Galatia,
and Titus to Dal-
matia.

βασιλείαν αὐτοῦ· 2 κήρυξον τὸν λόγον, ἐπίστηθι εὐκαίρως ἀκαίρως,
kingdom: *his* preach the word. Be prepared when it is opportune or inopportune;
993 899 3062 3836 3364 2392 2323 178
n.asf r.gsm.3 v.aam.2s d.asm n.asm v.aam.2s adv adv

ἔλεγξον, ἐπιτίμησον, παρακάλεσον, ἐν πάσῃ μακροθυμίᾳ καὶ διδαχῇ. 3
confront, rebuke, and exhort, with complete patience and teaching. For a
1794 2203 4151 1877 4246 3429 2779 1439 1142
v.aam.2s v.aam.2s v.aam.2s p.d a.dsf n.dsf cj n.dsf

ἔσται γὰρ καιρὸς ὅτε τῆς ὑγιαινούσης διδασκαλίας
time will come *For time* when they will not put up with *{the}* healthy teaching,
2789 1639 1142 2789 4021 462 462 4024 462 462 462 3836 5617 1436
v.fmi.3s cj n.nsm cj d.gsf pt.pa.gsf n.gsf

οὐκ ἀνέξονται ἀλλὰ κατὰ τὰς ἰδίας ἐπιθυμίας ἑαυτοῖς
not they will put up with but ⌊in accordance with⌋ *{the}* their own lust *for themselves*
4024 462 247 2848 3836 2625 2123 1571
pl v.fmi.3p cj p.a d.apf a.apf n.apf r.dpm.3

ἐπισωρεύσουσιν διδασκάλους κνηθόμενοι τὴν ἀκοὴν 4 καὶ
they will heap up teachers for themselves, having itching *{the}* ears, and they will
2197 1437 1571 1571 3117 3836 198 2779 695 695
v.fai.3p n.apm pt.pp.npm d.asf n.asf cj

ἀπὸ μὲν τῆς ἀληθείας τὴν ἀκοὴν ἀποστρέψουσιν,
turn away from ~ listening to the truth *{the} listening to they will turn away* and wander
695 695 608 3525 198 198 3836 237 3836 198 695 1254 1762
p.g pl d.gsf n.gsf d.asf n.asf v.fai.3p

ἐπὶ δὲ τοὺς μύθους ἐκτραπήσονται. 5 σὺ δὲ νῆφε ἐν πᾶσιν,
off into *and* the myths. *wander off* But you, *But* be clear-minded in everything.
1762 2093 1254 3836 3680 1762 1254 5148 1254 3768 1877 4246
p.a cj d.apm n.apm v.fpi.3p r.ns.2 cj v.pam.2s p.d a.dpn

κακοπάθησον, ἔργον ποίησον → εὐαγγελιστοῦ, τὴν διακονίαν
Suffer evil. Do the work *Do* of an evangelist. Complete *{the}* your ministry.
2802 4472 2240 4472 2296 4442 3836 5148 1355
v.aam.2s n.asn v.aam.2s n.gsm d.asf n.asf

σου πληροφόρησον. 6 ἐγὼ γὰρ ↱ ἤδη σπένδομαι, καὶ
your Complete For I *For* am already ⌊being poured out like a drink offering,⌋ and
5148 4442 1142 1609 1142 5064 2453 5064 2779
r.gs.2 v.aam.2s r.ns.1 cj adv v.ppi.1s cj

ὁ καιρὸς τῆς ἀναλύσεώς μου ἐφέστηκεν. 7 τὸν καλὸν ἀγῶνα ἠγώνισμαι, τὸν
the time of my departure *my* has arrived. The good fight I have fought, the
3836 2789 3836 1609 385 1609 2392 3836 2819 74 76 3836
d.nsm n.nsm d.gsf n.gsf r.gs.1 v.rai.3s d.asm a.asm n.asm v.rmi.1s d.asm

δρόμον τετέλεκα, τὴν πίστιν τετήρηκα· 8 λοιπὸν ἀπόκειταί μοι ὁ τῆς
race I have completed, the faith I have kept. Now is reserved ⌊for me⌋ the crown of
1536 5464 3836 4411 5498 3370 641 1609 3836 5109 3836
n.asm v.rai.1s d.asf n.asf v.rai.1s adv v.pmi.3s r.ds.1 d.nsm d.gsf

δικαιοσύνης στέφανος, ὃν ἀποδώσει μοι ὁ κύριος
righteousness, *crown* which the Lord, the righteous judge, will give to me *the Lord*
1466 5109 4005 3836 3261 3836 1465 3216 625 1609 3836 3261
n.gsf n.nsm r.asm v.fai.3s r.ds.1 d.nsm n.nsm

ἐν ἐκείνῃ τῇ ἡμέρᾳ, ὁ δίκαιος κριτής, οὐ μόνον δὲ ἐμοὶ ἀλλὰ καὶ
on that *{the}* Day, *the righteous judge* but not only *but* to me but also
1877 1697 3836 2465 3836 1465 3216 1254 4024 3667 1254 1609 247 2779
p.d r.dsf d.dsf n.dsf d.nsm a.nsm n.nsm pl adv cj r.ds.1 cj adv

πᾶσι τοῖς ἠγαπηκόσι τὴν ἐπιφάνειαν αὐτοῦ. 9 σπούδασον ἐλθεῖν πρός με
to everyone who has loved *{the}* his appearing. *his* Do your best to come to me
4246 3836 26 3836 899 2211 899 5079 2262 4639 1609
a.dpm d.dpm pt.ra.dpm d.asf n.asf r.gsm.3 v.aam.2s f.aa p.a r.as.1

ταχέως· 10 Δημᾶς γάρ με ἐγκατέλιπεν ἀγαπήσας τὸν νῦν αἰῶνα
soon, for Demas *for* deserted me *deserted* ⌊because he loved⌋ the present age
5441 1142 1318 1142 1593 1609 1593 26 3836 3814 172
adv n.nsm cj r.as.1 v.aai.3s pt.aa.nsm d.asm adv n.asm

καὶ ἐπορεύθη εἰς Θεσσαλονίκην, Κρήσκης εἰς Γαλατίαν, Τίτος εἰς Δαλματίαν·
and has gone to Thessalonica, Crescens to Galatia, Titus to Dalmatia.
2779 4513 1650 2553 3206 1650 1130 5519 1650 1237
cj v.api.3s p.a n.asf n.nsm p.a n.asf n.nsm p.a n.asf

NASB

kingdom: 2 preach
the word; be ready
in season *and* out
of season; reprove,
rebuke, exhort,
with great patience
and instruction.
3 For the time will
come when they
will not endure
sound doctrine; but
wanting to have
their ears tickled,
they will accumu-
late for themselves
teachers in accor-
dance to their own
desires, 4 and will
turn away their ears
from the truth and
will turn aside to
myths. 5 But you, be
sober in all things,
endure hardship,
do the work of an
evangelist, fulfill
your ministry.
6 For I am already
being poured out
as a drink offer-
ing, and the time
of my departure
has come. 7 I have
fought the good
fight, I have fin-
ished the course,
I have kept the
faith; 8 in the future
there is laid up
for me the crown
of righteousness,
which the Lord, the
righteous Judge,
will award to me
on that day; and
not only to me,
but also to all who
have loved His ap-
pearing.

Personal Concerns

9 Make every ef-
fort to come to me
soon; 10 for Demas,
having loved this
present world, has
deserted me and
gone to Thessalon-
ica; Crescens *has
gone* to Galatia,
Titus to Dalmatia.

NIV

[11]Only Luke is
with me. Get Mark
and bring him with
you, because he is
helpful to me in
my ministry. [12]I
sent Tychicus to
Ephesus. [13]When
you come, bring
the cloak that I left
with Carpus at Tro-
as, and my scrolls,
especially the
parchments.
[14]Alexander the
metalworker did
me a great deal of
harm. The Lord
will repay him for
what he has done.
[15]You too should
be on your guard
against him, be-
cause he strongly
opposed our mes-
sage.
[16]At my first de-
fense, no one came
to my support, but
everyone desert-
ed me. May it not
be held against
them. [17]But the
Lord stood at my
side and gave me
strength, so that
through me the
message might be
fully proclaimed
and all the Gen-
tiles might hear
it. And I was de-
livered from the
lion's mouth. [18]The
Lord will rescue
me from every evil
attack and will
bring me safely to
his heavenly king-
dom. To him be
glory for ever and
ever. Amen.

Final Greetings

[19]Greet Priscil-
la[a] and Aquila
and the household
of Onesiphorus.
[20]Erastus stayed in
Corinth, and I left
Trophimus sick in
Miletus.

[a] 19 Greek *Prisca*, a variant of *Priscilla*

11 Λουκᾶς ἐστιν μόνος μετ᾽ ἐμοῦ. Μᾶρκον ἀναλαβὼν ἄγε μετὰ
Luke alone is *alone* with me. Get Mark *Get* and bring him with
3371 3668 1639 3668 3552 1609 377 3453 377 72 3552
n.nsm v.pai.3s a.nsm p.g r.gs.1 n.asm pt.aa.nsm v.pam.2s p.g

σεαυτοῦ, ἔστιν γάρ μοι εὔχρηστος εἰς διακονίαν. 12 Τύχικον
you, for he is *for* useful to me *useful* for ministry. And I sent Tychicus
4932 1142 1639 1142 2378 1609 2378 1650 1355 1254 690 690 5608
r.gsm.2 v.pai.3s cj r.ds.1 a.nsm p.a n.asf n.asm

δὲ ἀπέστειλα εἰς Ἔφεσον. 13 τὸν φαιλόνην ὃν ἀπέλιπον ἐν Τρῳάδι παρὰ
And I sent to Ephesus. Bring the cloak that I left in Troas with
1254 690 1650 2387 5770 3836 5742 4005 657 1877 5590 4123
cj v.aai.1s p.a n.asf d.asm n.asm r.asm v.aai.1s p.d n.dsf p.d

Κάρπῳ ἐρχόμενος φέρε, καὶ τὰ βιβλία μάλιστα τὰς μεμβράνας. 14 Ἀλέξανδρος
Carpus when you come *Bring* and the books, especially the parchments. Alexander
2842 2262 5770 2779 3836 1046 3436 3836 3521 235
n.dsm pt.pm.nsm v.pam.2s cj d.apn n.apn adv.s d.apf n.apf n.nsm

ὁ χαλκεὺς πολλά μοι κακὰ ἐνεδείξατο· ἀποδώσει αὐτῷ ὁ
the coppersmith did me great *me* harm; *did* the Lord will repay him *the*
3836 5906 1892 1609 4498 1609 2805 1892 3836 3261 625 899 3836
d.nsm n.nsm a.apn r.ds.1 a.apn v.ami.3s v.fai.3s r.dsm.3 d.nsm

κύριος κατὰ τὰ ἔργα αὐτοῦ· 15 ↱ ὃν καὶ σὺ
Lord ⌊according to⌋ *{the}* his deeds, *his* against whom also you
3261 2848 3836 899 2240 899 5875 4005 2779 5148
n.nsm p.a d.apn n.apn r.gsm.3 r.asm adv r.ns.2

φυλάσσου, ↱ λίαν γὰρ ἀντέστη τοῖς ἡμετέροις λόγοις. 16 ἐν
⌊should be on your guard,⌋ for he vehemently *for* opposed *{the}* our words. At
5875 1142 468 3336 1142 468 3836 2466 3364 1877
v.pmm.2s adv cj v.aai.3s d.dpm r.dpm.1 n.dpm p.d

τῇ πρώτῃ μου ἀπολογίᾳ οὐδείς μοι παρεγένετο, ἀλλὰ πάντες
{the} my first *my* defense no one came forward ⌊for me,⌋ *came forward* but everyone
3836 1609 4755 1609 665 4029 4134 4134 1609 4134 247 4246
d.dsf a.dsf r.gs.1 n.dsf a.nsm r.ds.1 v.ami.3s cj a.npm

με ἐγκατέλιπον· μὴ αὐτοῖς λογισθείη· 17 ὁ
deserted me; *deserted* may it not be held ⌊against them.⌋ *may it be held* But the
1593 1609 1593 3357 3357 3590 3357 3357 899 3357 1254 3836
r.as.1 v.aai.3p pl r.dpm.3 v.apo.3s d.nsm

δέ κύριός μοι παρέστη καὶ ἐνεδυνάμωσέν με, ἵνα δι᾽ ἐμοῦ τὸ
But Lord stood by me *stood by* and strengthened me, so that through me the
1254 3261 4225 4225 1609 4225 2779 1904 1609 2671 1328 1609 3836
cj n.nsm r.ds.1 v.aai.3s cj v.aai.3s r.as.1 cj p.g r.gs.1 d.nsn

κήρυγμα πληροφορηθῇ καὶ ἀκούσωσιν πάντα τὰ ἔθνη, καὶ
proclamation might be fulfilled, namely, all the Gentiles might hear, *all the Gentiles* and
3060 4442 2779 4246 3836 1620 201 4246 3836 1620 2779
n.nsn v.aps.3s cj v.aas.3p a.npn d.npn n.npn cj

ἐρρύσθην ἐκ στόματος → λέοντος. 18 ῥύσεταί με ὁ κύριος ἀπὸ
I was rescued from the mouth of a lion. The Lord will rescue me *The Lord* from
4861 1666 5125 3329 3836 3261 4861 1609 3836 3261 608
v.api.1s p.g n.gsn n.gsm v.fmi.3s r.as.1 d.nsm n.nsm p.g

παντὸς ἔργου πονηροῦ καὶ σώσει εἰς τὴν βασιλείαν
every evil deed *evil* and ⌊will bring me safely⌋ into *{the}* his heavenly kingdom,
4246 4505 2240 4505 2779 5392 1650 3836 899 2230 993
a.gsn n.gsn a.gsn cj v.fai.3s p.a d.asf n.asf

αὐτοῦ τὴν ἐπουράνιον· ᾧ ἡ δόξα εἰς τοὺς ⌊αἰῶνας τῶν αἰώνων,⌋ ἀμήν.
his {the} heavenly ⌊to whom⌋ be *{the}* glory for all time. Amen.
899 3836 2230 4005 3836 1518 1650 3836 172 3836 172 297
r.gsm.3 d.asf a.asf r.dsm d.nsf n.nsf p.a d.apm n.apm d.gpm n.gpm pl

19 ἄσπασαι Πρίσκαν καὶ Ἀκύλαν καὶ τὸν Ὀνησιφόρου οἶκον.
Greet Prisca and Aquila and the household of Onesiphorus. *household*
832 4571 2779 217 2779 3836 3875 3947 3875
v.amm.2s n.asf cj n.asm cj d.asm n.gsm n.asm

20 Ἔραστος ἔμεινεν ἐν Κορίνθῳ, ↱ ↱ Τρόφιμον δὲ ἀπέλιπον ἐν Μιλήτῳ
Erastus remained in Corinth, and I left Trophimus *and* behind in Miletus
2235 3531 1877 3172 1254 657 657 5576 1254 657 1877 3626
n.nsm v.aai.3s p.d n.dsf n.asm cj v.aai.1s p.d n.dsf

NASB

[11]Only Luke is with
me. Pick up Mark
and bring him
with you, for he
is useful to me for
service. [12]But Ty-
chicus I have sent
to Ephesus. [13]When
you come bring
the cloak which I
left at Troas with
Carpus, and the
books, especially
the parchments.
[14]Alexander the
coppersmith did
me much harm;
the Lord will repay
him according to
his deeds. [15]Be on
guard against him
yourself, for he
vigorously opposed
our teaching.
[16]At my first
defense no one
supported me,
but all deserted
me; may it not be
counted against
them. [17]But the
Lord stood with me
and strengthened
me, so that through
me the proclama-
tion might be fully
accomplished, and
that all the Gentiles
might hear; and I
was rescued out of
the lion's mouth.
[18]The Lord will res-
cue me from every
evil deed, and will
bring me safely to
His heavenly king-
dom; to Him *be* the
glory forever and
ever. Amen.
[19]Greet Prisca
and Aquila, and
the household
of Onesiphorus.
[20]Erastus remained
at Corinth, but Tro-
phimus I left sick
at Miletus.

NIV

[21] Do your best to get here before winter. Eubulus greets you, and so do Pudens, Linus, Claudia and all the brothers and sisters.[a]
[22] The Lord be with your spirit. Grace be with you all.

ἀσθενοῦντα. [21] σπούδασον πρὸ χειμῶνος ἐλθεῖν. ἀσπάζεταί
⌞because he was sick.⌟ Do your best to come before winter. *to come* Eubulus greets
820 5079 2262 2262 4574 5930 2262 2300 832
pt.pa.asm v.aam.2s p.g n.gsm f.aa v.pmi.3s

σε Εὔβουλος καὶ Πούδης καὶ Λίνος καὶ Κλαυδία καὶ οἱ ἀδελφοὶ πάντες.
you *Eubulus* as do Pudens and Linus and Claudia and all the brethren. *all*
5148 2300 2779 4545 2779 3352 2779 3086 2779 4246 3836 81 4246
r.as.2 n.nsm cj n.nsm cj n.nsm cj n.nsf cj d.npm n.npm a.npm

[22] ὁ κύριος μετὰ τοῦ πνεύματός σου. ἡ χάρις μεθ᾽ ὑμῶν.[a]
The Lord be with *{the}* your spirit. *your* *{the}* Grace be with ⌞you all.⌟
3836 3261 3552 3836 5148 4460 5148 3836 5921 3552 7007
d.nsm n.nsm p.g d.gsn n.gsn r.gs.2 d.nsf n.nsf p.g r.gp.2

NASB

[21] Make every effort to come before winter. Eubulus greets you, also Pudens and Linus and Claudia and all the brethren.
[22] The Lord be with your spirit. Grace be with you.

[a] 21 The Greek word for *brothers and sisters* (*adelphoi*) refers here to believers, both men and women, as part of God's family.

[a] ἀμήν. πρὸς Τιμόθεον δευτέρα τῆς Ἐφεσίων ἐκκλησίας πρῶτον ἐπίσκοπον χειροτονηθέντα. ἐγράφη ἀπὸ Ῥώμης ὅτε ἐκ δευτέρου παρέστη Παῦλος τῷ Καίσαρι Νερώνι included by TR after ὑμῶν.

Titus

NIV

1 Paul, a servant
of God and an
apostle of Jesus
Christ to further
the faith of God's
elect and their
knowledge of the
truth that leads to
godliness— 2 in
the hope of eter-
nal life, which
God, who does
not lie, promised
before the begin-
ning of time, 3 and
which now at his
appointed season
he has brought to
light through the
preaching entrust-
ed to me by the
command of God
our Savior,
4 To Titus, my
true son in our
common faith:

Grace and peace
from God the Fa-
ther and Christ
Jesus our Savior.

Appointing Elders Who Love What Is Good

5 The reason I left
you in Crete was
that you might put
in order what was
left unfinished and
appoint[a] elders
in every town, as
I directed you.
6 An elder must be
blameless, faithful
to his wife, a man
whose children be-
lieve[b] and are not
open to the charge
of being wild
and disobedient.
7 Since an overseer
manages God's
household, he must
be blameless—not
overbearing, not

1:1 Παῦλος δοῦλος θεοῦ, ἀπόστολος δὲ Ἰησοῦ Χριστοῦ κατὰ πίστιν
Paul, a servant of God and an apostle *and* of Jesus Christ, for the faith
4263 1529 2536 1254 693 1254 2652 5986 2848 4411
n.nsm n.nsm n.gsm n.nsm cj n.gsm n.gsm p.a n.asf

→ ἐκλεκτῶν θεοῦ καὶ ἐπίγνωσιν → ἀληθείας τῆς κατ' εὐσέβειαν
of the elect of God and the knowledge of the truth that produces godliness,
1723 2536 2779 2106 237 3836 2848 2354
a.gpm n.gsm cj n.asf n.gsf d.gsf p.a n.asf

2 ἐπ' ἐλπίδι → ζωῆς αἰωνίου, ἣν
⌞for the sake of⌟ the hope of eternal life, *eternal* which God, who does not lie,
2093 1828 173 2437 173 4005 2536 3836 950 950 950
p.d n.dsf n.gsf a.gsf r.asf

ἐπηγγείλατο ὁ ἀψευδὴς θεὸς πρὸ χρόνων αἰωνίων, 3 ἐφανέρωσεν δὲ
promised *who* *does not lie* *God* before times eternal, and revealed *and* his
2040 3836 950 2536 4574 5989 173 1254 5746 1254 899
v.ami.3s d.nsm a.nsm n.nsm p.g n.gpm a.gpm v.aai.3s cj

→ καιροῖς ἰδίοις τὸν λόγον αὐτοῦ ἐν κηρύγματι, ↱ ὃ
word at the proper time *proper* *{the}* *word* *his* in the proclamation, with which I
3364 2625 2789 2625 3836 3364 899 1877 3060 4409 4005 1609
n.dpm a.dpm d.asm n.asm r.gsm.3 p.d n.dsn r.asn

ἐπιστεύθην ἐγὼ κατ' ἐπιταγὴν τοῦ σωτῆρος ἡμῶν θεοῦ, 4 Τίτῳ
have been entrusted *I* by the command of God our Savior, *our* *God* to Titus, a
4409 1609 2848 2198 3836 2536 7005 5400 7005 2536 5519
v.api.1s r.ns.1 p.a n.asf d.gsm n.gsm r.gp.1 n.gsm n.dsm

γνησίῳ τέκνῳ κατὰ κοινὴν πίστιν, χάρις καὶ εἰρήνη ἀπὸ θεοῦ πατρὸς καὶ
true son in a common faith: Grace and peace from God the Father and
1188 5451 2848 3123 4411 5921 2779 1645 608 2536 4252 2779
a.dsn n.dsn p.a a.asf n.asf n.nsf cj n.nsf p.g n.gsm n.gsm cj

Χριστοῦ Ἰησοῦ τοῦ σωτῆρος ἡμῶν. 5 τούτου χάριν ἀπέλιπόν σε ἐν
Christ Jesus *{the}* our Savior. *our* For this reason *For* I left you in
5986 2652 3836 7005 5400 7005 5920 4047 5920 657 5148 1877
n.gsm n.gsm d.gsm n.gsm r.gp.1 r.gsn p.g v.aai.1s r.as.2 p.d

Κρήτῃ, ἵνα τὰ λείποντα ἐπιδιορθώσῃ καὶ καταστήσῃς
Crete, so that you might put right the ⌞remaining things⌟ *you might put right* and appoint
3207 2671 2114 2114 2114 2114 3836 3309 2114 2779 2770
n.dsf cj d.apn pt.pa.apn v.ams.2s cj v.aas.2s

κατὰ πόλιν πρεσβυτέρους, ὡς ἐγώ σοι διεταξάμην, 6 εἴ τις
elders in every town, *elders* as I directed you *directed* — if anyone
4565 2848 4484 4565 6055 1609 1411 5148 1411 1623 5516
p.a n.asf a.apm cj r.ns.1 r.ds.2 v.ami.1s cj r.nsm

ἐστιν ἀνέγκλητος, μιᾶς γυναικὸς ἀνήρ, τέκνα ἔχων πιστά,
is above reproach, a man of one woman, *man* having believing children, *having* *believing*
1639 441 467 1651 1222 467 2400 4412 5451 2400 4412
v.pai.3s a.nsm a.gsf n.gsf n.nsm n.apn pt.pa.nsm a.apn

μὴ ἐν κατηγορίᾳ ἀσωτίας ἢ ἀνυπότακτα. 7 δεῖ γάρ
not ⌞open to⌟ the charge of debauchery or being rebellious. For ⌞it is necessary⌟ *For* for
3590 1877 2990 861 2445 538 1142 1256 1142
pl p.d n.dsf n.gsf cj a.apn v.pai.3s cj

τὸν ἐπίσκοπον ἀνέγκλητον εἶναι ὡς θεοῦ οἰκονόμον, μὴ
an overseer to be above reproach *to be* as a steward of God, *steward* not
3836 2176 1639 1639 441 1639 6055 3874 2536 3874 3590
d.asm n.asm a.asm f.pa pl n.gsm n.asm pl

NASB

Salutation

1:1 Paul, a bond-
servant of God
and an apostle of
Jesus Christ, for
the faith of those
chosen of God and
the knowledge of
the truth which
is according to
godliness, 2 in the
hope of eternal life,
which God, who
cannot lie, prom-
ised long ages ago,
3 but at the proper
time manifested,
even His word, in
the proclamation
with which I was
entrusted according
to the command-
ment of God our
Savior,
4 To Titus, my true
child in a common
faith: Grace and
peace from God
the Father and
Christ Jesus our
Savior.

Qualifications of Elders

5 For this reason I
left you in Crete,
that you would set
in order what re-
mains and appoint
elders in every city
as I directed you,
6 *namely,* if any man
is above reproach,
the husband of
one wife, having
children who be-
lieve, not accused
of dissipation or
rebellion. 7 For the
overseer must be
above reproach as
God's steward, not

[a] 5 Or *ordain*
[b] 6 Or *children are trustworthy*

NIV

quick-tempered, not
given to drunken-
ness, not violent, not
pursuing dishonest
gain. [8]Rather, he
must be hospita-
ble, one who loves
what is good, who
is self-controlled,
upright, holy and
disciplined. [9]He
must hold firmly
to the trustworthy
message as it has
been taught, so that
he can encourage
others by sound
doctrine and refute
those who oppose it.

Rebuking Those Who Fail to Do Good

[10]For there are
many rebellious
people, full of
meaningless talk
and deception, es-
pecially those of
the circumcision
group. [11]They must
be silenced, because
they are disrupting
whole households
by teaching things
they ought not to
teach—and that
for the sake of dis-
honest gain. [12]One
of Crete's own
prophets has said it:
"Cretans are always
liars, evil brutes,
lazy gluttons."[a]
[13]This saying is true.
Therefore rebuke
them sharply, so that
they will be sound
in the faith [14]and
will pay no attention
to Jewish myths or
to the merely hu-
man commands of
those who reject the
truth. [15]To the pure,
all things are pure,
but to those who are
corrupted and do
not believe, nothing
is pure. In fact, both
their minds and
consciences are cor-
rupted. [16]They claim
to know God, but
by their actions they
deny him. They are
detestable, disobedi-
ent and unfit for

[a] 12 From the Cretan philosopher Epimenides

αὐθάδη, μὴ ὀργίλον, μὴ πάροινον, μὴ πλήκτην, μὴ αἰσχροκερδῆ, [8]ἀλλὰ
arrogant, not quick-tempered, not a drunkard, not violent, not greedy for gain, but
881 3590 3975 3590 4232 3590 4438 3590 153 247
a.asm pl a.asm pl n.asm pl n.asm pl a.asm cj

φιλόξενον φιλάγαθον σώφρονα δίκαιον ὅσιον ἐγκρατῆ, [9]ἀντεχόμενον τοῦ
hospitable, ⌊loving what is good,⌋ self-controlled, just, holy, disciplined, holding fast to the
5811 5787 5409 1465 4008 1604 504 3836
a.asm a.asm a.asm a.asm a.asm a.asm pt.pm.asm d.gsm

κατὰ τὴν διδαχὴν πιστοῦ λόγου, ἵνα
trustworthy word that is ⌊in accordance with⌋ the teaching, *trustworthy* *word* so that he might
4412 3364 2848 3836 1439 4412 3364 2671 1639 1639
p.a d.asf n.asf a.gsm n.gsm cj

δυνατὸς ᾖ καὶ παρακαλεῖν ἐν τῇ διδασκαλίᾳ τῇ ὑγιαινούσῃ
be able *he might be* both to exhort with *{the}* healthy doctrine *{the}* *healthy*
1639 1543 1639 2779 4151 1877 3836 5617 1436 3836 5617
a.nsm v.pas.3s cj f.pa p.d d.dsf n.dsf d.dsf pt.pa.dsf

καὶ τοὺς ἀντιλέγοντας ἐλέγχειν. [10] εἰσὶν γὰρ πολλοὶ[a]
and to rebuke those who oppose it. *to rebuke* For ⌊there are⌋ *For* many
2779 1794 1794 3836 515 1794 1142 1639 1142 4498
cj d.apm pt.pa.apm f.pa v.pai.3p cj a.npm

ἀνυπότακτοι, ματαιολόγοι καὶ φρεναπάται, μάλιστα οἱ ἐκ τῆς περιτομῆς,
rebellious people, senseless babblers and deceivers, especially those of the circumcision.
538 3468 2779 5855 3436 3836 1666 3836 4364
a.npm n.npm cj n.npm adv.s d.npm p.g d.gsf n.gsf

[11]οὓς → → δεῖ ἐπιστομίζειν, οἵτινες ὅλους οἴκους
those It is therefore necessary to muzzle those who are upsetting entire households
4005 1256 2187 4005 4015 426 426 3910 3875
r.apm v.pai.3s f.pa r.npm a.apm n.apm

ἀνατρέπουσιν διδάσκοντες ἃ ↱ μὴ δεῖ αἰσχροῦ κέρδους χάριν. [12] εἶπέν
are upsetting by teaching what is not proper for shameful gain. *for* *said*
426 1438 4005 1256 3590 1256 5920 156 3046 5920 3306
v.pai.3p pt.pa.npm r.apn pl v.pai.3s a.gsn n.gsn p.g v.aai.3s

τις ἐξ αὐτῶν ἴδιος αὐτῶν προφήτης· Κρῆτες ἀεὶ ψεῦσται, κακὰ θηρία,
One of them, their own prophet, said, "Cretans are always liars, evil beasts,
5516 1666 899 2625 899 4737 3306 3205 107 6026 2805 2563
r.nsm p.g r.gpm.3 a.nsm r.gpm.3 n.nsm n.npm adv n.npm a.npn n.npn

γαστέρες ἀργαί. [13] ἡ μαρτυρία αὕτη ἐστὶν ἀληθής. δι’ ἣν αἰτίαν ἔλεγχε
lazy gluttons." *lazy* *{the}* This testimony *This* is true, for which reason rebuke
734 1143 734 3836 4047 3456 4047 1639 239 1328 4005 162 1794
n.npf n.npf d.nsf n.nsf r.nsf v.pai.3s a.nsf p.a r.asf n.asf v.pam.2s

αὐτοὺς ἀποτόμως, ἵνα ὑγιαίνωσιν ἐν τῇ πίστει, [14] μὴ προσέχοντες
them sharply, so that they may be healthy in the faith, not ⌊being devoted to⌋
899 705 2671 5617 1877 3836 4411 3590 4668
r.apm.3 adv cj v.pas.3p p.d d.dsf n.dsf pl pt.pa.npm

Ἰουδαϊκοῖς μύθοις καὶ ἐντολαῖς ἀνθρώπων ἀποστρεφομένων τὴν
Jewish myths and commandments of people ⌊who are turning away from⌋ the
2679 3680 2779 1953 476 695 3836
a.dpm n.dpm cj n.dpf n.gpm pt.pm.gpm d.asf

ἀλήθειαν. [15] πάντα καθαρὰ τοῖς καθαροῖς· τοῖς δὲ μεμιαμμένοις καὶ
truth. All things are clean to the clean, but to the *but* defiled and
237 4246 2754 3836 2754 1254 3836 1254 3620 2779
n.asf a.npn a.npn d.dpm a.dpm d.dpm cj pt.rp.dpm cj

ἀπίστοις οὐδὲν καθαρόν, ἀλλὰ μεμίανται αὐτῶν καὶ ὁ νοῦς καὶ ἡ
unbelieving nothing is clean, but *are defiled* both their *both* *{the}* mind and *{the}*
603 4029 2754 247 3620 2779 899 2779 3836 3808 2779 3836
a.dpm a.nsn a.nsn cj v.rpi.3s r.gpm.3 cj d.nsm n.nsm cj d.nsf

συνείδησις. [16] θεὸν ὁμολογοῦσιν εἰδέναι, τοῖς
conscience are defiled. They profess to know God, *They profess* *to know* but by their
5287 3620 3620 3933 3933 3857 3857 2536 3933 3857 1254 3836
n.nsf n.asm v.pai.3p f.ra cj d.dpn

δὲ ἔργοις ἀρνοῦνται, βδελυκτοὶ ὄντες καὶ ἀπειθεῖς καὶ πρὸς
but deeds they deny him, being abominable *being* and disobedient and worthless for
1254 2240 766 1639 1008 1639 2779 579 2779 99 4639
cj n.dpn v.pmi.3p a.npm pt.pa.npm cj a.npm cj p.a

[a] καὶ included by UBS after πολλοὶ.

NASB

self-willed, not
quick-tempered,
not addicted to
wine, not pugna-
cious, not fond
of sordid gain,
[8]but hospitable,
loving what is
good, sensible,
just, devout, self-
controlled, [9]holding
fast the faithful
word which is in
accordance with
the teaching, so
that he will be able
both to exhort in
sound doctrine and
to refute those who
contradict.
[10]For there are
many rebellious
men, empty talk-
ers and deceivers,
especially those of
the circumcision,
[11]who must be
silenced because
they are upsetting
whole families,
teaching things
they should not
teach for the sake
of sordid gain.
[12]One of them-
selves, a prophet
of their own,
said, "Cretans are
always liars, evil
beasts, lazy glut-
tons." [13]This testi-
mony is true. For
this reason reprove
them severely so
that they may be
sound in the faith,
[14]not paying at-
tention to Jewish
myths and com-
mandments of men
who turn away
from the truth.
[15]To the pure, all
things are pure; but
to those who are
defiled and unbe-
lieving, nothing is
pure, but both their
mind and their con-
science are defiled.
[16]They profess to
know God, but by
their deeds they
deny *Him,* being
detestable and
disobedient and
worthless for

NIV

doing anything
good.

Doing Good for the Sake of the Gospel

2 You, howev-
er, must teach
what is appropriate
to sound doctrine.
2 Teach the older
men to be tem-
perate, worthy of
respect, self-con-
trolled, and sound
in faith, in love
and in endurance.
3 Likewise, teach
the older women
to be reverent in
the way they live,
not to be slander-
ers or addicted to
much wine, but
to teach what is
good. 4 Then they
can urge the youn-
ger women to love
their husbands and
children, 5 to be
self-controlled and
pure, to be busy at
home, to be kind,
and to be subject
to their husbands,
so that no one will
malign the word
of God.
6 Similarly, en-
courage the young
men to be self-
controlled. 7 In ev-
erything set them
an example by do-
ing what is good.
In your teaching
show integrity,
seriousness 8 and
soundness of
speech that cannot
be condemned,
so that those who
oppose you may
be ashamed be-
cause they have
nothing bad to say
about us.
9 Teach slaves to
be subject to their
masters in every-
thing, to try to
please them, not to
talk back to them,
10 and not to steal
from them, but to
show that they can
be fully trusted, so
that in every way
they will make
the teaching about
God our

πᾶν ἔργον ἀγαθὸν ἀδόκιμοι.
any good work. *good* *worthless*
4246 19 2240 19 99
a.asn n.asn a.asn a.npm

2:1 σὺ δὲ λάλει ἃ πρέπει τῇ ὑγιαινούσῃ διδασκαλίᾳ. 2 πρεσβύτας
But you, *But* speak what is fitting for healthy teaching. Older men
1254 5148 1254 3281 4005 4560 3836 5617 1436 4566
r.ns.2 cj v.pam.2s r.npn v.pai.3s d.dsf pt.pa.dsf n.dsf n.apm

νηφαλίους εἶναι, σεμνούς, σώφρονας, ὑγιαίνοντας τῇ πίστει, τῇ
should be clear-minded, *should be* dignified, self-controlled, healthy in faith, in
1639 1639 3767 1639 4948 5409 5617 3836 4411 3836
a.apm f.pa a.apm a.apm pt.pa.apm d.dsf n.dsf d.dsf

ἀγάπῃ, τῇ ὑπομονῇ· 3 πρεσβύτιδας ὡσαύτως ἐν καταστήματι
love, and in steadfastness. Elderly women, likewise, are to be reverent in demeanor,
27 3836 5705 4567 6058 2640 1877 2949
n.dsf d.dsf n.dsf n.apf adv p.d n.dsn

ἱεροπρεπεῖς, μὴ διαβόλους μὴ → οἴνῳ πολλῷ δεδουλωμένας,
reverent not slanderers, and not enslaved to much wine, *much* *enslaved*
2640 3590 1333 3590 1530 4498 3885 4498 1530
a.apf pl a.apf cj n.dsm a.dsm pt.rp.apf

καλοδιδασκάλους, 4 ἵνα σωφρονίζωσιν τὰς νέας φιλάνδρους
teaching what is good, and so encourage the ⌊younger women⌋ to love their husbands
2815 2671 5405 3836 3742 5791
a.apf cj v.pas.3p d.apf a.apf a.apf

εἶναι, φιλοτέκνους 5 σώφρονας ἁγνὰς οἰκουργοὺς ἀγαθάς,
{to be} and children, to be self-controlled, pure, working at home, kind,
1639 5817 5409 54 3877 19
f.pa a.apf a.apf a.apf a.apf a.apf

ὑποτασσομένας τοῖς ἰδίοις ἀνδράσιν, ἵνα ↱ μὴ ὁ λόγος
submissive to their own husbands that the word of God may not *the* *word*
5718 3836 2625 467 2671 3836 3364 3836 2536 1059 3590 3836 3364
pt.pp.apf d.dpm a.dpm n.dpm cj pl d.nsm n.nsm

τοῦ θεοῦ βλασφημῆται. 6 τοὺς νεωτέρους ὡσαύτως παρακάλει σωφρονεῖν
of *God* be blasphemed. Urge the younger men, likewise, *Urge* to be self-controlled
3836 2536 1059 4151 3836 3742 6058 4151 5404
d.gsm n.gsm v.pps.3s d.apm a.apm.c adv v.pam.2s f.pa

7 περὶ πάντα, σεαυτὸν παρεχόμενος τύπον καλῶν ἔργων,
in all things, showing yourself *showing* to be an example of good works, pure and
4309 4246 4218 4932 4218 5596 2819 2240 917
p.a a.apn r.asm.2 pt.pm.nsm n.asm a.gpn n.gpn

ἐν τῇ διδασκαλίᾳ ἀφθορίαν, σεμνότητα, 8
dignified in your teaching, *pure* *dignified* beyond reproach in your healthy
4949 1877 3836 1436 917 4949 183 183 5618
p.d d.dsf n.dsf n.asf n.asf

λόγον ὑγιῆ ἀκατάγνωστον, ἵνα ὁ ⌊ἐξ ἐναντίας⌋ ἐντραπῇ
instruction, *healthy* *beyond reproach* so that the opponent ⌊may be put to shame⌋
3364 5618 183 2671 3836 1666 1885 1956
n.asm a.asm a.asm cj d.nsm p.g a.gsf v.aps.3s

μηδὲν ἔχων λέγειν περὶ ἡμῶν φαῦλον. 9 δούλους
because he has nothing *because he has* evil to say against us. *evil* Urge slaves
2400 2400 2400 3594 2400 5765 3306 4309 7005 5765 1529
a.asn pt.pa.nsm f.pa p.g r.gp.1 a.asn n.apm

ἰδίοις δεσπόταις ὑποτάσσεσθαι ἐν πᾶσιν, εὐαρέστους
to be subject ⌊to their own⌋ masters *to be subject* in all things, to be pleasing,
5718 5718 5718 2625 1305 5718 1877 4246 1639 1639 2298
a.dpm n.dpm f.pp p.d a.dpn a.apm

εἶναι, μὴ ἀντιλέγοντας, 10 μὴ νοσφιζομένους, ἀλλὰ πᾶσαν πίστιν
to be not talking back, not pilfering but showing completely good faithfulness
1639 3590 515 3590 3802 247 1892 4246 19 4411
f.pa pl pt.pa.apm pl pt.pm.apm cj a.asf n.asf

ἐνδεικνυμένους ἀγαθήν, ἵνα τὴν διδασκαλίαν τὴν τοῦ
showing *good* so that they might adorn the teaching *{the}* of God our
1892 19 2671 3175 3175 3175 3836 1436 3836 3836 2536 7005
pt.pm.apm a.asf cj d.asf n.asf d.asf d.gsm

NASB

any good deed.

Duties of the Older and Younger

2:1 But as for you,
speak the things
which are fitting
for sound doctrine.
2 Older men are
to be temperate,
dignified, sensible,
sound in faith, in
love, in persever-
ance.
3 Older women
likewise are to be
reverent in their
behavior, not mali-
cious gossips nor
enslaved to much
wine, teaching
what is good, 4 so
that they may en-
courage the young
women to love
their husbands, to
love their children,
5 *to be* sensible,
pure, workers at
home, kind, being
subject to their
own husbands, so
that the word of
God will not be
dishonored.
6 Likewise urge
the young men to
be sensible; 7 in all
things show your-
self to be an exam-
ple of good deeds,
with purity in
doctrine, dignified,
8 sound *in* speech
which is beyond
reproach, so that
the opponent will
be put to shame,
having nothing bad
to say about us.
9 *Urge* bondslaves
to be subject to
their own masters
in everything, to
be well-pleasing,
not argumentative,
10 not pilfering, but
showing all good
faith so that they
will adorn the doc-
trine of God

NIV

Savior attractive.
11For the grace
of God has ap-
peared that offers
salvation to all
people. 12It teaches
us to say "No" to
ungodliness and
worldly passions,
and to live self-
controlled, upright
and godly lives in
this present age,
13while we wait
for the blessed
hope—the appear-
ing of the glory
of our great God
and Savior, Jesus
Christ, 14who gave
himself for us to
redeem us from all
wickedness and to
purify for himself
a people that are
his very own, ea-
ger to do what is
good.
15These, then,
are the things
you should teach.
Encourage and
rebuke with all
authority. Do not
let anyone despise
you.

Saved in Order to Do Good

3 Remind the
people to be
subject to rulers
and authorities, to
be obedient, to be
ready to do what-
ever is good, 2to
slander no one, to
be peaceable and
considerate, and
always to be gentle
toward everyone.
3At one time we
too were fool-
ish, disobedient,
deceived and
enslaved by all
kinds of passions
and pleasures. We
lived in malice and
envy, being hated
and hating one an-
other. 4But when
the kindness and
love of God our
Savior

σωτῆρος ἡμῶν θεοῦ κοσμῶσιν ἐν πᾶσιν. 11 ἐπεφάνη γὰρ ἡ χάρις τοῦ θεοῦ
Savior *our* *God* *they might adorn* in all things. *has appeared* For the grace of God
5400 7005 2536 3175 1877 4246 2210 1142 3836 5921 3836 2536
n.gsm r.gp.1 n.gsm v.pas.3p p.d a.dpn v.api.3s cj d.nsf n.nsf d.gsm n.gsm

σωτήριος πᾶσιν ἀνθρώποις 12 παιδεύουσα ἡμᾶς, ἵνα ἀρνησάμενοι
has appeared, bringing salvation for all people, teaching us that, having denied
2210 2210 5402 4246 476 4084 7005 2671 766
a.nsf a.dpm n.dpm pt.pa.nsf r.ap.1 cj pt.am.npm

τὴν ἀσέβειαν καὶ τὰς κοσμικὰς ἐπιθυμίας σωφρόνως
the ungodliness and the worldly passions, we should live ⌞in a self-controlled manner⌟
3836 813 2779 3836 3176 2123 2409 2409 2409 5407
d.asf n.asf cj d.apf a.apf n.apf adv

καὶ δικαίως καὶ εὐσεβῶς ζήσωμεν ἐν τῷ νῦν αἰῶνι, 13 προσδεχόμενοι τὴν
and justly and reverently *we should live* in the present age, waiting for the
2779 1469 2779 2357 2409 1877 3836 3814 172 4657 3836
cj adv cj adv v.aas.1p p.d d.dsm adv n.dsm pt.pm.npm d.asf

μακαρίαν ἐλπίδα καὶ ἐπιφάνειαν τῆς δόξης τοῦ μεγάλου θεοῦ καὶ
blessed hope, *{even}* the appearing of the glory of our great God and
3421 1828 2779 2211 3836 1518 3836 7005 3489 2536 2779
a.asf n.asf cj n.asf d.gsf n.gsf d.gsm a.gsm n.gsm cj

σωτῆρος ἡμῶν Ἰησοῦ Χριστοῦ, 14 ὃς ἔδωκεν ἑαυτὸν ὑπὲρ ἡμῶν, ἵνα λυτρώσηται
Savior *our* Jesus Christ, who gave himself for us so that he might redeem
5400 7005 2652 5986 4005 1443 1571 5642 7005 2671 3390
n.gsm r.gp.1 n.gsm n.gsm r.nsm v.aai.3s r.asm.3 p.g r.gp.1 cj v.ams.3s

ἡμᾶς ἀπὸ πάσης ἀνομίας καὶ καθαρίσῃ ἑαυτῷ λαὸν περιούσιον,
us from all lawlessness and cleanse for himself a special people, *special* a
7005 608 4246 490 2779 2751 1571 4342 3295 4342
r.ap.1 p.g a.gsf n.gsf cj v.aas.3s r.dsm.3 n.asm a.asm

ζηλωτὴν καλῶν ἔργων. 15 ταῦτα λάλει καὶ παρακάλει καὶ ἔλεγχε μετὰ
zealot for good works. Speak these things *Speak* and encourage and rebuke with
2421 2819 2240 3281 4047 3281 2779 4151 2779 1794 3552
n.asm a.gpn n.gpn r.apn v.pam.2s cj v.pam.2s cj v.pam.2s p.g

πάσης ἐπιταγῆς· μηδείς σου περιφρονείτω.
all authority; let no one disregard you. *let disregard*
4246 2198 4368 3594 4368 5148 4368
a.gsf n.gsf a.nsm r.gs.2 v.pam.3s

3:1 ὑπομίμνῃσκε αὐτοὺς ἀρχαῖς ἐξουσίαις ὑποτάσσεσθαι,
Remind them to be subject to rulers, to authorities, *to be subject*
5703 899 5718 5718 5718 794 2026 5718
v.pam.2s r.apm.3 n.dpf n.dpf f.pp

πειθαρχεῖν, πρὸς πᾶν ἔργον ἀγαθὸν ἑτοίμους εἶναι, 2
to be obedient, to be ready for any good work, *good* *ready* *to be* to blaspheme
4272 1639 1639 2289 4639 4246 19 2240 19 2289 1639 1059 1059
f.pa p.a a.asn n.asn a.asn a.apm f.pa

μηδένα βλασφημεῖν, ἀμάχους εἶναι, ἐπιεικεῖς, πᾶσαν ἐνδεικνυμένους
no one, *to blaspheme* to be peaceable, *to be* gracious, showing complete *showing*
3594 1059 1639 1639 285 1639 2117 1892 4246 1892
a.asm f.pa a.apm f.pa a.apm a.asf pt.pm.apm

πραΰτητα πρὸς πάντας ἀνθρώπους. 3 → ἦμεν γάρ ποτε καί
gentleness toward all people. For once we ourselves also were *For* *once* *also*
4559 4639 4246 476 1142 4537 7005 2779 1639 1142 4537 2779
n.asf p.a a.apm n.apm v.iai.1p cj adv adv

ἡμεῖς ἀνόητοι, ἀπειθεῖς, πλανώμενοι, δουλεύοντες ἐπιθυμίαις καὶ ἡδοναῖς
ourselves foolish, disobedient, being led astray, being enslaved by desires and various pleasures,
7005 485 579 4414 1526 2123 2779 4476 2454
r.np.1 a.npm a.npm pt.pp.npm pt.pa.npm n.dpf cj n.dpf

ποικίλαις, ἐν κακίᾳ καὶ φθόνῳ διάγοντες, στυγητοί, μισοῦντες
various living a life of evil and envy, *living a life* detestable, hating
4476 1341 1341 1341 1877 2798 2779 5784 1341 5144 3631
a.dpf p.d n.dsf cj n.dsm pt.pa.npm a.npm pt.pa.npm

ἀλλήλους. 4 ὅτε δὲ ἡ χρηστότης καὶ ἡ φιλανθρωπία
one another. But when *But* the goodness and *{the}* loving kindness of God our Savior
253 1254 4021 1254 3836 5983 2779 3836 5792 3836 2536 7005 5400
r.apm cj cj d.nsf n.nsf cj d.nsf n.nsf

NASB

our Savior in every
respect.
11For the grace of
God has appeared,
bringing salva-
tion to all men,
12instructing us to
deny ungodliness
and worldly desires
and to live sensi-
bly, righteously
and godly in the
present age, 13look-
ing for the blessed
hope and the
appearing of the
glory of our great
God and Savior,
Christ Jesus, 14who
gave Himself for
us to redeem us
from every lawless
deed, and to pu-
rify for Himself a
people for His own
possession, zealous
for good deeds.
15These things
speak and exhort
and reprove with
all authority. Let no
one disregard you.

Godly Living

3:1Remind them to
be subject to rul-
ers, to authorities,
to be obedient, to
be ready for every
good deed, 2to ma-
lign no one, to be
peaceable, gentle,
showing every con-
sideration for all
men. 3For we also
once were foolish
ourselves, disobe-
dient, deceived,
enslaved to various
lusts and pleasures,
spending our life
in malice and envy,
hateful, hating one
another. 4But when
the kindness of
God our Savior and
His love for

NIV

appeared, [5]he
saved us, not be-
cause of righteous
things we had
done, but because
of his mercy. He
saved us through
the washing of re-
birth and renewal
by the Holy Spirit,
[6]whom he poured
out on us gen-
erously through
Jesus Christ our
Savior, [7]so that,
having been justi-
fied by his grace,
we might become
heirs having the
hope of eternal life.
[8]This is a trust-
worthy saying.
And I want you to
stress these things,
so that those who
have trusted in God
may be careful to
devote themselves
to doing what is
good. These things
are excellent and
profitable for ev-
eryone.
[9]But avoid fool-
ish controversies
and genealogies
and arguments
and quarrels about
the law, because
these are unprof-
itable and useless.
[10]Warn a divisive
person once, and
then warn them a
second time. After
that, have nothing
to do with them.
[11]You may be sure
that such people
are warped and
sinful; they are
self-condemned.

Final Remarks

[12]As soon as I
send Artemas or
Tychicus to you,
do your best to
come to me at Ni-
copolis, because
I have decided to
winter there. [13]Do
everything you
can to help Zenas
the lawyer and
Apollos on their
way and see that
they have every-
thing they need.

ἐπεφάνη τοῦ σωτῆρος ἡμῶν θεοῦ, [5]οὐκ ἐξ ἔργων τῶν ἐν δικαιοσύνῃ ἃ
appeared, *of* *Savior* *our* *God* not ˪because of˩ works of *{in}* righteousness that
2210 3836 5400 7005 2536 4024 1666 2240 3836 1877 1466 4005
v.api.3s d.gsm n.gsm r.gp.1 n.gsm pl p.g n.gpn d.gpn p.d n.dsf r.apn

ἐποιήσαμεν ἡμεῖς ἀλλὰ κατὰ τὸ αὐτοῦ ἔλεος ἔσωσεν ἡμᾶς διὰ
we did *we* but ˪according to˩ *{the}* his mercy, he saved us, through the
7005 4472 7005 247 2848 3836 899 1799 5392 7005 1328
v.aai.1p r.np.1 cj p.a d.asn r.gsm.3 n.asn v.aai.3s r.ap.1 p.g

λουτροῦ παλιγγενεσίας καὶ ἀνακαινώσεως → πνεύματος ἁγίου, [6]οὗ →
washing of regeneration and renewal of the Holy Spirit, *Holy* whom he
3373 4098 2779 364 41 4460 41 4005
n.gsn n.gsf cj n.gsf n.gsn a.gsn r.gsn

ἐξέχεεν ἐφ' ἡμᾶς πλουσίως διὰ Ἰησοῦ Χριστοῦ τοῦ σωτῆρος ἡμῶν,
richly poured out for us *richly* through Jesus Christ *{the}* our Savior, *our*
4455 1772 2093 7005 4455 1328 2652 5986 3836 7005 5400 7005
v.aai.3s p.a r.ap.1 adv p.g n.gsm n.gsm d.gsm n.gsm r.gp.1

[7]ἵνα δικαιωθέντες τῇ ἐκείνου χάριτι κληρονόμοι
so that having been justified by his grace, we might become heirs
2671 1467 3836 1697 5921 1181 1181 1181 3101
cj pt.ap.npm d.dsf r.gsm n.dsf n.npm

γενηθῶμεν κατ' ἐλπίδα → ζωῆς αἰωνίου. [8]πιστὸς ὁ λόγος,
we might become ˪according to˩ the hope of eternal life. *eternal* Trustworthy is the saying,
1181 2848 1828 173 2437 173 4412 3836 3364
v.aps.1p p.a n.asf n.gsf a.gsf a.nsm d.nsm n.nsm

καὶ περὶ τούτων βούλομαί σε διαβεβαιοῦσθαι,
and I want you to insist emphatically on these things *I want* *you* *to insist emphatically*
2779 1089 1089 5148 1331 1331 1331 4309 4047 1089 5148 1331
cj p.g r.gpn v.pmi.1s r.as.2 f.pm

ἵνα φροντίζωσιν καλῶν
so that those who have believed in God ˪might be intent on˩ devoting themselves to good
2671 3836 4409 4409 4409 4409 2536 5863 4613 4613 4613 2819
cj v.pas.3p a.gpn

ἔργων προΐστασθαι οἱ πεπιστευκότες θεῷ· ταῦτά ἐστιν καλὰ καὶ ὠφέλιμα
works. *devoting themselves to* *those* *who have believed in* *God* These are good and profitable
2240 4613 3836 4409 2536 4047 1639 2819 2779 6068
n.gpn f.pm d.npm pt.ra.npm n.dsm r.npn v.pai.3s a.npn cj a.npn

τοῖς ἀνθρώποις. [9] μωρὰς δὲ ζητήσεις καὶ γενεαλογίας καὶ ἔρεις καὶ
for people. But shun foolish *But* speculations and genealogies and strife and
3836 476 1254 4325 3704 1254 2428 2779 1157 2779 2251 2779
d.dpm n.dpm a.apf cj n.apf cj n.apf cj n.apf cj

μάχας → νομικὰς περιΐστασο· εἰσὶν γὰρ ἀνωφελεῖς καὶ μάταιοι. [10]
quarrels about the law, *shun* for they are *for* harmful and useless. Avoid
3480 3788 4325 1142 1639 1142 543 2779 3469 4148
n.apf a.apf v.pmm.2s v.pai.3p cj a.npf cj a.npf

αἱρετικὸν ἄνθρωπον μετὰ μίαν καὶ δευτέραν νουθεσίαν παραιτοῦ, [11]εἰδὼς ὅτι
the factious person after a first and second warning, *Avoid* knowing that
148 476 3552 1651 2779 1311 3804 4148 3857 4022
a.asm n.asm p.a a.asf cj a.asf n.asf v.pmm.2s pt.ra.nsm cj

ἐξέστραπται ὁ τοιοῦτος καὶ ἁμαρτάνει ὢν αὐτοκατάκριτος.
such a person has been warped *{the}* *such a person* and is sinning, being self-condemned.
5525 5525 5525 1750 3836 5525 2779 279 1639 896
v.rpi.3s d.nsm r.nsm cj v.pai.3s pt.pa.nsm a.nsm

[12]ὅταν πέμψω Ἀρτεμᾶν πρὸς σὲ ἢ Τύχικον, σπούδασον ἐλθεῖν πρός με εἰς
When I send Artemas to you or Tychicus, do your best to come to me in
4020 4287 782 4639 5148 2445 5608 5079 2262 4639 1609 1650
cj v.aas.1s n.asm p.a r.as.2 cj n.asm v.aam.2s f.aa p.a r.as.1 p.a

Νικόπολιν, ἐκεῖ γὰρ κέκρικα παραχειμάσαι. [13] ↱ ↱
Nicopolis, *there* for I have decided to winter there. Do your best to help
3776 1695 1142 3212 4199 1695 5081 5081 5081 4636 4636
n.asf adv cj v.rai.1s f.aa

Ζηνᾶν τὸν νομικὸν καὶ Ἀπολλῶν σπουδαίως πρόπεμψον, ἵνα μηδὲν
Zenas the lawyer and Apollos *Do your best* on their journey, so that they lack nothing.
2424 3836 3788 2779 663 5081 4636 2671 899 3309 3594
n.asm d.asm n.asm cj n.asm adv v.aam.2s cj a.nsn

NASB

mankind appeared,
[5]He saved us,
not on the basis
of deeds which
we have done in
righteousness,
but according to
His mercy, by the
washing of regen-
eration and renew-
ing by the Holy
Spirit, [6]whom He
poured out upon
us richly through
Jesus Christ our
Savior, [7]so that be-
ing justified by His
grace we would be
made heirs accord-
ing to *the* hope of
eternal life. [8]This
is a trustworthy
statement; and
concerning these
things I want you
to speak confident-
ly, so that those
who have believed
God will be care-
ful to engage in
good deeds. These
things are good and
profitable for men.
[9]But avoid foolish
controversies and
genealogies and
strife and disputes
about the Law, for
they are unprofit-
able and worth-
less. [10]Reject a
factious man after
a first and second
warning, [11]knowing
that such a man is
perverted and is
sinning, being self-
condemned.

Personal Concerns

[12]When I send Ar-
temas or Tychicus
to you, make every
effort to come to
me at Nicopolis,
for I have decided
to spend the winter
there. [13]Diligently
help Zenas the law-
yer and Apollos on
their way so that
nothing is lacking

NIV

[14]Our people must
learn to devote
themselves to do-
ing what is good,
in order to provide
for urgent needs
and not live unpro-
ductive lives.
[15]Everyone with
me sends you
greetings. Greet
those who love us
in the faith.
Grace be with
you all.

αὐτοῖς λείπη. 14 → μανθανέτωσαν δὲ καὶ οἱ ἡμέτεροι
they *lack* And let our people learn *And* *{also}* *{the}* *our people* to be
899 3309 1254 2466 2466 3443 1254 2779 3836 2466 4613 4613
r.dpm.3 v.pas.3s v.pam.3p cj adv d.npm r.npm.1

καλῶν ἔργων προΐστασθαι εἰς τὰς ἀναγκαίας χρείας, ⌊ἵνα μὴ⌋
devoted to good deeds, *to be devoted to* specifically the urgent needs, lest
4613 4613 2819 2240 4613 1650 3836 338 5970 2671 3590
a.gpn n.gpn f.pm p.a d.apf a.apf n.apf cj pl

ὦσιν ἄκαρποι. 15 ἀσπάζονταί σε οἱ μετ᾽ ἐμοῦ πάντες. ἄσπασαι
they be fruitless. All those with me greet you. *those* *with* *me* *All* Greet
1639 182 4246 3836 3552 1609 832 5148 3836 3552 1609 4246 832
v.pas.3p a.npm v.pmi.3p r.as.2 d.npm p.g r.gs.1 a.npm v.amm.2s

τοὺς φιλοῦντας ἡμᾶς ἐν πίστει. ἡ χάρις μετὰ πάντων ὑμῶν.[a]
those who love us in the faith. *{the}* Grace be with all of you.
3836 5797 7005 1877 4411 3836 5921 3552 4246 7007
d.apm pt.pa.apm r.ap.1 p.d n.dsf d.nsf n.nsf p.g a.gpm r.gp.2

NASB

for them. [14]Our
people must also
learn to engage in
good deeds to meet
pressing needs, so
that they will not
be unfruitful.
[15]All who are
with me greet you.
Greet those who
love us in *the* faith.
Grace be with
you all.

[a] ἀμήν. πρὸς Τίτον τῆς Κρητῶν ἐκκλησίας πρῶτον ἐπίσκοπον χειροτονηθέντα. ἐγράφη ἀπὸ Νικοπόλεως τῆς Μακεδονίας included by TR after ὑμῶν.

Philemon

NIV

1 Paul, a prisoner
of Christ Jesus,
and Timothy our
brother,
To Philemon our
dear friend and
fellow worker—
2 also to Apphia
our sister and Ar-
chippus our fellow
soldier—and to
the church that
meets in your
home:
3 Grace and peace
to you[a] from God
our Father and the
Lord Jesus Christ.

Thanksgiving and Prayer

4 I always thank
my God as I re-
member you in my
prayers, 5 because
I hear about your
love for all his holy
people and your
faith in the Lord
Jesus. 6 I pray that
your partnership
with us in the faith
may be effective
in deepening your
understanding of
every good thing
we share for the
sake of Christ.
7 Your love has
given me great joy
and encourage-
ment, because you,
brother, have re-
freshed the hearts
of the Lord's
people.

Paul's Plea for Onesimus

8 Therefore, al-
though in Christ I
could be bold and
order you to do
what you ought to
do, 9 yet I prefer

[a] 3 The Greek is plural; also in verses 22 and 25; elsewhere in this letter "you" is singular.

1:1 Παῦλος δέσμιος Χριστοῦ Ἰησοῦ καὶ Τιμόθεος ὁ ἀδελφὸς Φιλήμονι τῷ
Paul, a prisoner of Christ Jesus, and Timothy our brother, to Philemon {the}
4263 1300 5986 2652 2779 5510 3836 81 5800 3836
n.nsm n.nsm n.gsm n.gsm cj n.nsm d.nsm n.nsm n.dsm d.dsm

ἀγαπητῷ καὶ συνεργῷ ἡμῶν 2 καὶ Ἀπφίᾳ τῇ ἀδελφῇ καὶ Ἀρχίππῳ τῷ
our dear friend and fellow worker, our {and} to Apphia our sister, {and} to Archippus {the}
7005 28 2779 5301 7005 2779 722 3836 80 2779 800 3836
a.dsm cj n.dsm r.gp.1 cj n.dsf d.dsf n.dsf cj n.dsm d.dsm

συστρατιώτῃ ἡμῶν καὶ τῇ κατʼ οἶκόν σου ἐκκλησίᾳ,
our fellow soldier, our and ⌊to the⌋ church ⌊that meets in⌋ your house: your church
7005 5369 7005 2779 3836 1711 2848 5148 3875 5148 1711
n.dsm r.gp.1 cj d.dsf p.a n.asm r.gs.2 n.dsf

3 χάρις ὑμῖν καὶ εἰρήνη ἀπὸ θεοῦ πατρὸς ἡμῶν καὶ κυρίου Ἰησοῦ Χριστοῦ.
Grace to you and peace from God our Father our and the Lord Jesus Christ.
5921 7007 2779 1645 608 2536 7005 4252 7005 2779 3261 2652 5986
n.nsf r.dp.2 cj n.nsf p.g n.gsm n.gsm r.gp.1 cj n.gsm n.gsm n.gsm

4 → εὐχαριστῶ τῷ θεῷ μου πάντοτε ↱ ↱ μνείαν σου ποιούμενος
I always thank {the} my God my always when I remember you {making}
4121 2373 3836 1609 2536 1609 4121 4472 4472 3644 5148 4472
v.pai.1s d.dsm n.dsm r.gs.1 adv n.asf r.gs.2 pt.pm.nsm

ἐπὶ τῶν προσευχῶν μου, 5 ἀκούων σου τὴν ἀγάπην
in {the} my prayers, my ⌊because I hear⌋ of your {the} love for all the saints
2093 3836 1609 4666 1609 201 5148 3836 27 1650 4246 3836 41
p.g d.gpf n.gpf r.gs.1 pt.pa.nsm r.gs.2 d.asf n.asf

καὶ τὴν πίστιν, ἣν ἔχεις πρὸς τὸν κύριον Ἰησοῦν καὶ εἰς πάντας τοὺς
and your faith {that} {you have} in the Lord Jesus. {and} for all the
2779 3836 4411 4005 2400 4639 3836 3261 2652 2779 1650 4246 3836
cj d.asf n.asf r.asf v.pai.2s p.a d.asm n.asm n.asm cj p.a a.apm d.apm

ἁγίους, 6 ὅπως ἡ κοινωνία τῆς πίστεώς σου ἐνεργὴς
saints And I pray that the sharing of your faith your may become effective
41 3968 3836 3126 3836 5148 4411 5148 1181 1181 1921
a.apm cj d.nsf n.nsf d.gsf n.gsf r.gs.2 a.nsf

γένηται ἐν ἐπιγνώσει παντὸς ἀγαθοῦ τοῦ ἐν ἡμῖν[a] εἰς Χριστόν.
may become in the knowledge of every good thing ⌊that belongs⌋ to us in Christ.
1181 1877 2106 4246 19 3836 1877 7005 1650 5986
v.ams.3s p.d n.dsf a.gsn a.gsn d.gsn p.d r.dp.1 p.a n.asm

7 χαρὰν γὰρ πολλὴν ἔσχον καὶ παράκλησιν ἐπὶ τῇ
For I have derived much joy For much I have derived and encouragement from {the}
1142 2400 2400 2400 4498 5915 1142 4498 2400 2779 4155 2093 3836
n.asf cj a.asf v.aai.1s cj n.asf p.d d.dsf

ἀγάπῃ σου, ὅτι τὰ σπλάγχνα τῶν ἁγίων ἀναπέπαυται διὰ
your love, your my brother, because the hearts of the saints have been refreshed by
5148 27 5148 81 81 4022 3836 5073 3836 41 399 1328
n.dsf r.gs.2 cj d.npn n.npn d.gpm a.gpm v.rpi.3s p.g

σοῦ, ἀδελφέ. 8 διὸ πολλὴν ἐν Χριστῷ παρρησίαν
you. my brother So, although in Christ I have sufficient in Christ freedom
5148 81 1475 2400 1877 5986 2400 2400 4498 1877 5986 4244
r.gs.2 n.vsm cj a.asf p.d n.dsm n.asf

ἔχων ἐπιτάσσειν σοι ↱ ↱ τὸ ἀνῆκον 9 ↱ διὰ τὴν ἀγάπην ↰ μᾶλλον
although I have to order you to do what you ought, yet for {the} love's sake I prefer
2400 2199 5148 465 465 3836 465 3437 1328 3836 27 1328 3437
pt.pa.nsm f.pa r.ds.2 d.asn pt.pa.asn p.a d.asf n.asf adv.c

[a] ἡμῖν UBS, TNIV. ὑμῖν NET.

NASB

Salutation

1:1 Paul, a prisoner
of Christ Jesus,
and Timothy our
brother,
To Philemon our
beloved *brother*
and fellow worker,
2 and to Apphia
our sister, and to
Archippus our fel-
low soldier, and
to the church in
your house: 3 Grace
to you and peace
from God our Fa-
ther and the Lord
Jesus Christ.

Philemon's Love and Faith

4 I thank my God
always, making
mention of you
in my prayers,
5 because I hear of
your love and of
the faith which you
have toward the
Lord Jesus and to-
ward all the saints;
6 *and I pray* that the
fellowship of your
faith may become
effective [a]through
the knowledge of
every good thing
which is in you
for Christ's sake.
7 For I have come
to have much joy
and comfort in
your love, because
the hearts of the
saints have been
refreshed through
you, brother.
8 Therefore,
though I have
enough confidence
in Christ to order
you *to do* what
is proper, 9 yet for
love's sake I rather

[a] Or *in*

NIV

to appeal to you on
the basis of love.
It is as none other
than Paul—an old
man and now also
a prisoner of Christ
Jesus— [10]that I
appeal to you for
my son Onesimus,[a]
who became my
son while I was in
chains. [11]Formerly
he was useless to
you, but now he
has become useful
both to you and
to me.
[12]I am sending
him—who is my
very heart—back
to you. [13]I would
have liked to keep
him with me so
that he could take
your place in help-
ing me while I
am in chains for
the gospel. [14]But
I did not want to
do anything with-
out your consent,
so that any favor
you do would not
seem forced but
would be volun-
tary. [15]Perhaps the
reason he was sep-
arated from you
for a little while
was that you might
have him back for-
ever— [16]no longer
as a slave, but
better than a slave,
as a dear brother.
He is very dear to
me but even dear-
er to you, both as
a fellow man and
as a brother in the
Lord.
[17]So if you con-
sider me a partner,
welcome him as
you would wel-
come me. [18]If he
has done you any
wrong or owes you
anything, charge it
to me.

[a] 10 *Onesimus* means *useful.*

παρακαλῶ, τοιοῦτος ὢν ὡς Παῦλος πρεσβύτης νυνὶ δὲ
to appeal to you — I, *{being}* *{as}* Paul, an old man and even now *and*
4151 5525 1639 6055 4263 4566 1254 2779 3815 1254
v.pai.1s r.nsm pt.pa.nsm pl n.nsm n.nsm adv cj

καὶ δέσμιος Χριστοῦ Ἰησοῦ· [10] παρακαλῶ σε περὶ τοῦ ἐμοῦ τέκνου,
even a prisoner for the sake of Christ Jesus — I appeal to you for *{the}* my child,
2779 1300 5986 2652 4151 5148 4309 3836 1847 5451
adv n.nsm n.gsm n.gsm v.pai.1s r.as.2 p.g d.gsn r.gsn.1 n.gsn

ὃν ἐγέννησα ἐν τοῖς δεσμοῖς, Ὀνήσιμον, [11] τόν ποτέ
Onesimus, whose father I became while in prison. *Onesimus* *{the}* Formerly he was of
3946 4005 1164 1877 3836 1301 3946 3836 4537 947
r.asm v.aai.1s p.d d.dpm n.dpm n.asm d.asm adv

σοι ἄχρηστον νυνὶ δὲ καὶ[a] σοὶ καὶ ἐμοὶ
no use to you, *of no use* but now *but* he has become useful both to you and to me.
947 947 5148 947 1254 3815 1254 2378 2779 5148 2779 1609
r.ds.2 a.asm adv cj cj r.ds.2 cj r.ds.1

εὔχρηστον, [12] ὃν ἀνέπεμψά ← σοι, αὐτόν, τοῦτ᾽ ἔστιν τὰ
useful *him* I am sending him back to you, that is, ⌞the one who⌟ is *that* *is* *{the}*
2378 4005 402 4005 5148 4047 1639 899 4047 1639 3836
a.asm r.asm v.aai.1s r.ds.2 r.asm.3 r.nsn v.pai.3s d.apn

ἐμὰ σπλάγχνα· [13] ὃν ἐγὼ ἐβουλόμην πρὸς ἐμαυτὸν κατέχειν,
⌞my own⌟ heart. I wanted to keep him *I* *wanted* with me, *to keep*
1847 5073 1609 1089 2988 2988 4005 1609 1089 4639 1831 2988
r.apn.1 n.apn r.asm r.ns.1 v.imi.1s p.a r.asm.1 f.pa

ἵνα ὑπὲρ σοῦ ↰ μοι διακονῇ ἐν τοῖς
so that he could minister to me on your behalf *to me* *he could minister* during my
2671 1354 1354 1354 1609 1609 5642 5148 5642 1609 1354 1877 3836
cj p.g r.gs.2 r.ds.1 v.pas.3s p.d d.dpm

δεσμοῖς τοῦ εὐαγγελίου, [14] χωρὶς δὲ
imprisonment ⌞for the⌟ gospel, but I did not want to do anything without *but*
1301 3836 2295 1254 2527 2527 4029 2527 4472 4472 4029 6006 1254
n.dpm d.gsn n.gsn p.g cj

τῆς σῆς γνώμης οὐδὲν ἠθέλησα ποιῆσαι, ἵνα μὴ ὡς
{the} your consent, *not anything* *I did want* *to do* so that your helpfulness might not be *{as}*
3836 5050 1191 4029 2527 4472 2671 5148 19 1639 3590 1639 6055
d.gsf r.gsf.2 n.gsf a.asn v.aai.1s f.aa cj pl pl

κατὰ ἀνάγκην τὸ ἀγαθόν σου ᾖ ἀλλὰ κατὰ ἑκούσιον. [15] τάχα
by compulsion *{the}* *helpfulness* *your* *might be* but by your own free will. Perhaps
2848 340 3836 19 5148 1639 247 2848 1730 5440
p.a n.asf d.nsn a.nsn r.gs.2 v.pas.3s cj p.a a.asn adv

γὰρ διὰ τοῦτο ἐχωρίσθη πρὸς
{for} he was separated from you for a while for this reason, *he was separated from* *for*
1142 6004 6004 6004 6004 4639 6052 6052 1328 4047 6004 4639
cj p.a r.asn v.api.3s p.a

ὥραν, ἵνα αἰώνιον αὐτὸν ἀπέχῃς, [16] οὐκέτι ὡς
a while that you might have him back forever, *him* *you might have back* no longer as a
6052 2671 600 600 600 899 600 173 899 600 4033 6055
n.asf cj a.asm r.asm.3 v.pas.2s adv pl

δοῦλον ἀλλ᾽ ὑπὲρ δοῦλον, ἀδελφὸν ἀγαπητόν, μάλιστα ἐμοί,
slave, but ⌞more than⌟ a slave, as a dear brother. *dear* He is ⌞especially so⌟ to me,
1529 247 5642 1529 28 81 28 3436 1609
n.asm cj p.a n.asm n.asm a.asm adv.s r.ds.1

πόσῳ δὲ μᾶλλον σοὶ καὶ ἐν σαρκὶ καὶ ἐν κυρίῳ. [17] εἰ
but how much *but* more to you, both in the flesh and in the Lord. So then if
1254 4531 1254 3437 5148 2779 1877 4922 2779 1877 3261 4036 4036 1623
r.dsn cj adv.c r.ds.2 cj p.d n.dsf cj p.d n.dsm cj

οὖν με ἔχεις → κοινωνόν, προσλαβοῦ αὐτὸν ὡς ἐμέ.
So then you regard me *you regard* as a partner, welcome him as you would me.
4036 2400 2400 1609 2400 3128 4689 899 6055 1609
cj r.as.1 v.pai.2s n.asm v.amm.2s r.asm.3 cj r.as.1

[18] εἰ δέ τι ἠδίκησέν σε ἢ ὀφείλει, ↱ τοῦτο ἐμοὶ
If *{and}* *anything* he has wronged you or owes you anything, charge that to my
1623 1254 5516 92 5148 2445 4053 5516 1824 4047 1609
cj cj r.asn v.aai.3s r.as.2 cj v.pai.3s r.asn r.ds.1

[a] [καὶ] UBS, omitted by NET.

NASB

appeal *to you*—
since I am such a
person as Paul, the
aged, and now also
a prisoner of Christ
Jesus—

Plea for Onesimus, a Free Man

[10]I appeal to you
for my child [a]One-
simus, whom I
have begotten in
my imprisonment,
[11]who formerly was
useless to you, but
now is useful both
to you and to me.
[12]I have sent him
back to you in per-
son, that is, *send-
ing* my very heart,
[13]whom I wished
to keep with me,
so that on your
behalf he might
minister to me in
my imprisonment
for the gospel; [14]but
without your con-
sent I did not want
to do anything, so
that your goodness
would not be, in
effect, by compul-
sion but of your
own free will. [15]For
perhaps he was for
this reason sepa-
rated *from you* for
a while, that you
would have him
back forever, [16]no
longer as a slave,
but more than a
slave, a beloved
brother, especially
to me, but how
much more to you,
both in the flesh
and in the Lord.
[17]If then you re-
gard me a partner,
accept him as *you
would* me. [18]But
if he has wronged
you in any way or
owes you anything,
charge that to my

[a] I.e. useful

NIV

[19]I, Paul, am writ-
ing this with my
own hand. I will
pay it back — not
to mention that
you owe me your
very self. [20]I do
wish, brother, that
I may have some
benefit from you
in the Lord; refresh
my heart in Christ.
[21]Confident of your
obedience, I write
to you, knowing
that you will do
even more than
I ask.
[22]And one thing
more: Prepare a
guest room for me,
because I hope to
be restored to you
in answer to your
prayers.

[23]Epaphras, my
fellow prisoner in
Christ Jesus, sends
you greetings.
[24]And so do Mark,
Aristarchus, De-
mas and Luke, my
fellow workers.
[25]The grace of the
Lord Jesus Christ
be with your spirit.

ἐλλόγα. [19] ἐγὼ Παῦλος ἔγραψα τῇ ἐμῇ χειρί, ἐγὼ → → ἀποτίσω·
account — I, Paul, am writing this with ⌊my own⌋ hand — I will pay it back.
1824 1609 4263 1211 3836 1847 5931 1609 702
v.pam.2s r.ns.1 n.nsm v.aai.1s d.dsf r.dsf.1 n.dsf r.ns.1 v.fai.1s

↱ ἵνα μὴ⌋ λέγω σοι ὅτι καὶ σεαυτόν μοι
I could also mention *{to you}* that *also* you owe me ⌊your very self!⌋ *me*
3306 2671 3590 2779 3306 5148 4022 2779 4695 4695 1609 4932 1609
cj pl v.pas.1s r.ds.2 cj adv r.asm.2 r.ds.1

προσοφείλεις. [20] ναὶ ἀδελφέ, ἐγώ σου ὀναίμην
you owe Yes, brother, I *from you* ⌊do wish that I may have some benefit⌋ from you
4695 3721 81 1609 5148 3949 5148 5148
v.pai.2s pl n.vsm r.ns.1 r.gs.2 v.amo.1s

ἐν κυρίῳ· ἀνάπαυσόν μου τὰ σπλάγχνα ἐν Χριστῷ. [21] πεποιθὼς τῇ
in the Lord. Refresh my *{the}* heart in Christ. Confident of your
1877 3261 399 1609 3836 5073 1877 5986 4275 3836 5148
p.d n.dsm v.aam.2s r.gs.1 d.apn n.apn p.d n.dsm pt.ra.nsm d.dsf

ὑπακοῇ σου ἔγραψά σοι, εἰδὼς ὅτι καὶ ὑπὲρ ἃ λέγω
obedience, *your* I write to you, knowing that you will do even ⌊more than⌋ *{what}* I say.
5633 5148 1211 5148 3857 4022 4472 4472 4472 2779 5642 4005 3306
n.dsf r.gs.2 v.aai.1s r.ds.2 pt.ra.nsm cj adv p.a r.apn v.pai.1s

ποιήσεις. [22] ἅμα δὲ καὶ ἑτοίμαζέ μοι ξενίαν·
you will do ⌊At the same time,⌋ *{and}* *{also}* prepare a guest room ⌊for me,⌋ *guest room* for
4472 275 1254 2779 2286 3825 3825 1609 3825 1142
v.fai.2s adv cj adv v.pam.2s r.ds.1 n.asf

ἐλπίζω γὰρ ὅτι διὰ τῶν προσευχῶν ὑμῶν χαρισθήσομαι ὑμῖν.
I am hoping *for* that through *{the}* your prayers *your* ⌊I will be graciously given⌋ to you.
1827 1142 4022 1328 3836 7007 4666 7007 5919 7007
v.pai.1s cj cj p.g d.gpf n.gpf r.gp.2 v.fpi.1s r.dp.2

[23] ἀσπάζεταί σε Ἐπαφρᾶς ὁ συναιχμάλωτός μου ἐν Χριστῷ Ἰησοῦ,
sends greetings *you* Epaphras, *{the}* my fellow prisoner *my* in Christ Jesus, sends
832 5148 2071 3836 1609 5257 1609 1877 5986 2652 832
v.pmi.3s r.as.2 n.nsm d.nsm n.nsm r.gs.1 p.d n.dsm n.dsm

[24] Μᾶρκος, Ἀρίσταρχος, Δημᾶς, Λουκᾶς, οἱ
you greetings, as do Mark, Aristarchus, Demas, and Luke, *{the}* my
5148 832 3453 752 1318 3371 3836 1609
n.nsm n.nsm n.nsm n.nsm d.npm

συνεργοί μου. [25] ἡ χάρις τοῦ κυρίου Ἰησοῦ Χριστοῦ μετὰ τοῦ
fellow workers. *my* The grace of the Lord Jesus Christ be with *{the}* your
5301 1609 3836 5921 3836 3261 2652 5986 3552 3836 7007
n.npm r.gs.1 d.nsf n.nsf d.gsm n.gsm n.gsm n.gsm p.g d.gsn

πνεύματος ὑμῶν.[a]
spirit. *your*
4460 7007
n.gsn r.gp.2

NASB

account; [19]I, Paul,
am writing this
with my own hand,
I will repay it (not
to mention to you
that you owe to
me even your own
self as well). [20]Yes,
brother, let me ben-
efit from you in the
Lord; refresh my
heart in Christ.
[21]Having con-
fidence in your
obedience, I write
to you, since I
know that you will
do even more than
what I say.
[22]At the same time
also prepare me a
lodging, for I hope
that through your
prayers I will be
given to you.
[23]Epaphras, my
fellow prisoner
in Christ Jesus,
greets you, [24]*as do*
Mark, Aristarchus,
Demas, Luke, my
fellow workers.
[25]The grace of the
Lord Jesus Christ
be with your spirit.[a]

[a] ἀμήν. πρὸς Φιλήμονα ἐγράφη ἀπὸ Ῥώμης διὰ Ὀνησίμου οἰκέτου included by TR after ὑμῶν.

[a] One early ms adds *Amen*

Hebrews

NIV

God's Final Word: His Son

1 In the past God
spoke to our an-
cestors through the
prophets at many
times and in various
ways, 2but in these
last days he has spo-
ken to us by his Son,
whom he appointed
heir of all things,
and through whom
also he made the
universe. 3The Son
is the radiance of
God's glory and the
exact representation
of his being, sus-
taining all things by
his powerful word.
After he had provid-
ed purification for
sins, he sat down at
the right hand of the
Majesty in heaven.
4So he became as
much superior to the
angels as the name
he has inherited is
superior to theirs.

The Son Superior to Angels

5For to which of
the angels did God
ever say,

"You are my Son;
today I have
become your
Father"[a]?

Or again,

"I will be his
Father,
and he will be
my Son"[b]?

6And again, when
God brings his
firstborn into the
world, he says,

"Let all God's
angels

1:1 πολυμερῶς καὶ πολυτρόπως πάλαι ὁ θεὸς λαλήσας τοῖς πατράσιν
at different times and in various ways In the past {the} God spoke to our fathers at
4495 2779 4502 4093 3836 2536 3281 3836 4252 4495
adv cj adv adv d.nsm n.nsm pt.aa.nsm d.dpm n.dpm

ἐν τοῖς προφήταις 2 ἐπ' ἐσχάτου τῶν
different times and in various ways through the prophets, but in these final {the}
4495 4495 2779 4502 4502 4502 1877 3836 4737 2093 4047 2274 3836
p.d d.dpm n.dpm p.g a.gsm d.gpf

ἡμερῶν τούτων ἐλάλησεν ἡμῖν ἐν υἱῷ, ὃν ἔθηκεν κληρονόμον
days these he has spoken to us by his Son, whom he appointed the heir
2465 4047 3281 7005 1877 5626 4005 5502 3101
n.gpf r.gpf v.aai.3s r.dp.1 p.d n.dsm r.asm v.aai.3s n.asm

πάντων, δι' οὗ ↱ καὶ ἐποίησεν τοὺς αἰῶνας· 3 ὃς ὢν
of all things, through whom he also created the material universe. This Son is the
4246 1328 4005 4472 2779 4472 3836 172 4005 1639
a.gpn p.g r.gsm adv v.aai.3s d.apm n.apm r.nsm pt.pa.nsm

ἀπαύγασμα τῆς δόξης καὶ χαρακτὴρ τῆς ὑποστάσεως αὐτοῦ,
radiance of his glory and the exact representation of his nature, *his* and
575 3836 1518 2779 5917 3836 899 5712 899 5445
n.nsn d.gsf n.gsf cj n.nsm d.gsf n.gsf r.gsm.3

φέρων τε τὰ πάντα τῷ ῥήματι τῆς δυνάμεως αὐτοῦ,
⌊although sustaining⌋ *and* *{the}* ⌊all there is⌋ ⌊by the⌋ word of his power, *his* yet made
5770 5445 3836 4246 3836 4839 3836 899 1539 899 4472 4472
pt.pa.nsm cj d.apn a.apn d.dsn n.dsn d.gsf n.gsf r.gsm.3

καθαρισμὸν τῶν ἁμαρτιῶν ποιησάμενος ἐκάθισεν ἐν δεξιᾷ τῆς
purification for sins, *yet made* and then sat down at the right hand of the
2752 3836 281 4472 2767 1877 1288 3836
n.asm d.gpf n.gpf pt.am.nsm v.aai.3s p.d a.dsf d.gsf

μεγαλωσύνης ἐν ὑψηλοῖς, 4 τοσούτῳ κρείττων γενόμενος τῶν
Majesty on high, having been exalted as far above *exalted* *having been* the
3488 1877 5734 1181 1181 3202 5537 3202 1181 3836
n.gsf p.d a.dpm r.dsn a.nsm.c pt.am.nsm d.gpm

ἀγγέλων → ὅσῳ διαφορώτερον παρ' αὐτοὺς κεκληρονόμηκεν
angels as the name he inherited is more noble than theirs. *he inherited*
34 3950 3099 3099 4012 1427 4123 899 3099
n.gpm r.dsn a.asn.c p.a r.apm.3 v.rai.3s

ὄνομα. 5 τίνι γὰρ → εἶπέν ποτε τῶν ἀγγέλων,
name For to which *For* of the angels did God ever say, *ever* *of the* *angels* "My
3950 1142 5515 1142 3836 3836 34 4537 3306 4537 3836 34 1609
n.asn r.dsm cj v.aai.3s adv d.gpm n.gpm

υἱός μου εἶ σύ, ἐγὼ σήμερον γεγέννηκά σε; καὶ πάλιν, ἐγὼ ἔσομαι αὐτῷ
Son *My* are you! Today I *Today* have fathered you"? Or again, "I will be to him
5626 1609 1639 5148 4958 1609 4958 1164 5148 2779 4099 1609 1639 899
n.nsm r.gs.1 v.pai.2s r.ns.2 r.ns.1 adv v.rai.1s r.as.2 cj adv r.ns.1 v.fmi.1s r.dsm.3

εἰς πατέρα, καὶ αὐτὸς ἔσται μοι εἰς υἱόν; 6 ὅταν δὲ πάλιν
{for} a father, and he shall be to me *{for}* a son"? And again, when *And* *again*
1650 4252 2779 899 1639 1609 1650 5626 1254 4099 4020 1254 4099
p.a n.asm cj r.nsm v.fmi.3s r.ds.1 p.a n.asm cj cj adv

εἰσαγάγῃ τὸν πρωτότοκον εἰς τὴν οἰκουμένην, λέγει, καὶ →
he brings the firstborn into the world, he says, *{and}* "Let all the angels of
1652 3836 4758 1650 3836 3876 3306 2779 4246 34 2536
v.aas.3s d.asm a.asm p.a d.asf n.asf v.pai.3s cj

NASB

God's Final Word in His Son

1:1God, after He
spoke long ago to
the fathers in the
prophets in many
portions and in
many ways, 2in
these last days has
spoken to us in
His Son, whom He
appointed heir of
all things, through
whom also He
made the world.
3And He is the
radiance of His
glory and the exact
representation of
His nature, and
upholds all things
by the word of His
power. When He
had made purifica-
tion of sins, He
sat down at the
right hand of the
Majesty on high,
4having become
as much better
than the angels, as
He has inherited
a more excellent
name than they.
5For to which of
the angels did He
ever say,
" You are My
Son,
Today I have
begotten
You"?
And again,
" I will be a Fa-
ther to Him
And He shall
be a Son to
Me"?
6And when He
again brings the
firstborn into the
world, He says,
" And let all
the angels of

[a] 5 Psalm 2:7
[b] 5 2 Samuel 7:14; 1 Chron. 17:13

NIV

worship
him."[a]
7 In speaking of the
angels he says,
"He makes his
angels
spirits,
and his servants
flames of
fire."[b]
8 But about the Son
he says,
"Your throne,
O God, will
last for ever
and ever;
a scepter of
justice
will be the
scepter
of your
kingdom.
9 You have loved
righteous-
ness and
hated
wickedness;
therefore God,
your God,
has set you
above your
companions
by anointing
you with the
oil of joy."[c]
10 He also says,
"In the beginning,
Lord, you
laid the
foundations
of the earth,
and the heavens
are the work
of your
hands.
11 They will perish,
but you
remain;
they will all
wear out like
a garment.
12 You will roll them
up like a
robe;
like a garment
they will be
changed.
But you remain
the same,
and your years
will never
end."[d]
13 To which of the
angels did God ever
say,

[a] 6 Deut. 32:43 (see Dead Sea Scrolls and Septuagint)
[b] 7 Psalm 104:4
[c] 9 Psalm 45:6,7
[d] 12 Psalm 102:25-27

προσκυνησάτωσαν αὐτῷ πάντες ἄγγελοι θεοῦ. 7 καὶ πρὸς μὲν τοὺς
God worship him." *all* *angels* *of God* *{and}* Regarding ~ the
2536 4686 899 4246 34 2536 2779 4639 3525 3836
v.aam.3p r.dsm.3 a.npm n.npm n.gsm cj p.a pl d.apm

ἀγγέλους λέγει, ὁ ποιῶν τοὺς ἀγγέλους αὐτοῦ πνεύματα καὶ τοὺς
angels he says, "He makes *{the}* his angels *his* winds, and *{the}* his
34 3306 3836 4472 3836 899 34 899 4460 2779 3836 899
n.apm v.pai.3s d.nsm pt.pa.nsm d.apm n.apm r.gsm.3 n.apn cj d.apm

λειτουργοὺς αὐτοῦ πυρὸς φλόγα. 8 πρὸς δὲ τὸν υἱόν· ὁ
ministers *his* a flame of fire." *flame* But regarding *But* the Son he says, *{the}*
3313 899 5825 4786 5825 1254 4639 1254 3836 5626 3836
n.apm r.gsm.3 n.gsn n.asf p.a cj d.asm n.asm d.nsm

θρόνος σου ὁ θεὸς εἰς τὸν ⌞αἰῶνα τοῦ αἰῶνος,⌟ καὶ ἡ ῥάβδος τῆς
"Your throne, *Your* O God, is for all time, and the scepter of
5148 2585 5148 3836 2536 1650 3836 172 3836 172 2779 3836 4811 3836
n.nsm r.gs.2 d.vsm n.vsm p.a d.asm n.asm d.gsm n.gsm cj d.nsf n.nsf d.gsf

εὐθύτητος ῥάβδος τῆς βασιλείας σου. 9 ἠγάπησας δικαιοσύνην καὶ
absolute justice is the scepter of your kingdom. *your* You have loved righteousness and
2319 4811 3836 5148 993 5148 26 1466 2779
n.gsf n.nsf d.gsf n.gsf r.gs.2 v.aai.2s n.asf cj

ἐμίσησας ἀνομίαν· ⌞διὰ τοῦτο⌟ ἔχρισέν σε ὁ θεὸς ὁ θεός σου
hated lawlessness; therefore *has anointed* *you* *{the}* God, *{the}* your God, *your* has
3631 490 1328 4047 5987 5148 3836 2536 3836 5148 2536 5148 5987
v.aai.2s n.asf p.a r.asn v.aai.3s r.as.2 d.nsm n.nsm d.nsm n.nsm r.gs.2

→ ἔλαιον ἀγαλλιάσεως παρὰ τοὺς μετόχους σου. 10 καί,
anointed you with the oil of gladness beyond *{the}* your companions." *your* And, "In
5987 5148 1778 21 4123 3836 5148 3581 5148 2779 2848
n.asn n.gsf p.a d.apm n.apm r.gs.2 cj

σὺ κατ᾽ ἀρχάς, κύριε, τὴν γῆν
the beginning, Lord, you *In* *beginning* *Lord* laid the foundation of the earth,
794 3261 5148 2848 794 3261 2530 2530 2530 3836 1178
r.ns.2 p.a n.apf n.vsm d.asf n.asf

ἐθεμελίωσας, καὶ ἔργα τῶν χειρῶν σού εἰσιν οἱ οὐρανοί·
laid the foundation and the heavens are the works of your hands. *your* *are* *the* *heavens*
2530 2779 3836 4041 1639 2240 3836 5148 5931 5148 1639 3836 4041
v.aai.2s cj n.npn d.gpf n.gpf r.gs.2 v.pai.3p d.npm n.npm

11 αὐτοὶ ἀπολοῦνται, σὺ δὲ διαμένεις, καὶ πάντες ὡς ἱμάτιον
They will perish; but you *but* continue. And all of them like a garment
899 660 1254 5148 1254 1373 2779 4246 6055 2668
r.npm v.fmi.3p r.ns.2 cj v.pai.2s cj a.npm pl n.nsn

παλαιωθήσονται, 12 καὶ ὡσεὶ περιβόλαιον ἑλίξεις αὐτούς, ↰ ὡς ἱμάτιον
will wear out, *{and}* like a robe ⌞you will fold⌟ them up, like a garment
4096 2779 6059 4316 1813 899 1813 6055 2668
v.fpi.3p cj pl n.asn v.fai.2s r.apm.3 pl n.nsn

↱ ↱ καὶ ἀλλαγήσονται· σὺ δὲ ὁ αὐτὸς εἶ καὶ τὰ ἔτη σου
they will also be changed. But you *But* are the same, *are* and *{the}* your years *your*
248 248 2779 248 1254 5148 1254 1639 3836 899 1639 2779 3836 5148 2291 5148
adv v.fpi.3p r.ns.2 cj d.nsm r.nsm v.pai.2s cj d.npn n.npn r.gs.2

↱ οὐκ ἐκλείψουσιν. 13 πρὸς τίνα δὲ τῶν ἀγγέλων → → εἴρηκέν ποτε,
will never end." And to which *And* of the angels has he ever said, *ever*
1722 4024 1722 1254 4639 5515 1254 3836 34 4537 3306 4537
pl v.fai.3p p.a r.asm cj d.gpm n.gpm v.rai.3s adv

NASB

GOD WORSHIP
HIM."
7 And of the angels
He says,
"WHO MAKES
HIS ANGELS
WINDS,
AND HIS MINIS-
TERS A FLAME
OF FIRE."
8 But of the Son *He*
says,
"YOUR THRONE,
O GOD, IS
FOREVER AND
EVER,
AND THE RIGH-
TEOUS SCEPTER
IS THE SCEPTER
OF [a]HIS KING-
DOM.
9 "YOU HAVE
LOVED RIGH-
TEOUSNESS
AND HATED
LAWLESSNESS;
THEREFORE
GOD, YOUR
GOD, HAS
ANOINTED YOU
WITH THE OIL
OF GLADNESS
ABOVE YOUR
COMPANIONS."
10 And,
"YOU, LORD, IN
THE BEGIN-
NING LAID THE
FOUNDATION
OF THE EARTH,
AND THE HEAV-
ENS ARE THE
WORKS OF
YOUR HANDS;
11 THEY WILL PER-
ISH, BUT YOU
REMAIN;
AND THEY ALL
WILL BECOME
OLD LIKE A
GARMENT,
12 AND LIKE A
MANTLE YOU
WILL ROLL
THEM UP;
LIKE A GAR-
MENT THEY
WILL ALSO BE
CHANGED.
BUT YOU ARE
THE SAME,
AND YOUR
YEARS WILL
NOT COME TO
AN END."
13 But to which of
the angels has He
ever said,

[a] Late mss read *Your*

NIV

"Sit at my right
hand
until I make
your enemies
a footstool for
your feet"[a]?
14 Are not all angels
ministering spirits
sent to serve those
who will inherit
salvation?

Warning to Pay Attention

2 We must
pay the most
careful attention,
therefore, to what
we have heard, so
that we do not drift
away. 2 For since
the message spo-
ken through angels
was binding, and
every violation
and disobedience
received its just
punishment, 3 how
shall we escape
if we ignore so
great a salvation?
This salvation,
which was first
announced by the
Lord, was con-
firmed to us by
those who heard
him. 4 God also
testified to it by
signs, wonders and
various miracles,
and by gifts of the
Holy Spirit distrib-
uted according to
his will.

Jesus Made Fully Human

5 It is not to angels
that he has sub-
jected the world to
come, about which
we are speaking.
6 But there is a
place where some-
one has testified:

"What is mankind
that you are
mindful of
them,
a son of man
that you care
for him?
7 You made them a
little[b] lower
than

[a] 13 Psalm 110:1
[b] 7 Or *them for a little while*

κάθου ἐκ δεξιῶν μου, ⌞ἕως ἂν⌟ θῶ τοὺς ἐχθρούς σου ὑποπόδιον
"Sit at my right hand *my* until I make *{the}* your enemies *your* a footstool
2764 1666 1609 1288 1609 2401 323 5502 3836 5148 2398 5148 5711
v.pmm.2s p.g a.gpf r.gs.1 cj pl v.aas.1s d.apm a.apm r.gs.2 n.asn

τῶν ποδῶν σου; 14 οὐχὶ πάντες εἰσὶν λειτουργικὰ πνεύματα
for your feet"? *your* Are they not all *Are they* ministering spirits sent out
3836 5148 4546 5148 1639 1639 4049 4246 1639 3312 4460 690 690
d.gpm n.gpm r.gs.2 pl a.npm v.pai.3p a.npn n.npn

εἰς διακονίαν ἀποστελλόμενα διὰ τοὺς μέλλοντας κληρονομεῖν σωτηρίαν;
to serve *sent out* ⌞for the sake of⌟ those who are to inherit salvation?
1650 1355 690 1328 3836 3516 3099 5401
p.a n.asf pt.pp.npn p.a d.apm pt.pa.apm f.pa n.asf

2:1 ⌞Διὰ τοῦτο⌟ δεῖ ↱ περισσοτέρως προσέχειν ἡμᾶς τοῖς
Therefore we must pay much closer attention *we* to what
1328 4047 7005 1256 4668 4359 4668 7005 3836
p.a r.asn v.pai.3s adv.c f.pa r.ap.1 d.dpn

ἀκουσθεῖσιν, μήποτε παραρυῶμεν. 2 εἰ γὰρ ὁ δι᾽
we have heard, lest we drift away from it. For if *For* the message spoken through
201 3607 4184 1142 1623 1142 3836 3364 3281 1328
pt.ap.dpn cj v.aps.1p cj cj d.nsm p.g

ἀγγέλων λαληθεὶς λόγος ἐγένετο βέβαιος καὶ πᾶσα παράβασις καὶ παρακοὴ
angels *spoken* *message* became firmly established and every transgression and disobedience
34 3281 3364 1181 1010 2779 4246 4126 2779 4157
n.gpm pt.ap.nsm n.nsm v.ami.3s a.nsm cj a.nsf n.nsf cj n.nsf

ἔλαβεν ἔνδικον μισθαποδοσίαν, 3 πῶς ↱ ἡμεῖς ἐκφευξόμεθα
received a just penalty, how will we escape if we neglect
3284 1899 3632 4802 1767 7005 1767 288 288 288
v.aai.3s a.asf n.asf pl r.np.1 v.fmi.1p

τηλικαύτης ἀμελήσαντες σωτηρίας, ἥτις ἀρχὴν ⌞λαβοῦσα λαλεῖσθαι⌟ διὰ τοῦ
such a great *if we neglect* salvation? Which at first was declared by the
5496 288 5401 4015 794 3284 3281 1328 3836
r.gsf pt.aa.npm n.gsf r.nsf n.asf pt.aa.nsf f.pp p.g d.gsm

κυρίου ὑπὸ τῶν ἀκουσάντων εἰς ἡμᾶς ἐβεβαιώθη,
Lord, and it was attested to us by those who heard, *to* *us* *it was attested*
3261 1011 1011 1011 1650 7005 5679 3836 201 1650 7005 1011
n.gsm p.g d.gpm pt.aa.gpm p.a r.ap.1 v.api.3s

4 → συνεπιμαρτυροῦντος τοῦ θεοῦ σημείοις τε καὶ τέρασιν καὶ ποικίλαις
while God supported their testimony *{the}* *God* by signs ~ and wonders and various
2536 5296 3836 2536 4956 5445 2779 5469 2779 4476
pt.pa.gsm d.gsm n.gsm n.dpn cj cj n.dpn cj a.dpf

δυνάμεσιν καὶ → πνεύματος ἁγίου μερισμοῖς κατὰ τὴν αὐτοῦ
miracles, and by gifts of the Holy Spirit *Holy* distributed ⌞according to⌟ *{the}* his
1539 2779 41 4460 41 3536 2848 3836 899
n.dpf cj n.gsn a.gsn n.dpm p.a d.asf r.gsm.3

θέλησιν; 5 Οὐ γὰρ ἀγγέλοις ὑπέταξεν τὴν οἰκουμένην τὴν
will. Now it was not *Now* to angels that God subjected the world *{the}*
2526 1142 4024 1142 34 5718 3836 3876 3836
n.asf pl cj n.dpm v.aai.3s d.asf n.asf d.asf

μέλλουσαν, περὶ ἧς λαλοῦμεν. 6 διεμαρτύρατο δέ πού
to come, about which we are speaking. But someone has testified *But* somewhere,
3516 4309 4005 3281 1254 5516 1371 1254 4543
pt.pa.asf p.g r.gsf v.pai.1p v.ami.3s cj adv

τις λέγων, τί ἐστιν ἄνθρωπος ὅτι μιμνῄσκῃ αὐτοῦ, ἢ υἱὸς
someone *{saying}* "What is man that you take thought for him, or the son
5516 3306 5515 1639 476 4022 3630 899 2445 5626
r.nsm pt.pa.nsm r.nsn v.pai.3s n.nsm cj v.ppi.2s r.gsm.3 cj n.nsm

ἀνθρώπου ὅτι ἐπισκέπτῃ αὐτόν; 7 ἠλάττωσας αὐτὸν → βραχύ τι ↰ παρ᾽
of man, that you care for him? You made him for a little while *a* lower than
476 4022 2170 899 1783 899 5516 1099 5516 1783 4123
n.gsm cj v.pmi.2s r.asm.3 v.aai.2s r.asm.3 adv r.asn p.a

NASB

" SIT AT MY
RIGHT HAND,
UNTIL I MAKE
YOUR ENEMIES
A FOOTSTOOL
FOR YOUR
FEET"?
14 Are they not all
ministering spirits,
sent out to render
service for the sake
of those who will
inherit salvation?

Give Heed

2:1 For this reason
we must pay much
closer attention
to what we have
heard, so that we
do not drift away
from it. 2 For if
the word spoken
through angels
proved unalterable,
and every trans-
gression and dis-
obedience received
a just penalty, 3 how
will we escape if
we neglect so great
a salvation? After
it was at the first
spoken through
the Lord, it was
confirmed to us by
those who heard,
4 God also testifying
with them, both by
signs and wonders
and by various
miracles and by
gifts of the Holy
Spirit according to
His own will.

Earth Subject to Man

5 For He did not
subject to angels
the world to come,
concerning which
we are speaking.
6 But one has testi-
fied somewhere,
saying,
" WHAT IS MAN,
THAT YOU RE-
MEMBER HIM?
OR THE SON
OF MAN, THAT
YOU ARE CON-
CERNED ABOUT
HIM?
7 " YOU HAVE MADE
HIM FOR A
LITTLE WHILE
LOWER THAN
THE ANGELS;

NIV

the angels;
you crowned them
with glory and
honor
8 and put
everything
under their
feet."[a,b]

In putting everything
under them,[c] God left
nothing that is not
subject to them.[d] Yet at
present we do not see
everything subject to
them.[e] 9But we do see
Jesus, who was made
lower than the angels
for a little while, now
crowned with glory
and honor because he
suffered death, so that
by the grace of God he
might taste death for
everyone.

10In bringing many
sons and daughters
to glory, it was fitting
that God, for whom
and through whom
everything exists,
should make the pio-
neer of their salvation
perfect through what
he suffered. 11Both
the one who makes
people holy and those
who are made holy are
of the same family. So
Jesus is not ashamed
to calling them broth-
ers and sisters.[f] 12He
says,

"I will declare your
name to my
brothers and
sisters;
in the assembly I
will sing your
praises."[g]

13And again,

"I will put my trust

[a] 6-8 Psalm 8:4-6
[b] 7,8 Or 7*You made him a little lower than the angels;/ you crowned him with glory and honor/ 8and put everything under his feet."*
[c] 8 Or *him*
[d] 8 Or *him*
[e] 8 Or *him*
[f] 11 The Greek word for *brothers and sisters* (*adelphoi*) refers here to believers, both men and women, as part of God's family; also in verse 12; and in 3:1, 12; 10:19; 13:22.
[g] 12 Psalm 22:22

ἀγγέλους, δόξῃ καὶ τιμῇ ἐστεφάνωσας αὐτόν,[a] 8
the angels; you crowned him ⌊with glory⌋ and honor, *you crowned* *him* You put
34 5110 5110 899 1518 2779 5507 5110 899 5718 5718
n.apm n.dsf cj n.dsf v.aai.2s r.asm.3

πάντα ὑπέταξας ὑποκάτω τῶν ποδῶν αὐτοῦ. ἐν τῷ γὰρ
everything in subjection under *{the}* his feet." *his* Now in ~ *Now* putting
4246 5718 5691 3836 899 4546 899 1142 1877 3836 1142
a.apn v.aai.2s p.g d.gpm n.gpm r.gsm.3 p.d d.dsn cj

ὑποτάξαι αὐτῷ[b] τὰ πάντα οὐδὲν ἀφῆκεν αὐτῷ
everything in subjection to him, *{the}* *everything* he left nothing *he left* outside his
4246 5718 899 3836 4246 918 918 4029 918 538 899
f.aa r.dsm.3 d.apn a.apn a.asn v.aai.3s r.dsm.3

ἀνυπότακτον. νῦν δὲ οὔπω ὁρῶμεν αὐτῷ τὰ πάντα
control. But in fact *But* we do not yet see everything under his *{the}* *everything*
538 1254 3814 1254 3972 3972 4037 3972 4246 5718 899 3836 4246
a.asn adv cj adv v.pai.1p r.dsm.3 d.apn a.apn

ὑποτεταγμένα· 9 τὸν δὲ βραχύ τι
control. But we do see Jesus, who *But* for a little while *a* was made lower
5718 1254 1063 1063 1063 2652 3836 1254 5516 1099 5516 1783 1783 1783
pt.rp.apn d.asm cj adv r.asn

παρ' ἀγγέλους ἠλαττωμένον βλέπομεν Ἰησοῦν
than the angels, *was made lower* *we do see* *Jesus* so that by the grace of God he
4123 34 1783 1063 2652 3968 3968 5921 5921 2536 2536 1174
p.a n.apm pt.rp.asm v.pai.1p n.asm

διὰ τὸ πάθημα τοῦ θανάτου δόξῃ
might taste death for everyone, ⌊because of⌋ the suffering of death crowned ⌊with glory⌋
1174 1174 2505 5642 4246 1328 3836 4077 3836 2505 5110 1518
p.a d.asn n.asn d.gsm n.gsm n.dsf

καὶ τιμῇ ἐστεφανωμένον, ὅπως χάριτι θεοῦ ὑπὲρ παντὸς γεύσηται θανάτου.
and honor. *crowned* *so that* *by grace* *of God* *for* *everyone* *he might taste* *death*
2779 5507 5110 3968 5921 2536 5642 4246 1174 2505
cj n.dsf pt.rp.asm cj n.dsf n.gsm p.g a.gsm v.ams.3s n.gsm

10 ἔπρεπεν γὰρ αὐτῷ, δι' ὃν τὰ πάντα καὶ δι' οὗ τὰ
For it was appropriate *For* that God, for whom *{the}* *{all things}* and through whom *{the}*
1142 4560 1142 899 1328 4005 3836 4246 2779 1328 4005 3836
v.iai.3s cj r.dsm.3 p.a r.asm d.npn a.npn cj p.g r.gsm d.npn

πάντα, πολλοὺς υἱοὺς εἰς δόξαν ἀγαγόντα τὸν ἀρχηγὸν
all things exist, in bringing many sons to glory, *in bringing* should make the champion
4246 72 72 4498 5626 1650 1518 72 5457 5457 3836 795
a.npn a.apm n.apm p.a n.asf pt.aa.asm d.asm n.asm

τῆς σωτηρίας αὐτῶν διὰ παθημάτων τελειῶσαι. 11 ὅ τε
of their salvation *their* perfect through suffering. *should make perfect* For the *{both}*
3836 899 5401 899 5457 1328 4077 5457 1142 3836 5445
d.gsf n.gsf r.gpm.3 p.g n.gpn f.aa d.nsm cj

γὰρ ἁγιάζων καὶ οἱ ἁγιαζόμενοι ἐξ ἑνὸς πάντες·
For one who sanctifies and those who are sanctified are all of one *all* origin.
1142 39 2779 3836 39 4246 1666 1651 4246
cj pt.pa.nsm cj d.npm pt.pp.npm p.g a.gsm a.npm

⌊δι' ἣν αἰτίαν⌋ οὐκ ἐπαισχύνεται ἀδελφοὺς αὐτοὺς
That is why Jesus is not ashamed to call them brothers, *them*
1328 4005 162 2049 4024 2049 2813 2813 899 81 899
p.a r.asf n.asf pl v.ppi.3s n.apm r.apm.3

καλεῖν 12 λέγων, ἀπαγγελῶ τὸ ὄνομά σου τοῖς ἀδελφοῖς μου, ἐν
to call ⌊when he says,⌋ "I will proclaim *{the}* your name *your* to my brothers; *my* in
2813 3306 550 3836 5148 3950 5148 3836 1609 81 1609 1877
f.pa pt.pa.nsm v.fai.1s d.asn n.asn r.gs.2 d.dpm n.dpm r.gs.1 p.d

μέσῳ ἐκκλησίας ὑμνήσω σε, 13 καὶ πάλιν, ἐγὼ ἔσομαι πεποιθὼς
the midst of the congregation I will sing your praise." And again, "I will put my trust
3545 1711 5630 5148 5630 2779 4099 1609 1639 4275
n.dsn n.gsf v.fai.1s r.as.2 cj adv r.ns.1 v.fmi.1s pt.ra.nsm

[a] καὶ κατέστησας αὐτὸν ἐπὶ τὰ ἔργα τῶν χειρῶν σου included by TR after αὐτόν.
[b] [αὐτῷ] UBS.

NASB

YOU HAVE
CROWNED HIM
WITH GLORY
AND HONOR,
[a]AND HAVE
APPOINTED
HIM OVER THE
WORKS OF
YOUR HANDS;
8 YOU HAVE PUT
ALL THINGS IN
SUBJECTION
UNDER HIS
FEET."
For in subjecting
all things to him,
He left nothing that
is not subject to
him. But now we
do not yet see all
things subjected
to him.

Jesus Briefly Humbled

9But we do see
Him who was
made for a little
while lower than
the angels, *namely,*
Jesus, because of
the suffering of
death crowned with
glory and honor, so
that by the grace of
God He might taste
death for everyone.
10For it was fitting
for Him, for whom
are all things, and
through whom are
all things, in bring-
ing many sons to
glory, to perfect the
author of their sal-
vation through suf-
ferings. 11For both
He who sanctifies
and those who are
sanctified are all
from one *Father;*
for which reason
He is not ashamed
to call them breth-
ren, 12saying,
"I WILL PRO-
CLAIM YOUR
NAME TO MY
BRETHREN,
IN THE MIDST OF
THE CONGRE-
GATION I WILL
SING YOUR
PRAISE."
13And again,
"I WILL PUT
MY TRUST IN
HIM."

[a] Two early mss do not contain *And... hands*

NIV

in him."[a]

And again he says,

"Here am I, and
the children
God has
given me."[b]

14 Since the children have flesh and blood, he too shared in their humanity so that by his death he might break the power of him who holds the power of death—that is, the devil— 15 and free those who all their lives were held in slavery by their fear of death. 16 For surely it is not angels he helps, but Abraham's descendants. 17 For this reason he had to be made like them,[c] fully human in every way, in order that he might become a merciful and faithful high priest in service to God, and that he might make atonement for the sins of the people. 18 Because he himself suffered when he was tempted, he is able to help those who are being tempted.

Jesus Greater Than Moses

3 Therefore, holy brothers and sisters, who share in the heavenly calling, fix your thoughts on Jesus, whom we acknowledge as our apostle and high priest. 2 He was faithful to the one who appointed him,

ἐπ᾽ αὐτῷ, καὶ πάλιν, ἰδοὺ ἐγὼ καὶ τὰ παιδία ἅ μοι ἔδωκεν
in him." And again, "Here I am and the children whom God has given me." *has given*
2093 899 2779 4099 2627 1609 2779 3836 4086 4005 2536 1443 1443 1609 1443
p.d r.dsm.3 cj adv j r.ns.1 cj d.npn n.npn r.apn r.ds.1 v.aai.3s

ὁ θεός. 14 ἐπεὶ οὖν τὰ παιδία κεκοινώνηκεν αἵματος καὶ σαρκός,
{the} *God* Therefore since *Therefore* the children share in blood and flesh,
3836 2536 4036 2075 4036 3836 4086 3125 135 2779 4922
d.nsm n.nsm cj cj d.npn n.npn v.rai.3s n.gsn cj n.gsf

↱ καὶ αὐτὸς παραπλησίως μετέσχεν τῶν αὐτῶν, ἵνα διὰ τοῦ θανάτου
he himself also, *himself* in the same way, shared the same things so that by his death
3576 899 2779 899 4181 3576 3836 899 2671 1328 3836 2505
adv r.nsm adv v.aai.3s d.gpn r.gpn cj p.g d.gsm n.gsm

καταργήσῃ τὸν τὸ κράτος ἔχοντα τοῦ θανάτου, τοῦτ᾽ ἔστιν
he might destroy the one who holds the power *one who holds* of death (that is,
2934 3836 2400 2400 2400 3836 3197 2400 3836 2505 4047 1639
v.aas.3s d.asm d.asn n.asn pt.pa.asm d.gsm n.gsm r.nsn v.pai.3s

τὸν διάβολον, 15 καὶ ἀπαλλάξῃ τούτους, ὅσοι
the devil), and liberate those who through all their life were held in
3836 1333 2779 557 4047 4012 1328 4246 3836 2409 1639 1944 1525
d.asm n.asm cj v.aas.3s r.apm r.npm

→ φόβῳ θανάτου διὰ παντὸς τοῦ ζῆν ἔνοχοι ἦσαν δουλείας. 16
slavery by their fear of death. *through* *all* *their* *life* *held* *were* *in slavery* For
1525 5832 2505 1328 4246 3836 2409 1944 1639 1525 1142
n.dsm n.gsm p.g a.gsn d.gsn f.pa a.npm v.iai.3p n.gsf

οὐ γὰρ δήπου ἀγγέλων ἐπιλαμβάνεται ἀλλὰ
surely he does not *For* *surely* reach out to help angels, *he does reach out to help* but
1327 2138 2138 4024 1142 1327 2138 2138 2138 2138 34 2138 247
pl cj adv n.gpm v.pmi.3s cj

σπέρματος Ἀβραὰμ ἐπιλαμβάνεται. 17 ὅθεν
he reaches out to help the seed of Abraham. *he reaches out to help* Therefore
2138 2138 2138 2138 2138 5065 11 2138 3854
n.gsn n.gsm v.pmi.3s cj

ὤφειλεν κατὰ πάντα τοῖς ἀδελφοῖς
he was obligated to become like his brothers in every respect, *his* *brothers*
4053 3929 3929 3929 3836 81 2848 4246 3836 81
v.iai.3s p.a a.apn d.dpm n.dpm

ὁμοιωθῆναι, ἵνα ἐλεήμων γένηται καὶ πιστὸς ἀρχιερεὺς τὰ
to become like so that he could become a merciful *he could become* and faithful high priest *{the}*
3929 2671 1181 1181 1181 1798 1181 2779 4412 797 3836
f.ap cj a.nsm v.ams.3s cj a.nsm n.nsm d.apn

πρὸς τὸν θεὸν εἰς τὸ ἱλάσκεσθαι τὰς ἁμαρτίας τοῦ λαοῦ.
⌊in the service of⌋ *{the}* God, to ~ ⌊make propitiation for⌋ the sins of the people.
4639 3836 2536 1650 3836 2661 3836 281 3836 3295
p.a d.asm n.asm p.a d.asn f.pm d.apf n.apf d.gsm n.gsm

18 ⌊ἐν ᾧ⌋ γὰρ → πέπονθεν αὐτὸς πειρασθείς, δύναται
For because *For* he himself suffered *himself* when tempted, he is able to come to
1142 1877 4005 1142 899 4248 899 4279 1538 1070 1070 1070
p.d r.dsn cj v.rai.3s r.nsm pt.ap.nsm v.ppi.3s

τοῖς πειραζομένοις βοηθῆσαι.
the aid of those who are being tempted. *to come to the aid of*
1070 1070 1070 3836 4279 1070
d.dpm pt.pp.dpm f.aa

3:1 ὅθεν, ἀδελφοὶ ἅγιοι, κλήσεως
⌊For this reason,⌋ holy brothers, *holy* you who share in the heavenly calling,
3854 41 81 41 3581 3581 3581 3581 2230 3104
cj n.vpm a.vpm n.gsf

ἐπουρανίου μέτοχοι, κατανοήσατε τὸν ἀπόστολον καὶ ἀρχιερέα τῆς
heavenly *you who share in* consider that the apostle and high priest of whom our
2230 3581 2917 3836 693 2779 797 3836 7005
a.gsf n.vpm v.aam.2p d.asm n.asm cj n.asm d.gsf

ὁμολογίας ἡμῶν Ἰησοῦν, 2 πιστὸν ὄντα τῷ ποιήσαντι αὐτὸν
confession *our* speaks, Jesus, was faithful *was* ⌊to the⌋ one who appointed him in
3934 7005 2652 1639 4412 1639 3836 4472 899 1877
n.gsf r.gp.1 n.asm a.asm pt.pa.asm d.dsm pt.aa.dsm r.asm.3

NASB

And again,

"BEHOLD, I AND
THE CHILDREN
WHOM GOD
HAS GIVEN
ME."

14 Therefore, since the children share in flesh and blood, He Himself likewise also partook of the same, that through death He might render powerless him who had the power of death, that is, the devil,
15 and might free those who through fear of death were subject to slavery all their lives. 16 For assuredly He does not give help to angels, but He gives help to the descendant of Abraham.
17 Therefore, He had to be made like His brethren in all things, so that He might become a merciful and faithful high priest in things pertaining to God, to make propitiation for the sins of the people.
18 For since He Himself was tempted in that which He has suffered, He is able to come to the aid of those who are tempted.

Jesus Our High Priest

3:1 Therefore, holy brethren, partakers of a heavenly calling, consider Jesus, the Apostle and High Priest of our confession; 2 He was faithful to Him who appointed

[a] *13* Isaiah 8:17
[b] *13* Isaiah 8:18
[c] *17* Or *like his brothers*

NIV

just as Moses was faithful in all God's house. [3]Jesus has been found worthy of greater honor than Moses, just as the builder of a house has greater honor than the house itself. [4]For every house is built by someone, but God is the builder of everything. [5]"Moses was faithful as a servant in all God's house,"[a] bearing witness to what would be spoken by God in the future. [6]But Christ is faithful as the Son over God's house. And we are his house, if indeed we hold firmly to our confidence and the hope in which we glory.

Warning Against Unbelief

[7]So, as the Holy Spirit says:

"Today, if you hear his voice,
[8] do not harden your hearts
as you did in the rebellion,
during the time of testing in the wilderness,
[9] where your ancestors tested and tried me,
though for forty years they saw what I did.
[10] That is why I was angry with that generation;
I said, 'Their hearts are always going astray,

[a] 5 Num. 12:7

ὡς καὶ Μωϋσῆς ἐν ὅλῳ[a] τῷ οἴκῳ αὐτοῦ. [3]
all his house, as Moses also *Moses* was. *in* *all* *{the}* *house* *his* For Jesus has
3910 899 3875 6055 3707 2779 3707 1877 3910 3836 3875 899 1142 4047 546
cj adv n.nsm p.d a.dsm d.dsm n.dsm r.gsm.3

πλείονος γὰρ οὗτος δόξης παρὰ Μωϋσῆν ἠξίωται, καθ'
been counted worthy of greater *For* *Jesus* glory than Moses, *has been counted worthy* just
546 546 546 4498 1142 4047 1518 4123 3707 546 2848
a.gsf.c cj r.nsm n.gsf p.a n.asm v.rpi.3s p.a

ὅσον πλείονα τιμὴν ἔχει τοῦ οἴκου ὁ
as the builder of a house has greater honor *has* ⌊than the⌋ house itself. *the*
4012 3836 2941 2941 2941 2941 2400 4498 5507 2400 3836 3875 899 3836
r.asn a.asf.c n.asf v.pai.3s d.gsm n.gsm d.nsm

κατασκευάσας αὐτόν· [4] πᾶς γὰρ οἶκος κατασκευάζεται ὑπό τινος, ὁ
builder of a house *itself* For every *For* house is built by someone, but the
2941 899 1142 4246 1142 3875 2941 5679 5516 1254 3836
pt.aa.nsm r.asm.3 a.nsm cj n.nsm v.ppi.3s p.g r.gsm d.nsm

δὲ πάντα κατασκευάσας θεός. [5]καὶ Μωϋσῆς μὲν πιστὸς ἐν
but one who built everything *one who built* is God. Now Moses ~ was faithful in
1254 2941 2941 2941 4246 2941 2536 2779 3707 3525 4412 1877
cj a.apn pt.aa.nsm n.nsm cj n.nsm pl a.nsm p.d

ὅλῳ τῷ οἴκῳ αὐτοῦ ὡς θεράπων εἰς μαρτύριον ↰ τῶν
all *{the}* God's household *God's* as a servant, bearing witness to ⌊those things⌋
3910 3836 899 3875 899 6055 2544 1650 3457 1650 3836
a.dsm d.dsm n.dsm r.gsm.3 pl n.nsm p.a n.asn d.gpn

λαληθησομένων, [6] Χριστὸς δὲ ὡς υἱὸς ἐπὶ τὸν
⌊that would be spoken later,⌋ but Christ *but* is faithful as the Son, presiding over *{the}*
3281 1254 5986 1254 6055 5626 2093 3836
pt.fp.gpn n.nsm cj pl n.nsm p.a d.asm

οἶκον αὐτοῦ· οὗ οἶκός ἐσμεν ἡμεῖς, ἐάνπερ[b]
God's household, *God's* and we are his household *are* *we* if indeed we hold firmly
899 3875 899 7005 1639 4005 3875 1639 7005 1570 2988 2988 2988
n.asm r.gsm.3 r.gsm n.nsm v.pai.1p r.np.1 cj

τὴν παρρησίαν καὶ τὸ καύχημα τῆς ἐλπίδος[c] κατάσχωμεν.
to our confidence and the hope of which we boast. *the* *hope* *we hold firmly to*
2988 3836 4244 2779 3836 1828 3836 3017 3836 1828 2988
d.asf n.asf cj d.asn n.asn d.gsf n.gsf v.aas.1p

[7]διό, καθὼς λέγει τὸ πνεῦμα τὸ ἅγιον, σήμερον ἐὰν
Therefore just as the Holy Spirit says, *the* *Spirit* *{the}* *Holy* "Today, if · you hear
1475 2777 3836 41 4460 3306 3836 4460 3836 41 4958 1569 201 201
cj cj v.pai.3s d.nsn n.nsn d.nsn a.nsn adv cj

τῆς φωνῆς αὐτοῦ ἀκούσητε, [8]↱ μὴ σκληρύνητε τὰς καρδίας ὑμῶν ὡς
{the} his voice, *his* *you hear* do not harden *{the}* your hearts *your* as
3836 899 5889 899 201 5020 3590 5020 3836 7007 2840 7007 6055
d.gsf n.gsf r.gsm.3 v.aas.2p pl v.aas.2p d.apf n.apf r.gp.2 cj

ἐν τῷ παραπικρασμῷ κατὰ τὴν ἡμέραν τοῦ πειρασμοῦ ἐν τῇ ἐρήμῳ,
you did in the rebellion, on the day of testing in the wilderness
1877 3836 4177 2848 3836 2465 3836 4280 1877 3836 2245
p.d d.dsm n.dsm p.a d.asf n.asf d.gsm n.gsm p.d d.dsf n.dsf

[9]οὗ ἐπείρασαν οἱ πατέρες ὑμῶν ἐν δοκιμασίᾳ
where your fathers put *{the}* *fathers* *your* me to the test through their
4023 7007 4252 4279 3836 4252 7007 1877 1508
adv v.aai.3p d.npm n.npm r.gp.2 p.d n.dsf

καὶ εἶδον τὰ ἔργα μου [10] τεσσεράκοντα ἔτη· διὸ
distrust, though ⌊they had seen⌋ *{the}* my works *my* for forty years. Therefore
2779 1625 3836 1609 2240 1609 5477 2291 1475
cj v.aai.3p d.apn n.apn r.gs.1 a.apn n.apn cj

προσώχθισα τῇ γενεᾷ ταύτῃ καὶ εἶπον, ↱ ↱ ἀεὶ πλανῶνται τῇ
I was angry with this generation *this* and said, 'They are always going astray ⌊in their⌋
4696 3836 4047 1155 4047 2779 3306 4414 4414 107 4414 3836
v.aai.1s d.dsf n.dsf r.dsf cj v.aai.1s adv v.ppi.3p d.dsf

[a] [ὅλῳ] UBS, omitted by NET.
[b] ἐάνπερ UBS, NET. ἐάν[περ] UBS.
[c] μέχρι τέλους βεβαίαν included by TR after ἐλπίδος.

NASB

Him, as Moses also was in all His house. [3]For He has been counted worthy of more glory than Moses, by just so much as the builder of the house has more honor than the house. [4]For every house is built by someone, but the builder of all things is God. [5]Now Moses was faithful in all His house as a servant, for a testimony of those things which were to be spoken later; [6]but Christ *was faithful* as a Son over His house—whose house we are, if we hold fast our confidence and the boast of our hope firm until the end.

[7]Therefore, just as the Holy Spirit says,

"TODAY IF YOU HEAR HIS VOICE,
[8] DO NOT HARDEN YOUR HEARTS AS WHEN THEY PROVOKED ME,
AS IN THE DAY OF TRIAL IN THE WILDERNESS,
[9] WHERE YOUR FATHERS TRIED *Me* BY TESTING *Me*,
AND SAW MY WORKS FOR FORTY YEARS.
[10]"THEREFORE I WAS ANGRY WITH THIS GENERATION,
AND SAID, 'THEY ALWAYS GO ASTRAY IN

NIV

and they have
not known
my ways.'
11 So I declared on
oath in my
anger,
'They shall
never enter
my rest.' "[a]

12 See to it, broth-
ers and sisters, that
none of you has a
sinful, unbelieving
heart that turns
away from the
living God. 13 But
encourage one
another daily, as
long as it is called
"Today," so that
none of you may
be hardened by
sin's deceitfulness.
14 We have come to
share in Christ, if
indeed we hold our
original conviction
firmly to the very
end. 15 As has just
been said:

"Today, if you
hear his
voice,
do not harden
your hearts
as you did in the
rebellion."[b]

16 Who were they
who heard and re-
belled? Were they
not all those Moses
led out of Egypt?
17 And with whom
was he angry for
forty years? Was
it not with those
who sinned, whose
bodies perished
in the wilderness?
18 And to whom
did God swear that
they would never
enter his rest if not
to those who dis-
obeyed? 19 So we
see that they were
not able to enter,
because of their
unbelief.

καρδίᾳ, αὐτοὶ δὲ ↱ οὐκ ἔγνωσαν τὰς ὁδούς μου, 11 ὡς ὤμοσα ἐν τῇ
hearts, and they *and* have not known *{the}* my ways.' *my* So I swore in *{the}*
2840 1254 899 1254 1182 4024 1182 3836 1609 3847 1609 6055 3923 1877 3836
n.dsf r.npm cj pl v.aai.3p d.apf n.apf r.gs.1 cj v.aai.1s p.d d.dsf

ὀργῇ μου, ↱ ↱ εἰ ⌊εἰσελεύσονται εἰς⌋ τὴν κατάπαυσίν μου.
my anger, *my* 'They shall ⌊certainly not⌋ enter *{the}* my rest.' *my*
1609 3973 1609 1656 1656 1623 1656 1650 3836 1609 2923 1609
n.dsf r.gs.1 cj v.fmi.3p p.a d.asf n.asf r.gs.1

12 βλέπετε, ἀδελφοί, μήποτε ἔσται ἔν τινι ὑμῶν καρδία πονηρὰ
Be careful, brothers, lest there be in any of you an evil, unbelieving heart *evil*
1063 81 3607 1639 1877 5516 7007 4505 602 2840 4505
v.pam.2p n.vpm cj v.fmi.3s p.d r.dsm r.gp.2 n.nsf a.nsf

ἀπιστίας ἐν τῷ ἀποστῆναι ἀπὸ θεοῦ ζῶντος, 13 ἀλλὰ παρακαλεῖτε
unbelieving that ~ turns away from the living God. *living* But encourage
602 1877 3836 923 608 2409 2536 2409 247 4151
n.gsf p.d d.dsn f.aa p.g n.gsm pt.pa.gsm cj v.pam.2p

ἑαυτοὺς ⌊καθ' ἑκάστην⌋ ἡμέραν, ⌊ἄχρις οὗ⌋ τὸ σήμερον καλεῖται,
one another every day, as long as it is called *{the}* "today," *it is called*
1571 2848 1667 2465 948 4005 2813 2813 2813 3836 4958 2813
r.apm.2 p.a r.asf n.asf p.g r.gsm d.nsn adv v.ppi.3s

ἵνα μὴ σκληρυνθῇ τις ἐξ ὑμῶν → ἀπάτῃ τῆς ἁμαρτίας
that none of you may be hardened *{one}* *of* *you* by the deceitfulness of sin.
2671 3590 1666 7007 5020 5516 1666 7007 573 3836 281
cj pl v.aps.3s r.nsm p.g r.gp.2 n.dsf d.gsf n.gsf

14 μέτοχοι γὰρ τοῦ Χριστοῦ γεγόναμεν, ἐάνπερ τὴν
For we have become partners *For* of Christ, *we have become* if in fact we hold the
1142 1181 1181 1181 3581 1142 3836 5986 1181 1570 2988 2988 3836
n.npm cj d.gsm n.gsm v.rai.1p cj d.asf

ἀρχὴν τῆς ὑποστάσεως μέχρι τέλους βεβαίαν κατάσχωμεν 15 ἐν τῷ
beginning of our confidence firm to the end. *firm* *we hold* As ~
794 3836 5712 1010 3588 5465 1010 2988 1877 3836
n.asf d.gsf n.gsf p.g n.gsn a.asf v.aas.1p p.d d.dsn

λέγεσθαι, σήμερον ἐὰν τῆς φωνῆς αὐτοῦ ἀκούσητε, ↱ μὴ σκληρύνητε
it is said, "Today, if you hear *{the}* his voice, *his* *you hear* do not harden
3306 4958 1569 201 201 3836 899 5889 899 201 5020 3590 5020
f.pp adv cj d.gsf n.gsf r.gsm.3 v.aas.2p pl v.aas.2p

τὰς καρδίας ὑμῶν ὡς ἐν τῷ παραπικρασμῷ. 16 τίνες γὰρ
{the} your hearts *your* as you did in the rebellion." For who *For* were they
3836 7007 2840 7007 6055 1877 3836 4177 1142 5515 1142
d.apf n.apf r.gp.2 cj p.d d.dsm n.dsm r.npm cj

ἀκούσαντες παρεπίκραναν; ἀλλ' οὐ πάντες οἱ ἐξελθόντες ἐξ
who heard and rebelled? Were they not really *not* all those who came ⌊out of⌋
201 4176 4024 247 4024 4246 3836 2002 1666
pt.aa.npm v.aai.3p cj pl a.npm d.npm pt.aa.npm p.g

Αἰγύπτου διὰ Μωϋσέως; 17 τίσιν δὲ προσώχθισεν τεσσεράκοντα ἔτη;
Egypt ⌊led by⌋ Moses? And with whom *And* was he angry for forty years?
131 1328 3707 1254 5515 1254 4696 5477 2291
n.gsf p.g n.gsm r.dpm cj v.aai.3s a.apn n.apn

οὐχὶ τοῖς ἁμαρτήσασιν, ὧν τὰ κῶλα ἔπεσεν ἐν τῇ ἐρήμῳ; 18
Was it not ⌊with those⌋ who sinned, whose *{the}* bodies fell in the wilderness? And
4049 3836 279 4005 3836 3265 4406 1877 3836 2245 1254
pl d.dpm pt.aa.dpm r.gpm d.npn n.npn v.aai.3s p.d d.dsf n.dsf

τίσιν δὲ ὤμοσεν ↱ ↱ μὴ ⌊εἰσελεύσεσθαι εἰς⌋ τὴν κατάπαυσιν
to whom *And* did he swear that they would not enter *{the}* his rest,
5515 1254 3923 1656 1656 3590 1656 1650 3836 899 2923
r.dpm cj v.aai.3s pl f.fm p.a d.asf n.asf

αὐτοῦ ⌊εἰ μὴ⌋ τοῖς ἀπειθήσασιν; 19 καὶ βλέπομεν ὅτι ⌊οὐκ
his except those ⌊who had refused to obey?⌋ So then we see that they were unable
899 1623 3590 3836 578 2779 1063 4022 4024
r.gsm.3 cj pl d.dpm pt.aa.dpm cj v.pai.1p cj pl

ἠδυνήθησαν⌋ εἰσελθεῖν δι' ἀπιστίαν.
to enter ⌊because of⌋ unbelief.
1538 1656 1328 602
v.api.3p f.aa p.a n.asf

NASB

THEIR HEART,
AND THEY DID
NOT KNOW MY
WAYS';
11 AS I SWORE IN
MY WRATH,
'THEY SHALL
NOT ENTER MY
REST.' "

The Peril of Unbelief

12 Take care, breth-
ren, that there not
be in any one of
you an evil, unbe-
lieving heart that
falls away from the
living God. 13 But
encourage one an-
other day after day,
as long as it is *still*
called "Today," so
that none of you
will be hardened
by the deceitful-
ness of sin. 14 For
we have become
partakers of Christ,
if we hold fast the
beginning of our
assurance firm until
the end, 15 while it
is said,
"TODAY IF YOU
HEAR HIS
VOICE,
DO NOT HARDEN
YOUR HEARTS,
AS WHEN THEY
PROVOKED
ME."
16 For who provoked
Him when they had
heard? Indeed, did
not all those who
came out of Egypt
led by Moses?
17 And with whom
was He angry for
forty years? Was
it not with those
who sinned, whose
bodies fell in the
wilderness? 18 And
to whom did He
swear that they
would not enter
His rest, but to
those who were
disobedient? 19 *So*
we see that they
were not able to
enter because of
unbelief.

[a] *11* Psalm 95:7-11
[b] *15* Psalm 95:7,8

NIV

A Sabbath-Rest for the People of God

4 Therefore, since the promise of entering his rest still stands, let us be careful that none of you be found to have fallen short of it. 2 For we also have had the good news proclaimed to us, just as they did; but the message they heard was of no value to them, because they did not share the faith of those who obeyed.[a] 3 Now we who have believed enter that rest, just as God has said,

> "So I declared on oath in my anger,
> 'They shall never enter my rest.' "[b]

And yet his works have been finished since the creation of the world. 4 For somewhere he has spoken about the seventh day in these words: "On the seventh day God rested from all his works."[c] 5 And again in the passage above he says, "They shall never enter my rest."

6 Therefore since it still remains for some to enter that rest, and since those who formerly had the good news proclaimed to them did not go in because of their disobedience, 7 God again set a certain day, calling it "Today." This he did when a long time later he spoke through David,

[a] 2 Some manuscripts *because those who heard did not combine it with faith*
[b] 3 Psalm 95:11; also in verse 5
[c] 4 Gen. 2:2

4:1 φοβηθῶμεν οὖν, μήποτε → καταλειπομένης
let us fear Therefore *lest* while the promise of entering his rest is still open,
5828 4036 3607 2039 1656 899 2923 2901
v.aps.1p cj cj pt.pp.gsf

ἐπαγγελίας εἰσελθεῖν εἰς τὴν κατάπαυσιν αὐτοῦ
promise *entering* *{into}* *{the}* *rest* *his* let us fear lest any one of you
2039 1656 1650 3836 2923 899 5828 5828 5828 3607 5516 1666 7007
n.gsf f.aa p.a d.asf n.asf r.gsm.3

δοκῇ τις ἐξ ὑμῶν ὑστερηκέναι. 2 ↱ καὶ γὰρ ἐσμεν
may seem *anyone* *of* *you* to be excluded from it. For we also *For* had
1506 5516 1666 7007 5728 1142 1639 2779 1142 1639
v.pas.3s r.nsm p.g r.gp.2 f.ra adv cj v.pai.1p

εὐηγγελισμένοι καθάπερ κἀκεῖνοι· ἀλλ' ↱ οὐκ
good news proclaimed to us just as they did; but the word they heard did not
2294 2749 2797 247 3836 3364 198 6067 4024
pt.rp.npm cj adv cj pl

ὠφέλησεν ὁ λόγος τῆς ἀκοῆς ἐκείνους ↱ ↱ μὴ συγκεκερασμένους
benefit *the* *word* *{the}* *heard* those who were not united with those
6067 3836 3364 3836 198 1697 5166 5166 3590 5166 3836 3836
v.aai.3s d.nsm n.nsm d.gsf n.gsf r.apm pl pt.rp.apm

τῇ πίστει τοῖς ἀκούσασιν. 3 εἰσερχόμεθα
who listened in faith *with those* *who listened* For we who have believed do enter
201 201 3836 4411 3836 201 1142 3836 3836 4409 4409 1656
d.dsf n.dsf d.dpm pt.aa.dpm v.pmi.1p

γὰρ εἰς τὴν[a] κατάπαυσιν οἱ πιστεύσαντες, καθὼς εἴρηκεν, ὡς ὤμοσα ἐν
For *{into}* that rest, *we who* *have believed* just as God has said, "As I swore in
1142 1650 3836 2923 3836 4409 2777 3306 6055 3923 1877
cj p.a d.asf n.asf d.npm pt.aa.npm cj v.rai.3s cj v.aai.1s p.d

τῇ ὀργῇ μου, ↱ ↱ εἰ ˻εἰσελεύσονται εἰς˼ τὴν κατάπαυσίν
{the} my anger, *my* 'They shall ˻certainly not˼ enter *{the}* my rest,' "
3836 1609 3973 1609 1656 1656 1623 1656 1650 3836 1609 2923
d.dsf n.dsf r.gs.1 cj v.fmi.3p p.a d.asf n.asf

μου, καίτοι τῶν ἔργων ἀπὸ καταβολῆς → κόσμου
my and yet his work has been completed since the foundation of the world
1609 2792 3836 2240 1181 1181 1181 608 2856 3180
r.gs.1 cj d.gpn n.gpn p.g n.gsf n.gsm

γενηθέντων. 4 εἴρηκεν γάρ που περὶ τῆς ἑβδόμης
has been completed For somewhere he has spoken *For* *somewhere* of the seventh day
1181 1142 4543 3306 1142 4543 4309 3836 1575
pt.ap.gpn v.rai.3s cj adv p.g d.gsf a.gsf

οὕτως, καὶ κατέπαυσεν ὁ θεὸς ἐν τῇ ἡμέρᾳ τῇ ἑβδόμῃ ἀπὸ
in this manner: "And God rested *{the}* *God* on the seventh day *{the}* *seventh* from
4048 2779 2536 2924 3836 2536 1877 3836 1575 2465 3836 1575 608
adv cj v.aai.3s d.nsm n.nsm p.d d.dsf n.dsf d.dsf a.dsf p.g

πάντων τῶν ἔργων αὐτοῦ, 5 καὶ ἐν τούτῳ πάλιν, ↱
all *{the}* his works." *his* And furthermore in this context *furthermore* he said, "They
4246 3836 899 2240 899 2779 4099 1877 4047 4099 1656
a.gpn d.gpn n.gpn r.gsm.3 cj p.d r.dsm adv

↱ εἰ ˻εἰσελεύσονται εἰς˼ τὴν κατάπαυσίν μου. 6 ἐπεὶ
shall ˻certainly not˼ enter *{the}* my rest." *my* Therefore since
1656 1623 1656 1650 3836 1609 2923 1609 4036 2075
cj v.fmi.3p p.a d.asf n.asf r.gs.1 cj

οὖν ἀπολείπεται τινὰς ˻εἰσελθεῖν εἰς˼ αὐτήν, καὶ οἱ πρότερον
Therefore it remains for some to enter it, and those who previously
4036 657 5516 1656 1650 899 2779 3836 4728
cj v.ppi.3s r.apm f.aa p.a r.asf.3 cj d.npm adv.c

εὐαγγελισθέντες οὐκ εἰσῆλθον δι' ἀπείθειαν, 7 πάλιν
˻had the good news proclaimed˼ to them failed to enter ˻because of˼ disobedience, God again
2294 4024 1656 1328 577 4099
pt.ap.npm pl v.aai.3p p.a n.asf adv

τινὰ ὁρίζει ἡμέραν, σήμερον, ἐν Δαυὶδ λέγων μετὰ
ordains a certain *ordains* day — "today" — saying through David, *saying* after
3988 5516 3988 2465 4958 3306 1877 1253 3306 3552
r.asf v.pai.3s n.asf adv p.d n.dsm pt.pa.nsm p.a

[a] [τὴν] UBS.

NASB

The Believer's Rest

4:1 Therefore, let us fear if, while a promise remains of entering His rest, any one of you may seem to have come short of it. 2 For indeed we have had good news preached to us, just as they also; but the word they heard did not profit them, because it was not united by faith in those who heard. 3 For we who have believed enter that rest, just as He has said,

> "As I swore in My wrath,
> They shall not enter My rest,"

although His works were finished from the foundation of the world. 4 For He has said somewhere concerning the seventh *day*: "And God rested on the seventh day from all His works"; 5 and again in this *passage*, "They shall not enter My rest." 6 Therefore, since it remains for some to enter it, and those who formerly had good news preached to them failed to enter because of disobedience, 7 He again fixes a certain day, "Today," saying through David after

NIV

as in the passage
already quoted:

“Today, if you
hear his
voice,
do not harden
your
hearts.”[a]

8 For if Joshua had
given them rest,
God would not
have spoken later
about another day.
9 There remains,
then, a Sabbath-
rest for the people
of God; 10 for any-
one who enters
God’s rest also
rests from their
works,[b] just as
God did from his.
11 Let us, therefore,
make every effort
to enter that rest,
so that no one will
perish by follow-
ing their example
of disobedience.
12 For the word of
God is alive and
active. Sharper
than any double-
edged sword, it
penetrates even to
dividing soul and
spirit, joints and
marrow; it judges
the thoughts and
attitudes of the
heart. 13 Nothing
in all creation is
hidden from God’s
sight. Everything
is uncovered and
laid bare before
the eyes of him
to whom we must
give account.

Jesus the Great High Priest

14 Therefore, since
we have a great
high priest who
has ascended into
heaven,[c] Jesus the
Son of God, let us
hold firmly to the
faith we profess.
15 For we do

[a] 7 Psalm 95:7,8
[b] 10 Or *labor*
[c] 14 Greek *has gone through the heavens*

τοσοῦτον χρόνον, καθὼς προείρηται, σήμερον ἐὰν τῆς φωνῆς
so long a time, just as ⌞it has been said before,⌟ “Today, if you hear *{the}* his voice,
5537 5989 2777 4597 4958 1569 201 201 3836 899 5889
r.asm n.asm cj v.rpi.3s adv cj d.gsf n.gsf

αὐτοῦ ἀκούσητε, ↱ μὴ σκληρύνητε τὰς καρδίας ὑμῶν. 8 εἰ γὰρ
his *you hear* do not harden *{the}* your hearts.” *your* For if *For* Joshua
899 201 5020 3590 5020 3836 7007 2840 7007 1142 1623 1142 2652
r.gsm.3 v.aas.2p pl v.aas.2p d.apf n.apf r.gp.2 cj cj

↱ ↱ αὐτοὺς Ἰησοῦς κατέπαυσεν, οὐκ ἂν περὶ ἄλλης
had given them *Joshua* rest, God would not *would* have spoken of another
2924 2924 899 2652 2924 323 4024 323 3281 3281 4309 257
r.apm.3 n.nsm v.aai.3s pl pl p.g r.gsf

ἐλάλει μετὰ ταῦτα ἡμέρας. 9 ἄρα ἀπολείπεται σαββατισμὸς τῷ
have spoken time after that. *time* Consequently there remains a Sabbath rest ⌞for the⌟
3281 2465 3552 4047 2465 726 657 4878 3836
v.iai.3s p.a r.apn n.gsf cj v.ppi.3s n.nsm d.dsm

λαῷ τοῦ θεοῦ. 10 ὁ γὰρ ⌞εἰσελθὼν εἰς⌟ τὴν κατάπαυσιν αὐτοῦ ↱
people of God. For the *For* one who enters *{the}* God’s rest *God’s* has
3295 3836 2536 1142 3836 1142 1656 1650 3836 899 2923 899 2924
n.dsm d.gsm n.gsm d.nsm cj pt.aa.nsm p.a d.asf n.asf r.gsm.3

καὶ αὐτὸς κατέπαυσεν ἀπὸ τῶν ἔργων αὐτοῦ ὥσπερ ἀπὸ τῶν ἰδίων ὁ
also *{he}* rested from *{the}* his works, *his* as God did from *{the}* his. *{the}*
2779 899 2924 608 3836 899 2240 899 6061 2536 608 3836 2625 3836
adv r.nsm v.aai.3s p.g d.gpn n.gpn r.gsm.3 cj p.g d.gpn a.gpn d.nsm

θεός. 11 → → σπουδάσωμεν οὖν ⌞εἰσελθεῖν εἰς⌟ ἐκείνην τὴν
God Let us, therefore, make every effort *therefore* to enter that *{the}*
2536 4036 5079 4036 1656 1650 1697 3836
n.nsm v.aas.1p cj f.aa p.a r.asf d.asf

καταπαυσιν, ⌞ἵνα μὴ⌟ ἐν τῷ αὐτῷ τις ὑποδείγματι
rest; otherwise one of you might fall by the same *one* sort
2923 2671 3590 5516 4406 4406 1877 3836 899 5516 5682
n.asf cj pl p.d d.dsn r.dsn r.nsm n.dsn

πέσῃ τῆς ἀπειθείας. 12 ζῶν γὰρ ὁ λόγος τοῦ θεοῦ καὶ ἐνεργὴς
might fall of disobedience. *is living* For the word of God is living and effective,
4406 3836 577 2409 1142 3836 3364 3836 2536 2409 2409 2779 1921
v.aas.3s d.gsf n.gsf pt.pa.nsm cj d.nsm n.nsm d.gsm n.gsm cj a.nsm

καὶ τομώτερος ὑπὲρ πᾶσαν μάχαιραν δίστομον καὶ διϊκνούμενος ἄχρι
{and} sharper than any two-edged sword, *two-edged* *{and}* cutting through ⌞so as to⌟
2779 5533 5642 4246 1492 3479 1492 2779 1459 948
cj a.nsm.c p.a a.asf n.asf a.asf cj pt.pm.nsm p.g

μερισμοῦ ψυχῆς καὶ πνεύματος, ἁρμῶν τε καὶ μυελῶν, καὶ κριτικὸς
divide soul from spirit, joints ~ from marrow. It is even able to discern the
3536 6034 2779 4460 765 5445 2779 3678 2779 3217
n.gsm n.gsf cj n.gsn n.gpm cj cj n.gpm cj a.nsm

ἐνθυμήσεων καὶ ἐννοιῶν → καρδίας· 13 καὶ οὐκ ἔστιν κτίσις
thoughts and deliberations of the heart. And nothing in creation is *creation*
1927 2779 1936 2840 2779 4024 3232 1639 3232
n.gpf cj n.gpf n.gsf cj pl v.pai.3s n.nsf

ἀφανὴς → ἐνώπιον αὐτοῦ, πάντα δὲ γυμνὰ καὶ τετραχηλισμένα
hidden from God’s sight, *God’s* but everything *but* is uncovered and exposed
905 899 1967 899 1254 4246 1254 1218 2779 5548
a.nsf p.g r.gsm.3 a.npn cj a.npn cj pt.rp.npn

τοῖς ὀφθαλμοῖς → αὐτοῦ, πρὸς ὃν ἡμῖν ὁ λόγος. 14
to the eyes of the one to whom we must give *{the}* account. Therefore
3836 4057 899 4639 4005 7005 3836 3364 4036
d.dpm n.dpm r.gsm.3 p.a r.asm r.dp.1 d.nsm n.nsm

ἔχοντες οὖν ἀρχιερέα μέγαν διεληλυθότα τοὺς οὐρανούς,
⌞since we have⌟ *Therefore* a great high priest *great* who has gone through the heavens,
2400 4036 3489 797 3489 1451 3836 4041
pt.pa.npm cj n.asm a.asm pt.ra.asm d.apm n.apm

Ἰησοῦν τὸν υἱὸν τοῦ θεοῦ, κρατῶμεν τῆς ὁμολογίας. 15 ↱ ↱
Jesus the Son of God, ⌞let us continue to hold fast to⌟ our confession. For we do
2652 3836 5626 3836 2536 3195 3836 3934 1142 2400 2400
n.asm d.asm n.asm d.gsm n.gsm v.pas.1p d.gsf n.gsf

NASB

so long a time just
as has been said
before,
“ TODAY IF YOU
HEAR HIS
VOICE,
DO NOT HARDEN
YOUR HEARTS.”
8 For if Joshua had
given them rest,
He would not have
spoken of another
day after that. 9 So
there remains a
Sabbath rest for
the people of God.
10 For the one who
has entered His
rest has himself
also rested from
his works, as God
did from His.
11 Therefore let us
be diligent to enter
that rest, so that
no one will fall,
through *following*
the same example
of disobedience.
12 For the word of
God is living and
active and sharper
than any two-
edged sword, and
piercing as far as
the division of soul
and spirit, of both
joints and marrow,
and able to judge
the thoughts and
intentions of the
heart. 13 And there is
no creature hidden
from His sight, but
all things are open
and laid bare to the
eyes of Him with
whom we have
to do.
14 Therefore, since
we have a great
high priest who has
passed through the
heavens, Jesus the
Son of God, let us
hold fast our con-
fession. 15 For we

NIV

not have a high
priest who is un-
able to empathize
with our weak-
nesses, but we
have one who has
been tempted in
every way, just as
we are—yet he
did not sin. [16]Let
us then approach
God's throne of
grace with confi-
dence, so that we
may receive mercy
and find grace to
help us in our time
of need.
5 Every high
priest is se-
lected from among
the people and is
appointed to rep-
resent the people
in matters related
to God, to offer
gifts and sacrific-
es for sins. [2]He is
able to deal gently
with those who are
ignorant and are
going astray, since
he himself is sub-
ject to weakness.
[3]This is why he
has to offer sacri-
fices for his own
sins, as well as for
the sins of the peo-
ple. [4]And no one
takes this honor
on himself, but he
receives it when
called by God, just
as Aaron was.
[5]In the same way,
Christ did not take
on himself the
glory of becoming
a high priest. But
God said to him,

"You are my Son;
today I have
become your
Father."[a]

[6]And he says in
another

οὐ γὰρ ἔχομεν ἀρχιερέα ⌊μὴ δυνάμενον⌋ συμπαθῆσαι ταῖς ἀσθενείαις
not *For* have a high priest who is unable to feel *{the}* our weaknesses,
4024 1142 2400 797 3590 1538 5217 3836 7005 819
pl cj v.pai.1p n.asm pl pt.pp.asm f.aa d.dpf n.dpf

ἡμῶν, πεπειρασμένον δὲ κατὰ πάντα ⌊καθ' ὁμοιότητα⌋
our but ⌊one who has been tempted⌋ *but* in every way just as we are — yet
7005 1254 4279 1254 2848 4246 2848 3928
r.gp.1 pt.rp.asm cj p.a a.apn p.a n.asf

χωρὶς ἁμαρτίας. [16] προσερχώμεθα οὖν μετὰ παρρησίας τῷ θρόνῳ τῆς
without sin. Therefore let us approach *Therefore* with confidence the throne of
6006 281 4036 4665 4036 3552 4244 3836 2585 3836
p.g n.gsf v.pms.1p cj p.g n.gsf d.dsm n.dsm d.gsf

χάριτος, ἵνα λάβωμεν ἔλεος καὶ χάριν εὕρωμεν εἰς εὔκαιρον
grace, so that we may receive mercy and find grace *find* for help ⌊when we need it.⌋
5921 2671 3284 1799 2779 2351 5921 2351 1650 1069 2322
n.gsf cj v.aas.1p n.asn cj n.asf v.aas.1p p.a a.asf

βοήθειαν.
help
1069
n.asf

5:1 πᾶς γὰρ ἀρχιερεὺς ἐξ ἀνθρώπων λαμβανόμενος
For every *For* high priest, being chosen ⌊from among⌋ men, *being chosen* is
1142 4246 1142 797 3284 3284 1666 476 3284 2770
a.nsm cj n.nsm p.g n.gpm pt.pp.nsm

ὑπὲρ ἀνθρώπων καθίσταται τὰ πρὸς τὸν
appointed ⌊on behalf of⌋ men *is appointed* to represent them in matters ⌊related to⌋ *{the}*
2770 5642 476 2770 3836 4639 3836
p.g n.gpm v.ppi.3s d.apn p.a d.asm

θεόν, ἵνα προσφέρῃ δῶρά τε καὶ θυσίας ὑπὲρ ἁμαρτιῶν, [2]
God, to offer gifts *{both}* and sacrifices for sins. He is able
2536 2671 4712 1565 5445 2779 2602 5642 281 1538 1538 1538
n.asm cj v.pas.3s n.apn cj cj n.apf p.g n.gpf

μετριοπαθεῖν δυνάμενος τοῖς ἀγνοοῦσιν καὶ πλανωμένοις, ἐπεὶ καὶ
to deal compassionately *He is able* ⌊with the⌋ ignorant and going astray, since he too
3584 1538 3836 51 2779 4414 2075 899 2779
f.pa pt.pp.nsm d.dpm pt.pa.dpm cj pt.pp.dpm cj adv

αὐτὸς περίκειται ἀσθένειαν [3]καὶ ⌊δι' αὐτὴν⌋ ὀφείλει,
he is subject to weakness. *{and}* That is why he is obligated to offer sacrifice
899 4329 819 2779 1328 899 4053 4712 4712
r.nsm v.pmi.3s n.asf cj p.a r.asf.3 v.pai.3s

καθὼς περὶ τοῦ λαοῦ, οὕτως καὶ περὶ αὑτοῦ
for his own sins, just as he does for the sins of the people. *{in this way}* *{also}* *for* *his own*
4309 899 899 281 2777 4309 3836 3295 4048 2779 4309 899
pl p.g d.gsm n.gsm adv adv p.g r.gsm.3

προσφέρειν περὶ ἁμαρτιῶν. [4]καὶ οὐχ ἑαυτῷ τις
to offer *{for}* *sins* And no one takes this honor ⌊on his own accord,⌋ *one*
4712 4309 281 2779 4024 5516 3284 3836 5507 1571 5516
f.pa p.g n.gpf cj pl r.dsm.3 r.nsm

λαμβάνει τὴν τιμὴν ἀλλὰ καλούμενος ὑπὸ τοῦ θεοῦ καθώσπερ καὶ
takes *this* *honor* but receives it when called by *{the}* God, just as Aaron also
3284 3836 5507 247 2813 5679 3836 2536 2778 2 2779
v.pai.3s d.asf n.asf cj pt.pp.nsm p.g d.gsm n.gsm cj adv

Ἀαρών. [5]οὕτως καὶ ὁ Χριστὸς οὐχ ἑαυτὸν ἐδόξασεν γενηθῆναι
Aaron was. So also *{the}* Christ did not exalt himself *did exalt* to become
2 4048 2779 3836 5986 1519 4024 1519 1571 1519 1181
n.nsm adv adv d.nsm n.nsm pl r.asm.3 v.aai.3s f.ap

ἀρχιερέα ἀλλ' ὁ λαλήσας πρὸς αὐτόν, υἱός μου
high priest, but was appointed by the one who said to him, "You are my Son, *my*
797 247 3836 3281 4639 899 5148 1639 1609 5626 1609
n.asm cj d.nsm pt.aa.nsm p.a r.asm.3 n.nsm r.gs.1

εἶ σύ, ἐγὼ σήμερον → → γεγέννηκά σε· [6]καθὼς καὶ ἐν ἑτέρῳ
are *You* today I *today* have become your Father"; *your* as also in another
1639 5148 4958 1609 4958 5148 1164 5148 2777 2779 1877 2283
v.pai.2s r.ns.2 r.ns.1 adv v.rai.1s r.as.2 cj adv p.d r.dsm

NASB

do not have a high
priest who cannot
sympathize with
our weaknesses,
but One who has
been tempted in
all things as *we*
are, yet without
sin. [16]Therefore let
us draw near with
confidence to the
throne of grace,
so that we may
receive mercy and
find grace to help
in time of need.

The Perfect High Priest

[5:1]For every high
priest taken from
among men is ap-
pointed on behalf
of men in things
pertaining to God,
in order to offer
both gifts and
sacrifices for sins;
[2]he can deal gently
with the ignorant
and misguided,
since he himself
also is beset with
weakness; [3]and
because of it he is
obligated to offer
sacrifices for sins,
as for the people,
so also for himself.
[4]And no one takes
the honor to him-
self, but *receives it*
when he is called
by God, even as
Aaron was.
[5]So also Christ did
not glorify Himself
so as to become a
high priest, but He
who said to Him,
"YOU ARE MY
SON,
TODAY I HAVE
BEGOTTEN
YOU";
[6]just as He says
also in another
passage,

[a] 5 Psalm 2:7

NIV

place,
"You are a priest
forever,
in the order
of Mel-
chizedek."[a]
7During the days
of Jesus' life on
earth, he offered
up prayers and pe-
titions with fervent
cries and tears to
the one who could
save him from
death, and he was
heard because of
his reverent sub-
mission. 8Son
though he was, he
learned obedience
from what he suf-
fered 9and, once
made perfect, he
became the source
of eternal salvation
for all who obey
him 10and was des-
ignated by God to
be high priest in
the order of Mel-
chizedek.

Warning Against Falling Away

11We have much
to say about this,
but it is hard to
make it clear to
you because you
no longer try to
understand. 12In
fact, though by
this time you
ought to be teach-
ers, you need
someone to teach
you the elemen-
tary truths of
God's word all
over again. You
need milk, not
solid food! 13Any-
one who lives on
milk, being still
an infant, is not
acquainted with
the teaching about
righteousness.
14But solid food
is for the mature,
who by constant
use

[a] 6 Psalm 110:4

λέγει, σὺ ἱερεὺς εἰς τὸν αἰῶνα κατὰ τὴν τάξιν Μελχισέδεκ,
place God says, "You are a priest for all time ⌊according to⌋ the order of Melchizedek."
3306 5148 2636 1650 3836 172 2848 3836 5423 3519
v.pai.3s r.ns.2 n.nsm p.a d.asm n.asm p.a d.asf n.asf n.gsm

7 ὃς ἐν ταῖς ἡμέραις τῆς σαρκὸς αὐτοῦ δεήσεις τε καὶ
Jesus In the days of his flesh, *his* Jesus offered up prayers *{both}* and
4005 1877 3836 2465 3836 899 4922 899 4005 4712 4712 1255 5445 2779
r.nsm p.d d.dpf n.dpf d.gsf n.gsf r.gsm.3 n.apf cj cj

ἱκετηρίας πρὸς τὸν δυνάμενον σῴζειν αὐτὸν ἐκ
supplications, with loud crying and tears, to the ⌊one who was able⌋ to save him from
2656 3552 2708 3199 2779 1232 4639 3836 1538 5392 899 1666
n.apf p.a d.asm pt.pp.asm f.pa r.asm.3 p.g

θανάτου μετὰ κραυγῆς ἰσχυρᾶς καὶ δακρύων προσενέγκας καὶ εἰσακουσθεὶς
death, *with crying loud and tears offered up* and he was heard
2505 3552 3199 2708 2779 1232 4712 2779 1653
n.gsm p.g n.gsf a.gsf cj n.gpn pt.aa.nsm cj pt.ap.nsm

ἀπὸ τῆς εὐλαβείας, 8 καίπερ ὢν υἱός, ἔμαθεν ἀφ' ὧν
⌊because of⌋ his godly fear. Although ⌊he was⌋ a son, he learned obedience from what
608 3836 2325 2788 1639 5626 3443 5633 608 4005
p.g d.gsf n.gsf cj pt.pa.nsm n.nsm v.aai.3s p.g r.gpn

ἔπαθεν τὴν ὑπακοήν, 9 καὶ τελειωθεὶς ἐγένετο πᾶσιν τοῖς ὑπακούουσιν
he suffered. *{the} obedience* And once made perfect, he became for all those who obey
4248 3836 5633 2779 5457 1181 4246 3836 5634
v.aai.3s d.asf n.asf cj pt.ap.nsm v.ami.3s a.dpm d.dpm pt.pa.dpm

αὐτῷ αἴτιος → σωτηρίας αἰωνίου, 10 προσαγορευθεὶς ὑπὸ τοῦ θεοῦ
him the source of eternal salvation, *eternal* having been designated by *{the}* God a
899 165 173 5401 173 4641 5679 3836 2536
r.dsm.3 n.nsm n.gsf a.gsf pt.ap.nsm p.g d.gsm n.gsm

ἀρχιερεὺς κατὰ τὴν τάξιν Μελχισέδεκ. 11 περὶ οὗ πολὺς ἡμῖν
high priest ⌊according to⌋ the order of Melchizedek. On ⌊this subject⌋ we have much *we*
797 2848 3836 5423 3519 4309 4005 7005 4498 7005
n.nsm p.a d.asf n.asf n.gsm p.g r.gsm a.nsm r.dp.1

ὁ λόγος καὶ δυσερμήνευτος λέγειν, ἐπεὶ νωθροὶ γεγόνατε
{the} to say and it is hard to explain, since you have become sluggish *you have become*
3836 3364 2779 1549 3306 2075 1181 1181 1181 3821 1181
d.nsm n.nsm cj a.nsm f.pa cj a.npm v.rai.2p

ταῖς ἀκοαῖς. 12 καὶ γὰρ → ὀφείλοντες εἶναι διδάσκαλοι διὰ
in understanding. *{also}* For though by this time you ought to be teachers, *by*
3836 198 2779 1142 1328 3836 5989 4053 1639 1437 1328
d.dpf n.dpf adv cj pt.pa.npm f.pa n.npm p.a

τὸν χρόνον, πάλιν χρείαν ἔχετε τοῦ
this time you have need of someone to teach you again *need you have {the}*
3836 5989 2400 2400 5970 5516 1438 1438 7007 4099 5970 2400 3836
d.asm n.asm adv n.asf v.pai.2p d.gsn

διδάσκειν ὑμᾶς τινὰ τὰ στοιχεῖα τῆς ἀρχῆς τῶν λογίων τοῦ θεοῦ
to teach you someone the basic elements *{the} basic* of God's revelation. *{the} God's*
1438 7007 5516 3836 794 5122 3836 794 3836 2536 3359 3836 2536
f.pa r.ap.2 r.asm d.apn n.apn d.gsf n.gsf d.gpn n.gpn d.gsm n.gsm

καὶ γεγόνατε χρείαν ἔχοντες γάλακτος[a] οὐ στερεᾶς τροφῆς.
{and} ⌊You have become⌋ people having need *people having* of milk, not solid food;
2779 1181 2400 2400 5970 2400 1128 4024 5104 5575
cj v.rai.2p n.asf pt.pa.npm n.gsn pl a.gsf n.gsf

13 πᾶς γὰρ ὁ μετέχων γάλακτος ἄπειρος → λόγου
for everyone *for* who lives on milk is inexperienced with the teaching
1142 4246 1142 3836 3576 1128 586 3364
a.nsm cj d.nsm pt.pa.nsm n.gsn a.nsm n.gsm

δικαιοσύνης, νήπιος γάρ ἐστιν· 14 →
about righteousness, since he is still a child. *since he is* But solid food is for the
1466 1142 1639 1639 3758 1142 1639 1254 5104 5575 1639
n.gsf a.nsm cj v.pai.3s

τελείων δέ ἐστιν ἡ στερεὰ τροφή, τῶν διὰ τὴν ἕξιν τὰ
mature, *But is {the} solid food* for those who ⌊by virtue of⌋ their maturity have *{the}*
5455 1254 1639 3836 5104 5575 3836 1328 3836 2011 2400 3836
a.gpm cj v.pai.3s d.nsf a.nsf n.nsf d.gpm p.a d.asf n.asf d.apn

[a] καὶ included by UBS after γάλακτος.

NASB

"You are a
priest for-
ever
According to
the order
of Melchi-
zedek."
7In the days of His
flesh, He offered
up both prayers
and supplications
with loud crying
and tears to the
One able to save
Him from death,
and He was heard
because of His
piety. 8Although
He was a Son, He
learned obedience
from the things
which He suffered.
9And having been
made perfect,
He became to all
those who obey
Him the source of
eternal salvation,
10being designated
by God as a high
priest according
to the order of
Melchizedek.
11Concerning [a]him
we have much to
say, and *it is* hard
to explain, since
you have become
dull of hearing.
12For though by this
time you ought to
be teachers, you
have need again for
someone to teach
you the elementary
principles of the
oracles of God, and
you have come to
need milk and not
solid food. 13For
everyone who par-
takes *only* of milk
is not accustomed
to the word of righ-
teousness, for he
is an infant. 14But
solid food is for the
mature, who be-
cause of practice

[a] Lit *whom* or *which*

NIV

have trained them-
selves to distin-
guish good from
evil.
6 Therefore
let us move
beyond the ele-
mentary teachings
about Christ and
be taken forward
to maturity, not
laying again the
foundation of re-
pentance from acts
that lead to death,[a]
and of faith in
God, 2 instruction
about cleansing
rites,[b] the laying
on of hands, the
resurrection of the
dead, and eternal
judgment. 3 And
God permitting,
we will do so.
4 It is impossible
for those who have
once been enlight-
ened, who have
tasted the heaven-
ly gift, who have
shared in the Holy
Spirit, 5 who have
tasted the good-
ness of the word
of God and the
powers of the com-
ing age 6 and who
have fallen[c] away,
to be brought back
to repentance. To
their loss they are
crucifying the Son
of God all over
again and subject-
ing him to public
disgrace. 7 Land
that drinks in the
rain often fall-
ing on it and that
produces a crop
useful to those for
whom it is farmed
receives the bless-
ing of God. 8 But
land that produces
thorns and thistles
is worthless and is
in danger of being
cursed. In the end
it will be burned.
9 Even though we
speak like this,
dear friends, we
are convinced of

[a] 1 Or *from useless rituals*
[b] 2 Or *about baptisms*
[c] 6 Or *age, 6if they fall*

αἰσθητήρια γεγυμνασμένα ἐχόντων πρὸς διάκρισιν καλοῦ τε καὶ κακοῦ.
senses that are trained *have* to distinguish good ~ from evil.
152 1214 2400 4639 1360 2819 5445 2779 2805
n.apn pt.rp.apn pt.pa.gpm p.a n.asf a.gsn cj cj a.gsn

6:1 διὸ ἀφέντες τὸν τῆς ἀρχῆς τοῦ Χριστοῦ λόγον
Therefore ⌊let us leave standing⌋ the *{the}* elementary teaching about Christ *teaching*
1475 918 3836 3836 794 3364 3836 5986 3364
cj pt.aa.npm d.asm d.gsf n.gsf d.gsm n.gsm n.asm

ἐπὶ τὴν τελειότητα φερώμεθα, μὴ πάλιν θεμέλιον
and let us move on to *{the}* maturity, *let us move on* not laying again a foundation
5770 5770 5770 5770 2093 3836 5456 5770 3590 2850 4099 2529
p.a d.asf n.asf v.pps.1p pl adv n.asm

καταβαλλόμενοι μετανοίας ἀπὸ νεκρῶν ἔργων καὶ πίστεως ἐπὶ θεόν, 2
laying of repentance from dead works and of faith in God, instruction
2850 3567 608 3738 2240 2779 4411 2093 2536 1439
pt.pm.npm n.gsf p.g a.gpn n.gpn cj n.gsf p.a n.asm

βαπτισμῶν διδαχῆς ἐπιθέσεώς τε χειρῶν, ἀναστάσεώς τε →
⌊about cleansing rites⌋ *instruction* and laying on *and* of hands, the resurrection ~ of the
968 1439 5445 2120 5445 5931 414 5445
n.gpm n.gsf n.gsf cj n.gpf n.gsf cj

νεκρῶν καὶ κρίματος αἰωνίου. 3 καὶ τοῦτο ποιήσομεν, ἐάνπερ
dead, and eternal judgment. *eternal* And we will do this, *we will do* if God
3738 2779 173 3210 173 2779 4472 4472 4472 4047 4472 1570 2536
a.gpm cj n.gsn a.gsn cj r.asn v.fai.1p cj

ἐπιτρέπῃ ὁ θεός. 4 ἀδύνατον γὰρ → τοὺς → → ἅπαξ φωτισθέντας,
permits. *{the}* *God* For it is impossible *For* when those who have once been enlightened
2205 3836 2536 1142 105 1142 5894 3836 5894 5894 562 5894
v.pas.3s d.nsm n.nsm a.nsn cj d.apm adv pt.ap.apm

γευσαμένους τε τῆς δωρεᾶς τῆς ἐπουρανίου καὶ μετόχους
and have tasted *and* the heavenly gift *{the}* *heavenly* and have become partakers
5445 1174 5445 3836 2230 1561 3836 2230 2779 1181 1181 3581
pt.am.apm cj d.gsf n.gsf d.gsf a.gsf cj n.apm

γενηθέντας → πνεύματος ἁγίου 5 καὶ καλὸν γευσαμένους
have become of the Holy Spirit *Holy* and have tasted the goodness *have tasted*
1181 41 4460 41 2779 1174 1174 2819 1174
pt.ap.apm n.gsn a.gsn cj a.asn pt.am.apm

θεοῦ ῥῆμα δυνάμεις τε → μέλλοντος αἰῶνος 6 καὶ παραπεσόντας,
of God's word and the powers *and* of the coming age and have committed apostasy,
2536 4839 5445 1539 5445 3516 172 2779 4178
n.gsm n.asn n.apf cj pt.pa.gsm n.gsm cj pt.aa.apm

πάλιν ἀνακαινίζειν εἰς μετάνοιαν, → ἀνασταυροῦντας
{again} to restore them to repentance, since to their own harm they are crucifying
4099 362 1650 3567 1571 1571 1571 416
adv f.pa p.a n.asf pt.pa.apm

ἑαυτοῖς τὸν υἱὸν τοῦ θεοῦ ← καὶ παραδειγματίζοντας. 7 γῆ γὰρ
to their own the Son of God again and exposing him to public shame. For the field *For*
1571 3836 5626 3836 2536 416 2779 4136 1142 1178 1142
r.dpm.3 d.asm n.asm d.gsm n.gsm cj pt.pa.apm n.nsf cj

ἡ πιοῦσα τὸν ἐπ᾽ αὐτῆς ἐρχόμενον πολλάκις ὑετὸν καὶ
that soaks up the frequent rain that falls on it *that falls* *frequent* *rain* and
3836 4403 3836 4490 5624 2262 2262 2093 899 2262 4490 5624 2779
d.nsf pt.aa.nsf d.asm p.g r.gsf.3 pt.pm.asm adv n.asm cj

τίκτουσα βοτάνην εὔθετον ἐκείνοις δι᾽ οὓς καὶ γεωργεῖται, μεταλαμβάνει
yields a crop useful for those for whom *{also}* it is cultivated, receives a
5503 1083 2310 1697 1328 4005 2779 1175 3561
pt.pa.nsf n.asf a.asf r.dpm p.a r.apm adv v.ppi.3s v.pai.3s

εὐλογίας ἀπὸ τοῦ θεοῦ· 8 ἐκφέρουσα δὲ ἀκάνθας καὶ τριβόλους, ἀδόκιμος καὶ
blessing from *{the}* God. But if it produces *But* thorns and thistles, it is useless and
2330 608 3836 2536 1254 1766 1254 180 2779 5560 99 2779
n.gsf p.g d.gsm n.gsm pt.pa.nsf cj n.apf cj n.apm a.nsf cj

κατάρας ἐγγύς, ἧς τὸ τέλος εἰς καῦσιν. 9 πεπείσμεθα
about to be cursed; *about to be* its *{the}* fate is to be burned. But ⌊we are convinced of⌋
1584 1584 1584 2932 1584 4005 3836 5465 1650 3011 1254 4275
n.gsf p.g r.gsf d.nsn n.nsn p.a n.asf v.rpi.1p

NASB

have their senses
trained to discern
good and evil.

The Peril of Falling Away

6:1 Therefore leav-
ing the elementary
teaching about the
Christ, let us press
on to maturity,
not laying again
a foundation of
repentance from
dead works and of
faith toward God,
2 of instruction
about washings
and laying on of
hands, and the
resurrection of the
dead and eternal
judgment. 3 And
this we will do, if
God permits. 4 For
in the case of those
who have once
been enlightened
and have tasted
of the heavenly
gift and have been
made partakers of
the Holy Spirit,
5 and have tasted
the good word of
God and the pow-
ers of the age to
come, 6 and *then*
have fallen away, it
is impossible to re-
new them again to
repentance, since
they again crucify
to themselves the
Son of God and
put Him to open
shame. 7 For ground
that drinks the rain
which often falls
on it and brings
forth vegetation
useful to those for
whose sake it is
also tilled, receives
a blessing from
God; 8 but if it
yields thorns and
thistles, it is worth-
less and close to
being cursed, and
it ends up being
burned.

Better Things for You

9 But, beloved, we
are convinced

NIV

better things in
your case—the
things that have
to do with salva-
tion. 10 God is not
unjust; he will not
forget your work
and the love you
have shown him
as you have helped
his people and con-
tinue to help them.
11 We want each of
you to show this
same diligence to
the very end, so
that what you hope
for may be fully
realized. 12 We do
not want you to
become lazy, but
to imitate those
who through faith
and patience inher-
it what has been
promised.

The Certainty of God's Promise

13 When God
made his promise
to Abraham, since
there was no one
greater for him to
swear by, he swore
by himself, 14 say-
ing, "I will surely
bless you and give
you many descen-
dants."[a] 15 And so
after waiting pa-
tiently, Abraham
received what was
promised.
16 People swear by
someone greater
than themselves,
and the oath con-
firms what is said
and puts an end to
all argument. 17 Be-
cause God wanted
to make the un-
changing nature of
his purpose very
clear to the heirs of
what was

δὲ περὶ ὑμῶν, ↰ ἀγαπητοί, τὰ κρείσσονα καὶ ἐχόμενα
But better things in your case, beloved *{the}* *better things* — *{and}* ⌊things that accompany⌋
1254 3202 3202 4309 7007 4309 28 3836 3202 2779 2400
cj p.g r.gp.2 a.vpm d.apn a.apn.c cj pt.pm.apn

σωτηρίας, εἰ καὶ οὕτως λαλοῦμεν. 10 οὐ γὰρ
salvation — even though *even* we speak as *we speak* we do. For God is not *For*
5401 2779 1623 2779 3281 3281 4048 3281 1142 2536 4024 1142
n.gsf cj adv adv v.pai.1p pl cj

ἄδικος ὁ θεὸς ἐπιλαθέσθαι τοῦ ἔργου ὑμῶν καὶ τῆς ἀγάπης ἧς
so unjust *{the}* *God* as to forget *{the}* your work *your* and the love *{that}*
96 3836 2536 2140 3836 7007 2240 7007 2779 3836 27 4005
a.nsm d.nsm n.nsm f.am d.gsn n.gsn r.gp.2 cj d.gsf n.gsf r.gsf

ἐνεδείξασθε εἰς τὸ ὄνομα αὐτοῦ, διακονήσαντες
you have demonstrated for *{the}* his cause, *his* when you served and continue to serve
1892 1650 3836 899 3950 899 1354 2779 1354 1354 1354
v.ami.2p p.a d.asn n.asn r.gsm.3 pt.aa.npm

τοῖς ἁγίοις καὶ διακονοῦντες. 11 ἐπιθυμοῦμεν δὲ ἕκαστον ὑμῶν
{the} fellow believers. *and* *continue to serve* But we want *But* each one of you to
3836 41 2779 1354 1254 2121 1254 1667 7007 1892
d.dpm a.dpm cj pt.pa.npm v.pai.1p cj r.asm r.gp.2

τὴν αὐτὴν ἐνδείκνυσθαι σπουδὴν πρὸς τὴν πληροφορίαν
demonstrate the same *to demonstrate* earnestness to the very end for the fulfillment
1892 3836 899 1892 5082 948 5465 5465 4639 3836 4443
d.asf r.asf f.pm n.asf p.a d.asf n.asf

τῆς ἐλπίδος ἄχρι τέλους, 12 ἵνα μὴ νωθροὶ γένησθε, μιμηταὶ
of your hope, *to* *very end* so that you will not be lazy, *you will be* but imitators
3836 1828 948 5465 2671 1181 1181 3590 1181 3821 1181 1254 3629
d.gsf n.gsf p.g n.gsn cj pl a.npm v.ams.2p n.npm

δὲ τῶν ↱ διὰ πίστεως καὶ μακροθυμίας κληρονομούντων τὰς ἐπαγγελίας.
but of those who by faith and perseverance inherit the promises.
1254 3836 3099 1328 4411 2779 3429 3099 3836 2039
cj d.gpm p.g n.gsf cj n.gsf pt.pa.gpm d.apf n.apf

13 τῷ γὰρ Ἀβραὰμ ἐπαγγειλάμενος ὁ θεός, ἐπεὶ κατ᾽
When God made a promise to *{for}* Abraham, *When made a promise* *{the}* *God* since *by*
2040 2536 2040 2040 2040 3836 1142 11 2040 3836 2536 2075 2848
d.dsm cj n.dsm pt.am.nsm d.nsm n.nsm cj p.g

οὐδενὸς εἶχεν μείζονος ὀμόσαι, ὤμοσεν καθ᾽ ἑαυτοῦ 14 λέγων,
he had no one *he had* greater by whom to swear, he swore by himself, saying,
2400 2400 4029 2400 3489 2848 3923 3923 2848 1571 3306
a.gsm v.iai.3s a.gsm.c f.aa v.aai.3s p.g r.gsm.3 pt.pa.nsm

⌊εἰ μὴν⌋ → → → ⌊εὐλογῶν εὐλογήσω⌋ σε καὶ →
"Surely I will bless you greatly *you* and increase your descendants
1623 3605 5148 2328 2328 5148 2779 5148 5148
cj pl pt.pa.nsm v.fai.1s r.as.2 cj

⌊πληθύνων πληθυνῶ⌋ σε· 15 καὶ οὕτως μακροθυμήσας
abundantly." *your descendants* And thus by patient endurance, Abraham
4437 4437 5148 2779 4048 3428
pt.pa.nsm v.fai.1s r.as.2 cj adv pt.aa.nsm

ἐπέτυχεν τῆς ἐπαγγελίας. 16 ἄνθρωποι γὰρ κατὰ τοῦ μείζονος
received what had been promised. For people *For* swear by *{the}* ⌊someone greater⌋
2209 3836 2039 1142 476 1142 3923 2848 3836 3489
v.aai.3s d.gsf n.gsf n.npm cj p.g d.gsm a.gsm.c

ὀμνύουσιν, καὶ πάσης
than themselves, *swear* and the oath confirms what is said and puts to an end all
3923 2779 3836 3992 1650 4306 4246
v.pai.3p cj a.gsf

αὐτοῖς ἀντιλογίας πέρας ⌊εἰς βεβαίωσιν⌋ ὁ ὅρκος· 17 ⌊ἐν ᾧ⌋
{to them} dispute. *end* *confirms* *the* *oath* Because God wanted
899 517 4306 1650 1012 3836 3992 1877 4005 2536 1089
r.dpm.3 n.gsf n.nsn p.a n.asf d.nsm n.nsm p.d r.dsn

↱ ↱ περισσότερον βουλόμενος ὁ θεὸς ἐπιδεῖξαι τοῖς κληρονόμοις τῆς
to show more *wanted* *{the}* *God* clearly to the heirs of the
2109 2109 4358 1089 3836 2536 2109 3836 3101 3836
adv.c pt.pm.nsm d.nsm n.nsm f.aa d.dpm n.dpm d.gsf

NASB

of better things
concerning you,
and things that
accompany salva-
tion, though we
are speaking in
this way. 10 For God
is not unjust so
as to forget your
work and the love
which you have
shown toward His
name, in having
ministered and in
still ministering to
the saints. 11 And
we desire that each
one of you show
the same diligence
so as to realize the
full assurance of
hope until the end,
12 so that you will
not be sluggish, but
imitators of those
who through faith
and patience inherit
the promises.
13 For when God
made the promise
to Abraham, since
He could swear by
no one greater, He
swore by Himself,
14 saying, "I WILL
SURELY BLESS YOU
AND I WILL SURELY
MULTIPLY YOU."
15 And so, having
patiently waited,
he obtained the
promise. 16 For men
swear by one great-
er *than themselves,*
and with them an
oath *given* as con-
firmation is an end
of every dispute.
17 In the same way
God, desiring even
more to show to
the heirs of the

[a] *14* Gen. 22:17

NIV

promised, he con-
firmed it with an
oath. [18]God did
this so that, by
two unchangeable
things in which it
is impossible for
God to lie, we who
have fled to take
hold of the hope
set before us may
be greatly encour-
aged. [19]We have
this hope as an
anchor for the soul,
firm and secure.
It enters the inner
sanctuary behind
the curtain, [20]where
our forerunner,
Jesus, has entered
on our behalf. He
has become a high
priest forever, in
the order of Mel-
chizedek.

Melchizedek the Priest

7 This Melchiz-
edek was king
of Salem and priest
of God Most High.
He met Abraham
returning from the
defeat of the kings
and blessed him,
[2]and Abraham
gave him a tenth of
everything. First,
the name Melchiz-
edek means "king
of righteousness";
then also, "king
of Salem" means
"king of peace."
[3]Without father or
mother, without
genealogy, without
beginning of days
or end of life, re-
sembling the Son
of God,

ἐπαγγελίας τὸ ἀμετάθετον τῆς βουλῆς αὐτοῦ ἐμεσίτευσεν → ὅρκῳ,
promise the unchanging nature of his purpose, *his* he confirmed it with an oath,
2039 3836 292 3836 899 1087 899 3541 3992
n.gsf d.asn a.asn d.gsf n.gsf r.gsm.3 v.aai.3s n.dsm

18 ἵνα διὰ δύο πραγμάτων ἀμεταθέτων, ἐν οἷς ἀδύνατον
so that through two unchangeable facts, *unchangeable* in which it is impossible for
2671 1328 1545 292 4547 292 1877 4005 105
cj p.g a.gpn n.gpn a.gpn p.d r.dpn a.nsn

ψεύσασθαι τὸν[a] θεόν, ἰσχυρὰν παράκλησιν
God to lie, *{the}* *God* we who have taken refuge might have strong incentive
2536 6017 3836 2536 2400 3836 2966 2966 2966 2400 2400 2708 4155
f.am d.asm n.asm a.asf n.asf

ἔχωμεν οἱ καταφυγόντες κρατῆσαι τῆς προκειμένης ἐλπίδος· 19
we might have *who* *have taken refuge* to hold fast to the hope set before us. *hope* We
2400 3836 2966 3195 3836 1828 4618 1828 2400
v.pas.1p d.npm pt.aa.npm f.aa d.gsf pt.pm.gsf n.gsf

ἣν ὡς ἄγκυραν ἔχομεν τῆς ψυχῆς ἀσφαλῆ τε καὶ βεβαίαν καὶ
have this hope as an anchor *We have* for life, both sure *both* and steadfast — *{and}*
2400 4005 6055 46 2400 3836 6034 5445 855 5445 2779 1010 2779
r.asf pl n.asf v.pai.1p d.gsf n.gsf a.asf cj cj a.asf cj

⌊εἰσερχομένην εἰς⌋ τὸ ἐσώτερον τοῦ καταπετάσματος, 20 ὅπου
a hope that enters the inner shrine ⌊behind the⌋ veil, where Jesus
1656 1650 3836 2278 3836 2925 3963 2652
pt.pm.asf p.a d.asn p.g d.gsn n.gsn cj

→ πρόδρομος ὑπὲρ ἡμῶν εἰσῆλθεν Ἰησοῦς,
has entered on our behalf as forerunner, *on behalf* *our* *has entered* *Jesus* having become a
1656 1656 5642 7005 5642 4596 5642 7005 1656 2652 1181 1181
n.nsm p.g r.gp.1 v.aai.3s n.nsm

κατὰ τὴν τάξιν Μελχισέδεκ ἀρχιερεὺς γενόμενος εἰς
high priest for all time ⌊according to⌋ the order of Melchizedek. *high priest* *having become* *for*
797 797 1650 3836 172 2848 3836 5423 3519 797 1181 1650
p.a d.asf n.asf n.gsm n.nsm pt.am.nsm p.a

τὸν αἰῶνα.
all *time*
3836 172
d.asm n.asm

7:1 οὗτος γὰρ ὁ Μελχισέδεκ, βασιλεὺς Σαλήμ, ἱερεὺς τοῦ θεοῦ
For this *For* *{the}* Melchizedek, king of Salem, priest of the Most High God,
1142 4047 1142 3836 3519 995 4889 2636 3836 5736 5736 2536
r.nsm cj d.nsm n.nsm n.nsm n.gsf n.nsm d.gsm n.gsm

τοῦ ὑψίστου, ὁ συναντήσας Ἀβραὰμ ὑποστρέφοντι ἀπὸ τῆς κοπῆς τῶν βασιλέων
{the} *Most High* *{the}* met Abraham returning from the defeat of the kings
3836 5736 3836 5267 11 5715 608 3836 3158 3836 995
d.gsm a.gsm.s d.nsm pt.aa.nsm n.dsm pt.pa.dsm p.g d.gsf n.gsf d.gpm n.gpm

καὶ εὐλογήσας αὐτόν, 2 ᾧ καὶ δεκάτην ἀπὸ πάντων
and blessed him, and ⌊to him⌋ *and* Abraham alloted a tenth part of everything.
2779 2328 899 2779 4005 2779 11 3532 1281 608 4246
cj pt.aa.nsm r.asm.3 r.dsm adv n.asf p.g a.gpn

ἐμέρισεν Ἀβραάμ, πρῶτον μὲν ἑρμηνευόμενος βασιλεὺς
alloted *Abraham* Translated, his name means first, ~ *Translated* "king
3532 11 2257 4754 3525 2257 995
v.aai.3s n.nsm adv pl pt.pp.nsm n.nsm

δικαιοσύνης ἔπειτα δὲ καὶ βασιλεὺς Σαλήμ, ὅ ἐστιν βασιλεὺς
of righteousness," then *{and}* it also means, "king of Salem," that is, "king
1466 2083 1254 2779 995 4889 4005 1639 995
n.gsf adv cj adv n.nsm n.gsf r.nsn v.pai.3s n.nsm

εἰρήνης, 3 ἀπάτωρ ἀμήτωρ ἀγενεαλόγητος, μήτε ἀρχὴν
of peace." He is without father, without mother, without genealogy, having neither beginning
1645 574 298 37 2400 3612 794
n.gsf n.nsm n.nsm a.nsm cj n.asf

ἡμερῶν μήτε ζωῆς τέλος ἔχων, ἀφωμοιωμένος δὲ τῷ υἱῷ τοῦ θεοῦ,
of days nor end of life; *end* *having* but like *but* the Son of God
2465 3612 5465 2437 5465 2400 1254 926 1254 3836 5626 3836 2536
n.gpf cj n.gsf n.asn pt.pa.nsm pt.rp.nsm cj d.dsm n.dsm d.gsm n.gsm

NASB

promise the
unchangeableness
of His purpose,
interposed with an
oath, [18]so that by
two unchangeable
things in which it
is impossible for
God to lie, we who
have taken refuge
would have strong
encouragement to
take hold of the
hope set before
us. [19]This hope we
have as an anchor
of the soul, a *hope*
both sure and
steadfast and one
which enters within
the veil, [20]where
Jesus has entered
as a forerunner for
us, having become
a high priest
forever accord-
ing to the order of
Melchizedek.

Melchizedek's Priesthood Like Christ's

[7:1]For this
Melchizedek, king
of Salem, priest
of the Most High
God, who met
Abraham as he was
returning from the
slaughter of the
kings and blessed
him, [2]to whom also
Abraham appor-
tioned a tenth part
of all *the spoils,*
was first of all,
by the translation
of his name, king
of righteousness,
and then also king
of Salem, which
is king of peace.
[3]Without father,
without mother,
without geneal-
ogy, having neither
beginning of days
nor end of life, but
made like the Son

[a] [τὸν] UBS, omitted by TNIV.

NIV

he remains a priest
forever.
[4]Just think how
great he was:
Even the patriarch
Abraham gave
him a tenth of the
plunder! [5]Now the
law requires the
descendants of
Levi who become
priests to collect
a tenth from the
people—that is,
from their fellow
Israelites—even
though they al-
so are descended
from Abraham.
[6]This man, how-
ever, did not trace
his descent from
Levi, yet he col-
lected a tenth from
Abraham and
blessed him who
had the promis-
es. [7]And without
doubt the lesser
is blessed by the
greater. [8]In the one
case, the tenth is
collected by peo-
ple who die; but
in the other case,
by him who is de-
clared to be living.
[9]One might even
say that Levi, who
collects the tenth,
paid the tenth
through Abraham,
[10]because when
Melchizedek met
Abraham, Levi
was still in the
body of his an-
cestor.

Jesus Like Melchizedek

[11]If perfection
could have been
attained through
the Levitical
priesthood—and
indeed the law
given to the people
established that
priesthood—why
was there still
need for another

μένει ἱερεὺς εἰς τὸ διηνεκές. [4] θεωρεῖτε δὲ πηλίκος οὗτος, ᾧ
he continues a priest for all time. But see *But* how great this man was ⌊to whom⌋
3531 2636 1650 3836 1457 1254 2555 1254 4383 4047 4005
v.pai.3s n.nsm p.a d.asn a.asn v.pam.2p cj r.nsm r.nsm r.dsm

καὶ [a] δεκάτην Ἀβραὰμ ἔδωκεν ἐκ τῶν ἀκροθινίων ὁ
{also} the patriarch Abraham gave a tithe *Abraham* *gave* of the finest plunder. *the*
2779 3836 4256 11 1443 1281 11 1443 1666 3836 215 3836
adv n.asf n.nsm v.aai.3s p.g d.gpn n.gpn d.nsm

πατριάρχης. [5] καὶ οἱ μὲν ἐκ τῶν υἱῶν Λευὶ τὴν ἱερατείαν
patriarch And those ~ of the sons of Levi who receive the priestly office
4256 2779 3836 3525 1666 3836 5626 3322 3284 3284 3836 2632
n.nsm cj d.npm pl p.g d.gpm n.gpm n.gsm d.asf n.asf

λαμβάνοντες ἐντολὴν ἔχουσιν ἀποδεκατοῦν τὸν
who receive have a mandate *have* according to the law ⌊to collect a tithe from⌋ the
3284 2400 1953 2400 2848 2848 3836 3795 620 3836
pt.pa.npm n.asf v.pai.3p f.pa d.asm

λαὸν κατὰ τὸν νόμον, τοῦτ᾽ ἔστιν τοὺς ἀδελφοὺς αὐτῶν,
people, *according to* *the* *law* that is, from *{the}* their fellow countrymen, *their*
3295 2848 3836 3795 4047 1639 3836 899 81 899
n.asm p.a d.asm n.asm r.nsn v.pai.3s d.apm n.apm r.gpm.3

καίπερ → ἐξεληλυθότας ἐκ τῆς ὀσφύος Ἀβραάμ· [6] ὁ δὲ ↱ ↱
although they too come from the loins of Abraham. But ⌊this man⌋ *But* who does
2788 2002 1666 3836 4019 11 1254 3836 1254 1156 1156
cj pt.ra.apm p.g d.gsf n.gsf n.gsm d.nsm cj

μὴ γενεαλογούμενος ἐξ αὐτῶν δεδεκάτωκεν Ἀβραὰμ καὶ τὸν
not trace his descent from them ⌊received tithes from⌋ Abraham and blessed the
3590 1156 1666 899 1282 11 2779 2328 3836
pl pt.pp.nsm p.g r.gpm.3 v.rai.3s n.gsm cj d.asm

ἔχοντα τὰς ἐπαγγελίας εὐλόγηκεν. [7] χωρὶς δὲ πάσης ἀντιλογίας τὸ
⌊one who had⌋ the promises. *blessed* It is without *{and}* any dispute that the
2400 3836 2039 2328 6006 1254 4246 517 3836
pt.pa.asm d.apf n.apf v.rai.3s p.g cj a.gsf n.gsf d.nsn

ἔλαττον ὑπὸ τοῦ κρείττονος εὐλογεῖται. [8] καὶ
⌊person of lesser status⌋ is blessed by the ⌊one of greater status.⌋ *is blessed* *{and}*
1781 2328 2328 5679 3836 3202 2328 2779
a.nsn.c p.g d.gsm a.gsm.c v.ppi.3s cj

ὧδε μὲν⌋ δεκάτας ἀποθνῄσκοντες ἄνθρωποι λαμβάνουσιν,
In the one case, *tithes* mortal men receive tithes, but
6045 3525 1281 633 476 3284 1281 1254
adv pl n.apf pt.pa.npm n.npm v.pai.3p

ἐκεῖ δὲ μαρτυρούμενος ὅτι ζῇ. [9] καὶ ὡς ἔπος
⌊in the other case,⌋ *but* ⌊by one of whom it is testified⌋ that ⌊he lives.⌋ And it could be said
1695 1254 3455 4022 2409 2779 6055 2229
adv cj pt.pp.nsm cj v.pai.3s cj cj n.asn

εἰπεῖν,⌋ δι᾽ Ἀβραὰμ καὶ Λευὶ ὁ
that Levi himself, who receives tithes, paid tithes through Abraham, *{and}* *Levi* *who*
3306 3322 3836 3284 1281 1282 1282 1328 11 2779 3322 3836
f.aa p.g n.gsm cj n.nsm d.nsm

δεκάτας λαμβάνων δεδεκάτωται· [10] ἔτι γὰρ ἐν τῇ ὀσφύϊ τοῦ πατρὸς
tithes *receives* *paid tithes* for he was still *for* in the loins of his ancestor
1281 3284 1282 1142 1639 1639 2285 1142 1877 3836 4019 3836 4252
n.apf pt.pa.nsm v.rpi.3s adv cj p.d d.dsf n.dsf d.gsm n.gsm

ἦν ὅτε συνήντησεν αὐτῷ Μελχισέδεκ. [11] εἰ μὲν οὖν τελείωσις
he was when Melchizedek met Abraham. *Melchizedek* If, ~ then, perfection
1639 4021 3519 5267 899 3519 1623 3525 4036 5459
v.iai.3s cj v.aai.3s r.dsm.3 n.nsm cj pl cj n.nsf

διὰ τῆς Λευιτικῆς ἱερωσύνης ἦν, ὁ λαὸς
had been attainable through the Levitical priesthood *had been* (for under it the people
1639 1639 1328 3836 3325 2648 1639 1142 2093 899 3836 3295
p.g d.gsf a.gsf n.gsf v.iai.3s d.nsm n.nsm

γὰρ ἐπ᾽ αὐτῆς νενομοθέτηται, τίς ἔτι χρεία
for *under* *it* had received the law), what further need would there have been for another kind
1142 2093 899 3793 5515 2285 5970 2283 2283
cj p.g r.gsf.3 v.rpi.3s r.nsf adv n.nsf

NASB

of God, he remains
a priest perpetually.
[4]Now observe
how great this man
was to whom Abra-
ham, the patriarch,
gave a tenth of the
choicest spoils.
[5]And those indeed
of the sons of Levi
who receive the
priest's office have
commandment in
the Law to collect
a tenth from the
people, that is,
from their brethren,
although these are
descended from
Abraham. [6]But
the one whose
genealogy is not
traced from them
collected a tenth
from Abraham and
blessed the one
who had the prom-
ises. [7]But without
any dispute the
lesser is blessed
by the greater. [8]In
this case mortal
men receive tithes,
but in that case
one *receives them,*
of whom it is
witnessed that he
lives on. [9]And, so
to speak, through
Abraham even
Levi, who received
tithes, paid tithes,
[10]for he was still
in the loins of
his father when
Melchizedek met
him.
[11]Now if perfec-
tion was through
the Levitical
priesthood (for on
the basis of it the
people received the
Law), what further
need *was there* for
another priest

[a] [καὶ] UBS.

NIV

priest to come,
one in the order
of Melchizedek,
not in the order of
Aaron? 12 For when
the priesthood is
changed, the law
must be changed
also. 13 He of whom
these things are
said belonged to
a different tribe,
and no one from
that tribe has ever
served at the altar.
14 For it is clear that
our Lord descend-
ed from Judah,
and in regard to
that tribe Moses
said nothing about
priests. 15 And what
we have said is
even more clear if
another priest like
Melchizedek ap-
pears, 16 one who
has become a priest
not on the basis of
a regulation as to
his ancestry but
on the basis of the
power of an inde-
structible life. 17 For
it is declared:

> "You are a priest
> forever,
> in the order
> of Mel-
> chizedek."[a]

18 The former reg-
ulation is set aside
because it was
weak and useless
19 (for the law made
nothing perfect),
and a better hope
is introduced, by
which we draw
near to God.
20 And it was not

κατὰ τὴν τάξιν Μελχισέδεκ ἕτερον ἀνίστασθαι ἱερέα καὶ
of priest to arise ⌊according to⌋ the order of Melchizedek, *another kind* *to arise* *priest* *{and}*
2636 482 482 2848 3836 5423 3519 2283 482 2636 2779
p.a d.asf n.asf n.gsm r.asm f.pm n.asm cj

οὐ κατὰ τὴν τάξιν Ἀαρὼν λέγεσθαι; 12 →
rather than one designated after the order of Aaron? *designated* For whenever the
4024 3306 2848 3836 5423 2 3306 1142 3836
pl p.a d.asf n.asf n.gsm f.pp

μετατιθεμένης γὰρ τῆς ἱερωσύνης ⌊ἐξ ἀνάγκης⌋
priesthood is altered, *For* *the* *priesthood* there is necessarily an alteration
2648 3572 1142 3836 2648 1181 1181 1666 340 3557
pt.pp.gsf cj d.gsf n.gsf p.g n.gsf

καὶ νόμου μετάθεσις γίνεται. 13 ἐφ᾽ ὃν γὰρ
in the law as well. *in law* *alteration* *there is* For the one of whom *For* these things
3795 3795 2779 3795 3557 1181 1142 2093 4005 1142 4047 4047
adv n.gsm n.nsf v.pmi.3s p.a r.asm cj

λέγεται ταῦτα, φυλῆς ἑτέρας μετέσχηκεν, ἀφ᾽ ἧς οὐδεὶς
are said *these things* belongs to a different tribe, *different* *belongs to* from which no one
3306 4047 3576 3576 2283 5876 2283 3576 608 4005 4029
v.ppi.3s r.npn n.gsf r.gsf v.rai.3s p.g r.gsf a.nsm

προσέσχηκεν τῷ θυσιαστηρίῳ· 14 πρόδηλον γὰρ ὅτι
has ever served ⌊at the⌋ altar. For it is perfectly clear *For* that our Lord is
4668 3836 2603 1142 4593 1142 4022 7005 3261 422
v.rai.3s d.dsn n.dsn a.nsn cj cj

ἐξ Ἰούδα ἀνατέταλκεν ὁ κύριος ἡμῶν, εἰς ἣν φυλὴν
descended from Judah, *is descended* *{the}* *Lord* *our* and ⌊in regard to⌋ that tribe Moses
422 1666 2683 422 3836 3261 7005 1650 4005 5876 3707
p.g n.gsm v.rai.3s d.nsm n.nsm r.gp.1 p.a r.asf n.asf

περὶ ἱερέων οὐδὲν Μωϋσῆς ἐλάλησεν. 15 καὶ περισσότερον
said nothing about priests. *nothing* *Moses* *said* And it is even more
3281 4029 4309 2636 4029 3707 3281 2779 1639 1639 2285 4358
p.g n.gpm a.asn n.nsm v.aai.3s cj adv.c

ἔτι κατάδηλόν ἐστιν, εἰ κατὰ τὴν ὁμοιότητα Μελχισέδεκ
even obvious *it is* that if, ⌊according to⌋ the likeness of Melchizedek, another priest
2285 2867 1639 1623 2848 3836 3928 3519 2283 2636
adv a.nsn v.pai.3s cj p.a d.asf n.asf n.gsm

ἀνίσταται ἱερεὺς ἕτερος, 16 ὃς οὐ κατὰ νόμον →
arises, *priest* *another* he does so not ⌊on the basis of⌋ a law expressed in a carnal
482 2636 2283 4005 4024 2848 3795 1181 4921
v.pmi.3s n.nsm r.nsm r.nsm pl p.a n.asm

ἐντολῆς σαρκίνης γέγονεν ἀλλὰ κατὰ δύναμιν → ζωῆς
commandment, *carnal* *expressed* but ⌊on the basis of⌋ the power of an indestructible life.
1953 4921 1181 247 2848 1539 186 2437
n.gsf a.gsf v.rai.3s cj p.a n.asf n.gsf

ἀκαταλύτου. 17 μαρτυρεῖται γὰρ ὅτι σὺ ἱερεὺς εἰς τὸν αἰῶνα
indestructible For it is attested *For* of him, ~ "You are a priest for all time,
186 1142 3455 1142 4022 5148 2636 1650 3836 172
a.gsf v.ppi.3s cj cj r.ns.2 n.nsm p.a d.asm n.asm

κατὰ τὴν τάξιν Μελχισέδεκ. 18 ἀθέτησις μὲν γὰρ γίνεται →
⌊according to⌋ the order of Melchizedek." For there is an annulment ~ *For* *there is* of a
2848 3836 5423 3519 1142 1181 1181 120 3525 1142 1181
p.a d.asf n.asf n.gsm n.nsf pl cj v.pmi.3s

προαγούσης ἐντολῆς διὰ τὸ αὐτῆς ἀσθενὲς καὶ ἀνωφελές 19
former commandment ⌊because of⌋ *{the}* its weakness and uselessness (for the law
4575 1953 1328 3836 899 822 2779 543 1142 3836 3795
pt.pa.gsf n.gsf p.a d.asn r.gsf.3 a.asn cj a.asn

↱ οὐδὲν γὰρ ἐτελείωσεν ὁ νόμος ἐπεισαγωγὴ δὲ → κρείττονος
made nothing *for* perfect); *the* *law* but the introduction *but* of a better
5457 4029 1142 5457 3836 3795 1254 2081 1254 3202
a.asn cj v.aai.3s d.nsm n.nsm n.nsf cj a.gsf.c

ἐλπίδος δι᾽ ἧς ἐγγίζομεν τῷ θεῷ. 20 καὶ ⌊καθ᾽ ὅσον⌋ οὐ
hope through which we draw near to God. And since this was not done
1828 1328 4005 1581 3836 2536 2779 2848 4012 4024
n.gsf p.g r.gsf v.pai.1p d.dsm n.dsm cj p.a r.asn pl

NASB

to arise accord-
ing to the order of
Melchizedek, and
not be designated
according to the
order of Aaron?
12 For when the
priesthood is
changed, of neces-
sity there takes
place a change of
law also. 13 For the
one concerning
whom these things
are spoken belongs
to another tribe,
from which no one
has officiated at the
altar. 14 For it is evi-
dent that our Lord
was descended
from Judah, a tribe
with reference to
which Moses spoke
nothing concern-
ing priests. 15 And
this is clearer still,
if another priest
arises according
to the likeness of
Melchizedek, 16 who
has become *such*
not on the basis of
a law of physi-
cal requirement,
but according to
the power of an
indestructible life.
17 For it is attested
of Him,

> "YOU ARE A
> PRIEST FOR-
> EVER
> ACCORDING TO
> THE ORDER
> OF MELCHI
> ZEDEK."

18 For, on the one
hand, there is a
setting aside of a
former command-
ment because of its
weakness and use-
lessness 19 (for the
Law made nothing
perfect), and on the
other hand there
is a bringing in
of a better hope,
through which we
draw near to God.
20 And inasmuch as
it was not without

[a] 17 Psalm 110:4

NIV

without an oath!
Others became
priests without any
oath, [21]but he be-
came a priest with
an oath when God
said to him:

"The Lord has
sworn
and will not
change his
mind:
'You are
a priest
forever.'"[a]

[22]Because of this
oath, Jesus has
become the guar-
antor of a better
covenant.
[23]Now there
have been many
of those priests,
since death pre-
vented them from
continuing in
office; [24]but be-
cause Jesus lives
forever, he has a
permanent priest-
hood. [25]Therefore
he is able to save
completely[b] those
who come to God
through him, be-
cause he always
lives to intercede
for them.
[26]Such a high
priest truly meets
our need—one
who is holy,
blameless, pure,
set apart from sin-
ners, exalted above
the heavens. [27]Un-
like the other high
priests, he does
not need to offer
sacrifices day after
day, first for his
own sins, and then
for the sins of the
people. He sacri-
ficed for their sins
once for all when
he offered

χωρὶς ὁρκωμοσίας· οἱ μὲν γὰρ χωρὶς ὁρκωμοσίας
without an oath (for others ~ *for* have become priests without an oath,
6006 3993 1142 3836 3525 1142 1639 1181 2636 6006 3993
p.g n.gsf d.npm pl cj p.g n.gsf

εἰσὶν ἱερεῖς γεγονότες, 21 ὁ δὲ μετὰ ὁρκωμοσίας διὰ τοῦ
have priests become but he *but* became a priest with an oath by the
1639 2636 1181 1254 3836 1254 3552 3993 1328 3836
v.pai.3p n.npm pt.ra.npm d.nsm cj p.g n.gsf p.g d.gsm

λέγοντος πρὸς αὐτόν, ὤμοσεν κύριος καὶ ↱ οὐ μεταμεληθήσεται· ←
one who said to him, "The Lord has sworn *Lord* and will not change his
3306 4639 899 3261 3923 3261 2779 3564 4024 3564
pt.pa.gsm p.a r.asm.3 v.aai.3s n.nsm cj pl v.fpi.3s

← σὺ ἱερεὺς εἰς τὸν αἰῶνα.[a] 22 ⌊κατὰ τοσοῦτο καὶ⌋[b]
mind, 'You are a priest for all time'" accordingly Jesus has become
5148 2636 1650 3836 172 2848 5537 2779 2652 1181 1181
r.ns.2 n.nsm p.a d.asm n.asm p.a r.asn adv

→ κρείττονος διαθήκης γέγονεν ἔγγυος Ἰησοῦς. 23 καὶ οἱ
the guarantor of a better covenant. *has become guarantor Jesus* Now *these*
1583 3202 1347 1181 1583 2652 2779 3836
a.gsf.c n.gsf v.rai.3s n.nsm n.nsm cj d.npm

μὲν πλείονές εἰσιν γεγονότες ἱερεῖς διὰ τὸ
⌊on the one hand,⌋ these many have become priests because ~ they were hindered
3525 3836 4498 1639 1181 2636 1328 3836 3266 3266 3266
pl a.npm.c v.pai.3p pt.ra.npm n.npm p.a d.asn

θανάτῳ κωλύεσθαι ← παραμένειν· 24 ὁ δὲ
by death *they were hindered* from ⌊continuing in office,⌋ *Jesus* ⌊but on the other hand,⌋ Jesus,
2505 3266 4169 3836 1254 3836
n.dsm f.pp f.pa d.nsm cj

διὰ τὸ μένειν αὐτὸν εἰς τὸν αἰῶνα ἀπαράβατον ἔχει
because ~ he remains *he* for all time, has a priesthood that is permanent. *has*
1328 3836 899 3531 899 1650 3836 172 2400 2648 563 2400
p.a d.asn f.pa r.asm.3 p.a d.asm n.asm a.asf v.pai.3s

τὴν ἱερωσύνην· 25 ⌊ὅθεν καὶ⌋ σῴζειν ⌊εἰς τὸ παντελὲς⌋
{the} priesthood Consequently, he is able to save completely
3836 2648 3854 2779 1538 1538 1538 5392 1650 3836 4117
d.asf n.asf cj adv f.pa p.a d.asn a.asn

δύναται τοὺς προσερχομένους δι' αὐτοῦ τῷ θεῷ, ↱ ↱ πάντοτε
he is able those who draw near to God through him, *to God* because he continually
1538 3836 4665 3836 2536 1328 899 3836 2536 2409 2409 4121
v.ppi.3s d.apm pt.pm.apm p.g r.gsm.3 d.dsm n.dsm adv

ζῶν εἰς τὸ ἐντυγχάνειν ὑπὲρ αὐτῶν. 26 τοιοῦτος γὰρ
lives to ~ intercede for them. For such *For* a high priest was
2409 1650 3836 1961 5642 899 1142 5525 1142 797 797 4560
pt.pa.nsm p.a d.asn f.pa p.g r.gpm.3 r.nsm cj

ἡμῖν καὶ ἔπρεπεν ἀρχιερεύς, ὅσιος ἄκακος ἀμίαντος,
appropriate for us, *{also} was appropriate high priest* ⌊one who is holy,⌋ innocent, undefiled;
4560 7005 2779 4560 797 4008 179 299
r.dp.1 adv v.iai.3s n.nsm a.nsm a.nsm a.nsm

κεχωρισμένος ἀπὸ τῶν ἁμαρτωλῶν καὶ ὑψηλότερος τῶν οὐρανῶν
having been separated from *{the}* sinners, *{and}* he became exalted above the heavens.
6004 608 3836 283 2779 1181 1181 5734 3836 4041
pt.rp.nsm p.g d.gpm a.gpm cj a.nsm.c d.gpm n.gpm

γενόμενος, 27 ὃς οὐκ ἔχει ⌊καθ' ἡμέραν⌋ ἀνάγκην,
he became He has no *has* need to offer up daily *need* sacrifices,
1181 4005 2400 4024 2400 340 429 429 429 2848 2465 340 2602
pt.am.nsm r.nsm pl v.pai.3s p.a n.asf n.asf

ὥσπερ οἱ ἀρχιερεῖς, πρότερον ὑπὲρ τῶν ἰδίων ἁμαρτιῶν θυσίας ἀναφέρειν
like those other high priests, first for *{the}* their own sins *sacrifices to offer up*
6061 3836 797 4728 5642 3836 2625 281 2602 429
pl d.npm n.npm adv.c p.g d.gpf a.gpf n.gpf n.apf f.pa

ἔπειτα τῶν τοῦ λαοῦ· τοῦτο γὰρ ἐποίησεν ἐφάπαξ
and then for the sins of the people, for this *for* he did ⌊once for all⌋ when he offered up
2083 3836 3836 3295 1142 4047 1142 4472 2384 429 429 429 429
adv d.gpf d.gsm n.gsm r.asn cj v.aai.3s adv

NASB

an oath [21](for they
indeed became
priests without an
oath, but He with
an oath through
the One who said
to Him,
"THE LORD HAS
SWORN
AND WILL NOT
CHANGE HIS
MIND,
[21]'YOU ARE A
PRIEST FOR-
EVER'");
[22]so much the more
also Jesus has
become the guar-
antee of a better
covenant.
[23]The *former*
priests, on the one
hand, existed in
greater numbers
because they were
prevented by death
from continuing,
[24]but Jesus, on the
other hand, be-
cause He continues
forever, holds His
priesthood perma-
nently. [25]Therefore
He is able also to
save forever those
who draw near to
God through Him,
since He always
lives to make inter-
cession for them.
[26]For it was fit-
ting for us to have
such a high priest,
holy, innocent, un-
defiled, separated
from sinners and
exalted above the
heavens; [27]who
does not need dai-
ly, like those high
priests, to offer up
sacrifices, first for
His own sins and
then for the *sins* of
the people, because
this He did once
for all when He

[a] 21 Psalm 110:4
[b] 25 Or *forever*

[a] κατὰ τὴν τάξιν Μελχισεδέκ included by TR after αἰῶνα.
[b] [καὶ] UBS, omitted by TNIV.

NIV

himself. [28]For the
law appoints as
high priests men in
all their weakness;
but the oath, which
came after the law,
appointed the Son,
who has been made
perfect forever.

The High Priest of a New Covenant

8 Now the main
point of what
we are saying is
this: We do have
such a high priest,
who sat down at
the right hand of
the throne of the
Majesty in heaven,
[2]and who serves in
the sanctuary, the
true tabernacle set
up by the Lord, not
by a mere human
being.
[3]Every high
priest is appointed
to offer both gifts
and sacrifices, and
so it was neces-
sary for this one
also to have some-
thing to offer. [4]If
he were on earth,
he would not be
a priest, for there
are already priests
who offer the gifts
prescribed by the
law. [5]They serve at
a sanctuary that is
a copy and shadow
of what is in heav-
en. This is why
Moses was warned
when he was about
to build the tab-
ernacle: "See to
it that you make
everything accord-
ing to the pattern
shown you on the
mountain."[a] [6]But
in fact

ἑαυτὸν ἀνενέγκας. 28 ὁ νόμος γὰρ ἀνθρώπους καθίστησιν
himself. *when he offered up* For the law *For* appoints men *appoints* as
1571 429 1142 3836 3795 1142 2770 476 2770
r.asm.3 pt.aa.nsm d.nsm n.nsm cj n.apm v.pai.3s

ἀρχιερεῖς ἔχοντας ἀσθένειαν, ὁ λόγος δὲ τῆς ὁρκωμοσίας τῆς
high priests who have weaknesses, but the word *but* of the oath, which came
797 2400 819 1254 3836 3364 1254 3836 3993 3836
n.apm pt.pa.apm n.asf d.nsm n.nsm cj d.gsf n.gsf d.gsf

μετὰ τὸν νόμον υἱὸν εἰς τὸν αἰῶνα
⌊later than⌋ the law, appoints the Son who has been made perfect for all time.
3552 3836 3795 5626 5457 5457 5457 5457 5457 1650 3836 172
p.a d.asm n.asm n.asm p.a d.asm n.asm

τετελειωμένον.
who has been made perfect
5457
pt.rp.asm

8:1 κεφάλαιον δὲ ἐπὶ τοῖς λεγομένοις,
Now the crowning affirmation *Now* to what we are saying is this: we do have
1254 3049 1254 2093 3836 3306 2400 2400 2400
n.nsn cj p.d d.dpn pt.pp.dpn

τοιοῦτον ἔχομεν ἀρχιερέα, ὃς ἐκάθισεν ἐν δεξιᾷ τοῦ θρόνου τῆς
such *we do have* a high priest, who ⌊has taken his seat⌋ at the right hand of the throne of the
5525 2400 797 4005 2767 1877 1288 3836 2585 3836
r.asm v.pai.1p n.asm r.nsm v.aai.3s p.d a.dsf d.gsm n.gsm d.gsf

μεγαλωσύνης ἐν τοῖς οὐρανοῖς, 2 τῶν ἁγίων λειτουργὸς καὶ
Majesty in *{the}* heaven, an officiating priest of holy things *officiating priest* and
3488 1877 3836 4041 3313 3313 3836 41 3313 2779
n.gsf p.d d.dpm n.dpm d.gpn a.gpn n.nsm cj

τῆς σκηνῆς τῆς ἀληθινῆς, ἣν ἔπηξεν ὁ κύριος, οὐκ ἄνθρωπος.
of the true tabernacle *{the} true* which the Lord put up, *the Lord* not man.
3836 240 5008 3836 240 4005 3836 3261 4381 3836 3261 4024 476
d.gsf n.gsf d.gsf a.gsf r.asf v.aai.3s d.nsm n.nsm pl n.nsm

3 πᾶς γὰρ ἀρχιερεὺς εἰς τὸ προσφέρειν δῶρά τε καὶ θυσίας
For every *For* high priest is appointed to ~ offer both gifts *both* and sacrifices;
1142 4246 1142 797 2770 2770 1650 3836 4712 5445 1565 5445 2779 2602
a.nsm cj n.nsm p.a d.asn f.pa n.apn cj cj n.apf

καθίσταται· ὅθεν ἀναγκαῖον ἔχειν τι καὶ τοῦτον
is appointed so it was necessary for this high priest also to have something *also this*
2770 3854 338 4047 2779 2400 5516 2779 4047
v.ppi.3s cj a.nsn f.pa r.asn adv r.asm

ὃ προσενέγκῃ. 4 εἰ μὲν οὖν ἦν ἐπὶ γῆς, ↱ οὐδ᾽ ἂν ἦν
{that} to offer. So if ~ *So* ⌊he had been⌋ on earth, he would not *would* be a
4005 4712 4036 1623 3525 4036 1639 2093 1178 1639 323 4028 323 1639
r.asn v.aas.3s cj pl cj v.iai.3s p.g n.gsf adv pl v.iai.3s

ἱερεύς, ὄντων τῶν προσφερόντων κατὰ νόμον τὰ
priest, ⌊since there are already⌋ those who offer the gifts ⌊prescribed by⌋ the law. *the*
2636 1639 3836 4712 3836 1565 2848 3795 3836
n.nsm pt.pa.gpm d.gpm pt.pa.gpm p.a n.asm d.apn

δῶρα· 5 οἵτινες ὑποδείγματι καὶ σκιᾷ λατρεύουσιν
gifts The place where they serve is a shadowy suggestion *{and} shadowy serve*
1565 4015 3302 5014 5682 2779 5014 3302
n.apn r.npm n.dsn cj n.dsf v.pai.3p

τῶν ἐπουρανίων, καθὼς κεχρημάτισται Μωϋσῆς
of the heavenly sanctuary, just as Moses was warned *Moses* by God
3836 2230 2777 3707 5976 3707
d.gpn a.gpn cj v.rpi.3s n.nsm

μέλλων ἐπιτελεῖν τὴν σκηνήν, ὅρα γάρ φησιν, ποιήσεις
⌊when he was about⌋ to erect the tabernacle; for he said, "See *for he said* that you make
3516 2200 3836 5008 1142 5774 5774 3972 1142 5774 4472
pt.pa.nsm f.pa d.asf n.asf v.pam.2s cj v.pai.3s v.fai.2s

πάντα κατὰ τὸν τύπον τὸν δειχθέντα σοι ἐν τῷ ὄρει· 6 νῦν[a]
everything ⌊according to⌋ the pattern *{the}* shown you on the mountain." But as it is,
4246 2848 3836 5596 3836 1259 5148 1877 3836 4001 1254 3814
a.apn p.a d.asm n.asm d.asm pt.ap.asm r.ds.2 p.d d.dsn n.dsn adv

NASB

offered up Himself.
[28]For the Law
appoints men as
high priests who
are weak, but the
word of the oath,
which came after
the Law, *appoints* a
Son, made perfect
forever.

A Better Ministry

[8:1]Now the main
point in what has
been said *is this:*
we have such a
high priest, who
has taken His seat
at the right hand
of the throne of
the Majesty in
the heavens, [2]a
minister in the
sanctuary and in
the true tabernacle,
which the Lord
pitched, not man.
[3]For every high
priest is appointed
to offer both gifts
and sacrifices; so
it is necessary that
this *high priest* also
have something
to offer. [4]Now if
He were on earth,
He would not be a
priest at all, since
there are those who
offer the gifts ac-
cording to the Law;
[5]who serve a copy
and shadow of the
heavenly things,
just as Moses was
warned *by God*
when he was about
to erect the taber-
nacle; for, "SEE,"
He says, "THAT YOU
MAKE all things
ACCORDING TO THE
PATTERN WHICH WAS
SHOWN YOU ON THE
MOUNTAIN." [6]But

[a] 5 Exodus 25:40

[a] νῦν TNIV, NET. νυν[ί] UBS.

NIV

the ministry Jesus has received is as superior to theirs as the covenant of which he is mediator is superior to the old one, since the new covenant is established on better promises.
[7] For if there had been nothing wrong with that first covenant, no place would have been sought for another. [8] But God found fault with the people and said[a]:

"The days are coming,
declares the Lord,
when I will make a new covenant
with the people of Israel
and with the people of Judah.
[9] It will not be like the covenant
I made with their ancestors
when I took them by the hand
to lead them out of Egypt,
because they did not remain faithful to my covenant,
and I turned away from them,
declares the Lord.
[10] This is the covenant I will establish with the people of Israel
after that time, declares the Lord.
I will put my laws in their minds
and write them on their hearts.

[a] 8 Some manuscripts may be translated *fault and said to the people.*

δὲ διαφορωτέρας τέτυχεν λειτουργίας,
But he has obtained a superior *he has obtained* ministry, since the covenant
1254 5593 5593 5593 1427 5593 3311 1347
cj a.gsf.c v.rai.3s n.gsf

ὅσῳ καὶ κρείττονός ἐστιν διαθήκης μεσίτης, ἥτις
of which *{also}* he is mediator is better, *is* *covenant* *mediator* since it has been
4012 2779 3542 1639 3202 1639 1347 3542 4015 3793 3793
r.dsn adv a.gsf.c v.pai.3s n.gsf n.nsm r.nsf

ἐπὶ κρείττοσιν ἐπαγγελίαις νενομοθέτηται. [7] εἰ γὰρ ἡ
enacted ⌊on the basis of⌋ better promises. *has been enacted* For if *For* *{the}* that
3793 2093 3202 2039 3793 1142 1623 1142 3836 1697
p.d a.dpf.c n.dpf v.rpi.3s cj cj d.nsf

πρώτη ἐκείνη ἦν ἄμεμπτος, οὐκ ἂν →
first *that* covenant ⌊had been⌋ blameless, then no occasion would have been sought for a
4755 1697 1639 289 4024 5536 323 2426 2426 2426
a.nsf r.nsf v.iai.3s a.nsf pl pl

δευτέρας ἐζητεῖτο τόπος. [8] μεμφόμενος γὰρ αὐτοὺς[a] λέγει,
second. *have been sought* *occasion* For finding fault, *For* God says to them, *says*
1311 2426 5536 1142 3522 1142 3306 899 3306
a.gsf v.ipi.3s n.nsm pt.pm.nsm cj r.apm.3 v.pai.3s

ἰδοὺ ἡμέραι ἔρχονται, λέγει κύριος, καὶ συντελέσω ἐπὶ τὸν
"Behold, days are coming, declares the Lord, when I will establish a new covenant with the
2627 2465 2262 3306 3261 2779 5334 2785 1347 2093 3836
j n.npf v.pmi.3p v.pai.3s n.nsm cj v.fai.1s p.a d.asm

οἶκον Ἰσραὴλ καὶ ἐπὶ τὸν οἶκον Ἰούδα διαθήκην καινήν, [9] οὐ κατὰ τὴν
house of Israel and with the house of Judah. *covenant* *new* It will not be like the
3875 2702 2779 2093 3836 3875 2683 1347 2785 4024 2848 3836
n.asm n.gsm cj p.a d.asm n.asm n.gsm n.asf a.asf pl p.a d.asf

διαθήκην, ἣν ἐποίησα τοῖς πατράσιν αὐτῶν ἐν ἡμέρᾳ →
covenant that I made with their fathers *their* on the day when I
1347 4005 4472 3836 899 4252 899 1877 2465 1609
n.asf r.asf v.aai.1s d.dpm n.dpm r.gpm.3 p.d n.dsf

ἐπιλαβομένου ← μου τῆς χειρὸς αὐτῶν ἐξαγαγεῖν αὐτοὺς ἐκ γῆς
took them by *I* the hand *them* to bring them ⌊out of⌋ the land
2138 899 1609 3836 5931 899 1974 899 1666 1178
pt.am.gsm r.gs.1 d.gsf n.gsf r.gpm.3 f.aa r.apm.3 p.g n.gsf

Αἰγύπτου, ὅτι αὐτοὶ ↱ οὐκ ἐνέμειναν ἐν τῇ διαθήκῃ μου, κἀγὼ ἠμέλησα
of Egypt, because they did not continue in *{the}* my covenant *my* and I abandoned
131 4022 899 1844 4024 1844 1877 3836 1609 1347 1609 2743 288
n.gsf cj r.npm pl v.aai.3p p.d d.dsf n.dsf r.gs.1 crasis v.aai.1s

αὐτῶν, λέγει κύριος· [10] ὅτι αὕτη ἡ διαθήκη, ἣν διαθήσομαι τῷ οἴκῳ
them, says the Lord. For this is the covenant that I will establish ⌊with the⌋ house
899 3306 3261 4022 4047 3836 1347 4005 1416 3836 3875
r.gpm.3 v.pai.3s n.nsm cj r.nsf d.nsf n.nsf r.asf v.fmi.1s d.dsm n.dsm

Ἰσραὴλ μετὰ τὰς ἡμέρας ἐκείνας, λέγει κύριος, διδοὺς νόμους μου
of Israel after *{the}* those days, *those* declares the Lord: I will put my laws *my*
2702 3552 3836 1697 2465 1697 3306 3261 1443 1609 3795 1609
n.gsm p.a d.apf n.apf r.apf v.pai.3s n.nsm pt.pa.nsm n.apm r.gs.1

εἰς τὴν διάνοιαν αὐτῶν καὶ ἐπὶ καρδίας αὐτῶν
in *{the}* their minds *their* and I will inscribe them on their hearts. *their*
1650 3836 899 1379 899 2779 2108 2108 2108 899 2093 899 2840 899
p.a d.asf n.asf r.gpm.3 cj p.a n.apf r.gpm.3

[a] αὐτοὺς UBS, TNIV. αὐτοῖς NET.

NASB

now He has obtained a more excellent ministry, by as much as He is also the mediator of a better covenant, which has been enacted on better promises.

A New Covenant

[7] For if that first *covenant* had been faultless, there would have been no occasion sought for a second. [8] For finding fault with them, He says,
"BEHOLD, DAYS ARE COMING, SAYS THE LORD,
WHEN I WILL EFFECT A NEW COVENANT
WITH THE HOUSE OF ISRAEL AND WITH THE HOUSE OF JUDAH;
[9] NOT LIKE THE COVENANT WHICH I MADE WITH THEIR FATHERS
ON THE DAY WHEN I TOOK THEM BY THE HAND
TO LEAD THEM OUT OF THE LAND OF EGYPT;
FOR THEY DID NOT CONTINUE IN MY COVENANT,
AND I DID NOT CARE FOR THEM, SAYS THE LORD.
[10] "FOR THIS IS THE COVENANT THAT I WILL MAKE WITH THE HOUSE OF ISRAEL
AFTER THOSE DAYS, SAYS THE LORD:
I WILL PUT MY LAWS INTO THEIR MINDS,
AND I WILL WRITE THEM ON THEIR HEARTS.

NIV

I will be their
God,
and they will be
my people.
11 No longer will
they teach
their
neighbor,
or say to one
another,
'Know the
Lord,'
because they will
all know me,
from the least
of them to
the greatest.
12 For I will forgive
their
wickedness
and will
remember
their sins no
more."[a]

13 By calling this
covenant "new," he
has made the first
one obsolete; and
what is obsolete
and outdated will
soon disappear.

Worship in the Earthly Tabernacle

9 Now the first
covenant had
regulations for
worship and also
an earthly sanctu-
ary. 2 A tabernacle
was set up. In its
first room were
the lampstand and
the table with its
consecrated bread;
this was called the
Holy Place. 3 Be-
hind the second
curtain was a room
called the Most
Holy Place, 4 which
had the golden al-
tar of incense and
the gold-covered
ark of the cov-
enant. This ark
contained the gold
jar of manna, Aar-
on's staff that had
budded, and the
stone tablets of the
covenant.

ἐπιγράψω αὐτούς, καὶ ἔσομαι αὐτοῖς εἰς θεόν, καὶ αὐτοὶ ἔσονταί μοι εἰς λαόν·
I will inscribe them *{and}* I will be their *{for}* God and they will be my *{for}* people.
2108 899 2779 1639 899 1650 2536 2779 899 1639 1609 1650 3295
v.fai.1s r.apm.3 cj v.fmi.1s r.dpm.3 p.a n.asm cj r.npm v.fmi.3p r.ds.1 p.a n.asm

11 καὶ ↱ ↱ ⌞οὐ μὴ⌟ διδάξωσιν ἕκαστος τὸν πολίτην αὐτοῦ καὶ ἕκαστος τὸν
And they will not teach each one *{the}* his neighbor *his* and each one *{the}*
2779 1438 1438 4024 3590 1438 1667 3836 899 4489 899 2779 1667 3836
cj pl pl v.aas.3p r.nsm d.asm n.asm r.gsm.3 cj r.nsm d.asm

ἀδελφὸν αὐτοῦ λέγων, γνῶθι τὸν κύριον, ὅτι ↱ ↱ πάντες εἰδήσουσίν με
his brother *his* saying, 'Know the Lord,' for they will all know me
899 81 899 3306 1182 3836 3261 4022 3857 3857 4246 3857 1609
n.asm r.gsm.3 pt.pa.nsm v.aam.2s d.asm n.asm cj a.npm v.fai.3p r.as.1

ἀπὸ μικροῦ ἕως μεγάλου αὐτῶν, 12 ὅτι ἵλεως ἔσομαι
from the least of them to the greatest. *of them* For I will be gracious *I will be*
608 3625 899 899 2401 3489 899 4022 1639 1639 1639 2664 1639
p.g a.gsm p.g a.gsm r.gpm.3 cj a.nsm v.fmi.1s

ταῖς ἀδικίαις αὐτῶν καὶ τῶν ἁμαρτιῶν αὐτῶν
toward their iniquities *their* and I will never again remember *{the}* their sins." *their*
3836 899 94 899 2779 3630 3630 4024 2285 3630 3836 899 281 899
d.dpf n.dpf r.gpm.3 cj d.gpf n.gpf r.gpm.3

⌞οὐ μὴ⌟ μνησθῶ ἔτι. 13 ἐν τῷ λέγειν καινὴν → →
never I will remember again In ~ speaking of a new covenant, he makes the first
4024 3590 3630 2285 1877 3836 3306 2785 3836 4755
pl pl v.aps.1s adv p.d d.dsn f.pa a.asf

πεπαλαίωκεν τὴν πρώτην· τὸ δὲ παλαιούμενον καὶ γηράσκον ἐγγὺς
one obsolete. *the first one* And what *And* is becoming obsolete and growing old is ready
4755 4096 3836 4755 1254 3836 1254 4096 2779 1180 1584
v.rai.3s d.asf a.asf d.nsn cj pt.pp.nsn cj pt.pa.nsn p.g

ἀφανισμοῦ.
to disappear.
907
n.gsm

9:1 εἶχε μὲν οὖν καὶ[a] ἡ πρώτη δικαιώματα λατρείας
had ~ Now the first covenant, in fact, *the first* had regulations for worship
2400 3525 4036 3836 4755 2779 3836 4755 2400 1468 3301
v.iai.3s pl cj adv d.nsf a.nsf n.apn n.gsf

τό τε ἅγιον κοσμικόν. 2 σκηνὴ γὰρ κατεσκευάσθη ἡ
{the} and also an earthly sanctuary. *earthly* For a tent *For* was set up. The
3836 5445 3176 41 3176 1142 5008 1142 2941 3836
d.asn cj a.asn a.asn n.nsf cj v.api.3s d.nsf

πρώτη ἐν ᾗ ἥ τε λυχνία καὶ ἡ τράπεζα καὶ ἡ πρόθεσις τῶν
outer room, in which were the ~ lampstand and the table and the consecrated *{the}*
4755 1877 4005 3836 5445 3393 2779 3836 5544 2779 3836 4606 3836
a.nsf p.d r.dsf d.nsf cj n.nsf cj d.nsf n.nsf cj d.nsf n.nsf d.gpm

ἄρτων, ἥτις λέγεται Ἅγια· 3 μετὰ δὲ τὸ δεύτερον
bread, *{which}* was called "the Holy Place." Behind *{and}* the curtain was a second room,
788 4015 3306 41 3552 1254 3836 2925 1311
n.gpm r.nsf v.ppi.3s a.npn p.a cj d.asn a.asn

καταπέτασμα σκηνὴ ἡ λεγομένη ⌞Ἅγια Ἁγίων,⌟ 4
curtain a shrine *{the}* called "the Most Holy Place." It contained the
2925 5008 3836 3306 41 41 2400 2400
n.asn n.nsf d.nsf pt.pp.nsf a.npn a.gpn

χρυσοῦν ἔχουσα θυμιατήριον καὶ τὴν κιβωτὸν τῆς διαθήκης περικεκαλυμμένην
golden *It contained* altar of incense and the ark of the covenant covered
5997 2400 2593 2779 3836 3066 3836 1347 4328
a.asn pt.pa.nsf n.asn cj d.asf n.asf d.gsf n.gsf pt.rp.asf

πάντοθεν χρυσίῳ, ἐν ᾗ στάμνος χρυσῆ ἔχουσα τὸ μάννα καὶ
on all sides with gold, in which were the golden urn *golden* containing the manna, *{and}*
4119 5992 1877 4005 5997 5085 5997 2400 3836 3445 2779
adv n.dsn p.d r.dsf n.nsf a.nsf pt.pa.nsf d.asn n.asn cj

ἡ ῥάβδος Ἀαρὼν ἡ βλαστήσασα καὶ αἱ πλάκες τῆς διαθήκης,
{the} Aaron's rod *Aaron's* that had budded, and the stone tablets of the covenant.
3836 2 4811 2 3836 1056 2779 3836 4419 3836 1347
d.nsf n.nsf n.gsm d.nsf pt.aa.nsf cj d.npf n.npf d.gsf n.gsf

NASB

AND I WILL BE
THEIR GOD,
AND THEY
SHALL BE MY
PEOPLE.
11 "AND THEY
SHALL NOT
TEACH EVERY-
ONE HIS FEL-
LOW CITIZEN,
AND EVERYONE
HIS BROTHER,
SAYING,
'KNOW THE
LORD,'
FOR ALL WILL
KNOW ME,
FROM THE
LEAST TO THE
GREATEST OF
THEM.
12 "FOR I WILL BE
MERCIFUL TO
THEIR INIQUI-
TIES,
AND I WILL
REMEMBER
THEIR SINS NO
MORE."
13 When He said, "A
new *covenant,*" He
has made the first
obsolete. But what-
ever is becoming
obsolete and grow-
ing old is ready to
disappear.

The Old and the New

9:1 Now even the
first *covenant* had
regulations of di-
vine worship and
the earthly sanc-
tuary. 2 For there
was a tabernacle
prepared, the outer
one, in which *were*
the lampstand and
the table and the
sacred bread; this
is called the holy
place. 3 Behind the
second veil there
was a tabernacle
which is called the
Holy of Holies,
4 having a golden
altar of incense
and the ark of the
covenant covered
on all sides with
gold, in which was
a golden jar hold-
ing the manna, and
Aaron's rod which
budded, and the
tables of the cov-
enant;

[a] 12 Jer. 31:31-34

[a] [καὶ] UBS.

NIV

⁵Above the ark
were the cheru-
bim of the Glory,
overshadowing the
atonement cover.
But we cannot dis-
cuss these things in
detail now.
⁶When every-
thing had been
arranged like this,
the priests entered
regularly into the
outer room to car-
ry on their minis-
try. ⁷But only the
high priest entered
the inner room,
and that only once
a year, and nev-
er without blood,
which he offered
for himself and for
the sins the people
had committed in
ignorance. ⁸The
Holy Spirit was
showing by this
that the way into
the Most Holy
Place had not yet
been disclosed as
long as the first
tabernacle was
still functioning.
⁹This is an illustra-
tion for the present
time, indicating
that the gifts and
sacrifices being
offered were not
able to clear the
conscience of the
worshiper. ¹⁰They
are only a mat-
ter of food and
drink and various
ceremonial wash-
ings—external
regulations apply-
ing until the time
of the new order.

The Blood of Christ

¹¹But when Christ
came as high
priest of the good
things that are now
already here,[a] he
went through the
greater and more
perfect

[a] *11* Some early manuscripts *are to come*

⁵ ὑπεράνω δὲ αὐτῆς χερουβὶν δόξης κατασκιάζοντα τὸ ἱλαστήριον·
Above *{and}* it were the cherubim of glory overshadowing the place of forgiveness.
5645 1254 899 5938 1518 2944 3836 2663
p.g cj r.gsf.3 n.npn n.gsf pt.pa.npn d.asn n.asn

περὶ ὧν ˻οὐκ ἔστιν˼ νῦν λέγειν κατὰ μέρος. ⁶ τούτων δὲ
Of ˻these things˼ we cannot now speak in detail. When these things *{and}* had
4309 4005 4024 1639 3814 3306 2848 3538 2941 4047 1254 2941
p.g r.gpn pl v.pai.3s adv f.pa p.a n.asn r.gpn cj

οὕτως κατεσκευασμένων εἰς μὲν
been prepared ˻in this way,˼ *When had been prepared* the priests used to enter regularly into ~
2941 2941 4048 2941 3836 2636 1655 1655 1655 1328 1650 3525
adv pt.rp.gpn p.a pl

τὴν πρώτην σκηνὴν ˻διὰ παντὸς˼ εἰσίασιν οἱ ἱερεῖς τὰς
the outer room *regularly* *used to enter* *the* *priests* to perform their
3836 4755 5008 1328 4246 1655 3836 2636 2200 2200 3836
d.asf a.asf n.asf p.g a.gsn v.pai.3p d.npm n.npm d.apf

λατρείας ἐπιτελοῦντες, ⁷ εἰς δὲ τὴν δευτέραν ἅπαξ τοῦ
ritual services; *to perform* however into *however* the second room *once* *{the}*
3301 2200 1254 1650 1254 3836 1311 562 3836
n.apf pt.pa.npm p.a cj d.asf a.asf adv d.gsm

ἐνιαυτοῦ μόνος ὁ ἀρχιερεύς, οὐ χωρὶς
year only the high priest entered, and that only once a year, and not without taking
1929 3668 3836 797 562 1929 4024 6006
n.gsm a.nsm d.nsm n.nsm pl p.g

αἵματος ὃ προσφέρει ὑπὲρ ἑαυτοῦ καὶ τῶν τοῦ
blood, which he offered for himself and for the sins committed unintentionally by the
135 4005 4712 5642 1571 2779 3836 52 52 52 3836
n.gsn r.asn v.pai.3s p.g r.gsm.3 cj d.gpn d.gsm

λαοῦ ἀγνοημάτων, ⁸ τοῦτο δηλοῦντος τοῦ πνεύματος τοῦ
people. *sins committed unintentionally* By this the Holy Spirit is showing *the* *Spirit* *{the}*
3295 52 4047 3836 41 4460 1317 3836 4460 3836
n.gsm n.gpn r.asn pt.pa.gsn d.gsn n.gsn d.gsn

ἁγίου, ↱ μήπω πεφανερῶσθαι τὴν τῶν ἁγίων
Holy that the way into the real sanctuary had not yet been disclosed *the* *the* *sanctuary*
41 3836 3847 3836 41 5746 3609 5746 3836 3836 41
a.gsn adv f.rp d.asf d.gpn a.gpn

ὁδὸν ἔτι τῆς πρώτης σκηνῆς ἐχούσης στάσιν, ⁹ ἥτις παραβολὴ εἰς
way ˻as long as˼ the first tent was standing. This is an illustration ˻pointing to˼
3847 2285 3836 4755 5008 2400 5087 4015 4130 1650
n.asf adv d.gsf a.gsf n.gsf pt.pa.gsf n.asf r.nsf n.nsf p.a

τὸν καιρὸν τὸν ἐνεστηκότα, καθ' ἣν δῶρά τε καὶ θυσίαι
the present time, *{the}* *present* during which the gifts ~ and sacrifices
3836 1931 2789 3836 1931 2848 4005 1565 5445 2779 2602
d.asm n.asm d.asm pt.ra.asm p.a r.asf n.npn cj cj n.npf

προσφέρονται ˻μὴ δυνάμεναι˼ κατὰ συνείδησιν
being offered cannot perfect the worshiper ˻so far as˼ his conscience is
4712 3590 1538 5457 3836 3302 2848 5287
v.ppi.3p pl pt.pp.npf p.a n.asf

τελειῶσαι τὸν λατρεύοντα, ¹⁰ μόνον ἐπὶ βρώμασιν καὶ πόμασιν καὶ
concerned, *perfect* *the* *worshiper* but deal only with food and drink and
5457 3836 3302 3667 2093 1109 2779 4503 2779
f.aa d.asm pt.pa.asm adv p.d n.dpn cj n.dpn cj

διαφόροις βαπτισμοῖς, δικαιώματα → σαρκὸς μέχρι καιροῦ
various ceremonial washings, regulations for the body imposed until the time
1427 968 1468 4922 2130 3588 2789
a.dpm n.dpm n.npn n.gsf p.g n.gsm

διορθώσεως ἐπικείμενα. ¹¹ ↱ Χριστὸς δὲ παραγενόμενος ἀρχιερεὺς τῶν
of correction. *imposed* But when Christ *But* appeared as high priest of the
1481 2130 1254 4134 5986 1254 4134 797 3836
n.gsf pt.pm.npn n.nsm cj pt.am.nsm n.nsm d.gpn

γενομένων[a] ἀγαθῶν διὰ τῆς μείζονος καὶ τελειοτέρας
good things ˻that have now come,˼ *good things* passing through the greater and more perfect
19 19 1181 19 1328 3836 3489 2779 5455
pt.am.gpn a.gpn p.g d.gsf a.gsf.c cj a.gsf.c

[a] μελλόντων included by TR after γενομένων.

NASB

⁵and above it *were*
the cherubim of
glory overshadow-
ing the mercy seat;
but of these things
we cannot now
speak in detail.
⁶Now when these
things have been
so prepared, the
priests are continu-
ally entering the
outer tabernacle
performing the di-
vine worship, ⁷but
into the second,
only the high priest
enters once a year,
not without *taking*
blood, which he
offers for himself
and for the sins of
the people commit-
ted in ignorance.
⁸The Holy Spirit *is*
signifying this, that
the way into the
holy place has not
yet been disclosed
while the outer
tabernacle is still
standing, ⁹which
is a symbol for the
present time. Ac-
cordingly both gifts
and sacrifices are
offered which can-
not make the wor-
shiper perfect in
conscience, ¹⁰since
they *relate* only to
food and drink and
various washings,
regulations for the
body imposed until
a time of reforma-
tion.
¹¹But when Christ
appeared *as* a high
priest of the good
things [a]to come, *He*
entered through the
greater and more
perfect

[a] Two early mss read *that have come*

NIV

tabernacle that is not made with human hands, that is to say, is not a part of this creation. 12He did not enter by means of the blood of goats and calves; but he entered the Most Holy Place once for all by his own blood, thus obtaining[a] eternal redemption. 13The blood of goats and bulls and the ashes of a heifer sprinkled on those who are ceremonially unclean sanctify them so that they are outwardly clean. 14How much more, then, will the blood of Christ, who through the eternal Spirit offered himself unblemished to God, cleanse our consciences from acts that lead to death,[b] so that we may serve the living God!

15For this reason Christ is the mediator of a new covenant, that those who are called may receive the promised eternal inheritance—now that he has died as a ransom to set them free from the sins committed under the first covenant.

16In the case of a will,[c] it is necessary to prove the death of the one who made it, 17because a will is in force only when

σκηνῆς οὐ χειροποιήτου, τοῦτ᾽ ἔστιν οὐ ταύτης τῆς κτίσεως, 12
tent (not made with hands, that is, not of this *of* creation), he entered
5008 4024 5935 4047 1639 4024 3836 4047 3836 3232 1656 1656
n.gsf pl a.gsf r.nsn v.pai.3s pl r.gsf d.gsf n.gsf

οὐδὲ δι᾽ αἵματος τράγων καὶ
once for all into the Most Holy Place, not ⌊by means of⌋ the blood of goats and
2384 2384 2384 1650 3836 41 41 41 4028 1328 135 5543 2779
cj p.g n.gsn n.gpm cj

μόσχων διὰ δὲ τοῦ ἰδίου αἵματος εἰσῆλθεν ἐφάπαξ εἰς τὰ
calves, but ⌊by means of⌋ *but* *{the}* his own blood, *he entered* *once for all* *into* *the*
3675 1254 1328 1254 3836 2625 135 1656 2384 1650 3836
n.gpm p.g cj d.gsn a.gsn n.gsn v.aai.3s adv p.a d.apn

ἅγια αἰωνίαν λύτρωσιν εὑράμενος. 13 εἰ γὰρ τὸ αἷμα
Most Holy Place thus obtaining an eternal redemption. *thus obtaining* For if *For* the blood
41 2351 2351 173 3391 2351 1142 1623 1142 3836 135
a.apn a.asf n.asf pt.am.nsm cj cj d.nsn n.nsn

τράγων καὶ ταύρων καὶ σποδὸς → δαμάλεως ῥαντίζουσα τοὺς
of goats and bulls, and the sprinkled ashes of a heifer, *sprinkled* sanctify those
5543 2779 5436 2779 4822 5075 1239 4822 39 3836
n.gpm cj n.gpm cj n.nsf n.gsf pt.pa.nsf d.apm

κεκοινωμένους ἁγιάζει πρὸς τὴν τῆς σαρκὸς καθαρότητα,
⌊who have been ceremonially defiled⌋ *sanctify* so that *{the}* their flesh is purified,
3124 39 4639 3836 3836 4922 2755
pt.rp.apm v.pai.3s p.a d.asf d.gsf n.gsf n.asf

14 πόσῳ μᾶλλον ↱ τὸ αἷμα τοῦ Χριστοῦ, ὃς διὰ πνεύματος
how much more will the blood of Christ, who through the eternal Spirit
4531 3437 2751 3836 135 3836 5986 4005 1328 173 4460
r.dsn adv.c d.nsn n.nsn d.gsm n.gsm r.nsm p.g n.gsn

αἰωνίου ἑαυτὸν προσήνεγκεν ἄμωμον τῷ θεῷ, καθαριεῖ τὴν
eternal offered himself *offered* without blemish to God, purify *{the}* our
173 4712 1571 4712 320 3836 2536 2751 3836 7005
a.gsn r.asm.3 v.aai.3s a.asm d.dsm n.dsm v.fai.3s d.asf

συνείδησιν ἡμῶν ἀπὸ νεκρῶν ἔργων εἰς τὸ λατρεύειν θεῷ ζῶντι. 15 καὶ
conscience *our* from dead works to ~ worship the living God! *living* And
5287 7005 608 3738 2240 1650 3836 3302 2409 2536 2409 2779
n.asf r.gp.1 p.g a.gpn n.gpn p.a d.asn f.pa n.dsm pt.pa.dsm cj

διὰ τοῦτο → διαθήκης καινῆς μεσίτης ἐστίν, ὅπως
for this reason he is the mediator of a new covenant, *new* *mediator* *he is* so that those
1328 4047 1639 1639 3542 2785 1347 2785 3542 1639 3968 3836
p.a r.asn n.gsf a.gsf n.nsm v.pai.3s cj

↱ θανάτου γενομένου εἰς
who are called may receive the promised eternal inheritance, since a death has occurred that
2813 2813 2813 3284 3284 3836 2039 173 3100 1181 2505 1181 1650
n.gsm pt.am.gsm p.a

ἀπολύτρωσιν τῶν ἐπὶ τῇ πρώτῃ διαθήκῃ
redeems them ⌊from the⌋ transgressions committed under that first covenant.
667 3836 4126 2093 3836 4755 1347
n.asf d.gpf p.d d.dsf a.dsf n.dsf

παραβάσεων τὴν ἐπαγγελίαν λάβωσιν οἱ κεκλημένοι τῆς αἰωνίου κληρονομίας.
transgressions *the* *promised* *may receive* *those* *who are called* *{the}* *eternal* *inheritance*
4126 3836 2039 3284 3836 2813 3836 173 3100
n.gpf d.asf n.asf v.aas.3p d.npm pt.rp.npm d.gsf a.gsf n.gsf

16 ὅπου γὰρ διαθήκη, θάνατον ἀνάγκη
For where *For* there is a covenant, it is required that the death *it is required* of the
1142 3963 1142 1347 340 340 340 2505 340 3836 3836
cj cj n.nsf n.asm n.nsf

φέρεσθαι τοῦ διαθεμένου· 17 διαθήκη γὰρ
one who made it be established. *of the* *one who made* For a will *For* takes effect
1416 1416 1416 5770 3836 1416 1142 1347 1142 1010 1010
f.pp d.gsm pt.am.gsm n.nsf cj

ἐπὶ νεκροῖς βεβαία, ⌊ἐπεὶ μήποτε⌋ ἰσχύει ὅτε
⌊only when⌋ a ⌊person has died;⌋ *takes effect* it cannot possibly be valid ⌊so long as⌋ the
2093 3738 1010 2075 3607 2710 4021 3836
p.d a.dpm a.nsf cj pl v.pai.3s cj

NASB

tabernacle, not made with hands, that is to say, not of this creation; 12and not through the blood of goats and calves, but through His own blood, He entered the holy place once for all, having obtained eternal redemption. 13For if the blood of goats and bulls and the ashes of a heifer sprinkling those who have been defiled sanctify for the cleansing of the flesh, 14how much more will the blood of Christ, who through the eternal Spirit offered Himself without blemish to God, cleanse your conscience from dead works to serve the living God?

15For this reason He is the mediator of a new covenant, so that, since a death has taken place for the redemption of the transgressions that were *committed* under the first covenant, those who have been called may receive the promise of the eternal inheritance. 16For where a covenant is, there must of necessity be the death of the one who made it. 17For a covenant is valid *only* when men are dead, [a]for it is never in force

[a] 12 Or *blood, having obtained*
[b] 14 Or *from useless rituals*
[c] 16 Same Greek word as *covenant*; also in verse 17

[a] Two early mss read *for is it then... lives?*

NIV

somebody has
died; it never takes
effect while the one
who made it is liv-
ing. [18]This is why
even the first cov-
enant was not put
into effect without
blood. [19]When Mo-
ses had proclaimed
every command of
the law to all the
people, he took the
blood of calves, to-
gether with water,
scarlet wool and
branches of hys-
sop, and sprinkled
the scroll and all
the people. [20]He
said, "This is the
blood of the cov-
enant, which God
has commanded
you to keep."[a]
[21]In the same way,
he sprinkled with
the blood both the
tabernacle and
everything used
in its ceremo-
nies. [22]In fact, the
law requires that
nearly everything
be cleansed with
blood, and without
the shedding of
blood there is no
forgiveness.
[23]It was neces-
sary, then, for
the copies of the
heavenly things to
be purified with
these sacrifices,
but the heavenly
things themselves
with better sacri-
fices than these.
[24]For Christ did
not enter a sanc-
tuary made with
human hands that
was only a copy
of the true one; he
entered heaven it-
self, now to appear
for us in God's
presence. [25]Nor did
he enter heaven to
offer himself again
and again,

ζῇ ὁ διαθέμενος. 18 ὅθεν οὐδὲ ἡ πρώτη
one who made it ⌞is still alive.⌟ *the* *one who made* Therefore not even the first covenant
1416 1416 1416 2409 3836 1416 3854 4028 3836 4755
v.pai.3s d.nsm pt.am.nsm cj adv d.nsf a.nsf

χωρὶς αἵματος ἐγκεκαίνισται· 19 λαληθείσης γὰρ πάσης
was inaugurated without blood. *was inaugurated* *when had been declared* For when every
1590 1590 6006 135 1590 3281 1142 3281 4246
p.g n.gsn v.rpi.3s pt.ap.gsf cj a.gsf

ἐντολῆς κατὰ τὸν νόμον ὑπὸ Μωϋσέως παντὶ τῷ λαῷ, λαβὼν
commandment of the law had been declared by Moses to all the people, taking
1953 2848 3836 3795 3281 3281 3281 5679 3707 4246 3836 3295 3284
n.gsf p.a d.asm n.asm p.g n.gsm a.dsm d.dsm n.dsm pt.aa.nsm

τὸ αἷμα τῶν μόσχων [a]καὶ τῶν τράγων μετὰ ὕδατος καὶ ἐρίου
the blood of calves and *{the}* goats ⌞together with⌟ water and scarlet wool
3836 135 3836 3675 2779 3836 5543 3552 5623 2779 3132 2250
d.asn n.asn d.gpm n.gpm cj d.gpm n.gpm p.g n.gsn cj n.gsn

κοκκίνου καὶ ὑσσώπου αὐτό τε τὸ βιβλίον καὶ πάντα
scarlet and hyssop, he sprinkled both the book itself *both* *the* *book* and all
3132 2779 5727 4822 4822 5445 3836 1046 899 5445 3836 1046 2779 4246
a.gsn cj n.gsf r.asn cj d.asn n.asn cj a.asm

τὸν λαὸν ἐρράντισεν 20 λέγων, τοῦτο τὸ αἷμα τῆς διαθήκης ἧς
the people, *he sprinkled* saying, "This is the blood of the covenant which God
3836 3295 4822 3306 4047 3836 135 3836 1347 4005 2536
d.asm n.asm v.aai.3s pt.pa.nsm r.nsn d.nsn n.nsn d.gsf n.gsf r.gsf

ἐνετείλατο πρὸς ὑμᾶς ὁ θεός. 21 καὶ
ordained for you." *{the}* *God* And in the same way he sprinkled with blood both
1948 4639 7007 3836 2536 1254 3931 3931 3931 3931 4822 4822 3836 135 2779
v.ami.3s p.a r.ap.2 d.nsm n.nsm cj

τὴν σκηνὴν δὲ καὶ πάντα τὰ σκεύη τῆς λειτουργίας τῷ αἵματι ὁμοίως
the tent *And* and all the vessels *{the}* used in worship. *with* *blood* *in the same way*
3836 5008 1254 2779 4246 3836 5007 3836 3311 3836 135 3931
d.asf n.asf cj cj a.apn d.apn n.apn d.gsf n.gsf d.dsn n.dsn adv

ἐρράντισεν. 22 καὶ σχεδὸν ἐν αἵματι
he sprinkled In fact, according to the law almost everything is sprinkled with blood,
4822 2779 2848 2848 3836 3795 5385 4246 2751 2751 1877 135
v.aai.3s cj adv p.d n.dsn

πάντα καθαρίζεται κατὰ τὸν νόμον καὶ χωρὶς αἱματεκχυσίας οὐ
everything *is sprinkled* *according to* *the* *law* and without the shedding of blood there is no
4246 2751 2848 3836 3795 2779 6006 136 1181 1181 4024
a.npn v.ppi.3s p.a d.asm n.asm cj p.g n.gsf pl

γίνεται ἄφεσις. 23 ἀνάγκη οὖν τὰ μὲν ὑποδείγματα τῶν ἐν τοῖς
there is forgiveness. Thus it was necessary *Thus* that *{the}* ~ earthly copies of the *{in}* *{the}*
1181 912 4036 340 4036 3836 3525 5682 3836 1877 3836
v.pmi.3s n.nsf n.nsf cj d.apn pl n.apn d.gpn p.d d.dpm

οὐρανοῖς τούτοις καθαρίζεσθαι,
heavenly realities be purified by these rites, *be purified* but the heavenly realities
4041 2751 2751 4047 2751 1254 3836 2230 2230
n.dpm r.dpn f.pp

αὐτὰ δὲ τὰ ἐπουράνια κρείττοσιν θυσίαις παρὰ ταύτας. 24
themselves *but* *the* *heavenly realities* with better sacrifices than these. For Christ did
899 1254 3836 2230 3202 2602 4123 4047 1142 5986 1656
r.apn cj d.apn a.apn a.dpf.c n.dpf p.a r.apf

οὐ γὰρ εἰς χειροποίητα εἰσῆλθεν ἅγια Χριστός,
not *For* *{into}* enter a sanctuary made with hands, *did enter* *sanctuary* *Christ* that was a
4024 1142 1650 1656 41 5935 1656 41 5986
pl cj p.a a.apn v.aai.3s a.apn n.nsm

ἀντίτυπα τῶν ἀληθινῶν, ἀλλ᾽ εἰς αὐτὸν τὸν οὐρανόν, νῦν ἐμφανισθῆναι
mere copy of the true one, but into heaven itself, *{the}* *heaven* now to appear
531 3836 240 247 1650 4041 899 3836 4041 3814 1872
n.apn d.gpn a.gpn cj p.a r.asm d.asm n.asm adv f.ap

τῷ προσώπῳ τοῦ θεοῦ ὑπὲρ ἡμῶν· ↰ 25 οὐδ᾽ ἵνα πολλάκις
⌞in the⌟ presence of God on our behalf. Nor was it to offer himself repeatedly,
3836 4725 3836 2536 5642 7005 5642 4028 2671 4712 1571 4490
d.dsn n.dsn d.gsm n.gsm p.g r.gp.1 cj cj adv

NASB

while the one
who made it lives.
[18]Therefore even
the first *covenant*
was not inaugurat-
ed without blood.
[19]For when every
commandment had
been spoken by
Moses to all the
people according
to the Law, he
took the blood of
the calves and the
goats, with water
and scarlet wool
and hyssop, and
sprinkled both the
book itself and all
the people, [20]say-
ing, "THIS IS THE
BLOOD OF THE COV-
ENANT WHICH GOD
COMMANDED YOU."
[21]And in the same
way he sprinkled
both the tabernacle
and all the vessels
of the ministry
with the blood.
[22]And according
to the Law, *one*
may almost *say,* all
things are cleansed
with blood, and
without shedding
of blood there is no
forgiveness.
[23]Therefore it was
necessary for the
copies of the things
in the heavens to
be cleansed with
these, but the
heavenly things
themselves with
better sacrifices
than these. [24]For
Christ did not
enter a holy place
made with hands,
a *mere* copy of the
true one, but into
heaven itself, now
to appear in the
presence of God
for us; [25]nor was it
that He would offer
Himself often,

[a] 20 Exodus 24:8

[a] [καὶ τῶν τράγων] UBS, omitted by TNIV.

NIV

the way the high
priest enters the
Most Holy Place
every year with
blood that is not
his own. 26Other-
wise Christ would
have had to suffer
many times since
the creation of the
world. But he has
appeared once for
all at the culmina-
tion of the ages to
do away with sin
by the sacrifice
of himself. 27Just
as people are des-
tined to die once,
and after that to
face judgment, 28so
Christ was sacri-
ficed once to take
away the sins of
many; and he will
appear a second
time, not to bear
sin, but to bring
salvation to those
who are waiting
for him.

Christ's Sacrifice Once for All

10 The law
is only a
shadow of the
good things that
are coming—not
the realities them-
selves. For this
reason it can nev-
er, by the same
sacrifices repeated
endlessly year
after year, make
perfect those who
draw near to wor-
ship. 2Otherwise,
would they not
have stopped being
offered? For the
worshipers would
have been cleansed
once for all, and
would no longer
have felt guilty for
their sins.

προσφέρῃ ἑαυτόν, ὥσπερ ὁ ἀρχιερεὺς ⌊εἰσέρχεται εἰς⌋ τὰ ἅγια κατ᾽
offer *himself* as the high priest enters the ⌊Most Holy Place⌋ every
4712 1571 6061 3836 797 1656 1650 3836 41 2848
v.pas.3s r.asm.3 cj d.nsm n.nsm v.pmi.3s p.a d.apn a.apn p.a

ἐνιαυτὸν ἐν αἵματι ἀλλοτρίῳ, 26 ἐπεὶ ἔδει αὐτὸν
year with blood not his own, for then he ⌊would have had⌋ *he* to suffer
1929 1877 135 259 2075 899 1256 899 4248 4248
n.asm p.d n.dsn a.dsn cj v.iai.3s r.asm.3

πολλάκις παθεῖν ἀπὸ καταβολῆς → κόσμου· νυνὶ δὲ
again and again *to suffer* since the foundation of the world. But ⌊as it is,⌋ *But* he has
4490 4248 608 2856 3180 1254 3815 1254 5746 5746
adv f.aa p.g n.gsf n.gsm adv cj

ἅπαξ ἐπὶ συντελείᾳ τῶν αἰώνων εἰς ἀθέτησιν τῆς[a] ἁμαρτίας διὰ
appeared ⌊once for all⌋ at the climax of the ages to put away *{the}* sin by
5746 562 2093 5333 3836 172 1650 120 3836 281 1328
adv p.d n.dsf d.gpm n.gpm p.a n.asf d.gsf n.gsf p.g

τῆς θυσίας αὐτοῦ πεφανέρωται. 27 καὶ καθ᾽ ὅσον ἀπόκειται τοῖς ἀνθρώποις
{the} his sacrifice. *his* *he has appeared* And just as it is appointed for mortals
3836 899 2602 899 5746 2779 2848 4012 641 3836 476
d.gsf n.gsf r.gsm.3 v.rpi.3s cj p.a r.asn v.pmi.3s d.dpm n.dpm

ἅπαξ ἀποθανεῖν, μετὰ δὲ τοῦτο κρίσις, 28 οὕτως καὶ ὁ
to die once, *to die* and after *and* that ⌊to experience judgment,⌋ so also *{the}*
633 633 562 633 1254 3552 1254 4047 3213 4048 2779 3836
adv f.aa p.a cj r.asn n.nsf adv adv d.nsm

Χριστὸς ἅπαξ προσενεχθεὶς εἰς τὸ πολλῶν
Christ, after having been offered once *after having been offered* to ~ bear the sins of many,
5986 4712 4712 4712 4712 562 4712 1650 3836 429 281 4498
n.nsm adv pt.ap.nsm p.a d.asn a.gpm

ἀνενεγκεῖν ἁμαρτίας ⌊ἐκ δευτέρου⌋
bear *sins* will appear a second time to those who are eagerly
429 281 3972 3972 1666 1311 3836 3836 587 587 587
f.aa n.apf p.g a.gsn

χωρὶς ἁμαρτίας ὀφθήσεται τοῖς αὐτὸν ἀπεκδεχομένοις
awaiting him, ⌊without reference to⌋ sin *will appear* *to those* *him* *who are eagerly awaiting*
587 899 6006 281 3972 3836 899 587
p.g n.gsf v.fpi.3s d.dpm r.asm.3 pt.pm.dpm

εἰς σωτηρίαν.
but for salvation.
1650 5401
p.a n.asf

10:1

σκιὰν γὰρ ἔχων ὁ νόμος τῶν
For since the law is but a shadow *For* *since is* *the* *law* of the good
1142 2400 3836 3795 2400 5014 1142 2400 3836 3795 3836 19
n.asf cj pt.pa.nsm d.nsm n.nsm d.gpn

μελλόντων ἀγαθῶν, οὐκ αὐτὴν τὴν εἰκόνα τῶν πραγμάτων, κατ᾽ ἐνιαυτὸν
things to come *good* and not the actual *the* form of those realities, *after* *year*
3516 19 4024 3836 899 3836 1635 3836 4547 2848 1929
pt.pa.gpn a.gpn pl r.asf d.asf n.asf d.gpn n.gpn p.a n.asm

ταῖς αὐταῖς θυσίαις ἃς προσφέρουσιν
it can never perfect those who draw near by the same sacrifices which they offer
1538 1538 4030 5457 3836 4665 4665 4665 3836 899 2602 4005 4712
d.dpf r.dpf n.dpf r.apf v.pai.3p

⌊εἰς τὸ διηνεκὲς⌋ οὐδέποτε δύναται τοὺς προσερχομένους
continuously year after year. *never* *it can* *those* *who draw near*
1650 3836 1457 2848 1929 4030 1538 3836 4665
p.a d.asn a.asn adv v.ppi.3s d.apm pt.pm.apm

τελειῶσαι· 2 ἐπεὶ ↱ οὐκ ἂν ἐπαύσαντο προσφερόμεναι διὰ τὸ
perfect For otherwise would they not *would* have ceased being offered, since ~ the
5457 2075 323 4264 4024 323 4264 4712 1328 3836 3836
f.aa cj pl pl v.ami.3p pt.pp.npf p.a d.asn

μηδεμίαν ἔχειν ἔτι συνείδησιν ἁμαρτιῶν
worshipers, once cleansed, would have no *would have* *{longer}* consciousness of sins?
3302 562 2751 2400 2400 3594 2400 2285 5287 281
a.asf f.pa adv n.asf n.gpf

[a] [τῆς] UBS.

NASB

as the high priest
enters the holy
place year by year
with blood that
is not his own.
26Otherwise, He
would have needed
to suffer often
since the founda-
tion of the world;
but now once at
the consummation
of the ages He has
been manifested
to put away sin
by the sacrifice
of Himself. 27And
inasmuch as it is
appointed for men
to die once and
after this *comes*
judgment, 28so
Christ also, having
been offered once
to bear the sins of
many, will appear
a second time for
salvation without
reference to sin, to
those who eagerly
await Him.

One Sacrifice of Christ Is Sufficient

10:1For the Law,
since it has *only* a
shadow of the good
things to come *and*
not the very form
of things, [a]can nev-
er, by the same sac-
rifices which they
offer continually
year by year, make
perfect those who
draw near. 2Other-
wise, would they
not have ceased to
be offered, because
the worshipers,
having once been
cleansed, would
no longer have had
consciousness of
sins?

[a] Two early mss read *they can*

NIV

3But those sacrifices are an annual reminder of sins. 4It is impossible for the blood of bulls and goats to take away sins.

5Therefore, when Christ came into the world, he said:

"Sacrifice and offering
you did not desire,
but a body you prepared for me;
6with burnt offerings and sin offerings
you were not pleased.
7Then I said, 'Here I am—it is written about me in the scroll—
I have come to do your will, my God.'"[a]

8First he said, "Sacrifices and offerings, burnt offerings and sin offerings you did not desire, nor were you pleased with them"—though they were offered in accordance with the law. 9Then he said, "Here I am, I have come to do your will." He sets aside the first to establish the second. 10And by that will, we have been made holy through the sacrifice of the body of Jesus Christ once for all.

11Day after day every priest stands and performs his religious duties; again and again he offers the same sacrifices, which can never take away sins. 12But when this priest had offered for all time one sacrifice

[a] 7 Psalm 40:6-8 (see Septuagint)

τοὺς λατρεύοντας ἅπαξ κεκαθαρισμένους; 3ἀλλ᾽ ἐν αὐταῖς
the worshipers once cleansed But in these sacrifices there is a
3836 3302 562 2751 247 1877 899
d.apm pt.pa.apm adv pt.rp.apm cj p.d r.dpf.3

ἀνάμνησις ἁμαρτιῶν κατ᾽ ἐνιαυτόν· 4ἀδύνατον γὰρ → αἷμα ταύρων
reminder of sins year after year. For it is impossible For for the blood of bulls
390 281 2848 1929 1142 105 1142 135 5436
n.nsf n.gpf p.a n.asm a.nsn cj n.asn n.gpm

καὶ τράγων ἀφαιρεῖν ἁμαρτίας. 5διὸ εἰσερχόμενος εἰς τὸν κόσμον λέγει,
and goats to take away sins. Therefore when he came into the world, he said,
2779 5543 904 281 1475 1656 1650 3836 3180 3306
cj n.gpm f.pa n.apf cj pt.pm.nsm p.a d.asm n.asm v.pai.3s

θυσίαν καὶ προσφορὰν ↱ ↱ οὐκ ἠθέλησας, σῶμα δὲ κατηρτίσω μοι·
"Sacrifice and offering you did not desire, but a body but you prepared for me.
2602 2779 4714 2527 2527 4024 2527 1254 5393 1254 2936 1609
n.asf cj n.asf pl v.aai.2s n.asn cj v.ami.2s r.ds.1

6 ὁλοκαυτώματα καὶ ⌊περὶ ἁμαρτίας⌋ οὐκ
You did not take pleasure in whole burnt offerings and sin-offerings. not
2305 2305 4024 2305 2305 2305 3906 2779 4309 281 4024
n.apn cj p.g n.gsf pl

εὐδόκησας. 7τότε εἶπον, ἰδοὺ ἥκω, ἐν κεφαλίδι → βιβλίου
You did take pleasure in Then I said, 'Behold, ⌊I have come⌋ — in the scroll of a book
2305 5538 3306 2627 2457 1877 3053 1046
v.aai.2s adv v.aai.1s j v.rai.1s p.d n.dsf n.gsn

γέγραπται περὶ ἐμοῦ, τοῦ ποιῆσαι ὁ θεὸς τὸ θέλημά σου. 8
it is written about me — ~ to do your will, O God.'" {the} will your After he
1211 4309 1609 3836 4472 5148 2525 3836 2536 3836 2525 5148 3306 3306
v.rpi.3s p.g r.gs.1 d.gsn f.aa d.vsm n.vsm d.asn n.asn r.gs.2

ἀνώτερον λέγων ὅτι θυσίας καὶ προσφορὰς καὶ ὁλοκαυτώματα
said ⌊what I just quoted,⌋ After he said ~ "Sacrifices and offerings and whole burnt offerings
3306 542 3306 4022 2602 2779 4714 2779 3906
adv.c pt.pa.nsm cj n.apf cj n.apf cj n.apn

καὶ ⌊περὶ ἁμαρτίας⌋ ↱ ↱ οὐκ ἠθέλησας οὐδὲ εὐδόκησας,
and sin-offerings you did not desire nor ⌊did you take pleasure in⌋ them"
2779 4309 281 2527 2527 4024 2527 4028 2305
cj p.g n.gsf pl v.aai.2s cj v.aai.2s

αἵτινες κατὰ νόμον προσφέρονται, 9τότε εἴρηκεν, ἰδοὺ
(namely those offered ⌊according to⌋ the law), offered then he added, "Behold,
4015 4712 2848 3795 4712 5538 3306 2627
r.npf p.a n.asm v.ppi.3p adv v.rai.3s j

ἥκω τοῦ ποιῆσαι τὸ θέλημά σου. ἀναιρεῖ τὸ πρῶτον
⌊I have come⌋ ~ to do {the} your will." your ⌊He does away with⌋ the first
2457 3836 4472 3836 5148 2525 5148 359 3836 4755
v.rai.1s d.gsn f.aa d.asn n.asn r.gs.2 v.pai.3s d.asn a.asn

ἵνα τὸ δεύτερον στήσῃ, 10ἐν ᾧ θελήματι ἡγιασμένοι
⌊in order to⌋ establish the second. establish By that will we have been made holy
2671 2705 3836 1311 2705 1877 4005 2525 1639 1639 1639 39
cj d.asn a.asn v.aas.3s p.d r.dsn n.dsn pt.rp.npm

ἐσμὲν διὰ τῆς προσφορᾶς τοῦ σώματος Ἰησοῦ Χριστοῦ ἐφάπαξ.
we have been through the offering of the body of Jesus Christ ⌊once for all.⌋
1639 1328 3836 4714 3836 5393 2652 5986 2384
v.pai.1p p.g d.gsf n.gsf d.gsn n.gsn n.gsm n.gsm adv

11καὶ πᾶς μὲν ἱερεὺς ἕστηκεν καθ᾽ ἡμέραν λειτουργῶν
Furthermore, every ~ priest stands day after day ⌊performing his religious duties,⌋
2779 4246 3525 2636 2705 2848 2465 3310
cj a.nsm pl n.nsm v.rai.3s p.a n.asf pt.pa.nsm

καὶ τὰς αὐτὰς πολλάκις προσφέρων θυσίας, αἵτινες οὐδέποτε
{and} offering repeatedly the same repeatedly offering sacrifices, which can never
2779 4712 4490 3836 899 4490 4712 2602 4015 1538 4030
cj d.apf r.apf adv pt.pa.nsm n.apf r.npf adv

δύνανται περιελεῖν ἁμαρτίας, 12 οὗτος δὲ μίαν
can take away sins. But when this priest But had offered a single sacrifice
1538 4311 281 1254 4712 4047 1254 4712 4712 1651 2602
v.ppi.3p f.aa n.apf r.nsm cj a.asf

NASB

3But in those *sacrifices* there is a reminder of sins year by year. 4For it is impossible for the blood of bulls and goats to take away sins.
5Therefore, when He comes into the world, He says,
"SACRIFICE AND OFFERING YOU HAVE NOT DESIRED,
BUT A BODY YOU HAVE PREPARED FOR ME;
6IN WHOLE BURNT OFFERINGS AND *sacrifices* FOR SIN YOU HAVE TAKEN NO PLEASURE.
7"THEN I SAID, 'BEHOLD, I HAVE COME
(IN THE SCROLL OF THE BOOK IT IS WRITTEN OF ME)
TO DO YOUR WILL, O GOD.'"
8After saying above, "SACRIFICES AND OFFERINGS AND WHOLE BURNT OFFERINGS AND *sacrifices* FOR SIN YOU HAVE NOT DESIRED, NOR HAVE YOU TAKEN PLEASURE *in them*" (which are offered according to the Law), 9then He said, "BEHOLD, I HAVE COME TO DO YOUR WILL." He takes away the first in order to establish the second.
10By this will we have been sanctified through the offering of the body of Jesus Christ once for all.
11Every priest stands daily ministering and offering time after time the same sacrifices, which can never take away sins;
12but He, having offered one sacrifice for sins for

NIV

for sins, he sat down at the right hand of God, 13 and since that time he waits for his enemies to be made his footstool. 14 For by one sacrifice he has made perfect forever those who are being made holy.

15 The Holy Spirit also testifies to us about this. First he says:

16 "This is the covenant I will make with them
after that time, says the Lord.
I will put my laws in their hearts,
and I will write them on their minds."[a]

17 Then he adds:

"Their sins and lawless acts
I will remember no more."[b]

18 And where these have been forgiven, sacrifice for sin is no longer necessary.

A Call to Persevere in Faith

19 Therefore, brothers and sisters, since we have confidence to enter the Most Holy Place by the blood of Jesus, 20 by a new and living way opened for us through the curtain, that is, his body, 21 and since we have a great priest over the house of God, 22 let us draw near to God with a sincere heart and with the full assurance that faith brings, having our hearts sprinkled to cleanse us from a guilty conscience

ὑπὲρ ἁμαρτιῶν προσενέγκας θυσίαν εἰς τὸ διηνεκὲς ἐκάθισεν ἐν δεξιᾷ
for sins *when had offered* *sacrifice* for all time, he sat down at the right hand
5642 281 4712 2602 1650 3836 1457 2767 1877 1288
p.g n.gpf pt.aa.nsm n.asf p.a d.asn a.asn v.aai.3s p.d a.dsf

τοῦ θεοῦ, 13 τὸ λοιπὸν ἐκδεχόμενος ἕως τεθῶσιν οἱ ἐχθροὶ
of God, waiting ⌊from that⌋ time *waiting* until his enemies are placed *{the}* *enemies*
3836 2536 1683 3836 3370 1683 2401 899 2398 5502 3836 2398
d.gsm n.gsm d.asn adv pt.pm.nsm cj v.aps.3p d.npm a.npm

αὐτοῦ → ὑποπόδιον τῶν ποδῶν αὐτοῦ. 14 → μιᾷ γὰρ προσφορᾷ
his as a footstool for his feet, *his* because by a single *because* offering
899 5711 3836 899 4546 899 1142 1651 1142 4714
r.gsm.3 n.asn d.gpm n.gpm r.gsm.3 a.dsf cj n.dsf

τετελείωκεν εἰς τὸ διηνεκὲς τοὺς ἁγιαζομένους. 15
he has perfected for all time those ⌊who are being made holy.⌋ And the Holy Spirit also
5457 1650 3836 1457 3836 39 1254 3836 41 4460 2779
v.rai.3s p.a d.asn a.asn d.apm pt.pp.apm

μαρτυρεῖ δὲ ἡμῖν καὶ τὸ πνεῦμα τὸ ἅγιον· μετὰ γὰρ τὸ εἰρηκέναι, 16 αὕτη
witnesses *And* to us, *also* *the* *Spirit* *{the}* *Holy* for after *for* ~ saying, "This is
3455 1254 7005 2779 3836 4460 3836 41 1142 3552 1142 3836 3306 4047
v.pai.3s cj r.dp.1 adv d.nsn n.nsn d.nsn a.nsn p.a cj d.asn f.ra r.nsf

ἡ διαθήκη ἣν διαθήσομαι πρὸς αὐτοὺς μετὰ τὰς ἡμέρας ἐκείνας, λέγει
the covenant that I will establish with them after *{the}* those days, *those* declares the
3836 1347 4005 1416 4639 899 3552 3836 1697 2465 1697 3306
d.nsf n.nsf r.asf v.fmi.1s p.a r.apm.3 p.a d.apf n.apf r.apf v.pai.3s

κύριος, διδοὺς νόμους μου ἐπὶ καρδίας αὐτῶν καὶ ἐπὶ
Lord; I will put my laws *my* in their hearts *their* and I will inscribe them on
3261 1443 1609 3795 1609 2093 899 2840 899 2779 2108 2108 2108 899 2093
n.nsm pt.pa.nsm n.apm r.gs.1 p.a n.apf r.gpm.3 cj p.a

τὴν διάνοιαν αὐτῶν ἐπιγράψω αὐτούς, 17 καὶ τῶν ἁμαρτιῶν
{the} their minds," *their* *I will inscribe* *them* then he says, *{the}* "Their sins
3836 899 1379 899 2108 899 2779 3836 899 281
d.asf n.asf r.gpm.3 v.fai.1s r.apm.3 cj d.gpf n.gpf

αὐτῶν καὶ τῶν ἀνομιῶν αὐτῶν ↱ ↱ ⌊οὐ μὴ⌋ μνησθήσομαι ἔτι.
Their and *{the}* their lawless acts *their* I will never again remember." *again*
899 2779 3836 899 490 899 3630 3630 4024 3590 2285 3630 2285
r.gpm.3 cj d.gpf n.gpf r.gpm.3 pl pl v.fpi.1s adv

18 ὅπου δὲ ἄφεσις τούτων, οὐκέτι προσφορὰ περὶ
Now where *Now* there is forgiveness of these, there is no longer any offering for
1254 3963 1254 912 4047 4033 4714 4309
cj cj n.nsf r.gpf adv n.nsf p.g

ἁμαρτίας. 19 ἔχοντες οὖν, ἀδελφοί, παρρησίαν εἰς τὴν
sin. Therefore, brothers, ⌊since we have⌋ *Therefore* *brothers* confidence to *{the}*
281 4036 81 2400 4036 81 4244 1650 3836
n.gsf pt.pa.npm cj n.vpm n.asf p.a d.asf

εἴσοδον τῶν ἁγίων ἐν τῷ αἵματι Ἰησοῦ, 20 ἣν
enter the holy place by the blood of Jesus, a way that is new and living, which
1658 3836 41 1877 3836 135 2652 3847 4710 2779 2409 4005
n.asf d.gpn a.gpn p.d d.dsn n.dsn n.gsm r.asf

ἐνεκαίνισεν ἡμῖν ὁδὸν πρόσφατον καὶ ζῶσαν διὰ τοῦ καταπετάσματος, τοῦτ᾽ ἔστιν
he opened for us *way* *new* *and* *living* through the curtain, that is,
1590 7005 3847 4710 2779 2409 1328 3836 2925 4047 1639
v.aai.3s r.dp.1 n.asf a.asf cj pt.pa.asf p.g d.gsn n.gsn r.nsn v.pai.3s

τῆς σαρκὸς αὐτοῦ, 21 καὶ ἱερέα μέγαν ἐπὶ τὸν
through his flesh, *his* and since we have a great priest *great* ⌊in charge of⌋ the
3836 899 4922 899 2779 3489 2636 3489 2093 3836
d.gsf n.gsf r.gsm.3 cj n.asm a.asm p.a d.asm

οἶκον τοῦ θεοῦ, 22 προσερχώμεθα μετὰ ἀληθινῆς καρδίας ἐν πληροφορίᾳ
house of God, ⌊let us continue to draw near⌋ with a sincere heart in full assurance
3875 3836 2536 4665 3552 240 2840 1877 4443
n.asm d.gsm n.gsm v.pms.1p p.g a.gsf n.gsf p.d n.dsf

πίστεως → ῥεραντισμένοι τὰς καρδίας ἀπὸ συνειδήσεως
of faith, since our hearts ⌊have been sprinkled clean⌋ *our* *hearts* from a guilty conscience
4411 3836 2840 4822 3836 2840 608 4505 5287
n.gsf pt.rp.npm d.apf n.apf p.g n.gsf

NASB

all time, SAT DOWN AT THE RIGHT HAND OF GOD, 13 waiting from that time onward UNTIL HIS ENEMIES BE MADE A FOOTSTOOL FOR HIS FEET. 14 For by one offering He has perfected for all time those who are sanctified. 15 And the Holy Spirit also testifies to us; for after saying,

16 "THIS IS THE COVENANT THAT I WILL MAKE WITH THEM
AFTER THOSE DAYS, SAYS THE LORD:
I WILL PUT MY LAWS UPON THEIR HEART,
AND ON THEIR MIND I WILL WRITE THEM,"

He then says,

17 "AND THEIR SINS AND THEIR LAWLESS DEEDS
I WILL REMEMBER NO MORE."

18 Now where there is forgiveness of these things, there is no longer *any* offering for sin.

A New and Living Way

19 Therefore, brethren, since we have confidence to enter the holy place by the blood of Jesus, 20 by a new and living way which He inaugurated for us through the veil, that is, His flesh, 21 and since *we have* a great priest over the house of God, 22 let us draw near with a sincere heart in full assurance of faith, having our hearts sprinkled *clean* from an evil conscience and

[a] 16 Jer. 31:33
[b] 17 Jer. 31:34

NIV

and having our
bodies washed with
pure water. 23 Let
us hold unswerv-
ingly to the hope
we profess, for he
who promised is
faithful. 24 And let
us consider how
we may spur one
another on toward
love and good
deeds, 25 not giving
up meeting togeth-
er, as some are in
the habit of doing,
but encouraging
one another—and
all the more as you
see the Day ap-
proaching.
26 If we delib-
erately keep on
sinning after we
have received the
knowledge of the
truth, no sacrifice
for sins is left,
27 but only a fear-
ful expectation of
judgment and of
raging fire that
will consume the
enemies of God.
28 Anyone who re-
jected the law of
Moses died with-
out mercy on the
testimony of two
or three witness-
es. 29 How much
more severely do
you think some-
one deserves to be
punished who has
trampled the Son
of God underfoot,
who has treated as
an unholy thing
the blood of the
covenant that sanc-
tified them, and
who has insulted
the Spirit of grace?
30 For we know him
who said, "It is
mine to avenge; I
will repay,"[a] and
again, "The Lord
will judge

πονηρᾶς καὶ λελουσμένοι τὸ σῶμα → ὕδατι καθαρῷ·
guilty and our bodies washed *our bodies* with clean water. *clean*
4505 2779 3836 5393 3374 3836 5393 2754 5623 2754
a.gsf cj pt.rp.npm d.asn n.asn n.dsn a.dsn

23 κατέχωμεν τὴν ὁμολογίαν τῆς ἐλπίδος ἀκλινῆ,
⌊Let us continue to hold fast⌋ the hope that we confess *the hope* without wavering,
2988 3836 1828 3836 3934 3836 1828 195
v.pas.1p d.asf n.asf d.gsf n.gsf a.asf

πιστὸς γὰρ ὁ ἐπαγγειλάμενος, 24 καὶ κατανοῶμεν
faithful for the ⌊one who made the promise⌋ is faithful. And let us take thought of how to
4412 1142 3836 2040 4412 2779 2917 4237 4237
a.nsm cj d.nsm pt.am.nsm cj v.pas.1p

ἀλλήλους εἰς παροξυσμὸν ἀγάπης καὶ καλῶν ἔργων, 25 μὴ ἐγκαταλείποντες
spur one another ⌊on to⌋ *how to spur* love and good works, not abandoning
4237 253 1650 4237 27 2779 2819 2240 3590 1593
r.apm p.a n.asm n.gsf cj a.gpn n.gpn pl pt.pa.npm

τὴν ἐπισυναγωγὴν ἑαυτῶν, καθὼς ἔθος τισίν, ἀλλὰ
{the} our own meetings, *our own* as is the habit of some, but rather
3836 1571 1571 2191 1571 2777 1621 5516 247
d.asf n.asf r.gpm.1 cj n.nsn r.dpm cj

παρακαλοῦντες, καὶ ⌊τοσούτῳ μᾶλλον⌋ ὅσῳ βλέπετε ἐγγίζουσαν
encouraging one another, and all the more since you see the Day drawing near.
4151 2779 5537 3437 4012 1063 3836 2465 1581
pt.pa.npm cj r.dsn adv.c r.dsn v.pai.2p pt.pa.asf

τὴν ἡμέραν. 26 ↱ ἑκουσίως γὰρ ἁμαρτανόντων ἡμῶν μετὰ τὸ λαβεῖν τὴν
the Day For if we deliberately *For* persist in sin *we* after ~ receiving the
3836 2465 1142 279 7005 1731 1142 279 7005 3552 3836 3284 3836
d.asf n.asf adv cj pt.pa.gpm r.gp.1 p.a d.asn f.aa d.asf

ἐπίγνωσιν τῆς ἀληθείας, οὐκέτι περὶ ἁμαρτιῶν ἀπολείπεται
knowledge of the truth, there is no longer any sacrifice for sins, *there is any*
2106 3836 237 657 657 4033 657 2602 4309 281 657
n.asf d.gsf n.gsf adv p.g n.gpf v.ppi.3s

θυσία, 27 φοβερὰ δέ τις ἐκδοχὴ κρίσεως καὶ → πυρὸς ζῆλος
sacrifice but only a terrifying *but a* expectation of judgment and of raging fire *raging*
2602 1254 5516 5829 1254 5516 1693 3213 2779 2419 4786 2419
n.nsf a.nsf cj r.nsf n.nsf n.gsf cj n.gsn n.nsm

ἐσθίειν μέλλοντος τοὺς ὑπεναντίους. 28 ἀθετήσας τις νόμον
ready to consume *ready* the adversaries. Anyone who violates *Anyone* the law
3516 2266 3516 3836 5641 5516 119 5516 3795
f.pa pt.pa.gsn d.apm a.apm pt.aa.nsm r.nsm n.asm

Μωϋσέως χωρὶς οἰκτιρμῶν ἐπὶ δυσὶν ἢ τρισὶν μάρτυσιν
of Moses dies without mercy on the testimony of two or three witnesses.
3707 633 6006 3880 2093 1545 2445 5552 3459
n.gsm p.g n.gpm p.d a.dpm cj a.dpm n.dpn

ἀποθνήσκει· 29 πόσῳ δοκεῖτε χείρονος ἀξιωθήσεται τιμωρίας
dies How much greater punishment do you think *greater* will be deserved *punishment*
633 4531 5937 5513 1506 5937 546 5513
v.pai.3s r.dsn v.pai.2p a.gsf.c v.fpi.3s n.gsf

ὁ ↱ ↱ ↱ ↱ τὸν υἱὸν τοῦ θεοῦ καταπατήσας καὶ τὸ
by the one who has trampled the Son of God underfoot, and has profaned the
3836 2922 2922 2922 2922 3836 5626 3836 2536 2922 2779 3123 3123 3836
d.nsm d.asm n.asm d.gsm n.gsm pt.aa.nsm cj d.asn

αἷμα τῆς διαθήκης ⌊κοινὸν ἡγησάμενος,⌋ ἐν ᾧ ἡγιάσθη, καὶ
blood of the covenant *has profaned* by which ⌊he was made holy,⌋ and has
135 3836 1347 3123 2451 1877 4005 39 2779 1964
n.asn d.gsf n.gsf a.asn pt.am.nsm p.d r.dsn v.api.3s cj

τὸ πνεῦμα τῆς χάριτος ἐνυβρίσας; 30 οἴδαμεν γὰρ τὸν εἰπόντα,
insulted the Spirit of grace? *has insulted* For we know *For* the one who said,
1964 3836 4460 3836 5921 1964 1142 3857 1142 3836 3306
d.asn n.asn d.gsf n.gsf pt.aa.nsm v.rai.1p cj d.asm pt.aa.asm

ἐμοὶ ἐκδίκησις, ἐγὼ ἀνταποδώσω. καὶ πάλιν, κρινεῖ
"Vengeance ⌊belongs to me,⌋ *Vengeance* I will repay," and again, "The Lord will judge
1689 1609 1689 1609 500 2779 4099 3261 3212
r.ds.1 n.nsf r.ns.1 v.fai.1s cj adv v.fai.3s

NASB

our bodies washed
with pure water.
23 Let us hold fast
the confession of
our hope without
wavering, for He
who promised is
faithful; 24 and let
us consider how
to stimulate one
another to love
and good deeds,
25 not forsaking our
own assembling
together, as is the
habit of some, but
encouraging *one*
another; and all the
more as you see the
day drawing near.

Christ or Judgment

26 For if we go on
sinning willfully
after receiving the
knowledge of the
truth, there no lon-
ger remains a sacri-
fice for sins, 27 but a
terrifying expecta-
tion of judgment
and THE FURY OF
A FIRE WHICH WILL
CONSUME THE AD-
VERSARIES. 28 Any-
one who has set
aside the Law of
Moses dies with-
out mercy on *the*
testimony of two
or three witnesses.
29 How much se-
verer punishment
do you think he
will deserve who
has trampled under
foot the Son of
God, and has re-
garded as unclean
the blood of the
covenant by which
he was sanctified,
and has insulted
the Spirit of grace?
30 For we know Him
who said, "VEN-
GEANCE IS MINE, I
WILL REPAY." And
again, "THE LORD
WILL JUDGE HIS

[a] 30 Deut. 32:35

NIV

his people."[a] 31 It is
a dreadful thing to
fall into the hands
of the living God.
32 Remember
those earlier days
after you had re-
ceived the light,
when you endured
in a great conflict
full of suffering.
33 Sometimes you
were publicly ex-
posed to insult
and persecution;
at other times you
stood side by side
with those who
were so treated.
34 You suffered
along with those in
prison and joyfully
accepted the con-
fiscation of your
property, because
you knew that you
yourselves had
better and lasting
possessions. 35 So
do not throw away
your confidence;
it will be richly re-
warded.
36 You need to
persevere so that
when you have
done the will of
God, you will re-
ceive what he has
promised. 37 For,

"In just a little
while,
he who is
coming will
come
and will not
delay."[b]

38 And,

"But my
righteous[c]
one will live
by faith.
And I take no
pleasure
in the one who
shrinks
back."[d]

39 But we do not
belong to those
who shrink back
and are destroyed,
but to

[a] 30 Deut. 32:36; Psalm 135:14
[b] 37 Isaiah 26:20; Hab. 2:3
[c] 38 Some early manuscripts *But the righteous*
[d] 38 Hab. 2:4 (see Septuagint)

κύριος τὸν λαὸν αὐτοῦ. 31 φοβερὸν τὸ ἐμπεσεῖν εἰς χεῖρας →
Lord *{the}* his people." *his* It is terrifying ~ to fall into the hands of the living
3261 3836 899 3295 899 5829 3836 1860 1650 5931 2409
n.nsm d.asm n.asm r.gsm.3 a.nsn d.nsn f.aa p.a n.apf

θεοῦ ζῶντος. 32 ἀναμιμνῄσκεσθε δὲ τὰς πρότερον ἡμέρας, ἐν αἷς
God. *living* Instead, remember *Instead* those former days in which,
2536 2409 1254 389 1254 3836 4728 2465 1877 4005
n.gsm pt.pa.gsm v.ppm.2p cj d.apf adv.c n.apf p.d r.dpf

φωτισθέντες → πολλὴν ἄθλησιν ὑπεμείνατε
⌞after you had received the light,⌟ you weathered such a difficult struggle *you weathered*
5894 5702 5702 4498 124 5702
pt.ap.npm a.asf n.asf v.aai.2p

παθημάτων, 33 τοῦτο μὲν ὀνειδισμοῖς τε
with suffering. Sometimes ~ you were made a public spectacle, both by insults *both*
4077 4047 3525 2518 2518 2518 2518 2518 2518 5445 3944 5445
n.gpn r.asn pl n.dpm cj

καὶ θλίψεσιν θεατριζόμενοι, τοῦτο δὲ κοινωνοὶ
and persecutions, *you were made a public spectacle* and ⌞at other times,⌟ *and* you became one with
2779 2568 2518 1254 4047 1254 1181 1181 3128
cj n.dpf pt.pp.npm r.asn pl n.npm

τῶν οὕτως ἀναστρεφομένων γενηθέντες. 34 καὶ γὰρ
those who were treated ⌞in that way,⌟ *who were treated* *you became* for in fact *for* you
3836 418 418 418 4048 418 1181 1142 2779 1142 5217
d.gpm adv pt.pp.gpm pt.ap.npm adv cj

τοῖς δεσμίοις συνεπαθήσατε καὶ τὴν
shared the sufferings of those in prison, *you shared the sufferings* and with joy accepted the
5217 5217 5217 3836 1300 5217 2779 3552 5915 4657 3836
d.dpm n.dpm v.aai.2p cj d.asf

ἁρπαγὴν τῶν ὑπαρχόντων ὑμῶν μετὰ χαρᾶς προσεδέξασθε γινώσκοντες →
confiscation of your belongings, *your* *with* *joy* *accepted* since you knew that you
771 3836 7007 5639 7007 3552 5915 4657 1182
n.asf d.gpn pt.pa.gpn r.gp.2 p.g n.gsf v.ami.2p pt.pa.npm

ἔχειν ἑαυτοὺς κρείττονα ὕπαρξιν καὶ μένουσαν. 35
yourselves had *yourselves* a better and lasting possession. *and* *lasting* Therefore
1571 2400 1571 3202 2779 3531 5638 2779 3531 4036
f.pa r.apm.2 a.asf.c n.asf cj pt.pa.asf

↱ μὴ ἀποβάλητε οὖν τὴν παρρησίαν ὑμῶν, ἥτις ἔχει μεγάλην
do not throw away *Therefore* *{the}* your boldness, *your* which has great
610 3590 610 4036 3836 7007 4244 7007 4015 2400 3489
pl v.aas.2p cj d.asf n.asf r.gp.2 r.nsf v.pai.3s a.asf

μισθαποδοσίαν. 36 ὑπομονῆς γὰρ ἔχετε χρείαν ἵνα
reward. *of endurance* *then* You have need of endurance, then, so that after you
3632 5705 1142 2400 5970 5705 5705 1142 2671 4472 4472
n.asf n.gsf cj v.pai.2p n.asf cj

τὸ θέλημα τοῦ θεοῦ ποιήσαντες κομίσησθε τὴν ἐπαγγελίαν.
have done the will of God, *after you have done* you may receive what was promised.
4472 4472 3836 2525 3836 2536 4472 3152 3836 2039
d.asn n.asn d.gsm n.gsm pt.aa.npm v.ams.2p d.asf n.asf

37 ἔτι γὰρ μικρὸν ⌞ὅσον ὅσον,⌟ ὁ ἐρχόμενος ἥξει καὶ ↱ ↱
For "just *For* a little longer, the ⌞one who is coming⌟ ⌞will arrive;⌟ *{and}* he will
1142 2285 1142 3625 4012 4012 3836 2262 2457 2779 5988 5988
adv cj a.asm r.asm r.asm d.nsm pt.pm.nsm v.fai.3s cj

οὐ χρονίσει· 38 ὁ δὲ δίκαιός μου ἐκ πίστεως ζήσεται, καὶ
not delay. *{the}* But my ⌞righteous one⌟ *my* will live by faithfulness. *will live* But
4024 5988 3836 1254 1609 1465 1609 2409 2409 1666 4411 2409 2779
pl v.fai.3s d.nsm cj a.nsm r.gs.1 p.g n.gsf v.fmi.3s cj

ἐὰν ὑποστείληται, ↱ ↱ οὐκ εὐδοκεῖ ἡ ψυχή μου ἐν αὐτῷ. 39
should he shrink back, my soul will take no pleasure *{the}* *soul* *my* in him." But
1569 5713 1609 6034 2305 2305 4024 2305 3836 6034 1609 1877 899 1254
cj v.ams.3s pl v.pai.3s d.nsf n.nsf r.gs.1 p.d r.dsm.3

ἡμεῖς δὲ οὐκ ἐσμὲν ὑποστολῆς εἰς ἀπώλειαν ἀλλὰ
we *But* are not *are* ⌞of those who shrink back⌟ and are lost, but are
7005 1254 1639 4024 1639 5714 1650 724 247
r.np.1 cj pl v.pai.1p n.gsf p.a n.asf cj

NASB

PEOPLE." 31 It is a ter-
rifying thing to fall
into the hands of
the living God.
32 But remember
the former days,
when, after being
enlightened, you
endured a great
conflict of suffer-
ings, 33 partly by be-
ing made a public
spectacle through
reproaches and
tribulations, and
partly by becom-
ing sharers with
those who were so
treated. 34 For you
showed sympathy
to the prisoners and
accepted joyfully
the seizure of your
property, know-
ing that you have
for yourselves a
better possession
and a lasting one.
35 Therefore, do not
throw away your
confidence, which
has a great reward.
36 For you have
need of endurance,
so that when you
have done the will
of God, you may
receive what was
promised.

37 FOR YET IN A
VERY LITTLE
WHILE,
HE WHO IS
COMING WILL
COME, AND
WILL NOT DE-
LAY.
38 BUT MY RIGH-
TEOUS ONE
SHALL LIVE BY
FAITH;
AND IF HE
SHRINKS BACK,
MY SOUL HAS
NO PLEASURE
IN HIM.

39 But we are not of
those who shrink
back to destruction,

NIV

those who have
faith and are
saved.

Faith in Action

11 Now faith is
confidence
in what we hope
for and assurance
about what we do
not see. [2]This is
what the ancients
were commend-
ed for.
[3]By faith we
understand that
the universe was
formed at God's
command, so that
what is seen was
not made out of
what was visible.
[4]By faith Abel
brought God a bet-
ter offering than
Cain did. By faith
he was commend-
ed as righteous,
when God spoke
well of his offer-
ings. And by faith
Abel still speaks,
even though he is
dead.
[5]By faith Enoch
was taken from
this life, so that he
did not experience
death: "He could
not be found, be-
cause God had
taken him away."[a]
For before he was
taken, he was
commended as
one who pleased
God. [6]And without
faith it is impossi-
ble to please God,
because anyone
who comes to him
must believe that
he exists and that
he rewards those
who earnestly seek
him.
[7]By faith Noah,
when warned
about things not
yet seen, in holy
fear built

πίστεως εἰς περιποίησιν ψυχῆς.
⌊of those who are faithful⌋ and so preserve their soul.
4411 1650 4348 6034
n.gsf p.a n.asf n.gsf

11:1 ἔστιν δὲ πίστις ἐλπιζομένων ὑπόστασις,
Now faith is *Now faith* the assurance ⌊of things hoped for,⌋ *assurance* the
1254 4411 1639 1254 4411 5712 1827 5712
v.pai.3s cj n.nsf pt.pp.gpn n.nsf

πραγμάτων ἔλεγχος οὐ βλεπομένων. 2 ἐν ταύτῃ γὰρ
conviction of things *conviction* not seen. For by it *For* the men of the
1793 4547 1793 4024 1063 1142 1877 4047 1142 3836 4565 4565 4565
n.gpn n.nsm pl pt.pp.gpn p.d r.dsf cj

ἐμαρτυρήθησαν οἱ πρεσβύτεροι. 3 πίστει νοοῦμεν
past were approved *the* *men of the past* by God. By faith we understand that the universe
4565 3455 3836 4565 4411 3783 3836 172
v.api.3p d.npm a.npm n.dsf v.pai.1p

κατηρτίσθαι τοὺς αἰῶνας → ῥήματι θεοῦ, εἰς τὸ μὴ
was created *the* *universe* by the word of God, ⌊so that⌋ ~ what is seen was not
2936 3836 172 4839 2536 1650 3836 3836 1063 1063 1181 3590
f.rp d.apm n.apm n.dsn n.gsm p.a d.asn pl

ἐκ φαινομένων τὸ βλεπόμενον γεγονέναι. 4 πίστει
brought into being from anything observable. *what is seen* *was brought into being* By faith
1181 1181 1181 1666 5743 3836 1063 1181 4411
p.g pt.pm.gpn d.asn pt.pp.asn f.ra n.dsf

πλείονα θυσίαν Ἅβελ παρὰ Κάϊν προσήνεγκεν τῷ θεῷ,
Abel offered to God a more acceptable sacrifice *Abel* than Cain, *offered* *to* *God*
6 4712 3836 2536 4498 2602 6 4123 2782 4712 3836 2536
a.asf.c n.asf n.nsm p.a n.asm v.aai.3s d.dsm n.dsm

δι' ἧς ἐμαρτυρήθη εἶναι δίκαιος, μαρτυροῦντος ἐπὶ
through which faith he was attested as righteous, God himself showing his approval by
1328 4005 3455 1639 1465 2536 3455 2093
p.g r.gsf v.api.3s f.pa a.nsm pt.pa.gsm p.d

τοῖς δώροις αὐτοῦ τοῦ θεοῦ, καὶ δι'
accepting *{the}* his gifts. *his* *{the}* *God* And though he died, he still speaks through
3836 899 1565 899 3836 2536 2779 633 633 633 3281 2285 3281 1328
d.dpn n.dpn r.gsm.3 d.gsm n.gsm cj p.g

αὐτῆς ἀποθανὼν ἔτι λαλεῖ. 5 πίστει Ἑνὼχ μετετέθη τοῦ ↱ ↱ μὴ
his faith. *though he died* *still* *he speaks* By faith Enoch ⌊was taken up⌋ so that he did not
899 633 2285 3281 4411 1970 3572 3836 1625 1625 3590
r.gsf.3 pt.aa.nsm adv v.pai.3s n.dsf n.nsm v.api.3s d.gsn pl

ἰδεῖν θάνατον, καὶ ↱ ↱ οὐχ ηὑρίσκετο διότι μετέθηκεν αὐτὸν ὁ θεός.
see death, and he could not be found, because God had taken him. *{the}* *God*
1625 2505 2779 2351 2351 4024 2351 1484 2536 3572 899 3836 2536
f.aa n.asm cj pl v.ipi.3s cj v.aai.3s r.asm.3 d.nsm n.nsm

πρὸ γὰρ τῆς μεταθέσεως μεμαρτύρηται εὐαρεστηκέναι τῷ θεῷ·
For before *For* he was taken he had been approved ⌊as one who had been pleasing⌋ to God,
1142 4574 1142 3836 3557 3455 2297 3836 2536
p.g cj d.gsf n.gsf v.rpi.3s f.ra d.dsm n.dsm

6 χωρὶς δὲ πίστεως ἀδύνατον εὐαρεστῆσαι·
and without *and* faith it is impossible to please him, for the one who approaches
1254 6006 1254 4411 105 2297 1142 3836 4665 4665 4665
p.g cj n.gsf a.nsn f.aa

πιστεῦσαι γὰρ δεῖ τὸν προσερχόμενον τῷ θεῷ ὅτι ἔστιν καὶ
God must believe *for* *must* *the* *one who approaches* *{the}* *God* that he exists and that he
2536 1256 4409 1142 1256 3836 4665 3836 2536 4022 1639 2779
f.aa cj v.pai.3s d.asm pt.pm.asm d.dsm n.dsm cj v.pai.3s cj

τοῖς ἐκζητοῦσιν αὐτὸν μισθαποδότης γίνεται. 7 πίστει χρηματισθεὶς
rewards those who seek him. *rewards* *{he is}* By faith Noah, having been warned
3633 3836 1699 899 3633 1181 4411 3820 5976
d.dpm pt.pa.dpm r.asm.3 n.nsm v.pmi.3s n.dsf pt.ap.nsm

Νῶε περὶ τῶν μηδέπω βλεπομένων, εὐλαβηθεὶς κατεσκεύασεν
Noah by God concerning events ⌊as yet unseen,⌋ took heed and built
3820 4309 3836 3596 1063 2326 2941
n.nsm p.g d.gpn adv pt.pp.gpn pt.ap.nsm v.aai.3s

NASB

but of those who
have faith to the
preserving of the
soul.

The Triumphs of Faith

[11:1]Now faith is the
assurance of *things*
hoped for, the con-
viction of things
not seen. [2]For by
it the men of old
gained approval.
[3]By faith we
understand that
the worlds were
prepared by the
word of God, so
that what is seen
was not made out
of things which
are visible. [4]By
faith Abel offered
to God a better
sacrifice than Cain,
through which
he obtained the
testimony that he
was righteous,
God testifying
about his gifts,
and through faith,
though he is dead,
he still speaks. [5]By
faith Enoch was
taken up so that
he would not see
death; AND HE WAS
NOT FOUND BECAUSE
GOD TOOK HIM UP;
for he obtained the
witness that before
his being taken up
he was pleasing to
God. [6]And without
faith it is impos-
sible to please
Him, for he who
comes to God must
believe that He is
and *that* He is a
rewarder of those
who seek Him. [7]By
faith Noah, being
warned *by God*
about things not
yet seen, in rever-
ence prepared an

[a] 5 Gen. 5:24

NIV

an ark to save his
family. By his faith
he condemned the
world and became
heir of the righ-
teousness that is in
keeping with faith.
8 By faith Abra-
ham, when called
to go to a place he
would later receive
as his inheritance,
obeyed and went,
even though he
did not know
where he was go-
ing. 9 By faith he
made his home in
the promised land
like a stranger in
a foreign country;
he lived in tents,
as did Isaac and
Jacob, who were
heirs with him of
the same prom-
ise. 10 For he was
looking forward to
the city with foun-
dations, whose ar-
chitect and builder
is God. 11 And by
faith even Sar-
ah, who was past
childbearing age,
was enabled to
bear children be-
cause she[a] consid-
ered him faithful
who had made the
promise. 12 And so
from this one man,
and he as good
as dead, came
descendants as nu-
merous as the stars
in the sky and as
countless as the
sand on the sea-
shore.
13 All these people
were still living
by faith when they
died.

κιβωτὸν εἰς σωτηρίαν τοῦ οἴκου αὐτοῦ δι' ἧς κατέκρινεν
an ark for the safety of his household. *his* By this act of faith he condemned
3066 1650 5401 3836 899 3875 899 1328 4005 2891
n.asf p.a n.asf d.gsm n.gsm r.gsm.3 p.g r.gsf v.aai.3s

τὸν κόσμον, καὶ τῆς κατὰ πίστιν δικαιοσύνης
{the} humanity and became an heir of the righteousness that ⌞comes by⌟ faith. *righteousness*
3836 3180 2779 1181 3101 3836 1466 2848 4411 1466
d.asm n.asm cj d.gsf p.a n.asf n.gsf

ἐγένετο κληρονόμος. 8 πίστει καλούμενος Ἀβραὰμ ὑπήκουσεν
became heir By faith Abraham obeyed ⌞when he was called⌟ *Abraham obeyed*
1181 3101 4411 11 5634 2813 11 5634
v.ami.3s n.nsm n.dsf pt.pp.nsm n.nsm v.aai.3s

ἐξελθεῖν εἰς τόπον ὃν ἤμελλεν λαμβάνειν εἰς κληρονομίαν, καὶ ἐξῆλθεν ↱
to go out to a place which he would receive as an inheritance. *{and}* He set out even
2002 1650 5536 4005 3516 3284 1650 3100 2779 2002 2179
f.aa p.a n.asm r.asm v.iai.3s f.pa p.a n.asf cj v.aai.3s

↱ ↱ ↱ μὴ ἐπιστάμενος ποῦ ἔρχεται. 9 πίστει παρῴκησεν εἰς γῆν
though he did not know where he was going. By faith he migrated to the land
2179 2179 2179 3590 2179 4543 2262 4411 4228 1650 1178
pl pt.pp.nsm cj v.pmi.3s n.dsf v.aai.3s p.a n.asf

τῆς ἐπαγγελίας ὡς ἀλλοτρίαν ἐν σκηναῖς κατοικήσας μετὰ
{the} he had been promised, as to a foreign land, living in tents *living* as did
3836 2039 6055 259 2997 1877 5008 2997 3552
d.gsf n.gsf pl a.asf p.d n.dpf pt.aa.nsm p.g

Ἰσαὰκ καὶ Ἰακὼβ τῶν συγκληρονόμων τῆς ἐπαγγελίας τῆς αὐτῆς· 10
Isaac and Jacob, *{the}* heirs with him of the same promise, *{the} same* for
2693 2779 2609 3836 5169 3836 899 2039 3836 899 1142
n.gsm cj n.gsf d.gpm n.gpm d.gsf n.gsf d.gsf r.gsf

ἐξεδέχετο γὰρ τὴν τοὺς θεμελίους ἔχουσαν πόλιν ἧς
⌞he was looking forward to⌟ *for* the city which has foundations, *has city* whose
1683 1142 3836 4484 3836 2400 2529 2400 4484 4005
v.imi.3s cj d.asf d.apm n.apm pt.pa.asf n.asf r.gsf

τεχνίτης καὶ δημιουργὸς ὁ θεός. 11 πίστει καὶ
designer and builder is *{the}* God. By faith *{also}* Abraham was enabled to become a
5493 2779 1321 3836 2536 4411 2779 3284 1539 3284 3284
n.nsm cj n.nsm d.nsm n.nsm n.dsf adv

αὐτὴ Σάρρα στεῖρα δύναμιν εἰς ⌞καταβολὴν
father — even though Sarah herself *Sarah* was sterile *enabled {for} father*
2856 4925 899 4925 5096 1539 1650 2856
r.nsf n.nsf a.nsf n.asf p.a n.asf

σπέρματος⌟ ἔλαβεν καὶ παρὰ ↱ καιρὸν ἡλικίας, ἐπεὶ
was to become and beyond the normal age of childbearing — because he
5065 3284 2779 4123 2461 2789 2461 2075 2451
n.gsn v.aai.3s adv p.a n.asm n.gsf cj

πιστὸν ἡγήσατο τὸν ἐπαγγειλάμενον. 12 διὸ καὶ
regarded as faithful *he regarded* the ⌞one who had made the promise.⌟ And so *And* it was that
2451 4412 2451 3836 2040 2779 1475 2779
a.asm v.ami.3s d.asm pt.am.asm cj adv

ἀφ' ἑνὸς ἐγεννήθησαν, καὶ ταῦτα
from this one man, and he was already impotent, there were born *{and}* descendants
608 1651 3739 3739 3739 3739 1164 2779 4047
p.g a.gsm v.api.3p cj r.apn

νενεκρωμένου, καθὼς τὰ ἄστρα τοῦ οὐρανοῦ τῷ πλήθει καὶ
he was already impotent as many as the stars of heaven in number and as
3739 2777 3836 849 3836 4041 3836 4436 2779
pt.rp.gsm pl d.npn n.npn d.gsm n.gsm d.dsn n.dsn cj

ὡς ἡ ἄμμος ἡ παρὰ τὸ χεῖλος τῆς θαλάσσης ἡ
innumerable as the ⌞grains of sand⌟ *{the}* along the shore of the sea *{the}*
410 6055 3836 302 3836 4123 3836 5927 3836 2498 3836
pl d.nsf n.nsf d.nsf p.a d.asn n.asn d.gsf n.gsf d.nsf

ἀναρίθμητος. 13 κατὰ πίστιν ἀπέθανον οὗτοι πάντες, μὴ λαβόντες
innumerable These all died in faith, *died These all* without receiving
410 4047 4246 633 2848 4411 633 4047 4246 3590 3284
a.nsf p.a n.asf v.aai.3p r.npm a.npm pl pt.aa.npm

NASB

ark for the salva-
tion of his house-
hold, by which he
condemned the
world, and became
an heir of the righ-
teousness which is
according to faith.
8 By faith Abra-
ham, when he was
called, obeyed by
going out to a place
which he was to re-
ceive for an inheri-
tance; and he went
out, not knowing
where he was go-
ing. 9 By faith he
lived as an alien in
the land of prom-
ise, as in a foreign
land, dwelling in
tents with Isaac
and Jacob, fellow
heirs of the same
promise; 10 for he
was looking for
the city which has
foundations, whose
architect and
builder is God. 11 By
faith even Sarah
herself received
ability to conceive,
even beyond the
proper time of life,
since she consid-
ered Him faithful
who had promised.
12 Therefore there
was born even of
one man, and him
as good as dead
at that, *as many
descendants* AS THE
STARS OF HEAVEN IN
NUMBER, AND IN-
NUMERABLE AS THE
SAND WHICH IS BY
THE SEASHORE.
13 All these died
in faith, without
receiving the

[a] 11 Or *By faith Abraham, even though he was too old to have children—and Sarah herself was not able to conceive—was enabled to become a father because he*

NIV

They did not re-
ceive the things
promised; they
only saw them and
welcomed them
from a distance,
admitting that they
were foreigners
and strangers on
earth. 14 People who
say such things
show that they are
looking for a coun-
try of their own.
15 If they had been
thinking of the
country they had
left, they would
have had oppor-
tunity to return.
16 Instead, they
were longing for a
better country—a
heavenly one.
Therefore God is
not ashamed to be
called their God,
for he has prepared
a city for them.
17 By faith Abra-
ham, when God
tested him, of-
fered Isaac as a
sacrifice. He who
had embraced
the promises was
about to sacri-
fice his one and
only son, 18 even
though God had
said to him, "It is
through Isaac that
your offspring will
be reckoned."[a]
19 Abraham rea-
soned that God
could even raise
the dead, and so in
a manner of speak-
ing he did receive
Isaac back from
death.
20 By faith Isaac
blessed Jacob and
Esau in regard to
their future.
21 By faith

τὰς ἐπαγγελίας ἀλλὰ πόρρωθεν αὐτὰς ἰδόντες καὶ
the fulfillment of the promises, but they saw them from a distance *them* *they saw* and
3836 2039 247 1625 1625 899 4523 899 1625 2779
d.apf n.apf cj adv r.apf.3 pt.aa.npm cj

ἀσπασάμενοι καὶ ὁμολογήσαντες ὅτι ξένοι καὶ παρεπίδημοί
greeted them. *{and}* They acknowledged that they were strangers and exiles
832 2779 3933 4022 1639 1639 3828 2779 4215
pt.am.npm cj pt.aa.npm cj n.npm cj n.npm

εἰσιν ἐπὶ τῆς γῆς. 14 οἱ γὰρ τοιαῦτα λέγοντες ἐμφανίζουσιν
they were in the land. For those *For* who speak ˻in such a way˼ *who speak* make it clear
1639 2093 3836 1178 1142 3836 1142 3306 3306 5525 3306 1872
v.pai.3p p.g d.gsf n.gsf d.npm cj r.apn pt.pa.npm v.pai.3p

ὅτι πατρίδα ἐπιζητοῦσιν. 15 καὶ εἰ μὲν
that they are seeking a ˻land of their own.˼ *they are seeking* *{and}* If ~ they had been
4022 2118 2118 2118 4258 2118 2779 1623 3525 3648 3648 3648
cj n.asf v.pai.3p cj cj pl

ἐκείνης ἐμνημόνευον ἀφ᾽ ἧς ἐξέβησαν, →
referring to that country *they had been referring to* from which ˻they had set out,˼ they would
3648 3648 1697 3648 608 4005 1674 323
r.gsf v.iai.3p p.g r.gsf v.aai.3p

εἶχον ἂν καιρὸν ἀνακάμψαι· 16 νῦν δὲ
have had *would* opportunity to return. But ˻as it is,˼ *But* they were longing for a
2400 323 2789 366 1254 3814 1254 3977 3977 3977 3977
v.iai.3p pl n.asm f.aa adv cj

κρείττονος ὀρέγονται, τοῦτ᾽ ἔστιν ἐπουρανίου. διὸ ↱
better homeland, *they were longing for* that is, a heavenly one. ˻For this reason˼ God is
3202 3977 4047 1639 2230 1475 2536 2049
a.gsf.c v.pmi.3p r.nsn v.pai.3s a.gsf cj

οὐκ ἐπαισχύνεται αὐτοὺς ὁ θεὸς θεὸς ἐπικαλεῖσθαι αὐτῶν·
not ashamed *{them}* *{the}* *God* to be called their God, *to be called* *their* for
4024 2049 899 3836 2536 2126 2126 2126 899 2536 2126 899 1142
pl v.ppi.3s r.apm.3 d.nsm n.nsm n.nsm f.pp r.gpm.3

ἡτοίμασεν γὰρ → αὐτοῖς πόλιν. 17 πίστει
he has prepared *for* a city to receive them. *city* By faith Abraham, when he was being
2286 1142 4484 899 4484 4411 11 4279 4279 4279 4279
v.aai.3s cj r.dpm.3 n.asf n.dsf

προσενήνοχεν Ἀβραὰμ τὸν Ἰσαὰκ πειραζόμενος καὶ
tested, offered up *Abraham* *{the}* Isaac; *when he was being tested* yes, he who had received
4279 4712 11 3836 2693 4279 2779 3836 346 346 346
v.rai.3s n.nsm d.asm n.asm pt.pp.nsm cj

τὸν μονογενῆ προσέφερεν, ὁ τὰς ἐπαγγελίας
the promises was offering his only son, *was offering* *he* *the* *promises*
3836 2039 4712 4712 3836 3666 4712 3836 3836 2039
d.asm a.asm v.iai.3s d.nsm d.apf n.apf

ἀναδεξάμενος, 18 πρὸς ὃν ἐλαλήθη ὅτι ἐν Ἰσαὰκ
who had received of whom ˻he had been told,˼ ~ "It is through Isaac that descendants
346 4639 4005 3281 4022 1877 2693 5065
pt.am.nsm p.a r.asm v.api.3s cj p.d n.dsm

κληθήσεταί σοι σπέρμα, 19 λογισάμενος ὅτι καὶ
will be named ˻for you."˼ *descendants* He considered that God was able to raise him up even
2813 5148 5065 3357 4022 2536 1543 1543 1586 1586 1586 2779
v.fpi.3s r.ds.2 n.nsn pt.am.nsm cj adv

ἐκ νεκρῶν ἐγείρειν δυνατὸς ὁ θεός, ὅθεν αὐτὸν καὶ ἐν παραβολῇ
from the dead, *to raise up* *was able* *{the}* *God* *from there* *him* and, in a sense,
1666 3738 1586 1543 3836 2536 3854 899 2779 1877 4130
p.g a.gpm f.pa a.nsm d.nsm n.nsm cj r.asm.3 adv p.d n.dsf

ἐκομίσατο. ← 20 πίστει καὶ
he did receive him back from there. By faith Isaac invoked blessings on Jacob and Esau, even
3152 899 3854 3854 4411 2693 2328 2328 2328 2609 2779 2481 2779
v.ami.3s n.dsf adv

περὶ μελλόντων εὐλόγησεν Ἰσαὰκ τὸν Ἰακὼβ καὶ τὸν Ἠσαῦ. 21 πίστει
regarding things to come. *invoked blessings on* *Isaac* *{the}* *Jacob* *and* *{the}* *Esau* By faith
4309 3516 2328 2693 3836 2609 2779 3836 2481 4411
p.g pt.pa.gpn v.aai.3s n.nsm d.asm n.asm cj d.asm n.asm n.dsf

NASB

promises, but hav-
ing seen them and
having welcomed
them from a dis-
tance, and having
confessed that they
were strangers and
exiles on the earth.
14 For those who say
such things make it
clear that they are
seeking a country
of their own. 15 And
indeed if they had
been thinking of
that *country* from
which they went
out, they would
have had opportu-
nity to return. 16 But
as it is, they desire
a better *country,*
that is, a heavenly
one. Therefore God
is not ashamed
to be called their
God; for He has
prepared a city for
them.
17 By faith Abra-
ham, when he was
tested, offered up
Isaac, and he who
had received the
promises was of-
fering up his only
begotten *son;* 18 *it*
was he to whom it
was said, "IN ISAAC
YOUR DESCENDANTS
SHALL BE CALLED."
19 He considered
that God is able to
raise *people* even
from the dead,
from which he also
received him back
as a type. 20 By faith
Isaac blessed Jacob
and Esau, even
regarding things to
come. 21 By faith

[a] 18 Gen. 21:12

NIV

Jacob, when he
was dying, blessed
each of Joseph's
sons, and wor-
shiped as he leaned
on the top of his
staff.
22By faith Joseph,
when his end was
near, spoke about
the exodus of the
Israelites from
Egypt and gave
instructions con-
cerning the burial
of his bones.
23By faith Moses'
parents hid him
for three months
after he was born,
because they saw
he was no ordinary
child, and they
were not afraid of
the king's edict.
24By faith Mo-
ses, when he had
grown up, refused
to be known as
the son of Phar-
aoh's daughter.
25He chose to be
mistreated along
with the people of
God rather than
to enjoy the fleet-
ing pleasures of
sin. 26He regarded
disgrace for the
sake of Christ as of
greater value than
the treasures of
Egypt, because he
was looking ahead
to his reward.
27By faith he left
Egypt, not fearing
the king's anger;
he persevered be-
cause he saw him
who is invisible.
28By faith he kept
the Passover and
the application of
blood, so that the
destroyer of the
firstborn would
not touch the first-
born of Israel.
29By faith

Ἰακὼβ ἀποθνῄσκων ἕκαστον τῶν υἱῶν Ἰωσὴφ εὐλόγησεν καὶ
Jacob, while dying, blessed each of the sons of Joseph, *blessed* and
2609 633 2328 1667 3836 5626 2737 2328 2779
n.nsm pt.pa.nsm r.asm d.gpm n.gpm n.gsm v.aai.3s cj

προσεκύνησεν ἐπὶ τὸ ἄκρον τῆς ῥάβδου αὐτοῦ. 22 πίστει Ἰωσὴφ
bowed in worship, leaning on the top of his staff. *his* By faith Joseph,
4686 2093 3836 216 3836 899 4811 899 4411 2737
v.aai.3s p.a d.asn n.asn d.gsf n.gsf r.gsm.3 n.dsf n.nsm

τελευτῶν περὶ τῆς ἐξόδου τῶν υἱῶν Ἰσραὴλ ἐμνημόνευσεν καὶ
⌞at the end of his life,⌟ spoke about the exodus of the sons of Israel *spoke* and gave
5462 3648 4309 3836 2016 3836 5626 2702 3648 2779 1948
pt.pa.nsm p.g d.gsf n.gsf d.gpm n.gpm n.gsm v.aai.3s cj

περὶ τῶν ὀστέων αὐτοῦ ἐνετείλατο. 23 πίστει Μωϋσῆς
instructions regarding the burial of his bones. *his* *gave instructions* By faith Moses,
1948 4309 3836 899 4014 899 1948 4411 3707
p.g d.gpn n.gpn r.gsm.3 v.ami.3s n.dsf n.nsm

γεννηθεὶς ἐκρύβη τρίμηνον ὑπὸ τῶν πατέρων αὐτοῦ, διότι εἶδον
⌞when he was born,⌟ was hidden for three months by *{the}* his parents, *his* because they saw
1164 3221 5564 5679 3836 899 4252 899 1484 1625
pt.ap.nsm v.api.3s n.asn p.g d.gpm n.gpm r.gsm.3 cj v.aai.3p

ἀστεῖον τὸ παιδίον καὶ ↱ ↱ οὐκ ἐφοβήθησαν τὸ
that he was an extraordinary *{the}* child, and they were not afraid of the king's
842 3836 4086 2779 5828 5828 4024 5828 3836 995
a.asn d.asn n.asn cj pl v.api.3p d.asn

διάταγμα τοῦ βασιλέως. 24 πίστει Μωϋσῆς μέγας γενόμενος
edict. *{the}* *king's* By faith Moses, when he was ⌞grown up,⌟ *when he was*
1409 3836 995 4411 3707 1181 1181 1181 3489 1181
n.asn d.gsm n.gsm n.dsf n.nsm a.nsm pt.am.nsm

ἠρνήσατο λέγεσθαι υἱὸς → θυγατρὸς Φαραώ, 25 μᾶλλον ἑλόμενος
disdained to be called the son of Pharaoh's daughter, *Pharaoh's* choosing rather *choosing*
766 3306 5626 5755 2588 5755 145 3437 145
v.ami.3s f.pp n.nsm n.gsf n.gsm adv.c pt.am.nsm

συγκακουχεῖσθαι τῷ λαῷ τοῦ θεοῦ ἢ πρόσκαιρον ἔχειν
⌞to suffer hardship along with⌟ the people of God than to enjoy the transient *to enjoy*
5156 3836 3295 3836 2536 2445 2400 2400 4672 2400
f.pm d.dsm n.dsm d.gsm n.gsm pl a.asf f.pa

ἁμαρτίας ἀπόλαυσιν, 26 μείζονα
pleasure of sin. *pleasure* He considered abuse for the sake of Christ greater
656 281 656 2451 2451 3944 3836 3836 3836 3836 5986 3489
n.gsf n.asf a.asm.c

πλοῦτον ἡγησάμενος τῶν Αἰγύπτου θησαυρῶν τὸν ὀνειδισμὸν
wealth *He considered* ⌞than the⌟ treasures of Egypt, *treasures* *{the}* *abuse*
4458 2451 3836 2565 131 2565 3836 3944
n.asm pt.am.nsm d.gpm n.gsf n.gpm d.asm n.asm

τοῦ Χριστοῦ· ἀπέβλεπεν γὰρ εἰς τὴν μισθαποδοσίαν. 27 πίστει
for the sake of *Christ* for ⌞he was looking ahead⌟ *for* to his reward. By faith
3836 5986 1142 611 1142 1650 3836 3632 4411
d.gsm n.gsm v.iai.3s cj p.a d.asf n.asf n.dsf

κατέλιπεν Αἴγυπτον μὴ φοβηθεὶς τὸν θυμὸν τοῦ βασιλέως·
he left Egypt, not fearing the anger of the king, for he endured as
2901 131 3590 5828 3836 2596 3836 995 1142 2846 2846 6055
v.aai.3s n.asf pl pt.ap.nsm d.asm n.asm d.gsm n.gsm

τὸν γὰρ ἀόρατον ὡς ὁρῶν ἐκαρτέρησεν. 28 πίστει
though seeing the *for* ⌞one who is invisible.⌟ *as though* *seeing* *he endured* By faith
6055 3972 3836 1142 548 6055 3972 2846 4411
d.asm cj a.asm pl pt.pa.nsm v.aai.3s n.dsf

πεποίηκεν τὸ πάσχα καὶ τὴν πρόσχυσιν τοῦ αἵματος, ἵνα
he kept the Passover and the sprinkling of blood, so that the destroying angel
4472 3836 4247 2779 3836 4717 3836 135 2671 3836 3905 3905
v.rai.3s d.asn n.asn cj d.asf n.asf d.gsn n.gsn cj

μὴ ὁ ὀλοθρεύων τὰ πρωτότοκα θίγῃ αὐτῶν. 29 πίστει
would not *the* *destroying angel* touch *{the}* their firstborn. *would touch* *their* By faith
2566 3590 3836 3905 2566 3836 899 4758 2566 899 4411
pl d.nsm pt.pa.nsm d.apn a.apn v.aas.3s r.gpm.3 n.dsf

NASB

Jacob, as he was
dying, blessed
each of the sons
of Joseph, and
worshiped, *leaning*
on the top of his
staff. 22By faith
Joseph, when he
was dying, made
mention of the
exodus of the sons
of Israel, and gave
orders concerning
his bones.
23By faith Mo-
ses, when he was
born, was hidden
for three months
by his parents,
because they saw
he was a beautiful
child; and they
were not afraid of
the king's edict.
24By faith Moses,
when he had grown
up, refused to be
called the son of
Pharaoh's daugh-
ter, 25choosing
rather to endure
ill-treatment with
the people of God
than to enjoy the
passing pleasures
of sin, 26consider-
ing the reproach
of Christ greater
riches than the
treasures of Egypt;
for he was looking
to the reward. 27By
faith he left Egypt,
not fearing the
wrath of the king;
for he endured, as
seeing Him who
is unseen. 28By
faith he kept the
Passover and the
sprinkling of the
blood, so that he
who destroyed the
firstborn would not
touch them.

NIV

the people passed
through the Red
Sea as on dry
land; but when the
Egyptians tried to
do so, they were
drowned.
[30]By faith the
walls of Jericho
fell, after the
army had marched
around them for
seven days.
[31]By faith the
prostitute Rahab,
because she wel-
comed the spies,
was not killed with
those who were
disobedient.[a]
[32]And what more
shall I say? I do
not have time to
tell about Gideon,
Barak, Samson and
Jephthah, about
David and Samuel
and the prophets,
[33]who through
faith conquered
kingdoms, admin-
istered justice, and
gained what was
promised; who shut
the mouths of li-
ons, [34]quenched the
fury of the flames,
and escaped the
edge of the sword;
whose weakness
was turned to
strength; and who
became powerful
in battle and rout-
ed foreign armies.
[35]Women received
back their dead,
raised to life again.
There were others
who were tortured,
refusing to be re-
leased so that they
might gain an even
better resurrection.
[36]Some faced jeers
and flogging, and
even chains and
imprisonment.
[37]They were put
to death by ston-
ing;[b] they were
sawed in two; they
were killed by the
sword. They went
about in sheepskins
and goatskins,

[a] 31 Or *unbelieving*
[b] 37 Some early manuscripts *stoning; they were put to the test;*

διέβησαν τὴν ἐρυθρὰν θάλασσαν ὡς διὰ ξηρᾶς γῆς, ἧς ⌊πεῖραν
they crossed the Red Sea ⌊as if⌋ on dry land; but when the Egyptians tried,
1329 3836 2261 2498 6055 1328 3831 1178 4005 3836 130 4278
v.aai.3p d.asf a.asf n.asf pl p.g a.gsf n.gsf r.gsf n.asf

λαβόντες⌋ οἱ Αἰγύπτιοι κατεπόθησαν. [30] πίστει τὰ τείχη Ἰεριχὼ ἔπεσαν
the *Egyptians* they were drowned. By faith the walls of Jericho fell down
3284 3836 130 2927 4411 3836 5446 2637 4406
pt.aa.npm d.npm n.npm v.api.3p n.dsf d.npn n.npn n.gsf v.aai.3p

κυκλωθέντα ἐπὶ ἑπτὰ ἡμέρας. [31] πίστει Ῥαὰβ ἡ πόρνη → οὐ
⌊after they had been encircled⌋ for seven days. By faith Rahab the prostitute did not
3240 2093 2231 2465 4411 4805 3836 4520 5272 4024
pt.ap.npn p.a a.apf n.apf n.dsf n.nsf d.nsf n.nsf pl

συναπώλετο τοῖς ἀπειθήσασιν δεξαμένη τοὺς κατασκόπους μετ᾽ εἰρήνης.
perish with the unbelievers, ⌊because she had received⌋ the spies with peace.
5272 3836 578 1312 3836 2946 3552 1645
v.ami.3s d.dpm pt.aa.dpm pt.am.nsf d.apm n.apm p.g n.gsf

[32] καὶ τί ἔτι λέγω; ἐπιλείψει με γὰρ διηγούμενον ὁ χρόνος περὶ
And what more ⌊shall I say?⌋ For time would fail me *For* if I told *{the}* *time* about
2779 5515 2285 3306 1142 5989 2142 1609 1142 1455 3836 5989 4309
cj r.asn adv v.pas.1s v.fai.3s r.as.1 cj pt.pm.asm d.nsm n.nsm p.g

Γεδεών, Βαράκ, Σαμψών, Ἰεφθάε, Δαυίδ τε καὶ Σαμουὴλ καὶ τῶν
Gideon, Barak, Samson, Jephthah, about both David *both* and Samuel and the
1146 973 4907 2650 5445 1253 5445 2779 4905 2779 3836
n.gsm n.gsm n.gsm n.gsm n.gsm cj cj n.gsm cj d.gpm

προφητῶν, [33] οἳ διὰ πίστεως κατηγωνίσαντο βασιλείας, εἰργάσαντο
prophets, who through faith conquered kingdoms, brought about
4737 4005 1328 4411 2865 993 2237
n.gpm d.npm p.g n.gsf v.ami.3p n.apf v.ami.3p

δικαιοσύνην, ἐπέτυχον ἐπαγγελιῶν, ἔφραξαν στόματα λεόντων, [34] ἔσβεσαν
justice, obtained what was promised; who shut the mouths of lions, extinguished
1466 2209 2039 5852 5125 3329 4931
n.asf v.aai.3p n.gpf v.aai.3p n.apn n.gpm v.aai.3p

δύναμιν πυρός, ἔφυγον στόματα → μαχαίρης, → ἐδυναμώθησαν
raging flames, escaped the edge of the sword; who after weakness were made strong,
1539 4786 5771 5125 3479 608 819 1540
n.asf n.gsn v.aai.3p n.apn n.gsf v.api.3p

ἀπὸ ἀσθενείας, ἐγενήθησαν ἰσχυροὶ ἐν πολέμῳ, → παρεμβολὰς ἔκλιναν
after *weakness* who became mighty in war and put foreign armies to flight.
608 819 1181 2708 1877 4483 3111 259 4213 3111
p.g n.gsf v.api.3p a.npm p.d n.dsm n.apf v.aai.3p

ἀλλοτρίων. [35] ἔλαβον γυναῖκες ἐξ ἀναστάσεως τοὺς νεκροὺς
foreign Women received *Women* their dead by resurrection. *{the}* *dead*
259 1222 3284 1222 899 3738 1666 414 3836 3738
n.gpm v.aai.3p n.npf p.g n.gsf d.apm a.apm

αὐτῶν· ἄλλοι δὲ ἐτυμπανίσθησαν → οὐ προσδεξάμενοι τὴν ἀπολύτρωσιν,
their But others *But* were tortured, after refusing to accept *{the}* release,
899 1254 257 1254 5594 4657 4024 4657 3836 667
r.gpf.3 r.npm pl v.api.3p pl pt.am.npm d.asf n.asf

ἵνα κρείττονος ἀναστάσεως τύχωσιν· [36] ἕτεροι δὲ
so that they might gain a better resurrection. *they might gain* Others *{and}* experienced
2671 5593 5593 5593 3202 414 5593 2283 1254 4278
cj a.gsf.c n.gsf v.aas.3p r.npm pl

ἐμπαιγμῶν καὶ μαστίγων ⌊πεῖραν ἔλαβον,⌋ ἔτι δὲ δεσμῶν καὶ φυλακῆς·
jeering and flogging, *experienced* and even *and* chains and prison.
1849 2779 3465 4278 3284 1254 2285 1254 1301 2779 5871
n.gpm cj n.gpf n.asf v.aai.3p adv cj n.gpm cj n.gsf

[37] ἐλιθάσθησαν, ἐπρίσθησαν,[a] ἐν φόνῳ → μαχαίρης
They were stoned; they were sawn in two; they were murdered by the sword.
3342 4569 1877 5840 633 633 633 3479
v.api.3p v.api.3p p.d n.dsm n.gsf

ἀπέθανον, περιῆλθον ἐν μηλωταῖς, ἐν ⌊αἰγείοις δέρμασιν,⌋
they were murdered They went about in sheepskins and *{in}* goatskins,
633 4320 1877 3603 1877 128 1293
v.aai.3p v.aai.3p p.d n.dpf p.d a.dpn n.dpn

[a] ἐπειράσθησαν included by TR after ἐπρίσθησαν.

NASB

[29]By faith they
passed through the
Red Sea as though
they were passing
through dry land;
and the Egyp-
tians, when they
attempted it, were
drowned.
[30]By faith the
walls of Jericho
fell down after they
had been encircled
for seven days.
[31]By faith Rahab
the harlot did not
perish along with
those who were
disobedient, after
she had welcomed
the spies in peace.
[32]And what more
shall I say? For
time will fail me
if I tell of Gideon,
Barak, Samson,
Jephthah, of Da-
vid and Samuel
and the prophets,
[33]who by faith con-
quered kingdoms,
performed *acts*
of righteousness,
obtained promises,
shut the mouths of
lions, [34]quenched
the power of fire,
escaped the edge
of the sword,
from weakness
were made strong,
became mighty in
war, put foreign
armies to flight.
[35]Women received
back their dead
by resurrection;
and others were
tortured, not ac-
cepting their
release, so that
they might obtain a
better resurrection;
[36]and others expe-
rienced mockings
and scourgings,
yes, also chains
and imprison-
ment. [37]They were
stoned, they were
sawn in two, [a]they
were tempted, they
were put to death
with the sword;
they went about
in sheepskins, in
goatskins,

[a] One early ms does not contain *they were tempted*

NIV

destitute, persecut-
ed and mistreat-
ed— [38]the world
was not worthy of
them. They wan-
dered in deserts
and mountains,
living in caves
and in holes in the
ground.
[39]These were all
commended for
their faith, yet
none of them re-
ceived what had
been promised,
[40]since God had
planned something
better for us so
that only together
with us would they
be made perfect.

12 Therefore,
since we
are surrounded
by such a great
cloud of witness-
es, let us throw off
everything that
hinders and the
sin that so easily
entangles. And
let us run with
perseverance the
race marked out
for us, [2]fixing our
eyes on Jesus, the
pioneer and per-
fecter of faith. For
the joy set before
him he endured
the cross, scorning
its shame, and sat
down at the right
hand of the throne
of God. [3]Consider
him who endured
such opposition
from sinners, so
that you will not

ὑστερούμενοι, θλιβόμενοι, κακουχούμενοι, [38] ὧν οὐκ ἦν
destitute, persecuted, mistreated ⌊(of whom⌋ the world was not *was*
5728 2567 2807 4005 3836 3180 1639 4024 1639
pt.pp.npm pt.pp.npm pt.pp.npm r.gpm pl v.iai.3s

ἄξιος ὁ κόσμος, ἐπὶ ἐρημίαις πλανώμενοι καὶ
worthy). *the* *world* They wandered aimlessly in deserts *They wandered aimlessly* and on
545 3836 3180 4414 4414 4414 2093 2244 4414 2779
a.nsm d.nsm n.nsm p.d n.dpf pt.pp.npm cj

ὄρεσιν καὶ σπηλαίοις καὶ ταῖς ὀπαῖς τῆς γῆς. [39] καὶ ↱ οὗτοι
mountains, *{and}* living in caves and *{the}* crevices in the ground, and although they
4001 2779 5068 2779 3836 3956 3836 1178 2779 3455 4047
n.dpn cj n.dpn cj d.dpf n.dpf d.gsf n.gsf cj r.npm

πάντες μαρτυρηθέντες διὰ τῆς πίστεως ↱ ↱ οὐκ ἐκομίσαντο τὴν
all had received commendation for their faith, they did not receive what
4246 3455 1328 3836 4411 3152 3152 4024 3152 3836
a.npm pt.ap.npm p.g d.gsf n.gsf pl v.ami.3p d.asf

ἐπαγγελίαν, [40] τοῦ θεοῦ περὶ ἡμῶν ↰ ↰
had been promised, for *{the}* God had provided something better with us in mind,
2039 3836 2536 4587 4587 5516 3202 4309 7005 4309 4309
n.asf d.gsm n.gsm p.g r.gp.1

κρεῖττόν τι προβλεψαμένου, ἵνα μὴ χωρὶς ἡμῶν
better *something* *had provided* so that they should not reach their goal apart from us.
3202 5516 4587 2671 5457 5457 3590 5457 5457 5457 6006 7005
a.asn.c r.asn pt.am.gsm cj pl p.g r.gp.1

τελειωθῶσιν.
they should reach their goal
5457
v.aps.3p

[12:1] τοιγαροῦν καὶ ἡμεῖς τοσοῦτον ἔχοντες
Therefore *also* since we ourselves have so great *since we have* a cloud of
5521 2779 2400 2400 7005 2400 5537 2400 3751 3459
cj cj r.np.1 r.asn pt.pa.npm

περικείμενον ἡμῖν νέφος μαρτύρων, ὄγκον → → ἀποθέμενοι πάντα
witnesses surrounding us, *cloud* *of witnesses* *impediment* let us also lay aside every
3459 4329 7005 3751 3459 3839 2779 700 4246
pt.pm.asn r.dp.1 n.asn n.gpm n.asm pt.am.npm a.asm

καὶ τὴν εὐπερίστατον ἁμαρτίαν, δι᾽ ὑπομονῆς
impediment, and the sin that so easily distracts, *sin* and let us run with endurance
3839 2779 3836 281 2342 281 5556 5556 5556 1328 5705
cj d.asf a.asf n.asf p.g n.gsf

τρέχωμεν τὸν προκείμενον ἡμῖν ἀγῶνα [2] ἀφορῶντες εἰς τὸν
let us run the race that is prescribed for us, *race* fixing our gaze upon Jesus, the pioneer
5556 3836 74 4618 7005 74 927 1650 2652 3836 795
v.pas.1p d.asm pt.pm.asm r.dp.1 n.asm pt.pa.npm p.a d.asm

τῆς πίστεως ἀρχηγὸν καὶ τελειωτὴν Ἰησοῦν, ὃς ἀντὶ τῆς
and perfecter of our faith, *pioneer* *and* *perfecter* *Jesus* who ⌊rather than⌋ the joy
2779 5460 3836 4411 795 2779 5460 2652 4005 505 3836 5915
d.gsf n.gsf n.asm cj n.asm n.asm r.nsm p.g d.gsf

προκειμένης αὐτῷ χαρᾶς ὑπέμεινεν σταυρὸν αἰσχύνης καταφρονήσας
set before him *joy* endured a cross, disregarding its shame, *disregarding* and
4618 899 5915 5702 5089 2969 158 2969 5445
pt.pm.gsf r.dsm.3 n.gsf v.aai.3s n.asm n.gsf pt.aa.nsm

ἐν δεξιᾷ τε τοῦ θρόνου τοῦ θεοῦ κεκάθικεν.
has now taken his seat at the right hand *and now* of the throne of God. *has taken his seat*
2767 5445 2767 2767 2767 1877 1288 5445 3836 2585 3836 2536 2767
p.d a.dsf cj d.gsm n.gsm d.gsm n.gsm v.rai.3s

[3] ἀναλογίσασθε γὰρ τὸν τοιαύτην
Consider *{for}* him who endured from sinners *{the}* such opposition
382 1142 5702 5702 5702 5679 283 3836 5525 517
v.amm.2p cj d.asm r.asf

ὑπομεμενηκότα ὑπὸ τῶν ἁμαρτωλῶν εἰς ἑαυτὸν ἀντιλογίαν, ἵνα ↱ ↱ μὴ
him who endured *from* *{the}* *sinners* against himself, *opposition* so that you may not
5702 5679 3836 283 1650 1571 517 2671 2827 2827 3590
pt.ra.asm p.g d.gpm a.gpm p.a r.asm.3 n.asf cj pl

NASB

being destitute,
afflicted, ill-treated
[38](*men* of whom
the world was not
worthy), wander-
ing in deserts and
mountains and
caves and holes in
the ground.
[39]And all these,
having gained
approval through
their faith, did not
receive what was
promised, [40]because
God had provided
something bet-
ter for us, so that
apart from us they
would not be made
perfect.

Jesus, the Example

[12:1]Therefore, since
we have so great a
cloud of witnesses
surrounding us, let
us also lay aside
every encumbrance
and the sin which
so easily entangles
us, and let us run
with endurance the
race that is set be-
fore us, [2]fixing our
eyes on Jesus, the
author and perfect-
er of faith, who for
the joy set before
Him endured the
cross, despising the
shame, and has sat
down at the right
hand of the throne
of God.
[3]For consider Him
who has endured
such hostility by
sinners against
Himself, so that
you will not grow

NIV

grow weary and
lose heart.

God Disciplines His Children

4 In your struggle
against sin, you
have not yet re-
sisted to the point
of shedding your
blood. 5 And have
you completely
forgotten this word
of encouragement
that addresses
you as a father ad-
dresses his son? It
says,

> "My son, do not make light of the Lord's discipline,
> and do not lose heart when he rebukes you,
> 6 because the Lord disciplines the one he loves,
> and he chastens everyone he accepts as his son."[a]

7 Endure hardship
as discipline; God
is treating you as
his children. For
what children are
not disciplined by
their father? 8 If
you are not disci-
plined—and ev-
eryone undergoes
discipline—then
you are not legiti-
mate, not true sons
and daughters at
all. 9 Moreover,
we have all had
human fathers
who disciplined us
and we respected
them for it. How
much more should
we submit to the
Father of spirits
and live! 10 They
disciplined us for a
little while as they
thought best; but
God disciplines
us for our good, in
order that we may
share in his holi-
ness. 11 No disci-
pline seems pleas-
ant at the time, but
painful. Later on,

[a] 5,6 Prov. 3:11,12 (see Septuagint)

κάμητε ταῖς ψυχαῖς ὑμῶν ἐκλυόμενοι. 4 οὔπω μέχρις
grow weary in your souls *your* and lose heart. You have not yet resisted to the point
2827 3836 7007 6034 7007 1725 510 510 4037 510 3588
v.aas.2p d.dpf n.dpf r.gp.2 pt.pp.npm adv p.g

αἵματος ἀντικατέστητε πρὸς τὴν ἁμαρτίαν ἀνταγωνιζόμενοι. 5 καὶ
of bloodshed *You have resisted* as you struggle against *{the}* sin. *as you struggle* And
135 510 497 497 497 4639 3836 281 497 2779
n.gsn v.aai.2p p.a d.asf n.asf pt.pm.npm cj

ἐκλέλησθε τῆς παρακλήσεως, ἥτις ὑμῖν ὡς υἱοῖς διαλέγεται·
have you forgotten the word of encouragement that speaks to you as sons? *speaks* "My
1720 3836 4155 4015 1363 7007 6055 5626 1363 1609
v.rmi.2p d.gsf n.gsf r.nsf r.dp.2 pl n.dpm v.pmi.3s

υἱέ μου, ↱ μὴ ὀλιγώρει παιδείας → κυρίου μηδὲ ἐκλύου
son, *My* do not regard lightly the discipline of the Lord, nor lose heart when corrected
5626 1609 3902 3590 3902 4082 3261 3593 1725 1794 1794
n.vsm r.gs.1 pl v.pam.2s n.gsf n.gsm cj v.ppm.2s

ὑπ' αὐτοῦ ἐλεγχόμενος· 6 ὃν γὰρ ἀγαπᾷ κύριος παιδεύει,
by him. *when corrected* For the Lord disciplines ⌊the one⌋ *For* he loves, *Lord* *disciplines*
5679 899 1794 1142 3261 4084 4005 1142 26 3261 4084
p.g r.gsm.3 pt.pp.nsm r.asm cj v.pai.3s n.nsm v.pai.3s

μαστιγοῖ δὲ πάντα → υἱὸν ὃν παραδέχεται.
and ⌊corrects with punishment⌋ *and* everyone whom he receives as a son." *whom* *he receives*
1254 3463 1254 4246 4005 4138 4138 5626 4005 4138
v.pai.3s cj a.asm n.asm r.asm v.pmi.3s

7 εἰς παιδείαν ὑπομένετε, ὡς υἱοῖς ὑμῖν
Endure your trials as divine discipline. *Endure trials* God is treating you as sons. *you*
5702 5702 1650 4082 5702 2536 4712 4712 7007 6055 5626 7007
p.a n.asf v.pai.2p pl n.dpm r.dp.2

προσφέρεται ὁ θεός. τίς γὰρ υἱὸς ὃν ↱ οὐ παιδεύει
is treating *{the}* *God* For what *For* son is there whom a father does not discipline?
4712 3836 2536 1142 5515 1142 5626 4005 4252 4084 4024 4084
v.ppi.3s d.nsm n.nsm r.nsm cj n.nsm r.asm pl v.pai.3s

πατήρ; 8 εἰ δὲ χωρίς ἐστε παιδείας ἧς ⌊μέτοχοι
father But if *But* you are left without *you are* discipline, ⌊in which⌋ all sons share,
4252 1254 1623 1254 1639 1639 6006 1639 4082 4005 4246 3581
n.nsm cj cj p.g v.pai.2p n.gsf r.gsf n.npm

γεγόνασιν⌋ πάντες, ἄρα νόθοι καὶ οὐχ υἱοί ἐστε. 9 εἶτα
all then you are ⌊illegitimate children⌋ and not sons. *you are* Furthermore,
1181 4246 726 1639 1639 3785 2779 4024 5626 1639 1663
v.rai.3p a.npm cj a.npm cj pl n.npm v.pai.2p adv

τοὺς μὲν τῆς σαρκὸς ἡμῶν πατέρας εἴχομεν παιδευτὰς καὶ
{the} ~ we had *{the}* our natural *our* fathers *we had* who disciplined us and
3836 3525 2400 2400 3836 7005 4922 7005 4252 2400 4083 2779
d.apm pl d.gsf n.gsf r.gp.1 n.apm v.iai.1p n.apm cj

ἐνετρεπόμεθα· ↱ ↱ οὐ πολὺ δὲ[a] μᾶλλον ὑποταγησόμεθα τῷ πατρὶ
we respected them. Should we not much *{and}* more submit ourselves ⌊to the⌋ Father
1956 5718 5718 4024 4498 1254 3437 5718 3836 4252
v.ipi.1p pl adv cj adv.c v.fpi.1p d.dsm n.dsm

τῶν πνευμάτων καὶ ζήσομεν; 10 οἱ μὲν γὰρ πρὸς ὀλίγας ἡμέρας
of spirits and live? For they ~ *For* disciplined us for a short time
3836 4460 2779 2409 1142 3836 3525 1142 4084 4639 3900 2465
d.gpn n.gpn cj v.fai.1p d.npm pl cj p.a a.apf n.apf

κατὰ τὸ δοκοῦν αὐτοῖς ἐπαίδευον, ὁ δὲ ἐπὶ τὸ συμφέρον
as it seemed best to them, *disciplined* but he *but* disciplines us for our benefit,
2848 3836 1506 899 4084 1254 3836 1254 2093 3836 5237
p.a d.asn pt.pa.asn r.dpm.3 v.iai.3p d.nsm cj p.a d.asn pt.pa.asn

εἰς τὸ μεταλαβεῖν τῆς ἁγιότητος αὐτοῦ. 11 πᾶσα δὲ παιδεία πρὸς μὲν
⌊so that⌋ ~ we may share *{the}* his holy character. *his* All *{and}* discipline at ~
1650 3836 3561 3836 899 42 899 4246 1254 4082 4639 3525
p.a d.asn f.aa d.gsf n.gsf r.gsm.3 a.nsf cj n.nsf p.a pl

τὸ παρὸν οὐ δοκεῖ χαρᾶς εἶναι ἀλλὰ λύπης, ὕστερον δὲ
the time seems not *seems* to be pleasant, *to be* but painful; but later *but* it
3836 4205 1506 4024 1506 1639 1639 5915 1639 247 3383 1254 5731 1254 625
d.asn pt.pa.asn pl v.pai.3s n.gsf f.pa cj n.gsf adv.c cj

[a] [δὲ] UBS, omitted by TNIV.

NASB

weary and lose
heart.

A Father's Discipline

4 You have not yet
resisted to the point
of shedding blood
in your striving
against sin; 5 and
you have forgot-
ten the exhortation
which is addressed
to you as sons,

> "My son, do not regard lightly the discipline of the Lord,
> Nor faint when you are reproved by Him;
> 6 For those whom the Lord loves He disciplines,
> And He scourges every son whom He receives."

7 It is for discipline
that you endure;
God deals with
you as with sons;
for what son is
there whom *his*
father does not
discipline? 8 But
if you are with-
out discipline, of
which all have
become partakers,
then you are il-
legitimate children
and not sons. 9 Fur-
thermore, we had
earthly fathers to
discipline us, and
we respected them;
shall we not much
rather be subject to
the Father of spir-
its, and live? 10 For
they disciplined
us for a short time
as seemed best
to them, but He
disciplines us for
our good, so that
we may share His
holiness. 11 All
discipline for the
moment seems not
to be joyful, but
sorrowful; yet to

NIV

however, it pro-
duces a harvest of
righteousness and
peace for those
who have been
trained by it.
12 Therefore,
strengthen your
feeble arms and
weak knees.
13 "Make level
paths for your
feet,"[a] so that the
lame may not be
disabled, but rath-
er healed.

Warning and Encouragement

14 Make every
effort to live in
peace with every-
one and to be holy;
without holiness
no one will see
the Lord. 15 See to
it that no one falls
short of the grace
of God and that no
bitter root grows
up to cause trouble
and defile many.
16 See that no one is
sexually immoral,
or is godless like
Esau, who for a
single meal sold
his inheritance
rights as the oldest
son. 17 Afterward,
as you know, when
he wanted to in-
herit this blessing,
he was rejected.
Even though he
sought the bless-
ing with tears, he
could not change
what he had done.

The Mountain of Fear and the Mountain of Joy

18 You have not
come to a moun-
tain that can be
touched and that
is burning with
fire; to darkness,
gloom and storm;
19 to a trumpet blast
or to such a voice
speaking words
that those who
heard it begged
that no further

καρπὸν εἰρηνικὸν τοῖς δι᾽
yields the peaceful fruit *peaceful* of righteousness to those who have been trained by
625 1646 2843 1646 1466 1466 3836 1214 1214 1214 1214 1328
n.asm a.asm d.dpm p.g

αὐτῆς γεγυμνασμένοις ἀποδίδωσιν δικαιοσύνης. 12 διὸ τὰς
it. *who have been trained* *it yields* *of righteousness* Therefore strengthen your
899 1214 625 1466 1475 494 3836
r.gsf.3 pt.rp.dpm v.pai.3s n.gsf cj d.apf

παρειμένας χεῖρας καὶ τὰ παραλελυμένα γόνατα ἀνορθώσατε, 13 καὶ
drooping hands and *{the}* weakened knees *strengthen* and make straight
4223 5931 2779 3836 4168 1205 494 2779 4472 3981
pt.rp.apf n.apf cj d.apn pt.rp.apn n.apn v.aam.2p cj

τροχιὰς ὀρθὰς ποιεῖτε τοῖς ποσὶν ὑμῶν, ἵνα ↱ μὴ τὸ χωλὸν
paths *straight make* for your feet, *your* so that what is lame may not *what is lame*
5579 3981 4472 3836 7007 4546 7007 2671 3836 6000 6000 1762 3590 3836 6000
n.apf a.apf v.pam.2p d.dpm n.dpm r.gp.2 cj pl d.nsn a.nsn

ἐκτραπῇ, ἰαθῇ δὲ μᾶλλον. 14 εἰρήνην διώκετε μετὰ πάντων
be dislocated, but rather healed. *but rather* Strive for peace *Strive for* with everyone,
1762 1254 3437 2615 1254 3437 1503 1503 1645 1503 3552 4246
v.aps.3s v.aps.3s cj adv.c n.asf v.pam.2p p.g a.gpm

καὶ τὸν ἁγιασμόν, οὗ χωρὶς οὐδεὶς ὄψεται τὸν κύριον,
and for the holiness without which *without* no one will see the Lord.
2779 3836 40 6006 4005 6006 4029 3972 3836 3261
cj d.asm n.asm r.gsm p.g a.nsm v.fmi.3s d.asm n.asm

15 ἐπισκοποῦντες μή τις ˻ὑστερῶν ἀπὸ˼ τῆς χάριτος τοῦ θεοῦ, μή
Take care that no one forfeits the grace of God; and that no
2174 3590 5516 5728 608 3836 5921 3836 2536 3590
pt.pa.npm cj r.nsm pt.pa.nsm p.g d.gsf n.gsf d.gsm n.gsm cj

τις ῥίζα πικρίας ἄνω φύουσα ἐνοχλῇ καὶ δι᾽ αὐτῆς
{one} root of bitterness grows up *grows* and causes trouble and by it many
5516 4844 4394 5886 539 5886 1943 2779 1328 899 4498
r.nsf n.nsf n.gsf adv pt.pa.nsf v.pas.3s cj p.g r.gsf.3

μιανθῶσιν πολλοί, 16 μή τις πόρνος ἢ βέβηλος ὡς Ἠσαῦ, ὃς
are defiled. *many* that no one becomes immoral and profane like Esau, who gave
3620 4498 3590 5516 4521 2445 1013 6055 2481 4005 625
v.aps.3p a.npm cj r.nsm n.nsm cj a.nsm pl n.nsm r.nsm

ἀντὶ βρώσεως μιᾶς ἀπέδετο τὰ πρωτοτόκια
up his inheritance rights ˻in return for˼ a single meal. *single gave up {the} inheritance rights*
625 1571 4757 4757 505 1651 1111 1651 625 3836 4757
p.g n.gsf a.gsf v.ami.3s d.apn n.apn

ἑαυτοῦ. 17 ἴστε γὰρ ὅτι καὶ μετέπειτα θέλων κληρονομῆσαι τὴν
his For ˻you know˼ *For* that even afterward, ˻when he wanted˼ to inherit the
1571 1142 3857 1142 4022 2779 3575 2527 3099 3836
r.gsm.3 v.rai.2p cj cj adv adv pt.pa.nsm f.aa d.asf

εὐλογίαν ἀπεδοκιμάσθη, μετανοίας γὰρ τόπον οὐχ
blessing, he was rejected, for he found no opportunity for repentance, *for opportunity no*
2330 627 1142 2351 2351 4024 5536 3567 1142 5536 4024
n.asf v.api.3s n.gsf cj n.asm pl

εὗρεν καίπερ μετὰ δακρύων ἐκζητήσας αὐτήν.
he found even though he sought the blessing earnestly with tears. *he sought earnestly blessing*
2351 2788 1699 1699 899 1699 3552 1232 1699 899
v.aai.3s cj p.g n.gpn pt.aa.nsm r.asf.3

18 ↱ ↱ οὐ γὰρ προσεληλύθατε ψηλαφωμένῳ καὶ κεκαυμένῳ
For you have not *For* come to ˻something that can be touched,˼ *{and}* to a blazing
1142 4665 4665 4024 1142 4665 6027 2779 2794
pl cj v.rai.2p pt.pp.dsn cj pt.rp.dsn

πυρὶ καὶ γνόφῳ καὶ ζόφῳ καὶ θυέλλῃ 19 καὶ → σάλπιγγος ἤχῳ
fire, and darkness, and gloom, and a whirlwind; *{and}* to the blast of a trumpet *to blast*
4786 2779 1190 2779 2432 2779 2590 2779 2491 2491 4894 2491
n.dsn cj n.dsm cj n.dsm cj n.dsf cj n.gsf n.dsm

καὶ φωνῇ ῥημάτων, ἧς ↱ οἱ ἀκούσαντες παρῃτήσαντο μὴ →
and a sound of words which made those who heard it beg that no further
2779 5889 4839 4005 4148 3836 201 4148 3590
cj n.dsf n.gpn r.gsf d.npm pt.aa.npm v.ami.3p pl

NASB

those who have
been trained by it,
afterwards it yields
the peaceful fruit
of righteousness.
12 Therefore,
strengthen the
hands that are
weak and the knees
that are feeble,
13 and make straight
paths for your feet,
so that *the limb*
which is lame may
not be put out of
joint, but rather be
healed.
14 Pursue peace
with all men, and
the sanctification
without which no
one will see the
Lord. 15 See to it
that no one comes
short of the grace
of God; that no
root of bitterness
springing up causes
trouble, and by it
many be defiled;
16 that *there be* no
immoral or god-
less person like
Esau, who sold
his own birthright
for a *single* meal.
17 For you know that
even afterwards,
when he desired to
inherit the blessing,
he was rejected, for
he found no place
for repentance,
though he sought
for it with tears.

Contrast of Sinai and Zion

18 For you have
not come to *a*
mountain that can
be touched and to
a blazing fire, and
to darkness and
gloom and whirl-
wind, 19 and to the
blast of a trumpet
and the sound of
words which *sound*
was such that those
who heard begged
that no further

[a] 13 Prov. 4:26

NIV

word be spoken
to them, 20 because
they could not bear
what was com-
manded: "If even
an animal touches
the mountain, it
must be stoned to
death."[a] 21 The sight
was so terrifying
that Moses said, "I
am trembling with
fear."[b]
22 But you have
come to Mount
Zion, to the city
of the living God,
the heavenly Jeru-
salem. You have
come to thousands
upon thousands
of angels in joy-
ful assembly, 23 to
the church of the
firstborn, whose
names are written
in heaven. You
have come to God,
the Judge of all, to
the spirits of the
righteous made
perfect, 24 to Jesus
the mediator of a
new covenant, and
to the sprinkled
blood that speaks
a better word than
the blood of Abel.
25 See to it that
you do not refuse
him who speaks.
If they did not es-
cape when they
refused him who
warned them on
earth, how much
less will we, if we
turn away from
him who warns us
from heaven? 26 At
that time his voice
shook the earth,
but now he has
promised, "Once
more I will shake
not only the earth
but also the heav-
ens."[c] 27 The words
"once more" indi-
cate the removing
of what can be
shaken—that is,
created things—
so that

[a] 20 Exodus 19:12,13
[b] 21 See Deut. 9:19.
[c] 26 Haggai 2:6

προστεθῆναι αὐτοῖς λόγον, 20 ↱ ↱ οὐκ ἔφερον γὰρ τὸ
message be given to them, *message* for they could not endure *for* the
3364 4707 899 3364 1142 5770 5770 4024 5770 1142 3836
f.ap r.dpm.3 n.asm pl v.iai.3p cj d.asn

διαστελλόμενον, κἂν θηρίον θίγῃ τοῦ ὄρους, λιθοβοληθήσεται·[a] 21 καί,
order that was given: "If even a wild animal touches the mountain, it shall be stoned." And
1403 2829 2563 2566 3836 4001 3344 2779
pt.pp.asn crasis n.nsn v.aas.3s d.gsn n.gsn v.fpi.3s cj

οὕτω φοβερὸν ἦν τὸ φανταζόμενον, Μωϋσῆς εἶπεν, ἔκφοβός εἰμι καὶ
so awesome was the spectacle that Moses said, "I am terrified *I am* and
4048 5829 1639 3836 5751 3707 3306 1639 1639 1769 1639 2779
adv a.nsn v.iai.3s d.nsn pt.pp.nsn n.nsm v.aai.3s a.nsm v.pai.1s cj

ἔντρομος. 22 ἀλλὰ προσεληλύθατε Σιὼν ὄρει καὶ → πόλει →
trembling." ⌊On the contrary,⌋ you have come to Mount Zion, *Mount* even to the city of the
1958 247 4665 4001 4994 4001 2779 4484
a.nsm cj v.rai.2p n.dsf n.dsn cj n.dsf

θεοῦ ζῶντος, Ἰερουσαλὴμ ἐπουρανίῳ, καὶ μυριάσιν ἀγγέλων, →
living God, *living* the heavenly Jerusalem, *heavenly* and to innumerable angels, to a
2409 2536 2409 2230 2647 2230 2779 3689 34
n.gsm pt.pa.gsm n.dsf a.dsf cj n.dpf n.gpm

πανηγύρει 23 καὶ → ἐκκλησίᾳ → πρωτοτόκων ἀπογεγραμμένων ἐν
joyful assembly, and to the assembly of the firstborn whose names are inscribed in
4108 2779 1711 4758 616 1877
n.dsf cj n.dsf a.gpm pt.rp.gpm p.d

οὐρανοῖς καὶ → κριτῇ θεῷ πάντων καὶ → πνεύμασι → δικαίων
heaven, and to God, the judge *God* of all, and to the spirits of the righteous
4041 2779 2536 3216 2536 4246 2779 4460 1465
n.dpm cj n.dsm n.dsm a.gpm cj n.dpn a.gpm

τετελειωμένων 24 καὶ → διαθήκης νέας μεσίτῃ
⌊who have been made perfect,⌋ and to Jesus, mediator of a new covenant, *new* *mediator*
5457 2779 2652 2652 3542 3742 1347 3742 3542
pt.rp.gpm cj n.gsf a.gsf n.dsm

Ἰησοῦ καὶ → αἵματι ῥαντισμοῦ κρεῖττον λαλοῦντι παρὰ τὸν
to Jesus and to sprinkled blood *sprinkled* speaking more effectively *speaking* than the
2652 2779 4823 135 4823 3281 3202 3281 4123 3836
n.dsm cj n.dsn n.gsm a.asn.c pt.pa.dsn p.a d.asm

Ἄβελ. 25 βλέπετε μὴ παραιτήσησθε τὸν λαλοῦντα· εἰ γὰρ
blood of Abel. Take care not to disregard the one who is speaking! For if *For*
6 1063 3590 4148 3836 3281 1142 1623 1142
n.asm v.pam.2p cj v.ams.2p d.asm pt.pa.asm cj cj

ἐκεῖνοι ↱ οὐκ ἐξέφυγον ἐπὶ γῆς
those did not escape when they disregarded the one who warned them on earth,
1697 1767 4024 1767 4148 4148 4148 3836 5976 5976 5976 2093 1178
r.npm pl v.aai.3p p.g n.gsf

παραιτησάμενοι τὸν χρηματίζοντα, πολὺ μᾶλλον ἡμεῖς οἱ τὸν
when they disregarded *the* *one who warned* how much less will we, if we reject the one
4148 3836 5976 4498 3437 7005 3836 695 3836
pt.am.npm d.asm pt.pa.asm adv adv.c r.np.1 d.npm d.asm

ἀπ' οὐρανῶν ἀποστρεφόμενοι, 26 οὗ ἡ φωνὴ τὴν
who warns from heaven. *reject* At that time his *{the}* voice shook the
608 4041 695 5538 5538 5538 4005 3836 5889 4888 3836
p.g n.gpm pt.pm.npm r.gsm d.nsf n.nsf d.asf

γῆν ἐσάλευσεν τότε, νῦν δὲ ἐπήγγελται λέγων, ἔτι ἅπαξ ↱ ἐγὼ
earth, *shook* *At that time* but now *but* he has promised, *{saying}* "Yet ⌊once more⌋ will I
1178 4888 5538 1254 3814 1254 2040 3306 2285 562 4940 1609
n.asf v.aai.3s adv adv cj v.rmi.3s pt.pa.nsm adv adv r.ns.1

σείσω οὐ μόνον τὴν γῆν ἀλλὰ καὶ τὸν οὐρανόν. 27 τὸ δὲ ἔτι ἅπαξ
shake not only the earth but also the heaven." The phrase, *{and}* "Yet ⌊once more,"⌋
4940 4024 3667 3836 1178 247 2779 3836 4041 3836 1254 2285 562
v.fai.1s pl adv d.asf n.asf cj adv d.asm n.asm d.nsn cj adv adv

δηλοῖ τὴν[b] τῶν σαλευομένων μετάθεσιν ὡς πεποιημένων, ἵνα
declares the removal of what can be shaken *removal* — ⌊that is,⌋ created things — so that
1317 3836 3557 3836 4888 3557 6055 4472 2671
v.pai.3s d.asf d.gpn pt.pp.gpn n.asf pl pt.rp.gpn cj

[a] ἢ βολίδι κατατοξευθήσεται included by TR after λιθοβοληθήσεται.
[b] [τὴν] UBS.

NASB

word be spoken to
them. 20 For they
could not bear the
command, "IF EVEN
A BEAST TOUCHES
THE MOUNTAIN, IT
WILL BE STONED."
21 And so terrible
was the sight, *that*
Moses said, "I AM
FULL OF FEAR and
trembling." 22 But
you have come to
Mount Zion and to
the city of the liv-
ing God, the heav-
enly Jerusalem,
and to myriads
of angels, 23 to the
general assembly
and church of the
firstborn who are
enrolled in heaven,
and to God, the
Judge of all, and
to the spirits of *the*
righteous made
perfect, 24 and to
Jesus, the mediator
of a new cov-
enant, and to the
sprinkled blood,
which speaks better
than *the blood* of
Abel.

The Unshaken Kingdom

25 See to it that you
do not refuse Him
who is speaking.
For if those did not
escape when they
refused him who
warned *them* on
earth, much less
will we *escape* who
turn away from
Him who *warns*
from heaven. 26 And
His voice shook
the earth then, but
now He has prom-
ised, saying, "YET
ONCE MORE I WILL
SHAKE NOT ONLY THE
EARTH, BUT ALSO THE
HEAVEN." 27 This *ex-
pression,* "Yet once
more," denotes the
removing of those
things which can
be shaken, as of
created things, so

NIV

what cannot be shaken may remain.

[28]Therefore, since we are receiving a kingdom that cannot be shaken, let us be thankful, and so worship God acceptably with reverence and awe, [29]for our "God is a consuming fire."[a]

Concluding Exhortations

13 Keep on loving one another as brothers and sisters. [2]Do not forget to show hospitality to strangers, for by so doing some people have shown hospitality to angels without knowing it. [3]Continue to remember those in prison as if you were together with them in prison, and those who are mistreated as if you yourselves were suffering.

[4]Marriage should be honored by all, and the marriage bed kept pure, for God will judge the adulterer and all the sexually immoral. [5]Keep your lives free from the love of money and be content with what you have, because God has said,

> "Never will I leave you;
> never will I forsake you."[b]

[6]So we say with confidence,

> "The Lord is my helper; I will not be afraid.
> What can mere mortals do to me?"[c]

[7]Remember your leaders, who spoke the word of God to you. Consider

[a] 29 Deut. 4:24
[b] 5 Deut. 31:6
[c] 6 Psalm 118:6,7

μεινη τὰ μὴ σαλευόμενα. [28] διὸ
what cannot be shaken may remain. *what cannot be shaken* Therefore since we are
3836 3590 4888 4888 3531 3836 3590 4888 1475 4161 4161 4161
v.aas.3s d.npn pl pt.pp.npn cj

βασιλείαν ἀσάλευτον παραλαμβάνοντες ἔχωμεν χάριν, δι'
receiving a kingdom ⌊that cannot be shaken,⌋ *since we are receiving* let us be thankful, and in
4161 993 810 4161 2400 5921 1328
n.asf a.asf pt.pa.npm v.pas.1p n.asf p.g

ἧς λατρεύωμεν εὐαρέστως τῷ θεῷ μετὰ εὐλαβείας καὶ δέους·
⌊this way⌋ worship God ⌊in an acceptable manner,⌋ *{the}* *God* with reverence and awe,
4005 3302 2536 2299 3836 2536 3552 2325 2779 1290
r.gsf v.pas.1p adv d.dsm n.dsm p.g n.gsf cj n.gsn

[29] καὶ γὰρ ὁ θεὸς ἡμῶν πῦρ καταναλίσκον.
for indeed *for* *{the}* our God *our* is a consuming fire. *consuming*
1142 2779 1142 3836 7005 2536 7005 2914 4786 2914
adv cj d.nsm n.nsm r.gp.1 n.nsn pt.pa.nsn

[13:1] ἡ φιλαδελφία μενέτω. [2] τῆς φιλοξενίας μὴ
{the} Brotherly love must continue. Do not neglect *{the}* ⌊hospitality to strangers,⌋ *not*
3836 5789 3531 2140 3590 2140 3836 5810 3590
d.nsf n.nsf v.pam.3s d.gsf n.gsf pl

ἐπιλανθάνεσθε, διὰ ταύτης γὰρ ἔλαθόν τινες ξενίσαντες
Do neglect for by this means *for* some have entertained *some* angels without knowing it.
2140 1142 1328 4047 1142 5516 3291 5516 34 3826
v.pmm.2p p.g r.gsf cj v.aai.3p r.npm pt.aa.npm

ἀγγέλους. [3] μιμνῄσκεσθε τῶν δεσμίων ὡς συνδεδεμένοι,
angels Continue to remember those in prison, ⌊as though⌋ ⌊you were in prison with⌋ them, and
34 3630 3836 1300 6055 5279
n.apm v.ppm.2p d.gpm n.gpm pl pt.rp.npm

τῶν κακουχουμένων ὡς καὶ ↱ αὐτοὶ ὄντες ⌊ἐν σώματι.⌋
those who are being mistreated, ⌊as though⌋ *{also}* you yourself were suffering bodily.
3836 2807 6055 2779 1639 899 1639 1877 5393
d.gpm pt.pp.gpm pl adv r.npm pt.pa.npm p.d n.dsn

[4] τίμιος ὁ γάμος ἐν πᾶσιν καὶ ἡ κοίτη
Marriage must be honored *{the}* *Marriage* by everyone and the ⌊marriage bed⌋ must be
1141 5508 3836 1141 1877 4246 2779 3836 3130
a.nsm d.nsm n.nsm p.d a.dpn cj d.nsf n.nsf

ἀμίαντος, πόρνους γὰρ καὶ μοιχοὺς κρινεῖ ὁ θεός.
undefiled, for God will judge the sexually immoral *for* and the adulterers. *will judge* *{the}* *God*
299 1142 2536 3212 3212 4521 1142 2779 3659 3212 3836 2536
a.nsf n.apm cj cj n.apm v.fai.3s d.nsm n.nsm

[5] ἀφιλάργυρος ὁ τρόπος, ἀρκούμενοι τοῖς
Your conduct must be ⌊free from the love of money,⌋ *Your* *conduct* and be content with what
3836 5573 921 3836 5573 758 3836
a.nsm d.nsm n.nsm pt.pp.npm d.dpn

παροῦσιν. αὐτὸς γὰρ εἴρηκεν, ⌊οὐ μή⌋ σε ἀνῶ οὐδ' ⌊οὐ
you have; for God himself *for* has said, "I will never leave you; *I will leave* *{nor}* never
4205 1142 899 1142 3306 479 479 4024 3590 479 5148 479 4028 4024
pt.pa.dpn r.nsm cj v.rai.3s pl pl r.as.2 v.aas.1s cj pl

μή⌋ σε ἐγκαταλίπω, [6] ὥστε θαρροῦντας ἡμᾶς λέγειν,
will I forsake you." *will I forsake* So we can say with confidence, *we* *can say*
3590 1593 1593 1593 5148 1593 6063 7005 3306 3306 2509 7005 3306
pl r.as.2 v.aas.1s cj pt.pa.apm r.ap.1 f.pa

κύριος ἐμοὶ βοηθός, ↱ ↱ [a]οὐ φοβηθήσομαι, τί → ποιήσει μοι
"The Lord is my helper, I will not be afraid. What can man do to me?"
3261 1609 1071 5828 5828 4024 5828 5515 476 4472 1609
n.nsm r.ds.1 n.nsm pl v.fpi.1s r.asn v.fai.3s r.ds.1

ἄνθρωπος; [7] Μνημονεύετε τῶν ἡγουμένων ὑμῶν, οἵτινες ἐλάλησαν
man Continue to remember *{the}* your leaders, *your* those who spoke God's
476 3648 3836 7007 2451 7007 4015 3281 2536
n.nsm v.pam.2p d.gpm pt.pm.gpm r.gp.2 r.npm v.aai.3p

ὑμῖν τὸν λόγον τοῦ θεοῦ, ὧν ἀναθεωροῦντες τὴν
message to you; *{the}* *message* *{the}* *God's* reflect on the outcome of their *reflect on* *{the}*
3364 7007 3836 3364 3836 2536 355 355 4005 355 3836
r.dp.2 d.asm n.asm d.gsm n.gsm r.gpm pt.pa.npm d.asf

[a] καὶ included by UBS before οὐ.

NASB

that those things which cannot be shaken may remain. [28]Therefore, since we receive a kingdom which cannot be shaken, let us show gratitude, by which we may offer to God an acceptable service with reverence and awe; [29]for our God is a consuming fire.

The Changeless Christ

[13:1]Let love of the brethren continue. [2]Do not neglect to show hospitality to strangers, for by this some have entertained angels without knowing it. [3]Remember the prisoners, as though in prison with them, *and* those who are ill-treated, since you yourselves also are in the body. [4]Marriage *is to be held* in honor among all, and the *marriage* bed *is to be* undefiled; for fornicators and adulterers God will judge. [5]*Make sure that* your character is free from the love of money, being content with what you have; for He Himself has said, "I WILL NEVER DESERT YOU, NOR WILL I EVER FORSAKE YOU," [6]so that we confidently say,

> "THE LORD IS MY HELPER, I WILL NOT BE AFRAID.
> WHAT WILL MAN DO TO ME?"

[7]Remember those who led you, who spoke the word of God to you; and considering the

NIV

the outcome of
their way of life
and imitate their
faith. [8]Jesus Christ
is the same yester-
day and today and
forever.
[9]Do not be car-
ried away by all
kinds of strange
teachings. It is
good for our hearts
to be strengthened
by grace, not by
eating ceremonial
foods, which is of
no benefit to those
who do so. [10]We
have an altar from
which those who
minister at the
tabernacle have no
right to eat.
[11]The high priest
carries the blood
of animals into the
Most Holy Place
as a sin offering,
but the bodies are
burned outside
the camp. [12]And
so Jesus also suf-
fered outside the
city gate to make
the people holy
through his own
blood. [13]Let us,
then, go to him
outside the camp,
bearing the dis-
grace he bore.
[14]For here we do
not have an endur-
ing city, but we are
looking for the city
that is to come.
[15]Through Jesus,
therefore, let us
continually offer
to God a sacrifice
of praise — the
fruit

ἔκβασιν τῆς ἀναστροφῆς μιμεῖσθε τὴν πίστιν. [8]Ἰησοῦς Χριστὸς
way of life, and imitate their faith. Jesus Christ is the same
1676 3836 419 3628 3836 4411 2652 5986 3836 899
n.asf d.gsf n.gsf v.pmm.2p d.asf n.asf n.nsm n.nsm

ἐχθὲς καὶ σήμερον ὁ αὐτὸς καὶ εἰς τοὺς αἰῶνας. [9]
yesterday and today *the same* and for all time! Do not be swept off your
2396 2779 4958 3836 899 2779 1650 3836 172 4195 3590 4195 4195 4195 4195
adv cj adv d.nsm r.nsm cj p.a d.apm n.apm

→ διδαχαῖς ποικίλαις καὶ ξέναις μὴ παραφέρεσθε·
feet by all sorts of strange teachings, *all sorts of {and} strange not Do be swept off your feet*
4195 4476 4476 4476 3828 1439 4476 2779 3828 3590 4195
n.dpf a.dpf cj a.dpf pl v.ppm.2p

καλὸν γὰρ χάριτι βεβαιοῦσθαι τὴν
for it is good *for* for the heart to be strengthened by grace, *to be strengthened the*
1142 2819 1142 3836 2840 1011 1011 1011 5921 1011 3836
a.nsn cj n.dsf f.pp d.asf

καρδίαν, οὐ βρώμασιν ἐν οἷς ↱ οὐκ ὠφελήθησαν οἱ
heart not by foods, with which their adherents are not benefited. *their*
2840 4024 1109 1877 4005 3836 4344 6067 4024 6067 3836
n.asf pl n.dpn p.d r.dpn pl v.api.3p d.npm

περιπατοῦντες. [10]ἔχομεν θυσιαστήριον ἐξ οὗ
adherents We have an altar from which those who serve in the tabernacle
4344 2400 2603 1666 4005 3836 3302 3302 3836 3836 5008
pt.pa.npm v.pai.1p n.asn p.g r.gsn

φαγεῖν ↱ οὐκ ἔχουσιν ἐξουσίαν οἱ τῇ σκηνῇ λατρεύοντες. [11]
to eat do not have the right to eat. *those in the tabernacle who serve* For
2266 2400 4024 2400 2026 2266 2266 3836 3836 5008 3302 1142
f.aa pl v.pai.3p n.asf d.npm d.dsf n.dsf pt.pa.npm

ὧν γὰρ εἰσφέρεται ζῴων τὸ αἷμα
while the blood of those *For* animals whose blood is brought *animals the blood* into the Most
3836 135 4005 1142 2442 135 1662 2442 3836 135 1650 3836 41
r.gpn cj v.ppi.3s n.gpn d.nsn n.nsn

περὶ ἁμαρτίας εἰς τὰ ἅγια διὰ
Holy Place by the high priest as a sacrifice for sin, *into the Most Holy Place by*
41 41 1328 3836 797 797 4309 281 1650 3836 41 1328
p.g n.gsf p.a d.apn a.apn p.g

τοῦ ἀρχιερέως, τούτων τὰ σώματα κατακαίεται ἔξω τῆς παρεμβολῆς. [12]διὸ
the high priest their *{the}* bodies are burned outside the camp. So Jesus
3836 797 4047 3836 5393 2876 2032 3836 4213 1475 2652
d.gsm n.gsm r.gpn d.npn n.npn v.ppi.3s p.g d.gsf n.gsf cj

καὶ Ἰησοῦς, ἵνα ἁγιάσῃ διὰ τοῦ
also *Jesus* suffered outside the city gate ⌞in order to⌟ sanctify the people through *{the}*
2779 2652 4248 2032 3836 4783 4783 2671 39 3836 3295 1328 3836
adv n.nsm cj v.aas.3s p.g d.gsn

ἰδίου αἵματος τὸν λαόν, ἔξω τῆς πύλης ἔπαθεν. [13]τοίνυν ἐξερχώμεθα πρὸς αὐτὸν
his own blood. *the people outside the city gate suffered* So then, let us go to him
2625 135 3836 3295 2032 3836 4783 4248 5523 2002 4639 899
a.gsn n.gsn d.asm n.asm p.g d.gsf n.gsf v.aai.3s cj v.pms.1p p.a r.asm.3

ἔξω τῆς παρεμβολῆς τὸν ὀνειδισμὸν αὐτοῦ φέροντες· [14]
outside the camp, bearing the reproach he bore. *bearing* For here we
2032 3836 4213 5770 3836 3944 899 5770 1142 6045 2400
p.g d.gsf n.gsf d.asm n.asm r.gsm.3 pt.pa.npm

οὐ γὰρ ἔχομεν ὧδε μένουσαν πόλιν ἀλλὰ τὴν
have no *For we have here* permanent city, but we are looking forward to the city that
2400 4024 1142 2400 6045 3531 4484 247 2118 2118 2118 2118 2118 3836
pl cj v.pai.1p adv pt.pa.asf n.asf cj d.asf

μέλλουσαν ἐπιζητοῦμεν. [15]δι᾽ αὐτοῦ οὖν[a] → → ἀναφέρωμεν
is to come. *we are looking forward to* Through him, therefore, let us continually offer up
3516 2118 1328 899 4036 1328 429
pt.pa.asf v.pai.1p p.g r.gsm.3 cj v.pas.1p

θυσίαν αἰνέσεως ⌞διὰ παντὸς⌟ τῷ θεῷ, τοῦτ᾽ ἔστιν καρπὸν
to God a sacrifice of praise, *continually to God* that is to say, the fruit
3836 2536 2602 139 1328 4246 3836 2536 4047 1639 2843
n.asf n.gsf p.g a.gsn d.dsm n.dsm r.nsn v.pai.3s n.asm

[a] [οὖν] UBS.

NASB

result of their con-
duct, imitate their
faith. [8]Jesus Christ
is the same yester-
day and today and
forever. [9]Do not be
carried away by
varied and strange
teachings; for it is
good for the heart
to be strengthened
by grace, not by
foods, through
which those who
were so occupied
were not benefited.
[10]We have an altar
from which those
who serve the
tabernacle have no
right to eat. [11]For
the bodies of those
animals whose
blood is brought
into the holy place
by the high priest
as an offering for
sin, are burned
outside the camp.
[12]Therefore Jesus
also, that He might
sanctify the people
through His own
blood, suffered
outside the gate.
[13]So, let us go out
to Him outside the
camp, bearing His
reproach. [14]For here
we do not have a
lasting city, but we
are seeking *the city*
which is to come.

God-pleasing Sacrifices

[15]Through Him
then, let us con-
tinually offer up a
sacrifice of praise
to God, that is, the

NIV

of lips that openly
profess his name.
[16]And do not forget
to do good and to
share with oth-
ers, for with such
sacrifices God is
pleased.
[17]Have confi-
dence in your
leaders and submit
to their authority,
because they keep
watch over you as
those who must
give an account.
Do this so that
their work will be
a joy, not a burden,
for that would be
of no benefit to
you.
[18]Pray for us. We
are sure that we
have a clear con-
science and desire
to live honorably
in every way. [19]I
particularly urge
you to pray so that
I may be restored
to you soon.

Benediction and Final Greetings

[20]Now may the
God of peace, who
through the blood
of the eternal cov-
enant brought back
from the dead our
Lord Jesus, that
great Shepherd of
the sheep, [21]equip
you with every-
thing good for
doing his will, and
may he work in us
what is pleasing to
him, through Jesus
Christ, to whom be
glory for ever and
ever. Amen.
[22]Brothers and
sisters, I urge you
to bear with my
word of

χειλέων ὁμολογούντων τῷ ὀνόματι αὐτοῦ. 16 τῆς δὲ
of lips acknowledging *{the}* his name. *his* And do not neglect *{the}* *And*
5927 3933 3836 899 3950 899 1254 2140 3590 2140 3836 1254
n.gpn pt.pa.gpn d.dsn n.dsn r.gsm.3 d.gsf cj

εὐποιΐας καὶ κοινωνίας μὴ ἐπιλανθάνεσθε· → τοιαύταις γὰρ
doing good and ⌊sharing with others,⌋ *not* *do neglect* for with sacrifices like that *for*
2343 2779 3126 3590 2140 1142 2602 5525 1142
n.gsf cj n.gsf pl v.pmm.2p r.dpf cj

θυσίαις εὐαρεστεῖται ὁ θεός. 17 πείθεσθε τοῖς ἡγουμένοις ὑμῶν
sacrifices God is pleased. *{the}* *God* ⌊Continue to obey⌋ *{the}* your leaders *your*
2602 2536 2297 3836 2536 4275 3836 7007 2451 7007
n.dpf v.ppi.3s d.nsm n.nsm v.ppm.2p d.dpm pt.pm.dpm r.gp.2

καὶ ὑπείκετε, αὐτοὶ γὰρ ἀγρυπνοῦσιν ὑπὲρ τῶν ψυχῶν ὑμῶν ὡς
and submit to them, for they *for* keep watch over *{the}* your souls *your* as
2779 5640 1142 899 1142 70 5642 3836 7007 6034 7007 6055
cj v.pam.2p r.npm cj v.pai.3p p.g d.gpf n.gpf r.gp.2 pl

λόγον ἀποδώσοντες, ἵνα μετὰ χαρᾶς τοῦτο
those who must give an account. *those who must give* Let them do this with joy, *this*
625 625 625 625 3364 625 2671 4472 4472 4047 3552 5915 4047
n.asm pt.fa.npm cj p.g n.gsf r.asn

ποιῶσιν καὶ μὴ στενάζοντες· ἀλυσιτελὲς γὰρ ὑμῖν τοῦτο.
them do and not with groaning, for that would be of no advantage *for* to you. *that*
4472 2779 3590 5100 1142 4047 269 1142 7007 4047
v.pas.3p cj pl pt.pa.npm a.nsn cj r.dp.2 r.nsn

18 προσεύχεσθε περὶ ἡμῶν, πειθόμεθα γὰρ ὅτι καλὴν συνείδησιν
Continue to pray for us, for we are convinced *for* that we have a clear conscience,
4667 4309 7005 1142 4275 1142 4022 2400 2400 2819 5287
v.pmm.2p p.g r.gp.1 v.ppi.1p cj cj a.asf n.asf

ἔχομεν, ἐν πᾶσιν καλῶς θέλοντες
we have desiring to conduct ourselves honorably in every way. *honorably* *desiring*
2400 2527 418 418 418 2822 1877 4246 2822 2527
v.pai.1p p.d a.dpn adv pt.pa.npm

ἀναστρέφεσθαι. 19 περισσοτέρως δὲ παρακαλῶ τοῦτο
to conduct ourselves I urge you to do this more than ever *{and}* *I urge* *this*
418 4151 4151 4472 4472 4047 4359 1254 4151 4047
f.pp adv.c cj v.pai.1s r.asn

ποιῆσαι, ἵνα τάχιον ἀποκατασταθῶ ὑμῖν. 20
to do so that I may be restored to you sooner. *I may be restored* *to you* And may
4472 2671 635 635 635 635 7007 7007 5441 635 7007 1254
f.aa cj adv.c v.aps.1s r.dp.2

ὁ δὲ θεὸς τῆς εἰρήνης, ὁ ἀναγαγὼν ἐκ
the *And* God of peace, who, by the blood of the eternal covenant, brought up from the
3836 1254 2536 3836 1645 3836 1877 135 1347 173 1347 343 1666
d.nsm cj n.nsm d.gsf n.gsf d.nsm pt.aa.nsm p.g

νεκρῶν τὸν ποιμένα τῶν προβάτων τὸν μέγαν ἐν αἵματι διαθήκης αἰωνίου,
dead the great shepherd of the sheep, *{the}* *great* *by* *blood* *of covenant* *eternal*
3738 3836 3489 4478 3836 4585 3836 3489 1877 135 1347 173
a.gpm d.asm n.asm d.gpn n.gpn d.asm a.asm p.d n.dsn n.gsf a.gsf

τὸν κύριον ἡμῶν Ἰησοῦν, 21 καταρτίσαι ὑμᾶς ↰ ἐν παντὶ ἀγαθῷ εἰς
{the} our Lord *our* Jesus, make you complete with everything good to
3836 7005 3261 7005 2652 2936 7007 2936 1877 4246 19 1650
d.asm n.asm r.gp.1 n.asm v.aao.3s r.ap.2 p.d a.dsn a.dsn p.a

τὸ ποιῆσαι τὸ θέλημα αὐτοῦ, ποιῶν ἐν ἡμῖν τὸ εὐάρεστον →
~ do *{the}* his will, *his* accomplishing *in* us that which is pleasing in his
3836 4472 3836 899 2525 899 4472 1877 7005 3836 2298 899
d.asn f.aa d.asn n.asn r.gsm.3 pt.pa.nsm p.d r.dp.1 d.asn a.asn

ἐνώπιον αὐτοῦ διὰ Ἰησοῦ Χριστοῦ, ᾧ ἡ δόξα εἰς τοὺς ⌊αἰῶνας [a]τῶν
sight, *his* through Jesus Christ, ⌊to whom⌋ be *{the}* glory for all time.
1967 899 1328 2652 5986 4005 3836 1518 1650 3836 172 3836
p.g r.gsm.3 p.g n.gsm n.gsm r.dsm d.nsf n.nsf p.a d.apm n.apm d.gpm

αἰώνων,⌋[b] ἀμήν. 22 παρακαλῶ δὲ ὑμᾶς, ἀδελφοί, ἀνέχεσθε τοῦ λόγου τῆς
Amen. I appeal to *{and}* you, brothers, bear with my word of
172 297 4151 1254 7007 81 462 3836 3364 3836
n.gpm pl v.pai.1s cj r.ap.2 n.vpm v.pmm.2p d.gsm n.gsm d.gsf

[a] [τῶν αἰώνων] UBS, , NET.
[b] αἰώνων omitted in NET.

NASB

fruit of lips that
give thanks to His
name. [16]And do not
neglect doing good
and sharing, for
with such sacrifices
God is pleased.
[17]Obey your lead-
ers and submit *to*
them, for they keep
watch over your
souls as those who
will give an ac-
count. Let them do
this with joy and
not with grief, for
this would be un-
profitable for you.
[18]Pray for us, for
we are sure that we
have a good con-
science, desiring to
conduct ourselves
honorably in all
things. [19]And I urge
you all the more
to do this, so that I
may be restored to
you the sooner.

Benediction

[20]Now the God of
peace, who brought
up from the dead
the great Shep-
herd of the sheep
through the blood
of the eternal cov-
enant, *even* Jesus
our Lord, [21]equip
you in every good
thing to do His
will, working in us
that which is pleas-
ing in His sight,
through Jesus
Christ, to whom *be*
the glory forever
and ever. Amen.
[22]But I urge you,
brethren, bear with
this word of

NIV

exhortation, for in
fact I have written
to you quite briefly.
[23]I want you to
know that our
brother Timothy
has been released.
If he arrives soon,
I will come with
him to see you.
[24]Greet all your
leaders and all
the Lord's people.
Those from Ita-
ly send you their
greetings.
[25]Grace be with
you all.

παρακλήσεως, καὶ γὰρ ⌞διὰ βραχέων⌟ ἐπέστειλα
exhortation, for in fact *for* I have written to you briefly. *I have written*
4155 1142 2779 1142 2182 2182 2182 7007 7007 1328 1099 2182
n.gsf adv cj p.g a.gpm v.aai.1s

ὑμῖν. 23 γινώσκετε τὸν ἀδελφὸν ἡμῶν Τιμόθεον ἀπολελυμένον,
to you Know that *{the}* our brother *our* Timothy has been set free. If he arrives
7007 1182 3836 7005 81 7005 5510 668 1569 2262 2262
r.dp.2 v.pai.2p d.asm n.asm r.gp.1 n.asm pt.rp.asm

μεθ᾽ οὗ ἐὰν τάχιον ἔρχηται ὄψομαι ὑμᾶς. 24 ἀσπάσασθε
soon, I will visit you with him. *If* *soon* *he arrives* *I will visit* *you* Greet
5441 3972 3972 3972 7007 3552 4005 1569 5441 2262 3972 7007 832
p.g r.gsm cj adv.c v.pms.3s v.fmi.1s r.ap.2 v.amm.2p

πάντας τοὺς ἡγουμένους ὑμῶν καὶ πάντας τοὺς ἁγίους.
all *{the}* your leaders *your* and all the saints. Those from Italy
4246 3836 7007 2451 7007 2779 4246 3836 41 3836 608 2712
a.apm d.apm pt.pm.apm r.gp.2 cj a.apm d.apm a.apm

ἀσπάζονται ὑμᾶς οἱ ἀπὸ τῆς Ἰταλίας. 25 ἡ χάρις μετὰ πάντων ὑμῶν.[a]
greet you. *Those* *from* *{the}* *Italy* *{the}* Grace be with all of you.
832 7007 3836 608 3836 2712 3836 5921 3552 4246 7007
v.pmi.3p r.ap.2 d.npm p.g d.gsf n.gsf d.nsf n.nsf p.g a.gpm r.gp.2

NASB

exhortation, for
I have written to
you briefly. [23]Take
notice that our
brother Timothy
has been released,
with whom, if he
comes soon, I will
see you. [24]Greet
all of your leaders
and all the saints.
Those from Italy
greet you.
[25]Grace be with
you all.

[a] ἀμήν. πρὸς Ἑβραίους ἐγράφη ἀπὸ τῆς Ἰταλίας διὰ Τιμοθέου included by TR after ὑμῶν.

James

NIV

1 James, a servant
of God and of the
Lord Jesus Christ,

To the twelve tribes
scattered among the
nations:

Greetings.

Trials and Temptations

2Consider it pure
joy, my brothers and
sisters,[a] whenever
you face trials of
many kinds, 3be-
cause you know
that the testing of
your faith produces
perseverance. 4Let
perseverance fin-
ish its work so that
you may be mature
and complete, not
lacking anything.
5If any of you lacks
wisdom, you should
ask God, who gives
generously to all
without finding
fault, and it will be
given to you. 6But
when you ask, you
must believe and
not doubt, because
the one who doubts
is like a wave of
the sea, blown and
tossed by the wind.
7That person should
not expect to receive
anything from the
Lord. 8Such a per-
son is double-mind-
ed and unstable in
all they do.

9Believers in hum-
ble circumstances
ought to take pride
in their high posi-
tion. 10But the rich
should take pride in
their humiliation—

[a] 2 The Greek word for *brothers and sisters* (*adelphoi*) refers here to believers, both men and women, as part of God's family; also in verses 16 and 19; and in 2:1, 5, 14; 3:10, 12; 4:11; 5:7, 9, 10, 12, 19.

1:1 Ἰάκωβος θεοῦ καὶ → κυρίου Ἰησοῦ Χριστοῦ δοῦλος ταῖς δώδεκα
James, a servant of God and of the Lord Jesus Christ, *servant* to the twelve
2610 1529 2536 2779 3261 2652 5986 1529 3836 1557
n.nsm n.gsm cj n.gsm n.gsm n.gsm n.nsm d.dpf a.dpf

φυλαῖς ταῖς ἐν τῇ διασπορᾷ χαίρειν. 2 πᾶσαν χαρὰν ἡγήσασθε,
tribes *{the}* in the dispersion: Greetings. Consider it sheer joy, *Consider* my
5876 3836 1877 3836 1402 5897 2451 4246 5915 2451 1609
n.dpf d.dpf p.d d.dsf n.dsf f.pa a.asf n.asf v.amm.2p

ἀδελφοί μου, ὅταν πειρασμοῖς περιπέσητε ποικίλοις,
brothers, *my* when you encounter various kinds of trials, *you encounter* *various kinds of*
81 1609 4020 4346 4346 4476 4476 4476 4280 4346 4476
n.vpm r.gs.1 cj n.dpm v.aas.2p a.dpm

3 γινώσκοντες ὅτι τὸ δοκίμιον ὑμῶν τῆς πίστεως κατεργάζεται ὑπομονήν.
because you know that the testing of your *of* faith produces endurance.
1182 4022 3836 1510 3836 7007 3836 4411 2981 5705
pt.pa.npm cj d.nsn n.nsn r.gp.2 d.gsf n.gsf v.pmi.3s n.asf

4 ἡ δὲ ὑπομονὴ ἔργον τέλειον ἐχέτω, ἵνα ἦτε τέλειοι
{the} And let endurance carry out its intended purpose, *let carry out* so that ⌊you may be⌋ mature
3836 1254 2400 5705 2400 2400 2240 5455 2400 2671 1639 5455
d.nsf cj n.nsf n.asn a.asn v.pam.3s cj v.pas.2p a.npm

καὶ ὁλόκληροι ἐν μηδενὶ λειπόμενοι. 5 εἰ δέ τις ὑμῶν λείπεται
and complete, lacking in nothing. *lacking* But if *But* any of you lacks
2779 3908 3309 1877 3594 3309 1254 1623 1254 5516 7007 3309
cj a.npm p.d a.dsn pt.pp.npm cj cj r.nsm r.gp.2 v.ppi.3s

σοφίας, αἰτείτω παρὰ τοῦ διδόντος θεοῦ πᾶσιν ἁπλῶς καὶ μὴ
wisdom, ⌊he should ask⌋ God, *{from}* who gives *God* to everyone generously, *{and}* not
5053 160 2536 4123 3836 1443 2536 4246 607 2779 3590
n.gsf v.pam.3s p.g d.gsm pt.pa.gsm n.gsm a.dpm adv cj pl

ὀνειδίζοντος καὶ δοθήσεται αὐτῷ. 6 αἰτείτω δὲ ἐν πίστει
⌊demanding something in return,⌋ and it will be given to him. But he must ask *But* in faith
3943 2779 1443 899 1254 160 1254 1877 4411
pt.pa.gsm cj v.fpi.3s r.dsm.3 v.pam.3s cj p.d n.dsf

μηδὲν διακρινόμενος, ὁ γὰρ διακρινόμενος ἔοικεν κλύδωνι → θαλάσσης
without doubting, for the *for* doubter is like a wave of the sea,
3594 1359 1142 3836 1142 1359 2036 3114 2498
a.asn pt.pm.nsm d.nsm cj pt.pm.nsm v.rai.3s n.dsm n.gsf

ἀνεμιζομένῳ καὶ ῥιπιζομένῳ. 7 ↱ μὴ γὰρ οἰέσθω ὁ ἄνθρωπος
driven by the wind and tossed about. For that person must not *For* imagine *{the}* *person*
448 2779 4847 1142 1697 476 3887 3590 1142 3887 3836 476
pt.pp.dsm cj pt.pp.dsm pl cj v.pmm.3s d.nsm n.nsm

ἐκεῖνος ὅτι λήμψεταί τι παρὰ τοῦ κυρίου, 8 ἀνὴρ
that that he will receive anything from the Lord; he is a double-minded man,
1697 4022 3284 5516 4123 3836 3261 1500 467
r.nsm cj v.fmi.3s r.asn p.g d.gsm n.gsm n.nsm

δίψυχος, ἀκατάστατος ἐν πάσαις ταῖς ὁδοῖς αὐτοῦ. 9 →
double-minded unstable in all *{the}* his ways. *his* Let the brother of limited
1500 190 1877 4246 3836 899 3847 899 3836 81 5424
a.nsm a.nsm p.d a.dpf d.dpf n.dpf r.gsm.3

καυχάσθω δὲ ὁ ἀδελφὸς ὁ ταπεινὸς ἐν τῷ ὕψει αὐτοῦ,
means take pride *{and}* *the* *brother* *{the}* *limited means* in *{the}* his ⌊high position,⌋ *his*
5424 3016 1254 3836 81 3836 5424 1877 3836 899 5737 899
v.pmm.3s cj d.nsm n.nsm d.nsm a.nsm p.d d.dsn n.dsn r.gsm.3

10 ὁ δὲ πλούσιος ἐν τῇ ταπεινώσει αὐτοῦ, ὅτι ὡς ἄνθος →
and the *and* wealthy brother in *{the}* his humiliation, *his* because like a flower in
1254 3836 1254 4454 1877 3836 899 5428 899 4022 6055 470
d.nsm cj a.nsm p.d d.dsf n.dsf r.gsm.3 cj pl n.nsn

NASB

Testing Your Faith

1:1James, a bond-
servant of God and
of the Lord Jesus
Christ,
To the twelve
tribes who are
dispersed abroad:
Greetings.
2Consider it all
joy, my brethren,
when you encoun-
ter various trials,
3knowing that the
testing of your
faith produces
endurance. 4And
let endurance have
its perfect result,
so that you may be
perfect and com-
plete, lacking in
nothing.
5But if any of you
lacks wisdom, let
him ask of God,
who gives to all
generously and
without reproach,
and it will be given
to him. 6But he
must ask in faith
without any doubt-
ing, for the one
who doubts is like
the surf of the sea,
driven and tossed
by the wind. 7For
that man ought
not to expect that
he will receive
anything from
the Lord, 8*being*
a double-minded
man, unstable in all
his ways.
9But the brother
of humble circum-
stances is to glory
in his high posi-
tion; 10and the rich
man *is to glory* in
his humiliation, be-
cause like flower-
ing grass he will

NIV

since they will
pass away like a
wild flower. [11]For
the sun rises with
scorching heat and
withers the plant;
its blossom falls
and its beauty is
destroyed. In the
same way, the rich
will fade away
even while they go
about their busi-
ness.
12 Blessed is the
one who perse-
veres under trial
because, having
stood the test, that
person will receive
the crown of life
that the Lord has
promised to those
who love him.
13 When tempted,
no one should say,
"God is tempt-
ing me." For God
cannot be tempted
by evil, nor does
he tempt anyone;
14 but each person
is tempted when
they are dragged
away by their own
evil desire and
enticed. [15]Then,
after desire has
conceived, it gives
birth to sin; and
sin, when it is full-
grown, gives birth
to death.
16 Don't be de-
ceived, my dear
brothers and sis-
ters. [17]Every good
and perfect gift is
from above, com-
ing down from the
Father of the heav-
enly lights, who
does not change
like shifting shad-
ows. [18]He chose
to give us birth
through the word
of truth, that we
might be a kind of
firstfruits

χόρτου παρελεύσεται. 11 ἀνέτειλεν γὰρ ὁ ἥλιος σὺν τῷ
the meadow he will pass away. For the sun rises *For the sun* with its
5965 4216 1142 3836 2463 422 1142 3836 2463 5250 3836
n.gsm v.fmi.3s v.aai.3s cj d.nsm n.nsm p.d d.dsm

καύσωνι καὶ ἐξήρανεν τὸν χόρτον καὶ τὸ ἄνθος αὐτοῦ ἐξέπεσεν καὶ ἡ
⌞scorching heat⌟ and withers the meadow; *{and} {the}* its flower *its* falls and *{the}*
3014 2779 3830 3836 5965 2779 3836 899 470 899 1738 2779 3836
n.dsm cj v.aai.3s d.asm n.asm cj d.nsn n.nsn r.gsm.3 v.aai.3s cj d.nsf

⌞εὐπρέπεια τοῦ προσώπου⌟ αὐτοῦ ἀπώλετο· οὕτως καὶ ὁ πλούσιος
its beauty *its* fades. ⌞In the same way⌟ *{also}* the rich man
899 2346 3836 4725 899 660 4048 2779 3836 4454
n.nsf d.gsn n.gsn r.gsm.3 v.ami.3s adv adv d.nsm a.nsm

ἐν ταῖς πορείαις αὐτοῦ μαρανθήσεται. 12 μακάριος ἀνὴρ
will fade away while pursuing his business. *his will fade away* Blessed is the man
3447 3447 3447 1877 3836 899 4512 899 3447 3421 467
p.d d.dpf n.dpf r.gsm.3 v.fpi.3s a.nsm n.nsm

ὃς ὑπομένει πειρασμόν, ὅτι δόκιμος
who remains steadfast when tested, because once he is shown to be genuine,
4005 5702 4280 4022 1181 1181 1181 1181 1181 1181 1511
r.nsm v.pai.3s n.asm cj a.nsm

γενόμενος λήμψεται τὸν στέφανον τῆς ζωῆς ὃν ἐπηγγείλατο
once he is shown to be he will receive the crown of life that the Lord has promised
1181 3284 3836 5109 3836 2437 4005 2040
pt.am.nsm v.fmi.3s d.asm n.asm d.gsf n.gsf r.asm v.ami.3s

τοῖς ἀγαπῶσιν αὐτόν. 13 μηδεὶς πειραζόμενος λεγέτω ὅτι
to those who love him. No one when tempted should say, ~ "I am being tempted
3836 26 899 3594 4279 3306 4022 4279 4279 4279 4279
d.dpm pt.pa.dpm r.asm.3 a.nsm pt.pp.nsm v.pam.3s cj

ἀπὸ θεοῦ πειράζομαι· ὁ γὰρ θεὸς ἀπείραστός ἐστιν κακῶν, →
by God"; *I am being tempted* *{the}* for God cannot be tempted to do evil, and he himself
608 2536 4279 3836 1142 2536 585 1639 2805 1254 899
p.g n.gsm v.ppi.1s d.nsm cj n.nsm a.nsm v.pai.3s a.gpn

πειράζει δὲ αὐτὸς οὐδένα. 14 ἕκαστος δὲ πειράζεται ↱ ὑπὸ τῆς
tempts *and himself* no one else. But each person *But* is tempted when by *{the}*
4279 1254 899 4029 1254 1667 1254 4279 1999 5679 3836
v.pai.3s cj r.nsm a.asm r.nsm cj v.ppi.3s p.g d.gsf

ἰδίας ἐπιθυμίας ἐξελκόμενος καὶ δελεαζόμενος· 15 εἶτα ἡ ἐπιθυμία
his own desire he is lured away and enticed. Then *{the}* desire,
2625 2123 1999 2779 1284 1663 3836 2123
a.gsf n.gsf pt.pp.nsm cj pt.pp.nsm adv d.nsf n.nsf

συλλαβοῦσα τίκτει ἁμαρτίαν, ἡ δὲ ἁμαρτία ἀποτελεσθεῖσα
when it has conceived, ⌞gives birth to⌟ sin; *{the}* and sin, when it is full-grown,
5197 5503 281 3836 1254 281 699
pt.aa.nsf v.pai.3s n.asf d.nsf cj n.nsf pt.ap.nsf

ἀποκύει θάνατον. 16 ↱ μὴ πλανᾶσθε, ἀδελφοί μου ἀγαπητοί. 17 πᾶσα
brings forth death. Do not be deceived, *brothers* my dear brothers. Every
652 2505 4414 3590 4414 81 1609 28 81 4246
v.pai.3s n.asm pl v.ppm.2p n.vpm r.gs.1 a.vpm a.nsf

δόσις ἀγαθὴ καὶ πᾶν δώρημα τέλειον ἄνωθέν ἐστιν καταβαῖνον
good gift *good* and every perfect gift *perfect* is from above, *is* coming down
19 1521 19 2779 4246 5455 1564 5455 1639 540 1639 2849
n.nsf a.nsf cj a.nsn n.nsn a.nsn adv v.pai.3s pt.pa.nsn

ἀπὸ τοῦ πατρὸς τῶν φώτων, παρ᾽ ᾧ οὐκ ἔνι παραλλαγὴ ἢ
from the Father of lights, with whom there is no *there is* variation or shadow
608 3836 4252 3836 5890 4123 4005 1928 1928 4024 1928 4164 2445 684
p.g d.gsm n.gsm d.gpn n.gpn p.d r.dsm pl v.pai.3s n.nsf cj

τροπῆς ἀποσκίασμα. 18 βουληθεὶς ἀπεκύησεν ἡμᾶς ↰
⌞caused by change.⌟ *shadow* ⌞According to his sovereign plan,⌟ he brought us into
5572 684 1089 652 7005 652
n.gsf n.nsn pt.ap.nsm v.aai.3s r.ap.1

↰ → λόγῳ ἀληθείας εἰς τὸ εἶναι ἡμᾶς ἀπαρχήν τινα
being through his word of truth, ⌞so that⌟ ~ we ⌞would be⌟ *we* a kind of first fruits *kind*
652 3364 237 1650 3836 7005 1639 7005 5516 569 5516
n.dsm n.gsf p.a d.asn f.pa r.ap.1 n.asf r.asf

NASB

pass away. [11]For
the sun rises with a
scorching wind and
withers the grass;
and its flower falls
off and the beauty
of its appearance
is destroyed; so
too the rich man
in the midst of his
pursuits will fade
away.
12 Blessed is a man
who perseveres
under trial; for
once he has been
approved, he will
receive the crown
of life which *the*
Lord has promised
to those who love
Him. [13]Let no one
say when he is
tempted, "I am
being tempted by
God"; for God
cannot be tempted
by evil, and He
Himself does not
tempt anyone.
14 But each one is
tempted when he
is carried away and
enticed by his own
lust. [15]Then when
lust has conceived,
it gives birth to
sin; and when sin
is accomplished, it
brings forth death.
16 Do not be de-
ceived, my beloved
brethren. [17]Every
good thing given
and every perfect
gift is from above,
coming down from
the Father of lights,
with whom there
is no variation or
shifting shadow.
18 In the exercise
of His will He
brought us forth by
the word of truth,
so that we would
be a kind of first

NIV

of all he created.

Listening and Doing

[19]My dear broth-
ers and sisters,
take note of this:
Everyone should
be quick to listen,
slow to speak and
slow to become
angry, [20]because
human anger does
not produce the
righteousness
that God desires.
[21]Therefore, get
rid of all moral
filth and the evil
that is so prevalent
and humbly accept
the word planted
in you, which can
save you.
[22]Do not mere-
ly listen to the
word, and so de-
ceive yourselves.
Do what it says.
[23]Anyone who lis-
tens to the word
but does not do
what it says is
like someone who
looks at his face
in a mirror [24]and,
after looking at
himself, goes away
and immediately
forgets what he
looks like. [25]But
whoever looks
intently into the
perfect law that
gives freedom, and
continues in it—
not forgetting what
they have heard,
but doing it—they
will be blessed in
what they do.
[26]Those who con-
sider themselves
religious and yet
do not keep a
tight rein on their
tongues deceive
themselves, and
their religion is
worthless. [27]Reli-
gion that God

τῶν αὐτοῦ κτισμάτων. [19] ἴστε, ἀδελφοί μου ἀγαπητοί·
of all he created. Understand this, *brothers* my dear brothers: everyone
3836 899 3233 3857 81 1609 28 81 4246
d.gpn r.gsm.3 n.gpn v.ram.2p n.vpm r.gs.1 a.vpm

ἔστω δὲ ⌞πᾶς ἄνθρωπος⌟ ταχὺς εἰς τὸ ἀκοῦσαι, βραδὺς εἰς τὸ λαλῆσαι,
⌞must be⌟ *{and}* *everyone* quick to ~ listen, slow to ~ speak,
1639 1254 4246 476 5444 1650 3836 201 1096 1650 3836 3281
v.pam.3s cj a.nsm n.nsm a.nsm p.a d.asn f.aa a.nsm p.a d.asn f.aa

βραδὺς εἰς ὀργήν· [20] ὀργὴ γὰρ ἀνδρὸς
and slow to ⌞become angry.⌟ For the anger *For* of man does not bring about the
1096 1650 3973 1142 3973 1142 467 2237 4024 2237 2237
a.nsm p.a n.asf n.nsf cj n.gsm

δικαιοσύνην θεοῦ οὐκ ἐργάζεται. [21] διὸ ἀποθέμενοι πᾶσαν
righteousness that ⌞God requires.⌟ *not* *does bring about* Therefore put aside all
1466 2536 4024 2237 1475 700 4246
n.asf n.gsm pl v.pmi.3s cj pt.am.npm a.asf

ῥυπαρίαν καὶ περισσείαν κακίας ἐν πραΰτητι, δέξασθε τὸν ἔμφυτον
filthiness and rampant wickedness, and receive with meekness *receive* the implanted
4864 2779 4353 2798 1312 1877 4559 1312 3836 1875
n.asf cj n.asf n.gsf p.d n.dsf v.amm.2p d.asm a.asm

λόγον τὸν δυνάμενον σῶσαι τὰς ψυχὰς ὑμῶν. [22] γίνεσθε δὲ ποιηταὶ →
word, which is able to save *{the}* your souls. *your* But be *But* doers of the
3364 3836 1538 5392 3836 7007 6034 7007 1254 1181 1254 4475
n.asm d.asm pt.pp.asm f.aa d.apf n.apf r.gp.2 v.pmm.2p cj n.npm

λόγου καὶ μὴ μόνον ἀκροαταὶ παραλογιζόμενοι ἑαυτούς. [23] ὅτι εἴ τις
word and not merely hearers, deceiving yourselves. For if someone is a
3364 2779 3590 3667 212 4165 1571 4022 1623 5516 1639
n.gsm cj pl adv n.npm pt.pm.npm r.apm.2 cj cj r.nsm

ἀκροατὴς → λόγου ἐστὶν καὶ οὐ ποιητής, οὗτος ἔοικεν ἀνδρὶ κατανοοῦντι
hearer of the word *is* and not a doer, he is like a person who looks at
212 3364 1639 2779 4024 4475 4047 2036 467 2917
n.nsm n.gsm v.pai.3s cj pl n.nsm r.nsm v.rai.3s n.dsm pt.pa.dsm

τὸ πρόσωπον τῆς γενέσεως αὐτοῦ ἐν ἐσόπτρῳ· [24] κατενόησεν
{the} his natural face *{the}* *natural* *his* in a mirror; then ⌞after looking at⌟
3836 899 1161 4725 3836 1161 899 1877 2269 1142 2917
d.asn n.asn d.gsf n.gsf r.gsm.3 p.d n.dsn v.aai.3s

γὰρ ἑαυτὸν καὶ ἀπελήλυθεν καὶ εὐθέως ἐπελάθετο → ὁποῖος ἦν.
then himself *{and}* he goes away and immediately forgets what he was like. *he was*
1142 1571 2779 599 2779 2311 2140 1639 1639 3961 1639
cj r.asm.3 cj v.rai.3s cj adv v.ami.3s r.nsm v.iai.3s

[25] ὁ δὲ παρακύψας εἰς νόμον τέλειον τὸν τῆς
But the *But* ⌞person who looks intently⌟ into the perfect law, *perfect* the law that
1254 3836 1254 4160 1650 5455 3795 5455 3836 3836
d.nsm cj pt.aa.nsm p.a n.asm a.asm d.asm d.gsf

ἐλευθερίας καὶ παραμείνας, οὐκ ἀκροατὴς ἐπιλησμονῆς
provides liberty, and continues in it, not having become a forgetful hearer *forgetful*
1800 2779 4169 4024 1181 1181 2144 212 2144
n.gsf cj pt.aa.nsm pl n.nsm n.gsf

γενόμενος ἀλλὰ ποιητὴς ἔργου, οὗτος μακάριος ἐν τῇ ποιήσει
having become but an active doer — he will be blessed in *{the}* his doing.
1181 247 4475 2240 4047 1639 1639 3421 1877 3836 899 4474
pt.am.nsm cj n.nsm n.gsn r.nsm a.nsm p.d d.dsf n.dsf

αὐτοῦ ἔσται. [26] εἴ τις δοκεῖ θρησκὸς εἶναι ↱ ↱ μὴ
his *will be* If someone thinks that he is religious, *he is* yet does not
899 1639 1623 5516 1506 1639 1639 2580 1639 5902 5902 3590
r.gsm.3 v.fmi.3s cj r.nsm v.pai.3s a.nsm f.pa pl

χαλιναγωγῶν γλῶσσαν αὐτοῦ ἀλλὰ ἀπατῶν καρδίαν αὐτοῦ, τούτου
bridle his tongue *his* but deceives his heart, *his* this person's religion
5902 899 1185 899 247 572 899 2840 899 4047 2579
pt.pa.nsm n.asf r.gsm.3 cj pt.pa.nsm n.asf r.gsm.3 r.gsm

μάταιος ἡ θρησκεία. [27] θρησκεία καθαρὰ καὶ ἀμίαντος παρὰ τῷ θεῷ
is worthless. *{the}* *religion* Religion that is pure and undefiled before *{the}* God
3469 3836 2579 2579 2754 2779 299 4123 3836 2536
a.nsf d.nsf n.nsf n.nsf a.nsf cj a.nsf p.d d.dsm n.dsm

NASB

fruits among His
creatures.
[19a]*This* you know,
my beloved breth-
ren. But everyone
must be quick to
hear, slow to speak
and slow to anger;
[20]for the anger
of man does not
achieve the righ-
teousness of God.
[21]Therefore, putting
aside all filthi-
ness and *all* that
remains of wicked-
ness, in humility
receive the word
implanted, which
is able to save your
souls. [22]But prove
yourselves doers of
the word, and not
merely hearers who
delude themselves.
[23]For if anyone is a
hearer of the word
and not a doer, he
is like a man who
looks at his natural
face in a mirror;
[24]for *once* he has
looked at himself
and gone away, he
has immediately
forgotten what
kind of person he
was. [25]But one who
looks intently at
the perfect law, the
law of liberty, and
abides by it, not
having become a
forgetful hearer but
an effectual doer,
this man will be
blessed in what he
does.
[26]If anyone thinks
himself to be
religious, and yet
does not bridle
his tongue but
deceives his *own*
heart, this man's
religion is worth-
less. [27]Pure and un-
defiled religion in
the sight of *our*

[a] Or *Know* this

NIV

our Father accepts
as pure and fault-
less is this: to look
after orphans and
widows in their
distress and to keep
oneself from be-
ing polluted by the
world.

Favoritism Forbidden

2 My brothers
and sisters, be-
lievers in our glo-
rious Lord Jesus
Christ must not
show favoritism.
[2]Suppose a man
comes into your
meeting wearing a
gold ring and fine
clothes, and a poor
man in filthy old
clothes also comes
in. [3]If you show
special attention
to the man wear-
ing fine clothes
and say, "Here's a
good seat for you,"
but say to the poor
man, "You stand
there" or "Sit on
the floor by my
feet," [4]have you
not discriminated
among yourselves
and become judges
with evil thoughts?
[5]Listen, my dear
brothers and sis-
ters: Has not God
chosen those who
are poor in the
eyes of the world
to be rich in faith
and to inherit the
kingdom he prom-
ised those who
love him? [6]But
you have dishon-
ored the poor. Is
it not the rich who
are exploiting
you? Are they not
the ones who are
dragging you into
court? [7]Are they
not the ones who
are blaspheming
the noble name of
him to whom you
belong?
[8]If you really
keep the royal

καὶ πατρὶ αὕτη ἐστίν, ἐπισκέπτεσθαι ὀρφανοὺς καὶ χήρας ἐν τῇ
{and} the Father is this: *is* to care for orphans and widows in *{the}* their
2779 4252 1639 4047 1639 2170 4003 2779 5939 1877 3836 899
cj n.dsm r.nsf v.pai.3s f.pm a.apm cj n.apf p.d d.dsf

θλίψει αὐτῶν, ἄσπιλον ἑαυτὸν τηρεῖν ἀπὸ τοῦ κόσμου.
⌊time of trouble,⌋ *their* and to keep oneself unstained *oneself* *to keep* by the world.
2568 899 5498 5498 1571 834 1571 5498 608 3836 3180
n.dsf r.gpm.3 a.asm r.asm.3 f.pa p.g d.gsm n.gsm

2:1 ἀδελφοί μου, μὴ ἐν προσωπολημψίαις ἔχετε
My brothers, *My* stop showing favoritism ⌊as you live out⌋ *favoritism* *showing*
1609 81 1609 3590 2400 4721 1877 4721 2400
n.vpm r.gs.1 pl p.d n.dpf v.pam.2p

τὴν πίστιν τοῦ κυρίου ἡμῶν Ἰησοῦ Χριστοῦ τῆς δόξης. 2 ἐὰν γὰρ
your faith in our glorious Lord *our* Jesus Christ. *{the}* *glorious* For if *For* a
3836 4411 3836 7005 1518 3261 7005 2652 5986 3836 1518 1142 1569 1142
d.asf n.asf d.gsm n.gsm r.gp.1 n.gsm n.gsm d.gsf n.gsf cj cj

εἰσέλθῃ εἰς συναγωγὴν ὑμῶν ἀνὴρ χρυσοδακτύλιος ἐν ἐσθῆτι λαμπρᾷ,
man comes into your congregation *your* *man* wearing a gold ring and fine clothes, *fine*
467 1656 1650 7007 5252 7007 467 5993 1877 3287 2264 3287
v.aas.3s p.a n.asf r.gp.2 n.nsm a.nsm p.d n.dsf a.dsf

εἰσέλθῃ δὲ καὶ πτωχὸς ἐν ῥυπαρᾷ ἐσθῆτι, 3
comes in and *also* a poor man in dirty clothes also comes in, and
1656 1254 2779 4777 1877 4865 2264 2779 1656 1656 1254
v.aas.3s cj adv a.nsm p.d a.dsf n.dsf

ἐπιβλέψητε δὲ ἐπὶ τὸν φοροῦντα τὴν ἐσθῆτα τὴν λαμπρὰν καὶ
⌊you pay special attention⌋ *and* to the one wearing the fine clothes *{the}* *fine* and
2098 1254 2093 3836 5841 3836 3287 2264 3836 3287 2779
v.aas.2p cj p.a d.asm pt.pa.asm d.asf n.asf d.asf a.asf cj

εἴπητε, σὺ κάθου ὧδε καλῶς, καὶ τῷ πτωχῷ εἴπητε, σὺ στῆθι
say, "You sit here ⌊in a good place,"⌋ but ⌊to the⌋ poor man you say, "You stand
3306 5148 2764 6045 2822 2779 3836 4777 3306 5148 2705
v.aas.2p r.ns.2 v.pmm.2s adv adv cj d.dsm a.dsm v.aas.2p r.ns.2 v.aam.2s

ἐκεῖ ἢ κάθου ὑπὸ τὸ ὑποπόδιόν μου, 4 ↱ ↱ οὐ διεκρίθητε
⌊over there,⌋ or sit down ⌊here at⌋ *{the}* my feet," *my* have you not made distinctions
1695 2445 2764 5679 3836 1609 5711 1609 1359 1359 4024 1359
adv cj v.pmm.2s p.a d.asn n.asn r.gs.1 pl v.api.2p

ἐν ἑαυτοῖς καὶ ἐγένεσθε κριταὶ → διαλογισμῶν πονηρῶν; 5 Ἀκούσατε,
among yourselves and become judges with evil motives? *evil* Listen,
1877 1571 2779 1181 3216 4505 1369 4505 201
p.d r.dpm.2 cj v.ami.2p n.npm n.gpm a.gpm v.aam.2p

ἀδελφοί μου ἀγαπητοί· ↱ οὐχ ὁ θεὸς ἐξελέξατο τοὺς →
brothers! my dear brothers! Did not *{the}* God choose those whom the world
81 1609 28 81 1721 4024 3836 2536 1721 3836 3836 3180
n.vpm r.gs.1 a.vpm pl d.nsm n.nsm v.ami.3s d.apm

πτωχοὺς τῷ κόσμῳ πλουσίους ἐν πίστει καὶ κληρονόμους τῆς βασιλείας
considers poor *the* *world* to be rich in faith and to inherit the kingdom,
4777 3836 3180 4454 1877 4411 2779 3101 3836 993
a.apm d.dsm n.dsm a.apm p.d n.dsf cj n.apm d.gsf n.gsf

ἧς ἐπηγγείλατο τοῖς ἀγαπῶσιν αὐτόν; 6 ὑμεῖς δὲ ἠτιμάσατε τὸν
which he promised to those who love him? But you *But* have dishonored the
4005 2040 3836 26 899 1254 7007 1254 869 3836
r.gsf v.ami.3s d.dpm pt.pa.dpm r.asm.3 r.np.2 cj v.aai.2p d.asm

πτωχόν. οὐχ οἱ πλούσιοι καταδυναστεύουσιν ὑμῶν καὶ αὐτοὶ
poor! Is it not the rich who oppress you? And are not they the ones
4777 4024 3836 4454 2872 7007 2779 899
a.asm pl d.npm a.npm v.pai.3p r.gp.2 cj r.npm

ἕλκουσιν ὑμᾶς εἰς κριτήρια; 7 οὐκ αὐτοὶ βλασφημοῦσιν τὸ
who drag you into court? Are they not *they* the ones who are blaspheming the
1816 7007 1650 3215 899 4024 899 1059 3836
v.pai.3p r.ap.2 p.a n.apn pl r.npm v.pai.3p d.asn

καλὸν ὄνομα ↱ τὸ ἐπικληθὲν ἐφ᾽ ὑμᾶς; 8 Εἰ μέντοι
honorable name by which you were called? *{over}* *you* If you really fulfill the royal
2819 3950 2126 3836 7007 2126 2093 7007 1623 5464 3530 5464 997
a.asn n.asn d.asn pt.ap.asn p.a r.ap.2 cj cj

NASB

God and Father
is this: to visit or-
phans and widows
in their distress,
and to keep oneself
unstained by the
world.

The Sin of Partiality

[2:1]My brethren, do
not hold your faith
in our glorious
Lord Jesus Christ
with *an attitude of*
personal favorit-
ism. [2]For if a man
comes into your as-
sembly with a gold
ring and dressed
in fine clothes, and
there also comes
in a poor man in
dirty clothes, [3]and
you pay special
attention to the one
who is wearing the
fine clothes, and
say, "You sit here
in a good place,"
and you say to the
poor man, "You
stand over there,
or sit down by my
footstool," [4]have
you not made dis-
tinctions among
yourselves, and
become judges
with evil motives?
[5]Listen, my be-
loved brethren: did
not God choose the
poor of this world
to be rich in faith
and heirs of the
kingdom which He
promised to those
who love Him?
[6]But you have dis-
honored the poor
man. Is it not the
rich who oppress
you and person-
ally drag you into
court? [7]Do they not
blaspheme the fair
name by which you
have been called?
[8]If, however, you
are fulfilling the

NIV

law found in
Scripture, "Love
your neighbor as
yourself,"[a] you
are doing right.
9 But if you show
favoritism, you sin
and are convict-
ed by the law as
lawbreakers. 10 For
whoever keeps the
whole law and yet
stumbles at just
one point is guilty
of breaking all of
it. 11 For he who
said, "You shall not
commit adultery,"[b]
also said, "You
shall not murder."[c]
If you do not com-
mit adultery but do
commit murder,
you have become a
lawbreaker.
12 Speak and act
as those who are
going to be judged
by the law that
gives freedom,
13 because judg-
ment without mer-
cy will be shown
to anyone who has
not been merciful.
Mercy triumphs
over judgment.

Faith and Deeds

14 What good is it,
my brothers and
sisters, if some-
one claims to have
faith but has no
deeds? Can such
faith save them?
15 Suppose a broth-
er or a sister is
without clothes
and daily food. 16 If
one of you says
to them, "Go in
peace; keep warm
and well fed," but
does nothing about
their physical
needs, what good
is it?

νόμον τελεῖτε βασιλικὸν κατὰ τὴν γραφήν· ἀγαπήσεις τὸν πλησίον
law *you fulfill* *royal* ⌊as set forth in⌋ this scripture, "You shall love *{the}* your neighbor
3795 5464 997 2848 3836 1210 26 3836 5148 4446
n.asm v.pai.2p a.asm p.a d.asf n.asf v.fai.2s d.asm adv

σου ὡς σεαυτόν, καλῶς ποιεῖτε· 9 εἰ δὲ προσωπολημπτεῖτε,
your as yourself," you are doing well. *you are doing* But if *But* you show favoritism,
5148 6055 4932 4472 4472 4472 2822 4472 1254 1623 1254 4719
r.gs.2 cj r.asm.2 adv v.pai.2p cj cj v.pai.2p

ἁμαρτίαν ἐργάζεσθε ἐλεγχόμενοι ὑπὸ τοῦ νόμου ὡς
you are committing sin *you are committing* and are convicted by the law as
2237 2237 2237 281 2237 1794 5679 3836 3795 6055
n.asf v.pmi.2p pt.pp.npm p.g d.gsm n.gsm pl

παραβάται. 10 ὅστις γὰρ ὅλον τὸν νόμον τηρήσῃ πταίσῃ δὲ ἐν
transgressors. For whoever *For* keeps the entire *the* law *keeps* yet fails *yet* at
4127 1142 4015 1142 5498 3836 3910 3836 3795 5498 1254 4760 1254 1877
n.npm r.nsm cj a.asm d.asm n.asm v.aas.3s v.aas.3s cj p.d

ἑνί, γέγονεν → πάντων ἔνοχος. 11 ὁ γὰρ εἰπών,
a ⌊single point⌋ has become guilty of the law as a whole. *guilty* For he *For* who said,
1651 1181 1944 4246 1944 1142 3836 1142 3306
a.dsn v.rai.3s a.gpn a.nsm d.nsm cj pt.aa.nsm

↱ μὴ μοιχεύσῃς, εἶπεν καί, ↱ μὴ φονεύσῃς· εἰ δὲ ↱ ↱
"Do not commit adultery," also said, *also* "Do not commit murder." Now if *Now* you do
3658 3590 3658 2779 3306 2779 5839 3590 5839 1254 1623 1254 3658 3658
pl v.aas.2s v.aai.3s adv pl v.aas.2s cj cj

οὐ μοιχεύεις φονεύεις δέ, γέγονας παραβάτης →
not commit adultery but ⌊do commit murder,⌋ *but* ⌊you have become⌋ a transgressor of the
4024 3658 1254 5839 1254 1181 4127
pl v.pai.2s v.pai.2s cj v.rai.2s n.nsm

νόμου. 12 οὕτως λαλεῖτε καὶ οὕτως ποιεῖτε ὡς διὰ
law. So speak and so act as those who are to be judged by the
3795 4048 3281 2779 4048 4472 6055 3516 3516 3516 3212 3212 3212 1328
n.gsm adv v.pam.2p cj adv v.pam.2p pl p.g

νόμου ἐλευθερίας μέλλοντες κρίνεσθαι. 13 ἡ γὰρ κρίσις ἀνέλεος
law that brings freedom. *those who are* *to be judged* *{the}* For judgment will be without mercy
3795 1800 3516 3212 3836 1142 3213 447
n.gsm n.gsf pt.pa.npm f.pp d.nsf cj n.nsf a.nsf

τῷ μὴ ποιήσαντι ἔλεος· κατακαυχᾶται ἔλεος κρίσεως.
⌊for one⌋ who has shown no *who has shown* mercy; mercy triumphs *mercy* over judgment.
3836 4472 4472 4472 3590 4472 1799 1799 2878 1799 3213
d.dsm pl pt.aa.dsm n.asn v.pmi.3s n.nsn n.gsf

14 τί τὸ ὄφελος, ἀδελφοί μου, ἐὰν πίστιν λέγῃ
What *{the}* good is it, my brothers, *my* if someone claims to have faith *claims*
5515 3836 4055 1609 81 1609 1569 5516 3306 2400 2400 4411 3306
r.nsn d.nsn n.nsn n.vpm r.gs.1 cj n.asf v.pas.3s

τις ἔχειν ἔργα δὲ μὴ ἔχῃ; μὴ δύναται ἡ πίστις
someone *to have* but has no works? *but* *no* *has* *{not}* Can ⌊that kind of⌋ faith
5516 2400 1254 2400 3590 2240 1254 3590 2400 3590 1538 3836 4411
r.nsm f.pa n.apn cj pl v.pas.3s pl v.ppi.3s d.nsf n.nsf

σῶσαι αὐτόν; 15 ἐὰν ἀδελφὸς ἢ ἀδελφὴ γυμνοὶ ὑπάρχωσιν καὶ
save him? If a brother or sister lacks ⌊adequate clothing⌋ *lacks* and
5392 899 1569 81 2445 80 5639 1218 5639 2779
f.aa r.asm.3 cj n.nsm cj n.nsf a.npm v.pas.3p cj

λειπόμενοι τῆς ἐφημέρου τροφῆς 16 εἴπῃ δέ τις αὐτοῖς ἐξ ὑμῶν·
is in need of daily food, and one of you says *and* *one* to them, *of* *you*
3309 3836 2390 5575 1254 5516 1666 7007 3306 1254 5516 899 1666 7007
pt.pp.npm d.gsf n.gsf n.gsf v.aas.3s cj r.nsm r.dpm.3 p.g r.gp.2

ὑπάγετε ἐν εἰρήνῃ, θερμαίνεσθε καὶ χορτάζεσθε, ↱ ↱ μὴ δῶτε δὲ
"Go in peace; stay warm and eat your fill," and yet you do not give *and yet*
5632 1877 1645 2548 2779 5963 1254 1254 1443 1443 3590 1443 1254
v.pam.2p p.d n.dsf v.pmm.2p cj v.ppm.2p pl v.aas.2p cj

αὐτοῖς τὰ ἐπιτήδεια τοῦ σώματος, τί τὸ ὄφελος;
them what their body needs, *their body* what *{the}* good is that?
899 3836 3836 5393 2201 3836 5393 5515 3836 4055
r.dpm.3 d.apn a.apn d.gsn n.gsn r.nsn d.nsn n.nsn

NASB

royal law accord-
ing to the Scrip-
ture, "YOU SHALL
LOVE YOUR NEIGH-
BOR AS YOURSELF,"
you are doing well.
9 But if you show
partiality, you are
committing sin
and are convicted
by the law as
transgressors. 10 For
whoever keeps
the whole law and
yet stumbles in
one *point,* he has
become guilty of
all. 11 For He who
said, "DO NOT COM-
MIT ADULTERY," also
said, "DO NOT COM-
MIT MURDER." Now
if you do not com-
mit adultery, but
do commit murder,
you have become a
transgressor of the
law. 12 So speak and
so act as those who
are to be judged by
the law of liberty.
13 For judgment *will
be* merciless to one
who has shown
no mercy; mercy
triumphs over
judgment.

Faith and Works

14 What use is it,
my brethren, if
someone says he
has faith but he has
no works? Can that
faith save him? 15 If
a brother or sister
is without cloth-
ing and in need of
daily food, 16 and
one of you says
to them, "Go in
peace, be warmed
and be filled," and
yet you do not
give them what is
necessary for *their*
body, what use is
that?

[a] *8* Lev. 19:18
[b] *11* Exodus 20:14; Deut. 5:18
[c] *11* Exodus 20:13; Deut. 5:17

NIV

17 In the same way,
faith by itself, if it
is not accompanied
by action, is dead.
18 But someone
will say, "You
have faith; I have
deeds."
Show me your
faith without
deeds, and I will
show you my
faith by my deeds.
19 You believe that
there is one God.
Good! Even the
demons believe
that—and shud-
der.
20 You foolish per-
son, do you want
evidence that faith
without deeds is
useless[a]? 21 Was
not our father
Abraham consid-
ered righteous for
what he did when
he offered his
son Isaac on the
altar? 22 You see
that his faith and
his actions were
working together,
and his faith was
made complete by
what he did. 23 And
the scripture was
fulfilled that says,
"Abraham believed
God, and it was
credited to him as
righteousness,"[b]
and he was called
God's friend.
24 You see that a
person is consid-
ered righteous by
what they do and
not by faith alone.
25 In the same
way, was not even
Rahab the pros-
titute considered
righteous for what
she did when she
gave lodging to
the spies and sent
them off in a dif-
ferent direction?
26 As the body
without the spirit

[a] 20 Some early manuscripts *dead*
[b] 23 Gen. 15:6

17 οὕτως καὶ ἡ πίστις, ἐὰν μὴ ἔχῃ ἔργα, νεκρά ἐστιν →
⌊In the same way⌋ *{also}* *{the}* faith, if it has no *it has* works, is dead, *is* since
4048 2779 3836 4411 1569 2400 2400 3590 2400 2240 1639 3738 1639
adv adv d.nsf n.nsf cj pl v.pas.3s n.apn a.nsf v.pai.3s

καθ᾽ ἑαυτήν. 18 ἀλλ᾽ ἐρεῖ τις, σὺ πίστιν ἔχεις, κἀγὼ
it is by itself. But someone ⌊will say,⌋ *someone* "You have faith *have* and I have
2848 1571 247 5516 3306 5516 5148 2400 4411 2400 2743 2400
p.a r.asf.3 cj v.fai.3s r.nsm r.ns.2 n.asf v.pai.2s crasis

ἔργα ἔχω· δεῖξόν μοι τὴν πίστιν σου χωρὶς τῶν ἔργων, κἀγώ σοι
works." *have* Show me *{the}* your faith *your* without *{the}* works, and I will show you
2240 2400 1259 1609 3836 5148 4411 5148 6006 3836 2240 2743 1259 1259 5148
n.apn v.pai.1s v.aam.2s r.ds.1 d.asf n.asf r.gs.2 p.g d.gpn n.gpn crasis r.ds.2

δείξω ἐκ τῶν ἔργων μου τὴν πίστιν. 19 σὺ πιστεύεις ὅτι
will show my faith by *{the}* my works. *my* *my* *faith* You believe that God is
1259 3836 4411 1666 3836 1609 2240 1609 3836 4411 5148 4409 4022 2536 1639
v.fai.1s p.g d.gpn n.gpn r.gs.1 d.asf n.asf r.ns.2 v.pai.2s cj

εἷς ἐστιν ὁ θεός, καλῶς ποιεῖς· καὶ τὰ δαιμόνια πιστεύουσιν καὶ
one; *is* *{the}* *God* you do well. *you do* Even the demons believe, and
1651 1639 3836 2536 4472 4472 2822 4472 2779 3836 1228 4409 2779
a.nsm v.pai.3s d.nsm n.nsm adv v.pai.2s adv d.npn n.npn v.pai.3p cj

φρίσσουσιν. 20 θέλεις δὲ γνῶναι, ὦ ἄνθρωπε κενέ, ὅτι ἡ
shudder. ⌊Would you like⌋ *{and}* to be shown, you shallow person, *shallow* that *{the}*
5857 2527 1254 1182 6043 3031 476 3031 4022 3836
v.pai.3p v.pai.2s cj f.aa j n.vsm a.vsm cj d.nsf

πίστις χωρὶς τῶν ἔργων ἀργή[a] ἐστιν; 21 Ἀβραὰμ ὁ πατὴρ ἡμῶν
faith without *{the}* works is useless? *is* Was not Abraham *{the}* our father *our*
4411 6006 3836 2240 1639 734 1639 1467 4024 11 3836 7005 4252 7005
n.nsf p.g d.gpn n.gpn a.nsf v.pai.3s n.nsm d.nsm n.nsm r.gp.1

οὐκ ἐξ ἔργων ἐδικαιώθη ἀνενέγκας Ἰσαὰκ τὸν υἱὸν αὐτοῦ ἐπὶ
not justified by works *Was justified* when he offered his son Isaac *{the}* *son* *his* on
4024 1467 1666 2240 1467 429 899 5626 2693 3836 5626 899 2093
pl p.g n.gpn v.api.3s pt.aa.nsm n.asm d.asm n.asm r.gsm.3 p.a

τὸ θυσιαστήριον; 22 βλέπεις ὅτι ἡ πίστις συνήργει τοῖς ἔργοις
the altar? You see that *{the}* faith ⌊was at work along with⌋ *{the}* his works
3836 2603 1063 4022 3836 4411 5300 3836 899 2240
d.asn n.asn v.pai.2s cj d.nsf n.nsf v.iai.3s d.dpn n.dpn

αὐτοῦ καὶ ἐκ τῶν ἔργων ἡ πίστις ἐτελειώθη,
his and that his faith was made complete by his works. *his* *faith* *was made complete*
899 2779 3836 4411 5457 5457 5457 1666 3836 2240 3836 4411 5457
r.gsm.3 cj p.g d.gpn n.gpn d.nsf n.nsf v.api.3s

23 καὶ ἐπληρώθη ἡ γραφὴ ἡ λέγουσα, ἐπίστευσεν δὲ
And the scripture was fulfilled *the* *scripture* that says, "And Abraham believed *And*
2779 3836 1210 4444 3836 1210 3836 3306 1254 11 4409 1254
cj v.api.3s d.nsf n.nsf d.nsf pt.pa.nsf v.aai.3s cj

Ἀβραὰμ τῷ θεῷ, καὶ ἐλογίσθη αὐτῷ εἰς δικαιοσύνην καὶ
Abraham *{the}* God, and it was credited to him as righteousness," and he was called the
11 3836 2536 2779 3357 899 1650 1466 2779 2813 2813 2813
n.nsm d.dsm n.dsm cj v.api.3s r.dsm.3 p.a n.asf cj

φίλος θεοῦ ἐκλήθη. 24 ὁρᾶτε ὅτι ἐξ ἔργων δικαιοῦται
friend of God. *he was called* You see that a person is justified by works *is justified*
5813 2536 2813 3972 4022 476 1467 1467 1666 2240 1467
n.nsm n.gsm v.api.3s v.pai.2p cj p.g n.gpn v.ppi.3s

ἄνθρωπος καὶ οὐκ ἐκ πίστεως μόνον. 25 ὁμοίως δὲ καὶ Ῥαὰβ
person and not by faith alone. And ⌊in the same way⌋ *And* was not also Rahab
476 2779 4024 1666 4411 3667 1254 3931 1254 1467 4024 2779 4805
n.nsm cj pl p.g n.gsf adv adv cj adv n.nsf

ἡ πόρνη οὐκ ἐξ ἔργων ἐδικαιώθη ὑποδεξαμένη τοὺς ἀγγέλους καὶ
the harlot *not* justified by works *was justified* ⌊when she took in⌋ the spies and sent
3836 4520 4024 1467 1666 2240 1467 5685 3836 34 2779 1675
d.nsf n.nsf pl p.g n.gpn v.api.3s pt.am.nsf d.apm n.apm cj

ἑτέρᾳ ὁδῷ ἐκβαλοῦσα; 26 ὥσπερ γὰρ τὸ σῶμα χωρὶς πνεύματος
them out by another way? *sent out* For just as *For* the body without the spirit
1675 2283 3847 1675 1142 6061 1142 3836 5393 6006 4460
r.dsf n.dsf pt.aa.nsf cj cj d.nsn n.nsn p.g n.gsn

[a] νεκρά included by TR after ἀργή.

NASB

17 Even so faith, if
it has no works,
is dead, *being* by
itself.
18 But someone
may *well* say,
"You have faith
and I have works;
show me your faith
without the works,
and I will show
you my faith by
my works." 19 You
believe that [a]God
is one. You do
well; the demons
also believe, and
shudder. 20 But are
you willing to rec-
ognize, you foolish
fellow, that faith
without works is
useless? 21 Was not
Abraham our father
justified by works
when he offered up
Isaac his son on the
altar? 22 You see that
faith was working
with his works, and
as a result of the
works, faith was
perfected; 23 and the
Scripture was ful-
filled which says,
"AND ABRAHAM
BELIEVED GOD, AND
IT WAS RECKONED TO
HIM AS RIGHTEOUS-
NESS," and he was
called the friend
of God. 24 You see
that a man is justi-
fied by works and
not by faith alone.
25 In the same way,
was not Rahab the
harlot also justified
by works when she
received the mes-
sengers and sent
them out by anoth-
er way? 26 For just
as the body without
the spirit is

[a] One early ms reads *there is one God*

NIV

is dead, so faith
without deeds is
dead.

Taming the Tongue

3 Not many of
you should be-
come teachers, my
fellow believers,
because you know
that we who teach
will be judged
more strictly. 2 We
all stumble in
many ways. Any-
one who is never at
fault in what they
say is perfect, able
to keep their whole
body in check.
3 When we put
bits into the
mouths of horses
to make them obey
us, we can turn the
whole animal. 4 Or
take ships as an
example. Although
they are so large
and are driven by
strong winds, they
are steered by a
very small rudder
wherever the pilot
wants to go. 5 Like-
wise, the tongue is
a small part of the
body, but it makes
great boasts. Con-
sider what a great
forest is set on fire
by a small spark.
6 The tongue also
is a fire, a world
of evil among the
parts of the body.
It corrupts the
whole body, sets
the whole course
of one's life on
fire, and is itself
set on fire by hell.
7 All kinds of an-
imals, birds, rep-
tiles and

νεκρόν ἐστιν, οὕτως καὶ ἡ πίστις χωρὶς ἔργων νεκρά ἐστιν.
is dead, *is* so also *{the}* faith devoid of works is dead. *is*
1639 3738 1639 4048 2779 3836 4411 6006 2240 1639 3738 1639
a.nsn v.pai.3s adv adv d.nsf n.nsf p.g n.gpn a.nsf v.pai.3s

3:1 μὴ πολλοὶ διδάσκαλοι γίνεσθε, ἀδελφοί μου,
Not many of you should become teachers, *you should become* my brothers, *my*
3590 4498 1181 1181 1181 1437 1181 1609 81 1609
pl a.npm n.npm v.pmm.2p n.vpm r.gs.1

εἰδότες ὅτι μεῖζον κρίμα λημψόμεθα.
⌞for you know⌟ that those of us who teach will be judged by a stricter standard. *will be judged*
3857 4022 3284 3284 3284 3284 3489 3210 3284
pt.ra.npm cj a.asn.c n.asn v.fmi.1p

2 πολλὰ γὰρ πταίομεν ἅπαντες. εἴ τις
For we all stumble ⌞in many ways.⌟ *For we stumble all* If someone does not stumble
1142 4760 570 4760 4498 1142 4760 570 1623 5516 4760 4024 4760
a.apn cj v.pai.1p a.npm cj r.nsm

ἐν λόγῳ οὐ πταίει, οὗτος τέλειος ἀνὴρ δυνατὸς χαλιναγωγῆσαι
in ⌞what he says,⌟ *not does stumble* he is a mature individual, able to bridle
1877 3364 4024 4760 4047 5455 467 1543 5902
p.d n.dsm pl v.pai.3s r.nsm a.nsm n.nsm a.nsm f.aa

καὶ ὅλον τὸ σῶμα. 3 εἰ δὲ τῶν
his whole body as well. *whole his body* Now if *Now* we put bits into the mouths of
3836 3910 5393 2779 3910 3836 5393 1254 1623 1254 965 965 5903 1650 3836 5125 3836
adv a.asn d.asn n.asn cj cj d.gpm

ἵππων τοὺς χαλινοὺς εἰς τὰ στόματα βάλλομεν εἰς τὸ πείθεσθαι αὐτοὺς
horses *{the} bits into the mouths we put* to ~ make them obey *them*
2691 3836 5903 1650 3836 5125 965 1650 3836 899 4275 899
n.gpm d.apm n.apm p.a d.apn n.apn v.pai.1p p.a d.asn f.pp r.apm.3

ἡμῖν, καὶ ὅλον τὸ σῶμα αὐτῶν μετάγομεν. 4 ἰδοὺ καὶ τὰ
us, then we guide their entire *{the}* body. *their we guide* Or consider *Or {the}*
7005 2779 3555 3555 899 3910 3836 5393 899 3555 2779 2627 2779 3836
r.dp.1 adv a.asn d.asn n.asn r.gpm.3 v.pai.1p j adv d.npn

πλοῖα τηλικαῦτα ὄντα καὶ ὑπὸ ἀνέμων
ships: though they are so large *though they are* and are driven by strong winds,
4450 1639 1639 1639 5496 1639 2779 1785 1785 5679 5017 449
n.npn r.npn pt.pa.npn cj p.g n.gpm

σκληρῶν ἐλαυνόμενα, μετάγεται ὑπὸ ἐλαχίστου πηδαλίου ὅπου ἡ ὁρμὴ
strong are driven they are steered by a very small rudder, wherever the impulse
5017 1785 3555 5679 1788 4382 3963 3836 3995
a.gpm pt.pp.npn v.ppi.3s p.g a.gsn.s n.gsn cj d.nsf n.nsf

τοῦ εὐθύνοντος βούλεται, 5 οὕτως καὶ ἡ γλῶσσα μικρὸν μέλος ἐστὶν καὶ
of the pilot directs. So also is the tongue a small member, *is* yet
3836 2316 1089 4048 2779 1639 3836 1185 3625 3517 1639 2779
d.gsm pt.pa.gsm v.pmi.3s adv adv d.nsf n.nsf a.nsn n.nsn v.pai.3s cj

μεγάλα αὐχεῖ. ἰδοὺ ἡλίκον πῦρ
it boasts of great things. *it boasts* See how large a forest is set on fire by such a small flame.
902 902 3489 902 2627 2462 2462 5627 409 409 409 409 2462 4786
a.apn v.pai.3s j a.nsn n.nsn

ἡλίκην ὕλην ἀνάπτει· 6 καὶ ἡ γλῶσσα πῦρ· ὁ κόσμος τῆς
how large forest is set on fire And the tongue is a fire! The tongue is a world of
2462 5627 409 2779 3836 1185 4786 3836 1185 3836 3180 3836
a.asf n.asf v.pai.3s cj d.nsf n.nsf n.nsn d.nsm n.nsm d.gsf

ἀδικίας ἡ γλῶσσα καθίσταται ἐν τοῖς μέλεσιν ἡμῶν, ἡ σπιλοῦσα
iniquity *The tongue* set among *{the}* our members; *our* it defiles the
94 3836 1185 2770 1877 3836 7005 3517 7005 3836 5071 3836
n.gsf d.nsf n.nsf v.ppi.3s p.d d.dpn n.dpn r.gp.1 d.nsf pt.pa.nsf

ὅλον τὸ σῶμα καὶ φλογίζουσα τὸν τροχὸν τῆς γενέσεως καὶ φλογιζομένη ὑπὸ
whole *the* body, *{and}* sets on fire the course of our life, and is set on fire by
3910 3836 5393 2779 5824 3836 5580 3836 1161 2779 5824 5679
a.asn d.asn n.asn cj pt.pa.nsf d.asm n.asm d.gsf n.gsf cj pt.pp.nsf p.g

τῆς γεέννης. 7 πᾶσα γὰρ φύσις θηρίων τε καὶ πετεινῶν, ἑρπετῶν τε καὶ
{the} hell. For every *For* species of beast *{both}* and bird, reptile *{both}* and
3836 1147 1142 4246 1142 5882 2563 5445 2779 4374 2260 5445 2779
d.gsf n.gsf a.nsf cj n.nsf n.gpn cj cj n.gpn n.gpn cj cj

NASB

dead, so also faith
without works is
dead.

The Tongue Is a Fire

3:1 Let not many *of*
you become teach-
ers, my brethren,
knowing that as
such we will incur
a stricter judgment.
2 For we all stumble
in many *ways.* If
anyone does not
stumble in what he
says, he is a perfect
man, able to bridle
the whole body as
well. 3 Now if we
put the bits into the
horses' mouths so
that they will obey
us, we direct their
entire body as well.
4 Look at the ships
also, though they
are so great and are
driven by strong
winds, are still
directed by a very
small rudder wher-
ever the inclination
of the pilot desires.
5 So also the tongue
is a small part of
the body, and *yet*
it boasts of great
things.
See how great a
forest is set aflame
by such a small
fire! 6 And the
tongue is a fire,
the *very* world of
iniquity; the tongue
is set among our
members as that
which defiles the
entire body, and
sets on fire the
course of *our* life,
and is set on fire
by hell. 7 For every
species of beasts
and birds, of rep-
tiles and creatures

NIV

sea creatures are
being tamed and
have been tamed
by mankind, 8but
no human be-
ing can tame the
tongue. It is a rest-
less evil, full of
deadly poison.
9With the tongue
we praise our Lord
and Father, and
with it we curse
human beings,
who have been
made in God's
likeness. 10Out of
the same mouth
come praise and
cursing. My broth-
ers and sisters,
this should not be.
11Can both fresh
water and salt
water flow from
the same spring?
12My brothers and
sisters, can a fig
tree bear olives, or
a grapevine bear
figs? Neither can a
salt spring produce
fresh water.

Two Kinds of Wisdom

13Who is wise
and understand-
ing among you?
Let them show it
by their good life,
by deeds done in
the humility that
comes from wis-
dom. 14But if you
harbor bitter envy
and selfish ambi-
tion in your hearts,
do not boast about
it or deny the truth.
15Such "wisdom"
does not come
down from heaven
but is earthly, un-
spiritual, demonic.
16For where you
have envy and
selfish ambition,
there you find dis-
order and every
evil practice.
17But the wisdom
that comes from
heaven

ἐναλίων δαμάζεται καὶ δεδάμασται τῇ φύσει τῇ ἀνθρωπίνῃ. 8
sea creature, can be tamed, and has been tamed ⌞by the⌟ human species. {the} human But
1879 1238 2779 1238 3836 474 5882 3836 474 1254
n.gpn v.ppi.3s cj v.rpi.3s d.dsf n.dsf d.dsf a.dsf

τὴν δὲ γλῶσσαν οὐδεὶς δαμάσαι δύναται ἀνθρώπων, ἀκατάστατον
the But tongue, no one is able to tame; is able {of men} it is a restless
3836 1254 1185 4029 1538 1538 1238 1538 476 190
d.asf cj n.asf a.nsm f.aa v.ppi.3s n.gpm a.nsn

κακόν, μεστὴ → ἰοῦ θανατηφόρου. 9 ἐν αὐτῇ εὐλογοῦμεν τὸν κύριον καὶ
evil, full of deadly poison. deadly With it we bless our Lord and
2805 3550 2504 2675 2504 1877 899 2328 3836 3261 2779
a.nsn a.nsf n.gsm a.gsm p.d r.dsf.3 v.pai.1p d.asm n.asm cj

πατέρα καὶ ἐν αὐτῇ καταρώμεθα τοὺς ἀνθρώπους τοὺς καθ' ὁμοίωσιν
Father, and with it we curse those {people} who are made in the likeness
4252 2779 1877 899 2933 3836 476 3836 1181 1181 2848 3932
n.asm cj p.d r.dsf.3 v.pmi.1p d.apm n.apm d.apm p.a n.asf

θεοῦ γεγονότας, 10 ἐκ τοῦ αὐτοῦ στόματος ἐξέρχεται εὐλογία καὶ κατάρα.
of God. are made From the same mouth come blessing and cursing. My
2536 1181 1666 3836 899 5125 2002 2330 2779 2932 1609
n.gsm pt.ra.apm p.g d.gsn r.gsn n.gsn v.pmi.3s n.nsf cj n.nsf

οὐ χρή, ἀδελφοί μου, ταῦτα οὕτως γίνεσθαι. 11 μήτι ἡ
brothers, this should not should brothers My this {so} happen. {not} Does a
81 4047 5973 4024 5973 81 1609 4047 4048 1181 3614 3836
pl v.pai.3s n.vpm r.gs.1 r.npn adv f.pm pl d.nsf

πηγὴ ἐκ τῆς αὐτῆς ὀπῆς βρύει τὸ γλυκὺ καὶ τὸ
spring pour forth water from the same opening pour forth that is both {the} fresh and {the}
4380 1108 1108 1666 3836 899 3956 1108 3836 1184 2779 3836
n.nsf p.g d.gsf r.gsf n.gsf v.pai.3s d.asn a.asn cj d.asn

πικρόν; 12 μὴ δύναται, ἀδελφοί μου, συκῆ ἐλαίας ποιῆσαι
brackish? {not} My brothers, can brothers My a fig tree produce olives, produce
4395 3590 1609 81 1538 81 1609 5190 4472 1777 4472
a.asn pl v.ppi.3s n.vpm r.gs.1 n.nsf n.apf f.aa

ἢ ἄμπελος σῦκα; οὔτε ἁλυκὸν γλυκὺ ποιῆσαι ὕδωρ. 13 τίς
or a grapevine figs? Neither can a salt spring supply fresh supply water. Who is
2445 306 5192 4046 266 4472 1184 4472 5623 5515
cj n.nsf n.apn cj a.nsn a.asn f.aa n.asn r.nsm

σοφὸς καὶ ἐπιστήμων ἐν ὑμῖν; δειξάτω ἐκ τῆς
wise and understanding among you? By his exemplary conduct let him show By his
5055 2779 2184 1877 7007 1666 3836 2819 419 1259 1666 3836
a.nsm cj a.nsm p.d r.dp.2 v.aam.3s p.g d.gsf

καλῆς ἀναστροφῆς τὰ ἔργα αὐτοῦ ἐν πραΰτητι σοφίας. 14
exemplary conduct {the} his works his done in the gentleness born of wisdom. But
2819 419 3836 899 2240 899 1877 4559 5053 1254
a.gsf n.gsf d.apn n.apn r.gsm.3 p.d n.dsf n.gsf

εἰ δὲ ζῆλον πικρὸν ἔχετε καὶ ἐριθείαν ἐν τῇ καρδίᾳ
if But you have bitter jealousy bitter you have and selfish ambition in {the} your heart,
1623 1254 2400 2400 4395 2419 4395 2400 2779 2249 1877 3836 7007 2840
cj cj n.asm a.asm v.pai.2p cj n.asn p.d d.dsf n.dsf

ὑμῶν, ↱ μὴ κατακαυχᾶσθε καὶ ψεύδεσθε κατὰ τῆς ἀληθείας. 15 οὐκ
your do not be arrogant and tell lies against the truth. This is not
7007 2878 3590 2878 2779 6017 2848 3836 237 4047 1639 4024
r.gp.2 pl v.pmm.2p cj v.pmm.2p p.g d.gsf n.gsf pl

ἔστιν αὕτη ἡ σοφία ἄνωθεν κατερχομένη ἀλλὰ ἐπίγειος,
is This the wisdom that comes down from above, that comes down but is earthly,
1639 4047 3836 5053 2982 2982 2982 540 2982 247 2103
v.pai.3s r.nsf d.nsf n.nsf adv pt.pm.nsf cj a.nsf

ψυχική, δαιμονιώδης. 16 ὅπου γὰρ ζῆλος καὶ ἐριθεία, ἐκεῖ
unspiritual, demonic. For where For jealousy and selfish ambition exist, there you will
6035 1229 1142 3963 1142 2419 2779 2249 1695
a.nsf a.nsf cj cj n.nsm cj n.nsf adv

ἀκαταστασία καὶ πᾶν φαῦλον πρᾶγμα. 17 ἡ δὲ ἄνωθεν σοφία
find disorder and every evil practice. But the But wisdom from above wisdom
189 2779 4246 5765 4547 1254 3836 1254 5053 540 5053
n.nsf cj a.nsn a.nsn n.nsn d.nsf cj adv n.nsf

NASB

of the sea, is tamed
and has been tamed
by the human race.
8But no one can
tame the tongue;
it is a restless evil
and full of deadly
poison. 9With it
we bless *our* Lord
and Father, and
with it we curse
men, who have
been made in the
likeness of God;
10from the same
mouth come *both*
blessing and curs-
ing. My brethren,
these things ought
not to be this way.
11Does a fountain
send out from the
same opening *both*
fresh and bitter
water? 12Can a fig
tree, my brethren,
produce olives, or a
vine produce figs?
Nor *can* salt water
produce fresh.

Wisdom from Above

13Who among
you is wise and
understanding? Let
him show by his
good behavior his
deeds in the gentle-
ness of wisdom.
14But if you have
bitter jealousy and
selfish ambition
in your heart, do
not be arrogant
and *so* lie against
the truth. 15This
wisdom is not that
which comes down
from above, but
is earthly, natural,
demonic. 16For
where jealousy
and selfish ambi-
tion exist, there is
disorder and every
evil thing. 17But the
wisdom from

NIV

is first of all pure;
then peace-loving,
considerate, sub-
missive, full of
mercy and good
fruit, impartial and
sincere. 18 Peace-
makers who sow
in peace reap a
harvest of righ-
teousness.

Submit Yourselves to God

4 What causes
fights and quar-
rels among you?
Don't they come
from your desires
that battle within
you? 2 You desire but
do not have, so you
kill. You covet but
you cannot get what
you want, so you
quarrel and fight.
You do not have
because you do not
ask God. 3 When
you ask, you do not
receive, because you
ask with wrong mo-
tives, that you may
spend what you get
on your pleasures.
4 You adulterous peo-
ple,[a] don't you know
that friendship with
the world means en-
mity against God?
Therefore, anyone
who chooses to be a
friend of the world
becomes an enemy
of God. 5 Or do you
think Scripture says
without reason that
he jealously longs
for the spirit he has
caused to dwell in
us[b]? 6 But he gives us
more grace. That is
why Scripture says:

> "God opposes the proud
> but shows favor to the humble."[c]

7 Submit your-
selves, then, to
God.

[a] 4 An allusion to covenant unfaithfulness; see Hosea 3:1.
[b] 5 Or *that the spirit he caused to dwell in us envies intensely;* or *that the Spirit he caused to dwell in us longs jealously*
[c] 6 Prov. 3:34

πρῶτον μὲν ἁγνή ἐστιν, ἔπειτα εἰρηνική, ἐπιεικής, εὐπειθής, μεστὴ ἐλέους καὶ
is first of all ~ pure, *is* then peaceable, gentle, open to reason, full of mercy and
1639 4754 3525 54 1639 2083 1646 2117 2340 3550 1799 2779
adv pl a.nsf v.pai.3s adv a.nsf a.nsf a.nsf a.nsf n.gsn cj

καρπῶν ἀγαθῶν, ἀδιάκριτος, ἀνυπόκριτος. 18 καρπὸς δὲ
good fruits, *good* free from prejudice and hypocrisy. And a harvest *And*
19 2843 19 88 537 1254 2843 1254
n.gpm a.gpm a.nsf a.nsf n.nsm cj

δικαιοσύνης ἐν εἰρήνῃ σπείρεται τοῖς ποιοῦσιν εἰρήνην.
of righteousness is sown in peace *is sown* by those who make peace.
1466 5062 5062 1877 1645 5062 3836 4472 1645
n.gsf p.d n.dsf v.ppi.3s d.dpm pt.pa.dpm n.asf

4:1 πόθεν πόλεμοι καὶ πόθεν μάχαι ἐν ὑμῖν; οὐκ
⌊What accounts for⌋ the quarrels and *{what accounts for}* disputes among you? Is it not
4470 4483 2779 4470 3480 1877 7007 4024
cj n.npm cj cj n.npf p.d r.dp.2 pl

ἐντεῦθεν, ἐκ τῶν ἡδονῶν ὑμῶν τῶν στρατευομένων ἐν τοῖς μέλεσιν
this — *{from}* *{the}* your desires *your* that are at war in *{the}* your members?
1949 1666 3836 7007 2454 7007 3836 5129 1877 3836 7007 3517
adv p.g d.gpf n.gpf r.gp.2 d.gpf pt.pm.gpf p.d d.dpn n.dpn

ὑμῶν; 2 ἐπιθυμεῖτε καὶ ↱ οὐκ ἔχετε, φονεύετε καὶ ζηλοῦτε καὶ ⌊οὐ δύνασθε⌋
your You desire and do not have; you murder and envy and cannot
7007 2121 2779 2400 4024 2400 5839 2779 2420 2779 4024 1538
r.gp.2 v.pai.2p cj pl v.pai.2p v.pai.2p cj v.pai.2p cj pl v.ppi.2p

ἐπιτυχεῖν, μάχεσθε καὶ πολεμεῖτε, ↱ ↱ οὐκ ἔχετε διὰ τὸ ↱ μὴ
obtain; you fight and quarrel. You do not have because ~ you do not
2209 3481 2779 4482 2400 2400 4024 2400 1328 3836 7007 160 3590
f.aa v.pmi.2p cj v.pai.2p pl v.pai.2p p.a d.asn pl

αἰτεῖσθαι ὑμᾶς, 3 αἰτεῖτε καὶ ↱ οὐ λαμβάνετε διότι κακῶς
ask. *you* You ask and do not receive because you ask ⌊for the wrong reason,⌋
160 7007 160 2779 3284 4024 3284 1484 160 160 2809
f.pm r.ap.2 v.pai.2p cj pl v.pai.2p cj adv

αἰτεῖσθε, ἵνα ἐν ταῖς ἡδοναῖς ὑμῶν δαπανήσητε.
you ask that you can spend it on *{the}* your pleasures. *your* *you can spend*
160 2671 1251 1251 1251 1877 3836 7007 2454 7007 1251
v.pmi.2p cj p.d d.dpf n.dpf r.gp.2 v.aas.2p

4 μοιχαλίδες, ↱ ↱ οὐκ οἴδατε ὅτι ἡ φιλία τοῦ κόσμου
⌊You adulterous people!⌋ Do you not know that *{the}* friendship ⌊with the⌋ world is
3655 3857 3857 4024 3857 4022 3836 5802 3836 3180 1639
n.vpf pl v.rai.2p cj d.nsf n.nsf d.gsm n.gsm

ἔχθρα τοῦ θεοῦ ἐστιν; ⌊ὃς ἐὰν⌋ οὖν βουληθῇ φίλος
hostility toward God? *is* Therefore whoever *Therefore* desires to be a friend
2397 3836 2536 1639 4036 4005 1569 4036 1089 1639 1639 5813
n.nsf d.gsm n.gsm v.pai.3s r.nsm pl cj v.aps.3s n.nsm

εἶναι τοῦ κόσμου, ἐχθρὸς τοῦ θεοῦ καθίσταται. 5 ἢ δοκεῖτε
to be of the world makes himself an enemy of God. *makes himself* Or do you imagine
1639 3836 3180 2770 2770 2398 3836 2536 2770 2445 1506
f.pa d.gsm n.gsm a.nsm d.gsm n.gsm v.ppi.3s cj v.pai.2p

ὅτι κενῶς ἡ γραφὴ λέγει, ↱ ⌊πρὸς φθόνον⌋
that scripture ⌊has no meaning⌋ *{the}* *scripture* when it says, "God yearns jealously
4022 1210 3036 3836 1210 3306 2160 4639 5784
cj adv d.nsf n.nsf v.pai.3s p.a n.asm

ἐπιποθεῖ τὸ πνεῦμα ὃ κατῴκισεν ἐν ἡμῖν, 6 μείζονα δὲ δίδωσιν
over the spirit that he has placed in us"? But he gives greater *But* *he gives*
2160 3836 4460 4005 3001 1877 7005 1254 1443 1443 3489 1254 1443
v.pai.3s d.asn n.asn r.asn v.aai.3s p.d r.dp.1 a.asf.c cj v.pai.3s

χάριν; διὸ λέγει, ὁ θεὸς ὑπερηφάνοις ἀντιτάσσεται,
grace. ⌊That is why⌋ scripture says, *{the}* "God opposes the proud *opposes* but
5921 1475 3306 3836 2536 530 5662 530 1254
n.asf cj v.pai.3s d.nsm n.nsm a.dpm v.pmi.3s

→ ταπεινοῖς δὲ δίδωσιν χάριν. 7 ὑποτάγητε οὖν τῷ θεῷ,
he gives grace to the humble." *but* *he gives* *grace* So submit yourselves *So* to God.
1443 1443 5921 5424 1254 1443 5921 4036 5718 4036 3836 2536
a.dpm cj v.pai.3s n.asf v.apm.2p cj d.dsm n.dsm

NASB

above is first pure,
then peaceable,
gentle, reasonable,
full of mercy and
good fruits, un-
wavering, without
hypocrisy. 18 And
the seed whose
fruit is righteous-
ness is sown in
peace by those who
make peace.

Things to Avoid

4:1 What is the
source of quar-
rels and conflicts
among you? Is not
the source your
pleasures that wage
war in your mem-
bers? 2 You lust and
do not have; *so* you
commit murder.
You are envious
and cannot obtain;
so you fight and
quarrel. You do not
have because you
do not ask. 3 You
ask and do not re-
ceive, because you
ask with wrong
motives, so that
you may spend *it*
on your pleasures.
4 You adulteresses,
do you not know
that friendship
with the world is
hostility toward
God? Therefore
whoever wishes
to be a friend of
the world makes
himself an enemy
of God. 5 Or do
you think that the
Scripture speaks to
no purpose: "[a]He
jealously desires
the Spirit which
He has made to
dwell in us"? 6 But
He gives a greater
grace. Therefore *it*
says, "GOD IS OP-
POSED TO THE PROUD,
BUT GIVES GRACE
TO THE HUMBLE."
7 Submit therefore
to God.

[a] Or *The spirit which He has made to dwell in us lusts with envy*

NIV

Resist the devil,
and he will flee
from you. 8 Come
near to God and
he will come near
to you. Wash your
hands, you sin-
ners, and purify
your hearts, you
double-minded.
9 Grieve, mourn and
wail. Change your
laughter to mourn-
ing and your joy to
gloom. 10 Humble
yourselves before
the Lord, and he
will lift you up.
11 Brothers and
sisters, do not
slander one anoth-
er. Anyone who
speaks against a
brother or sister[a]
or judges them
speaks against the
law and judges it.
When you judge
the law, you are
not keeping it, but
sitting in judgment
on it. 12 There is
only one Lawgiv-
er and Judge, the
one who is able to
save and destroy.
But you—who are
you to judge your
neighbor?

Boasting About Tomorrow

13 Now listen, you
who say, "Today
or tomorrow we
will go to this or
that city, spend a
year there, carry on
business and make
money." 14 Why,
you do not even
know what will
happen tomorrow.
What is your life?
You are a mist that
appears for a lit-
tle while and then
vanishes. 15 Instead,
you ought to say,
"If it is the Lord's
will, we will live
and do this or
that."

[a] 11 The Greek word for *brother or sister* (*adelphos*) refers here to a believer, whether man or woman, as part of God's family.

ἀντίστητε δὲ τῷ διαβόλῳ καὶ φεύξεται ἀφ᾽ ὑμῶν, 8 ἐγγίσατε τῷ θεῷ καὶ
Resist *{and}* the devil and he will flee from you. Draw near to God and
468 1254 3836 1333 2779 5771 608 7007 1581 3836 2536 2779
v.aam.2p cj d.dsm n.dsm cj v.fmi.3s p.g r.gp.2 v.aam.2p d.dsm n.dsm cj

ἐγγιεῖ ὑμῖν. καθαρίσατε χεῖρας, ἁμαρτωλοί, καὶ ἁγνίσατε καρδίας,
⌊he will draw near⌋ to you. Cleanse your hands, you sinners, and purify your hearts,
1581 7007 2751 5931 283 2779 49 2840
v.fai.3s r.dp.2 v.aam.2p n.apf a.vpm cj v.aam.2p n.apf

δίψυχοι. 9 ταλαιπωρήσατε καὶ πενθήσατε καὶ κλαύσατε. ὁ
you double-minded. Be miserable and mourn and weep; let *{the}* your
1500 5415 2779 4291 2779 3081 3573 3836 7007
a.vpm v.aam.2p cj v.aam.2p cj v.aam.2p d.nsm

γέλως ὑμῶν εἰς πένθος μετατραπήτω καὶ ἡ χαρὰ εἰς κατήφειαν.
laughter *your* be turned into mourning *let be turned* and your joy into gloom.
1152 7007 3573 3573 1650 4292 3573 2779 3836 5915 1650 2993
n.nsm r.gp.2 p.a n.asn v.apm.3s cj d.nsf n.nsf p.a n.asf

10 ταπεινώθητε ἐνώπιον → κυρίου καὶ ὑψώσει ὑμᾶς. ↰ 11 ↱ μὴ
Humble yourselves in the presence of the Lord and he will lift you up. Do not
5427 1967 3261 2779 5738 7007 5738 2895 3590
v.apm.2p p.g n.gsm cj v.fai.3s r.ap.2 pl

καταλαλεῖτε ἀλλήλων, ἀδελφοί. ὁ καταλαλῶν ἀδελφοῦ ἢ κρίνων τὸν
speak against one another, my brothers. Whoever speaks against a brother or judges *{the}*
2895 253 81 3836 2895 81 2445 3212 3836
v.pam.2p r.gpm n.vpm d.nsm pt.pa.nsm n.gsm cj pt.pa.nsm d.asm

ἀδελφὸν αὐτοῦ καταλαλεῖ νόμου καὶ κρίνει νόμον· εἰ δὲ
his brother, *his* speaks against the law and judges the law; but if *but* you judge
899 81 899 2895 3795 2779 3212 3795 1254 1623 1254 3212 3212
n.asm r.gsm.3 v.pai.3s n.gsm cj v.pai.3s n.asm cj cj

νόμον κρίνεις, οὐκ εἶ ποιητὴς → νόμου ἀλλὰ κριτής.
the law, *you judge* you are not *you are* a doer of the law but a judge of it.
3795 3212 1639 1639 4024 1639 4475 3795 247 3216
n.asm v.pai.2s pl v.pai.2s n.nsm n.gsm cj n.nsm

12 εἷς ἐστιν ὁ[a] νομοθέτης καὶ κριτὴς ὁ δυνάμενος
There is only one *There is* who is the lawgiver and judge — the one who is able
1639 1639 1651 1639 3836 3794 2779 3216 3836 1538
a.nsm v.pai.3s d.nsm n.nsm cj n.nsm d.nsm pt.pp.nsm

σῶσαι καὶ ἀπολέσαι· σὺ δὲ τίς εἶ ὁ κρίνων τὸν πλησίον;
to save and to destroy; so who are you *so who are* *{the}* to be judging your neighbor?
5392 2779 660 1254 5515 1639 5148 1254 5515 1639 3836 3212 3836 4446
f.aa cj f.aa r.ns.2 cj r.nsm v.pai.2s d.vsm pt.pa.vsm d.asm adv

13 Ἄγε νῦν οἱ λέγοντες, σήμερον ἢ αὔριον πορευσόμεθα εἰς τήνδε τὴν
Come now, ⌊you who⌋ say, "Today or tomorrow we will go to some *{the}*
72 3814 3836 3306 4958 2445 892 4513 1650 3840 3836
v.pam.2s adv d.vpm pt.pa.vpm adv cj adv v.fmi.1p p.a r.asf d.asf

πόλιν καὶ ποιήσομεν ἐκεῖ ἐνιαυτὸν καὶ ἐμπορευσόμεθα καὶ κερδήσομεν·
city and spend a year there *year* and engage in business and make a profit."
4484 2779 4472 1929 1695 1929 2779 1864 2779 3045
n.asf cj v.fai.1p adv n.asm cj v.fmi.1p cj v.fai.1p

14 οἵτινες ↱ οὐκ ἐπίστασθε τὸ τῆς αὔριον
You have no idea *{the}* what your life will be like *{the}* tomorrow.
4015 2179 4024 2179 3836 4481 7007 2437 4481 4481 4481 3836 892
r.npm pl v.ppi.2p d.asn d.gsf adv

ποία ἡ ζωὴ ὑμῶν· ἀτμὶς γάρ ἐστε ἡ πρὸς
what will be like *{the}* *life* *your* For you are but a mist *For* *you are* that appears for a
4481 3836 2437 7007 1142 1639 1639 874 1142 1639 3836 5743 4639
r.nsf d.nsf n.nsf r.gp.2 n.nsf cj v.pai.2p d.nsf p.a

ὀλίγον φαινομένη, ἔπειτα καὶ ἀφανιζομένη. 15 ἀντὶ τοῦ λέγειν
brief moment *appears* and then *and* disappears. Instead, ~ you ⌊ought to say,⌋
3900 5743 2779 2083 2779 906 505 3836 7007 3306
a.asn pt.pp.nsf adv cj pt.pp.nsf p.g d.gsn f.pa

ὑμᾶς, ἐὰν ὁ κύριος θελήσῃ καὶ ζήσομεν καὶ ποιήσομεν τοῦτο ἢ ἐκεῖνο.
you "If the Lord so decrees, then we will live and do this or that."
7007 1569 3836 3261 2527 2779 2409 2779 4472 4047 2445 1697
r.ap.2 cj d.nsm n.nsm v.aas.3s cj v.fai.1p cj v.fai.1p r.asn cj r.asn

[a] [ὁ] UBS, omitted by TNIV.

NASB

Resist the devil
and he will flee
from you. 8 Draw
near to God and
He will draw near
to you. Cleanse
your hands, you
sinners; and purify
your hearts, you
double-minded.
9 Be miserable and
mourn and weep;
let your laughter be
turned into mourn-
ing and your joy to
gloom. 10 Humble
yourselves in the
presence of the
Lord, and He will
exalt you.
11 Do not speak
against one an-
other, brethren. He
who speaks against
a brother or judges
his brother, speaks
against the law and
judges the law;
but if you judge
the law, you are
not a doer of the
law but a judge *of*
it. 12 There is *only*
one Lawgiver and
Judge, the One
who is able to save
and to destroy; but
who are you who
judge your neigh-
bor?
13 Come now, you
who say, "Today
or tomorrow we
will go to such and
such a city, and
spend a year there
and engage in busi-
ness and make a
profit." 14 Yet you
do not know what
your life will be
like tomorrow. You
are *just* a vapor that
appears for a little
while and then
vanishes away.
15 Instead, *you ought*
to say, "If the Lord
wills, we will live
and also do this or

NIV

[16]As it is, you boast in your arrogant schemes. All such boasting is evil. [17]If anyone, then, knows the good they ought to do and doesn't do it, it is sin for them.

Warning to Rich Oppressors

5 Now listen, you rich people, weep and wail because of the misery that is coming on you. [2]Your wealth has rotted, and moths have eaten your clothes. [3]Your gold and silver are corroded. Their corrosion will testify against you and eat your flesh like fire. You have hoarded wealth in the last days. [4]Look! The wages you failed to pay the workers who mowed your fields are crying out against you. The cries of the harvesters have reached the ears of the Lord Almighty. [5]You have lived on earth in luxury and self-indulgence. You have fattened yourselves in the day of slaughter.[a] [6]You have condemned and murdered the innocent one, who was not opposing you.

Patience in Suffering

[7]Be patient, then, brothers and sisters, until the Lord's coming. See how the farmer waits for the land to yield

[a] 5 Or *yourselves as in a day of feasting*

16 νῦν δὲ → → → καυχᾶσθε ἐν ταῖς ἀλαζονείαις ὑμῶν· πᾶσα
But ˻as it is,˼ *But* you are making arrogant boasts; *{in}* *{the}* *arrogant* *{your}* all
1254 3814 1254 224 3016 1877 3836 224 7007 4246
adv cj v.pmi.2p p.d d.dpf n.dpf r.gp.2 a.nsf

καύχησις τοιαύτη πονηρά ἐστιν. 17 εἰδότι οὖν καλὸν
such boasting *such* is evil. *is* So the ˻person who knows˼ *So* ˻what is right˼
5525 3018 5525 1639 4505 1639 4036 3857 4036 2819
n.nsf r.nsf a.nsf v.pai.3s pt.ra.dsm cj a.asn

ποιεῖν καὶ μὴ ποιοῦντι, ἁμαρτία αὐτῷ ἐστιν.
to do and fails to do it, for him it is sin. *for him* *it is*
4472 2779 3590 4472 899 899 1639 1639 281 899 1639
f.pa cj pl pt.pa.dsm n.nsf r.dsm.3 v.pai.3s

5:1 ἄγε νῦν οἱ πλούσιοι, κλαύσατε ὀλολύζοντες ἐπὶ ταῖς ταλαιπωρίαις
Come now, you rich people, weep and wail over the miseries
72 3814 3836 4454 3081 3909 2093 3836 5416
v.pam.2s adv d.vpm a.vpm v.aam.2p pt.pa.npm p.d d.dpf n.dpf

ὑμῶν ταῖς ἐπερχομέναις. 2 ὁ πλοῦτος ὑμῶν σέσηπεν καὶ
that are coming your way. *that* *are coming* *{the}* Your riches *Your* have rotted and
3836 2088 2088 7007 3836 2088 3836 7007 4458 7007 4960 2779
r.gp.2 d.dpf pt.pm.dpf d.nsm n.nsm r.gp.2 v.rai.3s cj

τὰ ἱμάτια ὑμῶν σητόβρωτα γέγονεν, 3 ὁ χρυσὸς ὑμῶν καὶ ὁ
{the} your clothes *your* are moth-eaten. *are* *{the}* Your gold *Your* and your
3836 7007 2668 7007 1181 4963 1181 3836 7007 5996 7007 2779 3836
d.npn n.npn r.gp.2 a.npn v.rai.3s d.nsm n.nsm r.gp.2 cj d.nsm

ἄργυρος κατίωται καὶ ὁ ἰὸς αὐτῶν εἰς μαρτύριον ὑμῖν
silver have rusted and *{the}* their rust *their* will be *{for}* a witness ˻against you,˼
738 2995 2779 3836 899 2675 899 1639 1639 1650 3457 7007
n.nsm v.rpi.3s cj d.nsm n.nsm r.gpm.3 p.a n.asn r.dp.2

ἔσται καὶ φάγεται τὰς σάρκας ὑμῶν ὡς πῦρ. ἐθησαυρίσατε ἐν
will be and it will consume *{the}* your flesh *your* like fire. ˻You have stored up treasure˼ for
1639 2779 2266 3836 7007 4922 7007 6055 4786 2564 1877
v.fmi.3s cj v.fmi.3s d.apf n.apf r.gp.2 pl n.nsn v.aai.2p p.d

ἐσχάταις ἡμέραις. 4 ἰδοὺ ὁ μισθὸς τῶν ἐργατῶν τῶν
the last days. Look, the wages you have held back ˻from the˼ workers who
2274 2465 2627 3836 3635 691 691 691 691 3836 2239 3836
a.dpf n.dpf j d.nsm n.nsm d.gpm n.gpm d.gpm

ἀμησάντων τὰς χώρας ὑμῶν ὁ ἀπεστερημένος ἀφ' ὑμῶν
mowed *{the}* your fields *your* *{the}* *you have held back* are crying out against you,
286 3836 7007 6001 7007 3836 691 3189 3189 3189 608 7007
pt.aa.gpm d.apf n.apf r.gp.2 d.nsm pt.rp.nsm p.g r.gp.2

κράζει, καὶ αἱ βοαὶ τῶν θερισάντων εἰς τὰ ὦτα → κυρίου
are crying out and the cries of the harvesters have reached *{to}* the ears of the Lord
3189 2779 3836 1068 3836 2545 1656 1656 1650 3836 4044 3261
v.pai.3s cj d.npf n.npf d.gpm pt.aa.gpm p.a d.apn n.apn n.gsm

σαβαὼθ εἰσεληλύθασιν. 5 ἐτρυφήσατε ἐπὶ τῆς γῆς ↰ ↰ καὶ
of Hosts. *have reached* You have lived on the earth in self-indulgence and
4877 1656 5587 2093 3836 1178 5587 5587 2779
n.gpm v.rai.3p v.aai.2p p.g d.gsf n.gsf cj

ἐσπαταλήσατε, ἐθρέψατε τὰς καρδίας ὑμῶν ἐν ἡμέρᾳ σφαγῆς,
luxury. You have fattened *{the}* your hearts *your* for a day of slaughter.
5059 5555 3836 7007 2840 7007 1877 2465 5375
v.aai.2p v.aai.2p d.apf n.apf r.gp.2 p.d n.dsf n.gsf

6 κατεδικάσατε, → ἐφονεύσατε τὸν δίκαιον, ↱ ↱ οὐκ
You condemn the innocent and put him to death; *the* *innocent* he does not
2868 3836 1465 5839 3836 1465 530 530 4024
v.aai.2p v.aai.2p d.asm a.asm pl

ἀντιτάσσεται ὑμῖν. 7 μακροθυμήσατε οὖν, ἀδελφοί, ἕως τῆς παρουσίας τοῦ
resist you. Be patient, therefore, dear friends, until the coming of the
530 7007 3428 4036 81 2401 3836 4242 3836
v.pmi.3s r.dp.2 v.aam.2p cj n.vpm p.g d.gsf n.gsf d.gsm

κυρίου. ἰδοὺ ὁ γεωργὸς ἐκδέχεται τὸν τίμιον καρπὸν τῆς γῆς
Lord. ˻Note how˼ the farmer waits for the precious harvest of the earth,
3261 2627 3836 1177 1683 3836 5508 2843 3836 1178
n.gsm j d.nsm n.nsm v.pmi.3s d.asm a.asm n.asm d.gsf n.gsf

NASB

that." [16]But as it is, you boast in your arrogance; all such boasting is evil. [17]Therefore, to one who knows *the* right thing to do and does not do it, to him it is sin.

Misuse of Riches

[5:1]Come now, you rich, weep and howl for your miseries which are coming upon you. [2]Your riches have rotted and your garments have become moth-eaten. [3]Your gold and your silver have rusted; and their rust will be a witness against you and will consume your flesh like fire. It is in the last days that you have stored up your treasure! [4]Behold, the pay of the laborers who mowed your fields, *and* which has been withheld by you, cries out *against you;* and the outcry of those who did the harvesting has reached the ears of the Lord of Sabaoth. [5]You have lived luxuriously on the earth and led a life of wanton pleasure; you have fattened your hearts in a day of slaughter. [6]You have condemned and put to death the righteous *man;* he does not resist you.

Exhortation

[7]Therefore be patient, brethren, until the coming of the Lord. The farmer waits for the precious produce of the soil,

NIV

its valuable crop,
patiently waiting
for the autumn and
spring rains. [8]You
too, be patient and
stand firm, because
the Lord's com-
ing is near. [9]Don't
grumble against
one another, broth-
ers and sisters, or
you will be judged.
The Judge is stand-
ing at the door!
[10]Brothers and
sisters, as an ex-
ample of patience
in the face of
suffering, take
the prophets who
spoke in the name
of the Lord. [11]As
you know, we
count as blessed
those who have
persevered. You
have heard of Job's
perseverance and
have seen what
the Lord finally
brought about.
The Lord is full of
compassion and
mercy.
[12]Above all,
my brothers and
sisters, do not
swear—not by
heaven or by earth
or by anything
else. All you need
to say is a simple
"Yes" or "No."
Otherwise you will
be condemned.

The Prayer of Faith

[13]Is anyone
among you in trou-
ble? Let them pray.
Is anyone happy?
Let them sing
songs of praise.
[14]Is anyone among
you sick? Let them
call the elders of
the church to pray
over them and
anoint them with
oil in the name of
the Lord. [15]And
the prayer offered
in faith will make
the

μακροθυμῶν ἐπ᾽ αὐτῷ ἕως λάβῃ πρόϊμον καὶ ὄψιμον. 8
being patient for it until it receives the early and latter rains. You too
3428 2093 899 2401 3284 4611 2779 4069 7007 2779
pt.pa.nsm p.d r.dsm.3 cj v.aas.3s n.asm cj n.asm

μακροθυμήσατε καὶ ὑμεῖς, στηρίξατε τὰς καρδίας ὑμῶν, ὅτι ἡ παρουσία τοῦ
must be patient; *too You* strengthen *{the}* your hearts, *your* for the coming of the
3428 2779 7007 5114 3836 7007 2840 7007 4022 3836 4242 3836
v.aam.2p adv r.np.2 v.aam.2p d.apf n.apf r.gp.2 cj d.nsf n.nsf d.gsm

κυρίου ἤγγικεν. 9 → μὴ στενάζετε, ἀδελφοί, κατ᾽ ἀλλήλων
Lord is near. Do not complain against one another, my brothers, *against one another*
3261 1581 5100 3590 5100 2848 253 253 81 2848 253
n.gsm v.rai.3s pl v.pam.2p n.vpm p.g r.gpm

⌞ἵνα μὴ⌟ κριθῆτε· ἰδοὺ ὁ κριτὴς πρὸ τῶν θυρῶν ἕστηκεν. 10 →
lest you be judged. Look, the judge is standing at the doors. *is standing* As an
2671 3590 3212 2627 3836 3216 2705 2705 4574 3836 2598 2705
cj pl v.aps.2p j d.nsm n.nsm p.g d.gpf n.gpf v.rai.3s

ὑπόδειγμα λάβετε, ἀδελφοί, τῆς κακοπαθίας καὶ
example of suffering and patience, brothers, take *brothers of suffering and*
5682 3836 2801 2779 3429 81 3284 81 3836 2801 2779
n.asn v.aam.2p n.vpm d.gsf n.gsf cj

τῆς μακροθυμίας τοὺς προφήτας οἳ ἐλάλησαν ἐν τῷ ὀνόματι → κυρίου.
{the} patience the prophets who spoke in the name of the Lord.
3836 3429 3836 4737 4005 3281 1877 3836 3950 3261
d.gsf n.gsf d.apm n.apm r.npm v.aai.3p p.d d.dsn n.dsn n.gsm

11 ἰδοὺ μακαρίζομεν τοὺς ὑπομείναντας· τὴν ὑπομονὴν Ἰὼβ
For sure, we regard as blessed those who persevered. You have heard of the perseverance of Job
2627 3420 3836 5702 201 201 201 201 3836 5705 2724
j v.pai.1p d.apm pt.aa.apm d.asf n.asf n.gsm

ἠκούσατε καὶ τὸ τέλος → κυρίου εἴδετε, ὅτι
You have heard of and have seen the result of the Lord's activity, *have seen* that the Lord is
201 2779 1625 1625 3836 5465 3261 1625 4022 3836 3261 1639
v.aai.2p cj d.asn n.asn n.gsm v.aai.2p cj

πολύσπλαγχνός ἐστιν ὁ κύριος καὶ οἰκτίρμων. 12 πρὸ πάντων δέ,
exceedingly compassionate *is the Lord* and merciful. Above all, *{and}* my
4499 1639 3836 3261 2779 3881 4574 4246 1254 1609
a.nsm v.pai.3s d.nsm n.nsm cj a.nsm p.g a.gpn cj

ἀδελφοί μου, μὴ ὀμνύετε μήτε τὸν οὐρανὸν μήτε τὴν γῆν μήτε ἄλλον τινὰ
brothers, *my* do not swear, either by heaven or by earth or by any other *any*
81 1609 3590 3923 3612 3836 4041 3612 3836 1178 3612 5516 257 5516
n.vpm r.gs.1 pl v.pam.2p cj d.asm n.asm cj d.asf n.asf cj r.asm r.asm

ὅρκον· → ἤτω δὲ ὑμῶν τὸ ναὶ ναὶ καὶ τὸ οὒ οὔ, ἵνα
oath. Rather let your "Yes" be *Rather your {the} Yes* yes and your "No," no, so that
3992 1254 7007 3721 1639 1254 7007 3836 3721 3721 2779 3836 4024 4024 2671
n.asm v.pam.3s cj r.gp.2 d.nsn pl pl cj d.nsn pl pl cj

μὴ ὑπὸ κρίσιν πέσητε. 13 → κακοπαθεῖ τις
you may not fall under judgment. *you may fall* Is anyone among you suffering? *anyone*
4406 4406 3590 4406 5679 3213 4406 5516 1877 7007 2802 5516
pl p.a n.asf v.aas.2p v.pai.3s r.nsm

ἐν ὑμῖν, προσευχέσθω· → εὐθυμεῖ τις, ψαλλέτω· 14 →
among you He should pray. Is anyone cheerful? *anyone* ⌞He should sing praises.⌟ Is anyone
1877 7007 4667 5516 2313 5516 6010 5516
p.d r.dp.2 v.pmm.3s v.pai.3s r.nsm v.pam.3s

ἀσθενεῖ τις ἐν ὑμῖν, προσκαλεσάσθω τοὺς πρεσβυτέρους τῆς
among you sick? *anyone among you* He should call for the elders of the
1877 7007 820 5516 1877 7007 4673 3836 4565 3836
v.pai.3s r.nsm p.d r.dp.2 v.amm.3s d.apm a.apm d.gsf

ἐκκλησίας καὶ προσευξάσθωσαν ἐπ᾽ αὐτὸν ἀλείψαντες αὐτὸν[a] ἐλαίῳ ἐν τῷ
church and have them pray over him, anointing him with oil in the
1711 2779 4667 2093 899 230 899 1778 1877 3836
n.gsf cj v.amm.3p p.a r.asm.3 pt.aa.npm r.asm.3 n.dsn p.d d.dsn

ὀνόματι τοῦ κυρίου. 15 καὶ ἡ εὐχὴ τῆς πίστεως σώσει τὸν
name of the Lord; and the prayer ⌞offered in⌟ faith will restore the
3950 3836 3261 2779 3836 2376 3836 4411 5392 3836
n.dsn d.gsm n.gsm cj d.nsf n.nsf d.gsf n.gsf v.fai.3s d.asm

[a] [αὐτὸν] UBS.

NASB

being patient about
it, until it gets
the early and late
rains. [8]You too be
patient; strengthen
your hearts, for
the coming of the
Lord is near. [9]Do
not complain,
brethren, against
one another, so
that you yourselves
may not be judged;
behold, the Judge
is standing right at
the door. [10]As an
example, brethren,
of suffering and
patience, take
the prophets who
spoke in the name
of the Lord. [11]We
count those blessed
who endured. You
have heard of the
endurance of Job
and have seen the
outcome of the
Lord's dealings,
that the Lord is full
of compassion and
is merciful.
[12]But above all,
my brethren, do
not swear, either by
heaven or by earth
or with any other
oath; but your yes
is to be yes, and
your no, no, so that
you may not fall
under judgment.
[13]Is anyone among
you suffering?
Then he must pray.
Is anyone cheer-
ful? He is to sing
praises. [14]Is anyone
among you sick?
Then he must call
for the elders of the
church and they are
to pray over him,
anointing him with
oil in the name of
the Lord; [15]and the
prayer offered in
faith will [a]restore

[a] Or *save*

NIV

sick person well;
the Lord will raise
them up. If they
have sinned, they
will be forgiven.
16 Therefore confess
your sins to each
other and pray for
each other so that
you may be healed.
The prayer of a
righteous person is
powerful and ef-
fective.
17 Elijah was a hu-
man being, even as
we are. He prayed
earnestly that it
would not rain,
and it did not rain
on the land for
three and a half
years. 18 Again he
prayed, and the
heavens gave rain,
and the earth pro-
duced its crops.
19 My brothers and
sisters, if one of
you should wander
from the truth and
someone should
bring that person
back, 20 remem-
ber this: Whoever
turns a sinner from
the error of their
way will save them
from death and
cover over a multi-
tude of sins.

κάμνοντα καὶ ἐγερεῖ αὐτὸν ↰ ὁ κύριος· κἂν
⌊one who is sick⌋ and the Lord will raise him up. *the* *Lord* ⌊And if⌋ he has committed
2827 2779 3836 3261 1586 899 1586 3836 3261 2829 1639 1639 4472
pt.pa.asm cj v.fai.3s r.asm.3 d.nsm n.nsm crasis

ἁμαρτίας ᾖ πεποιηκώς, ἀφεθήσεται αὐτῷ. 16 ἐξομολογεῖσθε οὖν
sins, *he has* *committed* he will be forgiven. *he* Therefore confess *Therefore*
281 1639 4472 899 918 899 4036 2018 4036
n.apf v.pas.3s pt.ra.nsm v.fpi.3s r.dsm.3 v.pmm.2p cj

ἀλλήλοις τὰς ἁμαρτίας καὶ εὔχεσθε ὑπὲρ ἀλλήλων ὅπως
your sins to one another *your* *sins* and pray for one another so that
3836 281 253 3836 281 2779 2377 5642 253 3968
r.dpm d.apf n.apf cj v.pmm.2p p.g r.gpm cj

ἰαθῆτε. ↱ πολὺ ἰσχύει δέησις
⌊you may be healed.⌋ The active prayer of a righteous person has great power. *prayer*
2615 1919 1255 1465 1465 1465 2710 4498 2710 1255
v.aps.2p adv v.pai.3s n.nsf

δικαίου ἐνεργουμένη. 17 Ἠλίας ἄνθρωπος ἦν ὁμοιοπαθὴς ἡμῖν, καὶ
of righteous person *active* Elijah was a man *was* exactly like us, and
1465 1919 2460 1639 476 1639 3926 7005 2779
a.gsm pt.pm.nsf n.nsm n.nsm v.iai.3s a.nsm r.dp.1 cj

⌊προσευχῇ προσηύξατο⌋ τοῦ ↱ ↱ ↱ μὴ βρέξαι, καὶ
he prayed earnestly ~ that it would not rain, and for three years and
4666 4667 3836 1101 1101 1101 3590 1101 2779 1929 5552 1929 2779
n.dsf v.ami.3s d.gsn pl f.aa cj

οὐκ ἔβρεξεν ἐπὶ τῆς γῆς ἐνιαυτοὺς τρεῖς καὶ μῆνας ἕξ· 18 καὶ
six months no rain fell on the earth. *for years* *three* *and* *months* *six* Then he
1971 3604 4024 1101 2093 3836 1178 1929 5552 2779 3604 1971 2779 4667
pl v.aai.3s p.g d.gsf n.gsf n.apm a.apm cj n.apm a.apm cj

πάλιν προσηύξατο, καὶ ὁ οὐρανὸς ὑετὸν ἔδωκεν καὶ ἡ γῆ
prayed again, *he prayed* and the heavens poured down rain *poured down* and the earth
4667 4099 4667 2779 3836 4041 1443 1443 5624 1443 2779 3836 1178
adv v.ami.3s cj d.nsm n.nsm n.asm v.aai.3s cj d.nsf n.nsf

ἐβλάστησεν τὸν καρπὸν αὐτῆς. 19 ἀδελφοί μου, ἐάν τις ἐν ὑμῖν
produced *{the}* its harvest. *its* My brothers, *My* if anyone among you
1056 3836 899 2843 899 1609 81 1609 1569 5516 1877 7007
v.aai.3s d.asm n.asm r.gsf.3 n.vpm r.gs.1 cj r.nsm p.d r.dp.2

πλανηθῇ ἀπὸ τῆς ἀληθείας καὶ → ἐπιστρέψῃ τις αὐτόν,
strays from the truth and someone brings him back, *someone* *him*
4414 608 3836 237 2779 5516 899 2188 5516 899
v.aps.3s p.g d.gsf n.gsf cj v.aas.3s r.nsm r.asm.3

20 γινωσκέτω ὅτι ὁ ἐπιστρέψας ἁμαρτωλὸν ↰ ἐκ πλάνης → ὁδοῦ
he should know that the one who brings a sinner back from the error of his way
1182 4022 3836 2188 283 2188 1666 4415 899 3847
v.pam.3s cj d.nsm pt.aa.nsm a.asm p.g n.gsf n.gsf

αὐτοῦ σώσει ψυχὴν αὐτοῦ ἐκ θανάτου καὶ καλύψει πλῆθος
his will save that person's soul *that person's* from death and cover a multitude
899 5392 899 899 6034 899 1666 2505 2779 2821 4436
r.gsm.3 v.fai.3s n.asf r.gsm.3 p.g n.gsm cj v.fai.3s n.asn

ἁμαρτιῶν.
of sins.
281
n.gpf

NASB

the one who is
sick, and the Lord
will raise him up,
and if he has com-
mitted sins, they
will be forgiven
him. 16 Therefore,
confess your sins
to one another,
and pray for one
another so that you
may be healed. The
effective prayer of
a righteous man
can accomplish
much. 17 Elijah was
a man with a nature
like ours, and he
prayed earnestly
that it would not
rain, and it did not
rain on the earth
for three years and
six months. 18 Then
he prayed again,
and the sky poured
rain and the earth
produced its fruit.
19 My brethren,
if any among you
strays from the
truth and one turns
him back, 20 let him
know that he who
turns a sinner from
the error of his way
will save his soul
from death and will
cover a multitude
of sins.

1 Peter

NIV

1 Peter, an apos-
tle of Jesus
Christ,

To God's elect,
exiles scattered
throughout the
provinces of Pon-
tus, Galatia, Cap-
padocia, Asia and
Bithynia, [2]who
have been chosen
according to the
foreknowledge of
God the Father,
through the sanc-
tifying work of the
Spirit, to be obedi-
ent to Jesus Christ
and sprinkled with
his blood:

Grace and peace
be yours in abun-
dance.

Praise to God for a Living Hope

[3]Praise be to the
God and Father
of our Lord Jesus
Christ! In his great
mercy he has giv-
en us new birth
into a living hope
through the res-
urrection of Jesus
Christ from the
dead, [4]and into an
inheritance that
can never perish,
spoil or fade. This
inheritance is kept
in heaven for you,
[5]who through faith
are shielded by
God's power un-
til the coming of
the salvation that
is ready to be re-
vealed in the last
time. [6]In all this
you greatly re-
joice, though now
for a little while
you may have had
to suffer grief in
all kinds of trials.
[7]These have come
so that the proven
genuineness of
your faith

1:1 Πέτρος ἀπόστολος Ἰησοῦ Χριστοῦ ἐκλεκτοῖς παρεπιδήμοις →
Peter, an apostle of Jesus Christ, {elect} ⌊to those who live as refugees⌋ of the
4377 693 2652 5986 1723 4215
n.nsm n.nsm n.gsm n.gsm a.dpm n.dpm

διασπορᾶς Πόντου, Γαλατίας, Καππαδοκίας, Ἀσίας καὶ Βιθυνίας, [2] κατὰ
dispersion in Pontus, Galatia, Cappadocia, Asia, and Bithynia, elect ⌊according to⌋
1402 4509 1130 2838 823 2779 1049 2848
n.gsf n.gsm n.gsf n.gsf n.gsf cj n.gsf p.a

πρόγνωσιν θεοῦ πατρὸς ἐν ἁγιασμῷ → πνεύματος εἰς ὑπακοὴν καὶ
the foreknowledge of God the Father by being set apart by the Spirit for obedience and
4590 2536 4252 1877 40 4460 1650 5633 2779
n.asf n.gsm n.gsm p.d n.dsm n.gsn p.a n.asf cj

ῥαντισμὸν → αἵματος Ἰησοῦ Χριστοῦ, ↱ χάρις ↱ ὑμῖν καὶ
for sprinkling with the blood of Jesus Christ. May grace and peace be yours *and*
4823 135 2652 5986 4437 5921 2779 1645 4437 7007 2779
n.asm n.gsn n.gsm n.gsm n.nsf r.dp.2 cj

εἰρήνη πληθυνθείη. [3]εὐλογητὸς ὁ θεὸς καὶ πατὴρ τοῦ κυρίου
peace ⌊in ever increasing measure.⌋ Blessed be the God and Father of our Lord
1645 4437 2329 3836 2536 2779 4252 3836 7005 3261
n.nsf v.apo.3s a.nsm d.nsm n.nsm cj n.nsm d.gsm n.gsm

ἡμῶν Ἰησοῦ Χριστοῦ, ὁ κατὰ τὸ πολὺ αὐτοῦ ἔλεος ἀναγεννήσας ἡμᾶς
our Jesus Christ, who ⌊according to⌋ {the} his great *his* mercy gave us
7005 2652 5986 3836 2848 3836 899 4498 899 1799 335 7005
r.gp.1 n.gsm n.gsm d.nsm p.a d.asn a.asn r.gsm.3 n.asn pt.aa.nsm r.ap.1

↰ ↰ εἰς ἐλπίδα ζῶσαν δι' ἀναστάσεως Ἰησοῦ Χριστοῦ ἐκ
new birth into a living hope *living* through the resurrection of Jesus Christ from the
335 335 1650 2409 1828 2409 1328 414 2652 5986 1666
p.a n.asf pt.pa.asf p.g n.gsf n.gsm n.gsm p.g

νεκρῶν, [4]εἰς κληρονομίαν ἄφθαρτον καὶ ἀμίαντον καὶ ἀμάραντον,
dead, to an inheritance that is imperishable, {and} undefiled, and unfading,
3738 1650 3100 915 2779 299 2779 278
a.gpm p.a n.asf a.asf cj a.asf cj a.asf

τετηρημένην ἐν οὐρανοῖς εἰς ὑμᾶς [5]τοὺς ἐν δυνάμει θεοῦ φρουρουμένους
being preserved in heaven for you, who by the power of God are being guarded
5498 1877 4041 1650 7007 3836 1877 1539 2536 5864
pt.rp.asf p.d n.dpm p.a r.ap.2 d.apm p.d n.dsf n.gsm pt.pp.apm

διὰ πίστεως εἰς σωτηρίαν ἑτοίμην ἀποκαλυφθῆναι ἐν καιρῷ ἐσχάτῳ.
through faith for a salvation ready to be revealed in the last time. *last*
1328 4411 1650 5401 2289 636 1877 2274 2789 2274
p.g n.gsf p.a n.asf a.asf f.ap p.d n.dsm a.dsm

[6]ἐν ᾧ ἀγαλλιᾶσθε, → ὀλίγον ἄρτι εἰ
In this you rejoice, even if now it is necessary for a short time *now* *if*
1877 4005 22 1623 785 1256 1256 1256 3900 785 1623
p.d r.dsm v.pmi.2p adv adv cj

δέον[a] λυπηθέντες ἐν ποικίλοις πειρασμοῖς, [7]ἵνα τὸ δοκίμιον
it is necessary to be made sorrowful by various trials, so that the genuineness of
1256 3382 1877 4476 4280 2671 3836 1510 3836
pt.pa.nsn pt.ap.npm p.d a.dpm n.dpm cj d.nsn n.nsn

ὑμῶν τῆς πίστεως πολυτιμότερον χρυσίου τοῦ ἀπολλυμένου
your *of* faith (which is more precious than gold that perishes), having been tested
7007 3836 4411 4501 5992 3836 660 1507 1507 1507
r.gp.2 d.gsf n.gsf a.nsn.c n.gsn d.gsn pt.pm.gsn

NASB

A Living Hope, and a Sure Salvation

1:1Peter, an apostle
of Jesus Christ,

To those who re-
side as aliens, scat-
tered throughout
Pontus, Galatia,
Cappadocia, Asia,
and Bithynia, who
are chosen [2]accord-
ing to the fore-
knowledge of God
the Father, by the
sanctifying work of
the Spirit, to obey
Jesus Christ and
be sprinkled with
His blood: May
grace and peace be
yours in the fullest
measure.

[3]Blessed be the
God and Father
of our Lord Jesus
Christ, who accord-
ing to His great
mercy has caused
us to be born again
to a living hope
through the resur-
rection of Jesus
Christ from the
dead, [4]to *obtain* an
inheritance *which*
is imperishable
and undefiled and
will not fade away,
reserved in heaven
for you, [5]who are
protected by the
power of God
through faith for a
salvation ready to
be revealed in the
last time. [6]In this
you greatly rejoice,
even though now
for a little while,
if necessary, you
have been dis-
tressed by various
trials, [7]so that the
proof of your faith,
being more pre-
cious than gold
which is perish-
able, even though
tested by fire, may

[a] ἐστὶν included by UBS after δέον.

NIV

—of greater worth
than gold, which
perishes even
though refined by
fire—may result
in praise, glory
and honor when
Jesus Christ is re-
vealed. [8]Though
you have not seen
him, you love him;
and even though
you do not see him
now, you believe
in him and are
filled with an inex-
pressible and glo-
rious joy, [9]for you
are receiving the
end result of your
faith, the salvation
of your souls.
[10]Concerning
this salvation, the
prophets, who
spoke of the grace
that was to come
to you, searched
intently and with
the greatest care,
[11]trying to find
out the time and
circumstances to
which the Spirit
of Christ in them
was pointing when
he predicted the
sufferings of the
Messiah and the
glories that would
follow. [12]It was
revealed to them
that they were not
serving themselves
but you, when they
spoke of the things
that have now been
told you by those
who have preached
the gospel to you
by the Holy Spirit
sent from heaven.
Even angels long
to look into these
things.

Be Holy

[13]Therefore, with
minds that are
alert and fully so-
ber, set your hope
on the grace to
be brought to you
when Jesus Christ
is revealed at his
coming. [14]As obe-
dient children,

διὰ πυρὸς δὲ δοκιμαζομένου, εὑρεθῇ εἰς ἔπαινον καὶ δόξαν καὶ τιμὴν
by fire, *{and}* *having been tested* ⌊may be found⌋ to your praise and glory and honor
1328 4786 1254 1507 2351 1650 2047 2779 1518 2779 5507
p.g n.gsn cj pt.pp.gsn v.aps.3s p.a n.asm cj n.asf cj n.asf

ἐν ἀποκαλύψει Ἰησοῦ Χριστοῦ· [8] ὃν ↱ ↱ ↱ οὐκ ἰδόντες ἀγαπᾶτε,
at the revelation of Jesus Christ. *him* Though you have not seen him, you love
1877 637 2652 5986 4005 1625 1625 1625 4024 1625 26
p.d n.dsf n.gsm n.gsm r.asm pl pt.aa.npm v.pai.2p

εἰς ὃν ἄρτι μὴ ὁρῶντες πιστεύοντες
him. Though not seeing him now, yet believing in him, *now* *not* *Though seeing* *believing*
4005 3972 3590 3972 785 1254 4409 1650 4005 785 3590 3972 4409
p.a r.asm adv pl pt.pa.npm pt.pa.npm

δὲ ἀγαλλιᾶσθε χαρᾷ ἀνεκλαλήτῳ καὶ δεδοξασμένῃ [9] κομιζόμενοι τὸ
yet you rejoice with joy unspeakable and filled with glory, ⌊because you are obtaining⌋ the
1254 22 5915 443 2779 1519 3152 3836
cj v.pmi.2p n.dsf a.dsf cj pt.rp.dsf pt.pm.npm d.asn

τέλος τῆς πίστεως ὑμῶν[a] σωτηρίαν → ψυχῶν. [10] περὶ ἧς
goal of your faith *your* — the salvation of your souls. Concerning this
5465 3836 7007 4411 7007 5401 6034 4309 4005
n.asn d.gsf n.gsf r.gp.2 n.asf n.gpf p.g r.gsf

σωτηρίας ἐξεζήτησαν καὶ ἐξηραύνησαν προφῆται οἱ περὶ τῆς
salvation, *investigated diligently* *and* *examined with care* the prophets who prophesied of the
5401 1699 2779 2001 4737 3836 4736 4309 3836
n.gsf v.aai.3p cj v.aai.3p n.npm d.npm p.g d.gsf

εἰς ὑμᾶς χάριτος προφητεύσαντες,
grace that would come to you *grace* *prophesied* investigated diligently and
5921 1650 7007 5921 4736 1699 1699 2779
p.a r.ap.2 n.gsf pt.aa.npm

[11] ἐραυνῶντες εἰς τίνα ἢ ποῖον καιρὸν
examined with care, trying to discover *{to}* what time or manner of time the Spirit of
2001 2001 2001 2236 1650 5515 2445 4481 2789 3836 4460 5986
pt.pa.npm p.a r.asm cj r.asm n.asm

ἐδήλου τὸ ἐν αὐτοῖς πνεῦμα Χριστοῦ προμαρτυρόμενον
Christ who was in them was indicating *the* *in* *them* *Spirit* *of Christ* when he predicted
5986 1877 899 1317 3836 1877 899 4460 5986 4626
v.iai.3s d.nsn p.d r.dpm.3 n.nsn n.gsm pt.pm.nsn

τὰ εἰς Χριστὸν παθήματα καὶ τὰς μετὰ ταῦτα δόξας.
the sufferings of Christ *sufferings* and the glories that ⌊would follow.⌋ *that* *glories*
3836 4077 1650 5986 4077 2779 3836 1518 4047 3552 4047 1518
d.apn p.a n.asm n.apn cj d.apf p.a r.apn n.apf

[12] οἷς ἀπεκαλύφθη ὅτι οὐχ ἑαυτοῖς ὑμῖν δὲ διηκόνουν
⌊To them⌋ it was revealed that not to themselves, but to you, *but* they were ministering
4005 636 4022 4024 1571 1254 7007 1254 1354
r.dpm v.api.3s cj pl r.dpm.3 r.dp.2 cj v.iai.3p

αὐτά, ἃ νῦν ἀνηγγέλη ὑμῖν διὰ τῶν εὐαγγελισαμένων ὑμᾶς ἐν[b]
these things that now ⌊have been announced⌋ to you through those who preached to you by
899 4005 3814 334 7007 1328 3836 2294 7007 1877
r.apn.3 r.npn adv v.api.3s r.dp.2 p.g d.gpm pt.am.gpm r.ap.2 p.d

πνεύματι ἁγίῳ ἀποσταλέντι ἀπ᾽ οὐρανοῦ, εἰς ἃ
the Holy Spirit *Holy* sent from heaven — things into which angels
41 4460 41 690 608 4041 1650 4005 34
n.dsn a.dsn pt.ap.dsn p.g n.gsm p.a r.apn

ἐπιθυμοῦσιν ἄγγελοι παρακύψαι. [13] διὸ ἀναζωσάμενοι τὰς ὀσφύας τῆς
long *angels* to look. Therefore gird up the loins of your
2121 34 4160 1475 350 3836 4019 3836 7007
v.pai.3p n.npm f.aa cj pt.am.npm d.apf n.apf d.gsf

διανοίας ὑμῶν νήφοντες τελείως ἐλπίσατε ἐπὶ τὴν
mind, *your* be sober-minded, and set your hope completely *set your hope* on the grace
1379 7007 3768 1827 1827 1827 5458 1827 2093 3836 5921
n.gsf r.gp.2 pt.pa.npm adv v.aam.2p p.a d.asf

φερομένην ὑμῖν χάριν ἐν ἀποκαλύψει Ἰησοῦ Χριστοῦ. [14] ὡς τέκνα
⌊that will be brought⌋ to you *grace* at the revelation of Jesus Christ. As children
5770 7007 5921 1877 637 2652 5986 6055 5451
pt.pp.asf r.dp.2 n.asf p.d n.dsf n.gsm n.gsm pl n.npn

[a] [ὑμῶν] UBS, omitted by TNIV.
[b] [ἐν] UBS.

NASB

be found to result
in praise and glory
and honor at the
revelation of Jesus
Christ; [8]and though
you have not seen
Him, you love
Him, and though
you do not see Him
now, but believe in
Him, you greatly
rejoice with joy in-
expressible and full
of glory, [9]obtaining
as the outcome
of your faith the
salvation of [a]your
souls.
[10]As to this salva-
tion, the prophets
who prophesied
of the grace that
would come to
you made careful
searches and inqui-
ries, [11]seeking to
know what person
or time the Spirit of
Christ within them
was indicating as
He predicted the
sufferings of Christ
and the glories to
follow. [12]It was re-
vealed to them that
they were not serv-
ing themselves, but
you, in these things
which now have
been announced to
you through those
who preached the
gospel to you by
the Holy Spirit sent
from heaven—
things into which
angels long to look.
[13]Therefore, pre-
pare your minds for
action, keep sober
in spirit, fix your
hope completely
on the grace to be
brought to you at
the revelation of
Jesus Christ. [14]As
obedient children,

[a] One early ms does not contain *your*

NIV

do not conform
to the evil desires
you had when you
lived in ignorance.
[15]But just as he
who called you is
holy, so be holy
in all you do; [16]for
it is written: "Be
holy, because I am
holy."[a]
[17]Since you call
on a Father who
judges each per-
son's work impar-
tially, live out your
time as foreigners
here in reverent
fear. [18]For you
know that it was
not with perish-
able things such
as silver or gold
that you were re-
deemed from the
empty way of life
handed down to
you from your an-
cestors, [19]but with
the precious blood
of Christ, a lamb
without blemish
or defect. [20]He
was chosen before
the creation of the
world, but was
revealed in these
last times for your
sake. [21]Through
him you believe in
God, who raised
him from the dead
and glorified him,
and so your faith
and hope are in
God.
[22]Now that you
have purified
yourselves by
obeying the truth
so that you have
sincere love for
each other,

[a] 16 Lev. 11:44,45; 19:2

ὑπακοῆς ↱ μὴ συσχηματιζόμενοι ταῖς πρότερον ἐν τῇ
of obedience, do not be conformed to the desires you used to have in {the} your
5633 5372 3590 5372 3836 2123 4728 1877 3836 7007
n.gsf pl pt.pp.npm d.dpf adv.c p.d d.dsf

ἀγνοίᾳ ὑμῶν ἐπιθυμίαις [15] ἀλλὰ κατὰ τὸν καλέσαντα ὑμᾶς ἅγιον καὶ
⌞time of ignorance⌟ *your* *desires* but, just as the one who called you is holy, so also
53 7007 2123 247 2848 3836 2813 7007 41 2779
n.dsf r.gp.2 n.dpf cj p.a d.asm pt.aa.asm r.ap.2 a.asm adv

αὐτοὶ ἅγιοι ἐν πάσῃ ἀναστροφῇ γενήθητε, [16] διότι γέγραπται ὅτι[a]
are you to be holy in all your conduct. *are to be* For it is written, ~
1181 899 1181 1181 41 1877 4246 419 1181 1484 1211 4022
r.npm a.npm p.d a.dsf n.dsf v.apm.2p cj v.rpi.3s cj

ἅγιοι ἔσεσθε, ὅτι ἐγὼ ἅγιός εἰμι.[b] [17] καὶ εἰ πατέρα
"Be holy, *Be* because I am holy." *am* And if you call upon him as Father
1639 41 1639 4022 1609 1639 41 1639 2779 1623 2126 2126 2126 4252
a.npm v.fmi.2p cj r.ns.1 a.nsm v.pai.1s cj cj n.asm

ἐπικαλεῖσθε τὸν ἀπροσωπολήμπτως κρίνοντα κατὰ τὸ ἑκάστου
you call upon who judges impartially *judges* ⌞according to⌟ the work of each,
2126 3836 3212 719 3212 2848 3836 2240 1667
v.pmi.2p d.asm adv pt.pa.asm p.a d.asn r.gsm

ἔργον, ἐν φόβῳ τὸν τῆς παροικίας ὑμῶν χρόνον
work conduct yourselves with fear ⌞during the⌟ time of your exile, *your* *time*
2240 418 418 1877 5832 3836 5989 3836 7007 4229 7007 5989
n.asn p.d n.dsm d.asm d.gsf n.gsf r.gp.2 n.asm

ἀναστράφητε, [18] εἰδότες ὅτι
conduct yourselves ⌞since you know⌟ that you were ransomed from the empty way of life
418 3857 4022 3390 3390 3390 1666 3836 3469 419 419 419
v.apm.2p pt.ra.npm cj

οὐ φθαρτοῖς, ἀργυρίῳ ἢ χρυσίῳ,
handed down from your ancestors, not ⌞by perishable things⌟ such as silver or gold,
4261 4261 4261 7007 4261 4024 5778 736 2445 5992
pl a.dpn n.dsn cj n.dsn

ἐλυτρώθητε ἐκ τῆς ματαίας ὑμῶν ἀναστροφῆς πατροπαραδότου [19] ἀλλὰ
you were ransomed *from* *the* *empty* *your* *way of life* *handed down from ancestors* but
3390 1666 3836 3469 7007 419 4261 247
v.api.2p p.g d.gsf a.gsf r.gp.2 n.gsf a.gsf cj

τιμίῳ αἵματι ὡς → ἀμνοῦ ἀμώμου καὶ ἀσπίλου Χριστοῦ,
by precious blood, as of a lamb without blemish or spot, the blood of Christ.
5508 135 6055 303 320 2779 834 5986
a.dsn n.dsn pl n.gsm a.gsm cj a.gsm n.gsm

[20] προεγνωσμένου μὲν πρὸ καταβολῆς → κόσμου φανερωθέντος
⌞He was chosen in advance,⌟ ~ before the foundation of the world, but was revealed
4589 3525 4574 2856 3180 1254 5746
pt.rp.gsm pl p.g n.gsf n.gsm pt.ap.gsm

δὲ ἐπ' ἐσχάτου τῶν χρόνων δι' ὑμᾶς [21] τοὺς δι' αὐτοῦ πιστοὺς εἰς θεὸν
but at the end of the times for you who through him believe in God,
1254 2093 2274 3836 5989 1328 7007 3836 1328 899 4412 1650 2536
cj p.g a.gsm d.gpm n.gpm p.a r.ap.2 d.apm p.g r.gsm.3 a.apm p.a n.asm

τὸν ἐγείραντα αὐτὸν ἐκ νεκρῶν καὶ δόξαν αὐτῷ δόντα, ὥστε τὴν
who raised him from the dead and gave him glory, *him* *gave* so that {the} your
3836 1586 899 1666 3738 2779 1443 899 1518 899 1443 6063 3836 7007
d.asm pt.aa.asm r.asm.3 p.g a.gpm cj n.asf r.dsm.3 pt.aa.asm cj d.asf

πίστιν ὑμῶν καὶ ἐλπίδα εἶναι εἰς θεόν. [22] τὰς ψυχὰς ὑμῶν
faith *your* and hope are in God. Since you have purified {the} your souls *your*
4411 7007 2779 1828 1639 1650 2536 49 49 49 49 3836 7007 6034 7007
n.asf r.gp.2 cj n.asf f.pa p.a n.asm d.apf n.apf r.gp.2

ἡγνικότες ἐν τῇ ὑπακοῇ τῆς ἀληθείας[c] εἰς
Since you have purified by {the} obedience to the truth ⌞so that⌟ there is a sincere
49 1877 3836 5633 3836 237 1650 537
pt.ra.npm p.d d.dsf n.dsf d.gsf n.gsf p.a

[a] [ὅτι] UBS.
[b] [εἰμι] UBS, omitted by TNIV.
[c] διὰ Πνεύματος included by TR after ἀληθείας.

NASB

do not be con-
formed to the
former lusts *which*
were yours in your
ignorance, [15]but
like the Holy One
who called you,
be holy yourselves
also in all *your*
behavior; [16]because
it is written, "YOU
SHALL BE HOLY, FOR
I AM HOLY."
[17]If you address
as Father the One
who impartially
judges according
to each one's work,
conduct yourselves
in fear during the
time of your stay
on earth; [18]know-
ing that you were
not redeemed
with perishable
things like silver
or gold from your
futile way of life
inherited from
your forefathers,
[19]but with precious
blood, as of a lamb
unblemished and
spotless, *the blood*
of Christ. [20]For He
was foreknown
before the founda-
tion of the world,
but has appeared
in these last times
for the sake of you
[21]who through Him
are believers in
God, who raised
Him from the dead
and gave Him
glory, so that your
faith and hope are
in God.
[22]Since you have
in obedience to the
truth purified your
souls for a sincere

NIV

love one another deeply, from the heart.[a] 23 For you have been born again, not of perishable seed, but of imperishable, through the living and enduring word of God. 24 For,

"All people are like grass,
and all their glory is like the flowers of the field;
the grass withers and the flowers fall,
25 but the word of the Lord endures forever."[b]

And this is the word that was preached to you.

2 Therefore, rid yourselves of all malice and all deceit, hypocrisy, envy, and slander of every kind.
2 Like newborn babies, crave pure spiritual milk, so that by it you may grow up in your salvation,
3 now that you have tasted that the Lord is good.

The Living Stone and a Chosen People

4 As you come to him, the living Stone—rejected by humans but chosen by God and precious to him—
5 you also, like living stones, are being built into a spiritual house[c] to be a holy priesthood, offering spiritual sacrifices acceptable to God

φιλαδελφίαν ἀνυπόκριτον, ἐκ καθαρᾶς[a] καρδίας
⌊love for other believers,⌋ sincere love one another fervently from a pure heart,
5789 537 26 253 253 1757 1666 2754 2840
n.asf a.asf p.g a.gsf n.gsf

ἀλλήλους ἀγαπήσατε ἐκτενῶς 23 ἀναγεγεννημένοι οὐκ ἐκ σπορᾶς
one another love fervently ⌊for you have been born again⌋ not of perishable seed
253 26 1757 335 4024 1666 5778 5076
r.apm v.aam.2p adv pt.rp.npm pl p.g n.gsf

φθαρτῆς ἀλλὰ ἀφθάρτου διὰ λόγου ζῶντος θεοῦ
perishable but of imperishable, ⌊by means of⌋ the living and enduring word living of God.
5778 247 915 1328 2409 2779 3531 3364 2409 2536
a.gsf cj a.gsf p.g n.gsm pt.pa.gsm n.gsm

καὶ μένοντος.[b] 24 διότι πᾶσα σὰρξ ὡς χόρτος καὶ πᾶσα δόξα αὐτῆς ὡς
and enduring For "All flesh is like grass, and all its glory its like the
2779 3531 1484 4246 4922 6055 5965 2779 4246 899 1518 899 6055
cj pt.pa.gsm cj a.nsf n.nsf pl n.nsm cj a.nsf n.nsf r.gsf.3 pl

ἄνθος χόρτου· ἐξηράνθη ὁ χόρτος καὶ τὸ ἄνθος ἐξέπεσεν· 25 τὸ δὲ
flower of grass; the grass dries up the grass and its flower falls; but the but
470 5965 3836 5965 3830 3836 5965 2779 3836 470 1738 1254 3836 1254
n.nsn n.gsm v.api.3s d.nsm n.nsm cj d.nsn n.nsn v.aai.3s d.nsn cj

ῥῆμα → κυρίου μένει εἰς τὸν αἰῶνα. τοῦτο δέ ἐστιν τὸ ῥῆμα τὸ
word of the Lord endures for all time." And this And is the word that
4839 3261 3531 1650 3836 172 1254 4047 1254 1639 3836 4839 3836
n.nsn n.gsm v.pai.3s p.a d.asm n.asm r.nsn cj v.pai.3s d.nsn n.nsn d.nsn

εὐαγγελισθὲν εἰς ὑμᾶς.
was preached to you.
2294 1650 7007
pt.ap.nsn p.a r.ap.2

2:1 ἀποθέμενοι οὖν πᾶσαν κακίαν καὶ πάντα δόλον καὶ
Therefore, having put away Therefore all malice and all deceit and
4036 700 4036 4246 2798 2779 4246 1515 2779
pt.am.npm cj a.asf n.asf cj a.asm n.asm cj

ὑποκρίσεις καὶ φθόνους καὶ πάσας καταλαλιάς, 2 ὡς ἀρτιγέννητα
hypocrisy and envy and slander ⌊of every kind,⌋ slander like newborn
5694 2779 5784 2779 2896 4246 2896 6055 786
n.apf cj n.apm cj a.apf n.apf pl a.npn

βρέφη τὸ λογικὸν ἄδολον γάλα ἐπιποθήσατε, ἵνα ἐν αὐτῷ
babes, crave the milk that is pure and spiritual, pure milk crave so that by it
1100 2160 3836 1128 100 3358 100 1128 2160 2671 1877 899
n.npn d.asn a.asn a.asn n.asn v.aam.2p cj p.d r.dsn.3

αὐξηθῆτε εἰς σωτηρίαν, 3 εἰ ἐγεύσασθε ὅτι χρηστὸς ὁ
⌊you may grow up⌋ to salvation, since you have tasted that the Lord is good. the
889 1650 5401 1623 1174 4022 3836 3261 5982 3836
v.aps.2p p.a n.asf cj v.ami.2p cj a.nsm d.nsm

κύριος. 4 πρὸς ὃν προσερχόμενοι λίθον ζῶντα ὑπὸ
Lord As you come to him, As you come a living stone living rejected by
3261 4665 4665 4665 4639 4005 4665 2409 3345 2409 627 5679
n.nsm p.a r.asm pt.pm.npm n.asm pt.pa.asm p.g

ἀνθρώπων μὲν ἀποδεδοκιμασμένον παρὰ δὲ θεῷ ἐκλεκτὸν ἔντιμον,
men ~ rejected but chosen by but God chosen and precious,
476 3525 627 1254 1723 4123 1254 2536 1723 1952
n.gpm pl pt.rp.asm p.d cj n.dsm a.asm a.asm

5 καὶ αὐτοὶ ὡς λίθοι ζῶντες οἰκοδομεῖσθε → οἶκος πνευματικὸς
you also, you like living stones, living are being built up as a spiritual house, spiritual
899 2779 899 6055 2409 3345 2409 3868 4461 3875 4461
cj r.npm pl n.npm pt.pa.npm v.ppi.2p n.nsm a.nsm

εἰς ἱεράτευμα ἅγιον ἀνενέγκαι πνευματικὰς θυσίας εὐπροσδέκτους τῷ[c] θεῷ
to be a holy priesthood holy to offer spiritual sacrifices acceptable to God
1650 41 2633 41 429 4461 2602 2347 3836 2536
p.a n.asn a.asn f.aa a.apf n.apf a.apf d.dsm n.dsm

NASB

love of the brethren, fervently love one another from [a]the heart, 23 for you have been born again not of seed which is perishable but imperishable, *that is,* through the living and enduring word of God. 24 For,

" ALL FLESH IS LIKE GRASS,
AND ALL ITS GLORY LIKE THE FLOWER OF GRASS.
THE GRASS WITHERS,
AND THE FLOWER FALLS OFF,
25 BUT THE WORD OF THE LORD ENDURES FOREVER."

And this is the word which was preached to you.

As Newborn Babes

2:1 Therefore, putting aside all malice and all deceit and hypocrisy and envy and all slander,
2 like newborn babies, long for the pure milk of the word, so that by it you may grow in respect to salvation,
3 if you have tasted the kindness of the Lord.

As Living Stones

4 And coming to Him as to a living stone which has been rejected by men, but is choice and precious in the sight of God,
5 you also, as living stones, are being built up as a spiritual house for a holy priesthood, to offer up spiritual sacrifices acceptable to God

[a] 22 Some early manuscripts *from a pure heart*
[b] 25 Isaiah 40:6-8 (see Septuagint)
[c] 5 Or *into a temple of the Spirit*

[a] [καθαρᾶς] UBS, omitted by TNIV.
[b] εἰς τὸν αἰῶνα included by TR after μένοντος.
[c] [τῷ] UBS, omitted by TNIV.

[a] Two early mss read *a clean heart*

NIV

through Jesus
Christ. 6For in
Scripture it says:

"See, I lay a stone
in Zion,
a chosen and
precious cornerstone,
and the one who
trusts in him
will never
be put to
shame."[a]

7Now to you who
believe, this stone is
precious. But to those
who do not believe,

"The stone the
builders
rejected
has become
the cornerstone,"[b]

8and,
"A stone that
causes
people to
stumble
and a rock that
makes them
fall."[c]

They stumble because they disobey
the message—which
is also what they
were destined for.
9But you are a
chosen people, a
royal priesthood,
a holy nation,
God's special possession, that you
may declare the
praises of him who
called you out of
darkness into his
wonderful light.
10Once you were
not a people, but
now you are the
people of God;
once you had not
received mercy,
but now you have
received mercy.

Living Godly Lives in a Pagan Society

11Dear friends,
I urge you, as
foreigners and
exiles, to abstain
from sinful desires, which wage
war against your
soul. 12Live such
good lives among
the pagans that,
though

[a] 6 Isaiah 28:16
[b] 7 Psalm 118:22
[c] 8 Isaiah 8:14

διὰ Ἰησοῦ Χριστοῦ. 6διότι περιέχει ἐν γραφῇ· ἰδοὺ τίθημι ἐν Σιὼν λίθον
through Jesus Christ. For it says in scripture, "Behold, I lay in Zion a stone,
1328 2652 5986 1484 4321 1877 1210 2627 5502 1877 4994 3345
p.g n.gsm n.gsm cj v.pai.3s p.d n.dsf j v.pai.1s p.d n.dsf n.asm

ἀκρογωνιαῖον ἐκλεκτὸν ἔντιμον καὶ ὁ πιστεύων ἐπ' αὐτῷ ↱ ⌊οὐ μὴ⌋
a cornerstone chosen and precious, and the one who believes in him will never
214 1723 1952 2779 3836 4409 2093 899 2875 4024 3590
a.asm a.asm a.asm cj d.nsm pt.pa.nsm p.d r.dsm.3 pl pl

καταισχυνθῇ. 7 ὑμῖν οὖν ἡ τιμὴ τοῖς
be put to shame." Therefore the great value is to you *Therefore* *the* *great value* who
2875 4036 3836 5507 5507 7007 4036 3836 5507 3836
v.aps.3s r.dp.2 cj d.nsf n.nsf d.dpm

πιστεύουσιν, ἀπιστοῦσιν δὲ λίθος ὃν
believe; but ⌊for those who do not believe,⌋ *but* "The stone that the builders
4409 1254 601 1254 3345 4005 3836 3868
pt.pa.dpm pt.pa.dpm cj n.nsm r.asm

ἀπεδοκίμασαν οἱ οἰκοδομοῦντες, οὗτος ἐγενήθη εἰς ⌊κεφαλὴν
rejected, *the* *builders* ⌊this very one⌋ has become *{for}* the cornerstone,"
627 3836 3868 4047 1181 1650 3051
v.aai.3p d.npm pt.pa.npm r.nsm v.api.3s p.a n.asf

γωνίας⌋ 8καὶ λίθος → → προσκόμματος καὶ πέτρα → →
and, "A stone that makes people stumble and a rock that makes them
1224 2779 3345 4682 2779 4376
n.gsf cj n.nsm n.gsn cj n.nsf

σκανδάλου· οἳ προσκόπτουσιν
fall." They stumble, as they were destined to do, since they do not obey
4998 4005 4684 5502 5502 5502 1650 4005 578 578 578 578 578
n.gsn r.npm v.pai.3p

τῷ λόγῳ ἀπειθοῦντες εἰς ὃ καὶ ἐτέθησαν. 9 ὑμεῖς δὲ
the word. *since they do not obey* *to* *do* *{also}* *they were destined* But you *But* are a chosen
3836 3364 578 1650 4005 2779 5502 1254 7007 1254 1723
d.dsm n.dsm pt.pa.npm p.a r.asn adv v.api.3p r.np.2 cj

γένος ἐκλεκτόν, βασίλειον ἱεράτευμα, ἔθνος ἅγιον, λαὸς εἰς
race, *chosen* a royal priesthood, a holy nation, *holy* a people for his own
1169 1723 994 2633 41 1620 41 3295 1650
n.nsn a.nsn a.nsn n.nsn n.nsn a.nsn n.nsm p.a

περιποίησιν, ὅπως τὰς ἀρετὰς ἐξαγγείλητε τοῦ
possession, so that you may declare the ⌊glorious deeds⌋ *you may declare* of the one who called
4348 3968 1972 1972 1972 3836 746 1972 3836 2813 2813 2813
n.asf cj d.apf n.apf v.aas.2p d.gsm

ἐκ σκότους ὑμᾶς καλέσαντος εἰς τὸ θαυμαστὸν αὐτοῦ φῶς· 10
you ⌊out of⌋ darkness *you* *one who called* into *{the}* his marvelous *his* light. At one
7007 1666 5030 7007 2813 1650 3836 899 2515 899 5890 4537 4537
p.g n.gsn r.ap.2 pt.aa.gsm p.a d.asn a.asn r.gsm.3 n.asn

οἵ ποτε οὐ λαὸς νῦν δὲ λαὸς θεοῦ, οἱ ↱
time you *At one time* were not a people, but now *but* you are the people of God. You were
4537 4005 4537 4024 3295 1254 3814 1254 3295 2536 3836 1796
r.npm adv pl n.nsm adv cj n.nsm n.gsm d.npm

↱ οὐκ ἠλεημένοι νῦν δὲ ἐλεηθέντες. 11ἀγαπητοί, παρακαλῶ ὡς
shown no mercy, but now *but* ⌊have received mercy.⌋ Dear friends, I urge you as
1796 4024 1796 1254 3814 1254 1796 28 4151 6055
pl pt.rp.npm adv cj pt.ap.npm a.vpm v.pai.1s pl

παροίκους καὶ παρεπιδήμους ἀπέχεσθαι τῶν σαρκικῶν ἐπιθυμιῶν αἵτινες
foreigners and exiles to abstain from desires of the flesh, *desires* which
4230 2779 4215 600 2123 3836 4920 2123 4015
n.apm cj n.apm f.pm d.gpf a.gpf n.gpf r.npf

στρατεύονται κατὰ τῆς ψυχῆς· 12 τὴν ἀναστροφὴν ὑμῶν
wage war against your soul, and maintain an honorable *{the}* lifestyle *{your}*
5129 2848 3836 6034 2400 2819 3836 419 7007
v.pmi.3p p.g d.gsf n.gsf d.asf n.asf r.gp.2

ἐν τοῖς ἔθνεσιν ἔχοντες καλήν, ἵνα ἐν ᾧ
among the Gentiles *maintain* *honorable* so that, ⌊with respect to⌋ ⌊the very things about which⌋
1877 3836 1620 2400 2819 2671 1877 4005
p.d d.dpn n.dpn pt.pa.npm a.asf cj p.d r.dsn

NASB

through Jesus
Christ. 6For *this*
is contained in
Scripture:
"BEHOLD, I LAY
IN ZION A
CHOICE STONE,
A PRECIOUS
CORNER *stone,*
AND HE WHO
BELIEVES IN
HIM WILL
NOT BE DISAPPOINTED."
7This precious
value, then, is for
you who believe;
but for those who
disbelieve,
"THE STONE
WHICH THE
BUILDERS REJECTED,
THIS BECAME
THE VERY CORNER *stone,*"
8and,
"A STONE OF
STUMBLING
AND A ROCK OF
OFFENSE";
for they stumble
because they are
disobedient to the
word, and to this
doom they were
also appointed.
9But you are A
CHOSEN RACE, A
royal PRIESTHOOD, A
HOLY NATION, A PEOPLE FOR *God's* OWN
POSSESSION, so that
you may proclaim
the excellencies
of Him who has
called you out of
darkness into His
marvelous light;
10for you once were
NOT A PEOPLE, but
now you are THE
PEOPLE OF GOD; you
had NOT RECEIVED
MERCY, but now
you have RECEIVED
MERCY.
11Beloved, I urge
you as aliens and
strangers to abstain from fleshly
lusts which wage
war against the
soul. 12Keep your
behavior excellent among the
Gentiles, so that in
the thing in which
they slander you as
evildoers, they may
because of your

NIV

they accuse you of
doing wrong, they
may see your good
deeds and glorify
God on the day he
visits us.
13 Submit your-
selves for the
Lord's sake to
every human au-
thority: whether
to the emperor,
as the supreme
authority, 14 or to
governors, who
are sent by him to
punish those who
do wrong and to
commend those
who do right. 15 For
it is God's will
that by doing good
you should silence
the ignorant talk
of foolish peo-
ple. 16 Live as free
people, but do not
use your freedom
as a cover-up for
evil; live as God's
slaves. 17 Show
proper respect to
everyone, love the
family of believ-
ers, fear God, hon-
or the emperor.
18 Slaves, in rev-
erent fear of God
submit yourselves
to your masters,
not only to those
who are good and
considerate, but
also to those who
are harsh. 19 For it
is commendable
if someone bears
up under the pain
of unjust suffer-
ing because they
are conscious of
God. 20 But how
is it to your credit
if you receive a
beating for doing
wrong and endure
it? But if you suf-
fer for doing good
and you endure it,
this is commend-
able before God.
21 To this you were
called, because
Christ suffered for
you,

καταλαλοῦσιν ὑμῶν ὡς κακοποιῶν ↱ ↱ ἐκ τῶν καλῶν ἔργων
they slander you as evildoers, they may, by observing your good works,
2895 7007 6055 2804 1519 1519 1666 2227 3836 2819 2240
v.pai.3p r.gp.2 pl n.gpm p.g d.gpn a.gpn n.gpn

ἐποπτεύοντες δοξάσωσιν τὸν θεὸν ἐν ἡμέρᾳ ἐπισκοπῆς. 13 ὑποτάγητε πάσῃ
observing glorify *{the}* God on the day of visitation. Submit to every
2227 1519 3836 2536 1877 2465 2175 5718 4246
pt.pa.npm v.aas.3p d.asm n.asm p.d n.dsf n.gsf v.apm.2p a.dsf

ἀνθρωπίνῃ κτίσει διὰ τὸν κύριον, εἴτε → βασιλεῖ ὡς ὑπερέχοντι,
human authority ⌊on account of⌋ the Lord, whether to the king as supreme,
474 3232 1328 3836 3261 1664 995 6055 5660
a.dsf n.dsf p.a d.asm n.asm cj n.dsm pl pt.pa.dsm

14 εἴτε ἡγεμόσιν ὡς δι᾽ αὐτοῦ πεμπομένοις εἰς ἐκδίκησιν
or to governors as those sent by him *those sent* for the punishment
1664 2450 6055 4287 4287 1328 899 4287 1650 1689
cj n.dpm pl p.g r.gsm.3 pt.pp.dpm p.a n.asf

κακοποιῶν ἔπαινον δὲ ἀγαθοποιῶν· 15 ὅτι οὕτως ἐστὶν τὸ
⌊of those who do evil⌋ and the praise *and* of those who do good. For this is the
2804 1254 2047 1254 18 4022 4048 1639 3836
n.gpm n.asm cj n.gpm cj adv v.pai.3s d.nsn

θέλημα τοῦ θεοῦ ἀγαθοποιοῦντας φιμοῦν τὴν τῶν ἀφρόνων ἀνθρώπων
will of God: by doing good to silence the ignorance of foolish men.
2525 3836 2536 16 5821 3836 57 3836 933 476
n.nsn d.gsm n.gsm pt.pa.apm f.pa d.asf d.gpm a.gpm n.gpm

ἀγνωσίαν, 16 ὡς ἐλεύθεροι καὶ μὴ ὡς → ἐπικάλυμμα
ignorance Live as free people, *{and}* not as those using freedom as a cover-up
57 6055 1801 2779 3590 6055 2400 2400 1800 2127
n.asf pl a.npm cj pl pl n.asn

ἔχοντες τῆς κακίας τὴν ἐλευθερίαν ἀλλ᾽ ὡς θεοῦ δοῦλοι. 17
those using for evil, *{the}* *freedom* but as servants of God. *servants* Honor
2400 3836 2798 3836 1800 247 6055 1529 2536 1529 5506
pt.pa.npm d.gsf n.gsf d.asf n.asf cj pl n.gsm n.npm

πάντας τιμήσατε, τὴν ἀδελφότητα ἀγαπᾶτε, τὸν θεὸν φοβεῖσθε,
everyone; *Honor* love the brotherhood; *love* reverence *{the}* God; *reverence* honor
4246 5506 26 3836 82 26 5828 3836 2536 5828 5506
a.apm v.aam.2p d.asf n.asf v.pam.2p d.asm n.asm v.ppm.2p

τὸν βασιλέα τιμᾶτε. 18 οἱ οἰκέται ὑποτασσόμενοι ἐν
the king. *honor* *{the}* ⌊Household servants⌋ should be subject to their masters with
3836 995 5506 3836 3860 5718 3836 3836 1305 1877
d.asm n.asm v.pam.2p d.npm n.npm pt.pp.npm p.d

παντὶ φόβῳ τοῖς δεσπόταις, οὐ μόνον τοῖς ἀγαθοῖς καὶ ἐπιεικέσιν ἀλλὰ καὶ τοῖς
all respect, *to their masters* not only to the good and kind but also to the
4246 5832 3836 1305 4024 3667 3836 19 2779 2117 247 2779 3836
a.dsm n.dsm d.dpm n.dpm pl adv d.dpm a.dpm cj a.dpm cj adv d.dpm

σκολιοῖς. 19 τοῦτο γὰρ χάρις εἰ διὰ συνείδησιν θεοῦ
unjust. For this *For* is commendable, if ⌊because of⌋ conscience ⌊toward God⌋
5021 1142 4047 1142 5921 1623 1328 5287 2536
a.dpm r.nsn cj n.nsf cj p.a n.asf n.gsm

ὑποφέρει τις λύπας πάσχων ἀδίκως. 20 ποῖον γὰρ κλέος
someone endures *someone* pain while suffering unjustly. For what *For* praise is there
5516 5722 5516 3383 4248 97 1142 4481 1142 3094
v.pai.3s r.nsm n.apf pt.pa.nsm adv r.nsn cj n.nsn

εἰ ἁμαρτάνοντες καὶ κολαφιζόμενοι ὑπομενεῖτε; ἀλλ᾽ εἰ ἀγαθοποιοῦντες
if, when you do wrong and are beaten for it, you endure it? But if when you do good
1623 279 2779 3139 5702 247 1623 16
cj pt.pa.npm cj pt.pp.npm v.fai.2p cj cj pt.pa.npm

καὶ πάσχοντες ὑπομενεῖτε, τοῦτο χάρις παρὰ θεῷ. ↰ 21 εἰς
and suffer for it you endure it, this is commendable in God's sight. For to
2779 4248 5702 4047 5921 4123 2536 4123 1142 1650
cj pt.pa.npm v.fai.2p r.nsn n.nsf p.d n.dsm p.a

τοῦτο γὰρ ἐκλήθητε, ὅτι καὶ Χριστὸς ἔπαθεν ὑπὲρ ὑμῶν
this *For* ⌊you have been called,⌋ because Christ also *Christ* suffered for you, leaving
4047 1142 2813 4022 5986 2779 5986 4248 5642 7007 5701
r.asn cj v.api.2p cj adv n.nsm v.aai.3s p.g r.gp.2

NASB

good deeds, as they
observe *them,* glo-
rify God in the day
of [a]visitation.

Honor Authority

13 Submit your-
selves for the
Lord's sake to
every human insti-
tution, whether to
a king as the one
in authority, 14 or to
governors as sent
by him for the pun-
ishment of evildo-
ers and the praise
of those who do
right. 15 For such is
the will of God that
by doing right you
may silence the ig-
norance of foolish
men. 16 *Act* as free
men, and do not
use your freedom
as a covering for
evil, but *use it* as
bondslaves of God.
17 Honor all people,
love the brother-
hood, fear God,
honor the king.
18 Servants, be
submissive to your
masters with all
respect, not only to
those who are good
and gentle, but also
to those who are
unreasonable. 19 For
this *finds* favor,
if for the sake of
conscience toward
God a person bears
up under sorrows
when suffering
unjustly. 20 For what
credit is there if,
when you sin and
are harshly treated,
you endure it with
patience? But if
when you do what
is right and suffer
for it you patiently
endure it, this *finds*
favor with God.

Christ Is Our Example

21 For you have
been called for
this purpose, since
Christ also suffered
for you, leaving

[a] I.e. Christ's com-
ing again in judgment

NIV

leaving you an
example, that you
should follow in
his steps.
[22]"He committed
no sin,
and no deceit
was found
in his
mouth."[a]
[23]When they
hurled their insults
at him, he did not
retaliate; when he
suffered, he made
no threats. In-
stead, he entrusted
himself to him
who judges justly.
[24]"He himself bore
our sins" in his
body on the cross,
so that we might
die to sins and live
for righteousness;
"by his wounds
you have been
healed." [25]For "you
were like sheep
going astray,"[b] but
now you have re-
turned to the Shep-
herd and Overseer
of your souls.
3 Wives, in the
same way
submit yourselves
to your own hus-
bands so that, if
any of them do not
believe the word,
they may be won
over without words
by the behavior of
their wives, [2]when
they see the purity
and reverence of
your lives. [3]Your
beauty should not
come from out-
ward adornment,
such as elaborate
hairstyles and the
wearing of gold
jewelry or fine
clothes. [4]Rather, it
should be that of
your inner self, the
unfading beauty of
a gentle and quiet

[a] 22 Isaiah 53:9
[b] 24,25 Isaiah 53:4,5,6 (see Septuagint)

ὑμῖν ὑπολιμπάνων ὑπογραμμὸν ἵνα ἐπακολουθήσητε τοῖς ἴχνεσιν
behind for you *leaving behind* an example so that you might follow in his footsteps.
5701 7007 5701 5681 2671 2051 3836 899 2717
r.dp.2 pt.pa.nsm n.asm cj v.aas.2p d.dpn n.dpn

αὐτοῦ, [22] ὃς ἁμαρτίαν οὐκ ἐποίησεν οὐδὲ → εὑρέθη δόλος
his He did not commit sin, *not* *did commit* nor was deceit found *deceit*
899 4005 4472 4024 4472 281 4024 4472 4028 1515 2351 1515
r.gsm.3 r.nsm n.asf pl v.aai.3s cj v.api.3s n.nsm

ἐν τῷ στόματι αὐτοῦ, [23] ↱ ὃς λοιδορούμενος ↱ ↱ οὐκ
in *{the}* his mouth. *his* When he was insulted, he did not
1877 3836 899 5125 899 3366 4005 3366 518 518 4024
p.d d.dsn n.dsn r.gsm.3 r.nsm pt.pp.nsm pl

ἀντελοιδόρει, πάσχων ↱ ↱ οὐκ ἠπείλει, παρεδίδου δὲ τῷ
⌊respond with an insult;⌋ ⌊when he suffered,⌋ he did not threaten, but entrusted himself *but* ⌊to the⌋
518 4248 580 580 4024 580 1254 4140 1254 3836
v.iai.3s pt.pa.nsm pl v.iai.3s v.iai.3s cj d.dsm

κρίνοντι δικαίως· [24] ὃς τὰς ἁμαρτίας ἡμῶν αὐτὸς ἀνήνεγκεν
one who judges justly. He himself bore *{the}* our sins *our* *himself* *bore*
3212 1469 4005 899 429 3836 7005 281 7005 899 429
pt.pa.dsm adv r.nsm d.apf n.apf r.gp.1 r.nsm v.aai.3s

ἐν τῷ σώματι αὐτοῦ ἐπὶ τὸ ξύλον, ἵνα ταῖς ἁμαρτίαις
in *{the}* his body *his* on the tree so that we, having died to sins,
1877 3836 899 5393 899 2093 3836 3833 2671 2409 614 614 3836 281
p.d d.dsn n.dsn r.gsm.3 p.a d.asn n.asn cj d.dpf n.dpf

ἀπογενόμενοι τῇ δικαιοσύνῃ ζήσωμεν, οὗ τῷ μώλωπι
having died might live to righteousness. *we might live* By his *By* wounds
614 2409 2409 3836 1466 2409 3836 4005 3836 3698
pt.am.npm d.dsf n.dsf v.aas.1p r.gsm d.dsm n.dsm

ἰάθητε. [25] ἦτε γὰρ ὡς πρόβατα πλανώμενοι, ἀλλὰ
⌊you were healed.⌋ For ⌊you were⌋ *For* like sheep, going astray, but now
2615 1142 1639 1142 6055 4585 4414 247 3814
v.api.2p v.iai.2p cj pl n.npn pt.pp.npm cj

ἐπεστράφητε νῦν ἐπὶ τὸν ποιμένα καὶ ἐπίσκοπον τῶν ψυχῶν ὑμῶν.
⌊you have turned back⌋ *now* to the shepherd and guardian of your souls. *your*
2188 3814 2093 3836 4478 2779 2176 3836 7007 6034 7007
v.api.2p adv p.a d.asm n.asm cj n.asm d.gpf n.gpf r.gp.2

[3:1] ὁμοίως αἱ[a] γυναῖκες, ὑποτασσόμεναι τοῖς ἰδίοις ἀνδράσιν, ἵνα
⌊In the same way,⌋ *{the}* wives should be subject to their own husbands, so that
3931 3836 1222 5718 3836 2625 467 2671
adv d.npf n.npf pt.pp.npf d.dpm a.dpm n.dpm cj

καὶ εἴ τινες ἀπειθοῦσιν τῷ λόγῳ, διὰ
even if some of them refuse to believe the word, they may be won without a word by
2779 1623 5516 578 3836 3364 3045 3045 3045 3045 459 3364 1328
adv cj r.npm v.pai.3p d.dsm n.dsm p.g

τῆς τῶν γυναικῶν ἀναστροφῆς ἄνευ λόγου κερδηθήσονται,
the conduct of their wives *conduct* *without* *word* *they may be won*
3836 419 3836 1222 419 459 3364 3045
d.gsf d.gpf n.gpf n.gsf p.g n.gsm v.fpi.3p

[2]ἐποπτεύσαντες τὴν ἐν φόβῳ ἁγνὴν ἀναστροφὴν ὑμῶν. [3] ↱
when they observe with respect the *with* *respect* purity of your life. *your* Do not
2227 1877 5832 3836 1877 5832 54 7007 419 7007 1639 4024
pt.aa.npm d.asf p.d n.dsm a.asf n.asf r.gp.2

↱ ὧν ἔστω οὐχ ὁ ἔξωθεν ἐμπλοκῆς τριχῶν καὶ περιθέσεως
let your beauty be *not* *{the}* external — such as braiding the hair, *{and}* wearing
1639 4005 3180 1639 4024 3836 2033 1862 2582 2779 4324
r.gpf v.pam.3s pl d.nsm p.g n.gsf n.gpf cj n.gsf

χρυσίων ἢ ἐνδύσεως → ἱματίων κόσμος [4]ἀλλ᾽ ὁ κρυπτὸς
gold jewelry, or dressing up in fine clothes *beauty* — but let it be the inner person
5992 2445 1906 2668 3180 247 3836 3220 476
n.gpn cj n.gsf n.gpn n.nsm cj d.nsm a.nsm

τῆς καρδίας ἄνθρωπος ἐν τῷ ἀφθάρτῳ τοῦ πραέως καὶ ἡσυχίου
of the heart, *person* *{in}* the unfading beauty of a gentle and tranquil
3836 2840 476 1877 3836 915 3836 4558 2779 2485
d.gsf n.gsf n.nsm p.d d.dsn a.dsn d.gsn a.gsn cj a.gsn

[a] [αἱ] UBS, omitted by TNIV.

NASB

you an example
for you to follow
in His steps, [22]WHO
COMMITTED NO SIN,
NOR WAS ANY DE-
CEIT FOUND IN HIS
MOUTH; [23]and while
being reviled, He
did not revile in
return; while suf-
fering, He uttered
no threats, but kept
entrusting *Himself*
to Him who judges
righteously; [24]and
He Himself bore
our sins in His
body on the cross,
so that we might
die to sin and live
to righteousness;
for by His wounds
you were healed.
[25]For you were con-
tinually straying
like sheep, but now
you have returned
to the Shepherd
and Guardian of
your souls.

Godly Living

[3:1]In the same
way, you wives, be
submissive to your
own husbands so
that even if any *of*
them are disobedi-
ent to the word,
they may be won
without a word
by the behavior
of their wives, [2]as
they observe your
chaste and respect-
ful behavior. [3]Your
adornment must
not be *merely*
external—braiding
the hair, and wear-
ing gold jewelry, or
putting on dresses;
[4]but *let it be* the
hidden person of
the heart, with the
imperishable qual-
ity of a gentle and
quiet spirit,

NIV

spirit, which is
of great worth in
God's sight. [5]For
this is the way the
holy women of the
past who put their
hope in God used
to adorn them-
selves. They sub-
mitted themselves
to their own hus-
bands, [6]like Sarah,
who obeyed Abra-
ham and called
him her lord. You
are her daughters
if you do what is
right and do not
give way to fear.
[7]Husbands, in the
same way be con-
siderate as you live
with your wives,
and treat them
with respect as the
weaker partner
and as heirs with
you of the gracious
gift of life, so that
nothing will hin-
der your prayers.

Suffering for Doing Good

[8]Finally, all of
you, be like-mind-
ed, be sympa-
thetic, love one
another, be com-
passionate and
humble. [9]Do not
repay evil with
evil or insult with
insult. On the con-
trary, repay evil
with blessing, be-
cause to this you
were called so that
you may inherit a
blessing. [10]For,

"Whoever would
love life
and see good
days
must keep their
tongue from
evil
and their
lips from
deceitful
speech.
[11]They must turn
from evil and
do good;
they must seek
peace and
pursue it.
[12]For the eyes of the
Lord are on
the righteous

πνεύματος, ὅ ἐστιν ἐνώπιον τοῦ θεοῦ πολυτελές. [5]
spirit, which in the sight of God is *in the sight of* *God* precious. For
4460 4005 1967 1967 1967 3836 2536 1639 1967 3836 2536 4500 1142
n.gsn r.nsn v.pai.3s p.g d.gsm n.gsm a.nsn

οὕτως γάρ ποτε καὶ αἱ ἅγιαι γυναῖκες αἱ
⌊in the same way,⌋ *For* ⌊at an earlier time,⌋ *{also}* the devout women — those
4048 1142 4537 2779 3836 41 1222 3836
adv cj adv adv d.npf a.npf n.npf d.npf

ἐλπίζουσαι εἰς θεὸν ἐκόσμουν ἑαυτὰς ὑποτασσόμεναι τοῖς ἰδίοις
⌊who put their hope⌋ in God — used to adorn themselves by being subject to their own
1827 1650 2536 3175 1571 5718 3836 2625
pt.pa.npf p.a n.asm v.iai.3p r.apf.3 pt.pp.npf d.dpm a.dpm

ἀνδράσιν, [6]ὡς Σάρρα ὑπήκουσεν τῷ Ἀβραάμ κύριον αὐτὸν
husbands, ⌊just as⌋ Sarah obeyed *{the}* Abraham, calling him "my lord." *him*
467 6055 4925 5634 3836 11 2813 899 3261 899
n.dpm cj n.nsf v.aai.3s d.dsm n.dsm n.asm r.asm.3

καλοῦσα, ἧς ἐγενήθητε τέκνα ἀγαθοποιοῦσαι καὶ ↱ μὴ φοβούμεναι
calling You are her *You are* daughters if you do what is right and do not fear
2813 1181 1181 4005 1181 5451 16 2779 5828 3590 5828
pt.pa.nsf r.gsf v.api.2p n.npn pt.pa.npf cj pl pt.pp.npf

μηδεμίαν πτόησιν. [7]οἱ ἄνδρες ὁμοίως, συνοικοῦντες κατὰ
any intimidation. *{the}* Husbands, ⌊in the same way,⌋ live with them with
3594 4766 3836 467 3931 5324 2848
a.asf n.asf d.npm n.npm adv pt.pa.npm p.a

γνῶσιν ὡς ἀσθενεστέρῳ σκεύει τῷ γυναικείῳ,
understanding, showing honor to the woman as a weaker vessel, *to the* *woman*
1194 671 5507 3836 3836 1221 6055 822 5007 3836 1221
n.asf pl a.dsn.c n.dsn d.dsn a.dsn

ἀπονέμοντες τιμὴν ὡς καὶ συγκληρονόμοις → χάριτος ζωῆς εἰς τὸ
showing *honor* since *{also}* you are joint heirs of the ⌊gracious gift⌋ of life, ⌊so that⌋ ~ your
671 5507 6055 2779 5169 5921 2437 1650 3836 7007
pt.pa.npm n.asf pl adv n.dpf n.gsf n.gsf p.a d.asn

↱ μὴ ἐγκόπτεσθαι τὰς προσευχὰς ὑμῶν. [8]τὸ δὲ τέλος πάντες
prayers may not be hindered. *{the}* *prayers* *your* *{the}* *{and}* Finally, all of you, be
4666 1601 3590 1601 3836 4666 7007 3836 1254 5465 4246
pl f.pp d.apf n.apf r.gp.2 d.asn cj n.asn a.npm

ὁμόφρονες, συμπαθεῖς, φιλάδελφοι, εὔσπλαγχνοι, ταπεινόφρονες,
of one mind, sympathetic, ⌊loving your believing brothers,⌋ compassionate, humble —
3939 5218 5790 2359 5426
a.npm a.npm a.npm a.npm a.npm

[9]μὴ ἀποδιδόντες κακὸν ἀντὶ κακοῦ ἢ λοιδορίαν ἀντὶ λοιδορίας, τοὐναντίον
not returning evil for evil or insult for insult, but on the contrary
3590 625 2805 505 2805 2445 3367 505 3367 1254 5539
pl pt.pa.npm a.asn p.g a.gsn cj n.asf p.g n.gsf crasis.asn

δὲ εὐλογοῦντες ὅτι εἰς τοῦτο ἐκλήθητε ἵνα εὐλογίαν
but blessing, because for this you were called that you might inherit a blessing.
1254 2328 4022 1650 4047 2813 2671 3099 3099 3099 2330
cj pt.pa.npm cj p.a r.asn v.api.2p cj n.asf

κληρονομήσητε. [10] ὁ γὰρ θέλων ζωὴν ἀγαπᾶν καὶ ἰδεῖν
you might inherit For "The *For* ⌊one who desires⌋ to love life *to love* and to see good
3099 1142 3836 1142 2527 26 26 2437 26 2779 1625 19
v.aas.2p d.nsm cj pt.pa.nsm n.asf f.pa cj f.aa

ἡμέρας ἀγαθὰς παυσάτω τὴν γλῶσσαν ἀπὸ κακοῦ καὶ χείλη τοῦ μὴ λαλῆσαι
days, *good* let him keep his tongue from evil and his lips ~ from speaking
2465 19 4264 3836 1185 608 2805 2779 5927 3836 3590 3281
n.apf a.apf v.aam.3s d.asf n.asf p.g a.gsn cj n.apn d.gsn pl f.aa

δόλον, [11] ἐκκλινάτω δὲ ἀπὸ κακοῦ καὶ ποιησάτω ἀγαθόν, ζητησάτω
deceit. And ⌊let him turn away⌋ *And* from evil and do good; let him seek
1515 1254 1712 1254 608 2805 2779 4472 19 2426
n.asm v.aam.3s cj p.g a.gsn cj v.aam.3s a.asn v.aam.3s

εἰρήνην καὶ διωξάτω αὐτήν· [12]ὅτι ὀφθαλμοὶ → κυρίου ἐπὶ δικαίους
peace and pursue it. For the eyes of the Lord are on the righteous,
1645 2779 1503 899 4022 4057 3261 2093 1465
n.asf cj v.aam.3s r.asf.3 cj n.npm n.gsm p.a a.apm

NASB

which is precious
in the sight of God.
[5]For in this way
in former times
the holy women
also, who hoped in
God, used to adorn
themselves, being
submissive to their
own husbands;
[6]just as Sarah
obeyed Abraham,
calling him lord,
and you have be-
come her children
if you do what is
right without being
frightened by any
fear.
[7]You husbands in
the same way, live
with *your wives* in
an understanding
way, as with some-
one weaker, since
she is a woman;
and show her
honor as a fellow
heir of the grace of
life, so that your
prayers will not be
hindered.
[8]To sum up, all of
you be harmonious,
sympathetic, broth-
erly, kindhearted,
and humble in
spirit; [9]not return-
ing evil for evil or
insult for insult,
but giving a bless-
ing instead; for you
were called for the
very purpose that
you might inherit a
blessing. [10]For,

"THE ONE WHO
DESIRES LIFE,
TO LOVE AND
SEE GOOD
DAYS,
MUST KEEP HIS
TONGUE FROM
EVIL AND HIS
LIPS FROM
SPEAKING DE-
CEIT.
[11]"HE MUST TURN
AWAY FROM
EVIL AND DO
GOOD;
HE MUST SEEK
PEACE AND
PURSUE IT.
[12]"FOR THE EYES
OF THE LORD
ARE TOWARD
THE RIGH-
TEOUS,

NIV

and his ears are
attentive to
their prayer,
but the face of
the Lord
is against
those who do
evil."[a]

13 Who is going
to harm you if you
are eager to do
good? 14 But even if
you should suffer
for what is right,
you are blessed.
"Do not fear their
threats[b]; do not be
frightened."[c] 15 But
in your hearts
revere Christ as
Lord. Always be
prepared to give an
answer to every-
one who asks you
to give the reason
for the hope that
you have. But do
this with gentle-
ness and respect,
16 keeping a clear
conscience, so
that those who
speak maliciously
against your good
behavior in Christ
may be ashamed of
their slander. 17 For
it is better, if it is
God's will, to suf-
fer for doing good
than for doing evil.
18 For Christ also
suffered once for
sins, the righteous
for the unrigh-
teous, to bring you
to God. He was
put to death in the
body but made
alive in the Spirit.
19 After being made
alive,[d] he went and
made proclamation
to the imprisoned
spirits— 20 to
those who were
disobedient long
ago when

καὶ ὦτα αὐτοῦ εἰς δέησιν αὐτῶν, πρόσωπον δὲ → κυρίου
and his ears *his* are open to their prayers; *their* but the face *but* of the Lord
2779 899 4044 899 1650 899 1255 899 1254 4725 1254 3261
cj n.npn r.gsm.3 p.a n.asf r.gpm.3 n.nsn cj n.gsm

ἐπὶ ποιοῦντας κακά. 13 καὶ τίς ὁ κακώσων ὑμᾶς ἐὰν
is against those who do evil." And who is the ⌊one who will harm⌋ you if you become
2093 4472 2805 2779 5515 3836 2808 7007 1569 1181 1181
p.a pt.pa.apm a.apn cj r.nsm d.nsm pt.fa.nsm r.ap.2 cj

τοῦ ἀγαθοῦ ζηλωταὶ γένησθε; 14 ἀλλ᾽ εἰ καὶ πάσχοιτε
zealots for what is good? *zealots* *you become* But even if *even* ⌊you should suffer⌋
2421 3836 19 2421 1181 247 2779 1623 2779 4248
d.gsn a.gsn n.npm v.ams.2p cj cj adv v.pao.2p

διὰ δικαιοσύνην, μακάριοι. τὸν δὲ φόβον
⌊because of⌋ righteousness, blessed are you. And do not fear *{the}* *And* their threats
1328 1466 3421 1254 5828 3590 5828 3836 1254 899 5832
p.a n.asf a.npm d.asm cj n.asm

αὐτῶν μὴ φοβηθῆτε μηδὲ ταραχθῆτε, 15 κύριον δὲ τὸν Χριστὸν ἁγιάσατε ἐν ταῖς
their *not* *do fear* or be troubled, *Lord* but *{the}* *Christ* *set apart* in *{the}*
899 3590 5828 3593 5429 3261 1254 3836 5986 39 1877 3836
r.gpm.3 pl v.aps.2p cj v.aps.2p n.asm cj d.asm n.asm v.aam.2p p.d d.dpf

καρδίαις ὑμῶν, ἕτοιμοι ἀεὶ πρὸς ἀπολογίαν
your hearts *your* set apart Christ as Lord, being ready ⌊at all times⌋ to make a defense
7007 2840 7007 39 39 5986 3261 2289 107 4639 665
n.dpf r.gp.2 a.npm adv p.a n.asf

παντὶ τῷ αἰτοῦντι ὑμᾶς ↰ λόγον περὶ τῆς ἐν ὑμῖν ἐλπίδος,
to all who ask you for a word concerning the hope that is in you. *hope*
4246 3836 160 7007 160 3364 4309 3836 1828 1877 7007 1828
a.dsm d.dsm pt.pa.dsm r.ap.2 n.asm p.g d.gsf p.d r.dp.2 n.gsf

16 ἀλλὰ μετὰ πραΰτητος καὶ φόβου, συνείδησιν ἔχοντες
But do it with gentleness and respect, maintaining a clear conscience, *maintaining*
247 3552 4559 2779 5832 2400 19 5287 2400
cj p.g n.gsf cj n.gsm n.asf pt.pa.npm

ἀγαθήν, ἵνα ἐν ᾧ καταλαλεῖσθε καταισχυνθῶσιν οἱ
clear so that in ⌊the very thing for which⌋ you are being slandered, *will be put to shame* those
19 2671 1877 4005 2895 2875 3836
a.asf cj p.d r.dsn v.ppi.2p v.aps.3p d.npm

ἐπηρεάζοντες ὑμῶν τὴν ἀγαθὴν ἐν Χριστῷ ἀναστροφήν.
who are reviling your *{the}* good conduct in Christ *conduct* will be put to
2092 7007 3836 19 419 1877 5986 419 2875 2875 2875 2875
pt.pa.npm r.gp.2 d.asf a.asf p.d n.dsm n.asf

17 κρεῖττον γὰρ ἀγαθοποιοῦντας, εἰ θέλοι τὸ
shame. For it is better *For* to suffer for doing good, if it is *{the}* God's
2875 1142 3202 1142 4248 4248 16 1623 2527 3836 2536
a.nsn.c cj pt.pa.apm cj v.pao.3s d.nsn

θέλημα τοῦ θεοῦ, πάσχειν ἢ κακοποιοῦντας. 18 ὅτι καὶ Χριστὸς
will, *{the}* *God's* *to suffer* than for doing evil. Because Christ also *Christ* suffered
2525 3836 2536 4248 2445 2803 4022 5986 2779 5986 4248
n.nsn d.gsm n.gsm f.pa pl pt.pa.apm cj adv n.nsm

ἅπαξ περὶ ἁμαρτιῶν ἔπαθεν, δίκαιος ὑπὲρ ἀδίκων, ἵνα
once for our sins, *suffered* the righteous ⌊on behalf of⌋ the unrighteous, that he might
562 4309 281 4248 1465 5642 96 2671 4642 4642
adv p.g n.gpf v.aai.3s a.nsm p.g a.gpm cj

ὑμᾶς προσαγάγῃ τῷ θεῷ θανατωθεὶς μὲν → σαρκὶ ζῳοποιηθεὶς
lead you *he might lead* to God. ⌊He was put to death⌋ ~ in the flesh but made alive
4642 7007 4642 3836 2536 2506 3525 4922 1254 2443
r.ap.2 v.aas.3s d.dsm n.dsm pt.ap.nsm pl n.dsf pt.ap.nsm

δὲ → πνεύματι· 19 ἐν ᾧ καὶ τοῖς ἐν φυλακῇ
but in the spirit, in which also he went and proclaimed to the spirits in prison,
1254 4460 1877 4005 2779 3062 4513 3062 3836 4460 1877 5871
cj n.dsn p.d r.dsn adv d.dpn p.d n.dsf

πνεύμασιν πορευθεὶς ἐκήρυξεν, 20 → ἀπειθήσασίν ποτε ὅτε
spirits *went* *he proclaimed* who once were disobedient *once* when the patience of
4460 4513 3062 4537 578 4537 4021 3836 3429 3836
n.dpn pt.ap.nsm v.aai.3s pt.aa.dpm adv cj

NASB

AND HIS EARS
ATTEND TO
THEIR PRAYER,
BUT THE FACE
OF THE LORD
IS AGAINST
THOSE WHO DO
EVIL."
13 Who is there to
harm you if you
prove zealous for
what is good? 14 But
even if you should
suffer for the sake
of righteousness,
you are blessed.
AND DO NOT FEAR
THEIR INTIMIDA-
TION, AND DO NOT
BE TROUBLED, 15 but
[a]sanctify Christ
as Lord in your
hearts, always *be-
ing* ready to make
a defense to every-
one who asks you
to give an account
for the hope that
is in you, yet with
gentleness and rev-
erence; 16 and keep
a good conscience
so that in the thing
in which you are
slandered, those
who revile your
good behavior in
Christ will be put
to shame. 17 For it
is better, if God
should will it so,
that you suffer for
doing what is right
rather than for do-
ing what is wrong.
18 For Christ also
died for sins once
for all, *the* just for
the unjust, so that
He might bring
us to God, having
been put to death in
the flesh, but made
alive in the spirit;
19 in which also He
went and made
proclamation to
the spirits *now* in
prison, 20 who once
were disobedient,
when the patience

[a] 12 Psalm 34:12-16
[b] 14 Or *fear what they fear*
[c] 14 Isaiah 8:12
[d] 18,19 Or *but made alive in the spirit, 19 in which also*

[a] I.e. set apart

NIV

God waited pa-
tiently in the days
of Noah while
the ark was being
built. In it only
a few people,
eight in all, were
saved through
water, 21and this
water symboliz-
es baptism that
now saves you
also—not the re-
moval of dirt from
the body but the
pledge of a clear
conscience toward
God.[a] It saves you
by the resurrection
of Jesus Christ,
22who has gone
into heaven and
is at God's right
hand—with an-
gels, authorities
and powers in sub-
mission to him.

Living for God

4 Therefore,
since Christ
suffered in his
body, arm your-
selves also with
the same attitude,
because whoever
suffers in the body
is done with sin.
2As a result, they
do not live the rest
of their earthly
lives for evil hu-
man desires, but
rather for the will
of God. 3For you
have spent enough
time in the past
doing what pagans
choose to do—liv-
ing in debauchery,
lust, drunkenness,
orgies, carousing
and detestable
idolatry. 4They are
surprised that you
do not

[a] 21 Or *but an appeal to God for a clear conscience*

ἀπεξεδέχετο ἡ τοῦ θεοῦ μακροθυμία ἐν ἡμέραις Νῶε →
God waited *the of God patience* in the days of Noah while the ark
2536 587 3836 3836 2536 3429 1877 2465 3820 3066
v.imi.3s d.nsf d.gsm n.gsm n.nsf p.d n.dpf n.gsm

κατασκευαζομένης κιβωτοῦ εἰς ἣν ὀλίγοι, τοῦτ' ἔστιν ὀκτὼ ψυχαί,
was being built, *ark* in which a few, that is eight souls,
2941 3066 1650 4005 3900 4047 1639 3893 6034
pt.pp.gsf n.gsf p.a r.asf a.npm r.nsn v.pai.3s a.npf n.npf

διεσώθησαν δι' ὕδατος. 21 ὃ καὶ
⌊were brought safely⌋ through water. This water prefigures baptism, which *{also}* now saves
1407 1328 5623 531 967 4005 2779 3814 5392
v.api.3p p.g n.gsn r.nsn adv

ὑμᾶς ἀντίτυπον νῦν σῴζει βάπτισμα, οὐ → σαρκὸς
you *prefigures now saves baptism* — not the removal of dirt from the body
7007 531 3814 5392 967 4024 629 4866 4866 4922
r.ap.2 a.nsn adv v.pai.3s n.nsn pl n.gsf

ἀπόθεσις ῥύπου ἀλλὰ συνειδήσεως ἀγαθῆς ἐπερώτημα εἰς θεόν,
removal of dirt but the answer of a good conscience *good answer* to God —
629 4866 247 2090 19 5287 19 2090 1650 2536
n.nsf n.gsm cj n.gsf a.gsf n.nsn p.a n.asm

δι' ἀναστάσεως Ἰησοῦ Χριστοῦ, 22 ὅς ἐστιν ἐν δεξιᾷ τοῦ[a] θεοῦ
by the resurrection of Jesus Christ, who is at the right hand of God,
1328 414 2652 5986 4005 1639 1877 1288 3836 2536
p.g n.gsf n.gsm n.gsm r.nsm v.pai.3s p.d a.dsf d.gsm n.gsm

πορευθεὶς εἰς οὐρανόν ὑποταγέντων αὐτῷ ἀγγέλων καὶ ἐξουσιῶν καὶ δυνάμεων.
having gone into heaven, *being made subject to him* all angels and authorities and powers
4513 1650 4041 5718 899 34 2779 2026 2779 1539
pt.ap.nsm p.a n.asm pt.ap.gpm r.dsm.3 n.gpm cj n.gpf cj n.gpf

being made subject to him.
5718 5718 5718 899 899

4:1 → Χριστοῦ οὖν παθόντος → σαρκὶ καὶ ὑμεῖς
Therefore since Christ *Therefore* suffered in the flesh, arm yourselves also *{you}*
4036 4248 5986 4036 4248 4922 3959 3959 2779 7007
n.gsm cj pt.aa.gsm n.dsf adv r.np.2

τὴν αὐτὴν ἔννοιαν ὁπλίσασθε, ὅτι ὁ παθὼν →
with the same way of thinking, *arm yourselves* that is, that the ⌊one who has suffered⌋ in the
3836 899 1936 3959 4022 3836 4248
d.asf r.asf n.asf v.amm.2p cj d.nsm pt.aa.nsm

σαρκὶ πέπαυται ἁμαρτίας 2 εἰς τὸ μηκέτι
flesh has finished with sin, ⌊so that⌋ ~ you no longer live your remaining days in the
4922 4264 281 1650 3836 3600 1051 3836 2145 5989 1877
n.dsf v.rmi.3s n.gsf p.a d.asn adv

→ ἀνθρώπων ἐπιθυμίαις ἀλλὰ → θελήματι θεοῦ τὸν
flesh concerned about human desires but about the will of God. *your*
4922 2123 476 2123 247 2525 2536 3836
n.gpm n.dpf cj n.dsn n.gsm d.asm

ἐπίλοιπον ἐν σαρκὶ βιῶσαι χρόνον. 3 ἀρκετὸς γὰρ ὁ παρεληλυθὼς χρόνος
remaining in flesh live days enough For the time already gone by *time* is
2145 1877 4922 1051 5989 757 1142 3836 5989 4216 5989
a.asm p.d n.dsf f.aa n.asm a.nsm cj d.nsm pt.ra.nsm n.nsm

τὸ βούλημα τῶν ἐθνῶν κατειργάσθαι
enough for you to have done what the pagans like *the pagans* to do,
757 3836 3836 1620 1088 3836 1620 2981
d.asn n.asn d.gpn n.gpn f.rm

πεπορευμένους ἐν ἀσελγείαις, ἐπιθυμίαις, οἰνοφλυγίαις, κώμοις, πότοις καὶ
carrying on in sensuality, passions, drunkenness, orgies, ⌊drinking parties,⌋ and
4513 1877 816 2123 3886 3269 4542 2779
pt.rm.apm p.d n.dpf n.dpf n.dpf n.dpm n.dpm cj

ἀθεμίτοις εἰδωλολατρίαις. 4 ἐν ᾧ ξενίζονται → μὴ
disgusting worship of idols. In ⌊all this,⌋ they are surprised that you do not
116 1630 1877 4005 3826 7007 5340 3590
a.dpf n.dpf p.d r.dsn v.ppi.3p pl

[a] [τοῦ] UBS, omitted by TNIV.

NASB

of God kept wait-
ing in the days of
Noah, during the
construction of the
ark, in which a few,
that is, eight per-
sons, were brought
safely through *the*
water. 21Corre-
sponding to that,
baptism now saves
you—not the re-
moval of dirt from
the flesh, but an
appeal to God for a
good conscience—
through the resur-
rection of Jesus
Christ, 22who is at
the right hand of
God, having gone
into heaven, after
angels and authori-
ties and powers
had been subjected
to Him.

Keep Fervent in Your Love

4:1Therefore, since
Christ has [a]suffered
in the flesh, arm
yourselves also
with the same pur-
pose, because he
who has suffered in
the flesh has ceased
from sin, 2so as to
live the rest of the
time in the flesh no
longer for the lusts
of men, but for the
will of God. 3For
the time already
past is sufficient
for you to have car-
ried out the desire
of the Gentiles,
having pursued a
course of sensual-
ity, lusts, drunken-
ness, carousing,
drinking parties
and abominable
idolatries. 4In *all*
this, they are sur-
prised that you do

[a] I.e. suffered death

NIV

join them in their
reckless, wild liv-
ing, and they heap
abuse on you. 5 But
they will have to
give account to
him who is ready
to judge the living
and the dead. 6 For
this is the reason
the gospel was
preached even to
those who are now
dead, so that they
might be judged
according to hu-
man standards in
regard to the body,
but live according
to God in regard to
the spirit.
7 The end of all
things is near.
Therefore be alert
and of sober mind
so that you may
pray. 8 Above all,
love each other
deeply, because
love covers over
a multitude of
sins. 9 Offer hos-
pitality to one
another without
grumbling. 10 Each
of you should use
whatever gift you
have received to
serve others, as
faithful stewards
of God's grace in
its various forms.
11 If anyone speaks,
they should do so
as one who speaks
the very words
of God. If any-
one serves, they
should do so with
the strength God
provides, so that in
all things God may
be praised through
Jesus Christ. To
him be the glo-
ry and the power
for ever and ever.
Amen.

Suffering for Being a Christian

12 Dear friends, do
not be surprised
at the fiery ordeal
that has come on
you to test you, as
though something
strange were hap-
pening

συντρεχόντων ὑμῶν εἰς τὴν αὐτὴν τῆς ἀσωτίας ἀνάχυσιν
plunge with them *you* into the same flood of debauchery, *flood* and
5340 7007 1650 3836 899 431 3836 861 431
pt.pa.gpm r.gp.2 p.a d.asf r.asf d.gsf n.gsf n.asf

βλασφημοῦντες, 5 οἳ ἀποδώσουσιν λόγον τῷ ἑτοίμως
they malign you. They will give an account to him who stands ready
1059 4005 625 3364 3836 2400 2400 2400 2290
pt.pa.npm r.npm v.fai.3p n.asm d.dsm adv

ἔχοντι κρῖναι ζῶντας καὶ νεκρούς. 6 εἰς τοῦτο γὰρ καὶ
him who stands to judge the living and the dead. It was for ⌊this very purpose⌋ *{for}* *{also}*
2400 3212 2409 2779 3738 1650 4047 1142 2779
pt.pa.dsm f.aa pt.pa.apm cj a.apm p.a r.asn cj adv

→ νεκροῖς εὐηγγελίσθη, ἵνα κριθῶσι
that the gospel was preached to the dead, *gospel was preached* so that though ⌊they were judged⌋
2294 2294 2294 3738 2294 2671 3525 3212
a.dpm v.api.3s cj v.aps.3p

μὲν κατὰ ἀνθρώπους → σαρκὶ ζῶσι δὲ κατὰ θεὸν → πνεύματι.
though as men in the flesh, ⌊they might live⌋ *{and}* as God in the Spirit.
3525 2848 476 4922 2409 1254 2848 2536 4460
pl p.a n.apm n.dsf v.pas.3p cj p.a n.asm n.dsn

7 πάντων δὲ τὸ τέλος ἤγγικεν. σωφρονήσατε οὖν καὶ
The end of all things *{and}* *The* *end* is at hand, so use sound judgment *so* and
3836 5465 4246 1254 3836 5465 1581 4036 5404 4036 2779
a.gpn cj d.nsn n.nsn v.rai.3s v.aam.2p cj cj

νήψατε εἰς προσευχάς· 8 πρὸ πάντων τὴν
be sober-minded ⌊for the sake of⌋ prayer. Above all, *{the}* maintain a fervent love
3768 1650 4666 4574 4246 3836 2400 1756 27
v.aam.2p p.a n.apf p.g a.gpn d.asf

εἰς ἑαυτοὺς ἀγάπην ἐκτενῆ ἔχοντες, ὅτι ἀγάπη καλύπτει πλῆθος ἁμαρτιῶν.
among yourselves, *love* *fervent* *maintain* for love covers a multitude of sins.
1650 1571 27 1756 2400 4022 27 2821 4436 281
p.a r.apm.2 n.asf a.asf pt.pa.npm cj n.nsf v.pai.3s n.asn n.gpf

9 φιλόξενοι εἰς ἀλλήλους ἄνευ γογγυσμοῦ, 10 ἕκαστος
Be hospitable to one another without grumbling. Each one should serve others
5811 1650 253 459 1198 1667 1354 1354 1571
a.npm p.a r.apm p.g n.gsm r.nsm

καθὼς ἔλαβεν χάρισμα εἰς ἑαυτοὺς αὐτὸ διακονοῦντες ὡς
⌊in respect to⌋ the gift he has received, *gift* *{for}* *others* *{it}* *should serve* as a
2777 5922 3284 5922 1650 1571 899 1354 6055
cj v.aai.3s n.asn p.a r.apm.3 r.asn.3 pt.pa.npm pl

καλοὶ οἰκονόμοι ποικίλης χάριτος θεοῦ. 11 εἴ τις
good steward of the grace of God ⌊in its various forms:⌋ *of grace* *of God* if someone
2819 3874 5921 5921 2536 2536 4476 5921 2536 1623 5516
a.npm n.npm a.gsf n.gsf n.gsm cj r.nsm

λαλεῖ, ὡς λόγια θεοῦ· εἴ τις διακονεῖ, ὡς ἐξ ἰσχύος ἧς
speaks, as speaking the oracles of God; if someone serves, as by the strength that God
3281 6055 3359 2536 1623 5516 1354 6055 1666 2709 4005 2536
v.pai.3s pl n.npn n.gsm cj r.nsm v.pai.3s pl p.g n.gsf r.gsf

χορηγεῖ ὁ θεός, ἵνα ἐν πᾶσιν δοξάζηται ὁ θεὸς διὰ Ἰησοῦ
supplies *{the}* *God* — so that in everything God may be glorified *{the}* *God* through Jesus
5961 3836 2536 2671 1877 4246 2536 1519 3836 2536 1328 2652
v.pai.3s d.nsm n.nsm cj p.d a.dpn v.pps.3s d.nsm n.nsm p.g n.gsm

Χριστοῦ, ᾧ ἐστιν ἡ δόξα καὶ τὸ κράτος εἰς τοὺς ⌊αἰῶνας τῶν αἰώνων,⌋
Christ. ⌊To him⌋ belong *{the}* glory and *{the}* power for all time.
5986 4005 1639 3836 1518 2779 3836 3197 1650 3836 172 3836 172
n.gsm r.dsm v.pai.3s d.nsf n.nsf cj d.nsn n.nsn p.a d.apm n.apm d.gpm n.gpm

ἀμήν. 12 ἀγαπητοί, → μὴ ξενίζεσθε τῇ ἐν ὑμῖν
Amen. Dear friends, do not be surprised that a trial by fire is taking place among you,
297 28 3826 3590 3826 4280 3836 4796 1181 1181 1181 1877 7007
pl a.vpm pl v.ppm.2p d.dsf p.d r.dp.2

πυρώσει πρὸς πειρασμὸν ὑμῖν γινομένῃ ὡς ξένου
fire *{for}* *trial* *{you}* *is taking place* ⌊as though⌋ ⌊something strange⌋ were happening
4796 4639 4280 7007 1181 6055 3828 5201 5201
n.dsf p.a n.asm r.dp.2 pt.pm.dsf pl a.gsn

NASB

not run with *them*
into the same
excesses of dissipa-
tion, and they ma-
lign *you;* 5 but they
will give account
to Him who is
ready to judge the
living and the dead.
6 For the gospel has
for this purpose
been preached even
to those who are
dead, that though
they are judged in
the flesh as men,
they may live in
the spirit according
to *the will of* God.
7 The end of all
things is near;
therefore, be of
sound judgment
and sober *spirit*
for the purpose
of prayer. 8 Above
all, keep fervent in
your love for one
another, because
love covers a
multitude of sins.
9 Be hospitable
to one another
without complaint.
10 As each one has
received a *special*
gift, employ it in
serving one another
as good stewards
of the manifold
grace of God.
11 Whoever speaks,
is to do so as one
who is speaking
the utterances of
God; whoever
serves *is to do so*
as one who is serv-
ing by the strength
which God sup-
plies; so that in all
things God may be
glorified through
Jesus Christ, to
whom belongs the
glory and dominion
forever and ever.
Amen.

Share the Sufferings of Christ

12 Beloved, do not
be surprised at the
fiery ordeal among
you, which comes
upon you for your
testing, as though
some strange thing
were happening

NIV

to you. 13 But rejoice inasmuch as you participate in the sufferings of Christ, so that you may be overjoyed when his glory is revealed. 14 If you are insulted because of the name of Christ, you are blessed, for the Spirit of glory and of God rests on you. 15 If you suffer, it should not be as a murderer or thief or any other kind of criminal, or even as a meddler. 16 However, if you suffer as a Christian, do not be ashamed, but praise God that you bear that name. 17 For it is time for judgment to begin with God's household; and if it begins with us, what will the outcome be for those who do not obey the gospel of God? 18 And,

"If it is hard
for the righteous
to be saved,
what will
become of
the ungodly
and the
sinner?"[a]

19 So then, those who suffer according to God's will should commit themselves to their faithful Creator and continue to do good.

To the Elders and the Flock

5 To the elders among you, I appeal as a fellow elder and a witness of Christ's sufferings who also will share in the glory

[a] 18 Prov. 11:31 (see Septuagint)

ὑμῖν συμβαίνοντος, 13 ἀλλὰ καθὸ κοινωνεῖτε τοῖς τοῦ Χριστοῦ
to you. *were happening* But rejoice ⌊insofar as⌋ you now share the sufferings of Christ,
7007 5201 247 5897 2771 3125 3836 4077 3836 5986
r.dp.2 pt.pa.gsn cj cj v.pai.2p d.dpn d.gsm n.gsm

παθήμασιν χαίρετε, ἵνα καὶ ἐν τῇ ἀποκαλύψει τῆς δόξης αὐτοῦ →
sufferings *rejoice* so that *also* when *{the}* his glory is revealed, *{the}* *glory* *his* you
4077 5897 2671 2779 1877 3836 899 1518 637 3836 1518 899
n.dpn v.pam.2p cj adv p.d d.dsf n.dsf d.gsf n.gsf r.gsm.3

→ χαρῆτε ἀγαλλιώμενοι. 14 εἰ ὀνειδίζεσθε ἐν ὀνόματι Χριστοῦ,
may also rejoice and be glad. If you are insulted for the name of Christ, you
2779 5897 22 1623 3943 1877 3950 5986
v.aps.2p pt.pm.npm cj v.ppi.2p p.d n.dsn n.gsm

μακάριοι, ὅτι τὸ τῆς δόξης καὶ τὸ τοῦ θεοῦ πνεῦμα
are blessed, because the Spirit of glory, ⌊that is,⌋ the Spirit of God, *Spirit* is resting
3421 4022 3836 3836 1518 2779 3836 4460 3836 2536 4460 399 399
a.npm cj d.nsn d.gsf n.gsf cj d.nsn d.gsm n.gsm n.nsn

ἐφ᾽ ὑμᾶς ἀναπαύεται.[a] 15 μὴ γάρ τις ὑμῶν πασχέτω ὡς φονεὺς ἢ
on you. *is resting* But not *But* one of you should suffer as a murderer or a
2093 7007 399 1142 3590 1142 5516 7007 4248 6055 5838 2445
p.a r.ap.2 v.pmi.3s pl cj r.nsm r.gp.2 v.pam.3s pl n.nsm cj

κλέπτης ἢ κακοποιὸς ἢ ὡς ἀλλοτριεπίσκοπος· 16 εἰ δὲ
thief or a criminal or as a ⌊meddler in the affairs of another;⌋ but if *but*
3095 2445 2804 2445 6055 258 1254 1623 1254
n.nsm cj n.nsm cj pl n.nsm cj cj

ὡς Χριστιανός, ↱ ↱ μὴ αἰσχυνέσθω, δοξαζέτω δὲ τὸν
someone suffers as a Christian, he should not be disgraced, but should glorify *but* *{the}*
6055 5985 159 159 3590 159 1254 1519 1254 3836
pl n.nsm pl v.pmm.3s v.pam.3s cj d.asm

θεὸν ἐν τῷ ὀνόματι τούτῳ. 17 ὅτι ὁ[b] καιρὸς τοῦ ἄρξασθαι τὸ
God by *{the}* this name. *this* Because the time has come ~ to begin *{the}*
2536 1877 3836 4047 3950 4047 4022 3836 2789 3836 806 3836
n.asm p.d d.dsn n.dsn r.dsn cj d.nsm n.nsm d.gsn f.am d.asn

κρίμα ἀπὸ τοῦ οἴκου τοῦ θεοῦ· εἰ δὲ πρῶτον ἀφ᾽ ἡμῶν, τί τὸ
judgment with the house of God, and if *and* first with us, what will be the
3210 608 3836 3875 3836 2536 1254 1623 1254 4754 608 7005 5515 3836
n.asn p.g d.gsm n.gsm d.gsm n.gsm cj cj adv p.g r.gp.1 r.nsn d.nsn

τέλος τῶν ἀπειθούντων τῷ τοῦ θεοῦ εὐαγγελίῳ; 18 καὶ εἰ ὁ
outcome for those who do not obey the gospel of God? *gospel* And "If the
5465 3836 578 3836 2295 3836 2536 2295 2779 1623 3836
n.nsn d.gpm pt.pa.gpm d.dsn d.gsm n.gsm n.dsn cj cj d.nsm

δίκαιος ↱ μόλις σῴζεται, ὁ ἀσεβὴς καὶ ἁμαρτωλὸς
⌊righteous person⌋ is barely saved, what will become of the ungodly and the sinner?"
1465 5392 3660 5392 4543 5743 5743 3836 815 2779 283
a.nsm adv v.ppi.3s d.nsm a.nsm cj a.nsm

ποῦ φανεῖται; 19 ὥστε καὶ οἱ πάσχοντες κατὰ τὸ θέλημα τοῦ
what will become So then, let those who are suffering ⌊according to⌋ the will of
4543 5743 6063 2779 4192 3836 4248 2848 3836 2525 3836
cj v.fmi.3s cj adv d.npm pt.pa.npm p.a d.asn n.asn d.gsm

θεοῦ → πιστῷ κτίστῃ παρατιθέσθωσαν τὰς ψυχὰς
God by doing good entrust their souls to a faithful Creator. *let entrust* *{the}* *souls*
2536 1877 17 17 4192 899 6034 4412 3234 4192 3836 6034
n.gsm a.dsm n.dsm v.pmm.3p d.apf n.apf

αὐτῶν ἐν ἀγαθοποιίᾳ.
their *by* *doing good*
899 1877 17
r.gpm.3 p.d n.dsf

5:1 πρεσβυτέρους οὖν ἐν ὑμῖν παρακαλῶ ← ὁ συμπρεσβύτερος καὶ
elders Therefore *among* *you* *exhort* I, a fellow elder and a
4565 4036 1877 7007 4151 3836 5236 2779
a.apm cj p.d r.dp.2 v.pai.1s d.nsm n.nsm cj

μάρτυς τῶν τοῦ Χριστοῦ παθημάτων, ὁ καὶ τῆς
witness of the sufferings of Christ, *sufferings* and a *and* partaker of the glory that
3459 3836 4077 3836 5986 4077 2779 3836 2779 3128 1518 1518 3836
n.nsm d.gpn d.gsm n.gsm n.gpn d.nsm adv d.gsf

[a] κατὰ μὲν αὐτοὺς βλασφημεῖται, κατὰ δὲ ὑμᾶς δοξάζεται included by TR after ἀναπαύεται.
[b] [ὁ] UBS.

NASB

to you; 13 but to the degree that you share the sufferings of Christ, keep on rejoicing, so that also at the revelation of His glory you may rejoice with exultation. 14 If you are reviled for the name of Christ, you are blessed, because the Spirit of glory and of God rests on you. 15 Make sure that none of you suffers as a murderer, or thief, or evildoer, or a troublesome meddler; 16 but if *anyone suffers* as a Christian, he is not to be ashamed, but is to glorify God in this name. 17 For *it is* time for judgment to begin with the household of God; and if *it begins* with us first, what *will be* the outcome for those who do not obey the gospel of God? 18 AND IF IT IS WITH DIFFICULTY THAT THE RIGHTEOUS IS SAVED, WHAT WILL BECOME OF THE GODLESS MAN AND THE SINNER? 19 Therefore, those also who suffer according to the will of God shall entrust their souls to a faithful Creator in doing what is right.

Serve God Willingly

5:1 Therefore, I exhort the elders among you, as *your* fellow elder and witness of the sufferings of Christ, and a partaker also of the glory that

NIV

to be revealed: 2Be
shepherds of God's
flock that is under
your care, watch-
ing over them—
not because you
must, but because
you are willing, as
God wants you to
be; not pursuing
dishonest gain,
but eager to serve;
3not lording it over
those entrusted
to you, but being
examples to the
flock. 4And when
the Chief Shepherd
appears, you will
receive the crown
of glory that will
never fade away.
5In the same
way, you who are
younger, submit
yourselves to your
elders. All of you,
clothe yourselves
with humility to-
ward one another,
because,

> "God opposes the
> proud
> but shows
> favor to the
> humble."[a]

6Humble your-
selves, therefore,
under God's
mighty hand, that
he may lift you up
in due time. 7Cast
all your anxiety
on him because he
cares for you.
8Be alert and of
sober mind. Your
enemy the dev-
il prowls around
like a roaring lion
looking for some-
one to devour. 9Re-
sist him, standing
firm in the faith,
because you know
that the family of
believers

[a] 5 Prov. 3:34

μελλούσης ἀποκαλύπτεσθαι δόξης κοινωνός· 2ποιμάνατε
is about to be revealed, *of glory* *partaker* exhort the elders among you: shepherd
3516 636 1518 3128 4151 4565 1877 7007 4477
pt.pa.gsf f.pp n.gsf n.nsm v.aam.2p

τὸ ἐν ὑμῖν ποίμνιον τοῦ θεοῦ ἐπισκοποῦντες[a] μὴ
the flock of God among you, *flock* *of* *God* watching over it — not
3836 4480 3836 2536 1877 7007 4480 3836 2536 2174 3590
d.asn p.d r.dp.2 n.asn d.gsm n.gsm pt.pa.npm pl

ἀναγκαστῶς ἀλλὰ ἑκουσίως κατὰ θεόν, μηδὲ αἰσχροκερδῶς ἀλλὰ
⌊because you have to,⌋ but voluntarily, as God would have it; not for shameful gain but
339 247 1731 2848 2536 3593 154 247
adv cj adv p.a n.asm cj adv cj

προθύμως, 3→ μηδ᾽ ὡς κατακυριεύοντες τῶν κλήρων ἀλλὰ
eagerly. Do not *{as}* domineer ⌊over those⌋ ⌊entrusted to your charge,⌋ but be
4610 2894 3593 6055 2894 3836 3102 247 1181
adv cj pl pt.pa.npm d.gpm n.gpm cj

τύποι γινόμενοι τοῦ ποιμνίου· 4καὶ → φανερωθέντος τοῦ
examples *be* to the flock. Then when the Chief Shepherd appears, *the*
5596 1181 3836 4480 2779 3836 799 799 5746 3836
n.npm pt.pm.npm d.gsn n.gsn cj pt.ap.gsm d.gsm

ἀρχιποίμενος κομιεῖσθε τὸν ἀμαράντινον τῆς δόξης στέφανον.
Chief Shepherd you will receive the glorious crown that will not tarnish. *{the}* *glorious* *crown*
799 3152 3836 1518 5109 277 3836 1518 5109
n.gsm v.fmi.2p d.asm a.asm d.gsf n.gsf n.asm

5ὁμοίως, νεώτεροι, ὑποτάγητε → πρεσβυτέροις· πάντες δὲ
Likewise, ⌊you who are younger,⌋ be subject to the elders. And all *And* of you,
3931 3742 5718 4565 1254 4246 1254
adv a.vpm.c v.apm.2p a.dpm a.vpm cj

ἀλλήλοις[b] τὴν ταπεινοφροσύνην ἐγκομβώσασθε, ὅτι
clothe yourselves with humility toward one another, *with* *humility* *clothe yourselves* for
1599 1599 3836 5425 253 3836 5425 1599 4022
r.dpm d.asf n.asf v.amm.2p cj

ὁ[c] θεὸς ὑπερηφάνοις ἀντιτάσσεται, → ταπεινοῖς δὲ
{the} "God opposes the proud *opposes* but gives grace to the humble." *but*
3836 2536 530 5662 530 1254 1443 5921 5424 1254
d.nsm n.nsm a.dpm v.pmi.3s a.dpm cj

δίδωσιν χάριν. 6ταπεινώθητε οὖν ὑπὸ τὴν κραταιὰν χεῖρα τοῦ θεοῦ, ἵνα
gives *grace* Humble yourselves *{then}* under the mighty hand of God that he
1443 5921 5427 4036 5679 3836 3193 5931 3836 2536 2671 5738
v.pai.3s n.asf v.apm.2p cj p.a d.asf a.asf n.asf d.gsm n.gsm cj

ὑμᾶς ὑψώσῃ ἐν καιρῷ, 7 πᾶσαν τὴν μέριμναν ὑμῶν
may exalt you *he may exalt* in due time, casting all *{the}* your anxieties *your*
5738 5738 7007 5738 1877 2789 2166 4246 3836 7007 3533 7007
r.ap.2 v.aas.3s p.d n.dsm a.asf d.asf n.asf r.gp.2

ἐπιρίψαντες ἐπ᾽ αὐτόν, ὅτι αὐτῷ μέλει περὶ ὑμῶν. 8νήψατε, γρηγορήσατε.
casting on him, because he cares about you. Be sober-minded! Be alert!
2166 2093 899 4022 899 3508 4309 7007 3768 1213
pt.aa.npm p.a r.asm.3 cj r.dsm.3 v.pai.3s p.g r.gp.2 v.aam.2p v.aam.2p

ὁ ἀντίδικος ὑμῶν διάβολος ὡς λέων ὠρυόμενος
the Your adversary *Your* the devil prowls around like a roaring lion *roaring*
3836 7007 508 7007 3836 1333 4344 4344 6055 6054 3329 6054
d.nsm n.nsm r.gp.2 n.nsm pl n.nsm pt.pm.nsm

περιπατεῖ ζητῶν τινα[d] καταπιεῖν· 9 ᾧ ἀντίστητε στερεοὶ τῇ πίστει
prowls around seeking someone to devour. Resist him, *Resist* steadfast ⌊in the⌋ faith,
4344 2426 5516 2927 468 4005 468 5104 3836 4411
v.pai.3s pt.pa.nsm r.asm f.aa r.dsm v.aam.2p a.npm d.dsf n.dsf

εἰδότες τὰ αὐτὰ τῶν παθημάτων τῇ
knowing that the ⌊same kind⌋ of sufferings are being endured by your fellow believers
3857 3836 899 3836 4077 2200 2200 2200 3836 7007 82 82
pt.ra.npm d.apn r.apn d.gpn n.gpn d.dsf

NASB

is to be revealed,
2shepherd the flock
of God among
you, exercising
oversight not
under compulsion,
but voluntarily,
according to *the*
will of God; and
not for sordid gain,
but with eagerness;
3nor yet as lording
it over those allot-
ted to your charge,
but proving to be
examples to the
flock. 4And when
the Chief Shepherd
appears, you will
receive the unfad-
ing crown of glory.
5You younger men,
likewise, be subject
to *your* elders; and
all of you, clothe
yourselves with
humility toward
one another, for
GOD IS OPPOSED
TO THE PROUD, BUT
GIVES GRACE TO THE
HUMBLE.
6Therefore
humble yourselves
under the mighty
hand of God, that
He may exalt you
at the proper time,
7casting all your
anxiety on Him,
because He cares
for you. 8Be of
sober *spirit,* be on
the alert. Your ad-
versary, the devil,
prowls around
like a roaring lion,
seeking someone to
devour. 9But resist
him, firm in *your*
faith, knowing that
the same experi-
ences of suffering
are being accom-
plished by your
brethren who are

[a] [ἐπισκοποῦντες] UBS.
[b] ὑποτασσόμενοι included by TR after ἀλλήλοις.
[c] [ὁ] UBS.
[d] [τινα] UBS.

NIV

throughout the
world is undergo-
ing the same kind
of sufferings.
10 And the God
of all grace, who
called you to his
eternal glory in
Christ, after you
have suffered a
little while, will
himself restore
you and make you
strong, firm and
steadfast. 11 To
him be the power
for ever and ever.
Amen.

Final Greetings

12 With the help
of Silas,[a] whom I
regard as a faith-
ful brother, I have
written to you
briefly, encour-
aging you and
testifying that this
is the true grace
of God. Stand fast
in it.
13 She who is in
Babylon, chosen
together with you,
sends you her
greetings, and so
does my son Mark.
14 Greet one anoth-
er with a kiss of
love.
Peace to all of
you who are in
Christ.

ἐν τῷ[a] κόσμῳ ὑμῶν ἀδελφότητι ἐπιτελεῖσθαι. 10 ὁ δὲ θεὸς πάσης
throughout the world. *your* *fellow believers* *are being endured* And the *And* God of all
1877 3836 3180 7007 82 2200 1254 3836 1254 2536 4246
p.d d.dsm n.dsm r.gp.2 n.dsf f.pp d.nsm cj n.nsm a.gsf

χάριτος, ὁ καλέσας ὑμᾶς εἰς τὴν αἰώνιον αὐτοῦ δόξαν ἐν Χριστῷ,[b]
grace, the ⌞one who has called⌟ you into *{the}* his eternal *his* glory in Christ,
5921 3836 2813 7007 1650 3836 899 173 899 1518 1877 5986
n.gsf d.nsm pt.aa.nsm r.ap.2 p.a d.asf a.asf r.gsm.3 n.asf p.d n.dsm

↱ ὀλίγον παθόντας αὐτὸς καταρτίσει, στηρίξει,
will, after you have suffered a little while, *after you have suffered* himself restore, confirm,
2936 4248 4248 4248 4248 3900 4248 899 2936 5114
adv pt.aa.apm r.nsm v.fai.3s v.fai.3s

σθενώσει, θεμελιώσει. 11 αὐτῷ τὸ κράτος εἰς τοὺς αἰῶνας, ἀμήν.
strengthen, and establish you. To him be *{the}* power for all time. Amen.
4964 2530 899 3836 3197 1650 3836 172 297
v.fai.3s v.fai.3s r.dsm.3 d.nsn n.nsn p.a d.apm n.apm pl

12 διὰ Σιλουανοῦ ὑμῖν τοῦ πιστοῦ ἀδελφοῦ, ὡς λογίζομαι,
By Silvanus, *to you* a faithful brother as I regard him, I have written
1328 4977 7007 3836 4412 81 6055 3357 1211 1211 1211
p.g n.gsm r.dp.2 d.gsm a.gsm n.gsm cj v.pmi.1s

⌞δι' ὀλίγων⌟ ἔγραψα παρακαλῶν καὶ ἐπιμαρτυρῶν ταύτην εἶναι
briefly *I have written* to you, exhorting and testifying that this is the
1328 3900 1211 7007 7007 4151 2779 2148 4047 1639
p.g a.gpn v.aai.1s pt.pa.nsm cj pt.pa.nsm r.asf f.pa

ἀληθῆ χάριν τοῦ θεοῦ εἰς ἣν στῆτε. 13 ἀσπάζεται ὑμᾶς ἡ ἐν
true grace of God. Stand fast in it. *Stand fast* *sends greetings* *you* She who is in
239 5921 3836 2536 2705 2705 1650 4005 2705 832 7007 3836 1877
a.asf n.asf d.gsm n.gsm p.a r.asf v.aam.2p v.pmi.3s r.ap.2 d.nsf p.d

Βαβυλῶνι συνεκλεκτὴ καὶ Μᾶρκος ὁ υἱός μου.
Babylon, ⌞chosen along with⌟ you, sends you greetings, as does Mark, *{the}* my son. *my*
956 5293 832 7007 832 2779 3453 3836 1609 5626 1609
n.dsf a.nsf cj n.nsm d.nsm n.nsm r.gs.1

14 ἀσπάσασθε ἀλλήλους ἐν φιλήματι ἀγάπης. εἰρήνη → ὑμῖν πᾶσιν
Greet one another with the kiss of love. Peace be with all of you *all*
832 253 1877 5799 27 1645 4246 7007 4246
v.amm.2p r.apm p.d n.dsn n.gsf n.nsf r.dp.2 a.dpm

τοῖς ἐν Χριστῷ.
who are in Christ.
3836 1877 5986
d.dpm p.d n.dsm

NASB

in the world.
10 After you have
suffered for a
little while, the
God of all grace,
who called you
to His eternal
glory in Christ, will
Himself perfect,
confirm, strengthen
and establish
you. 11 To Him *be*
dominion forever
and ever. Amen.
12 Through Sil-
vanus, our faithful
brother (for so I
regard *him*), I have
written to you
briefly, exhort-
ing and testifying
that this is the
true grace of God.
Stand firm in it!
13 She who is in
Babylon, chosen
together with you,
sends you greet-
ings, and *so does*
my son, Mark.
14 Greet one another
with a kiss of love.
Peace be to you
all who are in
Christ.

[a] 12 Greek *Silvanus*, a variant of *Silas*

[a] [τῷ] UBS.
[b] Ἰησοῦ included by UBS after Χριστῷ.

2 Peter

NIV

1 Simon Peter,
a servant and
apostle of Jesus
Christ,
To those who
through the righ-
teousness of our
God and Savior
Jesus Christ have
received a faith as
precious as ours:
2 Grace and peace
be yours in abun-
dance through the
knowledge of God
and of Jesus our
Lord.

Confirming One's Calling and Election

3 His divine pow-
er has given us
everything we
need for a godly
life through our
knowledge of him
who called us
by his own glo-
ry and goodness.
4 Through these he
has given us his
very great and pre-
cious promises, so
that through them
you may partici-
pate in the divine
nature, having es-
caped the corrup-
tion in the world
caused by evil
desires.
5 For this very
reason, make ev-
ery effort to add
to your faith good-
ness; and to good-
ness, knowledge;
6 and to knowledge,
self-control; and
to self-control,
perseverance; and
to perseverance,
godliness; 7 and to
godliness, mutual
affection; and to

1:1 Συμεὼν Πέτρος δοῦλος καὶ ἀπόστολος Ἰησοῦ Χριστοῦ τοῖς ἰσότιμον
Simon Peter, a servant and apostle of Jesus Christ, to those *equal privilege*
5208 4377 1529 2779 693 2652 5986 3836 2700
n.nsm n.nsm n.nsm cj n.nsm n.gsm n.gsm d.dpm a.asf

ἡμῖν λαχοῦσιν πίστιν ἐν δικαιοσύνῃ τοῦ θεοῦ ἡμῶν καὶ
with ours who have received a faith that through the justice of our God *our* and
7005 3275 4411 1877 1466 3836 7005 2536 7005 2779
r.dp.1 pt.aa.dpm n.asf p.d n.dsf d.gsm n.gsm r.gp.1 cj

σωτῆρος Ἰησοῦ Χριστοῦ, 2 ↱ χάρις ↱ ὑμῖν
Savior Jesus Christ is of equal privilege with ours: May grace and peace be yours
5400 2652 5986 2700 2700 7005 7005 4437 5921 2779 1645 4437 7007
n.gsm n.gsm n.gsm n.nsf r.dp.2

καὶ εἰρήνη πληθυνθείη ἐν ἐπιγνώσει τοῦ θεοῦ καὶ Ἰησοῦ τοῦ
and *peace* ⌞in ever increasing measure⌟ through knowledge of God and of Jesus {the} our
2779 1645 4437 1877 2106 3836 2536 2779 2652 3836 7005
cj n.nsf v.apo.3s p.d n.dsf d.gsm n.gsm cj n.gsm d.gsm

κυρίου ἡμῶν. 3 ὡς πάντα ἡμῖν τῆς θείας
Lord. *our* {as} His divine power has freely given to us everything *to us* {the} *divine*
3261 7005 6055 899 2521 1539 1563 1563 1563 7005 7005 4246 7005 3836 2521
n.gsm r.gp.1 pl a.apn r.dp.1 d.gsf a.gsf

δυνάμεως αὐτοῦ τὰ πρὸς ζωὴν καὶ εὐσέβειαν δεδωρημένης διὰ τῆς
power *His* we need {the} for a life of godliness, *has freely given* through the
1539 899 3836 4639 2437 2779 2354 1563 1328 3836
n.gsf r.gsm.3 d.apn p.a n.asf cj n.asf pt.rm.gsf p.g d.gsf

ἐπιγνώσεως τοῦ καλέσαντος ἡμᾶς ἰδίᾳ δόξῃ καὶ ἀρετῇ, 4 δι' ὧν
knowledge of him who called us ⌞by his own⌟ glory and might, ⌞by means⌟ of which
2106 3836 2813 7005 2625 1518 2779 746 1328 4005
n.gsf d.gsm pt.aa.gsm r.ap.1 a.dsf n.dsf cj n.dsf p.g r.gpn

τὰ τίμια καὶ μέγιστα ἡμῖν ἐπαγγέλματα
he has freely given to us his precious and splendid *to us* promises,
1563 1563 1563 1563 7005 7005 3836 5508 2779 3492 7005 2041
d.apn a.apn cj a.apn.s r.dp.1 n.apn

δεδώρηται, ἵνα διὰ τούτων γένησθε θείας κοινωνοὶ φύσεως
he has freely given so that through them *you may become* *of divine* *partakers* *nature* you may
1563 2671 1328 4047 1181 2521 3128 5882 1181 1181
v.rmi.3s cj p.g r.gpn v.ams.2p a.gsf n.npm n.gsf

ἀποφυγόντες τῆς ἐν τῷ κόσμῳ ἐν ἐπιθυμίᾳ
escape the corruption that is in the world ⌞caused by⌟ sinful desire and become
709 3836 5785 1877 3836 3180 1877 2123 1181
pt.aa.npm d.gsf p.d d.dsm n.dsm p.d n.dsf

φθορᾶς. 5 καὶ ↱ αὐτὸ τοῦτο δὲ
partakers of the divine nature. *corruption* {also} For this very reason, {and} make every
3128 2521 2521 5882 5785 2779 4047 899 4047 1254 4210 4246
n.gsf adv r.asn r.asn cj

σπουδὴν πᾶσαν παρεισενέγκαντες ἐπιχορηγήσατε ἐν τῇ πίστει ὑμῶν
effort *every* *make* *to produce* by {the} your faith *your* to
5082 4246 4210 2220 1877 3836 7007 4411 7007 2220
n.asf a.asf pt.aa.npm v.aam.2p p.d d.dsf n.dsf r.gp.2

τὴν ἀρετήν, ἐν δὲ τῇ ἀρετῇ τὴν γνῶσιν, 6 ἐν δὲ τῇ γνώσει τὴν
produce {the} virtue, by {and} {the} virtue {the} knowledge, by {and} {the} knowledge {the}
2220 3836 746 1877 1254 3836 746 3836 1194 1877 1254 3836 1194 3836
d.asf n.asf p.d cj d.dsf n.dsf d.asf n.asf p.d cj d.dsf n.dsf d.asf

ἐγκράτειαν, ἐν δὲ τῇ ἐγκρατείᾳ τὴν ὑπομονήν, ἐν δὲ τῇ ὑπομονῇ τὴν
self-control, by {and} {the} self-control {the} steadfastness, by {and} {the} steadfastness {the}
1602 1877 1254 3836 1602 3836 5705 1877 1254 3836 5705 3836
n.asf p.d cj d.dsf n.dsf d.asf n.asf p.d cj d.dsf n.dsf d.asf

εὐσέβειαν, 7 ἐν δὲ τῇ εὐσεβείᾳ τὴν φιλαδελφίαν, ἐν δὲ τῇ
godliness, by {and} {the} godliness {the} brotherly affection, and by *and* {the}
2354 1877 1254 3836 2354 3836 5789 1254 1877 1254 3836
n.asf p.d cj d.dsf n.dsf d.asf n.asf p.d cj d.dsf

NASB

Growth in Christian Virtue

1:1 Simon Peter, a
bond-servant and
apostle of Jesus
Christ,
To those who
have received a
faith of the same
kind as ours, by the
righteousness of
our God and Sav-
ior, Jesus Christ:
2 Grace and peace
be multiplied to
you in the knowl-
edge of God and
of Jesus our Lord;
3 seeing that His
divine power has
granted to us ev-
erything pertaining
to life and godli-
ness, through the
true knowledge of
Him who called us
by His own glory
and excellence.
4 For by these He
has granted to us
His precious and
magnificent prom-
ises, so that by
them you may be-
come partakers of
the divine nature,
having escaped the
corruption that is in
the world by lust.
5 Now for this very
reason also, apply-
ing all diligence,
in your faith sup-
ply moral excel-
lence, and in *your*
moral excellence,
knowledge, 6 and in
your knowledge,
self-control, and in
your self-control,
perseverance, and
in *your* persever-
ance,

NIV

mutual affection, love. 8 For if you possess these qualities in increasing measure, they will keep you from being ineffective and unproductive in your knowledge of our Lord Jesus Christ. 9 But whoever does not have them is nearsighted and blind, forgetting that they have been cleansed from their past sins.

10 Therefore, my brothers and sisters,[a] make every effort to confirm your calling and election. For if you do these things, you will never stumble, 11 and you will receive a rich welcome into the eternal kingdom of our Lord and Savior Jesus Christ.

Prophecy of Scripture

12 So I will always remind you of these things, even though you know them and are firmly established in the truth you now have. 13 I think it is right to refresh your memory as long as I live in the tent of this body, 14 because I know that I will soon put it aside, as our Lord Jesus Christ has made clear to me. 15 And I will make every effort to see that after my departure you will always be able to remember these things.

φιλαδελφίᾳ τὴν ἀγάπην. 8 ταῦτα γὰρ ὑμῖν ὑπάρχοντα
brotherly affection *{the}* love. For if you possess these qualities *For* *you* *if possess*
5789 3836 27 1142 5639 7007 5639 4047 1142 7007 5639
n.dsf d.asf n.asf r.npn cj r.dp.2 pt.pa.npn

καὶ πλεονάζοντα ⌞οὐκ ἀργοὺς⌟ ⌞οὐδὲ ἀκάρπους⌟
{and} in increasing measure, they will make you effective and productive
2779 4429 2770 2770 2770 4024 734 4028 182
cj pt.pa.npn pl a.apm cj a.apm

καθίστησιν εἰς τὴν τοῦ κυρίου ἡμῶν Ἰησοῦ Χριστοῦ ἐπίγνωσιν·
they will make in your knowledge of our Lord *our* Jesus Christ. *knowledge*
2770 1650 3836 2106 3836 7005 3261 7005 2652 5986 2106
v.pai.3s p.a d.asf d.gsm n.gsm r.gp.1 n.gsm n.gsm n.asf

9 ᾧ γὰρ ➔ μὴ πάρεστιν ταῦτα, τυφλός ἐστιν μυωπάζων,
For the ⌞one who⌟ *For* does not have these qualities is blind; *is* he is nearsighted,
1142 4005 1142 4205 3590 4205 4047 1639 5603 1639 3697
r.dsm cj pl v.pai.3s r.npn a.nsm v.pai.3s pt.pa.nsm

λήθην λαβὼν τοῦ καθαρισμοῦ τῶν πάλαι αὐτοῦ ἁμαρτιῶν. 10 διὸ
having forgotten *having* that he was cleansed from his past *his* sins. Therefore,
3284 3330 3284 3836 2752 3836 899 4093 899 281 1475
n.asf pt.aa.nsm d.gsm n.gsm d.gpf adv r.gsm.3 n.gpf cj

μᾶλλον, ἀδελφοί, σπουδάσατε βεβαίαν ὑμῶν τὴν κλῆσιν καὶ ἐκλογὴν
my brothers, be all the more *brothers* eager to confirm your *{the}* call and election.
81 3437 81 5079 1010 7007 3836 3104 2779 1724
adv.c n.vpm v.aam.2p a.asf r.gp.2 d.asf n.asf cj n.asf

ποιεῖσθαι· ταῦτα γὰρ ποιοῦντες ➔ ➔ ⌞οὐ μὴ⌟ πταίσητέ ποτε.
{to make} For by doing these things *For* *by doing* you will never come to ruin. *{ever}*
4472 1142 4472 4472 4047 1142 4472 4760 4760 4024 3590 4760 4537
f.pm r.apn cj pt.pa.npm pl pl v.aas.2p adv

11 οὕτως γὰρ πλουσίως ἐπιχορηγηθήσεται ὑμῖν ἡ εἴσοδος εἰς τὴν αἰώνιον
For ⌞in this way⌟ *For* *richly* *will be provided* *for you* *{the}* entry into the eternal
1142 4048 1142 4455 2220 7007 3836 1658 1650 3836 173
adv cj adv v.fpi.3s r.dp.2 d.nsf n.nsf p.a d.asf a.asf

βασιλείαν τοῦ κυρίου ἡμῶν καὶ σωτῆρος Ἰησοῦ Χριστοῦ.
kingdom of our Lord *our* and Savior Jesus Christ will be richly provided
993 3836 7005 3261 7005 2779 5400 2652 5986 2220 2220 4455 2220
n.asf d.gsm n.gsm r.gp.1 cj n.gsm n.gsm n.gsm

12 διὸ μελλήσω ἀεὶ ὑμᾶς ὑπομιμνῄσκειν περὶ τούτων
for you. Therefore I intend ⌞to keep on⌟ reminding you *reminding* of these things,
7007 7007 1475 3516 107 5703 7007 5703 4309 4047
cj v.fai.1s adv r.ap.2 f.pa p.g r.gpn

καίπερ εἰδότας καὶ ἐστηριγμένους ἐν τῇ παρούσῃ ἀληθείᾳ.
even though you know them and are established in the truth ⌞that you now have.⌟ *truth*
2788 3857 2779 5114 1877 3836 237 4205 237
cj pt.ra.apm cj pt.rp.apm p.d d.dsf pt.pa.dsf n.dsf

13 δίκαιον δὲ ἡγοῦμαι, ἐφ᾽ ὅσον εἰμὶ ἐν τούτῳ
Indeed, I consider it the right thing *Indeed* *I consider* to do, as long as I am in this
1254 2451 2451 1465 1254 2451 2093 4012 1639 1877 4047
a.asn cj v.pmi.1s p.a r.asm v.pai.1s p.d r.dsn

τῷ σκηνώματι, διεγείρειν ὑμᾶς ἐν ὑπομνήσει, 14 εἰδὼς ὅτι
{the} body, to keep refreshing your *{in}* memory, ⌞since I know⌟ that my body
3836 5013 1444 7007 1877 5704 3857 4022 1609 5013
d.dsn n.dsn f.pa r.ap.2 p.d n.dsf pt.ra.nsm cj

➔ ταχινή ἐστιν ἡ ἀπόθεσις τοῦ σκηνώματός μου καθὼς καὶ ὁ κύριος
will soon be *{the}* put aside *{the}* *body* *my* as *{also}* *{the}* our Lord
1639 5442 1639 3836 629 3836 5013 1609 2777 2779 3836 7005 3261
a.nsf v.pai.3s d.nsf n.nsf d.gsn n.gsn r.gs.1 cj adv d.nsm n.nsm

ἡμῶν Ἰησοῦς Χριστὸς ἐδήλωσέν μοι, 15 ➔ ➔ σπουδάσω δὲ καὶ
our Jesus Christ made clear to me. And I will also do my best *And* *also* to see that
7005 2652 5986 1317 1609 1254 2779 5079 1254 2779
r.gp.1 n.nsm n.nsm v.aai.3s r.ds.1 v.fai.1s cj adv

➔ ἑκάστοτε ἔχειν ὑμᾶς μετὰ τὴν ἐμὴν ἔξοδον τὴν τούτων
you will always be able *you* to recall these things after *{the}* my decease. *{the}* *these things*
7007 2400 1668 2400 7007 3647 4047 4047 3552 3836 1847 2016 3836 4047
adv f.pa r.ap.2 p.a d.asf r.asf.1 n.asf d.asf r.gpn

NASB

godliness, 7 and in *your* godliness, brotherly kindness, and in *your* brotherly kindness, love. 8 For if these *qualities* are yours and are increasing, they render you neither useless nor unfruitful in the true knowledge of our Lord Jesus Christ. 9 For he who lacks these *qualities* is blind *or* short-sighted, having forgotten *his* purification from his former sins. 10 Therefore, brethren, be all the more diligent to make certain about His calling and choosing you; for as long as you practice these things, you will never stumble; 11 for in this way the entrance into the eternal kingdom of our Lord and Savior Jesus Christ will be abundantly supplied to you.

12 Therefore, I will always be ready to remind you of these things, even though you *already* know *them,* and have been established in the truth which is present with *you.* 13 I consider it right, as long as I am in this *earthly* dwelling, to stir you up by way of reminder, 14 knowing that the laying aside of my *earthly* dwelling is imminent, as also our Lord Jesus Christ has made clear to me. 15 And I will also be diligent that at any

[a] *10* The Greek word for *brothers and sisters* (*adelphoi*) refers here to believers, both men and women, as part of God's family.

NIV

16For we did not
follow cleverly de-
vised stories when
we told you about
the coming of our
Lord Jesus Christ
in power, but we
were eyewitnesses
of his majesty. 17He
received honor and
glory from God
the Father when
the voice came
to him from the
Majestic Glory,
saying, "This is my
Son, whom I love;
with him I am well
pleased."[a] 18We
ourselves heard
this voice that
came from heaven
when we were with
him on the sacred
mountain.
19We also have
the prophetic
message as some-
thing completely
reliable, and you
will do well to pay
attention to it, as
to a light shining
in a dark place, un-
til the day dawns
and the morning
star rises in your
hearts. 20Above
all, you must un-
derstand that no
prophecy of Scrip-
ture came about
by the prophet's
own interpreta-
tion of things.
21For prophecy
never had its ori-
gin in the human
will, but prophets,
though human,
spoke from God as
they were carried
along by the Holy
Spirit.

False Teachers and Their Destruction

2 But there were
also false
prophets among
the people, just as
there will

μνήμην ποιεῖσθαι. 16 οὐ γὰρ σεσοφισμένοις μύθοις
recall {to make} For we did not For follow cunningly crafted stories
3647 4472 1142 1979 1979 4024 1142 1979 5054 3680
n.asf f.pm pl cj pt.rp.dpm n.dpm

ἐξακολουθήσαντες ἐγνωρίσαμεν ὑμῖν τὴν τοῦ κυρίου ἡμῶν Ἰησοῦ
we did follow ⌞when we made known⌟ to you the coming of our Lord our Jesus
1979 1192 7007 3836 4242 3836 7005 3261 7005 2652
pt.aa.npm v.aai.1p r.dp.2 d.asf d.gsm n.gsm r.gp.1 n.gsm

Χριστοῦ δύναμιν καὶ παρουσίαν ἀλλ᾽ ἐπόπται γενηθέντες τῆς ἐκείνου
Christ in power, {and} coming but we were eyewitnesses we were of his
5986 1539 2779 4242 247 1181 1181 2228 1181 3836 1697
n.gsm n.asf cj n.asf cj n.npm pt.ap.npm d.gsf r.gsm

μεγαλειότητος. 17 λαβὼν γὰρ παρὰ θεοῦ πατρὸς τιμὴν καὶ
majesty. For he received For honor and glory from God the Father honor and
3484 1142 3284 1142 5507 2779 1518 4123 2536 4252 5507 2779
n.gsf pt.aa.nsm cj p.g n.gsm n.gsm n.asf cj

δόξαν ↱ φωνῆς ἐνεχθείσης αὐτῷ τοιᾶσδε ὑπὸ τῆς μεγαλοπρεποῦς δόξης,
glory when a voice borne to him {such} by the Majestic Glory
1518 5770 5889 5770 899 5524 5679 3836 3485 1518
n.asf n.gsf pt.ap.gsf r.dsm.3 r.gsf p.g d.gsf a.gsf n.gsf

ὁ υἱός μου ὁ ἀγαπητός μου οὗτός ἐστιν εἰς ὃν
proclaimed: "This is {the} my Son, my {the} my Beloved, my This is on whom
4047 1639 3836 1609 5626 1609 3836 1609 28 1609 4047 1639 1650 4005
d.nsm n.nsm r.gs.1 d.nsm a.nsm r.gs.1 r.nsm v.pai.3s p.a r.asm

ἐγὼ εὐδόκησα, 18 καὶ ταύτην τὴν φωνὴν ἡμεῖς ἠκούσαμεν
my favor rests." {and} We ourselves heard this {the} voice ourselves We heard borne
1609 2305 2779 201 7005 201 4047 3836 5889 7005 201 5770
r.ns.1 v.aai.1s cj r.asf d.asf n.asf r.np.1 v.aai.1p

ἐξ οὐρανοῦ ἐνεχθεῖσαν σὺν αὐτῷ ὄντες ἐν τῷ ἁγίῳ ὄρει.
from heaven, borne for we were with him for we were on the holy mountain.
1666 4041 5770 1639 1639 1639 5250 899 1639 1877 3836 41 4001
p.g n.gsm pt.ap.asf p.d r.dsm.3 pt.pa.npm p.d d.dsn a.dsn n.dsn

19 καὶ ἔχομεν βεβαιότερον τὸν προφητικὸν λόγον, ᾧ
Moreover, we hold the prophetic word to be reliable, the prophetic word and to it you
2779 2400 3836 4738 3364 1010 3836 4738 3364 4005 4472
cj v.pai.1p a.asm.c d.asm a.asm n.asm r.dsm

καλῶς ποιεῖτε προσέχοντες ὡς → λύχνῳ φαίνοντι ἐν
will do well you will do to pay attention to it as you would to a lamp shining in
4472 4472 2822 4472 4668 4005 4005 6055 3394 5743 1877
adv v.pai.2p pt.pa.npm pl n.dsm pt.pa.dsm p.d

αὐχμηρῷ τόπῳ, ⌞ἕως οὗ⌟ ἡμέρα διαυγάσῃ καὶ φωσφόρος ἀνατείλῃ ἐν ταῖς
a gloomy place, until the day dawns and the morning star arises in {the}
903 5536 2401 4005 2465 1419 2779 5892 422 1877 3836
a.dsm n.dsm p.g r.gsm n.nsf v.aas.3s cj n.nsm v.aas.3s p.d d.dpf

καρδίαις ὑμῶν, 20 τοῦτο πρῶτον γινώσκοντες ὅτι πᾶσα προφητεία
your hearts. your {this} Above all, you must understand that {each} no prophecy
7007 2840 7007 4047 4754 1182 4022 4246 4024 4735
n.dpf r.gp.2 r.asn adv pt.pa.npm cj a.nsf n.nsf

γραφῆς → ἰδίας ἐπιλύσεως οὐ γίνεται· 21 οὐ
of scripture arises from the prophet's own interpretation, no arises for prophecy never
1210 1181 2625 2146 4024 1181 1142 4735 4024
n.gsf a.gsf n.gsf pl v.pmi.3s pl

γὰρ → θελήματι ἀνθρώπου ἠνέχθη προφητεία ποτέ, ἀλλὰ
for had its origin in the will of man, had its origin prophecy {ever} but men
1142 5770 5770 5770 2525 476 5770 4735 4537 247 476
cj n.dsn n.gsm v.api.3s n.nsf adv cj

ὑπὸ πνεύματος ἁγίου φερόμενοι ἐλάλησαν ἀπὸ θεοῦ ἄνθρωποι.
borne along by the Holy Spirit Holy borne along spoke from God. men
5770 5770 5679 41 4460 41 5770 3281 608 2536 476
p.g n.gsn a.gsn pt.pp.npm v.aai.3p p.g n.gsm n.npm

2:1 ἐγένοντο δὲ καὶ ψευδοπροφῆται ἐν τῷ λαῷ, ὡς καὶ
But there were But also false prophets among the people, ⌞just as⌟ {also} there will
1254 1181 1254 2779 6021 1877 3836 3295 6055 2779 1639 1639
v.ami.3p cj adv n.npm p.d d.dsm n.dsm cj adv

NASB

time after my
departure you will
be able to call these
things to mind.

Eyewitnesses

16For we did not
follow cleverly
devised tales when
we made known
to you the power
and coming of our
Lord Jesus Christ,
but we were eye-
witnesses of His
majesty. 17For when
He received honor
and glory from
God the Father,
such an utterance
as this was made
to Him by the Ma-
jestic Glory, "This
is My beloved Son
with whom I am
well-pleased"—
18and we ourselves
heard this utterance
made from heaven
when we were with
Him on the holy
mountain.
19*So* we have the
prophetic word
made more sure, to
which you do well
to pay attention as
to a lamp shining
in a dark place,
until the day dawns
and the morning
star arises in your
hearts. 20But know
this first of all, that
no prophecy of
Scripture is *a mat-
ter* of one's own
interpretation, 21for
no prophecy was
ever made by an
act of human will,
but men moved
by the Holy Spirit
spoke from God.

The Rise of False Prophets

2:1But false proph-
ets also arose
among the people,
just as there will

[a] *17* Matt. 17:5; Mark 9:7; Luke 9:35

NIV

be false teachers
among you. They
will secretly intro-
duce destructive
heresies, even de-
nying the sovereign
Lord who bought
them — bringing
swift destruction
on themselves.
2 Many will fol-
low their depraved
conduct and will
bring the way of
truth into disrepute.
3 In their greed
these teachers will
exploit you with
fabricated stories.
Their condemna-
tion has long been
hanging over them,
and their destruc-
tion has not been
sleeping.
4 For if God did
not spare angels
when they sinned,
but sent them to
hell,[a] putting them
in chains of dark-
ness[b] to be held
for judgment; 5 if
he did not spare
the ancient world
when he brought
the flood on its un-
godly people, but
protected Noah, a
preacher of righ-
teousness, and
seven others; 6 if
he condemned the
cities of Sodom
and Gomorrah by
burning them to
ashes, and made
them an example
of what is going
to happen to the
ungodly; 7 and if
he rescued Lot,
a righteous man,
who was dis-
tressed by the
depraved conduct
of the lawless 8 (for
that

ἐν ὑμῖν ἔσονται ψευδοδιδάσκαλοι, οἵτινες παρεισάξουσιν
be false teachers among you, *there will be* *false teachers* who will bring in
1639 6015 6015 1877 7007 1639 6015 4015 4206
p.d r.dp.2 v.fmi.3p n.npm r.npm v.fai.3p

αἱρέσεις ἀπωλείας καὶ τὸν ἀγοράσαντα αὐτοὺς δεσπότην
destructive heresies, *destructive* even denying the Master who bought them, *Master*
724 146 724 2779 766 3836 1305 60 899 1305
n.apf n.gsf adv d.asm pt.aa.asm r.apm.3 n.asm

ἀρνούμενοι. ἐπάγοντες ἑαυτοῖς ταχινὴν ἀπώλειαν, 2 καὶ πολλοὶ ἐξακολουθήσουσιν
denying bringing on themselves swift destruction. *{and}* Many will follow
766 2042 1571 5442 724 2779 4498 1979
pt.pm.npm pt.pa.npm r.dpm.3 a.asf n.asf cj a.npm v.fai.3p

αὐτῶν ταῖς ἀσελγείαις δι' οὓς ἡ ὁδὸς τῆς ἀληθείας
their *{the}* immoral lifestyle, and ⌊because of⌋ them the way of truth
899 3836 816 1328 4005 3836 3847 3836 237
r.gpm.3 d.dpf n.dpf p.a r.apm d.nsf n.nsf d.gsf n.gsf

βλασφημηθήσεται, 3 καὶ ἐν πλεονεξίᾳ → πλαστοῖς
will be maligned. And in their greed they will exploit you with their fabricated
1059 2779 1877 4432 1864 1864 1864 7007 4422
v.fpi.3s cj p.d n.dsf a.dpm

λόγοις ὑμᾶς ἐμπορεύσονται, οἷς τὸ κρίμα ↱ ἔκπαλαι οὐκ
stories. *you* *they will exploit* Their *{the}* condemnation has not ⌊from ancient times⌋ *not*
3364 7007 1864 4005 3836 3210 733 4024 1732 4024
n.dpm r.ap.2 v.fmi.3p r.dpm d.nsn n.nsn adv pl

ἀργεῖ καὶ ἡ ↱ ἀπώλεια αὐτῶν οὐ νυστάζει. 4 εἰ γὰρ ὁ
been idle, *{and}* nor *{the}* has their destruction *their* *nor* been sleeping. For if *For* *{the}*
733 2779 4024 3836 3818 899 724 899 4024 3818 1142 1623 1142 3836
v.pai.3s cj d.nsf n.nsf r.gpm.3 pl v.pai.3s cj cj d.nsm

θεὸς ἀγγέλων ἁμαρτησάντων οὐκ ἐφείσατο ἀλλὰ
God did not spare the angels when they sinned *not* *did spare* but cast them into hell,
2536 5767 4024 5767 34 279 4024 5767 247 5434 5434 5434
n.nsm n.gpm pt.aa.gpm pl v.ami.3s cj

σειραῖς ζόφου ταρταρώσας παρέδωκεν εἰς
committing them to chains ⌊of utter darkness,⌋ *cast into hell* *committing* there to be kept until
4140 4937 2432 5434 4140 5498 5498 5498 1650
n.dpf n.gsm pt.aa.nsm v.aai.3s p.a

κρίσιν τηρουμένους, 5 καὶ ἀρχαίου κόσμου οὐκ ἐφείσατο
the judgment; *to be kept* and if he did not spare the ancient world *not* *he did spare*
3213 5498 2779 5767 5767 4024 5767 792 3180 4024 5767
n.asf pt.pp.apm cj a.gsm n.gsm pl v.ami.3s

ἀλλὰ ὄγδοον Νῶε δικαιοσύνης κήρυκα ἐφύλαξεν
(but preserved Noah, the eighth, *Noah* a herald of righteousness) *herald* *preserved* when he
247 5875 3820 3838 3820 3061 1466 3061 5875 2042 2042
cj a.asm n.asm n.gsf n.asm v.aai.3s

κατακλυσμὸν → κόσμῳ ἀσεβῶν ἐπάξας, 6 καὶ ↱ ↱
brought the deluge on an ungodly world; *ungodly* *when he brought* *{and}* if by
2042 2886 815 3180 815 2042 2779 5491 5491
n.asm n.dsm a.gpm pt.aa.nsm cj

↱ πόλεις Σοδόμων καὶ Γομόρρας τεφρώσας καταστροφῇ[a]
reducing the cities of Sodom and Gomorrah to ashes he condemned them to extinction,
5491 4484 5047 2779 1202 5491 2891 2891 2953
n.apf n.gpn cj n.gsf pt.aa.nsm n.dsf

κατέκρινεν ὑπόδειγμα μελλόντων → ἀσεβέσιν[b] τεθεικώς,
he condemned making them an example of ⌊what is going to happen⌋ to the ungodly, *making*
2891 5502 5682 3516 815 5502
v.aai.3s n.asn pt.pa.gpn a.dpm pt.ra.nsm

7 καὶ δίκαιον Λὼτ καταπονούμενον ὑπὸ τῆς τῶν
and rescued the ⌊righteous man⌋ Lot, who was distressed by the immoral lifestyle of
2779 4861 1465 3397 2930 5679 3836 816 419 3836
cj a.asm n.asm pt.pp.asm p.g d.gsf d.gpm

ἀθέσμων ἐν ἀσελγείᾳ ἀναστροφῆς ἐρρύσατο· 8 βλέμματι γὰρ καὶ ἀκοῇ ↱ ὁ
lawless men *{in}* *immoral* *lifestyle* *rescued* *saw* (for *and* *heard* while that
118 1877 816 419 4861 1062 1142 2779 198 1594 3836
a.gpm p.d n.dsf n.gsf v.ami.3s n.dsn cj cj n.dsf d.nsm

NASB

also be false teach-
ers among you,
who will secretly
introduce destruc-
tive heresies, even
denying the Master
who bought them,
bringing swift
destruction upon
themselves. 2 Many
will follow their
sensuality, and
because of them
the way of the truth
will be maligned;
3 and in *their* greed
they will exploit
you with false
words; their judg-
ment from long
ago is not idle, and
their destruction is
not asleep.
4 For if God did
not spare angels
when they sinned,
but cast them into
hell and commit-
ted them to pits of
darkness, reserved
for judgment; 5 and
did not spare the
ancient world, but
preserved Noah, a
preacher of righ-
teousness, with
seven others, when
He brought a flood
upon the world of
the ungodly; 6 and
if He condemned
the cities of Sodom
and Gomorrah
to destruction by
reducing *them* to
ashes, having made
them an example to
those who would
live ungodly *lives*
thereafter; 7 and
if He rescued
righteous Lot,
oppressed by the
sensual conduct

[a] 4 Greek *Tartarus*
[b] 4 Some manuscripts *in gloomy dungeons*

[a] [καταστροφῇ] UBS.
[b] ἀσεβέσιν TNIV, NET. ἀσεβέ[σ]ιν UBS.

NIV

righteous man, liv-
ing among them
day after day, was
tormented in his
righteous soul
by the lawless
deeds he saw and
heard)— 9 if this is
so, then the Lord
knows how to res-
cue the godly from
trials and to hold
the unrighteous for
punishment on the
day of judgment.
10 This is especially
true of those who
follow the corrupt
desire of the flesh[a]
and despise au-
thority.
Bold and arro-
gant, they are not
afraid to heap
abuse on celestial
beings; 11 yet even
angels, although
they are stronger
and more power-
ful, do not heap
abuse on such be-
ings when bring-
ing judgment on
them from[b] the
Lord. 12 But these
people blaspheme
in matters they do
not understand.
They are like un-
reasoning animals,
creatures of in-
stinct, born only
to be caught and
destroyed, and like
animals they too
will perish.
13 They will be
paid back with
harm for the harm
they have done.
Their idea of plea-
sure is to carouse
in broad daylight.
They are blots and
blemishes, revel-
ing in their plea-
sures while they

[a] 10 In contexts like this, the Greek word for *flesh* (*sarx*) refers to the sinful state of human beings, often presented as a power in opposition to the Spirit; also in verse 18.
[b] 11 Many manuscripts *beings in the presence of*

δίκαιος ἐγκατοικῶν ἐν αὐτοῖς ἡμέραν ἐξ ἡμέρας
⌞righteous man⌟ was living among them day after day, he was tormented in his
1465 1594 1877 899 2465 1666 2465 989 989 989
a.nsm pt.pa.nsm p.d r.dpm.3 n.asf p.g n.gsf

ψυχὴν δικαίαν → ἀνόμοις ἔργοις ἐβασάνιζεν·
righteous soul *righteous* by the lawless deeds *he was tormented* that he saw and heard);
1465 6034 1465 491 2240 989 1062 2779 198
n.asf a.asf a.dpn n.dpn v.iai.3s

9 οἶδεν κύριος εὐσεβεῖς ἐκ πειρασμοῦ ῥύεσθαι,
then the Lord knows *Lord* how to rescue the godly from trial, *to rescue* but
3261 3857 3261 4861 4861 2356 1666 4280 4861 1254
v.rai.3s n.nsm a.apm p.g n.gsm f.pm

ἀδίκους δὲ εἰς ἡμέραν κρίσεως
to keep the unrighteous *but* under guard awaiting punishment on the day of judgment,
5498 5498 96 1254 5498 5498 3134 3134 1650 2465 3213
a.apm cj p.a n.asf n.gsf

κολαζομένους τηρεῖν, 10 μάλιστα δὲ τοὺς ↱ ὀπίσω σαρκὸς ἐν
awaiting punishment *to keep under guard* especially *{and}* those who *{after}* *flesh* in polluting
3134 5498 3436 1254 3836 4513 3958 4922 1877 3622
pt.pp.apm f.pa adv.s cj d.apm p.g n.gsf p.d

ἐπιθυμίᾳ μιασμοῦ πορευομένους καὶ κυριότητος καταφρονοῦντας.
lust *polluting* indulge the flesh and despise authority. *despise*
2123 3622 4513 4922 2779 2969 3262 2969
n.dsf n.gsm pt.pm.apm cj n.gsf pt.pa.apm

τολμηταὶ αὐθάδεις, δόξας ↱ οὐ τρέμουσιν βλασφημοῦντες,
These bold and insolent people *glorious ones* are not afraid to slander the
5532 881 1518 5554 4024 5554 1059
n.npm a.npm n.apf pl v.pai.3p pt.pa.npm

11 ὅπου ἄγγελοι ἰσχύϊ καὶ δυνάμει μείζονες ὄντες
glorious ones, whereas angels, although greater in strength and power, *greater* *although*
1518 1518 3963 34 1639 3489 2709 2779 1539 3489 1639
cj n.npm n.dsf cj n.dsf a.npm.c pt.pa.npm

↱ οὐ φέρουσιν κατ᾽ αὐτῶν παρὰ κυρίου[a] βλάσφημον
do not bring a slanderous judgment against them before the Lord. *slanderous*
5770 4024 5770 1061 3213 2848 899 4123 3261 1061
pl v.pai.3p p.g r.gpm.3 p.g n.gsm a.asf

κρίσιν. 12 οὗτοι δὲ ὡς ἄλογα ζῷα γεγεννημένα φυσικὰ εἰς
judgment But these people, *But* like irrational animals, born ⌞creatures of instinct⌟ to be
3213 1254 4047 1254 6055 263 2442 1164 5879 1650
n.asf r.npm cj pl a.npn n.npn pt.rp.npn a.npn p.a

ἅλωσιν καὶ φθορὰν ἐν οἷς ἀγνοοῦσιν βλασφημοῦντες, ἐν τῇ
captured and destroyed, are ignorant of those *are ignorant* whom they slander, and in *{the}* their
274 2779 5785 51 51 1877 4005 51 1059 1877 3836 899
n.asf cj n.asf p.d r.dpn v.pai.3p pt.pa.npm p.d d.dsf

φθορᾷ αὐτῶν ↱ ↱ καὶ φθαρήσονται 13 ἀδικούμενοι → μισθὸν →
destruction *their* will themselves also be destroyed, suffering harm as the reward for the
5785 899 5780 5780 2779 5780 92 3635
n.dsf r.gpm.3 adv v.fpi.3p pt.pp.npm n.asm

ἀδικίας, ἡδονὴν ἡγούμενοι τὴν ἐν ἡμέρᾳ τρυφήν,
harm they have done. They consider indulgence *They consider* *{the}* in the daytime a pleasure.
94 2451 2451 2454 2451 3836 1877 2465 5588
n.gsf n.asf pt.pm.npm d.asf p.d n.dsf n.asf

σπίλοι καὶ μῶμοι ἐντρυφῶντες ἐν ταῖς ἀπάταις αὐτῶν
They are spots and blemishes, reveling in *{the}* their ⌞deceitful pleasures⌟ *their*
5070 2779 3700 1960 1877 3836 899 573 899
n.npm cj n.npm pt.pa.npm p.d d.dpf n.dpf r.gpm.3

συνευωχούμενοι ὑμῖν, 14 ὀφθαλμοὺς ἔχοντες μεστοὺς μοιχαλίδος καὶ
while they feast with you. They have eyes *They have* full of adultery *{and}*
5307 7007 2400 2400 4057 2400 3550 3655 2779
pt.pp.npm r.dp.2 n.apm pt.pa.npm a.apm n.gsf cj

ἀκαταπαύστους ἁμαρτίας, δελεάζοντες ψυχὰς ἀστηρίκτους, καρδίαν
that do not stop sinning. They seduce unstable souls *unstable* and have hearts
188 281 1284 844 6034 844 2400 2840
a.apm n.gsf pt.pa.npm n.apf a.apf n.asf

[a] κυρίου UBS, TNIV. κυρίῳ NET.

NASB

of unprincipled
men 8(for by what
he saw and heard
that righteous
man, while living
among them, felt
his righteous soul
tormented day after
day by *their* law-
less deeds), 9 *then*
the Lord knows
how to rescue the
godly from tempta-
tion, and to keep
the unrighteous
under punishment
for the day of
judgment, 10 and
especially those
who indulge the
flesh in *its* corrupt
desires and despise
authority.
Daring, self-
willed, they do not
tremble when they
revile angelic maj-
esties, 11 whereas
angels who are
greater in might
and power do not
bring a reviling
judgment against
them before the
Lord. 12 But these,
like unreasoning
animals, born as
creatures of instinct
to be captured and
killed, reviling
where they have
no knowledge, will
in the destruction
of those creatures
also be destroyed,
13 suffering wrong
as the wages of
doing wrong. They
count it a pleasure
to revel in the
daytime. They are
stains and blemish-
es, reveling in their
[a]deceptions, as they
carouse with you,
14 having eyes full
of adultery that

[a] One early ms reads *love feasts*

NIV

feast with you.[a]
14 With eyes full
of adultery, they
never stop sinning;
they seduce the
unstable; they are
experts in greed—
an accursed brood!
15 They have left
the straight way
and wandered off
to follow the way
of Balaam son of
Bezer,[b] who loved
the wages of wick-
edness. 16 But he
was rebuked for
his wrongdoing
by a donkey—an
animal without
speech—who
spoke with a hu-
man voice and re-
strained the proph-
et's madness.
17 These people are
springs without
water and mists
driven by a storm.
Blackest dark-
ness is reserved
for them. 18 For
they mouth empty,
boastful words and,
by appealing to
the lustful desires
of the flesh, they
entice people who
are just escaping
from those who
live in error. 19 They
promise them free-
dom, while they
themselves are
slaves of deprav-
ity—for "people
are slaves to what-
ever has mastered
them." 20 If they
have escaped the
corruption of the
world by know-
ing our Lord and
Savior Jesus Christ
and are again en-
tangled in it and
are overcome, they
are worse off at the
end than they were
at the beginning.
21 It would have
been better for
them not to have
known the way of
righteousness, than
to have known it

[a] 13 Some manuscripts *in their love feasts*
[b] 15 Greek *Bosor*

γεγυμνασμένην πλεονεξίας ἔχοντες, κατάρας τέκνα· 15 καταλείποντες εὐθεῖαν ὁδὸν
well trained in greed. *have* Accursed brood! Forsaking the right way,
1214 4432 2400 2932 5451 2901 2318 3847
pt.rp.asf n.gsf pt.pa.npm n.gsf n.npn pt.pa.npm a.asf n.asf

ἐπλανήθησαν, ἐξακολουθήσαντες τῇ ὁδῷ τοῦ Βαλαὰμ τοῦ Βοσόρ, ὃς
they have gone astray, following the way of Balaam, the son of Beor, who
4414 1979 3836 3847 3836 962 3836 1082 4005
v.api.3p pt.aa.npm d.dsf n.dsf d.gsm n.gsm d.gsm n.gsm r.nsm

μισθὸν ἀδικίας ἠγάπησεν 16 ἔλεγξιν δὲ ἔσχεν ἰδίας
loved the reward of wrongdoing. *loved* But he was rebuked *But* *he was* ⌊for his own⌋
26 3635 94 26 1254 2400 2400 1792 1254 2400 2625
n.asm n.gsf v.aai.3s n.asf cj v.aai.3s a.gsf

παρανομίας· ὑποζύγιον ἄφωνον ἐν → ἀνθρώπου φωνῇ
transgression — a dumb donkey, *dumb* speaking with the voice of a man, *voice*
4175 936 5689 936 5779 1877 5889 476 5889
n.gsf n.nsn a.nsn p.d n.gsm n.dsf

φθεγξάμενον ἐκώλυσεν τὴν τοῦ προφήτου παραφρονίαν. 17 οὗτοί
speaking restrained the madness of the prophet. *madness* ⌊These people⌋
5779 3266 3836 4197 3836 4737 4197 4047
pt.am.nsn v.aai.3s d.asf d.gsm n.gsm n.asf r.npm

εἰσιν πηγαὶ ἄνυδροι καὶ ὁμίχλαι ὑπὸ λαίλαπος ἐλαυνόμεναι, οἷς
are wells without water, *{and}* mists driven by a squall. *driven* ⌊For them⌋
1639 4380 536 2779 3920 1785 5679 3278 1785 4005
v.pai.3p n.npf a.npf cj n.npf p.g n.gsf pt.pp.npf r.dpm

ὁ ζόφος τοῦ σκότους τετήρηται. 18 ὑπέρογκα γὰρ
the gloom of darkness has been reserved. For by speaking pompous *For* words
3836 2432 3836 5030 5498 1142 5779 5779 5665 1142 5779
d.nsm n.nsm d.gsn n.gsn v.rpi.3s a.apn cj

ματαιότητος φθεγγόμενοι δελεάζουσιν ἐν ἐπιθυμίαις → σαρκὸς ἀσελγείαις
of vanity, *by speaking words* they entice, by lusts of the flesh and debauchery,
3470 5779 1284 1877 2123 4922 816
n.gsf pt.pm.npm v.pai.3p p.d n.dpf n.gsf n.dpf

τοὺς ὀλίγως ἀποφεύγοντας τοὺς ἐν πλάνῃ
those who are just escaping from those who are living in error.
3836 3903 709 3836 418 418 418 1877 4415
d.apm adv pt.pa.apm d.apm p.d n.dsf

ἀναστρεφομένους, 19 ἐλευθερίαν αὐτοῖς ἐπαγγελλόμενοι,
who are living They promise them freedom, *them* *They promise* but they
418 2040 2040 899 1800 899 2040
pt.pp.apm n.asf r.dpm.3 pt.pm.npm

αὐτοὶ δοῦλοι ὑπάρχοντες τῆς φθορᾶς· ᾧ γάρ τις ἥττηται,
themselves are slaves *are* of corruption; for ⌊by whatever⌋ *for* a man is overcome,
899 5639 1529 5639 3836 5785 1142 4005 1142 5516 2487
r.npm n.npm pt.pa.npm d.gsf n.gsf r.dsn cj r.nsm v.rpi.3s

τούτῳ δεδούλωται. 20 εἰ γὰρ ἀποφυγόντες τὰ μιάσματα τοῦ κόσμου
to this he is enslaved. For if *For* ⌊after they have escaped⌋ the defilements of the world
4047 1530 1142 1623 1142 709 3836 3621 3836 3180
r.dsn v.rpi.3s cj cj pt.aa.npm d.apn n.apn d.gsm n.gsm

ἐν ἐπιγνώσει τοῦ κυρίου ἡμῶν[a] καὶ σωτῆρος Ἰησοῦ Χριστοῦ, ↱ ↱
through the knowledge of our Lord *our* and Savior Jesus Christ, they are
1877 2106 3836 7005 3261 7005 2779 5400 2652 5986 2487 2487
p.d n.dsf d.gsm n.gsm r.gp.1 cj n.gsm n.gsm n.gsm

τούτοις δὲ πάλιν ἐμπλακέντες ἡττῶνται, γέγονεν
again entangled in them *{and}* *again* *entangled* and overcome, the last state has become
4099 1861 4047 1254 4099 1861 2487 3836 2274 1181
r.dpn cj adv pt.ap.npm v.ppi.3p v.rai.3s

αὐτοῖς τὰ ἔσχατα χείρονα τῶν πρώτων. 21 κρεῖττον γὰρ ἦν
for them *the* *last* worse ⌊than the⌋ first. *better* For ⌊it would have been⌋ better
899 3836 2274 5937 3836 4755 3202 1142 1639 3202
r.dpm.3 d.npn a.npn a.npn.c d.gpn a.gpn a.nsn.c cj v.iai.3s

αὐτοῖς μὴ ἐπεγνωκέναι τὴν ὁδὸν τῆς δικαιοσύνης ἢ ἐπιγνοῦσιν
for them never ⌊to have come to know⌋ the way of righteousness than, ⌊having come to know⌋ it,
899 3590 2105 3836 3847 3836 1466 2445 2105
r.dpm.3 pl f.ra d.asf n.asf d.gsf n.gsf pl pt.aa.dpm

[a] [ἡμῶν] UBS.

NASB

never cease from
sin, enticing un-
stable souls, having
a heart trained in
greed, accursed
children; 15 forsak-
ing the right way,
they have gone
astray, having
followed the way
of Balaam, the
son of Beor, who
loved the wages of
unrighteousness;
16 but he received
a rebuke for his
own transgres-
sion, *for* a mute
donkey, speaking
with a voice of a
man, restrained
the madness of the
prophet.
17 These are
springs without
water and mists
driven by a storm,
for whom the black
darkness has been
reserved. 18 For
speaking out ar-
rogant *words* of
vanity they entice
by fleshly desires,
by sensuality, those
who barely escape
from the ones
who live in error,
19 promising them
freedom while they
themselves are
slaves of corrup-
tion; for by what a
man is overcome,
by this he is en-
slaved. 20 For if,
after they have
escaped the defile-
ments of the world
by the knowledge
of the Lord and
Savior Jesus
Christ, they are
again entangled in
them and are over-
come, the last state
has become worse
for them than the
first. 21 For it would
be better for

NIV

and then to turn their backs on the sacred command that was passed on to them. [22]Of them the proverbs are true: "A dog returns to its vomit,"[a] and, "A sow that is washed returns to her wallowing in the mud."

The Day of the Lord

3 Dear friends, this is now my second letter to you. I have written both of them as reminders to stimulate you to wholesome thinking. [2]I want you to recall the words spoken in the past by the holy prophets and the command given by our Lord and Savior through your apostles.
[3]Above all, you must understand that in the last days scoffers will come, scoffing and following their own evil desires. [4]They will say, "Where is this 'coming' he promised? Ever since our ancestors died, everything goes on as it has since the beginning of creation." [5]But they deliberately forget that long ago by God's word the heavens came into being and the earth was formed out of water and by water. [6]By these waters also the world of that time

ὑποστρέψαι ἐκ τῆς παραδοθείσης αὐτοῖς ἁγίας ἐντολῆς.
to turn back from the holy commandment that was delivered to them. *holy commandment*
5715 1666 3836 41 1953 4140 899 41 1953
f.aa p.g d.gsf pt.ap.gsf r.dpm.3 a.gsf n.gsf

22 συμβέβηκεν αὐτοῖς τὸ τῆς ἀληθοῦς παροιμίας, κύων ἐπιστρέψας
What has happened to them illustrates the *{the}* true proverb: "A dog returns
5201 899 3836 3836 239 4231 3264 2188
v.rai.3s r.dpm.3 d.nsn d.gsf a.gsf n.gsf n.nsm pt.aa.nsm

ἐπὶ τὸ ἴδιον ἐξέραμα, καί, ὗς λουσαμένη εἰς κυλισμὸν →
to *{the}* its own vomit, and a sow, ⌊after washing herself,⌋ returns to wallow in the
2093 3836 2625 2000 2779 5725 3374 1650 3243
p.a d.asn a.asn n.asn cj n.nsf pt.am.nsf p.a n.asm

βορβόρου.
mire."
1079
n.gsm

3:1 ταύτην ἤδη, ἀγαπητοί, δευτέραν ὑμῖν
This, dear friends, is now *dear friends* the second letter I have written to you
4047 28 28 2453 28 1311 2186 1211 1211 1211 7007
r.asf adv a.vpm a.asf r.dp.2

γράφω ἐπιστολήν, ἐν αἷς διεγείρω ὑμῶν ἐν
I have written letter (in ⌊both of them⌋ ⌊I have been trying to arouse⌋ your pure minds with a
1211 2186 1877 4005 1444 7007 1637 1379 1877
v.pai.1s n.asf p.d r.dpf v.pai.1s r.gp.2 p.d

ὑπομνήσει τὴν εἰλικρινῆ διάνοιαν 2 μνησθῆναι τῶν προειρημένων ῥημάτων
reminder) *{the} pure minds* to remember the words spoken beforehand *words*
5704 3836 1637 1379 3630 3836 4839 4597 4839
n.dsf d.asf a.asf n.asf f.ap d.gpn pt.rp.gpn n.gpn

ὑπὸ τῶν ἁγίων προφητῶν καὶ τῆς τῶν ἀποστόλων ὑμῶν ἐντολῆς τοῦ κυρίου
by the holy prophets and the *through apostles your* commandment of the Lord
5679 3836 41 4737 2779 3836 3836 693 7007 1953 3836 3261
p.g d.gpm a.gpm n.gpm cj d.gsf d.gpm n.gpm r.gp.2 n.gsf d.gsm n.gsm

καὶ σωτῆρος, 3 τοῦτο πρῶτον γινώσκοντες ὅτι
and Savior spoken through your apostles. *{this}* Above all you must understand that in
2779 5400 3836 7007 693 4047 4754 1182 4022 2093
cj n.gsm r.asn adv pt.pa.npm cj

ἐλεύσονται ἐπ' ἐσχάτων τῶν ἡμερῶν ἐν[a] ἐμπαιγμονῇ ἐμπαῖκται
the last days scoffers will come *in last the days* with scoffing, *scoffers*
3836 2274 2465 1851 2262 2093 2274 3836 2465 1877 1848 1851
v.fmi.3p p.g a.gpf d.gpf n.gpf p.d n.dsf n.npm

κατὰ τὰς ἰδίας ἐπιθυμίας αὐτῶν πορευόμενοι 4 καὶ λέγοντες, ποῦ
following *{after} {the}* their own lusts *their following* and saying, "Where
4513 2848 3836 899 2625 2123 899 4513 2779 3306 4543
p.a d.apf a.apf n.apf r.gpm.3 pt.pm.npm cj pt.pa.npm cj

ἐστιν ἡ ἐπαγγελία τῆς παρουσίας αὐτοῦ; ἀφ' ἧς γὰρ οἱ πατέρες
is the promise of his coming? *his* For ever since *For* our fathers
1639 3836 2039 3836 899 4242 899 1142 608 4005 1142 3836 4252
v.pai.3s d.nsf n.nsf d.gsf n.gsf r.gsm.3 p.g r.gsf cj d.npm n.npm

ἐκοιμήθησαν, πάντα οὕτως διαμένει ἀπ' ἀρχῆς κτίσεως.
fell asleep, everything has gone along as it has *has gone along* from the beginning of creation."
3121 4246 1373 1373 1373 4048 1373 608 794 3232
v.api.3p a.npn adv v.pai.3s p.g n.gsf n.gsf

5 λανθάνει γὰρ αὐτοὺς τοῦτο θέλοντας ὅτι
For in maintaining this, they ⌊overlook the fact⌋ *For they this in maintaining* that by
1142 2527 2527 4047 899 3291 1142 899 4047 2527 4022 3836
v.pai.3s cj r.apm.3 r.nsn pt.pa.apm cj

οὐρανοὶ ἦσαν ἔκπαλαι καὶ γῆ ἐξ ὕδατος καὶ
the word of God heavens existed long ago and an earth was formed ⌊out of⌋ water and
3836 3364 3836 2536 4041 1639 1732 2779 1178 5319 5319 1666 5623 2779
n.npm v.iai.3p adv cj n.nsf p.g n.gsn cj

δι' ὕδατος συνεστῶσα τῷ τοῦ θεοῦ λόγῳ, 6 δι' ὧν ὁ τότε
⌊by means of⌋ water. *was formed by the of God word* By these the world ⌊of that time⌋
1328 5623 5319 3836 3836 2536 3364 1328 4005 3836 3180 5538
p.g n.gsn pt.ra.nsf d.dsm d.gsm n.gsm n.dsm p.g r.gpn d.nsm adv

NASB

them not to have known the way of righteousness, than having known it, to turn away from the holy commandment handed on to them. [22]It has happened to them according to the true proverb, "A DOG RETURNS TO ITS OWN VOMIT," and, "A sow, after washing, *returns* to wallowing in the mire."

Purpose of This Letter

[3:1]This is now, beloved, the second letter I am writing to you in which I am stirring up your sincere mind by way of reminder, [2]that you should remember the words spoken beforehand by the holy prophets and the commandment of the Lord and Savior *spoken* by your apostles.

The Coming Day of the Lord

[3]Know this first of all, that in the last days mockers will come with *their* mocking, following after their own lusts, [4]and saying, "Where is the promise of His coming? For *ever* since the fathers fell asleep, all continues just as it was from the beginning of creation." [5]For when they maintain this, it escapes their notice that by the word of God *the* heavens existed long ago and *the* earth was formed out of water and

[a] 22 Prov. 26:11

[a] [ἐν] UBS.

NIV

was deluged and
destroyed. [7]By
the same word the
present heavens
and earth are re-
served for fire, be-
ing kept for the day
of judgment and
destruction of the
ungodly.
[8]But do not for-
get this one thing,
dear friends: With
the Lord a day is
like a thousand
years, and a thou-
sand years are like
a day. [9]The Lord is
not slow in keep-
ing his promise, as
some understand
slowness. Instead
he is patient with
you, not wanting
anyone to perish,
but everyone to
come to repen-
tance.
[10]But the day of
the Lord will come
like a thief. The
heavens will dis-
appear with a roar;
the elements will
be destroyed by
fire, and the earth
and everything
done in it will be
laid bare.[a]
[11]Since every-
thing will be
destroyed in this
way, what kind of
people ought you
to be? You ought
to live holy and
godly lives [12]as
you look forward
to the day of God
and speed its com-
ing.[b] That day will
bring about the
destruction of the
heavens by fire,
and the elements
will melt in the
heat. [13]But in keep-
ing with his prom-
ise we are looking
forward to a new

[a] 10 Some manu-
scripts *be burned up*
[b] 12 Or *as you wait
eagerly for the day of
God to come*

κόσμος ὕδατι κατακλυσθεὶς ἀπώλετο· [7]
world was destroyed, being deluged with water. *being deluged* *was destroyed* But by the
3180 660 660 2885 2885 5623 2885 660 1254 3836 3836
n.nsm n.dsn pt.ap.nsm v.ami.3s

οἱ δὲ νῦν οὐρανοὶ καὶ ἡ γῆ τῷ αὐτῷ λόγῳ
same word the *But* present heavens and *{the}* earth *by the* *same* *word* have been
899 3364 3836 1254 3814 4041 2779 3836 1178 3836 899 3364 1639 1639
d.npm cj adv n.npm cj d.nsf n.nsf d.dsm r.dsm n.dsm

τεθησαυρισμένοι εἰσὶν πυρὶ τηρούμενοι εἰς ἡμέραν κρίσεως καὶ ἀπωλείας
reserved *have been* for fire, kept for the day of judgment and destruction
2564 1639 4786 5498 1650 2465 3213 2779 724
pt.rp.npm v.pai.3p n.dsn pt.pp.npm p.a n.asf n.gsf cj n.gsf

τῶν ἀσεβῶν ἀνθρώπων. [8]ἓν δὲ ↱ ↱ τοῦτο μὴ λανθανέτω
of ungodly men. *one thing* But do not let this one thing *not* escape
3836 815 476 1651 1254 3291 3590 3291 4047 1651 1651 3590 3291
d.gpm a.gpm n.gpm a.nsn cj r.nsn pl v.pam.3s

ὑμᾶς, ↰ ἀγαπητοί, ὅτι μία ἡμέρα παρὰ κυρίῳ ὡς χίλια ἔτη καὶ
your notice, dear friends, that one day with the Lord is as a thousand years and a
7007 3291 28 4022 1651 2465 4123 3261 6055 5943 2291 2779
r.ap.2 a.vpm cj a.nsf n.nsf p.d n.dsm pl a.npn n.npn cj

χίλια ἔτη ὡς ἡμέρα μία. [9] ↱ οὐ βραδύνει κύριος
thousand years are as a single day. *single* The Lord is not late *Lord* in fulfilling
5943 2291 6055 1651 2465 1651 3261 1094 4024 1094 3261
a.npn n.npn pl n.nsf a.nsf pl v.pai.3s n.nsm

τῆς ἐπαγγελίας, ὥς τινες βραδύτητα ἡγοῦνται, ἀλλὰ μακροθυμεῖ εἰς ὑμᾶς,
his promise, as some regard lateness, *regard* but is patient toward you,
3836 2039 6055 5516 2451 1097 2451 247 3428 1650 7007
d.gsf n.gsf cj r.npm n.asf v.pmi.3p cj v.pai.3s p.a r.ap.2

μὴ βουλόμενός τινας ἀπολέσθαι ἀλλὰ πάντας εἰς μετάνοιαν
not willing that anyone should perish, but that all should come to repentance.
3590 1089 5516 660 247 4246 6003 6003 1650 3567
pl pt.pp.nsm r.apm f.am cj a.apm p.a n.asf

χωρῆσαι. [10] ἥξει δὲ ἡμέρα → κυρίου ὡς κλέπτης, ἐν ᾗ
should come *will come* But the Day of the Lord will come like a thief, in which
6003 2457 1254 2465 3261 2457 2457 6055 3095 1877 4005
f.aa v.fai.3s cj n.nsf n.gsm pl n.nsm p.d r.dsf

οἱ οὐρανοὶ ῥοιζηδὸν παρελεύσονται στοιχεῖα δὲ
the heavens will pass away ⌞with a rushing noise,⌟ *will pass away* the elements *{and}* will
3836 4041 4216 4216 4216 4853 4216 5122 1254 3395
d.npm n.npm adv v.fmi.3p n.npn cj

καυσούμενα λυθήσεται καὶ γῆ καὶ τὰ ἐν αὐτῇ ἔργα
melt in the intense heat, *will melt* and the earth and the works in it *works*
3395 3012 3395 2779 1178 2779 3836 2240 1877 899 2240
pt.pp.npn v.fpi.3s cj n.nsf cj d.npn p.d r.dsf.3 n.npn

εὑρεθήσεται. [11] ↱ τούτων ↱ οὕτως πάντων λυομένων
will be exposed. Since all these things are thus *all* to be dissolved,
2351 3395 4246 4047 3395 4048 4246 3395
v.fpi.3s r.gpn adv a.gpn pt.pp.gpn

ποταποὺς δεῖ ὑπάρχειν ὑμᾶς[a] ἐν ἁγίαις ἀναστροφαῖς καὶ εὐσεβείαις,
⌞what kind of people⌟ ought you to be *you* in holy conduct and godliness,
4534 1256 7007 5639 7007 1877 41 419 2779 2354
r.apm v.pai.3s f.pa r.ap.2 p.d a.dpf n.dpf cj n.dpf

[12] προσδοκῶντας καὶ σπεύδοντας τὴν παρουσίαν τῆς τοῦ θεοῦ ἡμέρας
waiting for and hastening the coming of the day of God, *day*
4659 2779 5067 3836 4242 3836 2465 3836 2536 2465
pt.pa.apm cj pt.pa.apm d.asf n.asf d.gsf d.gsm n.gsm n.gsf

δι' ἣν οὐρανοὶ πυρούμενοι λυθήσονται καὶ στοιχεῖα
⌞because of⌟ which the heavens ⌞will be set on fire⌟ and dissolved, and the elements will melt
1328 4005 4041 4792 3395 2779 5122 5494 5494
p.a r.asf n.npm pt.pp.npm v.fpi.3p cj n.npn

καυσούμενα τήκεται. [13] καινοὺς δὲ
in the heat. *will melt* But according to his promise we are waiting for new *But*
3012 5494 1254 2848 2848 899 2041 4659 4659 4659 4659 2785 1254
pt.pp.npn v.ppi.3s a.apm cj

[a] [ὑμᾶς] UBS, omitted by NET.

NASB

by water, [6]through
which the world
at that time was
destroyed, being
flooded with water.
[7]But by His word
the present heavens
and earth are being
reserved for fire,
kept for the day
of judgment and
destruction of
ungodly men.
[8]But do not let
this one *fact* es-
cape your notice,
beloved, that with
the Lord one day
is like a thousand
years, and a thou-
sand years like one
day. [9]The Lord is
not slow about His
promise, as some
count slowness, but
is patient toward
you, not wishing
for any to perish
but for all to come
to repentance.

A New Heaven and Earth

[10]But the day of
the Lord will come
like a thief, in
which the heavens
will pass away
with a roar and the
elements will be
destroyed with in-
tense heat, and the
earth and its works
will be [a]burned up.
[11]Since all these
things are to be de-
stroyed in this way,
what sort of people
ought you to be in
holy conduct and
godliness, [12]looking
for and hastening
the coming of the
day of God, be-
cause of which the
heavens will be de-
stroyed by burning,
and the elements
will melt with

[a] Two early mss
read *discovered*

NIV

heaven and a new
earth, where righ-
teousness dwells.
14So then, dear
friends, since you
are looking for-
ward to this, make
every effort to be
found spotless,
blameless and at
peace with him.
15Bear in mind
that our Lord's
patience means
salvation, just as
our dear brother
Paul also wrote
you with the wis-
dom that God gave
him. 16He writes
the same way in
all his letters,
speaking in them
of these matters.
His letters contain
some things that
are hard to under-
stand, which igno-
rant and unstable
people distort, as
they do the other
Scriptures, to their
own destruction.
17Therefore, dear
friends, since you
have been fore-
warned, be on
your guard so that
you may not be
carried away by
the error of the
lawless and fall
from your secure
position. 18But
grow in the grace
and knowledge of
our Lord and Sav-
ior Jesus Christ.
To him be glory
both now and for-
ever! Amen.

οὐρανοὺς καὶ γῆν καινὴν κατὰ τὸ ἐπάγγελμα αὐτοῦ προσδοκῶμεν, ἐν
heavens and a new earth *new* *according to* *{the}* *promise* *his* *we are waiting for* in
4041 2779 2785 1178 2785 2848 3836 2041 899 4659 1877
n.apm cj n.asf a.asf p.a d.asn n.asn r.gsm.3 v.pai.1p p.d

οἷς δικαιοσύνη κατοικεῖ. 14 διό, ἀγαπητοί, ταῦτα
which righteousness will be at home. So then, dear friends, since you await these things,
4005 1466 2997 1475 28 4659 4659 4659 4047
r.dpm n.nsf v.pai.3s cj a.vpm r.apn

προσδοκῶντες σπουδάσατε ἄσπιλοι καὶ ἀμώμητοι αὐτῷ εὑρεθῆναι
since you await strive to be found without spot or blemish, *in him* *to be found*
4659 5079 2351 2351 2351 834 2779 318 899 2351
pt.pa.npm v.aam.2p a.npm cj a.npm r.dsm.3 f.ap

ἐν εἰρήνῃ 15 καὶ τὴν τοῦ κυρίου ἡμῶν μακροθυμίαν
at peace in him. And consider the patience of our Lord *our* *patience* as
1877 1645 899 899 2779 2451 3836 3429 3836 7005 3261 7005 3429
p.d n.dsf cj d.asf d.gsm n.gsm r.gp.1 n.asf

σωτηρίαν ἡγεῖσθε, καθὼς καὶ ὁ ἀγαπητὸς ἡμῶν ἀδελφὸς Παῦλος
salvation, *consider* just as also *{the}* our dear *our* brother Paul wrote to you
5401 2451 2777 2779 3836 7005 28 7005 81 4263 1211 7007 7007
n.asf v.pmm.2p cj adv d.nsm a.nsm r.gp.1 n.nsm n.nsm

κατὰ τὴν δοθεῖσαν αὐτῷ σοφίαν ἔγραψεν ὑμῖν, 16 ὡς καὶ ἐν
⌊according to⌋ the wisdom given to him, *wisdom* *wrote* *to you* as *{also}* he does in
2848 3836 5053 1443 899 5053 1211 7007 6055 2779 1877
p.a d.asf pt.ap.asf r.dsm.3 n.asf v.aai.3s r.dp.2 cj adv p.d

πάσαις ἐπιστολαῖς λαλῶν ἐν αὐταῖς περὶ τούτων, ἐν αἷς ἐστιν
all his letters, speaking in them of these matters, in which are some things
4246 2186 3281 1877 899 4309 4047 1877 4005 1639 5516 5516
a.dpf n.dpf pt.pa.nsm p.d r.dpf.3 p.g r.gpn p.d r.dpf v.pai.3s

δυσνόητά τινα, ἃ οἱ ἀμαθεῖς καὶ ἀστήρικτοι στρεβλοῦσιν
hard to understand, *some things* ⌊things that⌋ the ignorant and unstable distort to
1554 5516 4005 3836 276 2779 844 5137 4639
a.npn r.npn r.apn d.npm a.npm cj a.npm v.pai.3p

ὡς καὶ τὰς λοιπὰς γραφὰς πρὸς τὴν ἰδίαν αὐτῶν
their own destruction, as *{also}* they do the other scriptures. *to* *{the}* *own* *their*
899 2625 724 6055 2779 3836 3370 1210 4639 3836 2625 899
cj adv d.apf a.apf n.apf p.a d.asf a.asf r.gpm.3

ἀπώλειαν. 17 ὑμεῖς οὖν, ἀγαπητοί, προγινώσκοντες φυλάσσεσθε, ἵνα ↱
destruction You therefore, dear friends, knowing this beforehand, be on your guard that you
724 7007 4036 28 4589 5875 2671 1738
n.asf r.np.2 cj a.vpm pt.pa.npm v.pmm.2p cj

μὴ τῇ τῶν ἀθέσμων πλάνῃ συναπαχθέντες ἐκπέσητε
are not led astray ⌊by the⌋ error of these lawless people *error* *are led astray* and fall
5270 3590 5270 5270 3836 4415 3836 118 4415 5270 1738
pl d.dsf d.gpm a.gpm n.dsf pt.ap.npm v.aas.2p

τοῦ ἰδίου στηριγμοῦ, 18 αὐξάνετε δὲ ἐν χάριτι καὶ γνώσει τοῦ
from your stable position. But grow *But* in the grace and knowledge of our
3836 2625 5113 1254 889 1254 1877 5921 2779 1194 3836 7005
d.gsm a.gsm n.gsm v.pam.2p cj p.d n.dsf cj n.dsf d.gsm

κυρίου ἡμῶν καὶ σωτῆρος Ἰησοῦ Χριστοῦ. αὐτῷ ἡ δόξα καὶ νῦν καὶ εἰς
Lord *our* and Savior Jesus Christ. To him be the glory both now and in the
3261 7005 2779 5400 2652 5986 899 3836 1518 2779 3814 2779 1650
n.gsm r.gp.1 cj n.gsm n.gsm n.gsm r.dsm.3 d.nsf n.nsf cj adv cj p.a

ἡμέραν αἰῶνος. ἀμήν.[a]
eternal day. *eternal* Amen.
172 2465 172 297
n.asf n.gsm pl

[a] [ἀμήν] UBS, omitted by NET.

NASB

intense heat! 13But
according to His
promise we are
looking for new
heavens and a new
earth, in which
righteousness
dwells.
14Therefore, be-
loved, since you
look for these
things, be diligent
to be found by Him
in peace, spotless
and blameless,
15and regard the
patience of our
Lord *as* salvation;
just as also our
beloved brother
Paul, according to
the wisdom given
him, wrote to you,
16as also in all *his*
letters, speaking
in them of these
things, in which
are some things
hard to understand,
which the untaught
and unstable dis-
tort, as *they do*
also the rest of the
Scriptures, to their
own destruction.
17You therefore,
beloved, knowing
this beforehand,
be on your guard
so that you are not
carried away by
the error of unprin-
cipled men and
fall from your own
steadfastness, 18but
grow in the grace
and knowledge of
our Lord and Sav-
ior Jesus Christ. To
Him *be* the glory,
both now and to
the day of eternity.
Amen.

1 John

NIV

The Incarnation of the Word of Life

1 That which
was from the
beginning, which
we have heard,
which we have
seen with our
eyes, which we
have looked at and
our hands have
touched—this
we proclaim con-
cerning the Word
of life. 2The life
appeared; we have
seen it and testi-
fy to it, and we
proclaim to you
the eternal life,
which was with
the Father and has
appeared to us.
3We proclaim to
you what we have
seen and heard, so
that you also may
have fellowship
with us. And our
fellowship is with
the Father and
with his Son, Jesus
Christ. 4We write
this to make our[a]
joy complete.

Light and Darkness, Sin and Forgiveness

5This is the
message we have
heard from him
and declare to
you: God is light;
in him there is no
darkness at all. 6If
we claim to have
fellowship with
him and yet walk
in the darkness, we
lie and do not live
out the truth. 7But
if we walk in the
light, as he is in the
light, we have
fellowship

[a] 4 Some manuscripts *your*

1:1 ὅ ἦν ἀπ' ἀρχῆς, ὃ ἀκηκόαμεν, ὃ ἑωράκαμεν
⌞That which⌟ ⌞has existed⌟ from the beginning, which we have heard, which we have seen
4005 1639 608 794 4005 201 4005 3972
r.nsn v.iai.3s p.g n.gsf r.asn v.rai.1p r.asn v.rai.1p

τοῖς ὀφθαλμοῖς ἡμῶν, ὃ ἐθεασάμεθα καὶ αἱ χεῖρες ἡμῶν ἐψηλάφησαν
with our eyes, *our* which we looked upon and *{the}* our hands *our* have touched,
3836 7005 4057 7005 4005 2517 2779 3836 7005 5931 7005 6027
d.dpm n.dpm r.gp.1 r.asn v.ami.1p cj d.npf n.npf r.gp.1 v.aai.3p

περὶ τοῦ λόγου τῆς ζωῆς — 2καὶ ἡ ζωὴ ἐφανερώθη, καὶ ἑωράκαμεν καὶ
concerning the word of life — *{and}* this life was revealed, and we have seen it and
4309 3836 3364 3836 2437 2779 3836 2437 5746 2779 3972 2779
p.g d.gsm n.gsm d.gsf n.gsf cj d.nsf n.nsf v.api.3s cj v.rai.1p cj

μαρτυροῦμεν καὶ ἀπαγγέλλομεν ὑμῖν τὴν ζωὴν τὴν αἰώνιον ἥτις ἦν
are bearing witness and proclaiming to you the eternal life *{the}* *eternal* that existed
3455 2779 550 7007 3836 173 2437 3836 173 4015 1639
v.pai.1p cj v.pai.1p r.dp.2 d.asf n.asf d.asf a.asf r.nsf v.iai.3s

πρὸς τὸν πατέρα καὶ ἐφανερώθη ἡμῖν 3ὃ ἑωράκαμεν καὶ ἀκηκόαμεν,
with the Father and was revealed to us — ⌞that which⌟ we have seen and heard
4639 3836 4252 2779 5746 7005 4005 3972 2779 201
p.a d.asm n.asm cj v.api.3s r.dp.1 r.asn v.rai.1p cj v.rai.1p

ἀπαγγέλλομεν καὶ ὑμῖν, ἵνα καὶ ὑμεῖς κοινωνίαν ἔχητε μεθ' ἡμῶν.
we proclaim also to you, so that you too *you* may have fellowship *may have* with us;
550 2779 7007 2671 7007 2779 7007 2400 2400 3126 2400 3552 7005
v.pai.1p adv r.dp.2 cj adv r.np.2 n.asf v.pas.2p p.g r.gp.1

καὶ ἡ κοινωνία δὲ ἡ ἡμετέρα μετὰ τοῦ πατρὸς καὶ μετὰ τοῦ
and indeed *{the}* our fellowship *and* *{the}* *our* is with the Father and with *{the}* his
1254 2779 3836 2466 3126 1254 3836 2466 3552 3836 4252 2779 3552 3836 899
adv d.nsf n.nsf cj d.nsf r.nsf.1 p.g d.gsm n.gsm cj p.g d.gsm

υἱοῦ αὐτοῦ Ἰησοῦ Χριστοῦ. 4καὶ ταῦτα γράφομεν ἡμεῖς, ἵνα ἡ
Son *his* Jesus Christ. *{and}* These things we are writing *we* that *{the}* our
5626 899 2652 5986 2779 4047 7005 1211 7005 2671 3836 7005
n.gsm r.gsm.3 n.gsm n.gsm cj r.apn v.pai.1p r.np.1 cj d.nsf

χαρὰ ἡμῶν[a] ᾖ πεπληρωμένη. 5καὶ ἔστιν αὕτη ἡ ἀγγελία ἣν
joy *our* ⌞may be⌟ complete. Now this is *this* the message that
5915 7005 1639 4444 2779 4047 1639 4047 3836 32 4005
n.nsf r.gp.1 v.pas.3s pt.rp.nsf cj v.pai.3s r.nsf d.nsf n.nsf r.asf

ἀκηκόαμεν ἀπ' αὐτοῦ καὶ ἀναγγέλλομεν ὑμῖν, ὅτι ὁ θεὸς φῶς ἐστιν καὶ
we have heard from him and are proclaiming to you: *{that}* *{the}* God is light, *is* and
201 608 899 2779 334 7007 4022 3836 2536 1639 5890 1639 2779
v.rai.1p p.g r.gsm.3 cj v.pai.1p r.dp.2 cj d.nsm n.nsm n.nsn v.pai.3s cj

σκοτία ἐν αὐτῷ οὐκ ἔστιν οὐδεμία. 6ἐὰν εἴπωμεν ὅτι
there is absolutely no darkness in him. *no* *there is* *absolutely* If we say that we
1639 1639 4029 4024 5028 1877 899 4024 1639 4029 1569 3306 4022 2400
n.nsf p.d r.dsm.3 pl v.pai.3s a.nsf cj v.aas.1p cj

κοινωνίαν ἔχομεν μετ' αὐτοῦ καὶ ἐν τῷ σκότει περιπατῶμεν,
have fellowship *we have* with him but continue to walk in *{the}* darkness, *continue to walk*
2400 3126 2400 3552 899 2779 4344 4344 4344 1877 3836 5030 4344
n.asf v.pai.1p p.g r.gsm.3 cj p.d d.dsn n.dsn v.pas.1p

ψευδόμεθα καὶ ↱ οὐ ποιοῦμεν τὴν ἀλήθειαν· ↰ ↰ 7 ἐὰν δὲ
we lie and are not putting the truth into practice. But if *But* we walk
6017 2779 4472 4024 4472 3836 237 4472 4472 1254 1569 1254 4344 4344
v.pmi.1p cj pl v.pai.1p d.asf n.asf cj cj

ἐν τῷ φωτὶ περιπατῶμεν ὡς αὐτός ἐστιν ἐν τῷ φωτί, κοινωνίαν ἔχομεν
in the light, *we walk* as he is in the light, we have fellowship *we have*
1877 3836 5890 4344 6055 899 1639 1877 3836 5890 2400 2400 3126 2400
p.d d.dsn n.dsn v.pas.1p cj r.nsm v.pai.3s p.d d.dsn n.dsn n.asf v.pai.1p

[a] ὑμῶν included by TR after ἡμῶν.

NASB

Introduction, The Incarnate Word

1:1What was from
the beginning,
what we have
heard, what we
have seen with
our eyes, what we
have looked at and
touched with our
hands, concern-
ing the Word of
Life— 2and the life
was manifested,
and we have seen
and testify and
proclaim to you the
eternal life, which
was with the Father
and was manifested
to us— 3what we
have seen and
heard we proclaim
to you also, so that
you too may have
fellowship with
us; and indeed our
fellowship is with
the Father, and
with His Son Jesus
Christ. 4These
things we write, so
that our joy may be
made complete.

God Is Light

5This is the mes-
sage we have heard
from Him and
announce to you,
that God is Light,
and in Him there
is no darkness at
all. 6If we say that
we have fellowship
with Him and *yet*
walk in the dark-
ness, we lie and
do not practice the
truth; 7but if we
walk in the Light
as He Himself is in
the Light, we have
fellowship with

NIV

with one anoth-
er, and the blood
of Jesus, his Son,
purifies us from
all[a] sin.
8 If we claim to
be without sin, we
deceive ourselves
and the truth is not
in us. 9 If we con-
fess our sins, he is
faithful and just
and will forgive us
our sins and purify
us from all unrigh-
teousness. 10 If we
claim we have not
sinned, we make
him out to be a liar
and his word is not
in us.

2 My dear chil-
dren, I write
this to you so that
you will not sin.
But if anybody
does sin, we have
an advocate with
the Father—Jesus
Christ, the Righ-
teous One. 2 He
is the atoning
sacrifice for our
sins, and not only
for ours but also
for the sins of the
whole world.

Love and Hatred for Fellow Believers

3 We know that
we have come to
know him if we
keep his com-
mands. 4 Whoever
says, "I know
him," but does not
do what he com-
mands is a liar,
and the truth is
not in that person.
5 But if anyone
obeys his word,
love for God[b]

[a] 7 Or *every*
[b] 5 Or *word, God's love*

μετ' ἀλλήλων καὶ τὸ αἷμα Ἰησοῦ τοῦ υἱοῦ αὐτοῦ καθαρίζει ἡμᾶς ἀπὸ πάσης
with one another, and the blood of Jesus *{the}* his Son *his* cleanses us from all
3552 253 2779 3836 135 2652 3836 899 5626 899 2751 7005 608 4246
p.g r.gpm cj d.nsn n.nsn n.gsm d.gsm n.gsm r.gsm.3 v.pai.3s r.ap.1 p.g a.gsf

ἁμαρτίας. 8 ἐὰν εἴπωμεν ὅτι ἁμαρτίαν οὐκ ἔχομεν,
sin. If we say that we are without sin, *without we are* we are deceiving
281 1569 3306 4022 2400 2400 4024 281 4024 2400 4414 4414 4414
n.gsf cj v.aas.1p cj n.asf pl v.pai.1p

ἑαυτοὺς πλανῶμεν καὶ ἡ ἀλήθεια οὐκ ἔστιν ἐν ἡμῖν. 9 ἐὰν ὁμολογῶμεν
ourselves *we are deceiving* and the truth is not *is* in us. If we confess
1571 4414 2779 3836 237 1639 4024 1639 1877 7005 1569 3933
r.apm.1 v.pai.1p cj d.nsf n.nsf pl v.pai.3s p.d r.dp.1 cj v.pas.1p

τὰς ἁμαρτίας ἡμῶν, πιστός ἐστιν καὶ δίκαιος, ἵνα ἀφῇ ἡμῖν
{the} our sins, *our* he is faithful *he is* and just and *{that}* ⌊will forgive⌋ us
3836 7005 281 7005 1639 1639 4412 1639 2779 1465 2671 918 7005
d.apf n.apf r.gp.1 a.nsm v.pai.3s cj a.nsm cj v.aas.3s r.dp.1

τὰς ἁμαρτίας καὶ καθαρίσῃ ἡμᾶς ἀπὸ πάσης ἀδικίας. 10 ἐὰν εἴπωμεν ὅτι ↱
our sins and cleanse us from all unrighteousness. If we say that we
3836 281 2779 2751 7005 608 4246 94 1569 3306 4022 279
d.apf n.apf cj v.aas.3s r.ap.1 p.g a.gsf n.gsf cj v.aas.1p cj

↱ οὐχ ἡμαρτήκαμεν, ψεύστην ποιοῦμεν αὐτὸν καὶ ὁ λόγος
have not sinned, we make him a liar *we make* *him* and *{the}* his word
279 4024 279 4472 4472 899 6026 4472 899 2779 3836 899 3364
pl v.rai.1p n.asm v.pai.1p r.asm.3 cj d.nsm n.nsm

αὐτοῦ οὐκ ἔστιν ἐν ἡμῖν.
his is not *is* in us.
899 1639 4024 1639 1877 7005
r.gsm.3 pl v.pai.3s p.d r.dp.1

2:1 τεκνία μου, ταῦτα γράφω ὑμῖν ἵνα ↱ ↱
My little children, *My* I am writing these things *I am writing* to you so that you may
1609 5448 1609 1211 1211 1211 4047 1211 7007 2671 279 279
n.vpn r.gs.1 r.apn v.pai.1s r.dp.2 cj

μὴ ἁμάρτητε. καὶ ἐάν τις ἁμάρτῃ, παράκλητον ἔχομεν πρὸς τὸν
not sin. But if anyone does sin, we have an advocate *we have* with the
3590 279 2779 1569 5516 279 2400 2400 4156 2400 4639 3836
pl v.aas.2p cj cj r.nsm v.aas.3s n.asm v.pai.1p p.a d.asm

πατέρα Ἰησοῦν Χριστὸν δίκαιον· 2 καὶ αὐτὸς ἱλασμός ἐστιν περὶ
Father, Jesus Christ the ⌊righteous one.⌋ *{and}* He is the propitiation *is* for
4252 2652 5986 1465 2779 899 1639 2662 1639 4309
n.asm n.asm n.asm a.asm cj r.nsm n.nsm v.pai.3s p.g

τῶν ἁμαρτιῶν ἡμῶν, οὐ περὶ τῶν ἡμετέρων δὲ μόνον ἀλλὰ καὶ περὶ
{the} our sins, *our* and not for *{the}* ours *and* only, but also for those
3836 7005 281 7005 1254 4024 4309 3836 2466 1254 3667 247 2779 4309
d.gpf n.gpf r.gp.1 pl p.g d.gpf r.gpf.1 cj adv cj adv p.g

ὅλου τοῦ κόσμου. 3 καὶ ἐν τούτῳ γινώσκομεν ὅτι ἐγνώκαμεν αὐτόν,
of the entire *the* world. Now this ⌊is how⌋ *this* we can be sure that we know God:
3836 3910 3836 3180 2779 4047 1877 4047 1182 4022 1182 899
a.gsm d.gsm n.gsm cj p.d r.dsn v.pai.1p cj v.rai.1p r.asm.3

ἐὰν τὰς ἐντολὰς αὐτοῦ τηρῶμεν. 4 ὁ λέγων ὅτι ἔγνωκα
if we keep *{the}* his commandments. *his* *we keep* The ⌊one who says,⌋ ~ "I know
1569 5498 5498 3836 899 1953 899 5498 3836 3306 4022 1182
cj d.apf n.apf r.gsm.3 v.pas.1p d.nsm pt.pa.nsm cj v.rai.1s

αὐτὸν καὶ τὰς ἐντολὰς αὐτοῦ μὴ τηρῶν, ψεύστης
God," yet does not keep *{the}* his commandments, *his* *not* *does keep* is a liar
899 2779 5498 3590 5498 3836 899 1953 899 3590 5498 1639 6026
r.asm.3 cj d.apf n.apf r.gsm.3 pl pt.pa.nsm n.nsm

ἐστὶν καὶ ἐν τούτῳ ἡ ἀλήθεια οὐκ ἔστιν· 5 ὃς δ' ἂν
is and the truth is not in him. *the* *truth* *not* *is* But whoever *But* ~
1639 2779 3836 237 1639 4024 1877 4047 3836 237 4024 1639 1254 4005 1254 323
v.pai.3s cj p.d r.dsm d.nsf n.nsf pl v.pai.3s r.nsm cj pl

τηρῇ αὐτοῦ τὸν λόγον, ἀληθῶς ἐν τούτῳ ἡ ἀγάπη τοῦ θεοῦ
keeps his *{the}* word, truly in that person is the love of God
5498 899 3836 3364 242 1877 4047 3836 27 3836 2536
v.pas.3s r.gsm.3 d.asm n.asm adv p.d r.dsm d.nsf n.nsf d.gsm n.gsm

NASB

one another, and
the blood of Jesus
His Son cleanses
us from all sin.
8 If we say that we
have no sin, we
are deceiving our-
selves and the truth
is not in us. 9 If we
confess our sins,
He is faithful and
righteous to forgive
us our sins and to
cleanse us from all
unrighteousness.
10 If we say that we
have not sinned,
we make Him a liar
and His word is not
in us.

Christ Is Our Advocate

2:1 My little chil-
dren, I am writing
these things to you
so that you may not
sin. And if anyone
sins, we have an
[a]Advocate with the
Father, Jesus Christ
the righteous; 2 and
He Himself is the
propitiation for our
sins; and not for
ours only, but also
for *those of* the
whole world.
3 By this we know
that we have come
to know Him, if
we keep His com-
mandments. 4 The
one who says, "I
have come to know
Him," and does
not keep His com-
mandments, is a
liar, and the truth
is not in him; 5 but
whoever keeps His
word, in him the
love of God has

[a] Gr *Paracletos,* one called alongside to help; or *Intercessor*

NIV

is truly made com-
plete in them. This
is how we know we
are in him: 6 Whoever
claims to live in him
must live as Jesus did.
7 Dear friends, I
am not writing you
a new command but
an old one, which
you have had since
the beginning. This
old command is the
message you have
heard. 8 Yet I am
writing you a new
command; its truth
is seen in him and
in you, because the
darkness is passing
and the true light is
already shining.
9 Anyone who claims
to be in the light but
hates a brother or sis-
ter[a] is still in the darkness. 10 Anyone who
loves their brother and
sister[b] lives in the light,
and there is nothing
in them to make them
stumble. 11 But anyone
who hates a brother or
sister is in the darkness
and walks around in
the darkness. They do
not know where they
are going, because the
darkness has blinded
them.

Reasons for Writing

12 I am writing to
you, dear
children,
because your
sins have
been forgiven
on account of
his name.
13 I am writing to
you, fathers,
because you
know him
who is
from the
beginning.

[a] 9 The Greek word for *brother or sister* (*adelphos*) refers here to a believer, whether man or woman, as part of God's family; also in verse 11; and in 3:15, 17; 4:20; 5:16.
[b] 10 The Greek word for *brother and sister* (*adelphos*) refers here to a believer, whether man or woman, as part of God's family; also in 3:10; 4:20, 21.

τετελείωται, ⌞ἐν τούτῳ⌟ γινώσκομεν ὅτι ἐν αὐτῷ ἐσμεν.
brought to fulfillment. This is how we can be sure that we are in him: *we are*
5457 1877 4047 1182 4022 1639 1639 1877 899 1639
v.rpi.3s p.d r.dsn v.pai.1p cj p.d r.dsm.3 v.pai.1p

6 ὁ λέγων ἐν αὐτῷ μένειν ὀφείλει καθὼς ἐκεῖνος
the ⌞one who claims⌟ to abide in God *to abide* ought to walk just as Jesus
3836 3306 3531 3531 1877 899 3531 4053 4344 4344 2777 1697
d.nsm pt.pa.nsm p.d r.dsm.3 f.pa v.pai.3s cj r.nsm

περιεπάτησεν καὶ αὐτὸς οὕτως[a] περιπατεῖν. 7 ἀγαπητοί, οὐκ ἐντολὴν
walked. *{also}* *{he}* *{thus}* *to walk* Dear friends, it is not a new commandment
4344 2779 899 4048 4344 28 4024 2785 1953
v.aai.3s adv r.nsm adv f.pa a.vpm pl n.asf

καινὴν γράφω ὑμῖν ἀλλ᾽ ἐντολὴν παλαιὰν ἣν εἴχετε
new that I write to you, but an old commandment *old* — one that ⌞you have had⌟
2785 1211 7007 247 4094 1953 4094 4005 2400
a.asf v.pai.1s r.dp.2 cj n.asf a.asf r.asf v.iai.2p

ἀπ᾽ ἀρχῆς· ἡ ἐντολὴ ἡ παλαιά ἐστιν ὁ λόγος ὃν
from the beginning. The old commandment *{the}* *old* is the message *{that}*
608 794 3836 4094 1953 3836 4094 1639 3836 3364 4005
p.g n.gsf d.nsf n.nsf d.nsf a.nsf v.pai.3s d.nsm n.nsm r.asm

ἠκούσατε. 8 πάλιν ἐντολὴν καινὴν γράφω ὑμῖν, ὅ
⌞you have already heard.⌟ Yet it is a new commandment *new* that I write to you, one
201 4099 2785 1953 2785 1211 7007 4005
v.aai.2p adv n.asf a.asf v.pai.1s r.dp.2 r.nsn

ἐστιν ἀληθὲς ἐν αὐτῷ καὶ ἐν ὑμῖν, ὅτι ἡ σκοτία παράγεται καὶ τὸ
that is true in him and in you, because the darkness is passing away and the true
1639 239 1877 899 2779 1877 7007 4022 3836 5028 4135 2779 3836 240
v.pai.3s a.nsn p.d r.dsm.3 cj p.d r.dp.2 cj d.nsf n.nsf v.ppi.3s cj d.nsn

φῶς τὸ ἀληθινὸν ↱ ἤδη φαίνει. 9 ὁ λέγων ἐν τῷ φωτὶ
light *{the}* *true* is already shining. The ⌞one who claims⌟ to be in the light
5890 3836 240 5743 2453 5743 3836 3306 1639 1639 1877 3836 5890
n.nsn d.nsn a.nsn adv v.pai.3s d.nsm pt.pa.nsm p.d d.dsn n.dsn

εἶναι καὶ τὸν ἀδελφὸν αὐτοῦ μισῶν ἐν τῇ
to be but goes on hating *{the}* his brother *his* *goes on hating* is still in the
1639 2779 3631 3631 3631 3836 899 81 899 3631 1639 2401 1877 3836
f.pa cj d.asm n.asm r.gsm.3 pt.pa.nsm p.d d.dsf

σκοτίᾳ ἐστὶν ⌞ἕως ἄρτι.⌟ 10 ὁ ἀγαπῶν τὸν ἀδελφὸν αὐτοῦ
darkness. *is* *still* The ⌞one who loves⌟ *{the}* his brother *his* is living
5028 1639 2401 785 3836 26 3836 899 81 899 3531 3531
n.dsf v.pai.3s p.g adv d.nsm pt.pa.nsm d.asm n.asm r.gsm.3

ἐν τῷ φωτὶ μένει καὶ σκάνδαλον ἐν αὐτῷ οὐκ ἔστιν·
in the light *is living* and *cause for stumbling* in him there is no *there is* cause for
1877 3836 5890 3531 2779 4998 1877 899 1639 1639 4024 1639 4998 4998
p.d d.dsn n.dsn v.pai.3s cj n.nsn p.d r.dsm.3 pl v.pai.3s

11 ὁ δὲ μισῶν τὸν ἀδελφὸν αὐτοῦ ἐν τῇ σκοτίᾳ
stumbling. But the *But* ⌞one who hates⌟ *{the}* his brother *his* is in the darkness;
4998 1254 3836 1254 3631 3836 899 81 899 1639 1877 3836 5028
d.nsm cj pt.pa.nsm d.asm n.asm r.gsm.3 p.d d.dsf n.dsf

ἐστὶν καὶ ἐν τῇ σκοτίᾳ περιπατεῖ καὶ ↱ οὐκ οἶδεν ποῦ ὑπάγει,
is *{and}* he walks in the darkness *he walks* and does not know where he is going,
1639 2779 4344 4344 1877 3836 5028 4344 2779 3857 4024 3857 4543 5632
v.pai.3s cj p.d d.dsf n.dsf v.pai.3s cj pl v.rai.3s cj v.pai.3s

ὅτι ἡ σκοτία ἐτύφλωσεν τοὺς ὀφθαλμοὺς αὐτοῦ. 12 γράφω ὑμῖν,
because the darkness has blinded *{the}* his eyes. *his* I am writing to you, my
4022 3836 5028 5604 3836 899 4057 899 1211 7007
cj d.nsf n.nsf v.aai.3s d.apm n.apm r.gsm.3 v.pai.1s r.dp.2

τεκνία, ὅτι ἀφέωνται ὑμῖν αἱ ἁμαρτίαι διὰ τὸ ὄνομα
children, because your sins are forgiven *your* *{the}* *sins* ⌞on account of⌟ *{the}* his name.
5448 4022 7007 281 918 7007 3836 281 1328 3836 899 3950
n.vpn cj v.rpi.3p r.dp.2 d.npf n.npf p.a d.asn n.asn

αὐτοῦ. 13 γράφω ὑμῖν, πατέρες, ὅτι ἐγνώκατε τὸν ἀπ᾽ ἀρχῆς.
his I am writing to you, fathers, because you know him who is from the beginning.
899 1211 7007 4252 4022 1182 3836 608 794
r.gsm.3 v.pai.1s r.dp.2 n.vpm cj v.rai.2p d.asm p.g n.gsf

[a] [οὕτως] UBS.

NASB

truly been per-
fected. By this we
know that we are in
Him: 6 the one who
says he abides in
Him ought himself
to walk in the same
manner as He
walked.
7 Beloved, I am
not writing a new
commandment to
you, but an old
commandment
which you have
had from the be-
ginning; the old
commandment is
the word which
you have heard.
8 On the other hand,
I am writing a new
commandment
to you, which is
true in Him and in
you, because the
darkness is passing
away and the true
Light is already
shining. 9 The one
who says he is in
the Light and *yet*
hates his brother
is in the darkness
until now. 10 The
one who loves his
brother abides in
the Light and there
is no cause for
stumbling in him.
11 But the one who
hates his brother
is in the darkness
and walks in the
darkness, and does
not know where he
is going because
the darkness has
blinded his eyes.
12 I am writing to
you, little children,
because your sins
have been forgiven
you for His name's
sake. 13 I am writ-
ing to you, fathers,
because you know
Him who has been
from the begin-
ning. I am writing

NIV

I am writing to
you, young
men,
because
you have
overcome the
evil one.
[14] I write to you, dear
children,
because you
know the
Father.
I write to you,
fathers,
because you
know him
who is
from the
beginning.
I write to you,
young men,
because you are
strong,
and the word of
God lives in
you,
and you have
overcome the
evil one.

On Not Loving the World

[15] Do not love the
world or anything
in the world. If
anyone loves the
world, love for
the Father[a] is not
in them. [16] For ev-
erything in the
world — the lust
of the flesh, the
lust of the eyes,
and the pride of
life — comes not
from the Father but
from the world.
[17] The world and its
desires pass away,
but whoever does
the will of God
lives forever.

Warnings Against Denying the Son

[18] Dear children,
this is the last hour;
and as you have
heard that the an-
tichrist is coming,
even now many
antichrists have
come. This is how
we know it is the
last hour. [19] They
went out from us,
but they did not
really belong to us.
For if they had be-
longed to us, they
would

[a] 15 Or *world, the Father's love*

γράφω ὑμῖν, νεανίσκοι, ὅτι νενικήκατε τὸν πονηρόν.[a] 14 ἔγραψα
I am writing to you, young men, because you have overcome the evil one. I have written
1211 7007 3734 4022 3771 3836 4505 1211
v.pai.1s r.dp.2 n.vpm cj v.rai.2p d.asm a.asm v.aai.1s

ὑμῖν, παιδία, ὅτι ἐγνώκατε τὸν πατέρα. ἔγραψα ὑμῖν, πατέρες, ὅτι
to you, my children, because you know the Father. I have written to you, fathers, because
7007 4086 4022 1182 3836 4252 1211 7007 4252 4022
r.dp.2 n.vpn cj v.rai.2p d.asm n.asm v.aai.1s r.dp.2 n.vpm cj

ἐγνώκατε τὸν ἀπ᾽ ἀρχῆς. ἔγραψα ὑμῖν, νεανίσκοι, ὅτι
you know him who is from the beginning. I have written to you, young men, because you are
1182 3836 608 794 1211 7007 3734 4022 1639 1639
v.rai.2p d.asm p.g n.gsf v.aai.1s r.dp.2 n.vpm cj

ἰσχυροί ἐστε καὶ ὁ λόγος τοῦ θεοῦ ἐν ὑμῖν μένει καὶ νενικήκατε
strong, *you are* and the word of God abides in you, *abides* and you have overcome
2708 1639 2779 3836 3364 3836 2536 3531 1877 7007 3531 2779 3771
a.npm v.pai.2p cj d.nsm n.nsm d.gsm n.gsm p.d r.dp.2 v.pai.3s cj v.rai.2p

τὸν πονηρόν. 15 ➜ μὴ ἀγαπᾶτε τὸν κόσμον μηδὲ τὰ ἐν τῷ κόσμῳ. ἐάν
the evil one. Do not love the world or ⌊the things⌋ in the world. If
3836 4505 26 3590 26 3836 3180 3593 3836 1877 3836 3180 1569
d.asm a.asm pl v.pam.2p d.asm n.asm cj d.apn p.d d.dsm n.dsm cj

τις ἀγαπᾷ τὸν κόσμον, οὐκ ἔστιν ἡ ἀγάπη τοῦ πατρὸς ἐν αὐτῷ·
anyone loves the world, *not is* the love of the Father is not in him.
5516 26 3836 3180 4024 1639 3836 27 3836 4252 1639 4024 1877 899
r.nsm v.pas.3s d.asm n.asm pl v.pai.3s d.nsf n.nsf d.gsm n.gsm p.d r.dsm.3

16 ὅτι πᾶν τὸ ἐν τῷ κόσμῳ, ἡ ἐπιθυμία τῆς σαρκὸς καὶ ἡ ἐπιθυμία
For all that is in the world — the desire of the flesh, *{and}* the desire
4022 4246 3836 1877 3836 3180 3836 2123 3836 4922 2779 3836 2123
cj a.nsn d.nsn p.d d.dsm n.dsm d.nsf n.nsf d.gsf n.gsf cj d.nsf n.nsf

τῶν ὀφθαλμῶν καὶ ἡ ἀλαζονεία τοῦ βίου, οὐκ ἔστιν ἐκ τοῦ πατρὸς
of the eyes, *{and}* the pride of possession — is not *is* from the Father
3836 4057 2779 3836 224 3836 1050 1639 4024 1639 1666 3836 4252
d.gpm n.gpm cj d.nsf n.nsf d.gsm n.gsm pl v.pai.3s p.g d.gsm n.gsm

ἀλλ᾽ ἐκ τοῦ κόσμου ἐστίν. 17 καὶ ὁ κόσμος παράγεται καὶ ἡ ἐπιθυμία
but from the world. *{is}* *{and}* The world is passing away with all its desires,
247 1666 3836 3180 1639 2779 3836 3180 4135 2779 3836 899 2123
cj p.g d.gsm n.gsm v.pai.3s cj d.nsm n.nsm v.ppi.3s cj d.nsf n.nsf

αὐτοῦ, ὁ δὲ ποιῶν τὸ θέλημα τοῦ θεοῦ μένει εἰς τὸν αἰῶνα.
its but the *but* ⌊one who does⌋ the will of God remains for all time.
899 1254 3836 1254 4472 3836 2525 3836 2536 3531 1650 3836 172
r.gsm.3 d.nsm cj pt.pa.nsm d.asn n.asn d.gsm n.gsm v.pai.3s p.a d.asm n.asm

18 παιδία, ἐσχάτη ὥρα ἐστίν, καὶ καθὼς ἠκούσατε ὅτι ἀντίχριστος
My children, it is the last hour! *it is* And just as you heard that the Antichrist
4086 1639 1639 2274 6052 1639 2779 2777 201 4022 532
n.vpn a.nsf n.nsf v.pai.3s cj cj v.aai.2p cj n.nsm

ἔρχεται, καὶ νῦν ἀντίχριστοι πολλοὶ γεγόνασιν, ὅθεν γινώσκομεν ὅτι
would come, even now many antichrists *many* have appeared. Therefore we know that
2262 2779 3814 4498 532 4498 1181 3854 1182 4022
v.pmi.3s adv adv n.npm a.npm v.rai.3p cj v.pai.1p cj

ἐσχάτη ὥρα ἐστίν. 19 ἐξ ἡμῶν ἐξῆλθαν ἀλλ᾽
it is the last hour. *it is* They went out from us *They went out* but they were
1639 1639 2274 6052 1639 2002 2002 2002 1666 7005 2002 247 1639 1639
a.nsf n.nsf v.pai.3s p.g r.gp.1 v.aai.3p cj

οὐκ ἦσαν ἐξ ἡμῶν· εἰ γὰρ ἐξ ἡμῶν ἦσαν, ➜
not *they were* of us; for if *for* they had been of us, *they had been* they would
4024 1639 1666 7005 1142 1623 1142 1639 1639 1639 1666 7005 1639 323
pl v.iai.3p p.g r.gp.1 cj cj p.g r.gp.1 v.iai.3p

[a] γράφω ὑμῖν, παιδία, ὅτι ἐγνώκατε τὸν πατέρα included by TR after πονηρόν.

NASB

to you, young men,
because you have
overcome the evil
one. I have written
to you, children,
because you know
the Father. [14] I have
written to you,
fathers, because
you know Him
who has been from
the beginning. I
have written to
you, young men,
because you are
strong, and the
word of God
abides in you, and
you have overcome
the evil one.

Do Not Love the World

[15] Do not love
the world nor the
things in the world.
If anyone loves the
world, the love of
the Father is not in
him. [16] For all that
is in the world, the
lust of the flesh and
the lust of the eyes
and the boastful
pride of life, is not
from the Father,
but is from the
world. [17] The world
is passing away,
and *also* its lusts;
but the one who
does the will of
God lives forever.
[18] Children, it is
the last hour; and
just as you heard
that antichrist is
coming, even now
many antichrists
have appeared;
from this we know
that it is the last
hour. [19] They went
out from us, but
they were not *re-
ally* of us; for if
they had been of
us, they would

NIV

have remained with
us; but their going
showed that none
of them belonged
to us.
[20]But you have an
anointing from the
Holy One, and all
of you know the
truth.[a] [21]I do not
write to you be-
cause you do not
know the truth,
but because you
do know it and be-
cause no lie comes
from the truth.
[22]Who is the liar?
It is whoever de-
nies that Jesus is
the Christ. Such a
person is the anti-
christ—denying
the Father and the
Son. [23]No one who
denies the Son has
the Father; whoev-
er acknowledges
the Son has the Fa-
ther also.
[24]As for you, see
that what you have
heard from the be-
ginning remains in
you. If it does, you
also will remain in
the Son and in the
Father. [25]And this
is what he prom-
ised us—eternal
life.
[26]I am writing
these things to you
about those who
are trying to lead
you astray. [27]As for
you, the anointing
you received from
him remains in
you, and you do
not need anyone
to teach you. But
as his anointing
teaches you about
all things and as
that anointing is
real, not counter-
feit—just as

[a] 20 Some manu-
scripts *and you know
all things*

μεμενήκεισαν ἂν μεθ᾽ ἡμῶν· ἀλλ᾽ ἵνα φανερωθῶσιν ὅτι
have continued *would* with us. But they went out from us that ⌞it might become plain⌟ that
3531 323 3552 7005 247 2671 5746 4022
v.lai.3p pl p.g r.gp.1 cj cj v.aps.3p cj

οὐκ εἰσὶν πάντες ἐξ ἡμῶν. 20 καὶ ὑμεῖς χρῖσμα ἔχετε ἀπὸ τοῦ
none of them are *{all}* of us. But you have an anointing *have* from the
4024 1639 4246 1666 7005 2779 7007 2400 5984 2400 608 3836
pl v.pai.3p a.npm p.g r.gp.1 cj r.np.2 n.asn v.pai.2p p.g d.gsm

ἁγίου καὶ → οἴδατε πάντες.[a] 21 οὐκ ἔγραψα ὑμῖν ὅτι ↱
Holy One, and you all know *all* the truth. *not* I write to you, not because you
41 2779 4246 3857 4246 4024 1211 7007 4024 4022 3857
a.gsm cj v.rai.2p a.npm pl v.aai.1s r.dp.2 cj

↱ οὐκ οἴδατε τὴν ἀλήθειαν ἀλλ᾽ ὅτι οἴδατε αὐτὴν καὶ ὅτι πᾶν
do not know the truth, but because ⌞you do know⌟ it and because *{every}* no
3857 4024 3857 3836 237 247 4022 3857 899 2779 4022 4246 4024
pl v.rai.2p d.asf n.asf cj cj v.rai.2p r.asf.3 cj cj a.nsn

ψεῦδος ἐκ τῆς ἀληθείας οὐκ ἔστιν. 22 τίς ἐστιν ὁ ψεύστης ⌞εἰ μὴ⌟ ὁ
lie comes from the truth. *no* *comes* Who is the liar but the
6022 1639 1666 3836 237 4024 1639 5515 1639 3836 6026 1623 3590 3836
n.nsn p.g d.gsf n.gsf pl v.pai.3s r.nsm v.pai.3s d.nsm n.nsm cj pl d.nsm

ἀρνούμενος ὅτι Ἰησοῦς οὐκ ἔστιν ὁ Χριστός; οὗτός ἐστιν ὁ ἀντίχριστος,
one who denies that Jesus *{not}* is the Christ? This one is the Antichrist,
766 4022 2652 4024 1639 3836 5986 4047 1639 3836 532
pt.pm.nsm cj n.nsm pl v.pai.3s d.nsm n.nsm r.nsm v.pai.3s d.nsm n.nsm

ὁ ἀρνούμενος τὸν πατέρα καὶ τὸν υἱόν. 23 πᾶς ὁ ἀρνούμενος τὸν υἱὸν
the one who denies the Father and the Son. No one who denies the Son
3836 766 3836 4252 2779 3836 5626 4028 4246 3836 766 3836 5626
d.nsm pt.pm.nsm d.asm n.asm cj d.asm n.asm a.nsm d.nsm pt.pm.nsm d.asm n.asm

οὐδὲ τὸν πατέρα ἔχει, ὁ ὁμολογῶν τὸν υἱὸν καὶ τὸν πατέρα
No has the Father. *has* The one who confesses the Son *also* has the Father also.
4028 2400 3836 4252 2400 3836 3933 3836 5626 2779 2400 3836 4252 2779
cj d.asm n.asm v.pai.3s d.nsm pt.pa.nsm d.asm n.asm adv d.asm n.asm

ἔχει. 24 ὑμεῖς ὃ ἠκούσατε ἀπ᾽ ἀρχῆς, ἐν ὑμῖν μενέτω. ἐὰν
has Let what you *what* heard from the beginning abide in you. *Let abide* If
2400 3531 4005 7007 4005 201 608 794 3531 1877 7007 3531 1569
v.pai.3s r.np.2 r.asn v.aai.2p p.g n.gsf p.d r.dp.2 v.pam.3s cj

ἐν ὑμῖν μείνῃ ὃ ἀπ᾽ ἀρχῆς ἠκούσατε, καὶ
what you heard from the beginning abides in you, *abides* *what* *from* *beginning* *you heard* then
4005 201 201 608 794 3531 1877 7007 3531 4005 608 794 201 2779
p.d r.dp.2 v.aas.3s r.asn p.g n.gsf v.aai.2p adv

ὑμεῖς ἐν τῷ υἱῷ καὶ ἐν τῷ πατρὶ μενεῖτε. 25 καὶ αὕτη ἐστὶν ἡ
you will abide in the Son and in the Father. *will abide* And this is the
7007 3531 3531 1877 3836 5626 2779 1877 3836 4252 3531 2779 4047 1639 3836
r.np.2 p.d d.dsm n.dsm cj p.d d.dsm n.dsm v.fai.2p cj r.nsf v.pai.3s d.nsf

ἐπαγγελία ἣν αὐτὸς ἐπηγγείλατο ἡμῖν, τὴν ζωὴν τὴν αἰώνιον. 26
promise that he made to us — *{the}* eternal life. *{the}* *eternal* I have
2039 4005 899 2040 7005 3836 173 2437 3836 173 1211 1211
n.nsf r.asf r.nsm v.ami.3s r.dp.1 d.asf n.asf d.asf a.asf

ταῦτα ἔγραψα ὑμῖν περὶ τῶν πλανώντων ὑμᾶς. 27 καὶ
written these things *I have written* to you concerning those ⌞who are trying to deceive⌟ you. But
1211 4047 1211 7007 4309 3836 4414 7007 2779
r.apn v.aai.1s r.dp.2 p.g d.gpm pt.pa.gpm r.ap.2 cj

ὑμεῖς τὸ χρῖσμα ὃ ἐλάβετε ἀπ᾽ αὐτοῦ, μένει ἐν ὑμῖν καὶ
the anointing you *the* *anointing* *{that}* received from him abides in you, and you have
3836 5984 7007 3836 5984 4005 3284 608 899 3531 1877 7007 2779 2400 2400
r.np.2 d.nsn n.nsn r.asn v.aai.2p p.g r.gsm.3 v.pai.3s p.d r.dp.2 cj

οὐ χρείαν ἔχετε ἵνα τις διδάσκῃ ὑμᾶς, ἀλλ᾽ ὡς τὸ αὐτοῦ χρῖσμα διδάσκει
no need *you have* that anyone teach you. But as *{the}* his anointing teaches
4024 5970 2400 2671 5516 1438 7007 247 6055 3836 899 5984 1438
pl n.asf v.pai.2p cj r.nsm v.pas.3s r.ap.2 cj cj d.nsn r.gsm.3 n.nsn v.pai.3s

ὑμᾶς περὶ πάντων καὶ ἀληθές ἐστιν καὶ οὐκ ἔστιν ψεῦδος, καὶ καθὼς
you about all things, and is true *is* and not *{is}* a lie, *{and}* just as
7007 4309 4246 2779 1639 239 1639 2779 4024 1639 6022 2779 2777
r.ap.2 p.g a.gpn cj a.nsn v.pai.3s cj pl v.pai.3s n.nsn cj cj

[a] πάντα included by TR after πάντες.

NASB

have remained
with us; but *they
went out,* so that it
would be shown
that they all are
not of us. [20]But you
have an anointing
from the Holy One,
and you all know.
[21]I have not written
to you because you
do not know the
truth, but because
you do know it,
and because no
lie is of the truth.
[22]Who is the liar
but the one who
denies that Jesus is
the Christ? This is
the antichrist, the
one who denies the
Father and the Son.
[23]Whoever denies
the Son does not
have the Father; the
one who confesses
the Son has the
Father also. [24]As
for you, let that
abide in you which
you heard from the
beginning. If what
you heard from the
beginning abides in
you, you also will
abide in the Son
and in the Father.

The Promise Is Eternal Life

[25]This is the prom-
ise which He Him-
self made to us:
eternal life.
[26]These things I
have written to you
concerning those
who are trying to
deceive you. [27]As
for you, the anoint-
ing which you
received from Him
abides in you, and
you have no need
for anyone to teach
you; but as His
anointing teaches
you about all
things, and is true
and is not a lie,

NIV

it has taught you,
remain in him.

God's Children and Sin

28 And now, dear
children, contin-
ue in him, so that
when he appears
we may be con-
fident and un-
ashamed before
him at his coming.
29 If you know
that he is righ-
teous, you know
that everyone who
does what is right
has been born of
him.
3 See what great
love the Father
has lavished on us,
that we should be
called children of
God! And that is
what we are! The
reason the world
does not know us
is that it did not
know him. 2 Dear
friends, now we
are children of
God, and what we
will be has not yet
been made known.
But we know that
when Christ ap-
pears,[a] we shall be
like him, for we
shall see him as he
is. 3 All who have
this hope in him
purify themselves,
just as he is pure.
4 Everyone who
sins breaks the
law; in fact, sin is
lawlessness. 5 But
you know that he
appeared so that
he might take
away our sins. And
in him is no sin.
6 No one who lives
in him keeps on
sinning. No one
who continues to
sin has

ἐδίδαξεν ὑμᾶς, μένετε ἐν αὐτῷ. 28 καὶ νῦν, τεκνία, μένετε ἐν αὐτῷ, ἵνα
it has taught you, abide in him. And now, dear children, abide in him, so that
1438 7007 3531 1877 899 2779 3814 5448 3531 1877 899 2671
v.aai.3s r.ap.2 v.pai.2p p.d r.dsm.3 cj adv n.vpn v.pam.2p p.d r.dsm.3 cj

ἐὰν φανερωθῇ σχῶμεν παρρησίαν καὶ μὴ αἰσχυνθῶμεν ἀπ' αὐτοῦ ↰ ἐν
when he appears ⌞we may have⌟ confidence and not be put to shame in his presence when
1569 5746 2400 4244 2779 3590 159 608 899 608 1877
cj v.aps.3s v.aas.1p n.asf cj pl v.aps.1p p.g r.gsm.3 p.d

τῇ παρουσίᾳ αὐτοῦ. 29 ἐὰν εἰδῆτε ὅτι δίκαιός ἐστιν, →
{the} he comes. *he* If you know that he is righteous, *he is* you also
3836 899 4242 899 1569 3857 4022 1639 1639 1465 1639 2779
d.dsf n.dsf r.gsm.3 cj v.ras.2p cj a.nsm v.pai.3s

γινώσκετε ὅτι καὶ πᾶς ὁ ποιῶν τὴν δικαιοσύνην ἐξ αὐτοῦ
know that *also* everyone who practices *{the}* righteousness has been born of him.
1182 4022 2779 4246 3836 4472 3836 1466 1164 1164 1164 1666 899
v.pai.2p cj adv a.nsm d.nsm pt.pa.nsm d.asf n.asf p.g r.gsm.3

γεγέννηται.
has been born
1164
v.rpi.3s

3:1 ἴδετε ποταπὴν ἀγάπην δέδωκεν ἡμῖν ὁ πατήρ, ἵνα
See what great love the Father has given to us, *the Father* that we should
1625 4534 27 3836 4252 1443 7005 3836 4252 2671 2813 2813
v.aam.2p r.asf n.asf v.rai.3s r.dp.1 d.nsm n.nsm cj

τέκνα θεοῦ κληθῶμεν, καὶ ἐσμέν. ⌞διὰ τοῦτο⌟ ὁ
be called children of God *we should be called* — ⌞and so⌟ we are! The reason the
2813 2813 5451 2536 2813 2779 1639 1328 4047 3836
n.npn n.gsm v.aps.1p cj v.pai.1p p.a r.asn d.nsm

κόσμος ↱ οὐ γινώσκει ἡμᾶς, ὅτι ↱ ↱ οὐκ ἔγνω αὐτόν. 2 ἀγαπητοί,
world does not know us is that it did not know him. Dear friends,
3180 1182 4024 1182 7005 4022 1182 1182 4024 1182 899 28
n.nsm pl v.pai.3s r.ap.1 cj pl v.aai.3s r.asm.3 a.vpm

νῦν τέκνα θεοῦ ἐσμεν, καὶ ↱ ↱ οὔπω ἐφανερώθη τί
⌞at the present time⌟ we are children of God, *we are* and it has not yet been revealed what
3814 1639 1639 5451 2536 1639 2779 5746 5746 4037 5746 5515
adv n.npn n.gsm v.pai.1p cj adv v.api.3s r.nsn

ἐσόμεθα. οἴδαμεν ὅτι ἐὰν φανερωθῇ, ὅμοιοι αὐτῷ ἐσόμεθα,
we will be. But we do know that when he is revealed we will be like him, *we will be*
1639 3857 4022 1569 5746 1639 1639 1639 3927 899 1639
v.fmi.1p v.rai.1p cj cj v.aps.3s a.npm r.dsm.3 v.fmi.1p

ὅτι ὀψόμεθα αὐτὸν καθώς ἐστιν. 3 καὶ πᾶς ὁ ἔχων τὴν ἐλπίδα
because we will see him just as he is. And everyone who has *{the}* this hope
4022 3972 899 2777 1639 2779 4246 3836 2400 3836 4047 1828
cj v.fmi.1p r.asm.3 cj v.pai.3s cj a.nsm d.nsm pt.pa.nsm d.asf n.asf

ταύτην ἐπ' αὐτῷ ἁγνίζει ἑαυτόν, καθὼς ἐκεῖνος ἁγνός ἐστιν. 4 πᾶς ὁ
this in him purifies himself, just as he is pure. *is* Everyone who
4047 2093 899 49 1571 2777 1697 1639 54 1639 4246 3836
r.asf p.d r.dsm.3 v.pai.3s r.asm.3 cj r.nsm a.nsm v.pai.3s a.nsm d.nsm

ποιῶν τὴν ἁμαρτίαν καὶ τὴν ἀνομίαν ποιεῖ, καὶ ἡ
⌞makes a practice of⌟ *{the}* sinning is also breaking the law; *is breaking* indeed, *{the}*
4472 3836 281 4472 2779 4472 3836 490 4472 2779 3836
pt.pa.nsm d.asf n.asf adv d.asf n.asf v.pai.3s cj d.nsf

ἁμαρτία ἐστὶν ἡ ἀνομία. 5 καὶ οἴδατε ὅτι ἐκεῖνος ἐφανερώθη, ἵνα
sin is *{the}* lawlessness. And you know that he appeared to take away
281 1639 3836 490 2779 3857 4022 1697 5746 2671 149 149
n.nsf v.pai.3s d.nsf n.nsf cj v.rai.2p cj r.nsm v.api.3s cj

τὰς ἁμαρτίας ἄρῃ, καὶ ἁμαρτία ἐν αὐτῷ οὐκ ἔστιν. 6 πᾶς
our sins, *take away* and that there is no sin in him. *no* *there is* No one
3836 281 149 2779 1639 1639 4024 281 1877 899 4024 1639 4024 4246
d.apf n.apf v.aas.3s cj n.nsf p.d r.dsm.3 pl v.pai.3s a.nsm

ὁ ἐν αὐτῷ μένων οὐχ ἁμαρτάνει· πᾶς ὁ ἁμαρτάνων οὐχ →
who abides in him *abides* *No* keeps on sinning; no one who continues to sin *no* has
3836 3531 1877 899 3531 4024 279 4024 4246 3836 279 4024
d.nsm p.d r.dsm.3 pt.pa.nsm pl v.pai.3s a.nsm d.nsm pt.pa.nsm pl

NASB

and just as it has
taught you, you
abide in Him.
28 Now, little chil-
dren, abide in Him,
so that when He
appears, we may
have confidence
and not shrink
away from Him in
shame at His com-
ing. 29 If you know
that He is righ-
teous, you know
that everyone also
who practices righ-
teousness is born
of Him.

Children of God Love One Another

3:1 See how great a
love the Father has
bestowed on us,
that we would be
called children of
God; and *such* we
are. For this reason
the world does not
know us, because it
did not know Him.
2 Beloved, now
we are children
of God, and it has
not appeared as
yet what we will
be. We know that
when He appears,
we will be like
Him, because we
will see Him just as
He is. 3 And every-
one who has this
hope *fixed* on Him
purifies himself,
just as He is pure.
4 Everyone who
practices sin also
practices lawless-
ness; and sin is
lawlessness. 5 You
know that He ap-
peared in order to
take away sins; and
in Him there is no
sin. 6 No one who
abides in Him sins;
no one who sins

[a] 2 Or *when it is made known*

NIV

either seen him or
known him.
7Dear children,
do not let anyone
lead you astray.
The one who does
what is right is
righteous, just as
he is righteous.
8The one who does
what is sinful is of
the devil, because
the devil has been
sinning from the
beginning. The
reason the Son of
God appeared was
to destroy the dev-
il's work. 9No one
who is born of God
will continue to
sin, because God's
seed remains in
them; they cannot
go on sinning, be-
cause they have
been born of God.
10This is how we
know who the chil-
dren of God are
and who the chil-
dren of the devil
are: Anyone who
does not do what is
right is not God's
child, nor is any-
one who does not
love their brother
and sister.

More on Love and Hatred

11For this is the
message you heard
from the begin-
ning: We should
love one another.
12Do not be like
Cain, who be-
longed to the evil
one and murdered
his brother. And
why did he mur-
der him? Because
his own actions
were evil and his
brother's were
righteous. 13Do not
be surprised, my
brothers and sis-
ters,[a] if the world
hates you.

[a] 13 The Greek word for *brothers and sisters* (*adelphoi*) refers here to believers, both men and women, as part of God's family; also in verse 16.

ἑώρακεν αὐτὸν οὐδὲ ἔγνωκεν αὐτόν. 7 τεκνία, ↱ μηδεὶς πλανάτω ὑμᾶς·
either seen him or known him. Little children, let no one deceive you.
3972 899 4028 1182 899 5448 4414 3594 4414 7007
v.rai.3s r.asm.3 cj v.rai.3s r.asm.3 n.vpn a.nsm v.pam.3s r.ap.2

ὁ ποιῶν τὴν δικαιοσύνην δίκαιός ἐστιν, καθὼς ἐκεῖνος
Whoever ⌊makes it a practice to do⌋ what is right is righteous, *is* just as he is
3836 4472 3836 1466 1639 1465 1639 2777 1697 1639
d.nsm pt.pa.nsm d.asf n.asf a.nsm v.pai.3s cj r.nsm

δίκαιός ἐστιν· 8 ὁ ποιῶν τὴν ἁμαρτίαν ἐκ τοῦ διαβόλου ἐστίν,
righteous. *is* The ⌊one who continues to⌋ *{the}* sin is of the devil, *is*
1465 1639 3836 4472 3836 281 1639 1666 3836 1333 1639
a.nsm v.pai.3s d.nsm pt.pa.nsm d.asf n.asf p.g d.gsm n.gsm v.pai.3s

ὅτι ἀπ' ἀρχῆς ὁ διάβολος ἁμαρτάνει.
because the devil has been sinning from the beginning. *the devil has been sinning* The Son
4022 3836 1333 279 279 279 608 794 3836 1333 279 3836 5626
cj p.g n.gsf d.nsm n.nsm v.pai.3s

εἰς τοῦτο ἐφανερώθη ὁ υἱὸς τοῦ θεοῦ, ἵνα
of God appeared for this purpose *appeared* *The Son of God* — that
3836 2536 5746 1650 4047 5746 3836 5626 3836 2536 2671
p.a r.asn v.api.3s d.nsm n.nsm d.gsm n.gsm cj

λύσῃ τὰ ἔργα τοῦ διαβόλου. 9 πᾶς ὁ γεγεννημένος ἐκ τοῦ θεοῦ
⌊he might destroy⌋ the works of the devil. No one *{the}* born of *{the}* God
3395 3836 2240 3836 1333 4024 4246 3836 1164 1666 3836 2536
v.aas.3s d.apn n.apn d.gsm n.gsm a.nsm d.nsm pt.rp.nsm p.g d.gsm n.gsm

ἁμαρτίαν οὐ ποιεῖ, ὅτι σπέρμα αὐτοῦ
makes a practice of sinning, *No makes a practice of* because God's seed *God's* abides
4472 4472 4472 4472 281 4024 4472 4022 899 5065 899 3531
n.asf pl v.pai.3s cj n.nsn r.gsm.3

ἐν αὐτῷ μένει, καὶ ⌊οὐ δύναται⌋ ἁμαρτάνειν, ὅτι ἐκ
in him. *abides {and}* He cannot keep on sinning, because he has been born of
1877 899 3531 2779 4024 1538 279 4022 1164 1164 1164 1164 1666
p.d r.dsm.3 v.pai.3s cj pl v.ppi.3s f.pa cj p.g

τοῦ θεοῦ γεγέννηται. 10 ἐν τούτῳ φανερά ἐστιν τὰ τέκνα τοῦ θεοῦ καὶ τὰ
{the} God. *he has been born* By this *revealed are* the children of God and the
3836 2536 1164 1877 4047 5745 1639 3836 5451 3836 2536 2779 3836
d.gsm n.gsm v.rpi.3s p.d r.dsn a.npn v.pai.3s d.npn n.npn d.gsm n.gsm cj d.npn

τέκνα τοῦ διαβόλου· πᾶς ὁ ↱ μὴ ποιῶν δικαιοσύνην
children of the devil are revealed: whoever *{the}* does not practice righteousness is
5451 3836 1333 1639 5745 4246 3836 4472 3590 4472 1466 1639
n.npn d.gsm n.gsm a.nsm d.nsm pl pt.pa.nsm n.asf

οὐκ ἔστιν ἐκ τοῦ θεοῦ, καὶ ὁ ↱ ↱ ↱ μὴ ἀγαπῶν τὸν ἀδελφὸν
not *is* of *{the}* God, nor is the one who does not love *{the}* his brother.
4024 1639 1666 3836 2536 2779 3836 26 26 26 3590 26 3836 899 81
pl v.pai.3s p.g d.gsm n.gsm adv d.nsm pl pt.pa.nsm d.asm n.asm

αὐτοῦ. 11 ὅτι αὕτη ἐστὶν ἡ ἀγγελία ἣν ἠκούσατε ἀπ' ἀρχῆς, ἵνα
his For this is the message that you heard from the beginning: that
899 4022 4047 1639 3836 32 4005 201 608 794 2671
r.gsm.3 cj r.nsf v.pai.3s d.nsf n.nsf r.asf v.aai.2p p.g n.gsf cj

ἀγαπῶμεν ἀλλήλους, 12 οὐ καθὼς Κάϊν ἐκ τοῦ πονηροῦ ἦν
we should love one another. We are not to be like Cain who was of the evil one *who was*
26 253 4024 2777 2782 1639 1639 1666 3836 4505 1639
v.pas.1p r.apm pl cj n.nsm p.g d.gsm a.gsm v.iai.3s

καὶ ἔσφαξεν τὸν ἀδελφὸν αὐτοῦ· καὶ ⌊χάριν τίνος⌋ ἔσφαξεν αὐτόν; ὅτι
and murdered *{the}* his brother. *his* And why did he murder him? Because
2779 5377 3836 899 81 899 2779 5920 5515 5377 899 4022
cj v.aai.3s d.asm n.asm r.gsm.3 cj p.g r.gsn v.aai.3s r.asm.3 cj

τὰ ἔργα αὐτοῦ πονηρὰ ἦν τὰ δὲ τοῦ ἀδελφοῦ αὐτοῦ
{the} his own deeds *his own* were evil *were* and those *and* of his brother *his* were
3836 899 899 2240 899 1639 4505 1639 1254 3836 1254 3836 899 81 899
d.npn n.npn r.gsm.3 a.npn v.iai.3s d.npn cj d.gsm n.gsm r.gsm.3

δίκαια. 13 καὶ[a] ↱ μὴ θαυμάζετε, ἀδελφοί, εἰ μισεῖ ὑμᾶς ὁ κόσμος.
righteous. So do not be surprised, brothers, if the world hates you. *the world*
1465 2779 2513 3590 2513 81 1623 3836 3180 3631 7007 3836 3180
a.npn cj pl v.pam.2p n.vpm cj v.pai.3s r.ap.2 d.nsm n.nsm

[a] [καὶ] UBS, omitted by TNIV.

NASB

has seen Him
or knows Him.
7Little children,
make sure no one
deceives you; the
one who practices
righteousness is
righteous, just as
He is righteous;
8the one who prac-
tices sin is of the
devil; for the devil
has sinned from the
beginning. The Son
of God appeared
for this purpose, to
destroy the works
of the devil. 9No
one who is born
of God practices
sin, because His
seed abides in him;
and he cannot sin,
because he is born
of God. 10By this
the children of God
and the children of
the devil are obvi-
ous: anyone who
does not practice
righteousness is not
of God, nor the one
who does not love
his brother.
11For this is the
message which you
have heard from
the beginning, that
we should love
one another; 12not
as Cain, *who* was
of the evil one and
slew his brother.
And for what
reason did he slay
him? Because his
deeds were evil,
and his brother's
were righteous.
13Do not be sur-
prised, brethren, if
the world hates

NIV

[14]We know that
we have passed
from death to life,
because we love
each other. Anyone
who does not love
remains in death.
[15]Anyone who
hates a brother or
sister is a murderer,
and you know that
no murderer has
eternal life residing
in him.
[16]This is how we
know what love is:
Jesus Christ laid
down his life for
us. And we ought
to lay down our
lives for our broth-
ers and sisters. [17]If
anyone has ma-
terial possessions
and sees a brother
or sister in need
but has no pity on
them, how can the
love of God be in
that person? [18]Dear
children, let us not
love with words
or speech but with
actions and in
truth.
[19]This is how we
know that we be-
long to the truth
and how we set our
hearts at rest in his
presence: [20]If our
hearts condemn
us, we know that
God is greater than
our hearts, and he
knows everything.
[21]Dear friends, if
our hearts do not
condemn us, we
have confidence
before God [22]and

---

14 ἡμεῖς οἴδαμεν ὅτι μεταβεβήκαμεν ἐκ τοῦ θανάτου εἰς τὴν ζωήν, ὅτι
We know that we have crossed over from {the} death to {the} life, because
7005 3857 4022 3553 1666 3836 2505 1650 3836 2437 4022
r.np.1 v.rai.1p cj v.rai.1p p.g d.gsm n.gsm p.a d.asf n.asf cj

ἀγαπῶμεν τοὺς ἀδελφούς· ὁ ↱ μὴ ἀγαπῶν μένει ἐν τῷ θανάτῳ.
we love the brothers. Whoever does not love remains in the realm of death.
26 3836 81 3836 26 3590 26 3531 1877 3836 2505
v.pai.1p d.apm n.apm d.nsm pl pt.pa.nsm v.pai.3s p.d d.dsm n.dsm

15 πᾶς ὁ μισῶν τὸν ἀδελφὸν αὐτοῦ ἀνθρωποκτόνος ἐστίν, καὶ
Everyone who hates {the} his brother his is a murderer, is and
4246 3836 3631 3836 899 81 899 1639 475 1639 2779
a.nsm d.nsm pt.pa.nsm d.asm n.asm r.gsm.3 n.nsm v.pai.3s cj

οἴδατε ὅτι πᾶς ἀνθρωποκτόνος οὐκ ἔχει ζωὴν αἰώνιον ἐν
you know that {every} no murderer no has eternal life eternal abiding in
3857 4022 4246 4024 475 4024 2400 173 2437 173 3531 1877
v.rai.2p cj a.nsm n.nsm pl v.pai.3s n.asf a.asf p.d

αὐτῷ μένουσαν. 16 ἐν τούτῳ ἐγνώκαμεν τὴν ἀγάπην, ὅτι ἐκεῖνος
him. abiding By this ⌞we have come to know⌟ {the} love: that he laid down
899 3531 1877 4047 1182 3836 27 4022 1697 5502 5502
r.dsm.3 pt.pa.asf p.d r.dsn v.rai.1p d.asf n.asf cj r.nsm

ὑπὲρ ἡμῶν ↰ τὴν ψυχὴν αὐτοῦ ἔθηκεν· καὶ ἡμεῖς ὀφείλομεν
his life on our behalf. {the} life his laid down And we are obligated to lay
899 6034 5642 7005 5642 3836 6034 899 5502 2779 7005 4053 5502 5502
p.g r.gp.1 d.asf n.asf r.gsm.3 v.aai.3s cj r.np.1 v.pai.1p

ὑπὲρ τῶν ἀδελφῶν τὰς ψυχὰς θεῖναι. 17 ὃς δ᾽ ἂν ἔχῃ
down our lives for the brothers. our lives to lay down But whoever But ~ has
5502 3836 6034 5642 3836 81 3836 6034 5502 1254 4005 1254 323 2400
p.g d.gpm n.gpm d.apf n.apf f.aa r.nsm cj pl v.pas.3s

τὸν βίον τοῦ κόσμου καὶ θεωρῇ τὸν ἀδελφὸν αὐτοῦ
this world's {the} resources this world's and sees {the} his fellow Christian his in
3836 3180 3836 1050 3836 3180 2779 2555 3836 899 81 899 2400
d.asm n.asm d.gsm n.gsm cj v.pas.3s d.asm n.asm r.gsm.3

χρείαν ἔχοντα καὶ κλείσῃ τὰ σπλάγχνα αὐτοῦ ἀπ᾽ αὐτοῦ, πῶς ↱ ἡ ἀγάπη
need in yet closes {the} his heart his against him, how does the love
5970 2400 2779 3091 3836 899 5073 899 608 899 4802 3531 3836 27
n.asf pt.pa.asm cj v.aas.3s d.apn n.apn r.gsm.3 p.g r.gsm.3 pl d.nsf n.nsf

τοῦ θεοῦ μένει ἐν αὐτῷ; 18 Τεκνία, μὴ ἀγαπῶμεν λόγῳ μηδὲ τῇ
of God abide in him? Little children, let us love, not let us love in word or {the}
3836 2536 3531 1877 899 5448 26 26 26 3590 26 3364 3593 3836
d.gsm n.gsm v.pai.3s p.d r.dsm.3 n.vpn pl v.pas.1p n.dsm cj d.dsf

γλώσσῃ ἀλλὰ ἐν ἔργῳ καὶ ἀληθείᾳ. 19 καὶ[a] ἐν τούτῳ γνωσόμεθα ὅτι
speech but in action and truth. And by this we will know that we are
1185 247 1877 2240 2779 237 2779 1877 4047 1182 4022 1639 1639
n.dsf cj p.d n.dsn cj n.dsf cj p.d r.dsn v.fmi.1p cj

ἐκ τῆς ἀληθείας ἐσμέν, καὶ ἔμπροσθεν αὐτοῦ
of the truth we are and will set our conscience at rest in his
1666 3836 237 1639 2779 4275 4275 7005 2840 4275 4275 1869 899
p.g d.gsf n.gsf v.pai.1p cj p.g r.gsm.3

↰ πείσομεν τὴν καρδίαν ἡμῶν, 20 ὅτι ἐὰν καταγινώσκῃ ἡμῶν
presence, will set at rest {the} conscience our that if our conscience condemns us,
1869 4275 3836 2840 7005 4022 1569 3836 2840 2861 7005
v.fai.1p d.asf n.asf r.gp.1 cj cj v.pas.3s r.gp.1

ἡ καρδία, ὅτι μείζων ἐστὶν ὁ θεὸς τῆς καρδίας ἡμῶν καὶ
our conscience that God is greater is {the} God than our conscience our and
3836 2840 4022 2536 1639 3489 1639 3836 2536 3836 7005 2840 7005 2779
d.nsf n.nsf cj a.nsm.c v.pai.3s d.nsm n.nsm d.gsf n.gsf r.gp.1 cj

γινώσκει πάντα. 21 ἀγαπητοί, ἐὰν ἡ καρδία ἡμῶν[b] ↱ μὴ καταγινώσκῃ,
knows all things. Dear friends, if {the} our conscience our does not condemn
1182 4246 28 1569 3836 7005 2840 7005 2861 3590 2861
v.pai.3s a.apn a.vpm cj d.nsf n.nsf r.gp.1 pl v.pas.3s

παρρησίαν ἔχομεν πρὸς τὸν θεόν 22 καὶ ⌞ὃ ἐὰν⌟ αἰτῶμεν
us, we have confidence we have ⌞in the presence of⌟ {the} God, and whatever we ask
2400 2400 4244 2400 4639 3836 2536 2779 4005 1569 160
n.asf v.pai.1p p.a d.asm n.asm cj r.asn pl v.pas.1p

[a] [καὶ] UBS, omitted by TNIV.
[b] [ἡμῶν] UBS.

NASB

you. [14]We know
that we have
passed out of death
into life, because
we love the breth-
ren. He who does
not love abides in
death. [15]Every-
one who hates
his brother is a
murderer; and you
know that no mur-
derer has eternal
life abiding in him.
[16]We know love by
this, that He laid
down His life for
us; and we ought to
lay down our lives
for the brethren.
[17]But whoever
has the world's
goods, and sees
his brother in need
and closes his heart
against him, how
does the love of
God abide in him?
[18]Little children,
let us not love
with word or with
tongue, but in deed
and truth. [19]We will
know by this that
we are of the truth,
and will assure our
heart before Him
[20]in whatever our
heart condemns us;
for God is greater
than our heart and
knows all things.
[21]Beloved, if our
heart does not
condemn us, we
have confidence
before God; [22]and
whatever we ask

NIV

receive from him
anything we ask,
because we keep
his commands and
do what pleases
him. [23]And this
is his command:
to believe in the
name of his Son,
Jesus Christ, and
to love one another
as he commanded
us. [24]The one who
keeps God's com-
mands lives in him,
and he in them.
And this is how we
know that he lives
in us: We know
it by the Spirit he
gave us.

On Denying the Incarnation

4 Dear friends,
do not believe
every spirit, but
test the spirits to
see whether they
are from God, be-
cause many false
prophets have gone
out into the world.
[2]This is how you
can recognize
the Spirit of God:
Every spirit that
acknowledges that
Jesus Christ has
come in the flesh
is from God, [3]but
every spirit that
does not acknowl-
edge Jesus is not
from God. This
is the spirit of the
antichrist, which
you have heard is
coming and even
now is already in
the world.
[4]You, dear chil-
dren, are from God
and have overcome
them, because the
one

λαμβάνομεν ἀπ' αὐτοῦ, ὅτι τὰς ἐντολὰς αὐτοῦ τηροῦμεν καὶ
we receive from him, because we keep *{the}* his commandments *his* *we keep* and
3284 608 899 4022 5498 5498 3836 899 1953 899 5498 2779
v.pai.1p p.g r.gsm.3 cj d.apf n.apf r.gsm.3 v.pai.1p cj

τὰ ἀρεστὰ ἐνώπιον αὐτοῦ ↰ ποιοῦμεν. [23] καὶ αὕτη ἐστὶν ἡ
do what is pleasing in his sight. *do* And this is *{the}* his
4472 3836 744 1967 899 1967 4472 2779 4047 1639 3836 899
d.apn a.apn p.g r.gsm.3 v.pai.1p cj r.nsf v.pai.3s d.nsf

ἐντολὴ αὐτοῦ, ἵνα πιστεύσωμεν τῷ ὀνόματι τοῦ υἱοῦ αὐτοῦ Ἰησοῦ
commandment: *his* that we believe ⌞in the⌟ name of his Son *his* Jesus
1953 899 2671 4409 3836 3950 3836 899 5626 899 2652
n.nsf r.gsm.3 cj v.aas.1p d.dsn n.dsn d.gsm n.gsm r.gsm.3 n.gsm

Χριστοῦ καὶ ἀγαπῶμεν ἀλλήλους, καθὼς ἔδωκεν ἐντολὴν ἡμῖν. [24] καὶ
Christ and love one another, just as he gave us the commandment. *us* And
5986 2779 26 253 2777 1443 7005 1953 7005 2779
n.gsm cj v.pas.1p r.apm cj v.aai.3s n.asf r.dp.1 cj

ὁ τηρῶν τὰς ἐντολὰς αὐτοῦ ἐν αὐτῷ μένει καὶ αὐτὸς ἐν
the ⌞one who keeps⌟ *{the}* his commandments *his* resides in him, *resides* and he in
3836 5498 3836 899 1953 899 3531 1877 899 3531 2779 899 1877
d.nsm pt.pa.nsm d.apf n.apf r.gsm.3 p.d r.dsm.3 v.pai.3s cj r.nsm p.d

αὐτῷ· καὶ ἐν τούτῳ γινώσκομεν ὅτι μένει ἐν ἡμῖν, ἐκ τοῦ πνεύματος οὗ
him. And by this we know that he abides in us: by the Spirit whom
899 2779 1877 4047 1182 4022 3531 1877 7005 1666 3836 4460 4005
r.dsm.3 cj p.d r.dsn v.pai.1p cj v.pai.3s p.d r.dp.1 p.g d.gsn n.gsn r.gsn

ἡμῖν ἔδωκεν.
he has given to us. *he has given*
1443 1443 1443 7005 1443
r.dp.1 v.aai.3s

[4:1] ἀγαπητοί, μὴ παντὶ πνεύματι πιστεύετε ἀλλὰ δοκιμάζετε τὰ
Dear friends, do not believe every spirit, *do believe* but test the
28 4409 3590 4409 4246 4460 4409 247 1507 3836
a.vpm pl a.dsn n.dsn v.pam.2p cj v.pam.2p d.apn

πνεύματα εἰ ἐκ τοῦ θεοῦ ἐστιν, ὅτι πολλοὶ
spirits to find out whether they are from *{the}* God, *they are* because many
4460 1623 1639 1639 1666 3836 2536 1639 4022 4498
n.apn cj p.g d.gsm n.gsm v.pai.3s cj a.npm

ψευδοπροφῆται ἐξεληλύθασιν εἰς τὸν κόσμον. [2] ⌞ἐν τούτῳ⌟ γινώσκετε
false prophets have gone out into the world. This is how you can recognize
6021 2002 1650 3836 3180 1877 4047 1182
n.npm v.rai.3p p.a d.asm n.asm p.d r.dsn v.pai.2p

τὸ πνεῦμα τοῦ θεοῦ· πᾶν πνεῦμα ὃ ὁμολογεῖ Ἰησοῦν Χριστὸν ἐν
the Spirit of God: every spirit that confesses that Jesus Christ has come in
3836 4460 3836 2536 4246 4460 4005 3933 2652 5986 2262 2262 1877
d.asn n.asn d.gsm n.gsm a.nsn n.nsn r.nsn v.pai.3s n.asm n.asm p.d

σαρκὶ ἐληλυθότα ἐκ τοῦ θεοῦ ἐστιν, [3] καὶ πᾶν πνεῦμα ὃ ↱ μὴ
the flesh *has come* is from *{the}* God, *is* but every spirit that does not
4922 2262 1639 1666 3836 2536 1639 2779 4246 4460 4005 3933 3590
n.dsf pt.ra.asm p.g d.gsm n.gsm v.pai.3s cj a.nsn n.nsn r.nsn pl

ὁμολογεῖ τὸν Ἰησοῦν[a] ἐκ τοῦ θεοῦ οὐκ ἔστιν· καὶ τοῦτό ἐστιν τὸ
confess *{the}* Jesus is not from *{the}* God. *not* *is* *{and}* This is the spirit
3933 3836 2652 1639 4024 1666 3836 2536 4024 1639 2779 4047 1639 3836
v.pai.3s d.asm n.asm p.g d.gsm n.gsm pl v.pai.3s cj r.nsn v.pai.3s d.nsn

τοῦ ἀντιχρίστου, ὃ ἀκηκόατε ὅτι ἔρχεται, καὶ νῦν ἐν τῷ
of the Antichrist, which you heard *{that}* was coming, and now is already in the
3836 532 4005 201 4022 2262 2779 3814 1639 2453 1877 3836
d.gsm n.gsm r.asn v.rai.2p cj v.pmi.3s cj adv p.d d.dsm

κόσμῳ ἐστὶν ἤδη. [4] ὑμεῖς ἐκ τοῦ θεοῦ ἐστε,
world. *is* *already* Little children, you have been born of *{the}* God *have been born*
3180 1639 2453 5448 5448 7007 1639 1639 1639 1666 3836 2536 1639
n.dsm v.pai.3s adv r.np.2 p.g d.gsm n.gsm v.pai.2p

τεκνία, καὶ νενικήκατε αὐτούς, ὅτι μείζων ἐστὶν ὁ ἐν ὑμῖν
Little children and have overcome them, because *greater* *is* the one who is in you
5448 2779 3771 899 4022 3489 1639 3836 1877 7007
n.vpn cj v.rai.2p r.apm.3 cj a.nsm.c v.pai.3s d.nsm p.d r.dp.2

NASB

we receive from
Him, because we
keep His com-
mandments and
do the things that
are pleasing in His
sight.
[23]This is His com-
mandment, that we
believe in the name
of His Son Jesus
Christ, and love
one another, just
as He commanded
us. [24]The one who
keeps His com-
mandments abides
in Him, and He in
him. We know by
this that He abides
in us, by the Spirit
whom He has
given us.

Testing the Spirits

[4:1]Beloved, do not
believe every spir-
it, but test the spir-
its to see whether
they are from God,
because many
false prophets have
gone out into the
world. [2]By this you
know the Spirit of
God: every spirit
that confesses that
Jesus Christ has
come in the flesh is
from God; [3]and ev-
ery spirit that does
not confess Jesus is
not from God; this
is the *spirit* of the
antichrist, of which
you have heard that
it is coming, and
now it is already
in the world. [4]You
are from God, little
children, and have
overcome them;
because greater is
He who is in you

[a] Χριστὸν ἐν σαρκὶ ἐληλυθότα included by TR after Ἰησοῦν.

NIV

who is in you is
greater than the
one who is in the
world. 5 They are
from the world and
therefore speak
from the viewpoint
of the world, and
the world listens to
them. 6 We are from
God, and whoever
knows God listens
to us; but whoever
is not from God
does not listen to
us. This is how we
recognize the Spir-
it[a] of truth and the
spirit of falsehood.

God's Love and Ours

7 Dear friends, let
us love one anoth-
er, for love comes
from God. Every-
one who loves has
been born of God
and knows God.
8 Whoever does not
love does not know
God, because God
is love. 9 This is
how God showed
his love among us:
He sent his one
and only Son into
the world that we
might live through
him. 10 This is love:
not that we loved
God, but that he
loved us and sent
his Son as an aton-
ing sacrifice for
our sins. 11 Dear
friends, since God
so loved us, we
also ought to love
one another. 12 No
one has ever seen
God; but if we love
one another, God
lives in us and his
love is

ἢ ὁ ἐν τῷ κόσμῳ. 5 αὐτοὶ ἐκ τοῦ κόσμου εἰσίν,
is greater than the one who is in the world. They are of the world; *are*
1639 3489 2445 3836 1877 3836 3180 899 1639 1666 3836 3180 1639
pl d.nsm p.d d.dsm n.dsm r.npm p.g d.gsm n.gsm v.pai.3p

⌞διὰ τοῦτο⌟ ἐκ τοῦ κόσμου λαλοῦσιν καὶ ὁ κόσμος
therefore they speak from the world's perspective *they speak* and the world listens
1328 4047 3281 3281 1666 3836 3180 3281 2779 3836 3180 201
p.a r.asn p.g d.gsm n.gsm v.pai.3p cj d.nsm n.nsm

αὐτῶν ἀκούει. 6 ἡμεῖς ἐκ τοῦ θεοῦ ἐσμεν, ὁ γινώσκων τὸν θεὸν
to them. *listens to* We are from *{the}* God. *are* The ⌞person who knows⌟ *{the}* God
201 899 201 7005 1639 1666 3836 2536 1639 3836 1182 3836 2536
r.gpm.3 v.pai.3s r.np.1 p.g d.gsm n.gsm v.pai.1p d.nsm pt.pa.nsm d.asm n.asm

ἀκούει ἡμῶν, ὃς οὐκ ἔστιν ἐκ τοῦ θεοῦ ↱ οὐκ ἀκούει ἡμῶν. ἐκ
listens to us, but whoever is not *is* from *{the}* God does not listen to us. By
201 7005 4005 1639 4024 1639 1666 3836 2536 201 4024 201 7005 1666
v.pai.3s r.gp.1 r.nsm pl v.pai.3s p.g d.gsm n.gsm pl v.pai.3s r.gp.1 p.g

τούτου γινώσκομεν τὸ πνεῦμα τῆς ἀληθείας καὶ τὸ πνεῦμα τῆς πλάνης.
this we know the Spirit of truth and the spirit of error.
4047 1182 3836 4460 3836 237 2779 3836 4460 3836 4415
r.gsn v.pai.1p d.asn n.asn d.gsf n.gsf cj d.asn n.asn d.gsf n.gsf

7 ἀγαπητοί, ἀγαπῶμεν ἀλλήλους, ὅτι ἡ ἀγάπη ἐκ τοῦ θεοῦ ἐστιν, καὶ
Dear friends, let us love one another, because *{the}* love is from *{the}* God, *is* and
28 26 253 4022 3836 27 1639 1666 3836 2536 1639 2779
a.vpm v.pas.1p r.apm cj d.nsf n.nsf p.g d.gsm n.gsm v.pai.3s cj

πᾶς ὁ ἀγαπῶν ἐκ τοῦ θεοῦ γεγέννηται καὶ γινώσκει τὸν θεόν.
everyone who loves has been born of *{the}* God *has been born* and knows *{the}* God.
4246 3836 26 1164 1164 1164 1666 3836 2536 1164 2779 1182 3836 2536
a.nsm d.nsm pt.pa.nsm p.g d.gsm n.gsm v.rpi.3s cj v.pai.3s d.asm n.asm

8 ὁ ↱ ↱ ↱ μὴ ἀγαπῶν ↱ οὐκ ἔγνω τὸν θεόν, ὅτι ὁ θεὸς
The person who does not love does not know *{the}* God, because *{the}* God is
3836 26 26 26 3590 26 1182 4024 1182 3836 2536 4022 3836 2536 1639
d.nsm pl pt.pa.nsm pl v.aai.3s d.asm n.asm cj d.nsm n.nsm

ἀγάπη ἐστίν. 9 ἐν τούτῳ ἐφανερώθη ἡ ἀγάπη τοῦ θεοῦ ἐν ἡμῖν,
love. *is* By this the love of God is revealed *the love of God* to us:
27 1639 1877 4047 3836 27 3836 2536 5746 3836 27 3836 2536 1877 7005
n.nsf v.pai.3s p.d r.dsn v.api.3s d.nsf n.nsf d.gsm n.gsm p.d r.dp.1

ὅτι τὸν υἱὸν αὐτοῦ τὸν μονογενῆ ἀπέσταλκεν ὁ
that God has sent *{the}* his one and only Son *his* *{the}* *one and only* *has sent* *{the}*
4022 2536 690 690 3836 899 3666 3666 3666 5626 899 3836 3666 690 3836
cj d.asm n.asm r.gsm.3 d.asm a.asm v.rai.3s d.nsm

θεὸς εἰς τὸν κόσμον ἵνα ζήσωμεν δι᾽ αὐτοῦ. 10 ἐν τούτῳ ἐστὶν ἡ
God into the world so that ⌞we might live⌟ through him. In this is *{the}*
2536 1650 3836 3180 2671 2409 1328 899 1877 4047 1639 3836
n.nsm p.a d.asm n.asm cj v.aas.1p p.g r.gsm.3 p.d r.dsn v.pai.3s d.nsf

ἀγάπη, οὐχ ὅτι ἡμεῖς ἠγαπήκαμεν τὸν θεὸν ἀλλ᾽ ὅτι αὐτὸς ἠγάπησεν ἡμᾶς καὶ
love, not that we have loved *{the}* God but that he loved us and
27 4024 4022 7005 26 3836 2536 247 4022 899 26 7005 2779
n.nsf pl cj r.np.1 v.rai.1p d.asm n.asm cj cj r.nsm v.aai.3s r.ap.1 cj

ἀπέστειλεν τὸν υἱὸν αὐτοῦ → ἱλασμὸν περὶ τῶν ἁμαρτιῶν ἡμῶν.
sent *{the}* his Son *his* as a propitiation for *{the}* our sins. *our*
690 3836 899 5626 899 2662 4309 3836 7005 281 7005
v.aai.3s d.asm n.asm r.gsm.3 n.asm p.g d.gpf n.gpf r.gp.1

11 ἀγαπητοί, εἰ οὕτως ὁ θεὸς ἠγάπησεν ἡμᾶς, καὶ ἡμεῖς
Dear friends, if God loved us like that, *{the}* *God* *loved* *us* we also *we*
28 1623 2536 26 7005 4048 3836 2536 26 7005 7005 2779 7005
a.vpm cj adv d.nsm n.nsm v.aai.3s r.ap.1 adv r.np.1

ὀφείλομεν ἀλλήλους ἀγαπᾶν. 12 θεὸν οὐδεὶς ↱ πώποτε τεθέαται. ἐὰν
ought to love one another. *to love* *God* No one has ever seen God. If
4053 26 26 253 26 2536 4029 2517 4799 2517 2536 1569
v.pai.1p r.apm f.pa n.asm a.nsm adv v.rmi.3s cj

ἀγαπῶμεν ἀλλήλους, ὁ θεὸς ἐν ἡμῖν μένει καὶ ἡ ἀγάπη αὐτοῦ
we love one another, *{the}* God abides in us, *abides* and *{the}* his love *his* has
26 253 3836 2536 3531 1877 7005 3531 2779 3836 899 27 899 1639
v.pas.1p r.apm d.nsm n.nsm p.d r.dp.1 v.pai.3s cj d.nsf n.nsf r.gsm.3

NASB

than he who is in
the world. 5 They
are from the world;
therefore they
speak *as* from
the world, and
the world listens
to them. 6 We are
from God; he who
knows God listens
to us; he who is not
from God does not
listen to us. By this
we know the spirit
of truth and the
spirit of error.

God Is Love

7 Beloved, let us
love one another,
for love is from
God; and everyone
who loves is born
of God and knows
God. 8 The one who
does not love does
not know God,
for God is love.
9 By this the love
of God was mani-
fested in us, that
God has sent His
only begotten Son
into the world so
that we might live
through Him. 10 In
this is love, not that
we loved God, but
that He loved us
and sent His Son
to be the propi-
tiation for our sins.
11 Beloved, if God
so loved us, we
also ought to love
one another. 12 No
one has seen God
at any time; if we
love one another,
God abides in us,
and His love is

[a] 6 Or *spirit*

NIV

made complete in us. [13]This is how we know that we live in him and he in us: He has given us of his Spirit. [14]And we have seen and testify that the Father has sent his Son to be the Savior of the world. [15]If anyone acknowledges that Jesus is the Son of God, God lives in them and they in God. [16]And so we know and rely on the love God has for us.

God is love. Whoever lives in love lives in God, and God in them. [17]This is how love is made complete among us so that we will have confidence on the day of judgment: In this world we are like Jesus. [18]There is no fear in love. But perfect love drives out fear, because fear has to do with punishment. The one who fears is not made perfect in love.

[19]We love because he first loved us. [20]Whoever claims to love God yet hates a brother or sister is a liar. For whoever does not love

ἐν ἡμῖν τετελειωμένη ἐστίν. [13] ἐν τούτῳ γινώσκομεν ὅτι
achieved its goal in us. *achieved its goal* *has* By this we know that we abide
5457 5457 5457 1877 7005 5457 1639 1877 4047 1182 4022 3531 3531
p.d r.dp.1 pt.rp.nsf v.pai.3s p.d r.dsn v.pai.1p cj

ἐν αὐτῷ μένομεν καὶ αὐτὸς ἐν ἡμῖν, ὅτι ἐκ τοῦ
in God *we abide* and he in us: because he has given us of *{the}* his
1877 899 3531 2779 899 1877 7005 4022 1443 1443 1443 7005 1666 3836 899
p.d r.dsm.3 v.pai.1p cj r.nsm p.d r.dp.1 cj p.g d.gsn

πνεύματος αὐτοῦ δέδωκεν ἡμῖν. [14] καὶ ἡμεῖς τεθεάμεθα καὶ μαρτυροῦμεν ὅτι ὁ
Spirit. *his* *he has given* *us* And we have seen and testify that the
4460 899 1443 7005 2779 7005 2517 2779 3455 4022 3836
n.gsn r.gsm.3 v.rai.3s r.dp.1 cj r.np.1 v.rmi.1p cj v.pai.1p cj d.nsm

πατὴρ ἀπέσταλκεν τὸν υἱὸν → σωτῆρα τοῦ κόσμου. [15] ὃς ἐὰν
Father has sent his Son as the Savior of the world. If anyone *If*
4252 690 3836 5626 5400 3836 3180 1569 4005 1569
n.nsm v.rai.3s d.asm n.asm n.asm d.gsm n.gsm r.nsm pl

ὁμολογήσῃ ὅτι Ἰησοῦς ἐστιν ὁ υἱὸς τοῦ θεοῦ, ὁ θεὸς ἐν αὐτῷ μένει
confesses that Jesus is the Son of God, *{the}* God abides in him *abides*
3933 4022 2652 1639 3836 5626 3836 2536 3836 2536 3531 1877 899 3531
v.aas.3s cj n.nsm v.pai.3s d.nsm n.nsm d.gsm n.gsm d.nsm n.nsm p.d r.dsm.3 v.pai.3s

καὶ αὐτὸς ἐν τῷ θεῷ. [16] καὶ ἡμεῖς ἐγνώκαμεν καὶ πεπιστεύκαμεν τὴν
and he in *{the}* God. And we ⌞have come to know⌟ and to trust the
2779 899 1877 3836 2536 2779 7005 1182 2779 4409 3836
cj r.nsm p.d d.dsm n.dsm cj r.np.1 v.rai.1p cj v.rai.1p d.asf

ἀγάπην ἣν ἔχει ὁ θεὸς ἐν ἡμῖν. ὁ θεὸς ἀγάπη ἐστίν, καὶ ὁ
love that God has *{the}* *God* for us. *{the}* God is love, *is* and the
27 4005 2536 2400 3836 2536 1877 7005 3836 2536 1639 27 1639 2779 3836
n.asf r.asf v.pai.3s d.nsm n.nsm p.d r.dp.1 d.nsm n.nsm n.nsf v.pai.3s cj d.nsm

μένων ἐν τῇ ἀγάπῃ ἐν τῷ θεῷ μένει καὶ ὁ θεὸς ἐν
⌞one who abides⌟ in *{the}* love abides in *{the}* God, *abides* and *{the}* God abides in
3531 1877 3836 27 3531 1877 3836 2536 3531 2779 3836 2536 3531 1877
pt.pa.nsm p.d d.dsf n.dsf p.d d.dsm n.dsm v.pai.3s cj d.nsm n.nsm p.d

αὐτῷ μένει. [17] ἐν τούτῳ τετελείωται ἡ ἀγάπη μεθ᾽ ἡμῶν, ἵνα
him. *abides* By this, love is fully realized *{the}* *love* among us, so that we may
899 3531 1877 4047 27 5457 3836 27 3552 7005 2671 2400 2400
r.dsm.3 v.pai.3s p.d r.dsn v.rpi.3s d.nsf n.nsf p.g r.gp.1 cj

παρρησίαν ἔχωμεν ἐν τῇ ἡμέρᾳ τῆς κρίσεως, ὅτι καθὼς ἐκεῖνός ἐστιν
have confidence *we may have* in the day of judgment; because just as he is,
2400 4244 2400 1877 3836 2465 3836 3213 4022 2777 1697 1639
n.asf v.pas.1p p.d d.dsf n.dsf d.gsf n.gsf cj cj r.nsm v.pai.3s

καὶ ἡμεῖς ἐσμεν ἐν τῷ κόσμῳ τούτῳ. [18] φόβος οὐκ ἔστιν
so also are we *are* in *{the}* this world. *this* There is no fear *no* *There is*
2779 1639 7005 1639 1877 3836 4047 3180 4047 1639 1639 4024 5832 4024 1639
adv r.np.1 v.pai.1p p.d d.dsm n.dsm r.dsm n.nsm pl v.pai.3s

ἐν τῇ ἀγάπῃ ἀλλ᾽ ἡ τελεία ἀγάπη ἔξω βάλλει τὸν φόβον, ὅτι ὁ
in *{the}* love, but *{the}* perfect love drives out *drives* *{the}* fear because *{the}*
1877 3836 27 247 3836 5455 27 965 2032 965 3836 5832 4022 3836
p.d d.dsf n.dsf cj d.nsf a.nsf n.nsf adv v.pai.3s d.asm n.asm cj d.nsm

φόβος κόλασιν ἔχει, ὁ δὲ φοβούμενος ↱ οὐ
fear has to do with punishment. *has to do with* So the *So* one who fears has not
5832 2400 2400 2400 2400 3136 2400 1254 3836 1254 5828 5457 4024
n.nsm n.asf v.pai.3s d.nsm cj pt.pp.nsm pl

τετελείωται ἐν τῇ ἀγάπῃ. [19] ἡμεῖς ἀγαπῶμεν, ὅτι αὐτὸς πρῶτος ἠγάπησεν
been perfected in *{the}* love. We love because he first loved
5457 1877 3836 27 7005 26 4022 899 4755 26
v.rpi.3s p.d d.dsf n.dsf r.np.1 v.pai.1p cj r.nsm a.nsm v.aai.3s

ἡμᾶς. [20] ἐὰν τις εἴπῃ ὅτι ἀγαπῶ τὸν θεὸν καὶ τὸν ἀδελφὸν αὐτοῦ
us. If someone says, ~ "I love *{the}* God," yet hates *{the}* his brother, *his*
7005 1569 5516 3306 4022 26 3836 2536 2779 3631 3836 899 81 899
r.ap.1 cj r.nsm v.aas.3s cj v.pai.1s d.asm n.asm cj d.asm n.asm r.gsm.3

μισῇ, ψεύστης ἐστίν· ὁ γὰρ ↱ ↱ ↱ μὴ ἀγαπῶν τὸν
hates he is a liar; *he is* for the *for* one who does not love *{the}* his
3631 1639 1639 6026 1639 1142 3836 1142 26 26 26 3590 26 3836 899
v.pas.3s n.nsm v.pai.3s d.nsm cj pl pt.pa.nsm d.asm

NASB

perfected in us. [13]By this we know that we abide in Him and He in us, because He has given us of His Spirit. [14]We have seen and testify that the Father has sent the Son *to be* the Savior of the world.

[15]Whoever confesses that Jesus is the Son of God, God abides in him, and he in God. [16]We have come to know and have believed the love which God has for us. God is love, and the one who abides in love abides in God, and God abides in him. [17]By this, love is perfected with us, so that we may have confidence in the day of judgment; because as He is, so also are we in this world. [18]There is no fear in love; but perfect love casts out fear, because fear involves punishment, and the one who fears is not perfected in love. [19]We love, because He first loved us. [20]If someone says, "I love God," and hates his brother, he is a liar; for the one who does not

NIV

their brother and
sister, whom they
have seen, cannot
love God, whom
they have not seen.
21 And he has given
us this command:
Anyone who loves
God must also love
their brother and
sister.

Faith in the Incarnate Son of God

5 Everyone who
believes that
Jesus is the Christ
is born of God,
and everyone who
loves the father
loves his child as
well. 2 This is how
we know that we
love the children
of God: by loving
God and carrying
out his commands.
3 In fact, this is
love for God: to
keep his com-
mands. And his
commands are not
burdensome, 4 for
everyone born of
God overcomes
the world. This is
the victory that
has overcome the
world, even our
faith. 5 Who is it
that overcomes the
world? Only the
one who believes
that Jesus is the
Son of God.
6 This is the one
who came by wa-
ter and blood—
Jesus Christ. He
did not come by
water only, but by
water and blood.
And it is the Spir-
it who testifies,
because the Spirit
is the

ἀδελφὸν αὐτοῦ ὃν ἑώρακεν, τὸν θεὸν ὃν ↱ ↱ οὐχ ἑώρακεν ⌊οὐ
brother *his* whom he has seen, cannot love *{the}* God whom he has not seen. *cannot*
81 899 4005 3972 4024 26 3836 2536 4005 3972 3972 4024 3972 4024
n.asm r.gsm.3 r.asm v.rai.3s d.asm n.asm r.asm pl v.rai.3s pl

δύναται⌋ ἀγαπᾶν. 21 καὶ ταύτην τὴν ἐντολὴν ἔχομεν ἀπ' αὐτοῦ, ἵνα
love And *this* the commandment we have from him is this: *{that}*
1538 26 2779 4047 3836 1953 2400 608 899 4047 2671
v.ppi.3s f.pa cj r.asf d.asf n.asf v.pai.1p p.g r.gsm.3 cj

ὁ ἀγαπῶν τὸν θεὸν → ἀγαπᾷ καὶ τὸν ἀδελφὸν αὐτοῦ.
the ⌊one who loves⌋ *{the}* God must also love *also* *{the}* his brother. *his*
3836 26 3836 2536 2779 26 2779 3836 899 81 899
d.nsm pt.pa.nsm d.asm n.asm v.pas.3s adv d.asm n.asm r.gsm.3

5:1 πᾶς ὁ πιστεύων ὅτι Ἰησοῦς ἐστιν ὁ Χριστὸς, ἐκ τοῦ
Everyone who believes that Jesus is the Christ has been born of *{the}*
4246 3836 4409 4022 2652 1639 3836 5986 1164 1164 1164 1666 3836
a.nsm d.nsm pt.pa.nsm cj n.nsm v.pai.3s d.nsm n.nsm p.g d.gsm

θεοῦ γεγέννηται, καὶ πᾶς ὁ ἀγαπῶν τὸν γεννήσαντα ἀγαπᾷ καὶ [a] τὸν
God, *has been born* and everyone who loves the father loves *{also}* *{the}* his
2536 1164 2779 4246 3836 26 3836 1164 26 2779 3836 899
n.gsm v.rpi.3s cj a.nsm d.nsm pt.pa.nsm d.asm pt.aa.asm v.pai.3s adv d.asm

γεγεννημένον ἐξ αὐτοῦ. 2 ἐν τούτῳ γινώσκομεν ὅτι ἀγαπῶμεν τὰ τέκνα τοῦ
child. *{from}* *his* By this we know that we love the children of
1164 1666 899 1877 4047 1182 4022 26 3836 5451 3836
pt.rp.asm p.g r.gsm.3 p.d r.dsn v.pai.1p cj v.pai.1p d.apn n.apn d.gsm

θεοῦ, ὅταν τὸν θεὸν ἀγαπῶμεν καὶ τὰς ἐντολὰς αὐτοῦ
God: whenever we love *{the}* God *we love* and obey *{the}* his commandments. *his*
2536 4020 26 26 3836 2536 26 2779 4472 3836 899 1953 899
n.gsm cj d.asm n.asm v.pas.1p cj d.apf n.apf r.gsm.3

ποιῶμεν. 3 αὕτη γάρ ἐστιν ἡ ἀγάπη τοῦ θεοῦ, ἵνα τὰς
obey For this *For* is the love of God: that we keep *{the}* his
4472 1142 4047 1142 1639 3836 27 3836 2536 2671 5498 5498 3836 899
v.pas.1p r.nsf cj v.pai.3s d.nsf n.nsf d.gsm n.gsm cj d.apf

ἐντολὰς αὐτοῦ τηρῶμεν, καὶ αἱ ἐντολαὶ αὐτοῦ βαρεῖαι
commandments. *his* *we keep* And *{the}* his commandments *his* are not burdensome,
1953 899 5498 2779 3836 899 1953 899 1639 4024 987
n.apf r.gsm.3 v.pas.1p cj d.npf n.npf r.gsm.3 a.npf

οὐκ εἰσίν. 4 ὅτι πᾶν τὸ γεγεννημένον ἐκ τοῦ θεοῦ νικᾷ τὸν κόσμον· καὶ
not *are* because everyone who has been born of *{the}* God conquers the world. And
4024 1639 4022 4246 3836 1164 1666 3836 2536 3771 3836 3180 2779
pl v.pai.3p cj a.nsn d.nsn pt.rp.nsn p.g d.gsm n.gsm v.pai.3s d.asm n.asm cj

αὕτη ἐστὶν ἡ νίκη ἡ νικήσασα τὸν κόσμον, ἡ πίστις
this is the ⌊victorious power⌋ that has conquered the world — *{the}* our faith.
4047 1639 3836 3772 3836 3771 3836 3180 3836 7005 4411
r.nsf v.pai.3s d.nsf n.nsf d.nsf pt.aa.nsf d.asm n.asm d.nsf n.nsf

ἡμῶν. 5 τίς δέ [b] ἐστιν ὁ νικῶν τὸν κόσμον ⌊εἰ μὴ⌋ ὁ πιστεύων ὅτι
our Who *{and}* is it that conquers the world, but the one who believes that
7005 5515 1254 1639 3836 3771 3836 3180 1623 3590 3836 4409 4022
r.gp.1 r.nsm cj v.pai.3s d.nsm pt.pa.nsm d.asm n.asm cj pl d.nsm pt.pa.nsm cj

Ἰησοῦς ἐστιν ὁ υἱὸς τοῦ θεοῦ; 6 οὗτός ἐστιν ὁ ἐλθὼν δι' ὕδατος καὶ
Jesus is the Son of God? This is the ⌊one who came⌋ by water and
2652 1639 3836 5626 3836 2536 4047 1639 3836 2262 1328 5623 2779
n.nsm v.pai.3s d.nsm n.nsm d.gsm n.gsm r.nsm v.pai.3s d.nsm pt.aa.nsm p.g n.gsn cj

αἵματος, Ἰησοῦς Χριστός, οὐκ ἐν τῷ ὕδατι μόνον ἀλλ' ἐν τῷ ὕδατι καὶ ἐν
blood — Jesus Christ; not by *{the}* water only but by *{the}* water and *{by}*
135 2652 5986 4024 1877 3836 5623 3667 247 1877 3836 5623 2779 1877
n.gsn n.nsm n.nsm pl p.d d.dsn n.dsn adv cj p.d d.dsn n.dsn cj p.d

τῷ αἵματι· καὶ τὸ πνεῦμά ἐστιν τὸ μαρτυροῦν, ὅτι τὸ πνεῦμά ἐστιν ἡ
{the} blood. And the Spirit is the one who testifies, because the Spirit is the
3836 135 2779 3836 4460 1639 3836 3455 4022 3836 4460 1639 3836
d.dsn n.dsn cj d.nsn n.nsn v.pai.3s d.nsn pt.pa.nsn cj d.nsn n.nsn v.pai.3s d.nsf

[a] [καὶ] UBS, omitted by NET.
[b] [δέ] UBS.

NASB

love his brother
whom he has seen,
cannot love God
whom he has not
seen. 21 And this
commandment we
have from Him,
that the one who
loves God should
love his brother
also.

Overcoming the World

5:1 Whoever be-
lieves that Jesus
is the [a]Christ is
born of God, and
whoever loves the
Father loves the
child born of Him.
2 By this we know
that we love the
children of God,
when we love
God and observe
His command-
ments. 3 For this is
the love of God,
that we keep His
commandments;
and His com-
mandments are not
burdensome. 4 For
whatever is born
of God overcomes
the world; and this
is the victory that
has overcome the
world—our faith.
5 Who is the one
who overcomes the
world, but he who
believes that Jesus
is the Son of God?
6 This is the One
who came by water
and blood, Jesus
Christ; not with
the water only, but
with the water and
with the blood. It is
the Spirit who tes-
tifies, because the
Spirit is the truth.

[a] I.e. Messiah

NIV

truth. [7]For there
are three that tes-
tify: [8]the[a] Spirit,
the water and the
blood; and the
three are in agree-
ment. [9]We accept
human testimony,
but God's testi-
mony is greater
because it is the
testimony of God,
which he has giv-
en about his Son.
[10]Whoever believes
in the Son of God
accepts this testi-
mony. Whoever
does not believe
God has made him
out to be a liar, be-
cause they have not
believed the testi-
mony God has giv-
en about his Son.
[11]And this is the
testimony: God has
given us eternal
life, and this life is
in his Son. [12]Who-
ever has the Son
has life; whoever
does not have the
Son of God does
not have life.

Concluding Affirmations

[13]I write these
things to you who
believe in the
name of the Son
of God so that you
may know that you
have eternal life.
[14]This is the confi-
dence we have in
approaching God:
that if we ask any-
thing according to
his will, he hears
us. [15]And if we
know that he hears
us—whatever we
ask—we know
that we have

[a] 7,8 Late manuscripts of the Vulgate *testify in heaven: the Father, the Word and the Holy Spirit, and these three are one.* [8]*And there are three that testify on earth: the* (not found in any Greek manuscript before the fourteenth century)

ἀλήθεια. [7]ὅτι τρεῖς εἰσιν οἱ μαρτυροῦντες,[a] [8]τὸ πνεῦμα καὶ τὸ
truth. For there are three *there are* that testify: the Spirit and the
237 4022 1639 1639 5552 1639 3836 3455 3836 4460 2779 3836
n.nsf cj a.npm v.pai.3p d.npm pt.pa.npm d.nsn n.nsn cj d.nsn

ὕδωρ καὶ τὸ αἷμα, καὶ οἱ τρεῖς εἰς τὸ ἕν εἰσιν. [9]εἰ τὴν
water and the blood; and the three are in *{the}* accord. *are* If we receive the
5623 2779 3836 135 2779 3836 5552 1639 1650 3836 1651 1639 1623 3284 3284 3836
n.nsn cj d.nsn n.nsn cj d.npm a.npm p.a d.asn a.asn v.pai.3p cj d.asf

μαρτυρίαν τῶν ἀνθρώπων λαμβάνομεν, ἡ μαρτυρία τοῦ θεοῦ μείζων ἐστίν·
testimony of men, *we receive* the testimony of God is greater, *is*
3456 3836 476 3284 3836 3456 3836 2536 1639 3489 1639
n.asf d.gpm n.gpm v.pai.1p d.nsf n.nsf d.gsm n.gsm a.nsf.c v.pai.3s

ὅτι αὕτη ἐστὶν ἡ μαρτυρία τοῦ θεοῦ ὅτι μεμαρτύρηκεν περὶ τοῦ υἱοῦ
because this is the testimony of God that he has borne concerning *{the}* his Son.
4022 4047 1639 3836 3456 3836 2536 4022 3455 4309 3836 899 5626
cj r.nsf v.pai.3s d.nsf n.nsf d.gsm n.gsm cj v.rai.3s p.g d.gsm n.gsm

αὐτοῦ. [10]ὁ πιστεύων εἰς τὸν υἱὸν τοῦ θεοῦ ἔχει τὴν μαρτυρίαν ἐν
his The one who believes in the Son of God has the testimony in
899 3836 4409 1650 3836 5626 3836 2536 2400 3836 3456 1877
r.gsm.3 d.nsm pt.pa.nsm p.a d.asm n.asm d.gsm n.gsm v.pai.3s d.asf n.asf p.d

ἑαυτῷ, ὁ ↱ ↱ ↱ μὴ πιστεύων τῷ θεῷ ψεύστην
himself; the one who does not believe *{the}* God has made him out to be a liar,
1571 3836 4409 4409 4409 3590 4409 3836 2536 4472 4472 899 6026
r.dsm.3 d.nsm pl pt.pa.nsm d.dsm n.dsm n.asm

πεποίηκεν αὐτόν, ὅτι ↱ ↱ οὐ πεπίστευκεν εἰς τὴν μαρτυρίαν ἣν
has made *him* because he has not believed in the testimony that God
4472 899 4022 4409 4409 4024 4409 1650 3836 3456 4005 2536
v.rai.3s r.asm.3 cj pl v.rai.3s p.a d.asf n.asf r.asf

μεμαρτύρηκεν ὁ θεὸς περὶ τοῦ υἱοῦ αὐτοῦ. [11]καὶ αὕτη ἐστὶν ἡ
has borne *{the}* *God* concerning *{the}* his Son. *his* And this is the
3455 3836 2536 4309 3836 899 5626 899 2779 4047 1639 3836
v.rai.3s d.nsm n.nsm p.g d.gsm n.gsm r.gsm.3 cj r.nsf v.pai.3s d.nsf

μαρτυρία, ὅτι ζωὴν αἰώνιον ἔδωκεν ἡμῖν ὁ θεός, καὶ αὕτη
testimony: *{that}* God gave us eternal life, *eternal* *gave* *us* *{the}* *God* and this
3456 4022 2536 1443 7005 173 2437 173 1443 7005 3836 2536 2779 4047
n.nsf cj n.asf a.asf v.aai.3s r.dp.1 d.nsm n.nsm cj r.nsf

ἡ ζωὴ ἐν τῷ υἱῷ αὐτοῦ ἐστιν. [12]ὁ ἔχων τὸν υἱὸν ἔχει τὴν
{the} life is in *{the}* his Son. *his* *is* The ⌊one who has⌋ the Son has *{the}*
3836 2437 1639 1877 3836 899 5626 899 1639 3836 2400 3836 5626 2400 3836
d.nsf n.nsf p.d d.dsm n.dsm r.gsm.3 v.pai.3s d.nsm pt.pa.nsm d.asm n.asm v.pai.3s d.asf

ζωήν· ὁ ↱ ↱ ↱ μὴ ἔχων τὸν υἱὸν τοῦ θεοῦ τὴν ζωὴν οὐκ
life; the one who does not have the Son of God does not have *{the}* life. *not*
2437 3836 2400 2400 2400 3590 2400 3836 5626 3836 2536 2400 4024 2400 3836 2437 4024
n.asf d.nsm pl pt.pa.nsm d.asm n.asm d.gsm n.gsm d.asf n.asf pl

ἔχει. [13] ταῦτα ἔγραψα ὑμῖν ἵνα εἰδῆτε ὅτι
does have I am writing these things *I am writing* to you so that ⌊you may know⌋ that you have
2400 1211 1211 1211 4047 1211 7007 2671 3857 4022 2400 2400
v.pai.3s r.apn v.aai.1s r.dp.2 cj v.ras.2p cj

ζωὴν ἔχετε αἰώνιον, τοῖς πιστεύουσιν εἰς τὸ ὄνομα τοῦ υἱοῦ τοῦ
eternal life *you have* *eternal* — you who believe in the name of the Son of
173 2437 2400 173 3836 4409 1650 3836 3950 3836 5626 3836
n.asf v.pai.2p a.asf d.dpm pt.pa.dpm p.a d.asn n.asn d.gsm n.gsm d.gsm

θεοῦ. [14]καὶ αὕτη ἐστὶν ἡ παρρησία ἣν ἔχομεν πρὸς αὐτὸν ὅτι ἐάν
God. And this is the confidence *{that}* we have ⌊as we approach⌋ him: that if we
2536 2779 4047 1639 3836 4244 4005 2400 4639 899 4022 1569 160
n.gsm cj r.nsf v.pai.3s d.nsf n.nsf r.asf v.pai.1p p.a r.asm.3 cj cj

τι αἰτώμεθα κατὰ τὸ θέλημα αὐτοῦ ἀκούει ἡμῶν. [15]καὶ ἐὰν
ask anything *we ask* ⌊according to⌋ *{the}* his will, *his* he hears us. And if
160 5516 160 2848 3836 899 2525 899 201 7005 2779 1569
r.asn v.pms.1p p.a d.asn n.asn r.gsm.3 v.pai.3s r.gp.1 cj cj

οἴδαμεν ὅτι ἀκούει ἡμῶν → ⌊ὃ ἐὰν⌋ αἰτώμεθα, οἴδαμεν ὅτι ἔχομεν τὰ
we know that he hears us regarding whatever we ask, we know that we have the
3857 4022 201 7005 4005 1569 160 3857 4022 2400 3836
v.rai.1p cj v.pai.3s r.gp.1 r.asn pl v.pms.1p v.rai.1p cj v.pai.1p d.apn

[a] ἐν τῷ οὐρανῷ, ὁ πατήρ, ὁ λόγος, καὶ τὸ Ἅγιον Πνεῦμα· καὶ οὗτοι οἱ τρεῖς ἕν εἰσι. [8] καὶ τρεῖς εἰσιν οἱ μαρτυροῦντες ἐν τῇ γῇ, included by TR after μαρτυροῦντες.

NASB

[7]For there are three
that testify: [8a]the
Spirit and the water
and the blood; and
the three are in
agreement. [9]If we
receive the testi-
mony of men, the
testimony of God
is greater; for the
testimony of God
is this, that He has
testified concerning
His Son. [10]The one
who believes in the
Son of God has the
testimony in him-
self; the one who
does not believe
God has made Him
a liar, because he
has not believed
in the testimony
that God has given
concerning His
Son. [11]And the
testimony is this,
that God has given
us eternal life, and
this life is in His
Son. [12]He who has
the Son has the
life; he who does
not have the Son of
God does not have
the life.

This Is Written That You May Know

[13]These things I
have written to you
who believe in the
name of the Son of
God, so that you
may know that you
have eternal life.
[14]This is the con-
fidence which we
have before Him,
that, if we ask any-
thing according to
His will, He hears
us. [15]And if we
know that He hears
us *in* whatever we
ask, we know that
we have the

[a] A few late mss add *...in heaven, the Father, the Word, and the Holy Spirit, and these three are one. And there are three that testify on earth, the Spirit*

NIV

what we asked of
him.
[16]If you see any
brother or sister
commit a sin that
does not lead to
death, you should
pray and God will
give them life. I re-
fer to those whose
sin does not lead
to death. There
is a sin that leads
to death. I am not
saying that you
should pray about
that. [17]All wrong-
doing is sin, and
there is sin that
does not lead to
death.
[18]We know that
anyone born of
God does not
continue to sin;
the One who was
born of God keeps
them safe, and the
evil one cannot
harm them. [19]We
know that we are
children of God,
and that the whole
world is under the
control of the evil
one. [20]We know
also that the Son
of God has come
and has given us
understanding, so
that we may know
him who is true.
And we are in him
who is true by
being in his Son
Jesus Christ. He is
the true God and
eternal life.
[21]Dear children,
keep yourselves
from idols.

αἰτήματα ἃ ᾐτήκαμεν ἀπ' αὐτοῦ. 16 ἐάν τις ἴδῃ τὸν ἀδελφὸν αὐτοῦ
requests that we have asked of him. If someone sees {the} his brother *his*
161 4005 160 608 899 1569 5516 1625 3836 899 81 899
n.apn r.apn v.rai.1p p.g r.gsm.3 cj r.nsm v.aas.3s d.asm n.asm r.gsm.3

ἁμαρτάνοντα ἁμαρτίαν ➝ μὴ πρὸς θάνατον, αἰτήσει καὶ δώσει
committing a sin that does not lead to death, ⌊he should ask⌋ and God will give
279 281 4639 3590 4639 2505 160 2779 1443
pt.pa.asm n.asf pl p.a n.asm v.fai.3s cj v.fai.3s

αὐτῷ ζωήν, τοῖς ἁμαρτάνουσιν ➝ μὴ πρὸς θάνατον. ἔστιν ἁμαρτία
him life — to those whose sins do not lead to death. ⌊There is⌋ sin that
899 2437 3836 279 4639 3590 4639 2505 1639 281
r.dsm.3 n.asf d.dpm pt.pa.dpm pl p.a n.asm v.pai.3s n.nsf

πρὸς θάνατον· οὐ περὶ ἐκείνης λέγω ἵνα
⌊leads to⌋ death; I do not say that he should pray about that. *I do say* *that*
4639 2505 3306 3306 4024 3306 2671 2263 2263 2263 4309 1697 3306 2671
p.a n.asm pl p.g r.gsf v.pai.1s cj

ἐρωτήσῃ. 17 πᾶσα ἀδικία ἁμαρτία ἐστίν, καὶ ἔστιν ἁμαρτία ➝ οὐ
he should pray All wrongdoing is sin, *is* but there is sin that does not
2263 4246 94 1639 281 1639 2779 1639 281 4639 4024
v.aas.3s a.nsf n.nsf n.nsf v.pai.3s cj v.pai.3s n.nsf pl

πρὸς θάνατον. 18 οἴδαμεν ὅτι πᾶς ὁ γεγεννημένος ἐκ τοῦ θεοῦ ➝ οὐχ
lead to death. We know that everyone who has been born of {the} God does not
4639 2505 3857 4022 4246 3836 1164 1666 3836 2536 279 4024
p.a n.asm v.rai.1p cj a.nsm d.nsm pt.rp.nsm p.g d.gsm n.gsm pl

ἁμαρτάνει, ἀλλ' ὁ γεννηθεὶς ἐκ τοῦ θεοῦ τηρεῖ αὐτὸν καὶ ὁ πονηρὸς
continue to sin, but the ⌊one who was born⌋ of {the} God protects him and the evil one
279 247 3836 1164 1666 3836 2536 5498 899 2779 3836 4505
v.pai.3s cj d.nsm pt.ap.nsm p.g d.gsm n.gsm v.pai.3s r.asm.3 cj d.nsm a.nsm

➝ οὐχ ἅπτεται αὐτοῦ. 19 οἴδαμεν ὅτι ἐκ τοῦ θεοῦ ἐσμεν καὶ
will not harm him. We know that we are children of {the} God, *we are* and that
721 4024 721 899 3857 4022 1639 1639 1666 3836 2536 1639 2779
pl v.pmi.3s r.gsm.3 v.rai.1p cj p.g d.gsm n.gsm v.pai.1p cj

ὁ κόσμος ὅλος ἐν τῷ πονηρῷ κεῖται. 20 οἴδαμεν δὲ
the whole world *whole* lies in the power of the evil one. *lies* And we know *And*
3836 3910 3180 3910 3023 1877 3836 4505 3023 1254 3857 1254
d.nsm n.nsm a.nsm p.d d.dsm a.dsm v.pmi.3s v.rai.1p cj

ὅτι ὁ υἱὸς τοῦ θεοῦ ἥκει καὶ δέδωκεν ἡμῖν διάνοιαν ἵνα γινώσκωμεν τὸν
that the Son of God has come and has given us discernment so that we may know him
4022 3836 5626 3836 2536 2457 2779 1443 7005 1379 2671 1182 3836
cj d.nsm n.nsm d.gsm n.gsm v.rai.3s cj v.rai.3s r.dp.1 n.asf cj v.pas.1p d.asm

ἀληθινόν, καὶ ἐσμὲν ἐν τῷ ἀληθινῷ, ἐν τῷ υἱῷ αὐτοῦ Ἰησοῦ Χριστῷ.
who is true; and we are in him who is true, in {the} his Son *his* Jesus Christ.
240 2779 1639 1877 3836 240 1877 3836 899 5626 899 2652 5986
a.asm cj v.pai.1p p.d d.dsm a.dsm p.d d.dsm n.dsm r.gsm.3 n.dsm n.dsm

οὗτός ἐστιν ὁ ἀληθινὸς θεὸς καὶ ζωὴ αἰώνιος. 21 τεκνία, φυλάξατε
This one is the true God and eternal life. *eternal* Little children, keep
4047 1639 3836 240 2536 2779 173 2437 173 5448 5875
r.nsm v.pai.3s d.nsm a.nsm n.nsm cj n.nsf a.nsf n.vpn v.aam.2p

ἑαυτὰ ἀπὸ τῶν εἰδώλων.
yourselves from {the} idols.
1571 608 3836 1631
r.apn.2 p.g d.gpn n.gpn

NASB

requests which we
have asked from
Him.
[16]If anyone sees
his brother com-
mitting a sin not
leading to death, he
shall ask and *God*
will for him give
life to those who
commit sin not
leading to death.
There is a sin *lead-
ing* to death; I do
not say that he
should make re-
quest for this. [17]All
unrighteousness is
sin, and there is a
sin not *leading* to
death.
[18]We know that
no one who is born
of God sins; but
He who was born
of God keeps him,
and the evil one
does not touch
him. [19]We know
that we are of
God, and that the
whole world lies
in *the power of* the
evil one. [20]And we
know that the Son
of God has come,
and has given us
understanding so
that we may know
Him who is true;
and we are in Him
who is true, in His
Son Jesus Christ.
This is the true
God and eternal
life.
[21]Little children,
guard yourselves
from idols.

2 John

NIV

[1]The elder,
To the lady cho-
sen by God and
to her children,
whom I love in
the truth—and
not I only, but also
all who know the
truth— [2]because
of the truth, which
lives in us and will
be with us forever:
[3]Grace, mercy
and peace from
God the Father and
from Jesus Christ,
the Father's Son,
will be with us in
truth and love.

[4]It has given me
great joy to find
some of your chil-
dren walking in
the truth, just as
the Father com-
manded us. [5]And
now, dear lady, I
am not writing you
a new command
but one we have
had from the be-
ginning. I ask that
we love one an-
other. [6]And this is
love: that we walk
in obedience to his
commands. As you
have heard from
the beginning, his
command is that
you walk in love.
[7]I say this be-
cause many de-
ceivers, who do
not acknowledge
Jesus Christ as
coming in the
flesh, have gone
out into the world.
Any such person
is the deceiver and
the antichrist.

1:1 ὁ πρεσβύτερος → ἐκλεκτῇ κυρίᾳ καὶ τοῖς τέκνοις αὐτῆς, οὓς ἐγὼ
The elder to the elect lady and *{the}* her children, *her* whom I
3836 4565 1723 3257 2779 3836 899 5451 899 4005 1609
d.nsm a.nsm a.dsf n.dsf cj d.dpn n.dpn r.gsf.3 r.apm r.ns.1

ἀγαπῶ ἐν ἀληθείᾳ, καὶ οὐκ ἐγὼ μόνος ἀλλὰ καὶ πάντες οἱ ἐγνωκότες τὴν
love in truth (and not I alone, but also all who know the
26 1877 237 2779 4024 1609 3668 247 2779 4246 3836 1182 3836
v.pai.1s p.d n.dsf cj pl r.ns.1 a.nsm cj adv a.npm d.npm pt.ra.npm d.asf

ἀλήθειαν, 2 διὰ τὴν ἀλήθειαν τὴν μένουσαν ἐν ἡμῖν καὶ μεθ᾽ ἡμῶν
truth), ⌞because of⌟ the truth that abides in us and will be with us
237 1328 3836 237 3836 3531 1877 7005 2779 1639 1639 3552 7005
n.asf p.a d.asf n.asf d.asf pt.pa.asf p.d r.dp.1 cj p.g r.gp.1

ἔσται εἰς τὸν αἰῶνα. 3 ἔσται μεθ᾽ ἡμῶν χάρις ἔλεος εἰρήνη
will be for all time: Grace, mercy, and peace will be with us, *Grace mercy peace*
1639 1650 3836 172 5921 1799 1645 1639 3552 7005 5921 1799 1645
v.fmi.3s p.a d.asm n.asm v.fmi.3s p.g r.gp.1 n.nsf n.nsn n.nsf

παρὰ θεοῦ πατρὸς καὶ παρὰ Ἰησοῦ Χριστοῦ τοῦ υἱοῦ τοῦ πατρὸς ἐν ἀληθείᾳ
from God the Father and from Jesus Christ the Son of the Father, in truth
4123 2536 4252 2779 4123 2652 5986 3836 5626 3836 4252 1877 237
p.g n.gsm n.gsm cj p.g n.gsm n.gsm d.gsm n.gsm d.gsm n.gsm p.d n.dsf

καὶ ἀγάπῃ. 4 ἐχάρην λίαν ὅτι εὕρηκα ἐκ τῶν τέκνων σου
and in love. I rejoiced greatly because I have found ⌞some of⌟ *{the}* your children *your*
2779 27 5897 3336 4022 2351 1666 3836 5148 5451 5148
cj n.dsf v.api.1s adv cj v.rai.1s p.g d.gpn n.gpn r.gs.2

περιπατοῦντας ἐν ἀληθείᾳ, καθὼς ἐντολὴν ἐλάβομεν παρὰ τοῦ
walking in the truth, just as we received commandment *we received* from the
4344 1877 237 2777 3284 3284 1953 3284 4123 3836
pt.pa.apm p.d n.dsf cj n.asf v.aai.1p p.g d.gsm

πατρός. 5 καὶ νῦν ἐρωτῶ σε, κυρία, οὐχ ὡς
Father. And now I ask you, dear lady — not ⌞as though⌟ I were writing a new
4252 2779 3814 2263 5148 3257 4024 6055 1211 1211 1211 2785
n.gsm cj adv v.pai.1s r.as.2 n.vsf pl pl

ἐντολὴν καινὴν γράφων σοι ἀλλὰ ἣν εἴχομεν ἀπ᾽ ἀρχῆς,
commandment *new* *I were writing* to you, but the one ⌞we have had⌟ from the beginning —
1953 2785 1211 5148 247 4005 2400 608 794
n.asf a.asf pt.pa.nsm r.ds.2 cj r.asf v.iai.1p p.g n.gsf

ἵνα ἀγαπῶμεν ἀλλήλους. 6 καὶ αὕτη ἐστὶν ἡ ἀγάπη, ἵνα περιπατῶμεν κατὰ
that we love one another. And this is *{the}* love: that we walk ⌞according to⌟
2671 26 253 2779 4047 1639 3836 27 2671 4344 2848
cj v.pas.1p r.apm cj r.nsf v.pai.3s d.nsf n.nsf cj v.pas.1p p.a

τὰς ἐντολὰς αὐτοῦ· αὕτη ἡ ἐντολή ἐστιν, καθὼς ἠκούσατε
{the} his commandments. *his* This is the commandment, *is* just as you have heard
3836 899 1953 899 4047 1639 3836 1953 1639 2777 201
d.apf n.apf r.gsm.3 r.nsf d.nsf n.nsf v.pai.3s cj v.aai.2p

ἀπ᾽ ἀρχῆς, ἵνα ἐν αὐτῇ περιπατῆτε. 7 ὅτι πολλοὶ πλάνοι
from the beginning, that you should walk in it. *you should walk* For many deceivers
608 794 2671 4344 4344 4344 1877 899 4344 4022 4498 4418
p.g n.gsf cj p.d r.dsf.3 v.pas.2p cj a.npm n.npm

ἐξῆλθον εἰς τὸν κόσμον, οἱ ↱ μὴ ὁμολογοῦντες Ἰησοῦν Χριστὸν
⌞have gone out⌟ into the world, people who do not confess that Jesus Christ
2002 1650 3836 3180 3836 3933 3590 3933 2652 5986
v.aai.3p p.a d.asm n.asm d.npm pl pt.pa.npm n.asm n.asm

ἐρχόμενον ἐν σαρκί· οὗτός ἐστιν ὁ πλάνος καὶ ὁ ἀντίχριστος.
has come in the flesh. ⌞Any such person⌟ is the deceiver and the Antichrist!
2262 1877 4922 4047 1639 3836 4418 2779 3836 532
pt.pm.asm p.d n.dsf r.nsm v.pai.3s d.nsm n.nsm cj d.nsm n.nsm

NASB

Walk According to His
Commandments

1:1The elder to the
chosen lady and
her children, whom
I love in truth; and
not only I, but also
all who know the
truth, [2]for the sake
of the truth which
abides in us and
will be with us
forever: [3]Grace,
mercy *and* peace
will be with us,
from God the Fa-
ther and from Jesus
Christ, the Son of
the Father, in truth
and love.
[4]I was very glad
to find *some* of
your children walk-
ing in truth, just as
we have received
commandment *to*
do from the Father.
[5]Now I ask you,
lady, not as though
I were writing to
you a new com-
mandment, but the
one which we have
had from the begin-
ning, that we love
one another. [6]And
this is love, that
we walk according
to His command-
ments. This is the
commandment,
just as you have
heard from the
beginning, that you
should walk in it.
[7]For many deceiv-
ers have gone out
into the world,
those who do not
acknowledge Jesus
Christ *as* coming
in the flesh. This
is the deceiver and
the antichrist.

NIV

[8]Watch out that
you do not lose
what we[a] have
worked for, but
that you may be
rewarded fully.
[9]Anyone who runs
ahead and does
not continue in the
teaching of Christ
does not have God;
whoever continues
in the teaching has
both the Father and
the Son. [10]If any-
one comes to you
and does not bring
this teaching, do
not take them into
your house or wel-
come them. [11]Any-
one who welcomes
them shares in their
wicked work.

[12]I have much to
write to you, but
I do not want to
use paper and ink.
Instead, I hope to
visit you and talk
with you face to
face, so that our
joy may be com-
plete.

[13]The children of
your sister, who
is chosen by God,
send their greet-
ings.

[a] 8 Some manu-
scripts *you*

8 → → βλέπετε ἑαυτούς, ἵνα ↱ ↱ μὴ ἀπολέσητε ἃ εἰργασάμεθα ἀλλὰ
Be on your guard, *your* so that we may not lose the things we worked for but
1571 1063 1571 2671 660 660 3590 660 4005 2237 247
v.pam.2p r.apm.2 cj pl v.aas.2p r.apn v.ami.1p cj

μισθὸν πλήρη ἀπολάβητε. 9 πᾶς ὁ προάγων καὶ ↱ μὴ
may receive a full reward. *full* *may receive* Everyone who goes on ahead and does not
655 655 4441 3635 4441 655 4246 3836 4575 2779 3531 3590
n.asm a.asm v.aas.2p a.nsm d.nsm pt.pa.nsm cj pl

μένων ἐν τῇ διδαχῇ τοῦ Χριστοῦ θεὸν οὐκ ἔχει· ὁ μένων
continue in the teaching of Christ, does not have God. *not* *does have* Whoever continues
3531 1877 3836 1439 3836 5986 2400 4024 2400 2536 4024 2400 3836 3531
pt.pa.nsm p.d d.dsf n.dsf d.gsm n.gsm n.asm pl v.pai.3s d.nsm pt.pa.nsm

ἐν τῇ διδαχῇ, οὗτος καὶ τὸν πατέρα καὶ τὸν υἱὸν ἔχει. 10 εἴ τις
in the teaching *{this one}* has both the Father and the Son. *has* If someone
1877 3836 1439 4047 2400 2779 3836 4252 2779 3836 5626 2400 1623 5516
p.d d.dsf n.dsf r.nsm cj d.asm n.asm cj d.asm n.asm v.pai.3s cj r.nsm

ἔρχεται πρὸς ὑμᾶς καὶ ταύτην τὴν διδαχὴν οὐ φέρει, ↱ μὴ
comes to you and does not bring this *{the}* teaching, *not* *does bring* do not
2262 4639 7007 2779 5770 4024 5770 4047 3836 1439 4024 5770 3284 3590
v.pmi.3s p.a r.ap.2 cj r.asf d.asf n.asf pl v.pai.3s pl

λαμβάνετε αὐτὸν εἰς οἰκίαν καὶ χαίρειν αὐτῷ μὴ λέγετε, 11
receive him into your house or give him any greeting, *him* *any* *give* for
3284 899 1650 3864 2779 3306 899 3590 5897 899 3590 3306 1142
v.pam.2p r.asm.3 p.a n.asf cj f.pa r.dsm.3 pl v.pam.2p

ὁ λέγων γὰρ αὐτῷ χαίρειν κοινωνεῖ τοῖς ἔργοις αὐτοῦ τοῖς
the ⌊one who gives⌋ *for* him a greeting ⌊becomes a partner⌋ in his evil deeds. *his* *{the}*
3836 3306 1142 899 5897 3125 3836 899 4505 2240 899 3836
d.nsm pt.pa.nsm cj r.dsm.3 f.pa v.pai.3s d.dpn n.dpn r.gsm.3 d.dpn

πονηροῖς. 12 πολλὰ ἔχων ὑμῖν γράφειν
evil Although I have ⌊many other things⌋ *Although I have* to write to you, *to write*
4505 2400 2400 2400 4498 2400 1211 1211 7007 1211
a.dpn a.apn pt.pa.nsm r.dp.2 f.pa

↱ ↱ οὐκ ἐβουλήθην διὰ χάρτου καὶ μέλανος, ἀλλὰ ἐλπίζω γενέσθαι πρὸς ὑμᾶς
I do not want to use paper and ink; instead, I hope to be with you
1089 1089 4024 1089 1328 5925 2779 3506 247 1827 1181 4639 7007
pl v.api.1s p.g n.gsm cj a.gsn cj v.pai.1s f.am p.a r.ap.2

καὶ στόμα πρὸς στόμα λαλῆσαι, ἵνα ἡ χαρὰ ἡμῶν
and speak face to face, *speak* so that *{the}* our joy *our* may be
2779 3281 5125 4639 5125 3281 2671 3836 7005 5915 7005 1639 1639
cj n.asn p.a n.asn f.aa cj d.nsf n.nsf r.gp.1

πεπληρωμένη ᾖ. 13 ἀσπάζεταί σε τὰ τέκνα τῆς ἀδελφῆς σου τῆς
complete. *may be* *send greetings* *you* The children of your elect sister *your* *{the}*
4444 1639 832 5148 3836 5451 3836 5148 1723 80 5148 3836
pt.rp.nsf v.pas.3s v.pmi.3s r.as.2 d.npn n.npn d.gsf n.gsf r.gs.2 d.gsf

ἐκλεκτῆς.
elect send you greetings.
1723 832 5148 832
a.gsf

NASB

[8]Watch yourselves,
that you do not
lose what we have
accomplished, but
that you may re-
ceive a full reward.
[9]Anyone who goes
too far and does
not abide in the
teaching of Christ,
does not have God;
the one who abides
in the teaching, he
has both the Father
and the Son. [10]If
anyone comes to
you and does not
bring this teaching,
do not receive him
into *your* house,
and do not give
him a greeting;
[11]for the one who
gives him a greet-
ing participates in
his evil deeds.

[12]Though I have
many things to
write to you, I do
not want to *do so*
with paper and ink;
but I hope to come
to you and speak
face to face, so that
your joy may be
made full.

[13]The children of
your chosen sister
greet you.

3 John

NIV

[1]The elder,

To my dear friend
Gaius, whom I love
in the truth.

[2]Dear friend, I
pray that you may
enjoy good health
and that all may
go well with you,
even as your soul is
getting along well.
[3]It gave me great
joy when some be-
lievers came and
testified about your
faithfulness to the
truth, telling how
you continue to
walk in it. [4]I have
no greater joy than
to hear that my
children are walk-
ing in the truth.
[5]Dear friend,
you are faithful in
what you are doing
for the brothers
and sisters,[a] even
though they are
strangers to you.
[6]They have told the
church about your
love. Please send
them on their way
in a manner that
honors God. [7]It
was for the sake of
the Name that they
went out, receiving
no help from the
pagans. [8]We ought
therefore to show
hospitality to such
people so that we
may work together
for the truth.
[9]I wrote to the
church, but Diot-
rephes, who loves
to be first, will not
welcome us. [1]

[a] 5 The Greek word for *brothers and sisters* (*adelphoi*) refers here to believers, both men and women, as part of God's family.

1:1 ὁ πρεσβύτερος Γαΐῳ τῷ ἀγαπητῷ, ὃν ἐγὼ ἀγαπῶ ἐν ἀληθείᾳ.
From the elder, to Gaius my dear brother, whom I love in truth.
3836 4565 1127 3836 28 4005 1609 26 1877 237
d.nsm a.nsm n.dsm d.dsm a.dsm r.asm r.ns.1 v.pai.1s p.d n.dsf

2 ἀγαπητέ, περὶ πάντων εὔχομαί σε εὐοδοῦσθαι καὶ ὑγιαίνειν,
Dear friend, I pray that in every way *I pray* you may prosper and be in good health,
28 2377 2377 4309 4246 2377 5148 2338 2779 5617
a.vsm p.g a.gpn v.pmi.1s r.as.2 f.pp cj f.pa

καθὼς εὐοδοῦταί σου ἡ ψυχή. 3 ἐχάρην γὰρ λίαν →
just as your soul is prospering. *your {the} soul* For I rejoiced *For* greatly when the brothers
2777 5148 6034 2338 5148 3836 6034 1142 5897 1142 3336 81
cj v.ppi.3s r.gs.2 d.nsf n.nsf v.api.1s cj adv

ἐρχομένων ἀδελφῶν καὶ μαρτυρούντων σου τῇ ἀληθείᾳ, καθὼς σὺ
came *brothers* and testified to your fidelity ⌊to the⌋ truth, as indeed you
2262 81 2779 3455 5148 3836 237 2777 5148
pt.pm.gpm n.gpm cj pt.pa.gpm r.gs.2 d.dsf n.dsf cj r.ns.2

ἐν ἀληθείᾳ περιπατεῖς. 4 μειζοτέραν τούτων οὐκ ἔχω
do walk in the truth. *do walk* I have no greater joy than this: *no I have*
4344 4344 1877 237 4344 2400 2400 4024 3504 5915 4047 4024 2400
p.d n.dsf v.pai.2s a.asf.c r.gpf pl v.pai.1s

χαράν, ἵνα ἀκούω τὰ ἐμὰ τέκνα ἐν τῇ ἀληθείᾳ περιπατοῦντα.
joy to hear that *{the}* my children are walking in the truth. *are walking*
5915 2671 201 3836 1847 5451 4344 4344 1877 3836 237 4344
n.asf cj v.pas.1s d.apn r.apn.1 n.apn p.d d.dsf n.dsf pt.pa.apn

5 ἀγαπητέ, πιστὸν ποιεῖς ὃ ἐὰν ἐργάσῃ εἰς τοὺς ἀδελφοὺς
Dear brother, you are faithful *you are* in what ~ you are doing for the brothers,
28 4472 4472 4412 4472 4005 1569 2237 1650 3836 81
a.vsm a.asn v.pai.2s r.asn pl v.ams.2s p.a d.apm n.apm

καὶ τοῦτο ξένους, 6 οἳ ἐμαρτύρησάν σου τῇ ἀγάπῃ ἐνώπιον
⌊even though⌋ they are strangers. They have testified to your *{the}* love before the
2779 4047 3828 4005 3455 5148 3836 27 1967
cj r.asn n.apm r.npm v.aai.3p r.gs.2 d.dsf n.dsf p.g

ἐκκλησίας, ↱ ↱ οὓς καλῶς ποιήσεις προπέμψας
church. You will do well to help them *well* *You will do* on their way
1711 4472 4472 4472 2822 4636 4636 4005 2822 4472 4636
n.gsf r.apm adv v.fai.2s pt.aa.nsm

ἀξίως τοῦ θεοῦ· 7 ὑπὲρ γὰρ τοῦ ὀνόματος
⌊in a manner worthy⌋ of God, because they set out ⌊for the sake⌋ *because* of the Name,
547 3836 2536 1142 2002 2002 2002 5642 1142 3836 3950
adv d.gsm n.gsm p.g cj d.gsn n.gsn

ἐξῆλθον μηδὲν λαμβάνοντες ἀπὸ τῶν ἐθνικῶν. 8 ἡμεῖς οὖν
they set out accepting nothing *accepting* from *{the}* nonbelievers. Therefore we *Therefore*
2002 3284 3594 3284 608 3836 1618 4036 7005 4036
v.aai.3p a.asn pt.pa.npm p.g d.gpm a.gpm r.np.1 cj

ὀφείλομεν ὑπολαμβάνειν τοὺς τοιούτους, ἵνα συνεργοὶ γινώμεθα
ought to show hospitality to such men, so that we may be coworkers *we may be*
4053 5696 3836 5525 2671 1181 1181 1181 5301 1181
v.pai.1p f.pa d.apm r.apm cj n.npm v.pms.1p

τῇ ἀληθείᾳ. 9 ἔγραψά τι ↰ τῇ ἐκκλησίᾳ, ἀλλ᾽ ὁ
⌊for the⌋ truth. I sent a letter ⌊to the⌋ church, but Diotrephes, who
3836 237 1211 5516 1211 3836 1711 247 1485 3836
d.dsf n.dsf v.aai.1s r.asn d.dsf n.dsf cj d.nsm

φιλοπρωτεύων αὐτῶν Διοτρέφης ↱ οὐκ ἐπιδέχεται ἡμᾶς. ↰ 10 διὰ
likes to be in charge, *{them}* *Diotrephes* does not acknowledge our authority. For
5812 899 1485 2110 4024 2110 7005 2110 1328
pt.pa.nsm r.gpm.3 n.nsm pl v.pmi.3s r.ap.1 p.a

NASB

You Walk in the Truth
[1:1]The elder to the
beloved Gaius,
whom I love in
truth.
[2]Beloved, I pray
that in all respects
you may prosper
and be in good
health, just as your
soul prospers. [3]For
I was very glad
when brethren
came and testified
to your truth, *that
is,* how you are
walking in truth. [4]I
have no greater joy
than this, to hear of
my children walk-
ing in the truth.
[5]Beloved, you are
acting faithfully
in whatever you
accomplish for the
brethren, and es-
pecially *when they
are* strangers; [6]and
they have testified
to your love before
the church. You
will do well to send
them on their way
in a manner worthy
of God. [7]For they
went out for the
sake of the Name,
accepting nothing
from the Gentiles.
[8]Therefore we
ought to support
such men, so that
we may be fellow
workers with the
truth.
[9]I wrote some-
thing to the church;
but Diotrephes,
who loves to be
first among them,
does not accept
what we say. [10]For

NIV

[0]So when I come,
I will call atten-
tion to what he is
doing, spreading
malicious nonsense
about us. Not sat-
isfied with that,
he even refuses
to welcome other
believers. He also
stops those who
want to do so and
puts them out of
the church.
[11]Dear friend, do
not imitate what
is evil but what is
good. Anyone who
does what is good
is from God. Any-
one who does what
is evil has not seen
God. [12]Demetrius
is well spoken of
by everyone—and
even by the truth it-
self. We also speak
well of him, and
you know that our
testimony is true.
[13]I have much to
write you, but I do
not want to do so
with pen and ink.
[14]I hope to see you
soon, and we will
talk face to face.

Peace to you. The
friends here send
their greetings.
Greet the friends
there by name.

τοῦτο, ἐὰν ἔλθω, ὑπομνήσω αὐτοῦ τὰ ἔργα ἃ ποιεῖ
this reason, should I come, ⌞I will bring up⌟ *{his}* the things *{that}* ⌞he is doing,⌟ disparaging us
4047 1569 2262 5703 899 3836 2240 4005 4472 5826 7005
r.asn cj v.aas.1s v.fai.1s r.gsm.3 d.apn n.apn r.apn v.pai.3s

→ λόγοις πονηροῖς φλυαρῶν ἡμᾶς, καὶ μὴ ἀρκούμενος ἐπὶ τούτοις
with malicious talk. *malicious* *disparaging us* And not satisfied with that, he
4505 3364 4505 5826 7005 2779 3590 758 2093 4047 899
n.dpm a.dpm pt.pa.nsm r.ap.1 cj pl pt.pp.nsm p.d r.dpn

οὔτε αὐτὸς ἐπιδέχεται τοὺς ἀδελφοὺς καὶ τοὺς βουλομένους
refuses *he* to welcome the brothers. He even prevents those ⌞who would like to⌟
4046 899 2110 3836 81 3266 2779 3266 3836 1089
cj r.nsm v.pmi.3s d.apm n.apm cj d.apm pt.pm.apm

κωλύει καὶ ἐκ τῆς ἐκκλησίας ἐκβάλλει. [11] ἀγαπητέ, ↱ μὴ μιμοῦ
He prevents and puts them ⌞out of⌟ the church. *puts* Dear friend, do not imitate
3266 2779 1675 1666 3836 1711 1675 28 3628 3590 3628
v.pai.3s cj p.g d.gsf n.gsf v.pai.3s a.vsm pl v.pmm.2s

τὸ κακὸν ἀλλὰ τὸ ἀγαθόν. ὁ ἀγαθοποιῶν ἐκ τοῦ θεοῦ ἐστιν· ὁ
what is evil but what is good. The ⌞one who does good⌟ is of *{the}* God; *is* the
3836 2805 247 3836 19 3836 16 1639 1666 3836 2536 1639 3836
d.asn a.asn cj d.asn a.asn d.nsm pt.pa.nsm p.g d.gsm n.gsm v.pai.3s d.nsm

κακοποιῶν ↱ οὐχ ἑώρακεν τὸν θεόν. [12]
⌞one who does evil⌟ has not seen *{the}* God. Everyone has testified favorably
2803 3972 4024 3972 3836 2536 4246 3455 3455
pt.pa.nsm pl v.rai.3s d.asm n.asm

Δημητρίῳ μεμαρτύρηται ὑπὸ πάντων καὶ ὑπὸ αὐτῆς τῆς
regarding Demetrius, *has testified* *{from}* *Everyone* ⌞and so⌟ has *{from}* the truth itself. *the*
1320 3455 5679 4246 2779 5679 3836 237 899 3836
n.dsm v.rpi.3s p.g a.gpm cj p.g r.gsf d.gsf

ἀληθείας· καὶ ἡμεῖς δὲ μαρτυροῦμεν, καὶ οἶδας ὅτι ἡ
truth And we testify for him as well, *we* *And* *testify* and you know that *{the}*
237 1254 7005 3455 2779 7005 1254 3455 2779 3857 4022 3836
n.gsf adv r.np.1 cj v.pai.1p cj v.rai.2s cj d.nsf

μαρτυρία ἡμῶν ἀληθής ἐστιν. [13] πολλὰ εἶχον γράψαι σοι ἀλλ᾽
our testimony *our* is true. *is* I have many things *I have* to write to you, but
7005 3456 7005 1639 239 1639 2400 2400 4498 2400 1211 5148 247
n.nsf r.gp.1 a.nsf v.pai.3s a.apn v.iai.1s f.aa r.ds.2 cj

↱ ↱ οὐ θέλω διὰ μέλανος καὶ καλάμου σοι γράφειν, [14] ἐλπίζω
I do not wish to write with ink and pen. *{to you}* *to write* But I hope
2527 2527 4024 2527 1211 1211 1328 3506 2779 2812 5148 1211 1254 1827
pl v.pai.1s p.g a.gsn cj n.gsm r.ds.2 f.pa v.pai.1s

δὲ εὐθέως σε ἰδεῖν, καὶ στόμα πρὸς στόμα
But to see you ⌞in the near future,⌟ *you* *to see* and we will speak face to face.
1254 1625 1625 5148 2311 5148 1625 2779 3281 3281 3281 5125 4639 5125
cj adv r.as.2 f.aa cj n.asn p.a n.asn

λαλήσομεν.[a] [15] εἰρήνη σοι. → ἀσπάζονταί σε οἱ φίλοι.
we will speak Peace to you. The friends here send you greetings. *you* *The* *friends*
3281 1645 5148 3836 5813 5148 832 5148 3836 5813
v.fai.1p n.nsf r.ds.2 v.pmi.3p r.as.2 d.npm n.npm

ἀσπάζου τοὺς φίλους κατ᾽ ὄνομα.
Greet the friends there by name.
832 3836 5813 2848 3950
v.pmm.2s d.apm n.apm p.a n.asn

NASB

this reason, if I
come, I will call at-
tention to his deeds
which he does,
unjustly accusing
us with wicked
words; and not
satisfied with this,
he himself does not
receive the breth-
ren, either, and he
forbids those who
desire *to do so* and
puts *them* out of
the church.
[11]Beloved, do not
imitate what is evil,
but what is good.
The one who does
good is of God; the
one who does evil
has not seen God.
[12]Demetrius has
received a *good*
testimony from
everyone, and from
the truth itself;
and we add our
testimony, and you
know that our testi-
mony is true.
[13]I had many
things to write to
you, but I am not
willing to write
them to you with
pen and ink; [14]but
I hope to see you
shortly, and we will
speak face to face.
[15]Peace *be* to you.
The friends greet
you. Greet the
friends by name.

[a] εἰρήνη σοι. ἀσπάζονταί σε οἱ φίλοι. ἀσπάζου τοὺς φίλους κατ᾽ ὄνομα included by TR after λαλήσομεν.

Jude

NIV

1 Jude, a servant
of Jesus Christ and
a brother of James,

To those who
have been called,
who are loved in
God the Father
and kept for[a] Jesus
Christ:

2 Mercy, peace
and love be yours
in abundance.

The Sin and Doom of Ungodly People

3 Dear friends, al-
though I was very
eager to write to
you about the sal-
vation we share, I
felt compelled to
write and urge you
to contend for the
faith that was once
for all entrusted
to God's holy peo-
ple. 4 For certain
individuals whose
condemnation was
written about[b]
long ago have se-
cretly slipped in
among you. They
are ungodly peo-
ple, who pervert
the grace of our
God into a license
for immorality and
deny Jesus Christ
our only Sovereign
and Lord.
5 Though you
already know all
this, I want to re-
mind you that the
Lord[c] at one time
delivered his peo-
ple out of Egypt,
but later destroyed
those who did not
believe.

[a] 1 Or *by*; or *in*
[b] 4 Or *individuals who were marked out for condemnation*
[c] 5 Some early manuscripts *Jesus*

1:1 Ἰούδας Ἰησοῦ Χριστοῦ δοῦλος, ἀδελφὸς δὲ Ἰακώβου, τοῖς
Jude, a servant of Jesus Christ *servant* and brother *and* of James, to those
2683 1529 2652 5986 1529 1254 81 1254 2610 3836
n.nsm n.gsm n.gsm n.nsm n.nsm cj n.gsm d.dpm

ἐν θεῷ πατρὶ ἠγαπημένοις καὶ Ἰησοῦ Χριστῷ
who are called, who are loved in God the Father *who are loved* and kept for Jesus Christ:
3105 3105 3105 26 26 26 1877 2536 4252 26 2779 5498 2652 5986
p.d n.dsm n.dsm pt.rp.dpm cj n.dsm n.dsm

τετηρημένοις κλητοῖς· 2 ἔλεος ὑμῖν καὶ εἰρήνη καὶ ἀγάπη
kept *who are called* May mercy, peace, and love be yours *{and}* *peace* *and* *love*
5498 3105 4437 1799 1645 2779 27 4437 7007 2779 1645 2779 27
pt.rp.dpm a.dpm n.nsn r.dp.2 cj n.nsf cj n.nsf

πληθυνθείη. 3 ἀγαπητοί, ⌞πᾶσαν σπουδὴν⌟ ποιούμενος
⌞in ever increasing measure.⌟ Dear friends, although I was eager *although I was*
4437 28 4472 4472 4472 4246 5082 4472
v.apo.3s a.vpm a.asf n.asf pt.pm.nsm

γράφειν ὑμῖν περὶ τῆς κοινῆς ἡμῶν σωτηρίας ἀνάγκην
to write to you about *{the}* our common *our* salvation, nevertheless I find it necessary
1211 7007 4309 3836 7005 3123 7005 5401 2400 2400 340
f.pa r.dp.2 p.g d.gsf a.gsf r.gp.1 n.gsf n.asf

ἔσχον γράψαι ὑμῖν παρακαλῶν ἐπαγωνίζεσθαι τῇ
I find to write and encourage you *encourage* to carry on the struggle ⌞for the⌟ faith that was
2400 1211 4151 7007 4151 2043 3836 4411 4140 4140
v.aai.1s f.aa r.dp.2 pt.pa.nsm f.pm d.dsf

ἅπαξ παραδοθείσῃ τοῖς ἁγίοις πίστει. 4 γάρ
⌞once for all⌟ delivered to the saints. *faith* For certain men have stolen in unawares *For*
562 4140 3836 41 4411 1142 5516 476 4208 1142
adv pt.ap.dsf d.dpm a.dpm n.dsf v.aai.3p cj

παρεισέδυσαν

τινες ἄνθρωποι, οἱ πάλαι προγεγραμμένοι εἰς τοῦτο τὸ κρίμα,
certain men — men who long ago were designated for this *{the}* condemnation —
5516 476 3836 4093 4592 1650 4047 3836 3210
r.npm n.npm d.npm adv pt.rp.npm p.a r.asn d.asn n.asn

ἀσεβεῖς, τὴν τοῦ θεοῦ ἡμῶν χάριτα μετατιθέντες
ungodly men who turn the grace of our God *our* *grace* *who turn* into an excuse
815 3572 3572 3836 5921 3836 7005 2536 7005 5921 3572
a.npm d.asf d.gsm n.gsm r.gp.1 n.asf pt.pa.npm

εἰς ἀσέλγειαν καὶ τὸν μόνον δεσπότην καὶ κύριον ἡμῶν Ἰησοῦν
for blatant immorality, and *{the}* deny our only Master and Lord, *our* Jesus
1650 816 2779 3836 766 7005 3668 1305 2779 3261 7005 2652
p.a n.asf cj d.asm adv n.asm cj n.asm r.gp.1 n.asm

Χριστὸν ἀρνούμενοι. 5 ὑπομνῆσαι δὲ ὑμᾶς βούλομαι,
Christ. *deny* Now I want to remind *Now* you, *I want* though you once
5986 766 1254 1089 1089 5703 1254 7007 1089 7007 562
n.asm pt.pm.npm f.aa cj r.ap.2 v.pmi.1s

εἰδότας ὑμᾶς[a] πάντα ὅτι ὁ[b] Ἰησοῦς[c] ἅπαξ[d] λαὸν ἐκ γῆς
knew *you* all this, that the Lord, *once* having saved his people ⌞out of⌟ *{land}*
3857 7007 4246 4022 3836 2652 562 5392 5392 3295 1666 1178
pt.ra.apm r.ap.2 a.apn cj d.nsm n.nsm adv n.asm p.g n.gsf

Αἰγύπτου σώσας τὸ δεύτερον τοὺς μὴ πιστεύσαντας
Egypt, *having saved* *{the}* afterward destroyed those who did not believe.
131 5392 3836 1311 660 3836 4409 4409 3590 4409
n.gsf pt.aa.nsm d.asn a.asn d.apm pl pt.aa.apm

[a] [ὑμᾶς] UBS.
[b] [ὁ] UBS.
[c] Ἰησοῦς NET. κύριος UBS, TNIV.
[d] ἅπαξ omitted in NET.

NASB

The Warnings of History to the Ungodly

1:1 Jude, a bond-
servant of Jesus
Christ, and brother
of James,
To those who are
the called, beloved
in God the Father,
and kept for Jesus
Christ: 2 May mercy
and peace and love
be multiplied to
you.
3 Beloved, while I
was making every
effort to write you
about our com-
mon salvation, I
felt the necessity
to write to you ap-
pealing that you
contend earnestly
for the faith which
was once for all
handed down to
the saints. 4 For cer-
tain persons have
crept in unnoticed,
those who were
long beforehand
marked out for
this condemnation,
ungodly persons
who turn the grace
of our God into
licentiousness and
deny our only Mas-
ter and Lord, Jesus
Christ.
5 Now I desire to
remind you, though
you know all
things once for all,
that [a]the Lord, after
saving a people
out of the land
of Egypt, subse-
quently destroyed
those who did not
believe.

[a] Two early mss read *Jesus*

NIV

[6]And the angels
who did not keep
their positions of
authority but aban-
doned their proper
dwelling — these
he has kept in
darkness, bound
with everlasting
chains for judg-
ment on the great
Day. [7]In a similar
way, Sodom and
Gomorrah and the
surrounding towns
gave themselves up
to sexual immoral-
ity and perversion.
They serve as an
example of those
who suffer the pun-
ishment of eternal
fire.
[8]In the very
same way, on the
strength of their
dreams these
ungodly people
pollute their own
bodies, reject au-
thority and heap
abuse on celestial
beings. [9]But even
the archangel Mi-
chael, when he
was disputing with
the devil about the
body of Moses, did
not himself dare to
condemn him for
slander but said,
"The Lord rebuke
you!"[a] [10]Yet these
people slander
whatever they do
not understand,
and the very things
they do understand
by instinct — as
irrational animals
do — will destroy
them.
[11]Woe to them!
They have taken
the way of Cain;
they have rushed
for profit into Ba-
laam's error;

ἀπώλεσεν, 6 ἀγγέλους τε τοὺς ↱ μὴ τηρήσαντας τὴν ἑαυτῶν ἀρχὴν ἀλλὰ
destroyed And the angels *And* who did not stay within *{the}* their own domain but
660 5445 34 5445 3836 5498 3590 5498 3836 1571 794 247
v.aai.3s n.apm cj d.apm pl pt.aa.apm d.asf r.gpm.3 n.asf cj

ἀπολιπόντας τὸ ἴδιον οἰκητήριον εἰς
abandoned their proper dwelling, he has kept in eternal chains in utter darkness for
657 3836 2625 3863 5498 5498 5498 1301 132 1301 5679 2432 2432 1650
pt.aa.apm d.asn a.asn n.asn p.a

κρίσιν → μεγάλης ἡμέρας δεσμοῖς ἀϊδίοις ὑπὸ ζόφον τετήρηκεν,
the judgment of the great day. *in chains eternal in utter darkness he has kept*
3213 3489 2465 1301 132 5679 2432 5498
n.asf a.gsf n.gsf n.dpm a.dpm p.a n.asm v.rai.3s

7 ὡς Σόδομα καὶ Γόμορρα καὶ αἱ ⌊περὶ αὐτὰς⌋ πόλεις
Likewise, Sodom and Gomorrah and the neighboring towns, which indulged in
6055 5047 2779 1202 2779 3836 4309 899 4484 1745 1745 4047
cj n.npn cj n.nsf cj d.npf p.a r.apf.3 n.npf

τὸν ὅμοιον τρόπον τούτοις ἐκπορνεύσασαι καὶ
sexual immorality in the same way *in sexual immorality which indulged* as the angels and
4047 4047 3836 3927 5573 4047 1745 2779
d.asm a.asm n.asm r.dpm pt.aa.npf cj

⌊ἀπελθοῦσαι ὀπίσω⌋ σαρκὸς ἑτέρας, πρόκεινται δεῖγμα
pursued unnatural desire, *unnatural* are exhibited as an example by undergoing
599 3958 2283 4922 2283 4618 1257 5674 5674
pt.aa.npf p.g n.gsf r.gsf v.pmi.3p n.asn

→ πυρὸς αἰωνίου δίκην ὑπέχουσαι. 8 ὁμοίως
the punishment of eternal fire. *eternal punishment by undergoing* Yet ⌊in the same way⌋
1472 173 4786 173 1472 5674 3530 3931
n.gsn a.gsn n.asf pt.pa.npf adv

μέντοι καὶ οὗτοι ἐνυπνιαζόμενοι σάρκα μὲν μιαίνουσιν
Yet also these people also, relying on their dreams, defile the flesh, ~ *defile* reject
3530 2779 4047 2779 1965 3620 4922 3525 3620 119
cj adv r.npm pt.pp.npm n.asf pl v.pai.3p

κυριότητα δὲ ἀθετοῦσιν δόξας δὲ βλασφημοῦσιν. 9 ὁ
authority, *{and} reject* and blaspheme the ⌊glorious ones.⌋ *and blaspheme* *{the}*
3262 1254 119 1254 1059 1518 1254 1059 3836
n.asf cj v.pai.3p n.apf cj v.pai.3p d.nsm

δὲ Μιχαὴλ ὁ ἀρχάγγελος, ὅτε τῷ διαβόλῳ διακρινόμενος
But when Michael the archangel, *when* in debate ⌊with the⌋ devil, *in debate*
1254 4021 3640 3836 791 4021 1359 1359 3836 1333 1359
cj n.nsm d.nsm n.nsm cj d.dsm n.dsm pt.pm.nsm

διελέγετο περὶ τοῦ Μωϋσέως σώματος, ↱ ↱ οὐκ ἐτόλμησεν ⌊κρίσιν
was arguing about the body of Moses, *body* he did not presume to condemn
1363 4309 3836 5393 3707 5393 5528 5528 4024 5528 3213
v.imi.3s p.g d.gsn n.gsm n.gsn pl v.aai.3s n.asf

ἐπενεγκεῖν⌋ βλασφημίας ἀλλὰ εἶπεν, ἐπιτιμήσαι σοι κύριος. 10
him for blasphemy, but said, "The Lord rebuke you!" *Lord* But
2214 1060 247 3306 3261 2203 5148 3261 1254
f.aa n.gsf cj v.aai.3s v.aao.3s r.ds.2 n.nsm

οὗτοι δὲ ὅσα μὲν ↱ ↱ οὐκ οἴδασιν βλασφημοῦσιν, ὅσα
these people *But* blaspheme whatever ~ they do not understand, *blaspheme* and what
4047 1254 1059 4012 3525 3857 3857 4024 3857 1059 1254 4012
r.npm cj r.apn pl pl v.rai.3p v.pai.3p r.apn

δὲ φυσικῶς ὡς τὰ ἄλογα ζῷα ἐπίστανται, ἐν τούτοις
and they do understand by instinct as *{the}* irrational beasts, *they do understand* by these
1254 2179 2179 2179 5880 6055 3836 263 2442 2179 1877 4047
cj adv pl d.npn a.npn n.npn v.ppi.3p p.d r.dpn

φθείρονται. 11 οὐαὶ αὐτοῖς, ὅτι τῇ ὁδῷ τοῦ Κάϊν ἐπορεύθησαν
⌊they are being destroyed.⌋ Woe to them! For they take the way of Cain, *they take*
5780 4026 899 4022 4513 4513 3836 3847 3836 2782 4513
v.ppi.3p j r.dpm.3 cj d.dsf n.dsf d.gsm n.gsm v.api.3p

καὶ τῇ πλάνῃ τοῦ Βαλαὰμ μισθοῦ ἐξεχύθησαν
and abandon themselves ⌊to the⌋ error of Balaam ⌊for the sake of gain,⌋ *abandon themselves*
2779 1773 1773 3836 4415 3836 962 3635 1773
cj d.dsf n.dsf d.gsm n.gsm n.gsm v.api.3p

NASB

[6]And angels who
did not keep their
own domain, but
abandoned their
proper abode, He
has kept in eternal
bonds under dark-
ness for the judg-
ment of the great
day, [7]just as Sodom
and Gomorrah and
the cities around
them, since they
in the same way
as these indulged
in gross immoral-
ity and went after
strange flesh, are
exhibited as an ex-
ample in undergo-
ing the punishment
of eternal fire.
[8]Yet in the same
way these men,
also by dreaming,
defile the flesh,
and reject author-
ity, and revile
angelic majesties.
[9]But Michael the
archangel, when he
disputed with the
devil and argued
about the body of
Moses, did not dare
pronounce against
him a railing judg-
ment, but said,
"The Lord rebuke
you!" [10]But these
men revile the
things which they
do not understand;
and the things
which they know
by instinct, like un-
reasoning animals,
by these things
they are destroyed.
[11]Woe to them! For
they have gone the
way of Cain, and
for pay they have
rushed headlong
into the error of
Balaam, and per-
ished in the

[a] 9 Jude is alluding to the Jewish *Testament of Moses* (approximately the first century A.D.).

NIV

they have been de-
stroyed in Korah's
rebellion.
12 These people
are blemishes at
your love feasts,
eating with you
without the slight-
est qualm — shep-
herds who feed
only themselves.
They are clouds
without rain,
blown along by
the wind; autumn
trees, without fruit
and uprooted —
twice dead. 13 They
are wild waves of
the sea, foaming
up their shame;
wandering stars,
for whom blackest
darkness has been
reserved forever.
14 Enoch, the sev-
enth from Adam,
prophesied about
them: "See, the
Lord is coming
with thousands
upon thousands of
his holy ones 15 to
judge everyone,
and to convict all
of them of all the
ungodly acts they
have committed in
their ungodliness,
and of all the defi-
ant words ungodly
sinners have spo-
ken against him."[a]
16 These people
are grumblers and
faultfinders; they
follow their own
evil desires; they
boast about them-
selves and flatter
others for their
own advantage.

A Call to Persevere

17 But, dear
friends, remember
what the apostles
of our Lord

[a] 14,15 From the Jewish *First Book of Enoch* (approximately the first century B.C.)

καὶ τῇ ἀντιλογίᾳ τοῦ Κόρε ἀπώλοντο. 12 οὗτοί εἰσιν οἱ
and perish ⌊in the⌋ rebellion of Korah. *perish* ⌊These people⌋ are *{the}* blemishes
2779 660 3836 517 3836 3169 660 4047 1639 3836 5069
cj d.dsf n.dsf d.gsm n.gsm v.ami.3p r.npm v.pai.3p d.npm

ἐν ταῖς ἀγάπαις ὑμῶν σπιλάδες συνευωχούμενοι ἀφόβως,
on *{the}* your love-feasts, *your* *blemishes* feasting with you without reverence, caring only
1877 3836 7007 27 7007 5069 5307 925 4477
p.d d.dpf n.dpf r.gp.2 n.npf pt.pp.npm adv

ἑαυτοὺς ποιμαίνοντες, νεφέλαι ἄνυδροι ὑπὸ ἀνέμων
for themselves. *caring for* They are waterless clouds, *waterless* swept along by winds;
4477 1571 4477 536 3749 536 4195 4195 5679 449
r.apm.3 pt.pa.npm n.npf a.npf p.g n.gpm

παραφερόμεναι, δένδρα φθινοπωρινὰ ἄκαρπα δὶς
swept along autumn trees *autumn* without fruit and uprooted — completely
4195 5781 1285 5781 182 1748 1489
pt.pp.npf n.npn a.npn a.npn adv

ἀποθανόντα ἐκριζωθέντα, 13 κύματα ἄγρια ➝ θαλάσσης ἐπαφρίζοντα τὰς
dead; *uprooted* wild waves *wild* of the sea, casting up *{the}*
633 1748 67 3246 67 2498 2072 3836
pt.aa.npn pt.ap.npn n.npn a.npn n.gsf pt.pa.npn d.apf

ἑαυτῶν αἰσχύνας, ↰ ↰ ἀστέρες πλανῆται οἷς ὁ ζόφος τοῦ
their shameful deeds like foam; wandering stars *wandering* ⌊for whom⌋ the gloom of
1571 158 2072 2072 4417 843 4417 4005 3836 2432 3836
r.gpn.3 n.apf n.npm n.npm r.dpm d.nsm n.nsm d.gsn

σκότους εἰς αἰῶνα τετήρηται. 14 προεφήτευσεν δὲ
utter darkness has been reserved for eternity. *has been reserved* *prophesied* *{and}* It was
5030 5498 5498 5498 1650 172 5498 4736 1254
n.gsn p.a n.asm v.rpi.3s v.aai.3s cj

καὶ τούτοις ἕβδομος ἀπὸ Ἀδὰμ Ἑνὼχ λέγων,
also about these that Enoch, the seventh in descent from Adam, *Enoch* prophesied, saying,
2779 4047 1970 1575 608 77 1970 4736 3306
adv r.dpm a.nsm p.g n.gsm n.nsm pt.pa.nsm

ἰδοὺ ἦλθεν κύριος ἐν ἁγίαις μυριάσιν αὐτοῦ
"Behold, the Lord comes *Lord* with ten thousands of his holy ones *ten thousands* *his*
2627 3261 2262 3261 1877 3689 3689 899 41 3689 899
j v.aai.3s n.nsm p.d a.dpf n.dpf r.gsm.3

15 ποιῆσαι κρίσιν κατὰ πάντων καὶ ἐλέγξαι πᾶσαν[a] ψυχὴν[b] περὶ πάντων τῶν
to execute judgment on all and to convict all the ungodly of all *{the}*
4472 3213 2848 4246 2779 1794 4246 6034 4309 4246 3836
f.aa n.asf p.g a.gpm cj f.aa a.asf n.asf p.g a.gpn d.gpn

ἔργων ἀσεβείας αὐτῶν ὧν ἠσέβησαν καὶ περὶ
their ungodly acts *ungodly* *their* that ⌊they have committed in their ungodliness,⌋ and of
899 813 2240 813 899 4005 814 2779 4309
n.gpn n.gsf r.gpm.3 r.gpn v.aai.3p cj p.g

πάντων τῶν σκληρῶν ὧν ἐλάλησαν κατ᾽ αὐτοῦ ἁμαρτωλοὶ ἀσεβεῖς.
all the harsh things that ungodly sinners have spoken against him." *sinners* *ungodly*
4246 3836 5017 4005 815 283 3281 2848 899 283 815
a.gpn d.gpn a.gpn r.gpn v.aai.3p p.g r.gsm.3 a.npm a.npm

16 οὗτοί εἰσιν γογγυσταὶ μεμψίμοιροι κατὰ τὰς
⌊These people⌋ are grumblers, malcontents who follow *{according to}* *{the}* their
4047 1639 1199 3523 4513 4513 2848 3836 1571
r.npm v.pai.3p n.npm a.npm p.a d.apf

ἐπιθυμίας ἑαυτῶν πορευόμενοι, καὶ τὸ στόμα αὐτῶν λαλεῖ ὑπέρογκα,
sinful desires; *their* *who follow* *{and}* *{the}* their speech *their* is arrogant,
2123 1571 4513 2779 3836 899 5125 899 3281 5665
n.apf r.gpm.3 pt.pm.npm cj d.nsn n.nsn r.gpm.3 v.pai.3s a.apn

θαυμάζοντες πρόσωπα ὠφελείας χάριν. 17 ὑμεῖς δέ, ἀγαπητοί,
they flatter others to gain advantage. *to* But you, *But* dear friends,
2513 4725 5920 6066 5920 1254 7007 1254 28
pt.pa.npm n.apn n.gsf p.g r.np.2 cj a.vpm

μνήσθητε τῶν ῥημάτων τῶν προειρημένων ὑπὸ τῶν ἀποστόλων τοῦ κυρίου
must remember the predictions *{the}* foretold by the apostles of our Lord
3630 3836 4839 3836 4597 5679 3836 693 3836 7005 3261
v.apm.2p d.gpn n.gpn d.gpn pt.rp.gpn p.g d.gpm n.gpm d.gsm n.gsm

[a] πᾶσαν UBS, NET. πάντας ψυχὴν τοῦ ἀσεβεῖς TNIV.
[b] ψυχὴν UBS, NET. τοῦ ἀσεβεῖς TNIV.

NASB

rebellion of Korah.
12 These are the men
who are hidden
reefs in your love
feasts when they
feast with you
without fear, caring
for themselves;
clouds without wa-
ter, carried along
by winds; autumn
trees without
fruit, doubly dead,
uprooted; 13 wild
waves of the sea,
casting up their
own shame like
foam; wandering
stars, for whom
the black darkness
has been reserved
forever.
14 *It was* also
about these men
that Enoch, *in* the
seventh *genera-
tion* from Adam,
prophesied, say-
ing, "Behold, the
Lord came with
many thousands
of His holy ones,
15 to execute judg-
ment upon all,
and to convict all
the ungodly of
all their ungodly
deeds which they
have done in an
ungodly way, and
of all the harsh
things which un-
godly sinners have
spoken against
Him." 16 These are
grumblers, finding
fault, following
after their *own*
lusts; they speak
arrogantly, flatter-
ing people for the
sake of *gaining an*
advantage.

Keep Yourselves in the Love of God

17 But you, be-
loved, ought to re-
member the words
that were spoken
beforehand by the
apostles of our

NIV

Jesus Christ fore-
told. [18]They said
to you, "In the last
times there will be
scoffers who will
follow their own
ungodly desires."
[19]These are the
people who divide
you, who follow
mere natural in-
stincts and do not
have the Spirit.
[20]But you, dear
friends, by build-
ing yourselves up
in your most holy
faith and praying
in the Holy Spirit,
[21]keep yourselves
in God's love as
you wait for the
mercy of our Lord
Jesus Christ to
bring you to eter-
nal life.
[22]Be merciful to
those who doubt;
[23]save others by
snatching them
from the fire; to
others show mercy,
mixed with fear—
hating even the
clothing stained by
corrupted flesh.[a]

Doxology

[24]To him who is
able to keep you
from stumbling
and to present you
before his glorious
presence with-
out fault and with
great joy— [25]to
the only God our
Savior be glory,
majesty, power and
authority, through
Jesus Christ our
Lord, before all
ages, now and for-
evermore! Amen.

[a] 22,23 The Greek manuscripts of these verses vary at several points.

ἡμῶν Ἰησοῦ Χριστοῦ 18 ὅτι ἔλεγον ὑμῖν, ὅτι[a] ἐπ' ἐσχάτου τοῦ[b] χρόνου
our Jesus Christ, how they said to you, ~ "In the final {the} age
7005 2652 5986 4022 3306 7007 4022 2093 2274 3836 5989
r.gp.1 n.gsm n.gsm cj v.iai.3p r.dp.2 cj p.g a.gsm d.gsm n.gsm

ἔσονται ἐμπαῖκται κατὰ τὰς ἑαυτῶν ἐπιθυμίας πορευόμενοι τῶν
⌞there will be⌟ scoffers driven by {the} their own ungodly desires." driven {the}
1639 1851 4513 2848 3836 1571 813 2123 4513 3836
v.fmi.3p n.npm p.a d.apf r.gpm.3 n.apf pt.pm.npm d.gpf

ἀσεβειῶν. 19 οὗτοί εἰσιν οἱ ἀποδιορίζοντες, ψυχικοί,
ungodly These are the ones causing division, worldly-minded, and devoid of the
813 4047 1639 3836 626 6035 3590 3590
n.gpf r.npm v.pai.3p d.npm pt.pa.npm a.npm

πνεῦμα ⌞μὴ ἔχοντες.⌟ 20 ὑμεῖς δέ, ἀγαπητοί, ἐποικοδομοῦντες ἑαυτοὺς
Spirit. devoid of But you, But dear friends, build yourselves up
4460 3590 2400 1254 7007 1254 28 2224 1571 2224
n.asn pl pt.pa.npm r.np.2 cj a.vpm pt.pa.npm r.apm.2

τῇ ἁγιωτάτῃ ὑμῶν πίστει, ἐν πνεύματι ἁγίῳ προσευχόμενοι,
in your most holy your faith and pray in the Holy Spirit. Holy pray
3836 7007 41 7007 4411 4667 1877 41 4460 41 4667
d.dsf a.dsf.s r.gp.2 n.dsf p.d n.dsn a.dsn pt.pm.npm

21 ἑαυτοὺς ἐν ἀγάπῃ θεοῦ τηρήσατε προσδεχόμενοι τὸ ἔλεος τοῦ
Keep yourselves in the love of God Keep as you wait for the mercy of our
5498 1571 1877 27 2536 5498 4657 3836 1799 3836 7005
r.apm.2 p.d n.dsf n.gsm v.aam.2p pt.pm.npm d.asn n.asn d.gsm

κυρίου ἡμῶν Ἰησοῦ Χριστοῦ εἰς ζωὴν αἰώνιον. 22 καὶ
Lord our Jesus Christ to grant you eternal life. eternal And have mercy on
3261 7005 2652 5986 1650 173 2437 173 2779 1790 1790 1790
n.gsm r.gp.1 n.gsm n.gsm p.a n.asf a.asf cj

⌞οὓς μὲν⌟ ἐλεᾶτε διακρινομένους, 23 ⌞οὓς δὲ⌟ σῴζετε
some have mercy on who are wavering; save others save by snatching them
4005 3525 1790 1359 5392 4005 1254 5392 773 773
r.apm pl v.pam.2p pt.pm.apm r.apm pl v.pam.2p

ἐκ πυρὸς ἁρπάζοντες, ⌞οὓς δὲ⌟ ἐλεᾶτε ἐν φόβῳ
⌞out of⌟ the fire; by snatching and have mercy on others have mercy on with fear,
1666 4786 773 1790 1790 1790 4005 1254 1790 1877 5832
p.g n.gsn pt.pa.npm r.apm pl v.pam.2p p.d n.dsm

μισοῦντες καὶ τὸν ἀπὸ τῆς σαρκὸς ἐσπιλωμένον χιτῶνα. 24 τῷ
hating even the garment stained by the flesh. stained garment Now ⌞to the⌟
3631 2779 3836 5945 5071 608 3836 4922 5071 5945 1254 3836
pt.pa.npm adv d.asm p.g d.gsf n.gsf pt.rp.asm n.asm d.dsm

δὲ δυναμένῳ φυλάξαι ὑμᾶς ἀπταίστους καὶ → → στῆσαι →
Now ⌞one who is able⌟ to keep you from stumbling, and to make you stand in his glorious
1254 1538 5875 7007 720 2779 2705 899 1518
cj pt.pp.dsm f.aa r.ap.2 a.apm cj f.aa

κατενώπιον τῆς δόξης αὐτοῦ ἀμώμους ἐν ἀγαλλιάσει, 25 → μόνῳ θεῷ
presence {the} glorious his without blame and with great joy — to the only God,
2979 3836 1518 899 320 1877 21 3668 2536
p.g d.gsf n.gsf r.gsm.3 a.apm p.d n.dsf a.dsm n.dsm

σωτῆρι ἡμῶν διὰ Ἰησοῦ Χριστοῦ τοῦ κυρίου ἡμῶν δόξα
our Savior, our through Jesus Christ {the} our Lord, our belong glory,
7005 5400 7005 1328 2652 5986 3836 7005 3261 7005 1518
n.dsm r.gp.1 p.g n.gsm n.gsm d.gsm n.gsm r.gp.1 n.nsf

μεγαλωσύνη κράτος καὶ ἐξουσία πρὸ παντὸς τοῦ αἰῶνος καὶ νῦν καὶ εἰς πάντας
majesty, power, and authority, before all {the} time, {and} now and for all
3488 3197 2779 2026 4574 4246 3836 172 2779 3814 2779 1650 4246
n.nsf n.nsn cj n.nsf p.g a.gsm d.gsm n.gsm cj adv cj p.a a.apm

τοὺς αἰῶνας, ἀμήν.
{the} time. Amen.
3836 172 297
d.apm n.apm pl

[a] [ὅτι] UBS, omitted by TNIV.
[b] [τοῦ] UBS.

NASB

Lord Jesus Christ,
[18]that they were
saying to you, "In
the last time there
will be mockers,
following after
their own ungodly
lusts." [19]These are
the ones who cause
divisions, worldly-
minded, devoid
of the Spirit. [20]But
you, beloved,
building yourselves
up on your most
holy faith, praying
in the Holy Spirit,
[21]keep yourselves
in the love of God,
waiting anxiously
for the mercy of
our Lord Jesus
Christ to eternal
life. [22]And have
mercy on some,
who are doubt-
ing; [23]save others,
snatching them out
of the fire; and on
some have mercy
with fear, hating
even the garment
polluted by the
flesh.
[24]Now to Him
who is able to
keep you from
stumbling, and to
make you stand in
the presence of His
glory blameless
with great joy, [25]to
the only God our
Savior, through
Jesus Christ our
Lord, *be* glory,
majesty, dominion
and authority, be-
fore all time and
now and forever.
Amen.

Revelation

NIV

Prologue

1 The revelation
from Jesus
Christ, which God
gave him to show
his servants what
must soon take
place. He made it
known by sending
his angel to his
servant John, [2]who
testifies to every-
thing he saw—
that is, the word
of God and the
testimony of Jesus
Christ. [3]Blessed is
the one who reads
aloud the words of
this prophecy, and
blessed are those
who hear it and
take to heart what
is written in it,
because the time
is near.

Greetings and Doxology

[4]John,

To the seven
churches in the
province of Asia:

Grace and peace
to you from him
who is, and who
was, and who is
to come, and from
the seven spirits[a]
before his throne,
[5]and from Jesus
Christ, who is the
faithful witness,
the firstborn from
the dead, and the
ruler of the kings
of the earth.

To him who loves
us and has freed
us from our sins
by his blood, [6]and
has made us to be
a kingdom and
priests to serve his
God and Father—
to him be glory
and power for ever
and ever! Amen.

[a] 4 That is, the sev-
enfold Spirit

1:1 ἀποκάλυψις Ἰησοῦ Χριστοῦ ἣν ἔδωκεν αὐτῷ ὁ θεὸς δεῖξαι τοῖς
The revelation of Jesus Christ, which God gave him *{the}* *God* to show to
637 2652 5986 4005 2536 1443 899 3836 2536 1259 3836
n.nsf n.gsm n.gsm r.asf v.aai.3s r.dsm.3 d.nsm n.nsm f.aa d.dpm

δούλοις αὐτοῦ ἃ δεῖ γενέσθαι ⌊ἐν τάχει,⌋ καὶ
his servants *his* the ⌊things that⌋ must soon take place. *soon* *{and}*
899 1529 899 4005 1256 1877 1181 1877 5443 2779
n.dpm r.gsm.3 r.apn v.pai.3s f.am p.d n.dsn cj

ἐσήμανεν ἀποστείλας διὰ τοῦ ἀγγέλου αὐτοῦ τῷ δούλῳ αὐτοῦ
⌊He made it known⌋ by sending *{through}* *{the}* his angel *his* to his servant *his*
4955 690 1328 3836 899 34 899 3836 899 1529 899
v.aai.3s pt.aa.nsm p.g d.gsm n.gsm r.gsm.3 d.dsm n.dsm r.gsm.3

Ἰωάννῃ, [2]ὃς ἐμαρτύρησεν τὸν λόγον τοῦ θεοῦ καὶ τὴν
John, who bore witness to everything he saw, the word of God and the
2722 4005 3455 4012 1625 1625 3836 3364 3836 2536 2779 3836
n.dsm r.nsm v.aai.3s d.asm n.asm d.gsm n.gsm cj d.asf

μαρτυρίαν Ἰησοῦ Χριστοῦ ὅσα εἶδεν. [3]μακάριος ὁ ἀναγινώσκων
testimony of Jesus Christ. *everything* *he saw* Blessed is the one who reads aloud the
3456 2652 5986 4012 1625 3421 3836 336 3836
n.asf n.gsm n.gsm r.apn v.aai.3s a.nsm d.nsm pt.pa.nsm

καὶ οἱ ἀκούοντες τοὺς λόγους τῆς προφητείας καὶ
words of this prophecy, and those who hear *the* *words* *of this* *prophecy* and
3364 3836 3836 4735 2779 3836 201 3836 3364 3836 4735 2779
cj d.npm pt.pa.npm d.apm n.apm d.gsf n.gsf cj

τηροῦντες τὰ ἐν αὐτῇ γεγραμμένα, ὁ γὰρ καιρὸς ἐγγύς.
keep what is written in it, *is written* for the *for* time is near.
5498 3836 1211 1211 1877 899 1211 1142 3836 1142 2789 1584
pt.pa.npm d.apn p.d r.dsf.3 pt.rp.apn d.nsm cj n.nsm adv

[4]Ἰωάννης ταῖς ἑπτὰ ἐκκλησίαις ταῖς ἐν τῇ Ἀσίᾳ· χάρις ὑμῖν καὶ εἰρήνη ἀπὸ
John to the seven churches that are in *{the}* Asia: Grace to you and peace from
2722 3836 2231 1711 3836 1877 3836 823 5921 7007 2779 1645 608
n.nsm d.dpf a.dpf n.dpf d.dpf p.d d.dsf n.dsf n.nsf r.dp.2 cj n.nsf p.g

ὁ ὢν καὶ ὁ ἦν καὶ ὁ ἐρχόμενος καὶ ἀπὸ τῶν ἑπτὰ πνευμάτων ἃ
the ⌊one who is,⌋ and who was, and who is to come, and from the seven spirits who
3836 1639 2779 3836 1639 2779 3836 2262 2779 608 3836 2231 4460 4005
d.nsm pt.pa.nsm cj d.nsm v.iai.3s cj d.nsm pt.pm.nsm cj p.g d.gpn a.gpn n.gpn r.npn

ἐνώπιον τοῦ θρόνου αὐτοῦ [5]καὶ ἀπὸ Ἰησοῦ Χριστοῦ, ὁ μάρτυς,
are before *{the}* his throne, *his* and from Jesus Christ the faithful witness,
1967 3836 899 2585 899 2779 608 2652 5986 3836 4412 3459
p.g d.gsm n.gsm r.gsm.3 cj p.g n.gsm n.gsm d.nsm n.nsm

ὁ πιστός, ὁ πρωτότοκος τῶν νεκρῶν καὶ ὁ ἄρχων τῶν βασιλέων τῆς
{the} *faithful* the firstborn of the dead, and the ruler of the kings of the
3836 4412 3836 4758 3836 3738 2779 3836 807 3836 995 3836
d.nsm a.nsm d.nsm a.nsm d.gpm a.gpm cj d.nsm n.nsm d.gpm n.gpm d.gsf

γῆς. τῷ ἀγαπῶντι ἡμᾶς καὶ λύσαντι ἡμᾶς ἐκ τῶν ἁμαρτιῶν ἡμῶν ἐν
world. ⌊To him⌋ who loves us and has freed us from *{the}* our sins *our* by
1178 3836 26 7005 2779 3395 7005 1666 3836 7005 281 7005 1877
n.gsf d.dsm pt.pa.dsm r.ap.1 cj pt.aa.dsm r.ap.1 p.g d.gpf n.gpf r.gp.1 p.d

τῷ αἵματι αὐτοῦ, [6]καὶ ἐποίησεν ἡμᾶς βασιλείαν, ἱερεῖς τῷ θεῷ καὶ
{the} his blood *his* and has made us a kingdom, priests to his God and
3836 899 135 899 2779 4472 7005 993 2636 3836 899 2536 2779
d.dsn n.dsn r.gsm.3 cj v.aai.3s r.ap.1 n.asf n.apm d.dsm n.dsm cj

πατρὶ αὐτοῦ, αὐτῷ ἡ δόξα καὶ τὸ κράτος εἰς τοὺς ⌊αἰῶνας [a]τῶν αἰώνων·⌋
Father, *his* to him be *{the}* glory and *{the}* dominion for all time.
4252 899 899 3836 1518 2779 3836 3197 1650 3836 172 3836 172
n.dsm r.gsm.3 r.dsm.3 d.nsf n.nsf cj d.nsn n.nsn p.a d.apm n.apm d.gpm n.gpm

[a] [τῶν αἰώνων] UBS.

NASB

The Revelation of Jesus Christ

[1:1]The Revelation
of Jesus Christ,
which God gave
Him to show to His
bond-servants, the
things which must
soon take place;
and He sent and
communicated *it*
by His angel to His
bond-servant John,
[2]who testified to the
word of God and
to the testimony of
Jesus Christ, *even*
to all that he saw.
[3]Blessed is he who
reads and those
who hear the words
of the prophecy,
and heed the things
which are written
in it; for the time
is near.

Message to the Seven Churches

[4]John to the seven
churches that are
in Asia: Grace to
you and peace,
from Him who is
and who was and
who is to come,
and from the seven
Spirits who are
before His throne,
[5]and from Jesus
Christ, the faithful
witness, the first-
born of the dead,
and the ruler of the
kings of the earth.
To Him who loves
us and released us
from our sins by
His blood— [6]and
He has made us
to be a kingdom,
priests to His God
and Father—to
Him *be* the glory
and the dominion
forever and ever.

NIV

7"Look, he is
coming with
the clouds,"[a]
and "every eye
will see him,
even those who
pierced him";
and all peoples
on earth
"will mourn
because of
him."[b]
So shall it
be! Amen.
8"I am the Alpha
and the Omega,"
says the Lord God,
"who is, and who
was, and who is
to come, the Al-
mighty."

John's Vision of Christ

9I, John, your
brother and com-
panion in the suf-
fering and king-
dom and patient
endurance that are
ours in Jesus, was
on the island of
Patmos because of
the word of God
and the testimony
of Jesus. 10On the
Lord's Day I was
in the Spirit, and
I heard behind me
a loud voice like a
trumpet, 11which
said: "Write on a
scroll what you see
and send it to the
seven churches: to
Ephesus, Smyr-
na, Pergamum,
Thyatira, Sardis,
Philadelphia and
Laodicea."
12I turned around
to see the voice
that was speak-
ing to me. And
when I turned I
saw seven gold-
en lampstands,
13and among the
lampstands was
someone like a son
of man,[c] dressed
in a robe reaching
down to his feet
and with a golden
sash around his
chest. 14The hair
on his head was

[a] 7 Daniel 7:13
[b] 7 Zech. 12:10
[c] 13 See Daniel 7:13.

ἀμήν. 7ἰδοὺ ἔρχεται μετὰ τῶν νεφελῶν, καὶ ὄψεται αὐτὸν πᾶς
Amen. Behold, he is coming with the clouds, and every eye will see him, *every*
297 2627 2262 3552 3836 3749 2779 4246 4057 3972 899 4246
pl j v.pmi.3s p.g d.gpf n.gpf cj v.fmi.3s r.asm.3 a.nsm

ὀφθαλμὸς καὶ οἵτινες αὐτὸν ἐξεκέντησαν, καὶ
eye even those who pierced him; *pierced* and all the tribes of earth
4057 2779 4015 1708 899 1708 2779 4246 3836 5876 3836 1178
n.nsm cj r.npm r.asm.3 v.aai.3p cj

κόψονται ἐπ' αὐτὸν πᾶσαι αἱ φυλαὶ τῆς γῆς. ναί, ἀμήν. 8ἐγώ
will wail ⌊on account of⌋ him. *all the tribes of earth* ⌊So shall it be!⌋ Amen. "I
3164 2093 899 4246 3836 5876 3836 1178 3721 297 1609
v.fmi.3p p.a r.asm.3 a.npf d.npf n.npf d.gsf n.gsf pl pl r.ns.1

εἰμι τὸ ἄλφα καὶ τὸ ὦ, λέγει κύριος ὁ θεός, ὁ ὢν καὶ ὁ
am the Alpha and the Omega," says the Lord *{the}* God, "the ⌊one who is,⌋ and who
1639 3836 270 2779 3836 6042 3306 3261 3836 2536 3836 1639 2779 3836
v.pai.1s d.nsn n.nsn cj d.nsn n.nsn v.pai.3s n.nsm d.nsm n.nsm d.nsm pt.pa.nsm cj d.nsm

ἦν καὶ ὁ ἐρχόμενος, ὁ παντοκράτωρ. 9ἐγὼ Ἰωάννης, ὁ ἀδελφὸς ὑμῶν
was, and who is to come, the Almighty." I, John, *{the}* your brother *your*
1639 2779 3836 2262 3836 4120 1609 2722 3836 7007 81 7007
v.iai.3s cj d.nsm pt.pm.nsm d.nsm n.nsm r.ns.1 n.nsm d.nsm n.nsm r.gp.2

καὶ συγκοινωνὸς ἐν τῇ θλίψει καὶ βασιλείᾳ καὶ ὑπομονῇ ἐν
and partner in the tribulation and kingdom and patient endurance that are in
2779 5171 1877 3836 2568 2779 993 2779 5705 1877
cj n.nsm p.d d.dsf n.dsf cj n.dsf cj n.dsf p.d

Ἰησοῦ, ἐγενόμην ἐν τῇ νήσῳ τῇ καλουμένῃ Πάτμῳ διὰ τὸν λόγον τοῦ
Jesus, was on the island *{the}* called Patmos ⌊on account of⌋ the word of
2652 1181 1877 3836 3762 3836 2813 4253 1328 3836 3364 3836
n.dsm v.ami.1s p.d d.dsf n.dsf d.dsf pt.pp.dsf n.dsm p.a d.asm n.asm d.gsm

θεοῦ καὶ τὴν μαρτυρίαν Ἰησοῦ. 10ἐγενόμην ἐν πνεύματι ἐν τῇ κυριακῇ
God and the testimony of Jesus. I was in the spirit on the Lord's
2536 2779 3836 3456 2652 1181 1877 4460 1877 3836 3258
n.gsm cj d.asf n.asf n.gsm v.ami.1s p.d n.dsn p.d d.dsf a.dsf

ἡμέρᾳ καὶ ἤκουσα ὀπίσω μου φωνὴν μεγάλην ὡς σάλπιγγος 11λεγούσης,
Day, and I heard behind me a loud voice *loud* like a trumpet, saying,
2465 2779 201 3958 1609 3489 5889 3489 6055 4894 3306
n.dsf cj v.aai.1s p.g r.gs.1 n.asf a.asf pl n.gsf pt.pa.gsf

ὃ βλέπεις γράψον εἰς βιβλίον καὶ πέμψον ταῖς ἑπτὰ ἐκκλησίαις, εἰς
"Write what you see *Write* on a scroll and send it to the seven churches — to
1211 4005 1063 1211 1650 1046 2779 4287 3836 2231 1711 1650
r.asn v.pai.2s v.aam.2s p.a n.asn cj v.aam.2s d.dpf a.dpf n.dpf p.a

Ἔφεσον καὶ εἰς Σμύρναν καὶ εἰς Πέργαμον καὶ εἰς Θυάτειρα καὶ εἰς Σάρδεις
Ephesus, *{and} {to}* Smyrna, *{and} {to}* Pergamum, *{and} {to}* Thyatira, *{and} {to}* Sardis,
2387 2779 1650 5044 2779 1650 4307 2779 1650 2587 2779 1650 4915
n.asf cj p.a n.asf cj p.a n.asf cj p.a n.apn cj p.a n.apf

καὶ εἰς Φιλαδέλφειαν καὶ εἰς Λαοδίκειαν. 12καὶ ἐπέστρεψα βλέπειν τὴν φωνὴν
{and} {to} Philadelphia, and *{to}* Laodicea." And I turned to see the voice
2779 1650 5788 2779 1650 3293 2779 2188 1063 3836 5889
cj p.a n.asf cj p.a n.asf cj v.aai.1s f.pa d.asf n.asf

ἥτις ἐλάλει μετ' ἐμοῦ, καὶ ἐπιστρέψας εἶδον ἑπτὰ λυχνίας χρυσᾶς
that was speaking to me, and when I had turned I saw seven golden lampstands, *golden*
4015 3281 3552 1609 2779 2188 1625 2231 5997 3393 5997
r.nsf v.iai.3s p.g r.gs.1 cj pt.aa.nsm v.aai.1s a.apf n.apf a.apf

13καὶ ἐν μέσῳ τῶν λυχνιῶν ὅμοιον υἱὸν ἀνθρώπου ἐνδεδυμένον ποδήρη
and in the midst of the lampstands one like a son of man, dressed in a long robe
2779 1877 3545 3836 3393 3927 5626 476 1907 4468
cj p.d n.dsn d.gpf n.gpf a.asm n.asm n.gsm pt.rp.asm n.asm

καὶ περιεζωσμένον πρὸς τοῖς μαστοῖς ζώνην χρυσᾶν. 14ἡ
and with a gold sash tied ⌊high across⌋ his chest. *sash gold {the}*
2779 5997 2438 4322 4639 3836 3466 2438 5997 3836
cj pt.rp.asm p.d d.dpm n.dpm n.asf a.asf d.nsf

δὲ κεφαλὴ αὐτοῦ καὶ αἱ τρίχες λευκαὶ ὡς ἔριον λευκὸν ὡς χιὼν
{and} His head *His* and his hair were white, like white wool, *white* like snow,
1254 899 3051 899 2779 3836 2582 3328 6055 3328 2250 3328 6055 5946
cj n.nsf r.gsm.3 cj d.npf n.npf a.npf pl n.nsn a.nsn pl n.nsf

NASB

Amen. 7BEHOLD, HE
IS COMING WITH THE
CLOUDS, and every
eye will see Him,
even those who
pierced Him; and
all the tribes of the
earth will mourn
over Him. So it is
to be. Amen.
8"I am the Alpha
and the Omega,"
says the Lord God,
"who is and who
was and who is
to come, the Al-
mighty."

The Patmos Vision

9I, John, your
brother and fel-
low partaker in
the tribulation
and kingdom and
perseverance *which
are* in Jesus, was
on the island called
Patmos because of
the word of God
and the testimony
of Jesus. 10I was [a]in
the Spirit on the
Lord's day, and I
heard behind me a
loud voice like *the
sound* of a trumpet,
11saying, "Write in
a book what you
see, and send *it* to
the seven churches:
to Ephesus and
to Smyrna and to
Pergamum and
to Thyatira and
to Sardis and to
Philadelphia and to
Laodicea."
12Then I turned to
see the voice that
was speaking with
me. And having
turned I saw seven
golden lampstands;
13and in the middle
of the lampstands *I
saw* one like [b]a son
of man, clothed in
a robe reaching to
the feet, and girded
across His chest
with a golden sash.
14His head and His
hair were white
like white wool,
like snow;

[a] Or *in spirit*
[b] Or *the Son of Man*

NIV

white like wool,
as white as snow,
and his eyes were
like blazing fire.
15 His feet were like
bronze glowing
in a furnace, and
his voice was like
the sound of rush-
ing waters. 16 In
his right hand he
held seven stars,
and coming out
of his mouth was
a sharp, double-
edged sword. His
face was like the
sun shining in all
its brilliance.
17 When I saw
him, I fell at his
feet as though
dead. Then he
placed his right
hand on me and
said: "Do not be
afraid. I am the
First and the Last.
18 I am the Living
One; I was dead,
and now look, I am
alive for ever and
ever! And I hold
the keys of death
and Hades.
19 "Write, there-
fore, what you
have seen, what
is now and what
will take place lat-
er. 20 The mystery
of the seven stars
that you saw in my
right hand and of
the seven golden
lampstands is this:
The seven stars
are the angels[a] of
the seven church-
es, and the seven
lampstands are the
seven churches.

To the Church in Ephesus

2 "To the angel[b]
of the church
in Ephesus write:

[a] 20 Or *messengers*
[b] 1 Or *messenger*; also in verses 8, 12 and 18

καὶ οἱ ὀφθαλμοὶ αὐτοῦ ὡς φλὸξ πυρὸς 15 καὶ οἱ πόδες αὐτοῦ
and *{the}* his eyes *his* were like a flame of fire. *{and}* *{the}* His feet *His*
2779 3836 899 4057 899 6055 5825 4786 2779 3836 899 4546 899
cj d.npm n.npm r.gsm.3 pl n.nsf n.gsn cj d.npm n.npm r.gsm.3

ὅμοιοι χαλκολιβάνῳ ὡς ἐν καμίνῳ πεπυρωμένης καὶ ἡ φωνὴ
were like burnished bronze, *{like}* refined in a furnace, *refined* and *{the}* his voice
3927 5909 6055 4792 1877 2825 4792 2779 3836 899 5889
a.npm n.dsn pl p.d n.dsf pt.rp.gsf cj d.nsf n.nsf

αὐτοῦ ὡς φωνὴ → ὑδάτων πολλῶν, 16 καὶ ἔχων ἐν τῇ δεξιᾷ
his was like the roar of many waters. *many* *{and}* *he held* In *{the}* his right
899 6055 5889 4498 5623 4498 2779 2400 1877 3836 899 1288
r.gsm.3 pl n.nsf n.gpn a.gpn cj pt.pa.nsm p.d d.dsf a.dsf

χειρὶ αὐτοῦ ἀστέρας ἑπτὰ καὶ ἐκ τοῦ στόματος αὐτοῦ
hand *his* he held seven stars, *seven* *{and}* from *{the}* his mouth *his* came a
5931 899 2400 2400 2231 843 2231 2779 1666 3836 899 5125 899 1744
n.dsf r.gsm.3 n.apm a.apm cj p.g d.gsn n.gsn r.gsm.3

ῥομφαία δίστομος ὀξεῖα ἐκπορευομένη καὶ ἡ ὄψις αὐτοῦ
sharp two-edged sword, *two-edged* *sharp* *came* and *{the}* his face *his* was
3955 1492 4855 1492 3955 1744 2779 3836 899 4071 899 5743
n.nsf a.nsf a.nsf pt.pm.nsf cj d.nsf n.nsf r.gsm.3

ὡς ὁ ἥλιος φαίνει ἐν τῇ δυνάμει αὐτοῦ. 17 καὶ ὅτε εἶδον αὐτόν,
shining like the sun *was shining* at *{the}* full strength. *full* And when I saw him,
5743 6055 3836 2463 5743 1877 3836 899 1539 899 2779 4021 1625 899
cj d.nsm n.nsm v.pai.3s p.d d.dsf n.dsf r.gsm.3 cj cj v.aai.1s r.asm.3

ἔπεσα πρὸς τοὺς πόδας αὐτοῦ ὡς νεκρός, καὶ ἔθηκεν τὴν δεξιὰν
I fell at *{the}* his feet *his* ⌊as though⌋ dead. And he laid *{the}* his right hand
4406 4639 3836 899 4546 899 6055 3738 2779 5502 3836 899 1288
v.aai.1s p.a d.apm n.apm r.gsm.3 pl a.nsm cj v.aai.3s d.asf a.asf

αὐτοῦ ἐπ' ἐμὲ λέγων, ↱ μὴ φοβοῦ· ἐγώ εἰμι ὁ πρῶτος καὶ ὁ ἔσχατος
his on me, saying, "Do not fear! I am the First and the Last,
899 2093 1609 3306 5828 3590 5828 1609 1639 3836 4755 2779 3836 2274
r.gsm.3 p.a r.as.1 pt.pa.nsm pl v.ppm.2s r.ns.1 v.pai.1s d.nsm a.nsm cj d.nsm a.nsm

18 καὶ ὁ ζῶν, καὶ ἐγενόμην νεκρὸς καὶ ἰδοὺ ζῶν εἰμι εἰς
{and} the ⌊Living One.⌋ *{and}* I was dead, but behold, I am alive *I am* for
2779 3836 2409 2779 1181 3738 2779 2627 1639 1639 2409 1639 1650
cj d.nsm pt.pa.nsm cj v.ami.1s a.nsm cj j pt.pa.nsm v.pai.1s p.a

τοὺς ⌊αἰῶνας τῶν αἰώνων⌋ καὶ ἔχω τὰς κλεῖς τοῦ θανάτου καὶ τοῦ ᾅδου.
all time! And I hold the keys of death and of Hades.
3836 172 3836 172 2779 2400 3836 3090 3836 2505 2779 3836 87
d.apm n.apm d.gpm n.gpm cj v.pai.1s d.apf n.apf d.gsm n.gsm cj d.gsm n.gsm

19 γράψον οὖν ἃ εἶδες καὶ ἃ εἰσὶν καὶ ἃ
Write therefore the ⌊things that⌋ ⌊you have seen,⌋ *{and}* ⌊those that⌋ are, and ⌊those that⌋
1211 4036 4005 1625 2779 4005 1639 2779 4005
v.aam.2s cj r.apn v.aai.2s cj r.npn v.pai.3p cj r.npn

μέλλει γενέσθαι μετὰ ταῦτα. 20 τὸ μυστήριον τῶν ἑπτὰ ἀστέρων οὓς εἶδες ἐπὶ
are to take place after this. The mystery of the seven stars that you saw in
3516 1181 3552 4047 3836 3696 3836 2231 843 4005 1625 2093
v.pai.3s f.am p.a r.apn d.nsn n.nsn d.gpm a.gpm n.gpm r.apm v.aai.2s p.g

τῆς δεξιᾶς μου καὶ τὰς ἑπτὰ λυχνίας τὰς χρυσᾶς· οἱ ἑπτὰ
{the} my right hand, *my* and the seven golden lampstands, *{the}* *golden* is this: the seven
3836 1609 1288 1609 2779 3836 2231 5997 3393 3836 5997 3836 2231
d.gsf a.gsf r.gs.1 cj d.apf a.apf n.apf d.apf a.apf d.npm a.npm

ἀστέρες ἄγγελοι τῶν ἑπτὰ ἐκκλησιῶν εἰσιν καὶ αἱ λυχνίαι αἱ ἑπτὰ
stars are the angels of the seven churches, *are* and the seven lampstands *{the}* *seven*
843 1639 34 3836 2231 1711 1639 2779 3836 2231 3393 3836 2231
n.npm n.npm d.gpf a.gpf n.gpf v.pai.3p cj d.npf n.npf d.npf a.npf

ἑπτὰ ἐκκλησίαι εἰσίν.
are the seven churches. *are*
1639 2231 1711 1639
a.npf n.npf v.pai.3p

2:1 τῷ ἀγγέλῳ τῆς ἐν Ἐφέσῳ ἐκκλησίας γράψον, τάδε λέγει ὁ
⌊"To the⌋ angel of the church in Ephesus *church* write: *this* *has to say* The
3836 34 3836 1711 1877 2387 1711 1211 3840 3306 3836
d.dsm n.dsm d.gsf p.d n.dsf n.gsf v.aam.2s r.apn v.pai.3s d.nsm

NASB

and His eyes were
like a flame of fire.
15 His feet *were* like
burnished bronze,
when it has been
made to glow in a
furnace, and His
voice *was* like the
sound of many
waters. 16 In His
right hand He held
seven stars, and out
of His mouth came
a sharp two-edged
sword; and His
face was like the
sun shining in its
strength.
17 When I saw
Him, I fell at His
feet like a dead
man. And He
placed His right
hand on me, say-
ing, "Do not be
afraid; I am the
first and the last,
18 and the living
One; and I was
dead, and behold,
I am alive forever-
more, and I have
the keys of death
and of Hades.
19 Therefore write
the things which
you have seen, and
the things which
are, and the things
which will take
place after these
things. 20 As for the
mystery of the sev-
en stars which you
saw in My right
hand, and the seven
golden lampstands:
the seven stars are
the angels of the
seven churches,
and the seven
lampstands are the
seven churches.

Message to Ephesus

2:1 "To the angel of
the church in Ephe-
sus write:

NIV

These are the
words of him who
holds the seven
stars in his right
hand and walks
among the seven
golden lamp-
stands. 2 I know
your deeds, your
hard work and
your persever-
ance. I know that
you cannot toler-
ate wicked peo-
ple, that you have
tested those who
claim to be apos-
tles but are not,
and have found
them false. 3 You
have persevered
and have endured
hardships for my
name, and have
not grown weary.
4 Yet I hold this
against you: You
have forsaken the
love you had at
first. 5 Consider
how far you have
fallen! Repent
and do the things
you did at first.
If you do not re-
pent, I will come
to you and re-
move your lamp-
stand from its
place. 6 But you
have this in your
favor: You hate
the practices of
the Nicolaitans,
which I also hate.
7 Whoever has
ears, let them
hear what the
Spirit says to the
churches. To the
one who is victo-
rious, I will give
the right to eat
from the tree of
life, which is in
the paradise of
God.

To the Church in Smyrna

8 "To the angel
of the church in
Smyrna write:

These are the
words of him
who is the First
and the Last, who
died and came to
life again.

κρατῶν τοὺς ἑπτὰ ἀστέρας ἐν τῇ δεξιᾷ αὐτοῦ, ὁ περιπατῶν ⌊ἐν
⌊one who holds⌋ the seven stars in *{the}* his right hand, *his* who walks among
3195 3836 2231 843 1877 3836 899 1288 899 3836 4344 1877
pt.pa.nsm d.apm a.apm n.apm p.d d.dsf a.dsf r.gsm.3 d.nsm pt.pa.nsm p.d

μέσῳ⌋ τῶν ἑπτὰ λυχνιῶν τῶν χρυσῶν· 2 οἶδα τὰ
the seven golden lampstands, *{the} golden* has this to say: I know *{the}* your
3545 3836 2231 5997 3393 3836 5997 3306 3840 3306 3306 3857 3836 5148
n.dsn d.gpf a.gpf n.gpf d.gpf a.gpf v.rai.1s d.apn

ἔργα σου καὶ τὸν κόπον καὶ τὴν ὑπομονήν σου καὶ ὅτι ⌊οὐ
works, *your {and}* your toil and *{the}* your patient endurance, *your* and that you cannot
2240 5148 2779 3836 3160 2779 3836 5148 5705 5148 2779 4022 4024
n.apn r.gs.2 cj d.asm n.asm cj d.asf n.asf r.gs.2 cj cj pl

δύνῃ⌋ βαστάσαι κακούς, καὶ ἐπείρασας τοὺς λέγοντας ἑαυτοὺς
put up with ⌊those who are evil,⌋ but have tested those who call themselves
1538 1002 2805 2779 4279 3836 3306 1571
v.ppi.2s f.aa a.apm cj v.aai.2s d.apm pt.pa.apm r.apm.3

ἀποστόλους καὶ οὐκ εἰσὶν καὶ εὗρες αὐτοὺς ψευδεῖς, 3 καὶ
apostles (but are not) *are* and found them to be false. I also know that you have
693 2779 1639 4024 1639 2779 2351 899 6014 2779 2400 2400
n.apm cj pl v.pai.3p cj v.aai.2s r.apm.3 a.apm cj

ὑπομονὴν ἔχεις καὶ ἐβάστασας διὰ τὸ ὄνομά μου ↰ καὶ
demonstrated your patience *you have* and borne hardship for *{the}* my name's *my* sake, and
5705 2400 2779 1002 1328 3836 1609 3950 1609 1328 2779
n.asf v.pai.2s cj v.aai.2s p.a d.asn n.asn r.gs.1 cj

↱ οὐ κεκοπίακες. 4 ἀλλὰ ἔχω κατὰ σοῦ ὅτι τὴν
have not grown weary. But ⌊I do have⌋ this against you, that you have left *{the}* your first
3159 4024 3159 247 2400 2848 5148 4022 918 918 918 3836 5148 4755
pl v.rai.2s cj v.pai.1s p.g r.gs.2 cj d.asf

ἀγάπην σου τὴν πρώτην ἀφῆκες. 5 μνημόνευε οὖν πόθεν
love! *your {the} first you have left* Therefore remember *Therefore* from where
27 5148 3836 4755 918 4036 3648 4036 4470
n.asf r.gs.2 d.asf a.asf v.aai.2s v.pam.2s cj cj

πέπτωκας καὶ μετανόησον καὶ τὰ πρῶτα ἔργα ποίησον· εἰ
you have fallen; *{and}* repent and do the works you did at first. *works do* If
4406 2779 3566 2779 4472 3836 2240 4755 2240 4472 1623
v.rai.2s cj v.aam.2s cj d.apn a.apn n.apn v.aam.2s cj

δὲ μή, ἔρχομαί σοι καὶ κινήσω τὴν λυχνίαν σου ἐκ τοῦ τόπου
{and} not, I will come to you and remove *{the}* your lampstand *your* from *{the}* its place,
1254 3590 2262 5148 2779 3075 3836 5148 3393 5148 1666 3836 899 5536
cj pl v.pmi.1s r.ds.2 cj v.fai.1s d.asf n.asf r.gs.2 p.g d.gsm n.gsm

αὐτῆς, ⌊ἐὰν μὴ⌋ μετανοήσῃς. 6 ἀλλὰ τοῦτο ἔχεις, ὅτι μισεῖς τὰ
its unless you repent. But you do have this: *you do have {that}* you hate the
899 1569 3590 3566 247 2400 2400 2400 4047 2400 4022 3631 3836
r.gsf.3 cj pl v.aas.2s cj r.asn v.pai.2s cj v.pai.2s d.apn

ἔργα τῶν Νικολαϊτῶν ἃ κἀγὼ μισῶ. 7 ὁ ἔχων οὖς ἀκουσάτω τί τὸ
practices of the Nicolaitans, which I also hate. He ⌊who has⌋ an ear, let him hear what the
2240 3836 3774 4005 2743 3631 3836 2400 4044 201 5515 3836
n.apn d.gpm n.gpm r.apn crasis v.pai.1s d.nsm pt.pa.nsm n.asn v.aam.3s r.asn d.nsn

πνεῦμα λέγει ταῖς ἐκκλησίαις. τῷ νικῶντι δώσω αὐτῷ
Spirit says to the churches. ⌊To the⌋ ⌊one who conquers,⌋ ⌊I will give the right⌋ *{to him}*
4460 3306 3836 1711 3836 3771 1443 899
n.nsn v.pai.3s d.dpf n.dpf d.dsm pt.pa.dsm v.fai.1s r.dsm.3

φαγεῖν ἐκ τοῦ ξύλου τῆς ζωῆς, ὅ ἐστιν ἐν τῷ παραδείσῳ τοῦ θεοῦ. 8 καὶ
to eat from the tree of life, which is in the paradise of God. *{and}*
2266 1666 3836 3833 3836 2437 4005 1639 1877 3836 4137 3836 2536 2779
f.aa p.g d.gsn n.gsn d.gsf n.gsf r.nsn v.pai.3s p.d d.dsm n.dsm d.gsm n.gsm cj

τῷ ἀγγέλῳ τῆς ἐν Σμύρνῃ ἐκκλησίας γράψον, τάδε λέγει ὁ
⌊"To the⌋ angel of the church in Smyrna *church* write: *this has to say* The
3836 34 3836 1711 1877 5044 1711 1211 3840 3306 3836
d.dsm n.dsm d.gsf p.d n.dsf n.gsf v.aam.2s r.apn v.pai.3s d.nsm

πρῶτος καὶ ὁ ἔσχατος, ὃς ⌊ἐγένετο νεκρὸς⌋ καὶ ἔζησεν·
⌊one who is the First⌋ and the Last, who died and ⌊came to life,⌋ has this
4755 2779 3836 2274 4005 1181 3738 2779 2409 3306 3840
a.nsm cj d.nsm a.nsm r.nsm v.ami.3s a.nsm cj v.aai.3s

NASB

The One who
holds the seven
stars in His right
hand, the One who
walks among the
seven golden lamp-
stands, says this:
2 'I know your
deeds and your toil
and perseverance,
and that you cannot
tolerate evil men,
and you put to
the test those who
call themselves
apostles, and they
are not, and you
found them *to be*
false; 3 and you
have perseverance
and have endured
for My name's
sake, and have not
grown weary. 4 But
I have *this* against
you, that you have
left your first love.
5 Therefore remem-
ber from where
you have fallen,
and repent and do
the deeds you did
at first; or else I am
coming to you and
will remove your
lampstand out of
its place—unless
you repent. 6 Yet
this you do have,
that you hate the
deeds of the Ni-
colaitans, which I
also hate. 7 He who
has an ear, let him
hear what the Spirit
says to the church-
es. To him who
overcomes, I will
grant to eat of the
tree of life which is
in the Paradise of
God.'

Message to Smyrna

8 "And to the angel
of the church in
Smyrna write:
The first and the
last, who was dead,
and has come to
life, says this:

NIV

9 I know your af-
flictions and your
poverty — yet
you are rich! I
know about the
slander of those
who say they are
Jews and are not,
but are a syna-
gogue of Satan.
10 Do not be afraid
of what you are
about to suffer. I
tell you, the devil
will put some of
you in prison to
test you, and you
will suffer per-
secution for ten
days. Be faithful,
even to the point
of death, and I
will give you life
as your victor's
crown.
11 Whoever has
ears, let them
hear what the
Spirit says to the
churches. The
one who is victo-
rious will not be
hurt at all by the
second death.

To the Church in Pergamum

12 "To the angel of
the church in Per-
gamum write:
These are the
words of him who
has the sharp,
double-edged
sword. 13 I know
where you live —
where Satan has
his throne. Yet
you remain true
to my name. You
did not renounce
your faith in me,
not even in the
days of Antipas,
my faithful wit-
ness, who was put
to death in your
city — where Sa-
tan lives.
14 Nevertheless, I
have a few things
against you:
There are some
among you who
hold to the teach-
ing of Balaam,

9 οἶδά σου τὴν θλῖψιν καὶ τὴν πτωχείαν, ἀλλὰ πλούσιος εἶ,
to say: I know your {the} affliction and your poverty (but you are rich), you are
3306 3306 3857 5148 3836 2568 2779 3836 4775 247 1639 1639 4454 1639
v.rai.1s r.gs.2 d.asf n.asf cj d.asf n.asf cj a.nsm v.pai.2s

καὶ τὴν βλασφημίαν ἐκ τῶν λεγόντων Ἰουδαίους εἶναι ἑαυτοὺς καὶ
and the slander against you by those who call themselves Jews {to be} themselves and
2779 3836 1060 1666 3836 3306 1571 2681 1639 1571 2779
cj d.asf n.asf p.g d.gpm pt.pa.gpm a.apm f.pa r.apm.3 cj

οὐκ εἰσὶν ἀλλὰ συναγωγὴ τοῦ σατανᾶ. 10 ↱ μηδὲν φοβοῦ ἃ
are not, are but are a synagogue of Satan. Do not fear what
1639 4024 1639 247 5252 3836 4928 5828 3594 5828 4005
pl v.pai.3p cj n.nsf d.gsm n.gsm a.asn v.ppm.2s r.apn

μέλλεις πάσχειν. ἰδοὺ μέλλει βάλλειν ὁ διάβολος ἐξ ὑμῶν
you are about to suffer. {behold} The devil is about to throw The devil ⌊some of⌋ you
3516 4248 2627 3836 1333 3516 965 3836 1333 1666 7007
v.pai.2s f.pa j v.pai.3s f.pa d.nsm n.nsm p.g r.gp.2

εἰς φυλακὴν ἵνα πειρασθῆτε καὶ ἕξετε θλῖψιν → ἡμερῶν δέκα.
into prison so that you may be tested, and ⌊you will have⌋ affliction for ten days. ten
1650 5871 2671 4279 2779 2400 2568 1274 2465 1274
p.a n.asf cj v.aps.2p cj v.fai.2p n.asf n.gpf a.gpf

γίνου πιστὸς ἄχρι θανάτου, καὶ δώσω σοι τὸν στέφανον τῆς ζωῆς. 11 ὁ
Be faithful until death, and I will give you the crown of life. He
1181 4412 948 2505 2779 1443 5148 3836 5109 3836 2437 3836
v.pmm.2s a.nsm p.g n.gsm cj v.fai.1s r.ds.2 d.asm n.asm d.gsf n.gsf d.nsm

ἔχων οὖς ἀκουσάτω τί τὸ πνεῦμα λέγει ταῖς ἐκκλησίαις. ὁ
⌊who has⌋ an ear, let him hear what the Spirit is saying to the churches. The
2400 4044 201 5515 3836 4460 3306 3836 1711 3836
pt.pa.nsm n.asn v.aam.3s r.asn d.nsn n.nsn v.pai.3s d.dpf n.dpf d.nsm

νικῶν ↱ ⌊οὐ μὴ⌋ ἀδικηθῇ ἐκ τοῦ θανάτου τοῦ δευτέρου.
⌊one who conquers⌋ will not be harmed by the second death. {the} second
3771 92 4024 3590 92 1666 3836 1311 2505 3836 1311
pt.pa.nsm pl pl v.aps.3s p.g d.gsm n.gsm d.gsm a.gsm

12 καὶ τῷ ἀγγέλῳ τῆς ἐν Περγάμῳ ἐκκλησίας γράψον, τάδε λέγει
{and} ⌊"To the⌋ angel of the church in Pergamum church write: this has to say
2779 3836 34 3836 1711 1877 4307 1711 1211 3840 3306
cj d.dsm n.dsm d.gsf p.d n.dsf n.gsf v.aam.2s r.apn v.pai.3s

ὁ ἔχων τὴν ῥομφαίαν τὴν δίστομον τὴν ὀξεῖαν·
The ⌊one who has⌋ the sharp two-edged sword {the} two-edged {the} sharp has this to
3836 2400 3836 3955 1492 4855 3836 1492 3836 3955 3306 3840 3306
d.nsm pt.pa.nsm d.asf n.asf d.asf a.asf d.asf a.asf

13 οἶδα ποῦ κατοικεῖς, ὅπου ὁ θρόνος τοῦ σατανᾶ, καὶ
say: I know where you live, where {the} Satan has his throne. his Satan Yet
3306 3857 4543 2997 3963 3836 4928 3836 2585 3836 4928 2779
v.rai.1s cj v.pai.2s cj d.nsm n.nsm d.gsm n.gsm cj

κρατεῖς τὸ ὄνομά μου καὶ ↱ ↱ οὐκ ἠρνήσω τὴν πίστιν μου καὶ
⌊you are holding fast to⌋ {the} my name, my and you did not deny your faith in me even
3195 3836 1609 3950 1609 2779 766 766 4024 766 3836 4411 1609 2779
v.pai.2s d.asn n.asn r.gs.1 cj pl v.ami.2s d.asf n.asf r.gs.1 adv

ἐν ταῖς ἡμέραις Ἀντιπᾶς ὁ μάρτυς μου ὁ πιστός μου, ὃς
in the days of Antipas {the} my faithful witness, my {the} faithful {my} who
1877 3836 2465 525 3836 1609 4412 3459 1609 3836 4412 1609 4005
p.d d.dpf n.dpf n.nsm d.nsm n.nsm r.gs.1 d.nsm a.nsm r.gs.1 r.nsm

ἀπεκτάνθη παρ' ὑμῖν, ὅπου ὁ σατανᾶς κατοικεῖ. 14 ἀλλ' ἔχω
was put to death in your city where {the} Satan lives. But I have several things
650 4123 7007 3963 3836 4928 2997 247 2400 3900 3900
v.api.3s p.d r.dp.2 cj d.nsm n.nsm v.pai.3s cj v.pai.1s

κατὰ σοῦ ὀλίγα ὅτι ἔχεις ἐκεῖ κρατοῦντας τὴν διδαχὴν Βαλαάμ,
against you, several things because you have among you those who follow the teaching of Balaam,
2848 5148 3900 4022 2400 1695 3195 3836 1439 962
p.g r.gs.2 a.apn cj v.pai.2s adv pt.pa.apm d.asf n.asf n.gsm

NASB

9 "I know your
tribulation and
your poverty (but
you are rich), and
the blasphemy by
those who say they
are Jews and are
not, but are a syna-
gogue of Satan.
10 Do not fear what
you are about to
suffer. Behold, the
devil is about to
cast some of you
into prison, so that
you will be tested,
and you will have
tribulation for ten
days. Be faithful
until death, and I
will give you the
crown of life. 11 He
who has an ear, let
him hear what the
Spirit says to the
churches. He who
overcomes will not
be hurt by the sec-
ond death.'

Message to Pergamum

12 "And to the an-
gel of the church in
Pergamum write:
The One who
has the sharp two-
edged sword says
this:
13 'I know where
you dwell, where
Satan's throne is;
and you hold fast
My name, and
did not deny My
faith even in the
days of Antipas,
My witness, My
faithful one, who
was killed among
you, where Satan
dwells. 14 But I
have a few things
against you, be-
cause you have
there some who
hold the teaching
of Balaam,

NIV

who taught Balak to entice the Israelites to sin so that they ate food sacrificed to idols and committed sexual immorality. 15 Likewise, you also have those who hold to the teaching of the Nicolaitans. 16 Repent therefore! Otherwise, I will soon come to you and will fight against them with the sword of my mouth.

17 Whoever has ears, let them hear what the Spirit says to the churches. To the one who is victorious, I will give some of the hidden manna. I will also give that person a white stone with a new name written on it, known only to the one who receives it.

To the Church in Thyatira

18 "To the angel of the church in Thyatira write:

These are the words of the Son of God, whose eyes are like blazing fire and whose feet are like burnished bronze. 19 I know your deeds, your love and faith, your service and perseverance, and that you are now doing more than you did at first.

20 Nevertheless, I have this against you: You tolerate that woman Jezebel, who calls herself a prophet. By her teaching she misleads my servants into sexual immorality and the eating of

ὃς ἐδίδασκεν τῷ Βαλὰκ βαλεῖν σκάνδαλον ἐνώπιον τῶν υἱῶν Ἰσραὴλ
the one who instructed {the} Balak to put a stumbling block before the sons of Israel
4005 1438 3836 963 965 4998 1967 3836 5626 2702
r.nsm v.iai.3s d.dsm n.dsm f.aa n.asn p.g d.gpm n.gpm n.gsm

φαγεῖν εἰδωλόθυτα καὶ πορνεῦσαι. 15 οὕτως →
⌞so they would eat⌟ ⌞food sacrificed to idols⌟ and ⌞commit sexual immorality.⌟ So also do you
2266 1628 2779 4519 4048 2779 5148
f.aa n.apn cj f.aa adv

ἔχεις καὶ σὺ κρατοῦντας τὴν διδαχὴν τῶν[a] Νικολαϊτῶν ὁμοίως. 16
have {also} {you} those who follow the teaching of the Nicolaitans. {same way} Therefore
2400 2779 5148 3195 3836 1439 3836 3774 3931 4036
v.pai.2s adv r.ns.2 pt.pa.apm d.asf n.asf d.gpm n.gpm adv

μετανόησον οὖν· ⌞εἰ δὲ μή,⌟ ἔρχομαί σοι ταχὺ καὶ πολεμήσω
repent! {Therefore} Otherwise, I will come to you ⌞without delay⌟ and will fight
3566 4036 1623 1254 3590 2262 5148 5444 2779 4482
v.aam.2s cj cj cj pl v.pmi.1s r.ds.2 adv cj v.fai.1s

μετ' αὐτῶν ἐν τῇ ῥομφαίᾳ τοῦ στόματός μου. 17 ὁ ἔχων οὖς
against them with the sword of my mouth. {my} He ⌞who has⌟ an ear,
3552 899 1877 3836 4855 3836 1609 5125 1609 3836 2400 4044
p.g r.gpm.3 p.d d.dsf n.dsf d.gsn n.gsn r.gs.1 d.nsm pt.pa.nsm n.asn

ἀκουσάτω τί τὸ πνεῦμα λέγει ταῖς ἐκκλησίαις. τῷ νικῶντι δώσω
let him hear what the Spirit is saying to the churches. ⌞To the⌟ ⌞one who conquers⌟ I will give
201 5515 3836 4460 3306 3836 1711 3836 3771 1443
v.aam.3s r.asn d.nsn n.nsn v.pai.3s d.dpf n.dpf d.dsm pt.pa.dsm v.fai.1s

αὐτῷ τοῦ μάννα τοῦ κεκρυμμένου καὶ δώσω αὐτῷ ψῆφον
{to him} ⌞some of the⌟ hidden manna. {the} {hidden} And I will give him a white stone,
899 3836 3221 3445 3836 3221 2779 1443 899 3328 6029
r.dsm.3 d.gsn n.gsn d.gsn pt.rp.gsn cj v.fai.1s r.dsm.3 n.asf

λευκήν, καὶ ἐπὶ τὴν ψῆφον ὄνομα καινὸν γεγραμμένον ὃ
{white} and on that stone will be written a new name {new} {will be written} which
3328 2779 2093 3836 6029 1211 1211 1211 2785 3950 2785 1211 4005
a.asf cj p.a d.asf n.asf n.asn a.asn pt.rp.asn r.asn

οὐδεὶς οἶδεν ⌞εἰ μὴ⌟ ὁ λαμβάνων. 18 καὶ τῷ ἀγγέλῳ τῆς
no one can understand except the one who receives it. {and} ⌞"To the⌟ angel of the
4029 3857 1623 3590 3836 3284 2779 3836 34 3836
a.nsm v.rai.3s cj pl d.nsm pt.pa.nsm cj d.dsm n.dsm d.gsf

ἐν Θυατείροις ἐκκλησίας γράψον, τάδε λέγει ὁ υἱὸς τοῦ θεοῦ, ὁ
church in Smyrna {church} write: {this} {has to say} The Son of God, who
1711 1877 2587 1711 1211 3840 3306 3836 5626 3836 2536 3836
p.d n.dpn n.gsf v.aam.2s r.apn v.pai.3s d.nsm n.nsm d.gsm n.gsm d.nsm

ἔχων τοὺς ὀφθαλμοὺς αὐτοῦ ὡς φλόγα πυρὸς καὶ οἱ πόδες αὐτοῦ
has {the} eyes {his} like a flame of fire and {the} whose feet {whose} are
2400 3836 4057 899 6055 5825 4786 2779 3836 899 4546 899
pt.pa.nsm d.apm n.apm r.gsm.3 pl n.asf n.gsn cj d.npm n.npm r.gsm.3

ὅμοιοι χαλκολιβάνῳ· 19 οἶδά σου τὰ ἔργα καὶ τὴν
like burnished bronze, has this to say: I know your {the} works, {and} {the} your
3927 5909 3306 3840 3306 3306 3857 5148 3836 2240 2779 3836 5148
a.npm n.dsn v.rai.1s r.gs.2 d.apn n.apn cj d.asf

ἀγάπην καὶ τὴν πίστιν καὶ τὴν διακονίαν καὶ τὴν ὑπομονήν σου, καὶ
love and {the} faith and {the} service and {the} steadfast endurance, {your} and that
27 2779 3836 4411 2779 3836 1355 2779 3836 5705 5148 2779
n.asf cj d.asf n.asf cj d.asf n.asf cj d.asf n.asf r.gs.2 cj

τὰ ἔργα σου τὰ ἔσχατα πλείονα τῶν πρώτων. 20 ἀλλὰ ἔχω
{the} your recent works {your} {the} {recent} are greater ⌞than the⌟ first. But I have this
3836 5148 2274 2240 5148 3836 2274 4498 3836 4755 247 2400
d.apn n.apn r.gs.2 d.apn a.apn a.apn.c d.gpn a.gpn cj v.pai.1s

κατὰ σοῦ ὅτι ἀφεῖς τὴν γυναῖκα Ἰεζάβελ, ἡ λέγουσα ἑαυτὴν προφῆτιν καὶ
against you, that you tolerate that woman Jezebel, who calls herself a prophetess and
2848 5148 4022 918 3836 1222 2630 3836 3306 1571 4739 2779
p.g r.gs.2 cj v.pai.2s d.asf n.asf n.asf d.nsf pt.pa.nsf r.asf.3 n.asf cj

διδάσκει καὶ πλανᾷ τοὺς ἐμοὺς δούλους πορνεῦσαι καὶ φαγεῖν
is teaching and seducing {the} my servants ⌞to practice sexual immorality⌟ and to eat
1438 2779 4414 3836 1847 1529 4519 2779 2266
v.pai.3s cj v.pai.3s d.apm r.apm.1 n.apm f.aa cj f.aa

NASB

who kept teaching Balak to put a stumbling block before the sons of Israel, to eat things sacrificed to idols and to commit *acts of* immorality. 15 So you also have some who in the same way hold the teaching of the Nicolaitans. 16 Therefore repent; or else I am coming to you quickly, and I will make war against them with the sword of My mouth. 17 He who has an ear, let him hear what the Spirit says to the churches. To him who overcomes, to him I will give *some* of the hidden manna, and I will give him a white stone, and a new name written on the stone which no one knows but he who receives it.'

Message to Thyatira

18 "And to the angel of the church in Thyatira write:

The Son of God, who has eyes like a flame of fire, and His feet are like burnished bronze, says this:

19 'I know your deeds, and your love and faith and service and perseverance, and that your deeds of late are greater than at first. 20 But I have *this* against you, that you tolerate the woman Jezebel, who calls herself a prophetess, and she teaches and leads My bond-servants astray so that they commit *acts of* immorality and eat

[a] [τῶν] UBS.

NIV

food sacrificed
to idols. 21 I have
given her time to
repent of her im-
morality, but she
is unwilling. 22 So
I will cast her on
a bed of suffer-
ing, and I will
make those who
commit adultery
with her suffer
intensely, unless
they repent of
her ways. 23 I will
strike her chil-
dren dead. Then
all the churches
will know that
I am he who
searches hearts
and minds, and I
will repay each of
you according to
your deeds.
24 Now I say to
the rest of you
in Thyatira, to
you who do not
hold to her teach-
ing and have not
learned Satan's
so-called deep
secrets, 'I will
not impose any
other burden on
you, 25 except to
hold on to what
you have until I
come.'
26 To the one
who is victori-
ous and does my
will to the end,
I will give au-
thority over the
nations— 27 that
one 'will rule
them with an
iron scepter and
will dash them to
pieces like pot-
tery'[a]—just as
I have received
authority from
my Father. 28 I
will also give that
one the morning
star. 29 Whoever
has ears, let them
hear what the
Spirit says to the
churches.

[a] 27 Psalm 2:9

εἰδωλόθυτα. 21 καὶ ἔδωκα αὐτῇ χρόνον ἵνα μετανοήσῃ, καὶ
⌞food sacrificed to idols.⌟ {and} I have given her time to repent, but
1628 2779 1443 899 5989 2671 3566 2779
n.apn cj v.aai.1s r.dsf.3 n.asm cj v.aas.3s cj

⌞οὐ θέλει⌟ μετανοῆσαι ἐκ τῆς πορνείας αὐτῆς. 22 ἰδοὺ
she is unwilling to repent of {the} her sexual immorality. her Beware,
4024 2527 3566 1666 3836 899 4518 899 2627
pl v.pai.3s f.aa p.g d.gsf n.gsf r.gsf.3 j

βάλλω αὐτὴν εἰς κλίνην καὶ τοὺς μοιχεύοντας μετ' αὐτῆς εἰς
I will throw her onto a bed of suffering, and those who commit adultery with her into great
965 899 1650 3109 2779 3836 3658 3552 899 1650 3489
v.pai.1s r.asf.3 p.a n.asf cj d.apm pt.pa.apm p.g r.gsf.3 p.a

θλῖψιν μεγάλην, ⌞ἐὰν μὴ⌟ μετανοήσωσιν ἐκ τῶν ἔργων αὐτῆς, 23 καὶ
affliction, great unless they repent of {the} her ways. her {and} I will
2568 3489 1569 3590 3566 1666 3836 899 2240 899 2779 650 650
n.asf a.asf cj pl v.aas.3p p.g d.gpn n.gpn r.gsf.3 cj

τὰ τέκνα αὐτῆς ἀποκτενῶ ἐν θανάτῳ. καὶ
kill {the} her children her I will kill with a fatal disease. Then all the churches
650 3836 899 5451 899 650 1877 2505 2779 4246 3836 1711
d.apn n.apn r.gsf.3 v.fai.1s p.d n.dsm cj

γνώσονται πᾶσαι αἱ ἐκκλησίαι ὅτι ἐγώ εἰμι ὁ ἐραυνῶν νεφροὺς καὶ
will understand all the churches that I am the one who searches minds and
1182 4246 3836 1711 4022 1609 1639 3836 2236 3752 2779
v.fmi.3p a.npf d.npf n.npf cj r.ns.1 v.pai.1s d.nsm pt.pa.nsm n.apm cj

καρδίας, καὶ δώσω → ὑμῖν ἑκάστῳ κατὰ τὰ ἔργα ὑμῶν.
hearts; and I will give to each of you each ⌞according to⌟ {the} your works. your
2840 2779 1443 1667 7007 1667 2848 3836 7007 2240 7007
n.apf cj v.fai.1s r.dp.2 r.dsm p.a d.apn n.apn r.gp.2

24 ὑμῖν δὲ λέγω τοῖς λοιποῖς τοῖς ἐν Θυατείροις, ὅσοι ↱ οὐκ ἔχουσιν
of you But I say to the rest of you {the} in Thyatira, who do not follow
7007 1254 3306 3836 3370 7007 7007 3836 1877 2587 4012 2400 4024 2400
r.dp.2 cj v.pai.1s d.dpm a.dpm d.dpm p.d n.dpn r.npm pl v.pai.3p

τὴν διδαχὴν ταύτην, οἵτινες ↱ οὐκ ἔγνωσαν τὰ βαθέα τοῦ σατανᾶ ὡς
{the} this teaching this (who have not learned 'the deep things of Satan,' as
3836 4047 1439 4047 4015 1182 4024 1182 3836 960 3836 4928 6055
d.asf n.asf r.asf r.npm pl v.aai.3p d.apn a.apn d.gsm n.gsm cj

λέγουσιν, οὐ βάλλω ἐφ' ὑμᾶς ἄλλο βάρος, 25 πλὴν
they call them), to you I say, no I lay on you no other burden, only hold fast
3306 3306 3306 4024 965 2093 7007 4024 257 983 4440 3195 3195
v.pai.3p pl v.pai.1s p.a r.ap.2 r.asn n.asn cj

ὃ ἔχετε κρατήσατε ἄχρις[a] οὗ ἂν ἥξω. 26 καὶ ὁ νικῶν
to what you have hold fast to until {when} ~ I come. As for the ⌞one who conquers,⌟
3195 4005 2400 3195 948 4005 323 2457 2779 3836 3771
r.asn v.pai.2p v.aam.2p p.g r.gsm pl v.aas.1s cj d.nsm pt.pa.nsm

καὶ ὁ τηρῶν ἄχρι τέλους τὰ ἔργα μου, δώσω αὐτῷ
{and} who keeps my works until the end, {the} works my to him I will give to him
2779 3836 5498 1609 2240 948 5465 3836 2240 1609 899 899 1443 899
cj d.nsm pt.pa.nsm p.g n.gsn d.apn n.apn r.gs.1 v.fai.1s r.dsm.3

ἐξουσίαν ἐπὶ τῶν ἐθνῶν 27 καὶ ποιμανεῖ αὐτοὺς ἐν ῥάβδῳ σιδηρᾷ ὡς τὰ
authority over the nations, and he will rule them with a rod of iron, ⌞as when⌟ {the}
2026 2093 3836 1620 2779 4477 899 1877 4811 4971 6055 3836
n.asf p.g d.gpn n.gpn cj v.fai.3s r.apm.3 p.d n.dsf a.dsf cj d.npn

σκεύη τὰ κεραμικὰ συντρίβεται, 28 ↱ ὡς κἀγὼ εἴληφα
earthen pots {the} earthen are broken to pieces, even as I myself have received authority
3039 5007 3836 3039 5341 2779 6055 2779 3284
n.npn d.npn a.npn v.ppi.3s cj crasis v.rai.1s

παρὰ τοῦ πατρός μου, ↱ ↱ καὶ δώσω αὐτῷ τὸν ἀστέρα τὸν
from {the} my Father. my I will also give him the morning star. {the}
4123 3836 1609 4252 1609 1443 1443 2779 1443 899 3836 4748 843 3836
p.g d.gsm n.gsm r.gs.1 cj v.fai.1s r.dsm.3 d.asm n.asm d.asm

πρωϊνόν. 29 ὁ ἔχων οὖς ἀκουσάτω τί τὸ πνεῦμα λέγει ταῖς
morning He ⌞who has⌟ an ear, let him hear what the Spirit is saying to the
4748 3836 2400 4044 201 5515 3836 4460 3306 3836
a.asm d.nsm pt.pa.nsm n.asn v.aam.3s r.asn d.nsn n.nsn v.pai.3s d.dpf

[a] ἄχρις UBS, NET. ἄχρι TNIV.

NASB

things sacrificed to
idols. 21 I gave her
time to repent, and
she does not want
to repent of her im-
morality. 22 Behold,
I will throw her on
a bed *of sickness,*
and those who
commit adultery
with her into great
tribulation, unless
they repent of
[a]her deeds. 23 And
I will kill her
children with pes-
tilence, and all the
churches will know
that I am He who
searches the minds
and hearts; and I
will give to each
one of you accord-
ing to your deeds.
24 But I say to you,
the rest who are
in Thyatira, who
do not hold this
teaching, who have
not known the deep
things of Satan, as
they call them—I
place no other
burden on you.
25 Nevertheless what
you have, hold fast
until I come. 26 He
who overcomes,
and he who keeps
My deeds until the
end, TO HIM I WILL
GIVE AUTHORITY
OVER THE NATIONS;
27 AND HE SHALL
RULE THEM WITH
A ROD OF IRON, AS
THE VESSELS OF THE
POTTER ARE BROKEN
TO PIECES, as I also
have received
authority from
My Father; 28 and I
will give him the
morning star. 29 He
who has an ear, let
him hear what the
Spirit says to the
churches.'

[a] One early ms reads *their*

NIV

To the Church in Sardis

3 "To the angel[a]
of the church
in Sardis write:
These are the
words of him
who holds the
seven spirits[b]
of God and the
seven stars. I
know your deeds;
you have a rep-
utation of being
alive, but you are
dead. 2 Wake up!
Strengthen what
remains and is
about to die, for I
have found your
deeds unfinished
in the sight of my
God. 3 Remember,
therefore, what
you have received
and heard; hold it
fast, and repent.
But if you do not
wake up, I will
come like a thief,
and you will not
know at what
time I will come
to you.
4 Yet you have
a few people in
Sardis who have
not soiled their
clothes. They
will walk with
me, dressed in
white, for they
are worthy. 5 The
one who is vic-
torious will, like
them, be dressed
in white. I will
never blot out
the name of that
person from the
book of life, but
will acknowledge
that name before
my Father and his
angels. 6 Whoever
has ears, let them
hear what the
Spirit says to the

[a] 1 Or *messenger*; also in verses 7 and 14
[b] 1 That is, the sevenfold Spirit

ἐκκλησίαις.
churches.
1711
n.dpf

3:1 καὶ τῷ ἀγγέλῳ τῆς ἐν Σάρδεσιν ἐκκλησίας γράψον, τάδε
{and} ⸤"To the⸥ angel of the church in Sardis *church* write: *this*
2779 3836 34 3836 1711 1877 4915 1711 1211 3840
cj d.dsm n.dsm d.gsf p.d n.dpf n.gsf v.aam.2s r.apn

λέγει ὁ ἔχων τὰ ἑπτὰ πνεύματα τοῦ θεοῦ καὶ τοὺς ἑπτὰ ἀστέρας·
has to say The ⸤one who has⸥ the seven Spirits of God and the seven stars has
3306 3836 2400 3836 2231 4460 3836 2536 2779 3836 2231 843 3306
v.pai.3s d.nsm pt.pa.nsm d.apn a.apn n.apn d.gsm n.gsm cj d.apm a.apm n.apm

οἶδά σου τὰ ἔργα ὅτι ὄνομα ἔχεις ὅτι ζῇς,
this to say: I know your *{the}* deeds; that you have a reputation *you have* that ⸤you are alive,⸥
3840 3306 3306 3857 5148 3836 2240 4022 2400 2400 3950 2400 4022 2409
v.rai.1s r.gs.2 d.apn n.apn cj n.asn v.pai.2s cj v.pai.2s

καὶ νεκρὸς εἶ. 2 ⸤γίνου γρηγορῶν⸥ καὶ στήρισον τὰ λοιπὰ
but you are dead. *you are* Wake up and strengthen the ⸤things that remain,⸥
2779 1639 1639 3738 1639 1181 1213 2779 5114 3836 3370
cj a.nsm v.pai.2s v.pmm.2s pt.pa.nsm cj v.aam.2s d.apn a.apn

ἃ ἔμελλον ἀποθανεῖν, ↱ ↱ οὐ γὰρ εὕρηκά σου τὰ ἔργα πεπληρωμένα
which are about to die; for I have not *for* found your *{the}* works fully completed
4005 3516 633 1142 2351 2351 4024 1142 2351 5148 3836 2240 4444
r.npn v.iai.3p f.aa pl cj v.rai.1s r.gs.2 d.apn n.apn pt.rp.apn

ἐνώπιον τοῦ θεοῦ μου. 3 μνημόνευε οὖν πῶς εἴληφας καὶ ἤκουσας καὶ
in the sight of my God. *my* Remember, then, what you received and heard; *{and}*
1967 3836 1609 2536 1609 3648 4036 4802 3284 2779 201 2779
p.g d.gsm n.gsm r.gs.1 v.pam.2s cj cj v.rai.2s cj v.aai.2s cj

τήρει καὶ μετανόησον. ἐὰν οὖν ↱ ↱ μὴ γρηγορήσῃς, ἥξω ὡς
obey it, and repent. But if *But* you do not wake up, ⸤I will come⸥ like a
5498 2779 3566 4036 1569 4036 1213 1213 3590 1213 2457 6055
v.pam.2s cj v.aam.2s cj cj pl v.aas.2s v.fai.1s pl

κλέπτης, καὶ ↱ ↱ ⸤οὐ μὴ⸥ γνῷς ποίαν ὥραν ἥξω ἐπὶ σέ. 4 ἀλλὰ
thief, and you will not know at what hour ⸤I will come⸥ against you. But
3095 2779 1182 1182 4024 3590 1182 4481 6052 2457 2093 5148 247
n.nsm cj pl pl v.aas.2s r.asf n.asf v.fai.1s p.a r.as.2 cj

ἔχεις ὀλίγα ὀνόματα ἐν Σάρδεσιν ἃ ↱ οὐκ ἐμόλυναν τὰ ἱμάτια
you have a few people in Sardis who have not soiled *{the}* their garments,
2400 3900 3950 1877 4915 4005 3662 4024 3662 3836 899 2668
v.pai.2s a.apn n.apn p.d n.dpf r.npn pl v.aai.3p d.apn n.apn

αὐτῶν, καὶ περιπατήσουσιν μετ᾽ ἐμοῦ ἐν λευκοῖς, ὅτι ἄξιοί εἰσιν. 5 ὁ
their and they will walk with me in white, for they are worthy. *they are* The
899 2779 4344 3552 1609 1877 3328 4022 1639 1639 545 1639 3836
r.gpm.3 cj v.fai.3p p.g r.gs.1 p.d a.dpn cj a.npm v.pai.3p d.nsm

νικῶν ↱ οὕτως περιβαλεῖται ἐν ἱματίοις λευκοῖς καὶ ↱ ↱
⸤one who conquers⸥ will, ⸤in this way,⸥ be dressed in white clothing, *white* and I will
3771 4314 4048 4314 1877 3328 2668 3328 2779 1981 1981
pt.pa.nsm adv v.fmi.3s p.d n.dpn a.dpn cj

⸤οὐ μὴ⸥ ἐξαλείψω τὸ ὄνομα αὐτοῦ ἐκ τῆς βίβλου τῆς ζωῆς καὶ
never erase *{the}* his name *his* from the Book of Life, but
4024 3590 1981 3836 899 3950 899 1666 3836 1047 3836 2437 2779
pl pl v.aas.1s d.asn n.asn r.gsm.3 p.g d.gsf n.gsf d.gsf n.gsf cj

ὁμολογήσω τὸ ὄνομα αὐτοῦ ἐνώπιον τοῦ πατρός μου καὶ ἐνώπιον τῶν
will acknowledge *{the}* his name *his* before *{the}* my Father *my* and before *{the}*
3933 3836 899 3950 899 1967 3836 1609 4252 1609 2779 1967 3836
v.fai.1s d.asn n.asn r.gsm.3 p.g d.gsm n.gsm r.gs.1 cj p.g d.gpm

ἀγγέλων αὐτοῦ. 6 ὁ ἔχων οὖς ἀκουσάτω τί τὸ πνεῦμα λέγει ταῖς
his angels. *his* He ⸤who has⸥ an ear, let him hear what the Spirit is saying to the
899 34 899 3836 2400 4044 201 5515 3836 4460 3306 3836
n.gpm r.gsm.3 d.nsm pt.pa.nsm n.asn v.aam.3s r.asn d.nsn n.nsn v.pai.3s d.dpf

---

NASB

Message to Sardis

3:1 "To the angel
of the church in
Sardis write:
He who has the
seven Spirits of
God and the seven
stars, says this: 'I
know your deeds,
that you have a
name that you are
alive, but you are
dead. 2 Wake up,
and strengthen the
things that remain,
which were about
to die; for I have
not found your
deeds completed
in the sight of
My God. 3 So re-
member what you
have received and
heard; and keep
it, and repent.
Therefore if you
do not wake up, I
will come like a
thief, and you will
not know at what
hour I will come
to you. 4 But you
have a few people
in Sardis who have
not soiled their
garments; and they
will walk with Me
in white, for they
are worthy. 5 He
who overcomes
will thus be clothed
in white garments;
and I will not erase
his name from the
book of life, and
I will confess his
name before My
Father and before
His angels. 6 He
who has an ear, let
him hear what the
Spirit says to the
churches.'

NIV

churches.

To the Church in Philadelphia

[7]"To the angel of the church in Philadelphia write:

These are the words of him who is holy and true, who holds the key of David. What he opens no one can shut, and what he shuts no one can open. [8]I know your deeds. See, I have placed before you an open door that no one can shut. I know that you have little strength, yet you have kept my word and have not denied my name. [9]I will make those who are of the synagogue of Satan, who claim to be Jews though they are not, but are liars—I will make them come and fall down at your feet and acknowledge that I have loved you. [10]Since you have kept my command to endure patiently, I will also keep you from the hour of trial that is going to come on the whole world to test the inhabitants of the earth.

[11]I am coming soon. Hold on to what you have, so that no one will take your crown. [12]The one who is victorious I will make a pillar in the temple of my God. Never again will they leave it. I will write on them the name of my God and the name of the city of my God,

ἐκκλησίαις. [7]καὶ τῷ ἀγγέλῳ τῆς ἐν Φιλαδελφείᾳ ἐκκλησίας γράψον,
churches. {and} ⌞"To the⌟ angel of the church in Philadelphia church write:
1711 2779 3836 34 3836 1711 1877 5788 1711 1211
n.dpf cj d.dsm n.dsm d.gsf p.d n.dsf n.gsf v.aam.2s

τάδε λέγει ὁ ἅγιος, ὁ ἀληθινός, ὁ ἔχων τὴν κλεῖν Δαυίδ, ὁ
this has to say The ⌞one who is holy,⌟ who is true, who has the key of David, who
3840 3306 3836 41 3836 240 3836 2400 3836 3090 1253 3836
r.apn v.pai.3s d.nsm a.nsm d.nsm a.nsm d.nsm pt.pa.nsm d.asf n.asf n.gsm d.nsm

ἀνοίγων καὶ οὐδεὶς κλείσει καὶ κλείων καὶ οὐδεὶς ἀνοίγει· [8]οἶδά
opens and no one can shut, who shuts and no one can open, has this to say: I know
487 2779 4029 3091 2779 3091 2779 4029 487 3306 3840 3306 3306 3857
pt.pa.nsm cj a.nsm v.fai.3s cj pt.pa.nsm cj a.nsm v.pai.3s v.rai.1s

σου τὰ ἔργα, ἰδοὺ δέδωκα ἐνώπιόν σου θύραν ἠνεῳγμένην, ἣν οὐδεὶς
your {the} works. Look, I have placed before you an open door, open which no one
5148 3836 2240 2627 1443 1967 5148 487 2598 487 4005 4029
r.gs.2 d.apn n.apn j v.rai.1s p.g r.gs.2 n.asf pt.rp.asf r.asf a.nsm

δύναται κλεῖσαι αὐτήν, ὅτι μικρὰν ἔχεις δύναμιν καὶ ἐτήρησάς
is able to shut. {it} I know that you have little you have strength, yet you have kept
1538 3091 899 4022 2400 2400 3625 2400 1539 2779 5498
v.ppi.3s f.aa r.asf.3 cj a.asf v.pai.2s n.asf cj v.aai.2s

μου τὸν λόγον καὶ ↱ οὐκ ἠρνήσω τὸ ὄνομά μου. [9]ἰδοὺ διδῶ
my {the} word and have not denied {the} my name. my Behold, ⌞I will make⌟ those
1609 3836 3364 2779 766 4024 766 3836 1609 3950 1609 2627 1443
r.gs.1 d.asm n.asm cj pl v.ami.2s d.asn n.asn r.gs.1 j v.pai.1s

ἐκ τῆς συναγωγῆς τοῦ σατανᾶ τῶν λεγόντων ἑαυτοὺς Ἰουδαίους εἶναι,
of the synagogue of Satan who claim {themselves} to be Jews to be
1666 3836 5252 3836 4928 3836 3306 1571 1639 1639 2681 1639
p.g d.gsf n.gsf d.gsm n.gsm d.gpm pt.pa.gpm r.apm.3 a.apm f.pa

καὶ οὐκ εἰσὶν ἀλλὰ ψεύδονται. ἰδοὺ ποιήσω αὐτοὺς ἵνα ἥξουσιν
and are not, are but lie — {behold} I will make them {in order to} come
2779 1639 4024 1639 247 6017 2627 4472 899 2671 2457
cj pl v.pai.3p cj v.pmi.3p j v.fai.1s r.apm.3 cj v.fai.3p

καὶ προσκυνήσουσιν ἐνώπιον τῶν ποδῶν σου καὶ γνῶσιν ὅτι ἐγὼ ἠγάπησά
and bow down before {the} your feet your and understand that I have loved
2779 4686 1967 3836 5148 4546 5148 2779 1182 4022 1609 26
cj v.fai.3p p.g d.gpm n.gpm r.gs.2 cj v.aas.3p cj r.ns.1 v.aai.1s

σε. [10]ὅτι ἐτήρησας τὸν λόγον τῆς ὑπομονῆς μου, κἀγώ
you. Because you have kept {the} my word about patient endurance, my I also will keep
5148 4022 5498 3836 1609 3364 3836 5705 1609 2743 5498 5498
r.as.2 cj v.aai.2s d.asm n.asm d.gsf n.gsf r.gs.1 crasis

σε τηρήσω ἐκ τῆς ὥρας τοῦ πειρασμοῦ τῆς μελλούσης ἔρχεσθαι ἐπὶ τῆς
you will keep from the hour of testing that is coming upon the whole
5148 5498 1666 3836 6052 3836 4280 3836 3516 2262 2093 3836 3910
r.as.2 v.fai.1s p.g d.gsf n.gsf d.gsm n.gsm d.gsf pt.pa.gsf f.pm p.g d.gsf

οἰκουμένης ὅλης πειράσαι τοὺς κατοικοῦντας ἐπὶ τῆς γῆς. [11]ἔρχομαι ταχύ·
world whole to test those who live on the earth. I am coming soon.
3876 3910 4279 3836 2997 2093 3836 1178 2262 5444
n.gsf a.gsf f.aa d.apm pt.pa.apm p.g d.gsf n.gsf v.pmi.1s adv

κράτει ὃ ἔχεις, ἵνα μηδεὶς λάβῃ τὸν στέφανόν σου. [12]ὁ
⌞Hold on to⌟ what you have, so that no one ⌞can take away⌟ {the} your crown. your The
3195 4005 2400 2671 3594 3284 3836 5148 5109 5148 3836
v.pam.2s r.asn v.pai.2s cj a.nsm v.aas.3s d.asm n.asm r.gs.2 d.nsm

νικῶν ποιήσω αὐτὸν στῦλον ἐν τῷ ναῷ τοῦ θεοῦ μου καὶ
⌞one who conquers,⌟ I will make him a pillar in the temple of my God my and
3771 4472 899 5146 1877 3836 3724 3836 1609 2536 1609 2779
pt.pa.nsm v.fai.1s r.asm.3 n.asm p.d d.dsm n.dsm d.gsm n.gsm r.gs.1 cj

ἔξω ↱ ↱ ⌞οὐ μὴ⌟ ἐξέλθῃ ἔτι καὶ γράψω ἐπ᾽ αὐτὸν τὸ ὄνομα
out of he will never go out of it, {again} and I will write on him the name
2032 2002 2002 4024 3590 2002 2032 2032 2285 2779 1211 2093 899 3836 3950
adv pl pl v.aas.3s adv cj v.fai.1s p.a r.asm.3 d.asn n.asn

τοῦ θεοῦ μου καὶ τὸ ὄνομα τῆς πόλεως τοῦ θεοῦ μου, τῆς καινῆς
of my God, my and the name of the city of my God my (the new
3836 1609 2536 1609 2779 3836 3950 3836 4484 3836 1609 2536 1609 3836 2785
d.gsm n.gsm r.gs.1 cj d.asn n.asn d.gsf n.gsf d.gsm n.gsm r.gs.1 d.gsf a.gsf

NASB

Message to Philadelphia

[7]"And to the angel of the church in Philadelphia write:

He who is holy, who is true, who has the key of David, who opens and no one will shut, and who shuts and no one opens, says this:

[8]'I know your [a]deeds. Behold, I have put before you an open door which no one can shut, because you have a little power, and have kept My word, and have not denied My name. [9]Behold, I will cause *those* of the synagogue of Satan, who say that they are Jews and are not, but lie—I will make them come and bow down at your feet, and *make them* know that I have loved you. [10]Because you have kept the word of My perseverance, I also will keep you from the hour of testing, that *hour* which is about to come upon the whole world, to test those who dwell on the earth. [11]I am coming quickly; hold fast what you have, so that no one will take your crown. [12]He who overcomes, I will make him a pillar in the temple of My God, and he will not go out from it anymore; and I will write on him the name of My God, and the name of the city of My God, the new

[a] Or *deeds (behold... shut), that you have*

NIV

the new Jeru-
salem, which is
coming down out
of heaven from
my God; and I
will also write
on them my new
name. 13 Whoever
has ears, let them
hear what the
Spirit says to the
churches.

To the Church in
Laodicea

14 "To the angel of
the church in La-
odicea write:

These are the
words of the
Amen, the faith-
ful and true wit-
ness, the ruler of
God's creation.
15 I know your
deeds, that you
are neither cold
nor hot. I wish
you were either
one or the other!
16 So, because you
are lukewarm—
neither hot nor
cold—I am about
to spit you out of
my mouth. 17 You
say, 'I am rich;
I have acquired
wealth and do not
need a thing.' But
you do not real-
ize that you are
wretched, pitiful,
poor, blind and
naked. 18 I counsel
you to buy from
me gold refined
in the fire, so you
can become rich;
and white clothes
to wear, so you
can cover your
shameful naked-
ness; and salve to
put on your eyes,
so you can see.
19 Those whom
I love I rebuke
and discipline.
So be earnest and
repent. 20 Here I
am! I stand at the
door and knock.
If anyone hears

Ἰερουσαλὴμ ἡ καταβαίνουσα ἐκ τοῦ οὐρανοῦ ἀπὸ τοῦ θεοῦ μου, καὶ
Jerusalem which comes down ⌊out of⌋ *{the}* heaven from *{the}* my God), *my* and
2647 3836 2849 1666 3836 4041 608 3836 1609 2536 1609 2779
n.gsf d.nsf pt.pa.nsf p.g d.gsm n.gsm p.g d.gsm n.gsm r.gs.1 cj

τὸ ὄνομά μου τὸ καινόν. 13 ὁ ἔχων οὖς ἀκουσάτω τί
{the} my own new name. *my own* *{the}* *new* He ⌊who has⌋ an ear, let him hear what
3836 1609 1609 2785 3950 1609 3836 2785 3836 2400 4044 201 5515
d.asn n.asn r.gs.1 d.asn a.asn d.nsm pt.pa.nsm n.asn v.aam.3s r.asn

τὸ πνεῦμα λέγει ταῖς ἐκκλησίαις. 14 καὶ τῷ ἀγγέλῳ τῆς ἐν
the Spirit is saying to the churches. *{and}* ⌊"To the⌋ angel of the church in
3836 4460 3306 3836 1711 2779 3836 34 3836 1711 1877
d.nsn n.nsn v.pai.3s d.dpf n.dpf cj d.dsm n.dsm d.gsf p.d

Λαοδικείᾳ ἐκκλησίας γράψον, τάδε λέγει ὁ ἀμήν, ὁ μάρτυς
Laodicea *church* write: *this* *has to say* The Amen, the faithful and true Witness,
3293 1711 1211 3840 3306 3836 297 3836 4412 2779 240 3459
n.dsf n.gsf v.aam.2s r.apn v.pai.3s d.nsm pl d.nsm n.nsm

ὁ πιστὸς καὶ ἀληθινός, ἡ ἀρχὴ τῆς κτίσεως τοῦ θεοῦ·
{the} *faithful* *and* *true* the Beginning of God's creation, *{the}* *God's* has this to
3836 4412 2779 240 3836 794 3836 2536 3232 3836 2536 3306 3840 3306
d.nsm a.nsm cj a.nsm d.nsf n.nsf d.gsf n.gsf d.gsm n.gsm

15 οἶδά σου τὰ ἔργα ὅτι οὔτε ψυχρὸς εἶ οὔτε ζεστός. ὄφελον
say: I know your *{the}* works, that you are neither cold *you are* nor hot. Would
3306 3857 5148 3836 2240 4022 1639 1639 4046 6037 1639 4046 2412 4054
v.rai.1s r.gs.2 d.apn n.apn cj cj a.nsm v.pai.2s cj a.nsm pt.aa.nsn

ψυχρὸς ἦς ἢ ζεστός. 16 οὕτως ὅτι χλιαρὸς
that you were either cold *you were* or hot! So because you are lukewarm,
1639 1639 6037 1639 2445 2412 4048 4022 1639 1639 5950
a.nsm v.iai.2s cj a.nsm adv cj a.nsm

εἶ καὶ οὔτε ζεστὸς οὔτε ψυχρός, μέλλω σε ἐμέσαι ἐκ τοῦ
you are *{and}* neither hot nor cold, I am about to vomit you *to vomit* ⌊out of⌋ *{the}* my
1639 2779 4046 2412 4046 6037 3516 1840 1840 5148 1840 1666 3836 1609
v.pai.2s cj cj a.nsm cj a.nsm v.pai.1s r.as.2 f.aa p.g d.gsn

στόματός μου. 17 ὅτι λέγεις ὅτι πλούσιός εἰμι καὶ πεπλούτηκα καὶ
mouth! *my* Because you say, ~ 'I am rich *I am* and have prospered; *{and}*
5125 1609 4022 3306 4022 1639 1639 4454 1639 2779 4456 2779
n.gsn r.gs.1 cj v.pai.2s cj a.nsm v.pai.1s cj v.rai.1s cj

↱ οὐδὲν χρείαν ἔχω, καὶ ↱ οὐκ οἶδας ὅτι σὺ εἶ ὁ ταλαίπωρος
I need nothing,' *need* *{have}* but do not realize that you are *{the}* wretched,
2400 5970 4029 5970 2400 2779 3857 4024 3857 4022 5148 1639 3836 5417
a.asn n.asf v.pai.1s cj pl v.rai.2s cj r.ns.2 v.pai.2s d.nsm a.nsm

καὶ ἐλεεινὸς καὶ πτωχὸς καὶ τυφλὸς καὶ γυμνός, 18 συμβουλεύω σοι ἀγοράσαι
{and} miserable, *{and}* poor, *{and}* blind, and naked, I counsel you to buy
2779 1795 2779 4777 2779 5603 2779 1218 5205 5148 60
cj a.nsm cj a.nsm cj a.nsm cj a.nsm v.pai.1s r.ds.2 f.aa

παρ᾽ ἐμοῦ χρυσίον πεπυρωμένον ἐκ πυρὸς ἵνα πλουτήσῃς, καὶ ἱμάτια λευκὰ
from me gold refined by fire so you can be rich; and white garments *white*
4123 1609 5992 4792 1666 4786 2671 4456 2779 3328 2668 3328
p.g r.gs.1 n.asn pt.rp.asn p.g n.gsn cj v.aas.2s cj n.apn a.apn

ἵνα περιβάλῃ καὶ ↱ μὴ φανερωθῇ ἡ αἰσχύνη τῆς
to clothe yourself so your shameful nakedness will not be exposed; *{the}* *shameful* *{the}*
2671 4314 2779 5148 158 1219 5746 3590 5746 3836 158 3836
cj v.ams.2s cj pl v.aps.3s d.nsf n.nsf d.gsf

γυμνότητός σου, καὶ κολλούριον[a] ἐγχρῖσαι τοὺς ὀφθαλμούς σου ἵνα βλέπῃς.
nakedness *your* and salve to put on *{the}* your eyes *your* so you can see!
1219 5148 2779 3141 1608 3836 5148 4057 5148 2671 1063
n.gsf r.gs.2 cj n.asn f.aa d.apm n.apm r.gs.2 cj v.pas.2s

19 ἐγὼ ὅσους ἐὰν φιλῶ ἐλέγχω καὶ παιδεύω· ζήλευε οὖν καὶ
As many as I *As many as* ~ love, I reprove and discipline; so be earnest *so* and
4012 4012 4012 1609 4012 1569 5797 1794 2779 4084 4036 2418 4036 2779
r.ns.1 r.apm pl v.pas.1s v.pai.1s cj v.pai.1s v.pam.2s cj cj

μετανόησον. 20 ἰδοὺ ἕστηκα ἐπὶ τὴν θύραν καὶ κρούω· ἐάν τις ἀκούσῃ
repent. ⌊Take note!⌋ I am standing at the door and knocking. If anyone hears
3566 2627 2705 2093 3836 2598 2779 3218 1569 5516 201
v.aam.2s j v.rai.1s p.a d.asf n.asf cj v.pai.1s cj r.nsm v.aas.3s

NASB

Jerusalem, which
comes down out of
heaven from My
God, and My new
name. 13 He who has
an ear, let him hear
what the Spirit says
to the churches.'

Message to Laodicea

14 "To the angel
of the church in
Laodicea write:
The Amen, the
faithful and true
Witness, the [a]Be-
ginning of the
creation of God,
says this:
15 'I know your
deeds, that you are
neither cold nor
hot; I wish that
you were cold or
hot. 16 So because
you are lukewarm,
and neither hot
nor cold, I will
spit you out of My
mouth. 17 Because
you say, "I am
rich, and have
become wealthy,
and have need of
nothing," and you
do not know that
you are wretched
and miserable and
poor and blind and
naked, 18 I advise
you to buy from
Me gold refined
by fire so that
you may become
rich, and white
garments so that
you may clothe
yourself, and *that*
the shame of your
nakedness will
not be revealed;
and eye salve to
anoint your eyes so
that you may see.
19 Those whom I
love, I reprove and
discipline; there-
fore be zealous and
repent. 20 Behold,
I stand at the door
and knock; if any-
one hears My voice

[a] κολλούριον UBS, NET. κολλύριον UBS, TNIV.

[a] I.e. Origin or Source

NIV

my voice and
opens the door,
I will come in
and eat with that
person, and they
with me.
[21] To the one who
is victorious, I
will give the right
to sit with me on
my throne, just
as I was victori-
ous and sat down
with my Father
on his throne.
[22] Whoever has
ears, let them
hear what the
Spirit says to the
churches."

The Throne in Heaven

4 After this I
looked, and
there before me
was a door stand-
ing open in heav-
en. And the voice
I had first heard
speaking to me
like a trumpet
said, "Come up
here, and I will
show you what
must take place af-
ter this." [2] At once
I was in the Spirit,
and there before
me was a throne
in heaven with
someone sitting
on it. [3] And the one
who sat there had
the appearance of
jasper and ruby. A
rainbow that shone
like an emerald en-
circled the throne.
[4] Surrounding
the throne were
twenty-four other
thrones, and seat-
ed on them were
twenty-four elders.
They were dressed
in white and had
crowns of gold
on their heads.
[5] From the throne
came flashes of
lightning, rum-
blings and peals of
thunder.

τῆς φωνῆς μου καὶ ἀνοίξῃ τὴν θύραν, καὶ [a] εἰσελεύσομαι πρὸς αὐτὸν καὶ
{the} my voice *my* and opens the door, {also} I will enter {to} his house and
3836 1609 5889 1609 2779 487 3836 2598 2779 1656 4639 899 2779
d.gsf n.gsf r.gs.1 cj v.aas.3s d.asf n.asf adv v.fmi.1s p.a r.asm.3 cj

δειπνήσω μετ᾽ αὐτοῦ καὶ αὐτὸς μετ᾽ ἐμοῦ. 21 ὁ νικῶν
eat with him, and he with me. As for the ⌊one who conquers,⌋ to him
1268 3552 899 2779 899 3552 1609 3836 3771 899 899
v.fai.1s p.g r.gsm.3 cj r.nsm p.g r.gs.1 d.nsm pt.pa.nsm

δώσω αὐτῷ καθίσαι μετ᾽ ἐμοῦ ἐν τῷ θρόνῳ μου, ὡς κἀγὼ
⌊I will give the right⌋ *to him* to sit with me on {the} my throne, *my* as I also
1443 899 2767 3552 1609 1877 3836 1609 2585 1609 6055 2743
v.fai.1s r.dsm.3 f.aa p.g r.gs.1 p.d d.dsm n.dsm r.gs.1 cj crasis

ἐνίκησα καὶ ἐκάθισα μετὰ τοῦ πατρός μου ἐν τῷ θρόνῳ αὐτοῦ. 22 ὁ
conquered and sat with {the} my Father *my* on {the} his throne. *his* He
3771 2779 2767 3552 3836 1609 4252 1609 1877 3836 899 2585 899 3836
v.aai.1s cj v.aai.1s p.g d.gsm n.gsm r.gs.1 p.d d.dsm n.dsm r.gsm.3 d.nsm

ἔχων οὖς ἀκουσάτω τί τὸ πνεῦμα λέγει ταῖς ἐκκλησίαις.
⌊who has⌋ an ear, let him hear what the Spirit is saying to the churches."
2400 4044 201 5515 3836 4460 3306 3836 1711
pt.pa.nsm n.asn v.aam.3s r.asn d.nsn n.nsn v.pai.3s d.dpf n.dpf

4:1 μετὰ ταῦτα εἶδον, καὶ ἰδοὺ θύρα ἠνεῳγμένη ἐν τῷ οὐρανῷ, καὶ ἡ
After this I looked, and behold, a door standing open in {the} heaven! And the
3552 4047 1625 2779 2627 2598 487 1877 3836 4041 2779 3836
p.a r.apn v.aai.1s cj j n.nsf pt.rp.nsf p.d d.dsm n.dsm cj d.nsf

φωνὴ ἡ πρώτη ἣν ἤκουσα ὡς σάλπιγγος λαλούσης μετ᾽
first voice, {the} *first* which I had heard speaking to me like a trumpet, *speaking* *to*
4755 5889 3836 4755 4005 201 3281 3552 1609 6055 4894 3281 3552
n.nsf d.nsf a.nsf r.asf v.aai.1s pl n.gsf pt.pa.gsf p.g

ἐμοῦ λέγων, ἀνάβα ὧδε, καὶ δείξω σοι ἃ δεῖ γενέσθαι μετὰ ταῦτα.
me said, ⌊"Come up⌋ here, and ⌊I will show⌋ you what must take place after this."
1609 3306 326 6045 2779 1259 5148 4005 1256 1181 3552 4047
r.gs.1 pt.pa.nsm v.aam.2s adv cj v.fai.1s r.ds.2 r.apn v.pai.3s f.am p.a r.apn

2 εὐθέως ἐγενόμην ἐν πνεύματι, καὶ ἰδοὺ θρόνος ἔκειτο ἐν τῷ
Immediately I was in the spirit, and behold, a throne was standing in {the}
2311 1181 1877 4460 2779 2627 2585 3023 1877 3836
adv v.ami.1s p.d n.dsn cj j n.nsm v.imi.3s p.d d.dsm

οὐρανῷ, καὶ ἐπὶ τὸν θρόνον καθήμενος, 3 καὶ ὁ καθήμενος ὅμοιος
heaven and one sitting on the throne! *one sitting* And the one sitting there had
4041 2779 2764 2764 2093 3836 2585 2764 2779 3836 2764 3927
n.dsm cj p.a d.asm n.asm pt.pm.nsm cj d.nsm pt.pm.nsm a.nsm

ὁράσει → λίθῳ ἰάσπιδι καὶ σαρδίῳ, καὶ ἶρις κυκλόθεν τοῦ
the appearance of a ⌊precious gem⌋ — jasper or carnelian — and a rainbow encircled the
3970 3345 2618 2779 4917 2779 2692 3239 3836
n.dsf n.dsm n.dsf cj n.dsn cj n.nsf p.g d.gsm

θρόνου ὅμοιος ὁράσει σμαραγδίνῳ. 4 καὶ κυκλόθεν τοῦ θρόνου
throne, in appearance like *in appearance* an emerald. {and} Around the throne
2585 3970 3970 3927 3970 5039 2779 3239 3836 2585
n.gsm a.nsm n.dsf a.dsm cj p.g d.gsm n.gsm

θρόνους ⌊εἴκοσι τέσσαρες,⌋ καὶ ἐπὶ τοὺς θρόνους
were twenty-four thrones, *twenty-four* and seated on those thrones were
1633 2585 1633 5475 2779 2764 2093 3836 2585
n.apm a.apm a.apm cj p.a d.apm n.apm

⌊εἴκοσι τέσσαρας⌋ πρεσβυτέρους καθημένους περιβεβλημένους ἐν ἱματίοις
twenty-four elders, *seated* clothed in white garments,
1633 5475 4565 2764 4314 1877 3328 2668
a.apm a.apm a.apm pt.pm.apm pt.rp.apm p.d n.dpn

λευκοῖς καὶ ἐπὶ τὰς κεφαλὰς αὐτῶν στεφάνους χρυσοῦς. 5 καὶ ἐκ
white and upon {the} their heads *their* were crowns of gold. {and} ⌊Out from⌋
3328 2779 2093 3836 899 3051 899 5109 5997 2779 1666
a.dpn cj p.a d.apf n.apf r.gpm.3 n.apm a.apm cj p.g

τοῦ θρόνου ἐκπορεύονται ἀστραπαὶ καὶ φωναὶ καὶ βρονταί, καὶ
the throne came flashes of lightning, {and} rumblings, and peals of thunder. {and}
3836 2585 1744 847 2779 5889 2779 1103 2779
d.gsm n.gsm v.pmi.3p n.npf cj n.npf cj n.npf cj

[a] [καὶ] UBS, omitted by TNIV.

NASB

and opens the door,
I will come in to
him and will dine
with him, and he
with Me. [21] He who
overcomes, I will
grant to him to
sit down with Me
on My throne, as
I also overcame
and sat down with
My Father on His
throne. [22] He who
has an ear, let
him hear what the
Spirit says to the
churches.'"

Scene in Heaven

4:1 After these
things I looked,
and behold, a door
standing open in
heaven, and the
first voice which I
had heard, like *the
sound* of a trumpet
speaking with me,
said, "Come up
here, and I will
show you what
must take place
after these things."
[2] Immediately I
was [a] in the Spirit;
and behold, a
throne was stand-
ing in heaven, and
One sitting on
the throne. [3] And
He who was sit-
ting *was* like a
jasper stone and a
sardius in appear-
ance; and *there
was* a rainbow
around the throne,
like an emerald
in appearance.
[4] Around the throne
were twenty-four
thrones; and upon
the thrones *I saw*
twenty-four elders
sitting, clothed in
white garments,
and golden crowns
on their heads.

The Throne and Worship of the Creator

[5] Out from the
throne come flash-
es of lightning and
sounds and peals of
thunder.

[a] Or *in spirit*

NIV

In front of the throne, seven lamps were blazing. These are the seven spirits[a] of God. 6 Also in front of the throne there was what looked like a sea of glass, clear as crystal.

In the center, around the throne, were four living creatures, and they were covered with eyes, in front and in back. 7 The first living creature was like a lion, the second was like an ox, the third had a face like a man, the fourth was like a flying eagle. 8 Each of the four living creatures had six wings and was covered with eyes all around, even under its wings. Day and night they never stop saying:

"'Holy, holy, holy
is the Lord God
Almighty,'[b]
who was, and is, and
is to come."

9 Whenever the living creatures give glory, honor and thanks to him who sits on the throne and who lives for ever and ever, 10 the twenty-four elders fall down before him who sits on the throne and worship him who lives for ever and ever. They

[a] 5 That is, the sevenfold Spirit
[b] 8 Isaiah 6:3

ἑπτὰ λαμπάδες πυρὸς καιόμεναι ἐνώπιον τοῦ
Seven torches of fire, which are the seven spirits of God, were burning before the
2231 3286 4786 4005 1639 3836 2231 4460 3836 2536 2794 1967 3836
a.npf n.npf n.gsn pt.pp.npf p.g d.gsm

θρόνου, ἅ εἰσιν τὰ ἑπτὰ πνεύματα τοῦ θεοῦ, 6 καὶ ἐνώπιον τοῦ θρόνου
throne, *which are the seven spirits of God* and before the throne there
2585 4005 1639 3836 2231 4460 3836 2536 2779 1967 3836 2585
n.gsm r.npn v.pai.3p d.npn a.npn n.npn d.gsm n.gsm cj p.g d.gsm n.gsm

ὡς θάλασσα ὑαλίνη ὁμοία κρυστάλλῳ. καὶ ⌊ἐν μέσῳ⌋ τοῦ θρόνου
was ⌊as it were⌋ a sea of glass, like crystal; and around the throne,
6055 2498 5612 3927 3223 2779 1877 3545 3836 2585
pl n.nsf a.nsf a.nsf n.dsm cj p.d n.dsn d.gsm n.gsm

καὶ κύκλῳ τοῦ θρόνου τέσσαρα ζῷα γέμοντα ὀφθαλμῶν ἔμπροσθεν
{and} close by the throne, were four ⌊living creatures⌋ full of eyes in front
2779 3241 3836 2585 5475 2442 1154 4057 1869
cj p.g d.gsm n.gsm a.npn n.npn pt.pa.npn n.gpm adv

καὶ ὄπισθεν. 7 καὶ τὸ ζῷον τὸ πρῶτον ὅμοιον λέοντι καὶ τὸ
and in back. *{and}* The first ⌊living creature⌋ *{the} first* was like a lion, *{and}* the
2779 3957 2779 3836 4755 2442 3836 4755 3927 3329 2779 3836
cj adv cj d.nsn n.nsn d.nsn a.nsn a.nsn n.dsm cj d.nsn

δεύτερον ζῷον ὅμοιον μόσχῳ καὶ τὸ τρίτον ζῷον ἔχων τὸ
second ⌊living creature⌋ like an ox, *{and}* the third ⌊living creature⌋ had a
1311 2442 3927 3675 2779 3836 5569 2442 2400 3836
a.nsn n.nsn a.nsn n.dsm cj d.nsn a.nsn n.nsn pt.pa.nsm d.asn

πρόσωπον ὡς ἀνθρώπου καὶ τὸ τέταρτον ζῷον ὅμοιον ἀετῷ
face like a man's, and the fourth ⌊living creature⌋ was like a flying eagle.
4725 6055 476 2779 3836 5480 2442 3927 4375 108
n.asn pl n.gsm cj d.nsn a.nsn n.nsn a.nsn n.dsm

πετομένῳ. 8 καὶ τὰ τέσσαρα ζῷα, ἓν καθ᾽ ἓν αὐτῶν ἔχων ἀνὰ
flying And the four ⌊living creatures,⌋ *{one} {by} {one}* each of them with *each*
4375 2779 3836 5475 2442 1651 2848 1651 324 899 2400 324
pt.pm.dsm cj d.npn a.npn n.npn a.nsn p.a a.asn r.gpn.3 pt.pa.nsm p.a

πτέρυγας ἕξ, κυκλόθεν καὶ ἔσωθεν γέμουσιν ὀφθαλμῶν, καὶ
six wings, *six* were full of eyes around and within. *were full of eyes* And
1971 4763 1971 1154 1154 4057 4057 3239 2779 2277 1154 4057 2779
n.apf a.apf adv cj adv v.pai.3p n.gpm cj

ἀνάπαυσιν οὐκ ἔχουσιν ἡμέρας καὶ νυκτὸς λέγοντες, ἅγιος
day or night they never rest, *never {have} day or night* saying: "Holy,
2465 2779 3816 2400 4024 398 4024 2400 2465 2779 3816 3306 41
n.asf pl v.pai.3p n.gsf cj n.gsf pt.pa.npm a.nsm

ἅγιος ἅγιος κύριος ὁ θεὸς ὁ παντοκράτωρ, ὁ ἦν καὶ ὁ ὢν καὶ ὁ
holy, holy, Lord *{the}* God *{the}* Almighty, who was, and who is, and who
41 41 3261 3836 2536 3836 4120 3836 1639 2779 3836 1639 2779 3836
a.nsm a.nsm n.nsm d.nsm n.nsm d.nsm n.nsm d.nsm v.iai.3s cj d.nsm pt.pa.nsm cj d.nsm

ἐρχόμενος. 9 καὶ ὅταν δώσουσιν τὰ ζῷα δόξαν καὶ
is to come!" And whenever the living creatures give *the living creatures* glory and
2262 2779 4020 3836 2442 2442 1443 3836 2442 1518 2779
pt.pm.nsm cj cj v.fai.3p d.npn n.npn n.asf cj

τιμὴν καὶ εὐχαριστίαν τῷ καθημένῳ ἐπὶ τῷ θρόνῳ τῷ ζῶντι εἰς
honor and thanks ⌊to the⌋ ⌊one who is seated⌋ on the throne, ⌊to the⌋ ⌊one who lives⌋ for
5507 2779 2374 3836 2764 2093 3836 2585 3836 2409 1650
n.asf cj n.asf d.dsm pt.pm.dsm p.d d.dsm n.dsm d.dsm pt.pa.dsm p.a

τοὺς ⌊αἰῶνας τῶν αἰώνων,⌋ 10 πεσοῦνται οἱ ⌊εἴκοσι
all time, the twenty-four elders fall down *the twenty-four*
3836 172 3836 172 3836 1633 4565 4406 3836 1633
d.apm n.apm d.gpm n.gpm v.fmi.3p d.npm a.npm

τέσσαρες⌋ πρεσβύτεροι ἐνώπιον τοῦ καθημένου ἐπὶ τοῦ θρόνου καὶ
elders before the one who is seated on the throne and
5475 4565 1967 3836 2764 2093 3836 2585 2779
a.npm a.npm p.g d.gsm pt.pm.gsm p.g d.gsm n.gsm cj

προσκυνήσουσιν τῷ ζῶντι εἰς τοὺς ⌊αἰῶνας τῶν αἰώνων⌋ καὶ βαλοῦσιν
worship the ⌊one who lives⌋ for all time. *{and}* They cast
4686 3836 2409 1650 3836 172 3836 172 2779 965
v.fai.3p d.dsm pt.pa.dsm p.a d.apm n.apm d.gpm n.gpm cj v.fai.3p

NASB

And *there were* seven lamps of fire burning before the throne, which are the seven Spirits of God; 6 and before the throne *there was something* like a sea of glass, like crystal; and in the center and around the throne, four living creatures full of eyes in front and behind. 7 The first creature *was* like a lion, and the second creature like a calf, and the third creature had a face like that of a man, and the fourth creature *was* like a flying eagle. 8 And the four living creatures, each one of them having six wings, are full of eyes around and within; and day and night they do not cease to say,

"HOLY, HOLY,
HOLY *is* THE
LORD GOD,
THE ALMIGHTY, WHO
WAS AND WHO
IS AND WHO IS
TO COME."

9 And when the living creatures give glory and honor and thanks to Him who sits on the throne, to Him who lives forever and ever, 10 the twenty-four elders will fall down before Him who sits on the throne, and will worship Him who lives forever and ever, and will cast

NIV

lay their crowns
before the throne
and say:
11 "You are worthy,
our Lord and
God,
to receive glory
and honor
and power,
for you created all
things,
and by your
will they
were created
and have their
being."

The Scroll and the Lamb

5 Then I saw
in the right
hand of him who
sat on the throne a
scroll with writing
on both sides and
sealed with seven
seals. 2 And I saw
a mighty angel
proclaiming in a
loud voice, "Who
is worthy to break
the seals and open
the scroll?" 3 But
no one in heav-
en or on earth or
under the earth
could open the
scroll or even look
inside it. 4 I wept
and wept because
no one was found
who was worthy
to open the scroll
or look inside.
5 Then one of the
elders said to me,
"Do not weep!
See, the Lion of
the tribe of Judah,
the Root of David,
has triumphed. He
is able to open the
scroll and its seven
seals."
6 Then I saw a
Lamb, looking
as if it had been
slain, standing at
the center of the
throne, encircled
by the four living
creatures and the
elders. The Lamb
had seven horns
and seven eyes,

τοὺς στεφάνους αὐτῶν ἐνώπιον τοῦ θρόνου λέγοντες, 11 ἄξιος εἶ, ὁ
{the} their crowns *their* before the throne, saying, "Worthy ⌊are you,⌋ {the}
3836 899 5109 899 1967 3836 2585 3306 545 1639 3836
d.apm n.apm r.gpm.3 p.g d.gsm n.gsm pt.pa.npm a.nsm v.pai.2s d.vsm

κύριος καὶ ὁ θεὸς ἡμῶν, λαβεῖν τὴν δόξαν καὶ τὴν τιμὴν καὶ τὴν δύναμιν,
our Lord and {the} God, *our* to receive {the} glory and {the} honor and {the} power,
7005 3261 2779 3836 2536 7005 3284 3836 1518 2779 3836 5507 2779 3836 1539
n.vsm cj d.vsm n.vsm r.gp.1 f.aa d.asf n.asf cj d.asf n.asf cj d.asf n.asf

ὅτι σὺ ἔκτισας τὰ πάντα καὶ διὰ τὸ θέλημά σου ἦσαν καὶ
for you created {the} all things, and ⌊because of⌋ {the} your will *your* they existed and
4022 5148 3231 3836 4246 2779 1328 3836 5148 2525 5148 1639 2779
cj r.ns.2 v.aai.2s d.apn a.apn cj p.a d.asn n.asn r.gs.2 v.iai.3p cj

ἐκτίσθησαν.
were created."
3231
v.api.3p

5:1 καὶ εἶδον ἐπὶ τὴν δεξιὰν τοῦ καθημένου ἐπὶ τοῦ θρόνου βιβλίον
Then I saw in the right hand of the ⌊one who was seated⌋ on the throne a scroll
2779 1625 2093 3836 1288 3836 2764 2093 3836 2585 1046
cj v.aai.1s p.a d.asf a.asf d.gsm pt.pm.gsm p.g d.gsm n.gsm n.asn

γεγραμμένον ἔσωθεν καὶ ὄπισθεν κατεσφραγισμένον → σφραγῖσιν ἑπτά.
written inside and on the back, sealed with seven seals. *seven*
1211 2277 2779 3957 2958 2231 5382 2231
pt.rp.asn adv cj adv pt.rp.asn n.dpf a.dpf

2 καὶ εἶδον ἄγγελον ἰσχυρὸν κηρύσσοντα ἐν φωνῇ μεγάλῃ, τίς
And I saw a powerful angel *powerful* proclaiming in a loud voice, *loud* "Who
2779 1625 2708 34 2708 3062 1877 3489 5889 3489 5515
cj v.aai.1s n.asm a.asm pt.pa.asm p.d n.dsf a.dsf r.nsm

ἄξιος ἀνοῖξαι τὸ βιβλίον καὶ λῦσαι τὰς σφραγῖδας αὐτοῦ; 3 καὶ οὐδεὶς
is worthy to open the scroll and break {the} its seals?" *its* But no one
545 487 3836 1046 2779 3395 3836 899 5382 899 2779 4029
a.nsm f.aa d.asn n.asn cj f.aa d.apf n.apf r.gsn.3 cj a.nsm

ἐδύνατο ἐν τῷ οὐρανῷ οὐδὲ ἐπὶ τῆς γῆς οὐδὲ ὑποκάτω τῆς γῆς ἀνοῖξαι
was able in {the} heaven or on {the} earth or under the earth was able to open
1538 1877 3836 4041 4028 2093 3836 1178 4028 5691 3836 1178 1538 1538 487
v.ipi.3s p.d d.dsm n.dsm cj p.g d.gsf n.gsf cj p.g d.gsf n.gsf f.aa

τὸ βιβλίον οὔτε βλέπειν αὐτό. 4 καὶ ἔκλαιον πολύ, ὅτι οὐδεὶς
the scroll or look into it. So ⌊I began to weep⌋ bitterly because no one was found
3836 1046 4046 1063 899 2779 3081 4498 4022 4029 2351 2351
d.asn n.asn cj f.pa r.asn.3 cj v.iai.1s adv cj a.nsm

ἄξιος εὑρέθη ἀνοῖξαι τὸ βιβλίον οὔτε βλέπειν αὐτό. 5 καὶ εἷς ἐκ τῶν
worthy *was found* to open the scroll or to look into it. Then one of the
545 2351 487 3836 1046 4046 1063 899 2779 1651 1666 3836
a.nsm v.api.3s f.aa d.asn n.asn cj f.pa r.asn.3 cj a.nsm p.g d.gpm

πρεσβυτέρων λέγει μοι, μὴ κλαῖε, ἰδοὺ ἐνίκησεν ὁ λέων ὁ ἐκ τῆς
elders said to me, "Stop weeping! Look, *has won the victory* the Lion {the} of the
4565 3306 1609 3590 3081 2627 3771 3836 3329 3836 1666 3836
a.gpm v.pai.3s r.ds.1 pl v.pam.2s j v.aai.3s d.nsm n.nsm d.nsm p.g d.gsf

φυλῆς Ἰούδα, ἡ ῥίζα Δαυίδ, ἀνοῖξαι τὸ βιβλίον καὶ
tribe of Judah, the root of David, has won the victory ⌊so that he can open⌋ the scroll and
5876 2683 3836 4844 1253 3771 3771 3771 3771 487 3836 1046 2779
n.gsf n.gsm d.nsf n.nsf n.gsm f.aa d.asn n.asn cj

τὰς ἑπτὰ σφραγῖδας αὐτοῦ. 6 καὶ εἶδον ⌊ἐν μέσῳ⌋ τοῦ θρόνου
{the} its seven seals." *its* And I saw standing there, between the throne
3836 899 2231 5382 899 2779 1625 2705 1877 3545 3836 2585
d.apf a.apf n.apf r.gsn.3 cj v.aai.1s p.d n.dsn d.gsm n.gsm

καὶ τῶν τεσσάρων ζῴων καὶ ⌊ἐν μέσῳ⌋ τῶν πρεσβυτέρων ἀρνίον
and the four ⌊living creatures⌋ and among the elders, a Lamb
2779 3836 5475 2442 2779 1877 3545 3836 4565 768
cj d.gpn a.gpn n.gpn cj p.d n.dsn d.gpm a.gpm n.asn

ἑστηκὸς ὡς ἐσφαγμένον ἔχων κέρατα ἑπτὰ καὶ ὀφθαλμοὺς
standing that appeared ⌊to have been killed,⌋ having seven horns *seven* and seven eyes,
2705 6055 5377 2400 2231 3043 2231 2779 2231 4057
pt.ra.asn pl pt.rp.asn pt.pa.nsm n.apn a.apn cj n.apm

NASB

their crowns before
the throne, saying,
11 "Worthy are
You, our Lord
and our God,
to receive
glory and
honor and
power; for
You created
all things,
and because
of Your will
they existed,
and were cre-
ated."

The Book with Seven Seals

5:1 I saw in the
right hand of Him
who sat on the
throne a book writ-
ten inside and on
the back, sealed up
with seven seals.
2 And I saw a strong
angel proclaiming
with a loud voice,
"Who is worthy to
open the book and
to break its seals?"
3 And no one in
heaven or on the
earth or under the
earth was able to
open the book or to
look into it. 4 Then
I *began* to weep
greatly because
no one was found
worthy to open the
book or to look
into it; 5 and one of
the elders *said to
me, "Stop weep-
ing; behold, the
Lion that is from
the tribe of Judah,
the Root of David,
has overcome so
as to open the
book and its seven
seals."
6 And I saw [a]be-
tween the throne
(with the four liv-
ing creatures) and
the elders a Lamb
standing, as if
slain, having seven
horns and seven
eyes, which are

[a] Lit *in the middle of the throne and of the four living creatures, and in the middle of the elders*

NIV

which are the sev-
en spirits[a] of God
sent out into all the
earth. 7He went
and took the scroll
from the right hand
of him who sat on
the throne. 8And
when he had taken
it, the four living
creatures and the
twenty-four elders
fell down before
the Lamb. Each
one had a harp and
they were holding
golden bowls full
of incense, which
are the prayers of
God's people. 9And
they sang a new
song, saying:

"You are worthy
to take the
scroll
and to open its
seals,
because you were
slain,
and with your
blood you
purchased
for God
persons from
every tribe
and language
and people
and nation.
10 You have made
them to be
a kingdom
and priests
to serve our
God,
and they will
reign[b] on the
earth."

11Then I looked
and heard the
voice of many an-
gels, numbering
thousands upon
thousands, and ten
thousand times
ten thousand.
They encircled
the throne and the
living creatures
and the elders. 12In
a loud voice they
were saying:

"Worthy is the
Lamb, who
was slain,

ἑπτὰ οἵ εἰσιν τὰ ἑπτὰ[a] πνεύματα τοῦ θεοῦ ἀπεσταλμένοι εἰς πᾶσαν τὴν γῆν.
seven which are the seven spirits of God sent out into all the earth.
2231 4005 1639 3836 2231 4460 3836 2536 690 1650 4246 3836 1178
a.apm r.npm v.pai.3p d.npn a.npn n.npn d.gsm n.gsm pt.rp.npm p.a a.asf d.asf n.asf

7 καὶ ἦλθεν καὶ εἴληφεν ἐκ τῆς δεξιᾶς τοῦ καθημένου ἐπὶ τοῦ
And he went and took the scroll from the right hand of the ⌊one who was seated⌋ on the
2779 2262 2779 3284 1666 3836 1288 3836 2764 2093 3836
cj v.aai.3s cj v.rai.3s p.g d.gsf a.gsf d.gsm pt.pm.gsm p.g d.gsm

θρόνου. 8 καὶ ὅτε ἔλαβεν τὸ βιβλίον, τὰ τέσσαρα ζῷα καὶ οἱ
throne. And when he had taken the scroll, the four ⌊living creatures⌋ and the
2585 2779 4021 3284 3836 1046 3836 5475 2442 2779 3836
n.gsm cj cj v.aai.3s d.asn n.asn d.npn a.npn n.npn cj d.npm

⌊εἴκοσι τέσσαρες⌋ πρεσβύτεροι ἔπεσαν ἐνώπιον τοῦ ἀρνίου ἔχοντες ἕκαστος
twenty-four elders fell down before the Lamb, each holding *each* a
1633 5475 4565 4406 1967 3836 768 1667 2400 1667
a.npm a.npm a.npm v.aai.3p p.g d.gsn n.gsn pt.pa.npm r.nsm

κιθάραν καὶ φιάλας χρυσᾶς γεμούσας θυμιαμάτων, αἵ εἰσιν αἱ προσευχαὶ
harp and golden bowls *golden* full of incense, which are the prayers
3067 2779 5997 5786 5997 1154 2592 4005 1639 3836 4666
n.asf cj n.apf a.apf pt.pa.apf n.gpn r.npf v.pai.3p d.npf n.npf

τῶν ἁγίων, 9 καὶ ᾄδουσιν ᾠδὴν καινὴν λέγοντες, ἄξιος εἶ λαβεῖν τὸ
of the saints. And they sang a new song, *new* saying, "Worthy ⌊are you⌋ to take the
3836 41 2779 106 2785 6046 2785 3306 545 1639 3284 3836
d.gpm a.gpm cj v.pai.3p n.asf a.asf pt.pa.npm a.nsm v.pai.2s f.aa d.asn

βιβλίον καὶ ἀνοῖξαι τὰς σφραγῖδας αὐτοῦ, ὅτι ἐσφάγης καὶ
scroll and to open *{the}* its seals, *its* for ⌊you were slain,⌋ and by your blood
1046 2779 487 3836 899 5382 899 4022 5377 2779 1877 5148 135
n.asn cj f.aa d.apf n.apf r.gsn.3 cj v.api.2s cj

ἠγόρασας τῷ θεῷ ἐν τῷ αἵματί σου ἐκ πάσης φυλῆς καὶ γλώσσης
you ransomed people for God *by* *{the}* *blood* *your* from every tribe, *{and}* language,
60 3836 2536 1877 3836 135 5148 1666 4246 5876 2779 1185
v.aai.2s d.dsm n.dsm p.d d.dsn n.dsn r.gs.2 p.g a.gsf n.gsf cj n.gsf

καὶ λαοῦ καὶ ἔθνους 10 καὶ ἐποίησας αὐτοὺς τῷ θεῷ
{and} people, and nation. And you have made them a kingdom and priests to our God,
2779 3295 2779 1620 2779 4472 899 993 2779 2636 3836 7005 2536
cj n.gsm cj n.gsn cj v.aai.2s r.apm.3 d.dsm n.dsm

ἡμῶν βασιλείαν καὶ ἱερεῖς, καὶ βασιλεύσουσιν ἐπὶ τῆς γῆς. 11 καὶ εἶδον, καὶ
our *kingdom* *and* *priests* and they will reign on the earth." Then I looked, and
7005 993 2779 2636 2779 996 2093 3836 1178 2779 1625 2779
r.gp.1 n.asf cj n.apm cj v.fai.3p p.g d.gsf n.gsf cj v.aai.1s cj

ἤκουσα φωνὴν → ἀγγέλων πολλῶν κύκλῳ τοῦ θρόνου καὶ τῶν
I heard the voice of many angels *many* surrounding the throne and the
201 5889 4498 34 4498 3241 3836 2585 2779 3836
v.aai.1s n.asf n.gpm a.gpm p.g d.gsm n.gsm cj d.gpn

ζῴων καὶ τῶν πρεσβυτέρων, καὶ ἦν ὁ ἀριθμὸς αὐτῶν
⌊living creatures⌋ and the elders; and their number was *{the}* *number* *their*
2442 2779 3836 4565 2779 899 750 1639 3836 750 899
n.gpn cj d.gpm a.gpm cj v.iai.3s d.nsm n.nsm r.gpm.3

μυριάδες μυριάδων καὶ χιλιάδες χιλιάδων 12 λέγοντες → φωνῇ
ten thousand times ten thousand and thousands of thousands, saying with a loud voice,
3689 3689 2779 5942 5942 3306 3489 5889
n.npf n.gpf cj n.npf n.gpf pt.pa.npm n.dsf

μεγάλῃ, ἄξιόν ἐστιν τὸ ἀρνίον τὸ ἐσφαγμένον λαβεῖν τὴν δύναμιν καὶ πλοῦτον
loud "Worthy is the Lamb who was slain, to receive *{the}* power and wealth
3489 545 1639 3836 768 3836 5377 3284 3836 1539 2779 4458
a.dsf a.nsn v.pai.3s d.nsn n.nsn d.nsn pt.rp.nsn f.aa d.asf n.asf cj n.asm

NASB

the seven Spirits
of God, sent out
into all the earth.
7And He came and
took the book out
of the right hand of
Him who sat on the
throne. 8When He
had taken the book,
the four living
creatures and the
twenty-four elders
fell down before
the Lamb, each one
holding a harp and
golden bowls full
of incense, which
are the prayers of
the saints. 9And
they *sang a new
song, saying,

"Worthy are
You to take
the book and
to break its
seals; for
You were
slain, and
purchased
for God with
Your blood
men from ev-
ery tribe and
tongue and
people and
nation.
10 "You have
made them *to
be* a kingdom
and priests
to our God;
and they will
reign upon
the earth."

Angels Exalt the Lamb

11Then I looked,
and I heard the
voice of many
angels around the
throne and the liv-
ing creatures and
the elders; and the
number of them
was myriads of
myriads, and thou-
sands of thousands,
12saying with a loud
voice,

"Worthy is the
Lamb that
was slain to
receive power
and riches

[a] 6 That is, the sev-
enfold Spirit
[b] 10 Some manu-
scripts *they reign*

[a] [ἑπτὰ] UBS.

NIV

to receive
power and
wealth and
wisdom and
strength
and honor and
glory and
praise!"
13 Then I heard
every creature
in heaven and on
earth and under
the earth and on
the sea, and all
that is in them,
saying:
"To him who sits
on the throne
and to the
Lamb
be praise and
honor and
glory and
power,
for ever and ever!"
14 The four living
creatures said,
"Amen," and the
elders fell down
and worshiped.

The Seals

6 I watched
as the Lamb
opened the first
of the seven seals.
Then I heard one
of the four living
creatures say in a
voice like thunder,
"Come!" 2 I looked,
and there before
me was a white
horse! Its rider
held a bow, and he
was given a crown,
and he rode out as
a conqueror bent
on conquest.
3 When the Lamb
opened the sec-
ond seal, I heard
the second liv-
ing creature say,
"Come!" 4 Then
another horse
came out, a fiery
red one. Its rider
was given power
to take peace from
the earth and to
make people kill
each other. To him
was given a large
sword.

καὶ σοφίαν καὶ ἰσχὺν καὶ τιμὴν καὶ δόξαν καὶ εὐλογίαν. 13 καὶ πᾶν
and wisdom and might and honor and glory and praise!" Then I heard every
2779 5053 2779 2709 2779 5507 2779 1518 2779 2330 2779 201 201 4246
cj n.asf cj n.asf cj n.asf cj n.asf cj n.asf cj a.asn

κτίσμα ὃ ἐν τῷ οὐρανῷ καὶ ἐπὶ τῆς γῆς καὶ ὑποκάτω τῆς γῆς καὶ ἐπὶ τῆς
creature {that} in {the} heaven and on {the} earth and under the earth and in the
3233 4005 1877 3836 4041 2779 2093 3836 1178 2779 5691 3836 1178 2779 2093 3836
n.asn r.nsn p.d d.dsm n.dsm cj p.d d.gsf n.gsf cj p.g d.gsf n.gsf cj p.g d.gsf

θαλάσσης καὶ τὰ ἐν αὐτοῖς πάντα ἤκουσα λέγοντας, τῷ καθημένῳ
sea, and {the} all that is in them, *all* *I heard* saying, ⌊"To the⌋ one seated
2498 2779 3836 4246 1877 899 4246 201 3306 3836 2764
n.gsf cj d.apn p.d r.dpm.3 a.apn v.aai.1s pt.pa.apm d.dsm pt.pm.dsm

ἐπὶ τῷ θρόνῳ καὶ τῷ ἀρνίῳ ἡ εὐλογία καὶ ἡ τιμὴ καὶ ἡ δόξα καὶ
on the throne and ⌊to the⌋ Lamb be {the} praise and {the} honor and {the} glory and
2093 3836 2585 2779 3836 768 3836 2330 2779 3836 5507 2779 3836 1518 2779
p.g d.dsm n.dsm cj d.dsn n.dsn d.nsf n.nsf cj d.nsf n.nsf cj d.nsf n.nsf cj

τὸ κράτος εἰς τοὺς ⌊αἰῶνας τῶν αἰώνων.⌋ 14 καὶ τὰ τέσσαρα ζῷα
{the} might for all time! And the four ⌊living creatures⌋
3836 3197 1650 3836 172 3836 172 2779 3836 5475 2442
d.nsn n.nsn p.a d.apm n.apm d.gpm n.gpm cj d.npn a.npn n.npn

ἔλεγον, ἀμήν. καὶ οἱ πρεσβύτεροι ἔπεσαν καὶ προσεκύνησαν.[a]
said, "Amen!" And the elders fell down and worshiped.
3306 297 2779 3836 4565 4406 2779 4686
v.iai.3p pl cj d.npm a.npm v.aai.3p cj v.aai.3p

6:1 καὶ εἶδον ὅτε ἤνοιξεν τὸ ἀρνίον μίαν ἐκ τῶν ἑπτὰ σφραγίδων,
Then I watched as the Lamb opened *the* *Lamb* one of the seven seals,
2779 1625 4021 3836 768 487 3836 768 1651 1666 3836 2231 5382
cj v.aai.1s cj v.aai.3s d.nsn n.nsn a.asf p.g d.gpf a.gpf n.gpf

καὶ ἤκουσα ἑνὸς ἐκ τῶν τεσσάρων ζῴων λέγοντος ὡς φωνὴ
and I heard one of the four ⌊living creatures⌋ say with a voice like *with voice*
2779 201 1651 1666 3836 5475 2442 3306 5889 5889 6055 5889
cj v.aai.1s a.gsn p.g d.gpn a.gpn n.gpn pt.pa.gsn pl n.dsf

βροντῆς, ἔρχου. 2 καὶ εἶδον, καὶ ἰδοὺ ἵππος λευκός, καὶ ὁ καθήμενος
thunder, "Come!" {and} I looked, and behold, a white horse! *white* And the one seated
1103 2262 2779 1625 2779 2627 3328 2691 3328 2779 3836 2764
n.gsf v.pmm.2s cj v.aai.1s cj j n.nsm a.nsm cj d.nsm pt.pm.nsm

ἐπ᾽ αὐτὸν ἔχων τόξον καὶ ἐδόθη αὐτῷ στέφανος καὶ ἐξῆλθεν
on it had a bow; and ⌊there was given⌋ to him a crown, and he went out
2093 899 2400 5534 2779 1443 899 5109 2779 2002
p.a r.asm.3 pt.pa.nsm n.asn cj v.api.3s r.dsm.3 n.nsm cj v.aai.3s

νικῶν καὶ ἵνα νικήσῃ. 3 καὶ ὅτε ἤνοιξεν τὴν σφραγῖδα τὴν δευτέραν,
conquering and to conquer. And when he opened the second seal, {the} *second*
3771 2779 2671 3771 2779 4021 487 3836 1311 5382 3836 1311
pt.pa.nsm cj cj v.aas.3s cj cj v.aai.3s d.asf n.asf d.asf a.asf

ἤκουσα τοῦ δευτέρου ζῴου λέγοντος, ἔρχου. 4 καὶ ἐξῆλθεν ἄλλος ἵππος
I heard the second ⌊living creature⌋ saying, "Come!" And out came another horse,
201 3836 1311 2442 3306 2262 2779 2002 257 2691
v.aai.1s d.gsn a.gsn n.gsn pt.pa.gsn v.pmm.2s cj v.aai.3s r.nsm n.nsm

πυρρός, καὶ τῷ καθημένῳ ἐπ᾽ αὐτὸν ἐδόθη αὐτῷ λαβεῖν τὴν εἰρήνην ἐκ
bright red; and {the} its rider {on} *its* was allowed {to him} to take {the} peace from
4794 2779 3836 899 2764 2093 899 1443 899 3284 3836 1645 1666
a.nsm cj d.dsm pt.pm.dsm p.a r.asm.3 v.api.3s r.dsm.3 f.aa d.asf n.asf p.g

τῆς γῆς καὶ ἵνα ἀλλήλους σφάξουσιν καὶ ἐδόθη
the earth {and} so that men should slay one another, *should slay* and a great sword was given
3836 1178 2779 2671 5377 5377 253 5377 2779 3489 3479 1443
d.gsf n.gsf cj cj r.apm v.fai.3p cj v.api.3s

[a] ζῶντι εἰς τοὺς αἰῶνας τῶν αἰώνων included by TR after προσεκύνησαν.

NASB

and wisdom
and might
and honor
and glory and
blessing."
13 And every created
thing which is in
heaven and on the
earth and under the
earth and on the
sea, and all things
in them, I heard
saying,
"To Him who
sits on the
throne, and
to the Lamb,
be blessing
and honor
and glory and
dominion
forever and
ever."
14 And the four liv-
ing creatures kept
saying, "Amen."
And the elders fell
down and wor-
shiped.

The Book Opened; The First Seal—Rider on the White Horse

6:1 Then I saw
when the Lamb
broke one of the
seven seals, and
I heard one of
the four living
creatures saying
as with a voice of
thunder, "Come."
2 I looked, and be-
hold, a white horse,
and he who sat on
it had a bow; and a
crown was given to
him, and he went
out conquering and
to conquer.

The Second Seal—War

3 When He broke
the second seal, I
heard the second
living creature
saying, "Come."
4 And another, a red
horse, went out;
and to him who sat
on it, it was grant-
ed to take peace
from the earth, and
that *men* would
slay one another;
and a great sword
was given to him.

NIV

[5]When the Lamb
opened the third
seal, I heard the
third living crea-
ture say, "Come!"
I looked, and there
before me was a
black horse! Its
rider was holding
a pair of scales in
his hand. [6]Then I
heard what sound-
ed like a voice
among the four
living creatures,
saying, "Two
pounds[a] of wheat
for a day's wages,[b]
and six pounds[c] of
barley for a day's
wages,[d] and do not
damage the oil and
the wine!"
[7]When the Lamb
opened the fourth
seal, I heard the
voice of the fourth
living creature say,
"Come!" [8]I looked,
and there before
me was a pale
horse! Its rider was
named Death, and
Hades was follow-
ing close behind
him. They were
given power over a
fourth of the earth
to kill by sword,
famine and plague,
and by the wild
beasts of the earth.
[9]When he opened
the fifth seal, I saw
under the altar the
souls of those who
had been slain be-
cause of the word
of God and the
testimony they had
maintained. [10]They
called out in a loud
voice, "How long,
Sovereign Lord,
holy and true, un-
til you judge the
inhabitants of the
earth and avenge

[a] 6 Or about 1 kilogram
[b] 6 Greek *a denarius*
[c] 6 Or about 3 kilograms
[d] 6 Greek *a denarius*

αὐτῷ μάχαιρα μεγάλη. [5]καὶ ὅτε ἤνοιξεν τὴν σφραγῖδα τὴν τρίτην, ἤκουσα
to him. *sword* *great* And when he opened the third seal, *{the}* *third* I heard
899 3479 3489 2779 4021 487 3836 5569 5382 3836 5569 201
r.dsm.3 n.nsf a.nsf cj cj v.aai.3s d.asf n.asf d.asf a.asf v.aai.1s

τοῦ τρίτου ζῴου λέγοντος, ἔρχου. καὶ εἶδον, καὶ ἰδοὺ ἵππος μέλας,
the third ⸤living creature⸥ saying, "Come!" And I looked, and behold, a black horse! *black*
3836 5569 2442 3306 2262 2779 1625 2779 2627 3506 2691 3506
d.gsn a.gsn n.gsn pt.pa.gsn v.pmm.2s cj v.aai.1s cj j n.nsm a.nsm

καὶ ὁ καθήμενος ἐπ' αὐτὸν ἔχων ζυγὸν ἐν τῇ χειρὶ αὐτοῦ.
And *{the}* its rider *{on}* *its* had a ⸤pair of scales⸥ in *{the}* his hand. *his*
2779 3836 899 2764 2093 899 2400 2433 1877 3836 899 5931 899
cj d.nsm pt.pm.nsm p.a r.asm.3 pt.pa.nsm n.asm p.d d.dsf n.dsf r.gsm.3

[6]καὶ ἤκουσα ὡς φωνὴν ἐν μέσῳ τῶν τεσσάρων ζῴων
And I heard ⸤what seemed to be⸥ a voice in the midst of the four ⸤living creatures,⸥
2779 201 6055 5889 1877 3545 3836 5475 2442
cj v.aai.1s pl n.asf p.d n.dsn d.gpn a.gpn n.gpn

λέγουσαν, χοῖνιξ σίτου → δηναρίου καὶ τρεῖς χοίνικες κριθῶν → δηναρίου,
saying, "A quart of wheat for a denarius, and three quarts of barley for a denarius,
3306 5955 4992 1324 2779 5552 5955 3208 1324
pt.pa.asf n.nsf n.gsm n.gsn cj a.npf n.npf n.gpf n.gsn

καὶ τὸ ἔλαιον καὶ τὸν οἶνον μὴ ἀδικήσῃς. [7]καὶ ὅτε ἤνοιξεν τὴν
but do not harm the oil and the wine!" *not* *do harm* And when he opened the
2779 92 3590 92 3836 1778 2779 3836 3885 3590 92 2779 4021 487 3836
cj d.asn n.asn cj d.asm n.asm pl v.aas.2s cj cj v.aai.3s d.asf

σφραγῖδα τὴν τετάρτην, ἤκουσα φωνὴν τοῦ τετάρτου ζῴου
fourth seal, *{the}* *fourth* I heard the voice of the fourth ⸤living creature⸥
5480 5382 3836 5480 201 5889 3836 5480 2442
n.asf d.asf a.asf v.aai.1s n.asf d.gsn a.gsn n.gsn

λέγοντος, ἔρχου. [8]καὶ εἶδον, καὶ ἰδοὺ ἵππος χλωρός, καὶ ὁ
saying, "Come!" And I looked, and behold, a pale horse! *pale* And *{the}* its
3306 2262 2779 1625 2779 2627 5952 2691 5952 2779 3836 899
pt.pa.gsn v.pmm.2s cj v.aai.1s cj j n.nsm a.nsm cj d.nsm

καθήμενος ἐπάνω αὐτοῦ ὄνομα αὐτῷ ὁ[a] θάνατος, καὶ ὁ ᾅδης ἠκολούθει
rider's *{upon}* *its* name *{to him}* was *{the}* Death, and *{the}* Hades was following
2764 2062 899 3950 899 3836 2505 2779 3836 87 199
pt.pm.nsm p.g r.gsm.3 n.nsn r.dsm.3 d.nsm n.nsm cj d.nsm n.nsm v.iai.3s

μετ' αὐτοῦ καὶ ἐδόθη αὐτοῖς ἐξουσία ἐπὶ τὸ τέταρτον τῆς γῆς
with him. And authority was given to them *authority* over a fourth of the earth,
3552 899 2779 2026 1443 899 2026 2093 3836 5480 3836 1178
p.g r.gsm.3 cj v.api.3s r.dpm.3 n.nsf p.a d.asn a.asn d.gsf n.gsf

ἀποκτεῖναι ἐν ῥομφαίᾳ καὶ ἐν λιμῷ καὶ ἐν θανάτῳ καὶ ὑπὸ τῶν θηρίων τῆς
to kill with sword and with famine and with pestilence and by *{the}* wild beasts of the
650 1877 4855 2779 1877 3350 2779 1877 2505 2779 5679 3836 2563 3836
f.aa p.d n.dsf cj p.d n.dsm cj p.d n.dsm cj p.g d.gpn n.gpn d.gsf

γῆς. [9]καὶ ὅτε ἤνοιξεν τὴν πέμπτην σφραγῖδα, εἶδον ὑποκάτω τοῦ θυσιαστηρίου
earth. And when he opened the fifth seal, I saw under the altar
1178 2779 4021 487 3836 4286 5382 1625 5691 3836 2603
n.gsf cj cj v.aai.3s d.asf a.asf n.asf v.aai.1s p.g d.gsn n.gsn

τὰς ψυχὰς τῶν ἐσφαγμένων διὰ τὸν λόγον τοῦ θεοῦ καὶ διὰ τὴν μαρτυρίαν
the souls of those ⸤who had been slain⸥ for the word of God and for the witness
3836 6034 3836 5377 1328 3836 3364 3836 2536 2779 1328 3836 3456
d.apf n.apf d.gpm pt.rp.gpm p.a d.asm n.asm d.gsm n.gsm cj p.a d.asf n.asf

ἣν εἶχον. [10]καὶ ἔκραξαν → φωνῇ μεγάλῃ λέγοντες, ἕως πότε,
{that} ⸤they had borne.⸥ And ⸤they cried out⸥ with a loud voice, *loud* saying, "How long,
4005 2400 2779 3189 3489 5889 3489 3306 2401 4537
r.asf v.iai.3p cj v.aai.3p n.dsf a.dsf pt.pa.npm p.g adv

ὁ δεσπότης ὁ ἅγιος καὶ ἀληθινός, οὐ κρίνεις καὶ ἐκδικεῖς
O ⸤Sovereign Lord,⸥ *{the}* holy and true, before ⸤you bring judgment⸥ and avenge
3836 1305 3836 41 2779 240 4024 3212 2779 1688
d.vsm n.vsm d.vsm a.vsm cj a.vsm pl v.pai.2s cj v.pai.2s

[a] [ὁ] UBS.

NASB

The Third Seal—Famine

[5]When He broke
the third seal, I
heard the third liv-
ing creature saying,
"Come." I looked,
and behold, a black
horse; and he who
sat on it had a pair
of scales in his
hand. [6]And I heard
something like a
voice in the center
of the four living
creatures saying,
"A [a]quart of wheat
for a [b]denarius, and
three quarts of bar-
ley for a denarius;
and do not damage
the oil and the
wine."

The Fourth Seal—Death

[7]When the Lamb
broke the fourth
seal, I heard the
voice of the fourth
living creature
saying, "Come." [8]I
looked, and behold,
an ashen horse;
and he who sat on
it had the name
Death; and Hades
was following with
him. Authority
was given to them
over a fourth of the
earth, to kill with
sword and with
famine and with
pestilence and by
the wild beasts of
the earth.

The Fifth Seal—Martyrs

[9]When the Lamb
broke the fifth seal,
I saw underneath
the altar the souls
of those who had
been slain because
of the word of
God, and because
of the testimony
which they had
maintained; [10]and
they cried out with
a loud voice, say-
ing, "How long,
O Lord, holy and
true, will You
refrain from judg-

[a] Gr *choenix;* i.e. a dry measure almost equal to a qt
[b] The denarius was equivalent to a day's wages

NIV

our blood?" 11Then each of them was given a white robe, and they were told to wait a little longer, until the full number of their fellow servants, their brothers and sisters,[a] were killed just as they had been.

12I watched as he opened the sixth seal. There was a great earthquake. The sun turned black like sackcloth made of goat hair, the whole moon turned blood red, 13and the stars in the sky fell to earth, as figs drop from a fig tree when shaken by a strong wind. 14The heavens receded like a scroll being rolled up, and every mountain and island was removed from its place.

15Then the kings of the earth, the princes, the generals, the rich, the mighty, and everyone else, both slave and free, hid in caves and among the rocks of the mountains. 16They called to the mountains and the rocks, "Fall on us and hide us[b] from the face of him who sits on the throne and from the wrath of the Lamb! 17For the great day of their[c] wrath has come,

τὸ αἷμα ἡμῶν ἐκ τῶν κατοικούντων ἐπὶ τῆς γῆς; 11 καὶ
{the} our blood *our* on those who dwell on the earth?" Then a white robe
3836 7005 135 7005 1666 3836 2997 2093 3836 1178 2779 3328 5124
d.asn n.asn r.gp.1 p.g d.gpm pt.pa.gpm p.g d.gsf n.gsf cj

ἐδόθη → αὐτοῖς ἑκάστῳ στολὴ λευκὴ καὶ ἐρρέθη αὐτοῖς ἵνα
was given to each of them *each* *robe* *white* and they were told *they* to
1443 1667 899 1667 5124 3328 2779 899 3306 899 2671
v.api.3s r.dpm.3 r.dsm n.nsf a.nsf cj v.api.3s r.dpm.3 cj

ἀναπαύσονται ἔτι χρόνον μικρόν, ἕως πληρωθῶσιν καὶ οἱ
rest *{still}* a little while, *little* until the number was reached *{also}* *{the}* of their
399 2285 3625 5989 3625 2401 4444 2779 3836 899
v.fmi.3p adv n.asm a.asm cj v.aps.3p adv d.npm

σύνδουλοι αὐτῶν καὶ οἱ ἀδελφοὶ αὐτῶν οἱ μέλλοντες ἀποκτέννεσθαι
fellow servants *their* and *{the}* their brothers *their* who were to be killed just
5281 899 2779 3836 899 81 899 3836 3516 650 2779
n.npm r.gpm.3 cj d.npm n.npm r.gpm.3 d.npm pt.pa.npm f.pp

ὡς καὶ αὐτοί. 12 καὶ εἶδον ὅτε ἤνοιξεν τὴν σφραγῖδα τὴν ἕκτην,
as *just* they had been. And *I looked* when he opened the sixth seal, *{the}* *sixth*
6055 2779 899 2779 1625 4021 487 3836 1761 5382 3836 1761
cj adv r.npm cj v.aai.1s cj v.aai.3s d.asf n.asf d.asf a.asf

καὶ σεισμὸς μέγας ἐγένετο καὶ ὁ ἥλιος ἐγένετο
I looked, and there was a great earthquake; *great* *there was* *{and}* the sun became as
1625 1625 2779 1181 1181 3489 4939 3489 1181 2779 3836 2463 1181
cj n.nsm a.nsm v.ami.3s cj d.nsm n.nsm v.ami.3s

μέλας ὡς σάκκος τρίχινος καὶ ἡ σελήνη ὅλη ἐγένετο ὡς αἷμα 13 καὶ
black as sackcloth made of hair, *{and}* the entire moon *entire* became like blood, and
3506 6055 4884 5570 2779 3836 3910 4943 3910 1181 6055 135 2779
a.nsm pl n.nsm a.nsm cj d.nsf n.nsf a.nsf v.ami.3s pl n.nsn cj

οἱ ἀστέρες τοῦ οὐρανοῦ ἔπεσαν εἰς τὴν γῆν, ὡς συκῆ βάλλει τοὺς
the stars of the sky fell to the earth as a fig tree drops *{the}* its
3836 843 3836 4041 4406 1650 3836 1178 6055 5190 965 3836 899
d.npm n.npm d.gsm n.gsm v.aai.3p p.a d.asf n.asf cj n.nsf v.pai.3s d.apm

ὀλύνθους αὐτῆς ὑπὸ ἀνέμου μεγάλου σειομένη, 14 καὶ ὁ
winter fruit *its* when shaken by a fierce wind. *fierce* *when shaken* *{and}* The
3913 899 4940 4940 5679 3489 449 3489 4940 2779 3836
n.apm r.gsf.3 p.g n.gsm a.gsm pt.pp.nsf cj d.nsm

οὐρανὸς ἀπεχωρίσθη ὡς βιβλίον ἑλισσόμενον καὶ πᾶν ὄρος καὶ νῆσος
sky vanished like a scroll being rolled up, and every mountain and island was
4041 714 6055 1046 1813 2779 4246 4001 2779 3762 3075
n.nsm v.api.3s pl n.nsn pt.pp.nsn cj a.nsn n.nsn cj n.nsf

ἐκ τῶν τόπων αὐτῶν ἐκινήθησαν. 15 καὶ οἱ βασιλεῖς τῆς γῆς καὶ
removed from *{the}* its place. *its* *was removed* Then the kings of the earth and
3075 1666 3836 899 5536 899 3075 2779 3836 995 3836 1178 2779
p.g d.gpm n.gpm r.gpn.3 v.api.3p cj d.npm n.npm d.gsf n.gsf cj

οἱ μεγιστᾶνες καὶ οἱ χιλίαρχοι καὶ οἱ πλούσιοι καὶ οἱ ἰσχυροὶ καὶ πᾶς
the princes and the generals and the rich and the powerful and everyone
3836 3491 2779 3836 5941 2779 3836 4454 2779 3836 2708 2779 4246
d.npm n.npm cj d.npm n.npm cj d.npm a.npm cj d.npm a.npm cj a.nsm

δοῦλος καὶ ἐλεύθερος ἔκρυψαν ἑαυτοὺς εἰς τὰ σπήλαια καὶ εἰς τὰς
— slave and free — hid themselves in the caves and among the
1529 2779 1801 3221 1571 1650 3836 5068 2779 1650 3836
n.nsm cj a.nsm v.aai.3p r.apm.3 p.a d.apn n.apn cj p.a d.apf

πέτρας τῶν ὀρέων 16 καὶ λέγουσιν τοῖς ὄρεσιν καὶ ταῖς πέτραις, πέσετε ἐφ'
rocks of the mountains. *{and}* They said to the mountains and the rocks, "Fall on
4376 3836 4001 2779 3306 3836 4001 2779 3836 4376 4406 2093
n.apf d.gpn n.gpn cj v.pai.3p d.dpn n.dpn cj d.dpf n.dpf v.aam.2p p.a

ἡμᾶς καὶ κρύψατε ἡμᾶς ἀπὸ προσώπου τοῦ καθημένου ἐπὶ τοῦ θρόνου καὶ
us and hide us from the face of the one who is seated on the throne and
7005 2779 3221 7005 608 4725 3836 2764 2093 3836 2585 2779
r.ap.1 cj v.aam.2p r.ap.1 p.g n.gsn d.gsm pt.pm.gsm p.g d.gsm n.gsm cj

ἀπὸ τῆς ὀργῆς τοῦ ἀρνίου, 17 ὅτι ἦλθεν ἡ ἡμέρα
from the wrath of the Lamb, because the great day of their wrath has come, *{the}* *day*
608 3836 3973 3836 768 4022 3489 2465 3836 899 3973 2262 3836 2465
p.g d.gsf n.gsf d.gsn n.gsn cj v.aai.3s d.nsf n.nsf

NASB

ing and avenging our blood on those who dwell on the earth?" 11And there was given to each of them a white robe; and they were told that they should rest for a little while longer, until *the number of* their fellow servants and their brethren who were to be killed even as they had been, would be completed also.

The Sixth Seal—Terror

12I looked when He broke the sixth seal, and there was a great earthquake; and the sun became black as sackcloth *made* of hair, and the whole moon became like blood; 13and the stars of the sky fell to the earth, as a fig tree casts its unripe figs when shaken by a great wind. 14The sky was split apart like a scroll when it is rolled up, and every mountain and island were moved out of their places. 15Then the kings of the earth and the great men and the [a]commanders and the rich and the strong and every slave and free man hid themselves in the caves and among the rocks of the mountains; 16and they *said to the mountains and to the rocks, "Fall on us and hide us from the presence of Him who sits on the throne, and from the wrath of the Lamb; 17for the great day of their wrath has come,

[a] *11* The Greek word for *brothers and sisters* (*adelphoi*) refers here to believers, both men and women, as part of God's family; also in 12:10; 19:10.
[b] *16* See Hosea 10:8.
[c] *17* Some manuscripts *his*

[a] I.e. chiliarchs, in command of one thousand troops

NIV

and who can with-
stand it?"

144,000 Sealed

7 After this I
saw four an-
gels standing at
the four corners
of the earth, hold-
ing back the four
winds of the earth
to prevent any
wind from blow-
ing on the land or
on the sea or on
any tree. 2 Then I
saw another angel
coming up from
the east, having
the seal of the liv-
ing God. He called
out in a loud voice
to the four angels
who had been
given power to
harm the land and
the sea: 3 "Do not
harm the land or
the sea or the trees
until we put a seal
on the foreheads
of the servants of
our God." 4 Then I
heard the number
of those who were
sealed: 144,000
from all the tribes
of Israel.

5 From the tribe
of Judah
12,000 were
sealed,
from the tribe
of Reuben
12,000,
from the tribe
of Gad
12,000,
6 from the tribe
of Asher
12,000,
from the tribe
of Naphtali
12,000,
from the tribe
of Manasseh
12,000,

ἡ μεγάλη τῆς ὀργῆς αὐτῶν, καὶ τίς δύναται σταθῆναι;
{the} great of wrath their and who is able to stand fast?"
3836 3489 3836 3973 899 2779 5515 1538 2705
d.nsf a.nsf d.gsf n.gsf r.gpm.3 cj r.nsm v.ppi.3s f.ap

7:1 Μετὰ τοῦτο εἶδον τέσσαρας ἀγγέλους ἑστῶτας ἐπὶ τὰς τέσσαρας γωνίας τῆς
After this I saw four angels standing at the four corners of the
3552 4047 1625 5475 34 2705 2093 3836 5475 1224 3836
p.a r.asn v.aai.1s a.apm n.apm pt.ra.apm p.a d.apf a.apf n.apf d.gsf

γῆς, κρατοῦντας τοὺς τέσσαρας ἀνέμους τῆς γῆς ἵνα μὴ πνέῃ ἄνεμος
earth holding back the four winds of the earth, so that no wind ⌊could blow⌋ *wind*
1178 3195 3836 5475 449 3836 1178 2671 3590 449 4463 449
n.gsf pt.pa.apm d.apm a.apm n.apm d.gsf n.gsf cj pl v.pas.3s n.nsm

ἐπὶ τῆς γῆς μήτε ἐπὶ τῆς θαλάσσης μήτε ἐπὶ πᾶν δένδρον. 2 καὶ εἶδον ἄλλον
on the earth or on the sea or against any tree. Then I saw another
2093 3836 1178 3612 2093 3836 2498 3612 2093 4246 1285 2779 1625 257
p.g d.gsf n.gsf cj p.g d.gsf n.gsf cj p.a a.asn n.asn cj v.aai.1s r.asm

ἄγγελον ἀναβαίνοντα ἀπὸ ἀνατολῆς → ἡλίου ἔχοντα σφραγῖδα →
angel ascending from the rising of the sun, with the seal of the living
34 326 608 424 2463 2400 5382 2409
n.asm pt.pa.asm p.g n.gsf n.gsm pt.pa.asm n.asf

θεοῦ ζῶντος, καὶ ἔκραξεν → φωνῇ μεγάλῃ τοῖς τέσσαρσιν ἀγγέλοις οἷς
God. *living* And ⌊he called out⌋ in a loud voice *loud* to the four angels who
2536 2409 2779 3189 3489 5889 3489 3836 5475 34 4005
n.gsm pt.pa.gsm cj v.aai.3s n.dsf a.dsf d.dpm a.dpm n.dpm r.dpm

ἐδόθη αὐτοῖς ἀδικῆσαι τὴν γῆν καὶ τὴν θάλασσαν 3 λέγων, ↱ μὴ
⌊had been given power⌋ *{to them}* to harm the earth and the sea, saying, "Do not
1443 899 92 3836 1178 2779 3836 2498 3306 92 3590
v.api.3s r.dpm.3 f.aa d.asf n.asf cj d.asf n.asf pt.pa.nsm pl

ἀδικήσητε τὴν γῆν μήτε τὴν θάλασσαν μήτε τὰ δένδρα, ἄχρι σφραγίσωμεν τοὺς
harm the earth or the sea or the trees until we have sealed the
92 3836 1178 3612 3836 2498 3612 3836 1285 948 5381 3836
v.aas.2p d.asf n.asf cj d.asf n.asf cj d.apn n.apn cj v.aas.1p d.apm

δούλους τοῦ θεοῦ ἡμῶν ἐπὶ τῶν μετώπων αὐτῶν. 4 καὶ ἤκουσα τὸν
servants of our God *our* on *{the}* their foreheads." *their* And I heard the
1529 3836 7005 2536 7005 2093 3836 899 3587 899 2779 201 3836
n.apm d.gsm n.gsm r.gp.1 p.g d.gpn n.gpn r.gpm.3 cj v.aai.1s d.asm

ἀριθμὸν τῶν ἐσφραγισμένων, ἑκατὸν ⌊τεσσεράκοντα τέσσαρες⌋ χιλιάδες,
number of those who were sealed, one hundred forty-four thousand,
750 3836 5381 1669 5477 5475 5942
n.asm d.gpm pt.rp.gpm a.npf a.npf a.npf n.npf

ἐσφραγισμένοι ἐκ πάσης φυλῆς → υἱῶν Ἰσραήλ· 5 ἐκ φυλῆς Ἰούδα δώδεκα
sealed from every tribe of the sons of Israel: from the tribe of Judah twelve
5381 1666 4246 5876 5626 2702 1666 5876 2683 1557
pt.rp.npm p.g a.gsf n.gsf n.gpm n.gsm p.g n.gsf n.gsm a.npf

χιλιάδες ἐσφραγισμένοι, ἐκ φυλῆς Ῥουβὴν δώδεκα χιλιάδες, ἐκ φυλῆς
thousand sealed, from the tribe of Reuben twelve thousand, from the tribe
5942 5381 1666 5876 4857 1557 5942 1666 5876
n.npf pt.rp.npm p.g n.gsf n.gsm a.npf n.npf p.g n.gsf

Γὰδ δώδεκα χιλιάδες, 6 ἐκ φυλῆς Ἀσὴρ δώδεκα χιλιάδες, ἐκ φυλῆς
of Gad twelve thousand, from the tribe of Asher twelve thousand, from the tribe
1122 1557 5942 1666 5876 818 1557 5942 1666 5876
n.gsm a.npf n.npf p.g n.gsf n.gsm a.npf n.npf p.g n.gsf

Νεφθαλὶμ δώδεκα χιλιάδες, ἐκ φυλῆς Μανασσῆ δώδεκα χιλιάδες, 7 ἐκ
of Naphtali twelve thousand, from the tribe of Manasseh twelve thousand, from the
3750 1557 5942 1666 5876 3442 1557 5942 1666
n.gsm a.npf n.npf p.g n.gsf n.gsm a.npf n.npf p.g

NASB

and who is able to
stand?"

An Interlude

7:1 After this I
saw four angels
standing at the
four corners of the
earth, holding back
the four winds of
the earth, so that
no wind would
blow on the earth
or on the sea or on
any tree. 2 And I
saw another angel
ascending from
the rising of the
sun, having the
seal of the living
God; and he cried
out with a loud
voice to the four
angels to whom
it was granted to
harm the earth and
the sea, 3 saying,
"Do not harm the
earth or the sea or
the trees until we
have sealed the
bond-servants of
our God on their
foreheads."

The 144,000

4 And I heard the
number of those
who were sealed,
one hundred and
forty-four thousand
sealed from every
tribe of the sons of
Israel:
5 from the tribe
of Judah,
twelve thou-
sand *were*
sealed, from
the tribe
of Reuben
twelve thou-
sand, from
the tribe of
Gad twelve
thousand,
6 from the tribe
of Asher
twelve thou-
sand, from
the tribe of
Naphtali
twelve thou-
sand, from
the tribe of
Manasseh
twelve thou-
sand,
7 from the tribe

NIV

7 from the tribe
of Simeon
12,000,
from the tribe
of Levi
12,000,
from the tribe
of Issachar
12,000,
8 from the tribe
of Zebulun
12,000,
from the tribe
of Joseph
12,000,
from the tribe
of Benjamin
12,000.

The Great Multitude in White Robes

9 After this I
looked, and there
before me was a
great multitude
that no one could
count, from every
nation, tribe, peo-
ple and language,
standing before the
throne and before
the Lamb. They
were wearing
white robes and
were holding palm
branches in their
hands. 10 And they
cried out in a loud
voice:

"Salvation belongs
to our God,
who sits on the
throne,
and to the Lamb."

11 All the angels
were standing
around the throne
and around the el-
ders and the four
living creatures.
They fell down on
their faces before
the throne and
worshiped God,
12 saying:

"Amen!
Praise and glory
and wisdom and
thanks and
honor
and power and
strength
be to our God for
ever and
ever.
Amen!"

13 Then one of the
elders asked me,
"These in

φυλῆς Συμεὼν δώδεκα χιλιάδες, ἐκ φυλῆς Λευὶ δώδεκα χιλιάδες, ἐκ
tribe of Simeon twelve thousand, from the tribe of Levi twelve thousand, from the
5876 5208 1557 5942 1666 5876 3322 1557 5942 1666
n.gsf n.gsm a.npf n.npf p.g n.gsf n.gsm a.npf n.npf p.g

φυλῆς Ἰσσαχὰρ δώδεκα χιλιάδες, 8 ἐκ φυλῆς Ζαβουλὼν δώδεκα χιλιάδες, ἐκ
tribe of Issachar twelve thousand, from the tribe of Zebulun twelve thousand, from
5876 2704 1557 5942 1666 5876 2404 1557 5942 1666
n.gsf n.gsm a.npf n.npf p.g n.gsf n.gsm a.npf n.npf p.g

φυλῆς Ἰωσὴφ δώδεκα χιλιάδες, ἐκ φυλῆς Βενιαμὶν δώδεκα χιλιάδες
the tribe of Joseph twelve thousand, from the tribe of Benjamin twelve thousand
5876 2737 1557 5942 1666 5876 1021 1557 5942
n.gsf n.gsm a.npf n.npf p.g n.gsf n.gsm a.npf n.npf

ἐσφραγισμένοι. 9 μετὰ ταῦτα εἶδον, καὶ ἰδοὺ ὄχλος πολύς, ὃν
sealed. After this I looked, and behold, a vast multitude *vast* that no one
5381 3552 4047 1625 2779 2627 4498 4063 4498 4005 4029 4029
pt.rp.npm p.a r.apn v.aai.1s cj j n.nsm a.nsm r.asm

ἀριθμῆσαι αὐτὸν οὐδεὶς ἐδύνατο, ἐκ παντὸς ἔθνους καὶ φυλῶν καὶ
could count, *{it}* *no one* *could* people from every nation, *{and}* tribe, *{and}*
1538 749 899 4029 1538 1666 4246 1620 2779 5876 2779
f.aa r.asm.3 a.nsm v.ipi.3s p.g a.gsn n.gsn cj n.gpf cj

λαῶν καὶ γλωσσῶν ἑστῶτες ἐνώπιον τοῦ θρόνου καὶ ἐνώπιον τοῦ ἀρνίου
⌞cultural group,⌟ and language, standing before the throne and before the Lamb,
3295 2779 1185 2705 1967 3836 2585 2779 1967 3836 768
n.gpm cj n.gpf pt.ra.npm p.g d.gsm n.gsm cj p.g d.gsn n.gsn

περιβεβλημένους στολὰς λευκάς καὶ φοίνικες ἐν ταῖς χερσὶν αὐτῶν,
dressed in white robes, *white* with palm branches in *{the}* their hands, *their*
4314 3328 5124 3328 2779 5836 1877 3836 899 5931 899
pt.rp.apm n.apf a.apf cj n.npm p.d d.dpf n.dpf r.gpm.3

10 καὶ κράζουσιν → φωνῇ μεγάλῃ λέγοντες, ἡ σωτηρία τῷ θεῷ
and they cried out in a loud voice, *loud* saying, *{the}* "Salvation belongs to our God
2779 3189 3489 5889 3489 3306 3836 5401 3836 7005 2536
cj v.pai.3p n.dsf a.dsf pt.pa.npm d.nsf n.nsf d.dsm n.dsm

ἡμῶν τῷ καθημένῳ ἐπὶ τῷ θρόνῳ καὶ τῷ ἀρνίῳ. 11 καὶ πάντες οἱ ἄγγελοι
our who is seated on the throne and ⌞to the⌟ Lamb!" And all the angels
7005 3836 2764 2093 3836 2585 2779 3836 768 2779 4246 3836 34
r.gp.1 d.dsm pt.pm.dsm p.d d.dsm n.dsm cj d.dsn n.dsn cj a.npm d.npm n.npm

εἱστήκεισαν κύκλῳ τοῦ θρόνου καὶ τῶν πρεσβυτέρων καὶ τῶν τεσσάρων
were standing around the throne and around the elders and the four
2705 3241 3836 2585 2779 3836 4565 2779 3836 5475
v.lai.3p p.g d.gsm n.gsm cj d.gpm a.gpm cj d.gpn a.gpn

ζῴων καὶ ἔπεσαν ἐνώπιον τοῦ θρόνου ἐπὶ τὰ πρόσωπα
⌞living creatures,⌟ and they fell on their faces before the throne *on* *{the}* *faces*
2442 2779 4406 2093 899 4725 1967 3836 2585 2093 3836 4725
n.gpn cj v.aai.3p p.g d.gsm n.gsm p.a d.apn n.apn

αὐτῶν καὶ προσεκύνησαν τῷ θεῷ 12 λέγοντες, ἀμήν, ἡ εὐλογία καὶ ἡ δόξα
their and worshiped *{the}* God, saying, "Amen! *{the}* Praise and *{the}* glory
899 2779 4686 3836 2536 3306 297 3836 2330 2779 3836 1518
r.gpm.3 cj v.aai.3p d.dsm n.dsm pt.pa.npm pl d.nsf n.nsf cj d.nsf n.nsf

καὶ ἡ σοφία καὶ ἡ εὐχαριστία καὶ ἡ τιμὴ καὶ ἡ δύναμις καὶ ἡ ἰσχὺς
and *{the}* wisdom and *{the}* thanksgiving and *{the}* honor and *{the}* power and *{the}* might
2779 3836 5053 2779 3836 2374 2779 3836 5507 2779 3836 1539 2779 3836 2709
cj d.nsf n.nsf cj d.nsf n.nsf cj d.nsf n.nsf cj d.nsf n.nsf cj d.nsf n.nsf

τῷ θεῷ ἡμῶν εἰς τοὺς ⌞αἰῶνας τῶν αἰώνων·⌟ ἀμήν. 13 καὶ ἀπεκρίθη
be to our God *our* for all time! Amen." Then *addressed*
3836 7005 2536 7005 1650 3836 172 3836 172 297 2779 646
d.dsm n.dsm r.gp.1 p.a d.apm n.apm d.gpm n.gpm pl cj v.api.3s

εἷς ἐκ τῶν πρεσβυτέρων λέγων μοι, οὗτοι οἱ περιβεβλημένοι τὰς
one of the elders addressed me, saying, *me* "These *{the}* dressed in *{the}*
1651 1666 3836 4565 646 1609 3306 1609 4047 3836 4314 3836
a.nsm p.g d.gpm a.gpm pt.pa.nsm r.ds.1 r.npm d.npm pt.rp.npm d.apf

NASB

of Simeon
twelve thou-
sand, from
the tribe of
Levi twelve
thousand,
from the tribe
of Issachar
twelve thou-
sand,
8 from the tribe
of Zebulun
twelve thou-
sand, from
the tribe of
Joseph twelve
thousand,
from the tribe
of Benjamin,
twelve thou-
sand *were*
sealed.

A Multitude from the Tribulation

9 After these things
I looked, and be-
hold, a great multi-
tude which no one
could count, from
every nation and
all tribes and peo-
ples and tongues,
standing before the
throne and before
the Lamb, clothed
in white robes,
and palm branches
were in their hands;
10 and they cry out
with a loud voice,
saying,
"Salvation to our
God who sits on
the throne, and to
the Lamb." 11 And
all the angels were
standing around
the throne and
around the elders
and the four living
creatures; and they
fell on their faces
before the throne
and worshiped
God, 12 saying,
"Amen, blessing
and glory and wis-
dom and thanks-
giving and honor
and power and
might, *be* to our
God forever and
ever. Amen."
13 Then one of the
elders answered,
saying to me,
"These who are
clothed in the

NIV

white robes—who are they, and where did they come from?"

[14]I answered, "Sir, you know."

And he said, "These are they who have come out of the great tribulation; they have washed their robes and made them white in the blood of the Lamb.

[15]Therefore,

"they are before the throne of God
and serve him day and night in his temple;
and he who sits on the throne
will shelter them with his presence.
[16]'Never again will they hunger;
never again will they thirst.
The sun will not beat down on them,'[a]
nor any scorching heat.
[17]For the Lamb at the center of the throne
will be their shepherd;
'he will lead them to springs of living water.'[b]
'And God will wipe away every tear from their eyes.'[c]"

The Seventh Seal and the Golden Censer

8 When he opened the seventh seal, there was silence in heaven for about half an hour.

[2]And I saw the seven angels who stand before God, and seven trumpets were given to them.

[3]Another angel, who had a golden censer, came and stood at the altar. He was given much incense to

---

στολὰς τὰς λευκὰς τίνες εἰσὶν καὶ πόθεν ἦλθον; ↰ [14]καὶ
white robes {the} white — who are they and where ⌞did they come⌟ from?" {and}
3328 5124 3836 3328 5515 1639 2779 4470 2262 4470 2779
n.apf d.apf a.apf r.npm v.pai.3p cj cj v.aai.3p cj

εἴρηκα αὐτῷ, κύριέ μου, σὺ οἶδας. καὶ εἶπέν μοι, οὗτοί εἰσιν
I said to him, "My lord, My you ⌞are the one who knows."⌟ Then he said to me, "These are
3306 899 1609 3261 1609 5148 3857 2779 3306 1609 4047 1639
v.rai.1s r.dsm.3 n.vsm r.gs.1 r.ns.2 v.rai.2s cj v.aai.3s r.ds.1 r.npm v.pai.3p

οἱ ἐρχόμενοι ἐκ τῆς θλίψεως τῆς μεγάλης καὶ ἔπλυναν
the ⌞ones who have come⌟ ⌞out of⌟ the great tribulation; {the} great {and} ⌞they have washed⌟
3836 2262 1666 3836 3489 2568 3836 3489 2779 4459
d.npm pt.pm.npm p.g d.gsf n.gsf d.gsf a.gsf cj v.aai.3p

τὰς στολὰς αὐτῶν καὶ → ἐλεύκαναν αὐτὰς ἐν τῷ αἵματι τοῦ ἀρνίου.
{the} their robes their and made them white them in the blood of the Lamb.
3836 899 5124 899 2779 899 3326 899 1877 3836 135 3836 768
d.apf n.apf r.gpm.3 cj v.aai.3p r.apf.3 p.d d.dsn n.dsn d.gsn n.gsn

[15]διὰ τοῦτό εἰσιν ἐνώπιον τοῦ θρόνου τοῦ θεοῦ καὶ λατρεύουσιν αὐτῷ ἡμέρας
For this reason they are before the throne of God, and serve him day
1328 4047 1639 1967 3836 2585 3836 2536 2779 3302 899 2465
p.a r.asn v.pai.3p p.g d.gsm n.gsm d.gsm n.gsm cj v.pai.3p r.dsm.3 n.gsf

καὶ νυκτὸς ἐν τῷ ναῷ αὐτοῦ, καὶ ὁ καθήμενος ἐπὶ τοῦ θρόνου
and night in {the} his temple, his and the one seated on the throne
2779 3816 1877 3836 899 3724 899 2779 3836 2764 2093 3836 2585
cj n.gsf p.d d.dsm n.dsm r.gsm.3 cj d.nsm pt.pm.nsm p.g d.gsm n.gsm

σκηνώσει ἐπ' αὐτούς. [16]οὐ πεινάσουσιν ἔτι οὐδὲ διψήσουσιν
will be a shelter over them. No longer will they go hungry, longer neither will they thirst
5012 2093 899 4024 2285 4277 2285 4028 1498
v.fai.3s p.a r.apm.3 pl v.fai.3p adv cj v.fai.3p

ἔτι οὐδὲ ↱ μὴ πέσῃ ἐπ' αὐτοὺς ὁ ἥλιος οὐδὲ πᾶν καῦμα,
again; {nor} the sun will not beat down upon them, the sun nor any ⌞scorching heat;⌟
2285 4028 3836 2463 4406 3590 4406 2093 899 3836 2463 4028 4246 3008
adv cj pl v.aas.3s p.a r.apm.3 d.nsm n.nsm cj a.nsn n.nsn

[17]ὅτι τὸ ἀρνίον τὸ ⌞ἀνὰ μέσον⌟ τοῦ θρόνου ποιμανεῖ αὐτοὺς καὶ ὁδηγήσει
for the Lamb ⌞at the⌟ center of the throne will shepherd them and guide
4022 3836 768 3836 324 3545 3836 2585 4477 899 2779 3842
cj d.nsn n.nsn d.nsn p.a n.asn d.gsm n.gsm v.fai.3s r.apm.3 cj v.fai.3s

αὐτοὺς ἐπὶ ζωῆς πηγὰς ὑδάτων, καὶ ἐξαλείψει ὁ θεὸς πᾶν
them to springs of living springs water, and God will wipe away {the} God every
899 2093 4380 2437 4380 5623 2779 2536 1981 3836 2536 4246
r.apm.3 p.a n.gsf n.apf n.gpn cj v.fai.3s d.nsm n.nsm a.asn

δάκρυον ἐκ τῶν ὀφθαλμῶν αὐτῶν.
tear from {the} their eyes." their
1232 1666 3836 899 4057 899
n.asn p.g d.gpm n.gpm r.gpm.3

[8:1]καὶ ὅταν ἤνοιξεν τὴν σφραγῖδα τὴν ἑβδόμην, ἐγένετο σιγὴ
{and} When the Lamb opened the seventh seal, {the} seventh there was silence
2779 4020 487 3836 1575 5382 3836 1575 1181 4968
cj cj v.aai.3s d.asf n.asf d.asf a.asf v.ami.3s n.nsf

ἐν τῷ οὐρανῷ ὡς ἡμιώριον. [2]καὶ εἶδον τοὺς ἑπτὰ ἀγγέλους οἳ
in {the} heaven ⌞for about⌟ half an hour. Then I saw the seven angels who stand
1877 3836 4041 6055 2469 2779 1625 3836 2231 34 4005 2705
p.d d.dsm n.dsm pl n.asn cj v.aai.1s d.apm a.apm n.apm r.npm

ἐνώπιον τοῦ θεοῦ ἑστήκασιν, καὶ ἐδόθησαν αὐτοῖς ἑπτὰ σάλπιγγες. [3]καὶ
before {the} God, stand and to them were given to them seven trumpets. And
1967 3836 2536 2705 2779 899 899 1443 899 2231 4894 2779
p.g d.gsm n.gsm v.rai.3p cj v.api.3p r.dpm.3 a.npf n.npf cj

ἄλλος ἄγγελος ἦλθεν καὶ ἐστάθη ἐπὶ τοῦ θυσιαστηρίου ἔχων λιβανωτὸν
another angel came and stood at the altar, holding a golden censer.
257 34 2262 2779 2705 2093 3836 2603 2400 5997 3338
r.nsm n.nsm v.aai.3s cj v.api.3s p.g d.gsn n.gsn pt.pa.nsm n.asm

χρυσοῦν, καὶ ἐδόθη αὐτῷ θυμιάματα πολλά, ἵνα
golden {and} To him was given To him a large quantity of incense large quantity to
5997 2779 899 899 1443 899 4498 4498 2592 4498 2671
a.asm cj v.api.3s r.dsm.3 n.npn a.npn cj

NASB

white robes, who are they, and where have they come from?" [14]I said to him, "My lord, you know." And he said to me, "These are the ones who come out of the great tribulation, and they have washed their robes and made them white in the blood of the Lamb. [15]For this reason, they are before the throne of God; and they serve Him day and night in His temple; and He who sits on the throne will spread His tabernacle over them. [16]They will hunger no longer, nor thirst anymore; nor will the sun beat down on them, nor any heat; [17]for the Lamb in the center of the throne will be their shepherd, and will guide them to springs of the water of life; and God will wipe every tear from their eyes."

The Seventh Seal—the Trumpets

[8:1]When the Lamb broke the seventh seal, there was silence in heaven for about half an hour. [2]And I saw the seven angels who stand before God, and seven trumpets were given to them.

[3]Another angel came and stood at the altar, holding a golden censer; and much incense was given to him, so

---

[a] 16 Isaiah 49:10
[b] 17 Isaiah 49:10
[c] 17 Isaiah 25:8

NIV

offer, with the
prayers of all
God's people, on
the golden altar in
front of the throne.
4 The smoke of the
incense, together
with the prayers
of God's people,
went up before
God from the an-
gel's hand. 5 Then
the angel took the
censer, filled it
with fire from the
altar, and hurled it
on the earth; and
there came peals
of thunder, rum-
blings, flashes of
lightning and an
earthquake.

The Trumpets

6 Then the seven
angels who had
the seven trumpets
prepared to sound
them.
7 The first an-
gel sounded his
trumpet, and there
came hail and fire
mixed with blood,
and it was hurled
down on the earth.
A third of the
earth was burned
up, a third of the
trees were burned
up, and all the
green grass was
burned up.
8 The second
angel sounded
his trumpet, and
something like a
huge mountain, all
ablaze, was thrown
into the sea. A
third of the sea
turned into blood,
9 a third of the liv-
ing creatures in
the sea died, and a
third of the ships
were destroyed.
10 The third angel
sounded his trum-
pet, and a great
star, blazing like a
torch,

δώσει ταῖς προσευχαῖς → τῶν ἁγίων πάντων ἐπὶ τὸ θυσιαστήριον
offer up, ⌊with the⌋ prayers of all the saints, *all* on the golden altar
1443 3836 4666 4246 3836 41 4246 2093 3836 5997 2603
v.fai.3s d.dpf n.dpf d.gpm a.gpm a.gpm p.a d.asn n.asn

τὸ χρυσοῦν τὸ ἐνώπιον τοῦ θρόνου. 4 καὶ ἀνέβη ὁ καπνὸς τῶν θυμιαμάτων
{the} *golden* that is before the throne. And *rose* the smoke of the incense,
3836 5997 3836 1967 3836 2585 2779 326 3836 2837 3836 2592
d.asn a.asn d.asn p.g d.gsm n.gsm cj v.aai.3s d.nsm n.nsm d.gpn n.gpn

ταῖς προσευχαῖς τῶν ἁγίων ἐκ χειρὸς τοῦ ἀγγέλου ἐνώπιον
⌊with the⌋ prayers of the saints, rose before God from the hand of the angel. *before*
3836 4666 3836 41 326 1967 2536 1666 5931 3836 34 1967
d.dpf n.dpf d.gpm a.gpm p.g n.gsf d.gsm n.gsm p.g

τοῦ θεοῦ. 5 καὶ εἴληφεν ὁ ἄγγελος τὸν λιβανωτὸν καὶ ἐγέμισεν αὐτὸν
{the} *God* Then the angel took *the* *angel* the censer and filled it
3836 2536 2779 3836 34 3284 3836 34 3836 3338 2779 1153 899
d.gsm n.gsm cj v.rai.3s d.nsm n.nsm d.asm n.asm cj v.aai.3s r.asm.3

ἐκ τοῦ πυρὸς τοῦ θυσιαστηρίου καὶ ἔβαλεν ← εἰς τὴν γῆν, καὶ ἐγένοντο
with *{the}* fire ⌊from the⌋ altar and threw it down on the earth, and there were
1666 3836 4786 3836 2603 2779 965 1650 3836 1178 2779 1181
p.g d.gsn n.gsn d.gsn n.gsn cj v.aai.3s p.a d.asf n.asf cj v.ami.3p

βρονταὶ καὶ φωναὶ καὶ ἀστραπαὶ καὶ σεισμός. 6 καὶ οἱ ἑπτὰ
peals of thunder, *{and}* rumblings, *{and}* flashes of lightning, and an earthquake. And the seven
1103 2779 5889 2779 847 2779 4939 2779 3836 2231
n.npf cj n.npf cj n.npf cj n.nsm cj d.npm a.npm

ἄγγελοι οἱ ἔχοντες τὰς ἑπτὰ σάλπιγγας ἡτοίμασαν αὑτοὺς ↰ ἵνα σαλπίσωσιν.
angels who had the seven trumpets made themselves ready to blow
34 3836 2400 3836 2231 4894 2286 899 2286 2671 4895
n.npm d.npm pt.pa.npm d.apf a.apf n.apf v.aai.3p r.apm.3 cj v.aas.3p

7 καὶ ὁ πρῶτος ἐσάλπισεν· καὶ ἐγένετο χάλαζα καὶ πῦρ
them. *{and}* The first angel blew his trumpet, and there followed hail and fire,
2779 3836 4755 4895 2779 1181 5898 2779 4786
cj d.nsm a.nsm v.aai.3s cj v.ami.3s n.nsf cj n.nsn

μεμιγμένα ἐν αἵματι καὶ ἐβλήθη εἰς τὴν γῆν, καὶ τὸ τρίτον τῆς γῆς
mixed with blood, and ⌊it was thrown down⌋ on the earth, and a third of the earth
3624 1877 135 2779 965 1650 3836 1178 2779 3836 5569 3836 1178
pt.rp.npn p.d n.dsn cj v.api.3s p.a d.asf n.asf cj d.nsn a.nsn d.gsf n.gsf

κατεκάη καὶ τὸ τρίτον τῶν δένδρων κατεκάη καὶ πᾶς χόρτος
⌊was burned up,⌋ and a third of the trees ⌊were burned up,⌋ and all the green grass
2876 2779 3836 5569 3836 1285 2876 2779 4246 5952 5965
v.api.3s cj d.nsn a.nsn d.gpn n.gpn v.api.3s cj a.nsm n.nsm

χλωρὸς κατεκάη. 8 καὶ ὁ δεύτερος ἄγγελος ἐσάλπισεν· καὶ ὡς
green ⌊was burned up.⌋ *{and}* The second angel blew his trumpet, and something like a
5952 2876 2779 3836 1311 34 4895 2779 6055
a.nsm v.api.3s cj d.nsm a.nsm n.nsm v.aai.3s cj pl

ὄρος μέγα πυρὶ καιόμενον ἐβλήθη εἰς τὴν θάλασσαν,
great mountain, *great* burning ⌊with fire,⌋ *burning* ⌊was thrown down⌋ into the sea,
3489 4001 3489 2794 4786 2794 965 1650 3836 2498
n.nsn a.nsn n.dsn pt.pp.nsn v.api.3s p.a d.asf n.asf

καὶ ἐγένετο τὸ τρίτον τῆς θαλάσσης αἷμα 9 καὶ ἀπέθανεν
and a third of the sea turned into *a* *third* *of the* *sea* blood, *{and}* *died*
2779 3836 5569 3836 3836 2498 1181 3836 5569 3836 2498 135 2779 633
cj v.ami.3s d.nsn a.nsn d.gsf n.gsf n.nsn cj v.aai.3s

τὸ τρίτον τῶν κτισμάτων τῶν ἐν τῇ θαλάσσῃ τὰ ⌊ἔχοντα ψυχάς⌋
a third of the living creatures *{the}* in the sea *{the}* *living* died,
3836 5569 3836 2400 3233 3836 1877 3836 2498 3836 2400 6034 633
d.nsn a.nsn d.gpn n.gpn d.gpn p.d d.dsf n.dsf d.npn pt.pa.npn n.apf

καὶ τὸ τρίτον τῶν πλοίων διεφθάρησαν. 10 καὶ ὁ τρίτος ἄγγελος ἐσάλπισεν·
and a third of the ships were destroyed. *{and}* The third angel blew his trumpet,
2779 3836 5569 3836 4450 1425 2779 3836 5569 34 4895
cj d.nsn a.nsn d.gpn n.gpn v.api.3p cj d.nsm a.nsm n.nsm v.aai.3s

καὶ ἔπεσεν ἐκ τοῦ οὐρανοῦ ἀστὴρ μέγας καιόμενος ὡς λαμπὰς καὶ
and there fell from *{the}* heaven a great star, *great* blazing like a torch, and
2779 4406 1666 3836 4041 3489 843 3489 2794 6055 3286 2779
cj v.aai.3s p.g d.gsm n.gsm n.nsm a.nsm pt.pp.nsm pl n.nsf cj

NASB

that he might add
it to the prayers of
all the saints on
the golden altar
which was before
the throne. 4 And
the smoke of the
incense, with the
prayers of the
saints, went up be-
fore God out of the
angel's hand. 5 Then
the angel took the
censer and filled it
with the fire of the
altar, and threw it
to the earth; and
there followed
peals of thunder
and sounds and
flashes of lightning
and an earthquake.
6 And the seven
angels who had the
seven trumpets pre-
pared themselves
to sound them.
7 The first sound-
ed, and there came
hail and fire, mixed
with blood, and
they were thrown
to the earth; and a
third of the earth
was burned up, and
a third of the trees
were burned up,
and all the green
grass was burned
up.
8 The second an-
gel sounded, and
something like a
great mountain
burning with fire
was thrown into
the sea; and a third
of the sea became
blood, 9 and a third
of the creatures
which were in the
sea and had life,
died; and a third
of the ships were
destroyed.
10 The third angel
sounded, and a
great star fell from
heaven, burning
like a torch, and

NIV

fell from the sky
on a third of the
rivers and on the
springs of water—
11 the name of the
star is Worm-
wood.[a] A third of
the waters turned
bitter, and many
people died from
the waters that had
become bitter.
12 The fourth an-
gel sounded his
trumpet, and a
third of the sun
was struck, a third
of the moon, and a
third of the stars,
so that a third of
them turned dark.
A third of the day
was without light,
and also a third of
the night.
13 As I watched,
I heard an eagle
that was flying in
midair call out in a
loud voice: "Woe!
Woe! Woe to the
inhabitants of the
earth, because of
the trumpet blasts
about to be sound-
ed by the other
three angels!"
9 The fifth angel
sounded his
trumpet, and I saw
a star that had fall-
en from the sky to
the earth. The star
was given the key
to the shaft of the
Abyss. 2 When he
opened the Abyss,
smoke rose from
it like the smoke
from a gigantic
furnace. The sun
and sky were dark-
ened by the smoke
from the Abyss.

[a] 11 Wormwood is a bitter substance.

ἔπεσεν ἐπὶ τὸ τρίτον τῶν ποταμῶν καὶ ἐπὶ τὰς πηγὰς τῶν ὑδάτων, 11 καὶ τὸ
it fell on a third of the rivers and on the springs of water. *{and}* The
4406 2093 3836 5569 3836 4532 2779 2093 3836 4380 3836 5623 2779 3836
v.aai.3s p.a d.asn a.asn d.gpm n.gpm cj p.a d.apf n.apf d.gpn n.gpn cj d.nsn

ὄνομα τοῦ ἀστέρος λέγεται ὁ Ἄψινθος, καὶ ἐγένετο τὸ τρίτον τῶν ὑδάτων
name of the star is *{the}* Wormwood. *{and}* *became* A third of the waters
3950 3836 843 3306 3836 952 2779 1181 3836 5569 3836 5623
n.nsn d.gsm n.gsm v.ppi.3s d.nsm n.nsm cj v.ami.3s d.nsn a.nsn d.gpn n.gpn

εἰς ἄψινθον καὶ πολλοὶ τῶν ἀνθρώπων ἀπέθανον ἐκ τῶν ὑδάτων ὅτι
became *{into}* wormwood, and many *{the}* people died from the waters because
1181 1650 952 2779 4498 3836 476 633 1666 3836 5623 4022
p.a n.asm cj a.npm d.gpm n.gpm v.aai.3p p.g d.gpn n.gpn cj

ἐπικράνθησαν. 12 καὶ ὁ τέταρτος ἄγγελος ἐσάλπισεν· καὶ ἐπλήγη τὸ
⌊they had been made bitter.⌋ *{and}* The fourth angel blew his trumpet, and *was struck* a
4393 2779 3836 5480 34 4895 2779 4448 3836
v.api.3p cj d.nsm a.nsm n.nsm v.aai.3s cj v.api.3s d.nsn

τρίτον τοῦ ἡλίου καὶ τὸ τρίτον τῆς σελήνης καὶ τὸ τρίτον τῶν
third of the sun was struck, and a third of the moon, and a third of the
5569 3836 2463 4448 4448 2779 3836 5569 3836 4943 2779 3836 5569 3836
a.nsn d.gsm n.gsm cj d.nsn a.nsn d.gsf n.gsf cj d.nsn a.nsn d.gpm

ἀστέρων, ἵνα σκοτισθῇ τὸ τρίτον αὐτῶν καὶ
stars, so that a third of them were darkened; *a* *third* *of them* *{and}* for a third of
843 2671 3836 5569 899 899 5029 3836 5569 899 2779 3836 3836 5569
n.gpm cj v.aps.3s d.nsn a.nsn r.gpm.3 cj

ἡ ἡμέρα ↱ ↱ μὴ φάνῃ τὸ τρίτον αὐτῆς καὶ ἡ νὺξ ὁμοίως.
the day there was no light, *for a third* *{of it}* and for a third of the night as well.
3836 2465 5743 5743 3590 5743 3836 5569 899 2779 3836 3816 3931
d.nsf n.nsf pl v.aas.3s d.asn a.asn r.gsf.3 cj d.nsf n.nsf adv

13 καὶ εἶδον, καὶ ἤκουσα ἑνὸς ἀετοῦ πετομένου ἐν
Then I looked, and I heard an eagle crying with a loud voice as it flew directly
2779 1625 2779 201 1651 108 3306 5889 3489 5889 4375 1877
cj v.aai.1s cj v.aai.1s a.gsm n.gsm pt.pm.gsm p.d

μεσουρανήματι λέγοντος φωνῇ μεγάλῃ, οὐαὶ οὐαὶ οὐαὶ τοὺς κατοικοῦντας ἐπὶ
overhead, *crying* *with voice* *loud* "Woe, woe, woe to those who live on
3547 3306 5889 3489 4026 4026 4026 3836 2997 2093
n.dsn pt.pa.gsm n.dsf a.dsf j j j d.apm pt.pa.apm p.g

τῆς γῆς ἐκ τῶν → λοιπῶν φωνῶν τῆς σάλπιγγος τῶν τριῶν
the earth ⌊because of⌋ the blasts of the other *blasts* *{the}* trumpets that the three
3836 1178 1666 3836 5889 3370 5889 3836 4894 3836 5552
d.gsf n.gsf p.g d.gpf a.gpf n.gpf d.gsf n.gsf d.gpm a.gpm

ἀγγέλων τῶν μελλόντων σαλπίζειν.
angels *{the}* are about to blow!"
34 3836 3516 4895
n.gpm d.gpm pt.pa.gpm f.pa

9:1 καὶ ὁ πέμπτος ἄγγελος ἐσάλπισεν· καὶ εἶδον ἀστέρα ἐκ τοῦ
{and} The fifth angel blew his trumpet, and I saw a star fallen from the
2779 3836 4286 34 4895 2779 1625 843 4406 1666 3836
cj d.nsm a.nsm n.nsm v.aai.3s cj v.aai.1s n.asm p.g d.gsm

οὐρανοῦ πεπτωκότα εἰς τὴν γῆν, καὶ ἐδόθη αὐτῷ ἡ κλεὶς τοῦ φρέατος
sky *fallen* to the earth; and he was given *he* the key to the shaft
4041 4406 1650 3836 1178 2779 899 1443 899 3836 3090 3836 5853
n.gsm pt.ra.asm p.a d.asf n.asf cj v.api.3s r.dsm.3 d.nsf n.nsf d.gsn n.gsn

τῆς ἀβύσσου 2 καὶ ἤνοιξεν τὸ φρέαρ τῆς ἀβύσσου, καὶ ἀνέβη
of the abyss. *{and}* He opened the shaft of the abyss, and from the shaft rose
3836 12 2779 487 3836 5853 3836 12 2779 1666 3836 5853 326
d.gsf n.gsf cj v.aai.3s d.asn n.asn d.gsf n.gsf cj v.aai.3s

καπνὸς ἐκ τοῦ φρέατος ὡς καπνὸς → καμίνου μεγάλης, καὶ ἐσκοτώθη
smoke *from the shaft* like the smoke of a giant furnace, *giant* and *were darkened*
2837 1666 3836 5853 6055 2837 3489 2825 3489 2779 5031
n.nsm p.g d.gsn n.gsn pl n.nsm n.gsf a.gsf cj v.api.3s

ὁ ἥλιος καὶ ὁ ἀὴρ ἐκ τοῦ καπνοῦ τοῦ φρέατος.
the sun and the air were darkened with smoke from *with* *smoke* the shaft.
3836 2463 2779 3836 113 5031 5031 3836 2837 1666 3836 2837 3836 5853
d.nsm n.nsm cj d.nsm n.nsm p.g d.gsm n.gsm d.gsn n.gsn

NASB

it fell on a third
of the rivers and
on the springs of
waters. 11 The name
of the star is called
Wormwood; and a
third of the waters
became worm-
wood, and many
men died from the
waters, because
they were made
bitter.
12 The fourth angel
sounded, and a
third of the sun and
a third of the moon
and a third of the
stars were struck,
so that a third of
them would be
darkened and the
day would not
shine for a third of
it, and the night in
the same way.
13 Then I looked,
and I heard an
eagle flying in
midheaven, saying
with a loud voice,
"Woe, woe, woe to
those who dwell on
the earth, because
of the remaining
blasts of the trum-
pet of the three an-
gels who are about
to sound!"

The Fifth Trumpet—the Bottomless Pit

9:1 Then the fifth
angel sounded, and
I saw a star from
heaven which had
fallen to the earth;
and the key of the
bottomless pit was
given to him. 2 He
opened the bottom-
less pit, and smoke
went up out of the
pit, like the smoke
of a great furnace;
and the sun and the
air were darkened
by the smoke of
the pit.

NIV

3And out of the
smoke locusts
came down on the
earth and were
given power like
that of scorpions
of the earth. 4They
were told not to
harm the grass of
the earth or any
plant or tree, but
only those people
who did not have
the seal of God on
their foreheads.
5They were not
allowed to kill
them but only to
torture them for
five months. And
the agony they
suffered was like
that of the sting of
a scorpion when
it strikes. 6During
those days people
will seek death but
will not find it;
they will long to
die, but death will
elude them.
7The locusts
looked like hors-
es prepared for
battle. On their
heads they wore
something like
crowns of gold,
and their faces
resembled human
faces. 8Their hair
was like women's
hair, and their
teeth were like li-
ons' teeth. 9They
had breastplates
like breastplates of
iron, and the sound
of their wings was
like the thundering
of many horses
and chariots rush-
ing into battle.
10They had tails

3καὶ ἐκ τοῦ καπνοῦ ἐξῆλθον ἀκρίδες εἰς τὴν γῆν, καὶ ἐδόθη αὐταῖς
Then ⌞out of⌟ the smoke came locusts onto the earth, and they were given *they*
2779 1666 3836 2837 2002 210 1650 3836 1178 2779 899 1443 899
cj p.g d.gsm n.gsm v.aai.3p n.npf p.a d.asf n.asf cj v.api.3s r.dpf.3

ἐξουσία ὡς ἔχουσιν ἐξουσίαν οἱ σκορπίοι τῆς γῆς. 4καὶ ἐρρέθη
power like *{they have}* the power of *{the}* scorpions of the earth. *{and}* They were told
2026 6055 2400 2026 3836 5026 3836 1178 2779 899 3306
n.nsf cj v.pai.3p n.asf d.npm n.npm d.gsf n.gsf cj v.api.3s

αὐταῖς ἵνα μὴ ἀδικήσουσιν τὸν χόρτον τῆς γῆς οὐδὲ πᾶν χλωρὸν οὐδὲ πᾶν
They *{that}* not to harm the grass of the earth or any green plant or any
899 2671 3590 92 3836 5965 3836 1178 4028 4246 5952 4028 4246
r.dpf.3 cj pl v.fai.3p d.asm n.asm d.gsf n.gsf cj a.asn a.asn cj a.asn

δένδρον, ⌞εἰ μὴ⌟ τοὺς ἀνθρώπους οἵτινες ↱ οὐκ ἔχουσι τὴν σφραγῖδα τοῦ θεοῦ
tree, but only those people who did not have the seal of God
1285 1623 3590 3836 476 4015 2400 4024 2400 3836 5382 3836 2536
n.asn cj pl d.apm n.apm r.npm pl v.pai.3p d.asf n.asf d.gsm n.gsm

ἐπὶ τῶν μετώπων. 5καὶ ἐδόθη αὐτοῖς ἵνα μὴ ἀποκτείνωσιν αὐτούς,
on their foreheads. *{and}* They were allowed *They* *{that}* not to kill them
2093 3836 3587 2779 899 1443 899 2671 3590 650 899
p.g d.gpn n.gpn cj v.api.3s r.dpm.3 cj pl v.aas.3p r.apm.3

ἀλλ' ἵνα βασανισθήσονται → μῆνας πέντε, καὶ ὁ βασανισμὸς
but *{that}* to torture them for five months, *five* and *{the}* their torture
247 2671 989 4297 3604 4297 2779 3836 899 990
cj cj v.fpi.3p n.apm a.apm cj d.nsm n.nsm

αὐτῶν ὡς βασανισμὸς → σκορπίου ὅταν παίσῃ ἄνθρωπον. 6καὶ ἐν ταῖς
their was like the torture of a scorpion when it stings a person. And in *{the}*
899 6055 990 5026 4020 4091 476 2779 1877 3836
r.gpf.3 pl n.nsm n.gsm cj v.aas.3s n.asm cj p.d d.dpf

ἡμέραις ἐκείναις ζητήσουσιν οἱ ἄνθρωποι τὸν θάνατον καὶ ↱ ⌞οὐ
those days *those* people will seek *{the}* *people* *{the}* death but will not
1697 2465 1697 476 2426 3836 476 3836 2505 2779 2351 4024
n.dpf r.dpf v.fai.3p d.npm n.npm d.asm n.asm cj pl

μὴ⌟ εὑρήσουσιν αὐτόν, καὶ ἐπιθυμήσουσιν ἀποθανεῖν καὶ φεύγει ὁ
find it; *{and}* they will long to die, but death will flee *{the}*
3590 2351 899 2779 2121 633 2779 2505 5771 3836
pl v.fai.3p r.asm.3 cj v.fai.3p f.aa cj v.pai.3s d.nsm

θάνατος ἀπ' αὐτῶν. 7καὶ τὰ ὁμοιώματα τῶν ἀκρίδων ὅμοια ἵπποις
death from them. *{and}* *{the}* In appearance the locusts were like horses
2505 608 899 2779 3836 3930 3836 210 3927 2691
n.nsm p.g r.gpm.3 cj d.npn n.npn d.gpf n.gpf a.npn n.dpm

ἡτοιμασμένοις εἰς πόλεμον, καὶ ἐπὶ τὰς κεφαλὰς αὐτῶν ὡς
prepared for battle. *{and}* On *{the}* their heads *their* were something like
2286 1650 4483 2779 2093 3836 899 3051 899 3927 6055
pt.rp.dpm p.a n.asm cj p.a d.apf n.apf r.gpm.3 pl

στέφανοι ὅμοιοι χρυσῷ, καὶ τὰ πρόσωπα αὐτῶν ὡς πρόσωπα
crowns *something* of gold, and *{the}* their faces *their* were like human faces.
5109 3927 5996 2779 3836 899 4725 899 6055 476 4725
n.npm a.npm n.dsm cj d.npn n.npn r.gpm.3 pl n.npn

ἀνθρώπων, 8καὶ εἶχον τρίχας ὡς τρίχας γυναικῶν, καὶ αἱ
human *{and}* ⌞They had⌟ hair like women's hair, *women's* and *{the}* their
476 2779 2400 2582 6055 1222 2582 1222 2779 3836 899
n.gpm cj v.iai.3p n.apf pl n.apf n.gpf cj d.npm

ὀδόντες αὐτῶν ὡς λεόντων ἦσαν, 9καὶ εἶχον θώρακας ὡς θώρακας
teeth *their* were like lions' teeth. *were* *{and}* ⌞They had⌟ breastplates like breastplates
3848 899 1639 6055 3329 1639 2779 2400 2606 6055 2606
n.npm r.gpf.3 pl n.gpm v.iai.3p cj v.iai.3p n.apm pl n.apm

σιδηροῦς, καὶ ἡ φωνὴ τῶν πτερύγων αὐτῶν ὡς φωνὴ →
of iron, and the sound of their wings *their* was like the sound of many horse-drawn
4971 2779 3836 5889 3836 899 4763 899 6055 5889 4498 2691
a.apm cj d.nsf n.nsf d.gpf n.gpf r.gpf.3 pl n.nsf

ἁρμάτων ἵππων πολλῶν τρεχόντων εἰς πόλεμον, 10καὶ ἔχουσιν οὐρὰς ὁμοίας
chariots *horse-drawn* *many* rushing into battle. *{and}* They had tails like
761 2691 4498 5556 1650 4483 2779 2400 4038 3927
n.gpn n.gpm a.gpm pt.pa.gpm p.a n.asm cj v.pai.3p n.apf a.apf

NASB

3Then out of the
smoke came
locusts upon the
earth, and power
was given them, as
the scorpions of the
earth have power.
4They were told not
to hurt the grass of
the earth, nor any
green thing, nor
any tree, but only
the men who do
not have the seal of
God on their fore-
heads. 5And they
were not permitted
to kill anyone, but
to torment for five
months; and their
torment was like
the torment of a
scorpion when it
stings a man. 6And
in those days men
will seek death
and will not find
it; they will long to
die, and death flees
from them.
7The appearance
of the locusts was
like horses pre-
pared for battle;
and on their heads
appeared to be
crowns like gold,
and their faces
were like the faces
of men. 8They had
hair like the hair of
women, and their
teeth were like
the teeth of lions.
9They had breast-
plates like breast-
plates of iron; and
the sound of their
wings was like the
sound of chariots,
of many horses
rushing to battle.
10They have tails

NIV

with stingers, like
scorpions, and in
their tails they had
power to torment
people for five
months. 11 They
had as king over
them the angel of
the Abyss, whose
name in Hebrew
is Abaddon and in
Greek is Apollyon
(that is, Destroyer).
12 The first woe
is past; two other
woes are yet to
come.
13 The sixth angel
sounded his trum-
pet, and I heard a
voice coming from
the four horns of
the golden altar
that is before God.
14 It said to the
sixth angel who
had the trumpet,
"Release the four
angels who are
bound at the great
river Euphrates."
15 And the four an-
gels who had been
kept ready for this
very hour and day
and month and
year were released
to kill a third of
mankind. 16 The
number of the
mounted troops
was twice ten
thousand times ten
thousand. I heard
their number.
17 The horses and
riders I saw in my
vision looked like
this: Their breast-
plates were fiery
red, dark blue, and
yellow as sulfur.
The heads of the
horses resembled
the heads of lions,
and out of their
mouths came fire,
smoke

σκορπίοις καὶ κέντρα, καὶ ἐν ταῖς οὐραῖς αὐτῶν ἡ ἐξουσία αὐτῶν ἀδικῆσαι
scorpions, with stingers; and *in* *{the}* *tails* *their* *{the}* their power *their* to hurt
5026 2779 3034 2779 1877 3836 4038 899 3836 899 2026 899 92
n.dpm cj n.apn cj p.d d.dpf n.dpf r.gpf.3 d.nsf n.nsf r.gpf.3 f.aa

τοὺς ἀνθρώπους → μῆνας πέντε, 11 ἔχουσιν ἐπ᾽ αὐτῶν
{the} people for five months *five* lies in their tails. They have as king over them
3836 476 4297 3604 4297 1877 899 4038 2400 995 995 2093 899
d.apm n.apm n.apm a.apm v.pai.3p p.g r.gpf.3

βασιλέα τὸν ἄγγελον τῆς ἀβύσσου, ὄνομα αὐτῷ Ἑβραϊστὶ Ἀβαδδών, καὶ
king the angel of the abyss, whose name *whose* in Hebrew is Abaddon, but
995 3836 34 3836 12 899 3950 899 1580 3 2779
n.asm d.asm n.asm d.gsf n.gsf n.nsn r.dsm.3 adv n.nsm cj

ἐν τῇ Ἑλληνικῇ ὄνομα ἔχει Ἀπολλύων. 12 ἡ οὐαὶ ἡ μία
in *{the}* Greek he has the name *he has* Apollyon. The first woe *{the}* *first*
1877 3836 1819 2400 2400 3950 2400 661 3836 1651 4026 3836 1651
p.d d.dsf a.dsf n.asn v.pai.3s n.nsm d.nsf j d.nsf a.nsf

ἀπῆλθεν· ἰδοὺ → ἔρχεται ἔτι δύο οὐαὶ μετὰ ταῦτα. 13 καὶ ὁ
has passed; behold, two woes are yet to come *yet* *two* *woes* after this. *{and}* The
599 2627 1545 4026 2285 2262 2285 1545 4026 3552 4047 2779 3836
v.aai.3s j v.pmi.3s adv a.npf j p.a r.apn cj d.nsm

ἕκτος ἄγγελος ἐσάλπισεν· καὶ ἤκουσα φωνὴν μίαν ἐκ τῶν τεσσάρων[a]
sixth angel blew his trumpet, and I heard a voice *a* from the four
1761 34 4895 2779 201 1651 5889 1651 1666 3836 5475
a.nsm n.nsm v.aai.3s cj v.aai.1s n.asf a.asf p.g d.gpn a.gpn

κεράτων τοῦ θυσιαστηρίου τοῦ χρυσοῦ τοῦ ἐνώπιον τοῦ θεοῦ, 14 λέγοντα
horns of the golden altar *{the}* *golden* that is before *{the}* God, saying
3043 3836 5997 2603 3836 5997 3836 1967 3836 2536 3306
n.gpn d.gsn n.gsn d.gsn a.gsn d.gsn p.g d.gsm n.gsm pt.pa.asm

τῷ ἕκτῳ ἀγγέλῳ, ὁ ἔχων τὴν σάλπιγγα, λῦσον τοὺς τέσσαρας ἀγγέλους τοὺς
⌊to the⌋ sixth angel who had the trumpet, "Release the four angels who
3836 1761 34 3836 2400 3836 4894 3395 3836 5475 34 3836
d.dsm a.dsm n.dsm d.nsm pt.pa.nsm d.asf n.asf v.aam.2s d.apm a.apm n.apm d.apm

δεδεμένους ἐπὶ τῷ ποταμῷ τῷ μεγάλῳ Εὐφράτῃ. 15 καὶ ἐλύθησαν οἱ
are bound at the great river *{the}* *great* Euphrates." So *were released* the
1313 2093 3836 3489 4532 3836 3489 2371 2779 3395 3836
pt.rp.apm p.d d.dsm n.dsm d.dsm a.dsm n.dsm cj v.api.3p d.npm

τέσσαρες ἄγγελοι οἱ ἡτοιμασμένοι εἰς τὴν ὥραν καὶ ἡμέραν καὶ μῆνα καὶ
four angels, who had been prepared for this hour, *{and}* day, *{and}* month, and
5475 34 3836 2286 1650 3836 6052 2779 2465 2779 3604 2779
a.npm n.npm d.npm pt.rp.npm p.a d.asf n.asf cj n.asf cj n.asm cj

ἐνιαυτόν, ἵνα ἀποκτείνωσιν τὸ τρίτον τῶν ἀνθρώπων. 16 καὶ ὁ
year, were released to kill a third of mankind. *{and}* The
1929 3395 3395 2671 650 3836 5569 3836 476 2779 3836
n.asm cj v.aas.3p d.asn a.asn d.gpm n.gpm cj d.nsm

ἀριθμὸς τῶν στρατευμάτων τοῦ ἱππικοῦ δισμυριάδες → μυριάδων,
number of mounted troops *{the}* *mounted* was twice ten thousand times ten thousand;
750 3836 2690 5128 3836 2690 1490 3689
n.nsm d.gpn n.gpn d.gsn n.gsn n.npf n.gpf

ἤκουσα τὸν ἀριθμὸν αὐτῶν. 17 καὶ οὕτως εἶδον τοὺς ἵππους ἐν τῇ ὁράσει
I heard *{the}* their number. *their* And this is how I saw the horses in my vision
201 3836 899 750 899 2779 4048 1625 3836 2691 1877 3836 3970
v.aai.1s d.asm n.asm r.gpn.3 cj adv v.aai.1s d.apm n.apm p.d d.dsf n.dsf

καὶ τοὺς ⌊καθημένους ἐπ᾽⌋ αὐτῶν, ἔχοντας θώρακας πυρίνους
and those who rode them: The riders wore breastplates that were fiery red,
2779 3836 2764 2093 899 2400 2606 4791
cj d.apm pt.pm.apm p.g r.gpm.3 pt.pa.apm n.apm a.apm

καὶ ὑακινθίνους καὶ θειώδεις, καὶ αἱ κεφαλαὶ τῶν ἵππων ὡς
{and} dark blue, and ⌊yellow like sulfur,⌋ and the heads of the horses were like lions'
2779 5610 2779 2523 2779 3836 3051 3836 2691 6055 3329
cj a.apm cj a.apm cj d.npf n.npf d.gpm n.gpm pl

κεφαλαὶ λεόντων, καὶ ἐκ τῶν στομάτων αὐτῶν ἐκπορεύεται πῦρ καὶ καπνὸς
heads, *lions'* and ⌊out of⌋ *{the}* their mouths *their* came fire and smoke
3051 3329 2779 1666 3836 899 5125 899 1744 4786 2779 2837
n.npf n.gpm cj p.g d.gpn n.gpn r.gpm.3 v.pmi.3s n.nsn cj n.nsm

NASB

like scorpions, and
stings; and in their
tails is their power
to hurt men for
five months. 11 They
have as king over
them, the angel
of the abyss; his
name in Hebrew is
[a]Abaddon, and in
the Greek he has
the name Apollyon.
12 The first woe
is past; behold,
two woes are still
coming after these
things.

The Sixth Trumpet—Army from the East

13 Then the sixth
angel sounded,
and I heard a voice
from the [b]four
horns of the golden
altar which is
before God, 14 one
saying to the sixth
angel who had the
trumpet, "Release
the four angels
who are bound at
the great river Eu-
phrates." 15 And the
four angels, who
had been prepared
for the hour and
day and month and
year, were released,
so that they would
kill a third of man-
kind. 16 The number
of the armies of the
horsemen was two
hundred million; I
heard the number
of them. 17 And this
is how I saw in the
vision the horses
and those who sat
on them: *the riders*
had breastplates
the color of fire
and of hyacinth
and of brimstone;
and the heads of
the horses are like
the heads of lions;
and out of their
mouths proceed
fire and smoke and
brimstone.

[a] [τεσσάρων] UBS, omitted by NET.

[a] I.e. destruction
[b] Two early mss do not contain *four*

NIV

and sulfur. 18 A
third of man-
kind was killed
by the three
plagues of fire,
smoke and sul-
fur that came out
of their mouths.
19 The power of
the horses was in
their mouths and
in their tails; for
their tails were
like snakes, having
heads with which
they inflict injury.
20 The rest of
mankind who
were not killed by
these plagues still
did not repent of
the work of their
hands; they did not
stop worshiping
demons, and idols
of gold, silver,
bronze, stone and
wood—idols that
cannot see or hear
or walk. 21 Nor did
they repent of their
murders, their
magic arts, their
sexual immorality
or their thefts.

The Angel and the Little Scroll

10 Then I saw
another
mighty angel com-
ing down from
heaven. He was
robed in a cloud,
with a rainbow
above his head;
his face was like
the sun, and his
legs were like fi-
ery pillars. 2 He
was holding a little
scroll, which lay
open in his hand.
He planted

καὶ θεῖον. 18 ἀπὸ τῶν τριῶν πληγῶν τούτων ἀπεκτάνθησαν τὸ τρίτον τῶν
and sulfur. By {the} these three plagues *these* *was killed* a third of
2779 2520 608 3836 4047 5552 4435 4047 650 3836 5569 3836
cj n.nsn p.g d.gpf a.gpf n.gpf r.gpf v.api.3p d.nsn a.nsn d.gpm

ἀνθρώπων, ἐκ τοῦ πυρὸς καὶ τοῦ καπνοῦ καὶ τοῦ θείου τοῦ
mankind was killed, by the fire and the smoke and the sulfur that
476 650 650 1666 3836 4786 2779 3836 2837 2779 3836 2520 3836
n.gpm p.g d.gsn n.gsn cj d.gsm n.gsm cj d.gsn n.gsn d.gsn

ἐκπορευομένου ἐκ τῶν στομάτων αὐτῶν. 19 ἡ γὰρ ἐξουσία τῶν ἵππων
came ⌞out of⌟ {the} their mouths. *their* For the *For* power of the horses
1744 1666 3836 899 5125 899 1142 3836 1142 2026 3836 2691
pt.pm.gsn p.g d.gpn n.gpn r.gpm.3 d.nsf cj n.nsf d.gpm n.gpm

ἐν τῷ στόματι αὐτῶν ἐστιν καὶ ἐν ταῖς οὐραῖς αὐτῶν, αἱ γὰρ
is in {the} their mouths *their* *is* and in {the} their tails, *their* {the} for their
1639 1877 3836 899 5125 899 1639 2779 1877 3836 899 4038 899 3836 1142 899
p.d d.dsn n.dsn r.gpm.3 v.pai.3s cj p.d d.dpf n.dpf r.gpm.3 d.npf cj

οὐραὶ αὐτῶν ὅμοιαι ὄφεσιν, ἔχουσαι κεφαλὰς καὶ ἐν αὐταῖς ἀδικοῦσιν. 20 καὶ
tails *their* are like serpents, having heads; and with them they inflict harm. {and}
4038 899 3927 4058 2400 3051 2779 1877 899 92 2779
n.npf r.gpm.3 a.npf n.dpm pt.pa.npf n.apf cj p.d r.dpf.3 v.pai.3p cj

οἱ λοιποὶ τῶν ἀνθρώπων, οἳ ↱ ↱ οὐκ ἀπεκτάνθησαν ἐν ταῖς πληγαῖς
The rest of mankind, those who were not killed by {the} these plagues,
3836 3370 3836 476 4005 650 650 4024 650 1877 3836 4047 4435
d.npm a.npm d.gpm n.gpm r.npm pl v.api.3p p.d d.dpf n.dpf

ταύταις, ↱ οὐδὲ μετενόησαν ἐκ τῶν ἔργων τῶν χειρῶν αὐτῶν, ἵνα μὴ
these did not repent of the works of their hands *their* so as ⌞to give up⌟
4047 3566 4028 3566 1666 3836 2240 3836 899 5931 899 2671 3590
r.dpf adv v.aai.3p p.g d.gpn n.gpn d.gpf n.gpf r.gpm.3 cj pl

προσκυνήσουσιν τὰ δαιμόνια καὶ τὰ εἴδωλα τὰ χρυσᾶ καὶ τὰ ἀργυρᾶ καὶ τὰ
worshiping {the} demons and {the} idols of gold and {the} silver and {the}
4686 3836 1228 2779 3836 1631 3836 5997 2779 3836 739 2779 3836
v.fai.3p d.apn n.apn cj d.apn n.apn d.apn a.apn cj d.apn a.apn cj d.apn

χαλκᾶ καὶ τὰ λίθινα καὶ τὰ ξύλινα, ἃ οὔτε βλέπειν δύνανται οὔτε
bronze and {the} stone and {the} wood, which are not able to see *are able* or
5911 2779 3836 3343 2779 3836 3832 4005 1538 4046 1538 1063 1538 4046
a.apn cj d.apn a.apn cj d.apn a.apn r.npn cj f.pa v.ppi.3p cj

ἀκούειν οὔτε περιπατεῖν, 21 ⌞καὶ οὐ⌟ μετενόησαν ἐκ τῶν φόνων αὐτῶν οὔτε
hear or walk. Neither did they repent of {the} their murders *their* or
201 4046 4344 2779 4024 3566 1666 3836 899 5840 899 4046
f.pa cj f.pa cj pl v.aai.3p p.g d.gpm n.gpm r.gpm.3 cj

ἐκ τῶν φαρμάκων αὐτῶν οὔτε ἐκ τῆς πορνείας αὐτῶν οὔτε ἐκ τῶν
{of} {the} their sorceries *their* or {of} {the} their sexual immorality *their* or {of} {the}
1666 3836 899 5760 899 4046 1666 3836 899 4518 899 4046 1666 3836
p.g d.gpn n.gpn r.gpm.3 cj p.g d.gsf n.gsf r.gpm.3 cj p.g d.gpn

κλεμμάτων αὐτῶν.
their stealing. *their*
899 3092 899
n.gpn r.gpm.3

10:1 καὶ εἶδον ἄλλον ἄγγελον ἰσχυρὸν καταβαίνοντα ἐκ τοῦ οὐρανοῦ
Then I saw another powerful angel *powerful* coming down from {the} heaven,
2779 1625 257 2708 34 2708 2849 1666 3836 4041
cj v.aai.1s r.asm n.asm a.asm pt.pa.asm p.g d.gsm n.gsm

περιβεβλημένον νεφέλην, καὶ ἡ ἶρις ἐπὶ τῆς κεφαλῆς αὐτοῦ καὶ τὸ
wrapped in a cloud, with a rainbow above {the} his head; *his* {and} {the} his
4314 3749 2779 3836 2692 2093 3836 899 3051 899 2779 3836 899
pt.rp.asm n.asf cj d.nsf n.nsf p.g d.gsf n.gsf r.gsm.3 cj d.nsn

πρόσωπον αὐτοῦ ὡς ὁ ἥλιος καὶ οἱ πόδες αὐτοῦ ὡς στῦλοι πυρός,
face *his* was like the sun, and {the} his legs *his* were like pillars of fire.
4725 899 6055 3836 2463 2779 3836 899 4546 899 6055 5146 4786
n.nsn r.gsm.3 pl d.nsm n.nsm cj d.npm n.npm r.gsm.3 pl n.npm n.gsn

2 καὶ ἔχων ἐν τῇ χειρὶ αὐτοῦ βιβλαρίδιον ἠνεῳγμένον. καὶ ἔθηκεν
{and} He held in {the} his hand *his* a little scroll that had been unrolled. {and} Placing
2779 2400 1877 3836 899 5931 899 1044 487 2779 5502
cj pt.pa.nsm p.d d.dsf n.dsf r.gsm.3 n.asn pt.rp.asn cj v.aai.3s

NASB

18 A third of man-
kind was killed by
these three plagues,
by the fire and the
smoke and the
brimstone which
proceeded out of
their mouths. 19 For
the power of the
horses is in their
mouths and in their
tails; for their tails
are like serpents
and have heads,
and with them they
do harm.
20 The rest of man-
kind, who were
not killed by these
plagues, did not
repent of the works
of their hands, so
as not to worship
demons, and the
idols of gold and of
silver and of brass
and of stone and of
wood, which can
neither see nor hear
nor walk; 21 and
they did not repent
of their murders
nor of their sorcer-
ies nor of their
immorality nor of
their thefts.

The Angel and the Little Book

10:1 I saw another
strong angel com-
ing down out of
heaven, clothed
with a cloud; and
the rainbow was
upon his head, and
his face was like
the sun, and his
feet like pillars of
fire; 2 and he had
in his hand a little
book which was
open. He placed

NIV

his right foot on
the sea and his
left foot on the
land, 3and he gave
a loud shout like
the roar of a lion.
When he shouted,
the voices of the
seven thunders
spoke. 4And when
the seven thunders
spoke, I was about
to write; but I
heard a voice from
heaven say, "Seal
up what the seven
thunders have said
and do not write it
down."
5Then the angel
I had seen stand-
ing on the sea and
on the land raised
his right hand to
heaven. 6And he
swore by him who
lives for ever and
ever, who created
the heavens and all
that is in them, the
earth and all that
is in it, and the sea
and all that is in it,
and said, "There
will be no more
delay! 7But in the
days when the
seventh angel is
about to sound his
trumpet, the mys-
tery of God will be
accomplished, just
as he announced
to his servants the
prophets."
8Then the voice
that I had heard
from heaven
spoke to me once
more: "Go, take
the scroll that lies
open in the hand
of the angel who is
standing on the sea
and on the land."
9So I went to the
angel and asked

τὸν πόδα αὐτοῦ τὸν δεξιὸν ἐπὶ τῆς θαλάσσης, τὸν δὲ εὐώνυμον ἐπὶ
{the} his right foot his {the} right on the sea {the} and his left foot on
3836 899 1288 4546 899 3836 1288 2093 3836 2498 3836 1254 2381 2093
d.asm n.asm r.gsm.3 d.asm a.asm p.g d.gsf n.gsf d.asm cj a.asm p.g

τῆς γῆς, 3καὶ ἔκραξεν → φωνῇ μεγάλῃ ὥσπερ λέων μυκᾶται. καὶ ὅτε
the land, {and} he shouted in a loud voice loud like a lion roaring. And when
3836 1178 2779 3189 3489 5889 3489 6061 3329 3681 2779 4021
d.gsf n.gsf cj v.aai.3s n.dsf a.dsf cj n.nsm v.pmi.3s cj cj

ἔκραξεν, ἐλάλησαν αἱ ἑπτὰ βρονταὶ τὰς ἑαυτῶν φωνάς. 4καὶ ὅτε
he shouted, sounded the seven thunders sounded {the} their voices. And when
3189 3281 3836 2231 1103 3281 3836 1571 5889 2779 4021
v.aai.3s v.aai.3p d.npf a.npf n.npf d.apf r.gpf.3 n.apf cj cj

ἐλάλησαν αἱ ἑπτὰ βρονταί, ἤμελλον γράφειν, καὶ ἤκουσα φωνὴν
had sounded the seven thunders had sounded, I was preparing to write but I heard a voice
3281 3836 2231 1103 3281 3281 3516 1211 2779 201 5889
v.aai.3p d.npf a.npf n.npf v.iai.1s f.pa cj v.aai.1s n.asf

ἐκ τοῦ οὐρανοῦ λέγουσαν, σφράγισον ἃ ἐλάλησαν αἱ ἑπτὰ βρονταί,
from {the} heaven saying, "Seal up what have said the seven thunders have said,
1666 3836 4041 3306 5381 4005 3281 3836 2231 1103 3281 3281
p.g d.gsm n.gsm pt.pa.asf v.aam.2s r.apn v.aai.3p d.npf a.npf n.npf

καὶ ↱ μὴ ↱ αὐτὰ γράψῃς. 5καὶ ὁ ἄγγελος, ὃν εἶδον ἑστῶτα ἐπὶ τῆς
and do not write it down." Then the angel that ⌊I had seen⌋ standing on the
2779 1211 3590 1211 899 1211 2779 3836 34 4005 1625 2705 2093 3836
cj pl r.apn.3 v.aas.2s cj d.nsm n.nsm r.asm v.aai.1s pt.ra.asm p.g d.gsf

θαλάσσης καὶ ἐπὶ τῆς γῆς, ἦρεν τὴν χεῖρα αὐτοῦ τὴν δεξιὰν εἰς τὸν
sea and on the land raised {the} his right hand his {the} right to {the}
2498 2779 2093 3836 1178 149 3836 899 1288 5931 899 3836 1288 1650 3836
n.gsf cj p.g d.gsf n.gsf v.aai.3s d.asf n.asf r.gsm.3 d.asf a.asf p.a d.asm

οὐρανὸν 6καὶ ὤμοσεν ἐν τῷ ζῶντι εἰς τοὺς ⌊αἰῶνας τῶν αἰώνων,⌋ ὃς
heaven and swore by the ⌊one who lives⌋ for all time, who
4041 2779 3923 1877 3836 2409 1650 3836 172 3836 172 4005
n.asm cj v.aai.3s p.d d.dsm pt.pa.dsm p.a d.apm n.apm d.gpm n.gpm r.nsm

ἔκτισεν τὸν οὐρανὸν καὶ τὰ ἐν αὐτῷ καὶ τὴν γῆν καὶ τὰ ἐν αὐτῇ καὶ
created {the} heaven and what is in it, {and} the earth and what is in it, and
3231 3836 4041 2779 3836 1877 899 2779 3836 1178 2779 3836 1877 899 2779
v.aai.3s d.asm n.asm cj d.apn p.d r.dsm.3 cj d.asf n.asf cj d.apn p.d r.dsf.3 cj

τὴν θάλασσαν καὶ τὰ ἐν αὐτῇ, ὅτι χρόνος οὐκέτι
the sea and what is in it, ~ "There will be no more delay! no more
3836 2498 2779 3836 1877 899 4022 1639 1639 1639 4033 4033 5989 4033
d.asf n.asf cj d.apn p.d r.dsf.3 cj n.nsm adv

ἔσται, 7ἀλλ᾽ ἐν ταῖς ἡμέραις τῆς φωνῆς τοῦ ἑβδόμου ἀγγέλου, ὅταν
There will be But in the days when {the} {sound} the seventh angel when
1639 247 1877 3836 2465 4020 3836 5889 3836 1575 34 4020
v.fmi.3s cj p.d d.dpf n.dpf d.gsf n.gsf d.gsm a.gsm n.gsm cj

μέλλῃ σαλπίζειν, καὶ ἐτελέσθη τὸ μυστήριον τοῦ θεοῦ,
is about ⌊to sound his trumpet,⌋ {also} will be fulfilled the mystery of God will be
3516 4895 2779 5464 3836 3696 3836 2536 5464 5464
v.pas.3s f.pa adv v.api.3s d.nsn n.nsn d.gsm n.gsm

ὡς εὐηγγέλισεν τοὺς ἑαυτοῦ δούλους τοὺς προφήτας. 8καὶ ἡ φωνὴ ἣν
fulfilled, ⌊just as⌋ he announced to his servants the prophets." Then the voice that
5464 6055 2294 3836 1571 1529 3836 4737 2779 3836 5889 4005
cj v.aai.3s d.apm r.gsm.3 n.apm d.apm n.apm cj d.nsf n.nsf r.asf

ἤκουσα ἐκ τοῦ οὐρανοῦ πάλιν λαλοῦσαν μετ᾽ ἐμοῦ καὶ λέγουσαν,
I had heard from {the} heaven spoke to me again, spoke to me {and} saying,
201 1666 3836 4041 3281 3552 1609 4099 3281 3552 1609 2779 3306
v.aai.1s p.g d.gsm n.gsm adv pt.pa.asf p.g r.gs.1 cj pt.pa.asf

ὕπαγε λάβε τὸ βιβλίον τὸ ἠνεῳγμένον ἐν τῇ χειρὶ τοῦ ἀγγέλου τοῦ ἑστῶτος
"Go, take the scroll that is open in the hand of the angel who is standing
5632 3284 3836 1046 3836 487 1877 3836 5931 3836 34 3836 2705
v.pam.2s v.aam.2s d.asn n.asn d.asn pt.rp.asn p.d d.dsf n.dsf d.gsm n.gsm d.gsm pt.ra.gsm

ἐπὶ τῆς θαλάσσης καὶ ἐπὶ τῆς γῆς. 9καὶ ἀπῆλθα πρὸς τὸν ἄγγελον λέγων
on the sea and on the land." So I went to the angel and told
2093 3836 2498 2779 2093 3836 1178 2779 599 4639 3836 34 3306
p.g d.gsf n.gsf cj p.g d.gsf n.gsf cj v.aai.1s p.a d.asm n.asm pt.pa.nsm

NASB

his right foot on
the sea and his left
on the land; 3and
he cried out with
a loud voice, as
when a lion roars;
and when he had
cried out, the seven
peals of thunder ut-
tered their voices.
4When the seven
peals of thunder
had spoken, I was
about to write;
and I heard a
voice from heaven
saying, "Seal up
the things which
the seven peals
of thunder have
spoken and do not
write them." 5Then
the angel whom
I saw standing
on the sea and on
the land lifted up
his right hand to
heaven, 6and swore
by Him who lives
forever and ever,
WHO CREATED HEAV-
EN AND THE THINGS
IN IT, AND THE EARTH
AND THE THINGS
IN IT, AND THE SEA
AND THE THINGS
IN IT, that there
will be delay no
longer, 7but in the
days of the voice
of the seventh
angel, when he is
about to sound,
then the mystery
of God is finished,
as He preached to
His servants the
prophets.
8Then the voice
which I heard from
heaven, *I heard*
again speaking
with me, and say-
ing, "Go, take the
book which is open
in the hand of the
angel who stands
on the sea and on
the land." 9So I
went to the angel,

NIV

him to give me
the little scroll. He
said to me, "Take
it and eat it. It will
turn your stomach
sour, but 'in your
mouth it will be
as sweet as hon-
ey.'[a]" 10I took the
little scroll from
the angel's hand
and ate it. It tasted
as sweet as hon-
ey in my mouth,
but when I had
eaten it, my stom-
ach turned sour.
11Then I was told,
"You must proph-
esy again about
many peoples,
nations, languages
and kings."

The Two Witnesses

11 I was given
a reed like
a measuring rod
and was told, "Go
and measure the
temple of God and
the altar, with its
worshipers. 2But
exclude the outer
court; do not mea-
sure it, because it
has been given to
the Gentiles. They
will trample on
the holy city for
42 months. 3And
I will appoint
my two witness-
es, and they will
prophesy for 1,260
days, clothed in
sackcloth." 4They
are "the two olive
trees" and the two
lampstands, and
"they stand before
the Lord of the
earth."[b] 5If anyone
tries to harm them,

[a] 9 Ezek. 3:3
[b] 4 See
Zech. 4:3,11,14.

αὐτῷ δοῦναί μοι τὸ βιβλαρίδιον. καὶ λέγει μοι, λάβε καὶ κατάφαγε αὐτό, καὶ
him to give me the little scroll. And he said to me, "Take it and eat it; {and}
899 1443 1609 3836 1044 2779 3306 1609 3284 2779 2983 899 2779
r.dsm.3 f.aa r.ds.1 d.asn n.asn cj v.pai.3s r.ds.1 v.aam.2s cj v.aam.2s r.asn.3 cj

πικρανεῖ σου τὴν κοιλίαν, ↰ ἀλλ' ἐν τῷ στόματί σου ἔσται γλυκὺ ὡς
it will make your {the} stomach bitter, but in {the} your mouth your ⌊it will be⌋ sweet as
4393 5148 3836 3120 4393 247 1877 3836 5148 5125 5148 1639 1184 6055
v.fai.3s r.gs.2 d.asf n.asf cj p.d d.dsn n.dsn r.gs.2 v.fmi.3s a.nsn pl

μέλι. 10 καὶ ἔλαβον τὸ βιβλαρίδιον ἐκ τῆς χειρὸς τοῦ ἀγγέλου καὶ κατέφαγον
honey." So I took the little scroll from the hand of the angel and ate
3510 2779 3284 3836 1044 1666 3836 5931 3836 34 2779 2983
n.nsn cj v.aai.1s d.asn n.asn p.g d.gsf n.gsf d.gsm n.gsm cj v.aai.1s

αὐτό, καὶ ἦν ἐν τῷ στόματί μου ὡς μέλι γλυκὺ καὶ
it. {and} it was In {the} my mouth my it was as sweet as honey, sweet but
899 2779 1639 1877 3836 1609 5125 1609 1639 1639 1184 6055 3510 1184 2779
r.asn.3 cj v.iai.3s p.d d.dsn n.dsn r.gs.1 pl n.nsn a.nsn cj

ὅτε ἔφαγον αὐτό, ἐπικράνθη ἡ κοιλία μου. 11 καὶ λέγουσίν μοι,
when I had eaten it, my stomach became bitter. {the} stomach my Then they said to me,
4021 2266 899 1609 3120 4393 3836 3120 1609 2779 3306 1609
cj v.aai.1s r.asn.3 v.api.3s d.nsf n.nsf r.gs.1 cj v.pai.3p r.ds.1

δεῖ σε πάλιν προφητεῦσαι ἐπὶ λαοῖς καὶ ἔθνεσιν καὶ
"You must You prophesy again prophesy about many peoples and nations and
5148 1256 5148 4736 4099 4736 2093 4498 3295 2779 1620 2779
v.pai.3s r.as.2 adv f.aa p.d n.dpm cj n.dpn cj

γλώσσαις καὶ βασιλεῦσιν πολλοῖς.
languages and kings." many
1185 2779 995 4498
n.dpf cj n.dpm a.dpm

11:1 καὶ ἐδόθη μοι κάλαμος ὅμοιος ῥάβδῳ,
Then a measuring rod like a staff was given to me; measuring rod like staff and
2779 2812 2812 3927 4811 1443 1609 2812 3927 4811
cj v.api.3s r.ds.1 n.nsm a.nsm n.dsf

λέγων, ἔγειρε καὶ μέτρησον τὸν ναὸν τοῦ θεοῦ καὶ τὸ θυσιαστήριον καὶ
someone said, "Rise and measure the temple of God and the altar and
3306 1586 2779 3582 3836 3724 3836 2536 2779 3836 2603 2779
pt.pa.nsm v.pam.2s cj v.aam.2s d.asm n.asm d.gsm n.gsm cj d.asn n.asn cj

τοὺς προσκυνοῦντας ⌊ἐν αὐτῷ.⌋ 2 καὶ τὴν αὐλὴν τὴν ἔξωθεν τοῦ ναοῦ
those who worship there, but exclude the court that is outside the temple;
3836 4686 1877 899 2779 1675 3836 885 3836 2033 3836 3724
d.apm pt.pa.apm p.d r.dsm.3 cj d.asf n.asf d.asf p.g d.gsm n.gsm

⌊ἔκβαλε ἔξωθεν⌋ καὶ μὴ αὐτὴν μετρήσῃς, ὅτι ἐδόθη τοῖς
exclude {and} do not measure it do measure because ⌊it has been given⌋ to the
1675 2033 2779 3582 3590 3582 899 3582 4022 1443 3836
v.aam.2s p.g cj pl r.asf.3 v.aas.2s cj v.api.3s d.dpn

ἔθνεσιν, καὶ τὴν πόλιν τὴν ἁγίαν πατήσουσιν →
nations. And they will trample the holy city {the} holy they will trample for forty-two
1620 2779 4251 4251 4251 3836 41 4484 3836 41 4251 5477
n.dpn cj d.asf n.asf d.asf a.asf v.fai.3p

μῆνας ⌊τεσσεράκοντα καὶ[a] δύο.⌋ 3 καὶ δώσω τοῖς δυσὶν μάρτυσίν
months. forty-two And ⌊I will give power⌋ to my two witnesses,
3604 5477 2779 1545 2779 1443 3836 1609 1545 3459
n.apm a.apm cj a.apm cj v.fai.1s d.dpm a.dpm n.dpm

μου καὶ προφητεύσουσιν ἡμέρας χιλίας διακοσίας ἑξήκοντα
my and they will prophesy days ⌊for one thousand⌋ two hundred and sixty days,
1609 2779 4736 2465 5943 1357 2008 2465
r.gs.1 cj v.fai.3p n.apf a.apf a.apf a.apf

περιβεβλημένοι σάκκους. 4 οὗτοί εἰσιν αἱ δύο ἐλαῖαι καὶ αἱ δύο λυχνίαι αἱ
clothed in sackcloth." (These are the two olive trees and the two lampstands that
4314 4884 4047 1639 3836 1545 1777 2779 3836 1545 3393 3836
pt.rp.npm n.apm r.npm v.pai.3p d.npf a.npf n.npf cj d.npf a.npf n.npf d.npf

ἐνώπιον τοῦ κυρίου τῆς γῆς ἑστῶτες. 5 καὶ εἴ τις αὐτοὺς
stand before the Lord of the earth.) stand And if anyone tries to harm them,
2705 1967 3836 3261 3836 1178 2705 2779 1623 5516 2527 92 92 899
p.g d.gsm n.gsm d.gsf n.gsf pt.ra.npm cj cj r.nsm r.apm.3

[a] [καὶ] UBS.

NASB

telling him to give
me the little book.
And he *said to me,
"Take it and eat it;
it will make your
stomach bitter, but
in your mouth it
will be sweet as
honey." 10I took the
little book out of
the angel's hand
and ate it, and in
my mouth it was
sweet as honey;
and when I had eat-
en it, my stomach
was made bitter.
11And they *said
to me, "You must
prophesy again
concerning many
peoples and nations
and tongues and
kings."

The Two Witnesses

11:1Then there
was given me a
measuring rod
like a staff; and
someone said, "Get
up and measure
the temple of God
and the altar, and
those who worship
in it. 2Leave out
the court which is
outside the temple
and do not measure
it, for it has been
given to the na-
tions; and they will
tread under foot
the holy city for
forty-two months.
3And I will grant
authority to my
two witnesses, and
they will prophesy
for twelve hundred
and sixty days,
clothed in sack-
cloth." 4These are
the two olive trees
and the two lamp-
stands that stand
before the Lord of
the earth. 5And if
anyone wants to
harm them, fire

NIV

fire comes from
their mouths and
devours their ene-
mies. This is how
anyone who wants
to harm them must
die. 6They have
power to shut up
the heavens so
that it will not rain
during the time
they are prophesy-
ing; and they have
power to turn the
waters into blood
and to strike the
earth with every
kind of plague as
often as they want.
7Now when they
have finished their
testimony, the
beast that comes
up from the Abyss
will attack them,
and overpower
and kill them.
8Their bodies will
lie in the pub-
lic square of the
great city—which
is figuratively
called Sodom and
Egypt—where
also their Lord
was crucified.
9For three and a
half days some
from every people,
tribe, language and
nation will gaze on
their bodies and
refuse them burial.
10The inhabitants
of the earth will
gloat over them
and will celebrate
by sending each
other gifts, be-
cause these two
prophets had tor-
mented those who
live on the earth.
11But after the

θέλει ἀδικῆσαι πῦρ ἐκπορεύεται ἐκ τοῦ στόματος αὐτῶν καὶ κατεσθίει τοὺς
tries *to harm* fire comes ⌊out of⌋ *{the}* their mouth *their* and devours *{the}*
2527 92 4786 1744 1666 3836 899 5125 899 2779 2983 3836
v.pai.3s f.aa n.nsn v.pmi.3s p.g d.gsn n.gsn r.gpm.3 cj v.pai.3s d.apm

ἐχθροὺς αὐτῶν· καὶ εἴ τις θελήσῃ αὐτοὺς ἀδικῆσαι,
their enemies. *their* And if anyone tries to harm them, *to harm* he must be killed
899 2398 899 2779 1623 5516 2527 92 92 899 92 899 1256 650 650
a.apm r.gpm.3 cj cj r.nsm v.aas.3s r.apm.3 f.aa

οὕτως δεῖ αὐτὸν ἀποκτανθῆναι. 6οὗτοι ἔχουσιν τὴν ἐξουσίαν
⌊in this way.⌋ *must* *he* *be killed* These two witnesses have the power
4048 1256 899 650 4047 2400 3836 2026
adv v.pai.3s r.asm.3 f.ap r.npm v.pai.3p d.asf n.asf

κλεῖσαι τὸν οὐρανόν, ἵνα μὴ ὑετὸς βρέχῃ τὰς ἡμέρας τῆς προφητείας
to shut the sky so that no rain will fall ⌊during the⌋ days of their prophesying,
3091 3836 4041 2671 3590 5624 1101 3836 2465 3836 899 4735
f.aa d.asm n.asm cj pl n.nsm v.pas.3s d.apf n.apf d.gsf n.gsf

αὐτῶν, καὶ ἐξουσίαν ἔχουσιν ἐπὶ τῶν ὑδάτων στρέφειν αὐτὰ εἰς αἷμα καὶ
their and they have power *they have* over the waters to turn them into blood and
899 2779 2400 2400 2026 2400 2093 3836 5623 5138 899 1650 135 2779
r.gpm.3 cj n.asf v.pai.3p p.g d.gpn n.gpn f.pa r.apn.3 p.a n.asn cj

πατάξαι τὴν γῆν ἐν πάσῃ πληγῇ ⌊ὁσάκις ἐὰν⌋ θελήσωσιν. 7καὶ ὅταν
to strike the earth with ⌊every kind of⌋ plague, as often as they wish. *{and}* When
4250 3836 1178 1877 4246 4435 4006 1569 2527 2779 4020
f.aa d.asf n.asf p.d a.dsf n.dsf adv pl v.aas.3p cj cj

τελέσωσιν τὴν μαρτυρίαν αὐτῶν, τὸ θηρίον τὸ ἀναβαῖνον ἐκ τῆς
they have finished *{the}* their testimony, *their* the beast that comes up from the
5464 3836 899 3456 899 3836 2563 3836 326 1666 3836
v.aas.3p d.asf n.asf r.gpm.3 d.nsn n.nsn d.nsn pt.pa.nsn p.g d.gsf

ἀβύσσου ποιήσει μετ᾽ αὐτῶν πόλεμον καὶ νικήσει αὐτοὺς καὶ ἀποκτενεῖ αὐτούς.
abyss will make war on them *war* and conquer them and kill them,
12 4472 4483 3552 899 4483 2779 3771 899 2779 650 899
n.gsf v.fai.3s p.g r.gpm.3 n.asm cj v.fai.3s r.apm.3 cj v.fai.3s r.apm.3

8καὶ τὸ πτῶμα αὐτῶν ἐπὶ τῆς πλατείας τῆς πόλεως τῆς
and *{the}* their dead bodies *their* will lie in the street of the great city, *{the}*
2779 3836 899 4773 899 2093 3836 4426 3836 3489 4484 3836
cj d.nsn n.nsn r.gpm.3 p.g d.gsf n.gsf d.gsf n.gsf d.gsf

μεγάλης, ἥτις καλεῖται πνευματικῶς Σόδομα καὶ Αἴγυπτος, ὅπου καὶ
great which symbolically is called *symbolically* Sodom, or Egypt, where also
3489 4015 4462 2813 4462 5047 2779 131 3963 2779
a.gsf r.nsf v.ppi.3s adv n.npn cj n.nsf cj adv

ὁ κύριος αὐτῶν ἐσταυρώθη. 9καὶ βλέπουσιν
{the} their Lord *their* was crucified. *{and}* *will gaze at* For three and a half days those
3836 899 3261 899 5090 2779 1063 2465 5552 2779 2468 2465
d.nsm n.nsm r.gpm.3 v.api.3s cj v.pai.3p

ἐκ τῶν λαῶν καὶ φυλῶν καὶ γλωσσῶν καὶ ἐθνῶν τὸ πτῶμα
from every people and tribe and language and nation will gaze at *{the}* their dead bodies
1666 3836 3295 2779 5876 2779 1185 2779 1620 1063 1063 1063 3836 899 4773
p.g d.gpm n.gpm cj n.gpf cj n.gpf cj n.gpn d.asn n.asn

αὐτῶν ἡμέρας τρεῖς καὶ ἥμισυ καὶ τὰ πτώματα αὐτῶν ⌊οὐκ
their *For days* *three* *and* *half* and refuse to let *{the}* *{dead bodies}* them *refuse to let*
899 2465 5552 2779 2468 2779 4024 4024 4024 3836 4773 899 4024
r.gpm.3 n.apf a.apf cj n.asn cj d.apn n.apn r.gpm.3 pl

ἀφίουσιν⌋ τεθῆναι εἰς μνῆμα. 10καὶ οἱ κατοικοῦντες ἐπὶ τῆς γῆς χαίρουσιν
be placed in a tomb. And those who dwell on the earth will rejoice
918 5502 1650 3645 2779 3836 2997 2093 3836 1178 5897
v.pai.3p f.ap p.a n.asn cj d.npm pt.pa.npm p.g d.gsf n.gsf v.pai.3p

ἐπ᾽ αὐτοῖς καὶ εὐφραίνονται καὶ δῶρα πέμψουσιν ἀλλήλοις, ὅτι οὗτοι
over them and celebrate and send gifts *send* to one another, because these
2093 899 2779 2370 2779 4287 1565 4287 253 4022 4047
p.d r.dpm.3 cj v.ppi.3p cj n.apn v.fai.3p r.dpm cj r.npm

οἱ δύο προφῆται ἐβασάνισαν τοὺς κατοικοῦντας ἐπὶ τῆς γῆς. 11καὶ μετὰ τὰς
{the} two prophets had tormented those who dwell on the earth. But after the
3836 1545 4737 989 3836 2997 2093 3836 1178 2779 3552 3836
d.npm a.npm n.npm v.aai.3p d.apm pt.pa.apm p.g d.gsf n.gsf cj p.a d.apf

NASB

flows out of their
mouth and devours
their enemies; so
if anyone wants
to harm them, he
must be killed in
this way. 6These
have the power to
shut up the sky, so
that rain will not
fall during the days
of their prophesy-
ing; and they have
power over the
waters to turn them
into blood, and
to strike the earth
with every plague,
as often as they
desire.
7When they have
finished their tes-
timony, the beast
that comes up out
of the abyss will
make war with
them, and over-
come them and kill
them. 8And their
dead bodies *will*
lie in the street
of the great city
which [a]mystically
is called Sodom
and Egypt, where
also their Lord was
crucified. 9Those
from the peoples
and tribes and
tongues and na-
tions *will* look at
their dead [b]bodies
for three and a half
days, and will not
permit their dead
bodies to be laid
in a tomb. 10And
those who dwell
on the earth *will*
rejoice over them
and celebrate; and
they will send gifts
to one another,
because these two
prophets tormented
those who dwell on
the earth.
11But after the

[a] Lit *spiritually*
[b] Lit *body*

NIV

three and a half
days the breath[a]
of life from God
entered them, and
they stood on their
feet, and terror
struck those who
saw them. 12 Then
they heard a loud
voice from heaven
saying to them,
“Come up here.”
And they went
up to heaven in a
cloud, while their
enemies looked on.
13 At that very
hour there was a
severe earthquake
and a tenth of the
city collapsed.
Seven thousand
people were killed
in the earthquake,
and the survivors
were terrified and
gave glory to the
God of heaven.
14 The second woe
has passed; the
third woe is com-
ing soon.

The Seventh Trumpet

15 The seventh
angel sounded his
trumpet, and there
were loud voices
in heaven, which
said:

“The kingdom of
the world has
become
the kingdom
of our Lord
and of his
Messiah,
and he will
reign for ever
and ever.”

16 And the twen-
ty-four elders,
who were seated
on their thrones
before God, fell
on their faces and
worshiped God,
17 saying:

“We give thanks
to you,
Lord God
Almighty,
the One who is
and who was,

[a] 11 Or *Spirit* (see Ezek. 37:5,14)

τρεῖς ἡμέρας καὶ ἥμισυ πνεῦμα ζωῆς ἐκ τοῦ θεοῦ ⸂εἰσῆλθεν ἐν⸃
three and a half days, *and* *half* the breath of life from *{the}* God entered
5552 2779 2468 2465 2779 2468 4460 2437 1666 3836 2536 1656 1877
a.apf n.apf cj n.asn n.nsn n.gsf p.g d.gsm n.gsm v.aai.3s p.d

αὐτοῖς, καὶ ἔστησαν ἐπὶ τοὺς πόδας αὐτῶν, καὶ φόβος μέγας ἐπέπεσεν ἐπὶ
them and they stood on *{the}* their feet; *their* and great fear *great* fell on
899 2779 2705 2093 3836 899 4546 899 2779 3489 5832 3489 2158 2093
r.dpm.3 cj v.aai.3p p.a d.apm n.apm r.gpm.3 cj n.nsm a.nsm v.aai.3s p.a

τοὺς θεωροῦντας αὐτούς. 12 καὶ ἤκουσαν φωνῆς μεγάλης ἐκ τοῦ
those who were watching them. Then they heard a loud voice *loud* from *{the}*
3836 2555 899 2779 201 3489 5889 3489 1666 3836
d.apm pt.pa.apm r.apm.3 cj v.aai.3p n.gsf a.gsf p.g d.gsm

οὐρανοῦ λεγούσης αὐτοῖς, ἀνάβατε ὧδε. καὶ ἀνέβησαν εἰς τὸν οὐρανὸν ἐν τῇ
heaven, saying to them, “Come up here!” And they arose to *{the}* heaven in a
4041 3306 899 326 6045 2779 326 1650 3836 4041 1877 3836
n.gsm pt.pa.gsf r.dpm.3 v.aam.2p adv cj v.aai.3p p.a d.asm n.asm p.d d.dsf

νεφέλῃ, καὶ ἐθεώρησαν αὐτοὺς οἱ ἐχθροὶ αὐτῶν. 13 καὶ ἐν ἐκείνῃ τῇ
cloud, and their enemies watched them. *{the}* *enemies* *their* And at that very
3749 2779 899 2398 2555 899 3836 2398 899 2779 1877 1697 3836
n.dsf cj v.aai.3p r.apm.3 d.npm a.npm r.gpm.3 cj p.d r.dsf d.dsf

ὥρᾳ ἐγένετο σεισμὸς μέγας καὶ τὸ δέκατον τῆς πόλεως ἔπεσεν καὶ
hour there was a great earthquake, *great* and a tenth of the city fell. *{and}* Seven
6052 1181 3489 4939 3489 2779 3836 1281 3836 4484 4406 2779 2231
n.dsf v.ami.3s n.nsm a.nsm cj d.nsn a.nsn d.gsf n.gsf v.aai.3s cj

ἀπεκτάνθησαν ἐν τῷ σεισμῷ ὀνόματα ἀνθρώπων χιλιάδες ἑπτὰ
thousand people were killed in the earthquake, *{names}* *people* *thousand* *Seven*
5942 476 650 1877 3836 4939 3950 476 5942 2231
v.api.3p p.d d.dsm n.dsm n.npn n.gpm n.npf a.npf

καὶ οἱ λοιποὶ ἔμφοβοι ἐγένοντο καὶ ἔδωκαν δόξαν τῷ θεῷ τοῦ οὐρανοῦ.
and the rest were terrified *were* and gave glory ⸂to the⸃ God of heaven.
2779 3836 3370 1181 1873 1181 2779 1443 1518 3836 2536 3836 4041
cj d.npm a.npm a.npm v.ami.3p cj v.aai.3p n.asf d.dsm n.dsm d.gsm n.gsm

14 ἡ οὐαὶ ἡ δευτέρα ἀπῆλθεν· ἰδοὺ ἡ οὐαὶ ἡ τρίτη ἔρχεται
The second woe *{the}* *second* has passed; *{behold}* the third woe *{the}* *third* is coming
3836 1311 4026 3836 1311 599 2627 3836 5569 4026 3836 5569 2262
d.nsf j d.nsf a.nsf v.aai.3s j d.nsf j d.nsf a.nsf v.pmi.3s

ταχύ. 15 καὶ ὁ ἕβδομος ἄγγελος ἐσάλπισεν· καὶ ἐγένοντο φωναὶ μεγάλαι
soon. Then the seventh angel blew his trumpet, and there were loud voices *loud*
5444 2779 3836 1575 34 4895 2779 1181 3489 5889 3489
adv cj d.nsm a.nsm n.nsm v.aai.3s cj v.ami.3p n.npf a.npf

ἐν τῷ οὐρανῷ λέγοντες, ἐγένετο ἡ βασιλεία τοῦ κόσμου
in *{the}* heaven, saying, *has become* “The kingdom of the world has become the
1877 3836 4041 3306 1181 3836 993 3836 3180 1181 1181
p.d d.dsm n.dsm pt.pa.npm v.ami.3s d.nsf n.nsf d.gsm n.gsm

τοῦ κυρίου ἡμῶν καὶ τοῦ χριστοῦ αὐτοῦ, καὶ βασιλεύσει εἰς τοὺς
kingdom of our Lord *our* and of his Christ, *his* and he will reign for all
3836 7005 3261 7005 2779 3836 899 5986 899 2779 996 1650 3836
d.gsm n.gsm r.gp.1 cj d.gsm n.gsm r.gsm.3 cj v.fai.3s p.a d.apm

⸂αἰῶνας τῶν αἰώνων.⸃ 16 καὶ οἱ ⸂εἴκοσι τέσσαρες⸃ πρεσβύτεροι οἱ[a]
time.” Then the twenty-four elders who were
172 3836 172 2779 3836 1633 5475 4565 3836 2764
n.apm d.gpm n.gpm cj d.npm a.npm a.npm a.npm d.npm

ἐνώπιον τοῦ θεοῦ καθήμενοι ἐπὶ τοὺς θρόνους αὐτῶν ἔπεσαν
seated on their thrones before *{the}* God *were seated* *on* *{the}* *thrones* *their* fell
2764 2093 899 2585 1967 3836 2536 2764 2093 3836 2585 899 4406
p.g d.gsm n.gsm pt.pm.npm p.a d.apm n.apm r.gpm.3 v.aai.3p

ἐπὶ τὰ πρόσωπα αὐτῶν καὶ προσεκύνησαν τῷ θεῷ 17 λέγοντες,
on *{the}* their faces *their* and worshiped *{the}* God, saying,
2093 3836 899 4725 899 2779 4686 3836 2536 3306
p.a d.apn n.apn r.gpm.3 cj v.aai.3p d.dsm n.dsm pt.pa.npm

εὐχαριστοῦμέν σοι, κύριε ὁ θεὸς ὁ παντοκράτωρ, ὁ ὢν καὶ ὁ ἦν,
“We give thanks to you, Lord *{the}* God *{the}* Almighty, who is and who was,
2373 5148 3261 3836 2536 3836 4120 3836 1639 2779 3836 1639
v.pai.1p r.ds.2 n.vsm d.vsm n.vsm d.vsm n.vsm d.vsm pt.pa.vsm cj d.vsm v.iai.3s

[a] [οἱ] UBS.

NASB

three and a half
days, the breath
of life from God
came into them,
and they stood on
their feet; and great
fear fell upon those
who were watch-
ing them. 12 And
they heard a loud
voice from heaven
saying to them,
“Come up here.”
Then they went up
into heaven in the
cloud, and their
enemies watched
them. 13 And in that
hour there was a
great earthquake,
and a tenth of the
city fell; seven
thousand people
were killed in the
earthquake, and the
rest were terrified
and gave glory to
the God of heaven.
14 The second woe
is past; behold, the
third woe is com-
ing quickly.

The Seventh Trumpet—Christ's Reign Foreseen

15 Then the seventh
angel sounded; and
there were loud
voices in heaven,
saying,
“**T**he kingdom
of the world has
become *the king-
dom* of our Lord
and of His [a]Christ;
and He will reign
forever and ever.”
16 And the twenty-
four elders, who
sit on their thrones
before God, fell
on their faces and
worshiped God,
17 saying,
“**W**e give You
thanks, O Lord
God, the Almighty,
who are and who

[a] I.e. Messiah

NIV

because you have
taken your
great power
and have begun
to reign.
18 The nations were
angry,
and your wrath
has come.
The time has come
for judging
the dead,
and for
rewarding
your servants
the prophets
and your people
who revere
your name,
both great and
small—
and for destroying
those who
destroy the
earth."

19 Then God's
temple in heaven
was opened, and
within his temple
was seen the ark of
his covenant. And
there came flashes
of lightning, rum-
blings, peals of
thunder, an earth-
quake and a severe
hailstorm.

The Woman and the Dragon

12 A great sign
appeared in
heaven: a woman
clothed with the
sun, with the moon
under her feet and
a crown of twelve
stars on her head.
2 She was pregnant
and cried out in
pain as she was
about to give birth.
3 Then another
sign appeared in
heaven: an enor-
mous red dragon
with seven heads
and ten horns and
seven crowns on
its heads. 4 Its tail
swept a

ὅτι εἴληφας τὴν δύναμίν σου τὴν μεγάλην καὶ ἐβασίλευσας.
because ⌊you have taken⌋ {the} your great power your {the} great and begun to reign.
4022 3284 3836 5148 3489 1539 5148 3836 3489 2779 996
cj v.rai.2s d.asf n.asf r.gs.2 d.asf a.asf cj v.aai.2s

18 καὶ τὰ ἔθνη ὠργίσθησαν, καὶ ἦλθεν ἡ ὀργή σου καὶ ὁ καιρὸς
{and} The nations raged, but your wrath came; {the} wrath your and the time
2779 3836 1620 3974 2779 5148 3973 2262 3836 3973 5148 2779 3836 2789
cj d.npn n.npn v.api.3p cj v.aai.3s d.nsf n.nsf r.gs.2 cj d.nsm n.nsm

τῶν νεκρῶν κριθῆναι καὶ ⌊δοῦναι τὸν μισθὸν⌋ τοῖς δούλοις σου
for the dead to be judged, and the time to reward {the} your servants, your
3836 3738 3212 2779 1443 3836 3635 3836 5148 1529 5148
d.gpm a.gpm f.ap cj f.aa d.asm n.asm d.dpm n.dpm r.gs.2

τοῖς προφήταις καὶ τοῖς ἁγίοις καὶ τοῖς φοβουμένοις τὸ ὄνομά σου, τοὺς
the prophets and {the} saints, and those who fear {the} your name, your both {the}
3836 4737 2779 3836 41 2779 3836 5828 3836 5148 3950 5148 3836
d.dpm n.dpm cj d.dpm a.dpm cj d.dpm pt.pp.dpm d.asn n.asn r.gs.2 d.apm

μικροὺς καὶ τοὺς μεγάλους, καὶ διαφθεῖραι τοὺς διαφθείροντας τὴν γῆν.
small and {the} great, and the time to destroy the destroyers of the earth."
3625 2779 3836 3489 2779 1425 3836 1425 3836 1178
a.apm cj d.apm a.apm cj f.aa d.apm pt.pa.apm d.asf n.asf

19 καὶ ἠνοίγη ὁ ναὸς τοῦ θεοῦ ὁ ἐν τῷ οὐρανῷ καὶ
Then was opened the temple of God, which is in {the} heaven, was opened, and
2779 487 3836 3724 3836 2536 3836 1877 3836 4041 487 487 2779
cj v.api.3s d.nsm n.nsm d.gsm n.gsm d.nsm p.d d.dsm n.dsm cj

ὤφθη ἡ κιβωτὸς τῆς διαθήκης αὐτοῦ ἐν τῷ ναῷ αὐτοῦ, καὶ
was seen the ark of his covenant his was seen within {the} his temple; his and
3972 3836 3066 3836 899 1347 899 3972 3972 1877 3836 899 3724 899 2779
v.api.3s d.nsf n.nsf d.gsf n.gsf r.gsm.3 p.d d.dsm n.dsm r.gsm.3 cj

ἐγένοντο ἀστραπαὶ καὶ φωναὶ καὶ βρονταὶ καὶ σεισμὸς καὶ
there were flashes of lightning, {and} rumblings, {and} peals of thunder, {and} an earthquake, and
1181 847 2779 5889 2779 1103 2779 4939 2779
v.ami.3p n.npf cj n.npf cj n.npf cj n.nsm cj

χάλαζα μεγάλη.
heavy hail. heavy
3489 5898 3489
n.nsf a.nsf

12:1 καὶ σημεῖον μέγα ὤφθη ἐν τῷ οὐρανῷ, γυνὴ περιβεβλημένη
Then a great sign great appeared in {the} heaven: a woman clothed with
2779 3489 4956 3489 3972 1877 3836 4041 1222 4314
cj n.nsn a.nsn v.api.3s p.d d.dsm n.dsm n.nsf pt.rp.nsf

τὸν ἥλιον, καὶ ἡ σελήνη ὑποκάτω τῶν ποδῶν αὐτῆς καὶ ἐπὶ τῆς
the sun, {and} with the moon under {the} her feet, her and on {the} her
3836 2463 2779 3836 4943 5691 3836 899 4546 899 2779 2093 3836 899
d.asm n.asm cj d.nsf n.nsf p.g d.gpm n.gpm r.gsf.3 cj p.g d.gsf

κεφαλῆς αὐτῆς στέφανος → ἀστέρων δώδεκα, 2 καὶ ⌊ἐν
head her was a crown of twelve stars. twelve {and} She was pregnant
3051 899 5109 1557 843 1557 2779 2400 2400 1877
n.gsf r.gsf.3 n.nsm n.gpm a.gpm cj p.d

γαστρὶ⌋ ἔχουσα, καὶ κράζει ὠδίνουσα καὶ βασανιζομένη τεκεῖν. 3 καὶ
She was and ⌊was crying out⌋ in labor pains as she struggled ⌊to give birth.⌋ Then
1143 2400 2779 3189 6048 2779 989 5503 2779
n.dsf pt.pa.nsf cj v.pai.3s pt.pa.nsf cj pt.pp.nsf f.aa cj

ὤφθη ἄλλο σημεῖον ἐν τῷ οὐρανῷ, καὶ ἰδοὺ δράκων
another sign appeared another sign in {the} heaven: {and} {behold} a huge red dragon
257 4956 3972 257 4956 1877 3836 4041 2779 2627 3489 4794 1532
v.api.3s r.nsn n.nsn p.d d.dsm n.dsm cj j n.nsm

μέγας πυρρὸς ἔχων κεφαλὰς ἑπτὰ καὶ κέρατα δέκα καὶ ἐπὶ τὰς
huge red that had seven heads seven and ten horns, ten and on {the} its
3489 4794 2400 2231 3051 2231 2779 1274 3043 1274 2779 2093 3836 899
a.nsm a.nsm pt.pa.nsm n.apf a.apf cj n.apn a.apn cj p.a d.apf

κεφαλὰς αὐτοῦ ἑπτὰ διαδήματα, 4 καὶ ἡ οὐρὰ αὐτοῦ σύρει τὸ
heads its were seven crowns. {and} {the} His tail His ⌊swept away⌋ a
3051 899 2231 1343 2779 3836 899 4038 899 5359 3836
n.apf r.gsm.3 a.apn n.apn cj d.nsf n.nsf r.gsm.3 v.pai.3s d.asn

NASB

were, because
You have taken
Your great power
and have begun to
reign. 18And the na-
tions were enraged,
and Your wrath
came, and the time
came for the dead
to be judged, and
the time to reward
Your bond-servants
the prophets and
the saints and those
who fear Your
name, the small
and the great, and
to destroy those
who destroy the
earth."
19And the temple
of God which is
in heaven was
opened; and the
ark of His cov-
enant appeared in
His temple, and
there were flashes
of lightning and
sounds and peals
of thunder and an
earthquake and a
great hailstorm.

The Woman, Israel

12:1A great sign ap-
peared in heaven:
a woman clothed
with the sun, and
the moon under
her feet, and on her
head a crown of
twelve stars; 2and
she was with child;
and she *cried out,
being in labor and
in pain to give
birth.

The Red Dragon, Satan

3Then another sign
appeared in heav-
en: and behold, a
great red dragon
having seven heads
and ten horns, and
on his heads *were*
seven diadems.
4And his tail *swept
away a third of

NIV

third of the stars
out of the sky and
flung them to the
earth. The dragon
stood in front of
the woman who
was about to give
birth, so that it
might devour her
child the moment
he was born. 5She
gave birth to a
son, a male child,
who "will rule all
the nations with
an iron scepter."[a]
And her child was
snatched up to God
and to his throne.
6The woman fled
into the wilderness
to a place prepared
for her by God,
where she might
be taken care of
for 1,260 days.
7Then war broke
out in heaven.
Michael and his
angels fought
against the drag-
on, and the dragon
and his angels
fought back. 8But
he was not strong
enough, and they
lost their place in
heaven. 9The great
dragon was hurled
down—that an-
cient serpent
called the devil, or
Satan, who leads
the whole world
astray. He was
hurled to the earth,
and his angels with
him.
10Then I heard a
loud voice in heav-
en say:

"Now have come
the salvation
and the

[a] 5 Psalm 2:9

τρίτον τῶν ἀστέρων τοῦ οὐρανοῦ καὶ ἔβαλεν αὐτοὺς εἰς τὴν γῆν. καὶ ὁ
third of the stars of heaven and hurled them to the earth. And the
5569 3836 843 3836 4041 2779 965 899 1650 3836 1178 2779 3836
a.asn d.gpm n.gpm d.gsm n.gsm cj v.aai.3s r.apm.3 p.a d.asf n.asf cj d.nsm

δράκων ἕστηκεν ἐνώπιον τῆς γυναικὸς τῆς μελλούσης τεκεῖν, ἵνα ὅταν τέκῃ
dragon stood before the woman who was about ⌊to give birth,⌋ so that when she bore
1532 2705 1967 3836 1222 3836 3516 5503 2671 4020 5503
n.nsm v.rai.3s p.g d.gsf n.gsf d.gsf pt.pa.gsf f.aa cj cj v.aas.3s

τὸ τέκνον αὐτῆς καταφάγῃ. 5 καὶ ἔτεκεν υἱὸν ἄρσεν,
{the} her child her he might devour it. So the woman ⌊gave birth to⌋ a son, a male child,
3836 899 5451 899 2983 2779 5503 5626 781
d.asn n.asn r.gsf.3 v.aas.3s cj v.aai.3s n.asm a.asn

ὃς μέλλει ποιμαίνειν πάντα τὰ ἔθνη ἐν ῥάβδῳ σιδηρᾷ. καὶ
who is going to rule all the nations with an iron rod; iron but her child
4005 3516 4477 4246 3836 1620 1877 4971 4811 4971 2779 899 5451
r.nsm v.pai.3s f.pa a.apn d.apn n.apn p.d n.dsf a.dsf cj

ἡρπάσθη τὸ τέκνον αὐτῆς πρὸς τὸν θεὸν καὶ πρὸς τὸν θρόνον αὐτοῦ.
⌊was taken up⌋ {the} child her to {the} God and to {the} his throne. his
773 3836 5451 899 4639 3836 2536 2779 4639 3836 899 2585 899
v.api.3s d.nsn n.nsn r.gsf.3 p.a d.asm n.asm cj p.a d.asm n.asm r.gsm.3

6 καὶ ἡ γυνὴ ἔφυγεν εἰς τὴν ἔρημον, ὅπου ἔχει ἐκεῖ τόπον
Then the woman fled into the wilderness where {she has} {there} a place
2779 3836 1222 5771 1650 3836 2245 3963 2400 1695 5536
cj d.nsf n.nsf v.aai.3s p.a d.asf n.asf cj v.pai.3s adv n.asm

ἡτοιμασμένον ἀπὸ τοῦ θεοῦ, ἵνα ἐκεῖ τρέφωσιν αὐτὴν ἡμέρας
had been prepared for her by {the} God, so there ⌊they can take care of⌋ her there days
2286 608 3836 2536 2671 1695 5555 899 1695 2465
pt.rp.asm p.g d.gsm n.gsm cj adv v.pas.3p r.asf.3 n.apf

χιλίας διακοσίας ἑξήκοντα. 7 καὶ ἐγένετο πόλεμος ἐν τῷ
⌊for one thousand⌋ two hundred and sixty days. Then war broke out war in {the}
5943 1357 2008 2465 2779 4483 1181 4483 1877 3836
a.apf a.apf a.apf cj v.ami.3s n.nsm p.d d.dsm

οὐρανῷ, ὁ Μιχαὴλ καὶ οἱ ἄγγελοι αὐτοῦ τοῦ πολεμῆσαι μετὰ τοῦ
heaven, {the} Michael and {the} his angels his ~ fought against the
4041 3836 3640 2779 3836 899 34 899 3836 4482 3552 3836
n.dsm d.nsm n.nsm cj d.npm n.npm r.gsm.3 d.gsn f.aa p.g d.gsm

δράκοντος. καὶ ὁ δράκων ἐπολέμησεν καὶ οἱ ἄγγελοι αὐτοῦ,
dragon. {and} The dragon and his angels fought back, and {the} angels his
1532 2779 3836 1532 2779 899 34 4482 2779 3836 34 899
n.gsm cj d.nsm n.nsm v.aai.3s cj d.npm n.npm r.gsm.3

8 καὶ ↱ ↱ οὐκ ἴσχυσεν οὐδὲ ↱ τόπος εὑρέθη αὐτῶν ἔτι ἐν τῷ
but he was not strong enough, and no longer was a place found for them longer in {the}
2779 2710 2710 4024 2710 4028 2285 2351 5536 2351 899 2285 1877 3836
cj pl v.aai.3s cj n.nsm v.api.3s r.gpm.3 adv p.d d.dsm

οὐρανῷ. 9 καὶ ἐβλήθη ὁ δράκων ὁ μέγας, ὁ
heaven. And the great dragon ⌊was thrown down,⌋ the dragon {the} great that ancient
4041 2779 3836 3489 1532 965 3836 1532 3836 3489 3836 792
n.dsm cj v.api.3s d.nsm n.nsm d.nsm a.nsm d.nsm

ὄφις ὁ ἀρχαῖος, ὁ καλούμενος διάβολος καὶ ὁ Σατανᾶς, ὁ πλανῶν
serpent, {the} ancient who is called the devil and {the} Satan, the deceiver of
4058 3836 792 3836 2813 1333 2779 3836 4928 3836 4414
n.nsm d.nsm a.nsm d.nsm pt.pp.nsm n.nsm cj d.nsm n.nsm d.nsm pt.pa.nsm

τὴν οἰκουμένην ὅλην, ἐβλήθη εἰς τὴν γῆν, καὶ οἱ ἄγγελοι
the whole world whole — ⌊he was thrown down⌋ to the earth, and {the} his angels
3836 3910 3876 3910 965 1650 3836 1178 2779 3836 899 34
d.asf n.asf a.asf v.api.3s p.a d.asf n.asf cj d.npm n.npm

αὐτοῦ μετ᾽ αὐτοῦ ἐβλήθησαν. 10 καὶ ἤκουσα φωνὴν
his were thrown down with him. were thrown down Then I heard a loud voice
899 965 965 965 3552 899 965 2779 201 3489 5889
r.gsm.3 p.g r.gsm.3 v.api.3p cj v.aai.1s n.asf

μεγάλην ἐν τῷ οὐρανῷ λέγουσαν, ἄρτι ἐγένετο ἡ σωτηρία καὶ ἡ
loud in {the} heaven saying, ⌊"Just now⌋ have come the salvation and the
3489 1877 3836 4041 3306 785 1181 3836 5401 2779 3836
a.asf p.d d.dsm n.dsm pt.pa.asf adv v.ami.3s d.nsf n.nsf cj d.nsf

NASB

the stars of heaven
and threw them
to the earth. And
the dragon stood
before the woman
who was about to
give birth, so that
when she gave
birth he might
devour her child.

The Male Child, Christ

5And she gave birth
to a son, a male
child, who is to
rule all the nations
with a rod of iron;
and her child was
caught up to God
and to His throne.
6Then the woman
fled into the wil-
derness where
she *had a place
prepared by God,
so that there she
would be nourished
for one thousand
two hundred and
sixty days.

The Angel, Michael

7And there was
war in heaven,
Michael and his
angels waging war
with the dragon.
The dragon and his
angels waged war,
8and they were not
strong enough, and
there was no longer
a place found for
them in heaven.
9And the great
dragon was thrown
down, the serpent
of old who is called
the devil and Satan,
who deceives the
whole world; he
was thrown down
to the earth, and
his angels were
thrown down with
him. 10Then I heard
a loud voice in
heaven, saying,
"Now the salva-
tion, and the

NIV

power
and the
kingdom of
our God,
and the
authority of
his Messiah.
For the accuser of
our brothers
and sisters,
who accuses
them before
our God day
and night,
has been hurled
down.
11 They triumphed
over him
by the blood of
the Lamb
and by the
word of their
testimony;
they did not love
their lives so
much
as to shrink
from death.
12 Therefore rejoice,
you heavens
and you who
dwell in
them!
But woe to the
earth and the
sea,
because the
devil has
gone down to
you!
He is filled with
fury,
because he
knows that
his time is
short."
13 When the drag-
on saw that he had
been hurled to the
earth, he pursued
the woman who
had given birth
to the male child.
14 The woman was
given the two
wings of a great
eagle, so that she
might fly to the
place prepared for
her in the wilder-
ness, where she
would be taken
care of for a time,
times and half a
time, out of the
serpent's reach.
15 Then from his
mouth the serpent
spewed water like
a river, to overtake
the woman and

δύναμις καὶ ἡ βασιλεία τοῦ θεοῦ ἡμῶν καὶ ἡ ἐξουσία τοῦ χριστοῦ
power and the kingdom of our God *our* and the authority of his Christ,
1539 2779 3836 993 3836 7005 2536 7005 2779 3836 2026 3836 899 5986
n.nsf cj d.nsf n.nsf d.gsm n.gsm r.gp.1 cj d.nsf n.nsf d.gsm n.gsm

αὐτοῦ, ὅτι ἐβλήθη ὁ κατήγωρ τῶν ἀδελφῶν ἡμῶν,
his because *has been thrown down* the accuser of our brothers *our* has been thrown
899 4022 965 3836 2992 3836 7005 81 7005 965 965 965
r.gsm.3 cj v.api.3s d.nsm n.nsm d.gpm n.gpm r.gp.1

ὁ κατηγορῶν αὐτοὺς ἐνώπιον τοῦ θεοῦ ἡμῶν ἡμέρας
down, the one who accuses them day and night before *{the}* our God. *our* *day*
965 3836 2989 899 2465 2779 3816 1967 3836 7005 2536 7005 2465
d.nsm pt.pa.nsm r.apm.3 p.g d.gsm n.gsm r.gp.1 n.gsf

καὶ νυκτός. 11 καὶ αὐτοὶ ἐνίκησαν αὐτὸν διὰ τὸ αἷμα τοῦ ἀρνίου καὶ διὰ τὸν
and night *{and}* They overcame him by the blood of the Lamb and by the
2779 3816 2779 899 3771 899 1328 3836 135 3836 768 2779 1328 3836
cj n.gsf cj r.npm v.aai.3p r.asm.3 p.a d.asn n.asn d.gsn n.gsn cj p.a d.asm

λόγον τῆς μαρτυρίας αὐτῶν καὶ ↱ ↱ οὐκ ἠγάπησαν τὴν ψυχὴν αὐτῶν
word of their testimony, *their* and they did not love *{the}* their lives *their*
3364 3836 899 3456 899 2779 26 26 4024 26 3836 899 6034 899
n.asm d.gsf n.gsf r.gpm.3 cj pl v.aai.3p d.asf n.asf r.gpm.3

ἄχρι θανάτου. 12 ⌞διὰ τοῦτο⌟ εὐφραίνεσθε, οἱ[a] οὐρανοὶ καὶ οἱ
⌞even to⌟ death. Therefore, rejoice, O heavens and all who dwell
948 2505 1328 4047 2370 3836 4041 2779 3836 5012
p.g n.gsm p.a r.asn v.ppm.2p d.vpm n.vpm cj d.vpm

ἐν αὐτοῖς σκηνοῦντες. οὐαὶ τὴν γῆν καὶ τὴν θάλασσαν, ὅτι
in them! *dwell* But woe to you, O earth and *{the}* sea, for the devil
1877 899 5012 4026 3836 1178 2779 3836 2498 4022 3836 1333
p.d r.dpm.3 pt.pa.vpm j d.asf n.asf cj d.asf n.asf cj

κατέβη ὁ διάβολος πρὸς ὑμᾶς ἔχων θυμὸν μέγαν, εἰδὼς
⌞has come down⌟ *the devil* to you having great wrath, *great* ⌞because he knows⌟
2849 3836 1333 4639 7007 2400 3489 2596 3489 3857
v.aai.3s d.nsm n.nsm p.a r.ap.2 pt.pa.nsm n.asm a.asm pt.ra.nsm

ὅτι ὀλίγον καιρὸν ἔχει. 13 καὶ ὅτε εἶδεν ὁ δράκων
that he has only a short time!" *he has* So when the dragon saw *the dragon*
4022 2400 2400 3900 2789 2400 2779 4021 3836 1532 1625 3836 1532
cj a.asm n.asm v.pai.3s cj cj v.aai.3s d.nsm n.nsm

ὅτι ἐβλήθη εἰς τὴν γῆν, ἐδίωξεν τὴν γυναῖκα ἥτις ἔτεκεν
that ⌞he had been thrown down⌟ to the earth, he pursued the woman who ⌞had given birth to⌟
4022 965 1650 3836 1178 1503 3836 1222 4015 5503
cj v.api.3s p.a d.asf n.asf v.aai.3s d.asf n.asf r.nsf v.aai.3s

τὸν ἄρσενα. 14 καὶ ἐδόθησαν τῇ γυναικὶ αἱ δύο πτέρυγες τοῦ
the male child. But the woman was given *the woman* the two wings of a great
3836 781 2779 3836 1222 1443 3836 1222 3836 1545 4763 3836 3489
d.asm a.asm cj v.api.3p d.dsf n.dsf d.npf a.npf n.npf d.gsm

ἀετοῦ τοῦ μεγάλου, ἵνα πέτηται εἰς τὴν ἔρημον εἰς τὸν τόπον αὐτῆς,
eagle *{the} great* so ⌞she could fly away⌟ into the wilderness to the place *{her}*
108 3836 3489 2671 4375 1650 3836 2245 1650 3836 5536 899
n.gsm d.gsm a.gsm cj v.pms.3s p.a d.asf n.asf p.a d.asm n.asm r.gsf.3

ὅπου τρέφεται ἐκεῖ → καιρὸν καὶ καιροὺς καὶ ἥμισυ καιροῦ
where ⌞she would be taken care of⌟ *{there}* for a time, and times, and half a time, safe
3963 5555 1695 2789 2779 2789 2779 2468 2789
cj v.ppi.3s adv n.asm cj n.apm cj a.asn n.gsm

ἀπὸ προσώπου τοῦ ὄφεως. 15 καὶ ἔβαλεν ὁ ὄφις
from the presence of the serpent. Then the serpent spouted *the serpent* water like a river
608 4725 3836 4058 2779 3836 4058 965 3836 4058 5623 6055 4532
p.g n.gsn d.gsm n.gsm cj v.aai.3s d.nsm n.nsm

ἐκ τοῦ στόματος αὐτοῦ ὀπίσω τῆς γυναικὸς ὕδωρ ὡς ποταμόν, ἵνα
⌞out of⌟ *{the}* his mouth *his* after the woman *water like river* to sweep
1666 3836 899 5125 899 3958 3836 1222 5623 6055 4532 2671 4472
p.g d.gsn n.gsn r.gsm.3 p.g d.gsf n.gsf n.asn pl n.asm cj

αὐτὴν ποταμοφόρητον ποιήσῃ. 16 καὶ ἐβοήθησεν ἡ γῆ τῇ
her away by a flood, *sweep away* but the earth ⌞came to the help of⌟ *the earth* the
899 4472 4533 4472 2779 3836 1178 1070 3836 1178 3836
r.asf.3 a.asf v.aas.3s cj v.aai.3s d.nsf n.nsf d.dsf

NASB

power, and the
kingdom of our
God and the
authority of His
Christ have come,
for the accuser of
our brethren has
been thrown down,
he who accuses
them before our
God day and night.
11 And they over-
came him because
of the blood of the
Lamb and because
of the word of their
testimony, and they
did not love their
life even when
faced with death.
12 For this reason,
rejoice, O heavens
and you who dwell
in them. Woe to the
earth and the sea,
because the devil
has come down to
you, having great
wrath, knowing
that he has *only* a
short time."
13 And when the
dragon saw that
he was thrown
down to the earth,
he persecuted the
woman who gave
birth to the male
child. 14 But the two
wings of the great
eagle were given
to the woman, so
that she could fly
into the wilder-
ness to her place,
where she *was
nourished for a
time and times and
half a time, from
the presence of the
serpent. 15 And the
serpent poured wa-
ter like a river out
of his mouth after
the woman, so that
he might cause her
to be swept away
with the flood.
16 But the earth
helped the

[a] [οἱ] UBS, omitted by TNIV.

NIV

sweep her away
with the torrent.
16 But the earth
helped the wom-
an by opening its
mouth and swal-
lowing the river
that the dragon had
spewed out of his
mouth. 17 Then the
dragon was en-
raged at the woman
and went off to
wage war against
the rest of her off-
spring—those who
keep God's com-
mands and hold
fast their testimony
about Jesus.

The Beast out of the Sea

13 The drag-
on[a] stood
on the shore of
the sea. And I saw
a beast coming
out of the sea. It
had ten horns and
seven heads, with
ten crowns on its
horns, and on each
head a blasphe-
mous name. 2 The
beast I saw resem-
bled a leopard, but
had feet like those
of a bear and a
mouth like that of
a lion. The drag-
on gave the beast
his power and his
throne and great
authority. 3 One of
the heads of the
beast seemed to
have had a fatal
wound, but the
fatal wound had
been healed. The
whole world was
filled with wonder
and followed the
beast. 4 People wor-
shiped the dragon
because he had
given authority to
the beast, and they
also worshiped the
beast and asked,
"Who is like the

[a] 1 Some manuscripts *And I*

γυναικὶ καὶ ἤνοιξεν ἡ γῆ τὸ στόμα αὐτῆς καὶ κατέπιεν τὸν
woman; *{and}* the ground opened up *the* *ground* *{the}* *{mouth}* *{its}* and swallowed the
1222 2779 3836 1178 487 3836 1178 3836 5125 899 2779 2927 3836
n.dsf cj v.aai.3s d.nsf n.nsf d.asn n.asn r.gsf.3 cj v.aai.3s d.asm

ποταμὸν ὃν ἔβαλεν ὁ δράκων ἐκ τοῦ στόματος αὐτοῦ. 17 καὶ
river that the dragon had spewed *the* *dragon* from *{the}* his mouth. *his* So
4532 4005 3836 1532 965 3836 1532 1666 3836 899 5125 899 2779
n.asm r.asm v.aai.3s d.nsm n.nsm p.g d.gsn n.gsn r.gsm.3 cj

ὠργίσθη ὁ δράκων ἐπὶ τῇ γυναικὶ καὶ ἀπῆλθεν ποιῆσαι πόλεμον
the dragon became furious *the* *dragon* with the woman and went off to make war
3836 1532 3974 3836 1532 2093 3836 1222 2779 599 4472 4483
v.api.3s d.nsm n.nsm p.d d.dsf n.dsf cj v.aai.3s f.aa n.asm

μετὰ τῶν λοιπῶν τοῦ σπέρματος αὐτῆς τῶν τηρούντων τὰς ἐντολὰς τοῦ
against the rest of her children, *her* those who keep the commandments of
3552 3836 3370 3836 899 5065 899 3836 5498 3836 1953 3836
p.g d.gpn a.gpm d.gsn n.gsn r.gsf.3 d.gpm pt.pa.gpm d.apf n.apf d.gsm

θεοῦ καὶ ἐχόντων τὴν μαρτυρίαν Ἰησοῦ.
God and hold to the testimony of Jesus.
2536 2779 2400 3836 3456 2652
n.gsm cj pt.pa.gpm d.asf n.asf n.gsm

13:1 καὶ εἶδον ἐκ τῆς θαλάσσης θηρίον ἀναβαῖνον, ἔχον κέρατα
And I saw, rising ⌊out of⌋ the sea, a beast *rising* with ten horns
2779 1625 326 1666 3836 2498 2563 326 2400 1274 3043
cj v.aai.1s p.g d.gsf n.gsf n.asn pt.pa.asn pt.pa.asn n.apn

δέκα καὶ κεφαλὰς ἑπτὰ καὶ ἐπὶ τῶν κεράτων αὐτοῦ δέκα
ten and seven heads. *seven* *{and}* On *{the}* his ten horns *his* were ten
1274 2779 2231 3051 2231 2779 2093 3836 899 3043 899 1274
a.apn cj n.apf a.apf cj p.g d.gpn n.gpn r.gsn.3 a.apn

διαδήματα καὶ ἐπὶ τὰς κεφαλὰς αὐτοῦ ὀνόματα[a]
crowns and on *{the}* his heads *his* were written blasphemous names.
1343 2779 2093 3836 899 3051 899 1060 3950
n.apn cj p.a d.apf n.apf r.gsn.3 n.asn

βλασφημίας. 2 καὶ τὸ θηρίον ὃ εἶδον ἦν ὅμοιον παρδάλει καὶ οἱ πόδες
blasphemous And the beast that I saw was like a leopard, *{and}* *{the}* his feet
1060 2779 3836 2563 4005 1625 1639 3927 4203 2779 3836 899 4546
n.gsf cj d.nsn n.nsn r.asn v.aai.1s v.iai.3s a.nsn n.dsf cj d.npm n.npm

αὐτοῦ ὡς ἄρκου καὶ τὸ στόμα αὐτοῦ ὡς στόμα λέοντος. καὶ
his were like a bear's, and *{the}* its mouth *its* was like a lion's mouth. *lion's* And
899 6055 759 2779 3836 899 5125 899 6055 3329 5125 3329 2779
r.gsn.3 pl n.gsm cj d.nsn n.nsn r.gsn.3 pl n.nsn n.gsm cj

ἔδωκεν αὐτῷ ὁ δράκων τὴν δύναμιν αὐτοῦ καὶ τὸν
to the beast the dragon gave *to beast the* *dragon* *{the}* his power *his* and *{the}* his
899 899 3836 1532 1443 899 3836 1532 3836 899 1539 899 2779 3836 899
v.aai.3s r.dsn.3 d.nsm n.nsm d.asf n.asf r.gsm.3 cj d.asm

θρόνον αὐτοῦ καὶ ἐξουσίαν μεγάλην. 3 καὶ μίαν ἐκ τῶν κεφαλῶν αὐτοῦ
throne *his* and great authority. *great* *{and}* One of the beast's heads *beast's*
2585 899 2779 3489 2026 3489 2779 1651 1666 3836 899 3051 899
n.asm r.gsm.3 cj n.asf a.asf cj a.asf p.g d.gpf n.gpf r.gsn.3

ὡς → → → ἐσφαγμένην ⌊εἰς θάνατον,⌋ καὶ ἡ πληγὴ
appeared to have been mortally wounded, *mortally* but *{the}* his deadly wound
6055 1650 5377 1650 2505 2779 3836 899 2505 4435
pl pt.rp.asf p.a n.asm cj d.nsf n.nsf

τοῦ θανάτου αὐτοῦ ἐθεραπεύθη. καὶ ἐθαυμάσθη ὅλη ἡ γῆ
{the} *deadly* *his* had been healed. *{and}* The whole world marveled *whole* *The* *world* as
3836 2505 899 2543 2779 3836 3910 1178 2513 3910 3836 1178
d.gsm n.gsm r.gsn.3 v.api.3s cj v.api.3s a.nsf d.nsf n.nsf

ὀπίσω τοῦ θηρίου 4 καὶ προσεκύνησαν τῷ δράκοντι, ὅτι ἔδωκεν τὴν
they followed the beast. *{and}* They worshiped the dragon because he had given *{the}*
3958 3836 2563 2779 4686 3836 1532 4022 1443 3836
p.g d.gsn n.gsn cj v.aai.3p d.dsm n.dsm cj v.aai.3s d.asf

ἐξουσίαν τῷ θηρίῳ, καὶ προσεκύνησαν τῷ θηρίῳ λέγοντες, τίς ὅμοιος τῷ
authority ⌊to the⌋ beast, and they worshiped the beast, saying, "Who is like the
2026 3836 2563 2779 4686 3836 2563 3306 5515 3927 3836
n.asf d.dsn n.dsn cj v.aai.3p d.dsn n.dsn pt.pa.npm r.nsm a.nsm d.dsn

[a] ὀνόμα TNIV, NET. ὀνόμα[τα] UBS.

NASB

woman, and the
earth opened its
mouth and drank
up the river which
the dragon poured
out of his mouth.
17 So the dragon was
enraged with the
woman, and went
off to make war
with the rest of her
children, who keep
the commandments
of God and hold
to the testimony of
Jesus.

The Beast from the Sea

13:1 And the dragon
stood on the sand
of the seashore.
Then I saw a
beast coming up
out of the sea,
having ten horns
and seven heads,
and on his horns
were ten diadems,
and on his heads
were blasphemous
names. 2 And the
beast which I saw
was like a leopard,
and his feet were
like *those* of a bear,
and his mouth
like the mouth of
a lion. And the
dragon gave him
his power and his
throne and great
authority. 3 *I saw*
one of his heads
as if it had been
slain, and his fatal
wound was healed.
And the whole
earth was amazed
and followed after
the beast; 4 they
worshiped the
dragon because he
gave his authority
to the beast; and
they worshiped
the beast, saying,
"Who is like the

NIV

beast? Who can
wage war against it?"
5The beast was
given a mouth to
utter proud words
and blasphemies
and to exercise its
authority for for-
ty-two months. 6It
opened its mouth
to blaspheme God,
and to slander his
name and his dwell-
ing place and those
who live in heaven.
7It was given power
to wage war against
God's holy peo-
ple and to conquer
them. And it was
given authority over
every tribe, peo-
ple, language and
nation. 8All inhab-
itants of the earth
will worship the
beast—all whose
names have not
been written in the
Lamb's book of life,
the Lamb who was
slain from the crea-
tion of the world.[a]
9Whoever has
ears, let them hear.

10"If anyone is to go
into captivity,
into captivity
they will go.
If anyone is to be
killed[b] with
the sword,
with the sword
they will be
killed."[c]

This calls for patient
endurance and faith-
fulness on the part of
God's people.

The Beast out of the Earth

11Then I saw a
second beast, com-
ing out of the earth.
It had two horns
like a lamb, but it
spoke like a drag-
on. 12It exercised
all the authority
of the first beast
on its behalf, and
made the earth

[a] 8 Or *written from the creation of the world in the book of life belonging to the Lamb who was slain*
[b] 10 Some manuscripts *anyone kills*
[c] 10 Jer. 15:2

θηρίῳ καὶ τίς δύναται πολεμῆσαι μετʼ αὐτοῦ; 5Καὶ ἐδόθη αὐτῷ
beast?" and, "Who is able to make war against him?" *{and}* The beast was given *beast* a
2563 2779 5515 1538 4482 3552 899 2779 899 1443 899
n.dsn cj r.nsm v.ppi.3s f.aa p.g r.gsn.3 cj v.api.3s r.dsn.3

στόμα λαλοῦν μεγάλα καὶ βλασφημίας καὶ ἐδόθη αὐτῷ
mouth to speak arrogant words and blasphemies, and he was allowed *he* to exercise
5125 3281 3489 2779 1060 2779 899 1443 899 4472 4472
n.nsn pt.pa.nsn a.apn cj n.apf cj v.api.3s r.dsn.3

ἐξουσία ποιῆσαι → μῆνας ⌞τεσσεράκοντα καὶ[a] δύο.⌟ 6καὶ ἤνοιξεν τὸ
authority *to exercise* for forty-two months. *forty-two* *{and}* He opened *{the}*
2026 4472 5477 3604 5477 2779 1545 2779 487 3836
n.nsf f.aa n.apm a.apm cj a.apm cj v.aai.3s d.asn

στόμα αὐτοῦ εἰς βλασφημίας πρὸς τὸν θεὸν βλασφημῆσαι τὸ ὄνομα αὐτοῦ
his mouth *his* in blasphemies against *{the}* God, to blaspheme *{the}* his name *his*
899 5125 899 1650 1060 4639 3836 2536 1059 3836 899 3950 899
n.asn r.gsn.3 p.a n.apf p.a d.asm n.asm f.aa d.asn n.asn r.gsm.3

καὶ τὴν σκηνὴν αὐτοῦ, τοὺς ἐν τῷ οὐρανῷ σκηνοῦντας.
and *{the}* his dwelling, *his* that is, those who live in *{the}* heaven. *who live*
2779 3836 899 5008 899 3836 5012 5012 1877 3836 4041 5012
cj d.asf n.asf r.gsm.3 d.apm p.d d.dsm n.dsm pt.pa.apm

7καὶ ἐδόθη αὐτῷ ποιῆσαι πόλεμον μετὰ τῶν ἁγίων καὶ νικῆσαι
{and} The beast was allowed *beast* to make war against the saints and to conquer
2779 899 1443 899 4472 4483 3552 3836 41 2779 3771
cj v.api.3s r.dsn.3 f.aa n.asm p.g d.gpm a.gpm cj f.aa

αὐτούς, καὶ ἐδόθη αὐτῷ ἐξουσία ἐπὶ πᾶσαν φυλὴν καὶ λαὸν καὶ γλῶσσαν καὶ
them. And he was given *he* authority over every tribe and people and language and
899 2779 899 1443 899 2026 2093 4246 5876 2779 3295 2779 1185 2779
r.apm.3 cj v.api.3s r.dsn.3 n.nsf p.a a.asf n.asf cj n.asm cj n.asf cj

ἔθνος. 8καὶ προσκυνήσουσιν αὐτὸν πάντες οἱ κατοικοῦντες ἐπὶ τῆς γῆς,
nation. And *will worship* *him* all those living on the earth will
1620 2779 4686 899 4246 3836 2997 2093 3836 1178 4686
n.asn cj v.fai.3p r.asm.3 a.npm d.npm pt.pa.npm p.g d.gsf n.gsf

οὗ ↱ οὐ γέγραπται τὸ ὄνομα αὐτοῦ ἐν τῷ βιβλίῳ
worship him, everyone whose name has not been written *{the}* *name* *{his}* in the Book
4686 899 4005 3950 1211 4024 1211 3836 3950 899 1877 3836 1046
r.gsm pl v.rpi.3s d.nsn n.nsn r.gsm.3 p.d d.dsn n.dsn

τῆς ζωῆς τοῦ ἀρνίου τοῦ ἐσφαγμένου ἀπὸ καταβολῆς → κόσμου. 9εἴ τις
of Life of the Lamb who was slain from the foundation of the world. If anyone
3836 2437 3836 768 3836 5377 608 2856 3180 1623 5516
d.gsf n.gsf d.gsn n.gsn d.gsn pt.rp.gsn p.g n.gsf n.gsm cj r.nsm

ἔχει οὖς ἀκουσάτω. 10εἴ τις εἰς αἰχμαλωσίαν, εἰς αἰχμαλωσίαν
has an ear, let him hear! If anyone is ⌞meant for⌟ captivity, into captivity
2400 4044 201 1623 5516 1650 168 1650 168
v.pai.3s n.asn v.aam.3s cj r.nsm p.a n.asf p.a n.asf

ὑπάγει· εἴ τις ἐν μαχαίρῃ ἀποκτανθῆναι αὐτὸν
he will go. If anyone is to be killed by the sword, *to be killed* by the sword he
5632 1623 5516 650 650 650 1877 3479 650 1877 3479 899
v.pai.3s cj r.nsm p.d n.dsf f.ap r.asm.3

ἐν μαχαίρῃ ἀποκτανθῆναι. ὧδέ ἐστιν ἡ ὑπομονὴ καὶ ἡ πίστις τῶν ἁγίων.
by *sword* will be killed. This calls for the endurance and *{the}* faithfulness of the saints.
1877 3479 650 6045 1639 3836 5705 2779 3836 4411 3836 41
p.d n.dsf f.ap adv v.pai.3s d.nsf n.nsf cj d.nsf n.nsf d.gpm a.gpm

11καὶ εἶδον ἄλλο θηρίον ἀναβαῖνον ἐκ τῆς γῆς, καὶ εἶχεν κέρατα δύο
Then I saw another beast rising ⌞out of⌟ the earth. *{and}* He had two horns *two*
2779 1625 257 2563 326 1666 3836 1178 2779 2400 1545 3043 1545
cj v.aai.1s r.asn n.asn pt.pa.asn p.g d.gsf n.gsf cj v.iai.3s n.apn a.apn

ὅμοια ἀρνίῳ καὶ ἐλάλει ὡς δράκων. 12καὶ τὴν ἐξουσίαν
like a lamb, but he spoke like a dragon. *{and}* He exercised all the authority
3927 768 2779 3281 6055 1532 2779 4472 4472 4246 3836 2026
a.apn n.dsn cj v.iai.3s pl n.nsm cj d.asf n.asf

τοῦ πρώτου θηρίου πᾶσαν ποιεῖ ἐνώπιον αὐτοῦ, ↞ καὶ ποιεῖ τὴν γῆν καὶ
of the first beast *all* *He exercised* on his behalf, and made the earth and
3836 4755 2563 4246 4472 1967 899 1967 2779 4472 3836 1178 2779
d.gsn a.gsn n.gsn a.asf v.pai.3s p.g r.gsn.3 cj v.pai.3s d.asf n.asf cj

[a] [καὶ] UBS.

NASB

beast, and who is
able to wage war
with him?" 5There
was given to him
a mouth speaking
arrogant words and
blasphemies, and
authority to act for
forty-two months
was given to him.
6And he opened
his mouth in blas-
phemies against
God, to blaspheme
His name and His
tabernacle, *that is,*
those who dwell in
heaven.
7It was also given
to him to make
war with the saints
and to overcome
them, and authority
over every tribe
and people and
tongue and nation
was given to him.
8All who dwell on
the earth will wor-
ship him, *everyone*
whose name has
not been [a]written
from the founda-
tion of the world
in the book of life
of the Lamb who
has been slain. 9If
anyone has an ear,
let him hear. 10If
anyone [b]*is destined*
for captivity, to
captivity he goes;
if anyone kills with
the sword, with
the sword he must
be killed. Here is
the perseverance
and the faith of the
saints.

The Beast from the Earth

11Then I saw an-
other beast coming
up out of the earth;
and he had two
horns like a lamb
and he spoke as a
dragon. 12He exer-
cises all the author-
ity of the first beast
in his presence.
And he makes the
earth and those

[a] Or *written in the book...slain from the foundation of the world*
[b] Or leads *into captivity*

NIV

and its inhabitants
worship the first
beast, whose fatal
wound had been
healed. 13 And it
performed great
signs, even caus-
ing fire to come
down from heaven
to the earth in full
view of the people.
14 Because of the
signs it was given
power to perform
on behalf of the
first beast, it de-
ceived the inhabi-
tants of the earth.
It ordered them to
set up an image in
honor of the beast
who was wounded
by the sword and
yet lived. 15 The
second beast was
given power to
give breath to the
image of the first
beast, so that the
image could speak
and cause all who
refused to wor-
ship the image to
be killed. 16 It also
forced all people,
great and small,
rich and poor, free
and slave, to re-
ceive a mark on
their right hands or
on their foreheads,
17 so that they could
not buy or sell un-
less they had the
mark, which is the
name of the beast
or the number of
its name.
18 This calls for

τοὺς ἐν αὐτῇ κατοικοῦντας ἵνα προσκυνήσουσιν τὸ θηρίον τὸ
those who live in it *who live* to worship the first beast, *{the}*
3836 2997 2997 1877 899 2997 2671 4686 3836 4755 2563 3836
d.apm p.d r.dsf.3 pt.pa.apm cj v.fai.3p d.asn n.asn d.asn

πρῶτον, οὗ ἐθεραπεύθη ἡ πληγὴ τοῦ θανάτου αὐτοῦ.
first the ⌞one whose⌟ deadly wound had been healed. *{the}* *wound* *{the}* *deadly* *{his}*
4755 4005 2505 4435 2543 3836 4435 3836 2505 899
a.asn r.gsn v.api.3s d.nsf n.nsf d.gsm n.gsm r.gsn.3

13 καὶ ποιεῖ σημεῖα μεγάλα, ἵνα καὶ πῦρ ποιῇ
{and} He performed impressive signs, *impressive* even *{also}* making fire *making* come down
2779 4472 3489 4956 3489 2671 2779 4472 4786 4472 2849 2849
cj v.pai.3s n.apn a.apn cj adv n.asn v.pas.3s

ἐκ τοῦ οὐρανοῦ καταβαίνειν εἰς τὴν γῆν ἐνώπιον τῶν ἀνθρώπων, 14 καὶ
from *{the}* heaven *come down* to *{the}* earth in the sight of everyone; and by
1666 3836 4041 2849 1650 3836 1178 1967 3836 476 2779 1328
p.g d.gsm n.gsm f.pa p.a d.asf n.asf p.g d.gpm n.gpm cj

πλανᾷ τοὺς
the signs he was allowed to perform on behalf of the beast, he deceived those
3836 4956 899 1443 1443 4472 4472 1967 1967 1967 3836 2563 4414 3836
v.pai.3s d.apm

κατοικοῦντας ἐπὶ τῆς γῆς διὰ τὰ σημεῖα ἃ ἐδόθη αὐτῷ ποιῆσαι ἐνώπιον
who live on the earth. *by* *the* *signs* *{that}* *was allowed* *he* *to perform* *on behalf of*
2997 2093 3836 1178 1328 3836 4956 4005 1443 899 4472 1967
pt.pa.apm p.g d.gsf n.gsf p.a d.apn n.apn r.npn v.api.3s r.dsn.3 f.aa p.g

τοῦ θηρίου, λέγων τοῖς κατοικοῦσιν ἐπὶ τῆς γῆς ποιῆσαι εἰκόνα τῷ
the *beast* He told those who live on the earth to make an image ⌞in honor of the⌟
3836 2563 3306 3836 2997 2093 3836 1178 4472 1635 3836
d.gsn n.gsn pt.pa.nsm d.dpm pt.pa.dpm p.g d.gsf n.gsf f.aa n.asf d.dsn

θηρίῳ, ὃς ἔχει τὴν πληγὴν τῆς μαχαίρης καὶ ἔζησεν. 15 καὶ
beast who ⌞had been⌟ *{the}* wounded ⌞by the⌟ sword yet lived. *{and}* The second beast
2563 4005 2400 3836 4435 3836 3479 2779 2409 2779 899
n.dsn r.nsm v.pai.3s d.asf n.asf d.gsf n.gsf cj v.aai.3s cj

ἐδόθη αὐτῷ ⌞δοῦναι πνεῦμα⌟ τῇ εἰκόνι τοῦ θηρίου, ἵνα καὶ
was allowed *beast* to animate the image of the first beast so that *{and}* the image
1443 899 1443 4460 3836 1635 3836 2563 2671 2779 3836 1635
v.api.3s r.dsn.3 f.aa n.asn d.dsf n.dsf d.gsn n.gsn cj cj

λαλήσῃ ἡ εἰκὼν τοῦ θηρίου καὶ ποιήσῃ ἵνα[a] ὅσοι ἐὰν
of the beast could speak, *the* *image* *of the* *beast* and could cause *{that}* ⌞all those who⌟ ~
3836 3836 2563 3281 3836 1635 3836 2563 2779 4472 2671 4012 1569
v.aas.3s d.nsf n.nsf d.gsn n.gsn cj v.aas.3s cj r.npm pl

↱ μὴ προσκυνήσωσιν τῇ εἰκόνι τοῦ θηρίου ἀποκτανθῶσιν. 16 ↱ καὶ ποιεῖ
would not worship the image of the beast to be killed. He also caused
4686 3590 4686 3836 1635 3836 2563 650 4472 2779 4472
pl v.aas.3p d.dsf n.dsf d.gsn n.gsn v.aps.3p cj v.pai.3s

πάντας, τοὺς μικροὺς καὶ τοὺς μεγάλους, καὶ τοὺς πλουσίους καὶ τοὺς πτωχούς,
everyone — *{the}* small and *{the}* great, *{and}* *{the}* rich and *{the}* poor,
4246 3836 3625 2779 3836 3489 2779 3836 4454 2779 3836 4777
a.apm d.apm a.apm cj d.apm a.apm cj d.apm a.apm cj d.apm a.apm

καὶ τοὺς ἐλευθέρους καὶ τοὺς δούλους, ἵνα δῶσιν αὐτοῖς χάραγμα ἐπὶ τῆς
{and} *{the}* free and *{the}* slave — to receive *{to them}* a mark on *{the}*
2779 3836 1801 2779 3836 1529 2671 1443 899 5916 2093 3836
cj d.apm a.apm cj d.apm n.apm cj v.aas.3p r.dpm.3 n.asn p.g d.gsf

χειρὸς αὐτῶν τῆς δεξιᾶς ἢ ἐπὶ τὸ μέτωπον αὐτῶν 17 καὶ ἵνα μή
their right hand *their* *{the}* *right* or on *{the}* their forehead. *their* And *{thus}* no
899 1288 5931 899 3836 1288 2445 2093 3836 899 3587 899 2779 2671 3590
n.gsf r.gpm.3 d.gsf a.gsf cj p.a d.asn n.asn r.gpm.3 cj cj pl

τις δύνηται ἀγοράσαι ἢ πωλῆσαι ⌞εἰ μὴ⌟ ὁ ἔχων τὸ χάραγμα
one was permitted to buy or to sell unless he bore the mark, that is,
5516 1538 60 2445 4797 1623 3590 3836 2400 3836 5916
r.nsm v.pps.3s f.aa cj f.aa cj pl d.nsm pt.pa.nsm d.asn n.asn

τὸ ὄνομα τοῦ θηρίου ἢ τὸν ἀριθμὸν τοῦ ὀνόματος αὐτοῦ. 18 ὧδε
the name of the beast or the number of his name. *his* This calls for
3836 3950 3836 2563 2445 3836 750 3836 899 3950 899 6045 1639 1639
d.asn n.asn d.gsn n.gsn cj d.asm n.asm d.gsn n.gsn r.gsn.3 adv

[a] [ἵνα] UBS.

NASB

who dwell in it to
worship the first
beast, whose fatal
wound was healed.
13 He performs great
signs, so that he
even makes fire
come down out of
heaven to the earth
in the presence
of men. 14 And he
deceives those who
dwell on the earth
because of the
signs which it was
given him to per-
form in the pres-
ence of the beast,
telling those who
dwell on the earth
to make an image
to the beast who
*had the wound of
the sword and has
come to life. 15 And
it was given to him
to give breath to
the image of the
beast, so that the
image of the beast
would even [a]speak
and cause as many
as do not worship
the image of the
beast to be killed.
16 And he causes
all, the small and
the great, and the
rich and the poor,
and the free men
and the slaves, to
be given a mark on
their right hand or
on their forehead,
17 and *he provides*
that no one will be
able to buy or to
sell, except the one
who has the mark,
either the name
of the beast or
the number of his
name. 18 Here is

[a] One early ms reads *speak, and he will cause*

NIV

wisdom. Let the
person who has
insight calculate
the number of the
beast, for it is the
number of a man.[a]
That number is
666.

The Lamb and the 144,000

14 Then I
looked, and
there before me
was the Lamb,
standing on Mount
Zion, and with
him 144,000 who
had his name and
his Father's name
written on their
foreheads. 2 And
I heard a sound
from heaven like
the roar of rush-
ing waters and
like a loud peal
of thunder. The
sound I heard was
like that of harp-
ists playing their
harps. 3 And they
sang a new song
before the throne
and before the four
living creatures
and the elders. No
one could learn the
song except the
144,000 who had
been redeemed
from the earth.
4 These are those
who did not defile
themselves with
women, for they
remained virgins.
They follow the
Lamb wherever he
goes. They were
purchased from
among mankind
and offered as
firstfruits to God
and the Lamb. 5 No
lie was found in
their mouths;

ἡ σοφία ἐστίν. ↱ ὁ ἔχων νοῦν ψηφισάτω τὸν ἀριθμὸν τοῦ θηρίου,
{the} wisdom: *calls for* let the ⌊one who has⌋ insight calculate the number of the beast,
3836 5053 1639 6028 3836 2400 3808 6028 3836 750 3836 2563
d.nsf n.nsf v.pai.3s d.nsm pt.pa.nsm n.asm v.aam.3s d.asm n.asm d.gsn n.gsn

ἀριθμὸς γὰρ → ἀνθρώπου ἐστίν, καὶ ὁ ἀριθμὸς αὐτοῦ
for it is the number *for* of a man, *it is* and *{the}* his number *his* is
1142 1639 1639 750 1142 476 1639 2779 3836 899 750 899
n.nsm cj n.gsm v.pai.3s cj d.nsm n.nsm r.gsn.3

ἑξακόσιοι ⌊ἑξήκοντα ἕξ.⌋
six hundred and sixty-six.
1980 2008 1971
a.npm a.npm a.npm

14:1 καὶ εἶδον, καὶ ἰδοὺ τὸ ἀρνίον ἑστὸς ἐπὶ τὸ ὄρος Σιὼν καὶ μετ'
Then I looked, and behold, I saw a Lamb standing on *{the}* Mount Zion; and with
2779 1625 2779 2627 3836 768 2705 2093 3836 4001 4994 2779 3552
cj v.aai.1s cj j d.nsn n.nsn pt.ra.nsn p.a d.asn n.asn n.asf cj p.g

αὐτοῦ ἑκατὸν ⌊τεσσεράκοντα τέσσαρες⌋ χιλιάδες ἔχουσαι τὸ ὄνομα
him were one hundred and forty-four thousand who had *{the}* his name
899 1669 5477 5475 5942 2400 3836 899 3950
r.gsm.3 a.npf a.npf a.npf n.npf pt.pa.npf d.asn n.asn

αὐτοῦ καὶ τὸ ὄνομα τοῦ πατρὸς αὐτοῦ γεγραμμένον ἐπὶ τῶν
his and *{the}* his Father's name *{the}* *Father's* *his* written on *{the}* their
899 2779 3836 899 4252 3950 3836 4252 899 1211 2093 3836 899
r.gsm.3 cj d.asn n.asn d.gsm n.gsm r.gsm.3 pt.rp.asn p.g d.gpn

μετώπων αὐτῶν. 2 καὶ ἤκουσα φωνὴν ἐκ τοῦ οὐρανοῦ ὡς φωνὴν →
foreheads. *their* And I heard a sound from *{the}* heaven like the roar of many
3587 899 2779 201 5889 1666 3836 4041 6055 5889 4498
n.gpn r.gpm.3 cj v.aai.1s n.asf p.g d.gsm n.gsm pl n.asf

ὑδάτων πολλῶν καὶ ὡς φωνὴν → βροντῆς μεγάλης, καὶ ἡ φωνὴ ἣν
waters *many* and like the sound of loud thunder. *loud* *{and}* The sound *{that}*
5623 4498 2779 6055 5889 3489 1103 3489 2779 3836 5889 4005
n.gpn a.gpn cj pl n.asf n.gsf a.gsf cj d.nsf n.nsf r.asf

ἤκουσα ὡς κιθαρῳδῶν κιθαριζόντων ἐν ταῖς κιθάραις αὐτῶν.
I heard was like the sound of harpists playing on *{the}* their harps, *their*
201 6055 3069 3068 1877 3836 899 3067 899
v.aai.1s pl n.gpm pt.pa.gpm p.d d.dpf n.dpf r.gpm.3

3 καὶ ᾄδουσιν[a] ᾠδὴν καινὴν ἐνώπιον τοῦ θρόνου καὶ ἐνώπιον τῶν
and they were singing a new song *new* before the throne and before the
2779 106 2785 6046 2785 1967 3836 2585 2779 1967 3836
cj v.pai.3p n.asf a.asf p.g d.gsm n.gsm cj p.g d.gpn

τεσσάρων ζῴων καὶ τῶν πρεσβυτέρων, καὶ οὐδεὶς ἐδύνατο μαθεῖν τὴν
four ⌊living creatures⌋ and the elders. *{and}* No one was able to learn the
5475 2442 2779 3836 4565 2779 4029 1538 3443 3836
a.gpn n.gpn cj d.gpm a.gpm cj a.nsm v.ipi.3s f.aa d.asf

ᾠδὴν ⌊εἰ μὴ⌋ αἱ ἑκατὸν ⌊τεσσεράκοντα τέσσαρες⌋ χιλιάδες, οἱ
song except the one hundred and forty-four thousand who
6046 1623 3590 3836 1669 5477 5475 5942 3836
n.asf cj pl d.npf a.npf a.npf a.npf n.npf d.npm

ἠγορασμένοι ἀπὸ τῆς γῆς. 4 οὗτοί εἰσιν οἳ μετὰ
had been redeemed from the earth. These are the ones who have not been defiled with
60 608 3836 1178 4047 1639 4005 3662 3662 3662 4024 3662 3662 3552
pt.rp.npm p.g d.gsf n.gsf r.npm v.pai.3p d.npm p.g

γυναικῶν οὐκ ἐμολύνθησαν, παρθένοι γάρ εἰσιν, οὗτοι οἱ
women, *not* *ones who have been defiled* for they are virgins. *for* *they are* These are the
1222 4024 3662 1142 1639 1639 4221 1142 1639 4047 3836
n.gpf pl v.api.3p n.npm cj v.pai.3p r.npm d.npm

ἀκολουθοῦντες τῷ ἀρνίῳ ⌊ὅπου ἂν⌋ ὑπάγῃ. οὗτοι ἠγοράσθησαν ἀπὸ τῶν
ones who follow the Lamb wherever he goes. These were redeemed from the
199 3836 768 3963 323 5632 4047 60 608 3836
pt.pa.npm d.dsn n.dsn cj pl v.pas.3s r.npm v.api.3p p.g d.gpm

ἀνθρώπων ἀπαρχὴ τῷ θεῷ καὶ τῷ ἀρνίῳ, 5 καὶ ἐν τῷ στόματι αὐτῶν
human race as firstfruits for God and ⌊for the⌋ Lamb, and in *{the}* their mouth *their*
476 569 3836 2536 2779 3836 768 2779 1877 3836 899 5125 899
n.gpm n.nsf d.dsm n.dsm cj d.dsn n.dsn cj p.d d.dsn n.dsn r.gpm.3

NASB

wisdom. Let him
who has under-
standing calculate
the number of
the beast, for the
number is that of a
man; and his num-
ber is [a]six hundred
and sixty-six.

The Lamb and the 144,000 on Mount Zion

14:1 Then I looked,
and behold, the
Lamb *was* standing
on Mount Zion,
and with Him one
hundred and forty-
four thousand,
having His name
and the name of
His Father written
on their foreheads.
2 And I heard a
voice from heaven,
like the sound of
many waters and
like the sound of
loud thunder, and
the voice which I
heard *was* like *the*
sound of harpists
playing on their
harps. 3 And they
*sang a new song
before the throne
and before the four
living creatures
and the elders; and
no one could learn
the song except the
one hundred and
forty-four thousand
who had been
purchased from the
earth. 4 These are
the ones who have
not been defiled
with women, for
they [b]have kept
themselves chaste.
These *are* the ones
who follow the
Lamb wherever He
goes. These have
been purchased
from among men
as first fruits to
God and to the
Lamb. 5 And no lie

[a] 18 Or *is humanity's number*

[a] ὡς included by UBS after ᾄδουσιν.

[a] One early ms reads 616
[b] Lit *are chaste men*

NIV

they are blameless.

The Three Angels

[6]Then I saw an-
other angel flying
in midair, and he
had the eternal
gospel to proclaim
to those who live
on the earth—to
every nation, tribe,
language and peo-
ple. [7]He said in a
loud voice, "Fear
God and give him
glory, because the
hour of his judg-
ment has come.
Worship him who
made the heavens,
the earth, the sea
and the springs of
water."
[8]A second an-
gel followed and
said, "'Fallen!
Fallen is Babylon
the Great,'[a] which
made all the na-
tions drink the
maddening wine
of her adulteries."
[9]A third angel
followed them
and said in a loud
voice: "If anyone
worships the beast
and its image and
receives its mark
on their forehead
or on their hand,
[10]they, too, will
drink the wine of
God's fury, which
has been poured
full strength into
the cup of his
wrath. They will
be tormented with
burning sulfur in
the presence of the
holy angels and of
the Lamb. [11]And
the smoke of their
torment will rise
for ever and ever.
There will be no
rest day or night
for those who wor-
ship the beast and

οὐχ εὑρέθη ψεῦδος, ἄμωμοί εἰσιν.[a] [6]καὶ εἶδον ἄλλον ἄγγελον
no lie was found; *lie* they are blameless. *they are* Then I saw another angel
4024 6022 2351 6022 1639 1639 320 1639 2779 1625 257 34
pl v.api.3s n.nsn a.npm v.pai.3p cj v.aai.1s r.asm n.asm

πετόμενον ἐν μεσουρανήματι, ἔχοντα εὐαγγέλιον αἰώνιον εὐαγγελίσαι
flying directly overhead, with an eternal gospel *eternal* to proclaim
4375 1877 3547 2400 173 2295 173 2294
pt.pm.asm p.d n.dsn pt.pa.asm n.asn a.asn f.aa

ἐπὶ τοὺς καθημένους ἐπὶ τῆς γῆς καὶ ἐπὶ πᾶν ἔθνος καὶ φυλὴν καὶ γλῶσσαν
to those who live on the earth — *{and}* to every nation, *{and}* tribe, *{and}* language,
2093 3836 2764 2093 3836 1178 2779 2093 4246 1620 2779 5876 2779 1185
p.a d.apm pt.pm.apm p.g d.gsf n.gsf cj p.a a.asn n.asn cj n.asf cj n.asf

καὶ λαόν, [7] λέγων ἐν φωνῇ μεγάλῃ, φοβήθητε τὸν θεὸν καὶ δότε αὐτῷ
and people. And he said with a loud voice, *loud* "Fear *{the}* God and give him
2779 3295 3306 1877 3489 5889 3489 5828 3836 2536 2779 1443 899
cj n.asm pt.pa.nsm p.d n.dsf a.dsf v.apm.2p d.asm n.asm cj v.aam.2p r.dsm.3

δόξαν, ὅτι ἦλθεν ἡ ὥρα τῆς κρίσεως αὐτοῦ, καὶ προσκυνήσατε
glory, because *has come* the hour of his judgment *his* has come, and worship
1518 4022 2262 3836 6052 3836 899 3213 899 2262 2262 2779 4686
n.asf cj v.aai.3s d.nsf n.nsf d.gsf n.gsf r.gsm.3 cj v.aam.2p

τῷ ποιήσαντι τὸν οὐρανὸν καὶ τὴν γῆν καὶ θάλασσαν καὶ πηγὰς ὑδάτων.
him who made *{the}* heaven and *{the}* earth, *{and}* the sea and the springs of water."
3836 4472 3836 4041 2779 3836 1178 2779 2498 2779 4380 5623
d.dsm pt.aa.dsm d.asm n.asm cj d.asf n.asf cj n.asf cj n.apf n.gpn

[8]καὶ ἄλλος ἄγγελος δεύτερος ἠκολούθησεν λέγων, ἔπεσεν ἔπεσεν Βαβυλὼν ἡ
Then another angel, a second, followed, saying, "Fallen, fallen is Babylon the
2779 257 34 1311 199 3306 4406 4406 956 3836
cj r.nsm n.nsm a.nsm v.aai.3s pt.pa.nsm v.aai.3s v.aai.3s n.nsf d.nsf

μεγάλη ἣ ἐκ τοῦ οἴνου τοῦ θυμοῦ τῆς
great! — she who has made all nations drink of the wine of her passionate *{the}*
3489 4540 4005 4540 4540 4246 1620 4540 1666 3836 3885 3836 899 2596 3836
a.nsf r.nsf p.g d.gsm n.gsm d.gsm n.gsm d.gsf

πορνείας αὐτῆς πεπότικεν πάντα τὰ ἔθνη. [9]καὶ ἄλλος ἄγγελος τρίτος
immorality." *her* *she has made drink* *all* *{the}* *nations* Then another angel, a third,
4518 899 4540 4246 3836 1620 2779 257 34 5569
n.gsf r.gsf.3 v.rai.3s a.apn d.apn n.apn cj r.nsm n.nsm a.nsm

ἠκολούθησεν αὐτοῖς λέγων ἐν φωνῇ μεγάλῃ, εἴ τις προσκυνεῖ τὸ
followed them, declaring in a loud voice, *loud* "If anyone worships the
199 899 3306 1877 3489 5889 3489 1623 5516 4686 3836
v.aai.3s r.dpm.3 pt.pa.nsm p.d n.dsf a.dsf cj r.nsm v.pai.3s d.asn

θηρίον καὶ τὴν εἰκόνα αὐτοῦ καὶ λαμβάνει χάραγμα ἐπὶ τοῦ μετώπου
beast and *{the}* his image, *his* and receives a mark on *{the}* his forehead
2563 2779 3836 899 1635 899 2779 3284 5916 2093 3836 899 3587
n.asn cj d.asf n.asf r.gsn.3 cj v.pai.3s n.asn p.g d.gsn n.gsn

αὐτοῦ ἢ ἐπὶ τὴν χεῖρα αὐτοῦ, [10] καὶ αὐτὸς πίεται ἐκ τοῦ οἴνου τοῦ
his or on *{the}* his hand, *his* he also *he* will drink of the wine of
899 2445 2093 3836 899 5931 899 899 2779 899 4403 1666 3836 3885 3836
r.gsm.3 cj p.a d.asf n.asf r.gsm.3 adv r.nsm v.fmi.3s p.g d.gsm n.gsm d.gsm

θυμοῦ τοῦ θεοῦ τοῦ κεκερασμένου ἀκράτου ἐν τῷ ποτηρίῳ τῆς ὀργῆς
God's wrath, *{the}* *God's* *{the}* poured full strength into the cup of his wrath,
2536 2596 3836 2536 3836 3042 204 1877 3836 4539 3836 899 3973
n.gsm d.gsm n.gsm d.gsm pt.rp.gsm a.gsm p.d d.dsn n.dsn d.gsf n.gsf

αὐτοῦ καὶ βασανισθήσεται ἐν πυρὶ καὶ θείῳ ἐνώπιον → ἀγγέλων
his and he will be tormented with fire and sulfur in the presence of the holy angels
899 2779 989 1877 4786 2779 2520 1967 41 34
r.gsm.3 cj v.fpi.3s p.d n.dsn cj n.dsn p.g n.gpm

ἁγίων καὶ ἐνώπιον τοῦ ἀρνίου. [11]καὶ ὁ καπνὸς τοῦ βασανισμοῦ αὐτῶν
holy and in the presence of the Lamb. And the smoke from their torture *their*
41 2779 1967 3836 768 2779 3836 2837 3836 899 990 899
a.gpm cj p.g d.gsn n.gsn cj d.nsm n.nsm d.gsm n.gsm r.gpm.3

⌞εἰς αἰῶνας⌟ αἰώνων ἀναβαίνει, καὶ
will go up forever and ever, *will go up* and those who worship the beast and
326 326 326 1650 172 172 326 2779 3836 4686 4686 3836 2563 2779
p.a n.apm n.gpm v.pai.3s cj

NASB

was found in their
mouth; they are
blameless.

Vision of the Angel with the Gospel

[6]And I saw an-
other angel flying
in midheaven,
having an eternal
gospel to preach to
those who live on
the earth, and to
every nation and
tribe and tongue
and people; [7]and
he said with a
loud voice, "Fear
God, and give Him
glory, because the
hour of His judg-
ment has come;
worship Him who
made the heaven
and the earth and
sea and springs of
waters."
[8]And another an-
gel, a second one,
followed, saying,
"Fallen, fallen is
Babylon the great,
she who has made
all the nations
drink of the wine
of the passion of
her immorality."

Doom for Worshipers of the Beast

[9]Then another
angel, a third one,
followed them,
saying with a loud
voice, "If anyone
worships the beast
and his image, and
receives a mark
on his forehead or
on his hand, [10]he
also will drink of
the wine of the
wrath of God,
which is mixed
in full strength
in the cup of His
anger; and he will
be tormented with
fire and brimstone
in the presence of
the holy angels and
in the presence of
the Lamb. [11]And
the smoke of their
torment goes up
forever and ever;
they have no rest
day and night,
those who worship
the beast and his

[a] 8 Isaiah 21:9

[a] ἐνώπιον τοῦ θρόνου τοῦ Θεοῦ included by TR after εἰσιν.

NIV

its image, or for
anyone who re-
ceives the mark of
its name." [12]This
calls for patient
endurance on the
part of the people
of God who keep
his commands and
remain faithful to
Jesus.
[13]Then I heard a
voice from heav-
en say, "Write
this: Blessed are
the dead who die
in the Lord from
now on."
"Yes," says the
Spirit, "they will
rest from their la-
bor, for their deeds
will follow them."

Harvesting the Earth and Trampling the Winepress

[14]I looked, and
there before me
was a white cloud,
and seated on the
cloud was one
like a son of man[a]
with a crown of
gold on his head
and a sharp sick-
le in his hand.
[15]Then another
angel came out
of the temple and
called in a loud
voice to him who
was sitting on the
cloud, "Take your
sickle and reap,
because the time
to reap has come,
for the harvest of
the earth is ripe."
[16]So he who was
seated on the cloud
swung his sickle
over the earth, and
the earth was har-
vested.
[17]Another angel
came out of the
temple in heaven,
and he too

[a] *14* See Daniel 7:13.

οὐκ ἔχουσιν ἀνάπαυσιν ἡμέρας καὶ νυκτός οἱ προσκυνοῦντες
his image will have no *will have* relief day or night, *those who worship*
899 1635 2400 2400 4024 2400 398 2465 2779 3816 3836 4686
pl v.pai.3p n.asf n.gsf cj n.gsf d.npm pt.pa.npm

τὸ θηρίον καὶ τὴν εἰκόνα αὐτοῦ καὶ εἴ τις λαμβάνει τὸ χάραγμα
the beast and {the} image his ⌞along with⌟ *{if}* ⌞anyone who⌟ receives the mark
3836 2563 2779 3836 1635 899 2779 1623 5516 3284 3836 5916
d.asn n.asn cj d.asf n.asf r.gsn.3 cj cj r.nsm v.pai.3s d.asn n.asn

τοῦ ὀνόματος αὐτοῦ. [12] ὧδε ἡ ὑπομονὴ τῶν ἁγίων ἐστίν,
of his name." *his* This calls for *{the}* endurance ⌞on the part of the⌟ saints, *calls for*
3836 899 3950 899 6045 1639 1639 3836 5705 3836 41 1639
d.gsn n.gsn r.gsn.3 adv d.nsf n.nsf d.gpm a.gpm v.pai.3s

οἱ τηροῦντες τὰς ἐντολὰς τοῦ θεοῦ καὶ ↰ ↰ ↰ τὴν πίστιν Ἰησοῦ.
those who keep the commandments of God and hold fast to their faith in Jesus.
3836 5498 3836 1953 3836 2536 2779 5498 5498 5498 3836 4411 2652
d.npm pt.pa.npm d.apf n.apf d.gsm n.gsm cj d.asf n.asf n.gsm

[13] καὶ ἤκουσα φωνῆς ἐκ τοῦ οὐρανοῦ λεγούσης, γράψον, μακάριοι οἱ
And I heard a voice from *{the}* heaven saying, "Write this: Blessed are the
2779 201 5889 1666 3836 4041 3306 1211 3421 3836
cj v.aai.1s n.gsf p.g d.gsm n.gsm pt.pa.gsf v.aam.2s a.npm d.npm

νεκροὶ οἱ ἐν κυρίῳ ἀποθνῄσκοντες ἀπ᾽ ἄρτι. ναί, λέγει τὸ
dead who die in the Lord *die* from now on." "Yes indeed!" says the
3738 3836 633 1877 3261 633 608 785 3721 3306 3836
a.npm d.npm p.d n.dsm pt.pa.npm p.g adv pl v.pai.3s d.nsn

πνεῦμα, ἵνα ἀναπαήσονται ἐκ τῶν κόπων αὐτῶν, τὰ γὰρ ἔργα αὐτῶν
Spirit, "so they can rest from *{the}* their labors, *their {the}* because their deeds *their*
4460 2671 399 1666 3836 899 3160 899 3836 1142 899 2240 899
n.nsn cj v.fpi.3p p.g d.gpm n.gpm r.gpm.3 d.npn cj n.npn r.gpm.3

ἀκολουθεῖ μετ᾽ αὐτῶν. [14] καὶ εἶδον, καὶ ἰδοὺ νεφέλη λευκή, καὶ
will follow *{after}* them!" Then I looked, and behold, a white cloud, *white* and seated
199 3552 899 2779 1625 2779 2627 3328 3749 3328 2779 2764
v.pai.3s p.g r.gpm.3 cj v.aai.1s cj j n.nsf a.nsf cj

ἐπὶ τὴν νεφέλην καθήμενον ὅμοιον υἱὸν ἀνθρώπου, ἔχων ἐπὶ
on the cloud *seated* was one like a son of man. He had a golden crown on
2093 3836 3749 2764 3927 5626 476 2400 5997 5109 2093
p.a d.asf n.asf pt.pm.asm a.asm n.asm n.gsm pt.pa.nsm p.g

τῆς κεφαλῆς αὐτοῦ στέφανον χρυσοῦν καὶ ἐν τῇ χειρὶ αὐτοῦ
{the} his head *his crown golden* and a sharp sickle in *{the}* his hand. *his*
3836 899 3051 899 5109 5997 2779 3955 1535 1877 3836 899 5931 899
d.gsf n.gsf r.gsm.3 n.asm a.asm cj p.d d.dsf n.dsf r.gsm.3

δρέπανον ὀξύ. [15] καὶ ἄλλος ἄγγελος ἐξῆλθεν ἐκ τοῦ ναοῦ κράζων ἐν
sickle sharp Then another angel came ⌞out of⌟ the temple, calling with a loud
1535 3955 2779 257 34 2002 1666 3836 3724 3189 1877 3489
n.asn a.asn cj r.nsm n.nsm v.aai.3s p.g d.gsm n.gsm pt.pa.nsm p.d

φωνῇ μεγάλῃ τῷ καθημένῳ ἐπὶ τῆς νεφέλης, πέμψον τὸ δρέπανόν
voice *loud* ⌞to the⌟ ⌞one who was sitting⌟ on the cloud, ⌞"Thrust in⌟ *{the}* your sickle
5889 3489 3836 2764 2093 3836 3749 4287 3836 5148 1535
n.dsf a.dsf d.dsm pt.pm.dsm p.g d.gsf n.gsf v.aam.2s d.asn n.asn

σου καὶ θέρισον, ὅτι ἦλθεν ἡ ὥρα θερίσαι, ὅτι ἐξηράνθη
your and reap, for the hour to reap has come, *the hour to reap* because *is ripe*
5148 2779 2545 4022 3836 6052 2545 2545 2262 3836 6052 2545 4022 3830
r.gs.2 cj v.aam.2s cj v.aai.3s d.nsf n.nsf f.aa cj v.api.3s

ὁ θερισμὸς τῆς γῆς. [16] καὶ ἔβαλεν ὁ καθήμενος ἐπὶ τῆς νεφέλης
the harvest of the earth is ripe." So *swung* the one who sat on the cloud
3836 2546 3836 1178 3830 3830 2779 965 3836 2764 2093 3836 3749
d.nsm n.nsm d.gsf n.gsf cj v.aai.3s d.nsm pt.pm.nsm p.g d.gsf n.gsf

τὸ δρέπανον αὐτοῦ ἐπὶ τὴν γῆν καὶ ἐθερίσθη ἡ γῆ.
swung *{the}* his sickle *his* across the earth, and the earth was reaped. *the earth*
965 3836 899 1535 899 2093 3836 1178 2779 3836 1178 2545 3836 1178
d.asn n.asn r.gsm.3 p.a d.asf n.asf cj v.api.3s d.nsf n.nsf

[17] καὶ ἄλλος ἄγγελος ἐξῆλθεν ἐκ τοῦ ναοῦ τοῦ ἐν τῷ οὐρανῷ
Then another angel came ⌞out of⌟ the temple *{the}* in *{the}* heaven, and he too
2779 257 34 2002 1666 3836 3724 3836 1877 3836 4041 899 2779
cj r.nsm n.nsm v.aai.3s p.g d.gsm n.gsm d.gsm p.d d.dsm n.dsm

NASB

image, and who-
ever receives the
mark of his name."
[12]Here is the per-
severance of the
saints who keep the
commandments of
God and their faith
in Jesus.
[13]And I heard a
voice from heaven,
saying, "Write,
'Blessed are the
dead who die in
the Lord from now
on!'" "Yes," says
the Spirit, "so that
they may rest from
their labors, for
their deeds follow
with them."

The Reapers

[14]Then I looked,
and behold, a white
cloud, and sitting
on the cloud *was*
one like [a]a son
of man, having
a golden crown
on His head and
a sharp sickle in
His hand. [15]And
another angel came
out of the temple,
crying out with a
loud voice to Him
who sat on the
cloud, "Put in your
sickle and reap, for
the hour to reap
has come, because
the harvest of
the earth is ripe."
[16]Then He who sat
on the cloud swung
His sickle over the
earth, and the earth
was reaped.
[17]And another an-
gel came out of the
temple which is in
heaven, and he

[a] Or *the Son of Man*

NIV

had a sharp sick-
le. 18 Still another
angel, who had
charge of the fire,
came from the al-
tar and called in
a loud voice to
him who had the
sharp sickle, "Take
your sharp sick-
le and gather the
clusters of grapes
from the earth's
vine, because its
grapes are ripe."
19 The angel swung
his sickle on the
earth, gathered its
grapes and threw
them into the great
winepress of God's
wrath. 20 They were
trampled in the
winepress outside
the city, and blood
flowed out of the
press, rising as
high as the hors-
es' bridles for a
distance of 1,600
stadia.[a]

Seven Angels With Seven Plagues

15 I saw in
heaven an-
other great and
marvelous sign:
seven angels with
the seven last
plagues—last,
because with them
God's wrath is
completed. 2 And
I saw what looked
like a sea of glass
glowing with fire
and, standing be-
side the sea, those
who had been
victorious over the
beast and its image
and over the num-
ber of its name.
They held harps
given them by

[a] *20* That is, about 180 miles or about 300 kilometers

ἔχων καὶ αὐτὸς δρέπανον ὀξύ. 18 καὶ ἄλλος ἄγγελος ἐξῆλθεν[a] ἐκ τοῦ
had *too* *he* a sharp sickle. *sharp* Then another angel, *came out* *from* *the*
2400 2779 899 3955 1535 3955 2779 257 34 2002 1666 3836
pt.pa.nsm adv r.nsm n.asn a.asn cj r.nsm n.nsm v.aai.3s p.g d.gsn

θυσιαστηρίου ὁ[b] ἔχων ἐξουσίαν ἐπὶ τοῦ πυρός, καὶ
altar the ⌊one who had⌋ authority over the fire, came out from the altar and
2603 3836 2400 2026 2093 3836 4786 2002 2002 1666 3836 2603 2779
n.gsn d.nsm pt.pa.nsm n.asf p.g d.gsn n.gsn cj

ἐφώνησεν → φωνῇ μεγάλῃ τῷ ἔχοντι τὸ δρέπανον τὸ ὀξὺ
called with a loud voice *loud* ⌊to the⌋ angel who had the sharp sickle, *{the}* *sharp*
5888 3489 5889 3489 3836 2400 3836 3955 1535 3836 3955
v.aai.3s n.dsf a.dsf d.dsm pt.pa.dsm d.asn n.asn d.asn a.asn

λέγων, πέμψον σου τὸ δρέπανον τὸ ὀξὺ καὶ τρύγησον τοὺς
{saying} ⌊"Thrust in⌋ your *{the}* sharp sickle *{the}* *sharp* and gather the
3306 4287 5148 3836 3955 1535 3836 3955 2779 5582 3836
pt.pa.nsm v.aam.2s r.gs.2 d.asn n.asn d.asn a.asn cj v.aam.2s d.apm

βότρυας τῆς ἀμπέλου τῆς γῆς, ὅτι ἤκμασαν αἱ σταφυλαὶ
⌊clusters of grapes⌋ ⌊from the⌋ vine of the earth, for its grapes are ripe." *{the}* *grapes*
1084 3836 306 3836 1178 4022 899 5091 196 3836 5091
n.apm d.gsf n.gsf d.gsf n.gsf cj v.aai.3p d.npf n.npf

αὐτῆς. 19 καὶ ἔβαλεν ὁ ἄγγελος τὸ δρέπανον αὐτοῦ εἰς τὴν γῆν
its So the angel swung *the* *angel* *{the}* his sickle *his* across the earth
899 2779 3836 34 965 3836 34 3836 899 1535 899 1650 3836 1178
r.gsf.3 cj v.aai.3s d.nsm n.nsm d.asn n.asn r.gsm.3 p.a d.asf n.asf

καὶ ἐτρύγησεν τὴν ἄμπελον τῆς γῆς καὶ ἔβαλεν εἰς τὴν ληνὸν τοῦ
and gathered the grape harvest of the earth and threw it into the great winepress of the
2779 5582 3836 306 3836 1178 2779 965 1650 3836 3489 3332 3836
cj v.aai.3s d.asf n.asf d.gsf n.gsf cj v.aai.3s p.a d.asf n.asf d.gsm

θυμοῦ τοῦ θεοῦ τὸν μέγαν. 20 καὶ ἐπατήθη ἡ ληνὸς ἔξωθεν τῆς
wrath of God. *{the}* *great* Then the winepress was trodden *the* *winepress* outside the
2596 3836 2536 3836 3489 2779 3836 3332 4251 3836 3332 2033 3836
n.gsm d.gsm n.gsm d.asm a.asm cj v.api.3s d.nsf n.nsf p.g d.gsf

πόλεως καὶ ἐξῆλθεν αἷμα ἐκ τῆς ληνοῦ ἄχρι τῶν
city, and blood poured out *blood* from the winepress, rising ⌊to the height⌋ of horses'
4484 2779 135 2002 135 1666 3836 3332 948 3836 2691
n.gsf cj v.aai.3s n.nsn p.g d.gsf n.gsf p.g d.gpm

χαλινῶν τῶν ἵππων ἀπὸ ⌊σταδίων χιλίων ἑξακοσίων.⌋
bridles *{the}* *horses'* ⌊for a distance of about⌋ two hundred miles.
5903 3836 2691 608 5084 5943 1980
n.gpm d.gpm n.gpm p.g n.gpm a.gpm a.gpm

15:1 καὶ εἶδον ἄλλο σημεῖον ἐν τῷ οὐρανῷ μέγα καὶ θαυμαστόν,
Then I saw another sign in *{the}* heaven, great and marvelous: seven
2779 1625 257 4956 1877 3836 4041 3489 2779 2515 2231
cj v.aai.1s r.asn n.asn p.d d.dsm n.dsm a.asn cj a.asn

ἀγγέλους ἑπτὰ ἔχοντας πληγὰς ἑπτὰ τὰς ἐσχάτας, ὅτι ἐν αὐταῖς
angels *seven* with seven plagues, *seven* which are the last, because with them
34 2231 2400 2231 4435 2231 3836 2274 4022 1877 899
n.apm a.apm pt.pa.apm n.apf a.apf d.apf a.apf cj p.d r.dpf.3

ἐτελέσθη ὁ θυμὸς τοῦ θεοῦ. 2 καὶ εἶδον ὡς
is finished the wrath of God is finished. And I saw ⌊what appeared to be⌋ a
5464 3836 2596 3836 2536 5464 5464 2779 1625 6055
v.api.3s d.nsm n.nsm d.gsm n.gsm cj v.aai.1s pl

θάλασσαν ὑαλίνην μεμιγμένην πυρὶ καὶ τοὺς νικῶντας ἐκ τοῦ θηρίου
sea of glass mixed ⌊with fire,⌋ and those who had conquered *{over}* the beast
2498 5612 3624 4786 2779 3836 3771 1666 3836 2563
n.asf a.asf pt.rp.asf n.dsn cj d.apm pt.pa.apm p.g d.gsn n.gsn

καὶ ἐκ τῆς εἰκόνος αὐτοῦ καὶ ἐκ τοῦ ἀριθμοῦ τοῦ ὀνόματος αὐτοῦ
and *{over}* *{the}* his image *his* and *{over}* the number of his name. *his*
2779 1666 3836 899 1635 899 2779 1666 3836 750 3836 899 3950 899
cj p.g d.gsf n.gsf r.gsn.3 cj p.g d.gsm n.gsm d.gsn n.gsn r.gsn.3

ἑστῶτας ἐπὶ τὴν θάλασσαν τὴν ὑαλίνην ἔχοντας κιθάρας τοῦ
⌊They were standing⌋ beside the sea of glass with harps given them by
2705 2093 3836 2498 3836 5612 2400 3067 3836
pt.ra.apm p.a d.asf n.asf d.asf a.asf pt.pa.apm n.apf d.gsm

[a] [ἐξῆλθεν] UBS.
[b] [ὁ] UBS.

NASB

also had a sharp
sickle. 18 Then
another angel, the
one who has power
over fire, came out
from the altar; and
he called with a
loud voice to him
who had the sharp
sickle, saying, "Put
in your sharp sickle
and gather the
clusters from the
vine of the earth,
because her grapes
are ripe." 19 So the
angel swung his
sickle to the earth
and gathered *the*
clusters from the
vine of the earth,
and threw them
into the great wine
press of the wrath
of God. 20 And the
wine press was
trodden outside
the city, and blood
came out from the
wine press, up to
the horses' bridles,
for a distance
of [a]two hundred
miles.

A Scene of Heaven

15:1 Then I saw
another sign in
heaven, great and
marvelous, seven
angels who had
seven plagues,
which are the last,
because in them
the wrath of God is
finished.
2 And I saw some-
thing like a sea of
glass mixed with
fire, and those who
had been victori-
ous over the beast
and his image and
the number of his
name, standing on
the sea of glass,
holding harps of

[a] Lit *sixteen hundred stadia;* a stadion was approx 600 ft

NIV

God 3 and sang the song of God's servant Moses and of the Lamb:

"Great and marvelous are your deeds,
Lord God Almighty.
Just and true are your ways,
King of the nations.[a]
4 Who will not fear you, Lord,
and bring glory to your name?
For you alone are holy.
All nations will come
and worship before you,
for your righteous acts have been revealed."[b]

5 After this I looked, and I saw in heaven the temple—that is, the tabernacle of the covenant law—and it was opened.
6 Out of the temple came the seven angels with the seven plagues. They were dressed in clean, shining linen and wore golden sashes around their chests.
7 Then one of the four living creatures gave to the seven angels seven golden bowls filled with the wrath of God, who lives for ever and ever.
8 And the temple was filled with smoke from the glory of God and from his power, and no one could enter the temple until the seven plagues of the seven angels were completed.

[a] 3 Some manuscripts *ages*
[b] 3,4 Phrases in this song are drawn from Psalm 111:2,3; Deut. 32:4; Jer. 10:7; Psalms 86:9; 98:2.

θεοῦ. 3 καὶ ᾄδουσιν τὴν ᾠδὴν Μωϋσέως τοῦ δούλου τοῦ θεοῦ καὶ τὴν ᾠδὴν τοῦ
God. And they sing the song of Moses the servant of God and the song of the
2536 2779 106 3836 6046 3707 3836 1529 3836 2536 2779 3836 6046 3836
n.gsm cj v.pai.3p d.asf n.asf n.gsm d.gsm n.gsm d.gsm n.gsm cj d.asf n.asf d.gsn

ἀρνίου λέγοντες, μεγάλα καὶ θαυμαστὰ τὰ ἔργα σου, κύριε ὁ θεὸς ὁ
Lamb, saying, "Great and marvelous are *{the}* your deeds, *your* O Lord *{the}* God *{the}*
768 3306 3489 2779 2515 3836 5148 2240 5148 3261 3836 2536 3836
n.gsn pt.pa.npm a.npn cj a.npn d.npn n.npn r.gs.2 n.vsm d.vsm n.vsm d.vsm

παντοκράτωρ· δίκαιαι καὶ ἀληθιναὶ αἱ ὁδοί σου, ὁ βασιλεὺς τῶν
Almighty! Just and true are *{the}* your ways, *your* O King of the
4120 1465 2779 240 3836 5148 3847 5148 3836 995 3836
n.vsm a.npf cj a.npf d.npf n.npf r.gs.2 d.vsm n.vsm d.gpn

ἐθνῶν· 4 τίς ↱ ⌞οὐ μὴ⌟ φοβηθῇ, κύριε, καὶ δοξάσει τὸ ὄνομά σου; ὅτι
nations! Who will not fear you, O Lord, and glorify *{the}* your name? *your* For
1620 5515 5828 4024 3590 5828 3261 2779 1519 3836 5148 3950 5148 4022
n.gpn r.nsm pl pl v.aps.3s n.vsm cj v.fai.3s d.asn n.asn r.gs.2 cj

μόνος ὅσιος, ὅτι πάντα τὰ ἔθνη ἥξουσιν καὶ προσκυνήσουσιν ἐνώπιόν
you alone are holy, for all *{the}* nations will come and worship before
3668 4008 4022 4246 3836 1620 2457 2779 4686 1967
a.nsm a.nsm cj a.npn d.npn n.npn v.fai.3p cj v.fai.3p p.g

σου, ὅτι τὰ δικαιώματά σου ἐφανερώθησαν. 5 καὶ μετὰ ταῦτα εἶδον, καὶ
you, for *{the}* your righteous acts *your* have been revealed." *{and}* After this I looked, and
5148 4022 3836 5148 1468 5148 5746 2779 3552 4047 1625 2779
r.gs.2 cj d.npn n.npn r.gs.2 v.api.3p cj p.a r.apn v.aai.1s cj

ἠνοίγη ὁ ναὸς τῆς σκηνῆς τοῦ μαρτυρίου ἐν τῷ οὐρανῷ,
was opened the temple, that is, the tent of witness, in *{the}* heaven was opened,
487 3836 3724 3836 5008 3836 3457 1877 3836 4041 487 487
v.api.3s d.nsm n.nsm d.gsf n.gsf d.gsn n.gsn p.d d.dsm n.dsm

6 καὶ ἐξῆλθον οἱ ἑπτὰ ἄγγελοι οἱ[a] ἔχοντες τὰς ἑπτὰ πληγὰς
and out of the temple came the seven angels who had the seven plagues.
2779 1666 1666 3836 3724 2002 3836 2231 34 3836 2400 3836 2231 4435
cj v.aai.3p d.npm a.npm n.npm d.npm pt.pa.npm d.apf a.apf n.apf

ἐκ τοῦ ναοῦ ἐνδεδυμένοι λίνον καθαρὸν λαμπρὸν καὶ περιεζωσμένοι
out of the temple ⌞They were clothed in⌟ linen, clean and bright, *{and}* wearing
1666 3836 3724 1907 3351 2754 3287 2779 4322
p.g d.gsm n.gsm pt.rp.npm n.asn a.asn a.asn cj pt.rp.npm

περὶ τὰ στήθη ζώνας χρυσᾶς. 7 καὶ ἓν ἐκ τῶν τεσσάρων
golden sashes across their chests. *sashes golden* Then one of the four
5997 2438 4309 3836 5111 2438 5997 2779 1651 1666 3836 5475
p.a d.apn n.apn n.apf a.apf cj a.nsn p.g d.gpn a.gpn

ζῴων ἔδωκεν τοῖς ἑπτὰ ἀγγέλοις ἑπτὰ φιάλας χρυσᾶς γεμούσας τοῦ
⌞living creatures⌟ gave the seven angels seven golden bowls *golden* full of the
2442 1443 3836 2231 34 2231 5997 5786 5997 1154 3836
n.gpn v.aai.3s d.dpm a.dpm n.dpm a.apf n.apf a.apf pt.pa.apf d.gsm

θυμοῦ τοῦ θεοῦ τοῦ ζῶντος εἰς τοὺς ⌞αἰῶνας τῶν αἰώνων.⌟ 8 καὶ
wrath of God who lives for all time; and the temple
2596 3836 2536 3836 2409 1650 3836 172 3836 172 2779 3836 3724
n.gsm d.gsm n.gsm d.gsm pt.pa.gsm p.a d.apm n.apm d.gpm n.gpm cj

ἐγεμίσθη ὁ ναὸς καπνοῦ ἐκ τῆς δόξης τοῦ θεοῦ καὶ ἐκ τῆς δυνάμεως
was filled *the temple* with smoke from the glory of God and from *{the}* his power,
1153 3836 3724 2837 1666 3836 1518 3836 2536 2779 1666 3836 899 1539
v.api.3s d.nsm n.nsm n.gsm p.g d.gsf n.gsf d.gsm n.gsm cj p.g d.gsf n.gsf

αὐτοῦ, καὶ οὐδεὶς ἐδύνατο ⌞εἰσελθεῖν εἰς⌟ τὸν ναὸν ἄχρι τελεσθῶσιν αἱ ἑπτὰ
his and no one could enter the temple until *had run their course* the seven
899 2779 4029 1538 1656 1650 3836 3724 948 5464 3836 2231
r.gsm.3 cj a.nsm v.ipi.3s f.aa p.a d.asm n.asm cj v.aps.3p d.npf a.npf

πληγαὶ τῶν ἑπτὰ ἀγγέλων.
plagues ⌞from the⌟ seven angels had run their course.
4435 3836 2231 34 5464 5464 5464 5464
n.npf d.gpm a.gpm n.gpm

[a] [οἱ] UBS.

NASB

God. 3 And they *sang the song of Moses, the bond-servant of God, and the song of the Lamb, saying,
"Great and marvelous are Your works,
O Lord God, the Almighty;
Righteous and true are Your ways,
King of the [a]nations!
4 "Who will not fear, O Lord, and glorify Your name?
For You alone are holy;
FOR ALL THE NATIONS WILL COME AND WORSHIP BEFORE YOU,
FOR YOUR RIGHTEOUS ACTS HAVE BEEN REVEALED."

5 After these things I looked, and the temple of the tabernacle of testimony in heaven was opened, 6 and the seven angels who had the seven plagues came out of the temple, clothed in [b]linen, clean *and* bright, and girded around their chests with golden sashes.
7 Then one of the four living creatures gave to the seven angels seven golden bowls full of the wrath of God, who lives forever and ever. 8 And the temple was filled with smoke from the glory of God and from His power; and no one was able to enter the temple until the seven plagues of the seven angels were finished.

[a] Two early mss read *ages*
[b] One early ms reads *stone*

NIV

The Seven Bowls of God's Wrath

16 Then I
heard a loud
voice from the
temple saying to
the seven angels,
"Go, pour out the
seven bowls of
God's wrath on the
earth."
[2]The first angel
went and poured
out his bowl on the
land, and ugly, fes-
tering sores broke
out on the people
who had the mark
of the beast and
worshiped its im-
age.
[3]The second an-
gel poured out his
bowl on the sea,
and it turned into
blood like that of
a dead person, and
every living thing
in the sea died.
[4]The third angel
poured out his
bowl on the riv-
ers and springs of
water, and they be-
came blood. [5]Then
I heard the angel in
charge of the wa-
ters say:

"You are just
in these
judgments,
O Holy One,
you who are
and who
were;
[6] for they have shed
the blood
of your
holy people
and your
prophets,
and you have
given them
blood to
drink as they
deserve."

[7]And I heard the
altar respond:

"Yes, Lord God
Almighty,
true and just
are your
judgments."

[8]The fourth an-
gel poured out his
bowl on the sun,
and the sun was
allowed to scorch
people

16:1 καὶ ἤκουσα μεγάλης φωνῆς ἐκ τοῦ ναοῦ λεγούσης τοῖς ἑπτὰ ἀγγέλοις,
Then I heard a loud voice from the temple declaring to the seven angels,
2779 201 3489 5889 1666 3836 3724 3306 3836 2231 34
cj v.aai.1s a.gsf n.gsf p.g d.gsm n.gsm pt.pa.gsf d.dpm a.dpm n.dpm

ὑπάγετε καὶ ἐκχέετε τὰς ἑπτὰ φιάλας τοῦ θυμοῦ τοῦ θεοῦ εἰς
"Go and pour out on the earth the seven bowls of God's wrath." *{the} God's on*
5632 2779 1772 1650 3836 1178 3836 2231 5786 3836 2536 2596 3836 2536 1650
v.pam.2p cj v.pam.2p d.apf a.apf n.apf d.gsm n.gsm d.gsm n.gsm p.a

τὴν γῆν. [2]καὶ ἀπῆλθεν ὁ πρῶτος καὶ ἐξέχεεν τὴν φιάλην
the earth So the first angel went *the first* and poured out *{the}* his bowl
3836 1178 2779 3836 4755 599 3836 4755 2779 1772 3836 899 5786
d.asf n.asf cj v.aai.3s d.nsm a.nsm cj v.aai.3s d.asf n.asf

αὐτοῦ εἰς τὴν γῆν, καὶ ἐγένετο ἕλκος κακὸν καὶ πονηρὸν ἐπὶ τοὺς
his on the earth, and *broke out sore* a repulsive and malignant sore broke out on *{the}*
899 1650 3836 1178 2779 1181 1814 2805 2779 4505 1814 1181 1181 2093 3836
r.gsm.3 p.a d.asf n.asf cj v.ami.3s n.nsn a.nsn cj a.nsn p.a d.apm

ἀνθρώπους τοὺς ἔχοντας τὸ χάραγμα τοῦ θηρίου καὶ τοὺς προσκυνοῦντας τῇ
everyone who bore the mark of the beast and who worshiped *{the}* his
476 3836 2400 3836 5916 3836 2563 2779 3836 4686 3836 899
n.apm d.apm pt.pa.apm d.asn n.asn d.gsn n.gsn cj d.apm pt.pa.apm d.dsf

εἰκόνι αὐτοῦ. [3]καὶ ὁ δεύτερος ἐξέχεεν τὴν φιάλην αὐτοῦ εἰς τὴν
image. *his* *{and}* The second angel poured out *{the}* his bowl *his* on the
1635 899 2779 3836 1311 1772 3836 899 5786 899 1650 3836
n.dsf r.gsm.3 cj d.nsm a.nsm v.aai.3s d.asf n.asf r.gsm.3 p.a d.asf

θάλασσαν, καὶ ἐγένετο αἷμα ὡς → νεκροῦ, καὶ πᾶσα ψυχὴ ζωῆς
sea and ⌞it turned into⌟ blood like that of a corpse, and every living creature *living* in
2498 2779 1181 135 6055 3738 2779 4246 2437 6034 2437 1877
n.asf cj v.ami.3s n.nsn pl a.gsm cj a.nsf n.nsf n.gsf

ἀπέθανεν τὰ ἐν τῇ θαλάσσῃ. [4]καὶ ὁ τρίτος ἐξέχεεν τὴν
the sea died. *{the} in the sea* *{and}* The third angel poured out *{the}* his
3836 2498 633 3836 1877 3836 2498 2779 3836 5569 1772 3836 899
v.aai.3s d.npn p.d d.dsf n.dsf cj d.nsm a.nsm v.aai.3s d.asf

φιάλην αὐτοῦ εἰς τοὺς ποταμοὺς καὶ τὰς πηγὰς τῶν ὑδάτων, καὶ ἐγένετο
bowl *his* on the rivers and the springs of water, and ⌞they turned into⌟
5786 899 1650 3836 4532 2779 3836 4380 3836 5623 2779 1181
n.asf r.gsm.3 p.a d.apm n.apm cj d.apf n.apf d.gpn n.gpn cj v.ami.3s

αἷμα. [5]καὶ ἤκουσα τοῦ ἀγγέλου τῶν ὑδάτων λέγοντος, δίκαιος
blood. Then I heard the angel in charge of the waters say, "You are just,
135 2779 201 3836 34 3836 5623 3306 1639 1639 1465
n.nsn cj v.aai.1s d.gsm n.gsm d.gpn n.gpn pt.pa.gsm a.nsm

εἶ, ὁ ὢν καὶ ὁ ἦν, ὁ ὅσιος, ὅτι ↱ ↱ ταῦτα
You are O Holy One, who is and who was, *O Holy One* because you brought these
1639 3836 4008 4008 3836 1639 2779 3836 1639 3836 4008 4022 3212 3212 4047
v.pai.2s d.vsm pt.pa.vsm cj d.vsm v.iai.3s d.vsm a.vsm cj r.apn

ἔκρινας, [6]ὅτι αἷμα ἁγίων καὶ προφητῶν ἐξέχεαν καὶ
judgments, because they shed the blood of saints and prophets, *they shed* and you have given
3212 4022 1772 1772 135 41 2779 4737 1772 2779 1443 1443 1443
v.aai.2s cj n.asn a.gpm cj n.gpm v.aai.3p cj

αἷμα αὐτοῖς δέδωκας[a] πιεῖν, ἄξιοί εἰσιν. [7]καὶ ἤκουσα
them blood *them* *you have given* to drink. It is ⌞what they deserve!"⌟ *It is* And I heard
899 135 899 1443 4403 1639 1639 545 1639 2779 201
n.asn r.dpm.3 v.rai.2s f.aa a.npm v.pai.3p cj v.aai.1s

τοῦ θυσιαστηρίου λέγοντος, ναὶ κύριε ὁ θεὸς ὁ παντοκράτωρ, ἀληθιναὶ
the altar saying, "Yes indeed, O Lord *{the}* God the Almighty, true
3836 2603 3306 3721 3261 3836 2536 3836 4120 240
d.gsn n.gsn pt.pa.gsn pl n.vsm d.vsm n.vsm d.vsm n.vsm a.npf

καὶ δίκαιαι αἱ κρίσεις σου. [8]καὶ ὁ τέταρτος ἐξέχεεν τὴν
and just are *{the}* your judgments!" *your* *{and}* The fourth angel poured out *{the}* his
2779 1465 3836 5148 3213 5148 2779 3836 5480 1772 3836 899
cj a.npf d.npf n.npf r.gs.2 cj d.nsm a.nsm v.aai.3s d.asf

φιάλην αὐτοῦ ἐπὶ τὸν ἥλιον, καὶ ἐδόθη αὐτῷ καυματίσαι τοὺς ἀνθρώπους
bowl *his* on the sun, and it was allowed *it* to scorch *{the}* people
5786 899 2093 3836 2463 2779 899 1443 899 3009 3836 476
n.asf r.gsm.3 p.a d.asm n.asm cj v.api.3s r.dsm.3 f.aa d.apm n.apm

[a] δέδωκας TNIV, NET. [δ]έδωκας UBS.

NASB

Six Bowls of Wrath

16:1Then I heard a
loud voice from the
temple, saying to
the seven angels,
"Go and pour out
on the earth the
seven bowls of the
wrath of God."
[2]So the first *angel*
went and poured
out his bowl on the
earth; and it be-
came a loathsome
and malignant sore
on the people who
had the mark of the
beast and who wor-
shiped his image.
[3]The second
angel poured out
his bowl into the
sea, and it became
blood like *that* of
a dead man; and
every living [a]thing
in the sea died.
[4]Then the third
angel poured out
his bowl into the
rivers and the
springs of waters;
and they became
blood. [5]And I
heard the angel
of the waters say-
ing, "Righteous
are You, who are
and who were, O
Holy One, because
You judged these
things; [6]for they
poured out the
blood of saints and
prophets, and You
have given them
blood to drink.
They deserve it."
[7]And I heard the
altar saying, "Yes,
O Lord God, the
Almighty, true and
righteous are Your
judgments."
[8]The fourth *angel*
poured out his
bowl upon the sun,
and it was given to
it to scorch men

[a] Lit *soul*

NIV

with fire. 9They
were seared by the
intense heat and
they cursed the
name of God, who
had control over
these plagues, but
they refused to
repent and glorify
him.
10The fifth an-
gel poured out
his bowl on the
throne of the beast,
and its kingdom
was plunged into
darkness. Peo-
ple gnawed their
tongues in agony
11and cursed the
God of heaven
because of their
pains and their
sores, but they
refused to repent
of what they had
done.
12The sixth an-
gel poured out his
bowl on the great
river Euphrates,
and its water was
dried up to pre-
pare the way for
the kings from the
East. 13Then I saw
three impure spir-
its that looked like
frogs; they came
out of the mouth
of the dragon, out
of the mouth of
the beast and out
of the mouth of
the false prophet.
14They are de-
monic spirits that
perform signs, and
they go out to the
kings of the whole
world, to gather
them for the battle
on the great day of
God Almighty.
15"Look, I come
like a thief!

ἐν πυρί. 9καὶ ἐκαυματίσθησαν οἱ ἄνθρωποι καῦμα μέγα καὶ
with fire. {and} Although scorched by the fierce heat the people heat fierce {and}
1877 4786 2779 3009 3489 3008 3836 476 3008 3489 2779
p.d n.dsn cj v.api.3p d.npm n.npm n.asn a.asn cj

ἐβλασφήμησαν τὸ ὄνομα τοῦ θεοῦ τοῦ ἔχοντος τὴν ἐξουσίαν ἐπὶ τὰς πληγὰς
cursed the name of God who had {the} authority over {the} these plagues,
1059 3836 3950 3836 2536 3836 2400 3836 2026 2093 3836 4047 4435
v.aai.3p d.asn n.asn d.gsm n.gsm d.gsm pt.pa.gsm d.asf n.asf p.a d.apf n.apf

ταύτας καὶ ↱ οὐ μετενόησαν δοῦναι αὐτῷ δόξαν. 10καὶ ὁ πέμπτος
these and would not repent and give him glory. {and} The fifth angel
4047 2779 3566 4024 3566 1443 899 1518 2779 3836 4286
r.apf cj pl v.aai.3p f.aa r.dsm.3 n.asf cj d.nsm a.nsm

ἐξέχεεν τὴν φιάλην αὐτοῦ ἐπὶ τὸν θρόνον τοῦ θηρίου, καὶ
poured out {the} his bowl his on the throne of the beast, and his kingdom
1772 3836 899 5786 899 2093 3836 2585 3836 2563 2779 899 993
v.aai.3s d.asf n.asf r.gsn.3 p.a d.asm n.asm d.gsn n.gsn cj

ἐγένετο ἡ βασιλεία αὐτοῦ ἐσκοτωμένη, καὶ ἐμασῶντο τὰς
⌞was plunged into⌟ {the} kingdom his darkness. {and} People gnawed {the} their
1181 3836 993 899 5031 2779 3460 3836 899
v.ami.3s d.nsf n.nsf r.gsm.3 pt.rp.nsf cj v.imi.3p d.apf

γλώσσας αὐτῶν ἐκ τοῦ πόνου, 11καὶ ἐβλασφήμησαν τὸν θεὸν τοῦ οὐρανοῦ ἐκ
tongues their in {the} pain and cursed the God of heaven for
1185 899 1666 3836 4506 2779 1059 3836 2536 3836 4041 1666
n.apf r.gpm.3 p.g d.gsm n.gsm cj v.aai.3p d.asm n.asm d.gsm n.gsm p.g

τῶν πόνων αὐτῶν καὶ ἐκ τῶν ἑλκῶν αὐτῶν καὶ ↱ ↱ οὐ μετενόησαν ἐκ
{the} their pain their and {for} {the} sores, {their} but they would not repent of
3836 899 4506 899 2779 1666 3836 1814 899 2779 3566 3566 4024 3566 1666
d.gpm n.gpm r.gpm.3 cj p.g d.gpn n.gpn r.gpm.3 cj pl v.aai.3p p.g

τῶν ἔργων αὐτῶν. 12καὶ ὁ ἕκτος ἐξέχεεν τὴν φιάλην αὐτοῦ ἐπὶ
{the} their deeds. their {and} The sixth angel poured out {the} his bowl his on
3836 899 2240 899 2779 3836 1761 1772 3836 899 5786 899 2093
d.gpn n.gpn r.gpm.3 cj d.nsm a.nsm v.aai.3s d.asf n.asf r.gsm.3 p.a

τὸν ποταμὸν τὸν μέγαν τὸν Εὐφράτην, καὶ ἐξηράνθη τὸ ὕδωρ
the great river {the} great {the} Euphrates, and its water ⌞was dried up⌟ {the} water
3836 3489 4532 3836 3489 3836 2371 2779 899 5623 3830 3836 5623
d.asm n.asm d.asm a.asm d.asm n.asm cj v.api.3s d.nsn n.nsn

αὐτοῦ, ἵνα ἑτοιμασθῇ ἡ ὁδὸς τῶν βασιλέων τῶν ἀπὸ ⌞ἀνατολῆς ἡλίου.⌟
its to prepare the way for the kings {the} from the east.
899 2671 2286 3836 3847 3836 995 3836 608 424 2463
r.gsm.3 cj v.aps.3s d.nsf n.nsf d.gpm n.gpm d.gpm p.g n.gsf n.gsm

13καὶ εἶδον ἐκ τοῦ στόματος τοῦ
And I saw three unclean spirits, which looked like frogs, coming ⌞out of⌟ the mouth of the
2779 1625 5552 176 4460 6055 1005 1666 3836 5125 3836
cj v.aai.1s p.g d.gsn n.gsn d.gsm

δράκοντος καὶ ἐκ τοῦ στόματος τοῦ θηρίου καὶ ἐκ τοῦ στόματος τοῦ
dragon, {and} ⌞out of⌟ the mouth of the beast, and ⌞out of⌟ the mouth of the
1532 2779 1666 3836 5125 3836 2563 2779 1666 3836 5125 3836
n.gsm cj p.g d.gsn n.gsn d.gsn n.gsn cj p.g d.gsn n.gsn d.gsm

ψευδοπροφήτου πνεύματα τρία ἀκάθαρτα ὡς βάτραχοι· 14εἰσὶν γὰρ
false prophet. spirits three unclean like frogs ⌞They were⌟ {for} demonic
6021 4460 5552 176 6055 1005 1639 1142 1228
n.gsm n.apn a.apn a.apn pl n.npm v.pai.3p cj

πνεύματα δαιμονίων ποιοῦντα σημεῖα, ἃ ἐκπορεύεται ἐπὶ τοὺς βασιλεῖς τῆς
spirits, demonic performing signs, who go out to the kings of the whole
4460 1228 4472 4956 4005 1744 2093 3836 995 3836 3910
n.npn n.gpn pt.pa.npn n.apn r.npn v.pmi.3s p.a d.apm n.apm d.gsf

οἰκουμένης ὅλης συναγαγεῖν αὐτοὺς εἰς τὸν πόλεμον τῆς ἡμέρας τῆς
world whole to assemble them for {the} battle ⌞on the⌟ great day {the}
3876 3910 5251 899 1650 3836 4483 3836 3489 2465 3836
n.gsf a.gsf f.aa r.apm.3 p.a d.asm n.asm d.gsf n.gsf d.gsf

μεγάλης τοῦ θεοῦ τοῦ παντοκράτορος. 15ἰδοὺ ἔρχομαι ὡς κλέπτης.
great of God the Almighty. ("Behold, I am coming like a thief!
3489 3836 2536 3836 4120 2627 2262 6055 3095
a.gsf d.gsm n.gsm d.gsm n.gsm j v.pmi.1s pl n.nsm

NASB

with fire. 9Men
were scorched with
fierce heat; and
they blasphemed
the name of God
who has the power
over these plagues,
and they did not
repent so as to give
Him glory.
10Then the fifth
angel poured out
his bowl on the
throne of the beast,
and his kingdom
became darkened;
and they gnawed
their tongues be-
cause of pain, 11and
they blasphemed
the God of heaven
because of their
pains and their
sores; and they did
not repent of their
deeds.
12The sixth *angel*
poured out his
bowl on the great
river, the Euphra-
tes; and its water
was dried up, so
that the way would
be prepared for the
kings from the east.

Armageddon

13And I saw *coming*
out of the mouth
of the dragon and
out of the mouth of
the beast and out
of the mouth of the
false prophet, three
unclean spirits like
frogs; 14for they are
spirits of demons,
performing signs,
which go out to the
kings of the whole
world, to gather
them together for
the war of the great
day of God, the Al-
mighty. 15("Behold,
I am coming like

NIV

Blessed is the
one who stays
awake and re-
mains clothed, so
as not to go naked
and be shameful-
ly exposed."
16 Then they gath-
ered the kings to-
gether to the place
that in Hebrew is
called Armaged-
don.
17 The seventh
angel poured out
his bowl into the
air, and out of the
temple came a
loud voice from
the throne, say-
ing, "It is done!"
18 Then there came
flashes of light-
ning, rumblings,
peals of thun-
der and a severe
earthquake. No
earthquake like it
has ever occurred
since mankind has
been on earth, so
tremendous was
the quake. 19 The
great city split into
three parts, and
the cities of the
nations collapsed.
God remembered
Babylon the Great
and gave her the
cup filled with the
wine of the fury of
his wrath. 20 Every
island fled away
and the moun-
tains could not
be found. 21 From
the sky huge
hailstones, each
weighing about a
hundred pounds,[a]
fell on people. And
they cursed God
on account of the
plague of hail, be-
cause the plague
was so terrible.

μακάριος ὁ γρηγορῶν καὶ τηρῶν τὰ ἱμάτια αὐτοῦ, ↰ ↰ ἵνα
Blessed is the ⌊one who stays awake⌋ and keeps {the} his clothes his at hand, so that
3421 3836 1213 2779 5498 3836 899 2668 899 5498 5498 2671
a.nsm d.nsm pt.pa.nsm cj pt.pa.nsm d.apn n.apn r.gsm.3 cj

μὴ γυμνὸς περιπατῇ καὶ βλέπωσιν τὴν
he will not be caught naked he will be caught and his shameful condition be seen.") {the}
4344 4344 3590 4344 4344 1218 4344 2779 899 859 859 1063 3836
pl a.nsm v.pas.3s cj v.pas.3p d.asf

ἀσχημοσύνην αὐτοῦ. 16 καὶ συνήγαγεν αὐτοὺς εἰς τὸν τόπον τὸν
shameful condition his And the spirits gathered the kings to the place that
859 899 2779 5251 899 1650 3836 5536 3836
n.asf r.gsm.3 cj v.aai.3s r.apm.3 p.a d.asm n.asm d.asm

καλούμενον Ἑβραϊστὶ Ἁρμαγεδών. 17 καὶ ὁ ἕβδομος ἐξέχεεν
in Hebrew is called in Hebrew Armageddon. Then the seventh angel poured out
1580 1580 2813 1580 762 2779 3836 1575 1772
pt.pp.asm adv n.asn cj d.nsm a.nsm v.aai.3s

τὴν φιάλην αὐτοῦ ἐπὶ τὸν ἀέρα, καὶ ἐξῆλθεν φωνὴ
{the} his bowl his on the air, and out of the temple came a loud voice
3836 899 5786 899 2093 3836 113 2779 1666 1666 3836 3724 2002 3489 5889
d.asf n.asf r.gsm.3 p.a d.asm n.asm cj v.aai.3s n.nsf

μεγάλη ἐκ τοῦ ναοῦ ἀπὸ τοῦ θρόνου λέγουσα, γέγονεν. 18 καὶ ἐγένοντο
loud out of the temple from the throne, saying, "It is done!" {and} There came
3489 1666 3836 3724 608 3836 2585 3306 1181 2779 1181
a.nsf p.g d.gsm n.gsm p.g d.gsm n.gsm pt.pa.nsf v.rai.3s cj v.ami.3p

ἀστραπαὶ καὶ φωναὶ καὶ βρονταὶ καὶ σεισμὸς ἐγένετο
flashes of lightning, {and} rumblings, {and} peals of thunder, and a violent earthquake {there came}
847 2779 5889 2779 1103 2779 3489 4939 1181
n.npf cj n.npf cj n.npf cj n.nsm v.ami.3s

μέγας, οἷος ↱ ↱ οὐκ ἐγένετο ⌊ἀφ' οὗ⌋ ἄνθρωπος ἐγένετο ἐπὶ τῆς γῆς
violent ⌊such as⌋ there had never been since man was on the earth,
3489 3888 1181 1181 4024 1181 608 4005 476 1181 2093 3836 1178
a.nsm r.nsm pl v.ami.3s p.g r.gsm n.nsm v.ami.3s p.g d.gsf n.gsf

τηλικοῦτος σεισμὸς οὕτω μέγας. 19 καὶ ἐγένετο
{so great} so violent was that earthquake. so violent {and} The great city was split
5496 4048 3489 4939 4048 3489 2779 3836 3489 4484 1181
r.nsm n.nsm adv a.nsm cj v.ami.3s

ἡ πόλις ἡ μεγάλη εἰς τρία μέρη καὶ αἱ πόλεις τῶν ἐθνῶν ἔπεσαν. καὶ
The city {the} great into three parts, and the cities of the nations fell. So
3836 4484 3836 3489 1650 5552 3538 2779 3836 4484 3836 1620 4406 2779
d.nsf n.nsf d.nsf a.nsf p.a a.apn n.apn cj d.npf n.npf d.gpn n.gpn v.aai.3p cj

Βαβυλὼν ἡ μεγάλη ἐμνήσθη ἐνώπιον τοῦ θεοῦ δοῦναι αὐτῇ τὸ
Babylon the great was remembered before {the} God and was given {to it} the
956 3836 3489 3630 1967 3836 2536 1443 899 3836
n.nsf d.nsf a.nsf v.api.3s p.g d.gsm n.gsm f.aa r.dsf.3 d.asn

ποτήριον τοῦ οἴνου τοῦ θυμοῦ τῆς ὀργῆς αὐτοῦ. 20 καὶ πᾶσα
cup ⌊filled with the⌋ wine of his fierce anger. {the} fierce his {and} Every
4539 3836 3885 3836 899 3973 2596 3836 3973 899 2779 4246
n.asn d.gsm n.gsm d.gsm n.gsm d.gsf n.gsf r.gsm.3 cj a.nsf

νῆσος ἔφυγεν καὶ ὄρη οὐχ εὑρέθησαν. 21 καὶ χάλαζα μεγάλη
island fled away and no mountains no could be found. And enormous hailstones, enormous
3762 5771 2779 4024 4001 4024 2351 2779 3489 5898 3489
n.nsf v.aai.3s cj n.npn pl v.api.3p cj n.nsf a.nsf

ὡς ταλαντιαία καταβαίνει ἐκ τοῦ οὐρανοῦ ἐπὶ τοὺς ἀνθρώπους, καὶ
about ⌊one hundred pounds each,⌋ fell from {the} heaven on {the} people, and
6055 5418 2849 1666 3836 4041 2093 3836 476 2779
pl a.nsf v.pai.3s p.g d.gsm n.gsm p.a d.apm n.apm cj

ἐβλασφήμησαν οἱ ἄνθρωποι τὸν θεὸν ἐκ τῆς πληγῆς τῆς χαλάζης, ὅτι
people blasphemed {the} people {the} God for the plague of hail, because
476 1059 3836 476 3836 2536 1666 3836 4435 3836 5898 4022
v.aai.3p d.npm n.npm d.asm n.asm p.g d.gsf n.gsf d.gsf n.gsf cj

μεγάλη ἐστὶν ἡ πληγὴ αὐτῆς σφόδρα.
devastating the plague was the plague {of it} so devastating.
3489 3836 4435 1639 3836 4435 899 5379 3489
a.nsf v.pai.3s d.nsf n.nsf r.gsf.3 adv

NASB

a thief. Blessed is
the one who stays
awake and keeps
his clothes, so that
he will not walk
about naked and
men will not see
his shame.") 16 And
they gathered
them together to
the place which in
Hebrew is called
[a]Har-Magedon.

Seventh Bowl of Wrath

17 Then the seventh
angel poured out
his bowl upon the
air, and a loud
voice came out of
the temple from
the throne, saying,
"It is done." 18 And
there were flashes
of lightning and
sounds and peals
of thunder; and
there was a great
earthquake, such as
there had not been
since man came to
be upon the earth,
so great an earth-
quake *was it, and*
so mighty. 19 The
great city was split
into three parts,
and the cities of the
nations fell. Baby-
lon the great was
remembered before
God, to give her
the cup of the wine
of His fierce wrath.
20 And every island
fled away, and the
mountains were
not found. 21 And
huge hailstones,
about [b]one hundred
pounds each, *came
down from heaven
upon men; and
men blasphemed
God because of the
plague of the hail,
because its plague
*was extremely
severe.

[a] 21 Or about 45 kilograms

[a] Two early mss read *Armagedon*
[b] Lit *the weight of a talent*

NIV

**Babylon, the Prostitute
on the Beast**

17 One of
the seven
angels who had
the seven bowls
came and said
to me, "Come, I
will show you the
punishment of the
great prostitute,
who sits by many
waters. 2 With her
the kings of the
earth committed
adultery, and the
inhabitants of the
earth were intox-
icated with the
wine of her adul-
teries."
3 Then the angel
carried me away
in the Spirit into a
wilderness. There
I saw a woman
sitting on a scar-
let beast that was
covered with blas-
phemous names
and had seven
heads and ten
horns. 4 The wom-
an was dressed in
purple and scarlet,
and was glittering
with gold, pre-
cious stones and
pearls. She held a
golden cup in her
hand, filled with
abominable things
and the filth of her
adulteries. 5 The
name written on
her forehead was a
mystery:

BABYLON THE GREAT
THE MOTHER OF
PROSTITUTES
AND OF THE
ABOMINATIONS OF
THE EARTH.

6 I saw that the
woman was drunk
with the blood of
God's holy people,
the blood of those
who bore testimo-
ny to Jesus.
When I saw her, I
was greatly aston-
ished. 7 Then the
angel

17:1 καὶ ἦλθεν εἷς ἐκ τῶν ἑπτὰ ἀγγέλων τῶν ἐχόντων τὰς ἑπτὰ φιάλας
Then *came* one of the seven angels who had the seven bowls came
2779 2262 1651 1666 3836 2231 34 3836 2400 3836 2231 5786 2262
cj v.aai.3s a.nsm p.g d.gpm a.gpm n.gpm d.gpm pt.pa.gpm d.apf a.apf n.apf

καὶ ἐλάλησεν μετ᾽ ἐμοῦ λέγων, δεῦρο, δείξω σοι τὸ κρίμα τῆς πόρνης
and talked with me, saying, "Come, ⌊I will show⌋ you the judgment of the great prostitute
2779 3281 3552 1609 3306 1306 1259 5148 3836 3210 3836 3489 4520
cj v.aai.3s p.g r.gs.1 pt.pa.nsm j v.fai.1s r.ds.2 d.asn n.asn d.gsf n.gsf

τῆς μεγάλης τῆς καθημένης ἐπὶ ὑδάτων πολλῶν, 2 μεθ᾽ ἧς
{the} great who is seated on many waters. *many* *with her*
3836 3489 3836 2764 2093 4498 5623 4498 3552 4005
d.gsf a.gsf d.gsf pt.pm.gsf p.g n.gpn a.gpn p.g r.gsf

ἐπόρνευσαν οἱ βασιλεῖς τῆς γῆς
committed acts of immorality The kings of the earth committed acts of immorality with her,
4519 3836 995 3836 1178 4519 4519 4519 4519 3552 4005
v.aai.3p d.npm n.npm d.gsf n.gsf

καὶ ἐμεθύσθησαν οἱ κατοικοῦντες τὴν γῆν ἐκ τοῦ οἴνου τῆς
and *became intoxicated* those who dwell upon the earth became intoxicated with the wine of
2779 3499 3836 2997 3836 1178 3499 3499 1666 3836 3885 3836
cj v.api.3p d.npm pt.pa.npm d.asf n.asf p.g d.gsm n.gsm d.gsf

πορνείας αὐτῆς. 3 καὶ ἀπήνεγκέν με ↰ εἰς ἔρημον ἐν
her immorality." *her* So he carried me away in the spirit into a wilderness, *in*
899 4518 899 2779 708 1609 708 1877 4460 1650 2245 1877
n.gsf r.gsf.3 cj v.aai.3s r.as.1 p.a n.asf p.d

πνεύματι. καὶ εἶδον γυναῖκα καθημένην ἐπὶ θηρίον κόκκινον,
spirit and there I saw a woman sitting on a scarlet beast *scarlet*
4460 2779 1625 1222 2764 2093 3132 2563 3132
n.dsn cj v.aai.1s n.asf pt.pm.asf p.a n.asn a.asn

γέμοντα[a] ὀνόματα βλασφημίας, ἔχων κεφαλὰς ἑπτὰ καὶ
covered with blasphemous names. *blasphemous* It had seven heads *seven* and ten
1154 1060 3950 1060 2400 2231 3051 2231 2779 1274
pt.pa.asm n.apn n.gsf pt.pa.nsm n.apf a.apf cj

κέρατα δέκα. 4 καὶ ἡ γυνὴ ἦν περιβεβλημένη πορφυροῦν καὶ κόκκινον καὶ
horns. *ten* *{and}* The woman was clothed in purple and scarlet, and
3043 1274 2779 3836 1222 1639 4314 4528 2779 3132 2779
n.apn a.apn cj d.nsf n.nsf v.iai.3s pt.rp.nsf a.asn cj a.asn cj

κεχρυσωμένη χρυσίῳ καὶ ⌊λίθῳ τιμίῳ⌋ καὶ μαργαρίταις, ἔχουσα
adorned with gold and jewels and pearls. In her hand she held a
5998 5992 2779 3345 5508 2779 3449 1877 899 5931 2400
pt.rp.nsf n.dsn cj n.dsm a.dsm cj n.dpm pt.pa.nsf

ποτήριον χρυσοῦν ἐν τῇ χειρὶ αὐτῆς γέμον βδελυγμάτων καὶ τὰ
golden cup *golden* *In* *{the}* *hand* *her* full of abominations, *{and}* the
5997 4539 5997 1877 3836 5931 899 1154 1007 2779 3836
n.asn a.asn p.d d.dsf n.dsf r.gsf.3 pt.pa.asn n.gpn cj d.apn

ἀκάθαρτα τῆς πορνείας αὐτῆς 5 καὶ ἐπὶ τὸ μέτωπον αὐτῆς
impurities of her fornication. *her* And on *{the}* her forehead *her* was written a
176 3836 899 4518 899 2779 2093 3836 899 3587 899 1211 1211
a.apn d.gsf n.gsf r.gsf.3 cj p.a d.asn n.asn r.gsf.3

ὄνομα γεγραμμένον, μυστήριον, Βαβυλὼν ἡ μεγάλη, ἡ μήτηρ τῶν πορνῶν καὶ
name, *was written* a mystery: "Babylon the great, *{the}* mother of prostitutes and
3950 1211 3696 956 3836 3489 3836 3613 3836 4520 2779
n.nsn pt.rp.nsn n.nsn n.nsf d.nsf a.nsf d.nsf n.nsf d.gpf n.gpf cj

τῶν βδελυγμάτων τῆς γῆς. 6 καὶ εἶδον τὴν γυναῖκα μεθύουσαν ἐκ τοῦ αἵματος
of the abominations of the earth." And I saw the woman drunk with the blood
3836 1007 3836 1178 2779 1625 3836 1222 3501 1666 3836 135
d.gpn n.gpn d.gsf n.gsf cj v.aai.1s d.asf n.asf pt.pa.asf p.g d.gsn n.gsn

τῶν ἁγίων καὶ ἐκ τοῦ αἵματος τῶν μαρτύρων Ἰησοῦ. καὶ
of the saints, *{and}* *{with}* the blood of those ⌊who bore witness to⌋ Jesus. *{and}*
3836 41 2779 1666 3836 135 3836 3459 2652 2779
d.gpm a.gpm cj p.g d.gsn n.gsn d.gpm n.gpm n.gsm cj

ἐθαύμασα ἰδὼν αὐτὴν ⌊θαῦμα μέγα.⌋ 7 καὶ
I was astounded ⌊When I saw⌋ her, I was greatly astounded. Then the angel
2513 1625 899 2513 2513 2512 3489 2513 2779 3836 34
v.aai.1s pt.aa.nsm r.asf.3 n.asn a.asn cj

[a] γέμοντα UBS, NET. γέμον TNIV.

NASB

The Doom of Babylon

17:1 Then one of
the seven angels
who had the seven
bowls came and
spoke with me,
saying, "Come
here, I will show
you the judgment
of the great harlot
who sits on many
waters, 2 with whom
the kings of the
earth committed
acts of immoral-
ity, and those who
dwell on the earth
were made drunk
with the wine of
her immorality."
3 And he carried me
away [a] in the Spirit
into a wilderness;
and I saw a woman
sitting on a scarlet
beast, full of blas-
phemous names,
having seven heads
and ten horns.
4 The woman was
clothed in purple
and scarlet, and
adorned with gold
and precious stones
and pearls, having
in her hand a gold
cup full of abomi-
nations and of the
unclean things
of her immoral-
ity, 5 and on her
forehead a name
was written, a mys-
tery, "BABYLON
THE GREAT, THE
MOTHER OF HAR-
LOTS AND OF THE
ABOMINATIONS
OF THE EARTH."
6 And I saw the
woman drunk with
the blood of the
saints, and with
the blood of the
witnesses of Jesus.
When I saw her, I
wondered greatly.
7 And the angel

[a] Or *in spirit*

NIV

said to me: "Why
are you astonished?
I will explain to
you the mystery of
the woman and of
the beast she rides,
which has the sev-
en heads and ten
horns. 8 The beast,
which you saw,
once was, now is
not, and yet will
come up out of the
Abyss and go to its
destruction. The
inhabitants of the
earth whose names
have not been writ-
ten in the book of
life from the cre-
ation of the world
will be astonished
when they see the
beast, because it
once was, now is
not, and yet will
come.
9 "This calls for
a mind with wis-
dom. The seven
heads are seven
hills on which the
woman sits. 10 They
are also seven
kings. Five have
fallen, one is, the
other has not yet
come; but when
he does come, he
must remain for
only a little while.
11 The beast who
once was, and now
is not, is an eighth
king. He belongs
to the seven and
is going to his de-
struction.
12 "The ten horns
you saw are ten
kings who have
not yet received a
kingdom, but who
for one hour will
receive authori-
ty as kings along
with the beast.
13 They

εἶπέν μοι ὁ ἄγγελος, ⌊διὰ τί⌋ ἐθαύμασας; ἐγὼ ἐρῶ σοι τὸ
said to me, *the* *angel* "Why are you astounded? I ⌊will explain⌋ to you the
3306 1609 3836 34 1328 5515 2513 1609 3306 5148 3836
v.aai.3s r.ds.1 d.nsm n.nsm p.a r.asn v.aai.2s r.ns.1 v.fai.1s r.ds.2 d.asn

μυστήριον τῆς γυναικὸς καὶ τοῦ θηρίου τοῦ
mystery of the woman and of the beast with seven heads and ten horns that
3696 3836 1222 2779 3836 2563 2400 2231 3051 2779 1274 3043 3836
n.asn d.gsf n.gsf cj d.gsn n.gsn d.gsn

βαστάζοντος αὐτὴν τοῦ ἔχοντος τὰς ἑπτὰ κεφαλὰς καὶ τὰ δέκα κέρατα. 8 τὸ
carries her. *{the}* *with* *{the}* *seven* *heads* *and* *{the}* *ten* *horns* The
1002 899 3836 2400 3836 2231 3051 2779 3836 1274 3043 3836
pt.pa.gsn r.asf.3 d.gsn pt.pa.gsn d.apf a.apf n.apf cj d.apn a.apn n.apn d.nsn

θηρίον ὃ εἶδες ἦν καὶ οὐκ ἔστιν καὶ μέλλει ἀναβαίνειν ἐκ τῆς
beast that you saw was, and now is not, *now is* but is about to rise from the
2563 4005 1625 1639 2779 1639 1639 4024 1639 2779 3516 326 1666 3836
n.nsn r.asn v.aai.2s v.iai.3s cj pl v.pai.3s cj v.pai.3s f.pa p.g d.gsf

ἀβύσσου καὶ εἰς ἀπώλειαν ὑπάγει, καὶ θαυμασθήσονται οἱ κατοικοῦντες ἐπὶ
abyss and go to destruction. *go* And *will be astounded* those who dwell on
12 2779 5632 1650 724 5632 2779 2513 3836 2997 2093
n.gsf cj p.a n.asf v.pai.3s cj v.fpi.3p d.npm pt.pa.npm p.g

τῆς γῆς, ὧν ↱ οὐ γέγραπται τὸ ὄνομα ἐπὶ τὸ βιβλίον τῆς ζωῆς ἀπὸ
the earth, whose names have not been written *{the}* *names* in the Book of Life from the
3836 1178 4005 3950 1211 4024 1211 3836 3950 2093 3836 1046 3836 2437 608
d.gsf n.gsf r.gpm pl v.rpi.3s d.nsn n.nsn p.a d.asn n.asn d.gsf n.gsf p.g

καταβολῆς → κόσμου, βλεπόντων τὸ θηρίον ὅτι ἦν καὶ
foundation of the world, will be astounded when they see the beast, because ⌊he was⌋ and
2856 3180 2513 2513 2513 1063 3836 2563 4022 1639 2779
n.gsf n.gsm pt.pa.gpm d.asn n.asn cj v.iai.3s cj

οὐκ ἔστιν καὶ παρέσται 9 ὧδε ὁ νοῦς ὁ ἔχων σοφίαν. αἱ ἑπτὰ
is not, *is* but is to come. "This calls for a mind *{the}* with wisdom. The seven
1639 4024 1639 2779 4205 6045 3836 3808 3836 2400 5053 3836 2231
pl v.pai.3s cj v.fmi.3s adv d.nsm n.nsm d.nsm pt.pa.nsm n.asf d.npf a.npf

κεφαλαὶ ἑπτὰ ὄρη εἰσίν, ὅπου ἡ γυνὴ κάθηται ἐπ᾽ αὐτῶν.
heads are seven mountains *are* *{where}* on which the woman sits. *on* *which*
3051 1639 2231 4001 1639 3963 2093 899 3836 1222 2764 2093 899
n.npf a.npn n.npn v.pai.3p cj d.nsf n.nsf v.pmi.3s p.g r.gpn.3

καὶ βασιλεῖς ἑπτά εἰσιν· 10 οἱ πέντε ἔπεσαν, ὁ εἷς ἔστιν, ὁ
They are also seven kings: *seven* *They are* *{the}* five have fallen, *{the}* one is, the
1639 1639 2779 2231 995 2231 1639 3836 4297 4406 3836 1651 1639 3836
cj n.npm a.npm v.pai.3p d.npm a.npm v.aai.3p d.nsm a.nsm v.pai.3s d.nsm

ἄλλος ↱ οὔπω ἦλθεν, καὶ ὅταν ἔλθῃ ὀλίγον
other has not yet come; and when ⌊he does come,⌋ he must remain ⌊for only a brief time.⌋
257 2262 4037 2262 2779 4020 2262 899 1256 3531 3900
r.nsm adv v.aai.3s cj cj v.aas.3s adv

αὐτὸν δεῖ μεῖναι. 11 καὶ τὸ θηρίον ὃ ἦν καὶ οὐκ ἔστιν καὶ
he *must* *remain* *{and}* The beast that was, and now is not, *now is* *{also}* is
899 1256 3531 2779 3836 2563 4005 1639 2779 1639 1639 4024 1639 2779 1639
r.asm.3 v.pai.3s f.aa cj d.nsn n.nsn r.nsn v.iai.3s cj pl v.pai.3s adv

αὐτὸς ὄγδοός ἐστιν καὶ ἐκ τῶν ἑπτά ἐστιν, καὶ εἰς
himself an eighth king, *is* ⌊but also⌋ ⌊one of⌋ the seven, *{he is}* and is on his way to
899 3838 1639 2779 1666 3836 2231 1639 2779 5632 5632 5632 5632 5632 1650
r.nsm a.nsm v.pai.3s cj p.g d.gpm a.gpm v.pai.3s cj p.a

ἀπώλειαν ὑπάγει. 12 καὶ τὰ δέκα κέρατα ἃ εἶδες δέκα βασιλεῖς εἰσιν,
destruction. *is on his way* And the ten horns that you saw are ten kings *are*
724 5632 2779 3836 1274 3043 4005 1625 1639 1274 995 1639
n.asf v.pai.3s cj d.npn a.npn n.npn r.apn v.aai.2s a.npm n.npm v.pai.3p

οἵτινες βασιλείαν οὔπω ἔλαβον, ἀλλὰ
who as yet have not received royal power, *as yet not* *have received* but will receive
4015 4037 4037 3284 4037 3284 993 4037 3284 247 3284 3284
r.npm n.asf adv v.aai.3p cj

ἐξουσίαν ὡς βασιλεῖς μίαν ὥραν λαμβάνουσιν μετὰ τοῦ θηρίου. 13 οὗτοι
ruling authority as kings for one hour, *will receive* ⌊along with⌋ the beast. These
2026 6055 995 1651 6052 3284 3552 3836 2563 4047
n.asf pl n.npm a.asf n.asf v.pai.3p p.g d.gsn n.gsn r.npm

NASB

said to me, "Why
do you wonder?
I will tell you the
mystery of the
woman and of the
beast that carries
her, which has the
seven heads and
the ten horns.
8 "The beast that
you saw was, and
is not, and is about
to come up out of
the abyss and [a]go
to destruction. And
those who dwell
on the earth, whose
name has not been
written in the book
of life from the
foundation of the
world, will wonder
when they see the
beast, that he was
and is not and will
come. 9 Here is the
mind which has
wisdom. The seven
heads are seven
mountains on
which the woman
sits, 10 and they are
seven kings; five
have fallen, one
is, the other has
not yet come; and
when he comes, he
must remain a little
while. 11 The beast
which was and is
not, is himself also
an eighth and is
one of the seven,
and he goes to
destruction. 12 The
ten horns which
you saw are ten
kings who have
not yet received a
kingdom, but they
receive authority
as kings with the
beast for one hour.

[a] One early ms reads *is going*

NIV

have one pur-
pose and will give
their power and
authority to the
beast. [14]They will
wage war against
the Lamb, but the
Lamb will triumph
over them be-
cause he is Lord of
lords and King of
kings—and with
him will be his
called, chosen and
faithful followers."
[15]Then the an-
gel said to me,
"The waters you
saw, where the
prostitute sits,
are peoples, mul-
titudes, nations
and languages.
[16]The beast and
the ten horns you
saw will hate the
prostitute. They
will bring her to
ruin and leave her
naked; they will
eat her flesh and
burn her with fire.
[17]For God has put
it into their hearts
to accomplish his
purpose by agree-
ing to hand over
to the beast their
royal authority,
until God's words
are fulfilled. [18]The
woman you saw
is the great city
that rules over the
kings of the earth."

Lament Over Fallen Babylon

18 After this I
saw anoth-
er angel coming
down from heav-
en. He had great
authority, and
the earth was il-
luminated by his
splendor.

μίαν γνώμην ἔχουσιν καὶ τὴν δύναμιν καὶ ἐξουσίαν αὐτῶν
are of one mind *are* and will hand over *{the}* their power and authority *their*
2400 1651 1191 2400 2779 1443 1443 1443 3836 899 1539 2779 2026 899
a.asf n.asf v.pai.3p cj d.asf n.asf cj n.asf r.gpm.3

τῷ θηρίῳ διδόασιν. 14 οὗτοι μετὰ τοῦ ἀρνίου πολεμήσουσιν καὶ
⌊to the⌋ beast. *will hand over* They will make war on the Lamb, *will make war* but
3836 2563 1443 4047 4482 4482 4482 3552 3836 768 4482 2779
d.dsn n.dsn v.pai.3p r.npm p.g d.gsn n.gsn v.fai.3p cj

τὸ ἀρνίον νικήσει αὐτούς, ὅτι κύριος κυρίων ἐστὶν καὶ βασιλεὺς
the Lamb will conquer them because he is Lord of lords *he is* and King
3836 768 3771 899 4022 1639 1639 3261 3261 1639 2779 995
d.nsn n.nsn v.fai.3s r.apm.3 cj n.nsm n.gpm v.pai.3s cj n.nsm

βασιλέων καὶ οἱ μετ᾽ αὐτοῦ κλητοὶ καὶ ἐκλεκτοὶ καὶ πιστοί.
of kings; and with him will be the *with him* called, *{and}* the chosen, and the faithful."
995 2779 3552 899 3836 3552 899 3105 2779 1723 2779 4412
n.gpm cj d.npm p.g r.gsm.3 a.npm cj a.npm cj a.npm

15 καὶ λέγει μοι, τὰ ὕδατα ἃ εἶδες οὗ ἡ πόρνη κάθηται,
Then the angel said to me, "The waters that you saw, where the prostitute is seated, are
2779 3306 1609 3836 5623 4005 1625 4023 3836 4520 2764 1639
cj v.pai.3s r.ds.1 d.npn n.npn r.apn v.aai.2s adv d.nsf n.nsf v.pmi.3s

λαοὶ καὶ ὄχλοι εἰσὶν καὶ ἔθνη καὶ γλῶσσαι. 16 καὶ τὰ δέκα κέρατα ἃ
peoples, *{and}* multitudes, *are* *{and}* nations, and languages. As for the ten horns that
3295 2779 4063 1639 2779 1620 2779 1185 2779 3836 1274 3043 4005
n.npm cj n.npm v.pai.3p cj n.npn cj n.npf cj d.npn a.npn n.npn r.apn

εἶδες ↱ καὶ τὸ θηρίον οὗτοι μισήσουσιν τὴν πόρνην καὶ ἠρημωμένην
you saw, they and the beast *{these}* will hate the prostitute and make her desolate
1625 3631 2779 3836 2563 4047 3631 3836 4520 2779 4472 899 2246
v.aai.2s cj d.nsn n.nsn r.npm v.fai.3p d.asf n.asf cj pt.rp.asf

ποιήσουσιν αὐτὴν καὶ γυμνὴν καὶ τὰς σάρκας αὐτῆς
make *her* and naked. *{and}* They will devour *{the}* her flesh *her*
4472 899 2779 1218 2779 2266 2266 2266 3836 899 4922 899
v.fai.3p r.asf.3 cj a.asf cj d.apf n.apf r.gsf.3

φάγονται καὶ αὐτὴν κατακαύσουσιν ← ἐν πυρί. 17 ὁ γὰρ θεὸς ἔδωκεν
They will devour and *her* burn her up with fire, *{the}* for God has put it
2266 2779 899 2876 899 1877 4786 3836 1142 2536 1443
v.fmi.3p cj r.asf.3 v.fai.3p p.d n.dsn d.nsm cj n.nsm v.aai.3s

εἰς τὰς καρδίας αὐτῶν ποιῆσαι τὴν γνώμην αὐτοῦ καὶ ⌊ποιῆσαι
into *{the}* their hearts *their* to carry out *{the}* his purpose *his* *{and}* by agreeing together
1650 3836 899 2840 899 4472 3836 899 1191 899 2779 4472
p.a d.apf n.apf r.gpm.3 f.aa d.asf n.asf r.gsm.3 cj f.aa

μίαν γνώμην⌋ καὶ δοῦναι τὴν βασιλείαν αὐτῶν τῷ θηρίῳ ἄχρι
{and} to turn over *{the}* their royal power *their* ⌊to the⌋ beast, until
1651 1191 2779 1443 3836 899 993 899 3836 2563 948
a.asf n.asf cj f.aa d.asf n.asf r.gpm.3 d.dsn n.dsn cj

τελεσθήσονται οἱ λόγοι τοῦ θεοῦ. 18 καὶ ἡ γυνὴ ἣν εἶδες
are fulfilled the words of God are fulfilled. And the woman *{that}* you saw
5464 3836 3364 3836 2536 5464 5464 2779 3836 1222 4005 1625
v.fpi.3p d.npm n.npm d.gsm n.gsm cj d.nsf n.nsf r.asf v.aai.2s

ἔστιν ἡ πόλις ἡ μεγάλη ἡ ἔχουσα βασιλείαν ἐπὶ τῶν βασιλέων τῆς
is the great city *{the}* *great* that has dominion over the kings of the
1639 3836 3489 4484 3836 3489 3836 2400 993 2093 3836 995 3836
v.pai.3s d.nsf n.nsf d.nsf a.nsf d.nsf pt.pa.nsf n.asf p.g d.gpm n.gpm d.gsf

γῆς.
earth."
1178
n.gsf

18:1 μετὰ ταῦτα εἶδον ἄλλον ἄγγελον καταβαίνοντα ἐκ τοῦ οὐρανοῦ ἔχοντα
After this I saw another angel coming down from *{the}* heaven, having
3552 4047 1625 257 34 2849 1666 3836 4041 2400
p.a r.apn v.aai.1s r.asm n.asm pt.pa.asm p.g d.gsm n.gsm pt.pa.asm

ἐξουσίαν μεγάλην, καὶ ἡ γῆ ἐφωτίσθη ἐκ τῆς δόξης αὐτοῦ. 2 καὶ
great authority, *great* and the earth was made bright with *{the}* his glory. *his* And
3489 2026 3489 2779 3836 1178 5894 1666 3836 899 1518 899 2779
n.asf a.asf cj d.nsf n.nsf v.api.3s p.g d.gsf n.gsf r.gsm.3 cj

NASB

[13]These have one
purpose, and they
give their power
and authority to the
beast.

Victory for the Lamb

[14]These will
wage war against
the Lamb, and
the Lamb will
overcome them,
because He is Lord
of lords and King
of kings, and those
who are with Him
are the called and
chosen and faith-
ful."
[15]And he *said to
me, "The waters
which you saw
where the harlot
sits, are peoples
and multitudes
and nations and
tongues. [16]And the
ten horns which
you saw, and the
beast, these will
hate the harlot
and will make her
desolate and naked,
and will eat her
flesh and will burn
her up with fire.
[17]For God has put
it in their hearts to
execute His pur-
pose by having a
common purpose,
and by giving
their kingdom to
the beast, until the
words of God will
be fulfilled. [18]The
woman whom you
saw is the great
city, which reigns
over the kings of
the earth."

Babylon Is Fallen

[18:1]After these
things I saw an-
other angel coming
down from heaven,
having great au-
thority, and the
earth was illumined
with his glory.

NIV

2 With a mighty voice he shouted:

"'Fallen! Fallen is Babylon the Great!'[a]
She has become a dwelling for demons
and a haunt for every impure spirit,
a haunt for every unclean bird,
a haunt for every unclean and detestable animal.
3 For all the nations have drunk
the maddening wine of her adulteries.
The kings of the earth committed adultery with her,
and the merchants of the earth grew rich from her excessive luxuries."

Warning to Escape Babylon's Judgment

4 Then I heard another voice from heaven say:

"'Come out of her, my people,'[b]
so that you will not share in her sins,
so that you will not receive any of her plagues;
5 for her sins are piled up to heaven,
and God has remembered her crimes.
6 Give back to her as she has given;
pay her back double for what she has done.
Pour her a double portion from her own cup.
7 Give her as much torment and grief
as the glory and luxury she gave herself.
In her heart

[a] 2 Isaiah 21:9
[b] 4 Jer. 51:45

ἔκραξεν ἐν ἰσχυρᾷ φωνῇ λέγων, Ἔπεσεν ἔπεσεν Βαβυλὼν ἡ μεγάλη, καὶ
⌊he called out⌋ with a powerful voice, saying, "Fallen, fallen is Babylon the great! *{and}*
3189 1877 2708 5889 3306 4406 4406 956 3836 3489 2779
v.aai.3s p.d a.dsf n.dsf pt.pa.nsm v.aai.3s v.aai.3s n.nsf d.nsf a.nsf cj

ἐγένετο κατοικητήριον δαιμονίων καὶ φυλακὴ παντὸς πνεύματος
⌊She has become⌋ a dwelling place for demons and a haunt for every unclean spirit,
1181 2999 1228 2779 5871 4246 176 4460
v.ami.3s n.nsn n.gpn cj n.nsf a.gsn n.gsn

ἀκαθάρτου καὶ φυλακὴ παντὸς ὀρνέου ἀκαθάρτου [a]καὶ φυλακὴ παντὸς
unclean *{and}* a haunt for every unclean bird, *unclean* *{and}* a haunt for every
176 2779 5871 4246 176 3997 176 2779 5871 4246
a.gsn cj n.nsf a.gsn n.gsn a.gsn cj n.nsf a.gsn

θηρίου ἀκαθάρτου καὶ μεμισημένου, 3ὅτι
unclean and detestable beast. *unclean* *and* *detestable* For all the nations have
176 2779 3631 2563 176 2779 3631 4022 4246 3836 1620 4403
n.gsn a.gsn cj pt.rp.gsn cj

ἐκ τοῦ οἴνου τοῦ θυμοῦ τῆς πορνείας αὐτῆς πέπωκαν[b] πάντα τὰ
drunk *{from}* the wine of her passionate *{the}* immorality, *her* *have drunk* *all* *the*
4403 1666 3836 3885 3836 899 2596 3836 4518 899 4403 4246 3836
p.g d.gsm n.gsm d.gsm n.gsm d.gsf n.gsf r.gsf.3 v.rai.3p a.npn d.npn

ἔθνη καὶ οἱ βασιλεῖς τῆς γῆς μετ᾽ αὐτῆς
nations and the kings of the earth have committed acts of immorality with her,
1620 2779 3836 995 3836 1178 4519 4519 4519 4519 4519 3552 899
n.npn cj d.npm n.npm d.gsf n.gsf p.g r.gsf.3

ἐπόρνευσαν καὶ οἱ ἔμποροι τῆς γῆς ἐκ τῆς
have committed acts of immorality and the merchants of the earth have grown rich from the
4519 2779 3836 1867 3836 1178 4456 4456 4456 1666 3836
v.aai.3p cj d.npm n.npm d.gsf n.gsf p.g d.gsf

δυνάμεως τοῦ στρήνους αὐτῆς ἐπλούτησαν. 4καὶ ἤκουσα ἄλλην φωνὴν
power of her excessive luxury." *her* *have grown rich* Then I heard another voice
1539 3836 899 5140 899 4456 2779 201 257 5889
n.gsf d.gsn n.gsn r.gsf.3 v.aai.3p cj v.aai.1s r.asf n.asf

ἐκ τοῦ οὐρανοῦ λέγουσαν, Ἐξέλθατε ὁ λαός μου ἐξ αὐτῆς
from *{the}* heaven saying, "Come out of her, *{the}* my people, *my* *out of* *her*
1666 3836 4041 3306 2002 1666 1666 899 3836 1609 3295 1609 1666 899
p.g d.gsm n.gsm pt.pa.asf v.aam.2p d.vsm n.vsm r.gs.1 p.g r.gsf.3

⌊ἵνα μὴ⌋ συγκοινωνήσητε ταῖς ἁμαρτίαις αὐτῆς, καὶ ἐκ τῶν
lest you share in her sins, *her* and lest you receive *{from}* *{the}*
2671 3590 5170 3836 899 281 899 2779 2671 3284 3284 1666 3836
cj pl v.aas.2p d.dpf n.dpf r.gsf.3 cj p.g d.gpf

πληγῶν αὐτῆς ⌊ἵνα μὴ⌋ λάβητε, 5ὅτι ἐκολλήθησαν αὐτῆς αἱ ἁμαρτίαι
her plagues; *her* *lest* *you receive* for her sins are heaped up *her* *{the}* *sins*
899 4435 899 2671 3590 3284 4022 899 281 3140 899 3836 281
n.gpf r.gsf.3 cj pl v.aas.2p cj v.api.3p r.gsf.3 d.npf n.npf

ἄχρι τοῦ οὐρανοῦ καὶ ἐμνημόνευσεν ὁ θεὸς τὰ ἀδικήματα αὐτῆς.
⌊as high as⌋ *{the}* heaven, and God has remembered *{the}* *God* *{the}* her crimes. *her*
948 3836 4041 2779 2536 3648 3836 2536 3836 899 93 899
p.g d.gsm n.gsm cj v.aai.3s d.nsm n.nsm d.apn n.apn r.gsf.3

6ἀπόδοτε αὐτῇ ↰ ὡς καὶ ↱ αὐτὴ ἀπέδωκεν καὶ διπλώσατε τὰ
Pay her back as *{also}* she herself has paid back others, and repay her *{the}*
625 899 625 6055 2779 625 899 625 2779 1488 3836
v.aam.2p r.dsf.3 cj adv r.nsf v.aai.3s cj v.aam.2p d.apn

διπλᾶ κατὰ τὰ ἔργα αὐτῆς, ἐν τῷ ποτηρίῳ ᾧ ἐκέρασεν κεράσατε
double ⌊according to⌋ *{the}* her works; *her* in the cup that she mixed, mix a
1487 2848 3836 899 2240 899 1877 3836 4539 4005 3042 3042
a.apn p.a d.apn n.apn r.gsf.3 p.d d.dsn n.dsn r.dsn v.aai.3s v.aam.2p

αὐτῇ διπλοῦν, 7ὅσα ἐδόξασεν αὐτὴν καὶ ἐστρηνίασεν,
double draught for her. *double draught* As she exalted herself and lived in luxury, give her an
1487 1487 899 1487 4012 1519 899 2779 5139 1443 899
r.dsf.3 a.asn r.apn v.aai.3s r.asf.3 cj v.aai.3s

τοσοῦτον δότε αὐτῇ βασανισμὸν καὶ πένθος. ὅτι ἐν τῇ καρδίᾳ
equal measure *give* *her* of torment and mourning; because in *{the}* her heart
5537 1443 899 990 2779 4292 4022 1877 3836 899 2840
r.asm v.aam.2p r.dsf.3 n.asm cj n.asn cj p.d d.dsf n.dsf

[a] [καὶ φυλακὴ παντὸς θηρίου ἀκαθάρτου] UBS.
[b] πέπωκαν UBS, TNIV. πέπτωκαν NET.

NASB

2And he cried out with a mighty voice, saying, "Fallen, fallen is Babylon the great! She has become a dwelling place of demons and a prison of every unclean spirit, and a prison of every unclean and hateful bird. 3For all the nations [a]have drunk of the wine of the passion of her immorality, and the kings of the earth have committed *acts of* immorality with her, and the merchants of the earth have become rich by the wealth of her sensuality."

4I heard another voice from heaven, saying, "Come out of her, my people, so that you will not participate in her sins and receive of her plagues; 5for her sins have piled up as high as heaven, and God has remembered her iniquities. 6Pay her back even as she has paid, and give back *to her* double according to her deeds; in the cup which she has mixed, mix twice as much for her. 7To the degree that she glorified herself and lived sensuously, to the same degree give her torment and mourning; for she says in her heart,

[a] Two early ancient mss read *have fallen by*

NIV

she boasts,
'I sit enthroned as queen.
I am not a widow;[a]
I will never mourn.'
[8] Therefore in one day her plagues will overtake her:
death, mourning and famine.
She will be consumed by fire,
for mighty is the Lord God who judges her.

Threefold Woe Over Babylon's Fall

[9] "When the kings of the earth who committed adultery with her and shared her luxury see the smoke of her burning, they will weep and mourn over her. [10] Terrified at her torment, they will stand far off and cry:

"'Woe! Woe to you, great city,
you mighty city of Babylon!
In one hour your doom has come!'

[11] "The merchants of the earth will weep and mourn over her because no one buys their cargoes anymore— [12] cargoes of gold, silver, precious stones and pearls; fine linen, purple, silk and scarlet cloth; every sort of citron wood, and articles of every kind made of ivory, costly wood, bronze, iron and marble; [13] cargoes of cinnamon and spice,

[a] 7 See Isaiah 47:7,8.

αὐτῆς λέγει ὅτι κάθημαι → βασίλισσα καὶ χήρα οὐκ εἰμὶ καὶ
her she said, ~ 'I sit as a queen, *{and}* I am no widow, *no* *I am* and
899 3306 4022 2764 999 2779 1639 1639 4024 5939 4024 1639 2779
r.gsf.3 v.pai.3s cj v.pmi.1s n.nsf cj n.nsf pl v.pai.1s cj

πένθος ↱ ↱ ⌞οὐ μὴ⌟ ἴδω. [8] ⌞διὰ τοῦτο⌟ ἐν μιᾷ
mourning I will never see.' Therefore her plagues will come in a single
4292 1625 1625 4024 3590 1625 1328 4047 899 4435 2457 2457 1877 1651
n.asn pl pl v.aas.1s p.a r.asn p.d a.dsf

ἡμέρᾳ ἥξουσιν αἱ πληγαὶ αὐτῆς, θάνατος καὶ πένθος καὶ λιμός, καὶ
day *will come* *{the}* *plagues* *her* — death and mourning and famine. And she will
2465 2457 3836 4435 899 2505 2779 4292 2779 3350 2779 2876 2876
n.dsf v.fai.3p d.npf n.npf r.gsf.3 n.nsm cj n.nsn cj n.nsm cj

ἐν πυρὶ κατακαυθήσεται, ὅτι ἰσχυρὸς κύριος ὁ θεὸς ὁ
be consumed with fire, *she will be consumed* for mighty is the Lord *{the}* God who
2876 2876 1877 4786 2876 4022 2708 3261 3836 2536 3836
p.d n.dsn v.fpi.3s cj a.nsm n.nsm d.nsm n.nsm d.nsm

κρίνας αὐτήν. [9] καὶ κλαύσουσιν καὶ κόψονται ἐπ' αὐτὴν οἱ βασιλεῖς τῆς
has judged her." Then *will weep* *and* *wail* *over* *her* the kings of the
3212 899 2779 3081 2779 3164 2093 899 3836 995 3836
pt.aa.nsm r.asf.3 cj v.fai.3p cj v.fmi.3p p.a r.asf.3 d.npm n.npm d.gsf

γῆς οἱ μετ' αὐτῆς πορνεύσαντες καὶ
earth, those who committed acts of immorality with her *who committed acts of immorality* and
1178 3836 4519 4519 4519 4519 4519 3552 899 4519 2779
n.gsf d.npm p.g r.gsf.3 pt.aa.npm cj

στρηνιάσαντες, ὅταν βλέπωσιν τὸν καπνὸν τῆς
shared her luxury, will weep and wail over her when they see the smoke of her
5139 3081 3081 2779 3164 2093 899 4020 1063 3836 2837 3836 899
pt.aa.npm cj v.pas.3p d.asm n.asm d.gsf

πυρώσεως αὐτῆς, [10] ἀπὸ μακρόθεν ἑστηκότες διὰ τὸν φόβον τοῦ
burning. *her* They will stand at a distance *They will stand* in *{the}* fear of
4796 899 2705 2705 2705 608 3427 2705 1328 3836 5832 3836
n.gsf r.gsf.3 p.g adv pt.ra.npm p.a d.asm n.asm d.gsm

βασανισμοῦ αὐτῆς λέγοντες, οὐαὶ οὐαί, ἡ πόλις ἡ μεγάλη, Βαβυλὼν
her torment, *her* and say, "Alas! Alas! O great city, *{the}* *great* Babylon
899 990 899 3306 4026 4026 3836 3489 4484 3836 3489 956
n.gsm r.gsf.3 pt.pa.npm j j d.vsf n.vsf d.vsf a.vsf n.vsf

ἡ πόλις ἡ ἰσχυρά, ὅτι → μιᾷ ὥρᾳ ἦλθεν ἡ κρίσις
the mighty city! *{the}* *mighty* For in a single hour your judgment has come." *{the}* *judgment*
3836 2708 4484 3836 2708 4022 1651 6052 5148 3213 2262 3836 3213
d.vsf n.vsf d.vsf a.vsf cj a.dsf n.dsf v.aai.3s d.nsf n.nsf

σου. [11] καὶ οἱ ἔμποροι τῆς γῆς κλαίουσιν καὶ πενθοῦσιν ἐπ' αὐτήν, ὅτι
your And the merchants of the earth will weep and mourn over her since no
5148 2779 3836 1867 3836 1178 3081 2779 4291 2093 899 4022 4029
r.gs.2 cj d.npm n.npm d.gsf n.gsf v.pai.3p cj v.pai.3p p.a r.asf.3 cj

τὸν γόμον αὐτῶν οὐδεὶς ἀγοράζει οὐκέτι [12] γόμον χρυσοῦ καὶ
one buys *{the}* their cargo *their* *no one* *buys* anymore, cargo such as gold, *{and}*
4029 60 3836 899 1203 899 4029 60 4033 1203 5996 2779
d.asm n.asm r.gpm.3 a.nsm v.pai.3s adv n.asm n.gsm cj

ἀργύρου καὶ λίθου τιμίου καὶ μαργαριτῶν καὶ βυσσίνου καὶ πορφύρας
silver, *{and}* precious stones, *precious* and pearls; *{and}* fine linen, *{and}* purple,
738 2779 5508 3345 5508 2779 3449 2779 1115 2779 4525
n.gsm cj n.gsm a.gsm cj n.gpm cj a.gsn cj n.gsf

καὶ σιρικοῦ καὶ κοκκίνου, καὶ πᾶν → → ξύλον θύϊνον καὶ
{and} silk, and scarlet cloth; *{and}* ⌞all kinds of things⌟ made of citron wood, *citron* *{and}*
2779 4986 2779 3132 2779 4246 2591 3833 2591 2779
cj n.gsn cj a.gsn cj a.asn n.asn a.asn cj

πᾶν σκεῦος ἐλεφάντινον καὶ πᾶν σκεῦος ἐκ ξύλου τιμιωτάτου
⌞all kinds of⌟ articles made of ivory, and ⌞all kinds of⌟ articles ⌞made of⌟ costly wood, *costly*
4246 5007 1804 2779 4246 5007 1666 5508 3833 5508
a.asn n.asn a.asn cj a.asn n.asn p.g n.gsn a.gsn.s

καὶ χαλκοῦ καὶ σιδήρου καὶ μαρμάρου, [13] καὶ κιννάμωμον καὶ ἄμωμον καὶ
{and} bronze, *{and}* iron, and marble; *{and}* cinnamon, *{and}* spice, *{and}*
2779 5910 2779 4970 2779 3454 2779 3077 2779 319 2779
cj n.gsm cj n.gsm cj n.gsm cj n.asn cj n.asn cj

NASB

'I SIT *as* A QUEEN AND I AM NOT A WIDOW, and will never see mourning.' [8] For this reason in one day her plagues will come, pestilence and mourning and famine, and she will be burned up with fire; for the Lord God who judges her is strong.

Lament for Babylon

[9] "And the kings of the earth, who committed *acts of* immorality and lived sensuously with her, will weep and lament over her when they see the smoke of her burning, [10] standing at a distance because of the fear of her torment, saying, 'Woe, woe, the great city, Babylon, the strong city! For in one hour your judgment has come.'

[11] "And the merchants of the earth weep and mourn over her, because no one buys their cargoes any more— [12] cargoes of gold and silver and precious stones and pearls and fine linen and purple and silk and scarlet, and every *kind of* citron wood and every article of ivory and every article *made* from very costly wood and bronze and iron and marble, [13] and cinnamon and spice and incense

NIV

of incense, myrrh
and frankincense,
of wine and olive
oil, of fine flour
and wheat; cattle
and sheep; horses
and carriages; and
human beings sold
as slaves.
14 "They will say,
'The fruit you
longed for is gone
from you. All your
luxury and splen-
dor have vanished,
never to be recov-
ered.' 15 The mer-
chants who sold
these things and
gained their wealth
from her will stand
far off, terrified
at her torment.
They will weep
and mourn 16 and
cry out:

"'Woe! Woe to
you, great
city,
dressed in fine
linen, purple
and scarlet,
and glittering
with gold,
precious
stones and
pearls!
17 In one hour such
great wealth
has been
brought to
ruin!'

"Every sea cap-
tain, and all who
travel by ship,
the sailors, and
all who earn their
living from the
sea, will stand far
off. 18 When they
see the smoke of
her burning, they
will exclaim, 'Was
there ever a city
like this great
city?' 19 They will
throw dust on
their heads, and
with weeping and
mourning cry out:

"'Woe! Woe to
you, great
city,

θυμιάματα καὶ μύρον καὶ λίβανον καὶ οἶνον καὶ ἔλαιον καὶ σεμίδαλιν καὶ
incense, {and} myrrh, and frankincense; {and} wine, {and} olive oil, {and} fine flour, and
2592 2779 3693 2779 3337 2779 3885 2779 1778 2779 4947 2779
n.apn cj n.asn cj n.asm cj n.asm cj n.asn cj n.asf cj

σῖτον καὶ κτήνη καὶ πρόβατα, καὶ ἵππων καὶ ῥεδῶν καὶ σωμάτων, καὶ
wheat; {and} cattle, {and} sheep, {and} horses, and chariots; and slaves, ⌊that is,⌋ human
4992 2779 3229 2779 4585 2779 2691 2779 4832 2779 5393 2779 476
n.asm cj n.apn cj n.apn cj n.gpm cj n.gpf cj n.gpn cj

ψυχὰς ἀνθρώπων. 14 καὶ ἡ ὀπώρα σου τῆς ἐπιθυμίας τῆς ψυχῆς
livestock. *human* {and} "The fruit that your soul {the} longed for {the} *soul*
6034 476 2779 3836 3967 5148 6034 3836 2123 3836 6034
n.apf n.gpm cj d.nsf n.nsf r.gs.2 d.gsf n.gsf d.gsf n.gsf

ἀπῆλθεν ἀπὸ σοῦ, καὶ πάντα τὰ λιπαρὰ καὶ τὰ λαμπρὰ ἀπώλετο ἀπὸ σοῦ
has gone from you, and all your delicacies and {the} ⌊splendid things⌋ are lost to you,
599 608 5148 2779 4246 3836 3353 2779 3836 3287 660 608 5148
v.aai.3s p.g r.gs.2 cj a.npn d.npn n.npn cj d.npn a.npn v.ami.3s p.g r.gs.2

καὶ ⌊οὐκέτι οὐ μὴ⌋ αὐτὰ εὑρήσουσιν. ↰ 15 οἱ ἔμποροι τούτων οἱ
{and} never {them} to be found again!" The merchants *these things* who
2779 4033 4024 3590 899 2351 4033 3836 1867 4047 3836
cj adv pl pl r.apn.3 v.fai.3p d.npm n.npm r.gpn d.npm

πλουτήσαντες ἀπ' αὐτῆς ἀπὸ μακρόθεν στήσονται
became rich by selling her these things will stand at a distance *will stand* weeping
4456 608 899 4047 4047 2705 2705 608 3427 2705 3081
pt.aa.npm p.g r.gsf.3 p.g adv v.fmi.3p

διὰ τὸν φόβον τοῦ βασανισμοῦ αὐτῆς κλαίοντες καὶ
and mourning because they {the} fear {the} her torment. *her* *weeping* *and*
2779 4291 1328 3836 5832 3836 899 990 899 3081 2779
p.a d.asm n.asm d.gsm n.gsm r.gsf.3 pt.pa.npm cj

πενθοῦντες 16 λέγοντες, οὐαὶ οὐαί, ἡ πόλις ἡ μεγάλη, ἡ
mourning ⌊They will lament,⌋ "Alas, alas, O great city, {the} *great* {the}
4291 3306 4026 4026 3836 3489 4484 3836 3489 3836
pt.pa.npm pt.pa.npm j j d.vsf n.vsf d.vsf a.vsf d.vsf

περιβεβλημένη βύσσινον καὶ πορφυροῦν καὶ κόκκινον καὶ κεχρυσωμένη ἐν[a]
clothed in fine linen, {and} purple, and scarlet, {and} glittering with
4314 1115 2779 4528 2779 3132 2779 5998 1877
pt.rp.vsf a.asn cj a.asn cj a.asn cj pt.rp.vsf p.d

χρυσίῳ καὶ λίθῳ τιμίῳ καὶ μαργαρίτῃ, 17 ὅτι → μιᾷ ὥρᾳ
gold, {and} precious stones, *precious* and pearls! For in a single hour such great
5992 2779 5508 3345 5508 2779 3449 4022 1651 6052 5537 4458
n.dsn cj n.dsm a.dsm cj n.dsm cj a.dsf n.dsf

ἠρημώθη ὁ τοσοῦτος πλοῦτος. καὶ πᾶς κυβερνήτης καὶ
wealth ⌊has been brought to ruin."⌋ {the} *such* *great wealth* And every sea captain and
4458 2246 3836 5537 4458 2779 4246 3237 2779
v.api.3s d.nsm r.nsm n.nsm cj a.nsm n.nsm cj

πᾶς ὁ ἐπὶ τόπον πλέων καὶ ναῦται καὶ ὅσοι
everyone who travels by sea, *travels* {and} sailors and ⌊those who⌋ make their living
4246 3836 4434 2093 5536 4434 2779 3731 2779 4012 2237 2237 2237
a.nsm d.nsm p.a n.asm pt.pa.nsm cj n.npm cj r.npm

τὴν θάλασσαν ἐργάζονται, ἀπὸ μακρόθεν ἔστησαν 18 καὶ ἔκραζον
⌊from the⌋ sea, *make their living* stood at a distance *stood* and cried out
3836 2498 2237 2705 608 3427 2705 2779 3189
d.asf n.asf v.pmi.3p p.g adv v.aai.3p cj v.iai.3p

βλέποντες τὸν καπνὸν τῆς πυρώσεως αὐτῆς λέγοντες, τίς → ὁμοία
as they saw the smoke of her burning, *her* exclaiming, "What city was ever like
1063 3836 2837 3836 899 4796 899 3306 5515 3927
pt.pa.npm d.asm n.asm d.gsf n.gsf r.gsf.3 pt.pa.npm r.nsf a.nsf

τῇ πόλει τῇ μεγάλῃ; 19 καὶ ἔβαλον χοῦν ἐπὶ τὰς κεφαλὰς αὐτῶν καὶ
the great city?" {the} *great* And they threw dust on {the} their heads *their* and
3836 3489 4484 3836 3489 2779 965 5967 2093 3836 899 3051 899 2779
d.dsf n.dsf d.dsf a.dsf cj v.aai.3p n.asm p.a d.apf n.apf r.gpm.3 cj

ἔκραζον κλαίοντες καὶ πενθοῦντες λέγοντες, οὐαὶ οὐαί, ἡ πόλις ἡ μεγάλη,
cried out as they wept and mourned, saying, "Alas, alas, O great city {the} *great*
3189 3081 2779 4291 3306 4026 4026 3836 3489 4484 3836 3489
v.iai.3p pt.pa.npm cj pt.pa.npm pt.pa.npm j j d.vsf n.vsf d.vsf a.vsf

[a] [ἐν] UBS.

NASB

and perfume and
frankincense and
wine and olive oil
and fine flour and
wheat and cattle
and sheep, and *car-
goes* of horses and
chariots and slaves
and human lives.
14 The fruit you long
for has gone from
you, and all things
that were luxuri-
ous and splendid
have passed away
from you and *men*
will no longer
find them. 15 The
merchants of
these things, who
became rich from
her, will stand at a
distance because of
the fear of her tor-
ment, weeping and
mourning, 16 saying,
'Woe, woe, the
great city, she who
was clothed in fine
linen and purple
and scarlet, and
adorned with gold
and precious stones
and pearls; 17 for in
one hour such great
wealth has been
laid waste!' And
every shipmaster
and every pas-
senger and sailor,
and as many as
make their living
by the sea, stood
at a distance, 18 and
were crying out as
they saw the smoke
of her burning, say-
ing, 'What *city* is
like the great city?'
19 And they threw
dust on their heads
and were crying
out, weeping and
mourning, saying,
'Woe, woe, the
great city, in which

NIV

where all who
had ships on
the sea
became rich
through her
wealth!
In one hour she
has been
brought to
ruin!'
20 "Rejoice over her,
you heavens!
Rejoice, you
people of
God!
Rejoice,
apostles and
prophets!
For God has
judged her
with the
judgment she
imposed on
you."

The Finality of Babylon's Doom

21 Then a mighty
angel picked up a
boulder the size of
a large millstone
and threw it into
the sea, and said:

"With such
violence
the great city of
Babylon will
be thrown
down,
never to be
found again.
22 The music of
harpists and
musicians,
pipers and
trumpeters,
will never be
heard in you
again.
No worker of any
trade
will ever be
found in you
again.
The sound of a
millstone
will never be
heard in you
again.
23 The light of a lamp
will never shine
in you again.
The voice of
bridegroom
and bride
will never be
heard in you
again.
Your merchants
were the
world's
important
people.

ἐν ᾗ ἐπλούτησαν πάντες οἱ ἔχοντες τὰ πλοῖα ἐν τῇ θαλάσσῃ ἐκ
by which *grew rich* all who had *{the}* ships at *{the}* sea grew rich from
1877 4005 4456 4246 3836 2400 3836 4450 1877 3836 2498 4456 4456 1666
p.d r.dsf v.aai.3p a.npm d.npm pt.pa.npm d.apn n.apn p.d d.dsf n.dsf p.g

τῆς τιμιότητος αὐτῆς, ὅτι → μιᾷ ὥρᾳ ἠρημώθη. 20 εὐφραίνου
{the} her prosperity! *her* For in a single hour ⌞she has been brought to ruin.⌟ Rejoice
3836 899 5509 899 4022 1651 6052 2246 2370
d.gsf n.gsf r.gsf.3 cj a.dsf n.dsf v.api.3s v.ppm.2s

ἐπ᾽ αὐτῇ, οὐρανὲ καὶ οἱ ἅγιοι καὶ οἱ ἀπόστολοι καὶ οἱ προφῆται, ὅτι
over her, O heaven, and you saints and *{the}* apostles and *{the}* prophets, for God
2093 899 4041 2779 3836 41 2779 3836 693 2779 3836 4737 4022 2536
p.d r.dsf.3 n.vsm cj d.vpm a.vpm cj d.vpm n.vpm cj d.vpm n.vpm cj

ἔκρινεν ὁ θεὸς τὸ κρίμα ὑμῶν ἐξ αὐτῆς. 21 καὶ
has pronounced *{the}* *God* *{the}* judgment for you against her!" Then a mighty angel
3212 3836 2536 3836 3210 7007 1666 899 2779 1651 2708 34
v.aai.3s d.nsm n.nsm d.asn n.asn r.gp.2 p.g r.gsf.3 cj

ἦρεν εἷς ἄγγελος ἰσχυρὸς λίθον ὡς μύλινον μέγαν καὶ ἔβαλεν
⌞picked up⌟ *a* *angel* *mighty* a stone ⌞the size of⌟ a huge millstone *huge* and hurled it
149 1651 34 2708 3345 6055 3489 3684 3489 2779 965
v.aai.3s a.nsm n.nsm a.nsm n.asm pl a.asm a.asm cj v.aai.3s

εἰς τὴν θάλασσαν λέγων, οὕτως ὁρμήματι βληθήσεται Βαβυλὼν ἡ
into the sea, saying, ⌞"With this kind of⌟ violence *will be thrown down* Babylon the
1650 3836 2498 3306 4048 3996 965 956 3836
p.a d.asf n.asf pt.pa.nsm adv n.dsn v.fpi.3s n.nsf d.nsf

μεγάλη πόλις καὶ ⌞οὐ μὴ⌟ εὑρεθῇ ἔτι. 22 καὶ
great city will be thrown down, and never again ⌞will it be found!⌟ *again* And the
3489 4484 965 965 965 965 2779 4024 3590 2285 2351 2285 2779
a.nsf n.nsf cj pl pl v.aps.3s adv cj

φωνὴ κιθαρῳδῶν καὶ μουσικῶν καὶ αὐλητῶν καὶ σαλπιστῶν ↱ ⌞οὐ μὴ⌟
sound of harpists and musicians, *{and}* flute players and trumpeters, will never again
5889 3069 2779 3676 2779 886 2779 4896 201 4024 3590 2285
n.nsf n.gpm cj n.gpm cj n.gpm cj n.gpm pl pl

ἀκουσθῇ ἐν σοὶ ἔτι, καὶ πᾶς τεχνίτης πάσης τέχνης ↱ ⌞οὐ μὴ⌟ εὑρεθῇ
be heard; *{in}* *{you}* *again* *{and}* *{every}* craftsman of any trade will never again be found
201 1877 5148 2285 2779 4246 5493 4246 5492 2351 4024 3590 2285 2351
v.aps.3s p.d r.ds.2 adv cj a.nsm n.nsm a.gsf n.gsf pl pl v.aps.3s

ἐν σοὶ ἔτι, καὶ φωνὴ → μύλου ↱ ⌞οὐ μὴ⌟ ἀκουσθῇ ἐν σοὶ ἔτι,
in you, *again* and the sound of the mill will never again be heard in you; *again*
1877 5148 2285 2779 5889 3685 201 4024 3590 2285 201 1877 5148 2285
p.d r.ds.2 adv cj n.nsf n.gsm pl pl v.aps.3s p.d r.ds.2 adv

23 καὶ φῶς → λύχνου ↱ ⌞οὐ μὴ⌟ φάνῃ ἐν σοὶ ἔτι, καὶ φωνὴ
{and} the light of a lamp will never again shine in you, *again* and the voice
2779 5890 3394 5743 4024 3590 2285 5743 1877 5148 2285 2779 5889
cj n.nsn n.gsm pl pl v.aas.3s p.d r.ds.2 adv cj n.nsf

νυμφίου καὶ νύμφης ↱ ⌞οὐ μὴ⌟ ἀκουσθῇ ἐν σοὶ ἔτι· ὅτι οἱ
of bridegroom and bride will never again be heard in you; *again* for *{the}* your
3812 2779 3811 201 4024 3590 2285 201 1877 5148 2285 4022 3836 5148
n.gsm cj n.gsf pl pl v.aps.3s p.d r.ds.2 adv cj d.npm

ἔμποροί σου ἦσαν οἱ μεγιστᾶνες τῆς γῆς, ὅτι ἐν τῇ
merchants *your* were the great ones of the earth, and all nations were deceived by *{the}*
1867 5148 1639 3836 3491 3836 1178 4022 4246 1620 4414 4414 1877 3836
n.npm r.gs.2 v.iai.3p d.npm n.npm d.gsf n.gsf cj p.d d.dsf

NASB

all who had ships
at sea became rich
by her wealth, for
in one hour she has
been laid waste!'
20 Rejoice over her,
O heaven, and you
saints and apostles
and prophets,
because God
has pronounced
judgment for you
against her."
21 Then a strong
angel took up a
stone like a great
millstone and
threw it into the
sea, saying, "So
will Babylon,
the great city, be
thrown down with
violence, and will
not be found any
longer. 22 And the
sound of harpists
and musicians and
flute-players and
trumpeters will not
be heard in you
any longer; and no
craftsman of any
craft will be found
in you any longer;
and the sound of
a mill will not be
heard in you any
longer; 23 and the
light of a lamp will
not shine in you
any longer; and
the voice of the
bridegroom and
bride will not be
heard in you any
longer; for your
merchants were the
great men of the
earth, because all
the nations were
deceived by your

NIV

By your magic
spell all the
nations were
led astray.
24 In her was found
the blood of
prophets and
of God's holy
people,
of all who
have been
slaughtered
on the earth."

Threefold Hallelujah Over Babylon's Fall

19 After this I
heard what
sounded like the
roar of a great
multitude in heav-
en shouting:

"Hallelujah!
Salvation and
glory and
power belong
to our God,
2 for true and
just are his
judgments.
He has condemned
the great
prostitute
who corrupted
the earth
by her
adulteries.
He has avenged
on her the
blood of his
servants."

3 And again they
shouted:

"Hallelujah!
The smoke from
her goes up
for ever and
ever."

4 The twenty-four
elders and the four
living creatures
fell down and wor-
shiped God, who
was seated on the
throne. And they
cried:

"Amen,
Hallelujah!"

5 Then a voice came
from the throne,
saying:

"Praise our God,
all you his
servants,
you who fear him,
both great and
small!"

6 Then I heard
what sounded like
a great multitude,

φαρμακείᾳ σου ἐπλανήθησαν πάντα τὰ ἔθνη, 24 καὶ ἐν αὐτῇ
your magic spells. *your* *were deceived* *all* *{the}* *nations* And in her was found the
5148 5758 5148 4414 4246 3836 1620 2779 1877 899 2351 2351
n.dsf r.gs.2 v.api.3p a.npn d.npn n.npn cj p.d r.dsf.3

αἷμα προφητῶν καὶ ἁγίων εὑρέθη καὶ πάντων τῶν ἐσφαγμένων ἐπὶ τῆς γῆς.
blood of prophets and of saints, *was found* and of all who have been slain on the earth."
135 4737 2779 41 2351 2779 4246 3836 5377 2093 3836 1178
n.nsn n.gpm cj a.gpm v.api.3s cj a.gpm d.gpm pt.rp.gpm p.g d.gsf n.gsf

19:1 μετὰ ταῦτα ἤκουσα ὡς ⌊φωνὴν μεγάλην⌋ → ὄχλου
After this I heard what sounded like the roar of a great throng
3552 4047 201 6055 5889 3489 4498 4063
p.a r.apn v.aai.1s pl n.asf a.asf n.gsm

πολλοῦ ἐν τῷ οὐρανῷ λεγόντων, ἀλληλουϊά· ἡ σωτηρία καὶ ἡ δόξα καὶ ἡ
great in *{the}* heaven, saying, "Hallelujah! *{the}* Salvation and *{the}* glory and *{the}*
4498 1877 3836 4041 3306 252 3836 5401 2779 3836 1518 2779 3836
a.gsm p.d d.dsm n.dsm pt.pa.gpm j d.nsf n.nsf cj d.nsf n.nsf cj d.nsf

δύναμις τοῦ θεοῦ ἡμῶν, 2 ὅτι ἀληθιναὶ καὶ δίκαιαι αἱ κρίσεις
power ⌊belong to⌋ our God, *our* because true and just are *{the}* his judgments.
1539 3836 7005 2536 7005 4022 240 2779 1465 3836 899 3213
n.nsf d.gsm n.gsm r.gp.1 cj a.npf cj a.npf d.npf n.npf

αὐτοῦ· ὅτι ἔκρινεν τὴν πόρνην τὴν μεγάλην ἥτις ἔφθειρεν τὴν γῆν ἐν τῇ
his For he has judged the great prostitute *{the}* *great* who corrupted the earth with *{the}*
899 4022 3212 3836 3489 4520 3836 3489 4015 5780 3836 1178 1877 3836
r.gsm.3 cj v.aai.3s d.asf n.asf d.asf a.asf r.nsf v.aai.3s d.asf n.asf p.d d.dsf

πορνείᾳ αὐτῆς, καὶ ἐξεδίκησεν τὸ αἷμα τῶν δούλων αὐτοῦ ἐκ
her immorality, *her* and has avenged the blood of his servants *his* shed by her
899 4518 899 2779 1688 3836 135 3836 899 1529 899 1666 899
n.dsf r.gsf.3 cj v.aai.3s d.asn n.asn d.gpm n.gpm r.gsm.3 p.g

χειρὸς αὐτῆς. 3 καὶ δεύτερον εἴρηκαν, ἀλληλουϊά, καὶ ὁ καπνὸς αὐτῆς
hand." *her* Then again ⌊they cried out,⌋ "Hallelujah! *{and}* The smoke from her
5931 899 2779 1311 3306 252 2779 3836 2837 899
n.gsf r.gsf.3 cj adv v.rai.3p j cj d.nsm n.nsm r.gsf.3

ἀναβαίνει εἰς τοὺς ⌊αἰῶνας τῶν αἰώνων.⌋ 4 καὶ ἔπεσαν οἱ
burning rises for all time!" And *fell down* the twenty-four
326 1650 3836 172 3836 172 2779 4406 3836 1633
v.pai.3s p.a d.apm n.apm d.gpm n.gpm cj v.aai.3p d.npm

πρεσβύτεροι οἱ ⌊εἴκοσι τέσσαρες⌋ καὶ τὰ τέσσαρα ζῷα καὶ
elders *{the}* *twenty-four* and the four ⌊living creatures⌋ fell down and
4565 3836 1633 5475 2779 3836 5475 2442 4406 4406 2779
a.npm d.npm a.npm a.npm cj d.npn a.npn n.npn cj

προσεκύνησαν τῷ θεῷ τῷ καθημένῳ ἐπὶ τῷ θρόνῳ λέγοντες, ἀμὴν ἀλληλουϊά.
worshiped *{the}* God who was seated on the throne, saying, "Amen! Hallelujah!"
4686 3836 2536 3836 2764 2093 3836 2585 3306 297 252
v.aai.3p d.dsm n.dsm d.dsm pt.pm.dsm p.d d.dsm n.dsm pt.pa.npm pl j

5 καὶ φωνὴ ἀπὸ τοῦ θρόνου ἐξῆλθεν λέγουσα, αἰνεῖτε τῷ θεῷ ἡμῶν
And *voice* from the throne came a voice saying, "Praise *{the}* our God, *our*
2779 5889 608 3836 2585 2002 5889 3306 140 3836 7005 2536 7005
cj n.nsf p.g d.gsm n.gsm v.aai.3s pt.pa.nsf v.pam.2p d.dsm n.dsm r.gp.1

πάντες οἱ δοῦλοι αὐτοῦ καὶ[a] οἱ φοβούμενοι αὐτόν, οἱ μικροὶ καὶ οἱ
all you his servants *his* and you who fear him, *{the}* small and *{the}*
4246 3836 899 1529 899 2779 3836 5828 899 3836 3625 2779 3836
a.vpm d.vpm n.vpm r.gsm.3 cj d.vpm pt.pp.vpm r.asm.3 d.vpm a.vpm cj d.vpm

μεγάλοι. 6 καὶ ἤκουσα ὡς φωνὴν → ὄχλου πολλοῦ καὶ
great." Then I heard what sounded like the voice of a great multitude *great* — *{and}* it
3489 2779 201 6055 5889 4498 4063 4498 2779
a.vpm cj v.aai.1s pl n.asf n.gsm a.gsm cj

NASB

sorcery. 24 And in
her was found the
blood of prophets
and of saints and of
all who have been
slain on the earth."

The Fourfold Hallelujah

19:1 After these
things I heard
something like a
loud voice of a
great multitude in
heaven, saying,
"**H**allelujah!
Salvation and
glory and power
belong to our God;
2 BECAUSE HIS JUDG-
MENTS ARE TRUE
AND RIGHTEOUS; for
He has judged the
great harlot who
was corrupting the
earth with her im-
morality, and HE
HAS AVENGED THE
BLOOD OF HIS BOND-
SERVANTS ON HER."
3 And a second time
they said, "Hal-
lelujah! HER SMOKE
RISES UP FOREVER
AND EVER." 4 And
the twenty-four
elders and the four
living creatures
fell down and wor-
shiped God who
sits on the throne
saying, "Amen.
Hallelujah!" 5 And
a voice came from
the throne, saying,
"**G**ive praise to
our God, all you
His bond-servants,
you who fear Him,
the small and the
great." 6 Then I
heard *something*
like the voice of a
great multitude

[a] [καὶ] UBS.

NIV

like the roar of
rushing waters and
like loud peals of
thunder, shouting:

"Hallelujah!
For our
Lord God
Almighty
reigns.
7 Let us rejoice and
be glad
and give him
glory!
For the wedding of
the Lamb has
come,
and his bride
has made
herself ready.
8 Fine linen, bright
and clean,
was given her
to wear."
(Fine linen stands
for the righteous
acts of God's holy
people.)

9 Then the angel
said to me, "Write
this: Blessed are
those who are
invited to the wed-
ding supper of the
Lamb!" And he
added, "These are
the true words of
God."
10 At this I fell at
his feet to worship
him. But he said to
me, "Don't do that!
I am a fellow ser-
vant with you and
with your brothers
and sisters who
hold to the tes-
timony of Jesus.
Worship God!
For it is the Spirit
of prophecy who
bears testimony to
Jesus."

The Heavenly Warrior Defeats the Beast

11 I saw heaven
standing open and
there before me
was a white horse,
whose rider is
called Faithful and
True. With jus-
tice he judges and
wages war. 12 His
eyes are like

ὡς φωνὴν → ὑδάτων πολλῶν καὶ ὡς φωνὴν → βροντῶν
was like the roar of many waters, *many* *{and}* like the sound of crashing thunder
6055 5889 4498 5623 4498 2779 6055 5889 2708 1103
pl n.asf n.gpn a.gpn cj pl n.asf n.gpf

ἰσχυρῶν λεγόντων, ἀλληλουϊά, ὅτι ἐβασίλευσεν κύριος ὁ θεὸς ἡμῶν[a]
crashing — crying out, "Hallelujah! For *reigns!* the Lord *{the}* our God *our*
2708 3306 252 4022 996 3261 3836 7005 2536 7005
a.gpf pt.pa.gpm j cj v.aai.3s n.nsm d.nsm n.nsm r.gp.1

ὁ παντοκράτωρ. 7 χαίρωμεν καὶ ἀγαλλιῶμεν καὶ δώσωμεν τὴν δόξαν
the Almighty reigns! Let us rejoice and be glad and give him the glory,
3836 4120 996 5897 2779 22 2779 1443 899 3836 1518
d.nsm n.nsm v.pas.1p cj v.pas.1p cj v.aas.1p d.asf n.asf

αὐτῷ, ὅτι ἦλθεν ὁ γάμος τοῦ ἀρνίου καὶ ἡ γυνὴ αὐτοῦ →
him for *has come* the marriage of the Lamb has come, and *{the}* his bride *his* has
899 4022 2262 3836 1141 3836 768 2262 2262 2779 3836 899 1222 899
r.dsm.3 cj v.aai.3s d.nsm n.nsm d.gsn n.gsn cj d.nsf n.nsf r.gsm.3

→ ἡτοίμασεν ἑαυτὴν 8 καὶ ἐδόθη αὐτῇ ἵνα περιβάληται
made herself ready. *herself* *{and}* To her ⌊it has been granted⌋ *To her* to be clothed in
1571 2286 1571 2779 899 899 1443 899 2671 4314
v.aai.3s r.asf.3 cj v.api.3s r.dsf.3 cj v.ams.3s

βύσσινον λαμπρὸν καθαρόν· τὸ γὰρ βύσσινον τὰ δικαιώματα τῶν
fine linen, bright and clean" — for the *for* fine linen is the righteous acts of the
1115 3287 2754 1142 3836 1142 1115 1639 3836 1468 3836
a.asn a.asn a.asn d.nsn cj a.nsn d.npn n.npn d.gpm

ἁγίων ἐστίν. 9 καὶ λέγει μοι, γράψον, μακάριοι οἱ εἰς
saints. *is* And the angel said to me, "Write, 'Blessed are those who are invited to
41 1639 2779 3306 1609 1211 3421 3836 2813 2813 2813 1650
a.gpm v.pai.3s cj v.pai.3s r.ds.1 v.aam.2s a.npm d.npm p.a

τὸ δεῖπνον τοῦ γάμου τοῦ ἀρνίου κεκλημένοι. ↱ καὶ λέγει μοι, οὗτοι
the marriage supper *{the}* *marriage* of the Lamb!'" *who are invited* He also said to me, "These
3836 1141 1270 3836 1141 3836 768 2813 3306 2779 3306 1609 4047
d.asn n.asn d.gsm n.gsm d.gsn n.gsn pt.rp.npm cj v.pai.3s r.ds.1 r.npm

οἱ λόγοι ἀληθινοὶ τοῦ θεοῦ εἰσιν. 10 καὶ ἔπεσα ἔμπροσθεν τῶν
are the true words *true* of God." *are* Then I fell down at *{the}* his
1639 3836 240 3364 240 3836 2536 1639 2779 4406 1869 3836 899
d.npm n.npm a.npm d.gsm n.gsm v.pai.3p cj v.aai.1s p.g d.gpm

ποδῶν αὐτοῦ προσκυνῆσαι αὐτῷ. καὶ λέγει μοι, ὅρα μή· ↰
feet *his* to worship him, but he said to me, "Do not do that! I am a
4546 899 4686 899 2779 3306 1609 3972 3590 3972 1639 1639
n.gpm r.gsm.3 f.aa r.dsm.3 cj v.pai.3s r.ds.1 v.pam.2s pl

σύνδουλός σού εἰμι καὶ τῶν ἀδελφῶν σου τῶν ἐχόντων τὴν μαρτυρίαν
fellow servant ⌊with you⌋ *I am* and *{the}* your brothers *your* who hold to the testimony
5281 5148 1639 2779 3836 5148 81 5148 3836 2400 3836 3456
n.nsm r.gs.2 v.pai.1s cj d.gpm n.gpm r.gs.2 d.gpm pt.pa.gpm d.asf n.asf

Ἰησοῦ· τῷ θεῷ προσκύνησον. ἡ γὰρ μαρτυρία Ἰησοῦ ἐστιν τὸ
about Jesus. Worship *{the}* God! *Worship* For the *For* testimony about Jesus is the
2652 4686 3836 2536 4686 1142 3836 1142 3456 2652 1639 3836
n.gsm d.dsm n.dsm v.aam.2s d.nsf cj n.nsf n.gsm v.pai.3s d.nsn

πνεῦμα τῆς προφητείας. 11 καὶ εἶδον τὸν οὐρανὸν ἠνεῳγμένον, καὶ ἰδοὺ
spirit of prophecy." Then I saw *{the}* heaven opened, and behold, a white
4460 3836 4735 2779 1625 3836 4041 487 2779 2627 3328
n.nsn d.gsf n.gsf cj v.aai.1s d.asm n.asm pt.rp.asm cj j

ἵππος λευκὸς καὶ ὁ ⌊καθήμενος ἐπ'⌋ αὐτὸν καλούμενος[b] πιστὸς καὶ ἀληθινός,
horse! *white* *{and}* The one riding it is called Faithful and True,
2691 3328 2779 3836 2764 2093 899 2813 4412 2779 240
n.nsm a.nsm cj d.nsm pt.pm.nsm p.a r.asm.3 pt.pp.nsm a.nsm cj a.nsm

καὶ ἐν δικαιοσύνῃ κρίνει καὶ πολεμεῖ. 12 οἱ δὲ ὀφθαλμοὶ αὐτοῦ ὡς[c]
and with justice he judges and makes war. *{the}* *{and}* His eyes *His* are like
2779 1877 1466 3212 2779 4482 3836 1254 899 4057 899 6055
cj p.d n.dsf v.pai.3s cj v.pai.3s d.npm cj n.npm r.gsm.3 pl

[a] [ἡμῶν] UBS.
[b] [καλούμενος] UBS.
[c] [ὡς] UBS.

NASB

and like the sound
of many waters
and like the sound
of mighty peals of
thunder, saying,
"**H**allelujah! For
the Lord our God,
the Almighty,
reigns.

Marriage of the Lamb

7 Let us rejoice and
be glad and give
the glory to Him,
for the marriage
of the Lamb has
come and His
bride has made
herself ready." 8 It
was given to her
to clothe herself in
fine linen, bright
and clean; for the
fine linen is the
righteous acts of
the saints.
9 Then he *said
to me, "Write,
'Blessed are those
who are invited to
the marriage sup-
per of the Lamb.'"
And he *said to me,
"These are true
words of God."
10 Then I fell at his
feet to worship
him. But he *said
to me, "Do not do
that; I am a fellow
servant of yours
and your brethren
who hold the tes-
timony of Jesus;
worship God. For
the testimony of
Jesus is the spirit
of prophecy."

The Coming of Christ

11 And I saw heav-
en opened, and be-
hold, a white horse,
and He who sat on
it *is* called Faithful
and True, and in
righteousness He
judges and wages
war. 12 His eyes

NIV

blazing fire, and
on his head are
many crowns. He
has a name writ-
ten on him that no
one knows but he
himself. 13 He is
dressed in a robe
dipped in blood,
and his name is
the Word of God.
14 The armies of
heaven were fol-
lowing him, riding
on white horses
and dressed in fine
linen, white and
clean. 15 Coming
out of his mouth is
a sharp sword with
which to strike
down the nations.
"He will rule them
with an iron scep-
ter."[a] He treads the
winepress of the
fury of the wrath
of God Almighty.
16 On his robe and
on his thigh he has
this name written:

KING OF KINGS AND
LORD OF LORDS.

17 And I saw an
angel standing in
the sun, who cried
in a loud voice to
all the birds flying
in midair, "Come,
gather together for
the great supper of
God, 18 so that you
may eat the flesh
of kings, generals,
and the mighty, of
horses and their
riders, and the
flesh of all peo-
ple, free and slave,
great and small."
19 Then I saw the
beast and

φλὸξ πυρός, καὶ ἐπὶ τὴν κεφαλὴν αὐτοῦ διαδήματα πολλά, ἔχων
a flame of fire, and on *{the}* his head *his* are many diadems, *many* and he has
5825 4786 2779 2093 3836 899 3051 899 4498 1343 4498 2400
n.nsf n.gsn cj p.a d.asf n.asf r.gsm.3 n.npn a.npn pt.pa.nsm

ὄνομα γεγραμμένον ὃ οὐδεὶς οἶδεν ⌊εἰ μὴ⌋ αὐτός, 13 καὶ περιβεβλημένος
a name written that no one knows except himself. *{and}* He is clothed in a
3950 1211 4005 4029 3857 1623 3590 899 2779 4314
n.asn pt.rp.asn r.asn a.nsm v.rai.3s cj pl r.nsm cj pt.rp.nsm

ἱμάτιον βεβαμμένον αἵματι, καὶ κέκληται τὸ ὄνομα αὐτοῦ
robe dipped in blood, and the name by which he is called *the name by which* is
2668 970 135 2779 3836 3950 899 899 2813 3836 3950 899
n.asn pt.rp.asn n.dsn cj v.rpi.3s d.nsn n.nsn r.gsm.3

ὁ λόγος τοῦ θεοῦ. 14 καὶ τὰ στρατεύματα τὰ[a] ἐν τῷ οὐρανῷ
the Word of God. And the armies *{the}* of *{the}* heaven, arrayed in fine
3836 3364 3836 2536 2779 3836 5128 3836 1877 3836 4041 1907 1907 1115
d.nsm n.nsm d.gsm n.gsm cj d.npn n.npn d.npn p.d d.dsm n.dsm

ἠκολούθει αὐτῷ ἐφ' ἵπποις λευκοῖς, ἐνδεδυμένοι
linen, white and clean, were following him on white horses. *white arrayed in*
1115 3328 2754 199 899 2093 3328 2691 3328 1907
v.iai.3s r.dsm.3 p.d n.dpm a.dpm pt.rp.npm

βύσσινον λευκὸν καθαρόν. 15 καὶ ἐκ τοῦ στόματος αὐτοῦ ἐκπορεύεται
fine linen white clean *{and}* From *{the}* his mouth *his* extends a sharp
1115 3328 2754 2779 1666 3836 899 5125 899 1744 3955
a.asn a.asn a.asn cj p.g d.gsn n.gsn r.gsm.3 v.pmi.3s

ῥομφαία ὀξεῖα, ἵνα ἐν αὐτῇ πατάξῃ τὰ ἔθνη, καὶ αὐτὸς ποιμανεῖ
sword *sharp* so that with it ⌊he can strike down⌋ the nations. *{and}* He will rule
4855 3955 2671 1877 899 4250 3836 1620 2779 899 4477
n.nsf a.nsf cj p.d r.dsf.3 v.aas.3s d.apn n.apn cj r.nsm v.fai.3s

αὐτοὺς ἐν ῥάβδῳ σιδηρᾷ, καὶ αὐτὸς πατεῖ τὴν ⌊ληνὸν τοῦ οἴνου⌋ τοῦ
them with a rod of iron. *{and}* He will tread the winepress of the
899 1877 4811 4971 2779 899 4251 3836 3332 3836 3885 3836
r.apm.3 p.d n.dsf a.dsf cj r.nsm v.pai.3s d.asf n.asf d.gsm n.gsm d.gsm

θυμοῦ τῆς ὀργῆς τοῦ θεοῦ τοῦ παντοκράτορος, 16 καὶ ἔχει ἐπὶ τὸ ἱμάτιον καὶ
furious *{the}* wrath of God the Almighty. *{and} he has* On his robe and
2596 3836 3973 3836 2536 3836 4120 2779 2400 2093 3836 2668 2779
n.gsm d.gsf n.gsf d.gsm n.gsm d.gsm n.gsm cj v.pai.3s p.a d.asn n.asn cj

ἐπὶ τὸν μηρὸν αὐτοῦ ὄνομα γεγραμμένον, Βασιλεὺς βασιλέων καὶ
on *{the}* his thigh *his* he has a name written, King of kings and
2093 3836 899 3611 899 2400 2400 3950 1211 995 995 2779
p.a d.asm n.asm r.gsm.3 n.asn pt.rp.asn n.nsm n.gpm cj

Κύριος κυρίων. 17 καὶ εἶδον ἕνα ἄγγελον ἑστῶτα ἐν τῷ ἡλίῳ καὶ ἔκραξεν ἐν[b]
Lord of lords. Then I saw an angel standing in the sun, and he called with a
3261 3261 2779 1625 1651 34 2705 1877 3836 2463 2779 3189 1877
n.nsm n.gpm cj v.aai.1s a.asm n.asm pt.ra.asm p.d d.dsm n.dsm cj v.aai.3s p.d

φωνῇ μεγάλῃ λέγων πᾶσιν τοῖς ὀρνέοις τοῖς πετομένοις ἐν μεσουρανήματι·
loud voice *loud {saying}* to all the birds *{the}* flying in midair,
3489 5889 3489 3306 4246 3836 3997 3836 4375 1877 3547
n.dsf a.dsf pt.pa.nsm a.dpn d.dpn n.dpn d.dpn pt.pm.dpn p.d n.dsn

δεῦτε συνάχθητε εἰς τὸ δεῖπνον τὸ μέγα τοῦ θεοῦ 18 ἵνα φάγητε
"Come, gather together for the great supper *{the} great* of God, to eat the
1307 5251 1650 3836 3489 1270 3836 3489 3836 2536 2671 2266
adv v.apm.2p p.a d.asn n.asn d.asn a.asn d.gsm n.gsm cj v.aas.2p

σάρκας βασιλέων καὶ σάρκας χιλιάρχων καὶ σάρκας ἰσχυρῶν καὶ
flesh of kings, *{and}* the flesh of captains, *{and}* the flesh ⌊of mighty warriors,⌋ *{and}*
4922 995 2779 4922 5941 2779 4922 2708 2779
n.apf n.gpm cj n.apf n.gpm cj n.apf a.gpm cj

σάρκας ἵππων καὶ τῶν καθημένων ἐπ' αὐτῶν καὶ σάρκας πάντων
the flesh of horses and those who ride on them — *{and}* the flesh of all, both
4922 2691 2779 3836 2764 2093 899 2779 4922 4246 5445
n.apf n.gpm cj d.gpm pt.pm.gpm p.g r.gpm.3 cj n.apf a.gpm

ἐλευθέρων τε καὶ δούλων καὶ μικρῶν καὶ μεγάλων. 19 καὶ εἶδον τὸ θηρίον καὶ
free *both* and slave, and small and great." Then I saw the beast and
1801 5445 2779 1529 2779 3625 2779 3489 2779 1625 3836 2563 2779
a.gpm cj cj n.gpm cj a.gpm cj a.gpm cj v.aai.1s d.asn n.asn cj

NASB

are a flame of
fire, and on His
head *are* many
diadems; and He
has a name written
on Him which no
one knows except
Himself. 13 *He is*
clothed with a robe
dipped in blood,
and His name is
called The Word
of God. 14 And the
armies which are
in heaven, clothed
in fine linen, white
and clean, were
following Him
on white horses.
15 From His mouth
comes a sharp
sword, so that with
it He may strike
down the nations,
and He will rule
them with a rod of
iron; and He treads
the wine press of
the fierce wrath of
God, the Almighty.
16 And on His robe
and on His thigh
He has a name
written, "KING OF
KINGS, AND LORD
OF LORDS."
17 Then I saw an
angel standing in
the sun, and he
cried out with a
loud voice, say-
ing to all the birds
which fly in mid-
heaven, "Come,
assemble for the
great supper of
God, 18 so that you
may eat the flesh of
kings and the flesh
of [a]commanders
and the flesh of
mighty men and
the flesh of horses
and of those who
sit on them and the
flesh of all men,
both free men and
slaves, and small
and great."
19 And I saw the

a 15 Psalm 2:9

a [τὰ] UBS.
b [ἐν] UBS.

a I.e. chiliarchs, in command of one thousand troops

NIV

the kings of the
earth and their
armies gathered
together to wage
war against the
rider on the horse
and his army. 20 But
the beast was cap-
tured, and with it
the false prophet
who had per-
formed the signs
on its behalf. With
these signs he had
deluded those who
had received the
mark of the beast
and worshiped its
image. The two of
them were thrown
alive into the fiery
lake of burning
sulfur. 21 The rest
were killed with
the sword coming
out of the mouth
of the rider on the
horse, and all the
birds gorged them-
selves on their
flesh.

The Thousand Years

20 And I saw
an angel
coming down out
of heaven, hav-
ing the key to the
Abyss and holding
in his hand a great
chain. 2 He seized
the dragon, that
ancient serpent,
who is the devil, or
Satan, and bound
him for a thou-
sand years. 3 He
threw him into the
Abyss, and locked
and sealed it over
him, to keep him
from deceiving the
nations anymore
until the thousand
years were ended.
After that, he must
be set free for a
short time.
4 I saw thrones

τοὺς βασιλεῖς τῆς γῆς καὶ τὰ στρατεύματα αὐτῶν συνηγμένα ποιῆσαι τὸν
the kings of the earth and *{the}* their armies *their* gathered to make *{the}*
3836 995 3836 1178 2779 3836 899 5128 899 5251 4472 3836
d.apm n.apm d.gsf n.gsf cj d.apn n.apn r.gpm.3 pt.rp.apn f.aa d.asm

πόλεμον μετὰ τοῦ ⌊καθημένου ἐπὶ⌋ τοῦ ἵππου καὶ μετὰ τοῦ στρατεύματος
war against the one who rode the horse and against *{the}* his army.
4483 3552 3836 2764 2093 3836 2691 2779 3552 3836 899 5128
n.asm p.g d.gsm pt.pm.gsm p.g d.gsm n.gsm cj p.g d.gsn n.gsn

αὐτοῦ. 20 καὶ ἐπιάσθη τὸ θηρίον καὶ μετ᾽ αὐτοῦ ὁ ψευδοπροφήτης
his And the beast was captured, *the* *beast* and with him the false prophet,
899 2779 3836 2563 4389 3836 2563 2779 3552 899 3836 6021
r.gsm.3 cj v.api.3s d.nsn n.nsn cj p.g r.gsn.3 d.nsm n.nsm

ὁ ποιήσας τὰ σημεῖα ἐνώπιον αὐτοῦ, ἐν οἷς ἐπλάνησεν τοὺς
who in his presence performed *{the}* signs *in presence* *his* by which he deceived those
3836 1967 899 1967 4472 3836 4956 1967 899 1877 4005 4414 3836
d.nsm pt.aa.nsm d.apn n.apn p.g r.gsn.3 p.d r.dpn v.aai.3s d.apm

λαβόντας τὸ χάραγμα τοῦ θηρίου καὶ τοὺς προσκυνοῦντας τῇ εἰκόνι
who had received the mark of the beast and those who worshiped *{the}* his image.
3284 3836 5916 3836 2563 2779 3836 4686 3836 899 1635
pt.aa.apm d.asn n.asn d.gsn n.gsn cj d.apm pt.pa.apm d.dsf n.dsf

αὐτοῦ· ζῶντες ἐβλήθησαν οἱ δύο εἰς τὴν λίμνην τοῦ πυρὸς
his These two were thrown alive *were thrown* *These* *two* into the lake of fire
899 3836 1545 965 965 2409 965 3836 1545 1650 3836 3349 3836 4786
r.gsn.3 pt.pa.npm v.api.3p d.npm a.npm p.a d.asf n.asf d.gsn n.gsn

τῆς καιομένης ἐν θείῳ. 21 καὶ οἱ λοιποὶ ἀπεκτάνθησαν ἐν τῇ ῥομφαίᾳ
{the} burning with sulfur. And the rest were killed by the sword that
3836 2794 1877 2520 2779 3836 3370 650 1877 3836 4855 3836
d.gsf pt.pp.gsf p.d n.dsn cj d.npm a.npm v.api.3p p.d d.dsf n.dsf

τοῦ ⌊καθημένου ἐπὶ⌋ τοῦ ἵππου τῇ ἐξελθούσῃ ἐκ τοῦ
extended from the mouth of the one who rode the horse; *that* *extended* *from* *the*
2002 1666 3836 5125 3836 2764 2093 3836 2691 3836 2002 1666 3836
d.gsm pt.pm.gsm p.g d.gsm n.gsm d.dsf pt.aa.dsf p.g d.gsn

στόματος αὐτοῦ, καὶ πάντα τὰ ὄρνεα ἐχορτάσθησαν ἐκ τῶν σαρκῶν αὐτῶν.
mouth *{his}* and all the birds gorged themselves with *{the}* their flesh. *their*
5125 899 2779 4246 3836 3997 5963 1666 3836 899 4922 899
n.gsn r.gsm.3 cj a.npn d.npn n.npn v.api.3p p.g d.gpf n.gpf r.gpm.3

20:1 καὶ εἶδον ἄγγελον καταβαίνοντα ἐκ τοῦ οὐρανοῦ ἔχοντα
Then I saw an angel coming down from *{the}* heaven, having in his hand
2779 1625 34 2849 1666 3836 4041 2400 2093 899 5931
cj v.aai.1s n.asm pt.pa.asm p.g d.gsm n.gsm pt.pa.asm

τὴν κλεῖν τῆς ἀβύσσου καὶ ἅλυσιν μεγάλην ἐπὶ τὴν χεῖρα αὐτοῦ. 2 καὶ
the key to the abyss and a great chain. *great* *in* *{the}* *hand* *his* *{and}*
3836 3090 3836 12 2779 3489 268 3489 2093 3836 5931 899 2779
d.asf n.asf d.gsf n.gsf cj n.asf a.asf p.a d.asf n.asf r.gsm.3 cj

ἐκράτησεν τὸν δράκοντα, ὁ ὄφις ὁ ἀρχαῖος, ὅς ἐστιν διάβολος
He seized the dragon, that ancient serpent *{the}* *ancient* (who is the devil
3195 3836 1532 3836 792 4058 3836 792 4005 1639 1333
v.aai.3s d.asm n.asm d.nsm n.nsm d.nsm a.nsm r.nsm v.pai.3s n.nsm

καὶ ὁ Σατανᾶς, καὶ ἔδησεν αὐτὸν → χίλια ἔτη 3 καὶ ἔβαλεν αὐτὸν εἰς τὴν
and *{the}* Satan), and bound him for a thousand years. Then he threw him into the
2779 3836 4928 2779 1313 899 5943 2291 2779 965 899 1650 3836
cj d.nsm n.nsm cj v.aai.3s r.asm.3 a.apn n.apn cj v.aai.3s r.asm.3 p.a d.asf

ἄβυσσον καὶ ἔκλεισεν καὶ ἐσφράγισεν ἐπάνω αὐτοῦ, ἵνα ↱ ↱ μὴ πλανήσῃ
abyss, *{and}* locked and sealed it over him, so he could not deceive
12 2779 3091 2779 5381 2062 899 2671 4414 4414 3590 4414
n.asf cj v.aai.3s cj v.aai.3s p.g r.gsm.3 cj pl v.aas.3s

ἔτι τὰ ἔθνη ἄχρι τελεσθῇ τὰ χίλια ἔτη.
the nations ⌊any longer,⌋ *the* *nations* until the thousand years were finished. *the* *thousand* *years*
3836 1620 2285 3836 1620 948 3836 5943 2291 5464 3836 5943 2291
adv d.apn n.apn cj v.aps.3s d.npn a.npn n.npn

μετὰ ταῦτα δεῖ λυθῆναι αὐτὸν → μικρὸν χρόνον. 4 καὶ εἶδον θρόνους καὶ
After that he must be set loose *he* for a short time. And I saw thrones, and
3552 4047 899 1256 3395 899 3625 5989 2779 1625 2585 2779
p.a r.apn v.pai.3s f.ap r.asm.3 a.asm n.asm cj v.aai.1s n.apm cj

NASB

beast and the
kings of the earth
and their armies
assembled to make
war against Him
who sat on the
horse and against
His army.

Doom of the Beast and False Prophet

20 And the beast
was seized, and
with him the false
prophet who per-
formed the signs
in his presence, by
which he deceived
those who had re-
ceived the mark of
the beast and those
who worshiped his
image; these two
were thrown alive
into the lake of fire
which burns with
brimstone. 21 And
the rest were killed
with the sword
which came from
the mouth of Him
who sat on the
horse, and all the
birds were filled
with their flesh.

Satan Bound

20:1 Then I saw
an angel coming
down from heaven,
holding the key
of the abyss and
a great chain in
his hand. 2 And he
laid hold of the
dragon, the serpent
of old, who is the
devil and Satan,
and bound him for
a thousand years;
3 and he threw him
into the abyss, and
shut *it* and sealed
it over him, so
that he would not
deceive the nations
any longer, until
the thousand years
were completed;
after these things
he must be released
for a short time.
4 Then I saw
thrones, and they

NIV

on which were
seated those who
had been given
authority to judge.
And I saw the souls
of those who had
been beheaded be-
cause of their testi-
mony about Jesus
and because of
the word of God.
They[a] had not wor-
shiped the beast
or its image and
had not received
its mark on their
foreheads or their
hands. They came
to life and reigned
with Christ a thou-
sand years. 5(The
rest of the dead did
not come to life
until the thousand
years were ended.)
This is the first res-
urrection. 6Blessed
and holy are those
who share in the
first resurrection.
The second death
has no power over
them, but they will
be priests of God
and of Christ and
will reign with
him for a thousand
years.

The Judgment of Satan

7When the thou-
sand years are
over, Satan will be
released from his
prison 8and will
go out to deceive
the nations in the
four corners of the
earth—Gog and
Magog—and to
gather them for
battle. In num-
ber they are like
the sand on the
seashore. 9They
marched across
the breadth of the
earth and sur-
rounded the camp
of God's people,
the city he loves.
But fire came
down from

[a] 4 Or *God; I also saw those who*

ἐκάθισαν ἐπ᾽ αὐτοὺς καὶ κρίμα ἐδόθη αὐτοῖς,
seated on them {and} to judge were those who ⌊had been given the authority⌋ those to
2767 2093 899 2779 3210 899 1443 899 3210
v.aai.3p p.a r.apm.3 cj n.nsn v.api.3s r.dpm.3

καὶ τὰς ψυχὰς τῶν πεπελεκισμένων διὰ τὴν μαρτυρίαν Ἰησοῦ καὶ
judge. I also saw the souls of those who had been beheaded for the testimony of Jesus and
3210 2779 3836 6034 3836 4284 1328 3836 3456 2652 2779
cj d.apf n.apf d.gpm pt.rp.gpm p.a d.asf n.asf n.gsm cj

διὰ τὸν λόγον τοῦ θεοῦ καὶ οἵτινες ↱ οὐ προσεκύνησαν τὸ θηρίον οὐδὲ τὴν
for the word of God. {and} These had not worshiped the beast or {the}
1328 3836 3364 3836 2536 2779 4015 4686 4024 4686 3836 2563 4028 3836
p.a d.asm n.asm d.gsm n.gsm cj r.npm pl v.aai.3p d.asn n.asn cj d.asf

εἰκόνα αὐτοῦ καὶ ↱ οὐκ ἔλαβον τὸ χάραγμα ἐπὶ τὸ μέτωπον καὶ ἐπὶ
its image its and had not received its mark on {the} their foreheads or {on}
899 1635 899 2779 3284 4024 3284 3836 5916 2093 3836 3587 2779 2093
n.asf r.gsn.3 cj pl v.aai.3p d.asn n.asn p.a d.asn n.asn cj p.a

τὴν χεῖρα αὐτῶν. καὶ ἔζησαν καὶ ἐβασίλευσαν μετὰ τοῦ Χριστοῦ →
{the} their hands. their {and} ⌊They came to life⌋ and reigned with {the} Christ for a
3836 899 5931 899 2779 2409 2779 996 3552 3836 5986
d.asf n.asf r.gpm.3 cj v.aai.3p cj v.aai.3p p.g d.gsm n.gsm

χίλια ἔτη. 5 οἱ λοιποὶ τῶν νεκρῶν ↱ οὐκ ἔζησαν ἄχρι
thousand years. (The rest of the dead did not ⌊come to life⌋ until the thousand years
5943 2291 3836 3370 3836 3738 2409 4024 2409 948 3836 5943 2291
a.apn n.apn d.npm a.npm d.gpm a.gpm pl v.aai.3p cj

τελεσθῇ τὰ χίλια ἔτη. αὕτη ἡ ἀνάστασις ἡ πρώτη. 6 μακάριος καὶ
were finished). the thousand years This is the first resurrection. {the} first Blessed and
5464 3836 5943 2291 4047 3836 4755 414 3836 4755 3421 2779
v.aps.3s d.npn a.npn n.npn r.nsf d.nsf n.nsf d.nsf a.nsf a.nsm cj

ἅγιος ὁ ἔχων μέρος ἐν τῇ ἀναστάσει τῇ πρώτῃ· ἐπὶ τούτων ὁ
holy is the ⌊one who has⌋ a part in the first resurrection! {the} first Over such the
41 3836 2400 3538 1877 3836 4755 414 3836 4755 2093 4047 3836
a.nsm d.nsm pt.pa.nsm n.asn p.d d.dsf n.dsf d.dsf a.dsf p.g r.gpm d.nsm

δεύτερος θάνατος οὐκ ἔχει ἐξουσίαν, ἀλλ᾽ ἔσονται ἱερεῖς τοῦ θεοῦ καὶ τοῦ
second death has no has power, but ⌊they will be⌋ priests of God and of
1311 2505 2400 4024 2400 2026 247 1639 2636 3836 2536 2779 3836
a.nsm n.nsm pl v.pai.3s n.asf cj v.fmi.3p n.npm d.gsm n.gsm cj d.gsm

Χριστοῦ καὶ βασιλεύσουσιν μετ᾽ αὐτοῦ τὰ[a] χίλια ἔτη. 7 καὶ ὅταν
Christ, and they will reign with him for a thousand years. {and} When the thousand
5986 2779 996 3552 899 3836 5943 2291 2779 4020 3836 5943
n.gsm cj v.fai.3p p.g r.gsm.3 d.apn a.apn n.apn cj cj

τελεσθῇ τὰ χίλια ἔτη, λυθήσεται ὁ Σατανᾶς ἐκ τῆς
years are finished, the thousand years Satan will be released {the} Satan from {the} his
2291 5464 3836 5943 2291 4928 3395 3836 4928 1666 3836 899
v.aps.3s d.npn a.npn n.npn v.fpi.3s d.nsm n.nsm p.g d.gsf

φυλακῆς αὐτοῦ 8 καὶ ἐξελεύσεται πλανῆσαι τὰ ἔθνη τὰ ἐν ταῖς τέσσαρσιν
prison his and will go out to deceive the nations {the} at the four
5871 899 2779 2002 4414 3836 1620 3836 1877 3836 5475
n.gsf r.gsm.3 cj v.fmi.3s f.aa d.apn n.apn d.apn p.d d.dpf a.dpf

γωνίαις τῆς γῆς, τὸν Γὼγ καὶ Μαγώγ, συναγαγεῖν αὐτοὺς εἰς τὸν πόλεμον,
corners of the earth, {the} Gog and Magog, to gather them for {the} battle.
1224 3836 1178 3836 1223 2779 3408 5251 899 1650 3836 4483
n.dpf d.gsf n.gsf d.asm n.asm cj n.asm f.aa r.apm.3 p.a d.asm n.asm

ὧν ὁ ἀριθμὸς αὐτῶν ὡς ἡ ἄμμος τῆς θαλάσσης. 9 καὶ
{of whom} {the} In number they are as the sand of the sea. And
4005 3836 750 899 6055 3836 302 3836 2498 2779
r.gpm d.nsm n.nsm r.gpm.3 pl d.nsf n.nsf d.gsf n.gsf cj

ἀνέβησαν ἐπὶ τὸ πλάτος τῆς γῆς καὶ ἐκύκλευσαν τὴν παρεμβολὴν τῶν
⌊they marched up⌋ on the broad plain of the earth and encircled the camp of the
326 2093 3836 4424 3836 1178 2779 3238 3836 4213 3836
v.aai.3p p.a d.asn n.asn d.gsf n.gsf cj v.aai.3p d.asf n.asf d.gpm

ἁγίων καὶ τὴν πόλιν τὴν ἠγαπημένην, καὶ κατέβη πῦρ ἐκ τοῦ
saints and the beloved city, {the} beloved but fire came down fire from {the}
41 2779 3836 26 4484 3836 26 2779 4786 2849 4786 1666 3836
a.gpm cj d.asf n.asf d.asf pt.rp.asf cj v.aai.3s n.nsn p.g d.gsm

[a] [τὰ] UBS.

NASB

sat on them, and
judgment was
given to them. And
I *saw* the souls
of those who had
been beheaded
because of their
testimony of Jesus
and because of
the word of God,
and those who
had not worshiped
the beast or his
image, and had not
received the mark
on their forehead
and on their hand;
and they came to
life and reigned
with Christ for a
thousand years.
5The rest of the
dead did not come
to life until the
thousand years
were completed.
This is the first res-
urrection. 6Blessed
and holy is the one
who has a part in
the first resurrec-
tion; over these the
second death has
no power, but they
will be priests of
God and of Christ
and will reign with
Him for a thousand
years.

Satan Freed, Doomed

7When the thou-
sand years are
completed, Satan
will be released
from his prison,
8and will come out
to deceive the na-
tions which are in
the four corners of
the earth, Gog and
Magog, to gather
them together
for the war; the
number of them
is like the sand of
the seashore. 9And
they came up on
the broad plain of
the earth and sur-
rounded the camp
of the saints and
the beloved city,
and fire came down

NIV

heaven and de-
voured them. 10And
the devil, who
deceived them,
was thrown into
the lake of burning
sulfur, where the
beast and the false
prophet had been
thrown. They will
be tormented day
and night for ever
and ever.

The Judgment of the Dead

11Then I saw a
great white throne
and him who was
seated on it. The
earth and the
heavens fled from
his presence, and
there was no place
for them. 12And
I saw the dead,
great and small,
standing before the
throne, and books
were opened. An-
other book was
opened, which is
the book of life.
The dead were
judged according
to what they had
done as record-
ed in the books.
13The sea gave up
the dead that were
in it, and death
and Hades gave
up the dead that
were in them, and
each person was
judged accord-
ing to what they
had done. 14Then
death and Hades
were thrown into
the lake of fire.
The lake of fire is
the second death.
15Anyone whose
name was not
found written in
the book of life
was thrown into
the lake of fire.

οὐρανοῦ καὶ κατέφαγεν αὐτούς. 10 καὶ ὁ διάβολος ὁ πλανῶν
heaven and consumed them. And the devil, the ˪one who had deceived˩
4041 2779 2983 899 2779 3836 1333 3836 4414
n.gsm cj v.aai.3s r.apm.3 cj d.nsm n.nsm d.nsm pt.pa.nsm

αὐτοὺς ἐβλήθη εἰς τὴν λίμνην τοῦ πυρὸς καὶ θείου ὅπου καὶ τὸ θηρίον καὶ ὁ
them, was thrown into the lake of fire and sulfur where both the beast and the
899 965 1650 3836 3349 3836 4786 2779 2520 3963 2779 3836 2563 2779 3836
r.apm.3 v.api.3s p.a d.asf n.asf d.gsn n.gsn cj n.gsn cj adv d.nsn n.nsn cj d.nsm

ψευδοπροφήτης, καὶ βασανισθήσονται ἡμέρας καὶ νυκτὸς εἰς τοὺς
false prophet are. *{and}* There they will suffer torment day and night for all
6021 2779 989 2465 2779 3816 1650 3836
n.nsm cj v.fpi.3p n.gsf cj n.gsf p.a d.apm

˪αἰῶνας τῶν αἰώνων.˩ 11 καὶ εἶδον θρόνον μέγαν λευκὸν καὶ τὸν
time. Then I saw a great white throne *great* *white* and the
172 3836 172 2779 1625 3489 3328 2585 3489 3328 2779 3836
n.apm d.gpm n.gpm cj v.aai.1s n.asm a.asm a.asm cj d.asm

καθήμενον ἐπ᾽ αὐτόν, οὗ ἀπὸ τοῦ προσώπου ἔφυγεν
˪one who was seated˩ on it. From his *From {the}* presence earth and heaven fled away,
2764 2093 899 608 4005 608 3836 4725 1178 2779 4041 5771
pt.pm.asm p.a r.asm.3 r.gsm p.g d.gsn n.gsn v.aai.3s

ἡ γῆ καὶ ὁ οὐρανὸς καὶ τόπος οὐχ εὑρέθη αὐτοῖς. 12 καὶ εἶδον τοὺς
{the} earth and {the} heaven and no place *no* was found for them. And I saw the
3836 1178 2779 3836 4041 2779 4024 5536 4024 2351 899 2779 1625 3836
d.nsf n.nsf cj d.nsm n.nsm cj n.nsm pl v.api.3s r.dpm.3 cj v.aai.1s d.apm

νεκρούς, τοὺς μεγάλους καὶ τοὺς μικρούς, ἑστῶτας ἐνώπιον τοῦ θρόνου. καὶ
dead, the great and the small, standing before the throne, and the
3738 3836 3489 2779 3836 3625 2705 1967 3836 2585 2779
a.apm d.apm a.apm cj d.apm a.apm pt.ra.apm p.g d.gsm n.gsm cj

βιβλία ἠνοίχθησαν, καὶ ἄλλο βιβλίον ἠνοίχθη, ὅ ἐστιν τῆς ζωῆς, καὶ
books were opened. Then another book was opened — the *{it is}* Book of Life. And
1046 487 2779 257 1046 487 4005 1639 3836 2437 2779
n.npn v.api.3p cj r.nsn n.nsn v.api.3s r.nsn v.pai.3s d.gsf n.gsf cj

ἐκρίθησαν οἱ νεκροὶ ἐκ τῶν γεγραμμένων ἐν τοῖς βιβλίοις κατὰ
the dead were judged *the* *dead* by what was written in the books, ˪according to˩
3836 3738 3212 3836 3738 1666 3836 1211 1877 3836 1046 2848
v.api.3p d.npm a.npm p.g d.gpn pt.rp.gpn p.d d.dpn n.dpn p.a

τὰ ἔργα αὐτῶν. 13 καὶ ἔδωκεν ἡ θάλασσα τοὺς νεκροὺς τοὺς
{the} their deeds. *their* And the sea gave up *the* *sea* the dead that were
3836 899 2240 899 2779 3836 2498 1443 3836 2498 3836 3738 3836
d.apn n.apn r.gpm.3 cj v.aai.3s d.nsf n.nsf d.apm a.apm d.apm

ἐν αὐτῇ καὶ ὁ θάνατος καὶ ὁ ᾅδης ἔδωκαν τοὺς νεκροὺς τοὺς ἐν
in it, and *{the}* death and *{the}* Hades gave up the dead that were in
1877 899 2779 3836 2505 2779 3836 87 1443 3836 3738 3836 1877
p.d r.dsf.3 cj d.nsm n.nsm cj d.nsm n.nsm v.aai.3p d.apm a.apm d.apm p.d

αὐτοῖς, καὶ ἐκρίθησαν ἕκαστος κατὰ τὰ ἔργα αὐτῶν. 14 καὶ ὁ
them, and they were judged, each one ˪according to˩ *{the}* his deeds. *his* Then *{the}*
899 2779 3212 1667 2848 3836 899 2240 899 2779 3836
r.dpm.3 cj v.api.3p r.nsm p.a d.apn n.apn r.gpm.3 cj d.nsm

θάνατος καὶ ὁ ᾅδης ἐβλήθησαν εἰς τὴν λίμνην τοῦ πυρός. οὗτος ὁ
death and *{the}* Hades were thrown into the lake of fire. This is the second
2505 2779 3836 87 965 1650 3836 3349 3836 4786 4047 1639 3836 1311
n.nsm cj d.nsm n.nsm v.api.3p p.a d.asf n.asf d.gsn n.gsn r.nsm d.nsm

θάνατος ὁ δεύτερός ἐστιν, ἡ λίμνη τοῦ πυρός. 15 καὶ ˪εἴ τις˩ ↱
death, *{the} second* *is* the lake of fire. And anyone whose name was
2505 3836 1311 1639 3836 3349 3836 4786 2779 1623 5516 2351
n.nsm d.nsm a.nsm v.pai.3s d.nsf n.nsf d.gsn n.gsn cj cj r.nsm

οὐχ εὑρέθη ἐν τῇ βίβλῳ τῆς ζωῆς γεγραμμένος, ἐβλήθη εἰς τὴν λίμνην
not found written in the Book of Life *written* was thrown into the lake
4024 2351 1211 1877 3836 1047 3836 2437 1211 965 1650 3836 3349
pl v.api.3s p.d d.dsf n.dsf d.gsf n.gsf pt.rp.nsm v.api.3s p.a d.asf n.asf

τοῦ πυρός.
of fire.
3836 4786
d.gsn n.gsn

NASB

from heaven and
devoured them.
10And the devil
who deceived them
was thrown into
the lake of fire and
brimstone, where
the beast and the
false prophet are
also; and they will
be tormented day
and night forever
and ever.

Judgment at the Throne of God

11Then I saw a
great white throne
and Him who
sat upon it, from
whose presence
earth and heaven
fled away, and no
place was found
for them. 12And I
saw the dead, the
great and the small,
standing before the
throne, and books
were opened; and
another book was
opened, which is
the book of life;
and the dead were
judged from the
things which were
written in the
books, according to
their deeds. 13And
the sea gave up the
dead which were
in it, and death
and Hades gave
up the dead which
were in them; and
they were judged,
every one *of them*
according to their
deeds. 14Then death
and Hades were
thrown into the
lake of fire. This is
the second death,
the lake of fire.
15And if anyone's
name was not
found written in
the book of life, he
was thrown into
the lake of fire.

NIV

A New Heaven and a New Earth

21 Then I saw
"a new
heaven and a new
earth,"[a] for the
first heaven and
the first earth had
passed away, and
there was no lon-
ger any sea. 2 I saw
the Holy City, the
new Jerusalem,
coming down out
of heaven from
God, prepared as
a bride beautiful-
ly dressed for her
husband. 3 And I
heard a loud voice
from the throne
saying, "Look!
God's dwell-
ing place is now
among the people,
and he will dwell
with them. They
will be his people,
and God himself
will be with them
and be their God.
4 'He will wipe ev-
ery tear from their
eyes. There will be
no more death'[b] or
mourning or cry-
ing or pain, for the
old order of things
has passed away."
5 He who was
seated on the
throne said, "I am
making everything
new!" Then he
said, "Write this
down, for these
words are trust-
worthy and true."
6 He said to me:
"It is done. I am
the Alpha and the
Omega, the Be-
ginning and the
End. To the thirsty
I will give water
without cost from
the spring of the
water of life.

[a] 1 Isaiah 65:17
[b] 4 Isaiah 25:8

21:1 καὶ εἶδον οὐρανὸν καινὸν καὶ γῆν καινήν. ὁ γὰρ
Then I saw a new heaven *new* and a new earth, *new* for the *for*
2779 1625 2785 4041 2785 2779 2785 1178 2785 1142 3836 1142
cj v.aai.1s n.asm a.asm cj n.asf a.asf d.nsm cj

πρῶτος οὐρανὸς καὶ ἡ πρώτη γῆ ἀπῆλθαν καὶ ἡ θάλασσα οὐκ ἔστιν
first heaven and the first earth ⌊had passed away,⌋ and the sea was no *was*
4755 4041 2779 3836 4755 1178 599 2779 3836 2498 1639 4024 1639
a.nsm n.nsm cj d.nsf a.nsf n.nsf v.aai.3p cj d.nsf n.nsf pl v.pai.3s

ἔτι. 2 καὶ[a] τὴν πόλιν τὴν ἁγίαν Ἰερουσαλὴμ καινὴν εἶδον
more. And I saw the holy city, *{the}* *holy* the new Jerusalem, *new* *I saw*
2285 2779 1625 1625 3836 41 4484 3836 41 2785 2647 2785 1625
adv cj d.asf n.asf d.asf a.asf n.asf a.asf v.aai.1s

καταβαίνουσαν ἐκ τοῦ οὐρανοῦ ἀπὸ τοῦ θεοῦ ἡτοιμασμένην ὡς νύμφην
coming down ⌊out of⌋ *{the}* heaven from *{the}* God, made ready like a bride
2849 1666 3836 4041 608 3836 2536 2286 6055 3811
pt.pa.asf p.g d.gsm n.gsm p.g d.gsm n.gsm pt.rp.asf pl n.asf

κεκοσμημένην τῷ ἀνδρὶ αὐτῆς. 3 καὶ ἤκουσα φωνῆς μεγάλης ἐκ τοῦ
adorned for her husband. *her* And I heard a loud voice *loud* from the
3175 3836 899 467 899 2779 201 3489 5889 3489 1666 3836
pt.rp.asf d.dsm n.dsm r.gsf.3 cj v.aai.1s n.gsf a.gsf p.g d.gsm

θρόνου λεγούσης, ἰδοὺ ἡ σκηνὴ τοῦ θεοῦ μετὰ τῶν ἀνθρώπων, καὶ
throne saying, "Behold, the ⌊dwelling place⌋ of God is with *{the}* man, and
2585 3306 2627 3836 5008 3836 2536 3552 3836 476 2779
n.gsm pt.pa.gsf j d.nsf n.nsf d.gsm n.gsm p.g d.gpm n.gpm cj

σκηνώσει μετ᾽ αὐτῶν, καὶ αὐτοὶ λαοὶ αὐτοῦ ἔσονται, καὶ αὐτὸς
he will dwell with them. *{and}* They will be his people, *his* *will be* and God himself
5012 3552 899 2779 899 1639 1639 899 3295 899 1639 2779 2536 899
v.fai.3s p.g r.gpm.3 cj r.npm n.npm r.gsm.3 v.fmi.3p cj r.nsm

ὁ θεὸς μετ᾽ αὐτῶν ἔσται ➔ [b]αὐτῶν θεός,[c] 4 καὶ ἐξαλείψει πᾶν
{the} *God* will be with them *will be* as their God. *{and}* ⌊He will wipe away⌋ every
3836 2536 1639 1639 3552 899 1639 2536 899 2536 2779 1981 4246
d.nsm n.nsm p.g r.gpm.3 v.fmi.3s r.gpm.3 n.nsm cj v.fai.3s a.asn

δάκρυον ἐκ τῶν ὀφθαλμῶν αὐτῶν, καὶ ὁ θάνατος οὐκ ἔσται ἔτι
tear from *{the}* their eyes. *their* *{and}* *{the}* Death will be no *will be* more,
1232 1666 3836 899 4057 899 2779 3836 2505 1639 1639 4024 1639 2285
n.asn p.g d.gpm n.gpm r.gpm.3 cj d.nsm n.nsm pl v.fmi.3s adv

οὔτε πένθος οὔτε κραυγὴ οὔτε πόνος οὐκ ἔσται ἔτι, ὅτι[d] τὰ πρῶτα
{and} mourning and crying and pain will be no *will be* more, for the ⌊former things⌋
4046 4292 4046 3199 4046 4506 1639 1639 4024 1639 2285 4022 3836 4755
cj n.nsn cj n.nsf cj n.nsm pl v.fmi.3s adv cj d.npn a.npn

ἀπῆλθαν. 5 καὶ εἶπεν ὁ καθήμενος ἐπὶ τῷ θρόνῳ, ἰδοὺ καινὰ
⌊have passed away."⌋ And *said* the one seated on the throne said, "Behold, *new*
599 2779 3306 3836 2764 2093 3836 2585 3306 2627 2785
v.aai.3p cj v.aai.3s d.nsm pt.pm.nsm p.d d.dsm n.dsm j a.apn

ποιῶ πάντα καὶ λέγει, γράψον, ὅτι οὗτοι οἱ λόγοι
I am making all things new." And he said, "Write it down, for these *{the}* words are
4472 4246 2785 2779 3306 1211 4022 4047 3836 3364 1639
v.pai.1s a.apn cj v.pai.3s v.aam.2s cj r.npm d.npm n.npm

πιστοὶ καὶ ἀληθινοί εἰσιν. 6 καὶ εἶπέν μοι, γέγοναν. ἐγώ εἰμι[e] τὸ ἄλφα καὶ
trustworthy and true." *are* And he said to me, "It is done! I am the Alpha and
4412 2779 240 1639 2779 3306 1609 1181 1609 1639 3836 270 2779
a.npm cj a.npm v.pai.3p cj v.aai.3s r.ds.1 v.rai.3p r.ns.1 v.pai.1s d.nsn n.nsn cj

τὸ ὦ, ἡ ἀρχὴ καὶ τὸ τέλος. ἐγὼ τῷ διψῶντι
the Omega, the beginning and the end. *I* ⌊To the⌋ ⌊one who thirsts⌋ I
3836 6042 3836 794 2779 3836 5465 1609 3836 1498 1609
d.nsn n.nsn d.nsf n.nsf cj d.nsn n.nsn r.ns.1 d.dsm pt.pa.dsm

δώσω ἐκ τῆς πηγῆς τοῦ ὕδατος τῆς ζωῆς
⌊will give permission⌋ to drink free of charge from the spring of the water of life.
1443 1562 1562 1562 1666 3836 4380 3836 5623 3836 2437
v.fai.1s p.g d.gsf n.gsf d.gsn n.gsn d.gsf n.gsf

[a] ἐγὼ Ἰωάννης included by TR after καὶ.
[b] [αὐτῶν θεός] UBS, , NET.
[c] θεός omitted in NET.
[d] [ὅτι] UBS.
[e] [εἰμι] UBS, omitted by TNIV.

NASB

The New Heaven and Earth

21:1 Then I saw a
new heaven and a
new earth; for the
first heaven and the
first earth passed
away, and there is
no longer *any* sea.
2 And I saw the holy
city, new Jerusa-
lem, coming down
out of heaven
from God, made
ready as a bride
adorned for her
husband. 3 And I
heard a loud voice
from the throne,
saying, "Behold,
the tabernacle of
God is among men,
and He will dwell
among them, and
they shall be His
people, and God
Himself will be
among them[a], 4 and
He will wipe away
every tear from
their eyes; and
there will no longer
be *any* death; there
will no longer be
any mourning, or
crying, or pain; the
first things have
passed away."
5 And He who
sits on the throne
said, "Behold, I
am making all
things new." And
He *said, "Write,
for these words are
faithful and true."
6 Then He said to
me, "It is done. I
am the Alpha and
the Omega, the
beginning and the
end. I will give to
the one who thirsts
from the spring of
the water of life
without cost.

[a] One early ms reads, and be *their God*

NIV

[7]Those who are
victorious will in-
herit all this, and I
will be their God
and they will be
my children. [8]But
the cowardly, the
unbelieving, the
vile, the murderers,
the sexually im-
moral, those who
practice magic arts,
the idolaters and all
liars — they will be
consigned to the fi-
ery lake of burning
sulfur. This is the
second death."

The New Jerusalem, the Bride of the Lamb

[9]One of the seven
angels who had the
seven bowls full
of the seven last
plagues came and
said to me, "Come,
I will show you
the bride, the wife
of the Lamb."
[10]And he carried
me away in the
Spirit to a moun-
tain great and
high, and showed
me the Holy City,
Jerusalem, com-
ing down out of
heaven from God.
[11]It shone with the
glory of God, and
its brilliance was
like that of a very
precious jewel,
like a jasper, clear
as crystal. [12]It had
a great, high wall
with twelve gates,
and with twelve
angels at the gates.
On the gates were
written the names
of the twelve tribes
of Israel.

δωρεάν. [7]ὁ νικῶν κληρονομήσει ταῦτα καὶ ἔσομαι αὐτῷ
free of charge The ⌊one who conquers⌋ will inherit these blessings, and I will be his
1562 3836 3771 3099 4047 2779 1639 899
adv d.nsm pt.pa.nsm v.fai.3s r.apn cj v.fmi.1s r.dsm.3

θεὸς καὶ αὐτὸς ἔσται μοι υἱός. [8]τοῖς δὲ δειλοῖς καὶ ἀπίστοις καὶ
God and he will be my son. But ⌊as for the⌋ *But* cowardly, *{and}* the faithless, *{and}*
2536 2779 899 1639 1609 5626 1254 3836 1254 1264 2779 603 2779
n.nsm cj r.nsm v.fmi.3s r.ds.1 n.nsm d.dpm cj a.dpm cj a.dpm cj

ἐβδελυγμένοις καὶ φονεῦσιν καὶ πόρνοις καὶ
the detestable, *{and}* ⌊those who commit murder,⌋ *{and}* the ⌊sexually immoral,⌋ *{and}*
1009 2779 5838 2779 4521 2779
pt.rp.dpm cj n.dpm cj n.dpm cj

φαρμάκοις καὶ εἰδωλολάτραις καὶ πᾶσιν τοῖς ψευδέσιν τὸ
⌊those who practice the occult,⌋ *{and}* idolaters, and all *{the}* liars — *{the}* their
5761 2779 1629 2779 4246 3836 6014 3836 899
n.dpm cj n.dpm cj a.dpm d.dpm a.dpm d.nsn

μέρος αὐτῶν ἐν τῇ λίμνῃ τῇ καιομένῃ πυρὶ καὶ θείῳ, ὅ ἐστιν ὁ
place *their* will be in the lake that burns ⌊with fire⌋ and sulfur. That is the
3538 899 1877 3836 3349 3836 2794 4786 2779 2520 4005 1639 3836
n.nsn r.gpm.3 p.d d.dsf n.dsf d.dsf pt.pp.dsf n.dsn cj n.dsn r.nsn v.pai.3s d.nsm

θάνατος ὁ δεύτερος. [9]καὶ ἦλθεν εἷς ἐκ τῶν ἑπτὰ ἀγγέλων τῶν ἐχόντων
second death." *{the}* *second* Then came one of the seven angels who had
1311 2505 3836 1311 2779 2262 1651 1666 3836 2231 34 3836 2400
n.nsm d.nsm a.nsm cj v.aai.3s a.nsm p.g d.gpm a.gpm n.gpm d.gpm pt.pa.gpm

τὰς ἑπτὰ φιάλας τῶν γεμόντων τῶν ἑπτὰ πληγῶν τῶν ἐσχάτων καὶ ἐλάλησεν
the seven bowls *{the}* full of the seven final plagues, *{the}* *final* and he spoke
3836 2231 5786 3836 1154 3836 2231 2274 4435 3836 2274 2779 3281
d.apf a.apf n.apf d.gpm pt.pa.gpf d.gpf a.gpf n.gpf d.gpf a.gpf cj v.aai.3s

μετ' ἐμοῦ λέγων, δεῦρο, δείξω σοι τὴν νύμφην τὴν γυναῖκα τοῦ ἀρνίου.
with me, saying, "Come, ⌊I will show⌋ you the Bride, the wife of the Lamb."
3552 1609 3306 1306 1259 5148 3836 3811 3836 1222 3836 768
p.g r.gs.1 pt.pa.nsm j v.fai.1s r.ds.2 d.asf n.asf d.asf n.asf d.gsn n.gsn

[10]καὶ ἀπήνεγκέν με ↰ ἐν πνεύματι ἐπὶ ὄρος μέγα καὶ
And he carried me away in the spirit ⌊up onto⌋ a great, lofty mountain, *great* *{and}*
2779 708 1609 708 1877 4460 2093 3489 5734 4001 3489 2779
cj v.aai.3s r.as.1 p.d n.dsn p.a n.asn a.asn cj

ὑψηλόν, καὶ ἔδειξέν μοι τὴν πόλιν τὴν ἁγίαν Ἰερουσαλὴμ καταβαίνουσαν
lofty and showed me the holy city *{the}* *holy* Jerusalem coming down
5734 2779 1259 1609 3836 41 4484 3836 41 2647 2849
a.asn cj v.aai.3s r.ds.1 d.asf n.asf d.asf a.asf n.asf pt.pa.asf

ἐκ τοῦ οὐρανοῦ ἀπὸ τοῦ θεοῦ [11]ἔχουσαν τὴν δόξαν τοῦ θεοῦ, ὁ φωστὴρ
⌊out of⌋ *{the}* heaven from *{the}* God. It had the glory of God; *{the}* its radiance
1666 3836 4041 608 3836 2536 2400 3836 1518 3836 2536 3836 899 5891
p.g d.gsm n.gsm p.g d.gsm n.gsm pt.pa.asf d.asf n.asf d.gsm n.gsm d.nsm n.nsm

αὐτῆς ὅμοιος λίθῳ τιμιωτάτῳ ὡς λίθῳ ἰάσπιδι
its was like that of a very precious jewel, *very precious* like a jasper stone, *jasper*
899 3927 5508 5508 3345 5508 6055 2618 3345 2618
r.gsf.3 a.nsm n.dsm a.dsm.s pl n.dsm n.dsf

κρυσταλλίζοντι. [12]ἔχουσα τεῖχος μέγα καὶ ὑψηλόν, ἔχουσα
clear as crystal. It had a great, high wall *great* *{and}* *high* with twelve
3222 2400 3489 5734 5446 3489 2779 5734 2400 1557
pt.pa.dsm pt.pa.nsf n.asn a.asn cj a.asn pt.pa.nsf

πυλῶνας δώδεκα καὶ ἐπὶ τοῖς πυλῶσιν ἀγγέλους δώδεκα καὶ
gates, *twelve* *{and}* with twelve angels at the gates, *angels* *twelve* and the
4784 1557 2779 1557 34 2093 3836 4784 34 1557 2779
n.apm a.apm cj p.d d.dpm n.dpm n.apm a.apm cj

ὀνόματα ἐπιγεγραμμένα, ἅ ἐστιν [a]τὰ ὀνόματα[b] τῶν δώδεκα φυλῶν → υἱῶν
names *were inscribed* *{that}* *{is}* *{the}* *{names}* of the twelve tribes of the nation
3950 2108 4005 1639 3836 3950 3836 1557 5876 5626
n.apn pt.rp.apn r.npn v.pai.3s d.npn n.npn d.gpf a.gpf n.gpf n.gpm

[a] [τὰ ὀνόματα] UBS, omitted by TNIV.
[b]

NASB

[7]He who over-
comes will inherit
these things, and I
will be his God and
he will be My son.
[8]But for the cow-
ardly and unbeliev-
ing and abominable
and murderers and
immoral persons
and sorcerers and
idolaters and all
liars, their part *will*
be in the lake that
burns with fire and
brimstone, which is
the second death."
[9]Then one of
the seven angels
who had the seven
bowls full of the
seven last plagues
came and spoke
with me, saying,
"Come here, I will
show you the bride,
the wife of the
Lamb."

The New Jerusalem

[10]And he carried
me away [a]in the
Spirit to a great
and high mountain,
and showed me the
holy city, Jerusa-
lem, coming down
out of heaven from
God, [11]having the
glory of God. Her
brilliance was
like a very costly
stone, as a stone of
crystal-clear jasper.
[12]It had a great and
high wall, with
twelve gates, and
at the gates twelve
angels; and names
were written on
them, which are
the names of the
twelve tribes of

[a] Or *in spirit*

NIV

[13]There were three
gates on the east,
three on the north,
three on the south
and three on the
west. [14]The wall of
the city had twelve
foundations, and
on them were
the names of the
twelve apostles of
the Lamb.
[15]The angel who
talked with me had
a measuring rod
of gold to mea-
sure the city, its
gates and its walls.
[16]The city was laid
out like a square,
as long as it was
wide. He measured
the city with the
rod and found it to
be 12,000 stadia[a]
in length, and as
wide and high as it
is long. [17]The an-
gel measured the
wall using human
measurement, and
it was 144 cu-
bits[b] thick.[c] [18]The
wall was made
of jasper, and the
city of pure gold,
as pure as glass.
[19]The foundations
of the city walls
were decorated
with every kind
of precious stone.
The first founda-
tion was jasper, the
second sapphire,
the

[a] 16 That is, about 1,400 miles or about 2,200 kilometers
[b] 17 That is, about 200 feet or about 65 meters
[c] 17 Or *high*

Ἰσραήλ· of Israel 2702 n.gsm | were inscribed on the gates. 2108 2108
13 There were three gates 5552 4784 | ἀπὸ on 608 p.g | ἀνατολῆς the east, 424 n.gsf | πυλῶνες *gates* 4784 n.npm
τρεῖς *three* 5552 a.npm | καὶ *{and}* 2779 cj | three gates 5552 4784 | ἀπὸ on 608 p.g | βορρᾶ the north, 1080 n.gsm | πυλῶνες *gates* 4784 n.npm | τρεῖς *three* 5552 a.npm | καὶ *{and}* 2779 cj | three gates 5552 4784 | ἀπὸ on 608 p.g | νότου the south, 3803 n.gsm
πυλῶνες *gates* 4784 n.npm | τρεῖς *three* 5552 a.npm | καὶ and 2779 cj | three gates 5552 4784 | ἀπὸ on 608 p.g | δυσμῶν the west. 1553 n.gpf | πυλῶνες *gates* 4784 n.npm | τρεῖς. *three* 5552 a.npm | 14 καὶ *{and}* 2779 cj | τὸ The 3836 d.nsn | τεῖχος wall 5446 n.nsn | τῆς of the 3836 d.gsf
πόλεως city 4484 n.gsf | ἔχων had 2400 pt.pa.nsm | twelve 1557 | θεμελίους foundations, 2529 n.apm | δώδεκα *twelve* 1557 a.apm | καὶ and 2779 cj | ἐπ᾽ on 2093 p.g | αὐτῶν them 899 r.gpm.3 | were the | δώδεκα twelve 1557 a.npn | ὀνόματα names 3950 n.npn
τῶν of the 3836 d.gpm | δώδεκα twelve 1557 a.gpm | ἀποστόλων apostles 693 n.gpm | τοῦ of the 3836 d.gsn | ἀρνίου. Lamb. 768 n.gsn | 15 καὶ *{and}* 2779 cj | ὁ The 3836 d.nsm | λαλῶν ⌞one who spoke⌟ 3281 pt.pa.nsm | μετ᾽ with 3552 p.g | ἐμοῦ me 1609 r.gs.1 | εἶχεν had 2400 v.iai.3s | a
golden 5997 | μέτρον measuring 3586 n.asn | κάλαμον rod 2812 n.asm | χρυσοῦν, *golden* 5997 a.asm | with which | ἵνα to 2671 cj | μετρήσῃ measure 3582 v.aas.3s | τὴν the 3836 d.asf | πόλιν city, 4484 n.asf | καὶ *{and}* 2779 cj | τοὺς *{the}* 3836 d.apm | its 899
πυλῶνας gates 4784 n.apm | αὐτῆς *its* 899 r.gsf.3 | καὶ and 2779 cj | τὸ *{the}* 3836 d.asn | its 899 | τεῖχος wall. 5446 n.asn | αὐτῆς. *its* 899 r.gsf.3 | 16 καὶ *{and}* 2779 cj | ἡ The 3836 d.nsf | πόλις city 4484 n.nsf | was laid out 3023 3023 3023 | → as a
τετράγωνος square, 5481 a.nsf | κεῖται *was laid out* 3023 v.pmi.3s | καὶ *{and}* 2779 cj | τὸ *{the}* 3836 d.nsn | its 899 | μῆκος length 3601 n.nsn | αὐτῆς *its* 899 r.gsf.3 | ⌞ὅσον the same as 4012 r.nsn | καὶ⌟[a] 2779 adv | τὸ its 3836 d.nsn | πλάτος. width. 4424 n.nsn | καὶ *{and}* 2779 cj
ἐμέτρησεν He measured 3582 v.aai.3s | τὴν the 3836 d.asf | πόλιν city 4484 n.asf | τῷ ⌞with the⌟ 3836 d.dsm | καλάμῳ ⌞measuring rod⌟ 2812 n.dsm | ἐπὶ at 2093 p.g | twelve thousand 1557 5942 | σταδίων stadia, 5084 n.gpn | δώδεκα *twelve* 1557 a.gpf
χιλιάδων, *thousand* 5942 n.gpf | τὸ *{the}* 3836 d.nsn | its 899 | μῆκος length, 3601 n.nsn | καὶ *{and}* 2779 cj | τὸ *{the}* 3836 d.nsn | πλάτος width, 4424 n.nsn | καὶ and 2779 cj | τὸ *{the}* 3836 d.nsn | ὕψος height 5737 n.nsn | αὐτῆς *its* 899 r.gsf.3 | being 1639 | ἴσα equal. 2698 a.npn | ἐστίν. *being* 1639 v.pai.3s
17 ↱ He 3582 | καὶ also 2779 cj | ἐμέτρησεν measured 3582 v.aai.3s | τὸ *{the}* 3836 d.asn | its 899 | τεῖχος wall, 5446 n.asn | αὐτῆς *its* 899 r.gsf.3 | ἑκατὸν one hundred and 1669 a.gpm | ⌞τεσσεράκοντα forty-four 5477 a.gpm | τεσσάρων⌟ 5475 a.gpm
πηχῶν cubits 4388 n.gpm | → by human 476 | μέτρον measurement, 3586 n.asn | ἀνθρώπου, *human* 476 n.gsm | ὅ which 4005 r.nsn | ἐστιν is 1639 v.pai.3s | also an | ἀγγέλου. angel's 34 n.gsm | measurement.
18 καὶ *{and}* 2779 cj | τοῦ The 3836 d.gsn | ἡ *{the}* 3836 d.nsf | ἐνδώμησις *was made of* 1908 n.nsf | city's 899 | τείχους wall 5446 n.gsn | αὐτῆς *city's* 899 r.gsf.3 | was made of 1908 1908 1908 | ἴασπις jasper 2618 n.nsf | καὶ and 2779 cj | ἡ the 3836 d.nsf | πόλις city 4484 n.nsf
was pure 2754 | χρυσίον gold, 5992 n.nsn | καθαρὸν *pure* 2754 a.nsn | as pure 2754 | ὅμοιον as 3927 a.nsn | ὑάλῳ glass. 5613 n.dsm | καθαρῷ. *pure* 2754 a.dsm | 19 οἱ The 3836 d.npm | θεμέλιοι foundations 2529 n.npm | τοῦ of the 3836 d.gsn
τείχους wall 5446 n.gsn | τῆς of the 3836 d.gsf | πόλεως city 4484 n.gsf | were adorned 3175 3175 | παντὶ ⌞with every kind of⌟ 4246 a.dsm | precious 5508 | λίθῳ stone: 3345 n.dsm | τιμίῳ *precious* 5508 a.dsm | κεκοσμημένοι· *were adorned* 3175 pt.rp.npm
ὁ *{the}* 3836 d.nsm | θεμέλιος *{foundation}* 2529 n.nsm | ὁ the 3836 d.nsm | πρῶτος first 4755 a.nsm | ἴασπις, was jasper, 2618 n.nsf | ὁ the 3836 d.nsm | δεύτερος second 1311 a.nsm | σάπφιρος, sapphire, 4913 n.nsf | ὁ the 3836 d.nsm | τρίτος third 5569 a.nsm

[a] [καὶ] UBS, omitted by TNIV.

NASB

the sons of Israel.
[13]*There were* three
gates on the east
and three gates on
the north and three
gates on the south
and three gates on
the west. [14]And the
wall of the city had
twelve founda-
tion stones, and
on them *were* the
twelve names of
the twelve apostles
of the Lamb.
[15]The one who
spoke with me had
a gold measuring
rod to measure the
city, and its gates
and its wall. [16]The
city is laid out as
a square, and its
length is as great as
the width; and he
measured the city
with the rod, [a]fif-
teen hundred miles;
its length and
width and height
are equal. [17]And
he measured its
wall, [b]seventy-two
yards, *according
to* human measure-
ments, which are
also angelic *mea-
surements.* [18]The
material of the wall
was jasper; and the
city was pure gold,
like clear glass.
[19]The foundation
stones of the city
wall were adorned
with every kind of
precious stone. The
first foundation
stone was jasper;
the second, sap-
phire; the third,

[a] Lit *twelve thousand stadia;* a stadion was approx 600 ft
[b] Lit *one hundred forty-four cubits*

NIV

third agate, the
fourth emerald,
20 the fifth onyx,
the sixth ruby, the
seventh chrysolite,
the eighth beryl,
the ninth topaz, the
tenth turquoise, the
eleventh jacinth,
and the twelfth
amethyst.[a] 21 The
twelve gates were
twelve pearls, each
gate made of a
single pearl. The
great street of the
city was of gold, as
pure as transparent
glass.
22 I did not see a
temple in the city,
because the Lord
God Almighty and
the Lamb are its
temple. 23 The city
does not need the
sun or the moon to
shine on it, for the
glory of God gives
it light, and the
Lamb is its lamp.
24 The nations will
walk by its light,
and the kings of
the earth will
bring their splen-
dor into it. 25 On no
day will its gates
ever be shut, for
there will be no
night there. 26 The
glory and hon-
or of the nations
will be brought
into it. 27 Nothing
impure will ever
enter it, nor will
anyone who does
what is shameful
or deceitful, but
only those whose
names are written
in the Lamb's book
of life.

χαλκηδών, ὁ τέταρτος σμάραγδος, 20 ὁ πέμπτος σαρδόνυξ, ὁ ἕκτος σάρδιον,
agate, the fourth emerald, the fifth onyx, the sixth carnelian,
5907 3836 5480 5040 3836 4286 4918 3836 1761 4917
n.nsm d.nsm a.nsm n.nsm d.nsm a.nsm n.nsf d.nsm a.nsm n.nsn

ὁ ἕβδομος χρυσόλιθος, ὁ ὄγδοος βήρυλλος, ὁ ἔνατος τοπάζιον, ὁ δέκατος
the seventh chrysolite, the eighth beryl, the ninth topaz, the tenth
3836 1575 5994 3836 3838 1039 3836 1888 5535 3836 1281
d.nsm a.nsm n.nsm d.nsm a.nsm n.nsm d.nsm a.nsm n.nsn d.nsm a.nsm

χρυσόπρασος, ὁ ἑνδέκατος ὑάκινθος, ὁ δωδέκατος ἀμέθυστος, 21 καὶ οἱ
chrysoprase, the eleventh jacinth, the twelfth amethyst. {and} The
5995 3836 1895 5611 3836 1558 287 2779 3836
n.nsm d.nsm a.nsm n.nsm d.nsm a.nsm n.nsf cj d.npm

δώδεκα πυλῶνες δώδεκα μαργαρῖται, ⸤ἀνὰ εἷς ἕκαστος⸥ τῶν πυλώνων
twelve gates were twelve pearls, each of the gates
1557 4784 1557 3449 324 1651 1667 3836 4784
a.npm n.npm a.npm n.npm p.a a.nsm r.nsm d.gpm n.gpm

ἦν ἐξ ἑνὸς μαργαρίτου. καὶ ἡ πλατεῖα τῆς πόλεως χρυσίον
⸤was made⸥ of a single pearl. And the main street of the city was pure gold,
1639 1666 1651 3449 2779 3836 4426 3836 4484 2754 5992
v.iai.3s p.g a.gsm n.gsm cj d.nsf n.nsf d.gsf n.gsf n.nsn

καθαρὸν ὡς ὕαλος διαυγής. 22 καὶ ναὸν οὐκ εἶδον ἐν
pure like transparent glass. *transparent* {and} I saw no temple *no* *I saw* in the
2754 6055 1420 5613 1420 2779 1625 1625 4024 3724 4024 1625 1877
a.nsn pl n.nsf a.nsf cj n.asm pl v.aai.1s p.d

αὐτῇ, ὁ γὰρ κύριος ὁ θεὸς ὁ παντοκράτωρ ναὸς αὐτῆς ἐστιν
city, for the *for* Lord {the} God {the} Almighty is its temple, *its* *is*
899 1142 3836 1142 3261 3836 2536 3836 4120 1639 899 3724 899 1639
r.dsf.3 d.nsm cj n.nsm d.nsm n.nsm d.nsm n.nsm n.nsm r.gsf.3 v.pai.3s

καὶ τὸ ἀρνίον. 23 καὶ ἡ πόλις οὐ χρείαν ἔχει τοῦ ἡλίου οὐδὲ τῆς σελήνης
and the Lamb. And the city has no need *has* of sun or {the} moon
2779 3836 768 2779 3836 4484 2400 4024 5970 2400 3836 2463 4028 3836 4943
cj d.nsn n.nsn cj d.nsf n.nsf pl n.asf v.pai.3s d.gsm n.gsm cj d.gsf n.gsf

ἵνα φαίνωσιν αὐτῇ, ἡ γὰρ δόξα τοῦ θεοῦ → ἐφώτισεν αὐτήν, καὶ ὁ
to shine on it, for the *for* glory of God floods it with light, *it* and {the}
2671 5743 899 1142 3836 1142 1518 3836 2536 899 5894 899 2779 3836
cj v.pas.3p r.dsf.3 d.nsf cj n.nsf d.gsm n.gsm v.aai.3s r.asf.3 cj d.nsm

λύχνος αὐτῆς τὸ ἀρνίον. 24 καὶ περιπατήσουσιν τὰ ἔθνη διὰ
its lamp *its* is the Lamb. {and} The nations will walk *The* *nations* by
899 3394 899 3836 768 2779 3836 1620 4344 3836 1620 1328
n.nsm r.gsf.3 d.nsn n.nsn cj v.fai.3p d.npn n.npn p.g

τοῦ φωτὸς αὐτῆς, καὶ οἱ βασιλεῖς τῆς γῆς φέρουσιν τὴν δόξαν αὐτῶν
{the} its light *its* and the kings of the earth will bring {the} their splendor *their*
3836 899 5890 899 2779 3836 995 3836 1178 5770 3836 899 1518 899
d.gsn n.gsn r.gsf.3 cj d.npm n.npm d.gsf n.gsf v.pai.3p d.asf n.asf r.gpm.3

εἰς αὐτήν, 25 καὶ ↱ ↱ οἱ πυλῶνες αὐτῆς ⸤οὐ μὴ⸥ κλεισθῶσιν
into it. {and} On no day will {the} its gates *its* ever be closed,
1650 899 2779 2465 4024 2465 3091 3836 899 4784 899 4024 3590 3091
p.a r.asf.3 cj d.npm n.npm r.gsf.3 pl pl v.aps.3p

ἡμέρας, νὺξ γὰρ οὐκ ἔσται ἐκεῖ, 26 καὶ οἴσουσιν τὴν
On day since there will be no night *since* *no* *there will be* there. And they will bring the
2465 1142 1639 1639 1639 4024 3816 1142 4024 1639 1695 2779 5770 3836
n.gsf n.nsf cj pl v.fmi.3s adv cj v.fai.3p d.asf

δόξαν καὶ τὴν τιμὴν τῶν ἐθνῶν εἰς αὐτήν. 27 καὶ ⸤οὐ μὴ⸥ ⸤εἰσέλθῃ εἰς⸥ αὐτὴν
splendor and {the} wealth of the nations into it. But *no* *will enter* *it*
1518 2779 3836 5507 3836 1620 1650 899 2779 4024 3590 1656 1650 899
n.asf cj d.asf n.asf d.gpn n.gpn p.a r.asf.3 cj pl pl v.aas.3s p.a r.asf.3

πᾶν κοινὸν καὶ ὁ[a] ποιῶν βδέλυγμα καὶ ψεῦδος ↰
nothing that is unclean — {and} no one who practices idolatry or falsehood — will ever
4246 3123 2779 4024 3836 4472 1007 2779 6022 1656 4024
a.nsn a.nsn cj d.nsm pt.pa.nsm n.asn cj n.asn

⸤εἰ μὴ⸥ οἱ γεγραμμένοι ἐν τῷ βιβλίῳ τῆς ζωῆς
enter it, but only those whose names are written in the Lamb's Book of Life.
1656 899 1623 3590 3836 1211 1877 3836 768 1046 3836 2437
cj pl d.npm pt.rp.npm p.d d.dsn n.dsn d.gsf n.gsf

NASB

chalcedony; the
fourth, emer-
ald; 20 the fifth,
sardonyx; the
sixth, sardius; the
seventh, chrysolite;
the eighth, beryl;
the ninth, topaz;
the tenth, chryso-
prase; the eleventh,
jacinth; the twelfth,
amethyst. 21 And the
twelve gates were
twelve pearls; each
one of the gates
was a single pearl.
And the street of
the city was pure
gold, like transpar-
ent glass.
22 I saw no temple
in it, for the Lord
God the Almighty
and the Lamb are
its temple. 23 And
the city has no
need of the sun
or of the moon to
shine on it, for the
glory of God has
illumined it, and its
lamp *is* the Lamb.
24 The nations will
walk by its light,
and the kings of
the earth will bring
their glory into it.
25 In the daytime
(for there will be
no night there) its
gates will never be
closed; 26 and they
will bring the glory
and the honor of
the nations into
it; 27 and nothing
unclean, and no
one who practices
abomination and
lying, shall ever
come into it, but
only those whose
names are written
in the Lamb's book
of life.

[a] 20 The precise identification of some of these precious stones is uncertain.

[a] [ὁ] UBS.

NIV

Eden Restored

22 Then the
angel
showed me the
river of the water
of life, as clear as
crystal, flowing
from the throne
of God and of the
Lamb [2]down the
middle of the great
street of the city.
On each side of
the river stood the
tree of life, bear-
ing twelve crops of
fruit, yielding its
fruit every month.
And the leaves of
the tree are for the
healing of the na-
tions. [3]No longer
will there be any
curse. The throne
of God and of the
Lamb will be in
the city, and his
servants will serve
him. [4]They will
see his face, and
his name will be
on their foreheads.
[5]There will be no
more night. They
will not need the
light of a lamp or
the light of the
sun, for the Lord
God will give
them light. And
they will reign for
ever and ever.

John and the Angel

[6]The angel said
to me, "These
words are trust-
worthy and true.
The Lord, the God
who inspires the
prophets, sent his
angel to show his
servants the things
that must soon
take place."
[7]"Look,

τοῦ ἀρνίου.
{the} Lamb's
3836 768
d.gsn n.gsn

22:1 καὶ ἔδειξέν μοι ποταμὸν → ὕδατος ζωῆς λαμπρὸν ὡς
Then the angel showed me a river of living water, living clear as
2779 1259 1609 4532 2437 5623 2437 3287 6055
cj v.aai.3s r.ds.1 n.asm n.gsn n.gsf a.asm pl

κρύσταλλον, ἐκπορευόμενον ἐκ τοῦ θρόνου τοῦ θεοῦ καὶ τοῦ ἀρνίου. [2]ἐν
crystal, flowing from the throne of God and of the Lamb, through the
3223 1744 1666 3836 2585 3836 2536 2779 3836 768 1877
n.asm pt.pm.asm p.g d.gsm n.gsm d.gsm n.gsm cj d.gsn n.gsn p.d

μέσῳ τῆς πλατείας αὐτῆς καὶ τοῦ ποταμοῦ ⌊ἐντεῦθεν καὶ
middle of the city's main street. city's {and} On each side of the river On each side
3545 3836 899 4426 899 2779 1949 1949 1949 3836 4532 1949 2779
n.dsn d.gsf n.gsf r.gsf.3 cj d.gsm n.gsm adv cj

ἐκεῖθεν⌋ ξύλον ζωῆς ποιοῦν καρποὺς δώδεκα,
was the tree of life producing twelve kinds of fruit, twelve yielding its fruit
1696 3833 2437 4472 1557 2843 1557 625 899 2843
adv n.nsn n.gsf pt.pa.nsn n.apm a.apm

⌊κατὰ μῆνα ἕκαστον⌋ ἀποδιδοῦν τὸν καρπὸν αὐτοῦ, καὶ τὰ φύλλα τοῦ
every month. yielding {the} fruit its And {the} its leaves {the}
2848 3604 1667 625 3836 2843 899 2779 3836 3833 5877 3836
p.a n.asm r.asm pt.pa.nsn d.asm n.asm r.gsn.3 cj d.npn n.npn d.gsn

ξύλου εἰς θεραπείαν τῶν ἐθνῶν. [3]καὶ πᾶν
its were for the healing of the nations. {and} No longer will anything be
3833 1650 2542 3836 1620 2779 4024 2285 1639 4246 1639
n.gsn p.a n.asf d.gpn n.gpn cj a.nsn

κατάθεμα οὐκ ἔσται ἔτι. καὶ ὁ θρόνος τοῦ θεοῦ καὶ τοῦ ἀρνίου
under a curse. No will be longer {and} The throne of God and of the Lamb will be
2873 4024 1639 2285 2779 3836 2585 3836 2536 2779 3836 768 1639 1639
n.nsn pl v.fmi.3s adv cj d.nsm n.nsm d.gsm n.gsm cj d.gsn n.gsn

ἐν αὐτῇ ἔσται, καὶ οἱ δοῦλοι αὐτοῦ λατρεύσουσιν αὐτῷ [4]καὶ
in the city, will be and {the} his servants his will worship him. {and}
1877 899 1639 2779 3836 899 1529 899 3302 899 2779
p.d r.dsf.3 v.fmi.3s cj d.npm n.npm r.gsm.3 v.fai.3p r.dsm.3 cj

ὄψονται τὸ πρόσωπον αὐτοῦ, καὶ τὸ ὄνομα αὐτοῦ ἐπὶ τῶν
⌊They will see⌋ {the} his face, his and {the} his name his will be on {the} their
3972 3836 899 4725 899 2779 3836 899 3950 899 2093 3836 899
v.fmi.3p d.asn n.asn r.gsm.3 cj d.nsn n.nsn r.gsm.3 p.g d.gpn

μετώπων αὐτῶν. [5]καὶ νὺξ οὐκ ἔσται ἔτι καὶ οὐκ
foreheads. their And night will be no will be more. {and} They will have no
3587 899 2779 3816 1639 1639 4024 1639 2285 2779 2400 2400 2400 4024
n.gpn r.gpm.3 cj n.nsf pl v.fmi.3s adv cj pl

ἔχουσιν χρείαν → φωτὸς → λύχνου καὶ φωτὸς → ἡλίου, ὅτι
They will have need for the light of a lamp or the light of the sun because the
2400 5970 5890 3394 2779 5890 2463 4022
v.pai.3p n.asf n.gsn n.gsm cj n.gsn n.gsm cj

κύριος ὁ θεὸς φωτίσει ἐπ' αὐτούς, καὶ βασιλεύσουσιν εἰς τοὺς ⌊αἰῶνας τῶν
Lord {the} God will shine on them, and they will reign for all time.
3261 3836 2536 5894 2093 899 2779 996 1650 3836 172 3836
n.nsm d.nsm n.nsm v.fai.3s p.a r.apm.3 cj v.fai.3p p.a d.apm n.apm d.gpm

αἰώνων.⌋ [6]καὶ εἶπέν μοι, οὗτοι οἱ λόγοι πιστοὶ καὶ ἀληθινοί, καὶ ὁ
And he said to me, "These {the} words are reliable and true. And the
172 2779 3306 1609 4047 3836 3364 4412 2779 240 2779 3836
n.gpm cj v.aai.3s r.ds.1 r.npm d.npm n.npm a.npm cj a.npm cj d.nsm

κύριος ὁ θεὸς τῶν πνευμάτων τῶν προφητῶν ἀπέστειλεν τὸν ἄγγελον αὐτοῦ
Lord, the God of the spirits of the prophets, has sent {the} his angel his
3261 3836 2536 3836 4460 3836 4737 690 3836 899 34 899
n.nsm d.nsm n.nsm d.gpn n.gpn d.gpm n.gpm v.aai.3s d.asm n.asm r.gsm.3

δεῖξαι τοῖς δούλοις αὐτοῦ ἃ δεῖ γενέσθαι ⌊ἐν τάχει.⌋ [7]καὶ ἰδοὺ
to show to his servants his what must soon take place." soon {and} "Behold,
1259 3836 899 1529 899 4005 1256 1877 1181 1877 5443 2779 2627
f.aa d.dpm n.dpm r.gsm.3 r.apn v.pai.3s f.am p.d n.dsn cj j

NASB

The River and the Tree of Life

22:1Then he
showed me a river
of the water of life,
clear as crystal,
coming from the
throne of God
and of [a]the Lamb,
[2]in the middle
of its street. On
either side of the
river was the tree
of life, bearing
twelve [b]*kinds of*
fruit, yielding its
fruit every month;
and the leaves of
the tree were for
the healing of the
nations. [3]There
will no longer be
any curse; and the
throne of God and
of the Lamb will
be in it, and His
bond-servants will
serve Him; [4]they
will see His face,
and His name *will*
be on their fore-
heads. [5]And there
will no longer be
any night; and they
will not have need
of the light of a
lamp nor the light
of the sun, because
the Lord God will
illumine them; and
they will reign for-
ever and ever.
[6]And he said to
me, "These words
are faithful and
true"; and the Lord,
the God of the spir-
its of the prophets,
sent His angel to
show to His bond-
servants the things
which must soon
take place.
[7]"And behold, I

[a] Or *the Lamb. In the middle of its street, and on either side of the river, was*
[b] Or *crops of fruit*

NIV

I am coming soon!
Blessed is the
one who keeps
the words of the
prophecy written in
this scroll."
8I, John, am the
one who heard and
saw these things.
And when I had
heard and seen
them, I fell down
to worship at the
feet of the angel
who had been
showing them to
me. 9But he said
to me, "Don't do
that! I am a fellow
servant with you
and with your fel-
low prophets and
with all who keep
the words of this
scroll. Worship
God!"
10Then he told
me, "Do not seal
up the words of the
prophecy of this
scroll, because the
time is near. 11Let
the one who does
wrong continue to
do wrong; let the
vile person con-
tinue to be vile; let
the one who does
right continue to
do right; and let
the holy person
continue to be
holy."

Epilogue: Invitation and Warning

12"Look, I am
coming soon! My
reward is with me,
and I will give to
each person ac-
cording to what
they have done. 13I
am the Alpha and
the Omega, the
First and the Last,
the Beginning and
the End.
14"Blessed are
those who wash
their robes, that
they may have the
right to the tree of
life and may go
through the gates
into the city. 15Out-
side are the dogs,
those who practice

ἔρχομαι ταχύ. μακάριος ὁ τηρῶν τοὺς λόγους τῆς προφητείας τοῦ
I am coming soon! Blessed is the ⌞one who keeps⌟ the words of the prophecy of
2262 5444 3421 3836 5498 3836 3364 3836 4735 3836
v.pmi.1s adv a.nsm d.nsm pt.pa.nsm d.apm n.apm d.gsf n.gsf d.gsn

βιβλίου τούτου. 8 κἀγὼ Ἰωάννης ὁ ἀκούων καὶ βλέπων ταῦτα.
this book." *this* I, John, am the ⌞one who heard⌟ and saw these things.
4047 1046 4047 2743 2722 3836 201 2779 1063 4047
n.gsn r.gsn crasis n.nsm d.nsm pt.pa.nsm cj pt.pa.nsm r.apn

καὶ ὅτε ἤκουσα καὶ ἔβλεψα, ἔπεσα προσκυνῆσαι ἔμπροσθεν τῶν ποδῶν
And when I heard and saw them, I fell down to worship at the feet
2779 4021 201 2779 1063 4406 4686 1869 3836 4546
cj cj v.aai.1s cj v.aai.1s v.aai.1s f.aa p.g d.gpm n.gpm

τοῦ ἀγγέλου τοῦ δεικνύοντός μοι ταῦτα. 9 καὶ λέγει μοι, ὅρα μή· ↰
of the angel who was showing them to me. *them* But he said to me, "Do not do
3836 34 3836 1260 4047 1609 4047 2779 3306 1609 3972 3590 3972
d.gsm n.gsm d.gsm pt.pa.gsm r.ds.1 r.apn cj v.pai.3s r.ds.1 v.pam.2s pl

σύνδουλός σού εἰμι καὶ τῶν ἀδελφῶν σου τῶν προφητῶν
that! I am a fellow servant ⌞with you⌟ *I am* and with your brothers *your* the prophets,
1639 1639 5281 5148 1639 2779 3836 5148 81 5148 3836 4737
n.nsm r.gs.2 v.pai.1s cj d.gpm n.gpm r.gs.2 d.gpm n.gpm

καὶ τῶν τηρούντων τοὺς λόγους τοῦ βιβλίου τούτου· τῷ θεῷ
and with those who keep the words of this book. *this* Worship *{the}* God!"
2779 3836 5498 3836 3364 3836 4047 1046 4047 4686 3836 2536
cj d.gpm pt.pa.gpm d.apm n.apm d.gsn n.gsn r.gsn d.dsm n.dsm

προσκύνησον. 10 καὶ λέγει μοι, ↱ μὴ σφραγίσῃς τοὺς λόγους τῆς προφητείας
Worship Then he said to me, "Do not seal up the words of the prophecy
4686 2779 3306 1609 5381 3590 5381 3836 3364 3836 4735
v.aam.2s cj v.pai.3s r.ds.1 pl v.aas.2s d.apm n.apm d.gsf n.gsf

τοῦ βιβλίου τούτου, ὁ καιρὸς γὰρ ἐγγύς ἐστιν. 11 ↱ ὁ ἀδικῶν
of this book, *this* for the time *for* is near. *is* Let the evildoer
3836 4047 1046 4047 1142 3836 2789 1142 1639 1584 1639 92 3836 92
d.gsn n.gsn r.gsn d.nsm n.nsm cj adv v.pai.3s d.nsm pt.pa.nsm

ἀδικησάτω ἔτι καὶ ὁ ῥυπαρὸς ῥυπανθήτω ἔτι, καὶ ὁ δίκαιος
continue to do evil, *continue* and the filthy be filthy still; *{and}* let the righteous
2285 92 2285 2779 3836 4865 4862 2285 2779 4472 3836 1465
v.aam.3s adv cj d.nsm a.nsm v.apm.3s adv cj d.nsm a.nsm

δικαιοσύνην ποιησάτω ἔτι καὶ ὁ ἅγιος ἁγιασθήτω ἔτι.
continue to act righteously, *let to act* *continue* and the holy be holy still."
2285 4472 4472 1466 4472 2285 2779 3836 41 39 2285
n.asf v.aam.3s adv cj d.nsm a.nsm v.apm.3s adv

12 ἰδοὺ ἔρχομαι ταχύ, καὶ ὁ μισθός μου μετ᾽ ἐμοῦ ἀποδοῦναι
"Behold, I am coming soon, and *{the}* my recompense *my* is with me, to repay
2627 2262 5444 2779 3836 1609 3635 1609 3552 1609 625
j v.pmi.1s adv cj d.nsm n.nsm r.gs.1 p.g r.gs.1 f.aa

ἑκάστῳ ὡς τὸ ἔργον ἐστὶν αὐτοῦ. 13 ἐγώ τὸ ἄλφα καὶ τὸ
everyone ⌞according to⌟ what he has done. *has* *he* I am the Alpha and the
1667 6055 3836 899 1639 2240 1639 899 1609 3836 270 2779 3836
r.dsm cj d.nsn n.nsn v.pai.3s r.gsm.3 r.ns.1 d.nsn n.nsn cj d.nsn

ὦ, ὁ πρῶτος καὶ ὁ ἔσχατος, ἡ ἀρχὴ καὶ τὸ τέλος. 14 μακάριοι
Omega, the first and the last, the beginning and the end." Blessed are
6042 3836 4755 2779 3836 2274 3836 794 2779 3836 5465 3421
n.nsn d.nsm a.nsm cj d.nsm a.nsm d.nsf n.nsf cj d.nsn n.nsn a.npm

οἱ πλύνοντες τὰς στολὰς αὐτῶν, ἵνα ἔσται ἡ ἐξουσία αὐτῶν ἐπὶ τὸ
those who wash *{the}* their robes, *their* so they will have the right *they* to the
3836 4459 3836 899 5124 899 2671 899 1639 3836 2026 899 2093 3836
d.npm pt.pa.npm d.apf n.apf r.gpm.3 cj v.fmi.3s d.nsf n.nsf r.gpm.3 p.a d.asn

ξύλον τῆς ζωῆς καὶ τοῖς πυλῶσιν ⌞εἰσέλθωσιν εἰς⌟ τὴν πόλιν.
tree of life and may enter the city by its gates. *may enter* *the* *city*
3833 3836 2437 2779 1656 1656 3836 4484 3836 4784 1656 1650 3836 4484
n.asn d.gsf n.gsf cj d.dpm n.dpm v.aas.3p p.a d.asf n.asf

15 ἔξω οἱ κύνες καὶ οἱ φάρμακοι καὶ οἱ πόρνοι
Outside are the dogs, *{and}* those ⌞who practice the occult,⌟ *{and}* the ⌞sexually immoral,⌟
2032 3836 3264 2779 3836 5761 2779 3836 4521
adv d.npm n.npm cj d.npm n.npm cj d.npm n.npm

NASB

am coming quickly.
Blessed is he who
heeds the words
of the prophecy of
this book."
8I, John, am the
one who heard and
saw these things.
And when I heard
and saw, I fell
down to worship
at the feet of the
angel who showed
me these things.
9But he *said to me,
"Do not do that. I
am a fellow servant
of yours and of
your brethren the
prophets and of
those who heed the
words of this book.
Worship God."

The Final Message

10And he *said
to me, "Do not
seal up the words
of the prophecy
of this book, for
the time is near.
11Let the one who
does wrong, still
do wrong; and the
one who is filthy,
still be filthy; and
let the one who
is righteous, still
practice righteous-
ness; and the one
who is holy, still
keep himself holy."
12"Behold, I am
coming quickly,
and My reward *is*
with Me, to render
to every man ac-
cording to what he
has done. 13I am
the Alpha and the
Omega, the first
and the last, the
beginning and the
end."
14Blessed are
those who wash
their robes, so that
they may have the
right to the tree of
life, and may enter
by the gates into
the city. 15Outside
are the dogs and
the sorcerers and
the immoral

NIV

magic arts, the
sexually immor-
al, the murderers,
the idolaters and
everyone who
loves and practices
falsehood.
16“I, Jesus, have
sent my angel to
give you[a] this
testimony for the
churches. I am
the Root and the
Offspring of Da-
vid, and the bright
Morning Star.”
17The Spirit and
the bride say,
“Come!” And let
the one who hears
say, “Come!” Let
the one who is
thirsty come; and
let the one who
wishes take the
free gift of the wa-
ter of life.

18I warn every-
one who hears
the words of the
prophecy of this
scroll: If anyone
adds anything to
them, God will
add to that per-
son the plagues
described in this
scroll. 19And if
anyone takes
words away from
this scroll of
prophecy, God will
take away from
that person any
share in the tree
of life and in the
Holy City, which
are described in
this scroll.
20He who testi-
fies to these things
says, “Yes, I am
coming soon.”
Amen. Come,
Lord Jesus.
21The grace of
the Lord Jesus be
with God’s people.
Amen.

[a] *16* The Greek is plural.

καὶ	οἱ	φονεῦς	καὶ	οἱ	εἰδωλολάτραι	καὶ	πᾶς	φιλῶν	καὶ	ποιῶν
{and}	*{the}*	murderers,	*{and}*	*{the}*	idolaters,	and	everyone	who loves	and	practices
2779	3836	5838	2779	3836	1629	2779	4246	5797	2779	4472
cj	d.npm	n.npm	cj	d.npm	n.npm	cj	a.nsm	pt.pa.nsm	cj	pt.pa.nsm

ψεῦδος.	16 ἐγὼ	Ἰησοῦς	ἔπεμψα	τὸν		ἄγγελόν	μου	μαρτυρῆσαι	ὑμῖν
falsehood.	“I,	Jesus,	have sent	*{the}*	my	angel	*my*	to bear witness	to you
6022	1609	2652	4287	3836	1609	34	1609	3455	7007
n.asn	r.ns.1	n.nsm	v.aai.1s	d.asm		n.asm	r.gs.1	f.aa	r.dp.2

ταῦτα	ἐπὶ	ταῖς	ἐκκλησίαις.	ἐγώ	εἰμι	ἡ	ῥίζα	καὶ	τὸ	γένος	Δαυίδ,
⌞about these things⌟	for	the	churches.	I	am	the	Root,	*{and}*	the	descendant	of David
4047	2093	3836	1711	1609	1639	3836	4844	2779	3836	1169	1253
r.apn	p.d	d.dpf	n.dpf	r.ns.1	v.pai.1s	d.nsf	n.nsf	cj	d.nsn	n.nsn	n.gsm

ὁ			ἀστὴρ	ὁ	λαμπρὸς	ὁ	πρωϊνός.	17 καὶ	τὸ	πνεῦμα	καὶ	ἡ
— the	bright	morning	star!”	*{the}*	*bright*	*{the}*	*morning*	*{and}*	The	Spirit	and	the
3836	3287	4748	843	3836	3287	3836	4748	2779	3836	4460	2779	3836
d.nsm			n.nsm	d.nsm	a.nsm	d.nsm	a.nsm	cj	d.nsn	n.nsn	cj	d.nsf

νύμφη	λέγουσιν,	ἔρχου.	καὶ	↱	ὁ	ἀκούων	εἰπάτω,	ἔρχου.	καὶ	ὁ
Bride	say,	“Come!”	And	let	the	⌞one who hears⌟	say,	“Come!”	*{and}*	Whoever
3811	3306	2262	2779	3306	3836	201	3306	2262	2779	3836
n.nsf	v.pai.3p	v.pmm.2s	cj		d.nsm	pt.pa.nsm	v.aam.3s	v.pmm.2s	cj	d.nsm

διψῶν	ἐρχέσθω,		ὁ	θέλων	λαβέτω	ὕδωρ	ζωῆς
is thirsty,	⌞let him come forward;⌟	and	whoever	so desires,	let him receive the	water	of life
1498	2262		3836	2527	3284	5623	2437
pt.pa.nsm	v.pmm.3s		d.nsm	pt.pa.nsm	v.aam.3s	n.asn	n.gsf

δωρεάν.	18	μαρτυρῶ	ἐγὼ	παντὶ	τῷ	ἀκούοντι	τοὺς	λόγους	τῆς
free of charge.	I	bear witness	*I*	to everyone	who	hears	the	words	of the
1562	1609	3455	1609	4246	3836	201	3836	3364	3836
adv		v.pai.1s	r.ns.1	a.dsm	d.dsm	pt.pa.dsm	d.apm	n.apm	d.gsf

προφητείας	τοῦ		βιβλίου	τούτου·	ἐάν	τις	ἐπιθῇ	ἐπ'	αὐτά,		ἐπιθήσει
prophecy	of	this	book:	*this*	if	anyone	⌞should add⌟	to	them,	God	will add
4735	3836	4047	1046	4047	1569	5516	2202	2093	899	2536	2202
n.gsf	d.gsn		n.gsn	r.gsn	cj	r.nsm	v.aas.3s	p.a	r.apn.3		v.fai.3s

ὁ	θεὸς	ἐπ'	αὐτὸν	τὰς	πληγὰς	τὰς	γεγραμμένας	ἐν	τῷ		βιβλίῳ	τούτῳ,
{the}	*God*	to	him	the	plagues	*{the}*	described	in	*{the}*	this	book;	*this*
3836	2536	2093	899	3836	4435	3836	1211	1877	3836	4047	1046	4047
d.nsm	n.nsm	p.a	r.asm.3	d.apf	n.apf	d.apf	pt.rp.apf	p.d	d.dsn		n.dsn	r.dsn

19 καὶ	ἐάν	τις	ἀφέλῃ	ἀπὸ	τῶν	λόγων	τοῦ	βιβλίου	τῆς		προφητείας
and	if	anyone	⌞should take away⌟	from	the	words	of the	book	of	this	prophecy,
2779	1569	5516	904	608	3836	3364	3836	1046	3836	4047	4735
cj	cj	r.nsm	v.aas.3s	p.g	d.gpm	n.gpm	d.gsn	n.gsn	d.gsf		n.gsf

ταύτης,		ἀφελεῖ	ὁ	θεὸς	τὸ		μέρος	αὐτοῦ	ἀπὸ	τοῦ	ξύλου	τῆς	ζωῆς
this	God	⌞will take away⌟	*{the}*	*God*	*{the}*	his	share	*his*	from	the	tree	of	life
4047	2536	904	3836	2536	3836	899	3538	899	608	3836	3833	3836	2437
r.gsf		v.fai.3s	d.nsm	n.nsm	d.asn		n.asn	r.gsm.3	p.g	d.gsn	n.gsn	d.gsf	n.gsf

καὶ	ἐκ	τῆς		πόλεως	τῆς	ἁγίας	τῶν	γεγραμμένων	ἐν	τῷ		βιβλίῳ	τούτῳ.
and	from	the	holy	city,	*{the}*	*holy*	which	are described	in	*{the}*	this	book.	*this*
2779	1666	3836	41	4484	3836	41	3836	1211	1877	3836	4047	1046	4047
cj	p.g	d.gsf		n.gsf	d.gsf	a.gsf	d.gpm	pt.rp.gpm	p.d	d.dsn		n.dsn	r.dsn

20 λέγει	ὁ	μαρτυρῶν	ταῦτα,		ναί,	ἔρχομαι	ταχύ.	ἀμήν,	ἔρχου
says	The	⌞one who testifies to⌟	these things	says:	“Yes,	I am coming	soon!”	Amen!	Come,
3306	3836	3455	4047	3306	3721	2262	5444	297	2262
v.pai.3s	d.nsm	pt.pa.nsm	r.apn		pl	v.pmi.1s	adv	pl	v.pmm.2s

κύριε	Ἰησοῦ.	21	ἡ	χάρις	τοῦ	κυρίου	Ἰησοῦ	μετὰ		πάντων.[a]
Lord	Jesus!	May	the	grace	of the	Lord	Jesus	be with	you	all.
3261	2652		3836	5921	3836	3261	2652	3552		4246
n.vsm	n.vsm		d.nsf	n.nsf	d.gsm	n.gsm	n.gsm	p.g		a.gpm

[a] πάντων UBS, NET. τῶν ἁγίων TNIV.

NASB

persons and the
murderers and
the idolaters, and
everyone who
loves and practices
lying.
16“I, Jesus, have
sent My angel
to testify to you
these things for the
churches. I am the
root and the de-
scendant of David,
the bright morning
star.”
17The Spirit and
the bride say,
“Come.” And let
the one who hears
say, “Come.” And
let the one who is
thirsty come; let
the one who wishes
take the water of
life without cost.
18I testify to ev-
eryone who hears
the words of the
prophecy of this
book: if anyone
adds to them, God
will add to him
the plagues which
are written in this
book; 19and if
anyone takes away
from the words of
the book of this
prophecy, God will
take away his part
from the tree of
life and from the
holy city, which
are written in this
book.
20He who testi-
fies to these things
says, “Yes, I am
coming quickly.”
Amen. Come, Lord
Jesus.

Greek-English Dictionary

The first number in bold brackets is the Goodrick-Kohlenberger number. Following it is the Greek word, its transliteration, frequency (i.e., the number of times it occurs in the New Testament) followed by an "x," and then its definition. The final smaller number in brackets is the corresponding Strong's number (e.g., [25]). If there is no corresponding Strong's number, then there are double asterisks ([**]). If the entry ends with an asterisk, then all occurrences of the word in the NT have been noted.

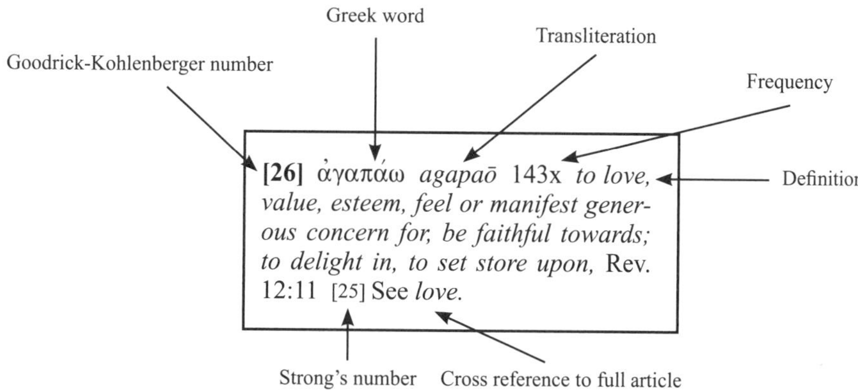

This dictionary includes all the Greek words that occur in the standard Greek NT. The frequencies are taken from the GNT-T database in the software program Accordance, which I helped develop.

This dictionary is not designed to replace a full dictionary (such as *A Greek-English Lexicon of the New Testament* by Frederick William Danker) or word study (such as *New International Dictionary of New Testament Theology: Abridged Edition* by Verlyn D. Verbrugge), but it will help for reference.

This is the same dictionary that is included in my *Mounce's Complete Expository Dictionary of Old and New Testament Words*. References such as "See *king; leader*" refer to the main entries in the *Expository Dictionary*.

Greek-English Dictionary

[2] Ἀαρών *Aarōn* 5x *Aaron,* pr. name, indecl, the brother of Moses (Exod. 4:14), Lk. 1:15; Acts 7:40; Heb. 5:4; 7:11; 9:4* [2]

[3] Ἀβαδδών *Abaddōn* 1x *Abaddon,* pr. name, indecl, alternate spelling: Ἀββαδών, the angel who rules in hell, Rev. 9:11* [3]

[4] ἀβαρής *abarēs* 1x literally: *weightless*; figurately: *not burdensome,* 2 Cor. 11:9* [4]

[5] ἀββά *abba* 3x *father,* Mk. 14:36; Rom. 8:15; Gal. 4:6* [5] See *abba; father.*

[6] Ἅβελ *Habel* 4x *Abel,* pr. name, indecl, Mt. 23:35; Lk. 11:51; Heb. 11:4; 12:24 [6]

[7] Ἀβιά *Abia* 3x *Abiajah,* pr. name, indecl. Hebrew is *Abijah*. (1) the son of Rehoboam (1 Chr. 3:10) Mt. 1:7. (2) the division of priests to which Zechariah belonged (1 Chr. 24:10) Lk. 1:5* [7]

[8] Ἀβιαθάρ *Abiathar* 1x *Abiathar,* pr. name, indecl, Mk. 2:26* [8]

[9] Ἀβιληνή *Abilēnē* 1x *Abilene,* a district of the Syrian Decapolis; from *Abila,* the chief town, Lk. 3:1* [9]

[10] Ἀβιούδ *Abioud* 2x *Abihud,* pr. name, indecl [10]

[11] Ἀβραάμ *Abraam* 73x *Abraham,* pr. name indecl [11]

[12] ἄβυσσος *abyssos* 9x *bottomless; place of the dead,* Lk. 8:31; Rom. 10:7 [12]

[13] Ἅγαβος *Hagabos* 2x *Agabus, pr. name,* Acts 11:28; 21:10* [13]

[14] ἀγαθοεργέω *agathoergeō* 2x *to do good, confer benefits,* Acts 14:17; 1 Tim. 6:18* [14]

[16] ἀγαθοποιέω *agathopoieō* 9x *to do good, do well; to do what is morally correct* (1 Pet. 2:15, 20) [15]

[17] ἀγαθοποιΐα *agathopoiia* 1x *well-doing,* 1 Pet. 4:19* [16]

[18] ἀγαθοποιός *agathopoios* 1x *doing good* or *right;* subst., *one who does good,* 1 Pet. 2:14* [17]

[19] ἀγαθός *agathos* 102x *good, profitable, generous, upright, virtuous* [18] See *good.*

[20] ἀγαθωσύνη *agathōsynē* 4x *goodness, virtue, beneficence,* Rom. 5:14; Eph. 5:9; 2 Thess. 1:11; *generosity,* Gal. 5:22* [19]

[21] ἀγαλλίασις *agalliasis* 5x *exultation, extreme joy* [20]

[22] ἀγαλλιάω *agalliaō* 11x *to celebrate, praise;* usually in the middle in the NT (ἀγαλλιάομαι) *to exult, rejoice exceedingly; to desire ardently,* Jn. 8:56 [21] See *exult; rejoice.*

[23] ἄγαμος *agamos* 4x *unmarried* (woman or man) 1 Cor. 7:8, 11, 32, 34* [22]

[24] ἀγανακτέω *aganakteō* 7x *to be pained; to be angry, vexed, indignant; to manifest indignation,* Mk. 14:4; Lk. 13:14 [23]

[25] ἀγανάκτησις *aganaktēsis* 1x *indignation,* 2 Cor. 7:11* [24]

[26] ἀγαπάω *agapaō* 143x *to love, value, esteem, feel or manifest generous concern for, be faithful towards; to delight in, to set store upon,* Rev. 12:11 [25] See *love.*

[27] ἀγάπη *agapē* 116x *love, generosity, kindly concern, devotedness;* pl. *love-feasts,* Jude 12 [26] See *love.*

[28] ἀγαπητός *agapētos* 61x *beloved, dear; worthy of love* [27] See *beloved; dear.*

[29] Ἁγάρ *Hagar* 2x pr. name, indecl, *Hagar* (Gen. 16), Gal. 4:24, 25* [28]

[30] ἀγγαρεύω *angareuō* 3x *to press,* or *compel* another to go somewhere, or carry some burden, Mt. 5:41; 27:32; Mk. 15:21* [29]

[31] ἀγγεῖον *angeion* 1x *a vessel, flask,* Mt. 25:4* [30]

[32] ἀγγελία *angelia* 2x *a messsage, doctrine,* or *precept,* delivered in the name of any one; *command,* 1 Jn. 1:5; 3:11* [31]

[33] ἀγγέλλω *angellō* 1x *to tell, to announce,* Jn. 20:18* [518]

[34] ἄγγελος *angelos* 175x *one sent, a messenger, angel* [32] See *angel; messenger.*

[35] ἄγγος *angos* 1x *vessel, container, basket,* Mt. 13:48* [30]

[36] ἀγέλη *agelē* 7x *flock, herd* [34]

[37] ἀγενεαλόγητος *agenealogētos* 1x *not included in a genealogy; independent of genealogy,* Heb. 7:3* [35]

[38] ἀγενής *agenēs* 1x lit., *without kin*; fig., *base, low, insignificant,* 1 Cor. 1:28* [36]

[39] ἁγιάζω *hagiazō* 28x *to separate, consecrate; cleanse, purify, sanctify; regard* or *reverence as holy* [37] See *consecrate; holy; make holy; sanctify.*

[40] ἁγιασμός *hagiasmos* 10x *sanctification, moral purity, sanctity* [38] See *holy.*

[41] ἅγιος *hagios* 233x *separate from common condition and use; dedicated.* Lk. 2:23; *hallowed;* used of things, τὰ ἅγια, *the sanctuary;* and of persons, *saints,* e.g., members of the first Christian communities; *pure, righteous,* ceremonially or morally; *holy* [39, 40] See *consecrate; holy; sacred; saint; sanctify.*

[42] ἁγιότης *hagiotēs* 1x *holiness, sanctity,* Heb. 12:10* [41]

[43] ἁγιωσύνη *hagiōsynē* 3x *sanctification, sanctity, holiness,* Rom. 1:4; 2 Cor. 7:1; 1 Thess. 3:13* [42]

[44] ἀγκάλη *ankalē* 1x *arm,* Lk. 2:28* [43]

[45] ἄγκιστρον *ankistron* 1x *a hook, fish-hook,* Mt. 17:27* [44]

[46] ἄγκυρα *ankyra* 4x *an anchor,* Acts 27:29, 30, 40; Heb. 6:19* [45]

[47] ἄγναφος *agnaphos* 2x *unshrunken; new,* Mt. 9:16; Mk. 2:21* [46]

[48] ἁγνεία *hagneia* 2x *purity, chastity,* 1 Tim. 4:12; 5:2* [47] See *innocent.*

[49] ἁγνίζω *hagnizō* 7x *to purify; to purify morally, reform, to live like one under a vow of abstinence,* as the Nazarites [48] See *purify.*

[50] ἁγνισμός *hagnismos* 1x *purification, abstinence,* Acts 21:26* [49]

[51] ἀγνοέω *agnoeō* 22x *to be ignorant; not to understand; sin through ignorance* [50] See *(be) ignorant; not know; not understand.*

[52] ἀγνόημα *agnoēma* 1x *error, sin of ignorance,* Heb. 9:7* [51]

[53] ἄγνοια *agnoia* 4x *ignorance, willfulness,* Acts 3:17; 17:30; Eph. 4:18; 1 Pet. 1:14* [52]

[54] ἁγνός *hagnos* 8x *pure, chaste, modest, innocent, blameless* [53] See *innocent; pure, purity.*

[55] ἁγνότης *hagnotēs* 2x *purity, life of purity,* 2 Cor. 6:6; 11:3* [54] See *pure, purity.*

[56] ἁγνῶς *hagnōs* 1x *purely, with sincerity,* Phil. 1:17* [55]

[57] ἀγνωσία *agnōsia* 2x *ignorance,* 1 Cor. 15:34; 1 Pet. 2:15* [56]

[58] ἄγνωστος *agnōstos* 1x *unknown,* Acts 17:23* [57]

[59] ἀγορά *agora* 11x *a place of public concourse, forum, market-place; the center of civic life; things said in the market, provision* [58] See *marketplace.*

[60] ἀγοράζω *agorazō* 30x *to buy; redeem, acquire* by a ransom or price paid [59] See *buy; purchase.*

[61] ἀγοραῖος *agoraios* 2x *one who visits the forum; a lounger, one who idles away his time in public places, rabble,* Acts 17:5; *pertaining to the forum, judicial;* ἀγόραιοι, *court days,* Acts 19:38* [60]

[62] ἄγρα *agra* 2x *a catching, thing taken, draught* of fishes, Lk. 5:4, 9* [61]

[63] ἀγράμματος *agrammatos* 1x *illiterate, unlearned,* Acts 4:13* [62]

[64] ἀγραυλέω *agrauleō* 1x *to remain in the open air, to live outside,* especially *by night,* Lk. 2:8* [63]

[65] ἀγρεύω *agreuō* 1x *to take in hunting, catch,* Mk. 12:13* [64]

[66] ἀγριέλαιος *agrielaios* 2x *a wild olive-tree, oleaster,* Rom. 11:17, 24* [65]

[67] ἄγριος *agrios* 3x *belonging to the field, wild; fierce, raging,* Mt. 3:4; Mk. 1:6; Jude 13* [66]

[68] Ἀγρίππας *Agrippas* 11x *Agrippa,* pr. name [67]

[69] ἀγρός *agros* 36x *a field,* especially *a cultivated field;* pl. *the country; lands, farms, villages* [68] See *countryside; field.*

[70] ἀγρυπνέω *agrypneō* 4x *to be awake, watch; to be watchful, vigilant* [69]

[71] ἀγρυπνία *agrypnia* 2x *want of sleep, watching,* 2 Cor. 6:5; 11:27* [70]

[72] ἄγω *agō* 67x *to lead. bring; lead away, drive off,* as a booty of cattle; *conduct, accompany; lead out, produce; conduct with force, drag, hurry away; guide, incite, entice; convey one's self, go, go away; pass* or *spend* as *time; celebrate* [33, 71] See *bring; go; lead.*

[73] ἀγωγή *agōgē* 1x *guidance, mode of instruction, discipline, course of life,* 2 Tim. 3:10* [72]

[74] ἀγών *agōn* 6x *place of contest, race-course, stadium; a contest, strife, contention; peril, toil* [73]

[75] ἀγωνία *agōnia* 1x *contest, violent struggle; agony, anguish,* Lk. 22:44* [74]

[76] ἀγωνίζομαι *agōnizomai* 8x *to be a combatant in the public games; to contend, fight, strive earnestly* [75]

[77] Ἀδάμ *Adam* 9x *Adam,* pr. name, indecl [76] See *Adam.*

[78] ἀδάπανος *adapanos* 1x *without expense, gratuitous,* 1 Cor. 9:18* [77]

[79] Ἀδδί *Addi* 1x *Addi,* pr. name, indecl Lk. 3:28* [78]

[80] ἀδελφή *adelphē* 26x *a sister; near kinswoman,* or *female relative, a female member of the Christian community* [79] See *sister.*

[81] ἀδελφός *adelphos* 343x *a brother, near kinsman* or *relative; one of the same nation* or *nature; one of equal rank and dignity; an associate, a member of the Christian community* [80] See *brother.*

[82] ἀδελφότης *adelphotēs* 2x *brotherhood, the body of the Christian brotherhood,* 1 Pet. 2:17; 5:9* [81]

[83] ἄδηλος *adēlos* 2x *not apparent* or *obvious; uncertain, not distinct,* Lk. 11:44; 1 Cor. 14:8* [82]

[84] ἀδηλότης *adēlotēs* 1x *uncertainty,* 1 Tim. 6:17* [83]

[85] ἀδήλως *adēlōs* 1x *uncertainly, dubiously, without a definite goal,* 1 Cor. 9:26* [84]

[86] ἀδημονέω *adēmoneō* 3x *to be depressed* or *dejected, full of anguish* or *sorrow,* Mt. 26:37; Mk. 14:33; Phil. 2:26* [85]

[87] ᾅδης *hadēs* 10x *the invisible abode* or *mansion of the dead; the place of punishment, hell; the lowest place* or *condition,* Mt. 11:23; Lk. 10:15 [86] See *grave; hades; hell.*

[88] ἀδιάκριτος *adiakritos* 1x *undistinguishing, impartial,* Jas. 3:17* [87]

[89] ἀδιάλειπτος *adialeiptos* 2x *unceasing, constant, settled,* Rom. 9:2; 2 Tim. 1:3* [88]

[90] ἀδιαλείπτως *adialeiptōs* 4x *unceasingly, by an unvarying practice,* Rom. 1:9; 1 Thess. 1:2; 2:13; 5:17* [89]

[92] ἀδικέω *adikeō* 28x *to act unjustly; wrong; injure; violate a law* [91] See *do wrong; harm; mistreat.*

[93] ἀδίκημα *adikēma* 3x *an act of injustice, crime,* Acts 18:14; 24:20; Rev. 18:5* [92]

[94] ἀδικία *adikia* 25x *injustice, wrong; iniquity, falsehood, deceitfulness* [93] See *evil; unrighteousness; wicked, wickedness; wrongdoing.*

[96] ἄδικος *adikos* 12x *unjust, unrighteous, dishonest, untrustworthy, vicious; deceitful,* [94] See *evildoer; unjust; unrighteous; wicked, wickedness.*

[97] ἀδίκως *adikōs* 1x *unjustly, undeservedly,* 1 Pet. 2:19* [95]

[98] Ἀδμίν *Admin* 1x *Admin,* pr. name, indecl, Lk. 3:33* [689]

[99] ἀδόκιμος *adokimos* 8x *unable to stand test, rejected, refuse, worthless* [96]

[100] ἄδολος *adolos* 1x *without deceit, sincere,* 1 Pet. 2:2* [97]

[101] Ἀδραμυττηνός *Adramyttēnos* 1x *of Adramyttium,* a Greek city on the coast of Aeolia, in Asia Minor, Acts 27:2* [98]

[102] Ἀδρίας *Adrias* 1x *the Adriatic sea,* Acts 27:27* [99]

[103] ἁδρότης *hadrotēs* 1x *abundance,* 2 Cor. 8:20* [100]

[104] ἀδυνατέω *adynateō* 2x *to not be able; to be impossible,* Mt. 17:20; Lk. 1:37* [101]

[105] ἀδύνατος *adynatos* 10x *impotent, weak; impossible* [102] See *crippled; impossible.*

[106] ᾄδω *adō* 5x *to sing,* Eph. 5:19; Col. 3:16; Rev. 5:9; 14:3; 15:3* [103] See *sing.*

[107] ἀεί *aei* 7x *always, for ever, constantly* [104]

[108] ἀετός *aetos* 5x *an eagle,* Rev. 12:14; or *vulture,* Lk. 17:37 [105]

[109] ἄζυμος *azymos* 9x *unleavened;* τὰ ἄζυμα, *the feast of unleavened bread;* met. *pure from foreign matter, unadulterated, genuine;* τὸ ἄζυμον, *genuineness,* 1 Cor. 5:7, 8 [106]

[110] Ἀζώρ *Azōr* 2x *Azor,* pr. name, indecl, Mt. 1:13f.* [107]

[111] Ἄζωτος *Azōtos* 1x *Azotus, Ashdod,* a seaport in Palestine, Acts 8:40* [108]

[113] ἀήρ *aēr* 7x *air, atmosphere* [109]

[114] ἀθανασία *athanasia* 3x *immortality,* 1 Cor. 15:53, 54; 1 Tim. 6:16* [110]

[116] ἀθέμιτος *athemitos* 2x *unlawful, criminal, wicked,* Acts 10:28; 1 Pet. 4:3* [111]

[117] ἄθεος *atheos* 1x *an atheist; godless, estranged from the knowledge and worship of the true God,* Eph. 2:12* [112]

[118] ἄθεσμος *athesmos* 2x *lawless, unrestrained, licentious,* 2 Pet. 2:7; 3:17* [113]

[119] ἀθετέω *atheteō* 16x pr. *to displace, set aside; to abrogate, annul, violate, swerve from; reject, condemn* [114] See *annul; nullify; reject; set aside.*

[120] ἀθέτησις *athetēsis* 2x *abrogation, annulling,* Heb. 7:18; 9:26* [115]

[122] Ἀθηναῖος *Athēnaios* 2x *Athenian, inhabiting* or *belonging to Athens,* Acts 17:21, 22* [117]

[123] ἀθλέω *athleō* 2x *to strive, contend, be a champion in the public games,* 2 Tim. 2:5* [118]

[124] ἄθλησις *athlēsis* 1x *contest, combat, struggle, conflict,* Heb. 10:32* [119]

[125] ἀθροίζω *athroizō* 1x *to collect, gather,* Lk. 24:33* [4867]

[126] ἀθυμέω *athumeō* 1x *to be discouraged, lose heart,* Col. 3:21* [120]

[127] ἀθῷος *athōos* 2x *unpunished;* met. *innocent,* Mt. 27:4, 24* [121]

[128] αἴγειος *aigeios* 1x *belonging to a goat,* Heb. 11:37* [122]

[129] αἰγιαλός *aigialos* 6x *seashore, beach,* Mt. 13:2, 48; Jn. 21:4; Acts 21:5; 27:39f.* [123]

[130] Αἰγύπτιος *Aigyptios* 5x *Egyptian* [124]

[131] Αἴγυπτος *Aigyptos* 25x *Egypt* [125]

[132] ἀΐδιος *aidios* 2x *always existing, eternal,* Rom. 1:20; Jude 6 [126]

[133] αἰδώς *aidōs* 1x *modesty, reverence,* 1 Tim. 2:9* [127]

[134] Αἰθίοψ *Aithiops* 2x *an Ethiopian,* Acts 8:27* [128]

[135] αἷμα *haima* 97x *blood; of the color of blood; bloodshed; blood-guiltiness; natural descent* [129] See *blood; death; killing.*

[136] αἱματεκχυσία *haimatekchusia* 1x *an effusion* or *shedding of blood,* Heb. 9:22* [130]

[137] αἱμορροέω *haimorroeō* 1x *to have a flow of blood,* Mt. 9:20* [131]

[138] Αἰνέας *Aineas* 2x *Aeneas,* pr. name, Acts 9:33f.* [132]

[139] αἴνεσις *ainesis* 1x *praise,* Heb. 13:15* [133]

[140] αἰνέω *aineō* 8x *to praise, celebrate* [134]

[141] αἴνιγμα *ainigma* 1x *an enigma, riddle, any thing obscurely expressed* or *intimated,* 1 Cor. 13:12* [135]

[142] αἶνος *ainos* 2x *praise,* Mt. 21:16; Lk. 18:43* [136]

[143] Αἰνών *Ainōn* 1x *Enon,* pr. name, indecl, where Jn. was baptizing, Jn. 3:23* [137]

[145] αἱρέω *haireō* 3x some list as deponent αἱρέομαι, *to take;* mid. *to choose* [138]

[146] αἵρεσις *hairesis* 9x strictly, *a choice* or *option;* hence, *a religious sect, faction;* by implication, *discord, contention* [139]

[147] αἱρετίζω *hairetizō* 1x *to choose, choose with delight* or *love,* Mt. 12:18* [140]

[148] αἱρετικός *hairetikos* 1x *one who creates* or *fosters factions,* Tit. 3:10* [141]

[149] αἴρω *airō* 101x *to take up, lift, raise; bear, carry; take away, remove; destroy, kill* [142] See *carry off; lift up; remove; take up.*

[150] αἰσθάνομαι *aisthanomai* 1x *to perceive, understand,* Lk. 9:45* [143]

[151] αἴσθησις *aisthēsis* 1x *perception, understanding,* Phil. 1:9* [144]

[152] αἰσθητήριον *aisthētērion* 1x *an organ of perception; internal sense,* Heb. 5:14* [145]

[153] αἰσχροκερδής *aischrokerdēs* 2x *eager for dishonorable gain, greedy,* 1 Tim. 3:8; Tit. 1:7* [146]

[154] αἰσχροκερδῶς *aischrokerdōs* 1x *for the sake of base gain, greedily,* 1 Pet. 5:2* [147]

[155] αἰσχρολογία *aischrologia* 1x *vile* or *obscene language, foul talk,* Col. 3:8* [148]

[156] αἰσχρός *aischros* 4x strictly, *deformed,* opposed to καλός; metaph. *shameful, indecent, dishonorable, vile,* 1 Cor. 11:6; 14:35; Eph. 5:12; Tit. 1:11* [149, 150]

[157] αἰσχρότης *aischrotēs* 1x *obscenity, indecency,* Eph. 5:4* [151]

[158] αἰσχύνη *aischunē* 6x *shame, disgrace; cause of shame, dishonorable conduct* [152]

[160] αἰτέω *aiteō* 70x *to ask, request; demand; desire,* Acts 7:46 [154] See *ask; demand; request.*

[161] αἴτημα *aitēma* 3x *a thing asked* or *sought for; petition, request,* Lk. 23:24; Phil. 4:6; 1 Jn. 5:15* [155]

[162] αἰτία *aitia* 20x *cause, motive, incitement; accusation, crime, case* [156] See *basis; cause; charge; reason.*

[165] αἴτιος *aitios* 5x *causative;* αἴτιος, *an author* or *causer,* Heb. 5:9; τὸ αἴτιον, equivalent to aijtiva [158, 159]

[166] αἰτίωμα *aitiōma* 1x *charge, accusation,* Acts 25:7* [157]

[167] αἰφνίδιος *aiphnidios* 2x *unforeseen, unexpected, sudden,* Lk. 21:34; 1 Thess. 5:3* [160]

[168] αἰχμαλωσία *aichmalōsia* 3x *captivity, state of captivity; captive multitude,* Eph. 4:8; Rev. 13:10* [161]

[169] αἰχμαλωτεύω *aichmalōteuō* 1x *to lead captive;* met. *to captivate,* Eph. 4:8* [162]

[170] αἰχμαλωτίζω *aichmalōtizō* 4x *to lead captive;* by impl. *to subject,* Lk. 21:24; Rom. 7:23; 2 Cor. 10:5; 2 Tim. 3:6* [163]

[171] αἰχμάλωτος *aichmalōtos* 1x *a captive,* Lk. 4:18* [164]

[172] αἰών *aiōn* 122x pr. *a very long time;* in the past, *ages long past,* Lk. 1:70; ἐκ τοῦ αἰῶνος, *since the world began,* Jn. 9:32; *life; an era; an age:* hence, *a state of things marking an age* or *era; the present order of nature; the natural condition of man, the world;* ὁ αἰών, *illimitable duration, eternity, without beginning or end;* as also, οἱ αἰῶνες ὁ αἰῶν τῶν αἰώνων, οἱ αἰῶνες τῶν αἰώνων; by an Aramaism οἱ αἰῶνες, *the material universe,* Heb. 1:2 [165] See *age; eternity; time.*

[173] αἰώνιος *aiōnios* 71x *indeterminate as to duration, eternal, everlasting* [166] See *eternal.*

[174] ἀκαθαρσία *akatharsia* 10x *uncleanness; lewdness; impurity* of motive, 1 Thess. 2:3 [167] See *impure; unclean.*

[176] ἀκάθαρτος *akathartos* 32x *impure, unclean; lewd; foul* [169] See *defiled; evil; impure; unclean.*

[177] ἀκαιρέομαι *akaireomai* 1x *to be without opportunity* or *occasion,* Phil. 4:10* [170]

[178] ἀκαίρως *akairōs* 1x *unseasonably,* 2 Tim. 4:2* [171]

[179] ἄκακος *akakos* 2x *free from evil, innocent, blameless; simple,* Rom. 16:18; Heb. 7:26* [172]

[180] ἄκανθα *akantha* 14x *a thorn, thornbush,* Mt. 7:16; 13:7; 27:29 [173] See *thorn.*

[181] ἀκάνθινος *akanthinos* 2x *thorny, made of thorns,* Mk. 15:17; Jn. 19:5* [174]

[182] ἄκαρπος *akarpos* 7x *without fruit, unfruitful, barren;* by impl. *noxious* [175]

[183] ἀκατάγνωστος *akatagnōstos* 1x pr. *not worthy of condemnation* by a judge; hence, *above reproach,* Tit. 2:8* [176]

[184] ἀκατακάλυπτος *akatakalyptos* 2x *uncovered, unveiled,* 1 Cor. 11:5, 13* [177]

[185] ἀκατάκριτος *akatakritos* 2x *uncondemned* in a public trial, Acts 16:37; 22:25* [178]

[186] ἀκατάλυτος *akatalytos* 1x *incapable of dissolution, indissoluble;* hence, *enduring, everlasting,* Heb. 7:16* [179]

[188] ἀκατάπαυστος *akatapaustos* 1x also spelled ἀκατάπαστος, *which cannot be restrained* from a thing, *unceasing,* 2 Pet. 2:14* [180]

[189] ἀκαταστασία *akatastasia* 5x pr. *instability;* hence, *an unsettled state; disorder, commotion, tumult, sedition,* Lk. 21:9; 1 Cor. 14:33; 2 Cor. 6:5; 12:20; Jas. 3:16* [181]

[190] ἀκατάστατος *akatastatos* 2x *unstable, inconstant; unquiet, turbulent,* Jas. 1:8; 3:8* [182]

[193] ἀκέραιος *akeraios* 3x pr. *unmixed:* hence, *without mixture of vice* or *deceit, sincere, blameless,* Mt. 10:16; Rom. 16:19; Phil. 2:15* [185]

[195] ἀκλινής *aklinēs* 1x *not declining, unwavering, steady,* Heb. 10:23* [186]

[196] ἀκμάζω *akmazō* 1x *to flourish, ripen, be in one's prime,* Rev. 14:18* [187]

[197] ἀκμήν *akmēn* 1x pr. *the point of a weapon; point of time:* ἀκμήν, for κατάκμήν, adv., *yet, still, even now,* Mt. 15:16* [188]

[198] ἀκοή *akoē* 24x *hearing; the act* or *sense of hearing,* 1 Cor. 12:17; 2 Pet. 2:8; *the instrument of hearing, the ear,* Mk. 7:35; *a thing heard;* announcement, *instruction, doctrine,* Jn. 12:38; Rom. 10:16; *report,* Mt. 4:24, et al [189] See *ear; hearing; message.*

[199] ἀκολουθέω *akoloutheō* 90x *to follow; follow* as a disciple; *imitate* [190] See *accompany; follow.*

[201] ἀκούω *akouō* 428x some list the future active as a middle deponent, ἀκούσομαι, *to hear; to heed, listen to,* Mk. 4:3; Lk. 19:48; *to heed, obey,* Mt. 18:15; Acts 4:19; *to understand,* 1 Cor. 14:2; *to take in* or *admit* to mental acceptance, Mk. 4:33; Jn. 8:43, 47 [191] See *hear.*

[202] ἀκρασία *akrasia* 2x *intemperance, self-indulgence,* Mt. 23:25; *unruly appetite, lustfulness,* 1 Cor. 7:5* [192]

[203] ἀκρατής *akratēs* 1x *without self-control, intemperate,* 2 Tim. 3:3 [193]

[204] ἄκρατος *akratos* 1x *unmixed, unmingled* wine, Rev. 14:10* [194]

[205] ἀκρίβεια *akribeia* 1x *accuracy, exactness; preciseness,* or *rigor, severe discipline,* Acts 22:3* [195]

[207] ἀκριβής *akribēs* 1x *exact, strict,* Acts 26:5* [**]

[208] ἀκριβόω *akriboō* 2x *to inquire accurately* or *diligently,* Mt. 2:7, 16 (see v. 8)* [198]

[209] ἀκριβῶς *akribōs* 9x *accurately, diligently,* Mt. 2:8; Lk. 1:3; Acts 18:25; *circumspectly, strictly,* Eph. 5:15; *precisely, distinctly,* 1 Thess. 5:2 [199, 197]

[210] ἀκρίς *akris* 4x *a locust,* Mt. 3:4; Mk. 1:6; Rev. 9:3, 7* [200]

[211] ἀκροατήριον *akroatērion* 1x *a place of audience,* Acts 25:23* [201]

[212] ἀκροατής *akroatēs* 4x *a hearer,* Rom. 2:13; Jas. 1:22, 23, 25* [202]

[213] ἀκροβυστία *akrobystia* 20x *foreskin; uncircumcision, the state of being uncircumcised,* Rom. 4:10; *uncircumcised men,* i.e., *Gentiles,* Rom. 4:9, et al [203] See *uncircumcised, uncircumcision.*

[214] ἀκρογωνιαῖος *akrogōniaios* 2x literally: *lying at the extreme corner*; with λίθος, *corner* or *foundation stone,* Eph. 2:20; 1 Pet. 2:6* [204]

[215] ἀκροθίνιον *akrothinion* 1x *the first-fruits* of the produce of the ground, which were taken from the top of the heap and offered to the gods; *the best and choicest of the spoils* of war, usually collected in a heap, Heb. 7:4* [205]

[216] ἄκρον *akron* 6x *the top, tip, end, extremity,* Mk. 13:27; Lk. 16:24; Heb. 11:21 [206]

[217] Ἀκύλας *Akylas* 6x *Aquila,* pr. name, Paul's friend and Priscilla's husband, Acts 18:2, 18, 26; Rom. 16:3; 1 Cor. 16:19; 2 Tim. 4:19* [207]

[218] ἀκυρόω *akyroō* 3x *to deprive of authority, annul, cancel,* Mt. 15:6; Mk. 7:13; Gal. 3:17* [208]

[219] ἀκωλύτως *akōlytōs* 1x *without hindrance, freely,* Acts 28:31* [209]

[220] ἄκων *akōn* 1x *unwilling,* 1 Cor. 9:17* [210]

[223] ἀλάβαστρος *alabastros* 4x can be masculine, feminine (2x), or neuter (ἀλάβαστρον, 2x), *an alabaster vase,* Mk. 14:3 (2x); 26:7; Lk. 7:37* [211]

[224] ἀλαζονεία *alazoneia* 2x *arrogance; presumptuous speech,* Jas. 4:16; *haughtiness,* 1 Jn. 2:16* [212]

[225] ἀλαζών *alazōn* 2x *prideful, arrogant, boasting,* Rom. 1:30; 2 Tim. 3:2* [213]

[226] ἀλαλάζω *alalazō* 2x pr. *wail loudly; utter loud sounds, Mk. 5:38; to raise the war-cry,* ἀλαλά: *to clash, clang,* 1 Cor. 13:1* [214]

[227] ἀλάλητος *alalētos* 1x *unutterable,* or, *unexpressed,* Rom. 8:26* [215]

[228] ἄλαλος *alalos* 3x *unable to speak* or *artilculate,* Mk. 7:37; 9:17, 25* [216]

[229] ἅλας *halas* 8x variant spellings of ἅλα and ἁλός, *salt,* Mt. 5:13; Mk. 9:50; met. *the salt* of wisdom and prudence, Col. 4:6 [217] See *salt.*

[230] ἀλείφω *aleiphō* 9x *to anoint* with oil or ointment [218] See *anoint.*

[231] ἀλεκτοροφωνία *alektorophōnia* 1x *the cock-crowing, the third watch of the night,* intermediate to mid-night and daybreak, and termed *cock-crow,* Mk. 13:35* [219]

[232] ἀλέκτωρ *alektōr* 12x *a cock, rooster,* Mt. 26:34; Mk. 14:30; Lk. 22:34; Jn. 13:38 [220] See *cock, rooster.*

[233] Ἀλεξανδρεύς *Alexandreus* 2x *a native of Alexandria, an Alexandrine,* Acts 6:9; 18:24 [221]

[234] Ἀλεξανδρῖνος *Alexandrinos* 2x *Alexandrian,* Acts 27:6; 28:11* [222]

[235] Ἀλέξανδρος *Alexandros* 6x *Alexander,* pr. name. (1) *The High Priest's kinsman,* Acts 4:6. (2) *A Jew of Ephesus,* Acts 19:33. (3) *The coppersmith,* 1 Tim. 1:20; 2 Tim. 4:14. (4) *Son of Simon of Cyrene,* Mk. 15:21* [223]

[236] ἄλευρον *aleuron* 2x *meal, flour,* Mt. 13:33; Lk. 13:21* [224]

[237] ἀλήθεια *alētheia* 109x *truth,* Mk. 5:33; *love of truth, sincerity,* 1 Cor. 5:8; divine *truth* revealed to man, Jn. 1:17; *practice in accordance with* Gospel *truth,* Jn. 3:21; 2 Jn. 4 [225] See *truth.*

[238] ἀληθεύω *alētheuō* 2x *to speak* or *maintain the truth; to act truly* or *sincerely,* Gal. 4:16; Eph. 4:15* [226]

[239] ἀληθής *alēthēs* 26x *true,* Jn. 4:18; *worthy of credit,* Jn. 5:31; *truthful,* Jn. 7:18 [227] See *truth.*

[240] ἀληθινός *alēthinos* 28x *sterling,* Lk. 16:11; *real,* Jn. 6:32; 1 Thess. 1:9; *unfeigned, trustworthy, true,* Jn. 19:35 [228] See *truth.*

[241] ἀλήθω *alēthō* 2x *to grind,* Mt. 24:41; Lk. 17:35* [229]

[242] ἀληθῶς *alēthōs* 18x *truly, really,* Mt. 14:33; *certainly, of a truth,* Jn. 17:8; Acts 12:11: *truly, actually,* Jn. 4:18 [230] See *really; surely; truly.*

[243] ἁλιεύς *halieus* 5x *a fisherman,* Mt. 4:18, 19; Mk. 1:16, 17; Lk. 5:2 [231]

[244] ἁλιεύω *halieuō* 1x *to fish,* Jn. 21:3* [232]

[245] ἁλίζω *halizō* 2x *to salt, season with salt, preserve by salting,* Mt. 5:13; Mk. 9:49* [233]

[246] ἀλίσγημα *alisgēma* 1x *pollution, defilement,* Acts 15:20* [234]

[247] ἀλλά *alla* 638x *but; however; but still more;* ἀλλάγε, *at all events;* ἀλλή, *unless, except.* Ἀλλά also serves to introduce a sentence with keenness and emphasis, Jn. 16:2; Rom. 6:5; 7:7; Phil. 3:8 [235]

[248] ἀλλάσσω *allassō* 6x *to change, alter, transform,* Acts 6:14; Rom. 1:23; 1 Cor. 15:51, 52; Gal. 4:20; Heb. 1:12 [236]

[249] ἀλλαχόθεν *allachothen* 1x *from another place* or *elsewhere,* Jn. 10:1* [237]

[250] ἀλλαχοῦ *allachou* 1x *elsewhere,* Mk. 1:38* [**]

[251] ἀλληγορέω *allēgoreō* 1x *to say what is either designed* or *fitted to convey a meaning other than the literal one, to allegorize;* ἀλληγορούμενος, *adapted to another meaning, otherwise significant,* Gal. 4:24* [238]

[252] ἁλληλουϊά *hallēlouia* 4x (Hebrew) *hallelujah, praise Yahweh* or *the Lord,* Rev. 19:1, 3, 4, 6* [239] See *alleluia; hallelujah.*

[253] ἀλλήλων *allēlōn* 100x *one another, each other* [240] See *each other; one another.*

[254] ἀλλογενής *allogenēs* 1x *of another race* or *nation,* i.e., not a Jew; *a stranger, foreigner,* Lk. 17:18* [241]

[256] ἅλλομαι *hallomai* 3x *to leap, jump, leap up,* Acts 3:8; 14:10; *to spring,* as water, Jn. 4:14* [242]

[257] ἄλλος *allos* 155x *another, some other;* ὁ ἄλλος, *the other;* οἱ ἄλλοι, *the others, the rest* [243] See *another; other.*

[258] ἀλλοτριεπίσκοπος *allotriepiskopos* 1x pr. *one who meddles with the affairs of others, a busybody in other men's matters; factious,* 1 Pet. 4:15* [244]

[259] ἀλλότριος *allotrios* 14x *belonging to another,* Lk. 16:12; *foreign,* Acts 7:6; Heb. 11:9; *a foreigner, alien,* Mt. 17:25 [245] See *foreign(er); other; someone else; strange(r).*

[260] ἀλλόφυλος *allophylos* 1x *of another race* or *nation,* i.e., not a Jew, *a Gentile, a foreigner,* Acts 10:28* [246]

[261] ἄλλως *allōs* 1x *otherwise,* 1 Tim. 5:25* [247]

[262] ἀλοάω *aloaō* 3x *to thresh; to tread,* 1 Cor. 9:9, 10; 1 Tim. 5:18* [248]

[263] ἄλογος *alogos* 3x *without speech* or *reason, irrational, brute,* 2 Pet. 2:12; Jude 10; *unreasonable, absurd,* Acts 25:27* [249]

[264] ἀλόη *aloē* 1x *aloe, lign-aloe,* a tree which grows in India and Cochin-China, the wood of which is soft and bitter, though highly aromatic. It is used by the Orientals as a perfume; and employed for the purposes of embalming, Jn. 19:39* [250]

[266] ἁλυκός *halykos* 1x *brackish, bitter, salt,* Jas. 3:12* [252]

[267] ἄλυπος *alypos* 1x *free from grief* or *sorrow,* Phil. 2:28* [253]

[268] ἅλυσις *halysis* 11x *a chain,* Mk. 5:3, 4 [254] See *chain.*

[269] ἀλυσιτελής *alysitelēs* 1x pr. *bringing in no revenue* or *profit;* hence, *unprofitable, useless; detrimental; ruinous, disastrous,* Heb. 13:17* [255]

[270] ἄλφα *alpha* 3x first letter of Greek alphabet, *Alpha,* Rev. 1:8.; 21:6; 22:13* [1] See *Alpha.*

[271] Ἁλφαῖος *Halphaios* 5x *Alphaeus,* pr. name. (1) *Father of Jas. the less,* Mt. 10:3; Mk. 3:18; Lk. 6:15; Acts 1:13. (2) *Father of Levi,* (or Matthew) Mk. 2:14* [256]

[272] ἅλων *halōn* 2x *a threshing-floor, a place where corn is trodden out;* meton. *the corn which is trodden out,* Mt. 3:12; Lk. 3:17* [257]

[273] ἀλώπηξ *alōpēx* 3x *a fox,* Mt. 8:20; Lk. 9:58; met. *a fox-like, crafty man,* Lk. 13:32* [258]

[274] ἅλωσις *halōsis* 1x *a taking, catching, capture,* 2 Pet. 2:12* [259]

[275] ἅμα *hama* 10x also functions as an improper preposition with the genitive (2x), *with, together with; at the same time* [260]

[276] ἀμαθής *amathēs* 1x *unlearned, uninstructed, rude,* 2 Pet. 3:16* [261]

[277] ἀμαράντινος *amarantinos* 1x *unfading;* hence, *enduring,* 1 Pet. 5:4* [262]

[278] ἀμάραντος *amarantos* 1x *unfading;* hence, *enduring,* 1 Pet. 1:4* [263]

[279] ἁμαρτάνω *hamartanō* 43x pr. *to miss a mark; to be in error,* 1 Cor. 15:34; Tit. 3:11; *to sin,* Jn. 5:14; *to be guilty of wrong,* Mt. 18:15 [264] See *sin.*

[280] ἁμάρτημα *hamartēma* 4x *an error; sin, offence,* Mk. 3:28; 4:12; Rom. 3:25; 1 Cor. 6:18 [265]

[281] ἁμαρτία *hamartia* 173x *error; offence, sin,* Mt. 1:21; *a principle* or *cause of sin,* Rom. 7:7; *proneness to sin, sinful propensity,* Rom. 7:17, 20; *guilt* or *imputation of sin,* Jn. 9:41; Heb. 9:26; *a guilty subject, sin-offering, expiatory victim,* 2 Cor. 5:21 [266] See *sin.*

[282] ἀμάρτυρος *amartyros* 1x *without testimony* or *witness, without evidence,* Acts 14:17* [267]

[283] ἁμαρτωλός *hamartōlos* 47x *one who deviates from the path of virtue, a sinner,* Mk. 2:17; *depraved,* Mk. 8:38; *sinful, detestable,* Rom. 7:13 [268] See *sinful; sinner.*

[285] ἄμαχος *amachos* 2x *not disposed to fight; not quarrelsome* or *contentious,* 1 Tim. 3:3; Tit. 3:2* [269]

[286] ἀμάω *amaō* 1x *to collect; to reap, mow* or *cut down,* Jas. 5:4* [270]

[287] ἀμέθυστος *amethustos* 1x *an amethyst,* a gem of a deep purple or violet color, Rev. 21:20* [271]

[288] ἀμελέω *ameleō* 4x *not to care for, to neglect, disregard,* Mt. 22:5; 1 Tim. 4:14; Heb. 2:3; 8:9* [272]

[289] ἄμεμπτος *amemptos* 5x *blameless, irreprehensible, without defect,* Lk. 1:6; Phil. 2:15; 3:6; 1 Thess. 3:13; Heb. 8:7* [273]

[290] ἀμέμπτως *amemptōs* 2x *blamelessly, unblamably, unexceptionably,* 1 Thess. 2:10; 5:23* [274]

[291] ἀμέριμνος *amerimnos* 2x *free from care* or *anxiety,* Mt. 28:14; 1 Cor. 7:32* [275]

[292] ἀμετάθετος *ametathetos* 2x *unchangeable,* Heb. 6:17, 18* [276]

[293] ἀμετακίνητος *ametakinētos* 1x *immovable, firm,* 1 Cor. 15:58* [277]

[294] ἀμεταμέλητος *ametamelētos* 2x *not to be repented of;* by impl. *irrevocable, enduring,* Rom. 11:29; 2 Cor. 7:10* [278]

[296] ἄμετρος *ametros* 2x *without* or *beyond measure, regardless of measure,* 2 Cor. 10:13, 15* [280]

[297] ἀμήν *amēn* 129x *in truth, most certainly; so be it;* ὁ ἀμήν, *the faithful and true one,* Rev. 3:14 [281] See *amen; truly.*

[298] ἀμήτωρ *amētōr* 1x pr. *without mother; independent of maternal descent,* Heb. 7:3* [282]

[299] ἀμίαντος *amiantos* 4x pr. *unstained, unsoiled;* met. *undefiled, chaste,* Heb. 7:26; 13:4; *pure, sincere,* Jas. 1:27; *undefiled, unimpaired,* 1 Pet. 1:4* [283]

[300] Ἀμιναδάβ *Aminadab* 3x *Aminadab,* pr. name, indecl, Mt. 1:4; Lk. 3:33* [284]

[302] ἄμμος *ammos* 5x *sand,* Mt. 7:26; Rom. 9:27; Heb. 11:12; Rev. 12:18, 20* [285]

[303] ἀμνός *amnos* 4x *a lamb,* Jn. 1:29, 36; Acts 8:32; 1 Pet. 1:19* [286]

[304] ἀμοιβή *amoibē* 1x (adequate) *return, recompense,* 1 Tim. 5:4* [287]

[306] ἄμπελος *ampelos* 9x *a vine, grape-vine* [288] See *vine.*

[307] ἀμπελουργός *ampelourgos* 1x *a vine-dresser, gardner,* Lk. 13:7* [289]

[308] ἀμπελών *ampelōn* 23x *a vineyard* [290] See *vineyard.*

[309] Ἀμπλιᾶτος *Ampliatos* 1x *Ampliatus,* pr. name, Rom. 16:8* [291]

[310] ἀμύνομαι *amynomai* 1x *to ward off; to help, assist; to repel from oneself, resist, make a defence; to assume the office of protector and avenger,* Acts 7:24* [292]

[311] ἀμφιβάλλω *amphiballō* 1x *to throw around; to cast* a net, Mk. 1:16* [906 + 293]

[312] ἀμφίβληστρον *amphiblēstron* 1x pr. *what is thrown around,* e.g., a garment; *a large kind of fishnet,* Mt. 4:18* [293]

[313] ἀμφιέζω *amphiezō* 1x *to clothe,* Lk. 12:28* [294]

[314] ἀμφιέννυμι *amphiennymi* 3x also spelled ἀμφιέζω and ἀμφιέννυμι, *to clothe, invest,* Mt. 6:30; 11:8; Lk. 7:25* [294]

[315] Ἀμφίπολις *Amphipolis* 1x *Amphipolis,* a city of Thrace, on the river Strymon, Acts 17:1* [295]

[316] ἄμφοδον *amphodon* 1x pr. *a road leading round a town* or *village; the street of a village,* Mk. 11:4* [296]

[317] ἀμφότεροι *amphoteroi* 14x *both.* Only plural in the NT. [297] See *both.*

[318] ἀμώμητος *amōmētos* 1x *blameless, unblemished,* 2 Pet. 3:14* [298]

[319] ἄμωμον *amōmon* 1x *amomum,* an odoriferous shrub, from which a precious ointment was prepared, Rev. 18:13* [**]

[322] Ἀμώς *Amōs* 3x *Amos,* pr. name, indecl, Mt. 1:10; Lk. 3:25* [301]

[323] ἄν *an* 166x For the various constructions of this particle, and their significance, consult a grammar. At the beginning of a clause, it is another form of ἐάν, *if,* Jn. 20:23 [302]

[324] ἀνά *ana* 13x prep. used in the NT only in certain forms. ἀνὰ μέρος, *in turn;* ἀνὰ μέσον, *through the midst, between;* ἀνὰ δηνάριον, *at the rate of a denarius;* with numerals, ἀνὰ ἑκατόν, *in parties of a hundred.* [303]

[325] ἀναβαθμός *anabathmos* 2x *the act of ascending; means of ascent, steps, stairs,* Acts 21:35, 40* [304]

[326] ἀναβαίνω *anabainō* 82x *to go up, ascend,* Mt. 5:1; *to climb,* Lk. 19:4; *to go on board,* Mk. 6:51; *to rise, mount upwards,* as smoke, Rev. 8:4; *to grow* or *spring up,* as plants, Mt. 13:7; *to spring up, arise,* as thoughts, Lk. 24:38 [305] See *ascend; go up.*

[327] ἀναβάλλω *anaballō* 1x *to throw back;* mid. *to put off, defer, adjourn,* Acts 24:22* [306]

[328] ἀναβιβάζω *anabibazō* 1x *to cause to come up* or *ascend, draw* or *bring up,* Mt. 13:48* [307]

[329] ἀναβλέπω *anablepō* 25x *to look upwards,* Mt. 14:19; *to see again, recover sight,* Mt. 11:5 [308] See *look up.*

[330] ἀνάβλεψις *anablepsis* 1x *recovery of sight,* Lk. 4:18* [309]

[331] ἀναβοάω *anaboaō* 1x *to cry out* or *aloud, exclaim,* Mt. 27:46* [310]

[332] ἀναβολή *anabolē* 1x *delay,* Acts 25:17* [311]

[333] ἀνάγαιον *anagaion* 2x *an upper room,* Mk. 14:15; Lk. 22:12* [508]

[334] ἀναγγέλλω *anangellō* 14x *to bring back word, announce, report,* Mk. 5:14; *to declare, set forth, teach,* Jn. 5:24 [312] See *report; tell.*

[335] ἀναγεννάω *anagennaō* 2x *to beget* or *bring forth again; to regenerate,* 1 Pet. 1:3, 23* [313]

[336] ἀναγινώσκω *anaginōskō* 32x *to gather exact knowledge of, recognize, discern;* especially, *to read* [314] See *read.*

[337] ἀναγκάζω *anankazō* 9x *to force, compel,* Acts 28:19; *to constrain, urge,* Lk. 14:23 [315] See *compel, compelled.*

[338] ἀναγκαῖος *anankaios* 8x *necessary, indispensable,* 1 Cor. 12:22; *necessary, needful, right, proper,* Acts 13:46; 2 Cor. 9:5; Phil. 1:24; 2:25; Heb. 8:3; *near, intimate, closely connected,* as friends, Acts 10:24 [316]

[339] ἀναγκαστῶς *anankastōs* 1x *by constraint* or *compulsion, unwillingly,* opposite to ἑκουσίως, 1 Pet. 5:2* [317]

[340] ἀνάγκη *anankē* 17x *necessity,* Mt. 18:7; *constraint, compulsion,* 2 Cor. 9:7; *obligation of duty,* moral or spiritual *necessity,* Rom. 13:5; *distress, trial, affliction,* Lk. 21:23; 1 Cor. 7:26; 2 Cor. 6:4; 12:10; 1 Thess. 3:7 [318] See *compelled; distress; must; necessary.*

[341] ἀναγνωρίζω *anagnōrizō* 1x *to recognize;* pass. *to be made known,* or *to cause one's self to be recognized,* Acts 7:13* [319]

[342] ἀνάγνωσις *anagnōsis* 3x *reading,* Acts 13:15; 2 Cor. 3:14; 1 Tim. 4:13* [320]

[343] ἀνάγω *anagō* 23x *to conduct; to lead* or *convey* up from a lower place to a higher, Lk. 4:5; *to offer up,* as a sacrifice, Acts 7:41; *to lead out, produce,* Acts 12:4; as a nautical term (in the middle or passive), *to set sail, put to sea,* Lk. 8:22 [321] See *bring up; lead up; put out to sea; sail.*

[344] ἀναδείκνυμι *anadeiknymi* 2x pr. *to show anything by raising it aloft,* as a torch; *to display, manifest, show plainly* or *openly,* Acts 1:24; *to mark out, constitute, appoint* by some outward sign, Lk. 10:1* [322]

[345] ἀνάδειξις *anadeixis* 1x *a showing forth, manifestation; public entrance upon the duty* or *office to which one is consecrated,* Lk. 1:80* [323]

[346] ἀναδέχομαι *anadechomai* 2x *to receive,* as opposed to shunning or refusing; *to receive* with hospitality, Acts 28:7; *to embrace* a proffer or promise, Heb. 11:17* [324]

[347] ἀναδίδωμι *anadidōmi* 1x *to give forth, up,* or *back; to deliver, present,* Acts 23:33* [325]

[348] ἀναζάω *anazaō* 3x *to live again, recover life, revive,* Rom. 7:9; met. *to live a new and reformed life,* Lk. 15:24, 32* [326]

[349] ἀναζητέω *anazēteō* 3x *to track; to seek diligently, inquire after, search for,* Lk. 2:44, 45; Acts 11:25* [327]

[350] ἀναζώννυμι *anazōnnymi* 1x *to gird* with a belt or girdle; *to gird one's self,* 1 Pet. 1:13* [328]

[351] ἀναζωπυρέω *anazōpyreō* 1x pr. *to kindle up a dormant fire;* met. *to revive, excite; to stir up, quicken* one's powers, 2 Tim. 1:6* [329]

[352] ἀναθάλλω *anathallō* 1x *to grow* or *bloom again*; *to renew*, Phil. 4:10* [330]

[353] ἀνάθεμα *anathema* 6x *a devoted thing,* ordinarily in a bad sense, *a person* or *thing accursed,* Rom. 9:3; 1 Cor. 12:3; 16:22; Gal. 1:8, 9; *a curse, execration, anathema,* Acts 23:14* [331] See *accursed; condemned; curse.*

[354] ἀναθεματίζω *anathematizō* 4x *to declare* any one *to be* ἀνάθεμα; *to curse, bind by a curse,* Mk. 14:71; Acts 23:12, 14, 21* [332]

[355] ἀναθεωρέω *anatheōreō* 2x *to view, behold attentively, contemplate,* Acts 17:23; Heb. 13:7* [333]

[356] ἀνάθημα *anathēma* 1x *a gift* or *offering consecrated to God,* Lk. 21:5* [334]

[357] ἀναίδεια *anaideia* 1x pr. *shamelessness;* hence, *persistence,* without regard to time, place, or person, Lk. 11:8* [335]

[358] ἀναίρεσις *anairesis* 1x *a taking up* or *away; a putting to death, murder,* Acts 8:1* [336]

[359] ἀναιρέω *anaireō* 24x pr. *to take up, lift,* as from the ground; *to take off, put to death, kill, murder,* Mt. 2:16; *to take away, abolish, abrogate,* Heb. 10:9; mid. *to take up* infants in order to bring them up, Acts 7:21 [337] See *abolish; kill; put to death; take away.*

[360] ἀναίτιος *anaitios* 2x *guiltless, innocent,* Mt. 12:5, 7* [338]

[361] ἀνακαθίζω *anakathizō* 2x *to set up;* intrans. *to sit up,* Lk. 7:15; Acts 9:40* [339]

[362] ἀνακαινίζω *anakainizō* 1x *to renovate, renew,* Heb. 6:6* [340] See *renew, renewal.*

[363] ἀνακαινόω *anakainoō* 2x *to invigorate, renew,* 2 Cor. 4:16; Col. 3:10* [341] See *renew, renewal.*

[364] ἀνακαίνωσις *anakainōsis* 2x *renovation, renewal,* Rom. 12:2; Tit. 3:5* [342] See *renew, renewal.*

[365] ἀνακαλύπτω *anakalyptō* 2x *to unveil, uncover;* pass. *to be unveiled,* 2 Cor. 3:18; met. *to be disclosed* in true character and condition, 2 Cor. 3:14* [343]

[366] ἀνακάμπτω *anakamptō* 4x pr. *to reflect, bend back;* hence, *to bend back* one's course, *return,* Mt. 2:12; Lk. 10:6; Acts 18:21; Heb. 11:15* [344]

[367] ἀνάκειμαι *anakeimai* 14x *to be laid up,* as offerings; later, *to lie, recline* at table, Mt. 9:10 [345] See *guest; recline.*

[368] ἀνακεφαλαιόω *anakephalaioō* 2x *to bring together several things under one, reduce under one head; to comprise,* Rom. 13:9; Eph. 1:10* [346]

[369] ἀνακλίνω *anaklinō* 6x *to lay down,* Lk. 2:7; *to cause to recline* at table, etc. Mk. 6:39; Lk. 9:15; 12:37; *to recline at table,* Mt. 8:11 [347]

[371] ἀνακράζω *anakrazō* 5x *to cry aloud, exclaim, shout,* Mk. 1:23; 6:49; Lk. 4:33; 8:28; 23:18* [349]

[373] ἀνακρίνω *anakrinō* 16x *to sift; to examine closely,* Acts 17:11; *to scrutinize, scan,* 1 Cor. 2:14, 15; 9:3; *to try* judicially, Lk. 23:14; *to judge, give judgment upon,* 1 Cor. 4:3, 4; *to put questions, be inquisitive,* 1 Cor. 10:25, 27; Acts 11:12 v.l [350] See *examine; investigate; judge.*

[374] ἀνάκρισις *anakrisis* 1x *investigation, judicial examination, hearing of a cause,* Acts 25:26* [351]

[376] ἀνακύπτω *anakyptō* 4x pr. *to raise up one's self, look up,* Lk. 13:11; Jn. 8:7, 10; met. *to look up* cheerily, *to be cheered,* Lk. 21:28* [352]

[377] ἀναλαμβάνω *analambanō* 13x *to take up, receive up,* Mk. 16:19; *to take up, carry,* Acts 7:43; *to take on board,* Acts 20:13, 14; *to take* in company, Acts 23:31; 2 Tim. 4:11 [353] See *lift up; take up.*

[378] ἀνάλημψις *analēmpsis* 1x *a taking up, receiving up,* Lk. 9:51* [354]

[381] ἀναλογία *analogia* 1x *analogy, ratio, proportion,* Rom. 12:6* [356]

[382] ἀναλογίζομαι *analogizomai* 1x *to consider attentively,* Heb. 12:3* [357]

[383] ἄναλος *analos* 1x *without saltiness, without the taste and pungency of salt, insipid,* Mk. 9:50 [358]

[384] ἀναλόω *analoō* 2x *to destroy,* Luke 9:54; Gal. 5:15 [355]

[385] ἀνάλυσις *analysis* 1x pr. *dissolution;* met. *departure, death,* 2 Tim. 4:6* [359]

[386] ἀναλύω *analyō* 2x trans. *to loose, dissolve;* intrans. *to loose* in order to departure; *to depart,* Lk. 12:36; *to depart* from life, Phil. 1:23* [360]

[387] ἀναμάρτητος *anamartētos* 1x *without sin, guiltless,* Jn. 8:7* [361]

[388] ἀναμένω *anamenō* 1x *to await, wait for, expect,* 1 Thess. 1:10* [362]

[389] ἀναμιμνῄσκω *anamimnēskō* 6x *to remind, cause to remember,* 1 Cor. 4:17; *to exhort,* 2 Tim. 1:6; *to call to mind, recollect, remember,* Mk. 11:21; 14:72; 2 Cor. 7:15; Heb. 10:32* [363]

[390] ἀνάμνησις *anamnēsis* 4x *remembrance; a commemoration, memorial,* Lk. 22:19; 1 Cor. 11:24, 25; Heb. 10:3* [364]

[391] ἀνανεόω *ananeoō* 1x also spelled ἀνανεόομαι, *to renew;* pass. *to be renewed, be renovated,* by inward reformation, Eph. 4:23* [365]

[392] ἀνανήφω *ananēphō* 1x *to become sober;* met. *to recover sobriety* of mind, 2 Tim. 2:26* [366]

[393] Ἁνανίας *Hananias* 11x *Ananias,* pr. name I. *A Christian of Jerusalem,* Acts 5:1, etc. II. *A Christian of Damascus,* Acts 9:12, etc. III. *High Priest,* Acts 23:2; 24:1 [367]

[394] ἀναντίρρητος *anantirrētos* 1x *not to be contradicted, indisputable,* Acts 19:36* [368]

[395] ἀναντιρρήτως *anantirrētōs* 1x pr. *without contradiction* or *disputing; without hesitation, promptly,* Acts 10:29* [369]

[396] ἀνάξιος *anaxios* 1x *inadequate, unworthy,* 1 Cor. 6:2* [370]

[397] ἀναξίως *anaxiōs* 1x *unworthily, in an improper manner,* 1 Cor. 11:27* [371]

[398] ἀνάπαυσις *anapausis* 5x *rest, intermission,* Mt. 11:29; Rev. 4:8; 14:11; meton. *place of rest, fixed habitation,* Mt. 12:43; Lk. 11:24* [372]

[399] ἀναπαύω *anapauō* 12x *to cause to rest, to soothe, refresh,* Mt. 11:28; mid. *to take rest, repose, refreshment,* Mt. 26:45; *to have a fixed place of rest, abide, dwell,* 1 Pet. 4:14 [373] See *refresh; rest.*

[400] ἀναπείθω *anapeithō* 1x *to persuade* to a different opinion, *to seduce,* Acts 18:13* [374]

[401] ἀνάπειρος *anapeiros* 2x also spelled ἀνάπηρος, *maimed, deprived of some member of the body,* or *at least of its use,* Lk. 14:13, 21 [376]

[402] ἀναπέμπω *anapempō* 5x *to send back,* Phlm. 12; *to send up, remit* to a tribunal, Lk. 23:7, 11, 15; Acts 25:21* [375]

[403] ἀναπηδάω *anapēdaō* 1x *to leap up, stand up,* Mk. 10:50* [450]

[404] ἀναπίπτω *anapiptō* 12x *to fall* or *recline backwards; to recline* at table, etc., Lk. 11:37; *to throw one's self back,* Jn. 21:20 [377] See *recline; sit down.*

[405] ἀναπληρόω *anaplēroō* 6x *to fill up, complete,* 1 Thess. 2:16; *to fulfil, confirm,* as a prophecy by the event, Mt. 13:14; *to fill* the place of any one, 1 Cor. 14:16; *to supply, make good,* 1 Cor. 16:17; Phil. 2:30; *to observe fully, keep* the law, Gal. 6:2* [378]

[406] ἀναπολόγητος *anapologētos* 2x *inexcusable,* Rom. 1:20; 2:1* [379]

[408] ἀναπτύσσω *anaptyssō* 1x *to roll back, unroll, unfold,* Lk. 4:17* [380]

[409] ἀνάπτω *anaptō* 2x *to light, kindle, set on fire,* Lk. 12:49; Jas. 3:5* [381]

[410] ἀναρίθμητος *anarithmētos* 1x *innumerable,* Heb. 11:12* [382]

[411] ἀνασείω *anaseiō* 2x pr. *to shake up;* met. *to stir up, instigate,* Mk. 15:11; Lk. 23:5* [383]

[412] ἀνασκευάζω *anaskeuazō* 1x pr. *to collect one's effects* or *baggage* (σκεύη) in order to remove; *to lay waste by carrying off* or *destroying* every thing; met. *to unsettle, pervert, subvert,* Acts 15:24* [384]

[413] ἀνασπάω *anaspaō* 2x *to draw up, to draw out,* Lk. 14:5; Acts 11:10* [385]

[414] ἀνάστασις *anastasis* 42x *a raising* or *rising up; resurrection,* Mt. 22:23; meton. *the author of resurrection,* Jn. 11:25; met. *an uprising* into a state of higher advancement and blessedness, Lk. 2:34 [386] See *resurrection.*

[415] ἀναστατόω *anastatoō* 3x *to lay waste, destroy; to disturb, throw into commotion,* Acts 17:6; *to excite to sedition and tumult,* Acts 21:38; *to disturb* the mind of any one by doubts, etc.; *to subvert, unsettle,* Gal. 5:12* [387]

[416] ἀνασταυρόω *anastauroō* 1x *to crucify again,* Heb. 6:6* [388]

[417] ἀναστενάζω *anastenazō* 1x *to sigh, groan deeply,* Mk. 8:12* [389]

[418] ἀναστρέφω *anastrephō* 9x *to overturn, throw down, to turn back, return,* Acts 5:22; 15:16; *to live, to conduct one's self,* 2 Cor. 1:12; Eph. 2:3; 1 Tim. 3:15; Heb. 13:18; 1 Pet. 1:17; 2 Pet. 2:18; *to gaze,* Heb. 10:33* [390] See *behave; conduct; live; turn back.*

[419] ἀναστροφή *anastrophē* 13x *conversation, mode of life, conduct, deportment,* Gal. 1:13 [391] See *conduct; life; way of life.*

[421] ἀνατάσσομαι *anatassomai* 1x pr. *to arrange;* hence, *to compose,* Lk. 1:1* [392]

[422] ἀνατέλλω *anatellō* 9x *to cause to rise,* Mt. 5:45; intrans. *to rise,* as the sun, stars, etc., Mt. 4:16; *to spring* by birth, Heb. 7:14 [393]

[423] ἀνατίθημι *anatithēmi* 2x in NT only mid., *to submit to* a person's *consideration, statement,* or *report* of matters, Acts 25:14; Gal. 2:2* [394]

[424] ἀνατολή *anatolē* 11x pr. *a rising* of the sun, etc.; *the place of rising, the east,* as also pl. ἀνατολαί, Mt. 2:1, 2; met. *the dawn* or *day-spring,* Lk. 1:78 [395] See *east; rising.*

[426] ἀνατρέπω *anatrepō* 3x pr. *to overturn, overthrow;* met. *to subvert, corrupt,* 2 Tim. 2:18; Tit. 1:11; Jn. 2:15* [396]

[427] ἀνατρέφω *anatrephō* 3x *to nurse,* as an infant, Acts 7:20; *to bring up, educate,* Acts 7:21; 22:3* [397]

[428] ἀναφαίνω *anaphainō* 2x *to bring to light, display;* mid. and pass. *to appear,* Lk. 19:11; a nautical term, *to come in sight of,* Acts 21:3* [398]

[429] ἀναφέρω *anapherō* 10x *to bear* or *carry upwards, lead up,* Mt. 17:1; *to offer* sacrifices, Heb. 7:27; *to bear aloft* or *sustain* a burden, as sins, 1 Pet. 2:24; Heb. 9:28 [399] See *bear (sins); lead up; offer up; take up.*

[430] ἀναφωνέω *anaphōneō* 1x *to exclaim, cry out,* Lk. 1:42* [400]

[431] ἀνάχυσις *anachusis* 1x *a pouring out;* met. *excess, stream, flood,* 1 Pet. 4:4* [401]

[432] ἀναχωρέω *anachōreō* 14x *to go backward; to depart, go away,* Mt. 2:12; *to withdraw, retire,* Mt. 9:24; Acts 23:19; 26:31 [402] See *depart; return.*

[433] ἀνάψυξις *anapsyxis* 1x pr. *a refreshing coolness* after heat; met. *refreshing, recreation, rest,* Acts 3:20* [403]

[434] ἀναψύχω *anapsychō* 1x *to recreate by fresh air; to refresh, cheer,* 2 Tim. 1:16* [404]

[435] ἀνδραποδιστής *andrapodistēs* 1x *a man-stealer, kidnapper,* 1 Tim. 1:10* [405]

[436] Ἀνδρέας *Andreas* 13x *Andrew,* pr. name [406]

[437] ἀνδρίζομαι *andrizomai* 1x *to render brave* or *manly;* mid. *to show* or *behave one's self like a man,* 1 Cor. 16:13* [407]

[438] Ἀνδρόνικος *Andronikos* 1x *Andronicus,* pr. name, Rom. 16:7* [408]

[439] ἀνδροφόνος *androphonos* 1x *a homicide, man-slayer, murderer,* 1 Tim. 1:9* [409]

[441] ἀνέγκλητος *anenklētos* 5x *unblamable, irreproachable,* 1 Cor. 1:8; Col. 1:22; 1 Tim. 3:10; Tit. 1:6, 7* [410]

[442] ἀνεκδιήγητος *anekdiēgētos* 1x *which cannot be related, inexpressible, unutterable, indescribable,* 2 Cor. 9:15* [411]

[443] ἀνεκλάλητος *aneklalētos* 1x *unspeakable, ineffable,* 1 Pet. 1:8* [412]

[444] ἀνέκλειπτος *anekleiptos* 1x *unfailing, exhaustless,* Lk. 12:33* [413]

[445] ἀνεκτός *anektos* 5x *tolerable, supportable,* Mt. 10:15; 11:22, 24; Lk. 10:12, 14* [414]

[446] ἀνελεήμων *aneleēmōn* 1x *unmerciful, uncompassionate, cruel,* Rom. 1:31* [415]

[447] ἀνέλεος *aneleos* 1x *merciless,* Jas. 2:13* [448]

[448] ἀνεμίζω *anemizō* 1x *to agitate with the wind;* pass. *to be agitated* or *driven by the wind,* Jas. 1:6* [416]

[449] ἄνεμος *anemos* 31x *the wind;* met. *a wind* of shifting doctrine, Eph. 4:14 [417] See *wind.*

[450] ἀνένδεκτος *anendektos* 1x *impossible, what cannot be,* Lk. 17:1* [418]

[451] ἀνεξεραύνητος *anexeraunētos* 1x also spelled ἀνεξερεύνητος, *unfathomable, incapable of human explanation,* Rom. 11:33* [419]

[452] ἀνεξίκακος *anexikakos* 1x *enduring* or *patient under evils and injuries,* 2 Tim. 2:24* [420]

[453] ἀνεξιχνίαστος *anexichniastos* 2x lit. 'not to be tracked out;' *inscrutable, incomprehensible, inexhaustible,* Rom. 11:33; Eph. 3:8* [421]

[454] ἀνεπαίσχυντος *anepaischuntos* 1x *without cause of shame, irreproachable,* 2 Tim. 2:15* [422]

[455] ἀνεπίλημπτος *anepilēmptos* 3x also spelled ἀνεπίληπρος. pr. *not to be laid hold of;* met. *beyond reproach, unblamable,* 1 Tim. 3:2; 5:7; 6:14* [423]

[456] ἀνέρχομαι *anerchomai* 3x *to ascend, go up,* Jn. 6:3; Gal. 1:17, 18* [424]

[457] ἄνεσις *anesis* 5x pr. *the relaxing* of a state of constraint; *relaxation* of rigor of confinement, Acts 24:23; met. *ease, rest, peace, tranquility,* 2 Cor. 2:13; 7:5; 8:13; 2 Thess. 1:7* [425]

[458] ἀνετάζω *anetazō* 2x *to examine thoroughly; to examine* by torture, Acts 22:24, 29* [426]

[459] ἄνευ *aneu* 3x some classify as an improper preposition, *without,* Mt. 10:29; 1 Pet. 3:1; 4:9* [427]

[460] ἀνεύθετος *aneuthetos* 1x *unfavorably situated, inconvenient,* Acts 27:12* [428]

[461] ἀνευρίσκω *aneuriskō* 2x *to find by diligent search,* Lk. 2:16; Acts 21:4* [429]

[462] ἀνέχομαι *anechōmai* 15x also listed as ἀνέχω, but it is always in the mid. in our literature, *to endure patiently*, 1 Cor. 4:12; 2 Cor. 11:20; 2 Thess. 1:4; *to bear with*, Matt 17:7; *to suffer, admit, permit*, Acts 18:14; 2 Cor. 11:4; 2 Tim. 4:3; Heb. 13:22 [430] See *bear with; endurance, endure; tolerate.*

[463] ἀνεψιός *anepsios* 1x *a nephew, cousin,* Col. 4:10* [431]

[464] ἄνηθον *anēthon* 1x *dill,* an aromatic plant, Mt. 23:23* [432]

[465] ἀνήκω *anēkō* 3x *to come up to, to pertain to;* ἀνήκει, impers. *it is fit, proper, becoming,* Col. 3:18; Eph. 5:4; Phlm. 8* [433]

[466] ἀνήμερος *anēmeros* 1x *savage, fierce, ferocious,* 2 Tim. 3:3* [434]

[467] ἀνήρ *anēr* 216x *a male person of full age and stature,* as opposed to a child or female, 1 Cor. 13:11; *a husband,* Mt. 1:16; *a man, human being, individual,* Lk. 11:31; used also pleonastically with other nouns and adjectives, Lk. 5:8; Acts 1:16 [435] See *husband; man.*

[468] ἀνθίστημι *anthistēmi* 14x *to oppose, resist, stand out against* [436] See *oppose; resist.*

[469] ἀνθομολογέομαι *anthomologeomai* 1x pr. *to come to an agreement;* hence, *to confess openly what is due; to confess, give thanks, render praise,* Lk. 2:38* [437]

[470] ἄνθος *anthos* 4x *a flower,* Jas. 1:10, 11; 1 Pet. 1:24 (2x)* [438]

[471] ἀνθρακιά *anthrakia* 2x *a mass* or *heap of live coals,* Jn. 18:18; 21:9 [439]

[472] ἄνθραξ *anthrax* 1x *a coal, burning coal,* Rom. 12:20* [440]

[473] ἀνθρωπάρεσκος *anthrōpareskos* 2x *desirous of pleasing men,* Eph. 6:6; Col. 3:22* [441]

[474] ἀνθρώπινος *anthrōpinos* 7x *human, belonging to man,* 1 Cor. 2:4, 13; 4:3; 10:13; Jas. 3:7; 1 Pet. 2:13; *suited to man,* Rom. 6:19* [442]

[475] ἀνθρωποκτόνος *anthrōpoktonos* 3x *a homicide, murderer,* Jn. 8:44; 1 Jn. 3:15* [443]

[476] ἄνθρωπος *anthrōpos* 550x *a human being,* Jn. 16:21; Phil. 2:7; *an individual,* Rom. 3:28, et al. freq.; used also pleonastically with other words, Mt. 11:19; et al.; met. *the* spiritual frame of the inner *man,* Rom. 7:22; Eph. 3:16; 1 Pet. 3:4 [444] See *human being; humankind; man; mankind; person.*

[478] ἀνθύπατος *anthupatos* 5x *a proconsul,* Acts 13:7, 8, 12; 19:38 [446]

[479] ἀνίημι *aniēmi* 4x. (1) *to loose, slacken,* Acts 27:40; *to unbind, unfasten,* Acts 16:26. (2) *to omit, dispense with,* Eph. 6:9. (3) *to leave* or *neglect,* Heb. 13:5* [447]

[481] ἄνιπτος *aniptos* 2x *unwashed*; *ceremonially unclean* Mt. 15:20; Mk. 7:2* [449]

[482] ἀνίστημι *anistēmi* 108x trans. *to cause to stand up* or *rise,* Acts 9:41; *to raise up,* as the dead, Jn. 6:39; *to raise up* into existence, Mt. 22:24; intrans. and mid., *to rise up,* Mt. 9:9; *to rise up* into existence, Acts 7:18; 20:30 [450] See *get up; raise up; stand up.*

[483] Ἅννα *Hanna* 1x *Anna,* pr. name, Lk. 2:26* [451]

[484] Ἅννας *Hannas* 4x *Annas,* pr. name, short version of Ἅνανος, Lk. 3:2; Jn. 18:13, 24; Acts 4:6* [452]

[485] ἀνόητος *anoētos* 6x *inconsiderate, unintelligent, unwise;* Lk. 24:25; Rom. 1:14; Gal. 3:1, 3; Tit. 3:3; *brutish,* 1 Tim. 6:9 [453]

[486] ἄνοια *anoia* 2x *want of understanding; folly, rashness, madness,* Lk. 6:11; 2 Tim. 3:9* [454]

[487] ἀνοίγω *anoigō* 77x trans. *to open,* Mt. 2:11; intrans. *to be opened, to be open,* Mt. 3:16; Jn. 1:52 [455] See *open; reveal; speak.*

[488] ἀνοικοδομέω *anoikodomeō* 2x *to rebuild,* Acts 15:16 (2x)* [456]

[489] ἄνοιξις *anoixis* 1x *an opening, act of opening,* Eph. 6:19* [457]

[490] ἀνομία *anomia* 15x *lawlessness; violation of law,* 1 Jn. 3:4; *iniquity, sin,* Mt. 7:23 [458] See *lawless, lawlessness; wicked, wickedness.*

[491] ἄνομος *anomos* 9x *lawless, without law, not subject to law,* 1 Cor. 9:21; *lawless, violating law, wicked, impious,* Acts 2:23; *a transgressor,* Mk. 15:28; Lk. 22:37 [459] See *lawless, lawlessness; wicked, wickedness.*

[492] ἀνόμως *anomōs* 2x *without* the intervention of *law,* Rom. 2:12 (2x) [460]

[494] ἀνορθόω *anorthoō* 3x *to restore to straightness* or *erectness,* Lk. 13:13; *to re-invigorate,* Heb. 12:12; *to re-erect,* Acts 15:16* [461]

[495] ἀνόσιος *anosios* 2x *impious, unholy,* 1 Tim. 1:9; 2 Tim. 3:2* [462]

[496] ἀνοχή *anochē* 2x *forbearance, patience,* Rom. 2:4; 3:26* [463]

[497] ἀνταγωνίζομαι *antagōnizomai* 1x *to contend, strive against,* Heb. 12:4* [464]

[498] ἀντάλλαγμα *antallagma* 2x *a price paid in exchange* for a thing; *compensation, equivalent ransom,* Mt. 16:26; Mk. 8:37* [465]

[499] ἀνταναπληρόω *antanaplēroō* 1x *to fill up, complete, supply,* Col. 1:24* [466]

[500] ἀνταποδίδωμι *antapodidōmi* 7x *to repay, give back, return, recompense,* Lk. 14:14 (2x); Rom. 11:35; 12:19; 1 Thess. 3:9; 2 Thess. 1:6; Heb. 10:30 [467]

[501] ἀνταπόδομα *antapodoma* 2x *repayment, recompense, retribution,* Lk. 14:12; Rom. 11:9* [468]

[502] ἀνταπόδοσις *antapodosis* 1x *recompense, reward,* Col. 3:24* [469]

[503] ἀνταποκρίνομαι *antapokrinomai* 2x occurs in the NT only in the mid., *to answer, speak in answer,* Lk. 14:6; *to reply against, contradict, dispute,* Rom. 9:20* [470]

[504] ἀντέχω *antechō* 4x *to hold firmly, cling* or *adhere to; to be devoted to* any one, Lk. 16:13; Tit. 1:9; *to exercise a zealous care for* any one, 1 Thess. 5:14; Mk. 6:24* [472]

[505] ἀντί *anti* 22x *over against;* hence, *in correspondence to, answering to,* Jn. 1:16; *in place of,* Mt. 2:22; *in retribution* or *return for,* Mt. 5:38; *in consideration of,* Heb. 12:2, 16; *on account of,* Mt. 17:27; ἀνθ᾽ ὧν, *because,* Lk. 1:20 [473]

[506] ἀντιβάλλω *antiballō* 1x pr. *to throw* or *toss from one to another;* met. *to agitate, to converse* or *discourse about,* Lk. 24:17* [474]

[507] ἀντιδιατίθημι *antidiatithēmi* 1x *to set opposite;* mid. (only in the NT) *to be of an opposite opinion, to be adverse; opponent,* 2 Tim. 2:25* [475]

[508] ἀντίδικος *antidikos* 5x *an opponent in a lawsuit,* Mt. 5:25 (2x); Lk. 12:58; 18:3; *an adversary,* 1 Pet. 5:8* [476]

[509] ἀντίθεσις *antithesis* 1x pr. *opposition;* hence, *a question proposed for dispute, disputation,* 1 Tim. 6:20* [477]

[510] ἀντικαθίστημι *antikathistēmi* 1x trans. *to set in opposition;* intrans. *to withstand, resist,* Heb. 12:4* [478]

[511] ἀντικαλέω *antikaleō* 1x *to invite in return,* Lk. 14:12* [479]

[512] ἀντίκειμαι *antikeimai* 8x pr. *occupy an opposite position;* met. *to oppose, be adverse to,* Gal. 5:17; 1 Tim. 1:10; *opponent, hostile,* Lk. 13:7 [480]

[513] ἄντικρυς *antikrys* 1x can function as an improper preposition with the gen., also spelled ἀντικρύ, *opposite to, over against,* Acts 20:15* [481]

[514] ἀντιλαμβάνω *antilambanō* 3x *to aid, assist, help,* Lk. 1:54; Acts 20:35; *to be a recipient,* 1 Tim. 6:2* [482]

[515] ἀντιλέγω *antilegō* 11x *to speak against, contradict; to dispute, deny,* Lk. 20:27; *to oppose,* Jn. 19:12; Acts 13:45; 28:19; Rom. 10:21; Tit. 1:9; 2:9; pass. *to be spoken against, decried,* Lk. 2:34; Acts 28:22* [471, 483] See *contradict; rebel; speak against.*

[516] ἀντίλημψις *antilēmpsis* 1x *aid, assistance;* meton, *one who aids* or *assists, a help,* 1 Cor. 12:28* [484]

[517] ἀντιλογία *antilogia* 4x *contradiction, question,* Heb. 6:16; 7:7; *opposition, rebellion,* Jude 11; *hostility,* Heb. 12:3* [485]

[518] ἀντιλοιδορέω *antiloidoreō* 1x *to reproach* or *revile again* or *in return,* 1 Pet. 2:23* [486]

[519] ἀντίλυτρον *antilytron* 1x *a ransom,* 1 Tim. 2:6* [487]

[520] ἀντιμετρέω *antimetreō* 1x *to measure in return,* Lk. 6:38* [488]

[521] ἀντιμισθία *antimisthia* 2x *a retribution, recompense,* Rom. 1:27; 2 Cor. 6:13* [489]

[522] Ἀντιόχεια *Antiocheia* 18x *Antioch,* pr. name I. *Antioch,* the metropolis of Syria, where the disciples first received the name of Christians II. *Antioch,* a city of Pisidia, Acts 13:14; 14:19; 2 Tim. 3:11 [490]

[523] Ἀντιοχεύς *Antiocheus* 1x *an inhabitant of Antioch,* Acts 6:5* [491]

[524] ἀντιπαρέρχομαι *antiparerchomai* 2x *to pass over against, to pass along* without noticing, Lk. 10:31, 32* [492]

[525] Ἀντιπᾶς *Antipas* 1x *Antipas,* pr. name, Rev. 2:13* [493]

[526] Ἀντιπατρίς *Antipatris* 1x *Antipatris,* pr. name, Acts 23:31* [494]

[527] ἀντιπέρα *antipera* 1x can function as an improper preposition with the gen., *opposite,* Lk. 8:26* [495]

[528] ἀντιπίπτω *antipiptō* 1x pr. *to fall upon, rush upon* any one; hence, *to resist by force, oppose, strive against,* Acts 7:51* [496]

[529] ἀντιστρατεύομαι *antistrateuomai* 1x *to war against; to contravene, oppose,* Rom. 7:23* [497]

[530] ἀντιτάσσω *antitassō* 5x *to post in adverse array,* as an army; mid. *to set oneself in opposition, resist,* Acts 18:6; Rom. 13:2; Jas. 5:6; *to be averse,* Jas. 4:6; 1 Pet. 5:5* [498]

[531] ἀντίτυπος *antitypos* 2x *of correspondent stamp* or *form; corresponding, in correspondent fashion,* 1 Pet. 3:21; τὸ ἀντίτυπον, *a copy, representation,* Heb. 9:24* [499]

[532] ἀντίχριστος *antichristos* 5x *antichrist, an opposer of Christ,* 1 Jn. 2:18, 22; 4:3; 2 Jn. 7; plural in 1 Jn. 2:18* [500] See *antichrist.*

[533] ἀντλέω *antleō* 4x *to draw,* e.g., wine, water, etc.; Jn. 2:8, 9; 4:7, 15* [501]

[534] ἄντλημα *antlēma* 1x pr. *that which is drawn; a bucket, vessel for drawing water,* Jn. 4:11* [502]

[535] ἀντοφθαλμέω *antophthalmeō* 1x pr. *to look in the face,* met. a nautical term, *to bear up against* the wind, Acts 27:15* [503]

[536] ἄνυδρος *anydros* 4x *without water, dry,* 2 Pet. 2:17; Jude 12; τόποι ἄνυδροι, *dry places,* and therefore, in the East, *barren, desert,* Mt. 12:43; Lk. 11:24* [504]

[537] ἀνυπόκριτος *anypokritos* 6x *unfeigned, real, sincere,* Rom. 12:9 [505]

[538] ἀνυπότακτος *anypotaktos* 4x *not subjected, not made subordinate,* Heb. 2:8; *insubordinate, refractory, disorderly, contumacious, lawless,* 1 Tim. 1:9; Tit. 1:6, 10 [506]

[539] ἄνω *anō* 9x *above,* Acts 2:19; Gal. 4:26; Col. 3:1; *up, upwards,* Jn. 11:41; ὁ, ἡ, τό, ἄνω, *that which is above,* Jn. 8:23; ἕως ἄνω, *to the top* [507]

[540] ἄνωθεν *anōthen* 13x *from above, from a higher place,* Jn. 3:31; of time, *from the first* or *beginning,* Acts 26:5; *from the source,* Lk. 1:33; *again, anew,* Jn. 3:3, 7; Gal. 4:9; with ἀπό, *from the top,* Mt. 27:51 [509] See *again; from above.*

[541] ἀνωτερικός *anōterikos* 1x *upper, higher, inland,* Acts 19:1* [510]

[543] ἀνωφελής *anōphelēs* 2x *useless, unprofitable,* Tit. 3:9; Heb. 7:18* [512]

[544] ἀξίνη *axinē* 2x *an axe,* Mt. 3:10; Lk. 3:9* [513]

[545] ἄξιος *axios* 41x pr. *of equal value; worthy, estimable,* Mt. 10:11, 13; *worthy of, deserving,* either good or evil, Mt. 10:10; *correspondent to,* Mt. 3:8; Lk. 3:8; Acts 26:20; *comparable, countervailing,* Rom. 8:18; *suitable, due,* Lk. 23:41 [514] See *deserving; worthy.*

[546] ἀξιόω *axioō* 7x *to judge* or *esteem worthy* or *deserving; to deem fitting, to require,* Acts 15:38; 28:22 [515] See *worthy.*

[547] ἀξίως *axiōs* 6x *worthily,* Col. 1:10; *suitably, in a manner becoming,* Rom. 16:2 [516]

[548] ἀόρατος *aoratos* 5x *invisible,* Rom. 1:20; Col. 1:15, 16; 1 Tim. 1:17; Heb. 11:27 [517]

[550] ἀπαγγέλλω *apangellō* 45x *to announce that with which a person is charged,* or *which is called for by circumstances; to carry back word,* Mt. 2:8; *to report,* Mt. 8:33; *to declare plainly,* Heb. 2:12; *to announce* formally, 1 Jn. 1:2, 3 [518] See *report; tell.*

[551] ἀπάγχω *apanchō* 1x *to strangle;* mid. *to choke* or *strangle one's self, hang one's self,* Mt. 27:5* [519]

[552] ἀπάγω *apagō* 15x *to lead away,* Mt. 26:57; *to conduct,* Mt. 7:13, 14; pass. *to be led off* to execution, Acts 12:19; met. *to be led astray, seduced,* 1 Cor. 12:1 [520] See *lead away.*

[553] ἀπαίδευτος *apaideutos* 1x *uninstructed, ignorant; silly, unprofitable,* 2 Tim. 2:23* [521]

[554] ἀπαίρω *apairō* 3x *to take away;* pass. *to be taken away; to be withdrawn,* Mt. 9:15; Mk. 2:20; Lk. 5:35* [522]

[555] ἀπαιτέω *apaiteō* 2x *to demand, require,* Lk. 12:20; *to demand back,* Lk. 6:30* [523]

[556] ἀπαλγέω *apalgeō* 1x pr. *to desist from grief;* hence, *to become insensible* or *callous,* Eph. 4:19* [524]

[557] ἀπαλλάσσω *apallassō* 3x *to set free, deliver, set at liberty,* Heb. 2:15; *to rid* judicially, Lk. 12:58; mid. *to depart, remove,* Acts 19:12* [525]

[558] ἀπαλλοτριόω *apallotrioō* 3x pass. *to be alienated from, be a stranger to; alien,* Eph. 2:12; 4:18; Col. 1:21* [526]

[559] ἁπαλός *hapalos* 2x *soft, tender,* Mt. 24:32; Mk. 13:28* [527]

[560] ἀπαντάω *apantaō* 2x *to meet, encounter,* Mk. 14:13; Lk. 17:12* [528]

[561] ἀπάντησις *apantēsis* 3x *a meeting, encounter;* εἰς ἀπάντησιν, *to meet,* Mt. 25:6; Acts 28:15; 1 Thess. 4:17* [529]

[562] ἅπαξ *hapax* 14x *once,* 2 Cor. 11:25; *once for all,* Heb. 6:4; 9:26, 28; 10:2; 1 Pet. 3:18, 20; Jude 3; εἰδὼς ἅπαξ, *knowing once for ever, unfailingly, constantly,* Jude 5 [530] See *once; once for all.*

[563] ἀπαράβατος *aparabatos* 1x *not transient; not to be superseded, unchangeable,* Heb. 7:24* [531]

[564] ἀπαρασκεύαστος *aparaskeuastos* 1x *unprepared,* 2 Cor. 9:4* [532]

[565] ἀπαρνέομαι *aparneomai* 11x *to deny, disown,* Mt. 26:34; *to renounce, disregard,* Mt. 16:24 [533] See *deny; disown; reject.*

[568] ἀπαρτισμός *apartismos* 1x *completion, perfection,* Lk. 14:28* [535]

[569] ἀπαρχή *aparchē* 9x pr. *the first act of a sacrifice;* hence, *the firstfruits, first portion, firstling,* Rom. 8:23 [536] See *firstfruits.*

[570] ἅπας *hapas* 34x *all, the whole* [537] See *all; everyone.*

[571] ἀπασπάζομαι *apaspazomai* 1x *to take leave of, say farwell to,* Acts 21:6* [782]

[572] ἀπατάω *apataō* 3x *to deceive, seduce into error,* Eph. 5:6; 1 Tim. 2:14; Jas. 1:26* [538]

[573] ἀπάτη *apatē* 7x *deceit, deception, delusion* [539]

[574] ἀπάτωρ *apatōr* 1x pr. *without a father, fatherless;* hence, *independent of paternal descent,* Heb. 7:3* [540]

[575] ἀπαύγασμα *apaugasma* 1x *a radiance,* Heb. 1:3* [541]

[577] ἀπείθεια *apeitheia* 7x *an uncompliant disposition; obstinacy, disobedience, unbelief,* Rom. 11:30, 32; Eph. 2:2; 5:6; Heb. 4:6, 11; Col. 3:6* [543]

[578] ἀπειθέω *apeitheō* 14x *to be uncompliant; to refuse belief, disbelieve,* Jn. 3:36; *to refuse belief and obedience,* Rom. 10:21; 1 Pet. 3:20; *to refuse conformity,* Rom. 2:8 [544] See *disobey; refuse to believe; reject.*

[579] ἀπειθής *apeithēs* 6x *who will not be persuaded, uncompliant; disobedient,* Lk. 1:17; Acts 26:19; Rom. 1:30; 2 Tim. 3:2; Tit. 1:16; 3:3 [545]

[580] ἀπειλέω *apeileō* 2x *to threaten, menace, rebuke,* Acts 4:17; 1 Pet. 2:23* [546]

[581] ἀπειλή *apeilē* 3x *threat, denunciation,* Acts 4:29; 9:1; *harshness of language,* Eph. 6:9* [547]

[582] ἄπειμι *apeimi* 7x *to be absent, away* 1 Cor. 5:3; 2 Cor. 10:1, 11; 13:2, 10; Phil. 1:27; Col. 2:5* [548]

[583] ἄπειμι *apeimi* 1x *to go away, depart, come* Acts 17:10* [549]

[584] ἀπεῖπον *apeipon* 1x *to refuse, forbid, to renounce, disclaim,* 2 Cor. 4:2* [550, 561]

[585] ἀπείραστος *apeirastos* 1x *inexperienced, untempted, incapable of being tempted,* Jas. 1:13* [551]

[586] ἄπειρος *apeiros* 1x *inexperienced, unskillful, ignorant,* Heb. 5:13* [552]

[587] ἀπεκδέχομαι *apekdechomai* 8x *to expect, wait* or *look for,* Rom. 8:19, 23, 25; 1 Cor. 1:7; Gal. 5:5; Phil. 3:20; Heb. 9:28 [553]

[588] ἀπεκδύομαι *apekdyomai* 2x *to put off, renounce,* Col. 3:9; *to despoil* a rival, Col. 2:15* [554]

[589] ἀπέκδυσις *apekdysis* 1x *a putting* or *stripping off, renunciation,* Col. 2:11* [555]

[590] ἀπελαύνω *apelaunō* 1x *to drive away,* Acts 18:16* [556]

[591] ἀπελεγμός *apelegmos* 1x pr. *refutation;* by impl. *disrepute. contempt,* Acts 19:27* [557]

[592] ἀπελεύθερος *apeleutheros* 1x *a freed-man,* 1 Cor. 7:22* [558]

[593] Ἀπελλῆς *Apellēs* 1x *Apelles,* proper name, Rom. 16:10* [559]

[594] ἀπελπίζω *apelpizō* 1x *to lay aside hope, despond, despair;* also, *to hope for* something *in return,* Lk. 6:35* [560]

[595] ἀπέναντι *apenanti* 5x some classify as an improper preposition, *opposite to, over against,* Mt. 27:61; *contrary to, in opposititີon to, against,* Acts 17:7; *before, in the presence of,* Mt. 27:24; Rom. 3:18; Acts 3:16* [561]

[596] ἀπέραντος *aperantos* 1x *unlimited, interminable, endless,* 1 Tim. 1:4* [562]

[597] ἀπερισπάστως *aperispastōs* 1x *without distraction, without care* or *anxiety,* 1 Cor. 7:35* [563]

[598] ἀπερίτμητος *aperitmētos* 1x pr. *uncircumcised;* met. *uncircumcised* in respect of untowardness and stubbornness, Acts 7:51* [564]

[599] ἀπέρχομαι *aperchomai* 117x *to go away, depart,* Mt. 8:18; *to go forth, pervade,* as a rumor, Mt. 4:24; *to arrive at* a destination, Lk. 23:33; *to pass away, disappear,* Rev. 21:4; ἀπέρχομαι ὀπίσω, *to follow,* Mk. 1:20 [565] See *go; go away; withdraw.*

[600] ἀπέχω *apechō* 19x trans. *to have in full* what is due or is sought, Mt. 6:2, 5, 16; Lk. 6:24; Phil. 4:18; *to have altogether,* Phlm. 15; hence, *it is enough,* Mk. 14:41; intrans. *to be distant,* Lk. 7:6; *to be estranged,* Mt. 15:8; Mk. 7:6, mid. *to abstain from,* Acts 14:20

[566, 567, 568] See *abstain from; (be) far; receive in full.*

[601] ἀπιστέω *apisteō* 8x *to refuse belief, be incredulous, disbelieve,* Mk. 16:11, 16; Lk. 24:11, 41; Acts 28:24; *to prove false, violate one's faith, be unfaithful,* Rom. 3:3; 2 Tim. 2:13 [569]

[602] ἀπιστία *apistia* 11x *unbelief, want of trust and confidence; a state of unbelief,* 1 Tim. 1:13; *violation of faith, faithlessness,* Rom. 3:3; Heb. 3:12, 19 [570] See *lack of faith; unbelief.*

[603] ἄπιστος *apistos* 23x *unbelieving, without confidence* in any one, Mt. 17:17; *violating one's faith, unfaithful, false, treacherous,* Lk. 12:46; *an unbeliever, infidel, pagan,* 1 Cor. 6:6; pass. *incredible,* Acts 26:8 [571] See *unbelieving, unbeliever.*

[605] ἁπλότης *haplotēs* 8x *simplicity, sincerity, purity* of mind, Rom. 12:8; 11:3; Eph. 6:5; Col. 3:22; *liberality,* as arising from simplicity and frankness of character, 2 Cor. 8:2; 9:11, 13; 11:3* [572]

[606] ἁπλοῦς *haplous* 2x pr. *single;* hence, *simple, uncompounded; sound, perfect,* Mt. 6:22; Lk. 11:34* [573]

[607] ἁπλῶς *haplōs* 1x *generously, in simplicity; sincerely, really,* or, *liberally, bountifully,* Jas. 1:5* [574]

[608] ἀπό *apo* 646x pr. *forth, from, away from;* hence, it variously signifies *departure; distance of time* or *place; avoidance; derivation from a quarter, source,* or *material; origination from agency* or *instrumentality* [575]

[609] ἀποβαίνω *apobainō* 4x *to step off; to disembark* from a ship, Lk. 5:2; Jn. 21:9; *to become, result, happen,* Lk. 21:13; Phil. 1:19* [576]

[610] ἀποβάλλω *apoballō* 2x *to cast* or *throw off, cast aside,* Mk. 10:50; Heb. 10:35* [577]

[611] ἀποβλέπω *apoblepō* 1x pr. *to look off from all other objects and at a single one;* hence, *to turn a steady gaze, to look with fixed and earnest attention,* Heb. 11:26* [578]

[612] ἀπόβλητος *apoblētos* 1x pr. *to be cast away;* met. *to be condemned, regarded as vile,* 1 Tim. 4:4* [579]

[613] ἀποβολή *apobolē* 2x *a casting off; rejection, reprobation,* Rom. 11:15; *loss, deprivation,* of life, etc., Acts 27:22* [580]

[614] ἀπογίνομαι *apoginomai* 1x *to be away from, unconnected with; to die;* met. *to die* to a thing by renouncing it, 1 Pet. 2:24* [581]

[615] ἀπογραφή *apographē* 2x *a register, inventory; registration, enrollment,* Lk. 2:2; Acts 5:37* [582]

[616] ἀπογράφω *apographō* 4x pr. *to copy;* hence, *to register, enroll,* Lk. 2:1; Heb. 12:23; mid. *to procure the registration of one's name, to give in one's name for registration,* Lk. 2:3, 5* [583]

[617] ἀποδείκνυμι *apodeiknymi* 4x *to point out, display; to prove, demonstrate,* Acts 25:7; *to designate, proclaim, hold forth,* 2 Thess. 2:4; *to constitute, appoint,* Acts 2:22; 1 Cor. 4:9* [584]

[618] ἀπόδειξις *apodeixis* 1x *manifestation, demonstration, indubitable proof,* 1 Cor. 2:4* [585]

[620] ἀποδεκατόω *apodekatoō* 4x *to pay* or *give tithes of,* Mt. 23:23; Lk. 11:42; 18:12; *to tithe, levy tithes upon,* Heb. 7:5* [586]

[621] ἀπόδεκτος *apodektos* 2x *acceptable, pleasant,* 1 Tim. 2:3; 5:4* [587]

[622] ἀποδέχομαι *apodechomai* 7x *to receive* kindly or heartily, *welcome,* Lk. 8:40; 9:11; Acts 18:27; 28:30; *to receive* with hearty assent, *embrace,* Acts 2:41; *to accept* with satisfaction, Acts 24:3* [588]

[623] ἀποδημέω *apodēmeō* 6x *to be absent from one's home* or *country; to go on travel,* Mt. 21:33; 25:14, 15; Mk. 12:1; Lk. 15:13; 20:9* [589]

[624] ἀπόδημος *apodēmos* 1x *absent* in foreign countries, Mk. 13:34* [590]

[625] ἀποδίδωμι *apodidōmi* 48x *to give in answer to a claim* or *expectation; to render* a due, Mt. 12:36; 16:27; 21:41; 22:21; *to recompense,* Mt. 6:4, 6, 18; *to discharge* an obligation, Mt. 5:33; *to pay* a debt, Mt. 5:26; *to render back, requite,* Rom. 12:17; *to give back, restore,* Lk. 4:20; 9:42; *to refund,* Lk. 10:35; 19:8; mid., *to sell,* Acts 5:8; 7:9; Heb. 12:16; pass., *to be sold,* Mt. 18:25; *to be given up* at a request, Mt. 27:58 [591] See *deliver; give (back); hand over; produce; reimburse; repay; reward; sell.*

[626] ἀποδιορίζω *apodiorizō* 1x pr. *to separate by intervening boundaries; to separate* or *divide,* Jude 19* [592]

[627] ἀποδοκιμάζω *apodokimazō* 9x *to reject upon trial; to reject,* Mt. 21:42; Mk. 12:10; Lk. 20:17; 1 Pet. 2:4, 7; pass., *to be disallowed* a claim, *declared useless,* Lk. 9:22; 17:25; Heb. 12:17 [593]

[628] ἀποδοχή *apodochē* 2x pr. *reception, welcome; acceptance approval;* met. *reception* of hearty assent, 1 Tim. 1:15; 4:9* [594]

[629] ἀπόθεσις *apothesis* 2x *a putting off* or *away, laying aside, removal, getting rid of,* a euphemism for death, 1 Pet. 3:21; 2 Pet. 1:14* [595]

[630] ἀποθήκη *apothēkē* 6x *a place where anything is laid up for preservation, repository, granary, storehouse, barn,* Mt. 3:12; 6:26; 13:30; Lk. 3:17; 12:18, 24 [596]

[631] ἀποθησαυρίζω *apothēsaurizō* 1x pr. *to lay up in store, hoard;* met. *to treasure up, secure,* 1 Tim. 6:19* [597]

[632] ἀποθλίβω *apothlibō* 1x pr. *to press out; to press close, press upon, crowd,* Lk. 8:45* [598]

[633] ἀποθνῄσκω *apothnēskō* 111x *to die,* Mt. 8:32; *to decay, rot,* as seeds, Jn. 12:24; 1 Cor. 15:36; *to wither, become dry,* as a tree, Jude 12; met. *to die* the death of final condemnation and misery, Jn. 6:50; 8:21, 24; *to die* to a thing by renunciation or utter separation, Rom. 6:2; 1 Cor. 15:31; Gal. 2;19; Col. 3:3 [599] See *die.*

[635] ἀποκαθίστημι *apokathistēmi* 8x also spelled ἀποκαθιστάνω, *to restore* a thing to its former place or state, *reestablish, bring back,* Mt. 12:13; 17:11; Mk. 3:5; 8:25 [600] See *restore, restoration.*

[636] ἀποκαλύπτω *apokalyptō* 26x pr. *uncover; to reveal,* Mt. 11:25; pass. *to be disclosed,* Lk. 2:35; Eph. 3:5; *to be plainly signified, distinctly declared,* Rom. 1:17, 18; *to be set forth, announced,* Gal. 3:23; *to be discovered* in true character, 1 Cor. 3:13; *to be manifested, appear,* Jn. 12:38;Rom. 8:18; 2 Thess. 2:3, 6, 8; 1 Pet. 1:5; 5:1 [601] See *disclose; reveal.*

[637] ἀποκάλυψις *apokalypsis* 18x *a disclosure, revelation,* Rom. 2:5; *manifestation, appearance,* Rom. 8:19; 1 Cor. 1:7; 2 Thess. 1:7; 1 Pet. 1:7, 13; 4:13; met. spiritual *enlightenment,* Lk. 2:32 [602] See *revelation.*

[638] ἀποκαραδοκία *apokaradokia* 2x *earnest expectation, eager hope,* Rom. 8:19; Phil. 1:20* [603]

[639] ἀποκαταλλάσσω *apokatallassō* 3x *to transfer from a certain state to another which is quite different;* hence, *to reconcile, restore to favor,* Eph. 2:16; Col. 1:20, 22* [604] See *reconcile.*

[640] ἀποκατάστασις *apokatastasis* 1x pr. *a restitution* or *restoration of* a thing to its former state; Acts 3:21* [605]

[641] ἀπόκειμαι *apokeimai* 4x *to be laid up, preserved,* Lk. 19:20; *to be stored up, be reserved, await* any one, Col. 1:5; 2 Tim. 4:8; Heb. 9:27* [606]

[642] ἀποκεφαλίζω *apokephalizō* 4x *to behead,* Mt. 14:10; Mk. 6:16, 28; Lk. 9:9 [607]

[643] ἀποκλείω *apokleiō* 1x *to close, shut up,* Lk. 13:25* [608]

[644] ἀποκόπτω *apokoptō* 6x *to cut off, cut loose,* Mk. 9:43, 45; Jn. 18:10, 26; Acts 27:32; *to castrate, make a eunuch,* Gal. 5:12* [609]

[645] ἀπόκριμα *apokrima* 1x *a judicial sentence, official report, decision,* 2 Cor. 1:9* [610]

[646] ἀποκρίνομαι *apokrinomai* 231x *to answer, reply,* Mt. 3:15; in NT *to respond* to certain present circumstances, *to avow,* Mt. 11:25 [611] See *answer; reply.*

[647] ἀπόκρισις *apokrisis* 4x *an answer, reply,* Lk. 2:47; 20:26; Jn. 1:22; 19:9 [612]

[648] ἀποκρύπτω *apokryptō* 4x *to hide away; to conceal, withhold from sight* or *knowledge,* Lk. 10:21; 1 Cor. 2:7; Eph. 3:9; Col. 1:26* [613]

[649] ἀπόκρυφος *apokryphos* 3x *hidden away; concealed, secret,* Mk. 4:22; Lk. 8:17; *stored up,* Col. 2:3* [614]

[650] ἀποκτείνω *apokteinō* 74x also spelled ἀποκτέννω or ἀποκτένω, *to kill,* Mt. 14:5; *to destroy, annihilate,* Mt. 10:28; *to destroy* a hostile principle, Eph. 2:16; met. *to kill* by spiritual condemnation, Rom. 7:11; 2 Cor. 3:6 [615] See *kill; put to death.*

[652] ἀποκυέω *apokyeō* 2x pr. *to bring forth, give birth, bring into being;* met. *to generate, produce,* Jas. 1:15; *to generate* by spiritual birth, Jas. 1:18* [616]

[653] ἀποκυλίω *apokyliō* 3x *to roll away,* Mt. 28:2; Mk. 16:3, 4; Lk. 24:2* [617]

[655] ἀπολαμβάνω *apolambanō* 10x *to receive* what is due, sought, or needed, Lk. 23:41; Rom. 1:27; Gal. 4:5; Col. 3:24; 2 Jn. 8; *to receive in full,* Lk. 16:25; *to receive back, recover,* Lk. 6:34; 15:27; 18:30; mid. *to take aside, lead away,* Mk. 7:33 [618] See *get back; receive; (be) repaid.*

[656] ἀπόλαυσις *apolausis* 2x *enjoyment, pleasure,* Heb. 11:25*; *beneficial participation,* 1 Tim. 6:17 [619]

[657] ἀπολείπω *apoleipō* 7x *to leave, leave behind;* pass. *to be left, remain,* 2 Tim. 4:13, 20; Heb. 4:6, 9; 10:26; *to relinquish, forsake, desert,* Tit. 1:5; Jude 6* [620]

[660] ἀπόλλυμι *apollymi* 90x *to destroy utterly; to kill,* Mt. 2:13; *to bring to nought, make void,* 1 Cor. 1:19; *to lose, be deprived of,* Mt. 10:42; *to be destroyed, perish,* Mt. 9:17; *to be put to death, to die,* Mt. 26:52; *to be lost, to stray,* Mt. 10:6 [622] See *destroy; lose; perish.*

[661] Ἀπολλύων *Apollyōn* 1x *Apollyon, Destroyer,* i.q. Ἀβαδδών, Rev. 9:11* [623]

[662] Ἀπολλωνία *Apollōnia* 1x *Apollonia,* a city of Macedonia, Acts 17:1* [624]

[663] Ἀπολλῶς *Apollōs* 10x *Apollos,* pr. name, Acts 18:24; 19:1; 1 Cor. 1:12; 3:4-6, 22; 4:6; 16:12; Tit. 3:13* [625]

[664] ἀπολογέομαι *apologeomai* 10x *to defend one's self against a charge, to make a defence,* Lk. 12:11; 21:14 [626] See *defend.*

[665] ἀπολογία *apologia* 8x *a verbal defence,* Acts 22:1; 25:16 [627]

[666] ἀπολούω *apolouō* 2x *to cleanse by bathing, to wash;* mid. *to cleanse one's self; to procure one's self to be cleansed;* met., of sin, Acts 22:16; 1 Cor. 6:11* [628] See *wash, washing.*

[667] ἀπολύτρωσις *apolytrōsis* 10x *redemption, release, a deliverance, procured by the payment of a ransom;* meton. the author of *redemption,* 1 Cor. 1:30; *deliverance,* simply, the idea of a ransom being excluded, Lk. 21:28; Heb. 11:35 [629] See *ransom; redemption.*

[668] ἀπολύω *apolyō* 66x pr. *to loose; to release* from a tie or burden, *set free, pardon,* Mt. 18:27; *to divorce,* Mt. 1:19; *to remit, forgive,* Lk. 6:37; *to liberate, discharge,* Mt. 27:15; *to dismiss,* Mt. 15:23; Acts 19:40; *to allow to depart, to send away,* Mt. 14:15; *to permit,* or, *signal departure* from life, Lk. 2:29; mid. *to depart,* Acts 28:25; pass. *to be rid,* Lk. 13:12 [630] See *divorce; release; send away.*

[669] ἀπομάσσω *apomassō* 1x *to wipe off* in protest*;* mid. *to wipe off one's self,* Lk. 10:11* [631]

[671] ἀπονέμω *aponemō* 1x *to portion off; to assign, bestow, pay,* 1 Pet. 3:7* [632]

[672] ἀπονίπτω *aponiptō* 1x *to cleanse* a part of the body *by washing, wash off;* mid., *wash* one's self, Mt. 27:24* [633]

[674] ἀποπίπτω *apopiptō* 1x *to fall off* or *from, drop from,* Acts 9:18* [634]

[675] ἀποπλανάω *apoplanaō* 2x *to cause to wander;* met. *to deceive, pervert, seduce,* Mk. 13:22; pass. *to wander;* met. *to swerve from, apostatize,* 1 Tim. 6:10* [635]

[676] ἀποπλέω *apopleō* 4x *to depart by ship, sail away,* Acts 13:4; 14:26; 20:15; 27:1* [636]

[678] ἀποπνίγω *apopnigō* 2x *to choke, suffocate,* Lk. 8:7; *to drown,* Lk. 8:33* [638]

[679] ἀπορέω *aporeō* 6x also spelled ἀπορρίπτω, pr. *to be without means;* met. *to hesitate, be at a stand, be in doubt and perplexity, at a loss, uncertain,* Jn. 13:22; Acts 25:20; 2 Cor. 4:8; Gal. 4:20 [639]

[680] ἀπορία *aporia* 1x *doubt, uncertainty, perplexity,* Lk. 21:25* [640]

[681] ἀπορίπτω *aporiptō* 1x *to throw off, throw down,* Acts 27:43* [641]

[682] ἀπορφανίζω *aporphanizō* 1x lit., *to make an orphan*; fig., *to deprive, bereave,* 1 Thess. 2:17* [642]

[684] ἀποσκίασμα *aposkiasma* 1x *a shadow cast;* met. *a shade, the slightest trace,* Jas. 1:17* [644]

[685] ἀποσπάω *apospaō* 4x *to draw away from; to draw out* or *forth,* Mt. 26:51; *to draw away, seduce,* Acts 20:30; *to separate one's self, to part,* Lk. 22:41; Acts 21:1* [645]

[686] ἀποστασία *apostasia* 2x *a falling away, a rebellion, apostasy,* Acts 21:21; 2 Thess. 2:3* [646]

[687] ἀποστάσιον *apostasion* 3x *defection, desertion,* as of a freedman from a patron; in NT *the act of putting away a wife, divorce,* Mt. 19:7; Mk. 10:4; meton. *a bill of repudiation, deed of divorce,* Mt. 5:31* [647]

[689] ἀποστεγάζω *apostegazō* 1x *to remove* or *break through a covering* or *roof* of a place, Mk. 2:4* [648]

[690] ἀποστέλλω *apostellō* 132x *to send forth* a messenger, agent, message, or command, Mt. 2:16; 10:5; *to put forth into action,* Mk. 4:29; *to liberate,* *rid,* Lk. 4:19; *to dismiss, send away,* Mk. 12:3 [649] See *send.*

[691] ἀποστερέω *apostereō* 6x *to deprive, detach, to steal, rob; to debar,* 1 Cor. 7:5; *to deprive* in a bad sense, *defraud,* Mk. 10:19; 1 Cor. 6:7; mid. *to suffer one's self to be deprived* or *defrauded,* 1 Cor. 6:8; pass. *to be destitute* or *devoid of,* 1 Tim. 6:5; *to be unjustly withheld,* Jas. 5:4* [650]

[692] ἀποστολή *apostolē* 4x *a sending, expedition; office* or *duty of one sent as a messenger* or *agent; office of an apostle, apostleship,* Acts 1:25; Rom. 1:5; 1 Cor. 9:2; Gal. 2:8* [651]

[693] ἀπόστολος *apostolos* 80x *one sent as a messenger* or *agent, the bearer of a commission, messenger,* Jn. 13:16; *an apostle,* Mt. 10:2 [652] See *apostle; delegate; messenger; send.*

[694] ἀποστοματίζω *apostomatizō* 1x pr. *to speak* or *repeat offhand;* also, *to interrogate or watch closely, to endeavor to entrap into unguarded language,* Lk. 11:53* [653]

[695] ἀποστρέφω *apostrephō* 9x *to turn away; to remove,* Acts 3:26; Rom. 11:26; 2 Tim. 4:4; *to turn* a people from their allegiance, to their sovereign, *pervert, incite to revolt,* Lk. 23:14; *to replace, restore,* Mt. 26:52; *to turn away from* any one, *to slight, reject, repulse,* Mt. 5:42; Tit. 1:14; Heb. 12:25; *to desert,* 2 Tim. 1:15 [654]

[696] ἀποστυγέω *apostygeō* 1x *to shrink from with abhorrence, detest, hate,* Rom. 12:9* [655]

[697] ἀποσυνάγωγος *aposynagōgos* 3x *expelled* or *excluded from the synagogue, excommunicated, cut off from the rights and privileges of a Jew, excluded from society,* Jn. 9:22; 12:42; 16:2* [656]

[698] ἀποτάσσω *apotassō* 6x middle: *to take leave of, bid farewell to,* Lk. 9:61; Acts 18:18, 21; 2 Cor. 2:13; *to dismiss, send away,* Mk. 6:46; fig: *to renounce, forsake,* Lk. 14:33 [657]

[699] ἀποτελέω *apoteleō* 2x *to bring to completion, perform;* pass. *to be perfected, to arrive at full stature* or *measure,* Lk. 13:32; Jas. 1:15* [658]

[700] ἀποτίθημι *apotithēmi* 9x mid: *to lay off, lay down* or *aside,* as garments, Acts 7:58; me [659]

[701] ἀποτινάσσω *apotinassō* 2x *to shake off,* Lk. 9:5; Acts 28:5* [660]

[702] ἀποτίνω *apotinō* 1x *to pay off* what is claimed or due; *to repay, refund, make good,* Phlm. 19* [661]

[703] ἀποτολμάω *apotolmaō* 1x *to dare* or *risk outright; to speak outright, without reserve* or *restraint,* Rom. 10:20 [662]

[704] ἀποτομία *apotomia* 2x pr. *abruptness;* met. *severity, rigor,* Rom. 11:22 (2x)* [663]

[705] ἀποτόμως *apotomōs* 2x *sharply, severely,* 2 Cor. 13:10; Tit. 1:13* [664]

[706] ἀποτρέπω *apotrepō* 1x mid: *to turn* any one *away* from a thing; mid. *to turn one's self away* from any one; *to avoid, shun,* 2 Tim. 3:5* [665]

[707] ἀπουσία *apousia* 1x *absence,* Phil. 2:12* [666]

[708] ἀποφέρω *apopherō* 6x *to bear* or *carry away, conduct away,* Mk. 15:1; Lk. 16:22; Acts 19:12; 1 Cor. 16:3; Rev. 17:3; 21:10* [667]

[709] ἀποφεύγω *apopheugō* 3x *to flee from, escape;* met. *to be rid, be freed from,* 2 Pet. 1:4; 2:18, 20* [668]

[710] ἀποφθέγγομαι *apophthengomai* 3x *to speak out, declare,* particularly solemn, weighty, or pithy sayings, Acts 2:4, 14; 26:25* [669]

[711] ἀποφορτίζομαι *apophortizomai* 1x *to unload,* Acts 21:3* [670]

[712] ἀπόχρησις *apochrēsis* 1x *a using up, consumimg,* or, *a discharge of an intended use,* Col. 2:22* [671]

[713] ἀποχωρέω *apochōreō* 3x *to go from* or *away, depart,* Mt. 7:23; Lk. 9:39; Acts 13:13* [672]

[714] ἀποχωρίζω *apochōrizō* 2x *to separate;* pass. *to be swept aside,* Rev. 6:14; mid. *to part,* Acts 15:39* [673]

[715] ἀποψύχω *apopsychō* 1x pr. *to breathe out, stop breathing, faint away, die;* met. *to be faint at heart, be dismayed,* Lk. 21:26* [674]

[716] Ἄππιος *Appios* 1x *the forum* or *marketplace, of Appius;* a village on the Appian road, near Rome, Acts 28:15* [675]

[717] ἀπρόσιτος *aprositos* 1x *unapproached, unapproachable,* 1 Tim. 6:16* [676]

[718] ἀπρόσκοπος *aproskopos* 3x *not stumbling* or *jarring;* met. *not stumbling* or *jarring* against moral rule, *blameless, clear,* Acts 24:16; Phil. 1:10; *free from offensiveness,* 1 Cor. 10:32* [677]

[719] ἀπροσωπολήμπτως *aprosōpo–lēmptōs* 1x *without respect of persons, impartially,* 1 Pet. 1:17* [678]

[720] ἄπταιστος *aptaistos* 1x *free from stumbling;* met. *free from* moral *stumbling, offence; blameless,* Jude 24* [679]

[721] ἅπτω *haptō* 39x pr. *to bring in contact, fit, fasten; to light, kindle,* Mk. 4:21; Lk. 8:16; *to touch,* Mt. 8:3; *to meddle, venture to partake,* Col. 2:21; *to have intercourse with, to know carnally,* 1 Cor. 7:1; by impl. *to harm,* 1 Jn. 5:18 [680, 681] See *cling; light; take hold; touch.*

[722] Ἀπφία *Apphia* 1x *Apphia,* pr. name, Phlm. 2* [682]

[723] ἀπωθέω *apōtheō* 6x *to thrust away, repel from one's self, repulse,* Acts 7:27; *to refuse, reject, cast off,* Acts 7:39; 13:46; Rom. 11:1, 2; 1 Tim. 1:19* [683]

[724] ἀπώλεια *apōleia* 18x *consumption, destruction; waste, annihilation,* Mt. 26:8; Mk. 14:4; *destruction, state of being destroyed,* Acts 25:6; eternal *ruin, perdition,* Mt. 7:13; Acts 8:20 [684] See *destruction; ruin; waste.*

[725] ἀρά *ara* 1x pr. *a prayer;* more commonly *a prayer for evil; curse, cursing, imprecation,* Rom. 3:14* [685]

[726] ἄρα *ara* 49x a particle which denotes, first, transition from one thing to another by natural sequence; secondly, logical inference; in which case the premises are either expressed, Mt. 12:28, or to be variously supplied, *so, therefore, then, consequently; as a result,* Acts 17:27 [686]

[727] ἆρα *ara* 3x inferential particle, used mainly in interrogations, *indicating anxiety or impatience,* Lk. 18:8; Acts 8:30; Gal. 2:17* [687]

[728] Ἀραβία *Arabia* 2x *Arabia,* Gal. 1:17; 4:25* [688]

[730] Ἀράμ *Aram* 2x *Aram,* pr. name, indecl, Mt. 1:3-4* [689]

[731] ἄραφος *araphos* 1x *not sewed, seamless,* Jn. 19:23* [729]

[732] Ἄραψ *Araps* 1x *an Arabian,* Acts 2:11* [690]

[733] ἀργέω *argeō* 1x pr. *to be unemployed; to be idle, to linger, to grow weary,* 2 Pet. 2:3* [691]

[734] ἀργός *argos* 8x pr. *inactive, unemployed,* Mt. 20:3, 6; *idle, averse from labor, lazy,* 1 Tim. 5:13; Tit. 1:12; met. 2 Pet. 1:8; *unprofitable, hollow,* or by impl., *injurious,* Mt. 12:36; Jas. 2:20* [692]

[736] ἀργύριον *argyrion* 20x *silver;* meton. *money,* Mt. 25:18, 27 [694] See *money; silver.*

[737] ἀργυροκόπος *argyrokopos* 1x *a forger of silver, silversmith,* Acts 19:24* [695]

[738] ἄργυρος *argyros* 5x *silver;* meton. *anything made of silver; money,* Jas. 5:3 [696]

[739] ἀργυροῦς *argyrous* 3x *made of silver,* Acts 19:24; 2 Tim. 2:20; Rev. 9:20* [693]

[741] Ἀρεοπαγίτης *Areopagitēs* 1x *a judge of the court of Areopagus,* Acts 17:34* [698]

[742] ἀρεσκεία *areskeia* 1x *a pleasing, desire of pleasing,* Col. 1:10* [699]

[743] ἀρέσκω *areskō* 17x *to please,* Mt. 14:6; *to be pleasing, acceptable,* Acts 6:5; *to consult the pleasure of* any one, Rom. 15:1, 2, 3; 1 Cor. 10:33; *to seek favor with, to strive to please,* Gal. 1:10; 1 Thess. 2:4 [700] See *please.*

[744] ἀρεστός *arestos* 4x *pleasing, acceptable,* Acts 12:3; 1 Jn. 3:22; 8:29, *deemed proper,* Acts 6:2 [701]

[745] Ἁρέτας *Haretas* 1x *Aretas,* pr. name, 2 Cor. 11:32* [702]

[746] ἀρετή *aretē* 5x *goodness, good quality* of any kind; *a gracious act* of God, 1 Pet. 2:9; 2 Pet. 1:3; *virtue, uprightness,* Phil. 4:8; 2 Pet. 1:5* [703]

[748] ἀρήν *arēn* 1x *a sheep, lamb,* Lk. 10:3* [704]

[749] ἀριθμέω *arithmeō* 3x *to count,* Mt. 10:30; Lk. 12:7; Rev. 7:9* [705]

[750] ἀριθμός *arithmos* 18x *a number,* Lk. 22:3; Jn. 6:10; Acts 4:4; Rev. 20:8; 13:18 [706] See *number.*

[751] Ἁριμαθαία *Harimathaia* 4x *Arimathea,* a town of Palestine, Mt. 27:57; Mk. 15:43; Lk. 23:51; Jn. 19:38* [707]

[752] Ἀρίσταρχος *Aristarchos* 5x *Aristarchus,* pr. name, Acts 19:29; 20:4; 27:2; Col. 4:10; Phlm. 24* [708]

[753] ἀριστάω *aristaō* 3x *to take the first meal, breakfast,* Jn. 21:12, 15; also, *to take a mid-day meal,* Lk. 11:37* [709]

[754] ἀριστερός *aristeros* 4x *the left hand,* Mt. 6:3; so ἐξ ἀριστερῶν, sc. μερῶν, Lk. 23:33; 2 Cor. 6:7; Mk. 10:37* [710]

[755] Ἀριστόβουλος *Aristoboulos* 1x *Aristobulus,* pr. name, Rom. 16:10* [711]

[756] ἄριστον *ariston* 3x pr. *the first meal, breakfast;* afterwards extended to signify also *a slight mid-day meal, luncheon,* Mt. 22:4; Lk. 11:38; 14:12* [712]

[757] ἀρκετός *arketos* 3x *sufficient, enough,* Mt. 6:34; 10:25; 1 Pet. 4:3* [713]

[758] ἀρκέω *arkeō* 8x pr. *to ward off;* thence; *to be of service, avail; to suffice, be enough,* Mt. 25:9; pass. *to be contented, satisfied,* Lk. 3:14; 1 Tim. 6:8; Heb. 13:5; 3 Jn. 10 [714]

[759] ἄρκος *arkos* 1x also spelled ἄρκτος, *a bear,* Rev. 13:2* [715]

[761] ἅρμα *harma* 4x *a chariot, vehicle,* Acts 8:28, 29, 38; Rev. 9:9* [716]

[762] Ἁρμαγεδών *Harmagedōn* 1x *Armageddon,* Rev. 16:16* [717]

[764] ἁρμόζω *harmozō* 1x *to fit together; to join, unite,* in marriage, *espouse, betroth,* 2 Cor. 11:2* [718]

[765] ἁρμός *harmos* 1x *a joint* Heb. 4:12* [719]

[766] ἀρνέομαι *arneomai* 33x *to deny, disclaim, disown,* Mt. 10:33; *to renounce,* Tit. 2:12; *to decline, refuse,* Heb. 11:24; absol. *to deny, contradict,* Lk. 8:15 [720] See *deny; disown; reject; renounce.*

[767] Ἀρνί *Arni* 1x *Arni,* pr. name, Lk. 3:33* [**]

[768] ἀρνίον *arnion* 30x *a young lamb, lamb,* Jn. 21:15; Rev. 5:6, 8 [721] See *lamb.*

[769] ἀροτριάω *arotriaō* 3x *to plow,* Lk. 17:7; 1 Cor. 9:10* [722]

[770] ἄροτρον *arotron* 1x *a plow,* Lk. 9:62* [723]

[771] ἁρπαγή *harpagē* 3x *plunder, pillage; the act of plundering,* Heb. 10:34; *prey, spoil,* Mt. 23:25; Lk. 11:39* [724]

[772] ἁρπαγμός *harpagmos* 1x *eager seizure;* in NT, *a thing retained with an eager grasp,* or *eagerly claimed and greatly desired,* Phil. 2:6* [725]

[773] ἁρπάζω *harpazō* 14x *to seize,* as a wild beast, Jn. 10:12; *take away by force, snatch away,* Mt. 13:19; Jn. 10:28, 29; Acts 23:10; Jude 23; met. *to seize on with avidity, eagerly, appropriate,* Mt. 11:12; *to convey away suddenly, transport hastily,* Jn. 6:15 [726] See *catch; snatch.*

[774] ἅρπαξ *harpax* 5x pr. *raveneous, ravening,* as a wild beast, Mt. 7:15; met. *rapacious, given to extortion and robbery, an extortioner,* Lk. 18:11; 1 Cor. 5:10, 11; 6:10* [727]

[775] ἀρραβών *arrabōn* 3x *a pledge, earnest,* 2 Cor. 1:22; 5:5; Eph. 1:14* [728] See *deposit; guarantee; pledge.*

[777] ἄρρητος *arrētos* 1x pr. *not spoken; what ought not to be spoken, secret; which cannot be spoken* or *uttered,* 2 Cor. 12:4* [731]

[779] ἄρρωστος *arrōstos* 5x *ill, sick, an invalid,* Mt. 14:14; Mk. 6:5, 13; 16:18; 1 Cor. 11:30 [732]

[780] ἀρσενοκοίτης *arsenokoitēs* 2x *a male engaging in same-gender sexual activity, a sodomite, pederast,* 1 Cor. 6:9; 1 Tim. 1:10* [733]

[781] ἄρσην *arsēn* 9x *male, of the male sex,* Mt. 19:4; Mk. 10:6; Lk. 2:23; Rom. 1:27; Gal. 3:28; Rev. 12:5, 13* [730] See *male.*

[782] Ἀρτεμᾶς *Artemas* 1x *Artemas,* pr. name, Tit. 3:12* [734]

[783] Ἄρτεμις *Artemis* 5x *Artemis* or *Diana,* Acts 19:24, 27, 28, 34, 35* [735]

[784] ἀρτέμων *artemōn* 1x *a topsail, foresail;* or, according to others, *the dolon* of Pliny and Pollux, a small sail near the bow of the ship, which was hoisted when the wind was too strong to use the larger sails, Acts 27:40* [736]

[785] ἄρτι *arti* 36x pr. *at the present moment, close upon it* either before of after; *now, at the present juncture,* Mt. 3:15; *forthwith, presently; just now, recently,* 1 Thess. 3:6; ἕως ἄρτι, *until now, hitherto,* Mt. 11:12; Jn. 2:10; ἀπ᾽ ἄρτι, or ἀπάρτι, *from this time, henceforth,* Mt. 23:39 [737] See *now.*

[786] ἀρτιγέννητος *artigennētos* 1x *just born, newborn,* 1 Pet. 2:2* [738]

[787] ἄρτιος *artios* 1x *entirely suited; capable, proficient, complete* in accomplishment, *ready,* 2 Tim. 3:17* [739]

[788] ἄρτος *artos* 97x *bread; a loaf* or *thin cake of bread,* Mt. 26:26; *food,* Mt. 15:2; Mk. 3:20; *bread, maintenance, living, necessities of life,* Mt. 6:11; Lk. 11:3; 2 Thess. 3:8 [740] See *bread; food; loaf.*

[789] ἀρτύω *artyō* 3x pr. *to fit, prepare; to season, make savoury,* Mk. 9:50; Lk. 14:34; Col. 4:6* [741]

[790] Ἀρφαξάδ *Arphaxad* 1x *Arphaxad,* pr. name, indecl, Lk. 3:36* [742]

[791] ἀρχάγγελος *archangelos* 2x *an archangel, chief angel,* 1 Thess. 4:16; Jude 9* [743]

[792] ἀρχαῖος *archaios* 11x *old, ancient, of former age,* Mt. 5:21, 33; *of long standing, old, veteran,* Acts 21:16; ἀφ᾽ ἡμερῶν ἀρχαίων, *from early days, from an early period,* of the Gospel, Acts 15:7 [744] See *ancient; old.*

[793] Ἀρχέλαος *Archelaos* 1x *Archelaus,* pr. name, Mt. 2:22* [745]

[794] ἀρχή *archē* 55x *a beginning,* Mt. 24:8; *an extremity, corner,* or, *an attached cord,* Acts 10:11; 11:5; *first place, headship; high estate, eminence,* Jude 6; *authority,* Lk. 20:20; *an authority, magistrate,* Lk. 12:11; *a principality, prince,* of spiritual existence, Eph. 3:10; 6:12; ἀπ᾽ ἀρχῆς, ἐξ ἀρχῆς, *from the first, originally,* Mt. 19:4, 8; Lk. 1:2; Jn. 6:64; 2 Thess. 2:13; 1 Jn. 1:1; 2:7; ἐν ἀρχῇ, κατ᾽ ἀρχάς, *in the beginning* of things, Jn. 1:1, 2; Heb. 1:10; ἐν ἀρχῇ, *at the first,* Acts 11:15; τὴν ἀρχήν, used adverbially, *wholly, altogether,* Jn. 8:25 [746] See *beginning; ruler.*

[795] ἀρχηγός *archēgos* 4x *a chief, leader, prince,* Acts 5:31; *a prime author,* Acts 3:15; Heb. 2:10; 12:2* [747]

[796] ἀρχιερατικός *archieratikos* 1x *belonging to* or *connected with the high-priest* or *his office,* Acts 4:6* [748]

[797] ἀρχιερεύς *archiereus* 122x *a high-priest, chief-priest* [749] See *chief priest; high priest.*

[799] ἀρχιποίμην *archipoimēn* 1x *chief shepherd,* 1 Pet. 5:4* [750]

[800] Ἄρχιππος *Archippos* 2x *Archippus,* pr. name, Col. 4:17; Phlm. 2, inscr. and subscr.* [751]

[801] ἀρχισυνάγωγος *archisynagōgos* 9x *a president* or *moderating elder of a synagogue,* Mk. 5:22, 35, 36, 38; Lk. 8:49 [752]

[802] ἀρχιτέκτων *architektōn* 1x *architect, head* or *master-builder,* 1 Cor. 3:10* [753]

[803] ἀρχιτελώνης *architelōnēs* 1x *a chief publican, chief collector of the customs* or *taxes,* Lk. 19:2* [754]

[804] ἀρχιτρίκλινος *architriklinos* 3x *master of a feast, headwaiter, butler,* Jn. 2:8, 9* [755]

[806] ἄρχω *archō* 86x pr. (act.) *to be first; to rule,* Mk. 10:42; Rom. 15:12; mid. *to begin,* Mt. 4:17; Lk. 24:27, 1 Pet. 4:17 [756, 757] See *begin; rule.*

[807] ἄρχων *archōn* 37x *one invested with power and dignity, chief, ruler, prince, magistrate,* Mt. 9:23; 20:25 [758] See *leader; prince; ruler.*

[808] ἄρωμα *arōma* 4x *an aromatic substance, spice,* etc., Mk. 16:1; Lk. 23:56; 24:1; Jn. 19:40* [759]

[810] ἀσάλευτος *asaleutos* 2x *unshaken, immovable,* Acts 27:41; met. *firm, stable, enduring,* Heb. 12:28* [761]

[811] Ἀσάφ *Asaph* 2x *Asaph,* pr. name, indecl, Mt. 1:7, 8* [760]

[812] ἄσβεστος *asbestos* 3x *unquenched; inextinguishable, unquenchable,* Mt. 3:12; Mk. 9:43; Lk. 3:17* [762]

[813] ἀσέβεια *asebeia* 6x *impiety, ungodliness; dishonesty, wickedness,* Rom. 1:18; 11:26; 2 Tim. 2:16; Tit. 2:12; Jude 15, 18* [763]

[814] ἀσεβέω *asebeō* 1x *to be impious, to act impiously* or *wickedly, live an impious life,* 2 Pet. 2:6; Jude 15* [764]

[815] ἀσεβής *asebēs* 9x *impious, ungodly; wicked, sinful,* Rom. 4:5; 5:6 [765] See *godless; ungodly; wicked, wickedness.*

[816] ἀσέλγεια *aselgeia* 10x *intemperance; licentiousness, lasciviousness,* Rom. 13:13; *insolence, outrageous behavior,* Mk. 7:22 [766] See *debauchery; lewdness; sensuality.*

[817] ἄσημος *asēmos* 1x pr. *not marked;* met. *not noted, not remarkable, unknown to fame, ignoble, mean, inconsiderable,* Acts 21:39* [767]

[818] Ἀσήρ *Asēr* 2x *Asher,* pr. name, indecl (Gen. 30:13; 49:20; 2 Chr. 30:11) Lk. 2:36; Rev. 7:6* [768]

[819] ἀσθένεια *astheneia* 24x *lack of strength, weakness, feebleness,* 1 Cor. 15:43; bodily *infirmity, state of ill health, sickness,* Mt. 8:17; Lk. 5:15; met. *infirmity, frailty, imperfection,* intellectual and moral, Rom. 6:19; 1 Cor. 2:3; Heb. 5:2; 7:28; *suffering, affliction, distress, calamity,* Rom. 8:26 [769] See *illness; sickness; weakness.*

[820] ἀσθενέω *astheneō* 33x *to be weak, deficient in strength; to be inefficient,* Rom. 8:3; 2 Cor. 13:3; *to* *be sick,* Mt. 25:36; met. *to be weak* in faith, *to doubt, hesitate, be unsettled, timid,* Rom. 14:1; 1 Cor. 8:9, 11, 12; 2 Cor. 11:29; *to be deficient in authority, dignity,* or *power, be contemptible,* 2 Cor. 11:21; 13:3, 9; *to be afflicted, distressed, needy,* Acts 20:35; 2 Cor. 12:10; 13:4, 9 [770] See *sick; weak.*

[821] ἀσθένημα *asthenēma* 1x pr. *weakness, infirmity,* met. *doubt, hesitation,* Rom. 15:1* [771]

[822] ἀσθενής *asthenēs* 26x *without strength, weak, infirm,* Mt. 26:41; Mk. 14:38; 1 Pet. 3:7; *helpless,* Rom. 5:6; *imperfect, inefficient,* Gal. 4:9; *feeble, without energy,* 2 Cor. 10:10; *infirm* in body, *sick, sickly,* Mt. 25:39, 43, 44; *weak,* mentally or spiritually, *dubious, hesitating,* 1 Cor. 8:7, 10; 9:22; 1 Thess. 5:14; *afflicted, distressed, oppressed with calamities,* 1 Cor. 4:10 [772] See *sick; weak.*

[823] Ἀσία *Asia* 18x *Asia,* the Roman province, Acts 19:27 [773]

[824] Ἀσιανός *Asianos* 1x *belonging to the Roman province of Asia,* Acts 20:4* [774]

[825] Ἀσιάρχης *Asiarchēs* 1x *an Asiarch,* an officer in the province of Asia, as in other eastern provinces of the Roman empire, selected, with others, from the more opulent citizens, to preside over the things pertaining to religious worship, and to exhibit annual public games at their own expense in honor of the gods, in the manner of the aediles at Rome, Acts 19:31* [775]

[826] ἀσιτία *asitia* 1x *abstinence from food, fasting, lack of appetite* Acts 27:21* [776]

[827] ἄσιτος *asitos* 1x *abstaining from food, fasting,* Acts 27:33* [777]

[828] ἀσκέω *askeō* 1x pr. *to work* materials, *to do one's best, practice;* absol. *to train* or *exert one's self, make endeavor,* Acts 24:16* [778]

[829] ἀσκός *askos* 12x *a leather bag* or *bottle, bottle of skin, wineskin,* Mt. 9:17; Mk. 2:22; Lk. 5:37, 38 [779] See *wineskin.*

[830] ἀσμένως *asmenōs* 1x *gladly, joyfully,* Acts 21:17* [780]

[831] ἄσοφος *asophos* 1x *unwise; destitute of* Christian *wisdom,* Eph. 5:15* [781]

[832] ἀσπάζομαι *aspazomai* 59x *to salute, greet, welcome, express good wishes, pay respects,* Mt. 10:12; Mk. 9:15, et al. freq.; *to bid farewell,* Acts 20:1; 21:6; *to treat with affection,* Mt. 5:47; met. *to embrace* mentally, *welcome* to the heart of understanding, Heb. 11:13 [782] See *greet; welcome.*

[833] ἀσπασμός *aspasmos* 10x *salutation, greeting,* Mt. 23:7; Mk. 12:38 [783] See *greeting.*

[834] ἄσπιλος *aspilos* 4x *spotless, unblemished, pure,* 1 Tim. 6:14; Jas. 1:27; 1 Pet. 1:19; 2 Pet. 3:14* [784]

[835] ἀσπίς *aspis* 1x *an asp,* a species of serpent of the most deadly venom, Rom. 3:13* [785]

[836] ἄσπονδος *aspondos* 1x pr. *unwilling to make a treaty;* hence, *implacable, irreconcilable,* 2 Tim. 3:3* [786]

[837] ἀσσάριον *assarion* 2x dimin. of the Latin, *as,* a Roman brass coin with the value of one-tenth of a denarius, or δραχμή, used to convey the idea of a trifle or very small sum, Mt. 10:29; Lk. 12:6* [787]

[839] ἆσσον *asson* 1x *nearer; very nigh, close;* used as the compar. of ἄγχι, Acts 27:13* [788]

[840] Ἆσσος *Assos* 2x *Assos,* a maritime city of Mysia, in Asia Minor, Acts 20:13-14* [789]

[841] ἀστατέω *astateō* 1x *to be unsettled, to be a wanderer, be homeless,* 1 Cor. 4:11* [790]

[842] ἀστεῖος *asteios* 2x pr. *belonging to a city; well bred, polite, polished;* hence, *elegant, fair, comely, beautiful,* Acts 7:20; Heb. 11:23* [791]

[843] ἀστήρ *astēr* 24x *a star, luminous body like a star, luminary,* Mt. 2:2, 7, 9, 10; Rev. 1:16 [792] See *star.*

[844] ἀστήρικτος *astēriktos* 2x *not made firm; unsettled, unstable, unsteady, weak,* 2 Pet. 2:14; 3:16* [793]

[845] ἄστοργος *astorgos* 2x *devoid of natural* or *instinctive affection, without affection to kindred, unloving,* Rom. 1:31; 2 Tim. 3:3* [794]

[846] ἀστοχέω *astocheō* 3x pr. *to miss the mark;* met. *to err, deviate, swerve from,* 1 Tim. 1:6; 6:21; 2 Tim. 2:18* [795]

[847] ἀστραπή *astrapē* 9x *lightning,* Mt. 24:27; *brightness, lustre,* Lk. 11:36 [796]

[848] ἀστράπτω *astraptō* 2x *to lighten, flash as lightning,* Lk. 17:24; *to be bright, shining,* Lk. 24:4* [797]

[849] ἄστρον *astron* 4x *a constellation; a star,* Lk. 21:25; Acts 7:43; 27:20; Heb. 11:12* [798] See *star.*

[850] Ἀσύγκριτος *Asynkritos* 1x *Asyncritus,* pr. name, Rom. 16:14* [799]

[851] ἀσύμφωνος *asymphōnos* 1x *discordant in sound;* met. *discordant, at variance,* Acts 28:25* [800]

[852] ἀσύνετος *asynetos* 5x *unintelligent, dull,* Mt. 15:16; Mk. 7:18; *reckless, perverse,* Rom. 1:21, 31; *unenlightened, heathenish,* Rom. 10:19 [801]

[853] ἀσύνθετος *asynthetos* 1x *unable to be trusted, undutiful, untrustworthy, faithless,* Rom. 1:31* [802]

[854] ἀσφάλεια *asphaleia* 3x pr. *state of security from falling, firmness; safety, security,* 1 Thess. 5:3; *certainty, truth,* Lk. 1:4; *means of security,* Acts 5:23* [803]

[855] ἀσφαλής *asphalēs* 5x pr. *firm, secure from falling; firm, sure, steady, immovable,* Heb. 6:19; met. *certain, sure,* Acts 21:34; 22:30; 25:26; *safe, making secure,* Phil. 3:1* [804]

[856] ἀσφαλίζω *asphalizō* 4x mid: *to make fast, safe,* or *secure, fasten,* Mt. 27:64, 65, 66; Acts 16:24* [805]

[857] ἀσφαλῶς *asphalōs* 3x *securely, safely; without fail, safely, under guard,* Mk. 14:44; Acts 16:23; *certainly, assuredly,* Acts 2:36* [806]

[858] ἀσχημονέω *aschēmoneō* 2x *to behave disgracefully, dishonorably, or indecently, or in an unbecoming manner,* 1 Cor. 13:5; *to behave in a manner open to censure,* 1 Cor. 7:36* [807]

[859] ἀσχημοσύνη *aschēmosynē* 2x pr. *shameless deed, indecent act; nakedness, shame, pudenda,* Rev. 16:15; *indecency, infamous lust* or *lewdness,* Rom. 1:27* [808]

[860] ἀσχήμων *aschēmōn* 1x *shameful, uncomely, indecent, the private parts,* 1 Cor. 12:23* [809]

[861] ἀσωτία *asōtia* 3x *dissipation, debauchery,* Eph. 5:18; Tit. 1:6; 1 Pet. 4:4* [810]

[862] ἀσώτως *asōtōs* 1x *dissolutely, loosely,* Lk. 15:13* [811]

[863] ἀτακτέω *atakteō* 1x pr. *to infringe* military *order;* met. *to be irregular, behave disorderly, to be lazy,* 2 Thess. 3:7* [812]

[864] ἄτακτος *ataktos* 1x pr. used of soldiers, *disorderly;* met. *irregular* in conduct, *disorderly, lazy,* 1 Thess. 5:14* [813]

[865] ἀτάκτως *ataktōs* 2x *disorderly, irresponsible, lazy,* 2 Thess. 3:6, 11* [814]

[866] ἄτεκνος *ateknos* 2x *childless,* Lk. 20:28, 29* [815]

[867] ἀτενίζω *atenizō* 14x *to fix one's eyes upon, look steadily, gaze intently,* Lk. 4:20 [816] See *gaze; look straight; stare.*

[868] ἄτερ *ater* 2x improper prep with the gen., *without,* Lk. 22:6, 35* [817]

[869] ἀτιμάζω *atimazō* 7x also spelled ἀτιμάω and ἀντιμόω, *to dishonor, slight,* Jn. 8:49; Rom. 2:23; Jas. 2:6; *to treat with indignity,* Mk. 12:4; Lk. 20:11; Acts 5:41; *to abuse, debase,* Rom. 1:24* [818]

[871] ἀτιμία *atimia* 7x *dishonor, infamy,* Rom. 1:26; *shame,* 1 Cor. 11:14; *meanness, vileness,* 1 Cor. 15:43; 2 Cor. 6:8; *a dishonorable use,* Rom. 9:21; 2 Tim. 2:20; κατὰ ἀτιμίαν, *slightingly, disparagingly,* 2 Cor. 11:21 [819]

[872] ἄτιμος *atimos* 4x *unhonored, without honor,* Mt. 13:57; Mk. 6:4; *despised,* 1 Cor. 4:10; 12:23* [820]

[874] ἀτμίς *atmis* 2x *an exhalation, vapor, smoke,* Acts 2:19; Jas. 4:14* [822]

[875] ἄτομος *atomos* 1x *indivisible,* and by impl. *exceedingly minute;* ἐν ἀτόμῳ, sc. χρόνῳ, *in an indivisible point of time, in an instant* or *moment,* 1 Cor. 15:52* [823]

[876] ἄτοπος *atopos* 4x pr. *out of place; inopportune, unsuitable, absurd; new, unusual, strange;* in NT *improper, amiss, wicked,* Lk. 23:41; Acts 25:5; 2 Thess. 3:2; *noxious, harmful,* Acts 28:6* [824]

[877] Ἀττάλεια *Attaleia* 1x *Attalia,* a city of Pamphylia, Acts 14:25* [825]

[878] αὐγάζω *augazō* 1x *to see distinctly, discern,* or possibly *to shine, give light* at 2 Cor. 4:4* [826]

[879] αὐγή *augē* 1x *radiance; daybreak, dawn,* Acts 20:11* [827]

[881] αὐθάδης *authadēs* 2x *one who pleases himself, willful, obstinate; arrogant, stubborn,* Tit. 1:7; 2 Pet. 2:10* [829]

[882] αὐθαίρετος *authairetos* 2x pr. *one who chooses his own course of action; acting spontaneously, of one's own accord,* 2 Cor. 8:3, 17* [830]

[883] αὐθεντέω *authenteō* 1x *to have authority over, domineer,* 1 Tim. 2:12* [831]

[884] αὐλέω *auleō* 3x *to play on a pipe* or *flute, pipe,* Mt. 11:17; Lk. 7:32; 1 Cor. 14:7* [832]

[885] αὐλή *aulē* 12x pr. *an unroofed enclosure; court-yard; sheepfold,* Jn. 10:1, 16; *an exterior court,* i.q. προαύλιον, an enclosed place between the door and the street, Rev. 11:2; *an interior court, quadrangle,* the open court in the middle of Oriental houses, which are commonly built in the form of a square enclosing this court, Mt. 26:58, 69; by synec. *a house, mansion, palace,* Mt. 26:3; Lk. 11:21 [833] See *courtyard; palace.*

[886] αὐλητής *aulētēs* 2x *a player on a pipe* or *flute,* Mt. 9:23; Rev. 18:22* [834]

[887] αὐλίζομαι *aulizomai* 2x pr. *to pass the time in a court-yard; to lodge;* hence, *to pass the night* in any place, *to lodge at night, pass* or *remain through the night,* Mt. 21:17; Lk. 21:37* [835]

[888] αὐλός *aulos* 1x *a pipe* or *flute,* 1 Cor. 14:7* [836]

[889] αὐξάνω *auxanō* 21x also spelled αὔξω, trans. *to cause to grow* or *increase;* pass. *to be increased, enlarged,* Mt. 13:32; 1 Cor. 3:6, 7; intrans. *to increase, grow,* Mt. 6:28; Mk. 4:8 [837] See *become greater; grow; increase.*

[890] αὔξησις *auxēsis* 2x *increase, growth,* Eph. 4:16; Col. 2:19* [838]

[891] αὔξω *auxō* 2x see αὐξάνω, Eph. 2:21; Col. 2:19* [837]

[892] αὔριον *aurion* 14x *tomorrow,* Mt. 6:30; ἡ αὔριον, sc. ἡμέρα, *the next day,* Mt. 6:34 [839] See *tomorrow.*

[893] αὐστηρός *austēros* 2x pr. *harsh, sour in flavor;* met. *harsh, rigid, ungenerous,* Lk. 19:21, 22* [840]

[894] αὐτάρκεια *autarkeia* 2x *sufficiency,* 2 Cor. 9:8; *contentment, self sufficiency,* 1 Tim. 6:6* [841]

[895] αὐτάρκης *autarkēs* 1x pr. *sufficient* or *adequate in one's self; contented with one's lot,* Phil. 4:11* [842]

[896] αὐτοκατάκριτος *autokatakritos* 1x *self-condemned,* Tit. 3:11* [843]

[897] αὐτόματος *automatos* 2x *self-excited, acting spontaneously, spontaneous, of his own accord,* Mk. 4:8; Acts 12:10* [844]

[898] αὐτόπτης *autoptēs* 1x *an eye-witness,* Lk. 1:2* [845]

[899] αὐτός *autos* 5,597x *self, very; alone,* Mk. 6:31; 2 Cor. 12:13; *of one's self, of one's own motion,* Jn. 16:27; used also in the oblique cases independently as a personal pron. of the third person; ὁ αὐτός, *the same; unchangeable,* Heb. 1:12; κατὰ τὸ αὐτό, *at the same time, together,* Acts 14:1; ἐπὶ τὸ αὐτό, *in one and the same place,* Mt. 22:34; *at the same time, together,* Acts 3:1 [846, 847, 848]

[7000] αὐτοῦ *autou* 4x *here*, Mt. 26:36; Lk. 9:27; *there*, Acts 18:19; 21:4*

[900] αὐτόφωρος *autophōros* 1x pr. *caught in the act of theft,* Jn. 8:4* [1888]

[901] αὐτόχειρ *autocheir* 1x *acting* or *doing anything with one's own hands,* Acts 27:19* [849]

[902] αὐχέω *aucheō* 1x *to boast,* Jas. 3:5* [3166]

[903] αὐχμηρός *auchmēros* 1x *squalid, filthy;* by impl. *dark, obscure, murky,* 2 Pet. 1:19* [850]

[904] ἀφαιρέω *aphaireō* 10x *to take away, remove,* Lk. 1:25; 10:42; *to take off, cut off, remove by cutting off,* Mt. 26:15; Mk. 14:47; Lk. 22:50 [851] See *cut off; take away.*

[905] ἀφανής *aphanēs* 1x *out of sight; invisible, hidden, concealed,* Heb. 4:13* [852]

[906] ἀφανίζω *aphanizō* 5x *to remove out of sight, cause to disappear;* pass. *to disappear, vanish,* Jas. 4:14; by impl. *to destroy, consume,* so that nothing shall be left visible, Mt. 6:19, 20; met. *to spoil, deform, disfigure,* Mt. 6:16; *to perish,* Acts 13:41* [853]

[907] ἀφανισμός *aphanismos* 1x *a disappearing, vanishing away;* met. *destruction, abolition, abrogation,* Heb. 8:13* [854]

[908] ἄφαντος *aphantos* 1x *not appearing, not seen, invisible;* hence, ἄφαντος γενέσθαι, *to disappear, vanish,* Lk. 24:31* [855]

[909] ἀφεδρών *aphedrōn* 2x *a latrine,* Mt. 15:17; Mk. 7:19* [856]

[910] ἀφειδία *apheidia* 1x pr. *the disposition of one who is* ἀφειδής, *unsparing;* hence, in NT *unsparingness* in the way of rigorous treatment, *non-indulgence,* Col. 2:23* [857]

[911] ἀφελότης *aphelotēs* 1x *sincerity, simplicity,* Acts 2:46 [858]

[912] ἄφεσις *aphesis* 17x *release, deliverance,* from captivity, Lk. 4:18 (2x); *remission, forgiveness, pardon,* Mt. 26:28 [859] See *forgiveness; freedom; release.*

[913] ἁφή *haphē* 2x *a fastening; a ligament,* by which the different members are connected, *commissure, joint,* Eph. 4:16; Col. 2:19* [860]

[914] ἀφθαρσία *aphtharsia* 7x *incorruptibility,* 1 Cor. 15:42, 53, 54; *immortality,* Rom. 2:7; 2 Tim. 1:10; *soundness, purity;* ἐν ἀφθαρσίᾳ, *purely, sincerely* or *constantly, unfailingly,* Eph. 6:24 [861]

[915] ἄφθαρτος *aphthartos* 8x *incorruptible, immortal, imperishable, undying, enduring,* Rom. 1:23; 1 Cor. 9:25; 15:52 [862]

[917] ἀφθορία *aphthoria* 1x pr. *incapability of decay;* met. *incorruptness, integrity, genuineness, purity,* Tit. 2:7* [90]

[918] ἀφίημι *aphiēmi* 143x *to send away, dismiss, suffer to depart; to emit, send forth;* τὴν φωνήν, *the voice, to cry out, utter an exclamation,* Mk. 15:37; τὸ πνεῦμα, *the spirit, to expire,* Mt. 27:50; *to omit, pass over* or *by; to let alone, care not for,* Mt. 15:14; 23:23; Heb. 6:1; *to permit, suffer, let, forbid not; to give up, yield, resign,* Mt. 5:40; *to remit, forgive, pardon; to relax, suffer to become less intense,* Rev. 2:4; *to leave, depart from; to desert, forsake; to leave remaining* or *alone; to leave behind,* sc. at one's death, Mk. 12:19, 20, 21, 22; Jn. 14:27 [863] See *divorce; forgive; leave.*

[919] ἀφικνέομαι *aphikneomai* 1x *to come, arrive at; to reach* as a report, Rom. 16:19* [864]

[920] ἀφιλάγαθος *aphilagathos* 1x *not a lover of good* and *good men,* 2 Tim. 3:3* [865]

[921] ἀφιλάργυρος *aphilargyros* 2x *not fond of money, not covetous, generous,* 1 Tim. 3:3; Heb. 13:5* [866]

[922] ἄφιξις *aphixis* 1x *arrival; departure,* Acts 20:29* [867]

[923] ἀφίστημι *aphistēmi* 14x trans. *to put away, separate; to draw off* or *away, withdraw, cause to revolt, mislead,* Acts 5:37; intrans., and mid., *to depart, go away from,* Lk. 2:37; met. *to desist* or *refrain from, let alone,* Acts 5:38; 22:29; 2 Cor. 12:8; *to make defection, fall away, apostatize,* Lk. 8:13; 1 Tim. 4:1; Heb. 3:12; *to withdraw from, have no intercourse with,* 1 Tim. 6:5; *to abstain from,* 2 Tim. 2:19 [868] See *abandon; depart; fall away; leave; take away; turn away.*

[924] ἄφνω *aphnō* 3x *suddenly, unexpectedly,* Acts 2:2; 16:26; 28:6* [869]

[925] ἀφόβως *aphobōs* 4x *fearlessly, boldly, intrepidly,* Phil. 1:14; *securely, peacefully, tranquilly,* Lk. 1:74; 1 Cor. 16:10; *boldly, shamelessly,* Jude 12* [870]

[926] ἀφομοιόω *aphomoioō* 1x *to assimilate, cause to resemble,* Heb. 7:3* [871]

[927] ἀφοράω *aphoraō* 2x *to view with undivided attention* by looking away from every other object; *to regard fixedly and earnestly,* Heb. 12:2; *to see distinctly,* Phil. 2:23* [542, 872]

[928] ἀφορίζω *aphorizō* 10x *to separate, take away, exclude; sever* from the rest, Mt. 13:49; *to separate* from society, *cut off from all intercourse, excommunicate,* Lk. 6:22; *to set apart, select,* Acts 13:2; Rom. 1:1; Gal. 1:15 [873] See *exclude; separate; set apart.*

[929] ἀφορμή *aphormē* 7x pr. *a starting point; means* to accomplish an object; *occasion, opportunity,* Rom. 7:8, 11 [874]

[930] ἀφρίζω *aphrizō* 2x *to froth, foam,* Mk. 9:18, 20* [875]

[931] ἀφρός *aphros* 1x *froth, foam,* Lk. 9:39* [876]

[932] ἀφροσύνη *aphrosynē* 4x *inconsiderateness, folly;* boastful *folly,* 2 Cor. 11:1, 17, 21; in NT *foolishness, levity, wickedness, impiety,* Mk. 7:22* [877]

[933] ἄφρων *aphrōn* 11x *unwise, inconsiderate, simple, foolish,* Lk. 11:40; 12:20; 1 Cor. 15:36; *ignorant,* religiously *unenlightened,* Rom. 2:20; Eph. 5:17; 1 Pet. 2:15; boastfully *foolish, vain,* 2 Cor. 11:16, 19 [878] See *fool; foolish.*

[934] ἀφυπνόω *aphypnoō* 1x *to awake from sleep;* in NT *to go off into sleep, fall asleep,* Lk. 8:23* [879]

[936] ἄφωνος *aphōnos* 4x *dumb, incapable of speech,* 1 Cor. 12:2; 2 Pet. 2:16; *silent, mute, uttering no voice,* Acts 8:32; *inarticulate, consisting of inarticulate sounds, unmeaning,* 1 Cor. 14:10* [880]

[937] Ἀχάζ *Achaz* 2x *Ahaz,* pr. name, indecl, Mt. 1:9* [881]

[938] Ἀχαΐα *Achaia* 10x *Achaia,* the Roman province, comprehending all Greece to the south of Thessaly [882]

[939] Ἀχαϊκός *Achaikos* 1x *Achaicus,* pr. name, 1 Cor. 16:17* [883]

[940] ἀχάριστος *acharistos* 2x *unthankful, ungrateful,* Lk. 6:35; 2 Tim. 3:2* [884]

[942] ἀχειροποίητος *acheiropoiētos* 3x *not made with hands,* Mk. 14:58; 2 Cor. 5:1; Col. 2:11* [886]

[943] Ἀχίμ *Achim* 2x *Achim,* pr. name, indecl, Mt. 1:14* [885]

[944] ἀχλύς *achlys* 1x *a mist; darkening, dimness,* of the sight, Acts 13:11* [887]

[945] ἀχρεῖος *achreios* 2x *useless, unprofitable, worthless,* Mt. 25:30; *unmeritorious,* Lk. 17:10* [888]

[946] ἀχρειόω *achreioō* 1x also ἀχρεόω, pas., *to render useless;* met., *to become corrupt, depraved,* Rom. 3:12* [889]

[947] ἄχρηστος *achrēstos* 1x *unuseful, useless, unprofitable,* and by impl. *detrimental, causing loss,* Phlm. 11* [890]

[948] ἄχρι *achri* 49x improper prep with the gen., also functioning as a conj, also spelled ἄχρις (Gal. 3:19; Heb. 3:13; Rev. 2:25), with respect to place, *as far as*; to time, *until, during*; as a conj., *until* [891]

[949] ἄχυρον *achuron* 2x *chaff, straw broken up* by treading out the grain, Mt. 3:12; Lk. 3:17* [892]

[950] ἀψευδής *apseudēs* 1x *free from falsehood; incapable of falsehood,* Tit. 1:2* [893]

[952] ἄψινθος *apsinthos* 2x see ἀψίνθιον [894]

[953] ἄψυχος *apsychos* 1x *void of life* or *sense, inanimate,* 1 Cor. 14:7* [895]

[955] Βάαλ *Baal* 1x *Baal,* (Hebrew for *Master*) pr. name, indecl., Rom. 11:4* [896]

[956] Βαβυλών *Babylōn* 12x *Babylon,* 1 Pet. 5:13 [897]

[957] βαθμός *bathmos* 1x pr. *a step, stair;* met. *grade* of dignity, *degree, rank, standing,* 1 Tim. 3:13* [898]

[958] βάθος *bathos* 8x *depth;* τὸ βάθος, *deep water,* Lk. 5:4; Mt. 13:5; met. *fullness, abundance, immensity,* Rom. 11:33; *an extreme degree,* 2 Cor. 8:2; pl. *profundities, deep-laid plans,* 1 Cor. 2:10; Rev. 2:24 [899]

[959] βαθύνω *bathunō* 1x *to deepen, excavate,* Lk. 6:48* [900]

[960] βαθύς *bathus* 4x *deep,* Jn. 4:11; met. *deep, profound,* Acts 20:9; Rev. 2:24; ὄρθρου βαθέος, lit. *at deep morning twilight, at the earliest dawn,* Lk. 24:1* [901]

[961] βάϊον *baion* 1x *a palm branch,* Jn. 12:13* [902]

[962] Βαλαάμ *Balaam* 3x *Balaam,* pr. name, indecl. [903]

[963] Βαλάκ *Balak* 1x *Balak,* pr. name, indecl., Rev. 2:14* [904]

[964] βαλλάντιον *ballantion* 4x also spelled βαλάντιον, *a bag, purse,* Lk. 10:4; 12:33; 22:35, 36* [905]

[965] βάλλω *ballō* 122x pluperfect, ἐβεβλήμην, *to throw, cast; to lay,* Rev. 2:22; Mt. 8:6, 14; *to put, place,* Jas. 3:3; *to place, deposit,* Mt. 27:6; Mk. 12:41-44; Lk. 21:1-4; Jn. 12:6; *to pour,* Jn. 13:5; *to thrust,* Jn. 18:11; 20:27; Mk. 7:33; Rev. 14:19; *to send forth,* Mt. 10:34; *to assault, strike,* Mk. 14:65; met. *to suggest,* Jn. 13:2; intrans. *to rush, beat,* as the wind, Acts 27:14 [906] See *throw.*

[966] βαπτίζω *baptizō* 77x pr. *to dip, immerse; to cleanse* or *purify by washing; to administer the rite of baptism, to baptize;* met. with various reference to the ideas associated with Christian baptism as an act of dedication, e.g. marked designation, devotion, trial, etc.; mid. *to procure baptism for one's self, to undergo baptism,* Acts 22:16 [907] See *baptize.*

[967] βάπτισμα *baptisma* 19x pr. *immersion; baptism, ordinance of baptism,* Mt. 3:7; Rom. 6:4; met. *baptism* in the trial of suffering, Mt. 20:22, 23; Mk. 10:38, 39 [908] See *baptism, baptist.*

[968] βαπτισμός *baptismos* 4x pr. *an act of dipping* or *immersion: a baptism,* Col. 2:12; Heb. 6:2; *an ablution,* Mk. 7:4; Heb. 9:10* [909] See *baptism; wash, washing.*

[969] βαπτιστής *baptistēs* 12x *one who baptizes, a baptist,* Mt. 3:1; 11:11, 12 [910] See *baptism, baptist.*

[970] βάπτω *baptō* 4x *to dip,* Jn. 13:26; Lk. 16:24; *to dye,* Rev. 19:13* [911]

[972] Βαραββᾶς *Barabbas* 11x *Barabbas,* pr. name [912]

[973] Βαράκ *Barak* 1x *Barak,* pr. name, indecl., Heb. 11:32* [913]

[974] Βαραχίας *Barachias* 1x *Barachias,* pr. name, Mt. 23:35 [914]

[975] βάρβαρος *barbaros* 6x pr. *one to whom a pure Greek dialect is not native; one who is not a proper Greek, a barbarian,* Rom. 1:14; Col. 3:11; Acts 28:2, 4; *a foreigner speaking a strange language,* 1 Cor. 14:11* [915]

[976] βαρέω *bareō* 6x *to be heavy upon, weigh down, burden, oppress,* as sleep, Mt. 26:43; Mk. 14:40; Lk. 9:32; *calamities,* 2 Cor. 1:8; 5:4; or, *trouble, care, expense,* etc. 1 Tim. 5:16* [916]

[977] βαρέως *bareōs* 2x *heavily;* met. *with difficulty, dully, stupidly,* Mt. 13:15; Acts 28:27* [917]

[978] Βαρθολομαῖος *Bartholomaios* 4x *Bartholomew,* pr. name [918]

[979] Βαριησοῦς *Bariēsous* 1x *Bar-jesus,* pr. name, Acts 13:6* [919]

[980] Βαριωνᾶ *Bariōna* 1x also Βὰρ Ἰωνᾶ or Βαριωνᾶς, *Bar-jona,* pr. name, Mt. 16:17* [920]

[982] Βαρναβᾶς *Barnabas* 28x *Barnabas,* pr. name, Acts 4:36; 13:1f.; 14:12; 15:2f.; 1 Cor. 9:6; Gal. 2:1, 9, 13; Col. 4:10 [921]

[983] βάρος *baros* 6x *weight, heaviness; a burden, anything grievous and hard to be borne,* Mt. 20:12; Acts 15:28; Gal. 6:2; Rev. 2:24; *burden, charge* or *weight, influence, dignity, honor,* 1 Thess. 2:7; with another noun in government, *fulness, abundance, excellence,* 2 Cor. 4:17* [922]

[984] Βαρσαββᾶς *Barsabbas* 2x *Bar-sabas,* pr. name. (1) *Joseph, surnamed Justus,* Acts 1:23. (2) *Judas,* Acts 15:22* [923]

[985] Βαρτιμαῖος *Bartimaios* 1x *Bartimaeus,* pr. name, Mk. 10:46* [924]

[987] βαρύς *barys* 6x *heavy;* met. *burdensome, oppressive* or *difficult of observance,* as precepts, Mt. 23:4; 1 Jn. 5:3; *weighty, important, momentous,* Mt. 23:23; Acts 25:7; *grievous, oppressive, afflictive, violent,* Acts 20:29; *authoritative, strict, stern, severe,* 2 Cor. 10:10* [926]

[988] βαρύτιμος *barytimos* 1x *of great price, precious,* Mt. 26:7* [927]

[989] βασανίζω *basanizō* 12x pr. *to press hard, torture;* met. *to examine, scrutinize, try,* either by words or torture; in NT *to afflict, torment;* pass. *to be afflicted, tormented, pained,* by diseases, Mt. 8:6, 29, 35; *to be tossed, agitated,* as by the waves, Mt. 14:24 [928] See *suffer; torment; torture.*

[990] βασανισμός *basanismos* 6x pr. *examination by torture; torment, torture,* Rev. 9:5; 14:11; 18:7, 10, 15* [929]

[991] βασανιστής *basanistēs* 1x pr. *an inquisitor, tormentor;* in NT *a keeper of a prison, jailer,* Mt. 18:34* [930]

[992] βάσανος *basanos* 3x pr. *lapis Lydius,* a species of stone from Lydia, which being applied to metals was thought to indicate any alloy which might be mixed with them, and therefore used in the trial of metals; hence, *examination* of a person, especially by torture; in NT *torture, torment, severe pain,* Mt. 4:24; Lk. 16:23, 28* [931]

[993] βασιλεία *basileia* 162x *a kingdom, realm,* the region or country governed by a king; *kingly power, authority, dominion, reign; royal dignity,* the title and honor of king; ἡ βασιλεία, Mt. 9:35, ἡ βασιλεία τοῦ θεοῦ, Rom. 14:17, or τοῦ Χριστου or τοῦ οὐρανοῦ or τῶν οὐρανῶν, *the reign* or *kingdom of the Messiah,* [932] See *dominion; kingdom; reign; rule.*

[994] βασίλειος *basileios* 2x *royal, regal;* met. *possessed of high prerogatives and distinction,* 1 Pet. 2:9; τὰ βαείλεια, sc. δώματα, *regal mansion, palaces,* Lk. 7:25* [933, 934]

[995] βασιλεύς *basileus* 115x *a king, monarch, one possessing regal authority* [935] See *king; rule; ruler.*

[996] βασιλεύω *basileuō* 21x *to possess regal authority, be a king, reign; to rule, govern,* Mt. 2:22; met. *to be in force, predominate, prevail,* Rom. 5:14, 17, 21; met. *to be in kingly case, fare royally,* 1 Cor. 4:8 [936] See *reign; rule; ruler.*

[997] βασιλικός *basilikos* 5x *royal, regal,* Acts 12:20, 21; βασιλικός, used as a subst. *a person attached to the king, courtier,* Jn. 4:46, 49; met. *royal, of the highest excellence,* Jas. 2:8* [937]

[999] βασίλισσα *basilissa* 4x *a queen,* Mt. 12:42; Lk. 11:31; Acts 8:27; Rev. 18:7* [938]

[1000] βάσις *basis* 1x pr. *a step; the foot,* Acts 3:7* [939]

[1001] βασκαίνω *baskainō* 1x pr. *to slander;* thence, *to bewitch* by spells, or by any other means; *to delude,* Gal. 3:1* [940]

[1002] βαστάζω *bastazō* 27x pr. *to lift, raise, bear aloft; to bear, carry* in the hands or about the person; *carry* as a message, Acts 9:15; *to take away, remove,*

Mt. 8:17; Jn. 20:15; *to take up,* Jn. 10:31; Lk. 14:27; *to bear* as a burden *endure, suffer; to sustain,* Rom. 11:18; *to bear with, tolerate; to sustain* mentally, *comprehend,* Jn. 16:12 [941] See *bear; carry.*

[1003] βάτος *batos* 5x *a thorn-bush,* Mk. 12:26; Lk. 6:44; 20:37; Acts 7:30, 35* [942]

[1004] βάτος *batos* 1x *a bath,* a measure for liquids, which is stated by Josephus (*Ant.* 8.57) to contain seventy-two sextarii, or about thirteen and one half gallons. Others estimate it to be nine gallons; and others, seven and one half gallons, Lk. 16:6* [943]

[1005] βάτραχος *batrachos* 1x *a frog,* Rev. 16:13 [944]

[1006] βατταλογέω *battalogeō* 1x also spelled βαττολογέω, pr. *to stammer;* hence, *to babble; to use vain repetitions,* Mt. 6:7* [945]

[1007] βδέλυγμα *bdelygma* 6x *an abomination, an abominable thing,* Mt. 24:15; Mk. 13:14; *idolatry with all its pollution,* Lk. 16:15; Rev. 17:4, 5; 21:27* [946]

[1008] βδελυκτός *bdelyktos* 1x *abominable, detestable,* Tit. 1:16* [947]

[1009] βδελύσσομαι *bdelyssomai* 2x *to abominate, loathe, detest, abhor,* Rom. 2:22; pass. *to be abominable, detestable,* Rev. 21:8* [948]

[1010] βέβαιος *bebaios* 8x *firm, stable, strong, secure, steadfast,* Heb. 3:14; 6:19; *sure, certain, established,* Rom. 4:16 [949]

[1011] βεβαιόω *bebaioō* 8x *to confirm, establish; to render constant and unwavering,* 1 Cor. 1:8; *to strengthen* or *establish* by arguments or proofs, *ratify,* Mk. 16:20; *to verify,* as promises, Rom. 15:8 [950]

[1012] βεβαίωσις *bebaiōsis* 2x *confirmation, firm establishment,* Phil. 1:7; Heb. 6:16* [951]

[1013] βέβηλος *bebēlos* 5x pr. *what is open and accessible to all;* hence, *profane, not religious, godless not connected with religion; unholy; a despiser, scorner,* 1 Tim. 1:9; 4:7 [952] See *profane.*

[1014] βεβηλόω *bebēloō* 2x *to profane, pollute, desecrate violate,* Mt. 12:5; Acts 24:6* [953]

[1015] Βεελζεβούλ *Beelzeboul* 7x variant spellings of Βεελζεβούβ and βεελζεβούλ, *Beelzeboul,* pr. name, indecl., Mt. 10:25 [954]

[1016] Βελιάρ *Beliar* 1x *Belial,* pr. name, indecl., 2 Cor. 6:15* [955]

[1017] βελόνη *belonē* 1x pr. *the point of a spear; a needle,* Lk. 18:25* [4476]

[1018] βέλος *belos* 1x *a missile weapon, dart, arrow,* Eph. 6:16* [956]

[1019] βελτίων *beltiōn* 1x *better;* βέλτιον, as an adv., *very well, too well to need informing,* 2 Tim. 1:18* [957]

[1021] Βενιαμίν *Beniamin* 4x *Benjamin,* pr. name, indecl. Acts 13:21; Rom. 11:1; Phil. 3:5; Rev. 7:8* [958]

[1022] Βερνίκη *Bernikē* 3x *Bernice,* pr. name, Acts 25:13, 23; 26:30* [959]

[1023] Βέροια *Beroia* 2x *Berea,* a town of Macedonia, Acts 17:10, 13* [960]

[1024] Βεροιαῖος *Beroiaios* 1x *belonging to Berea,* Acts 20:4* [961]

[1029] Βηθανία *Bēthania* 12x *Bethany.* (1) A village near Jerusalem, at the Mount of Olives, Mt. 21:17; Mk. 11:1. (2) A village beyond the Jordan, Jn. 1:28 [963]

[1031] Βηθεσδά *Bēthesda* 1x *Bethesda,* indecl., Jn. 5:2* [964]

[1033] Βηθλέεμ *Bēthleem* 8x *Bethlehem,* indecl., a town in Palestine [965]

[1034] Βηθσαϊδά *Bēthsaida* 7x also spelled Βηθσαϊδάν (1035) *Bethsaida,* indecl. (1) A city of Galilee, Mt. 11:21; Mk. 6:45. (2) A city of Lower Gaulanitis, near the Lake of Gennesareth, Lk. 9:10 [966]

[1036] Βηθφαγή *Bēthphagē* 3x *Bethphage,* indecl., a part of the Mount of Olives, Mt. 21:1; Mk. 11:1; Lk. 19:29* [967]

[1037] βῆμα *bēma* 12x *a step, footstep, foot-breadth, space to set the foot on,* Acts 7:5; *an elevated place ascended by steps, tribunal, throne,* Mt. 27:19; Acts 12:21 [968] See *court; judgment seat; throne.*

[1039] βήρυλλος *bēryllos* 1x *a beryl,* a precious stone of a sea-green color, found chiefly in India, Rev. 21:20* [969]

[1040] βία *bia* 3x *force, impetus, violence,* Acts 5:26; 21:35; 27:41* [970] See *violence.*

[1041] βιάζω *biazō* 2x also written as a middle deponent, βιάζομαι, *to urge, constrain, overpower by force; to press earnestly forward, to rush,* Lk. 16:16;

pass. *to be an object of a forceful movement,* Mt. 11:12* [971]

[1042] βίαιος *biaios* 1x *violent, strong,* Acts 2:2* [972]

[1043] βιαστής *biastēs* 1x *one who uses violence,* or *is impetuous; one who is forceful* in eager pursuit, Mt. 11:12* [973]

[1044] βιβλαρίδιον *biblaridion* 3x *a small volume* or *scroll, a little book,* Rev. 10:2, 9, 10* [974]

[1046] βιβλίον *biblion* 34x *a written volule* or *roll, book,* Lk. 4:17, 20; *a scroll, bill, billet,* Mt. 19:7; Mk. 10:4 [975] See *book; scroll; write, writing.*

[1047] βίβλος *biblos* 10x pr. *the inner bark* or *rind of the papyrus,* which was anciently used instead of paper; hence, *a written volume* or *roll, scroll, book, catalogue, account,* Mt. 1:1; Mk. 12:26 [976] See *book; scroll; write, writing.*

[1048] βιβρώσκω *bibrōskō* 1x *to eat,* Jn. 6:13* [977]

[1049] Βιθυνία *Bithunia* 2x *Bithynia,* a province of Asia Minor, Acts 16:7; 1 Pet. 1:1* [978]

[1050] βίος *bios* 10x *life; means of living; sustenance, maintenance, substance, goods,* Mk. 12:44, Lk. 8:14, 43; 15:12, 30; 21:4; 1 Tim. 2:2; 2 Tim. 2:4; 1 Jn. 2:16; 3:17* [979] See *life; possess, possessions; property.*

[1051] βιόω *bioō* 1x *to live,* 1 Pet. 4:2* [980]

[1052] βίωσις *biōsis* 1x *manner of life,* Acts 26:4* [981]

[1053] βιωτικός *biōtikos* 3x *pertaining to this life* or *the things of this life,* Lk. 21:34; 1 Cor. 6:3, 4* [982]

[1054] βλαβερός *blaberos* 1x *hurtful, harmful,* 1 Tim. 6:9* [983]

[1055] βλάπτω *blaptō* 2x pr. *to weaken, hinder, disable; to hurt, harm, injure,* Mk. 16:18; Lk. 4:35* [984]

[1056] βλαστάνω *blastanō* 4x also spelled βλαστάω, intrans. *to germinate, bud, sprout, spring up,* Mt. 13:26; Mk. 4:27; Heb. 9:4; trans. and causative, *to cause to shoot, to produce, yield,* Jas. 5:18* [985]

[1058] Βλάστος *Blastos* 1x *Blastus,* pr. name, Acts 12:20* [986]

[1059] βλασφημέω *blasphēmeō* 34x *to defame, revile, slander,* Mt. 27:39; *to speak of God* or *divine things in terms of impious irreverence, to blaspheme,* Mt. 9:3; 26:65 [987] See *blaspheme; insult; revile; slander.*

[1060] βλασφημία *blasphēmia* 18x *slander, railing, reproach,* Mt. 15:19; Mk. 7:22; *blasphemy,* Mt. 12:31; 26:65 [988] See *blasphemy; mockery.*

[1061] βλάσφημος *blasphēmos* 4x *slanderous, railing, reproachful,* 2 Tim. 3:2; 2 Pet. 2:11; *blasphemous,* Acts 6:11, 13; 1 Tim. 1:13 [989]

[1062] βλέμμα *blemma* 1x *a look; the act of seeing, sight,* 2 Pet. 2:8* [990]

[1063] βλέπω *blepō* 133x *to have the faculty of sight, to see,* Mt. 12:22; *to exercise sight, to see,* Mt. 6:4; *to look* towards or at, Mt. 22:16; *to face,* Acts 27:12; *to take heed,* Mt. 24:4; in NT, βλέπειν ἀπό, *to beware of, shun,* Mk. 8:15; trans., *to cast a look on,* Mt. 5:28; *to see, behold,* Mt. 13:17; *to observe,* Mt. 7:3; *to have an eye to, see to,* Mk. 13:9; Col. 4:17; 2 Jn. 8; *to discern* mentally, *perceive,* Rom. 7:23; 2 Cor. 7:8; Jas. 2:22; *to guard against,* Phil. 3:2; pass., *to be an object of sight, be visible,* Rom. 8:24 [991] See *look at; see; watch.*

[1064] βλητέος *blēteos* 1x *requiring to be cast* or *put,* Lk. 5:38* [992]

[1065] Βοανηργές *Boanērges* 1x *Boanerges,* pr. name, indecl., Mk. 3:17* [993]

[1066] βοάω *boaō* 12x *to cry out; to exclaim, proclaim,* Mt. 3:3; 15:34; Acts 8:7; πρός τινα, *to invoke, implore the aid of any one,* Lk. 18:7 [994] See *call; cry out; shout.*

[1067] Βόες *Boes* 2x *Boaz,* pr. name, indecl., Mt. 1:5* [1003]

[1068] βοή *boē* 1x *a cry, outcry, exclamation,* Jas. 5:4* [995]

[1069] βοήθεια *boētheia* 2x *help,* Heb. 4:16; meton. pl. *helps, supports,* Acts 27:17* [996]

[1070] βοηθέω *boētheō* 8x *to run to the aid of those who cry for help; to advance to the assistance of any one, help, aid, succor,* Mt. 15:25; Mk. 9:22, 24 [997]

[1071] βοηθός *boēthos* 1x *a helper,* Heb. 13:6* [998]

[1073] βόθυνος *bothunos* 3x *a pit, well* or *cistern,* Mt. 12:11; 15:14; Lk. 6:39* [999]

[1074] βολή *bolē* 1x *a cast, a throw; the distance to which a thing can be thrown,* Lk. 22:41* [1000]

[1075] βολίζω *bolizō* 2x *to take soundings, sound* Acts 27:28* [1001]

[1078] Βόος *Boos* 1x also spelled Βόοζ, *Boaz,* pr. name, indecl., Lk. 3:32* [1003]

[1079] βόρβορος *borboros* 1x *mud, mire, dung, filth,* 2 Pet. 2:22* [1004]

[1080] βορρᾶς *borras* 2x pr. *the north* or *N.N.E. wind;* meton. *the north,* Lk. 13:29; Rev. 21:13* [1005]

[1081] βόσκω *boskō* 9x *to feed, pasture, tend while grazing;* βόσκομαι, *to feed, be feeding,* Mt. 8:30, 33; Lk. 8:32, 34 [1006] See *feed.*

[1082] Βοσόρ *Bosor* 1x *Bosor,* pr. name, indecl., 2 Pet. 2:15* [1007]

[1083] βοτάνη *botanē* 1x *herb, herbage, produce of the earth,* Heb. 6:7* [1008]

[1084] βότρυς *botrys* 1x *a bunch* or *cluster of grapes,* Rev. 14:18* [1009]

[1085] βουλευτής *bouleutēs* 2x *a counsellor, senator; member of the Sanhedrin,* Mk. 15:43; Lk. 23:50* [1010]

[1086] βουλεύω *bouleuō* 6x mid., *to give counsel; to deliberate,* Lk. 14:31; Jn. 12:10; 11:53; *to purpose, determine,* Acts 27:39; 2 Cor. 1:17 (2x)* [1011]

[1087] βουλή *boulē* 12x *counsel, purpose, design, determination, decree,* Lk. 7:30; 23:51, et al. freq.; by impl. *secret thoughts, cogitations* of the mind, 1 Cor. 4:5 [1012] See *counsel; purpose.*

[1088] βούλημα *boulēma* 3x *purpose, will, determination,* Acts 27:43; Rom. 9:19; 1 Pet. 4:3* [1013]

[1089] βούλομαι *boulomai* 37x *to be willing, disposed,* Mk. 15:15; Acts 25:20; 28:18; *to intend,* Mt. 1:19; Acts 5:28; 12:4; 2 Cor. 1:15; *to desire,* 1 Tim. 6:9; *to choose, be pleased,* Jn. 18:39; Acts 18:15; Jas. 3:4; *to will, decree, appoint,* Lk. 22:42; Jas. 1:18; 1 Cor. 12:11; 1 Tim. 2:8; 5:14; ἐβουλόμην, *I could wish,* Acts 25:22 [1014] See *choose; desire; intend; plan; want; will.*

[1090] βουνός *bounos* 2x *a hill, rising ground,* Lk. 3:5; 23:30* [1015]

[1091] βοῦς *bous* 8x *an ox, a bull* or *cow,* an animal of the ox kind, Lk. 13:15 [1016]

[1092] βραβεῖον *brabeion* 2x *a prize* bestowed on victors in the public games, such as a crown, wreath, chaplet, garland, etc., 1 Cor. 9:24; Phil. 3:14* [1017]

[1093] βραβεύω *brabeuō* 1x pr. *to be a director* or *arbiter in the public games;* in NT *to preside, direct, rule, govern, be predominate,* Col. 3:15* [1018]

[1094] βραδύνω *bradynō* 2x *to be slow, to delay,* 1 Tim. 3:15; 2 Pet. 3:9* [1019]

[1095] βραδυπλοέω *bradyploeō* 1x *to sail slowly,* Acts 27:7* [1020]

[1096] βραδύς *bradys* 3x *slow, not hasty,* Jas. 1:19; *slow* of understanding, *heavy, stupid,* Lk. 24:25* [1021]

[1097] βραδύτης *bradytēs* 1x *slowness, tardiness, delay,* 2 Pet. 3:9* [1022]

[1098] βραχίων *brachiōn* 3x *the arm; the arm* as a symbol of power, Lk. 1:51; Jn. 12:38; Acts 13:17* [1023] See *arm.*

[1099] βραχύς *brachus* 7x *short, brief; few, small,* Lk. 22:58; Jn. 6:7; Acts 5:34; 27:28; Heb. 2:7, 9; 13:22* [1024]

[1100] βρέφος *brephos* 8x *a child;* whether unborn, *an embryo, fetus,* Lk. 1:41, 44; or just born, *an infant,* Lk. 2:12, 16; Acts 7:19; or partly grown, Lk. 18:15; 2 Tim. 3:15; met. *a babe* in simplicity of faith, 1 Pet. 2:2* [1025]

[1101] βρέχω *brechō* 7x *to wet, moisten,* Lk. 7:38; *to rain, cause* or *send rain,* Mt. 5:45; Lk. 17:29 [1026]

[1103] βροντή *brontē* 12x *thunder,* Mk. 3:17; Jn. 12:29 [1027] See *thunder.*

[1104] βροχή *brochē* 2x *rain,* Mt. 7:25, 27* [1028]

[1105] βρόχος *brochos* 1x *a cord, noose,* 1 Cor. 7:35* [1029]

[1106] βρυγμός *brygmos* 7x *gnashing* of teeth together, Mt. 8:12, 13, 42, 50; 22:13; 24:51; 25:30; Lk. 13:28* [1030]

[1107] βρύχω *brychō* 1x *to grate* or *gnash* the teeth, Acts 7:54* [1031]

[1108] βρύω *bryō* 1x pr. *to be full, to swell* with anything; *to emit, send forth,* Jas. 3:11* [1032]

[1109] βρῶμα *brōma* 17x *food,* Mt. 14:15; Mk. 7:19; *solid food,* 1 Cor. 3:2 [1033] See *food.*

[1110] βρώσιμος *brōsimos* 1x *eatable, that may be eaten,* Lk. 24:41* [1034]

[1111] βρῶσις *brōsis* 11x *eating, the act of eating,* Rom. 14:17; 1 Cor. 8:4; *meat, food,* Jn. 6:27; Heb.

12:16; *a canker* or *rust,* Mt. 6:19, 20 [1035] See *eating; food.*

[1112] βυθίζω *bythizō* 2x *to immerse, submerge, cause to sink,* Lk. 5:7; *to plunge deep, drown,* 1 Tim. 6:9* [1036]

[1113] βυθός *bythos* 1x *the bottom, lowest part; the deep, sea,* 2 Cor. 11:25* [1037]

[1114] βυρσεύς *byrseus* 3x *a tanner, leather-dresser,* Acts 9:43; 10:6, 32* [1038]

[1115] βύσσινος *byssinos* 5x *made of fine linen* or *fine cotton,* Rev. 18:16; 18:8 (2x), 14* [1039]

[1116] βύσσος *byssos* 1x *byssus,* a species of fine cotton highly prized by the ancients, Lk. 16:19* [1040]

[1117] βωμός *bōmos* 1x pr. *a slightly-elevated spot, base, pedestal;* hence, *an altar,* Acts 17:23* [1041]

[1119] Γαββαθᾶ *Gabbatha* 1x *Gabbatha,* pr. name, indecl., Jn. 19:13* [1042]

[1120] Γαβριήλ *Gabriēl* 2x *Gabriel,* pr. name, indecl., Lk. 1:19, 26* [1043]

[1121] γάγγραινα *gangraina* 1x *gangrene, mortification,* 2 Tim. 2:17* [1044]

[1122] Γάδ *Gad* 1x *Gad,* pr. name, indecl., Rev. 7:5* [1045]

[1123] Γαδαρηνός *Gadarēnos* 1x *an inhabitant of Gadara,* the chief city of Perea, Mt. 8:28* [1046]

[1124] Γάζα *Gaza* 1x *Gaza,* a strong city of Palestine, Acts 8:26* [1048]

[1125] γάζα *gaza* 1x *treasure, treasury,* Acts 8:27* [1047]

[1126] γαζοφυλάκιον *gazophylakion* 5x also spelled γαζοφυλακεῖον, *a treasury; the sacred treasure,* Mk. 12:41, 43; Lk. 21:1; Jn. 8:20* [1049]

[1127] Γάϊος *Gaios* 5x *Gaius,* pr. name. (1) Of Macedonia, Acts 19:29. (2) Of Corinth, 1 Cor. 1:14. (3) Of Derbe, Acts 20:4. (4) A Christian to whom John addressed his third Epistle, 3 Jn. 1; Rom. 16:23* [1050]

[1128] γάλα *gala* 5x *milk,* 1 Cor. 9:7; met. spiritual *milk,* consisting in the elements of Christian instruction, 1 Cor. 3:2; Heb. 5:12, 13; spiritual *nutriment,* 1 Pet. 2:2* [1051]

[1129] Γαλάτης *Galatēs* 1x *a Galatian, inhabitant of Galatia,* Gal. 3:1* [1052]

[1130] Γαλατία *Galatia* 4x *Galatia* or *Gallo-Graecia,* a province of Asia Minor, 1 Cor. 6:1; Gal. 1:2; 2 Tim. 4:10; 1 Pet. 1:1* [1053]

[1131] Γαλατικός *Galatikos* 2x *Galatian,* Acts 16:6; 18:23* [1054]

[1132] γαλήνη *galēnē* 3x *tranquillity of the sea, a calm,* Mt. 8:26; Mk. 4:39; Lk. 8:24* [1055]

[1133] Γαλιλαία *Galilaia* 61x *Galilee,* a district of Palestine north of Samaria, Mt. 4:15 [1056]

[1134] Γαλιλαῖος *Galilaios* 11x *a native of Galilee,* Mt. 26:69; Mk. 14:70; Lk. 13:1; Jn. 4:45; Acts 1:11 [1057]

[1136] Γαλλίων *Galliōn* 3x *Gallio,* pr. name, Acts 18:12, 14, 17* [1058]

[1137] Γαμαλιήλ *Gamaliēl* 2x *Gamaliel,* pr. name, indecl. [1059]

[1138] γαμέω *gameō* 28x *to marry,* Mt. 5:32, et al.; absol. *to marry, enter the marriage state,* Mt. 19:10, et al.; mid. *to marry, be married,* Mk. 10:12; 1 Cor. 7:39 [1060] See *marry, marriage; wedding.*

[1139] γαμίζω *gamizō* 7x also spelled γαμίσκω, *to give in marriage, permit to marry,* 1 Cor. 7:38 [1061]

[1140] γαμίσκω *gamiskō* 1x see γαμίζω [1061]

[1141] γάμος *gamos* 16x *a wedding; nuptial festivities, a marriage festival,* Mt. 22:2; 25:10; Jn. 2:1, 2; Rev. 19:7, 9; any *feast* or *banquet,* Lk. 12:36; 14:8; *the marriage state,* Heb. 13:4 [1062] See *marry, marriage; wedding.*

[1142] γάρ *gar* 1,041x *for.* (1) Cause or reason, *for,* Mt. 1:20; Jn 2:25. (2) Explanation or clarification such as the details of a circumstance, *for, you see, now,* Mt. 1:18; 12:40; Mk. 7:3. (3) Inference, *so, then,* Jas. 1:17 [1063]

[1143] γαστήρ *gastēr* 9x *the belly, stomach; the womb,* Lk. 1:31; ἐν γαστρὶ ἔχειν, *to be with child,* Mt. 1:18, 23; 24:19, et al.; γαστέρες, *gluttons,* Tit. 1:12 [1064]

[1145] γε *ge* 24x an enclitic particle imparting emphasis, translated with various terms and its force is often so weak that it cannot be translated; *at least, indeed, even;* often used with other words; εἴ γε, *if indeed,* Gal 3:4, [1065]

[1146] Γεδεών *Gedeōn* 1x *Gideon* (Judges 6-8), pr. name, indecl., Heb. 11:32* [1066]

[1147] γέεννα *geenna* 12x *Gehenna,* pr. *the valley of Hinnom,* south of Jerusalem, once celebrated for the horrid worship of Moloch, and afterwards polluted with every species of filth, as well as the carcasses of animals, and dead bodies of malefactors; to consume which, in order to avert the pestilence which such a mass of corruption would occasion, constant fires were kept burning; hence, *hell, the fires of Tartarus, the place of punishment in Hades,* Mt. 5:22, 29, 30; 10:28; 18:9, et al. [1067] See *hell.*

[1149] Γεθσημανί *Gethsēmani* 2x *Gethsemane,* pr. name, indecl., Mt. 26:36; Mk. 14:32* [1068]

[1150] γείτων *geitōn* 4x *a neighbor,* Lk. 14:12; 15:6, 9; Jn. 9:8* [1069]

[1151] γελάω *gelaō* 2x *to laugh, smile;* by impl. *to be merry, happy, to rejoice,* Lk. 6:21, 25* [1070]

[1152] γέλως *gelōs* 1x *laughter;* by impl. *mirth, joy, rejoicing,* Jas. 4:9* [1071]

[1153] γεμίζω *gemizō* 8x *to fill,* Mt. 4:37; 15:36, et al. [1072]

[1154] γέμω *gemō* 11x *to be full,* Mt. 23:27; Lk. 11:39, et al. [1073] See *(to be) covered; (to be) full.*

[1155] γενεά *genea* 43x pr. *birth;* hence, *progeny; a generation* of mankind, Mt. 11:16; 23:36, et al.; *a generation,* a step in a genealogy, Mt. 1:17; *a generation,* an interval of time, *an age;* in NT *course of life,* in respect of its events, interests, or character, Lk. 16:8; Acts 13:36 [1074] See *age; generation; race.*

[1156] γενεαλογέω *genealogeō* 1x *to reckon one's descent, derive one's origin,* Heb. 7:6* [1075]

[1157] γενεαλογία *genealogia* 2x *genealogy, catalogue of ancestors, history of descent,* 1 Tim. 1:4; Tit. 3:9* [1076]

[1160] γενέσια *genesia* 2x pr. *a day observed in memory of the dead;* in NT equivalent to γενέθλια, *celebration of one's birthday, birthday-festival,* Mt. 14:6; Mk. 6:21* [1077]

[1161] γένεσις *genesis* 5x *birth, nativity,* Mt. 1:18; Lk. 1:14; Jas. 1:23; *successive generation, descent, lineage,* Mt. 1:1; meton. *life,* Mt. 1:18; Jas. 3:6* [1078]

[1162] γενετή *genetē* 1x *birth,* Jn. 9:1* [1079]

[1163] γένημα *genēma* 4x *natural produce, fruit, increase,* Mt. 26:29; Mk. 14:25; Lk. 12:18; 22:18; 2 Cor. 9:10* [1081]

[1164] γεννάω *gennaō* 97x *to beget, generate,* Mt. 1:2-16, et al.; of women, *to bring forth, bear, give birth to,* Lk. 1:13, 57, et al.; pass. *to be born, produced,* Mt. 2:1, 4, et al.; met. *to produce, excite, give occasion to, effect,* 2 Tim. 2:23; from the Hebrew, *to constitute as son, to constitute as king,* or *as the representative* or *viceregent of God,* Acts 13:33; Heb. 1:5; 5:5; by impl. *to be a parent to* any one; pass. *to be a son* or *child to* any one, Jn. 1:13; 1 Cor. 4:15, et al. [1080] See *bear a child; born; father; give birth.*

[1165] γέννημα *gennēma* 4x *what is born* or *produced, offspring, progeny, brood,* Mt. 3:7; 12:34, et al.; *fruit, produce,* Mt. 26:29; Mk. 14:25, et al.; *fruit, increase,* Lk. 12:18; 2 Cor. 9:10 [1081]

[1166] Γεννησαρέτ *Gennēsaret* 3x *Gennesaret,* a lake of Palestine, called also the *Sea of Tiberias,* Mt. 14:34; Mk. 6:53; Lk. 5:1* [1082]

[1168] γεννητός *gennētos* 2x *born* or *produced of,* Mt. 11:11; Lk. 7:28* [1084]

[1169] γένος *genos* 20x *offspring, progeny,* Acts 17:28, 29; *family, kindred, lineage,* Acts 7:13, et al.; *race, nation, people,* Mk. 7:26; Acts 4:36, et al.; *kind, sort, species,* Mt. 13:47, et al. [1085] See *family; kind; offspring; people.*

[1170] Γερασηνός *Gerasēnos* 3x also spelled Γεργεσηνός, *from Gerasene,* belonging to the city of Gerasa, Mk. 5:1; Lk. 8:26, 37* [1086]

[1172] γερουσία *gerousia* 1x *a senate, assembly of elders; the elders* of Israel collectively, Acts 5:21* [1087]

[1173] γέρων *gerōn* 1x *an old man,* Jn. 3:4* [1088]

[1174] γεύομαι *geuomai* 15x *to taste,* Mt. 27:34; Jn. 2:9; absol. *to eat,* Acts 10:10, et al.; met. *to have perception of, experience,* Heb. 6:4, 5; 1 Pet. 2:3; θανάτου γεύεσθαι, *to experience death, to die,* Mt. 16:28, et al. [1089] See *eat; partake; taste.*

[1175] γεωργέω *geōrgeō* 1x *to cultivate, till the earth,* Heb. 6:7* [1090]

[1176] γεώργιον *geōrgion* 1x *cultivated field* or *ground, a farm,* 1 Cor. 3:9* [1091]

[1177] γεωργός *geōrgos* 19x *a farmer, one who tills the earth,* 2 Tim. 2:6; Jas. 5:7; in NT spc. *a vine-dresser, keeper of a vineyard,* i.q. ἀμπελουργός, Mt. 21:33, 34, et al. [1092] See *farmer; tenant farmer.*

[1178] γῆ *gē* 250x *earth, soil,* Mt. 13:5; Mk. 4:8, et al.; *the ground, surface of the earth,* Mt. 10:29; Lk.

6:49, et al.; *the land,* as opposed to the sea or a lake, Lk. 5:11; Jn. 21:8, 9, 11; *the earth, world,* Mt. 5:18, 35, et al.; by synec. *the inhabitants of the earth,* Mt. 5:13; 6:10; 10:34; *a land, region, tract, country, territory,* Mt. 2:20; 14:34;by way of eminence, *the* chosen *land,* Mt. 5:5; 24:30; 27:45; Eph. 6:3; *the inhabitants of a region* or *country,* Mt. 10:15; 11:24, et al. [1093] See *earth; ground; land; soil.*

[1179] γῆρας *gēras* 1x gen. *old age,* Lk. 1:36* [1094]

[1180] γηράσκω *gēraskō* 2x *to be* or *become old,* Jn. 21:18; Heb. 8:13* [1095]

[1181] γίνομαι *ginomai* 669x pluperfect, ἐγενόει (3rd sg), *to come into existence; to be created, exist by creation,* Jn. 1:3, 10; Heb. 11:3; Jas. 3:9; *to be born, produced, grow,* Mt. 21:19; Jn. 8:58, et al.; *to arise, come on, occur,* as the phenomena of nature, etc.; Mt. 8:24, 26; 9:16, et al.; *to come, approach,* as morning or evening, Mt. 8:16; 14:15, 23; *to be appointed, constituted, established,* Mk. 2:27; Gal. 3:17, et al.; *to take place, come to pass, happen, occur,* Mt. 1:22; 24:6, 20, 21, 34, et al. freq.; *to be done, performed, effected,* Mt. 21:42, et al.; *to be fulfilled, satisfied,* Mt. 6:10; 26:42, et al.; *to come into a particular state* or *condition; to become, assume the character and appearance* of anything, Mt. 5:45, et al.; *to become* or *be made* anything, *be changed* or *converted,* Mt. 4:3; 21:42; Mk. 1:17, et al.; *to be,* Mt. 11:26; 19:8; γίνεσθαι ὑπό τινα, *to be subject to,* Gal. 4:4; γίνεσθαι ἐν ἑαυτῷ, *to come to one's self, to recover from a trance* or *surprise,* Acts 12:11; μὴ γένοιτο, *let it not be, far be it from, God forbid,* Lk. 20:16; Rom. 3:4, 31, et al.; *to be kept, celebrated, solemnized,* as festivals, Mt. 26:2, et al.; *to be finished, completed,* Heb. 4:3 [1096] See *be; become.*

[1182] γινώσκω *ginōskō* 222x *to know,* whether the action be inceptive or complete and settled; *to perceive,* Mt. 22:18; Mk. 5:29; 8:17; 12:12; Lk. 8:46; *to mark, discern,* Mt. 25:24; Lk. 19:44; *to ascertain by examination,* Mk. 6:38; Jn. 7:51; Acts 23:28; *to understand,* Mk. 4:13; Lk. 18:34; Jn. 12:16; 13:7; Acts 8:30; 1 Cor. 14:7, 9; *to acknowledge,* Mt. 7:23; 2 Cor. 3:2; *to resolve, conclude,* Lk. 16:4; Jn. 7:26; 17:8; *to be assured,* Lk. 21:20; Jn. 6:69; 8:52; 2 Pet. 1:20; *to be skilled, to be master of* a thing, Mt. 16:3; Acts 21:37; *to know* carnally, Mt. 1:25; Lk. 1:34; from the Hebrew, *to view with favor,* 1 Cor. 8:3; Gal. 4:9 [1097] See *know; realize; understand.*

[1183] γλεῦκος *gleukos* 1x pr. *the unfermented juice of grapes;* hence, *sweet new wine,* Acts 2:13* [1098]

[1184] γλυκύς *glykys* 4x *sweet,* Jas. 3:11-12; Rev. 10:9, 10* [1099]

[1185] γλῶσσα *glōssa* 50x *the tongue,* Mk. 7:33, 35, et al.; meton. *speech, talk,* 1 Jn. 3:18; *a tongue, language,* Acts 2:11; 1 Cor. 13:1, et al.; meton. *a language not proper to a speaker, a gift* or *faculty of such language,* Mk. 16:17; 1 Cor. 14:13, 14, 26, et al.; from Hebrew, *a nation,* as defined by its language, Rev. 5:9, et al.; let. *a tongue-shaped flale,* Acts 2:3 [1100] See *language; tongue.*

[1186] γλωσσόκομον *glōssokomon* 2x pr. *a box for keeping the tongues, mouth-pieces,* or *reeds* of musical instruments; hence, genr. *any box* or *receptacle;* in NT *a purse, money-bag,* Jn. 12:6; 13:29* [1101]

[1187] γναφεύς *gnapheus* 1x *a fuller, a bleacher,* one who cleans woolen cloth, Mk. 9:3* [1102]

[1188] γνήσιος *gnēsios* 4x *lawful, legitimate,* as children; *genuine,* in faith, etc.; 1 Tim. 1:2; Tit. 1:4; *true, sincere,* 2 Cor. 8:8; Phil. 4:3* [1103]

[1189] γνησίως *gnēsiōs* 1x *genuinely, sincerely,* Phil. 2:20* [1104]

[1190] γνόφος *gnophos* 1x *a thick cloud, darkness,* Heb. 12:18* [1105]

[1191] γνώμη *gnōmē* 9x *the mind,* as the means of knowing and judging; *assent,* Phlm. 14; *purpose, resolution,* Acts 20:3; *opinion, judgment,* 1 Cor. 1:10; 7:40; *suggestion, suggested advice,* as distinguished from positive injunction, Acts 20:3; 1 Cor. 7:25; 2 Cor. 8:10 [1106]

[1192] γνωρίζω *gnōrizō* 25x *to make known, reveal, declare,* Jn. 15:15; 17:26, et al.; *to know,* Phil. 1:22 [1107] See *make known; tell.*

[1194] γνῶσις *gnōsis* 29x *knowledge,* Lk. 1:77; *knowledge* of a special kind and relatively high character, Lk. 11:52; Rom. 2:20; 1 Tim. 6:20; more particularly in respect of Christian enlightenment, Rom. 15:14; 1 Cor. 8:10; 12:8; 2 Cor. 11:6, et al. [1108] See *knowledge.*

[1195] γνώστης *gnōstēs* 1x *one acquainted with* a thing, *knowing, skillful,* Acts 26:3* [1109]

[1196] γνωστός *gnōstos* 15x *known,* Jn. 18:15, 16, et al.; *certain, incontrovertible,* Acts 4:16; τὸ γνωστόν, *that which is known* or *is cognizable, the unquestionable attributes,* Rom. 1:19; subst. *an acquaintance,*

Lk. 2:44; 23:49 [1110] See *friend; known; outstanding.*

[1197] γογγύζω *gongyzō* 8x *to speak privately and in a low voice, mutter,* Jn. 7:32; *to utter secret and sullen discontent, express indignant complaint, murmur, grumble,* Mt. 20:11; Lk. 5:30; Jn. 6:41, 43, 61; 1 Cor. 10:10* [1111] See *grumble; murmur.*

[1198] γογγυσμός *gongysmos* 4x *a muttering, murmuring, low and suppressed discourse,* Jn. 7:12; *the expression of secret and sullen discontent, murmuring, complaint,* Acts 6:1; Phil. 2:14; 1 Pet. 4:9* [1112]

[1199] γογγυστής *gongystēs* 1x *a murmurer, grumbler,* Jude 16* [1113]

[1200] γόης *goēs* 1x *a juggler, diviner;* hence, by impl. *an impostor, cheat,* 2 Tim. 3:13* [1114]

[1201] Γολγοθᾶ *Golgotha* 3x *Golgotha,* pr. name, Mt. 27:33; Mk. 15:22; Jn. 19:17* [1115]

[1202] Γόμορρα *Gomorra* 4x *Gomorrha* (Gen. 19), pr. name, Mt. 10:15; Rom. 9:29; 2 Pet. 2:6; Jude 7* [1116]

[1203] γόμος *gomos* 3x *the cargo* of a ship, Acts 21:3; by impl. *merchandise,* Rev. 18:11, 12* [1117]

[1204] γονεύς *goneus* 20x *a father;* pl. in NT *parents,* Mt. 10:21; Lk. 2:27, 41; 2 Cor. 12:14 [1118] See *parents.*

[1205] γόνυ *gony* 12x *the knee,* Lk. 22:41; Heb. 12:12, et al. [1119] See *knee.*

[1206] γονυπετέω *gonypeteō* 4x *to fall upon one's knees, to kneel before,* Mt. 17:14; 27:29; Mk. 1:40; 10:17* [1120]

[1207] γράμμα *gramma* 14x pr. *that which is written* or *drawn; a letter, character of the alphabet, a writing, book,* Jn. 5:47; *an acknowledgment of debt, an account, a bill, note,* Lk. 16:6, 7; *an epistle, letter,* Acts 28:21; Gal. 6:11; ἱερὰ γράμματα, *the sacred books of the Old Testament, the Jewish Scriptures,* 2 Tim. 3:15; spc. *the letter* of the law of Moses, *the bare literal sense,* Rom. 2:27, 29; 7:6; 2 Cor. 3:6, 7; pl. *letters, learning,* Jn. 7:15; Acts 26:24* [1121] See *learning; letters; write, writing.*

[1208] γραμματεύς *grammateus* 63x *a scribe; a clerk, town-clerk, registrar, recorder,* Acts 19:35; *one skilled in the Jewish law, a teacher* or *interpreter of the law,* Mt. 2:4; 5:20, et al. freq.; genr. *a religious teacher,* Mt. 13:52; by synec. *any one distinguished for learning* or *wisdom,* 1 Cor. 1:20 [1122] See *scribe; teacher of the law.*

[1209] γραπτός *graptos* 1x *written,* Rom. 2:15* [1123]

[1210] γραφή *graphē* 50x *a writing;* in NT *the Holy Scriptures, the Jewish Scriptures,* or *Books of the Old Testament,* Mt. 21:42; Jn. 5:39, et al.; by synec. *doctrines, declarations, oracles,* or *promises* contained in the sacred books, Mt. 22:29; Mk. 12:24, et al.; spc. *a prophecy,* Mt. 26:54; Mk. 14:49; Lk. 4:21; 24:27, 32; with the addition of προφητική, Rom. 16:26; of τῶν προφητῶν, Mt. 26:56 [1124] See *Scripture.*

[1211] γράφω *graphō* 191x *to engrave, write,* according to the ancient method of writing on plates of metal, waxes tables, etc., Jn. 8:6, 8; *to write* on parchment, paper, etc., generally, Mt. 27:37, et al.; *to write letters to another,* Acts 23:25; 2 Cor. 2:9; 13:10, et al.; *to describe in writing,* Jn. 1:46; Rom. 10:5; *to inscribe* in a catalogue, etc., Lk. 10:20; Rev. 13:8; 17:8, et al.; *to write* a law, *command,* or *enact in writing,* Mk. 10:5; 12:19; Lk. 2:23, et al. [1125] See *Scripture; write, writing.*

[1212] γραώδης *graōdēs* 1x *old-womanish;* by impl. *silly, absurd,* 1 Tim. 4:7* [1126]

[1213] γρηγορέω *grēgoreō* 22x *to be awake, to watch,* Mt. 26:38, 40, 41; Mk. 14:34; 37, 38; *to be alive,* 1 Thess. 5:10; met. *to be watchful, attentive, vigilant, circumspect,* Mt. 25:13; Mk. 13:35, et al. [1127] See *guard; keep watch; wake, wake up; watch.*

[1214] γυμνάζω *gymnazō* 4x pr. *to train in gymnastic discipline;* hence, *to exercise* in anything, *train to use, discipline,* 1 Tim. 4:7; Heb. 5:14; 12:11; 2 Pet. 2:14* [1128]

[1215] γυμνασία *gymnasia* 1x pr. *gymnastic exercise;* hence, *bodily discipline* of any kind, 1 Tim. 4:8* [1129]

[1217] γυμνιτεύω *gymniteuō* 1x *to be poorly clad,* 1 Cor. 4:11* [1130]

[1218] γυμνός *gymnos* 15x *naked, without clothing,* Mk. 14:51, 52; *without the upper garment, and clad only with an inner garment* or *tunic,* Jn. 21:7; *poorly* or *meanly clad, destitute of proper and sufficient clothing,* Mt. 25:36, 38, 43, 44; Acts 19:16; Jas. 2:15; met. *unclothed* with a body, 2 Cor. 5:3; *not covered, uncovered, open, manifest,* Heb. 4:13; *bare, mere,* 1 Cor. 15:37; *naked of* spiritual *clothing,* Rev. 3:17; 16:15; 17:16 [1131] See *naked; unclothed.*

[1219] γυμνότης *gymnotēs* 3x *nakedness; want of proper and sufficient clothing,* Rom. 8:35; 2 Cor. 11:27; spiritual *nakedness, being destitute of* spiritual *clothing,* Rev. 3:18* [1132]

[1220] γυναικάριον *gynaikarion* 1x *a little woman; a trifling, weak, silly woman,* 2 Tim. 3:6* [1133]

[1221] γυναικεῖος *gynaikeios* 1x *pertaining to women, female,* 1 Pet. 3:7* [1134]

[1222] γυνή *gynē* 215x *a woman,* Mt. 5:28, et al.; *a* married *woman, wife,* Mt. 5:31, 32; 14:3, et al.; in the voc. ὦ γύναι, *O woman!* an ordinary mode of addressing females under every circumstance; met. used of the Church, as united to Christ, Rev. 19:7; 21:9 [1135] See *wife; woman.*

[1223] Γώγ *Gōg* 1x *Gog,* pr. name of a nation, indecl., Rev. 20:8* [1136]

[1224] γωνία *gōnia* 9x *an* exterior *angle, projecting corner,* Mt. 6:5; 21:42; *an* interior *angle;* by impl. *a* dark *corner, obscure place,* Acts 26:26; *corner, extremity,* or *quarter* of the earth, Rev. 7:1; 20:8 [1137] See *capstone; corner; cornerstone.*

[1227] δαιμονίζομαι *daimonizomai* 13x in NT *to be possessed, afflicted, vexed, by a demon* or *evil spirit,* i.q. δαιμόνιον ἔχειν, Mt. 4:24; 8:16, 28, 33 [1139] See *demon-possessed.*

[1228] δαιμόνιον *daimonion* 63x *a* heathen *god, deity,* Acts 17:18; 1 Cor. 10:20, 21; Rev. 9:20; in NT, *a demon, evil spirit,* Mt. 7:22; 9:33, 34; 10:8; 12:24 [1140] See *demon.*

[1229] δαιμονιώδης *daimoniōdēs* 1x *pertaining to* or *proceeding from demons; demonic, devilish,* Jas. 3:15* [1141]

[1230] δαίμων *daimōn* 1x *a god, a superior power;* in NT *a malignant demon, evil angel,* Mt. 8:31* [1142]

[1231] δάκνω *daknō* 1x *to bite, sting;* met. *to molest, vex, injure,* Gal. 5:15* [1143]

[1232] δάκρυον *dakryon* 10x also spelled δάκρυ, *a tear* [1144] See *tears.*

[1233] δακρύω *dakryō* 1x *to shed tears, weep,* Jn. 11:35* [1145]

[1234] δακτύλιος *daktylios* 1x *a ring for the finger,* Lk. 15:22* [1146]

[1235] δάκτυλος *daktylos* 8x *a finger,* Mt. 23:4; Mk. 7:33; from Hebrew, *power,* Lk. 11:20 [1147]

[1236] Δαλμανουθά *Dalmanoutha* 1x *Dalmanutha,* indecl., a small town on the shore of the Sea of Tiberias, Mk. 8:10* [1148]

[1237] Δαλματία *Dalmatia* 1x *Dalmatia,* 2 Tim. 4:10* [1149]

[1238] δαμάζω *damazō* 4x also spelled δανείζω, *to subdue, tame,* Mk. 5:4; Jas. 3:7; met. *to restrain within proper limits,* Jas. 3:8* [1150]

[1239] δάμαλις *damalis* 1x *a heifer, young cow,* Heb. 9:13* [1151]

[1240] Δάμαρις *Damaris* 1x *Damaris,* pr. name, Acts 17:34* [1152]

[1241] Δαμασκηνός *Damaskēnos* 1x *A Damascene, a native of Damascus,* 2 Cor. 11:32* [1153]

[1242] Δαμασκός *Damaskos* 15x *Damascus,* the capital city of Syria [1154]

[1244] δανείζω *daneizō* 4x see δανίζω [1155]

[1245] δάνειον *daneion* 1x *a loan, debt,* Mt. 18:27* [1156]

[1248] Δανιήλ *Daniēl* 1x *Daniel,* pr. name, indecl., Mt. 24:15* [1158]

[1250] δανιστής *danistēs* 1x *a money-lender, creditor,* Lk. 7:41* [1157]

[1251] δαπανάω *dapanaō* 5x *to expend, be at expense,* Mk. 5:26; Acts 21:24; 2 Cor. 12:15; *to spend, waste, consume by extravagance,* Lk. 15:14; Jas. 4:3* [1159]

[1252] δαπάνη *dapanē* 1x *expense, cost,* Lk. 14:28* [1160]

[1253] Δαυίδ *Dauid* 59x also spelled Δανείδ and Δαβίδ, *David,* pr. name, indecl., Mt. 1:6; Lk. 1:27; Acts 2:29; Rom. 1:3; 2 Tim. 2:28 [1138]

[1254] δέ *de* 2,792x a particle with a slight adversative force, closer in meaning to καί than to ἀλλά, sometimes translated by punctuation such as a period or comma, *and,* Mt. 1:2–16; 5:31; linking a series without any necessary adversative force, *and, now, then,* Acts 4:5; Rom. 8:28; *now,* resuming an interrupted discourse, Mt 3:4; Lk. 4:1; 2 Cor. 2:10; Gal. 2:6; *but* with a slight adversative force, Mt. 6:1; 2 Cor. 2:15 [1161]

[1255] δέησις *deēsis* 18x *entreaty; prayer, supplication,* Lk. 1:13; 2:37; 5:33 [1162] See *petition; prayer; request; supplication.*

[1256] δεῖ *dei* 101x *it is binding, it is necessary, it is proper; it is inevitable,* Acts 21:22 [1163] See *must; necessary; ought; should.*

[1257] δεῖγμα *deigma* 1x pr. *that which is shown, a specimen, sample;* met. *an example* by way of warning, Jude 7* [1164]

[1258] δειγματίζω *deigmatizō* 2x *to make a public show* or *spectacle of,* Mt. 1:19; Col. 2:15* [1165]

[1259] δείκνυμι *deiknymi* 30x also formed δεικνύω 3x, *to show, point out, present to the sight,* Mt. 4:8; 8:4; *to exhibit, permit to see, cause to be seen,* Jn. 2:18; 10:32; 1 Tim. 6:15; *to demonstrate, prove,* Jas. 2:18; 3:13; met. *to teach, make known, declare, announce,* Mt. 16:21; Jn. 5:20; Acts 10:28 [1166] See *demonstrate; show.*

[1260] δεικνύω *deiknyō* 3x see δείκνυμι, Mt. 16:21; Jn. 2:18; Rev. 22:8* [**]

[1261] δειλία *deilia* 1x *timidity,* 2 Tim. 1:7* [1167]

[1262] δειλιάω *deiliaō* 1x *to be timid, be in fear,* Jn. 14:27* [1168]

[1264] δειλός *deilos* 3x *timid, fearful, cowardly,* Mt. 8:26; Mk. 4:40; Rev. 21:8* [1169]

[1265] δεῖνα *deina* 1x *such a one, a certain one,* Mt. 26:18* [1170]

[1267] δεινῶς *deinōs* 2x *dreadfully, grievously, greatly, terribly,* Mt. 8:6; Lk. 11:53* [1171]

[1268] δειπνέω *deipneō* 4x *to eat* or *dine,* Lk. 17:8; 22:20; 1 Cor. 11:25; Rev. 3:20 [1172]

[1270] δεῖπνον *deipnon* 16x pr. *a meal; supper, the principal meal taken in the evening,* Lk. 14:12; Jn. 13:2, 4; meton. *food,* 1 Cor. 11:21; *a feast, banquet,* Mt. 23:6; Mk. 6:21; 12:39 [1173] See *banquet; feast; supper.*

[1272] δεισιδαιμονία *deisidaimonia* 1x *fear of the gods;* in a bad sense, *superstition; a form of religious belief,* Acts 25:19* [1175]

[1273] δεισιδαίμων *deisidaimōn* 1x *reverencing the gods and divine things, religious;* in a bad sense, *superstitious;* in NT *careful and precise in the discharge of religious services,* Acts 17:22* [1174]

[1274] δέκα *deka* 25x *ten,* Mt. 20:24; 25:1; ἡμερῶν δέκα, *ten days, a few days, a short time,* Rev. 2:10 [1176] See *ten.*

[1277] δεκαοκτώ *dekaoktō* 2x *eighteen,* Lk. 13:4, 11* [1176 + 2532 + 3638]

[1278] δεκαπέντε *dekapente* 3x *fifteen,* indecl., Jn. 11:18; Acts 27:28; Gal. 1:18* [1178]

[1279] Δεκάπολις *Dekapolis* 3x *Decapolis,* a district of Palestine beyond Jordan, Mk. 5:20; 7:31; Mt. 4:25* [1179]

[1280] δεκατέσσαρες *dekatessares* 5x *fourteen,* Mt. 1:17; 2 Cor. 12:2; Gal. 2:1* [1180]

[1281] δέκατος *dekatos* 7x *tenth,* Jn. 1:39; Rev. 11:13; 21:20; δεκάτη, sc. μερίς, *a tenth part, tithe,* Heb. 7:2, 4, 8, 9* [1181, 1182] See *tenth; tithe.*

[1282] δεκατόω *dekatoō* 2x *to cause to pay tithes;* pass. *to be tithed, pay tithes,* Heb. 7:6, 9* [1183]

[1283] δεκτός *dektos* 5x *accepted, acceptable, agreeable, approved,* Lk. 4:24; Acts 10:35; Phil. 4:18; by impl. when used of a certain time, *marked by* divine *acceptance, propitious,* Lk. 4:19; 2 Cor. 6:2* [1184]

[1284] δελεάζω *deleazō* 3x pr. *to entrap, take* or *catch* with a bait; met. *allure, entice,* Jas. 1:14; 2 Pet. 2:14, 18* [1185]

[1285] δένδρον *dendron* 25x *a tree,* Mt. 3:10; 7:17; 13:32 [1186] See *tree.*

[1287] δεξιολάβος *dexiolabos* 1x *one posted on the right hand; a flank guard; a light armed spearman,* Acts 23:23* [1187]

[1288] δεξιός *dexios* 54x *right,* as opposed to left, Mt. 5:29, 30; Lk. 6:6; ἡ δεξιά, sc. χείρ, *the right hand,* Mt. 6:3; 27:29; τὰ δεξιά, sc. μέρη, *the parts towards the right hand, the right hand side;* καθίζειν, or, καθῆσθαι, or, ἑστάναι, ἐκ δεξιῶν [μερῶν] τινος, *to sit* or *stand at the right hand of any one,* as a mark of the highest honor and dignity which he can bestow, Mt. 20:20; 26:64; εἶνι ἐκ δεξιῶν [μερῶν] τινος, *to be at one's right hand,* as a helper, Acts 2:25; δεξιὰς (χεῖρας) διδόναι, *to give the right hand* to any one, as a pledge of sincerity in one's promises, Gal. 2:9 [1188] See *right; right hand; right side.*

[1289] δέομαι *deomai* 22x *to be in want, to need; to ask, request,* Mt. 9:38; Lk. 5:12; 8:28, 38; in NT absol. *to pray, offer prayer, beseech, supplicate,* Lk. 21:36; 22:32; Acts 4:31; 8:22, 24 [1189] See *ask; beg; beseech; plead; pray.*

[1290] δέος *deos* 1x *fear,* Heb. 12:28* [127]

[1291] Δερβαῖος *Derbaios* 1x *an inhabitant of Derbe,* Acts 20:4* [1190]

[1292] Δέρβη *Derbē* 3x *Derbe,* a city of Lycaonia, Acts 14:6, 20; 16:0* [1191]

[1293] δέρμα *derma* 1x *the skin* of an animal, Heb. 11:37* [1192]

[1294] δερμάτινος *dermatinos* 2x *made of skin, leathern,* Mt. 3:4; Mk. 1:6* [1193]

[1296] δέρω *derō* 15x *to skin, flay;* hence, *to eat, scourge, beat,* Mt. 21:35; Mk. 12:3, 5; 13:9 [1194] See *beat; strike.*

[1297] δεσμεύω *desmeuō* 3x *to bind, bind up,* as a bundle, Mt. 23:4; *to bind, confine,* Lk. 8:29; Acts 22:4* [1195]

[1299] δέσμη *desmē* 1x *a bundle,* as of tares, Mt. 13:30* [1197]

[1300] δέσμιος *desmios* 16x *one bound, a prisoner,* Mt. 27:15, 16; Mk. 15:6 [1198] See *prisoner.*

[1301] δεσμός *desmos* 18x *a bond, anything by which one is bound, a cord, chain, fetters,* etc.; and by meton. *imprisonment,* Lk. 8:29; Acts 16:26; 20:23; *a string* or *ligament,* as of the tongue, Mk. 7:35; met. *an impediment, infirmity,* Lk. 13:16 [1199] See *bond; chain; fetter.*

[1302] δεσμοφύλαξ *desmophylax* 3x *a keeper of a prison, jailer,* Acts 16:23, 27, 36* [1200]

[1303] δεσμωτήριον *desmōtērion* 4x *a prison,* Mt. 11:2; Acts 5:21, 23; 16:26* [1201]

[1304] δεσμώτης *desmōtēs* 2x *a prisoner,* i.q. δέσμιος, Acts 27:1, 42* [1202]

[1305] δεσπότης *despotēs* 10x *a lord, master,* especially of slaves, 1 Tim. 6:1, 2; 2 Tim. 2:21; Tit. 2:9; 1 Pet. 2:18; by impl. as denoting the possession of supreme authority, *Lord, sovereign,* used of God, Lk. 2:29; Acts 4:24; Rev. 6:10; and of Christ, 2 Pet. 2:1; Jude 4 [1203] See *lord; master.*

[1306] δεῦρο *deuro* 9x *here;* used also as a sort of imperative, *come, Come here!* Mt. 19:21; Mk. 10:21; used of time, ἄχρι τοῦ δεῦρο, sc. χρόνου, *to the present time,* Rom. 1:13 [1204]

[1307] δεῦτε *deute* 12x *come,* Mt. 4:19; 11:28; as a particle of exhortation, incitement, etc., and followed by an imperative, *come now,* etc., Mt. 21:38; 28:6 [1205] See *come.*

[1308] δευτεραῖος *deuteraios* 1x *on the second day* of a certain state or process, and used as an epithet of the subject or agent, Acts 28:13* [1206]

[1311] δεύτερος *deuteros* 43x *second,* Mt. 22:26; τὸ δεύτερον, *again, the second time, another time,* Jude 5; so ἐκ δευτέρου, Mt. 26:42; and ἐν τῷ δευτέρῳ, Acts 7:13 [1208] See *second.*

[1312] δέχομαι *dechomai* 56x *to take* into one's hands, etc., Lk. 2:28; 16:6, 7; *to receive,* Acts 22:5; 28:21; Phil. 4:18; *to receive into and retain, contain,* Acts 3:21; met. *to receive* by the hearing, *learn, acquire a knowledge of,* 2 Cor. 11:4; Jas. 1:21; *to receive, admit, grant access to, receive kindly, welcome,* Mt. 10:40, 41; 18:5; *to receive* in hospitality, *entertain,* Lk. 9:53; Heb. 11:31; *to bear with, bear patiently,* 2 Cor. 11:16; met. *to receive, approve, assent to,* Mt. 11:14; Lk. 8:13; Acts 8:14; 11:1; *to admit,* and by impl. *to embrace, follow,* 1 Cor. 2:14; 2 Cor. 8:17 [1209] See *receive; welcome.*

[1313] δέω *deō* 43x *to bind, tie,* Mt. 13:30; 21:2; *to bind, confine,* Mt. 27:2; 14:3; *to impede, hinder,* 2 Tim. 2:9; *to bind* with infirmity, Lk. 13:16; *to bind* by a legal or moral tie, as marriage, Rom. 7:2; 1 Cor. 7:27, 39; by impl. *to impel, compel,* Acts 20:22; in NT *to pronounce* or *declare to be binding* or *obligatory,* or, *to declare to be prohibited and unlawful,* Mt. 16:19; 18:18 [1210] See *bind; tie, tie up.*

[1314] δή *dē* 5x a particle that adds an intensity of expression to a term or clause. Its simplest and most ordinary uses are when it gives impressiveness to an affirmation, *indeed, really, doubtless, now, then, therefore,* Mt. 13:23; or earnestness to a call, injunction, or entreaty, Lk. 2:15; Acts 13:2; 15:36; 1 Cor. 16:20* [1211]

[1316] δῆλος *dēlos* 3x pr. *clearly visible; plain, manifest, evident,* Mt. 26:73; 1 Cor. 15:27; Gal. 3:11* [1212]

[1317] δηλόω *dēloō* 7x *to render manifest* or *evident; to make known, to tell, relate, declare,* 1 Cor. 1:11; Col. 1:8; *to show, point out, bring to light,* 1 Cor. 3:13; *to indicate, signify,* Heb. 9:8; 12:27; 1 Pet. 1:11 [1213]

[1318] Δημᾶς *Dēmas* 3x *Demas,* pr. name, Col. 4:14; 2 Tim. 4:10; Phlm. 24* [1214]

[1319] δημηγορέω *dēmēgoreō* 1x *to address a public assembly, to deliver a public oration,* Acts 12:21* [1215]

[1320] Δημήτριος *Dēmētrios* 3x *Demetrius,* pr. name. (1) *The Ephesian silversmith,* Acts 19:24, 38. (2) *A certain Christian,* 3 Jn. 12* [1216]

[1321] δημιουργός *dēmiourgos* 1x pr. *one who labors for the public,* or, *exercises some public calling;*

an architect, especially, the Divine *Architect* of the universe, Heb. 11:10 [1217]

[1322] δῆμος *dēmos* 4x *the people,* Acts 12:22; 17:5; 19:30, 33* [1218]

[1323] δημόσιος *dēmosios* 4x *public, belonging to the public,* Acts 5:18; δημοσίᾳ, *publicly,* Acts 16:37; 18:28; 20:20* [1219]

[1324] δηνάριον *dēnarion* 16x Latin *denarius,* a Roman silver coin; the name originally meant *ten asses,* Mt. 18:28; Mk. 6:37; Rev. 6:6 [1220] See *coin; days wage; denarius.*

[1327] δήπου *dēpou* 1x *now in some way, surely,* Heb. 2:16* [1222]

[1328] διά *dia* 667x. (1) gen., *through,* used of place or medium, Mt. 7:13; Lk. 6:1; 2 Cor. 11:33; *through,* of time, *during, in the course of,* Heb. 2:15; Acts 5:19; *through,* of immediate agency, causation, instrumentality, *by means of, by,* Jn. 1:3; Acts 3:18; of means or manner, *through, by, with,* Lk. 8:4; 2 Cor. 5:7; 8:8; of state or condition, *in a state of,* Rom. 4:11.

(2) acc., used of causation which is not direct and immediate in the production of a result, *on account of, because of, for the sake of, with a view to,* Mk. 2:27; Jn. 1:31; rarely, *through, while subject to* a state of untoward circumstances, Gal. 4:13 [1223]

[1329] διαβαίνω *diabainō* 3x *to pass through* or *over,* Lk. 16:26; Acts 16:9; Heb. 11:29* [1224]

[1330] διαβάλλω *diaballō* 1x *to throw* or *convey through* or *over; to thrust through; to defame, inform against,* Lk. 16:1* [1225]

[1331] διαβεβαιόομαι *diabebaioomai* 2x *to assert strongly, insist,* 1 Tim. 1:7; Tit. 3:8* [1226]

[1332] διαβλέπω *diablepō* 3x *to look through; to view steadily,* Mk. 8:25*; to see clearly* or *steadily,* Mt. 7:5; Lk. 6:42* [1227]

[1333] διάβολος *diabolos* 37x *slanderer,* 1 Tim. 3:11; 2 Tim. 3:3; Tit. 2:3; *a treacherous informer, traitor,* Jn. 6:70; ὁ διάβολος, *the devil* [1228] See *devil.*

[1334] διαγγέλλω *diangellō* 3x *to publish abroad, to proclaim far and wide,* Lk. 9:60; Rom. 9:17; *to certify* to the public, *give notice,* Acts 21:26* [1229]

[1335] διαγίνομαι *diaginomai* 3x pas., *to continue through; to intervene, elapse* of time, Mk. 16:1; Acts 25:13; 27:9* [1230]

[1336] διαγινώσκω *diaginōskō* 2x pr. *to distinguish; to resolve determinately; to examine, inquire into,* judicially, Acts 23:15; 24:22* [1231]

[1338] διάγνωσις *diagnōsis* 1x pr. *an act of distinguishing* or *discernment; a determination; examination* judicially, *hearing, trial,* Acts 25:21* [1233]

[1339] διαγογγύζω *diagongyzō* 2x *to murmur, mutter, complain, grumble,* Lk. 15:2; 19:7* [1234]

[1340] διαγρηγορέω *diagrēgoreō* 1x *to remain awake; to wake thoroughly,* Lk. 9:32* [1235]

[1341] διάγω *diagō* 2x *to conduct* or *carry through* or *over; to pass* or *spend* time, *live,* 1 Tim. 2:2; Tit. 3:3* [1236]

[1342] διαδέχομαι *diadechomai* 1x *to receive by transmission; to receive in return,* Acts 7:45* [1237]

[1343] διάδημα *diadēma* 3x pr. *a band* or *crown; a diadem,* the badge of a sovereign, Rev. 12:3; 13:1; 19:12* [1238]

[1344] διαδίδωμι *diadidōmi* 4x *to deliver from hand to hand; to distribute, divide,* Lk. 11:22; 18:22; Jn. 6:11; Acts 4:35* [1239]

[1345] διάδοχος *diadochos* 1x *a successor,* Acts 24:27* [1240]

[1346] διαζώννυμι *diazōnnymi* 3x *to gird firmly round,* Jn. 13:4, 5; mid. *to gird round one's self, to put on,* Jn. 21:7* [1241]

[1347] διαθήκη *diathēkē* 33x *a testamentary disposition, will; a covenant,* Heb. 9:16, 17; Gal. 3:15; in NT, *a covenant* of God with men, Gal. 3:17; 4:24; Heb. 9:4; Mt. 26:28; *the writings of the old covenant,* 2 Cor. 3:14 [1242] See *covenant; testament; will.*

[1348] διαίρεσις *diairesis* 3x *a division; a distinction, difference, diversity,* 1 Cor. 12:4, 5, 6* [1243]

[1349] διαιρέω *diaireō* 2x *to divide, to divide out, distribute,* Lk. 15:12; 1 Cor. 12:11* [1244]

[1350] διακαθαίρω *diakathairō* 1x *to cleanse thoroughly,* Lk. 3:17* [1245]

[1351] διακαθαρίζω *diakatharizō* 1x *to cleanse thoroughly,* Mt. 3:12 [1245]

[1352] διακατελέγχομαι *diakatelenchomai* 1x *to maintain discussion strenuously and thoroughly, to totally refute,* Acts 18:28* [1246]

[1354] διακονέω *diakoneō* 37x *to wait, attend upon, serve,* Mt. 8:15; Mk. 1:31; Lk. 4:39; *to be an attendant* or *assistant,* Acts 19:22; *to minister to, relieve, assist,* or *supply with the necessaries of life, provide the means of living,* Mt. 4:11; 27:55; Mk. 1:13; 15:41; Lk. 8:3; *to fill the office of* διάκονος, *deacon, perform the duties of deacon,* 1 Tim. 3:10, 13; 1 Pet. 4:11; *to convey in charge, administer,* 2 Cor. 3:3; 8:19, 20; 1 Pet. 1:12; 4:10; pass. *to receive service,* Mt. 20:28; Mk. 10:45 [1247] See *serve.*

[1355] διακονία *diakonia* 34x *serving, service, waiting, attendance, the act of rendering friendly offices,* Lk. 10:40; 2 Tim. 4:11; Heb. 1:14; *relief, aid,* Acts 6:1; 11:29; 2 Cor. 8:4; 9:1, 12, 13; *a commission,* Acts 12:25; Rom. 15:31; *a commission* or *ministry* in the service of the Gospel, Acts 1:17, 25; 20:24; Rom. 11:13; 2 Cor. 4:1; 5:18; 1 Tim. 1:12; *service* in the Gospel, Acts 6:4; 21:19; 1 Cor. 16:15; 2 Cor. 6:3; 11:8; Eph. 4:12; Rev. 2:19; *a function, ministry,* or *office* in the Church, Rom. 12:7; 1 Cor. 12:5; Col. 4:17; 2 Tim. 4:5; *a ministering* in the conveyance of a revelation from God, 2 Cor. 3:7, 8, 9 [1248] See *ministry; service.*

[1356] διάκονος *diakonos* 29x *one who renders service* to another; *an attendant, servant,* Mt. 20:26; 22:13; Jn. 2:5, 9; *one who executes a commission, a deputy,* Rom. 13:4; Χριστοῦ, Θεοῦ, ἐν κυρίῳ, etc. *a* commissioned *minister* or *preacher* of the Gospel, 1 Cor. 3:5; 2 Cor. 6:4; *a minister* charged with an announcement or sentence, 2 Cor. 3:6; Gal. 2:17; Col. 1:23; *a minister* charged with a significant characteristic, Rom. 15:8; *a servitor, devoted follower,* Jn. 12:26; *a deacon* or *deaconess,* whose official duty was to superintend the alms of the Church, with other kindred services, Rom. 16:1; Phil. 1:1; 1 Tim. 3:8, 12 [1249] See *deacon; minister; servant.*

[1357] διακόσιοι *diakosioi* 8x *two hundred,* Mk. 6:37; Jn. 6:7; 21:8; Acts 23:23f.* [1250]

[1358] διακούω *diakouō* 1x *to hear* a thing *through; to hear* judicially, Acts 23:35* [1251]

[1359] διακρίνω *diakrinō* 19x *to separate, sever; to make a distinction* or *difference,* Acts 15:9; 1 Cor. 11:29; *to make to differ, distinguish, prefer, confer a superiority,* 1 Cor. 4:7; *to examine, scrutinize, estimate,* 1 Cor. 11:31; 14:29; *to discern, discriminate,* Mt. 16:3; *to judge, to decide a cause,* 1 Cor. 6:5; *to dispute, contend,* Acts 11:2; Jude 9; *to make a distinction* mentally, Jas. 2:4; Jude 22; in NT *to hesitate, be in doubt, doubt,* Mt. 21:21; Mk. 11:23 [1252] See *distinguish; doubt; evaluate; judge; waver.*

[1360] διάκρισις *diakrisis* 3x *a separation; a distinction,* or, *doubt,* Rom. 14:1; *a discerning, the act of discerning* or *distinguishing,* Heb. 5:14; *the faculty of distinguishing and estimating,* 1 Cor. 12:10* [1253]

[1361] διακωλύω *diakōlyō* 1x *to hinder, restrain, prohibit,* Mt. 3:14* [1254]

[1362] διαλαλέω *dialaleō* 2x *to talk with;* by impl. *to consult, deliberate,* Lk. 6:11; *to divulge, publish, spread by rumor,* Lk. 1:65* [1255]

[1363] διαλέγομαι *dialegomai* 13x *to discourse, argue, reason,* Acts 17:2, 17; 24:12; *to address, speak to,* Heb. 12:5; *to contend, dispute,* Mk. 9:34; Jude 9 [1256] See *argue; persuade; prove; reason.*

[1364] διαλείπω *dialeipō* 1x *to leave an interval; to stop, cease,* Lk. 7:45* [1257]

[1365] διάλεκτος *dialektos* 6x *speech; manner of speaking; peculiar language* of a nation, *dialect, vernacular idiom,* Acts 1:19; 2:6, 8; 21:40; 22:2; 26:14 [1258]

[1367] διαλλάσσομαι *diallassomai* 1x *to be reconciled* to another, Mt. 5:24* [1259]

[1368] διαλογίζομαι *dialogizomai* 16x pr. *to make a settlement of accounts; to reason, deliberate, ponder, consider,* Mt. 16:7, 8; Mk. 2:6, 8; Jn. 11:50; *to dispute, contend,* Mk. 9:33 [1260] See *argue; consider; discuss; wonder.*

[1369] διαλογισμός *dialogismos* 14x *reasoning, thought, cogitation, purpose,* Mt. 15:19; Mk. 7:21; *discourse, dispute, disputation, contention,* Lk. 9:46; *doubt, hesitation, scruple,* Lk. 24:38 [1261] See *argument; discussion; thought.*

[1370] διαλύω *dialyō* 1x *to dissolve, dissipate, disperse,* Acts 5:36* [1262]

[1371] διαμαρτύρομαι *diamartyromai* 15x *to make solemn affirmation, protest; to make a solemn and earnest charge,* Lk. 16:28; Acts 2:40; *to declare solemnly and earnestly,* Acts 8:25; 18:5 [1263] See *testify; warn.*

[1372] διαμάχομαι *diamachomai* 1x *to fight out, to fight resolutely;* met. *to contend vehemently, insist,* Acts 23:9* [1264]

[1373] διαμένω *diamenō* 5x *to continue throughout; to continue, be permanent* or *unchanged,* Lk. 1:22; Gal. 2:5; Heb. 1:11; 2 Pet. 3:4; *to continue, remain constant,* Lk. 22:28 [1265]

[1374] διαμερίζω *diamerizō* 11x *to divide into parts and distribute,* Mt. 27:35; Mk. 15:24; Acts 2:3; pass. in NT *to be in a state of dissension,* Lk. 11:17, 18; 12:52, 53 [1266] See *divide; part.*

[1375] διαμερισμός *diamerismos* 1x *division;* met. in NT *disunion, dissension,* Lk. 12:51* [1267]

[1376] διανέμω *dianemō* 1x *to distribute; to divulge, spread abroad,* Acts 4:17* [1268]

[1377] διανεύω *dianeuō* 1x *to signify by a nod, beckon, make signs,* Lk. 1:22* [1269]

[1378] διανόημα *dianoēma* 1x *thought,* Lk. 11:17* [1270]

[1379] διάνοια *dianoia* 12x pr. *thought, intention; the mind, intellect, understanding,* Mt. 22:37; Mk. 12:30; Lk. 10:27; *an operation of the understanding, thought, imagination,* Lk. 1:51; *insight, comprehension,* 1 Jn. 5:20; *mode of thinking and feeling, disposition of mind and heart, the affection,* Eph. 2:3; Col. 1:21 [1271] See *mind; thought; understanding.*

[1380] διανοίγω *dianoigō* 8x *to open,* Mk. 7:34, 35; Lk. 2:23; 24:31; Acts 7:56; met. *to open* the sense of a thing, *explain, expound,* Lk. 24:32; Acts 17:3; διανοίγειν τὸν νοῦν, τὴν καρδίαν, *to open the mind, the heart,* so as to understand and receive, Lk. 24:45; Acts 16:14* [1272]

[1381] διανυκτερεύω *dianyktereuō* 1x *to pass the night, spend the whole night,* Lk. 6:12* [1273]

[1382] διανύω *dianyō* 1x *to complete, finish,* Acts 21:7* [1274]

[1384] διαπαρατριβή *diaparatribē* 1x *constant disputation,* 1 Tim. 6:5* [3859]

[1385] διαπεράω *diaperaō* 6x *to pass through* or *over,* Mt. 9:1; 14:34; Mk. 5:21; 6:53; Lk. 16:26; Acts 21:2* [1276]

[1386] διαπλέω *diapleō* 1x *to sail through* or *over,* Acts 27:5* [1277]

[1387] διαπονέομαι *diaponeomai* 2x pr. *to be thoroughly exercised with labor; to be wearied; to be vexed,* Acts 4:2; 16:18* [1278]

[1388] διαπορεύομαι *diaporeuomai* 5x *to go* or *pass through,* Lk. 6:1; 13:22; Acts 16:4; *to pass by,* Lk. 18:36 [1279]

[1389] διαπορέω *diaporeō* 4x *to be utterly at a loss; to be in doubt and perplexity,* Lk. 9:7; Acts 2:12; 5:24; 10:17 [1280]

[1390] διαπραγματεύομαι *diapragmateuomai* 1x *to despatch a matter thoroughly; to make profit in business, gain in trade,* Lk. 19:15* [1281]

[1391] διαπρίω *diapriō* 2x *to divide with a saw, saw asunder; to grate* the teeth in a rage; pass. met. *to be cut* to the heart, *to be enraged,* Acts 5:33; 7:54* [1282]

[1395] διαρπάζω *diarpazō* 3x *to plunder, spoil, pillage,* Mt. 12:29; Mk. 3:27 (2x)* [1283]

[1397] διασαφέω *diasapheō* 2x *to make known, declare, tell plainly,* or *fully,* Mt. 13:36; 18:31* [1285]

[1398] διασείω *diaseiō* 1x pr. *to shake thoroughly* or *violently; to harass, intimidate, extort from,* Lk. 3:14* [1286]

[1399] διασκορπίζω *diaskorpizō* 9x *to disperse, scatter,* Mt. 26:31; Mk. 14:27; *to dissipate, waste,* Lk. 15:13; 16:1; *to winnow,* or, *to strew,* Mt. 25:24, 26 [1287] See *scatter.*

[1400] διασπάω *diaspaō* 2x *to pull* or *tear asunder* or *in pieces, burst,* Mk. 5:4; Acts 23:10* [1288]

[1401] διασπείρω *diaspeirō* 3x *to scatter abroad* or *in every direction,* as seen; *to disperse,* Acts 8:1, 4; 11:19* [1289] See *scatter.*

[1402] διασπορά *diaspora* 3x pr. *a scattering,* as of seed; *dispersion;* in NT meton. *the dispersed portion* of the Jews, specially termed *the dispersion,* Jn. 7:35; Jas. 1:1; 1 Pet. 1:1* [1290]

[1403] διαστέλλω *diastellō* 8x *to determine, issue a decision; to state* or *explain distinctly and accurately;* hence, *to admonish, direct, charge, command,* Acts 15:24; Heb. 12:20; when followed by a negative clause, *to interdict, prohibit,* Mt. 16:30; Mk. 5:43 [1291] See *command; order; warn.*

[1404] διάστημα *diastēma* 1x *interval, space, distance,* Acts 5:7 [1292]

[1405] διαστολή *diastolē* 3x *distinction, difference,* Rom. 3:22; 10:12; 1 Cor. 14:7* [1293]

[1406] διαστρέφω *diastrephō* 7x *to distort, turn away;* met. *to pervert, corrupt,* Mt. 17:17; Lk. 9:41; *to turn out of the way, cause to make defection,* Lk. 23:2; Acts 13:8; διεστραμμένος, *perverse, corrupt, erroneous* [1294]

[1407] διασῴζω *diasōzō* 8x *to bring safely through; to convey in safety,* Acts 23:24; pass. *to reach a place* or *state of safety,* Acts 27:43, 44; 28:1, 4; 1 Pet. 3:20; *to heal, to restore to health,* Mt. 14:36; Lk. 7:3* [1295]

[1408] διαταγή *diatagē* 2x *an injunction, institute, ordinance,* Rom. 13:2; Acts 7:53* [1296]

[1409] διάταγμα *diatagma* 1x *a mandate, commandment, ordinance,* Heb. 11:23* [1297] See *commandment.*

[1410] διαταράσσω *diatarassō* 1x *to confuse, perplex, to move* or *trouble greatly,* Lk. 1:29* [1298]

[1411] διατάσσω *diatassō* 16x pr. *to arrange, make a precise arrangement; to prescribe,* 1 Cor. 11:34; 16:1; Tit. 1:5; *to direct,* Lk. 8:55; Acts 20:13; *to charge,* Mt. 11:1; *to command,* Acts 18:2; *to ordain,* Gal. 3:19 [1299] See *command; direct; instruct; order.*

[1412] διατελέω *diateleō* 1x *to complete, finish;* intrans. *to continue, persevere,* in a certain state or course of action, Acts 27:33* [1300]

[1413] διατηρέω *diatēreō* 2x *to watch carefully, guard with vigilance; to treasure up,* Lk. 2:51; ἑαυτὸν ἐκ, *to keep one's self from, to abstain wholly from,* Acts 15:29* [1301]

[1416] διατίθημι *diatithēmi* 7x in NT only mid., so some list as διατίθεμαι, *to arrange; to arrange according to one's own mind; to make a disposition, to make a will; to settle the terms of a covenant, to ratify,* Acts 3:25; Heb. 8:10; 10:16; *to assign,* Lk. 22:29 [1303]

[1417] διατρίβω *diatribō* 9x pr. *to rub, wear away by friction;* met. *to pass* or *spend* time, *to remain, stay, tarry, continue,* Jn. 3:22; 11:54; Acts 12:19; 14:3, 28 [1304]

[1418] διατροφή *diatrophē* 1x *food, sustenance,* 1 Tim. 6:8* [1305]

[1419] διαυγάζω *diaugazō* 1x *to shine through, shine out, dawn,* 2 Pet. 1:19* [1306]

[1420] διαυγής *diaugēs* 1x *translucent, transparent,* Rev. 21:21* [1307]

[1422] διαφέρω *diapherō* 13x *to convey through, across,* Mk. 11:16; *to carry different ways* or *into different parts, separate;* pass. *to be borne, driven,* or *tossed hither and thither,* Acts 27:27; *to be proclaimed, published,* Acts 13:49; intrans. met. *to differ,* 1 Cor. 15:41; *to excel, be better* or *of greater value, be superior,* Mt. 6:26; 10:31; impers. διαφέρει, *it makes a difference, it is of consequence;* with οὐδέν, *it makes no difference, it is nothing,* Gal. 2:6 [1308] See *carry through; differ; spread out; valuable; (have) value.*

[1423] διαφεύγω *diapheugō* 1x *to flee through, escape by flight,* Acts 27:42* [1309]

[1424] διαφημίζω *diaphēmizō* 3x *to report, proclaim, publish, spread abroad,* Mt. 9:31; 28:15; Mk. 1:45* [1310]

[1425] διαφθείρω *diaphtheirō* 6x *to corrupt* or *destroy utterly; to waste, bring to decay,* Lk. 12:33; 2 Cor. 4:16; *to destroy,* Rev. 8:9; 11:18 (2x); met. *to corrupt, pervert utterly,* 1 Tim. 6:5* [1311] See *corrupt, corruption; destroy.*

[1426] διαφθορά *diaphthora* 6x *corruption, dissolution,* Acts 2:27, 31; 13:34, 35, 36, 37* [1312]

[1427] διάφορος *diaphoros* 4x *different, diverse, of different kinds,* Rom. 12:6; Heb. 9:10; *excellent, superior,* Heb. 1:4; 8:6* [1313]

[1428] διαφυλάσσω *diaphylassō* 1x *to keep* or *guard carefully* or *with vigilance; to guard, protect,* Lk. 4:10* [1314]

[1429] διαχειρίζω *diacheirizō* 2x pr. *to have in the hands, to manage;* mid. later, *to kill,* Acts 5:30; 26:21* [1315]

[1430] διαχλευάζω *diachleuazō* 1x *to jeer outright, deride,* Acts 2:13* [5512]

[1431] διαχωρίζω *diachōrizō* 1x *to depart, go away,* Lk. 9:33* [1316]

[1434] διδακτικός *didaktikos* 2x *apt* or *qualified to teach,* 1 Tim. 3:2; 2 Tim. 2:24* [1317]

[1435] διδακτός *didaktos* 3x pr. *taught, teachable,* of things; in NT *taught,* of person, Jn. 6:45; 1 Cor. 2:13* [1318]

[1436] διδασκαλία *didaskalia* 21x *the act* or *occupation of teaching,* Rom. 12:7; 1 Tim. 4:13; *information, instruction,* Rom. 15:4; 2 Tim. 3:16; *matter taught, precept, doctrine,* Mt. 15:9; 1 Tim. 1:10 [1319] See *doctrine; teaching.*

[1437] διδάσκαλος *didaskalos* 59x *a teacher, master,* Rom. 2:20; in NT as an equivalent, to ῥαββί, Jn. 1:39 [1320] See *rabbi; teacher.*

[1438] διδάσκω *didaskō* 97x *to teach,* Mt. 4:23; 22:16; *to teach* or *speak in a public assembly,* 1 Tim. 2:12; *to direct, admonish,* Mt. 28:15; Rom. 2:21 [1321] See *instruct; teach.*

[1439] διδαχή *didachē* 30x *instruction, the giving of instruction, teaching,* Mk. 4:2; 12:38; *instruction, what is taught, doctrine,* Mt. 16:12; Jn. 7:16, 17;

meton. *mode of teaching and kind of doctrine taught,* Mt. 7:28; Mk. 1:27 [1322] See *doctrine; instruction; teaching.*

[1440] δίδραχμον *didrachmon* 2x *a didrachmon* or *double drachma,* a silver coin equal to the drachma of Alexandria, to two Attic drachmas, to two Roman denarii, and to the half-shekel of the Jews, Mt. 17:24 (2x)* [1323]

[1441] Δίδυμος *Didymos* 3x *a twin; Didymus,* the Greek equivalent to the name Thomas, Jn. 11:16; 20:24; 21:2* [1324]

[1443] δίδωμι *didōmi* 415x pluperfect, ἐδεδώκειν, *to give, bestow, present,* Mt. 4:9; 6:11; Jn. 3:16; 17:2, et al. freq.; *to give, cast, throw,* Mt. 7:6; *to supply, suggest,* Mt. 10:19; Mk. 13:11; *to distribute* alms, Mt. 19:21; Lk. 11:41; *to pay* tribute, etc., Mt. 22:17; Mk. 12:14; Lk. 20:22; *to be the author* or *source* of a thing, Lk. 12:51; Rom. 11:8; *to grant, permit, allow,* Acts 2:27; 13:35; Mt. 13:11; 19:11; *to deliver to, entrust, commit to the charge* of anyone, Mt. 25:15; Mk. 12:9; *to give* or *deliver up,* Lk. 22:19; Jn. 6:51; *to reveal, teach,* Acts 7:38; *to appoint, constitute,* Eph. 1:22; 4:11; *to consecrate, devote, offer in sacrifice,* 2 Cor. 8:5; Gal. 1:4; Rev. 8:3; *to present, expose* one's self in a place, Acts 19:31; *to recompense,* Rev. 2:23; *to attribute, ascribe,* Jn. 9:24; Rev. 11:13; from the Hebrew, *to place, put, fix, inscribe,* Heb. 8:10; 10:16; *to infix, impress,* 2 Cor. 12:7; Rev. 13:16; *to inflict,* Jn. 18:22; 19:3; 2 Thess. 1:8; *to give in charge, assign,* Jn. 5:36; 17:4; Rev. 9:5; *to exhibit, put forth,* Mt. 24:24; Acts 2:19; *to yield, bear* fruit, Mt. 13:8; διδόναι ἐργασίαν, *to endeavor, strive,* Lk. 12:58; διδόναι ἀπόκρισιν, *to answer, reply,* Jn. 1:22; διδόναι τόπον, *to give place, yield,* Lk. 14:9; Rom. 12:19 [1325] See *give; grasp; permit; yield.*

[1444] διεγείρω *diegeirō* 6x *to arouse* or *awake thoroughly,* Mt. 1:24; Mk. 4:38, 39; Lk. 8:24; pass. *to be raised, excited, agitated,* as a sea, Jn. 6:18; met. *to stir up, arouse, animate,* 2 Pet. 1:13; 3:1 [1326]

[1445] διενθυμέομαι *dienthumeomai* 1x *to revolve thoroughly in the mind, consider carefully, ponder, reflect,* Acts 10:19* [1760]

[1447] διέξοδος *diexodos* 1x *a passage throughout; a line of road, a thoroughfare,* Mt. 22:9* [1327]

[1449] διερμηνευτής *diermēneutēs* 1x *an interpreter,* 1 Cor. 14:28* [1328]

[1450] διερμηνεύω *diermēneuō* 6x *to explain, interpret, translate,* Lk. 24:27; Acts 9:36; 1 Cor. 14:5, 13, 27; *to be able to interpret,* 1 Cor. 12:30* [1329]

[1451] διέρχομαι *dierchomai* 43x *to pass through,* Mk. 10:25; Lk. 4:30; *to pass over, cross,* Mk. 4:35; Lk. 8:22; *to pass along,* Lk. 19:4; *to proceed,* Lk. 2:15; Acts 9:38; *to travel through* or *over* a country, *wander about,* Mt. 12:43; Lk. 9:6; *to transfix, pierce,* Lk. 2:35; *to spread abroad, be prevalent,* as a rumor, Lk. 5:15; met. *to extend to,* Rom. 5:12 [1330] See *come through; go through; pass through.*

[1452] διερωτάω *dierōtaō* 1x *to sift by questioning,* of persons; in NT, of things, *to ascertain by inquiry,* Acts 10:17* [1331]

[1453] διετής *dietēs* 1x *of two years; of the age of two years,* Mt. 2:16* [1332]

[1454] διετία *dietia* 2x *the space of two years,* Acts 24:27; 28:30* [1333]

[1455] διηγέομαι *diēgeomai* 8x pr. *to lead throughout; to declare thoroughly, detail, recount, relate, tell,* Mk. 5:16; 9:9; Lk. 8:39; Acts 8:33; Heb. 11:32 [1334]

[1456] διήγησις *diēgēsis* 1x *a narration, relation, history,* Lk. 1:1* [1335]

[1457] διηνεκής *diēnekēs* 4x *continuous, uninterrupted;* εἰς τὸ διηνεκές, *perpetually,* Heb. 7:3; 10:1, 12, 14* [1336]

[1458] διθάλασσος *dithalassos* 1x *surrounded on both sides by the sea;* τόπος διθάλασσος, *a shoal* or *sand-bank formed by the confluence of opposite currents,* Acts 27:41* [1337]

[1459] διϊκνέομαι *diikneomai* 1x *to go* or *pass through; to penetrate,* Heb. 4:12* [1338]

[1460] διΐστημι *diistēmi* 3x *to set at an interval, apart; to station at an interval* from a former position, Acts 27:28; intrans. *to stand apart; to depart, be parted,* Lk. 24:51; of time, *to intervene, be interposed,* Lk. 22:59* [1339]

[1462] διϊσχυρίζομαι *diischurizomai* 2x *to feel* or *express reliance; to affirm confidently, insist,* Lk. 22:59; Acts 12:15* [1340]

[1464] δικαιοκρισία *dikaiokrisia* 1x *just* or *righteous judgment,* Rom. 2:5* [1341]

[1465] δίκαιος *dikaios* 79x *just, equitable, fair,* Mt. 20:4; Lk. 12:57; Jn. 5:30; Col. 4:1; of persons, *just, righteous,* absolutely, Jn. 17:25; Rom. 3:10, 26; 2 Tim. 4:8; 1 Pet. 3:18; 1 Jn. 1:9; 2:1, 29; Rev. 16:5;

righteous by account and acceptance, Rom. 2:13; 5:19; in ordinary usage, *just, upright, innocent, pious,* Mt. 5:45; 9:13, et al. freq.; ὁ δίκαιος, *the Just One,* one of the distinctive titles of the Messiah, Acts 3:14; 7:52; 22:14 [1342] See *innocent; just; righteous, righteousness; upright.*

[1466] δικαιοσύνη *dikaiosynē* 92x *fair and equitable dealing, justice,* Acts 17:31; Heb. 11:33; Rom. 9:28; *integrity, virtue,* Lk. 1:75; Eph. 5:9; in NT *generosity, alms,* 2 Cor. 9:10, v.r.; Mt. 6:1; *piety, godliness,* Rom. 6:13; *investiture with the attribute of righteousness, acceptance as righteous, justification,* Rom. 4:11; 10:4, et al. freq.; *a provision* or *mean for justification,* Rom. 1:17; 2 Cor. 3:9; *an instance of justification,* 2 Cor. 5:21 [1343] See *innocence; justice; justification; righteous, righteousness.*

[1467] δικαιόω *dikaioō* 39x pr. *to make* or *render right* or *just;* mid. *to act with justice,* Rev. 22:11; *to avouch to be good and true, to vindicate,* Mt. 11:19; Lk. 7:29; *to set forth as good and just,* Lk. 10:29; 16:15; in NT *to hold as guiltless, to accept as righteous, to justify,* Rom. 3:26, 30; 4:5; 8:30, 33; pass. *to be held acquitted, to be cleared,* Acts 13:39; Rom. 3:24; 6:7; *to be approved, to stand approved, to stand accepted,* Rom. 2:13; 3:20, 28 [1344] See *justify; righteous, righteousness.*

[1468] δικαίωμα *dikaiōma* 10x pr. *a rightful act, act of justice, equity; a sentence,* of condemnation, Rev. 15:4; in NT, of acquittal, *justification,* Rom. 5:16; *a decree, law, ordinance,* Lk. 1:6; Rom. 1:32; 2:26; 8:4; Heb. 9:1, 10; *a meritorious act, an instance of perfect righteousness,* Rom. 5:18; Rev. 19:8* [1345] See *regulations; righteous, righteousness; righteous deeds.*

[1469] δικαίως *dikaiōs* 5x *justly, with strict justice,* 1 Pet. 2:23; *deservedly,* Lk. 23:41; *as it is right, fit* or *proper,* 1 Cor. 15:34; *uprightly, honestly, piously, religiously,* 1 Thess. 2:10; Tit. 2:12* [1346]

[1470] δικαίωσις *dikaiōsis* 2x pr. *a making right* or *just; a declaration of right* or *justice; a judicial sentence;* in NT, *acquittal, acceptance, justification,* Rom. 4:25; 5:18* [1347]

[1471] δικαστής *dikastēs* 2x *a judge,* Acts 7:27, 35* [1348]

[1472] δίκη *dikē* 3x *right, justice;* in NT *judicial punishment, vengeance,* 2 Thess. 1:9; Jude 7; *sentence of punishment, judgment,* Acts 25:15; personified, *the goddess of justice* or *vengeance, Nemesis, Paena,* Acts 28:4 [1349]

[1473] δίκτυον *diktyon* 12x *a net, fishing-net,* Mt. 4:20, 21 [1350] See *net.*

[1474] δίλογος *dilogos* 1x pr. *saying the same thing twice;* in NT *double-tongued, speaking one thing and meaning another, deceitful in words,* 1 Tim. 3:8* [1351]

[1475] διό *dio* 53x inferential conj., *on which account, wherefore, therefore, for this reason,* Mt. 27:8; 1 Cor. 12:3 [1352]

[1476] διοδεύω *diodeuō* 2x *to travel through* a place, *traverse,* Lk. 8:1; Acts 17:1 [1353]

[1477] Διονύσιος *Dionysios* 1x *Dionysius,* pr. name, Acts 17:34* [1354]

[1478] διόπερ *dioper* 2x inferential conj., *on this very account, for this very reason, wherefore,* 1 Cor. 8:13; 10:14* [1355]

[1479] διοπετής *diopetēs* 1x *which fell from Jupiter,* or *heaven;* τοῦ διοπετοῦς, sc. ἀγάλματος, *image* or *statue*; for discussion of ellipsis see grammars, Acts 19:35* [1356]

[1480] διόρθωμα *diorthōma* 1x *correction, emendation, reformation,* Acts 24:2* [2735]

[1481] διόρθωσις *diorthōsis* 1x *a complete rectification, reformation,* Heb. 9:10 [1357]

[1482] διορύσσω *dioryssō* 4x *to dig* or *break through,* Mt. 6:19, 20; 24:43; Lk. 12:39* [1358]

[1483] Διόσκουροι *Dioskouroi* 1x *the Dioscuri, Castor and Pollux,* sons of Jupiter by Leda, and patrons of sailors, Acts 28:11* [1359]

[1484] διότι *dioti* 23x *on the account that, because,* Lk. 2:7; 21:28; *in as much as,* Lk. 1:13; Acts 18:10 [1360]

[1485] Διοτρέφης *Diotrephēs* 1x *Diotrephes,* pr. name, 3 Jn. 9* [1361]

[1487] διπλοῦς *diplous* 4x *double,* Mt. 23:15; 1 Tim. 5:17; Rev. 18:6 [1362]

[1488] διπλόω *diploō* 1x *to double; to render back double,* Rev. 18:6* [1363]

[1489] δίς *dis* 6x *twice,* Mk. 14:30, 72; in the sense of *entirely, utterly,* Jude 12; ἅπαξ καὶ δίς, *once and again, repeatedly,* Phil. 4:16 [1364]

[1490] δισμυριάς *dismyrias* 1x *twice ten thousand, two myriads,* Rev. 9:16* [1417 + 3461]

[1491] διστάζω *distazō* 2x *to doubt, waver, hesitate,* Mt. 14:31; 28:17* [1365]

[1492] δίστομος *distomos* 3x pr. *having two mouths; two-edged,* Heb. 4:12; Rev. 1:16; 2:12* [1366]

[1493] δισχίλιοι *dischilioi* 1x *two thousand,* Mk. 5:13* [1367]

[1494] διϋλίζω *diylizō* 1x *to strain, filter thoroughly; to strain out* or *off,* Mt. 23:24* [1368]

[1495] διχάζω *dichazō* 1x *to cut asunder, disunite;* met. *to cause to disagree, set at variance,* Mt. 10:35* [1369]

[1496] διχοστασία *dichostasia* 2x *a standing apart; a division, dissension,* Rom. 16:17; Gal. 5:20* [1370]

[1497] διχοτομέω *dichotomeō* 2x pr. *to cut into two parts, cut asunder;* in NT *to inflict a punishment of extreme severity,* Mt. 24:51; Lk. 12:46* [1371]

[1498] διψάω *dipsaō* 16x *to thirst, be thirsty,* Mt. 25:35, 37, 42, 44; met. *to thirst after* in spirit, *to desire* or *long for ardently,* Mt. 5:6; Jn. 4:14; 6:35 [1372] See *thirst.*

[1499] δίψος *dipsos* 1x *thirst,* 2 Cor. 11:27* [1373]

[1500] δίψυχος *dipsychos* 2x *double-minded, inconstant, fickle,* Jas. 1:8; 4:8* [1374]

[1501] διωγμός *diōgmos* 10x pr. *chase, pursuit; persecution* (specifically for religious reasons), Mt. 13:21; Mk. 4:17; 10:30 [1375] See *persecution.*

[1502] διώκτης *diōktēs* 1x *a persecutor,* 1 Tim. 1:13* [1376]

[1503] διώκω *diōkō* 45x *to put in rapid motion; to pursue; to follow, pursue the direction of,* Lk. 17:23; *to follow eagerly, endeavor earnestly to acquire,* Rom. 9:30, 31; 12:13; *to press forwards,* Phil. 3:12, 14; *to pursue* with malignity, *persecute,* Mt. 5:10, 11, 12, 44 [1377] See *persecute; pursue.*

[1504] δόγμα *dogma* 5x *a decree, statute, ordinance,* Lk. 2:1; Acts 16:4; 17:7; Eph. 2:15; Col. 2:14* [1378]

[1505] δογματίζω *dogmatizō* 1x *to decree, prescribe an ordinance;* mid. *to suffer laws to be imposed on one's self, to submit to, bind one's self by, ordinances,* Col. 2:20* [1379]

[1506] δοκέω *dokeō* 62x *to think, imagine, suppose, presume,* Mt. 3:9; 6:7; *to seem, appear,* Lk. 10:36; Acts 17:18; *it seems; it seems good, best,* or *right, it pleases,* Lk. 1:3; Acts 15:22, 25 [1380] See *believe; suppose; think.*

[1507] δοκιμάζω *dokimazō* 22x *to test, assay* metals, 1 Pet. 1:7; *to prove, try, examine, scrutinize,* Lk. 14:19; Rom. 12:2; *to put to the proof, tempt,* Heb. 3:9; *to approve* after trial, *judge worthy, choose,* Rom. 14:22; 1 Cor. 16:3; 2 Cor. 8:22; *to decide upon* after examination, *judge of, distinguish, discern,* Lk. 12:56; Rom. 2:18; Phil. 1:10 [1381] See *approve; discern; test.*

[1508] δοκιμασία *dokimasia* 1x *proof, probation, testing, examination,* Heb. 3:9* [1381]

[1509] δοκιμή *dokimē* 7x *trial, proof by trial,* 2 Cor. 8:2; *the state* or *disposition of that which has been tried and approved, approved character* or *temper,* Rom. 5:4; 2 Cor. 2:9; Phil. 2:22; *proof, document, evidence,* 2 Cor. 8:2; 13:3* [1382]

[1510] δοκίμιον *dokimion* 2x *that by means of which anything is tried, proof, criterion, test; trial, the act of trying* or *putting to proof,* Jas. 1:3; *approved character,* 1 Pet. 1:7* [1383]

[1511] δόκιμος *dokimos* 7x *proved, tried; approved* after examination and trial, Rom. 16:10; Jas. 1:12; by impl. *acceptable,* Rom. 14:18 [1384]

[1512] δοκός *dokos* 6x *a beam* or *spar* of timber, Mt. 7:3, 4, 5; Lk. 6:41, 42* [1385]

[1513] δόλιος *dolios* 1x *fraudulent, deceitful,* 2 Cor. 11:13* [1386]

[1514] δολιόω *dolioō* 1x *to deceive, use fraud* or *deceit,* Rom. 3:13* [1387]

[1515] δόλος *dolos* 11x pr. *a bait* or *contrivance for entrapping, fraud, deceit, cunning, guile,* Mt. 26:4; Mk. 7:22; 14:1 [1388] See *deceit.*

[1516] δολόω *doloō* 1x pr. *to entrap, beguile; to adulterate, corrupt, falsify,* 2 Cor. 4:2* [1389]

[1517] δόμα *doma* 4x *a gift, present,* Mt. 7:11; Lk. 11:13; Eph. 4:8; Phil. 4:17* [1390]

[1518] δόξα *doxa* 166x pr. *a seeming; brightness, radiance, splendor; appearance; a notion, imagination, opinion; the opinion which obtains respecting one; reputation, credit, honor, glory;* in NT *honorable consideration,* Lk. 14:10; *praise, glorification, honor,* Jn. 5:41, 44; Rom. 4:20; 15:7; *dignity, majesty,* Rom. 1:23; 2 Cor. 3:7; *a glorious manifestation, glorious working,* Jn. 11:40; 2 Pet. 1:3; pl. *dignitaries,* 2 Pet. 2:10; Jude 8; *glorification in a future state of bliss,*

2 Cor. 4:17; 2 Tim. 2:10; *pride, ornament,* 1 Cor. 11:15; *reflection,* 1 Cor. 11:7; 1 Thess. 2:20; *splendid array, pomp, magnificence,* Mt. 6:29; 19:28; *radiance, dazzling lustre,* Lk. 2:9; Acts 22:11 [1391] See *glory; honor; splendor.*

[1519] δοξάζω *doxazō* 61x *to think, suppose, judge; to extol, magnify,* Mt. 6:2; Lk. 4:15; in NT *to adore, worship,* Rom. 1:21; *to invest with dignity* or *majesty,* 2 Cor. 3:10; Heb. 5:5; *to display with a manifestation of dignity, excellence,* or *majesty,* Jn. 12:28; 13:32; *to glorify* by admission to a state of bliss, *to beatify,* Rom. 8:30 [1392] See *give honor; glorify; praise.*

[1520] Δορκάς *Dorkas* 2x *Dorcas,* pr. name, signifying a *gazelle* or *antelope,* Acts 9:36, 39* [1393]

[1521] δόσις *dosis* 2x pr. *giving, outlay; giving and receiving,* Phil. 4:15; *a donation, gift,* Jas. 1:17* [1394]

[1522] δότης *dotēs* 1x *a giver,* 2 Cor. 9:7* [1395]

[1524] δουλαγωγέω *doulagōgeō* 1x pr. *to bring into slavery; to treat as a slave; to discipline into subjection,* 1 Cor. 9:27* [1396]

[1525] δουλεία *douleia* 5x *slavery, bondage, servile condition;* in NT met. with reference to degradation and unhappiness, Rom. 8:15, 21; Gal. 4:24; 5:1; Heb. 2:15* [1397]

[1526] δουλεύω *douleuō* 25x *to be a slave* or *servant; to be in slavery* or *subjection,* Jn. 8:33; Acts 7:7; Rom. 9:12; *to discharge the duties of a slave* or *servant,* Eph. 6:7; 1 Tim. 6:2; *to serve, be occupied in the service of, be devoted, subservient,* Mt. 6:24; Lk. 15:29; Acts 20:19; Rom. 14:18; 16:18; met. *to be enthralled, involved in a slavish service,* spiritually or morally, Gal. 4:9, 25; Tit. 3:3 [1398] See *(be) enslaved; serve.*

[1527] δούλη *doulē* 3x *female slave, bondmaid,* Lk. 1:38, 48; Acts 2:18* [1399]

[1528] δοῦλος *doulos* 126x *a male slave,* or *servant,* of various degrees, Mt. 8:9, et al. freq.; *a servitor, person of mean condition,* Phil. 2:7; fem. δούλη, *a female slave; a handmaiden,* Lk. 1:38, 48; Acts 2:18; δοῦλος, used figuratively, in a bad sense, *one involved in* moral or spiritual *bondage,* Jn. 8:34; Rom. 6:17, 20; 1 Cor. 7:23; 2 Pet. 2:19; in a good sense, *a* devoted *servant* or *minister,* Acts 16:17; Rom. 1:1; *one pledged* or *bound to serve,* 1 Cor. 7:22; 2 Cor. 4:5 [1400, 1401] See *servant; slave.*

[1530] δουλόω *douloō* 8x *to reduce to servitude, enslave, oppress by retaining in servitude,* Acts 7:6; 2 Pet. 2:19; met. *to render subservient,* 1 Cor. 9:19; pass. *to be under restraint,* 1 Cor. 7:15; *to be in bondage,* spiritually or morally, Gal. 4:3; Tit. 2:3; *to become devoted to the service of,* Rom. 6:18, 22* [1402]

[1531] δοχή *dochē* 2x pr. *reception* of guests; in NT *a banquet, feast,* Lk. 5:29; 14:13 [1403]

[1532] δράκων *drakōn* 13x *a dragon* or *large serpent;* met. *the devil* or *Satan,* Rev. 12:3, 4, 7, 9, 13, 16, 17; 13:2, 4, 11; 16:13; 20:2 [1404] See *dragon.*

[1533] δράσσομαι *drassomai* 1x pr. *to grasp with the hand, clutch; to lay hold of, seize, take, catch,* 1 Cor. 3:19* [1405]

[1534] δραχμή *drachmē* 3x *a drachma,* an Attic silver coin of nearly the same value as the Roman *denarius,* Lk. 15:8, 9* [1406]

[1535] δρέπανον *drepanon* 8x *an instrument with a curved blade,* as *a sickle,* Mk. 4:29; Rev. 14:14, 15, 16, 17, 18, 19* [1407]

[1536] δρόμος *dromos* 3x *a course, race, racecourse;* met. *course* of life or ministry, *career,* Acts 13:25; 20:24; 2 Tim. 4:7* [1408]

[1537] Δρούσιλλα *Drousilla* 1x *Drusilla,* pr. name, Acts 24:24* [1409]

[1538] δύναμαι *dynamai* 210x *to be able,* either intrinsically and absolutely, which is the ordinary signification; or, for specific reasons, Mt. 9:15; Lk. 16:2 [1410] See *ability; (be) able; can.*

[1539] δύναμις *dynamis* 119x *power; strength, ability,* Mt. 25:15; Heb. 11:11; *efficacy,* 1 Cor. 4:19, 20; Phil. 3:10; 1 Thess. 1:5; 2 Tim. 3:5; *energy,* Col. 1:29; 2 Tim. 1:7; *meaning, purport* of language, 1 Cor. 14:11; *authority,* Lk. 4:36; 9:1; *might, power, majesty,* Mt. 22:29; 24:30; Acts 3:12; Rom. 9:17; 2 Thess. 1:7; 2 Pet. 1:16; in NT *a manifestation* or *instance of power, mighty means,* Acts 8:10; Rom. 1:16; 1 Cor. 1:18, 24; ἡ δύναμις, *omnipotence,* Mt. 26:64; Lk. 22:69; Mt. 14:62; pl. *authorities,* Rom. 8:38; Eph. 1:21; 1 Pet. 3:22; *miraculous power,* Mk. 5:30; Lk. 1:35; 5:17; 6:19; 8:46; 24:49; 1 Cor. 2:4; *a miracle,* Mt. 11:20, 21, et al. freq.; *a worker of miracles,* 1 Cor. 12:28, 29; from the Hebrew αἱ δυνάμεις τῶν οὐρανῶν, *the heavenly luminaries,* Mt. 24:29; Mk. 13:25; Lk. 21:26; αἱ δυνάμεις, *the* spiritual *powers,* Mt. 14:2; Mk. 6:14 [1411] See *ability; miracle; power.*

[1540] δυναμόω *dynamoō* 2x *to strengthen, confirm,* Col. 1:11; Heb. 11:34* [1412]

[1541] δυνάστης *dynastēs* 3x *a potentate, sovereign; prince,* Lk. 1:52; 1 Tim. 6:15; *a person of rank and authority,* Acts 8:27* [1413]

[1542] δυνατέω *dynateō* 3x *to be powerful, mighty, to show one's self powerful,* 2 Cor. 9:8; 13:3; Rom. 14:4* [1414]

[1543] δυνατός *dynatos* 32x *able, having power, powerful, mighty;* δυνατὸς εἶναι, *to be able,* i.q. δύνασθαι, Lk. 14:31; Acts 11:17; ὁ δυνατός, *the Mighty One, God,* Lk. 1:49; τὸ δυνατόν, *power,* i.q. δύναμις, Rom. 9:22; *valid, powerful, efficacious,* 2 Cor. 10:4; *distinguished for rank, authority,* or *influence,* Acts 25:5; 1 Cor. 1:26; *distinguished for skill* or *excellence,* Lk. 24:19; Acts 7:22; Rom. 15:1; δυνατόν and δυνατά, *possible, capable of being done,* Mt. 19:26; 24:24 [1415] See *ability; mighty; possible.*

[1544] δύνω *dynō* 2x *to sink, go down, set* as the sun, Mk. 1:32; Lk. 4:40* [1416]

[1545] δύο *dyo* 135x *two,* Mt. 6:24; 21:38, 31, et al. freq.; οἱ δύο, *both,* Jn. 20:4; δύο ἢ τρεῖς, *two* or *three, some, a few,* Mt. 18:20; from the Hebrew, δύο δύο, *two and two,* Mk. 6:7, i.q. ἀνὰ δύο, Lk. 10:1, and κατὰ δύο, 1 Cor. 14:27 [1417] See *two.*

[1546] δυσβάστακτος *dysbastaktos* 1x *difficult* or *grievous to be borne, oppressive,* Lk. 11:46 [1419]

[1548] δυσεντέριον *dysenterion* 1x *dysentery,* Acts 28:8* [1420]

[1549] δυσερμήνευτος *dysermēneutos* 1x *difficult to be explained, hard to be understood,* Heb. 5:11* [1421]

[1550] δύσις *dysis* 1x *west,* Mk. 16:8 (shorter ending) [**]

[1551] δύσκολος *dyskolos* 1x pr. *peevish about food; hard to please, disagreeable;* in NT, *difficult,* Mk. 10:24* [1422]

[1552] δυσκόλως *dyskolōs* 3x *with difficulty, hardly,* Mt. 19:23; Mk. 10:23; Lk. 18:24* [1423]

[1553] δυσμή *dysmē* 5x *a sinking* or *setting;* pl. δυσμαί, *the setting of the sun;* hence, *the west,* Mt. 8:11; 24:27 [1424]

[1554] δυσνόητος *dysnoētos* 1x *hard to be understood,* 2 Pet. 3:16* [1425]

[1555] δυσφημέω *dysphēmeō* 1x pr. *to use ill words; to reproach, revile,* 1 Cor. 4:13* [987]

[1556] δυσφημία *dysphēmia* 1x *ill words; words of ill omen; reproach, slander,* 2 Cor. 6:8* [1426]

[1557] δώδεκα *dōdeka* 75x *twelve,* Mt. 9:20; 10:1; οἱ δώδεκα, *the twelve* apostles, Mt. 26:14, 20 [1427] See *twelve.*

[1558] δωδέκατος *dōdekatos* 1x *the twelfth,* Rev. 21:20* [1428]

[1559] δωδεκάφυλον *dōdekaphylon* 1x *twelve tribes,* Acts 26:7* [1429]

[1560] δῶμα *dōma* 7x pr. *a house;* synec. *a roof,* Mt. 10:27; 24:17 [1430]

[1561] δωρεά *dōrea* 11x *a gift, free gift, benefit,* Jn. 4:10; Acts 2:38 [1431] See *gift.*

[1562] δωρεάν *dōrean* 9x *gratis, gratuitously, freely,* Mt. 10:8; Rom. 3:24; in NT *undeservedly, without cause,* Jn. 15:25; *in vain,* Gal. 2:21 [1432]

[1563] δωρέομαι *dōreomai* 3x *to give freely, grant,* Mk. 15:45; 2 Pet. 1:3, 4* [1433]

[1564] δώρημα *dōrēma* 2x *a gift, free gift,* Rom. 5:16; Jas. 1:17* [1434]

[1565] δῶρον *dōron* 19x *a gift, present,* Mt. 2:11; Eph. 2:8; Rev. 11:10; *an offering, sacrifice,* Mt. 5:23, 24; 8:4; δῶρον, sc. ἐστι[ν], *it is consecrated to God,* Mt. 15:5; Mk. 7:11; *contribution* to the temple, Lk. 21:1, 4 [1435] See *gift; offering; present.*

[1568] ἔα *ea* 1x *Ha!* an expression of surprise or displeasure, Lk. 4:34* [1436]

[1569] ἐάν *ean* 350x *if,* ἐὰν μή, *except, unless;* also equivalent to ἀλλά, Gal. 2:16. Ἐάν, in NT as in the later Greek, is substituted for ἄν after relative words, Mt. 5:19. Tends to be an indicator for the subjunctive mood. [1437]

[1570] ἐάνπερ *eanper* 3x *if it be that, if indeed, if at all events,* Heb. 3:6, 14; 6:3 [1437 + 4007]

[1571] ἑαυτοῦ *heautou* 319x *himself, herself, itself,* Mt. 8:22; 12:26; 9:21; also used for the first and second persons, Rom. 8:23; Mt. 23:31; also equivalent to ἀλλήλων, Mk. 10:26; Jn. 12:19; ἀφʼ ἑαυτοῦ, ἀφʼ ἑαυτῶν, *of himself, themselves, voluntarily, spontaneously,* Lk. 12:57; 21:30; *of one's own will merely,* Jn. 5:19; διʼ ἑαυτοῦ, *of itself, in its own nature,* Rom. 14:14; ἐξ ἑαυτῶν, *of one's own self,* 2 Cor. 3:5; καθʼ ἑαυτόν, *by one's self, alone,*

Acts 28:16; Jas. 2:17; παρ᾽ ἑαυτῷ, *with one's self, at home,* 1 Cor. 16:2; πρὸς ἑαυτόν, *to one's self, to one's home,* Lk. 24:12; Jn. 20:10; or, *with one's self,* Lk. 18:11 [1438]

[1572] ἐάω *eaō* 11x *to let, allow, permit, suffer to be done,* Mt. 24:43; Lk. 4:41; *to let be, let alone, desist from, stop,* Lk. 22:51; *to commit* a ship to the sea, *let* her *drive,* Acts 27:40 [1439] See *allow; let.*

[1573] ἑβδομήκοντα *hebdomēkonta* 5x *seventy,* indecl., Acts 7:14; οἱ ἑβδομήκοντα, *the seventy* disciples, Lk. 10:1, 17; Acts 23:23* [1440]

[1574] ἑβδομηκοντάκις *hebdomēkontakis* 1x indecl, *seventy times,* Mt. 18:22* [1441]

[1575] ἕβδομος *hebdomos* 9x *seventh,* Jn. 4:52; Heb. 4:4; Jude 14; Rev. 8:1 [1442]

[1576] Ἔβερ *Eber* 1x *Heber,* pr. name, indecl., Lk. 3:35* [1443]

[1578] Ἑβραῖος *Hebraios* 4x *a Hebrew, one descended from Abraham the Hebrew,* 2 Cor. 11:22; Phil. 3:5; in NT, *a Jew of Palestine, one speaking Aramaic,* opp. to Ἑλληνιστής, Acts 6:1* [1445]

[1579] Ἑβραΐς *Hebrais* 3x *the Hebrew* dialect, i.e., the Hebrew-Aramaic dialect of Palestine, Acts 21:40; 22:2; 26:14* [1446]

[1580] Ἑβραϊστί *Hebraisti* 7x *in Hebrew* or *Aramaic,* Jn. 5:2; 19:13, 17, 20; 20:16; Rev. 9:11; 16:16* [1447]

[1581] ἐγγίζω *engizō* 42x pr. *to cause to approach;* in NT intrans. *to approach, draw near,* Mt. 21:1; Lk. 18:35; met. *to be at hand,* Mt. 3:2; 4:17; μέχρι θανάτου ἐγγίζειν, *to be at the point of death,* Phil. 2:30; from Hebrew *to draw near* to God, *to offer* Him *reverence and worship,* Mt. 15:8; Heb. 7:19; Jas. 4:8; used of God, *to draw near* to men, *assist* them, *bestow favors* on them, Jas. 4:8 [1448] See *approach; come near; draw near.*

[1582] ἐγγράφω *engraphō* 3x *to engrave, inscribe,* Lk. 10:20; met. ἐγγεγραμμένος, *imprinted,* 2 Cor. 3:2, 3* [1449]

[1583] ἔγγυος *engyos* 1x *a guarantee, sponsor,* Heb. 7:22* [1450]

[1584] ἐγγύς *engys* 31x some view as an improper prep., followed by gen. or dat., *near,* as to place, Lk. 19:11; *close at hand,* Rom. 10:8; *near,* in respect of ready interposition, Phil. 4:5; *near,* as to time, Mt. 24:32, 33; *near* to God, as being in covenant with him, Eph. 2:13; οἱ ἐγγύς, *the people near* to God, the Jews, Eph. 2:17 [1451] See *near; nigh.*

[1586] ἐγείρω *egeirō* 144x *to excite, arouse, awaken,* Mt. 8:25; mid. *to awake,* Mt. 2:13, 20, 21; met. mid. *to rouse one's self* to a better course of conduct, Rom. 13:11; Eph. 5:14; *to raise* from the dead, Jn. 12:1; and mid. *to rise* from the dead, Mt. 27:52; Jn. 5:21; met. *to raise* as it were from the dead, 2 Cor. 4:14; *to raise up, cause to rise up* from a prone posture, Acts 3:7; and mid. *to rise up,* Mt. 17:7; *to restore to health,* Jas. 5:15; met. et seq. ἐπῄ, *to excite* to war; mid. *to rise up against,* Mt. 24:7; *to raise up again, rebuild,* Jn. 2:19, 20; *to raise up* from a lower place, *to draw up* or *out of* a ditch, Mt. 12:10; from Hebrew, *to raise up, to cause to arise* or *exist,* Acts 13:22, 23; mid. *to arise, exist, appear,* Mt. 3:9; 11:11 [1453] See *raise; rise up; waken.*

[1587] ἔγερσις *egersis* 1x pr. *the act of waking* or *rising up; resurrection resuscitation,* Mt. 27:53* [1454]

[1589] ἐγκαίνια *enkainia* 1x *initiation, consecration;* in NT *the feast of rededication,* an annual festival of eight days in the month Kislev, Jn. 10:22* [1456]

[1590] ἐγκαινίζω *enkainizō* 2x *to initiate, consecrate, dedicate, renovate; to institute,* Heb. 9:18; 10:20* [1457]

[1592] ἐγκαλέω *enkaleō* 7x can be followed by a dative, *to bring a charge against, accuse; to institute judicial proceedings,* Acts 19:38, 40; 23:28, 29; 26:2, 7; Rom. 8:33 [1458] See *accuse.*

[1593] ἐγκαταλείπω *enkataleipō* 10x *to leave, leave behind; to forsake, abandon,* Mt. 27:46; Mk. 15:34; Acts 2:27, 30; Rom. 9:29; 2 Cor. 4:9; 2 Tim. 4:10, 16; Heb. 10:25; 13:5* [1459] See *abandon; desert; forsake.*

[1594] ἐγκατοικέω *enkatoikeō* 1x *to dwell in,* or *among,* 2 Pet. 2:8* [1460]

[1595] ἐγκαυχάομαι *enkauchaomai* 1x *to boast in,* or *of,* 2 Thess. 1:4* [2620]

[1596] ἐγκεντρίζω *enkentrizō* 6x *to ingraft;* met. Rom. 11:17, 19, 23, 24* [1461]

[1598] ἔγκλημα *enklēma* 2x *an accusation, charge, crimination,* Acts 23:29; 25:16* [1462]

[1599] ἐγκομβόομαι *enkomboomai* 1x pr. *to put on a garment which is to be tied;* in NT *to put on, clothe one's self with;* met. 1 Pet. 5:5* [1463]

[1600] ἐγκοπή *enkopē* 1x alsn spelled ἐκκοπή, pr. *an incision,* e.g. a trench, etc., cut in the way of an enemy; *an impediment, hindrance,* 1 Cor. 9:12* [1464]

[1601] ἐγκόπτω *enkoptō* 5x pr. *to cut* or *strike in;* hence, *to impede, interrupt, hinder,* Rom. 15:22; 1 Thess. 2:18; 1 Pet. 3:7; Gal. 5:7; Acts 24:4* [1465]

[1602] ἐγκράτεια *enkrateia* 4x *self-control, continence, temperance,* Acts 24:25; Gal. 4:23; 2 Pet. 1:6* [1466]

[1603] ἐγκρατεύομαι *enkrateuomai* 2x *to possess the power of self-control* or *continence,* 1 Cor. 7:9; *to practice abstinence,* 1 Cor. 9:25* [1467]

[1604] ἐγκρατής *enkratēs* 1x *strong, stout; possessed of mastery; master of self,* Tit. 1:8* [1468]

[1605] ἐγκρίνω *enkrinō* 1x *to judge* or *reckon among, consider as belonging to, adjudge to the number of; class with, place in the same rank,* 2 Cor. 10:12* [1469]

[1606] ἐγκρύπτω *enkryptō* 2x *to conceal in* anything; *to mix, intermix,* Mt. 13:33; Lk. 13:21* [1470]

[1608] ἐγχρίω *enchriō* 1x *to rub in, anoint,* Rev. 3:18* [1472]

[1609] ἐγώ *egō* 2,666x *I,* gen., ἐμοῦ [μου], dat., ἐμοί [μοι], acc., ἐμέ [με]. The plural ἡμεῖς is listed as its own form, 7005. [1473, 1691, 1698, 1700, 2248, 2249, 2254, 2257, 3165, 3427, 3450] See *I.*

[1610] ἐδαφίζω *edaphizō* 1x pr. *to form a level and firm surface; to level with the ground, overthrow, raze, destroy,* Lk. 19:44* [1474]

[1611] ἔδαφος *edaphos* 1x pr. *a bottom, base;* hence, *the ground,* Acts 22:7* [1475]

[1612] ἑδραῖος *hedraios* 3x *sedentary;* met. *settled, steady, firm, steadfast, constant,* 1 Cor. 7:37; 15:58; Col. 1:23* [1476]

[1613] ἑδραίωμα *hedraiōma* 1x *a basis, foundation,* 1 Tim. 3:15* [1477]

[1614] Ἑζεκίας *Hezekias* 2x *Hezekiah,* pr. name, Mt. 1:9f.* [1478]

[1615] ἐθελοθρησκία *ethelothrēskia* 1x also spelled ἐθελοθρησκεία, *self-made religion,* Col. 2:23* [1479]

[1616] ἐθίζω *ethizō* 1x *to accustom;* pass. *to be customary,* Lk. 2:27* [1480]

[1617] ἐθνάρχης *ethnarchēs* 1x *a governor, chief* of any tribe or nation, 2 Cor. 11:32* [1481]

[1618] ἐθνικός *ethnikos* 4x *national;* in NT *Gentile, heathen, not Israelites,* Mt. 5:47; 6:7; 18:17; 3 Jn. 7* [1482]

[1619] ἐθνικῶς *ethnikōs* 1x *like a Gentile,* Gal. 2:14* [1483]

[1620] ἔθνος *ethnos* 162x *a multitude, company,* Acts 17:26; 1 Pet. 2:9; Rev. 21:24; *a nation, people,* Mt. 20:25; 21:43; pl. ἔθνη, from the Hebrew, *nations* or *people* as distinguished from the Jews, *the heathen, Gentiles,* Mt. 4:15; 10:5; Lk. 2:32 [1484] See *Gentile; nation.*

[1621] ἔθος *ethos* 12x *a custom, usage, habit,* Lk. 2:42; 22:39; *an institute, rite,* Lk. 1:9; Acts 6:14; 15:1 [1485] See *custom; habit.*

[1623] εἰ *ei* 502x *if,* Mt. 4:6; 12:7; Acts 27:39, often with the sense of *since* esp. in first class conditional sentences, Mt. 4:3, Acts 4:9; with direct and indirect questions, *that,* 1 Jn 3:13; by a suppression of the apodosis of a sentence, εἰ serves to express a wish; *O if! O that!* Lk. 19:42; 22:42; also a strong negation, Mk. 8:12; Heb. 3:11; 4:3; in conjunction with other words, εἰ καί, *if even, though, although,* Lk. 18:4; εἰ μή, *unless, except,* Mt. 11:27; also equivalent to ἀλλά, *but,* Mt. 12:4; Mk. 13:32; Lk. 4:26, 27; εἰ μήτι, *unless perhaps, unless it be,* Lk. 9:13; εἴ τις, εἴ τι, pr. *if any one; whosoever, whatsoever,* Mt. 18:28 [1487]

[1624] εἰδέα *eidea* 1x *appearance, face,* Mt. 28:3* [2397]

[1626] εἶδος *eidos* 5x *form, external appearance,* Lk. 3:22; 9:29; Jn. 5:37; *kind, species,* 1 Thess. 5:22; *sight, perception,* 2 Cor. 5:7* [1491]

[1627] εἰδωλεῖον *eidōleion* 1x *a heathen temple,* 1 Cor. 8:10* [1493]

[1628] εἰδωλόθυτος *eidōlothutos* 9x as a noun *meat offered to an idol,* Acts 15:29; 21:25; 1 Cor. 8:1, 4, 7, 10; 10:19; Rev. 2:14, 20* [1494]

[1629] εἰδωλολάτρης *eidōlolatrēs* 7x *an idolater, worshipper of idols,* 1 Cor. 5:10, 11; 6:9; 10:7; Eph. 5:5; Rev. 21:8; 22:15* [1496] See *idolater, idolatry.*

[1630] εἰδωλολατρία *eidōlolatria* 4x *idolatry, worship of idols,* 1 Cor. 10:14; Gal. 5:20; Col. 3:5; 1 Pet. 4:3* [1495] See *idolater, idolatry.*

[1631] εἴδωλον *eidōlon* 11x pr. *a form, shape, figure; image* or *statue;* hence, *an idol, image of a god,* Acts 7:41; *a heathen god,* 1 Cor. 8:4, 7; for εἰδωλόθυτον, *the flesh of victims sacrificed to idols,* Acts 15:20;

Rom. 2:22; 1 Cor. 10:19; 12:12; 2 Cor. 6:16; 1 Thess. 1:9; 1 Jn. 5:21; Rev. 9:20* [1497] See *idol; image.*

[1632] εἰκῇ *eikē* 6x *without plan* or *system; without cause, rashly,* Col. 2:18; *to no purpose, in vain,* Rom. 13:4; 1 Cor. 15:2; Gal. 3:4 (2x); 4:11* [1500]

[1633] εἴκοσι *eikosi* 11x *twenty,* Lk. 14:31; Acts 27:28 [1501] See *twenty.*

[1634] εἴκω *eikō* 1x. (1) *to yield, give place, submit,* Gal. 2:5. (2) the perfect form ἔοικα (2036) is from this same root and functions as a present, Jm 1:6, 23 (ἔοικεν, 3 sg). Some list it as a separate word, but see the discussion in Liddell and Scott* [1502]

[1635] εἰκών *eikōn* 23x *a material image, likeness, effigy,* Mt. 22:20; Mk. 12:16; *a representation, exact image,* 1 Cor. 11:7; 15:49; Rev. 13:14f.; *resemblance,* Rom. 1:23; 8:29; Col. 3:10; Heb. 10:1 [1504] See *image; liken.*

[1636] εἰλικρίνεια *eilikrineia* 3x *clearness, purity;* met. *sincerity, integrity, ingenuousness,* 1 Cor. 5:8; 2 Cor. 1:12; 2:17* [1505]

[1637] εἰλικρινής *eilikrinēs* 2x pr. *that which being viewed in the sunshine is found clear and pure;* met. *spotless, sincere, ingenuous,* Phil. 1:10; 2 Pet. 3:1* [1506]

[1639] εἰμί *eimi* 2,462x *to be, to exist,* Jn. 1:1; 17:5; Mt. 6:30; Lk. 4:25, freq.; ἐστί[ν], *it is possible, proper,* Heb. 9:5; a simple linking verb ("copula") to the subject and predicate, and therefore in itself affecting the force of the sentence only by its tense, mood, etc., Jn. 1:1; 15:1, freq.; it also forms a frequent circumlocution with the participles of the present and perfect of other verbs, Mt. 19:22; Mk. 2:6 [1488, 1498, 1510, 1511, 1526, 2070, 2071, 2252, 2258, 2277, 2468, 5600, 5607] See *be.*

[1641] εἵνεκεν *heineken* 2x see ἕνεκα, *on account of,* Lk. 4:18; Acts 28:20; 2 Cor. 3:10* [1752]

[1642] εἴπερ *eiper* 6x *if indeed, if it be so that, granted,* Rom. 8:9; 1 Cor. 15:15; *since indeed, since,* 2 Thess. 1:6; 1 Pet. 2:3; *although indeed,* 1 Cor. 8:5 [1512]

[1644] εἰρηνεύω *eirēneuō* 4x *to be at peace; to cultivate peace, concord,* or *harmony,* Mt. 9:50; Rom. 12:18; 2 Cor. 13:11; 1 Thess. 5:13* [1514]

[1645] εἰρήνη *eirēnē* 92x *peace,* Lk. 14:32; Acts 12:20; *tranquillity,* Lk. 11:21; Jn. 16:33; 1 Thess. 5:3; *concord, unity, love of peace,* Mt. 10:34; Lk. 12:51; meton. *the author of peace,* Eph. 2:14; from the Hebrew *every kind of blessing and good,* Lk. 1:79; 2:14, 29; meton. *a salutation expressive of good wishes, a benediction, blessing,* Mt. 10:13 [1515] See *peace.*

[1646] εἰρηνικός *eirēnikos* 2x *pertaining to peace; peaceable, disposed to peace,* Jas. 3:17; from the Hebrew, *profitable, blissful,* Heb. 12:11* [1516]

[1647] εἰρηνοποιέω *eirēnopoieō* 1x *to make peace,* Col. 1:20* [1517]

[1648] εἰρηνοποιός *eirēnopoios* 1x *a peace-maker, one who cultivates peace and concord,* Mt. 5:9* [1518]

[1650] εἰς *eis* 1,767x *to, as far as, to the extent of,* Mt. 2:23; 4:24; *until,* Jn. 13:1; *against,* Mt. 18:15; Lk. 12:10; *before, in the presence of,* Acts 22:30; *in order to, for, with a view to,* Mk. 1:38; *for the use* or *service of,* Jn. 6:9; Lk. 9:13; 1 Cor. 16:1; *with reference to,* 2 Cor. 10:13, 16; *in accordance with,* Mt. 12:41; Lk. 11:32; 2 Tim. 2:26; also equivalent to ejn, Jn. 1:18; *by,* in forms of swearing, Mt. 5:35; from the Hebrew, εἶναι, γίνεσθαι εἰς, *to become, result in, amount to,* Mt. 19:5; 1 Cor. 4:3; εἰς τί, *why, wherefore,* Mt. 26:8 [1519]

[1651] εἷς *heis* 345x numeral *one,* Mt. 10:29, freq.; *only,* Mk. 12:6; *one* virtually by union, Mt. 19:5, 6; Jn. 10:30; *one and the same,* Lk. 12:52; Rom. 3:30; *one* in respect of office and standing, 1 Cor. 3:8; equivalent to τις, *a certain one,* Mt. 8:19; 16:14; *a, an,* Mt. 21:19; Jas. 4:13; εἷς ἕκαστος, *each one, every one,* Lk. 4:40; Acts 2:3; εἷς τὸν ἕνα, *one another,* 1 Thess. 5:11; εἷς καὶ εἷς, *the one- and the other,* Mt. 20:21; εἷς καθ᾽ εἷς and ὁδὲ καθ᾽ εἷς, *one by one, one after another, in succession,* Mk. 14:19; Jn. 8:9; as an ordinal, *first,* Mt. 28:1 [1520, 3391] See *one.*

[1652] εἰσάγω *eisagō* 11x *to lead* or *bring in, introduce, conduct* or *usher in* or *to* a place or person, Lk. 2:27; 14:21; 22:54; Jn. 18:16; Acts 9:8; 21:28f., 37; Heb. 1:6 [1521] See *bring in.*

[1653] εἰσακούω *eisakouō* 5x *to hear* or *hearken to, to heed,* 1 Cor. 14:21; *to listen to* the prayers of any one, *accept one's petition,* Mt. 6:7; Lk. 1:13; Acts 10:31; Heb. 5:7* [1522]

[1654] εἰσδέχομαι *eisdechomai* 1x *to admit; to receive into favor, receive kindly, accept with favor,* 2 Cor. 6:17* [1523]

[1655] εἴσειμι *eiseimi* 4x *to go in, enter,* Acts 3:3; 21:18, 26; Heb. 9:6* [1524]

[1656] εἰσέρχομαι *eiserchomai* 194x *to go* or *come in, enter,* Mt. 7:13; 8:5, 8; spc. *to enter* by force, *break in,* Mk. 3:27; Acts 20:29; met. with εἰς κόσμον, *to begin to exist, come into existence,* Rom. 5:12; 2 Jn. 7; or, *to make one's appearance on earth,* Heb. 10:5; *to enter into* or *take possession of,* Lk. 22:3; Jn. 13:27; *to enter into, enjoy, partake of,* Mt. 19:23, 24; *to enter into* any one's labor, *be* his *successor,* Jn. 4:38; *to fall into, be placed in* certain circumstances, Mt. 26:41; *to be put into,* Mt. 15:11; Acts 11:8; *to present one's self before,* Acts 19:30; met. *to arise, spring up,* Lk. 9:46; from the Hebrew, εἰσέρχεσθαι καὶ ἐξέρχεσθαι, *to go in and out, to live, discharge the ordinary functions of life,* Acts 1:21 [1525] See *enter.*

[1657] εἰσκαλέομαι *eiskaleomai* 1x *to call in; to invite in,* Acts 10:23* [1528]

[1658] εἴσοδος *eisodos* 5x *a place of entrance; the act of entrance,* Heb. 10:19; *admission, reception,* 1 Thess. 1:9; 2 Pet. 1:11; *a coming, approach, access,* 1 Thess. 2:1; *entrance* upon office, *commencement* or *beginning* of ministry, Acts 13:24* [1529]

[1659] εἰσπηδάω *eispēdaō* 1x *to leap* or *spring in, rush in eagerly,* Acts 16:29* [1530]

[1660] εἰσπορεύομαι *eisporeuomai* 18x *to go* or *come in, enter,* Mk. 1:21; 5:40; *to come to, visit,* Acts 28:30; *to be put in,* Mt. 15:17; Mk. 7:15, 18, 19; *to intervene,* Mk. 4:19 [1531] See *enter; go in.*

[1661] εἰστρέχω *eistrechō* 1x *to run in,* Acts 12:14* [1532]

[1662] εἰσφέρω *eispherō* 8x *to bring in* or *into,* Lk. 5:18, 19; 1 Tim. 6:7; Heb. 13:11; *to bring to* the ears of any one, *to announce,* Acts 17:20; *to lead into,* Mt. 6:13; Lk. 11:4; *drag in,* Lk. 12:11* [1533]

[1663] εἶτα *eita* 15x *then, afterwards,* Mk. 4:17, 28; Lk. 8:12; *in the next place,* 1 Cor. 12:28; *besides, furthermore,* Heb. 12:9 [1534]

[1664] εἴτε *eite* 65x *whether,* Rom. 12:6, 7, 8; 1 Cor. 3:22; 2 Cor. 1:6; 1 Thess. 5:10 [1535]

[1665] εἴωθα *eiōtha* 4x perfect of an obsolete present ἔθω, pluperfect is εἰώθειν, *to be accustomed, to be usual,* Mt. 27:15; Mk. 10:1; Lk. 4:16; Acts 17:2* [1486]

[1666] ἐκ *ek* 915x ἐξ before vowels, with genitive, *from, out of,* a place, Mt. 2:15; 3:17; *of, from, out of,* denoting origin or source, Mt. 1:3; 21:19; *of, from* some material, Mt. 3:9; Rom. 9:21; *of, from, among,* partitively, Mt. 6:27; 21:31; Mk. 9:17; *from,* denoting cause, Rev. 8:11; 17:6; means or instrument, Mt. 12:33, 37; *by, through,* denoting the author or efficient cause, Mt. 1:18; Jn. 10:32; *of,* denoting the distinguishing mark of a class, Rom. 2:8; Gal. 3:7; of time, *after,* 2 Cor. 4:6; Rev. 17:11; *from, after, since,* Mt. 19:12; Lk. 8:27; *for, with,* denoting a rate of payment, price, Mt. 20:2; 27:7; *at,* denoting position, Mt. 20:21, 23; after passive verbs, *by, of, from,* marking the agent, Mt. 15:5; Mk. 7:11; forming with certain words a periphrasis for an adverb, Mt. 26:42, 44; Mk. 6:51; Lk. 23:8; put after words of freeing, Rom. 7:24; 2 Cor. 1:10; used partitively after verbs of eating, drinking, etc., Jn. 6:26; 1 Cor. 9:7 [1537]

[1667] ἕκαστος *hekastos* 82x *each (one), every (one) separately,* Mt. 16:27; Lk. 13:15 [1538] See *each; every.*

[1668] ἑκάστοτε *hekastote* 1x *always,* 2 Pet. 1:15* [1539]

[1669] ἑκατόν *hekaton* 17x *one hundred,* Mt. 13:8; Mk. 4:8 [1540] See *hundred.*

[1670] ἑκατονταετής *hekatontaetēs* 1x *a hundred years old,* Rom. 4:19* [1541]

[1671] ἑκατονταπλασίων *hekatontaplasiōn* 3x *a hundredfold,* Mt. 19:29; Mk. 10:30; Lk. 8:8* [1542]

[1672] ἑκατοντάρχης *hekatontarchēs* 20x the text varies between this form and ἑκατόνταρχος, *commander of a hundred men, a centurion,* Lk. 23:47; Acts 10:1; 27:1ff. [1543] See *centurion.*

[1674] ἐκβαίνω *ekbainō* 1x *to go forth, go out of,* Heb. 11:15* [1831]

[1675] ἐκβάλλω *ekballō* 81x pluperfect, ἐκβεβλήκειν, *to cast out, eject by force,* Mt. 15:17; Acts 27:38; *to expel, force away,* Lk. 4:29; Acts 7:58; *to refuse,* Jn. 6:37; *to extract,* Mt. 7:4; *to reject with contempt, despise, contemn,* Lk. 6:22; in NT *to send forth, send out,* Mt. 9:38; Lk. 10:2; *to send away, dismiss,* Mt. 9:25; Mk. 1:12; met. *to spread abroad,* Mt. 12:20; *to bring out, produce,* Mt. 12:35; 13:52 [1544] See *drive out; eject; expel.*

[1676] ἔκβασις *ekbasis* 2x *a way out, egress;* hence, *result, issue,* Heb. 13:7; *means of clearance* or *successful endurance,* 1 Cor. 10:13* [1545]

[1678] ἐκβολή *ekbolē* 1x *a casting out;* especially, *a throwing overboard* of a cargo, Acts 27:18* [1546]

[1681] ἔκγονος *ekgonos* 1x *born of, descended from;* as a noun ἔκγονα, *descendants, grandchildren,* 1 Tim. 5:4* [1549]

[1682] ἐκδαπανάω *ekdapanaō* 1x *to expend, consume, exhaust,* 2 Cor. 12:15* [1550]

[1683] ἐκδέχομαι *ekdechomai* 6x pr. *to receive from* another; *to expect, look for,* Acts 17:16; *to wait for, to wait,* 1 Cor. 11:33; 16:11; Heb. 11:10; 10:13; Jas. 5:7* [1551]

[1684] ἔκδηλος *ekdēlos* 1x *clearly manifest, evident,* 2 Tim. 3:9* [1552]

[1685] ἐκδημέω *ekdēmeō* 3x pr. *to be absent from home, go abroad, travel;* hence, *to be absent from* any place or person, 2 Cor. 5:6, 8, 9* [1553]

[1686] ἐκδίδωμι *ekdidōmi* 4x middle, *to give out, to give up; to lease, to put out* at interest; in NT *to let out* to tenants, Mt. 21:33, 41; Lark 12:1; Lk. 20:9* [1554]

[1687] ἐκδιηγέομαι *ekdiēgeomai* 2x *to narrate fully, detail,* Acts 13:14; 15:3* [1555]

[1688] ἐκδικέω *ekdikeō* 6x pr. *to execute right and justice; to punish,* 2 Cor. 10:6; Rev. 6:10; 19:2; in NT *to right, avenge* a person, Lk. 18:3, 5; Rom. 12:9* [1556] See *avenge; punish, punishment; seek justice; vengeance.*

[1689] ἐκδίκησις *ekdikēsis* 9x *vengeance, punishment, retributive justice,* Lk. 21:22; Rom. 12:19; 2 Cor. 7:11; 1 Pet. 2:14; ἐκδίκησιν ποιεῖν, *to vindicate, avenge,* Lk. 18:7, 8; διδόναι ἐκδίκησιν, *to inflict vengeance,* Acts 7:24; 2 Thess. 1:8; Heb. 10:30* [1557]

[1690] ἔκδικος *ekdikos* 2x *an avenger, one who inflicts punishment,* Rom. 13:4; 1 Thess. 4:6* [1558]

[1691] ἐκδιώκω *ekdiōkō* 1x pr. *to chase away, drive out;* in NT *to persecute, vex, harass,* 1 Thess. 2:15* [1559]

[1692] ἔκδοτος *ekdotos* 1x *delivered up,* Acts 2:23* [1560]

[1693] ἐκδοχή *ekdochē* 1x *a looking for, expectation,* Heb. 10:27* [1561]

[1694] ἐκδύω *ekdyō* 6x pr. *to go out from; to take off, strip, unclothe,* Mt. 27:28, 31; mid. *to lay aside, to put off,* Mk. 15:20; Lk. 10:30; 2 Cor. 5:3f.* [1562]

[1695] ἐκεῖ *ekei* 105x *there, in that place,* Mt. 2:13, 15; *to that place,* Mt. 2:22; 17:20 [1563]

[1696] ἐκεῖθεν *ekeithen* 37x *from there,* Mt. 4:21; 5:26 [1564]

[1697] ἐκεῖνος *ekeinos* 265x demonstrative adjective or noun, *that, this, he,* etc., Mt. 17:27; 10:14; 2 Tim. 4:8; in contrast with οὗτος, referring to the former of two things previously mentioned, Lk. 18:14 [1565]

[1698] ἐκεῖσε *ekeise* 2x *there, at that place,* Acts 21:3; 22:5* [1566]

[1699] ἐκζητέω *ekzēteō* 7x *to seek out, investigate diligently, scrutinize,* 1 Pet. 1:10; *to ask for, beseech earnestly,* Heb. 12:17; *to seek diligently* or *earnestly after,* Acts 15:17; Rom. 3:11; Heb. 10:6; from the Hebrew, *to require, exact, demand,* Lk. 11:50, 51; Heb. 12:07* [1567]

[1700] ἐκζήτησις *ekzētēsis* 1x *useless speculation,* 1 Tim. 1:4* [2214]

[1701] ἐκθαμβέω *ekthambeō* 4x pas., *to be amazed, astonished, awe-struck,* Mk. 9:15; 14:33; 16:5, 6* [1568]

[1703] ἐκθαυμάζω *ekthaumazō* 1x *to wonder at, wonder greatly,* Mk. 12:17* [2296]

[1704] ἔκθετος *ekthetos* 1x *exposed, cast out, abandoned,* Acts 7:18* [1570]

[1705] ἐκκαθαίρω *ekkathairō* 2x *to cleanse thoroughly, purify,* 2 Tim. 2:21; *to purge out, eliminate,* 1 Cor. 5:7* [1571]

[1706] ἐκκαίω *ekkaiō* 1x pas., *to blaze out, to be inflamed,* Rom. 1:27* [1572]

[1708] ἐκκεντέω *ekkenteō* 2x *to stab, pierce deeply,* Jn. 19:37; Rev. 1:7* [1574]

[1709] ἐκκλάω *ekklaō* 3x *to break off,* pas., *be broken,* Rom. 11:17, 19, 20* [1575]

[1710] ἐκκλείω *ekkleiō* 2x *to shut out, exclude; to shut of, separate, insulate;* Gal. 4:17; *to leave no place for, eliminate,* Rom. 3:27* [1576]

[1711] ἐκκλησία *ekklēsia* 114x *a popular assembly,* Acts 19:32, 39, 41; in NT *the congregation* of the children of Israel, Acts 7:38; transferred to the Christian body, of which the congregation of Israel was a figure, *the Church,* 1 Cor. 12:28; Col. 1:18; a local portion of the *Church,* a local *church,* Rom. 16:1; *a* Christian *congregation,* 1 Cor. 14:4 [1577] See *church.*

[1712] ἐκκλίνω *ekklinō* 3x *to deflect, deviate,* Rom. 3:12; *to decline* or *turn away from, avoid,* Rom. 16:17; 1 Pet. 3:11 [1578]

[1713] ἐκκολυμβάω *ekkolymbaō* 1x *to swim out* to land, Acts 27:42* [1579]

[1714] ἐκκομίζω *ekkomizō* 1x *to carry out, bring out;* especially, *to carry out* a corpse for burial, Lk. 7:12* [1580]

[1716] ἐκκόπτω *ekkoptō* 10x *to cut out; to cut off,* Mt. 3:10; 5:30; met. *to cut off* an occasion, *remove, prevent,* 2 Cor. 11:12; *to render ineffectual,* Mt. 7:19; 18:8; Lk. 3:9; 12:7, 9; Rom. 11:22, 24; 1 Pet. 3:7* [1581] See *cut.*

[1717] ἐκκρεμάννυμι *ekkremannymi* 1x mid., *to hang upon* a speaker, *fondly listen to, be earnestly attentive,* Lk. 19:48* [1582]

[1718] ἐκλαλέω *eklaleō* 1x *to speak out; to tell, utter, divulge,* Acts 23:22* [1583]

[1719] ἐκλάμπω *eklampō* 1x *to shine out* or *forth,* Mt. 13:43* [1584]

[1720] ἐκλανθάνομαι *eklanthanomai* 1x *to make to forget; to forget entirely,* Heb. 12:5* [1585]

[1721] ἐκλέγομαι *eklegomai* 22x *to pick out;* in NT *to choose, select,* Lk. 6:13; 10:42; in NT *to choose out* as the recipients of special favor and privilege, Acts 13:17; 1 Cor. 1:27 [1586] See *choose; elect; set apart.*

[1722] ἐκλείπω *ekleipō* 4x *to fail, die out,* Lk. 22:32; *to come to an end,* Heb. 1:12; *to be defunct,* Lk. 16:9; 23:45* [1587]

[1723] ἐκλεκτός *eklektos* 22x *chosen out, selected;* in NT *chosen* as a recipient of special privilege, *elect,* Col. 3:12; *specially beloved,* Lk. 23:35; *possessed of prime excellence, exalted,* 1 Tim. 5:21; *choice, precious,* 1 Pet. 2:4, 6 [1588] See *chosen; elect; set apart.*

[1724] ἐκλογή *eklogē* 7x *the act of choosing out, election;* in NT *election* to privilege by divine grace, Rom. 9:11; 11:5, 28; 1 Thess. 1:4; 2 Pet. 1:10; ἡ ἐκλογή, *the elect,* Rom. 11:7; ἐκλογῆς, equivalent to ἐκλεκτόν, by Hebraism, Acts 9:15* [1589]

[1725] ἐκλύω *eklyō* 5x *to be weary, exhausted, faint,* Mt. 15:32; Mk. 8:3; Gal. 6:9; *to lose courage, to faint,* Heb. 12:3, 5* [1590]

[1726] ἐκμάσσω *ekmassō* 5x *to wipe off; to wipe dry,* Lk. 7:38, 44; Jn. 11:2; 12:3; 13:5* [1591]

[1727] ἐκμυκτηρίζω *ekmyktērizō* 2x *to mock, deride, scoff at,* Lk. 16:14; 23:35* [1592]

[1728] ἐκνεύω *ekneuō* 1x pr. *to swim out, to escape by swimming;* hence, generally, *to escape, get clear of* a place, Jn. 5:13; though ἐκνεύσας, in this place, may be referred to ἐκνεύω, *to deviate, withdraw** [1593]

[1729] ἐκνήφω *eknēphō* 1x pr. *to awake sober after intoxication;* met. *to shake off mental bewilderment, to wake up* from delusion and folly, 1 Cor. 15:34* [1594]

[1730] ἑκούσιος *hekousios* 1x *voluntary, spontaneous,* Phlm. 14* [1595]

[1731] ἑκουσίως *hekousiōs* 2x *voluntarily, spontaneously,* Heb. 10:26; 1 Pet. 5:2* [1596]

[1732] ἔκπαλαι *ekpalai* 2x *of old, long since,* 2 Pet. 2:3; 3:5* [1597]

[1733] ἐκπειράζω *ekpeirazō* 4x *to tempt, put to the test,* Mt. 4:7; Lk. 4:12; 1 Cor. 10:9; *to try, sound,* Lk. 10:25* [1598]

[1734] ἐκπέμπω *ekpempō* 2x *to send out,* or *away,* Acts 13:4; 17:10* [1599]

[1735] ἐκπερισσῶς *ekperissōs* 1x *exceedingly, vehemently,* Mk. 14:31* [1537 + 4053]

[1736] ἐκπετάννυμι *ekpetannymi* 1x pluperfect, ἐκπεπετάκειν, *to stretch forth, expand, extend,* Rom. 10:21* [1600]

[1737] ἐκπηδάω *ekpēdaō* 1x *to leap forth, rush out,* Acts 14:14* [1530]

[1738] ἐκπίπτω *ekpiptō* 10x *to fall off* or *from,* Acts 12:7; 27:32; met. *to fall from, forfeit, lose,* Gal. 5:4; 2 Pet. 3:17; *to be cast ashore,* Acts 27:17, 26, 29; *to fall to the ground, be fruitless, ineffectual,* Rom. 9:6; *to cease, come to an end,* Jas. 1:11; 1 Pet. 1:24* [1601] See *fail; fall; fall away.*

[1739] ἐκπλέω *ekpleō* 3x *to sail out of* or *from a place,* Acts 15:39; 18:18; 20:6* [1602]

[1740] ἐκπληρόω *ekplēroō* 1x *to fill out, complete, fill up;* met. *to fulfil, perform, accomplish,* Acts 13:33* [1603]

[1741] ἐκπλήρωσις *ekplērōsis* 1x pr. *a filling up, completion;* hence, *a fulfilling, accomplishment,* Acts 21:26* [1604]

[1742] ἐκπλήσσω *ekplēssō* 13x pr. *to strike out of;* hence, *to strike out of* one's wits, *to astound, amaze;*

pass., *overwhelmed,* Mt. 7:28; 13:54 [1605] See *(be) amazed; astonish; astound.*

[1743] ἐκπνέω *ekpneō* 3x *to breathe out; to expire, die,* Mk. 15:37, 39; Lk. 23:46* [1606]

[1744] ἐκπορεύομαι *ekporeuomai* 33x *to go from* or *out of* a place, *depart from,* Mk. 11:19; 13:1; *to be voided,* Mk. 7:19; *to be cast out,* Mt. 17:21; *to proceed from, be spoken,* Mt. 4:4; 15:11; *to burst forth,* Rev. 4:5; *to be spread abroad,* Lk. 4:37; *to flow out,* Rev. 22:1; from the Hebrew, ἐκπορεύομαι καὶ εἰσπορεύομαι. see εἰσέρχομαι, Acts 9:28 [1607] See *come out; go out.*

[1745] ἐκπορνεύω *ekporneuō* 1x *to be given to fornication, indulge in immorality,* Jude 7* [1608]

[1746] ἐκπτύω *ekptyō* 1x lit., *to spit out*; met. *to reject,* Gal. 4:14* [1609]

[1748] ἐκριζόω *ekrizoō* 4x *to root up, eradicate, pull out by the roots,* Mt. 13:29; 15:13; Lk. 17:6; Jude 12* [1610]

[1749] ἔκστασις *ekstasis* 7x pr. *a displacement;* hence, *a displacement of the mind from its ordinary state and self-possession; amazement, astonishment,* Mk. 5:42; *excess of fear; fear, terror,* Mk. 16:8; Lk. 5:26; Acts 3:10; in NT *an ecstasy, a trance,* Acts 10:10; 11:5; 22:17* [1611]

[1750] ἐκστρέφω *ekstrephō* 1x pr. *to turn out of, to turn inside out;* hence, *to change entirely;* in NT pass. *to be perverted,* Tit. 3:11* [1612]

[1752] ἐκταράσσω *ektarassō* 1x *to disturb, disquiet, throw into confusion,* Acts 16:20* [1613]

[1753] ἐκτείνω *ekteinō* 16x *to stretch out,* Mt. 8:3; 12:13; *to lay* hands on any one, Lk. 22:53; *to exert* power and energy, Acts 4:30; *to cast out, let down* an anchor, Acts 27:30 [1614] See *stretch out.*

[1754] ἐκτελέω *ekteleō* 2x *to bring to an end, to finish, complete,* Lk. 14:29, 30* [1615]

[1755] ἐκτένεια *ekteneia* 1x pr. *extension;* in NT *intenseness, intentness;* ἐν ἐκτενείᾳ, *intently, perseverance, earnestness,* Acts 26:7* [1616]

[1756] ἐκτενής *ektenēs* 1x pr. *extended;* met. *intense, earnest, fervent, eager,* 1 Pet. 4:8* [1618]

[1757] ἐκτενῶς *ektenōs* 3x *intensely, fervently, earnestly,* Lk. 22:44; Acts 12:5; 1 Pet. 1:22* [1617, 1619]

[1758] ἐκτίθημι *ektithēmi* 4x pr. *to place outside, put forth; to expose* an infant, Acts 7:21; met. *to set forth, declare, explain,* Acts 11:4; 18:26; 28:23* [1620]

[1759] ἐκτινάσσω *ektinassō* 4x *to shake out, shake off,* Mt. 10:14; Mk. 6:11; Acts 13:51; 18:6* [1621]

[1760] ἐκτός *ektos* 8x also functions as an improper prep. (4x), *without, on the outside;* τὸ ἐκτός, *the exterior, outside,* Mt. 23:26; met. *besides,* Acts 26:22; 1 Cor. 15:27; ἐκτὸς εἰ μή, *unless, except,* 1 Cor. 14:5 [1622]

[1761] ἕκτος *hektos* 14x *sixth,* Mt. 20:5; 27:45 [1623] See *sixth.*

[1762] ἐκτρέπω *ektrepō* 5x mid. and pas., *to turn out* or *aside,* Heb. 12:13; *to turn aside* or *away, swerve,* 1 Tim. 1:6; 5:15; 2 Tim. 4:4; *to turn from, avoid,* 1 Tim. 6:20* [1624]

[1763] ἐκτρέφω *ektrephō* 2x *to nourish, promote health and strength,* Eph. 5:29; *to bring up, educate,* Eph. 6:4* [1625]

[1765] ἔκτρωμα *ektrōma* 1x *an abortion, baby prematurely born,* 1 Cor. 15:8* [1626]

[1766] ἐκφέρω *ekpherō* 8x *to bring forth, carry out,* Lk. 15:22; Acts 5:15; 1 Tim. 6:7; *to carry out* for burial, Acts 5:6, 9, 10; *to produce, yield,* Mk. 8:23; Heb. 6:8* [1627]

[1767] ἐκφεύγω *ekpheugō* 8x intrans. *to flee out, to make an escape,* Acts 16:27; 19:16; trans. *to escape, avoid,* Lk. 21:36; Rom. 2:3 [1628]

[1768] ἐκφοβέω *ekphobeō* 1x *to terrify,* 2 Cor. 10:9* [1629]

[1769] ἔκφοβος *ekphobos* 2x *frightened, horrified,* Mk. 9:6; Heb. 12:21* [1630]

[1770] ἐκφύω *ekphyō* 2x lit. *to cause to grow, to generate; to put forth, shoot,* Mt. 24:32; Mk. 13:28* [1631]

[1772] ἐκχέω *ekcheō* 16x also formed as ἐκχύννομαι (11x), *to pour out,* Rev. 16:1, 2, 3; *to shed* blood, Mt. 26:28; Mk. 14:24; pass. *to gush out,* Acts 1:18; *to spill, scatter,* Mt. 9:17; Jn. 2:15; met. *to give largely, bestow liberally,* Acts 2:17, 18, 33; 10:45; pass. *to rush headlong* into anything, *be abandoned to,* Jude 11 [1632] See *pour out; shed.*

[1773] ἐκχύννομαι *ekchunnomai* 11x some list as the active ἐκχύννω; see ἐκχέω (*1772*) [1632] See *pour out; shed.*

[1774] ἐκχωρέω *ekchōreō* 1x *to go out, depart from, flee,* Lk. 21:21* [1633]

[1775] ἐκψύχω *ekpsychō* 3x *to expire, give up one's spirit,* Acts 5:5, 10; 12:23* [1634]

[1776] ἑκών *hekōn* 2x *willing, voluntary,* Rom. 8:20; 1 Cor. 9:17* [1635]

[1777] ἐλαία *elaia* 15x *an olive tree,* Mt. 21:1; 24:3; *an olive, fruit of the olive tree,* Jas. 3:12, ὄρος τῶν ἐλαιῶν, *the Mount of Olives,* Mt. 21:1 [1636] See *olive.*

[1778] ἔλαιον *elaion* 11x *olive oil, oil,* Mt. 25:3, 4, 8; Mk. 6:13 [1637] See *oil; olive oil.*

[1779] ἐλαιών *elaiōn* 1x *an olive garden;* in NT the mount *Olivet,* Lk. 19:29; 21:37; Acts 1:12* [1638]

[1780] Ἐλαμίτης *Elamitēs* 1x *an Elamite; an inhabitant of Elam,* a province of Persia, Acts 2:9* [1639]

[1781] ἐλάσσων *elassōn* 4x ἐλάττων (1784) is the Attic form of this word. Twice it is used with σσ (Jn. 2:10; Rom. 9:12) and twice with ττ (1 Tim. 5:9; Heb. 7:7). It is used as the comparative of μικρός, *less; less* in age, *younger,* Rom. 9:12; *less* in dignity, *inferior,* Heb. 7:7; *less* in quality, *inferior, worse,* Jn. 2:10; 1 Tim. 5:9* [1640]

[1782] ἐλαττονέω *elattoneō* 1x trans. *to make less;* intrans. *to be less, inferior; to have too little, want, lack,* 2 Cor. 8:15* [1641]

[1783] ἐλαττόω *elattoō* 3x *to make less* or *inferior,* Heb. 2:7; pass. *to be made less* or *inferior,* Heb. 2:9; *to decline* in importance, Jn. 3:30* [1642]

[1785] ἐλαύνω *elaunō* 5x *to drive, urge forward, spur on,* Lk. 8:29; Jas. 3:4; 2 Pet. 2:17; *to impel* a vessel by oars, *to row,* Mk. 6:48; Jn. 6:19* [1643]

[1786] ἐλαφρία *elaphria* 1x *lightness* in weight; hence, *lightness of mind, levity,* 2 Cor. 1:17* [1644]

[1787] ἐλαφρός *elaphros* 2x *light, not heavy,* Mt. 11:30; 2 Cor. 4:17* [1645]

[1788] ἐλάχιστος *elachistos* 14x used as the superlative of μικρός, *smallest, least,* Mt. 2:6; 5:19 [1646, 1647] See *least.*

[1789] Ἐλεάζαρ *Eleazar* 2x *Eleazar,* pr. name, indecl., Mt. 1:15* [1648]

[1790] ἐλεάω *eleaō* 4x see ἐλεέω, *have mercy on,* Rom. 9:16; 12:8; Jude 22, 23* [1653]

[1791] ἐλεγμός *elegmos* 1x *reproof,* 2 Tim. 3:16, a later equivalent to ἔλεγχος* [1650]

[1792] ἔλεγξις *elenxis* 1x *reproof, rebuke,* 2 Pet. 2:16* [1649]

[1793] ἔλεγχος *elenchos* 1x pr. *a trial in order to proof, a proof;* meton. *a certain persuasion,* Heb. 11:1* [1650]

[1794] ἐλέγχω *elenchō* 17x *to put to proof, to test; to convict,* Jn. 8:46; Jas. 2:9; *to refute, confute,* 1 Cor. 14:24; Tit. 1:9; *to detect, lay bare, expose,* Jn. 3:20; Eph. 5:11, 13; *to reprove, rebuke,* Mt. 18:15; Lk. 3:19; 1 Tim. 5:20; *to discipline, chastise,* Heb. 12:5; Rev. 3:19; pass. *to experience conviction,* Jn. 3:20; 1 Cor. 14:24 [1651] See *rebuke; refute.*

[1795] ἐλεεινός *eleeinos* 2x *pitiable, wretched, miserable,* 1 Cor. 15:19; Rev. 3:17* [1652]

[1796] ἐλεέω *eleeō* 28x also formed as ἐλεάω 4x, *to pity, have compassion on;* pass. *to receive pity, experience compassion,* Mt. 5:7; 9:27; 15:22; *to be gracious to* any one, *show gracious favor and saving mercy towards;* pass. *to be an object of gracious favor and saving mercy,* Rom. 11:30, 31; spc. *to obtain pardon and forgiveness,* 1 Tim. 1:13, 16 [1653] See *mercy; pity.*

[1797] ἐλεημοσύνη *eleēmosynē* 13x *pity, compassion;* in NT *an act of kindness, alms, almsgiving,* Mt. 6:2, 3, 4; Lk. 11:41 [1654] See *alms; gift.*

[1798] ἐλεήμων *eleēmōn* 2x *merciful, pitiful, compassionate,* Mt. 5:7; Heb. 2:17* [1655]

[1799] ἔλεος *eleos* 27x *pity, mercy, compassion,* Mt. 9:13; 12:7; Lk. 1:50, 78; meton. *benefit* which results from compassion, *kindness, mercies, blessing,* Lk. 1:54, 58, 72; 10:37; Rom. 9:23 [1656] See *compassion; mercy.*

[1800] ἐλευθερία *eleutheria* 11x *liberty, freedom,* 1 Cor. 10:29; Gal. 2:4 [1657] See *freedom.*

[1801] ἐλεύθερος *eleutheros* 23x *free, in a state of freedom* as opposed to slavery, 1 Cor. 12:13; Gal. 3:28; *free, exempt,* Mt. 17:26; 1 Cor. 7:39; *unrestricted, unfettered,* 1 Cor. 9:1; *free* from the dominion of sin, etc., Jn. 8:36; Rom. 6:20; *free* in the possession of Gospel privileges, 1 Pet. 2:16 [1658] See *free; freedom; independent.*

[1802] ἐλευθερόω *eleutheroō* 7x *to free, set free,* Jn. 8:32, 36; Rom. 6:18, 22; 8:2, 21; Gal. 5:1* [1659]

[1803] ἔλευσις *eleusis* 1x *a coming, advent,* Acts 7:52* [1660]

[1804] ἐλεφάντινος *elephantinos* 1x *ivory, made of ivory,* Rev. 18:12* [1661]

[1806] Ἐλιακίμ *Eliakim* 3x also spelled Ἐλιακείμ, *Eliakim,* pr. name, indecl., Mt. 1:13; Lk. 3:30* [1662]

[1808] Ἐλιέζερ *Eliezer* 1x *Eliezer,* pr. name, indecl., Lk. 3:29* [1663]

[1809] Ἐλιούδ *Elioud* 2x *Eliud,* the father of Eleazar, Mt. 1:14, 15* [1664]

[1810] Ἐλισάβετ *Elisabet* 9x *Elizabeth,* the wife of Zechariah and mother of John the Baptist, Lk. 1:5, 13, 24, 36, 57 [1665]

[1811] Ἐλισαῖος *Elisaios* 1x also spelled Ἐλισσαῖος, *Elisha,* pr. name, Lk. 4:27* [1666]

[1813] ἑλίσσω *helissō* 2x *to roll, fold up,* as garments, Heb. 1:12; Rev. 6:14* [1507, 1667]

[1814] ἕλκος *helkos* 3x pr. *a wound;* hence, *an ulcer, sore,* Lk. 16:21; Rev. 16:2, 11* [1668]

[1815] ἑλκόω *helkoō* 1x pass. *to be afflicted with ulcers,* Lk. 16:20* [1669]

[1817] Ἑλλάς *Hellas* 1x *Hellas, Greece;* in NT *the southern portion of Greece* as distinguished from Macedonia, Acts 20:2* [1671]

[1818] Ἕλλην *Hellēn* 25x *a Greek,* Acts 18:17; Rom. 1:14; *one not a Jew, a Gentile,* Acts 14:1; 16:1, 3 [1672] See *Greeks.*

[1819] Ἑλληνικός *Hellēnikos* 1x *Greek, Grecian,* Rev. 9:11* [1673]

[1820] Ἑλληνίς *Hellēnis* 2x *a female Greek,* Mk. 7:26; Acts 17:12* [1674]

[1821] Ἑλληνιστής *Hellēnistēs* 3x pr. *one who uses the language and follows the customs of the Greeks;* in NT *a Jew by blood, but a native of a Greek-speaking country, Hellenist,* Acts 6:1; 9:29; 11:20* [1675]

[1822] Ἑλληνιστί *Hellēnisti* 2x *in the Greek language,* Jn. 19:20; Acts 21:37* [1676]

[1824] ἐλλογέω *ellogeō* 2x *to enter in an account, to put* or *charge to one's account,* Phlm. 18; in NT *to impute,* Rom. 5:13* [1677]

[1825] Ἐλμαδάμ *Elmadam* 1x also spelled Ἐλμωδάμ, *Elmadam,* pr. name, indecl., Lk. 3:28* [1678]

[1827] ἐλπίζω *elpizō* 31x *to hope, expect,* Lk. 23:8; 24:21; *to repose hope and confidence in, trust, confide,* Mt. 12:21; Jn. 5:45 [1679] See *desire; hope; wish.*

[1828] ἐλπίς *elpis* 53x pr. *expectation; hope,* Acts 24:15; Rom. 5:4; meton. *the object of hope, thing hoped for,* Rom. 8:24; Gal. 5:5; *the author* or *source of hope,* Col. 1:27; 1 Tim. 1:1; *trust, confidence,* 1 Pet. 1:21; ἐπ᾽ ἐλπίδι, *in security, with a guarantee,* Acts 2:26; Rom. 8:20 [1680] See *confident expectation; desire; hope; wish.*

[1829] Ἐλύμας *Elymas* 1x *Elymas,* pr. name, Acts 13:8* [1681]

[1830] ἐλωΐ *elōi* 2x Aramaic for, *my God,* Mk. 15:34* [1682]

[1831] ἐμαυτοῦ *emautou* 37x *myself, my own,* Lk. 7:7; Jn. 5:31 [1683]

[1832] ἐμβαίνω *embainō* 16x *to step in; to go on board* a ship, *embark,* Mt. 8:23; 9:1; 13:2 [1684] See *get into (a boat).*

[1833] ἐμβάλλω *emballō* 1x *to cast into,* Lk. 12:5* [1685]

[1835] ἐμβάπτω *embaptō* 2x *to dip in,* Mt. 26:23; *to dip* for food in a dish, Mk. 14:20* [1686]

[1836] ἐμβατεύω *embateuō* 1x pr. *to step into* or *upon;* met. *to search into, investigate; to pry into intrusively,* Col. 2:18* [1687]

[1837] ἐμβιβάζω *embibazō* 1x *to cause to step into* or *upon; to set in* or *upon;* especially, *to put on board,* Acts 27:6* [1688]

[1838] ἐμβλέπω *emblepō* 11x *to look attentively, gaze earnestly,* at an object, followed by εἰς, Mk. 6:26; Acts 1:11; *to direct a glance, to look searchingly* or *significantly,* at a person, followed by the dat., Mk. 10:21; 14:67; Lk. 22:61; absol. *to see clearly,* Mk. 8:25; Acts 22:11 [1689] See *look at.*

[1839] ἐμβριμάομαι *embrimaomai* 5x Attic spelling, ἐμβριμόομαι, *to be greatly agitated,* Jn. 11:33, 38; *to charge* or *forbid sternly* or *vehemently,* Mt. 9:30; Mk. 1:43; *to express indignation, to censure,* Mk. 14:5* [1690]

[1840] ἐμέω *emeō* 1x *to vomit,* Rev. 3:16* [1692]

[1841] ἐμμαίνομαι *emmainomai* 1x *to be mad against, be furious toward,* Acts 26:11* [1693]

[1842] Ἐμμανουήλ *Emmanouēl* 1x *Emmanuel,* pr. name, indecl., Mt. 1:23* [1694] See *Immanuel.*

[1843] Ἐμμαοῦς *Emmaous* 1x *Emmaus,* pr. name, indecl., of a village near Jerusalem, Lk. 24:13* [1695]

[1844] ἐμμένω *emmenō* 4x pr. *to remain in* a place; met. *to abide by, to continue firm in, persevere in,* Acts 14:22; 28:30; Gal. 3:10; Heb. 8:9* [1696]

[1846] Ἑμμώρ *Hemmōr* 1x also spelled Ἑμμόρ, *Hamor,* pr. name, indecl., Acts 7:16 [1697]

[1847] ἐμός *emos* 76x *my, mine,* Jn. 7:16; 8:37 [1699]

[1848] ἐμπαιγμονή *empaigmonē* 1x *mocking, scoffing, derision,* 2 Pet. 3:3* [**]

[1849] ἐμπαιγμός *empaigmos* 1x *mocking, scoffing, scorn,* Heb. 11:36* [1701]

[1850] ἐμπαίζω *empaizō* 13x *to play upon, deride, mock, treat with scorn, ridicule,* Mt. 20:19; 27:29; by impl. *to delude, deceive,* Mt. 2:16 [1702] See *deceive; mock.*

[1851] ἐμπαίκτης *empaiktēs* 2x *a mocker, derider, scoffer,* 2 Pet. 3:3; Jude 18* [1703]

[1853] ἐμπεριπατέω *emperipateō* 1x pr. *to walk about in* a place; met. in NT *to live among, be conversant with,* 2 Cor. 6:16* [1704]

[1858] ἐμπίπλημι *empiplēmi* 5x also spelled ἐμπίμπλημι (1855) and ἐμπιμπλάω (1857), *to fill,* Acts 14:17; pass. *to be satisfied, satiated, full,* Lk. 1:53; 6:25; Jn. 6:12; met. *to have the full enjoyment of,* Rom. 15:24* [1705]

[1859] ἐμπίμπρημι *empimprēmi* 1x also spelled ἐμπίπρημι and ἐμπρήθω, *to set on fire, burn down,* Mt. 22:7* [1714]

[1860] ἐμπίπτω *empiptō* 7x *to fall into,* Mt. 12:11; Lk. 14:5; *to encounter,* Lk. 10:36; *to be involved in,* 1 Tim. 3:6, 7; 6:9; εἰς χεῖρας, *to fall under the chastisement of,* Heb. 10:31 [1706]

[1861] ἐμπλέκω *emplekō* 2x pr. *to intertwine;* met. *to implicate, entangle, involve;* pass. *to be implicated, involved,* or *to entangle one's self in,* 2 Tim. 2:4; 2 Pet. 2:20* [1707]

[1862] ἐμπλοκή *emplokē* 1x *braiding* or *plaiting* of hair, 1 Pet. 3:3* [1708]

[1863] ἐμπνέω *empneō* 1x gen., *to breathe into* or *upon; to respire, breathe;* met. *to breathe of, be animated with the spirit of,* Acts 9:1* [1709]

[1864] ἐμπορεύομαι *emporeuomai* 2x *to travel; to travel for business' sake; to trade, traffic,* Jas. 4:13; by impl., trans., *to make a gain of, deceive for one's own advantage,* 2 Pet. 2:3* [1710]

[1865] ἐμπορία *emporia* 1x *business, trade,* Mt. 22:5* [1711]

[1866] ἐμπόριον *emporion* 1x *a mart, marketplace, emporium;* met. *traffic,* Jn. 2:16* [1712]

[1867] ἔμπορος *emporos* 5x pr. *a passenger by sea; a traveller; one who travels about for traffic, a merchant,* Mt. 13:45; Rev. 18:3, 11, 15, 23* [1713]

[1869] ἔμπροσθεν *emprosthen* 48x also an improper prep., *before, in front of,* Lk. 19:4; Phil. 3:14; *before, in the presence of, in the face of,* Mt. 5:24; 23:14; *before, previous to,* Jn. 1:15, 27, 30; from the Hebrew, *in the sight* or *estimation of,* Mt. 11:26; 18:14 [1715]

[1870] ἐμπτύω *emptyō* 6x followed by the dat., or εἰς and the acc., *to spit upon,* Mt. 26:67; 27:30 [1716]

[1871] ἐμφανής *emphanēs* 2x *apparent, conspicuous, visible,* Acts 10:40; met. *manifest, known, comprehended, revealed,* Rom. 10:20* [1717]

[1872] ἐμφανίζω *emphanizō* 10x *to cause to appear clearly; to communicate, report,* Acts 23:15, 22; *to bring charges against,* Acts 24:1; 25:2, 15, *to manifest, explain,* Heb. 11:14; *to reveal, make known,* Jn. 14:21, 22; pass. *to appear, be visible,* Mt. 27:53; *to present one's self,* Heb. 9:24* [1718] See *disclose; show.*

[1873] ἔμφοβος *emphobos* 5x *terrible;* in NT *terrified,* Lk. 24:5, 37; Acts 10:4; 24:25; Rev. 11:13* [1719]

[1874] ἐμφυσάω *emphysaō* 1x *to blow* or *breathe into, inflate;* in NT *to breathe upon,* Jn. 20:22* [1720]

[1875] ἔμφυτος *emphytos* 1x *implanted, ingrafted,* Jas. 1:21* [1721]

[1877] ἐν *en* 2,752x followed by the dat., *in,* Mt. 8:6; Mk. 12:26; Rev. 6:6; *upon,* Lk. 8:32; *among,* Mt. 11:11; *before, in the presence of,* Mk. 8:38; *in the sight, estimation of,* 1 Cor. 14:11; *before,* judicially, 1 Cor. 6:2; *in,* of state, occupation, habit, Mt. 21:22; Lk. 7:25; Rom. 4:10; *in the case of,* Mt. 17:12; *in respect of,* Lk. 1:7; 1 Cor. 1:7; *on occasion of, on the ground of,* Mt. 6:7; Lk. 1:21; of the instrument, means, efficient cause, Rom. 12:21; Acts 4:12; *equipped with, furnished with,* 1 Cor. 4:21; Heb. 9:25; *arrayed with, accompanied by,* Lk. 14:31; Jude 14; of time, *during, in the course of,* Mt. 2:1; in NT of demonic possession, *possessed by,* Mk. 5:2 [1722]

[1878] ἐναγκαλίζομαι *enankalizomai* 2x *to take into* or *embrace in one's arms,* Mk. 9:36; 10:16* [1723]

[1879] ἐνάλιος *enalios* 1x *marine, living in the sea,* Jas. 3:7* [1724]

[1882] ἔναντι *enanti* 2x also an improper prep, *over against, in the presence of,* Lk. 1:8; Acts 8:21* [1725]

[1883] ἐναντίον *enantion* 8x acc sg neut of ἐναντίος used adverbially; the adj. does not appear in the NT, improper prep., *before, in the presence of,* Lk. 1:6; 20:26; Acts 8:32; 2 Cor. 2:7; Gal. 2:7; 1 Pet. 3:9; from the Hebrew, *in the sight* or *estimation of,* Acts 7:10; with τοῦ θεοῦ, an intensive expression, Lk. 24:19* [1726]

[1885] ἐναντίος *enantios* 8x *opposite to, over against,* Mk. 15:39; *contrary,* as the wind, Mt. 14:24; Acts 26:9; 28:17; ὁ ἐξ ἐναντίας, *an adverse party, enemy,* Tit. 2:8; *adverse, hostile, counter,* 1 Thess. 2:15 [1727]

[1887] ἐνάρχομαι *enarchomai* 2x *to begin, commence,* Gal. 3:3; Phil. 1:6* [1728]

[1888] ἔνατος *enatos* 10x *the ninth,* Mt. 20:5; 27:45f.; Mk. 15:33f.; Lk. 23:44; Acts 3:1; 10:3, 30; Rev. 21:20* [1766] See *ninth.*

[1890] ἐνδεής *endeēs* 1x *indigent, poor, needy,* Acts 4:34* [1729]

[1891] ἔνδειγμα *endeigma* 1x *a token, evidence, proof,* 2 Thess. 1:5* [1730]

[1892] ἐνδείκνυμι *endeiknymi* 11x *to manifest, display, show, demonstrate,* Rom. 9:17, 22; Heb. 6:10; *to give outward proof of,* Rom. 2:15; *to display* a certain bearing towards a person; hence, *to perpetrate openly,* 2 Tim. 4:14* [1731] See *demonstrate; show.*

[1893] ἔνδειξις *endeixis* 4x *a pointing out;* met. *manifestation, public declaration,* Rom. 3:25, 26; *a token, sign, proof,* i.q. ἔνδειγμα, 2 Cor. 8:24; Phil. 1:28* [1732]

[1894] ἕνδεκα *hendeka* 6x *eleven,* indecl. numeral, Mt. 28:16; Mk. 16:14; Lk. 24:9, 33; Acts 1:26; 2:14* [1733]

[1895] ἑνδέκατος *hendekatos* 3x *eleventh,* Mt. 20:6, 9; Rev. 21:20* [1734]

[1896] ἐνδέχομαι *endechomai* 1x *to admit, approve; to be possible,* impersonal, *it is possible,* Lk. 13:33* [1735]

[1897] ἐνδημέω *endēmeō* 3x *to dwell in* a place, *be at home,* 2 Cor. 5:6, 8, 9* [1736]

[1898] ἐνδιδύσκω *endidyskō* 2x a later form, equivalent to ἐνδύω, *to dress (oneself),* Mark 15:17; 16:19* [1737]

[1899] ἔνδικος *endikos* 2x *fair, just,* Rom. 3:8; Heb. 2:2* [1738]

[1901] ἐνδοξάζομαι *endoxazomai* 2x *to invest with glory;* pass. *to be glorified, to be made a subject of glorification,* 2 Thess. 1:10, 12* [1740]

[1902] ἔνδοξος *endoxos* 4x *honored,* 1 Cor. 4:10; *notable, memorable,* Lk. 13:17; *splendid, gorgeous,* Lk. 7:25; *in unsullied array,* Eph. 5:27* [1741]

[1903] ἔνδυμα *endyma* 8x *clothing, a garment,* Mt. 6:25, 28; 22:11, 12; in particular, *an outer garment, cloak, mantle,* Mt. 3:4; 7:15; 28:3; Lk. 12:23* [1742]

[1904] ἐνδυναμόω *endynamoō* 7x *to empower, invigorate,* Phil. 4:13; 1 Tim. 1:12; 2 Tim. 4:17; mid. *to summon up vigor, put forth energy,* Eph. 6:10; 2 Tim. 2:1; pass. *to acquire strength, be invigorated, be strong,* Acts 9:22; Rom. 4:20* [1743]

[1905] ἐνδύνω *endynō* 1x *enter, creep in,* 2 Tim. 3:6* [1744]

[1906] ἔνδυσις *endysis* 1x *a putting on,* or *wearing* of clothes, 1 Pet. 3:3* [1745]

[1907] ἐνδύω *endyō* 27x *to enter,* 2 Tim. 3:6; *to put on, clothe, invest, array,* Mt. 27:31; Mk. 15:17, 20; mid. *clothe one's self, be clothed,* Mt. 22:11, 27, 31; trop. *to be clothed* with spiritual gifts, graces, or character, Lk. 24:49; Rom. 13:14 [1746] See *clothe; put on; wear.*

[1908] ἐνδώμησις *endōmēsis* 1x *construction, material,* Rev. 21:18* [1739]

[1909] ἐνέδρα *enedra* 2x pr. *a sitting in* or *on a* spot; *an ambush,* or *lying in wait,* Acts 23:16; 25:3* [1747]

[1910] ἐνεδρεύω *enedreuō* 2x *to lie in wait* or *ambush for,* Acts 23:21; *to endeavor to entrap,* Lk. 11:54* [1748]

[1912] ἐνειλέω *eneileō* 1x *to envelope, to wrap up,* Mk. 15:46* [1750]

[1913] ἔνειμι *eneimi* 7x *to be in* or *within;* τὰ ἐνόντα, *those things which are within,* Lk. 11:41* [1751]

[1915] ἕνεκεν *heneken* 24x also spelled ἕνεκα, with the genitive, *on account of, for the sake of, by reason of.* Our text has ἕνεκεν 20x, ἕνεκα 4x (Mt. 19:5; Lk. 6:2; Acts 19:32; 26:21)* [1752]

[1916] ἐνενήκοντα *enenēkonta* 4x indecl, *ninety,* Mt. 18:12, 13; Lk. 15:4, 7* [1768]

[1917] ἐνεός *eneos* 1x *dumb, speechless,* Acts 9:7* [1769]

[1918] ἐνέργεια *energeia* 8x *energy, efficacy, power,* Phil. 3:21; Col. 2:12; *active energy, operation,* Eph. 1:19; 3:7; 4:16; Col. 1:29; 2 Thess. 2:9, 11* [1753]

[1919] ἐνεργέω *energeō* 21x *to effect,* 1 Cor. 12:6, 11; Gal. 3:5; Eph. 1:11; Phil. 2:13; *to put into operation,* Eph. 1:20; absol. *to be active,* Mt. 14:2; Mk. 6:14; Eph. 2:2; in NT *to communicate energy and efficiency,* Gal. 2:8; pass. or mid. *to come into activity, be actively developed; to be active, be in operation,* towards a result, 2 Cor. 4:12; 2 Thess. 2:7; *to be an active power* or *principle,* Rom. 7:5; 1 Thess. 2:12; *instinct with activity; in action, operative,* 2 Cor. 1:6; Gal. 5:6; Eph. 3:20; Col. 1:29; *earnest,* Jas. 5:16 [1754] See *operate; work.*

[1920] ἐνέργημα *energēma* 2x *an effect, thing effected, activity,* 1 Cor. 12:6; *operation, working,* 1 Cor. 12:10* [1755]

[1921] ἐνεργής *energēs* 3x *active,* Phlm. 6; *efficient, energetic,* Heb. 4:12; *adapted to accomplish* a thing, *effectual,* 1 Cor. 16:9* [1756]

[1922] ἐνευλογέω *eneulogeō* 2x *to bless in respect of,* or *by means of,* Acts 3:25; Gal. 3:8* [1757]

[1923] ἐνέχω *enechō* 3x *to hold within; to fix upon;* in NT intrans. (sc. χόλον) *to entertain a grudge against,* Mk. 6:19; *to be exasperated against,* Lk. 11:53; pass. *to be entangled, held fast in,* Gal. 5:1* [1758]

[1924] ἐνθάδε *enthade* 8x pr. *to this place,* Jn. 4:15, 16; also, *here, in this place,* Lk. 24:41; Acts 10:8; 16:28; 17:6; 25:17, 24* [1759]

[1925] ἔνθεν *enthen* 2x *from this place,* Mt. 17:20; Lk. 16:26* [1782]

[1926] ἐνθυμέομαι *enthumeomai* 2x *to ponder in one's mind, think of, meditate on,* Mt. 1:20; 9:4* [1760]

[1927] ἐνθύμησις *enthumēsis* 4x *the act of thought, reflection,* Mt. 9:4; 12:25; Heb. 4:12; *the result of thought, invention, device; idea,* Acts 17:29* [1761]

[1929] ἐνιαυτός *eniautos* 14x *a year,* more particularly as being a cycle of seasons, and in respect of its revolution, Jn. 11:49, 51; 18:13; in NT *an era,* Lk. 4:19 [1763] See *year.*

[1931] ἐνίστημι *enistēmi* 7x *to place in* or *upon;* intrans., *to stand close upon; to be at hand, impend, to be present,* Rom. 8:38; 2 Thess. 2:2; Heb. 9:9 [1764] See *present.*

[1932] ἐνισχύω *enischuō* 2x *to strengthen, impart strength and vigor,* Lk. 22:43; intrans. *to gain, acquire,* or *recover strength and vigor, be strengthened,* Acts 9:19* [1765]

[1933] ἐννέα *ennea* 5x indecl, *nine,* Mt. 18:12f.; Lk. 15:4, 7; 17:17* [1767]

[1935] ἐννεύω *enneuō* 1x *to nod at, signify by a nod; to make signs; to intimate by signs,* Lk. 1:62* [1770]

[1936] ἔννοια *ennoia* 2x *notion, idea; thought, purpose, intention,* Heb. 4:12; 1 Pet. 4:1* [1771]

[1937] ἔννομος *ennomos* 2x *within law; lawful, legal,* Acts 19:39; in NT *subject* or *under a law, obedient to a law,* 1 Cor. 9:21* [1772]

[1939] ἔννυχος *ennychos* 1x *nocturnal, while still dark,* Mk. 1:35* [1773]

[1940] ἐνοικέω *enoikeō* 5x *to dwell in, live, inhabit;* in NT met. *to be indwelling* spiritually, Rom. 8:11; Col. 3:16; 2 Tim. 1:14; *to be infixed* mentally, 2 Tim. 1:5; of the Deity, *to indwell,* by special presence, 2 Cor. 6:16* [1774]

[1941] ἐνορκίζω *enorkizō* 1x *to adjure,* 1 Thess. 5:27* [3726]

[1942] ἑνότης *henotēs* 2x *oneness, unity,* Eph. 4:3, 13* [1775]

[1943] ἐνοχλέω *enochleō* 2x *to trouble, annoy; to be a trouble,* Lk. 6:18; Heb. 12:15* [1776]

[1944] ἔνοχος *enochos* 10x *held in* or *by; subjected to,* Heb. 2:15; *subject to, liable to, guilty, deserving,* Mt. 5:21, 22; 26:66; Mk. 3:29; 14:64; *an offender against,* 1 Cor. 11:27; Jas. 2:10* [1777] See *guilty; liable; subject to; worthy.*

[1945] ἔνταλμα *entalma* 3x *a precept, commandment, ordinance,* Mt. 15:9; Mk. 7:7; Col. 2:22* [1778]

[1946] ἐνταφιάζω *entaphiazō* 2x *to prepare* a body *for burial,* Mt. 26:12; absol. *to make the ordinary preparations for burial,* Jn. 19:40* [1779]

[1947] ἐνταφιασμός *entaphiasmos* 2x *preparation* of a corpse *for burial, burial* itself, Mk. 14:8; Jn. 12:7* [1780]

[1948] ἐντέλλω *entellō* 15x some list as ἐντέλλομαι, mid., *to enjoin, charge, command,* Mt. 4:6; 15:4; 17:9; *to direct,* Mt. 19:7; Mk. 10:3 [1781] See *command; instruct; order.*

[1949] ἐντεῦθεν *enteuthen* 10x *hence, from this place,* Mt. 17:20; Lk. 4:9; ἐντεῦθεν καὶ ἐντεῦθεν, *on each side,* Rev. 22:2; *hence, from this cause,* Jas. 4:1 [1782]

[1950] ἔντευξις *enteuxis* 2x pr. *a meeting with;* hence *address; prayer, supplication, intercession,* 1 Tim. 2:1; 4:5* [1783]

[1952] ἔντιμος *entimos* 5x *honored, estimable, dear,* Lk. 7:2; 14:8; Phil. 2:29; *highly-valued, precious, costly,* 1 Pet. 2:4, 6* [1784]

[1953] ἐντολή *entolē* 67x *an injunction; a precept, commandment, law,* Mt. 5:19; 15:3, 6; *an order, direction,* Acts 17:15; *an edict,* Jn. 11:57; *a direction,* Mk. 10:5; *a commission,* Jn. 10:18, *a charge* of matters to be proclaimed or received, Jn. 12:49, 50; 1 Tim. 6:14; 2 Pet. 2:21 [1785] See *commandment; order.*

[1954] ἐντόπιος *entopios* 1x *in* or *of a place; an inhabitant, citizen,* Acts 21:12* [1786]

[1955] ἐντός *entos* 2x improper prep., gen., *inside, within,* Lk. 17:21; τὸ ἐντός, *the interior, inside,* Mt. 23:26* [1787]

[1956] ἐντρέπω *entrepō* 9x mid., *to revere, reverence, regard,* Mt. 21:37; Mk. 12:6; absol. *to feel shame, be put to shame,* 2 Thess. 3:14; Tit. 2:8; pass., *be put to shame,* 2 Thess. 3:14; Tit. 3:8 [1788]

[1957] ἐντρέφω *entrephō* 1x *to nourish in, bring up* or *educate in,* 1 Tim. 4:6* [1789]

[1958] ἔντρομος *entromos* 3x *trembling, terrified,* Acts 7:32; 16:29; Heb. 12:21* [1790]

[1959] ἐντροπή *entropē* 2x *humiliation;* in NT *shame,* 1 Cor. 6:5; 15:34* [1791]

[1960] ἐντρυφάω *entryphaō* 1x *to live luxuriously, riot, revel,* 2 Pet. 2:13* [1792]

[1961] ἐντυγχάνω *entynchanō* 5x *to fill in with, meet; to have conversation with, address; to address* or *apply to* any one, Acts 25:24; ὑπέρ τινος, *to intercede for any one, plead the cause of,* Rom. 8:27, 34; Heb. 7:25; κατά τινος, *to address a representation* or *suit against any one, to accuse, complain of,* Rom. 11:2* [1793]

[1962] ἐντυλίσσω *entylissō* 3x *to wrap up in, inwrap, envelope,* Mt. 27:59; Lk. 23:53; *to wrap up, roll* or *fold together,* Jn. 20:7* [1794]

[1963] ἐντυπόω *entypoō* 1x *to impress a figure, instamp, engrave,* 2 Cor. 3:7* [1795]

[1964] ἐνυβρίζω *enybrizō* 1x *to insult, outrage,* Heb. 10:29* [1796]

[1965] ἐνυπνιάζομαι *enypniazomai* 2x *to dream,* in NT *to dream* under supernatural impression, Acts 2:17; *to dream* delusion, *have visions,* Jude 8* [1797]

[1966] ἐνύπνιον *enypnion* 1x *a dream;* in NT *a supernatural suggestion* or *impression received during sleep, a sleep-vision,* Acts 2:17* [1798]

[1967] ἐνώπιον *enōpion* 94x gen., *before, in the presence of,* Lk. 5:25; 8:47; *in front of,* Rev. 4:5, 6; *immediately preceding* as a forerunner, Lk. 1:17; Rev. 16:19; from the Hebrew, *in the presence of,* metaphysically, *i.e.* in the sphere of sensation or thought, Lk. 12:9; 15:10; Acts 10:31; *in the eyes of, in the judgment of,* Lk. 16:15; 24:11; Acts 4:19 [1799]

[1968] Ἐνώς *Enōs* 1x *Enos,* pr. name, indecl., Lk. 3:38* [1800]

[1969] ἐνωτίζομαι *enōtizomai* 1x *to give ear, listen, pay attention to,* Acts 2:14* [1801]

[1970] Ἑνώχ *Henōch* 3x *Enoch,* pr. name, indecl., Lk. 3:37; Heb. 11:5; 1 Pet. 3:19; Jude 14* [1802]

[1971] ἕξ *hex* 13x *six,* indecl., Mt. 17:1; Mk. 9:2 [1803] See *six.*

[1972] ἐξαγγέλλω *exangellō* 2x *to tell forth, divulge, publish; to declare abroad, celebrate,* 1 Pet. 2:9, shorter ending of Mark* [1804]

[1973] ἐξαγοράζω *exagorazō* 4x *to buy out* of the hands of a person; *to redeem, set free,* Gal. 3:13; 4:5; mid. *to redeem, buy off, to secure for one's self* or *one's own use; to rescue* from loss or misapplication, Eph. 5:16; Col. 4:5* [1805] See *redeem.*

[1974] ἐξάγω *exagō* 12x *to bring* or *lead out, conduct out of,* Mk. 8:23; 15:20; Lk. 24:50 [1806] See *lead out.*

[1975] ἐξαιρέω *exaireō* 8x *to take out of; to pluck out, tear out,* Mt. 5:29; 18:9; mid. *to take out of, select, choose,* Acts 26:17; *to rescue, deliver,* Acts 7:10, 34; 12:11; 23:27; Gal. 1:4* [1807]

[1976] ἐξαίρω *exairō* 1x pr. *to lift up out of;* in NT *to remove, eject,* 1 Cor. 5:13* [1808]

[1977] ἐξαιτέω *exaiteō* 1x *to ask for; to demand;* mid. *to demand for one's self,* Lk. 22:31; also, *to obtain by asking** [1809]

[1978] ἐξαίφνης *exaiphnēs* 5x *suddenly, unexpectedly,* Mk. 13:36; Lk. 2:13; 9:39; Acts 9:3; 22:6* [1810]

[1979] ἐξακολουθέω *exakoloutheō* 3x *to follow out; to imitate,* 2 Pet. 2:2, 15; *to observe as a guide,* 2 Pet. 1:16* [1811]

[1980] ἑξακόσιοι *hexakosioi* 2x *six hundred,* Rev. 13:18; 14:20* [1812]

[1981] ἐξαλείφω *exaleiphō* 5x pr. *to anoint* or *smear over;* hence, *to wipe off* or *away,* Rev. 7:17; 21:4; *to blot out, obliterate,* Col. 2:14; Rev. 3:5; met. *to wipe out* guilt, Acts 3:19* [1813] See *blot out; wipe out.*

[1982] ἐξάλλομαι *exallomai* 1x *to leap* or *spring up* or *forth,* Acts 3:8* [1814]

[1983] ἐξανάστασις *exanastasis* 1x *a raising up; a dislodgment; a rising up; a resurrection from* the dead, Phil. 3:11* [1815]

[1984] ἐξανατέλλω *exanatellō* 2x *to raise up, make to spring up;* intrans. *to rise up, sprout, spring up* or *forth,* Mt. 13:5; Mk. 4:5* [1816]

[1985] ἐξανίστημι *exanistēmi* 3x *to cause to rise up, raise up;* from the Hebrew, *to raise up* into existence, Mk. 12:19; Lk. 20:28; intrans. *to rise up from, stand forth,* Acts 15:5* [1817]

[1987] ἐξαπατάω *exapataō* 6x pr. *to deceive thoroughly; to deceive, delude,* Rom. 7:11; 16:18; 1 2 Cor. 3:18; 11:3; 2 Thess. 2:3; 1 Tim. 2:14* [1818]

[1988] ἐξάπινα *exapina* 1x *suddenly, immediately, unexpectedly,* Mk. 9:8* [1819]

[1989] ἐξαπορέω *exaporeō* 2x some list as a deponent ἐξαπορέομαι, pas., *to be in the utmost perplexity* or *despair,* 2 Cor. 1:8; 4:8* [1820]

[1990] ἐξαποστέλλω *exapostellō* 13x *to send out* or *forth; to send away, dismiss,* Lk. 1:53; *to dispatch* on a service or agency, Acts 7:12; *to send forth* as a pervading influence, Gal. 4:6 [1821] See *send.*

[1992] ἐξαρτίζω *exartizō* 2x *to equip* or *furnish completely,* 2 Tim. 3:17; *to complete* time, Acts 21:5* [1822]

[1993] ἐξαστράπτω *exastraptō* 1x pr. *to flash forth;* hence, *to glisten as lightning,* Lk. 9:29* [1823]

[1994] ἐξαυτῆς *exautēs* 6x *at the very time; presently, instantly, immediately,* Mk. 6:25; Acts 10:33; 11:11 [1824]

[1995] ἐξεγείρω *exegeirō* 2x *to raise up* from the dead, 1 Cor. 6:14; *to raise up* into existence, or into a certain condition, Rom. 9:17* [1825]

[1996] ἔξειμι *exeimi* 4x *to go out* or *forth,* Acts 13:42; *to depart,* Acts 17:15; 20:7; ἐπὶ τὴν γῆν, *to get to land,* from the water, Acts 27:43 [1826]

[1999] ἐξέλκω *exelkō* 1x *to draw* or *drag out;* met. *to withdraw, allure, hurry away,* Jas. 1:14* [1828]

[2000] ἐξέραμα *exerama* 1x *vomit,* 2 Pet. 2:22* [1829]

[2001] ἐξεραυνάω *exeraunaō* 1x *to search out, to examine closely,* 1 Pet. 1:10* [1830]

[2002] ἐξέρχομαι *exerchomai* 218x *to go* or *come out of; to come out,* Mt. 5:26; 8:34; *to proceed, emanate, take rise from,* Mt. 2:6; 15:18; 1 Cor. 14:36; *to come abroad,* 1 Jn. 4:1; *to go forth, go away, depart,* Mt. 9:31; Lk. 5:8; *to escape,* Jn. 10:39; *to pass away, come to an end,* Acts 16:19 [1831] See *come out; go out.*

[2003] ἔξεστιν *exestin* 31x 3rd person sing of the unused ἔξειμι (#1997) used impersonally, *it is possible; it is permitted, it is lawful,* Mt. 12:2, 4; Mk. 3:4; Lk. 6:9; Acts 22:25; 1 Cor. 6:12 [1832] See *lawful; (to be) permitted.*

[2004] ἐξετάζω *exetazō* 3x *to search out; to inquire by interrogation, examine strictly,* Mt. 2:8; 10:11; *to interrogate,* Jn. 21:12* [1833]

[2007] ἐξηγέομαι *exēgeomai* 6x *to be a leader; to detail, to set forth in language; to tell, narrate, recount,* Lk. 24:35; Acts 10:8; *to make known, reveal,* Jn. 1:18; Acts 15:12, 14; 21:19* [1834]

[2008] ἑξήκοντα *hexēkonta* 9x indecl, *sixty,* Mt. 13:8, 23 [1835]

[2009] ἑξῆς *hexēs* 5x *successively, in order;* in NT with the article ὁ, ἡ, τό, ἑξῆς, *next,* Lk. 7:11; 9:37; Acts 21:1; 25:17; 27:18* [1836]

[2010] ἐξηχέω *exēcheō* 1x act., *to make to sound forth;* pas., *to sound forth,* 1 Thess. 1:8* [1837]

[2011] ἕξις *hexis* 1x *a condition of body* or *mind,* strictly, as resulting from practice; *habit,* Heb. 5:14* [1838]

[2014] ἐξίστημι *existēmi* 17x pr. *to put out of its place; to astonish, amaze,* Lk. 24:22; Acts 8:9, 11; intrans. *to be astonished,* Mt. 12:23; *to be beside one's self,* Mk. 3:21; 2 Cor. 5:13 [1839] See *(be) amazed; astonish; astound; terrify.*

[2015] ἐξισχύω *exischuō* 1x *to be fully able, be strong,* Eph. 3:18* [1840]

[2016] ἔξοδος *exodos* 3x *a way out, a going out; a going out, departure, the exodus,* Heb. 11:22; met. *a departure* from life, *decease, death,* Lk. 9:31; 2 Pet. 1:15* [1841]

[2017] ἐξολεθρεύω *exolethreuō* 1x *to destroy utterly, root out,* Acts 3:23* [1842]

[2018] ἐξομολογέομαι *exomologeomai* 10x *to agree, bind one's self, promise,* Lk. 22:6; mid. *to confess,* Mt. 3:6; *to profess openly,* Phil. 2:11; Rev. 3:5; *to make open avowal* of benefits; *to praise, celebrate,* Mt. 11:25; Lk. 10:21 [1843] See *confess; praise; profess.*

[2019] ἐξορκίζω *exorkizō* 1x *to put an oath* to a person, *to adjure,* Mt. 26:63* [1844]

[2020] ἐξορκιστής *exorkistēs* 1x pr. *one who puts an oath;* in NT *an exorcist, one who by various kinds of incantations,* etc., *pretended to expel demons,* Acts 19:13* [1845]

[2021] ἐξορύσσω *exoryssō* 2x *to dig out* or *through, force up,* Mk. 2:4; *to pluck out* the eyes, Gal. 4:15* [1846]

[2022] ἐξουδενέω *exoudeneō* 1x also spelled ἐξουδενόω, *to treat with contempt,* Mk. 9:12* [1847]

[2024] ἐξουθενέω *exoutheneō* 11x also spelled ἐξουθενόω, *to make light of, despise, treat with contempt and scorn,* Lk. 18:9; *to neglect, disregard,* 1 Thess. 5:20; ἐξουθενημένος, *contemptible, amount to nothing,* 2 Cor. 10:10; *of small account,* 1 Cor. 1:28; 6:4; by impl. *to reject with contempt,* Acts 4:11 [1848] See *despise; hold in contempt; look down on; ridicule.*

[2026] ἐξουσία *exousia* 102x *power, ability, faculty,* Mt. 9:8; 10:1; *efficiency, energy,* Lk. 4:32; *liberty, license,* Jn. 10:18; Acts 5:4; *authority, rule, dominion, jurisdiction,* Mt. 8:9; 28:18; meton. pl. *authorities, potentates, powers,* Lk. 12:11; 1 Cor. 15:24; Eph. 1:21; *right, authority, full power,* Mt. 9:6; 21:23; *privilege, prerogative,* Jn. 1:12; perhaps, *a veil,* 1 Cor. 11:10 [1849] See *authority; power; right.*

[2027] ἐξουσιάζω *exousiazō* 4x *to have* or *exercise power* or *authority over* anyone, Lk. 22:25; *to possess independent control over,* 1 Cor. 7:4 (2x); pass. *to be subject to, under the power* or *influence of,* 1 Cor. 6:12* [1850]

[2029] ἐξοχή *exochē* 1x pr. *prominence, anything prominent;* in NT *eminence, distinction,* Acts 25:23* [1851]

[2030] ἐξυπνίζω *exypnizō* 1x *to awake, arouse* from sleep, Jn. 11:11* [1852]

[2031] ἔξυπνος *exypnos* 1x *awake, aroused from sleep,* Acts 16:27* [1853]

[2032] ἔξω *exō* 63x can function as an improper prep., *without, out of doors;* Mt. 12:46, 47; ὁ, ἡ, τὸ ἔξω, *outer, external, foreign,* Acts 26:11; 2 Cor. 4:16; met. *not belonging to one's community,* Mk. 4:11; 1 Cor. 5:12, 13; *out, away,* from a place or person, Mt. 5:13; 13:48; as a prep., *out of,* Mk. 5:10 [1854] See *outdoors; outside.*

[2033] ἔξωθεν *exōthen* 13x can function as an improper prep., *outwardly, externally,* Mt. 23:27, 28; Mk. 7:15; ὁ, ἡ, τὸ ἔξωθεν, *outer, external,* Mt. 23:25; Lk. 11:39; τὸ ἔξωθεν, *the exterior,* Lk. 11:40; οἱ ἔξωθεν, *those who are without* the Christian community, 1 Tim. 3:7 [1855]

[2034] ἐξωθέω *exōtheō* 2x *to expel, drive out,* Acts 7:45; *to propel, urge forward,* Acts 27:39* [1856]

[2035] ἐξώτερος *exōteros* 3x comparative in form but used as a superlative, *outer, exterior, external,* Mt. 8:12; 22:13; 25:30* [1857]

[2036] ἔοικα *eoika* 2x see εἴκω (1634a), dat., *to be like,* Jas. 1:6, 23* [1503]

[2037] ἑορτάζω *heortazō* 1x *to keep a feast, celebrate a festival,* 1 Cor. 5:8* [1858]

[2038] ἑορτή *heortē* 25x *a solemn feast, public festival,* Lk. 2:41; 22:1; Jn. 13:1; spc. used of *the passover,* Mt. 26:5; 27:15 [1859] See *feast.*

[2039] ἐπαγγελία *epangelia* 52x *annunciation,* 2 Tim. 1:1; *a promise, act of promising,* Acts 13:23, 32; 23:21; meton. *the thing promised, promised favor and blessing,* Lk. 24:49; Acts 1:4 [1860] See *promise.*

[2040] ἐπαγγέλλομαι *epangellomai* 15x *to declare, to promise, undertake,* Mk. 14:11; Rom. 4:21; *to profess,* 1 Tim. 2:10 [1861] See *profess; promise.*

[2041] ἐπάγγελμα *epangelma* 2x *a promise,* 2 Pet. 3:13; meton. *promised favor* or *blessing,* 2 Pet. 1:4* [1862]

[2042] ἐπάγω *epagō* 3x *to bring upon, cause to come upon,* 2 Pet. 2:1, 5; met. *to cause to be imputed* or *attributed to, to bring* guilt *upon,* Acts 5:28* [1863]

[2043] ἐπαγωνίζομαι *epagōnizomai* 1x *to contend strenuously in defence of,* Jude 3* [1864]

[2044] ἐπαθροίζω *epathroizō* 1x act., *to gather together, to collect close upon,* or *beside*; pas., *to crowd upon,* Lk. 11:29* [1865]

[2045] Ἐπαίνετος *Epainetos* 1x *Epaenetus,* pr. name, Rom. 16:5* [1866]

[2046] ἐπαινέω *epaineō* 6x *to praise, commend, applaud,* Lk. 16:8; Rom. 15:11; 1 Cor. 11:2, 17, 22 (2x)* [1867]

[2047] ἔπαινος *epainos* 11x *praise, applause, honor paid,* Rom. 2:29; 2 Cor. 8:18; meton. *ground* or *reason of praise* or *commendation,* Phil. 4:8; *approval,* Rom. 13:3; 1 Pet. 2:14; 1 Cor. 4:5 [1868] See *commendation; praise.*

[2048] ἐπαίρω *epairō* 19x *to lift up, raise, elevate; to hoist,* Acts 27:40; τὴν φωνήν, *to lift up the voice, to speak in a loud voice,* Lk. 11:27; τὰς χεῖρας, *to lift up the hands* in prayer, Lk. 24:50; 1 Tim. 2:8; τοὺς ὀφθαλμούς, *to lift up the eyes, to look,* Mt. 17:8; τὴν κεφαλήν, *to lift up the head, to be encouraged, animated,* Lk. 21:28; τὴν πτέρναν, *to lift up the heel, to attack, assault;* or, *to seek one's overthrow* or *destruction,* Jn. 13:18; pass. *to be borne upwards,* Acts 1:9; met. mid. *to exalt one's self, assume consequence, be elated,* 2 Cor. 10:5 [1869] See *lift up; look up.*

[2049] ἐπαισχύνομαι *epaischunomai* 11x *to be ashamed of,* Mk. 8:38; Lk. 9:26; Rom. 1:16; 6:21; 2 Tim. 1:8, 12, 16; Heb. 2:11; 11:16* [1870] See *ashamed; embarrass, (be) embarrassed; (be) fearful.*

[2050] ἐπαιτέω *epaiteō* 2x *to prefer a suit* or *request in respect of certain circumstances; to ask alms, beg,* Lk. 16:3; 18:35* [1871]

[2051] ἐπακολουθέω *epakoloutheō* 4x *to follow upon; to accompany, be attendant,* Mk. 16:20; *to appear later,* 1 Tim. 5:24; met. *to follow* one's steps, *to imitate,* 1 Pet. 2:21; *to follow* a work, *pursue, prosecute, be studious of, devoted to,* 1 Tim. 5:10* [1872]

[2052] ἐπακούω *epakouō* 1x gen., *to listen* or *hearken to; to hear with favor,* 2 Cor. 6:2* [1873]

[2053] ἐπακροάομαι *epakroaomai* 1x gen., *to hear, hearken, listen to,* Acts 16:25* [1874]

[2054] ἐπάν *epan* 3x with subj., *whenever, as soon as,* Mt. 2:8; Lk. 11:22, 34* [1875]

[2055] ἐπάναγκες *epanankes* 1x *of necessity, necessarily;* τὰ ἐπάναγκες, *necessary things,* Acts 15:28* [1876]

[2056] ἐπανάγω *epanagō* 3x *to bring up* or *back;* intrans. *to return,* Mt. 21:18; a nautical term, *to put off from shore,* Lk. 5:3, 4* [1877]

[2057] ἐπαναμιμνῄσκω *epanamimnēskō* 1x *to remind, put in remembrance,* Rom. 15:15* [1878]

[2058] ἐπαναπαύομαι *epanapauomai* 2x pr. *to make to rest upon;* mid. *to rest upon; to abide with,* Lk. 10:6; *to rely on, confide in, abide by confidingly,* Rom. 2:17* [1879]

[2059] ἐπανέρχομαι *epanerchomai* 2x *to come back, return,* Lk. 10:35; 19:15* [1880]

[2060] ἐπανίστημι *epanistēmi* 2x *to raise up against;* mid. *to rise up against in rebellion,* Mt. 10:21; Mk. 13:12* [1881]

[2061] ἐπανόρθωσις *epanorthōsis* 1x *correction, reformation, improvement,* 2 Tim. 3:16* [1882]

[2062] ἐπάνω *epanō* 19x can function as an improper prep., *above, over, upon,* of place, Mt. 2:9; 5:14; *over,* of authority, Lk. 19:17, 19; *above, more than,* Mk. 14:5 [1883]

[2063] ἐπάρατος *eparatos* 1x *accursed,* Jn. 7:49* [1944]

[2064] ἐπαρκέω *eparkeō* 3x dat., pr. *to ward off; to assist, relieve, succor;* 1 Tim. 5:10, 16 (2x)* [1884]

[2065] ἐπαρχεία *eparcheia* 2x *province,* Acts 23:34; 25:1* [1885]

[2068] ἔπαυλις *epaulis* 1x pr. *a place to pass the night in; cottage, farm;* in NT *a dwelling, habitation, farm,* Acts 1:20* [1886]

[2069] ἐπαύριον *epaurion* 17x *tomorrow;* ἡ ἐπαύριον, sc. ἡμέρα, *the next* or *following day,* Mt. 27:62; Mk. 11:12 [1887]

[2071] Ἐπαφρᾶς *Epaphras* 3x *Epaphras,* pr. name, Col. 1:7; 4:12; Phlm. 23* [1889]

[2072] ἐπαφρίζω *epaphrizō* 1x *to foam out; to pour out like foam, vomit forth,* Jude 13* [1890]

[2073] Ἐπαφρόδιτος *Epaphroditos* 2x *Epaphroditus,* pr. name, Phil. 2:25; 4:18* [1891]

[2074] ἐπεγείρω *epegeirō* 2x *to raise* or *stir up against, excite* or *instigate against,* Acts 13:50; 14:2* [1892]

[2075] ἐπεί *epei* 26x *when, after, since, because, in as much as,* Mt. 18:32; 27:6; *for, for then, for else, since in that case,* Rom. 3:6; 11:6 [1893]

[2076] ἐπειδή *epeidē* 10x *since, because, in as much as,* Mt. 21:46; Lk. 11:6; Acts 13:46 [1894]

[2077] ἐπειδήπερ *epeidēper* 1x *since now, since indeed, considering that,* Lk. 1:1* [1895]

[2079] ἔπειμι *epeimi* 5x *to come upon; to come after; to succeed immediately,* Acts 7:26; 16:11; 20:15; 21:18; 23:11* [1966]

[2081] ἐπεισαγωγή *epeisagōgē* 1x *a superinduction, a further introduction,* whether by way of addition or substitution, *bringing in,* Heb. 7:19* [1898]

[2082] ἐπεισέρχομαι *epeiserchomai* 1x *to come in upon, invade, surprise,* Lk. 21:35* [1904]

[2083] ἔπειτα *epeita* 16x *thereupon, then, after that, in the next place, afterwards,* Mk. 7:5; Lk. 16:7 [1899]

[2084] ἐπέκεινα *epekeina* 1x *BAGD* say it is an adverb with the gen.; others classify it as an improper prep., gen., *on yonder side, beyond, farther on* Acts 7:43* [1900]

[2085] ἐπεκτείνομαι *epekteinomai* 1x pr. *to stretch out farther;* in NT mid. *to reach out towards, strain for,* Phil. 3:13* [1901]

[2086] ἐπενδύομαι *ependyomai* 2x *to put on over* or *in addition to;* mid. *to put on one's self in addition; to be further invested,* 2 Cor. 5:2, 4* [1902]

[2087] ἐπενδύτης *ependytēs* 1x *the outer* or *upper tunic,* worn between the inner tunic and the external garments, Jn. 21:7* [1903]

[2088] ἐπέρχομαι *eperchomai* 9x *to come to,* Acts 14:19; *to come upon,* Lk. 1:35; 21:26; Acts 1:8; Jas. 5:1; *to be coming on, to succeed,* Eph. 2:7; *to occur, happen to,* Acts 8:24; 13:40; *to come against, attack,* Lk. 11:22* [1904]

[2089] ἐπερωτάω *eperōtaō* 56x *to interrogate, question, ask,* Mt. 12:10; 17:10; in NT *to request, require,* Mt. 16:1; ἐπερωτᾶν τὸν θεόν, *to seek after, desire an acquaintance with God,* Rom. 10:20 [1905] See *ask; interrogate; question.*

[2090] ἐπερώτημα *eperōtēma* 1x pr. *an interrogation, question;* in NT *profession, pledge,* 1 Pet. 3:21* [1906]

[2091] ἐπέχω *epechō* 5x trans. *to hold out, present, exhibit, display,* Phil. 2:16; intrans. *to observe, take heed to, attend to,* Lk. 14:7; Acts 3:5; 1 Tim. 4:16; *to stay, delay,* Acts 19:22* [1907]

[2092] ἐπηρεάζω *epēreazō* 2x *to harass, insult,* Lk. 6:28; *to mistreat, abuse,* 1 Pet. 3:16* [1908]

[2093] ἐπί *epi* 890x. (1) with the gen., *upon, on,* Mt. 4:6; 9:2; 27:19; *in,* of locality, Mk. 8:4; *near upon, by, at,* Mt. 21:19; Jn. 21:1; *upon, over,* of authority, Mt. 2:22; Acts 8:27; *in the presence of,* especially in a judicial sense, 2 Cor. 7:14; Acts 25:9; *in the case of, in respect of,* Jn. 6:2; Gal. 3:16; *in the time of, at the time of,* Acts 11:28; Rom. 1:10; ἐπ᾽ ἀληθείας, *really, bona fide,* Mk. 12:32.

(2) with the dat., *upon, on,* Mt. 14:8; Mk. 2:21; Lk. 12:44; *close upon, by,* Mt. 24:33; Jn. 4:6; *in the neighborhood* or *society of,* Acts 28:14; *over,* of authority, Mt. 24:47; *to,* of addition, *besides,* Mt. 25:20; Eph. 6:16; Col. 3:14; supervening *upon, after,* 2 Cor. 1:4; 7:4; *immediately upon,* Jn. 4:27; *upon,* of the object of an act, *towards, to,* Mk. 5:33; Lk. 18:7; Acts 5:35; *against,* of hostile posture or disposition, Lk. 12:52; *in dependence upon,* Mt. 4:4; Lk. 5:5; Acts 14:3; *upon the ground of,* Mt. 19:9; Lk. 1:59; Phil. 1:3; Heb. 7:11; 8:6; 9:17; *with a view to,* Gal. 5:13; 1 Thess. 4:7.

(3) with the acc., *upon,* with the idea of previous or present motion, Mt. 4:5; 14:19, 26; *towards,* of place, *to,* Mt. 3:13; 22:34; *towards,* of the object of an action, Lk. 6:35; 9:38; *against,* of hostile movement, Mt. 10:21; *over,* of authority, Lk. 1:33; *to the extent of,* both of place and time, Rev. 21:16; Rom. 7:1; *near, by,* Mt. 9:9; *about, at, of time,* Acts 3:1; *in order to, with a view to, for the purpose of,* Mt. 3:7; Lk. 7:44 [1909]

[2094] ἐπιβαίνω *epibainō* 6x pr. *to step upon; to mount,* Mt. 21:5; *to go on board,* Acts 21:2; 27:2, *to enter,* Acts 20:18; *to enter upon,* Acts 21:4; 25:1* [1910]

[2095] ἐπιβάλλω *epiballō* 18x *to cast* or *throw upon,* Mk. 11:7; 1 Cor. 7:35; *to lay on, apply to,* Lk. 9:62; *to put on, sew on,* Mt. 9:16; Lk. 5:36; τὰς χεῖρας, *to lay hands on, offer violence to, seize,* Mt. 26:50; also, *to lay hand to, undertake, commence,* Acts 12:1; intrans. *to rush, dash, beat into,* Mk. 4:37; *to ponder, reflect* *on,* Mk. 14:72; *to fall to one's share, pertain to,* Lk. 15:12 [1911] See *arrest; break; lay on; sew on.*

[2096] ἐπιβαρέω *epibareō* 3x *to burden;* met. *to be burdensome, chargeable to,* 1 Thess. 2:9; 2 Thess. 3:8; *to bear hard upon, overcharge, weigh down,* 2 Cor. 2:5* [1912]

[2097] ἐπιβιβάζω *epibibazō* 3x *to cause to ascend* or *mount, to set upon,* Lk. 10:34; 19:35; Acts 23:24* [1913]

[2098] ἐπιβλέπω *epiblepō* 3x *to look upon; to regard* with partiality, Jas. 2:3; *to regard* with kindness and favor, Lk. 1:48; 9:38* [1914]

[2099] ἐπίβλημα *epiblēma* 4x *that which is put over* or *upon;* in NT *a patch,* Mt. 9:16; Mk. 2:21; Lk. 5:36 (2x)* [1915]

[2101] ἐπιβουλή *epiboulē* 4x *a purpose* or *design against* any one; *conspiracy, plot,* Acts 9:24; 20:3, 19; 23:30* [1917]

[2102] ἐπιγαμβρεύω *epigambreuō* 1x *to marry* a wife *by the law of affinity,* Mt. 22:24* [1918]

[2103] ἐπίγειος *epigeios* 7x pr. *on the earth,* Phil. 2:10; *earthly, terrestrial,* Jn. 3:12; 1 Cor. 15:40; 2 Cor. 5:1; Phil. 3:19; *earthly, low, grovelling,* Jas. 3:15* [1919]

[2104] ἐπιγίνομαι *epiginomai* 1x *to come on, spring up,* as the wind, Acts 28:13* [1920]

[2105] ἐπιγινώσκω *epiginōskō* 44x pr. *to make* a thing *a subject of observation;* hence, *to arrive at knowledge from preliminaries; to attain to a knowledge of,* Mt. 11:27; *to ascertain,* Lk. 7:37; 23:7; *to perceive,* Mk. 2:8; 5:30; *to discern, detect,* Mt. 7:16, 20; *to recognize,* Mk. 6:33; Lk. 24:16, 31; Acts 3:10; *to acknowledge, admit,* 1 Cor. 14:37; 1 Tim. 4:3; pass. *to have one's character discerned and acknowledged,* 2 Cor. 6:9; from the Hebrew, *to regard* with favor and kindness, 1 Cor. 16:18 [1921] See *know; perceive; recognize; understand.*

[2106] ἐπίγνωσις *epignōsis* 20x *the coming at the knowledge* of a thing, *ascertainment,* Rom. 3:20; *a distance perception* or *impression, acknowledgment, insight, recognition, consciousness,* Col. 2:2 [1922] See *knowledge; understanding.*

[2107] ἐπιγραφή *epigraphē* 5x *an inscription; a legend* of a coin, Mt. 22:20; Mk. 12:16; Lk. 20:24; *a label* of a criminal's name and offence, Mk. 15:26; Lk. 23:38* [1923]

[2108] ἐπιγράφω *epigraphō* 5x pluperfect pass., ἐπεγεγράμμην, *to imprint a mark on; to inscribe, engrave, write on,* Mk. 15:26; Acts 17:23; Rev. 21:12; met. *to imprint, impress deeply on,* Heb. 8:10; 10:16* [1924]

[2109] ἐπιδείκνυμι *epideiknymi* 7x *to exhibit,* Mt. 16:1; Acts 9:39; *to show,* Mt. 22:19; Lk. 17:14; *to point out,* Mt. 24:1; *to demonstrate, prove,* Acts 18:28; Heb. 6:17* [1925]

[2110] ἐπιδέχομαι *epidechomai* 2x *to admit; to receive kindly, welcome, entertain,* 3 Jn. 10; met. *to admit, approve, assent to,* 3 Jn. 9* [1926]

[2111] ἐπιδημέω *epidēmeō* 2x *to dwell among a people; to be at home among one's own people;* and in NT *to sojourn as a stranger among another people,* Acts 2:10; 17:21* [1927]

[2112] ἐπιδιατάσσομαι *epidiatassomai* 1x *to enjoin* anything *additional, superadd an injunction,* Gal. 3:15* [1928]

[2113] ἐπιδίδωμι *epididōmi* 9x *to give in addition;* also, *to give to, deliver to, give into one's hands,* Mt. 7:9, 10; Lk. 4:17; 11:11f.; 24:30, 42; Acts 15:30; intrans. probably a nautical term, *to commit a ship to the wind, let her drive,* Acts 27:15* [1929]

[2114] ἐπιδιορθόω *epidiorthoō* 1x *to set further to rights, to carry on an amendment, correct,* Tit. 1:5* [1930]

[2115] ἐπιδύω *epidyō* 1x *to set upon, to set during,* Eph. 4:26* [1931]

[2116] ἐπιείκεια *epieikeia* 2x also spelled ἐπιεικία, *reasonableness, equity;* in NT *gentleness, mildness,* 2 Cor. 10:1; *clemency,* Acts 24:4* [1932]

[2117] ἐπιεικής *epieikēs* 5x pr. *suitable; fair, reasonable; gentle, mild, patient,* 1 Tim. 3:3; Tit. 3:2; Jas. 3:17; 1 Pet. 2:18; τὸ ἐπιεικές, *mildness, gentleness,* Phil. 4:5* [1933]

[2118] ἐπιζητέω *epizēteō* 13x *to seek for, make search for,* Acts 12:19; *to require, demand,* Mt. 12:39; 16:4; Acts 19:39; *to desire, endeavor to obtain,* Rom. 11:7; Heb. 11:14; *to seek with care and anxiety,* Mt. 6:32 [1934] See *desire; look for; strive for.*

[2119] ἐπιθανάτιος *epithanatios* 1x *condemned to death, under sentence of death,* 1 Cor. 4:9* [1935]

[2120] ἐπίθεσις *epithesis* 4x *the act of placing upon, imposition* of hands, Acts 8:18; 1 Tim. 4:14; 2 Tim. 1:6; Heb. 6:2* [1936]

[2121] ἐπιθυμέω *epithumeō* 16x with the gen. or acc., *to set the heart upon; to desire, long for, have earnest desire,* Mt. 13:17; Lk. 15:16; *to lust after,* Mt. 5:28; spc. *to covet,* Rom. 13:9 [1937] See *covet; desire; lust.*

[2122] ἐπιθυμητής *epithumētēs* 1x *one who has an ardent desire for* anything, 1 Cor. 10:6* [1938]

[2123] ἐπιθυμία *epithumia* 38x *earnest desire,* Lk. 22:15; *irregular* or *violent desire,* Mk. 4:19; spc. impure *desire, lust,* Rom. 1:24; met. *the object of desire, what enkindles desire,* 1 Jn. 2:16, 17 [1939] See *desire; lust.*

[2125] ἐπικαθίζω *epikathizō* 1x *to cause to sit upon, seat upon,* Mt. 21:7 (where some mss read ἐπεκάθισεν, intrans. *to sit upon*)* [1940]

[2126] ἐπικαλέω *epikaleō* 30x pluperfect, ἐπεκέκλητο (3 sg), *to call on; to attach* or *connect a name,* Acts 15:17; Jas. 2:7; *to attach an additional name, to surname,* Mt. 10:3; pass. *to receive an appellation* or *surname,* Heb. 11:16; mid. *to call upon, invoke,* 2 Cor. 1:23; *to appeal to,* Acts 25:11, 12, 21 [1941] See *appeal; call; call on.*

[2127] ἐπικάλυμμα *epikalymma* 1x *a covering, veil;* met. *a cloak,* 1 Pet. 2:16* [1942]

[2128] ἐπικαλύπτω *epikalyptō* 1x *to cover over;* met. *to cover* or *veil* by a pardon, Rom. 4:7* [1943]

[2129] ἐπικατάρατος *epikataratos* 2x *cursed, accursed; subject to the curse* of condemnation, Gal. 3:10; *infamous,* Gal. 3:13* [1944]

[2130] ἐπίκειμαι *epikeimai* 7x *to lie upon, be placed upon,* Jn. 11:38; 21:9; *to press, urge upon,* Lk. 5:1; Acts 27:20; *be urgent, importunate upon,* Lk. 23:23; *to be imposed upon, be imposed* by law, Heb. 9:10; by necessity, 1 Cor. 9:16 [1945]

[2131] ἐπικέλλω *epikellō* 1x *to push* a ship *to shore,* Acts 27:41* [2027]

[2134] Ἐπικούρειος *Epikoureios* 1x *an Epicurean, follower of the philosophy of Epicurus,* Acts 17:18* [1946]

[2135] ἐπικουρία *epikouria* 1x *help, assistance,* Acts 26:22* [1947]

[2137] ἐπικρίνω *epikrinō* 1x *to decide; to decree,* Lk. 23:24* [1948]

[2138] ἐπιλαμβάνομαι *epilambanomai* 19x *to take hold of,* Mt. 14:31; Mk. 8:23; *to lay hold of, seize,* Lk. 23:26; Acts 16:19; met. *to seize on* as a ground of accusation, Lk. 20:20, 26; *to grasp, obtain* as if by seizure, 1 Tim. 6:12, 19; *to assume a portion of, to assume the nature of,* or, *to attach* or *ally one's self to,* Heb. 2:16 [1949] See *arrest; seize; take hold.*

[2140] ἐπιλανθάνομαι *epilanthanomai* 8x *to forget,* Mt. 16:5; *to be forgetful, neglectful of, to disregard,* Phil. 3:13; Heb. 6:10; in NT in a passive sense, *forgotten,* Lk. 12:6 [1950] See *forget.*

[2141] ἐπιλέγω *epilegō* 2x *to call,* Jn. 5:2; mid. *to select for one's self, choose,* Acts 15:40* [1951]

[2142] ἐπιλείπω *epileipō* 1x *to be insufficient, to run short, to fail,* Heb. 11:32* [1952]

[2143] ἐπιλείχω *epileichō* 1x *to lick,* Lk. 16:21* [621]

[2144] ἐπιλησμονή *epilēsmonē* 1x *forgetfulness, oblivion,* Jas. 1:25* [1953]

[2145] ἐπίλοιπος *epiloipos* 1x *remaining, still left,* 1 Pet. 4:2* [1954]

[2146] ἐπίλυσις *epilysis* 1x *a loosing, liberation;* met. *interpretation of* what is enigmatical and obscure, 2 Pet. 1:20* [1955]

[2147] ἐπιλύω *epilyō* 2x *to loose* what has previously been fastened or entangled, as a knot; met. *to solve, to explain,* what is enigmatical, as a parable, Mk. 4:34; *to settle, put an end to* a matter of debate, Acts 19:39* [1956]

[2148] ἐπιμαρτυρέω *epimartyreō* 1x *to bear testimony to; to testify solemnly,* 1 Pet. 5:12* [1957]

[2149] ἐπιμέλεια *epimeleia* 1x *care, attention,* Acts 27:3* [1958]

[2150] ἐπιμελέομαι *epimeleomai* 3x gen., *to take care of,* Lk. 10:34f.; 1 Tim. 3:5* [1959]

[2151] ἐπιμελῶς *epimelōs* 1x *carefully, diligently,* Lk. 15:8* [1960]

[2152] ἐπιμένω *epimenō* 16x *to stay longer, prolong a stay, remain on,* Acts 10:48; 15:34; *to continue, persevere,* Jn. 8:7; Acts 12:16; *to adhere to, continue to embrace,* Acts 13:43; Rom. 11:22; *to persist in,* Rom. 6:1; 1 Cor. 16:8 [1961] See *continue; remain; stay.*

[2153] ἐπινεύω *epineuō* 1x *to nod to;* met. *to assent to, consent,* Acts 18:20* [1962]

[2154] ἐπίνοια *epinoia* 1x *thought, purpose, device, intent,* Acts 8:22* [1963]

[2155] ἐπιορκέω *epiorkeō* 1x *to forswear one's self, to fail of observing one's oath,* Mt. 5:33* [1964]

[2156] ἐπίορκος *epiorkos* 1x *one who violates his oath, perjured,* 1 Tim. 1:10* [1965]

[2157] ἐπιούσιος *epiousios* 2x This word occurs nowhere else in Greek literature except in the context of the Lord's prayer. Guesses include, *necessary for today, necessary for tomorrow, daily, sufficient,* Mt. 6:11; Lk. 11:3* [1967]

[2158] ἐπιπίπτω *epipiptō* 11x *to fall upon; to throw one's self upon,* Lk. 15:20; Jn. 13:25; Acts 20:10, 37; *to press, urge upon,* Mk. 3:10; *to light upon,* Rom. 15:3; *to come over,* Acts 13:11; *to come upon, fall upon* mentally or spiritually, Lk. 1:12; Acts 8:16; 10:10, 44; 11:15; 19:17 [1968] See *come upon; embrace; fall upon.*

[2159] ἐπιπλήσσω *epiplēssō* 1x pr. *to inflict blows upon;* met. *to chide, reprove,* 1 Tim. 5:1* [1969]

[2160] ἐπιποθέω *epipotheō* 9x *to desire besides;* also, *to desire earnestly, long for,* 2 Cor. 5:2; *to have a strong bent,* Jas. 4:5; by impl. *to love, have affection for,* 2 Cor. 9:14 [1971]

[2161] ἐπιπόθησις *epipothēsis* 2x *earnest desire, strong affection,* 2 Cor. 7:7, 11* [1972]

[2162] ἐπιπόθητος *epipothētos* 1x *earnestly desired, longed for,* Phil. 4:1* [1973]

[2163] ἐπιποθία *epipothia* 1x *earnest desire,* Rom. 15:23* [1974]

[2164] ἐπιπορεύομαι *epiporeuomai* 1x *to travel to; to come to,* Lk. 8:4* [1975]

[2165] ἐπιράπτω *epiraptō* 1x also ἐπιρράπτω, *to sew on,* Mk. 2:21* [1976]

[2166] ἐπιρίπτω *epiriptō* 2x *to throw upon, cast upon,* Lk. 19:35; 1 Pet. 5:7* [1977]

[2168] ἐπίσημος *episēmos* 2x pr. *bearing a distinctive mark* or *device; noted, eminent,* Rom. 16:7; *notorious,* Mt. 27:16* [1978]

[2169] ἐπισιτισμός *episitismos* 1x *supply of food, provisions,* Lk. 9:12* [1979]

[2170] ἐπισκέπτομαι *episkeptomai* 11x *to look at observantly, to inspect; to look out, select,* Acts 6:3; *to go see, visit,* Lk. 1:68, 78, Acts 7:23; 15:36; *to visit* for the purpose of comfort and relief, Mt. 25:36, 43; Jas. 1:27; [1980] See *look after; take care of; visit.*

[2171] ἐπισκευάζομαι *episkeuazomai* 1x *to prepare for a journey,* Acts 21:15* [643]

[2172] ἐπισκηνόω *episkēnoō* 1x *to quarter in* or *at;* met. *to abide upon,* 2 Cor. 12:9* [1981]

[2173] ἐπισκιάζω *episkiazō* 5x *to overshadow,* Mt. 17:5; met. *to shed influence upon,* Lk. 1:35 [1982]

[2174] ἐπισκοπέω *episkopeō* 2x *to look at, inspect;* met. *to be circumspect, heedful,* Heb. 12:15; *to oversee, to exercise the office of* ἐπίσκοπος, 1 Pet. 5:2* [1983]

[2175] ἐπισκοπή *episkopē* 4x *inspection, oversight, visitation;* of God, *visitation, interposition,* whether in mercy or judgment, Lk. 19:44; 1 Pet. 2:12; *the office of an ecclesiastical overseer,* 1 Tim. 3:1; from the Hebrew, *charge, function,* Acts 1:20* [1984]

[2176] ἐπίσκοπος *episkopos* 5x pr. *an inspector, overseer; a watcher, guardian,* 1 Pet. 2:25; in NT *an* ecclesiastical *overseer,* Acts 20:28; Phil. 1:1; 1 Tim. 3:2; Tit. 1:7* [1985] See *bishop; overseer.*

[2177] ἐπισπάομαι *epispaomai* 1x *to draw upon* or *after;* in NT mid. *to obliterate circumcision* by artificial extension of the foreskin, 1 Cor. 7:18* [1986]

[2178] ἐπισπείρω *epispeirō* 1x *to sow in* or *among,* Mt. 13:25* [4687]

[2179] ἐπίσταμαι *epistamai* 14x *to be versed in, to be master of,* 1 Tim. 6:4; *to be acquainted with,* Acts 18:25; 19:15; Jude 10: *to know,* Acts 10:28; *to remember, comprehend, understand,* Mk. 14:68 [1987] See *know; understand.*

[2180] ἐπίστασις *epistasis* 2x pr. *care of, attention to,* 2 Cor. 11:28 [1999]

[2181] ἐπιστάτης *epistatēs* 7x pr. *one who stands by; one who is set over;* in NT in voc., equivalent to διδάσκαλε, or ῥαββί, *master, doctor,* Lk. 5:5; 8:24, 45; 9:33, 49; 17:13* [1988]

[2182] ἐπιστέλλω *epistellō* 3x *to send word to, to send injunctions,* Acts 15:20; 21:25; *to write to, write* a letter, Heb. 13:22* [1989]

[2184] ἐπιστήμων *epistēmōn* 1x *knowing, discreet, understanding,* Jas. 3:13* [1990]

[2185] ἐπιστηρίζω *epistērizō* 4x pr. *to cause to rest* or *lean on, to settle upon;* met. *to conform, strengthen, establish,* 14:22; 15:32, 41; 18:23* [1991]

[2186] ἐπιστολή *epistolē* 24x *word sent; an order, command; an epistle, letter,* Acts 9:2; 15:30 [1992] See *epistle; letter.*

[2187] ἐπιστομίζω *epistomizō* 1x *to apply a curb* or *muzzle;* met. *to put to silence,* Tit. 1:11* [1993]

[2188] ἐπιστρέφω *epistrephō* 36x trans. *to turn towards; to turn round; to bring back, convert,* Lk. 1:16, 17; Jas. 5:19, 20; intrans. and mid. *to turn one's self upon* or *towards,* Acts 9:40; Rev. 1:12; *to turn about,* Mt. 9:22; *to turn back, return,* Mt. 12:44; met. *to be converted,* Acts 28:27 [1994] See *return; turn.*

[2189] ἐπιστροφή *epistrophē* 1x *a turning towards, a turning about;* in NT met. *conversion,* Acts 15:3* [1995]

[2190] ἐπισυνάγω *episynagō* 8x *to gather to* a place; *to gather together, assemble, convene,* Mt. 23:37; 24:31; Lk. 17:37 [1996]

[2191] ἐπισυναγωγή *episynagōgē* 2x *the act of being gathered together* or *assembled,* 2 Thess. 2:1; *an assembling together,* Heb. 10:25* [1997]

[2192] ἐπισυντρέχω *episyntrechō* 1x *to run together* to a place, Mk. 9:25* [1998]

[2195] ἐπισφαλής *episphalēs* 1x *on the verge of falling, unsteady;* met. *insecure, hazardous, dangerous,* Acts 27:9* [2000]

[2196] ἐπισχύω *epischuō* 1x *to strengthen;* intrans. *to gather strength;* met. *to be urgent, to press on* a point, *insist,* Lk. 23:5* [2001]

[2197] ἐπισωρεύω *episōreuō* 1x *to heap up, accumulate largely;* met. *to procure in abundance,* 2 Tim. 4:3* [2002]

[2198] ἐπιταγή *epitagē* 7x *injunction,* 1 Cor. 7:6, 25; 2 Cor. 8:8; *a decree,* Rom. 16:26; 1 Tim. 1:1; Tit. 1:3; *authoritativeness, strictness,* Tit. 2:15* [2003]

[2199] ἐπιτάσσω *epitassō* 10x with dat., *to set over* or *upon; to enjoin, charge,* Mk. 1:27; 6:39; Lk. 4:36 [2004] See *command; order.*

[2200] ἐπιτελέω *epiteleō* 10x *to bring to an end; to finish, complete, perfect,* Rom. 15:28; 2 Cor. 8:6, 11; *to perform,* Lk. 13:32; *to carry into practice, to realize,* 2 Cor. 7:1; *to discharge,* Heb. 9:6; *to execute,* Heb. 8:5; *to carry out to completion,* Phil. 1:6; mid. *to end, make an end,* Gal. 3:3; pass. *to be fully undergone, endured,* 1 Pet. 5:9 [2005] See *complete.*

[2201] ἐπιτήδειος *epitēdeios* 1x *fit, suitable, necessary,* Jas. 2:16* [2006]

[2202] ἐπιτίθημι *epitithēmi* 39x *to put, place,* or *lay upon,* Mt. 9:18; Lk. 4:40; *to impose* a name, Mk. 3:16, 17; *to inflict,* Acts 16:23; Lk. 10:30; Rev. 22:18; mid. *to impose* with authority, Acts 15:28; 28:10; *to set* or *fall upon, assail, assault, attack,* Acts 18:10 [2007] See *put on.*

[2203] ἐπιτιμάω *epitimaō* 29x pr. *to set a value upon; to assess a penalty; to allege as a crimination;* hence, *to reprove, chide, censure, rebuke, reprimand, warn,* Mt. 19:13; Lk. 23:40; in NT *to admonish strongly, enjoin strictly,* Mt. 12:16; Lk. 17:3 [2008] See *rebuke.*

[2204] ἐπιτιμία *epitimia* 1x *a punishment, penalty,* 2 Cor. 2:6* [2009]

[2205] ἐπιτρέπω *epitrepō* 18x *to give over, to leave to the entire trust* or *management of* any one; hence, *to permit, allow, suffer,* Mt. 8:21; Mk. 5:13 [2010] See *allow: let; permit; suffer.*

[2207] ἐπιτροπή *epitropē* 1x *a trust; a commission, permission,* Acts 26:12* [2011]

[2208] ἐπίτροπος *epitropos* 3x *one to whose charge* or *control a thing is left; a steward, bailiff, agent, manager,* Mt. 20:8; *steward* or *overseer* of the revenue, *treasurer,* Lk. 8:3; *a guardian* of children, Gal. 4:2* [2012]

[2209] ἐπιτυγχάνω *epitynchanō* 5x *to light upon, find; to hit, reach; to acquire, obtain, attain,* Rom. 11:7 (2x); Heb. 6:15; 11:33; Jas. 4:2* [2013]

[2210] ἐπιφαίνω *epiphainō* 4x *to make to appear, to display;* pass. *to be manifested, revealed,* Tit. 2:11; 3:4; intrans. *to give light, shine,* Lk. 1:79; Acts 27:20* [2014]

[2211] ἐπιφάνεια *epiphaneia* 6x *appearance, manifestation,* 1 Tim. 6:14; 2 Tim. 1:10; *glorious display,* 2 Thess. 2:8; 2 Tim. 4:1, 8; Tit. 2:13* [2015]

[2213] ἐπιφαύσκω *epiphauskō* 1x *to shine upon, give light to, enlighten,* Eph. 5:14* [2017]

[2214] ἐπιφέρω *epipherō* 2x *to bring upon* or *against,* Jude 9; *to inflict,* Rom. 3:5* [2018]

[2215] ἐπιφωνέω *epiphōneō* 4x *to cry aloud, raise a shout* at a speaker, whether applaudingly, Acts 12:22; or the contrary, *to clamor at,* Lk. 23:21; Acts 21:34; 22:24* [2019]

[2216] ἐπιφώσκω *epiphōskō* 2x *to dawn, shine forth,* Mt. 28:1; hence, used of the reckoned commencement of the day, *to be near commencing, to dawn on,* Lk. 23:54* [2020]

[2217] ἐπιχειρέω *epicheireō* 3x *to put hand to* a thing; *to undertake, attempt,* Lk. 1:1; Acts 9:29; 19:13* [2021]

[2219] ἐπιχέω *epicheō* 1x *to pour upon,* Lk. 10:34* [2022]

[2220] ἐπιχορηγέω *epichorēgeō* 5x *to supply further; to superadd,* 2 Pet. 1:5; *to supply, furnish, give,* 2 Cor. 9:10; Gal. 3:5; 2 Pet. 1:11; pass. *to gather vigor,* Col. 2:19* [2023]

[2221] ἐπιχορηγία *epichorēgia* 2x *supply, aid, support,* Eph. 4:16; Phil. 1:19* [2024]

[2222] ἐπιχρίω *epichriō* 2x *to smear upon, to anoint,* Jn. 9:6, 11* [2025]

[2224] ἐποικοδομέω *epoikodomeō* 7x *to build upon,* 1 Cor. 3:10, 12, 14; pass. met. *to be built upon* as parts of a spiritual structure, Eph. 2:20; *to build up, carry up a building;* met. *to build up in spiritual advancement,*Col. 2:7; Jude 20* [2026]

[2226] ἐπονομάζω *eponomazō* 1x *to attach a name to;* pass. *to be named,* Rom. 2:17* [2028]

[2227] ἐποπτεύω *epopteuō* 2x *to look upon, observe, watch; to witness, be an eye-witness of,* 1 Pet. 2:12; 3:2* [2029]

[2228] ἐπόπτης *epoptēs* 1x *a looker-on, eye-witness,* 2 Pet. 1:16* [2030]

[2229] ἔπος *epos* 1x *a word, that which is expressed by words;* ὡς ἔπος εἰπεῖν, *so to say, if the expression may be allowed,* Heb. 7:9* [2031]

[2230] ἐπουράνιος *epouranios* 19x *heavenly,* in respect of locality, Eph. 1:20; Phil. 2:10; τὰ ἐπουράνια, *the upper regions* of the air, Eph. 6:12; *heavenly,* in respect of essence and character, *unearthly,* 1 Cor. 15:48, 49; met. *divine, spiritual,* Jn. 3:12 [2032] See *heavenly.*

[2231] ἑπτά *hepta* 88x *seven,* indecl. numeral, Mt. 15:34, 37; by Jewish usage for a round number, Mt. 12:45; Lk. 11:26 [2033] See *seven.*

[2232] ἑπτάκις *heptakis* 4x *seven times,* Mt. 18:21, 22; Lk. 17:4 (2x)* [2034]

[2233] ἑπτακισχίλιοι *heptakischilioi* 1x *seven thousand,* Rom. 11:4* [2035]

[2235] Ἔραστος *Erastos* 3x *Erastus,* pr. name, Acts 19:22; Rom. 16:23; 2 Tim. 4:20* [2037]

[2236] ἐραυνάω *eraunaō* 6x *to search, examine, investigate,* Jn. 5:39; 7:52; Rom. 8:27; 1 Cor. 2:10; 1 Pet. 1:11; Rev. 2:23* [2045]

[2237] ἐργάζομαι *ergazomai* 41x intrans. *to work, labor,* Mt. 21:28; Lk. 13:14; *to trade, traffic, do business,* Mt. 25:16; Rev. 18:17; *to act, exert one's power, be active,* Jn. 5:17; trans. *to do, perform, commit,* Mt. 26:10; Jn. 6:28; *to be engaged in, occupied upon,* 1 Cor. 9:13; Rev. 18:17; *to acquire, gain by one's labor,* Jn. 6:27 [2038] See *do; perform; produce; work.*

[2238] ἐργασία *ergasia* 6x *work, labor;* in NT ἐργασίαν διδόναι, *to endeavor, strive,* Lk. 12:58; *performance, practice,* Eph. 4:19; *a trade, business, craft,* Acts 19:25, *gain* acquired by labor or trade, *profit,* Acts 16:16, 19; 19:24* [2039]

[2239] ἐργάτης *ergatēs* 16x *a workman, laborer,* Mt. 9:37, 38; 20:1, 2, 8; met. *a* spiritual *workman* or *laborer,* 2 Cor. 11:13; *an artisan, artificer,* Acts 19:25; *a worker, practicer,* Lk. 13:27 [2040] See *laborer; worker.*

[2240] ἔργον *ergon* 169x *anything done* or *to be done; a deed, work, action,* Jn. 3:21; Eph. 2:10; 2 Cor. 9:8, et al. freq.; *duty enjoined, office, charge, business,* Mk. 13:34; Jn. 4:34, et al. freq.; *a process, course of action,* Jas. 1:4; *a work, product of an action* or *process,* Acts 7:41; Heb. 1:10; *substance in effect,* Rom. 2:15 [2041] See *work.*

[2241] ἐρεθίζω *erethizō* 2x *to provoke, to irritate, exasperate,* Col. 3:21; *to incite, stimulate,* 2 Cor. 9:2* [2042]

[2242] ἐρείδω *ereidō* 1x *to make to lean upon; to fix firmly;* intrans. *to become firmly fixed, stick fast,* Acts 27:41* [2043]

[2243] ἐρεύγομαι *ereugomai* 1x *to vomit;* met. *to utter, declare openly,* Mt. 13:35* [2044]

[2244] ἐρημία *erēmia* 4x *a solitude, uninhabited region, waste, desert,* Mt. 15:33; Mk. 8:4; 2 Cor. 11:26; Heb. 11:38* [2047]

[2245] ἔρημος *erēmos* 48x *lone, desert, waste, uninhabited,* Mt. 14:13, 15; Mk. 6:31, 32, 35; *lone, abandoned* to ruin, Mt. 23:38; Lk. 13:35; met. *lone, unmarried,* Gal. 4:27; as a subst. *a desert, uninhabited region, waste,* Mt. 3:1; 24:26; Acts 7:36 [2048] See *barren; desert; desolate; secluded; wilderness.*

[2246] ἐρημόω *erēmoō* 5x *to lay waste, make desolate, bring to ruin,* Mt. 12:25; Lk. 11:17; Rev. 17:16; 18:17, 19* [2049]

[2247] ἐρήμωσις *erēmōsis* 3x *desolation, devastation,* Mt. 24:15; Mk. 13:14; Lk. 21:20* [2050]

[2248] ἐρίζω *erizō* 1x *to quarrel; to wrangle; to use the harsh tone of a wrangler* or *brawler, to grate,* Mt. 12:19* [2051]

[2249] ἐριθεία *eritheia* 7x *the service of a party, party spirit; feud, faction,* 2 Cor. 12:20; *contentious disposition, selfish ambition,* Gal. 5:20; Phil. 1:17; 2:3; Jas. 3:14; by impl. *untowardness, disobedience,* Rom. 2:8; Jas. 3:16* [2052] See *ambition.*

[2250] ἔριον *erion* 2x *wool,* Heb. 9:19; Rev. 1:14* [2053]

[2251] ἔρις *eris* 9x *altercation, strife,* Rom. 13:13; *contentious disposition,* Rom. 1:29; Phil. 1:15 [2054] See *strife.*

[2252] ἐρίφιον *eriphion* 1x *a goat, kid,* Mt. 25:33* [2055]

[2253] ἔριφος *eriphos* 2x *a goat, kid,* Mt. 25:32; Lk. 15:29* [2056]

[2254] Ἑρμᾶς *Hermas* 1x *Hermas,* pr. name, Rom. 16:14* [2057]

[2255] ἑρμηνεία *hermēneia* 2x *interpretation, explanation,* 1 Cor. 14:26; meton. *the power* or *faculty of interpreting,* 1 Cor. 12:10* [2058]

[2257] ἑρμηνεύω *hermēneuō* 3x *to explain, interpret, translate,* Jn. 1:42; 9:7; Heb. 7:2* [2059]

[2258] Ἑρμῆς *Hermēs* 2x *Hermes* or *Mercury,* son of Jupiter and Maia, the messenger and interpreter of the gods, and the patron of eloquence, learning, etc., Acts 14:12; Rom. 16:14* [2060]

[2259] Ἑρμογένης *Hermogenēs* 1x *Hermogenes,* pr. name, 2 Tim. 1:15* [2061]

[2260] ἑρπετόν *herpeton* 4x *a creeping animal, a reptile,* Acts 10:12; 11:6; Rom. 1:23; Jas. 3:7* [2062]

[2261] ἐρυθρός *erythros* 2x *red,* Acts 7:36; Heb. 11:29* [2063]

[2262] ἔρχομαι *erchomai* 632x *to come, to go, to pass.* By the combination of this verb with other terms, a variety of meaning results, which, however, is due, not to a change of meaning in the verb, but to the adjuncts. Ὁ ἐρχόμενος, *He who is coming, the expected Messiah,* Mt. 11:3 [2064] See *arrive; come; go.*

[2263] ἐρωτάω *erōtaō* 63x *to ask, interrogate, inquire of,* Mt. 21:24; Lk. 20:3; in NT *to ask, request, beg, beseech,* Mt. 15:23; Lk. 4:38; Jn. 14:16 [2065] See *ask; inquire; request.*

[2264] ἐσθής *esthēs* 8x also spelled ἔσθησις, *a robe, vestment, raiment, garment,* Lk. 23:11; 24:4; Acts 1:10; 10:30; 12:21; Jas. 2:2, 3* [2066]

[2266] ἐσθίω *esthiō* 158x *to eat,* Mt. 12:1; 15:27; ἐσθίειν καὶ πίνειν, *to eat and drink, to eat and drink* in the usual manner, *follow the common mode of living,* Mt. 11:18; also with the associated notion of supposed security, Lk. 17:27; *to feast, banquet,* Mt. 24:49; met. *to devour, consume,* Heb. 10:27; Jas. 5:3; from the Hebrew, ἄρτον ἐσθίειν, *to eat bread, to take food, take the usual meals,* Mt. 15:2 [2068, 5315] See *eat.*

[2268] Ἑσλί *Hesli* 1x *Esli,* pr. name, indecl., Lk. 3:25* [2069]

[2269] ἔσοπτρον *esoptron* 2x *mirror,* Jas. 1:23; 1 Cor. 13:12* [2072]

[2270] ἑσπέρα *hespera* 3x *evening,* Lk. 24:29; Acts 4:3; 28:23* [2073]

[2272] Ἑσρώμ *Hesrōm* 3x *Hezron,* pr. name, indecl., Mt. 1:3; Lk. 3:33* [2074]

[2274] ἔσχατος *eschatos* 52x *farthest; last, latest,* Mt. 12:45; Mk. 12:6; *lowest,* Mt. 19:30; 20:16; *in the lowest plight,* 1 Cor. 4:9 [2078] See *last.*

[2275] ἐσχάτως *eschatōs* 1x *to be in the last extremity, most insignificant,* Mk. 5:23* [2079]

[2276] ἔσω *esō* 9x can function as an improper prep., *in, within, in the interior of,* Mt. 26:58; Jn. 20:26; ὁ, ἡ, τὸ ἔσω, *inner, interior, internal;* met. *within* the pale of community, 1 Cor. 5:12; ὁ ἔσω ἄνθρωπος, *the inner man, the mind, soul,* Rom. 7:22 [2080]

[2277] ἔσωθεν *esōthen* 12x *from within, from the interior,* Mk. 7:21, 23; *within, in the internal parts,* Mt. 7:15; ὁ, ἡ, τὸ ἔσωθεν, *interior, internal,* Lk. 11:39, 40; ὁ ἔσωθεν ἄνθρωπος, *the mind, soul,* 2 Cor. 4:16 [2081]

[2278] ἐσώτερος *esōteros* 2x *inner, interior,* Acts 16:24; Heb. 6:19* [2082]

[2279] ἑταῖρος *hetairos* 3x *a companion, associate, fellow-comrade, friend,* Mt. 20:13; 22:12; 26:50* [2083]

[2280] ἑτερόγλωσσος *heteroglōssos* 1x *one who speaks another* or *foreign language,* 1 Cor. 14:21* [2084]

[2281] ἑτεροδιδασκαλέω *heterodidaskaleō* 2x *to teach other* or *different doctrine,* and spc. *what is foreign to the Christian religion,* 1 Tim. 1:3; 6:3* [2085]

[2282] ἑτεροζυγέω *heterozygeō* 1x *to be unequally yoked* or *matched,* 2 Cor. 6:14* [2086]

[2283] ἕτερος *heteros* 98x *other,* Mt. 12:45; *another, some other,* Mt. 8:21; *besides,* Lk. 23:32; ὁ ἕτερος, *the other* of two, Mt. 6:24; τῇ ἑτέρᾳ, *on the next* day, Acts 20:15; 27:3; ὁ ἕτερος, *one's neighbor,* Rom. 13:8; *different,* Lk. 9:29; *foreign, strange,* Acts 2:4; 1 Cor. 14:21; *illicit,* Jude 7 [2087] See *another; other.*

[2284] ἑτέρως *heterōs* 1x *otherwise, differently,* Phil. 3:15* [2088]

[2285] ἔτι *eti* 93x *yet, still,* Mt. 12:46; *still, further, longer,* Lk. 16:2; *further, besides, in addition,* Mt. 18:16; with a compar. *yet, still,* Phil. 1:9 [2089]

[2286] ἑτοιμάζω *hetoimazō* 40x *to make ready, prepare,* Mt. 22:4; 26:17 [2090] See *prepare.*

[2288] ἑτοιμασία *hetoimasia* 1x *preparation; preparedness, readiness,* Eph. 6:15* [2091]

[2289] ἕτοιμος *hetoimos* 17x *ready, prepared,* Mt. 22:4, 8; Mk. 14:15 [2092] See *ready.*

[2290] ἑτοίμως *hetoimōs* 3x *in readiness, preparedly,* Acts 21:13; 2 Cor. 2:14; 1 Pet. 4:5* [2093]

[2291] ἔτος *etos* 49x *a year,* Lk. 2:41; 3:23 [2094] See *year.*

[2293] Εὕα *heua* 2x *Eve,* pr. name, 2 Cor. 11:3; 1 Tim. 2:13* [2096]

[2294] εὐαγγελίζω *euangelizō* 54x *to address with good tidings,* Rev. 10:7; 14:6; but elsewhere *to proclaim as good tidings, to announce good tidings of,* Lk. 1:19; *to address with good tidings,* Acts 13:32; 14:15; *to address with the Gospel teaching, evangelize,* Acts 16:10; Gal. 1:9; absol. *to announce the good tidings* of the Gospel, Lk. 4:18; 9:6; pass. *to be announced as good tidings,* Lk. 16:16; *to be addressed with good tidings,* Mt. 11:5; Lk. 7:22; Heb. 4:2 [2097] See *evangelize; preach.*

[2295] εὐαγγέλιον *euangelion* 76x *glad tidings, good* or *joyful news,* Mt. 4:23; 9:35; *the Gospel; doctrines of the Gospel,* Mt. 26:13; Mk. 8:35; meton. *the preaching of,* or *instruction in, the Gospel,* 1 Cor. 4:15; 9:14 [2098] See *good news; Gospel.*

[2296] εὐαγγελιστής *euangelistēs* 3x pr. *one who announces glad tidings; an evangelist, preacher of the Gospel, teacher of the Christian religion,* Acts 21:8; Eph. 4:11; 2 Tim. 4:5* [2099] See *evangelist.*

[2297] εὐαρεστέω *euaresteō* 3x *to please,* Heb. 11:5, 6; pass. *to take pleasure in, be well pleased with,* Heb. 13:16* [2100]

[2298] εὐάρεστος *euarestos* 9x *well-pleasing, acceptable, grateful,* Rom. 12:1, 2 [2101] See *acceptable; pleasing.*

[2299] εὐαρέστως *euarestōs* 1x *acceptably,* Heb. 12:28 [2102]

[2300] Εὔβουλος *euboulos* 1x *Eubulus,* pr. name, 2 Tim. 4:21* [2103]

[2301] εὖγε *euge* 1x *Well done!* Lk. 19:17* [2095]

[2302] εὐγενής *eugenēs* 3x *well-born, of high rank, honorable,* Lk. 19:12; 1 Cor. 1:26; *generous, candid,* Acts 17:11* [2104]

[2304] εὐδία *eudia* 1x *serenity of the heavens, a cloudless sky, fair* or *fine weather,* Mt. 16:2* [2105]

[2305] εὐδοκέω *eudokeō* 21x *to think well, approve, consent, take delight* or *pleasure,* Mt. 3:17; 17:5; Mk. 1:11; Lk. 3:22; 12:32 [2106] See *(be) pleased; prefer; well pleased.*

[2306] εὐδοκία *eudokia* 9x *good will, favor,* Lk. 2:14; *good pleasure, purpose, intention,* Mt. 11:26; Lk. 10:21; Eph. 1:5, 9; Phil. 2:13; by impl. *desire,* Rom. 10:1; Phil. 1:15; 2 Thess. 1:11* [2107] See *desire; pleasure; purpose.*

[2307] εὐεργεσία *euergesia* 2x *well-doing, a good deed, benefit conferred,* Acts 4:9; *duty, good offices,* 1 Tim. 6:2* [2108]

[2308] εὐεργετέω *euergeteō* 1x *to do good, exercise beneficence,* Acts 10:38* [2109]

[2309] εὐεργέτης *euergetēs* 1x *a well-doer; a benefactor,* Lk. 22:25* [2110]

[2310] εὔθετος *euthetos* 3x pr. *well arranged, rightly disposed; fit, proper, adapted,* Lk. 9:62; 14:35; *useful,* Heb. 6:7* [2111]

[2311] εὐθέως *eutheōs* 36x *immediately, instantly, at once,* Mt. 8:3; 13:5 [2112] See *immediately.*

[2312] εὐθυδρομέω *euthudromeō* 2x *to run on a straight course; to sail on a direct course,* Acts 16:11; 21:1* [2113]

[2313] εὐθυμέω *euthumeō* 3x *to be cheerful, be in good spirits, take courage,* Acts 27:22, 25; Jas. 5:13* [2114]

[2314] εὔθυμος *euthumos* 1x *good cheer* or *courage, cheerful,* Acts 27:36* [2115]

[2315] εὐθύμως *euthumōs* 1x *cheerfully,* Acts 24:10* [2115]

[2316] εὐθύνω *euthunō* 2x *to guide straight; to direct, guide, steer* a ship, Jas. 3:4; *to make straight,* Jn. 1:23* [2116]

[2317] εὐθύς *euthus* 59x *straight forwards; directly, immediately, instantly,* Mt. 3:16; 13:20, 21 [2117] See *immediately.*

[2319] εὐθύτης *euthutēs* 1x *righteousness, uprightness, equity,* Heb. 1:8* [2118]

[2320] εὐκαιρέω *eukaireō* 3x *to have convenient time* or *opportunity, have leisure,* Mk. 6:31; 1 Cor. 16:12; *to be at leisure* for a thing, *to be disposed to attend, to give time,* Acts 17:21* [2119]

[2321] εὐκαιρία *eukairia* 2x *convenient opportunity, favorable occasion,* Mt. 26:16; Lk. 22:6* [2120]

[2322] εὔκαιρος *eukairos* 2x *timely, opportune, seasonable, convenient,* Mk. 6:21; Heb. 4:16* [2121]

[2323] εὐκαίρως *eukairōs* 2x *opportunely, seasonable, conveniently,* Mk. 14:11; 2 Tim. 4:2* [2122]

[2324] εὔκοπος *eukopos* 7x *easy,* Mt. 9:5; 19:24; Mk. 2:9; 10:25; Lk. 5:3; 16:17; 18:25 [2123]

[2325] εὐλάβεια *eulabeia* 2x *the disposition of one who is* εὐλαβής, *caution, circumspection;* in NT *reverence* to God, *piety, fear, awe,* Heb. 5:7; 12:28* [2124]

[2326] εὐλαβέομαι *eulabeomai* 1x *to fear, be afraid* or *apprehensive;* in NT absol. *to reverence* God, *to be influenced by pious awe,* Heb. 11:7* [2125]

[2327] εὐλαβής *eulabēs* 4x pr. *taking hold of well,* i.e., *warily;* hence, *cautious, circumspect; full of reverence* towards God, *devout, pious, religious,* Lk. 2:25; Acts 2:5; 8:2; 22:12* [2126]

[2328] εὐλογέω *eulogeō* 41x pr. *to speak well of,* in NT *to bless, ascribe praise and glorification,* Lk. 1:64; *to bless, invoke a blessing upon,* Mt. 5:44; *to bless, confer a favor* or *blessing upon,* Eph. 1:3; Heb. 6:14; pass. *to be blessed, to be an object of favor* or *blessing,* Lk. 1:28 [2127] See *bless; praise; thank.*

[2329] εὐλογητός *eulogētos* 8x *worthy of praise* or *blessing, blessed,* Mk. 14:61; Lk. 1:68 [2128] See *blessed; praise, praised.*

[2330] εὐλογία *eulogia* 16x pr. *good speaking; fair speech, flattery,* Rom. 16:18; in NT *blessing, praise, celebration,* 1 Cor. 10:16; Rev. 5:12, 13; *invocation of good, benediction,* Jas. 3:10; *a divine blessing,* Rom. 15:29; *a gift, benevolence,* 2 Cor. 9:5; *a frank gift,* as opposed to πλεονεξία, 2 Cor. 9:5; ἐπ᾽ εὐλογίαις, *liberally,* 2 Cor. 9:6 [2129] See *blessing; gift; praise.*

[2331] εὐμετάδοτος *eumetadotos* 1x *liberal, bountiful, generous,* 1 Tim. 6:18* [2130]

[2332] Εὐνίκη *eunikē* 1x *Eunice,* pr. name, 2 Tim. 1:5* [2131]

[2333] εὐνοέω *eunoeō* 1x *to have kind thoughts, be well affected* or *kindly disposed* towards, *make friends,* Mt. 5:25* [2132]

[2334] εὔνοια *eunoia* 1x *good will, kindliness; heartiness, enthusiasm,* Eph. 6:7* [2133]

[2336] εὐνοῦχος *eunouchos* 8x pr. *one who has charge of the bedchamber;* hence, *a eunuch, one emasculated,* Mt. 19:12; as eunuchs in the East often rose to places of power and trust, hence, *a minister of a court,* Acts 8:27, 34, 36, 38f.* [2135]

[2337] Εὐοδία *euodia* 1x *Euodia,* pr. name, Phil. 4:2* [2136]

[2338] εὐοδόω *euodoō* 4x *to give a prosperous journey; cause to prosper* or *be successful;* pass. *to have a prosperous journey, to succeed in a journey,* Rom. 1:10; met. *to be furthered, to prosper,* temporally or spiritually, 1 Cor. 16:2; 3 Jn. 2 (2x)* [2137]

[2339] εὐπάρεδρος *euparedros* 1x *constantly attending; devoted to;* τὸ εὐπάρεδρον, *devotedness,* 1 Cor. 7:35* [2145]

[2340] εὐπειθής *eupeithēs* 1x *easily persuaded, compliant,* Jas. 3:17* [2138]

[2342] εὐπερίστατος *euperistatos* 1x *easily* or *constantly distracted,* Heb. 12:1* [2139]

[2343] εὐποιΐα *eupoiia* 1x *doing good, beneficence,* Heb. 13:16* [2140]

[2344] εὐπορέω *euporeō* 1x *to be in prosperous circumstances, enjoy plenty,* Acts 11:29* [2141]

[2345] εὐπορία *euporia* 1x *wealth, abundance,* Acts 19:25* [2142]

[2346] εὐπρέπεια *euprepeia* 1x *grace, beauty,* Jas. 1:11* [2143]

[2347] εὐπρόσδεκτος *euprosdektos* 5x *acceptable, grateful, pleasing,* Rom. 15:16, 31; 2 Cor. 6:2; 8:12; 1 Pet. 2:5; in NT *gracious** [2144]

[2349] εὐπροσωπέω *euprosōpeō* 1x *to carry* or *make a good showing,* Gal. 6:12* [2146]

[2350] εὐρακύλων *eurakylōn* 1x *the northeaster*, Acts 27:14* [2148]

[2351] εὑρίσκω *heuriskō* 176x *to find, to meet with;* Mt. 18:28; 20:6; *to find out, to detect, discover,* Lk. 23:2, 4, 14; *to acquire, obtain, win, gain,* Lk. 1:30; 9:12; *to find* mentally, *to comprehend, recognize,* Acts 17:27; Rom. 7:21; *to find* by experience, *observe, gather,* Rom. 7:18; *to devise* as feasible, Lk. 5:19; 19:48 [2147] See *discover; find; obtain.*

[2352] εὐρακύλων *eurakylōn* 1x also spelled εὐρυκλύδων and εὐροκλύδων, which *BAGD* says was probably due to scribal error, *euracylon,* the name of a tempestuous southeast wind, Acts 27:14* [2148]

[2353] εὐρύχωρος *eurychōros* 1x *spacious; broad, wide,* Mt. 7:13* [2149]

[2354] εὐσέβεια *eusebeia* 15x *reverential feeling; piety, devotion, godliness,* Acts 3:12; 1 Tim. 2:2; 4:7, 8; *religion, the* Christian *religion,* 1 Tim. 3:16 [2150] See *devotion; godliness.*

[2355] εὐσεβέω *eusebeō* 2x *to exercise piety;* towards a deity, *to worship,* Acts 17:23; towards relatives, *to be dutiful towards,* 1 Tim. 5:4* [2151]

[2356] εὐσεβής *eusebēs* 3x *reverent; pious, devout, religious,* Acts 10:2, 7; 2 Pet. 2:9* [2152]

[2357] εὐσεβῶς *eusebōs* 2x *piously, religiously,* 2 Tim. 3:12; Tit. 2:12* [2153]

[2358] εὔσημος *eusēmos* 1x pr. *well marked, strongly marked;* met. *significant, intelligible,* 1 Cor. 14:9* [2154]

[2359] εὔσπλαγχνος *eusplanchnos* 2x *tender-hearted, compassionate,* Eph. 4:32; 1 Pet. 3:8* [2155]

[2361] εὐσχημόνως *euschēmonōs* 3x *in a becoming manner, with propriety, decently, gracefully,* Rom. 13:13; 1 Cor. 14:40; 1 Thess. 4:12* [2156]

[2362] εὐσχημοσύνη *euschēmosynē* 1x *comeliness, gracefulness;* artificial *comeliness, ornamental array, embellishment,* 1 Cor. 12:23* [2157]

[2363] εὐσχήμων *euschēmōn* 5x *of good appearance, pleasing to look upon, comely,* 1 Cor. 12:24; met. *becoming, decent,* τὸ εὔσχημον, *decorum, propriety,* 1 Cor. 7:35; *honorable, reputable, of high standing and influence,* Mk. 15:43; Acts 13:50; 17:12* [2158]

[2364] εὐτόνως *eutonōs* 2x *intensely, vehemently, strenuously,* Lk. 23:10; Acts 18:28* [2159]

[2365] εὐτραπελία *eutrapelia* 1x *facetiousness, pleasantry;* hence, *buffoonery, coarse laughter,* Eph. 5:4* [2160]

[2366] Εὔτυχος *eutychos* 1x *Eutychus,* pr. name, Acts 20:9* [2161]

[2367] εὐφημία *euphēmia* 1x pr. *use of words of good omen;* hence, *favorable expression, praise, commendation, good report,* 2 Cor. 6:8* [2162]

[2368] εὔφημος *euphēmos* 1x pr. *of good omen, auspicious;* hence, *of good report, commendable, laudable, reputable, appealing,* Phil. 4:8* [2163]

[2369] εὐφορέω *euphoreō* 1x *to bear* or *bring forth well* or *plentifully, yield abundantly,* Lk. 12:16* [2164]

[2370] εὐφραίνω *euphrainō* 14x *to gladden,* 2 Cor. 2:2; pass. *to be glad, exult, rejoice,* Lk. 12:19; Acts 2:26; mid. *to feast in token of joy, keep a day of rejoicing,* Lk. 15:23, 24, 29, 32 [2165] See *celebrate; gladden; rejoice.*

[2371] Εὐφράτης *euphratēs* 2x the river *Euphrates,* Rev. 9:14; 16:12* [2166]

[2372] εὐφροσύνη *euphrosynē* 2x *joy, gladness, rejoicing,* Acts 2:28; 14:17* [2167]

[2373] εὐχαριστέω *eucharisteō* 38x *to thank,* Lk. 17:16; absol. *to give thanks,* Mt. 15:36; 26:27; pass. *to be made a matter of thankfulness,* 2 Cor. 1:11 [2168] See *give thanks; thanks.*

[2374] εὐχαριστία *eucharistia* 15x *gratitude, thankfulness,* Acts 24:3; *thanks, the act of giving thanks, thanksgiving,* 1 Cor. 14:16; *conversation marked by the gentle cheerfulness of a grateful heart,* as contrasted with the unseemly mirth of εὐτραπελία, Eph. 5:4 [2169] See *thanksgiving.*

[2375] εὐχάριστος *eucharistos* 1x *grateful, pleasing; mindful of benefits, thankful,* Col. 3:15* [2170]

[2376] εὐχή *euchē* 3x *a wish, prayer,* Jas. 5:15; *a vow,* Acts 21:23; Acts 18:18* [2171]

[2377] εὔχομαι *euchomai* 7x *to pray, offer prayer,* Acts 26:29; 2 Cor. 13:7, 9; Jas. 5:16; *to wish, desire,* Acts 27:29; Rom. 9:3; 3 Jn. 2* [2172]

[2378] εὔχρηστος *euchrēstos* 3x *highly useful, very profitable,* 2 Tim. 2:21; 4:11; Phlm. 11* [2173]

[2379] εὐψυχέω *eupsycheō* 1x *to be animated, encouraged, in good spirits,* Phil. 2:19* [2174]

[2380] εὐωδία *euōdia* 3x *a sweet smell, grateful odor, fragrance,* 2 Cor. 2:15; Eph. 5:2; Phil. 4:18* [2175] See *aroma.*

[2381] εὐώνυμος *euōnymos* 9x *of good name* or *omen;* used also as an euphemism by the Greeks instead of ἀριστερός, which was a word of bad import, as all omens on the left denoted misfortune; *the left,* Mt. 20:21, 23; 25:33, 41 [2176]

[2383] ἐφάλλομαι *ephallomai* 1x *to leap* or *spring upon, assault,* Acts 19:16* [2177]

[2384] ἐφάπαξ *ephapax* 5x *once for all,* Rom. 6:10; Heb. 7:27; 9:12; 10:10; *at once,* 1 Cor. 15:6* [2178]

[2386] Ἐφέσιος *Ephesios* 5x *Ephesian,* belonging to Ephesus, Acts 19:28, 34, 35; 21:29* [2180]

[2387] Ἔφεσος *Ephesos* 16x *Ephesus,* a celebrated city of Asia Minor, Acts 18:19, 21, 24; 1 Cor. 15:32* [2181]

[2388] ἐφευρετής *epheuretēs* 1x *an inventor, deviser,* Rom. 1:30* [2182]

[2389] ἐφημερία *ephēmeria* 2x pr. *daily course; the daily service* of the temple; *a class* of priests to which the daily service for a week was allotted in rotation, Lk. 1:5, 8* [2183]

[2390] ἐφήμερος *ephēmeros* 1x *lasting for a day; daily sufficient for a day, necessary for every day,* Jas. 2:15* [2184]

[2391] ἐφικνέομαι *ephikneomai* 2x *to come* or *reach to, to reach* a certain point or end; *to reach, arrive at,* 2 Cor. 10:13, 14* [2185]

[2392] ἐφίστημι *ephistēmi* 21x trans. *to place upon, over, close by;* intrans. *to stand by* or *near,* Lk. 2:38; 4:39; *to come suddenly upon,* Lk. 2:9; 24:4; *to come upon, assault,* Acts 6:12; 17:5; *to come near, approach,* Lk. 10:40; *to impend, be instant, to be at hand,* 1 Thess. 5:3; *to be present,* Acts 28:2; *to be pressing, urgent, earnest,* 2 Tim. 4:2 [2186] See *appear.*

[2393] ἐφοράω *ephoraō* 2x a proposed lexical form for the second aorist ἐπεῖδον [1896]

[2394] Ἐφραίμ *Ephraim* 1x *Ephraim,* pr. name, indecl. Jn. 11:54* [2187]

[2395] ἐφφαθά *ephphatha* 1x Aramaic, *be thou opened,* Mk. 7:34* [2188]

[2396] ἐχθές *echthes* 3x *yesterday,* Jn. 4:52; Acts 7:28; Heb. 13:8* [5504]

[2397] ἔχθρα *echthra* 6x *enmity, discord, feud,* Lk. 23:12; Gal. 5:20; *alienation,* Eph. 2:14, 16; *a principle* or *state of enmity,* Rom. 8:7; Jas. 4:4* [2189]

[2398] ἐχθρός *echthros* 32x *hated, under disfavor,* Rom. 11:28; *inimical, hostile,* Mt. 13:28; Col. 1:21; as a subst., *an enemy, adversary,* Mt. 5:43, 44; 10:36; Lk. 27:35 [2190] See *enemy.*

[2399] ἔχιδνα *echidna* 5x *a viper, poisonous serpent,* Acts 28:3; used also fig. of persons, Mt. 3:7; 12:34; 23:33; Lk. 3:7* [2191]

[2400] ἔχω *echō* 708x pluperfect., ἐσχήκειν, *to hold,* Rev. 1:16; *to seize, possess* a person, Mk. 16:8; *to have, possess,* Mt. 7:29, et al. freq.; *to have, have ready, be furnished with,* Mt. 5:23; Jn. 5:36; 6:68; *to have* as a matter of crimination, Mt. 5:23; Mk. 11:25; *to have* at command, Mt. 27:65; *to have* the power, *be able,* Mt. 18:25; Lk. 14:14; Acts 4:14; *to have* in marriage, Mt. 14:4; *to have, be affected by, subjected to,* Mt. 3:14; 12:10; Mk. 3:10; Jn. 12:48; 15:22, 24; 16:21, 22; Acts 23:29; 1 Tim. 5:12; Heb. 7:28; 1 Jn. 1:8; 4:18; χάραν ἔχειν, *to feel gratitude, be thankful,* 1 Tim. 1:12; 2 Tim. 1:3; Phlm. 7; *to hold, esteem, regard,* Mt. 14:5; Lk. 14:18, 19; *to have* or *hold* as an object of knowledge, faith, or practice, Jn. 5:38, 42; 14:21; 1 Jn. 5:12; 2 Jn. 9; *to hold on* in entire possession, *to retain,* Rom. 15:4; 2 Tim. 1:13; Heb. 12:28; intrans. with adverbs or adverbial expression, *to be, to fare,* Mt. 9:12; Mk. 2:17; 5:23; Lk. 5:31; Jn. 4:52; Acts 7:1; 12:15; 15:36; 21:13; 2 Cor. 10:6; 12:14; 1 Tim. 5:25; 1 Pet. 4:5; τὸ νῦν ἔχον, *for the present;* in NT ἔχειν ἐν γαστρί, *to be pregnant,* Mt. 1:18; as also ἔχειν κοίτην, Rom. 9:10; ἔχειν δαιμόνιον, *to be possessed,* Mt. 11:18; of time, *to have continued, to have lived,* Jn. 5:5, 6; 8:57; of space, *to embrace, be distant,* Acts 1:12; mid. pr. *to hold by, cling to;* hence, *to border upon, be next,* Mk. 1:38; Lk. 13:33; Acts 20:15; 21:26; *to tend immediately to,* Heb. 6:9 [2192] See *have; possess, possessions.*

[2401] ἕως *heōs* 146x can function as an improper prep., *while, as long as,* Jn. 9:4; *until,* Mt. 2:9; Lk. 15:4; as also in NT ἕως οὗ, ἕως ὅτου, Mt. 5:18, 26; ἕως ἄρτι, *until now,* Mt. 11:12; ἕως πότε, *until when,* *how long,* Mt. 17:17; ἕως σήμερον, *until this day, to this time,* 2 Cor. 3:15; as a prep. of time, *until,* Mt. 24:21; of place, *unto, even to,* Mt. 11:23; Lk. 2:15; ἕως ἄνω, *to the brim,* Jn. 2:7; ἕως εἰς, *even to, as far as,* Lk. 24:50; ἕως κάτω, *to the bottom;* ἕως ὧδε, *to this place,* Lk. 23:5; of state, *unto, even to,* Mt. 26:38; of number, *even, so much as,* Rom. 3:12, et al. freq. [2193]

[2404] Ζαβουλών *Zaboulōn* 3x *Zebulun,* pr. name, indecl., an Israelite tribe, Mt. 4:13, 15; Rev. 7:8* [2194]

[2405] Ζακχαῖος *Zakchaios* 3x *Zaccheus,* pr. name, Lk. 19:2, 5, 8* [2195]

[2406] Ζάρα *Zara* 1x *Zerah,* pr. name, indecl., Mt. 1:3* [2196]

[2408] Ζαχαρίας *Zacharias* 11x *Zacharias,* pr. name. (1) *Son of Barachias,* Mt. 23:35; Lk. 11:51. (2) *Father of Jn. the Baptist,* Lk. 1:5 [2197]

[2409] ζάω *zaō* 140x *to live, to be possessed of vitality, to exercise the functions of life,* Mt. 27:63; Acts 17:28; τὸ ζῆν, *life,* Heb. 2:15; *to have means of subsistence,* 1 Cor. 9:14; *to live, to pass existence* in a specific manner, Lk. 2:36; 15:13; *to be instinct with life and vigor;* hence, ζῶν, *living,* an epithet of God, in a sense peculiar to Himself; ἐλπὶς ζῶσα, *a living hope* in respect of vigor and constancy, 1 Pet. 1:3; ὕδωρ ζῶν, *living water* in respect of a full and unfailing flow, Jn. 4:10, 11; *to be alive* with cheered and hopeful feelings, 1 Thess. 3:8; *to be alive* in a state of salvation from spiritual death, 1 Jn. 4:9 [2198] See *alive; live.*

[2411] Ζεβεδαῖος *Zebedaios* 12x *Zebedee,* pr. name, the father of Jas. and John, Mt. 4:21; Mk. 10:35; Lk. 5:10; Jn. 21:1* [2199]

[2412] ζεστός *zestos* 3x pr. *boiled; boiling, boiling hot;* met. *glowing with zeal, fervent,* Rev. 3:15, 16* [2200]

[2414] ζεῦγος *zeugos* 2x *a yoke* of animals; *a pair, couple,* Lk. 2:24; 14:19* [2201]

[2415] ζευκτηρία *zeuktēria* 1x *a fastening, band,* Acts 27:40* [2202]

[2416] Ζεύς *Zeus* 2x the supreme god of the Greeks answering to the *Jupiter* of the Romans, Acts 14:12, 13* [2203]

[2417] ζέω *zeō* 2x *to boil, to be hot,* in NT met. *to be fervent, ardent, zealous,* Acts 18:25; Rom. 12:11* [2204]

[2418] ζηλεύω *zēleuō* 1x *to be zealous, earnest, eager,* Rev. 3:19* [2206]

[2419] ζῆλος *zēlos* 16x *generous rivalry; noble aspiration;* in NT *zeal, ardor in behalf of, ardent affection,* Jn. 2:17; Rom. 10:2; in a bad sense, *jealousy, envy, malice,* Acts 13:45; Rom. 13:13; *indignation, wrath,* Acts 5:17 [2205] See *earnestness; envy; jealousy; zeal.*

[2420] ζηλόω *zēloō* 11x *to have strong affection towards, be ardently devoted to,* 2 Cor. 11:2; *to make a show of affection and devotion towards,* Gal. 4:17; *to desire earnestly, aspire eagerly after,* 1 Cor. 12:31; 14:1, 39; absol. *to be fervent, to be zealous,* Rev. 3:19; *to be jealous, envious, spiteful,* Acts 7:9; 17:5; 1 Cor. 13:4; Jas. 4:2; pass. *to be an object of warm regard and devotion,* Gal. 4:18 [2206] See *desire eagerly; envy; jealous; zealous.*

[2421] ζηλωτής *zēlōtēs* 8x pr. *a generous rival, an imitator;* in NT *an aspirant,* 1 Cor. 14:12; Tit. 2:14; *a devoted adherent, a zealot,* Acts 21:20; 22:3; Gal. 1:14 [2207, 2208]

[2422] ζημία *zēmia* 4x *damage, loss, detriment,* Acts 27:10, 21; Phil. 3:7, 8* [2209]

[2424] Ζηνᾶς *Zēnas* 1x *Zenas,* pr. name, Tit. 3:13* [2211]

[2426] ζητέω *zēteō* 117x *to seek, look for,* Mt. 18:12; Lk. 2:48, 49; *to search after,* Mt. 13:45; *to be on the watch for,* Mt. 26:16; *to pursue, endeavor to obtain,* Rom. 2:7; 1 Pet. 3:11; *to desire, wish, want,* Mt. 12:47; *to seek, strive for,* Mt. 6:33; *to endeavor,* Mt. 21:46; *to require, demand, ask for,* Mk. 8:11; Lk. 11:16; 12:48; *to inquire* or *ask questions, question,* Jn. 16:19; *to deliberate,* Mk. 11:18; Lk. 12:29; ζητεῖν τὴν ψυχήν, *to seek the life* of any one, *to seek to kill,* Mt. 2:20 [2212] See *search; seek.*

[2427] ζήτημα *zētēma* 5x *a question; a subject of debate* or *controversy,* Acts 15:2; 18:15; 23:29; 25:19; 26:3* [2213]

[2428] ζήτησις *zētēsis* 7x *a seeking; an inquiry, a question; a dispute, debate, discussion,* Jn. 3:25; 1 Tim. 6:4; *a subject of dispute* or *controversy,* Acts 15:2, 7; 25:20; 2 Tim. 2:23; Tit. 3:9 [2214]

[2429] ζιζάνιον *zizanion* 8x *zizanium, darnel, spurious wheat,* a plant found in Palestine, which resembles wheat both in its stalk and grain, but is worthless, Mt. 13:25, 26, 27, 29, 30, 36, 38, 40* [2215]

[2431] Ζοροβαβέλ *Zorobabel* 3x *Zorobabel,* pr. name, indecl. (Ezra 2:2; 3:8), Mt. 1:12, 13; Lk. 3:27* [2216]

[2432] ζόφος *zophos* 5x *gloom, thick darkness,* Heb. 12:18; 2 Pet. 2:4, 17; Jude 6, 13* [2217]

[2433] ζυγός *zygos* 6x also spelled ζυγόν, ου, τό (n-2c), pr. *a cross bar* or *band; a yoke;* met. *a yoke* of servile condition, 1 Tim. 6:1; *a yoke* of service or obligation, Mt. 11:29, 30; Acts 15:10; Gal. 5:1; *the beam* of a balance; *a balance,* Rev. 6:5* [2218]

[2434] ζύμη *zymē* 13x *leaven, yeast,* Mt. 16:12; 13:33; met. *leaven* of the mind and conduct, by a system of doctrine or morals, used in a bad sense, Mt. 16:6, 11; 1 Cor. 5:6 [2219] See *leaven; yeast.*

[2435] ζυμόω *zymoō* 4x *to leaven, cause to ferment,* Mt. 13:33; Lk. 13:21; 1 Cor. 5:6; Gal. 5:9* [2220]

[2436] ζωγρέω *zōgreō* 2x pr. *to take alive, take prisoner in war* instead of killing; *to take captive, enthral,* 2 Tim. 2:26; also, *to catch* animals, as fish; in which sense it is used figuratively, Lk. 5:10* [2221]

[2437] ζωή *zōē* 135x *life, living existence,* Lk. 16:25; Acts 17:25; in NT spiritual *life* of deliverance from the proper penalty of sin, which is expressed by θάνατος, Jn. 6:51; Rom. 5:18; 6:4; the final *life* of the redeemed, Mt. 25:46; *life, source of* spiritual *life,* Jn. 5:39; 11:25; Col. 3:4 [2222] See *life.*

[2438] ζώνη *zōnē* 8x *a zone, belt, girdle,* Mt. 3:4; 10:9; Mk. 1:6; 6:8; Acts 21:11; Rev. 1:13; 15:6* [2223]

[2439] ζώννυμι *zōnnymi* 3x also spelled ζωννύω, *to gird, gird on, put on one's girdle,* Jn. 21:18 (2x), Acts 12:8* [2224]

[2441] ζῳογονέω *zōiogoneō* 3x pr. *to bring forth living creatures;* in NT *to preserve alive, save,* Lk. 17:33; Acts 7:19; 1 Tim. 6:13* [2225]

[2442] ζῷον *zōon* 23x *a living creature, animal,* Heb. 13:11; 2 Pet. 2:12 [2226] See *living creature.*

[2443] ζῳοποιέω *zōiopoieō* 11x pr. *to engender living creatures; to quicken, make alive,* Rom. 4:17; 8:11; 1 Cor. 15:36; in NT met. *to quicken* with the life of salvation, Jn. 6:63; 2 Cor. 3:6 [2227] See *give life.*

[2445] ἤ *ē* 343x can function as a conj (298t), *either, or,* Mt. 6:24; after comparatives, and ἄλλος, ἕτερος, expressed or implied, *than,* Mt. 10:15; 18:8; Acts 17:21; 24:21; intensive after ἀλλά and πρίν, Lk. 12:51; Mt. 1:18; it also serves to point an interrogation, Rom. 3:29 [2228]

[2448] ἡγεμονεύω *hēgemoneuō* 2x *to be a guide, leader, chief;* in NT *to hold the office of a Roman provincial governor,* Lk. 2:2; 3:1* [2230]

[2449] ἡγεμονία *hēgemonia* 1x *leadership, sovereignty;* in NT *a reign,* Lk. 3:1* [2231]

[2450] ἡγεμών *hēgemōn* 20x *a guide; a leader; a chieftain, prince,* Mt. 2:6; *a Roman provincial governor,* under whatever title, Mt. 10:18; 27:2; Lk. 20:20; Acts 23:24 [2232] See *governor; leader; ruler.*

[2451] ἡγέομαι *hēgeomai* 28x *to lead the way; to take the lead,* Acts 14:12; *to be chief, to preside, govern, rule,* Mt. 2:6; Acts 7:10; ἡγούμενος, *a chief officer* in the church, Heb. 13:7, 17, 24; also, *to think, consider, count, esteem, regard,* Acts 26:2; 2 Cor. 9:5 [2233] See *consider; regard; think.*

[2452] ἡδέως *hēdeōs* 5x *with pleasure, gladly, willingly,* Mk. 6:20; 12:37; 2 Cor. 11:19 [2234, 2236]

[2453] ἤδη *ēdē* 62x *before now, now, already,* Mt. 3:10; 5:28; ἤδη ποτέ, *at length,* Rom. 1:10; Phil. 4:10 [2235]

[2454] ἡδονή *hēdonē* 5x *pleasure, gratification;* esp. *sensual pleasure,* Lk. 8:14; Tit. 3:3; Jas. 4:3; 2 Pet. 2:13; *a passion,* Jas. 4:1* [2237]

[2455] ἡδύοσμον *hēdyosmon* 2x *garden mint,* Mt. 23:23; Lk. 11:42* [2238]

[2456] ἦθος *ēthos* 1x pr. *a place of customary resort;* hence, *a settled habit of mind and manners,* 1 Cor. 15:33* [2239]

[2457] ἥκω *hēkō* 26x *to become, have arrived,* Mt. 8:11; Mk. 8:3; Lk. 15:27; Rev. 15:4* [2240] See *come.*

[2458] ἠλί *ēli* 2x Aramaic for *My God!,* Mt. 27:46 (2x)* [2241]

[2459] Ἠλί *ēli* 1x *Heli,* the father of Joseph, Lk. 3:23* [2242]

[2460] Ἠλίας *ēlias* 29x *Elijah,* pr name, (1 Ki. 17-20), Mt. 11:14; 17:3f.; Mk. 15:35f.; Lk. 1:7; Jn. 1:21; Jas. 5:17 [2243]

[2461] ἡλικία *hēlikia* 8x *a particular period of life; the period fitted for a particular function, prime,* Heb. 11:11; *full age, years of discretion,* Jn. 9:21, 23; perhaps, *the whole duration of life,* Mt. 6:27; Lk. 12:25; otherwise, *stature,* Lk. 2:52; 19:3; Eph. 4:13* [2244]

[2462] ἡλίκος *hēlikos* 3x *as great as; how great,* Col. 2:1; Jas. 3:5 (2x)* [2245]

[2463] ἥλιος *hēlios* 32x *the sun,* Mt. 13:43; 17:2; Mk. 1:32; meton. *light of the sun, light,* Acts 13:11 [2246] See *sun.*

[2464] ἧλος *hēlos* 2x *a nail,* Jn. 20:25 (2x)* [2247]

[7005] ἡμεῖς *hēmeis* 864x plural of ἐγώ

[2465] ἡμέρα *hēmera* 389x *day, a day, the interval from sunrise to sunset,* opp. to νύξ, Mt. 4:2; 12:40; Lk. 2:44; *the interval of twenty-four hours,* comprehending day and night, Mt. 6:34; 15:32; from the Hebrew, ἡμέρᾳ καὶ ἡμέρᾳ, *day by day, every day,* 2 Cor. 4:16; ἡμέραν ἐξ ἡμέρας, *from day to day, continually,* 2 Pet. 2:8; καθ᾽ ἡμέραν, *every day, daily,* Acts 17:17; Heb. 3:13; *a point* or *period of time,* Lk. 19:42; Acts 15:7; Eph. 6:13; *a judgement, trial,* 1 Cor. 4:3 [2250] See *day.*

[2466] ἡμέτερος *hēmeteros* 7x *our,* Lk. 16:12; Acts 2:11; 24:6; 26:5; Rom. 15:4; 2 Tim. 4:15; Tit. 3:14; 1 Jn. 1:3; 2:2* [2251]

[2467] ἡμιθανής *hēmithanēs* 1x *half dead,* Lk. 10:30* [2253]

[2468] ἥμισυς *hēmisys* 5x *half,* Mk. 6:23; Lk. 19:8; Rev. 11:9, 11; 12:14* [2255]

[2469] ἡμιώριον *hēmiōrion* 1x also spelled ἡμίωρον, *half an hour,* Rev. 8:1* [2256]

[2471] ἡνίκα *hēnika* 2x *when,* 2 Cor. 3:15, 16* [2259]

[2472] ἤπερ *ēper* 1x strengthened form of ἤ, *than,* Jn. 12:43* [2260]

[2473] ἤπιος *ēpios* 2x *mild, gentle, kind,* 2 Tim. 2:24; 1 Thess. 2:7* [2261]

[2474] Ἤρ *ēr* 1x *Er,* pr. name, indecl., Lk. 3:28* [2262]

[2475] ἤρεμος *ēremos* 1x *tranquil, quiet,* 1 Tim. 2:2* [2263]

[2476] Ἡρῴδης *hērōdēs* 43x *Herod,* pr. name. (1) *Herod the Great,* Mt. 2:1. (2) *Herod Antipas,* tetrarch of Galilee and Peraea, Mt. 14:1. (3) *Herod Agrippa,* Acts 12:1 [2264]

[2477] Ἡρῳδιανοί *hērōidianoi* 3x *Herodians,* partisans of Ἡρῴδης, *Herod Antipas,* Mt. 22:16; Mk. 3:6; 12:13* [2265]

[2478] Ἡρῳδιάς *hērōidias* 6x *Herodias,* pr. name, the wife of Herod Antipas, Mt. 14:3, 6; Mk. 6:17, 19, 22; Lk. 3:19* [2266]

[2479] Ἡρῳδίων *hērōidiōn* 1x *Herodian,* pr. name, Rom. 16:11* [2267]

[2480] Ἠσαΐας *ēsaias* 22x *Isaiah,* pr. name, Mt. 3:3; 13:14; Mk. 1:2; Lk. 4:17; Jn. 1:23; 12:38, 39, 41; Acts 8:28; Rom. 9:27, 29 [2268]

[2481] Ἠσαῦ *ēsau* 3x *Esau,* pr. name, indecl. (Gen. 27-28), Rom. 9:13; Heb. 11:20; 12:16* [2269]

[2482] ἥσσων *hēssōn* 2x *lesser, inferior, weaker,* 1 Cor. 11:17; 2 Cor. 12:15* [2276]

[2483] ἡσυχάζω *hēsychazō* 5x *to be still, at rest; to live peaceably, be quiet,* 1 Thess. 4:11; *to rest* from labor, Lk. 23:56; *to be silent* or *quiet, acquiesce, to desist* from discussion, Lk. 14:4; Acts 11:18; 21:14* [2270]

[2484] ἡσυχία *hēsychia* 4x *rest, quiet, tranquillity; a quiet, tranquil life,* 2 Thess. 3:12; *silence, silent attention,* Acts 22:2; 1 Tim. 2:11, 12* [2271]

[2485] ἡσύχιος *hēsychios* 2x *quiet, tranquil, peaceful,* 1 Tim. 2:2; 1 Pet. 3:4* [2272]

[2486] ἤτοι *ētoi* 1x *whether,* with an elevated tone, Rom. 6:16* [2273]

[2487] ἡττάομαι *hēttaomai* 2x *to be less, inferior to; to fare worse*; by impl. *to be overcome, vanquished,* 2 Pet. 2:19, 20* [2274]

[2488] ἥττημα *hēttēma* 2x *an inferiority,* to a particular standard; *default, defeat, failure, shortcoming,* Rom. 11:12; 1 Cor. 6:7* [2275]

[2490] ἠχέω *ēcheō* 1x *to sound, ring,* 1 Cor. 13:1* [2278]

[2491] ἦχος *ēchos* 3x *roar, sound, noise,,* Heb. 12:19; *report,* Lk. 4:37; Acts 2:2* [2279]

[2492] ἦχος *ēchos* 1x *sound, noise,* Lk. 21:25* [2279]

[2497] Θαδδαῖος *Thaddaios* 2x *Thaddaeus,* pr. name, Mt. 10:3; Mk. 3:18* [2280]

[2498] θάλασσα *thalassa* 91x *the sea,* Mt. 23:15, Mk. 9:42; *a sea,* Acts 7:36; *an inland sea, lake,* Mt. 8:24 [2281] See *sea.*

[2499] θάλπω *thalpō* 2x *to impart warmth;* met. *to cherish, nurse, foster, comfort,* Eph. 5:29; 1 Thess. 2:7* [2282]

[2500] Θαμάρ *Thamar* 1x *Tamar,* (Gen. 38), pr. name, indecl., Mt. 1:3* [2283]

[2501] θαμβέω *thambeō* 3x *to be astonished, amazed, awestruck* Mt. 1:27; 10:24, 32* [2284]

[2502] θάμβος *thambos* 3x *astonishment, amazement, awe,* Lk. 4:36; 5:9; Acts 3:10* [2285]

[2503] θανάσιμος *thanasimos* 1x *deadly, mortal, fatal,* Mk. 16:18* [2286]

[2504] θανατηφόρος *thanatēphoros* 1x *bringing* or *causing death, deadly, fatal,* Jas. 3:8* [2287]

[2505] θάνατος *thanatos* 120x *death, the extinction of life,* whether naturally, Lk. 2:26; Mk. 9:1; or violently, Mt. 10:21; 15:4; *imminent danger of death,* 2 Cor. 4:11, 12; 11:23; in NT spiritual *death,* as opposed to ζωή in its spiritual sense, in respect of a forfeiture of salvation, Jn. 8:51; Rom. 6:16 [2288] See *death.*

[2506] θανατόω *thanatoō* 11x *to put to death, deliver to death,* Mt. 10:21; 26:59; Mk. 13:12; pass. *to be exposed to imminent danger of death,* Rom. 8:36; in NT met. *to subdue,* Rom. 8:13; [2289] See *kill; put to death.*

[2507] θάπτω *thaptō* 11x *to bury,* Mt. 8:21, 22; 14:12 [2290] See *bury.*

[2508] Θάρα *Thara* 1x *Terah,* Abraham's father, pr. name, indecl., Lk. 3:34* [2291]

[2509] θαρρέω *tharreō* 6x *to be confident, courageous,* 2 Cor. 5:6, 8; 7:16; 10:1, 2; Heb. 13:6* [2292]

[2510] θαρσέω *tharseō* 7x *to be of good courage, be of good cheer,* Mt. 9:2; *to be confident, hopeful*; *to be bold, maintain a bold bearing,* Mt. 9:22; 14:27; Mk. 6:50; 10:49; Jn. 16:33; Acts 23:11* [2293]

[2511] θάρσος *tharsos* 1x *courage, confidence,* Acts 28:15* [2294]

[2512] θαῦμα *thauma* 2x *a wonder; wonder, admiration, astonishment,* 2 Cor. 11:14; Rev. 17:6* [2295]

[2513] θαυμάζω *thaumazō* 43x *to admire, regard with admiration, wonder at,* Lk. 7:9; Acts 7:31; *to reverence, adore,* 2 Thess. 1:10; absol. *to wonder, be filled with wonder, admiration,* or *astonishment,* Mt. 8:10; Lk. 4:22 [2296] See *(be) amazed; astound; marvel; wonder.*

[2514] θαυμάσιος *thaumasios* 1x *wonderful, admirable, marvellous;* τὸ θαυμάσιον, *a wonder, wonderful work,* Mt. 21:15* [2297]

[2515] θαυμαστός *thaumastos* 6x *wondrous, glorious,* 1 Pet. 2:9; Rev. 15:1; *marvellous, strange, uncommon,* Mt. 21:42; Mk. 12:11; Jn. 9:30; Rev. 15:3* [2298]

[2516] θεά *thea* 1x *a goddess,* Acts 19:27* [2299]

[2517] θεάομαι *theaomai* 22x *to gaze upon,* Mt. 6:1; 23:5; Lk. 7:24; *to see, discern with the eyes,* Mk. 16:11, 14; Lk. 5:27; Jn. 1:14, 32, 38; *to see, visit,* Rom. 15:24 [2300] See *behold; observe; see.*

[2518] θεατρίζω *theatrizō* 1x *to be exposed as in a theater, to be made a gazing-stock, object of scorn,* Heb. 10:33* [2301]

[2519] θέατρον *theatron* 3x *a theater, a place where public games and spectacles are exhibited,* Acts 19:29, 31; meton. *a show, gazing-stock,* 1 Cor. 4:9* [2302]

[2520] θεῖον *theion* 7x *brimstone, sulphur,* Lk. 17:29; Rev. 9:17; 14:10; 19:20; 20:10; 21:8* [2303]

[2521] θεῖος *theios* 3x *divine, pertaining to God,* 2 Pet. 1:3, 4; τὸ θεῖον, *the divine nature, divinity,* Acts 17:29* [2304]

[2522] θειότης *theiotēs* 1x *divinity, deity, godhead, divine majesty,* Rom. 1:20* [2305]

[2523] θειώδης *theiōdēs* 1x *of brimstone, sulphurous,* Rev. 9:17* [2306]

[2525] θέλημα *thelēma* 62x *will, bent, inclination,* 1 Cor. 16:12; Eph. 2:3; 1 Pet. 4:3; *resolve,* 1 Cor. 7:37; *will, purpose, design,* 2 Tim. 2:26; 2 Pet. 1:21; *will, sovereign pleasure, behest,* Mt. 18:14; Lk. 12:47; Acts 13:22, et al. freq.; ἐν τῷ θελήματι θεοῦ, *Deo permittente, if God please* or *permit,* Rom. 1:10 [2307] See *will.*

[2526] θέλησις *thelēsis* 1x *will, pleasure,* Heb. 2:4* [2308]

[2527] θέλω *thelō* 208x *to exercise the will,* properly by an unimpassioned operation; *to be willing,* Mt. 17:4; *to be inclined, disposed,* Rom. 13:3; *to choose,* Lk. 1:62; *to intend, design,* Lk. 14:28; *to will,* Jn. 5:21; 21:22; ἤθελον, *I could wish,* Gal. 4:20 [2309] See *desire; want; will.*

[2528] θεμέλιον *themelion* 1x in Acts 16:26 *themelion* is used as a neuter noun from *themelios* (*2529*), *foundation* such as the foundation of a prison* [2310] See *foundation.*

[2529] θεμέλιος *themelios* 15x see θεμέλιον (*2528*) *a foundation,* Lk. 6:48, 49; Heb. 11:10; met. *a foundation* laid in elementary instruction, Heb. 6:1; *a foundation* of a superstructure of faith, doctrine, or hope, 1 Cor. 3:10, 11, 12; Eph. 2:20; 1 Tim. 6:19; *a foundation* laid in the commencement of the preaching of the Gospel, Rom. 15:20* [2310] See *foundation.*

[2530] θεμελιόω *themelioō* 5x *to found, lay the foundation of,* Mt. 7:25; Heb. 1:10; met. *to ground, establish, render firm and unwavering,* Eph. 3:17; Col. 1:23; 1 Pet. 5:10* [2311]

[2531] θεοδίδακτος *theodidaktos* 1x *taught of God, divinely instructed,* 1 Thess. 4:9* [2312]

[2534] θεομάχος *theomachos* 1x *fighting against God, in conflict with God,* Acts 5:39* [2314]

[2535] θεόπνευστος *theopneustos* 1x *divinely inspired,* 2 Tim. 3:16* [2315]

[2536] θεός *theos* 1,317x used mostly in N.T. of the true *God*, Mt. 3:9; 3:16; 4:10; including Jesus, Jn. 1:1; Rom. 9:5; Tit. 2:13; also of a false *god, a deity,* Acts 7:43; 1 Cor. 8:5; *an idol,* Acts 7:40 [2316] See *God.*

[2537] θεοσέβεια *theosebeia* 1x *worshipping of God, reverence towards God, piety,* 1 Tim. 2:10* [2317]

[2538] θεοσεβής *theosebēs* 1x *reverencing God, pious, godly, devout, a sincere worshipper of God,* Jn. 9:31* [2318]

[2539] θεοστυγής *theostygēs* 1x *God-hated;* in NT *a hater and despiser of God,* Rom. 1:30* [2319]

[2540] θεότης *theotēs* 1x *divinity, deity, godhead,* Col. 2:9* [2320]

[2541] Θεόφιλος *Theophilos* 2x *Theophilus,* pr. name, Lk. 1:3; Acts 1:1* [2321]

[2542] θεραπεία *therapeia* 3x *service, attendance; healing, cure,* Lk. 9:11; Rev. 22:2; meton. *those who render service, servants, domestics, family household,* Lk. 12:42* [2322]

[2543] θεραπεύω *therapeuō* 43x *to heal, cure,* Mt. 4:23, 24; 8:16; pass. *to receive service,* Acts 17:25; *to serve, minister to, render service and attendance; to render* divine *service, worship,* Acts 17:25 [2323] See *cure; heal.*

[2544] θεράπων *therapōn* 1x *an attendant, a servant; a minister,* Heb. 3:5* [2324]

[2545] θερίζω *therizō* 21x *to gather in harvest, reap,* Mt. 6:26; 25:24, 26; met. *to reap* the reward of labor, 1 Cor. 9:11; 2 Cor. 9:6; *to reap* the harvest of vengeance, Rev. 14:15, 16 [2325] See *harvest; reap.*

[2546] θερισμός *therismos* 13x *a harvest, the act of gathering in the harvest, reaping,* Jn. 4:35; met. *the harvest* of the Gospel, Mt. 9:37, 38; Lk. 10:2; *a crop;* met. *the crop* of vengeance, Rev. 14:15 [2326] See *harvest.*

[2547] θεριστής *theristēs* 2x *one who gathers in the harvest, a reaper,* Mt. 13:30, 39* [2327]

[2548] θερμαίνω *thermainō* 6x *to warm;* mid. *to warm one's self,* Mt. 14:54, 67; Jn. 18:18, 25; Jas. 2:16* [2328]

[2549] θέρμη *thermē* 1x also formed as θέρμα, *heat, warmth,* Acts 28:3* [2327]

[2550] θέρος *theros* 3x *the warm season of the year, summer,* Mt. 24:32; Mk. 13:28; Lk. 21:30* [2330]

[2552] Θεσσαλονικεύς *Thessalonikeus* 4x *Thessalonian, of Thessalonica,* Acts 20:4; 27:2; inscription to 1 and 2 Thess.* [2331]

[2553] Θεσσαλονίκη *Thessalonikē* 5x *Thessalonica,* a city of Macedonia, Acts 17:1, 11, 13; Phil. 4:16; 2 Tim. 4:10* [2332]

[2554] Θευδᾶς *Theudas* 1x *Theudas,* pr. name, Acts 5:36* [2333]

[2555] θεωρέω *theōreō* 58x *to be a spectator, to gaze on, contemplate; to behold, view* with interest and attention, Mt. 27:55; 28:1; *to contemplate* mentally, *consider,* Heb. 7:4; in NT *to see, perceive,* Mk. 3:11; *to come to a knowledge of,* Jn. 6:40; from the Hebrew, *to experience, undergo,* Jn. 8:51 [2334] See *perceive; see; watch.*

[2556] θεωρία *theōria* 1x *a beholding; a sight, spectacle,* Lk. 23:48* [2335]

[2557] θήκη *thēkē* 1x *a repository, receptacle; a case, sheath, scabbard,* Jn. 18:11* [2336]

[2558] θηλάζω *thēlazō* 5x *to suckle, give suck,* Mt. 24:19; Mk. 13:17; Lk. 21:23; *to suck,* Mt. 21:16; Lk. 11:27* [2337]

[2559] θῆλυς *thēlys* 5x *female;* τὸ θῆλυ, sc. γένος, *a female,* Mt. 19:4; Mk. 10:6; Gal. 3:28; ἡ θήλεια, *woman,* Rom. 1:26, 27* [2338]

[2560] θήρα *thēra* 1x *hunting, the chase;* met. *means of capture, a cause of destruction,* Rom. 11:9* [2339]

[2561] θηρεύω *thēreuō* 1x *to hunt, catch;* met. *to seize on, lay hold of,* Lk. 11:54* [2340]

[2562] θηριομαχέω *thēriomacheō* 1x *to fight with wild beasts;* met. *to be exposed to furious hostility,* 1 Cor. 15:32* [2341]

[2563] θηρίον *thērion* 46x *a beast, wild animal,* Mk. 1:13; Acts 10:12; met. *a brute, brutish man,* Tit. 1:12 [2342] See *beast.*

[2564] θησαυρίζω *thēsaurizō* 8x *to collect and lay up stores* or *wealth, treasure,* Mt. 6:19, 20; Lk. 12:21; 2 Cor. 12:14; Jas. 5:3; *to heap up, accumulate,* Rom. 2:5; 1 Cor. 16:2; *to reserve, keep in store,* 2 Pet. 3:7 [2343]

[2565] θησαυρός *thēsauros* 17x *a treasury, a store, treasure, precious deposit,* Mt. 6:19, 20, 21; *a receptacle in which precious articles are kept, a casket,* Mt. 2:11; *a storehouse,* Mt. 12:35 [2344] See *storeroom; treasure.*

[2566] θιγγάνω *thinganō* 3x *to touch,* Col. 2:21; Heb. 12:20; *to harm,* Heb. 11:28* [2345]

[2567] θλίβω *thlibō* 10x *to squeeze, press; to press upon, encumber, throng, crowd,* Mk. 3:9; met. *to distress, afflict,* 2 Cor. 1:6; 4:8; pass. *to be compressed, narrow,* Mt. 7:14 [2346] See *persecute; press; trouble.*

[2568] θλῖψις *thlipsis* 45x pr. *pressure, compression;* met. *affliction, distress* of mind, 2 Cor. 2:4; *distressing circumstances, trial, affliction,* Mt. 25:9 [2347] See *affliction; distress; tribulation; trouble.*

[2569] θνῄσκω *thnēskō* 9x *to die;* in NT *to be dead,* Mt. 2:20; Mk. 15:44 [2348]

[2570] θνητός *thnētos* 6x *mortal, subject to death,* Rom. 6:12; 8:11; 2 Cor. 4:11; τὸ θνητόν, *mortality,* 1 Cor. 15:53, 54; 2 Cor. 5:4* [2349] See *mortal.*

[2571] θορυβάζω *thorybazō* 1x *to be troubled, disturbed,* Lk. 10:41* [5182]

[2572] θορυβέω *thorybeō* 4x *to make a din, uproar;* trans. *to disturb, throw into commotion,* Acts 17:5; in NT mid. *to manifest agitation of mind, to raise a lament,* Mt. 9:23; Mk. 5:39; Acts 20:10* [2350]

[2573] θόρυβος *thorybos* 7x *an uproar, din; an outward expression of mental agitation, outcry,* Mk. 5:38; *a tumult, commotion,* Mt. 26:5 [2351]

[2575] θραύω *thrauō* 1x *to break, shiver;* met., *shattered, crushed* by cruel oppression, Lk. 4:18* [2352]

[2576] θρέμμα *thremma* 1x *that which is reared* (especially sheep and goats); pl. *cattle,* Jn. 4:12* [2353]

[2577] θρηνέω *thrēneō* 4x *to lament, bewail,* Mt. 11:17; Lk. 7:32; 23:27; Jn. 16:20* [2354]

[2579] θρησκεία *thrēskeia* 4x *religious worship,* Col. 2:18; *religion, a religious system,* Acts 26:5; *religion, piety,* Jas. 1:26, 27* [2356]

[2581] θριαμβεύω *thriambeuō* 2x pr. *to celebrate a triumph;* trans. *to lead in triumph, celebrate a triumph over,* Col. 2:15; in NT *to cause to triumph,* or, *to render conspicuous,* 2 Cor. 2:14* [2358]

[2582] θρίξ *thrix* 15x *a hair; the hair* of the head, Mt. 5:36; 10:30; of an animal, Mt. 3:4; Mk. 1:6 [2359] See *hair.*

[2583] θροέω *throeō* 3x *to cry aloud;* in NT pass., *to be disturbed, disquieted, alarmed, terrified,* Mt. 24:6; Mk. 13:7; 2 Thess. 2:2* [2360]

[2584] θρόμβος *thrombos* 1x *a lump;* espec. *a clot* of blood, *drop,* Lk. 22:44* [2361]

[2585] θρόνος *thronos* 62x *a seat, a throne,* Mt. 5:34; 19:28; Lk. 1:52; meton. *power, dominion,* Lk. 1:32; Heb. 1:8; *a potentate,* Col. 1:16 [2362] See *throne.*

[2587] Θυάτειρα *Thuateira* 4x *Thyatira,* a city of Lydia, Acts 16:14; Rev. 1:11; 2:18, 24* [2363]

[2588] θυγάτηρ *thugatēr* 28x *a daughter,* Mt. 9:18; 10:35, 37; in the vocative, an expression of affection and kindness, Mt. 9:22; from the Hebrew, *one of the female posterity* of any one, Lk. 1:5; met. *a city,* Mt. 21:5; Jn. 12:15; pl. *female inhabitants,* Lk. 23:28 [2364] See *daughter.*

[2589] θυγάτριον *thugatrion* 2x *a little daughter, female child,* Mk. 5:23; 7:25* [2365]

[2590] θύελλα *thuella* 1x *a tempest, whirlwind, hurricane,* Heb. 12:18* [2366]

[2591] θύϊνος *thuinos* 1x *thyme,* of θυΐα, *thya,* an aromatic evergreen tree, arbor vitae, resembling the cedar, and found in Libya, Rev. 18:12* [2367]

[2592] θυμίαμα *thumiama* 6x *incense, any odoriferous substance burnt in religious worship,* Rev. 5:8; 8:3, 4; 18:13; or, *the act of burning incense,* Lk. 1:10, 11* [2368]

[2593] θυμιατήριον *thumiatērion* 1x *an altar* of burning incense, Heb. 9:4* [2369]

[2594] θυμιάω *thumiaō* 1x *to burn incense,* Lk. 1:9* [2370]

[2595] θυμομαχέω *thumomacheō* 1x *to wage war fiercely; to be warmly hostile to, be enraged against,* Acts 12:20* [2371]

[2596] θυμός *thumos* 18x pr. *the soul, mind;* hence, *a strong passion* or *emotion of the mind; anger, wrath,* Lk. 4:28; Acts 19:28; pl. *swellings of anger,* 2 Cor. 12:20; Gal. 5:20 [2372] See *anger; fury; rage; wrath.*

[2597] θυμόω *thumoō* 1x *to provoke to anger;* pass. *to be angered, enraged,* Mt. 2:16* [2373]

[2598] θύρα *thura* 39x *a door, gate,* Mt. 6:6; Mk. 1:33; *an entrance,* Mt. 27:60; in NT met. *an opening, occasion, opportunity,* Acts 14:27; 1 Cor. 16:9; meton. *a medium* or *means of entrance,* Jn. 10:7, 9 [2374] See *door.*

[2599] θυρεός *thureos* 1x *a stone* or *other material employed to close a doorway;* later, *a large oblong shield,* Eph. 6:16* [2375]

[2600] θυρίς *thuris* 2x *a small opening; a window,* Acts 20:9; 2 Cor. 11:33* [2376]

[2601] θυρωρός *thurōros* 4x *a door-keeper, porter,* Mk. 13:34; Jn. 10:3; 18:16, 17* [2377]

[2602] θυσία *thusia* 28x *sacrifice, the act of sacrificing,* Heb. 9:26; *the thing sacrificed, a victim,* Mt. 9:13; 12:7; *the flesh of victims* eaten by the sacrificers, 1 Cor. 10:18; in NT *an offering* or *service* to God, Phil. 4:18 [2378] See *offering; sacrifice.*

[2603] θυσιαστήριον *thusiastērion* 23x *an altar,* Mt. 5:23, 24; Lk. 1:11; spc. *the altar of burnt-offering,* Mt. 23:35; Lk. 11:51; meton. *a class of sacrifices,* Heb. 13:10 [2379] See *altar.*

[2604] θύω *thuō* 14x *to offer; to kill in sacrifice, sacrifice, immolate,* Acts 14:13, 18; in NT *to slaughter* for food, Mt. 22:4 [2380] See *kill; sacrifice.*

[2605] Θωμᾶς *Thōmas* 11x *Thomas,* pr. name, Mt. 10:3; Mk. 3:18; Lk. 6:15; Jn. 11:16; 14:5; 20:24, 26, 27, 28; 21:2; Acts 1:13* [2381]

[2606] θώραξ *thōrax* 5x *a breast-plate, armor for the body,* consisting of two parts, one covering the breast and the other the back, Eph. 6:14; 1 Thess. 5:8; Rev. 9:9, 17* [2382]

[2608] Ἰάϊρος *Iairos* 2x also spelled Ἰάειρος, *Jairus,* pr. name, Mk. 5:22; Lk. 8:41* [2383]

[2609] Ἰακώβ *Iakōb* 27x *Jacob,* pr. name, indecl. (1) Son of Issac, Matt 1:2. (2) Father of Joseph, Mary's husband, Matt 1:15, 16 [2384]

[2610] Ἰάκωβος *Iakōbos* 42x *James,* pr. name. (1) *Son of Zebedee,* Mt. 4:21. (2) *Son of Alphaeus and Mary, brother of Jude,* Mt. 10:3. (3) *James the less, brother of Jesus,* Gal. 1:19 [2385]

[2611] ἴαμα *iama* 3x *healing, cure,* 1 Cor. 12:9, 28, 30* [2386]

[2612] Ἰαμβρῆς *Iambrēs* 1x *Jambres,* pr. name, 2 Tim. 3:8* [2387]

[2613] Ἰανναί *Iannai* 1x *Jannai,* pr. name, indecl., Lk. 3:24* [2388]

[2614] Ἰάννης *Iannēs* 1x *Jannes,* pr. name, 2 Tim. 3:8* [2389]

[2615] ἰάομαι *iaomai* 26x *to heal, cure,* Mt. 8:8; Lk. 9:2; met. *to heal,* spiritually, *restore from a state of sin and condemnation,* Mt. 13:15; Heb. 12:13 [2390] See *cure; heal.*

[2616] Ἰάρετ *Iaret* 1x *Jared,* pr. name, indecl., Lk. 3:37* [2391]

[2617] ἴασις *iasis* 3x *healing, cure,* Lk. 13:32; Acts 4:22, 30* [2392]

[2618] ἴασπις *iaspis* 4x *jasper,* a precious stone of various colors, as purple, cerulian green, etc. Rev. 4:3; 21:11, 18, 19* [2393]

[2619] Ἰάσων *Iasōn* 5x *Jason,* Acts 17:5-7 (3x), 9; Rom. 16:21* [2394]

[2620] ἰατρός *iatros* 7x *physician,* Mt. 9:12; Mk. 2:17; 5:26; Lk. 4:23; 5:31; 8:43; Col. 4:14* [2395]

[2623] ἴδε *ide* 29x the imperative of εἶδον used as a particle, *Lo! Behold!* Jn. 16:29; 19:4, 5 [2396] See *look.*

[2625] ἴδιος *idios* 114x *one's own,* Mk. 15:20; Jn. 7:18; *due, proper, specially assigned,* Gal. 6:9; 1 Tim. 2:6; 6:15; Tit. 1:3; also used in NT as a simple possessive, Eph. 5:22; τὰ ἴδια, *one's home, household, people,* Jn. 1:11; 16:32; 19:17; οἱ ἴδιοι, *members of one's own household, friends,* Jn. 1:11; Acts 24:23; ἰδίᾳ, adverbially, *respectively,* 1 Cor. 12:11; κατ᾽ ἰδίαν, adv., *privately, aside, by one's self, alone,* Mt. 14:13, 23 [2398] See *one's own.*

[2626] ἰδιώτης *idiōtēs* 5x pr. *one in private life, one devoid of special learning* or *gifts, a plain person,*

Acts 4:13; 2 Cor. 11:6; *ungifted,* 1 Cor. 14:16, 23, 24* [2399]

[2627] ἰδού *idou* 200x aorist middle imperative of εἶδον used as an interjection, *Look! See! Lo!* Mt. 1:23; Lk. 1:38; Acts 8:36 [2400] See *behold; look.*

[2628] Ἰδουμαία *Idoumaia* 1x *Idumaea,* a country south of Judea, Mk. 3:8* [2401]

[2629] ἱδρώς *hidrōs* 1x *sweat,* Lk. 22:44* [2402]

[2630] Ἰεζάβελ *Iezabel* 1x *Jezebel,* (1 Ki. 16:31), pr. name, indecl., Rev. 2:20* [2403]

[2631] Ἱεράπολις *Hierapolis* 1x *Hierapolis,* a city of Phrygia, Col. 4:13* [2404]

[2632] ἱερατεία *hierateia* 2x *priesthood, sacerdotal office,* Lk. 1:9; Heb. 7:5* [2405]

[2633] ἱεράτευμα *hierateuma* 2x *a priesthood;* meton. *a body of priests,* 1 Pet. 2:5, 9* [2406]

[2634] ἱερατεύω *hierateuō* 1x *to officiate as a priest, perform sacred rites,* Lk. 1:8* [2407]

[2635] Ἰερεμίας *Ieremias* 3x *Jeremiah,* pr. name, Mt. 2:17; 16:14; 27:9* [2408]

[2636] ἱερεύς *hiereus* 31x *a priest, one who performs sacrificial rites,* Mt. 8:4; Lk. 1:5; Jn. 1:19 [2409] See *priest.*

[2637] Ἰεριχώ *Ierichō* 7x *Jericho,* a city of Palestine, Mt. 20:29; Mk. 10:46; Lk. 10:30; 18:35; 19:1; Heb. 11:30* [2410]

[2638] ἱερόθυτος *hierothutos* 1x *offered in sacrifice,* 1 Cor. 10:28* [1494]

[2639] ἱερόν *hieron* 72x *temple, sanctuary,* Mt. 4:5; Lk. 4:9; Acts 19:27 [2411] See *temple.*

[2640] ἱεροπρεπής *hieroprepēs* 1x *reverent*, Tit. 2:13* [2412]

[2641] ἱερός *hieros* 2x *holy, divine, set apart,* 2 Tim. 3:15; τὰ ἱερά, *sacred rites,* 1 Cor. 9:13* [2413]

[2642] Ἱεροσόλυμα *Hierosolyma* 62x see Ἰερουσαλήμ [2414]

[2643] Ἱεροσολυμίτης *Hierosolymitēs* 2x *a native of Jerusalem,* Mk. 1:5; Jn. 7:25* [2415]

[2644] ἱεροσυλέω *hierosyleō* 1x *to despoil temples, commit sacrilege,* Rom. 2:22* [2416]

[2645] ἱερόσυλος *hierosylos* 1x *one who despoils temples, commits sacrilege,* Acts 19:37* [2417]

[2646] ἱερουργέω *hierourgeō* 1x *to officiate as priest, perform sacred rites;* in NT *to minister* in a divine commission, Rom. 15:16* [2418]

[2647] Ἰερουσαλήμ *Ierousalēm* 77x *Jerusalem,* pr. name, indecl., also spelled Ἱεροσόλυμα 62x in our text [2419]

[2648] ἱερωσύνη *hierōsynē* 3x *a priesthood, sacerdotal office,* Heb. 7:11, 12, 24* [2420]

[2649] Ἰεσσαί *Iessai* 5x *Jesse,* father of David (1 Sam. 16), pr. name, indecl., Mt. 1:5f.; Lk. 3:32; Acts 13:22; Rom. 15:12* [2421]

[2650] Ἰεφθάε *Iephthae* 1x *Jephthah,* (Jdg. 11f.), pr. name, indecl., Heb. 11:32* [2422]

[2651] Ἰεχονίας *Iechonias* 2x *Jechoniah,* pr. name, Mt. 1:11, 12; Lk. 3:23ff.* [2423]

[2652] Ἰησοῦς *Iēsous* 917x *a Savior, Jesus,* Mt. 1:21, 25; 2:1, et al. freq.; *Joshua,* Acts 7:45; Heb. 4:8; *Jesus,* a Jewish Christian, Col. 4:11 [2424] See *Jesus.*

[2653] ἱκανός *hikanos* 39x *befitting; sufficient, enough,* Lk. 22:38; ἱκανὸν ποιεῖν τινί, *to satisfy, gratify,* Mk. 15:15; τὸ ἱκανὸν λαμβάνειν, *to take security* or *bail* of any one, Acts 17:9; or persons, *adequate, competent, qualified,* 2 Cor. 2:16; *fit, worthy,* Mt. 3:11; 8:8; of number or quantity, *considerable, large, great, much,* and pl. *many,* Mt. 28:12; Mk. 10:46 [2425] See *adequate; deserve; sufficient.*

[2654] ἱκανότης *hikanotēs* 1x *sufficiency, ability, fitness, qualification,* 2 Cor. 3:5* [2426]

[2655] ἱκανόω *hikanoō* 2x *to make sufficient* or *competent, qualify,* 2 Cor. 3:6; Col. 1:12* [2427]

[2656] ἱκετηρία *hiketēria* 1x pr. *an olive branch* borne by suppliants in their hands; *prayer, supplication,* Heb. 5:7* [2428]

[2657] ἰκμάς *ikmas* 1x *moisture,* Lk. 8:6* [2429]

[2658] Ἰκόνιον *Ikonion* 6x *Iconium,* a city of Lycaonia, in Asia Minor, Acts 13:51; 14:1, 19, 21; 16:2; 2 Tim. 3:11* [2430]

[2659] ἱλαρός *hilaros* 1x *cheerful, not grudging,* 2 Cor. 9:7* [2431]

[2660] ἱλαρότης *hilarotēs* 1x *cheerfulness, graciousness,* Rom. 12:8* [2432]

[2661] ἱλάσκομαι *hilaskomai* 2x *to appease, render propitious;* in NT *to propitiate, make an atonement* or *propitiation for,* Heb. 2:17; ἱλάσθητι, *be gracious,* *show mercy, pardon,* Lk. 18:13* [2433] See *atone; (have) mercy; propitiate, propitiation,*

[2662] ἱλασμός *hilasmos* 2x *atoning sacrifice, sin offering, propitiation, expiation; one who makes propitiation/expiation,* 1 Jn. 2:2; 4:10* [2434] See *atonement, atoning sacrifice; propitiate, propitiation.*

[2663] ἱλαστήριον *hilastērion* 2x *the cover of the ark of the covenant, the mercy-seat, the place of propitiation,* Rom. 3:25; Heb. 9:5* [2435] See *atonement, atoning sacrifice; propitiate, propitiation.*

[2664] ἵλεως *hileōs* 2x *propitious, favorable, merciful, gracious,* Heb. 8:12; from the Hebrew, ἵλεως σοι (ὁ θεός) *God have mercy on you, God forbid, far be it from you,* Mt. 16:22* [2436]

[2665] Ἰλλυρικόν *Illyrikon* 1x *Illyricum,* a country between the Adriatic and the Danube, Rom. 15:19* [2437]

[2666] ἱμάς *himas* 4x *a strap* or *thong of leather,* Acts 22:25; *a shoe-latchet,* Mk. 1:7; Lk. 3:16; Jn. 1:27* [2438]

[2667] ἱματίζω *himatizō* 2x *to clothe;* pass. *to be clothed,* Mk. 5:15; Lk. 8:35* [2439]

[2668] ἱμάτιον *himation* 60x *a garment; the upper garment, mantle,* Mt. 5:40; 9:16, 20, 21; pl. *the mantle and tunic together,* Mt. 26:65; pl. genr. *garments, raiment,* Mt. 11:8; 24:18 [2440] See *cloak; clothes; robe.*

[2669] ἱματισμός *himatismos* 5x *garment; raiment, apparel, clothing,* Lk. 7:25; 9:29; Jn. 19:24; Acts 20:33; 1 Tim. 2:9* [2441]

[2671] ἵνα *hina* 663x *that, in order that,* Mt. 19:13; Mk. 1:38; Jn. 1:22; 3:15; 17:1; ἵνα μή, *that not, lest,* Mt. 7:1; in NT equivalent to ὥστε, *so that, so as that,* Jn. 9:2; also, marking a simple circumstance, *the circumstance that,* Mt. 10:25; Jn. 4:34; 6:29; 1 Jn. 4:17; 5:3 [2443]

[2672] ἱνατί *hinati* 6x *Why is it that? For what reason? Why?* Mt. 9:4; 27:46; Lk. 13:7; Acts 4:25; 7:26; 1 Cor. 10:29* [2444]

[2673] Ἰόππη *Ioppē* 10x *Joppa,* a city of Palestine, Acts 9:36, 38, 42f.; 10:5, 8, 23, 32; 11:5, 13* [2445]

[2674] Ἰορδάνης *Iordanēs* 15x *the river Jordan,* Mt. 3:5; Mk. 10:1; Lk. 4:1; Jn. 3:26 [2446]

[2675] ἰός *ios* 3x *a missile weapon, arrow, dart; venom, poison,* Rom. 3:13; Jas. 3:8; *rust,* Jas. 5:3* [2447]

[2677] Ἰουδαία *Ioudaia* 44x *Judea,* the southern party of the country, below Samaria, Mt. 2:1, 5, 22; 3:1; meton. *the inhabitants of Judea* [2449]

[2679] Ἰουδαϊκός *Ioudaikos* 1x *Jewish, current among the Jews,* Tit. 1:14* [2451]

[2680] Ἰουδαϊκῶς *Ioudaikōs* 1x *in the manner of Jews, according to Jewish custom,* Gal. 2:14* [2452]

[2681] Ἰουδαῖος *Ioudaios* 194x *Jewish,* Mk. 1:5; Jn. 3:22; Acts 16:1; 24:24; pr. *one sprung from the tribe of Judah,* or *a subject of the kingdom of Judah;* in NT *a descendant of Jacob, a Jew,* Mt. 28:15; Mk. 7:3; Acts 19:34; Rom. 2:28, 29 [2453] See *Jews.*

[2682] Ἰουδαϊσμός *Ioudaismos* 2x *Judaism, the character and condition of a Jew; practice of the Jewish religion,* Gal. 1:13, 14* [2454]

[2683] Ἰούδας *Ioudas* 44x *Judas, Jude,* pr. name. (1) *Judah, son of Jacob; the tribe of Judah,* Mt. 1:2; Lk. 1:39. (2) *Juda, son of Joseph, of the ancestry of Jesus,* Lk. 3:30. (3) *Juda, son of Joanna, of the ancestry of Jesus,* Lk. 3:26. (4) *Judas, brother of James, Jude,* Lk. 6:16; Jude 1. (5) *Judas Iscariot, son of Simon,* Mt. 10:4; Jn. 6:71. (6) *Judas, brother of Jesus,* Mt. 13:55; Mk. 6:3. (7) *Judas of Galilee,* Acts 5:37. (8) *Judas, surnamed Barsabas,* Acts 15:22. (9) *Judas of Damascus,* Acts 9:11 [2455]

[2684] Ἰουλία *Ioulia* 1x *Julia,* pr. name, Rom. 16:15* [2456]

[2685] Ἰούλιος *Ioulios* 2x *Julius,* pr. name, Acts 27:1, 3* [2457]

[2687] Ἰουνιᾶς *Iounias* 1x *Junia,* pr. name, Rom. 16:7* [2458]

[2688] Ἰοῦστος *Ioustos* 3x *Justus,* pr. name. (1) *Joseph Barsabas,* Acts 1:23. (2) *Justus of Corinth,* Acts 18:7. (3) *Jesus, called Justus,* Col. 4:11* [2459]

[2689] ἱππεύς *hippeus* 2x *a horseman;* pl. ἱππεῖς, *horsemen, cavalry,* Acts 23:23, 32* [2460]

[2690] ἱππικός *hippikos* 1x *equestrian;* τὸ ἱππικόν, *cavalry, horse,* Rev. 9:16* [2461]

[2691] ἵππος *hippos* 17x *a horse,* Jas. 3:3; Rev. 6:2, 4, 5, 8; 9:7, 17; 18:13; 19:11, 14 [2462] See *horse.*

[2692] ἶρις *iris* 2x *a rainbow, iris,* Rev. 4:3; 10:1* [2463]

[2693] Ἰσαάκ *Isaak* 20x *Isaac,* pr. name, indecl., Mt. 1:2; 8:11; 23:32; Acts 3:13;. Rom. 9:7f.; Gal. 4:28; Heb. 11:9ff.; Jas. 2:21 [2464]

[2694] ἰσάγγελος *isangelos* 1x *equal* or *similar to angels,* Lk. 20:36* [2465]

[2696] Ἰσκαριώθ *Iskariōth* 3x see Ἰσκαριώτης [2469]

[2697] Ἰσκαριώτης *Iskariōtēs* 8x *Iscariot,* surname of Judas, Mt. 10:4; 26:14; Lk. 22:3; Jn. 6:71; Jn. 12:4; 13:2, 26; 14:22. Also spelled Ἰσκαριώθ in our text 3x (Mk. 3:19; 14:10; Lk. 6:16), which is indeclinable.* [2469]

[2698] ἴσος *isos* 8x *equal, like,* Mt. 20:12; Lk. 6:34; *on an equality,* Phil. 2:6; met. *correspondent, consistent,* Mk. 14:56, 59 [2470]

[2699] ἰσότης *isotēs* 3x *equality, equal proportion,* 2 Cor. 8:13, 14; *fairness, equity, what is equitable,* Col. 4:1* [2471]

[2700] ἰσότιμος *isotimos* 1x *of equal price, equally precious* or *valuable,* 2 Pet. 1:1* [2472]

[2701] ἰσόψυχος *isopsychos* 1x *likeminded, of the same mind and spirit,* Phil. 2:20* [2473]

[2702] Ἰσραήλ *Israēl* 68x *Israel,* pr. name, indecl. [2474] See *Israel.*

[2703] Ἰσραηλίτης *Israēlitēs* 9x *an Israelite, a descendant of* Ἰσραήλ, *Israel* or *Jacob,* Jn. 1:47; Acts 2:22 [2475]

[2704] Ἰσσαχάρ *Issachar* 1x *Issachar,* pr. name, indecl., Rev. 7:7* [2466]

[2705] ἵστημι *histēmi* 154x pluperfect, ἑστάμην, also formed as στήκω 10x, trans. *to make to stand, set, place,* Mt. 4:5; *to set forth, appoint,* Acts 1:23; *to fix, appoint,* Acts 17:31; *to establish, confirm,* Rom. 10:3; Heb. 10:9; *to set down, impute,* Acts 7:60; *to weigh out, pay,* Mt. 26:15; intrans. *to stand,* Mt. 12:46; *to stand fast, be firm, be permanent, endure,* Mt. 12:25; Eph. 6:13; *to be confirmed, proved,* Mt. 18:16; 2 Cor. 13:1; *to stop,* Lk. 7:14; 8:44; Acts 8:38 [2476] See *appear; establish; place; propose; set; stand.*

[2707] ἱστορέω *historeō* 1x *to ascertain by inquiry and examination; to inquire of;* in NT *to visit* in order to become acquainted with, Gal. 1:18* [2477]

[2708] ἰσχυρός *ischuros* 29x *strong, mighty, robust,* Mt. 12:29; Lk. 11:21; *powerful, mighty,* 1 Cor. 1:27; 4:10; 1 Jn. 2:14; *strong, fortified,* Rev. 18:10; *vehement,* Mt. 14:20; *energetic,* 2 Cor. 10:10; *sure, firm,* Heb. 6:18 [2478] See *mighty; powerful; strong.*

[2709] ἰσχύς *ischus* 10x *strength, might, power,* Rev. 18:2; Eph. 1:19; *faculty, ability,* 1 Pet. 4:11; Mk. 12:30, 33; Lk. 10:27 [2479] See *might; power; strength.*

[2710] ἰσχύω *ischuō* 28x *to be strong, be well, be in good health,* Mt. 9:12; *to have power, be able,* Mt. 8:28; 26:40; *to have power* or *efficiency, avail, be valid,* Gal. 5:6; Heb. 9:17; *to be of service, be serviceable,* Mt. 5:13; meton. *to prevail,* Acts 19:16; Rev. 12:8 [2480] See *(be) able; overpower; prevail; (be) strong.*

[2711] ἴσως *isōs* 1x *equally; perhaps, it may be that,* Lk. 20:13* [2481]

[2712] Ἰταλία *Italia* 4x *Italy,* Acts 18:2; 27:1, 6; Heb. 13:24* [2482]

[2713] Ἰταλικός *Italikos* 1x *Italian,* Acts 10:1* [2483]

[2714] Ἰτουραῖος *Itouraios* 1x *Ituraea,* a district of Palestine beyond Jordan, Lk. 3:1* [2484]

[2715] ἰχθύδιον *ichthudion* 2x *a small fish,* Mt. 15:34; Mk. 8:7* [2485]

[2716] ἰχθύς *ichthus* 20x *a fish,* Mt. 15:36; 17:27; Lk. 5:6 [2486] See *fish.*

[2717] ἴχνος *ichnos* 3x *a footstep, track;* in NT pl. *footsteps, line of conduct,* Rom. 4:12; 2 Cor. 12:18; 1 Pet. 2:21* [2487]

[2718] Ἰωαθάμ *Iōatham* 2x *Joatham,* pr. name, indecl., Mt. 1:9* [2488]

[2720] Ἰωανάν *Iōanan* 1x *Joanan,* pr. name, indecl., Lk. 3:27* [2489]

[2721] Ἰωάννα *Iōanna* 2x also spelled Ἰωάνα, *Joanna,* pr. name, Lk. 8:3; 24:10* [2489, 2490]

[2722] Ἰωάννης *Iōannēs* 135x also spelled Ἰωάνης, *Joannes, John,* pr. name. (1) *John the Baptist,* Mt. 3:1, et al. (2) *John, son of Zebedee, the apostle,* Mt. 4:21, et al. (3) *John, surnamed Mark,* Acts 12:12, et al. (4) *John, the high-priest,* Acts 4:6 [2491]

[2724] Ἰώβ *Iōb* 1x *Job,* pr. name, indecl., Jas. 5:11* [2492]

[2725] Ἰωβήδ *Iōbēd* 3x *Obed,* David's grandfather, pr. name, indecl., Mt. 1:5; Lk. 3:32* [5601]

[2726] Ἰωδά *Iōda* 1x *Joda,* pr. name, indecl., Lk. 3:26* [2455]

[2727] Ἰωήλ *Iōēl* 1x *Joel,* an Old Testament prophet, pr. name, indecl., Acts 2:16* [2493]

[2729] Ἰωνάμ *Iōnam* 1x *Jonam,* pr. name, indecl., Lk. 3:30* [2494]

[2731] Ἰωνᾶς *Iōnas* 9x *Jonas,* pr. name *Jonah, the prophet,* Mt. 12:39; Lk. 11:29 [2495]

[2732] Ἰωράμ *Iōram* 2x *Joram,* king of Judah (2 Ki. 8:16ff.), pr. name, indecl., Mt. 1:8* [2496]

[2733] Ἰωρίμ *Iōrim* 1x *Jorim,* pr. name, indecl., Lk. 3:29* [2497]

[2734] Ἰωσαφάτ *Iōsaphat* 2x *Josaphat,* king of Judah (1 Ki. 22:41), pr. name, indecl., Mt. 1:8* [2498]

[2736] Ἰωσῆς *Iōsēs* 4x *Joses, Joseph* pr. name Mt. 27:56; Mk. 6:3; 15:40, 47* [2500]

[2737] Ἰωσήφ *Iōsēph* 35x *Joseph,* pr. name, indecl. (1) *Joseph, son of Jacob,* Jn. 4:5. (2) *Joseph, son of Jonan,* Lk. 3:30. (3) *Joseph, son of Judas,* Lk. 3:26. (4) *Joseph, son of Mattathias,* Lk. 3:24. (5) *Joseph, the husband of Mary,* Mt. 1:16. (6) *Joseph of Arimathea,* Mt. 27:57. (7) *Joseph Barsabas,* Acts 1:23. (8) *Joseph Barnabas,* Acts 4:36 [2501]

[2738] Ἰωσήχ *Iōsēch* 1x *Josech,* pr. name, indecl., Lk. 3:26* [2501]

[2739] Ἰωσίας *Iōsias* 2x *Josiah,* king of Judah (2 Ki. 22), Mt. 1:10, 11* [2502]

[2740] ἰῶτα *iōta* 1x *iota;* in NT used like the Hebrew/Aramaic *yod*, the smallest letter in the Hebrew/ Aramaic alphabet, as an expression for *the least* or *minutest part; a jot,* Mt. 5:18* [2503]

[2743] κἀγώ *kagō* 84x *and I, I also, but I,* a crasis of καί and ἐγώ, dat., κἀμοί, acc., κἀμέ [2504]

[2745] καθά *katha* 1x can function as an adverb, *just as,* Mt. 27:10* [2505]

[2746] καθαίρεσις *kathairesis* 3x *tearing down, destruction,* 2 Cor. 10:4, 8; 13:10* [2506]

[2747] καθαιρέω *kathaireō* 9x *take* or *bring down,* Mk. 15:36, 46; Lk. 1:52; 23:53; Acts 13:29; *tear down, destroy,* Lk. 12:18; Acts 13:19; 19:27; 2 Cor. 10:4* [2507]

[2748] καθαίρω *kathairō* 1x *to cleanse* from filth; *to clear* by pruning, *prune,* Jn. 15:2; met. *to cleanse* from sin, *make expiation* [2508]

[2749] καθάπερ *kathaper* 13x can function as an adverb, *even as, just as,* Rom. 3:4; 4:6; 9:13; 10:15; 11:8; 12:4; 1 Cor. 10:10; 12:12; 2 Cor. 1:14; 3:13, 18; 8:11; 1 Thess. 2:11; 3:6, 12; 4:5; Heb. 4:2* [2509]

[2750] καθάπτω *kathaptō* 1x trans. *to fasten* or *fit to;* in NT equivalent to καθάπτομαι, *to fix one's self upon, fasten upon, take hold of, seize,* Acts 28:3* [2510]

[2751] καθαρίζω *katharizō* 31x *to cleanse, render pure, purify,* Mt. 23:25; Lk. 11:39; *to cleanse* from leprosy, Mt. 8:2, 3; 10:8; met. *to cleanse* from sin, *purify by an expiatory offering, make expiation for,* Heb. 9:22, 23; 1 Jn. 1:7; *to cleanse* from sin, *free from the influence of error and sin,* Acts 15:9; 2 Cor. 7:1; *to pronounce* ceremonially *clean,* Acts 10:15; 11:9 [2511] See *cleanse; make clean.*

[2752] καθαρισμός *katharismos* 7x ceremonial *cleansing, purification,* Lk. 2:22; 5:14; *mode of purification,* Jn. 2:6; 3:25; *cleansing* of lepers, Mk. 1:44; met. *expiation,* Heb. 1:3; 2 Pet. 1:9* [2512]

[2754] καθαρός *katharos* 27x *clean, pure, unsoiled,* Mt. 23:26; 27:59; met. *clean* from guilt, *guiltless, innocent,* Acts 18:6; 20:26; *sincere, upright, virtuous, void of evil,* Mt. 5:8; Jn. 15:3; *clean* ceremonially and morally, Lk. 11:41 [2513] See *clean.*

[2755] καθαρότης *katharotēs* 1x *cleanness;* ceremonial *purity,* Heb. 9:13* [2514]

[2756] καθέδρα *kathedra* 3x *chair, seat,* Mt. 21:12; 23:2; Mk. 11:15* [2515]

[2757] καθέζομαι *kathezomai* 7x *to seat one's self, sit down,* Mt. 26:55; Lk. 2:46; Jn. 4:6; 1:20; 20:12; Acts 6:15; 20:9* [2516]

[2759] καθεξῆς *kathexēs* 5x *in a continual order* or *series, successively, consecutively,* Lk. 1:3; Acts 11:4; 18:23; ὁ, ἡ, καθεξῆς, *succeeding, subsequent,* Lk. 8:1; Acts 3:24* [2517]

[2761] καθεύδω *katheudō* 22x *to sleep, be fast asleep,* Mt. 8:24; 9:24; met. *to sleep* in spiritual sloth, Eph. 5:14; 1 Thess. 5:6; *to sleep* the sleep of death, *to die,* 1 Thess. 5:10 [2518] See *sleep.*

[2762] καθηγητής *kathēgētēs* 2x pr. *a guide, leader;* in NT *a teacher, instructor,* Mt. 23:10* [2519]

[2763] καθήκω *kathēkō* 2x *to reach, extend to;* καθήκει, impers. *it is fitting, meet,* Acts 22:22; τὸ καθῆκον, *what is fit, right, duty*; τὰ μὴ καθήκοντα, by litotes for *what is abominable* or *detestable,* Rom. 1:28* [2520]

[2764] κάθημαι *kathēmai* 91x *to sit, be sitting,* Mt. 9:9; Lk. 10:13; *to be seated,* 1 Cor. 14:30; *to be* *enthroned,* Rev. 18:7; *to dwell, reside,* Mt. 4:16; Lk. 1:79; 21:35 [2521] See *reside; seated; sit.*

[2766] καθημερινός *kathēmerinos* 1x *daily, day by day,* Acts 6:1* [2522]

[2767] καθίζω *kathizō* 46x. (1) trans. *to cause to sit, place;* καθίζομαι, *to be seated, sit,* Mt. 19:28; Lk. 22:30; *to cause to sit* as judges, *place, appoint,* 1 Cor. 6:4. (2) intrans. *to sit, sit down,* Mt. 13:48; 26:36; *to remain, settle, stay, continue, live,* Lk. 24:49 [2523] See *sit.*

[2768] καθίημι *kathiēmi* 4x *to let down, lower,* Lk. 5:19; Acts 9:25; 10:11; 11:5* [2524]

[2770] καθίστημι *kathistēmi* 21x also formed as καθιστάνω, *to place, set,* Jas. 3:6; *to set, constitute, appoint,* Mt. 24:45, 47; Lk. 12:14; *to set down* in a place, *conduct,* Acts 17:15; *to make, render,* or *cause to be,* 2 Pet. 1:8; pass. *to be rendered,* Rom. 5:19 [2525] See *appoint; become; escort; put in charge.*

[2771] καθό *katho* 4x *as,* Rom. 8:26; *according as, in proportion as, to the degree that,* 2 Cor. 8:12; 1 Pet. 4:13* [2526]

[2773] καθόλου *katholou* 1x *on the whole, entirely, in general, altogether, completely;* with a negative, *not at all,* Acts 4:18* [2527]

[2774] καθοπλίζω *kathoplizō* 1x middle, *to arm oneself (completely),* Lk. 11:21* [2528]

[2775] καθοράω *kathoraō* 1x pr. *to look down upon,* in the NT *to mark, perceive, discern,* Rom. 1:20* [2529]

[2776] καθότι *kathoti* 6x *as, just as, according as, in proportion as,* Acts 2:45; 4:35; *inasmuch as,* Lk. 1:7; 19:9; Acts 2:24; 17:31* [2530]

[2777] καθώς *kathōs* 182x *as, just as, in the manner that,* Mt. 21:6; 26:24; *how, in what manner,* Acts 15:14; *according as,* Mk. 4:33; *inasmuch as,* Jn. 17:2; of time, *when,* Acts 7:17 [2531]

[2778] καθώσπερ *kathōsper* 1x *just as, exactly as,* Heb. 5:4* [2509]

[2779] καί *kai* 9,160x. (1) *and,* Mt. 2:2, 3, 11; 4:22. (2) καί ... καί, *both ... and.* (3) as a cumulative particle, *also, too,* Mt. 5:39; Jn. 8:19; 1 Cor. 11:6. (4) emphatic, *even, also,* Mt. 10:30; 1 Cor. 2:10; in NT adversative, *but,* Mt. 11:19; also introductory of the apodosis of a sentence, Gal. 3:28; Jas. 2:4 [2532]

[2780] Καϊάφας *Kaiaphas* 9x *Caiaphas,* pr. name, the high priest from A.D. 18-36, Mt. 26:3, 57; Lk. 3:2; Jn. 11:49; 18:13f., 24, 28; Acts 4:6* [2533]

[2782] Κάϊν *Kain* 3x *Cain,* pr. name, indecl., Heb. 11:4; 1 Jn. 3:12; Jude 11* [2535]

[2783] Καϊνάμ *Kainam* 2x *Cainan,* pr. name, indecl., Lk. 3:36, 37* [2536]

[2785] καινός *kainos* 41x *new, recently made,* Mt. 9:17; Mk. 2:22; *new* in species, character, or mode, Mt. 26:28, 29; Mk. 14:24, 25; Lk. 22:20; Jn. 13:34; 2 Cor. 5:17; Gal. 6:15; Eph. 2:15; 4:24; 1 Jn. 2:7; Rev. 3:12; *novel, strange,* Mk. 1:27; Acts 17:19; *new* to the possessor, Mk. 16:17; *unheard of, unusual,* Mk. 1:27; Acts 17:19; met. *renovated, better, of higher excellence,* 2 Cor. 5:17; Rev. 5:9 [2537] See *new.*

[2786] καινότης *kainotēs* 2x *newness,* Rom. 6:4; 7:6* [2538]

[2788] καίπερ *kaiper* 5x *though, although;* Phil. 3:4; Heb. 5:8; 7:5; 12:17; 2 Pet. 1:12* [2539]

[2789] καιρός *kairos* 85x pr. *fitness, proportion, suitableness; a fitting situation, suitable place,* 1 Pet. 4:17; *a limited period of time marked by a suitableness of circumstances, a fitting season,* 1 Cor. 4:5; 1 Tim. 2:6; 6:15; Tit. 1:3; *opportunity,* Acts 24:25; Gal. 6:10; Heb. 11:15; *a limited period of time marked by characteristic circumstances, a signal juncture, a marked season,* Mt. 16:3; Lk. 12:56; 21:8; 1 Pet. 1:11; *a destined time,* Mt. 8:29; 26:18; Mk. 1:15; Lk. 21:24; 1 Thess. 5:1; *a season* in ordinary succession, equivalent to ὥρα, Mt. 13:30; Acts 14:17; in NT *a limited time, a short season,* Lk. 4:13; simply, *a point of time,* Mt. 11:25; Lk. 13:1 [2540] See *season; time.*

[2790] Καῖσαρ *Kaisar* 29x *Caesar,* pr. name [2541]

[2791] Καισάρεια *Kaisareia* 17x *Caesarea.* (1) *Caesarea Philippi,* Mt. 16:13; Mk. 8:27. (2) *Caesarea Augusta,* Acts 8:40 [2542]

[2792] καίτοι *kaitoi* 2x *and yet, though, although,* Acts 14:17; Heb. 4:3* [2543]

[2793] καίτοιγε *kaitoige* 1x *although indeed, and yet,* Jn. 4:2* [2544]

[2794] καίω *kaiō* 11x *to cause to burn, kindle, light,* Mt. 5:15; pass. *to be kindled, burn, flame,* Lk. 12:35; met. *to be kindled* into emotion, Lk. 24:32; *to consume with fire,* Jn. 15:6; 1 Cor. 13:3 [2545] See *burn.*

[2795] κἀκεῖ *kakei* 10x crasis, *and there,* Mt. 5:23; 10:11; *there also,* Acts 17:13 [2546]

[2796] κἀκεῖθεν *kakeithen* 10x crasis, *and there,* Mk. 10:1; Acts 7:4; 14:26; 20:15; 21:1; 27:4, 12; 28:15; *and then, afterwards,* Acts 13:21 [2547]

[2797] κἀκεῖνος *kakeinos* 22x crasis, *and he, she, it; and this, and that,* Mt. 15:18; 23:23; *he, she, it also; this also, that also,* Mt. 20:4 [2548]

[2798] κακία *kakia* 11x *malice, malignity,* Rom. 1:29; Eph. 4:31; *wickedness, depravity,* Acts 8:22; 1 Cor. 5:8; in NT *evil, trouble, calamity, misfortune,* Mt. 6:34 [2549] See *evil; malice; wicked, wickedness.*

[2799] κακοήθεια *kakoētheia* 1x *disposition for mischief, misfortune, malignity,* Rom. 1:29* [2550]

[2800] κακολογέω *kakologeō* 4x *to speak evil of, revile, abuse, insult,* Mk. 9:39; Acts 19:9; *to address with offensive language, to treat with disrespect,* Matt, 15:4; Mk. 7:10* [2551]

[2801] κακοπάθεια *kakopatheia* 1x *a state of suffering, affliction, trouble,* in NT *endurance in affliction, perseverance,* Jas. 5:10* [2552]

[2802] κακοπαθέω *kakopatheō* 3x *to suffer evil* or *afflictions,* 2 Tim. 2:9; *to be afflicted, troubled, dejected,* Jas. 5:13; in NT *to show endurance in trials and afflictions,* 2 Tim. 4:5* [2553]

[2803] κακοποιέω *kakopoieō* 4x *to cause evil, injure, do harm,* Mk. 3:4; Lk. 6:9; *to do evil, commit sin,* 1 Pet. 3:17; 3 Jn. 11* [2554]

[2804] κακοποιός *kakopoios* 3x *an evil-doer,* 1 Pet. 2:12, 14; 4:15* [2555]

[2805] κακός *kakos* 50x *bad, of a bad quality* or *disposition, worthless, corrupt, depraved,* Mt. 21:41; 24:48; Mk. 7:21; *wicked, criminal, morally bad;* τὸ κακόν, *evil, wickedness, crime,* Mt. 27:23; Acts 23:9; *deceitful,* 1 Pet. 3:10; *mischievous, harmful, destructive;* τὸ κακόν, *evil mischief, harm, injury,* Tit. 1:12; *afflictive;* τὸ κακόν, *evil, misery, affliction, suffering,* Lk. 16;25 [2556] See *bad; evil; wicked, wickedness; wrong.*

[2806] κακοῦργος *kakourgos* 4x *an evil-doer, malefactor, criminal,* Lk. 23:32, 33, 39; 2 Tim. 2:9* [2557]

[2807] κακουχέω *kakoucheō* 2x *to torment, afflict, harass;* pass. *to be afflicted, be oppressed with evils,* Heb. 11:37 13:3* [2558]

[2808] κακόω *kakoō* 6x *to harm, mistreat, cause evil to, oppress,* Acts 7:6, 19; 12:1; 18:10; 1 Pet. 3:13; in NT *to make angry, embitter,* Acts 14:2* [2559]

[2809] κακῶς *kakōs* 16x *ill, badly;* physically *ill, sick,* Mt. 4:24; 8:16; *grievously, vehemently,* Mt. 15:22; *wretchedly, miserably,* Mt. 21:41; *wickedly, reproachfully,* Acts 23:5; *wrongly, criminally,* Jn. 18:23; *amiss,* Jas. 4:3 [2560] See *evil; sick; wrong.*

[2810] κάκωσις *kakōsis* 1x *ill treatment, affliction, oppression, misery,* Acts 7:34* [2561]

[2811] καλάμη *kalamē* 1x *the stalk* of grain, *straw, stubble,* 1 Cor. 3:12* [2562]

[2812] κάλαμος *kalamos* 12x *a reed, cane,* Mt. 11:7; 12:20; Lk. 7:24; *a reed* in its various appliances, as, a wand, a staff, Mt. 27:29, 30, 48; Mk. 15:19, 36; *a measuring-rod,* Rev. 11:1; 21:15f.; a writer's *reed,* 3 Jn. 13* [2563] See *reed.*

[2813] καλέω *kaleō* 148x *to call, call to,* Jn. 10:3; *to call* into one's presence, *send for* a person, Mt. 2:7; *to summon,* Mt. 2:15; 25:14; *to invite,* Mt. 22:9; *to call* to the performance of a certain thing, Mt. 9:13; Heb. 11:8; *to call* to a participation in the privileges of the Gospel, Rom. 8:30; 9:24; 1 Cor. 1:9; 7:18; *to call* to an office or dignity, Heb. 5:4; *to name, style,* Mt. 1:21; pass. *to be styled, regarded,* Mt. 5:9, 19 [2564] See *call; invite; summon.*

[2814] καλλιέλαιος *kallielaios* 1x pr. adj. *productive of good oil;* as subst. *a cultivated olive tree,* Rom. 11:24* [2565]

[2815] καλοδιδάσκαλος *kalodidaskalos* 1x *teaching what is good; a teacher of good,* Tit. 2:3* [2567]

[2818] καλοποιέω *kalopoieō* 1x *to do well, do good, do what is right,* 2 Thess. 3:13* [2569]

[2819] καλός *kalos* 101x pr. *beautiful; good, of good quality* or *disposition; fertile, rich,* Mt. 13:8, 23; *useful, profitable,* Lk. 14:34; καλόν ἐστι[ν], *it is profitable, it is well,* Mt. 18:8, 9; *excellent, choice, select, goodly,* Mt. 7:17, 19; καλόν ἐστι[ν], *it is pleasant, delightful,* Mt. 17:4; *just, full* measure, Lk. 6:38; *honorable, distinguished,* Jas. 2:7; *good, possessing moral excellence, worthy, upright, virtuous,* Jn. 10:11, 14; 1 Tim. 4:6; τὸ καλόν, and τὸ καλόν ἔργον, *what is good and right, a good deed, rectitude, virtue,* Mt. 5:16; Rom. 7:18, 21; *right, duty, propriety,* Mt. 15:26; *benefit, favor,* Jn. 10:32, 33 [2566, 2570] See *beautiful; good.*

[2820] κάλυμμα *kalymma* 4x *a covering; a veil,* 2 Cor. 3:13; met. *a veil, a blind* to spiritual vision, 2 Cor. 3:14, 15, 16* [2571]

[2821] καλύπτω *kalyptō* 8x *to cover,* Mt. 8:24; Lk. 8:16; 23:30; *to hide, conceal,* Mt. 10:26; 2 Cor. 4:3; met. *to cover, throw a veil* of oblivion *over,* Jas. 5:20; 1 Pet. 4:8 [2572]

[2822] καλῶς *kalōs* 37x *well, rightly, suitable, with propriety, becomingly,* 1 Cor. 7:37; 14:17; Gal. 4:17; 5:7; *truly, justly, correctly,* Mk. 12:32; Lk. 20:39; Jn. 4:17; *appositely,* Mt. 15:7; Mk. 7:6; *becomingly, honorably,* Jas. 2:3; *well, effectually,* Mk. 7:9, 37; καλῶς εἰπεῖν, *to speak well, praise, applaud,* Lk. 6:26; καλῶς ἔχειν, *to be convalescent,* Mk. 16:18; καλῶς ποιεῖν, *to do good, confer benefits,* Mt. 5:44; 12:12; *to do well, act virtuously,* Phil. 4:14 [2573] See *good; right; well.*

[2823] κάμηλος *kamēlos* 6x *a camel,* Mt. 3:4; 23:24 [2574] See *camel.*

[2825] κάμινος *kaminos* 4x *a furnace, oven, kiln,* Mt. 13:42, 50; Rev. 1:15; 9:2* [2575]

[2826] καμμύω *kammyō* 2x *to shut, close* the eyes, Mt. 13:15; Acts 28:27* [2576]

[2827] κάμνω *kamnō* 2x *to tire with exertion, labor to weariness; to be wearied, tired out, exhausted, be discouraged,* Heb. 12:3; *to labor* under disease, *be sick,* Jas. 5:15* [2577]

[2828] κάμπτω *kamptō* 4x trans. *to bend, inflect* the knee, Rom. 11:4; Eph. 3:14 intrans. *to bend, bow,* Rom. 14:11; Phil. 2:10* [2578]

[2829] κἄν *kan* 17x crasis, *and if,* Mk. 16:18; *also if,* Mt. 21:21; *even if, if even, although,* Jn. 10:38; *if so much as,* Heb. 12:20; also in NT simply equivalent to καί, as a particle of emphasis, by a pleonasm of ἄν, *at least, at all events,* Mk. 6:56; Acts 5:15; 2 Cor. 11:16 [2579]

[2830] Κανά *Kana* 4x indecl. *Cana,* a town in Galilee, Jn. 2:1, 11; 4:46; 21:2* [2580]

[2831] Καναναῖος *Kananaios* 2x *a Canaanite,* Mt. 10:4; Mk. 3:18* [2581]

[2833] Κανδάκη *Kandakē* 1x *Candace,* pr. name, Acts 8:27* [2582]

[2834] κανών *kanōn* 4x *a measure, rule;* in NT *prescribed range* of action or duty, 2 Cor. 10:13, 15, 16; met. *rule* of conduct or doctrine, Gal. 6:16* [2583]

[2836] καπηλεύω *kapēleuō* 1x pr. *to be* κάπηλος, *a retailer; to peddle with; to corrupt, adulterate,* 2 Cor. 2:17* [2585]

[2837] καπνός *kapnos* 13x *smoke,* Acts 2:19; Rev. 8:4 [2586] See *smoke.*

[2838] Καππαδοκία *Kappadokia* 2x *Cappadocia,* a district of Asia Minor, Acts 2:9; 1 Pet. 1:1* [2587]

[2840] καρδία *kardia* 156x *the heart,* regarded as the seat of feeling, impulse, affection, desire, Mt. 6:21; 22:37; Phil. 1:7; *the heart,* as the seat of intellect, Mt. 13:15; Rom. 1:21; *the heart,* as the inner and mental frame, Mt. 5:8; Lk. 16:15; 1 Pet. 3:4; *the conscience,* 1 Jn. 3:20, 21; *the heart, the inner part, middle, center,* Mt. 12:40 [2588] See *heart.*

[2841] καρδιογνώστης *kardiognōstēs* 2x *heart-knower, searcher of hearts,* Acts 1:24; 15:8* [2589]

[2842] Κάρπος *Karpos* 1x *Carpus,* pr. name, 2 Tim. 4:13* [2591]

[2843] καρπός *karpos* 66x *fruit,* Mt. 3:10; 21:19, 34; from the Hebrew, καρπὸς κοιλίας, *fruit of the womb, offspring,* Lk. 1:42; καρπὸς ὀσφύος, *fruit of the loins, offspring, posterity,* Acts 2:30; καρπὸς χειλέων, *fruit of the lips, praise,* Heb. 13:15; met. *conduct, actions,* Mt. 3:8; 7:16; Rom. 6:22; *benefit, profit,* Rom. 1:13; 6:21; *reward,* Phil. 4:17 [2590] See *crop; fruit.*

[2844] καρποφορέω *karpophoreō* 8x *to bear fruit, yield,* Mk. 4:28; met, *to bring forth the fruit* of action or conduct, Mt. 13:23; Rom. 7:5; mid. *to expand by fruitfulness, to develop itself by success,* Col. 1:6, 10 [2592]

[2845] καρποφόρος *karpophoros* 1x *fruitful, adapted to bring forth fruit,* Acts 14:17* [2593]

[2846] καρτερέω *kartereō* 1x *to be stout; to endure patiently, persevere, bear up with fortitude,* Heb. 11:27* [2594]

[2847] κάρφος *karphos* 6x *any small dry thing,* as *chaff, stubble, splinter*; Mt. 7:3, 4, 5; Lk. 6:41, 42* [2595]

[2848] κατά *kata* 473x *down from,* Mt. 8:32; *down upon, upon,* Mk. 14:3; Acts 27:14; *down into;* κατὰ βάθους, *profound, deepest,* 2 Cor. 8:2; *down over, throughout* a space, Lk. 4:14; 23:5; *concerning,* in cases of pointed allegation, 1 Cor. 15:15; *against,* Mt. 12:30; *by,* in oaths, Mt. 26:63; with an acc. of place, *in the quarter of, about, near, at,* Lk. 10;32; Acts 2:10; *throughout,* Lk. 8:39; *in,* Rom. 16:5;

among, Acts 21:21; *in the presence of,* Lk. 2:31; *in the direction of, towards,* Acts 8:26; Phil. 3:14; of time, *within the range of; during, in the course of, at, about,* Acts 12:1; 27:27; distributively, κατ᾽ οἶκον, *by houses, from house to house,* Acts 2:46; kata; duvo, *two and two,* 1 Cor. 14:27; καθ᾽ ἡμέραν, *daily,* Mt. 26:55; trop., *according to, conformable to, in proportion to,* Mt. 9:29; 25:15; *after the fashion* or *likeness of.* Heb. 5:6; *in virtue of,* Mt. 19:3; *as respects,* Rom. 11:3; Acts 25;14; Heb. 9:9 [2596]

[2849] καταβαίνω *katabainō* 81x *to come* or *go down, descend,* Mt. 8:1; 17:9; *to lead down,* Acts 8:26; *to come down, fall,* Mt. 7:25, 27; *to be let down,* Acts 10:11; 11:5 [2597] See *come down; descend; go down.*

[2850] καταβάλλω *kataballō* 2x *to cast down,* 2 Cor. 4:9; mid. *to lay down, lay* a foundation, Heb. 6:1* [2598]

[2851] καταβαρέω *katabareō* 1x pr. *to weigh down,* met. *to burden, be burdensome to,* 2 Cor. 12:16* [2599]

[2852] καταβαρύνω *katabarynō* 1x *to weigh down, depress,* pass., *be heavy,* Mk. 14:40* [925]

[2853] κατάβασις *katabasis* 1x *the act of descending; a way down, descent,* Lk. 19:37* [2600]

[2856] καταβολή *katabolē* 11x pr. *a casting down; laying the foundation, foundation; beginning, commencement,* Mt. 13:35; 25:34; *conception* in the womb, Heb. 11:11 [2602] See *creation; foundation.*

[2857] καταβραβεύω *katabrabeuō* 1x pr. *to give an unfavorable decision as respects a prize;* hence, *to decide against,* Col. 2:18* [2603]

[2858] καταγγελεύς *katangeleus* 1x *one who announces* anything, *a proclaimer, publisher,* Acts 17:18* [2604]

[2859] καταγγέλλω *katangellō* 18x *to announce, proclaim,* Acts 13:38; in NT *to laud, celebrate,* Rom. 1:8 [2605] See *announce; make public; proclaim.*

[2860] καταγελάω *katagelaō* 3x *to deride, laugh at, jeer,* Mt. 9:24; Mk. 5:40; Lk. 8:53* [2606]

[2861] καταγινώσκω *kataginōskō* 3x *to determine against, condemn, blame, reprehend,* Gal. 2:11; 1 Jn. 3:20, 21 [2607]

[2862] κατάγνυμι *katagnymi* 4x *to break in pieces, crush, break in two,* Mt. 12:20; Jn. 19:31, 32, 33* [2608]

[2863] καταγράφω *katagraphō* 1x *to trace, draw in outline, write,* Jn. 8:6* [1125]

[2864] κατάγω *katagō* 9x *to lead, bring,* or *conduct down,* Acts 9:30; 22:30; 23:15, 20, 28; *to bring* a ship *to land;* pass. κατάγομαι, aor. κατήχθην, *to come to land, land, touch,* Lk. 5:11 [2609]

[2865] καταγωνίζομαι *katagōnizomai* 1x *to subdue, vanquish, overcome, conquer,* Heb. 11:33* [2610]

[2866] καταδέω *katadeō* 1x *to bind up; to bandage* a wound, Lk. 10:34* [2611]

[2867] κατάδηλος *katadēlos* 1x *quite clear* or *evident,* Heb. 7:15* [2612]

[2868] καταδικάζω *katadikazō* 5x *to give judgment against, condemn,* Mt. 12:7, 37; Lk. 6:37; Jas. 5:6* [2613]

[2869] καταδίκη *katadikē* 1x *condemnation, sentence of condemnation,* Acts 25:15* [1349]

[2870] καταδιώκω *katadiōkō* 1x *to follow hard upon; to track, search for, follow perseveringly,* Mk. 1:36* [2614]

[2871] καταδουλόω *katadouloō* 2x *to reduce to absolute servitude, make a slave of,* 2 Cor. 11:20; Gal. 2:4* [2615]

[2872] καταδυναστεύω *katadynasteuō* 2x *to tyrannize over, oppress, exploit,* Acts 10:38; Jas. 2:6* [2616]

[2873] κατάθεμα *katathema* 1x *an execration, curse;* by meton. *what is worthy of cursing* or *condemnation, an accursed thing,* Rev. 22:3* [2652]

[2874] καταθεματίζω *katathematizō* 1x *to curse,* Mt. 26:74* [2653]

[2875] καταισχύνω *kataischunō* 13x *to humiliate, shame, put to shame,* 1 Cor. 1:27; pass. *to be ashamed, be put to shame,* Lk. 13:17; *to dishonor, disgrace,* 1 Cor. 11:4, 5; from the Hebrew, *to frustrate, disappoint,* Rom. 5:5; 9:33; 1 Pet. 2:6 [2617] See *ashamed; disappoint; embarrass, (be) embarrassed; humiliate.*

[2876] κατακαίω *katakaiō* 12x *to burn up, consume with fire,* Mt. 3:12; 13:30, 40 [2618] See *burn.*

[2877] κατακαλύπτω *katakalyptō* 3x *to veil;* mid. *to veil one's self, be veiled* or *covered,* 1 Cor. 11:6, 7. In the pres act ind., 2nd sg, the personal ending σαι does not simplify as normal, κατακαυχᾶσαι* [2619]

[2878] κατακαυχάομαι *katakauchaomai* 4x *to boast, glory over, assume superiority over,* Rom. 11:18 (2x); Jas. 2:13; 3:14* [2620]

[2879] κατάκειμαι *katakeimai* 12x *to lie, be in a recumbent position, be laid down,* Mk. 1:30; 2:4; Lk. 5:25; Jn. 5:3, 6; Acts 9:33; 28:8; *to recline* at table, Mk. 2:15; 14:3; Lk. 5:29; 7:37; 1 Cor. 8:10* [2621] See *lie down; recline.*

[2880] κατακλάω *kataklaō* 2x *to break, break in pieces,* Mk. 6:41; Lk. 9:16* [2622]

[2881] κατακλείω *katakleiō* 2x *to close, shut fast; to shut up, confine,* Lk. 3:20; Acts 26:10* [2623]

[2883] κατακληρονομέω *kataklēronomeō* 1x *to give as inheritance,* Acts 13:19* [2624]

[2884] κατακλίνω *kataklinō* 5x *to cause to lie down, cause to recline* at table, Lk. 9:14, 15; mid. *to lie down, recline,* Lk. 7:36; 14:8; 24:30* [2625]

[2885] κατακλύζω *kataklyzō* 1x *to inundate, flood, deluge,* 2 Pet. 3:6* [2626]

[2886] κατακλυσμός *kataklysmos* 4x *flood, deluge,* Mt. 24:38, 39; Lk. 17:27; 2 Pet. 2:5* [2627]

[2887] κατακολουθέω *katakoloutheō* 2x *to follow closely* or *earnestly,* Lk. 23:55; Acts 16:17* [2628]

[2888] κατακόπτω *katakoptō* 1x *to cut* or *dash in pieces; to mangle, wound,* Mk. 5:5* [2629]

[2889] κατακρημνίζω *katakrēmnizō* 1x *to cast down headlong,* Lk. 4:29* [2630]

[2890] κατάκριμα *katakrima* 3x *punishment, condemnation, condemning sentence,* Rom. 5:16, 18; 8:1* [2631]

[2891] κατακρίνω *katakrinō* 18x *to give judgment against, condemn,* Mt. 27:3; Jn. 8:10, 11; *to condemn, to place in a guilty light* by contrast, Mt. 12:41, 42; Lk. 11:31, 32; Heb. 11:7 [2632] See *condemn; judge guilty.*

[2892] κατάκρισις *katakrisis* 2x *condemnation,* 2 Cor. 3:9; *censure,* 2 Cor. 7:3* [2633]

[2893] κατακύπτω *katakyptō* 1x *to bend down,* Jn. 8:8* [2596 + 2955]

[2894] κατακυριεύω *katakyrieuō* 4x *to get into one's power;* in NT *to bring under, master, overcome,* Acts 19:16; *to domineer over,* Mt. 20:25; Mk. 10:42; 1 Pet. 5:3* [2634]

[2895] καταλαλέω *katalaleō* 5x *to blab out; to speak against, slander,* Jas. 4:11; 1 Pet. 2:12; 3:16* [2635]

[2896] καταλαλιά *katalalia* 2x *evil-speaking, detraction, backbiting, slandering,* 2 Cor. 12:20; 1 Pet. 2:1* [2636]

[2897] κατάλαλος *katalalos* 1x *slanderous; a detractor, slanderer,* Rom. 1:30* [2637]

[2898] καταλαμβάνω *katalambanō* 15x *to lay hold of, grasp; to obtain, attain,* Rom. 9:30; 1 Cor. 9:24; Phil. 3:12, 13; *to seize, to take possession of,* Mk. 9:18; *to come suddenly upon; overtake, surprise,* Jn. 12:35; 1 Thess. 5:4; *to detect in the act, seize,* Jn. 8:3, 4; met. *to comprehend, apprehend,* Jn. 1:5; mid. *to understand, perceive,* Acts 4:13; 10:34; 25:25; Eph. 3:18* [2638] See *catch; grasp; obtain; seize; understand.*

[2899] καταλέγω *katalegō* 1x *to select, enter in a list* or *catalog, enroll,* 1 Tim. 5:9* [2639]

[2901] καταλείπω *kataleipō* 24x *to leave behind; to leave behind* at death, Mk. 12:19; *to relinquish, let remain,* Mk. 14:52; *to quit, depart from, forsake,* Mt. 4:13; 16:4; *to neglect,* Acts 6:2; *to leave alone,* or *without assistance,* Lk. 10:40; *to reserve,* Rom. 11:4 [2641] See *depart; leave behind.*

[2902] καταλιθάζω *katalithazō* 1x *to stone, kill by stoning,* Lk. 20:6* [2642]

[2903] καταλλαγή *katallagē* 4x pr. *an exchange; reconciliation, restoration to favor,* Rom. 5:11; 11:15; 2 Cor. 5:18, 19* [2643] See *reconciliation.*

[2904] καταλλάσσω *katallassō* 6x *to change, exchange; to reconcile;* pass. *to be reconciled,* Rom. 5:10 (2x); 1 Cor. 7:11; 2 Cor. 5:18, 19, 20* [2644] See *reconcile.*

[2905] κατάλοιπος *kataloipos* 1x *remaining;* οἱ κατάλοιποι, *the rest,* Acts 15:17* [2645]

[2906] κατάλυμα *katalyma* 3x *lodging, inn,* Lk. 2:7; *a guest-chamber,* Mk. 14:14; Lk. 22:11* [2646]

[2907] καταλύω *katalyō* 17x *to dissolve; to destroy, demolish, overthrow, throw down,* Mt. 24:2; 26:61; met. *to nullify, abrogate,* Mt. 5:17; Acts 5:38, 39; absol. *to unloose* harness, etc., *to halt, to stop for the night, lodge,* Lk. 9:12 [2647] See *destroy.*

[2908] καταμανθάνω *katamanthanō* 1x *to learn* or *observe thoroughly; to consider accurately and diligently, contemplate,* Mt. 6:28* [2648]

[2909] καταμαρτυρέω *katamartyreō* 3x *to witness* or *testify against,* Mt. 26:62; 27:13; Mk. 14:60* [2649]

[2910] καταμένω *katamenō* 1x *to remain; to abide, dwell,* Acts 1:13* [2650]

[2914] καταναλίσκω *katanaliskō* 1x *to consume,* as fire, Heb. 12:29* [2654]

[2915] καταναρκάω *katanarkaō* 3x in NT *to be burdensome to the disadvantage of* any one, *to be a dead weight upon;* by impl. *to be troublesome, burdensome to,* in respect of maintenance, 2 Cor. 11:9; 12:13, 14* [2655]

[2916] κατανεύω *kataneuō* 1x pr. *to nod, signify assent by a nod;* genr. *to make signs, beckon,* Lk. 5:7* [2656]

[2917] κατανοέω *katanoeō* 14x *to perceive, understand, apprehend,* Lk. 20:23; *to observe, consider, contemplate,* Lk. 12:24, 27; *to discern, detect,* Mt. 7:3; *to have regard to, make account of,* Rom. 4:19 [2657] See *consider; look; perceive.*

[2918] καταντάω *katantaō* 13x *to come to, arrive at,* Acts 16:1; 20:15; of an epoch, *to come upon,* 1 Cor. 10:11; met. *to reach, attain to,* Acts 26:7 [2658] See *arrive.*

[2919] κατάνυξις *katanyxis* 1x in NT *deep sleep, stupor, dullness,* Rom. 11:8* [2659]

[2920] κατανύσσομαι *katanyssomai* 1x *to pierce through; to pierce* with compunction and pain of heart, Acts 2:37* [2660]

[2921] καταξιόω *kataxioō* 3x *to consider worthy of,* Lk. 20:35; Acts 5:41; 2 Thess. 1:5* [2661]

[2922] καταπατέω *katapateō* 5x *to trample upon, tread down* or *under feet,* Mt. 5:13; 7:6; Lk. 8:5; 12:1; met. *to trample on* by indignity, *spurn,* Heb. 10:29* [2662]

[2923] κατάπαυσις *katapausis* 9x pr. *the act of giving rest; a state of settled* or *final rest,* Heb. 3:11, 18; 4:1, 3, 4, 5, 11; *a place of rest, place of abode, dwelling, habitation,* Acts 7:49* [2663]

[2924] καταπαύω *katapauō* 4x *to cause to cease, restrain,* Acts 14:18; *to cause to rest, give final rest to, settle finally,* Heb. 4:8; intrans. *to rest, desist from,* Heb. 4:4, 10* [2664]

[2925] καταπέτασμα *katapetasma* 6x *a veil, curtain,* Mt. 27:51; Mk. 15:38; Lk. 23:45; Heb. 6:19; 9:3; 10:20* [2665] See *veil.*

[2927] καταπίνω *katapinō* 7x *to drink, swallow, gulp down,* Mt. 23:24; *to swallow up, absorb,* Rev. 12:16; 2 Cor. 5:4; *to engulf, submerge, overwhelm,* Heb. 11:29; *to swallow greedily, devour,* 1 Pet. 5:8; *to destroy, annihilate,* 1 Cor. 15:54; 2 Cor. 2:7* [2666]

[2928] καταπίπτω *katapiptō* 3x *to fall down, fall prostrate,* Lk. 8:6; Acts 26:14; 28:6* [2667]

[2929] καταπλέω *katapleō* 1x *to sail towards land, to come to land,* Lk. 8:26* [2668]

[2930] καταπονέω *kataponeō* 2x *to exhaust by labor* or *suffering; to wear out,* 2 Pet. 2:7; *to overpower, oppress,* Acts 7:24* [2669]

[2931] καταποντίζω *katapontizō* 2x *to sink in the sea;* pass. *to sink,* Mt. 14:30; *to be plunged, submerged, drowned,* Mt. 18:6* [2670]

[2932] κατάρα *katara* 6x *a cursing, execration, imprecation,* Jas. 3:10; from the Hebrew, *condemnation, doom,* Gal. 3:10; Heb. 6:8; 2 Pet. 2:14; meton., *a doomed one, one on whom condemnation falls,* Gal. 3:13* [2671]

[2933] καταράομαι *kataraomai* 5x *to curse, to wish evil to, imprecate evil upon,* Mk. 11:21; Lk. 6:28; Rom. 12:14; Jas. 3:9; in NT pass. *to be cursed,* Mt. 25:41* [2672]

[2934] καταργέω *katargeō* 27x *to render useless* or *unproductive, occupy unprofitable,* Lk. 13:7; *to render powerless,* Rom. 6:6; *to make empty and unmeaning,* Rom. 4:14; *to render null, to abrogate, cancel,* Rom. 3:3, 31; Eph. 2:15; *to bring to an end,* 1 Cor. 2:6; 13:8; 15:24, 26; 2 Cor. 3:7; *to destroy, annihilate,* 2 Thess. 2:8; Heb. 2:14; *to free from, dissever from,* Rom. 7:2, 6; Gal. 5:4 [2673] See *destroy; nullify; release.*

[2935] καταριθμέω *katarithmeō* 1x *to enumerate, number with, count with,* Acts 1:17* [2674]

[2936] καταρτίζω *katartizō* 13x *to adjust thoroughly; to knit together, unite completely,* 1 Cor. 1:10; *to frame,* Heb. 11:3; *to prepare, provide,* Mt. 21:16; Heb. 10:5; *to qualify fully, to complete* in character, Lk. 6:40; Heb. 13:21; 1 Pet. 5:10; perf. pass. κατηρτισμένα, *fit, ripe,* Rom. 9:22; *to repair, refit,* Mt. 4:21; Mk. 1:19; *to supply, make good,* 1 Thess. 3:10; *to restore* to a forfeited condition, *to reinstate,* Gal. 6:1; 2 Cor. 13:11* [2675] See *prepare; put in order; restore.*

[2937] κατάρτισις *katartisis* 1x pr. *a complete adjustment; completeness* of character, *perfection,* 2 Cor. 13:9* [2676]

[2938] καταρτισμός *katartismos* 1x *a perfectly adjusted adaptation; complete qualification* for a specific purpose, Eph. 4:12* [2677]

[2939] κατασείω *kataseiō* 4x *to shake down* or *violently,* Acts 19:33; τὴν χεῖρα, or τῇ χειρί, *to wave the hand, beckon; to signal silence by waving the hand,* Acts 12:17; 13:16; 21:40* [2678]

[2940] κατασκάπτω *kataskaptō* 2x pr. *to dig down under, undermine;* by impl. *to overthrow; demolish, raze,* Rom. 11:3; τὰ κατεσκαμμένα, *ruins,* Acts 15:16* [2679]

[2941] κατασκευάζω *kataskeuazō* 11x *to prepare, put in readiness,* Mt. 11:10; Mk. 1:2; Lk. 1:17; 7:27; *to construct, form, build,* Heb. 3:3, 4; 9:2, 6; 11:7; 1 Pet. 3:20* [2680] See *build, build up; prepare.*

[2942] κατασκηνόω *kataskēnoō* 4x *to pitch one's tent;* in NT *to rest in* a place, *settle, abide,* Acts 2:26; *to haunt, roost,* Mt. 13:32; Mk. 4:32; Lk. 13:19* [2681]

[2943] κατασκήνωσις *kataskēnōsis* 2x pr. *the pitching a tent; a tent;* in NT *a dwelling place,* Mt. 8:20; Lk. 9:58* [2682]

[2944] κατασκιάζω *kataskiazō* 1x *to overshadow,* Heb. 9:5* [2683]

[2945] κατασκοπέω *kataskopeō* 1x *to view closely and accurately; to spy out,* Gal. 2:4* [2684]

[2946] κατάσκοπος *kataskopos* 1x *a scout, spy,* Heb. 11:31* [2685]

[2947] κατασοφίζομαι *katasophizomai* 1x *to exercise cleverness to the detriment of* any one, *to outwit; to make a victim of subtlety, to practice on the insidious dealing,* Acts 7:19* [2686]

[2948] καταστέλλω *katastellō* 2x *to arrange, dispose in regular order; to appease, quiet, pacify,* Acts 19:35, 36* [2687]

[2949] κατάστημα *katastēma* 1x *behavior, condition; personal appearance, demeanor,* Tit. 2:3* [2688]

[2950] καταστολή *katastolē* 1x pr. *an arranging in order; adjustment of dress;* in NT *apparel, dress,* 1 Tim. 2:9* [2689]

[2951] καταστρέφω *katastrephō* 2x *to invert; to overturn, upset, overthrow, throw down,* Mt. 21:12; Mk. 11:15* [2690]

[2952] καταστρηνιάω *katastrēniaō* 1x *to be headstrong* or *wanton towards,* 1 Tim. 5:11* [2691]

[2953] καταστροφή *katastrophē* 2x *an overthrow, destruction,* 2 Pet. 2:6; met. *overthrow* of right principle or faith, *utter detriment, perversion,* 2 Tim. 2:14* [2692]

[2954] καταστρώννυμι *katastrōnnymi* 1x *to lay flat;* pass. *to be laid prostrate* in death, 1 Cor. 10:5* [2693]

[2955] κατασύρω *katasyrō* 1x *to drag down, to drag away* by force, Lk. 12:58* [2694]

[2956] κατασφάζω *katasphazō* 1x also spelled κατασφάττω, *to slaughter, slay,* Lk. 19:27* [2695]

[2958] κατασφραγίζω *katasphragizō* 1x *to seal up,* Rev. 5:1* [2696]

[2959] κατάσχεσις *kataschesis* 2x *a possession, thing possessed,* Acts 7:5, 45* [2697]

[2960] κατατίθημι *katatithēmi* 2x mid. *to lay up for one's self;* χάριν, or χάριτας, *to lay up a store of favor for one's self, earn a title to favor* at the hands of a person, *to curry favor with,* Acts 24:27; 25:9* [2698]

[2961] κατατομή *katatomē* 1x *mutilation,* Phil. 3:2* [2699]

[2963] κατατρέχω *katatrechō* 1x *to run down,* Acts 21:32* [2701]

[2965] καταφέρω *katapherō* 4x *to bear down; to overpower,* as sleep, Acts 20:9; καταφέρειν ψῆφον, *to give a vote* or *verdict,* Acts 26:10; *to bring charges,* Acts 25:7* [2702]

[2966] καταφεύγω *katapheugō* 2x *to flee to* for refuge, Acts 14:6; Heb. 6:18* [2703]

[2967] καταφθείρω *kataphtheirō* 1x *to destroy, corrupt, deprave,* 2 Tim. 3:8* [2704]

[2968] καταφιλέω *kataphileō* 6x *to kiss affectionately* or *with a semblance of affection, to kiss with earnest gesture,* Mt. 26:49; Mk. 14:45; Lk. 7:38, 45; 15:20; Acts 20:37* [2705]

[2969] καταφρονέω *kataphroneō* 9x pr. *to look down on; to scorn, despise,* Mt. 18:10; Rom. 2:4; *to slight,* Mt. 6:24; Lk. 16:13; 1 Cor. 11:22; 1 Tim. 4:12; 6:2; 2 Pet. 2:10; *to disregard,* Heb. 12:2* [2706]

[2970] καταφρονητής *kataphronētēs* 1x *despiser, scorner,* Acts 13:41* [2707]

[2972] καταχέω *katacheō* 2x *to pour out* or *down upon,* Mt. 26:7; Mk. 14:3* [2708]

[2973] καταχθόνιος *katachthonios* 1x *under the earth, subterranean, infernal,* Phil. 2:10* [2709]

[2974] καταχράομαι *katachraomai* 2x *to use downright; to use up, consume; to make an unrestrained use of, use eagerly,* 1 Cor. 7:31; *to use to the full, stretch to the utmost, exploit,* 1 Cor. 9:18* [2710]

[2976] καταψύχω *katapsychō* 1x *to cool, refresh,* Lk. 16:24* [2711]

[2977] κατείδωλος *kateidōlos* 1x *rife with idols, sunk in idolatry, grossly idolatrous,* Acts 17:16* [2712]

[2978] κατέναντι *katenanti* 8x can function as an improper prep., *over against, opposite to,* Mk. 11:2; 12:41; 13:3; ὁ, ἡ, τό, κατέναντι, *opposite,* Lk. 19:30; *before, in the presence of, in the sight of,* Rom. 4:17 [2713]

[2979] κατενώπιον *katenōpion* 3x can function as an improper prep., *in the presence of, in the sight of, before*; Eph. 1:4; Col. 1:22; Jude 24* [2714]

[2980] κατεξουσιάζω *katexousiazō* 2x *to exercise lordship* or *authority over, domineer over,* Mt. 20:25; Mk. 10:42* [2715]

[2981] κατεργάζομαι *katergazomai* 22x *to work out; to effect, produce, bring out as a result,* Rom. 4:15; 5:3; 7:13; 2 Cor. 4:17; 7:10; Phil. 2:12; 1 Pet. 4:3; Jas. 1:3; *to work, practice, realize in practice,* Rom. 1:27; 2:9; *to work* or *mould into fitness,* 2 Cor. 5:5, *despatch,* Eph. 6:13 [2716] See *bring about; do; produce.*

[2982] κατέρχομαι *katerchomai* 16x *to come* or *go down,* Lk. 4:31; 9:37; Acts 8:5; 9:32; *to land at, touch at,* Acts 18:22; 27:5 [2718] See *come down, go down; land.*

[2983] κατεσθίω *katesthiō* 14x also spelled κατέσθω, *to eat up, devour,* Mt. 13:4; *to consume,* Rev. 11:5, *to expend, squander,* Lk. 15:30; met. *to make a prey of, plunder,* Mt. 23:13; Mk. 12:40; Lk. 20:47; 2 Cor. 11:20; *to annoy, injure,* Gal. 5:15 [2719] See *devour; eat.*

[2985] κατευθύνω *kateuthunō* 3x optative, κατευθύναι (3rd sg), *to make straight; to direct, guide aright,* Lk. 1:79; 1 Thess. 3:11; 2 Thess. 3:5* [2720]

[2986] κατευλογέω *kateulogeō* 1x *to bless,* Mk. 10:16* [2127]

[2987] κατεφίσταμαι *katephistamai* 1x *to come upon suddenly, rush upon, assault,* Acts 18:12* [2721]

[2988] κατέχω *katechō* 17x. (1) transitive, *to hold down; to detain, retain,* Lk. 4:42; Rom. 1:18; Phlm. 13; *to hinder, restrain,* 2 Thess. 2:6, 7; *to hold downright, hold in a firm grasp, to have in full and secure possession,* 1 Cor. 7:30; 2 Cor. 6:10; *to come into full possession of, seize upon*; *to keep, retain,* 1 Thess. 5:21; *to occupy,* Lk. 14:9; met. *to hold fast* mentally, *retain,* Lk. 8:15; 1 Cor. 11:2; 15:2; *to maintain,* Heb. 3:6, 14; 10:23.

(2) intransitive, a nautical term, *to land, touch,* Acts 27:40; pass. *to be in the grasp of, to be bound by,* Rom. 7:6* [2722] See *hold; restrain.*

[2989] κατηγορέω *katēgoreō* 23x *to speak against, accuse,* Mt. 12:10; 27:12; Jn. 5:45 [2723] See *accuse.*

[2990] κατηγορία *katēgoria* 3x *an accusation, crimination,* Jn. 18:29; 1 Tim. 5:19; Tit. 1:6* [2724]

[2991] κατήγορος *katēgoros* 4x *an accuser,* Acts 23:30, 35; Acts 25:16, 18* [2725]

[2992] κατήγωρ *katēgōr* 1x *an accuser,* Rev. 12:10, a barbarous form for κατήγορος* [2725]

[2993] κατήφεια *katēpheia* 1x *dejection, sorrow,* Jas. 4:9* [2726]

[2994] κατηχέω *katēcheō* 8x pr. *to sound in the ears, make the ears ring; to instruct orally, to instruct, inform,* 1 Cor. 14:19; pass. *to be taught, be instructed,* Lk. 1:4; Rom. 2:18; Gal. 6:6; *to be made acquainted,* Acts 18:25; *to receive information, hear report,* Acts 21:21, 24* [2727] See *inform; instruct; teach.*

[2995] κατιόω *katioō* 1x *to cover with rust;* pass. *to rust, become rusty* or *tarnished,* Jas. 5:3* [2728]

[2996] κατισχύω *katischuō* 3x *to overpower,* Mt. 16:18; absol. *to predominate, get the upper hand,* Lk. 21:36; 23:23* [2729]

[2997] κατοικέω *katoikeō* 44x trans. *to inhabit,* Acts 1:19; absol. *to have an abode, dwell,* Lk. 13:4; Acts 11:29; *to take up* or *find an abode,* Acts 7:2; *to indwell,* Eph. 3:17; Jas. 4:5 [2730] See *dwell; live.*

[2998] κατοίκησις *katoikēsis* 1x *an abode, dwelling, habitation,* Mk. 5:3* [2731]

[2999] κατοικητήριον *katoikētērion* 2x *an abode, dwelling, habitation,* the same as κατοίκησις, Eph. 2:22; Rev. 18:2* [2732]

[3000] κατοικία *katoikia* 1x *habitation,* i.q. κατοίκησις, Acts 17:26* [2733]

[3001] κατοικίζω *katoikizō* 1x *to cause to dwell,* Jas. 4:5* [2730]

[3002] κατοπτρίζω *katoptrizō* 1x *to show in a mirror; to present a clear and correct image of* a thing, mid. *to have presented in a mirror, to have a clear image presented,* or, *to reflect,* 2 Cor. 3:18* [2734]

[3004] κάτω *katō* 9x. (1) *down, downwards,* Mt. 4:6; Lk. 4:9; Jn. 8:6; Acts 20:9. (2) *beneath, below, under,* Mt. 27:51; Mk. 14:66; 15:38; Acts 2:19; ὁ, ἡ, τό, κάτω, *what is below, earthly,* Jn. 8:23* [2736]

[3005] κατώτερος *katōteros* 1x *lower,* Eph. 4:9* [2737]

[3006] κατωτέρω *katōterō* 1x *lower, farther down;* of time, *under,* Mt. 2:16* [2736]

[3007] Καῦδα *Kauda* 1x also spelled Κλαῦδα (3084) and Κλαῦδη (3085), *Cauda,* indecl. prop. name of an island, Acts 27:16* [2802]

[3008] καῦμα *kauma* 2x *heat, scorching* or *burning heat,* Rev. 7:16; 16:9* [2738]

[3009] καυματίζω *kaumatizō* 4x *to scorch, burn,* Mt. 13:6; Mk. 4:6; Rev. 16:8, 9* [2739]

[3011] καῦσις *kausis* 1x *burning, being burned,* Heb. 6:8* [2740]

[3012] καυσόω *kausoō* 2x *to be on fire, burn intensely,* 2 Pet. 3:10, 12* [2741]

[3013] καυστηριάζω *kaustēriazō* 1x also spelled καυτηριάζω, *to cauterize, brand;* pass. met. *to be branded* with marks of guilt, or, *to be seared* into insensibility, 1 Tim. 4:2* [2743]

[3014] καύσων *kausōn* 3x *fervent scorching heat; the scorching* of the sun, Mt. 20:12; *hot weather, a hot time,* Lk. 12:55; *the scorching wind of the East, Eurus,* Jas. 1:11* [2742]

[3016] καυχάομαι *kauchaomai* 37x *to glory, boast,* Rom. 2:17, 23; ὑπέρ τινος, *to boast of* a person or thing, *to undertake a complimentary testimony to,* 2 Cor. 12:5; *to rejoice, exult,* Rom. 5:2, 3, 11 [2744] See *boast; brag; rejoice.*

[3017] καύχημα *kauchēma* 11x *a glorying, boasting,* 1 Cor. 5:6; *a ground* or *matter of glorying* or *boasting,* Rom. 4:2; *joy, exultation,* Phil. 1:26; *complimentary testimony,* 1 Cor. 9:15, 16; 2 Cor. 9:3 [2745] See *boast; pride.*

[3018] καύχησις *kauchēsis* 11x *boasting, pride,* a later equivalent to καύχημαι, Rom. 3:27; 2 Cor. 7:4, 14; 11:10 [2746] See *boast; glory; pride.*

[3019] Καφαρναούμ *Kapharnaoum* 16x indecl. pr. name, *Capernaum* [2584]

[3020] Κεγχρεαί *Kenchreai* 2x *Cenchreae,* the port of Corinth on the Saronic Gulf; Acts 18:18; Rom. 16:1* [2747]

[3022] Κεδρών *Kedrōn* 1x indecl. pr. name, *Kidron,* a valley near Jerusalem, Jn. 18:1* [2748]

[3023] κεῖμαι *keimai* 24x *to lie, to be laid; to recline, to be lying, to have been laid down,* Mt. 28:6; Lk. 2:12; *to have been laid, placed, set,* Mt. 3:10; Lk. 3:9; Jn. 2:6; *to be situated,* as a city, Mt. 5:14; Rev. 21:16; *to be in store,* Lk. 12:19; met. *to be constituted, established* as a law, 1 Tim. 1:9; in NT of persons, *to be specially set, solemnly appointed, destined,* Lk. 2:34; Phil. 1:16; 1 Thess. 3:3; *to lie* under an influence, *to be involved in,* 1 Jn. 5:19 [2749] See *lie down.*

[3024] κειρία *keiria* 1x *a bandage, swath,* in NT pl. *graveclothes,* Jn. 11:44* [2750]

[3025] κείρω *keirō* 4x *to cut off* the hair, *shear, shave,* Acts 8:32; 18:18; 1 Cor. 11:6 (2x)* [2751]

[3026] κέλευσμα *keleusma* 1x *a word of command; a mutual cheer;* hence, in NT *a loud shout, an arousing outcry,* 1 Thess. 4:16* [2752]

[3027] κελεύω *keleuō* 25x *to order, command, direct, bid,* Mt. 8:18; 14:19, 28 [2753] See *command; order.*

[3029] κενοδοξία *kenodoxia* 1x *empty conceit,* Phil. 2:3* [2754]

[3030] κενόδοξος *kenodoxos* 1x *boastful,* Gal. 5:26* [2755]

[3031] κενός *kenos* 18x *empty; having nothing, empty-handed,* Mk. 12:3; met. *vain, fruitless, void of effect,* Acts 4:25; 1 Cor. 15:10; εἰς κενόν, *in vain, to no purpose,* 2 Cor. 6:1; *hollow, fallacious, false,* Eph. 5:6; Col. 2:8; *inconsiderate, foolish,* 1 Thess. 3:5; Jas. 2:20 [2756] See *empty; empty-handed; futile; useless; vain.*

[3032] κενοφωνία *kenophōnia* 2x *vain, empty babbling, vain disputation, fruitless discussion,* 1 Tim. 6:20; 2 Tim. 2:16* [2757]

[3033] κενόω *kenoō* 5x *to empty, evacuate;* ἑαυτόν, *to divest one's self of one's prerogatives, abase one's self,* Phil. 2:7; *to deprive a thing* of its proper functions, Rom. 4:14; 1 Cor. 1:17; *to show to be without foundation, falsify,* 1 Cor. 9:15; 2 Cor. 9:3* [2758]

[3034] κέντρον *kentron* 4x *a sharp point; a sting* of an animal, Rev. 9:10; *a prick, stimulus, goad,* Acts 26:14; met. of death, *destructive power, deadly venom,* 1 Cor. 15:55, 56* [2759]

[3035] κεντυρίων *kentyriōn* 3x in its original signification, *a commander of a hundred* foot-soldiers, *a centurion,* Mk. 15:39, 44, 45* [2760]

[3036] κενῶς *kenōs* 1x *in vain, to no purpose,* Jas. 4:5* [2761]

[3037] κεραία *keraia* 2x pr. *a horn-like projection, a point, extremity;* in NT *an apex,* or *fine point;* as of letters, used for *the minutest part, a tittle,* Mt. 5:18; Lk. 16:17* [2762]

[3038] κεραμεύς *kerameus* 3x *a potter,* Mt. 27:7, 10; Rom. 9:21* [2763]

[3039] κεραμικός *keramikos* 1x *made by a potter, earthen,* Rev. 2:27* [2764]

[3040] κεράμιον *keramion* 2x *an earthenware vessel, a pitcher, jar,* Mk. 14:13; Lk. 22;10* [2765]

[3041] κέραμος *keramos* 1x *potter's clay; earthenware; a roof, tile, tiling,* Lk. 5:19* [2766]

[3042] κεράννυμι *kerannymi* 3x *to mix, mingle,* drink; *to prepare* for drinking, Rev. 14:10; 18:6 (2x)* [2767]

[3043] κέρας *keras* 11x *a horn,* Rev. 5:6; 12:3; *a horn-like projection* at the corners of an altar, Rev. 9:13; *a horn* as a symbol of power, Lk. 1:69 [2768] See *horn.*

[3044] κεράτιον *keration* 1x pr. *a little horn;* in NT *a pod, the pod of the carob tree,* or *Ceratonia siliqua* of Linnaeus, a common tree in the East and the south of Europe, growing to a considerable size, and producing long slender pods, with a pulp of a sweetish taste, and several brown shining seeds like beans, sometimes eaten by the poorer people in Syria and Palestine, and commonly used for fattening swine, Lk. 15:16* [2769]

[3045] κερδαίνω *kerdainō* 17x *to gain* as a matter of profit, Mt. 25:17; *to win, acquire possession of,* Mt. 16:26; *to profit in the avoidance of, to avoid,* Acts 27:21; in NT Χριστόν, *to win* Christ, *to become possessed of* the privileges of the Gospel, Phil. 3:8; *to win over* from estrangement, Mt. 18:15; *to win over* to embrace the Gospel, 1 Cor. 9:19, 20, 21, 22; 1 Pet. 3:1; absol. *to make gain,* Jas. 4:13 [2770] See *gain; win.*

[3046] κέρδος *kerdos* 3x *gain, profit,* Phil. 1:21; 3:7; Tit. 1:11* [2771]

[3047] κέρμα *kerma* 1x *something clipped small; small change, small pieces of money, coin,* Jn. 2:15* [2772]

[3048] κερματιστής *kermatistēs* 1x *a money changer,* Jn. 2:14* [2773]

[3049] κεφάλαιον *kephalaion* 2x *a sum total; a sum of money, capital,* Acts 22:28; *the crowning* or *ultimate point* to preliminary matters, Heb. 8:1* [2774]

[3051] κεφαλή *kephalē* 75x *the head,* Mt. 5:36; 6:17; *the head, top;* κεφαλὴ γωνίας, *the head of the corner, the chief corner-stone,* Mt. 21:42; Lk. 20:17; met. *the head, superior, chief, principal, one to whom others are subordinate,* 1 Cor. 11:3; Eph. 1:22 [2776] See *head.*

[3052] κεφαλιόω *kephalioō* 1x *to hit the head,* Mk. 12:4* [2775]

[3053] κεφαλίς *kephalis* 1x in NT *a roll, volume, division* of a book, Heb. 10:7* [2777]

[3055] κημόω *kēmoō* 1x *to muzzle,* 1 Cor. 9:9* [5392]

[3056] κῆνσος *kēnsos* 4x *a census, assessment, enumeration of the people and a valuation of their property;* in NT *tribute, tax,* Mt. 17:25; *poll-tax,* Mt. 22:17, 19; Mk. 12:14* [2778]

[3057] κῆπος *kēpos* 5x *a garden, any place planted with trees and herbs,* Lk. 13:19; Jn. 18:1, 26; 19:41* [2779]

[3058] κηπουρός *kēpouros* 1x *a garden-keeper, gardener,* Jn. 20:15* [2780]

[3060] κήρυγμα *kērygma* 9x *proclamation, proclaiming, public annunciation,* Mt. 12:41; *public inculcation, preaching,* 1 Cor. 2:4; 15:14; meton. *what is publicly inculcated, doctrine,* Rom. 16:25; Tit. 1:3* [2782]

[3061] κῆρυξ *kēryx* 3x *a herald, public messenger;* in NT *a proclaimer, publisher, preacher,* 1 Tim. 2:7; 2 Tim. 1:11; 2 Pet. 2:5* [2783]

[3062] κηρύσσω *kēryssō* 61x *to publish, proclaim,* as a herald, 1 Cor. 9:27; *to announce openly and publicly,* Mk. 1:4; Lk. 4:18; Mk. 1:45; 7:36; *to announce* as a matter of doctrine, *inculcate, preach,* Mt. 24:14; Mk. 1:38; 13:10; Acts 15:21; Rom. 2:21 [2784] See *preach; proclaim; tell.*

[3063] κῆτος *kētos* 1x *a large fish, sea monster, whale,* Mt. 12:40* [2785]

[3064] Κηφᾶς *Kēphas* 9x *Cephas, Rock,* rendered into Greek by Πέτρος, Jn. 1:42; 1 Cor. 1:12; 3:22; 9:5; 15:5; Gal. 1:18; 2:9, 11, 14* [2786]

[3066] κιβωτός *kibōtos* 6x *a chest, coffer; the ark* of the covenant, Heb. 9:4; Rev. 11:19; *the ark* of Noah, Mt. 24:38; Lk. 17:27; Heb. 11:7; 1 Pet. 3:20* [2787]

[3067] κιθάρα *kithara* 4x *a lyre, harp,* 1 Cor. 14:7; Rev. 5:8; 14:2; 15:2* [2788]

[3068] κιθαρίζω *kitharizō* 2x *to play on a lyre* or *harp,* 1 Cor. 14:7; Rev. 14:2* [2789]

[3069] κιθαρῳδός *kitharōidos* 2x *one who plays on the lyre and accompanies it with his voice,* Rev. 14:2; 18:22* [2790]

[3070] Κιλικία *Kilikia* 8x *Cilicia,* a province of Asia Minor, Gal. 1:21 [2791]

[3073] κινδυνεύω *kindyneuō* 4x *to be in danger* or *peril,* Lk. 8:23; Acts 19:27, 40; 1 Cor. 15:30* [2793]

[3074] κίνδυνος *kindynos* 9x *danger, peril,* Rom. 8:35; 2 Cor. 11:26* [2794]

[3075] κινέω *kineō* 8x *to move,* Mt. 23:4; *to excite, agitate,* Acts 21:30; 24:5; *to remove,* Rev. 2:5; 6:14; in NT κεφαλήν, *to shake the head* in derision, Mt. 27:39; Mk. 15:29; mid., *to move, possess the faculty of motion, exercise the functions of life,* Acts 17:28* [2795] See *arouse; move; stir.*

[3077] κιννάμωμον *kinnamōmon* 1x *cinnamon,* Rev. 18:13* [2792]

[3078] Κίς *Kis* 1x *Kish,* the father of Saul, pr. name, indecl., Acts 13:21* [2797]

[3079] κίχρημι *kichrēmi* 1x *to lend,* Lk. 11:5* [5531]

[3080] κλάδος *klados* 11x *a bough, branch, shoot,* Mt. 13:32; 21:8; met. *a branch* of a family stock, Rom. 11:16, 21 [2798] See *branch.*

[3081] κλαίω *klaiō* 40x intrans. *to weep, shed tears,* Mt. 26:75; Mk. 5:38, 39; Lk. 19:41; 23:28; trans. *to weep for, bewail,* Mt. 2:18 [2799] See *cry; mourn; wail; weep.*

[3082] κλάσις *klasis* 2x *a breaking, the act of breaking,* Lk. 24:35; Acts 2:42 [2800]

[3083] κλάσμα *klasma* 9x *a piece broken off, fragment,* Mt. 14:20; 15:37; Mk. 6:43; 8:8, 19, 20; Lk. 9:17; Jn. 6:12f.* [2801]

[3086] Κλαυδία *Klaudia* 1x *Claudia,* pr. name, 2 Tim. 4:21* [2803]

[3087] Κλαύδιος *Klaudios* 3x *Claudius,* pr. name. (1) *The fourth Roman Emperor,* Acts 11:28; 18:2. (2) *Claudius Lysias, a Roman captain,* Acts 23:26* [2804]

[3088] κλαυθμός *klauthmos* 9x *weeping, crying,* Mt. 2:18; 8:12 [2805]

[3089] κλάω *klaō* 14x *to break off;* in NT *to break* bread, Mt. 14:19; with figurative reference to the violent death of Christ, 1 Cor. 11:24 [2806] See *break.*

[3090] κλείς *kleis* 6x *a key,* used in NT as the symbol of power, authority, etc. Mt. 16:19; Rev. 1:18; 3:7; 9:1; 20:1; met. *the key* of entrance into knowledge, Lk. 11:52* [2807]

[3091] κλείω *kleiō* 16x *to close, shut,* Mt. 6:6; 25:10; *to shut up* a person, Rev. 20:3; met. of the heavens, Lk. 4:25; Rev. 11:6; κλεῖσαι τὰ σπλάγχνα, *to shut one's bowels, to be hard-hearted, void of compassion,* 1 Jn. 3:17; κλείειν τὴν βασιλεία τῶν οὐρανῶν, *to endeavor to prevent entrance into the kingdom of heaven,* Mt. 23:13 [2808] See *shut.*

[3092] κλέμμα *klemma* 1x *theft,* Rev. 9:21* [2809]

[3093] Κλεοπᾶς *Kleopas* 1x *Cleopas,* pr. name, Lk. 24:18* [2810]

[3094] κλέος *kleos* 1x pr. *rumor, report; good report, praise, credit,* 1 Pet. 2:20* [2811]

[3095] κλέπτης *kleptēs* 16x *a thief,* Mt. 6:19, 20; 24:43; trop. *a thief* by imposture, Jn. 10:8 [2812] See *thief.*

[3096] κλέπτω *kleptō* 13x *to steal,* Mt. 6:19, 20; 19:18; *to take away stealthily, remove secretly,* Mt. 27:64; 28:13 [2813] See *steal.*

[3097] κλῆμα *klēma* 4x *a branch, shoot, twig,* esp. of the vine, Jn. 15:2, 4-6* [2814]

[3098] Κλήμης *Klēmēs* 1x *Clemens, Clement,* pr. name, Latin, Phil. 4:3* [2815]

[3099] κληρονομέω *klēronomeō* 18x pr. *to acquire by lot; to inherit, obtain by inheritance;* in NT *to obtain, acquire, receive possession of,* Mt. 5:5; 19:29; absol. *to be heir,* Gal. 4:30 [2816] See *inherit.*

[3100] κληρονομία *klēronomia* 14x *an inheritance, patrimony,* Mt. 21:38; Mk. 12:7; *a possession, portion, property,* Acts 7:5; 20:32; in NT *a share, participation* in privileges, Acts 20:32; Eph. 1:14; 5:5 [2817] See *inheritance.*

[3101] κληρονόμος *klēronomos* 15x *an heir,* Mt. 21:38; Gal. 4:1; *a possessor,* Rom. 4:13; Heb. 11:7; Jas. 2:5 [2818] See *heir.*

[3102] κλῆρος *klēros* 11x *a lot, die, a thing used in determining chances,* Mt. 27:35; Mk. 15:24; Lk. 23:34; Jn. 19:24; Acts 1:26; *assignment, investiture,* Acts 1:17; *allotment, destination,* Col. 1:12; *a part, portion, share,* Acts 8:21; 26:18; *a* constituent *portion* of the Church, 1 Pet. 5:3* [2819] See *inheritance; lot; share.*

[3103] κληρόω *klēroō* 1x *to obtain by lot* or *assignment; to obtain a portion, receive a share,* Eph. 1:11* [2820]

[3104] κλῆσις *klēsis* 11x *a call, calling, invitation;* in NT *the call* or *invitation* to the privileges of the Gospel, Rom. 11:29; Eph. 1:18; *the favor and privilege of the invitation,* 2 Thess. 1:11; 2 Pet. 1:10; *the temporal condition in which the call found a person,* 1 Cor. 1:26; 7:20 [2821] See *calling.*

[3105] κλητός *klētos* 10x *called, invited,* in NT *called* to privileges or function, Mt. 20:16; 22:14; Rom. 1:1, 6, 7; 8:28; 1 Cor. 1:1, 2, 24; Jude 1; Rev. 17:14 [2822] See *called.*

[3106] κλίβανος *klibanos* 2x *an oven,* Mt. 6:30; Lk. 12:28* [2823]

[3107] κλίμα *klima* 3x pr. *a slope; a portion of the* ideal *slope* of the earth's surface; *a tract* or *region* of country, Rom. 15:23; 2 Cor. 11:10; Gal. 1:21* [2824]

[3108] κλινάριον *klinarion* 1x *a small bed* or *couch,* Acts 5:15* [2825]

[3109] κλίνη *klinē* 9x *a couch, bed,* Mt. 9:2, 6; Mk. 4:21; Rev. 2:22 [2825]

[3110] κλινίδιον *klinidion* 2x *a small couch* or *bed,* Lk. 5:19, 24* [2826]

[3111] κλίνω *klinō* 7x pr. trans. *to cause to slope* or *bend; to bow down,* Lk. 24:5; Jn. 19:30; *to lay down* to rest, Mt. 8:20; Lk. 9:58; *to put to flight* troops, Heb. 11:34; intrans. of the day, *to decline,* Lk. 9:12; 24:29* [2827]

[3112] κλισία *klisia* 1x pr. *a place for reclining; a tent, seat, couch;* in NT *a group of persons reclining* at a meal. Lk. 9:14* [2828]

[3113] κλοπή *klopē* 2x *theft,* Mt. 15:19; Mk. 7:21* [2829]

[3114] κλύδων *klydōn* 2x *a wave, billow, surge,* Lk. 8:24; Jas. 1:6* [2830]

[3115] κλυδωνίζομαι *klydōnizomai* 1x *to be tossed by waves;* met. *to fluctuate* in opinion, *be agitated, tossed to and fro,* Eph. 4:14* [2831]

[3116] Κλωπᾶς *Klōpas* 1x *Cleopas,* pr. name, Jn. 19:25* [2832]

[3117] κνήθω *knēthō* 1x *to scratch; to tickle, cause titillation;* in NT mid. met. *to procure pleasurable excitement for, to indulge an itching,* 2 Tim. 4:3* [2833]

[3118] Κνίδος *Knidos* 1x *Cnidus,* a city of Caria, in Asia Minor, Acts 27:7* [2834]

[3119] κοδράντης *kodrantēs* 2x *a Roman brass coin,* equivalent to the *fourth part* of an *as,* or ἀσσάριον, or to δύο λεπτά, Mt. 5:26; Mk. 12:42* [2835]

[3120] κοιλία *koilia* 22x *a cavity; the belly,* Mt. 15:17; Mk. 7:19; *the stomach,* Mt. 12:40; Lk. 15:16; *the womb,* Mt. 19:12; Lk. 1:15; *the inner self,* Jn. 7:38 [2836] See *appetite; belly; stomach; womb.*

[3121] κοιμάω *koimaō* 18x *to lull to sleep;* pass. *to fall asleep, be asleep,* Mt. 28:13; Lk. 22:45; met. *to sleep* in death, Acts 7:60; 13:36; 2 Pet. 3:4 [2837] See *asleep; fall asleep.*

[3122] κοίμησις *koimēsis* 1x *sleep;* meton. *rest, repose,* Jn. 11:13* [2838]

[3123] κοινός *koinos* 14x *common, belonging equally to several,* Acts 2:44; 4:32; in NT *common, profane,* Heb. 10:29; Rev. 21:27; ceremonially *unclean,* Mk. 7:2; Acts 10:14 [2839] See *common; impure; profane.*

[3124] κοινόω *koinoō* 14x *to make common,* in NT *to profane, desecrate,* Acts 21:28; *to render* ceremonially *unclean, defile, pollute,* Mt. 15:11, 18, 20; 7:15, 18, 20, 23; Heb. 9:13; *to pronounce unclean* ceremonially, Acts 10:15; 11:9* [2840] See *defile; make impure.*

[3125] κοινωνέω *koinōneō* 8x *to have in common, share,* Heb. 2:14; *to be associated in, to become a sharer in,* Rom. 15:27; 1 Pet. 4:13; *to become implicated in, be a party to,* 1 Tim. 5:22; 2 Jn. 11; *to associate one's self with* by sympathy and assistance, *to* *communicate with* in the way of aid and relief, Rom. 12:13; Gal. 6:6; Phil. 4:15* [2841] See *participate in; share.*

[3126] κοινωνία *koinōnia* 19x *fellowship, partnership,* Acts 2:42; 2 Cor. 6:14; 13:13; Gal. 2:9; Phil. 3:10; 1 Jn. 1:3; *participation, communion,* 1 Cor. 10:16; *aid, relief,* Heb. 13:16; *contribution in aid,* Rom. 15:26 [2842] See *communion; fellowship; participation; sharing.*

[3127] κοινωνικός *koinōnikos* 1x *social;* in NT *generous, liberal, beneficent,* 1 Tim. 6:18* [2843]

[3128] κοινωνός *koinōnos* 10x *a fellow, partner, companion,* Mt. 23:30; Lk. 5:10; 1 Cor. 10:18, 20; 2 Cor. 8:23; Phlm. 17; Heb. 10:33; *a sharer, partaker,* 2 Cor. 1:7; 1 Pet. 5:1; 2 Pet. 1:4* [2844] See *participant; partner.*

[3130] κοίτη *koitē* 4x *a bed,* Lk. 11:7; *the* conjugal *bed,* Heb. 13:4; meton. *sexual intercourse, concubitus;* hence, *lewdness, whoredom, chambering,* Rom. 13:13; in NT *conception,* Rom. 9:10* [2845]

[3131] κοιτών *koitōn* 1x *a bed-chamber,* Acts 12:20* [2846]

[3132] κόκκινος *kokkinos* 6x *dyed with coccus, crimson, scarlet,* Mt. 27:28; Heb. 9:19; Rev. 17:3, 4; 18:12, 16* [2847]

[3133] κόκκος *kokkos* 7x *a kernel, grain, seed,* Mt. 13:31; 17:20; Mk. 4:31; Lk. 13:19; 17:6; Jn. 12:24; 1 Cor. 15:37* [2848]

[3134] κολάζω *kolazō* 2x pr. *to curtail, to coerce; to chastise, punish,* Acts 4:21; 2 Pet. 2:9* [2849]

[3135] κολακεία *kolakeia* 1x *flattery, adulation, obsequiousness,* 1 Thess. 2:5* [2850]

[3136] κόλασις *kolasis* 2x *chastisement, punishment,* Mt. 25:46; *painful disquietude, torment,* 1 Jn. 4:18* [2851]

[3139] κολαφίζω *kolaphizō* 5x *to beat with the fist, buffet,* Mt. 26:67; Mk. 14:65; met. *to maltreat, treat with excessive force,* 1 Cor. 4:11; *to punish,* 1 Pet. 2:20; *to buffet, fret, afflict,* 2 Cor. 12:7* [2852]

[3140] κολλάω *kollaō* 12x *to glue* or *weld together;* mid. *to adhere to,* Lk. 10:11; met. *to attach one's self to, unite with, associate with,* Lk. 15:15; Acts 5:13; Rev. 18:5 [2853] See *cling; join; unite.*

[3141] κολλούριον *kollourion* 1x also spelled κολλύριον, *collyrium, eye-salve,* Rev. 3:18* [2854]

[3142] κολλυβιστής *kollybistēs* 3x *a money-changer,* Mt. 21:12; Mk. 11:15; Jn. 2:15* [2855]

[3143] κολοβόω *koloboō* 4x in NT of time, *to cut short, shorten,* Mt. 24:22; Mk. 13:20* [2856]

[3145] Κολοσσαί *Kolossai* 1x also spelled Κολασσαεύς, *Colossae,* a city of Phrygia, Col. 1:2* [2857]

[3146] κόλπος *kolpos* 6x *the bosom,* Lk. 16:22, 23; Jn. 1:18; 13:23; *the bosom of a garment,* Lk. 6:38; *a bay, creek, inlet,* Acts 27:39* [2859]

[3147] κολυμβάω *kolymbaō* 1x *to dive;* in NT *to swim,* Acts 27:43* [2860]

[3148] κολυμβήθρα *kolymbēthra* 3x *a place where any one may swim; a pond, pool,* Jn. 5:2, 4, 7; 9:7* [2861]

[3149] κολωνία *kolōnia* 1x *a Roman colony,* Acts 16:12* [2862]

[3150] κομάω *komaō* 2x *to have long hair, wear the hair long,* 1 Cor. 11:14, 15* [2863]

[3151] κόμη *komē* 1x *the hair; a head of long hair,* 1 Cor. 11:15* [2864]

[3152] κομίζω *komizō* 10x pr. *to take into kindly keeping, to provide for; to convey, bring,* Lk. 7:37; mid. *to bring for one's self; to receive, obtain,* 2 Cor. 5:10; Eph. 6:8; *to receive again, recover,* Mt. 25:27; Heb. 11:19 [2865] See *pay back; receive.*

[3153] κομψότερον *kompsoteron* 1x in NT *in better health,* Jn. 4:52* [2866]

[3154] κονιάω *koniaō* 2x *to whitewash,* or, *plaster,* Mt. 23:27; Acts 23:3* [2867]

[3155] κονιορτός *koniortos* 5x *dust,* Mt. 10:14; Lk. 9:5; 10:11; Acts 13:51; 22:23* [2868]

[3156] κοπάζω *kopazō* 3x pr. *to grow weary, suffer exhaustion; to abate, be stilled,* Mt. 14:32; Mk. 4:39; 6:51* [2869]

[3157] κοπετός *kopetos* 1x pr. *a beating* of the breast, etc., in token of grief; *a wailing, lamentation,* Acts 8:2* [2870]

[3158] κοπή *kopē* 1x *a stroke, smiting;* in NT *slaughter,* Heb. 7:1* [2871]

[3159] κοπιάω *kopiaō* 23x *to be wearied* or *spent with labor, faint from weariness,* Mt. 11:28; Jn. 4:6; in NT *to labor hard, to toil,* Lk. 5:5; Jn. 4:38 [2872] See *labor; toil.*

[3160] κόπος *kopos* 18x *trouble, difficulty, uneasiness,* Mt. 26:10; Mk. 14:6; *labor, wearisome labor, travail, toil,* 1 Cor. 3:8; 15:58; meton. *the fruit* or *consequence of labor,* Jn. 4:38; 2 Cor. 10:15 [2873] See *labor; toil.*

[3161] κοπρία *kopria* 1x *dung, manure,* Lk. 14:35* [2874]

[3162] κόπριον *koprion* 1x *dung, manure,* Lk. 13:8* [2874]

[3164] κόπτω *koptō* 8x *to smite, cut; to cut off* or *down,* Mt. 21:8; Mk. 11:8; mid. *to beat one's self* in mourning, *lament, bewail,* Mt. 11:17; 24:30; Lk. 8:52; 23:27; Rev. 1:7; 18:9* [2875]

[3165] κόραξ *korax* 1x *a raven, crow,* Lk. 12:24* [2876]

[3166] κοράσιον *korasion* 8x *a girl, damsel, maiden,* Mt. 9:24, 25; 14:11; Mk. 5:41, 42; 6:22, 28* [2877]

[3167] κορβᾶν *korban* 1x *corban, a gift, offering, oblation, anything consecrated to God,* Mk. 7:11* [2878]

[3168] κορβανᾶς *korbanas* 1x *temple treasury, the sacred treasury,* Mt. 27:6* [2878]

[3169] Κόρε *Kore* 1x *Korah,* Jude 11* [2879]

[3170] κορέννυμι *korennymi* 2x *to satisfy,* Acts 27:38; 1 Cor. 4:8* [2880]

[3171] Κορίνθιος *Korinthios* 2x *Corinthian; an inhabitant of* Κόρινθος, *Corinth,* Acts 18:8; 2 Cor. 6:11* [2881]

[3172] Κόρινθος *Korinthos* 6x *Corinth,* a celebrated city of Greece, Acts 18:1; 19:1: 1 Cor. 1:2; 2 Cor. 1:1, 23; 2 Tim. 4:20* [2882]

[3173] Κορνήλιος *Kornēlios* 8x *Cornelius,* a Latin pr. name, Acts 10:1, 3, 17, 22, 24f., 30f.* [2883]

[3174] κόρος *koros* 1x *a cor,* the largest Jewish measure for things dry, equal to the homer, and about fifteen bushels English, according to Josephus, Lk. 16:7* [2884]

[3175] κοσμέω *kosmeō* 10x pluperfect, ἐκεκόσμητο (3 sg), *to arrange, set in order; to adorn, decorate, embellish,* Mt. 12:44; 23:29; *to prepare, put in readiness, trim,* Mt. 25:7; met. *to honor, dignify,* Tit. 2:10 [2885] See *adorn; decorate; make attractive; put in order; trim.*

[3176] κοσμικός *kosmikos* 2x pr. *belonging to the universe,* in NT *accommodated to the present state of things, adapted to this world, worldly,* Tit. 2:12; τὸ κοσμικόν, as a subst. *the apparatus* for the service of the tabernacle, Heb. 9:1* [2886]

[3177] κόσμιος *kosmios* 2x *decorous, respectable, well-ordered,* 1 Tim. 2:9; 3:2* [2887]

[3179] κοσμοκράτωρ *kosmokratōr* 1x pr. *monarch of the world;* in NT *a worldly prince, a power paramount in the world* of the unbelieving and ungodly, Eph. 6:12* [2888]

[3180] κόσμος *kosmos* 186x. (1) Pr. *order, regular disposition; ornament, decoration, embellishment,* 1 Pet. 3:3. (2) *The world, the material universe,* Mt. 13:35; *the world, the aggregate of sensitive existence,* 1 Cor. 4:9; *the* lower *world, the earth,* Mk. 16:15; *the world, the aggregate of mankind,* Mt. 5:14; *the world, the public,* Jn. 7:4; in NT *the present order of things, the* secular *world,* Jn. 18:36; *the human race* external to the Jewish nation, *the* heathen *world,* Rom. 11:12, 15; *the world* external to the Christian body, 1 Jn. 3:1, 13; *the world* or *material system* of the Mosaic covenant, Gal. 4:3; Col. 2:8, 20 [2889] See *universe; world.*

[3181] Κούαρτος *Kouartos* 1x *Quartus,* a Latin pr. name, Rom. 16:23* [2890]

[3182] κοῦμ *koum* 1x an Aramaic imperative, also spelled κοῦμι, *stand up,* Mk. 5:41* [2891]

[3184] κουστωδία *koustōdia* 3x *a watch, guard,* Mt. 27:65, 66; 28:11* [2892]

[3185] κουφίζω *kouphizō* 1x *to lighten, make light* or *less heavy,* Acts 27:38* [2893]

[3186] κόφινος *kophinos* 6x *a large basket,* Mt. 14:20; 16:9; Mk. 6:43; 8:19; Lk. 9:17; Jn. 6:13* [2894]

[3187] κράβαττος *krabattos* 11x also spelled κράββατος, *mattress, pallet, bed,* Mk. 2:4, 9, 11f.; 6:55; Jn. 5:8-11; Acts 5:15; 9:33* [2895] See *bed; cot; mat.*

[3189] κράζω *krazō* 55x *to utter a cry,* Mt. 14:26; *to exclaim, cry out,* Mt. 9:27; Jn. 1:15; *to cry* for vengeance, Jas. 5:4; *to cry* in supplication, Rom. 8:15; Gal. 4:6 [2896] See *cry out; shout.*

[3190] κραιπάλη *kraipalē* 1x also spelled κρεπάλη, *drunken dissipation,* Lk. 21:34* [2897]

[3191] κρανίον *kranion* 4x *a skull,* Mt. 27:33; Mk. 15:22; Lk. 23:33; Jn. 19:17* [2898] See *Calvary*; *Golgatha*; *skull.*

[3192] κράσπεδον *kraspedon* 5x *a margin, border, edge,* in NT *a fringe, tuft, tassel,* Mt. 9:20; 14:36; 23:5; Mk. 6:56; Lk. 8:44* [2899]

[3193] κραταιός *krataios* 1x *strong, mighty, powerful,* 1 Pet. 5:6* [2900]

[3194] κραταιόω *krataioō* 4x *to strengthen, render strong, corroborate, confirm;* pass. *to grow strong, acquire strength,* Lk. 1:80; 2:40; Eph. 3:16; *to be firm, resolute,* 1 Cor. 16:13* [2901]

[3195] κρατέω *krateō* 47x pr. *to be strong; to be superior* to any one, *subdue, vanquish,* Acts 2:24; *to get into one's power, lay hold of, seize, apprehend,* Mt. 14:3; 18:28; 21:46; *to gain, compass, attain,* Acts 27:13; in NT *to lay hold of, grasp, clasp,* Mt. 9:25; Mk. 1:31; 5:41; *to retain, keep under reserve,* Mk. 9:10; met, *to hold fast, observe,* Mk. 7:3, 8; 2 Thess. 2:15; *to hold to, adhere to,* Acts 3:11; Col. 2:19; *to restrain, hinder, repress,* Lk. 24:16; Rev. 7:1; *to retain, not to remit,* sins, Jn. 20:23 [2902] See *arrest; grasp; hold; seize.*

[3196] κράτιστος *kratistos* 4x *strongest;* in NT κράτιστε, a term of respect, *most excellent, noble,* or *illustrious,* Lk. 1:3; Acts 23:26; 24:3; 26:25* [2903]

[3197] κράτος *kratos* 12x *strength, power, might, force,* Acts 19:20; Eph. 1:19; meton. *a display of might,* Lk. 1:51; *power, sway, dominion,* Heb. 2:14; 1 Pet. 4:11; 5:11 [2904] See *might; power; strength.*

[3198] κραυγάζω *kraugazō* 9x *to cry out, exclaim, shout,* Mt. 12:19; Acts 22:23 [2905]

[3199] κραυγή *kraugē* 6x *a cry, outcry, clamor, shouting,* Mt. 25:6; Lk. 1:42; Acts 23:9; Eph. 4:31; *a cry* of sorrow, *wailing, lamentation,* Rev. 21:4; *a cry* for help, *earnest supplication,* Heb. 5:7* [2906]

[3200] κρέας *kreas* 2x *flesh, meat,* a later form of κρέατος, Rom. 14:21; 1 Cor. 8:13* [2907]

[3202] κρείττων *kreittōn* 19x can also be spelled κρείσσων, *better, more useful* or *profitable, more conducive to good,* 1 Cor. 7:8, 38; *superior, more excellent, of a higher nature, more valuable,* Heb. 1:4; 6:9; 7:7, 19, 22 [2908, 2909] See *better.*

[3203] κρεμάννυμι *kremannymi* 7x also spelled κρέμαμαι and κρεμάζω, *to hang, suspend,* Acts 5:30; 10:39; pass. *to be hung, suspended,* Mt. 18:6; Lk. 23:39; mid. κρέμαμαι, *to hang, be suspended,* Acts 28:4; Gal. 3:13; met. κρέμαμαι ἐν, *to hang upon, to be referable to* as an ultimate principle, Mt. 22:40 [2910]

[3204] κρημνός *krēmnos* 3x *a cliff, precipice, a steep bank,* Mt. 8:32; Mk. 5:13; Lk. 8:33* [2911]

[3205] Κρής *Krēs* 2x *a Cretan, an inhabitant of* Κρήτη, Acts 2:11; Tit. 1:12* [2912]

[3206] Κρήσκης *Krēskēs* 1x *Crescens,* a Latin pr. name, 2 Tim. 4:10* [2913]

[3207] Κρήτη *Krētē* 5x *Crete,* a large island in the eastern part of the Mediterranean, Acts 27:7, 12f., 21, Tit. 1:5* [2914]

[3208] κριθή *krithē* 1x *barley,* Rev. 6:6* [2915]

[3209] κρίθινος *krithinos* 2x *made of barley,* Jn. 6:9, 13* [2916]

[3210] κρίμα *krima* 27x *judgment; a sentence, award,* Mt. 7:2; *a judicial sentence,* Lk. 23:40; 24:20; Rom. 2:2; 5:16; *an* adverse *sentence,* Mt. 23:14; Rom. 13:2; 1 Tim. 5:12; Jas. 3:1; *judgment, administration of justice,* Jn. 9:39; Acts 24:25; *execution of justice,* 1 Pet. 4:17; *a lawsuit;* 1 Cor. 6:7; in NT *judicial visitation,* 1 Cor. 11:29; 2 Pet. 2:3; *an* administrative *decree,* Rom. 11:33 [2917] See *condemnation; judgment; punishment.*

[3211] κρίνον *krinon* 2x *a lily,* Mt. 6:28; Lk. 12:27* [2918]

[3212] κρίνω *krinō* 114x pluperfect, κεκρίκει (3 sg), pr. *to separate; to make a distinction between; to exercise judgment upon; to estimate,* Rom. 14:5; *to judge, to assume censorial power over, to call to account,* Mt. 7:1; Lk. 6:37; Rom. 2:1, 3; 14:3, 4, 10, 13; Col. 2:16; Jas. 4:11, 12; *to bring under question,* Rom. 14:22; *to judge* judicially, *to try* as a judge, Jn. 18:31; *to bring to trial,* Acts 13:27; *to sentence,* Lk. 19:22; Jn. 7:51; *to resolve on, decree,* Acts 16:4; Rev. 16:5; absol. *to decide, determine, resolve,* Acts 3:13; 15:19; 27:1; *to deem,* Acts 13:46; *to form a judgment, pass judgment,* Jn. 8:15; pass. *to be brought to trial,* Acts 25:10, 20; Rom. 3:4; *to be brought to account, to incur arraignment, be arraigned,* 1 Cor. 10:29; mid. *to go to law, litigate,* Mt. 5:40; in NT *to judge, to visit judicially,* Acts 7:7; 1 Cor. 11:31, 32; 1 Pet. 4:6; *to judge, to right, to vindicate,* Heb. 10:30; *to administer government over, to govern,* Mt. 19:28; Lk. 22:30 [2919] See *consider; decide; judge.*

[3213] κρίσις *krisis* 47x pr. *distinction; discrimination; judgment, decision, award,* Jn. 5:30; 7:24; 8:16; *a* judicial *sentence,* Jn. 3:19; Jas. 2:13; *an* adverse *sentence,* Mt. 23:33; Mk. 3:29; *judgment, judicial process, trial,* Mt. 10:15; Jn. 5:24; 12:31; 16:8; *judgment,* *administration of justice,* Jn. 5:22, 27; in NT *a court of justice, tribunal,* Mt. 5:21, 22; *an impeachment,* 2 Pet. 2:11; Jude 9; from the Hebrew, *justice, equity,* Mt. 12:18, 20; 23:23; Lk. 11:42 [2920] See *condemnation; judgment; justice.*

[3214] Κρίσπος *Krispos* 2x *Crispus,* a Latin pr. name, Acts 18:8; 1 Cor. 1:14* [2921]

[3215] κριτήριον *kritērion* 3x pr. *a standard* or *means by which to judge, criterion; a court of justice, tribunal,* Jas. 2:6; *a cause, controversy,* 1 Cor. 6:2, 4* [2922]

[3216] κριτής *kritēs* 19x *a judge,* Mt. 5:25; from the Hebrew, *a magistrate, ruler,* Acts 13:20; 24:10 [2923] See *judge.*

[3217] κριτικός *kritikos* 1x *able* or *quick to discern* or *judge,* Heb. 4:12* [2924]

[3218] κρούω *krouō* 9x *to knock* at a door, Mt. 7:7, 8; Lk. 11:9, 10; 12:36; 13:25; Acts 12:13, 16; Rev. 3:20* [2925]

[3219] κρύπτη *kryptē* 1x *a vault* or *closet, a cell* for storage, *dark secret place,* Lk. 11:33* [2926]

[3220] κρυπτός *kryptos* 17x *hidden, concealed, secret, clandestine,* Mt. 6:4, 6; τὰ κρυπτά, *secrets,* Rom. 2:16; 1 Cor. 14:25 [2927] See *hidden; secret.*

[3221] κρύπτω *kryptō* 18x *to hide, conceal,* Mt. 5:14; in NT *to lay up in store,* Col. 3:3; Rev. 2:17; κεκρυμμέμος, *concealed, secret,* Jn. 19:38 [2928] See *conceal; hide.*

[3222] κρυσταλλίζω *krystallizō* 1x *to be clear, brilliant like crystal,* Rev. 21:11* [2929]

[3223] κρύσταλλος *krystallos* 2x pr. *clear ice; crystal,* Rev. 4:6; 22:1* [2930]

[3224] κρυφαῖος *kryphaios* 2x *secret, hidden,* Mt. 6:18* [2927]

[3225] κρυφῇ *kryphē* 1x *in secret, secretly, not openly,* Eph. 5:12* [2931]

[3227] κτάομαι *ktaomai* 7x *to get, procure, provide,* Mt. 10:9; *to make gain, gain,* Lk. 18:12; *to purchase,* Acts 8:20; 22:28; *to be the cause* or *occasion of purchasing,* Acts 1:18; *to preserve, save,* Lk. 21:19; *to get under control, to be winning the mastery over,* 1 Thess. 4:4; perf. κέκτημαι, *to possess** [2932]

[3228] κτῆμα *ktēma* 4x *a possession, property, field,* Mt. 19:22; Mk. 10:22; Acts 2:45; 5:1* [2933]

[3229] κτῆνος *ktēnos* 4x pr. *property,* generally used in the plural, τὰ κτήνη; *property* in animals; *a beast of burden, domesticated animal,* Lk. 10:34; Acts 23:24; *beasts, cattle,* 1 Cor. 15:39; Rev. 18:13* [2934]

[3230] κτήτωρ *ktētōr* 1x *a possessor, owner,* Acts 4:34* [2935]

[3231] κτίζω *ktizō* 15x pr. *to reduce from a state of disorder and wildness;* in NT *to call into being, to create,* Mk. 13:19; *to call into individual existence, to frame,* Eph. 2:15; *to create* spiritually, *to invest with a* spiritual *frame,* Eph. 2:10; 4:24 [2936] See *create.*

[3232] κτίσις *ktisis* 19x. (1) pr. *a framing, founding.* (2) in NT *creation, the act of creating,* Rom. 1:20; *creation, the material universe,* Mk. 10:6; 13:19; Heb. 9:11; 2 Pet. 3:4; *a created thing, a creature,* Rom. 1:25; 8:39; Col. 1:15; Heb. 4:13; *the* human *creation,* Mk. 16:15; Rom. 8:19, 20, 21, 22; Col. 1:23; *a* spiritual *creation,* 2 Cor. 5:17; Gal. 6:15. (3) *an institution, ordinance,* 1 Pet. 2:13 [2937] See *creation.*

[3233] κτίσμα *ktisma* 4x pr. *a thing founded;* in NT *a created being, creature,* 1 Tim. 4:4; Jas. 1:18; Rev. 5:13; 8:9* [2938]

[3234] κτίστης *ktistēs* 1x *a founder;* in NT *a creator,* 1 Pet. 4:19* [2939]

[3235] κυβεία *kybeia* 1x also spelled κυβία, pr. *dice playing;* met. *craftiness, trickery,* Eph. 4:14* [2940]

[3236] κυβέρνησις *kybernēsis* 1x *government, office of a governor* or *director;* meton. *a director,* 1 Cor. 12:28* [2941]

[3237] κυβερνήτης *kybernētēs* 2x *a pilot, helmsman,* Acts 27:11; Rev. 18:17* [2942]

[3238] κυκλεύω *kykleuō* 1x *to encircle, surround, encompass,* Rev. 20:9* [2944]

[3239] κυκλόθεν *kyklothen* 3x *all around, round about,* Rev. 4:3, 4, 8* [2943]

[3240] κυκλόω *kykloō* 4x *to encircle, surround, encompass, come around.* Jn. 10:24; Acts 14:20; spc. *to lay siege to,* Lk. 21:20; *to march round,* Heb. 11:30* [2944]

[3241] κύκλῳ *kyklōi* 8x from κύκλος, functions in the NT only as an improper prep., *a circle;* in NT κύκλῳ functions adverbially, *round, round about, around,* Mk. 3:34; 6:6, 36 [2945]

[3243] κυλισμός *kylismos* 1x also spelled κύλισμα, a rolling, wallowing, 2 Pet. 2:22* [2946]

[3244] κυλίω *kyliō* 1x *to roll*; mid. *to roll one's self, to wallow,* Mk. 9:20 [2947]

[3245] κυλλός *kyllos* 4x pr. *crooked, bent, maimed, lame, crippled,* Mt. 18:8; Mk. 9:43, used as a noun meaning *cripple,* Mt. 15:30ff.* [2948]

[3246] κῦμα *kyma* 5x *a wave, surge, billow,* Mt. 8:24; 14:24; Mk. 4:37; Acts 27:41; Jude 13* [2949]

[3247] κύμβαλον *kymbalon* 1x *a cymbal,* 1 Cor. 13:1* [2950]

[3248] κύμινον *kyminon* 1x *cumin, cuminum salivum* of Linnaeus, a plant, a native of Egypt and Syria, whose seeds are of an aromatic, warm, bitterish taste, with a strong but not disagreeable smell, and used by the ancients as a condiment, Mt. 23:23* [2951]

[3249] κυνάριον *kynarion* 4x *a little* or *worthless dog,* Mt. 15:26, 27; Mk. 7:27, 28* [2952]

[3250] Κύπριος *Kyprios* 3x *a Cypriot, an inhabitant of Cyprus,* Acts 4:36; 11:20; 21:16* [2953]

[3251] Κύπρος *Kypros* 5x *Cyprus,* an island in the eastern part of the Mediterranean, Acts 11:19; 13:4; 15:39; 21:3; 27:4* [2954]

[3252] κύπτω *kyptō* 2x *to bend forwards, stoop down,* Mk. 1:7; Jn. 8:6* [2955]

[3254] Κυρηναῖος *Kyrēnaios* 6x *a Cyrenian, an inhabitant of Cyrene,* Mt. 27:32; Mk. 15:21; Lk. 23:26; Acts 6:9; 11:20; 13:1* [2956]

[3255] Κυρήνη *Kyrēnē* 1x *Cyrene,* a city founded by a colony of Greeks, in Northern Africa, Acts 2:10* [2957]

[3256] Κυρήνιος *Kyrēnios* 1x *Cyrenius* (perhaps *Quirinus*) pr. name, the governor of Syria, Lk. 2:2* [2958]

[3257] κυρία *kyria* 2x *a lady,* 2 Jn. 1:1, 5* [2959]

[3258] κυριακός *kyriakos* 2x *pertaining to the Lord Jesus Christ, the Lord's,* 1 Cor. 11:20; Rev. 1:10* [2960]

[3259] κυριεύω *kyrieuō* 7x *to be lord over, to be possessed of, mastery over,* Rom. 6:9, 14; 7:1; 14:9; 2 Cor. 1:24; 1 Tim. 6:15; *to exercise control over,* Lk. 22:25* [2961]

[3261] κύριος *kyrios* 717x *a lord, master,* Mt. 12:8; *an owner, possessor,* Mt. 20:8; *a potentate, sovereign,* Acts 25:26; *a power, deity,* 1 Cor. 8:5; *the Lord, Yahweh,* Mt. 1:22; *the Lord* Jesus Christ, Mt. 24:42; Mk. 16:19; Lk. 10:1; Jn. 4:1; 1 Cor. 4:5; freq.; κύριε, a term of respect of various force, *Sir, Lord,* Mt. 13:27; Acts 9:6, et al. freq. [2962] See *lord; master; sir.*

[3262] κυριότης *kyriotēs* 4x *lordship; constituted authority,* Eph. 1:21; 2 Pet. 2:10; Jude 8; pl. *authorities, potentates,* Col. 1:16. The Ephesian and Colossian passage could also be speaking about angelic powers.* [2963]

[3263] κυρόω *kyroō* 2x *to confirm, ratify,* Gal. 3:15; *to reaffirm, assure,* 2 Cor. 2:8* [2964]

[3264] κύων *kyōn* 5x *a dog,* Mt. 7:6; Lk. 16:21; 2 Pet. 2:22; met. *a dog, a religious corrupter,* Phil. 3:2; *miscreant,* Rev. 22:15* [2965]

[3265] κῶλον *kōlon* 1x lit., *a member* or *limb of the body,* fig., *dead body, corpse,* Heb. 3:17* [2966]

[3266] κωλύω *kōlyō* 23x *to hinder, restrain, prevent,* Mt. 19:14; Acts 8:36; Rom. 1:13 [2967] See *forbid; hinder; oppose; stop.*

[3267] κώμη *kōmē* 27x *a village, a country town,* Mt. 9:35; 10:11; Lk. 8:1 [2968] See *village.*

[3268] κωμόπολις *kōmopolis* 1x *a large village, market town,* Mk. 1:38* [2969]

[3269] κῶμος *kōmos* 3x pr. *a festive procession, a merry-making;* in NT *a revel, lewd, immoral feasting,* Rom. 13:13; Gal. 5:21; 1 Pet. 4:3* [2970]

[3270] κώνωψ *kōnōps* 1x *a gnat, mosquito,* which is found in wine when becoming sour, Mt. 23:24* [2971]

[3272] Κωσάμ *Kōsam* 1x *Cosam,* pr. name, indecl., Lk. 3:28* [2973]

[3273] κωφός *kōphos* 14x pr. *blunt, dull,* as a weapon; *dull* of hearing, *deaf,* Mt. 11:5; Mk. 7:32, 37; 9:25; Lk. 7:22; *dumb, mute,* Mt. 9:32, 33; 12:22; 15:30, 31; Lk. 1:22; meton. *making dumb, causing dumbness,* Lk. 11:14* [2974] See *deaf; mute.*

[3275] λαγχάνω *lanchanō* 4x *to have assigned to one, to obtain, receive,* Acts 1:17; 2 Pet. 1:1; *to have fall to one by lot,* Lk. 1:9; absol. *to cast lots,* Jn. 19:24* [2975]

[3276] Λάζαρος *Lazaros* 15x *Lazarus,* pr. name [2976]

[3277] λάθρα *lathrai* 4x *secretly, privately,* Mt. 1:19; 2:7; Jn. 11:28; Acts 16:37* [2977]

[3278] λαῖλαψ *lailaps* 3x *a squall of wind, a hurricane,* Mk. 4:37; Lk. 8:23; 2 Pet. 2:17* [2978]

[3279] λακάω *lakaō* 1x *burst open,* Acts 1:18* [2997]

[3280] λακτίζω *laktizō* 1x *to kick,* Acts 26:14* [2979]

[3281] λαλέω *laleō* 296x *to make vocal utterance; to babble, to talk;* in NT absol. *to exercise the faculty of speech,* Mt. 9:33; *to speak,* Mt. 10:20; *to hold converse with, to talk with,* Mt. 12:46; Mk. 6:50; Rev. 1:12; *to discourse, to make an address,* Lk. 11:37; Acts 11:20; 21:39; *to make announcement, to make a declaration,* Lk. 1:55; *to make mention,* Jn. 12:41; Acts 2:31; Heb. 4:8; 2 Pet. 3:16; trans. *to speak, address, preach,* Mt. 9:18; Jn. 3:11; Tit. 2:1; *to give utterance to, utter,* Mk. 2:7; Jn. 3:34; *to declare, announce, reveal,* Lk. 24:25 et al.; *to disclose,* 2 Cor. 12:4 [2980] See *say; speak.*

[3282] λαλιά *lalia* 3x *talk, speech;* in NT *matter of discourse,* Jn. 4:42; 8:43; *language, dialect,* Mt. 26:73* [2981]

[3284] λαμβάνω *lambanō* 258x. (1) *to take, take up, take in the hand,* Mt. 10:38; 13:31, 33; *to take on one's self, sustain,* Mt. 8:17; *to take, seize, seize upon,* Mt. 5:40; 21:34; Lk. 5:26; 1 Cor. 10:13; *to catch,* Lk. 5:5; 2 Cor. 12:16; *to assume, put on,* Phil. 2:7; *to make a rightful* or *successful assumption of,* Jn. 3:27; *to conceive,* Acts 28:15; *to take* by way of provision, Mt. 16:5; *to get, get together,* Mt. 16:9.

(2) *to receive* as payment, Mt. 17:24; Heb. 7:8; *to take* to wife, Mk. 12:19; *to admit, give reception to,* Jn. 6:21; 2 Jn. 10; met. *to give* mental *reception to,* Jn. 3:11; *to be* simply *recipient of, to receive,* Mt. 7:8; Jn. 7:23, 39; 19:30; Acts 10:43.

(3) used idiomatically with other words; λαμβάνειν πεῖραν, *to make encounter of* a matter of difficulty or trial, Heb. 11:29, 36; λαμβάνειν ἀρχήν, *to begin,* Heb. 2:3; λαμβάνειν συμβούλιον, *to take counsel, consult,* Mt. 12:14; λαμβάνειν λήθην, *to forget,* 2 Pet. 1:9; λαμβάνειν ὑπόμνησιν, *to recollect, call to mind,* 2 Tim. 1:5; λαμβάειν περιτομήν, *to receive circumcision, be circumcised,* Jn. 7:23; λαμβάνειν καταλλαγήν, *to be reconciled,* Rom. 5:11; λαμβάνειν κρίμα, *to receive condemnation* or *punishment, be punished,* Mk. 12:40; from the Hebrew, πρόσωπον λαμβάνειν, *to accept the person* of any one, *show partiality towards,* Lk. 20:21 [2983] See *get; receive; seize; take.*

[3285] Λάμεχ *Lamech* 1x *Lamech,* pr. name, indecl., Lk. 3:36* [2984]

[3286] λαμπάς *lampas* 9x *a light,* Acts 20:8; *a lamp,* Rev. 4:5; 8:10, *a* portable *lamp, lantern, torch,* Mt. 25:1, 3, 4, 7, 8; Jn. 18:3* [2985]

[3287] λαμπρός *lampros* 9x *bright, resplendent, shining,* Rev. 22:16; *clear, transparent,* Rev. 22:1; *white, glistening,* Acts 10:30; Rev. 15:6; Rev. 19:8; *of a bright color, gaudy,* Lk. 23:11; by impl. *splendid, magnificent, sumptuous,* Jas. 2:2, 3; Rev. 18:14* [2986]

[3288] λαμπρότης *lamprotēs* 1x *brightness, splendor,* Acts 26:13* [2987]

[3289] λαμπρῶς *lamprōs* 1x *splendidly; magnificently, sumptuously,* Lk. 16:19* [2988]

[3290] λάμπω *lampō* 7x *to shine, give light,* Mt. 5:15, 16; 17:2; *to flash, shine,* Lk. 17:24; Acts 12:7; 2 Cor. 4:6* [2989]

[3291] λανθάνω *lanthanō* 6x *to be unnoticed; to escape the knowledge* or *observation of* a person, Acts 26:26; 2 Pet. 3:5, 8; absol. *to be concealed* or *hidden, escape detection,* Mk. 7:24; Lk. 8:47; with a participle of another verb, *to be unconscious* of an action while being the subject or object of it, Heb. 13:2* [2990]

[3292] λαξευτός *laxeutos* 1x *cut in stone, hewn out of stone* or *rock,* Lk. 23:53* [2991]

[3293] Λαοδίκεια *Laodikeia* 6x *Laodicea,* a city of Phrygia in Asia Minor, Rev. 3:14* [2993]

[3294] Λαοδικεύς *Laodikeus* 1x *a Laodicean, an inhabitant of Laodicea,* Col. 4:16* [2994]

[3295] λαός *laos* 142x *a body of people; a concourse of people, a multitude,* Mt. 27:25; Lk. 8:47; *the common people,* Mt. 26:5; *a people, nation,* Mt. 2:4; Lk. 2:32; Tit. 2:14; ὁ λαός, *the people* of Israel, Lk. 2:10 [2992] See *people.*

[3296] λάρυγξ *larynx* 1x *the throat, gullet,* Rom. 3:13* [2995]

[3297] Λασαία *Lasaia* 1x *Lasaea,* also spelled Λασέα, a maritime town in Crete, Acts 27:8 [2996]

[3300] λατομέω *latomeō* 2x *to hew stones; to cut out of stone, hew from stone,* Mt. 27:60; Mk. 15:46; Lk. 23:53* [2998]

[3301] λατρεία *latreia* 5x *service, servitude; religious service, worship,* Jn. 16:2; Rom. 9:4; 12:1; Heb. 9:1, 6* [2999]

[3302] λατρεύω *latreuō* 21x *to be a servant, to serve,* Acts 27:23; *to render religious service and* *homage, worship,* Mt. 4:10; Lk. 1:74; spc. *to offer sacrifices, present offerings,* Heb. 8:5; 9:9 [3000] See *serve; worship.*

[3303] λάχανον *lachanon* 4x *a garden herb, vegetable,* Mt. 13:32; Mk. 4:32; Lk. 11:42; Rom. 14:2* [3001]

[3305] λεγιών *legiōn* 4x also spelled λεγεών, *a* Roman *legion;* in NT used indefinitely for a great number, Mt. 26:53; Mk. 5:9, 15, Lk. 8:30* [3003]

[3306] λέγω *legō* 2,353x *to say, speak.* (1) *to say* in general terms; Mt. 1:20; *to say* mentally, in thought, Mt. 3:9; Lk. 3:8; *to say,* as distinguished from acting, Mt. 23:3; *to mention, speak of,* Mk. 14:71; Lk. 9:31; Jn. 8:27; *to tell, declare, narrate,* Mt. 21:27; Mk. 10:32; *to express,* Heb. 5:11; *to put forth, propound,* Lk. 5:36; 13:6; Jn. 16:29; *to mean, to intend to signify,* 1 Cor. 1:12; 10:29; *to say, declare, affirm, maintain,* Mt. 3:9; 5:18; Mk. 12:18; Acts 17:7; 26:22; 1 Cor. 1:10; *to enjoin,* Acts 15:24; 21:21; Rom. 2:22.

(2) *to speak* in more specific terms; *to make an address* or *speech,* Acts 26:1; *to say* in written language, Mk. 15:28; Lk. 1:63; Jn. 19:37; *to ask,* Mt. 9:14; *to answer,* Mt. 4:10; *to term, designate, cull,* Mt. 19:17; Mk. 12:37; Lk. 20:37; 23:2; 1 Cor. 8:5; *to call* by a name, Mt. 2:23; *to command,* Mk. 13:37; pass. *to be further named, to be surnamed,* Mt. 1:16; *to be explained, interpreted,* Jn. 4:25; 20:16, 24; in NT σὺ λέγεις, *you say,* a form of affirmative answer to a question Mt. 27:11; Mk. 15:2; Jn. 18:37 [2036, 2046, 3004, 4483] See *call; name; say; speak; talk; tell.*

[3307] λεῖμμα *leimma* 1x pr. *a remnant;* in NT *a small residue,* Rom. 11:5* [3005] See *remnant.*

[3308] λεῖος *leios* 1x *smooth, level, plain,* Lk. 3:5* [3006]

[3309] λείπω *leipō* 6x trans. *to leave, forsake;* pass. *to be left, deserted;* by impl. *to be destitute of, deficient in,* Jas. 1:4, 5; 2:15; intrans. *to fail, be wanting, be deficient,* Lk. 18:22; Tit. 1:5; 3:13* [3007]

[3310] λειτουργέω *leitourgeō* 3x pr. *to perform some public service at one's own expense;* in NT *to officiate* as a priest, Heb. 10:11; *to minister* in the Christian Church, Acts 13:2; *to minister to, assist, succor,* Rom. 15:27* [3008]

[3311] λειτουργία *leitourgia* 6x pr. *a public service discharged by a citizen at his own expense;* in NT *a* sacred *ministration,* Lk. 1:23; Phil. 2:17; Heb. 8:6; 9:21; *a kind office, aid, relief,* 2 Cor. 9:12; Phil. 2:30* [3009]

[3312] λειτουργικός *leitourgikos* 1x *ministering; engaged in holy service,* Heb. 1:14* [3010]

[3313] λειτουργός *leitourgos* 5x pr. *a person of property who performed a public duty* or *service to the state at his own expense;* in NT *a minister* or *servant,* Rom. 13:6; 15:16; Heb. 1:7; 8:2; *one who ministers relief,* Phil. 2:25* [3011]

[3316] λεμά *lema* 2x Aramaic for *Why? Wherefore?* Mt. 27:46; Mk. 15:34* [2982]

[3317] λέντιον *lention* 2x *a coarse cloth,* with which servants were girded, *a towel, napkin, apron,* Jn. 13:4, 5* [3012]

[3318] λεπίς *lepis* 1x *a scale, shell, rind, crust, incrustation,* Acts 9:18* [3013]

[3319] λέπρα *lepra* 4x *the leprosy,* Mt. 8:3; Mk. 1:42; Lk. 5:12, 13* [3014]

[3320] λεπρός *lepros* 9x *leprous; a leper,* Mt. 8:2; 10:8 [3015]

[3322] Λευί *Leui* 8x *Levi,* also spelled Λευίς (3323), pr. name. When the NT refers to the Λευί of the OT, the word is indecl. (n-3g[2]); when it refers to a NT person, it is partially declined (n-3g[1]): Λευίς (nom); Λευίν (acc). (1) *Levi, son of Jacob,* Heb. 7:5, 9; Rev. 7:7. (2) *Levi, son of Symeon,* Lk. 3:29. (3) *Levi, son of Melchi,* Lk. 3:24 [3017]

[3324] Λευίτης *Leuitēs* 3x *a Levite, one of the posterity of Levi,* Jn. 1:19; Lk. 10:32; Acts 4:36* [3019]

[3325] Λευιτικός *Leuitikos* 1x *Levitical, pertaining to the Levites,* Heb. 7:11* [3020]

[3326] λευκαίνω *leukainō* 2x *to brighten, to make white,* Mk. 9:3; Rev. 7:14* [3021]

[3328] λευκός *leukos* 25x pr. *light, bright; white,* Mt. 5:36; 17:2; *whitening, growing white,* Jn. 4:35 [3022] See *white.*

[3329] λέων *leōn* 9x *a lion,* Heb. 11:33; 1 Pet. 5:8; Rev. 4:7; 9:8, 17; 10:3; 13:2; met. *a lion, cruel adversary, tyrant,* 2 Tim. 4:17; *a lion, a hero, deliverer,* Rev. 5:5* [3023]

[3330] λήθη *lēthē* 1x *forgetfulness, oblivion,* 2 Pet. 1:9* [3024]

[3331] λῆμψις *lēmpsis* 1x also spelled λῆψις, *taking, receiving,* Phil. 4:15* [3028]

[3332] ληνός *lēnos* 5x pr. *a tub. trough; a winepress,* into which grapes were cast and trodden, Rev. 14:19, 20; 19:15; *a wine-vat,* i.q. ὑπολήνιον, the lower vat into which the juice of the trodden grapes flowed, Mt. 21:33* [3025]

[3333] λῆρος *lēros* 1x *idle talk; an empty tale, nonsense,* Lk. 24:11* [3026]

[3334] λῃστής *lēstēs* 15x *a plunderer, robber, highwayman,* Mt. 21:13; 26:55; Mk. 11:17; Lk. 10:30; 2 Cor. 11:26; *a bandit, brigand,* Mt. 27:38, 44; Mk. 15:27; Jn. 18:40; trop. *a robber, rapacious imposter,* Jn. 10:1, 8 [3027] See *bandit; insurrectionist; robber.*

[3336] λίαν *lian* 12x *much, greatly, exceedingly,* Mt. 2:16; 4:8; 8:28 [3029]

[3337] λίβανος *libanos* 2x *arbor thurifera,* the tree producing frankincense, growing in Arabia and Mount Lebanon; in NT *frankincense,* the transparent gum that distils from incisions in the tree, Mt. 2:11; Rev. 18:13* [3030]

[3338] λιβανωτός *libanōtos* 2x *frankincense;* in NT *a censer,* Rev. 8:3, 5* [3031]

[3339] Λιβερτῖνος *Libertinos* 1x *a freedman, one who having been a slave has obtained his freedom,* or *whose father was a freed-man;* in NT the λιβερτῖνοι probably denote Jews who had been carried captive to Rome, and subsequently manumitted, Acts 6:9* [3032]

[3340] Λιβύη *Libyē* 1x *Libya,* a part of Africa, bordering on the west of Egypt, Acts 2:10* [3033]

[3342] λιθάζω *lithazō* 9x *to stone, pelt* or *kill with stones,* Jn. 8:5; 10:31, 32, 33; 11:8; Acts 5:26; 14:19; 2 Cor. 11:25; Heb. 11:37* [3034]

[3343] λίθινος *lithinos* 3x *made of stone,* Jn. 2:6; 2 Cor. 3:3; Rev. 9:20* [3035]

[3344] λιθοβολέω *lithoboleō* 7x *to stone, pelt with stones,* in order to kill, Mt. 21:35; 23:37 [3036]

[3345] λίθος *lithos* 59x *a stone,* Mt. 3:9; 4:3, 6; used figuratively, of Christ, Eph. 2:20; 1 Pet. 2:6; of believers, 1 Pet. 2:5; meton. *a tablet of stone,* 2 Cor. 3:7; *a precious stone,* Rev. 4:3 [3037] See *rock; stone.*

[3346] λιθόστρωτος *lithostrōtos* 1x *a pavement made of blocks of stone,* Jn. 19:13* [3038]

[3347] λικμάω *likmaō* 2x pr. *to winnow grain;* in NT *to scatter like chaff, crush,* Mt. 21:44; Lk. 20:18* [3039]

[3348] λιμήν *limēn* 3x *a port, haven, harbor,* Καλὰ Λιμένες, Acts 27:8, 12* [3040]

[3349] λίμνη *limnē* 11x *a tract of standing water; a lake,* Lk. 5:1; Rev. 20:14 [3041] See *lake; pond.*

[3350] λιμός *limos* 12x *famine, scarcity of food, want of grain,* Mt. 24:7; *famine, hunger, famishment,* Lk. 15:17; Rom. 8:35 [3042] See *famine; hunger.*

[3351] λίνον *linon* 2x *flax;* by meton. *a flaxen wick,* Mt. 12:20; *linen,* Rev. 15:6* [3043]

[3352] Λίνος *Linos* 1x some accent as Λῖνος, *Linus,* pr. name, 2 Tim. 4:21* [3044]

[3353] λιπαρός *liparos* 1x lit., *fat;* fig., *rich, sumptuous,* Rev. 18:14* [3045]

[3354] λίτρα *litra* 2x *a pound, libra,* equivalent to about twelve ounces (American), Jn. 12:3; 19:39* [3046]

[3355] λίψ *lips* 1x pr. *the south-west wind;* meton. *the south-west quarter of the heavens,* Acts 27:12* [3047]

[3356] λογεία *logeia* 2x *collection* of money, 1 Cor. 16:1f.* [3048]

[3357] λογίζομαι *logizomai* 40x. (1) pr. *to count, calculate; to count, enumerate,* Mk. 15:28; Lk. 22:37; *to set down* as a matter of account, 1 Cor. 13:5; 2 Cor. 3:5; 12:6; *to impute,* Rom. 4:3; 2 Cor. 5:19; 2 Tim. 4:16; *to account,* Rom. 2:26; 8:36; εἰς οὐδὲν λογισθῆναι, *to be set at nought, despised,* Acts 19:27; *to regard, deem, consider,* Rom. 6:11; 14:14; 1 Cor. 4:1; 2 Cor. 10:2; Phil. 3:13. (2) *to infer, conclude, presume,* Rom. 2:3; 3:28; 8:18; 2 Cor. 10:2, 7, 11; Heb. 11:19; 1 Pet. 5:12. (3) *to think upon, ponder,* Phil. 4:8; absol. *to reason,* Mk. 11:31; 1 Cor. 13:11 [3049] See *consider; credit; regard; think.*

[3358] λογικός *logikos* 2x *pertaining to speech; pertaining to reason;* in NT *rational, spiritual, pertaining to the mind and soul,* Rom. 12:1; 1 Pet. 2:2* [3050]

[3359] λόγιον *logion* 4x *an oracle, a divine communication* or *revelation,* Acts 7:38; Rom. 3:2; Heb. 5:12; 1 Pet. 4:11* [3051] See *oracle.*

[3360] λόγιος *logios* 1x *gifted with learning* or *eloquence,* Acts 18:24* [3052]

[3361] λογισμός *logismos* 2x pr. *a computation, act of computing; a thought, cogitation,* Rom. 2:15; *a conception, device,* 2 Cor. 10:4* [3053]

[3362] λογομαχέω *logomacheō* 1x *to contend about words;* by impl. *to dispute about trivial things,* 2 Tim. 2:14* [3054]

[3363] λογομαχία *logomachia* 1x *contention* or *strife about words;* by impl. *a dispute about trivial things, unprofitable controversy,* 1 Tim. 6:4* [3055]

[3364] λόγος *logos* 330x *a word, a thing uttered,* Mt. 12:32, 37; 1 Cor. 14:19; *speech, language, talk,* Mt. 22:15; Lk. 20:20; 2 Cor. 10:10; Jas. 3:2; *converse,* Lk. 24:17; mere *talk, wordy show,* 1 Cor. 4:19, 20; Col. 2:23; 1 Jn. 3:18; *language, mode of discourse, style of speaking,* Mt. 5:37; 1 Cor. 1:17; 1 Thess. 2:5; *a saying, a speech,* Mk. 7:29; Eph. 4:29; *an expression, form of words, formula,* Mt. 26:44; Rom. 13:9; Gal. 5:14; *a saying, a thing propounded in discourse,* Mt. 7:24; 19:11; Jn. 4:37; 6:60; 1 Tim. 1:15; *a message, announcement,* 2 Cor. 5:19; *a* prophetic *announcement,* Jn. 12:38; *an account, statement,* 1 Pet. 3:15; *a story, report,* Mt. 28:15; Jn. 4:39; 21:23; 2 Thess. 2:2; *a* written *narrative, a treatise,* Acts 1:1; *a set discourse,* Acts 20:7; *doctrine,* Jn. 8:31, 37; 2 Tim. 2:17; *subject-matter,* Acts 15:6; *reckoning, account,* Mt. 12:36; 18:23; 25:19; Lk. 16:2; Acts 19:40; 20:24; Rom. 9:28; Phil. 4:15, 17; Heb. 4:13; *a plea,* Mt. 5:32; Acts 19:38; *a motive,* Acts 10:29; *reason,* Acts 18:14; ὁ λόγος, *the word* of God, especially in the Gospel, Mt. 13:21, 22; Mk. 16:20; Lk. 1:2; Acts 6:4; ὁ λόγος, *the* divine *Word,* or *Logos,* Jn. 1:1 [3056] See *message; report; word.*

[3365] λόγχη *lonchē* 1x pr. *the head of a javelin; a spear, lance,* Jn. 19:34* [3057]

[3366] λοιδορέω *loidoreō* 4x *to revile, rail at, abuse,* Jn. 9:28; Acts 23:4; 1 Cor. 4:12; 1 Pet. 2:23* [3058]

[3367] λοιδορία *loidoria* 3x *reviling, railing, verbal abuse,* 1 Tim. 5:14; 1 Pet. 3:9* [3059]

[3368] λοίδορος *loidoros* 2x *reviling, railing;* as a subst. *a reviler, railer,* 1 Cor. 5:11; 6:10* [3060]

[3369] λοιμός *loimos* 2x *a pestilence, plague,* Lk. 21:11; met. *a pest, pestilent fellow,* Acts 24:5* [3061]

[3370] λοιπός *loipos* 55x *remaining; the rest, remainder*, Mt. 22:6; as an adv., οὗ λοιποῦ, *henceforth*, Gal. 6:17; τὸ λοιπόν, or λοιπόν, *henceforward*, Mt. 26:45; 2 Tim. 4:8; Acts 27:20; *as to the rest, besides*, 1 Cor. 1:16; *finally*, Eph. 6:10; ὃ δὲ λοιπόν, *but, now, furthermore*, 1 Cor. 4:2 [3062, 3063, 3064] See *left over; remaining.*

[3371] Λουκᾶς *Loukas* 3x *Luke,* pr. name [3065]

[3372] Λούκιος *Loukios* 2x *Lucius,* pr. name. (1) a person from Cyrene of Antioch, Acts 13:1. (2) a person who sends his greeting with Paul, Rom. 16:21* [3066]

[3373] λουτρόν *loutron* 2x *a bath, water for bathing; a bathing, washing, ablution,* Eph. 5:26; Tit. 3:5* [3067] See *wash, washing.*

[3374] λούω *louō* 5x pr. *to bathe the body,* as distinguished from washing only the extremities, Jn. 13:10; *to bathe, wash,* Acts 9:37; 16:33; Heb. 10:22; 2 Pet. 2:22* [3068] See *wash, washing.*

[3375] Λύδδα *Lydda* 3x *Lydda,* a town in Palestine, Acts 9:32, 35, 38* [3069]

[3376] Λυδία *Lydia* 2x *Lydia,* pr. name of a woman, Acts 16:14, 40* [3070]

[3377] Λυκαονία *Lykaonia* 1x *Lycaonia,* a province of Asia Minor, Acts 14:6* [3071]

[3378] Λυκαονιστί *Lykaonisti* 1x *in the dialect of Lycaonia,* Acts 14:11* [3072]

[3379] Λυκία *Lykia* 1x *Lycia,* a province of Asia Minor, Acts 27:5* [3073]

[3380] λύκος *lykos* 6x *a wolf,* Mt. 10:16; Lk. 10:3; Jn. 10:12; met. *a person of wolf-like character,* Mt. 7:15; Acts 20:29* [3074]

[3381] λυμαίνω *lymainō* 1x some list as a deponent, λυμαίνομαι, *to outrage, harm, violently maltreat;* in NT *to make havoc of, ruin,* Acts 8:3* [3075]

[3382] λυπέω *lypeō* 26x *to occasion grief* or *sorrow to, to distress,* 2 Cor. 2:2, 5; 7:8; pass. *to be grieved, pained, distressed, sorrowful,* Mt. 17:23; 19:22; *to aggrieve, cross, vex,* Eph. 4:30; pass. *to feel pained,* Rom. 14:15 [3076] See *sorrow.*

[3383] λύπη *lypē* 16x *pain, distress,* Jn. 16:21; *grief, sorrow,* Jn. 16:6, 20, 22; meton. *cause of grief, trouble, affliction,* 1 Pet. 2:19 [3077] See *grief; pain; sorrow.*

[3384] Λυσανίας *Lysanias* 1x *Lyssanias,* pr. name, Lk. 3:1* [3078]

[3385] Λυσίας *Lysias* 2x *Lysias,* pr. name, Acts 23:26; 24:7, 22* [3079]

[3386] λύσις *lysis* 1x *a loosing;* in NT *a release* from the marriage bond, *a divorce,* 1 Cor. 7:27* [3080]

[3387] λυσιτελέω *lysiteleō* 1x pr. *to compensate for incurred expense;* by impl. *to be advantageous to, to profit, advantage;* impers. Lk. 17:2* [3081]

[3388] Λύστρα *Lystra* 6x *Lystra,* a city of Lycaonia, in Asia Minor, Acts 14:6, 8, 21; 16:1f.; 2 Tim. 3:11* [3082]

[3389] λύτρον *lytron* 2x pr. *price paid; a ransom,* Mt. 20:28; Mk. 10:45* [3083] See *ransom.*

[3390] λυτρόω *lytroō* 3x *to release for a ransom;* mid, *to ransom, redeem, deliver, liberate,* Lk. 24:21; Tit. 2:14; 1 Pet. 1:18* [3084] See *redeem.*

[3391] λύτρωσις *lytrōsis* 3x *redemption,* Heb. 9:12; *liberation, deliverance,* Lk. 1:68; 2:38* [3085] See *redemption.*

[3392] λυτρωτής *lytrōtēs* 1x *a redeemer; a deliverer,* Acts 7:35* [3086]

[3393] λυχνία *lychnia* 12x *a candlestick, lampstand,* Mt. 5:15; met. *a candlestick,* as a figure of a Christian church, Rev. 1:12, 13, 20; of a teacher or prophet, Rev. 11:4 [3087] See *candle, candlestick; lamp, lampstand.*

[3394] λύχνος *lychnos* 14x *a light, lamp, candle,* etc., Mt. 5:15; Mk. 4:21; met. *a lamp,* as a figure of a distinguished teacher, Jn. 5:35 [3088] See *candle, candlestick; lamp, lampstand.*

[3395] λύω *lyō* 42x *to loosen, unbind, unfasten,* Mk. 1:7; *to loose, untie,* Mt. 21:2; Jn. 11:44; *to disengage,* 1 Cor. 7:27; *to set free, set at liberty, deliver,* Lk. 13:16; *to break,* Acts 27:41; Rev. 5:2, 5; *to break up, dismiss,* Acts 13:43; *to destroy, demolish,* Jn. 2:19; Eph. 2:14; met *to infringe,* Mt. 5:19; Jn. 5:18; 7:23; *to make void, nullify,* Jn. 10:35; in NT *to declare free,* of privileges, or, in respect of lawfulness, Mt. 16:19 [3089] See *break; destroy; free; loose; untie.*

[3396] Λωΐς *Lōis* 1x *Lois,* pr. name of a woman, 2 Tim. 1:5* [3090]

[3397] Λώτ *Lōt* 4x *Lot,* pr. name, indecl., Lk. 17:28, 29, 32; 2 Pet. 2:7* [3091]

[3399] Μάαθ *Maath* 1x *Maath,* pr. name, indecl., Lk. 3:26* [3092]

[3400] Μαγαδάν *Magadan* 1x *Magadan,* pr. name, indecl., Mt. 15:39* [3093]

[3402] Μαγδαληνή *Magdalēnē* 12x *Magdalene,* pr. name (*of Magdala*), Jn. 20:18 [3094]

[3404] μαγεία *mageia* 1x pr. *the system of the magians; magic,* Acts 8:11* [3095]

[3405] μαγεύω *mageuō* 1x *to be a magician; to use magical arts, practise magic, sorcery,* Acts 8:9* [3096]

[3407] μάγος *magos* 6x. (1) *a magus, sage of the magician religion, magician, astrologer, wise man,* Mt. 2:1, 7, 16. (2) *a magician, sorcerer,* Acts 13:6, 8* [3097]

[3408] Μαγώγ *Magōg* 1x *Magog,* pr. name, indecl., Rev. 20:8* [3098]

[3409] Μαδιάμ *Madiam* 1x *Madian,* a district of Arabia Petra, Acts 7:29* [3099]

[3411] μαθητεύω *mathēteuō* 4x intrans. *to be a disciple, follow as a disciple,* Mt. 27:57; in NT trans. *to make a disciple of, to train in discipleship,* Mt. 28:19; Acts 14:21; pass. *to be trained, disciplined, instructed,* Mt. 13:52* [3100]

[3412] μαθητής *mathētēs* 261x *a disciple,* Mt. 10:24, 42, et al. [3101] See *disciple.*

[3413] μαθήτρια *mathētria* 1x *a female disciple; a female Christian,* Acts 9:36* [3102]

[3415] Μαθθάτ *Maththat* 2x also spelled Ματθάτ, *Mathat,* pr. name, indecl., Lk. 3:24, 29* [3158]

[3416] Μαθθίας *Maththias* 2x also spelled Ματθίας, *BAGD* suggest it is a shortened form of Ματταθίας, *Matthias,* pr. name, Acts 1:23, 26* [3159]

[3419] μαίνομαι *mainomai* 5x *to be disordered in mind, mad,* Jn. 10:20; Acts 12:15; 26:24, 25; 1 Cor. 14:23* [3105]

[3420] μακαρίζω *makarizō* 2x *to pronounce happy, fortunate,* Lk. 1:48; Jas. 5:11* [3106]

[3421] μακάριος *makarios* 50x *happy, blessed,* as a noun it can depict someone who receives divine favor, Mt. 5:3, 4, 5, 7; Lk. 1: 45 [3107] See *blessed; favored; fortunate; happy; privileged.*

[3422] μακαρισμός *makarismos* 3x *a happy calling, the act of pronouncing happy,* Rom. 4:6, 9; *self-congratulation,* Gal. 4:15* [3108]

[3423] Μακεδονία *Makedonia* 22x *Macedonia,* Acts 16:9; Rom. 15:26; 1 Cor. 16:5; 1 Thess. 1:7; 1 Tim. 1:3 [3109]

[3424] Μακεδών *Makedōn* 5x *a native of Macedonia,* Acts 16:9; 19:29; 27:2; 2 Cor. 9:2, 4* [3110]

[3425] μάκελλον *makellon* 1x *meat market, marketplace, slaughter house,* 1 Cor. 10:25* [3111]

[3426] μακράν *makran* 10x *far, far off, at a distance, far distant,* Mt. 8:30; Mk. 12:34; met. οἱ μακράν, *remote, alien,* Eph. 2:13, 17; so οἱ εἰς μακράν, Acts 2:39 [3112] See *distant; far.*

[3427] μακρόθεν *makrothen* 14x *far off, at a distance, from afar, from a distance,* Mk. 8:3; 11:13; preceded by ἀπό, in the same sense, Mt. 26:58 [3113]

[3428] μακροθυμέω *makrothumeō* 10x *to be slow towards, be long-enduring; to exercise patience, be long-suffering, clement,* or *indulgent, to forbear,* Mt. 18:26, 29; 1 Cor. 13:4; 1 Thess. 5:14; 2 Pet. 3:9; *to have patience, endure patiently, wait with patient expectation,* Heb. 6:15; Jas. 5:7, 8; *to bear long* with entreaties for deliverance and avengement, Lk. 18:7* [3114] See *endurance, endure; patience, (be) patient; slow to anger.*

[3429] μακροθυμία *makrothumia* 14x *patience; patient enduring of evil, fortitude,* Col. 1:11; Col. 3:12; 1 Tim. 1:16; 1 Pet. 3:20; *slowness of avenging injuries, long-suffering, forbearance, clemency,* Rom. 2:4; 9:22; 2 Cor. 6:6; Gal. 5:22; Eph. 4:2; 2 Tim. 4:2; Jas. 5:10; *patient expectation,* 2 Tim. 3:10; Heb. 6:12; 2 Pet. 3:15* [3115] See *endurance, endure; patience, (be) patient; slow to anger.*

[3430] μακροθύμως *makrothumōs* 1x *patiently,* Acts 26:3* [3116]

[3431] μακρός *makros* 4x *long;* of space, *far, distant, remote,* Lk. 15:13; 19:12; of time, *of long duration,* Mk. 12:40; Lk. 20:47* [3117]

[3432] μακροχρόνιος *makrochronios* 1x *of long duration; long-lived,* Eph. 6:3* [3118]

[3433] μαλακία *malakia* 3x *softness; listlessness, indisposition, weakness, infirmity of body,* Mt. 4:23; 9:35; 10:1* [3119]

[3434] μαλακός *malakos* 4x *soft; soft to the touch, delicate,* Mt. 11:8; Lk. 7:25; met. *an instrument of unnatural lust, effeminate,* 1 Cor. 6:9* [3120]

[3435] Μαλελεήλ *Maleleēl* 1x *Maleleel,* pr. name, indecl., Lk. 3:37* [3121]

[3436] μάλιστα *malista* 12x *most, most of all, chiefly, especially,* Acts 20:38; 25:26 [3122]

[3437] μᾶλλον *mallon* 81x *more, to a greater extent, in a higher degree,* Mt. 18:13; 27:24; Jn. 5:18; 1 Cor. 14:18; *rather, in preference,* Mt. 10:6; Eph. 4:28; used in a periphrasis for the comparative, Acts 20:35; as an intensive with a comparative term, Mt. 6:26; Mk. 7:36; 2 Cor. 7:13; Phil. 1:23; μᾶλλον δέ, *yea rather,* or, *more properly speaking,* Rom. 8:34; Gal. 4:9; Eph. 5:11 [3123] See *instead; more; rather.*

[3438] Μάλχος *Malchos* 1x *Malchus,* pr. name, Jn. 18:10* [3124]

[3439] μάμμη *mammē* 1x *a mother;* later, *a grandmother,* 2 Tim. 1:5* [3125]

[3440] μαμωνᾶς *mamōnas* 4x *wealth, riches,* Lk. 16:9, 11; personified, like the Greek Πλοῦτος, *Mammon,* Mt. 6:24; Lk. 16:13* [3126]

[3441] Μαναήν *Manaēn* 1x *Manaen,* pr. name, indecl., Acts 13:1* [3127]

[3442] Μανασσῆς *Manassēs* 3x *Manasses,* pr. name. (1) *the tribe of Manasseh,* Rev. 7:6. (2) *Manasseh, king of Judah,* Mt. 1:10* [3128]

[3443] μανθάνω *manthanō* 25x *to learn, be taught,* Mt. 9:13; 11:29; 24:32; *to learn* by practice or experience, *acquire a custom* or *habit,* Phil. 4:11; 1 Tim. 5:4, 13; *to ascertain, be informed,* Acts 23:27; *to understand, comprehend,* Rev. 14:3 [3129] See *learn.*

[3444] μανία *mania* 1x *madness, insanity,* Acts 26:24* [3130]

[3445] μάννα *manna* 4x *manna,* the miraculous food of the Israelites while in the desert, Jn. 6:31, 49; Heb. 9:4; Rev. 2:17* [3131] See *manna.*

[3446] μαντεύομαι *manteuomai* 1x *to speak oracles, to divine,* Acts 16:16* [3132]

[3447] μαραίνω *marainō* 1x *to quench, cause to decay, fade,* or *wither;* pass. *to wither, waste away,* met. *to fade away, disappear, perish,* Jas. 1:11* [3133]

[3449] μαργαρίτης *margaritēs* 9x *a pearl,* Mt. 7:6; 13:45, 46; 1 Tim. 2:9; Rev. 17:4; 18:12, 16; 21:21* [3135]

[3450] Μάρθα *Martha* 13x *Martha,* pr. name, Jn. 12:2 [3136]

[3451] Μαρία *Maria* 27x *Mary,* pr. name. (1) The mother of Jesus, Mt. 1:16; Acts 1:14. (2) *Mary,* wife of Clopas, mother of James, Mk. 15:40; Lk. 24:10; Jn. 19:25. (3) *Mary Magdalene,* Mt. 27:56; Lk. 20:18. (4) Sister of Martha and Lazarus, Lk. 10:39; Jn. 11:1; 12:3. (5) Mother of Jn. surnamed Mark, Acts 12:12 (6) A Christian at Rome, Rom. 16:6 [3137]

[3452] Μαριάμ *Mariam* 27x the indeclinable form of Μαρία [3137]

[3453] Μᾶρκος *Markos* 8x *Mark,* pr. name [3138]

[3454] μάρμαρος *marmaros* 1x *a white glistening stone; marble,* Rev. 18:12* [3139]

[3455] μαρτυρέω *martyreō* 76x trans. *to testify, depose,* Jn. 3:11, 32; 1 Jn. 1:2; Rev. 1:2; 22:20; absol. *to give evidence,* Jn. 18:23; *to bear testimony, testify,* Lk. 4:22; Jn. 1:7, 8; *to bear testimony* in confirmation, Acts 14:3; *to declare* distinctly and formally, Jn. 4:44; pass. *to be the subject of testimony, to obtain attestation* to character, Acts 6:3; 10:22; 1 Tim. 5:10; Heb. 11:2, 4; mid. equivalent to μαρτύρομαι, *to make a solemn appeal,* Acts 26:22; 1 Thess. 2:12 [3140] See *confirm; testify; witness.*

[3456] μαρτυρία *martyria* 37x judicial *evidence,* Mk. 14:55, 56, 59; Lk. 22:71; *testimony* in general, Tit. 1:13; 1 Jn. 5:9 *testimony, declaration* in a matter of fact or doctrine, Jn. 1:19; 3:11; Acts 22:18; *attestation* to character, Jn. 5:34, 36; *reputation,* 1 Tim. 3:7 [3141] See *testimony; witness.*

[3457] μαρτύριον *martyrion* 19x *testimony, evidence,* Acts 4:33; 2 Cor. 1:12; Jas. 5:3; in NT *testimony, mode of solemn declaration,* Mt. 8:4; Lk. 9:5; *testimony, matter of solemn declaration,* 1 Cor. 1:6; 2:1; 1 Tim. 2:6; σκηνὴ τοῦ μαρτυρίου, a title of the Mosaic tabernacle, Acts 7:44; Rev. 15:5 [3142] See *testimony; witness.*

[3458] μαρτύρομαι *martyromai* 5x *to call to witness;* intrans. *to make a solemn affirmation* or *declaration,* Acts 20:26; 26:22; Gal. 5:3; *to make a solemn appeal,* Eph. 4:17; 1 Thess. 2:12* [3143]

[3459] μάρτυς *martys* 35x. (1) a judicial *witness, deponent,* Mt. 18:16; Heb. 10:28. (2) generally, *a witness* to a circumstance, Lk. 24:48; Acts 10:41; in NT *a witness, a testifier,* of a doctrine, Rev. 1:5; 3:14; 11:3. (3) *a martyr,* Acts 22:20; Rev. 2:13 [3144] See *witness.*

[3460] μασάομαι *masaomai* 1x *to chew, masticate,* in NT *to gnaw,* Rev. 16:10* [3145]

[3463] μαστιγόω *mastigoō* 7x *to scourge, whip,* Mt. 10:17; 20:19; 23:34; Mk. 10:34; Lk. 18:33; Jn. 19:1; met. *to chastise,* Heb. 12:6* [3146]

[3464] μαστίζω *mastizō* 1x *to scourge,* Acts 22:25* [3147]

[3465] μάστιξ *mastix* 6x *a scourge, whip,* Acts 22:24; Heb. 11:36; met. *a scourge* of disease, Mk. 3:10; 5:29, 34; Lk. 7:21* [3148]

[3466] μαστός *mastos* 3x *the breast, pap,* Lk. 11:27; 23:29; Rev. 1:13* [3149]

[3467] ματαιολογία *mataiologia* 1x *vain talking, idle disputation,* 1 Tim. 1:6* [3150]

[3468] ματαιολόγος *mataiologos* 1x *a vain talker, given to vain talking* or *trivial disputation,* Tit. 1:10* [3151]

[3469] μάταιος *mataios* 6x *idle, ineffective, worthless,* 1 Cor. 3:20; *groundless, deceptive, fallacious,* 1 Cor. 15:17; *useless, fruitless, unprofitable,* Tit. 3:9; Jas. 1:26; from the Hebrew, *erroneous* in principle, *corrupt, perverted,* 1 Pet. 1:18; τὰ μάταια, *superstition, idolatry,* Acts 14:15* [3152]

[3470] ματαιότης *mataiotēs* 3x *vanity, folly, futility,* from the Hebrew, religious *error,* Eph. 4:17; 2 Pet. 2:18; *false religion,* Rom. 8:20* [3153]

[3471] ματαιόω *mataioō* 1x *to make vain;* from the Hebrew, pass. *to fall into religious error, to be perverted,* Rom. 1:21* [3154]

[3472] μάτην *matēn* 2x *in vain, fruitlessly, without profit,* Mt. 15:9; Mk. 7:7* [3155]

[3474] Ματθάν *Matthan* 2x *Matthan,* pr. name, indecl., Mt. 1:15 (2x)* [3157]

[3477] Ματταθά *Mattatha* 1x *Mattatha,* pr. name, indecl.; Lk. 3:31* [3160]

[3478] Ματταθίας *Mattathias* 2x see also Μαθθίας, *Mattathias,* pr. name, Lk. 3:25, 26* [3161]

[3479] μάχαιρα *machaira* 29x *a large knife, dagger; a sword,* Mt. 26:47, 51; *the sword* of the executioner, Acts 12:2; Rom. 8:35; Heb. 11:37; hence, φορεῖν μάχαιραν, *to bear the sword, to have the power of life and death,* Rom. 13:4; meton. *war,* Mt. 10:34 [3162] See *sword.*

[3480] μάχη *machē* 4x *a fight, battle, conflict;* in NT *contention, dispute, strife, controversy,* 2 Cor. 7:5; 2 Tim. 2:23; Tit. 3:9; Jas. 4:1* [3163]

[3481] μάχομαι *machomai* 4x *to fight; to quarrel,* Acts 7:26; 2 Tim. 2:24; *to contend, dispute,* Jn. 6:52; Jas. 4:2* [3164]

[3483] μεγαλεῖος *megaleios* 1x *magnificent, splendid;* τὰ μεγαλεῖα, *great things, wonderful works,* Acts 2:11* [3167]

[3484] μεγαλειότης *megaleiotēs* 3x *majesty, magnificence, glory,* Lk. 9:43; Acts 19:27; 2 Pet. 1:16* [3168]

[3485] μεγαλοπρεπής *megaloprepēs* 1x pr. *becoming a great man; magnificent, glorious, most splendid,* 2 Pet. 1:17* [3169]

[3486] μεγαλύνω *megalynō* 8x lit., *to enlarge, amplify,* Mt. 23:5; 2 Cor. 10:15; *to manifest in an extraordinary degree,* Lk. 1:58; fig., *to magnify, exalt, extol,* Lk. 1:46; Acts 5:13; Acts 10:46; 19:17; Phil. 1:20* [3170] See *exalt; magnify.*

[3487] μεγάλως *megalōs* 1x *greatly, very much, vehemently,* Phil. 4:10* [3171]

[3488] μεγαλωσύνη *megalōsynē* 3x *greatness, majesty,* Heb. 1:3; 8:1; ascribed *majesty,* Jude 25* [3172]

[3489] μέγας *megas* 243x *great, large in size,* Mt. 27:60; Mk. 4:32; *great, much, numerous,* Mk. 5:11; Heb. 11:26; *great, grown up, adult,* Heb. 11:24; *great, vehement, intense,* Mt. 2:10; 28:8; *great, sumptuous,* Lk. 5:29; *great, important, weighty, of high importance,* 1 Cor. 9:11; 13:13; *great, splendid, magnificent,* Rev. 15:3; *extraordinary, wonderful,* 2 Cor. 11:15; *great, solemn,* Jn. 7:37; 19:31; *great* in rank, *noble,* Rev. 11:18; 13:16; *great* in dignity, *distinguished, eminent, illustrious, powerful,* Mt. 5:19; 18:1, 4; *great, arrogant, boastful,* Rev. 13:5 [3173] See *great; large; loud.*

[3490] μέγεθος *megethos* 1x *greatness, vastness,* Eph. 1:19* [3174]

[3491] μεγιστάν *megistan* 3x *great men, lords, chiefs, nobles, princes,* Mk. 6:21; Rev. 6:15; 18:23* [3175]

[3493] μεθερμηνεύω *methermēneuō* 8x *to translate, interpret,* Mt. 1:23; Mk. 5:41; 15:22, 34; Jn. 1:38, 41; Acts 4:36; 13:8* [3177]

[3494] μέθη *methē* 3x *strong drink; drunkenness,* Lk. 21:34; *an indulgence in drinking,* Rom. 13:13; Gal. 5:21* [3178]

[3496] μεθίστημι *methistēmi* 5x *to cause a change of position; to remove, transport,* 1 Cor. 13:2; *to transfer,* Col. 1:13; met. *to cause to change sides;* by impl. *to pervert, mislead,* Acts 19:26; *to remove* from office, *dismiss, discard,* Lk. 16:4; Acts 13:22* [3179]

[3497] μεθοδεία *methodeia* 2x *wile, scheme, scheming, craftiness,* Eph. 4:14; 6:11* [3180]

[3499] μεθύσκω *methuskō* 5x *to inebriate, make drunk;* pass. *to be intoxicated, to be drunk,* Lk. 12:45; Eph. 5:18; 1 Thess. 5:7; Rev. 17:2; *to drink freely,* Jn. 2:10* [3182]

[3500] μέθυσος *methusos* 2x *drunken; a drunkard,* 1 Cor. 5:11; 6:10* [3183]

[3501] μεθύω *methuō* 5x *to be intoxicated, be drunk,* Mt. 24:49; Acts 2:15; 1 Cor. 11:21; 1 Thess. 5:7; Rev. 17:6* [3184]

[3505] μείζων *meizōn* 48x *greater,* comparative of μέγας [3185, 3187] See *greater; greatest.*

[3506] μέλας *melas* 6x *black,* Mt. 5:36; Rev. 6:5, 12, the form μέλαν means *ink,* 2 Cor. 3:3; 2 Jn. 12; 3 Jn. 13 [3188, 3189]

[3507] Μελεά *Melea* 1x *Melea,* indecl. pr. name, Lk. 3:31* [3190]

[3508] μέλει *melei* 10x *there is a care, it concerns,* Mt. 22:16; Acts 18:17; 1 Cor. 7:21; 9:9 [3199] See *care about; concerned.*

[3509] μελετάω *meletaō* 2x *to care for; to bestow careful thought upon, to give painful attention to, be earnest in,* 1 Tim. 4:15; *to devise,* Acts 4:25* [3191]

[3510] μέλι *meli* 4x *honey,* Mt. 3:4; Mk. 1:6; Rev. 10:9, 10* [3192]

[3514] Μελίτη *Melitē* 1x also spelled Μελιτήνη, *Malta,* an island in the Mediterranean, Acts 28:1* [3194]

[3516] μέλλω *mellō* 109x *to be about to, be on the point of,* Mt. 2:13; Jn. 4:47; it serves to express in general a settled futurity, Mt. 11:14; Lk. 9:31; Jn. 11:51; *to intend,* Lk. 10:1; participle μέλλων, μέλλουσα, μέλλον, *future* as distinguished from past and present, Mt. 12:32; Lk. 13:9; *to be always, as it were, about to do, to delay, linger,* Acts 22:16 [3195] See *about to; going to; intend to.*

[3517] μέλος *melos* 34x *a member, limb, any part of the body,* Mt. 5:29, 30; Rom. 12:4; 1 Cor. 6:15; 12:12 [3196] See *member; part.*

[3518] Μελχί *Melchi* 2x *Melchi,* pr. name, indecl., Lk. 3:24, 28* [3197]

[3519] Μελχισέδεκ *Melchisedek* 8x *Melchisedek,* pr. name, indecl., Heb. 5:6, 10; 6:20; 7:1, 10f., 15, 17* [3198]

[3521] μεμβράνα *membrana* 1x *parchment, vellum,* 2 Tim. 4:13* [3200]

[3522] μέμφομαι *memphomai* 2x *to find fault with, blame, censure; to intimate dissatisfaction with,* Heb. 8:8; absol. *to find fault,* Rom. 9:19* [3201]

[3523] μεμψίμοιρος *mempsimoiros* 1x *finding fault* or *being discontented with one's lot, querulous; a discontented, querulous person, a complainer,* Jude 16* [3202]

[3525] μέν *men* 179x a particle serving to indicate that the term or clause with which it is used stands distinguished from another, usually in a sequence, and then mostly with δέ, Mt. 3:11; 9:39; Acts 1:1; ὁ μὲν ... ὁ δέ, *this ... that, the one ... the other*, Phil. 1:16, 17; *one ... another*, οἱ μὲν ... οἱ δέ, *some ... others*, Matt 22:5; ὅλλος μὲν ... ὅλλος δέ, *one ... another*, pl. *some ... others*, Matt 13:8; 21:35; ὅλλος μὲν ... ὅλλος δέ, *one ... another*, 1 Cor. 15:39; ὧδε μὲν ... ἐκεῖ δέ, *here ... there*, Heb. 7:8; τοῦτο μὲν ... τοῦτο δέ, *partly ... partly*, Heb. 10:33 [3303]

[3527] Μεννά *Menna* 1x *Menna,* pr. name, indecl., Lk. 3:31* [**]

[3528] μενοῦν *menoun* 1x see μενοῦνγε [3304]

[3529] μενοῦνγε *menounge* 3x also spelled as two words, μενοῦν γε (Lk. 11:28), a combination of particles serving to take up what has just preceded, with either emphasize or to correct; *indeed, really, truly, rather,* Rom. 9:20; 10:18; Phil. 3:8* [3304]

[3530] μέντοι *mentoi* 8x *truly, certainly, sure,* Jn. 4:27; Jude 8 [3305]

[3531] μένω *menō* 118x pluperfect, μεμενήκειν, *to stay,* Mt. 26:38; Acts 27:31; *to continue;* 1 Cor. 7:11; 2 Tim. 2:13; *to dwell, lodge, sojourn,* Jn. 1:39; Acts 9:43; *to remain,* Jn. 9:41; *to rest, settle,* Jn. 1:32, 33; 3:36; *to last, endure,* Mt. 11:23; Jn. 6:27; 1 Cor. 3:14; *to survive,* 1 Cor. 15:6; *to be existent,* 1 Cor. 13:13; *to continue unchanged,* Rom. 9:11; *to be permanent,* Jn. 15:16; 2 Cor. 3:11; Heb. 10:34; 13:14; 1 Pet. 1:23; *to persevere, be constant, be steadfast,* 1 Tim. 2:15; 2 Tim. 3:14; *to abide, to be in close and settled union,* Jn. 6:56; 14:10; 15:4; *to indwell,* Jn. 5:38; 1 Jn. 2:14; trans. *to wait for,* Acts 20:5, 23 [3306] See *abide; await; remain; stay; wait for.*

[3532] μερίζω *merizō* 14x *to divide; to divide out, distribute,* Mk. 6:41; *to assign, bestow,* Rom. 12:3; 1 Cor. 7:17; 2 Cor. 10:13; Heb. 7:2; mid. *to share,* Lk. 12:13; pass. *to be subdivided, to admit distinctions,* Mk. 3:24-26; 1 Cor. 1:13; *to be severed* by discord, *be at variance,* Mt. 12:25, 26; *to differ,* 1 Cor. 7:34* [3307] See *assign; divide.*

[3533] μέριμνα *merimna* 6x *care,* Mt. 13:22; Mk. 4:19; Lk. 8:14; 21:34; *anxiety, anxious interest,* 2 Cor. 11:28; 1 Pet. 5:7* [3308] See *anxiety; concern; worry.*

[3534] μεριμνάω *merimnaō* 19x *to be anxious,* or *solicitous,* Phil. 4:6; *to expend careful thought,* Mt. 6:27, 28, 31, 34a; 10:19; Lk. 10:41; 12:11, 22, 25, 26; *to concern one's self,* Mt. 6:25; 1 Cor. 12:25; *to have the thoughts occupied with,* 1 Cor. 7:32, 33, 34; *to feel an interest in,* Phil. 2:20* [3309] See *concerned; worry.*

[3535] μερίς *meris* 5x *a part; a division* of a country, *district, region, tract,* Acts 16:12; *a portion,* Lk. 10:42; *an* allotted *portion,* Col. 1:12; *a portion* in common, *share,* Acts 8:21; 2 Cor. 6:15* [3310]

[3536] μερισμός *merismos* 2x *a dividing, act of dividing,* Heb. 4:12; *distribution, gifts distributed,* Heb. 2:4* [3311]

[3537] μεριστής *meristēs* 1x *a divider, arbitrator,* Lk. 12:14* [3312]

[3538] μέρος *meros* 42x *a part, portion, division,* of a whole, Lk. 11:36; 15:12; Acts 5:2; Eph. 4:16; *a piece, fragment,* Lk. 24:42; Jn. 19:23; *a party, faction,* Acts 23:9; allotted *portion, lot, destiny,* Mt. 24:51; Lk. 12:46; *a calling, craft,* Acts 19:27; *a* partner's *portion, partnership, fellowship,* Jn. 13:8; pl. μέρη, a local *quarter, district, region,* Mt. 2:22; 16:13; Acts 19:1; Eph. 4:9; *side* of a ship, Jn. 21:6; ἐν μέρει, *in respect,* 2 Cor. 3:10; 9:3; Col. 2:16; 1 Pet. 4:16; μέρος τι, *partly, in some part,* 1 Cor. 11:18; ἀνὰ μέρος, *alternately, one after another,* 1 Cor. 14:27; ἀπὸ μέρους, *partly, in some part* or *measure,* 2 Cor. 1:14; ἐκ μέρους, *individually,* 1 Cor. 12:27; *partly, imperfectly,* 1 Cor. 13:9; κατὰ μέρος, *particularly, in detail,* Heb. 9:5 [3313] See *place; region; share.*

[3540] μεσημβρία *mesēmbria* 2x *mid-day, noon,* Acts 22:6; meton. *the south,* Acts 8:26* [3314]

[3541] μεσιτεύω *mesiteuō* 1x *to mediate; to intervene, interpose, guarantee,* Heb. 6:17* [3315]

[3542] μεσίτης *mesitēs* 6x *one that acts between two parties; a mediator, one who interposes to reconcile two adverse parties,* 1 Tim. 2:5; *an arbitrator, one who is the medium of communication between two parties, a mid-party,* Gal. 3:19, 20; Heb. 8:6; 9:15; 12:24* [3316] See *mediator.*

[3543] μεσονύκτιον *mesonyktion* 4x *midnight,* Mk. 13:35; Acts 16:25; 20:7* [3317]

[3544] Μεσοποταμία *Mesopotamia* 2x *Mesopotamia,* the country lying between the rivers Tigris and Euphrates, Acts 2:9; 7:2* [3318]

[3545] μέσος *mesos* 58x *mid, middle,* Mt. 25:6; Acts 26:13; ἀνὰ μέσον, *in the midst;* from the Hebrew, *in, among,* Mt. 13:25; *between,* 1 Cor. 6:5; διὰ μέσου, *through the midst of,* Lk. 4:30; εἰς τὸ μέσον, *into,* or *in the midst,* Mk. 3:3; Lk. 6:8; ἐκ μέσου, *from the midst, out of the way,* Col. 2:14; 2 Thess. 2:7; from the Hebrew, *from, from among,* Mt. 13:49; ἐν τῷ μέσῳ, *in the midst,* Mt. 10:16; *in the midst, in public, publicly,* Mt. 14:6 ἐν μέσῳ, *in the midst of; among,* Mt. 18:20; κατὰ μέσον τῆς νυκτός, *about midnight,* Acts 27:27 [3319] See *among; middle.*

[3546] μεσότοιχον *mesotoichon* 1x *a middle wall; a partition wall, a barrier,* Eph. 2:14* [3320]

[3547] μεσουράνημα *mesouranēma* 3x *the mid-heaven, mid-air,* Rev. 8:13; 14:6; 19:17* [3321]

[3548] μεσόω *mesoō* 1x *to be in the middle* or *midst; to be advanced midway,* Jn. 7:14* [3322]

[3549] Μεσσίας *Messias* 2x *the Messiah, the Anointed One,* i.q. ὁ Χριστός, Jn. 1:42, 4:25* [3323]

[3550] μεστός *mestos* 9x *full, full of, filled with,* Jn. 19:29; 21:11; *replete,* Mt. 23:28; Rom. 1:29; 15:14; Jas. 3:8, 17; 2 Pet. 2:14* [3324]

[3551] μεστόω *mestoō* 1x *to fill;* pass. *to be filled, be full,* Acts 2:13* [3325]

[3552] μετά *meta* 469x. (1) gen., *with, together with,* Mt. 16:27; 12:41; 26:55; *with, on the same side* or *party with, in aid of,* Mt. 12:30; 20:20; *with, by means of,* Acts 13:17; *with,* of conflict, Rev. 11:7; *with, among,* Lk. 24:5; *with, to, towards,* Lk. 1:58, 72.

(2) acc., *after,* of place, *behind,* Heb. 9:3; of time, *after,* Mt. 17:1; 24:29; followed by an infin. with the neut. article, *after, after that,* Mt. 26:32; Lk. 22:20 [3326]

[3553] μεταβαίνω *metabainō* 12x *to go* or *pass from one place to another,* Jn. 5:24; *to pass away, be removed,* Mt. 17:20; *to go away, depart,* Mt. 8:34 [3327] See *depart; leave; pass on.*

[3554] μεταβάλλω *metaballō* 1x *to change;* mid. *to change one's mind,* Acts 28:6* [3328]

[3555] μετάγω *metagō* 2x *to lead* or *move from one place to another; to change direction, turn about,* Jas. 3:3, 4* [3329]

[3556] μεταδίδωμι *metadidōmi* 5x *to give a part, to share,* Lk. 3:11; *to impart, bestow,* Rom. 1:11; 12:8; Eph. 4:28; 1 Thess. 2:8* [3330]

[3557] μετάθεσις *metathesis* 3x *a removal, translation,* Heb. 11:5; 12:27; *a transmutation, transformation, change by the abolition of one thing, and the substitution of another,* Heb. 7:12* [3331]

[3558] μεταίρω *metairō* 2x *to remove, transfer;* in NT intrans. *to go away, depart,* Mt. 13:53; 19:1* [3332]

[3559] μετακαλέω *metakaleō* 4x *to call from one place into another;* mid. *to call* or *send for, invite to come to oneself,* Acts 7:14; 10:32; 20:17; 24:25* [3333]

[3560] μετακινέω *metakineō* 1x *to move away, remove;* pass. met. *to stir away from, to swerve,* Col. 1:23* [3334]

[3561] μεταλαμβάνω *metalambanō* 7x *to partake of, share in,* Acts 2:46; 27:33f.; 2 Tim. 2:6; Heb. 6:7; 12:10; *to get, obtain, find,* Acts 24:25* [3335]

[3562] μετάλημψις *metalēmpsis* 1x *a partaking of, a being partaken of,* 1 Tim. 4:3* [3336]

[3563] μεταλλάσσω *metallassō* 2x *to exchange, change for* or *into, transmute,* Rom. 1:25, 26* [3337]

[3564] μεταμέλομαι *metamelomai* 6x *to change one's judgment on past points of conduct; to change one's mind and purpose,* Heb. 7:21; *to repent, regret,* Mt. 21:29, 32; 27:3; 2 Cor. 7:8* [3338]

[3565] μεταμορφόω *metamorphoō* 4x *to change the external form, transfigure;* mid. *to change one's form, be transfigured,* Mt. 17:2; Mk. 9:2; *to undergo a* spiritual *transformation* Rom. 12:2; 2 Cor. 3:18* [3339] See *transfigure; transform.*

[3566] μετανοέω *metanoeō* 34x *to undergo a change in frame of mind and feeling, to repent,* Lk. 17:3, 4; *to make a change of principle and practice, to reform,* Mt. 3:2 [3340] See *repent, repentance; turn.*

[3567] μετάνοια *metanoia* 22x *a change of mode of thought and feeling, repentance,* Mt. 3:8; Acts 20:21; 2 Tim. 2:25; practical *reformation,* Lk. 15:7; *reversal* of the past, Heb. 12:17 [3341] See *repent, repentance; turn.*

[3568] μεταξύ *metaxy* 9x can function as an improper prep., *between,* Mt. 23:35; Lk. 11:51; 16:26; Acts 15:9; ἐν τῷ μεταξύ, sc. χρόνῳ, *in the meantime, meanwhile,* Jn. 4:31; in NT ὁ μεταξύ, *following, succeeding,* Acts 13:42 [3342]

[3569] μεταπέμπω *metapempō* 9x *to send after;* mid. *to send after* or *for* any one, *invite to come to* *one's self,* Acts 10:5, 22, 29; 11:13; 20:1; 24:24, 26; 25:3* [3343]

[3570] μεταστρέφω *metastrephō* 2x *to turn about; convert* into something else, *change,* Acts 2:20; by impl. *to pervert,* Gal. 1:7* [3344]

[3571] μετασχηματίζω *metaschēmatizō* 5x *to remodel, transfigure,* Phil. 3:21; mid. *to transform one's self,* 2 Cor. 11:13, 14, 15; *to transfer* an imagination, 1 Cor. 4:6* [3345]

[3572] μετατίθημι *metatithēmi* 6x *to transport,* Acts 7:16; *to transfer,* Heb. 7:12; *to translate* out of the world, Heb. 11:5; met. *to transfer* to other purposes, *to pervert,* Jude 4; mid. *to transfer one's self, to change over,* Gal. 1:6* [3346]

[3573] μετατρέπω *metatrepō* 1x *to turn around, change, alter,* Jas. 4:9* [3344]

[3575] μετέπειτα *metepeita* 1x *afterwards,* Heb. 12:17* [3347]

[3576] μετέχω *metechō* 8x *to share in, partake,* 1 Cor. 9:10, 12; 10:17, 21; 1 Cor. 10:30; Heb. 2:14; 5:13; *to be a member of,* Heb. 7:13* [3348] See *partake; share.*

[3577] μετεωρίζομαι *meteōrizomai* 1x *to raise aloft;* met. *to unsettle in mind;* pass. *to be excited with anxiety, be in anxious suspense, worry,* Lk. 12:29* [3349]

[3578] μετοικεσία *metoikesia* 4x *change of abode* or *country, migration,* Mt. 1:11, 12, 17* [3350]

[3579] μετοικίζω *metoikizō* 2x *to cause to change abode, cause to emigrate,* Acts 7:4, 43* [3351]

[3580] μετοχή *metochē* 1x *a sharing, partaking; communion, fellowship,* 2 Cor. 6:14* [3352]

[3581] μέτοχος *metochos* 6x *a partaker,* Heb. 3:1, 14; 6:4; 12:8; *an associate, partner, fellow,* Lk. 5:7; Heb. 1:9* [3353]

[3582] μετρέω *metreō* 11x *to allot, measure,* Mt. 7:2; Mk. 4:24; Lk. 6:38; Rev. 11:1, 2; 21:15-17; met. *to estimate,* 2 Cor. 10:12* [3354] See *measure.*

[3583] μετρητής *metrētēs* 1x pr. *a measurer;* also, *metretes,* Latin *metreta,* equivalent to the Attic ἀμφορεύς, i.e., three-fourths of the Attic μέδιμνος, and therefore equal to about nine gallons, Jn. 2:6* [3355]

[3584] μετριοπαθέω *metriopatheō* 1x *to moderate one's passions; to be gentle, compassionate,* Heb. 5:2* [3356]

[3585] μετρίως *metriōs* 1x *moderately; slightly;* οὐ μετρίως *no little, not a little, much, greatly,* Acts 20:12* [3357]

[3586] μέτρον *metron* 14x *measure,* Mt. 7:2; Mk. 4:24; Lk. 6:38; Rev. 21:17; *measure, standard,* Eph. 4:13; *extent, compass,* 2 Cor. 10:13; allotted *measure, specific portion,* Rom. 12:3; Eph. 4:7, 16; ἐκ μέτρον, *by measure, with definite limitation,* Jn. 3:34 [3358] See *measure.*

[3587] μέτωπον *metōpon* 8x *forehead, front,* Rev. 7:3; 9:4; 13:16; 14:1, 9; 17:5; 20:4; 22:4* [3359]

[3588] μέχρι *mechri* 17x improper prep. and a conj (*until*), can also spelled μέχρις, *unto, even to,* Rom. 15:19; of time, *until, till,* Mt. 11:23; Mk. 13:30 [3360]

[3590] μή *mē* 1,042x a negative particle, *not.* (1) Particle, *not,* Mt. 18:25; Mk. 3:9; Col 2:21. (2) Conj., *lest,* Mt. 5:29, 30; 18:10; 24:6; Mk. 13:36. (3) interogative particle indicating the speaker expects a negative answer, μή, μήτι, or μήποτε, Mt. 12:23; 1 Cor. 12:29-30. (4) οὐ μή strengthens the negation, Mt. 5:18, 20; 10:23; 10:42. For the particulars of its usage, especially as distinguished from that of οὐ, consult a grammar [3361]

[3592] μηδαμῶς *mēdamōs* 2x *by no means,* Acts 10:14; 11:8* [3365]

[3593] μηδέ *mēde* 56x negative disjunctive particle, can function as an adverb and a conj, *neither,* and repeated, *neither-nor,* Mt. 6:25; 7:6; 10:9, 10; *not even, not so much as,* Mk. 2:2 [3366]

[3594] μηδείς *mēdeis* 90x *not one, none, no one,* Mt. 8:4 [3367]

[3595] μηδέποτε *mēdepote* 1x *not at any time, never,* 2 Tim. 3:7* [3368]

[3596] μηδέπω *mēdepō* 1x *not yet, not as yet,* Heb. 11:7* [3369]

[3597] Μῆδος *Mēdos* 1x *a Mede, a native of Media* in Asia, Acts 2:9* [3370]

[3600] μηκέτι *mēketi* 22x *no more, no longer,* Mk. 1:45; 2:2 [3371]

[3601] μῆκος *mēkos* 2x *length,* Eph. 3:18; Rev. 21:16* [3372]

[3602] μηκύνω *mēkynō* 1x *to lengthen, prolong;* mid. *to grow up,* as plants, Mk. 4:27* [3373]

[3603] μηλωτή *mēlōtē* 1x *a sheepskin,* Heb. 11:37* [3374]

[3604] μήν *mēn* 18x *a month,* Lk. 1:24, 26, 36, 56; in NT *the new moon, the day of the new moon,* Gal. 4:10 [3375] See *month.*

[3606] μηνύω *mēnyō* 4x *to disclose* what is secret, Jn. 11:57; Acts 23:30; 1 Cor. 10:28; *to declare, indicate,* Lk. 20:37* [3377]

[3607] μήποτε *mēpote* 25x *never, in order that...not;* can function as an adverb, *BAGD* lists it as a negative part., conj., and interrogative part., same signif. and usage as μή, Mt. 4:6; 13:15; Heb. 9:17; also, *whether,* Lk. 3:15 [3379]

[3609] μήπω *mēpō* 2x *not yet, not as yet,* Rom. 9:11; Heb. 9:8* [3380]

[3611] μηρός *mēros* 1x *the thigh,* Rev. 19:16* [3382]

[3612] μήτε *mēte* 34x *neither;* μήτε ... μήτε, or μὴ ... μήτε, or μηδὲ ... μητέ, *neither ... nor,* Mt. 5:34, 35, 36; Acts 23:8; 2 Thess. 2:2; in NT also equivalent to μηδέ, *not even, not so much as,* Mk. 3:20 [3383]

[3613] μήτηρ *mētēr* 83x *a mother,* Mt. 1:18; 12:49, 50, et al. freq.; *a parent* city, Gal. 4:26; Rev. 17:5 [3384] See *mother.*

[3614] μήτι *mēti* 18x interrogative particle, used in questions expecting a negative answer, often left untranslated; has the same use as μή in the form εἰ μήτε, Lk. 9:3; also when prefixed to an interrogative clause, Mt. 7:16; Jn. 4:29 [3385, 3387]

[3616] μήτρα *mētra* 2x *the womb,* Lk. 2:23; Rom. 4:19* [3388]

[3618] μητρολῴας *mētrolōas* 1x *one who murders* or *strikes his mother, matricide,* 1 Tim. 1:9* [3389]

[3620] μιαίνω *miainō* 5x pr. *to tinge, dye, stain; to pollute, defile,* ceremonially, Jn. 18:28; *to corrupt, deprave,* Tit. 1:15 (2x); Heb. 12:15; Jude 8* [3392]

[3621] μίασμα *miasma* 1x *pollution,* moral *defilement, corruption, 2 Pet. 2:20** [3393]

[3622] μιασμός *miasmos* 1x *pollution, corruption, defiling,* 2 Pet. 2:10* [3394]

[3623] μίγμα *migma* 1x *a mixture,* Jn. 19:39* [3395]

[3624] μίγνυμι *mignymi* 4x also spelled μείγνυμι, *to mix, mingle,* Mt. 27:34; Lk. 13:1; Rev. 8:7 [3396]

[3625] μικρός *mikros* 46x *little, small* in size quantity, etc. Mt. 13:32; Lk. 12:32; Rev. 3:8; *small, little* in age, *young, not adult,* Mk. 15:40; *little, short* in time, Jn. 7:33; μικρόν, sc. χρόνον, *a little while, a short time,* Jn. 13:33; μετὰ μικρόν, *after a little while, a little while afterwards,* Mt. 26:73; *little* in number, Lk. 12:32; *small, little in dignity, low, humble,* Mt. 10:42; 11:11; μικρόν, as an adv., *little, a little,* Mt. 26:39 [3397, 3398] See *insignificant; little; small.*

[3626] Μίλητος *Milētos* 3x *Miletus,* a seaport city of Caria, on the west coast of Asia Minor, Acts 20:15, 17; 2 Tim. 4:20* [3399]

[3627] μίλιον *milion* 1x *a Roman mile,* which contained *mille passuum,* 1000 paces, or 8 stadia, 4,854 feet, Mt. 5:41* [3400]

[3628] μιμέομαι *mimeomai* 4x *to imitate, follow* as an example, *strive to resemble,* 2 Thess. 3:7, 9; Heb. 13:7; 3 Jn. 11* [3401] See *imitate, imitator.*

[3629] μιμητής *mimētēs* 6x *an imitator, follower,* 1 Cor. 4:16; 11:1; Eph. 5:1; 1 Thess. 1:6; 2:14; Heb. 6:12* [3402] See *imitate, imitator.*

[3630] μιμνῄσκομαι *mimnēskomai* 23x *to remember, recollect, call to mind,* Mt. 26:75; Lk. 1:54, 72; 16:25; in NT, in a passive sense, *to be called to mind, be borne in mind,* Acts 10:31; Rev. 16:19 [3403] See *remember.*

[3631] μισέω *miseō* 40x *to hate, regard with ill-will,* Mt. 5:43, 44; 10:22; *to detest, abhor,* Jn. 3:20; Rom. 7:15; in NT *to regard with less affection, love less, esteem less,* Mt. 6:24; Lk. 14:26 [3404] See *hate.*

[3632] μισθαποδοσία *misthapodosia* 3x pr. *the discharge of wages; requital; reward,* Heb. 10:35; 11:26; *punishment,* Heb. 2:2* [3405]

[3633] μισθαποδότης *misthapodotēs* 1x *a bestower of remuneration; recompenser, rewarder,* Heb. 11:6* [3406]

[3634] μίσθιος *misthios* 2x *hired;* as a subst., *a hired servant, hireling,* Lk. 15:17, 19* [3407]

[3635] μισθός *misthos* 29x *hire, wages,* Mt. 20:8; Jas. 5:4; *reward,* Mt. 5:12, 46; 6:1, 2, 5, 16; *punishment,* 2 Pet. 2:13 [3408] See *reward; wage.*

[3636] μισθόω *misthoō* 2x *to hire out, let out to hire;* mid. *to hire,* Mt. 20:1, 7* [3409]

[3637] μίσθωμα *misthōma* 1x *hire, rent;* in NT *a hired dwelling,* Acts 28:30* [3410]

[3638] μισθωτός *misthōtos* 3x *a hireling,* Mk. 1:20; Jn. 10:12, 13* [3411]

[3639] Μιτυλήνη *Mitylēnē* 1x *Mitylene,* the capital city of Lesbos, in the Aegean sea, Acts 20:14* [3412]

[3640] Μιχαήλ *Michaēl* 2x *Michael, the archangel,* indecl., Jude 9; Rev. 12:7* [3413]

[3641] μνᾶ *mna* 9x Latin *mina; a weight,* equivalent to 100 drachmas; also *a sum,* equivalent to 100 drachmas and the sixtieth part of a talent, Lk. 19:13, 16, 18, 20, 24f.* [3414]

[3643] Μνάσων *Mnasōn* 1x *Mnason,* pr. name, Acts 21:16* [3416]

[3644] μνεία *mneia* 7x *remembrance, recollection,* Phil. 1:3; 1 Thess. 3:6; 2 Tim. 1:3; *mention;* μνείαν ποιεῖσθαι, *to make mention,* Rom. 1:9; Eph. 1:16; 1 Thess. 1:2; Phlm. 4* [3417]

[3645] μνῆμα *mnēma* 8x pr. *a memorial, monument; a tomb, sepulchre,* Mk. 5:3, 5; Lk. 8:27; 23:53; 24:1; Acts 2:29; 7:16; Rev. 11:9* [3418]

[3646] μνημεῖον *mnēmeion* 40x *monument, memorial,* Lk. 11:47; *grave, tomb,* Mt. 23:39; Mk. 5:2; Lk. 11:44; Jn. 11:17, 31, 38; Acts 13:29 [3419] See *grave; tomb.*

[3647] μνήμη *mnēmē* 1x *remembrance, recollection, memory;* μνήμην ποιεῖσθαι, *to make mention,* 2 Pet. 1:15* [3420]

[3648] μνημονεύω *mnēmoneuō* 21x *to remember, recollect, call to mind,* Mt. 16:9; Lk. 17:32; Acts 20:31; *to be mindful of, to fix the thoughts upon,* Heb. 11:15; *to make mention, mention, speak of,* Heb. 11:22 [3421] See *remember.*

[3649] μνημόσυνον *mnēmosynon* 3x *a record, memorial,* Acts 10:4; honorable *remembrance,* Mt. 26:13; Mk. 14:9* [3422]

[3650] μνηστεύω *mnēsteuō* 3x *to ask in marriage; to betroth;* pass. *to be betrothed, engaged,* Mt. 1:18; Lk. 1:27; 2:5* [3423]

[3652] μογιλάλος *mogilalos* 1x *having an impediment in one's speech, speaking with difficulty, a stammerer,* Mk. 7:32* [3424]

[3653] μόγις *mogis* 1x *with difficulty, scarcely, hardly,* Lk. 9:39* [3425]

[3654] μόδιος *modios* 3x *a modius,* a Roman measure for things dry, containing 16 sextarii, and equivalent to about *a peck* (8.75 liters); in NT *a corn measure,* Mt. 5:15; Mk. 4:21; Lk. 11:33* [3426]

[3655] μοιχαλίς *moichalis* 7x *an adulteress,* Rom. 7:3; Jas. 4:4; by meton., *an adulterous appearance, lustful significance,* 2 Pet. 2:14; from the Hebrew, spiritually *adulterous, faithless, ungodly,* Mt. 12:39; 16:4; Mk. 8:38* [3428]

[3656] μοιχάω *moichaō* 4x act., *to cause to commit adultery,* pass., *to commit* or *be guilty of adultery,* Mt. 5:32; 19:9; Mk. 10:11f.* [3429]

[3657] μοιχεία *moicheia* 3x *adultery,* Mt. 15:19; Mk. 7:22; Jn. 8:3* [3430]

[3658] μοιχεύω *moicheuō* 15x trans. *to commit adultery with, debauch,* Mt. 5:28; absol. and mid. *to commit adultery,* Mt. 5:27; Jn. 8:4; *to commit* spiritual *adultery, be guilty of idolatry,* Rev. 2:22 [3431] See *adultery; commit adultery.*

[3659] μοιχός *moichos* 3x *an adulterer,* Lk. 18:11; 1 Cor. 6:9; Heb. 13:4* [3432]

[3660] μόλις *molis* 6x *with difficulty, scarcely, hardly,* Acts 14:18; 27:7, 8, 16; Rom. 5:7; 1 Pet. 4:18* [3433]

[3661] Μολόχ *Moloch* 1x *Moloch,* pr. name, indecl., Acts 7:43* [3434]

[3662] μολύνω *molynō* 3x pr. *to stain, sully; to defile, contaminate* morally, 1 Cor. 8:7; Rev. 14:4; *to soil,* Rev. 3:4* [3435]

[3663] μολυσμός *molysmos* 1x *pollution, defilement,* 2 Cor. 7:1* [3436]

[3664] μομφή *momphē* 1x *a complaint, cause* or *ground of complaint,* Col. 3:13* [3437]

[3665] μονή *monē* 2x *a stay in any place; an abode, dwelling, mansion,* Jn. 14:2, 23* [3438]

[3666] μονογενής *monogenēs* 9x *only-begotten, only-born,* Lk. 7:12; 8:42; 9:38; Heb. 11:17; *only-begotten* in respect of peculiar generation, *unique,* Jn. 1:14, 18; 3:16, 18; 1 Jn. 4:9* [3439]

[3667] μόνον *monon* 70x the accusative singular form of *monos* (*3668*) used as an adverb meaning *only, alone* [3331] See *only.*

[3668] μόνος *monos* 44x *without accompaniment, alone,* Mt. 14:23; 18:15; Lk. 10:40; *singly existent, sole, only,* Jn. 17:3; *lone solitary,* Jn. 8:29; 16:32; *alone* in respect of restriction, *only,* Mt. 4:4; 12:4; *alone* in respect of circumstances, *only,* Lk. 24:18; *not multiplied by reproduction, lone, barren,* Jn. 12:24 [3332] See *alone; only.*

[3669] μονόφθαλμος *monophthalmos* 2x *one-eyed; deprived of an eye,* Mt. 18:9; Mk. 9:47* [3442]

[3670] μονόω *monoō* 1x *to leave alone;* pass. *to be left alone, be lone,* 1 Tim. 5:5* [3443]

[3671] μορφή *morphē* 3x *form, outward appearance,* Mk. 16:12; Phil. 2:6, 7* [3444] See *form; nature.*

[3672] μορφόω *morphoō* 1x *to give shape to, mold, fashion,* Gal. 4:19* [3445]

[3673] μόρφωσις *morphōsis* 2x pr. *a shaping, molding;* in NT *external form, appearance,* 2 Tim. 3:5; a settled *form,* prescribed *system,* Rom. 2:20* [3446]

[3674] μοσχοποιέω *moschopoieō* 1x *to form an image of a calf,* Acts 7:41* [3447]

[3675] μόσχος *moschos* 6x pr. *a tender branch, shoot; a young animal; a calf, young bull,* Lk. 15:23, 27, 30; Heb. 12:19; Rev. 4:7* [3448]

[3676] μουσικός *mousikos* 1x pr. *devoted to the arts of the Muses; a musician;* in NT, perhaps, *a singer,* Rev. 18:22* [3451]

[3677] μόχθος *mochthos* 3x *wearisome labor, toil, travail,* 2 Cor. 11:27; 1 Thess. 2:9; 2 Thess. 3:8* [3449]

[3678] μυελός *myelos* 1x *marrow,* Heb. 4:12* [3452]

[3679] μυέω *myeō* 1x *to initiate, instruct* in the sacred mysteries; in NT pass. *to be disciplined* in a practical lesson, *to learn* a lesson, Phil. 4:12* [3453]

[3680] μῦθος *mythos* 5x *a word, speech, a tale; a fable, figment,* 1 Tim. 1:4; 4:7; 2 Tim. 4:4; Tit. 1:14; 2 Pet. 1:16* [3454] See *myth.*

[3681] μυκάομαι *mykaomai* 1x *to low, bellow,* as a bull; also, *to roar,* as a lion, Rev. 10:3* [3455]

[3682] μυκτηρίζω *myktērizō* 1x *to contract the nose in contempt and derision, toss up the nose; to mock, deride,* Gal. 6:7* [3456]

[3683] μυλικός *mylikos* 1x *of a mill, belonging to a mill,* Lk. 17:2* [3457]

[3684] μύλινος *mylinos* 1x *belonging to a mill,* Rev. 18:21* [3458]

[3685] μύλος *mylos* 4x *a millstone,* Mt. 18:6; 24:41; Mk. 9:42; Rev. 18:22* [3458]

[3688] Μύρα *Myra* 1x neuter plural, *Myra,* a city of Lycia, Acts 27:5* [3460]

[3689] μυριάς *myrias* 8x *a myriad, ten thousand,* Acts 19:19; indefinitely, *a vast multitude,* Lk. 12:1; Acts 21:20; Heb. 12:22; Jude 14; Rev. 5:11; 9:16* [3461]

[3690] μυρίζω *myrizō* 1x *to anoint,* Mk. 14:8* [3462]

[3691] μύριοι *myrioi* 1x indefinitely, *a great number*; specifically, μύριοι, *a myriad, ten thousand,* Mt. 18:24* [3463]

[3692] μυρίος *myrios* 2x *innumerable,* 1 Cor. 4:15; 14:19* [3463]

[3693] μύρον *myron* 14x pr. *aromatic juice which distills from trees; ointment, unguent,* usually perfumed, Mt. 26:7, 12; Mk. 14:3, 4 [3464] See *ointment; perfume.*

[3695] Μυσία *Mysia* 2x *Mysia,* a province of Asia Minor, Acts 16:7f.* [3465]

[3696] μυστήριον *mystērion* 28x *a matter to the knowledge of which initiation is necessary; a secret* which would remain such but for revelation, Mt. 3:11; Rom. 11:25; Col. 1:26; *a concealed power* or *principle,* 2 Thess. 2:7; *a hidden meaning* of a symbol, Rev. 1:20: 17:7 [3466] See *mystery; secret.*

[3697] μυωπάζω *myōpazō* 1x pr. *to close the eyes, contract the eyelids, wink; to be nearsighted, partially blinded, slow to understand,* 2 Pet. 1:9* [3467]

[3698] μώλωψ *mōlōps* 1x *the mark of a blow; a stripe, a wound,* 1 Pet. 2:24* [3468]

[3699] μωμάομαι *mōmaomai* 2x *to find fault with, censure, blame,* 2 Cor. 8:20; passively, 2 Cor. 6:3* [3469]

[3700] μῶμος *mōmos* 1x *blame, ridicule; a disgrace* to society, *a stain,* 2 Pet. 2:13* [3470]

[3701] μωραίνω *mōrainō* 4x *to be foolish, to play the fool;* in NT trans. *to make foolish, convict of folly,* 1 Cor. 1:20; pass. *to be convicted of folly, to incur the character of folly,* Rom. 1:22; *to be rendered insipid,* Mt. 5:13; Lk. 14:34* [3471]

[3702] μωρία *mōria* 5x *foolishness,* 1 Cor. 1:18, 21, 23; 2:14; 3:19* [3472]

[3703] μωρολογία *mōrologia* 1x *foolish talk,* Eph. 5:4* [3473]

[3704] μωρός *mōros* 12x pr. *dull; foolish,* Mt. 7:26; 23:17; 25:2f., 8; 1 Cor. 1:25, 27; 3:18; 4:10; 2 Tim.

2:23; Tit. 3:9; from the Hebrew, *a fool* in senseless wickedness, Mt. 5:22* [3474] See *fool; foolish.*

[3707] Μωϋσῆς *Mōysēs* 80x also spelled Μωσῆς, *Moses,* pr. name, Mt. 8:4; Jn. 1:17; Rom. 5:14 [3475]

[3709] Ναασσών *Naassōn* 3x *Naasson,* pr. name, indecl., Mt. 1:4; Lk. 3:32* [3476]

[3710] Ναγγαί *Nangai* 1x *Naggai, Nagge,* pr. name, indecl., Lk. 3:25* [3477]

[3711] Ναζαρά *Nazara* 2x see Ναζαρέθ, Mt. 4:13; Lk. 4:16* [3478]

[3714] Ναζαρέθ *Nazareth* 6x an indeclinable form, *Nazareth,* is spelled Ναζαρέτ (4x) and Ναζαρά (2x) [3478]

[3715] Ναζαρέτ *Nazaret* 4x see Ναζαρέθ, Mt. 2:23; Mk. 1:9; Jn. 1:45, 46* [3478]

[3716] Ναζαρηνός *Nazarēnos* 6x *an inhabitant of Nazareth,* Mk. 1:24; 10:47; 4:67; 16:6; Lk. 4:34; 24:19* [3479]

[3717] Ναζωραῖος *Nazōraios* 13x also spelled Ναζαρηνός, *a Nazarite; an inhabitant of Nazareth,* Mt. 2:23; 26:71; Lk. 18:37; Jn. 18:5, 7; 19:19; Acts 2:22; 3:6; 4:10; 6:14; 22:8; 24:5; 26:9* [3480]

[3718] Ναθάμ *Natham* 1x also spelled Ναθάν, *Nathan,* pr. name, indecl., Lk. 3:31* [3481]

[3720] Ναθαναήλ *Nathanaēl* 6x *Nathanael,* pr. name, indecl., Jn. 1:45-49; 21:2 [3482]

[3721] ναί *nai* 33x a particle, used to strengthen an affirmation, *certainly,* Rev. 22:20; to make an affirmation, or express an assent, *yea, yes,* Mt. 5:37; Acts 5:8 [3483]

[3722] Ναιμάν *Naiman* 1x also spelled Νεεμάν, *Naaman,* pr. name, indecl., Lk. 4:27* [3497]

[3723] Ναΐν *Nain* 1x *Nain,* a town of Palestine, indecl., Lk. 7:11* [3484]

[3724] ναός *naos* 45x pr. *a dwelling; the dwelling* of a deity, *a temple,* Mt. 26:61; Acts 7:48; used figuratively of individuals, Jn. 2:19; 1 Cor. 3:16; spc. *the cell of a temple;* hence, *the Holy Place* of the Temple of Jerusalem, Mt. 23:35; Lk. 1:9; *a model of a temple, a shrine,* Acts 19:24 [3485] See *temple.*

[3725] Ναούμ *Naoum* 1x *Naum,* pr. name, indecl., Lk. 3:25* [3486]

[3726] νάρδος *nardos* 2x *spikenard,* a species of aromatic plant with grassy leaves and a fibrous root, of which the best and strongest grows in India; in NT *oil of spikenard,* an oil extracted from the plant, which was highly prized and used as an ointment either pure or mixed with other substances, Mk. 14:3; Jn. 12:3* [3487]

[3727] Νάρκισσος *Narkissos* 1x *Narcissus,* pr. name, Rom. 16:11* [3488]

[3728] ναυαγέω *nauageō* 2x *to make shipwreck, be shipwrecked,* 2 Cor. 11:25; 1 Tim. 1:19* [3489]

[3729] ναύκληρος *nauklēros* 1x *the master* or *owner of a ship,* Acts 27:11* [3490]

[3730] ναῦς *naus* 1x *a ship, vessel,* Acts 27:41* [3491]

[3731] ναύτης *nautēs* 3x *sailor, seaman,* Acts 27:27, 30; Rev. 18:17* [3492]

[3732] Ναχώρ *Nachōr* 1x *Nachor,* pr. name, indecl., Lk. 3:34* [3493]

[3733] νεανίας *neanias* 3x *a young man, youth,* Acts 20:9; 23:17; used of *one who is in the prime of life,* Acts 7:58* [3494]

[3734] νεανίσκος *neaniskos* 11x *a young man, youth,* Mk. 14:51; 16:5; used of *one in the prime of life,* Mt. 19:20, 22; νεανίσκοι, *soldiers,* Mk. 14:51 [3495] See *young man.*

[3735] Νέα πόλις *Neapolis* 1x *Neapolis,* a city of Thrace on the Strymonic gulf, Acts 16:11* [3496]

[3738] νεκρός *nekros* 128x *dead, without life,* Mt. 11:5; 22:31; met. νεκρός τινι, *dead to a thing, no longer devoted to,* or *under the influence of a thing,* Rom. 6:11; *dead* in respect of fruitlessness, Jas. 2:17, 20, 26; morally or spiritually *dead,* Rom. 6:13; Eph. 5:14; *dead* in alienation from God, Eph. 2:1, 5; Col. 2:13; *subject to death, mortal,* Rom. 8:10; *causing death and misery, fatal, having a destructive power,* Heb. 6:1; 9:14 [3498] See *dead.*

[3739] νεκρόω *nekroō* 3x pr. *to put to death, kill;* in NT met. *to deaden, mortify,* Col. 3:5; pass. *to be rendered impotent,* Rom. 4:19; Heb. 11:12* [3499]

[3740] νέκρωσις *nekrōsis* 2x pr. *a putting to death; dying, abandonment to death,* 2 Cor. 4:10; *deadness, impotency,* Rom. 4:19* [3500]

[3741] νεομηνία *neomēnia* 1x *new moon, first of the month,* Col. 2:16* [3561]

[3742] νέος *neos* 24x *recent, new, fresh,* Mt. 9:17; 1 Cor. 5:7; Col. 3:10; Heb. 12:24; *young, youthful,* Tit.

2:4. In Acts 16:11 is used in the name Νέαν πόλις, which some lexicons list as its own lexical form. This occurrence is not included in the word's frequency count. [3501] See *young.*

[3744] νεότης *neotēs* 4x *youth,* Mt. 19:20 [3503]

[3745] νεόφυτος *neophytos* 1x *newly* or *recently planted* met. *a neophyte, one newly implanted* into the Christian Church, *a new convert,* 1 Tim. 3:6* [3504]

[3748] νεύω *neuō* 2x *to nod; to intimate by a nod* or *significant gesture,* Jn. 13:24; Acts 24:10* [3506]

[3749] νεφέλη *nephelē* 25x *a cloud,* Mt. 17:5; 24:30; 26:64 [3507] See *cloud.*

[3750] Νεφθαλίμ *Nephthalim* 3x *Nephthalim,* pr. name, indecl., Mt. 4:13, 15; Rev. 5:6* [3508]

[3751] νέφος *nephos* 1x *a cloud;* trop. *a cloud, a throng* of persons, Heb. 12:1* [3509]

[3752] νεφρός *nephros* 1x *a kidney;* pl. νεφροί, *the kidneys, the reins* regarded as a seat of desire and affection, Rev. 2:23* [3510]

[3753] νεωκόρος *neōkoros* 1x pr. *one who sweeps* or *cleanses a temple;* generally, *one who has the charge of a temple;* in NT *a devotee* city, as having specially dedicated a temple to some deity, Acts 19:35* [3511]

[3754] νεωτερικός *neōterikos* 1x *juvenile, natural to youth, youthful,* 2 Tim. 2:22* [3512]

[3755] νή *nē* 1x *by, BAGD* calls it a "particle of strong affirmation," and is followed by the person or thing (in the acc) by which the person swears, *by,* 1 Cor. 15:31* [3513]

[3756] νήθω *nēthō* 2x *to spin,* Mt. 6:28; Lk. 12:27* [3514]

[3757] νηπιάζω *nēpiazō* 1x *to be childlike,* 1 Cor. 14:20* [3515]

[3758] νήπιος *nēpios* 15x pr. *not speaking,* Latin *infans; an infant, babe, child,* Mt. 21:16; 1 Cor. 13:11; *one below the age of manhood, a minor,* Gal. 4:1; met. *a babe* in knowledge, *unlearned, simple,* Mt. 11:25; Rom. 2:20 [3516] See *child; infant.*

[3759] Νηρεύς *Nēreus* 1x *Nereus,* pr. name, Rom. 16:15* [3517]

[3760] Νηρί *Nēri* 1x *Neri,* pr. name, indecl., Lk. 3:27* [3518]

[3761] νησίον *nēsion* 1x *a small island,* Acts 27:16* [3519]

[3762] νῆσος *nēsos* 9x *an island,* Acts 13:6; 27:26 [3520]

[3763] νηστεία *nēsteia* 5x *fasting, want of food,* 2 Cor. 6:5; 11:27; *a fast,* religious *abstinence from food,* Mt. 17:21; Lk. 2:37; spc. *the annual public fast of the Jews, the great day of atonement,* occurring in the month Tisri, corresponding to the new moon of October, Acts 27:9* [3521]

[3764] νηστεύω *nēsteuō* 20x *to fast,* Mt. 4:2; 6:16, 17, 18; 9:15 [3522] See *fast.*

[3765] νῆστις *nēstis* 2x can also be masc. with a gen. in ιδος (n-3c[2]), *fasting, hungry,* Mt. 15:32; Mk. 8:3* [3523]

[3767] νηφάλιος *nēphalios* 3x *somber, temperate, abstinent in respect to wine,* etc.; in NT met., *vigilant, circumspect, self-controlled,* 1 Tim. 3:2, 11; Tit. 2:2* [3524]

[3768] νήφω *nēphō* 6x *to be sober, not intoxicated;* in NT met., *to be vigilant, circumspect,* 1 Thess. 5:6, 8 [3525]

[3769] Νίγερ *Niger* 1x *Niger,* pr. name, probably not declined, Acts 13:1* [3526]

[3770] Νικάνωρ *Nikanōr* 1x *Nicanor,* pr. name, Acts 6:5* [3527]

[3771] νικάω *nikaō* 28x *to conquer, overcome, vanquish, subdue,* Lk. 1:22; Jn. 16:33; absol. *to overcome, prevail,* Rev. 5:5; *to come off superior* in a judicial cause, Rom. 3:4 [3528] See *overcome; (be) victorious.*

[3772] νίκη *nikē* 1x *victory;* meton. *a victorious principle,* 1 Jn. 5:4* [3529]

[3773] Νικόδημος *Nikodēmos* 5x *Nicodemus,* pr. name, Jn. 3:1, 4, 9; 7:50; 19:39* [3530]

[3774] Νικολαΐτης *Nikolaitēs* 2x *a Nicolaitan,* or follower of Nicolaus, a heresy of the Apostolic age, Rev. 2:6, 15* [3531]

[3775] Νικόλαος *Nikolaos* 1x *Nicolaus,* pr. name, Acts 6:5* [3532]

[3776] Νικόπολις *Nikopolis* 1x *Nicopolis,* a city of Macedonia, Tit. 3:12* [3533]

[3777] νῖκος *nikos* 4x *victory,* Mt. 12:20; 1 Cor. 15:54, 55, 57* [3534]

[3780] Νινευίτης *Nineuitēs* 3x *a Ninevite, an inhabitant of Nineveh,* Mt. 12:41; Lk. 11:30, 32* [3536]

[3781] νιπτήρ *niptēr* 1x *a basin* for washing some part of the person, Jn. 13:5* [3537]

[3782] νίπτω *niptō* 17x *to wash;* spc. *to wash* some part of the person, as distinguished from λούω, Mt. 6:17; Jn. 13:8 [3538] See *wash.*

[3783] νοέω *noeō* 14x *to perceive, observe; to mark* attentively, Mt. 24:15; Mk. 13:14; 2 Tim. 2:7; *to understand, comprehend,* Mt. 15:17; *to conceive,* Eph. 3:20 [3539] See *reflect on; see; understand.*

[3784] νόημα *noēma* 6x *the mind, the understanding, intellect,* 2 Cor. 3:14; 4:4; Phil. 4:7; *the heart, soul, affections, feelings, disposition,* 2 Cor. 11:3; *a conception of the mind, thought, purpose, device,* 2 Cor. 2:11; 10:5* [3540]

[3785] νόθος *nothos* 1x *spurious, bastard,* Heb. 12:8* [3541]

[3786] νομή *nomē* 2x *pasture, pasturage,* Jn. 10:9; ἔχειν νομήν, *to eat its way, spread corrosion,* 2 Tim. 2:17* [3542]

[3787] νομίζω *nomizō* 15x *to own as settled and established; to deem,* 1 Cor. 7:26; 1 Tim. 6:5; *to suppose, presume,* Mt. 5:17; 20:10; Lk. 2:44; *to be usual, customary,* Acts 16:13 [3543] See *think; suppose.*

[3788] νομικός *nomikos* 9x *pertaining to law; relating to the* Mosaic *law,* Tit. 3:9; as a subst., *one skilled in law, a jurist, lawyer,* Tit. 3:13; spc. *an interpreter and teacher of the* Mosaic *law,* Mt. 22:35 [3544]

[3789] νομίμως *nomimōs* 2x *lawfully, agreeably to law* or *custom, rightfully,* 1 Tim. 1:8; 2 Tim. 2:5* [3545]

[3790] νόμισμα *nomisma* 1x pr. *a thing sanctioned by law* or *custom; lawful money, coin,* Mt. 22:19* [3546]

[3791] νομοδιδάσκαλος *nomodidaskalos* 3x *a teacher and interpreter of the* Mosaic *law,* Lk. 5:17; Acts 5:34; 1 Tim. 1:7 [3547]

[3792] νομοθεσία *nomothesia* 1x *legislation;* ἡ νομοθεσία, *the gift of the* Divine *law,* or *the* Mosaic *law* itself, Rom. 9:4* [3548]

[3793] νομοθετέω *nomotheteō* 2x *to impose a law, give laws;* in NT pass., *to have a law imposed on one's self, receive a law,* Heb. 7:11; *to be enacted, constituted,* Heb. 8:6* [3549]

[3794] νομοθέτης *nomothetēs* 1x *a legislator, lawgiver,* Jas. 4:12* [3550]

[3795] νόμος *nomos* 194x *a law,* Rom. 4:15; 1 Tim. 1:9; *the* Mosaic *law,* Mt. 5:17, et al. freq.; *the Old Testament Scripture,* Jn. 10:34; *a legal tie,* Rom. 7:2, 3; *a law, a rule, standard,* Rom. 3:27; *a rule* of life and conduct, Gal. 6:2, Jas. 1:25 [3551] See *law.*

[3796] νοσέω *noseō* 1x *to be sick;* met. *to have a diseased appetite* or *craving for* a thing, *have an excessive and vicious fondness for* a thing, 1 Tim. 6:4* [3552]

[3798] νόσος *nosos* 11x *a disease, sickness, distemper,* Mt. 4:23, 24; 8:17; 9:35 [3554] See *illness; sickness.*

[3799] νοσσιά *nossia* 1x *a brood* of young birds, Lk. 13:34* [3555]

[3800] νοσσίον *nossion* 1x *the young of birds, a chick;* pl. *a brood* of young birds, Mt. 23:37* [3556]

[3801] νοσσός *nossos* 1x also spelled νεοσσός, *the young of birds, a young bird, chick,* Lk. 2:24* [3502]

[3802] νοσφίζω *nosphizō* 3x *to deprive, rob;* mid. *to misappropriate; to make secret reservation,* Acts 5:2, 3; *to purloin,* Tit. 2:10* [3557]

[3803] νότος *notos* 7x *the south wind,* Lk. 12:55; Acts 27:13; 28:13; meton. *the south, the southern quarter of the heavens,* Mt. 12:42; Lk. 11:31; 13:29; Rev. 21:13* [3558]

[3804] νουθεσία *nouthesia* 3x *warning, admonition,* 1 Cor. 10:11; Eph. 6:4; Tit. 3:10* [3559]

[3805] νουθετέω *noutheteō* 8x pr. *instruct; to admonish, warn,* Acts 20:31; Rom. 15:14 [3560] See *admonish; warn.*

[3807] νουνεχῶς *nounechōs* 1x *understandingly, sensibly, discreetly,* Mk. 12:34* [3562]

[3808] νοῦς *nous* 24x *the mind, intellect,* 1 Cor. 14:15, 19; *understanding, intelligent faculty,* Lk. 24:45; *intellect, judgment,* Rom. 7:23, 25; *opinion, sentiment,* Rom. 14:5; 1 Cor. 1:10; *mind, thought, conception,* Rom. 11:34; 1 Cor. 2:16; Phil. 4:7; *settled state of mind,* 2 Thess. 2:2; *frame of mind,* Rom. 1:28; 12:2; Col. 2:18; Eph. 4:23; 1 Tim. 6:5; 2 Tim. 3:8; Tit. 1:15 [3563] See *intellect; mind; understanding.*

[3811] νύμφη *nymphē* 8x *a bride,* Jn. 3:29; Rev. 18:23; 21:2, 9; 22:17; opposed to πενθερά, *a daughter-in-law,* Mt. 10:35; Lk. 12:53* [3565] See *bride.*

[3812] νυμφίος *nymphios* 16x *a bridegroom,* Mt. 9:15; 25:1, 5, 6, 10 [3566] See *bridegroom.*

[3813] νυμφών *nymphōn* 3x *a bridal-chamber;* in NT υἱοὶ τοῦ νυμφῶνος, *sons of the bridal-chamber, the bridegroom's attendant friends, groomsmen,* Mt. 9:15; Mk. 2:19; Lk. 5:34* [3567]

[3814] νῦν *nyn* 147x *now, at the present time,* Mk. 10:30; Lk. 6:21, et al. freq.; *just now,* Jn. 11:8; *forthwith,* Jn. 12:31; καὶ νῦν, *even now, as matters stand,* Jn. 11:22; *now,* expressive of a marked tone of address, Acts 7:34; 13:11; Jas. 4:13; 5:1; τὸ νῦν, *the present time,* Lk. 1:48; τανῦν, or τὰ νῦν, *now,* Acts 4:29 [3568] See *now; present time.*

[3815] νυνί *nyni* 20x of time, *now, at this very moment,* an emphatic form of νῦν although it now carries the same meaning [3570] See *now.*

[3816] νύξ *nyx* 61x *night,* Mt. 2:14; 28:13; Jn. 3:2; met. spiritual *night,* moral *darkness,* Rom. 13:12; 1 Thess. 5:5 [3571] See *night.*

[3817] νύσσω *nyssō* 1x *to prick* or *pierce,* Jn. 19:34* [3572] See *pierce.*

[3818] νυστάζω *nystazō* 2x *to nod; to nod in sleep; to sink into a sleep,* Mt. 25:5; *to slumber* in inactivity, 2 Pet. 2:3* [3573]

[3819] νυχθήμερον *nychthēmeron* 1x *a day and night, twenty-four hours,* 2 Cor. 11:25* [3574]

[3820] Νῶε *Nōe* 8x *Noah,* pr. name, indecl., Mt. 24:37ff; Lk. 3:36; 17:26f.; Heb. 11:7; 1 Pet. 3:20; 2 Pet. 2:25* [3575]

[3821] νωθρός *nōthros* 2x *slow, sluggish, lazy,* Heb. 5:11; 6:12* [3576]

[3822] νῶτος *nōtos* 1x *the back* of men or animals, Rom. 11:10* [3577]

[3825] ξενία *xenia* 2x pr. *state of being a guest;* then, *the reception of a guest* or *stranger, hospitality,* in NT *a lodging,* Acts 28:23; Phlm. 22* [3578]

[3826] ξενίζω *xenizō* 10x *to receive as a guest, entertain,* Acts 10:23; 28:7; Heb. 13:2; pass. *to be entertained as a guest, to lodge* or *reside with,* Acts 10:6, 18, 32; 21:16; *to strike with a feeling of strangeness, to surprise;* pass. or mid. *to be struck with surprise, be staggered, be amazed,* 1 Pet. 4:4, 12; intrans. *to be strange;* ξενίζοντα, *strange matters, novelties,* Acts 17:20* [3579] See *entertain; show hospitality; strange(r); (be) surprised.*

[3827] ξενοδοχέω *xenodocheō* 1x *to receive and entertain strangers, exercise hospitality,* 1 Tim. 5:10* [3580]

[3828] ξένος *xenos* 14x *strange, foreign, alien,* Eph. 2:12, 19; *strange, unexpected, surprising,* 1 Pet. 4:12; *novel,* Heb. 13:9; subst. *a stranger,* Mt. 25:35, et al.; *a host,* Rom. 16:23 [3581] See *alien; foreign(er); host; strange(r).*

[3829] ξέστης *xestēs* 1x *a sextarius,* a Roman measure, containing about one pint English; in NT used for *a small vessel, cup, pot,* Mk. 7:4* [3582]

[3830] ξηραίνω *xērainō* 15x *to dry up, parch,* Jas. 1:11; pass. *to be parched,* Mt. 13:6, et al.; *to be ripened* as corn, Rev. 14:15; *to be withered, to wither,* Mk. 11:20; of parts of the body, *to be withered,* Mk. 3:1, 3; *to pine,* Mk. 9:18 [3583] See *dry up; scorch; wither.*

[3831] ξηρός *xēros* 8x *dry, withered,* Lk. 23:31; ἡ ξηρά, sc. γῆ, *the dry land, land,* Mt. 23:15; Heb. 11:29; of parts of the body, *withered,* Mt. 12:10 [3584]

[3832] ξύλινος *xylinos* 2x *wooden, of wood, made of wood,* 2 Tim. 2:20; Rev. 9:20* [3585]

[3833] ξύλον *xylon* 20x *wood, timber,* 1 Cor. 3:12; Rev. 18:12; *stocks,* Acts 16:24; *a club,* Mt. 26:47, 55; *a post, cross, gibbet,* Acts 5:30; 10:29; 13:29; *a tree,* Lk. 23:31; Rev. 2:7 [3586] See *club; stocks; tree; wood.*

[3834] ξυράω *xyraō* 3x *to cut off the hair, shear, shave,* Acts 21:24; 1 Cor. 11:5, 6* [3587]

[3836] ὁ *ho* 19,867x the prepositive article, answering, to a considerable extent, to the English definite article; but, for the principle and facts of its usage, consult a grammar; ὁ μὲν ... ὁ δέ, *the one ... the other,* Phil. 1:16, 17; Heb. 7:5, 6, 20, 21, 23, 24; pl. *some ... others,* Mt. 13:23; 22:5, 6; ὁ δέ, *but he,* Mt. 4:4; 12:48; οἱ δέ, *but others,* Mt. 28:17; used, in a poetic quotation, for a personal pronoun, Acts 17:28 [3588, 5120]

[3837] ὀγδοήκοντα *ogdoēkonta* 2x indecl. numeral, *eighty,* Lk. 2:37; 16:7* [3589]

[3838] ὄγδοος *ogdoos* 5x *the eighth,* Lk. 1:59; Acts 7:8; 2 Pet. 2:5; Rev. 17:11; 21:20* [3590]

[3839] ὄγκος *onkos* 1x pr. *bulk, weight; a burden, impediment,* Heb. 12:1* [3591]

[3840] ὅδε *hode* 10x *this, that, he, she, it,* Lk. 10:39; 16:25; Acts 15:23 [3592]

[3841] ὁδεύω *hodeuō* 1x *to journey, travel,* Lk. 10:33* [3593]

[3842] ὁδηγέω *hodēgeō* 5x *to lead, guide,* Mt. 15:14; Lk. 6:39; Rev. 7:17; met. *to instruct, teach,* Jn. 16:13; Acts 8:31* [3594]

[3843] ὁδηγός *hodēgos* 5x *a guide, leader,* Acts 1:16; met. *an instructor, teacher,* Mt. 15:14; 23:16, 24; Rom. 2:19* [3595]

[3844] ὁδοιπορέω *hodoiporeō* 1x *to journey, travel,* Acts 10:9* [3596]

[3845] ὁδοιπορία *hodoiporia* 2x *to journey, journeying, travel,* Jn. 4:6; 2 Cor. 11:26* [3597]

[3847] ὁδός *hodos* 101x *a way, road,* Mt. 2:12; 7:13, 14; 8:28; 22:9, 10; *means of access, approach, entrance,* Jn. 14:6; Heb. 9:8; *direction, quarter, region,* Mt. 4:15; 10:5 *the act of journeying, a journey, way, course,* Mt. 10:10; Mk. 2:23; 1 Thess. 3:11; *a journey,* as regards extent, Acts 1:12; met. *a way,* systematic *course* of pursuit, Lk. 1:79; Acts 2:28; 16:17; *a way,* systematic *course* of action or conduct, Mt. 21:32; Rom. 11:33; 1 Cor. 4:17; *a way, system of doctrine,* Acts 18:26; ἡ ὁδός, *the way of the Christian faith,* Acts 19:9, 23, 24:22 [3598] See *journey; path; road; way.*

[3848] ὀδούς *odous* 12x *a tooth,* Mt. 5:38; 8:12 [3599] See *tooth.*

[3849] ὀδυνάω *odynaō* 4x *to pain* either bodily or mentally; pass. *to be in an agony, be tormented,* Lk. 2:48; 16:24, 25; *to be distressed, grieved,* Acts 20:38* [3600]

[3850] ὀδύνη *odynē* 2x *pain* of body of mind; *sorrow, grief,* Rom. 9:2; 1 Tim. 6:10* [3601]

[3851] ὀδυρμός *odyrmos* 2x *bitter lamentation, wailing,* Mt. 2:18; meton. *sorrow, mourning,* 2 Cor. 7:7* [3602]

[3852] Ὀζίας *Ozias* 2x *Uzziah,* pr. name, indeclinable, Lk. 3:23ff.* [3604]

[3853] ὄζω *ozō* 1x *to smell, emit an odor; to have an offensive smell, stink,* Jn. 11:39* [3605]

[3854] ὅθεν *hothen* 15x *whence,* Mt. 12:44; Acts 14:26; *from the place where,* Mt. 25:24, 26; *whence, from which circumstance,* 1 Jn. 2:18; *wherefore, whereupon,* Mt. 14:7 [3606]

[3855] ὀθόνη *othonē* 2x pr. *fine linen; a linen cloth; a sheet,* Acts 10:11; 11:5* [3607]

[3856] ὀθόνιον *othonion* 5x *a linen cloth;* in NT *a swath, bandage* for a corpse, Lk. 24:12 [3608]

[3857] οἶδα *oida* 318x *to know,* Mt. 6:8; *to know how,* Mt. 7:11; from the Hebrew, *to regard with favor,* 1 Thess. 5:12. οἶδα is actually a perfect form functioning as a present, and ᾔδειν is actually a pluperfect form functioning as an aorist. [1492] See *understand.*

[3858] οἰκεῖος *oikeios* 3x *belonging to a house, domestic;* pl. *members of a family, immediate kin,* 1 Tim. 5:8; *members of* a spiritual *family,* Eph. 2:19; *members of a* spiritual *brotherhood,* Gal. 6:10* [3609]

[3859] οἰκετεία *oiketeia* 1x *the members, of a household,* Mt. 24:45* [2322]

[3860] οἰκέτης *oiketēs* 4x pr. *an inmate of a house; a domestic servant, household slave,* Lk. 16:13; Acts 10:7; Rom. 14:4; 1 Pet. 2:18* [3610]

[3861] οἰκέω *oikeō* 9x *to dwell in, inhabit,* 1 Tim. 6:16; intrans. *to dwell, live; to cohabit,* 1 Cor. 7:12, 13; *to be indwelling, indwell,* Rom. 7:17, 18, 20; 8:9, 11; 1 Cor. 3:16* [3611]

[3862] οἴκημα *oikēma* 1x *a dwelling;* used in various conventional senses, and among them, *a prison, cell,* Acts 12:7* [3612]

[3863] οἰκητήριον *oikētērion* 2x *a habitation, dwelling, an abode,* Jude 6; trop. *the* personal *abode* of the soul, 2 Cor. 5:2* [3613]

[3864] οἰκία *oikia* 93x *a house, dwelling, an abode,* Mt. 2:11; 7:24, 27; trop. *the* bodily *abode* of the soul, 2 Cor. 5:1; meton. *a household, family,* Mt. 10:13; 12:25; meton. *goods, property, means,* Mt. 23:13 [3614] See *house.*

[3865] οἰκιακός *oikiakos* 2x *belonging to a house;* pl. *the members of a household* or *family, kindred,* Mt. 10:25, 36* [3615]

[3866] οἰκοδεσποτέω *oikodespoteō* 1x pr. *to be master of a household; to occupy one's self in the management of a household,* 1 Tim. 5:14* [3616]

[3867] οἰκοδεσπότης *oikodespotēs* 12x *the master* or *head of a house* or *family,* Mt. 10:25; 13:27, 52 [3617] See *landowner; master; owner.*

[3868] οἰκοδομέω *oikodomeō* 40x pluperfect, ᾠκοδόμητο (3 sg), *to build a house; to build,* Mt. 7:24; *to repair, embellish, and amplify* a building, Mt. 23:29; *to construct, establish,* Mt. 16:18; met. *to contribute to advancement* in religious knowledge, *to edify,* 1 Cor. 14:4, 17; *to advance* a person's spiritual condition, *to edify,* 1 Cor. 8:1; pass. *to make spiritual* advancement, *be edified,* Acts 9:31; *to advance* in presumption, 1 Cor. 8:10 [3618] See *edify; strengthen.*

[3869] οἰκοδομή *oikodomē* 18x pr. *the act of building; a building, structure,* Mt. 24:1; in NT *a* spiritual *structure,* as instanced in the Christian body, 1 Cor. 3:9; Eph. 2:21; religious *advancement, edification,* Rom. 14:19; 1 Cor. 14:3 [3619] See *building, building up; edification.*

[3871] οἰκοδόμος *oikodomos* 1x *a builder, architect,* Acts 4:11* [3618]

[3872] οἰκονομέω *oikonomeō* 1x *to manage a household; to manage the affairs* of any one, *be steward,* Lk. 16:2* [3621]

[3873] οἰκονομία *oikonomia* 9x pr. *the management of a household; a stewardship,* Lk. 16:2, 3, 4; in NT *an* apostolic *stewardship, a* ministerial *commission* in the publication and furtherance of the Gospel, 1 Cor. 9:17; 3:2; Col. 1:25; or, *an arranged plan, a scheme,* Eph. 1:10; *a due discharge of a commission,* 1 Tim. 1:4, Eph. 3:9* [3622]

[3874] οἰκονόμος *oikonomos* 10x *the manager of a household; a steward,* Lk. 12:42; 16:1, 3, 8; 1 Cor. 4:2; *a manager, trustee,* Gal. 4:2; *a* public *steward, treasurer,* Rom. 16:23; *a* spiritual *steward, the holder of a commission* in the service of the Gospel, 1 Cor. 4:1; Tit. 1:7; 1 Pet. 4:10* [3623] See *manager; steward.*

[3875] οἶκος *oikos* 114x *a house, dwelling,* Mt. 9:6, 7; Mk. 2:1, 11; 3:20; *place of abode, seat, site,* Mt. 23:38; Lk. 13:35; met. *a* spiritual *house* or *structure,* 1 Pet. 2:5; meton. *a household, family,* Lk. 10:5; 11:17; *a* spiritual *household,* 1 Tim. 3:15; Heb. 3:6; *family, lineage,* Lk. 1:27, 69; 2:4; from the Hebrew, *a people, nation,* Mt. 10:6; 15:24 [3624] See *family; house; temple.*

[3876] οἰκουμένη *oikoumenē* 15x some list as a participle, *the habitable earth, world,* Matt 24:14; Rom. 10:18; Heb. 1:6; used, however, with various restrictions of meaning, according to the context, Lk. 2:1; Acts 17:6; meton. *the inhabitants of the earth, the whole human race, mankind,* Acts 17:31; 19:27; Rev. 3:10. Some view this word as a participial form of οἰκέω. [3625] See *humankind; inhabited earth.*

[3877] οἰκουργός *oikourgos* 1x *one who is occupied in domestic affairs,* Tit. 2:5* [3626]

[3880] οἰκτιρμός *oiktirmos* 5x *compassion; kindness,* in relieving sorrow and want, Phil. 2:1; Col. 3:12; Heb. 10:28; *favor, grace, mercy,* Rom. 12:1; 2 Cor. 1:3* [3628]

[3881] οἰκτίρμων *oiktirmōn* 3x *compassionate, merciful,* Lk. 6:36; Jas. 5:11* [3629]

[3882] οἰκτίρω *oiktirō* 2x also spelled οἰκτείρω, *to have compassion on, exercise grace* or *favor towards,* Rom. 9:15* [3627]

[3884] οἰνοπότης *oinopotēs* 2x *wine-drinking;* in a bad sense, *a wine-bibber, drunkard,* Mt. 11:19; Lk. 7:34* [3630]

[3885] οἶνος *oinos* 34x *wine,* Mt. 9:17; Mk. 2:22; meton. *the vine and its clusters,* Rev. 6:6 met. οἶνος, *a potion,* οἶνος τοῦ θυμοῦ, *a potion of passion,* Rev. 14:8, 10; 16:19; 17:2, 18:3 [3631] See *wine.*

[3886] οἰνοφλυγία *oinophlygia* 1x *drunkenness,* 1 Pet. 4:3* [3632]

[3887] οἴομαι *oiomai* 3x *to think, suppose, imagine, presume,* Jn. 21:25; Phil. 1:17. οἰέσθω in Jas. 1:7 formed from the contracted form οἶμαι* [3633]

[3888] οἷος *hoios* 14x *what, of what kind* or *sort, as,* Mt. 24:21; Mk. 9:3; οὐχ, οἷον, *not so as, not as implying,* Rom. 9:6 [3634]

[3890] ὀκνέω *okneō* 1x *to be slow; to delay, hesitate,* Acts 9:38* [3635]

[3891] ὀκνηρός *oknēros* 3x *slow; slothful, indolent, idle,* Mt. 25:26; Rom. 12:11; *tedious, troublesome,* Phil. 3:1* [3636]

[3892] ὀκταήμερος *oktaēmeros* 1x *on the eighth day,* Phil. 3:5* [3637]

[3893] ὀκτώ *oktō* 8x *eight,* Lk. 2:21; 9:28 [3638]

[3897] ὄλεθρος *olethros* 4x *perdition, destruction,* 1 Cor. 5:5, 1 Thess. 5:3; 2 Thess. 1:9; 1 Tim. 6:9* [3639]

[3898] ὀλιγοπιστία *oligopistia* 1x *littleness* or *imperfectness of faith,* Mt. 17:20* [570]

[3899] ὀλιγόπιστος *oligopistos* 5x *scant of faith, of little faith, one whose faith is small and weak,* Mt. 6:30; 8:26; 14:31; 16:18; Lk. 12:28* [3640]

[3900] ὀλίγος *oligos* 40x *little, small,* in number, etc.; pl. *few,* Mt. 7:14; 9:37; 20:16; Lk. 13:23; δι' ὀλίγων, sc. λόγων, *in a few words, briefly,* 1 Pet. 5:12; *little* in time, *short, brief,* Acts 14:28; Rev. 12:12; πρὸς ὀλίγον, sc. χρόνον, *for a short time, for a little while,* Jas. 4:14; *little, small, light,* etc., in magnitude, amount, etc., Lk. 7:47; Acts 12:18; 15:2; ἐν ὀλίγῳ, *concisely, briefly,* Eph. 3:3; *almost,* Acts 26:28, 29 [3641] See *few; little; short; small.*

[3901] ὀλιγόψυχος *oligopsychos* 1x *fainthearted,* 1 Tim. 5:14* [3642]

[3902] ὀλιγωρέω *oligōreō* 1x *to neglect, regard slightly, make light of, despise,* Heb. 12:5* [3643]

[3903] ὀλίγως *oligōs* 1x *little, scarcely,* 2 Pet. 2:18* [3689]

[3904] ὀλοθρευτής *olothreutēs* 1x *a destroyer,* 1 Cor. 10:10* [3644]

[3905] ὀλοθρεύω *olothreuō* 1x also spelled ὀλεθρεύω, *to destroy, cause to perish,* Heb. 11:28* [3645]

[3906] ὁλοκαύτωμα *holokautōma* 3x *a holocaust, whole burnt-offering,* Mk. 12:33; Heb. 10:6, 8* [3646]

[3907] ὁλοκληρία *holoklēria* 1x *perfect soundness,* Acts 3:16* [3647]

[3908] ὁλόκληρος *holoklēros* 2x *whole, having all its parts, sound, perfect, complete in every part;* in NT *the whole,* 1 Thess. 5:23; morally, *perfect, faultless, blameless,* Jas. 1:4* [3648]

[3909] ὀλολύζω *ololyzō* 1x pr. *to cry aloud in invocation; to howl, utter cries of distress, lament, bewail,* Jas. 5:1* [3649]

[3910] ὅλος *holos* 109x *all, whole, entire,* Mt. 1:22; 4:23, 24 [3650] See *all; whole.*

[3911] ὁλοτελής *holotelēs* 1x *complete; all, the whole,* 1 Thess. 5:23* [3651]

[3912] Ὀλυμπᾶς *Olympas* 1x *Olympas,* pr. name, Rom. 16:15* [3652]

[3913] ὄλυνθος *olynthos* 1x *an unripe* or *unseasonable fig,* such as, shaded by the foliage, does not ripen at the usual season, but hangs on the trees during winter, Rev. 6:13* [3653]

[3914] ὅλως *holōs* 4x *wholly, altogether; actually, really,* 1 Cor. 5:1; 6:7; 15:29; with a negative, *at all,* Mt. 5:34* [3654]

[3915] ὄμβρος *ombros* 1x *rain, a storm of rain,* Lk. 12:54* [3655]

[3916] ὁμείρομαι *homeiromai* 1x also spelled ἱμείρομαι, *to desire earnestly, have a strong affection for,* 1 Thess. 2:8* [2442]

[3917] ὁμιλέω *homileō* 4x *to be in company with, associate with; to converse with, talk with,* Lk. 24:14, 15; Acts 20:11; 24:26* [3656]

[3918] ὁμιλία *homilia* 1x *intercourse, communication, converse,* 1 Cor. 15:33* [3657]

[3920] ὁμίχλη *homichlē* 1x *a mist, fog, a cloud,* 2 Pet. 2:17* [**]

[3921] ὄμμα *omma* 2x *the eye,* Mt. 20:34; Mk. 8:23* [3659]

[3923] ὀμνύω *omnyō* 26x *to swear,* Mt. 5:34; *to promise with an oath,* Mk. 6:23; Acts 2:30; 7:17 [3660] See *swear.*

[3924] ὁμοθυμαδόν *homothumadon* 11x *with one mind, with one accord, unanimously,* Acts 1:14; Rom. 15:6; *together, at once, at the same time,* Acts 2:1, 46; 4:24 [3661] See *together; unanimous.*

[3926] ὁμοιοπαθής *homoiopathēs* 2x *being affected in the same way* as another, *subject to the same incidents, of like infirmities, subject to the same frailties and evils,* Acts 14:15; Jas. 5:17* [3663]

[3927] ὅμοιος *homoios* 45x *like, similar, resembling,* Mt. 11:16; 13:31, 33, 44, 45, 47, 52; Jn. 8:55, et al. freq.; *like, of similar drift and force,* Mt. 22:39 [3664] See *like, liken; similar.*

[3928] ὁμοιότης *homoiotēs* 2x *likeness, similitude,* Heb. 4:15; 7:15* [3665]

[3929] ὁμοιόω *homoioō* 15x *to make like, cause to be like* or *resemble, assimilate;* pass. *to be made like, become like, resemble,* Mt. 6:8; 13:24; 18:23; *to liken, compare,* Mt. 7:24, 26; 11:16 [3666] See *compare; like, liken; similar.*

[3930] ὁμοίωμα *homoiōma* 6x pr. *that which is conformed* or *assimilated; form, shape, figure,* Rev. 9:7; *likeness, resemblance, similitude,* Rom. 1:23; 5:14; 6:5; 8:3; Phil. 2:7* [3667] See *image; liken; similarity.*

[3931] ὁμοίως *homoiōs* 30x *likewise, in a similar manner,* Mt. 22:26; 27:41 [3668] See *likewise; similar.*

[3932] ὁμοίωσις *homoiōsis* 1x pr. *assimilation; likeness, resemblance,* Jas. 3:9* [3669]

[3933] ὁμολογέω *homologeō* 26x *to speak in accordance, adopt the same terms of language; to engage, promise,* Mt. 14:7; *to admit, avow frankly,* Jn. 1:20; Acts 24:14; *to confess,* 1 Jn. 1:9; *to profess, confess,* Jn. 9:22; 12:42; Acts 23:8; *to avouch, declare openly and solemnly,* Mt. 7:23; in NT ὁμολογεῖν ἐν, *to accord* *belief,* Mt. 10:32; Lk. 12:8; *to accord approbation,* Lk. 12:8; from the Hebrew, *to accord praise,* Heb. 13:15 [3670] See *acknowledge; confess; promise.*

[3934] ὁμολογία *homologia* 6x *assent, consent; profession,* 2 Cor. 9:13; 1 Tim. 6:12, 13; Heb. 3:1; 4:14; 10:23* [3671]

[3935] ὁμολογουμένως *homologoumenōs* 1x *confessedly, avowedly, without controversy,* 1 Tim. 3:16* [3672]

[3937] ὁμότεχνος *homotechnos* 1x *to the same trade* or *occupation,* Acts 18:3* [3673]

[3938] ὁμοῦ *homou* 4x *together; in the same place,* Jn. 21:2; *together at the same time,* Jn. 4:36; 20:4; Acts 2:1* [3674]

[3939] ὁμόφρων *homophrōn* 1x *of like mind, of the same mind, like-minded,* 1 Pet. 3:8* [3675]

[3940] ὅμως *homōs* 3x *yet, nevertheless;* with μέντοι, *but nevertheless, but for all that,* Jn. 12:42; *even, though it be but,* 1 Cor. 14:7; Gal. 3:15* [3676]

[3941] ὄναρ *onar* 6x *a dream,* Mt. 1:20; 2:12, 13, 19, 22; 27:19* [3677]

[3942] ὀνάριον *onarion* 1x *a young donkey, a donkey's colt,* Jn. 12:14* [3678]

[3943] ὀνειδίζω *oneidizō* 9x *to censure, inveigh against,* Mt. 11:20; Mk. 16:14; *to reproach* or *revile,* Jas. 1:5; *to revile, insult with insulting language,* Mt. 5:11 [3679] See *insult; reproach.*

[3944] ὀνειδισμός *oneidismos* 5x *censure,* 1 Tim. 3:7; *reproach, reviling,* Rom. 15:3 [3680] See *insult; reproach.*

[3945] ὄνειδος *oneidos* 1x pr. *fame, report, character;* usually, *reproach, disgrace,* Lk. 1:25* [3681]

[3946] Ὀνήσιμος *Onēsimos* 2x *Onesimus,* pr. name, Col. 4:9; Phlm. 10* [3682]

[3947] Ὀνησίφορος *Onēsiphoros* 2x *Onesiphorus,* pr. name, 2 Tim. 1:16; 4:19* [3683]

[3948] ὀνικός *onikos* 2x *pertaining to a donkey;* μύλος ὀνικός, *a millstone turned by a donkey, a large* or *an upper millstone,* Mt. 18:6; Mk. 9:42* [3684]

[3949] ὀνίνημι *oninēmi* 1x optative, ὀναίμην, *to receive profit, pleasure,* etc.; with a gen., *to have joy of,* Phlm. 20* [3685]

[3950] ὄνομα *onoma* 231x *a name; the proper name* of a person, etc., Mt. 1:23, 25; 10:2; 27:32; *a mere name* or *reputation,* Rev. 3:1; in NT *a name* as the representative of a person, Mt. 6:9; Lk. 6:22; 11:2; *the name* of the author of a commission, delegated authority, or religious profession, Mt. 7:22; 10:22; 12:21; 18:5, 20; 19:29; 21:9; 28:19; Acts 3:16; 4:7, 12; εἰς ὄνομα, ἐν ὀνόματι, *on the score of being* possessor of a certain character, Mt. 10:41, 42; Mk. 9:41 [3686] See *name.*

[3951] ὀνομάζω *onomazō* 10x *to name,* Lk. 6:14; *to style, entitle,* Lk. 6:13; 1 Cor. 5:11; *to make mention of,* Eph. 5:3; *to make known,* Rom. 15:20; *to pronounce* in exorcism, Acts 19:13; in NT *to profess,* 2 Tim. 2:19 [3687] See *designate; name.*

[3952] ὄνος *onos* 5x *donkey, ass,* male or female, Mt. 21:2, 5, 7 [3688]

[3953] ὄντως *ontōs* 10x *really, in truth, truly,* Mk. 11:32; Lk. 23:47. [3689]

[3954] ὄξος *oxos* 6x *vinegar; a wine of sharp flavor, posca,* which was an ordinary beverage, and was often mixed with bitter herbs, etc., and this given to the condemned criminals in order to stupefy them, and lessen their sufferings, Mt. 27:48; Mk. 15:36; Lk. 23:36; Jn. 19:29, 30 [3690]

[3955] ὀξύς *oxys* 8x *sharp, keen,* Rev. 1:16; 2:12; 14:14, 17, 18; 19:15; *swift, nimble,* Rom. 3:15* [3691]

[3956] ὀπή *opē* 2x *a hole; a hole, vent, opening,* Jas. 3:11; *a hole, cavern,* Heb. 11:38* [3692]

[3957] ὄπισθεν *opisthen* 7x can function as an improper prep., *from behind, behind, after, at the back of,* Mt. 9:20; 15:23 [3693]

[3958] ὀπίσω *opisō* 35x can function as an improper prep., *behind, after, at one's back,* Mt. 4:10; Lk. 7:38; Rev. 1:10; τὰ ὀπίσω, *the things which are behind,* Phil. 3:13; ὀπίσω and εἰς τὰ ὀπίσω, *back, backwards,* Mt. 24:18; Mk. 13:16; Lk. 9:62, when an improper prep., takes the gen. [3694]

[3959] ὁπλίζω *hoplizō* 1x *to arm, equip;* mid. *to arm one's self, equip one's self,* 1 Pet. 4:1* [3695]

[3960] ὅπλον *hoplon* 6x *an implement,* Rom. 6:13; pl. τὰ ὅπλα, *arms, armor, weapons,* whether offensive or defensive, Jn. 18:3; Rom. 13:12; 2 Cor. 6:7; 10:4* [3696]

[3961] ὁποῖος *hopoios* 5x *what, of what sort* or *manner,* 1 Cor. 3:13; Gal. 2:6; 1 Thess. 1:9; Jas. 1:24; after τοιοῦτος, *as,* Acts 26:29* [3697]

[3963] ὅπου *hopou* 82x *where, in which place, in what place,* Mt. 6:19, 20, 21; Rev. 2:13; *whither, to what place,* Jn. 8:21; 14:4; ὅπου ἄν, or ἐάν, *wherever, in whatever place,* Mt. 24:28; *whithersoever,* Mt. 8:19; Jas. 3:4; met. *where, in which thing, state,* etc., Col. 3:11; *whereas,* 1 Cor. 3:3; 2 Pet. 2:11 [3699]

[3964] ὀπτάνομαι *optanomai* 1x *to be seen, appear,* Acts 1:3* [3700]

[3965] ὀπτασία *optasia* 4x *a vision, apparition,* Lk. 1:22; 24:23; Acts 26:19; 2 Cor. 12:1* [3701]

[3966] ὀπτός *optos* 1x *broiled, roasted,* etc., Lk. 24:42* [3702]

[3967] ὀπώρα *opōra* 1x *autumn; the fruit season;* meton. *fruits,* Rev. 18:14* [3703]

[3968] ὅπως *hopōs* 53x can function as a conj., *how, in what way* or *manner, by what means,* Mt. 22:5; Lk. 24:20; conj. *that, in order that,* and ὅπως μή, *that not, lest,* Mt. 6:2, 4, 5, 16, 18; Acts 9:2, et al. freq. [3704]

[3969] ὅραμα *horama* 12x *a thing seen, sight, appearance,* Acts 7:31; *a vision,* Mt. 17:9; Acts 9:10, 12 [3705] See *vision.*

[3970] ὅρασις *horasis* 4x *seeing, sight; appearance, aspect, a vision,* Acts 2:17; Rev. 9:17; 4:3* [3706]

[3971] ὁρατός *horatos* 1x *visible,* Col. 1:16* [3707]

[3972] ὁράω *horaō* 454x pluperfect, ἑωράκειν, some list εἶδον as the second aorist of ὁράω, *to see, behold,* Mt. 2:2, et al. freq.; *to look,* Jn. 19:37; *to visit,* Jn. 16:22; Heb. 13:23; *to mark, observe,* Acts 8:23; Jas. 2:24; *to be admitted to witness,* Lk. 17:22; Jn. 3:36; Col. 2:18; with θεόν, *to be admitted into the more immediate presence of God,* Mt. 5:8; Heb. 12:14; *to attain to a true knowledge of God,* 3 Jn. 11; *to see to* a thing, Mt. 27:4; Acts 18:15; ὅρα, *see, take care,* Mt. 8:4; Heb. 8:5; pass. *to appear,* Lk. 1:11; Acts 2:3; *to reveal one's self,* Acts 26:16; *to present one's self,* Acts 7:26 [3708] See *appear; consider; perceive; see.*

[3973] ὀργή *orgē* 36x pr. *mental bent, impulse; anger, indignation, wrath,* Eph. 4:31; Col. 3:8; μετ᾽ ὀργῆς, *indignantly,* Mk. 3:5; *vengeance, punishment,* Mt. 3:7; Lk. 3:7; 21:23; Rom. 13:4, 5 [3709] See *anger; wrath.*

[3974] ὀργίζω *orgizō* 8x some list as deponent, ὀργίζομαι, *to provoke to anger, irritate;* pass. *to be angry, indignant, enraged,* Mt. 5:22; 18:34 [3710]

[3975] ὀργίλος *orgilos* 1x *prone to anger, irascible, passionate,* Tit. 1:7* [3711]

[3976] ὀργυιά *orgyuia* 2x *the space measured by the arms outstretched; a fathom,* Acts 27:28 (2x)* [3712]

[3977] ὀρέγω *oregō* 3x *to extend, stretch out;* mid. *to stretch one's self out, to reach forward to,* met. *to desire earnestly, long after,* 1 Tim. 3:1; Heb. 11:16; by impl. *to indulge in, be devoted to,* 1 Tim. 6:10* [3713]

[3978] ὀρεινός *oreinos* 2x *mountainous, hilly,* Lk. 1:39, 65* [3714]

[3979] ὄρεξις *orexis* 1x *desire, longing; lust, concupiscence,* Rom. 1:27* [3715]

[3980] ὀρθοποδέω *orthopodeō* 1x *to walk in a straight course; to be straightforward* in moral conduct, Gal. 2:14* [3716]

[3981] ὀρθός *orthos* 2x *erect, upright,* Acts 14:10; *plain, level, straight,* Heb. 12:13* [3717]

[3982] ὀρθοτομέω *orthotomeō* 1x *to cut straight; to set forth truthfully, without perversion* or *distortion,* 2 Tim. 2:15* [3718]

[3983] ὀρθρίζω *orthrizō* 1x *to rise early in the morning; to come with the dawn,* Lk. 21:38* [3719]

[3984] ὀρθρινός *orthrinos* 1x a later form of ὄρθριος, *of* or *belonging to the morning, morning,* Lk. 24:22* [3720]

[3986] ὄρθρος *orthros* 3x *the dawn; the morning,* Jn. 8:2; Acts 5:21; ὄρθος βαθύς, *the first streak of dawn, the early dawn,* Lk. 24:1* [3722]

[3987] ὀρθῶς *orthōs* 4x *straightly; rightly, correctly,* Mk. 7:35; Lk. 7:43; 10:28; 20:21* [3723]

[3988] ὁρίζω *horizō* 8x *to set bounds to, to bound; to restrict,* Heb. 4:7; *to settle, appoint definitively,* Acts 17:26; *to fix determinately,* Acts 2:23; *to decree, destine,* Lk. 22:22; *to constitute, appoint,* Acts 10:42; 17:31; *to characterize with precision, to set forth distinctively,* Rom. 1:4; absol. *to resolve,* Acts 11:29* [3724] See *appoint; decide; determine; set.*

[3990] ὅριον *horion* 12x *a limit, bound, border of a territory* or *country;* pl. τὰ ὅρια, *region, territory, district,* Mt. 2:16; 4:13; 8:34 [3725] See *region; vicinity.*

[3991] ὁρκίζω *horkizō* 2x *to put to an oath; to implore, adjure, conjure,* Mk. 5:7; Acts 19:13* [3726]

[3992] ὅρκος *horkos* 10x *an oath,* Mt. 14:7, 9; 26:72; meton. *that which is solemnly promised, a vow,* Mt. 5:33 [3727] See *oath.*

[3993] ὁρκωμοσία *horkōmosia* 4x *the act of taking an oath; an oath,* Heb. 7:20, 21, 28* [3728]

[3994] ὁρμάω *hormaō* 5x pr. trans. *to put in motion, incite;* intrans. *to rush,* Mt. 8:32; Mk. 5:13; Lk. 8:33 [3729]

[3995] ὁρμή *hormē* 2x *impetus, impulse; assault, violent attempt,* Acts 14:5; met. *impulse of mind, purpose, will,* Jas. 3:4 [3730]

[3996] ὅρμημα *hormēma* 1x *violent* or *impetuous motion; violence,* Rev. 18:21* [3731]

[3997] ὄρνεον *orneon* 3x *a bird, fowl,* Rev. 18:2; 19:17, 21* [3732]

[3998] ὄρνις *ornis* 2x *bird, fowl;* domestic *hen,* Mt. 23:37; Lk. 13:34* [3733]

[3999] ὁροθεσία *horothesia* 1x pr. *the act of fixing boundaries; a bound set, certain bound, fixed limit,* Acts 17:26* [3734]

[4001] ὄρος *oros* 63x *a mountain, hill,* Mt. 5:1, 14; 8:1; 17:20 [3735] See *hill; mountain.*

[4002] ὀρύσσω *oryssō* 3x *to dig, excavate,* Mt. 21:33; 25:18; Mk. 12:1* [3736]

[4003] ὀρφανός *orphanos* 2x *bereaved* of parents, *orphan,* Jas. 1:27; *bereaved, desolate,* Jn. 14:18 [3737]

[4004] ὀρχέομαι *orcheomai* 4x *to dance,* Mt. 11:6, 17; Mk. 6:22; Lk. 7:32* [3738]

[4005] ὅς *hos* 1,407x *who, which, what, that,* Mt. 1:16, 23, 25; in NT interrog. ἐφ᾽ ὅ, *wherefore, why,* Mt. 26:50; in NT ὅς μὲν ... ὅς δέ, for ὁ μὲν ... ὁ δέ, Mt. 21:35; 2 Cor. 2:16 [3739]

[4006] ὁσάκις *hosakis* 3x *as often as,* 1 Cor. 11:25, 26; Rev. 11:6* [3740]

[4008] ὅσιος *hosios* 8x pr. *sanctioned by the supreme law of God, and nature; pious, devout,* Tit. 1:8; *pure,* 1 Tim. 2:8; supremely *holy,* Acts 2:27; 13:35; Heb. 7:26; Rev. 15:4; 16:5; τὰ ὅσια, *pledged bounties, mercies,* Acts 13:34* [3741] See *holy.*

[4009] ὁσιότης *hosiotēs* 2x *piety, sacred observance of all duties towards God, holiness,* Lk. 1:75; Eph. 4:24* [3742]

[4010] ὁσίως *hosiōs* 1x *piously,* 1 Thess. 2:10* [3743]

[4011] ὀσμή *osmē* 6x *smell, odor; fragrant odor,* Jn. 12:3; Eph. 5:2; Phil. 4:18; met. 2 Cor. 2:14, 16* [3744] See *aroma; odor.*

[4012] ὅσος *hosos* 110x *as great, as much,* Mk. 7:36; Jn. 6:11; Heb. 1:4; 8:6; 10:25; ἐφ᾽ ὅσον χρόνον, *for how long a time, while, as long as,* Rom. 7:1; so, ἐφ᾽ ὅσον, sc. χρόνον, Mt. 9:15; ὅσον χρόνον, *how long,* Mk. 2:19; neut. ὅσον repeated, ὅσον ὅσον, used to give intensity to other qualifying words, e.g., μικρόν, *the very least, a very little while,* Heb. 10:37; ἐφ᾽ ὅσον, *in as much as,* Mt. 25:40, 45; καθ᾽ ὅσον, *by how much, so far as,* Heb. 3:3; or, *in as much as, as, so,* Heb. 7:20; 9:27; pl. ὅσα, *so far as, as much as,* Rev. 1:2; 18:7; *how great, how much, how many, what,* Mk. 3:8; 5:19, 20; *how many, as many as, all who,* 2 Cor. 1:20; Phil. 3:15; 1 Tim. 6:1; ὅσος ἄν, or ἐάν, *whoever, whatsoever,* Mt. 7:12; 18:18 [3745]

[4014] ὀστέον *osteon* 4x contracted form, ὀστοῦν, οῦ, τό, *a bone,* Mt. 23:27; Lk. 24:39; Jn. 19:36; Heb. 11:22* [3747]

[4015] ὅστις *hostis* 144x *whoever, whatever; whosoever, whatsoever,* Mt. 5:39, 41; 13:12; 18:4; its use in place of the simple relative is also required in various cases, which may be learned from the grammars; ἕως ὅτου, sc. χρόνου, *until,* Lk. 13:8; *while,* Mt. 5:25 [3748, 3755]

[4017] ὀστράκινος *ostrakinos* 2x *earthen, of earthenware,* 2 Cor. 4:7; 2 Tim. 2:20* [3749]

[4018] ὄσφρησις *osphrēsis* 1x *smell, the sense of smelling,* 1 Cor. 12:17* [3750]

[4019] ὀσφῦς *osphys* 8x *the loins,* Mt. 3:4; Mk. 1:6. On the accent see BDF, 13. [3751]

[4020] ὅταν *hotan* 123x *when, whenever,* Mt. 5:11; 6:2; Mk. 3:11; Rev. 4:9, et al. freq.; in NT *in case of, on occasion of,* Jn. 9:5; 1 Cor. 15:27; Heb. 1:6 [3752]

[4021] ὅτε *hote* 103x *when, at the time that, at what time,* Mt. 7:28; 9:25; Lk. 13:35, et al. freq. [3753]

[4022] ὅτι *hoti* 1,296x originally was the neuter of ὅστις, *that,* Mt. 2:16, 22, 23; 6:5, 16; often used pleonastically in reciting another's words, Mt. 9:18; Lk. 19:42; Acts 5:23; as a causal particle, *for that, for, because,* Mt. 2:18; 5:3, 4, 5; 13:13; *because, seeing that, since,* Lk. 23:40; Acts 1:17 [3754]

[4023] οὗ *hou* 24x *where, in what place,* Mt. 2:9; 18:20; *whither, to what place,* Lk. 10:1; 22:10; 24:28; οὗ ἐάν, *whithersoever,* 1 Cor. 16:6 [3757]

[4024] οὐ *ou* 1,623x negative adverb, originally the gen. of ὅς, spelled οὐκ if followed by a word beginning with a vowel and a smooth breathing, οὐχ if followed by a vowel and rough breathing, *not, no,* Mt. 5:37; 12:43; 23:37; for the peculiarities of its usage (especially as distinct from μή) consult a grammar [3756]

[4025] οὐά *oua* 1x expressive of insult and derision, *Ah! Ah!,* Mk. 15:29* [3758]

[4026] οὐαί *ouai* 46x *Wo! Alas!* Mt. 11:21; 18:7; 23:13, 14, 15, 16; ἡ οὐαί, subst., *a woe, calamity,* Rev. 9:12; 11:14 [3759] See *alas; woe.*

[4027] οὐδαμῶς *oudamōs* 1x *by no means,* Mt. 2:6* [3760]

[4028] οὐδέ *oude* 143x negative conj., *neither, nor, and not, also not,* Mt. 5:15; 6:15, 20, 26, 28; when single, *not even* Mt. 6:29; 8:10 [3761]

[4029] οὐδείς *oudeis* 227x latter form, οὐθείς (4032), *not one, no one, none, nothing,* Mt. 5:13; 6:24; 19:17; met. οὐδέν, *nothing, of no account, naught,* Jn. 8:54; Acts 21:24 [3762]

[4030] οὐδέποτε *oudepote* 16x *never,* Mt. 7:23; 21:16, 42, et al. freq. [3763]

[4031] οὐδέπω *oudepō* 4x *not yet, never yet, never,* Jn. 7:39; 19:41; 20:9; Acts 8:16* [3764]

[4032] οὐθείς *outheis* 7x see οὐδείς [3762]

[4033] οὐκέτι *ouketi* 47x *no longer, no more,* Mt. 22:46 [3765]

[4034] οὐκοῦν *oukoun* 1x *then, therefore;* used interrogatively, Jn. 18:37* [3766]

[4036] οὖν *oun* 499x *then, now then,* Mt. 13:18; Jn. 19:29; *then, thereupon,* Lk. 15:28; Jn. 6:14; *therefore, consequently,* Mt. 5:48: Mk. 10:9; it also serves to mark the resumption of discourse after an interruption by a parenthesis, 1 Cor. 8:4. Sometimes it is not translated. [3767]

[4037] οὔπω *oupō* 26x *not yet,* Mt. 15:17; 16:9; 24:6 Jn. 2:4 [3768]

[4038] οὐρά *oura* 5x *a tail,* Rev. 9:10 (2x), 19 (2x); 12:4* [3769]

[4039] οὐράνιος *ouranios* 9x *heavenly, celestial,* Mt. 6:14, 26, 32; 15:13 [3770] See *heaven, heavens; heavenly.*

[4040] οὐρανόθεν *ouranothen* 2x *from heaven,* Acts 14:17; 26:13* [3771]

[4041] οὐρανός *ouranos* 273x *heaven, the heavens, the visible heavens and all their phenomena,* Mt. 5:18; 16:1; 24:29, et al. freq.; *the air, atmosphere,* in which the clouds and tempests gather, the birds fly, etc., Mt. 6:26; 16:2, 3; *heaven* as the peculiar seat and abode of God, of angels, of glorified spirits, etc., Mt. 5:34, 45, 48; 6:1, 9, 10; 12:50; Jn. 3:13, 31; 6:32, 38, 41, 42, 50, 51, 58; in NT *heaven* as a term expressive of the Divine Being, His administration, etc., Mt. 19:14; 21:25; Lk. 20:4, 5; Jn. 3:27 [3772] See *heaven, heavens; sky.*

[4042] Οὐρβανός *ourbanos* 1x *Urbanus, Urban,* pr. name, Rom. 16:9* [3773]

[4043] Οὐρίας *ourias* 1x *Urias, Uriah,* pr. name (2 Sam. 11; 12:24), Mt. 1:6* [3774]

[4044] οὖς *ous* 36x *the ear,* Mt. 10:27; Mk. 7:33; Lk. 22:50; Acts 7:57 [3775] See *ear.*

[4045] οὐσία *ousia* 2x *substance, property, goods, fortune,* Lk. 15:12, 13* [3776]

[4046] οὔτε *oute* 87x *neither, nor,* Lk. 20:36; οὔτε ... οὔτε, or οὐτὲ ... οὔτε, *neither ... nor,* Lk. 20:35; Gal. 1:12; in NT also used singly in the sense of οὐδέ, *not even,* Mk. 5:3; Lk. 12:26; 1 Cor. 3:2 [3777]

[4047] οὗτος *houtos* 1,387x *this, this* person or thing, Mt. 3:3, 9, 17; 8:9; 10:2; 24:34, et al. freq.; used by way of contempt, *this fellow,* Mt. 13:55; 27:47; αὐτὸ τοῦτο, *this very thing, this same thing,* 2 Cor. 2:3; 7:11; εἰς αὐτὸ τοῦτο, and elliptically, αὐτὸ τοῦτο, *for this same purpose, on this account,* Eph. 6:18, 22; 2 Pet. 1:5; καὶ οὗτος, *and moreover,* Lk. 7:12; 16:1; 20:30; καὶ τοῦτο, *and that too,* 1 Cor. 6:6, 8; τοῦτο μὲν ... τοῦτο δέ, *partly ... partly,* Heb. 10:33 [3778, 5023, 5025, 5026, 5123, 5124, 5125, 5126, 5127, 5128, 5129, 5130]

[4048] οὕτως *houtōs* 208x *thus, in this way,* Mt. 1:18; 2:5; 5:16; et al. freq.; ὃς μὲν οὕτως, ὃς δὲ οὕτως, *one so, and another so, one in one way, and another in another,* 1 Cor. 7:7; *so,* Mt. 7:12; 12:40; 24:27, 37, et al. freq.; *thus, under such circumstances,* Acts 20:11; *in such a condition,* viz., one previously mentioned, Acts 27:17; 1 Cor. 7:26, 40; and, perhaps, Jn. 4:6; *in an ordinary way, at ease,* like Latin *sic,* perhaps, Jn. 4:6 [3779]

[4049] οὐχί *ouchi* 54x a strengthened form of οὐ, *not,* Jn. 13:10, 11; when followed by ἀλλά, *nay, not so, by no means,* Lk. 1:60; 12:51; used also in negative interrogations, Mt. 5:46, 47; 6:25 [3780]

[4050] ὀφειλέτης *opheiletēs* 7x *a debtor, one who owes,* Mt. 18:24; met. *one who is in any way bound,* or *under obligation* to perform any duty, Rom. 1:14; 8:12; 15:27; Gal. 5:3; in NT *one who fails in duty, a delinquent, offender,* Mt. 6:12; *a sinner,* Lk. 13:4, cf. v. 2* [3781] See *debtor; obligation.*

[4051] ὀφειλή *opheilē* 3x *a debt,* Mt. 18:32; met. *a duty, due,* Rom. 13:7; 1 Cor. 7:3* [3782]

[4052] ὀφείλημα *opheilēma* 2x *a debt; a due,* Rom. 4:4, in NT *a delinquency, offence, fault, sin,* Mt. 6:12, cf. v. 14* [3783]

[4053] ὀφείλω *opheilō* 35x *to owe, be indebted,* Mt. 18:28, 30, 34; *to incur a bond, to be bound to make discharge,* Mt. 23:16, 18; *to be bound* or *obliged* by what is due or fitting or consequently necessary, Lk. 17:10; Jn. 13:14; *to deserve,* Jn. 19:7; *to be due* or *fitting,* 1 Cor. 7:3, 36; from the Aramaic, *to be delinquent,* Lk. 11:4 [3784] See *ought; owe.*

[4054] ὄφελον *ophelon* 4x originally a ptcp (aor act ptcp nom sg neut) from ὀφείλω, used in NT as an interj. to introduce a wish that cannot be attained, *O that! Would that!* 1 Cor. 4:8; 2 Cor. 11:1; Gal. 5:12; Rev. 3:15* [3785]

[4055] ὄφελος *ophelos* 3x *profit, benefit, advantage,* 1 Cor. 15:32; Jas. 2:14, 16* [3786]

[4056] ὀφθαλμοδουλία *ophthalmodoulia* 2x also written ὀφθαλμοδουλεία, *eye-service, service rendered only while under inspection,* Eph. 6:6; Col. 3:22* [3787]

[4057] ὀφθαλμός *ophthalmos* 100x *an eye,* Mt. 5:29, 38; 6:23; 7:3, 4, 5; ὀφθαλμὸς πονηρός, *an evil eye, an envious eye, envy,* Mt. 20:15; Mk. 7:22; met. *the* intellectual *eye,* Mt. 13:15; Mk. 8:18; Jn. 12:40; Acts 26:18 [3788] See *eye.*

[4058] ὄφις *ophis* 14x *a serpent,* Mt. 7:10; 10:16; *an* artificial *serpent,* Jn. 3:14; used of *the devil* or *Satan,* Rev. 12:9, 14, 15; 20:2; met. *a man of serpentine character,* Mt. 23:33 [3789] See *serpent; snake.*

[4059] ὀφρῦς *ophrys* 1x *a brow, eye-brow; the brow* of a mountain, *edge* of a precipice, Lk. 4:29* [3790]

[4061] ὀχλέω *ochleō* 1x pr. *to mob; to disturb, trouble,* Acts 5:16* [3791]

[4062] ὀχλοποιέω *ochlopoieō* 1x *to collect a mob, create a tumult,* Acts 17:5* [3792]

[4063] ὄχλος *ochlos* 175x *a crowd, a confused multitude of people,* Mt. 4:25; 5:1; 7:28; spc. *the common people,* Jn. 7:49; *a multitude, great number,* Lk. 5:29; 6:17; Acts 1:15; by impl. *tumult, uproar,* Lk. 22:6; Acts 24:18 [3793] See *crowd; mob; multitude; number.*

[4065] ὀχύρωμα *ochurōma* 1x *a stronghold;* met. *an* opposing *bulwark* of error or vice, 2 Cor. 10:4* [3794]

[4066] ὀψάριον *opsarion* 5x *a little fish,* Jn. 6:9, 11; 21:9, 10, 13* [3795]

[4067] ὀψέ *opse* 3x can function as an improper prep., *late;* put for *the first watch, at evening,* Mk. 11:19; 13:35; ὀψὲ σαββάτων, *after the close of the Sabbath,* Mt. 28:1 [3796]

[4068] ὀψία *opsia* 15x *evening,* either before or after sundown [3798]

[4069] ὄψιμος *opsimos* 1x *late; latter,* Jas. 5:7; poetic and later prose for ὄψιος* [3797] See *evening.*

[4071] ὄψις *opsis* 3x *a sight; the face, countenance,* Jn. 11:44; Rev. 1:16; *external appearance,* Jn. 7:24* [3799]

[4072] ὀψώνιον *opsōnion* 4x *provisions; a stipend* or *pay* of soldiers, Lk. 3:14; 1 Cor. 9:7; *wages* of any kind, 2 Cor. 11:8; due *wages, a* stated *recompense,* Rom. 6:23* [3800]

[4074] παγιδεύω *pagideuō* 1x *to ensnare, entrap, entangle,* Mt. 22:15* [3802]

[4075] παγίς *pagis* 5x *a snare, trap,* Lk. 21:35; met. *device, wile,* 1 Tim. 3:7; 6:9; 2 Tim. 2:26; met. *a trap* of ruin, Rom. 11:9* [3803]

[4076] πάγος *pagos* 2x *a hill,* Ἄρειος πάγος, *Areopagus, the hill of Mars,* at Athens, Acts 17:19, 22 [697]

[4077] πάθημα *pathēma* 16x *what is suffered; suffering, affliction,* Rom. 8:18; 2 Cor. 1:5, 6, 7; Phil. 3:10; *emotion, passion,* Rom. 7:5; Gal. 5:24 [3804] See *suffering.*

[4078] παθητός *pathētos* 1x *passible, capable of suffering, liable to suffer;* in NT *destined to suffer,* Acts 26:23* [3805]

[4079] πάθος *pathos* 3x *suffering; an affection, passion,* especially sexual, Rom. 1:26 [3806]

[4080] παιδαγωγός *paidagōgos* 3x *a pedagogue, childtender,* a person, usually a slave or freedman, to whom the care of the boys of a family was committed, whose duty it was to attend them at their play, lead them to and from the public school, and exercise a constant superintendence over their conduct and safety; in NT an ordinary *director* or *minister* contrasted with an Apostle, as a pedagogue occupies an inferior position to a parent, 1 Cor. 4:15; a term applied to the Mosaic law, as dealing with men as in a state of mere childhood and tutelage, Gal. 3:24, 25* [3807]

[4081] παιδάριον *paidarion* 1x *a little boy, child; a boy, lad,* Jn. 6:9* [3808]

[4082] παιδεία *paideia* 6x *education, training up, nurture* of children, Eph. 6:4; *instruction, discipline,* 2 Tim. 3:16; in NT *correction, chastisement,* Heb. 12:5, 7, 8, 11* [3809]

[4083] παιδευτής *paideutēs* 2x *a preceptor, instructor, teacher,* pr. of boys; gener. Rom. 2:20; in NT *a chastiser,* Heb. 12:9* [3810]

[4084] παιδεύω *paideuō* 13x *to educate, instruct* children, Acts 7:22; 22:3; genr. παιδεύομαι, t*o be taught, learn,* 1 Tim. 1:20; *to admonish, instruct by admonition,* 2 Tim. 2:25; Tit. 2:12; in NT *to chastise, chasten,* 1 Cor. 11:32; 2 Cor. 6:9; Heb. 12:6, 7, 10; Rev. 3:19; of criminals, *to scourge,* Lk. 23:16, 22* [3811] See *discipline; educate; punish; teach.*

[4085] παιδιόθεν *paidiothen* 1x *from childhood, from a child,* Mk. 9:21* [3812]

[4086] παιδίον *paidion* 52x *an infant, babe,* Mt. 2:8; but usually in NT as equiv. to παῖς, Mt. 14:21; Mk. 7:28, et al. freq.; pl. voc. used by way of endearment, *my dear children,* 1 Jn. 2:18; also as a term of familiar address, *children, my lads,* Jn. 21:5 [3813] See *child; little child.*

[4087] παιδίσκη *paidiskē* 13x *a girl, damsel, maiden; a female slave* or *servant,* Mt. 26:69; Mk. 14:66, 69 [3814] See *girl; servant girl.*

[4089] παίζω *paizō* 1x *to play in the manner of children; to sport, to practise the festive gestures* of idolatrous worship, 1 Cor. 10:7* [3815]

[4090] παῖς *pais* 24x *a child* in relation to parents, of either sex, Jn. 4:51; *a child* in respect of age, either male or female, and of all ages from infancy up to manhood, *a boy, youth, girl, maiden,* Mt. 2:16; 17:18; Lk. 2:43; 8:54; *a servant, slave,* Mt. 8:6, 8, 13, cf. v. 9; Lk. 7:7, cf. v. 3, 10; *an attendant, minister,* Mt. 14:2; Lk. 1:69; Acts 4:25; also, Lk. 1:54; or, perhaps, *a child* in respect of fatherly regard [3816] See *child.*

[4091] παίω *paiō* 5x *to strike, smite,* with the fist, Mt. 26:68; Lk. 22:64; with a sword, Mk. 14:47; Jn. 18:10; *to strike* as a scorpion, *to sting,* Rev. 9:5* [3817]

[4093] πάλαι *palai* 6x *of old, long ago,* Mt. 11:21; Lk. 10:13; Heb. 1:1; Jude 4; οἱ πάλαι, *old, former,* 2 Pet. 1:9; *some time since, already,* Mk. 15:44 [3819]

[4094] παλαιός *palaios* 19x *old, not new* or *recent,* Mt. 9:16, 17; 13:52; Lk. 5:36 [3820] See *old.*

[4095] παλαιότης *palaiotēs* 1x *oldness, obsoleteness,* Rom. 7:6* [3821]

[4096] παλαιόω *palaioō* 4x *to make old;* pass. *to grow old, to become worn,* Lk. 12:33; Heb. 1:11; met. *to treat as antiquated, to abrogate, supersede,* Heb. 8:13* [3822]

[4097] πάλη *palē* 1x *wrestling; struggle, contest,* Eph. 6:12* [3823]

[4098] παλιγγενεσία *palingenesia* 2x *a new birth; regeneration, renovation,* Mt. 19:28; Tit. 3:5. See unpublished Ph.D. dissertation, William D. Mounce, *The Origin of the New Testament Metaphor of Rebirth,* University of Aberdeen, Scotland* [3824] See *regeneration.*

[4099] πάλιν *palin* 141x pr. *back; again, back again,* Jn. 10:17; Acts 10:16; 11:10; *again* by repetition, Mt. 26:43; *again* in continuation, *further,* Mt. 5:33; 13:44, 45, 47, 18:19; *again, on the other hand,* 1 Jn. 2:8 [3825]

[4101] παμπληθεί *pamplēthei* 1x *the whole multitude together, all at once,* Lk. 23:18* [3826]

[4103] Παμφυλία *Pamphylia* 5x *Pamphylia,* a country of Asia Minor, Acts 2:10; 13:13; 14:24; 15:38; 27:5* [3828]

[4106] πανδοχεῖον *pandocheion* 1x *a public inn, place where travelers may lodge,* called in the East by the name of *menzil, khan, caravanserai,* Lk. 10:34* [3829]

[4107] πανδοχεύς *pandocheus* 1x *the keeper of a public inn* or *caravanserai, a host,* Lk. 10:35* [3830]

[4108] πανήγυρις *panēgyris* 1x pr. *an assembly of an entire people; a solemn gathering at a festival; a festive convocation,* Heb. 12:22* [3831]

[4109] πανοικεί *panoikei* 1x also spelled πανοικί, *with one's whole household* or *family,* Acts 16:34* [3832]

[4110] πανοπλία *panoplia* 3x *panoply, complete armor, a complete suit of armor,* both offensive and defensive, as the shield, sword, spear, helmet, breastplate, etc., Lk. 11:22; Eph. 6:11, 13* [3833]

[4111] πανουργία *panourgia* 5x *craft, cunning,* Lk. 20:23; 1 Cor. 3:19 [3834]

[4112] πανοῦργος *panourgos* 1x pr. *ready to do anything;* hence, *crafty, cunning, artful, wily,* 2 Cor. 12:16* [3835]

[4114] πανταχῇ *pantachē* 1x *everywhere,* Acts 21:28* [3837]

[4116] πανταχοῦ *pantachou* 7x *in all places, everywhere,* Mk. 16:20; Lk. 9:6 [3837]

[4117] παντελής *pantelēs* 2x *perfect, complete;* εἰς τὸ παντελές, adverbially, *throughout, through all time, ever,* Heb. 7:25; with a negative, *at all,* Lk. 13:11* [3838]

[4118] πάντῃ *pantē* 1x *everywhere; in every way, in every instance,* Acts 24:3* [3839]

[4119] πάντοθεν *pantothen* 3x *from every place, from all parts, on all sides, on every side, round about,* Mk. 1:45; Lk. 19:43; Heb. 9:4* [3840]

[4120] παντοκράτωρ *pantokratōr* 10x *almighty, omnipotent,* 2 Cor. 6:18; Rev. 1:8; 4:8 [3841] See *almighty.*

[4121] πάντοτε *pantote* 41x *always, at all times, ever,* Mt. 26:11; Mk. 14:7; Lk. 15:31; 18:1 [3842]

[4122] πάντως *pantōs* 8x *wholly, altogether; at any rate, by all means,* 1 Cor. 9:22; by impl. *surely, assuredly, certainly,* Lk. 4:23; Acts 21:22; 28:4; 1 Cor. 9:10; οὐ πάντως, *in nowise, not in the least,* Rom. 3:9; 1 Cor. 5:10; 16:12* [3843]

[4123] παρά *para* 194x. (1) gen., *from,* indicating source or origin, Mt. 2:4, 7; Mk. 8:11; Lk. 2:1; οἱ παρ᾽ αὐτοῦ, *his relatives* or *kinsmen,* Mk. 3:21; τὰ παρ᾽ αὐτῆς πάντα, *all her substance, property,* etc., Mk. 5:26.

(2) dat., *with, in, among,* etc., Mt. 6:1; 19:26; 21:25; 22:25; παρ᾽ ἑαυτῷ, at *home,* 1 Cor. 16:2; *in the sight of, in the judgment* or *estimation of,* 1 Cor. 3:19; 2 Pet. 2:11; 3:8.

(3) acc., motion, *by, near to, along,* Mt. 4:18; motion, *towards, to, at,* Mt. 15:30; Mk. 2:13; motion terminating in rest, *at, by, near, by the side of,* Mk. 4:1, 4; Lk. 5:1; 8:5; *in deviation from, in violation of, inconsistently with,* Acts 18:13; Rom. 1:26; 11:24; *above, more than,* Lk. 13:2, 4; Rom. 1:25.

(4) Misc., after comparatives, Lk. 3:13; 1 Cor. 3:11; *except, save,* 2 Cor. 11:24; *beyond, past,* Heb. 11:11; *in respect of, on the score of,* 1 Cor. 12:15, 16 [3844]

[4124] παραβαίνω *parabainō* 3x pr. *to step by the side of; to deviate;* met. *to transgress, violate,* Mt. 15:2, 3; *to incur forfeiture,* Acts 1:25* [3845]

[4125] παραβάλλω *paraballō* 1x *to cast* or *throw by the side of;* absol., a nautical term, *to bring to, land,* Acts 20:15* [3846]

[4126] παράβασις *parabasis* 7x *a stepping by the side, deviation; a transgression, violation of law,* Rom. 2:23; 4:15 [3847] See *transgression.*

[4127] παραβάτης *parabatēs* 5x *transgressor, violator of law,* Rom. 2:25, 27; Gal. 2:18; Jas. 2:9, 11* [3848]

[4128] παραβιάζομαι *parabiazomai* 2x *to force; to urge strongly, prevail upon,* Lk. 24:29; Acts 16:15* [3849]

[4129] παραβολεύομαι *paraboleuomai* 1x also spelled παραβουλεύομαι, *to stake* or *risk one's self,* Phil. 2:30* [3851]

[4130] παραβολή *parabolē* 50x *a placing one thing by the side of another; a comparing; a parallel case cited in illustration; a comparison, simile, similitude,* Mk. 4:30; Heb. 11:19; *a parable,* a short relation under which something else is figured, or in which that which is fictitious is employed to represent that which is real, Mt. 13:3, 10, 13, 18, 24, 31, 33, 34, 36, 53; 21:33, 45; 22:1; 24:32; in NT *a type, pattern, emblem,* Heb. 9:9; *a sentiment, grave and significant precept, maxim,* Lk. 14:7; *an obscure and enigmatical saying, anything expressed in remote and ambiguous terms,* Mt. 13:35; Mk. 7:17; *a proverb, adage,* Lk. 4:23 [3850] See *illustration; parable; proverb.*

[4132] παραγγελία *parangelia* 5x *a command, order, charge,* Acts 5:28; 16:24; *direction, precept,* 1 Thess. 4:2; 1 Tim. 1:5, 18* [3852]

[4133] παραγγέλλω *parangellō* 32x *to announce, notify; to command, direct, charge,* Mt. 10:5; Mk. 6:8, 8:6; Lk. 9:21; *to charge, entreat solemnly,* 1 Tim. 6:13 [3853] See *command; instruct; order.*

[4134] παραγίνομαι *paraginomai* 37x pluperfect, παραγεγόνει (3 sg), *to be by the side of; to come, ap-*

proach, arrive, Mt. 2:1; 3:13; Mk. 14:43; Lk. 7:4; seq. ἐπί, *to come upon* in order to seize, Lk. 22:52; *to come forth in public, make appearance,* Mt. 3:1; Heb. 9:11 [3854] See *arrive; come.*

[4135] παράγω *paragō* 10x *to lead beside;* intrans. *to pass along* or *by,* Mt. 20:30; Jn. 9:1; *to pass on,* Mt. 9:9, 27; intrans. and mid. *to pass away, be in a state of transition,* 1 Cor. 7:31; 1 Jn. 2:8, 17 [3855] See *pass.*

[4136] παραδειγματίζω *paradeigmatizō* 1x *to make an example of; to expose to ignominy and shame,* Heb. 6:6* [3856]

[4137] παράδεισος *paradeisos* 3x *a park, a forest where wild beasts were kept for hunting; a pleasure-park, a garden of trees of various kinds;* used in the LXX for *the Garden of Eden;* in NT the celestial *paradise,* Lk. 23:43; 2 Cor. 12:4; Rev. 2:7* [3857]

[4138] παραδέχομαι *paradechomai* 6x *to accept, receive,* met. *to receive, admit, yield assent to,* Mk. 4:20; Acts 15:4; 16:21; 22:18; 1 Tim. 5:19; in NT *to receive* or *embrace with favor, approve, love,* Heb. 12:6* [3858]

[4140] παραδίδωμι *paradidōmi* 119x pluperfect, παραδεδώκεισαν (3 pl), *to give over, hand over, deliver up,* Mt. 4:12; 5:25; 10:4, 17; *to commit, intrust,* Mt. 11:27; 25:14; *to commit, commend,* Acts 14:26; 15:40; *to yield up,* Jn. 19:30; 1 Cor. 15:24; *to abandon,* Acts 7:42; Eph. 4:19; *to stake, hazard,* Acts 15:26; *to deliver* as a matter of injunction, instruction, etc., Mk. 7:13; Lk. 1:2; Acts 6:14; absol. *to render a yield, to be matured,* Mk. 4:29 [3860] See *betray; hand over; pass down.*

[4141] παράδοξος *paradoxos* 1x *unexpected; strange, wonderful, astonishing,* Lk. 5:26* [3861]

[4142] παράδοσις *paradosis* 13x *delivery, handing over, transmission;* in NT *what is transmitted* in the way of teaching, *precept, doctrine,* 1 Cor. 11:2; 2 Thess. 2:15; 3:6; *tradition, traditionary law,* handed down from age to age, Mt. 15:2, 3, 6 [3862] See *tradition.*

[4143] παραζηλόω *parazēloō* 4x *to provoke to jealousy,* Rom. 10:19; *to excite to emulation,* Rom. 11:11, 14; *to provoke to indignation,* 1 Cor. 10:22* [3863]

[4144] παραθαλάσσιος *parathalassios* 1x *by the sea-side, situated on the sea-coast, maritime,* Mt. 4:13* [3864]

[4145] παραθεωρέω *paratheōreō* 1x *to look at things placed side by side,* as in comparison, *to regard less in comparison, overlook, neglect,* Acts 6:1* [3865]

[4146] παραθήκη *parathēkē* 3x *a deposit, a thing committed to one's charge, a trust,* 1 Tim. 6:20; 2 Tim. 1:12; 2 Tim. 1:14* [3866]

[4147] παραινέω *paraineō* 2x *to advise, exhort,* Acts 27:9, 22* [3867]

[4148] παραιτέομαι *paraiteomai* 12x *to ask for, request, intercede for, entreat; to beg off, excuse one's self,* Lk. 14:18, 19; *to deprecate, entreat against,* Acts 25:11; Heb. 12:19; *to decline receiving, refuse, reject,* 1 Tim. 4:7; 5:11; Tit. 3:10; Heb. 12:25; *to decline, avoid, shun,* 2 Tim. 2:23 [3868] See *make excuses; reject; request.*

[4149] παρακαθέζομαι *parakathezomai* 1x *to sit down by,* Lk. 10:39* [3869]

[4151] παρακαλέω *parakaleō* 109x *to call for, invite to come, send for,* Acts 28:20; *to call upon, exhort, admonish, persuade,* Lk. 3:18; Acts 2:40; 11:23; *to beg, beseech, entreat, implore,* Mt. 8:5, 31; 18:29; Mk. 1:40; *to animate, encourage, comfort, console,* Mt. 2:18; 5:4; 2 Cor. 1:4, 6; pass. *to be cheered, comforted,* Lk. 16:25; Acts 20:12; 2 Cor. 7:13 [3870] See *ask; comfort; exhort; implore; summon.*

[4152] παρακαλύπτω *parakalyptō* 1x *to cover over, veil;* met. pass. *to be veiled* from comprehension, Lk. 9:45* [3871]

[4154] παράκειμαι *parakeimai* 2x *to lie near, be adjacent;* met. *to be at hand, be present,* Rom. 7:18, 21* [3873]

[4155] παράκλησις *paraklēsis* 29x *a calling upon, exhortation, incitement, persuasion,* Rom. 12:8; 1 Cor. 14:3; *hortatory instruction,* Acts 13:15; 15:31; *entreaty, importunity, earnest supplication,* 2 Cor. 8:4; *solace, consolation,* Lk. 2:25; Rom. 15:4, 5; 2 Cor. 1:3, 4, 5, 6, 7; *cheering and supporting influence,* Acts 9:31; *joy, gladness, rejoicing,* 2 Cor. 7:13; *cheer, joy, enjoyment,* Lk. 6:24 [3874] See *comfort; consolation; encouragement.*

[4156] παράκλητος *paraklētos* 5x *one called* or *sent for to assist another; an advocate, one who pleads the cause of another,* 1 Jn. 2:1; genr. *one present to render various beneficial service,* and thus *the Paraclete,* whose influence and operation were to compensate for the departure of Christ himself, Jn. 14:16, 26; 15:26; 16:7* [3875] See *advocate; counselor; helper.*

[4157] παρακοή *parakoē* 3x *an erroneous* or *imperfect hearing; disobedience,* Rom. 5:19; *a deviation from obedience,* 2 Cor. 10:6; Heb. 2:2* [3876]

[4158] παρακολουθέω *parakoloutheō* 3x *to follow* or *accompany closely; to accompany, attend, characterize,* Mk. 16:17; *to follow* with the thoughts, *trace, investigate,* Lk. 1:3; *to conform to,* 1 Tim. 4:6; 2 Tim. 3:10* [3877]

[4159] παρακούω *parakouō* 3x *to overhear,* Mk. 5:36; *to hear amiss, to fail to listen, neglect to obey, disregard,* Mt. 18:17 (2x)* [3878]

[4160] παρακύπτω *parakyptō* 5x *to stoop beside; to stoop down* in order to take a view, Lk. 24:12; Jn. 20:5, 11; *to bestow a close and attentive look, to look intently, to penetrate,* Jas. 1:25; 1 Pet. 1:12* [3879]

[4161] παραλαμβάνω *paralambanō* 49x pr. *to take to one's side; to take, receive to one's self,* Mt. 1:20; Jn. 14:3; *to take* with one's self, Mt. 2:13, 14, 20, 21; 4:5, 8; *to receive* in charge or possession, Col. 4:17; Heb. 12:28; *to receive* as a matter of instruction, Mk. 7:4; 1 Cor. 11:23; 15:3; *to receive, admit, acknowledge,* Jn. 1:11; 1 Cor. 15:1; Col. 2:6; pass. *to be carried off,* Mt. 24:40, 41; Lk. 17:34, 35, 36 [3880] See *accept; receive.*

[4162] παραλέγομαι *paralegomai* 2x *to sail by, coast along,* Acts 27:8, 13* [3881]

[4163] παράλιος *paralios* 1x *adjacent to the sea, maritime;* ἡ παράλιος, sc. χώρα, *the sea coast,* Lk. 6:17* [3882]

[4164] παραλλαγή *parallagē* 1x *a shifting, mutation, change,* Jas. 1:17* [3883]

[4165] παραλογίζομαι *paralogizomai* 2x *to misreckon, make a false reckoning; to impose upon, deceive, delude, circumvent,* Col. 2:4; Jas. 1:22* [3884]

[4166] παραλυτικός *paralytikos* 10x *lame, palsied,* used only as a noun in NT, *paralytic,* Mt. 4:24; 8:6; 9:2, 6 [3885] See *lame; paralytic.*

[4168] παραλύω *paralyō* 5x *to undo, weaken, disable; to paralyze* the body or limbs; pass. *to be weakened,* Heb. 12:12; pass. perf. part. παραλελυμένος, *paralytic,* Lk. 5:18, 24 [3886]

[4169] παραμένω *paramenō* 4x *to stay beside; to continue, stay, abide,* 1 Cor. 16:6; Heb. 7:23; met. *to remain constant in, persevere in,* Phil. 1:25; Jas. 1:25* [3887]

[4170] παραμυθέομαι *paramytheomai* 4x *to exercise a gentle influence by words; to soothe, comfort, console,* Jn. 11:19, 31; 1 Thess. 5:14; *to cheer, exhort,* 1 Thess. 2:12* [3888]

[4171] παραμυθία *paramythia* 1x *comfort, encouragement,* 1 Cor. 14:3* [3889]

[4172] παραμύθιον *paramythion* 1x *gentle cheering, encouragement,* Phil. 2:1* [3890]

[4174] παρανομέω *paranomeō* 1x *to violate* or *transgress the law,* Acts 23:3* [3891]

[4175] παρανομία *paranomia* 1x *violation of the law, transgression,* 2 Pet. 2:16* [3892]

[4176] παραπικραίνω *parapikrainō* 1x pr. *to incite to bitter feelings; to provoke;* absol. *to act provokingly, be rebellious,* Heb. 3:16* [3893]

[4177] παραπικρασμός *parapikrasmos* 2x *exasperation, provocation; rebellion,* Heb. 3:8, 15* [3894]

[4178] παραπίπτω *parapiptō* 1x pr. *to fall by the side of;* met. *to fall off* or *away from, make defection from,* Heb. 6:6* [3895]

[4179] παραπλέω *parapleō* 1x *to sail by* or *past* a place, Acts 20:16* [3896]

[4180] παραπλήσιος *paraplēsios* 1x pr. *near alongside;* met. *like, similar;* neut. παραπλήσιον, adverbially, *near to, nearly, with a near approach to,* Phil. 2:27* [3897]

[4181] παραπλησίως *paraplēsiōs* 1x *like, in the same* or *like manner,* Heb. 2:14* [3898]

[4182] παραπορεύομαι *paraporeuomai* 5x *to pass by the side of; to pass along,* Mt. 27:39; Mk. 2:23; 9:30; 11:20; 15:29* [3899]

[4183] παράπτωμα *paraptōma* 19x pr. *a stumbling aside, a false step;* in NT *a trespass, fault, offence, transgression,* Mt. 6:14, 15; Mk. 11:25, 26; Rom. 4:25; *a fall* in faith, Rom. 11:11, 12 [3900] See *sin; transgression; trespass.*

[4184] παραρρέω *pararreō* 1x *to flow beside; to glide aside from; to fall off* from profession, *decline* from steadfastness, *make forfeit* of faith, Heb. 2:1* [3901]

[4185] παράσημος *parasēmos* 1x *a distinguishing mark; an ensign* of a ship, Acts 28:11* [3902]

[4186] παρασκευάζω *paraskeuazō* 4x *to prepare, make ready,* 2 Cor. 9:2, 3; mid. *to prepare one's self,* *put one's self in readiness,* Acts 10:10; 1 Cor. 14:8* [3903]

[4187] παρασκευή *paraskeuē* 6x *a getting ready, preparation,* in NT *preparation* for a feast, *day of preparation,* Mt. 27:62; Mk. 15:42 [3904]

[4189] παρατείνω *parateinō* 1x *to extend, stretch out; to prolong, continue,* Acts 20:7* [3905]

[4190] παρατηρέω *paratēreō* 6x *to watch closely,* Acts 9:24; *to observe* or *watch insidiously,* Mk. 3:2; Lk. 6:7; 14:1; 20:20; *to observe scrupulously,* Gal. 4:10* [3906]

[4191] παρατήρησις *paratērēsis* 1x *careful watching, intent observation,* Lk. 17:20* [3907]

[4192] παρατίθημι *paratithēmi* 19x *to place by the side of,* or *near; to set before,* Mk. 6:41; 8:6, 7; Lk. 9:16; met. *to set* or *lay before, propound,* Mt. 13:24, 31; *to inculcate,* Acts 17:3; *to deposit, commit to the charge of, entrust,* Lk. 12:48; 23:46; *to commend,* Acts 14:23 [3908] See *commit; set before.*

[4193] παρατυγχάνω *paratynchanō* 1x *to happen, to chance upon, chance to meet,* Acts 17:17* [3909]

[4194] παραυτίκα *parautika* 1x *instantly, immediately;* ὁ, ἡ, τό, παραυτίκα, *momentary, transient,* 2 Cor. 4:17* [3910]

[4195] παραφέρω *parapherō* 4x *to carry past; to cause to pass away,* Mk. 14:36; Lk. 22:42; pass. *to be swept along,* Jude 12; *to be led away, misled, seduced,* Heb. 13:9* [3911]

[4196] παραφρονέω *paraphroneō* 1x *to be beside oneself;* παραφρονῶν, *in foolish style,* 2 Cor. 11:23* [3912]

[4197] παραφρονία *paraphronia* 1x *madness, folly,* 2 Pet. 2:16* [3913]

[4199] παραχειμάζω *paracheimazō* 4x *to winter, spend the winter,* Acts 27:12; 28:11; 1 Cor. 16:6; Tit. 3:12* [3914]

[4200] παραχειμασία *paracheimasia* 1x *a wintering* in a place, Acts 27:12* [3915]

[4202] παραχρῆμα *parachrēma* 18x *at once, immediately,* Mt. 21:19, 20; Lk. 1:64 [3916] See *immediately.*

[4203] πάρδαλις *pardalis* 1x *a leopard* or *panther,* Rev. 13:2* [3917]

[4204] παρεδρεύω *paredreuō* 1x *to sit near; to attend, serve,* 1 Cor. 9:13* [4332]

[4205] πάρειμι *pareimi* 24x *to be beside; to be present,* Lk. 13:1; *to have come,* Mt. 26:50; Jn. 7:6; 11:28; Col. 1:6; *to be in possession,* Heb. 13:5; 2 Pet. 1:9, 12; part. παρών, οὖσα, όν, *present,* 1 Cor. 5:3; τὸ παρόν, *the present time, the present,* Heb. 12:11 [3918] See *(be) present.*

[4206] παρεισάγω *pareisagō* 1x *to introduce stealthily,* 2 Pet. 2:1* [3919]

[4207] παρείσακτος *pareisaktos* 1x *secretly introduced, brought in stealthily,* Gal. 2:4* [3920]

[4209] παρεισέρχομαι *pareiserchomai* 2x *to slip in, come in* as a side issue, Rom. 5:20; *to steal in,* Gal. 2:4* [3922]

[4210] παρεισφέρω *pareispherō* 1x *to bring in beside; to bring into play, exhibit in addition,* 2 Pet. 1:5* [3923]

[4211] παρεκτός *parektos* 3x can function as an improper prep., *without, on the outside; except,* Mt. 5:32; Acts 26:29; τὰ παρεκτός, *other matters,* 2 Cor. 11:28 [3924]

[4212] παρεμβάλλω *paremballō* 1x *to cast up, set up, throw up* a palisade, Lk. 19:43* [4016]

[4213] παρεμβολή *parembolē* 10x *an insertion besides;* later, *a marshalling* of an army; *an array* of battle, *army,* Heb. 11:34; *a camp,* Heb. 13:11, 13; Rev. 20:9; *a standing camp, fortress, citadel, castle,* Acts 21:34, 37; 22:24; 23:10, 16, 32* [3925] See *barracks; camp.*

[4214] παρενοχλέω *parenochleō* 1x *to trouble, harass,* Acts 15:19* [3926]

[4215] παρεπίδημος *parepidēmos* 3x *residing in a country not one's own, a sojourner, stranger,* Heb. 11:13; 1 Pet. 1:1; 2:11* [3927] See *alien; strange(r).*

[4216] παρέρχομαι *parerchomai* 29x *to pass beside, pass along, pass by,* Mt. 8:28; Mk. 6:48; *to pass, elapse,* as time, Mt. 14:15; Acts 27:19; *to pass away, be removed,* Mt. 26:39, 42; Mk. 14:35; met. *to pass away, disappear, vanish, perish,* Mt. 5:18; 24:34, 35; *to become vain, be rendered void,* Mt. 5:18; Mk. 13:31; trans. *to pass by, disregard, neglect,* Lk. 11:42; 15:29; *to come to the side of, come to,* Lk. 12:37; 17:7 [3928] See *disappear; pass away; pass by.*

[4217] πάρεσις *paresis* 1x *a letting pass; a passing over,* Rom. 3:25* [3929]

[4218] παρέχω *parechō* 16x *to hold beside; to hold out to, offer, present,* Lk. 6:29; *to confer, render,* Lk.

7:4; Acts 22:2; 28:2; Col. 4:1; *to afford, furnish,* Acts 16:16; 17:31; 19:24; 1 Tim. 6:17; *to exhibit,* Tit. 2:7; *to be the cause of, occasion,* Mt. 26:10; Mk. 14:6; Lk. 11:7 [3930] See *bother; provide.*

[4219] παρηγορία *parēgoria* 1x *exhortation; comfort, solace, consolation,* Col. 4:11* [3931]

[4220] παρθενία *parthenia* 1x *virginity,* Lk. 2:36* [3932]

[4221] παρθένος *parthenos* 15x *a virgin, maid,* Mt. 1:23; 25:1, 7, 11; Acts 21:9; in NT also masc., *chaste,* Rev. 14:4 [3933] See *virgin.*

[4222] Πάρθοι *Parthoi* 1x *a Parthian, a native of Parthia, in central Asia,* Acts 2:9 [3934]

[4223] παρίημι *pariēmi* 2x *to let pass beside, let fall beside; to relax,* Lk. 11:42; perf. pass. part. παρειμένος, *hanging down helplessly, unstrung, feeble,* Heb. 12:12* [3935]

[4225] παρίστημι *paristēmi* 41x pluperfect, παρειστήκειν, also formed as παριστάνω. (1) Trans. *to place beside; to have in readiness, provide,* Acts 23:24; *to range beside, to place at the disposal of,* Mt. 26:53; Acts 9:41; *to present* to God, *dedicate, consecrate, devote,* Lk. 2:22; Rom. 6:13, 19; *to prove, demonstrate, show,* Acts 1:3; 24:13; *to commend, recommend,* 1 Cor. 8:8.

(2) Intrans. (all mid. forms, perfect and pluperfect, second aorist act.) perf. παρέστηκα, part. παρεστώς, pluperf. παρειστήκειν, 2 aor. παρέστην, and mid., *to stand by* or *before,* Acts 27:24; Rom. 14:10; *to stand by, to be present,* Mk. 14:47, 69, 70; *to stand in attendance, attend,* Lk. 1:19; 1:24; of time, *to be present, have come,* Mk. 4:29; *to stand by* in aid, *assist, support,* Rom. 16:2 [3936] See *offer; place; present; stand.*

[4226] Παρμενᾶς *Parmenas* 1x *Parmenas,* pr. name, Acts 6:5* [3937]

[4227] πάροδος *parodos* 1x *a way by; a passing by;* ἐν παρόδῳ, *in passing, by the way,* 1 Cor. 16:7* [3938]

[4228] παροικέω *paroikeō* 2x *to dwell beside;* later, *to reside in a place as a stranger, sojourn, be a stranger* or *sojourner,* Lk. 24:18; Heb. 11:9* [3939]

[4229] παροικία *paroikia* 2x *a sojourning, temporary residence in a foreign land,* Acts 13:17; 1 Pet. 1:17* [3940]

[4230] πάροικος *paroikos* 4x *a neighbor;* later, *a sojourner, temporary resident, stranger,* Acts 7:6, 29; Eph. 2:19; 1 Pet. 2:11* [3941] See *alien; foreign(er); strange(r).*

[4231] παροιμία *paroimia* 5x *a by-word, proverb, adage,* 2 Pet. 2:22; in NT *an obscure saying, enigma,* Jn. 16:25, 29; *a parable, similitude, figurative discourse,* Jn. 10:6* [3942]

[4232] πάροινος *paroinos* 2x pr. *pertaining to wine, drunken;* hence, *quarrelsome, insolent, overbearing,* 1 Tim. 3:3; Tit. 1:7* [3943]

[4233] παροίχομαι *paroichomai* 1x *to have gone by;* perf. part. παρῳχημένος, *by-gone,* Acts 14:16* [3944]

[4234] παρομοιάζω *paromoiazō* 1x *to be like, to resemble,* Mt. 23:27* [3945]

[4235] παρόμοιος *paromoios* 1x *nearly resembling, similar, like,* Mk. 7:13* [3946]

[4236] παροξύνω *paroxynō* 2x *to sharpen;* met. *to incite, stir up,* Acts 17:16; *to irritate, provoke,* 1 Cor. 13:5* [3947]

[4237] παροξυσμός *paroxysmos* 2x *an inciting, incitement,* Heb. 10:24; *a sharp fit of anger, sharp contention, angry dispute,* Acts 15:39* [3948]

[4239] παροργίζω *parorgizō* 2x *to provoke to anger, irritate, exasperate,* Rom. 10:19; Eph. 6:4* [3949]

[4240] παροργισμός *parorgismos* 1x *provocation to anger; anger excited, indignation, wrath,* Eph. 4:26* [3950]

[4241] παροτρύνω *parotrynō* 1x *to stir up, incite, instigate,* Acts 13:50* [3951]

[4242] παρουσία *parousia* 24x *presence,* 2 Cor. 10:10; Phil. 2:12; *a coming, arrival, advent,* Phil. 1:26; Mt. 24:3, 27, 37, 39; 1 Cor. 15:23 [3952] See *coming; presence.*

[4243] παροψίς *paropsis* 1x pr. *a dainty side dish;* meton. *a plate, platter,* Mt. 23:25* [3953]

[4244] παρρησία *parrēsia* 31x *freedom in speaking, boldness of speech,* Acts 4:13; παρρησίᾳ, as an adv., *freely, boldly,* Jn. 7:13, 26; so μετὰ παρρησίας, Acts 2:29; 4:29, 31; *license, authority,* Phlm. 8; *confidence, assurance,* 2 Cor. 7:4; Eph. 3:12; Heb. 3:6; 10:19; *openness, frankness,* 2 Cor. 3:12; παρρησίᾳ, and ἐν παρρησίᾳ, adverbially, *openly, plainly, perspicuously, unambiguously,* Mk. 8:32; Jn. 10:24; *publicly,* *before all,* Jn. 7:4 [3954] See *assurance; boldness; certainty; confidence.*

[4245] παρρησιάζομαι *parrēsiazomai* 9x *to speak plainly, freely, boldly, and confidently,* Acts 13:46; 14:3 [3955]

[4246] πᾶς *pas* 1,243x *all;* in the sg. *the whole, entire,* usually when the substantive has the article, Mt. 6:29; 8:32; Acts 19:26; *every,* only with an anarthrous subst., Mt. 3:10; 4:4; pl. *all,* Mt. 1:17, et al. freq.; πάντα, *in all respects,* Acts 20:35; 1 Cor. 9:25; 10:33; 11:2; by a Hebraism, a negative with πᾶς is sometimes equivalent to οὐδείς or μηδείς, Mt. 24:22; Lk. 1:37; Acts 10:14; Rom. 3:20; 1 Cor. 1:29; Eph. 4:29 [3956] See *all; each; every.*

[4247] πάσχα *pascha* 29x *the passover, the paschal lamb,* Mt. 26:17; Mk. 14:12; met. used of Christ, the true *paschal lamb,* 1 Cor. 5:7; *the feast of the passover, the day on which the paschal lamb was slain and eaten,* the 14th of Nisan, Mt. 26:18; Mk. 14:1; Heb. 11:28; more genr. *the whole paschal festival,* including the seven days of *the feast of unleavened bread,* Mt. 26:2; Lk. 2:41; Jn. 2:13 [3957] See *passover.*

[4248] πάσχω *paschō* 42x *to be affected by* a thing, whether good or bad, *to suffer, endure* evil, Mt. 16:21; 17:12, 15; 27:19; absol. *to suffer* death, Lk. 22:15; 24:26 [3958] See *suffer.*

[4249] Πάταρα *Patara* 1x *Patara,* a city on the seacoast of Lycia, in Asia Minor, Acts 21:1* [3959]

[4250] πατάσσω *patassō* 10x *to strike, beat upon; to smite, wound,* Mt. 26:51; Lk. 22:49, 50; by impl. *to kill, slay,* Mt. 26:31; Mk. 14:27; Acts 7:24; *to strike gently,* Acts 12:7; from the Hebrew, *to smite* with disease, plagues, etc., Acts 12:23; Rev. 11:6; 19:15* [3960] See *hit; strike.*

[4251] πατέω *pateō* 5x intrans. *to tread,* Lk. 10:19; trans. *to tread* the winepress, Rev. 14:20; 19:15; *to trample,* Lk. 21:24; Rev. 11:2* [3961]

[4252] πατήρ *patēr* 413x *a father,* Mt. 2:22; 4:21, 22; spc. used of God, as the *Father* of man by creation, preservation, etc., Mt. 5:16, 45, 48; and peculiarly as the *Father* of our Lord Jesus Christ, Mt. 7:21; 2 Cor. 1:3; *the founder of a race, remote progenitor, forefather, ancestor,* Mt. 3:9; 23:30, 32; *an elder, senior, father* in age, 1 Jn. 2:13, 14; *a* spiritual *father,* 1 Cor. 4:15; *father* by origination, Jn. 8:44; Heb. 12:9; used as an appellation of honor, Mt. 23:9; Acts 7:2 [3962] See *ancestor; father.*

[4253] Πάτμος *Patmos* 1x *Patmos,* an island in the Aegean sea, Rev. 1:9* [3963]

[4255] πατριά *patria* 3x *descent, lineage; a family, tribe, race,* Lk. 2:4; Acts 3:25; Eph. 3:15* [3965]

[4256] πατριάρχης *patriarchēs* 4x *a patriarch, head* or *founder of a family,* Acts 2:29; 7:8, 9; Heb. 7:4* [3966]

[4257] πατρικός *patrikos* 1x *from fathers* or *ancestors, ancestral, paternal,* Gal. 1:14* [3967]

[4258] πατρίς *patris* 8x *one's native place, country,* or *city,* Mt. 13:54, 57; Mk. 6:1, 4; Lk. 4:23, 24; Jn. 4:44; *a* heavenly *country,* Heb. 11:14* [3968]

[4259] Πατροβᾶς *Patrobas* 1x *Patrobas,* pr. name, Rom. 16:14* [3969]

[4260] πατρολῴας *patrolōas* 1x also spelled πατραλῴας, *one who kills one's father, a patricide,* 1 Tim. 1:9* [3964]

[4261] πατροπαράδοτος *patroparadotos* 1x *handed down* or *received by tradition from one's fathers* or *ancestors,* 1 Pet. 1:18* [3970]

[4262] πατρῷος *patrōos* 3x *received from one's ancestors, paternal, ancestral,* Acts 22:3; 24:14; 28:17* [3971]

[4263] Παῦλος *Paulos* 158x *Paulus, Paul,* pr. name. (1) *Paul, the Apostle,* Acts 13:9, et al. freq. (2) *Sergius Paulus, the deputy* or *proconsul of Cyprus,* Acts 13:7 [3972]

[4264] παύω *pauō* 15x *to cause to pause* or *cease, restrain, prohibit,* 1 Pet. 3:10; mid. perf. πέπαυται, *to cease, stop, leave off, desist, refrain,* 1 Pet. 4:1 [3973] See *finish; stop.*

[4265] Πάφος *Paphos* 2x *Paphos,* the chief city in the island of Cyprus [3974]

[4266] παχύνω *pachunō* 2x *to fatten, make gross;* met. pass. *to be rendered gross, dull, unfeeling,* Mt. 13:15; Acts 28:27* [3975]

[4267] πέδη *pedē* 3x *a fetter, shackle,* Mk. 5:4; Lk. 8:29* [3976]

[4268] πεδινός *pedinos* 1x *level, flat,* Lk. 6:17* [3977]

[4269] πεζεύω *pezeuō* 1x pr. *to travel on foot; to travel by land,* Acts 20:13* [3978]

[4270] πεζῇ *pezē* 2x *on foot,* or, *by land,* Mt. 14:13; Mk. 6:33 [3979]

[4272] πειθαρχέω *peitharcheō* 4x *to obey* one *in authority,* Acts 5:29, 32; Tit. 3:1; genr. *to obey, follow,* or *conform to advice,* Acts 27:21* [3980]

[4273] πειθός *peithos* 1x also spelled πιθός, *persuasive, skillful,* 1 Cor. 2:4* [3981]

[4275] πείθω *peithō* 52x pluperfect, ἐπεποίθειν, *to persuade, seek to persuade, endeavor to convince,* Acts 18:4; 19:8, 26; 28:23; *to persuade, influence by persuasion,* Mt. 27:20; Acts 13:43; 26:28; *to incite, instigate,* Acts 14:19; *to appease, render tranquil, to quiet,* 1 Jn. 3:19; *to strive to conciliate, aspire to the favor of,* Gal. 1:10; *to pacify, conciliate, win over,* Mt. 28:14; Acts 12:20; pass. and mid. *to be persuaded of, be confident of,* Lk. 20:6; Rom. 8:38; Heb. 6:9; *to suffer one's self to be persuaded, yield to persuasion, to be induced,* Acts 21:14; *to be convinced, to believe, yield belief,* Lk. 16:31; Acts 17:4; *to assent, listen to, obey, follow,* Acts 5:36, 37, 40; 2 perf. πέποιθα, to *be assured, be confident,* 2 Cor. 2:3; Phil. 1:6; Heb. 13:18; *to confide in, trust, rely on, place hope and confidence in,* Mt. 27:43; Mk. 10:24; Rom. 2:19 [3982] See *convince; persuade.*

[4277] πεινάω *peinaō* 23x *to hunger, be hungry,* Mt. 4:2; Mk. 11:12; *to be exposed to hunger, be famished,* 1 Cor. 4:11; Phil. 4:12; met. *to hunger after, desire earnestly, long for,* Mt. 5:6 [3983] See *hungry.*

[4278] πεῖρα *peira* 2x *a trial, attempt, endeavor;* λαμβάνειν πεῖραν, *to attempt,* Heb. 11:29; also, *to experience,* Heb. 11:36* [3984]

[4279] πειράζω *peirazō* 38x *to make proof* or *trial of, put to the proof,* whether with good or mischievous intent, Mt. 16:1; 22:35; absol. *to attempt,* Acts 16:7; 24:6; in NT *to tempt,* Mt. 4:1; *to try, subject to trial,* 1 Cor. 10:13 [3985] See *attempt; tempt; test; try.*

[4280] πειρασμός *peirasmos* 21x *a test, proof, trial,* 1 Pet. 4:12; Heb. 3:8; direct *temptation* to sin, Lk. 4:13; *trial, temptation,* Mt. 6:13; 26:41; 1 Cor. 10:13; *trial, calamity, affliction,* Lk. 22:28 [3986] See *temptation; trial.*

[4281] πειράω *peiraō* 1x *to try, attempt, essay, endeavor,* Acts 26:21* [3987]

[4282] πεισμονή *peismonē* 1x *a yielding to persuasion, assent,* Gal. 5:8* [3988]

[4283] πέλαγος *pelagos* 2x *the deep, the open sea,* Mt. 18:6; *a sea,* distinguished from the sea in general, and named from an adjacent country, Acts 27:5* [3989]

[4284] πελεκίζω *pelekizō* 1x *to strike* or *cut with an axe; to behead,* Rev. 20:4* [3990]

[4286] πέμπτος *pemptos* 4x *fifth,* Rev. 6:9; 9:1; 16:10; 21:20* [3991]

[4287] πέμπω *pempō* 79x *to send, to dispatch on any message, embassy, business,* etc., Mt. 2:8; 11:2; 14:10; *to transmit,* Acts 11:29; Rev. 1:11; *to dismiss, permit to go,* Mk. 5:12; *to send in* or *among,* 2 Thess. 2:11; *to thrust in,* or *put forth,* Rev. 14:15, 18 [3992] See *send.*

[4288] πένης *penēs* 1x pr. *one who labors for his bread; poor, needy,* 2 Cor. 9:9* [3993]

[4289] πενθερά *penthera* 6x *a mother-in-law,* Mt. 8:14; 10:35; Mk. 1:30; Lk. 4:38; 12:53* [3994]

[4290] πενθερός *pentheros* 1x *a father-in-law,* Jn. 18:13* [3995]

[4291] πενθέω *pentheō* 10x trans. *to lament over,* 2 Cor. 12:21; absol. *to lament, be sad, mourn,* Mt. 5:4; 9:15; Mk. 16:10; mid. *to be sad, grieve, to feel guilt,* 1 Cor. 5:2 [3996] See *bewail; mourn.*

[4292] πένθος *penthos* 5x *mourning, sorrow, sadness, grief,* Jas. 4:9 [3997]

[4293] πενιχρός *penichros* 1x *poor, needy,* Lk. 21:2* [3998]

[4294] πεντάκις *pentakis* 1x *five times,* 2 Cor. 11:24* [3999]

[4295] πεντακισχίλιοι *pentakischilioi* 6x *five times one thousand, five thousand,* Mt. 14:21; 16:9 [4000]

[4296] πεντακόσιοι *pentakosioi* 2x *five hundred,* Lk. 7:41; 1 Cor. 15:6* [4001]

[4297] πέντε *pente* 38x *five,* Mt. 14:17, 19; 16:9 [4002] See *five.*

[4298] πεντεκαιδέκατος *pentekaidekatos* 1x *fifteenth,* Lk. 3:1* [4003]

[4299] πεντήκοντα *pentēkonta* 7x *fifty,* Mk. 6:40; Lk. 7:41 [4004]

[4300] πεντηκοστή *pentēkostē* 3x *Pentecost,* or *the Feast of Weeks;* one of the three great Jewish festivals, so called because it was celebrated on the *fiftieth* day, reckoning from the second day of the feast of unleavened bread, i.e., from the 16th day of Nisan, Acts 2:1; 20:16; 1 Cor. 16:8* [4005] See *Pentecost.*

[4301] πεποίθησις *pepoithēsis* 6x *trust, confidence, reliance,* 2 Cor. 1:15 [4006]

[4304] περαιτέρω *peraiterō* 1x compar. adv. of πέραν, Acts 19:39* [4012 + 2087]

[4305] πέραν *peran* 23x can function as an improper prep., *across, beyond, over, on the other side,* Mt. 4:15, 25; 19:1; Jn. 6:1, 17; ὁ, ἡ, τό, πέραν, *farther, on the farther side,* and τὸ πέραν, *the farther side, the other side,* Mt. 8:18, 28; 14:22 [4008]

[4306] πέρας *peras* 4x *an extremity, end,* Mt. 12:42; Lk. 11:31; Rom. 10:18; *an end, conclusion, termination,* Heb. 6:16* [4009]

[4307] Πέργαμος *Pergamos* 2x *Pergamus,* a city of Mysia, in Asia Minor, Rev. 1:11; 2:12* [4010]

[4308] Πέργη *Pergē* 3x *Perga,* the chief city of Pamphylia, in Asia Minor, Acts 13:13f.; 14:25 [4011]

[4309] περί *peri* 333x pr. of place. (1) gen., *about, around; about, concerning, respecting,* Mt. 2:8; 11:10; 22:31; Jn. 8:18; Rom. 8:3, et al. freq.

(2) acc., of place, *about, around, round about,* Mt. 3:4; Mk. 3:34; Lk. 13:8; οἱ περί τινα, *the companions* of a person, Lk. 22:49; *a person and his companions,* Acts 13:13; simply *a person,* Jn. 11:19; τὰ περί τινα, *the condition, circumstances of* any one, Phil. 2:23; of time, *about,* Mt. 20:3, 5, 6, 9; *about, concerning, respecting, touching,* Lk. 10:40; 1 Tim. 1:19; 6:21; Tit. 2:7 [4012]

[4310] περιάγω *periagō* 6x *to lead around, carry about* Acts 13:11 in one's company, 1 Cor. 9:5; *to traverse,* Mt. 4:23; 9:35; 23:15; Mk. 6:6 [4013]

[4311] περιαιρέω *periaireō* 5x *to take off, lift off, remove,* 2 Cor. 3:16; *to cast off,* Acts 27:40; met. *to cut off* hope, Acts 27:20; met. *to take away* sin, *remove the guilt* of sin, *make expiation for* sin, Heb. 10:11 [4014]

[4312] περιάπτω *periaptō* 1x *to light a fire, kindle,* Lk. 22:55* [681]

[4313] περιαστράπτω *periastraptō* 2x *to lighten around, shine like lightning around,* Acts 9:3; 22:6* [4015]

[4314] περιβάλλω *periballō* 23x *to cast around; to clothe,* Mt. 25:36, 38, 43; mid. *to clothe one's self, to be clothed,* Mt. 6:29, 31; Lk. 23:11; Jn. 19:2; Acts 12:8; Rev. 4:4 [4016] See *clothe; dress; wear.*

[4315] περιβλέπω *periblepō* 7x trans. *to look around upon,* Mk. 3:5, 34; 11:11; Lk. 6:10; absol. *to look around,* Mk. 5:32; 9:8; 10:23* [4017]

[4316] περιβόλαιον *peribolaion* 2x *that which is thrown around* any one, *clothing, covering; a cloak,* Heb. 1:12; *a covering,* 1 Cor. 11:15* [4018]

[4317] περιδέω *perideō* 1x pluperfect, περιεδέδετο (pass., 3 sg), *to bind round about;* pass. *to be bound around, be bound up,* Jn. 11:44* [4019]

[4318] περιεργάζομαι *periergazomai* 1x *to do a thing with excessive* or *superfluous care; to be a busybody,* 2 Thess. 3:11* [4020]

[4319] περίεργος *periergos* 2x *over careful; officious, a busybody,* 1 Tim. 5:13; in NT περίεργα, *magic arts, sorcery,* Acts 19:19* [4021]

[4320] περιέρχομαι *perierchomai* 3x *to go about, wander about, rove,* Acts 19:13; Heb. 11:37; *to go about, visit* from house to house, 1 Tim. 5:13* [4022]

[4321] περιέχω *periechō* 2x *to encompass, enclose;* met. *to encompass, seize on* the mind, Lk. 5:9; περιέχει, impers. *it is contained, it is among the contents* of a writing, 1 Pet. 2:6* [4023]

[4322] περιζώννυμι *perizōnnymi* 6x also spelled περιζωννύω, *to bind around with a girdle, gird;* in NT mid. *to gird one's self* in preparation for bodily motion and exertion, Lk. 12:37; 17:8; *to wear a girdle,* Rev. 1:13; 15:6 [4024]

[4324] περίθεσις *perithesis* 1x *a putting on, wearing* of dress, etc., 1 Pet. 3:3* [4025]

[4325] περιΐστημι *periistēmi* 4x *to place around;* intrans. 2 aor. περιέστην, perf. part. περιεστώς, *to stand around,* Jn. 11:42; Acts 25:7; mid. *to keep aloof from, avoid, shun,* 2 Tim. 2:16; Tit. 3:9* [4026]

[4326] περικάθαρμα *perikatharma* 1x pr. *filth;* met. *refuse, outcast,* 1 Cor. 4:13* [4027]

[4328] περικαλύπτω *perikalyptō* 3x *to cover round about, cover over; to cover* the face, Mk. 14:65; *to blindfold,* Lk. 22:64; pass. *to be overlaid,* Heb. 9:4* [4028]

[4329] περίκειμαι *perikeimai* 5x *to lie around, surround,* Heb. 12:1; *to be hung around,* Mk. 9:42; Lk. 17:2; *to have around one's self, to wear,* Acts 28:20; *to be in submission to,* Heb. 5:2* [4029]

[4330] περικεφαλαία *perikephalaia* 2x *a helmet,* Eph. 6:17; 1 Thess. 5:8* [4030]

[4331] περικρατής *perikratēs* 1x *overpowering;* περικρατὴς γενέσθαι, *to become master of, to secure,* Acts 27:16* [4031]

[4332] περικρύβω *perikrybō* 1x also spelled περικρύπτω, *to hide* or *keep from sight, to conceal by envelopment; to conceal,* Lk. 1:24* [4032]

[4333] περικυκλόω *perikykloō* 1x *to encircle, surround,* Lk. 19:43* [4033]

[4334] περιλάμπω *perilampō* 2x *to shine around,* Lk. 2:9; Acts 26:13* [4034]

[4335] περιλείπομαι *perileipomai* 2x *to leave remaining;* pass. *to remain, survive,* 1 Thess. 4:15, 17* [4035]

[4337] περίλυπος *perilypos* 5x *greatly grieved, exceedingly sorrowful,* Mt. 26:38; Mk. 14:34 [4036]

[4338] περιμένω *perimenō* 1x *to await, wait for,* Acts 1:4* [4037]

[4339] πέριξ *perix* 1x *neighboring,* Acts 5:16* [4038]

[4340] περιοικέω *perioikeō* 1x *to dwell around,* or *in the vicinity; to be a neighbor,* Lk. 1:65* [4039]

[4341] περίοικος *perioikos* 1x *one who dwells in the vicinity, a neighbor,* Lk. 1:58* [4040]

[4342] περιούσιος *periousios* 1x *chosen; peculiar, special,* Tit. 2:14* [4041]

[4343] περιοχή *periochē* 1x lit., *a compass, circumference, contents;* fig., *a section, a portion* of Scripture, Acts 8:32* [4042]

[4344] περιπατέω *peripateō* 95x pluperfect, περι[ε]πεπατήκει (3 sg), *to walk, walk about,* Mt. 9:5; 11:5; 14:25, 26, 29; *to rove, roam,* 1 Pet. 5:8; with μετά, *to accompany, follow,* Jn. 6:66; Rev. 3:4; *to walk, frequent* a locality, Jn. 7:1; 11:54; from the Hebrew, *to maintain a* certain *walk* of life and conduct, Gal. 5:16; Eph. 2:10 [4043] See *behave; live; walk.*

[4345] περιπείρω *peripeirō* 1x *to put on a spit, transfix;* met. *to pierce, wound deeply,* 1 Tim. 6:10* [4044]

[4346] περιπίπτω *peripiptō* 3x *to fall around* or *upon, to fall in with,* Lk. 10:30; *to fall into, light upon,* Acts 27:41; *to be involved in,* Jas. 1:2* [4045]

[4347] περιποιέω *peripoieō* 3x *to cause to remain over and above, to reserve, save,* Lk. 17:33; mid. *to acquire, gain, earn,* 1 Tim. 3:13; *to purchase,* Acts 20:28* [4046]

[4348] περιποίησις *peripoiēsis* 5x *a laying up, keeping; an acquiring* or *obtaining, acquisition,* 1 Thess. 5:9; 2 Thess. 2:14; *a saving, preservation,* Heb. 10:39; *a peculiar possession, specialty,* Eph. 1:14; 1 Pet. 2:9* [4047]

[4351] περιρήγνυμι *perirēgnymi* 1x also spelled περιρρήγνυμι, *to break* or *tear all around; to strip off,* Acts 16:22* [4048]

[4352] περισπάω *perispaō* 1x *to draw off from around; to wheel about; to distract;* pass. *to be distracted, over busied,* Lk. 10:40* [4049]

[4353] περισσεία *perisseia* 4x *superabundance,* Rom. 5:17; 2 Cor. 8:2; 10:15; Jas. 1:21* [4050]

[4354] περίσσευμα *perisseuma* 5x *more than enough, residue over and above,* Mk. 8:8; *abundance, exuberance,* Mt. 12:34; Lk. 6:45; *superabundance, affluence,* 2 Cor. 8:14* [4051]

[4355] περισσεύω *perisseuō* 39x *to be over and above, to be superfluous,* Mt. 14:20; Mk. 12:44; Lk. 21:4; *to exist in full quantity, to abound, be abundant,* Rom. 5:15; 2 Cor. 1:5; *to increase, be augmented,* Acts 16:5; *to be advanced, be rendered more prominent,* Rom. 3:7; of persons, *to be abundantly gifted, richly furnished, abound,* Lk. 15:17; Rom. 15:13; 1 Cor. 14:12; 2 Cor. 8:7; *to be possessed of a full sufficiency,* Phil. 4:12, 18; *to abound* in performance, 1 Cor. 15:58; *to be a gainer,* 1 Cor. 8:8; in NT trans., *to cause to be abundant,* 2 Cor. 4:15; 9:8; Eph. 1:8; *to cause to be abundantly furnished, cause to abound,* 1 Thess. 3:12; pass. *to be gifted with abundance,* Mt. 13:12; 25:29 [4052] See *abound; exceed; left over; overflow.*

[4356] περισσός *perissos* 6x *over and above,* Mt. 5:37; *superfluous,* 2 Cor. 9:1; *extraordinary,* Mt. 5:47; compar. *more, greater,* Mt. 11:9; 23:14; *excessive,* 2 Cor. 2:7; adverbially, περισσόν, *in full abundance,* Jn. 10:10; περισσότερον, and ἐκ περισσοῦ, *exceedingly, vehemently,* Mk. 6:51; 7:36; 1 Cor. 15:10; Eph. 3:20; τὸ περισσόν, *preeminence, advantage,* Rom. 3:1 [4053]

[4358] περισσότερος *perissoteros* 16x comparative adj. from περισσός, *greater, more,* Mk. 12:40; Lk. 20:47; *even more,* Lk. 12:48; 1 Cor. 15:10; *even more, so much more,* Mk. 7:36 [4055] See *greater; more.*

[4359] περισσοτέρως *perissoterōs* 12x *more, more abundantly, more earnestly, more vehemently,* 2 Cor. 7:13; *exceedingly,* Gal. 1:14 [4056] See *beyond measure; exceedlingly.*

[4360] περισσῶς *perissōs* 4x *much, abundantly, vehemently,* Acts 26:11; *more, more abundantly,* Mt. 27:23; Mk. 10:26; 15:14* [4057]

[4361] περιστερά *peristera* 10x *a dove, pigeon,* Mt. 3:16; 10:16 [4058] See *dove; pigeon.*

[4362] περιτέμνω *peritemnō* 17x *to cut around; to circumcise, remove the prepuce,* Lk. 1:59; 2:21; met. Col. 2:11; mid. *to submit to circumcision,* Acts 15:1 [4059] See *circumcise.*

[4363] περιτίθημι *peritithēmi* 8x *to place around, put about* or *around,* Mt. 21:33; 27:28; met. *to attach, bestow,* 1 Cor. 12:23 [4060]

[4364] περιτομή *peritomē* 36x *circumcision, the act* or *custom of circumcision,* Jn. 7:22, 23; Acts 7:8; *the state of being circumcised, the being circumcised,* Rom. 2:25, 26, 27; 4:10; meton. *the circumcision, those who are circumcised,* Rom. 3:30; 4:9 met. spiritual *circumcision* of the heart and affection, Rom. 2:29; Col. 2:11; meton. *persons* spiritually *circumcised,* Phil. 3:3 [4061] See *circumcision.*

[4365] περιτρέπω *peritrepō* 1x *to turn about; to bring round* into any state, Acts 26:24* [4062]

[4366] περιτρέχω *peritrechō* 1x *to run about, run up and down,* Mk. 6:55* [4063]

[4367] περιφέρω *peripherō* 3x *to bear* or *carry about,* Mk. 6:55; 2 Cor. 4:10; pass. *to be borne about hither and thither, driven to and fro,* Eph. 4:14* [4064]

[4368] περιφρονέω *periphroneō* 1x *to contemplate, reflect on; to despise, disregard,* Tit. 2:15* [4065]

[4369] περίχωρος *perichōros* 9x *neighboring;* ἡ περίχωρος, sc. γῆ, *an adjacent region, country round about,* Mt. 14:35; Mk. 1:28; meton. *inhabitants of the region round about,* Mt. 3:5 [4066]

[4370] περίψημα *peripsēma* 1x *filth which is wiped off;* met. 1 Cor. 4:13* [4067]

[4371] περπερεύομαι *perpereuomai* 1x *to vaunt one's self,* 1 Cor. 13:4* [4068]

[4372] Περσίς *Persis* 1x *Persis,* pr. name, Rom. 16:12* [4069]

[4373] πέρυσι *perysi* 2x *last year, a year ago,* 2 Cor. 8:10; 9:2* [4070]

[4374] πετεινόν *peteinon* 14x *a bird, fowl,* Mt. 6:26; 8:20 [4071] See *bird.*

[4375] πέτομαι *petomai* 5x also spelled πετάομαι, *to fly,* Rev. 4:7; 8:13; 12:14; 14:6; 19:17* [4072]

[4376] πέτρα *petra* 15x *a rock,* Mt. 7:24, 25; met. Rom. 9:33; 1 Pet. 2:8; *crags, clefts,* Rev. 6:15, 16; *stony ground,* Lk. 8:6, 13 [4073] See *rock.*

[4377] Πέτρος *Petros* 156x *a stone;* in NT the Greek rendering of the surname Cephas, given to the Apostle Simon, and having, therefore, the same sense as πέτρα, *Peter,* Mt. 4:18; 8:14 [4074]

[4378] πετρώδης *petrōdēs* 4x *like rock; stony, rocky,* Mt. 13:5, 20; Mk. 4:5, 16* [4075]

[4379] πήγανον *pēganon* 1x *rue,* a plant, *ruta graveolens* of Linnaeus, Lk. 11:42* [4076]

[4380] πηγή *pēgē* 11x *a source, spring, fountain,* Jas. 3:11, 12; *a well,* Jn. 4:6; *an issue, flux, flow,* Mk. 5:29; met. Jn. 4:14 [4077] See *fountain; spring; well.*

[4381] πήγνυμι *pēgnymi* 1x *to fasten; to pitch* a tent, Heb. 8:2* [4078]

[4382] πηδάλιον *pēdalion* 2x *a rudder,* Acts 27:40; Jas. 3:4* [4079]

[4383] πηλίκος *pēlikos* 2x *how large,* Gal. 6:11; *how great* in dignity, Heb. 7:4* [4080]

[4384] πηλός *pēlos* 6x *moist earth, mud, slime,* Jn. 9:6, 11, 14, 15; *clay,* potter's *clay,* Rom. 9:21* [4081]

[4385] πήρα *pēra* 6x *a leather bag* or *sack* for provisions, *wallet,* Mt. 10:10; Mk. 6:8 [4082]

[4388] πῆχυς *pēchus* 4x pr. *cubitus, the forearm;* hence, *a cubit,* a measure of length, equal to the distance from the elbow to the extremity of the middle finger, usually considered as equivalent to a foot and one half, or 17 inches and one half, Jn. 21:8; Rev. 21:17; met. of time, *a span,* Mt. 6:27; Lk. 12:25* [4083]

[4389] πιάζω *piazō* 12x *to press;* in NT *to take* or *lay hold of,* Acts 3:7; *to take, catch* fish, etc., Jn. 21:3, 10; Rev. 19:20; *to take, seize, apprehend, arrest,* Jn. 7:30, 32, 44 [4084] See *arrest; catch.*

[4390] πιέζω *piezō* 1x *to press, to press* or *squeeze down, make compact by pressure,* Lk. 6:38* [4085]

[4391] πιθανολογία *pithanologia* 1x *persuasive speech, plausible discourse,* Col. 2:4* [4086]

[4393] πικραίνω *pikrainō* 4x *to embitter, render bitter,* Rev. 10:9; pass. *to be embittered, be made bitter,* Rev. 8:11; 10:10; met. pass. *to be embittered, to grow angry, harsh,* Col. 3:19* [4087]

[4394] πικρία *pikria* 4x *bitterness,* Acts 8:23; Heb. 12:15; met. *bitterness* of spirit and language, *harshness,* Rom. 3:14; Eph. 4:31* [4088]

[4395] πικρός *pikros* 2x *bitter,* Jas. 3:11; met. *bitter, harsh,* Jas. 3:14* [4089]

[4396] πικρῶς *pikrōs* 2x *bitterly,* Mt. 26:75; Lk. 22:62* [4090]

[4397] Πιλᾶτος *Pilatos* 55x *Pilate,* pr. name [4091]

[4398] πίμπλημι *pimplēmi* 24x *to fill,* Mt. 27:48; pass. *to be filled* mentally, *be under full influence,* Lk. 1:15; 4:28; *to be fulfilled,* Lk. 21:22; of stated time, *to be brought to a close, arrive at its close,* Lk. 1:23, 57; 2:6, 21, 22 [4130] See *complete; fill; fulfill.*

[4399] πίμπρημι *pimprēmi* 1x *to set on fire, burn, inflame;* in NT pass., *to swell from inflamation,* Acts 28:6* [4092]

[4400] πινακίδιον *pinakidion* 1x *a small tablet* for writing, Lk. 1:63* [4093]

[4402] πίναξ *pinax* 5x pr. *a board* or *plank;* in NT *a plate, platter, dish* on which food was served, Mk. 14:8, 11 [4094]

[4403] πίνω *pinō* 73x *to drink,* Mt. 6:25, 31; 26:27, 29, et al. freq.; trop. of the earth, *to drink in, imbibe,* Heb. 6:7 [4095] See *drink.*

[4404] πιότης *piotēs* 1x *fatness, richness,* Rom. 11:17* [4096]

[4405] πιπράσκω *pipraskō* 9x *to sell,* Mt. 13:46; 18:25; met. with ὑπό, pass. *to be sold under, to be a slave to, be devoted to,* Rom. 7:14 [4097]

[4406] πίπτω *piptō* 90x *to fall,* Mt. 15:27; Lk. 10:18; *to fall, fall prostrate, fall down,* Mt. 17:6; 18:29; Lk. 17:16; *to fall down* dead, Lk. 21:24; *to fall, fall in ruins,* Mt. 7:25, 27; Lk. 11:17; met. *to fall, come by chance,* as a lot, Acts 1:26; *to fall, to fail, become null and void, fall to the ground,* Lk. 16:17; *to fall* into a worse state, Rev. 2:5; *to come to ruin,* Rom. 11:11; Heb. 4:11; *to fall* into sin, Rom. 11:22; 1 Cor. 10:2; *to fall* in judgment, by condemnation, Rev. 14:8; *to fall* upon, *seize,* Rev. 11:11; *to light* upon, Rev. 7:16; *to fall* under, *incur,* Jas. 5:12 [4098] See *bow down; collapse; fall.*

[4407] Πισιδία *Pisidia* 1x *Pisidia,* a country of Asia Minor, Acts 14:24* [4099]

[4409] πιστεύω *pisteuō* 241x pluperfect, πεπιστεύκειν, *to believe, give credit to,* Mk. 1:15; 16:13; Lk. 24:25; intrans. *to believe, have a mental persuasion,* Mt. 8:13; 9:28; Jas. 2:19; *to believe, be of opinion,* Rom. 14:2; in NT πιστεύειν ἐν, εἰς, ἐπί, *to believe in* or *on,* Mt. 18:6; 27:42; Jn. 3:15, 16, 18; absol. *to believe, be a believer,* Acts 2:44; 4:4, 32; 13:48; trans. *to intrust, commit to the charge* or *power of,* Lk. 16:11; Jn. 2:24; pass. *to be intrusted with,* Rom. 3:2; 1 Cor. 9:17 [4100] See *believe; convince; entrust; trust.*

[4410] πιστικός *pistikos* 2x *genuine, unadulterated, pure,* Mk. 14:3; Jn. 12:3* [4101]

[4411] πίστις *pistis* 243x *faith, belief, firm persuasion,* 2 Cor. 5:7; Heb. 11:1; *assurance, firm conviction,* Rom. 14:23; *ground of belief, guarantee, assurance,* Acts 17:31; *good faith, honesty, integrity,* Mt. 23:23; Gal. 5:22; Tit. 2:10; *faithfulness, truthfulness,* Rom. 3:3; in NT *faith* in God and Christ, Mt. 8:10; Acts 3:16, et al. freq.; ἡ πίστις, *the* matter of Gospel *faith,* Acts 6:7; Jude 3 [4102] See *faith; faithfulness; trustworthiness.*

[4412] πιστός *pistos* 67x *faithful, true, trustworthy,* Mt. 24:45; 25:21, 23; Lk. 12:42; 2 Tim. 2:2; *put in trust,* 1 Cor. 7:25; *true, veracious,* Rev. 1:5; 2:13; *credible, sure, certain, indubitable,* Acts 13:34; 1 Tim. 1:15; *believing, yielding belief and confidence,* Jn. 20:27; Gal. 3:9; spc. *a* Christian *believer,* Acts 10:45; 16:1, 15; 2 Cor. 6:15; πιστόν, *in a true-hearted manner, right-mindedly,* 3 Jn. 5 [4103] See *dependable; faithful; reliable; trustworthy.*

[4413] πιστόω *pistoō* 1x *to make trustworthy;* pass. *to be assured, feel sure belief,* 2 Tim. 3:14* [4104]

[4414] πλανάω *planaō* 39x *to lead astray, cause to wander;* pass. *to go astray, wander about, stray,* Mt. 18:12, 13; 1 Pet. 2:25; met. *to mislead, deceive,* Mt. 24:4, 5, 11, 24; pass. *to be deceived, err, mistake,* Mt. 22:29; *to seduce, delude,* Jn. 7:12; pass. *to be seduced* or *wander* from the path of virtue, *to sin, transgress,* Tit. 3:3; Heb. 5:2; Jas. 5:19 [4105] See *deceive; go astray; lead astray; wander.*

[4415] πλάνη *planē* 10x *a wandering; deceit, deception, delusion, imposture, fraud,* Mt. 27:64; 1 Thess. 2:3; *seduction, deceiving,* Eph. 4:14; 2 Thess. 2:11; 1 Jn. 4:6; *error, false opinion,* 2 Pet. 3:17; *wandering* from the path of truth and virtue, *perverseness, wickedness, sin,* Rom. 1:27; Jas. 5:20; 2 Pet. 2:18; Jude 11* [4106] See *deceit; deception; error.*

[4417] πλανήτης *planētēs* 1x *a rover, roving, a wanderer, wandering;* ἀστὴρ πλανήτης, *a wandering star,* Jude 13* [4107]

[4418] πλάνος *planos* 5x *a wanderer, vagabond;* also act. *deceiving, seducing; a deceiver, impostor,* Mt. 27:63; 2 Cor. 6:8; 1 Tim. 4:1; 2 Jn. 7* [4108]

[4419] πλάξ *plax* 3x *a flat broad surface;* a *table, tablet,* 2 Cor. 3:3; Heb. 9:4* [4109]

[4420] πλάσμα *plasma* 1x *a thing formed* or *fashioned;* spc. *a potter's vessel,* Rom. 9:20* [4110]

[4421] πλάσσω *plassō* 2x *to form, fashion, mould,* Rom. 9:20; 1 Tim. 2:13* [4111]

[4422] πλαστός *plastos* 1x *formed, fashioned, molded;* met. *fabricated, counterfeit, delusive,* 2 Pet. 2:3* [4112]

[4423] πλατεῖα *plateia* 9x *a street, broad way,* Mt. 6:5; 12:19; Lk. 10:10 [4113] See *street.*

[4424] πλάτος *platos* 4x *breadth,* Eph. 3:18; Rev. 20:9; 21:16* [4114]

[4425] πλατύνω *platynō* 3x *to make broad, widen, enlarge,* Mt. 23:5; pass. met. of the heart, from the Hebrew, *to be expanded* with kindly and genial feelings, 2 Cor. 6:11, 13* [4115]

[4426] πλατύς *platys* 1x *broad, wide,* Mt. 7:13* [4116]

[4427] πλέγμα *plegma* 1x *anything plaited* or *intertwined; a braid* of hair, 1 Tim. 2:9* [4117]

[4428] πλέκω *plekō* 3x *to interweave, weave, braid, plait,* Mt. 27:29; Mk. 15:17; Jn. 19:2* [4120]

[4429] πλεονάζω *pleonazō* 9x *to be more than enough; to have more than enough, to have in abundance,* 2 Cor. 8:15; *to abound, be abundant,* 2 Thess. 1:3; 2 Pet. 1:8; *to increase, be augmented,* Rom. 5:20; *to come into wider action, be more widely spread,* Rom. 6:1; 2 Cor. 4:15; in NT trans. *to cause to abound* or *increase, to augment,* 1 Thess. 3:12 [4121]

[4430] πλεονεκτέω *pleonekteō* 5x *to have more* than another; *to take advantage of; to overreach, make gain of,* 2 Cor. 7:2; 12:17, 18; *to wrong,* 1 Thess. 4:6; *to get the better,* or *an advantage of,* 2 Cor. 2:11* [4122]

[4431] πλεονέκτης *pleonektēs* 4x *one who has* or *claims to have more than his share; a covetous, avaricious person, one who defrauds for the sake of gain,* 1 Cor. 5:10, 11; 6:10; Eph. 5:5* [4123]

[4432] πλεονεξία *pleonexia* 10x *some advantage which one possesses over another; an inordinate desire of riches, covetousness,* Lk. 12:15; *grasping, overreaching, extortion,* Rom. 1:29; 1 Thess. 2:5; *a gift exacted by importunity and conferred with grudging, a hard-wrung gift,* 2 Cor. 9:5; *a scheme of extortion,* Mk. 7:22 [4124] See *covetousness; greed.*

[4433] πλευρά *pleura* 5x pr. *a rib; the side* of the body, Jn. 19:34; 20:20, 25, 27; Acts 12:7* [4125]

[4434] πλέω *pleō* 6x *to sail,* Lk. 8:23; Acts 21:3; 27:2, 6, 24; Rev. 18:17* [4126]

[4435] πληγή *plēgē* 22x *a blow, stroke, stripe,* Lk. 10:30; 12:48; meton. *a wound,* Acts 16:33; Rev. 13:3, 12, 14; from the Hebrew, *a plague, affliction, calamity,* Rev. 9:20; 11:6 [4127] See *beating; plague; wound.*

[4436] πλῆθος *plēthos* 31x *fullness, amplitude, magnitude; a multitude, a great number,* Lk. 1:10; 2:13; 5:6; *a multitude, a crowd, throng,* Mk. 3:7, 8; Lk. 6:17 [4128] See *crowd; multitude; number.*

[4437] πληθύνω *plēthunō* 12x optative, πληθύναι (3 sg), trans. *to multiply, cause to increase, augment,* 2 Cor. 9:10; Heb. 6:14; pass. *to be multiplied, increase, be accumulated,* Mt. 24:12; Acts 6:7; 7:17; intrans. *to multiply, increase, be augmented,* Acts 6:1 [4129] See *grow; increase; multiply.*

[4438] πλήκτης *plēktēs* 2x *a striker, one apt to strike; a quarrelsome, violent person,* 1 Tim. 3:3; Tit. 1:7* [4131]

[4439] πλήμμυρα *plēmmyra* 1x *the flood-tide; a flood,* Lk. 6:48* [4132]

[4440] πλήν *plēn* 31x can function as an improper prep., *besides, except,* Mk. 12:32; Acts 8:1; 20:23; as a conj. *but, however, nevertheless,* Mt. 18:7; Lk. 19:27; Eph. 5:33; equivalent to ἀλλά, Lk. 6:35; 12:31; Acts 27:22 [4133]

[4441] πλήρης *plērēs* 16x *full, filled,* Mt. 14:20; 15:37; *full* of disease, Lk. 5:12; met. *full of, abounding in, wholly occupied with, completely under the influence of,* or *affected by,* Lk. 4:1; Jn. 1:14; Acts 9:36; *full, complete, perfect,* Mk. 4:28 [4134] See *filled; full.*

[4442] πληροφορέω *plērophoreō* 6x *to bring full measure, to give in full; to carry out fully, to discharge completely,* 2 Tim. 4:5, 17; pass. of things, *to be fully established* as a matter of certainty, Lk. 1:1; of persons, *to be fully convinced, assured,* Rom. 4:21; 14:15; Col. 4:12* [4135]

[4443] πληροφορία *plērophoria* 4x *full conviction, firm persuasion, assurance,* 1 Thess. 1:5; Col. 2:2 [4136]

[4444] πληρόω *plēroō* 86x pluperf., πεπληρώκει (3 sg), *to fill, make full, fill up,* Mt. 13:48; 23:32; Lk. 3:5; *to fill up* a deficiency, Phil. 4:18, 19; *to pervade,* Jn. 12:3; Acts 2:2; *to pervade* with an influence, *to influence fully, possess fully,* Jn. 16:6; Acts 2:28; 5:3; Rom. 1:29; Eph. 5:18; *to complete, perfect,* Jn. 3:29; Eph. 3:19; *to bring to an end,* Lk. 7:1; *to perform fully, discharge,* Mt. 3:15; Acts 12:25; 13:25; 14:26; Rom. 13:8; Col. 4:17; *to consummate,* Mt. 5:17; *to realize, accomplish, fulfil,* Lk. 1:20; 9:31; Acts 3:18; 13:27; from the Hebrew; *to set forth fully,* Rom. 15:19; Col. 1:25; pass. of time, *to be fulfilled, come to an end, be fully arrived,* Mk. 1:15; Lk. 21:24; Jn. 7:8; of prophecy, *to receive fulfillment,* Mt. 1:22, et al. freq. [4137] See *fill; fulfill.*

[4445] πλήρωμα *plērōma* 17x *that which fills up; full measure, entire content,* Mk. 8:20; 1 Cor. 10:26, 28; *complement, full extent, full number,* Gal. 4:4; Eph. 1:10; *that which fills up a deficiency, a supplement, a patch,* Mt. 9:16; *fulness, abundance,* Jn. 1:16; *full measure,* Rom. 15:29; *a fulfilling, perfect performance,* Rom. 13:10; *complete attainment* of entire belief, *full acceptance,* Rom. 11:12; *full development, plenitude,* Eph. 4:13; Col. 1:19; 2:9 [4138] See *fulfillment; fullness.*

[4446] πλησίον *plēsion* 17x can function as an improper prep., *near, near by,* Jn. 4:5; ὁ πλησίον, *a neighbor,* Mt. 19:19; Rom. 15:2; a friendly *neighbor,* Mt. 5:43 [4139] See *near; neighbor.*

[4447] πλησμονή *plēsmonē* 1x *a filling up;* met. *gratification, satisfaction,* Col. 2:23* [4140]

[4448] πλήσσω *plēssō* 1x also spelled πλήττω, *to strike, smite;* from the Hebrew, *to smite, to plague, blast,* Rev. 8:12 [4141]

[4449] πλοιάριον *ploiarion* 5x *a small vessel, boat,* Mk. 3:9; Jn. 6:22, 23, 24 [4142]

[4450] πλοῖον *ploion* 67x *a vessel, ship, bark,* whether large or small, Mt. 4:21, 22; Acts 21:2, 3 [4143] See *boat; ship.*

[4454] πλούσιος *plousios* 28x *rich, opulent, wealthy;* and pl. οἱ πλούσιοι, *the rich,* Mt. 19:23, 24; 27:57; met. *rich, abounding in, distinguished for,* Eph. 2:4; Jas. 2:5; Rev. 2:9; 3:17; *rich* in glory, dignity, bliss, etc., 2 Cor. 8:9 [4145] See *rich, riches; wealth.*

[4455] πλουσίως *plousiōs* 4x *rich, largely, abundantly,* Col. 3:16 [4146]

[4456] πλουτέω *plouteō* 12x *to be* or *become rich,* Lk. 1:25; 1 Tim. 6:9; trop. Lk. 12:21; met. *to abound in, be abundantly furnished with,* 1 Tim. 6:18; *to be* spiritually *enriched,* 2 Cor. 8:9 [4147] See *rich, riches; wealth.*

[4457] πλουτίζω *ploutizō* 3x *to make rich, enrich;* met. *to enrich* spiritually, 1 Cor. 1:5; 2 Cor. 6:10; 9:11* [4148]

[4458] πλοῦτος *ploutos* 22x *riches, wealth, opulence,* Mt. 13:22; Lk. 8:14; in NT, πλοῦτος τοῦ Θεοῦ, or Χριστοῦ, *those rich benefits, those abundant blessings which flow from God* or *Christ,* Eph. 3:8; Phil. 4:19; meton. *richness, abundance,* Rom. 2:4; 11:33; 2 Cor. 8:2; meton. *a* spiritual *enriching,* Rom. 11:12 [4149] See *rich, riches; wealth.*

[4459] πλύνω *plynō* 3x *to wash* garments, Lk. 5:1; Rev. 7:14; 22:14* [4150]

[4460] πνεῦμα *pneuma* 379x *wind, air in motion,* Jn. 3:8; *breath,* 2 Thess. 2:8; the substance *spirit,* Jn. 3:6; *a spirit, spiritual being,* Jn. 4:24; Acts 23:8, 9; Heb. 1:14; *a* bodiless *spirit, specter,* Lk. 24:37; *a* foul *spirit,* δαιμόνιον, Mt. 8:16; Lk. 10:20; *spirit,* as a vital principle, Jn. 6:63; 1 Cor. 15:45; *the* human *spirit, the soul,* Mt. 26:41; 27:50; Acts 7:59; 1 Cor. 7:34; Jas. 2:26; *the spirit* as the seat of thought and feeling, *the mind,* Mk. 8:12; Acts 19:21; *spirit, mental frame,* 1 Cor. 4:21; 1 Pet. 3:4; *a* characteristic *spirit, an influential principle,* Lk. 9:55; 1 Cor. 2:12; 2 Tim. 1:7; *a pervading influence,* Rom. 11:8; *spirit, frame of mind,* as distinguished from outward circumstances and action, Mt. 5:3; *spirit* as distinguished from outward show and form. Jn. 4:23; *spirit, a* divinely bestowed *spiritual frame,* characteristic of true believers, Rom. 8:4; Jude 19; *spirit,* latent *spiritual import, spiritual significance,* as distinguished from the mere letter, Rom. 2:29; 7:6; 2 Cor. 3:6, 17; *spirit,* as a term for a process superior to a merely natural or carnal course of things, by the operation of the Divine Spirit, Rom. 8:4; Gal. 4:29; *a spiritual dispensation,* or *a* sealing energy of the Holy *Spirit,* Heb. 9:14; the Holy Spirit, Mt. 3:16; 12:31; Jn. 1:32, 33; *a gift of the Holy Spirit,* Jn. 7:39; Acts 19:2; 1 Cor. 14:12; *an operation* or *influence of the Holy Spirit,* 1 Cor. 12:3; *a spiritual influence, an inspiration,* Mt. 22:43; Lk. 2:27; Eph. 1:17; *a professedly divine communication,* or, *a professed possessor of a spiritual communication,* 1 Cor. 12:10; 2 Thess. 2:2; 1 Jn. 4:1, 2, 3 [4151] See *spirit.*

[4461] πνευματικός *pneumatikos* 26x *spiritual, pertaining to the soul,* as distinguished from what concerns the body, Rom. 15:27; 1 Cor. 9:11; *spiritual, pertaining to the nature of spirits,* 1 Cor. 15:44; τὰ πνευματικα; τῆς πονηρίας, i.q. τὰ πνεύματα τὰ πονηρά, *evil spirits,* Eph. 6:12; *spiritual, pertaining* or *relating to the influences of the Holy Spirit,* of things, Rom. 1:11; 7:14; τὰ πνευματικά, *spiritual gifts,* 1 Cor. 12:1; 14:1; *superior in process to the natural course of things, miraculous,* 1 Cor. 10:3; of persons, *gifted with a spiritual frame of mind, spiritually affected,* 1 Cor. 2:13, 15; *endowed with spiritual gifts, inspired,* 1 Cor. 14:37 [4152] See *spiritual.*

[4462] πνευματικῶς *pneumatikōs* 2x *spiritually, through spiritual views and affections,* 1 Cor. 2:14; *spiritually, in a spiritual sense, allegorically,* Rev. 11:8* [4153]

[4463] πνέω *pneō* 7x *to breathe; to blow,* as the wind, Mt. 7:25, 27 [4154]

[4464] πνίγω *pnigō* 3x *to stifle, suffocate, choke,* Mk. 5:13; *to seize by the throat,* Mk. 13:17; 18:28* [4155]

[4465] πνικτός *pniktos* 3x *strangled, suffocated;* in NT τὸ πνικτόν, *the flesh of animals killed by strangulation* or *suffocation,* Acts 15:20, 29; 21:25* [4156]

[4466] πνοή *pnoē* 2x *breath, respiration,* Acts 17:25; *a wind, a blast of wind, breeze,* Acts 2:2* [4157]

[4468] ποδήρης *podērēs* 1x *reaching to the feet;* as subst. sc. ἐσθής, *a long, flowing robe reaching down to the feet,* Rev. 1:13* [4158]

[4470] πόθεν *pothen* 29x *whence? from where,* used of place, etc., Mt. 15:33; met. of a state of dignity, Rev. 2:5; used of origin, Mt. 21:25; of cause, source, author, etc., Mt. 13:27, 54, 56; Lk. 1:43; *how? in what way?* Mk. 8:4; 12:37 [4159]

[4472] ποιέω *poieō* 568x pluperf., πεποιήκειν, *to make, form, construct,* Mt. 17:4; Mk. 9:5; Jn. 2:15; of God, *to create,* Mt. 19:4; Acts 4:24; *to make, prepare* a feast, etc., Mt. 22:2; Mk. 6:21; met. *to make, establish, ratify,* a covenant, Heb. 8:9; *to make, assume, consider, regard,* Mt. 12:33; *to make, effect, bring to pass, cause to take place, do, accomplish,* Mt. 7:22; 21:21; Mk. 3:8; 6:5; 7:37; met. *to perfect, accomplish, fulfil, put in execution* a purpose, promise, etc., Lk. 16:4; 19:48; *to cause, make,* Mt. 5:32; Jn. 11:37; Acts 24:12; *to make* gain, *gain, acquire,* Mt. 25:16; Lk. 19:18; *to get, procure,* Lk. 12:33; *to make, to cause to be* or *become* a thing, Mt. 21:13; 23:15; *to use, treat,* Lk. 15:19; *to make, constitute, appoint* to some office, Mt. 4:19; Mk. 3:14; *to make, declare to be,* 1 Jn. 1:10; 5:10; *to do, to perform, execute, practise, act,* Mt. 5:46, 47, 6:2, 3; *to commit* evil, Mt. 13:41; 27:23; *to be devoted to, follow, practise,* Jn. 3:21; 5:29; Rom. 3:12; *to do, execute, fulfil, keep, observe, obey,* precepts, etc., Mt. 1:24; 5:19; 7:21, 24, 26; *to bring* evil *upon, inflict,* Acts 9:13; *to keep, celebrate* a festival, Mt. 26:18; *to institute the celebration of* a festival, Heb. 11:28; ποιεῖν τινα ἔξω, *to cause to leave* a place, i.q. ἔξω ἄγειν, *to lead* or *conduct out,* Acts 5:34; *to pass, spend* time, *continue for* a time, Mt. 20:12; Acts 15:33; 18:23; Jas. 4:13; *to bear,* as trees, *yield, produce,* Mt. 3:8, 10; 7:17, 18, 19.

With a substantive or adjective it forms a periphrasis for the verb corresponding to the noun or adjective, e.g. δῆλον ποιεῖν, i.q. δηλοῦν, *to make manifest, betray,* Mt. 26:73; ἐκδίκησιν ποιεῖν, i.q. ἐδικεῖν, *to vindicate, avenge,* Lk. 18:7, 8; ἔκθετον ποιεῖν, i.q. ἐκτιθέναι, *to expose* infants, Acts 7:19; ἐνέδραν ποιεῖν, i.q. ἐνεδρεύειν, *to lie in wait,* Acts 25:3; ἐξουσίαν ποιεῖν, i.q. ἐξουσιάζειν, *to exercise power* or *authority,* Rev. 13:12; κρίσιν ποιεῖν, i.q. κρίνειν, *to judge, act as judge,* Jn. 5:27; λύτρωσιν ποιεῖν, i.q. λυτροῦν, *to deliver, set free,* Lk. 1:68; μονὴν ποιεῖν, i.q. μένειν, *to remain, dwell,* Jn. 14:23; πόλεμον ποιεῖν, i.q. πολεμεῖν, *to make* or *wage war, fight,* Rev. 11:7; συμβούλοιν ποιεῖν, i.q. συμβουλεύεσθαι, *to consult together, deliberate,* Mk. 3:6; συνωμοσίαν ποιεῖν, i.q. συνομνύναι, and συστροφὴν ποιεῖν, i.q. συστρέφεσθαι, *to conspire together, form a conspiracy,* Acts 23:12, 13; φανερὸν ποιεῖν, i.q. φανεροῦν, *to make known, betray,* Mt. 12:16; ἀναβολὴν ποῖεσθαι, i.q. ἀναβάλλεσθαι, *to delay, procrastinate,* Acts 25:17; βέβαιον ποιεῖσθαι, i.q. βεβαιοῦν, *to confirm, render firm and sure,* 2 Pet. 1:10; δεήσεις ποιεῖσθαι, i.q. δεῖσθαι, *to pray, offer prayer,* Lk. 5:33; ἐκβολὴν ποιεῖσθαι, i.q. ἐκβάλλειν, *to cast out, throw overboard,* Acts 27:18; καθαρισμὸν ποιεῖσθαι, i.q. καθαρίζειν, *to cleanse* from sin, Heb. 1:3; κοινωνίαν ποιεῖσθαι, i.q. κοινωνεῖν, *to communicate in liberality, bestow alms,* Rom. 15:26; κοπετὸν ποιεῖν, i.q. κόπτεσθαι, *to lament, bewail,* Acts 8:2; λόγον ποιεῖσθαι, *to regard, make account of,* Acts 20:24; μνείαν ποιεῖσθαι, i.q. μνησθῆναι, *to call to mind,* Rom. 1:9; μνήμην ποιεῖσθαι, *to remember, retain in memory,* 2 Pet. 1:15; πορείαν ποιεῖσθαι, i.q. πορεύεσθαι, *to go, journey, travel,* Lk. 13:22; πρόνοιαν ποιεῖσθαι, i.q. προνοεῖσθαι, *to take care of, provide for,* Rom. 13:14; σπουδὴν ποιεῖσθαι, *to act with diligence and earnestness*, Jude 3 [4160] See *accomplish; appoint; create; do; make.*

[4473] ποίημα *poiēma* 2x *that which is made* or *done; a work, workmanship, creation,* Rom. 1:20; met. Eph. 2:10* [4161]

[4474] ποίησις *poiēsis* 1x *a making; an acting, doing, performance; observance* of a law, Jas. 1:25* [4162]

[4475] ποιητής *poiētēs* 6x *a maker; the maker* or *author* of a song or poem, *a poet,* Acts 17:28; *a doer; a performer* of the enactments of a law, Rom. 2:13 [4163]

[4476] ποικίλος *poikilos* 10x *of various colors, variegated, checkered; various, diverse, manifold,* Mt. 4:24 [4164] See *various.*

[4477] ποιμαίνω *poimainō* 11x *to feed, pasture, tend a flock,* Lk. 17:7; 1 Cor. 9:7; trop. *to feed* with selfish indulgence, *to pamper,* Jude 12; met. *to tend, direct, superintend,* Mt. 2:6; Jn. 21:16; *to rule,* Rev. 2:27 [4165] See *shepherd.*

[4478] ποιμήν *poimēn* 18x *one who tends flocks* or *herds, a shepherd, herdsman,* Mt. 9:36; 25:32; met. *a pastor, superintendent, guardian,* Jn. 10:11, 14, 16 [4166] See *pastor; shepherd.*

[4479] ποίμνη *poimnē* 5x *a flock* of sheep, Lk. 2:8; 1 Cor. 9:7; meton. *a flock* of disciples, Mt. 26:31; Jn. 10:16* [4167]

[4480] ποίμνιον *poimnion* 5x *a flock;* met. *a flock* of Christian disciples, Lk. 12:32; Acts 20:28, 29; 1 Pet. 5:2, 3* [4168]

[4481] ποῖος *poios* 33x *of what kind, sort* or *species,* Jn. 12:33; 21:19; *what? which?* Mt. 19:18; 21:23, 24, 27 [4169]

[4482] πολεμέω *polemeō* 7x *to make* or *wage war, fight,* Rev. 2:16; 12:7; *to battle, quarrel,* Jas. 4:2 [4170]

[4483] πόλεμος *polemos* 18x *war,* Mt. 24:6; Mk. 13:7; *battle, engagement, combat,* 1 Cor. 14:8; Heb. 11:34; *battling, strife,* Jas. 4:1 [4171] See *battle; fight; war.*

[4484] πόλις *polis* 162x *a city, an enclosed and walled town,* Mt. 10:5, 11; 11:1; meton. *the inhabitants of a city,* Mt. 8:34; 10:15; with a gen. of person, or a personal pronoun, *the city* of any one, *the city* of one's birth or residence, Mt. 9:1; Lk. 2:4, 11; ἡ πόλις, *the city,* κατ᾽ ἐξοχήν, *Jerusalem,* Mt. 21:18; 28:11; met. *a place of permanent residence, abode, home,* Heb. 11:10, 16; 13:14. The frequency count does not include its occurrence in the name Νέαν πόλιν in Acts 16:11 [4172] See *city; town; village.*

[4485] πολιτάρχης *politarchēs* 2x *a ruler* or *prefect of a city, city magistrate,* Acts 17:6, 8* [4173]

[4486] πολιτεία *politeia* 2x *the state of being a citizen; citizenship, the right* or *privilege of being a citizen, freedom of a city* or *state,* Acts 22:28; *a commonwealth, community,* Eph. 2:12* [4174]

[4487] πολίτευμα *politeuma* 1x *the administration of a commonwealth;* in NT equivalent to πολιτεία, *a community, commonwealth,* Phil. 3:20* [4175]

[4488] πολιτεύομαι *politeuomai* 2x intrans. *to be a citizen;* trans. *to govern a city* or *state, administer the affairs of a state;* pass. *to be governed;* in NT *to order one's life and conduct, converse, live,* in a certain manner as to habits and principles, Acts 23:1; Phil. 1:27* [4176]

[4489] πολίτης *politēs* 4x *a citizen,* Lk. 15:15; 19:14; Acts 21:39; Heb. 8:11* [4177]

[4490] πολλάκις *pollakis* 18x *many times, often, frequently,* Mt. 17:15; Mk. 5:4; 9:22 [4178] See *often.*

[4491] πολλαπλασίων *pollaplasiōn* 1x *manifold, many times more,* Lk. 18:30* [4179]

[4494] πολυλογία *polylogia* 1x *wordiness, loquacity,* Mt. 6:7* [4180]

[4495] πολυμερῶς *polymerōs* 1x *in many parts* or *ways,* Heb. 1:1* [4181]

[4497] πολυποίκιλος *polypoikilos* 1x *exceedingly various, multiform, manifold;* by impl. *immense, infinite,* Eph. 3:10* [4182]

[4498] πολύς *polys* 416x *great* in magnitude or quantity, *much, large,* Mt. 13:5; Jn. 3:23; 15:8; pl. *many,* Mt. 3:7; in time, *long,* Mt. 25:19; Mk. 6:35; Jn. 5:6; οἱ πολλοί, *the many, the mass,* Rom. 5:15; 12:5; 1 Cor. 10:33; τὸ πολύ, *much,* 2 Cor. 8:15; πολύ, as an adv., *much, greatly,* Mk. 12:27; Lk. 7:47; of time, ἐπὶ πολύ, *a long time,* Acts 28:6; μετ᾽ οὐ πολὺ, *not long after,* Acts 27:14; followed by a compar., *much,* 2 Cor. 8:22; πολλῷ, *much, by much,* Mt. 6:30; Mk. 10:48; τὰ πολλά, as an adv., *most frequently, generally,* Rom. 15:22; πολλά, as an adv., *much, greatly, vehemently,* Mk. 1:45; 3:12; of time, *many times, frequently, often,* Mt. 9:14 [4118, 4119, 4183] See *great; large; many.*

[4499] πολύσπλαγχνος *polysplanchnos* 1x *very merciful, very compassionate,* Jas. 5:11* [4184]

[4500] πολυτελής *polytelēs* 3x *expensive, costly,* Mk. 14:3; 1 Tim. 2:9; *of great value, very precious,* 1 Pet. 3:4* [4185]

[4501] πολύτιμος *polytimos* 3x *of great price, costly, precious,* Mt. 13:46; Jn. 12:3; 1 Pet. 1:7* [4186]

[4502] πολυτρόπως *polytropōs* 1x *in many ways, in various modes,* Heb. 1:1* [4187]

[4503] πόμα *poma* 2x *drink,* 1 Cor. 10:4; Heb. 9:10* [4188]

[4504] πονηρία *ponēria* 7x pr. *badness, bad condition;* in NT *evil disposition* of mind, *wickedness, mischief, malignity,* Mt. 22:18; pl. πονηρίαι, *wicked deeds, villanies,* Mk. 7:23; Acts 3:26 [4189]

[4505] πονηρός *ponēros* 78x *bad, unsound,* Mt. 6:23; 7:17, 18; *evil, afflictive,* Eph. 5:16; 6:13; Rev. 16:2; *evil, wrongful, malignant, malevolent,* Mt. 5:11, 39; Acts 28:21; *evil, wicked, impious,* and τὸ πονηρόν, *evil, wrong, wickedness,* Mt. 5:37, 45; 9:4; *slothful, inactive,* Mt. 25:26; Lk. 19:22; ὁ πονηρός, *the evil one, the devil,* Mt. 13:19, 38; Jn. 17:15; *evil* eye, i.q. φθονερός *envious,* Mt. 20:15; Mk. 7:22; impl. *covetous,* Mt. 7:11 [4190, 4191] See *bad; evil; wicked, wickedness.*

[4506] πόνος *ponos* 4x *labor, travail; pain, misery, anguish,* Col. 4:13; Rev. 16:10, 11; 21:4* [4192]

[4507] Ποντικός *Pontikos* 1x *belonging to* or *an inhabitant of Pontus,* Acts 18:2* [4193]

[4508] Πόντιος *Pontios* 3x *Pontius,* pr. name, Acts 4:27 [4194]

[4509] Πόντος *Pontos* 1x *Pontus,* country of Asia Minor, Acts 2:9; 1 Pet. 1:1* [5117]

[4511] Πόπλιος *Poplios* 2x *Publius,* pr. name, Acts 28:7, 8* [4196]

[4512] πορεία *poreia* 2x *a going, progress; a journey, travel,* Lk. 13:22; from the Hebrew, *way* of life, *business, occupation,* Jas. 1:11* [4197]

[4513] πορεύω *poreuō* 153x also listed as a deponent, πορεύομαι, *to go, pass from one place to another,* Mt. 17:27; 18:12; *to go away, depart,* Mt. 24:1; 25:41; Jn. 14:2, 3; trop. *to go away, depart,* from life, *to die,* Lk. 22:22; *to go, pass on one's way, journey, travel,* Mt. 2:8, 9; Lk. 1:39; 2:41; πορεύομαι ὀπίσω, *to go after, to become a follower* or *partisan,* Lk. 21:8; or, *to pursue after, be devoted to,* 2 Pet. 2:10; from the Hebrew, *to go* or *proceed* in any way or course of life, *live* in any manner, Lk. 1:6; 8:14; Acts 9:31 [4198] See *go; travel; walk.*

[4514] πορθέω *portheō* 3x *to lay waste, destroy;* impl. *to harass, ravage,* Acts 9:21; Gal. 1:13, 23* [4199]

[4516] πορισμός *porismos* 2x *a providing, procuring;* meton. *source of gain,* 1 Tim. 6:5, 6* [4200]

[4517] Πόρκιος *Porkios* 1x *Porcius,* pr. name, Acts 24:27* [4201]

[4518] πορνεία *porneia* 25x *fornication, whoredom,* Mt. 15:19; Mk. 7:21; Acts 15:20, 29; *concubinage,* Jn. 8:41; *adultery,* Mt. 5:32; 19:9; *incest,* 1 Cor. 5:1; *lewdness, uncleanness,* genr., Rom. 1:29; from the Hebrew, put symbolically for *idolatry,* Rev. 2:21; 14:8 [4202] See *fornication; sexual immorality.*

[4519] πορνεύω *porneuō* 8x *to commit fornication,* 1 Cor. 6:18; 10:8; Rev. 2:14, 20; from the Hebrew, *to commit* spiritual *fornication, practise idolatry,* Rev. 17:2; 18:3, 9* [4203] See *commit sexual immorality; fornication; sexual immorality.*

[4520] πόρνη *pornē* 12x *a prostitute, a whore, harlot, an unchaste female,* Mt. 21:31, 32; from the Hebrew, a*n idolatress,* Rev. 17:1, 5, 15 [4204] See *harlot; prostitute.*

[4521] πόρνος *pornos* 10x *one who practices sexual immorality;* in NT *a fornicator, impure person,* 1 Cor. 5:9, 10, 11; 6:9 [4205] See *fornicator; sexual immorality.*

[4522] πόρρω *porrō* 4x *in advance, far advanced; far, far off, at a distance,* Mt. 15:8; Mk. 7:6; Lk. 14:32, can be an improper prep. with the gen. The comparative form of the adverb appears as πορρώτερον at Lk. 24:28.* [4206]

[4523] πόρρωθεν *porrōthen* 2x *from a distance, from afar,* Heb. 11:13; *at a distance, far, far off,* Lk. 17:12* [4207]

[4525] πορφύρα *porphyra* 4x *purpura, murex,* a species of shellfish that yielded the purple dye, highly esteemed by the ancients, its tint being a bright crimson; in NT *a purple garment, robe of purple,* Lk. 16:19; Rev. 18:12 [4209]

[4527] πορφυρόπωλις *porphyropōlis* 1x *a female seller of purple cloths,* Acts 16:4* [4211]

[4528] πορφυροῦς *porphyrous* 4x contracted form is πορφύρεος, *purple,* Jn. 19:2, 5; *purple clothing,* Rev. 17:4; 18:16* [4210]

[4529] ποσάκις *posakis* 3x *How many times? How often?* Mt. 18:21; 23:37; Lk. 13:34* [4212]

[4530] πόσις *posis* 3x *drinking; drink, beverage,* Jn. 6:55; Rom. 14:17; Col. 2:16* [4213]

[4531] πόσος *posos* 27x *How great? How much?* Mt. 6:23; Lk. 16:5, 7; 2 Cor. 7:11; πόσῳ, adverbially before a comparative, *How much? By how much?* Mt. 7:11; 10:25; Heb. 10:29; of time, *How long?* Mk. 9:21; of number, pl. *How many?* Mt. 15:34; 16:9, 10 [4214]

[4532] ποταμός *potamos* 17x *a river, stream,* Mk. 1:5; Acts 16:13; met. and allegor. Jn. 7:38; Rev. 22:1, 2; *a flood, winter torrent,* for χείμαρρος ποταμός, Mt. 7:25, 27 [4215] See *river; stream.*

[4533] ποταμοφόρητος *potamophorētos* 1x *borne along* or *carried away by a flood* or *torrent,* Rev. 12:15* [4216]

[4534] ποταπός *potapos* 7x *Of what country?* in NT equivalent to ποῖος, *What? Of what manner? Of what kind* or *sort?* Lk. 1:29; 7:37; denoting admiration, *What? What kind of? How great?* Mt. 8:27; Mk. 13:1 [4217]

[4536] πότε *pote* 19x interrogative adverb, *When? At what time?* Mt. 24:3; 25:37, 38, 39, 44; ἕως πότε, *until when? how long?* Mt. 17:17 [4219]

[4537] ποτε *pote* 29x enclitic particle, *once, some time* or *other,* either past or future; *formerly,* Jn. 9:13; *at length,* Lk. 22:32; *at any time, ever,* Eph. 5:29; Heb. 2:1; intensive after interrogatives, *ever,* 1 Cor. 9:7; Heb. 1:5 [4218]

[4538] πότερον *poteron* 1x interrogative of πότερος, α, ον, which never occurs in NT other than in this form, *whether?,* Jn. 7:17* [4220]

[4539] ποτήριον *potērion* 31x *a vessel for drinking, cup,* Mt. 10:42; 23:25, 26; meton. *the contents of a cup, liquor contained in a cup,* Lk. 22:20; 1 Cor. 10:16; from the Hebrew, *the cup* or *potion* of what God's administration deals out, Mt. 20:22, 23; Rev. 14:10 [4221] See *cup.*

[4540] ποτίζω *potizō* 15x *to cause to drink, give drink to,* Mt. 10:42; met. 1 Cor. 3:2; Rev. 14:8; *to water, irrigate,* met. 1 Cor. 3:6, 7, 8 [4222] See *give to drink; water.*

[4541] Ποτίολοι *Potioloi* 1x *Puteoli,* a town of Italy, Acts 28:13* [4223]

[4542] πότος *potos* 1x *a drinking; a drinking together, drinking bout,* 1 Pet. 4:3* [4224]

[4543] που *pou* 4x enclitic, *somewhere, in a certain place,* Heb. 2:6; 4:4; with numerals, *thereabout,* Rom. 4:19* [4225]

[4544] ποῦ *pou* 48x interrogative, *where? In what place?* direct, Mt. 2:2; Lk. 8:25; Jn. 1:39; indirect, Mt. 2:4; Jn. 1:40; *whither,* Jn. 3:8; 7:35; 13:36 [4226]

[4545] Πούδης *Poudēs* 1x *Pudens,* pr. name, Latin, 2 Tim. 4:21* [4227]

[4546] πούς *pous* 93x *the foot,* Mt. 4:6; 5:35; 7:6; 22:44; 28:9; Lk. 1:79; Acts 5:9; Rom. 3:15 [4228] See *feet; foot.*

[4547] πρᾶγμα *pragma* 11x *a thing done, fact, deed, work, transaction,* Lk. 1:1; Jas. 3:16; *a matter, affair,* Mt. 18:19; Rom. 16:2; *a matter* of dispute, 1 Cor. 6:1; *a thing,* genr., Heb. 10:1; 11:1; τὸ πρᾶγμα, a euphemism for *unlawful sexual conduct,* perhaps, 1 Thess. 4:6 [4229] See *matter; thing.*

[4548] πραγματεία *pragmateia* 1x *an application to a matter of business;* in NT *business, affair, transaction,* 2 Tim. 2:4* [4230]

[4549] πραγματεύομαι *pragmateuomai* 1x *to be occupied with* or *employed in any business, do business; to trade traffic,* Lk. 19:13* [4231]

[4550] πραιτώριον *praitōrion* 8x when used in reference to a camp, *the tent of the general* or *commander-in-chief;* hence, in reference to a province, *the palace in which the governor of the province resided,* Mt. 27:27; Mk. 15:16; Acts 23:35; *the camp occupied by the praetorian cohorts at Rome, the praetorian camp,* or, *the Roman emperor's palace,* Phil. 1:13 [4232] See *palace.*

[4551] πράκτωρ *praktōr* 2x *an exactor of dues* or *penalties; an officer* who enforced payment of debts by imprisonment, Lk. 12:58* [4233]

[4552] πρᾶξις *praxis* 6x *operation, business, office,* Rom. 12:4; πρᾶξις and πράξεις, *actions, mode of acting, ways, deeds, practice, behavior,* Mt. 16:27; Lk. 23:51 [4234]

[4555] πρασιά *prasia* 2x *a small area* or *bed in a garden;* trop. *a company of persons disposed in squares;* from the Hebrew, πρασιαὶ πρασιαί, *by ar-*

eas, by squares, like beds in a garden, *group by group,* Mk. 6:40* [4237]

[4556] πράσσω *prassō* 39x *to do, execute, perform, practise, act, transact,* and of evil, *to commit,* Lk. 22:23; 23:15; Jn. 3:20; Acts 26:9, 20, 26, 31; *to fulfil, obey, observe* a law, Rom. 2:25; *to do to* any one, Acts 16:28; 5:35; *to occupy one's self with, be engaged in, busy one's self about,* Acts 19:19; 1 Thess. 4:11; absol. *to fare,* Acts 15:29; Eph. 6:21; *to exact, require, collect* tribute, money lent, etc., Lk. 3:13; 19:23 [4238] See *act; do; practice.*

[4557] πραϋπάθεια *praupatheia* 1x *meekness, gentleness of mind, kindness,* 1 Tim. 6:11* [4236]

[4558] πραΰς *praus* 4x also spelled πρᾶος, *meek, gentle, kind, forgiving,* Mt. 5:5; *mild, benevolent, humane,* Mt. 11:29; 21:5; 1 Pet. 3:4* [4239]

[4559] πραΰτης *prautēs* 11x also spelled πραότης, ητος, ἡ, *meekness, mildness, forbearance,* 1 Pet. 3:15; *gentleness, kindness,* Jas. 1:21; 3:13; Gal. 5:23 [4240] See *gentleness; humility*

[4560] πρέπω *prepō* 7x *it becomes, it is fitting, it is proper, it is right,* etc., and part. πρέπον, *becoming, suitable, decorous,* etc., Mt. 3:15; 1 Cor. 11:13; Eph. 5:3; 1 Tim. 2:10 [4241]

[4561] πρεσβεία *presbeia* 2x *eldership, seniority; an embassy, legation; a body of ambassadors, legates,* Lk. 14:32; 19:14* [4242]

[4563] πρεσβεύω *presbeuō* 2x *to be elder; to be an ambassador, perform the duties of an ambassador,* 2 Cor. 5:20; Eph. 6:20* [4243]

[4564] πρεσβυτέριον *presbyterion* 3x *a body of old men, an assembly of elders; the Jewish Sanhedrin,* Lk. 22:66; Acts 22:5; *a body of elders* in the Christian church, *a presbytery,* 1 Tim. 4:14* [4244]

[4565] πρεσβύτερος *presbyteros* 66x *elder, senior; older, more advanced in years,* Lk. 15:25; Jn. 8:9; Acts 2:17; *an elder* in respect of age, *person advanced in years,* 1 Tim. 5:1, 2; pl. spc. *ancients, ancestors, fathers,* Mt. 15:2; Heb. 11:2; as a title of dignity, *an elder,* local *dignitary,* Lk. 7:3; *an elder, member of the Jewish Sanhedrin,* Mt. 16:21; 21:23; 26:3, 47, 57, 59; *an elder* or *presbyter* of the Christian church, Acts 11:30; 14:23, et al. freq. [4245] See *elder; older.*

[4566] πρεσβύτης *presbytēs* 3x *an old man, aged person,* Lk. 1:18; Tit. 2:2; Phlm. 9* [4246]

[4567] πρεσβῦτις *presbytis* 1x *an aged woman,* Tit. 2:3* [4247]

[4568] πρηνής *prēnēs* 1x *prone, head-first;* πρηνὴς γενόμενος, *falling head-long,* Acts 1:18* [4248]

[4569] πρίζω *prizō* 1x also spelled πρίω, *to saw, saw in two,* Heb. 11:37* [4249]

[4570] πρίν *prin* 13x can function as a temporal conj. and an improper prep., *before,* of time, Mt. 26:34, 75; Mk. 14:72; πρὶν ἤ, *sooner than, before,* Mt. 1:18; Lk. 2:26 [4250]

[4571] Πρίσκα *Priska* 3x see also Πρόσκιλλα, *Prisca,* pr. name, Rom. 16:3; 1 Cor. 16:19; 2 Tim. 4:19* [4251]

[4572] Πρίσκιλλα *Priskilla* 3x *Priscilla,* pr. name, the diminutive form of Πρίσκα, the wife of Aquila, Acts 18:2, 18, 26* [4252]

[4574] πρό *pro* 47x *before,* of place, *in front of, in advance of,* Mt. 11:10; Lk. 1:76; Acts 5:23; *before,* of time, Mt. 5:12; Lk. 11:38; before an infin. with the gen. of the article, *before, before that,* Mt. 6:8; Lk. 2:21; *before, above, in preference,* Jas. 5:12; 1 Pet. 4:8 [4253]

[4575] προάγω *proagō* 20x *to lead, bring,* or *conduct forth, produce,* Acts 12:6; 16:30; 25:26; intrans. *to go before, to go first,* Mt. 2:9; 21:9; Mk. 6:45; 1 Tim. 5:24; part. προάγων, ουσα, ον, *preceding, previous, antecedent,* 1 Tim. 1:18; Heb. 7:18; hence, in NT, trans. *to precede,* Mt. 14:22; *to be in advance of,* Mt. 21:31 [4254] See *go ahead.*

[4576] προαιρέω *proaireō* 1x *to prefer, choose;* met. *to purpose, intend considerately,* 2 Cor. 9:7* [4255]

[4577] προαιτιάομαι *proaitiaomai* 1x pr. *to charge beforehand; to convince beforehand,* Rom. 3:9, since the charges in the case in question were drawn from Scripture.* [4256]

[4578] προακούω *proakouō* 1x *to hear beforehand* or *already,* Col. 1:5* [4257]

[4579] προαμαρτάνω *proamartanō* 2x *to sin before;* perf., *to have already sinned, have sinned heretofore,* 2 Cor. 12:21; 13:2* [4258]

[4580] προαύλιον *proaulion* 1x *the exterior court* before an edifice, Mk. 14:68* [4259]

[4581] προβαίνω *probainō* 5x *to go forward, advance,* Mt. 4:21; Mk. 1:19; *to advance* in life, Lk. 1:7, 18; 2:36* [4260]

[4582] προβάλλω *proballō* 2x *to cast before, project; to put* or *urge forward,* Acts 19:33; *to put forth,* as a tree its blossoms, etc., Lk. 21:30* [4261]

[4583] προβατικός *probatikos* 1x *belonging* or *pertaining to sheep;* ἡ προβατικὴ, (πύλη) *the sheep gate,* Jn. 5:2* [4262]

[4585] πρόβατον *probaton* 39x *a sheep,* Mt. 7:15; 9:36; 10:16; met. Mt. 10:6; 15:24 [4263] See *sheep.*

[4586] προβιβάζω *probibazō* 1x *to cause* any one *to advance, to lead forward;* met. *to incite, instigate,* Mt. 14:8* [4264]

[4587] προβλέπω *problepō* 1x *to foresee;* mid. *to provide beforehand,* Heb. 11:40* [4265]

[4588] προγίνομαι *proginomai* 1x *to be* or *happen before, be previously done* or *committed;* προγεγονώς, *bygone, previous,* Rom. 3:25 [4266]

[4589] προγινώσκω *proginōskō* 5x *to know beforehand, to be previously acquainted with,* Acts 26:5; 2 Pet. 3:17; *to determine on beforehand, to foreordain,* 1 Pet. 1:20; in NT, from the Hebrew, *to foreknow, to appoint as the subject of future privileges,* Rom. 8:29; 11:2* [4267] See *foreknow, foreknowledge.*

[4590] πρόγνωσις *prognōsis* 2x *foreknowledge;* in NT *previous determination, purpose,* Acts 2:23; 1 Pet. 1:2* [4268] See *foreknow, foreknowledge.*

[4591] πρόγονος *progonos* 2x *born earlier, elder; a progenitor,* pl. *progenitors; parents,* 1 Tim. 5:4; *forefathers, ancestors,* 2 Tim. 1:3* [4269]

[4592] προγράφω *prographō* 4x *to write before,* Rom. 15:4; Eph. 3:3; *to make a subject of public notice; to set forth unreservedly and distinctly,* Gal. 3:1; *to designate clearly,* Jude 4* [4270]

[4593] πρόδηλος *prodēlos* 3x *previously manifest, evident, known to all; plainly manifest, very clear, prominently conspicuous,* 1 Tim. 5:24, 25; Heb. 7:14* [4271]

[4594] προδίδωμι *prodidōmi* 1x *to give before, precede in giving;* Rom. 11:35* [4272]

[4595] προδότης *prodotēs* 3x *a betrayer, traitor,* Lk. 6:16; Acts 7:52; 2 Tim. 3:4* [4273]

[4596] πρόδρομος *prodromos* 1x *a precursor, forerunner, one who advances to explore and prepare the way,* Heb. 6:20* [4274]

[4598] προελπίζω *proelpizō* 1x *to have hope and confidence* in a person or thing *beforehand,* Eph. 1:12* [4276]

[4599] προενάρχομαι *proenarchomai* 2x *to begin before* a particular time, 2 Cor. 8:6, 10* [4278]

[4601] προέρχομαι *proerchomai* 9x *to go forwards, advance, proceed,* Mt. 26:39; Mk. 14:35; Acts 12:10; *to precede, go before* any one, Lk. 22:47; *to precede* in time, *be a forerunner* or *precursor,* Lk. 1:17; *to outgo, outstrip in going,* Mk. 6:33; *to travel in advance of* any one, *precede,* 20:5, 13; 2 Cor. 9:5* [4281]

[4602] προετοιμάζω *proetoimazō* 2x *to prepare beforehand;* in NT *to appoint beforehand,* Rom. 9:23; Eph. 2:10* [4282]

[4603] προευαγγελίζομαι *proeuangelizomai* 1x *to announce joyful tidings beforehand,* Gal. 3:8* [4283]

[4604] προέχω *proechō* 1x *to have* or *hold before;* intrans. and mid. *to excel, surpass, have advantage* or *preeminence,* Rom. 3:9* [4284]

[4605] προηγέομαι *proēgeomai* 1x *to go before, precede, lead onward;* met. *to endeavor to take the lead of, vie with,* or, *to give precedence to, to prefer,* Rom. 12:10* [4285]

[4606] πρόθεσις *prothesis* 12x *a setting forth* or *before;* οἱ ἄρτοι τῆς προθέσεως, and ἡ πρόθεσις τῶν ἄρτων, *the shewbread,* the twelve loaves of bread, corresponding to the twelve tribes, which were *set out* in two rows upon the golden table in the sanctuary, Mt. 12:4; Mk. 2:26; Lk. 6:4; Heb. 9:2; *predetermination, purpose,* Acts 11:23; 27:13; Rom. 8:28; 2 Tim. 3:10 [4286] See *purpose.*

[4607] προθεσμία *prothesmia* 1x *a time before appointed, set* or *appointed time,* Gal. 4:2* [4287]

[4608] προθυμία *prothumia* 5x *promptness, readiness, eagerness of mind, willingness,* Acts 17:11; 2 Cor. 8:11, 12, 19; 9:2* [4288]

[4609] πρόθυμος *prothumos* 3x *ready in mind, prepared, prompt, willing,* Mt. 26:41; Mk. 14:38; τὸ πρόθυμον, i.q. ἡ προθυμία, *readiness, eagerness of mind,* Rom. 1:15* [4289]

[4610] προθύμως *prothumōs* 1x *promptly, readily, willingly, heartily, cheerfully,* 1 Pet. 5:2* [4290]

[4611] πρόϊμος *proimos* 1x also spelled πρώϊμος, *early,* Jas. 5:7* [4406]

[4613] προΐστημι *proistēmi* 8x *to set before;* met. *to set over, appoint with authority;* intrans. 2 aor.

προύστην, perf. προέστηκα, part. προεστώς, and mid. προΐσταμαι, *to preside, govern, superintend,* Rom. 12:8; 1 Thess. 5:12; 1 Tim. 3:4, 5, 12; 5:17; mid. *to undertake resolutely, to practise diligently, to maintain the practice of,* Tit. 3:8, 14* [4291]

[4614] προκαλέω *prokaleō* 1x *to call out, challenge to fight; to provoke, irritate, with feelings of ungenerous rivalry,* Gal. 5:26* [4292]

[4615] προκαταγγέλλω *prokatangellō* 2x *to declare* or *announce beforehand, foretell, predict,* Acts 3:18; 7:52* [4293]

[4616] προκαταρτίζω *prokatartizō* 1x *to make ready, prepare,* or *complete beforehand,* 2 Cor. 9:5* [4294]

[4618] πρόκειμαι *prokeimai* 5x *to lie* or *be placed before;* met. *to be proposed* or *set before,* as a duty, example, reward, etc., Heb. 6:18; 12:1, 2; Jude 7; *to be at hand, be present,* 2 Cor. 8:12* [4295]

[4619] προκηρύσσω *prokēryssō* 1x *to announce publicly;* in NT *to announce before,* Acts 13:24* [4296]

[4620] προκοπή *prokopē* 3x *advance upon a way;* met. *progress, advancement, furtherance,* Phil. 1:12, 25; 1 Tim. 4:15* [4297]

[4621] προκόπτω *prokoptō* 6x pr. *to cut* a passage *forward; to advance, make progress; to advance,* as time, *to be far spent,* Rom. 13:12; met. *to advance* in wisdom, age, or stature, Lk. 2:52; seq. ἐν, *to make progress* or *proficiency in,* Gal. 1:14; προκόπτω ἐπὶ πλεῖον, *to proceed* or *advance* further, 2 Tim. 2:16; 3:9; προκόπτω ἐπὶ τὸ χεῖρον, *to grow* worse and worse, 2 Tim. 3:13* [4298]

[4622] πρόκριμα *prokrima* 1x *previous judgment, prejudice,* or, *preference, partiality,* 1 Tim. 5:21* [4299]

[4623] προκυρόω *prokyroō* 1x *to sanction and establish previously, ratify and confirm before,* Gal. 3:17* [4300]

[4624] προλαμβάνω *prolambanō* 3x *to take before* another, 1 Cor. 11:21; trop. *to anticipate, do beforehand,* Mk. 14:8; *to take by surprise;* pass. *be taken unexpectedly, be overtaken, be taken by surprise,* Gal. 6:1* [4301]

[4625] προλέγω *prolegō* 15x *to tell beforehand, to foretell,* Mt. 24:25; Acts 1:16; Rom. 9:29; 2 Cor. 13:2; Gal. 5:21; 1 Thess. 3:4 [4302, 4277, 4280] See *say before; warn.*

[4626] προμαρτύρομαι *promartyromai* 1x pr. *to witness* or *testify beforehand; to declare beforehand, predict,* 1 Pet. 1:11* [4303]

[4627] προμελετάω *promeletaō* 1x *to practise beforehand; to premeditate,* Lk. 21:14* [4304]

[4628] προμεριμνάω *promerimnaō* 1x *to be anxious* or *solicitous beforehand, to ponder beforehand,* Mk. 13:11* [4305]

[4629] προνοέω *pronoeō* 3x *to perceive beforehand, foresee; to provide for,* 1 Tim. 5:8; mid. *to provide for one's self;* by impl. *to apply one's self to* a thing, *practice, strive to exhibit,* Rom. 12:17; 2 Cor. 8:21* [4306]

[4630] πρόνοια *pronoia* 2x *forethought; providence, provident care,* Acts 24:2; *provision,* Rom. 13:14* [4307]

[4632] προοράω *prooraō* 4x *to foresee,* Acts 2:31; Gal. 3:8; *to see before,* Acts 21:29; in NT *to have vividly present to the mind, to be mindful of,* Acts 2:25* [4275, 4308]

[4633] προορίζω *proorizō* 6x *to limit* or *mark out beforehand; to design definitely beforehand, ordain beforehand, predestine,* Acts 4:28; Rom. 8:29, 30 [4309] See *predestine.*

[4634] προπάσχω *propaschō* 1x *to experience previously,* of ill treatment, 1 Thess. 2:2* [4310]

[4635] προπάτωρ *propatōr* 1x *a grandfather; a progenitor,* or *ancestor,* Rom. 4:1* [3962]

[4636] προπέμπω *propempō* 9x *to send on before; to accompany* or *attend out of respect, escort, accompany for a certain distance on setting out on a journey,* Acts 15:3; 20:38; 21:5; *to furnish with things necessary for a journey,* Tit. 3:13; 3 Jn. 6 [4311]

[4637] προπετής *propetēs* 2x *falling forwards;* meton. *precipitate, rash,* Acts 19:36; 2 Tim. 3:4* [4312]

[4638] προπορεύομαι *proporeuomai* 2x *to precede, go before,* Acts 7:40; Lk. 1:76* [4313]

[4639] πρός *pros* 700x *from;* met. *for the benefit of,* Acts 27:34. (1) With a dative, *near, by, at, by the side of, in the vicinity of,* Mk. 5:11; Lk. 19:37.

(2) With an accusative, used of the place to which anything tends, *to, unto, towards,* Mt. 2:12; 3:5, 13; *at, close upon,* Mt. 3:10; Mk. 5:22; *near to, in the vicinity of,* Mk. 6:45; after verbs of speaking, pray-

ing, answering to a charge, etc., *to,* Mt. 3:15; 27:14; of place where, *with, in, among, by, at,* etc., Mt. 26:55; Mk. 11:4; Lk. 1:80; of time, *for, during,* Lk. 8:13; 1 Cor. 7:5; *near, towards,* Lk. 24:29; of the end, object, purpose for which an action is exerted, or to which any quality, etc., has reference, *to,* Jn. 4:35; Acts 3:10; 27:12; before an infin. with τό, *in order to, that, in order that,* Mt. 6:1; 13:30; 26:12; *so as to, so that,* Mt. 5:28; of the relation which any action, state, quality, etc., bears to any person or thing, *in relation to, of, concerning, in respect to, with reference to,* Mt. 19:8; Lk. 12:41; 18:1; 20:19; *as it respects, as it concerns, with relation to,* Mt. 27:4; Jn. 21:22, 23; *according to, in conformity with,* Lk. 12:47; 2 Cor. 5:10; *in comparison with,* Rom. 8:18; *in attention to,* Eph. 3:4; of the actions, dispositions, etc., exhibited with respect to any one, whether friendly, *towards,* Gal. 6:10; Eph. 6:9; or unfriendly, *with, against,* Lk. 23:12; Acts 23:30; after verbs signifying to converse, dispute, make a covenant, etc., *with,* Lk. 24:14; Acts 2:7; 3:25 [4314]

[4640] προσάββατον *prosabbaton* 1x *the day before the sabbath, sabbath-eve,* Mk. 15:42* [4315]

[4641] προσαγορεύω *prosagoreuō* 1x *to speak to, accost, to name, declare,* Heb. 5:10* [4316]

[4642] προσάγω *prosagō* 4x *to lead* or *conduct to, bring,* Lk. 9:41; Acts 16:20; *to conduct to the presence of, to procure access for,* 1 Pet. 3:18; *to bring near; to near,* in a nautical sense, Acts 27:27* [4317]

[4643] προσαγωγή *prosagōgē* 3x *approach; access, admission,* to the presence of any one, Rom. 5:2; Eph. 2:18; 3:12* [4318] See *access.*

[4644] προσαιτέω *prosaiteō* 1x *to ask for in addition; to ask earnestly, beg; to beg* alms, Jn. 9:8* [4319]

[4645] προσαίτης *prosaitēs* 2x *a beggar, mendicant,* Mk. 10:46; Jn. 9:8* [4319]

[4646] προσαναβαίνω *prosanabainō* 1x *to go up further,* Lk. 14:10* [4320]

[4649] προσαναλόω *prosanaloō* 1x *to spend,* Lk. 8:43* [4321]

[4650] προσαναπληρόω *prosanaplēroō* 2x *to fill up by addition; to supply* deficiencies, 2 Cor. 9:12; 11:9* [4322]

[4651] προσανατίθημι *prosanatithēmi* 2x occurs in the NT only as a middle, *to lay upon over and above;* mid. *to put one's self in free communication with, to confer with,* Gal. 1:16; *to confer upon, to propound as a matter of consideration,* Gal. 2:6* [4323]

[4653] προσαπειλέω *prosapeileō* 1x *to threaten in addition, utter additional threats,* Acts 4:21* [4324]

[4655] προσδαπανάω *prosdapanaō* 1x *to spend besides, expend over and above,* Lk. 10:35* [4325]

[4656] προσδέομαι *prosdeomai* 1x *to want besides* or *in addition, need,* Acts 17:25* [4326]

[4657] προσδέχομαι *prosdechomai* 14x *to receive, accept; to receive, admit, grant access to,* Lk. 15:2; *to receive, admit, accept,* and with οὐ, *to reject,* Heb. 11:35; *to submit to,* Heb. 10:34; *to receive kindly,* as a guest, *entertain,* Rom. 16:2; *to receive, admit,* as a hope, Acts 24:15; *to look* or *wait for, expect, await,* Mk. 15:43; Lk. 2:25 [4327] See *await; expect; receive; wait for; welcome.*

[4659] προσδοκάω *prosdokaō* 16x *to look for, be expectant of,* Mt. 11:3; Lk. 7:19, 20; Acts 3:5; 2 Pet. 3:12, 13, 14; *to expect,* Acts 28:6; *to wait for,* Lk. 1:21; 8:40; Acts 10:24; 27:33; absol. *to think, anticipate,* Mt. 24:50; Lk. 12:46 [4328] See *expect; look for; wait for.*

[4660] προσδοκία *prosdokia* 2x *a looking for, expectation, anticipation,* Lk. 21:26; meton. *expectation, what is expected* or *anticipated,* Acts 12:11* [4329]

[4661] προσεάω *proseaō* 1x *to permit to go farther,* Acts 27:7* [4330]

[4664] προσεργάζομαι *prosergazomai* 1x pr. *to work in addition; to gain in addition* in trade, Lk. 19:16* [4333]

[4665] προσέρχομαι *proserchomai* 86x *to come* or *go to* any one, *approach,* Mt. 4:3, 11; 5:1; 8:19, 25, et al. freq.; trop. *to come* or *go to, approach, draw near,* spiritually, Heb. 7:25; 11:6; 4:16; 1 Pet. 2:4; met. *to assent to, accede to, concur in,* 1 Tim. 6:3 [4334] See *approach; come to.*

[4666] προσευχή *proseuchē* 36x *prayer,* Mt. 17:21; 21:13, 22; Lk. 6:12; Acts 1:14; meton. *a place where prayer is offered, an oratory,* perhaps, Acts 16:13, 16 [4335] See *prayer.*

[4667] προσεύχομαι *proseuchomai* 85x *to pray, offer prayer,* Mt. 5:44; 6:5, 6 [4336] See *pray.*

[4668] προσέχω *prosechō* 24x *to have in addition; to hold to, bring near;* absol. *to apply* the mind to a thing, *to give heed to, attend to, observe, consider,* Acts 5:35; Heb. 2:1; 2 Pet. 1:19; *to take care of, pro-*

vide for, Acts 20:28; when followed by ἀπό, μή, or μήποτε, *to beware of, take heed of, guard against,* Mt. 6:1; 7:15; *to assent to, yield credence to, follow, adhere* or *be attached to,* Acts 8:6, 10, 11; 16:14; *to give one's self up to, be addicted to, engage in, be occupied with,* 1 Tim. 1:4, 3:8 [4337] See *guard; pay attention; watch out.*

[4669] προσηλόω *prosēloō* 1x *to nail to, affix with nails,* Col. 2:14* [4338]

[4670] προσήλυτος *prosēlytos* 4x pr. *a newcomer, a stranger;* in NT *a proselyte, convert from paganism to Judaism,* Mt. 23:15; Acts 2:11; 6:5; 13:43* [4339]

[4672] πρόσκαιρος *proskairos* 4x *opportune,* in NT *continuing for a limited time, temporary, transient,* Mt. 13:21; Mk. 4:17; 2 Cor. 4:18; Heb. 11:25* [4340]

[4673] προσκαλέω *proskaleō* 29x *to call to one's self, summon,* Mt. 10:1; 15:10, 32; 18:2; *to invite,* Acts 2:39; *to call* to the performance of a thing, *appoint,* Acts 13:2; 16:10 [4341] See *summon.*

[4674] προσκαρτερέω *proskartereō* 10x *to persist in adherence to* a thing; *to be intently engaged in, attend constantly to,* Acts 1:14; 2:42; Rom. 13:6; *to remain constantly* in a place, Acts 2:46; *to constantly attend upon, continue near to, be at hand,* Mk. 3:9; Acts 8:13; 10:7 [4342] See *attend to; (be) devoted to.*

[4675] προσκαρτέρησις *proskarterēsis* 1x *perseverance, unremitting continuance in* a thing, Eph. 6:18* [4343]

[4676] προσκεφάλαιον *proskephalaion* 1x pr. *a cushion for the head, pillow;* also, *a boat cushion,* Mk. 4:38* [4344]

[4677] προσκληρόω *posklēroō* 1x pr. *to assign by lot;* in NT, *to adjoin one's self to, associate with, follow as a disciple,* Acts 17:4* [4345]

[4679] προσκλίνω *prosklinō* 1x pr. *to make to lean upon* or *against* a thing; met., to *join one's self to, follow as an adherent,* Acts 5:36* [4347]

[4680] πρόσκλισις *prosklisis* 1x pr. *a leaning upon* or *towards* a thing; met. *a leaning towards* any one, *inclination* of mind *towards, partiality,* 1 Tim. 5:21* [4346]

[4681] προσκολλάω *proskollaō* 2x pr. *to glue to; to cleave closely to,* Mk. 10:7; Eph. 5:31* [4347]

[4682] πρόσκομμα *proskomma* 6x *a stumbling,* Rom. 9:32, 33; 1 Pet. 2:8; met. *a stumbling block, an occasion of sinning, means of inducing to sin,* Rom. 14:13; 1 Cor. 8:9; met. *a* moral *stumbling, a shock* to the moral or religious sense, *a* moral *embarrassment,* Rom. 14:20* [4348] See *offense; stumbling block.*

[4683] προσκοπή *proskopē* 1x pr. *a stumbling; offense;* in NT *an offense, shock, ground of exception,* 2 Cor. 6:3* [4349]

[4684] προσκόπτω *proskoptō* 8x *to dash against, to beat upon,* Mt. 7:27; *to strike* the foot *against,* Mt. 4:6; Lk. 4:11; *to stumble,* Jn. 11:9, 10; met. *to stumble at, to take offense at,* Rom. 9:32; 14:21; 1 Pet. 2:8* [4350]

[4685] προσκυλίω *proskyliō* 2x *to roll to* or *against,* Mt. 27:60; Mk. 15:46* [4351]

[4686] προσκυνέω *proskyneō* 60x *to do reverence* or *homage by kissing the hand;* in NT *to do reverence* or *homage by prostration,* Mt. 2:2, 8, 11; 20:20; Lk. 4:7; 24:52; *to pay* divine *homage, worship, adore,* Mt. 4:10; Jn. 4:20, 21; Heb. 1:6; *to bow one's self in adoration,* Heb. 11:21 [4352] See *fall down before; worship.*

[4687] προσκυνητής *proskynētēs* 1x *a worshiper,* Jn. 4:23* [4353]

[4688] προσλαλέω *proslaleō* 2x *to speak to, converse with,* Acts 13:43; 28:20* [4354]

[4689] προσλαμβάνω *proslambanō* 12x *to take to one's self, assume, take as a companion* or *associate,* Acts 17:5; 18:26; *to take,* as food, Acts 27:33, 36; *to receive kindly* or *hospitably, admit to one's society and friendship, treat with kindness,* Acts 28:2; Rom. 14:1, 3; 15:7; Phlm. 17; *to take aside* as a preliminary to an address of admonition, Mt. 16:22; Mk. 8:32* [4355] See *accept; take aside; welcome.*

[4691] πρόσλημψις *proslēmpsis* 1x also spelled πρόσληψις, *acceptance,* Rom. 11:15* [4356]

[4693] προσμένω *prosmenō* 7x *to continue, remain, stay* in a place, 1 Tim. 1:3; *to remain* or *continue with* any one, Mt. 15:32; Mk. 8:2; Acts 18:18; *to adhere to,* Acts 11:23; met. *to remain constant in, persevere in,* Acts 13:43; 1 Tim. 5:5* [4357]

[4694] προσορμίζω *prosormizō* 1x *to bring a ship to its station* or *to land;* mid. *to come to the land,* Mk. 6:53* [4358]

[4695] προσοφείλω *prosopheilō* 1x *to owe besides* or *in addition,* Phlm. 19* [4359]

[4696] προσοχθίζω *prosochthizō* 2x *to be vexed* or *angry at,* Heb. 3:10, 17* [4360]

[4698] πρόσπεινος *prospeinos* 1x *very hungry,* Acts 10:10* [4361]

[4699] προσπήγνυμι *prospēgnymi* 1x *to fix to, affix to,* Acts 2:23* [4362]

[4700] προσπίπτω *prospiptō* 8x *to fall* or *impinge upon* or *against* a thing; *to fall down to* any one, Mk. 3:11; 7:25; *to rush violently upon, beat against,* Mt. 7:25 [4363]

[4701] προσποιέω *prospoieō* 1x *to add* or *attach;* mid. *to attach to one's self; to take notice; to assume the appearance of, make a show of, pretend,* Lk. 24:28* [4364]

[4702] προσπορεύομαι *prosporeuomai* 1x *to go* or *come to* any one, Mk. 10:35* [4365]

[4704] προσρήσσω *prosrēssō* 2x also spelled προσρήγνυμι, *to break* or *burst upon, dash against,* Lk. 6:48, 49* [4366]

[4705] προστάσσω *prostassō* 7x pr. *to place* or *station at* or *against; to enjoin, command, direct,* Mt. 1:24; 8:4; Mk. 1:44; *to assign, constitute, appoint,* Acts 17:26 [4367] See *command; instruct.*

[4706] προστάτις *prostatis* 1x *a patroness, protectress,* Rom. 16:2* [4368]

[4707] προστίθημι *prostithēmi* 18x *to put to* or *near; to lay with* or *by the side of,* Acts 13:36; *to add, adjoin,* Mt. 6:27, 33; Lk. 3:20; Acts 2:41; from the Hebrew, denote *continuation,* or *repetition,* Lk. 19:11; 20:11, 12; Acts 12:3 [4369] See *add; increase.*

[4708] προστρέχω *prostrechō* 3x *to run to,* or *up,* Mk. 9:15; 10:17; Acts 8:30* [4370]

[4709] προσφάγιον *prosphagion* 1x *what is eaten besides;* hence, genr. *victuals, food,* Jn. 21:5* [4371]

[4710] πρόσφατος *prosphatos* 1x pr. *recently killed;* hence, genr. *recent, new, newly* or *lately made,* Heb. 10:20* [4372]

[4711] προσφάτως *prosphatōs* 1x *newly, recently, lately,* Acts 18:2* [4373]

[4712] προσφέρω *prospherō* 47x *to bear* or *bring to,* Mt. 4:24; 25:20; *to bring to* or *before* magistrates, Lk. 12:11; 23:14; *to bring near to, apply to,* Jn. 19:29; *to offer, tender, proffer,* as money, Acts 8:18; *to offer, present,* as gifts, oblations, etc., Mt. 2:11; 5:23; Heb. 5:7; *to offer* in sacrifice, Mk. 1:44; Lk. 5:14; *to offer up* any one as a sacrifice to God, Heb. 9:25, 28; 11:17; mid. *to bear one's self towards, behave* or *conduct one's self towards, to deal with, treat* any one, Heb. 12:7 [4374] See *bring; offer.*

[4713] προσφιλής *prosphilēs* 1x *friendly, grateful, acceptable,* Phil. 4:8* [4375]

[4714] προσφορά *prosphora* 9x pr. *a bringing to;* in NT *an offering, an act of offering up* or *sacrificing,* Heb. 10:10, 14, 18; trop. Rom. 15:16; *an offering, oblation, a thing offered,* Eph. 5:2; Heb. 10:5, 8; *a sacrifice, victim offered,* Acts 21:26; 24:17* [4376]

[4715] προσφωνέω *prosphōneō* 7x *to speak to, address,* Mt. 11:16; Lk. 7:32; 13:12; *to address, harangue,* Acts 22:2; *to call* to one's self, Lk. 6:13 [4377]

[4717] πρόσχυσις *proschusis* 1x *an effusion, sprinkling,* Heb. 11:28* [4378]

[4718] προσψαύω *prospsauō* 1x *to touch upon, touch lightly,* with the dative, Lk. 11:46* [4379]

[4719] προσωπολημπτέω *prosōpolēmpteō* 1x *show partiality,* Jas. 2:9* [4380]

[4720] προσωπολήμπτης *prosōpolēmptēs* 1x *one who shows partiality,* Acts 10:34* [4381]

[4721] προσωπολημψία *prosōpolēmpsia* 4x *respect of persons, partiality,* Rom. 2:11; Eph. 6:9; Col. 3:25; Jas. 2:1* [4382]

[4725] πρόσωπον *prosōpon* 76x *the face, countenance, visage,* Mt. 6:16, 17; 17:2, 6; according to late usage, *a person, individual,* 2 Cor. 1:11; hence, *a personal presence,* 1 Thess. 2:17; from the Hebrew, πρόσωπον πρὸς πρόσωπον, *face to face, clearly, perfectly,* 1 Cor. 13:12; *face, surface, external form, figure, appearance,* Mt. 16:3; Lk. 12:56; *external circumstances,* or *condition* of any one, Mt. 22:16; Mk. 12:14; πρόσωπον λαμβάνειν, *to have respect to the external circumstances* of any one, Lk. 20:21; Gal. 2:6; ἐν προσώπῳ, *in presence of,* 2 Cor. 2:10; ἀπὸ προσώπου, *from the presence of, from,* Acts 3:19; also, *from before,* Acts 7:45; εἰς πρόσωπον, and κατὰ πρόσωπον, *in the presence of, before,* Acts 3:13; 2 Cor. 8:24; also, *openly,* Gal. 2:11; κατὰ πρόσωπον, ἔχειν, *to have before one's face, to have* any one *present,* Acts 25:16; ἀπὸ προσώπου, *from,* Rev. 12:14; πρὸ προσώπου, *before,* Acts 13:24 [4383] See *countenance; face.*

[4727] προτείνω *proteinō* 1x *to extend before; to stretch out,* Acts 22:25* [4385]

[4728] πρότερος *proteros* 11x *former, prior,* Eph. 4:22; *before, formerly,* Jn. 6:62 [4386, 4387] See *earlier; former.*

[4729] προτίθημι *protithēmi* 3x *to place before; to set forth, propose publicly,* Rom. 3:25; mid. προτίθεμαι, *to purpose, determine, design beforehand,* Rom. 1:13; Eph. 1:9* [4388] See *plan; present.*

[4730] προτρέπω *protrepō* 1x *to turn forwards; to impel; to excite, urge, exhort,* Acts 18:27* [4389]

[4731] προτρέχω *protrechō* 2x *to run before,* or *in advance,* Lk. 19:4; Jn. 20:4* [4390]

[4732] προϋπάρχω *prouparchō* 2x *to be before,* or *formerly,* Lk. 23:12; Acts 8:9* [4391]

[4733] πρόφασις *prophasis* 6x pr. *that which appears in front, that which is put forward to hide the true state of things, an alleged motive; a fair show* or *pretext,* Acts 27:30; *a specious cloak,* Mt. 23:13; 1 Thess. 2:5; *a valid excuse,* Jn. 15:22 [4392]

[4734] προφέρω *propherō* 2x *to bring before, present; to bring forth* or *out, produce,* Lk. 6:45 (2x)* [4393]

[4735] προφητεία *prophēteia* 19x *prophecy, a prediction of future events,* Mt. 13:14; 2 Pet. 1:20, 21; *prophecy, a gifted faculty of setting forth and enforcing revealed truth,* 1 Cor. 12:10; 13:2; *prophecy, matter of divine teaching set forth by special gift,* 1 Tim. 1:18 [4394] See *prophecy.*

[4736] προφητεύω *prophēteuō* 28x *to exercise the function of a* προφήτης; *to prophesy, to foretell the future,* Mt. 11:13; *to divine,* Mt. 26:68; Mk. 14:65; Lk. 22:64; *to prophesy, to set forth matter of divine teaching by special faculty,* 1 Cor. 13:9; 14:1 [4395] See *prophesy.*

[4737] προφήτης *prophētēs* 144x pr. *a spokesman for* another; spc. *a spokesman* or *interpreter* for a deity; *a prophet, seer,* Tit. 1:12; in NT *a prophet, a divinely commissioned and inspired person,* Mt. 14:5; Lk. 7:16, 39; Jn. 9:17; *a prophet* in the Christian church, *a person gifted for the exposition of divine truth,* 1 Cor. 12:28, 29; *a prophet, a foreteller of the future,* Mt. 1:22, et al. freq.; οἱ προφῆται, *the prophetic scriptures of the Old Testament,* Lk. 16:29 [4396] See *prophet.*

[4738] προφητικός *prophētikos* 2x *prophetic, uttered by prophets,* Rom. 16:26; 2 Pet. 1:19* [4397]

[4739] προφῆτις *prophētis* 2x *a prophetess, a divinely gifted female teacher,* Lk. 2:36; Rev. 2:20* [4398]

[4740] προφθάνω *prophthanō* 1x *to outstrip, anticipate; to anticipate* any one in doing or saying a thing, *be beforehand with,* Mt. 17:25* [4399]

[4741] προχειρίζω *procheirizō* 3x also listed as a deponent, προχειρίζομαι, *to take into the hand, to make ready for use* or *action; to choose for oneself, select, appoint,* Acts 3:20; 22:14; 26:16* [4400] See *appoint; choose.*

[4742] προχειροτονέω *procheirotoneō* 1x pr. *to elect before* Acts 10:41* [4401]

[4743] Πρόχορος *Prochoros* 1x *Prochorus,* pr. name, Acts 6:5* [4402]

[4744] πρύμνα *prymna* 3x *the hinder part of a vessel, stern,* Mk. 4:38; Acts 27:29, 41* [4403]

[4745] πρωΐ *prōi* 12x *in the morning, early,* Mt. 16:3; 20:1; Mk. 15:1; Acts 28:23; *the morning watch,* which ushers in the dawn, Mk. 13:35 [4404] See *dawn; early; morning.*

[4746] πρωΐα *prōia* 2x *morning, the morning hour,* Mt. 27:1; Jn. 21:4* [4405]

[4748] πρωϊνός *prōinos* 2x *belonging to the morning, morning,* Rev. 2:28; 22:16* [4407]

[4749] πρῷρα *prōra* 2x *the forepart of a vessel, prow,* Acts 27:30, 41* [4408]

[4750] πρωτεύω *prōteuō* 1x *to be first, to hold the first rank* or *highest dignity, have the preeminence, be chief,* Col. 1:18* [4409]

[4751] πρωτοκαθεδρία *prōtokathedria* 4x *the first* or *uppermost seat, the most honorable seat,* Mt. 23:6; Mk. 12:39; Lk. 11:43; 20:46* [4410]

[4752] πρωτοκλισία *prōtoklisia* 5x *the first place of reclining* at table, *the most honorable place at table,* Mt. 23:6; Mk. 12:39; Lk. 14:7, 8; 20:46 [4411]

[4754] πρῶτον *prōton* 60x an accusative singular neuter form of πρῶτος (*4755*) that became solidified in function as an adverb, *first* in time, *in the first place*, Mk. 4:28; 16:9; τὸ πρῶτον, *at the first, formerly*, Jn. 12:16; 19:39; *first* in dignity, importance, etc., *before all things*, Mt. 6:33 [4412] See *first.*

[4755] πρῶτος *prōtos* 95x *first* in time, order, etc., Mt. 10:2; 26:17; *first* in dignity, importance, etc., *chief, principal, most important,* Mk. 6:21; Lk. 19:47;

Acts 13:50; 16:12; as an equivalent to the compar. πρότερος (*4754*), *prior,* Jn. 1:5, 30; 15:18; Mt. 27:64; adverbially, *first,* Jn. 1:42; 5:4; 8:7 [4413] See *first.*

[4756] πρωτοστάτης *prōtostatēs* 1x pr. *one stationed in the first rank* of an army; *a leader; a chief, ringleader,* Acts 24:5* [4414]

[4757] πρωτοτόκια *prōtotokia* 1x *the rights of primogeniture, birthright,* Heb. 12:16 [4415]

[4758] πρωτότοκος *prōtotokos* 8x *first-born,* Lk. 2:7; Heb. 11:28; in NT *prior in generation,* Col. 1:15; *a firstborn* head of a spiritual family, Rom. 8:29; Heb. 1:6; *firstborn,* as possessed of the peculiar privilege of spiritual generation, Heb. 12:23 [4416] See *firstborn.*

[4759] πρώτως *prōtōs* 1x *for the first time,* Acts 11:26* [4412]

[4760] πταίω *ptaiō* 5x *to cause to stumble;* intrans. *to stumble, stagger, fall; to make a false step;* met. *to err, transgress,* Rom. 11:11; Jas. 2:10; 3:2 (2x); met. *to fail* of an object, 2 Pet. 1:10* [4417]

[4761] πτέρνα *pterna* 1x *the heel,* Jn. 13:18* [4418]

[4762] πτερύγιον *pterygion* 2x *a little wing; the extremity, the extreme point* of a thing; *a pinnacle,* or *apex* of a building, Mt. 4:5; Lk. 4:9* [4419]

[4763] πτέρυξ *pteryx* 5x *a wing, pinion,* Mt. 23:37; Lk. 13:34 [4420]

[4764] πτηνός *ptēnos* 1x as adj., *winged, with feathers;* as noun, *a bird, fowl,* 1 Cor. 15:39* [4421]

[4765] πτοέω *ptoeō* 2x *to terrify, affright;* pass. *to be terrified,* Lk. 21:9; 24:37* [4422]

[4766] πτόησις *ptoēsis* 1x *consternation, dismay,* 1 Pet. 3:6* [4423]

[4767] Πτολεμαΐς *Ptolemais* 1x *Ptolemais,* a city on the seacoast of Galilee: the modern *Acre,* Acts 21:7* [4424]

[4768] πτύον *ptyon* 2x *a fan, winnowing fork,* Mt. 3:12; Lk. 3:17* [4425]

[4769] πτύρω *ptyrō* 1x *to scare, terrify;* pass. *to be terrified, be in consternation,* Phil. 1:28* [4426]

[4770] πτύσμα *ptysma* 1x *spittle, saliva,* Jn. 9:6* [4427]

[4771] πτύσσω *ptyssō* 1x *to fold; to roll up* a scroll, Lk. 4:20* [4428]

[4772] πτύω *ptyō* 3x *to spit, spit out,* Mk. 7:33; 8:23; Jn. 9:6 [4429]

[4773] πτῶμα *ptōma* 7x *a fall; a dead body, carcass, corpse,* Mt. 24:28; Mk. 6:29 [4430]

[4774] πτῶσις *ptōsis* 2x *a fall, crash, ruin,* Mt. 7:27; met. *downfall, ruin,* Lk. 2:34* [4431]

[4775] πτωχεία *ptōcheia* 3x *begging; beggary; poverty,* 2 Cor. 8:2, 9; Rev. 2:9* [4432]

[4776] πτωχεύω *ptōcheuō* 1x *to be a beggar; to be* or *become poor, be in poverty,* 2 Cor. 8:9* [4433]

[4777] πτωχός *ptōchos* 34x *reduced to beggary, mendicant; poor, indigent,* Mt. 19:21; 26:9, 11; met. spiritually *poor,* Rev. 3:17; by impl. *a person of low condition,* Mt. 11:4; Lk. 4:18; 7:22; met. *beggarly, sorry,* Gal. 4:9; met. *lowly,* Mt. 5:3; Lk. 6:20 [4434] See *poor.*

[4778] πυγμή *pygmē* 1x *together with the forearm,* or, *with care, carefully,* Mk. 7:3* [4435]

[4781] πυκνός *pyknos* 3x *dense, thick; frequent,* 1 Tim. 5:23; πυκνά, as an adverb, *frequently, often,* Lk. 5:33; so the compar. πυκνότερον, *very frequently,* Acts 24:26* [4437]

[4782] πυκτεύω *pykteuō* 1x *to box, fight as a boxer,* 1 Cor. 9:26* [4438]

[4783] πύλη *pylē* 10x *a gate,* Mt. 7:13, 14; Lk. 7:12; Acts 12:10; πύλαι ᾅδου, *the gates of hades, the nether world and its powers, the powers of destruction, dissolution,* Mt. 16:18 [4439] See *door; gate.*

[4784] πυλών *pylōn* 18x *a gateway, vestibule,* Mt. 26:71; Lk. 16:20; *a gate,* Acts 14:13; Rev. 21:12, 13, 15, 21, 25 [4440] See *gate.*

[4785] πυνθάνομαι *pynthanomai* 12x *to ask, inquire,* Mt. 2:4; Lk. 15:26; *to investigate, examine* judicially, Acts 23:20; *to ascertain by inquiry, understand,* Acts 23:34 [4441] See *ask.*

[4786] πῦρ *pyr* 71x *fire,* Mt. 3:10; 7:19; 13:40, et al. freq.; πυρός, used by Hebraism with the force of an adjective, *fiery, fierce,* Heb. 10:27; *fire* used figuratively to express various circumstances of severe trial, Lk. 12:49; 1 Cor. 3:13; Jude 23 [4442] See *fire.*

[4787] πυρά *pyra* 2x *a fire, heap of combustibles,* Acts 28:2, 3* [4443]

[4788] πύργος *pyrgos* 4x *a tower,* Mt. 21:33; Mk. 12:1; Lk. 13:4; genr. *a castle, palace,* Lk. 14:28* [4444]

[4789] πυρέσσω *pyressō* 2x *to be feverish, be sick of a fever,* Mt. 8:14; Mk. 1:30* [4445]

[4790] πυρετός *pyretos* 6x *scorching and noxious heat; a fever,* Mt. 8:15; Mk. 1:31 [4446]

[4791] πύρινος *pyrinos* 1x pr. *of fire, fiery, burning; shining, glittering,* Rev. 9:17* [4447]

[4792] πυρόω *pyroō* 6x *to set on fire, burn;* pass. *to be kindled, be on fire, burn, flame,* Eph. 6:16; 2 Pet. 3:12; Rev. 1:15; met. *to fire* with distressful feelings, 2 Cor. 11:29; of lust, *to be inflamed, burn,* 1 Cor. 7:9; *to be tried with fire,* as metals, Rev. 3:18* [4448]

[4793] πυρράζω *pyrrazō* 2x *to be fiery red,* Mt. 16:2, 3* [4449]

[4794] πυρρός *pyrros* 2x *of the color of fire, fiery red,* Rev. 6:4; 12:3* [4450]

[4795] Πύρρος *Pyrros* 1x *Pyrrhus,* pr. name, Acts 20:4* [**]

[4796] πύρωσις *pyrōsis* 3x *a burning, conflagration,* Rev. 18:9, 18; met. *a fiery test* of trying circumstances, 1 Pet. 4:12* [4451]

[4797] πωλέω *pōleō* 22x *to sell,* Mt. 10:29; 13:44 [4453] See *sell.*

[4798] πῶλος *pōlos* 12x *a youngling; a foal* or *colt,* Mt. 21:2, 5, 7; Mk. 11:2 [4454] See *colt.*

[4799] πώποτε *pōpote* 6x *ever yet, ever, at any time,* Lk. 19:30; Jn. 1:18 [4455]

[4800] πωρόω *pōroō* 5x *to petrify; to harden;* in NT *to harden* the feelings, Jn. 12:40; pass. *to become callous, unimpressible,* Mk. 6:52; 8:17; Rom. 11:7; 2 Cor. 3:14* [4456]

[4801] πώρωσις *pōrōsis* 3x *a hardening;* met. *hardness* of heart, *callousness, insensibility,* Mk. 3:5; Rom. 11:25; Eph. 4:18* [4457]

[4802] πῶς *pōs* 103x interrogative particle, *How? In what manner? By what means?* Mt. 7:4; 22:12; Jn. 6:52; used in interrogations which imply a negative, Mt. 12:26, 29, 34; 22:45; 23:33; Acts 8:31; put concisely for *How is it that? How does it come to pass that?* Mt. 16:11; 22:43; Mk. 4:40; Jn. 7:15; with an indirect interrogation, *how, in what manner,* Mt. 6:28; 10:19; Mk. 11:18; put for τί, *What?* Lk. 10:26; put for ὡς, as a particle of exclamation, *how, how much, how greatly,* Mk. 10:23, 24 [4459]

[4803] πως *pōs* 15x enclitic particle, *in any way, by any means,* Acts 27:12; Rom. 1:10 [4452, 4458]

[4805] Ῥαάβ *Rhaab* 2x *Rahab,* pr. name, indecl (Jsh. 2; 6:17, 25) Heb. 11:31; Jas. 2:25* [4460]

[4806] ῥαββί *rhabbi* 15x also spelled ῥαββεί, *rabbi, my master, teacher,* Mt. 23:7, 8; 26:25, 49 [4461] See *master; rabbi; sir.*

[4808] ῥαββουνί *rhabbouni* 2x a form of ῥαββί, *my teacher,* Mk. 10:51; Jn. 20:16 [4462]

[4810] ῥαβδίζω *rhabdizō* 2x *to beat with rods,* Acts 16:22; 2 Cor. 11:25* [4463]

[4811] ῥάβδος *rhabdos* 12x *a rod, wand,* Heb. 9:4; Rev. 11:1; *a rod* of correction, 1 Cor. 4:21; *a staff,* Mt. 10:10; Heb. 11:21; *a scepter,* Heb. 1:8; Rev. 2:27 [4464] See *rod; scepter; staff.*

[4812] ῥαβδοῦχος *rhabdouchos* 2x *the bearer of a wand* of office; *a lictor, sergeant,* a public servant who bore a bundle or rods before the magistrates as insignia of their office, and carried into execution the sentences they pronounced, Acts 16:35, 38* [4465]

[4814] Ῥαγαύ *Rhagau* 1x *Ragau,* pr. name, indecl. Lk. 3:35* [4466]

[4815] ῥᾳδιούργημα *rhadiourgēma* 1x pr. *anything done lightly, levity; reckless conduct, crime,* Acts 18:14* [4467]

[4816] ῥᾳδιουργία *rhadiourgia* 1x *wickedness, unscrupulousness; recklessness,* Acts 13:10* [4468]

[4818] Ῥαιφάν *Rhaiphan* 1x pr. name., *Rephan,* Acts 7:43* [4481]

[4819] ῥακά *rhaka* 1x *raca,* an Aramaic term of bitter contempt, *worthless fellow, fool,* Mt. 5:22* [4469]

[4820] ῥάκος *rhakos* 2x *a piece torn off; a bit of cloth, cloth,* Mt. 9:16; Mk. 2:21* [4470]

[4821] Ῥαμά *Rhama* 1x *Rama,* a city of Judea [4471]

[4822] ῥαντίζω *rhantizō* 4x *to sprinkle,* Heb. 9:13, 19, 21; met. and by impl. *to cleanse by sprinkling, purify, free from pollution,* Heb. 10:22* [4472]

[4823] ῥαντισμός *rhantismos* 2x pr. *a sprinkling;* met. *a cleansing, purification,* Heb. 12:24; 1 Pet. 1:2* [4473]

[4824] ῥαπίζω *rhapizō* 2x *to beat with rods; to strike with the palm of the hand, cuff, clap,* Mt. 5:39; 26:67* [4474]

[4825] ῥάπισμα *rhapisma* 3x *a blow with the palm of the hand, cuff, slap,* Mk. 14:65; Jn. 18:22; 19:3* [4475]

[4827] ῥαφίς *rhaphis* 2x *a needle,* Mt. 19:24; Mk. 10:25* [4476]

[4829] Ῥαχάβ *Rhachab* 1x *Rachab,* pr. name, indecl., Mt. 1:5* [4477]

[4830] Ῥαχήλ *Rhachēl* 1x *Rachel,* pr. name, indecl., Mt. 2:18* [4478]

[4831] Ῥεβέκκα *Rhebekka* 1x *Rebecca,* pr. name, Rom. 9:10* [4479]

[4832] ῥέδη *rhedē* 1x *a carriage with four wheels* for travelling, *a chariot,* Rev. 18:13* [4480]

[4835] ῥέω *rheō* 1x *flow, overflow with,* Jn. 7:38* [4482]

[4836] Ῥήγιον *Rhēgion* 1x *Rhegium,* a city at the southwestern extremity of Italy, Acts 28:13* [4484]

[4837] ῥῆγμα *rhēgma* 1x *a rent; a crash, ruin,* Lk. 6:49* [4485]

[4838] ῥήγνυμι *rhēgnymi* 1x see ῥήσσω [4486]

[4839] ῥῆμα *rhēma* 68x *that which is spoken; declaration, saying, speech, word,* Mt. 12:36; 26:75; Mk. 9:32; 14:72; *a command, mandate, direction,* Lk. 3:2; 5:5; *a promise,* Lk. 1:38; 2:29; *a prediction, prophecy,* 2 Pet. 3:2; *a doctrine* of God or Christ, Jn. 3:34; 5:47; 6:63, 68; Acts 5:20; *an accusation, charge, crimination,* Mt. 5:11; 27:14; from the Hebrew, *a thing,* Mt. 4:4; Lk. 4:4; *a matter, affair, transaction, business,* Mt. 18:16; Lk. 1:65; 2 Cor. 13:1 [4487] See *event; matter; word.*

[4840] Ῥησά *Rhēsa* 1x *Rhesa,* pr. name, indecl., Lk. 3:27* [4488]

[4841] ῥήσσω *rhēssō* 6x also spelled ῥήγνυμι 1x in our text (Mt. 9:17). *to rend, shatter; to break* or *burst in pieces* Mt. 9:17; Mk. 2:22; Lk. 5:37; *to rend, lacerate,* Mt. 7:6; *to cast* or *dash* upon the ground, *convulse,* Mk. 9:18; Lk. 9:42; absol. *to break forth* into exclamation, Gal. 4:27 [4486]

[4842] ῥήτωρ *rhētōr* 1x *an orator, advocate,* Acts 24:1* [4489]

[4843] ῥητῶς *rhētōs* 1x *in express words, expressly,* 1 Tim. 4:1* [4490]

[4844] ῥίζα *rhiza* 17x *a root* of a tree, Mt. 3:10; 13:6; met. ἔχειν ῥίζαν, or ἔχειν ῥίζαν ἐν ἑαυτῷ, *to be rooted* in faith, Mt. 13:21; Mk. 4:17; Lk. 8:13; met. *cause, source, origin,* 1 Tim. 6:10; Heb. 12:15; by synec. *the trunk, stock* of a tree, met. Rom. 11:16, 17, 18; met. *offspring, progeny, a descendant,* Rom. 15:12; Rev. 5:5; 22:16 [4491] See *root.*

[4845] ῥιζόω *rhizoō* 2x *to root, cause to take root; firmly rooted, strengthened with roots;* met. *firm, constant, firmly fixed,* Eph. 3:17; Col. 2:7* [4492]

[4846] ῥιπή *rhipē* 1x pr. *a rapid sweep, jerk; a wink, twinkling* of the eye, 1 Cor. 15:52* [4493]

[4847] ῥιπίζω *rhipizō* 1x *to fan, blow, ventilate; to toss, agitate,* e.g. the ocean by the wind, Jas. 1:6* [4494]

[4848] ῥιπτέω *rhipteō* 1x also spelled ῥίπτω, frequent and repeated action, *to toss repeatedly, toss up* with violent gesture, Acts 22:23 (ῥιπτούντων)* [4495]

[4849] ῥίπτω *rhiptō* 7x also spelled ῥιπτέω, *to hurl, throw, cast; to throw* or *cast down,* Mt. 27:5; Lk. 4:35; 17:2; *to throw* or *cast* out, Acts 27:19, 29; *to lay down, set down,* Mt. 15:30; pass. *to be dispersed, scattered,* Mt. 9:36* [4496]

[4850] Ῥοβοάμ *Rhoboam* 2x *Roboam,* pr. name, indecl., Mt. 1:7* [4497]

[4851] Ῥόδη *Rhodē* 1x *Rhoda,* pr. name, Acts 12:13* [4498]

[4852] Ῥόδος *Rhodos* 1x *Rhodes,* an island in the Mediterranean, south of Caria, Acts 21:1* [4499]

[4853] ῥοιζηδόν *rhoizēdon* 1x *with a noise, with a crash,* etc., 2 Pet. 3:10* [4500]

[4855] ῥομφαία *rhomphaia* 7x pr. *a* Thracian *broadsword; a sword,* Rev. 1:16; 2:12; by meton. *war,* Rev. 6:8; met. *a thrill of anguish,* Lk. 2:35 [4501]

[4857] Ῥουβήν *Rhoubēn* 1x *Reuben,* pr. name, indecl., Rev. 7:5* [4502]

[4858] Ῥούθ *Rhouth* 1x *Ruth,* pr. name, indecl., Mt. 1:5* [4503]

[4859] Ῥοῦφος *Rhouphos* 2x *Rufus,* pr. name, Mk. 15:21; Rom. 16:13* [4504]

[4860] ῥύμη *rhymē* 4x pr. *a street,* Acts 9:11; 12:10; *a narrow street, lane, alley,* as distinguished from πλατεῖα, Mt. 6:2; Lk. 14:21* [4505]

[4861] ῥύομαι *rhyomai* 17x *to drag* out of danger, *to rescue, save,* Mt. 6:13; 27:43; *to be rescued, delivered,* Lk. 1:74; Rom. 15:31; 2 Thess. 3:2; 2 Tim. 4:17 [4506] See *deliver; rescue.*

[4862] ῥυπαίνω *rhypainō* 1x *to make filthy, defile,* Rev. 22:11* [4510]

[4864] ῥυπαρία *rhyparia* 1x *filth;* met. moral *filthiness, uncleanness, pollution,* Jas. 1:21* [4507]

[4865] ῥυπαρός *rhyparos* 2x *filthy, squalid, sordid, dirty,* Jas. 2:2; met. *defiled, polluted,* Rev. 22:11* [4508]

[4866] ῥύπος *rhypos* 1x *filth, squalor,* 1 Pet. 3:21* [4509]

[4868] ῥύσις *rhysis* 3x *a flowing; a* morbid *flux,* Mk. 5:25; Lk. 8:43, 44* [4511]

[4869] ῥυτίς *rhytis* 1x *a wrinkle;* met. *a* disfiguring *wrinkle, flaw, blemish,* Eph. 5:27* [4512]

[4871] Ῥωμαῖος *Rhōmaios* 12x *Roman; a Roman citizen,* Jn. 11:48; Acts 2:10; 16:21 [4514]

[4872] Ῥωμαϊστί *Rhōmaisti* 1x *in the Roman language, in Latin,* Jn. 19:20* [4515]

[4873] Ῥώμη *Rhōmē* 8x *Rome,* Acts 18:2; 19:21; 23:11; 28:14, 16; Rom. 1:7, 15; 2 Tim. 1:17* [4516]

[4874] ῥώννυμι *rhōnnymi* 1x *to strengthen, render firm; to be well, enjoy firm health;* at the end of letters, like the Latin *vale, farewell,* Acts 15:29* [4517]

[4876] σαβαχθάνι *sabachthani* 2x (Aramaic) *sabacthani, you have forsaken me;* interrogatively, *have you forsaken me?* preceded with λαμᾶ, *Why?* Mt. 27:46; Mk. 15:34* [4518]

[4877] Σαβαώθ *Sabaōth* 2x (Hebrew) *hosts, armies,* indecl., Rom. 9:29; Jas. 5:4* [4519]

[4878] σαββατισμός *sabbatismos* 1x pr. *a keeping of a sabbath; a state of rest, a sabbath-state,* Heb. 4:9* [4520]

[4879] σάββατον *sabbaton* 68x pr. *cessation from labor, rest; the* Jewish *sabbath,* both in the sg. and pl., Mt. 12:2, 5, 8; 28:1; Lk. 4:16; *a week,* sg. and pl., Mt. 28:1; Mk. 16:9; pl. *sabbaths,* or *times of sacred rest,* Col. 2:16 [4521] See *sabbath.*

[4880] σαγήνη *sagēnē* 1x *a large net,* Mt. 13:47* [4522]

[4881] Σαδδουκαῖος *Saddoukaios* 14x *a Sadducee, one belonging to the sect of the Sadducees,* which, according to the Talmudists, was founded by one, *Sadoc,* about three centuries before the Christian era: they were directly opposed in sentiments to the Pharisees, Mt. 3:7; 16:1, 6, 11, 12; 22:23, 34; Mk. 12:18; Lk. 20:27; Acts 4:1; 5:17; 23:6-8* [4523]

[4882] Σαδώκ *Sadōk* 2x *Zadok,* pr. name, indecl., Mt. 1:14* [4524]

[4883] σαίνω *sainō* 1x pr. *to wag* the tail; *to fawn, flatter, cajole;* pass. *to be cajoled; to be wrought upon, to be perturbed,* 1 Thess. 3:3* [4525]

[4884] σάκκος *sakkos* 4x *sackcloth,* a coarse black cloth made of hair (goat or camel), Rev. 6:12; a mourning garment of *sackcloth,* Mt. 11:21; Lk. 10:13; Rev. 11:3* [4526]

[4885] Σαλά *Sala* 2x *Sala,* pr. name, indecl., Lk. 3:32, 35* [4527]

[4886] Σαλαθιήλ *Salathiēl* 3x *Shealtiel,* pr. name, indecl., Mt. 1:12; Lk. 3:27* [4528]

[4887] Σαλαμίς *Salamis* 1x *Salamis,* a city in the island of Cyprus, Acts 13:5* [4529]

[4887.5] Σαλείμ *Saleim* 1x *Saleim,* also formed as Σαλίμ (*4890*). John was baptizing at Aenon near Saleim, Jn. 3:26* [4529]

[4888] σαλεύω *saleuō* 15x *to make to rock, to shake,* Mt. 11:7; 24:29; Mk. 13:25; Lk. 6:38, 48; 7:24; 21:26; Acts 4:31; 16:26; Heb. 12:26; met. *to stir up, excite* the people, Acts 17:13; *to agitate, disturb* mentally, Acts 2:25; 2 Thess. 2:2; pass. impl. *to totter, be ready to fall, be near to ruin,* met. Heb. 12:36, 27* [4531] See *agitate; shake.*

[4889] Σαλήμ *Salēm* 2x (Hebrew, meaning *peace*), *Salem,* pr. name, indecl., Heb. 7:1f.* [4532]

[4891] Σαλμών *Salmōn* 2x *Salmon,* pr. name, indecl., Mt. 1:4f.* [4533]

[4892] Σαλμώνη *Salmōnē* 1x *Salmone,* a promontory, the eastern extremity of Crete, Acts 27:7* [4534]

[4893] σάλος *salos* 1x *agitation, tossing, rolling,* spc. of the sea, Lk. 21:25* [4535]

[4894] σάλπιγξ *salpinx* 11x *trumpet,* 1 Cor. 14:8; Heb. 12:19; Rev. 1:10; 4:1; 8:2, 6; 13:9; 1 Thess. 4:16; *sound of the trumpet,* Mt. 24:31; 1 Cor. 15:52; 1 Thess. 4:16* [4536] See *trumpet.*

[4895] σαλπίζω *salpizō* 12x *to sound a trumpet,* Mt. 6:2; 1 Cor. 5:52; Rev. 8:6, 7, 8, 10, 12, 13; 9:1, 13; 10:7; 11:15* [4537] See *sound (a trumpet).*

[4896] σαλπιστής *salpistēs* 1x *a trumpeter,* Rev. 18:22* [4538]

[4897] Σαλώμη *Salōmē* 2x *Salome,* pr. name, a Galilean woman who followed Jesus, Mt. 27:56; Mk. 15:40; 16:1* [4539]

[4899] Σαμάρεια *Samareia* 11x *Samaria,* the city and region so called, Acts 8:14 [4540]

[4901] Σαμαρίτης *Samaritēs* 9x *a Samaritan, an inhabitant of the city* or *region of Samaria,* applied by the Jews as a term of reproach and contempt, Mt. 10:5; Jn. 4:9, 39f.; 8:48; Lk. 9:52; 10:33; 17:16; Acts 8:25* [4541]

[4902] Σαμαρῖτις *Samaritis* 2x *a Samaritan woman,* Jn. 4:9* [4542]

[4903] Σαμοθρᾴκη *Samothrakē* 1x *Samothrace,* an island in the northern part of the Aegean sea, Acts 16:11* [4543]

[4904] Σάμος *Samos* 1x *Samos,* a celebrated island, in the Aegean sea, Acts 20:15* [4544]

[4905] Σαμουήλ *Samouēl* 3x (1 Sam. 1:1-25:1), *Samuel,* pr. name, indecl., Acts 3:24; 13:20; Heb. 11:32* [4545]

[4907] Σαμψών *Sampsōn* 1x (Jdg. 13-16), *Samson,* pr. name, indecl., Heb. 11:32* [4546]

[4908] σανδάλιον *sandalion* 2x *a sandal,* a sole of wood or hide, covering the bottom of the foot, and bound on with leathern thongs, Mk. 6:9, Acts 12:8* [4547]

[4909] σανίς *sanis* 1x *a board, plank,* Acts 27:44* [4548]

[4910] Σαούλ *Saoul* 9x *Saul,* pr. name, indecl. I. *Saul, king of Israel,* Acts 13:21; II. *The Apostle Paul,* Acts 9:4, 17; 22:7, 13; 26:14* [4549]

[4911] σαπρός *sapros* 8x pr. *rotten, putrid;* hence, *bad, of a bad quality,* Mt. 7:17, 18; 12:33; Lk. 6:43; *refuse,* Mt. 13:48; met. *corrupt, depraved, vicious, foul, impure,* Eph. 4:29* [4550]

[4912] Σάπφιρα *Sapphira* 1x *Sapphira,* wife of Ananias and a member of the Jerusalem church, Acts 5:1* [4551]

[4913] σάπφιρος *sapphiros* 1x *a sapphire,* a precious stone of a blue color in various shades, next in hardness and value to the diamond, Rev. 21:19 [4552]

[4914] σαργάνη *sarganē* 1x *twisted* or *plaited work; a netword of cords like a basket, basket of ropes,* etc. 2 Cor. 11:33* [4553]

[4915] Σάρδεις *Sardeis* 3x *Sardis,* the capital city of Lydia, in Asia Minor Rev. 1:11; 3:1, 4* [4554]

[4917] σάρδιον *sardion* 2x *carnelian,* a reddish precious stone, Rev. 4:3; 21:20* [4556]

[4918] σαρδόνυξ *sardonyx* 1x *sardonyx,* a gem exhibiting the color of the carnelian and the white of the calcedony, intermingled in alternate layers, Rev. 21:20* [4557]

[4919] Σάρεπτα *Sarepta* 1x *Sarepta,* a city of Phoenicia, between Tyre and Sidon, Lk. 4:26* [4558]

[4920] σαρκικός *sarkikos* 7x *fleshly; pertaining to the body, corporeal, physical,* Rom. 15:27; 1 Cor. 9:11; *carnal, pertaining to the flesh,* 1 Pet. 2:11; *carnal, low in spiritual knowledge and frame,* 1 Cor. 3:3 (2x); *carnal, human* as opposed to divine, 2 Cor. 1:12; 10:4* [4559] See *fleshly; worldly;*

[4921] σάρκινος *sarkinos* 4x *of flesh, fleshly,* 2 Cor. 3:3; Rom. 7:14; 1 Cor. 3:1; Heb. 7:16* [4560]

[4922] σάρξ *sarx* 147x *flesh,* Lk. 24:39; Jn. 3:6; *the* human *body,* 2 Cor. 7:5; *flesh, human nature, human frame,* Jn. 1:13, 14; 1 Pet. 4:1; 1 Jn. 4:2; *kindred,* Rom. 11:14; *lineage,* Rom. 1:3; 9:3; *flesh, humanity, human beings,* Mt. 24:22; Lk. 3:6; Jn. 17:2; *the circumstances of the body, material condition,* 1 Cor. 5:5; 7:28; Phlm. 16; *flesh, mere humanity, human fashion,* 1 Cor. 1:26; 2 Cor. 1:17; *flesh* as the seat of passion and frailty, Rom. 8:1, 3, 5; *carnality,* Gal. 5:24; *materiality, material circumstance,* as opposed to the spiritual, Phil. 3:3, 4; Col. 2:18; *a material system* or *mode,* Gal. 3:3; Heb. 9:10 [4561] See *body; flesh; sinful nature.*

[4924] σαρόω *saroō* 3x *to sweep, to clean with a broom,* Mt. 12:44; Lk. 11:25; 15:8* [4563]

[4925] Σάρρα *Sarra* 4x *Sara, Sarah,* pr. name, the wife of Abraham, Rom. 4:19; 9:9; Heb. 11:11; 1 Pet. 3:6* [4564]

[4926] Σαρών *Sarōn* 1x *Saron,* a level tract of Palestine, between Caesarea and Joppa, Acts 9:35* [4565]

[4928] Σατανᾶς *Satanas* 36x *an adversary, opponent, enemy,* perhaps, Mt. 16:23; Mk. 8:33; Lk. 4:8; elsewhere, *Satan, the devil,* Mt. 4:10; Mk. 1:13 [4567] See *Satan.*

[4929] σάτον *saton* 2x *a satum* or *seah,* a Hebrew measure for things dry, containing, as Josephus testifies, (*Ant.* 9.85) an Italian modius and one half, or 24 sextarii, and therefore equivalent to somewhat less than three gallons English, Mt. 13:33; Lk. 13:21* [4568]

[4930] Σαῦλος *Saulos* 15x *Saul,* the Hebrew name of the Apostle Paul, Σαούλ with a Greek termination, Acts 7:58; 8:1, 3; 9:1 [4569]

[4931] σβέννυμι *sbennymi* 6x *to extinguish, quench,* Mt. 12:20; 25:8; Mk. 9:44, 46, 48; Eph. 6:16; Heb. 11:34; met. *to quench, damp, hinder, thwart,* 1 Thess. 5:19* [4570] See *quench.*

[4932] σεαυτοῦ *seautou* 43x *of yourself, to yourself,* etc. Mt. 4:6; 8:4; 19:19 [4572]

[4933] σεβάζομαι *sebazomai* 1x *to feel dread of* a thing; *to venerate, adore, worship,* Rom. 1:25* [4573]

[4934] σέβασμα *sebasma* 2x *an object of religious veneration and worship,* Acts 17:23; 2 Thess. 2:4* [4574]

[4935] σεβαστός *sebastos* 3x pr. *venerable, august;* ὁ Σεβαστός, i.q. Latin *Augustus,* Acts 25:21, 25; *Augustan,* or, *Sebastan,* named from the city Sebaste, Acts 27:1* [4575]

[4936] σέβω *sebō* 10x mid., *to stand in awe; to venerate, reverence, worship, adore,* Mt. 15:9; Mk. 7:7; Acts 18:13; 19:27; part. σεβόμενος, η, ον, *worshiping, devout, pious,* a term applied to proselytes to Judaism, Acts 13:43; 16:14; 18:7; 13:50; 17:4, 17* [4576] See *worship.*

[4937] σειρά *seira* 1x *a cord, rope, band;* in NT *a chain,* 2 Pet. 2:4* [4577]

[4939] σεισμός *seismos* 14x pr. *a shaking, agitation, concussion; an earthquake,* Mt. 24:7; 27:54; *a tempest,* Mt. 8:24 [4578] See *earthquake; storm.*

[4940] σείω *seiō* 5x *to shake, agitate,* Heb. 12:26; pass. *to quake,* Mt. 27:51; 28:4; Rev. 6:13; met. *to put in commotion, agitate,* Mt. 21:10 [4579]

[4941] Σεκοῦνδος *Sekoundos* 1x *Secundus,* pr. name, Acts 20:4* [4580]

[4942] Σελεύκεια *Seleukeia* 1x *Seleucia,* a city of Syria, west of Antioch, on the Orontes, Acts 13:4* [4581]

[4943] σελήνη *selēnē* 9x *the moon,* Mt. 24:29; Mk. 13:24 [4582] See *moon.*

[4944] σεληνιάζομαι *selēniazomai* 2x *to be a lunatic,* Mt. 4:24; 17:15* [4583]

[4946] Σεμεΐν *Semein* 1x *Semei,* pr. name, indecl., Lk. 3:26* [4584]

[4947] σεμίδαλις *semidalis* 1x *the finest flour,* Rev. 18:13* [4585]

[4948] σεμνός *semnos* 4x *august, venerable; honorable, reputable,* Phil. 4:8; *grave, serious, dignified,* 1 Tim. 3:8, 11; Tit. 2:2* [4586]

[4949] σεμνότης *semnotēs* 3x pr. *majesty; gravity, dignity, dignified seriousness,* 1 Tim. 2:2; 3:4; Tit. 2:7* [4587]

[4950] Σέργιος *Sergios* 1x *Sergius,* pr. name, Acts 13:7* [4588]

[4952] Σερούχ *Serouch* 1x *Serug,* proper name, Lk. 3:35* [4562]

[4953] Σήθ *Sēth* 1x *Seth,* (Gen. 4:25f.) pr. name, indecl., Lk. 3:38* [4589]

[4954] Σήμ *Sēm* 1x *Shem,* (Gen. 5:32) pr. name, indecl., Lk. 3:36* [4590]

[4955] σημαίνω *sēmainō* 6x *to indicate by a sign, to signal; to indicate, intimate,* Jn. 12:33; 18:32; 21:19; *to make known, communicate,* Acts 11:28; Rev. 1:1; *to specify,* Acts 25:27* [4591]

[4956] σημεῖον *sēmeion* 77x *a sign, a mark, token,* by which anything is known or distinguished, Mt. 16:3; 24:3; 2 Thess. 3:17; *a token, pledge, assurance,* Lk. 2:12; *a proof, evidence, convincing token,* Mt. 12:38; 16:1; Jn. 2:18; in NT *a sign, wonder, remarkable event, wonderful appearance, extraordinary phenomenon,* 1 Cor. 14:22; Rev. 12:1, 3; 15:1; *a portent, prodigy,* Mt. 24:30; Acts 2:19; *a wonderful work, miraculous operation, miracle,* Mt. 24:24; Mk. 16:17, 20; meton. *a sign, a signal character,* Lk. 2:34 [4592] See *miracle; sign.*

[4957] σημειόω *sēmeioō* 1x mid., *to mark, inscribe marks upon;* mid. *to mark for one's self, note,* 2 Thess. 3:14* [4593]

[4958] σήμερον *sēmeron* 41x *today, this day,* Mt. 6:11, 30; 16:3; 21:28; *now, at present,* Heb. 13:8; 2 Cor. 3:15; ἡ σήμερον, sc. ἡμέρα, sometimes expressed, *this day, the present day,* Acts 20:26; ἕως or ἄχρι τῆς σήμερον, *until this day, until our times,* Mt. 11:23; 27:8 [4594] See *today.*

[4960] σήπω *sēpō* 1x *to cause to putrify, rot, be corrupted* or *rotten,* Jas. 5:2* [4595]

[4962] σής *sēs* 3x *a moth,* Lk. 12:33; Mt. 6:19f.* [4597]

[4963] σητόβρωτος *sētobrōtos* 1x *moth-eaten,* Jas. 5:2* [4598]

[4964] σθενόω *sthenoō* 1x *to strengthen, impart strength,* 1 Pet. 5:10* [4599]

[4965] σιαγών *siagōn* 2x *the jawbone;* in NT *the cheek,* Mt. 5:39; Lk. 6:29* [4600]

[4967] σιγάω *sigaō* 10x *to be silent, keep silence,* Lk. 9:36; 20:26; Acts 15:12f.; 1 Cor. 14:28, 30, 34; Lk. 18:39; trans. *to keep in silence, not to reveal, to conceal;* pass. *to be concealed, not to be revealed,* Rom. 16:25* [4601] See *quiet; silent.*

[4968] σιγή *sigē* 2x *silence,* Acts 21:40; Rev. 8:1* [4602]

[4970] σίδηρος *sidēros* 1x *iron,* Rev. 18:12* [4604]

[4971] σιδηροῦς *sidērous* 5x *made of iron,* Acts 12:10; Rev. 2:27; 9:9; 12:5; 19:15* [4603]

[4972] Σιδών *Sidōn* 9x *Sidon,* a celebrated city of Phoenicia, Mt. 11:21f.; Mk. 3:8; 7:31; Lk. 6:17; Acts 27:3 [4605]

[4973] Σιδώνιος *Sidōnios* 2x *Sidonian; an inhabitant of* Σιδών, *Sidon,* Acts 12:20; Lk. 4:26* [4606]

[4974] σικάριος *sikarios* 1x *an assassin, bandit, robber,* Acts 21:38* [4607]

[4975] σίκερα *sikera* 1x *strong* or *inebriating drink,* Lk. 1:15* [4608]

[4976] Σίλας *Silas* 12x *Silas,* pr. name, in Luke, Acts 15:22; see Σιλουανός [4609]

[4977] Σιλουανός *Silouanos* 4x *Silvanus,* pr. name, 2 Cor. 1:19; 1 Thess. 1:1; 2 Thess. 1:1; 1 Pet. 5:12, see Σίλας* [4610]

[4978] Σιλωάμ *Silōam* 3x *Siloam,* a pool or fountain near Jerusalem, Lk. 13:4; Jn. 9:7, 11* [4611]

[4980] σιμικίνθιον *simikinthion* 1x *an apron,* Acts 19:12* [4612]

[4981] Σίμων *Simōn* 75x *Simon,* pr. name. (1) *Simon Peter,* Mt. 4:18. (2) *Simon (the Canaanite) the Zealot,* Mt. 10:4; Acts 1:13 . (3) *Simon, brother of Jesus,* Mt. 13:55; Mk. 6:3. (4) *Simon, the leper,* Mt. 26:6; Mk. 14:3. (5) *Simon, the Pharisee,* Lk. 7:40. (6) *Simon of Cyrene,* Mt. 27:32. (7) *Simon, father of Judas Iscariot,* Jn. 6:71. (8) *Simon, the sorcerer,* Acts 8:9. (9) *Simon, the tanner, of Joppa,* Acts 9:43; 10:6 [4613]

[4982] Σινά *Sina* 4x *Mount Sinai,* in Arabia, Acts 7:30, 38; Gal. 4:24, 25* [4614]

[4983] σίναπι *sinapi* 5x *mustard;* in NT probably the shrub, not the herb, *Khardal, Salvadora Persica L.,* the fruit of which possesses the pungency of mustard, Mt. 13:31; 17:20; Mk. 4:31; Lk. 13:19; 17:6* [4615]

[4984] σινδών *sindōn* 6x *sindon;* pr. *fine Indian cloth; fine linen;* in NT *a linen garment, an upper garment* or *wrapper of fine linen,* worn in summer by night, and used to envelope dead bodies, Mt. 27:59; Mk. 14:51, 52; 15:46; Lk. 23:53* [4616]

[4985] σινιάζω *siniazō* 1x *to sift;* met. *to sift* by trials and temptations, Lk. 22:31* [4617]

[4986] σιρικός *sirikos* 1x see also σηρικός, *silk, of silk, silken;* τὸ σηρικόν, *silken stuff,* Rev. 18:12* [4596]

[4988] σιτευτός *siteutos* 3x *fed, fatted,* Lk. 15:23, 27, 30* [4618]

[4989] σιτίον *sition* 1x *provision of corn, food,* Acts 7:12* [4621]

[4990] σιτιστός *sitistos* 1x *fatted, a fatling, cattle,* Mt. 22:4* [4619]

[4991] σιτομέτριον *sitometrion* 1x *a certain measure of grain* distributed for food at set times to the slaves of a family, *a ration,* Lk. 12:42* [4620]

[4992] σῖτος *sitos* 14x *corn, grain, wheat,* Mt. 3:12; 13:25, 29, 30; Mk. 4:28 [4621] See *grain; wheat.*

[4994] Σιών *Siōn* 7x *Zion, Mt. Zion, a hill within the city of Jerusalem,* indecl., Heb. 12:22; Rev. 14:1; *poetic use,* Mt. 21:5; Jn. 12:15; *people of Israel,* Rom. 9:33; 11:26; *new Jerusalem of Christianity,* 1 Pet. 2:6* [4622]

[4995] σιωπάω *siōpaō* 10x *to be silent, keep silence, hold one's peace,* Mt. 20:31; 26:63; Mk. 3:4; 9:34; 10:48; 14:61; Lk. 19:40; Acts 18:9; σιωπῶν, *silent, dumb,* Lk. 1:20; met. *to be silent, still, hushed, calm,* as the sea, Mk. 4:39* [4623] See *quiet; silent.*

[4997] σκανδαλίζω *skandalizō* 29x pr. *to cause to stumble;* met. *offend,* Mt. 17:27; *to offend, shock, excite feeling of repugnance,* Jn. 6:61; 1 Cor. 8:13; pass. *to be offended, shocked, pained,* Mt. 15:12; Rom. 14:21; 2 Cor. 11:29; σκανδαλίζεσθαι ἔν τινι, *to be affected with scruples of repugnance towards any one* as respects his claims or pretensions, Mt. 11:6; 13:57; met. *to cause to stumble* morally, *to cause to falter* or *err,* Mt. 5:29; 18:6; pass. *to falter, fall away,* Mt. 13:21 [4624] See *cause to sin; offend.*

[4998] σκάνδαλον *skandalon* 15x pr. *a trap-spring;* also genr. *a stumbling block, anything against which one stumbles, an impediment;* met. *a cause of ruin, destruction, misery,* etc., Rom. 9:33; 11:9; 1 Pet. 2:8; *a cause* or *occasion of sinning,* Mt. 16:23; 18:7 (3x); Lk. 17:1; Rom. 14:13; 16:17; Rev. 2:14; *scandal, offense, cause of indignation,* Mt. 13:41; 1 Cor. 1:23;

Gal. 5:11; 1 Jn. 2:10* [4625] See *cause of sin; obstacle; offense; stumbling block.*

[4999] σκάπτω *skaptō* 3x *to dig, excavate,* Lk. 6:48; 13:8; 16:3* [4626]

[5002] σκάφη *skaphē* 3x pr. *anything excavated* or *hollowed; a boat, skiff,* Acts 27:16, 30, 32* [4627]

[5003] σκέλος *skelos* 3x *the leg,* Jn. 19:31, 32, 33* [4628]

[5004] σκέπασμα *skepasma* 1x *covering; clothing, raiment,* 1 Tim. 6:8* [4629]

[5005] Σκευᾶς *Skeuas* 1x *Sceva,* pr. name, Acts 19:14* [4630]

[5006] σκευή *skeuē* 1x *apparatus; tackle, equipment, ship's gear,* Acts 27:19* [4631]

[5007] σκεῦος *skeuos* 23x *a vessel, utensil* for containing anything, Mk. 11:16; Lk. 8:16; Rom. 9:21; *any utensil, instrument;* σκεύη, *household stuff, furniture, goods,* etc., Mt. 12:29; Mk. 3:27; *the mast of a ship,* or, *the sail,* Acts 27:17; met. *an instrument, means, organ, minister,* Acts 9:15; σκεύη ὀργῆς and σκεύη ἐλέους, *vessels of wrath,* or, *of mercy, persons visited by punishment,* or, *the divine favor,* Rom. 9:22, 23; *the vessel* or *frame* of the human individual, 1 Thess. 4:4; 1 Pet. 3:7 [4632] See *container; instrument; jar.*

[5008] σκηνή *skēnē* 20x *a tent, tabernacle;* genr. *any temporary dwelling; a tent, booth,* Mt. 17:4; Heb. 11:9; *the tabernacle* of the covenant, Heb. 8:5; 9:1, 21; 13:10; allegor. *the* celestial or true *tabernacle,* Heb. 8:2; 9:11; *a division* or *compartment of the tabernacle,* Heb. 9:2, 3, 6; *a* small portable *tent* or *shrine,* Acts 7:43; *an abode* or *seat* of a lineage, Acts 15:16; *a mansion, habitation, abode, dwelling,* Lk. 16:9; Rev. 13:6 [4633] See *tabernacle; tent.*

[5009] σκηνοπηγία *skēnopēgia* 1x pr. *a pitching of tents* or *booths;* hence, *the feast of tabernacles* or *booths,* instituted in memory of the forty years' wandering of the Israelites in the desert, and as a season of gratitude for the ingathering of harvest, celebrated for eight days, commencing on the 15th of Tisri, Jn. 7:2* [4634]

[5010] σκηνοποιός *skēnopoios* 1x *a tent-maker,* Acts 18:3* [4635]

[5011] σκῆνος *skēnos* 2x *a tent, tabernacle, lodging;* met. *the* corporeal *tabernacle,* 2 Cor. 5:1, 4* [4636]

[5012] σκηνόω *skēnoō* 5x *to pitch tent, encamp; to tabernacle, dwell in a tent; to dwell, have one's abode,* Jn. 1:14; Rev. 7:15; 12:12; 13:6; 21:3* [4637] See *dwell; live; pitch (a tent).*

[5013] σκήνωμα *skēnōma* 3x *a habitation, abode, dwelling,* Acts 7:46; *the* corporeal *tabernacle* of the soul, 2 Pet. 1:13, 14* [4638]

[5014] σκιά *skia* 7x *a shade, shadow,* Mk. 4:32; Acts 5:15; met. *a shadow, a foreshadowing, a vague outline,* in distinction from ἡ εἰκών, the perfect image or delineation, and τὸ σῶμα, the reality, Col. 2:17; Heb. 8:5; 10:1; *gloom;* σκιὰ θανάτου, *death shade, the thickest darkness,* Mt. 4:16; Lk. 1:79* [4639]

[5015] σκιρτάω *skirtaō* 3x *to leap,* Lk. 1:41, 44; *to leap, skip, bound* for joy, Lk. 6:23* [4640]

[5016] σκληροκαρδία *sklērokardia* 3x *hardness of heart, obstinacy, perverseness,* Mt. 19:8; Mk. 10:5; 16:14* [4641]

[5017] σκληρός *sklēros* 5x *dry, hard* to the touch; met. *harsh, severe, stern,* Mt. 25:24; *vehement, violent, fierce,* Jas. 3:4; *grievous, painful,* Acts 26:14; *grating* to the mind, *repulsive, offensive,* Jn. 6:60; *stubborn, resistance to authority,* Jude 15* [4642]

[5018] σκληρότης *sklērotēs* 1x *hardness;* met. σκληρότης τῆς καρδίας, *hardness of heart, obstinacy, perverseness,* Rom. 2:5* [4643]

[5019] σκληροτράχηλος *sklērotrachēlos* 1x *stiff-necked, obstinate,* Acts 7:51* [4644]

[5020] σκληρύνω *sklērynō* 6x *to harden;* met. *to harden* morally, *to make stubborn,* Heb. 3:8, 15; 4:7; as a negation of ἐλεεῖν, *to leave to stubbornness and contumacy,* Rom. 9:18; mid. and pass. *to put on a stubborn frame,* Acts 19:9; Heb. 3:13* [4645]

[5021] σκολιός *skolios* 4x *crooked, tortuous,* Lk. 3:5; met. *perverse, wicked,* Acts 2:40; Phil. 2:15; *crooked, peevish, morose,* 1 Pet. 2:18* [4646]

[5022] σκόλοψ *skolops* 1x *anything pointed;* met. *a thorn, a plague,* 2 Cor. 12:7* [4647]

[5023] σκοπέω *skopeō* 6x *to view attentively, watch; to see, observe, take care, beware,* Lk. 11:35; Gal. 6:1; *to regard, have respect to,* 2 Cor. 4:18; Phil. 2:4; *to mark, note,* Rom. 16:17; Phil. 3:17* [4648]

[5024] σκοπός *skopos* 1x *a watcher;* also, *a distant object on which the eye is kept fixed; a mark, goal,* Phil. 3:14* [4649]

[5026] σκορπίος *skorpios* 5x *a scorpion,* a large insect, sometimes several inches in length, shaped somewhat like a crab and furnished with a tail terminating in a stinger from which it emits a dangerous poison, Lk. 10:19; 11:12; Rev. 9:3, 5, 10* [4651]

[5027] σκοτεινός *skoteinos* 3x *dark,* Mt. 6:23; Lk. 11:34, 36* [4652]

[5028] σκοτία *skotia* 16x *darkness,* Jn. 6:17; 20:1; *privacy,* Mt. 10:27; Lk. 12:3; met. moral or spiritual *darkness,* Jn. 1:5 (2x); 8:12; 12:35, 46; 1 Jn. 1:5; 2:8, 9, 11* [4653] See *darkenss.*

[5030] σκότος *skotos* 31x *darkness,* Mt. 27:45; Acts 2:20; *gloom* of punishment and misery, Mt. 8:12; 2 Pet. 2:17; met. moral or spiritual *darkness,* Mt. 4:16; Jn. 3:19; Eph. 5:11; *a realm of* moral *darkness,* Eph. 5:8; 6:12 [4655] See *darkness.*

[5031] σκοτόω *skotoō* 3x *to darken, shroud in darkness,* Eph. 4:18; Rev. 9:2; 16:10 [4656]

[5032] σκύβαλον *skybalon* 1x *dung, sweepings, refuse, rubbish,* Phil. 3:8* [4657]

[5033] Σκύθης *Skythēs* 1x *A Scythian, a native of Scythia,* the modern Mongolia and Tartary, Col. 3:11* [4658]

[5034] σκυθρωπός *skythrōpos* 2x *of a stern, morose, sour, gloomy,* or *dejected countenance,* Mt. 6:16; Lk. 24:17* [4659]

[5035] σκύλλω *skyllō* 4x *to flay, lacerate;* met. *to vex, trouble, annoy,* Mk. 5:35; Lk. 7:6; 8:49; pass. met. ἐσκυλμένοι, *in sorry plight,* Mt. 9:36* [4660]

[5036] σκῦλον *skylon* 1x *spoils stripped off an enemy;* σκῦλα, *spoil, plunder, booty,* Lk. 11:22* [4661]

[5037] σκωληκόβρωτος *skōlēkobrōtos* 1x *eaten of worms, consumed by worms,* Acts 12:23* [4662]

[5038] σκώληξ *skōlēx* 1x *a worm;* met. *gnawing anguish,* Mk. 9:48* [4663]

[5039] σμαράγδινος *smaragdinos* 1x *of smaragdus* or *emerald,* Rev. 4:3* [4664]

[5040] σμάραγδος *smaragdos* 1x *smaragdus, the emerald,* a gem of a pure green color; but under this name the ancients probably comprised all stones of a fine green color, Rev. 21:19* [4665]

[5043] σμύρνα *smyrna* 2x *myrrh,* an aromatic bitter resin, or gum, issuing by incision, and sometimes spontaneously, from the trunk and larger branches of a small thorny tree growing in Egypt, Arabia, and Abyssinia, much used by the ancients in unguents, Mt. 2:11; Jn. 19:39* [4666]

[5044] Σμύρνα *Smyrna* 2x *Smyrna,* a maritime city of Ionia, in Asia Minor, Rev. 1:11; 2:8* [4667]

[5046] σμυρνίζω *smyrnizō* 1x *to mingle* or *flavor with myrrh,* Mk. 15:23* [4669]

[5047] Σόδομα *Sodoma* 9x *Sodom,* (Gen. 19:24) one of the four cities of the vale of Siddim, now covered by the Dead sea, Mt. 11:23f.; Lk. 17:29; Rom. 9:29; 2 Pet. 2:6; Rev. 11:8 [4670]

[5048] Σολομών *Solomōn* 12x *Solomon,* also spelled Σολομῶν, pr. name, son and successor of David, Mt. 1:6f.; 6:29; Lk. 11:31; Jn. 10:23; Acts 3:11; 7:47 [4672]

[5049] σορός *soros* 1x *a coffer; an urn for receiving the ashes of the dead; a coffin;* in NT *a bier,* Lk. 7:14* [4673]

[5050] σός *sos* 26x *yours,* Mt. 7:3, 22; οἱ σοί, *your kindred, friends,* etc., Mk. 5:19; τὸ σόν and τὰ σά, *what is yours, your property, goods,* etc., Mt. 20:14; 25:25; Lk. 6:30 [4674]

[5051] σουδάριον *soudarion* 4x *a handkerchief, napkin,* etc., Lk. 19:20; Jn. 11:44; 20:7; Acts 19:12* [4676]

[5052] Σουσάννα *Sousanna* 1x *Susanna,* pr. name, Lk. 8:3* [4677]

[5053] σοφία *sophia* 51x *wisdom* in general, *knowledge,* Mt. 12:42; Lk. 2:40, 52; 11:31; Acts 7:10; *ability,* Lk. 21:15; Acts 6:3, 10; practical *wisdom, prudence,* Col. 4:5; *learning, science,* Mt. 13:54; Mk. 6:2; Acts 7:22; scientific *skill,* 1 Cor. 1:17; 2:1; professed *wisdom,* human *philosophy,* 1 Cor. 1:19, 20, 22; 2:4, 5, 6; superior *knowledge and enlightenment,* Col. 2:23; in NT divine *wisdom,* Rom. 11:33; Eph. 3:10; Col. 2:3; revealed *wisdom,* Mt. 11:19; Lk. 11:49; 1 Cor. 1:24, 30; 2:7; Christian *enlightenment,* 1 Cor. 12:8; Eph. 1:8, 17; Col. 1:9, 28, 3:16; Jas. 1:5; 3:13 [4678] See *wisdom.*

[5054] σοφίζω *sophizō* 2x *to make wise, enlighten,* 2 Tim. 3:15; mid. *to invent skilfully, devise artfully,* pass. 2 Pet. 1:16* [4679]

[5055] σοφός *sophos* 20x *wise* generally, 1 Cor. 1:25; *shrewd, clever,* Rom. 16:19; 1 Cor. 3:10; 6:5; *learned, intelligent,* Mt. 11:25; Rom. 1:14, 22; 1 Cor. 1:19, 20, 26, 27; 3:18; in NT divinely *instructed,* Mt. 23:34; *furnished with* Christian *wisdom,* spiritually *enlightened,* Jas. 3:13; *all wise,* Rom. 16:27; 1 Tim. 1:17; Jude 25 [4680] See *wisdom.*

[5056] Σπανία *Spania* 2x *Spain,* Rom. 15:24, 28* [4681]

[5057] σπαράσσω *sparassō* 3x pr. *to tear, lacerate;* by impl. *to agitate greatly, convulse, distort by convulsion,* Mk. 1:26; 9:26; Lk. 9:39* [4682]

[5058] σπαργανόω *sparganoō* 2x *to swathe, wrap in swaddling cloths,* Lk. 2:7, 12* [4683]

[5059] σπαταλάω *spatalaō* 2x *to live luxuriously, voluptuously, wantonly,* 1 Tim. 5:6; Jas. 5:5* [4684]

[5060] σπάω *spaō* 2x *to draw, pull; to draw* a sword, Mk. 14:47; Acts 16:27* [4685]

[5061] σπεῖρα *speira* 7x *anything twisted* or *wreathed, a cord, coil, band,* etc.; *a band of soldiers, company, troop;* used for a Roman *cohort,* about 600 soldiers, Mt. 27:27; Acts 10:1; *the* temple *guard,* Mk. 15:16; Jn. 18:3, 12; Acts 21:31; 27:1* [4686]

[5062] σπείρω *speirō* 52x *to sow* seed, Mt. 6:26; 13:3, 4, 18, 24, 25, 27, 37, 3 [4687] See *sow.*

[5063] σπεκουλάτωρ *spekoulatōr* 1x *a sentinel, life-guardsman,* a kind of soldiers who formed the body-guard of princes, etc., one of whose duties was to put criminals to death, Mk. 6:27* [4688]

[5064] σπένδω *spendō* 2x *to pour out a libation* or *drink-offering;* in NT mid. *to make a libation of one's self* by expending energy and life in the service of the Gospel, Phil. 2:17; pass. *to be in the act of being sacrificed* in the cause of the Gospel, 2 Tim. 4:6* [4689]

[5065] σπέρμα *sperma* 43x *seed,* Mt. 13:24, 27, 37, 38; *semen virile,* Heb. 11:11; *offspring, posterity,* Mt. 22:24, 25; Jn. 7:42; *a seed* of future generations, Rom. 9:29; in NT met. *a seed* or *principle* of spiritual life, 1 Jn. 3:9 [4690] See *descendant; seed.*

[5066] σπερμολόγος *spermologos* 1x pr. *seed-picking; one who picks up and retails scraps of information; a gossip; a babbler,* Acts 17:18* [4691]

[5067] σπεύδω *speudō* 6x trans. *to urge on, impel, quicken; to quicken* in idea, *to be eager for the arrival of,* 2 Pet. 3:12; intrans. *to hasten, make haste,* Acts 20:16; 22:18; the part. has the force of an adverb, *quickly, hastily,* Lk. 2:16; 19:5, 6* [4692]

[5068] σπήλαιον *spēlaion* 6x *a cave, cavern, den, hideout,* Mt. 21:13; Mk. 11:17; Lk. 19:46; Jn. 11:38; Heb. 11:38; Rev. 6:5* [4693]

[5069] σπιλάς *spilas* 1x *a sharply-cleft portion of rock;* in NT *a flaw, stigma,* Jude 12* [4694]

[5070] σπίλος *spilos* 2x *a spot, stain, blot;* a moral *blemish,* Eph. 5:27; 2 Pet. 2:13* [4696]

[5071] σπιλόω *spiloō* 2x *to spot, soil; to contaminate, defile,* Jas. 3:6; Jude 23* [4695]

[5072] σπλαγχνίζομαι *splanchnizomai* 12x *to be moved with pity* or *compassion,* Mt. 9:36; 14:14; 20:34; Lk. 7:13; *to be compassionate,* Mt. 18:27 [4697] See *(have) compassion; show compassion.*

[5073] σπλάγχνον *splanchnon* 11x *the chief intestines, viscera; the entrails, bowels,* Acts 1:18; met. *the heart, the affections of the heart, the tender affections,* Lk. 1:78; 2 Cor. 6:12; 7:15; Phil. 1:8, 2:1; Col. 3:12; Phlm. 7, 20; 1 Jn. 3:17; meton. *a cherished one, dear as one's self,* Phlm. 12* [4698] See *affection; compassion; pity; tenderness.*

[5074] σπόγγος *spongos* 3x *a sponge,* Mt. 27:48; Mk. 15:36; Jn. 19:29* [4699]

[5075] σποδός *spodos* 3x *ashes,* Mt. 11:21; Lk. 10:13; Heb. 9:13* [4700]

[5076] σπορά *spora* 1x *a sowing; seed sown;* met. generative *seed, generation,* 1 Pet. 1:23* [4701]

[5077] σπόριμος *sporimos* 3x *sown, fit to be sown;* in NT τὰ σπόριμα, *fields which are sown, fields of grain, cornfields,* Mt. 12:1; Mk. 2:23; Lk. 6:1* [4702]

[5078] σπόρος *sporos* 6x *a sowing;* in NT *seed, that which is sown,* Mk. 4:26, 27; Lk. 8:5, 11; met. *the seed sown* in almsgiving, 2 Cor. 9:10* [4703]

[5079] σπουδάζω *spoudazō* 11x *to hurry; be bent upon,* Gal. 2:10; *to endeavor earnestly, strive,* Eph. 4:3 [4704] See *make effort; strive.*

[5080] σπουδαῖος *spoudaios* 3x *earnest, eager, forward, zealous,* 2 Cor. 8:17, 22 (2x)* [4705, 4706, 4707]

[5081] σπουδαίως *spoudaiōs* 4x *earnestly, eagerly, diligently,* Lk. 7:4; 2 Tim. 1:17; Tit. 3:13; compar. σπουδαιοτέρως, *more earnestly, with special urgency,* Phil. 2:28 [4708, 4709]

[5082] σπουδή *spoudē* 12x *haste;* μετὰ σπουδῆς, *with haste, hastily, quickly,* Mk. 6:25; Lk. 1:39; *earnestness, earnest application, diligence, enthusiasm,* Rom. 12:8, 11; 2 Cor. 7:11, 12; 8:16; 8:7f. [4710] See *concern; eagerness; earnestness.*

[5083] σπυρίς *spyris* 5x also spelled σφυρίς, *a basket, handbasket* for provision, Mt. 15:37; 16:10; Mk. 8:8, 20; Acts 9:25* [4711]

[5084] στάδιον *stadion* 7x pr. *a fixed standard of measure; a stadium,* the eighth part of a Roman mile, and nearly equal to a furlong, containing 201.45 yards, *about 192 meters,* Lk. 24:13; Mt. 14:24; Jn. 6:19; 11:18; Rev. 14:20; 21:16; *a race-course, a race,* 1 Cor. 9:24* [4712]

[5085] στάμνος *stamnos* 1x can be masculine, but not in the NT, *a wine jar; a pot, jar, urn, vase,* Heb. 9:4* [4713]

[5086] στασιαστής *stasiastēs* 1x *a partisan, rebel, revolutionary,* Mt. 15:7* [4955]

[5087] στάσις *stasis* 9x *a setting; a standing; an* effective *position, an* unimpaired *standing* or *dignity,* Heb. 9:8; *a gathered party, a group;* hence, *a tumultuous assemblage, popular outbreak,* Mk. 15:7; Acts 19:40; Lk. 23:19, 25; *seditious movement,* Acts 24:5; *discord, dispute, dissension,* Acts 15:2; 23:7, 10* [4714]

[5088] στατήρ *statēr* 1x pr. *a weight; a stater,* an Attic silver coin, equal in value to the Jewish shekel, or to four Attic or two Alexandrian drachmas, Mt. 17:27* [4715]

[5089] σταυρός *stauros* 27x *a stake; a cross,* Mt. 27:32, 40, 42; Phil. 2:8; by impl. *the punishment of the cross, crucifixion,* Eph. 2:16; Heb. 12:2; meton. *the crucifixion* of Christ in respect of its import, *the doctrine of the cross,* 1 Cor. 17:18; Gal. 5:11; 6:12, 14; met. *to take up,* or *bear one's cross, to be ready to encounter any hardship,* Mt. 10:38; 16:24 [4716] See *cross.*

[5090] σταυρόω *stauroō* 46x *to fix stakes;* later, *to crucify, affix to the cross,* Mt. 20:19; 23:34; met. *to crucify, to mortify, to deaden, to make a sacrifice of,* Gal. 5:24; pass. *to be cut off* from a thing, as by a violent death, *to be come dead to,* Gal. 6:14 [4717] See *crucify.*

[5091] σταφυλή *staphylē* 3x *a cluster* or *bunch of grapes,* Mt. 7:16; Lk. 6:44, Rev. 14:18* [4718]

[5092] στάχυς *stachus* 5x *an ear of corn, head of grain,* Mt. 12:1; Mk. 2:23; 4:28; Lk. 6:1* [4719]

[5093] Στάχυς *Stachus* 1x *Stachys,* pr. name, Rom. 16:9* [4720]

[5094] στέγη *stegē* 3x *a roof, flat roof* of a house, Mt. 8:8; Mk. 2:4; Lk. 7:6* [4721]

[5095] στέγω *stegō* 4x *to cover; to hold off, to hold in;* hence, *to hold out against, to endure patiently,* 1 Cor. 9:12; 13:7; absol. *to contain one's self,* 1 Thess. 3:1, 5* [4722]

[5096] στεῖρα *steira* 5x *barren, incapable of bearing children,* Lk. 1:7, 36; 23:29; Gal. 4:27; Heb. 11:11* [4723]

[5097] στέλλω *stellō* 2x pr. *to place in set order, to arrange; to equip; to despatch; to stow;* mid. *to contract one's self, to shrink; to withdraw from, avoid, shun,* 2 Cor. 8:20; 2 Thess. 3:6* [4724]

[5098] στέμμα *stemma* 1x *a crown, wreath,* Acts 14:13* [4725]

[5099] στεναγμός *stenagmos* 2x *a sighing, groaning, groan,* Acts 7:34; an inward *sighing,* Rom. 8:26* [4726]

[5100] στενάζω *stenazō* 6x *to groan, sigh,* Rom. 8:23; 2 Cor. 5:2, 4; Heb. 13:17; *to sigh* inwardly, Mk. 7:34; *to complain,* Jas. 5:9* [4727]

[5101] στενός *stenos* 3x *narrow, strait,* Mt. 7:13, 14; Lk. 13:24* [4728]

[5102] στενοχωρέω *stenochōreō* 3x *to crowd together into a narrow place, straiten;* pass. met. *to be in straits, to be cooped up, to be cramped* from action, 2 Cor. 4:8; *to be cramped* in feeling, 2 Cor. 6:12* [4729]

[5103] στενοχωρία *stenochōria* 4x pr. *narrowness of place, a narrow place;* met. *straits, distress, anguish,* Rom. 2:9; 8:35; 2 Cor. 6:4; 12:10* [4730]

[5104] στερεός *stereos* 4x *stiff, hard;* of food, *solid,* as opposed to what is liquid and light, Heb. 5:12, 14; *firm, steadfast,* 2 Tim. 2:19; 1 Pet. 5:9* [4731]

[5105] στερεόω *stereoō* 3x *to make firm; to strengthen,* Acts 3:7, 16; *to settle,* Acts 16:5* [4732]

[5106] στερέωμα *stereōma* 1x pr. *what is solid and firm;* met. *firmness, steadfastness, constancy,* Col. 2:5* [4733]

[5107] Στεφανᾶς *Stephanas* 3x *Stephanas,* pr. name, 1 Cor. 1:16; 16:15, 17* [4734]

[5108] Στέφανος *Stephanos* 7x *Stephen,* pr. name, Acts 6:5, 8f.; 7:59; 8:2; 11:19; 22:20* [4736]

[5109] στέφανος *stephanos* 18x *that which forms an encirclement; a crown,* Mt. 27:29; Rev. 4:4, 10; *wreath,* conferred on a victor in the public games, 1 Cor. 9:25; met. *a crown, reward, prize,* 2 Tim. 4:8; Jas. 1:12; *a crown, ornament, honor, glory* [4735] See *crown; wreath.*

[5110] στεφανόω *stephanoō* 3x *to crown; to crown* as victor in the games, [4737]

[5111] στῆθος *stēthos* 5x *the breast, chest,* Lk. 18:13; 23:48; Jn. 13:25; 21:20; Rev. 15:6* [4738]

[5112] στήκω *stēkō* 9x *to stand,* Mk. 3:31; 11:25; met. *to stand* when under judgment, *to be approved,* Rom. 14:4; *to stand firm, be constant, persevere,* 1 Cor. 16:13; Gal. 5:1; Phil. 1:27; 4:1; 1 Thess. 3:8; 2 Thess. 2:15* [4739] See *stand firm.*

[5113] στηριγμός *stērigmos* 1x pr. *a fixing, settling; a state of firmness, fixedness;* met. *firmness* of belief, *settle frame* of mind, 2 Pet. 3:17* [4740]

[5114] στηρίζω *stērizō* 13x *to set fast; to set* in a certain position or direction, Lk. 9:51; met. *to render* mentally *steadfast, to settle, confirm,* Lk. 22:32; Rom. 1:11; *to stand immovable,* Lk. 16:26; met. *to be* mentally *settled,* 2 Pet. 1:12 [4741] See *establish; fix; strengthen.*

[5115] στιβάς *stibas* 1x *a stuffing of leaves, boughs,* etc., meton. *a bough, branch,* Mk. 11:8* [4746]

[5116] στίγμα *stigma* 1x *a mark, brand,* Gal. 6:17* [4742]

[5117] στιγμή *stigmē* 1x pr. *a point;* met. *a point* of time, *moment, instant,* Lk. 4:5* [4743]

[5118] στίλβω *stilbō* 1x *to shine, glisten, be radiant,* Mk. 9:3* [4744]

[5119] στοά *stoa* 4x *a colonnade, cloister, covered walk supported by columns,* Jn. 5:2; 10:23; Acts 3:11; 5:12* [4745] See *porch.*

[5121] Στοϊκός *Stoikos* 1x *Stoic,* Acts 17:18* [4770]

[5122] στοιχεῖον *stoicheion* 7x *an element; an element* of the natural universe, 2 Pet. 3:10, 12; *an element* or *rudiment* of any intellectual or religious system, Gal. 4:3, 9; Col. 2:8, 20; Heb. 5:12* [4747]

[5123] στοιχέω *stoicheō* 5x pr. *to advance in a line;* met. *to frame one's conduct* by a certain rule, Acts 21:24; Rom. 4:12; Gal. 5:25; 6:16; Phil. 3:16* [4748]

[5124] στολή *stolē* 9x *equipment; dress; a long garment, flowing robe,* worn by priests, kings, and persons of distinction, Mt. 12:38; 16:5; Lk. 15:22; Rev. 6:11 [4749]

[5125] στόμα *stoma* 78x *the mouth,* Mt. 12:34; 15:11, 17, 18; 21:16; *speech, words,* Mt. 18:16; 2 Cor. 13:1; *command of speech, facility of language,* Lk. 21:15; from the Hebrew, ἀνοίγειν τὸ στόμα, *to utter, to speak,* Mt. 5:2, 13:35; also, used of the earth, *to rend, yawn,* Rev. 12:16; στόμα πρὸς στόμα λαλεῖν, *to speak mouth to mouth, face to face,* 2 Jn. 12; 3 Jn. 14; *the edge* or *point* of a weapon, Lk. 21:24; Heb. 11:34 [4750] See *edge; mouth; testimony.*

[5126] στόμαχος *stomachos* 1x pr. *the gullet* leading to the stomach; hence, later, *the stomach* itself, 1 Tim. 5:23* [4751]

[5127] στρατεία *strateia* 2x *a military expedition, campaign;* and genr. *military service, warfare;* met. *the* Christian *warfare,* 2 Cor. 10:4; *fight,* 1 Tim. 1:18* [4752]

[5128] στράτευμα *strateuma* 8x *an army,* Mt. 22:7; Rev. 19:14, 19; *an armed force, corps,* Acts 23:10, 27; *troops, guards,* Lk. 23:11; Rev. 9:16* [4753] See *army.*

[5130] στρατηγός *stratēgos* 10x *a leader* or *commander of an army, general; a* Roman *praetor, provincial magistrate,* Acts 16:20, 22, 35, 36, 38; στρατηγός τοῦ ἱεροῦ, *the captain* or *prefect of the temple,* the chief of the Levites who kept guard in and around the temple, Lk. 22:4, 52; Acts 4:1; 5:24, 26* [4755] See *magistrate.*

[5131] στρατιά *stratia* 2x *an army, host;* from the Hebrew, στρατιὰ οὐράνιος, or τοῦ οὐρανοῦ, *the heavenly host, the host of heaven, the hosts of angels,* Lk. 2:13; *the stars,* Acts 7:42* [4756]

[5132] στρατιώτης *stratiōtēs* 26x *a soldier,* Mt. 8:9; 27:27; met. *a soldier* of Christ, 2 Tim. 2:3 [4757] See *soldier.*

[5133] στρατολογέω *stratologeō* 1x *to collect* or *gather an army, enlist troops,* 2 Tim. 2:4* [4758]

[5136] στρατόπεδον *stratopedon* 1x pr. *the site of an encampment; an encampment;* meton. *an army,* Lk. 21:20* [4760]

[5137] στρεβλόω *strebloō* 1x pr. *to distort* the limbs *on a rack;* met. *to wrench, distort, pervert,* 2 Pet. 3:16* [4761]

[5138] στρέφω *strephō* 21x *to twist; to turn,* Mt. 5:39; *to make a change* of substance, *to change,* Rev. 11:6; absol. *to change* or *turn* one's course of dealing, Acts 7:42; mid. *to turn one's self about,* Mt. 16:23; Lk. 7:9; *to turn back,* Acts 7:39; *to change one's direction, to turn* elsewhere, Acts 13:46; *to change one's course of principle and conduct, to be converted,* Mt. 18:3 [4762] See *change; return; turn.*

[5139] στρηνιάω *strēniaō* 2x *to be wanton, to revel, riot,* Rev. 18:7, 9* [4763]

[5140] στρῆνος *strēnos* 1x *luxury, sensuality,* Rev. 18:3* [4764]

[5141] στρουθίον *strouthion* 4x *any small bird,* spc. *a sparrow,* Mt. 10:29, 31; Lk. 12:6, 7* [4765]

[5143] στρωννύω *strōnnyō* 6x the thematic form of στρώννυμι, the μι form never being visible in the NT, *to spread, to strew,* Mt. 21:8; Mk. 11:8; *to spread* a couch, *make your own bed,* Acts 9:34; used of a supper-chamber, pass. *to have the couches spread, to be prepared, furnished,* Mk. 14:15; Lk. 22:12* [4766]

[5144] στυγητός *stygētos* 1x *hateful, disgusting, detested,* Tit. 3:3* [4767]

[5145] στυγνάζω *stygnazō* 2x *to put on a gloomy and downcast look, to be shocked, appalled,* Mk. 10:22; of the sky, *to lower,* Mt. 16:3* [4768]

[5146] στῦλος *stylos* 4x *a pillar, column,* Rev. 10:1; used of persons of authority, influence, etc., *a support* or *pillar* of the Church, Gal. 2:9; Rev. 3:12; *a support* of true doctrine, 1 Tim. 3:15* [4769] See *pillar.*

[5148] σύ *sy* 2,906x *you,* gen., σοῦ, dat., σοί, acc., σε, Mt. 1:20; 2:6. The plural ὑμεῖς is listed as its own form, 7007. [4571, 4671, 4675, 4771, 5209, 5210, 5213, 5216]

[5149] συγγένεια *syngeneia* 3x *kindred; kinsfolk, kinsmen, relatives,* Lk. 1:61; Acts 7:3, 14* [4772]

[5150] συγγενής *syngenēs* 11x *kindred, akin;* as a subst. *a kinsman* or *kinswoman, relative;* Mk. 6:4; Lk. 1:58; 2:44; 14:12; 21:16; Jn. 18:26; Acts 10:24; *one* nationally *akin, a fellow countryman,* Rom. 9:3; 16:7, 11, 21* [4773] See *relative.*

[5151] συγγενίς *syngenis* 1x *a kinswoman, female relative,* Lk. 1:36* [4773]

[5152] συγγνώμη *syngnōmē* 1x *pardon; concession, leave, permission,* 1 Cor. 7:6* [4774]

[5153] συγκάθημαι *synkathēmai* 2x *to sit in company with,* Mk. 14:54; Acts 26:30* [4775]

[5154] συγκαθίζω *synkathizō* 2x trans. *to cause to sit down with, seat in company with,* Eph. 2:6; intrans. *to sit in company with; to sit down together,* Lk. 22:55* [4776]

[5155] συγκακοπαθέω *synkakopatheō* 2x *to suffer evils together with* someone; *to be enduringly adherent,* 2 Tim. 1:8; 2:3* [4777]

[5156] συγκακουχέομαι *synkakoucheomai* 1x *to encounter adversity along with* any one, Heb. 11:25* [4778]

[5157] συγκαλέω *synkaleō* 8x *to call together,* Mk. 15:16; Lk. 15:6, 9; Acts 5:21; mid. *to call around one's self,* Lk. 9:1; 23:13; Acts 10:24; 28:17* [4779]

[5158] συγκαλύπτω *synkalyptō* 1x *to cover completely, to cover up;* met. *to conceal,* Lk. 12:2* [4780]

[5159] συγκάμπτω *synkamptō* 1x *to bend* or *bow together; to bow down* the back of any one afflictively, Rom. 11:10* [4781]

[5160] συγκαταβαίνω *synkatabainō* 1x *to go down with* anyone, Acts 25:5* [4782]

[5161] συγκατάθεσις *synkatathesis* 1x *assent;* in NT *accord, alliance, agreement,* 2 Cor. 6:16* [4783]

[5163] συγκατατίθημι *synkatatithēmi* 1x *to set down together with;* mid. *to agree, accord,* Lk. 23:51* [4784]

[5164] συγκαταψηφίζομαι *synkatapsēphizomai* 1x *to count, number with, be chosen together with,* Acts 1:26* [4785]

[5166] συγκεράννυμι *synkerannymi* 2x pluperf., συνεκέκρατο (3 sg), *to mix with, mingle together; to blend,* 1 Cor. 12:24; pass. *to be combined, united,* Heb. 4:2* [4786]

[5167] συγκινέω *synkineō* 1x *to agitate, put in turmoil; to excite,* Acts 6:12* [4787]

[5168] συγκλείω *synkleiō* 4x *to shut up together, to hem in; to enclose,* Lk. 5:6; met. *to band* under a sweeping sentence, Rom. 11:32; Gal. 3:22; pass. *to be banded* under a bar of disability, Gal. 3:23* [4788]

[5169] συγκληρονόμος *synklēronomos* 4x pr. *a coheir,* Rom. 8:17; *a fellow participant,* Eph. 3:6; Heb. 11:9; 1 Pet. 3:7* [4789]

[5170] συγκοινωνέω *synkoinōneō* 3x *to be a joint partaker, participate with* a person; in NT *to mix one's self up* in a thing, *to involve one's self, be an accomplice in,* Eph. 5:11; Rev. 18:4; *to sympathize actively in, to relieve,* Phil. 4:14* [4790]

[5171] συγκοινωνός *synkoinōnos* 4x *one who partakes jointly; a coparticipant,* Rom. 11:17; *a copartner* in service, *fellow,* 1 Cor. 9:23; Phil. 1:7; *a sharer,* 1 Cor. 9:23; Rev. 1:9* [4791]

[5172] συγκομίζω *synkomizō* 1x *to prepare for burial, take charge of the funeral* of any one, *bury,* Acts 8:2* [4792]

[5173] συγκρίνω *synkrinō* 3x *to combine, compound; to compare, to estimate by comparing with* something else, or, *to match,* 2 Cor. 10:12 (2x); *to explain, to illustrate,* or, *to suit,* 1 Cor. 2:13* [4793]

[5174] συγκύπτω *synkyptō* 1x *to bend* or *bow together; to be bowed together, bent over,* Lk. 13:11* [4794]

[5175] συγκυρία *synkyria* 1x *concurrence, coincidence, chance, accident;* κατὰ συγκρυίαν, *by chance, accidentally,* Lk. 10:31* [4795]

[5176] συγχαίρω *synchairō* 7x *to rejoice with* any one, *sympathize in joy,* Lk. 1:58; 15:6, 9; Phil. 2:17, 18; met. 1 Cor. 12:26; *to sympathize in the advancement of, congratulate,* 1 Cor. 13:6* [4796]

[5177] συγχέω *syncheō* 5x *to pour together, mingle by pouring together;* hence, *to confound, perplex, amaze,* Acts 2:6; *to confound* in dispute, Acts 9:22; *to throw into confusion, fill with uproar,* Acts 19:32; 21:27, 31* [4797]

[5178] συγχράομαι *synchraomai* 1x *use in common; associate with, have dealings with,* Jn. 4:9* [4798]

[5180] σύγχυσις *synchusis* 1x pr. *a pouring together;* hence, *confusion, commotion, tumult, uproar,* Acts 19:29* [4799]

[5182] συζάω *syzaō* 3x *to live with; to continue in life with* someone, 2 Cor. 7:3; *to coexist in life with* another, Rom. 6:8; 2 Tim. 2:11* [4800]

[5183] συζεύγνυμι *syzeugnymi* 2x *to join together;* trop. *join together, unite,* Mt. 19:6; Mk. 10:9* [4801]

[5184] συζητέω *syzēteō* 10x *to seek, ask,* or *inquire with* another; *to deliberate, debate,* Mk. 1:27; 9:10; Lk. 24:15; *to hold discourse with, argue, reason,* Mk. 8:11; 12:28; Lk. 22:23; Acts 6:9; 9:29; *to question, dispute, quibble,* Mk. 9:14, 16* [4802] See *debate; discuss.*

[5186] συζητητής *syzētētēs* 1x *a disputant, controversial reasoner, sophist, debater,* 1 Cor. 1:20* [4804]

[5187] σύζυγος *syzygos* 1x *an associate, comrade, fellow laborer,* or it could be the person's name, Phil. 4:3* [4805]

[5188] συζωοποιέω *syzōopoieō* 2x *to make alive together with another; to make a sharer in the quickening of another,* Eph. 2:5; Col. 2:13* [4806]

[5189] συκάμινος *sykaminos* 1x *a sycamore tree, mulberry tree,* i.q. συκομοραία, q.v., Lk. 17:6* [4807]

[5190] συκῆ *sykē* 16x *a fig tree,* Mt. 21:19 [4808] See *fig tree.*

[5191] συκομορέα *sykomorea* 1x *the fig mulberry tree, sycamore fig,* Lk. 19:4* [4809]

[5192] σῦκον *sykon* 4x *a fig, a ripe fig,* Mt. 7:16; Mk. 11:13; Lk. 6:44; Jas. 3:12* [4810]

[5193] συκοφαντέω *sykophanteō* 2x *to inform against; to accuse falsely;* by impl. *to wrong by false accusations; to extort* money *by false informations,* Lk. 3:14; 19:8* [4811]

[5194] συλαγωγέω *sylagōgeō* 1x *to carry off as a prey* or *booty;* met. *to make victims of fraud,* Col. 2:8* [4812]

[5195] συλάω *sylaō* 1x *to strip; to rob,* 2 Cor. 11:8* [4813]

[5196] συλλαλέω *syllaleō* 6x *to talk, converse,* or *discuss with,* Mt. 17:3; Mk. 9:4; Lk. 4:36; 9:30; 22:4; Acts 25:12* [4814]

[5197] συλλαμβάνω *syllambanō* 16x *to catch; to seize, apprehend,* Mt. 26:55; Acts 1:16; *to catch,* as prey, Lk. 5:9; *to conceive, become pregnant,* Lk. 1:24, 31, 36; 2:21; met. Jas. 1:15; mid. *to help, aid, assist,* Lk. 5:7; Phil. 4:3 [4815] See *arrest; catch; conceive; seize.*

[5198] συλλέγω *syllegō* 8x *to collect, gather,* Mt. 7:16, 13:28-30, 40f., 48; Lk. 6:44* [4816]

[5199] συλλογίζομαι *syllogizomai* 1x *to reason together; to consider, deliberate, reason,* Lk. 20:5* [4817]

[5200] συλλυπέω *syllypeō* 1x *to be grieved together with; to be grieved,* Mk. 3:5* [4818]

[5201] συμβαίνω *symbainō* 8x *to step* or *come together; to happen, meet, fall out, come about*, Mk. 10:32; Lk. 24:14 ; Acts 3:10; 20:19; 21:35; 1 Cor. 10:11; 1 Pet. 4:12; 2 Pet. 2:22* [4819]

[5202] συμβάλλω *symballō* 6x pr. *to throw together;* absol. *to meet and join,* Acts 20:14; *to meet* in war, *to encounter, engage with,* Lk. 14:31; *to encounter* in discourse or dispute, Acts 17:18; *to consult together,* Acts 4:15; mid. *to contribute, be of service to, to aid,* Acts 18:27; συμβάλλειν ἐν τῇ καρδίᾳ, *to revolve in mind, ponder upon,* Lk. 2:19* [4820]

[5203] συμβασιλεύω *symbasileuō* 2x *to reign with;* met. *to enjoy honor with,* 1 Cor. 4:8; 2 Tim. 2:12* [4821]

[5204] συμβιβάζω *symbibazō* 7x pr. *to cause to come together; to unite, knit together,* Eph. 4:16; Col. 2:2, 19; *to infer, conclude,* Acts 16:10; by impl. *to prove, demonstrate,* Acts 9:22; in NT *to teach, instruct,* Acts 19:33; 1 Cor. 2:16* [4822]

[5205] συμβουλεύω *symbouleuō* 4x *to counsel, advise, exhort,* Jn. 18:14; Rev. 3:18; mid. *to consult together, plot,* Mt. 26:4; Acts 9:23* [4823]

[5206] συμβούλιον *symboulion* 8x *counsel, consultation, mutual consultation,* Mt. 12:14; 22:15; 27:1, 7; 28:12; Mk. 3:6; Acts 27:1, 7; 28:12; *a council of counsellors,* Acts 25:12* [4824]

[5207] σύμβουλος *symboulos* 1x *a counsellor; advisor, one who shares one's counsel,* Rom. 11:34* [4825]

[5208] Συμεών *Symeōn* 7x *Symeon, Simeon,* pr. name. indecl. (1) *Simeon,* son of Juda, Lk. 3:30. (2) *Simeon,* son of Jacob, Rev. 7:7. (3) *Simeon,* a prophet of Jerusalem, Lk. 2:25, 34. (4) *Simeon,* or *Simon Peter,* Acts 15:14; 2 Pet. 1:1. (5) *Simeon,* called Niger, Acts 13:1* [4826]

[5209] συμμαθητής *symmathētēs* 1x *a fellow disciple,* Jn. 11:16* [4827]

[5210] συμμαρτυρέω *symmartyreō* 3x *to testify* or *bear witness together with* another, *confirm, add testimony,* Rom. 2:15; 8:16; 9:1* [4828]

[5211] συμμερίζω *symmerizō* 1x *to divide with* another so as to receive a part to one's self, *share with, partake with,* 1 Cor. 9:13* [4829]

[5212] συμμέτοχος *symmetochos* 2x *a partaker with* any one, *a joint partaker,* Eph. 3:6; 5:7* [4830]

[5213] συμμιμητής *symmimētēs* 1x *an imitator together with* any one, *a joint imitator,* Phil. 3:17* [4831]

[5214] συμμορφίζω *symmorphizō* 1x *to conform to, take on the same form as,* Phil. 3:10* [4833]

[5215] σύμμορφος *symmorphos* 2x *of like form, assimilated, conformed, similar in form,* Rom. 8:29; Phil. 3:21* [4832]

[5217] συμπαθέω *sympatheō* 2x *to sympathize with,* Heb. 4:15; *to be compassionate,* Heb. 10:34* [4834]

[5218] συμπαθής *sympathēs* 1x *sympathizing, compassionate,* 1 Pet. 3:8* [4835]

[5219] συμπαραγίνομαι *symparaginomai* 1x *to be present together with; to come together, convene,* Lk. 23:48* [4836]

[5220] συμπαρακαλέω *symparakaleō* 1x *to invite, exhort* along with others; pass. *to share in mutual encouragement,* Rom. 1:12* [4837]

[5221] συμπαραλαμβάνω *symparalambanō* 4x *to take along with, take as a companion,* Acts 12:25; 15:37, 38; Gal. 2:1* [4838]

[5223] συμπάρειμι *sympareimi* 1x *to be present with* any one, Acts 25:24* [4840]

[5224] συμπάσχω *sympaschō* 2x *to suffer with, sympathize,* 1 Cor. 12:26; *to suffer as* another, *endure corresponding sufferings,* Rom. 8:17* [4841]

[5225] συμπέμπω *sympempō* 2x *to send with* any one, 2 Cor. 8:18, 22* [4842]

[5227] συμπεριλαμβάνω *symperilambanō* 1x *to embrace together; to embrace,* Acts 20:10* [4843]

[5228] συμπίνω *sympinō* 1x *to drink with* any one, Acts 10:41* [4844]

[5229] συμπίπτω *sympiptō* 1x *fall together, collapse,* Lk. 6: 49* [4098]

[5230] συμπληρόω *symplēroō* 3x *to fill, fill up,* Lk. 8:23; pass., of time, *to be completed, have fully come,* Lk. 9:51; Acts 2:1* [4845]

[5231] συμπνίγω *sympnigō* 5x *to throttle, choke;* trop. *to choke* the growth or increase of seed or plants, Mt. 13:22; Mk. 4:7, 19; Lk. 8:14; *to press upon, crowd,* Lk. 8:42* [4846]

[5232] συμπολίτης *sympolitēs* 1x *a fellow citizen,* met. Eph. 2:19* [4847]

[5233] συμπορεύομαι *symporeuomai* 4x *to go with, accompany,* Lk. 7:11; 14:25; 24:15; *to come together, assemble,* Mk. 10:1* [4848]

[5235] συμπόσιον *symposion* 2x *a drinking together; a feast, banquet; a festive company;* in NT, pl. συμπόσια, *eating party,* Mk. 6:39 (2x)* [4849]

[5236] συμπρεσβύτερος *sympresbyteros* 1x *a fellow elder, fellow presbyter,* 1 Pet. 5:1* [4850]

[5237] συμφέρω *sympherō* 15x *to bring together, collect,* Acts 19:19; absol. *be for the benefit* of any one, *be profitable, advantageous, expedient,* 1 Cor.

6:12; *to suit best, be appropriate,* 2 Cor. 8:10; *good, benefit, profit, advantage,* Acts 20:20; 1 Cor. 7:35; *it is profitable, advantageous, expedient,* Mt. 5:29, 30; 19:10 [4851] See *(be) beneficial.*

[5238] σύμφημι *symphēmi* 1x pr. *to agree with,* Rom. 7:16* [4852]

[5239] σύμφορος *symphoros* 2x *profitable, expedient,* 1 Cor. 7:35; 10:33* [4851]

[5241] συμφυλέτης *symphyletēs* 1x pr. *one of the same tribe; a fellow citizen, fellow countryman,* 1 Thess. 2:14* [4853]

[5242] σύμφυτος *symphytos* 1x pr. *planted together, grown together;* in NT met. *grown together, closely entwined* or *united with,* Rom. 6:5* [4854]

[5243] συμφύω *symphyō* 1x *to make to grow together;* pass. *to grow* or *spring up with,* Lk. 8:7* [4855]

[5244] συμφωνέω *symphōneō* 6x *to sound together, to be in unison, be in accord;* trop. *to agree with, accord with* in purport, Acts 15:15; *to harmonize with, suit with,* Lk. 5:36; *to agree with, make an agreement,* Mt. 18:19; 20:2, 13; Acts 5:9* [4856] See *agree.*

[5245] συμφώνησις *symphōnēsis* 1x *unison, accord; agreement,* 2 Cor. 6:15* [4857]

[5246] συμφωνία *symphōnia* 1x *symphony, harmony of sounds, concert of instruments, music,* Lk. 15:25* [4858]

[5247] σύμφωνος *symphōnos* 1x *agreeing in sound;* met. *harmonious, agreeing, accord, agreement,* 1 Cor. 7:5* [4859]

[5248] συμψηφίζω *sympsēphizō* 1x *to calculate together, compute, count up,* Acts 19:19* [4860]

[5249] σύμψυχος *sympsychos* 1x *united in mind, at unity,* Phil. 2:2 [4861]

[5250] σύν *syn* 128x *with, together with,* Mt. 25:27; 26:35; 27:38; *attendant on,* 1 Cor. 15:10; *besides,* Lk. 24:21; *with, with the assistance of,* 1 Cor. 5:4; *with, in the same manner as,* Gal. 3:9; εἶναι σύν τινι, *to be with any one, to be in company with, accompany,* Lk. 2:13; 8:38; *to be on the side of, be a partisan of any one,* Acts 4:13; 14:4; οἱ σύν τινι, *those with any one, the companions of any one,* Mk. 2:26; Acts 22:9; *the colleagues, associates of any one,* Acts 5:17, 21 [4862]

[5251] συνάγω *synagō* 59x *to bring together, collect, gather,* as grain, fruits, etc., Mt. 3:12 6:26; 13:30, 47; *to collect* an assembly; pass. *to convene, come together, meet,* Mt. 2:4; 13:2; 18:20; 22:10; in NT *to receive with kindness and hospitality, to entertain,* Mt. 25:35, 38, 43 [4863] See *gather; harvest.*

[5252] συναγωγή *synagōgē* 56x *a collecting, gathering; a* Christian *assembly* or *congregation,* Jas. 2:2; *the congregation* of a synagogue, Acts 9:2; hence, the place itself, *a synagogue,* Lk. 7:5 [4864] See *assembly; congregation; synagogue.*

[5253] συναγωνίζομαι *synagōnizomai* 1x *to combat in company with* any one; *to exert one's strength with, to be earnest in aiding, help,* Rom. 15:30* [4865]

[5254] συναθλέω *synathleō* 2x pr. *to fight* or *work on the side of* any one; in NT *to cooperate vigorously with* a person, Phil. 4:3; *to make effort in the cause of, in support of* a thing, Phil. 1:27* [4866]

[5255] συναθροίζω *synathroizō* 2x *to gather; to bring together,* Acts 19:25; pass. *to come together, convene,* Acts 12:12* [4867]

[5256] συναίρω *synairō* 3x *to take up* a thing *with* any one; in NT συναίρειν λόγον, *to settle accounts, reckon* in order to payment, Mt. 18:23, 24; 25:19* [4868]

[5257] συναιχμάλωτος *synaichmalōtos* 3x *a fellow captive,* Rom. 16:7; Col. 4:10; Phlm. 23* [4869]

[5258] συνακολουθέω *synakoloutheō* 3x *to follow in company with, accompany,* Mk. 5:37; 14:51; Lk. 23:49* [4870]

[5259] συναλίζω *synalizō* 1x *to cause to come together, collect, assemble, congregate;* mid. *to convene to one's self,* Acts 1:4* [4871]

[5261] συναλλάσσω *synallassō* 1x *to negotiate* or *bargain with* someone; *to reconcile,* Acts 7:26* [4900]

[5262] συναναβαίνω *synanabainō* 2x *to go up, ascend with* someone, Mk. 15:41; Acts 13:31* [4872]

[5263] συνανάκειμαι *synanakeimai* 7x *to recline with* someone at table, Mt. 9:10; 14:9; Mk. 2:15; 6:22; Lk. 7:49; 14:10, 15* [4873]

[5265] συναναπαύομαι *synanapauomai* 1x *to experience refreshment* or *rest in company with* someone, Rom. 15:32* [4875]

[5267] συναντάω *synantaō* 6x *to meet with, fall in with, encounter,* Lk. 9:37; 22:10; Acts 10:25; Heb. 7:1, 10; *to occur, happen to, befall,* Acts 20:22* [4876]

[5269] συναντιλαμβάνομαι *synantilambanomai* 2x pr. *to take hold of with* someone; *to support, help, aid,* Lk. 10:40; Rom. 8:26* [4878]

[5270] συναπάγω *synapagō* 3x *to lead* or *carry away with; to seduce;* pass. *to be led away* [4879]

[5271] συναποθνῄσκω *synapothnēskō* 3x *to die together with* any one, Mk. 14:31; 2 Cor. 7:3; met. *to die with,* in respect of a spiritual likeness, 2 Tim. 2:11* [4880]

[5272] συναπόλλυμι *synapollymi* 1x *to destroy together with* others; mid. *to perish* or *be destroyed with* others, Heb. 11:31* [4881]

[5273] συναποστέλλω *synapostellō* 1x *to send forth together with* someone, 2 Cor. 12:18* [4882]

[5274] συναρμολογέω *synarmologeō* 2x *to join together fitly, fit* or *frame together, compact,* Eph. 2:21; 4:16* [4883]

[5275] συναρπάζω *synarpazō* 4x pluperf., συνηρπάκειν, *to snatch up, clutch; to seize and carry off suddenly,* Acts 6:12; *to seize with force and violence,* Lk. 8:29; Acts 19:29; pass. of a ship, *to be caught and swept on* by the wind, Acts 27:15* [4884]

[5277] συναυξάνω *synauxanō* 1x pas., *to grow together* in company, Mt. 13:30* [4885]

[5278] σύνδεσμος *syndesmos* 4x *that which binds together,* Col. 2:19; *a band* of union, Eph. 4:3; Col. 3:14; *a bundle,* or, *bond,* Acts 8:23* [4886]

[5279] συνδέω *syndeō* 1x *to bind together;* in NT pass. *to be in bonds together,* Heb. 13:3* [4887]

[5280] συνδοξάζω *syndoxazō* 1x in NT *to glorify together with, to exalt to a state of dignity and happiness in company with, to make to partake in the glorification* of another, Rom. 8:17* [4888]

[5281] σύνδουλος *syndoulos* 10x *a fellow-slave, fellow-servant,* Mt. 24:49; 18:28f., 31, 33; Col. 4:7; Rev. 6:11; 19:10; 22:9; *a fellow-minister* of Christ, Col. 1:7* [4889] See *fellow servant; fellow slave.*

[5282] συνδρομή *syndromē* 1x *a running together, forming a mob,* Acts 21:30* [4890]

[5283] συνεγείρω *synegeirō* 3x *to raise up with* any one; *to raise up with* Christ by spiritual resemblance of His resurrection, Eph. 2:6; Col. 2:12; 3:1* [4891]

[5284] συνέδριον *synedrion* 22x pr. *a sitting together, assembly,* etc., in NT *the Sanhedrin,* the supreme council of the Jewish nation, Mt. 5:22; 26:59; meton. *the Sanhedrin,* as including the members and place of meeting, Lk. 22:66; Acts 4:15; genr. *a* judicial *council, tribunal,* Mt. 10:17; Mk. 13:9 [4892] See *council; Sanhedrin.*

[5287] συνείδησις *syneidēsis* 30x *consciousness,* Heb. 10:2; *a present idea, persisting notion, impression of reality,* 1 Pet. 2:19; *conscience,* as an inward moral impression of one's actions and principles, Acts 23:1; 24:16; Rom. 9:1; 2 Cor. 1:12; *conscience,* as the inward faculty of moral judgment, Rom. 2:15; 13:5; 1 Cor. 8:7b, 10, 12; 10:25, 27, 28, 29; 2 Cor. 4:2; 5:11; 1 Tim. 1:5, 19; 3:9; 4:2; 2 Tim. 1:3; *conscience,* as the inward moral and spiritual frame, Tit. 1:15; Heb. 9:9, 14; 10:22; 13:18; 1 Pet. 3:16, 21* [4893] See *conscience, consciousness.*

[5289] σύνειμι *syneimi* 2x from εἰμί, *to be with, be in company with,* Lk. 9:18; Acts 22:11* [4895]

[5290] σύνειμι *syneimi* 1x from εἶμι, *to come together,* Lk. 8:4* [4896]

[5291] συνεισέρχομαι *syneiserchomai* 2x *to enter with* someone, Jn. 18:15; *to embark with,* Jn. 6:22* [4897]

[5292] συνέκδημος *synekdēmos* 2x *one who accompanies* another *to foreign countries, fellow traveller,* Acts 19:29; 2 Cor. 8:19* [4898]

[5293] συνεκλεκτός *syneklektos* 1x *chosen along with* others; *elected* to Gospel privileges *along with,* 1 Pet. 5:13* [4899]

[5296] συνεπιμαρτυρέω *synepimartyreō* 1x *to join in according testimony; to support by testimony, to confirm, sanction,* Heb. 2:4* [4901]

[5298] συνεπιτίθημι *synepitithēmi* 1x can also be spelled συνεπιτίθεμαι, mid., *to set upon along with, join with others* in an attack; *to unite in impeaching,* Acts 24:9* [4934]

[5299] συνέπομαι *synepomai* 1x *to follow with, attend, accompany,* Acts 20:4* [4902]

[5300] συνεργέω *synergeō* 5x *to work together with, to cooperate,* etc., 1 Cor. 16:16; 2 Cor. 6:1; *to assist, afford aid to,* Mk. 16:20; Jas. 2:22; absol. *to conspire actively* to a result, Rom. 8:28* [4903]

[5301] συνεργός *synergos* 13x *a fellow laborer, associate, helper,* Rom. 16:3, 9, 21; 2 Cor. 1:24 [4904] See *coworker; fellow worker.*

[5302] συνέρχομαι *synerchomai* 30x pluperf., συνεληλύθεισαν (3 pl), *to come together; to assem-*

ble, Mk. 3:20; 6:33; 14:53; *to cohabit* matrimonially, Mt. 1:18; 1 Cor. 7:5; *to go* or *come with* any one, *to accompany,* Lk. 23:55; Acts 9:39; *to company with, associate with,* Acts 1:21 [4905] See *assemble; come together; gather.*

[5303] συνεσθίω *synesthiō* 5x *to eat with,* Acts 10:41; 11:3; 1 Cor. 5:11; by impl. *to associate with, live on familiar terms with,* Lk. 15:2; Gal. 2:12* [4906]

[5304] σύνεσις *synesis* 7x pr. *a sending together, a junction,* as of streams; met. *understanding, intelligence, discernment,* Lk. 2:47; 1 Cor. 1:19; meton. *the understanding, intellect, mind,* Mk. 12:33; Eph. 3:4; Col. 1:9; 2:2; 2 Tim. 2:7* [4907] See *insight; understanding.*

[5305] συνετός *synetos* 4x *intelligent, discerning, wise, prudent,* Mt. 11:25; Lk. 10:21; Acts 13:7; 1 Cor. 1:19* [4908]

[5306] συνευδοκέω *syneudokeō* 6x *to approve with* another; *to agree with in principle,* Rom. 1:32; *to stamp approval,* Lk. 11:48; Acts 8:1; 22:20; *to be willing, agreeable,* 1 Cor. 7:12, 13* [4909]

[5307] συνευωχέομαι *syneuōcheomai* 2x *to feast together with,* 2 Pet. 2:13; Jude 12* [4910]

[5308] συνεφίστημι *synephistēmi* 1x *to set together upon, join in an attack,* Acts 16:22* [4911]

[5309] συνέχω *synechō* 12x pr. *to hold together; to confine, shut up, close;* τὰ ωτα, *to stop the ears,* Acts 7:57; *to confine,* as a besieged city, Lk. 19:43; *to hold, hold fast, have the custody of* any one, Lk. 22:63; *to hem in, urge, press upon,* Lk. 8:45; *to exercise a constraining influence on,* 2 Cor. 5:14; pass. *to be seized with, be affected with,* as fear, disease, etc., Mt. 4:24; Lk. 4:38; 8:37; Acts 28:8; *to be in a state of* mental *constriction, to be hard pressed* by urgency of circumstances, Lk. 12:50; Acts 18:5; Phil. 1:23* [4912] See *compel; suffer.*

[5310] συνήδομαι *synēdomai* 1x *to be pleased along with* others; *to congratulate; to delight in, approve cordially,* Rom. 7:22* [4913]

[5311] συνήθεια *synētheia* 3x *use, custom; an established custom, practice,* Jn. 18:39; 1 Cor. 8:7; 11:16* [4914]

[5312] συνηλικιώτης *synēlikiōtēs* 1x *one of the same age, an equal in age,* Gal. 1:14* [4915]

[5313] συνθάπτω *synthaptō* 2x *to bury with;* pass. in NT *to be buried with* Christ symbolically, Rom. 6:4; Col. 2:12* [4916]

[5314] συνθλάω *synthlaō* 2x *to crush together; to break in pieces, shatter,* Mt. 21:44; Lk. 20:18* [4917]

[5315] συνθλίβω *synthlibō* 2x *to press together; to press upon, crowd,* Mk. 5:24, 31* [4918]

[5316] συνθρύπτω *synthryptō* 1x *to crush to pieces;* met. *to break* the heart of any one, *to make to recoil in fear,* Acts 21:13* [4919]

[5317] συνίημι *syniēmi* 26x also συνίω, see *BAGD* for a discussion, pr. *to send together;* met. *to understand, comprehend thoroughly,* Mt. 13:51; Lk. 2:50; 18:34; 24:45; *to perceive clearly,* Mt. 16:12; 17:13; Acts 7:25; Rom. 15:21; Eph. 5:17; absol. *to be well judging, sensible,* 2 Cor. 10:12; *to be* spiritually *intelligent,* Mt. 13:13, 14, 15; Acts 28:26, 27; *to be* religiously *wise,* Rom. 3:11 [4920] See *realize; understand.*

[5319] συνίστημι *synistēmi* 16x also spelled συνιστάνω and συνιστάω, *to place together; to recommend to favorable attention,* Rom. 16:1; 2 Cor. 3:1; 10:18; *to place in a striking point of view,* Rom. 3:5; 5:8; Gal. 2:18; *to stand beside,* Lk. 9:32; *to have been permanently framed,* Col. 1:17; *to be composed,* 2 Pet. 3:5 [4921] See *commend; hold together.*

[5321] συνοδεύω *synodeuō* 1x *to journey* or *travel with, accompany on a journey,* Acts 9:7* [4922]

[5322] συνοδία *synodia* 1x pr. *a journeying together;* meton. *a company of fellow travellers, caravan,* Lk. 2:44* [4923]

[5323] σύνοιδα *synoida* 2x a defective verb that is actually perfect in form but present in meaning, *to share in the knowledge of* a thing; *to be privy to,* Acts 5:2; *to be conscious;* οὐδέν σύνοιδα, *to have a clear conscience,* 1 Cor. 4:4* [4894]

[5324] συνοικέω *synoikeō* 1x *to dwell with; to live* or *cohabit with,* 1 Pet. 3:7* [4924]

[5325] συνοικοδομέω *synoikodomeō* 1x *to build in company with* someone; pass. *to be built up, form a constituent part of a structure,* Eph. 2:22* [4925]

[5326] συνομιλέω *synomileō* 1x pr. *to be in company with; to talk* or *converse with,* Acts 10:27* [4926]

[5327] συνομορέω *synomoreō* 1x *to be next to, be next door,* Acts 18:7* [4927]

[5328] συνοράω *synoraō* 2x *perceive, become aware of, realize,* Acts 12:12; 14:6* [4894]

[5330] συνοχή *synochē* 2x pr. *a being held together; compression;* in NT met. *distress of mind, anxiety, anguish,* Lk. 21:25; 2 Cor. 2:4 [4928]

[5332] συντάσσω *syntassō* 3x pr. *to arrange* or *place in order together;* in NT *to order, charge, direct,* Mt. 21:6, 26:19; 27:10* [4929] See *command; instruct.*

[5333] συντέλεια *synteleia* 6x *a complete combination, a completion, consummation, end,* Mt. 13:39, 40, 49; 24:3; 28:20; Heb. 9:26* [4930]

[5334] συντελέω *synteleō* 6x pr. *to bring to an end altogether; to finish, end,* Lk. 4:13; *to consummate,* Rom. 9:28; *to ratify* a covenant, Heb. 8:8; pass. *to be terminated,* Lk. 4:2; Acts 21:27; *to be fully realized,* Mk. 13:4* [4931]

[5335] συντέμνω *syntemnō* 1x pr. *to cut short, contract by cutting off;* met. *to execute speedily,* or from the Hebrew, *to determine, decide, decree,* Rom. 9:28 (2x)* [4932]

[5337] συντηρέω *syntēreō* 3x *to keep safe and sound,* Mt. 9:17; *to observe strictly,* or, *to secure from harm, protect,* Mk. 6:20; *to preserve in memory, keep carefully in mind,* Lk. 2:19* [4933]

[5338] συντίθημι *syntithēmi* 3x *to agree together, come to a mutual understanding,* Jn. 9:22; Acts 23:20; *to bargain, to pledge one's self,* Lk. 22:5* [4934]

[5339] συντόμως *syntomōs* 1x *concisely, briefly,* Acts 24:4* [4935]

[5340] συντρέχω *syntrechō* 3x *to run together, flock together,* Mk. 6:33; Acts 3:11; *to run in company with* others, met. 1 Pet. 4:4* [4936]

[5341] συντρίβω *syntribō* 7x *to rub together; to shiver,* Mk. 14:3; Rev. 2:27; *to break, break in pieces,* Mk. 5:4; Jn. 19:36; *to break down, crush, bruise,* Mt. 12:20; met. *to break the power of* any one, *deprive of strength, debilitate,* Lk. 9:39; Rom. 16:20* [4937]

[5342] σύντριμμα *syntrimma* 1x *a breaking, bruising;* in NT *destruction, ruin,* Rom. 3:16* [4938]

[5343] σύντροφος *syntrophos* 1x *nursed with* another; *one brought up* (*NIV*) or *educated with* another, *intimate friend, friend of the court* (*RSV*) Acts 13:1* [4939]

[5344] συντυγχάνω *syntynchanō* 1x *to meet* or *fall in with; join,* in NT *to get to, approach,* Lk. 8:19* [4940]

[5345] Συντύχη *Syntychē* 1x *Syntyche,* pr. name, Phil. 4:2* [4941]

[5347] συνυποκρίνομαι *synypokrinomai* 1x *to dissemble, feign with,* or *in the same manner as* another, *join in the playing of the hypocrite,* Gal. 2:13* [4942]

[5348] συνυπουργέω *synypourgeō* 1x *to aid along with* another, *help together,* 2 Cor. 1:11* [4943]

[5349] συνωδίνω *synōdinō* 1x pr. *to travail at the same time with;* trop. *suffer together,* Rom. 8:22* [4944]

[5350] συνωμοσία *synōmosia* 1x *a banding by oath; a combination, conspiracy, plot,* Acts 23:13* [4945]

[5352] Συράκουσαι *Syrakousai* 1x *Syracuse,* a celebrated city of Sicily, Acts 28:12* [4946]

[5353] Συρία *Syria* 8x *Syria,* an extensive country of Asia, Mt. 4:24; Lk. 2:2; Acts 15:23 [4947]

[5354] Σύρος *Syros* 1x *a Syrian,* Lk. 4:27* [4948]

[5355] Συροφοινίκισσα *Syrophoinikissa* 1x *a Syrophoenician woman,* Phoenicia being included in Syria, Mk. 7:26* [4949]

[5358] Σύρτις *Syrtis* 1x *a shoal, sand-bank, a place dangerous on account of shoals,* two of which were particularly famous on the northern coast of Africa, one lying near Carthage, and the other, *the syrtis major,* lying between Cyrene and Leptis, which is probably referred to in Acts 27:17* [4950]

[5359] σύρω *syrō* 5x *to draw, drag,* Jn. 21:8; Rev. 12:4; *to force away, hale* before magistrates, etc., Acts 8:3; 14:19; 17:6* [4951]

[5360] συσπαράσσω *sysparassō* 2x *to tear to pieces; to convulse altogether,* Mk. 9:20; Lk. 9:42* [4952]

[5361] σύσσημον *syssēmon* 1x *a signal,* Mk. 14:44* [4953]

[5362] σύσσωμος *syssōmos* 1x *united in the same body;* met. pl. *joint members* in a spiritual body, Eph. 3:6* [4954]

[5364] συστατικός *systatikos* 1x *commendatory, recommendatory, letter of recommendation,* 2 Cor. 3:1* [4956]

[5365] συσταυρόω *systauroō* 5x *to crucify with* another, Mt. 27:44; Mk. 15:32; Jn. 19:32; pass. met.

to be crucified with another in a spiritual resemblance, Rom. 6:6; Gal. 2:20* [4957]

[5366] συστέλλω *systellō* 2x *to draw together, contract, straiten; to enwrap;* hence, i.q. περιστέλλω, *to lay out, prepare for burial,* Acts 5:6; pass. *to be shortened,* 1 Cor. 7:29* [4958]

[5367] συστενάζω *systenazō* 1x *to groan* or *lament together,* Rom. 8:22* [4959]

[5368] συστοιχέω *systoicheō* 1x pr. *to be in the same row with;* met. *to correspond to,* Gal. 4:25* [4960]

[5369] συστρατιώτης *systratiōtēs* 2x *a fellow soldier, co-militant,* in the service of Christ, Phil. 2:25; Phlm. 2* [4961]

[5370] συστρέφω *systrephō* 2x *to turn* or *roll together; to collect, gather,* Acts 28:3; Mt. 17:22* [4962]

[5371] συστροφή *systrophē* 2x *a gathering, tumultuous assembly,* Acts 19:40; *a combination, conspiracy,* Acts 23:12* [4963]

[5372] συσχηματίζω *syschēmatizō* 2x *to fashion in accordance with;* mid/pass. *to conform* or *assimilate one's self to,* met. Rom. 12:2; 1 Pet. 1:14* [4964]

[5373] Συχάρ *Sychar* 1x *Sychar,* indecl., a city of Samaria, Jn. 4:5* [4965]

[5374] Συχέμ *Sychem* 2x *Shechem,* indecl., fem., a city of Samaria, Acts 7:16* [4966]

[5375] σφαγή *sphagē* 3x *slaughter,* Acts 8:32; Rom. 8:36; Jas. 5:5* [4967]

[5376] σφάγιον *sphagion* 1x *a victim* slaughtered in sacrifice, *offering,* Acts 7:42* [4968]

[5377] σφάζω *sphazō* 10x also spelled σφάττω, *to slaughter, kill, slay;* pr. used of animals killed in sacrifice, etc., Rev. 5:6, 9, 12; 13:8; of persons, etc., 1 Jn. 3:12; Rev. 6:4, 9; 18:24; *to wound mortally,* Rev. 13:3* [4969] See *slay.*

[5379] σφόδρα *sphodra* 11x *much, greatly, exceedingly,* Mt. 2:10; 17:6; Mk. 16:4; Lk. 18:23; Acts 6:7 [4970] See *greatly.*

[5380] σφοδρῶς *sphodrōs* 1x *exceedingly, vehemently,* Acts 27:18* [4971]

[5381] σφραγίζω *sphragizō* 15x *to seal, stamp with a seal,* Mt. 27:66; Rev. 20:3; *to seal up, to close up, conceal,* Rev. 10:4; 22:10; *to set a mark upon, distinguish by a mark,* Eph. 1:13; 4:30; Rev. 7:3, 4, 5, 8; *to seal, to mark distinctively* as invested with a certain character, Jn. 6:27; mid. *to set one's own mark upon, seal as one's own, to impress with a mark of acceptance,* 2 Cor. 1:22; *to deliver over safely to* someone, Rom. 15:28; absol. *to set to one's seal, to make a solemn declaration,* Jn. 3:33* [4972] See *seal.*

[5382] σφραγίς *sphragis* 16x *a seal, a signet ring,* Rev. 7:2; *an inscription on a seal, motto,* 2 Tim. 2:19; *a seal, the impression of a seal,* Rev. 5:1, 2, 5, 9, 6:1, 3, 5, 7, 9, 12; 8:1; *a seal, a distinctive mark,* Rev. 9:4; *a seal, a token, proof,* 1 Cor. 9:2; *a token* of guarantee, Rom. 4:11* [4973] See *seal.*

[5383] σφυδρόν *sphydron* 1x *ankle,* Acts 3:7* [4974]

[5385] σχεδόν *schedon* 3x pr. *near,* of place; hence, *nearly, almost,* Acts 13:44; 19:26; Heb. 9:22* [4975]

[5386] σχῆμα *schēma* 2x *fashion, form; fashion, external show,* 1 Cor. 7:31; Phil. 2:7* [4976] See *appearance; figure; form.*

[5387] σχίζω *schizō* 11x *to split,* Mt. 27:51; Mk. 15:38; *to rend, tear asunder,* Mt. 27:51; Lk. 5:36; 23:45; Jn. 19:24; 21:11); mid. *to open* or *unfold* with a chasm, Mk. 1:10; pass. met. *to be divided* into parties or factions, Acts 14:4; 23:7* [4977] See *divide; split; tear.*

[5388] σχίσμα *schisma* 8x *a split,* Mt. 9:16; Mk. 2:21; met. *a division* into parties, *schism,* Jn. 7:43; 9:16; 10:19; 1 Cor. 1:10; 11:18; 12:25* [4978] See *division.*

[5389] σχοινίον *schoinion* 2x pr. *a cord made of rushes;* genr. *a rope, cord,* Jn. 2:15; Acts 27:32* [4979]

[5390] σχολάζω *scholazō* 2x *to be unemployed, to be at leisure; to be at leisure* for a thing, *to devote one's self entirely* to a thing, 1 Cor. 7:5; *to be unoccupied, empty,* Mt. 12:44* [4980]

[5391] σχολή *scholē* 1x *freedom from occupation;* later, *ease, leisure; a school,* Acts 19:9* [4981]

[5392] σῴζω *sōzō* 106x *to save, rescue; to preserve safe and unharmed,* Mark. 8:25; 10:22; 24:22; 27:40, 42, 49; 1 Tim. 2:15; σῴζειν εἰς, *to bring safely to,* 2 Tim. 4:18; *to cure, heal, restore to health,* Mt. 9:21, 22; Mk. 5:23, 28, 34; 6:56; *to save, preserve* from being lost, Mt. 16:25; Mk. 3:4; 8:35; σῴζειν ἀπό, *to deliver from, set free from,* Mt. 1:21; Jn. 12:27; Acts 2:40; in NT *to rescue* from unbelief, *convert,* Rom. 11:14; 1 Cor. 1:21; 7:16; *to bring within the pale of saving privilege,* Tit. 3:5; 1 Pet. 3:21; *to save* from final ruin, 1 Tim. 1:15; pass. *to be brought within the* *pale of saving privilege,* Acts 2:47; Eph. 2:5, 8; *to be in the way of salvation,* 1 Cor. 15:2; 2 Cor. 2:15 [4982] See *heal; rescue; save.*

[5393] σῶμα *sōma* 142x *the body* of an animal; *a* living *body,* Mt. 5:29, 30; 6:22, 23, 25; Jas. 3:3; *a person, individual,* 1 Cor. 6:16; *a* dead *body; corpse, carcass,* Mt. 14:12; 27:52, 58; Heb. 13:11; *the* human *body* considered as the seat and occasion of moral imperfection, as inducing to sin through its appetites and passions, Rom. 7:24; 8:13; genr. *a body, a material substance,* 1 Cor. 15:37, 38, 40; *the substance, reality,* as opposed to ἡ σκιά, Col. 2:17; in NT met., *the* aggregate *body* of believers, *the body* of the Church, Rom. 12:5; Col. 1:18 [4983] See *body.*

[5394] σωματικός *sōmatikos* 2x *bodily, of* or *belonging to the body,* 1 Tim. 4:8; *corporeal, material,* Lk. 3:22* [4984]

[5395] σωματικῶς *sōmatikōs* 1x *bodily, in a bodily frame,* Col. 2:9* [4985]

[5396] Σώπατρος *Sōpatros* 1x *Sopater,* pr. name, Acts 20:4* [4986]

[5397] σωρεύω *sōreuō* 2x *to heap* or *pile up,* Rom. 12:20; met. pass. *to be filled* with sins, 2 Tim. 3:6* [4987]

[5398] Σωσθένης *Sōsthenēs* 2x *Sosthenes,* pr. name, Acts 18:17; 1 Cor. 1:1* [4988]

[5399] Σωσίπατρος *Sōsipatros* 1x *Sosipater,* pr. name, Rom. 16:21* [4989]

[5400] σωτήρ *sōtēr* 24x *a savior, preserver, deliverer,* Lk. 1:47; 2:11; Acts 5:31 [4990] See *savior.*

[5401] σωτηρία *sōtēria* 46x *a saving, preservation,* Acts 27:34; Heb. 11:7; *deliverance,* Lk. 1:69, 71; Acts 7:25; *salvation,* spiritual and eternal, Lk. 1:77; 19:9; Acts 4:12; Rev. 7:10; *a being placed in a condition of salvation* by an embracing of the Gospel, Rom. 10:1, 10; 2 Tim. 3:15; *means* or *opportunity of salvation,* Acts 13:26; Rom. 11:11; Heb. 2:3; ἡ σωτηρία, *the* promised *deliverance* by the Messiah, Jn. 4:22 [4991] See *salvation.*

[5403] σωτήριος *sōtērios* 1x *imparting salvation, saving,* Lk. 2:30; 3:6; Acts 28:28; Eph. 6:17; Tit. 2:11* [4992]

[5404] σωφρονέω *sōphroneō* 6x *to be of a sound mind, be in one's right mind, be sane,* Mk. 5:15; Lk. 8:35; *to be calm,* 2 Cor. 5:13; *to be sober-minded, sedate,* Tit. 2:6; 1 Pet. 4:7; *to be of a modest, humble mind,* Rom. 12:3* [4993]

[5405] σωφρονίζω *sōphronizō* 1x *encourage, to restore to a right mind; to make sober-minded, to steady* by exhortation and guidance, Tit. 2:4* [4994]

[5406] σωφρονισμός *sōphronismos* 1x *self discipline, prudence,* 2 Tim. 1:7* [4995]

[5407] σωφρόνως *sōphronōs* 1x *in the manner of a person in his right mind; soberly, temperately,* Tit. 2:12* [4996]

[5408] σωφροσύνη *sōphrosynē* 3x *sanity, soundness of mind, a sane mind,* Acts 26:25; female *modesty,* 1 Tim. 2:9, 15* [4997]

[5409] σώφρων *sōphrōn* 4x *of a sound mind, sane; temperate, discreet,* 1 Tim. 3:2; Tit. 1:8; 2:2; *modest, chaste,* Tit. 2:5* [4998]

[5411] ταβέρναι *tabernai* 1x *taverns,* used in the NT only in the transliterated Latin name of "Three Taverns" (Τριῶν ταβερνῶν), see 5553, Acts 28:15* [4999]

[5412] Ταβιθά *Tabitha* 2x *antelope, Tabitha,* pr. name, Acts 9:36, 40* [5000]

[5413] τάγμα *tagma* 1x pr. *anything placed in order;* in NT *order of* succession, *class, group,* 1 Cor. 15:23* [5001]

[5414] τακτός *taktos* 1x pr. *arranged; fixed, appointed, set,* Acts 12:21* [5002]

[5415] ταλαιπωρέω *talaipōreō* 1x *to endure severe labor and hardship; to be harassed; complain,* Jas. 4:9* [5003]

[5416] ταλαιπωρία *talaipōria* 2x *toil, difficulty, hardship; calamity, misery, distress,* Rom. 3:16; Jas. 5:1* [5004]

[5417] ταλαίπωρος *talaipōros* 2x pr. *enduring severe effort and hardship;* hence, *wretched, miserable, afflicted,* Rom. 7:24; Rev. 3:17* [5005]

[5418] ταλαντιαῖος *talantiaios* 1x *of a talent weight, weighing a talent,* Rev. 16:21* [5006]

[5419] τάλαντον *talanton* 14x *the scale of a balance; a talent,* which as a weight was among the Jews equivalent to 3000 shekels, i.e., as usually estimated, 114 lbs. 15 dwts. Troy; while the Attic talent, on the usual estimate, was only equal to 56 lbs. 11 oz. Troy, Mt. 18:24; 25:15, 16, 20, 22, 24, 25, 28* [5007] See *talent.*

[5420] ταλιθά *talitha* 1x Aramaic, *(little) girl,* Mk. 5:41* [5008]

[5421] ταμεῖον *tameion* 4x *a storehouse, granary, barn,* Lk. 12:24; *a chamber, closet, place of retirement and privacy,* Mt. 6:6; 24:26; Lk. 12:3* [5009]

[5423] τάξις *taxis* 9x *order, regular disposition, arrangement; order, series, succession,* Lk. 1:8; *an order, distinctive class,* as of priests, Heb. 5:6, 10; 6:20; 7:11(2x), 17; *order, good order,* 1 Cor. 14:40; *orderliness, well-regulated conduct,* Col. 2:5* [5010]

[5424] ταπεινός *tapeinos* 8x *low* in situation; of condition, *humble, poor, mean, depressed,* Lk. 1:52; 2 Cor. 7:6; Jas. 1:9; met. of the mind, *humble, lowly, modest,* Mt. 11:29; Rom. 12:16; 2 Cor. 10:1; Jas. 4:6; 1 Pet. 5:5* [5011]

[5425] ταπεινοφροσύνη *tapeinophrosynē* 7x *lowliness* or *humility of mind, modesty,* Acts 20:19; Eph. 4:2; Phil. 2:3; Col. 2:18, 23; 3:12; 1 Pet. 5:5* [5012]

[5426] ταπεινόφρων *tapeinophrōn* 1x *humble-minded,* 1 Pet. 3:8* [5391]

[5427] ταπεινόω *tapeinoō* 14x *to bring low, depress, level,* Lk. 3:5; met. *to humble, abase,* Phil. 2:8; mid. *to descend to,* or *live in, a humble condition,* 2 Cor. 11:7; Phil. 4:12; *to humble, depress the pride of,* any one, Mt. 18:4; mid. *to humble one's self, exhibit humility and contrition,* Jas. 4:10; 1 Pet. 5:6; *to humble* with respect to hopes and expectations, *to depress* with disappointment, Mt. 23:12; Lk. 14:11; 18:14; 2 Cor. 12:21* [5013] See *humble; humiliate; make low.*

[5428] ταπείνωσις *tapeinōsis* 4x *depression; low estate, abject condition,* Lk. 1:48; Acts 8:33; Phil. 3:21; Jas. 1:10* [5014]

[5429] ταράσσω *tarassō* 17x *to agitate, trouble,* as water, Jn. 5:7; met. *to agitate, trouble* the mind; with fear, *to terrify, put in consternation,* Mt. 2:3; 14:26; with grief, etc., *affect with grief, anxiety,* etc., Jn. 12:27; 13:21; with doubt, etc., *to unsettle, perplex,* Acts 15:24; Gal. 1:7 [5015] See *distress; disturb; trouble.*

[5431] τάραχος *tarachos* 2x *agitation, commotion; consternation, terror,* Acts 12:18; *excitement, tumult, public contention,* Acts 19:23* [5017]

[5432] Ταρσεύς *Tarseus* 2x *of,* or *a native of* Ταρσός, *Tarsus,* the metropolis of Cilicia, Acts 9:11; 21:39* [5018]

[5433] Ταρσός *Tarsos* 3x *Tarsus,* the chief city of Cilicia, and birth-place of the Apostle Paul, Acts 9:30; 11:25; 22:3* [5019]

[5434] ταρταρόω *tartaroō* 1x *to cast* or *thrust down to Tartarus* or *Gehenna,* 2 Pet. 2:4* [5020]

[5435] τάσσω *tassō* 8x *to arrange; to set, appoint,* in a certain station, Lk. 7:8; Rom. 13:1; *to set, devote,* to a pursuit, 1 Cor. 16:15; *to belong to, to dispose, frame,* for an object, Acts 13:48; *to arrange, appoint,* place or time, Mt. 28:16; Acts 28:23; *to allot, assign,* Acts 22:10; *to settle, decide,* Acts 15:2* [5021]

[5436] ταῦρος *tauros* 4x *a bull, ox,* Mt. 22:4; Acts 14:13; Heb. 9:13; 10:4* [5022]

[5438] ταφή *taphē* 1x *burial, the act of burying, burial place,* Mt. 27:7* [5027]

[5439] τάφος *taphos* 7x *a sepulchre, grave, tomb,* Mt. 23:27, 29; 27:61, 64, 66; 28:1; met. Rom. 3:13* [5028]

[5440] τάχα *tacha* 2x pr. *quickly, soon; perhaps, possibly,* Rom. 5:7; Phlm. 15* [5029]

[5441] ταχέως *tacheōs* 15x adverb of ταχύς, *quickly, speedily; soon, shortly,* 1 Cor. 4:19; Gal. 1:6; *hastily,* Lk. 14:21; 16:6; *with inconsiderate haste,* 1 Tim. 5:22 [5030, 5032, 5033] See *quickly; soon.*

[5442] ταχινός *tachinos* 2x *swift, speedy,* 2 Pet. 2:1; *near at hand, impending,* 2 Pet. 1:14* [5031]

[5443] τάχος *tachos* 8x *swiftness, speed, quickness;* ἐν τάχει, *with speed, quickly, speedily; soon, shortly,* Lk. 18:8; Acts 25:4; *hastily, immediately,* Acts 12:7; 22:18; Rom. 16:20; 1 Tim. 3:14; Rev. 1:1; 22:6* [5034]

[5444] ταχύς *tachus* 13x *swift, fleet, quick;* met. *ready, prompt,* Jas. 1:19; Mt. 28:7f.; Mk. 9:39; Lk. 15:22; Jn. 11:29 [5035, 5036] See *quickly; soon.*

[5445] τε *te* 215x enclitic, can function as a conj., serving either as a lightly-appending link, Acts 1:15; *and,* Acts 2:3; or as an inclusive prefix, Lk. 12:45; *both,* Lk. 24:20; Acts 26:16 [5037]

[5446] τεῖχος *teichos* 9x *a wall* of a city, Acts 9:25; 2 Cor. 11:33; Heb. 11:30; Rev. 21:12, 14f., 17-19* [5038]

[5447] τεκμήριον *tekmērion* 1x *a sign, indubitable token, clear proof,* Acts 1:3* [5039]

[5448] τεκνίον *teknion* 8x *a little child;* τεκνία, an endearing appellation, *my dear children,* Jn. 13:33; 1 Jn. 2:1, 12, 28; 3:7, 18; 4:4; 5:21* [5040]

[5449] τεκνογονέω *teknogoneō* 1x *to bear children, to rear a family,* 1 Tim. 5:14* [5041]

[5450] τεκνογονία *teknogonia* 1x *the bearing of children, the rearing of a family,* 1 Tim. 2:15* [5042]

[5451] τέκνον *teknon* 99x *a child, a son* or *daughter,* Mt. 2:18; Lk. 1:7; pl. *descendants, posterity,* Mt. 3:9; Acts 2:39; *child, son,* as a term of endearment, Mt. 9:2; Mk. 2:5; 10:24; pl. *children, inhabitants, people,* of a city, Mt. 23:37; Lk. 19:44; from the Hebrew, met. *a child* or *son* who is a disciple, follower, 1 Cor. 4:17; 1 Tim. 1:2; 2 Tim. 1:2; Tit. 1:4; Phlm. 10; 3 Jn. 4; *a child* in virtue of gracious acceptance, Jn. 1:12; 11:52; Rom. 8:16, 21; 1 Jn. 3:1; *a child* in virtue of spiritual conformity, Jn. 8:39; Phil. 2:15; 1 Jn. 3:10; *a child of, one characterized by* some condition or quality, Mt. 11:19; Eph. 2:3; 5:8; 1 Pet. 1:14; 2 Pet. 2:14 [5043] See *children.*

[5452] τεκνοτροφέω *teknotropheō* 1x *to rear a family,* 1 Tim. 5:10* [5044]

[5454] τέκτων *tektōn* 2x *an artisan;* and spc. *one who works with wood, a carpenter,* Mt. 13:55; Mk. 6:3* [5045]

[5455] τέλειος *teleios* 19x *brought to completion; fully accomplished, fully developed,* Jas. 1:4a; *fully realized, thorough,* 1 Jn. 4:18; *complete, entire,* as opposed to what is partial and limited, 1 Cor. 13:10; *full grown of ripe age,* 1 Cor. 14:20; Eph. 4:13; Heb. 5:14; *fully accomplished* in Christian enlightenment, 1 Cor. 2:6; Phil. 3:15; Col. 1:28; *perfect* in some point of character, *without shortcoming* in respect of a certain standard, Mt. 5:48; 19:21; Col. 4:12; Jas. 1:4b; 3:2; *perfect, consummate,* Rom. 12:2; Jas. 1:17, 25; compar. *of higher excellence and efficiency,* Heb. 9:11* [5046] See *end; mature; perfect.*

[5456] τελειότης *teleiotēs* 2x *completeness, perfectness,* Col. 3:14; *ripeness* of knowledge or practice, *maturity,* Heb. 6:1* [5047]

[5457] τελειόω *teleioō* 23x *to execute fully, discharge,* Jn. 4:34; 5:36; 17:4; *to reach the end of, run through, finish,* Lk. 2:43; Acts 20:24; *to consummate, place in a condition of finality,* Heb. 7:19; *to perfect* a person, *advance* a person *to final completeness* of character, Heb. 2:10; 5:9; 7:28; *to perfect* a person, *advance* a person *to a completeness* of its kind, which needs no further provision, Heb. 9:9; 10:1, 14; pass. *to receive fulfillment,* Jn. 19:28; *to be brought to the goal, to reach the end of one's course,* Lk. 13:32; Phil. 3:12; Heb. 11:40; 12:23; *to be fully developed,* 2 Cor. 12:9; Jas. 2:22; 1 Jn. 2:5; 4:12, 17; *to be completely organized, to be closely embodied,* Jn. 17:23 [5048] See *complete; end; fulfill; perfect.*

[5458] τελείως *teleiōs* 1x *perfectly, completely,* 1 Pet. 1:13* [5049]

[5459] τελείωσις *teleiōsis* 2x *a completing; a fulfillment, an accomplishment* of predictions, promised, etc., Lk. 1:45; *finality* of function, *completeness* of operation and effect, Heb. 7:11* [5050]

[5460] τελειωτής *teleiōtēs* 1x *a finisher, one who completes and perfects* a thing; *one who brings through to final attainment, perfecter,* Heb. 12:2* [5051]

[5461] τελεσφορέω *telesphoreō* 1x *to bring to maturity,* as fruits, etc.; met. Lk. 8:14* [5052]

[5462] τελευτάω *teleutaō* 11x *to end, finish, complete;* absol. *to end* [5053] See *die.*

[5463] τελευτή *teleutē* 1x *a finishing, end;* hence, *end* of life, *death, decease,* Mt. 2:15* [5054]

[5464] τελέω *teleō* 28x *to finish, complete, conclude,* an operation, Mt. 11:1; 13:53; 19:1; *to finish* a circuit, Mt. 10:23; *to fulfil, to carry out into full operation,* Rom. 2:27; Gal. 5:16; Jas. 2:8; *to pay* dues, Mt. 17:24; pass. *to be fulfilled, realized,* Lk. 12:50; 18:31; of time, *to be ended, elapse,* Rom. 15:8; 20:3, 5, 7 [5055] See *complete; end.*

[5465] τέλος *telos* 40x *an end attained, consummation; an end, closing act,* Mt. 24:6, 14; 1 Cor. 15:24; *full performance, perfect discharge,* Rom. 10:4; *fulfillment, realization,* Lk. 22:37; *final dealing,* developed *issue,* Jas. 5:11; *issue, final stage,* 1 Cor. 10:11; *issue, result,* Mt. 26:58; Rom. 6:21, 22; 1 Pet. 1:9; antitypical *issue,* 2 Cor. 3:13; practical *issue,* 1 Tim. 1:5; *ultimate destiny,* Phil. 3:19; Heb. 6:8; 1 Pet. 4:17; *a tax* or *dues,* Mt. 17:25; Rom. 13:7; εἰς τέλος, *to the full,* 1 Thess. 2:16; εἰς τέλος, *continually,* Lk. 18:5; εἰς τέλος, μέχρι, ἄχρι τέλους, *throughout,* Mt. 10:22; Mk. 13:13; Jn. 13:1; Heb. 3:6, 14; 6:11; Rev. 2:26 [5056] See *end.*

[5467] τελώνης *telōnēs* 21x *one who farms the public revenues;* in NT *a publican, collector of imposts, revenue officer, tax gatherer,* Mt. 5:46; 9:10, 11; 10:3; Mk. 2:15f.; Lk. 3:12 [5057] See *tax collector.*

[5468] τελώνιον *telōnion* 3x *a custom-house, toll house; collector's office,* Mt. 9:9; Mk. 2:14; Lk. 5:27* [5058]

[5469] τέρας *teras* 16x *a prodigy, portent,* Acts 2:19; *a signal act, wonder, miracle,* Mt. 13:22; Jn. 4:48; Acts 2:43 [5059] See *miracle; wonders.*

[5470] Τέρτιος *Tertios* 1x *Tertius,* pr. name, a helper of Paul, Rom. 16:22* [5060]

[5472] Τέρτυλλος *Tertyllos* 2x *Tertullus,* pr. name, an attorney, Acts 24:1f.* [5061]

[5475] τέσσαρες *tessares* 41x *four,* Mt. 24:31; Mk. 2:3 [5064] See *four.*

[5476] τεσσαρεσκαιδέκατος *tessareskaidekatos* 2x *the fourteenth,* Acts 27:27, 33* [5065]

[5477] τεσσεράκοντα *tesserakonta* 22x *forty,* indecl., Mt. 4:2; Jn. 2:20; Acts 1:3; 23:13, 21; Heb. 3:9; Rev. 11:2; 21:17 [5062] See *forty.*

[5478] τεσσερακονταετής *tesserakontaetēs* 2x *forty years,* Acts 7:23; 13:18* [5063]

[5479] τεταρταῖος *tetartaios* 1x *on the fourth day,* Jn. 11:39* [5066]

[5480] τέταρτος *tetartos* 10x *fourth,* Mt. 14:25; *the fourth part, quarter,* Rev. 6:8 [5067] See *fourth.*

[5481] τετράγωνος *tetragōnos* 1x *four-angled, quadrangular, square,* Rev. 21:16* [5068]

[5482] τετράδιον *tetradion* 1x *a set of four; a detachment of four* men, Acts 12:4* [5069]

[5483] τετρακισχίλιοι *tetrakischilioi* 5x *four thousand,* Mt. 15:38; 16:10; Mk. 8:9, 20; Acts 21:38* [5070]

[5484] τετρακόσιοι *tetrakosioi* 4x *four hundred,* Acts 5:36; 7:6; 13:20; Gal. 3:17* [5071]

[5485] τετράμηνος *tetramēnos* 1x *of four months, four months in duration,* Jn. 4:35* [5072]

[5487] τετραπλοῦς *tetraplous* 1x contracted form of τετραπλόος, *four times (as much), fourfold, quadruple,* Lk. 19:8* [5073]

[5488] τετράπους *tetrapous* 3x *four-footed; quadrupeds,* Acts 10:12; 11:6; Rom. 1:23* [5074]

[5489] τετρααρχέω *tetraarcheō* 3x also spelled τετραρχέω, *be tetrarch,* Lk. 3:1 (3x)* [5075]

[5490] τετραάρχης *tetraarchēs* 4x also spelled τετράρχης, *a tetrarch,* title of a prince, whose rank was lower than a king, Mt. 14:1; Lk. 3:19; 9:7; Acts 13:1* [5076]

[5491] τεφρόω *tephroō* 1x *to reduce to ashes, to consume, destroy,* 2 Pet. 2:6* [5077]

[5492] τέχνη *technē* 3x *art, skill,* Acts 17:29; *an art, trade, craft,* Acts 18:3; Rev. 18:22* [5078]

[5493] τεχνίτης *technitēs* 4x *an artisan; workman, mechanic,* Acts 19:24, 38; Rev. 18:22; *an architect, builder,* Heb. 11:10* [5079]

[5494] τήκω *tēkō* 1x *to dissolve;* pass. *to melt,* 2 Pet. 3:12* [5080]

[5495] τηλαυγῶς *tēlaugōs* 1x *clearly, plainly, distinctly,* Mk. 8:25* [5081]

[5496] τηλικοῦτος *tēlikoutos* 4x *so great, large, important,* 2 Cor. 1:10; Heb. 2:3; Jas. 3:4; Rev. 16:18* [5082]

[5498] τηρέω *tēreō* 70x *to keep watch upon, guard,* Mt. 27:36, 54; 28:4; Acts 12:6; *to watch over* protectively, *guard,* 1 Jn. 5:18; Rev. 16:15; *to mark attentively, to heed,* Rev. 1:3; *to observe* practically, *keep strictly,* Mt. 19:17; 23:3; 28:20; Mk. 7:9; Jn. 8:51; *to preserve, shield,* Jn. 17:15; *to store up, reserve,* Jn. 2:10; 12:7; 1 Pet. 1:4; 2 Pet. 2:4, 9, 17; *to keep in custody,* Acts 12:5; 16:23; *to maintain,* Eph. 4:3; 2 Tim. 4:7; *to keep* in a condition, Jn. 17:11, 12; 1 Cor. 7:37; 2 Cor. 11:9; 1 Tim. 5:22; Jas. 1:27 [5083] See *keep; obey.*

[5499] τήρησις *tērēsis* 3x *a keeping, custody;* meton. *a place of custody, prison, ward,* Acts 4:3; 5:18; met. practical *observance, strict performance,* 1 Cor. 7:19* [5084]

[5500] Τιβεριάς *Tiberias* 3x *Tiberias,* a city of Galilee, built by Herod Antipas, and named in honor of Tiberius, Jn. 6:1, 23; 21:1* [5085]

[5501] Τιβέριος *Tiberios* 1x *Tiberius,* the third Roman emperor, *14-37 A.D.,* Lk. 3:1* [5086]

[5502] τίθημι *tithēmi* 100x by-form of τιθέω, *to place, set, lay,* Mt. 5:15; Mk. 6:56; Lk. 6:48; *to produce* at table, Jn. 2:10; *to deposit, lay,* Mt. 27:60; Lk. 23:53; Acts 3:2; *to lay down,* Lk. 19:21, 22; Jn. 10:11, 15, 17, 18; 1 Jn. 3:16; *to lay aside, put off,* Jn. 13:4; *to allocate, assign,* Mt. 24:51; Lk. 12:46; *to set, appoint,* Jn. 15:16; Acts 13:47; Heb. 1:2; *to render, make,* Mt. 22:44; Rom. 4:17; 1 Cor. 9:18; mid. *to put* in custody, Mt. 14:3; Acts 4:3; *to reserve,* Acts 1:7; *to commit* as a matter of charge, 2 Cor. 5:19; *to set,* with design, in a certain arrangement or position, Acts 20:28; 1 Cor. 12:18, 28; 1 Thess. 5:9; 1 Tim. 1:12; pass. 1 Tim. 2:7; 2 Tim. 1:11; 1 Pet. 2:8

τιθέναι τὰ γόνατα, *to kneel down,* Mk. 15:19; Lk. 22:41; Acts 7:60; 9:40; 20:36; 21:5; τίθεσθαι ἐν τῇ καρδίᾳ, *to lay to heart, ponder,* Lk. 1:66; also, εἰς τὰς καρδίας, Lk. 21:14; *to design, resolve,* Acts 5:4; also, ἐν πνεύματι, Acts 19:21; also, βουλήν, Acts 17:12; τίθεσθαι εἰς τὰ ὦτα, *to give attentive audience to, to listen to retentively,* Lk. 9:44 [5087] See *appoint; lay down; place; put.*

[5503] τίκτω *tiktō* 18x *to bear, bring forth* children, Mt. 1:21, 23; trop. *to bear, produce,* as the earth, *yield,* Heb. 6:7; met. *to give birth to,* Jas. 1:15 [5088] See *bring forth; give birth; produce.*

[5504] τίλλω *tillō* 3x *to pull, pluck off,* Mt. 12:1; Mk. 2:23; Lk. 6:1* [5089]

[5505] Τιμαῖος *Timaios* 1x *Timaeus,* pr. name, Mk. 10:46* [5090]

[5506] τιμάω *timaō* 21x *to estimate in respect of worth; to hold in estimation, respect, honor, reverence,* Mt. 15:4, 5, 8; 19:19; Mk. 7:10; *to honor* with reverent service, Jn. 5:23 (4x); 8:49; *to treat with honor, manifest consideration towards,* Acts 28:10; *to treat graciously, visit with marks of favor,* Jn. 12:26; mid. *to price,* Mt. 27:9 [5091] See *honor; value.*

[5507] τιμή *timē* 41x *a pricing, estimate of worth; price, value,* Mt. 27:9; *price* paid, Mt. 27:6; meton. *a thing of price,* and collectively, *precious things,* Rev. 21:24, 26; *preciousness,* 1 Pet. 2:7; substantial *value,* real *worth,* Col. 2:23; *careful regard, honor, state of honor, dignity,* Rom. 9:21; Heb. 5:4; *honor* conferred, *observance, veneration,* Rom. 2:7, 10; 12:10; *mark of favor and consideration,* Acts 28:10, *honorarium, compensation,* 1 Tim. 5:7 [5092] See *honor; price; respect; value.*

[5508] τίμιος *timios* 13x *precious, costly, of great price,* 1 Cor. 3:12; Rev. 18:12; *precious, dear, valuable,* Acts 20:24; 1 Pet. 1:7, 19; *honored, esteemed, respected,* Acts 5:34; Heb. 13:4 [5093] See *honorable; precious; valuable.*

[5509] τιμιότης *timiotēs* 1x *preciousness, costliness;* meton. *precious things, valuable merchandise,* Rev. 18:19* [5094]

[5510] Τιμόθεος *Timotheos* 24x *Timotheus, Timothy,* pr. name, *son of Eunice, traveling companion of Paul,* Acts 16:1; Rom. 16:21; 1 Cor. 4:17; 2 Cor. 1:1; Phil. 1:1; Col. 1:1; 1 Thess. 1:1; 1 Tim. 1:2, 18; 6:20; 2 Tim. 1:2 [5095]

[5511] Τίμων *Timōn* 1x *Timon,* pr. name, Acts 6:5* [5096]

[5512] τιμωρέω *timōreō* 2x *to avenge,* someone; in NT *to punish,* Acts 22:5; 26:11* [5097]

[5513] τιμωρία *timōria* 1x *punishment,* Heb. 10:29* [5098]

[5514] τίνω *tinō* 1x *to pay; to pay* a penalty, *incur* punishment, 2 Thess. 1:9* [5099]

[5515] τίς *tis* 555x *Who? What?* Mt. 3:7; 5:13; 19:27; equivalent to πότερος, *Whether? which* of two things? Mt. 9:5; Mk. 2:9; Phil. 1:22; *Why?* Mt. 8:26; 9:11, 14; τί ὅτι, *Why is it that?* Mk. 2:16; Jn. 14:22; *What?* as an emphatic interrogative, Acts 26:8; τί, *How very!* Mt. 7:14; in indirect question, Mt. 10:11 [5101]

[5516] τις *tis* 534x enclitic, indefinite pronoun, *a certain one, someone,* Mt. 12:47; pl. *some, certain, several,* Lk. 8:2; Acts 9:19; 2 Pet. 3:16; *one, a person,* Mt. 12:29; Lk. 14:8; Jn. 6:50; combined with the name of an individual, *one,* Mk. 15:21; *as it were in a manner, a kind of,* Heb. 10:27; Jas. 1:18; *any* whatever, Mt. 8:28; Lk. 11:36; Rom. 8:39; τις, *somebody* of consequence, Acts 5:36; τι, *something* of consequence, Gal. 2:6; 6:3; τι, *anything* at all, *anything* worth account, 1 Cor. 3:7; 10:19; τι *at all,* Phil. 3:15; Phlm. 18 [5100]

[5517] Τίτιος *Titios* 1x *Titius,* pr. name, Acts 18:7* [2459]

[5518] τίτλος *titlos* 2x *an inscribed roll, superscription,* Jn. 19:19, 20* [5102]

[5519] Τίτος *Titos* 13x *Titus,* pr. name, friend and helper of Paul, 2 Cor. 2:13; 7:6; Gal. 2:1; 2 Tim. 4:10; Tit. 1:4 [5103]

[5521] τοιγαροῦν *toigaroun* 2x *well then, so then, wherefore, for that reason,* 1 Thess. 4:8; Heb. 12:1* [5105]

[5524] τοιόσδε *toiosde* 1x *such as this; such as follows,* 2 Pet. 1:17* [5107]

[5525] τοιοῦτος *toioutos* 57x *such, such like, of this kind* or *sort,* Mt. 18:5; 19:14; *such, so great,* Mt. 9:8; Mk. 6:2; ὁ τοιοῦτος, *such a fellow,* Acts 22:22; also, *the one alluded to,* 1 Cor. 1:5; 2 Cor. 2:6, 7; 12:2, 3, 5 [5108]

[5526] τοῖχος *toichos* 1x *a wall* of a building, as distinct from a city wall or fortification (τεῖχος) Acts 23:3* [5109]

[5527] τόκος *tokos* 2x *a bringing forth; offspring;* met. *produce* of money lent, *interest, usury,* Mt. 25:27; Lk. 19:23* [5110]

[5528] τολμάω *tolmaō* 16x *to assume resolution* to do a thing, Mk. 15:43; Rom. 5:7; Phil. 1:14; *to make up the mind,* 2 Cor. 10:12; *to dare,* Acts 5:13; 7:32; *to presume,* Mt. 22:46; Mk. 12:34; Lk. 20:40; Jn. 21:12; Rom. 15:18; Jude 9; *to have the face,* 1 Cor. 6:1; absol. *to assume a bold bearing, courageous,* 2 Cor. 10:2; 11:21* [5111] See *(have) courage; dare.*

[5529] τολμηρός *tolmēros* 1x *bold, daring*, Rom. 15:15* [5112]

[5532] τολμητής *tolmētēs* 1x *one who is bold;* in a bad sense, *a presumptuous, audacious person,* 2 Pet. 2:10* [5113]

[5533] τομός *tomos* 1x *cutting, sharp, sharper,* Heb. 4:12* [5114]

[5534] τόξον *toxon* 1x *a bow,* Rev. 6:2* [5115]

[5535] τοπάζιον *topazion* 1x *a topaz,* a gem of a yellowish color, different from the modern topaz, Rev. 21:20* [5116]

[5536] τόπος *topos* 94x *a place, locality,* Mt. 12:43; Lk. 6:17; *a* limited *spot* or *ground,* Mt. 24:15; 27:33; Jn. 4:20; Acts 6:13; *a* precise *spot* or *situation,* Mt. 28:6; Mk. 16:6; Lk. 14:9; *a dwelling place, abode, mansion, dwelling, seat,* Jn. 14:2, 3; Acts 4:31; *a place* of ordinary deposit, Mt. 26:52; *a place, passage* in a book, Lk. 4:17; *place* occupied, *room, space,* Lk. 2:7; 14:9, 22; *place, opportunity,* Acts 25:16; Heb. 12:17; *place, condition, position,* 1 Cor. 14:16 [5117] See *district; place; region.*

[5537] τοσοῦτος *tosoutos* 20x *so great, so much,* Mt. 8:10; 15:33; *so long,* of time, Jn. 14:9; pl. *so many,* Mt. 15:33 [5118]

[5538] τότε *tote* 160x *then, at that time,* Mt. 2:17; 3:5; 11:20; *then,* Mt. 12:29; 13:26; 25:31; ἀπὸ τότε, *from that time,* Mt. 4:17; 16:21; ὁ τότε, *which then was,* 2 Pet. 3:6 [5119]

[5543] τράγος *tragos* 4x *a male goat,* Heb. 9:12, 13, 19; 10:4* [5131]

[5544] τράπεζα *trapeza* 15x *a table, an eating table,* Mt. 15:27; Mk. 7:28; Heb. 9:2; by impl. *a meal, feast,* Rom. 11:9; 1 Cor. 10:21; *a table* or *counter* of a money changer, Mt. 21:12; *a bank,* Lk. 19:23; by impl. pl. *money matters,* Acts 6:2 [5132] See *table.*

[5545] τραπεζίτης *trapezitēs* 1x *a money changer, broker, banker,* who exchanges or loans money for a premium, Mt. 25:27* [5133]

[5546] τραῦμα *trauma* 1x *a wound,* Lk. 10:34* [5134]

[5547] τραυματίζω *traumatizō* 2x *to wound,* Lk. 20:12; Acts 19:16* [5135]

[5548] τραχηλίζω *trachēlizō* 1x pr. *to grip the neck; to bend the neck back,* so as to make bare or expose the throat, as in slaughtering animals, etc.; met. *to lay bare in view,* Heb. 4:13* [5136]

[5549] τράχηλος *trachēlos* 7x *the neck,* Mt. 18:6; Mk. 9:42; Lk. 15:20; 17:2; ἐπιθεῖναι ζυγὸν ἐπὶ τὸν τράχηλον, *to put a yoke upon the neck* of someone, met. *to bind to a burdensome observance,* Acts 15:10; 20:37; ὑποτιθέναι τὸν τράχηλον, *to lay down one's neck* under the axe of the executioner, *to imperil one's life,* Rom. 16:4* [5137]

[5550] τραχύς *trachus* 2x *rough, rugged, uneven,* Lk. 3:5; εἰς τραχεῖς τόπους, *on a rocky shore,* Acts 27:29* [5138]

[5551] Τραχωνῖτις *Trachōnitis* 1x *Trachonitis,* part of the tetrarchy of Herod Antipas, the north-easternmost habitable district east of the Jordan, Lk. 3:1* [5139]

[5552] τρεῖς *treis* 68x *three,* Mt. 12:40. The frequency count does not include its occurrence in the name Τριῶν ταβερνῶν in Acts 28:15 (5553) [5140] See *three.*

[5553] Τρει ς ταβέρναι *treis tabernai* 1x *Three Taverns,* the name of a station on the Appian Way in Acts 28:15 (Τριῶν ταβερνῶν). The Latin *taberna* is an inn or shop [5992]

[5554] τρέμω *tremō* 3x *to tremble, be agitated from fear,* Mk. 5:33; Lk. 8:47; by impl. *to fear, be afraid,* 2 Pet. 2:10* [5141]

[5555] τρέφω *trephō* 9x *to nourish; to feed, support, cherish, provide for,* [5142]

[5556] τρέχω *trechō* 20x *to run,* Mt. 27:48; 28:8; *to run a race,* 1 Cor. 9:24; met. 1 Cor. 9:24, 26; Heb. 12:1; in NT *to run* a certain course of conduct, Gal. 5:7; *to run* a course of exertion, Rom. 9:16; Gal. 2:2; Phil. 2:16; *to run, to progress freely, to advance rapidly,* 2 Thess. 3:1 [5143] See *run.*

[5557] τρῆμα *trēma* 1x *an aperture, hole, eye of a needle,* Lk. 18:25* [5169]

[5558] τριάκοντα *triakonta* 11x *thirty,* indecl., Mt. 13:8, 23; Mk. 4:8; Lk. 3:23 [5144] See *thirty.*

[5559] τριακόσιοι *triakosioi* 2x *three hundred,* Mk. 14:5; Jn. 12:5* [5145]

[5560] τρίβολος *tribolos* 2x pr. *three-pronged; a thistle, thorn,* Mt. 7:16; Heb. 6:8* [5146]

[5561] τρίβος *tribos* 3x *a beaten track; a road, highway,* Mt. 3:3; Mk. 1:3; Lk. 3:4* [5147]

[5562] τριετία *trietia* 1x *the space of three years,* Acts 20:31* [5148]

[5563] τρίζω *trizō* 1x *to creak, grating sound; to gnash, grind* the teeth, Mk. 9:18* [5149]

[5564] τρίμηνος *trimēnos* 1x *the space of three months,* Heb. 11:23* [5150]

[5565] τρίς *tris* 12x *three times, thrice,* Mt. 26:34, 75; ἐπὶ τρίς, *to the extent of thrice, as many as three times,* Acts 10:16; 11:10 [5151] See *three times.*

[5566] τρίστεγον *tristegon* 1x *the third floor, third story,* Acts 20:9* [5152]

[5567] τρισχίλιοι *trischilioi* 1x *three thousand,* Acts 2:41* [5153]

[5568] τρίτον *triton* 8x the accusative singular neuter form of *tritos* (*5569*) used adverbially *the third time, for the third time,* Mk. 14:41; Lk. 23:22 [5154] See *third.*

[5569] τρίτος *tritos* 48x *third,* Mt. 20:3; 27:64; ἐκ τρίτου, *the third time, for the third time,* Mt. 26:44; τὸ τρίτον, sc. μέρος, *the third part,* Rev. 8:7, 12; [5154] See *third.*

[5570] τρίχινος *trichinos* 1x *of hair, made of hair,* Rev. 6:12* [5155]

[5571] τρόμος *tromos* 5x pr. *a trembling, quaking; trembling* from fear, *fear, terror, agitation of mind,* Mk. 16:8; *anxious,* under solemn responsibility, 1 Cor. 2:3; *reverence, veneration, awe,* 2 Cor. 7:15; Eph. 6:5; Phil. 2:12* [5156]

[5572] τροπή *tropē* 1x *a turning round; a turning back, change, mutation,* Jas. 1:17* [5157]

[5573] τρόπος *tropos* 13x *a turn; mode, manner, way,* Jude 7; ὃν τρόπον, + καθ᾽ ὃν τρόπον, *in which manner, as, even as,* Mt. 23:37; Acts 15:11; κατὰ μηδένα τρόπον, *in no way, by no means,* 2 Thess. 2:3; ἐν παντὶ τρόπῳ, and παντὶ τρόπῳ *in every way, by every means,* Phil. 1:18; 2 Thess. 3:16; *turn* of mind or action, *habit, disposition,* Heb. 13:5 [5158]

[5574] τροποφορέω *tropophoreō* 1x *to bear with the disposition, manners, and conduct of* any one, *to put up with,* Acts 13:18* [5159]

[5575] τροφή *trophē* 16x *nourishment, food,* Mt. 3:4; Lk. 12:23; Jn. 4:8; Acts 9:19; Jas. 2:15; *provision,* Mt. 24:45; *sustenance, maintenance,* Mt. 10:10; met. *nourishment* of the mind, *of spiritual nourishment,* Heb. 5:12, 14 [5160] See *food.*

[5576] Τρόφιμος *Trophimos* 3x *Trophimus,* pr. name, of Ephesus, a friend of Paul, Acts 20:4; 21:29; 2 Tim. 4:20* [5161]

[5577] τροφός *trophos* 1x *a nurse,* 1 Thess. 2:7* [5162]

[5579] τροχιά *trochia* 1x *a track, way, path,* met. Heb. 12:13* [5163]

[5580] τροχός *trochos* 1x pr. *a runner; anything spherical, a wheel; drift, course,* with which signification the word is usually written τρόχος, Jas. 3:6* [5164]

[5581] τρύβλιον *tryblion* 2x *a bowl, dish,* Mt. 26:23; Mk. 14:20* [5165]

[5582] τρυγάω *trygaō* 3x *to harvest, gather,* fruits, and spc. grapes, Lk. 6:44; Rev. 14:18, 19* [5166]

[5583] τρυγών *trygōn* 1x *a turtledove,* Lk. 2:24* [5167]

[5584] τρυμαλιά *trymalia* 1x *a hole, perforation; eye* of a needle, Mk. 10:25* [5168]

[5585] τρύπημα *trypēma* 1x *a hole; eye* of a needle, Mt. 19:24* [5169]

[5586] Τρύφαινα *Tryphaina* 1x *Tryphaena,* pr. name, Rom. 16:12* [5170]

[5587] τρυφάω *tryphaō* 1x *to live self-indulgently, luxuriously,* Jas. 5:5* [5171]

[5588] τρυφή *tryphē* 2x *indulgent living, luxury,* Lk. 7:25; 2 Pet. 2:13* [5172]

[5589] Τρυφῶσα *Tryphōsa* 1x *Tryphosa,* pr. name, Rom. 16:12* [5173]

[5590] Τρῳάς *Trōias* 6x *Troas,* a city on the coast of Phrygia, near the site of ancient Troy, Acts 16:8, 11; 20:5f.; 2 Cor. 2:12; 2 Tim. 4:13* [5174]

[5592] τρώγω *trōgō* 6x pr. *to crunch; to eat,* Mt. 24:38; from the Hebrew, ἄρτον τρώγειν, *to take food, partake of a meal,* Jn. 6:54, 56-58; 13:18* [5176]

[5593] τυγχάνω *tynchanō* 12x *to hit* an object; *to attain to, to obtain, acquire, enjoy,* Lk. 20:35; Acts 24:2; 26:22; 27:3; 2 Tim. 2:10; Heb. 8:6; 11:35; intrans. *to happen, fall out, chance; common, ordinary,* Acts 19:11; 28:2; as an adv., *it may be, perchance, perhaps,* 1 Cor. 16:6; εἰ τύχοι, *as it so happens, as the case may be,* 1 Cor. 14:10; 15:37* [5177] See *happen; turn out.*

[5594] τυμπανίζω *tympanizō* 1x pr. *to beat a drum; to drum upon;* in NT *to torture, beat to death with rods and clubs,* Heb. 11:35* [5178]

[5595] τυπικῶς *typikōs* 1x *figuratively, typically,* 1 Cor. 10:11* [5179]

[5596] τύπος *typos* 15x pr. *an impress; a print, mark,* of a wound inflicted, Jn. 20:25; *a delineation; an image, statue,* Acts 7:43; *a formula, scheme,* Rom. 6:17; *form,* Acts 23:25; *a figure, counterpart,* 1 Cor. 10:6; *an* anticipative *figure, type,* Rom. 5:14; *a model pattern,* Acts 7:44; Heb. 8:5; *a* moral *pattern,* Phil. 3:17; 1 Thess. 1:7; 2 Thess. 3:9; 1 Tim. 4:12; Tit. 2:7; 1 Pet. 5:3* [5179] See *example; model; pattern.*

[5597] τύπτω *typtō* 13x *to beat, strike, smite,* Mt. 24:49; 27:30; *to beat* the breast, as expressive of grief or strong emotion, Lk. 18:13; 23:48; in NT met. *to wound* or *shock* the conscience of any one, 1 Cor. 8:12; from the Hebrew, *to smite* with evil, *punish,* Acts 23:3 [5180] See *beat; strike.*

[5598] Τύραννος *Tyrannos* 1x *Tyrannus,* an Ephesian, Acts 19:9* [5181]

[5601] Τύριος *Tyrios* 1x *a Tyrian, an inhabitant of Tyre,* Acts 12:20* [5183]

[5602] Τύρος *Tyros* 11x *Tyre,* a celebrated and wealthy commercial city of Phoenicia, Mt. 11:21; 15:21; Mk. 7:24; Acts 21:3, 7 [5184]

[5603] τυφλός *typhlos* 50x *blind,* Mt. 9:27, 28; 11:5; 12:22; met. mentally *blind,* Mt. 15:14; 23:16 [5185] See *blind.*

[5604] τυφλόω *typhloō* 3x *to blind, render blind;* met. Jn. 12:40; 2 Cor. 4:4; 1 Jn. 2:11* [5186]

[5605] τυφόω *typhoō* 3x *to besmoke;* met. *to possess with the fumes* of conceit; pass. *to be demented with conceit, puffed up,* 1 Tim. 3:6; 6:4; 2 Tim. 3:4; 1 Tim. 6:4* [5187]

[5606] τύφω *typhō* 1x *to raise a smoke;* pass. *to emit smoke, smoke, smoulder,* Mt. 12:20* [5188]

[5607] τυφωνικός *typhōnikos* 1x *stormy, tempestuous;* with ἄνεμος it means *hurricane, typhoon, whirlwind,* Acts 27:14* [5189]

[5608] Τυχικός *Tychikos* 5x *Tychicus,* pr. name, a friend or companion of Paul, Acts 20:4; Eph. 6:21; Col. 4:7; 2 Tim. 4:12; Tit. 3:12; Eph. subscr.; Col. subscr.* [5190]

[5610] ὑακίνθινος *hyakinthinos* 1x *hyacinthine, resembling the hyacinth in color, dark blue,* Rev. 9:17* [5191]

[5611] ὑάκινθος *hyakinthos* 1x *a hyacinth,* a gem resembling the color of the *hyacinth flower, dark blue,* Rev. 21:20* [5192]

[5612] ὑάλινος *hyalinos* 3x *made of glass; glassy, translucent,* Rev. 4:6; 15:2* [5193]

[5613] ὕαλος *hyalos* 2x *a transparent stone, crystal;* also, *glass,* Rev. 21:18, 21* [5194]

[5614] ὑβρίζω *hybrizō* 5x *to run riot;* trans. *to outrage, to treat in an arrogant* or *spiteful manner, scoff at, insult,* Mt. 22:6; Lk. 11:45; 18:32; Acts 14:5; 1 Thess. 2:2* [5195]

[5615] ὕβρις *hybris* 3x *insolence; shame, insult, outrage,* 2 Cor. 12:10; *damage* by sea, Acts 27:10, 21* [5196]

[5616] ὑβριστής *hybristēs* 2x *an overbearing, violent person,* Rom. 1:30; 1 Tim. 1:13* [5197]

[5617] ὑγιαίνω *hygiainō* 12x *to be sound, in health,* Lk. 5:31; 7:10; *to be safe and sound,* Lk. 15:27; 3 Jn. 2; met. *to be healthful* or *sound* in faith, doctrine, etc., Tit. 1:9, 13; 2:1, 2; *sound, pure, uncorrupted,* 1 Tim. 1:10; 6:3; 2 Tim. 1:13; 4:3* [5198] See *(be) healthy; (be) sound.*

[5618] ὑγιής *hygiēs* 11x *sound, in health,* Mt. 12:13; 15:31; met. of doctrine, *sound, pure, wholesome,* Tit. 2:8 [5199] See *well; whole.*

[5619] ὑγρός *hygros* 1x pr. *wet, moist, humid;* used of a tree, *full of sap, fresh, green,* Lk. 23:31* [5200]

[5620] ὑδρία *hydria* 3x *a water pot pitcher,* Jn. 2:6, 7; *a bucket, pail,* Jn. 4:28* [5201]

[5621] ὑδροποτέω *hydropoteō* 1x *to be only a water drinker,* 1 Tim. 5:23* [5202]

[5622] ὑδρωπικός *hydrōpikos* 1x *dropsical, suffering from dropsey,* Lk. 14:2* [5203]

[5623] ὕδωρ *hydōr* 76x *water,* Mt. 3:11, 16; 14:28, 29; 17:15; Jn. 5:3, 4, 7; *watery fluid,* Jn. 19:34; ὕδωρ ζῶν, *living water, fresh flowing water,* Jn. 4:11; met. of spiritual refreshment, Jn. 4:10; 7:38 [5204] See *water.*

[5624] ὑετός *hyetos* 5x *rain,* Acts 14:17; 28:2; Heb. 6:7; Jas. 5:18; Rev. 11:6* [5205]

[5625] υἱοθεσία *hyiothesia* 5x *adoption, a placing in the condition of a son,* Rom. 8:15, 23; 9:4; Gal. 4:5; Eph. 1:5* [5206] See *adoption.*

[5626] υἱός *hyios* 377x *a son,* Mt. 1:21, 25; 7:9; 13:55 freq.; *a* legitimate *son,* Heb. 12:8; *a son* artificially constituted, Acts 7:21; Heb. 11:24; *a descendant,* Mt. 1:1, 20; Mk. 12:35; in NT *the young* of an animal, Mt. 21:5; *a* spiritual *son* in respect of conversion or discipleship, 1 Pet. 5:13; from the Hebrew, *a disciple,* perhaps, Mt. 12:27; *a son* as implying connection in respect of membership, service, resemblance, manifestation, destiny, etc., Mt. 8:12; 9:15; 13:38; 23:15; Mk. 2:29; 3:17; Lk. 5:34; 10:6; 16:8; 20:34, 36; Jn. 17:12; Acts 2:25; 4:36; 13:10; Eph. 2:2; 5:6; Col. 3:6; 1 Thess. 5:5; 2 Thess. 2:3; υἱὸς θεοῦ, κ.τ.λ., *son of God* in respect of divinity, Mt. 4:3, 6; 14:33; Rom. 1:4; also, in respect of privilege and character, Mt. 5:9, 45; Lk. 6:35; Rom. 8:14, 19; 9:26; Gal. 3:26; ὁ υἱὸς τοῦ θεοῦ, κ.τ.λ., a title of the Messiah, Mt. 26:63; Mk. 3:11; 14:61; Jn. 1:34, 50; 20:31; υἱὸς ἀνθρώπου, *a son of man, a man,* Mk. 3:28; Eph. 3:5; Heb. 2:6; ὁ υἱὸς τοῦ ἀνθρώπου, a title of the Messiah, Mt. 8:20 freq.; as also, ὁ υἱὸς Δαβίδ, (Δαυὶδ) Mt. 12:23 [5207] See *child; son.*

[5627] ὕλη *hylē* 1x *wood, a forest;* in NT *firewood, a mass of fuel,* Jas. 3:5* [5208]

[7007] ὑμεῖς *hymeis* 1,840x plural of σύ

[5628] Ὑμέναιος *Hymenaios* 2x *Hymenaeus,* pr. name, 1 Tim. 1:20; 2 Tim. 2:17* [5211]

[5629] ὑμέτερος *hymeteros* 11x *your, yours,* Lk. 6:20; Jn. 7:6; 15:20 [5212]

[5630] ὑμνέω *hymneō* 4x *to hymn, praise, celebrate* or *worship with hymns,* Acts 16:25; Heb. 2:12; absol. *to sing a hymn,* Mt. 26:30; Mk. 14:26* [5214]

[5631] ὕμνος *hymnos* 2x *a song; a hymn, song of praise* to God, Eph. 5:19; Col. 3:16* [5215]

[5632] ὑπάγω *hypagō* 79x *to lead* or *bring under; to lead* or *bring from under; draw on* or *away;* in NT intrans. *to go away, depart,* Mt. 8:4, 13; 9:6; ὕπαγε ὀπίσω μου, *Get behind me! Away! Begone!* Mt. 4:10; 16:23; *to go,* Mt. 5:41; Lk. 12:58; *to depart* life, Mt. 26:24 [5217] See *depart; go.*

[5633] ὑπακοή *hypakoē* 15x *a hearkening to; obedience,* Rom. 5:19; 6:16; 1 Pet. 1:14; *submissiveness,* Rom. 16:19; 2 Cor. 7:15; *submission,* Rom. 1:5; 15:18; 16:26; 2 Cor. 10:5; Heb. 5:8; 1 Pet. 1:2, 22; *compliance,* Phlm. 21 [5218] See *obedience.*

[5634] ὑπακούω *hypakouō* 21x *to give ear; to listen,* Acts 12:13; *to obey,* Mt. 8:27; Mk. 1:27; in NT *to render submissive acceptance,* Acts 6:7; Rom. 6:17; 2 Thess. 1:8; Heb. 5:9; absol. *to be submissive,* Phil. 2:12 [5219] See *obey.*

[5635] ὕπανδρος *hypandros* 1x *bound to a man, married,* Rom. 7:2* [5220]

[5636] ὑπαντάω *hypantaō* 10x *to meet,* Mt. 8:28; Lk. 8:27; Jn. 11:20, 30; 12:18 [5221] See *oppose.*

[5637] ὑπάντησις *hypantēsis* 3x *a meeting, act of meeting,* Mt. 8:34; 25:1; Jn. 12:13* [5222]

[5638] ὕπαρξις *hyparxis* 2x *goods possessed, substance, property,* Acts 2:45; Heb. 10:34* [5223]

[5639] ὑπάρχω *hyparchō* 60x *to begin; to come into existence; to exist; to be, subsist,* Acts 19:40; 28:18; *to be in possession, to belong,* Acts 3:6; 4:37; *goods, possessions, property,* Mt. 19:21; Lk. 8:3; *to be,* Lk. 7:25; 8:41 [5224, 5225] See *be; exist; possess, possessions.*

[5640] ὑπείκω *hypeikō* 1x *to yield, give way;* absol. *to be submissive,* Heb. 13:17* [5226]

[5641] ὑπεναντίος *hypenantios* 2x *over against; contrast, adverse,* Col. 2:14; ὁ ὑπεναντίος, *an opponent, adversary,* Heb. 10:27* [5227]

[5642] ὑπέρ *hyper* 150x (1) gen., *above, over;* met. *in behalf of,* Mt. 5:44; Mk. 9:40; Jn. 17:19; *instead of* beneficially, Phlm. 13; *in maintenance of,* Rom. 15:8; *for the furtherance of,* Jn. 11:4; 2 Cor. 1:6, 8; *for the realization of,* Phil. 2:13; equivalent to περί, *about, concerning,* with the further signification of interest or concern in the subject, Acts 5:41; Rom. 9:27; 2 Cor. 5:12; 8:23; 2 Thess. 2:1.

(2) acc., *over, beyond;* met. *beyond, more than,* Mt. 10:37; 2 Cor. 1:8; used after comparative terms, Lk. 16:8; 2 Cor. 12:13; Heb. 4:12.

(3) in NT as an adv., *in a higher degree, in fuller measure,* 2 Cor. 11:23 [5228]

[5643] ὑπεραίρω *hyperairō* 3x *to raise* or *lift up above* or *over;* mid. *to lift up one's self;* met. *to be* *over-elated,* 2 Cor. 12:7 (2x); *to bear one's self arrogantly, to rear a haughty front,* 2 Thess. 2:4* [5229]

[5644] ὑπέρακμος *hyperakmos* 1x *past the bloom of life, past one's prime,* 1 Cor. 7:36* [5230]

[5645] ὑπεράνω *hyperanō* 3x can function as an improper prep., *above, over, far above;* of place, Eph. 4:10; Heb. 9:5; of rank, dignity, Eph. 1:21* [5231]

[5647] ὑπεραυξάνω *hyperauxanō* 1x *to increase exceedingly,* 2 Thess. 1:3* [5232]

[5648] ὑπερβαίνω *hyperbainō* 1x *to overstep; to wrong, transgress,* 1 Thess. 4:6* [5233]

[5649] ὑπερβαλλόντως *hyperballontōs* 1x *exceedingly, above measure,* 2 Cor. 11:23* [5234]

[5650] ὑπερβάλλω *hyperballō* 5x pr. *to cast* or *throw over* or *beyond, to overshoot;* met. *to surpass, excel; surpassing,* 2 Cor. 3:10; 9:14; Eph. 1:19; 2:7; 3:19* [5235]

[5651] ὑπερβολή *hyperbolē* 8x pr. *a throwing beyond, an overshooting; extraordinary amount* or *character, transcendency, excess,* 2 Cor. 12:7; 4:7; καθ᾿ ὑπερβολήν, adverbially, *exceedingly, extremely,* Rom. 7:13; 2 Cor. 1:8; Gal. 1:13; *a far better way,* 1 Cor. 12:31; *beyond all measure,* 2 Cor. 4:17* [5236]

[5654] ὑπερέκεινα *hyperekeina* 1x *BAGD* list as an adverb used with the gen., others list as an improper prep., *beyond,* 2 Cor. 10:16* [5238]

[5655] ὑπερεκπερισσοῦ *hyperekperissou* 3x *in over abundance; beyond all measure, superabundantly,* Eph. 3:20; 1 Thess. 3:10; 5:13* [5240]

[5657] ὑπερεκτείνω *hyperekteinō* 1x *to overextend, overstretch,* 2 Cor. 10:14* [5239]

[5658] ὑπερεκχύννω *hyperekchunnō* 1x *to pour out above measure* or *in excess;* pass. *to run over, overflow,* Lk. 6:38* [5240]

[5659] ὑπερεντυγχάνω *hyperentynchanō* 1x *to intercede for,* Rom. 8:26* [5241]

[5660] ὑπερέχω *hyperechō* 5x *to hold above;* intrans. *to stand out above, to overtop;* met. *to surpass, excel,* Phil. 2:3; 4:7; τὸ ὑπερέχον, *excellence, preeminence,* Phil. 3:8; *to be higher, superior,* Rom. 13:1; 1 Pet. 2:13* [5242]

[5661] ὑπερηφανία *hyperēphania* 1x *haughtiness, arrogance,* Mk. 7:22* [5243]

[5662] ὑπερήφανος *hyperēphanos* 5x *assuming, haughty, arrogant,* Lk. 1:51; Rom. 1:30; 2 Tim. 3:2; Jas. 4:6; 1 Pet. 5:5* [5244]

[5663] ὑπερλίαν *hyperlian* 2x *in the highest degree, preeminently, especially, superlatively,* 2 Cor. 11:5; 12:11* [5244]

[5664] ὑπερνικάω *hypernikaō* 1x *to overpower in victory; to be abundantly victorious, prevail mightily,* Rom. 8:37* [5245]

[5665] ὑπέρογκος *hyperonkos* 2x pr. *swollen, overgrown;* of language, *swelling, pompous, boastful,* 2 Pet. 2:18; Jude 16* [5246]

[5666] ὑπεροράω *hyperoraō* 1x *overlook, disregard,* Acts 17:30* [5237]

[5667] ὑπεροχή *hyperochē* 2x *prominence;* met., *excellence, rare quality,* 1 Cor. 2:1; *eminent station, authority,* 1 Tim. 2:2* [5247]

[5668] ὑπερπερισσεύω *hyperperisseuō* 2x *to superabound; to abound still more,* Rom. 5:20; mid. *to be abundantly filled, overflow,* 2 Cor. 7:4* [5248]

[5669] ὑπερπερισσῶς *hyperperissōs* 1x *superabundantly, most vehemently, above all measure,* Mk. 7:37* [5249]

[5670] ὑπερπλεονάζω *hyperpleonazō* 1x *to superabound, be in exceeding abundance, over exceed,* 1 Tim. 1:14* [5250]

[5671] ὑπερυψόω *hyperypsoō* 1x *to exalt supremely,* Phil. 2:9* [5251]

[5672] ὑπερφρονέω *hyperphroneō* 1x *to have lofty thoughts, be elated, haughty,* Rom. 12:3* [5252]

[5673] ὑπερῷον *hyperōon* 4x *the upper part of a house, upper room,* or *chamber,* Acts 1:13; 9:37, 39; 20:8* [5253]

[5674] ὑπέχω *hypechō* 1x pr. *to hold under; to render, undergo, suffer,* Jude 7* [5254]

[5675] ὑπήκοος *hypēkoos* 3x *giving ear; obedient, submissive,* Acts 7:39; 2 Cor. 2:9; Phil. 2:8* [5255]

[5676] ὑπηρετέω *hypēreteō* 3x *to subserve,* Acts 13:36; *to relieve, supply,* Acts 20:34; *to render service, be helpful,* Acts 24:23* [5256]

[5677] ὑπηρέτης *hypēretēs* 20x pr. *an under-rower, a rower, one of a ship's crew; a minister, attendant, servant; an attendant* on a magistrate, *officer,* Mt. 5:25; *an attendant* or *officer* of the Sanhedrin, Mt. 26:58; *an attendant,* or *servant* of a synagogue, Lk.

4:20; *a minister, attendant, assistant* in any work, Lk. 1:2; Jn. 18:36 [5257] See *guard; minister; official.*

[5678] ὕπνος *hypnos* 6x *sleep,* Mt. 1:24; Lk. 9:32; Jn. 11:13; Acts 20:9; met. spiritual *sleep,* religious *slumber,* Rom. 13:11* [5258]

[5679] ὑπό *hypo* 220x (1) gen., *under;* hence, used to express influence, causation, agency; *by,* Mt. 1:22 freq.; *by the agency of, at the hands of,* 2 Cor. 11:24; Heb. 12:3.

(2) acc., *under,* with the idea of motion associated, Mt. 5:15; *under,* Jn. 1:49; 1 Cor. 10:1; *under* subjection to, Rom. 6:14; 1 Tim. 6:1; of time, *at, about,* Acts 5:21 [5259]

[5680] ὑποβάλλω *hypoballō* 1x *to cast under;* met. *to suggest, instigate,* Acts 6:11* [5260]

[5681] ὑπογραμμός *hypogrammos* 1x pr. *a copy to write after;* met. *an example for imitation, pattern,* 1 Pet. 2:21* [5261]

[5682] ὑπόδειγμα *hypodeigma* 6x *a token, intimation; an example, model,* proposed for imitation or admonition, Jn. 13:15; Heb. 4:11; Jas. 5:10; 2 Pet. 2:6; *a copy,* Heb. 8:5; 9:23* [5262] See *copy; example.*

[5683] ὑποδείκνυμι *hypodeiknymi* 6x also spelled ὑποδεικνύω, *to indicate,* Acts 20:35; *to intimate, suggest, show, prove,* Mt. 3:7; Lk. 3:7; 6:47; 12:5; Acts 9:16* [5263]

[5685] ὑποδέχομαι *hypodechomai* 4x *to give reception to; to receive as a guest, welcome, entertain,* Lk. 10:38; 19:6; Acts 17:7; Jas. 2:25* [5264]

[5686] ὑποδέω *hypodeō* 3x *to bind under,* mid. *to bind under one's self, put on one's own feet,* Acts 12:8; *to shoe,* Eph. 6:15; pass. *to be shod,* Mk. 6:9* [5265]

[5687] ὑπόδημα *hypodēma* 10x *anything bound under; a sandal,* Mt. 3:11; 10:10 [5266] See *sandal.*

[5688] ὑπόδικος *hypodikos* 1x *under a legal process;* also, *under a judicial sentence; under verdict* to an opposed party in a suit, *liable to penalty,* Rom. 3:19* [5267]

[5689] ὑποζύγιον *hypozygion* 2x *an animal subject to the yoke, a beast of burden;* in NT spc. *an ass, donkey,* Mt. 21:5; 2 Pet. 2:16* [5268]

[5690] ὑποζώννυμι *hypozōnnymi* 1x *to gird under,* of persons; *to undergird* a ship with cables, chains, etc., Acts 27:17* [5269]

[5691] ὑποκάτω *hypokatō* 11x can function as an improper prep., *under, beneath, underneath,* Mk. 6:11; 7:28; met. Heb. 2:8 [5270]

[5693] ὑποκρίνομαι *hypokrinomai* 1x *to answer, respond; to act a part* upon the stage; hence, *to assume a counterfeit character; to pretend, feign, make believe,* Lk. 20:20* [5271]

[5694] ὑπόκρισις *hypokrisis* 6x *a response, answer; an over-acting personification, acting; hypocrisy, simulation,* Mt. 23:28; Mk. 12:15; Lk. 12:1; Gal. 2:13; 1 Tim. 4:2; 1 Pet. 2:1* [5272] See *hypocrisy.*

[5695] ὑποκριτής *hypokritēs* 17x *the giver of an answer* or *response; a stageplayer, actor;* in NT *a* moral or religious *counterfeit, a hypocrite, pretender,* Mt. 6:2, 5, 16; 7:5 [5273] See *hypocrite.*

[5696] ὑπολαμβάνω *hypolambanō* 5x *to take up,* by placing one's self underneath what is taken up; *to catch away, withdraw,* Acts 1:9; *to take up* discourse by continuation; hence, *to answer,* Lk. 10:30; *to take up* a notion, *to think, suppose,* Lk. 7:43; Acts 2:15; *receive as a guest,* 3 Jn. 8* [5274]

[5698] ὑπόλειμμα *hypoleimma* 1x *a remnant,* Rom. 9:27* [2640] See *remnant.*

[5699] ὑπολείπω *hypoleipō* 1x *to leave remaining, leave behind;* pass. *to be left surviving,* Rom. 11:3* [5275]

[5700] ὑπολήνιον *hypolēnion* 1x *a vat,* placed under the press, ληνός, to receive the juice, Mk. 12:1* [5276]

[5701] ὑπολιμπάνω *hypolimpanō* 1x *to leave behind,* 1 Pet. 2:21* [5277]

[5702] ὑπομένω *hypomenō* 17x intrans. *to remain* or *stay behind,* when others have departed, Lk. 2:43; trans. *to bear up under, endure, suffer patiently,* 1 Cor. 13:7; Heb. 10:32; absol. *to continue firmly, hold out, remain constant, persevere,* Mt. 10:22; 24:13 [5278] See *endurance, endure; persevere; stand firm; stay.*

[5703] ὑπομιμνῄσκω *hypomimnēskō* 7x *remember, remind,* Jn. 14:26; Tit. 3:1; 2 Pet. 1:12; Jude 5; *to suggest recollection of, remind* others *of,* 2 Tim. 2:14; 3 Jn. 10; *to call to mind, recollect, remember,* Lk. 22:61* [5279]

[5704] ὑπόμνησις *hypomnēsis* 3x *a putting in mind, act of reminding,* 2 Pet. 1:13; 3:1; *remembrance, recollection,* 2 Tim. 1:5* [5280]

[5705] ὑπομονή *hypomonē* 32x *patient endurance,* 2 Cor. 12:12; Col. 1:11; *patient awaiting,* Lk. 21:19; *a patient frame of mind, patience,* Rom. 5:3, 4; 15:4, 5; Jas. 1:3; *perseverance,* Rom. 2:7; *endurance* in adherence to an object, 1 Thess. 1:3; 2 Thess. 3:5; Rev. 1:9; ἐν ὑπομονῇ and δι᾽ ὑπομονῆς, *constantly, perseveringly,* Lk. 8:15; Rom. 8:25; Heb. 12:1; *an enduring* of affliction, etc., *the act of suffering, undergoing,* etc., 2 Cor. 1:6; 6:4 [5281] See *endurance, endure; perseverance.*

[5706] ὑπονοέω *hyponoeō* 3x *to suspect; to suppose, deem,* Acts 13:25; 25:18; 27:27* [5282]

[5707] ὑπόνοια *hyponoia* 1x *suspicion, surmise,* 1 Tim. 6:4* [5283]

[5709] ὑποπλέω *hypopleō* 2x *to sail under; to sail under* the lee, or, *to the south of,* an island, etc., Acts 27:4, 7* [5284]

[5710] ὑποπνέω *hypopneō* 1x *to blow gently,* as the wind, Acts 27:13* [5285]

[5711] ὑποπόδιον *hypopodion* 7x *a footstool,* Jas. 2:3 [5286] See *footstool.*

[5712] ὑπόστασις *hypostasis* 5x pr. *a standing under; a taking* of a thing *upon one's self; an assumed position, an assumption* of a specific character, *essence, reality,* 2 Cor. 11:17; *an engagement undertaken* with regard to the conduct of others, *a vouching, confidence, conviction, assurance, steadfastness,* 2 Cor. 9:4; or of one's self, *a pledged profession,* Heb. 3:14; *an assured impression, a mental realizing,* Heb. 11:1; *a substructure, basis; subsistence, essence,* Heb. 1:3* [5287]

[5713] ὑποστέλλω *hypostellō* 4x pr. *to let down, to stow away; to draw back, withdraw,* Gal. 2:12; mid. *to shrink back, recoil,* Heb. 10:38; *to keep back, suppress, conceal,* Acts 20:20, 27* [5288]

[5714] ὑποστολή *hypostolē* 1x *a shrinking back,* Heb. 10:39* [5289]

[5715] ὑποστρέφω *hypostrephō* 35x *to turn back, return,* Mk. 14:40; Lk. 1:56; 2:39, 43, 45 [5290] See *return.*

[5716] ὑποστρωννύω *hypostrōnnyō* 1x *to stow under, spread underneath,* Lk. 19:36* [5291]

[5717] ὑποταγή *hypotagē* 4x *subordination,* 1 Tim. 3:4; *submissiveness, obedience,* 2 Cor. 9:13; Gal. 2:5; 1 Tim. 2:11* [5292]

[5718] ὑποτάσσω *hypotassō* 38x *to place* or *arrange under; to subordinate,* 1 Cor. 15:27; *to bring under influence,* Rom. 8:20; pass. *to be subordinated,* 1 Cor. 14:32; *to be brought under a state* or *influence,* Rom. 8:20; mid. *to submit one's self, render obedience, be submissive,* Lk. 2:51; 10:17 [5293] See *(be) subject; submit.*

[5719] ὑποτίθημι *hypotithēmi* 2x *to place under; to lay down* the neck beneath the sword of the executioner, *to set on imminent risk,* Rom. 16:4; mid. *to suggest, recommend to attention,* 1 Tim. 4:6* [5294]

[5720] ὑποτρέχω *hypotrechō* 1x *to run under;* as a nautical term, *to sail under* the lee of, Acts 27:16* [5295]

[5721] ὑποτύπωσις *hypotypōsis* 2x *a sketch, delineation; a form, formula, presentment, sample,* 2 Tim. 1:13; *a pattern, a model representation,* 1 Tim. 1:16* [5296]

[5722] ὑποφέρω *hypopherō* 3x *to bear under; to bear up under, support, sustain,* 1 Cor. 10:13; *to endure patiently,* 1 Pet. 2:19; *to undergo,* 2 Tim. 3:11* [5297]

[5723] ὑποχωρέω *hypochōreō* 2x *to withdraw, retire, retreat,* Lk. 5:16; 9:10* [5298]

[5724] ὑπωπιάζω *hypōpiazō* 2x pr. *to strike one upon the parts beneath the eye; to beat black and blue;* hence, *to discipline by hardship, coerce, torment,* 1 Cor. 9:27; met. *to weary* by continual importunities, *pester,* Lk. 18:5* [5299]

[5725] ὗς *hys* 1x *a hog, swine, boar, sow,* 2 Pet. 2:22* [5300]

[5727] ὕσσωπος *hyssōpos* 2x *hyssop,* in NT, however, not the plant usually so named, but probably the caper plant; *a bunch of hyssop,* Heb. 9:19; *a hyssop stalk,* Jn. 19:29* [5301]

[5728] ὑστερέω *hystereō* 16x *to be behind* in place or time, *to be in the rear; to fall short of, be inferior to,* 2 Cor. 11:5; 12:11; *to fail of, fail to attain,* Heb. 4:1; *to be in want of, lack,* Lk. 22:35; *to be wanting,* Mk. 10:21; absol. *to be defective, in default,* Mt. 19:20; 1 Cor. 12:24; *to run short,* Jn. 2:3; mid. *to come short of* a privilege or standard, *to miss,* Rom. 3:23; absol. *to come short, be below standard,* 1 Cor. 1:7; *to come short* of sufficiency, *to be in need, want,* Lk. 15:14; 2 Cor. 11:9; Phil. 4:12; Heb. 11:37; *to be a loser, suffer detriment,* 1 Cor. 8:8; in NT ὑστερεῖν ἀπό, *to* *be backwards with respect to, to slight,* Heb. 12:15* [5302] See *fall short; lack.*

[5729] ὑστέρημα *hysterēma* 9x *a shortcoming, defect;* personal *shortcoming,* 1 Cor. 16:17; Phil. 2:30; Col. 1:24; 1 Thess. 3:10; *want, need, poverty, penury,* Lk. 21:4; 2 Cor. 8:14; 9:12; 11:9* [5303] See *lacking.*

[5730] ὑστέρησις *hysterēsis* 2x *want, need,* Mk. 12:44; Phil. 4:11* [5304]

[5731] ὕστερος *hysteros* 12x *posterior* in place or time; *subsequent, later, last, finally,* Mt. 21:31; 1 Tim. 4:1 [5305, 5306] See *afterward; finally; later.*

[5733] ὑφαντός *hyphantos* 1x *woven,* Jn. 19:23* [5307]

[5734] ὑψηλός *hypsēlos* 11x *high, lofty, elevated,* Mt. 4:8; 17:1; τὰ ὑψηλά, *the highest* heaven, Heb. 1:3; *upraised,* Acts 13:17; met. *highly esteemed,* Lk. 16:15; φρονεῖν τὰ ὑψηλά, *to have lofty thoughts, be proud, arrogant,* Rom. 12:16 [5308] See *exalted; high; proud.*

[5735] ὑψηλοφρονέω *hypsēlophroneō* 1x *to have lofty thoughts, be proud, haughty,* 1 Tim. 6:17* [5309]

[5736] ὕψιστος *hypsistos* 13x *highest, loftiest, most elevated;* τὰ ὕψιστα, from the Hebrew, *the highest* heaven, Mt. 21:9; Mk. 11:10; met. ὁ ὕψιστος, *the Most High,* Mk. 5:7 [5310] See *high; most high.*

[5737] ὕψος *hypsos* 6x *height,* Eph. 3:18; Rev. 21:16; met. *exaltation, dignity, eminence,* Jas. 1:9; from the Hebrew, *the height* of heaven, Lk. 1:78; 24:49; Eph. 4:8* [5311] See *exalted; high.*

[5738] ὑψόω *hypsoō* 20x *to raise aloft, lift up,* Jn. 3:14; 8:28; met. *to elevate* in condition, *uplift, exalt,* Mt. 11:23; 23:12; Lk. 1:52 [5312] See *exalt; lift up.*

[5739] ὕψωμα *hypsōma* 2x *height,* Rom. 8:39; *a towering* of self-conceit, *presumption, exaltation, pride,* 2 Cor. 10:5* [5313]

[5741] φάγος *phagos* 2x *a glutton,* Mt. 11:19; Lk. 7:34* [5314]

[5742] φαιλόνης *phailonēs* 1x *a thick cloak* for travelling, with a hood, 2 Tim. 4:13* [5341]

[5743] φαίνω *phainō* 31x *to cause to appear, bring to light;* absol. *to shine,* Jn. 1:5; 5:35; 2 Pet. 1:19; 1 Jn. 2:8; Rev. 1:16; 8:12; 21:23; mid./pass. *to be seen, appear, be visible,* Mt. 1:20; 2:7, 13, 19; τὰ φαινόμενα, *things visible, things obvious to the senses,* Heb. 11:3; φαίνομαι, *to appear, seen, be in appearance,* Mt. 23:27; Lk. 24:11; *to appear* in thought, *seen* in idea, *be a notion,* Mk. 14:64 [5316] See *appear; shine.*

[5744] Φάλεκ *Phalek* 1x *Peleg,* also spelled Φάλεγ, pr. name, indecl., Lk. 3:35* [5317]

[5745] φανερός *phaneros* 18x *apparent, manifest, clear, known, well-known,* Mk. 4:22; 6:14; Gal. 5:19; *in outward guise, externally,* Rom. 2:28 [5318] See *known; obvious; plain.*

[5746] φανερόω *phaneroō* 49x *to bring to light, to set in a clear light; to manifest, display,* Jn. 2:11; 7:4; 9:3; *to show,* Rom. 1:19; 2 Cor. 7:12; *to declare, make known,* Jn. 17:6; *to disclose,* Mk. 4:22; 1 Cor. 4:5; Col. 4:4; *to reveal,* Rom. 3:21; 16:26; Col. 1:26; *to present to view,* Jn. 21:1, 14; pass. *to make an appearance,* Mk. 16:12, 14; spc. of Christ, *to be* personally *manifested,* Jn. 1:31; Col. 3:4; 1 Pet. 1:20; 5:4; 1 Jn. 3:5; *to be laid bare, appear in true character,* 2 Cor. 5:10, 11 [5319] See *appear; disclose; reveal.*

[5747] φανερῶς *phanerōs* 3x *manifestly; clearly, plainly, distinctly,* Acts 10:3; *openly, publicly,* Mk. 1:45; Jn. 7:10* [5320] See *openly; publicly.*

[5748] φανέρωσις *phanerōsis* 2x *a disclosure, clear display,* 2 Cor. 4:2; *an* outward *evidencing* of a latent principle, active *exhibition,* 1 Cor. 12:7* [5321]

[5749] φανός *phanos* 1x *a torch, lantern, light,* Jn. 18:3* [5322]

[5750] Φανουήλ *Phanouēl* 1x *Phanuel,* pr. name, indecl., Lk. 2:36* [5323]

[5751] φαντάζω *phantazō* 1x *to render visible, cause to appear;* pass. *to appear, be seen;* τὸ φανταζόμενον, *the sight, spectacle,* Heb. 12:21* [5324]

[5752] φαντασία *phantasia* 1x pr. *a rendering visible; a display; pomp, parade,* Acts 25:23* [5325]

[5753] φάντασμα *phantasma* 2x *a phantom, specter,* Mt. 14:26; Mk. 6:49* [5326]

[5754] φάραγξ *pharanx* 1x *a cleft, ravine, valley,* Lk. 3:5* [5327]

[5755] Φαραώ *Pharaō* 5x *Pharaoh,* pr. name, indecl., Acts 7:10, 13, 21; Rom. 9:17; Heb. 11:24* [5328]

[5756] Φαρές *Phares* 3x *Perezs,* pr. name, indecl., Mt. 1:3; Lk. 3:33* [5329]

[5757] Φαρισαῖος *Pharisaios* 98x *a Pharisee, a follower of the sect of the Pharisees,* a numerous and powerful sect of the Jews, distinguished for their ceremonial observances, and apparent sanctity of life, and for being rigid interpreters of the Mosaic law; but who frequently violated its spirit by their traditional interpretations and precepts, to which they ascribed nearly an equal authority with the OT Scriptures, Mt. 5:20; 12:2; 23:14 [5330] See *Pharisee.*

[5758] φαρμακεία *pharmakeia* 2x *employment of drugs* for any purpose; *sorcery, magic, enchantment,* Rev. 18:23; Gal. 5:20* [5331]

[5760] φάρμακον *pharmakon* 1x *a drug; an enchantment; magic potion, charm,* Rev. 9:21* [5331]

[5761] φάρμακος *pharmakos* 2x *a sorcerer, magician,* Rev. 21:8; 22:15* [5333]

[5762] φάσις *phasis* 1x *report, information,* Acts 21:31* [5334]

[5763] φάσκω *phaskō* 3x *to assert, affirm,* Acts 24:9; 25:19; Rom. 1:22* [5335]

[5764] φάτνη *phatnē* 4x *a manger, stall,* Lk. 2:7, 12, 16; 13:15* [5336]

[5765] φαῦλος *phaulos* 6x *vile, refuse; evil, wicked;* Jn. 3:20; 5:29; Rom. 9:11; 2 Cor. 5:10; Tit. 2:8; Jas. 3:16* [5337]

[5766] φέγγος *phengos* 2x *light, splendor, radiance,* Mt. 24:29; Mk. 13:24* [5338]

[5767] φείδομαι *pheidomai* 10x *to spare; to be tender of,* Rom. 8:32; *to spare,* in respect of hard dealing, Acts 20:29; Rom. 11:21; 1 Cor. 7:28; 2 Cor. 1:23; 13:2; 2 Pet. 2:4, 5; absol. *to forbear, abstain,* 2 Cor. 12:6* [5339] See *spare.*

[5768] φειδομένως *pheidomenōs* 2x *sparingly,* 2 Cor. 9:6 (2x)* [5340]

[5770] φέρω *pherō* 66x *to bear, carry,* Mk. 2:3; *to bring,* Mt. 14:11, 18; *to conduct,* Mt. 17:17; Jn. 21:18; *to bear, endure,* Rom. 9:22; Heb. 12:20; 13:13; *to uphold, maintain, conserve,* Heb. 1:3; *to bear, bring forth, produce,* Mk. 4:8; Jn. 12:24; 15:2; *to bring forward, advance, allege,* Jn. 18:29; Acts 25:7; 2 Pet. 2:11; *to offer, ascribe,* Rev. 21:24, 26; absol. used of a gate, *to lead,* Acts 12:10; pass. *to be brought* within reach, *offered,* 1 Pet. 1:13; *to be brought in, to enter,* Heb. 9:16; *to be under a moving influence, to be moved,* 2 Pet. 1:21; mid. *to rush, sweep,* Acts 2:2; *to proceed, come forth, have utterance,* 2 Pet. 1:17, 18, 21; *to proceed, make progress,* Heb. 6:1; used of a ship, *to drive* before the wind, Acts 27:15, 17 [5342] See *bring; carry; endurance, endure; present; sustain.*

[5771] φεύγω *pheugō* 29x absol. *to flee, take to flight,* Mt. 2:13; 8:33; *to shrink, stand fearfully aloof,* 1 Cor. 10:14; *to make escape,* Mt. 23:33; trans. *to shun,* 1 Cor. 6:18; 1 Tim. 6:11; 2 Tim. 2:22; *to escape,* Heb. 11:34 [5343] See *escape; flee; run away.*

[5772] Φῆλιξ *Phēlix* 9x *Felix,* pr. name, Acts 23:24, 26; 24:3, 22, 24f., 27; 25:14* [5344]

[5773] φήμη *phēmē* 2x pr. *a celestial* or *oracular utterance; an utterance; fame, rumor, report,* Mt. 9:26; Lk. 4:14* [5345]

[5774] φημί *phēmi* 66x *to utter; to say, speak,* Mt. 8:8; 14:8; 26:34, 61; *to say, allege, affirm,* Rom. 3:8 [5346] See *answer; declare; reply; say.*

[5776] Φῆστος *Phēstos* 13x *Festus,* pr. name, Acts 24:27; 25:1, 4, 12ff., 22ff.; 26:24f., 32* [5347]

[5777] φθάνω *phthanō* 7x *come before, precede,* 1 Thess. 4:15; absol. *to advance, make progress,* 2 Cor. 10:14; Phil. 3:16; *to come up* with, *come* upon, *be close at hand,* Mt. 12:28; Lk. 11:20; 1 Thess. 2:16; *to attain* an object of pursuit, Rom. 9:31* [5348]

[5778] φθαρτός *phthartos* 6x *corruptible, perishable,* Rom. 1:23; 1 Cor. 9:25; 15:53f.; 1 Pet. 1:18, 23* [5349] See *corrupt; corruption.*

[5779] φθέγγομαι *phthengomai* 3x *to emit a sound; to speak,* Acts 4:18; 2 Pet. 2:16, 18* [5350]

[5780] φθείρω *phtheirō* 9x *to spoil, ruin,* 1 Cor. 3:17; 2 Cor. 7:2; *to corrupt,* morally *deprave,* 1 Cor. 15:33; 2 Cor. 11:3 [5351] See *corrupt, corruption; destroy.*

[5781] φθινοπωρινός *phthinopōrinos* 1x *belonging to late autumn, bare,* Jude 12* [5352]

[5782] φθόγγος *phthongos* 2x *a* vocal *sound,* Rom. 10:18; 1 Cor. 14:7* [5353]

[5783] φθονέω *phthoneō* 1x *to envy,* Gal. 5:26* [5354]

[5784] φθόνος *phthonos* 9x *envy, jealously, spite,* Mt. 27:18; Mk. 15:10; Rom. 1:29; Gal. 5:21; Phil. 1:15; 1 Tim. 6:4; Tit. 3:3; Jas. 4:5; 1 Pet. 2:1* [5355] See *envy.*

[5785] φθορά *phthora* 9x *corruption, decay, ruin, corruptibility, mortality,* Rom. 8:21; 1 Cor. 15:42; meton. *corruptible, perishable substance,* 1 Cor. 15:50; *killing, slaughter,* 2 Pet. 2:12; spiritual *ruin,* Gal. 6:8; Col. 2:22; met. moral *corruption, depravity,* 2 Pet. 1:4; 2:19* [5356] See *corrupt, corruption; destruction.*

[5786] φιάλη *phialē* 12x *a bowl, shallow cup,* Rev. 5:8; 15:7; 16:1, 2, 3, 4 [5357] See *bowl.*

[5787] φιλάγαθος *philagathos* 1x *a lover of goodness,* or, *of the good, a fosterer of virtue,* Tit. 1:8* [5358]

[5788] Φιλαδέλφεια *Philadelpheia* 2x *Philadelphia,* a city of Lydia, near Mount Tmolus, Rev. 1:11; 3:7* [5359]

[5789] φιλαδελφία *philadelphia* 6x *brotherly love;* in NT *love of the* Christian *brotherhood,* Rom. 12:10; 1 Thess. 4:9; Heb. 13:1; 1 Pet. 1:22; 2 Pet. 1:7* [5360]

[5790] φιλάδελφος *philadelphos* 1x *brother-loving;* in NT *loving the members of the* Christian *brotherhood,* 1 Pet. 3:8* [5361]

[5791] φίλανδρος *philandros* 1x *husband-loving; conjugal,* Tit. 2:4* [5362]

[5792] φιλανθρωπία *philanthrōpia* 2x *philanthropy, love of mankind,* Tit. 3:4; *benevolence, humanity,* Acts 28:2* [5363]

[5793] φιλανθρώπως *philanthrōpōs* 1x *humanely, benevolently, kindly,* Acts 27:3* [5364]

[5794] φιλαργυρία *philargyria* 1x *love of money, covetousness,* 1 Tim. 6:10* [5365]

[5795] φιλάργυρος *philargyros* 2x *money-loving, covetous,* Lk. 16:14; 2 Tim. 3:2* [5366]

[5796] φίλαυτος *philautos* 1x *self-loving; selfish,* 2 Tim. 3:2* [5367]

[5797] φιλέω *phileō* 25x pr. *to manifest some act* or *token of kindness* or *affection; to kiss,* Mt. 26:48; Mk. 14:44; Lk. 22:47; *to love, regard with affection, have affection for,* Mt. 10:37; Jn. 5:20; *to like, be fond of, delight in* a thing, Mt. 23:6; Rev. 22:15; *to cherish inordinately, set store by,* Jn. 12:25 [5368] See *love.*

[5798] φιλήδονος *philēdonos* 1x *pleasure-loving; a lover of pleasure,* 2 Tim. 3:4* [5369]

[5799] φίλημα *philēma* 7x *a kiss,* Lk. 7:45; 22:48; Rom. 16:16; 1 Cor. 16:20; 2 Cor. 13:12; 1 Thess. 5:26; 1 Pet. 5:14* [5370]

[5800] Φιλήμων *Philēmōn* 1x *Philemon,* pr. name, Phlm. 1; subscr. and title* [5371]

[5801] Φίλητος *Philētos* 1x *Philetus,* pr. name, 2 Tim. 2:17* [5372]

[5802] φιλία *philia* 1x *affection, fondness, love,* Jas. 4:4* [5373]

[5803] Φιλιππήσιος *Philippēsios* 1x *a Philippian, a citizen of* Φίλιπποι, *Philippi,* Phil. 4:15; title* [5374]

[5804] Φίλιπποι *Philippoi* 4x *Philippi,* a considerable city of Macedonia, east of Amphipolis, Acts 16:12; 20:6; Phil. 1:1; 1 Thess. 2:2; 1 & 2 Cor. subscr.* [5375]

[5805] Φίλιππος *Philippos* 36x *Philip,* pr. name . (1) *Philip, the Apostle,* Mt. 10:3. (2) *Philip, the Evangelist,* Acts 6:5. (3) *Philip, son of Herod the Great and Mariamne,* Mt. 14:3 . (4) *Philip, son of Herod the Great and Cleopatra,* Mt. 16:13; Lk. 3:1 [5376]

[5806] φιλόθεος *philotheos* 1x *God-loving, pious; a lover of God,* 2 Tim. 3:4* [5377]

[5807] Φιλόλογος *Philologos* 1x *Philologus,* pr. name, Rom. 16:15* [5378]

[5808] φιλονεικία *philoneikia* 1x *a love of contention; rivalry, contention,* Lk. 22:24* [5379]

[5809] φιλόνεικος *philoneikos* 1x *fond of contention; contentious, disputatious,* 1 Cor. 11:16* [5380]

[5810] φιλοξενία *philoxenia* 2x *kindness to strangers, hospitality,* Rom. 12:13; Heb. 13:2* [5381]

[5811] φιλόξενος *philoxenos* 3x *kind to strangers, hospitable,* 1 Tim. 3:2; Tit. 1:8; 1 Pet. 4:9* [5382]

[5812] φιλοπρωτεύω *philoprōteuō* 1x *to love* or *desire to be first* or *chief, affect pre-eminence,* 3 Jn. 9* [5383]

[5813] φίλος *philos* 29x *loved, dear; devoted;* Acts 19:31; as a subst., *a friend,* Lk. 7:6; 11:5, 6, 8; *a congenial associate,* Mt. 11:19; Lk. 7:34; Jas. 4:4; used as a word of courteous appellation, Lk. 14:10 [5384] See *friend.*

[5814] φιλοσοφία *philosophia* 1x *a love of science;* systematic *philosophy;* in NT *the philosophy* of the Jewish gnosis, Col. 2:8* [5385]

[5815] φιλόσοφος *philosophos* 1x pr. *a lover of science, a* systematic *philosopher,* Acts 17:18* [5386]

[5816] φιλόστοργος *philostorgos* 1x *tenderly affectionate,* Rom. 12:10* [5387]

[5817] φιλότεκνος *philoteknos* 1x *loving one's children, duly parental,* Tit. 2:4* [5388]

[5818] φιλοτιμέομαι *philotimeomai* 3x pr. *to be ambitious of honor;* by impl. *to exert one's self* to accomplish a thing, *use one's utmost efforts, endeavor earnestly,* Rom. 15:20; 2 Cor. 5:9; 1 Thess. 4:11* [5389]

[5819] φιλοφρόνως *philophronōs* 1x *with kindly feeling* or *manner, courteously,* Acts 28:7* [5390]

[5821] φιμόω *phimoō* 7x *to muzzle,* 1 Tim. 5:18; met. and by impl. *to silence, put to silence;* pass. *to be silent, speechless,* Mt. 22:12, 34; 1 Pet. 2:15; Mk. 1:25; trop. pass. *to be hushed,* as winds and waves, Mk. 4:39; Lk. 4:35* [5392] See *muzzle; quiet; speechless.*

[5823] Φλέγων *Phlegōn* 1x *Phlegon,* pr. name, Rom. 16:14* [5393]

[5824] φλογίζω *phlogizō* 2x *to set in a flame, kindle, inflame,* Jas. 3:6 (2x)* [5394]

[5825] φλόξ *phlox* 7x *a flame,* Lk. 16:24; Acts 7:30 [5395]

[5826] φλυαρέω *phlyareō* 1x *to talk folly* or *nonsense;* in NT trans., *bring unjustified charges against,* 3 Jn. 10* [5396]

[5827] φλύαρος *phlyaros* 1x *a gossip, tattler,* 1 Tim. 5:13* [5397]

[5828] φοβέομαι *phobeomai* 95x has an active form, φοβέω (5828), but only occurs as a passive (deponent) in our literature, *to fear, dread,* Mt. 10:26; 14:5; *to fear reverentially, to reverence,* Mk. 6:20; Lk. 1:50; Acts 10:2; Eph. 5:33; Rev. 11:18; *to be afraid* to do a thing, Mt. 2:22; Mk. 9:32; *to be reluctant, to scruple,* Mt. 1:20; *to fear, be apprehensive,* Acts 27:17; 2 Cor. 11:3; 12:20; *to be fearfully anxious,* Heb. 4:1; absol. *to be fearful, afraid, alarmed,* Mt. 14:27; 17:6, 7; Mk. 16:8; *to be fearfully impressed,* Rom. 11:20 [5399] See *(be) afraid; fear; respect; stand in awe.*

[5829] φοβερός *phoberos* 3x *fearful; terrible,* Heb. 10:27, 31; 12:21* [5398]

[5831] φόβητρον *phobētron* 1x *something which inspires terror; terrible sight* or *event,* Lk. 21:11* [5400]

[5832] φόβος *phobos* 47x *fear, terror, affright,* Mt. 14:26; Lk. 1:12; *astonishment, amazement,* Mt. 28:8; Mk. 4:41; *trembling concern,* 1 Cor. 2:3; 2 Cor. 7:15; meton. *a terror, an object* or *cause of terror,* Rom. 13:5; *reverential fear, awe,* Acts 9:31; Rom. 3:18; *respect, deference,* Rom. 13:7; 1 Pet. 2:18 [5401] See *alarm; awe; fear; fright; respect.*

[5833] Φοίβη *Phoibē* 1x *Phoebe,* pr. name, Rom. 16:1* [5402]

[5834] Φοινίκη *Phoinikē* 3x *Phoenice, Phoenicia,* a country on the east of the Mediterranean, between Palestine and Syria, anciently celebrated for commerce, Acts 11:19; 15:3; 21:2* [5403]

[5836] φοῖνιξ *phoinix* 2x *the palm tree, the date palm,* Jn. 12:13; Rev. 7:9. Identical in form to the word meaning *phoenix,* the Egyptian bird.* [5404]

[5837] Φοῖνιξ *Phoinix* 1x *Phoenix, Phoenice,* a city, with a harbor, on the southeast coast of Crete, Acts 27:12* [5405]

[5838] φονεύς *phoneus* 7x *a homicide, murderer,* Mt. 22:7; Acts 3:14; 7:52; 28:4; 1 Pet. 4:15; Rev. 21: 8; 22:15* [5406]

[5839] φονεύω *phoneuō* 12x *to put to death, kill, stay,* Mt. 23:31, 35; absol. *to commit murder,* Mt. 5:21 [5407] See *murder.*

[5840] φόνος *phonos* 9x *a killing, slaughter, murder,* Mt. 15:19; Mk. 7:21; 15:7 [5408]

[5841] φορέω *phoreō* 6x *to bear; to wear,* Mt. 11:8; Jn. 19:5; Rom. 13:4; 1 Cor. 15:49; Jas. 2:3 [5409]

[5842] φόρον *phoron* 1x *a forum, marketplace;* Φόρον Ἀππίου, *Forum Appii,* the name of a small town on the Appian way, according to Antoninus, forty-three Roman miles from Rome, or about forty English miles, Acts 28:15* [5410]

[5843] φόρος *phoros* 5x *tribute, tax,* strictly such as is laid on dependent and subject people, Lk. 20:22; 23:2; Rom. 13:6, 7* [5411]

[5844] φορτίζω *phortizō* 2x *to load, burden;* met. Mt. 11:28; Lk. 11:46* [5412]

[5845] φορτίον *phortion* 6x *a load, burden;* of a ship, *freight, cargo,* Acts 27:10; met. *a burden* of imposed precepts, etc., Mt. 11:30; 23:4; Lk. 11:46 (2x); of faults, sins, etc., Gal. 6:5* [5413]

[5847] Φορτουνᾶτος *Phortounatos* 1x *Fortunatus,* pr. name, 1 Cor. 16:17* [5415]

[5848] φραγέλλιον *phragellion* 1x *a whip, scourge,* Jn. 2:15* [5416]

[5849] φραγελλόω *phragelloō* 2x *to scourge,* Mt. 27:26; Mk. 15:15* [5417]

[5850] φραγμός *phragmos* 4x *a fence, hedge; a hedgeside path,* Mt. 21:33; Mk. 12:1; Lk. 14:23; met. *a parting fence,* Eph. 2:14* [5418]

[5851] φράζω *phrazō* 1x pr. *to propound in distinct terms, to tell;* in NT *to explain, interpret, expound,* Mt. 15:15* [5419]

[5852] φράσσω *phrassō* 3x *to fence in;* by impl. *to obstruct, stop, close up,* Heb. 11:33; met. *to silence, put to silence,* Rom. 3:19; 2 Cor. 11:10* [5420]

[5853] φρέαρ *phrear* 7x *a well, cistern,* Lk. 14:5; Jn. 4:11, 12; *a pit,* Rev. 9:1, 2* [5421] See *pit.*

[5854] φρεναπατάω *phrenapataō* 1x *to deceive the mind; to deceive, impose on,* Gal. 6:3* [5422]

[5855] φρεναπάτης *phrenapatēs* 1x *a deceiver, seducer,* Tit. 1:10* [5423]

[5856] φρήν *phrēn* 2x pr. *the diaphragm, midriff; the mind, intellect, understanding,* 1 Cor. 14:20 (2x)* [5424]

[5857] φρίσσω *phrissō* 1x *to be ruffled, to bristle; to shiver, shudder* from fear, Jas. 2:19* [5425]

[5858] φρονέω *phroneō* 26x *to think, to mind; to be of opinion,* Acts 28:22; Phil. 1:7; *to take thought, be considerate,* Phil. 4:10; *to entertain sentiments* or *inclinations* of a specific kind, *to be minded,* Rom. 12:16; 15:5; 1 Cor. 13:11; 2 Cor. 13:11; Gal. 5:10; Phil. 2:2; 3:16; 4:2; *to be in a* certain *frame of mind,* Rom. 12:3; Phil. 2:5; *to imagine, entertain conceit,* 1 Cor. 4:6; *to heed, pay regard to,* Rom. 14:6; *to incline to, be set upon, mind,* Mt. 16:23; Mk. 8:33; Rom. 8:5; Phil. 3:15, 19; Col. 3:2 [5426] See *set the mind on; think.*

[5859] φρόνημα *phronēma* 4x *frame of thought, will, aspirations,* Rom. 8:6, 7, 27* [5427]

[5860] φρόνησις *phronēsis* 2x *a thoughtful frame, understanding, insight, sense, rightmindedness,* Lk. 1:17; *intelligence,* Eph. 1:8* [5428]

[5861] φρόνιμος *phronimos* 14x *considerate, thoughtful, prudent, discreet,* Mt. 7:24; 10:16; 24:45; 25:2, 4, 8, 9; Lk. 12:42; *sensible, wise,* Rom. 11:25; 12:16; 1 Cor. 4:10; 10:15; 2 Cor. 11:19* [5429] See *intelligent; prudent; shrewd; wise, skillful.*

[5862] φρονίμως *phronimōs* 1x *considerately, providently,* Lk. 16:8* [5430]

[5863] φροντίζω *phrontizō* 1x *to be considerate, be careful,* Tit. 3:8* [5431]

[5864] φρουρέω *phroureō* 4x *to keep watch;* trans. *to guard, watch,* with a military guard, 2 Cor. 11:32; *to keep* in a condition of restraint, Gal. 3:23; *to keep* in a state of settlement or security, Phil. 4:7; 1 Pet. 1:5* [5432]

[5865] φρυάσσω *phryassō* 1x pr. *to snort, neigh, stamp,* etc.; as a high-spirited horse; hence, *to be noisy, fierce, insolent, and tumultuous, to rage, tumultuate,* Acts 4:25* [5433]

[5866] φρύγανον *phryganon* 1x *a dry twig, branch,* etc., Acts 28:3* [5434]

[5867] Φρυγία *Phrygia* 3x *Phrygia,* an inland province of Asia Minor, Acts 2:10; 16:6; 18:23; 1 Tim. subscr.* [5435]

[5869] Φύγελος *Phygelos* 1x *Phygellus,* pr. name, 2 Tim. 1:15* [5436]

[5870] φυγή *phygē* 1x *a fleeing, flight,* Mt. 24:20* [5437]

[5871] φυλακή *phylakē* 47x *a keeping watch, ward, guard,* Lk. 2:8; *a place of watch,* Rev. 18:2; *a watch, guard, body of guards,* Acts 12:10; *ward, custody, imprisonment,* 2 Cor. 6:5; 11:23; Heb. 11:36; *prison,* 1 Pet. 3:19; *a place of custody, prison,* Mt. 14:10; 25:39, 44; *a watch* or *division,* of the night, which in the time of our Savior was divided into watches of three hours each, called ὀψέ, μεσονύκτιον, ἀλεκτοροφωνία and πρωΐα, or πρωΐ, Mt. 14:25; 24:43; Mk. 6:48; Lk. 12:38 (2x) [5438] See *jail; prison; watch.*

[5872] φυλακίζω *phylakizō* 1x *to deliver into custody, put in prison, imprison,* Acts 22:19* [5439]

[5873] φυλακτήριον *phylaktērion* 1x *the station of a guard* or *watch; a preservative, safeguard;* hence, *a phylactery* or *amulet,* worn about the person; from which circumstance the word is used in the NT as a term for the Jewish *Tephillin* or *prayer-case,* which took their rise from the injunction in Deut. 6:8; 11:18; Mt. 23:5* [5440]

[5874] φύλαξ *phylax* 3x *a watchman, guard, sentinel,* Acts 5:23; 12:6, 19* [5441]

[5875] φυλάσσω *phylassō* 31x *to be on watch, keep* watch, Lk. 2:8; *to have in keeping,* Acts 20:20; *to have in custody,* Acts 28:16; *to keep* under restraint, *confine,* Lk. 8:29; Acts 12:4; 23:35; *to guard, defend,* Lk. 11:21; *to keep safe, preserve,* Jn. 12:25; 17:12; 2 Thess. 3:3; 2 Pet. 2:5; Jude 24; *to keep* in abstinence, Acts 21:25; 1 Jn. 5:21; *to observe* a matter of injunction or duty, Mk. 10:20; Lk. 11:28; Acts 7:53; 16:4; 21:24; mid. *to be on one's guard, beware,* Lk. 12:15; 2 Tim. 4:15; 2 Pet. 3:17 [5442] See *beware; guard; keep; obey; observe.*

[5876] φυλή *phylē* 31x *a tribe,* Mt. 19:28; 24:30; Lk. 2:36; *a people, nation,* Rev. 1:7; 5:9 [5443] See *people; tribe.*

[5877] φύλλον *phyllon* 6x *a leaf,* Mt. 21:19 [5444]

[5878] φύραμα *phyrama* 5x *that which is mingled and reduced to a uniform consistence, by kneading, beating, treading,* etc.; *a mass* of potter's clay, Rom. 9:21; of dough, 1 Cor. 5:6, 7; Gal. 5:9; met. Rom. 11:16* [5445]

[5879] φυσικός *physikos* 3x *natural, agreeable to nature,* Rom. 1:26, 27; *following the instinct of nature,* as animals, 2 Pet. 2:12* [5446]

[5880] φυσικῶς *physikōs* 1x *naturally, by natural instinct,* Jude 10* [5447]

[5881] φυσιόω *physioō* 7x *to inflate puff up;* met. *to inflate* with pride and vanity, 1 Cor. 8:1; pass. *to be inflated* with pride, *to be proud, vain, arrogant,* 1 Cor. 4:6, 18, 19; 5:2; 13:4; Col. 2:18* [5448]

[5882] φύσις *physis* 14x *essence,* Gal. 4:8; *native condition, birth,* Rom. 2:27; 11:21, 24; Gal. 2:15; Eph. 2:3; *native species, kind,* Jas. 3:7; *nature, natural frame,* 2 Pet. 1:4; *nature, native instinct,* Rom. 2:14; 1 Cor. 11:14; *nature, prescribed course of nature,* Rom. 1:26* [5449] See *kind; natural condition; nature.*

[5883] φυσίωσις *physiōsis* 1x pr. *inflation;* met. *inflation* of mind, *pride,* 2 Cor. 12:20* [5450]

[5884] φυτεία *phyteia* 1x *plantation, the act of planting; a plant,* met. Mt. 15:13* [5451]

[5885] φυτεύω *phyteuō* 11x *to plant, set,* Mt. 21:33; Lk. 13:6; 17:6, 28; 20:9; met. Mt. 15:13; Mk. 12:1; *to plant* the Gospel, 1 Cor. 3:6, 7, 8; 9:7* [5452] See *plant.*

[5886] φύω *phyō* 3x *to generate, produce;* pass. *to be generated, produced;* of plants, *to germinate, sprout,* Lk. 8:6, 8; intrans. *to germinate, spring* or *grow up,* Heb. 12:15* [5453]

[5887] φωλεός *phōleos* 2x *a den, lair, burrow,* Mt. 8:20; Lk. 9:58* [5454]

[5888] φωνέω *phōneō* 43x *to sound, utter a sound;* of the cock, *to crow,* Mt. 26:34, 74, 75; *to call,* or *cry out, exclaim,* Lk. 8:8, 54; 16:24; 23:46; *to call to,* Mt. 27:47; Mk. 3:31; *to call,* Jn. 13:13; *to call, summon,* Mt. 20:32; *to invite* to a feast, Lk. 14:12 [5455] See *call; crow; invite; make a noise; summon.*

[5889] φωνή *phōnē* 139x *a sound,* Mt. 24:31; Jn. 3:8; Rev. 4:5; 8:5; *a cry,* Mt. 2:18; *an* articulate *sound, voice,* Mt. 3:3, 17; 17:5; 27:46, 50; *voice, speech, discourse,* Jn. 10:16, 27; Acts 7:31; 12:22; 13:27; Heb. 3:7, 15; *tone* of address, Gal. 4:20; *language, tongue, dialect,* 1 Cor. 14:10 [5456] See *language; sound; speech; voice.*

[5890] φῶς *phōs* 73x *light,* Mt. 17:2; 2 Cor. 4:6; *daylight, broad day,* Mt. 10:27; Lk. 12:3; *radiance, blaze of light,* Mt. 4:16; Acts 9:3; 12:7; *an instrument* or *means of light, a light,* Mt. 6:23; Acts 16:29; *a fire,* Mk. 14:54; Lk. 22:56; from the Hebrew, *the light* of God's presence, 2 Cor. 11:14; 1 Tim. 6:16; met. *the light* of Divine truth, spiritual *illumination,* Lk. 16:8; Jn. 3:19; Rom. 13:12; Eph. 5:8; 1 Pet. 2:9; 1 Jn. 1:7; 2:8, 9, 10; *a source* or *dispenser of* spiritual *light,* Mt. 5:14; Jn. 1:4, 5, 7, 8, 9; 8:12; 9:5; pure *radiance,* perfect *brightness,* 1 Jn. 1:5 [5457] See *light.*

[5891] φωστήρ *phōstēr* 2x *a cause of light, illuminator; a light, luminary, star,* Phil. 2:15; *radiance,* or, *luminary,* Rev. 21:11* [5458]

[5892] φωσφόρος *phōsphoros* 1x *light-bringing;* sc. ἀστήρ, *Lucifer, the morning star,* met. 2 Pet. 1:19* [5459]

[5893] φωτεινός *phōteinos* 5x *radiant, lustrous,* Mt. 17:5; *enlightened, illuminated,* Mt. 6:22; Lk. 11:34, 36 (2x)* [5460]

[5894] φωτίζω *phōtizō* 11x *to light, give light to, illuminate, shine upon,* Lk. 11:36; Rev. 18:1; 21:23; met. *to enlighten* spiritually, Jn. 1:9; Eph. 1:18; 3:9; Heb. 6:4; 10:32; *to reveal, to bring to light, make known,* 1 Cor. 4:5; 2 Tim. 1:10; intrans. *shine,* Rev. 22:5* [5461] See *enlighten; (give) light.*

[5895] φωτισμός *phōtismos* 2x *illumination; a shining forth, bringing to light, enlightenment,* 2 Cor. 4:4, 6* [5462]

[5897] χαίρω *chairō* 74x *to rejoice, be glad, be joyful, be full of joy,* Mt. 2:10; 5:12; 18:13; Mk. 14:11; Rom. 12:12; 2 Cor. 2:3; a term of salutation, *Hail!* Mt. 26:49; λέγω χαίρειν, *to greet,* 2 Jn. 10:11; an epistolary greeting, *Health!* Acts 15:23 [5463] See *rejoice.*

[5898] χάλαζα *chalaza* 4x *hail,* Rev. 8:7; 11:19; 16:21 (2x)* [5464]

[5899] χαλάω *chalaō* 7x *to slacken; to let down, lower,* Mk. 2:4; Lk. 5:4, 5; Acts 9:25; 27:17, 30; 1 Cor. 11:33* [5465]

[5900] Χαλδαῖος *Chaldaios* 1x *a Chaldean, a native of Chaldea,* a country of central Asia, which seems to have included Mesopotamia, Acts 7:4* [5466]

[5901] χαλεπός *chalepos* 2x *hard, rugged; furious, ferocious,* Mt. 8:28; *difficult, trying,* 2 Tim. 3:1* [5467]

[5902] χαλιναγωγέω *chalinagōgeō* 2x pr. *to guide with a bridle;* met. *to bridle, control, sway,* Jas. 1:26; 3:2* [5468]

[5903] χαλινός *chalinos* 2x *a bridle, bit,* Jas. 3:3; Rev. 14:20* [5469]

[5906] χαλκεύς *chalkeus* 1x pr. *a coppersmith;* hence, genr. *a worker in metals, smith,* 2 Tim. 4:14* [5471]

[5907] χαλκηδών *chalkēdōn* 1x *chalcedony,* the name of a gem, generally of a whitish, bluish, or gray color, susceptible of a high and beautiful polish, and of which there are several varieties, as the onyx, modern carnelian, etc., Rev. 21:19* [5472]

[5908] χαλκίον *chalkion* 1x *a vessel, copper, brazen utensil,* Mk. 7:4* [5473]

[5909] χαλκολίβανον *chalkolibanon* 2x *orichalcum, fine bronze,* a factitious metal of which there were several varieties, the white being of the highest repute, or, *deep-tinted frankincense,* Rev. 1:15; 2:18* [5474]

[5910] χαλκός *chalkos* 5x *copper,* also, *bronze,* Rev. 18:12; *a brazen musical instrument,* 1 Cor. 13:1; *copper money,* Mt. 10:9; *money* in general, Mk. 6:8; 12:41* [5475]

[5911] χαλκοῦς *chalkous* 1x contracted form of χάλκεος, *made of copper, brass,* or *bronze,* Rev. 9:20* [5470]

[5912] χαμαί *chamai* 2x *on the ground, to the earth,* Jn. 9:6; 18:6* [5476]

[5913] Χανάαν *Chanaan* 2x *Canaan,* the ancient name of Palestine, Acts 7:11; 13:19 [5477]

[5914] Χαναναῖος *Chananaios* 1x *Canaanitish, of Canaan,* Mt. 15:22* [5478]

[5915] χαρά *chara* 59x *joy, gladness, rejoicing,* Mt. 2:10; 13:20, 44; 28:8; meton, *joy, cause of joy, occasion of rejoicing,* Lk. 2:10; Phil. 4:1; 1 Thess. 2:19, 20; *bliss,* Mt. 25:21, 23 [5479] See *gladness; happiness; joy.*

[5916] χάραγμα *charagma* 8x *an imprinted mark,* Rev. 13:16, 17; 14:9, 11; 16:2; 19:20; 20:4; *sculpture,* Acts 17:29* [5480]

[5917] χαρακτήρ *charaktēr* 1x *an impress, exact expression, reproduction, exact representation,* Heb. 1:3* [5481]

[5918] χάραξ *charax* 1x *a stake; a* military *palisade, rampart,* formed from the earth thrown out of the ditch, and stuck with sharp stakes or palisades, Lk. 19:43* [5482]

[5919] χαρίζομαι *charizomai* 23x *to gratify; to bestow* in kindness, *grant* as a free favor, Lk. 7:21; Rom. 8:32; *to grant the deliverance* of a person in favor to the desire of others, Acts 3:14; 27:24; Phlm. 22; *to sacrifice* a person to the demand of enemies, Acts 25:11; *to remit, forgive,* Lk. 7:42; 2 Cor. 2:7, 10 [5483] See *forgive; give.*

[5920] χάριν *charin* 9x the acc. sg form of the noun χάριν which can be used as an improper prep., *on account of,* Lk. 7:47; Eph. 3:1, 14; 1 Jn. 3:12; *for the sake of, in order to,* Gal. 3:19; Tit. 1:5, 11; Jude 16; *on the score of,* 1 Tim. 5:14* [5484]

[5921] χάρις *charis* 155x *pleasing show, charm; beauty, attractiveness, gracefulness; a pleasing circumstance, matter of approval,* 1 Pet. 2:19, 20; *kindly bearing, graciousness,* Lk. 4:22; *a beneficial opportunity, benefit,* 2 Cor. 1:15; Eph. 4:29; *a charitable act, generous gift,* 1 Cor. 16:3; 2 Cor. 8:4, 6; *an act of favor,* Acts 25:3; *favor, acceptance,* Lk. 1:30, 52; Acts 2:47; 7:10, 46; *free favor, free gift, grace,* Jn. 1:14, 16, 17; Rom. 4:4, 16; 11:5, 6; Eph. 2:5, 8; 1 Pet. 3:7; *free favor* specially manifested by God towards man in the Gospel scheme, *grace,* Acts 15:11; Rom. 3:24; 5:15, 17, 20, 21; 6:1; 2 Cor. 4:15; *a gracious provision, gracious scheme, grace,* Rom. 6:14, 15; Heb. 2:9; 12:28; 13:9; *gracious dealing* from God, *grace,* Acts 14:26; 15:40; Rom. 1:7; 1 Cor. 1:4; 15:10; Gal. 1:15; *a commission graciously devolved* by God upon a human agent, Rom. 1:5; 12:3; 15:15; 1 Cor. 3:10; 2 Cor. 1:12; Gal. 2:9; Eph. 3:8; *grace, graciously bestowed* divine *endowment* or *influence,* Lk. 2:40; Acts 4:33; 11:23; Rom. 12:6; 2 Cor. 12:9; *grace,* Acts 11:43; Rom. 5:2; Gal. 5:4; 2 Pet. 3:18; *an emotion correspondent to what is pleasing* or *kindly; sense of obligation,* Lk. 17:9; *a grateful frame of mind,* 1 Cor. 10:30; *thanks,* Lk. 6:32, 33, 34; Rom. 6:17; 1 Cor. 15:57; χάριν or χάριτας καταθέσθαι, *to oblige, gratify,* Acts 24:27; 25:9 [5485] See *favor; grace.*

[5922] χάρισμα *charisma* 17x *a free favor, free gift,* Rom. 5:15, 16; 6:23; 2 Cor. 1:11; *benefit,* Rom. 1:11; a divinely conferred *endowment,* 1 Cor. 12:4, 9, 28, 30, 31 [5486] See *gift; spiritual endowment.*

[5923] χαριτόω *charitoō* 2x *to favor, visit with favor, to make an object of favor, to gift,* Eph. 1:6; pass. *to be visited with free favor, be an object of gracious visitation,* Lk. 1:28* [5487]

[5924] Χαρράν *Charran* 2x *Charran,* a city in the northern part of Mesopotamia, Acts 7:2, 4* [5488]

[5925] χάρτης *chartēs* 1x *paper,* 2 Jn. 12* [5489]

[5926] χάσμα *chasma* 1x *a chasm, gulf,* Lk. 16:26* [5490]

[5927] χεῖλος *cheilos* 7x *a lip,* and pl. τὰ χείλη, *the lips,* Mt. 15:8; Mk. 7:6; Rom. 3:13; Heb. 13:15; 1 Pet. 3:10; trop. χεῖλος τῆς θαλάσσης, *the seashore,* Heb. 11:12; meton. *language, dialect,* 1 Cor. 14:21* [5491]

[5928] χειμάζω *cheimazō* 1x *to excite a tempest, toss with a tempest;* pass. *to be storm-tossed,* Acts 27:18* [5492]

[5930] χειμών *cheimōn* 6x *stormy weather,* Mt. 16:3; *a storm, tempest,* Acts 27:20; *winter,* Mt. 24:20; Mk. 13:18; Jn. 10:22; 2 Tim. 4:21* [5494]

[5931] χείρ *cheir* 177x *a hand,* Mt. 3:12; 4:6; 8:15 freq.; from the Hebrew, χεὶρ Κυρίου, *a* special *operation of God,* Acts 11:21; 13:3; ἐν χειρί, *by agency,* Acts 7:35; Gal. 3:19 [5495] See *hand.*

[5932] χειραγωγέω *cheiragōgeō* 2x *to lead by the hand,* Acts 9:8; 22:11* [5496]

[5933] χειραγωγός *cheiragōgos* 1x *one who leads another by the hand,* Acts 13:11* [5497]

[5934] χειρόγραφον *cheirographon* 1x *handwriting; a written form, literal instrument,* as distinguished from a spiritual dispensation, Col. 2:14* [5498]

[5935] χειροποίητος *cheiropoiētos* 6x *made by hand, artificial, material,* Mk. 14:58; Acts 7:48; 17:24; Eph. 2:11; Heb. 9:11, 24* [5499]

[5936] χειροτονέω *cheirotoneō* 2x *to stretch out the hand; to constitute by voting; to appoint, constitute, choose or elect by raising hands,* Acts 14:23; 2 Cor. 8:19* [5500]

[5937] χείρων *cheirōn* 11x *worse,* Mt. 9:16; *more severe,* Jn. 5:14; Heb. 10:29 [5501] See *worse.*

[5938] Χερούβ *Cheroub* 1x also spelled Χερουβείν and Χερουβίμ, indecl. *cherub, a two-winged figure over the ark of the covenant,* Heb. 9:5* [5502]

[5939] χήρα *chēra* 26x *a widow,* Mt. 23:14; Lk. 4:26 [5503] See *widow.*

[5941] χιλίαρχος *chiliarchos* 21x *commander of a thousand men;* hence, genr. *a commander, military chief,* Mk. 6:21; Rev. 6:15; 19:18; spc. *a* legionary *tribune,* Acts 21:31, 32, 33, 37; *the prefect* of the temple, Jn. 18:12 [5506] See *commander.*

[5942] χιλιάς *chilias* 23x the number *one thousand, a thousand,* Lk. 14:31; Acts 4:4 [5505] See *thousand.*

[5943] χίλιοι *chilioi* 11x *a thousand,* 2 Pet. 3:8; Rev. 11:3; 12:6; 14:20; 20:2-7* [5507] See *thousand.*

[5945] χιτών *chitōn* 11x *a tunic, vest,* the inner garment which fitted close to the body, having armholes, and sometimes sleeves, and reaching below the knees, worn by both sexes, Mt. 5:40; 10:10; pl. χιτῶνες, *clothes, garments* in general, Mk. 14:63 [5509] See *garment; tunic.*

[5946] χιών *chiōn* 2x *snow,* Mt. 28:3; Rev. 1:14* [5510]

[5948] χλαμύς *chlamys* 2x *chlamys,* a type of *cloak;* a Roman military commander's *cloak,* Mt. 27:28, 31* [5511]

[5949] χλευάζω *chleuazō* 1x *to jeer, scoff,* Acts 17:32* [5512]

[5950] χλιαρός *chliaros* 1x *warm, tepid; lukewarm,* Rev. 3:16* [5513]

[5952] χλωρός *chlōros* 4x *pale green; green, verdent,* Mk. 6:39; Rev. 8:7; 9:4; *pale, sallow,* Rev. 6:8* [5515]

[5954] χοϊκός *choikos* 4x *of earth, earthy,* 1 Cor. 15:47, 48, 49* [5517]

[5955] χοῖνιξ *choinix* 2x *a choenix,* an Attic measure for things dry, being the 48th part of a medimnus, consequently equal to the 8th part of the Roman modius, and nearly equivalent to about one quart, being considered a sufficient daily allowance for the sustenance of one man, Rev. 6:6 (2x)* [5518]

[5956] χοῖρος *choiros* 12x pr. *a young swine; a swine, hog,* or *sow,* Mt. 8:30, 31, 32 [5519] See *pig.*

[5957] χολάω *cholaō* 1x pr. *to be melancholy;* used later as an equivalent to χολοῦμαι, *to be angry, incensed,* Jn. 7:23* [5520]

[5958] χολή *cholē* 2x *the bile, gall;* in NT *a bitter ingredient,* as *wormwood,* Mt. 27:34; χολὴ πικρίας, *intense bitterness,* met. *thorough disaffection* to divine truth, *utter estrangement,* Acts 8:23* [5521]

[5960] Χοραζίν *Chorazin* 2x also spelled Χωραζίν and Χοραζείν, *Chorazin,* a town of Galilee, probably near Bethsaida and Capernaum, indecl., Mt. 11:21; Lk. 10:13* [5523]

[5961] χορηγέω *chorēgeō* 2x *to lead a chorus;* at Athens, *to defray the cost of a chorus;* hence, *to supply funds; to supply, furnish,* 2 Cor. 9:10; 1 Pet. 4:11* [5524]

[5962] χορός *choros* 1x *dancing* with music, Lk. 15:25* [5525]

[5963] χορτάζω *chortazō* 16x pr. *to feed* or *fill with grass, herbage,* etc., *to fatten;* used of animals of prey, *to satiate, gorge,* Rev. 19:21; of persons, *to satisfy with food,* Mt. 14:20; 15:33, 37; met. *to satisfy* the desire of any one, Mt. 5:6 [5526] See *satisfy.*

[5964] χόρτασμα *chortasma* 1x *pasture, provender* for cattle; *food, provision, sustenance,* for men, Acts 7:11* [5527]

[5965] χόρτος *chortos* 15x *an enclosure; pasture ground; fodder* for beasts; in NT *herbage, grass,* Mt. 6:30; 14:19; *a plant* of corn, Mt. 13:26; Mk. 4:28 [5528] See *grass.*

[5967] χοῦς *chous* 2x uncontracted form χόος, *dust,* acc., χοῦν, Mk. 6:11; Rev. 18:19* [5522]

[5968] χράομαι *chraomai* 11x *to use, make use of, employ,* Acts 27:17; 1 Cor. 7:31; *to take advantage of,* 1 Cor. 7:21; 9:12, 15; *to use, to treat, behave towards,* Acts 27:3; 2 Cor. 13:10 [5530] See *use.*

[5970] χρεία *chreia* 49x *use; need, necessity, requisiteness,* Eph. 4:29; Heb. 7:11; personal *need, an* individual *want,* Acts 20:34; Rom. 12:13; Phil. 2:25; 4:16, 19; χρείαν ἔχω, *to need, require, want,* Mt. 6:8; 14:16; Mk. 2:25; Jn. 2:25; ἐστὶ χρεία, *there is need,* Lk. 10:42; τὰ πρὸς τὴν χρείαν, *necessary things,* Acts 28:10; *a necessary business, affair,* Acts 6:3 [5532] See *need.*

[5971] χρεοφειλέτης *chreopheiletēs* 2x *debtor,* Lk. 7:41; 16:5* [5533]

[5973] χρή *chrē* 1x impersonal verb, *there is need* or *occasion, it is necessary, it is requisite; it becomes, it is proper,* Jas. 3:10* [5534]

[5974] χρῄζω *chrēzō* 5x *to need, want, desire,* Mt. 6:32; Lk. 11:8; 12:30; Rom. 16:2; 2 Cor. 3:1* [5535]

[5975] χρῆμα *chrēma* 6x *anything useful,* or *needful;* pl. *wealth, riches,* Mk. 10:23; Lk. 18:24; *money,* Acts 8:18, 20; 24:26; sg. *price,* Acts 4:37* [5536]

[5976] χρηματίζω *chrēmatizō* 9x *to have dealings, transact business; to negotiate; to give answer on deliberation;* in NT *to utter a divine communication,* Heb. 12:25; pass. *to be divinely instructed, receive a revelation* or *warning from God,* Mt. 2:12, 22; Lk. 2:26; Acts 10:22; Heb. 8:5; 11:7; intrans. *to receive an appellation,* Acts 11:26; Rom. 7:3* [5537]

[5977] χρηματισμός *chrēmatismos* 1x in NT *a response from God, a divine communication, oracle,* Rom. 11:4* [5538]

[5978] χρήσιμος *chrēsimos* 1x *useful, profitable,* 2 Tim. 2:14* [5539]

[5979] χρῆσις *chrēsis* 2x *use, employment; manner of using,* Rom. 1:26, 27* [5540]

[5980] χρηστεύομαι *chrēsteuomai* 1x *to be gentle, benign, kind,* 1 Cor. 13:4* [5541]

[5981] χρηστολογία *chrēstologia* 1x *bland address, fair speaking,* Rom. 16:18* [5542]

[5982] χρηστός *chrēstos* 7x *useful, profitable; good, agreeable,* Lk. 5:39; *easy,* as a yoke, Mt. 11:30; *gentle, benign, kind, obliging, gracious,* Lk. 6:35; Eph. 4:32; Rom. 2:4; 1 Pet. 2:3; *good* in character, disposition, etc., *virtuous,* 1 Cor. 15:33* [5543] See *kind.*

[5983] χρηστότης *chrēstotēs* 10x pr. *goodness, kindness, gentleness,* Rom. 2:4; 11:22(3x); 2 Cor. 6:6; Gal. 5:22; Col. 3:12; Tit. 3:4; *kindness* shown, *beneficence,* Eph. 2:7; *goodness, virtue,* Rom. 3:12* [5544] See *goodness; kindness.*

[5984] χρῖσμα *chrisma* 3x pr. *anything which is applied by smearing; ointment;* in NT *an anointing,* in the reception of spiritual privileges, 1 Jn. 2:20, 27* [5545]

[5985] Χριστιανός *Christianos* 3x *a Christian, follower of Christ,* Acts 11:26; 26:28; 1 Pet. 4:16* [5546] See *Christian.*

[5986] Χριστός *Christos* 529x pr. *anointed;* ὁ Χριστός, *the Christ, the Anointed One,* i.q. Μεσσίας, *the Messiah,* Mt. 1:16, 17; Jn. 1:20, 25, 42; meton. *Christ, the word* or *doctrine of Christ,* 2 Cor. 1:19; 21; Eph. 4:20; *Christ, a* truly *Christian frame* of doctrine and affection, Rom. 8:10; Gal. 4:19; *Christ,* *the Church of Christ,* 1 Cor. 12:12; *Christ the* distinctive *privileges of the Gospel of Christ,* Gal. 3:27; Phil. 3:8; Heb. 3:14 [5547] See *anointed one; Christ; Messiah.*

[5987] χρίω *chriō* 5x *to anoint;* in NT *to anoint,* by way of instituting to a dignity, function, or privilege, Lk. 4:18; Acts 4:27; 10:38; 2 Cor. 1:21; Heb. 1:9* [5548] See *anoint.*

[5988] χρονίζω *chronizō* 5x *to spend time; to linger, delay, be long,* Mt. 24:48; 25:5; Lk. 1:21; 12:45; Heb. 10:37* [5549]

[5989] χρόνος *chronos* 54x *time,* whether in respect of duration or a definite point of its lapse, Mt. 2:7; 25:19 freq.; *an epoch, era,* marked *duration,* Acts 1:7; 1 Thess. 5:1 [5550] See *time.*

[5990] χρονοτριβέω *chronotribeō* 1x *to spend time, waste time, linger, delay,* Acts 20:16* [5551]

[5992] χρυσίον *chrysion* 12x *gold,* Heb. 9:4; 1 Pet. 1:7; Rev. 3:18; 21:18, 21; spc. *gold when coined* or *manufactured; golden ornaments,* 1 Tim. 2:9; 1 Pet. 3:3; Rev. 17:4; 18:16; *gold coin, money,* Acts 3:6; 20:33; 1 Pet. 1:18* [5553] See *gold.*

[5993] χρυσοδακτύλιος *chrysodaktylios* 1x *having rings of gold on the fingers,* Jas. 2:2* [5554]

[5994] χρυσόλιθος *chrysolithos* 1x *chrysolite,* a name applied by the ancients to all gems of a gold color; spc. the modern *topaz,* Rev. 21:10* [5555]

[5995] χρυσόπρασος *chrysoprasos* 1x *a chrysoprase,* a species of gem of a golden green color like that of a leek, Rev. 21:20* [5556]

[5996] χρυσός *chrysos* 10x *gold,* Mt. 2:11; 23:16, 17; meton. *gold ornaments,* 1 Tim. 2:9; *gold coin, money,* Mt. 10:9 [5557] See *gold.*

[5997] χρυσοῦς *chrysous* 18x *golden, made of* or *adorned with gold,* 2 Tim. 2:20; Heb. 9:4; Rev. 1:12, 13, 20; 9:13, 20, 21:15 [5552] See *gold.*

[5998] χρυσόω *chrysoō* 2x *to gild, overlay with gold, adorn* or *deck with gold,* Rev. 17:4; 18:16* [5558]

[5999] χρώς *chrōs* 1x *the skin; the body surface;* Acts 19:12* [5559]

[6000] χωλός *chōlos* 14x *crippled in the feet, limping, halting, lame,* Mt. 11:5; 15:30, 31; met. *limping, weak,* spiritually, Heb. 12:13; *maimed, deprived of a foot,* for ἀναπηρός, Mk. 9:45 [5560] See *crippled; lame.*

[6001] χώρα *chōra* 28x *space, room; a country, region, tract, province,* Mk. 5:10; Lk. 2:8; *a district, territory, suburbs,* Mt. 8:28; meton. *the inhabitants of a country, region,* etc., Mk. 1:5; Acts 12:20; *the country,* as opposed to the city or town, Lk. 21:21; *a field, farm,* Lk. 12:16; Jn. 4:35 [5561] See *country; field; region.*

[6003] χωρέω *chōreō* 10x *to make room,* either by motion or capacity; *to move, pass,* Mt. 15:17; *to proceed, go on,* 2 Pet. 3:9; *to progress, make way,* Jn. 8:37; trans. *to hold* as contents, *contain, afford room for,* Mk. 2:2; Jn. 2:6; 21:25; met. *to give* mental *admittance to, to yield accordance,* Mt. 19:11, 12; *to admit* to approbation and esteem, *to regard cordially,* 2 Cor. 7:2* [5562] See *accept; hold; (have) room for.*

[6004] χωρίζω *chōrizō* 13x *to divide, separate,* Mt. 19:6; Mk. 10:9; Rom. 8:35, 39; *to dissociate one's self, to part,* 1 Cor. 7:10, 11, 15; *to withdraw, depart,* Acts 1:4; 18:1, 2; Phlm. 15; *to be aloof,* Heb. 7:26* [5563] See *divorce; separate.*

[6005] χωρίον *chōrion* 10x *a place, spot;* Mt. 26:36; Mk. 14:32; *a field, farm, estate, domain,* Jn. 4:5; Acts 1:18, 19(2x); 4:34; 5:3, 8; 28:7* [5564] See *field; place.*

[6006] χωρίς *chōris* 41x can function as an improper prep., *apart,* Jn. 20:7; *apart from, parted from,* Jn. 15:5; Jas. 2:18, 20, 26; *alien from,* Eph. 2:12; *apart from, on a distinct footing from,* 1 Cor. 11:11; *apart from, distinct from, without the intervention of,* Rom. 3:21, 28; 4:6; *apart from* the company of, *independently of,* 1 Cor. 4:8; Heb. 11:40 *without* the presence of, Heb. 9:28; *without* the agency of, Jn. 1:3; Rom. 10:14; *without* the employment of, Mt. 13:34; Mk. 4:34; Heb. 7:20, 21; 9:7, 18, 22; *without,* Lk. 6:49; Phil. 2:14; 1 Tim. 2:8; 5:21; Phlm. 14; Heb. 10:28; 11:6; 12:8, 14; *clear from,* Heb. 7:7; *irrespectively of,* Rom. 7:8, 9; *without reckoning, besides,* Mt. 14:21; 15:38; 2 Cor. 11:28; *with the exception of,* Heb. 4:15 [5565]

[6008] χῶρος *chōros* 1x *Corus,* or *Caurus, the northwest wind;* meton, *the northwest* quarter of the heavens, Acts 27:12* [5566]

[6010] ψάλλω *psallō* 5x *to move by a touch, to twitch; to touch, strike* the strings or chords of an instrument; absol. *to play on a stringed instrument; to sing to music;* in NT *to sing praises,* Rom. 15:9; 1 Cor. 14:15; Eph. 5:19; Jas. 5:13* [5567] See *sing.*

[6011] ψαλμός *psalmos* 7x *impulse, touch* of the chords of a stringed instrument; in NT *a sacred song, psalm,* Lk. 20:42; 24:44; Acts 1:20; 13:33; 1 Cor. 14:26; Eph. 5:19; Col. 3:16* [5568] See *psalm.*

[6012] ψευδάδελφος *pseudadelphos* 2x *a false brother, a pretend Christian,* 2 Cor. 11:26; Gal. 2:4* [5569]

[6013] ψευδαπόστολος *pseudapostolos* 1x *a false apostle, pretend minister of Christ,* 2 Cor. 11:13* [5570]

[6014] ψευδής *pseudēs* 3x *false, lying,* Acts 6:13; Rev. 2:2; in NT pl. *maintainers of* religious *falsehood, corrupters of the truth* of God, Rev. 21:8* [5571]

[6015] ψευδοδιδάσκαλος *pseudodidaskalos* 1x *a false teacher, one who teaches false doctrines,* 2 Pet. 2:1* [5572]

[6016] ψευδολόγος *pseudologos* 1x *false-speaking,* 1 Tim. 4:2* [5573]

[6017] ψεύδομαι *pseudomai* 12x *lie,* Mt. 5:11; Acts 5:4; Rom. 9:1; 2 Cor. 11:31 [5574] See *lie.*

[6018] ψευδομαρτυρέω *pseudomartyreō* 5x *to bear false witness, give false testimony,* Mt. 19:18; Mk. 10:19; 14:56, 57; Lk. 18:20* [5576]

[6019] ψευδομαρτυρία *pseudomartyria* 2x *false witness, false testimony,* Mt. 15:19; 26:59* [5577]

[6020] ψευδόμαρτυς *pseudomartys* 2x *a false witness,* Mt. 26:60 (2x); 1 Cor. 15:15* [5575]

[6021] ψευδοπροφήτης *pseudoprophētēs* 11x *a false prophet, one who falsely claims to speak by divine inspiration,* whether as a foreteller of future events, or as a teacher of doctrines, Mt. 7:15; 24:24; Mk. 13:22; Acts 13:6; 1 Jn. 4:1; Rev. 16:13 [5578] See *false prophet.*

[6022] ψεῦδος *pseudos* 10x *falsehood,* Jn. 8:44; Eph. 4:25; 2 Thess. 2:9, 11; 1 Jn. 2:21, 27; in NT religious *falsehood, perversion* of religious truth, *false religion,* Rom. 1:25; *the practices of false religion,* Rev. 14:15; 21:27; 22:15* [5579] See *deception; falsehood; lie.*

[6023] ψευδόχριστος *pseudochristos* 2x *a false Christ, pretend Messiah,* Mt. 24:24; Mk. 13:22* [5580]

[6024] ψευδώνυμος *pseudōnymos* 1x *falsely named, falsely called,* 1 Tim. 6:20* [5581]

[6025] ψεῦσμα *pseusma* 1x *a falsehood, lie;* in NT *untruthfulness,* Rom. 3:7* [5582]

[6026] ψεύστης *pseustēs* 10x *one who utters a falsehood, a liar,* Jn. 8:44, 55; Rom. 3:4; 1 Tim. 1:10; Tit. 1:12; 1 Jn. 1:10; 2:4, 22; 4:20; 5:10* [5583] See *liar.*

[6027] ψηλαφάω *psēlaphaō* 4x *to feel, handle,* Lk. 24:39; *to feel* or *grope for* or *after,* as persons in the dark, Acts 17:27; Heb. 12:18; 1 Jn. 1:1* [5584]

[6028] ψηφίζω *psēphizō* 2x *to reckon by means of pebbles, compute by counters;* hence genr. *to compute, reckon, calculate,* Lk. 14:28; Rev. 13:18* [5585]

[6029] ψῆφος *psēphos* 3x *a small stone, pebble; a pebble* variously employed, especially in a ballot; hence, *a vote, suffrage,* Acts 26:10; *a pebble* or *stone;* probably given as a token, Rev. 2:17 (2x)* [5586]

[6030] ψιθυρισμός *psithurismos* 1x *a whispering; a* calumnious *whispering, gossip,* 2 Cor. 12:20* [5587]

[6031] ψιθυριστής *psithuristēs* 1x *a whisperer; a whisperer, gossip,* Rom. 1:29* [5588]

[6033] ψιχίον *psichion* 2x *a morsel, crumb, bit,* Mt. 15:27; Mk. 7:28* [5589]

[6034] ψυχή *psychē* 103x *breath; the principle of animal life; the life,* Mt. 2:20; 6:25; Mk. 3:4; Lk. 21:19; Jn. 10:11; *an inanimate being,* 1 Cor. 15:45; *a* human *individual, soul,* Acts 2:41; 3:23; 7:14; 27:37; Rom. 13:1; 1 Pet. 3:20; *the* immaterial *soul,* Mt. 10:28; 1 Pet. 1:9; 2:11, 25; 4:19; *the soul* as the seat of religious and moral sentiment, Mt. 11:29; Acts 14:2, 22; 15:24; Eph. 6:6; *the soul,* as a seat of feeling, Mt. 12:18; 26:38; *the soul, the* inner *self,* Lk. 12:19 [5590] See *life; mind; person; soul.*

[6035] ψυχικός *psychikos* 6x *pertaining to the life* or *soul;* in NT *animal,* as distinguished from spiritual subsistence, 1 Cor. 15:44, 46; *occupied with mere animal things, animal, sensual,* 1 Cor. 2:14; Jas. 3:15; Jude 19* [5591]

[6036] ψῦχος *psychos* 3x *cold,* Jn. 18:18; Acts 28:2; 2 Cor. 11:27* [5592]

[6037] ψυχρός *psychros* 4x *cool, cold,* Mt. 10:42; met. Rev. 3:15, 16* [5593]

[6038] ψύχω *psychō* 1x *to breathe; to cool;* pass. *to be cooled;* met. of affection, Mt. 24:12* [5594]

[6039] ψωμίζω *psōmizō* 2x pr. *to feed by morsels;* hence, genr. *to feed, supply with food,* Rom. 12:20; *to bestow in supplying food,* 1 Cor. 13:3* [5595]

[6040] ψωμίον *psōmion* 4x *a bit, morsel, mouthful,* Jn. 13:26, 27, 30* [5596]

[6041] ψώχω *psōchō* 1x *to rub in pieces,* as the ears of grain, Lk. 6:1* [5597]

[6042] Ὦ *ō* 3x *Omega,* the last letter of the Greek alphabet, hence, met. τὸ Ω, *the last,* Rev. 1:8; 21:6; 22:13* [5598] See *Alpha; Omega.*

[6043] ὦ *ō* 17x *O!,* Mt. 15:28; Mk. 9:19; Acts 1:1; Rom. 2:1, 3; 11:33 [5599]

[6045] ὧδε *hōde* 61x *here, in this place,* Mt. 12:6, 41; ὧδε ἢ ὧδε, *here* or *there,* Mt. 24:23; τὰ ὧδε, *the state of things here,* Col. 4:9; met. *herein, in this thing,* Rev. 13:10, 18; *to this place,* Mt. 8:29; 14:18 [5602]

[6046] ᾠδή *ōdē* 7x *an ode, song, hymn,* Eph. 5:19; Col. 3:16; Rev. 5:9; 14:3; 15:3* [5603]

[6047] ὠδίν *ōdin* 4x *the spasms* or *pains,* of a woman in travail, *a birth pang,* 1 Thess. 5:3; pl. met. *birth throes, preliminary troubles* to the development of a catastrophe, Mt. 24:8; Mk. 13:8; from the Hebrew, *a stringent band, a snare, noose,* Acts 2:24* [5604]

[6048] ὠδίνω *ōdinō* 3x *to be in travail,* Gal. 4:27; Rev. 12:2; met. *to travail with, suffer birth pangs, to make effort to bring to* spiritual birth, Gal. 4:19* [5605] See *birth pangs; travail.*

[6049] ὦμος *ōmos* 2x *the shoulder,* Mt. 23:4; Lk. 15:5* [5606]

[6050] ὠνέομαι *ōneomai* 1x *to buy, purchase,* Acts 7:16* [5608]

[6051] ᾠόν *ōon* 1x *an egg,* Lk. 11:12* [5609]

[6052] ὥρα *hōra* 106x *a limited portion of time,* marked out by part of a settled routine or train of circumstances; *a season of the year; time of day,* Mt. 14:15; Mk. 6:35; 11:11; *an hour,* Mt. 20:3; Jn. 11:9; in NT *an* eventful *season,* 1 Jn. 2:18 (2x); Rev. 3:10; 14:7; *due time,* Jn. 16:21; Rom. 13:11; *a* destined *period, hour,* Mt. 26:45; Mk. 14:35; Jn. 2:4; 7:30; *a short period,* Mt. 26:40; Jn. 5:35; 2 Cor. 7:8; Gal. 2:5; 1 Thess. 2:17; Phlm. 15; *a point of time, time,* Mt. 8:13; 24:42; Lk. 2:38 [5610] See *hour.*

[6053] ὡραῖος *hōraios* 4x *timely, seasonable; in prime, blooming;* in NT *beautiful,* Mt. 23:27; Acts 3:2, 10; Rom. 10:15* [5611]

[6054] ὠρύομαι *ōryomai* 1x *to howl; to roar,* as a lion, 1 Pet. 5:8* [5612]

[6055] ὡς *hōs* 504x conjunction formed from the relative pronoun ὅς, used as a comparative part. and conj., *as,* correlatively, Mk. 4:26; Jn. 7:46; Rom. 5:15; *as, like as,* Mt. 10:16; Eph. 5:8; *according as,* Gal. 6:10; *as, as it were,* Rev. 8:8; *as,* Lk. 16:1; Acts 3:12; before numerals, *about,* Mk. 5:13; conj. *that,* Acts 10:28; *how,* Rom. 11:2; *when,* Mt. 28:9; Phil. 2:23; as an exclamatory particle, *how,* Rom. 10:15; equivalent to ὥστε, *accordingly,* Heb. 3:11; also, *on condition that, provided that,* Acts 20:24; ὡς εἰπεῖν, *so to speak,* Heb. 7:9 [5613]

[6057] ὡσαννά *hōsanna* 6x *Hosanna! save now, help now,* Mt. 21:9, 15; Mk. 11:9, 10; Jn. 12:13* [5614] See *hosanna.*

[6058] ὡσαύτως *hōsautōs* 17x *just so, in just the same way* or *manner, likewise,* Mt. 20:5; 21:30 [5615]

[6059] ὡσεί *hōsei* 21x *as if; as it were, as, like,* Mt. 3:16; 9:36; with terms of number or quantity, *about,* Mt. 14:21; Lk. 1:56; 22:41, 59 [5616]

[6060] Ὡσηέ *hōsēe* 1x *Hosea,* pr. name, indecl., Rom. 9:25* [5617]

[6061] ὥσπερ *hōsper* 36x *just as, as,* Mt. 6:2; 24:37; 1 Thess. 5:3 [5618]

[6062] ὡσπερεί *hōsperei* 1x *just as if; as it were,* 1 Cor. 15:8* [5619]

[6063] ὥστε *hōste* 83x *so that, so as that, so as to,* Mt. 8:24; Mk. 2:12; Acts 14:1; Gal. 2:13; as an illative particle, *therefore, consequently,* Mt. 12:12; 23:31 [5620]

[6064] ὠτάριον *ōtarion* 2x *an ear,* Mt. 14:47; Jn. 18:10* [5621]

[6065] ὠτίον *ōtion* 3x in NT simply equivalent to οὖς, *an ear,* Mt. 26:51; Lk. 22:51; Jn. 18:26* [5621]

[6066] ὠφέλεια *ōpheleia* 2x *help; profit, gain, advantage, benefit,* Rom. 3:1; Jude 16* [5622]

[6067] ὠφελέω *ōpheleō* 15x *to help, profit, benefit, accomplish,* Mt. 27:24; Mk. 7:11; Rom. 2:25; *be of value,* Jn. 6:63 [5623] See *gain; profit; value.*

[6068] ὠφέλιμος *ōphelimos* 4x *profitable, useful, beneficial; serviceable,* 1 Tim. 4:8 (2x); 2 Tim. 3:16; Tit. 3:8* [5624]

[7000] αὐτοῦ *autou* 4x *here,* Mt. 26:36; Lk. 9:27; *there,* Acts 18:19; 21:4. See also 899*

[7005] ἡμεῖς *hēmeis* 864x plural of ἐγώ (1609)

[7007] ὑμεῖς *hymeis* 1,840x plural of σύ (5148)

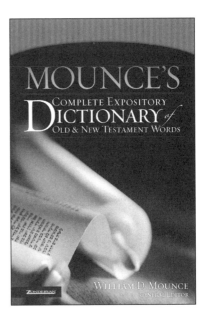

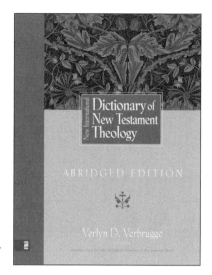

We want to hear from you. Please send your comments about this book to us in care of zreview@zondervan.com. Thank you.